Children's Books In Print®

2021

This edition of

CHILDREN'S BOOKS IN PRINT® 2021
was prepared by R.R. Bowker's Database Publishing Group
in collaboration with the Information Technology Department.

Oren Beit-Arie, President ProQuest Books
Beat Barblan, Vice President Product Management
Mark Van Orman, Senior Director Content Operations

International Standard Book Number/Standard Address Number Agency
John Purcell, Manager, ISBN Agency
Richard Smith, Product Manager, Identifier Services
Raymond Reynolds, Victer Basurco, Tim Conboy, Publisher Relations
Representatives

Books Content Operations
Margot Cronin, Lisa Heft, Michael Hild, Senior Managers Content Operations
Adrene Allen, Manager Content Operations
Ekaterina Boehm, Ila Joseph, Halyna Testerman, Senior Content Data Analysts
Mark Ahmad, Edward Albright, Jr, Ron Butkiewicz, Vivian Chen,
Teresa Gibbons, Marc Guerino,
Latonia Hall, Jillian Heyman, Lynda Keller, Zack Laubernds, Tom Lucas,
Nicholas Mak, Charu Mehta, Ryan Oberti, Felix Offei, Lynese Pegram,
Richard Sakul, Daniel Smith, Content Data Analysts
Rosemary Walker, Content Editor

Provider Relations
Patricia Payton, Senior Manager Provider Relations
Ralph Coviello, Suzanne Franks, Engagement Managers
Michael Olenick, Content Business Analyst Senior
Matt O'Connell, Content Business Analyst Lead

Data Services Production
Andy K. Haramasz, Manager Data Distribution & QA

Editorial Systems Group
Mark Heinzelman, Chief Data Architect

Computer Operations Group
Ed Albright, UNIX Administrator
John Nesselt, UNIX Administrator

Bowker®

Children's Books In Print® 2021

An Author, Title, and Illustrator Index to Books for Children and Young Adults

VOLUME 3

- **Authors O-Z**
- **Illustrators**
- **Publishers, Wholesalers & Distributors**

GREY HOUSE PUBLISHING

ProQuest LLC
789 E. Eisenhower Parkway
P.O. Box 1346
Ann Arbor, MI 48106-1346
Phone: 734-761-4700
Toll-free: 1-800-521-0600
E-mail:
customerservice@proquest.com
URL: http://www.proquest.com

Grey House Publishing, Inc.
4919 Route 22
Amenia, NY 12501
Phone: 518-789-8700
Toll-free: 1-800-562-2139
Fax: 518-789-0545
E-mail: books@greyhouse.com
URL: http://www.greyhouse.com

Pep Carrera, President, ProQuest Books

Children's Books In Print® 2021 is published by Grey House Publishing, Inc. under exclusive license from ProQuest, LLC.

Publishers may update or add to their listings by accessing one of Bowker's online portals: **BowkerLink** for international publishers at http://www.bowkerlink.com and **MyIdentifiers** for USA publishers at http://www.myidentifiers.com.

No payment is either solicited or accepted for the inclusion of entries in this publication.

International Standard Book Numbers

ISBN 13: 978-1-64265-526-1 (set)
ISBN 13: 978-1-64265-527-8 (Vol. 1)
ISBN 13: 978-1-64265-528-5 (Vol. 2)
ISBN 13: 978-1-64265-719-7 (Vol. 3)

International Standard Serial Number

0069-3480

Library of Congress Control Number

70-101705

Printed and bound in Canada

CONTENTS

How To Use CHILDREN'S BOOKS IN PRINT®

This 52nd edition of R.R. Bowker's ***Children's Books In Print***® is produced from the Books In Print database. Volumes 1 and 2 contain the Title Index to approximately 275,00 books available from some 20,000 United States publishers. Volume 1 includes books published after 2003. Volumes 2 and 3 includes the Author and Illustrator indexes, with listings for approximately 60,000 contributors. The Name Publishers index with full contact information for all of the publishers listed in the bibliographic entries is included at the end of the book, followed by a separate index to wholesalers and distributors.

RELATED PRODUCTS

In addition to the printed version, the entire Books In Print database (more than 50 million records, including OP/OSI titles, ebooks, audio books and videos) can be searched by customers on Bowker's Web site, http://www.booksinprint.com. For further information about subscribing to this online service, please contact Bowker at 1-888-269-5372.

The Books In Print database is also available in an array of other formats such as online access through Books In Print site licensing. Database vendors such as OVID Technologies, Inc. make the Books In Print database available to their subscribers.

COMPILATION

In order to be useful to subscribers, the information contained in ***Children's Books In Print***® must be complete and accurate. Publishers are asked to review and correct their entries prior to each publication, providing current price, publication date, availability status, and ordering information, as well as recently published and forthcoming titles. Tens of thousands of entries are added or updated for each edition.

DATA ACQUISITION

Bowker aggregates bibliographic information via ONIX, excel and text data feeds from publishers, national libraries, distributors, and wholesalers. Publishers may also add to or update their listings using one of Bowker's online portals: **BowkerLink** for international publishers at http://www.bowkerlink.com and **MyIdentifiers** for USA publishers at http://www.myidentifiers.com.

Larger publishing houses can submit their bibliographic information to the Books In Print database from their own databases. Bowker's system accepts publisher data 24 hours a day, 7 days a week via FTP. The benefits to this method are: no paper intervention, reduced costs, increased timeliness, and less chance of human error that can occur when re-keying information.

To communicate new title information to Books In Print, the quality of the publisher's textual data must be up to—or extremely close to—reference book standards. Publishers interested in setting up a data feed are invited to access the Bowker Title Submission Guide at http://www.bowker.com or contact us at Data.Submissions@Bowker.com.

Updated information or corrections to the listings in *Books In Print* can now be submitted at any time via email at Data.Submissions@bowker.com. Publishers can also submit updates and new titles to ***Children's Books In Print®*** through one of Bowker's online portals: **BowkerLink** for international publishers at http://www.bowkerlink.com and **MyIdentifiers** for USA publishers at http://www.myidentifiers.com.

To ensure the accuracy, timeliness and comprehensiveness of data in ***Children's Books In Print®***, Bowker has initiated discussions with the major publishers. This outreach entails analyzing the quality of all publisher submissions to the Books In Print database, and working closely with the publisher to improve the content and timeliness of the information. This outreach also lays the groundwork for incorporating new valuable information into ***Children's Books In Print®***. We are now collecting cover art, descriptive jacket and catalog copy, tables of contents, and contributor biographies, as well as awards won, bestseller listings, and review citations.

Bowker will make this important additional information available to customers who receive *Books In Print* in specific electronic formats and through subscriptions to http://www.booksinprint.com.

ALPHABETICAL ARRANGEMENT OF AUTHOR, TITLE, AND ILLUSTRATOR INDEXES

Within each index, entries are filed alphabetically by word with the following exception:

Initial articles of titles in English, French, German, Italian, and Spanish are deleted from both author and title entries.

Numerals, including years, are written out in some cases and are filed alphabetically.

As a general rule, U.S., UN, Dr., Mr., and St. are filed in strict alphabetical order unless the author/publisher specifically requests that the abbreviation be filed as if it were spelled out.

Proper names beginning with "Mc" and "Mac" are filed in strict alphabetical order. For example, entries for contributor's names such as MacAdam, MacAvory, MacCarthy, MacDonald, and MacLean are located prior to the pages with entries for names such as McAdams, McCarthy, McCoy, and McDermott.

Entries beginning with initial letters (whether authors' given names, or titles) are filed first, e.g., Smith, H.C., comes before Smith, Harold A.; B is for Betsy comes before Babar, etc.

Compound names are listed under the first part of the name, and cross references appear under the last part of the name.

SPECIAL NOTE ON HOW TO FIND AN AUTHOR'S OR ILLUSTRATOR'S LISTING

In sorting author and illustrator listings by computer, it is not possible to group the entire listing for an individual together unless a standard spelling and format for each name is used. The information in R.R. Bowker's ***Children's Books In Print®*** is based on data received from the publishers. If a name appears in various forms in this data, the listing in the index may be divided into several groups.

INFORMATION INCLUDED IN AUTHOR, TITLE, AND ILLUSTRATOR ENTRIES

Entries in the Title and Illustrator indexes include the following bibliographic information, when available: author, co-author, editor, co-editor, translator, co-translator, illustrator, co-illustrator, photographer, co-photographer, title, title supplement, sub-title, number of volumes, edition, series information, language if other than English, whether or not illustrated, number of pages, (orig.) if an original paperback, grade range, year of publication, price, International Standard Book Number, publisher's order number, imprint, and publisher name.

Titles new to this edition are indicated by bolding the ISBN. Information on the International Standard Book Numbering System is available from R.R. Bowker.

Author Index entries provide the contributor(s) name(s), title, subtitle, title supplement, and a page number cross reference to the full bibliographic entry in the Title Index (in Volume 1).

The prices cited are those provided by the publishers and generally refer to either the trade edition or the Publisher's Library Bound edition. The abbreviation "lib. bdg." is used whenever the price cited is for a publisher's library bound edition.

ISBN AGENCY

Each title included in **Children's Books In Print®** has been assigned an International Standard Book Number (ISBN) by the publisher. All ISBNs listed in this directory have been validated by using the check digit control, ensuring accuracy. ISBNs allow order transmission and bibliographic information updating using publishing industry supported EDI formats (e.g., ONIX). Publishers not currently participating in the ISBN system may request the assignment of an ISBN Publisher Prefix from the ISBN Agency by calling 877-310-7333, faxing 908-219-0195, or through the ISBN Agency's web site at **http://www.myidentifiers.com**. Please note: The ISBN prefix 0-615 is for decentralized use by the U.S. ISBN Agency and has been assigned to many publishers. It is not unique to one publisher.

SAN AGENCY

Another listing feature in **Children's Books In Print®** is the Standard Address Number (SAN), a unique identification number assigned to each address of an organization in or served by the publishing industry; it facilitates communications and transactions with other members of the industry.

The SAN identifies either a bill to or ship to address for purchasing, billing, shipping, receiving, paying, crediting, and refunding, and can be used for any other communication or transaction between participating companies and organizations in the publishing supply chain.

To obtain an application or further information on the SAN system, please email the SAN Agency at **SAN@bowker.com,** or visit **www.myidentifiers.com**

PUBLISHER NAME INDEX

A key to the abbreviated publisher names (e.g., "Middle Atlantic Pr.") used in the bibliographic entries of ***Children's Books In Print®*** is found after the Illustrator Index in Volume 2. Entries in this index contain each publisher's abbreviated name, followed by its ISBN prefix(es), business affiliation (e.g., "Div. of International Publishing")when available, ordering address(es), SAN (Standard Address Number), telephone, fax, and toll-free numbers. Editorial address(es) (and associated contact numbers) follows. Addresses without a specific label are for editorial offices rather than ordering purposes.

Abbreviations used to identify publishers' imprints are followed by the full name of the imprint. E-mail and Web site addresses are then supplied. A listing of distributors associated with the publisher concludes each entry; each distributor symbol is in bold type, followed by its abbreviated name.

A dagger preceding an entry and the note "CIP" at the end of the entry both indicate that the publisher participates in the Cataloging in Publication Program of the Library of Congress.

Foreign publishers with U.S. distributors are listed, followed by their three-character ISO (International Standards Organization) country code ("GBR," "CAN," etc.), ISBN prefix(es), when available, and a cross-reference to their U.S. distributor, as shown below:

Atrium (GBR) *(0-9535353) Dist by* **Dufour**.

Publishers with like or similar names are referenced by a "Do not confuse with . . ." notation at the end of the entry. In addition, cross-references are provided from imprints and former company names to the new name.

WHOLESALER & DISTRIBUTOR NAME INDEX

Full information on distributors as well as wholesalers is provided in this index. Note that those publishers who also serve as distributors may be listed both here and in the Publisher Name Index.

SAMPLE ENTRY TITLE INDEX

1 Anti-Boredom Book: 2 133 Completely Unboring Things to Do!
3 Owl & Chikadee Magazines Editors 4 rev. ed 5 2000 6 128 p.
7 (J) 8 (gr. k-4). 9 (Illus.). 10 pap. 11 12.95 12 (978-1-8956889-9-3(X)); 13 22.95
14 (1-894379-00-4) 15 GDPD 16 CAN 17 (Owl Greey). 18 *Dist:* Firefly Bks Limited

Note: Items containing a distributor symbol should be ordered from the distributor, not the publisher.

KEY

1 Title
2 Subtitle
3 Contributor
4 Edition information
5 Publication year
6 Number of pages
7 Audience
8 Grade information
9 Illustrated
10 Binding type
11 Price
12 International Standard Book Number
13 Additional price
14 Corresponding ISBN
15 Publisher symbol
16 Foriegn publisher ISO code
17 Imprint symbol
18 U.S. distributor symbol- see note

SAMPLE ENTRY PUBLISHER NAME INDEX

1 † 2 **Mosby, Inc.,** 3 *(0-323; 0-7234; 0-8016; 0-8151; 0-88416; 0-941158; 1-55664; 1-56815),* 4 Div. of Harcourt, Inc., A Harcourt Health Sciences Co., 5 Orders Addr.: 6227 Sea Harbor Dr., Orlando, FL 32887 6 Toll Free Fax: 800-235-0256 7 Toll Free: 800-543-1918 8 Edit Addr.: 11830 Westline Industrial Dr., Saint Louis, MO 63146
9 (SAN 200-2280) 10 Toll Free: 800-325-4177
11 Web site: http://www.mosby.com/
12 Dist(s): ***PennWell Corp.*** 13 *CIP.*

KEY

1 CIP Identifier
2 Publisher Name
3 ISBN Prefixes
4 Division of
5 Orders Address
6 Orders Fax
7 Orders Telephone
8 Editorial Address
9 SAN
10 Toll-Free
11 Web site
12 Distributors
13 Cataloging in Publication

SAMPLE ENTRY WHOLESALER & DISTRIBUTOR NAME INDEX

1 **New Leaf Distributing Co., Inc.,** 2 *(0-9627209),* 3 Div. of Al-Wali Corp.,
4 401 Thornton Rd., Lithia Springs, GA 30122-1557 5 (SAN 169-1449)
6 Tel: 770-948-7845; 7 Fax: 770-944-2313; 8 Toll Free Fax: 800-326-1066;
9 Toll Free: 800-326-2665
10 Email: NewLeaf-dist.com
11 Web site: http://www.NewLeaf-dist.com

KEY

1 Distributor name
2 ISBN prefix
3 Division of
4 Editorial address
5 SAN
6 Telephone
7 Fax
8 Toll free fax
9 Toll free
10 E-mail
11 Web site

PUBLISHER COUNTRY CODES

Foreign Publishers are listed with the three letter International Standards Organization (ISO) code for their country of domicile. This is the complete list of ISO codes though not all countries may be represented. The codes are mnemonic in most cases. The country names here may be shortened to a more common usage form.

AFG	AFGHANISTAN
AGO	ANGOLA
ALB	ALBANIA
AND	ANDORRA
ANT	NETHERLANDS ANTILLES
ARE	UNITED ARAB EMIRATES
ARG	ARGENTINA
ARM	ARMENIA
ASM	AMERICAN SAMOA
ATA	ANTARCTICA
ATG	ANTIGUA & BARBUDA
AUS	AUSTRALIA
AUT	AUSTRIA
AZE	AZERBAIJAN
BDI	BURUNDI
BEL	BELGIUM
BEN	BENIN
BFA	BURKINA FASO
BGD	BANGLADESH
BGR	BULGARIA
BHR	BAHRAIN
BHS	BAHAMAS
BIH	BOSNIA & HERZEGOVINA
BLR	BELARUS
BLZ	BELIZE
BMU	BERMUDA
BOL	BOLIVIA
BRA	BRAZIL
BRB	BARBADOS
BRN	BRUNEI DARUSSALAM
BTN	BHUTAN
BWA	BOTSWANA
BWI	BRITISH WEST INDIES
CAF	CENTRAL AFRICAN REP
CAN	CANADA
CH2	CHINA
CHE	SWITZERLAND
CHL	CHILE
CHN	CHINA
CIV	IVORY COAST
CMR	CAMEROON
COD	ZAIRE
COG	CONGO (BRAZZAVILLE)
COL	COLOMBIA
COM	COMOROS
CPV	CAPE VERDE
CRI	COSTA RICA
CS	CZECHOSLOVAKIA
CUB	CUBA
CYM	CAYMAN ISLANDS
CYP	CYPRUS
CZE	CZECH REPUBLIC
DEU	GERMANY
DJI	DJIBOUTI
DMA	DOMINICA
DNK	DENMARK
DOM	DOMINICAN REPUBLIC
DZA	ALGERIA
ECU	ECUADOR
EG	East Germany
EGY	EGYPT
EI	EUROPEAN UNION
EN	England
ESP	SPAIN
EST	ESTONIA
ETH	ETHIOPIA
FIN	FINLAND
FJI	FIJI
FLK	FALKLAND ISLANDS
FRA	FRANCE
FRO	FAEROE ISLANDS
FSM	MICRONESIA
GAB	GABON
GBR	UNITED KINGDOM
GEO	GEORGIA
GHA	GHANA
GIB	GIBRALTAR
GIN	GUINEA
GLP	GUADELOUPE
GMB	GAMBIA
GNB	GUINEA-BISSAU
GNQ	EQUATORIAL GUINEA
GRC	GREECE
GRD	GRENADA
GRL	GREENLAND
GTM	GUATEMALA
GUF	FRENCH GUIANA
GUM	GUAM
GUY	GUYANA
HKG	HONG KONG
HND	HONDURAS
HRV	Croatia
HTI	HAITI
HUN	HUNGARY
IDN	INDONESIA
IND	INDIA
IRL	IRELAND
IRN	IRAN
IRQ	IRAQ
ISL	ICELAND
ISR	ISRAEL
ITA	ITALY
JAM	JAMAICA
JOR	JORDAN
JPN	JAPAN
KAZ	KAZAKSTAN
KEN	KENYA
KGZ	KYRGYZSTAN
KHM	CAMBODIA
KNA	ST. KITTS-NEVIS
KO	Korea
KOR	SOUTH KOREA
KOS	KOSOVA
KWT	KUWAIT
LAO	LAOS
LBN	LEBANON
LBR	LIBERIA
LBY	LIBYA
LCA	ST. LUCIA
LIE	LIECHTENSTEIN
LKA	SRI LANKA
LSO	LESOTHO
LTU	LITHUANIA
LUX	LUXEMBOURG
LVA	LATVIA
MAC	MACAO
MAR	MOROCCO
MCO	MONACO
MDA	MOLDOVA
MDG	MALAGASY REPUBLIC
MDV	MALDIVE ISLANDS
MEX	MEXICO
MHL	MARSHALL ISLANDS
MKD	MACEDONIA
MLI	MALI
MLT	MALTA
MMR	UNION OF MYANMAR
MNE	MONTENEGRO
MNG	MONGOLIA
MOZ	MOZAMBIQUE
MRT	MAURITANIA
MSR	MONTESERRAT
MTQ	MARTINIQUE
MUS	MAURITIUS
MWI	MALAWI
MYS	MALAYSIA
NAM	NAMIBIA
NCL	NEW CALEDONIA
NER	NIGER
NGA	NIGERIA
NIC	NICARAGUA
NLD	THE NETHERLANDS
NOR	NORWAY
NPL	NEPAL
NRU	NAURU
NZL	NEW ZEALAND
OMN	SULTANATE OF OMAN
PAK	PAKISTAN
PAN	PANAMA
PER	PERU
PHL	PHILIPPINES
PNG	PAPUA NEW GUINEA
POL	POLAND
PRI	Puerto Rico
PRK	NORTH KOREA
PRT	PORTUGAL
PRY	PARAGUAY
PYF	FRENCH POLYNESIA
REU	REUNION
ROM	RUMANIA
RUS	RUSSIA
RWA	RWANDA
SAU	SAUDI ARABIA
SC	Scotland
SCG	SERBIA & MONTENEGRO
SDN	SUDAN
SEN	SENEGAL
SGP	SINGAPORE
SLB	SOLOMON ISLANDS
SLE	SIERRA LEONE
SLV	EL SALVADOR
SMR	SAN MARINO
SOM	SOMALIA

PUBLISHER COUNTRY CODES

STP	SAO TOME E PRINCIPE
SU	Soviet Union
SUR	SURINAM
SVK	Slovakia
SVN	SLOVENIA
SWE	SWEDEN
SWZ	SWAZILAND
SYC	SEYCHELLES
SYN	SYNDETICS
SYR	SYRIA
TCA	TURKS NDS
TCD	CHAD
TGO	TOGO
THA	THAILAND
TKM	TURKMENISTAN
TON	TONGA
TTO	TRINIDAD AND TOBAGO
TUN	TUNISIA
TUR	TURKEY
TWN	TAIWAN
TZA	TANZANIA
UGA	UGANDA
UI	UNITED KINGDOM
UKR	UKRAINE
UN	UNITED NATIONS
URY	URUGUAY
USA	UNITED STATES
UZB	UZBEKISTAN
VAT	VATICAN CITY
VCT	ST. VINCENT
VEN	VENEZUELA
VGB	BRITISH VIRGIN ISLANDS
VIR	U.S. VIRGIN ISLANDS
VNM	VIETNAM
VUT	VANUATU
WA	Wales
WSM	WESTERN SAMOA
YEM	REPUBLIC OF YEMEN
YUG	YUGOSLAVIA
ZAF	SOUTH AFRICA
ZMB	ZAMBIA
ZWE	ZIMBABWE

COUNTRY SEQUENCE

AFGHANISTAN	AFG
ALBANIA	ALB
ALGERIA	DZA
AMERICAN SAMOA	ASM
ANDORRA	AND
ANGOLA	AGO
ANGUILLA	AIA
ANTARCTICA	ATA
ANTIGUA & BARBUDA	ATG
ARGENTINA	ARG
ARMENIA	ARM
ARUBA	ABW
AUSTRALIA	AUS
AUSTRIA	AUT
AZERBAIJAN	AZE
BAHAMAS	BHS
BAHRAIN	BHR
BANGLADESH	BGD
BARBADOS	BRB
BELARUS	BLR
BELGIUM	BEL
BELIZE	BLZ
BENIN	BEN
BERMUDA	BMU
BHUTAN	BTN
BOLIVIA	BOL
BOSNIA & HERZEGOVINA	BIH
BOTSWANA	BWA
BOUVET ISLAND	BVT
BRAZIL	BRA
BRITISH INDIAN OCEAN TERRITORY	IOT
BRITISH WEST INDIES	BWI
BRUNEI DARUSSALAM	BRN
BULGARIA	BGR
BURKINA FASO	BFA
BURUNDI	BDI
CAMBODIA	KHM
CAMEROON	CMR
CANADA	CAN
CAPE VERDE	CPV
CAYMAN ISLANDS	CYM
CENTRAL AFRICAN REPUBLIC	CAF
CHAD	TCD
CHILE	CHL
CHINA	CHN
CHRISTMAS ISLAND	CXR
COCOS (KEELING) ISLANDS	CCK
COLOMBIA	COL
COMOROS	COM
CONGO	COG

CONGO, THE DEMOCRATIC REPUBLIC OF THE CONGO	COD
COOK ISLANDS	COK
COSTA RICA	CRI
COTE' D' IVOIRE	CIV
CROATIA	HRV
CUBA	CUB
CYPRUS	CYP
CZECH REPUBLIC	CZE
CZECHOSLOVAKIA	CSK
DENMARK	DNK
DJIBOUTI	DJI
DOMINICA	DMA
DOMINICAN REPUBLIC	DOM
EAST TIMOR	TMP
ECUADOR	ECU
EGYPT (ARAB REPUBLIC OF EGYPT)	EGY
EL SALVADOR	SLV
EQUATORIAL GUINEA	GNQ
ERITREA	ERI
ESTONIA	EST
ETHIOPIA	ETH
EAST GERMANY	DDR
FALKLAND ISLANDS	FLK
FAROE ISLANDS	FRO
FEDERATED STATES OF MICRONESIA	FSM
FIJI	FJI
FINLAND	FIN
FRANCE	FRA
FRENCH GUIANA	GUF
FRENCH POLYNESIA	PYF
FRENCH SOUTHERN TERRITORIES	ATF
GABON	GAB
GAMBIA	GMB
GEORGIA	GEO
GERMANY	DEU
GHANA	GHA
GIBRALTAR	GIB
GREECE	GRC
GREENLAND	GRL
GRENADA	GRD
GUADELOUPE	GLP
GUAM	GUM
GUATEMALA	GTM
GUINEA	GIN
GUINEA-BISSAU	GNB
GUYANA	GUY
HAITI	HTI
HEARD ISLAND & MCDONALD ISLANDS	HMD

HONDURAS	HND
HONG KONG	HKG
HUNGARY	HUN
ICELAND	ISL
INDIA	IND
INDONESIA	IDN
IRAN, ISLAMIC REPUBLIC OF	IRN
IRAQ	IRQ
IRELAND	IRL
ISRAEL	ISR
ITALY	ITA
JAMAICA	JAM
JAPAN	JPN
JORDAN	JOR
KAZAKSTAN	KAZ
KENYA	KEN
KIRIBATI	KIR
KOREA, DEMOCRATIC PEOPLE'S REPUBLIC OF	PRK
KOREA, REPUBLIC OF	KOR
KUWAIT	KWT
KYRGYZSTAN	KGZ
KOSOVA	KOS
LAO PEOPLE'S DEMOCRATIC REPUBLIC	LAO
LATVIA	LVA
LEBANON	LBN
LESOTHO	LSO
LIBERIA	LBR
LIBYAN ARAB JAMAHIRIYA	LBY
LIECHTENSTEIN	LIE
LITHUANIA	LTU
LUXEMBOURG	LUX
MACAU	MAC
MACEDONIA, THE FORMER YUGOSLAV REPUBLIC OF	MKD
MADAGASCAR	MDG
MALAWI	MWI
MALAYSIA	MYS
MALDIVE ISLANDS	MDV
MALI	MLI
MALTA	MLT
MARSHALL ISLANDS	MHL
MARTINIQUE	MTQ
MAURITANIA	MRT
MAURITIUS	MUS
MAYOTTE	MYT
MEXICO	MEX
MOLDOVA, REPUBLIC OF	MDA
MONACO	MCO

COUNTRY SEQUENCE

MONGOLIA	MNG
MONTENEGRO	MNE
MONTSERRAT	MSR
MOROCCO	MAR
MOZAMBIQUE	MOZ
MYANMAR	MMR
NAMIBIA	NAM
NAURU	NRU
NEPAL	NPL
NETHERLANDS	NLD
NETHERLANDS ANTILLES	ANT
NEW CALEDONIA	NCL
NEW ZEALAND	NZL
NICARAGUA	NIC
NIGER	NER
NIGERIA	NGA
NIUE	NIU
NORFOLK ISLAND	NFK
NORTHERN MARIANA ISLANDS	MNP
NORWAY	NOR
OMAN	OMN
OCCUPIED PALESTINIAN TERRITORY	PSE
PAKISTAN	PAK
PALAU	PLW
PANAMA	PAN
PAPUA NEW GUINEA	PNG
PARAGUAY	PRY
PERU	PER
PHILIPPINES	PHL
PITCAIRN	PCN
POLAND	POL
PORTUGAL	PRT
PUERTO RICO	PRI
QATAR	QAT
REUNION	REU
ROMANIA	ROM
RUSSIAN FEDERATION	RUS
RWANDA	RWA
SAINT HELENA	SHN
SAINT KITTS & NEVIS	KNA
SAINT PIERRE & MIQUELON	SPM
SAINT VINCENT & THE GRENADINES	VCT
SAMOA	WSM
SAN MARINO	SMR
SAO TOME E PRINCIPE	STP
SAUDI ARABIA	SAU
SENEGAL	SEN
SERBIA	SRB
SERBIA & MONTENEGRO	SCG
SEYCHELLES	SYC
SIERRA LEONE	SLE
SINGAPORE	SGP
SLOVAKIA	SVK
SLOVENIA	SVN
SOLOMON ISLANDS	SLB
SOMALIA	SOM
SOUTH AFRICA	ZAF
SOUTH GEORGIA & THE SANDWICH ISLANDS	SGS
SPAIN	ESP
SRI LANKA	LKA
ST. LUCIA	LCA
SUDAN	SDN
SURINAME	SUR
SVALBARD & JAN MAYEN	SJM
SWAZILAND	SWZ
SWEDEN	SWE
SWITZERLAND	CHE
SYRIAN ARAB REPUBLIC	SYR
TAIWAN, REPUBLIC OF CHINA	TWN
TAJIKISTAN	TJK
TANZANIA, UNITED REPUBLIC OF	TZA
THAILAND	THA
TOGO	TGO
TOKELAU	TKL
TONGA	TON
TRINIDAD & TOBAGO	TTO
TUNISIA	TUN
TURKEY	TUR
TURKMENISTAN	TKM
TURKS & CAICOS ISLANDS	TCA
TUVALU	TUV
U.S.S.R.	SUN
UGANDA	UGA
UKRAINE	UKR
UNITED ARAB EMIRATES	UAE
UNITED KINGDOM	GBR
UNITED STATES	USA
UNITED STATES MINOR OUTLYING ISLANDS	UMI
URUGUAY	URY
UZBEKISTAN	UZB
VANUATU	VUT
VATICAN CITY STATE (HOLY SEE)	VAT
VENEZUELA	VEN
VIET NAM	VNM
VIRGIN ISLANDS, BRITISH	VGB
VIRGIN ISLANDS, U. S.	VIR
WALLIS & FUTUNA	WLF
WESTERN SAHARA	ESH
West Germany	BRD
YEMEN	YEM
YUGOSLAVIA	YUG
ZAMBIA	ZMB
ZIMBABWE	ZWE
ZAIRE	ZAR

LANGUAGE CODES

ACE	Achioli
AFA	Afro-Asiatic
AFR	Afrikaans
AKK	Akkadian
ALB	Albanian
ALE	Aleut
ALG	Algonquin
AMH	Amharic
ANG	Anglo-Saxon
APA	Apache
ARA	Arabic
ARC	Aramaic
ARM	Armenian
ARN	Araucanian
ARP	Arapaho
ARW	Arawak
ASM	Assamese
AVA	Avar
AVE	Avesta
AYM	Aymara
AZE	Azerbaijani
BAK	Bashkir
BAL	Baluchi
BAM	Bambara
BAQ	Basque
BAT	Baltic
BEJ	Beja
BEL	Belorussian
BEM	Bemba
BEN	Bengali
BER	Berber Group
BIH	Bihari
BLA	Blackfoot
BRE	Breton
BUL	Bulgarian
BUR	Burmese
CAD	Caddo
CAI	Central American
CAM	Cambodian
CAR	Carib
CAT	Catalan
CAU	Caucasian
CEL	Celtic Group
CHB	Chibcha
CHE	Chechen
CHI	Chinese
CHN	Chinook
CHO	Choctaw
CHR	Cherokee
CHU	Church Slavic
CHV	Chuvash
CHY	Cheyenne
COP	Coptic
COR	Cornish
CRE	Cree
CRO	Croatian
CRP	Creoles and Pidgins
CUS	Cushitic
CZE	Czech
DAK	Dakota
DAN	Danish
DEL	Delaware
DIN	Dinka
DOI	Dogri
DRA	Dravidian
DUA	Duala
DUT	Dutch
EFI	Efik
EGY	Egyptian
ELX	Elamite
ENG	English
ENM	English, Middle
ESK	Eskimo
RUM	Romanian
RUN	Rundi
RUS	Russian
SAD	Sandawe
SAG	Sango
SAI	South American
SAM	Samaritan
SAN	Sanskrit
SAO	Sampan
SBC	Serbo-Croatian
SCO	Scots
SEL	Selkup
SEM	Semitic
SER	Serbian
SHN	Shan
SHO	Shona
SID	Sidamo
SIO	Siouan Languages
SIT	Sino-Tibetan
SLA	Slavic
SLO	Slovak
SLV	Slovenian
SMO	Samoan
SND	Sindhi
SNH	Singhalese
SOG	Sogdian
SOM	Somali
SON	Songhai
ESP	Esperanto
EST	Estonian
ETH	Ethiopic
EWE	Ewe
FAN	Fang
FAR	Faroese
FEM	French, Middle
FIJ	Fijian
FIN	Finnish
FIU	Finno-Ugrian
FLE	Flemish
FON	Fon
FRE	French
FRI	Frisian
FRO	French, Old
GAA	Ga
GAE	Gaelic
GAG	Gallegan
GAL	Galla
GEC	Greek, Classical
GEH	German, Middle h
GEM	Germanic
GEO	Georgian
GER	German
GLG	Galician
GOH	German, Old High
GON	Gondi
GOT	Gothic
GRE	Greek
GUA	Guarani
GUJ	Gujarati
HAU	Hausa
HAW	Hawaiian
HEB	Hebrew
HER	Herero
HIL	Hiligaynon
HIN	Hindi
HUN	Hungarian
HUP	Hupa
IBA	Iban
IBO	Igbo
ICE	Icelandic
IKU	Inuktitut
ILO	Ilocano
INC	Indic
IND	Indonesian
INE	Indo-European
INT	Interlingua
IRA	Iranian
IRI	Irish
IRO	Iroquois
ITA	Italian
JAV	Javanese
JPN	Japanese
KAA	Karakalpak
KAC	Kachin
KAM	Kamba
KAN	Kannada
KAR	Karen
KAS	Kashmiri
KAU	Kanuri
KAZ	Kazakh
KHA	Khasi
KHM	Khmer, Central
KIK	Kikuyu
KIN	Kinyarwanda
KIR	Kirghiz
KOK	Konkani
KON	Kongo
KOR	Korean
KPE	Kpelle
KRO	Kru
KRU	Kurukh
SOT	Sotho, Southern
SPA	Spanish
SRD	Sardinian
SRR	Serer
SSA	Sub-Saharan
SUK	Sukuma
SUN	Sundanese
SUS	Susu
SUX	Sumerian
SWA	Swahili
SWE	Swedish
SYR	Syriac
TAG	Tagalog
TAJ	Tajik
TAM	Tamil
TAR	Tatar
TEL	Telugu
TEM	Temne
TER	Tereno
THA	Thai
TIB	Tibetan
TIG	Tigre
TIR	Tigrinya
TOG	Tonga, Nyasa

LANGUAGE CODES

TON	Tonga, Tonga
TSI	Tsimshian
TSO	Tsonga
TSW	Tswana
KUA	Kwanyama
KUR	Kurdish
LAD	Ladino
LAH	Lahnda
LAM	Lamba
LAO	Laotian
LAP	Lapp
LAT	Latin
LAV	Latvian
LIN	Lingala
LIT	Lithuanian
LOL	Lolo
LUB	Luba
LUG	Luganda
LUI	Luiseno
MAC	Macedonian
MAI	Maithili
MAL	Malayalam
MAN	Mandingo
MAO	Maori
MAP	Malayo-Polynesian
MAR	Marathi
MAS	Masai
MAY	Malay
MEN	Mende
MIC	Micmac
MIS	Miscellaneous
MLA	Malagasy
MLT	Malteses
MNO	Manobo
MOL	Moldavian
MON	Mongol
MOS	Mossi
MUL	Multiple Languages
MUS	Muskogee
MYN	Mayan
NAI	North American
NAV	Navaho
NBL	Ndebele, Southern
NDE	Ndebele, Northern
NEP	Nepali
NEW	Newari
NIC	Niger-Congo
NNO	Norwegian
NOB	Norwegian Bokmal
NOR	Norwegian
NSO	Sotho, Northern
NUB	Nubian
NYA	Nyanja
NYM	Nyamwezi
NYO	Nyoro Group
OES	Ossetic
OJI	Ojibwa
ORI	Oriya
OSA	Osage
OTO	Otomi
PAA	Papuan-Australian
PAH	Pahari
PAL	Pahlavi
PAN	Panjabi
PEO	Persian, Old
PER	Persian, Modern
PLI	Pali
POL	Polish
POR	Portuguese
PRA	Prakrit
PRO	Provencal
PUS	Pushto
QUE	Quechua
RAJ	Rajasthani
ROA	Romance
ROH	Romanish
ROM	Romany
TUK	Turkmen
TUR	Turkish
TUT	Turko-Tataric
TWI	Twi
UGA	Ugaritic
UIG	Uigur
UKR	Ukrainian
UMB	Umbundu
UND	Undetermined
URD	Urdu
UZB	Uzbek
VIE	Vietnamese
VOT	Votic
WAL	Walamo
WAS	Washo
WEL	Welsh
WEN	Wendic
WOL	Wolof
XHO	Xhosa
YAO	Yao
YID	Yiddish
YOR	Yoruba
ZAP	Zapotec
ZEN	Zenaga
ZUL	Zulu
ZUN	Zuni

LIST OF ABBREVIATIONS

Abr.	abridged
act. bk.	activity book
adapt.	adapted
aft.	afterword
alt.	alternate
Amer.	American
anniv.	anniversary
anno.	annotated by
annot.	annotation(s)
ans.	answer(s)
app.	appendix
Apple II	Apple II disk
approx.	approximately
assn.	association
audio	analog audio cassette
auth.	author
bd.	bound
bdg.	binding
bds.	boards
bibl(s).	bibliography(ies)
bk(s).	book(s)
bklet(s).	booklet(s)
boxed	boxed set, slipcase or caseboard
Bro.	Brother
C	college audience level
co.	company
comm.	commission, committee
comment.	commentaries
comp.	complied
cond.	condensed
contrib.	contributed
corp.	corporation
dept.	department
des	designed
diag(s).	diagram(s)
digital audio	digital audio cassette
dir.	director
disk	software disk or diskette
dist.	distributed
Div.	Division
doz.	dozen
ea.	each
ed.	edited, edition, editor
eds.	editions, editors
educ.	education
elem.	elementary
ency.	encyclopedia
ENG	English
enl.	enlarged
epil.	epilogue
exp.	expanded
expr.	experiments
expurg.	expurgated
fac.	facsimile
fasc.	fascicule
fict.	fiction
fig(s).	figure(s)
flmstrp.	filmstrip
footn.	
for.	foreign
frwd.	foreword
gen.	general
gr.	grade(s)
hndbk.	handbook
illus.	Illustrated, illustration(s), Illustrator(s)
in prep.	in preparation
incl.	includes, including
info.	information
inst.	institute
intro.	introduction
ISBN	International Standard Book Number
ISO	International Standards Organization
ITA	Italian
i.t.a.	initial teaching alphabet
J.	juvenile audience level
JPN	Japanese
Jr.	Junior
jt. auth.	joint author
jt. ed.	joint editor
k	kindergarten audience level
lab	laboratory
lang(s).	language(s)
LC	Library of Congress
lea.	leather
lib.	library
lib. bdg.	library binding
lit.	literature, literary
lp	record, album, long playing
l.t.	large type
ltd.	limited
ltd. ed.	limited edition
mac hd	144M, Mac
mac ld	800K, Mac
mass mkt.	mass market paperbound
math.	mathematics
mic. film	microfilm
mic form	microform
mod.	modern
MS(S)	manuscript(s)
natl.	national
net	net price
no(s).	number(s)
o.p.	out of print
orig.	original text, not a reprint (paperback)
o.s.i.	out of stock indefinitely
p.	pages
pap.	paper
per.	perfect binding
photos	photographer, photographs
pop. ed.	Popular edition
prep.	preparation
probs.	problems
prog. bk.	programmed books
ps.	preschool audience level
pseud.	pseudonym
pt(s).	part(s)
pub.	published, publisher publishing
pubn.	publication
ref(s).	reference(s)
rep.	reprint
reprod(s).	reproduction(s)
ret.	retold by
rev.	revised
rpm.	revolution per minute (phono records)
SAN	Standard Address Number
S&L	signed and limited
sec.	section
sel.	selected
ser.	series
Soc.	society
sols.	solutions
s.p.	school price
Sr. (after given name)	Senior
Sr. (before given name	Sister
St.	Saint
stu.	student manual, study guide, etc.
subs.	subsidiary
subsc.	subscription
suppl.	supplement
tech.	technical
text ed.	text edition
tr.	translated, translation translator
trans.	transparencies
unabr.	unabridged
unexpurg.	unexpurgated
univ.	university
var.	variorum
vdisk	videodisk
VHS	video, VHS format
vol(s).	volume(s)
wkbk.	workbook
YA	Young adult audience level
yrbk.	yearbook
3.5 hd	1.44M, 3.5 disk, DOS
3.5 ld	720, 3.5 Disk, DOS
5.25 hd	1.2M, 5.25 Disk, DOS
5.25 ld	360K, 5.25 Disk, DOS

AUTHOR INDEX

Volume 3

O – Z

O

O

—Maine. (p. 1383)
—Massachusetts. (p. 1417)
—Mexico/México. (p. 1454)
—Mexico/México. Benson, Megan, tr. (p. 1454)
—Michigan. (p. 1458)
—Missouri. (p. 1482)
—Nevada. (p. 1589)
—New Mexico. (p. 1595)
—New York / Nueva York. (p. 1598)
—Puerto Rico. (p. 1811)
Obregon, Jose Maria. Ronaldhino. (p. 1902)
Obregón, José María. Texas. (p. 2209)
—Utah. (p. 2342)
—Wisconsin. (p. 2477)
Obregon, Jose Maria, illus. see Daning, Tom.
Obregón, José María, illus. see Faust, Daniel R.
Obregon, Jose Maria, illus. see Herdling, Glenn.
Obregón, José María, jt. auth. see Daning, Tom.
Obregón, José María, jt. auth. see Faust, Daniel R.
Obregón, José María, jt. auth. see Herdling, Glenn.
Obregón, José María, jt. auth. see Nelson, John.
Obregon, Jose Maria, tr. see Daning, Tom.
Obregón, José María, tr. see DeMolay, Jack.
Obregon, Jose Maria, tr. see Twine, Alice.
O'Brian, Matt. Bill Arp's Peace Papers (Classic Reprint) (p. 226)
O'Brian, Pliny. Empires, Crusaders, & Invasions Through the Middle Ages. (p. 645)
—Feudalism in Medieval Europe. (p. 721)
—Knights: Warriors of the Middle Ages. (p. 1228)
—Myths of the Ancient Romans. (p. 1572)
O'Brian, Virginia. Librarian's Job. (p. 1284)
O'Brien, Alex. Comeback. (p. 428)
—Playmaker. (p. 1761)
O'Brien, Andrew & O'Brien, Emma. Little Bubishi: A History of Karate for Children. (p. 1313)
O'Brien, Anne. Patches in Her Dreams: An Alaskan Children's Story. (p. 1704)
O'Brien, Anne Sibley. Hocus Pocus, It's Fall! Gal, Susan, illus. (p. 986)
—I'm New Here. (p. 1098)
—I'm New Here. O'Brien, Anne Sibley, Illus. (p. 1098)
—In the Shadow of the Sun. (p. 1111)
—Path of Stars. O'Brien, Anne Sibley, illus. (p. 1704)
—Someone New. O'Brien, Anne Sibley, illus. (p. 2060)
O'Brien, Anne Sibley, illus. see Avraham, Kate Aver.
O'Brien, Anne Sibley, illus. see Coburn, Jewell Reinhart & Lee, Tzexa Cherta.
O'Brien, Anne Sibley, illus. see Havill, Juanita.
O'Brien, Anne Sibley, illus. see Knight, Margy Burns.
O'Brien, Anne Sibley, jt. auth. see Gal, Susan.
O'Brien, Anne Sibley & O'Brien, Perry Edmond. After Gandhi: One Hundred Years of Nonviolent Resistance. (p. 33)
—After Gandhi: One Hundred Years of Nonviolent Resistance. O'Brien, Anne Sibley & O'Brien, Perry Edmond, illus. (p. 33)
O'Brien, Annemarie. Lara's Gift. (p. 1244)
O'Brien, Bob, illus. see Christine, Medicus.
O'Brien, Bob, illus. see Medicus, Christine.
O'Brien, Bridget. Alligators: Level 1. (p. 56)
—Alligators Eat & Grow: Level 2. (p. 56)
—Alligators in the Swamp: Level 3. (p. 56)
—Deer. Keimig, Candice & LaViolette, Renee, illus. (p. 525)
—Deer Eat & Grow. Keimig, Candice & LaViolette, Renee, illus. (p. 525)
—Deer in the Woods. Keimig, Candice & LaViolette, Renee, illus. (p. 525)
O'Brien, Caragh M. Birthmarked. (p. 234)
—Keep of Ages. (p. 1207)
—Prized. (p. 1802)
—Promised: The Birthmarked Trilogy. (p. 1806)
O'Brien, Carola. Bobby Dazzler & the Three Rubies of Ishmalan. (p. 252)
O'Brien, Christine, illus. see Heiss, Renee & Stewart, Gary a.
O'Brien, Cynthia. Amazing Brain Mysteries. (p. 64)
—Bringing Back the American Alligator. (p. 282)
—Bringing Back the Gray Wolf. (p. 282)
—Cultural Traditions in Iceland. (p. 484)
—Cultural Traditions in Sri Lanka. (p. 484)
—Dream Jobs in Green & Sustainable Living. (p. 601)
—Dream Jobs in Transportation, Distribution & Logistics. (p. 601)
—Explore with Christopher Columbus. (p. 680)
—Explore with Francisco Pizarro. (p. 680)
—Explore with Giovanni Da Verrazzano. (p. 680)
—Explore with John Franklin. (p. 680)
—Explore with Marquette & Jolliet. (p. 680)
—Explore with Ponce de León. (p. 680)
—Explore with Samuel de Champlain. (p. 680)
—Explore with Sieur de la Salle. (p. 680)
—Explore with Stanley & Livingstone. (p. 680)
—Fairy Myths. (p. 697)
—Go West: First Contact with Native Nations. (p. 849)
—Go West with Merchants & Traders. (p. 849)
—Go West with Miners, Prospectors, & Loggers. (p. 849)
—Innovations in Communication. (p. 1121)
—Innovations in Safety. (p. 1121)
—Lost Treasures. (p. 1356)
—Mermaid Myths. (p. 1449)
—Myths & Legends of North America: Canada & the Northern United States. (p. 1571)
—Parts Work Together. (p. 1702)
—Pathways Through North America. (p. 1705)
—Polar Animals. Bracken, Carolyn, illus. (p. 1769)
—Searching for Extraterrestrials. (p. 1971)
—Technology & You! (p. 2197)
—Technology Then & Now. (p. 2198)
—What Is Technology? (p. 2416)
—Your Guide to Knights & the Age of Chivalry. (p. 2533)
—Your Guide to the Arts in the Middle Ages. (p. 2533)
O'Brien, Cynthia, jt. auth. see Corporate Contributor Staff.
O'Brien, Cynthia, jt. auth. see Dalrymple, Lisa.
O'Brien, Cynthia, contrib. by. Fairy Myths. (p. 697)
O'Brien, Cynthia, et al. Best & Buzzworthy 2017: World Records, Trending Topics, & Viral Moments. (p. 205)
Obrien, Cynthia Kern. I Used to Be a Fairy... A True Story by Granny. Gillen, Rosemarie, illus. (p. 1083)
O'Brien, Daniel. Your Presidential Fantasy Dream Team. Rowntree, Winston, illus. (p. 2534)
O'Brien, Derek. Bournvita Quiz Contest Collector's Edition. (p. 265)
O'Brien, Derek, intro. Great Indian Speeches for Children. (p. 887)
O'Brien, Dillon. Dalys of Dalystown (Classic Reprint) (p. 498)
O'Brien, Duncan. Matson the Mouse. Drage, Robyn, illus. (p. 1425)
O'Brien, Edward J. Best Short Stories of 1922 & the Yearbook of the American Short Story (Classic Reprint) (p. 207)
—Great Modern English Stories an Anthology Compiled & Edited: With an Introduction (Classic Reprint) (p. 887)
O'Brien, Edward Joseph. Best British Short Stories of 1922 (Classic Reprint) (p. 205)
—Best Short Stories Of 1919: And the Yearbook of the American Short Story (Classic Reprint) (p. 207)
—Best Short Stories of 1919, & the Yearbook of the American Short Story (Classic Reprint) (p. 207)
—Great Modern English Stories: An Anthology (Classic Reprint) (p. 887)
O'Brien, Edward Joseph Harrington. 50 Best American Short Stories, 1915-1939 (Classic Reprint) (p. 2555)
O'Brien, Edward L. Best Short Stories Of 1915: And the Yearbook of the American Short Story (Classic Reprint) (p. 207)
O'Brien, Fitz James. Poems & Stories of Fitz-James O'Brien: Collected & Edited, with a Sketch of the Author (Classic Reprint) (p. 1765)
O'Brien, Frances. Lasell Leaves, Vol. 44: October, 1918 (Classic Reprint) (p. 1246)
O'Brien, Frederick. Atolls of the Sun (Classic Reprint) (p. 134)
—Mystic Isles of the South Seas (Classic Reprint) (p. 1571)
O'Brien, Georgina. Twentieth-Century Hero (Classic Reprint) (p. 2304)
O'Brien, Gregory, illus. see De Goldi, Kate.
O'Brien, Gretchen. Education in California (California) (p. 626)
O'Brien, Howard Vincent. New Men for Old (Classic Reprint) (p. 1595)
—Thirty (Classic Reprint) (p. 2223)
O'Brien, Joe. Alfie Green & the Conker King. Texier, Jean, illus. (p. 43)
—Beyond the Cherry Tree. McGann, Oisín, illus. (p. 212)
—Curious Elf. (p. 486)
—Legends' Lair. (p. 1263)
—Tiger Boots. (p. 2241)
O'Brien, John, illus. see Bader, Bonnie & Who HQ.
O'Brien, John, illus. see Branley, Franklyn M.
O'Brien, John, illus. see Buckley, James, Jr., et al.
O'Brien, John, illus. see Castrovilla, Selene.
O'Brien, John, illus. see D'Agnese, Joseph.
O'Brien, John, illus. see Demuth, Patricia Brennan & Who HQ.
O'Brien, John, illus. see Edgers, Geoff & Who HQ.
O'brien, John, illus. see Edgers, Geoff.
O'Brien, John, illus. see Edwards, Roberta & Who HQ.
O'Brien, John, illus. see Fradin, Dennis Brindell & Who HQ.
O'brien, John, illus. see Fradin, Dennis Brindell.
O'Brien, John, illus. see Frith, Margaret & Who HQ.
O'brien, John, illus. see Frith, Margaret.
O'Brien, John, illus. see Herman, Gail & Who HQ.
O'brien, John, illus. see Herman, Gail.
O'Brien, John, illus. see Holub, Joan & Who HQ.
O'brien, John, illus. see Holub, Joan.
O'Brien, John, illus. see Jones, Charlotte Foltz.
O'Brien, John, illus. see Kelley, True & Who HQ.
O'Brien, John, illus. see Mannis, Celeste & Who HQ.
O'Brien, John, illus. see McDonough, Yona Zeldis & Who HQ.
O'brien, John, illus. see Pollack, Pam & Belviso, Meg.
O'Brien, John, illus. see Pollack, Pam, et al.
O'Brien, John, illus. see Prince, April Jones & Who HQ.
O'brien, John, illus. see Prince, April Jones.
O'Brien, John, illus. see Rau, Dana Meachen & Who HQ.
O'brien, John, illus. see Rau, Dana Meachen.
O'Brien, John, illus. see Reed, Avery & Who HQ.
O'brien, John, illus. see Reed, Avery.
O'Brien, John, illus. see Rosenstock, Barb.
O'brien, John, illus. see Schroeder, Alan.
O'Brien, John, illus. see Stine, Megan & Who HQ.
O'Brien, John, illus. see Who HQ & O'Connor, Jim.
O'Brien, John A. Elves, Gnomes, & Other Little People Coloring Book. (p. 640)
O'Brien, Johnny. Day of Deliverance. Hardcastle, Nick, illus. (p. 513)
—Day of the Assassins: A Jack Christie Novel Hardcastle, Nick, illus. (p. 514)
—Day of the Assassins. Hardcastle, Nick, illus. (p. 514)
O'Brien, Josh, illus. see Syswerda, Jean E.
O'Brien, Kathryn. Be Still. Flint, Gillian, illus. (p. 177)
—Give Thanks. Flint, Gillian, illus. (p. 840)
—I Can. Flint, Gillian, illus. (p. 1061)
Obrien, Kathryn & Kathryn, Obrien. World Spinning Adventures of Brianna & Nicole. (p. 2505)
O'Brien, Keith. Fly Girls Young Readers' Edition: How Five Daring Women Defied All Odds & Made Aviation History. (p. 754)
O'Brien, Kelan. I Couldn't Find the Morning Time. (p. 1064)
O'Brien, Kim. Caballos Paint. Strictly Spanish Translation Services Staff, tr. (p. 307)
—Caballos Pura Sangre. Strictly Spanish Translation Services Staff, tr. (p. 307)
O'Brien, Lara. Chesca & the Spirit of Grace. (p. 366)
O'Brien, Leila. Candy Land Is in Trouble! (p. 322)
O'Brien, Liam & O'Brien, Noreen. Unstoppable Jimmy. Berg, Jessica, illus. (p. 2336)
O'Brien, Lindsy. Chipmunks. (p. 379)
—Communication Long Ago & Today (p. 431)
—Frogs. (p. 790)
—Squirrels. (p. 2095)
—Tarantula vs. Tarantula Hawk: Clash of the Giants. (p. 2191)
—World's Weirdest Animals. (p. 2508)
O'Brien, Lindsy, et al. Bug Battles. (p. 291)
O'Brien, Lindsy J. Chipmunks. (p. 379)
—Frogs. (p. 790)
—Squirrels. (p. 2095)
O'Brien M Ed, Jeanne B. Finding Shapes in Nature: A Discovery Book for Children. (p. 730)
O'Brien, Mandie. Molly's Christmas Gift. (p. 1490)
O'Brien, May L. Legend of the Seven Sisters: A Traditional Aboriginal Story from Western Australia. Wyatt, Sue, illus. (p. 1263)
O'Brien, Melanie. My Belly Button. (p. 1532)
—No More Diapers. (p. 1613)
O'Brien, Msgr Raymond J. Midget: The Story of a Boy Who Was Always Goin' Alone. Bartholomew, Erin, illus. (p. 1461)
—Nice Going, Red: The Story of a Boy Who Couldn't Take It. Bartholomew, Erin, illus. (p. 1602)
O'Brien Novak, Patty. Engineering the ABCs. (p. 652)
O'Brien, Pat. Outwitting the Hun: My Escape from a German Prison Camp (Classic Reprint) (p. 1686)
O'Brien, Patrick. You Are the First Kid on Mars. O'Brien, Patrick, illus. (p. 2525)
O'Brien, Patrick, illus. see O'Malley, Kevin.
O'Brien, Patrick, jt. auth. see O'Malley, Kevin.
O'Brien, Patrick Joseph. Will Rogers: Ambassador of Good Will, Prince of Wit & Wisdom (Classic Reprint) (p. 2467)
O'Brien, Perry Edmond, jt. auth. see O'Brien, Anne Sibley.
O'Brien, Private Jack. Into the Jaws of Death (Classic Reprint) (p. 1128)
O'Brien, Renee McMullen. Amazing Mocha & His Courageous Journey. O'Brien, Renee McMullen, illus. (p. 66)
O'Brien, Richard. Christopher & Joshua Go Fishing. (p. 388)
O'Brien, Seumas. Blind: A Comedy in One Act (Classic Reprint) (p. 244)
—Whale & the Grasshopper: And Other Fables (Classic Reprint) (p. 2403)
O'Brien, Sophie Raffalovich. Under Croagh Patrick (Classic Reprint) (p. 2321)
O'Brien, Terry. Little Red Book English Vocabulary Today. (p. 1326)
—Little Red Book Idioms & Phrases. (p. 1326)
—Little Red Book of Phrasal Verbs. (p. 1326)
O'Brien, Terry, ed. see Henry, O.
O'Brien, Thomas E. Magic of Finbar. (p. 1378)
O'Brien, Timothy J. Rheemer the Rhymer Rhinoceros. (p. 1874)
O'Brien, William. 'neath Silver Mask, or the Cloudland of Life (Classic Reprint) (p. 1584)
—When We Were Boys: A Novel (Classic Reprint) (p. 2434)
O'Brien-Palmer, Michelle. Life of Riley: A Solve-It Book, Repetitive Version. Engle, Amber Lena, illus. (p. 1295)
—Life of Riley: A Solve-It Book: Repetitive Edition. Engle, Amber Lena, illus. (p. 1295)
Observatory, Lick, jt. auth. see Trustees, Lick Observatory.
Observatory, Madras. Results of Observations of the Fixed Stars: Made with the Meridian Circle at the Government Observatory, Madras, in the Years 1862, 1863 & 1864 (Classic Reprint) (p. 1870)
Observatory, Manila, jt. auth. see Maso, Miguel Saderra.
Observatory, Oxford Radcliffe. Astronomical & Meteorological Observations Made at the Radcliffe Observatory, Oxford, in the Year 1864, Vol. 24 (Classic Reprint) (p. 129)
Obyn, E. A. St. Sowing & Reaping: A Story for Boys (Classic Reprint) (p. 2070)
O'Byrne, Chelsea, illus. see Heidbreder, Robert.
O'Byrne, Chelsea, illus. see Savage, Candace.
O'Byrne, Dermot. Red Owen (Classic Reprint) (p. 1858)
O'Byrne, M. L. Leixlip Castle: A Romance of the Penal Days of 1690 (Classic Reprint) (p. 1266)
O'Byrne, Nicola. Use Your Imagination. O'Byrne, Nicola, illus. (p. 2341)
—What's Next Door? O'Byrne, Nicola, illus. (p. 2425)
—Where Is Home, Daddy Bear? (p. 2437)
O'Byrne, Nicola, illus. see Bromley, Nick.
O'Byrne, Nicola, illus. see O'Dare, Helen.
O'Byrne, Nicola, illus. see Strathie, Chae.
O'Cain, Leeana, jt. auth. see Odd Dot.
O'Callaghan, Gemma, illus. see Morpurgo, Michael.
O'callaghan I Duch, Elena. color de la arena. (p. 420)
O'Callaghan i Duch, Elena. Mi Supercamión. (p. 1456)
O'Callaghan, Joanne. Found in Melbourne. Song, Kori, illus. (p. 771)
O'Callaghan, Jonathan. Basher STEM Junior: Engineering. Basher, Simon, illus. (p. 169)
—Basher STEM Junior: Math. Basher, Simon, illus. (p. 169)
—Basher STEM Junior: Science. Basher, Simon, illus. (p. 169)
—Basher STEM Junior: Technology. Basher, Simon, illus. (p. 169)
O'Campo, Allicia. Tinky Goes to North Americ. (p. 2248)
Ocampo, Jonna. On My Way to the Lilikoi Tree. (p. 1653)
Ocampo, Jonna Amato. Henry el Astronauta. (p. 955)
Ocampo, L. A. Cardboard Sisters Save the World: An Activity Storybook. (p. 328)
Ocando, Jose, tr. see Edwards, Nneka.
O'Casey, Sean. Drums of Father Ned (Classic Reprint) (p. 606)
Ocasio, Carlos, illus. see Bernart, Patrick.
Ocaya, Carlo. Mystical Tales: The Knight. (p. 1571)
—Mystical Tales: The Cursed Queen. (p. 1571)
Ocba Exam Secrets Test Prep, ed. Ohio American Government Success Strategies Study Guide: Ocba Test Review for the Ohio Computer Based Assessments. (p. 1642)
—Ohio American History Success Strategies Study Guide: Ocba Test Review for the Ohio Computer Based Assessments. (p. 1642)
—Ohio Grade 5 Science Success Strategies Study Guide: Ocba Test Review for the Ohio Computer Based Assessments. (p. 1642)
—Ohio Grade 8 Science Success Strategies Study Guide: Ocba Test Review for the Ohio Computer Based Assessments. (p. 1642)
—Ohio Physical Science Success Strategies Study Guide: Ocba Test Review for the Ohio Computer Based Assessments. (p. 1642)
Ocean, Davy. Boy Who Cried Shark. Blecha, Aaron, illus. (p. 270)
—Deep-Sea Disaster. Blecha, Aaron, illus. (p. 524)
—Deep-Sea Treasury: Deep-Sea Disaster; Lights! Camera! Hammerhead!; Squid-Napped; the Boy Who Cried Shark. Blecha, Aaron, illus. (p. 524)
—Fishin' Impossible Blecha, Aaron, illus. (p. 742)
—Fishin': Impossible. Blecha, Aaron, illus. (p. 742)
—Long Fin Silver. Blecha, Aaron, illus. (p. 1343)
—Shark Party. Blecha, Aaron, illus. (p. 2002)
—Shark School 3-Books-In-1! #2: The Boy Who Cried Shark; a Fin-Tastic Finish; Splash Dance. Blecha, Aaron, illus. (p. 2002)
—Shark School Fin-Tastic Collection Books 1-10: Deep-Sea Disaster; Lights! Camera! Hammerhead!; Squid-Napped!; the Boy Who Cried Shark; a Fin-tastic Finish; Splash Dance; Tooth or Dare; Fishin': Impossible; Long Fin Silver; Space Invaders. Blecha, Aaron, illus. (p. 2002)
—Shark School Shark-Tacular Collection Books 1-8: Deep-Sea Disaster; Lights! Camera! Hammerhead!; Squid-Napped!; the Boy Who Cried Shark; a Fin-tastic Finish; Splash Dance; Tooth or Dare; Fishin': Impossible. Blecha, Aaron, illus. (p. 2002)
—Space Invaders. Blecha, Aaron, illus. (p. 2071)
—Splash Dance. Blecha, Aaron, illus. (p. 2084)
—Tooth or Dare. Blecha, Aaron, illus. (p. 2262)
Oceanak, Karla. All Me, All the Time: The Authorized Art-O-Biography Of... Spanjer, Kendra, illus. (p. 52)
—Artsy-Fartsy. Spanjer, Kendra, illus. (p. 124)
—Bogus: An Aldo Zelnick Comic Novel. Spanjer, Kendra, illus. (p. 254)
—Cahoots: An Aldo Zelnick Comic Novel. Spanjer, Kendra, illus. (p. 308)
—Cahoots. Spanjer, Kendra, illus. (p. 308)
—Dumbstruck: An Aldo Zelnick Comic Novel. Spanjer, Kendra, illus. (p. 610)
—Dumbstruck. Spanjer, Kendra, illus. (p. 610)
—Egghead: An Aldo Zelnick Comic Novel. Spanjer, Kendra, illus. (p. 628)
—Egghead. Spanjer, Kendra, illus. (p. 628)
—Finicky: An Aldo Zelnick Comic Novel. Spanjer, Kendra, illus. (p. 731)
—Finicky. Spanjer, Kendra, illus. (p. 731)
—Glitch: An Aldo Zelnick Comic Novel. Spanjer, Kendra, illus. (p. 843)
—Glitch. Spanjer, Kendra, illus. (p. 843)
—Goodnight Unicorn: A Magical Parody. Spanjer, Kendra, illus. (p. 868)
—Hotdogger: An Aldo Zelnick Comic Novel. Spanjer, Kendra, illus. (p. 1007)
—Hotdogger. Spanjer, Kendra, illus. (p. 1007)
—Ignoramus: An Aldo Zelnick Comic Novel. Spanjer, Kendra, illus. (p. 1094)
—Ignoramus. Spanjer, Kendra, illus. (p. 1094)
—Jackpot: An Aldo Zelnick Comic Novel. Spanjer, Kendra, illus. (p. 1153)
—Kerfuffle: An Aldo Zelnick Comic Novel. Spanjer, Kendra, illus. (p. 1210)
—Kerfuffle. Spanjer, Kendra, illus. (p. 1210)
—Logjam: Book 12. Spanjer, Kendra, illus. (p. 1339)
—Logjam. Spanjer, Kendra, illus. (p. 1339)
—Mooch. Spanjer, Kendra, illus. (p. 1500)
Ocegueda, Aleida. Ópatas, Tarahumaras, Yaquis y Seris. Gutiérrez, Lorena, illus. (p. 1665)
Ocegueda, Aleida, illus. see Gutiérrez Schott, Lorena.
Oceguera, Aracely, tr. see Turk, Cheri.
Ocello, Salvatore, illus. see Nelligan, Patty.
Ochiltree, Dianne. Molly, by Golly! The Legend of Molly Williams, America's First Female Firefighter. Kemly, Kathleen, illus. (p. 1489)
Ochiltree, Henry. Redburn (Classic Reprint) (p. 1859)
Ochoa, Ana, illus. see Brozo, Patty.
Ochoa, Ana, illus. see Neasi, Barbara J.
Ochoa, Ana, illus. see Rosa-Mendoza, Gladys.
Ochoa, Ana, jt. auth. see Neasi, Barbara J.
Ochoa, Edna, tr. see Villaseñor, Victor.
Ochoa, Louisa & Benchmark Education Co., LLC Staff. Know about Storms. (p. 1229)
Ochoa, Louisa, et al. Know about Storms - Paul Takes a Walk - City Lights: BuildUp Unit 10 Lap Book. Jennings, Sarah, illus. (p. 1229)
Ochs, Tom. Day on the Farm Playing Along Dindar, Kubra, illus. (p. 514)
Ochsenheimer, Ferdinand. Die Schmetterlinge Von Europa, Vol. 5: Zweyte Abtheilung (Classic Reprint) (p. 544)
Ochsner, Gina. Hidden Letters of Velta B. (p. 966)
Ocker, J. W. Death & Douglas. (p. 521)
Ockler, Sarah. Bittersweet. (p. 235)
—Book of Broken Hearts. (p. 258)
—Pacte des Coeurs Bris's(le) (p. 1691)
—#scandal. (p. 1941)
—Summer of Chasing Mermaids. (p. 2149)
—Twenty Boy Summer. (p. 2304)
Ockside, Knight Russ. History & Records of the Elephant Club: Compiled from Authentic Documents Now in Possession of the Zoological Society (Classic Reprint) (p. 976)
Oclon, Kim. Man Up. (p. 1395)
O'Concheanainn, Toms, jt. auth. see MacManus, Seumas.
Oconis, Sandra Quinn. Adventures in Quinnland. (p. 20)
O'Connell, Bailey. Earth's Rainiest Places. (p. 618)
O'Connell, Caitlin. Baby Elephant in the Wild. O'Connell, Caitlin & Rodwell, Timothy, illus. (p. 150)
—Bridge to the Wild: Behind the Scenes at the Zoo. (p. 280)
O'Connell, Caitlin, jt. auth. see Jackson, Donna M.
O'Connell, Caitlin & Jackson, Donna M. Elephant Scientist. Rodwell, Timothy, illus. (p. 634)

O'Connell, Catherine M. Excursions in Ireland During 1844 And 1850: With a Visit to the Late Daniel o'Connell, M. P (Classic Reprint) (p. 676)
O'Connell, Daniel. Their Majesties Abroad, or Ferdinand & Isabella: An Historical Extravaganza in Two Acts (Classic Reprint) (p. 2215)
O'Connell, Dave, illus. see Krivitzky, Nathan & Nathan, Krivitzky.
O'Connell, David, illus. see Bird, Pip.
O'Connell, David, illus. see Packiam Alloway, Tracy Packiam.
O'Connell, David, illus. see Watkins, Sam.
O'Connell, David, jt. auth. see McIntyre, Sarah.
O'Connell, Díóg. Under the Moon, over the Stars: Irish Urban Street Games. (p. 2322)
O'Connell, Eleanor. Homes Around the World. (p. 998)
—Schools Around the World. (p. 1947)
—Transportation Around the World. (p. 2278)
O'Connell, Emma. We Love Blue! (p. 2391)
—We Love Green! (p. 2391)
—We Love Orange! (p. 2391)
O'Connell, Isabel. Gypsy. Scott, Susan, illus. (p. 907)
O'Connell, Jennifer. Eye of the Whale: A Rescue Story O'Connell, Jennifer, illus. (p. 688)
—It's Halloween Night! Morris, Jennifer E., illus. (p. 1145)
O'Connell, Jennifer Barrett. It's Halloween Night! (p. 1145)
O'Connell, Kay. Swanky Spider Meets Professor Pendulum. (p. 2167)
O'Connell, Kim A. Discover Ancient Greece. (p. 554)
O'Connell, Lorraine, illus. see Random House Staff.
O'Connell, Mary. Dear Reader: A Novel. (p. 520)
O'Connell, Rebecca. Baby Goes Beep. Wilson-Max, Ken, illus. (p. 150)
—Baby Parade. Poole, Susie, illus. (p. 152)
—Baby Party. Poole, Susie, illus. (p. 152)
—Penina Levine Is a Hard-boiled Egg. Lue Sue, Majella, illus. (p. 1716)
O'Connell, S. L. Short Stories to Tickle the Imagination. (p. 2010)
O'connell, Tyne. Royal Match. (p. 1910)
O'Connell, Tyne. Royal Mess. (p. 1910)
O'Connon, Jane & Harper Collins/Leap Frog. LeapReader Book, Fancy Nancy Explorer Extraordinaire! Glasser, Robin Preiss, illus. (p. 1255)
O'Connor, Alison. Amazing Animals from a to Z. (p. 63)
O'Connor, Bailey, illus. see Ceballos, Jacalyn Martin.
O'Connor, Barbara. Fantastic Secret of Owen Jester. (p. 707)
—How to Steal a Dog: A Novel. (p. 1044)
—On the Road to Mr. Mineo's. (p. 1655)
—On the Road to Mr. Mineo's. (p. 1655)
—Small Adventure of Popeye & Elvis. (p. 2039)
—Wish. (p. 2478)
O'connor, Barbara. Wish. (p. 2478)
O'Connor, Barbara. Wonderland: A Novel. (p. 2490)
—Wonderland. (p. 2490)
O'Connor, Barry. Turf-Fire Stories & Fairy Tales of Ireland (Classic Reprint) (p. 2299)
O'Connor, Clare. Skateboard Sibby (p. 2029)
O'Connor, Constance & Rojas, Natalia. Every Family Is Different: Even Animal Families! Poley, Lucy, illus. (p. 670)
O'Connor, Daniel & Barrie, J. M. Peter Pan Picture Book. Woodward, Alice B., illus. (p. 1729)
O'Connor, Deborah, illus. see Yates, Brad.
O'Connor, Fergal, illus. see Leavy, Una.
O'Connor, Flannery. Good Man Is Hard to Find & Other Stories. (p. 863)
O'Connor, Frances. History of Islam. (p. 978)
—Understanding Islam: History of Islam. (p. 2325)
O-Connor, Frankie. Ants Go Marching One by One: Read with Me. Groot, Nicole, illus. (p. 103)
O'Connor, Frankie. Ants Go Marching One by One. Paiva, Johannah Gilman, ed. (p. 103)
O'Connor, George. Aphrodite: Goddess of Love. (p. 105)
—Aphrodite: Goddess of Love. O'Connor, George, illus. (p. 105)
—Athena: Grey-Eyed Goddess. Bk. 2 O'Connor, George, illus. (p. 132)
—Captain Awesome Gets a Hole-In-One. (p. 324)
—Hades: Lord of the Dead. O'Connor, George, illus. (p. 909)
—Hera: The Goddess & Her Glory. O'Connor, George, illus. (p. 957)
—If I Had a Raptor. O'Connor, George, illus. (p. 1091)
—If I Had a Triceratops. O'Connor, George, illus. (p. 1091)
—Ker-Splash! O'Connor, George, illus. (p. 1210)
—Olympians: Apollo: The Brilliant One. (p. 1651)
—Olympians: Ares: Bringer of War. O'Connor, George, illus. (p. 1651)
—Olympians: Artemis: Wild Goddess of the Hunt. (p. 1651)
—Olympians: Athena: Grey-Eyed Goddess. Bk. 2 O'Connor, George, illus. (p. 1651)
—Olympians: Hephaistos: God of Fire. (p. 1651)
—Olympians: Hermes: Tales of the Trickster. (p. 1651)
—Olympians: Zeus: King of the Gods. O'Connor, George, illus. (p. 1651)
—Poseidon: Earth Shaker. O'Connor, George, illus. (p. 1779)
O'Connor, George, illus. see Abela, Deborah.
O'Connor, George, illus. see Kirby, Lee.
O'Connor, George, illus. see Kirby, Stan.
O'Connor, George, illus. see Lee, Jack, et al.
O'Connor, Gr, illus. see O'Connor, Karen.
O'Connor, Heather. Betting Game (p. 209)
O'Connor, Jane. Apples Galore! (p. 107)
O'connor, Jane. Best Reading Buddies. (p. 207)
—Bubbles, Bubbles, & More Bubbles! (p. 289)
O'Connor, Jane. Budding Ballerina. (p. 290)
—Every Day Is Earth Day. (p. 670)
—Fancy Day in Room 1-A. (p. 705)
—Fancy Nancy: Jojo & Daddy Bake a Cake. (p. 705)
—Fancy Nancy: Nancy Clancy, Super Sleuth. (p. 705)
—Fancy Nancy: Bubbles, Bubbles, & More Bubbles! Enik, Ted, illus. (p. 705)
—Fancy Nancy: The Dazzling Book Report. Glasser, Robin Preiss & Enik, Ted, illus. (p. 705)
—Fancy Nancy: 5-Minute Fancy Nancy Stories. Glasser, Robin Preiss, illus. (p. 705)
—Fancy Nancy: a Flutter of Butterflies Reusable Sticker Book. Glasser, Robin Preiss, illus. (p. 705)
—Fancy Nancy & the Dazzling Jewels. Glasser, Robin Preiss, illus. (p. 705)
—Fancy Nancy & the Delectable Cupcakes. Glasser, Robin Preiss, illus. (p. 705)
—Fancy Nancy & the Fabulous Fashion Boutique. Glasser, Robin Preiss, illus. (p. 705)
—Fancy Nancy & the Fall Foliage. Glasser, Robin Preiss, illus. (p. 705)
—Fancy Nancy & the Late, Late, Late Night. (p. 705)
—Fancy Nancy & the Late, Late, LATE Night. Glasser, Robin Preiss, illus. (p. 705)
—Fancy Nancy & the Mean Girl. Glasser, Robin Preiss, illus. (p. 705)
—Fancy Nancy & the Mermaid Ballet. Glasser, Robin Preiss, illus. (p. 705)
—Fancy Nancy & the Missing Easter Bunny. (p. 705)
—Fancy Nancy & the Missing Easter Bunny. Glasser, Robin Preiss, illus. (p. 705)
—Fancy Nancy & the Quest for the Unicorn: Includes over 30 Stickers! Glasser, Robin Preiss, illus. (p. 705)
O'connor, Jane. Fancy Nancy & the Quest for the Unicorn. (p. 705)
O'Connor, Jane. Fancy Nancy & the Sensational Babysitter. (p. 705)
—Fancy Nancy & the Sensational Babysitter. Glasser, Robin Preiss et al, illus. (p. 705)
—Fancy Nancy & the Too-Loose Tooth. (p. 705)
—Fancy Nancy & the Too-Loose Tooth. Glasser, Robin Preiss, illus. (p. 705)
—Fancy Nancy & the Wedding of the Century. Glasser, Robin Preiss, illus. (p. 705)
—Fancy Nancy: Apples Galore! Glasser, Robin Preiss, illus. (p. 705)
—Fancy Nancy: Aspiring Artist. Glasser, Robin Preiss, illus. (p. 705)
—Fancy Nancy: Best Reading Buddies. Glasser, Robin Preiss, illus. (p. 705)
—Fancy Nancy Big Book. Glasser, Robin Preiss, illus. (p. 705)
—Fancy Nancy: Bubbles, Bubbles, & More Bubbles! Glasser, Robin Preiss, illus. (p. 705)
—Fancy Nancy: Budding Ballerina. Glasser, Robin Preiss, illus. (p. 705)
—Fancy Nancy: Candy Bonanza. Glasser, Robin Preiss, illus. (p. 705)
—Fancy Nancy Collector's Quintet. Glasser, Robin Preiss, illus. (p. 705)
—Fancy Nancy: Every Day Is Earth Day. Glasser, Robin Preiss et al, illus. (p. 705)
—Fancy Nancy: Explorer Extraordinaire! Glasser, Robin Preiss, illus. (p. 705)
—Fancy Nancy: Express Yourself! A Doodle & Draw Book. Glasser, Robin Preiss, illus. (p. 705)
—Fancy Nancy: Fanciest Doll in the Universe. Glasser, Robin Preiss, illus. (p. 705)
—Fancy Nancy: Fancy Day in Room 1-A. Glasser, Robin Preiss, illus. (p. 705)
—Fancy Nancy: Fashionista: a Coloring & Activity Book. Glasser, Robin Preiss, illus. (p. 705)
—Fancy Nancy: Girl on the Go: A Doodle & Draw Book. Glasser, Robin Preiss & Ivanov, Olga, illus. (p. 705)
—Fancy Nancy: Hair Dos & Hair Don'ts. Glasser, Robin Preiss, illus. (p. 705)
—Fancy Nancy: Halloween... or Bust! Glasser, Robin Preiss, illus. (p. 705)
—Fancy Nancy: Heart to Heart: With Fancy Stickers! Glasser, Robin Preiss, illus. (p. 705)
—Fancy Nancy: It's Backward Day! Glasser, Robin Preiss, illus. (p. 705)
—Fancy Nancy: Jojo & Daddy Bake a Cake. Glasser, Robin Preiss, illus. (p. 705)
—Fancy Nancy: Jojo & the Big Mess. Glasser, Robin Preiss, illus. (p. 705)
—Fancy Nancy: Jojo & the Magic Trick. Glasser, Robin Preiss, illus. (p. 705)
—Fancy Nancy: Jojo & the Twins. Glasser, Robin Preiss, illus. (p. 705)
—Fancy Nancy: Just My Luck! Glasser, Robin Preiss, illus. (p. 705)
—Fancy Nancy: My Family History. Glasser, Robin Preiss, illus. (p. 705)
—Fancy Nancy: Nancy Clancy Bind-Up: Books 1 And 2: Super Sleuth & Secret Admirer. Glasser, Robin Preiss, illus. (p. 705)
—Fancy Nancy: Nancy Clancy Bind-Up: Books 3 And 4: Sees the Future & Secret of the Silver Key. Glasser, Robin Preiss, illus. (p. 705)
—Fancy Nancy: Nancy Clancy, Late-Breaking News! Glasser, Robin Preiss, illus. (p. 705)
—Fancy Nancy: Nancy Clancy: My Secret Diary. Glasser, Robin Preiss, illus. (p. 705)
—Fancy Nancy: Nancy Clancy, Secret Admirer. Glasser, Robin Preiss, illus. (p. 705)
—Fancy Nancy: Nancy Clancy, Secret of the Silver Key. Glasser, Robin Preiss, illus. (p. 705)
—Fancy Nancy: Nancy Clancy Seeks a Fortune. Glasser, Robin Preiss & Bracken, Carolyn, illus. (p. 705)
—Fancy Nancy: Nancy Clancy, Soccer Mania. Glasser, Robin Preiss, illus. (p. 705)
—Fancy Nancy: Nancy Clancy, Star of Stage & Screen. Glasser, Robin Preiss, illus. (p. 705)
—Fancy Nancy: Nancy Clancy's Astounding Chapter Book Quartet: Books 5-8. Glasser, Robin Preiss, illus. (p. 705)
—Fancy Nancy: Nancy Clancy's Tres Charming Chapter Book Box Set: Books 1-3 Glasser, Robin Preiss, illus. (p. 705)
—Fancy Nancy: Nancy Clancy's Ultimate Chapter Book Quartet: Books 1 Through 4. Glasser, Robin Preiss, illus. (p. 705)
—Fancy Nancy: Oodles of Kittens. Glasser, Robin Preiss, illus. (p. 705)
—Fancy Nancy: Ooh la la! It's Beauty Day. Glasser, Robin Preiss, illus. (p. 705)
—Fancy Nancy: Our Thanksgiving Banquet. Glasser, Robin Preiss, illus. (p. 705)
—Fancy Nancy: Pajama Day. Glasser, Robin Preiss et al, illus. (p. 705)
—Fancy Nancy: Peanut Butter & Jellyfish. Glasser, Robin Preiss, illus. (p. 705)
—Fancy Nancy Petite Library: 4 Mini Books. Glasser, Robin Preiss, illus. (p. 705)
—Fancy Nancy: Poet Extraordinaire! Glasser, Robin Preiss, illus. (p. 705)
—Fancy Nancy: Puppy Party. Glasser, Robin Preiss, illus. (p. 705)
—Fancy Nancy: Puzzle-Palooza. Glasser, Robin Preiss, illus. (p. 705)
—Fancy Nancy: Sand Castles & Sand Palaces. Glasser, Robin Preiss, illus. (p. 705)
—Fancy Nancy: Saturday Night Sleepover. Glasser, Robin Preiss, illus. (p. 705)
—Fancy Nancy: Spectacular Spectacles. Glasser, Robin Preiss, illus. (p. 705)
—Fancy Nancy: Splendid Speller. Glasser, Robin Preiss, illus. (p. 705)
—Fancy Nancy: Splendiferous Christmas. Glasser, Robin Preiss, illus. (p. 705)
—Fancy Nancy: Splendiferous Christmas. Glasser, Robin Preiss, illus. (p. 706)
—Fancy Nancy: Spring Fashion Fling. Glasser, Robin Preiss, illus. (p. 706)
—Fancy Nancy: Stellar Stargazer! Glasser, Robin Preiss, illus. (p. 706)
—Fancy Nancy Storybook Favorites. Glasser, Robin Preiss, illus. (p. 706)
—Fancy Nancy Storybook Treasury. Glasser, Robin Preiss, illus. (p. 706)
—Fancy Nancy: Super Secret Surprise Party. Glasser, Robin Preiss, illus. (p. 706)
—Fancy Nancy: Tea for Two. Glasser, Robin Preiss, illus. (p. 706)
—Fancy Nancy: Tea Parties. Glasser, Robin Preiss, illus. (p. 706)
—Fancy Nancy: the 100th Day of School. Glasser, Robin Preiss, illus. (p. 706)
—Fancy Nancy: the Dazzling Book Report. Glasser, Robin Preiss, illus. (p. 706)
—Fancy Nancy: the Show Must Go On. Glasser, Robin Preiss, illus. (p. 706)
—Fancy Nancy: the Worst Secret Keeper Ever. Glasser, Robin Preiss, illus. (p. 706)
—Fancy Nancy - There's No Day Like a Snow Day. (p. 705)
—Fancy Nancy: There's No Day Like a Snow Day. Glasser, Robin Preiss, illus. (p. 706)
—Fancy Nancy: Time for Puppy School. Glasser, Robin Preiss, illus. (p. 706)
—Fancy Nancy: Too Many Tutus. Glasser, Robin Preiss, illus. (p. 706)
—Fancy Nancy's 12-Book Fantastic Phonics Fun! Includes 12 Mini-Books Featuring Short & Long Vowel Sounds Glasser, Robin Preiss, illus. (p. 706)
—Fancy Nancy's Absolutely Stupendous Sticker Book. Glasser, Robin Preiss, illus. (p. 706)
—Fancy Nancy's Elegant Easter. Glasser, Robin Preiss, illus. (p. 706)
—Fancy Nancy's Fabulous Fall Storybook Collection. Glasser, Robin Preiss, illus. (p. 706)
—Fancy Nancy's Fabulously Fancy Treasury. Glasser, Robin Preiss, illus. (p. 706)
—Fancy Nancy's Gloriously Gigantic Sticker-Tivity Book. Glasser, Robin Preiss, illus. (p. 706)
—Fancy Nancy's Haunted Mansion: a Reusable Sticker Book for Halloween. Glasser, Robin Preiss, illus. (p. 706)
—Fancy Nancy's Marvelous Mother's Day Brunch. Glasser, Robin Preiss, illus. (p. 706)
—Fancy Nancy's Perfectly Pink Playtime Purse. Glasser, Robin Preiss, illus. (p. 706)
—Fancy Nancy's Perfectly Posh Paper Doll Book. Glasser, Robin Preiss, illus. (p. 706)
—Fancy Nancy's Sticker-Doodle Book. (p. 706)
—Hidden Army: Clay Soldiers of Ancient China. (p. 965)
—It's Backward Day! (p. 1144)
—Jojo & Daddy Bake a Cake. (p. 1175)
—JoJo & the Big Mess. (p. 1175)
—JoJo & the Magic Trick. (p. 1175)
—JoJo & the Twins. (p. 1175)
—Just My Luck! (p. 1194)
—Lulu & the Witch Baby. Sinclair, Bella, illus. (p. 1367)
—Lulu Goes to Witch School. Sinclair, Bella, illus. (p. 1367)
—My Family History. (p. 1538)
—Nancy Clancy, Secret Admirer. (p. 1574)
—Nancy Clancy, Secret of the Silver Key. (p. 1574)
—Nancy Clancy Sees the Future. (p. 1574)
—Nancy Clancy, Soccer Mania. Glasser, Robin Preiss, illus. (p. 1574)
—Nancy Clancy, Star of Stage & Screen. (p. 1574)
—Nancy la Elegante y la Perrita Popoff: Fancy Nancy & the Posh Puppy (Spanish Edition) Glasser, Robin Preiss, illus. (p. 1574)
—Nancy Makes Her Mark. (p. 1574)
—Peanut Butter & Jellyfish. (p. 1710)
—Puppy Party. (p. 1815)
—Sand Castles & Sand Palaces. (p. 1930)
—Spring Fashion Fling. (p. 2092)
—Super Secret Surprise Party. (p. 2156)
—Tea for Two. Glasser, Robin Preiss, illus. (p. 2194)
—Time for Puppy School. (p. 2244)
O'connor, Jane. Time for Puppy School. (p. 2244)
O'Connor, Jane. Time for Puppy School. Glasser, Robin Preiss & Enik, Ted, illus. (p. 2244)
—Too Many Tutus. (p. 2261)
O'connor, Jane. Who Is Ralph Lauren? (p. 2448)
O'Connor, Jane. Worst Secret Keeper Ever. (p. 2509)
O'Connor, Jane, jt. auth. see Who HQ.
O'Connor, Jane & Glasser, Robin Preiss. It's Backward Day! Enik, Ted, illus. (p. 1144)
—JoJo & Daddy Bake a Cake. Whipple, Rick, illus. (p. 1175)
O'Connor, Jeff, illus. see Mackall, Dandi Daley.
O'Connor, Jenny. Grand Goblin Ball. Willis-Crowley, Kate, illus. (p. 876)
—Smoky the Dragon Baby. Willis-Crowley, Kate, illus. (p. 2043)
O'Connor, Jim. What Is Rock & Roll? Copeland, Gregory, illus. (p. 2416)
—What Was Pompeii? (p. 2421)
—What Was the Battle of Gettysburg? (p. 2421)
—What Were the Twin Towers? (p. 2422)
O'connor, Jim. Where Is the Colosseum? (p. 2438)
—Where Is the Grand Canyon? (p. 2438)
O'Connor, Jim. Who Is Bob Dylan? (p. 2447)
O'Connor, Jim, jt. auth. see Who HQ.
O'Connor, Jim & Who Hq. What Was the Battle of Gettysburg? Mantha, John, illus. (p. 2421)
O'Connor, John, illus. see McPhail, David.
O'Connor, Jon. Drex Harding: Versus the Middle School Mafia. (p. 604)
O'Connor, Kaitlyn Shea, illus. see Calkhoven, Laurie.
O'Connor, Karen. Animals on the Verge of Extinction. (p. 95)
—Santa's Wish. O'Connor, Gr, illus. (p. 1934)
—Threat of Invasive Species. (p. 2231)
O'Connor, Laura E., ed. see Moyle, William.
O'Connor, Len. They Talked to a Stranger (Classic Reprint) (p. 2219)
O'Connor, Marcy, illus. see Ceballos, Jacalyn Martin.
O'Connor, Mary Hamilton. Vanishing Swede: A Tale of Adventure & Pluck in the Pine Forests of Oregon (Classic Reprint) (p. 2347)
O'Connor, Matt. Sky Knight & the Lost Knights. (p. 2033)
—Sky Knight & the Pirate Problem. (p. 2033)
—Sky Knight & the Raptor Trials. (p. 2033)
O'Connor, Miles. Tree That Moved. (p. 2284)
O'Connor, Pat. Secret Visions. (p. 1979)
O'Connor, Percival C. Scott. Indian Countryside: A Calendar & Diary (Classic Reprint) (p. 1116)
O'Connor, Rachel. Halloween / Halloween. (p. 912)
O'Connor, Shannon, illus. see Jackson, Ann.
O'Connor, Sheila. Sparrow Road. (p. 2075)
—Until Tomorrow, Mr. Marsworth. (p. 2336)
O'Connor, Sophia. Watership Down. (p. 2386)
—Watership down the Coloring Book. (p. 2386)
O'Connor, T. P. Dog Stars Three Luminaries in the Dog World (Classic Reprint) (p. 576)
—Herself-Ireland (Classic Reprint) (p. 963)
—I Myself (Classic Reprint) (p. 1079)
—My Beloved South (Classic Reprint) (p. 1532)
O'Connor, Tara. Altered History of Willow Sparks. (p. 60)
—Roots. (p. 1903)
O'Connor, Tara, illus. see Priest, Cherie.
O'Connor, Tim. Rhyme of the Ontiphant. (p. 1875)
O'Connor, Tim, illus. see Elkins, Stephen.
O'Connor, Tim, illus. see Holmes, Andy.
O'Connor, Tim, illus. see Larsen, Carolyn.
O'Connor, V.C.Scott. Scene of War (Classic Reprint) (p. 1943)
O'Connor, William Douglas. Harrington: A Story of True Love (Classic Reprint) (p. 933)
—Three Tales: The Ghost; the Brazen Android; the Carpenter (Classic Reprint) (p. 2235)
O'Connor, William Frederick. Folk Tales from Tibet: With Illustrations by a Tibetan Artist & Some Verses from Tibetan Love-Songs, Collected & Translated (Classic Reprint) (p. 757)
O'Connor, William Van. Campus on the River (Classic Reprint) (p. 316)
O'Connor, Wm. D. Ghost (Classic Reprint) (p. 827)
Octobre, Sylvie. ¿Quién Teme a Las Culturas Juveniles? Las Culturas Juveniles en la Era Digital. (p. 1827)
Oczkus, Lori. Close Reading with Paired Texts (p. 407)
—Close Reading with Paired Texts Level 1: Engaging Lessons to Improve Comprehension (p. 407)
—Close Reading with Paired Texts, Level 5 (p. 407)
—Disappearing Rainforests Level 2 (p. 553)
Oda, Eiichiro. One Piece Vol. 66. (p. 1661)
—One Piece Vol. 74. (p. 1661)
—One Piece Vol. 80. (p. 1661)
Oda, Eiichiro, jt. auth. see Steele, Michael Anthony.
Oda, Kancho, illus. see McCarthy, Ralph F.
Oda, Matthew K. Time MacHine: Mario's Box A Journey into Creativity. (p. 2245)
Oda, Mayumi. Happy Veggies. (p. 924)
Oda, Mayumi, illus. see Herbert, Anne & Pavel, Margaret Paloma.
Odanaka, Barbara. Construction Cat. Hanson, Sydney, illus. (p. 443)
—Crazy Day at the Critter Café. White, Lee, illus. (p. 469)
O'Dare, Helen. Love. O'Byrne, Nicola, illus. (p. 1358)
O'Day, John. Reggie Bush: Superstar on Offense. (p. 1861)
O'Day, John Christopher. Oil Wells in the Woods (Classic Reprint) (p. 1643)
Odd Dot. 20 First Words in 20 Languages. (p. 2553)
—Baby Beats: Let's Learn 2/4 Time! Stubbings, Ellen, illus. (p. 149)
—Eyeball Everything. (p. 688)
—Secret Message Origami: Pass Secret Notes That Only Your Friends Can Read! (with 120 Origami Sheets) Cide, Jane, illus. (p. 1977)
Odd Dot, jt. auth. see Krasner, Justin.
Odd Dot, jt. auth. see Ray, Meg.
Odd Dot, jt. auth. see Venable, Colleen Af.
Odd Dot & O'Cain, Leeana. Tiny World: Soap! O'Cain, Leeana, illus. (p. 2250)
Oddi, Sara, illus. see Coe, Jonathan.
Oddo, Jennifer M. Asim the Awesome Possum: Asim Gets His Awesome. Lamb, T. S., illus. (p. 126)
Ode, Eric. Bigfoot Does Not Like Birthday Parties. Temairik, Jaime, illus. (p. 224)
—Boy & the Dragon Harris, Jim, illus. (p. 268)
—Busy Trucks on the Go. (p. 302)
—Dan, the Taxi Man. (p. 499)
—Paulina & the Pirate's Hat Ode, Eric, illus. (p. 1707)
—Sea Star Wishes: Poems from the Coast. Brooks, Erik, illus. (p. 1968)
—Sea Star Wishes. Brooks, Erik, illus. (p. 1968)
—Too Many Tomatoes. Culotta, Kent, illus. (p. 2261)
—When You're a Pirate Dog & Other Pirate Poems Harris, Jim, illus. (p. 2435)
Ode, Eric, jt. auth. see Skewes, John.

Numeric

O'Dea, Lori. Super Dog. Greenhead, Bill, illus. (p. 2154)

—Tools for Seeing. (p. 2261)

O'Dea, Mark. Red Bud Women: Four Dramatic Episodes (Classic Reprint) (p. 1856)

O'Dea, Michael, Rory and Cavanaugh & Benchmark Education Co. Staff. Wall. (p. 2372)

O'Dea, Rory & Benchmark Education Co. Staff. Books That Changed My Life. (p. 261)

—Opinions about Art - a Study of Paintings from the Romantic Era. (p. 1666)

O'Dea, Tierney, jt. auth. see Gendell, Megan.

Odedele, Joseph. Joseph & His Three Friends. (p. 1178)

Odell, Amy-Brooke. Silo Boys. (p. 2019)

O'Dell, Angela. America's Story. (p. 75)

—America's Story 3 Set. (p. 75)

—Math Lessons for a Living Education Level 6: Level 6. (p. 1424)

—World's Story 1: Creation to the Roman Empire: the Ancients. (p. 2508)

—World's Story 1 (Teacher Guide) The Ancients: Creation to the Roman Empire. (p. 2508)

O'Dell, Angela & Carlson, Kyrsten. Math Lessons for a Living Education Level 2. (p. 1424)

Odell Bright, Monyue. First Day of School. (p. 736)

Odell, Carol. Once upon a Time in the Kitchen. Pignataro, Anna, illus. (p. 1658)

Odell, Catherine Lazar, illus. see McLellan, Gretchen Brandenburg.

O'Dell, Dalton & Hinckley Barnes, Reed. Secret Santa Volume One. (p. 1979)

Odell, Eva Beede. Roxy's Good Angel: And Other New England Tales (Classic Reprint) (p. 1909)

O'Dell, Kathleen. Aviary. (p. 143)

O'Dell, Kathryn. Bright Lights on Broadway. (p. 281)

—Life Online: the Digital Age Low Intermediate Book with Online Access. (p. 1295)

—Science of Light Low Intermediate Book with Online Access. (p. 1958)

O'Dell, Kathryn L. American Authors E. B. White & Gary Soto. (p. 70)

—From Wagon to Train. Chalik, Chris, illus. (p. 794)

—Oklahoma Fame! Jim Thorpe, Will Rogers, Maria Tallchief. (p. 1644)

O'Dell, Kathryn L., et al. My Coast Is Better Than Yours! (p. 1535)

O'Dell, Kevin. Mother Earth, Brother Sun, Sister Moon. (p. 1509)

O'Dell, Kevin M. Mother Earth, Brother Sun, Sister Moon. (p. 1509)

O'Dell, Nicole. 30-Day Prayer Challenge for Teen Girls. (p. 2554)

O'Dell, Patrick Timothy Wayne. Elvin. (p. 640)

O'Dell, Scott. Black Pearl. (p. 239)

—Black Star, Bright Dawn. (p. 239)

—Island of the Blue Dolphins: The Complete Reader's Edition. Schwebel, Sara L., ed. (p. 1139)

—Island of the Blue Dolphins. (p. 1139)

—Island of the Blue Dolphins. Lewin, Ted, illus. (p. 1139)

—King's Fifth. (p. 1223)

—Perla Negra = the Black Pearl. (p. 1724)

—Sing down the Moon. (p. 2023)

—Thunder Rolling in the Mountains. (p. 2238)

—Zia (p. 2540)

—Zia. (p. 2540)

O'DellKathryn. SCIENCE OF DARKNESS LOW INTERMEDIATE BOOK WITH ONLINE ACCESS. (p. 1957)

—SHARK ATTACK LOW INTERMEDIATE BOOK WITH ONLINE ACCESS. (p. 2001)

—SHOOT TO KILL: WHY WE HUNT HIGH BEGINNING BOOK WITH ONLINE ACCESS. (p. 2009)

—SURVIVAL GUIDE: LOST IN THE MOUNTAINS LOW INTERMEDIATE BOOK WITH ONLINE ACCESS. (p. 2164)

Odenthal, Amy. Butterfly Wings Are Not Just Beautiful Things. (p. 304)

Odentz, Howard. Bloody Bloody Apple. (p. 246)

—Bottle Toss. (p. 265)

—Dead. (p. 517)

—Dead (a Lot) (p. 517)

—Dead End. (p. 517)

—Wicked Dead. (p. 2460)

Odermatt, Jonas. Action Auf Dem Pferdehof. (p. 12)

Odets, Clifford. Three Dramas of American Individualism: Golden Boy; High Tor; the Magnificent Yankee (Classic Reprint) (p. 2232)

Odg, Fuse. Nana Yaa & the Golden Stool. Shroom, Rahima, illus. (p. 1573)

Odgers, Darrel, jt. auth. see Odgers, Sally.

Odgers, Darrel & Odgers, Sally. Blue Stealer. Dawson, Janine, illus. (p. 249)

—Bush Rescue. Dawson, Janine, illus. (p. 301)

—Cranky Paws. Dawson, Janine, illus. (p. 467)

—Farm Rescue. Dawson, Janine, illus. (p. 710)

—Ham Heist. Dawson, Janine, illus. (p. 913)

—Inspector Jacques. Dawson, Janine, illus. (p. 1124)

—Kitten's Tale. Dawson, Janine, illus. (p. 1226)

—Mare's Tale. Dawson, Janine, illus. (p. 1403)

—Python Problem. Dawson, Janine, illus. (p. 1819)

Odgers, Darrel & Sally. Pup's Tale: Pet Vet Book 6. Dawson, Janine, illus. (p. 1815)

Odgers, Sally. Felix & His Flying Machine (p. 719)

—Good Night, Truck. McKenzie, Heath, illus. (p. 865)

—Journey to the Center of the Earth (p. 1182)

—Pearl the Flying Unicorn. Thomas, Adele K., illus. (p. 1710)

—Pearl the Magical Unicorn. Thomas, Adele K., illus. (p. 1710)

—Silver Skateboard. (p. 2020)

—Untold Story of Ms. Mirabella (p. 2336)

—Where Did the Dinosaurs Go? (p. 2436)

—Wintersong. (p. 2476)

Odgers, Sally, ed. see Winter, Isobelle.

Odgers, Sally, jt. auth. see Steck-Vaughn Company.

Odgers, Sally & Darrel. Bush Rescue: Pup Patrol. Dawson, Janine, illus. (p. 301)

—Farm Rescue: Pup Patrol. Dawson, Janine, illus. (p. 710)

—Storm Rescue: Pup Patrol. Dawson, Janine, illus. (p. 2126)

Odhiambo, Eucabeth. Auma's Long Run. (p. 136)

Odierno, Lisa. Bunny Hide-and-Seek. (p. 298)

—Kitten & Her Sister. (p. 1225)

Odierno, Lisa, jt. auth. see Galvin, Laura Gates.

Odierno, Lisa & Soundprints Staff. Bunny Hide-and-Seek. (p. 298)

Odin, Jey. Chicken Fighter. (p. 368)

Odjick, Jay, illus. see Munsch, Robert.

Odjick, Jay & Tenascon, Patrick. Kagagi: the Raven: The Raven. O'Reilly, Sean Patrick, ed. (p. 1201)

O'Doherty, Carolyn. Rewind. (p. 1874)

—Unleashed. (p. 2333)

O'Doherty, David. Danger Is Everywhere: A Handbook for Avoiding Danger. Judge, Chris, illus. (p. 501)

—Danger Is Still Everywhere: Beware of the Dog! Judge, Chris, illus. (p. 501)

—Danger Is Totally Everywhere: School of Danger. (p. 501)

O'Doherty, Owen. Bright Sparks: Amazing Discoveries, Inventions & Designs by Women. (p. 281)

Odoi-Atsem, Victoria. Lwanda & the Sun Compass. (p. 1369)

—Water & Sky. (p. 2384)

Odom, Kelly, illus. see Parrish, Edith E.

Odom, Matthew. My Very First Our World Book IR. (p. 1564)

Odom, McKenzie. Clockwork Witch. (p. 406)

Odom, Mel. Conspiracy Revealed. (p. 443)

—His Legacy Avenged. (p. 974)

Odom, Rebecca. Grandpa & the Raccoon. Tebbit, Jake, illus. (p. 879)

Odone, Jamison. Alice's Adventures in Wonderland. Odone, Jamison, illus. (p. 46)

O'Donnell, Allison. I Burn. (p. 1061)

O'Donnell, Elizabeth. Maggie Does Not Want to Move. (p. 1376)

O'Donnell, Elliot. Banshee (Classic Reprint) (p. 164)

—Haunted Places in England (Classic Reprint) (p. 938)

—More Haunted Houses of London (Classic Reprint) (p. 1505)

O'Donnell, Elliott. Meaning of Dreams (Classic Reprint) (p. 1434)

—Mrs. E. M. Ward's Reminiscences (Classic Reprint) (p. 1522)

—Some Haunted Houses: Of England Wales (Classic Reprint) (p. 2059)

—Sorcery Club (Classic Reprint) (p. 2065)

O'Donnell, F. Hugh. Ruin of Education in Ireland & the Irish Fanar. (p. 1913)

O'Donnell, Jessica. Egyptian Cobra. (p. 628)

—Leontyne Price: First Lady of Opera. (p. 1267)

O'Donnell, K. So Many Seeds: Learning the S Sound. (p. 2050)

O'Donnell, Kayla. What Do Carpenters Do? Relate Addition & Subtraction to Length (p. 2408)

O'Donnell, Kerri. Ancient Civilizations of Greece & Rome: Solving Algebraic Equations. (p. 80)

—Aves: Dinosaurios de nuestros días (Birds: Modern-Day Dinosaurs) (p. 143)

—Bats. (p. 173)

—Denali National Park: An Alaskan Ecosystem: Creating Graphical Representations of Data. (p. 528)

—Explorers in North America: Solving Addition & Subtraction Problems Using Timelines. (p. 680)

—Galileo: Man of Science. (p. 806)

—How Chocolate Is Made: From Natural Resource to Finished Product. (p. 1027)

—Komodo Dragons. (p. 1231)

—Moons of Our Solar System. (p. 1503)

—Natural Wonders of the World: Converting Distance Measurements to Metric Units. (p. 1580)

—Natural Wonders of the World: Understanding & Representing Numbers in the Billions. (p. 1580)

—Sir Isaac Newton: Using the Laws of Motion to Solve Problems. (p. 2025)

—Snakes of the World: Learning to Use Inches & Feet to Measure an Object. (p. 2044)

—Timeline of the California Gold Rush. (p. 2246)

—Trip Around the World: Using Expanded Notation to Represent Numbers. (p. 2288)

—Ugly Bugs. (p. 2313)

—Ugly Sea Creatures. (p. 2314)

—Vultures. (p. 2369)

O'Donnell, Laura, jt. auth. see O'Donnell, Liam.

O'Donnell, Liam. Crack the Pirate Code. (p. 466)

—Escape from the End: An Unofficial Minecraft Adventure for Children Ages 8 - 14. (p. 661)

—Food Fight Deas, Mike, illus. (p. 759)

—Ganked: Geeked Out Mysteries #1. (p. 808)

—Get into Pirate Gear. (p. 824)

—Hop on the Pirate History Boat. (p. 1001)

—Media Meltdown: A Graphic Guide Adventure Deas, Mike, illus. (p. 1436)

—Pirates! (p. 1750)

—Power Play Deas, Mike, illus. (p. 1783)

—Shocking World of Electricity with Max Axiom Super Scientist: An Augmented Reading Science Experience. Dominguez, Richard, illus. (p. 2008)

—Shocking World of Electricity with Max Axiom Super Scientist: 4D an Augmented Reading Science Experience. Dominguez, Richard, illus. (p. 2008)

—Sink or Swim with Pirate Ships. (p. 2024)

—Soccer Sabotage: A Graphic Guide Adventure Deas, Mike, illus. (p. 2052)

—Tank & Fizz: The Case of Firebane's Folly Deas, Mike, illus. (p. 2190)

—Tank & Fizz: the Case of the Battling Bots Deas, Mike, illus. (p. 2190)

—Tank & Fizz: the Case of the Missing Mage Deas, Mike, illus. (p. 2190)

—Tank & Fizz: the Case of the Slime Stampede Deas, Mike, illus. (p. 2190)

—Tank & Fizz: the Case of the Tentacle Terror Deas, Mike, illus. (p. 2190)

—Understanding Photosynthesis with Max Axiom Super Scientist: An Augmented Reading Science Experience. Dominguez, Richard, illus. (p. 2325)

—Understanding Photosynthesis with Max Axiom Super Scientist: 4D an Augmented Reading Science Experience. Dominguez, Richard, illus. (p. 2325)

—West Meadows Detectives: the Case of the Berry Burglars. Grand, Aurélie, illus. (p. 2402)

—World of Food Chains with Max Axiom Super Scientist: An Augmented Reading Science Experience. Martin, Cynthia, illus. (p. 2503)

—World of Food Chains with Max Axiom Super Scientist: 4D an Augmented Reading Science Experience. Martin, Cynthia, illus. (p. 2503)

—World of Food Chains with Max Axiom, Super Scientist. Martin, Cynthia, illus. (p. 2503)

O'Donnell, Liam & Barnett, Charles, III. Cómo Comprender la Fotosíntesis con Max Axiom, Supercientífico. Dominguez, Richard, illus. (p. 432)

O'Donnell, Liam, et al. Graphic Science 4D: 4D an Augmented Reading Science Experience. Martin, Cynthia & Dominguez, Richard, illus. (p. 880)

O'Donnell, Mabel. Alice & Jerry Basic Readers Reading Foundation Program: Guidebook for Teachers for the New down the River Road (Classic Reprint) (p. 44)

—Alice & Jerry Basic Readers; Reading Foundation Program: Guidebook for Teachers for the New Day in & Day Out (Classic Reprint) (p. 44)

—Alice & Jerry Books: Round about (Classic Reprint) (p. 44)

—Alice & Jerry Books: Day in & Day Out (Classic Reprint) (p. 44)

—Alice & Jerry Books: The Companion Book for Round about (Classic Reprint) (p. 44)

—Companion Book for Day in & Day Out: The Alice & Jerry Books (Classic Reprint) (p. 433)

—Companion Book for down the River Road (Classic Reprint) (p. 433)

—Companion Book for Friendly Village (Classic Reprint) (p. 433)

—Companion Book for If I Were Going (Classic Reprint) (p. 433)

—Companion Book for Through the Green Gate (Classic Reprint) (p. 433)

—Down the River Road (Classic Reprint) (p. 590)

—Engine Whistles (Classic Reprint) (p. 651)

—First Reading Readiness Book: Here We Go (Classic Reprint) (p. 739)

—Friendly Village (Classic Reprint) (p. 786)

—Guidebook for Teachers for the Basic Preprimer Programme: To Accompany Skip along & Open the Door (Classic Reprint) (p. 904)

—Guidebook for Teachers for the Preprimer Program (Classic Reprint) (p. 904)

—Here & There (Classic Reprint) (p. 957)

—High on a Hill (Classic Reprint) (p. 968)

—If I Were Going (Classic Reprint) (p. 1091)

—Open the Door: The New Alice & Jerry Books Reading Foundation Series (Classic Reprint) (p. 1665)

—Rides & Slides (Classic Reprint) (p. 1878)

—Singing Wheels (Classic Reprint) (p. 2024)

—Through the Green Gate (Classic Reprint) (p. 2237)

—Vocabulary First Reader Workbook: To Be Used with the First Reader Workbook (Classic Reprint) (p. 2364)

—Workbook for Singing Wheels (Classic Reprint) (p. 2495)

—Workbook for the New down the River Road (Classic Reprint) (p. 2495)

—Workbook for the New Friendly Village (Classic Reprint) (p. 2495)

—Workbook for Through the Green Gate (Classic Reprint) (p. 2495)

O'Donnell, Mabel C. Companion Book for Rides & Slides: The Alice & Jerry Books (Classic Reprint) (p. 433)

O'Donnell, Patrick. Did Dinosaurs Have Dentists? Mehlen, Erik, illus. (p. 542)

—Do Penguins Have Pediatricians? Mehlen, Erik, illus. (p. 570)

O'Donnell, Shannon. Lion's Son. (p. 1307)

O'Donnell, Steven & Bendixsen, Stephanie. Dig World (Pixel Raiders #1) Kennett, Chris, illus. (p. 545)

—Dragon Land. Kennett, Chris, illus. (p. 594)

O'Donnell, Tom. Hamstersaurus Rex. Miller, Tim, illus. (p. 914)

—Hamstersaurus Rex Gets Crushed. Miller, Tim, illus. (p. 914)

—Hamstersaurus Rex vs. Squirrel Kong. Miller, Tim, illus. (p. 914)

—Hamstersaurus Rex vs. the Cutepocalypse. Miller, Tim, illus. (p. 914)

—Homerooms & Hall Passes. (p. 997)

O'Donnell Tubb, Kristin, jt. auth. see Tubb, Kristin O'Donnell.

O'Donoghue, Chris. Charlie's Reading Rescue: Improve an Older Child's Reading. (p. 360)

O'Donoghue, D. J. Humour of Ireland: Selected, with Introduction, Biographical Index & Notes (Classic Reprint) (p. 1051)

O'Donoghue, D. J., jt. auth. see Lover, Samuel.

O'Donoghue, Francis Talbot. St. Knighton's Keive: A Cornish Tale; with a PostScript & Glossary (Classic Reprint) (p. 2097)

O'Donoghue, Sean. Create a Quilt: Understand Concepts of Area. (p. 469)

—Disaster of the Irish Potato Famine: Irish Immigrants Arrive in America (1845-1850) (p. 553)

—Thomas Jefferson & the Louisiana Purchase. (p. 2228)

O'Donoghue Sullivan, Margaret. In the Light of Other Days. (p. 1109)

O'Donovan, Catherine. Millie Malone Receives a Mysterious Present. (p. 1467)

O'Donovan, Gerald. Conquest (Classic Reprint) (p. 442)

—Father Ralph (Classic Reprint) (p. 714)

—Holy Tree (Classic Reprint) (p. 995)

—Vocations (Classic Reprint) (p. 2364)

—Waiting (Classic Reprint) (p. 2370)

O'Donovan, Peter. Imperfectly Proper (Classic Reprint) (p. 1102)

O'Dowd, Chris & Murphy, Nick V. Fish Detective. (p. 741)

Odriozola, Elena, illus. see Chandler, Susan.

Odriozola, Elena, illus. see Wolff, Ferida & Savitz, Harriet May.

O'Duffy, Eimar. Bricriu's Feast: A Comedy in Three Acts, with an Epilogue (Classic Reprint) (p. 280)

—Lion & the Fox (Classic Reprint) (p. 1305)

—Printer's Errors (Classic Reprint) (p. 1800)

—Wasted Island (Classic Reprint) (p. 2382)

Odum, Howard Washington. Negro Workaday Songs (Classic Reprint) (p. 1585)

Oduwole, Ben. Flying Tortoise. (p. 755)

O'Dwyer, Edward. Rain on Cruise's Street (p. 1835)

O'Dwyer, Frank. Little Fish Who Liked to Wish. (p. 1316)

—Meelygrat the Scalycat & the Moonlight Ball. (p. 1437)

O'Dwyer, Suzanne. Bart the Dog. (p. 168)

Odynski, Tay, illus. see Andrejcin, Brittany.

Oechsle, Michael. Lost Cipher. (p. 1353)

Oechsli, Helen. In My Garden. (p. 1106)

Oeda, Shiro. Moon Phase Calender Picturebook. (p. 1502)

Oehlers, Adam, illus. see LaFleur, Leo.

Oehlert, Mark, illus. see Taylor, Patricia.

Oehm, Kent, illus. see Hall, Francie.

Oehmichen, Ariel. Chosen Last. Du Pont, Brittany, illus. (p. 382)

Oehrle, Richard T., jt. ed. see Kruijff, Geert-Jan M.

Oehschlaeger, J. C. Key to Ahn's Practical & Easy Method of Learning the German Language (Classic Reprint) (p. 1211)

Oehschlger, J. C. Key to Ahn's Practical & Easy Method of Learning the German Language (Classic Reprint) (p. 1211)

Oelke, Lianne. Nice Try, Jane Sinner. (p. 1602)

Oelofsen, Vian, illus. see Hay, Sam.

Oelofsen, Vian, illus. see Stinson, Kathy.

Oelrich, Josh. Lithegol: The Prophecy: a Futuristic Sequel to the King Arthur Legend. Bruno, Beth, ed. (p. 1309)

Oelschig, Marius. Jak of the Bushveld. (p. 1155)

—Jessi: The Everyday Adventures of a Nature-Loving South African Girl. (p. 1165)

—Wishing Stone. (p. 2479)

Oelschlager, Vanita. Ariel Bradley, Spy for General Washington. (p. 115)

—Birds of a Feather: A Book of Idioms & Silly Pictures. Hegan, Robin, illus. (p. 232)

—Birds of a Feather. Hegan, Robin, illus. (p. 232)

—Bonyo Bonyo. Blackwood, Kristin & Blanc, Mike, illus. (p. 256)

—Carrot. Blackwood, Kristin, illus. (p. 334)

—Elefante. Blackwood, Kristin, illus. (p. 632)

—Farfalla: A Story of Loss & Hope. Blackwood, Kristin, illus. (p. 709)

—I Came from the Water: One Haitian Boy's Incredible Tale of Survival. Blanc, Mike, illus. (p. 1061)

—Ivan's Great Fall: Poetry for Summer & Autumn from Great Poets & Writers of the Past. Blackwood, Kristin, illus. (p. 1149)

—Ivy in Bloom: The Poetry of Spring from Great Poets & Writers from the Past. Blackwood, Kristin, illus. (p. 1150)

—Knees: The Mixed up World of a Boy with Dyslexia. Rossi, Joe, illus. (p. 1227)

—Life Is a Bowl Full of Cherries. (p. 1293)

—Magic Words: From the Ancient Oral Tradition of the Inuit. Blanc, Mike, illus. (p. 1379)

—Out of the Blue: A book of color idioms & silly Pictures. Hegan, Robin, illus. (p. 1682)

—Porcupette Finds a Family. Blanc, Mike, illus. (p. 1778)

—Postcards from a War. Blanc, Mike & Bauknight, Wilfred, illus. (p. 1780)

—Tale of Two Daddies. Blackwood, Kristin, illus. (p. 2180)

—Tale of Two Mommies. Blanc, Mike, illus. (p. 2180)

Oelschlager, Vanita & Blackwood, Kristin. Farfalla: A Story of Loss & Hope. (p. 709)

Oelschlager, Vanita & Blanc, Mike. I Came from the Water: One Haitian Boy's Incredible Tale of Survival. (p. 1061)

Oeltjenbruns, Joni, illus. see Bullard, Lisa.

Oeltjenbruns, Joni, illus. see Clairmont, Patsy.

Oelze, Don, illus. see Bouchard, David.

Oeming, Michael Avon, illus. see Bendis, Brian Michael.

Oeming, Michael Avon & Glass, Bryan J. L. Legend. (p. 1261)

Oemler, Marie Conway. Purple Heights, Vol. 1 (Classic Reprint) (p. 1816)

—Slippy Mcgee, Sometimes Known As the Butterfly Man (Classic Reprint) (p. 2038)

—Two Shall Be Born (Classic Reprint) (p. 2309)

—Where the Young Child Was & Also the Spirit of the House, the Youngest, Officer, Linden Goes Home, the Little Brown House, That Makes, the World Go Round (Classic Reprint) (p. 2440)

—Woman Named Smith (Classic Reprint) (p. 2485)

Oeppen, Ceri. Hopes, Needs, Rights, & Laws: How Do Governments & Citizens Manage Migration & Settlement? (p. 1002)

Oertel, Andreas. In Too Deep: The Shenanigans Series, Book Five (p. 1112)

—Panama Pursuit: The Shenanigans Series, Book Four. (p. 1695)

Oertel, J. a. Hand in Hand, Through the Happy Valley (Classic Reprint) (p. 914)

Oertel, Jennifer, illus. see Hall, Jacque.

Oesch, Brian, illus. see Turner, Juliette.

Oesterley, Herman. Hundred Mery Talys: From the Only Perfect Copy Known (Classic Reprint) (p. 1051)

Oesterley, Hermann. Shakespeare's Jest Book: A Hundred Mery Talys, from the Only Perfect Copy Known; Edited with Introduction & Notes (Classic Reprint) (p. 1999)

—Shakespeare's Jest Book. (p. 1999)

Oestreich, Laurie. Gluten Free Is Part of Me. (p. 845)

Oestreicher, David M. Algonquian of New York. (p. 44)

Oestreicher, Mark & Lindsey, Brooklyn. 99 Thoughts for Junior Highers: Biblical Truths in Bite-Sized Pieces. (p. 2556)

Oettinger, Ludwig. Geometrische Aufgaben Zum Gebrauch Bei Vorlesungen, Beim Unterricht an Höheren Lehranstalten und Zum Selbst-Studium, Vol. 1 (Classic Reprint) (p. 818)

Oetzel, Shawn. Adventures of Captain Kitchen. (p. 22)

of, American Society. ASME 2014 International Mechanical Engineering Congress & Exposition: Volume 1: Advances in Aerospace & Technology. (p. 126)
Of, Author. In Tent & Bungalow (Classic Reprint) (p. 1107)
—Ladye Nancye, Vol. 1 Of 3: A Novel (Classic Reprint) (p. 1239)
Of Education, State Board. California State Series of School Text-Books. Advanced Arithmetic. (p. 311)
—California State Series of School Text-Books; First Reader. (p. 311)
Of the United States, National Education. Addresses & Journal of Proceedings of the National Educational Association, Session of the Year 1875, at Minneapolis, Minnesota. (p. 15)
Of York, Sarah Duchess. Genie Gems: Mission to Devon. (p. 815)
Ofanansky, Allison. How It's Made: Hanukkah Menorah. Alpern, Eliyahu, photos by. (p. 1032)
—How It's Made: Torah Scroll Alpern, Andrew, photos by. (p. 1033)
—How It's Made Matzah. Alpern, Andrew, photos by. (p. 1033)
—Sukkot Treasure Hunt Alpern, Eliyahu, illus. (p. 2148)
—What's the Buzz? Honey for a Sweet New Year. Alpern, Eliyahu, illus. (p. 2426)
Ofanansky, Allison Maile. New Month, New Moon. Alpern, Eliyahu, photos by. (p. 1595)
—Patchwork Torah. Oriol, Elsa, illus. (p. 1704)
—Tisha B'Av: A Jerusalem Journey. Alpern, Eliyahu, photos by. (p. 2251)
O'Farrell, S. P. Simone Lafray & the Chocolatiers' Ball. (p. 2021)
O'Farrell, Suma. Rangoli: An Indian Art Activity Book. (p. 1841)
Ofelia, Jahde. Blue Crystal. (p. 248)
Ofer, Avi, illus. see Argaman, Iris.
Ofer, Avi, illus. see Shem-Tov, Tami & Sandbank, Rachella.
O'Ferrall, Zoe More, illus. see Prager, Sarah.
Offermann, Andrea, illus. see Anderson, M. T.
Offermann, Andrea, illus. see Hartnett, Sonya.
Offermann, Andrea, illus. see Milford, Kate.
Offermann, Andrea, illus. see White, J. A.
Offermann, Andrea, illus. see Yeomans, Ellen.
Office, Bancroft Library. Regional Oral. Builders & Sustainers of the Independent Living Movement in Berkeley, Vol. 4 (Classic Reprint) (p. 294)
Office, Canadian War Records. Canada in Khaki 1917: A Tribute to the Officers & Men Now Serving in the Canadian Expeditionary Force (Classic Reprint) (p. 320)
Office, Library Of Congress Copyright. Catalog of Copyright Entries, Third Series, Parts 7-11 a, Number 1, Vol. 2: Works of Art; Reproductions of Works of Art; Scientific & Technical Drawings; Photographic Works; Prints & Pictorial Illustrations; January-June, 1948 (Classic Reprint) (p. 342)
—Catalog of Copyright Entries, Vol. 3: Part 6; Maps; January-June, 1949 (Classic Reprint) (p. 342)
—Catalog of Copyright Entries, Vol. 4: Engravings, Cuts, & Prints; Chromos & Lithographs; Photographs; Fine Arts; January, 1909 (Classic Reprint) (p. 342)
—Catalog of Copyright Entries, Vol. 41: Part 4; Works of Art; Reproductions of a Work of Art; Drawings of Plastic Works of a Scientific or Technical Character; Photographs; Prints & Pictorial Illustrations, Including Prints & Labels Used for Articles O. (p. 342)
—Catalogue of Copyright Entries, Vol. 10: Part 4; for the Year 1915; Nos. 1-4 (Classic Reprint) (p. 342)
—Works of Art, Reproductions of Works of Art, Scientific & Technical Drawings, Photographic Works, Prints & Pictorial Illustrations: January-June, 1949 (Classic Reprint) (p. 2496)
Office, Massachusetts. Attorney. Official Report of the Trial of John o'Neil for the Murder of Hattie Evelyn Mccloud, in the Superior Court of Massachusetts: From Notes of the Official Stenographers (Classic Reprint) (p. 1641)
Office, Massachusetts Attorney 'S. Official Report of the Trial of John o'Neil for the Murder of Hattie Evelyn Mccloud, in the Superior Court of Massachusetts: From Notes of the Official Stenographers (Classic Reprint) (p. 1641)
Officer, A. Flag. Arthur Montague, or an Only Son at Sea, Vol. 3 of 3 (Classic Reprint) (p. 122)
Officer, A. Naval. Petrel, Vol. 2 Of 3: A Tale of the Sea (Classic Reprint) (p. 1731)
Officer, Robyn, illus. see Setzer, Lee Ann.
Official Roblox, Official. Inside the World of Roblox. (p. 1124)
—Roblox Character Encyclopedia. (p. 1892)
—Roblox Top Adventure Games. (p. 1892)
—Roblox Top Battle Games. (p. 1892)
—Roblox Top Role-Playing Games. (p. 1892)
—Roblox Ultimate Avatar Sticker Book. (p. 1892)
—Roblox Ultimate Guide Collection: Top Adventure Games, Top Role-Playing Games, Top Battle Games. Official Roblox, Official, illus. (p. 1892)
—Roblox: Where's the Noob? (p. 1892)
Offill, Jenny. 11 Experiments That Failed. Carpenter, Nancy, illus. (p. 2550)
—17 Things I'm Not Allowed to Do Anymore. Carpenter, Nancy, illus. (p. 2552)
—Sparky! Appelhans, Chris, illus. (p. 2075)
Offit, Sidney. Adventures of Homer Fink. Galdone, Paul, illus. (p. 24)
Offord, Alexander. Causes of World War II. (p. 347)
—Communication Inventions: The Talk of the Town. (p. 431)
—What Is Environmental Entrepreneurship? (p. 2415)
Offord, Roszella, illus. see Roberson, Melondy.
Offutt, Jason. Ella Ewing: The Missouri Giantess. (p. 637)
—Helen Stephens: The Fulton Flash. Hare, John, illus. (p. 949)
—J. C. Penney: The Man with a Thousand Partners. (p. 1150)
Ofiesh, Nicole, jt. auth. see Watson, Philip.
O'Flahertie Wills Wilde, Oscar Fingal, jt. auth. see Wilde, Oscar.
O'Flaherty, Liam. Informer (Classic Reprint) (p. 1119)
Ofoche, Uzo. Monte & Me. (p. 1499)
Oftedal, Kristin, illus. see Norac, Carl.
Ogaki, Philippe, et al. Mythics #1: Heroes Reborn. Picard, Alice et al, illus. (p. 1571)
O'Gallagher, Felix. Essay on the Investigation of the First Principles of Nature, Vol. 2: Together with the Application Thereof to Solve the PHænomena of the Physical System; in Which the Nature & Fuel of the Sun Are Physically Investigated; the Real Principles of Cold. (p. 663)
—Essay on the Investigation of the First Principles of Nature, Vol. 2: Together with the Application Thereof to Solve the Phaenomena of the Physical System; in Which the Nature & Fuel of the Sun Are Physically Investigated; the Real Principles of Cold. (p. 663)
—Essay on the Investigation of the First Principles of Nature, Vol. 1: Together with the Application Thereof to Solve the Phenomena of the Physical System; Containing a New Philosophical Theory Whereby First Principles, with Their Material Substances An. (p. 663)
Ogasawara, Tomofumi, illus. see Sumizawa, Katsuyuki.
Ogata, Michael. New Friend for Nai'a. (p. 1593)
Ogawa, Evan, jt. auth. see Ogawa, Grace.
Ogawa, Grace. Angeldevil V: Tales, Tools, Pawns & Fools. Ogawa, Grace, illus. (p. 86)
Ogawa, Grace & Ogawa, Evan. Iron Wizard II: Only Fear What You Do Not Know. (p. 1136)
Ogawa, Suharu. Piece It Together Family Puzzle: Catstronauts. (p. 1742)
Ogawa, Suharu, illus. see Vermond, Kira.
Ogbe, Joe-Jesimiel. Pathways to Academic Success. (p. 1705)
Ogborn, Dorothy. Aurora, 1922 (Classic Reprint) (p. 137)
Ogburn, Jacqueline. Unicorn in the Barn. Green, Rebecca, illus. (p. 2328)
Ogden, Antoinette. Christmas Stories from French & Spanish Writers. (p. 387)
—Christmas Stories from French & Spanish Writers (Classic Reprint) (p. 387)
Ogden, Bill, illus. see Christopher, Matt.
Ogden, C. K. Library of the University of California Los Angeles (Classic Reprint) (p. 1285)
Ogden, Charles, ed. Edgar & Ellen Graphic Novelty: A Comics Collection. (p. 625)
Ogden, Charlie. Censorship & Privacy. (p. 351)
—Equality & Diversity. (p. 659)
—Fair Trade & Global Economy. (p. 695)
—Government & Democracy. (p. 872)
—Human Rights & Liberty. (p. 1050)
—Identity & Gender. (p. 1089)
—Insects. (p. 1122)
—Law & Justice. (p. 1253)
—Peace & War. (p. 1709)
—Surviving a Killer Virus. (p. 2164)
—Surviving a Robot Revolution. (p. 2164)
—Surviving a Zombie Apocalypse. (p. 2164)
—Surviving an Alien Invasion. (p. 2165)
Ogden, Deborah. Mackensie Butterfly Lark in Central Park. (p. 1372)
Ogden, Dennis. Saving Spade: WWI Has Ended but the Battle to Save a Horse Has Just Begun. (p. 1939)
Ogden, G. W. Rustler of Wind River (Classic Reprint) (p. 1917)
Ogden, George W. Claim Number One (Classic Reprint) (p. 397)
Ogden, George Washington. Bondboy (Classic Reprint) (p. 255)
—Flockmaster of Poison Creek (Classic Reprint) (p. 750)
—Land of Last Chance (Classic Reprint) (p. 1241)
—Long Fight (Classic Reprint) (p. 1343)
Ogden, Harriet V. C. Then Came Molly (Classic Reprint) (p. 2215)
Ogden, Julen. Passed On. (p. 1703)
Ogden, Lesley Evans. Canada's Flag. (p. 320)
Ogden, Ruth. Courage a Story Wherein Every One Comes to the Conclusion That the Courage in Question Proved a Courage Worth Having (Classic Reprint) (p. 462)
—His Little Royal Highness. (p. 974)
—His Little Royal Highness (Classic Reprint) (p. 974)
—Little Homespun (Classic Reprint) (p. 1318)
—Little Queen of Hearts: An International Story (Classic Reprint) (p. 1325)
—Loyal Hearts & True (Classic Reprint) (p. 1363)
—Loyal Little Red-Coat: A Story of Child-Life in New York a Hundred Years Ago. (p. 1363)
—Loyal Little Red-Coat: A Story of Child-Life in New York a Hundred Years Ago (Classic Reprint) (p. 1363)
—Tattine (Classic Reprint) (p. 2193)
Oge, Eugene. Carnet Blanc a Qui Dois-Je Mon Chic ? (p. 332)
—Carnet Ligne a Qui Dois-Je Mon Chic ? (p. 332)
Oge-E, Eugene. Carnet Blanc Biere de L'Eclair. (p. 332)
—Carnet Ligne Biere de L'Eclair. (p. 332)
Ogeerally, Maggie. Do You Ever Have Bad Thoughts That Keep You up at Night. (p. 571)
—On the Eve of My Birthday. (p. 1654)
Ogilvie, Campbell Patrick. Argentina from a British Point of View: And Notes on Argentine Life (Classic Reprint) (p. 114)
Ogilvie, David Douglas. Fife & Forfar Yeomanry: And 14th (F. & F. Yeo.) Battn. R. H. 1914-1919. (p. 724)
Ogilvie, J. G., tr. see Verne, Jules.
Ogilvie, John. Imperial Dictionary of the English Language, Vol. 3: A Complete Encyclopedic Lexicon, Literary, Scientific, & Technological; I-Screak (Classic Reprint) (p. 1102)
—Imperial Dictionary of the English Language, Vol. 1: A Complete Encyclopedic Lexicon, Literary, Scientific, & Technological; a-Depascent (Classic Reprint) (p. 1102)
—Imperial Dictionary of the English Language, Vol. 4: A Complete Encyclopaedic Lexicon, Literary, Scientific, & Technological; Scream-Zythum (Classic Reprint) (p. 1102)
—Imperial Dictionary the English Language, Vol. 2: A Complete Encyclopedic Lexicon, Literary, Scientific, & Technological; Depasture-Kythe (Classic Reprint) (p. 1102)
Ogilvie, John Stuart. American Temperance Speaker, Vol. 1: A Choice Collection of Dialogues, Prose & Poetry, Especially Adapted for Use in All Adult & Juvenile Temperance Organizations, Sabbath & Day Schools, & for Public & Private Readings, Recitations & Addre. (p. 74)
Ogilvie, Samuel J. Tiger, Vol. 10: The California School of Mechanical Arts; March 1913 (Classic Reprint) (p. 2241)
Ogilvie, Sara, illus. see Bently, Peter.
Ogilvie, Sara, illus. see Crompton, Richmal.
Ogilvie, Sara, illus. see Donaldson, Julia.
Ogilvie, Sara, illus. see Jennings, Garth.
Ogilvie, Sara, illus. see Jones, Pip.
Ogilvie, Sara, illus. see Kemp, Anna.
Ogilvie, Sara, illus. see Price, Susan.
Ogilvie, Sara, illus. see Sparkes, Amy.
Ogilvie, Shane, illus. see Leys, Dave.
Ogilvie, Shane, illus. see Tabain, Dave & Worland, Nadia.
Ogilvie, Yolanda. Nana: A Portrait of Inspiration. (p. 1573)
Ogintz, Eileen. Acadia National Park (p. 9)
—Kid's Guide to Chicago (p. 1215)
—Kid's Guide to Denver, Boulder & Colorado's Ski Country (p. 1215)
OGINTZ, Eileen. Kids Guide to Maine (p. 1215)
Ogintz, Eileen. Kid's Guide to San Diego. (p. 1215)
—Kid's Guide to the Great Smoky Mountains (p. 1215)
—Los Angeles County - Kid's Guide. (p. 1349)
Ogle, Bonnie T. Golden Frogs / Las Ranas Doradas: Bilingual English Spanish. (p. 857)
Ogle, David B., jt. ed. see Little, Thomas Hamilton.
Ogle, Nancy Gray, illus. see Hodge, Deborah.
Ogle, Nancy Gray, illus. see Mason, Adrienne.
Ogle, Nathaniel. Mariamne, Vol. 1: An Historical Novel of Palestine (Classic Reprint) (p. 1404)
Ogle, Ponsonby. Selections from the Writings of Ponsonby Ogle (Classic Reprint) (p. 1986)
Ogle, Rex. Free Lunch. (p. 782)
Ogle, William. Trinity College School Record, Vol. 32: December 15th, 1928 (Classic Reprint) (p. 2288)
Ogle, Wm. Trinity College School Courier: November 15th, 1928 (Classic Reprint) (p. 2288)
—Trinity College School Record, Vol. 32: March 15th, 1929 (Classic Reprint) (p. 2288)
—Trinity College School Record, Vol. 32: February 1st, 1929 (Classic Reprint) (p. 2288)
—Trinity College School Record, Vol. 32: November 15th, 1928 (Classic Reprint) (p. 2288)
Ogle-Graham, Laura. No-No Nona & No-No Nit. (p. 1614)
Oglesby, Maria, illus. see April, Elyse & Ryan, Regina Sara.
Oglesby, Tamsin. Mouse & His Child. (p. 1514)
Ogletree, Chanelle. Reader. Johnson, Larry, ed. (p. 1845)
Ogmios, illus. see Keeney, Kenneth.
Ognibene, Edward. Strength in Differences. (p. 2140)
Ogonor, Fyne. Baby Eagle & the Chicks: The Similarity Between Tom & the Baby Eagle. (p. 150)
Ogorek, Elchanan. As Bs CS Oh My! Ogorek, Elchanan, illus. (p. 124)
O'Gorman, Cookie. Adorkable. (p. 17)
O'Gorman, Neil. Plants & Their Environments. (p. 1757)
O'Gorman, Sarah, ed. see Hill, Sarah.
O'Grady, Alice. Story Teller's Book (Classic Reprint) (p. 2135)
O'Grady, Laurie, illus. see David, Sophia.
O'Grady, O'Grady. Lost on du-Corrig or Twixt Earth & Ocean (Classic Reprint) (p. 1355)
—Teacher's Story Teller's Book (Classic Reprint) (p. 2195)
O'Grady, Standish. Chain of Gold: A Tale of Adventure on the West Coast of Ireland (Classic Reprint) (p. 353)
—Flight of the Eagle (Classic Reprint) (p. 748)
—In the Wake of King James: Or Dun-Randal on the Sea (Classic Reprint) (p. 1111)
—In the Wake of King James or Dun-Randal on the Sea. (p. 1111)
—Ulrick the Ready (Classic Reprint) (p. 2314)
Oguchi, Stephanie. Colors of Me: Chi-Chi's Hair. (p. 426)
O'Guilin, Peadar. Call. (p. 311)
—Invasion (the Call, Book 2) (p. 1130)
Ogunkoya, Olukayode. Godly Children, Praying Children. (p. 853)
Ogunnaike, Oludamini. Meet Our New Student from Mali. (p. 1439)
Oh, Charlotte, illus. see Gates Galvin, Laura.
Oh, DaYun. We Are Brothers. Godeassi, Anna, illus. (p. 2389)
Oh, Ellen. Flying Lessons & Other Stories. (p. 755)
—Prophecy. (p. 1807)
—Spirit Hunters. (p. 2083)
—Spirit Hunters #2: the Island of Monsters. (p. 2083)
—Warrior. (p. 2379)
Oh, Ellen, ed. Flying Lessons & Other Stories. (p. 755)
Oh, Ellen, et al. Thousand Beginnings & Endings. (p. 2231)
Oh, H. Too. Super Duper Water Balloon Launcher Kit: Ready! Aim! Splash! (p. 2155)
Oh, Ha Rim. Sunjai & Kiwon. (p. 2152)
Oh, Hyeon-Gyeong. How Does It Protect Itself? Camouflage. Choi, Cheol-Min, illus. (p. 1030)
Oh, Joowon. Our Favorite Day. Oh, Joowon, illus. (p. 1678)
Oh, Lee, illus. see Joo, Mi-hwa.
Oh, Seung-min, illus. see Jang, Ki-hwa & Kim, In-sook.
Oh, Seung-min, illus. see Jang, Ki-hwa.
O'Hagan, Jeanette. Blood Crystal: A Novella. (p. 246)
—Heart of the Mountain: A Short Novella. (p. 945)
—Shadow Crystals: A Novella. (p. 1996)
—Stone of the Sea: A Short Novella. (p. 2121)
O'Hagan, Katie, illus. see Levenson, Eleanor.
O'Hailey, Tina. When Darkness Begins. (p. 2429)
O'Hair, Margaret. My Pup Lyon, Tammie, illus. (p. 1559)
O'Halloran, Rohahiio Richard. Cortney Christina Rae's First Day of School. (p. 456)
Ohanesian, Diane. ABCs of Thanks & Please. Chamberlain, Margaret, illus. (p. 5)
—Hugga Bugga Love. Flint, Gillian, illus. (p. 1048)
—Snuggle down Deep. Bornoff, Emily, illus. (p. 2050)
Ohanesian, Diane, jt. auth. see Daronco, Mickey.
O'Hanlon, Alice. Diamond in the Rough, Vol. 1 of 3 (Classic Reprint) (p. 538)
O'Hannrachain, Micheal. Swordsman of the Brigade (Classic Reprint) (p. 2171)
O'Hanrahan, Michael. Swordsman of the Brigade (Classic Reprint) (p. 2171)
O'Haodha, Tomas. Cainnt Scoile, (School Talk), Vol. 2: An Irish-English Conversation Book for Use in Elementary Schools & Gaelic League Classes (Classic Reprint) (p. 309)
O'Hara, Bernard Francis. Artemisia, 1903 (Classic Reprint) (p. 122)
O'Hara, Cynthia, illus. see Neuhofer, Sheri L.
O'Hara, Jack. Diary of a Scotty-Dog! Cactus Joe. (p. 539)
O'Hara, John. Big Laugh: A Novel (Classic Reprint) (p. 221)
O'Hara, John Myers. Embers. (p. 641)
O'Hara, Katrina. Cat Food. (p. 341)
—Lemur & the Mermaid. (p. 1266)
O'Hara, Lauren, illus. see Dahl, Sophie.
O'Hara, M. Herbe Verte du Wyoming. (p. 957)
O'Hara, Megan. Plains Communities Past & Present (p. 1754)
O'Hara, Michael Brian. Adventures of Alexander T. Frog. (p. 21)
—Short Tale of a Long, Long Tail. (p. 2011)
O'Hara, Mo. Agent Moose. Bradley, Jess, illus. (p. 35)
—Any Fin Is Possible: My Big Fat Zombie Goldfish. Jagucki, Marek, illus. (p. 104)
—Cats in the Crater: My FANGtastically Evil Vampire Pet. Jagucki, Marek, illus. (p. 346)
—Fins of Fury: My Big Fat Zombie Goldfish. Jagucki, Marek, illus. (p. 731)
—Fin-Tastic Fish-Sitter. Jagucki, Marek, illus. (p. 727)
—Jurassic Carp: My Big Fat Zombie Goldfish. Jagucki, Marek, illus. (p. 1192)
—Legend of King Arthur-A-tops. Joyner, Andrew, illus. (p. 1262)
—My Big Fat Zombie Goldfish. Jagucki, Marek, illus. (p. 1532)
—My FANGtastically Evil Vampire Pet. Jagucki, Marek, illus. (p. 1538)
—Romeosaurus & Juliet Rex. Joyner, Andrew, illus. (p. 1901)
—SeaQuel: My Big Fat Zombie Goldfish. Jagucki, Marek, illus. (p. 1970)
—Space Cat-Astrophe: My FANGtastically Evil Vampire Pet. Jagucki, Marek, illus. (p. 2071)
O'Hara, Natalia. Hortense & the Shadow. (p. 1005)
O'Hara, Nicholas. Sonidos / Sort It by Sound. de la Vega, Eida, tr. (p. 2064)
—Sort It by Sound. (p. 2066)
—Sort It by Texture. (p. 2066)
—Sort It by Weight. (p. 2066)
—Textura / Sort It by Texture. de la Vega, Eida, tr. (p. 2210)
O'Hara, Susan. Christie Plays Softball. Barrett, Rebecca, illus. (p. 383)
—Tim's First Soccer Game. Barrett, Rebecca, illus. (p. 2247)
O'Hare, Michael, illus. see Van Lente, Fred.
Ohare, Ted. Boas. Rourke Publishing Staff, ed. (p. 251)
—Cobras. Rourke Publishing Staff, ed. (p. 410)
—Rattlesnakes. Rourke Publishing Staff, ed. (p. 1843)
O'Hart, Sinéad. Eye of the North. (p. 688)
—Starspun Web. (p. 2107)
Ohayon, Jaci. Food Dancer: Traveling, Tasting & Twirling Around the World. (p. 759)
O'Hearn, Darcee. Wendy the Whitebark Pine. Young, Adam, illus. (p. 2400)
O'Hearn, Kate. End of Olympus. (p. 648)
—Flame of Olympus. (p. 746)
—Missing. (p. 1480)
—New Olympians. (p. 1596)
—Olympus at War. (p. 1651)
—Origins of Olympus. (p. 1672)
—Pegasus Mythic Collection Books 1-6: The Flame of Olympus; Olympus at War; the New Olympians; Origins of Olympus; Rise of the Titans; the End of Olympus. (p. 1714)
—Rise of the Titans. (p. 1885)
—Runaway. (p. 1914)
—Titans. (p. 2251)
—Valkyrie. (p. 2344)
—Valkyrie Complete Collection: Valkyrie; the Runaway; War of the Realms. (p. 2344)
—War of the Realms. (p. 2376)
O'Hearn, Michael. Allosaurus vs. Brachiosaurus: Might Against Height. Renne, Philip K., illus. (p. 57)
—Awesome Space Robots. (p. 145)
—Deinonychus vs. Styracosaurus: When Claws & Spikes Collide Renne, Philip K., illus. (p. 526)
—el Dorado Map. (p. 630)
—Ghosts vs. Witches: Tussle of the Tricksters. Moffet, Patricia, illus. (p. 830)
—Monster Wars. Moffet, Patricia et al, illus. (p. 1497)
—Sea Monsters vs. Dragons: Showdown of the Legends Altmann, Scott, illus. (p. 1968)
—Story of the New England Patriots. (p. 2134)
—This or That History Debate: A Rip-Roaring Game of Either/or Questions. (p. 2226)
—Triceratops vs. Stegosaurus: When Horns & Plates Collide. Renne, Philip K., illus. (p. 2287)
—Tyrannosaurus Rex vs. Velociraptor: Power Against Speed. Renne, Philip K., illus. (p. 2311)
—Vampires vs. Werewolves: Battle of the Bloodthirsty Beasts. Kendree, McLean, illus. (p. 2346)
—Zombies vs. Mummies: Clash of the Living Dead. Moffet, Patricia, illus. (p. 2542)
O'Hearn, Michael, et al. This or That? (p. 2226)
O'Hely, Eileen. P. E. P. Squad. (p. 1690)
—Penny in Space. Phelan, Nicky, illus. (p. 1717)
—Penny on Safari. Phelan, Nicky, illus. (p. 1717)
O'Hern, Ashley. Braelynn. (p. 274)
O'Hern, Kerri, jt. auth. see Anderson, Dale.
O'Hern, Kerri, jt. auth. see Holland, Gini.
O'Hern, Kerri, jt. auth. see Mayo, Gretchen Will.
O'Hern, Kerri, jt. auth. see Raatma, Lucia.
O'Hern, Kerri, jt. auth. see Riehecky, Janet.
Ohi, Debbie Ridpath. Sam & Eva. Ohi, Debbie Ridpath, illus. (p. 1926)
—Where Are My Books? Ohi, Debbie Ridpath, illus. (p. 2435)
Ohi, Debbie Ridpath, illus. see Black, Michael Ian.
Ohi, Debbie Ridpath, illus. see Blume, Judy.
Ohi, Debbie Ridpath, illus. see McLaughlin, Lauren.
Ohi, Debbie Ridpath, illus. see Park, Linda Sue.
Ohi, Debbie Ridpath, illus. see Reynolds, Aaron.
Ohi, Debbie Ridpath, illus. see Sanders, Rob.
Ohi, Ruth. Chicken, Pig, Cow & the Class Pet. (p. 368)

Numeric

—Chicken, Pig, Cow & the Purple Problem. (p. 368)
—Chicken, Pig, Cow Horse Around. (p. 368)
—Chicken, Pig, Cow on the Move. (p. 368)
—Chicken, Pig, Cow's First Fight. (p. 368)
—Fox & Squirrel. Ohi, Ruth, illus. (p. 774)
—Kenta & the Big Wave. (p. 1209)
—Shh! My Brother's Napping. Ohi, Ruth, illus. (p. 2006)
Ohi, Ruth, illus. see Jennings, Sharon.
Ohi, Ruth, illus. see Kogawa, Joy.
Ohi, Ruth, illus. see Page, P. K. & Ellis, Sarah.
O'Higgins, Harvey. Some Distinguished Americans: Imaginary Portraits (Classic Reprint) (p. 2059)
O'Higgins, Harvey J. Don-A-Dreams: A Story of Love & Youth (Classic Reprint) (p. 580)
—Grand Army Man (Classic Reprint) (p. 876)
—Silent Sam: And Other Stories of Our Day (Classic Reprint) (p. 2017)
O'Higgins, Harvey Jerrold. His Mother (Classic Reprint) (p. 974)
Ohio, Ada High School. Cn Yor Hi, Vol. 7: The Official Annual of the Student Body of ADA High School, May, 1915 (Classic Reprint) (p. 409)
Ohkubo, Atsushi, creator. Soul Eater, Vol. 2. (p. 2066)
—Soul Eater, Vol. 3. (p. 2066)
Ohlenroth, Pat, jt. auth. see Sohn, Emily.
Ohlenroth, Patricia, jt. auth. see Sohn, Emily.
Ohlin, Nancy. Always, Forever. (p. 61)
—American Revolution. Larkum, Adam, illus. (p. 73)
—Ancient Egypt. Larkum, Adam, illus. (p. 80)
—Ancient Greece. Larkum, Adam, illus. (p. 81)
—Beauty. (p. 184)
—Civil Rights Movement. Simó, Roger, illus. (p. 396)
—Civil War. Larkum, Adam, illus. (p. 396)
—Consent. (p. 442)
—Pearl Harbor. Simó, Roger, illus. (p. 1710)
—Space Race. Simó, Roger, illus. (p. 2072)
—Statue of Liberty. Simó, Roger, illus. (p. 2109)
—Thorn Abbey. (p. 2230)
—Titanic. Larkum, Adam, illus. (p. 2251)
—Vikings. Larkum, Adam, illus. (p. 2357)
—Women's Suffrage. Simó, Roger, illus. (p. 2488)
—World War II. Simó, Roger, illus. (p. 2505)
Ohlin, Nancy, jt. auth. see McKenzie, Paige.
Ohlms, Sharon. Children's Stories. (p. 375)
Ohlsen, Erik. Forest of Fire: A Wildfire Story. (p. 766)
—Living Playground. (p. 1334)
Ohlson, E. E. Pippa at Brighton (Classic Reprint) (p. 1749)
Ohnaka, Kathryn. Do Immigrants Have the Right to Come to the United States? (p. 570)
—Key Civil Rights Laws (p. 1210)
—Key Civil Rights Laws. (p. 1210)
—Key Immigration Laws (p. 1211)
—Key Immigration Laws. (p. 1211)
Ohnet, Georges. Cloud & Sunshine: Noir et Rose; Two Love Stories (Classic Reprint) (p. 407)
—Woman of Mystery (Classic Reprint) (p. 2485)
O'Hollaren, William. Creighton Quarterly Shadows, Vol. 30: The Student Magazine of the Creighton University, Omaha; April, 1939 (Classic Reprint) (p. 473)
—Creighton Quarterly Shadows, Vol. 30: The Student Magazine of the Creighton University, Omaha; February, 1939 (Classic Reprint) (p. 473)
OHora, Zachariah. My Cousin Momo. (p. 1536)
—Niblet & Ralph. (p. 1602)
—No Fits, Nilson! OHora, Zachariah, illus. (p. 1612)
—Not So Quiet Library. (p. 1623)
—Stop Snoring, Bernard! OHora, Zachariah, illus. (p. 2122)
OHora, Zachariah, illus. see Bardhan-Quallen, Sudipta.
OHora, Zachariah, illus. see Dyckman, Ame.
OHora, Zachariah, illus. see Higgins, Carter.
OHora, Zachariah, illus. see Shea, Bob.
OHora, Zachariah, illus. see Vega, Denise.
OHora, Zachariah, illus. see Wheeler, Lisa.
Ohotmu Team & O'Sullivan, Mike, texts. Marvel Cinematic Universe Guidebook: It's All Connected. (p. 1412)
Ohrt, Kate. Dancing Dreams. Valiant, Kristi, illus. (p. 500)
—Rainbow Book. (p. 1836)
Ohrt, Kate, jt. auth. see Accord Publishing Staff.
Ohtaka, Shinobu, creator. Sumomomo, Momomo, Vol. 12: The Strongest Bride on Earth (p. 2150)
Oie, Brantley. Panda Loves. (p. 1695)
Oien, Jennifer, illus. see Grandma Poo Poo.
Oja, L. G. Little Miss Izzy's Adventures - Miss Izzy & the Monsters. (p. 1322)
Ojakorotu, Victor, ed. see Baughan, Brian.
Ojakorotu, Victor, ed. see Friedenthal, Lora & Kavanaugh, Dorothy.
Ojakorotu, Victor, ed. see Gelletly, LeeAnne.
Ojakorotu, Victor, ed. see Habeeb, William Mark.
Ojakorotu, Victor, ed. see Lewis, Susan Grant.
Ojakorotu, Victor, ed. see Marcovitz, Hal.
Ojakorotu, Victor, ed. see Obadina, Elizabeth.
Ojakorotu, Victor, ed. see Obadina, Tunde.
Ojakorotu, Victor, ed. see Rotberg, Robert I.
Ojakorotu, Victor, ed. see Shah, Anup.
Ojala, Eiko, illus. see Eggers, Dave.
Ojala, Eiko, illus. see Katz, Susan B.
Ojeda, Carlos, illus. see Perks, Joseph M.
Ojo, LaMuriel. Phenix City Story, Bertha's Confession. (p. 1733)
Ojo, Loyce. Bath Time. (p. 172)
Ojoye-Adebayo, Ibitola. My Name Is Lizzy Adams. (p. 1557)
Ok, SeoJeong, illus. see Kim, JeongHo.
Okab, Baaraaha. If the Light Can Find Its Way. (p. 1092)
Okabe, Akiko, illus. see Pouatcha, Pearly.
Okada, Chiaki, illus. see Newson, Karl.
Okafor, Michelle Relerford. Khi Has Fun at Home. (p. 1212)
Okamoto, Alan, illus. see Bennett, Jeffrey.
Okamoto, Nadya. Power to the Period (wt) A Menstruation Manifesto. Elfast, Rebecca, illus. (p. 1783)
O'Kane, Walter Collins. Jim & Peggy at Meadowbrook Farm (Classic Reprint) (p. 1168)
Okawa, Bkub. Pop Team Epic. (p. 1775)
—Pop Team Epic, Second Season. (p. 1775)
Oke, Ikeogu. Tortoise & the Princess. (p. 2266)
Okeden, Fitzmaurice. Felicia's Dowry, Vol. 1 of 3 (Classic Reprint) (p. 719)
Okee Dokee Brothers Staff. Can You Canoe? & Other Adventure Songs. Reese, Brandon, illus. (p. 318)
—Thousand Star Hotel. Reese, Brandon, illus. (p. 2231)
Okeefe, Cameron Killian. Little Book of Simple Sayings. (p. 1312)
O'Keefe, Emily. Crop Circles. (p. 477)
—Eyewitness to the Assassination of Archduke Francis Ferdinand. (p. 689)
—Eyewitness to World War I Medicine. (p. 689)
—Humpback Whale. (p. 1051)
—Investigating Crop Circles. (p. 1131)
—UFOs. (p. 2313)
O'Keefe, Kathy Della Torre. Child's Guide to the Beatitudes. (p. 376)
O'Keefe, Laurie, illus. see Jennings, Terry Catasús.
OKeefe, Raven, illus. see Lofficier, Randy.
O'Keefe, Sherry. Aung San Suu Kyi. (p. 136)
—From China to America: The Story of Amy Tan. (p. 791)
—Spin: The Story of Michael Jackson. (p. 2082)
O'Keefe, Vivien. Short & Sweet. (p. 2010)
O'Keeffe, Adelaide. Dudley, Vol. 1 of 3 (Classic Reprint) (p. 609)
—Dudley, Vol. 2 of 3 (Classic Reprint) (p. 609)
—Dudley, Vol. 3 of 3 (Classic Reprint) (p. 609)
O'Keeffe, Alejandro, illus. see Heos, Bridget.
O'Keeffe, Alejandro, illus. see Nadin, Joanna.
O'Keeffe, Frank. Harry Flammable. (p. 934)
O'Keeffe, John. Dramatic Works of John O'Keeffe. (p. 597)
—Dramatic Works of John o'Keeffe, Esq. , Vol. 3 Of 4: Published under the Gracious Patronage of His Royal Highness the Prince of Wales (Classic Reprint) (p. 597)
—Dramatic Works of John o'Keeffe, Esq. , Vol. 3 of 4 (Classic Reprint) (p. 597)
—London Hermit, or Rambles in Dorsetshire: A Comedy, As Performed with Universal Applause at the Theatres Royal (Classic Reprint) (p. 1341)
—Recollections of the Life of John o'Keeffe, Vol. 2 Of 2: Written by Himself (Classic Reprint) (p. 1854)
O'Keeffe, Stuart. Quick Six Fix: 100 No-Fuss, Full-Flavor Recipes - Six Ingredients, Six Minutes Prep, Six Minutes Cleanup. (p. 1827)
Okeke, Nike. No Space for Junk: Inspired by a True Life Journey to Finding Happiness (p. 1615)
Okeley, William. Eben-Ezer, or a Small Monument of Great Mercy: Appearing in the Miraculous Deliverance of William Okeley, William Adams, John Anthony, John Jephs, John-Carpenter from the Miserable Slavery of Algiers (Classic Reprint) (p. 622)
O'Kelly, C. S. Adventures of Gracie & Monkeybear: Book 2: Winter. Callahan, Tricia, ed. (p. 23)
—Las Aventuras de Gracie y OsoMono: Libro 1: Verano. Callahan, Tricia, ed. (p. 1245)
O'Kelly, O'Kelly. Bribe: A Play in Three Acts (Classic Reprint) (p. 280)
O'Kelly, Seumas. Golden Barque & the Weaver's Grave. (p. 856)
—Golden Barque & the Weaver's Grave (Classic Reprint) (p. 856)
—Lady of Deerpark (Classic Reprint) (p. 1237)
—Leprechaun of Killmeen (Classic Reprint) (p. 1268)
—Matchmakers: A Comedy in One Act (Classic Reprint) (p. 1420)
—Waysiders: Stories of Connacht (Classic Reprint) (p. 2388)
—Wet Clay (Classic Reprint) (p. 2403)
Oketani, Shogo, jt. auth. see Lowitz, Leza.
Oketch, Alphonce Omondi, illus. see Carlson, Martin D.
Oki, Morihiro. Maza Teresa: Afureru Al. (p. 1430)
Okido. Head to Toe: My Body & How It Works. (p. 942)
OKIDO & Anon. Head to Toe: My Body & How It Works. (p. 942)
—My Animal Book: Facts & Fun, Questions & Answers, Things to Make & Do. (p. 1531)
Okido Staff. Color Me In! An Activity Book. (p. 420)
—How Things Work: Facts & Fun, Questions & Answers, Things to Make & Do. (p. 1036)
—My Animal Book: Facts & Fun, Questions & Answers, Things to Make & Do. (p. 1531)
—My Big World: Facts & Fun Questions & Answers Things to Make & Do. (p. 1533)
—What's Inside? See-Through Pages & Magic Surprises! (p. 2424)
Okido Staff, creator. Let's Play a Game: All You Need to Play Six Board Games. (p. 1276)
O'Kif, illus. see Benjamin, A. H.
O'Kif, Alejandro. Beauty & the Beast (Tales to Grow By) A Story about Trust. (p. 185)
Okito. World & the Mysteries: A Dog Asks, Why? (p. 2501)
Oklejak, Marianna, illus. see Wechterowicz, Przemystaw.
Okobia, Desiri. I AM Bodel. (p. 1058)
—I Am Bodel. (p. 1058)
Okon, Jodi, jt. auth. see Mills, Nathan.
Okonji, Azuka, illus. see Chukwumerije, Dikeogu.
Okonowski, Anne. Standing in the CIA Director's Shoes. (p. 2101)
—Who Are Nationalists & What Do They Believe In? (p. 2446)
Okorafor, Nnedi. Akata Warrior. (p. 38)
—Akata Witch. (p. 38)
—Ikenga. (p. 1094)
Oksner, Judith, illus. see Milton, Edith.
Oksner, Judith, illus. see Montgomery, Sy.
Okstad, Ella, illus. see Crowe, Caroline.
Okstad, Ella, illus. see Grabill, Rebecca.
Okstad, Ella, illus. see Hood, Morag.
Okstad, Ella, illus. see Jones, Pip.
Okstad, Ella, illus. see Metzger, Steve.
Okstad, Ella, illus. see Nesbit, E.
Oku, Makiko, tr. see ZOO, La.
Olabi, Adriana. Fine Motor Activities. (p. 730)
Oladele, Wealth Samuel. Youth Desire. (p. 2536)
Oladokun, Alexander. Acrux Manor: The Prodigal's Curse (Hardcover) (p. 12)
Oladosu, Folake. Ajayi lo Si Ile-Eko. Lowe, Wesley, illus. (p. 38)
—Ajayi lo Si Oko Isu. Lowe, Wesley, illus. (p. 38)
Olafsdottir, Linda, illus. see Cech, John & Namm, Diane.
Olafsdottir, Linda, illus. see Namm, Diane & Andersen, Hans.
Olafsdottir, Linda, illus. see Olmstead, Kathleen.
Olafsdottir, Linda, jt. auth. see Olmstead, Kathleen.
Olah, Tina, illus. see Dobson, Julie M.
Olan, Agnieszka, illus. see Lenington, Paula.
Olander, Johan. Field Guide to Aliens: Intergalactic Worrywarts, Bubblonauts, Silver-Slurpers, & Other Extraterrestria (p. 723)
—Field Guide to Monsters: Googly-Eyed Wart Floppers, Shadow-Casters, Toe-Eaters, & Other Creatures (p. 723)
Olanin, Cynthia E. Adventures of Emistine. (p. 23)
Olasky, Susan. Annie Henry & the Birth of Liberty. (p. 100)
—Annie Henry & the Mysterious Stranger. (p. 100)
—Annie Henry & the Redcoats. (p. 100)
—Annie Henry & the Secret Mission. (p. 100)
O'Laughlin, Ann. Amazing Bi-Ski Rescue. Foster-Fell, Jeremy, ed. (p. 64)
Olazagasti-Segovia, Elena, tr. see Cofer, Judith Ortiz.
Olberg, Henry. Magical Tooth Fairies: A Surprise in Mexico. (p. 1380)
—Magical Tooth Fairies: The Secret of the Magic Dust. (p. 1380)
Olbey, Arpad, illus. see Bradman, Tom and Tony.
Olbey, Arpad, illus. see Watson, J. A.
Olbrys, Brooks. Adventures of Blue Ocean Bob: Blue Ocean Bob Discovers His Purpose. Hamilton, Emma Walton, ed. (p. 22)
Olcott, Alison, jt. auth. see Hudd, Emily.
Olcott, Charles S. Lure of the Camera (Classic Reprint) (p. 1369)
Olcott, Frances Jenkins. Book of Elves & Fairies: For Story-Telling & Reading Aloud & for the Children's Own Reading (Classic Reprint) (p. 258)
—Children's Reading (Classic Reprint) (p. 374)
—Fairy Tales for Children (Classic Reprint) (p. 697)
—Good Stories for Great Holidays, Arranged for Story-Telling & Reading Aloud & for the Children's Own Reading (Classic Reprint) (p. 866)
—Red Indian Fairy Book for the Children's Own Reading & for Story-Tellers (Classic Reprint) (p. 1857)
—Wonder Garden: Nature Myths & Tales from All the World over for Story-Telling & Reading Aloud & for the Children's Own Reading (Classic Reprint) (p. 2488)
Olcott, Harriet A. Torchlight: Or, Through the Wood (Classic Reprint) (p. 2264)
Olcott, Harriet A. Hinsdale. Isora's Child (Classic Reprint) (p. 1140)
Olcott, Virginia. Holiday Plays for Home, School & Settlement (Classic Reprint) (p. 988)
—Patriotic Plays for Young People (Classic Reprint) (p. 1705)
—Plays for Home, School & Settlement: Flowers in the Palace Garden, & Other Plays (Classic Reprint) (p. 1761)
Olcott, William Tyler. Field Book of the Stars. (p. 723)
Old Farmer's Almanac Staff. Old Farmer's Almanac for Kids. (p. 1645)
Old Farmer's Almanac Staff, ed. Old Farmer's Almanac for Kids (p. 1645)
Old, Kenneth G. & West, Patty Old. Return of the Twith: The Twith Logue Chronicles. (p. 1871)
—Secret Quest: The Twith Logue Chronicles. (p. 1978)
Old Nana. Santa's Team. Kalpart, illus. (p. 1934)
Old, Wendie C. Life of Duke Ellington: Giant of Jazz. (p. 1294)
—Life of Louis Armstrong: King of Jazz. (p. 1294)
—Wright Brothers: Aviation Pioneers & Inventors. (p. 2511)
Oldberg, Oscar. Manual of Weights, Measures, & Specific Gravity: Including Principles of Metrology; the Weights & Measures Now in Use; Weight & Volume, & Their Reciprocal Relations; Weighing & Measuring; Balances (Scales) & Weights; Measures of Capacity; Sp. (p. 1399)
Oldenburg, Richard. How the Quail Earned His Topknot. (p. 1036)
—Three Little Green Pigs, Llc: A Recycling Pig Tale. Samantha May Cerney, illus. (p. 2233)
—Three Little Green Pigs, Llc: A Recycling Pig Tale. Cerney, Samantha May, illus. (p. 2233)
Older, Daniel Jose. Dactyl Hill Squad (p. 494)
Older, Daniel José. Dactyl Hill Squad. (p. 494)
—Freedom Fire. (p. 782)
—Shadowhouse Fall. (p. 1997)
—Shadowshaper. (p. 1998)
—Shadowshaper - Legacy. (p. 1998)
Older, Fremont. Socialist & the Prince (Classic Reprint) (p. 2053)
Older, Jules. Snowmobile: Bombardier's Dream Machine. Lauritano, Michael, illus. (p. 2049)
Oldershaw, Daisy. Lonely Planet. (p. 1342)
Oldfield, Dawn Bluemel. Abyssinians: Egyptian Royalty? (p. 9)
—English Mastiff: The World's Heaviest Dog. (p. 654)
—Killer Whale: Water Bullet! (p. 1217)
—Leaping Ground Frogs. (p. 1255)
—Newfoundland: Water Rescuer. (p. 1600)
—Tarsier. (p. 2192)
—Venus: Super Hot. (p. 2351)
—Venus: Supercaliente. (p. 2351)
—Water Frog Polliwogs. (p. 2384)
Oldfield, F. F. W. Illustrated Films Monthly, Vol. 2: March-August, 1914 (Classic Reprint) (p. 1096)
Oldfield, Jenny. Crazy Horse. (p. 469)
Oldfield, Matt & Oldfield, Tom. Aguero. (p. 36)
—Bale: Real Madrid. (p. 161)
—Beckham. (p. 187)
—Figo. (p. 726)
—Gerrard: Liverpool F.C. (p. 823)
—Hazard: From the Playground to the Pitch. (p. 941)
—Iniesta: FC Barcelona. (p. 1120)
—Klinsmann. (p. 1227)
—Luis Suarez: el Pistolero. (p. 1366)
—Maradona. (p. 1402)
—Messi. (p. 1452)
—Neuer. (p. 1589)
—Neymar. (p. 1601)
—Pogba: Manchester United. (p. 1767)
—Pogba. (p. 1767)
—Road to the World Cup. (p. 1888)
—Ronaldo. (p. 1902)
—Rooney: Manchester United. (p. 1903)
—Sanchez. (p. 1930)
—Sterling. (p. 2115)
—Suarez: F.C. Barcelona. (p. 2145)
—Zidane. (p. 2540)
—Zlatan. (p. 2541)
Oldfield, Rachel. Up up Up. Reed, Susan, illus. (p. 2338)
Oldfield, Rachel, illus. see Nelson, Sarah.
Oldfield, Rachel, illus. see Reed, Susan.
Oldfield, Rachel, illus. see Williams, Brenda.
Oldfield, Tom, jt. auth. see Seton, Ernest Thompson.
Oldfield, Tom & Oldfield, Matt. Jamie Carragher: Liverpool's Legacy. (p. 1157)
—Lukaku. (p. 1366)
—Neymar: From the Playground to the Pitch. (p. 1601)
—Philippe Coutinho - The Kid: A Great Future for Liverpool's Little Magician. (p. 1734)
—Raheem Sterling: Red Lightning. (p. 1834)
—Steven Gerrard. (p. 2116)
—Wayne Rooney: Captain of England. (p. 2388)
—Zinedine Zidane: One of the Greats. (p. 2540)
Oldham, Bethenia McLemore. Practical Plans for Primary Teachers in Public or Private Schools (Classic Reprint) (p. 1784)
Oldham, Brad. Witch in My House. (p. 2479)
Oldham, Cindi, illus. see Williams, Annie Morris.
Oldham, E. S. By the Trent (Classic Reprint) (p. 306)
Oldham, Marion, illus. see Molesworth, Mary Louisa.
Oldham, Matthew. Mi Primer Libro Sobre el Cuerpo Humano: My Very First Body Book. (p. 1455)
—Mi Primer Libro Sobre Nuestro Planeta(My Very 1St Our World Book) (p. 1455)
—My Very First Body Book IR. (p. 1564)
—See Inside a Museum IR. (p. 1981)
Oldham, Matthew, jt. auth. see Cullis, Megan.
Oldham, Oliver. Humorous Speaker: Being a Choice Collection of Amusing Pieces, Both in Prose & Verse, Original & Selected; Consisting of Dialogues, Soliloquies, Parodies, &C (Classic Reprint) (p. 1051)
—Oldham's Amusing & Instructive Reader: A Course of Reading, Original & Selected, in Prose & Poetry, Wherein Wit, Humor, & Mirth Are Made the Means of Awakening Interest, & Imparting Instruction; for the Use of Schools & Academies. (p. 1649)
Olding, Lori. Origami Nun. (p. 1671)
Oldland, Nicholas. Big Bear Hug. (p. 216)
—Big Bear Hug. Oldland, Nicholas, illus. (p. 216)
—Busy Beaver. Oldland, Nicholas, illus. (p. 302)
—Dinosaur Countdown. Oldland, Nicholas, illus. (p. 548)
—Hockey in the Wild. Oldland, Nicholas, illus. (p. 985)
—Making the Moose Out of Life. Oldland, Nicholas, illus. (p. 1390)
—One Wild Christmas. Oldland, Nicholas, illus. (p. 1663)
Oldman, James. Superhighway. Ingram, Chris, illus. (p. 2160)
Oldmeadow, Ernest. Antonio (Classic Reprint) (p. 103)
—Susan (Classic Reprint) (p. 2166)
—Virginie (Classic Reprint) (p. 2361)
Oldpath, Obadish. Lin: Or, Notable People & Notable Things in the Early History of Lynn, the Third Plantation of Massachusetts Colony (Classic Reprint) (p. 1303)
Oldroyd, Mark, illus. see Jarman, Julia.
Oldroyd, Mark, illus. see Jones, Carrie.
Oldroyd, Mark, illus. see Knudsen, Shannon.
Oldroyd, Mark, illus. see Krensky, Stephen.
Olds, Charles Louis. Wood-Pile Recollections (Classic Reprint) (p. 2491)
Olea, Francisco, illus. see Maturana, Andrea.
Olearnick, Jan. Louisa Moo Alcott. (p. 1357)
O'Leary Brown, Erin, illus. see Curry, Don L.
O'Leary Brown, Erin, illus. see Hoffmann, Catherine E. & Hoffmann, Dana Marie.
O'Leary Brown, Erin, jt. auth. see Curry, Don L.
O'Leary, Chris, illus. see Miranda, Patricia J.
O'Leary, Denyse. What Are Newton's Laws of Motion? (p. 2405)
O'Leary, John. Goldilocks: A Pop-Up Book. O'Leary, John, illus. (p. 860)
O'Leary, Michael. Hampshire Folk Tales for Children. (p. 913)
O'Leary, Peter Canon. Shiana (Classic Reprint) (p. 2007)
O'Leary, Sara. Boy & the Blue Moon. Crowley, Ashley, illus. (p. 268)
—Family Is a Family Is a Family Leng, Qin, illus. (p. 702)
—Night Walk Arscott, Ellie, illus. (p. 1608)
—Owls Are Good at Keeping Secrets. Grant, Jacob, illus. (p. 1689)
—This Is Sadie. Morstad, Julie, illus. (p. 2225)
—When I Was Small. Morstad, Julie, illus. (p. 2431)
—When You Were Small. Morstad, Julie, illus. (p. 2434)
—You Are One. Klassen, Karen, illus. (p. 2524)
O'Leary, Sara & Opal, Paola. Zingy. Morstad, Julie, illus. (p. 2540)
O'Leary, Stephanie. If I Get to Heaven Before You. (p. 1091)
O'Leary, Tony. Canal Pirates. Kelly, Zac, illus. (p. 321)
O'Leary, Wendy, jt. auth. see Willard, Christopher.
Oleck, Joan. Graphic Design & Desktop Publishing. (p. 880)
Olek, Lisa B. Naked Cat With The Velvet Paws. Gruenfelder, Robin, illus. (p. 1573)
—Yoshka's Journey to Christmas. Gruenfelder, Robin, illus. (p. 2523)
Oleksiw, Mark Paul. Boys Who Danced with the Moon. (p. 273)
—Munching on the Sun. (p. 1526)
—Time's Musicians. (p. 2247)
Oleksy, Walter. Choosing a Career in Agriculture. (p. 381)
—Circulatory System. (p. 393)
Oleksy, Walter G., jt. auth. see Nathan, Jacintha.
Olena Rudge. Adventures of Sophie & Katia in the Enchanted Forest. (p. 28)
Olesen, Andrew. George Washington: The First President of the United States. (p. 819)

Olesen, Demetria Vassiliou. Lambyro. Forcada, Adiela & Giron, Elizabeth, illus. (p. 1240)
Olexa, Keith. Gross Science of Lice & Other Parasites. (p. 898)
—Working As a School Safety Officer. (p. 2495)
Oleynikov, Igor, illus. see Andersen, Hans.
Oleynikov, Igor, illus. see Lithgow, John.
Oleynikov, Igor, illus. see Lloyd-Jones, Sally.
Olguin Loza, Victor. Invento de Las Aves. (p. 1130)
—Spiderboy. (p. 2081)
Olien, Becky, jt. auth. see Olien, Rebecca.
Olien, Jessica. Adrift: An Odd Couple of Polar Bears. Olien, Jessica, illus. (p. 17)
—Blobfish Book. Olien, Jessica, illus. (p. 245)
—Right Now. Olien, Jessica, illus. (p. 1882)
—Shark Detective! Olien, Jessica, illus. (p. 2002)
—When a Tiger Comes to Dinner. Olien, Jessica, illus. (p. 2429)
Olien, Jessica, illus. see Root, Andrew.
Olien, Rebecca. Cleaning Water. (p. 402)
—How Do We Know about Dinosaurs? A Fossil Mystery McDee, Katie, illus. (p. 1029)
—Longitude & Latitude. (p. 1344)
—Looking at Maps & Globes. (p. 1347)
—Map Keys. (p. 1400)
—Saving Water. (p. 1939)
—Water Cycle at Work. (p. 2384)
—Water in Our World. (p. 2384)
—Water Sources. (p. 2385)
—Where Do the Birds Go? A Migration Mystery McDee, Katie, illus. (p. 2436)
Olien, Rebecca, jt. auth. see Hansen, Amy S.
Olien, Rebecca & Olien, Becky. Rescue Helicopters in Action (p. 1868)
Olin, Marilyn. Mom, Mac & Cheese, Please! Pantic, Dunja, illus. (p. 1490)
Olin, Nicki. God Made Me Special, Just Like You! (p. 852)
Olin, Sean. Reckless Hearts. (p. 1853)
—Wicked Games. (p. 2460)
Olinger, Heidi. Leonardo's Science Workshop: Invent, Create, & Make STEAM Projects Like a Genius. (p. 1267)
Oliphant. Curate in Charge (Classic Reprint) (p. 485)
—Harry Joscelyn, Vol. 1 of 3 (Classic Reprint) (p. 934)
—He That Will Not When He May, Vol. 3 of 3 (Classic Reprint) (p. 942)
—Innocent: A Tale of Modern Life (Classic Reprint) (p. 1121)
—Joyce (Classic Reprint) (p. 1184)
—Little Pilgrim in the Unseen (Classic Reprint) (p. 1324)
—Madonna Mary, Vol. 2 of 2 (Classic Reprint) (p. 1375)
—Neighbours on the Green (Classic Reprint) (p. 1586)
—Railway Man & His Children (Classic Reprint) (p. 1835)
—Railway Man & His Children, Vol. 1 of 3 (Classic Reprint) (p. 1835)
—Two Strangers (Classic Reprint) (p. 2309)
—Unjust Steward: Or the Minister's Debt (Classic Reprint) (p. 2333)
—Ways of Life: Two Stories (Classic Reprint) (p. 2388)
—Whiteladies, Vol. 1 of 3 (Classic Reprint) (p. 2445)
—Within the Precincts (Classic Reprint) (p. 2482)
Oliphant, Allan. To Arms! Being Some Passages from the Early Life of Allan Oliphant, Chirurgeon (Classic Reprint) (p. 2252)
Oliphant, Laurence. Masollam a Problem of the Period, Vol. 1 Of 3: A Novel (Classic Reprint) (p. 1417)
—Masollam; a Problem of the Period, Vol. 3 Of 3: A Novel (Classic Reprint) (p. 1417)
Oliphant, M. O. W. Kirsteen: The Story of a Scotch Family Seventy Years Ago (Classic Reprint) (p. 1224)
—Story of a Governess (Classic Reprint) (p. 2128)
—Story of Valentine & His Brother (Classic Reprint) (p. 2135)
Oliphant, Manelle, illus. see Spurr, Elizabeth.
Oliphant, Margaret. At His Gates: A Novel (Classic Reprint) (p. 129)
—At His Gates, Vol. 1 Of 3: A Novel (Classic Reprint) (p. 129)
—At His Gates, Vol. 2 Of 3: A Novel (Classic Reprint) (p. 129)
—Athelings, or the Three Gifts (Classic Reprint) (p. 132)
—Athelings, or the Three Gifts, Vol. 1 of 3 (Classic Reprint) (p. 132)
—Athelings; or, the Three Gifts, Vol. III. (p. 132)
—Autobiography & Letters of Mrs. M. O. W. Oliphant (Classic Reprint) (p. 139)
—Carità, Vol. 1 of 3 (Classic Reprint) (p. 331)
—Carita, Vol. 2 of 3 (Classic Reprint) (p. 331)
—Duke's Daughter & the Fugitives, Vol. 2 of 3 (Classic Reprint) (p. 609)
—Effie Ogilvie, Vol. 2 Of 2: The Story of a Young Life (Classic Reprint) (p. 627)
—For Love & Life, Vol. 1 of 3 (Classic Reprint) (p. 763)
—Fugitives (Classic Reprint) (p. 797)
—Greatest Heiress in England, Vol. 1 of 2 (Classic Reprint) (p. 891)
—Harry Muir: A Story of Scottish Life (Classic Reprint) (p. 934)
—He That Will Not When He May, Vol. 1 of 3 (Classic Reprint) (p. 942)
—Heir Presumptive & the Heir Apparent, Vol. 1 of 2 (Classic Reprint) (p. 949)
—House on the Moor (Classic Reprint) (p. 1024)
—John: A Love Story (Classic Reprint) (p. 1171)
—John Drayton, Vol. 1 Of 2: Being a History of the Early Life & Development of a Liverpool Engineer (Classic Reprint) (p. 1172)
—Katie Stewart, a True Story: And Other Tales (Classic Reprint) (p. 1205)
—Kirsteen, Vol. 2 Of 3: The Story of a Scotch Family Seventy Years Ago (Classic Reprint) (p. 1224)
—Ladies Lindores, Vol. 1 of 3 (Classic Reprint) (p. 1236)
—Last of the Mortimers: A Story in Two Voices (Classic Reprint) (p. 1249)
—Last of the Mortimers, Vol. 2 Of 3: A Story in Two Voices (Classic Reprint) (p. 1249)
—Lilliesleaf: Being a Concluding Series of Passages in the Life of Mrs. Margaret Maitland (Classic Reprint) (p. 1301)
—Lilliesleaf, Vol. 3 Of 3: Being a Concluding Series of Passages in the Life of Mrs. Margaret Maitland, of Sunnyside (Classic Reprint) (p. 1301)
—Madam: A Novel (Classic Reprint) (p. 1373)
—Madonna Mary, Vol. 1 of 3 (Classic Reprint) (p. 1375)
—Madonna Mary, Vol. 2 of 3 (Classic Reprint) (p. 1375)
—May, Vol. 1 (Classic Reprint) (p. 1429)
—Miss. Marjoribanks, Vol. 2 of 3 (Classic Reprint) (p. 1479)
—Old Mr. Tredgold, Vol. 1 of 2 (Classic Reprint) (p. 1647)
—Ombra, Vol. 1 of 3 (Classic Reprint) (p. 1651)
—Perpetual Curate, Vol. 1 of 3 (Classic Reprint) (p. 1724)
—Prodigals, Vol. 2 Of 2: And Their Inheritance (Classic Reprint) (p. 1804)
—Rector & the Doctor's Family (Classic Reprint) (p. 1855)
—Rose in June (Classic Reprint) (p. 1905)
—Salem Chapel (Classic Reprint) (p. 1924)
—Second Son, Vol. 1 of 3 (Classic Reprint) (p. 1974)
—Sir Robert's Fortune: A Novel (Classic Reprint) (p. 2026)
—Son of the Soil: A Novel (Classic Reprint) (p. 2062)
—Sorceress, Vol. 1 Of 2: A Novel (Classic Reprint) (p. 2065)
—Sorceress, Vol. 3 Of 3: A Novel (Classic Reprint) (p. 2065)
—Within the Precincts, Vol. 1 of 3 (Classic Reprint) (p. 2482)
—Young Musgrave (Classic Reprint) (p. 2531)
—Zaidee: A Romance. in Three Volumes, Vol. I. (p. 2538)
—Zaidee: A Romance from Blackwood's Magazine (Classic Reprint) (p. 2538)
—Zaidee, Vol. 1 Of 3: A Romance (Classic Reprint) (p. 2538)
—Zaidee, Vol. 3 Of 3: A Romance (Classic Reprint) (p. 2538)
Oliphant, Margaret & Walker, Annie Louisa. Autobiography & Letters of Mrs. M. O. W. Oliphant. (p. 139)
Oliphant, Margaret O. Chronicles of Carlingford, Vol. 3: Miss. Marjoribanks (Classic Reprint) (p. 388)
—Little Pilgrim: In the Seen & the Unseen (Classic Reprint) (p. 1324)
Oliphant, Margaret O. W. At His Gates, Vol. 1 Of 3: A Novel (Classic Reprint) (p. 129)
—At His Gates, Vol. 2 Of 3: A Novel (Classic Reprint) (p. 129)
—At His Gates, Vol. 3 Of 3: A Novel (Classic Reprint) (p. 129)
—Athelings, or the Three Gifts, Vol. 1 of 3 (Classic Reprint) (p. 132)
—Autobiography & Letters of Mrs. M. O. W. Oliphant (Classic Reprint) (p. 139)
—Brownlows: A Novel (Classic Reprint) (p. 287)
—Brownlows, Vol. 1 of 3 (Classic Reprint) (p. 287)
—Brownlows, Vol. 2 of 3 (Classic Reprint) (p. 287)
—Brownlows, Vol. 3 of 3 (Classic Reprint) (p. 287)
—Carità (Classic Reprint) (p. 331)
—Carita, Vol. 1 of 3 (Classic Reprint) (p. 331)
—Carita, Vol. 2 of 3 (Classic Reprint) (p. 331)
—Carita, Vol. 3 of 3 (Classic Reprint) (p. 331)
—Chronicles of Carlingford, Vol. 3: Miss. Marjoribanks (Classic Reprint) (p. 389)
—Country Gentleman & His Family (Classic Reprint) (p. 461)
—Country Gentleman & His Family, Vol. 1 of 3 (Classic Reprint) (p. 461)
—Country Gentleman, Vol. 2 Of 3: And His Family (Classic Reprint) (p. 461)
—Cuckoo in the Nest, Vol. 1 of 2 (Classic Reprint) (p. 482)
—Curate in Charge (Classic Reprint) (p. 485)
—Days of My Life: An Autobiography (Classic Reprint) (p. 515)
—Diana Trelawny (Classic Reprint) (p. 538)
—Duke's Daughter & the Fugitives, Vol. 2 of 3 (Classic Reprint) (p. 609)
—Effie Ogilvie, Vol. 1 Of 2: The Story of a Young Life (Classic Reprint) (p. 627)
—For Love & Life, Vol. 1 of 2 (Classic Reprint) (p. 763)
—Greatest Heiress in England, Vol. 1 of 3 (Classic Reprint) (p. 891)
—Harry Joscelyn, Vol. 2 of 3 (Classic Reprint) (p. 934)
—Harry Muir, Vol. 1 Of 3: A Story of Scottish Life (Classic Reprint) (p. 934)
—Harry Muir, Vol. 2 Of 3: A Story of Scottish Life (Classic Reprint) (p. 934)
—Harry Muir, Vol. 3 Of 3: A Story of Scottish Life (Classic Reprint) (p. 934)
—He That Will Not When He May (Classic Reprint) (p. 942)
—He That Will Not When He May, Vol. 2 of 3 (Classic Reprint) (p. 942)
—Heir Presumptive, Vol. 1 Of 3: And the Heir Apparent (Classic Reprint) (p. 949)
—House on the Moor (Classic Reprint) (p. 1024)
—Innocent: A Tale of Modern Life (Classic Reprint) (p. 1121)
—Innocent, Vol. 1 Of 3: A Tale of Modern Life (Classic Reprint) (p. 1121)
—Innocent, Vol. 2 Of 3: A Tale of Modern Life (Classic Reprint) (p. 1121)
—Innocent, Vol. 3 Of 3: A Tale of Modern Life (Classic Reprint) (p. 1121)
—It Was a Lover & His Lass (Classic Reprint) (p. 1142)
—It Was a Lover & His Lass, Vol. 1 of 3 (Classic Reprint) (p. 1142)
—John: A Love Story (Classic Reprint) (p. 1171)
—John Drayton, Vol. 1 Of 2: Being a History of the Early Life & Development of a Liverpool Engineer (Classic Reprint) (p. 1172)
—John Drayton, Vol. 2: Being a History of the Early Life & Development of a Liverpool Engineer (Classic Reprint) (p. 1172)
—John, Vol. 2 Of 2: A Love Story (Classic Reprint) (p. 1174)
—Kirsteen, Vol. 2 Of 3: The Story of a Scotch Family Seventy Years Ago (Classic Reprint) (p. 1224)
—Ladies Lindores, Vol. 1 of 3 (Classic Reprint) (p. 1236)
—Lady William (Classic Reprint) (p. 1238)
—Laird of Norlaw: A Scottish Story (Classic Reprint) (p. 1240)
—Laird of Norlaw, Vol. 2 Of 3: A Scottish Story (Classic Reprint) (p. 1240)
—Last of the Mortimers: A Story in Two Voices (Classic Reprint) (p. 1249)
—Last of the Mortimers, Vol. 1 Of 3: A Story in Two Voices (Classic Reprint) (p. 1249)
—Lilliesleaf: Being a Concluding Series of Passages in the Life of Mrs. Margaret Maitland (Classic Reprint) (p. 1301)
—Lilliesleaf, Vol. 2 Of 3: Being a Concluding Series of Passages in the Life of Mrs. Margaret Maitland, of Sunnyside (Classic Reprint) (p. 1301)
—Madam: A Novel (Classic Reprint) (p. 1374)
—Madam, Vol. 1 of 3 (Classic Reprint) (p. 1374)
—Madam, Vol. 3 of 3 (Classic Reprint) (p. 1374)
—Madonna Mary, Vol. 1 of 2 (Classic Reprint) (p. 1375)
—Madonna Mary, Vol. 2 of 2 (Classic Reprint) (p. 1375)
—Madonna Mary, Vol. 3 (Classic Reprint) (p. 1375)
—Melvilles, Vol. 3 of 3 (Classic Reprint) (p. 1443)
—Memoirs & Resolutions of Adam Graeme of Mossgray, Vol. 3 Of 3: Including Some Chronicles of the Borough of Fendie (Classic Reprint) (p. 1444)
—Memoirs & Resolutions of Adam Graeme, of Mossgray, Vol. 1 Of 3: Including Some Chronicles of the Borough of Fendie (Classic Reprint) (p. 1444)
—Miss. Marjoribanks (Classic Reprint) (p. 1479)
—Miss. Marjoribanks, Vol. 2 of 3 (Classic Reprint) (p. 1479)
—Mrs. Arthur, Vol. 2 of 3 (Classic Reprint) (p. 1521)
—Neighbours on the Green (Classic Reprint) (p. 1586)
—Neighbours on the Green, Vol. 1 of 3 (Classic Reprint) (p. 1586)
—Ombra (Classic Reprint) (p. 1651)
—Ombra, Vol. 1 of 3 (Classic Reprint) (p. 1651)
—Ombra, Vol. 2 of 3 (Classic Reprint) (p. 1651)
—Ombra, Vol. 3 of 3 (Classic Reprint) (p. 1651)
—Passages in the Life of Mrs. Margaret Maitland, of Sunnyside, Vol. 2 of 3 (Classic Reprint) (p. 1703)
—Perpetual Curate, Vol. 1 of 3 (Classic Reprint) (p. 1724)
—Phoebe, Junior, Vol. 1 Of 3: A Last Chronicle of Carlingford (Classic Reprint) (p. 1735)
—Poor Gentleman, Vol. 1 of 3 (Classic Reprint) (p. 1774)
—Primrose Path: A Chapter in the Annals of the Kingdom of Fife (Classic Reprint) (p. 1793)
—Primrose Path. (p. 1793)
—Primrose Path, a Chapter, 1878, Vol. 3 Of 3: In the Annals of the Kingdom of Fife (Classic Reprint) (p. 1793)
—Primrose Path, Vol. 1 Of 3: A Chapter in the Annals of the Kingdom of Fife (Classic Reprint) (p. 1793)
—Prodigals, Vol. 1 Of 2: And Their Inheritance (Classic Reprint) (p. 1804)
—Prodigals, Vol. 2 Of 2: And Their Inheritance (Classic Reprint) (p. 1804)
—Railway Man & His Children (Classic Reprint) (p. 1835)
—Railway Man & His Children, Vol. 1 of 3 (Classic Reprint) (p. 1835)
—Rector & the Doctor's Family (Classic Reprint) (p. 1855)
—Rose in June, Vol. 1 of 2 (Classic Reprint) (p. 1905)
—Rose in June, Vol. 2 of 2 (Classic Reprint) (p. 1905)
—Salem Chapel (Classic Reprint) (p. 1924)
—Salem Chapel, Vol. 1 of 2 (Classic Reprint) (p. 1924)
—Salem Chapel, Vol. 2 of 2 (Classic Reprint) (p. 1924)
—Second Son, Vol. 1 of 3 (Classic Reprint) (p. 1974)
—Sir Tom (Classic Reprint) (p. 2026)
—Sir Tom, Vol. 1 (Classic Reprint) (p. 2026)
—Sir Tom, Vol. 2 (Classic Reprint) (p. 2026)
—Sir Tom, Vol. 3 (Classic Reprint) (p. 2026)
—Son of His Father, Vol. 1 of 3 (Classic Reprint) (p. 2061)
—Son of the Soil: A Novel (Classic Reprint) (p. 2062)
—Son of the Soil, Vol. 1 (Classic Reprint) (p. 2062)
—Sorceress, Vol. 1 Of 3: A Novel (Classic Reprint) (p. 2065)
—Sorceress, Vol. 2 Of 3: A Novel (Classic Reprint) (p. 2065)
—Sorceress, Vol. 3 Of 3: A Novel (Classic Reprint) (p. 2065)
—Story of Valentine & His Brother (Classic Reprint) (p. 2135)
—Three Brothers, Vol. 1 of 3 (Classic Reprint) (p. 2232)
—Two Strangers (Classic Reprint) (p. 2309)
—Unjust Steward: Or the Minister's Debt (Classic Reprint) (p. 2333)
—Whiteladies, Vol. 1 of 3 (Classic Reprint) (p. 2445)
—Who Was Lost & Is Found: A Novel (Classic Reprint) (p. 2451)
—Widow's Tale: And Other Stories (Classic Reprint) (p. 2461)
—Within the Precincts, Vol. 1 of 3 (Classic Reprint) (p. 2482)
—Young Musgrave, Vol. 1 of 3 (Classic Reprint) (p. 2531)
—Zaidee, Vol. 2 Of 3: A Romance (Classic Reprint) (p. 2538)
Oliphant, Oliphant. Chronicles of Carlingford: A Novel (Classic Reprint) (p. 388)
—Laird of Norlaw, Vol. 1 Of 3: A Scottish Story (Classic Reprint) (p. 1240)
—Phoebe Junior, Vol. 2 (Classic Reprint) (p. 1735)
Oliphant, Philip Laurence. River of Vengeance (Classic Reprint) (p. 1887)
Oliphant, William. Little Alfred: Or, the Influence of Home Training. (p. 1310)
—Little Alfred: Or the Influence of Home Training (Classic Reprint) (p. 1310)
Olitzky, Kerry. Where's the Potty on This Ark? Tompkins, Abigail, illus. (p. 2441)
Oliva, Octavio, illus. see Smith, Michael & Wang, Emily.
Oliva, Octavio, illus. see Smith, Michael.
Oliva, Octavio, jt. auth. see Smith, Michael.
Olivarez, Ernest. Jose the Reindeer: Jose el Venadito. Illustrations, Blueberry, illus. (p. 1178)
Olivarez, Marlynn. Snuffy's Star. (p. 2050)
Olivaria, Dawn. Bear Who Wanted to Be a Mouse. (p. 180)
Olivas, Daniel. Benjamin & the Word: Benjamín y la Palabra. Baeza Ventura, Gabriela, tr. (p. 200)
Olivas, John D. Endeavour's Long Journey: Celebrating 19 Years of Space Exploration. Roski, Gayle Garner, illus. (p. 649)
—Endeavour's Long Journey. Roski, Gayle Garner, illus. (p. 649)
—Endeavour's Long Journey/la Larga Travesía de Endeavour. Roski, Gayle G., illus. (p. 649)
Olivas, Silvia, jt. auth. see Disney Book Group.
Olivas, Silvia, jt. auth. see RH Disney Staff.
Olive, Aylett. Bad Day. (p. 157)
—People Just Like You. (p. 1718)
Olive, Gloria D. My Hat! My Hat! Where Is My Hat? Barge III, John, illus. (p. 1549)
Olive, Guillaume & He, Zihong. My First Book of Chinese Calligraphy. (p. 1542)
Olive, M. Foster. Morphine. (p. 1506)
—Understanding Drugs: Ecstasy. (p. 2324)
Olive, Miss, jt. auth. see Marie, Susan.
Olive, Teresa, et al. Best-Loved Christmas Stories. Munger, Nancy et al, illus. (p. 206)
Olive, William. In-Between. (p. 1104)
Oliveira, De. Aniki Bobo. Enfants Dans la Ville. (p. 87)
Oliveira, Jô, illus. see Roscoe, Alessandra Pontes.
Oliveira, Jô de. Kuarup, a Festa DOS Mortos: Lendas DOS Povos Indigenas Do Xingu. (p. 1233)
Oliveira, Luis. Children of Hope 3. (p. 371)
—DogMan 2. (p. 577)
Oliveira, Thais. Princesas Adoradoras: Um Chamado para a Realeza. Francisco, Eneas, ed. (p. 1795)
Oliver, Alison. Be Bold, Baby: J. K. Rowling. (p. 176)
—Be Bold, Baby: Michelle Obama. (p. 176)
—Be Bold, Baby: Oprah. (p. 176)
—Be Bold, Baby: Sonia Sotomayor. (p. 176)
—Cat Tote (p. 342)
—Moon. (p. 1501)
—Sun. (p. 2150)
Oliver, Alison, illus. see Adams, Jennifer.
Oliver, Alison, illus. see Colleen, Marcie.
Oliver, Ben. Loop. (p. 1348)
Oliver, Butterworth. Enormous Egg. (p. 655)
Oliver, Carmen. Bears Make the Best Math Buddies. Claude, Jean, illus. (p. 181)
—Bears Make the Best Reading Buddies. Claude, Jean, illus. (p. 181)
—Cuentos Ilustrados de Ficción. Claude, Jean, illus. (p. 483)
—No Hay Nada Más Chistoso Que Leer con un Oso. Claude, Jean, illus. (p. 1613)
—Voice for the Spirit Bears: How One Boy Inspired Millions to Save a Rare Animal. Dockrill, Katy, illus. (p. 2365)
Oliver, Catherine E., jt. auth. see Warwick, Michael Andrew.
Oliver, Clare. Great Britain. (p. 884)
OLIVER, Clare. Weather. (p. 2393)
Oliver, Daniel. First Lines of Physiology: Designed for the Use of Students of Medicine (Classic Reprint) (p. 738)
Oliver, E. L. Brujita of Washington Heights: Book II Blood Ties. (p. 287)
Oliver, Frederic L. Give That Child a Mouth. (p. 840)
Oliver, Ig. Butterfly Bee Lady & the Bee. (p. 304)
—Butterfly Bee Lady - Part 2. (p. 304)
Oliver, Ilanit. Olivia & the Best Teacher Ever. (p. 1650)
—Ten Flying Brooms. Poling, Kyle, illus. (p. 2204)
Oliver, Jan. Heart of Fire. (p. 945)
Oliver, Jana. Briar Rose. (p. 280)
—Demon Trapper's Daughter. (p. 528)
—Foretold. (p. 767)
Oliver, Jane. Birthday Surprise. Raga, Silvia, illus. (p. 234)
Oliver, Joyce, ed. see Oliver, Peter M.
Oliver, Juan, illus. see Lindeen, Mary.
Oliver, Juan, illus. see Schmauss, Judy Kentor.
Oliver, Juan Bautista Juan. How the Camel Got Its Hump - 6 Pack: Set of 6 with Common Core Teacher Materials. (p. 1035)
—Who Will Bell the Cat? - 6 Pack: Set of 6 with Common Core Teacher Materials. (p. 2452)
Oliver, Juan Bautista Juan, illus. see Daniel, Claire.
Oliver, Juan Bautista Juan, illus. see Garcia, Ellen.
Oliver, Juan Bautista Juan, illus. see Giachetti, Julia.
Oliver, Juan Bautista Juan, illus. see Koons, Linda.
Oliver, Juan Bautista Juan, illus. see Linde, Barbara M.
Oliver, Juan Bautista Juan, illus. see Pippin, Jessica.
Oliver, Juan Bautista Juan, illus. see Schmauss, Judy Kentor.
Oliver, Juan Bautista Juan, illus. see Sparks, Stacey.
Oliver, Juanbjuan. Prince & the Three Oranges a Fairy Tale from Mexico. (p. 1794)
Oliver, Juanbjuan, illus. see Bradman, Tony.
Oliver, Juanbjuan, illus. see Carrington, Jim.
oliver, juanbjuan, illus. see Coyle, Becky.
Oliver, Julia, illus. see Darens, Cat.
Oliver, June a. Kai's Pie. Montano, Andrea, illus. (p. 1201)
Oliver, Karen. Secret of the Elves. (p. 1977)
Oliver, Katherine Elspeth. Claw (Classic Reprint) (p. 402)
Oliver, Keith B. Inspirational Adventures of Princess Jewels & Faceless: Dare2dream. (p. 1124)
Oliver, Kelly. Kassy o'Roarke, Cub Reporter. (p. 1204)
Oliver, Laetitia Selwyn. Expiation of the Lady Anne (Classic Reprint) (p. 679)
Oliver, Lauren. Before I Fall. (p. 190)
—Broken Things. (p. 285)
—Dara & Nick. (p. 504)
—Delirium (p. 527)
—Delirium. (p. 527)
—Delirium Stories: Hana, Annabel, Raven & Alex. (p. 527)
—Delirium Stories: Hana, Annabel, & Raven. (p. 527)
—Delirium Stories: Hana, Annabel, Raven, & Alex. (p. 527)
—Delirium: the Special Edition. (p. 527)
—Liesl & Po. (p. 1287)
—Liesl & Po. Acedera, Kei, illus. (p. 1287)
—Magnificent Monsters of Cedar Street. (p. 1382)
—Pandemonium. (p. 1696)
—Panic. (p. 1696)
—Replica. (p. 1866)
—Requiem. (p. 1868)
—Ringer. (p. 1883)
—Si No Despierto / Before I Fall. (p. 2014)
—Spindlers. Bruno, Iacopo, illus. (p. 2082)
—Vanishing Girls. (p. 2347)
—Whistling Willy. (p. 2443)
Oliver, Lauren & Chester, H. C. Curiosity House: the Fearsome Firebird. (p. 486)
—Curiosity House: the Screaming Statue. (p. 486)
—Curiosity House: the Shrunken Head. Lacombe, Benjamin, illus. (p. 486)
—Screaming Statue. (p. 1964)
Oliver, Liana, illus. see Adams, Paul Robert.
Oliver, Lin. Almost Identical. (p. 57)
—Attack of the Growling Eyeballs. Gilpin, Stephen, illus. (p. 134)
—Beware! Shadows in the Night #3. Kallis, Samantha, illus. (p. 211)
—Danger! Tiger Crossing #1. Kallis, Samantha, illus. (p. 501)
—Double-Crossed #3. (p. 588)
—Double-Crossed #3 (HC) (p. 588)
—Escape of the Mini-Mummy. Gilpin, Stephen, illus. (p. 661)
—Little Poems for Tiny Ears. dePaola, Tomie, illus. (p. 1324)
—Look Out! Ghost Mountain Below #4. Kallis, Samantha, illus. (p. 1346)

—Revenge of the Itty-Bitty Brothers Gilpin, Stephen, illus. (p. 1872)
—Revenge of the Itty-Bitty Brothers. Gilpin, Stephen, illus. (p. 1872)
—Secret of the Super-Small Superstar. Gilpin, Stephen, illus. (p. 1978)
—Splat! Another Messy Sunday #2. Kallis, Samantha, illus. (p. 2084)
—Twice as Nice. (p. 2304)
—Two-Faced (p. 2307)
—Warning! Journey to Forever #5. Kimbell, Emily & Kallis, Samantha, illus. (p. 2379)
Oliver, Lin, jt. auth. see Winkler, Henry.
Oliver, Lin & Baker, Theo. Shadow Mask (p. 1996)
—Sound Bender. (p. 2067)
Oliver, Lin & Winkler, Henry. My Book of Pickles... Oops, I Mean Lists. (p. 1534)
—There's a Zombie in My Bathtub. (p. 2218)
—There's a Zombie in My Bathtub #5. Garrett, Scott, illus. (p. 2218)
Oliver, - Linda. Very Best Me. McGilp, Tina, illus. (p. 2352)
Oliver, Marilyn Tower. Infamous Alcatraz Prison in United States History. (p. 1118)
Oliver, Maritza. Be Kind to Every Kind. (p. 177)
—Pig Is a Dog Is a Kid. (p. 1743)
Oliver, Mark, illus. see Ewart, Franzeska G.
Oliver, Mark, illus. see Fuerst, Jeffrey B.
Oliver, Mark, illus. see Harris, Brooke.
Oliver, Mark, illus. see Kloepfer, John.
Oliver, Martin. Boys' Miscellany. Phillips, Mike, illus. (p. 272)
—Boys Only: How to Survive Anything! Ecob, Simon, illus. (p. 273)
—Off with Their Heads! Pinder, Andrew, illus. (p. 1640)
—Spycraft: Buster Book of Know-How. (p. 2093)
Oliver, Martin, jt. auth. see Stride, Lottie.
Oliver Miguel Montoya, Jose. Tecnicas de Pesca Recreativa Continental. (p. 2198)
Oliver, N. W. Sephora, Vol. 1 Of 2: A Hebrew Tale, Descriptive of the Country of Palestine, & of the Manners & Customs of the Ancient Israelites (Classic Reprint) (p. 1989)
Oliver, Narelle. Sand Swimmers: The Secret Life of Australia's Desert Wilderness. Oliver, Narelle, illus. (p. 1930)
—Tide Pool Secrets. Oliver, Narelle, illus. (p. 2240)
Oliver, Peru. Haut Conteurs T1- la Voix des Rois(les) (p. 939)
—Haut - Conteurs T2. Roi Vampire(les) (p. 939)
—Haut-Conteurs T4. Treize Damn's. (p. 939)
Oliver, Peter M. Fred's Challenge. Oliver, Joyce, ed. (p. 782)
Oliver, Sarah. Best World Book Week Ever. (p. 208)
Oliver, Sheila. Tinky Turtle Finds the Word. McQuitty, LaVonia Corbin, illus. (p. 2248)
Oliver, Simone G. Tools Make Work Easier. (p. 2261)
Oliver, Sw. Mike at the Aquarium. Crawley, Ceron, illus. (p. 1464)
Oliver, Tamara. Mystery of Phebe's Phamous Cupcakes. (p. 1569)
Oliver, Tamara Krenek. Lenny Lizard Learns a Lesson. (p. 1266)
Oliver, Temple. Forest Idyl (Classic Reprint) (p. 766)
Oliver, Wm H. Roughing It with the Regulars (Classic Reprint) (p. 1907)
Olivera, Fernando, illus. see Zubizarreta, Rosalma, et al.
Olivera, M., jt. auth. see Hazelton, N.
Olivera, Ramon. ABCs on Wheels. Olivera, Ramon, illus. (p. 5)
—ABCs on Wings. Olivera, Ramon, illus. (p. 5)
Oliveri, Lisa L. Last Pacifier. Fisher, Marianne, illus. (p. 1249)
Oliveros, Jessie. Remember Balloons. Wulfekotte, Dana, illus. (p. 1864)
Oliver-Pullins, Latasha. Devil's Deeds. (p. 536)
Oliveto, Michelle. My Dog the Faker. (p. 1537)
Olivetti, Ariel, illus. see Brooks, Mark.
Olivetti, Ariel, et al. Cable: the Last Hope. (p. 307)
Olivia, Asha. Message from God: A Book Journal for Children to Connect, Write, & Release. Jasmine, Mills, illus. (p. 1451)
Olivia, Cosneau. Animaux de la Fort(les) (p. 96)
—Attrape ! (p. 135)
—Au Temps des Dinosaures. (p. 135)
—CA Flotte ? CA Coule ? Plouf ! (p. 307)
—Grenouille(la) (p. 895)
—Oiseau(l') (p. 1643)
—Papillon(le) (p. 1698)
—Papillons du Monde(les) (p. 1698)
Olivier, Abbe. Memoirs of the Life & Adventures of Signor Rozelli, Late of the Hague, Vol. 1: Giving a Particular Account of His Birth, Education, Slavery, Monastic State, Imprisonment in the Inquisition at Rome, & the Different Figures He Has since Made, As Well In. (p. 1445)
Olivier, Charbonnel. Ma Station Spatiale. (p. 1371)
Olivier, Cherine. Shadow Love. (p. 1996)
Olivier, Jacques. Alphabet de l'Imperfection et Malice des Femmes: Reveu, Corrige, et Augmente d'un Friand Dessert et de Plusieurs Histoires Pour les Courtisans et Partisans de la Femme Mondaine (Classic Reprint) (p. 59)
—Alphabet de l'Imperfection et Malice des Femmes: Reveu, Corrigé, et Augmenté d'un Friand Dessert et de Plusieurs Histoires Pour les Courtisans et Partisans de la Femme Mondaine (Classic Reprint) (p. 59)
Olivier, Jonty. Nine Lives & Times of Mr. Hyde: Those Who Do Bad Deeds Always Get Their Comeuppance. (p. 1609)
Olivier, Latyk. Blanche-Neige. (p. 242)
Olivier, Lauren. Réplica / Replica. (p. 1866)
Olivier, Malie. Jessie Die Kameelperd Soek Werk. Ndlovu, Busisiwe, illus. (p. 1165)
—Ryno Die Klein Renoster. Ndlovu, Busisiwe, illus. (p. 1919)
—Ryno the Little Rhino. (p. 1919)
—Thabo en Die Klein Drakie (Afrikaans) Naidoo, Melvyn, illus. (p. 2210)
Olivier-Argyle, Daniel, illus. see Thornton, Stephen.
Olivotti, Sergio. Zoohablador. (p. 2543)
Olizon-Chikiamco, Norma. Pan de Sal Saves the Day: An Award-Winning ChildrenAEs Story from the Philippines [New Bilingual English & Tagalog Edition]. Salvatus, Mark, illus. (p. 1695)
Ollendorff, H. G. Clef de la Nouvelle Methode Pour Apprendre a Lire, Ecrire et a Parler une Langue en Six Mois, Appliquee a l'Anglais (Classic Reprint) (p. 403)
Oller, Erika, illus. see Newman, Lesléa & Newman, Lesléa.
Oller, Erika, illus. see Newman, Lesléa.
Ollhoff, Jim. African Mythology (p. 33)
—African-American History (p. 32)
—Alaska (p. 39)
—Arizona (p. 116)
—Black Death. (p. 237)
—Brain. (p. 274)
—Captain Cook. (p. 325)
—Chinese Mythology (p. 378)
—Christopher Columbus. (p. 388)
—Civil Rights Movement (p. 396)
—Civil War (p. 396)
—Civil War: Turning Points. (p. 397)
—Colorado (p. 421)
—Conflicts & Independence (p. 440)
—Connecticut (p. 441)
—Conquistadors. (p. 442)
—Courage & Growth (p. 462)
—Delaware (p. 526)
—Digestive System. (p. 545)
—Ear, Nose, & Throat. (p. 613)
—Early Battles. (p. 614)
—Egyptian Mythology (p. 628)
—EMT. (p. 645)
—European Mythology (p. 667)
—Ferdinand Magellan. (p. 720)
—Final Years. (p. 727)
—Firefighter. (p. 733)
—Florida (p. 751)
—Flu. (p. 753)
—Fossil Fuels (p. 770)
—Freedom & the Future (p. 782)
—Future Energy (p. 802)
—Geothermal, Biomass, & Hydrogen (p. 821)
—Germ Detectives. (p. 821)
—Greek Mythology (p. 892)
—Hawaii (p. 940)
—Hazmat. (p. 941)
—Heart. (p. 944)
—Idaho (p. 1089)
—Identity & Civil Rights (p. 1089)
—Jacques Cousteau. (p. 1154)
—Japanese Mythology (p. 1160)
—Leaders & Generals. (p. 1254)
—Living in a Warmer World (p. 1333)
—Malaria (p. 1391)
—Marco Polo. (p. 1403)
—Mayan & Aztec Mythology (p. 1429)
—Middle Eastern Mythology (p. 1460)
—Missouri (p. 1482)
—Montana (p. 1499)
—Muscles & Bones. (p. 1528)
—Myths & Controversies (p. 1571)
—Native American Mythology (p. 1578)
—Nebraska (p. 1584)
—Neil Armstrong. (p. 1586)
—Norse Mythology (p. 1620)
—North Dakota (p. 1621)
—Nuclear Energy (p. 1628)
—Pioneers of Equality (p. 1748)
—Puerto Rico (p. 1811)
—Roots of Humanity (p. 1903)
—Science. (p. 1948)
—Skin. (p. 2032)
—Slavery. (p. 2035)
—Smallpox (p. 2040)
—Social Solutions (p. 2053)
—Solar Power (p. 2055)
—South Carolina (p. 2068)
—South Dakota (p. 2068)
—Swat. (p. 2167)
—Technological Solutions (p. 2197)
—Tennessee (p. 2206)
—Texas (p. 2209)
—Utah (p. 2342)
—Washington, D. C (p. 2381)
—Water & Ice (p. 2384)
—West Virginia (p. 2402)
—What Are Germs? (p. 2405)
—Wind & Water (p. 2471)
—World in Crisis (p. 2502)
—World of Mythology (p. 2503)
—Wyoming (p. 2515)
—Years of Slavery (p. 2520)
Ollhoff, Jim, jt. auth. see ABDO Publishing Company Staff.
Ollier, Charles. Fallacy of Ghosts, Dreams, & Omens: With Stories of Witchcraft, Life-In-Death, & Monomania (Classic Reprint) (p. 700)
—Ferrers, Vol. 1 Of 3: A Romance of the Reign of George the Second (Classic Reprint) (p. 721)
—Ferrers, Vol. 2 Of 3: A Romance of the Reign of George the Second (Classic Reprint) (p. 721)
Olliffe, Pat, jt. illus. see Frenz, Ron.
Ollivant, Alfred. Bob, Son of Battle (Classic Reprint) (p. 252)
—Boy Woodburn a Story of the Sussex Downs (Classic Reprint) (p. 271)
—Brown Mare: And Other Studies of England under the Cloud (Classic Reprint) (p. 287)
—Danny (Classic Reprint) (p. 504)
—Gentleman: A Romance of the Sea (Classic Reprint) (p. 816)
—One Woman: Being the Second Part of a Romance of Sussex (Classic Reprint) (p. 1663)
—Owd Bob: The Grey Dog of Kenmuir. (p. 1688)
—Redcoat Captain a Story of That Country (Classic Reprint) (p. 1859)
—Royal Road: Being the Story of the Life, Death, & Resurrection of Edward Hankey of London (Classic Reprint) (p. 1910)
—Taming of John Blunt (Classic Reprint) (p. 2189)
—Two Men: A Romance of Sussex (Classic Reprint) (p. 2308)
Olliver, Linda, illus. see Fries-Gaither, Jessica.
Ollivier, Reina & Claes, Karel. Builders. Padmos, Steffie, illus. (p. 294)
Ol'mak, Tatjana. Cherry Princess. (p. 366)
Olmanson, Shaina. Coco Idea Lab. Olmanson, Shaina, photos by. (p. 411)
—Lion King Idea Lab. Olmanson, Shaina, photos by. (p. 1306)
Olmedillas, Cathy, jt. compiled by see Anorak Press Staff.
Olmedillas, Cathy, compiled by. Anorak. (p. 100)
Olmis, Elisabeth. Sylvester Quarry: Sequel to over at Little Acorns (Classic Reprint) (p. 2173)
Olmstead, Becky. Best News Ever/la Major Noticia en el Mundo (Spanish Edition) (p. 207)
Olmstead, Emma Gertrude. Ned & Nan in Holland (Classic Reprint) (p. 1584)
Olmstead, Florence. Anchorage (Classic Reprint) (p. 79)
Olmstead, James Munson. Noah & His Times: Embracing the Consideration of Various Inquiries Relative to the Antediluvian & Earlier Postdiluvian Periods, with Discussions of Several of the Leading Questions of the Present Day (Classic Reprint) (p. 1615)
Olmstead, Kathleen. Enormous Turnip. Olafsdottir, Linda, illus. (p. 655)
—Fox & the Grapes. Brannen, Sarah S., illus. (p. 774)
—King Midas. Quarello, Maurizio A. C., illus. (p. 1220)
—Lion & the Mouse. Wakefield, Scott, illus. (p. 1305)
—Pied Piper of Hamelin. Brannen, Sarah S., illus. (p. 1742)
—Sorcerer's Apprentice. Olafsdottir, Linda, illus. (p. 2065)
Olmstead, Kathleen & Andersen, Hans. Little Match Girl. Kim, Jin-Woo, illus. (p. 1321)
—Steadfast Tin Soldier. Calo, Marcos, illus. (p. 2110)
Olmstead, Kathleen & Olafsdottir, Linda. Beauty & the Beast. (p. 185)
Olmstead, Kathleen, et al. Thumbelina. Sokolava, Valerie, illus. (p. 2238)
Olmstead, Mark. Adventures of the True Sunbeam. (p. 28)
Olmsted, Denison. Compendium of Astronomy: Adapted to the Use of Schools & Academies (Classic Reprint) (p. 433)
—Compendium of Astronomy: Containing the Elements of the Science, Familiarly Explained & Illustrated, Adapted to the Use of Schools & Academies, & of the General Reader (Classic Reprint) (p. 433)
—Compendium of Astronomy: Containing the Elements of the Science, Familiarly Explained & Illustrated; Adapted to the Use of High Schools & Academies, & of the General Reader (Classic Reprint) (p. 433)
—Compendium of Astronomy: Containing the Elements of the Science, Familiarly Explained & Illustrated; Adapted to the Use of High Schools & Academies, & of the General Reader; a New & Greatly Improved Edition, Containing the Latest Discoveries. (p. 433)
—Rudiments of Natural Philosophy & Astronomy: Designed for the Younger Classes in Academies, & for Common Schools, with Numerous Engravings, Illustrative of Philosophical Experiments (Classic Reprint) (p. 1912)
Olmsted, Frederick Law. Cotton Kingdom, Vol. 1 Of 2: A Traveller's Observations on Cotton & Slavery in the American Slave States (Classic Reprint) (p. 457)
—Journey in the Back Country, Vol. 1 Of 2: In the Winter of 1853-4 (Classic Reprint) (p. 1181)
—Walks & Talks of an American Farmer in England; Part II. (p. 2372)
—Walks & Talks of an American Farmer in England (Classic Reprint) (p. 2372)
Olmsted, Frederick Law, jt. auth. see Dunlap, Julie.
Olney, Edward. Introduction to Algebra: Designed for Use in Our Public Schools, by Pupils Not Having Sufficient Maturity to Enter at Once upon the Author's Complete School Algebra, & for Preparatory Departments of Colleges (Classic Reprint) (p. 1129)
—Introduction to Algebra: Designed for Use in Our Public Schools, by Pupils Not Having Sufficient Maturity to Enter at Once upon the Author's Complete Algebra, & for Preparatory Departments of Colleges, Where This Book Can Be Followed Immediately by Th. (p. 1129)
Olney, Ellen W. Love in Idleness: A Summer Story (Classic Reprint) (p. 1359)
Olney, J. Easy Reader, or Introduction to the National Preceptor: Consisting of Familiar & Progressive Lessons, Designed to Aid in Thinking, Spelling, Defining, & Correct Reading (Classic Reprint) (p. 621)
Olney, Ross R. Time Dial (p. 2244)
Olnhausen, Mary Phinney von. Adventures of an Army Nurse in Two Wars (Classic Reprint) (p. 21)
Olofsdotter, Marie, illus. see Adler, David A. & Adler, Michael S.
O'Loghlin, James. New Kid: Very Popular Me. Martin, Matthew, illus. (p. 1595)
Oloja, Ene. Why the Tortoise Has a Patchy Back: A Nigerian Folktale. (p. 2459)
—Why the Tortoise Has a Patchy Back: A Famous Nigerian Folktale. (p. 2459)
Olortegui, Diego. X-23 Vol. 2: X-Assassin (p. 2515)
Olorunlowo, Teresa. Adventures of Moyin: Moyin Goes to Hawaii. (p. 25)
O'Loughlin, Declan & McKenna, Donna, eds. Fone a Friend: A Prayer Book by Children for Children. (p. 758)
O'Loughlin, Mary A. Irish Emigrant: An Irish-American Drama, in Five Acts (Classic Reprint) (p. 1134)
Olsen, Alana. Day at Work with a Molecular Biologist (p. 512)
—Firefighters to the Rescue. (p. 734)
—It's Summer. (p. 1147)
—Look Out for the Blue-Ringed Octopus! (p. 1346)
—What Do You Know about Bugs? Understand Place Value. (p. 2409)
Olsen, Bevan. Innkeeper's Christmas. (p. 1121)
—Magi. (p. 1376)
Olsen, Brittany Long. Magic in the Valley: The Story of Moira Green, Witch. (p. 1377)
Olsen, Charles. Hero's Tale. (p. 963)
Olsen, Dag, tr. see Darling, Jeanne.
Olsen, Eric. Adventures of Bunny Ted. (p. 22)
Olsen, Erik. Cobble Cavern. (p. 410)
—Garden of the Lost Souls. (p. 809)
—Quest & Honor (Flin's Destiny 4) (p. 1825)
Olsen, Grant Orrin. Rhino Trouble. Carpenter, Mike, illus. (p. 1874)
Olsen, Jan Z. Mat Man on the Go. Delaney, Molly, illus. (p. 1420)
—Mat Man Opposites. Delaney, Molly, illus. (p. 1420)
Olsen, Jan Z., creator. Color Print & Number Wall Cards. (p. 421)
Olsen, John Charles. Van Nostrand's Chemical Annual 1913: A Hand-Book of Useful Data for Analytical, Manufacturing, & Investigating Chemists, & Chemical Students (Classic Reprint) (p. 2347)
Olsen, Kaki. Swan & Shadow: A Swan Lake Story. (p. 2167)
Olsen, Kent Johnson. Anti-Injustice Squad: The Cacomistle Team. (p. 102)
Olsen, Kirstin. Daily Life of Women in the Progressive Era (p. 496)
Olsen, Leigh. Adventure to Wishing Star Waterfall. (p. 19)
—Charlie & the Chocolate Factory Mad Libs. (p. 359)
—Percy Jackson Mad Libs. (p. 1721)
—Stars in the Sky. (p. 2107)
—Stocking Stuffer Mad Libs. (p. 2120)
Olsen, Leigh & S. I. International. What Do You Say? A Book about Manners. (p. 2409)
Olsen, Nora. Frenemy of the People. (p. 784)
—Maxine Wore Black. (p. 1428)
—Swans & Klons. (p. 2167)
Olsen, Rodger, jt. auth. see Frankowski, Leo.
Olsen, S. R. When Dogs Dream. Showalter, Kristin, illus. (p. 2430)
Olsen, Shea & Craft, Elizabeth. Flower. (p. 752)
Olsen, Suzie. Annie Aardvark, Mathematician. Kinney, Davina "Viv", illus. (p. 99)
Olsen, Sylvia. Different Game (p. 545)
—Molly's Promise (p. 1490)
—Neekah's Knitting Needles. Lott, Sheena, illus. (p. 1585)
—Yetsa's Sweater Larson, Joan, illus. (p. 2521)
Olsen, Sylvia & Charko, Kasia. Sebastian Sasquatch (p. 1973)
Olshan, Matthew. Mighty Lalouche. Blackall, Sophie, illus. (p. 1463)
—Voyage in the Clouds: The (Mostly) True Story of the First International Flight by Balloon in 1785. Blackall, Sophie, illus. (p. 2368)
Olson, Abbey. When I Grow up I Want to Be Perfect. Rothfuss, Nina Marie, illus. (p. 2431)
Olson, Amy. What's Bugging Camo the Chameleon. (p. 2423)
Olson, Bethany. Baby Cats. (p. 149)
—Baby Deer. (p. 149)
—Baby Horses. (p. 151)
—Baby Pandas. (p. 152)
—Baby Rabbits. (p. 152)
—Baby Wolves. (p. 153)
Olson, Charlotte. Sammy Goes on an Aeroplane. (p. 1928)
—Suzie & Cruzie. (p. 2166)
—Suzie Goes to School. (p. 2166)
—Suzie Goes to the Dentist. (p. 2166)
—Suzie's Christmas Time. (p. 2166)
Olson, Cynthia J. Kiera's Cry (p. 1216)
Olson, D. A. Treasure Map. (p. 2282)
Olson, David. Don't Be Like Trump. (p. 582)
Olson, Doug & Olson, Doug, Jr. Stefon Diggs: The Maker of Football Miracles. (p. 2112)
Olson, E. M. My Math Monster. (p. 1555)
—Oliver the Toaster. (p. 1650)
Olson, Ed, illus. see Carvin, Rose-Mae.
Olson, Ed, illus. see Greiner, Ruth B.
Olson, Ed, illus. see Greiner, Ruth B., et al.
Olson, Ed, illus. see King, Emily.
Olson, Ed, illus. see Lyster, R. Iona, et al.
Olson, Ed, illus. see Martonyi, E. Andrew.
Olson, Elsie. Animal Builder Brawl. (p. 88)
—Animal Predator Smackdown. (p. 91)
—Animal Speed Showdown. (p. 91)
—Are You Psychic? Facts, Trivia, & Quizzes. (p. 113)
—Astrological Signs: Facts, Trivia, & Quizzes. (p. 128)
—Be Aware!: a Hero's Guide to Being Smart & Staying Safe. (p. 176)
—Be Bold!: a Hero's Guide to Being Brave. (p. 176)
—Be Kind!: a Hero's Guide to Beating Bullying. (p. 177)
—Be Respectful!: a Hero's Guide to Being Courteous. (p. 177)
—Be Strong!: a Hero's Guide to Being Resilient. (p. 177)
—Be Well!: a Hero's Guide to a Healthy Mind & Body. (p. 178)
—Biofuel Energy. (p. 228)
—Breakthroughs in Moon Exploration. (p. 278)
—Build a Shelter Your Way!: Constructing Weatherproof Structures. (p. 293)
—Building the Empire State Building. (p. 295)
—Building the Golden Gate Bridge. (p. 295)
—Building the Hoover Dam. (p. 295)
—Coal Energy. (p. 410)
—Connect It! Circuits You Can Squish, Bend, & Twist. (p. 440)
—Dams. (p. 499)
—Design Survival Clothing Your Way!: Crafting Weatherproof Wearables. (p. 532)
—Dreams & What They Mean: Facts, Trivia, & Quizzes. (p. 603)
—Drones. (p. 605)
—Exploring Earthquakes: Seismologists at Work! (p. 681)
—Exploring Fossils: Paleontologists at Work! (p. 681)
—Exploring Minerals: Mineralogists at Work! (p. 682)
—Exploring the Rock Cycle: Petrologists at Work! (p. 683)
—Exploring Volcanoes: Volcanologists at Work! (p. 684)
—Exploring Weather: Meteorologists at Work! (p. 684)
—Geothermal Energy. (p. 821)
—Levi Strauss: Blue Jean Genius. (p. 1282)
—Magic Disappearing Acts. (p. 1377)
—Magic Tricks with Cards. (p. 1379)
—Magic Tricks with Optical Illusions. (p. 1379)
—Magic Tricks with Props. (p. 1379)
—Make a Creepy Costume Your Way! (p. 1385)
—Make a Dinosaur Your Way! (p. 1385)
—Make a Mini Monster Your Way! (p. 1385)
—Make a Mini UFO Your Way! (p. 1385)
—Make a Pack Your Way!: Building Bags to Haul Your Gear. (p. 1386)

O'Neal, Shaquille. Little Shaq. Taylor, Theodore, illus. (p. 1327)
—Little Shaq. Taylor, Theodore, III, illus. (p. 1327)
—Little Shaq: Star of the Week. Taylor, Theodore, III, illus. (p. 1327)
—Little Shaq Takes a Chance. Taylor, Theodore, III, illus. (p. 1327)
O'Neal-Thorpe, Rochelle. Adventures of Captain Remarkable: Companion chapter book to Captain Remarkable. Tamang, Mayan, illus. (p. 22)
—Doll at the Christmas Bazaar: Christmas Miracles. Penn, Karen V., illus. (p. 578)
—Gabe & the Bike: Riding the Minuteman Trail. O'Neal-Thorpe, Rochelle, illus. (p. 804)
—Gabe & the Park & his Big Toy Box: The Adventures of Gabe Series. O'Neal-Thorpe, Rochelle, illus. (p. 804)
Onefam. Just Dad & Me - a Father Son Journal. (p. 1192)
O'Neil, Arthur W. Traveling School of Seven Abroad: Study, Work & Pleasure in Foreign Lands; the Rewritten Diary of an American Student & Sightseer (Classic Reprint) (p. 2280)
O'Neil, Daniel. Big Dan Runs the Marathon. (p. 219)
—Coach Jenn the Life Changer. (p. 409)
O'Neil, Dennis, ed. see Starlin, Jim, et al.
O'Neil, Dennis, ed. see Starlin, Jim.
O'Neil, J. B. Fart Book: The Disgusting Adventures of Milo Snotrocket. (p. 711)
—Ninja Farts: The Disgusting Adventures of Milo Snotrocket. (p. 1610)
O'Neil, Jane. Kimberly et la Bête de Feu. Phelipon, Laure, illus. (p. 1218)
—Predator. (p. 1786)
O'Neil, Juliana. Discover Halloween: Level 1 Reader. (p. 554)
O'Neil, Kristy, illus. see Gunn, Sharyn.
O'Neil, Owen Rowe. Adventures in Swaziland: The Story the of a South African Boer (Classic Reprint) (p. 20)
O'Neil, Rose. Kewpie Primer: With Illustrations (Classic Reprint) (p. 1210)
O'Neil, Sharron, illus. see Rosa-Mendoza, Gladys.
O'Neil, Terry. N. A. R. T. A Concise History of the North American Racing Team 1957 To 1983. (p. 1572)
O'Neill. Bondman: A Story of the Times of Wat Tyler (Classic Reprint) (p. 255)
O'Neill, Agatha, illus. see Davis, Mandie.
O'Neill, Alexis. Jacob Riis's Camera: Bringing Light to Tenement Children. Kelley, Gary, illus. (p. 1154)
—Recess Queen. (p. 1853)
O'Neill, Amanda. I Wonder Why Snakes Shed Their Skin. (p. 1086)
—I Wonder Why Spiders Spin Webs: And Other Questions about Creepy Crawlies. (p. 1086)
O'Neill, Catharine. Annie & Simon: The Sneeze & Other Stories. O'Neill, Catharine, illus. (p. 99)
—Annie & Simon: Banana Muffins & Other Stories. O'Neill, Catharine, illus. (p. 99)
O'Neill, Corey. Creatures #3 Mitchell, Laura, illus. (p. 471)
—Main Event #2 Mitchell, Laura, illus. (p. 1383)
—Revolt #6 Mitchell, Laura, illus. (p. 1873)
—Triangle #4 Mitchell, Laura, illus. (p. 2286)
—War Design #5 Mitchell, Laura, illus. (p. 2376)
O'Neill, Dan. Stubborn Gal: The True Story of an Undefeated Sled Dog Racer. Maisch, Klara, illus. (p. 2143)
O'Neill, Daniel K. Junk Yard Dog. (p. 1191)
O'Neill, Dave, illus. see Shankman, Ed.
O'Neill, Elizabeth. Alfred Visits Connecticut. (p. 43)
—Alfred Visits Hawaii. (p. 43)
—Alfred Visits Idaho. (p. 43)
—Alfred Visits Montana. (p. 43)
—Alfred Visits New Mexico. (p. 43)
—Alfred Visits Utah. (p. 43)
—Alfred Visits Washington State. (p. 43)
Oneill, Elizabeth. Alfred Visits West Virginia. (p. 43)
O'Neill, Elizabeth. Alfred Visits Wisconsin. (p. 43)
—World's Story. (p. 2508)
O'Neill, Eugene. Anna Christie. (p. 97)
—Emperor Jones. (p. 644)
—Hairy Ape: Anna Christie; the First Man (Classic Reprint) (p. 910)
—Plays: First Series: the Straw, the Emperor Jones, & Diff'rent (Classic Reprint) (p. 1761)
O'Neill, Eugene G. Before Breakfast: A Play in One Act (Classic Reprint) (p. 190)
—Beyond the Horizon: A Play in Three Acts (Classic Reprint) (p. 212)
—Gold: A Play in Four Acts (Classic Reprint) (p. 855)
—Moon of the Caribbees: And Six Other Plays of the Sea (Classic Reprint) (p. 1502)
—Thirst: And Other One Act Plays (Classic Reprint) (p. 2223)
O'Neill, Ewa, illus. see Jackson, Amber L.
O'Neill, Ewa, illus. see Jackson, Amber.
O'Neill, Gemma. Monty's Magnificent Mane. O'Neill, Gemma, illus. (p. 1500)
—Oh Dear, Geoffrey! O'Neill, Gemma, illus. (p. 1641)
O'Neill, H.C. Devonshire Idyls (Classic Reprint) (p. 536)
O'Neill, Ian. Jimmy First & Destiny's Watch. (p. 1168)
O'Neill, Jacquie. Figure Skating. (p. 726)
O'Neill, James. Garrison Tales from Tonquin (Classic Reprint) (p. 810)
O'Neill, Joe. Legends of the Rif Addicott, Sara & Walton, Bedelia C., eds. (p. 1264)
O'Neill, John R. Mahatma Gandhi, Nelson Mandela. (p. 1382)
O'Neill, John R. & Benchmark Education Co., LLC Staff. Mahatma Gandhi y Nelson Mandela: Set of 6 with Common Core Teacher Materials. (p. 1382)
O'neill, Joseph. Great Wall of China (p. 890)
O'Neill, Joseph. Movie Director. (p. 1516)
O'Neill, Joseph R. Bolshevik Revolution (p. 254)
—Irish Potato Famine (p. 1135)
O'Neill, Joy. Why Do We Have to Move? (p. 2457)
O'Neill, Juliana. Bug & the Bugs. Graves, Lisa, illus. (p. 291)
—Discover London: Level 3 Reader. (p. 554)
—Discover Nests: Level 1 Reader. (p. 554)
—Discover Thanksgiving: Level 2 Reader. (p. 555)
—Doy Gracias: (I Say Thanks) Kincaid, Olivia, illus. (p. 591)
—Good Pet. (p. 865)
—Hello. Bartolomé, Soraya, illus. (p. 950)
—I Say Thanks. Kincaid, Olivia, illus. (p. 1081)
—I Say Thanks / Doy Gracias. Kincaid, Olivia, illus. (p. 1081)
—If I Had a Cat. Nikiel, Laura, illus. (p. 1091)
—If I Had a Cat / Si Tuviera un Gato. Nikiel, Laura, illus. (p. 1091)
—If I Had a Dog. Nikiel, Laura, illus. (p. 1091)
—If I Had a Dog / Si Tuviera un Perro. Nikiel, Laura, illus. (p. 1091)
—Monsters Move. Pryce, Adam, illus. (p. 1498)
—Pick a Pup. Johnston, Jenna, illus. (p. 1738)
—Say Boo. (p. 1940)
—Si Tuviera un Gato. Nikiel, Laura, illus. (p. 2014)
—Si Tuviera un Perro. Nikiel, Laura, illus. (p. 2014)
—That Is My Kitten. (p. 2213)
O'Neill, Katie. Aquicorn Cove. O'Neill, Katie, illus. (p. 108)
—Dewdrop. O'Neill, Katie, illus. (p. 536)
—Princess Princess Ever After. (p. 1799)
—Princess Princess Ever After. O'Neill, Katie, illus. (p. 1799)
—Tea Dragon Festival. (p. 2194)
—Tea Dragon Society. (p. 2194)
—Tea Dragon Society. O'Neill, Katie, illus. (p. 2194)
O'Neill, Katie, illus. see Gwynne, Penelope.
O'Neill, Katie, illus. see Toole, Anne.
O'Neill, Kelly, illus. see Casey, Catherine.
O'Neill, Lauren, illus. see Webb, Sarah.
O'Neill, Louise. Surface Breaks. (p. 2162)
O'Neill, M. J. How He Does It: Sam. T Jack, Twenty Years a King in the Realm of Burlesque (Classic Reprint) (p. 1031)
O'Neill, Martin, illus. see Rhodes, James.
O'Neill, Michael Patrick. Wild Waters: Photo Journal. (p. 2465)
O'Neill, Moira. Elf-Errant (Classic Reprint) (p. 635)
O'Neill, O'Neill. Physical Training for Special Classes of the Elementary Schools (Classic Reprint) (p. 1737)
—Travels of John Wryland, Being an Account of His Journey to Tibet, of His Founding a Kingdom on the Island of Palti, & of His War Against the Ne-AR-Bians (Classic Reprint) (p. 2281)
O'Neill, Philomena. Willa & the Bear. (p. 2468)
O'Neill, Philomena, illus. see Kroll, Virginia.
O'Neill, Philomena, illus. see Morgan, Cindy.
O'Neill, Philomena, illus. see Morrisette, Sharon.
O'Neill, Philomena, illus. see Stolberg, Tina.
O'Neill, Poppy. Believing in Me: A Child's Guide to Self-Confidence & Self-Esteem. (p. 196)
—Sometimes I'm Anxious: A Child's Guide to Overcoming Anxiety. (p. 2061)
O'Neill, Rachael. My First Library: With Nine Colorful Books. (p. 1544)
O'Neill, Rachael, illus. see Davies, Gill.
O'Neill, Richard. Lost Homework. Beautyman, Kirsti, illus. (p. 1353)
—Polonius the Pit Pony. Parker-Thomas, Feronia, illus. (p. 1772)
O'Neill, Robert, ed. see Engle, Stephen Douglas.
O'Neill, Robert John. World War II: Essential Histories (p. 2505)
O'Neill, Robert John & Gallagher, Gary W. Civil War: Bull Run & Other Eastern Battles, 1861-May 1863. (p. 396)
O'Neill, Robert John & Glatthaar, Joseph T. Civil War: Sherman's Capture of Atlanta & Other Western Battles, 1863-1865. (p. 397)
O'Neill, Robert John, et al. World War II: Northwest Europe, 1944-1945. (p. 2505)
O'Neill, Robert L. Sammy the Flying Purple Baby Elephant: Remembering the Old Ways of the Elephant. (p. 1928)
O'Neill, S. J. How He Does It: Sam. T Jack, Twenty Years a King in the Realm of Burlesque (Classic Reprint) (p. 1031)
O'Neill, Sean. 50 Things You Didn't Know about Ancient Egypt. O'Neill, Sean, illus. (p. 2556)
—50 Things You Didn't Know about Ancient Greece. O'Neill, Sean, illus. (p. 2556)
—50 Things You Didn't Know about Ancient Rome. O'Neill, Sean, illus. (p. 2556)
—50 Things You Didn't Know about Colonial America. O'Neill, Sean, illus. (p. 2556)
—50 Things You Didn't Know about the Middle Ages. O'Neill, Sean, illus. (p. 2556)
—Rocket Robinson & the Pharaoh's Fortune. O'Neill, Sean, illus. (p. 1895)
—Rocket Robinson & the Secret of the Saint. O'Neill, Sean, illus. (p. 1895)
O'Neill, Sean, illus. see Bailer, Darice.
O'Neill, Sean, illus. see Blevins, Wiley.
O'Neill, Sean, illus. see Yomtov, Nel.
O'Neill, Sean, illus. see Yomtov, Nelson.
O'Neill, Terence & Williams, Josh. 3D Printing. (p. 2547)
—Arduino. (p. 112)
O'Neill, Todd, illus. see Cohen, Mary.
O'Neill, Tom. Old Friends. (p. 1645)
O'Neill-Sheehan, Betsy. Goldivine. (p. 860)
Oneka, Angelo O. Mary & Jackie Discovered Jupiter. (p. 1414)
Ong, Cristina, illus. see Bryant, Megan E.
Ong, Cristina, tr. see Bryant, Megan E.
Ong, Gelyn. Forest Fable. (p. 766)
Ong, Jacqueline, jt. auth. see Sheehan, Patricia.
Ong, Olivia, illus. see Etheridge, M. C. D.
Ong, Wilson, illus. see James, Helen Foster & Loh, Virginia Shin-Mui.
Ong, Wilson, illus. see Rodriguez, Sonia & Browning, Kurt.
Ongaro, Isabella, illus. see Niner, Holly L.
Ongren, Olof Gustaf, jt. auth. see Berzelius, Jöns Jakob.
Onions, Oliver. Back o' the Moon: And Other Stories (Classic Reprint) (p. 155)
—Case in Camera (Classic Reprint) (p. 336)
—Compleat Bachelor (Classic Reprint) (p. 434)
—Crooked Mile (Classic Reprint) (p. 477)
—Debit Account (Classic Reprint) (p. 522)
—Drakestone (Classic Reprint) (p. 596)
—Gray Youth the Story of a Very Modern Courtship, & a Very Modern Marriage (Classic Reprint) (p. 883)
—In Accordance with the Evidence (Classic Reprint) (p. 1104)
—Mushroom Town (Classic Reprint) (p. 1528)
—Story of Louie (Classic Reprint) (p. 2131)
—Tower of Oblivion (Classic Reprint) (p. 2269)
Onishi, Mika, tr. see Clamp Staff.
Onishi, Satoru. Who's Hiding? Onishi, Satoru, illus. (p. 2453)
Onley, Sandra. Hailey the Sheepdog. (p. 911)
Onlyanose & Kelly, Charlene. My Neighbors Are All Cats: Collecting Stars. Hu, Tiger, illus. (p. 1557)
Ono, Fuyumi. Twelve Kingdoms (p. 2303)
Ono, Kenji, illus. see Chin, Oliver.
Ono, Mari. Fun Origami for Children: Pets! 12 Amazing Animals to Fold. (p. 799)
Ono, Mari & Ono, Roshin. Fun Origami for Children: Flight! 12 Paper Planes & Other Flying Objects to Fold for Fun! (p. 799)
—Origami for Children: Book & Paper Pack with 35 Projects (p. 1671)
Ono, Mari & Shingu, Fumiaki. Fun Origami for Children: Wild! 12 Amazing Animals to Fold. (p. 799)
Ono, Mari & Takai, Hiroaki. Fun Origami for Children: Dino! 12 Daring Dinosaurs to Fold. (p. 799)
Ono, Roshin, jt. auth. see Ono, Mari.
Onoda, Yuta, illus. see Barnhill, Kelly.
Onoda, Yuta, illus. see Lewis, Gill.
Onodera, Maya. Robin's Christmas Journey. (p. 1891)
Onsgard, Bethany. Asia (p. 126)
—Life During the California Gold Rush (p. 1291)
—Life on the Frontier (p. 1295)
—Making a City Smart. (p. 1388)
Ont, Grand Opera House London. Season '94-95 (Classic Reprint) (p. 1972)
Ontario, Grand Opera House London. Grand Opera House, London, Ont. , Programme: Tuesday, Oct. 9th; the Favorite Romantic Actor Robert Mantell, under the Management of Augustus Pitou, in Dumas' Great Play in Six Acts, the Corsican Brothers (Classic Reprint) (p. 877)
Ontario, London Normal School. Year Book of Class 1927-1928 (Classic Reprint) (p. 2518)
Onuoha, Chinwe. Climate Change & Life on Earth. (p. 405)
Onus, Katie. Island of the Wolves. (p. 1140)
Onwuemene, Toyosi. Mi Cabello Se Llama Bella. Galicia, Diana, illus. (p. 1454)
Onwusilikam, Ify Chinedum. Drama Queen. (p. 596)
Onyebuchi, Tochi. Beasts Made of Night. (p. 182)
—Bestias de la Noche. (p. 208)
—Crown of Thunder. (p. 479)
—War Girls. (p. 2376)
Onyefulu, Ifeoma. Deron Goes to Nursery School. (p. 530)
Onyett, Nicola & Williams, Tennessee. Streetcar Named Desire. (p. 2140)
Onyumbe, Jacob. Kevin the Wild Boy: The Diaries of a Survivor (p. 1210)
Oollah, Einaiut. Bahar-Danush, or Garden of Knowledge, Vol. 2 Of 3: An Oriental Romance, Translated from the Persic (Classic Reprint) (p. 159)
Oort, Henricus, jt. auth. see Wicksteed, Philip Henry.
Oostendorp, Leila Kadri. Animal Asanas: Yoga for Children. Bahia, Elsa, illus. (p. 88)
Oosthuizen, Sarah & Groenewald, Catherine. Nosipho Comes to Stay. (p. 1622)
Ooten, Tara Broeckel & Cooke, C. W. Fame: Justin Bieber. (p. 701)
Opal, Paola. Bitsy. (p. 235)
—Dotty. (p. 588)
—Emma. (p. 642)
—Ollie. (p. 1650)
—Perry. (p. 1724)
—Pippy. (p. 1749)
—Rokko. (p. 1897)
—Saffy & Ollie. (p. 1922)
—Saffy Looks for Rain. (p. 1922)
—Totty. (p. 2267)
—Zingy. (p. 2540)
Opal, Paola, illus. see Winters, Kari-Lynn.
Opal, Paola, jt. auth. see O'Leary, Sara.
Oparin, Alejandro. Origen de la Vida. (p. 1671)
Opatz, Shane, illus. see Holtz, Monica Stauber.
Opatz, Shane, photos by see Holtz, Monica Stauber.
Opdyke, Irene Gut. In My Hands: Memories of a Holocaust Rescuer. (p. 1106)
Opdyke, Irene Gut & Armstrong, Jennifer. In My Hands: Memories of a Holocaust Rescuer. (p. 1106)
Opel, Andrew. Bobhouse: A Winnipesaukee Christmas. Hayes, Karel & Gorey, John, illus. (p. 252)
Opel, Andy. Witches: A Winnipesaukee Adventure. Hayes, Karel, illus. (p. 2480)
Open Court Staff. Breaking Code Sentence Strips. (p. 278)
Openshaw, Mary. Loser Pays: A Story of the French Revolution (Classic Reprint) (p. 1352)
Opie. Madeline, Vol. 2: A Tale (Classic Reprint) (p. 1375)
—New Tales, Vol. 1 of 4 (Classic Reprint) (p. 1597)
—New Tales, Vol. 2 of 4 (Classic Reprint) (p. 1597)
—New Tales, Vol. 3 of 4 (Classic Reprint) (p. 1597)
—New Tales, Vol. 4 of 4 (Classic Reprint) (p. 1597)
—Simple Tales, Vol. 1 of 2 (Classic Reprint) (p. 2022)
—Simple Tales, Vol. 3 of 4 (Classic Reprint) (p. 2022)
—Simple Tales, Vol. 4 of 4 (Classic Reprint) (p. 2022)
—Tales of Real Life (Classic Reprint) (p. 2185)
—Tales of the Heart, Vol. 2 of 4 (Classic Reprint) (p. 2186)
—Valentine's Eve, Vol. 1 of 3 (Classic Reprint) (p. 2344)
Opie, Amelia. Father & Daughter: A Tale (Classic Reprint) (p. 714)
—Tales of the Heart, Vol. 4 of 4 (Classic Reprint) (p. 2186)
—Temper, or Domestic Scenes, Vol. 1 Of 3: A Tale (Classic Reprint) (p. 2202)
—Works of Mrs. Amelia Opie, Vol. 2 of 3 (Classic Reprint) (p. 2499)
Opie, Amelia Alderson. Illustrations of Lying, in All Its Branches, Vol. 1 of 2 (Classic Reprint) (p. 1097)
—Madeline, Vol. 1: A Tale (Classic Reprint) (p. 1375)
—Simple Tales, Vol. 1 of 4 (Classic Reprint) (p. 2022)
—Tales of Real Life, Vol. 3 of 3 (Classic Reprint) (p. 2185)
—Tales of the Heart, Vol. 1 Of 4: Love, Mystery, & Superstition (Classic Reprint) (p. 2186)
—Works of Mrs. Amelia Opie, Vol. 1 of 3 (Classic Reprint) (p. 2499)
—Works of Mrs. Amelia Opie, Vol. 3 Of 3: Complete (Classic Reprint) (p. 2499)
Opie, David, illus. see Levy, Debbie & Panza, Rosana.
Opie, David, illus. see Smith, Molly.
Opie, Iona. My Very First Mother Goose. Wells, Rosemary, illus. (p. 1564)
—One, Two, Three, Mother Goose. Wells, Rosemary, illus. (p. 1663)
—Very Best Mother Goose Book Tower. Wells, Rosemary, illus. (p. 2352)
Opie, Iona, ed. Snuggle up with Mother Goose. Wells, Rosemary, illus. (p. 2050)
Opini, Bathseba & Lee, Richard B. Africans Thought of It: Amazing Innovations. (p. 33)
Opio, Leoncio. Adventures of Mr. Nimbus & the School House Bullies. (p. 25)
Opitz, Todd. Football & the Fly. (p. 761)
Opler, Morris Edward. Apache Life-Way: The Economic, Social, & Religious Institutions of the Chiricahua Indians (Classic Reprint) (p. 105)
O'Porter, Dawn. Goose. (p. 869)
Oppatt, Karen, jt. auth. see Gabolinscy, Jack.
Oppedisano, Robert & McCoy, Lisa. Internet. (p. 1127)
Oppegaard, David. Firebug of Balrog County. (p. 733)
—Town Built on Sorrow. (p. 2270)
Oppel, Karl. Thiergeschichten: Erzählungen und Schilderungen Aus Dem Leben der Thiere (Classic Reprint) (p. 2220)
Oppel, Kenneth. Bloom. (p. 246)
—Boundless. Tierney, Jim, illus. (p. 265)
—Every Hidden Thing. (p. 670)
—Inkling. Smith, Sydney, illus. (p. 1120)
—King's Taster. Johnson, Steve & Fancher, Lou, illus. (p. 1223)
—Nest. Klassen, Jon, illus. (p. 1588)
—Silverwing Collection: Silverwing; Sunwing; Firewing. (p. 2020)
—Starclimber. (p. 2106)
—Such Wicked Intent: The Apprenticeship of Victor Frankenstein, Book Two (p. 2146)
—Such Wicked Intent. (p. 2146)
—This Dark Endeavor: The Apprenticeship of Victor Frankenstein. (p. 2224)
Oppel, Kenneth & Klassen, Jon. Nest. Klassen, Jon, illus. (p. 1588)
—Nido. (p. 1604)
Oppen, Mark van & Marvano. Berlin: The Seven Dwarves. (p. 203)
Oppenheim, Donald. Robert Kwong at the Yeshiva. (p. 1890)
Oppenheim, E. Phillips. Anna the Adventuress (Classic Reprint) (p. 97)
—Berenice (Classic Reprint) (p. 202)
—Betrayal (Classic Reprint) (p. 208)
—Box with Broken Seals (Classic Reprint) (p. 266)
—Enoch Strone: A Master of Men (Classic Reprint) (p. 655)
—Hillman (Classic Reprint) (p. 972)
—Jacob's Ladder (Classic Reprint) (p. 1154)
—Kingdom of the Blind (Classic Reprint) (p. 1222)
—Malefactor (Classic Reprint) (p. 1392)
—Master Mummer (Classic Reprint) (p. 1418)
—Missioner (Classic Reprint) (p. 1481)
—Mr. Grex of Monte Carlo (Classic Reprint) (p. 1518)
—Nobody's Man. (p. 1617)
—Nobody's Man (Classic Reprint) (p. 1617)
—Passionate Quest (Classic Reprint) (p. 1703)
—Pawns Count (Classic Reprint) (p. 1708)
—Peer & the Woman (Classic Reprint) (p. 1714)
—People's Man (Classic Reprint) (p. 1719)
—Postmaster of Market Deignton (Classic Reprint) (p. 1780)
—Prince of Sinners (Classic Reprint) (p. 1794)
—Seven Conundrums (Classic Reprint) (p. 1993)
—Sleeping Memory (Classic Reprint) (p. 2037)
—Tempting of Tavernake (Classic Reprint) (p. 2203)
—Traitors (Classic Reprint) (p. 2276)
—Vanished Messenger (Classic Reprint) (p. 2347)
—Wicked Marquis (Classic Reprint) (p. 2460)
—Works of E. Phillips Oppenheim: Mysterious Mr. Sabin (Classic Reprint) (p. 2497)
—World's Great Snare (Classic Reprint) (p. 2507)
—Wrath to Come (Classic Reprint) (p. 2510)
—Yellow House, Master of Men, Vol. 1 (Classic Reprint) (p. 2520)
—Zeppelin's Passenger (Classic Reprint) (p. 2539)
Oppenheim, Edward Phillips. Falling Star (Classic Reprint) (p. 701)
—Light Beyond (Classic Reprint) (p. 1298)
—Mr. Grex of Monte Carlo. (p. 1518)
—Survivor (Classic Reprint) (p. 2165)
—Those Other Days (Classic Reprint) (p. 2230)
Oppenheim, James. Nine-Tenths. (p. 1609)
—Nine-Tenths: A Novel (Classic Reprint) (p. 1610)
—Olympian: A Story of the City (Classic Reprint) (p. 1651)
—Pay Envelopes: Tales of the Mill, the Mine & the City Street (Classic Reprint) (p. 1708)
—Wild Oats (Classic Reprint) (p. 2464)
Oppenheim, Joanne. Christmas Witch, an Italian Legend: Level 3. Mitra, Annie, illus. (p. 388)
—Could It Be? Level 2. Schindler, S. D., illus. (p. 458)
—Donkey's Tale: Level 2. Demarest, Chris, illus. (p. 582)
—Knish War on Rivington Street. Davis, Jon, illus. (p. 1229)
—Not Now! Said the Cow. Demarest, William, illus. (p. 1623)
—Prince's Bedtime. Latimer, Miriam, illus. (p. 1795)
—Prince's Breakfast. Latimer, Miriam, illus. (p. 1795)
—Wake up, Baby! Lynn, Sweat, illus. (p. 2371)
Oppenheim, Joanne F. & Barefoot Books. Desayuno Del Principe. Latimer, Miriam, illus. (p. 530)
Oppenheim, Joanne F. & Barefoot Books Staff. Prince's Breakfast. Latimer, Miriam, illus. (p. 1795)
—Principe No Duerme. Latimer, Miriam, illus. (p. 1800)
Oppenheim, Shulamith. Where Do I End & You Begin? Felix, Monique, illus. (p. 2436)
Oppenheimer, Nancy, illus. see Rouss, Sylvia A.
Oppenlander, Annette. Escape from the Past: The Kid. (p. 661)
—Escape from the Past: At Witches' End. (p. 661)
—Escape from the Past: The Duke's Wrath. (p. 661)

—Everything We Lose: A Civil War Novel of Hope, Courage & Redemption. (p. 673)
Opper, F. Mother Goose's Nursery Rhymes: With 250 Pictures (Classic Reprint) (p. 1509)
Opper, Frederick. Museum of Wonders, & What the Young Folks Saw There: Explained in Many Pictures (Classic Reprint) (p. 1528)
Optebeeck, E. Charleston Earthquake: Spectacular Drama, in Three Acts (Classic Reprint) (p. 359)
Optic, Oliver, jt. auth. see Ballantyne, R. M.
Optic, Oliver, pseud. All Aboard: Or Life on the Lake (Classic Reprint) (p. 48)
—All Aboard. (p. 48)
—All Taut or Rigging the Boat (Classic Reprint) (p. 53)
—Bear & Forbear: Or the Young Skipper of Lake Ucayga (Classic Reprint) (p. 179)
—Birthday Party: A Story for Little Folks (Classic Reprint) (p. 233)
—Bivouac & Battle, or the Struggles of a Soldier (Classic Reprint) (p. 235)
—Boat Club: Or, the Bunkers of Rippleton, a Tale for Boys (Classic Reprint) (p. 251)
—Boat Club. (p. 251)
—Brake Up: The Young Peacemakers. (p. 275)
—Brake Up: Or the Young Peacemakers (Classic Reprint) (p. 275)
—Brave Old Salt. (p. 276)
—Breaking Away: The Fortunes of a Student. (p. 278)
—Breaking Away: Or, the Fortunes of a Student (Classic Reprint) (p. 278)
—Breaking Away: Or, the Fortunes of a Student - Scholar's Choice Edition. (p. 278)
—Breaking Away. (p. 278)
—Brother Against Brother, or the War on the Border (Classic Reprint) (p. 286)
—Careless Kate: A Story for Little Folks (Classic Reprint) (p. 330)
—Careless Kate. (p. 330)
—Desk & Debit: Or, the Catastrophes of a Clerk (Classic Reprint) (p. 533)
—Dolly & I: A Story for Little Folks. (p. 579)
—Dolly & I: A Story for Little Folks (Classic Reprint) (p. 579)
—Dolly & I. (p. 579)
—Dorcas Club: Or Our Girls Afloat (Classic Reprint) (p. 586)
—Do-Somethings: A Story for Little Folks (Classic Reprint) (p. 571)
—Down the Rhine: Young America in Germany. (p. 590)
—Down the Rhine; or Young America in Germany: A Story of Travel & Adventure (Classic Reprint) (p. 590)
—Down the River: Or Buck Bradford & His Tyrants (Classic Reprint) (p. 590)
—Fanny Grant among the Indians: A Story for Young People (Classic Reprint) (p. 706)
—Field & Forest, or the Fortunes of a Farmer (Classic Reprint) (p. 722)
—Fighting for the Right. (p. 725)
—Fighting Joe: The Fortunes of a Staff Officer. (p. 725)
—Fighting Joe: Or the Fortunes of a Staff Officer; a Story of Great Rebellion (Classic Reprint) (p. 725)
—Fighting Joe, or the Fortunes of a Staff Officer: A Story of the Great Rebellion (Classic Reprint) (p. 725)
—Four Young Explorers: Sight-Seeing in the Tropics. (p. 773)
—Great Bonanza: Illustrated Narrative of Adventure & Discovery in Gold Mining, Silver Mining, among the Raftsmen, in the Oil Regions, Whaling, Hunting, Fishing & Fighting (Classic Reprint) (p. 884)
—In School & Out: Or the Conquest of Richard Grant, a Story for Young People (Classic Reprint) (p. 1107)
—In School & Out. (p. 1107)
—Just His Luck (Classic Reprint) (p. 1193)
—Lightning Express: Or, the Rival Academies (Classic Reprint) (p. 1300)
—Little Bobtail: Or, the Wreck of the Penobscot (Classic Reprint) (p. 1312)
—Little by Little. (p. 1313)
—Little Merchant: A Story for Little Folks (Classic Reprint) (p. 1321)
—Make or Break: Or, the Rich Man's Daughter (Classic Reprint) (p. 1386)
—Now or Never. (p. 1628)
—Oliver Optic's Magazine, 1875, Vol. 17: Our Boys & Girls (Classic Reprint) (p. 1649)
—On Time: Or, the Young Captain of the Ucayga Steamer (Classic Reprint) (p. 1656)
—On Time. (p. 1656)
—Or, the Young Pilot of Lake Champlain: A Story for Young People (Classic Reprint) (p. 1668)
—Our Boys & Girls, 1871 (Classic Reprint) (p. 1676)
—Out West, or Roughing It on the Great Lakes (Classic Reprint) (p. 1683)
—Outward Bound: Young America Afloat. (p. 1686)
—Plane & Plank: Or, the Mishaps of a Mechanic (Classic Reprint) (p. 1754)
—Poor & Proud. (p. 1774)
—Rich & Humble, or the Mission of Bertha Grant: A Story for Young People (Classic Reprint) (p. 1876)
—Seek & Find: The Adventures of a Smart Boy. (p. 1984)
—Seek & Find: Or the Adventures of a Smart Boy (Classic Reprint) (p. 1984)
—Shamrock & Thistle: Young America in Ireland & Scotland. (p. 1999)
—Shamrock & Thistle: Or, Young America in Ireland & Scotland; a Story of Travel & Adventure (Classic Reprint) (p. 1999)
—Snug Harbor. (p. 2050)
—Snug Harbor, or the Champlain Mechanics (Classic Reprint) (p. 2050)
—Soldier Boy: Tom Somers in the Army. (p. 2056)
—Soldier Boy: Or, Tom Somers in the Army. (p. 2056)
—Soldier Boy. (p. 2056)
—Soldier Boy, or Tom Somers in the Army: A Story of the Great Rebellion (Classic Reprint) (p. 2056)
—Soldier Boy; or, Tom Somers in the Army. (p. 2056)
—Starry Flag: Or, the Young Fisherman of Cape Ann (Classic Reprint) (p. 2106)
—Switch off, or the War of the Students (Classic Reprint) (p. 2171)
—Through by Daylight: Or, the Young Engineer of the Lake Shore Railroad (Classic Reprint) (p. 2236)
—Try Again. (p. 2297)
—Try Again, or the Trials & Triumphs of Harry West: A Story for Young Folks (Classic Reprint) (p. 2297)
—Uncle Ben: A Story for Little Folks (Classic Reprint) (p. 2318)
—Up & down the Nile, or Young Adventurers in Africa (Classic Reprint) (p. 2337)
—Victorious Union: The Blue & the Gray-Afloat Book 6. (p. 2356)
—Work & Win: Noddy Newman on a Cruise. (p. 2495)
—Work & Win: Or, Noddy Newman on a Cruise; a Story for Young People (Classic Reprint) (p. 2495)
—Yacht Club: The Young Boat-Builder. (p. 2516)
—Yacht Club: Or the Young Boat-Builder (Classic Reprint) (p. 2516)
—Yacht Club. (p. 2516)
—Young Lieutenant: Or, the Adventures of an Army Officer, a Story of Great Rebellion (Classic Reprint) (p. 2531)
Optic, Oliver, pseud & Lee and, Shepard. Now or Never. (p. 1628)
Optic, Oliver, pseud & Sayer, Reimunt. Lightning Express. (p. 1300)
Optic, Oliver, pseud & Shute, A. Burnham. Four Young Explorers. (p. 773)
Optic, Oliver, pseud & Wilmer, Richard Hooker. Brother Against Brother. (p. 286)
—Fighting for the Right. (p. 725)
—On the Blockade. (p. 1653)
—Soldier Boy. (p. 2056)
Optometry, Massachusetts School of. Scope: June 1940 (Classic Reprint) (p. 1961)
—Scope: May, 1938 (Classic Reprint) (p. 1961)
—Scope: February 1942 (Classic Reprint) (p. 1961)
—Scope: February, 1941 (Classic Reprint) (p. 1961)
—Scope: September 1939 (Classic Reprint) (p. 1961)
—Scope: September 1940 (Classic Reprint) (p. 1961)
O'Quinn, Amy M. Marie Curie for Kids: Her Life & Scientific Discoveries, with 21 Activities & Experiments. (p. 1405)
—Nikola Tesla for Kids: His Life, Ideas, & Inventions, with 21 Activities. (p. 1609)
O'Quinn, Lynne R. God Made You & God Made Me. (p. 852)
—Jesus Christ: The One. (p. 1166)
Or, Elbert, illus. see Torres, J.
Or Silat, Tammara. Tree Who Didn't Want to Grow. (p. 2284)
Ora, Vania, illus. see Kone, Kevin D.
Oraegbunem, Annastasia Onyinyechukwuka. Super Agnes. (p. 2154)
Oral, Feridun. Friend in Winter. Oral, Feridun, illus. (p. 786)
—Rice Porridge & the Little Dragon. (p. 1876)
—When the Moon Came Down. Oral, Feridun, illus. (p. 2433)
Oral, Feridun, illus. see Lamour-Crochet, Céline.
Oral, Feridun, illus. see Weineger, Brigitte.
Oral, Feridun, illus. see Westerlund, Kate.
Oral, Osman. I Believe in Allah. (p. 1060)
—I Believe in the Angels. (p. 1060)
—I Believe in the Books. (p. 1060)
—I Believe in the Divine Destiny & Decree. (p. 1060)
—I Believe in the Hereafter. (p. 1060)
—I Believe in the Prophets. (p. 1060)
Oram, Hiawyn. Filbert, the Good Little Fiend. Liao, Jimmy, illus. (p. 726)
—In the Attic. Kitamura, Satoshi, illus. (p. 1107)
—My Friend Fred. Reeve, Rosie, illus. (p. 1547)
—Snowboy & the Last Tree Standing. Sif, Birgitta, illus. (p. 2049)
Oram, Nina. Emerald Tree. (p. 641)
—Joining. (p. 1175)
Oramas, Jennifer. Peter's Purpose. Huseman, Ryan, illus. (p. 1730)
Orange County Association Staff, jt. auth. see Field, Shelly.
Orange Shirt Society, Orange Shirt. Orange Shirt Day. Webstad, Phyllis & Sorley, Joan, eds. (p. 1668)
Oranje, Corien. Rhino & Narwhal. Ten Berge, Marieke, illus. (p. 1874)
Oransky Wittenstein, Vicki. Reproductive Rights: Who Decides? (p. 1867)
Orazzini, Francesco, illus. see Pere, Tuula.
Orback, Craig, illus. see Brill, Marlene Targ.
Orback, Craig, illus. see Deutsch, Stacia & Cohon, Rhody.
Orback, Craig, illus. see Dokey, Cameron.
Orback, Craig, illus. see Figley, Marthy Rhodes & Figley, Marty Rhodes.
Orback, Craig, illus. see Figley, Marthy Rhodes.
Orback, Craig, illus. see Figley, Marty Rhodes.
Orback, Craig, illus. see Hill, Lee Sullivan.
Orback, Craig, illus. see Hopkinson, Deborah.
Orback, Craig, illus. see Jazynka, Kitson & Tripp, Valerie.
Orback, Craig, illus. see Jazynka, Kitson.
Orback, Craig, illus. see Krensky, Stephen.
Orback, Craig, illus. see Lehman-Wilzig, Tami.
Orback, Craig, illus. see Ludwig, Trudy.
Orback, Craig, illus. see Thomas, Patricia.
Orback, Craig, illus. see Wadsworth, Ginger.
Orback, Craig, illus. see Waxman, Laura Hamilton.
Orback, Craig, jt. auth. see Williams, Laura E.
Orban, Jani, illus. see Johnson, Terry Lynn.
Orbe, Alex, illus. see Schachter, Esty.
Orbeck-Nilssen, Constance. I'm Right Here. Düzakin, Akin, illus. (p. 1099)
—Vanishing Colors. Düzakin, Akin, illus. (p. 2347)
Orbie. Clothesline. Li, Karen, tr. from FRE. (p. 407)
Orbie, illus. see Dubé, Pierrette.
Orca Book Publishers, ed. 2018 Orca French Currents & Soundings (p. 2561)
—2018 Orca Soundings Essential (p. 2561)
—2018 Orca Spanish Soundings (p. 2561)
—Orca Young Readers Collection (p. 1669)
—Secrets Goreader Collection (p. 1980)
—Secrets Goreader Volume 1. (p. 1980)
Orcel, Nande. Rise of Jmugea: Book Two of the Omordion Trilogy. (p. 1885)
—Secret of Omordion: Book One of the Omordion Trilogy. (p. 1977)
Orchard, Ben L. Interesting Facts about US Presidents: Weird, Strange & Fun Facts of America's Greatest Presidents That Will Make You Rethink about History. (p. 1126)
Orchard, Eric. Bera the One-Headed Troll. (p. 202)
—Maddy Kettle Book 1: the Adventure of the Thimblewitch. (p. 1374)
Orchard, Eric, illus. see Halsey, Jacqueline.
Orchard, Eric, illus. see Inglis, Kate.
Orchard, Eric, illus. see Muller, Carrie & Halsey, Jacqueline.
Orchard, Fleur, illus. see Fisher, Cat & Fisher, Stu.
Orchard, Harry. Confessions & Autobiography of Harry Orchard (Classic Reprint) (p. 439)
Orchard, Heather. My Super Family: A Book for Blended Families. Matiashevsky, Angela, illus. (p. 1562)
Orchard, Kerry. How Danny Found His Brave. Gonzalez, Roberto, illus. (p. 1027)
—How to Tame Dragons & Hush Hyenas. Gonzalez, Roberto, illus. (p. 1044)
—No Trolls Allowed Guidebook. Gonzalez, Roberto, illus. (p. 1615)
Orchid Publishing, prod. Sleeping Beauty Ballet by Aleksandra. (p. 2037)
Orciari, Emanuela, illus. see Mazzucco, Melania G.
Orcutt, Emma Louise. Divine Seal (Classic Reprint) (p. 566)
Orcutt, William Dana. Balance: A Novel of Today (Classic Reprint) (p. 160)
—Flower of Destiny: An Episode (Classic Reprint) (p. 752)
—Lever: A Novel (Classic Reprint) (p. 1282)
—Moth a Novel (Classic Reprint) (p. 1509)
Orczy, Baroness. Old Hungarian Fairy Tales: (Illustrated & Unabridged Classic Edition) Barstow, Montagu, illus. (p. 1646)
Orczy, Emmuska. Bride of the Plains (Classic Reprint) (p. 280)
—Bronze Eagle: A Story of the Hundred Days (Classic Reprint) (p. 285)
—Gallant Pimpernel - Unabridged - Lord Tony's Wife, the Way of the Scarlet Pimpernel, Sir Percy Leads the Band, the Triumph of the Scarlet Pimperne. (p. 806)
—Laughing Cavalier (Classic Reprint) (p. 1252)
—Lord Tony's Wife: An Adventure of the Scarlet Pimpernel (Classic Reprint) (p. 1349)
—Meadowsweet (Classic Reprint) (p. 1434)
—Nest of the Sparrowhawk: A Romance of the 17th Century (Classic Reprint) (p. 1588)
—Nicolette: A Tale of Old Provence (Classic Reprint) (p. 1604)
—Scarlet Pimpernell. (p. 1942)
—Son of the People: A Romance of the Hungarian Plains (Classic Reprint) (p. 2062)
—True Woman (Classic Reprint) (p. 2295)
Ord, G. W., illus. see Selous, Edmund.
Ord, Mandy, illus. see Wild, Margaret.
Ordas, Emi, illus. see Gillespie, L.
Ordas, Emi, illus. see Gillespie, Lisa Jane.
Ordas, Emi, illus. see Tiger Tales.
Ordaz, Francisco, illus. see Maier, Paul L.
Ordaz, Frank, illus. see Doherty, Patrick.
Ordaz, Frank, illus. see Warner, Michael N.
Ordoñez, Alejandro. Amar(se) Es de Valientes / Loving Yourself Is for the Brave. (p. 62)
—Nadie Sale Ileso Del Amor / No One Gets Out of Love Unscathed. (p. 1572)
Ordonez, Ana Isabel. Aye Aye & Euricoty Go to Space: Vol VII. (p. 145)
—Fedor, the Tsunami & Cinico Forest. (p. 718)
Ordonez Cuadrado, Rafael. Pedo Más Grande Del Mundo. du Fay, Laure, illus. (p. 1712)
—World's Biggest Fart. du Fay, Laure, illus. (p. 2506)
Ordóñez, María Antonia, illus. see Landrón, Rafael & Landrón, José Rafael.
Ordóñez, Miguel, illus. see Elya, Susan Middleton.
Ordóñez, Miguel, illus. see Fallon, Jimmy.
Ordonez, Miguel, illus. see Stanton, Andy.
Ordonez Rodas, Azucena. ANTONELA y la Estrella Del Amor. (p. 103)
—Jardín de Nina. (p. 1160)
—Luz de Luna (Leyenda) (p. 1369)
—Nina Tiene un Hermanito. (p. 1609)
—Yhoren la Isla Encantada. (p. 2521)
Ordonneau, Maurice. Poupee Souvenir (Classic Reprint) (p. 1781)
Ordoobadi, Lucy. Captain Gets in Shape! (p. 325)
—Captain Goes to School! (p. 325)
—Captain Takes a Vacation! (p. 326)
Ordway, Edith B. Handbook of Conundrums (Classic Reprint) (p. 915)
Ore, Simon, ed. see Clark, David A.
Ore, Stephen. Round Trip: A Novel. (p. 1908)
Orea, Lucia, tr. see Zak, Monica.
Orecchia, Giulia, tr. see Mantegazza, Giovanna.
Oredola, Aisha. Rid Me of This. (p. 1877)
O'Reilly, Avril. Fairy in the Family. (p. 696)
—Fairy in the Family Again - the School Science Competition. (p. 696)
—My First Holy Communion Keepsake Journal. (p. 1544)
O'Reilly, Bill. Day the President Was Shot. (p. 514)
—Day the World Went Nuclear: Dropping the Atom Bomb & the End of World War II in the Pacific. (p. 514)
—Hitler's Last Days: The Death of the Nazi Regime & the World's Most Notorious Dictator. (p. 982)
—Hitler's Last Days. (p. 982)
—Kennedy's Last Days: The Assassination That Defined a Generation. (p. 1209)
—Last Days of Jesus: His Life & Times. Low, William & Cobalt Illustrations Studio Staff, illus. (p. 1247)
—Últimos Días de Jesús. Uxó, Carlos, tr. (p. 2316)
O'Reilly, Bill, jt. auth. see Patterson, James.
O'Reilly, Bill, jt. auth. see Zimmerman, Dwight Jon.
O'Reilly, Bill & Patterson, James. Give Please a Chance. (p. 840)
O'Reilly, Bill & Zimmerman, Dwight Jon. Lincoln's Last Days: The Shocking Assassination That Changed America Forever. (p. 1303)
—Lincoln's Last Days. (p. 1303)
O'Reilly, Dowell. Fivecorners (Classic Reprint) (p. 745)
O'Reilly, Gertrude M. Just Stories (Classic Reprint) (p. 1194)
O'Reilly, Gillian, jt. auth. see Lee, Cora.
O'Reilly, Jane. Notations of Cooper Cameron. (p. 1624)
—Secret of Goldenrod. (p. 1977)
O'Reilly, John, illus. see Mewburn, Kyle.
O'Reilly, John Boyle. Moondyne: A Story of Convict Life in Australia (Classic Reprint) (p. 1502)
O'Reilly, Phillip. Theology for Young Christians: Preparing for Spiritual Battle with Lessons from Genesis (p. 2216)
O'Reilly, Sean. Missing Mummy (p. 1480)
—Monster Beach (p. 1495)
—Monster Beach Arcana Studio Staff, illus. (p. 1495)
—Monster Crooks (p. 1495)
—Monster Crooks Arcana Studio Staff, illus. (p. 1495)
—Scare Fair (p. 1941)
—Scare Fair Arcana Studio Staff, illus. (p. 1941)
—Toy Snatcher (p. 2270)
—Wolfboy's Wish (p. 2484)
—Wolfboy's Wish Arcana Studio Staff, illus. (p. 2484)
O'Reilly, Sean Patrick. Gwaii. Chastain, Grant, ed. (p. 907)
O'Reilly, Sean Patrick, ed. see Adams, Matthew R.
O'Reilly, Sean Patrick, ed. see Blaylock, Josh.
O'Reilly, Sean Patrick, ed. see Brown, Bruce.
O'Reilly, Sean Patrick, ed. see Kinney, Scott.
O'Reilly, Sean Patrick, ed. see Kirkham, Tyler & Kirkham, Rian.
O'Reilly, Sean Patrick, ed. see MacPherson, Dwight L.
O'Reilly, Sean Patrick, ed. see Marz, Ron & Poulton, Mark.
O'Reilly, Sean Patrick, ed. see Najman, Alexander.
O'Reilly, Sean Patrick, ed. see Odjick, Jay & Tenascon, Patrick.
O'Reilly, Sean Patrick, ed. see Patterson, Michael.
O'Reilly, Sean Patrick, ed. see Pell, Jason.
O'Reilly, Sean Patrick, ed. see Raymond, Roger & Savoy, Darryl.
O'Reilly, Sean Patrick, ed. see Rodriguez, Alfredo.
O'Reilly, Sean Patrick, ed. see Sherman, M. Zachary & Martinek, Tom.
O'Reilly, Sean Patrick, ed. see Tra, Frank.
O'Reilly, Zoe, illus. see Clarke, Gail.
Orejon Plaza, Virginia. Cielo Sobre ADA. (p. 391)
Orel, Brigita. Pirate Tree. Poh, Jennie, illus. (p. 1750)
O'Rell, Max. John Bull, Junior: Or French As She Is Traduced (Classic Reprint) (p. 1172)
Orellana, Marjorie Faulstich, jt. auth. see Persano, Thomas.
Orellana, Nery, illus. see Gillooly, Jessica B.
Orelli, Konrad von. Alt-Französische Grammatik, Worin Die Conjugation Vorzugsweise Berücksichtigt Ist: Nebst Einem Anhang Von Alten Fabliaux et Contes Welche Schiller's Gang Nach Dem Eisenhammer, Wieland's Wasserkufe, Bürger's Lied Von Treue, Langbein's Kirschbaum Entspre. (p. 60)
Oren, Rony. Animaged Haggadah. (p. 87)
Orender, Donna. Wowsdom! the Girl's Guide to the Positive & the Possible. (p. 2510)
Orenstein, Denise Gosliner. Dirt. (p. 552)
Orenstein, Ronald. Weird Butterflies & Moths. Marent, Thomas, photos by. (p. 2397)
Orfield, Matthias Nordberg. Federal Land Grants to the States with Special Reference to Minnesota (Classic Reprint) (p. 717)
Orford, Margie. Little Red Hen. Lilje, Karen, illus. (p. 1326)
—Magic Fish. Littlewort, Lizza, illus. (p. 1377)
Orgain, Kate Alma. Waif from Texas (Classic Reprint) (p. 2370)
Organ, Betty. Peter's Christmas Eve Adventure Martin, Shawn, illus. (p. 1730)
Organization, Jenny Appleseed. Finmore's Humongous Talking Worm. (p. 731)
Orgill, Roxane. Footwork: The Story of Fred & Adele Astaire. Jorisch, Stéphane, illus. (p. 762)
—Jazz Day: The Making of a Famous Photograph. Vallejo, Francis, illus. (p. 1162)
—Siege: How General Washington Kicked the British Out of Boston & Launched a Revolution. (p. 2015)
—Skit-Scat Raggedy Cat: Ella Fitzgerald. Qualls, Sean, illus. (p. 2033)
Orgullo, Marisa. Celebrating Carnival! (p. 349)
—Celebrating Christmas! (p. 349)
—Celebrating Day of the Dead! (p. 349)
—Celebrating Hispanic Heritage Month! (p. 349)
—I Want to Draw Dinosaurs. (p. 1085)
—What Happens When My Parents Get Divorced? (p. 2412)
Orie, London. My Emojis. (p. 1537)
Origami, jt. auth. see Maekawa, Jun.
Origami, jt. auth. see Robinson, Nick.
Original Story, Unabridged -, jt. auth. see Stoker, Bram.
Original Story, Unabridged -, jt. auth. see Wells, H. G.
Oriol, Elsa, illus. see Ofanansky, Allison Maile.
Oriole, Beth. Hannah's Zoo. (p. 918)
O'Riordan, Aileen & Triggs, Pat. Following in Darwin's Footsteps. (p. 758)
Oritz, Orlando, jt. auth. see Ortiz, Orlando.
Orkrania, Alexia, illus. see Graham, Oakley.
Orkrania, Alexia, illus. see Reasoner, Charles.
Orkrania, Alexia, illus. see Rose, Eilidh.
Orlandi, Lorenzo, illus. see Rock, Lois.
Orlando, Jade, illus. see Fang, Vicky.
Orlando, Kristen. No Sabes Mi Nombre. (p. 1614)
—You Don't Know My Name. (p. 2527)
—You Won't See Me Coming. (p. 2528)
Orlando, Martha Jane. Trip, a Tryst & a Terror. (p. 2288)
Orlean, Susan & Bradford, Chris. Young Samurai the Way of the Warrior. (p. 2532)
Orlebar, Frederica St. John. Adventures of Her Serene Limpness, the Moon-Faced Princess, Dulcet & Debonaire (Classic Reprint) (p. 24)
Orlen, Amy. Nantucket Elves. (p. 1574)
Orlinsky, Lori. Being Small (Isn't So Bad after All) (p. 195)

Orloff, Karen Kaufman. Miles of Smiles. Lozano, Luciano, illus. (p. 1465)
—Mystery at the Aquarium (a Nightlight Detective Book) Smith, Jamie, illus. (p. 1568)
—Nightlight Detective: Mystery at the Museum. Smith, Jamie, illus. (p. 1608)
—Nightlight Detective: Big Top Circus Mystery. Smith, Jamie, illus. (p. 1608)
—Some Days. Chen, Ziyue, illus. (p. 2058)
Orloff, Shelly M. You & Me & Allergies: Bringing Awareness to Environmental & Food Allergies Sensitivities. (p. 2524)
Orloffsky, R. Nadia, or Out of the Beaten Track, Vol. 2 (Classic Reprint) (p. 1572)
—Nadia, Vol. 3: Or, Out of the Beaten Track (Classic Reprint) (p. 1572)
Orloffsky, R. & Langenau. Nadia, or, Out of the Beaten Track, Vol. I. (p. 1572)
Orman, Roscoe. Ricky & Mobo. (p. 1877)
Ormand, Kate. Dark Days. (p. 506)
—Pack. (p. 1691)
—Wanderers. (p. 2375)
Ormand, Kate & Louise, Kate. Dark Days. (p. 506)
Orme, David. Amazing Gadgets. (p. 65)
—Ancient Mysteries. (p. 81)
—Bugs & Spiders. (p. 292)
—Bugs & Spiders. Mongiovi, Jorge, illus. (p. 292)
—Comets. (p. 429)
—Dinosaurs! (p. 550)
—Endangered Animals. (p. 649)
—Extreme Science. (p. 687)
—Extreme Sports. (p. 687)
—Fantastic Feats (Don't Do This at Home) (p. 707)
—Fear. (p. 716)
—Great Disasters. (p. 885)
—Great Journeys. (p. 887)
—How to Be a Pop Star. (p. 1037)
—Life in Space. (p. 1292)
—Lost Animals. Mongiovi, Jorge, illus. (p. 1352)
—Mummies. (p. 1526)
—Plagues. (p. 1754)
—Science Fiction. (p. 1955)
—Sea Killers. (p. 1967)
—Speed. (p. 2078)
—Spies. (p. 2081)
—Spies. Martin, Jan, illus. (p. 2081)
—Strange Creatures. (p. 2137)
—Strange Creatures. Lindblad, Stefan, illus. (p. 2137)
—UFOs: Are They Real? (p. 2313)
—Vampires. (p. 2346)
—Vampires. Hovland, Oivind, illus. (p. 2346)
—Weird Places. (p. 2397)
Orme, David, jt. auth. see Orme, David.
Orme, David, jt. auth. see Orme, Helen.
Orme, David, jt. auth. see Ruffell, Ann.
Orme, Eve. Dual Reflection (Classic Reprint) (p. 607)
Orme, Harinani, illus. see Crowl, Janice.
Orme, Helen. 800 Words. (p. 2560)
—Body Art. (p. 253)
—Healthy Eating. (p. 943)
—Magic. (p. 1376)
—Seeds, Bulbs, Plants & Flowers: The Best Start in Science. (p. 1983)
—Seeds, Bulbs, Plants & Flowers. (p. 1983)
—Sharks. (p. 2002)
—Solar System. (p. 2056)
—Weather. (p. 2393)
—What Things Are Made Of. (p. 2420)
Orme, Helen, jt. auth. see Orme, David.
Orme, Helen, jt. auth. see Randall, Ronne.
Orme, Nicholas. Fleas, Flies, & Friars: Children's Poetry from the Middle Ages (p. 747)
Orme, Robert. Biblical Literacy. (p. 214)
—Christianity. (p. 382)
Orme, Robert, jt. auth. see Lewis, Andy.
Ormerod, Edward Latham. British Social Wasps: An Introduction to Their Anatomy & Physiology, Architecture, & General Natural History, with Illustrations of the Different Species & Their Nests (Classic Reprint) (p. 283)
Ormerod, Jan. Baby Swap. Joyner, Andrew, illus. (p. 153)
—Bike Ride. Blackwood, Freya, illus. (p. 225)
—Lizzie Nonsense. Ormerod, Jan, illus. (p. 1337)
—Making Up. Blackwood, Freya, illus. (p. 1390)
—Snack. Blackwood, Freya, illus. (p. 2044)
Ormerod, Jan, illus. see Applegate, Katherine.
Ormerod, Jan, illus. see Ashman, Linda.
Ormerod, Jan, illus. see Calmenson, Stephanie.
Ormerod, Jan, illus. see Harris, Robie H.
Ormerod, Nicola. Roxy May, Help My Boyfriend Is a Fairy. (p. 1909)
Ormes, Jane, illus. see Haworth, Katie.
Ormes, Jane, illus. see Nosy Crow.
Ormond, Frederic. Three Keys (Classic Reprint) (p. 2233)
Ormond, Jennifer. DJ's Allergies. Walstead, Curt, illus. (p. 567)
Ormondroyd, Edward. David & the Phoenix. (p. 510)
—David & the Phoenix. Raysor, Joan, illus. (p. 510)
—Time at the Top & All in Good Time: Two Novels. Ericksen, Barb et al, illus. (p. 2243)
Ormsbee, K. E. Doorway & the Deep. (p. 585)
—House in Poplar Wood. (p. 1022)
—Midnight on Strange Street. (p. 1461)
—Water & the Wild. (p. 2384)
—Water & the Wild. Mora, Elsa, illus. (p. 2384)
Ormsbee, Kathryn. Great Unknowable End. (p. 890)
—Lucky Few. (p. 1364)
—Sullivan Sisters. (p. 2148)
—Tash Hearts Tolstoy. (p. 2192)
Ormsby, Anne. Soldier's Family, or Guardian Genii, Vol. 1 Of 4: A Romance (Classic Reprint) (p. 2057)
Ormsby, Lawrence, illus. see Plumb, Sally.
Orne, Martha Russell. Black Diamond: A Comic Drama in Two Acts (Classic Reprint) (p. 237)
—Donation Party, or Thanksgiving Eve at the Parsonage: A Comedy in Three Acts (Classic Reprint) (p. 581)
Orne, Philip. Simply a Love-Story (Classic Reprint) (p. 2022)
Ornelas, Lourdes. I Am Proud! (p. 1059)
—So Can I. (p. 2050)
Ornia-Blanco, Miguel, illus. see Dahl, Michael.
Ornitz, Samuel. Haunch Paunch & Jowl: An Anonymous Autobiography (Classic Reprint) (p. 937)
Orno, Don. Revolt Against Sentimental Scruples: The Sock, a Play of Protest; Together with a Foreward on Marital Morality & Unmoral Murder (Classic Reprint) (p. 1873)
Ornot, R. D. Hide-And-Seek: A First Book of Position Words. Mangal, Sakshi, illus. (p. 967)
Ornstein, Esther. Middos Man Book & CD. Judowitz, Yoel, illus. (p. 1461)
Ornstein, Mike. Kindergarrrten Bus. Barry, Kevin M., illus. (p. 1218)
Orodan, Mike. Farm. (p. 709)
—Peek-A-Baby: Ocean. (p. 1712)
Oron, Hagit R. Bravo & Elphie. (p. 277)
—Elphie Goes Trick or Treating. (p. 639)
Oron, Judie. Cry of the Giraffe. (p. 480)
Oron, Marian & Marciniak, Eliza. Detective Nosegoode & the Music Box Mystery. (p. 534)
Orona-Ramirez, Kristy. Kiki's Journey. Warm Day, Jonathan, illus. (p. 1217)
Oronoz, Alan, illus. see Alva, C.
O'Rourke, Davey. American Artists Help Keep America Beautiful. (p. 70)
O'Rourke, Erica. Resonance. (p. 1869)
O'Rourke, Kathryn Maureen. Head to Heart: Fixing Failure, Grief, & Anger: Finding Love, Grace, & Mercy: Josh & Emily. (p. 942)
—Superhero Heart Rescue: The Solution When Feeling Guilty & Afraid. (p. 2159)
—Superhero Heart Rescue: The Solution When Feeling Worthless & Rejected. (p. 2159)
—Superhero Heart Rescue: The Solution, When Feeling Lonely, Insecure, & Unwanted. (p. 2159)
O'Rourke, Kristin. There's a Bully in My Brain. (p. 2217)
O'Rourke, Molly. Adventures of Gleeson & Cormac: Why Do People Cry? (p. 23)
O'Rourke, Page Eastburn, illus. see Driscoll, Laura.
O'Rourke, Page Eastburn, illus. see Hayward, Linda.
O'Rourke, Page Eastburn, illus. see Skinner, Daphne.
O'Rourke, Ryan. Bella Lost & Found. O'Rourke, Ryan, illus. (p. 197)
—Bella up, up, & Away. O'Rourke, Ryan, illus. (p. 197)
O'Rourke, Ryan, illus. see Crum, Shutta.
O'Rourke, Ryan, illus. see Gray, Rita.
O'Rourke, Ryan, illus. see McReynolds, Linda.
O'Rourke, Ryan, illus. see Sayres, Brianna Caplan.
O'Rourke, Ryan, illus. see Suen, Anastasia.
O'Rourke, Ryan, illus. see Vamos, Samantha R.
O'Rourke, Ryan, illus. see Vamos, Samantha R., et al.
O'Rourke, Ryan, illus. see Vanderwater, Amy Ludwig.
O'Rourke, Ryan, jt. auth. see McReynolds, Linda.
O'Rourke, Tim. Flashes. (p. 747)
Oroz, Joyce, illus. see Weitzel, Nancy.
Orozco, Fa & Fernandez, Pedro J. Había una Vez... mexicanas Que Hicieron Historia / Once upon a Time... Mexican Women Who Made History. (p. 908)
Orozco, Jose-Luis. Diez Deditos. (p. 544)
Orozco, Rebeca. It's Our Nature. Cottin, Menena, illus. (p. 1147)
Orozco-Velasquez, Diana Maria & Orozco Velasquez, Gina Marcela. Animales en Peligro de Extinción. (p. 93)
—Cómo Cuidar Nuestro Planeta. (p. 432)
Orpen. Perfection City (Classic Reprint) (p. 1723)
Orpen, Adela E. Jay-Hawkers: A Story of Free Soil & Border Ruffian Days (Classic Reprint) (p. 1161)
Orpen, William. Onlooker in France: 1917 1919 (Classic Reprint) (p. 1664)
Orpinas, Jean-Paul, illus. see Kidd, Rob.
Orpinas, Jean-Paul, illus. see Lagonegro, Melissa.
Orpinas, Jean-Paul, illus. see Saxon, Victoria & RH Disney Staff.
Orr, Anne. Tatting with Anne Orr. (p. 2193)
Orr, Bobby, jt. auth. see Kootstra, Kara.
Orr, Deborah Murphy. Smarter Balanced - Math, Grade 8. (p. 2041)
Orr, Diane. My Name Is Merlin: A de Good Life Farm Book. (p. 1557)
—My Name Is Mocha. (p. 1557)
—My Name Is Odin: A de Good Life Farm Book. (p. 1557)
—We Are Mocha's Family. (p. 2389)
Orr, J. Rainbows. (p. 1837)
Orr, James Lee. Ned Dawson in Wilful Land (Classic Reprint) (p. 1585)
Orr, Jennifer. Rating Your Bunkmates & Other Camp Crimes. (p. 1842)
Orr, Katherine. Master Dao & the Energy of Life. Orr, Katherine, illus. (p. 1418)
Orr, Katherine, illus. see Cook, Mauliola.
Orr, Katherine, jt. auth. see Cook, Mauliola.
Orr, Lucinda Lee. Journal of a Young Lady of Virginia, 1782 (Classic Reprint) (p. 1180)
Orr, Nicole. Backyard Jungle Safari Foxes. (p. 157)
Orr, Ronalee Bennett. Windy Rafters Roughnecks: Mystery at the Barn. (p. 2472)
Orr, Tamara. Emily Osment. (p. 642)
Orr, Tamara B. Extreme Skysurfing. (p. 687)
—Extreme Wakeboarding. (p. 687)
Orr, Tamra. Aardvark or Anteater. (p. 2)
—Alpaca or Llama. (p. 58)
—Amenorrhea: Why Your Period Stops. (p. 69)
—Amy Tan: Author Extraordinaire (p. 77)
—Ancient Egypt. (p. 80)
—AnnaSophia Robb. (p. 98)
—Avian Flu. (p. 143)
—Aztecs. (p. 146)
—Backyard Insects: Walking Sticks. (p. 157)
—Bangladesh. (p. 163)
—Barbados Henderson, James D., ed. (p. 165)
—Barbados. (p. 165)
—Blogging. (p. 245)
—Brenda Song. (p. 279)
—Butterfly or Moth. (p. 304)
—Career As an Aircraft Mechanic & Service Technician. (p. 328)
—Career as an Auto Mechanic. (p. 328)
—Careers in Glasswork (p. 329)
—Careers in Sheet Metal & Ironwork (p. 330)
—Carstensz Pyramid. (p. 335)
—Chinese Heritage. (p. 378)
—Chris Johnson. (p. 382)
—Civil Rights Movement: Advocating for Equality. (p. 396)
—Combatting Body Shaming. (p. 428)
—Community Sites. (p. 432)
—Coping with Racial Inequality. (p. 451)
—Crocodile or Alligator. (p. 477)
—Crowdfunding. (p. 479)
—Cuban Heritage. (p. 482)
—Day by Day with Dwayne the Rock Johnson. (p. 512)
—Day by Day with Selena Gomez. (p. 513)
—Day by Day with Willow Smith. (p. 513)
—Department of Transportation. (p. 529)
—Digital Privacy: Securing Your Data. (p. 546)
—Dominican Heritage. (p. 580)
—Ecstasy. (p. 624)
—Environmentalist. (p. 657)
—Experiment with Weather. (p. 678)
—Filipino Heritage. (p. 726)
—Frequently Asked Questions about Bone Cancer. (p. 784)
—Frog or Toad. (p. 789)
—Growing Nutritious Food. (p. 899)
—History of Voting Rights. (p. 981)
—Home & Family Relationships. (p. 995)
—How Did They Build That? Zoo. (p. 1027)
—How to Research Your Ancestry. (p. 1043)
—Hydrogen Bomb: Unleashing the Nuclear Age & Arms Race. (p. 1055)
—I Have Been Shamed on the Internet, Now What? (p. 1066)
—I Spy in the Sky the Clouds. (p. 1082)
—I Spy in the Sky the Moon. (p. 1082)
—I Spy in the Sky the Stars. (p. 1082)
—I Spy in the Sky the Sun. (p. 1082)
—Image Sharing. (p. 1100)
—Indian Heritage. (p. 1116)
—Indonesia. (p. 1117)
—Iran & Nuclear Weapons. (p. 1133)
—Jennifer Lawrence. (p. 1164)
—Jonas Brothers. (p. 1177)
—Kid's Guide to the Economy. (p. 1215)
—Korean Heritage. (p. 1231)
—Kristen Stewart. (p. 1232)
—Liver Cancer: Current & Emerging Trends in Detection & Treatment. (p. 1332)
—Liver Cancer. (p. 1332)
—Long Ago & Far Away Mesopotamia: Mesopotamia. (p. 1342)
—Louis Armstrong. (p. 1357)
—Markus (Notch) Persson. (p. 1407)
—Memorial Day/Día de los Caídos. de la Vega, Eida, tr. from ENG. (p. 1445)
—Mexican Heritage. (p. 1454)
—Microblogging. (p. 1459)
—Miles Davis. (p. 1465)
—Money Matters: A Kid's Guide to Money (p. 1493)
—Monsters of Hercules. (p. 1498)
—Motion & Forces. (p. 1511)
—My Friend Is Buddhist. (p. 1547)
—National Zoo. (p. 1578)
—Native American Medicine. Johnson, Troy, ed. (p. 1578)
—Organic Farmer. (p. 1670)
—Ovarian Tumors & Cysts. (p. 1686)
—Porpoise or Dolphin. (p. 1778)
—Praying Mantis. (p. 1785)
—Primary Source History of the Colony of New Jersey. (p. 1792)
—Racial Profiling (p. 1832)
—Railroad & the Civil War (1860s) (p. 1835)
—Robert Pattison. (p. 1890)
—Seal or Sea Lion. (p. 1970)
—Sharing Economy. (p. 2001)
—Shia Labeouf. (p. 2007)
—Sirens. (p. 2026)
—Social Networking. (p. 2053)
—Southwest. (p. 2069)
—Stephanie Meyer. (p. 2115)
—Story of the Constitution. (p. 2133)
—Studying Sinkholes. (p. 2144)
—Super Cool Science Experiments: Circulation. (p. 2154)
—Tenth Amendment: Limiting Federal Powers. (p. 2206)
—Thailand. (p. 2211)
—Truth about Cocaine. (p. 2296)
—Understanding Economic Systems. (p. 2324)
—Understanding Sound. (p. 2325)
—Unearthing Fossils. (p. 2326)
—Video Sharing. (p. 2356)
—Vietnamese Heritage. (p. 2357)
—Wasp or Bee. (p. 2382)
—Ways to Help the Elderly: A Guide to Giving Back. (p. 2388)
—We Visit Afghanistan. (p. 2392)
—We Visit Chile. (p. 2392)
—What Degree Do I Need to Pursue a Career in Business? (p. 2407)
—What's So Great about the Buffalo Soldiers. (p. 2425)
—What's So Great about the Tuskegee Airmen. (p. 2425)
—Windward Islands Henderson, James D., ed. (p. 2472)
—Working at the Zoo. (p. 2495)
—Your Career in the Coast Guard. (p. 2533)
—Your Career in the Navy. (p. 2533)
—Zest. (p. 2540)
Orr, Tamra, jt. auth. see Peters, Jennifer.
Orr, Tamra, jt. auth. see Uhl, Xina M.
Orr, Tamra & Cooley Peterson, Megan. Smithsonian Field Trips. (p. 2042)
Orr, Tamra & Sommers, Michael A. Avi (p. 143)
Orr, Tamra B. African Americans in the Armed Forces (p. 32)
—Air. (p. 37)
—Alaska (Revised Edition) (p. 40)
—Amelia Earhart. (p. 69)
—Anger. (p. 86)
—Animal Discoveries. (p. 89)
—Animals Helping to Keep the Peace. (p. 94)
—Antibiotics. (p. 102)
—Bald Eagle: All about the American Symbol. (p. 160)
—Bangladesh. (p. 163)
—Battling Extinction. (p. 175)
—Bermuda. (p. 203)
—California. (p. 310)
—Coping with Breakups & Jealousy. (p. 451)
—Crime Scene Investigator. (p. 474)
—Erosion. (p. 660)
—Excitement. (p. 676)
—Extreme in-Line Skating. (p. 686)
—Extreme Skysurfing. (p. 687)
—Extreme Street Luge. (p. 687)
—Extreme Wakeboarding. (p. 687)
—Fear. (p. 716)
—Florida. (p. 751)
—Food of China. (p. 760)
—Food of Greece. (p. 760)
—Forecasting a Flood. (p. 765)
—Forensic Science Investigator. (p. 765)
—Friendliness. (p. 786)
—Growing Nutritious Food. (p. 899)
—Harlem Renaissance: An African American Cultural Movement. (p. 930)
—How Did They Build That? Lighthouse. (p. 1027)
—I See Falling Stars. (p. 1081)
—Indiana. (p. 1116)
—Investigating a Crime Scene. (p. 1131)
—Israeli-Palestinian Conflict: the Struggle for Middle East Peace (p. 1141)
—It Snows. (p. 1142)
—It's Cool to Learn about the United States Midwest. (p. 1144)
—It's Cool to Learn about the United States Southwest. (p. 1144)
—Joy. (p. 1184)
—Leonardo Da Vinci: Renaissance Genius. (p. 1267)
—Liberty Bell: Introducing Primary Sources. (p. 1284)
—Madagascar. (p. 1373)
—Manga Artists. (p. 1397)
—Marvelous Discoveries. (p. 1413)
—Michelangelo: Master of the Renaissance. (p. 1458)
—Midwest. (p. 1462)
—Money-Making Opportunities for Teens Who Like Working Outside. (p. 1492)
—Ocean Discoveries. (p. 1635)
—Oklahoma. (p. 1643)
—Oprah Winfrey. (p. 1667)
—Planet Earth Discoveries. (p. 1755)
—Poison Dart Frog. (p. 1767)
—Polar Bears. (p. 1769)
—Pondering Pollution. (p. 1773)
—Red-Eyed Tree Frog. (p. 1857)
—Reticulated Python. (p. 1870)
—Rocks. (p. 1896)
—Sadness. (p. 1921)
—Science of a Fastball. (p. 1957)
—Science of a Flip Turn. (p. 1957)
—Searching the Sky. (p. 1971)
—Selfies from Space: How Satellites Help Science on Earth. (p. 1987)
—Shyness. (p. 2013)
—Space Discoveries. (p. 2071)
—Space, Incorporated: The Future of Commercial Space Travel. (p. 2071)
—Star-Spangled Banner: Introducing Primary Sources. (p. 2103)
—Statue of Liberty: Introducing Primary Sources. (p. 2109)
—Super Cool Science Experiments: Weather. (p. 2154)
—Super Cool Science Experiments: Digestion. (p. 2154)
—Super Cool Science Experiments: Respiration. (p. 2154)
—Surprise. (p. 2163)
—Tornadoes. (p. 2265)
—Tracking an Epidemic. (p. 2272)
—Tsunamis. (p. 2298)
—Turkey. (p. 2299)
—Undersea World. (p. 2324)
—Understanding Insects. (p. 2325)
—Understanding Sound. (p. 2325)
—Unearthing Fossils. (p. 2326)
—USMC Special Reaction Teams. (p. 2342)
—Vo-Tech Track to Success in Law, Public Safety, Corrections, & Security. (p. 2364)
—Walt Disney. (p. 2373)
—Walt Disney: The Man Behind the Magic. (p. 2374)
—We Have Hurricanes. (p. 2391)
—Wildfires. (p. 2466)
—Wind Blows. (p. 2471)
—Working with Tech in Construction (p. 2496)
—Zest. (p. 2540)
—Zion. (p. 2541)
Orr, Tamra B., jt. auth. see Brown, Jonatha A.
Orr, Tamra B., jt. auth. see Given-Wilson, Rachel.
Orr, Tamra B., jt. auth. see Gunderson, Jessica.
Orr, Tamra B., jt. auth. see King, David C.
Orr, Tamra B., jt. auth. see LeVert, Suzanne.
Orr, Tamra B., jt. auth. see Mezzanotte, Jim.
Orr, Tamra B., jt. auth. see NgCheong-Lum, Roseline.
Orr, Tamra B., jt. auth. see Orr, Tamra.
Orr, Tamra B. & Sipperley, Keli. Earth Materials & Systems. (p. 617)
Orr, Tamra B., VIII, jt. auth. see Moragne, Wendy.
Orr, Tasso VanCe. Applied Mental Efficiency. (p. 107)
Orr, Wendy. ABANDONED! a Lion Called Kiki. Castelao, Patricia, illus. (p. 2)
—DISCOVERED! a Beagle Called Bella Castelao, Patricia, illus. (p. 555)
—Dragonfly Song. (p. 595)
—Princess & Her Panther. Stringer, Lauren, illus. (p. 1795)
—Raven's Mountain. (p. 1844)
—STOLEN! a Pony Called Pebbles. Castelao, Patricia, illus. (p. 2120)
—Stolen! - A Pony Called Pebbles. (p. 2120)

—Swallow's Dance. (p. 2167)
—Wanted! - A Guinea Pig Called Henry. Castelao, Patricia, illus. (p. 2375)
Orred, Meta. Honour's Worth or the Cost of a Vow. (p. 1000)
—Honour's Worth, or the Cost of a Vow, Vol. 1 Of 2: A Novel (Classic Reprint) (p. 1000)
Orrego, Marcela, tr. see Kerr, Christiane.
Orrelle, Yael Kimhi, illus. see Cohen, Deborah Bodin.
Orsak, Lane Rockford. Keiko the Fairy, the Kujiki. (p. 1208)
Orser-Mokelky, Jacqueline. If I Had ... (p. 1091)
Orshoski, Paul. We Both Read Bilingual Edition-The Mouse in My House/un Raton en Mi Casa. Canetti, Yanitzia, tr. from ENG. (p. 2389)
—We Both Read-My Sitter Is a T-Rex! (Level 1-2) Ebbeler, Jeffrey, illus. (p. 2389)
—We Both Read-The Mouse in My House. Ebbeler, Jeffrey, illus. (p. 2390)
—We Read Phonics-Ant in Her Pants. Ebbeler, Jeffrey, illus. (p. 2392)
—We Read Phonics-Bugs on the Bus. Noiset, Michele, illus. (p. 2392)
—We Read Phonics-Dad Does It All. Ebbeler, Jeffrey, illus. (p. 2392)
—We Read Phonics-I Do Not Like Greens! Ebbeler, Jeffrey, illus. (p. 2392)
—We Read Phonics-Robot Man. Ebbeler, Jeffrey, illus. (p. 2392)
—We Read Phonics-Sports Dream. Ebbeler, Jeffrey, illus. (p. 2392)
—We Read Phonics-Talent Night. Kulka, Joe, illus. (p. 2392)
—We Read Phonics-Who Took the Cookbook? Light, Kelly, illus. (p. 2392)
Orshoski, Paul & Max, Dave. We Both Read-The Ant & the Pancake. (p. 2390)
Orsi, Tea. Tinker Bell & Her Magical Friends. (p. 2248)
—Tinker Bell & the Legend of the NeverBeast. (p. 2248)
—Tinker Bell & the Pirate Fairy. (p. 2248)
—Tinker Bell & the Secret of the Wings. (p. 2248)
Orsi, Tea, jt. auth. see Ferrari, Alessandro.
Orsi, Tea, jt. auth. see RH Disney Staff.
Orsinger-Olson, Ann Kathryn. When Father Sun Moved to the Sky. Landreau, Sarah, illus. (p. 2430)
Orsini, Cheryl, illus. see Prior, Natalie Jane.
Orsini, Cheryl, jt. auth. see Reilly, Carmel.
Orsini, Janice, illus. see Moller, Tommie.
Orsolini, Laura. Maddalena. (p. 1374)
Orsolini, Laura, illus. see Jeong, SoYun.
Ort, Kathleen, ed. see Horn, Elizabeth L.
Ort, Kathleen, ed. see Taylor, Ronald J.
Ort, Kathleen, ed. see Taylor, Ronald J. & Douglas, George.
Ortac, Arda. Sharp Kids Activity. Ortac, Feride, illus. (p. 2003)
Ortac, Feride, illus. see Ortac, Arda.
Ortakales, Denise, illus. see Brenner, Barbara.
Ortas, Rachel. Messy Monster Book. (p. 1452)
Ortbals, Janet. Making of an Angel. (p. 1389)
—Ziggy's Chocolate Bar. (p. 2540)
Ortberg, John. Your Magnificent Chooser. Dunn, Robert, illus. (p. 2534)
Ortega, Claribel A. Ghost Squad. (p. 828)
Ortega, Damian, illus. see French, Vivian.
Ortega, Gemma Rovira, tr. see Rowling, J. K.
Ortega, Hilary. Majesta the Monarch Butterfly. Bowie, Maliana, illus. (p. 1384)
Ortega, James, illus. see Ortiz, Andrea.
Ortega, Jose, illus. see Mora, Pat.
Ortega, Julian G. Warrior Inspiration. (p. 2379)
Ortega, Mirelle, illus. see Kyle, Tracey.
Ortega, Mirelle, illus. see Meriano, Anna.
Ortega, Mirelle, illus. see Smith, Emma Bland.
Ortega, Nathalie, illus. see Clarke, Zoe.
Ortego, Sotheary. Soulful Journey. (p. 2066)
Ortells, Estela. En Africa. (p. 646)
Orth, Jack. Happy Days: Book 1. Sunshine, Mary Lou, illus. (p. 921)
—Happy Days: Book 2. Sunshine, Mary Lou, illus. (p. 921)
—Happy Days: Book 3. Sunshine, Mary Lou, illus. (p. 921)
Orth, Lizett Emma. Sixty Songs from Mother Goose (Classic Reprint) (p. 2029)
Orthwein, Edith Hall. Love in the Weaving (Classic Reprint) (p. 1360)
Ortiz, Abimael, illus. see Felicie-Soto, Ada.
Ortiz, Andrea. Snowflakes in June. Ortega, James, illus. (p. 2049)
Ortiz, Antonio. Lo Que Nunca Te Dije. (p. 1338)
Ortiz, Associate Professor Enrique. Ten Elephants & a Spider's Web: A Traditional Latin American Counting Rhyme & Other Activities: Spanish/English. (p. 2204)
Ortiz Bello, Frank J., ed. see Hernandez Gonzalez, Ana M.
Ortiz Bello, Frank Joseph. ¡mamá, Hay una Nube en la Cocina! de Sousa, Isis, illus. (p. 1392)
—¡un Rato para Divertirme! Actividades para niños y Niñas. (p. 2317)
Ortiz Bello, Frank Joseph, ed. see Colon Pena, Eduardo.
Ortiz Bello, Frank Joseph, ed. see Terron Tamez, Irma Ilia.
Ortiz Bello, Frank Joseph, illus. see Terron Tamez, Irma Ilia.
Ortiz Bello, Frank Joseph & Ortiz Bello, Mayra a, eds. Rebelión en Celestya. González Chico, Norberto, illus. (p. 1852)
Ortiz Bello, Frank Joseph, ed. Ana & Her Dog Nana. Marcano, Edgar J., tr. (p. 78)
Ortiz Bello, Mayra a, jt. ed. see Ortiz Bello, Frank Joseph.
Ortiz de Zárate, Marisol. Canción de Shao Li. (p. 321)
Ortiz, Edgar, illus. see Fortson, Dorris.
Ortiz, Elvira, tr. see Cregg, R. J.
Ortiz, Elvira, tr. see Stack, Stevie.
Ortiz, Elvira, tr. Disney Frozen: Movie Storybook / Libro Basado en la Película (English-Spanish) Disney Storybook Art Team, illus. (p. 560)
—Disney Moana: Movie Storybook / Libro Basado en la Película (English-Spanish) (p. 561)
—Disney Tangled: Movie Storybook / Libro Basado en la Película (English-Spanish) Disney Storybook Art Team, illus. (p. 563)
—Disney/Pixar Coco: Movie Storybook / Libro Basado en la Película (English-Spanish) (p. 564)
Ortiz, Enrique. Playing with Shapes. (p. 1761)
—Ten Elephants & a Spider's Web: A Traditional Latin American Counting Rhyme & Other Activities Spanish/English Second Edition. (p. 2204)
Ortiz, Esther, tr. see Buckingham, Piper.
Ortiz, Esther, tr. see Hendricks, Jamal.
Ortiz, Esther, tr. see Markham, Helena.
Ortiz, Esther, tr. see Stiles, Sara.
Ortiz, Estrella. Bailar: Let's Dance. Valdivia, Paloma, illus. (p. 159)
—De Paseo: Out & About. Valdivia, Paloma, illus. (p. 517)
Ortiz, Jennifer Anne. Dragonfly Farms: The Great Adventure. (abby Zechman), Zechmana, illus. (p. 595)
Ortiz, Jhon, illus. see Dinardo, Jeff.
Ortiz, Lars. Explore Mexico: A Coco Discovery Book. (p. 680)
Ortiz, Luz. Luzia. (p. 1369)
Ortiz, Lydia, illus. see Galison.
Ortiz, Lydia, illus. see Kleinman, Emily & Mudpuppy.
Ortiz, Lydia, illus. see Mudpuppy & Alpert, Yelena Moroz.
Ortiz, Lydia, illus. see Mudpuppy.
Ortiz, Maria. Meet Creative Cat. (p. 1438)
Ortiz, Miguel, illus. see Chimal, Carlos.
Ortiz, Miguel Antonia. Mario & the Cow. (p. 1406)
Ortiz, Miguel Antonio. Mario y la Vaca. (p. 1406)
Ortiz, Nívea, illus. see Eliot, Hannah.
Ortiz, Orlando. Los Casos de Chelo Gómez. (p. 1350)
Ortiz, Oscar, illus. see Cofer, Judith Ortiz.
Ortiz, Phillip, illus. see Russell, Reba.
Ortiz, Rafael. Road Trip Across America. (p. 1888)
Ortiz, Raquel M. & Ventura, Gabriela Baeza. Sofi & the Magic, Musical Mural. Dominguez, Maria, illus. (p. 2054)
—When Julia Danced Bomba / Cuando Julia Bailaba Bomba. De Vita, Flor, illus. (p. 2431)
Ortiz, Simon J. Good Rainbow Road. Lacapa, Michael, illus. (p. 865)
—People Shall Continue Graves, Sharol, illus. (p. 1719)
Ortiz, Simon J. & Graves, Sharol. Pueblo Seguirá Graves, Sharol, illus. (p. 1810)
Ortiz, Tracy. As Dreamtime Unfolds. (p. 124)
Ortiz, Victoria. Dissenter on the Bench: Ruth Bader Ginsburg's Life & Work. (p. 564)
Ortiz, Victoria, tr. see Christelow, Eileen.
Ortler, Brett. Animal Tracks Activity Book Christenson, Anna et al, illus. (p. 92)
—Outer Space Activity Book. Juliano, Phil, illus. (p. 1684)
Ortlund, Jani. Child's First Book about Marriage: God's Way Is Always Best! (p. 375)
Ortman, Blanche Sellers. New York to Peking (Classic Reprint) (p. 1599)
—Old House, & Other Stories (Classic Reprint) (p. 1646)
Ortner, Nick & Taylor, Alison. My Magic Breath: Finding Calm Through Mindful Breathing. Ortner, Nick & Polizzi, Michelle, illus. (p. 1555)
Orton, Helen Fuller. Bobby: Cloverfield Farm (Classic Reprint) (p. 252)
—Prince & Rover of Cloverfield Farm (Classic Reprint) (p. 1793)
Orton, James. Comparative Zoology: Structural & Systematic, for Use in Schools & Colleges (Classic Reprint) (p. 433)
Orton, Katharine. Nevertell. (p. 1590)
Orton, Marian. Detective Nosegoode & the Kidnappers. Marciniak, Eliza, tr. (p. 534)
Orton, Rebecca Rose. Minds & Signs. (p. 1470)
Ortu, Davide, illus. see Askew, Amanda.
Ortu, Davide, illus. see Atkins, Jill.
Ortu, Davide, illus. see Eeles, Alex.
Ortuno, Antonio. Ojo de Vidrio. (p. 1643)
Oru, Gideon. Walking Garden. (p. 2372)
Orum, Pernille, illus. see Carbone, Courtney.
Orum, Pernille, illus. see Hitchcock, Laura.
Orum, Pernille, illus. see Webster, Christy.
Orum-Nielsen, Pernille, illus. see Carbone, Courtney.
Orus Lacort, Mercedes. Mis Juegos de L?gica. (p. 1476)
—MIS Primeras Sumas y Restas. (p. 1476)
—MIS Primeros Sudokus. (p. 1476)
—My First Sudoku. (p. 1546)
—My First Sums & Subtractions. (p. 1546)
—My Logic Games. (p. 1554)
Orwell, George. 1987. (p. 2561)
—Rebelion en la Granja. (p. 1852)
Orwig, P. G. Founders Four Folder, Vol. 2: March, 1926 (Classic Reprint) (p. 771)
—Founders' Four Folder, Vol. 2: June, 1926 (Classic Reprint) (p. 771)
—Founders' Four Folder, Vol. 2: Come to Camp Number; May, 1926 (Classic Reprint) (p. 771)
—Founders' Four-Folder, Vol. 1: June, 1925 (Classic Reprint) (p. 771)
—Founders' Four-Folder, Vol. 1: November, 1924 (Classic Reprint) (p. 771)
—Founders' Four-Folder, Vol. 2: April, 1926 (Classic Reprint) (p. 771)
—Founders' Four-Folder, Vol. 2: December 1925 (Classic Reprint) (p. 771)
—Founders' Four-Folder, Vol. 2: November, 1925 (Classic Reprint) (p. 771)
Ory, Lucie, illus. see Ferre, Gil.
O'Ryan, Ellie. Belle: The Charming Gift. Liu, Chun & Melaranci, Elisabetta, illus. (p. 197)
—Case of the Digital Deception. (p. 337)
—Case of the Digital Deception. (p. 337)
—Cinderella: The Great Mouse Mistake. Studio IBOIX Staff, illus. (p. 392)
—George & the Dragon. (p. 818)
—Ghostly Tales of Connecticut. (p. 829)
—How to Raise Three Dragons. (p. 1043)
—Jasmine: The Jewel Orchard. (p. 1160)
—Merida: Legend of the Emeralds. Disney Storybook Artists, illus. (p. 1448)
—Phineas & Ferb: Lights, Camera, Perry? Jeff, Marsh & Povenmire, Dan, illus. (p. 1735)
—Sugary Secrets Behind Candy. McClurkan, Rob, illus. (p. 2147)
O'Ryan, Ellie, jt. auth. see Disney Book Group.
O'Ryan, Ellie & Lewman, David. Case of the Disappearing Dogs. (p. 337)
O'Ryan, Ray. Annoying Crush. (p. 100)
—Cosmic Blackout! Kraft, Jason, illus. (p. 456)
—Drake Makes a Splash! Jack, Colin, illus. (p. 596)
—Galactic Easter! (p. 805)
—Galactic Easter! Jack, Colin, illus. (p. 805)
—Galaxy Zack 3 Books In 1! Hello, Nebulon!; Journey to Juno; the Prehistoric Planet. Jack, Colin, illus. (p. 805)
—Green Christmas! (p. 893)
—Green Christmas! Jack, Colin, illus. (p. 893)
—Haunted Halloween. Kraft, Jason, illus. (p. 937)
—Hello, Nebulon! (p. 951)
—Hello, Nebulon! Jack, Colin, illus. (p. 951)
—Journey to Juno. (p. 1182)
—Journey to Juno. Jack, Colin, illus. (p. 1182)
—Monsters in Space! (p. 1498)
—Monsters in Space! Jack, Colin, illus. (p. 1498)
—Operation Twin Trouble. Kraft, Jason, illus. (p. 1666)
—Prehistoric Planet. (p. 1787)
—Prehistoric Planet. Jack, Colin, illus. (p. 1787)
—Ready, Set, Blast Off! (p. 1848)
—Ready, Set, Blast Off! Kraft, Jason, illus. (p. 1848)
—Return to Earth! Kraft, Jason, illus. (p. 1871)
—Science Fair Disaster! Kraft, Jason, illus. (p. 1954)
—Snow Place Like Home. Kraft, Jason, illus. (p. 2047)
—Space Camp. Kraft, Jason, illus. (p. 2071)
—Three's a Crowd! (p. 2236)
—Three's a Crowd! Jack, Colin, illus. (p. 2236)
Orzechowski, Shawneen. Sarah's Secret: Civil War Deserter at Fredericksburg. (p. 1935)
Orzeszko, Eliza. Argonauts (Classic Reprint) (p. 114)
Orzeszkowa, Eliza. Meir Ezofovitch: A Novel (Classic Reprint) (p. 1442)
Osa, Nancy. Battalion Banished: Defenders of the Overworld #2. (p. 173)
—Battle of Zombie Hill: Defenders of the Overworld #1. (p. 175)
—Cuba 15. (p. 482)
—Deep Ocean Six: Defenders of the Overworld #4. (p. 524)
—Spawn Point Zero: Defenders of the Overworld #3. (p. 2076)
Osada, Ryuta, illus. see Shakespeare, William.
Osadchuk, Alexey. Tägliche Grind - Im Virtuellen Hamsterrad (Spiegelwelt Buch #1) LitRPG-Serie. (p. 2176)
Osadchuk, Keit, illus. see Kaplan, Debbie.
Osamor, Michelle & Osamor, Siobhan. Things We Love. (p. 2221)
Osamu, Soda. Our Great Escape. (p. 1678)
Osbert, Shabamukama, illus. see Lewis, Ophelia S.
Osbert, Shabamukama, illus. see Logan, L. M.
Osborn, Anna. Cambridge English Qualifications - Practice Tests for A1 Movers. (p. 313)
—Flyers: Three Practice Tests for Cambridge English. (p. 754)
—Lower Secondary English As a Second Language Student's Book: Stage 8 (Collins Cambridge Lower Secondary English As a Second Language) (p. 1363)
—Lower Secondary English As a Second Language Workbook: Stage 8 (Collins Cambridge Lower Secondary English As a Second Language) (p. 1363)
—Practice Tests for A2 Flyers (Cambridge English Qualifications) (p. 1784)
—Practice Tests for Movers: YLE (Collins Cambridge English) (p. 1784)
Osborn, Carolyn. Where We Are Now. (p. 2440)
Osborn, D. W. Why Can't I Ribbit? (p. 2455)
Osborn, Hayley. Outlasted. (p. 1685)
—Outlawed. (p. 1685)
—Outplayed. (p. 1685)
Osborn, Henry Fairfield, jt. auth. see Scudder, Samuel Hubbard.
Osborn, Karen Delette. Miss Oak & the Weather Balloon: Life, Love, Divorce & Everything in Between. (p. 1479)
Osborn, Laughton. Confessions of a Poet, Vol. 2 (Classic Reprint) (p. 439)
—Sixty Years of the Life of Jeremy Levis, Vol. 1 of 2 (Classic Reprint) (p. 2029)
—Sixty Years of the Life of Jeremy Levis, Vol. 2 (Classic Reprint) (p. 2029)
Osborn, Norris G. Moriartys of Yale (Classic Reprint) (p. 1506)
Osborn, Russell Wright. Californian Through Connecticut & the Berkshires (Classic Reprint) (p. 311)
Osborn, Tonia Benington, illus. see Kyrja.
Osborn, Tonia Bennington, illus. see Kyrja.
Osborn, Traci, illus. see McPhail, J. A.
Osborne, A., jt. auth. see Field, Rachel.
Osborne, Edward, jt. auth. see Manning, Anne.
Osborne, Elise. Life & Its Aims: In Two Parts; Part First, Ideal Life; Part Second, Actual Life (Classic Reprint) (p. 1289)
Osborne, Erin. Spy Recruit Simmons, Bethany, illus. (p. 2093)
Osborne, F. M. Motion Picture Magazine, Vol. 29: February, 1925 (Classic Reprint) (p. 1511)
Osborne, Florence M. Motion Picture, Vol. 30: September, 1925 (Classic Reprint) (p. 1511)
Osborne, Harry. When Smith Stepped Out: A Comedy in Three Acts (Classic Reprint) (p. 2433)
Osborne, Jill. Riley Mae & the Sole Fire Safari (p. 1883)
Osborne, Joey N. Boxes, Boxes, Everywhere Boxes (p. 267)
Osborne, John Walter. Putnam's Monthly, Vol. 5: A Magazine of American Literature, Science, & Art; January to July, 1855 (Classic Reprint) (p. 1818)
Osborne, Josie. Mermaid's First Quest. (p. 1449)
Osborne, Kent. Adventure Time: Banana Guard Academy. (p. 19)
Osborne, Leo. Cat & the Coracle. (p. 341)
Osborne, Linda Barrett. Come on in, America: The United States in World War I. (p. 428)
—Miles to Go for Freedom: Segregation & Civil Rights in the Jim Crow Years. (p. 1465)
—This Land Is Our Land: A History of American Immigration. (p. 2226)
Osborne, M. K. Atletismo. (p. 134)
—Baloncesto. (p. 162)
—Basketball. (p. 170)
—Chicago Bears. (p. 367)
—Combat Sports. (p. 428)
—Dallas Cowboys. (p. 498)
—Denver Broncos. (p. 529)
—Gimnasia. (p. 833)
—Green Bay Packers. (p. 893)
—Gymnastics. (p. 907)
—Houston Texans. (p. 1025)
—Indianapolis Colts. (p. 1116)
—Indianapolis Colts. (p. 1117)
—Los Deportes de Combate. (p. 1350)
—Natación y Saltos Ornamentales. (p. 1576)
—New England Patriots. (p. 1593)
—New York Giants. (p. 1598)
—Superstars of the Chicago Bears: By M.K. Osborne. (p. 2161)
—Superstars of the Dallas Cowboys. (p. 2161)
—Superstars of the Denver Broncos. (p. 2161)
—Superstars of the Green Bay Packers. (p. 2161)
—Superstars of the New England Patriots. (p. 2161)
—Superstars of the New York Giants. (p. 2161)
—Swimming & Diving. (p. 2170)
—Track & Field. (p. 2272)
—Voleibol. (p. 2366)
—Volleyball. (p. 2367)
Osborne, Mark. Hugsky. (p. 1048)
Osborne, Mary A. Last of the Magicians. (p. 1248)
—Nonna's Book of Mysteries. (p. 1618)
Osborne, Mary P. Crazy Day with Cobras. (p. 469)
—Ghost Tale for Christmas Time. (p. 828)
—Magic Tree House 37: Dragon of the Red Dawn. (p. 1379)
—Magic Tree House #48: A Perfect Time for Pandas. (p. 1379)
—Magic Tree House #50: Hurry up, Houdini! (p. 1379)
—Magic Tree House #51: High Time for Heroes. (p. 1379)
—Magic Tree House Fact Tracker: Abraham Lincoln: a Nonfiction Companion to Magic Tree House #47: Abe Lincoln at Last! (p. 1379)
—Magic Tree House Research Guide #1: Dinosaurs. (p. 1379)
—Magic Tree House Research Guide #12: Sabertooths & the Ice Age. (p. 1379)
—Magic Tree House Research Guide #16: Polar Bears & the Arctic. (p. 1379)
—Magic Tree House#47: Abe Lincoln at Last! (p. 1379)
—Magic Tree House#49: Stallion by Starlight. (p. 1379)
Osborne, Mary Pope. Abe Lincoln at Last! (p. 5)
—Abe Lincoln at Last! Murdocca, Sal, illus. (p. 5)
—Afternoon on the Amazon (p. 34)
—Balto of the Blue Dawn. Murdocca, Sal, illus. (p. 162)
—Big Day for Baseball (p. 219)
—Big Day for Baseball. Ford, A. G., illus. (p. 219)
—Big Day for Baseball. Murdocca, Sal, illus. (p. 219)
—Big Day for Baseball. Murdocca, Sal & Ford, A. G., illus. (p. 219)
—Buffalo Before Breakfast (p. 291)
—Castillo Embrujado en la Noche de Halloween. (p. 340)
—Christmas in Camelot. (p. 385)
—Christmas in Camelot. Murdocca, Sal, illus. (p. 385)
—Civil War on Sunday (p. 397)
—Crazy Day with Cobras. (p. 469)
—Crazy Day with Cobras. Murdocca, Sal, illus. (p. 469)
—Danger in the Darkest Hour. Murdocca, Sal, illus. (p. 501)
—Dark Day in the Deep Sea. (p. 506)
—Dark Day in the Deep Sea. Murdocca, Sal, illus. (p. 506)
—Day of the Dragon King (p. 514)
—Dia Negro en el Fondo Del Mar (Dark Day in the Deep Sea) (p. 537)
—Dingoes at Dinnertime (p. 547)
—Dinosaurs Before Dark (p. 551)
—Dogs in the Dead of Night Murdocca, Sal, illus. (p. 578)
—Dogs in the Dead of Night. (p. 578)
—Dolphins at Daybreak (p. 580)
—Earthquake in the Early Morning (p. 617)
—Ghost Tale for Christmas Time. (p. 828)
—Ghost Tale for Christmas Time. Murdocca, Sal, illus. (p. 828)
—Ghost Town at Sundown (p. 828)
—Gigante de un Solo Ojo / Tales from the Odyssey: The One-Eyed Giant (Sol y Luna) Spanish Edition. (p. 832)
—Good Morning, Gorillas (p. 863)
—Good Night for Ghosts. (p. 864)
—Good Night for Ghosts. Murdocca, Sal, illus. (p. 864)
—Haunted Castle on Hallows Eve. (p. 937)
—Haunted Castle on Hallows Eve. Murdocca, Sal, illus. (p. 937)
—High Tide in Hawaii (p. 969)
—High Time for Heroes. (p. 969)
—High Time for Heroes. Murdocca, Sal, illus. (p. 969)
—Hour of the Olympics (p. 1022)
—Hurricane Heroes in Texas (p. 1054)
—Hurricane Heroes in Texas. Ford, A. G., illus. (p. 1054)
—Hurry up, Houdini! (p. 1055)
—Hurry up, Houdini! Murdocca, Sal, illus. (p. 1055)
—Invierno Del Hechicero Del Hielo. (p. 1132)
—Knight at Dawn (p. 1228)
—Late Lunch with Llamas. Ford, A. G., illus. (p. 1250)
—Leprechaun in Late Winter: Magic Tree House. Murdocca, Sal, illus. (p. 1268)
—Leprechaun in Late Winter. (p. 1268)
—Leprechaun in Late Winter. Murdocca, Sal, illus. (p. 1268)
—Lions at Lunchtime (p. 1307)
—Magic Tree House 45-Copy Warriors Tree House Floor Display (p. 1379)
—Magic Tree House 49. (p. 1379)
—Magic Tree House 50. (p. 1379)
—Magic Tree House 51. (p. 1379)
—Magic Tree House Books 17-20 Boxed Set: The Mystery of the Enchanted Dog Murdocca, Sal, illus. (p. 1379)
—Magic Tree House Books 21-24 Boxed Set: American History Quartet Murdocca, Sal, illus. (p. 1379)
—Magic "Tree House" Christmas in Camelot Display (p. 1379)
—Magic Tree House Deluxe Holiday Edition: Christmas in Camelot. Caparo, Antonio Javier, illus. (p. 1379)
—Magic Tree House Holiday 6-Copy Clip Strip Fall 2019 (p. 1379)
—Magic Tree House Merlin Missions Books 1-25 Boxed Set (p. 1379)
—Magic Tree House Merlin Missions Books 1-4 Boxed Set (p. 1379)

—Magic Tree House Thanksgiving 6-Copy Clip Strip Fall 2019 (p. 1379)
—Magic Tree House Wild West Ghost Town Clip Struo Spring 2018 (p. 1379)
—Midnight on the Moon (p. 1461)
—Monday with a Mad Genius. (p. 1492)
—Moonhorse. Saelig, S. M., illus. (p. 1502)
—Moonlight on the Magic Flute Murdocca, Sal, illus. (p. 1502)
—Mummies in the Morning (p. 1526)
—Narwhal on a Sunny Night (p. 1575)
—Narwhal on a Sunny Night. Ford, A. G., illus. (p. 1575)
—Navidad en Camelot. (p. 1582)
—Night of the Ninjas (p. 1607)
—Night of the Ninth Dragon. Murdocca, Sal, illus. (p. 1607)
—Perfect Time for Pandas Murdocca, Sal, illus. (p. 1723)
—Perfect Time for Pandas. (p. 1723)
—Pirates Past Noon (p. 1751)
—Polar Bears Past Bedtime (p. 1769)
—Revolutionary War on Wednesday (p. 1874)
—Season of the Sandstorms. (p. 1972)
—Shadow of the Shark. Murdocca, Sal, illus. (p. 1997)
—Soccer on Sunday. Murdocca, Sal, illus. (p. 2052)
—Stage Fright on a Summer Night (p. 2099)
—Stallion by Starlight. (p. 2099)
—Stallion by Starlight. Murdocca, Sal, illus. (p. 2099)
—Summer of the Sea Serpent Murdocca, Sal, illus. (p. 2150)
—Sunset of the Sabertooth (p. 2153)
—Tales from the Odyssey: Part One (p. 2183)
—Tales from the Odyssey: Part Two (p. 2183)
—Tales from the Odyssey, Part 1 (p. 2183)
—Thanksgiving on Thursday (p. 2212)
—Tigers at Twilight (p. 2242)
—To the Future, Ben Franklin! (p. 2253)
—To the Future, Ben Franklin! Ford, A. G., illus. (p. 2253)
—Tonight on the Titanic (p. 2260)
—Twister on Tuesday (p. 2306)
—Vacation under the Volcano (p. 2343)
—Verano de la Serpiente Marina. (p. 2351)
—Viking Ships at Sunrise (p. 2357)
—Warriors in Winter (p. 2380)
—Warriors in Winter. Ford, A. G., illus. (p. 2380)
—Winter of the Ice Wizard. Murdocca, Sal, illus. (p. 2475)
—World at War 1944. Murdocca, Sal, illus. (p. 2501)
Osborne, Mary Pope & Boyce, Natalie Pope. Abraham Lincoln: A Nonfiction Companion to Magic Tree House Merlin Mission #19: Abe Lincoln at Last. Murdocca, Sal, illus. (p. 7)
—Amazing Animals! Magic Tree House Fact Tracker Boxed Set: Dolphins & Sharks; Polar Bears & the Arctic; Penguins & Antarctica; Pandas & Other Endangered Species Murdocca, Sal, illus. (p. 63)
—Animal Games & Puzzles. Murdocca, Sal, illus. (p. 89)
—Baseball: A Nonfiction Companion to Magic Tree House #29: a Big Day for Baseball. Molinari, Carlo, illus. (p. 168)
—Benjamin Franklin: To the Future, Ben Franklin! Mones, Isidre, illus. (p. 200)
—China: Land of the Emperor's Great Wall: a Nonfiction Companion to Magic Tree House #14: Day of the Dragon King. (p. 377)
—China: Land of the Emperor's Great Wall: A Nonfiction Companion to Magic Tree House #14: Day of the Dragon King. Molinari, Carlo, illus. (p. 378)
—Dog Heroes: Magic Tree House Fact Tracker. Murdocca, Sal, illus. (p. 576)
—Dogsledding & Extreme Sports: A Nonfiction Companion to Magic Tree House Merlin Mission #26: Balto of the Blue Dawn. Molinari, Carlo, illus. (p. 578)
—Dogsledding & Extreme Sports. (p. 578)
—Games & Puzzles from the Tree House: Over 200 Challenges! Murdocca, Sal, illus. (p. 807)
—Ghosts: A Nonfiction Companion to a Good Night for Ghosts. (p. 829)
—Ghosts: A Nonfiction Companion to Magic Tree House Merlin Mission #14: a Good Night for Ghosts. Murdocca, Sal, illus. (p. 829)
—Heroes for All Times: Magic Tree House Fact Tracker. Murdocca, Sal, illus. (p. 961)
—Heroes for All Times. (p. 961)
—Horse Heroes: Magic Tree House Fact Tracker. Murdocca, Sal, illus. (p. 1004)
—Leonardo Da Vinci: A Nonfiction Companion to Monday with a Mad Genius. (p. 1267)
—Leonardo Da Vinci: A Nonfiction Companion to Magic Tree House Merlin Mission #10: Monday with a Mad Genius. Murdocca, Sal, illus. (p. 1267)
—Leprechauns & Irish Folklore: A Nonfiction Companion to Leprechaun in Late Winter. (p. 1268)
—Leprechauns & Irish Folklore: A Nonfiction Companion to Magic Tree House Merlin Mission #15: Leprechaun in Late Winter. Murdocca, Sal, illus. (p. 1268)
—Magic Tree House Box of Puzzles, Games, & Activities (3 Book Set) Murdocca, Sal, illus. (p. 1379)
—Magic Tree House Incredible Fact Book. Murdocca, Sal, illus. (p. 1379)
—Magic Tree House Survival Guide. Murdocca, Sal, illus. (p. 1379)
—Magic Tricks from the Tree House: A Fun Companion to Magic Tree House 50: Hurry up, Houdini! (p. 1379)
—Magic Tricks from the Tree House: A Fun Companion to Magic Tree House Merlin Mission #22: Hurry up, Houdini! Murdocca, Sal & Vilela, Luiz, illus. (p. 1379)
—Narwhals & Other Whales. Mones, Isidre, illus. (p. 1575)
—Ninjas & Samurai: A Nonfiction Companion to Magic Tree House #5: Night of the Ninjas. (p. 1610)
—Ninjas & Samurai: A Nonfiction Companion to Magic Tree House #5: Night of the Ninjas. Murdocca, Sal, illus. (p. 1610)
—Pandas & Other Endangered Species: A Perfect Time for Pandas. (p. 1696)
—Pandas & Other Endangered Species: A Nonfiction Companion to Magic Tree House Merlin Mission #20: a Perfect Time for Pandas. Murdocca, Sal, illus. (p. 1696)
—Sharks & Other Predators. Molinari, Carlo, illus. (p. 2002)
—Snakes & Other Reptiles: Magic Tree House Research Guide. Murdocca, Sal, illus. (p. 2044)
—Soccer. (p. 2051)
—Soccer: Soccer on Sunday. Murdocca, Sal, illus. (p. 2052)
—Texas: A Nonfiction Companion to Magic Tree House #30: Hurricane Heroes in Texas. Mones, Isidre, illus. (p. 2209)
—Texas: A Nonfiction Companion to Magic Tree House #30 - Hurricane Heroes in Texas. Mones, Isidre, illus. (p. 2209)
—Vikings: Magic Tree House Fact Tracker. Molinari, Carlo, illus. (p. 2358)
—Vikings: A Nonfiction Companion to Magic Tree House 15 Viking Ships at Sunrise. (p. 2358)
—Warriors. Mones, Isidre, illus. (p. 2379)
—Warriors: A Nonfiction Companion to Magic Tree House #31: Warriors in Winter. Mones, Isidre, illus. (p. 2380)
—Wild West: A Nonfiction Companion to Magic Tree House #10: Ghost Town at Sundown. Molinari, Carlo, illus. (p. 2465)
—Wild West. (p. 2465)
—Wild West. Mones, Isidre, illus. (p. 2465)
—World War II: A Nonfiction Companion to Magic Tree House Super Edition #1: World at War 1944. Molinari, Carlo, illus. (p. 2505)
Osborne, Mary Pope & Ford, A. G. To the Future, Ben Franklin! (p. 2253)
Osborne, Mary Pope & Natalie Pope Boyce. World War II: A Nonfiction Companion to Magic Tree House Super Edition #1 World at War 1944. (p. 2505)
Osborne, Mary Pope, et al. Buenos Días, Gorilas. Murdocca, Sal, illus. (p. 291)
—Carnaval a Media Luz. Murdocca, Sal, illus. (p. 332)
—Día Negro en el Fondo Del Mar. Murdocca, Sal, illus. (p. 537)
—Dragon Del Amanecer Rojo. Murdocca, Sal, illus. (p. 593)
—Estación de Las Tormentas de Arena. Murdocca, Sal, illus. (p. 664)
—Favorite Series Starters Boxed Set: A Collection of First Books from Five Favorite Series for Early Chapter Book Readers (p. 716)
—Fun Starts Here! Four Favorite Chapter Books in One. Murdocca, Sal, illus. (p. 800)
—Horse Heroes. (p. 1004)
—Jueves de Acción de Gracias. Murdocca, Sal, illus. (p. 1186)
—Lunes con un Genio Loco. Murdocca, Sal, illus. (p. 1369)
—Maremoto en Hawái. Murdocca, Sal, illus. (p. 1403)
—Miedo Escénico en una Noche de Verano. Murdocca, Sal, illus. (p. 1462)
—Noche de Los Nuevos Magos. Murdocca, Sal, illus. (p. 1617)
—Regalo Del Pingüino Emperador. Murdocca, Sal, illus. (p. 1861)
—Tormenta de Nieve en Luna Azul. Murdocca, Sal, illus. (p. 2265)
Osborne, Melissa Jane Osborne, jt. auth. see Fish, Veronica.
Osborne, Michael. OZ One Fine Adventure One: A Not So Short Walk. (p. 1690)
Osborne, Naomi. Should All Children Get Vaccines? (p. 2011)
Osborne, Richard, illus. see Carter, Russell Gordon.
Osborne, Thomas Mott. Within Prison Walls: Being a Narrative of Personal, Experience During a Confinement of Voluntary Confinement in the State Prison York Auburn, New York (Classic Reprint) (p. 2482)
Osborne, Will, jt. auth. see Osborne, Mary Pope.
Osborne, William. Hitler's Secret. (p. 982)
—Winter's Bullet. (p. 2476)
Osborne, William Hamilton. Red Mouse: A Mystery Romance (Classic Reprint) (p. 1857)
—Running Fight (Classic Reprint) (p. 1915)
Osbourne, Katharine Durham. Robert Louis Stevenson in California (Classic Reprint) (p. 1890)
Osbourne, Lloyd. Adventurer (Classic Reprint) (p. 19)
—Baby Bullet: The Bubble of Destiny (Classic Reprint) (p. 149)
—Infatuation (Classic Reprint) (p. 1118)
—Love, the Fiddler (Classic Reprint) (p. 1361)
—Motormaniacs (Classic Reprint) (p. 1512)
—Person of Some Importance (Classic Reprint) (p. 1725)
—Queen Versus Billy: And Other Stories (Classic Reprint) (p. 1824)
—Three Speeds Forward: An Automobile Love Story with One Reverse (Classic Reprint) (p. 2235)
—Tin Diskers: The Story of an Invasion That All but Failed (Classic Reprint) (p. 2247)
—Wild Justice (Classic Reprint) (p. 2463)
Osbourne, Lloyd, jt. auth. see Stevenson, Robert Louis.
Osburn, Mary Rose. I Know Body Parts. (p. 1067)
—I Know Colors. (p. 1067)
Osburn, Raymond Carroll, jt. auth. see Sumner, Francis Bertody.
Osburn, William. Chapter from the Insect World: Butterflies & Moths (Classic Reprint) (p. 357)
Oscar, Hijuelos, jt. auth. see Hijuelos, Oscar.
Oscar, W. N. Cruise of the Golden Wave (Classic Reprint) (p. 479)
Oscar, Wilde. Fantme de Canterville(le) (p. 708)
Osczepinski, Robert. Altar Boy. (p. 60)
Osdel, Janet Thomas Van. Betty Barker, a Little Girl with a Big Heart (Classic Reprint) (p. 209)
Oseghale, Angela. I Love to Read Two Letter Words. (p. 1076)
Osei, Joyce. Adventures of Amma & Kwessi - in Barbados: In the Sparkling Rainbow Teacup & Saucer. (p. 21)
Osei, Leah. Boy Who Cried Wolf & Other Aesop Fables (p. 270)
—Bremen Town Musicians: A Retelling of the Story by the Brothers Grimm (p. 279)
—Why Anansi Has Eight Thin Legs: A Tale from West Africa (p. 2455)
Osei, Leah, et al. Pastorcito Mentiroso y Otras Fabulas de Esopo. Donaera, Patrizia, illus. (p. 1704)
Oseid, Kelsey, illus. see Bailer, Darice.
Oseid, Kelsey, illus. see Howard, Jules.
Oseid, Kelsey, illus. see Lunde, Darrin.
Oselska-Nikitskiy, Veronika. Letter to My Niece Carta a Mi Sobrina. (p. 1279)
Oseman, Alice. Heartstopper (Heartstopper #1) Oseman, Alice, illus. (p. 946)
—Radio Silence. (p. 1833)
—Solitaire. (p. 2057)
Osgard, Lisa. Kahwallawallapoopoo: Maynard's Big, Bad Adventure. (p. 1201)
Osgood, Erastus. Bunch of Fun: A Farce in Three Acts (Classic Reprint) (p. 297)
Osgood, Harry O. Mrs. Compton's Manager: A Comedy in Three Acts (Classic Reprint) (p. 1521)
Osgood, Irene. Servitude (Classic Reprint) (p. 1992)
—Shadow of Desire (Classic Reprint) (p. 1997)
Osgood, Lucius. Osgood's Progressive Second Reader: Embracing Progressive Lessons in Reading & Spelling (Classic Reprint) (p. 1673)
Osgood, Phillips Endecott. Church Year Sermons for Children (Classic Reprint) (p. 390)
Osgood, William F. Introduction to Infinite Series. (p. 1129)
O'Shaughnessy, Darren, see Shan, Darren, pseud.
O'Shaughnessy, Edith. Alsace in Rust & Gold (Classic Reprint) (p. 60)
—Diplomatic Days (Classic Reprint) (p. 552)
—My Lorraine Journal (Classic Reprint) (p. 1554)
O'Shaughnessy, Kate. Lonely Heart of Maybelle Lane. (p. 1342)
O'Shaughnessy, N. E. Eleanor Shaw & the Tempest Rescue. (p. 630)
O'Shaughnessy, Ruth. Bats after Dark. (p. 173)
—Big Cats after Dark. (p. 219)
—Crocodiles & Alligators after Dark. (p. 477)
—Owls after Dark. (p. 1689)
—Raccoons after Dark. (p. 1830)
—Snakes after Dark. (p. 2044)
O'Shaughnessy, Tam. Sally Ride: A Photobiography of America's Pioneering Woman in Space. (p. 1925)
—Sally Ride: a Photobiography of America's Pioneering Woman in Space. (p. 1925)
O'Shaughnessy, Tam E., jt. auth. see Ride, Sally.
Oshaughnessy, Tom. Terence o'Dowd; or Romanism To-Day: An Irish Story, Founded on Facts (Classic Reprint) (p. 2206)
O'Shea, Bonnie, illus. see Winter, Christopher.
O'Shea, Clare, jt. auth. see Llewellyn, Claire.
O'Shea, Clare, jt. auth. see Powell, Jillian.
O'Shea, Ellen Margaret. Adventures of Thunder the Wonder Puppy: Book One in the Series - the Collies of Chimacum Valley. (p. 29)
—Piper & the Red Boat Coloring Book. O'Shea, Ellen Margaret, illus. (p. 1748)
O'Shea, Jocelyn, ed. see Copham, K. M.
O'Shea, John. Timid Tim & the Bright Red Toolbox. (p. 2247)
O'Shea, John Augustus. Mated from the Morgue: A Tale of the Second Empire. (p. 1420)
—Mated from the Morgue: A Tale of the Second Empire (Classic Reprint) (p. 1420)
—Romantic Spain, Vol. 1 Of 2: A Record of Personal Experiences (Classic Reprint) (p. 1901)
O'Shea, Katharine. Charles Stewart Parnell, Vol. 1: His Love Story & Political Life (Classic Reprint) (p. 359)
O'Shea, Keri Margaret. Brother Bears' Tragic Day. (p. 286)
O'Shea, M. V. Every-Day Speller, Vol. 2: Grades Three & Four (Classic Reprint) (p. 670)
O'Shea, Maria & Spilling, Michael. Kuwait. (p. 1233)
O'Shea, Mark. Exploring Nature: Incredible Lizards - Discover the Astonishing World of Chameleons, Geckos, Iguanas & More, with over 190 Pictures. (p. 682)
O'Shea, Mark, jt. auth. see Taylor, Barbara.
O'Shea, Melissa. Summer of the Would-Be Sister. (p. 2150)
O'Shea, Michael Vincent. Six Nursery Classics (Classic Reprint) (p. 2028)
O'Shea, Mick. Beyond District 12: The Stars of the Hunger Games. (p. 211)
—One Direction: No Limits. (p. 1659)
O'Shea, M.J. Blood Moon. (p. 246)
—Blood Moon [Library Edition]. (p. 246)
—Cold Moon. (p. 413)
—Cold Moon [Library Edition]. (p. 413)
—Hunter's Moon. (p. 1053)
—Loveblood. (p. 1361)
O'Shei, Tim. Bone-Chilling Myths (p. 255)
—Creepy Urban Legends (p. 473)
—Kendo [Scholastic]. (p. 1209)
—Secrets of Pompeii: Buried City of Ancient Rome (p. 1980)
—World's Zaniest Sports. (p. 2508)
Osheim, Tammy. Horse Tale of Friendship: Great Plains Magic Series. (p. 1005)
—Melody: A Tale of a Show Horse: Great Plains Magic Series. (p. 1443)
Oshel, Susie L., ed. see Willowtree, Sabbath Oshel.
Oshida, Tim. Society's Traitor. (p. 2054)
Oshida, Tim, illus. see Finnish, V. K.
Oshiro, Beverly & Sachs, Ruth. Adolf Eichmann (p. 16)
Oshiro, Kimberley. Saga of Simon the Skinny Pig: Simon Saves the Day. Yee, Jeanne, illus. (p. 1922)
Oshiro, Mark. Anger Is a Gift: A Novel. (p. 86)
—Each of Us a Desert. (p. 613)
Osial, Heather L. Californians Who Made a Difference. (p. 311)
Osier, Dan. Backhoes (p. 156)
—Basketball's MVPs (p. 171)
—Bulldozers (p. 296)
—Cement Mixers (p. 351)
—Cranes (p. 467)
—Dirk Nowitzki. (p. 552)
—Dump Trucks (p. 610)
—Forklifts (p. 768)
—Kevin Garnett. (p. 1210)
—Kobe Bryant. (p. 1230)
—LeBron James. (p. 1260)
—Steve Nash. (p. 2116)
—Tim Duncan. (p. 2243)
Osier, Peter. History of Western Sculpture. (p. 981)
Osier, Peter, ed. History of Western Sculpture. (p. 981)
Osio, Raymundo, ed. see Bradshaw, Felisha.
Oskarsson, Bárdur. Flat Rabbit. (p. 747)
—Where Are You, Wilbert? Thomsen, Marita, tr. from FAO. (p. 2435)
Osle, Janessa & Walter Foster Jr. Creative Team. Animals Around the World. Legendre, Philippe, illus. (p. 94)
—Planes, Trains & Moving Machines. Legendre, Philippe, illus. (p. 1755)
—Sea Creatures & Other Favorite Animals: Learn to Draw Land & Sea Animals Step by Step! Legendre, Philippe, illus. (p. 1967)
Oslizlo, Roksana, illus. see Dortch, Stephanie.
Oslizlo, Roksana, illus. see Thompson, Beth.
Osman, Azrah. Lulu & the Tiny Elephants. (p. 1367)
Osment, Philip, et al. Class Acts. (p. 399)
O'Smiles, Myles. Awesome Riddles for Awesome Kids: Trick Questions, Riddles & Brain Teasers for Kids Age 8-12. Berneri, Camilo, illus. (p. 145)
—Awesome Riddles for Awesome Kids: Trick Questions, Riddles & Brain Teasers for Kids Age 8-12. Berneri, Camilo Luis, illus. (p. 145)
—Clever Scenarios for Clever Kids: Thinking Questions for Kids, a Would You Rather Children's Game Book for Kids 8-12. Berneri, Camilo Luis, illus. (p. 404)
—Fun Jokes for Funny Kids: Jokes, Riddles & Brain-Teasers for Kids 6-10. Berneri, Camilo Luis, illus. (p. 799)
—More Jokes, Riddles & Scenarios for Happy Kids: A Children's Activity Book for Kids 8-12. Berneri, Camilo Luis, illus. (p. 1505)
—Myles & the Telling Bee. Berneri, Camilo Luis, illus. (p. 1566)
—Stinky Facts for Stinky Kids: Smelly, Stinky & Silly Facts for Kids 8 To 12. Berneri, Camilo Luis, illus. (p. 2120)
—Would You Rather? Silly, Challenging & Hilarious Questions for Kids 8-12. Berneri, Camilo Luis, illus. (p. 2510)
O'Smiles, Myles & Berneri, Camilo Luis. More Jokes, Riddles & Scenarios for Happy Kids: A Children's Activity Book for Kids 8-12. (p. 1505)
—Stinky Facts for Stinky Kids: Smelly, Stinky & Silly Facts for Kids 8 To 12. (p. 2120)
Osmond, Jack, illus. see Osmond, Joanne H.
Osmond, Jimmy. Awesome Possum Family Band. (p. 145)
Osmond, Joanne H. Fishy Adventure. Osmond, Jack, illus. (p. 742)
Osmond, Marion. Owl & the Moon (Classic Reprint) (p. 1688)
Osmond, Sophie. Australian Wooing (Classic Reprint) (p. 139)
Osmun, Leighton Graves. Clutch of Circumstance (Classic Reprint) (p. 409)
Osmundson, Linda. How the West Was Drawn: Women's Art (p. 1036)
—How the West Was Drawn: Cowboy Charlie's Art (p. 1036)
Osmundson, Linda L. How the West Was Drawn: Frederic Remington's Art (p. 1036)
Osnaya, Ricardo, illus. see Manning, Matthew K.
Osorio, Rick. Great Adventure of Sally Rock & the Secret of Man (p. 883)
Osorio, Samir. Buscando el Sotano. (p. 301)
Osorio, Sergio, illus. see Kidder, Harvey.
Osornio, Catherine L. Declaration of Independence from A to Z Johnson, Layne, illus. (p. 523)
O'Sorus, Roman. Eminem. (p. 642)
O'sorus, Roman, jt. auth. see O'Sorus, Roman.
O'Sorus, Roman & O'sorus, Roman. Eminem. (p. 642)
Ospringe, Emily. Punctuality, Sensibility, & Disappointment: Instructive & Entertaining Stories for Young People (Classic Reprint) (p. 1814)
Ossio, Fico, illus. see Dawson, Delilah S.
Ossio, Fico, illus. see Marz, Ron & Rodriguez, David A.
Ossipova, Irina, tr. see King, Dedie.
Ost, Janis. Frances, This Time You've Gone Too Far. (p. 776)
Ostapyk, Dennis. If Spiders Wore Shoes. (p. 1092)
Ostashevsky, Eugene. Fire Horse: Children's Poems by Vladimir Mayakovsky, Osip Mandelstam & Daniil Kharms. (p. 732)
Osteen, Victoria. Gifts from the Heart Palmisciano, Diane, illus. (p. 832)
—My Happy Heart Books: A Touch-And-Feel Book Boxed Set Day, Betsy, illus. (p. 1549)
—Unexpected Treasures. Palmisciano, Diane, illus. (p. 2327)
Osten-Sacken, Carl Robert. Western Diptera. (p. 2402)
Ostenso Moore, Anna V. We Gather at This Table. Krueger, Peter, illus. (p. 2390)
Oster, Grigorii. Kotenok Po Imeni Gav. Shvart?s?man, L., illus. (p. 1231)
Osterheld, Dudley Oliver. What the Wild Flowers Tell Us: Nature Talks with Young People (Classic Reprint) (p. 2420)
Osterhold, Jared, illus. see Falconer, Ian, et al.
Osterhold, Jared, illus. see Hillert, Margaret.
Osterhold, Jared, illus. see McCurry, Kristen.
Osterhold, Jared, illus. see Shaw, Natalie.
Osterlund, Anne. Academy 7. (p. 9)
Ostermann, Riley. So Big. (p. 2050)
Ostermann, Ruby. Willie Tucker & His Gramma: The Life of a Dog. (p. 2469)
Ostermeyer Phoitography. Frosty & Snowy's Arctic Adventures. (p. 795)
Ostermeyer, Tim. Snowball's Antarctic Adventures. (p. 2048)
Ostermeyer, Tim, photos by. Titus & Tiana: Lesson for Baby Tigers. (p. 2251)
Ostertag, Blanche, jt. auth. see Mabie, Hamilton Wright.
Ostertag, Molly Knox. Hidden Witch. Ostertag, Molly Knox, illus. (p. 966)
—Witch Boy. (p. 2479)
Ostertag, Molly Knox, et al. Regular Show: Parks & Wreck. Rupert, Mad & Syph, Rian, illus. (p. 1862)
Osterweil, Adam. Cooper & the Enchanted Metal Detector. (p. 451)
Ostler, Alan. Arabs in Tripoli (Classic Reprint) (p. 109)
Ostler, Heather. Siren's Secret. (p. 2026)
Ostlere, Cathy. Karma. (p. 1204)
Ostlere, May. Dead! (Classic Reprint) (p. 517)
Oston, M. Queer Patients (Classic Reprint) (p. 1825)
Ostopowich, Melanie. Oceans, Lakes, & Rivers. (p. 1636)
—Rock Cycle. (p. 1894)
—Waste. (p. 2382)
—Water Pollution. (p. 2385)
Ostow, David, jt. auth. see Ostow, Micol.
Ostow, Micol. Day Before. (p. 512)
—Death of a Cheerleader (Riverdale, Novel #4) (p. 521)
—Get Out of Town. (p. 824)
—GoldenGirl. (p. 860)

Numeric

—Rodeo: Conteo. (p. 1897)
—Spectacular Sports: Rodeo: Counting (Grade 1) (p. 2078)
—Stem: Robots: 3-D Shapes (Grade 1) (p. 2113)
Otterman, Joseph, jt. auth. see Rice, Dona.
Ottersley, Martha T. Dora & the Winter Games (Dora the Explorer) Hall, Susan, illus. (p. 585)
Ottersley, Martha T., adapted by. Nickelodeon Shimmer & Shine: What's Your Wish?: Book & Magnetic Playset. (p. 1603)
Ottina, Laura. In the Arctic. Ranchetti, Sebastiano, illus. (p. 1107)
—In the Forest. Ranchetti, Sebastiano, illus. (p. 1109)
—In the Jungle. Ranchetti, Sebastiano, illus. (p. 1109)
—In the Sea. Ranchetti, Sebastiano, illus. (p. 1110)
—On the Farm. Ranchetti, Sebastiano, illus. (p. 1654)
—On the Savanna. Ranchetti, Sebastiano, illus. (p. 1655)
Ottinger, Jon, illus. see Pugliano-Martin, Carol.
Ottley, Matt, illus. see Estela, Lucy.
Ottley, Matt, illus. see Morgan, Sally & Kwaymullina, Ezekiel.
Ottley, Matt, illus. see Parker, Danny.
Ottley, Matt, illus. see Young, Rebecca.
Ottley, Ryan. Amazing Spider-Man by Nick Spencer Vol. 1: Back to Basics (p. 66)
—Amazing Spider-Man by Nick Spencer Vol. 3: Lifetime Achievement. (p. 66)
—Amazing Spider-Man by Nick Spencer Vol. 5: Behind the Scenes. (p. 66)
—Amazing Spider-Man by Nick Spencer Vol. 6: Absolute Carnage. (p. 66)
—Amazing Spider-Man: Hunted (Vol. 4) TPB. (p. 66)
Ottley, Ryan & Coello, Iban. Amazing Spider-Man by Nick Spencer Vol. 8: Threats & Menaces. (p. 66)
Ottman, Margaret B. Lonely Loon. (p. 1342)
Otto, Emil. Exercises for Translating, English into German (Classic Reprint) (p. 676)
—Materials for Translating English into French: With Grammatical Notes & a Vocabulary (Classic Reprint) (p. 1421)
Otto, Jean. Story of the Stuck Jesus. (p. 2134)
Otto, Jessica, jt. auth. see Bauer, Susan Wise.
Otto, Joanne. You-Song. (p. 2528)
Otto, Madison. Steadfast Heart. (p. 2110)
Ottolenghi, Carol. Princess & the Pea: La Princesa y el Guisante. (p. 1796)
—Princess & the Pea. (p. 1796)
—Puss in Boots (El Gato Con Botas) (p. 1817)
—Sleeping Beauty. (p. 2036)
—Sleeping Beauty (La Bella Durmiente) (p. 2037)
—Three Billy Goats Gruff. (p. 2232)
—Three Billy Goats Gruff (Los Tres Chivitos) (p. 2232)
Ottolengui, Rodrigues. Crime of the Century (Classic Reprint) (p. 474)
Ottolengul, Daniel. Behind the Seams: By a Nigger Woman Who Took in Work from Mrs. Lincoln & Mrs. Davis (Classic Reprint) (p. 193)
Ottolini, Horacio, jt. auth. see Fisch, Sholly.
Ottway, T. News from the Invisible World 1853: A Collection of Remarkable Narratives on the Certainty of Supernatural Visitations from the Dead to the Living; Impartially Compiled from the Works of Baxter, Wesley, Simpson, & Other Writers of Indisputable Veracity. (p. 1600)
Otukile, Mpho. Lion's Deceit. Dow, S. B., illus. (p. 1307)
Otway, Caesar. Sketches in Ireland: Descriptive of Interesting Portions of the Counties of Donegal, Cork, & Kerry (Classic Reprint) (p. 2031)
—Tour in Connaught: Comprising Sketches of Clonmacnoise, Joyce Country, & Achill (Classic Reprint) (p. 2268)
Otway, Helen. Bible Tales Puzzle & Activity Book: Activity Fun with Your Best-Loved Bible Stories. (p. 214)
—Life of Jesus Puzzle & Activity Book: Activity Fun with Your Best-Loved Bible Stories. (p. 1294)
—Stories from the New Testament Puzzle & Activity Book: Activity Fun with Your Best-Loved Bible Stories. (p. 2124)
—Stories from the Old Testament Puzzle & Activity Book: Activity Fun with Your Best-Loved Bible Stories. (p. 2124)
Ou, Yi. Solar Coaster. (p. 2055)
Oubre, Glenn. Twelve Days of a Berry Christmas. (p. 2303)
Ouchley, Amy Griffin. Swamper: Letters from a Louisiana Swamp Rabbit. (p. 2167)
Oud, Pauline. But I Wanted a Little Sister. (p. 302)
—Christmas with Lily & Milo. (p. 388)
—Counting Animals with Lily & Milo. (p. 459)
—Eating with Lily & Milo. (p. 622)
—Fall with Lily & Milo. (p. 700)
—Spring with Lily & Milo. (p. 2092)
Oudinot, Wanda, photos by see Sedlacek, Jan Gill.
Ouellet, Alexander. Tools of a+ Students: The a Students Toolbox for Success. (p. 2261)
Ouellet, Joanne, illus. see MacDonald, Anne Louise.
Ouellette, Daniel E. Jason Stone (Book VIII) the Final Chapter. (p. 1161)
Ouellette, Michelle, illus. see Harrison, Paula.
Ouellette, Troy David. Giant Declan & Snugglight's Christmas. Ouellette, Troy David, illus. (p. 830)
—Giant Declan & the Candy Treasure. (p. 830)
Ouerghi, Rida. My First Book of Gymnastics: Movement Exercises for Young Children. Fouquier, Elsa, illus. (p. 1542)
—My First Book of Pilates: Pilates for Children. Fouquier, Elsa, illus. (p. 1543)
Oughton, Taylor, illus. see Galvin, Laura Gates.
Oughton, Taylor, illus. see Pfeffer, Wendy.
Oui Love Books. Amour de Cassatt / Cassatt's Love: Learn Family Relationships in French & English. Cassatt, Mary, illus. (p. 77)
—Points de Seurat / Seurat's Dots: Learn Shapes in French & English. Seurat, Georges, illus. (p. 1767)
Ouida. Dog of Flanders. (p. 576)
—Held in Bondage, or Granville de Vigne: A Tale of the Day (Classic Reprint) (p. 949)
—In Maremma, Vol. 2 Of 3: A Story (Classic Reprint) (p. 1106)
—Moths, Vol. 1 Of 3: A Novel (Classic Reprint) (p. 1511)
—Village Commune (Classic Reprint) (p. 2358)
Ouida, jt. auth. see de la Ramée, Louise.
Ouida, Ouida. Ariadne, Vol. 1 Of 3: The Story of a Dream (Classic Reprint) (p. 115)
—Bimbi: Stories for Children (Classic Reprint) (p. 228)
—Cecil Castlemaine's Gage: And Other Novelettes (Classic Reprint) (p. 348)
—Cecil Castlemaine's Gage, and, Lady Marabout's Troubles: And Other Stories (Classic Reprint) (p. 348)
—Child of Urbino & Moufflou (Classic Reprint) (p. 370)
—Dog of Flanders; the Numberg Stove; & Other Stories (Classic Reprint) (p. 576)
—Frescoes, Dramatic Sketches (Classic Reprint) (p. 784)
—Friendship: A Story (Classic Reprint) (p. 787)
—Friendship, Vol. 1 Of 3: A Story (Classic Reprint) (p. 788)
—Friendship, Vol. 2 Of 2: A Story (Classic Reprint) (p. 788)
—Held in Bondage, or Granville de Vigne: A Tale of the Day (Classic Reprint) (p. 949)
—Held in Bondage, or Granville de Vigne, Vol. 1 Of 2: A Tale of the Day (Classic Reprint) (p. 949)
—Helianthus: A Novel (Classic Reprint) (p. 950)
—House Party (Classic Reprint) (p. 1024)
—In a Winter City: A Story of the Day (Classic Reprint) (p. 1104)
—In Maremma, Vol. 1 Of 3: A Story (Classic Reprint) (p. 1106)
—In Maremma, Vol. 2 Of 3: A Story (Classic Reprint) (p. 1106)
—Madame la Marquise, & Other Novelettes (Classic Reprint) (p. 1374)
—Massarenes: A Novel (Classic Reprint) (p. 1418)
—Moths, Vol. 1 Of 3: A Novel (Classic Reprint) (p. 1511)
—Moths, Vol. 3 Of 3: A Novel (Classic Reprint) (p. 1511)
—Othmar: A Novel (Classic Reprint) (p. 1675)
—Pascarel, Vol. 1 Of 3: Only a Story (Classic Reprint) (p. 1702)
—Pipistrello: And Other Stories (Classic Reprint) (p. 1749)
—Princess Napraxine (Classic Reprint) (p. 1798)
—Princess Napraxine, Vol. 1 of 3 (Classic Reprint) (p. 1798)
—Puck: His Vicissitudes, Adventures, Observations, Conclusions, Friendships, & Philosophies (Classic Reprint) (p. 1810)
—Puck: His Vicissitudes, Adventures, Observations, Conclusions, Friendships, & Philosophies, Vol. 2 of 3 (Classic Reprint) (p. 1810)
—Puck, Vol. 1 Of 3: His Vicissitudes, Adventures, Observations, Conclusions, Friendships, & Philosophies (Classic Reprint) (p. 1810)
—Rainy June: And Other Stories (Classic Reprint) (p. 1837)
—Rinaldo (Classic Reprint) (p. 1883)
—Ruffino C (Classic Reprint) (p. 1912)
—Santa Barbara (Classic Reprint) (p. 1931)
—Selve (Classic Reprint) (p. 1987)
—Signa, Vol. 1 Of 3: A Story (Classic Reprint) (p. 2016)
—Street Dust: And Other Stories (Classic Reprint) (p. 2140)
—Strega & Other Stories (Classic Reprint) (p. 2140)
—Syrlin (Classic Reprint) (p. 2174)
—Syrlin, Vol. 1 of 3 (Classic Reprint) (p. 2174)
—Syrlin, Vol. 2 of 3 (Classic Reprint) (p. 2174)
—Tower of Taddeo (Classic Reprint) (p. 2269)
—Tower of Taddeo, Vol. 1 (Classic Reprint) (p. 2269)
—Tower of Taddeo, Vol. 2 of 3 (Classic Reprint) (p. 2269)
—Toxin: A Sketch (Classic Reprint) (p. 2270)
—Toxin: A Story of Venice (Classic Reprint) (p. 2270)
—Tricotrin the Story of a Waif & Stray (Classic Reprint) (p. 2288)
—Tricotrin, Vol. 1 Of 3: The Story of a Waif & Stray (Classic Reprint) (p. 2288)
—Two Little Wooden Shoes: A Sketch (Classic Reprint) (p. 2308)
—Under Two Flags (Classic Reprint) (p. 2323)
—Under Two Flags, Vol. 1 Of 3: A Story of the Household & the Desert (Classic Reprint) (p. 2323)
—Under Two Flags, Vol. 2: A Story of the Household & the Desert (Classic Reprint) (p. 2323)
—Village Commune (Classic Reprint) (p. 2358)
—Wanda (Classic Reprint) (p. 2374)
—Wanda, Vol. 1 of 3 (Classic Reprint) (p. 2374)
—Wanda, Vol. 2 of 3 (Classic Reprint) (p. 2374)
—Wanda, Vol. 3 of 3 (Classic Reprint) (p. 2374)
—Warda; Ariadne, Vol. 7: The General's Match-Making (Classic Reprint) (p. 2378)
Ouimet, David. I Go Quiet. (p. 1065)
Ouimet, David, illus. see San Souci, Robert D.
Ouimet, Lindsey. (Not Quite) the Same Old Song. (p. 1623)
—Perdition. (p. 1721)
—What's a Soulmate? (p. 2423)
Ould, Hermon. Between Sunset & Dawn: A Play in Four Scenes (Classic Reprint) (p. 210)
Oulton, Harry. Heather's Piglets. (p. 946)
—Return of a Pig Called Heather. (p. 1870)
Oum, Siya, jt. illus. see Henderson, Erica.
Ouren, Todd. Patriotic Songs (p. 1705)
Ouren, Todd, illus. see Blair, Eric, et al.
Ouren, Todd, illus. see Blair, Eric.
Ouren, Todd, illus. see Britton, Tamara L.
Ouren, Todd, illus. see Dahl, Michael.
Ouren, Todd, illus. see Doering Tourville, Amanda.
Ouren, Todd, illus. see Hall, M. C.
Ouren, Todd, illus. see Loewen, Nancy.
Ouren, Todd, illus. see Salas, Laura Purdie.
Ouren, Todd, illus. see Shaskan, Trisha Speed.
Ouren, Todd, illus. see Stille, Darlene R.
Ouren, Todd, illus. see Stockland, Patricia M.
Ouren, Todd, illus. see Tourville, Amanda Doering.
Ouriou, Susan, tr. see Cathon.
Ouriou, Susan, tr. see Chartrand, Lili.
Ouriou, Susan, tr. see Gingras, Charlotte.
Ouriou, Susan, tr. see Jacob, André.
Ouriou, Susan, tr. see Luján, Jorge.
Ourious, Susan, tr. see Britt, Fanny.
Ourious, Susan, tr. see Serrano, Francisco.
Oursler, Fulton. Behold This Dreamer! (Classic Reprint) (p. 193)
Ouseley, Deryk, illus. see Thomas, Keltie.
Ouston, Elaine J. Barben's Magic Quest: Book One the Magic Begins. (p. 165)
—Bush Tails Book 2: A Close Call & Jake to the Rescue. (p. 301)
Outhwaite, R. L. Wisdom of Esau (Classic Reprint) (p. 2477)
Outlaw, Meena Dhanjal. Mattie Has Wheels Rides a Magic School Bus. (p. 1426)
Outlaw, Pat. Torchlight, Vol. 2: November 1944 (Classic Reprint) (p. 2264)
Outram, Evelyn. Sav & Josh O Lucky's Christmas Adventure & Magic Street. (p. 1937)
Ouvry, M. H. Lady's Diary: Before & During the Indian Mutiny (Classic Reprint) (p. 1239)
Ouyessad, Myriam. Magical Tree: A Children's Book Inspired by Gustav Klimt (p. 1380)
—Wolf Will Not Come Badel, Ronan, illus. (p. 2484)
Ouzoun-Andreou, Calliope. To Magiko Ftero. Gibbins, Amy, illus. (p. 2253)
Ovadia, Ron, jt. auth. see Grant, Ron.
Ovakimyan, Liza, illus. see Perry, Melanie Denise.
Ovalle Nu, ed. see Carrasco Gallegos, Catalina.
Ovalle Nunez, Maximo & Carrasco Gallegos, Catalina. Diario de MIS Primeros Ciclos Femeninos. (p. 538)
Ovenden, Bob. Muttly's Farmyard Adventures. (p. 1530)
Over, Arthur. Scratch & Draw Construction Site. Green, Barry, illus. (p. 1963)
—Scratch & Draw Farm Animals. Green, Barry, illus. (p. 1963)
—Sticker Dress-Up Dolls Playful Mermaids: 200 Reusable Stickers! Hinton, Steph, illus. (p. 2117)
Over, Arthur & Green, Barry. Halloween. (p. 911)
Over, John, illus. see Howard, Debbie.
Overbey, Allene. Colonnade, Vol. 3: March, 1941 (Classic Reprint) (p. 419)
—Colonnade, Vol. 3: January, 1941 (Classic Reprint) (p. 419)
—Colonnade, Vol. 4: March, 1942 (Classic Reprint) (p. 419)
—Colonnade, Vol. 4: January, 1942 (Classic Reprint) (p. 419)
—Colonnade, Vol. 4: November, 1941 (Classic Reprint) (p. 419)
Overcash, Lisa. My Fur-Ever Family. (p. 1548)
Overdeck, Laura. Bedtime Math: a Fun Excuse to Stay up Late. Paillot, Jim, illus. (p. 188)
—Bedtime Math: the Truth Comes Out. Paillot, Jim, illus. (p. 188)
—Bedtime Math: This Time It's Personal: This Time It's Personal. Paillot, Jim, illus. (p. 188)
—How Many Guinea Pigs Can Fit on a Plane? Answers to Your Most Clever Math Questions. (p. 1033)
Overend, Jody. Bessie: Life & Death. (p. 204)
Overend, William Heysham, jt. auth. see Henty, George.
Overett, A. M. Amelia & the Magic Jungle: 2nd Edition. (p. 68)
—Amelia & the Magic Jungle. Overett, A. M, illus. (p. 68)
Overholser, Dustin J. Imaginary Ninjas. (p. 1100)
Overington, Marcus. Lost on Bodmin Moor. (p. 1355)
Overley, Kristen V., illus. see Manwiller, S. A.
Overman, Britani, ed. see Young, Tiffany.
Overman, Mary N. Overman's Exhibition & School: Dialogues (Classic Reprint) (p. 1688)
Overmeer, Jenna Layne. City Lights. (p. 395)
Overmeer, Suzan. Ella the Swinging Duck. Berenschot, Myriam, illus. (p. 637)
Overmyer-Velazquez, Mark, ed. see Katchur, Matthew & Sterngass, Jon.
Overmyer-Velazquez, Mark, ed. see Seidman, David.
Overs, John. Evenings of a Working Man: Being the Occupation of His Scanty Leisure (Classic Reprint) (p. 669)
Overstake, Grant. Real Education of Tj Crowley. (p. 1849)
Overstreet, Chase. You Will Save the World. (p. 2528)
Overstreet, Karen LaFaye. Passed Away: Helping Young Children with Expressions of Family Loss - Adult Guide Included. Valente, Gianna Josephina & Valente, Peter Isaiah, illus. (p. 1703)
Overstreet, Tommy & Vest, Dale G. Graham Cracker Kid & the Calico Girl. Anderson, Jesse, illus. (p. 875)
Overton, Carrie. Was Ist das? Animals. (p. 2381)
Overton, Grant. Answerer (Classic Reprint) (p. 101)
—World Without End (Classic Reprint) (p. 2506)
Overton, Grant M. World's One Hundred Best Short Stories, Vol. 10 Of 10: Humor (Classic Reprint) (p. 2508)
Overton, Gwendolen. Captain's Daughter (Classic Reprint) (p. 326)
—Golden Chain (Classic Reprint) (p. 857)
—Heritage of Unrest (Classic Reprint) (p. 959)
Overton, Hollie. Baby Doll. (p. 150)
Overton, John. My Lady April (Classic Reprint) (p. 1551)
Overton, Kim, illus. see Cheney, Polly.
Overton, Kim G. Nathan & Father: A Walk of Wonder. (p. 1576)
Overton, Mark. Jack Winters' Gridiron Chums. (p. 1153)
Overton, Robert. King's Pardon: A Story of Land & Sea (Classic Reprint) (p. 1223)
—Overton Reciter: Character Sketches for Recitation (Classic Reprint) (p. 1688)
Overwater, Georgien, illus. see Daynes, Katie.
Ovid. Ovid - the Metamorphoses: 'Tears at Times Have the Weight of Speech" (p. 1688)
Ovid, Ovid. Metamorphoses d'Ovide, Avec des Explications À la Fin de Chaque Fable, Vol. 2: Augmentées du Jugement de Pâris, et de la Metamorphose des Abeilles (Classic Reprint) (p. 1452)
—Metamorphoses d'Ovide, en Latin et François, Divisées en XV. Livres: Avec de Nouvelles Explications Historiques, Morales et Politiques Sur Toutes les Fables, Chacune Selon Son Sujet (Classic Reprint) (p. 1452)
—Metamorphoses d'Ovide, Vol. 3 (Classic Reprint) (p. 1452)
—Oeuvres Completes d'Ovide, Vol. 1: Traduction Nouvelle (Classic Reprint) (p. 1639)
—Oeuvres Complètes d'Ovide, Vol. 3 (Classic Reprint) (p. 1639)
—Oeuvres Complettes d'Ovide, Vol. 7: Traduites en Français; Auxquelles on a Ajouté la Vie de Ce Poëte; les Hymnes de Callimaque; le Pervigilium Veneris; l'Epître de Lingendes Sur l'Exil d'Ovide (Classic Reprint) (p. 1639)
—P. Ovidii Nasonis Metamorphoseon Libri XV (Classic Reprint) (p. 1690)
—P. Ovidii Nasonis Metamorphoseon Libri XV. Cum Versione Anglica, Ad Verbum, Quantum Fieri Potuit, Sacta, or Ovid's Metamorphoses with an English Translation As Literal As Possible (Classic Reprint) (p. 1690)
—P. Ovidii Nasonis Metamorphoseon Libri XV, Vol. 1: Cum Appositis Italico Carmine Interpretationibus AC Notis (Classic Reprint) (p. 1690)
—P. Ovidii Nasonis Metamorphoseon Libri XV, Vol. 3: Cum Appositis Italico Carmine Interpretationibus, AC Notis (Classic Reprint) (p. 1690)
Ovide, Ovide. Metamorphose d'Ovide Figurée (Classic Reprint) (p. 1452)
—Metamorphoses d'Ovide (Classic Reprint) (p. 1452)
—Métamorphoses d'Ovide, Vol. 1: Traduites en Vers, Avec des Remarques et des Notes (Classic Reprint) (p. 1452)
—Metamorphoses d'Ovide, Vol. 1: Avec des Explications À la Fin de Chaque Fable; Augmentées du Jugement de Pâris, et de la Métamorphose des Abeilles (Classic Reprint) (p. 1452)
—Métamorphoses d'Ovide, Vol. 1 (Classic Reprint) (p. 1452)
—Metamorphoses d'Ovide, Vol. 2: Mises en Vers François (Classic Reprint) (p. 1452)
—Métamorphoses d'Ovide, Vol. 2: Traduction Nouvelle Avec le Texte Latin, Suivie d'une Analyse de l'Explication des Fables, de Notes Géographiques, Historiques, Mythologiques, et Critiques (Classic Reprint) (p. 1452)
—Metamorphoses d'Ovide, Vol. 3: En Latin et en Francois (Classic Reprint) (p. 1452)
—Métamorphoses d'Ovide, Vol. 3: Traduction Nouvelle Avec le Texte Latin, Suivie d'une Analyse de l'Explication des Fables, de Notes Géographiques, Historiques, Mythologiques et Critiques (Classic Reprint) (p. 1452)
—Metamorphoses d'Ovide, Vol. 3 (Classic Reprint) (p. 1452)
—Oeuvres d'Ovide, Vol. 7: Traduction Nouvelle; Contenant les Six Livres des Fastes (Classic Reprint) (p. 1639)
—Oeuvres d'Ovide, Vol. 8: Traduction Nouvelle; Contenant les Cinq Livres des Tristes (Classic Reprint) (p. 1639)
Ovington, Adelaide. Aviator's Wife (Classic Reprint) (p. 143)
Ovington, Mary White. Shadow (Classic Reprint) (p. 1996)
Ovocheva, Zhanna, illus. see George, Joshua.
Ovocheva, Zhanna, illus. see Lily, Amber.
Ovocheva, Zhanna, illus. see Linn, Susie.
Ovreas, Hakon. Brown. Dickson, Kari, tr. (p. 286)
—Brown. Torseter, Oyvind, illus. (p. 286)
Ovresat, Laura, illus. see Gerver, Jane E.
Ovresat, Laura, illus. see Shepherd, Jodie.
Ovresat, Laura, illus. see Yee, Wong Herbert.
Ovstedal, Barbara, see Douglas, Barbara, pseud.
Owaki, Takashi. Dreams Around the World. (p. 603)
Owen, jt. auth. see Giddens, Sandra.
Owen, Adeline. Night Before Christmas... the Rest of the Story: A True Story Based on New Testament Scripture. (p. 1605)
Owen, Andy, jt. auth. see Llewellyn, Claire.
Owen, Ashford. Lost Love (Classic Reprint) (p. 1355)
Owen, B. G. Who Will I Be? (p. 2452)
Owen, Caroline Dale. Seth Way a Romance of the New Harmony Community (Classic Reprint) (p. 1993)
Owen, Catherine. Day Cat, Night Cat. Keith, Jenny, illus. (p. 513)
—Molly Bishop's Family (Classic Reprint) (p. 1489)
Owen, Daniel. Rhys Lewis, Minister of Bethel: An Autobiography (Classic Reprint) (p. 1876)
Owen, Denise. Why Does God Pull Teeth? Wicker, Jo, illus. (p. 2457)
Owen, Dorothy Tudor. Child Vision: Being a Study in Mental Development & Expression (Classic Reprint) (p. 370)
Owen, Edward. Hyde Park: Select Narratives, Annual Events, etc;, During Twenty Years' Police Service in Hyde Park (Classic Reprint) (p. 1055)
Owen, Elizabeth, illus. see Bellingham, Brenda.
Owen, Ellen. Inkey Dinkey Land. (p. 1120)
Owen, Emily. Mechanical Maestro. (p. 1435)
Owen, Erich. Fruit Ninja. (p. 796)
Owen, Erich, illus. see Batterson, Jason.
Owen, Erich, illus. see Halfbrick Studios Staff.
Owen, Erich, illus. see Studios, Halfbrick.
Owen, Farleigh. Aden Power: Or, the Cost of a Scheme (Classic Reprint) (p. 16)
Owen, Frank. Actress (Classic Reprint) (p. 13)
Owen, Franklin S. Silas Marner: A Drama in Four Acts, Adapted from George Eliot's Novel (Classic Reprint) (p. 2017)
Owen, Gary. Mrs Reynolds & the Ruffian. (p. 1523)
Owen, George R. Truths Illustrated (Classic Reprint) (p. 2297)
Owen, George W. Leech Club; Or. The Mysteries of the Catskills (Classic Reprint) (p. 1261)
Owen, George Washington. Leech Club, or the Mysteries of the Catskills (Classic Reprint) (p. 1261)
Owen, Grace Arlington. Wonderful Story of Illinois: A Pageant (Classic Reprint) (p. 2490)
Owen, Harle Oren. Welsh Rarebit Tales (Classic Reprint) (p. 2400)
Owen, Harry Collinson. Adventures of Antoine (Classic Reprint) (p. 21)
Owen, Hyun Jung. Hodder Cambridge Primary Science Story Book C Foundation Stage Dinosaur Adventure (p. 986)
Owen, J. A. Annals of a Fishing Village: Drawn from the Notes of a Son of the Marshes (Classic Reprint) (p. 98)
—Candalaria: A Heroine of the Wild West (Classic Reprint) (p. 321)
—From Spring to Fall: Or When Life Stirs (Classic Reprint) (p. 793)
—Within an Hour of London Town: Among Wild Birds & Their Haunts (Classic Reprint) (p. 2482)
Owen, James A. Dawn of the Dragons: Here, There Be Dragons; the Search for the Red Dragon. (p. 512)
—Dragon's Apprentice. Owen, James A., illus. (p. 595)
—Dragons of Winter. Owen, James A., illus. (p. 596)
—Fall of the Dragons: The Dragon's Apprentice; the Dragons of Winter; the First Dragon. (p. 700)
—First Dragon. Owen, James A., illus. (p. 736)
—Indigo King. Owen, James A., illus. (p. 1117)
—Shadow Dragons. Owen, James A., illus. (p. 1996)
Owen, James A. & Owen, Jeremy. Lost Treasures of the Pirates of the Caribbean. Owen, James A., illus. (p. 1356)
Owen, James A., ed. Secrets of the Dragon Riders: Your Favorite Authors on Christopher Paolini's Inheritance Cycle: Completely Unauthorized. (p. 1980)

—Learn about Authors & Illustrators. (p. 1255)
—Learning about Australia. (p. 1257)
—Lebanon. (p. 1260)
—Malaysia. (p. 1391)
—Marilyn Monroe: Hollywood Icon (p. 1405)
—Mermaids. (p. 1449)
—Moose Attack. (p. 1503)
—Mountain Lion Attack. (p. 1513)
—Mummy's Curse. (p. 1526)
—Nepal. (p. 1587)
—Netherlands. (p. 1588)
—Nicaragua. (p. 1602)
—Nigeria. (p. 1604)
—Peru. (p. 1725)
—Poison Dart Frogs. (p. 1767)
—Polar Bear. (p. 1769)
—Pripyat: The Chernobyl Ghost Town. (p. 1801)
—Pro Gaming. (p. 1802)
—Proboscis Monkey. (p. 1803)
—Punishing Bullies: Zero Tolerance vs. Working Together. (p. 1814)
—Rat Attack. (p. 1842)
—Rev up Your Writing in Blogs. Gallagher-Cole, Mernie, illus. (p. 1872)
—Robot Uprising. (p. 1892)
—Saudi Arabia. (p. 1937)
—Seeing. (p. 1984)
—Share Your Book Report. (p. 2001)
—Singapore. (p. 2024)
—Smelling. (p. 2041)
—Snake Attack. (p. 2044)
—Somalia. (p. 2058)
—South Africa. (p. 2068)
—South Sudan. (p. 2069)
—Star-Nosed Mole. (p. 2102)
—Stay Safe Online. (p. 2109)
—Stonehenge. (p. 2121)
—Taiwan. (p. 2176)
—Tasting. (p. 2192)
—Tiger Attack. (p. 2241)
—Touching. (p. 2268)
—Turkey. (p. 2299)
—Unicorns. (p. 2329)
—West Virginia. (p. 2402)
—What Are Legends, Folktales, & Other Classic Stories? (p. 2405)
—What Are Plays? (p. 2405)
—What Protects Us During Natural Disasters? (p. 2419)
—What We Get from Egyptian Mythology. (p. 2422)
—Wheels. Butler, Reginald, illus. (p. 2427)
—Wild Dog Attack. (p. 2463)
—World of ESports. (p. 2503)
—YouTube. (p. 2536)
Owings, Lisa & Borgert-Spaniol, Megan. Ukraine. (p. 2314)
Owings, Lisa & Leaf, Christina. Tarsier. (p. 2192)
Owings, Lisa & Nelson, Robin. From Sea to Salt. (p. 793)
Owings, Osmond Young. David's Heritage: A Novel (Classic Reprint) (p. 511)
Owl, Grey. Adventures of Sajo & Her Beaver People. (p. 27)
—Adventures of Sajo & Her Beaver People (Classic Reprint) (p. 27)
—Adventures of Sajo & Her Beaver People - with Original Bw Illustrations & a Glossary of Ojibway Indian Words. (p. 27)
Owoeye, Erica. Understanding Supply & Demand (p. 2325)
Owsley, Anthony, illus. see Brown, Jordan D.
Owsley, Anthony, illus. see Rhatigan, Joe.
Owsley, Anthony, jt. auth. see Rhatigan, Joe.
Owusu-Akyeampong, Pauline Katufwa. Meet Tuku & Mumba the Elephant. (p. 1441)
Oxberry, W. Theatrical Banquet, or the Actor's Budget, Vol. 2 Of 2: Consisting of Monologues, Prologues, Addresses, Tales, &C. &C. , Serious & Comic (Classic Reprint) (p. 2215)
Oxberry, William. Actors Budget (Classic Reprint) (p. 13)
—Flowers of Literature, Vol. 1 Of 4: Consisting of Selections from History, Biography, Poetry & Romance; Jeux d'Esprit, Traditionary Relics, & Essays, with Translations from Approved Authors (Classic Reprint) (p. 753)
Oxelstrand, Sofia, illus. see Morley, J. S.
Oxenbury, Helen. Baby Love: All Fall down - Clap Hands - Say Goodnight - Tickle, Tickle. Set Oxenbury, Helen, illus. (p. 151)
—El Auto. (p. 630)
—El Restaurante de Mis Tios. (p. 630)
—It's My Birthday. Oxenbury, Helen, illus. (p. 1146)
—Pig Tale. Oxenbury, Helen, illus. (p. 1743)
Oxenbury, Helen, illus. see Bently, Peter.
Oxenbury, Helen, illus. see Burningham, John.
Oxenbury, Helen, illus. see Carroll, Lewis, pseud.
Oxenbury, Helen, illus. see Cooke, Trish.
Oxenbury, Helen, illus. see Donaldson, Julia.
Oxenbury, Helen, illus. see Fox, Mem.
Oxenbury, Helen, illus. see Hest, Amy.
Oxenbury, Helen, illus. see Knapman, Timothy.
Oxenbury, Helen, illus. see Krauss, Ruth.
Oxenbury, Helen, illus. see Potter, Beatrix.
Oxenbury, Helen, illus. see Root, Phyllis.
Oxenbury, Helen, illus. see Rosen, Michael.
Oxenbury, Helen, illus. see Trivizas, Eugene.
Oxenbury, Helen, illus. see Waddell, Martin.
Oxenbury, Helen, jt. illus. see Rosen, Michael.
Oxenford, John. Tales from the German, Comprising Specimens from the Most Celebrated Authors (Classic Reprint) (p. 2183)
Oxenham, John. 1914 (Classic Reprint) (p. 2561)
—Broken Shackles (Classic Reprint) (p. 285)
—Coil of Carne (Classic Reprint) (p. 413)
—Flowers of the Dust (Classic Reprint) (p. 753)
—Long Road (Classic Reprint) (p. 1343)
—Man of Sark (Classic Reprint) (p. 1394)
—Pearl of Pearl Island (Classic Reprint) (p. 1710)
—Profit & Loss (Classic Reprint) (p. 1805)
—Queen of the Guarded Mounts (Classic Reprint) (p. 1824)
—Rising Fortunes: The Story of a Man's Beginnings (Classic Reprint) (p. 1886)
—Song of Hyacinth, & Other Stories (Classic Reprint) (p. 2062)
Oxfam Staff, illus. see Cave, Kathryn.
Oxford Bible Staff, illus. see Rand, Casey.
Oxford Bible Staff, illus. see Raum, Elizabeth.
Oxford, ed. First Language English for IGCSERG (p. 738)
—Graphic Library - Science Complete Program. (p. 880)
—Oxford Picture Dictionary Content Areas for Kids: Reproducibles Collection. Pack (p. 1689)
—This Is My Dad. (p. 2225)
Oxford Editors. Earth. Geatches, Hazel, ed. (p. 615)
—Electricity. Geatches, Hazel, ed. (p. 631)
—Word Problems Interactive Years 5 & 6 (p. 2493)
Oxford Editors, jt. auth. see Northcott, Richard.
Oxford, Joe. Ned Clinton, Vol. 1 Of 3: Or the Commissary (Classic Reprint) (p. 1585)
Oxford Languages, Oxford. Oxford Roald Dahl Dictionary. (p. 1689)
—Oxford School Dictionary. (p. 1689)
Oxford University Press. Children's Visual Dictionary, French-English. (p. 375)
—Children's Visual Dictionary, Spanish-English. (p. 375)
Oxford University Press Staff. Oxford American Desk Dictionary & Thesaurus. (p. 1689)
Oxford University Press Staff, ed. see Duckworth, Michael.
Oxford University Press Staff, ed. see Henry, O.
Oxford University Press Staff, ed. see Nesbit, E. & Mowat, Diane.
Oxford University Press Staff, ed. see Vicary, Tim.
Oxlade, Chris. 150 Amazing Science Experiments: Fascinating Projects Using Everyday Materials, Demonstrated. (p. 2559)
—150 Great Science Experiments: Ingenious, Easy-To-Do Projects Explore & Explain the Wonders of Science & Technology. (p. 2559)
—Airplanes Inside & Out. (p. 37)
—Animal Infographics (p. 90)
—Be a Tracker. Sassin, Eva, illus. (p. 176)
—Be an Adventurer. Sassin, Eva, illus. (p. 176)
—Be an Explorer. Sassin, Eva, illus. (p. 176)
—Cameras: How They Work, Film, Digital, Filters, Effects - With 9 Easy-to-Do Experiments & 230 Exciting Pictures. (p. 314)
—Cars Inside & Out. (p. 335)
—Circulatory System: Where Do I Get My Energy? (p. 393)
—Climate Change. (p. 405)
—Climbing Trees & Muddy Knees: The Kids Guide to Getting Unplugged & Getting Outside. Sassin, Eva, illus. (p. 405)
—Conductors & Insulators (p. 438)
—Construction Machines. (p. 443)
—Cool Machines: Ten Fire Engines & Emergency Vehicles. (p. 449)
—Cool Machines: Ten Trucks. (p. 449)
—Design Line: Planes, Trains, & Automobiles. Lemanski, Mike, illus. (p. 532)
—Earth: Find Out about the Planet, Earthquakes, Volcanoes & Weather with 50 Great Experiments & Projects. (p. 615)
—Electricity (p. 631)
—Emergency Machines. (p. 641)
—Environment Infographics (p. 657)
—Excellent Science Experiments (p. 676)
—Experiments with Air & Water (p. 678)
—Experiments with Electricity & Magnets (p. 678)
—Experiments with Matter & Materials (p. 678)
—Experiments with Sound & Light (p. 679)
—Find Out about Machines. (p. 728)
—Gadgets & Games (p. 805)
—Gaming Technology. (p. 808)
—Garbage & Recycling (p. 808)
—Global Warming. (p. 844)
—Growth (p. 900)
—Gunpowder (p. 905)
—Heating (p. 946)
—History of Computers. (p. 977)
—History of Robots. (p. 979)
—History of Telecommunications. (p. 980)
—History of Transportation. (p. 981)
—Homes (p. 998)
—Igneous Rocks (p. 1094)
—Infographics (p. 1119)
—Inside Battleships. Viana, Tatio, illus. (p. 1122)
—Inside Fighter Planes. (p. 1123)
—Inside Submarines. Viana, Tatio, illus. (p. 1123)
—Inside Tanks & Heavy Artillery. Viana, Tatio, illus. (p. 1123)
—Introducing Africa (p. 1128)
—Introducing Europe (p. 1128)
—Introducing North America (p. 1129)
—Inventors' Secret Scrapbook. (p. 1130)
—Journey Through Transport. Haslam, John, illus. (p. 1182)
—Levers. (p. 1282)
—Light Bulb (p. 1298)
—Making a Circuit (p. 1388)
—Making Machines with Levers. (p. 1389)
—Making Machines with Pulleys. (p. 1389)
—Making Machines with Ramps & Wedges. (p. 1389)
—Mars (p. 1409)
—Metamorphic Rocks (p. 1452)
—Minerals. (p. 1471)
—Mobile Continent White Band. (p. 1485)
—Moon (p. 1501)
—Moon Edwards, Jeff, illus. (p. 1501)
—Moon. (p. 1501)
—Motorcycles. (p. 1512)
—Motorcycles Inside & Out. (p. 1512)
—Mountain Rescue (p. 1514)
—Mountains (p. 1514)
—Nuclear Energy (p. 1628)
—Nuclear Power. (p. 1628)
—Population Infographics (p. 1777)
—Pulleys. (p. 1812)
—Readers L3: Robots. (p. 1846)
—Rescue at Sea (p. 1868)
—Rocas Ígneas. (p. 1893)
—Rocas Metamórficas. (p. 1894)
—Rocas Sedimentarias. (p. 1894)
—Rocks. (p. 1896)
—Rocks & Minerals (p. 1896)
—Screws. (p. 1964)
—Screws. (p. 1965)
—Sedimentary Rocks (p. 1981)
—Ships & Boats: Sail; Navigation; Radar; Anchor; Keel. (p. 2008)
—Simple Experiments with Inclined Planes. (p. 2021)
—Simple Experiments with Levers. (p. 2021)
—Simple Experiments with Pulleys. (p. 2021)
—Simple Experiments with Wheels & Axles. (p. 2021)
—Simple Machine Projects. (p. 2021)
—Skyscrapers 3 Explorers. (p. 2034)
—Soil. (p. 2055)
—Solar Power (p. 2055)
—Space Watch: The Sun. (p. 2072)
—Sports (p. 2088)
—Sports Skills: Cricket. (p. 2089)
—Super Science Air & Water Experiments: 10 Amazing Experiments with Step by Step Photographs - For. (p. 2156)
—Super Science Experiments. Kelly, Richard, ed. (p. 2156)
—Super Science Light & Sound Experiments: 10 Amazing Experiments with Step-By-Step Photographs. (p. 2156)
—Top Ten Battles That Changed the World. (p. 2264)
—Top Ten Inventions That Changed the World. (p. 2264)
—Top Ten Scientific Discoveries That Changed the World. (p. 2264)
—Trains. (p. 2276)
—Trucks. (p. 2293)
—Trucks Inside & Out. (p. 2293)
—Using Batteries (p. 2341)
—Using Electricity (p. 2341)
—Volcanoes (p. 2366)
—Volcanoes. (p. 2366)
—Water (p. 2384)
—Way Little Engines Work (Thomas & Friends) (p. 2387)
—Weather Infographics (p. 2394)
—Wedges & Ramps. (p. 2395)
—Wheels. (p. 2427)
—Why Why Why... Do Astronauts Float in Space? (p. 2459)
—Why Why Why... Do Magnets Push & Pull? (p. 2459)
—Why Why Why... Do Tornadoes Spin? (p. 2460)
—Why Why Why... Does My Heart Begin to Race? (p. 2460)
—Wild Weather. (p. 2465)
Oxlade, Chris, jt. auth. see Ganeri, Anita.
Oxlade, Chris, jt. auth. see Gifford, Clive.
Oxlade, Chris, jt. auth. see Labrecque, Ellen.
Oxlade, Chris, jt. auth. see Loveless, Antony.
Oxlade, Chris, jt. auth. see Parker, Steve.
Oxlade, Chris & Farndon, John. Stickmen's Guide to Aircraft. Pyke, Jerry & Quay, John Paul de, illus. (p. 2118)
—Stickmen's Guide to Gigantic Machines. Pyke, Jerry & Quay, John Paul de, illus. (p. 2118)
—Stickmen's Guide to Trains & Automobiles. Pyke, Jerry & Quay, John Paul de, illus. (p. 2118)
—Stickmen's Guide to Watercraft. Pyke, Jerry & Quay, John Paul de, illus. (p. 2118)
Oxlade, Chris & Ganeri, Anita. Camera (p. 314)
—Car (p. 327)
—Computer (p. 437)
Oxlade, Chris & Jennings, Terry. Energy. (p. 650)
Oxlade, Chris & Jennings, Terry J. Energy. (p. 650)
Oxlade, Chris & Peacock, Graham. Machines: Gears, Levers, Pulleys, Engines. (p. 1372)
Oxlade, Chris & West, David. Apollo Missions & Other Adventures in Space. (p. 106)
Oxlade, Chris, et al. Science: Practical Projects (p. 1948)
—Science & History Project Book: 300 Step-By-Step Fun Science Experiments & History Craft Projects for Home Learning & School Study. (p. 1953)
Oxley, J. Macdonald. Bert Lloyd's Boyhood: A Story from Nova Scotia (Classic Reprint) (p. 204)
—Fergus Mactavish or Portage & Prairie: A Story of the Hudson's Bay Company (Classic Reprint) (p. 720)
—My Strange Rescue: And Other Stories of Sport & Adventure in Canada (Classic Reprint) (p. 1562)
—Norman's Nugget (Classic Reprint) (p. 1620)
—Specimen Hunters (Classic Reprint) (p. 2077)
Oxley, James Macdonald. Chore Boy of Camp Kippewa (Classic Reprint) (p. 381)
—Christmas Portfolio (Classic Reprint) (p. 386)
—Terry S Trials & Triumphs (Classic Reprint) (p. 2208)
—Young Woodsman, or Life in the Forests of Canada (Classic Reprint) (p. 2532)
Oxley, Jennifer, illus. see Aronson, Billy.
Oxley, Jennifer, illus. see Rusu, Meredith.
Oxley, Jennifer, jt. auth. see Aronson, Billy.
Oxley, Jennifer & Aronson, Billy. Big Dog Problem. (p. 219)
—Camp Problem. (p. 316)
—Peg + Cat: The Pizza Problem. (p. 1714)
—Peg + Cat: The Penguin Problem. (p. 1714)
—Peg + Cat: The Race Car Problem. (p. 1714)
—Peg + Cat: Math in the Bath: a Level 1 Reader. (p. 1714)
—Peg + Cat: Peg's Messy Room. (p. 1714)
—Peg + Cat: the Lemonade Problem. (p. 1714)
—Peg + Cat: the Penguin Problem. (p. 1714)
—Peg + Cat: the Pizza Problem. (p. 1714)
—Peg + Cat: the Puddle. (p. 1714)
—Peg + Cat: the Sleepover. (p. 1714)
—Peg up a Tree a Level 1 Reader. (p. 1714)
—Pirate Problem. (p. 1750)
—Race Car Problem. (p. 1831)
Oxley, Wayne. Rune Stone. (p. 1915)
Oxnard, Robert. Our Trip Around the World, 1919-20 (Classic Reprint) (p. 1681)
Oxridge, Panama. Justin Thyme. (p. 1195)
—Justin Thyme. Poxmage, Adrian, illus. (p. 1195)
—Thyme Running Out. (p. 2239)
Oxton, Alex, illus. see Laura, Gehl & Gehl, Laura.
Oxtra, Cristina. Red Riding Hood. Rivas, Miguel Díaz, illus. (p. 1858)
—Stan Lee: Get to Know the Comics Creator. (p. 2100)
—Stephen Hawking: Get to Know the Man Behind the Theory. (p. 2115)
—Tae Kwon Do Test. Erb, Amanda, illus. (p. 2175)
—Tara & the Towering Wave: An Indian Ocean Tsunami Survival Story. Ficorilli, Francesca, illus. (p. 2191)
Oyaga, Irene, tr. see Agin, Élodie, et al.
Oyague, Ralph. Adventures of a Dog Named Sam. (p. 21)
Oyakhilome, Chris. Let's Pray: A Beginner Guide to Prayer for Kids. (p. 1277)
Oyama, Misuzu. Rue de la Nuit: Labyrinth. (p. 1912)
Oyebanji, Moyinoluwa. Musings in a Moment. (p. 1529)
Oyen, Henry. Big Flat (Classic Reprint) (p. 220)
—Gaston Olaf (Classic Reprint) (p. 811)
—Joey the Dreamer: A Tale of Clay Court (Classic Reprint) (p. 1171)
—Plunderer (Classic Reprint) (p. 1763)
—Snow-Burner (Classic Reprint) (p. 2047)
—Tarrant of Tin Spout (Classic Reprint) (p. 2192)
—Twisted Trails (Classic Reprint) (p. 2306)
Oyewopo, Femi Emmanuel. Ten Types of Courtship. (p. 2205)
Oyler, Amy. Pop, Sizzle, Boom! 101 Science Experiments for the Mad Scientist in Every Kid. Brack, Amanda, illus. (p. 1775)
—Spectacular Science for Smart Kids: Clever Experiments & STEM Activities for Hours of Screen-Free Fun at Home. Brack, Amanda, illus. (p. 2077)
Oyola, Milta, tr. see Jingling, Kathy, ed.
Oz, Galia. Dog Trouble! (p. 576)
Oz, Galia & Kahn-Hoffman, Gilah. Dog Trouble! (p. 576)
Oz, Robin, illus. see Boegehold, Betty D.
Ozaki, Madame Yukio. Romances of Old Japan: Rendered into English, from Japanese Sources (Classic Reprint) (p. 1900)
Ozaki, Yei. Buddha's Crystal: And Other Fairy Stories (Classic Reprint) (p. 290)
—Buddha's Crystal, & Other Fairy Stories (Classic Reprint) (p. 290)
Ozaki, Yei Theodora. Japanese Fairy Book (Classic Reprint) (p. 1160)
—Warriors of Old Japan: And Other Stories (Classic Reprint) (p. 2380)
Ozaki, Yei Theodora & Sato, Take. Japanese Fairy Book. (p. 1160)
Ozalis-Graham, Lisa. Adventures of Finley & Cisco. (p. 23)
Ozcan, Pervin, illus. see Ball, Erin.
Ozdemir, Oktay, illus. see Ozdemir, Kelly G.
Oze, Ozkan. I Wonder about Allah Ayduz, Selma, tr. (p. 1086)
—I Wonder about the Prophet. Ayduz, Selma, tr. (p. 1086)
Ozee, Aaron. My Darling Child Shiloh. (p. 1536)
—Regulus. (p. 1862)
Ozgur, Lynne Emily. Darryl & the Mountain. Abay, Ismail, illus. (p. 508)
Ozment, Jones. Tree. (p. 2283)
Ozmore, Kia Kelly. Don't Give a Tiger Shark Indigestion. Ruble, Eugene, illus. (p. 583)
Ozoude, Marie, illus. see Ozoude, Alexander.
Ozunal, Berna, ed. see Paruzel-Gibson, Natalia.
Ozzie & Butler, Kevin. Geeze Louise / Paperback. (p. 813)
—SQUAWK SQUAWK... That's How I Talk. (p. 2094)
Ozzy, illus. see Smyth, Jimmy.

P

P, E. Ashmeads: Or, Scenes in Northern Europe (Classic Reprint) (p. 125)
P, F. H. Castle of Caithness, Vol. 1 Of 2: A Romance of the Thirteenth Century (Classic Reprint) (p. 340)
P, G. H. Artificial Mother: A Marital Fantasy (Classic Reprint) (p. 123)
P, G. y. Chiffon's Marriage (Classic Reprint) (p. 369)
p i kids. 20 Storybooks. (p. 2553)
—24 Mini Book Block! Gavin, Carolyn et al, illus. (p. 2554)
—Active Minds: Begin to Read. (p. 12)
—Baby Einstein: Let's Learn! 12 Book Block. (p. 150)
—Disney Baby: Read & Play with My Disney Friends! Disney Storybook Art Team, illus. (p. 558)
—Disney Frozen: Write-And-Erase Look & Find. (p. 559)
—Disney Mickey & Friends: Read & Play with Mickey & Minnie. Disney Storybook Art Team et al, illus. (p. 561)
—Disney Mickey & Friends. Jaime Diaz Studios, illus. (p. 561)
—Disney Minnie: Write-And-Erase Look & Find. (p. 561)
—Nickelodeon: 8-Book Set. (p. 1602)
—Nickelodeon. (p. 1602)
—Nickelodeon PAW Patrol: Read & Play with the PAW Patrol. Petrossi, Fabrizio & Moore, Harry, illus. (p. 1603)
—Precious Moments: Baby's First Year. (p. 1786)
—World of Eric Carle. Carle, Eric, illus. (p. 2502)
p i kids, jt. auth. see Publications International Ltd. Staff.
p i kids, P. i. Baby Einstein: Look & See with Me! (p. 150)
—Baby Einstein: Bedtime for Baby Animals. (p. 150)
—Baby Einstein: Goodnight, Little Mozart. (p. 150)
—Baby Einstein: Let's Look, Let's Learn, Let's Listen, Let's Move. (p. 150)
—Beat Bugs: With a Little Help from My Friends. (p. 182)
—Cars 3. (p. 334)
—Disney: Toy Story, Finding Nemo, Cars, Friends & Heroes. (p. 558)
—Disney: Finding Nemo, Best Friends, the Lion Guard, Finding Nemo & Finding Dory. (p. 558)
—Disney: Disney Princess Magic, Disney Princess, Minnie Mouse: Best Friends, Sofia the First. (p. 558)
—Disney Baby: Sleepy Stories. (p. 558)
—Disney Baby: Book & Phone Set. (p. 558)
—Disney Baby: Sound Storybook Treasury. (p. 558)
—Disney Baby: Skidamarink-A-Doo, I Love You! (p. 558)
—Disney Baby: Disney Princess: Come Out to Play! (p. 558)
—Disney Baby. (p. 558)
—Disney Mickey & Friends: Sing-Along Set. (p. 561)
—Disney Mickey Mouse Clubhouse. (p. 561)
—Disney Minnie: Ding Dong, It's Daisy! (p. 561)
—Disney Minnie: Pretty Piano Play Along. (p. 561)
—Disney Minnie. (p. 561)

—Look at Me! (p. 1345)
—Who Am I? An Animal Guessing Game. (p. 2446)
Page, Sheri Lee. Bubble Booh & the Land of Virtues. (p. 288)
Page, Skylar. Golden Flute. (p. 857)
—My Heavenly Diary. (p. 1549)
—My Heavenly Journal. (p. 1549)
—Where Is Katherine's Angel? (p. 2438)
Page, Stefan. ABC Farmers' Market Flash Cards. (p. 4)
—We're Going to the Farmers' Market. (p. 2400)
Page, Steve, illus. see Corrigan, Stacey.
Page, Steve, illus. see Hammond, Jenna.
Page, Steve, illus. see Lotz, Sally.
Page, Thomas Manning. Bohemian Life: Or the Autobiography of a Tramp (Classic Reprint) (p. 254)
Page, Thomas Nelson. Among the Camps: Or Young People's Stories of the War (Classic Reprint) (p. 76)
—Among the Camps. (p. 76)
—Bred in the Bone (Classic Reprint) (p. 279)
—Burial of the Guns (Classic Reprint) (p. 299)
—Burial, the Guns (Classic Reprint) (p. 299)
—Captured Santa Claus (Classic Reprint) (p. 327)
—Elsket: And Other Stories (Classic Reprint) (p. 640)
—In OLE Virginia (Classic Reprint) (p. 1106)
—In OLE Virginia, or Marse Chan & Other Stories (Classic Reprint) (p. 1106)
—John Marvel, Assistant (Classic Reprint) (p. 1173)
—John Marvel, Assistant, Vol. 2 (Classic Reprint) (p. 1173)
—Land of the Spirit (Classic Reprint) (p. 1242)
—Novels, Stories, Sketches & Poems of Thomas Nelson Page: Two Little Confederates; among the Camps; Two Prisoners (Classic Reprint) (p. 1627)
—Novels, Stories, Sketches & Poems of Thomas Nelson Page (Classic Reprint) (p. 1627)
—Old Gentleman of the Black Stock (Classic Reprint) (p. 1645)
—Old Gentleman of the Black Stock, and, Santa Claus's Partner (Classic Reprint) (p. 1645)
—On Newfound River (Classic Reprint) (p. 1653)
—Pastime Stories (Classic Reprint) (p. 1704)
—Polly: A Christmas Recollection (Classic Reprint) (p. 1771)
—Red Rock: A Chronicle of Reconstruction (Classic Reprint) (p. 1858)
—Red Rock, a Chronicle of Reconstruction, Vol. 1 (Classic Reprint) (p. 1858)
—Red Rock, Vol. 2: A Chronicle of Reconstruction (Classic Reprint) (p. 1858)
—Santa Claus's Partner (Classic Reprint) (p. 1932)
—Shepherd Who, Watched by Night (Classic Reprint) (p. 2006)
—Social Life in Old Virginia: Before the War (Classic Reprint) (p. 2053)
—Stories by American Authors, Vol. 9: Marse Chan; Mr. Bixby's Christmas Visitor; Eli; Young Strong of the Clarion; How Old Wiggins Wore Ship; Mas Has Come (Classic Reprint) (p. 2123)
—Tommy Trot's Visit to Santa Claus (Classic Reprint) (p. 2259)
—Tommy Trot's Visit to Santa Claus, and, a Captured Santa Claus (Classic Reprint) (p. 2259)
—Two Little Confederates (Classic Reprint) (p. 2308)
—Two Little Confederates - Scholar's Choice Edition. (p. 2308)
—Two Prisoners (Classic Reprint) (p. 2309)
—Under the Crust (Classic Reprint) (p. 2321)
Page, Tyler, illus. see Doerrfeld, Cori.
Page, Tyler, jt. auth. see Doerrfeld, Cori.
Page, Victor Wilfred. Aviation Engines: Design, Construction, Operation, & Repair (Classic Reprint) (p. 143)
—How to Run an Automobile: A Concise, Practical Treatise Written in Simple Language, Explaining the Functions of Modern Gasoline Automobile Parts with Complete Instructions for Driving & Care (Classic Reprint) (p. 1044)
Page, William P., jt. auth. see Bucke, Charles.
Page, Winter. Breaking Free. (p. 278)
Page-Clay, Mary. Mouse in the House. (p. 1515)
—Preacher's Coming to Dinner. (p. 1786)
Pagel-Hogan, Elizabeth. Gadget Disasters: Learning from Bad Ideas. (p. 805)
—Medical Mishaps: Learning from Bad Ideas. (p. 1436)
—So You Want to Be President of the United States. (p. 2051)
Pagel-Hogan, Elizabeth, jt. auth. see Leavitt, Amie Jane.
Pagel-Hogan, Elizabeth, et al. Being in Government. (p. 194)
Pagels, Douglas. Required Reading for All Teenagers: (or at Least One Who Is Very Important to Me!) Sheldon, Kristen, illus. (p. 1868)
Pages, Christina. Lucy in Her Secret Wood. (p. 1366)
—Woodland Adventures of Lucy & Will: A Story Inspired by Wordsworth's Wild Child Lucy Gray, Book 2. (p. 2491)
Pages, Coloring, jt. auth. see Manning, James.
Paget, Francis E. Warden of Berkinghot: Or, Rich & Poor (Classic Reprint) (p. 2378)
Paget, Francis Edward. Curate of Cumberworth, and, the Vicar of Roost: Tales (Classic Reprint) (p. 485)
—Owlet of Owlstone Edge: His Travels, His Experience, & His Lucubrations. (p. 1689)
—Owlet of Owlstone Edge: His Travels, His Experience, & His Lucubrations, Pp. 2-235. (p. 1689)
Paget, Gerald. Going Through the Mill (Classic Reprint) (p. 855)
Paget, R. L. Cap & Gown in Prose: Short Sketches Selected from Undergraduate Periodicals of Recent Years (Classic Reprint) (p. 323)
Paget, Sidney, jt. auth. see Doyle, Arthur Conan.
Paget, Walburga Lady. Scenes & Memories (Classic Reprint) (p. 1943)
Paget, Walter, jt. auth. see Dafoe, Daniel.
Paget, Walter Stanley, illus. see Defoe, Daniel.
Pagkaihang, Katesalin. Hermit Crab. (p. 959)
—Monkey. (p. 1493)
—Orangutan. (p. 1668)
Paglia, Isabella & Cavallaro, Francesca. Que Grande Eres Papa! (p. 1822)
Paglia, Rhonda. Little Lambs & the Very Special Mission. Paglia, Rhonda & Galaska, Taylor, illus. (p. 1320)
Pagni, Gianpaolo. Gianpaolo Pagni: Double Face. (p. 830)
Pagnoni, Roberta. Humpty Dumpty's Nursery Rhymes. (p. 1051)
—It's Easter Time. (p. 1145)
Pagnoni, Roberta, illus. see Auerbach, Annie.
Pagnoni, Roberta, illus. see Barron's Editorial Staff.
Pagnoni, Roberta, illus. see Caviezel, Giovanni & Lorini, Andrea.
Pagnoni, Roberta, illus. see Ravera, Giuseppe.
Pagnoni, Roberta & Rigo, Laura. My Princess Bag. (p. 1559)
Pagot, Franz. Knight, the Princess & the Invisible Virus. de Martin, Cinzia, ed. (p. 1228)
Pagratis, Magdalene. Jesus in Town. Casipit, Mel, illus. (p. 1166)
—What Would Jesus Do? Book 2 of the Jesus Series. Casipit, Mel, illus. (p. 2422)
Pagulayan, Carlo, illus. see Parker, Jeff.
Pahel, Carey. I Wish I Had an Otter. (p. 1086)
Pahel, Carey W. Rufus the Mild Mannered Bull: Rufus Saves the Day. (p. 1912)
Pahetti, Antonio, illus. see Blum, Ingo.
Pahl, John. Noctilucents Volume One: Martian Blood. (p. 1617)
Pahlow, Gertrude. Cross of the Heart's Desire (Classic Reprint) (p. 478)
—Gilded Chrysalis: A Novel (Classic Reprint) (p. 833)
—Glory of Going on (Classic Reprint) (p. 844)
Pahls, Stevie Kay. Dream Come True. Aerilyn Books, ed. (p. 601)
Pai, Roopa. From Leeches to Slug Glue. (p. 792)
Pai, Roopa, intro. On Your Marks: The Book of Crazy Exam Stories. (p. 1656)
Paiba, Helen. Animal Stories for 5 Year Olds. (p. 91)
—Animal Stories for 6 Year Olds. (p. 91)
—Bedtime Stories for 5 Year Olds. (p. 188)
—Funny Stories for 5 Year Olds. (p. 801)
—Funny Stories for 6 Year Olds. (p. 801)
—Scary Stories for 7 Year Olds. (p. 1943)
Paiba, Helen, ed. Animal Stories for 7 Year Olds. (p. 91)
—Funny Stories for 10 Year Olds. (p. 801)
—Funny Stories for 9 Year Olds. (p. 801)
Paidge, Emma. Nutsi Veut Attraper la Lune. Paidge, Emma, illus. (p. 1632)
Paige, Coren, illus. see Green, DeWana.
Paige, D. M. Box-Office Smash. (p. 266)
—Chart Topper. (p. 361)
—Going to Press. (p. 855)
—Size 0. (p. 2029)
Paige, Danielle. Baldosas Amarillas en Guerra. (p. 161)
—Dorothy Must Die. (p. 587)
—Dorothy Must Die 2-Book Box Set: Dorothy Must Die, the Wicked Will Rise. (p. 587)
—Dorothy Must Die Stories: No Place Like Oz, the Witch Must Burn, the Wizard Returns. (p. 587)
—Dorothy Must Die Stories Volume 2: Heart of Tin, the Straw King, Ruler of Beasts. (p. 587)
—Dorothy Must Die Stories Volume 3: Order of the Wicked, Dark Side of the Rainbow, the Queen of Oz. (p. 587)
—End of Oz. (p. 648)
—Mera: Tidebreaker. Byrne, Stephen, illus. (p. 1447)
—Stealing Snow. (p. 2110)
—Wicked Will Rise. (p. 2460)
—Yellow Brick War. (p. 2520)
Paige, David O. Cupid in Grandma's Garden: A Story-Poem (Classic Reprint) (p. 485)
Paige, Joy. Blue Whale: World's Largest Mammal. (p. 249)
—Cool Careers Without College for People Who Love to Build Things. (p. 447)
—Giraffe: World's Tallest Animal. (p. 834)
—Hummingbird: World's Smallest Bird. (p. 1050)
—Record-Breaking Animals (p. 1854)
—Sloth: World's Slowest Mammal. (p. 2038)
—Sloth / el Perezoso: The World's Slowest Mammal / el mamífero más lento del Mundo. (p. 2038)
—Stick Insect: World's Longest Insect. (p. 2117)
—Stick Insect / el insecto Palo: The World's Longest Insect / el insecto más largo del Mundo. (p. 2117)
Paige, Kenna. Through the Redwood Hollow. (p. 2237)
Paige, Nancy. Myrtle the Turtle Green, Megan, illus. (p. 1566)
Paige, Scotty D., Sr., jt. auth. see Thomas Nelson, Thomas.
Paige Slone Plagenz. Cookie Moon. (p. 446)
Paikai, Tammy. Too Many Mangos. Robinson, Don, illus. (p. 2261)
Pailey, Robtel Neajai. Jaadeh! Gbaa Sr, Amos W., tr. (p. 1151)
Pailler, Jeremy, illus. see Chng, Joyce.
Paillot, Jim, illus. see Blevins, Wiley.
Paillot, Jim, illus. see Cleary, Brian P.
Paillot, Jim, illus. see Gutman, Dan.
Paillot, Jim, illus. see Huffman, Julie.
Paillot, Jim, illus. see Metzger, Steve.
Paillot, Jim, illus. see Overdeck, Laura.
Paillot, Jim, illus. see Trueit, Trudi.
Pain, Barry. Collected Tales, Vol. 1 (Classic Reprint) (p. 414)
—Eliza (Classic Reprint) (p. 636)
—Exchange of Souls (Classic Reprint) (p. 676)
—Exiles of Faloo (Classic Reprint) (p. 677)
—If Winter Don't: A B C d e F, Notsomuchinson (Classic Reprint) (p. 1092)
—In a Canadian Canoe: The Nine Muses Minus One, & Other Stories (Classic Reprint) (p. 1103)
—In a Canadian Canoe. (p. 1103)
—Lindley Kays (Classic Reprint) (p. 1303)
—Marge Askinforit (Classic Reprint) (p. 1403)
—Memoirs of Constantine Dix (Classic Reprint) (p. 1444)
—More Short Plays: For Amateurs (Classic Reprint) (p. 1505)
—New Gulliver & Other Stories (Classic Reprint) (p. 1594)
—Octave of Claudius (Classic Reprint) (p. 1636)
—One Before: A Novel (Classic Reprint) (p. 1658)
—One Before (Classic Reprint) (p. 1658)
—Playthings & Parodies (Classic Reprint) (p. 1761)
—Short Plays: For Amateur Acting (Classic Reprint) (p. 2010)
—Stories & Interludes (Classic Reprint) (p. 2122)
—Stories in Grey (Classic Reprint) (p. 2124)
—Stories Without Tears (Classic Reprint) (p. 2126)
—Wilmay: And Other Stories of Women (Classic Reprint) (p. 2470)
—Wilmay & Other Stories of Women - Scholar's Choice Edition. (p. 2470)
Paine, Alan. Tamarack, Vol. 4: June, 1913 (Classic Reprint) (p. 2188)
Paine, Albert Bigelow. Arkansaw Bear: A Tale of Fanciful Adventure. (p. 116)
—Arkansaw Bear: A Tale of Fanciful Adventure (Classic Reprint) (p. 116)
—Arkansaw Bear. (p. 116)
—Bread Line: A Story of a Paper (Classic Reprint) (p. 277)
—Car That Went Abroad: Motoring Through the Golden Age (Classic Reprint) (p. 327)
—Dwellers in Arcady: The Story of an Abandoned Farm (Classic Reprint) (p. 611)
—From Van Dweller to Commuter: The Story of a Strenuous Quest for a Home & a Little Hearth & Garden (Classic Reprint) (p. 794)
—Hollow Tree & Deep Woods Book: Being a New Edition in One Volume of the Hollow Tree & in the Deep Woods with Several New Stories & Pictures Added (Classic Reprint) (p. 988)
—Hollow Tree & Deep Woods Book, Being a New Edition in One Volume of the Hollow Tree & in the Deep Woods with Several New Stories & Pictu. Condé, J. M., illus. (p. 988)
—Hollow Tree Nights & Days, Being a Continuation of the Stories about, the Hollow Tree & Deep Woods People (Classic Reprint) (p. 988)
—Hollow Tree Snowed-In Book: Being a Continuation of the Stories about the Hollow Tree & Deep Woods People. (p. 988)
—Hollow Tree Snowed-In Book: Being a Continuation of the Stories about, the Hollow Tree & in the Deep Woods People (Classic Reprint) (p. 988)
—How Mr. Rabbit Lost His Tail: Hollow Tree Stories (Classic Reprint) (p. 1034)
—How Mr. Rabbit Lost His Tail. (p. 1034)
—Life & Lillian Gish (Classic Reprint) (p. 1289)
—Little Garden Calendar: For Boys & Girls (Classic Reprint) (p. 1317)
—Lucky Piece: A Tale of the North Woods (Classic Reprint) (p. 1365)
—Making up with Mr. Dog: Hollow Tree Stories. (p. 1390)
—Making up with Mr. Dog: Hollow Tree Stories (Classic Reprint) (p. 1390)
—Mr. Rabbit's Wedding. (p. 1520)
—Mr. Rabbit's Wedding (Classic Reprint) (p. 1520)
—Mr. Turtle's Flying Adventure: Hollow Tree Stories (Classic Reprint) (p. 1521)
—Mr. Turtle's Flying Adventure. (p. 1521)
—Peanut: The Story of a Boy (Classic Reprint) (p. 1709)
—Ship-Dwellers: A Story of a Happy Cruise (Classic Reprint) (p. 2007)
—Tent Dwellers (Classic Reprint) (p. 2206)
—Van Dwellers: A Strenuous Quest for a Home. (p. 2347)
—Van Dwellers: A Strenuous Quest for a Home (Classic Reprint) (p. 2347)
Paine, Albert Bigelow 1861-1937, jt. auth. see Paine, Albert Bigelow.
Paine, Albert Bigelow & Fogarty, Thomas. Dwellers in Arcady: The Story of an Abandoned Farm. (p. 611)
Paine, Dorothy C. Maid of the Mountains (Classic Reprint) (p. 1383)
Paine, Jed. Ferrari (p. 721)
—Porsche (p. 1778)
Paine, Marion D. Barnard Language Reader. (p. 167)
—Bernard Language Reader (Classic Reprint) (p. 204)
Paine, Penelope Golville. Flower Girl A to Z. (p. 752)
Paine, Ralph D. Blackbeard: Buccaneer. (p. 240)
—Steam-Shovel Man (Classic Reprint) (p. 2110)
Paine, Ralph Delahaye. Campus Days (Classic Reprint) (p. 316)
—College Years (Classic Reprint) (p. 416)
—Head Coach (Classic Reprint) (p. 942)
—Sons of Eli (Classic Reprint) (p. 2064)
Paine, Thomas. Common Sense & Other Works. (p. 431)
Paino, Christina. Dog for a Month. (p. 576)
Paino, Francine. Mama's Little Lady: A Special Pony. (p. 1393)
Painted Daisies Inc. Staff & Borgatti, Katherine. Shermit's Adventure to Sprinkle Island. Painted Daisies Inc. Staff, illus. (p. 2006)
Painter, Andrew, illus. see Rickards, Lynne.
Painter, Brian. Rising of Dawn & Her Vampire Crew: Riding with the Devil. (p. 1886)
Painter, Brian & Benson, Kim. Rising of Dawn & Her Vampire Crew: Enter the Egyptian Gods. (p. 1886)
Painter, Grace. Harry Bear Story. Kacer, Stephen, illus. (p. 934)
Painter, Lucy. 100 Fantastic Things to Make, Do & Play: Simple, Fun Projects That Use Easy Everyday Materials - Cooking, Growing, Science, Music, Painting, Crafts & Party Games! (p. 2557)
—Outrageously Big Activity, Play & Project Book: Cookery, Painting, Crafts, Science, & Much More. (p. 1685)
Painter, Lucy, jt. auth. see Walton, Sally.
Painter, Mike. Pumposaurus. (p. 1813)
Painter, Peter. Picture-Room: Containing the Original Drawings of Eighteen Little Masters & Misses; to Which Are Added, Moral & Historical Explanations (Classic Reprint) (p. 1741)
Painton, Edith F. A. U. As a Woman Thinketh: A Comedy of the Period; in Three Acts (Classic Reprint) (p. 124)
—Laughing Cure: A Comedy in Two Acts (Classic Reprint) (p. 1252)
—Polly in History-Land: Or Glimpses of Washington (Classic Reprint) (p. 1772)
—Prize Essay: Or Boy Wanted, a Comedy for Girls, in Two Acts (Classic Reprint) (p. 1802)
—Star Bright a Comedy Drama in Three Acts (Classic Reprint) (p. 2102)
Painton, Edith Palmer. Crimson & the Blue: A Class Play in Four Acts & an Epilog (Classic Reprint) (p. 475)
Pair, Regether. Little Rock Island & a Little Rock Named Sam Who Doesn't Think He Fits In. (p. 1327)
Paisley, Erinne. Can Your Conversation Change the World? (p. 319)
—Can Your Outfit Change the World? (p. 319)
—Can Your Smartphone Change the World? (p. 319)
Paisley, Nc. Return to Kandar. (p. 1871)
—Wimbourne Twins. (p. 2470)
Paiva, Johannah Gilman. Guess How Much I Love Indiana. Kummer, Mark, illus. (p. 902)
—Guess How Much I Love Texas. Kummer, Mark, illus. (p. 902)
—Is There a Monster in My Closet? Long, Paulette Rich, illus. (p. 1137)
—Story of Esther. M., Dhanya, illus. (p. 2130)
—Story of Ruth. M., Dhanya, illus. (p. 2132)
Paiva, Johannah Gilman, ed. see Aladdin Books.
Paiva, Johannah Gilman, ed. see Benton, Michael.
Paiva, Johannah Gilman, ed. see Everett, Melissa.
Paiva, Johannah Gilman, ed. see Farndon, John.
Paiva, Johannah Gilman, ed. see Flowerpot Press Staff.
Paiva, Johannah Gilman, ed. see Kennelly, Sean & Carpenter, Dan.
Paiva, Johannah Gilman, ed. see Kennelly, Sean.
Paiva, Johannah Gilman, ed. see O'Connor, Frankie.
Paiva, Johannah Gilman, ed. see Petty, Kate.
Paiva, Johannah Gilman, ed. see Shand, Jennifer & Fabbri, Daniele.
Paiva, Johannah Gilman, ed. see Shand, Jennifer.
Paiva, Johannah Gilman, ed. Awesome Book of Monsters of the Deep. Various, illus. (p. 144)
—Awesome Book of Prehistoric Animals. Various, illus. (p. 144)
—Awesome Book of the Universe. Various, illus. (p. 144)
—Awesome Book of Volcanoes. Various, illus. (p. 144)
—Child's Book of Prayers: Please. (p. 375)
—Child's Book of Prayers: Thank You. (p. 375)
—Crazy Critters. Gardiner, Lisa M., illus. (p. 468)
—Farm Find. Gardiner, Lisa M., illus. (p. 710)
—My First Colors Book: Illustrated. (p. 1543)
—My First Counting Book: Illustrated. (p. 1543)
—My First Letters Book: Illustrated. (p. 1544)
—My First Shapes Book: Illustrated. (p. 1546)
—Really Big Awesome Book: Monsters of the Deep, the Universe, Volcanoes, Prehistoric Animals, & Tornadoes: Really Big Books. (p. 1851)
—Wheels on the Bus: Read with Me. (p. 2428)
—Zoo Friends. (p. 2543)
Paiva, Stela Maris Rezende. Poesia Da Primeira Vez. Cardon, Laurent, illus. (p. 1765)
Paizee, Daphne, et al. International Primary Science Student's Book 5. Miller, Jonathan & Pilling, Anne, eds. (p. 1127)
Paizee, Kati. Information Technology for CSEC 2nd Edition. (p. 1119)
Paizo Publishing (Pathfinder Roleplaying Game). Conflict PvP Tactics & Teams Rulebook. (p. 440)
Paj, Eduardo, illus. see Macalino, Damien.
Pajalunga, Lorena V. Yoga for Kids: Simple Animal Poses for Any Age. Forlati, Anna, illus. (p. 2523)
Pajalunga, Lorena Valentina. Good Morning Yoga: Relaxing Poses for Children. Láng, Anna, illus. (p. 863)
Pajkowski, Victoria. Gift. (p. 831)
Pajot, Astrid. Mincha. (p. 1469)
Pajot, Lauren, illus. see Segel, Robert G.
Pak, Greg. Hulk: World War Hulk. Romita, John & Romita, John, Jr., illus. (p. 1048)
—Totally Awesome Hulk, Volume 1. (p. 2266)
Pak, Greg, text. Hulk: Planet Hulk Prose Novel. (p. 1048)
Pak, Jiyeon. Finding Grandma's Memories. (p. 729)
—My Grandpa's Chair. (p. 1549)
Pak, Kenard. Goodbye Autumn, Hello Winter. Pak, Kenard, illus. (p. 866)
—Goodbye Summer, Hello Autumn. Pak, Kenard, illus. (p. 867)
—Goodbye Winter, Hello Spring. Pak, Kenard, illus. (p. 867)
—How to Count 1 to 5 in Five Languages. (p. 1039)
Pak, Kenard, illus. see Brill, Calista.
Pak, Kenard, illus. see Gray, Rita.
Pak, Kenard, illus. see Holt, Kari Anne.
Pak, Kenard, illus. see Lowry, Lois.
Pak, Kenard, illus. see MacLachlan, Patricia.
Pak, Kenard, illus. see MacLear, Kyo.
Pakarnyk, Alan, illus. see Loewen, Iris.
Pakkala, Christine. Jasmine & Maddie. (p. 1160)
—Last-But-Not-Least Lola & a Knot the Size of Texas. Hoppe, Paul, illus. (p. 1247)
—Last-But-Not-Least Lola & the Cupcake Queens. Hoppe, Paul, illus. (p. 1247)
—Last-But-Not-Least Lola & the Wild Chicken. Hoppe, Paul, illus. (p. 1247)
—Last-But-Not-Least Lola Going Green. Hoppe, Paul, illus. (p. 1247)
Pal, Ed. In the Beginning! The Truth of the Bible. (p. 1107)
Pal, Srijita C., ed. Development, Land Use, & Environmental Impact (p. 535)
Palache, Charles. Jottings from Russia (Classic Reprint) (p. 1179)
Palacio, R. J. 365 Days of Wonder: Mr. Browne's Precepts. (p. 2560)
—Auggie & Me: Three Wonder Stories. (p. 136)
—Auggie & Me: Three Wonder Stories. (p. 136)
—Pájaro Blanco / White Bird. (p. 1693)
—We're All Wonders. (p. 2400)
—We're All Wonders: Read Together Edition. (p. 2400)
—White Bird 9-Copy Floor Display (p. 2443)
—White Bird: a Wonder Story. (p. 2443)
—Wonder. (p. 2488)
—Wonder: la Historia de Julián / the Julian Chapter: a Wonder Story. (p. 2489)
Palacio, R. J., jt. auth. see Palacio, R. J.
Palacio, R. J. & Palacio, R. J. Lección de August (Movie Tie-In Edition) Wonder (Spanish-Language Edition) (p. 1260)
Palacio, R. J., intro. Share Your Rainbow: 18 Artists Draw Their Hope for the Future. (p. 2001)
Palacios. Guardians of the Galaxy Hallo-Scream Spook-tacular!!! Disney Storybook Art Team, illus. (p. 902)
Palacios, Argentina, tr. see Cleary, Beverly.
Palacios, Argentina, tr. see Goring, Ruth.
Palacios G., Sara Helena, illus. see Segovia, Silvia.

Palacios, John. Readers' Theater: Scripts for Young Readers: How the Tiger Got Its Stripes. (p. 1846)
Palacios, John, illus. see Stewart, Kelly, ed.
Palacios, Laura. Ten Hardworking Elves. (p. 2204)
Palacios, Sara, illus. see Akers, Martin, et al.
Palacios, Sara, illus. see Bartles, Veronica.
Palacios, Sara, illus. see Bennett, Liza & Ling, Lei.
Palacios, Sara, illus. see Brown, Monica.
Palacios, Sara, illus. see Charara, Hayan & Brown, Monica.
Palacios, Sara, illus. see Engle, Margarita.
Palacios, Sara, illus. see Funk, Josh.
Palacios, Sara, illus. see Griffin, Adele & Sheinmel, Courtney.
Palacios, Sara, illus. see Harshman, Marc.
Palacios, Sara, illus. see Hassan, Miriam, et al.
Palacios, Sara, illus. see McCarthy, Jenna.
Palacios, Sara, illus. see Perkins, Mitali.
Palacios, Sara, illus. see Steinberg, D. J.
Palacios, Sara, illus. see Theule, Larissa.
Palacios, Sara, illus. see Williams, Karen Lynn.
Palacios, Sara Helena, illus. see Leon, Georgina Lazaro.
Palacios, Sarah, illus. see Schmauss, Judy Kentor.
Palacios, Tomas. Angry Birds Movie 2: Best Enemies. (p. 87)
—Avengers: Age of Ultron: Friends & Foes. (p. 142)
—Best Enemies. (p. 205)
—Guardians of the Galaxy Hallo-Scream Spook-Tacular!!! (p. 902)
—Guardians of the Galaxy: the Story of the Guardians. Lim, Ron & Pinto, Marcelo, illus. (p. 902)
—I Am Ant-Man. (p. 1058)
—Lance Saves the World. (p. 1241)
—Spies in Disguise: Lance Saves the World. (p. 2081)
—These Are the Guardians of the Galaxy. (p. 2218)
Palacios, Tomas & Wright, Edgar. Ant-Man: I Am Ant-Man. (p. 101)
Palacios, Vicente. Origami Animals. (p. 1670)
Palacios, William, illus. see Shakespeare, William.
Palacious, John. Readers' Theater Paul Bunyan: Scripts for Young Readers. (p. 1846)
Palagonia, Peter, illus. see Akselrad, January & Young, Jennifer.
Palahicky, Sophia. Kid's Reading Craze - a Collection of 20 Short Stories. (p. 1216)
Palatini, Margie. Bad Boys Get Henpecked! Cole, Henry, illus. (p. 157)
—Boo-Hoo Moo. Graves, Keith, illus. (p. 256)
—Goldie & the Three Hares. Davis, Jack E., illus. (p. 860)
—Hogg, Hogg, & Hog. Palatini, Margie, illus. (p. 986)
—Isabella for Real. (p. 1138)
—Isabella for Real. Pham, Leuyen, illus. (p. 1138)
—Lousy Rotten Stinkin' Grapes. Moser, Barry, illus. (p. 1358)
—Stuff. Jones, Noah Z., illus. (p. 2144)
—Sweet Tooth. (p. 2169)
—Under a Pig Tree: A History of the Noble Fruit (a Mixed-Up Book) Groenink, Chuck, illus. (p. 2320)
Palatini, Margie, jt. auth. see Davis, Jack E.
Palavics, Sue. Being Benjamin. Putri, Putut, illus. (p. 194)
Palazeti, Toulla. Seed Was Planted. (p. 1983)
—Seed Was Planted/Sembré una Semilla. Barcita, Pamela, illus. (p. 1983)
Palazetti, Toulla. Seed Was Planted. Barcita, Pamela, illus. (p. 1983)
Palazzo-Craig, Janet. Making of the American Flag: Betsy Ross & George Washington. (p. 1390)
Palazzolo, Fran. Wise Owl's First Sounds & Sight Words. (p. 2478)
—Wise Owl's Vowels. (p. 2478)
Palecek, Josef, illus. see Andersen, Hans Christian.
Paleja, Shaker. Native Americans: A Visual Exploration. (p. 1578)
—Power Up! A Visual Exploration of Energy. (p. 1783)
Palen, Debbie, illus. see Blevins, Wiley.
Palen, Debbie, illus. see Calkhoven, Laurie.
Palen, Debbie, illus. see Gravelle, Karen & Gravelle, Jennifer.
Palen, Debbie, illus. see Hapka, Catherine A. & Vandenberg, Ellen.
Palen, Debbie, illus. see Hapka, Catherine A., et al.
Palermo, Sharon Gibson. Winter, Winter, Cold & Snow. Song, Christina, illus. (p. 2476)
Paley, Allison. Sky Is Burning. (p. 2033)
Paley, Caitlyn. King Lear. (p. 1220)
—Merchant of Venice. (p. 1447)
—Pros & Cons of Nuclear Power. (p. 1807)
—Slave Narratives & the Writings of Freedmen. (p. 2035)
—Strategic Inventions of the Revolutionary War. (p. 2139)
Paley, Dan. Rubio & Julienne: A Sweet & Cheesy Tale Gallegos, Lauren, illus. (p. 1911)
Paley, Daniel & Boyd, Aaron. Luigi & the Barefoot Races (p. 1366)
Paley, F. A. Greek Wit: A Collection of Smart Sayings & Anecdotes. (p. 893)
—Greek Wit: A Collection of Smart Sayings & Anecdotes, Translated from Greek Prose Writers (Classic Reprint) (p. 893)
—Greek Wit; a Collection of Smart Sayings & Anecdotes, First & Second Series. (p. 893)
—Greek Wit a Collection of Smart Sayings & Anecdotes Translated from Greek Prose Writers (Classic Reprint) (p. 893)
Paley, Frederick Apthorp. Fragments of the Greek Comic Poets: With Renderings in English Verse (Classic Reprint) (p. 775)
—Greek Wit: A Collection of Smart Sayings & Anecdotes Translated from Greek Prose Writers (Classic Reprint) (p. 893)
—Greek Wit: A Collection of Smart Sayings & Anecdotes; Translated from Greek Prose Writers (Classic Reprint) (p. 893)
Paley, Jane. Hooper Finds a Family: A Hurricane Katrina Dog's Survival Tale. (p. 1000)
Paley, Joan, illus. see Guiberson, Brenda Z.
Paley, Joan, illus. see Halfmann, Janet.
Paley, Joan, illus. see Pringle, Laurence.
Paley, Rebecca & Manwill, Melissa, contrib. by. Girl Named Hillary: the True Story of Hillary Clinton (American Girl: a Girl Named) (p. 836)
Paley, Rebecca, et al. Body Book for Boys. Sung Ku, Min, illus. (p. 253)
Paley-Phillips, Giles. Superchimp. Newson, Karl, illus. (p. 2159)
Palfrey, Bernard. No Match for Uncle Charlie. (p. 1613)
Palfrey, Jeanie. All about Stasia: Stories of the Sticks Episode One. Smith, Katharine, ed. (p. 50)
Palfrey, John Gorham. Youth's Prayer Book. (p. 2536)
Palfreyman, Anna. Climb On. (p. 405)
Palgrave, Francis Turner. Five Days Entertainments at Wentworth Grange (Classic Reprint) (p. 743)
Palgrave, Francis Turner, jt. auth. see Shakespeare, William.
Palgrave, Mary E. Between Two Opinions (Classic Reprint) (p. 210)
Palika, Liz & Miller, Katherine A. Animals at Work. (p. 94)
Palin, Cindy. To Willow's House for Tea. Abt-Tomkow, Desiree, illus. (p. 2254)
—Willow's Lullaby. Abt-Tomkow, Desiree, illus. (p. 2470)
Palin, Nicki, illus. see Goldsmith, Mike.
Palin, Tim, illus. see Armstrong, Thomas.
Palin, Tim, illus. see Berne, Emma Carlson.
Palin, Tim, illus. see Hoena, Blake.
Palin, Tim, illus. see Lotowycz, Randall.
Paling, Chris. Adventures of Rumble, Tumble, & Titch: Uncertain Times. (p. 27)
Palka, Yvonne. Dragon Fire Ocean Mist. (p. 593)
—Super Simple Sumi-E: Easy Asian Brush Painting for All Ages. (p. 2157)
Palladius, Rutilius Taurus Aemilianus. Palladius on Husbondrie: Edited from the Unique Ms. of about 1420 A. D. in Colchester Castle (Classic Reprint) (p. 1694)
Pallander, Edwin. Log of an Island Wanderer: Notes of Travel in the Eastern Pacific (Classic Reprint) (p. 1339)
Pallant, Katrina. Star Wars Deluxe Where's the Wookiee? Farinas, Ulises, illus. (p. 2104)
Pallares, Jose Miguel, tr. see Meyer, Stephenie.
Pallas, Norvin. Games with Codes & Ciphers. (p. 808)
Pallasch, Tina. Ever Atom: One. (p. 669)
Palleschi, Sarah. Did I Really Dream Last Night? (p. 543)
Pallis, Mark, jt. auth. see Kerr, Christiane.
Pallis, Mark & Kerr, Christiane. Crab & Whale: A New Way to Experience Mindfulness for Kids. Vol 1: Kindness. (p. 465)
Palliser, Rebecca. Love the Stationery in Your Classroom. (p. 1361)
Pallister, John, jt. auth. see Bowen, Ann.
Pallister, John C. In the Steps of the Great American Entomologist. Elgin, Kathleen, illus. (p. 1111)
Pallmer, Elisa, illus. see Coombs, Kate.
Pallmer, Elisa, jt. auth. see Raby, Meg.
Pallock, Ruth. Planet Mazol: Book 2 of World Adventures of Jayden. (p. 1755)
Pallotta, Jerry. Butterfly Colors & Counting. Bersani, Shennen, illus. (p. 304)
—Butterfly Counting. Bersani, Shennen, illus. (p. 304)
—Crab. Leonard, Tom, illus. (p. 465)
—Dinosaur Christmas. McWilliam, Howard, illus. (p. 548)
—Eyeball Alphabet Book. Bersani, Shennen, illus. (p. 688)
—F Is for Fenway Park: America's Oldest Major League Ballpark. (p. 689)
—Giraffe Did One Way up High. (p. 834)
—Hammerhead vs. Bull Shark. Bolster, Rob, illus. (p. 913)
—How Will I Get to School This Year? Biedrzycki, David, illus. (p. 1046)
—Jaguar vs. Skunk. Bolster, Rob, illus. (p. 1155)
—Killer Whale vs. Great White Shark. Bolster, Rob, illus. (p. 1217)
—Komodo Dragon vs. King Cobra. Bolster, Rob, illus. (p. 1231)
—Lion vs. Tiger. Bolster, Rob, illus. (p. 1306)
Pallotta Jerry. Not a Butterfly Alphabet Book. (p. 1622)
Pallotta, Jerry. Polar Bear vs. Grizzly Bear. Bolster, Rob, illus. (p. 1769)
—Santa Pups. (p. 1933)
—Santa Pups. Terry, Will, illus. (p. 1933)
—Sea Mammal Alphabet Book. (p. 1967)
—Sea Mammal Alphabet Book. Leonard, Tom, illus. (p. 1967)
—Tarantula vs. Scorpion. Bolster, Rob, illus. (p. 2191)
—Tyrannosaurus Rex vs. Velociraptor. Bolster, Rob, illus. (p. 2311)
—Very Berry Counting Book. Newton, Joy, illus. (p. 2352)
—Whale vs. Giant Squid. Bolster, Rob, illus. (p. 2403)
—What I Saw in the Teachers' Lounge. McWilliam, Howard, illus. (p. 2412)
—Who Will Plant a Tree? Leonard, Tom, illus. (p. 2452)
—Who Would Win?: Battle Royale. Bolster, Rob, illus. (p. 2452)
Pallotta, Jerry & Bolster, Rob. Construction Alphabet. (p. 443)
Pallotta, Jerry & Garnett, Sammie. U. S. Army Alphabet Book. (p. 2311)
Palma, Douglas. Double Gifted. (p. 589)
Palmarini, I. M. Continental Classics, Vol. 14: Spanish, Italian & Oriental Tales (Classic Reprint) (p. 445)
Palmen, Johan Axel. Festschrift Herrn Professor Dr. J. A. Palmen Zu Seinem 60. Geburtstage Am 7. November 1905 Gewidmet, Vol. 1: Von Schurlem und Kollegen (Classic Reprint) (p. 721)
—Festschrift Herrn Professor Dr. J. A. Palmén Zu Seinem 60. Geburtstage Am 7. November 1905 Gewidmet, Vol. 1: Von Schürlem und Kollegen (Classic Reprint) (p. 721)
Palmer, Abram Smythe, jt. auth. see Trench, Richard Chenevix.
Palmer, Agnes L. Salvage of Men: Stories of Humanity Touched by Divinity. (p. 1926)
—Salvage of Men: Stories of Humanity, Touched by Divinity (Classic Reprint) (p. 1926)
Palmer, Albert W. Mountain Trail & Its Message (Classic Reprint) (p. 1514)
Palmer, Alfred Herbert. Life of Joseph Wolf, Animal Painter (Classic Reprint) (p. 1294)
Palmer, Alicia Tyndal. Daughters of Isenberg, Vol. 1 Of 4: A Bavarian Romance (Classic Reprint) (p. 509)
Palmer, Alison. Simply Singing Time. (p. 2023)
Palmer, Andrea. Cats & Dogs! (p. 345)
—Mohave. (p. 1488)
—We're Going Freshwater Fishing. (p. 2400)
Palmer, Anne M. At the Depot: A Character Play, in One Act (Classic Reprint) (p. 130)
—Buying a Suit for Jimmy (Classic Reprint) (p. 304)
Palmer, Anthony. Soldier's Gift. Tanner, Jane, illus. (p. 2057)
Palmer, Barbara A. Clue Book for Boo-Boo. (p. 409)
—Journey of Cattail. (p. 1181)
Palmer, Barbara E. Recoverbee Says Learn with Me. (p. 1855)
Palmer, Bell Elliott. Men Not Wanted: An One-Act Comedy (Classic Reprint) (p. 1446)
—Single-Code Girl: A Novel (Classic Reprint) (p. 2024)
—What Can We Do with Aunt Sally? a Comedy in Two Acts (Classic Reprint) (p. 2407)
Palmer, Bill. And to All a Good Night: Christmas Folklore. (p. 83)
—And to All a Good Night: Christmas Folklore. Jabbour, Alan, ed. (p. 83)
—Gallup Guides for Youth Facing Persistent Prejudice. (p. 806)
—New Generation of Homosexuality: Modern Trends in Gay & Lesbian Communities. (p. 1594)
—Trailblazing Latino Americans. (p. 2275)
—Trailblazing Latino Americans. Limón, José E., ed. (p. 2275)
—What Causes Sexual Orientation? Genetics, Biology, Psychology. (p. 2407)
Palmer, C. Everard. Wooing of Beppo Tate. (p. 2492)
Palmer, Carolin D. David & Carolin Discover Coloring with Kindness. (p. 510)
Palmer, Charly, illus. see McDivitt, Lindsay.
Palmer, Charly, illus. see Sheppard, Markette.
Palmer, Charly, illus. see Taylor, Dorothea.
Palmer, Claude Irwin. Analytic Geometry: With Introductory Chapter on the Calculus (Classic Reprint) (p. 79)
Palmer, Connie. I Will Run Free No More (p. 1085)
Palmer, Dandi. Angelo & the Sunbeam Jewel. (p. 86)
—Barnaby Bell's Hot Air Balloon. (p. 167)
—Beaky & Squeaky. (p. 178)
—Bumblechunk & Tangle-Toof. (p. 297)
—Children's Colouring Book. (p. 373)
—Ganesha, the Elephant Faced God. (p. 808)
—Grunnick. (p. 901)
—King of Dolphin Island. (p. 1220)
—Love for Three Oranges. (p. 1359)
—Odd Alphabet. (p. 1637)
—Possomly's Bomb. (p. 1780)
—Short Stories for Older Children. (p. 2010)
—Sorcerer's Apprentice. (p. 2065)
Palmer, Douglas. Firefly Encyclopedia of Dinosaurs & Prehistoric Animals. (p. 734)
Palmer, Douglas, jt. auth. see Morgan, Ben.
Palmer, Edward. Freddy the Fan: The Fan That Wanted to Fly. (p. 781)
Palmer, Erin. Egyptian Mythology. Forsyth, Matt, illus. (p. 628)
—Greek Mythology. Forsyth, Matt, illus. (p. 892)
—School Dances, Yes or No. (p. 1945)
—Summer School, Yes or No. (p. 2150)
—U. S. Presidents. (p. 2312)
Palmer, Fiona. Deception: MTG Agency Series. (p. 523)
—Mission. (p. 1481)
—Recruit. (p. 1855)
Palmer, Florence U. One Year of Sunday School Lessons for Young Children: A Manual for Teachers & Parents, Presenting a Series of Sunday School Lessons Selected, Arranged, & Adapted for the Use of the Youngest Classes (Classic Reprint) (p. 1663)
Palmer, Florence Ursula. Second Year of Sunday School Lessons for Young Children: A Manual for Teachers & Parents; Presenting a Series of Lessons Selected, Arranged, & Adapted for the Use of Young Children (Classic Reprint) (p. 1974)
Palmer, Frederic. Ring & the Book: Written for the Christmas Festival 1907 (Classic Reprint) (p. 1883)
—Ring & the Book. (p. 1883)
Palmer, Frederick. Big Fellow (Classic Reprint) (p. 220)
—Danbury Rodd Aviator (Classic Reprint) (p. 499)
—In the Klondyke: Including an Account of a Winter's Journey to Dawson (Classic Reprint) (p. 1109)
—In the Klondyke. (p. 1109)
—Last Shot (Classic Reprint) (p. 1249)
—Lucy of the Stars (Classic Reprint) (p. 1366)
—Old Blood (Classic Reprint) (p. 1644)
—Over the Pass (Classic Reprint) (p. 1686)
—Vagabond (Classic Reprint) (p. 2343)
—Ways of the Service (Classic Reprint) (p. 2388)
Palmer, Frederick C. Saddle Room Songs & Hunting Ballads (Classic Reprint) (p. 1921)
Palmer, Gary, illus. see Crane, Carol.
Palmer, Gary, illus. see Young, Judy.
Palmer, Ingrid. All Out of Pretty. (p. 53)
Palmer, Iva-Marie. Gabby Garcia's Ultimate Playbook. Kissi, Marta, illus. (p. 804)
—Gabby Garcia's Ultimate Playbook #2: MVP Summer. Kissi, Marta, illus. (p. 804)
—Gabby Garcia's Ultimate Playbook #3: Sidelined. Kissi, Marta, illus. (p. 804)
—Gimme Everything You Got. (p. 833)
—Summers (p. 2150)
Palmer, Ivor. Rosa & the Wind Chimes. (p. 1904)
Palmer, J. Bean. Elsbeth & the Freedom Fighters: Book II in the Cape Cod Witch Series. Therrien, Melanie, illus. (p. 639)
Palmer, James, illus. see Collodi, Carlo & Barrie, J. M.
Palmer, James, illus. see Collodi, Carlo, et al.
Palmer, James, illus. see Smith, Carrie.
Palmer, James, illus. see Strom, Laura Layton.
Palmer, Jan, illus. see Gruelle, Johnny.
Palmer, Jennie. Wompananny Witches Make One Mean Pizza. (p. 2488)
Palmer, John. Like Master Like Man, Vol. 1 Of 2: A Novel (Classic Reprint) (p. 1301)
—Over the Hills: A Comedy in One Act (Classic Reprint) (p. 1686)
—Peter Paragon: A Tale of Youth (Classic Reprint) (p. 1729)
Palmer, John Williamson. New & the Old, or California & India in Romantic Aspects (Classic Reprint) (p. 1591)
Palmer, Judd. Umbrella. (p. 2316)
Palmer, Judd, illus. see Davidge, James.
Palmer, Julie. Kaye's Quilt. (p. 1207)
Palmer, Kate B. Twelve Songs: For Kindergarten & Primary Schools (Classic Reprint) (p. 2303)
Palmer, Kate S., illus. see Geddes, Diana E.
Palmer, Kate Salley, illus. see Mader, Jan.
Palmer, Kimmy, illus. see Flatley, Paula Chorman.
Palmer, Kris. Hot Wheels: From 0 to 50 at 1:64 Scale. (p. 1007)
Palmer, Kristen. Wild Weather Trivia. (p. 2465)
Palmer, Kristine. Eigenoids Episode 2: Momentum Sphere Coaster. (p. 629)
Palmer, Kristine M. Eigenoids Episode 1: Aqua Quest. (p. 629)
Palmer, Larry Schwarz,Iva-Marie. Romeo, Juliet & Jim: Book 1 (p. 1901)
Palmer, Libbi. PTSD Workbook for Teens: Simple, Effective Skills for Healing Trauma. (p. 1810)
Palmer, Lin. You Can't Hang a Man with a Wooden Leg. (p. 2526)
Palmer, Liza. Captain Marvel: Higher, Further, Faster. (p. 325)
—Captain Marvel: Higher, Further, Faster. Templer, Hannah, illus. (p. 325)
Palmer, Lois Sedgwick. Lesson Stories for the Kindergarten Grades of the Bible School: General Subject: God the Workman; the Creator & His Works (Classic Reprint) (p. 1268)
Palmer, Luella A. Play Life in the First Eight Years (Classic Reprint) (p. 1759)
Palmer, Lynde. Drifting & Steering (Classic Reprint) (p. 604)
—Helps over Hard Places: Stories for Boys (Classic Reprint) (p. 953)
—Honorable Club: And Other Tales (Classic Reprint) (p. 999)
—Honorable Club. (p. 999)
—John-Jack (Classic Reprint) (p. 1173)
—Where Honour Leads (Classic Reprint) (p. 2437)
Palmer, Mary. Devonshire Courtship: In Four Parts, to Which Is Added a Glossary (Classic Reprint) (p. 536)
Palmer, Mary A. Marian: A Story of the South (Classic Reprint) (p. 1404)
Palmer, Mary S. Tourism Writing: A New Literary Genre Unveiling the History, Mystery, & Economy of Places & Events. (p. 2269)
Palmer, Mary Towels, jt. auth. see Palmer, Frederic.
Palmer, Pat. Liking Myself. Shondeck, Betty, illus. (p. 1301)
—Mouse, the Monster & Me: Assertiveness for Young People. Shondeck, Betty, illus. (p. 1515)
Palmer, Priscilla, jt. auth. see Hoffman, Don.
Palmer, Priscilla & Hoffman, Don. Tony the Ferry Riding Pigeon. Goldberger, Dylan, illus. (p. 2260)
Palmer, R. E. Cloud Cuckoo. (p. 407)
—Gates of Dawn. (p. 811)
—Never Dawn. (p. 1589)
Palmer, Robert Manning. All about Airedales: A Book of General Information Valuable to Dog Lovers & Owners, Breeders & Fanciers, Illustrated from Selected Photographs of Noted Dogs & Rare Scenes; the Airedale Terrier Reviewed (Classic Reprint) (p. 48)
Palmer, Robin. Geek Charming. (p. 813)
—Girl vs. Superstar (p. 837)
—Little Miss Red. (p. 1322)
—Love You Like a Sister. (p. 1361)
—Wicked Jealous: A Love Story. (p. 2460)
—Yours Truly, Lucy B. Parker: for Better or for Worse (p. 2535)
—Yours Truly, Lucy B. Parker: Take My Advice: Book 4 (p. 2535)
Palmer, Ruth, illus. see Gamble, Adam & Jasper, Mark.
Palmer, Ruth, illus. see Jasper, Mark.
Palmer, Ruth, illus. see Kelly, Mij.
Palmer, Ruth, illus. see Knudsen, Shannon.
Palmer, Ruth, illus. see Potter, Beatrix.
Palmer, S. Y. Fortis Mission. (p. 769)
—May's Moon. (p. 1430)
Palmer, Sarah A. Story of Aunt Becky's Army-Life (Classic Reprint) (p. 2129)
Palmer, Stuart, et al. Cambridge Mathematics NSW Syllabus for the Australian Curriculum, Year 8. (p. 313)
—Cambridge Mathematics NSW Syllabus for the Australian Curriculum, Year 10. (p. 313)
—Cambridge Maths NSW Syllabus for the Australian Curriculum, Year 10. (p. 313)
Palmer, Thomas H. Moral Instructor, Vol. 3: Or Culture of the Heart, Affections, & Intellect, While Learning to Read (Classic Reprint) (p. 1503)
Palmer, Tom. Boys United. (p. 273)
—Gus the Famous Football Cat. Paterson, Alex, illus. (p. 906)
—Real Thing (p. 1850)
—Striking Out. (p. 2141)
Palmer, Tom, et al. Star Wars Legends Epic Collection: the Original Marvel Years Vol. 4. (p. 2104)
Palmer, Walter. Heart Throbs & Hoof Beats: Poems of Track, Stable & Fireside (Classic Reprint) (p. 945)
Palmer, Wayne. Growing in Faith Bible Storybook. (p. 899)
Palmer, William Thomas. English Lakes (Classic Reprint) (p. 654)
Palmero, Ana. OPUESTOS. (p. 1667)
Palmieri, Alice L. Ten Baby Berners Laying on the Bed. (p. 2203)
Palmieri, Kathryn & Palmieri, Patricia. GYPSY McPHEE: The New Kid in Town. (p. 907)
Palmieri-Cooney, Liz. Lizzie & the Flying Yoga Mat. (p. 1336)
Palmiotti, Jimmy. Best of Looney Tunes (p. 207)
Palmisciano, Diane, illus. see Conford, Ellen.
Palmisciano, Diane, illus. see Dussling, Jennifer.
Palmisciano, Diane, illus. see Giff, Patricia Reilly.
Palmisciano, Diane, illus. see Hayward, Linda.
Palmisciano, Diane, illus. see May, Eleanor.
Palmisciano, Diane, illus. see Osteen, Victoria.
Palmisciano, Diane, illus. see Walker, Nan.
Palmquist, Eric, illus. see Lindgren, Astrid.
Palmtag, Nele, illus. see Steinhöfel, Andreas.
Palo, Jefte, et al. Taskmaster: the Right Price. (p. 2192)

P

Paloma, Valdivia. Mes Dix Petits Chiens. (p. 1451)
—Quand la Grenouille Se Met a Chanter. (p. 1822)
Palomar, Eva. Bienvenida, Lupe. (p. 215)
Palomares, Susanna, et al. Hearts & Minds: An Afterschool Program for Developing Reading Literacy & Emotional Intelligence. (p. 946)
Palomino, Juan, illus. see Aridjis, Homero.
Palomo, Gabriela M., illus. see Weinberg, Bruce P.
Palone, Terry, photos by see Hooke, R. Schuyler.
Palova, Mariana. Nación de Las Bestias: El Señor Del Sabbath. (p. 1572)
Palser, Barb. Choosing News: What Gets Reported & Why (p. 381)
—Selling Ourselves: Marketing Body Images (p. 1987)
Palski, Leona M. Dimples the Snowman & the Ice Pond. (p. 547)
Palsson, Olafur, jt. auth. see Symington, Andrew James.
Paltock, Robert. Life & Adventures of Peter Wilkins: A Cornish Man (Classic Reprint) (p. 1288)
—Life & Adventures of Peter Wilkins, a Cornish Man, Vol. 2 Of 2: Relating Particularly, His Shipwreck near the South Pole; His Wonderful Passage Through a Subterraneous Cavern into a Kind of New World; His There Meeting with a Gawry, or Flying Woman, (p. 1288)
—Life & Adventures of Peter Wilkins, Vol. 1 (Classic Reprint) (p. 1288)
—Life & Adventures of Peter Wilkins; Volume I. (p. 1288)
Paltock, Robert & Bullen, Arthur H. Life & Adventures of Peter Wilkins. (p. 1288)
Paltock, Robert & Bullen, Arthur Henry. Life & Adventures of Peter Wilkins. (p. 1288)
Paltro, Piera. Learning My Prayers Daughters of St. Paul Staff, tr. (p. 1258)
Paltsits, Victor Hugo 1867-1952, jt. auth. see Frizzell, Lodisa.
Paluch, Beily. Braid the Challah: A Playful Action Rhyme. Argoff, Patti, illus. (p. 274)
—I Am a Torah: A Playful Action Rhyme. Agroff, Patti, illus. (p. 1057)
Palumbo, Lisa. Lots of Hugs & Kisses. (p. 1356)
Palumbo, Nancy L. Jindo & the Mailman. Fraser, John, illus. (p. 1169)
Palumbo, S. Violette, illus. see Mishriky, Mireille.
Palumbo, Violette S., illus. see Mishriky, Mireille.
Palund, Linda. Little Black Dress. (p. 1311)
Paluseka, Julia, illus. see Wellings, Chris.
Pam, Miss. Never Never Be a Bully. Stutz, Chris, illus. (p. 1590)
Pamela M Tuck. Mother of Many. (p. 1510)
Pamintuan, Angelo, illus. see Chase, Poppy.
Pamintuan, Macky, illus. see ABDO Publishing Company Staff & Keene, Carolyn.
Pamintuan, Macky, illus. see Ball, Nate.
Pamintuan, Macky, illus. see Brown, Jeff.
Pamintuan, Macky, illus. see Crouse, Livingstone.
Pamintuan, Macky, illus. see Crow, Kristyn.
Pamintuan, Macky, illus. see Egan, Kate.
Pamintuan, Macky, illus. see Greenburg, Dan.
Pamintuan, Macky, illus. see Houran, Lori Haskins.
Pamintuan, Macky, illus. see Keene, Carolyn.
Pamintuan, Macky, illus. see McCall Smith, Alexander.
Pamintuan, Macky, illus. see Nussbaum, Ben.
Pamintuan, Macky, illus. see Ryan, Candace.
Pamintuan, Macky, illus. see Schnell, David.
Pamintuan, Macky, illus. see Schwaeber, Barbie.
Pamintuan, Macky, illus. see Zondervan Staff.
Pamment, Katie, illus. see Dodd, Emily.
Pamment, Katie, illus. see Twain, Mark, pseud.
Pammer, Victoria. Katelyn & the Crooked Tooth. (p. 1204)
Pamphlets, Talbot Collection of British. Goddesses in Congress at Olympus-On-Spree (Classic Reprint) (p. 852)
Pamplico, John. Rebellion of the Beasts: Or, the Ass Is Dead! Long Live the Ass!! (Classic Reprint) (p. 1852)
Pamplona, Alberto Hernández. Visual Guide to Energy & Movement. (p. 2363)
—Visual Guide to Technology. (p. 2363)
—Visual Guide to the Universe. (p. 2363)
Pan, Emily X. R. Astonishing Color of After. (p. 128)
Pan, Hsinping. Baby's First Kind Words: A Board Book. (p. 154)
Pan, Hsinping, illus. see Ignatow, Amy.
Pan, Hsinping, illus. see Patterson, James & Patterson, Susan.
Pan, Hsinping, illus. see Patterson, Susan & Patterson, James.
Pan, Hsinping, illus. see Shulman, Naomi.
Pan, Michelle. Bella Should Have Dumped Edward: Controversial Views on the Twilight Series. (p. 197)
Pana, Andra, illus. see McWood, Allison.
Panaccione, Nancy. Mine! Diary: My Ideas Need Expressing. (p. 1470)
Panaccione, Nancy, illus. see Dakota, Heather.
Panafieu, De. Btes Biscornues, Saugrenues, Toutes Nues(les) (p. 288)
—Btes Qui Crachent, Qui Collent, Qui Croquent. a la Mer(les) (p. 288)
—Nucl'aire, Pour Quoi Faire ? (p. 1628)
Panafieu, Jean-Baptiste. Btes Qui Rdent, Qui Rongent, Qui Rampent la Ville(les) (p. 288)
Panagariya, Ananth, jt. auth. see Ota, Yuko.
Panagarry, Rachelle, illus. see Metcalf, Dan.
Pană, Andra, illus. see McWood, Allison.
Panaro, Carlo & Stabile, Vito. Uncle Scrooge: the World of Ideas. De Lorenzi, Paolo et al, illus. (p. 2319)
Pancheshnaya, Dasha, illus. see Forest, Jim.
Pancholy, Maulik. Best at It. (p. 205)
Panchyk, Richard. Baseball History for Kids: America at Bat from 1900 to Today, with 21 Activities. (p. 168)
—Boston History for Kids: From Red Coats to Red Sox, with 21 Activities. (p. 264)
—Charting the World: Geography & Maps from Cave Paintings to GPS with 21 Activities. (p. 361)
—Keys to American History: Understanding Our Most Important Historic Documents. (p. 1212)
—New York City History for Kids: From New Amsterdam to the Big Apple with 21 Activities. (p. 1598)
—Washington, DC History for Kids: The Making of a Capital City, with 21 Activities. (p. 2382)
Panchyshyn, Roksolana, illus. see McGee, Tori.
Panchyshyn, Roksolana, illus. see Pere, Tuula.
Panciroli, Fulvia. Varco Tra Due Epoche. (p. 2348)
Panckoucke, Andre-Joseph. Dictionnaire des Proverbes François et de Façons de Parler Comiques, Burlesques et Familières, &c: Avec l'Explication, et les Étymologies les Plus Avérées (Classic Reprint) (p. 542)
—Dictionnaire des Proverbes Francois, et de Facons de Parler Comiques, Burlesques et Familieres, &C: Avec l'Explication, et les Etymologies les Plus Averees (Classic Reprint) (p. 542)
—Dictionnaire des Proverbes François, et des Façons de Parler Comiques, Burlesques et Familières, &c: Avec l'Explication et les Étymologies les Plus Avérées (Classic Reprint) (p. 542)
—Dictionnaire des Proverbes François, et des Façons de Parler Comiques, Burlesques et Familières, &c: Avec l'Explication, et les Étymologies les Plus Avérées. P. J. P. D. L. N. D. L. E. F (Classic Reprint) (p. 542)
Panckridge, Michael. 44 Hours. (p. 2555)
—Cursed. (p. 489)
—Vanishings. (p. 2347)
P�rez, Soraya Bartolom�, illus. see English, Patrick.
Panda, Jake G. Case of the Cursed Dodo. (p. 337)
Pandanas, Ms L. A. Slinky Luminescence: Two Plus Who? (p. 2038)
—Zar-Zar the Russian Ladybeetle: Easter Beetle. (p. 2538)
—Zar-Zar the Russian Ladybeetle: Bull Ants, Bindies & Bees. (p. 2538)
—Zar-Zar the Russian Ladybeetle: The Land of Black & White. (p. 2538)
Pandelis, Bloomin' Harmony Judy E. Bloomin' Harmony. (p. 247)
Panders, Wendy, illus. see Ter Horst, Marc.
Pandey, Pooja. Little Monk's Buddha. (p. 1322)
—Little Monk's Hanuman. (p. 1322)
—Little Monk's Krishna. (p. 1323)
Pandey, Vibha. Big Banyan Tree. (p. 216)
Pandora. Ankh: Conquering the Seven Deadly Sins. (p. 96)
Pandu, Lingtang, illus. see Brigger, Laura.
Panec, D. J. How Many? A Counting Book. Blackmore, Katherine, illus. (p. 1033)
—How Many? (We Both Read - Level Pk-K) A Counting Book. Blackmore, Katherine, illus. (p. 1033)
—How Many? Cuantos Hay? A Counting Book: Spanish/English Bilingual Edition (We Both Read - Level Pk-K) Blackmore, Katherine, illus. (p. 1033)
—Riddle Rhymes (We Both Read - Level Pk-K) (p. 1878)
—We Both Read - Changing Places. Elkerton, Andy, illus. (p. 2389)
Paneck, Becky. Enchanted Paradise of Sugar Creek. Colbert, Megan Benham, illus. (p. 647)
Panetta, Kevin. Bloom. Ganucheau, Savanna, illus. (p. 246)
Panetta, Kevin & Ganucheau, Savanna. Bloom. (p. 247)
Pang, Alex, illus. see Daynes, Katie.
Pang, Alex, illus. see Gilpin, Daniel & West, David.
Pang, Alex, illus. see Gilpin, Daniel.
Pang, Alex, illus. see Parker, Steve.
Pang, Bonnie, illus. see Acampora, Courtney & Fischer, Maggie.
Pang, Bonnie, illus. see Feldman, Thea.
Pang, Bonnie, illus. see Greenberg, Mike & Greenberg, Stacy Steponate.
Pang, Bonnie, illus. see Myers, Tim J.
Pang, Guek Cheng, jt. auth. see Toth, Henrietta.
Pang, Guek Cheng & Nevins, Debbie. Grenada (p. 895)
Pang, Guek-Cheng. Grenada. (p. 895)
—Mongolia. (p. 1493)
Pang, Hannah. Wilderness: An Interactive Atlas of Animals. Wren, Jenny, illus. (p. 2466)
Pang, Mandy. Heart of a Mouse. Corrigan, Sophie, illus. (p. 945)
Pang, Ophelia. Ophelia Pang's Interactive Art Book. (p. 1666)
Pang, YaWen Ariel, illus. see Wargin, Kathy-jo.
Pangan, Catherine Hagerman. No Peanuts for Me! Warf, Gracie, illus. (p. 1614)
Pangborn, Frederic W. Perdida: A Round Unvarnished Tale Truthfully Delivered (Classic Reprint) (p. 1721)
Pangborn, Georgia Wood. Interventions (Classic Reprint) (p. 1127)
—Roman Biznet (Classic Reprint) (p. 1899)
Pangburn, Shane, illus. see Bosch, Pseudonymous.
Paniagua, Kelly. Bedtime for Sarah Sullivan. Warrick, Jessica, illus. (p. 188)
Panian, Angie & Panian, Tyler. Creature Clash! Mix & Match Coloring Book. (p. 471)
Paniaq, Herve. Takannaaluk Arnaktauyok, Germaine, illus. (p. 2176)
—Walrus Shannon, Ben, illus. (p. 2373)
Paniccia, Mark, ed. see Parker, Jeff.
Paniccia, Mark, ed. see Van Lente, Fred.
Panicker, Hari & Nair, Deepti. Seekers. (p. 1984)
Panigrahy, Sonia. Nina la Ninja Del Vecindario. (p. 1609)
—Nina the Neighborhood Ninja. Quintanilla, Hazel, illus. (p. 1609)
Panikkar, Raimon. Gota de Agua: Según Raimon Panikkar. Castel-Branco, Ines, illus. (p. 872)
Panini Publishing, creator. Scooby Doo! Summer Annual. (p. 1961)
Panitch, Amanda. Never Missing, Never Found. (p. 1590)
Panizzo, Caren. Giuliana's Fairy Door. (p. 839)
Panju, Sakeena, illus. see Kermalli, Shelina.
Pankey, Elena. Cats Memorials in Russia & World. (p. 346)
Pankey, Jill, illus. see McBeth, Mary G. & Stokes, Fraye.
Pankhurst, Kate. Mariella Mystery: el caso del fantasma del Conejillo de Indias: Vol. 1. (p. 1405)
—Mariella Mystery Investigates a Cupcake Conundrum. (p. 1405)
—Mariella Mystery Investigates a Kitty Calamity. (p. 1405)
—Mariella Mystery Investigates the Disappearing Dinner Lady. (p. 1405)
—Mariella Mystery Investigates the Ghostly Guinea Pig. (p. 1405)
—Mariella Mystery Investigates the Mystery of the Cursed Poodle. (p. 1405)
—Mariella Mystery Investigates the Spaghetti Yeti. (p. 1405)
Pankhurst, Kate, illus. see Fine, Anne.
Pankhurst, Kate, illus. see Jarman, Julia.
Pankhurst, Kate, illus. see Tiger Tales.
Pankhust, Kate, et al. Mariella Mystery: El Enigma Del Cupcake. (p. 1405)
Pankova, Yuliya, ed. Numbers - Guess What? (p. 1630)
—Veggies - Guess What? (p. 2349)
Panks, Cynthia F. Eulahlie Enchanted (a Child's Hurricane Katrina Story) (p. 667)
Pankuch, Leanne M. Dragon's Truth. (p. 596)
Pannell, Jack, jt. auth. see Levin, Michael.
Pannell, Nick, illus. see Mann, Scott.
Pannemaker, And Other Stories of Old Aut. Letters Everywhere: Stories & Rhymes for Children (Classic Reprint) (p. 1279)
Panno, Joseph. Aging. (p. 35)
—Animal Cloning: The Science of Nuclear Transfer. (p. 88)
—Cell: Nature's First Life-Form. (p. 350)
Pannone, Frank, ed. see Morinaga, Ai.
Panosian, Dan, illus. see Behling, Steve.
Panosian, Dan, illus. see West, Tracey.
Panova, Vera. Looking Ahead (Classic Reprint) (p. 1347)
Panse, Rudolf. Pathologische Anatomie des Ohres (Classic Reprint) (p. 1704)
Panse, Sonal, illus. see Miller, Judith J.
Panske, Andy, illus. see Rippel, Marie & LaTulippe, Renée.
Pansler Lam M a J D, Karen. Children's Illustrated Bible Primer with Commentary. (p. 374)
Pansy. Three People. (p. 2234)
Pansy, Pansy. Aunt Hannah & Martha & John (Classic Reprint) (p. 137)
—Chautauqua Girls at Home (Classic Reprint) (p. 363)
—Cunning Workmen (Classic Reprint) (p. 485)
—Eighty-Seven (Classic Reprint) (p. 629)
—Esther Reid (Classic Reprint) (p. 664)
—Gertrude's Diary: And the Cube (Classic Reprint) (p. 823)
—Grandpa's Darlings (Classic Reprint) (p. 879)
—Her Associate Members (Classic Reprint) (p. 956)
—Household Puzzles (Classic Reprint) (p. 1024)
—Interrupted (Classic Reprint) (p. 1127)
—Judge Burnham's Daughters (Classic Reprint) (p. 1185)
—Little Fishers: And Their Nets (Classic Reprint) (p. 1316)
—Little Minnie: And Other Stories (Classic Reprint) (p. 1322)
—Mary Burton & Other Stories: A Book for Girls (Classic Reprint) (p. 1414)
—Miss. Priscilla Hunter: And My Daughter Susan (Classic Reprint) (p. 1479)
—Mrs. Solomon Smith Looking on (Classic Reprint) (p. 1523)
—New Year's Tangles: And Other Stories (Classic Reprint) (p. 1598)
—One Commonplace Day (Classic Reprint) (p. 1659)
—Pocket Measure (Classic Reprint) (p. 1764)
—Ruth Erskine's Crosses (Classic Reprint) (p. 1918)
—Sevenfold Trouble (Classic Reprint) (p. 1994)
—Sydney Martin's Christmas (Classic Reprint) (p. 2172)
—Tip Lewis & His Lamp (Classic Reprint) (p. 2250)
—Wise & Otherwise (Classic Reprint) (p. 2477)
Pantaleo, Steve. DK Reader Level 2: WWE Sheamus. (p. 568)
—DK Reader Level 2: WWE the Rock. (p. 568)
—Meet the Champions. (p. 1439)
—WWE Ronda Rousey. (p. 2514)
—WWE Tag Teams & Team-Ups. (p. 2514)
Pantaleo, Steven. WWE: the World of the Rock. (p. 2514)
Pantalleresco, Joshua. Wandering God. Chan, Florence, illus. (p. 2375)
Pantazis, Pete, illus. see Wong, Clarissa.
Pantazis, Peter, illus. see Wong, Clarissa.
Pantazz, Ethel Greening. Roumania in Light Shadow (Classic Reprint) (p. 1907)
Panteleakos, Nicole. Planet Earth Is Blue. (p. 1755)
Pantermüller, Alice & Kohl, Daniela. My Life As Lotta: a House Full of Rabbits (Book 1) (p. 1551)
—My Life As Lotta: How Lamb Is That? (Book 2) (p. 1551)
Pantic, Dunja, illus. see Olin, Marilyn.
Pantoja, Maria Kristina, illus. see Thielbar, Melinda.
Pantoja, Maria Kristina Sb., illus. see Thielbar, Melinda.
Pantoja, Olivia. Big Apples & Lone Stars. (p. 216)
—Joan of Orc. (p. 1170)
Pantoja, Stephen. Amalaganimals: Ability Not Disability. (p. 61)
—Amalaganimals: Eracism Sc. (p. 61)
Pantoja, Tintin, illus. see Heagerty, Mat.
Pantoja, Tintin, illus. see Thielbar, Melinda.
Panton, J. E. Bypaths & Cross-Roads (Classic Reprint) (p. 306)
—Having & Holding, Vol. 1 Of 3: A Story of Country Life (Classic Reprint) (p. 940)
—Tangled Chain, Vol. 1 of 2 (Classic Reprint) (p. 2190)
Panton, Jane Ellen. Having & Holding, Vol. 3 Of 3: A Story of Country Life (Classic Reprint) (p. 940)
Panton, Jane Ellen (Frith). Fresh Leaves & Green Pastures (Classic Reprint) (p. 785)
—Having & Holding, Vol. 3 Of 3: A Story of Country Life (Classic Reprint) (p. 940)
Pantone. Pantone: Box of Colour: 6 Mini Board Books! (p. 1696)
—Pantone: Color Cards: 18 Oversized Flash Cards. Gibbs, Andrew, illus. (p. 1696)
—Pantone: Color Puzzles: 6 Color-Matching Puzzles. Carpenter, Tad, illus. (p. 1696)
—Pantone: Colors. (p. 1696)
—Pantone: Sticker Book with Posters. (p. 1696)
Pantoya, Michelle L., jt. auth. see Hunt, Emily M.
Panza, Rosana, jt. auth. see Levy, Debbie.
Panzieri, Lucia. Cocodrilo Amable. (p. 411)
Panzini, Alfredo. Wanted, a Wife: IO Cerco Moglie (Classic Reprint) (p. 2375)
Paola, Tomie de, see Berg, Jean Horton & dePaola, Tomie.
Paola, Tomie de, see Butler, Dori Hillestad & dePaola, Tomie.
Paola, Tomie de, see dePaola, Tomie.
Paola, Tomie de, see Flory, Jane & dePaola, Tomie.
Paola, Tomie de, see Goebel, Jenny & dePaola, Tomie.
Paola, Tomie de, see Grosset & Dunlap & dePaola, Tomie.
Paola, Tomie de, see Grosset and Dunlap Staff & dePaola, Tomie.
Paola, Tomie de, see Krulik, Nancy & dePaola, Tomie.
Paola, Tomie de, see Krulik, Nancy & dePaola, Tomie.
Paola, Tomie de, see Krulik, Nancy & dePaola, Tomie.
Paola, Tomie de, see Krulik, Nancy & dePaola, Tomie.
Paola, Tomie de, see Piper, Watty & dePaola, Tomie.
Paola, Tomie de, see Shaw, Gina & dePaola, Tomie.
Paola, Tomie de, see Wilde, Irma & dePaola, Tomie.
Paola, Tomie de, see Young, Karen Romano & dePaola, Tomie.
Paoletti, Laura, illus. see Smith, Ali.
Paoli, Xavier. My Royal Clients (Classic Reprint) (p. 1560)
Paolicchi, Daniel & Springer, Alice G. AP Spanish Language & Culture Premium: With 5 Practice Tests. (p. 105)
Paolicchi, Daniel & Springer, Alice Gericke. AP Spanish Language & Culture: With 2 Practice Tests. (p. 105)
Paolilli, Paul & Brewer, Dan. Nightlights. Brereton, Alice, illus. (p. 1608)
—Silver Seeds. (p. 2020)
Paolini, Alison, illus. see Hall, Kirk.
Paolini, Christopher. Brisingr. (p. 282)
—Brisingr: Inheritance Book 3 Vol. 4 Of 4. (p. 282)
—Brisingr. (p. 282)
—Eldest. (p. 630)
—Eragon (p. 659)
—Fork, the Witch, & the Worm: Tales from Alagaësia (Volume 1: Eragon) (p. 768)
—Inheritance: Book IV. (p. 1120)
—Inheritance (Inheritance Cycle, Book 4) (p. 1120)
Paolo, Domeniconi, illus. see Riggs, Kate.
Paolucci, Anthony. Creatureton High. (p. 472)
—Creatureton University. (p. 472)
—Rose in the Devil's Garden. (p. 1905)
Pap, Mary. Potty Fairy. (p. 1781)
—Potty Fairy French Version. (p. 1781)
Papa Bee. There's a Flower in Our Vegetable Garden. (p. 2217)
Papa, Marcia. Wee Bees & the Bee Attitudes. (p. 2395)
Papademetriou, Lisa. Accidentally Fooled. (p. 10)
—Accidentally Friends. (p. 10)
—Apartment 1986. (p. 105)
—Confectionately Yours #4: Something New. (p. 438)
—Dreamway. (p. 603)
—Rosetta's Daring Day. Clarke, Judith et al, illus. (p. 1906)
—Save the Cupcake! (p. 1937)
—Taking the Cake! (p. 2178)
—Tale of Highly Unusual Magic. (p. 2179)
Papademetriou, Lisa, illus. see Patterson, James, et al.
Papademetriou, Lisa, jt. auth. see Patterson, James.
Papademetriou, Lisa & Morris, Kimberly. Rani: Two Friendship Tales. Disney Storybook Artists Staff, illus. (p. 1841)
Papadopoulou, Demetra, tr. see Russ-Ayon, Angela.
Papakosta, Irene, tr. see Pere, Tuula.
Papaleo, Antonio, illus. see Williams, Simon.
Papalia, Roberta, illus. see Maddox, Jake.
Papaloizois Publications Inc. Eéa ×ánU! L3 STUDENT'S BOOK. (p. 627)
Papaloizos Publications Inc. Eéá ×ánU! L3 Activity Book. (p. 627)
—GEIA XARA L4 STUDENT'S BOOK. (p. 813)
Papandopol, Bogdan. I Love My Friends. a Book for Kids Only. (p. 1071)
—Look at the Skies Second Edition. (p. 1345)
—Zina & the Brave. (p. 2540)
Paparone, Pam, illus. see Macken, JoAnn Early.
Paparone, Pam, illus. see Sklansky, Amy E.
Paparone, Pamela, illus. see Butler, Kristi T.
Paparone, Pamela, illus. see Lindbergh, Reeve.
Paparone, Pamela, illus. see Polette, Nancy.
Paparone, Pamela, illus. see Roth, Carol.
Paparone-Donadio, Crystal. Glamma's Pajamas. (p. 841)
Papas, William. Tasso. (p. 2192)
Papatheodoulou, Antonis. última Carta. (p. 2314)
Pape, Catherine, illus. see Cooper, Howard.
Pape, Catherine Noel, illus. see MacKenzie, Carine & Motyer, Alec.
Pape, Frank, illus. see Vairous.
Pape, Frank C., illus. see Wilson, Richard.
Pape, Frank Cheyne. Diamond Fairy Book (Classic Reprint) (p. 538)
Pape, Jane, illus. see Blyton, Enid.
Pape, Lee. Bravest Thing in the World: A Comedy of Childhood in One Act (Classic Reprint) (p. 277)
Paper Dolls, jt. auth. see Rechlin, Ted.
Paper Dolls, jt. auth. see Swanson, Maggie.
Paper Dolls for Grownups Staff, jt. auth. see Lum, Kwei-lin.
Paper Dolls for Grownups Staff, jt. auth. see Mattox, Brenda Sneathen.
Paper Dolls for Grownups Staff, jt. auth. see Roytman, Arkady.
Paper Dolls for Grownups Staff, jt. auth. see Tierney, Tom.
Paperman, Ross, illus. see Litwin, Suzanne Reisler.
Papierowska, Marta, illus. see Speer, Wendell.
Papillion, Allison, illus. see Ibrahim, Benita & Ibrahim, Joshua.
Papineau, Lucie. Leon the Raccoon: Explores the Arctic. Doyle, Tommy, illus. (p. 1267)
—Lucy & the Dragonfly. Hamel, Caroline, illus. (p. 1365)
Papini, Giovanni. Libro Negro. (p. 1287)
Papish, Ram. Little Seal: An Alaska Adventure. (p. 1327)
Paplinksie, Cecilia, illus. see Harris, Sally M.
Paplow, Paula. Hands upon the Rock. (p. 916)
Papoulas, Ted, illus. see Uhlberg, Myron.
Papp, Kathy, jt. illus. see Papp, Robert.
Papp, Lisa. Madeline Finn & the Library Dog. Papp, Lisa, illus. (p. 1375)

Papp, Lisa, illus. see Bunting, Eve.
Papp, Lisa, illus. see Layne, Deborah & Layne, Steven.
Papp, Lisa, illus. see Noble, Trinka Hakes.
Papp, Lisa & Noble, Trinka Hakes. Battles. Papp, Robert, illus. (p. 175)
Papp, Lisa & Papp, Robert. Town That Fooled the British: A War of 1812 Story. Papp, Lisa & Papp, Robert, illus. (p. 2270)
Papp, Robert. Amazing Mystery Show. (p. 66)
—Clue in the Recycling Bin. (p. 409)
—Cupcake Caper. (p. 485)
—Great Turkey Heist. (p. 890)
—Monkey Trouble. (p. 1494)
—Pumpkin Head Mystery (p. 1812)
—Spooktacular Special. (p. 2086)
—Spy Game. (p. 2093)
—Spy in the Bleachers. (p. 2093)
—Zombie Project. (p. 2542)
Papp, Robert, illus. see Karwoski, Gail Langer.
Papp, Robert, illus. see Kurtz, Jane.
Papp, Robert, illus. see Layne, Deborah & Layne, Steven.
Papp, Robert, illus. see Medearis, Angela Shelf.
Papp, Robert, illus. see Noble, Trinka Hakes.
Papp, Robert, illus. see Papp, Lisa & Noble, Trinka Hakes.
Papp, Robert, illus. see Shefelman, Janice Jordan.
Papp, Robert, illus. see Sobol, Donald J.
Papp, Robert, illus. see Wilbur, Helen L.
Papp, Robert, jt. auth. see Papp, Lisa.
Papp, Robert & Papp, Kathy. Pumpkin Head Mystery. (p. 1812)
Papp, Robert L. Dog-Gone Mystery. (p. 576)
—Spy Game. (p. 2093)
—Superstar Watch. (p. 2161)
—Vampire Mystery. (p. 2346)
Pappal, Barbara. Thanksgiving of Surprises. (p. 2212)
Pappas, Charles. Tree That Loved the Eagle. Schlueter, Rachel, illus. (p. 2284)
Pappas, M. G. Hotel Pennsylvania: This Is the Beginning of the Dreamcatcher Gang As They Get Together, Go on Adventures & Learn How to Make Their Dreams Come True (the Dreamcatchers Book 1) (p. 1007)
Pappas, Theoni. Do the Math! Math Challenges to Exercise Your Mind. (p. 571)
—More Math Adventures with Penrose the Mathematical Cat. (p. 1505)
Pappin Hunt, Debbie. If I Were an Animal. (p. 1091)
Pappworth, Sara. Life & Art of Claude Monet. Ryn, Aude van, illus. (p. 1288)
Paprocki, Beth. Storyland: the Marvelous Mccrittersons — Road Trip to Grandma's: A Story Coloring Book. Paprocki, Greg, illus. (p. 2136)
Paprocki, Greg. A Is for Atom: A Midcentury Alphabet (p. 1)
—C Is for Castle: A Medieval Primer (p. 306)
—D Is for Dreidel: A Hanukkah Alphabet (p. 494)
—E Is for Easter (p. 612)
—G Is for Go-Go: A Sixties Alphabet (p. 804)
—Halloween Alphabet (p. 912)
—Harajuku Paper Dolls: Japanese Street Fashions! (p. 924)
—J Is for Jazz: A Roaring Twenties Alphabet (p. 1150)
—L Is for Love: A Heartfelt Alphabet (p. 1234)
—M Is for Monocle - Victorian Alphabet (p. 1370)
—R Is for Railway: An Industrial Revolution Alphabet (p. 1829)
—R Is for Ramadan (p. 1829)
—S Is for Sabertooth: a Stone Age Alphabet (p. 1919)
—S Is for Santa Claus: A Christmas Alphabet (p. 1919)
—S Is for School: A Classroom Alphabet (p. 1919)
—Wild West Alphabet (p. 2465)
Paprocki, Greg, illus. see Cooper, Bob.
Paprocki, Greg, illus. see King, Bart.
Paprocki, Greg, illus. see Lord, Cynthia.
Paprocki, Greg, illus. see Paprocki, Beth.
Paprocki, Greg, illus. see Spiro, Ruth.
Paprocki, Ray. Eli Manning. (p. 635)
Paprocki, Sherry Beck. Anita Roddick. (p. 96)
—Diana, Princess of Wales. (p. 538)
—Ellen Degeneres: Entertainer. (p. 637)
Papson, Kylie, illus. see Robinson, Beatriz M.
Paquet, Claudine. Antonio y la Bibliotecaria. (p. 103)
Paquet, Laura Byrne. Environment in Contemporary Africa. (p. 657)
Paquette, Ammi-Joan. Bunny Bus. Breen Withrow, Lesley, illus. (p. 298)
—Elf in the House. (p. 635)
—Elf in the House. Record, Adam, illus. (p. 635)
—Ghost in the House. (p. 827)
—Ghost in the House. Record, Adam, illus. (p. 827)
—Ghost in the House: a Lift-The-Flap Book. Record, Adam, illus. (p. 827)
—Paradox. (p. 1698)
—Petey & Pru & the Hullabaloo. Ang, Joy, illus. (p. 1730)
—Tiptoe Guide to Tracking Fairies. Unzner, Christa, illus. (p. 2250)
—Tiptoe Guide to Tracking Fairies. LeTourneau, Marie, illus. (p. 2250)
—Tiptoe Guide to Tracking Mermaids. LeTourneau, Marie, illus. (p. 2250)
—Train of Lost Things. (p. 2275)
Paquette, Ammi-Joan & Thompson, Laurie Ann. Two Truths & a Lie: Forces of Nature. (p. 2309)
—Two Truths & a Lie: Histories & Mysteries. (p. 2309)
—Two Truths & a Lie: It's Alive! Weber, Lisa K., illus. (p. 2309)
Paquette, Denise, illus. see Lavallee, Jeannie.
Paquette, Heather. Kammy the Chameleon Goes to School. Paquette Jr., Edward D., illus. (p. 1202)
Paquette, John R., illus. see Rowley, Julie P.
Paquette Jr., Edward D., illus. see Paquette, Heather.
Paquin, Pauline, illus. see Devine, Monica.
Parachini, Jodie. Complete Guide to U.S. Presidents. (p. 434)
—Half a Giraffe? Smythe, Richard, illus. (p. 910)
—This Is a Serious Book. Rieley, Daniel, illus. (p. 2224)
Parachini-Deny, Juliette & Dupin, Olivier. Unicornio Misterioso. (p. 2329)
—¡el Hámster Se Escapo! (p. 630)
—¡el Pequeño Panda Está Libre! (p. 630)
Paraclete Press, Paraclete. My First Heaven Book. Bartolomé, Soraya Pérez, illus. (p. 1544)
Paraclete Press Staff. Praying with My Fingers: An Easy Way to Talk with God. (p. 1786)
—Tarjeta Del Padre Nuestro - Prayer Card. (p. 2191)
Paraclete Video Productions Staff. Praying with My Fingers: An Easy Way to Talk with God. (p. 1786)
Parada, Jorge. Pacoso. (p. 1691)
Paradis. Texas Monsters. Paradis & Legdani, Sanaa, illus. (p. 2209)
Paradis, Anne. Caillou, Emma's Extra Snacks: Living with Diabetes. Sévigny, Eric, illus. (p. 308)
—Caillou, Fun Tracing & Pen Control: Preschool Writing Activities. Sévigny, Eric, illus. (p. 308)
—Caillou Goes to School. (p. 309)
—Caillou Makes a Meal. (p. 309)
—Caillou, My First French Word Book: Learn a New Language with Caillou! Brignaud, Pierre & Sévigny, Éric, illus. (p. 309)
—Caillou, My First Spanish Word Book. Brignaud, Pierre & Sévigny, Éric, illus. (p. 309)
—Caillou, My House: Includes 4 Chunky Board Books. Brignaud, Pierre, illus. (p. 309)
—Caillou Plays Hockey. (p. 309)
—Caillou Takes the Train. (p. 309)
—Caillou: the Little Christmas Artist. Sévigny, Eric, illus. (p. 309)
—Caillou Waits for Santa: Christmas Special Edition with Advent Calendar. Sévigny, Éric, illus. (p. 309)
—New Soccer Coach. (p. 1597)
—New York Monsters: A Search-And-Find Book. Danis Drouot, Lucile, illus. (p. 1599)
Paradis, Anne, jt. auth. see Chouette Publishing Staff.
Paradis, Anne, jt. auth. see Publishing, Chouette.
Paradis, Anne & Johnson, Marion. Caillou: Le Jardin de Carottes. Sévigny, Éric, illus. (p. 308)
Paradise, Elizabeth. Lost Dreamer. (p. 1353)
Paradiso, Tapesh. Magical Adventures of Mr. Balloon: Story Book. (p. 1379)
Parain, Nathalie. My Cut-Out Pictures. (p. 1536)
Parajes, Danilo, illus. see Roseberg, Anders.
Paramonova, Lea, illus. see Wildsmith, Sarah.
Paramore, Leslie, illus. see The Sparkler Princess.
Paramore, Scott, ed. see The Sparkler Princess.
Paranjpye, Kesava Balakrishna. Vikramorvasiyam: With Sanskrit Text, English Translation, Copious Notes, & an Elaborate Introduction (Classic Reprint) (p. 2358)
—Vikramorvasíyam: With Sanskrit Text, English Translation, Copious Notes, & an Elaborate Introduction (Classic Reprint) (p. 2358)
Paranuzzi, Fred. Babak the Beetle. Prigent, Andree, illus. (p. 147)
Paraschiv, Doina, illus. see Parr, Susan Sherwood.
Paraschiv, Doina, illus. see Wilhoite, Joellen.
Parasciuc, Natalia. Beaverlini & Rodney Are Having Fun! (p. 186)
Parashar, Sujata. In Pursuit of Ecstasy. (p. 1106)
Paraskevas, Michael. Mr. Moon. (p. 1519)
Paraskevas, Michael, illus. see Frost, Robert.
Paratore, Coleen Murtagh. Big Book about Being Big. Fennell, Clare, illus. (p. 217)
—Catching the Sun. (p. 344)
—Kip Campbell's Gift. (p. 1223)
—Mack Mcginn's Big Win. (p. 1372)
—Willa by Heart. (p. 2468)
Parbhoo, Bhijal. My Shining Little Star. (p. 1560)
Parchow, Marc, illus. see Golding, Elizabeth.
Parchow, Marc, illus. see Poitier, Anton.
Parchow, Marc, et al. Incredible Dot to Dot: Over 75 Timed Puzzles to Test Your Skills. (p. 1113)
Parcus, Stephanie. Jupiter Storm. (p. 1192)
Parcus, Stephanie, illus. see Helms, Melissa Hines.
Parda, Piotr. Graduation Day. Parda, Piotr, illus. (p. 875)
Pardee, Lucius Crocker. Folk of the Woods (Classic Reprint) (p. 757)
Pardew, David. Quincey's Questions: A French Bulldog Story. Suggs, Elizabeth, ed. (p. 1828)
Pardi, Charlotte, illus. see Ringtved, Glenn.
Pardo DeLange, Alex, illus. see Lachtman, Ofelia Dumas.
Pardo DeLange, Alex, illus. see Mercado-López, Larissa.
Pardo, Juan. When the Morning Comes Smith, Vernon, illus. (p. 2433)
Pardoe, Hiles. Gospel among the Boys & Girls: Dedicated to the Children at Chautauqua (Classic Reprint) (p. 870)
Pardoe, Julia. Flies in Amber, Vol. 1 of 3 (Classic Reprint) (p. 748)
—Miss. Pardoe's Complete Works: Comprising the Confessions of a Pretty Woman, the Jealous Wife, the Rival Beauties, the Wife's Trials, the Romance of the Harem (Classic Reprint) (p. 1479)
—Romance of the Harem, Vol. 3 of 3 (Classic Reprint) (p. 1900)
Pardoe, Miss. Flies in Amber, Vol. 3 Of 3: By Miss. Pardoe (Classic Reprint) (p. 748)
—Hungarian Castle, Vol. 3 of 3 (Classic Reprint) (p. 1052)
—Poor Relation, Vol. 1: A Novel (Classic Reprint) (p. 1774)
—Traits & Traditions of Portugal, Vol. 1 Of 2: Collected During a Residence in That Country (Classic Reprint) (p. 2276)
Pardoe, Pardoe. Thousand & One Days: A Companion to the Arabian Nights (Classic Reprint) (p. 2231)
—Traits & Traditions of Portugal, Vol. 2 Of 2: Collected During a Residence in That Country (Classic Reprint) (p. 2276)
Pardossi-Sarno, Beatrice. Petits Moments Littéraires: Édition Spéciale Partir en Livre 2018. Livio Editions, ed. (p. 1731)
Paré, Jean. Kids Cook! (p. 1214)
—Kids Do Baking: Sweet & Savoury Baked Delights (p. 1214)
—Kids Snack 'n Bake (p. 1216)
Paredes, Donna, illus. see Jackson, Amy.
Pareja, Alejandro, ed. see Doyle, A. Conan.
Parekh, Erin Nelson. Behowl the Moon: An Ageless Story from Shakespeare's a Midsummer Night's Dream. Amini, Mehrdokht, illus. (p. 193)
Parel, Gerald. Iron Man: Invincible Origins. (p. 1135)
Parent, Dan. Betty & Veronica: Best Friends Forever. (p. 209)
—Kevin Keller - Drive Me Crazy. (p. 1210)
—Your Pal Archie Vol. 1. (p. 2534)
Parent, Dan, illus. see Aguirre-Sacasa, Roberto.
Parent, Dan & Ruiz, Fernando. Die Kitty Die Hollywood or Bust. (p. 544)
Parent, David D. Drummers Forward! Marching with Angels: The Exciting Tale of a Drummer Boy Serving with the First Vermont Brigade & His Adventures During the Americ. (p. 606)
Parent, Meaghan B. Fall of Beth Anderson. (p. 700)
Parent, Nancy. Blippi: It's Time to Play: All-Star Reader Pre-Level 1. (p. 244)
—Blippi: It's Time to Play: All-Star Reader Pre-Level 1 (Library Binding) (p. 244)
—Disney Junior Fancy Nancy: The Case of the Disappearing Doll. (p. 560)
—Disney Junior Fancy Nancy: Chez Nancy. Disney Storybook Art Team, Disney Storybook, illus. (p. 560)
—Disney Junior Fancy Nancy: Mademoiselle Mom. Disney Storybook Art Team, Disney Storybook, illus. (p. 560)
—Disney Junior Fancy Nancy: Meet Fancy Nancy. Imaginism Studios, Imaginism, illus. (p. 560)
—Disney Junior Fancy Nancy: Nancy & the Mermaid Ballet. Disney Storybook Art Team, Disney Storybook, illus. (p. 560)
—Disney Junior Fancy Nancy: Nancy Makes Her Mark. Disney Storybook Art Team, Disney Storybook, illus. (p. 560)
—Disney Junior Fancy Nancy: Operation Fix Marabelle. Disney Storybook Art Team, Disney Storybook, illus. (p. 560)
—Disney Junior Fancy Nancy: School de Fancy. Disney Storybook Art Team, Disney Storybook, illus. (p. 560)
—Disney Junior Fancy Nancy: the Case of the Disappearing Doll. Disney Storybook Art Team, Disney Storybook, illus. (p. 560)
—Disney Mickey & Friends: Learning Time. (p. 561)
—Disney Mickey: No Nap for Pluto. Asaro, Massimo, illus. (p. 561)
—Disney: Minnie's Starry, Starry Night. Soffritti, Donald, illus. (p. 561)
—Disney Sweet Dreams, Mickey. Cangialosi, Ciro et al, illus. (p. 563)
—I Am Alexander Hamilton. (p. 1057)
—I Am Susan B. Anthony. (p. 1060)
—Mademoiselle Mom. (p. 1375)
—Operation Fix Marabelle. (p. 1666)
—Vampire for President. (p. 2346)
Parent, Nancy, jt. auth. see Golden Books.
Parent, Nancy, adapted by. Chez Nancy. (p. 367)
—DreamWorks Trolls World Tour: Magnetic Playset. (p. 603)
—DreamWorks Trolls World Tour: Music Speaker. (p. 603)
—DreamWorks Trolls World Tour: Together in Harmony. (p. 603)
Parent, Samuel, illus. see Quintin, Michel & Bergeron, Alain M.
Parente, Robin W., jt. auth. see Athans, Sandra K.
Parenteau, Shirley. Bears & Blossoms. Walker, David, illus. (p. 180)
—Bears & Boos. Walker, David, illus. (p. 180)
—Bears in a Band. Walker, David, illus. (p. 180)
—Bears in Beds. Walker, David, illus. (p. 180)
—Bears in the Bath. Walker, David, illus. (p. 180)
—Bears in the Snow. Walker, David, illus. (p. 180)
—Bears on Chairs: Book & Toy Gift Set. Walker, David, illus. (p. 181)
—Bears on Chairs. Walker, David, illus. (p. 181)
—Bears on Chairs/Osos en Sillas. Walker, David, illus. (p. 181)
—Dolls of Hope. (p. 579)
—Dolls of War. (p. 579)
—Ship of Dolls. (p. 2008)
Parenteau Shirley, Shirley. Bears in a Band. Walker, David, illus. (p. 180)
Parenting Press Staff & Cain, Janan. Asi Me Siento Yo. Canetti, Yanitzia, tr. (p. 125)
Paretzky, Leah. Doda Golda Comes for Pesach. David, Racheli, illus. (p. 574)
Parfitt, Rebecca, tr. see Luján, Jorge.
Parfumer, Clifford. Romance of Perfume Lands: Or, the Search for Capt. Jacob Cole (Classic Reprint) (p. 1900)
Pargment, Lila. Beginner's Russian Reader: With Conversational Exercises (Classic Reprint) (p. 192)
Parhad, Elisa. Los Angeles Is. Vidal, Alexander, illus. (p. 1349)
Parham, Donna, jt. auth. see Nuzzolo, Deborah.
Parham, Donna Potter. Discovering Sharks. Csotonyi, Julius T., illus. (p. 556)
Parham, Melanie. Sassy Feet. (p. 1936)
Parihar, Parul. Sociology of Conflict Studies: From Alienation to Alignment: a Situational Analysis of Kashmir Crisis. (p. 2054)
Parini, Jay, ed. see Frost, Robert.
Paris, American Art Association Of. Quartier Latin, Vol. 5: June & July, 1898 (Classic Reprint) (p. 1822)
Paris, David. Fantastic Kids: Young Artists (Level 4) (p. 707)
—History of Video Games (Grade 6) (p. 981)
—Niños Fantásticos: Jóvenes Artistas. (p. 1611)
Paris, Gaston. Lai de L'Oiselet: Poeme Francais du Xiiie Siecle (Classic Reprint) (p. 1239)
—Lai de L'Oiselet: Poème Français du Xiiie Siècle (Classic Reprint) (p. 1239)
Paris, Harper. Mystery Across the Secret Bridge. Calo, Marcos, illus. (p. 1568)
—Mystery at the Coral Reef. Calo, Marcos, illus. (p. 1568)
—Mystery in the Forbidden City. Calo, Marcos, illus. (p. 1569)
—Mystery of the Gold Coin. (p. 1570)
—Mystery of the Gold Coin. Calo, Marcos, illus. (p. 1570)
—Mystery of the Icy Paw Prints. Calo, Marcos, illus. (p. 1570)
—Mystery of the Mosaic. Calo, Marcos, illus. (p. 1570)
—Mystery of the Secret Society. Calo, Marcos, illus. (p. 1570)
—Mystery of the Stolen Painting. Calo, Marcos, illus. (p. 1570)
—Mystery of the Suspicious Spices. Calo, Marcos, illus. (p. 1570)
Paris, John. Kimono (Classic Reprint) (p. 1218)
Paris, John Ayrton. Philosophy in Sport Made Science in Earnest: Being an Attempt to Illustrate the First Principles of Natural Philosophy by the Aid of the Popular Toys & Sports. Cruikshank, George, illus. (p. 1735)
—Philosophy in Sport Made Science in Earnest: Being an Attempt to Implant in the Young Mind the First Principles of Natural Philosophy by the Aid of the Popular Toys & Sports of Youth (Classic Reprint) (p. 1735)
—Philosophy in Sport Made Science in Earnest, Vol. 1 Of 3: Being an Attempt to Illustrate the First Principles of Natural Philosophy by the Aid of Popular Toys & Sports (Classic Reprint) (p. 1735)
—Philosophy in Sport Made Science in Earnest, Vol. 3 Of 3: Being an Attempt to Illustrate the First Principles of Natural Philosophy by the Aid of the Popular Toys & Sports (Classic Reprint) (p. 1735)
—Sports & Amusements for the Juvenile Philosopher, Vol. 1: A Present for the Young (Classic Reprint) (p. 2088)
Paris, John Ayrton 1785-1856, jt. auth. see Routledge, Robert.
París, Mertxe, jt. auth. see Fatus, Sophie.
Paris, Morgaine. Composition of Matter. (p. 436)
Paris, Pat, illus. see Rottmann, Erik.
Paris, Stephanie. 20th Century: Race to the Moon (p. 2554)
—21st Century: Mysteries of Deep Space (p. 2554)
—Drag! Friction & Resistance (p. 592)
—Drugs & Alcohol (p. 606)
—Engineering Feats & Failures (p. 651)
—Forming a New Government (America's Early Years) (p. 768)
—Garden Invasion. (p. 809)
—Hablemos Claro: Alcohol y Drogas. (p. 908)
—Hablemos Claro: Fumar. (p. 908)
—Hablemos Claro: la Verdad Sobre la Comida. (p. 908)
—Ingeniería: Hazañas y Fracasos. (p. 1119)
—Pecos Bill & Slue-Foot Sue (p. 1711)
—Pop! Air & Water Pressure (p. 1775)
—Siglo Xxi: Misterios Del Espacio Sideral. (p. 2016)
—Straight Talk: Smoking (p. 2136)
—Straight Talk: Drugs & Alcohol (p. 2136)
—Straight Talk: The Truth about Food (p. 2136)
—Straight Talk - The Truth about Food (p. 2136)
—Technology Feats & Failures (p. 2197)
—Tecnología: Hazañas y Fracasos. (p. 2198)
—Vroom! Speed & Acceleration (p. 2368)
—¡Brumm! Velocidad y Aceleración. (p. 287)
—¡Fsst! Fricción y Resistencia. (p. 796)
Paris, Stephanie, jt. auth. see Herwick Rice, Dona.
Paris, Stephanie, jt. auth. see Kuligowski, Stephanie.
Paris, Stephanie & Kuligowski, Stephanie. 22nd Century - Future of Space (p. 2554)
Paris, Stephanie Herweck. Cells. (p. 350)
—Jonathan Clarkson Gibbs: Reconstruction Revolutionary. (p. 1177)
Paris, Val'rie. Fan de Bracelets Br'siliens. (p. 705)
—Fan de Scoubidous. (p. 705)
Parise, Anna Maria, ed. see Renzoni, Phil.
Pariseau, Chanel. Boy in the Blue Boots. (p. 269)
Parise-Peterson, Amanda. American Quarter Horses. (p. 73)
—Shetland Ponies. (p. 2006)
Parish, Alex. Peter & the Flying Sergeant. (p. 1728)
Parish, Annals of the. Stanley Buxton, Vol. 2 Of 3: Or, the Schoolfellows (Classic Reprint) (p. 2101)
Parish, Herman. Amelia Bedelia 12-Book Boxed Set: Amelia Bedelia by the Dozen. Avril, Lynne, illus. (p. 68)
—Amelia Bedelia 5-Minute Stories. Avril, Lynne, illus. (p. 68)
—Amelia Bedelia & Friends #1: Amelia Bedelia & Friends Beat the Clock. Avril, Lynne, illus. (p. 68)
—Amelia Bedelia & Friends #3: Amelia Bedelia & Friends Arise & Shine. Avril, Lynne, illus. (p. 68)
—Amelia Bedelia & Friends Chapter Book Boxed Set #1: All Boxed In [Books 1-4]. Avril, Lynne, illus. (p. 68)
—Amelia Bedelia Bakes Off. Sweat, Lynn, illus. (p. 68)
—Amelia Bedelia Bind-Up: Books 1 And 2: Amelia Bedelia Means Business; Amelia Bedelia Unleashed. Avril, Lynne, illus. (p. 68)
—Amelia Bedelia by the Yard. Avril, Lynne, illus. (p. 68)
—Amelia Bedelia Chalks One Up. (p. 68)
—Amelia Bedelia Chalks One Up. Avril, Lynne, illus. (p. 68)
—Amelia Bedelia Chapter Book #1: Amelia Bedelia Means Business. Avril, Lynne, illus. (p. 68)
—Amelia Bedelia Chapter Book 10-Book Box Set Avril, Lynne, illus. (p. 68)
—Amelia Bedelia Chapter Book #11: Amelia Bedelia Makes a Splash. Avril, Lynne, illus. (p. 68)
—Amelia Bedelia Chapter Book #2: Amelia Bedelia Unleashed (Special Edition) (p. 68)
—Amelia Bedelia Chapter Book #2: Amelia Bedelia Unleashed. Avril, Lynne, illus. (p. 68)
—Amelia Bedelia Chapter Book #3: Amelia Bedelia Road Trip! (Special Edition) (p. 68)
—Amelia Bedelia Chapter Book #4: Amelia Bedelia Goes Wild! (Special Edition) (p. 68)
—Amelia Bedelia Chapter Book #5. Avril, Lynne, illus. (p. 68)
—Amelia Bedelia Chapter Book #8: Amelia Bedelia Dances Off. Avril, Lynne, illus. (p. 68)
—Amelia Bedelia, Cub Reporter. Sweat, Lynn, illus. (p. 68)
—Amelia Bedelia Dances Off. (p. 68)
—Amelia Bedelia Digs In. (p. 68)
—Amelia Bedelia Gets a Break. Avril, Lynne, illus. (p. 68)
—Amelia Bedelia Gets the Picture. (p. 68)
—Amelia Bedelia Gets the Picture. Avril, Lynne, illus. (p. 68)
—Amelia Bedelia Goes Wild! (p. 68)
—Amelia Bedelia Hits the Trail. (p. 68)
—Amelia Bedelia Hits the Trail. Avril, Lynne, illus. (p. 68)
—Amelia Bedelia I Can Read Box Set #2: Books Are a Ball. Avril, Lynne, illus. (p. 68)
—Amelia Bedelia Is for the Birds. Avril, Lynne, illus. (p. 68)
—Amelia Bedelia Joins the Club. (p. 68)
—Amelia Bedelia Joins the Club. Avril, Lynne, illus. (p. 68)
—Amelia Bedelia Lost & Found. (p. 68)
—Amelia Bedelia Makes a Friend. Avril, Lynne, illus. (p. 68)
—Amelia Bedelia Means Business. Avril, Lynne, illus. (p. 68)
—Amelia Bedelia on the Job. (p. 68)
—Amelia Bedelia on the Move. (p. 68)
—Amelia Bedelia on the Move. Avril, Lynne, illus. (p. 68)
—Amelia Bedelia Road Trip! (p. 68)
—Amelia Bedelia Sleeps Over. (p. 68)
—Amelia Bedelia Sleeps Over. Avril, Lynne, illus. (p. 68)
—Amelia Bedelia Special Edition Holiday Chapter Book #1: Amelia Bedelia Wraps It Up. Avril, Lynne, illus. (p. 68)

P

—Amelia Bedelia Storybook Favorites: Includes 5 Stories Plus Stickers! Avril, Lynne, illus. (p. 68)
—Amelia Bedelia Storybook Treasury: Amelia Bedelia's First Day of School; Amelia Bedelia's First Field Trip; Amelia Bedelia Makes a Friend; Amelia Bedelia Sleeps over; Amelia Bedelia Hits the Trail. Avril, Lynne, illus. (p. 68)
—Amelia Bedelia Storybook Treasury #2 (Classic) Calling Doctor Amelia Bedelia; Amelia Bedelia & the Cat; Amelia Bedelia Bakes Off. Sweat, Lynn, illus. (p. 68)
—Amelia Bedelia Takes the Cake. Avril, Lynne, illus. (p. 68)
—Amelia Bedelia Talks Turkey. (p. 68)
—Amelia Bedelia Ties the Knot. (p. 68)
—Amelia Bedelia Tries Her Luck. (p. 68)
—Amelia Bedelia Tries Her Luck. Avril, Lynne, illus. (p. 68)
—Amelia Bedelia under the Weather. (p. 68)
—Amelia Bedelia under the Weather. Avril, Lynne, illus. (p. 68)
—Amelia Bedelia Unleashed. Avril, Lynne, illus. (p. 68)
—Amelia Bedelia's Backpack Bundle. Sweat, Lynn, illus. (p. 68)
—Amelia Bedelia's First Apple Pie. Avril, Lynne, illus. (p. 68)
—Amelia Bedelia's First Day of School. Avril, Lynne, illus. (p. 68)
—Amelia Bedelia's First Day of School Holiday. Avril, Lynne, illus. (p. 68)
—Amelia Bedelia's First Field Trip. (p. 68)
—Amelia Bedelia's First Field Trip. Avril, Lynne, illus. (p. 68)
—Amelia Bedelia's First Library Card. Avril, Lynne, illus. (p. 68)
—Amelia Bedelia's First Valentine. (p. 68)
—Amelia Bedelia's First Vote. Avril, Lynne, illus. (p. 68)
—Go West, Amelia Bedelia! Sweat, Lynn, illus. (p. 849)
Parish, Herman, jt. auth. see Parish, Peggy.
Parish, Jessica. Adventures of Pugalugs: Walkies. (p. 27)
—Adventures of Pugalugs: The Magic Bone. (p. 27)
—Adventures of Pugalugs: Trick or Treat. (p. 27)
—Adventures of Pugalugs: A Christmas 'Furry-Tail' (p. 27)
Parish, Julia Royce. Diadama Van Dyne (Classic Reprint) (p. 537)
Parish, Peggy. Amelia Bedelia. Siebel, Fritz, illus. (p. 68)
—Amelia Bedelia 50th Anniversary Library: Amelia Bedelia, Amelia Bedelia & the Surprise Shower, & Play Ball, Amelia Bedelia. (p. 68)
—Amelia Bedelia I Can Read Box Set #1: Amelia Bedelia Hit the Books Siebel, Fritz et al, illus. (p. 68)
Parish, Peggy & Parish, Herman. Amelia Bedelia Celebration: Four Stories Tall. Sweat, Lynn & Siebel, Fritz, illus. (p. 68)
Parish, Steve, illus. see Johnson, Rebecca.
Parish, W. D. Dictionary of the Kentish Dialect & Provincialisms: In Use in the County of Kent (Classic Reprint) (p. 542)
—Dictionary Sussex Dialect: And Collection of Provincialisms in Use in the County of Sussex (Classic Reprint) (p. 542)
Parish, William Douglas. Dictionary of the Kentish Dialect & Provincialisms in Use in the County of Kent (Classic Reprint) (p. 542)
Parisi, Andrea, illus. see Millici, Nate.
Parisi, Anthony. Baby Harp Seal's Snowy Day. (p. 151)
—First Look at Space. Pindroh, Paula, illus. (p. 738)
Parisi, Anthony, ed. see Galvin, Laura Gates.
Parisi, Anthony, illus. see Pollock, Hal.
Parisi, Mark. Marty Pants #1: Do Not Open! Parisi, Mark, illus. (p. 1411)
—Marty Pants #2: Keep Your Paws Off! Parisi, Mark, illus. (p. 1411)
—Marty Pants #3: How to Defeat a Wizard. Parisi, Mark, illus. (p. 1411)
Parisot, Felicite, illus. see Perry, Caroline.
Park, Alexander. Thunderbolts & the Circle of Power. (p. 2238)
Park, Angeland. Wherever I Am, I Am Home. (p. 2441)
Park, Barbara. Back to School with Junie B. 6-Copy Clip Strip Summer 2019 (p. 155)
—Junie B. Jones #25: Jingle Bells, Batman Smells! (P. S. So Does May.) Brunkus, Denise, illus. (p. 1190)
—Junie B. Jones #27: Dumb Bunny. Brunkus, Denise, illus. (p. 1190)
—Junie B. Jones #28: Turkeys We Have Loved & Eaten (and Other Thankful Stuff) Brunkus, Denise, illus. (p. 1190)
—Junie B. Jones Books in a Bus: Books 1-28 Brunkus, Denise, illus. (p. 1190)
—Junie B. Jones Complete Kindergarten Collection: Books 1-17 with Paper Dolls in Boxed Set Brunkus, Denise, illus. (p. 1190)
—Junie B. Jones Deluxe Holiday Edition: Jingle Bells, Batman Smells! (P. S. So Does May.) Brunkus, Denise, illus. (p. 1190)
—Junie B. Jones Holiday 6-Copy Clip Strip Fall 2019 (p. 1190)
—Junie B. Jones Springtime Ha-Ha-Holiday Set: Junie B. Jones & the Mushy Gushy Valentime; Junie B. Jones Dumb Bunny; Junie B. Jones Is a Graduation Girl (p. 1190)
—Junie B. My Valentime. Brunkus, Denise, illus. (p. 1190)
—Junie B. 's Essential Survival Guide to School (Junie B. Jones) Brunkus, Denise, illus. (p. 1190)
—Junie B.'s These Puzzles Hurt My Brain! Brunkus, Denise, illus. (p. 1190)
—Psssst! It's Me ... the Bogeyman. Kroninger, Stephen, illus. (p. 1809)
—Turkeys We Have Loved & Eaten (and Other Thankful Stuff) (p. 2300)
Park, Charlie, ed. see Bauer, Susan Wise.
Park, Christian J., tr. see Chul-heon, Chung.
Park, Christian J., tr. see Hye-sook, Lee.
Park, Christian J., tr. see Seong-eun, Kim.
Park, Darcie, illus. see Coerr, Eleanor.
Park, Devin & Lee, Claudia. Howl Michigan. (p. 1047)
Park, Dorothea. Here Comes the Postman (Classic Reprint) (p. 958)
Park, Frances & Park, Ginger. My Freedom Trip: A Child's Escape from North Korea. Jenkins, Debra Reid, illus. (p. 1547)
—My Freedom Trip. (p. 1547)
Park, Hannah & Park, Annette. Sylvester the Snail. (p. 2173)
Park, Hyeondo, illus. see Croall, Marie P.
Park, Hyeondo, illus. see Teer, Samuel.
Park, Hyeonhee. Classic Is My Power: Reading Soceity. (p. 400)
Park, J. G. Language Lessons: Including Composition & Inductive Grammar (Classic Reprint) (p. 1243)
Park, James F. Alfie. (p. 43)
—Charlie. (p. 359)
—Danny. (p. 503)
—Nicki. (p. 1604)
Park, Janie Jaehyun, illus. see Haskins, Jim & Benson, Kathleen.
Park, Jennifer. Shadows We Know by Heart. (p. 1998)
Park, JinJun, creator. Raiders, Vol. 2 (p. 1835)
Park, John Edgar. Children's Bread (Classic Reprint) (p. 373)
—How I Spent My Million: A Christmas Story (Classic Reprint) (p. 1032)
—Return of Our Boys: A Tale of Great Days (Classic Reprint) (p. 1871)
Park, Jong Jin. There Is Hair on the Snake's Head. (p. 2216)
Park, Julia E. Trail for the Murder of the King's English (Classic Reprint) (p. 2274)
Park, Jung-a, illus. see Subramaniam, Manasi.
Park, Junghwa, illus. see Danis, Naomi.
Park, Kathy, illus. see Lee, Jc.
Park, Ken. Americans from India & Other South Asian Countries. (p. 75)
Park, Keun, illus. see Kim, Cecil.
Park, Kyubyong & Amen, Henry J. My First Book of Korean Words: An ABC Rhyming Book of Korean Language & Culture. Padron, Aya, illus. (p. 1542)
Park, Laura, illus. see Eggers, Dave.
Park, Laura, illus. see Grabenstein, Chris & Patterson, James.
Park, Laura, illus. see Grabenstein, Chris.
Park, Laura, illus. see Patterson, James & Grabenstein, Chris.
Park, Laura, illus. see Patterson, James & Tebbetts, Chris.
Park, Laura, illus. see Patterson, James & Tebbetts, Christopher.
Park, Laura, illus. see Rex, Adam.
Park, Laura, illus. see Tebbetts, Chris & Patterson, James.
Park, Linda Sue. Archer's Quest. (p. 110)
—Firekeeper's Son. Downing, Julie, illus. (p. 734)
—Gondra's Treasure. Reinhardt, Jennifer Black, illus. (p. 861)
—Gurple & Preen: A Broken Crayon Cosmic Adventure. Ohi, Debbie Ridpath, illus. (p. 906)
—Keeping Score. (p. 1208)
—Kite Fighters. (p. 1225)
—Long Walk to Water: Based on a True Story. (p. 1343)
—Nya's Long Walk: A Step at a Time. Pinkney, Brian, illus. (p. 1632)
—Prairie Lotus. (p. 1785)
—Project Mulberry. (p. 1806)
—Seesaw Girl. Tseng, Mou-Sien & Tseng, Jean, illus. (p. 1985)
—Single Shard. (p. 2024)
—Storm Warning. (p. 2127)
—Tap Dancing on the Roof: Sijo (Poems) Banyai, Istvan, illus. (p. 2191)
—Third Gift. Ibatoulline, Bagram, illus. (p. 2222)
—Trust No One. (p. 2296)
—What Does Bunny See? (p. 2409)
—What Does Bunny See? A Book of Colors & Flowers. Smith, Maggie, illus. (p. 2410)
—When My Name Was Keoko. (p. 2432)
—Wing & Claw #1: Forest of Wonders. Madsen, Jim, illus. (p. 2473)
—Wing & Claw #2: Cavern of Secrets. Madsen, Jim, illus. (p. 2473)
—Wing & Claw #3: Beast of Stone. Madsen, Jim, illus. (p. 2473)
—Xander's Panda Party. Phelan, Matt, illus. (p. 2516)
—Yaks Yak: Animal Word Pairs. Reinhardt, Jennifer Black, illus. (p. 2517)
Park, Linda Sue & Knowlton, Ginger. Long Walk to Water: Based on a True Story. (p. 1343)
Park, Louise. Ancient Cities. (p. 80)
—Ancient Greece. (p. 81)
—Blood in the Arena: Gladiators of Ancient Rome. (p. 246)
—Extreme Fashions. (p. 686)
—Life in the Middle Ages. (p. 1292)
—Pharaohs' Armies. (p. 1733)
—Sinking of the Titanic. (p. 2024)
Park, Louise & Love, Timothy. Japanese Samurai. (p. 1160)
—Medieval Knights. (p. 1437)
—Roman Gladiators. (p. 1899)
—Scandinavian Vikings. (p. 1941)
—Spartan Hoplites. (p. 2075)
Park, Mac. Big Stink: D-Bot Squad 4. Hart, James, illus. (p. 223)
—D-Bot Squad Complete Collection (slipcase) Hart, James, illus. (p. 494)
—Deep Dive: D-Bot Squad 6. Hart, James, illus. (p. 524)
—Dino Corp: D-Bot Squad 8. Hart, James, illus. (p. 547)
—Dino Hunter: D-Bot Squad 1. Hart, James, illus. (p. 547)
—Double Trouble: D-Bot Squad 3. Hart, James, illus. (p. 589)
—Mega Hatch: D-Bot Squad 7. Hart, James, illus. (p. 1441)
—Sky High: D-Bot Squad 2. Hart, James, illus. (p. 2033)
—Stack Attack: D-Bot Squad 5. Hart, James, illus. (p. 2099)
Park, Meg, illus. see Rissi, Anica Mrose.
Park, Meg, illus. see Rylant, Cynthia.
Park, Mi-Ok, illus. see Roh, Grace S.
Park, Molly, illus. see Ly, Ginger.
Park, Noah. I Can Hear. (p. 1062)
Park, Peggy J. Is the Death Penalty Just? (p. 1137)
Park, Sang-Sun. Tarot Cafe (p. 2192)
—Tarot Cafe Manga Collection: Volume 1. (p. 2192)
Park, Scott, illus. see Hidalgo, Pablo.
Park, So Hee, creator. Goong, Vol. 13: The Royal Palace (p. 869)
—Goong, Vol. 14: The Royal Palace. (p. 869)
—Goong, Vol. 16: The Royal Palace (p. 869)
Park, Su-jeong, illus. see Yang, Dae-seung.
Park, Sun, illus. see Schmauss, Judy Kentor.
Park, Suzanne. Perfect Escape. (p. 1722)
Park, Tania. Road Trip. (p. 1888)
—Stalked. (p. 2099)
Park, Trip, illus. see Sayre, April Pulley.
Park, Trip, illus. see Stine, R. L.
Park, Ung Hyeon. Snow. (p. 2046)
Park, Wan-Seo. 7 Nyeon Donganui Jam. (p. 2549)
Park, Yeong Jin, illus. see Borin & Rin, Bo.
Park, Yeong-jin, illus. see Gam Do, Rin Bo.
Parke, John. Belonging. (p. 198)
—Far Away in the Misty Hills. (p. 708)
—Feather Beds Are Soft. (p. 717)
—Flood Fiddles & Fantasies. (p. 750)
—Freddy Bush Boy. (p. 781)
Parke, John G. Laws of the United States Relating to the Improvement of Rivers & Harbors from August 11, 1790, to March 3 1887: With a Tabulated Statement of Appropriations & Allotments (Classic Reprint) (p. 1253)
Parker, Al, illus. see Miller, Arthur.
Parker, Alana. Tess of the Locks. (p. 2208)
Parker, Amy. Biblia Del Plan Asombroso de Dios: El Precio Que Pagó para Ganar Tu Amor (p. 214)
—Christmas Prayer (p. 386)
—Five-Minute Bedtime Bible Stories. Carzon, Walter, illus. (p. 744)
—God Is Love. Kaulitzki, Ramona, illus. (p. 851)
—God Is with Us. Kaulitzki, Ramona, illus. (p. 851)
—How Big Is Love? (padded Board Book) Brookshire, Breezy, illus. (p. 1026)
—How Far Is Faith? (padded Board Book) Brookshire, Breezy, illus. (p. 1031)
—How High Is Hope? (padded Board Book) Brookshire, Breezy, illus. (p. 1031)
—How to Get a Daddy to Sleep Moore, Natalia, illus. (p. 1042)
—How to Get a Mommy to Sleep Moore, Natalia, illus. (p. 1042)
—My Christmas Prayer Endersby, Frank, illus. (p. 1535)
—Night Night Bible Stories: 30 Stories for Bedtime Allyn, Virginia, illus. (p. 1606)
—Night Night, Bunny Allyn, Virginia, illus. (p. 1606)
—Night Night, Daddy (p. 1606)
—Night Night Devotions: 90 Devotions for Bedtime Allyn, Virginia, illus. (p. 1606)
—Night Night, Farm Allyn, Virginia, illus. (p. 1606)
—Night Night, Farm Touch & Feel Allyn, Virginia, illus. (p. 1606)
—Night Night, Jungle Allyn, Virginia, illus. (p. 1606)
—Night Night, Mommy (p. 1606)
—Night Night Prayer Pedler, Caroline, illus. (p. 1606)
—Night Night, Pumpkin Allyn, Virginia, illus. (p. 1606)
—Night Night, Sleepytown Allyn, Virginia, illus. (p. 1606)
—Night Night, Train Allyn, Virginia, illus. (p. 1606)
—Night Night, Zoo Allyn, Virginia, illus. (p. 1607)
—Plans I Have for You Newton, Vanessa & Brantley Newton, Vanessa, illus. (p. 1756)
—Plans I Have for You Journal Brantley Newton, Vanessa, illus. (p. 1756)
—Thank You, God, for Grandma (p. 2211)
—Thank You, God, for Grandma (Mini Edition) (p. 2211)
—This Is the Day! Hernandez, Leeza, illus. (p. 2225)
—This Is the Day! / ¡Este Es el Día! Hernandez, Leeza, illus. (p. 2225)
—Tiny Blessings: for a Merry Christmas. Walsh, Sarah, illus. (p. 2248)
—Tiny Blessings: for All Seasons. Walsh, Sarah, illus. (p. 2248)
—Tiny Blessings: for Mealtime. Walsh, Sarah, illus. (p. 2248)
—Tiny Blessings: for My Family. Walsh, Sarah, illus. (p. 2248)
Parker, Amy & Edgson, Alison. Easter Prayer Touch & Feel (p. 620)
Parker, Amy & Powell, Doug. Big Book of Bible Questions. Tempest, Annabel, illus. (p. 217)
Parker, Amy & Walsh, Sarah. Tiny Blessings: for Giving Thanks. (p. 2248)
Parker, Amy Christine. Astray. (p. 128)
—Astray (Gated Sequel) (p. 128)
—Gated. (p. 811)
Parker, Andy, illus. see Goodhart, Pippa.
Parker, Anna. Sefer, 2013 (Classic Reprint) (p. 1985)
Parker, Anne-Marie. Rigby Reading Sails: Leveled Reader Silver Grades 4-5 Book 17: Mammals under Water. (p. 1881)
Parker, Annette L., jt. auth. see Parker, Keith W.
Parker, Ann-Marie. Rigby Reading Sails: Leveled Reader Emerald Grades 4-5 Book 1: Extreme Journeys. (p. 1881)
—Rigby Reading Sails: Leveled Reader Emerald Grades 4-5 Book 24: Amazing Predators. (p. 1881)
Parker, Ant. Amazing Airplanes Sound Book: A Very Noisy Book. (p. 62)
—Amazing Machines First Concepts: Colors. (p. 65)
—Amazing Machines First Concepts: Opposites. (p. 65)
Parker, Ant, illus. see Clarke, Jane.
Parker, Ant, illus. see Denchfield, Nick & Denchdfield, Nick.
Parker, Ant, illus. see Denchfield, Nick.
Parker, Ant, illus. see Mitton, Tony.
Parker, Ant, jt. auth. see Denchfield, Nick.
Parker, Ant, jt. auth. see Mitton, Tony.
Parker, Arnold. Ping-Pong: (Registered Trademark U. S. No. 36,854). the Game & How to Play It. (p. 1745)
Parker, Ashlyn. Ernie the Eraser. (p. 660)
Parker, Augusta Bethell Adamson. Among the Fairies (Classic Reprint) (p. 76)
Parker, Aura. Twig. Parker, Aura, illus. (p. 2304)
Parker, Ben. My First Guitar - Learn to Play: Kids. (p. 1544)
—My First Keyboard - Learn to Play: Kids. (p. 1544)
—My First Recorder - Learn to Play: Kids. (p. 1545)
Parker, Bertha Morris. Matter, Molecules, & Atoms (Yesterday's Classics) (p. 1425)
Parker, Beryl. Exploring New Fields (Classic Reprint) (p. 682)
Parker, Beth. Tale of Tom Turtle (p. 2180)
—Tom Turtle Visits Grandma's Farm. (p. 2258)
—Tom Turtle's Fishing Tail (p. 2258)
Parker, Bridget. South Carolina. (p. 2068)
—South Dakota. (p. 2068)
—Tennessee. (p. 2206)
—Texas. (p. 2209)
—Vermont. (p. 2352)
—Virginia. (p. 2360)
—Washington. (p. 2381)
—Washington, D.C. (p. 2382)
—West Virginia. (p. 2402)
—Wisconsin. (p. 2477)
—Wyoming. (p. 2515)
Parker, Burford. My Dad at My Age: List of Rules. (p. 1536)
Parker, Buzz, illus. see Reger, Rob & Gruner, Jessica.
Parker, Caroline H. Our Friends, the Birds (Classic Reprint) (p. 1678)
Parker, Cassie. Dream BIG! Carr, Bethany, illus. (p. 601)
—Follow Your Rainbow! Carr, Bethany, illus. (p. 758)
Parker, Chance. Kid's Guide to Drugs & Alcohol. (p. 1215)
—Nutrition & Science. (p. 1632)
—Volcanoes, Earthquakes, & Tsunamis. (p. 2366)
Parker, Clara. Eventful Night: A Comedy of a Western Mining Town (Classic Reprint) (p. 669)
Parker, Cornelia Stratton. Working with the Working Woman (Classic Reprint) (p. 2496)
Parker, Curtis, illus. see Hyde, Margaret E.
Parker, Curtis, illus. see Hyde, Margaret.
Parker, Daniel. April. (p. 107)
—August. (p. 136)
—December. (p. 523)
—February. (p. 717)
—January. (p. 1159)
—July. (p. 1187)
—June. (p. 1189)
—March. (p. 1402)
—May. (p. 1429)
—November. (p. 1627)
—October. (p. 1636)
—September. (p. 1989)
Parker, Danny. día Perfecto. (p. 537)
—Parachute. Ottley, Matt, illus. (p. 1698)
—Perfect. Blackwood, Freya, illus. (p. 1722)
—Road Trip. Eckstrom, Nathaniel, illus. (p. 1888)
—Sarah & the Steep Slope. Ottley, Matt, illus. (p. 1935)
—Treasure Trove (p. 2282)
—Tree: A Little Story about Big Things. Ottley, Matt, illus. (p. 2283)
Parker, Danny & Bodman, Charlotte. Molly & Mae: A Friendship Journey. Blackwood, Freya, illus. (p. 1489)
Parker, Danny & Shield, Guy. Plastic Palace (p. 1758)
Parker, David & Lyon, Tammie. ¡Soy Optimista! Lyon, Tammie, illus. (p. 2070)
Parker, Derek. Children of Zone. (p. 372)
Parker, Donald. Aaron Donald. (p. 2)
—Alvin Kamara. (p. 60)
—Chris Paul. (p. 382)
—Giannis Antetokounmpo. (p. 830)
—James Harden. (p. 1157)
—Kevin Durant. (p. 1210)
—Khalil Mack. (p. 1212)
—LeBron James. (p. 1260)
—Max Scherzer. (p. 1428)
—Paul George. (p. 1707)
—Russell Westbrook. (p. 1917)
—Sidney Crosby. (p. 2015)
—Stephen Curry. (p. 2115)
—Todd Gurley. (p. 2255)
Parker, Dorothy. High Society: Advice As to Social Campaigning, & Hints on the Management of Dowagers, Dinners, Debutantes, Dances, & the Thousand & One Diversions of Persons of Quality (Classic Reprint) (p. 969)
—Men I'm Not Married To. (p. 1446)
—Men I'm Not Married to (Classic Reprint) (p. 1446)
Parker, Dudrea. Pig Iron (Classic Reprint) (p. 1743)
Parker, Ed. Discover Brazil. (p. 554)
Parker, Edward. Brazil. (p. 277)
Parker, Edward, photos by see Bowden, Rob.
Parker, Eliza. Coquetterie, or Sketches of Society in France & Belgium, Vol. 2 of 3 (Classic Reprint) (p. 452)
Parker, Elizabeth, jt. auth. see Blackstone, Stella.
Parker, Emma. Albert & the Dragon. (p. 40)
—All Aboard! (p. 48)
—Aretas, Vol. 1 Of 4: A Novel (Classic Reprint) (p. 114)
—Aretas, Vol. 2 Of 4: A Novel; in 4 Vol (Classic Reprint) (p. 114)
—Aretas, Vol. 3 Of 4: A Novel (Classic Reprint) (p. 114)
—At the Circus. (p. 130)
—At the Farm. (p. 130)
—Bath Time. (p. 172)
—Bill Hides Acorns. (p. 226)
—Billy & the Deep Sea Monster. (p. 227)
—Birthday Surprise. (p. 234)
—Blah the Bacteria. (p. 242)
—Butterfly on the Subway. (p. 304)
—Can Your Dog? (p. 319)
—Captain Gold. (p. 325)
—Carousel. (p. 333)
—Cat on the High Seas. (p. 342)
—Cecil the Caterpillar. (p. 348)
—Chuck the Chilli. (p. 389)
—Dancing Class. (p. 500)
—Davey Dory. (p. 510)
—Delia Dynamite. (p. 526)
—Fluffiest Chicken. (p. 753)
—Frog That Did Not Like Water. (p. 789)
—Fruity Girls. (p. 796)
—Granny Odd Legs. (p. 880)
—Groat & the Coat. (p. 897)
—Guerrilla Chief, Vol. 2 Of 3: A Novel (Classic Reprint) (p. 902)
—How Many Fish? (p. 1033)
—How Shall I Get to School Today? (p. 1035)
—Jack & the Beanstalk. (p. 1151)
—Karaoke Colin. (p. 1203)
—Lightning Game. (p. 1300)
—Little Red Riding Hood. (p. 1332)
—Lucky Pearl. (p. 1365)
—Lulu & the Seed. (p. 1367)
—Magic Show. (p. 1379)
—Magic Snow Globe. (p. 1379)
—Missy Hip Hoppo. (p. 1482)
—Monkey in the Tree. (p. 1493)
—Mr Grumpy Bunny. (p. 1518)
—Naughty Puppy. (p. 1582)

—Little Mouse's New Friend: A Sharing & Caring Storybook. (p. 1323)
—Rainbow Fairies. (p. 1836)
—Sleep, Little Pup. Parry, Jo, illus. (p. 2036)
—Under the Rainbow. (p. 2322)
Parry, Jo, illus. see Baxter, Nicola & Francis, Jan.
Parry, Jo, illus. see Baxter, Nicola.
Parry, Jo, illus. see David, Juliet.
Parry, Jo, illus. see DePrisco, Dorothea.
Parry, Jo, illus. see Freedman, Claire.
Parry, Jo, illus. see Grover, Lorie Ann.
Parry, Jo, illus. see Ranson, Erin.
Parry, Jo, illus. see Thomas Nelson Publishing Staff.
Parry Jones, Terence Graham, see Fairgray, Richard & Jones, Terry.
Parry Jones, Terence Graham, see Jones, Terry.
Parry, Launie, illus. see Hanson, Jean.
Parry, Michael. Nanobot. (p. 1574)
Parry, Richard. Empire's Rogues: Volume 1: a Space Opera Adventure Collection. (p. 645)
Parry, Richard Hawley Grey. Pilbara Contract. (p. 1744)
Parry, Rosanne. Heart of a Shepherd. (p. 945)
—Last of the Name. (p. 1249)
—Second Fiddle. (p. 1973)
—Turn of the Tide. (p. 2300)
—Whale of the Wild. Moore, Lindsay, illus. (p. 2403)
—Wolf Called Wander. Armiño, Mónica, illus. (p. 2483)
—Written in Stone. (p. 2514)
Parry, Thomas Wood. When Daddy Was a Boy (Classic Reprint) (p. 2429)
Parry, Tom. P. P. , or the Man & the Tiger: A Highly Popular Farce, in One Act (Classic Reprint) (p. 1690)
Parshley, Matilda Allen. Stories of Bird Island (Classic Reprint) (p. 2124)
Parsley, Elise. If You Ever Want to Bring a Circus to the Library, Don't! (p. 1092)
—If You Ever Want to Bring a Piano to the Beach, Don't! (p. 1092)
—If You Ever Want to Bring a Pirate to Meet Santa, Don't! (p. 1092)
—Neck & Neck. (p. 1584)
Parsley, Elise, illus. see Barnett, Mac.
Parsloe, Alismarie, illus. see Brown, Kathy.
Parson, Colin R. Gamer. Peake, Nicola, ed. (p. 807)
Parson, Kirk. Fast Game (Classic Reprint) (p. 713)
—On the Mountain Division (Classic Reprint) (p. 1655)
Parsonage, Max. Simple Introduction to Chemistry. (p. 2021)
Parsons, Alfred. Notes in Japan (Classic Reprint) (p. 1624)
Parsons, Ash. Girls Save the World in This One. (p. 839)
—Holding on to You. (p. 987)
Parsons, Azariah Worthington. Rhymes, Rambles & Reminiscences (Classic Reprint) (p. 1875)
Parsons Battles, Louise. Lola the Lizard & Friends. (p. 1340)
Parsons, Colin R. D. I. S. C. Direct Interface Shadow Control. (p. 494)
—Ghosted. (p. 829)
—Wizards' Exile. (p. 2483)
Parsons, Cornelia Mitchell. Quaker Cross: A Story of the Old Bowne House (Classic Reprint) (p. 1821)
Parsons, E. Bryham. Pot-Pourri Parisien (Classic Reprint) (p. 1780)
Parsons, Elsie Clews. Folk-Lore from the Cape Verde Islands, Vol. 1 (Classic Reprint) (p. 757)
Parsons, Elsie Worthington Clews. Folk-Tales of Andros Island, Bahamas, Vol. 13 (Classic Reprint) (p. 757)
Parsons, Francis. As They Looked to the Children (Classic Reprint) (p. 124)
Parsons, Garry. Wrong Kind of Bark. Donaldson, Julia, illus. (p. 2514)
Parsons, Garry, illus. see Bently, Peter.
Parsons, Garry, illus. see Clarke, Jane.
Parsons, Garry, illus. see Donaldson, Julia.
Parsons, Garry, illus. see Doyle, Malachy.
Parsons, Garry, illus. see Fletcher, Tom & Poynter, Dougie.
Parsons, Garry, illus. see Grabham, Tim, et al.
Parsons, Garry, illus. see Gray, Kes.
Parsons, Garry, illus. see Guillain, Adam & Guillain, Charlotte.
Parsons, Garry, illus. see Hawking, Lucy & Hawking, Stephen.
Parsons, Garry, illus. see Hawking, Lucy.
Parsons, Garry, illus. see Hawking, Stephen & Hawking, Lucy.
Parsons, Garry, illus. see Jones, Gareth P.
Parsons, Garry, illus. see Lacey, Josh.
Parsons, Garry, illus. see Mayfield, Sue.
Parsons, Garry, illus. see Whybrow, Ian.
Parsons, Garry, jt. auth. see Doyle, Malachy.
Parsons, Garry, jt. auth. see Gray, Kes.
Parsons, Gary, illus. see Agnew, Kate.
Parsons, George Frederic. Middle Ground; or Between East & West: A Christmas Story (Classic Reprint) (p. 1460)
Parsons, Gladys. Cub, 1923 (Classic Reprint) (p. 482)
Parsons, James F. Fun in a Vaudeville Agency (Classic Reprint) (p. 799)
Parsons, James Franklin. Original Humorous Readings (Classic Reprint) (p. 1671)
Parsons, John. Ten Quests. (p. 2204)
Parsons, Julie. Gissitback. Price, Guy J., illus. (p. 839)
Parsons, Karyn. How High the Moon. (p. 1031)
Parsons, Kitty. Ancestral Timber (Classic Reprint) (p. 79)
Parsons, Laura Matilda Stephenson. Scenes in the Union Depot: A Humorous Entertainment in One Scene (Classic Reprint) (p. 1944)
Parsons, Leif. Only Fish Fall from the Sky. (p. 1664)
Parsons, Lucy. Ten Step Guide to Acing Every Exam You Ever Take. (p. 2205)
Parsons, Margaret Colby. Red Letter Day Plays (Classic Reprint) (p. 1857)
Parsons, Mark Huntley. Road Rash. (p. 1888)
Parsons, Marnie & Parsons, Marnie. PB's Comet Tomova, Veselina & Tomova, Veselina, illus. (p. 1709)
Parsons, Martin. History Detective Investigates: Evacuation in World War II. (p. 977)
Parsons, Nell. Little Burma Girl (Classic Reprint) (p. 1313)
Parsons, Stephen & Emond, Wes Lee. Sounding Alphabet & Colouring Book. (p. 2067)
Parsons, Terry. Horace the Impatient Rain-Drop. (p. 1003)
Parsons, Wendelin Van Draanen. Secret Life of Lincoln Jones. (p. 1976)
Part, Michael. Balotelli - the Untold Story. (p. 162)
—Cristiano Ronaldo: The Rise of a Winner. (p. 475)
—Flea: The Amazing Story of Leo Messi. (p. 747)
—James the Incredible Number 10. (p. 1157)
—Luis Suarez - a Striker's Story. (p. 1366)
—Neymar the Wizard. (p. 1601)
—Thomas Muller der Strahlende Sieger. (p. 2229)
Part, Michael, ed. see Masannak, Joachim.
Parthav Basu Shergill. India's Trident: Policies for Progress. (p. 1117)
Partheniou Grasso, Stella. Five Busy Beavers. Battuz, Christine, illus. (p. 743)
Parthenope, Frances. Grey Pool: And Other Stories (Classic Reprint) (p. 896)
Partho Acharya. Kidzztale: Tales of Kings, Queens, Witches & Amazing Creatures of Virpur. (p. 1216)
Parthum, Tess, tr. see Admont, Shelley & Books, Kidkiddos.
Parthum, Tess, tr. see Books, Kidkiddos & Nusinsky, Inna.
Particelli, Brice, jt. ed. see Mazer, Anne.
Partil, Sravan. Measuring Quilts: Understand Concepts of Area (p. 1435)
Partington, Blanche. Hale's Magazine, Vol. 6: December, 1899 (Classic Reprint) (p. 910)
Partington, Charles Frederick, jt. auth. see Newton, William.
Partington, Deborah, illus. see Burns, Hazlette H.
Partington, Deborah, illus. see Raby, Charlotte & Guille-Marrett, Emily.
Partington, Violet. French Fables in Action (Classic Reprint) (p. 783)
—French Fables in Action (Yesterday's Classics) (p. 784)
Partis, Joanne. Oh, No, Bear! (p. 1642)
—Oh, No, Bear! Partis, Joanne, illus. (p. 1642)
Partis, Joanne, illus. see Nilsen, Anna.
Partlan, Iris. Ash's Outdoors Discoveries. (p. 125)
Partner, Daniel, ed. see Hurlbut, Jesse Lyman.
Partner, Junior, jt. auth. see Eric, Allan.
Parton, Daron. Alligator in an Anorak. (p. 56)
Parton, Daron, illus. see Budge, Donald.
Parton, Daron, illus. see Kelly, Deborah.
Parton, Daron, jt. auth. see Brasch, Nicolas.
Parton, James. Captains of Industry or Men of Business Who Did Something Besides Making Money. (p. 326)
Parton, Margaret. Laughter on the Hill (Classic Reprint) (p. 1252)
Parton, Matthew R. My Closet Monster Ate My Homework (p. 1535)
Parton, Paua, illus. see Parton, Paula.
Parton, Paula. China Dahl. Parton, Paula, illus. (p. 378)
—I Always Wondered. Parton, Paula, illus. (p. 1056)
—Room 17 - Where History Comes Alive - Missions. Parton, Paula, illus. (p. 1903)
—We Love Christmas! Parton, Paula, illus. (p. 2391)
Parton, Sara Payson. Fern Leaves from Fanny's Port-Folio (Classic Reprint) (p. 720)
Partridge, Anthony. Kingdom of Earth (Classic Reprint) (p. 1222)
Partridge, Elizabeth. Boots on the Ground: America's War in Vietnam. (p. 262)
—Marching for Freedom: Walk Together Children & Don't You Grow Weary. (p. 1402)
Partridge, Emelyn Newcomb. Glooscap the Great, Chief & Other Stories: Legends of the Micmacs (Classic Reprint) (p. 844)
—Story-Telling in School & Home: A Study in Educational Aesthetics (Classic Reprint) (p. 2135)
Partridge, J. Bernard, jt. auth. see Jerome, Jerome.
Partridge, Kenneth. Louis Armstrong. (p. 1357)
Partridge, Magda, illus. see White, Dave & White, Barbi.
Partridge, Rose. On the Farm. Cottage Door Press, ed. (p. 1654)
—Whiskers & Tails: Animal Flip a Flap Board Book. Cottage Door Press, ed. (p. 2442)
Partridge, William Ordway. Czar's Gift (Classic Reprint) (p. 493)
Partridge-Johnson, Tracy. Golden Telescope. (p. 859)
Partrige, Sydney. Rocky Section: An Australian Romance (Classic Reprint) (p. 1896)
Paruit, Marie, illus. see Nielman, Louison.
Paruzel-Gibson, Natalia. Something Lost Something Found. Ozunal, Berna, ed. (p. 2060)
Parva, Blondel. Blondel Parva, Vol. 1 of 2 (Classic Reprint) (p. 245)
Parvela, Timo. Bicycling to the Moon. Talvitie, Virpi, illus. (p. 215)
Parvensky, Mary T., ed. see Parvensky Barwell, Catherine A.
Parvis, Sarah. Taylor Lautner. (p. 2193)
Parvis, Sarah E. Ghost Towns. (p. 828)
Parys, Sabrina. Everything You Need to Know about Stress & Depression. (p. 674)
—Helping a Friend with an Eating Disorder. (p. 953)
—Road to Marriage Equality. (p. 1888)
Pasachoff, Jay M. Peterson First Guide to Astronomy. (p. 1730)
Pasachoff, Naomi. Reading & Interpreting the Works of T. S. Eliot. (p. 1846)
—Reading & Interpreting the Works of the Brontë Sisters. (p. 1846)
Pasachoff, Naomi E. Student's Guide to T. S. Eliot. (p. 2143)
—Student's Guide to the Brontë Sisters. (p. 2143)
Pasadena, Calif Basket Fraternity. Basket, or the Journal of the Basket Fraternity or Lovers of Indian, 1903 (Classic Reprint) (p. 170)
Pasagic, Sara. I Love Art. (p. 1068)
Pasamar, Concha, illus. see Lopez Avila, Pilar & Merlan, Paula.
Pascal, Carlo. Studii Di Antichita e Mitologia (Classic Reprint) (p. 2144)
Pascal, Coatanlem. Doli, Indienne Pikuni. (p. 578)
Pascal, Erinn. Marauder's Map Guide to Hogwarts (Harry Potter) Cann, Helen, illus. (p. 1402)
Pascal, Francine. Betrayed. (p. 208)
—Fearless: Fearless; Sam; Run. (p. 716)
—Fearless 2: Twisted; Kiss; Payback. (p. 717)
—Fearless 3: Rebel; Heat; Blood. (p. 717)
—My First Love & Other Disasters: My First Love & Other Disasters; Love & Betrayal & Hold the Mayo; My Mother Was Never a Kid. (p. 1544)
—Ruling Class. (p. 1913)
Pascal, Janet. What Is the Panama Canal? (p. 2416)
—What Was the Great Chicago Fire? (p. 2421)
—What Was the Great Depression? (p. 2421)
—Where Is the Empire State Building? (p. 2438)
—Who Was Isaac Newton? (p. 2451)
—Who Was Maurice Sendak? (p. 2451)
Pascal, Janet B. What Was the Hindenburg? (p. 2421)
—What Was the Wild West? (p. 2421)
—Where Is the Tower of London? (p. 2438)
—Who Was Isaac Newton? (p. 2451)
Pascal, Janet B. & Who HQ. What Is the Panama Canal? Foley, Tim, illus. (p. 2416)
—What Was the Great Chicago Fire? Foley, Tim, illus. (p. 2421)
—What Was the Great Depression? Putra, Dede, illus. (p. 2421)
—What Was the Hindenburg? Groff, David, illus. (p. 2421)
—What Was the Wild West? Marchesi, Stephen, illus. (p. 2421)
—Where Is the Empire State Building? Colon, Daniel, illus. (p. 2438)
—Where Is the Tower of London? Malan, David, illus. (p. 2438)
—Who Was Dr. Seuss? Harrison, Nancy, illus. (p. 2450)
—Who Was Isaac Newton? Foley, Tim, illus. (p. 2451)
—Who Was Maurice Sendak? Marchesi, Stephen, illus. (p. 2451)
Pascale, Estellon. Doux Comme? (p. 590)
—Joueur Comme? (p. 1179)
Pascale, Hedelin. Gros Mensonge de Nino - Petites Histoires Naturelles(le) (p. 898)
Pascale, Vdauria. En SC'ne ! (p. 646)
Pascaretti, Vicki & Wilkie, Sara. Super Smart Information Strategies: Team Up Online. (p. 2158)
—Super Smart Information Strategies: Team up Online. (p. 2158)
Pascascio, Alethea, ed. see Pascascio, Alexis.
Pascascio, Alexis. I Am Me. Pascascio, Alethea, ed. (p. 1059)
Paschall, Ann S. Friend's Family: Intended for the Amusement & Instruction of Children (Classic Reprint) (p. 787)
—Home Circle (Classic Reprint) (p. 996)
Paschen, Elise & Raccah, Dominique. Poetry Speaks Who I Am: Poems of Discovery, Inspiration, Independence, & Everything Else. (p. 1767)
Paschkis, Julie. Flutter & Hum / Aleteo y Zumbido: Animal Poems / Poemas de Animales. Paschkis, Julie, illus. (p. 753)
—Kalinka & Grakkle Paschkis, Julie, illus. (p. 1202)
—Magic Spell. Paschkis, Julie, illus. (p. 1379)
—Mooshka, a Quilt Story Paschkis, Julie, illus. (p. 1503)
—P. Zonka Lays an Egg Paschkis, Julie, illus. (p. 1690)
—Vivid: Poems & Notes about Color. Paschkis, Julie, illus. (p. 2364)
—Where Lily Isn't. Chodos-Irvine, Margaret, illus. (p. 2439)
Paschkis, Julie, illus. see Brown, Monica.
Paschkis, Julie, illus. see Engle, Margarita.
Paschkis, Julie, illus. see Fleischman, Paul.
Paschkis, Julie, illus. see Khan, Hena.
Paschkis, Julie, illus. see Larios, Julie.
Paschkis, Julie, illus. see Lord, Janet.
Paschkis, Julie, illus. see MacDonald, Margaret Read.
Paschkis, Julie, illus. see Paye, Won-Ldy & Lippert, Margaret H.
Paschkis, Julie, illus. see Wong, Janet S.
Paschkis, Julie, jt. auth. see Shannon, George.
PASCO Scientific Staff, prod. Advanced Biology. (p. 17)
Pascoe, Bruce. Sea Horse. (p. 1967)
Pascoe, Charlotte Champion. Walks about St. Hilary: Chiefly among the Poor (Classic Reprint) (p. 2372)
Pascoe, Charlotte Champion, et al. Walks about St. Hilary. (p. 2372)
Pascoe, Elaine. Animals with Backbones. (p. 96)
—Ecosystem of a Stream. (p. 624)
Pascoe, Elaine, ed. see Corwin, Jeff.
Pascoe, Jed, illus. see Kempton, Clive & Atkin, Alan.
Pascoe, Jed, illus. see Moses, Brian, ed.
Pascoe, Jim. Cottons: the Secret of the Wind. Arnhold, Heidi, illus. (p. 457)
—Cottons: the White Carrot. Arnhold, Heidi, illus. (p. 457)
Pascoe, Matt. Chaos Island: A Daisy Albright Adventure. (p. 357)
Pascoe, Pete, illus. see Bowater, Alan.
Pascoe, Sara. Being a Witch, & Other Things I Didn't Ask For. Lindsey, Alexander, ed. (p. 194)
Pascual, Dennis Mark. Adventures of Dj the Butterfly & Friends Series Presents Dj's Birthday Party. (p. 23)
Pascucci, Adele. Duck on a Dock. (p. 608)
Pascuzzo, Phil, illus. see Marlowe, Sara.
Pasek, Benj & Paul, Justin. Greatest Showman - Recorder Fun! With Easy Instructions & Fingering Chart. (p. 892)
Pasek, Joanna, illus. see Deats, Dorie.
Pasek, Joanna, illus. see Laipid, Yossi.
Pasek, Joanna, illus. see Lapid, Yossi.
Pasek, Joanna, illus. see Sanchez, Shayla.
Pashayan, Laura. Clover's Voice. (p. 408)
Pashilk, Meri. Pearl the Turtle. (p. 1710)
Pashley, Hilton. Sammael's Wings. (p. 1928)
Pashley, Sue-Ellen. No Ordinary Jacket. Baker, Thea, illus. (p. 1614)
Pasiadis, Vanessa. Don't Call Me Cookie. Lowenstein, Anna, illus. (p. 582)
Pasishnychenko, Oksana, illus. see Everett, Melissa.
Paskalenko, Olga. Selfish Elf. Cervadiku, Ylber, illus. (p. 1987)
Paskey Gill, Jacqueline, illus. see Spalding, Brenda M.
Pasko, Martin & Loughridge, Lee. Prankster of Prime Time Burchett, Rick, illus. (p. 1785)
Pasnak, William. Ginger Princess (p. 833)
Pasquali, Elena. Lion Nursery Bible. Lamont, Priscilla, illus. (p. 1306)
—Two-Minute Bedtime Stories. Smee, Nicola, illus. (p. 2308)
Pasquali, Elena, retold by. Story of the Nativity: Retold from the Bible. (p. 2134)
Pasqualotto, Chiara, illus. see Levine, Anna.
Pasqualotto, Chiara, illus. see Meyer, Jane G.
Pasque, Peter. Better Electronic Invention. (p. 209)
Pasques, Patrick. Savanna Animals. (p. 1937)
Pasquet, Jacques. My Wounded Island Watson, Sophie, tr. from FRE. (p. 1565)
—Our Environment: Everything You Need to Know. Tanaka, Shelley, tr. from FRE. (p. 1677)
Pasquin, Anthony. Eccentricities of John Edwin, Comedian, Vol. 1 Of 2: Collected from His Manuscripts; & Enriched with Several Hundred Original Anecdotes (Classic Reprint) (p. 622)
—New Brighton Guide: Involving a Complete, Authentic, & Honorable Solution of the Recent Mysteries of Carlton House (Classic Reprint) (p. 1591)
—New Brighton Guide. (p. 1591)
Pasricha, Neil. Awesome Is Everywhere. (p. 144)
Pass, Elizabeth. Lillian's First Year. (p. 1301)
—Making of Rosalie. (p. 1390)
Pass, Erica. Hooray for Dads! (p. 1000)
Pass, Stuart. Squiggy Family: Adventure of the Giant Magic Bulb. (p. 2094)
—Squiggys' Return to Earth. (p. 2094)
Passaniti, Connie. Fairy Garden Zodiac Adventure. (p. 696)
Passaris, Debra. Fairatella. (p. 695)
Passaro, John. Frederick Douglass. (p. 781)
Passchier, Anne. She'll Be Coming 'Round the Mountain. (p. 2005)
Passchier, Anne, illus. see Genhart, Michael.
Passchier, Anne, illus. see Gryta, Thomas.
Passchier, Anne, illus. see Houghton Mifflin Harcourt, Houghton Mifflin.
Passchier, Anne, illus. see Lambert, Nancy.
Passchier, Anne, illus. see Pitman, Gayle E.
Passchier, Maja. Abracadabra Strings - Abracadabra Cello (Pupil's Book + 2 CDs): the Way to Learn Through Songs & Tunes. (p. 7)
Passen, Lisa. Dweezil. (p. 611)
—Monkey Mountain. (p. 1494)
Passmore, Ace. Red Stocking Society (p. 1859)
Passmore, Ruth. Roary the Lion. (p. 1889)
Passos, John Dos. One Man's Initiation 1917. (p. 1660)
—One Man's Initiation 1917 (Classic Reprint) (p. 1660)
—Rosinante to the Road Again (Classic Reprint) (p. 1906)
—Three Soldiers (Classic Reprint) (p. 2235)
Passos, John Dos, see Passos, John Dos.
Passturner, Ambroes. Rex's Journey: Helping Children Understand & Cope with Emotions. (p. 1874)
Passudetti, Christopher. Being Sara. (p. 195)
Passy, Paul. Conversations Francaises: En Transcription Phonetique Avec Traductions Anglaises (Classic Reprint) (p. 446)
Pastan, Amy. First Ladies. (p. 737)
Pastars, Chris, illus. see O'Neil, Patrick.
Pasteau, Delphine. Francis of Assisi: Wolf Tamer of the Middle Ages. Costa, Violaine, illus. (p. 776)
Pastel, Elyse, illus. see Bergen, Lara.
Pasternack, Sofiya. Anya & the Dragon. (p. 104)
Pasternack, Susan, ed. see Mahony, Mary.
Pasternak, Boris Leonidovich. Adolescence of Zhenya Luvers (Classic Reprint) (p. 16)
Pasternak, Carol. How to Raise Monarch Butterflies: A Step-by-Step Guide for Kids. (p. 1043)
Pastis, Stephan. Beginning Pearls. (p. 192)
—Cat Stole My Pants. (p. 342)
—Croc Ate My Homework. (p. 476)
—Mistakes Were Made (p. 1482)
—Mistakes Were Made. (p. 1482)
—Mistakes Were Made. Pastis, Stephan, illus. (p. 1482)
—Now Look What You've Done. (p. 1628)
—Now Look What You've Done. Pastis, Stephan, illus. (p. 1628)
—Skip School, Fly to Space: A Pearls Before Swine Collection. (p. 2032)
—Stephan's Web: A Pearls Before Swine Collection. (p. 2115)
—Suit Your Selfie: A Pearls Before Swine Collection. (p. 2148)
—Timmy Failure: Mistakes Were Made. Pastis, Stephan, illus. (p. 2247)
—Timmy Failure: It's the End When I Say It's the End. Pastis, Stephan, illus. (p. 2247)
—Timmy Failure It's the End When I Say It's the End. Pastis, Stephan, illus. (p. 2247)
—Timmy Failure: Now Look What Mistakes Were Made. Pastis, Stephan, illus. (p. 2247)
—Timmy Failure: Now Look What You've Done. Pastis, Stephan, illus. (p. 2247)
—Timmy Failure: Sanitized for Your Protection. Pastis, Stephan, illus. (p. 2247)
—Timmy Failure: the Book You're Not Supposed to Have. Pastis, Stephan, illus. (p. 2247)
—Timmy Failure: the Cat Stole My Pants. Pastis, Stephan, illus. (p. 2247)
—Timmy Failure: the Maximum Greatness Collection. Pastis, Stephan, illus. (p. 2247)
—Timmy Failure: the Movie. Pastis, Stephan, illus. (p. 2247)
—Timmy Failure: We Meet Again. Pastis, Stephan, illus. (p. 2247)
—Timmy Failure: Zero to Hero (Timmy Failure Prequel) (p. 2247)
—When Crocs Fly: A Pearls Before Swine Collection. (p. 2429)
Pastis, Stephan & Schulz, Charles M. Happiness Is a Warm Blanket, Charlie Brown! Scott, Bob, illus. (p. 919)
—Peanuts Happiness Is a Warm Blanket, Charlie Brown. Scott, Bob, illus. (p. 1710)
Pastnor, Paul. Dorcas Society, & Other Sketches (Classic Reprint) (p. 586)
Paston, George. Career of Candida (Classic Reprint) (p. 329)

—Feed the Brute (Classic Reprint) (p. 718)
—Naked Truth: A Farcical Comedy in Three Acts (Classic Reprint) (p. 1573)
—Parents Progress (Classic Reprint) (p. 1699)
—Study in Prejudices (Classic Reprint) (p. 2144)
Pastor, Leanne. All the Things You Could Be. (p. 54)
Pastor, Luis, tr. see Nöstlinger, Christine.
Pastor, Terry, illus. see Bone, Emily.
Pastor, Terry, illus. see Hawcock, David.
Pastor, Tony. Tony Pastor's Complete Budget of Comic Songs: Containing a Collection of Several Hundred Original Local Lays, Eccentric Lyrics, Comic Songs, Humorous Irish Ballads, Patriotic Vocal Gems, Stump Speeches, & Burlesque Orations; As Written, Sung, & Delive. (p. 2260)
Pastrana, Miguel. Teotihuacanos, Toltecas y Tarascos. Torralba, Enrique, illus. (p. 2206)
Pastrovicchio, Alessandro, illus. see Ferrari, Alessandro.
Pastrovicchio, Lorenzo, illus. see Alvarez, Miguel, et al.
Pastrovicchio, Lorenzo, illus. see Ambrosio, Stefano.
Pasture, Henry De La. Catherine's Child (Classic Reprint) (p. 345)
—Cornelius (Classic Reprint) (p. 454)
—Grey Knight (Classic Reprint) (p. 896)
—Honourable Mrs. Garry (Classic Reprint) (p. 1000)
—Lonely Lady of Grosvenor Square (Classic Reprint) (p. 1342)
—Man from America: A Sentimental Comedy (Classic Reprint) (p. 1394)
—Master Christopher (Classic Reprint) (p. 1418)
—Michael (Classic Reprint) (p. 1457)
—Peter's Mother (Classic Reprint) (p. 1730)
—Tyrant (Classic Reprint) (p. 2311)
Pat-A-Cake. Llamaste & Friends: Being Kind Through Yoga. Tempest, Annabel, illus. (p. 1338)
Patachitra, Studio, illus. see Peterson, M. S. Natasha C.
Pataki, Allison & Myers, Marya. Nelly Takes New York: A Little Girl's Adventures in the Big Apple. Valiant, Kristi, illus. (p. 1586)
Pataky, Steven H. Appaloosa Horse Tales: Polka Dot & Spirit of Thunder. (p. 106)
—Benny the Beagle. Fox, Charlotte L., ed. (p. 201)
Pataky Tunde. Pamacs Mesek. (p. 1694)
Patarava, Tamar, tr. see Pere, Tuula.
Patch, Edith M. Bird Stories (Yesterday's Classics) Sim, Robert J., illus. (p. 230)
—First Lessons in Nature Study (Yesterday's Classics) Sim, Robert J., illus. (p. 738)
—Hexapod Stories (Yesterday's Classics) Sim, Robert J., illus. (p. 963)
—Holiday Pond (Yesterday's Classics) (p. 988)
—Little Gateway to Science: Hexapod Stories. (p. 1317)
—Little Gateways to Science: Bird Stories (Classic Reprint) (p. 1317)
—Outdoor Visits: The Lives of Animals, Insects & Plants in Nature, Illustrated for Children in Storybook Style. (p. 1684)
Patch, Edith M. & Howe, Harrison E. Outdoor Visits (Yesterday's Classics) Richards, George M., illus. (p. 1684)
—Through Four Seasons. Eadie, Eleanor O., illus. (p. 2236)
Patch, Edith Marion. First Lessons in Nature Study (Classic Reprint) (p. 738)
—Hexapod Stories (Classic Reprint) (p. 963)
Patch, Kate Whiting. Sensitive Child (Classic Reprint) (p. 1989)
Patch, Lisa. Tales of the Lush Green Woods. Patch, Michael, illus. (p. 2186)
Patch, Michael, illus. see Amdahl Elco, Anita & Weikert Stelmach, Katherine.
Patch, Michael, illus. see Patch, Lisa.
Patch, Richard. Trial of Richard Patch for the Wilful Murder of Isaac Blight, at Rotherhithe, on the 23rd of September, 1805, at the Session House, Newington, Surrey, on Saturday the Fifth of April, 1806 (Classic Reprint) (p. 2286)
—Trial of Richard Patch, for the Wilful Murder of Mr. Isaac Blight, September 23, 1805, at Rotherhithe, in the County of Surry: Before the Right Hon. Sir A. MacDonald, Knt. , Lord Chief Baron of His Majesty's Court of Exchequer, at the Sessions House, N. (p. 2286)
Patch, Sebastion, illus. see Thimble The Fairy.
Patch, Sophia, illus. see Dunbar, L. J.
Patcha, El & Odd Dot. Tiny World: Embroidery! Patcha, El, illus. (p. 2250)
Patchen, Jacob Paul. At Daddy's Hands: Courage Knows No Age. (p. 129)
Patchett, Angela. Dragon Cottage. (p. 593)
Patchett, Ann . Escape Goat. Glasser, Robin Preiss, illus. (p. 661)
Patchett, Ann. Lambslide. Glasser, Robin Preiss, illus. (p. 1240)
Patchett, F. Plane Fun. (p. 1754)
Patchett, Fiona. Children's Baking Kit. (p. 372)
—Little Sparkly Sticker Book. (p. 1328)
—Little Sparkly Sticker Book Christmas. (p. 1328)
—Ponies (First Sticker Book) Finn, Rebecca, illus. (p. 1773)
Patchett, Terry. Nation. (p. 1577)
Patchin, Frank Gee. Pony Rider Boys in New Mexico: Or the End of the Silver Trail (Classic Reprint) (p. 1773)
—Pony Rider Boys in the Grand Canyon: The Mystery of Bright Angel Gulch. (p. 1773)
—Pony Rider Boys, in the Ozarks or the Secret of Ruby Mountain (Classic Reprint) (p. 1773)
Pate, Alexs. Being You. Soud, illus. (p. 195)
Pate, Gail. Halo. (p. 913)
—Light. (p. 1298)
Pate, Ginger. Look Left, Look Right, Look Left Again. Pennell, Rhett / R., illus. (p. 1346)
—Would You Invite a Skunk to Your Wedding? Blanski, Maribeth, illus. (p. 2509)
Pate, Jeremy, illus. see Sutton, Jake.
Pate, Rodney, illus. see Miller, William.
Pate, Rodney, tr. see Miller, William.
Pate, Rodney S., illus. see Miller, William.
Pate, Rodney S., illus. see Patrick, Denise Lewis.
Pate, Rodney S., illus. see Walker, Sally M.
Pate, Traci. Prodigal Pups. (p. 1804)
Patel, Axay. Alex & the Horse. (p. 42)
Patel, K. T. Stop the World Spinning Away! (p. 2122)
Patel, Kalpna, illus. see Metcalfe-Chenail, Danielle.
Patel, Krina, illus. see Riley, Peter.
Patel, Reena. Jessica's Dream Job. (p. 1165)
Patel, Sanjay & Haynes, Emily. Ganesha's Sweet Tooth. (p. 808)
Patel, Sasha. Coral: A Shelter Dog Adventure Book #1. (p. 453)
Patel, Sharad, et al. Bear with Big Feet. (p. 180)
Patel, Shilpa. Billy & Bella Bongo's Us Adventure: Michigan. (p. 226)
Patel, Shobhna & Anon. Nutcracker: A Papercut Pop-Up Book. (p. 1632)
Patel, Sonia. Bloody Seoul. (p. 246)
—Jaya & Rasa: A Love Story. (p. 1161)
—Rani Patel in Full Effect. (p. 1841)
Patel, T. Dench. Light. (p. 1298)
—South African: Roamer. (p. 2068)
Patel, T. M. Immigrant: Stargazer. (p. 1100)
Pateman, Matthew. Julian Barnes. (p. 1187)
Pateman, Robert & Elias, Josie. Kenya. (p. 1210)
Pateman, Robert & Sullivan, Laura L. Denmark. (p. 529)
Pateman, Robert, et al. Belgium. (p. 195)
—Egypt. (p. 628)
Patenaude, Danielle. Caillou Goes Apple Picking. Sévigny, Eric, illus. (p. 308)
Patenaude, Danielle & L'Heureux, Christine. Caillou Tries New Foods. Dupuis, Karina, illus. (p. 309)
Patenaude, Jeremy, et al. Playful Puppy. (p. 1760)
Patent, Dorothy Hinshaw. Call of the Osprey. Muñoz, William, illus. (p. 311)
—Camas & Sage: A Story of Bison Life on the Prairie Wald, Christina, illus. (p. 313)
—Decorated Horses. Brett, Jeannie, illus. (p. 523)
—Dogs on Duty: Soldiers' Best Friends on the Battlefield & Beyond. (p. 578)
—Flashy Fantastic Rain Forest Frogs. Jubb, Kendahl Jan, illus. (p. 747)
—Homesteading: Settling America's Heartland. Munoz, William, photos by. (p. 998)
—Made for Each Other: Why Dogs & People Are Perfect Partners. Munoz, William, photos by. (p. 1374)
—Made for Each Other: Why Dogs & People Are Perfect Partners. Munoz, William, photos by. (p. 1374)
—Saving the Tasmanian Devil: How Science Is Helping the World's Largest Marsupial Carnivore Survive. (p. 1939)
—Super Sniffers: Dog Detectives on the Job. (p. 2158)
Patent, Dorothy Hinshaw & Young, Jeffrey. Dog on Board: The True Story of Eclipse, the Bus-Riding Dog. Munoz, William, illus. (p. 576)
Pater, Erra. Book of Knowledge, Treating of the Wisdom of the Ancients, in Four Parts: Shewing the Various & Wonderful Operations of the Signs & Planets, an Other Celestial Constellations, of the Bodies of Men, &C. ; Prognostications for Ever Necessary to Keep. (p. 259)
Pater, Walter. Imaginary Portrait (Classic Reprint) (p. 1100)
Paterakis, Paul. Henry the Friendly Shark. (p. 955)
Paterno, Heather. Pj Bird. (p. 1752)
Paternoster, G. Sidney. Motor Pirate (Classic Reprint) (p. 1512)
Paternoster, George Sidney. Lady of the Blue Motor (Classic Reprint) (p. 1238)
Paterson, A. B. Collected Verse of a B. Paterson, Containing the Man from Snowy River, Rio Grande Saltbush Bill (Classic Reprint) (p. 414)
—Man from Snowy River: And Other Verse (Classic Reprint) (p. 1394)
—Old Bush Songs: Composed & Sung in the Bushranging, Digging, & Overlanding Days (Classic Reprint) (p. 1644)
—Outback Marriage (Classic Reprint) (p. 1684)
—Rio Grande's Last Race: And Other Verses (Classic Reprint) (p. 1883)
—Rio Grande's Last Race & Other Verses. (p. 1884)
—Three Elephant Power & Other Stories (Classic Reprint) (p. 2232)
Paterson, Alex, illus. see Hemming, Alice.
Paterson, Alex, illus. see Joyce, Melanie.
Paterson, Alex, illus. see Palmer, Tom.
Paterson, Alex, illus. see Sky Pony Press.
Paterson, Alys, illus. see Sperring, Mark.
Paterson, Arthur. For Freedom's Sake (Classic Reprint) (p. 762)
—Gospel Writ in Steel, a Story of the American Civil War (Classic Reprint) (p. 872)
—John Glynn: A Novel of Social Work (Classic Reprint) (p. 1173)
—King's Agent (Classic Reprint) (p. 1222)
—Son of the Plains (Classic Reprint) (p. 2062)
Paterson, Diane, illus. see McElroy, Lisa Tucker.
Paterson, Huntley, tr. see Salten, Felix.
Paterson, Isabel. Magpie's Nest (Classic Reprint) (p. 1382)
—Shadow Riders (Classic Reprint) (p. 1997)
Paterson, John. I Am the Rain Paterson, John, illus. (p. 1060)
Paterson, John, jt. auth. see Paterson, Katherine.
Paterson, John B., Jr. & Paterson, John B., Sr. Roberto's Trip to the Top. Alarcao, Renato, illus. (p. 1891)
Paterson, John B., Sr., jt. auth. see Paterson, John B., Jr.
Paterson Jr., John B. & Paterson Sr, John B. Roberto's Trip to the Top. Alarcao, Renato, illus. (p. 1891)
Paterson, Judy. Scottish Folk Tales for Children. (p. 1962)
Paterson, Katherine. Bridge to Terabithia. Diamond, Donna, illus. (p. 280)
—Bridge to Terabithia 40th Anniversary Edition. Diamond, Donna, illus. (p. 280)
—Bridge to Terabithia: a Harper Classic. Diamond, Donna, illus. (p. 280)
—Brother Sun, Sister Moon. Dalton, Pamela, illus. (p. 286)
—Day of the Pelican. (p. 514)
—Jacob Have I Loved. (p. 1154)
—My Brigadista Year. (p. 1534)
—Night of His Birth. Aisato, Lisa, illus. (p. 1607)
—Preacher's Boy. (p. 1786)
—Puente a Terabitia / Bridge to Terabithia (Serie Azul) Spanish Edition. (p. 1811)
—Same Stuff As Stars. (p. 1927)
—Stubborn Sweetness & Other Stories for the Christmas Season. (p. 2143)
—Tale of the Mandarin Ducks. (p. 2180)
—Who Am I? Exploring What It Means to Be a Child of God. (p. 2446)
Paterson, Katherine & Paterson, John. Flint Heart. Rocco, John, illus. (p. 749)
Paterson, Kimberley. Frankie the Ferret. (p. 778)
Paterson, Peter. Behind the Scenes: Being the Confessions of a Strolling Player. (p. 193)
—Behind the Scenes: Being the Confessions of a Strolling Player (Classic Reprint) (p. 193)
paterson, richard. Mango Chutney. (p. 1397)
—Mango Chutney & the Accidental Dog Biscuit Invention. (p. 1397)
Paterson, Roz. Sadie & the Snow Globe: A Mermaid Adventure. Paterson, Roz, illus. (p. 1921)
Paterson Sr, John B., jt. auth. see Paterson Jr., John B.
Paterson, Wendy, illus. see Noakes-Dobson, Candice.
Paterson, Wendy, jt. auth. see Noakes-Dobson, Candice.
Paterson, William. Golden Rod, Vol. 41: Mar. , 1929 (Classic Reprint) (p. 859)
Paterson, William Romaine. Old Dance Master (Classic Reprint) (p. 1645)
Pates Wilson, Carmen. New Brother Trouble: A Fostering Love Series. (p. 1592)
Patey, Nicola. Aspireland & the story of George. (p. 126)
Path, Michelle. Corallai. (p. 453)
—Cowboy Who Was Scared of Horses. (p. 464)
—Kandy Hamm & the Lost White Owl. (p. 1202)
—Marty & Maggie's Day at the Rodeo. (p. 1411)
—Most Splendidly Spectacular Circus of Starzborough: The City of Smogg. (p. 1508)
—Phantasmagorical Phobias. (p. 1732)
—Xalien the Purple Alien: Xalien Visits the Farm. (p. 2516)
—Xalien the Purple Alien: Xalien Goes to the Beach. (p. 2516)
Pathak, Rupesh & Bhatia, Vaishali. 'I Did It' Mathematics 8 Primary Teacher's Manual. (p. 1064)
Pathak, Varun, illus. see Zorn, Frederick J.
Paticoff, Melanie. Sophie's Tales: Overcoming Obstacles. Vales, Chrissie, illus. (p. 2065)
Patience, John. Favourite Stories from Fern Hollow. Patience, John, illus. (p. 716)
Patients from East Tennessee Children's Hospital, illus. see McMillan, Jenna.
Patil, Amruta, illus. see Wolfe, Carolyn.
Patil Kumar, Neha. Look up, Little One. (p. 1346)
Patiño, Carlos. Dave Loves Chickens (p. 510)
Patino, Ernesto. Boy Who Wouldn't Smile! (p. 271)
—When I Grow Up. (p. 2431)
Patkau, Karen. Triceratops Stomp. Patkau, Karen, illus. (p. 2287)
—Who Needs a Desert? A Desert Ecosystem. (p. 2449)
—Who Needs a Jungle? (p. 2449)
—Who Needs a Prairie? A Grassland Ecosystem. (p. 2449)
—Who Needs a Reef? A Coral Reef Ecosystem. (p. 2449)
—Who Needs a Swamp? (p. 2449)
—Who Needs an Iceberg? (p. 2449)
Patkau, Karen, illus. see Beck, Carolyn.
Patkau, Karen, illus. see Fullerton, Alma.
Patkau, Karen, illus. see Gamblin, Kate Moss.
Patkau, Karen, illus. see Lottridge, Celia.
Patlan, Alyssa A., illus. see Banda, Rey A.
Patmore. Childrens Garland - Scholar's Choice Edition. (p. 374)
Patmore, Coventry Kersey Dighton. Children's Garland. (p. 374)
—Children's Garland from the Best Poets: Selected & Arranged (Classic Reprint) (p. 374)
Patmore, P. G. Chatsworth or the Romance of a Week, Vol. 1 of 3 (Classic Reprint) (p. 362)
Paton, A. A. Mamelukes, Vol. 1 Of 3: A Romance of Life in Grand Cairo (Classic Reprint) (p. 1393)
—Mamelukes, Vol. 2 Of 3: A Romance of Life in Grand Cairo (Classic Reprint) (p. 1393)
—Mamelukes, Vol. 3 Of 3: A Romance of Life in Grand Cairo (Classic Reprint) (p. 1393)
Paton, Chris. Embers of the Raven: A Fantasy Adventure Story from Greenland. (p. 641)
—Ravenmind: A Fantasy Adventure Story of Dogs, Wolves & Magic in the Arctic. (p. 1844)
Paton, Frank H. L. Lomai of Lenakel: A Hero of the New Hebrides; a Fresh Chapter in the Triumph of the Gospel (Classic Reprint) (p. 1340)
Paton, Maggie Whitecross. Letters & Sketches from the New Hebrides (Classic Reprint) (p. 1279)
Paton, Raymond. Drummer of the Dawn (Classic Reprint) (p. 606)
Patradol Kitcharoen, illus. see Alfred Sole.
Patri, Angelo. Child Training (Classic Reprint) (p. 370)
—Schoolmaster of the Great City (Classic Reprint) (p. 1947)
Patriarche, Valance. Tag or the Chien Boule Dog (Classic Reprint) (p. 2176)
Patricelli, Leslie. Baby Happy Baby Sad/Bebè Feliz Bebè Triste. Patricelli, Leslie, illus. (p. 151)
—Be Quiet, Mike! (p. 177)
—Best Buds under Frogs. Patricelli, Leslie, illus. (p. 205)
—Big Kid Bed. Patricelli, Leslie, illus. (p. 221)
—Big Little / Grande Pequeño. Patricelli, Leslie, illus. (p. 221)
—Bigger! Bigger! Patricelli, Leslie, illus. (p. 224)
—Birthday Box. Patricelli, Leslie, illus. (p. 233)
—Blankie/Mantita. Patricelli, Leslie, illus. (p. 243)
—Boo! Patricelli, Leslie, illus. (p. 256)
—Boo! / ¡Bu! Patricelli, Leslie, illus. (p. 256)
—Doggie Gets Scared. Patricelli, Leslie, illus. (p. 577)
—Fa la La. Patricelli, Leslie, illus. (p. 690)
—Fa la La/Tra-La-la. Patricelli, Leslie, illus. (p. 690)
—Faster! Faster! Patricelli, Leslie, illus. (p. 713)
—Faster! Faster!/Mas Rapido! Mas Rapido! Patricelli, Leslie, illus. (p. 713)
—Hair. Patricelli, Leslie, illus. (p. 909)
—Higher! Higher! Patricelli, Leslie, illus. (p. 969)
—Hop! Hop! Patricelli, Leslie, illus. (p. 1001)
—Hop! Hop!/¡Salto! ¡Salto! Patricelli, Leslie, illus. (p. 1001)
—Huggy Kissy. Patricelli, Leslie, illus. (p. 1048)
—Huggy Kissy/Abrazos y Besitos. Patricelli, Leslie, illus. (p. 1048)
—Mad, Mad, MAD. Patricelli, Leslie, illus. (p. 1373)
—Nighty-Night. Patricelli, Leslie, illus. (p. 1608)
—No No Yes Yes/No No Sí Sí. Patricelli, Leslie, illus. (p. 1614)
—Patterson Puppies & the Midnight Monster Party. Patricelli, Leslie, illus. (p. 1706)
—Patterson Puppies & the Rainy Day. Patricelli, Leslie, illus. (p. 1706)
—Potty. Patricelli, Leslie, illus. (p. 1781)
—Potty/Bacinica. Patricelli, Leslie, illus. (p. 1781)
—Quiet Loud / Silencioso Ruidoso. Patricelli, Leslie, illus. (p. 1828)
—Tickle. Patricelli, Leslie, illus. (p. 2239)
—Toot. Patricelli, Leslie, illus. (p. 2262)
—Tooth. Patricelli, Leslie, illus. (p. 2262)
—Tubby. Patricelli, Leslie, illus. (p. 2298)
—Tubby/Bañito. Patricelli, Leslie, illus. (p. 2298)
—Yummy Yucky/¡Ñam! ¡Puaj! Patricelli, Leslie, illus. (p. 2537)
Patricelli, Leslie, illus. see Holub, Joan.
Patricia, Geis. Illusions D'Optique. (p. 1096)
Patricia Hutchison. Forgotten History of Everyday Inventions. (p. 768)
Patricia, MacLachlan. Sarah, Plain & Tall. (p. 1935)
Patricia, Prevosti. Betsy Did It. Amber, Malone, illus. (p. 209)
Patrick. Coloring Book for 7+ Year Olds (Gingerbread Man & Houses) (p. 423)
Patrick, Alex, illus. see Fischer, Maggie.
Patrick, Bernard. Basic Kindergarten Lined Paper for Children Aged 3 to 6 (Extra Wide Lines) 100 Basic Handwriting Practice Sheets for Children Aged 3 to 6: This Book Contains Suitable Handwriting Paper for Children Who Would Like to Practice Their Writing. (p. 169)
—Coloring Book for 2 Year Olds (Fitness) (p. 423)
—Coloring Book for 2 Year Olds (Fruit & Vegetables) (p. 423)
—Coloring Book for 2 Year Olds (Healthy Living) (p. 423)
—Coloring Book for 2 Year Olds (Jigsaw Pieces) (p. 423)
—Coloring Book for 2 Year Olds (Monsters) (p. 423)
—Coloring Book for 2 Year Olds (Office) (p. 423)
—Coloring Book for 2 Year Olds (Parks) (p. 423)
—Coloring Book for 2 Year Olds (Playground) (p. 423)
—Coloring Book for 2 Year Olds (Vegetarian Food) (p. 423)
—Coloring Book for 3 Year Olds (Kites) (p. 423)
—Coloring Book for 4-5 Year Olds (Ancient Egypt) (p. 423)
—Coloring Book for 4-5 Year Olds (Ancient Greece) (p. 423)
—Coloring Book for 4-5 Year Olds (Baby Animals) (p. 423)
—Coloring Book for 4-5 Year Olds (Ballet) (p. 423)
—Coloring Book for 4-5 Year Olds (Bathtime) (p. 423)
—Coloring Book for 4-5 Year Olds (Birds) (p. 423)
—Coloring Book for 4-5 Year Olds (Cats) (p. 423)
—Coloring Book for 4-5 Year Olds (Christmas Stockings) (p. 423)
—Coloring Book for 4-5 Year Olds (Christmas Trees) (p. 423)
—Coloring Book for 4-5 Year Olds (Cookies) (p. 423)
—Coloring Book for 4-5 Year Olds (Dinosaurs) (p. 423)
—Coloring Book for 4-5 Year Olds (Easter Eggs) (p. 423)
—Coloring Book for 4-5 Year Olds (Emergency Services) (p. 423)
—Coloring Book for 4-5 Year Olds (Gingerbread Man & Houses) (p. 423)
—Coloring Book for 7+ Year Olds (Ancient Rome) (p. 423)
—Coloring Book for 7+ Year Olds (Animal Selfies) (p. 423)
—Coloring Book for 7+ Year Olds (Ballet) (p. 423)
—Coloring Book for 7+ Year Olds (Balloons) (p. 423)
—Coloring Book for 7+ Year Olds (Bonfire Night) (p. 423)
—Coloring Book for 7+ Year Olds (Breakfast) (p. 423)
—Coloring Book for 7+ Year Olds (Cakes) (p. 423)
—Coloring Book for 7+ Year Olds (Farting Animals) (p. 423)
—Coloring Book for 7+ Year Olds (Gingerbread Man & Houses) (p. 423)
—Coloring Book for 7+ Year Olds (Landscapes) (p. 423)
—Coloring Books for 2 Year Olds (Alphabet & Numbers) (p. 424)
—Coloring Books for 2 Year Olds (Animals) (p. 424)
—Coloring Books for 2 Year Olds (Birds) (p. 424)
—Coloring Books for 2 Year Olds (Birthday) (p. 424)
—Coloring Books for 2 Year Olds (Bows) (p. 424)
—Coloring Books for 2 Year Olds (Christmas Stockings) (p. 424)
—Coloring Books for 2 Year Olds (Christmas Trees) (p. 424)
—Coloring Books for 2 Year Olds (Dinosaurs) (p. 424)
—Coloring Books for 2 Year Olds (Easter Eggs) (p. 424)
—Coloring Books for 2 Year Olds (Faces) (p. 424)
—Coloring Books for 2 Year Olds (UK Road Signs) (p. 424)
—Coloring Books for 2 Year Olds (USA Road Signs) (p. 424)
—Coloring Books for 4-5 Year Olds (Bees) (p. 424)
—Coloring Books for 4-5 Year Olds (Chicks) (p. 424)
—Coloring Books for 4-5 Year Olds (Dancing) (p. 424)
—Coloring Books for 4-5 Year Olds (Frogs) (p. 424)
—Coloring Books for 4-5 Year Olds (Penguins) (p. 424)
—Coloring Books for 4-5 Year Olds (People Around the World) (p. 424)
—Coloring Books for 4-5 Year Olds (Professions) (p. 424)
—Coloring Books for 7 Year Olds (Ancient Egypt) (p. 424)
—Coloring Books for 7+ Year Olds (Cat Lover Phrases) (p. 424)
—Coloring Books for 7+ Year Olds (Chicks) (p. 424)
—Coloring Books for 7+ Year Olds (Flags Volume 1) (p. 424)
—Coloring Books for 7+ Year Olds (Hats) (p. 424)
—Coloring Pages for 2 Year Olds (Musical Instruments) (p. 425)
—Feuilles de Travail Pratique d'Écriture Manuscrite Pour les Enfants: 100 Pages de Pratique d'Écriture Manuscrite Pour les Enfants Âgés de 3 À 6 Ans: Ce Livre Contient un Papier d'Écriture Approprié Avec des Lignes Très Épaisses Pour les Enfants désireux D. (p. 721)
—Fiches de Pratique d'Écriture Manuscrite Pour les Enfants Âgés de 3 À 5 ANS: 100 Pages de Pratique d'Écriture Manuscrite Pour les Enfants Âgés de 3 À 6 Ans: Ce Livre Contient un Papier d'Écriture Approprié Avec des Lignes Très Épaisses Pour les Enfants Dé. (p. 722)

—Woods Runner. (p. 2492)
Paulsen, Gary & Paulsen, Jim. Road Trip. (p. 1888)
Paulsen, Haley, illus. see Crescitelli, Mike & Crescitelli, John.
Paulsen, Jim, jt. auth. see Paulsen, Gary.
Paulsen, Rosalie. My Ferrets. (p. 1540)
Paulsen, Ruth Wright, illus. see Paulsen, Gary.
Paulsen, Thomas and Oliver. Attack Baby. (p. 134)
Paulson, Arlie, illus. see Nix, Pamela.
Paulson, Elizabeth. Dead upon a Time. (p. 518)
Paulson, Ingrid. Valkyrie Rising. (p. 2344)
—Why I Loathe Sterling Lane. (p. 2458)
Paulton, Edward A. Madame Moselle: Produced under Direction of Chase & Everall (Classic Reprint) (p. 1374)
Paultyn, Tony, illus. see Edwards, Irene.
Paulus, Rajdeep. Most Influential Women in Politics. (p. 1508)
Pauly, Alphonse. Oeuvres de J. de la Fontaine: D'Après les Textes Originaux Suivies d'une Notice Sur Sa Vie Ses Ouvrages, d'une Étude Bibliographique, de Notes, de Variantes d'un Glossaire (Classic Reprint) (p. 1639)
Pauly, Robert J. Speech, Media, & Protest Lansford, Tom, ed. (p. 2078)
Pauly, Ruby. R. I. P. (p. 1829)
Pauncey, Campbell. Englishwoman in the Philippines (Classic Reprint) (p. 655)
Pauphilet, Albert. Queste Del Saint Graal: Roman du Xiiie Siecle (Classic Reprint) (p. 1826)
Paur, Carol L. Isasnora Snores. (p. 1138)
Pause, Michael. Animals Being Colors: An ABC Collection of Animals & Colors. (p. 94)
Pausf, Kelly. Vieille Dame et Ses Chats ^ la Conqute de la Fort. (p. 2356)
Pauwels, Jess, illus. see Dillard, Sheri.
Pauwels, Jess, illus. see Jason June, Jason.
Pauwels, Jess, illus. see Yanish, Brian.
Pavan, Toni. Egypt, Nubia, & Kush: Set Of 6. (p. 628)
Pavanello, Roberto. Dancing Vampire. Zeni, Marco, tr. (p. 500)
—Midnight Witches Zeni, Marco, tr. (p. 1461)
Paver, Michelle. Chronicles of Ancient Darkness #4: Outcast Taylor, Geoff, illus. (p. 388)
—Chronicles of Ancient Darkness #5: Oath Breaker. Taylor, Geoff, illus. (p. 388)
—Chronicles of Ancient Darkness #6: Ghost Hunter Taylor, Geoff, illus. (p. 388)
—Gods & Warriors. (p. 853)
Pavese, Candace. Caught in the Net. Holroyd, Geraldine, illus. (p. 346)
Pavey, Peter. One Dragon's Dream. Pavey, Peter, illus. (p. 1659)
Pavey, Sue. Where Are You Hiding Charlie Dog? (p. 2435)
Pavia, Audrey & Schultz, Jacque Lynn. Having Fun with Your Dog. (p. 940)
Pavick, Sandy Mitchell. Decorative Arts. (p. 523)
Pavitte, Thomas. Querkles: Animals. (p. 1825)
Pavlet, Terry, illus. see Reed, Gary.
Pavlic, Dusan, illus. see Ganeri, Anita.
Pavlic, Dusan, illus. see Stride, Lottie.
Pavlicin, Karen. Summer of Courage. (p. 2149)
PAVLICK, A. N. N. M., jt. auth. see Pavlick, Leon E.
Pavlick, Leon E. & PAVLICK, A. N. N. M. Foxes on the Ridge. Calvert, Lissa, illus. (p. 774)
Pavlicko, Marie A., jt. auth. see Farr, Michael.
Pavlou, Stel. Daniel Coldstar #1: the Relic War. (p. 502)
—Daniel Coldstar #2: the Betrayer. (p. 502)
Pavlova, Chrisi E. da. Animal Stories from Green Lane Estate: Series Six. (p. 91)
Pavlova, Chrisi É. da. Animal Stories from Green Lane Estate: Series Four. (p. 91)
—Animal Stories from Green Lane Estate: Series Three. (p. 91)
Pavlova, Chrisi E. da. Animal Stories from Green Lane Estate Series 5. (p. 91)
Pavlova, Vera, illus. see Johnson, Vincent L.
Pavlova, Xenia. Best Friends Forever. (p. 206)
Pavlovi?, Milan, illus. see Renaud, Anne.
Pavlović, Milan, illus. see Fagan, Cary.
Pavlović, Milan, illus. see Hartt-Sussman, Heather.
Pavlović, Milan, illus. see Huser, Glen.
Pavlovic, Milan, illus. see Fagan, Cary.
Pavlovic, Milan, illus. see Leatherdale, Mary Beth.
Pavlovic, Zoran. Changing Global Economy. (p. 356)
—Terrorism & Security. (p. 2208)
Pavlovic, Zoran, et al. Spain. (p. 2073)
Pavolich, Deborah. Last Chance for Outside. (p. 1247)
Pavolino, Amy. When I Grow Up. (p. 2431)
Pavon, David, illus. see Swift, Ginger.
Pavon, Mar. Clucky & the Magic Kettle. Brokenbrow, Jon, tr. (p. 409)
—Clucky in the Garden of Mirrors. Brokenbrow, Jon, tr. (p. 409)
—Clucky the Hen. Brokenbrow, Jon, tr. (p. 409)
—Could It Happen to Anyone? Brokenbrow, Jon, tr. (p. 458)
—Gallina Cocorina. Carretero, Mónica, illus. (p. 806)
—I Want to Be Philberta. Brokenbrow, Jon, tr. (p. 1085)
Pavón, Mar. Lovely Man. Vaz De Carvalho, Joao, illus. (p. 1362)
Pavon, Mar. Very, Very Noisy Tractor. Brokenbrow, Jon, tr. (p. 2354)
—Zaira y los Delfines. Coco, Cha, illus. (p. 2538)
Pavone, Bree. Drawing a Butterfly with Circles. (p. 598)
—If I Were a Butterfly. (p. 1091)
Pawelak, Lydia, photos by see Bowes, Deborah & Kain, Karen.
Pawl, Jacqueline. Merciless. (p. 1448)
Pawlak, Debra Ann. Bruce Lee. (p. 287)
Pawlett, Mark. Tae Kwon Do Handbook. (p. 2175)
Pawlett, Ray, jt. auth. see Pawlett, Mark.
Pawlitz, Gail E., jt. ed. see Engelbrecht, Edward A.
Pawlitz, Gail E. & Engelbrecht, Edward A., eds. Moses, Gods Chosen Leader: Drawn directly from the Bible. (p. 1507)
Pawlowska, Yoi. Year of Strangers (Classic Reprint) (p. 2519)
Paws, Inc., Inc., illus. see Nickel, Scott, et al.
Pax, H. H., illus. see World Peace, Metta & McBride, Heddrick.
Pax, Hh, illus. see McIntyre, Madison G.
Paxen Learning Staff. Career Pathways Doc Lit: Document Literacy. (p. 329)
Paxmann, Christine. Flower Power: The Magic of Nature's Healers. Hajek, Olaf, illus. (p. 752)
—From Mud Huts to Skyscrapers. Ibelings, Anne, illus. (p. 792)
Paxson, Jillip Naysinthe, told to. First Thirty. (p. 740)
Paxson, William Alpha. Buckeye Baron: A Rural Story of a Buckeye Boy (Classic Reprint) (p. 289)
Paxton, Alexander S. Memory Days: In Which the Shenandoah Valley Is Seen in Retrospection, with Glimpses of School Days & the Life of Virginia People of Fifty Years Ago (Classic Reprint) (p. 1446)
Paxton, Cameron L., illus. see Cromwell, Daisy.
Paxton, Jennifer Z. Anatomicum: Welcome to the Museum. Wiedemann, Katy, illus. (p. 79)
Paxton, Kirsty. Chalk Giraffe. Lotter, Megan, illus. (p. 354)
Paxton, Mary W. Miss. Elvester's Girls, Vol. 3 Of 3: A Novel (Classic Reprint) (p. 1478)
Paxton, Philip. Piney Woods Tavern, or Sam Slick in Texas (Classic Reprint) (p. 1745)
—Wonderful Adventures of Captain Priest: A Tale of but Few Incidents, & No Plot in Particular (Classic Reprint) (p. 2489)
Paxton, Tom. Marvelous Toy. Cox, Steve, illus. (p. 1413)
Payan, Gregory. Federalists & Anti-Federalists: How & Why Political Parties Were Formed in Young America. (p. 717)
Payan, Michael. In the Ring with Bret Hart. (p. 1110)
—In the Ring with Diamond Dallas Page. (p. 1110)
—In the Ring with Goldberg. (p. 1110)
—In the Ring with Kevin Nash. (p. 1110)
—In the Ring with Scott Steiner. (p. 1110)
—In the Ring with Sting. (p. 1110)
Paye, Won-Ldy & Lippert, Margaret H. Mrs. Chicken & the Hungry Crocodile. Paschkis, Julie, illus. (p. 1521)
Payen-Payne, V. French Idioms & Proverbs: A Companion to Deshumbert's Dictionary of Difficulties (Classic Reprint) (p. 784)
Payette, Eveline. Rock Mammoth. Simon, Karen, tr. from FRE. (p. 1894)
Payette, John C. Nitam: The First. (p. 1611)
Payette, Marie-Christine, tr. see Anderson, Teddy.
Payette, Marie-Christine, tr. see Jaadee, Kung.
Payette, Marie-Christine, tr. see Larsen-Jonasson, Theresa.
Payette, Marie-Christine, tr. see Locke, Kevin.
Payette, Marie-Christine, tr. see Spiller, Trudy.
Payette, Marie-Christine, tr. see Webstad, Phyllis.
Payment, Felicity & Nair, Shanti. Teddy & the Power Within. (p. 2198)
Payment, Simone. American Women Spies of World War II. (p. 74)
—Bass Fishing. (p. 171)
—Biologists at Work. (p. 229)
—Black Ops & Other Special Missions of the U. S. Navy Seals. (p. 239)
—Bryce Harper. (p. 288)
—Buck Leonard. (p. 289)
—Calvin "Megatron" Johnson: Superstar Wide Receiver. (p. 313)
—Career as a Plumber. (p. 328)
—Careers in Restaurants. (p. 330)
—Cool Careers Without College for People Who Love to Travel. (p. 448)
—Extreme Rock Climbing (p. 687)
—Friendship, Dating, & Relationships. (p. 787)
—Getting to Know Python. (p. 826)
—Kyle Busch: NASCAR Driver. (p. 1234)
—LeBron James. (p. 1260)
—Meghan Markle & Prince Harry (p. 1442)
—Pony Express: A Primary Source History of the Race to Bring Mail to the American West. (p. 1773)
—Robotics Careers: Preparing for the Future. (p. 1893)
—Saving the Endangered Blue Whale (p. 1939)
—Taking Your Band Online. (p. 2178)
—What Happens to Your Body When You Run. (p. 2411)
Payn, F. W. Secrets of Lawn Tennis. (p. 1980)
Payn, James. Beggar on Horseback, or a County Family (Classic Reprint) (p. 191)
—Bred in the Bone, or Like Father, Like Son: A Novel (Classic Reprint) (p. 279)
—Bred in the Bone; or, Like Father, Like Son. a Novel, Pp. 1-137. (p. 279)
—Burnt Million, Vol. 1 of 2 (Classic Reprint) (p. 300)
—By Proxy, Vol. 1 of 2 (Classic Reprint) (p. 305)
—By Proxy, Vol. 2 of 2 (Classic Reprint) (p. 305)
—Canon's Ward, Vol. 3 of 3 (Classic Reprint) (p. 322)
—Carlyon's Year: A Novel (Classic Reprint) (p. 332)
—Carlyon's Year. (p. 332)
—Cecilis Tryst, Vol. 2 of 3 (Classic Reprint) (p. 348)
—Cecil's Tryst: A Novel (Classic Reprint) (p. 348)
—Cecil's Tryst. (p. 348)
—Cecil's Tryst, Vol. 1 Of 3: A Novel (Classic Reprint) (p. 348)
—Clyffards of Clyffe (Classic Reprint) (p. 409)
—Confidential Agent, Vol. 1 of 2 (Classic Reprint) (p. 439)
—Cornish Harbour (Classic Reprint) (p. 455)
—Eavesdropper: An Unparalleled Experience (Classic Reprint) (p. 622)
—Fallen Fortunes: A Novel (Classic Reprint) (p. 700)
—Fallen Fortunes, Vol. 1 Of 3: A Novel (Classic Reprint) (p. 700)
—Fallen Fortunes, Vol. 2: A Novel (Classic Reprint) (p. 700)
—Family Scapegrace, or Richard Arbour (Classic Reprint) (p. 703)
—For Cash Only, Vol. 1 Of 3: A Novel (Classic Reprint) (p. 762)
—Glow-Worm Tales: Second Series (Classic Reprint) (p. 845)
—Grape from a Thorn (Classic Reprint) (p. 880)
—Gwendoline's Harvest: A Novel (Classic Reprint) (p. 907)
—Gwendoline's Harvest. (p. 907)
—Halves, Vol. 1: A Novel (Classic Reprint) (p. 913)
—Halves, Vol. 2 Of 3: A Novel (Classic Reprint) (p. 913)
—Halves, Vol. 3 Of 3: And Other Tales (Classic Reprint) (p. 913)
—Heir of the Ages (Classic Reprint) (p. 948)
—Heir of the Ages, Vol. 1 of 3 (Classic Reprint) (p. 948)
—Heir of the Ages, Vol. 2 (Classic Reprint) (p. 948)
—Holiday Tasks: Being Essays Written in Vacation Time (Classic Reprint) (p. 988)
—In Market Overt: A Novel (Classic Reprint) (p. 1106)
—Kit: A Memory, Vol. 1 of 3 (Classic Reprint) (p. 1225)
—Kit, Vol. 2 Of 3: A Memory (Classic Reprint) (p. 1225)
—Leaves from Lakeland (Classic Reprint) (p. 1259)
—Less Black Than We're Painted: A Novel (Classic Reprint) (p. 1268)
—Less Black Than We're Painted, Vol. 1 of 3 (Classic Reprint) (p. 1268)
—Lights & Shadows of London Life, Vol. 1 of 2 (Classic Reprint) (p. 1300)
—Lost Sir Massingberd: A Romance of Real Life (Classic Reprint) (p. 1355)
—Lost Sir Massingberd. (p. 1355)
—Married Beneath Him: A Novel (Classic Reprint) (p. 1408)
—Mirk Abbey, Vol. 3 of 3 (Classic Reprint) (p. 1475)
—Modern Dick Whittington: Or a Patron of Letters (Classic Reprint) (p. 1486)
—Modern Dick Whittington, Vol. 1: Or a Patron of Letters (Classic Reprint) (p. 1486)
—Modern Dick Whittington, Vol. 2 Of 2: Or a Patron of Letters (Classic Reprint) (p. 1486)
—Murphy's Master: And Other Stories (Classic Reprint) (p. 1527)
—Mystery of Mirbridge (Classic Reprint) (p. 1569)
—People, Places & Things (Classic Reprint) (p. 1719)
—Prince of the Blood (Classic Reprint) (p. 1794)
—Prince of the Blood, Vol. 1: A Novel (Classic Reprint) (p. 1794)
—Prince of the Blood, Vol. 3 Of 3: A Novel (Classic Reprint) (p. 1794)
—Stumble on the Threshold, Vol. 1 of 2 (Classic Reprint) (p. 2144)
—Talk of the Town (Classic Reprint) (p. 2187)
—Talk of the Town, Vol. 1 of 2 (Classic Reprint) (p. 2187)
—Thicker Than Water: A Novel (Classic Reprint) (p. 2219)
—Thicker Than Water, Vol. 1 of 3 (Classic Reprint) (p. 2220)
—Under One Roof: An Episode in a Family History (Classic Reprint) (p. 2321)
—Under One Roof, Vol. 1 Of 3: An Episode in a Family History (Classic Reprint) (p. 2321)
—Under One Roof, Vol. 3: An Episode in a Family History (Classic Reprint) (p. 2321)
—Walter's Word, Vol. 1 Of 3: A Novel (Classic Reprint) (p. 2374)
—What He Cost Her, Vol. 1 of 3 (Classic Reprint) (p. 2412)
—Woman's Vengeance: A Novel (Classic Reprint) (p. 2486)
—Woman's Vengeance. (p. 2486)
—Woman's Vengeance, Vol. 2 Of 3: A Novel (Classic Reprint) (p. 2486)
—Word & the Will, Vol. 1 Of 2: A Novel (Classic Reprint) (p. 2493)
Payne, Anna. Extra Sepcial: For When Someone You Love Dies. (p. 685)
Payne, C. C. Lula Bell on Geekdom, Freakdom, & the Challenges of Bad Hair (p. 1367)
—Thing about Leftovers. (p. 2220)
Payne, C. F., illus. see Bildner, Phil.
Payne, C. F., illus. see Bunting, Eve.
Payne, C. F., illus. see Frederick, Heather Vogel.
Payne, C. F., illus. see Howe, James.
Payne, C. F., illus. see Kelly, Mark.
Payne, C. F., illus. see Lithgow, John.
Payne, C. F., illus. see Macy, Sue.
Payne, C. F., illus. see Moss, Marissa.
Payne, C. F., illus. see Nash, Ogden.
Payne, C. F., illus. see Rappaport, Doreen.
Payne, C. F., illus. see Thayer, Ernest L.
Payne, C. F., illus. see Winter, Jonah.
Payne, C. F., illus. see Yolen, Jane.
Payne, C. H. McGill Outlook Christmas, Vol. 8: December 18, 1905 (Classic Reprint) (p. 1432)
Payne, Dutton. Mistress Penwick (Classic Reprint) (p. 1483)
Payne, Ed & Johnson, Vail. Vail's Tales. Sekulic, Britt, illus. (p. 2343)
Payne, Elizabeth. Pharoahs of Ancient Egypt. (p. 1733)
Payne, Emily 'Madge'. Rucklestone. Payne, Emily 'Madge', illus. (p. 1912)
Payne, F. Ursula. Winning an Heiress: A Trace in One Art Seven Male Characters (Classic Reprint) (p. 2474)
Payne, Francis Loring. Story of Versailles. (p. 2135)
Payne, Frank. Webster the Beagle. (p. 2395)
Payne, Frank Owen. How to Teach about Aquatic Life: Fishes, Shellfish, Reptiles & Their Life-History (Classic Reprint) (p. 1044)
Payne, Gaynell. I Go Exploring. Buffinet, Jacqueline, illus. (p. 1065)
Payne, George Henry. Great Part: And Other Stories of the Stage (Classic Reprint) (p. 888)
Payne, Gregory. Chase to the Brazen Head. (p. 361)
Payne, Henry, illus. see Perkins, Al.
Payne, Jan, et al. Attila the Hun Was Killed by a Nosebleed: And Other Facts about History. (p. 135)
—It Can Rain Frogs & Fish: And Other Facts about Planet Earth. (p. 1141)
—Penicillin Was Discovered by Accident: The Truth about Inventions & Discoveries. (p. 1716)
—Rabbits Eat Their Own Poop: And Other Facts about Animals. (p. 1830)
Payne, Jody. Miss Spellin' Helen. Payne, Rachel & Song, Danielle, illus. (p. 1480)
Payne, John. New & Complete System of Universal Geography, Vol. 4 Of 4: Describing Asia, Africa, Europe & America; with Their Subdivisions of Republics, States, Empires, & Kingdoms; Extent, Boundaries, & Remarkable Appearances of Each Country, Cities, Towns, (p. 1591)
Payne, John, ed. see Kingsley, Kaza.
Payne, K. E. 365 Days. (p. 2560)
—Another 365 Days. (p. 100)
—Because of Her. (p. 186)
—Before. (p. 190)
—Me@You.com. (p. 1454)
Payne, Katie, illus. see Carter, Molly.
Payne, Kevin, illus. see Colombe, Rose.
Payne, Kimberley J. Trees of the Book: Learning from God's Creation. (p. 2284)
Payne, Lauren Murphy. Just Because I Am: A Child's Book of Affirmation. Iwai, Melissa, illus. (p. 1192)
—Just Because I Am. (p. 1192)
—Just Because I Am / Solo Porque Soy Yo: A Child's Book of Affirmation / un Libro de Afirmaciones para Niños. Iwai, Melissa, illus. (p. 1192)
—We Can Get Along: A Child's Book of Choices. Iwai, Melissa, illus. (p. 2390)
—We Can Get along / Podemos Llevarnos Bien: A Child's Book of Choices / un Libro de Alternativas para Niños. Iwai, Melissa, illus. (p. 2390)
Payne, M. D. What Is the Story of Scooby-Doo? (p. 2417)
—Who Is R. L. Stine? (p. 2448)
Payne, M. D. & Who HQ. What Is the Story of Scooby-Doo? Thomson, Andrew, illus. (p. 2417)
—Who Is R. L. Stine? Murray, Jake, illus. (p. 2448)
Payne, M. E. Buzz the Bee in Bee Smart. (p. 305)
Payne, Mark, illus. see Lebachen, Medyhne.
Payne, Mary Jennifer. Darkness Rising: Daughters of Light. (p. 508)
—Finding Jade. (p. 729)
—Since You've Been Gone. (p. 2023)
—Solomon's Ring: Daughters of Light. (p. 2058)
Payne, Matt. Secret Agent Gear: Spy Tools & Tech: Past, Present, & Future. (p. 1974)
Payne, Miriam. Greyt Christmas Tail. (p. 896)
—Greyt Pirate Tail. (p. 896)
Payne, Philip. Duchess of Few Clothes: A Comedy (Classic Reprint) (p. 607)
Payne, R. J. Woman in the Yellow Hat. (p. 2485)
Payne, Rachael. Cats Don't Take Karate. (p. 346)
—Charlie's Journey Home. (p. 360)
—Penguins Adrift. (p. 1716)
—Will You Be My Friend? (p. 2467)
—Zeke Can't Swim. (p. 2539)
Payne, Rachel, illus. see Payne, Jody.
Payne, Reina. Scent of the Ocean. (p. 1944)
Payne, Sally, illus. see Brooks, Susie.
Payne, Sandy. Find Your Magic. Goodpaster, Nancy, illus. (p. 728)
Payne, Trip. Crossword Puzzles for a Road Trip. (p. 478)
—Crossword Puzzles for Smart Kids. (p. 478)
—Crossword Puzzles for Vacation. (p. 478)
—Crossword Puzzles for Your Backpack. (p. 478)
Payne, Will. Losing Game a Novel (Classic Reprint) (p. 1352)
—Money Captain (Classic Reprint) (p. 1492)
—Mr. Salt: A Novel (Classic Reprint) (p. 1520)
—On Fortune's Road, Stories of Business (Classic Reprint) (p. 1652)
—Overlook House (Classic Reprint) (p. 1688)
—Scarred Chin (Classic Reprint) (p. 1942)
—When Love Speaks (Classic Reprint) (p. 2432)
Payne, William. Introduction to Geometry: Containing the Most Useful Propositions in Euclid, & Other Authors; Demonstrated in a Clear & Easy Method, for the Use of Learners (Classic Reprint) (p. 1129)
Payne-Gallwey, Ralph, jt. auth. see Hawker, Peter.
Payne-Sylvester, Linda. Here Comes Christmas & the Teddy Bears Get Ready. (p. 958)
Payno, Manuel. Los Bandidos de Rio Frio. (p. 1350)
Paynter, Mary Moncure. Caleb, the Irrepressible (Classic Reprint) (p. 310)
Payol, Faythe. Drake & Daphne Make a Discovery. (p. 596)
Payot Karpathakis, Emmanuelle. Nova Casa Da Pixie. (p. 1626)
—Nuevo Hogar de Pixie. (p. 1629)
—Pixie Déménage. (p. 1752)
—Pixie en Vacaciones. (p. 1752)
—Pixie's Holidays. (p. 1752)
—Pixies Neue Heimat. (p. 1752)
—Pixie's New Home. (p. 1752)
Payson, Edward. Doctor Tom (Classic Reprint) (p. 573)
Payson, George. Totemwell (Classic Reprint) (p. 2267)
Payson, Howard. Boy Scouts: At the Panama-Pacific Exposition (Classic Reprint) (p. 269)
—Boy Scouts at the Panama Canal (Classic Reprint) (p. 269)
—Boy Scouts of the Eagle Patrol. (p. 270)
—Boy Scouts of the Eagle Patrol (Classic Reprint) (p. 270)
—Boy Scouts on Belgian Battlefields (Classic Reprint) (p. 270)
—Boy Scouts on the Range (Classic Reprint) (p. 270)
—Boy Scouts under Fire in Mexico (Classic Reprint) (p. 270)
Payson, Stella T. Society Column (Classic Reprint) (p. 2053)
Payson, William Farquhar. Copy-Maker (Classic Reprint) (p. 452)
—Debonnaire (Classic Reprint) (p. 522)
—Novel (Classic Reprint) (p. 1626)
—Periwinkle: An Idyl of the Dunes (Classic Reprint) (p. 1723)
—Title-Mongers (Classic Reprint) (p. 2251)
Payton, Belle. Are You Thinking What I'm Thinking? (p. 114)
—Even the Score. (p. 669)
—May the Best Twin Win. (p. 1429)
—'Tis the Off-Season. (p. 2251)
—Twice the Talent. (p. 2304)
—Two Cool for School. (p. 2307)
—Two Steps Back. (p. 2309)
—Whole New Ball Game. (p. 2452)
Payton, Charles Alfred. Diamond Diggings of South Africa: A Personal & Practical Account (Classic Reprint) (p. 538)
Paytras, C. J. Littlest Homeless Angel: Darby's Story. (p. 1331)
Paz, Diana. Timespell. (p. 2247)
Paz, Myrna J. De La, see De La Paz, Myrna J.
Paz, Naomi. At the Hardware Store: Understand Place Value. (p. 131)
—At the Hardware Store. (p. 131)
Pazos, Carlos. Evolution for Smart Kids: A Little Scientist's Guide to the Origins of Life. (p. 675)
—Genetics for Smart Kids: A Little Scientist's Guide to Cells, DNA, Genes, & More! (p. 815)
—Quantum Physics for Smart Kids: A Little Scientist's Guide to Atoms, Molecules, Matter, & More. (p. 1822)

P

—Service in Servia under the Red Cross (Classic Reprint) (p. 1991)
Pearson, Francis B. Reveries of a Schoolmaster (Classic Reprint) (p. 1873)
Pearson, Henry Carr. Essentials of English: Lower Grades (Classic Reprint) (p. 664)
—Essentials of Spelling: Lower Grades (Classic Reprint) (p. 664)
—Essentials of Spelling. (p. 664)
Pearson, Henry Clemens. Her Opportunity (Classic Reprint) (p. 956)
—His Opportunity (Classic Reprint) (p. 974)
Pearson, Isseate. Our Lady of the Green: A Book of Ladies' Golf. (p. 1678)
Pearson, J. J. Anita & Ing: Garden Adventure. (p. 96)
Pearson, Jaci Conrad. Adams A to Z. Nelson, Darrel, illus. (p. 14)
Pearson, Joanna. Rites & Wrongs of Janice Wills. (p. 1886)
Pearson, John. Notes Made During a Journey in 1821 in the United States of America, from Philadelphia to the Neighbourhood of Lake Erie: Through Lancaster, Harrisburgh, Carlisle Pittsburgh, & Back to Philadelphia; Through Louis Town, Huntingdon,& New Holland; in Searc. (p. 1624)
Pearson, Jo-Lynn. I Grew You in My Heart. (p. 1065)
Pearson, Judith Frank. Chester the Christmas Church Mouse. (p. 366)
Pearson, Kit. Be My Love. (p. 177)
—Lights Go on Again: The Puffin Classics. (p. 1300)
—Magic Boat. (p. 1377)
—Puffin Classics Looking at the Moon. (p. 1811)
—Sky Is Falling: Puffin Classics. (p. 2033)
Pearson, Kit & Farris, Katherine. Bateau Magique Martinez, Rachel, tr. from ENG. (p. 172)
—Magic Boat Grimard, Gabrielle, illus. (p. 1377)
Pearson, Leslie. Flip & Flop. (p. 749)
Pearson, Luke. Hilda & the Bird Parade: Hilda Book 3. (p. 971)
—Hilda & the Black Hound: Hilda Book 4. (p. 971)
—Hilda & the Mountain King: Hilda Book 6 (p. 971)
—Hilda & the Stone Forest: Hilda Book 5. (p. 971)
—Hilda & the Troll: Hilda Book 1. (p. 971)
Pearson, Luke, illus. see Pope, Paul, et al.
Pearson, Luke & Davies, Stephen. Hilda & the Great Parade: Hilda Netflix Tie-In 2. Miller, Seaerra, illus. (p. 971)
—Hilda & the Hidden People: Hilda Netflix Tie-In 1. Miller, Seaerra, illus. (p. 971)
—Hilda & the Nowhere Space: Hilda Netflix Tie-In 3. Miller, Seaerra, illus. (p. 971)
Pearson, Maggie. Magic & Misery: Traditional Tales from Around the World. Greenwood, Francesca, illus. (p. 1376)
—Pop Star Pirates. (p. 1775)
—Rumpelstiltskin Returns. Stone, Steve, illus. (p. 1914)
—Short & Shocking! (p. 2010)
Pearson, Marie. Agility Dogs. (p. 35)
—Bulldogs. (p. 296)
—Dexters Adventures. (p. 536)
—Dog Trainer. (p. 576)
—Dolphins & Porpoises. (p. 580)
—Football. (p. 761)
—Frankenstein's Monster. (p. 778)
—Leopards & Cheetahs. (p. 1268)
—Loch Ness Monster. (p. 1338)
—Mummies. (p. 1526)
—Pet Groomer. (p. 1726)
—Wasps & Bees. (p. 2382)
—Werewolves. (p. 2401)
—Yorkshire Terriers. (p. 2523)
Pearson, Marie, contrib. by. Bulldogs. (p. 296)
—Yorkshire Terriers. (p. 2523)
Pearson, Marline E. Love Notes Instructor's Guide: Relationship Skills for Love, Life & Work. (p. 1360)
—Love Notes Participant's Workbook: Relationship Skills for Love, Life & Work. (p. 1360)
Pearson, Mary E. Adoration of Jenna Fox. (p. 17)
—Beauty of Darkness: The Remnant Chronicles, Book Three. (p. 185)
—Dance of Thieves. (p. 500)
—Fox Inheritance (p. 774)
—Generous Me. Krejca, Gary, illus. (p. 814)
—Heart of Betrayal: The Remnant Chronicles, Book Two. (p. 945)
—Heart of Betrayal. (p. 945)
—I Can Do It All. Shelly, Jeff, illus. (p. 1062)
—I Can Do It All. Shelley, Jeff, illus. (p. 1062)
—Kiss of Deception: The Remnant Chronicles, Book One. (p. 1224)
—Kiss of Deception. (p. 1224)
—Miles Between. (p. 1465)
—Vow of Thieves. (p. 2368)
Pearson, Mary E. & Shelly, Jeff. Puedo Hacer de Todo. Shelly, Jeff, illus. (p. 1811)
Pearson, Michael. Tracing Your Black Country Ancestors: A Guide for Family Historians. (p. 2272)
Pearson, Millie. Out of the Fire. (p. 1682)
Pearson, P. O'Connell. Fighting for the Forest: How FDR's Civilian Conservation Corps Helped Save America. (p. 725)
—Fly Girls: The Daring American Women Pilots Who Helped Win WWII. (p. 754)
Pearson, Pastor Vera M. These Two Foxes. (p. 2219)
Pearson, Paul M. Humorous Speaker: A Book of Humorous Selections for Reading & Speaking (Classic Reprint) (p. 1051)
—Speaker, Vol. 1: A Quarterly Magazine (Classic Reprint) (p. 2076)
Pearson, Peter. How to Eat an Airplane. Catusanu, Mircea, illus. (p. 1042)
—How to Walk a Dump Truck. Catusanu, Mircea, illus. (p. 1045)
Pearson, Randell, illus. see Wills, Cheryl.
Pearson, Ridley. Dark Passage. (p. 506)
—Foxglove Mission (p. 774)
—Foxglove Mission. Gonzalez, Ileana, illus. (p. 774)
—Kingdom Keepers: Disney after Dark. (p. 1221)
—Kingdom Keepers: Disney after Dark. Disney Storybook Art Team, illus. (p. 1221)
—Kingdom Keepers (Kingdom Keepers) Disney after Dark. Elwell, Tristan, illus. (p. 1222)
—Kingdom Keepers Adventure the Syndrome. (p. 1221)
—Kingdom Keepers Boxed Set: Featuring Kingdom Keepers I, II, & III. (p. 1221)
—Kingdom Keepers II: Disney at Dawn. (p. 1221)
—Kingdom Keepers III: Disney in Shadow. Disney Storybook Art Team, illus. (p. 1221)
—Kingdom Keepers III: Disney In Shadow. Elwell, Tristan, illus. (p. 1222)
—Kingdom Keepers New Series Book #1. (p. 1222)
—Kingdom Keepers: the Return Book Two Legacy of Secrets. (p. 1222)
—Kingdom Keepers V (Kingdom Keepers, Book V) Shell Game. (p. 1222)
—Kingdom Keepers VI: Dark Passage. (p. 1222)
—Legacy of Secrets. (p. 1261)
—Lock & Key: The Final Step. (p. 1338)
—Lock & Key: the Downward Spiral. (p. 1339)
—Lock & Key: the Initiation. (p. 1339)
—Polarshield Project (p. 1770)
—Power Play. (p. 1783)
—Shell Game. (p. 2005)
—Super Sons: the PolarShield Project. Gonzalez, Ile, illus. (p. 2158)
Pearson, Ridley, jt. auth. see Barry, Dave.
Pearson, Scott. Africanized Honeybees. (p. 33)
—Kudzu. (p. 1233)
—Red Fire Ants. (p. 1857)
—Zebra Mussels. (p. 2538)
Pearson, Scott, illus. see Neville, Ann.
Pearson, Shelley M. Book Smarts & Tender Hearts. (p. 260)
Pearson, Susan. How to Teach a Slug to Read Slonim, David, illus. (p. 1044)
—Slugger Slonim, David, illus. (p. 2039)
—Slugs in Love O'Malley, Kevin, illus. (p. 2039)
—We're Going on a Ghost Hunt Schindler, S. D., illus. (p. 2400)
—Who Swallowed Harold? And Other Poems about Pets Slonim, David, illus. (p. 2450)
Pearson, T. Gilbert. Stories of Bird Life (Classic Reprint) (p. 2124)
—Tales from Birdland (Classic Reprint) (p. 2182)
Pearson, Thomas Gilbert. Bird Study Book. (p. 230)
Pearson, Tracey Campbell. Elephant's Story. Pearson, Tracey Campbell, illus. (p. 634)
Pearson, William. Papers, Letters & Journals of William Pearson: Edited by His Widow (Classic Reprint) (p. 1698)
Pearson, William Winstanley. Shantiniketan the Bolpur School of off Tagore (Classic Reprint) (p. 2000)
Pearson, Yvonne. 12 Great Tips on Writing Poetry. (p. 2551)
—Amazing Animal Architects of the Water: A 4D Book. (p. 63)
—Bird in a Nest in a Tree: Teaching Nouns. (p. 230)
—Celebrate Constitution Day. (p. 348)
—Celebrate Presidents' Day. (p. 349)
—Concrete Poems. Petelinsek, Kathleen, illus. (p. 438)
—Cows, Horses, & Sheep: Teaching Plural Words. (p. 465)
—In & Out: Teaching Prepositions. (p. 1104)
—Limericks. Petelinsek, Kathleen, illus. (p. 1302)
—Narrative Poems. Petelinsek, Kathleen, illus. (p. 1575)
—Prose Poems. Petelinsek, Kathleen, illus. (p. 1807)
—Rev up Your Writing in Fictional Stories. Gallagher-Cole, Mernie, illus. (p. 1872)
—Sadie Braves the Wilderness. Ritz, Karen, illus. (p. 1921)
—Smelly, Stinky Skunk: Teaching Adjectives. (p. 2041)
Peart, Emily. Maude Maynard, Vol. 1 of 3 (Classic Reprint) (p. 1426)
Peary, Josephine. Children of the Arctic (Classic Reprint) (p. 371)
—Snow Baby: A True Story with True Pictures (Classic Reprint) (p. 2047)
Peary, Marie Ahnighito. Ootah & His Puppy (Classic Reprint) (p. 1665)
Peary, Robert E. Snowland Folk: The Eskimos, the Bears, the Dogs, the Musk Oxen, & Other Dwellers in the Frozen North (Classic Reprint) (p. 2049)
Pease, Alfred E. Badger: A Monograph (Classic Reprint) (p. 158)
Pease, Allen W. Defender of Babylon. (p. 525)
Pease, D. Robert. Noah Zarc: Omnibus. (p. 1616)
—Noah Zarc: Cataclysm. (p. 1616)
—Noah Zarc: Declaration. (p. 1616)
—Noah Zarc: Mammoth Trouble. (p. 1616)
—Noah Zarc: Omnibus. Diamond, Lane, ed. (p. 1616)
—Noah Zarc: Cataclysm. Diamond, Lane, ed. (p. 1616)
—Noah Zarc: Declaration. Diamond, Lane, ed. (p. 1616)
—Noah Zarc: Mammoth Trouble. Diamond, Lane, ed. (p. 1616)
Pease, Elaine. Tallie's Christmas Lights Surprise! Crum, Anna-Maria, illus. (p. 2188)
Pease, Howard. Border Ghost Stories (Classic Reprint) (p. 262)
—Borderland Studies (Classic Reprint) (p. 262)
—Tales of Northumbria (Classic Reprint) (p. 2184)
—White-Faced Priest: And Other Northumbrian Episodes (Classic Reprint) (p. 2443)
Pease, Karen Bessey. Grumble Bluff. (p. 900)
Pease, Lute. Pacific Monthly, Vol. 21: January to June, 1909 (Classic Reprint) (p. 1691)
Pease, Pamela. Design Dossier: Graphic Design. (p. 532)
—Design Dossier: The World of Design. (p. 532)
—Design Dossier: Architecture. Pease, Pamela, illus. (p. 532)
—Design Dossier. (p. 532)
—Pop-up Tour de France: The World's Greatest Bike Race. (p. 1775)
Pease, Verne S. In the Wake of War: A Tale of the South, under Carpet-Bagger Administration (Classic Reprint) (p. 1111)
Peaseland, John. Cat & the Moon. (p. 341)
Peasgood, Amy & Peasgood, Ruby. Robot Music: A Story for Kids with Li-Fraumeni Syndrome & Other Cancer Predispositions. (p. 1892)
Peaslee, Jessilyn Stewart. Ella. (p. 637)
Peaslee Levine, Martha. Twelve Days of Christmas in Pennsylvania. Dougherty, Rachel, illus. (p. 2303)
Peason, Sweetie. Bangladesh. (p. 163)
—Nicaragua. (p. 1602)
Peastitute, John. Kachimayichasuw: The Sneaks Who Stole the Sugar. (p. 1201)
—Kachimayichasuw: The Sneaks Who Stole the Sugar (2. 0) (p. 1201)
Peat, Fern Bisel. 5 Minute Holiday Classics. (p. 2548)
Peat, Fern Bisel, illus. see Clinton, Althea L. & Madsen, Eleanor.
Peat, Fern Bisel, illus. see Field, Eugene.
Peat, Fern Bisel, illus. see Stevenson, Robert Louis.
Peat, Private. Mrs. Private Peat (Classic Reprint) (p. 1523)
Peattie, Cindy. Cinderella Atlas. Mountford, Karl, illus. (p. 392)
Peattie, Cindy & Benchmark Education Co. Staff. Secret Language of Elephants. (p. 1976)
Peattie, Elia W. Annie Laurie & Azalea (Classic Reprint) (p. 100)
—Azalea: The Story of a Girl in the Blue Ridge Mountains (Classic Reprint) (p. 145)
—Azalea's Silver Web (Classic Reprint) (p. 145)
—Lotta Embury's Career (Classic Reprint) (p. 1356)
—Painted Windows (Classic Reprint) (p. 1693)
—Precipice: A Novel (Classic Reprint) (p. 1786)
—Precipice a Novel (Classic Reprint) (p. 1786)
—Shape of Fear: And Other Ghostly Tales (Classic Reprint) (p. 2000)
Peattie, Elia Wilkinson. Angel with a Broom (Classic Reprint) (p. 85)
—Edge of Things (Classic Reprint) (p. 625)
—Judge (Classic Reprint) (p. 1185)
—Mountain Woman (Classic Reprint) (p. 1514)
—Newcomers (Classic Reprint) (p. 1599)
—Pippins & Cheese: Being the Relation of How a Number of Persons Ate a Number of Dinners at Various Times & Places (Classic Reprint) (p. 1749)
Peavoy, Abbie. College Greetings, Vol. 17: October, 1913 (Classic Reprint) (p. 415)
—College Greetings, Vol. 17: December, 1913 (Classic Reprint) (p. 415)
Pebay-Maes, Eliette, tr. see Kloss, K.
Pecastaing, Camille, ed. see Aman, Israa.
Pecastaing, Camille, ed. see Mahdi, Nasreen.
Pecastaing, Camille, ed. see Mansoor, Musheer.
Pecastaing, Camille, ed. see Omar, Tayyib.
Pecastaing, Camille, ed. see Tamer, Abdul Hakeem.
Pecastaing, Camille, ed. see Wali, Anbara.
Pecastaing, Camille, ed. see Zaidi, Anbara.
Pecchioni Cummings, Deirdre. My Dad's Job. (p. 1536)
Pecchioni Cummings, Deirdre & Busse, Erika. I Want to Be a Bennett Belle. (p. 1084)
Pechova, Janina. Sock Rat. (p. 2054)
Pechter, Alese & Pechter, Morton. Skyward Bound: Hot-Air Ballooning. (p. 2034)
Peck, Anne. Children Will Save You. (p. 372)
Peck, Audrey. Helen Keller: Miracle Child. (p. 949)
Peck, Audrey, jt. auth. see Mills, Nathan.
Peck, Beth, illus. see Bryant, Jen.
Peck, Beth, illus. see Johnson, Angela.
Peck, Beth, illus. see Jones, Rebecca C.
Peck, Beth, illus. see Whelan, Gloria.
Peck, Ellen. Ecce Femina: Or, the Woman Zoe (Classic Reprint) (p. 622)
—Mary Brandegee: An Autobiography (Classic Reprint) (p. 1414)
—Renshawe: A Novel (Classic Reprint) (p. 1866)
Peck, Frances. Vaga, or a View of Nature, Vol. 1 Of 3: A Novel (Classic Reprint) (p. 2343)
—Vaga; or a View of Nature, Vol. 2 Of 3: A Novel (Classic Reprint) (p. 2343)
Peck, Geo W. Peck's Bad Boy & His Pa: First & Only Complete Edition (Classic Reprint) (p. 1711)
—Peck's Bad Boy with the Circus (Classic Reprint) (p. 1711)
Peck, George W. Grocery Man & Peck's Bad Boy Peck's Bad Boy & His Pa, No. 2 - 1883. (p. 897)
—How Private Geo; W. Peck Put down the Rebellion: Or the Funny Experiences of a Raw Recruit (Classic Reprint) (p. 1034)
—How Private George W. Peck Put down the Rebellion or, the Funny Experiences of a Raw Recruit - 1887. (p. 1034)
—Peck's Bad Boy Abroad (Classic Reprint) (p. 1711)
—Peck's Bad Boy Abroad Being a Humorous Description of the Bad Boy & His Dad in Their Journeys Through Foreign Lands - 1904. (p. 1711)
—Peck's Bad Boy & His Pa. (p. 1711)
—Peck's Bad Boy & His Pa 1883. (p. 1711)
—Peck's Bad Boy & the Grocery Man (Classic Reprint) (p. 1711)
—Peck's Bad Boy at the Circus. (p. 1711)
—Peck's Bad Boy in an Airship: In an Airship (Classic Reprint) (p. 1711)
—Peck's Bad Boy with the Cowboys. (p. 1711)
—Peck's Compendium of Fun. (p. 1711)
—Peck's Fun: Being Extracts from the la Crosse Sun, & Peck's Sun, Milwaukee Carefully Selected with Object of Affording the Public in One Volume, the Cream of Mr. Peck's Writings of the Past Ten Years (Classic Reprint) (p. 1711)
—Peck's Sunshine: Being a Collection of Articles Written for Peck's Sun, Milwaukee, Wis;, Generally Calculated to Throw Sunshine Instead of Clouds on the Faces of Those Who Read Them (Classic Reprint) (p. 1711)
—Peck's Sunshine Being a Collection of Articles Written for Peck's Sun, Milwaukee, Wis. - 1882. (p. 1711)
—Peck's Uncle Ike & the Red Headed Boy: Also, Sunbeams; Humor, Sarcasm & Sense (Classic Reprint) (p. 1711)
—Peck's Uncle Ike & the Red Headed Boy (Classic Reprint) (p. 1711)
—Peck's Uncle Ike & the Red Headed Boy 1899. (p. 1711)
Peck, George Wilbur. Peck's Bad Boy with the Cowboys (Classic Reprint) (p. 1711)
—Will He Marry Her? A Domestic Drama for Home Reading, Performed by Major Penny & a Numerous Staff of Auxiliaries; with Portraits of the Principal Performers, & Pictures of the Many Thrilling Incidents (Classic Reprint) (p. 2467)
Peck, Harry Thurston. Adventures of Mabel: The Illustrated Children's Classic; Mabel's Journeys with Her Animal Friends. (p. 25)
—Adventures of Mabel (Classic Reprint) (p. 25)
—Greystone & Porphyry. (p. 896)
—International Library of Masterpieces, Literature, Art & Rare Manuscripts, Vol. 22 Of 30: History, Biography, Science, Philosophy, Poetry, the Drama, Travel, Adventure, Fiction, & Rare & Little-Known Literature from the Archives of the Great Lib. (p. 1126)
—Masterpieces of the World's Literature, Ancient & Modern: The Great Authors of the World with Their Master Productions (Classic Reprint) (p. 1419)
—Masterpieces of the World's Literature, Ancient & Modern, Vol. 1: The Great Authors of the World with Their Master Productions (Classic Reprint) (p. 1419)
—Masterpieces of the World's Literature, Ancient & Modern, Vol. 10: The Great Authors of the World with Their Master Productions (Classic Reprint) (p. 1419)
—New Baedeker: Being Casual Notes of an Irresponsible Traveller (Classic Reprint) (p. 1591)
—World's Great Masterpieces, Vol. 23 (Classic Reprint) (p. 2507)
—World's Great Masterpieces, Vol. 29: History, Biography, Science, Philosophy (Classic Reprint) (p. 2507)
—World's Great Masterpieces, Vol. 5: History, Biography, Science, Philosophy, Poetry, the Drama, Travel, Adventure, Fiction, etc; a Record of the Great Things That Have Been Said & Thought & Done from the Beginning of History (Classic Reprint) (p. 2507)
—World's Great Masterpieces, Vol. 9: History, Biography, Science, Philosophy, Poetry, the Drama, Travel Adventure, Fiction, etc. ; a Record of the Great Things That I Have Been Said & Thought & Done from the Beginning of History (Classic Reprint) (p. 2507)
Peck, Ira. Screenland Plus TV-Land, Vol. 59: July 1955 (Classic Reprint) (p. 1964)
—Screenland Plus TV-Land, Vol. 60: July, 1957 (Classic Reprint) (p. 1964)
—Screenland Plus TV-Land, Vol. 61: July, 1959 (Classic Reprint) (p. 1964)
Peck, Jan. Giant Peach Yodel Root, Barry, illus. (p. 831)
—Way Out West on My Little Pony Leonhard, Herb, illus. (p. 2387)
Peck, Leanne. Mama Loves You More. (p. 1392)
Peck, Lillian Hoban, illus. see Hoban, Russell.
Peck, Madeline. Parker the Planner. (p. 1700)
Peck, Marshall H., III, jt. auth. see Berger, Melvin.
Peck, Michael. Booger Train (p. 257)
Peck, Michael J. Good Twin, Bad Twin. (p. 866)
Peck, Richard. Amanda/Miranda. (p. 62)
—Are You in the House Alone? (p. 113)
—Best Man. (p. 206)
—Mouse with the Question Mark Tail. (p. 1515)
—Season of Gifts. (p. 1972)
—Secrets at Sea. (p. 1980)
—Three Quarters Dead. (p. 2235)
Peck, Robert Morris. Wolf Hunters: A Story of the Buffalo Plains (Classic Reprint) (p. 2484)
Peck, Samuel Mintum. Alabama Sketches (Classic Reprint) (p. 39)
—Maybloom & Myrtle. (p. 1430)
Peck, Seth. Realm Volume 1. (p. 1851)
Peck, Steven L. Rifts of Rime (Quickened Chronicles) (p. 1879)
Peck, Tiler & Harris, Kyle. Katarina Ballerina. Collina, Sumiti, illus. (p. 1204)
Peck, Wallace. Golden Age of Patents: A Parody on Yankee Inventiveness (Classic Reprint) (p. 856)
—Story of a Train of Cars: A Tale of Travel (Classic Reprint) (p. 2128)
Peck, William Guy. Text-Book of Popular Astronomy for the Use of Colleges, Academies, & High Schools (Classic Reprint) (p. 2210)
Peck, William H. Mcdonalds; or the Ashes of Southern Homes: A Tale of Sherman's March (Classic Reprint) (p. 1431)
Peckahm, Lori, ed. 60 Years of Guide: Anniversary Story Collection. (p. 2556)
Peckham, Kim. Sensational Quotational Devotional: Youthful Devotionals Found in Famous, Funny, & Inspiring Quotes. (p. 1988)
Peckham, L. Fortnightly Philistine, Vol. 4: Oct; 29, 1897 (Classic Reprint) (p. 769)
—Fortnightly Philistine, Vol. 5: November 4, 1898 (Classic Reprint) (p. 769)
Peckham, Lori. Guide's Greatest Amazing Rescue Stories. (p. 904)
—Guide's Greatest Discovery Stories. (p. 904)
—Guide's Greatest Faith Stories. (p. 904)
—Guide's Greatest Friendship Stories. (p. 904)
—Guide's Greatest Hero Stories. (p. 904)
—Guide's Greatest Hope Stories. (p. 904)
—Guide's Greatest Mischief Stories. (p. 904)
—Guide's Greatest Mission Stories. (p. 904)
Peckham, Lori, ed. Guide's Greatest Funny Stories. (p. 904)
Peckover, Lyn. Sparkling Gold Dust. (p. 2075)
Pecorella, Jane. How a Quilt Is Built: Learning to Measure an Object Using Inches. (p. 1025)
Pedder, Digby Cotes. Where Men Decay: A Survey of Present Rural Conditions (Classic Reprint) (p. 2439)
Pedder, Pamela a. Moving Day. Hardcastle, E. Rachael, ed. (p. 1516)
—Queen's Visit. Edwards, Mark & Moss, Chris, illus. (p. 1825)
peddi, radhika. Kichkide. (p. 1212)
Peden, Margaret Sayers, tr. see Allende, Isabel.
Pedersen, David J. Clod Makes a Friend. Schmidt, Bryan Thomas & Fine, Danielle, eds. (p. 406)
Pedersen, Emma. Looking for Friends (English) (p. 1347)
Pedersen, Emma, illus. see Holden, Sarabeth.
Pedersen, Emma, illus. see Ittusardjuat, Monica.
Pedersen, Emma, illus. see Sammurtok, Nadia.
Pedersen, Emma, illus. see Whittingham, Jane.
Pedersen, Hilary. My Pacific Star. (p. 1558)
Pedersen, Janet, illus. see Clements, Andrew.

—Fuerzas de la Tierra - 6 Pack: Set of 6 Common Core Edition. (p. 797)
—George Washington. (p. 819)
—Inside the Corn Industry. (p. 1123)
—Juan Ponce de Leon. (p. 1184)
—Life of a Colonial Innkeeper. (p. 1293)
—Life of a Colonial Schoolteacher. (p. 1293)
—Maddie Ziegler. (p. 1374)
—Máquinas Simples y Complejas. (p. 1402)
—Máquinas Simples y Complejas - 6 Pack: Set of 6 Common Core Edition. (p. 1402)
—Mathematician & Computer Scientist Grace Hopper. (p. 1424)
—Naturaleza Del Movimiento. (p. 1580)
—Naturaleza Del Movimiento - 6 Pack: Set of 6 Common Core Edition. (p. 1580)
—Nature of Motion: Set Of 10. Solari, Kylee, illus. (p. 1581)
—Nature of Motion: Prime Bridges Edition. Solari, Kylee, illus. (p. 1581)
—Nature of Motion: Bridges Edition, Set Of 10. Solari, Kylee, illus. (p. 1581)
—Neil & Nan Build Narrative Nonfiction. Han, Yu-Mei, illus. (p. 1586)
—Olivia & Oscar Build an Opinion Piece. Hu, Caroline, illus. (p. 1650)
—Russia (p. 1917)
—Samuel de Champlain. (p. 1929)
—Simple & Complex Machines: Set Of 10. Solari, Kylee, illus. (p. 2021)
—Simple & Complex Machines: Prime Bridges Edition. Solari, Kylee, illus. (p. 2021)
—Simple & Complex Machines: Bridges Edition, Set Of 10. Solari, Kylee, illus. (p. 2021)
—Thomas Jefferson. (p. 2228)
Pelletier, Christina. Tale of the Little Green Tomato. Mangal, Sakshi, illus. (p. 2180)
Pelletier, Cynthia L. & Rabin, Shri. She Who Walks with Tigers (p. 2004)
Pelletier, Denise. Emma's Skiing Adventure. (p. 644)
Pelletier, Gilles, illus. see London, Jonathan.
Pelletier, Jennifer. Wonderful Imagination of Alish. (p. 2489)
Pelletier, Mia. Children's Guide to Arctic Birds Christopher, Danny, illus. (p. 374)
—Children's Guide to Arctic Butterflies Christopher, Danny, illus. (p. 374)
Pelletier, Ninon, illus. see Hughes, Alison.
Pelletier, Paul, et al. Guardians of the Galaxy: Somebody's Got to Do It Marvel Select Edition. (p. 902)
Pellett, Frank C. Our Backdoor Neighbors (Classic Reprint) (p. 1676)
Pelley, Kathleen T. Mamis Felices. Harper, Ruth E., illus. (p. 1393)
—Raj the Bookstore Tiger. Keiser, Paige, illus. (p. 1838)
—Sandal Artist Sprague, Lois, illus. (p. 1930)
Pelley, William Dudley. Fog: A Novel (Classic Reprint) (p. 756)
—Greater Glory (Classic Reprint) (p. 891)
Pelliccioni, Sanna, illus. see Pere, Tuula.
Pellicer, Carlos. Arbol Del Tropico. Suzan, Gerardo, illus. (p. 109)
Pellico, Silvio. Mie Prigioni, Memorie: My Imprisonments, Memoirs (Classic Reprint) (p. 1462)
—Mie Prigioni Memorie (Classic Reprint) (p. 1462)
Pellissier, M. Raoul. Complete Writings of Alfred de Musset, Vol. 7: The White Blackbird the Grisette Croisilles Pierre & Camille the Secret of Javotte the Baeuty Spot (Classic Reprint) (p. 436)
Pellissier-Lush, Julie. Mi'kmaq Campfire Stories of Prince Edward Island Ann Marie Martin, Laurie, illus. (p. 1465)
Pellisson, Georges. Miscellany of Divers Problems: Containing Ingenuous Solutions of Sundry Questions, Partly Moral, Partly of Other Subjects (Classic Reprint) (p. 1477)
Pellizzari, Barbara, illus. see Clement, Emily.
Pellizzari, Barbara, illus. see Stilton, Thea & Pizzelli, Anna.
Pellizzari, Barbara, illus. see Stilton, Thea & Schaffer, Andrea.
Pellowski, Anne & Sharpe, Roseanne. Stairstep Farm: Anna Roses's Story. (p. 2099)
Pellowski, Michael J. Joke & Riddle Bonanza. Hoffman, Sanford, illus. (p. 1176)
—Joke & Riddle Jackpot. (p. 1176)
—Joke & Riddle Jackpot. Reed, Chris, illus. (p. 1176)
—Mega Funny Jokes & Riddles. (p. 1441)
—Mega-Funny Jokes & Riddles. (p. 1441)
—Out of This World Jokes & Riddles. (p. 1683)
—Scared Silly Jokes & Riddles. (p. 1941)
—Wild & Wacky Pet Jokes & Riddles. (p. 2462)
Pells, T., jt. auth. see Sommerville, L.
Peloquin, Lili. Innocents (p. 1121)
Pelos, Rebecca & Greenberger, Robert. Cool Careers Without College for People Who Love Planning & Organizing. (p. 447)
Pelos, Rebecca & Roza, Greg. Cool Careers Without College for People Who Love Writing & Blogging. (p. 448)
Pelosi, Catherine. Quark's Academy. (p. 1822)
Pelouze, Edmond. Secrets Modernes des Arts et Métiers: Ouvrage Comprenant les découvertes les Plus Récentes Dans les Arts Industriels, et Leurs Applications, la Description des Brevêts d'Inventions Obtenus Depuis Plus Vingt Ans, les Procédés Employés Dans les Plus. (p. 1980)
—Secrets Modernes des Arts et Métiers, Vol. 1: Ouvrage Comprenant les découvertes les Plus Récentes Dans les Arts Industriels, et Leurs Applications; la Description des Brevêts d'Inventions Obtenus Depuis Plus de Vingt ANS (Classic Reprint) (p. 1980)
Pelouze, J. Traite de Chimie Generale, Vol. 1: Comprenant les Applications de Cette Science a l'Analyse Chimique, a l'Industrie, a l'Agriculture et a l'Histoire Naturelle (Classic Reprint) (p. 2276)
Pelta, Kathy. California. (p. 310)
—Idaho. (p. 1089)
—Texas. (p. 2209)
Pelto, Debra S. Schutzman E. Zoe, tr. see Love, Preston & Love, Portia.
Pelton, Agnes, illus. see Gale, Zona.
Pelton, Bonnie L., illus. see Ball Sr., Frank J.
Pelton, Deena. My Turtle. (p. 1563)
Pelton, Gerald. Purple & Gold of 1921, Vol. 7: Year Book of Morrison R. Waite High School (Classic Reprint) (p. 1816)
Pelton, Jonathan, illus. see Pelton, Joy.
Pelton, Joy. Elephant Moo. Pelton, Jonathan, illus. (p. 634)
Pelton, Mabell Shippie Clarke. Tar Heel Baron (Classic Reprint) (p. 2191)
Peltz, George A. Delightful Stories, or Home Talks Out of the Wonderful Book: A Series of One Hundred Delightful Fireside Stories, in the Chatty, Conversational Style (Classic Reprint) (p. 527)
Peltz, Jason. Who Is Hanukah Heshie? (p. 2448)
Pelusey, Jane, jt. auth. see Pelusey, Michael.
Pelusey, Michael. Giraffes & Zebras. (p. 834)
—Zoo Animals (p. 2543)
Pelusey, Michael & Pelusey, Jane. Apes & Monkeys. (p. 105)
—Bears. (p. 180)
—Elephants. (p. 634)
—Lions & Tigers. (p. 1307)
—Rhinoceroses & Hippopotamuses. (p. 1875)
Peluso, Martina, illus. see Brereton, Libby.
Peluso, Martina, illus. see Crebbin, June.
Peluso, Martina, illus. see DePalma, Kate.
Peluso, Martina, illus. see Finch, Mary & Barefoot Books.
Peluso, Martina, illus. see Flanagan, Liz, et al.
Peluso, Martina, illus. see Marks, Allison & Marks, Wayne.
Peluso, Martina, illus. see Marta Zafrilla, Marta.
Peluso, Martina, illus. see Pirotta, Saviour.
Peluso, Martina, illus. see Spyri, Johanna & Ladybird Books Staff.
Peluso, Martina, illus. see Zafrilla, Marta.
Pember, Arthur. Mysteries & Miseries of the Great Metropolis, with Some Adventures in the Country 1874: Being the Disguises & Surprises of a New-York Journalist, by the Amateur Vagabond, with Illustrations from Photographs by Gurney (Classic Reprint) (p. 1566)
Pember, Julia. Kateri Tekakwitha: The Lily of the Mohawks (Classic Reprint) (p. 1204)
Pember, Karl Albrecht. Goin' Swimmin' Day Before Yesterday (Classic Reprint) (p. 854)
Pember, Phoebe Yates. Southern Woman's Story (Classic Reprint) (p. 2069)
Pemberton. Will Is the Cause of Woe, Vol. 1 Of 3: A Novel (Classic Reprint) (p. 2467)
—World's Furniture, Vol. 1 Of 3: A Novel (Classic Reprint) (p. 2507)
Pemberton, Bert. Three for Adventure. (p. 2233)
Pemberton, Caroline H. Your Little Brother James. (p. 2534)
—Your Little Brother James (Classic Reprint) (p. 2534)
Pemberton, Delia. Civilization of Ancient Egypt. (p. 397)
Pemberton, Harriet L. Childe. Twenty Minutes: Drawing-Room Duologues, etc (Classic Reprint) (p. 2304)
Pemberton, Max. Aladdin of London: Or Lodestar (Classic Reprint) (p. 39)
—Beatrice of Venice (Classic Reprint) (p. 183)
—Doctor Xavier (Classic Reprint) (p. 574)
—Feo: A Romance (Classic Reprint) (p. 720)
—Fortunate Prisoner (Classic Reprint) (p. 769)
—Garden of Swords (Classic Reprint) (p. 809)
—Gentleman's Gentleman (Classic Reprint) (p. 816)
—Gold Wolf (Classic Reprint) (p. 856)
—Great White Army (Classic Reprint) (p. 891)
—Hundred Days (Classic Reprint) (p. 1051)
—I Crown Thee King: A Romance (Classic Reprint) (p. 1064)
—Little Huguenot: A Romance of Fountainebleau (Classic Reprint) (p. 1319)
—Love, the Harvester: Being a Story of the Gleaners in the Winter, of the Year, & of Those That Went a Hunting in the Days When George the Third Was King (Classic Reprint) (p. 1361)
—Mid the Thick Arrows (Classic Reprint) (p. 1460)
—My Sword for Lafayette: Being the Story of a Great Friendship; & of Certain Episodes in the Wars Waged for Liberty, Both in France & America by One Who Took No Mean Part Therein (Classic Reprint) (p. 1562)
—Phantom Army: Being the Story of a Man & a Mystery (Classic Reprint) (p. 1732)
—Pro Patriâ (Classic Reprint) (p. 1802)
—Puritan's Wife (Classic Reprint) (p. 1816)
—Romance (Classic Reprint) (p. 1899)
—Swords Reluctant: Published in London under the Title of War & the Woman (Classic Reprint) (p. 2171)
—White Motley (Classic Reprint) (p. 2444)
Pemberton, Max & Dadd, Frank. Love, the Harvester: Being a Story of the Gleaners in the Winter of the Year, & of Those That Went a Hunting in the Days When George the Third Was King. (p. 1361)
Pemberton, Max Joseph. Hindoo Khan: The Story of How an English Soldier Made Good in the Face of an Uphill Fight (Classic Reprint) (p. 972)
Pemberton, May. Christmas Plays for Children (Classic Reprint) (p. 386)
Pemberton, Morton Hord. Ruben, His Book: From Plow Shoe to Patent Leather with Variations, and, Reuben's European Travels, a Missouri Farmer in a Foreign Land (Classic Reprint) (p. 1911)
Pemberton, Rose. Inheritance & Variation of Traits. (p. 1120)
—Why Do We Have to Do Chores? (p. 2457)
Pemberton, Sir Max. Red Mom (Classic Reprint) (p. 1857)
Pemberton, Sue. Cambridge International AS & A Level Mathematics Pure Mathematics 1 Coursebook with Cambridge Online Mathematics (2 Years) Gilbey, Julian, ed. (p. 313)
Pemberton, T. Edgar. Bret Harte: A Treatise & a Tribute (Classic Reprint) (p. 279)
—Lord Dundreary: A Memoir of Edward Askew Sothern (Classic Reprint) (p. 1348)
—Very Old Question a Novel, Vol. 2 of 3 (Classic Reprint) (p. 2353)
—Very Old Question, Vol. 1 Of 3: A Novel (Classic Reprint) (p. 2353)
Pemberton, Virginia Carroll. Letters from Italy, Switzerland & Germany (Classic Reprint) (p. 1279)
Pen, Stub. Saw-Mill Science (Classic Reprint) (p. 1939)
Pena, Elizabeth. Matthew the Grumpy Baby Walrus. (p. 1426)
Peña, Karla, illus. see Siegal, Ida.
Pena, Nico. Hanazuki: Full of Treasures. (p. 914)
Pena, Nico, illus. see Ball, Georgia & Gudsnuk, Kristen.
Peña, Zeke, illus. see Quintero, Isabel & Iturbide, Graciela.
Peña, Zeke, illus. see Quintero, Isabel.
Peña, Zeke, illus. see Wetzel, Dan.
Penado, Martha. Star Stuff. (p. 2103)
Penaflor, Lygia Day. All of This Is True: a Novel. (p. 53)
Penashue, Mary Ann, illus. see Bartel, Bob.
Pence, Charlotte. Marlon Bundo's Best Christmas Ever. Pence, Karen, illus. (p. 1408)
—Marlon Bundo's Day in the Life of the Vice President. Pence, Karen, illus. (p. 1408)
Pence, Karen, illus. see Pence, Charlotte.
Pencil, Mark. White Sulphur Papers: Or Life at the Springs of Western Virginia (Classic Reprint) (p. 2445)
Penciller, Harry. Rural Life: Or Prose & Poetry of the Woods & Fields (Classic Reprint) (p. 1916)
Pender, Frederick W. Werner's Readings & Recitations, Vol. 35: Cats & Kittens (Classic Reprint) (p. 2401)
Pender, John, illus. see Reid, Stuart.
Pender, Lionel. Spy vs. Spy: Intelligence Organizations. (p. 2093)
—To Serve & Protect: The History of Policing. (p. 2253)
Pender, Margaret T. Last of the Irish Chiefs (Classic Reprint) (p. 1248)
—Outlaw (Classic Reprint) (p. 1685)
Pendered, Mary L. Dust & Laurel: A Study in Nineteenth Century Womanhood (Classic Reprint) (p. 610)
Pendergast, George. At the Crop Farm. (p. 130)
—At the Dairy Farm. (p. 130)
—Butterfly's Life Cycle. (p. 304)
—Deep-Sea Fishing. (p. 524)
—Deer Hunting. (p. 525)
—Duck Hunting. (p. 608)
—Fly Fishing. (p. 754)
—Freshwater Fishing. (p. 785)
—Rock Cycle at Work. (p. 1894)
—Turkey Hunting. (p. 2300)
—Water Cycle at Work. (p. 2384)
—Year of Seasons. (p. 2519)
Pendergraft, Cameron. Story about Tigger. Berner Coble, Lynn, ed. (p. 2127)
—Story about Tigger & Elsa. Berner Coble, Lynn, ed. (p. 2127)
Pendergraph, H. a. Messenger, Vol. 5: March, 1909 (Classic Reprint) (p. 1452)
—Messenger, Vol. 5: January, 1909 (Classic Reprint) (p. 1452)
—Messenger, Vol. 5: Published Monthly During the School Year, September, 1908 (Classic Reprint) (p. 1452)
Pendergrass, Daphne. Daniel Plays at School. (p. 503)
—It's Their World Now! (p. 1148)
—KleptoComs: Official Guide. (p. 1227)
—Meet the Penguins! Style Guide Staff, illus. (p. 1440)
—Owlette & the Giving Owl. (p. 1689)
—Owlette & the Giving Owl. Style Guide, illus. (p. 1689)
—PJ Masks Save the Library! (p. 1753)
—Riders of Berk: A Fiery Discovery. (p. 1878)
—Secrets of the Secret Panda Village. (p. 1981)
—Time to Be a Hero. (p. 2245)
Pendergrass, Daphne, adapted by. Time to Be a Hero. (p. 2245)
Pendergrass, Daphne & Ballard, Jenna. Honeydukes: A Scratch & Sniff Adventure. (p. 999)
Pendergrass, Mark D., illus. see Daubenspeck, Julie & Daubenspeck, Vince.
Penders, Ken, et al. Sonic - The Hedgehog (p. 2063)
Pendexter, Hugh. As Chronicled by His Right-Hand Man Billy Campbell (Classic Reprint) (p. 124)
—Gentlemen of the North (Classic Reprint) (p. 817)
—Kings of Missouri (Classic Reprint) (p. 1223)
—Red Belts (Classic Reprint) (p. 1856)
—Virginia Scout (Classic Reprint) (p. 2361)
Pendle, Lyn. George Saves the Rainforest. (p. 819)
Pendleton, Andrew Lewis. Silly Syclopedia: Containing Daffynishuns of the Words of the Slang Language Spoken by Midshipmen of the U. S. Naval Academy; Together with a Few Allusions to Ye Ancient City of Annapolis (Classic Reprint) (p. 2019)
Pendleton, Claudette M. I'm Mommy's Little Helper. Scott, Christopher L., illus. (p. 1098)
Pendleton, Edmund. Inheritance a Novel (Classic Reprint) (p. 1120)
Pendleton, Louis. Carita: A Cuban Romance. (p. 331)
—Carita: A Cuban Romance (Classic Reprint) (p. 331)
—Corona of the Nantahalas: A Romance (Classic Reprint) (p. 456)
—Forest Drama (Classic Reprint) (p. 766)
—Sons of Ham: A Tale of the New South (Classic Reprint) (p. 2064)
Pendleton, Thomas, jt. auth. see Petrucha, Stefan.
Pendry, Louise. Grandmas Can't Trampoline. (p. 878)
Pendziwol, Jean E. I Found Hope in a Cherry Tree Dion, Nathalie, illus. (p. 1065)
—Me & You & the Red Canoe Phil, illus. (p. 1433)
—Once upon a Northern Night Arsenault, Isabelle, illus. (p. 1657)
Pene J. Tales of Woodland Village - Melissa Mouse. (p. 2186)
Penfeather, Amabel. Elinor Wyllys, or the Young Folk of Longbridge, Vol. 2 Of 2: A Tale (Classic Reprint) (p. 635)
Penfield, Edward. Holland Sketches (Classic Reprint) (p. 988)
—Spanish Sketches (Classic Reprint) (p. 2074)
Penfield, Frederic Courtland. Motor That, Went to Court, a Fact-Story: With Random Illustrations (Classic Reprint) (p. 1512)
Penfield, James, illus. see Baltzer, Rochelle.
Penfield, Shiloh, illus. see Errico, Daniel.
Penfield, Shiloh, illus. see Wray, Brian.
Penfield, Shiloh, jt. auth. see Wray, Brian.
Penfield, Wilder. Galahad School Scrap Book (1905-1918) (Classic Reprint) (p. 805)
Penfold, Alexandra. All Are Welcome. Kaufman, Suzanne, illus. (p. 51)
—Eat, Sleep, Poop. Massey, Jane, illus. (p. 621)
—Food Truck Fest! Dutton, Mike, illus. (p. 760)
—Littlest Viking. Roxas, Isabel, illus. (p. 1332)
Peng, Cathy, illus. see Louie, Ai-Ling.
Peng, Chao, illus. see Chen, Wei Dong.
Peng, Chao, illus. see Dong Chen, Wei.
Peng, Chao, jt. auth. see Dong Chen, Wei.
Peng, Tan Huay. PENG's Fun with Chinese Characters for Children: Help Your Child Learn Chinese the Fun Way! (p. 1715)
Pengilly, Gordon, ed. see Unger-Pengilly, Elaine.
Penguin / LeapFrog, jt. auth. see Piper, Watty.
Penguin, Izy. Grandma Bendy. Penguin, Izy, illus. (p. 877)
Penguin Random House Australia. Puffin Little Cook: Snacks. (p. 1811)
Penguin Random House Grupo Editorial. Trolls. la Fiesta de Arcoíris / Rainbow Party (DreamWorks) Laguna, Fabio, illus. (p. 2290)
Penguin UK & British Broadcasting Company Staff. Doctor Who - The Essential Guide. (p. 574)
Penguin Workshop, Penguin. Queer Eye Guide: How to Love Yourself the Fab Five Way. Murray, Dale Edwin, illus. (p. 1825)
Penguin Young Readers. Llama Llama & the Lucky Pajamas. (p. 1337)
Penguin Young Readers & Buster Books Staff. Odd One Out. (p. 1637)
Penguin Young Readers Licenses. Hatch Bright! Sticker Activity Book. (p. 936)
—Hatch Friends Forever! Sticker Activity Book. (p. 936)
—Hatchy Birthday Party (Sticker Stories) (p. 936)
—Hatchy Vacation! (p. 936)
—Hello, Little Egg! An Oona & Baba Adventure. (p. 951)
—History Class: A Companion Quiz Book. (p. 976)
—Let's Go Fishing! (p. 1273)
—Magical Adventures: Sticker Activity Book. (p. 1379)
—Math Class: A Companion Quiz Book. (p. 1421)
—Me & My Hatchimal. (p. 1433)
—Meet Sonic! (p. 1439)
—Meet Sonic! A Sonic the Hedgehog Storybook. (p. 1439)
—Sonic & Friends Sticker Activity Book. (p. 2063)
—Ultimate Companion Quiz Book. (p. 2314)
Penguin Young Readers Licenses & Godbey, Cory. Aughra's Words of Wisdom. (p. 136)
Penguin Young Readers Licenses Staff. Good Night, Beautiful Moon. (p. 864)
Penguin Young Readers Staff. Little Book of Little Activists. (p. 1312)
Penh, Bophal, tr. see Reicherter, Daryn.
Penhale, Douglas, illus. see Swanson, Diane.
Penhall, Kym. Wall That Wasn't. (p. 2373)
Peniche, Fernando, illus. see Marz, Ron & Rodriguez, David A.
Penina, M. Ant & the Wheat Kernel: For Young Readers. Kaufman, Yaki, illus. (p. 101)
—Dove Builds a Nest: For Young Readers. Kaufman, Yaki, illus. (p. 590)
Penland, Annie. I'm Not Coming Out! (p. 1098)
Penley, Maegan, illus. see Seigle, Marilyn.
Penlington, Nathan. Boy in the Book. (p. 269)
Penman, Satella Jaques. Child-Rhymes & Other Recitations (Classic Reprint) (p. 370)
Penn, A. Town That Told a Story. (p. 2270)
Penn, Alexandra. Letter Mage: First Quarto. (p. 1278)
—Letter Mage: Third Quarto. (p. 1278)
—Letter Mage: Fourth Quarto. (p. 1278)
—Letter Mage: Second Quarto. (p. 1278)
Penn, Arial. S. O. L. (p. 1919)
Penn, Arthur A. Lass of Limerick Town: A Romantic Comic Opera in Two Acts (Classic Reprint) (p. 1246)
—Lass of Limerick Town: A Romantic Comic Opera in Two Acts; with Piano or Orchestral Accompaniment (Classic Reprint) (p. 1246)
Penn, Astor. All the Devils Here. (p. 54)
Penn, Audrey. Chester Raccoon & the Acorn Full of Memories. Gibson, Barbara, illus. (p. 366)
—Chester Raccoon & the Almost Perfect Sleepover. Gibson, Barbara, illus. (p. 366)
—Chester the Brave. Gibson, Barbara, illus. (p. 366)
—Color Game for Chester Raccoon. Gibson, Barbara, illus. (p. 420)
—Kai to the Rescue. Yamada, Mike, illus. (p. 1201)
—Kissing Hand. (p. 1225)
—Kissing Hand for Chester Raccoon. Gibson, Barbara, illus. (p. 1225)
—Miracle Jar: A Hanukkah Story. Lyon, Lea, illus. (p. 1474)
Penn, Audrey, et al. Kissing Hand. (p. 1225)
Penn, Barbra. Susan B. Anthony: Pioneering Leader of the Women's Rights Movement. (p. 2166)
Penn, Carlotta. Dream a Rainbow. Avelino, Joelle, illus. (p. 601)
Penn, Farrah. Twelve Steps to Normal. (p. 2303)
Penn, James. Farmer's Daughter, of Essex (Classic Reprint) (p. 711)
Penn, Jefferson. My Black Mammy: A True Story of the Southland (Classic Reprint) (p. 1533)
Penn, Jim, jt. auth. see Doeden, Matt.
Penn, Karen V., illus. see O'Neal-Thorpe, Rochelle.
Penn, Linda M. Clayton's Birding Adventure: A Young Boy Learns the Secret Ways of Birds. (p. 402)
—Is Kentucky in the Sky? (p. 1137)
Penn, M. W. 2 Lines. Firos, Daphne, illus. (p. 2546)
—Comparing Numbers! (p. 433)
—Counting Money! (p. 460)
—It's a Pattern! (p. 1143)
—It's a Shape! (p. 1143)
—It's Addition! (p. 1144)
—It's Subtraction! (p. 1147)
—Pebble Math. (p. 1711)
—Square Bear Meets Round Hound: A Fairytale of Shapes. Firos, Daphne, illus. (p. 2094)
Penn, Maya S. You Got This! Unleash Your Awesomeness, Find Your Path, & Change Your World. (p. 2527)
Penn, Mw. Pe'lerin of the Orb. (p. 1714)
—Sidney the Silly Who Only Eats 6. Tommer, Sarah, illus. (p. 2015)

P

—Ravi's Roar. (p. 1844)
—Ruby Finds a Worry. (p. 1911)
—Secret Mountain (p. 1977)
—Secret Mountain. (p. 1977)
—Spell Thief (p. 2079)
—Story Tree (p. 2136)
—Story Tree. (p. 2136)
Percival, Tom, illus. see Brezenoff, Steve.
Percival, Tom, illus. see Landy, Derek.
Percival, Tom, illus. see Marsh, Robert.
Percival, Tom, illus. see Nosy Crow.
Percival, Tom Robert James, illus. see Marsh, Robert.
Percivale, Tommaso, jt. auth. see Baccalario, Pierdomenico.
Percivall, Alfred. Somerset Neighbours (Classic Reprint) (p. 2060)
Percy, Adrian. Twice Outlawed, a Personal History of Ed & Loin Maxwell Alias the Williams Brothers: A Record of Highway Robbery, Horse Stealing, Romance, & Murder; to Which Is Added a Detailed & Graphic Account of the Arrest & Lynching of Edward Maxwell at Duran. (p. 2304)
Percy, Gilbert. Piccalilli: A Mixture. (p. 1738)
—Piccalilli: A Mixture (Classic Reprint) (p. 1738)
Percy, Graham. Tales from Around the World. (p. 2182)
Percy, J. P. Cool Machines: Ten Diggers & Digging Machines. (p. 449)
—Cool Machines: Ten Tractors & Farm Machines. (p. 449)
Percy, John. Metallurgy: The Art of Extracting Metals from Their Ores, & Adapting Them to Various Purposes of Manufacture; Iron & Steel (Classic Reprint) (p. 1452)
Percy, J.P. Animals. (p. 93)
—At Home. (p. 129)
—In the Street. (p. 1111)
—Nature. (p. 1580)
Percy, Sholto. Percy Anecdotes: Original & Select Sholto & Reuben (Classic Reprint) (p. 1721)
Percy, Stephen. Robin Hood & His Merry Foresters (Classic Reprint) (p. 1891)
Percy, Tasha. Official IRB Rugby World Cup 2015 Activity Book. (p. 1641)
Percy, Thomas. Hau Kiou Choaan, or the Pleasing History, Vol. 3: A Translation from the Chinese Language; to Which Are Added, I. the Argument or Story of a Chinese Play, II. a Collection of Chinese Provebs, & III. Fragments of Chinese Poetry (Classic Reprint) (p. 937)
—Hau Kiou Choaan, or the Pleasing History, Vol. 4: A Translation from the Chinese Language; to Which Are Added, I. the Argument or Story of a Chinese Play; II. a Collection of Chinese Proverbs; & III. Fragments of Chinese Poetry; with Notes. (p. 937)
Perdew, Laura. 12 Worst Fires of All Time. (p. 2552)
—12 Worst Floods of All Time. (p. 2552)
—Animal Conservationists. (p. 88)
—Animal Rights Movement (p. 91)
—Asking Questions about Food Advertising. (p. 126)
—Biodiversity: Explore the Diversity of Life on Earth with Environmental Science Activities for Kids. Casteel, Tom, illus. (p. 228)
—Bringing Back Our Wetlands. (p. 282)
—Bullying (p. 297)
—California Drought. (p. 310)
—Crazy Contraptions: Build Rube Goldberg Machines That Swoop, Spin, Stack, & Swivel: With Hands-On Engineering Activities. Rauch, Micah, illus. (p. 468)
—Deserts. (p. 532)
—Eating Local. (p. 622)
—Extinction: What Happened to the Dinosaurs, Mastodons, & Dodo Birds? with 25 Projects. Casteel, Tom, illus. (p. 685)
—Great Pacific Garbage Patch. (p. 888)
—History of Art (p. 977)
—How the Toilet Changed History (p. 1036)
—Information Literacy in the Digital Age (p. 1119)
—Internet Addiction (p. 1127)
—Islands. (p. 1140)
—Online Identity (p. 1663)
—Race to Discover Energy Independence. (p. 1831)
—Race to Renewable Energy. (p. 1831)
—Spit Nests, Puke Power, & Other Brilliant Bird Adaptations. Mazeika, Katie, illus. (p. 2084)
—Stink Fights, Earwax, & Other Marvelous Mammal Adaptations. Mazeika, Katie, illus. (p. 2119)
—Understanding Jordan Today. (p. 2325)
—Understanding Lebanon Today. (p. 2325)
—Water-Walking, Sidewinding, & Other Remarkable Reptile Adaptations. Mazeika, Katie, illus. (p. 2385)
Perdomo, Adolfo Perez, tr. see Eastman, P. D.
Perdomo, Juliana, illus. see Knowles, Laura.
Perdomo, Juliana, illus. see words&pictures.
Perdomo, Luis German. Cajita de Las Palabras Todas. (p. 309)
Perdue, H. Avis. Language Through Nature, Literature, & Art. (p. 1243)
—Language Through Nature, Literature, & Art (Classic Reprint) (p. 1243)
—New Century: First Reader (Classic Reprint) (p. 1592)
Perdue, H. Avis, jt. auth. see Allison, Samuel B.
Perdue, Hannah Avis. New Century First Reader (Classic Reprint) (p. 1592)
Perdue Henderson, D. Hayden Heyer: At Radcliff Manor. (p. 941)
Perdue II, D. Smile Made for Christmas. Rondo, Glenn, illus. (p. 2041)
Perdziak, Jeffrey, illus. see Klaiber, Sarah.
Perdziak, Jeffrey Scott, illus. see Everett, Engelic.
Pere, Tuula. Ang Manananambal Nga Iring: Cebuano Edition of the Healer Cat. Recina, Kris, tr. (p. 85)
—Ang Manggagamot Na Pusa: Tagalog Edition of the Healer Cat. Azarcon, Raymond, tr. (p. 85)
—Avulias Taskurapu: Finnish Edition of the Caring Crab. Panchyshyn, Roksolana, illus. (p. 143)
—Best Summer Guest. Korman, Susan, ed. (p. 208)
—Between the Walls. Korman, Susan, ed. (p. 210)
—Birch Tree's Year. Korman, Susan, ed. (p. 230)
—Bisad Bogsan: Somali Edition of the Healer Cat. Iman, Noor, tr. (p. 234)
—Björkens År: Swedish Edition of a Birch Tree's Year. Nikolowski-Bogomoloff, Angelika, tr. (p. 236)
—Blåsångarens Berättelser: Swedish Edition of a Bluebird's Memories. Torstensson, Elisabeth, tr. (p. 243)
—Bluebird's Memories. Korman, Susan, ed. (p. 249)
—Cannellonin Sirkus Perinteiden Pauloissa: Finnish Edition of Circus Cannelloni Invades Britain. (p. 322)
—Caring Crab. Korman, Susan, ed. (p. 331)
—Christmas Switcheroo. Korman, Susan, ed. (p. 387)
—Circus Cannelloni Invades Britain: English Edition. Korman, Susan, ed. (p. 393)
—Circus Cannelloni Invades Britain. Korman, Susan, ed. (p. 393)
—Circus Dogs Roscoe & Rolly. Korman, Susan, ed. (p. 393)
—Cirkus Cannelloni I Traditionens Snara: Swedish Edition of Circus Cannelloni Invades Britain. Wahlstrom, Mai-Le, tr. (p. 394)
—Cirkushundarna Rufus Och Ruffe: Swedish Edition of Circus Dogs Roscoe & Rolly. Nikolowski-Bogomoloff, Angelika, tr. (p. 394)
—Colin the Crab Falls in Love. Korman, Susan, ed. (p. 414)
—Colin the Crab Finds a Treasure. Korman, Susan, ed. (p. 414)
—Colin the Crab Gets Married. Korman, Susan, ed. (p. 414)
—Compagnons de Voyage: French Edition of Traveling Companions. Girval, Edith, tr. (p. 433)
—De Geneeskat: Dutch Edition of the Healer Cat. Van Eekelen, Mariken, tr. (p. 516)
—De Uil en de Herdersjongen: Dutch Edition of the Owl & the Shepherd Boy. Van Eekelen, Mariken, tr. (p. 517)
—Den Allerbedste Feriegæst: Danish Edition of the Best Summer Guest. Lundbeck, Merete, tr. (p. 528)
—Den Helbredende Kat: Danish Edition of the Healer Cat. Agerskov Christensen, Lisbeth, tr. (p. 528)
—Den Hjälpsamma Krabban: Swedish Edition of the Caring Crab. Torstensson, Elisabeth, tr. (p. 528)
—Die Geneser Kat: Afrikaans Edition of the Healer Cat. Stols, Victor, tr. (p. 543)
—Die Gesundmacherkatze: German Edition of the Healer Cat. Wenzel, Werner, tr. (p. 543)
—Du Kan Flyga, Lilla Fågel: You Can Fly, Little Bird, Swedish Edition. Torstensson, Elisabeth, tr. (p. 607)
—Et Medicus Cattus: Latin Edition of the Healer Cat. Udraoni, Rose, tr. (p. 665)
—Fox's City. Korman, Susan, ed. (p. 774)
—Fox's Palace. Vuoriaro, Paivi, tr. (p. 774)
—Gata Curadora: Galician Edition of the Healer Cat. Guede, Damian, tr. (p. 811)
—Gata Que Curava: Portuguese Edition of the Healer Cat. Jagnow, Dieter, tr. (p. 811)
—Gata Sanadora: Spanish Edition of the Healer Cat. Fuentes, María, tr. (p. 811)
—Gata Sanadora: Catalan Edition of the Healer Cat. Displas, Mireia, tr. (p. 811)
—Gered Uit de Vlammen: Dutch Edition of Saved from the Flames. Van Eekelen, Mariken, tr. (p. 821)
—Gnome's Garden. Korman, Susan, ed. (p. 845)
—Græðikisan: Icelandic Edition of the Healer Cat. Baroason, Helgi Mar, tr. (p. 896)
—Gyógyító Macska: Hungarian Edition of the Healer Cat. Czuczor, Tamas, tr. (p. 907)
—Hadurree Fayyistuu: Oromo Edition of the Healer Cat. Fayyistuu, Hadurree, tr. (p. 909)
—Hallonröd: Swedish Edition of Raspberry Red. Nikolowski-Bogomoloff, Angelika, tr. (p. 911)
—Healer Cat: Greek Edition of the Healer Cat. Papakosta, Irene, tr. (p. 942)
—Healer Cat. Korman, Susan, ed. (p. 942)
—Healer Cat (Oriya) Oriya Edition of the Healer Cat. Mahapatro, Gouri Sankar, tr. (p. 942)
—Healer Cat (Sinhala) Sinhala Edition of the Healer Cat. Jayasinghe, L. Sankha, ed. (p. 942)
—Helbrederkatten Heka: Norwegian Edition of the Healer Cat. Dore, Lisbeth, tr. (p. 949)
—Helmi, Perhosemme: Finnish Edition of Pearl, Our Butterfly. Flores, Catty, illus. (p. 952)
—Helmin Elämää: Finnish Edition of Pearl's Life. Flores, Catty, illus. (p. 952)
—Herr Cannellonis Cirkus: Swedish Edition of Mr. Cannelloni's Circus. Wahlstrom, Mai-Le, tr. (p. 963)
—Herra Cannellonin Sirkus: Finnish Edition of Mr. Cannelloni's Circus. (p. 963)
—Hurjat Hampaat: Finnish Edition of Terrific Teeth. Korman, Susan, ed. (p. 1054)
—Hurjat Hampaat: Finnish Edition of Terrific Teeth. Flores, Catty, illus. (p. 1054)
—I Gcás Cneisil Cit: Irish Edition of the Healer Cat. Stanler, Marina, tr. (p. 1065)
—IKati Eyayinothando: XhosaEdition of the Healer Cat. Matyobeni, Sindiswa Gloria, tr. (p. 1094)
—IKati Eyayinothando: Xhosa Edition of the Healer Cat. Matyobeni, Sindiswa Gloria, tr. (p. 1094)
—Ilay Saka Mpanasitrana: Malagasy Edition of the Healer Cat. Ralaivao, Zafimamy Gabriella, tr. (p. 1095)
—Isbjörnarnas Resa: Swedish Edition of the Polar Bears' Journey. Nikolowski-Bogomoloff, Angelika, tr. (p. 1138)
—Jääkarhujen Matka: Finnish Edition of the Polar Bears' Journey. Panchyshyn, Roksolana, illus. (p. 1151)
—Jonte SOM Sommargäst: Swedish Edition of the Best Summer Guest. Nikolowski-Bogomoloff, Angelika, tr. (p. 1177)
—Jonttu Kesävieraana: Finnish Edition of the Best Summer Guest. Radeva, Milena, illus. (p. 1177)
—Jule-Bytteri: Danish Edition of Christmas Switcheroo. Lundbeck, Merete, tr. (p. 1186)
—Kaj Krabba Blir Förälskad: Swedish Edition of Colin the Crab Falls in Love. Torstensson, Elisabeth, tr. (p. 1201)
—Kaj Krabba Finner en Skatt: Swedish Edition of Colin the Crab Finds a Treasure. Torstensson, Elisabeth, tr. (p. 1201)
—Kaj Krabba Gifter Sig: Swedish Edition of Colin the Crab Gets Married. Torstensson, Elisabeth, tr. (p. 1201)
—Katten Gottis: Swedish Edition of the Healer Cat. Nikolowski-Bogomoloff, Angelika, tr. (p. 1206)
—Katu Sendatzailea: Basque Edition of the Healer Cat. Ibarra, Galder, tr. (p. 1206)
—Ketun Kaupunki: Finnish Edition of the Fox's City. Alemanno, Andrea, illus. (p. 1210)
—Ketun Palatsi: Finnish Edition of the Fox's Palace. Alemanno, Andrea, illus. (p. 1210)
—Koivun Vuosi: Finnish Edition of a Birch Tree's Year. Rautkallio, Outi, illus. (p. 1230)
—Kucing Penyembuh Ajaib: Malay Edition of the Healer Cat. Bezak, Klaudia, illus. (p. 1233)
—Kucing Tukang Tamba: Javanese Edition of the Healer Cat. Anggarini, Dyah D., tr. (p. 1233)
—Kul Jul: Swedish Edition of Christmas Switcheroo. Nikolowski-Bogomoloff, Angelika, tr. (p. 1233)
—Kummat Lahjat: Finnish Edition of Christmas Switcheroo. (p. 1233)
—Kuracanto Kato: Esperanto Edition of the Healer Cat. Kiyani, Usman, tr. (p. 1233)
—Laakson Kehtolaulu: Finnish Edition of Lullaby of the Valley. Alemanno, Andrea, illus. (p. 1235)
—Labarin Magen Waraka: Hausa Edition of the Healer Cat. Abubakar, Mansur, tr. (p. 1235)
—Lars - Den Lille Vandraren: Swedish Edition of Leo, the Little Wanderer. Nikolowski-Bogomoloff, Angelika, tr. (p. 1245)
—Lauri - Pikku Matkamies: Finnish Edition of Leo, the Little Wanderer. Nieminen, Virpi, illus. (p. 1252)
—Leo, the Little Wanderer. Korman, Susan, ed. (p. 1267)
—Lub Kho Neeg Lub Siab Miv: Hmong Edition of the Healer Cat. Eldorka, Thainas, tr. (p. 1363)
—Lullaby of the Valley: Pacifistic Book about War & Peace. Korman, Susan, ed. (p. 1367)
—Maca Iscjeliteljka: Bosnian Edition of the Healer Cat. Karamustafic, Irma, tr. (p. 1371)
—Maca Iscjeljiteljka: Croatian Edition of the Healer Cat. Karamustafic, Irma, tr. (p. 1371)
—Macja Shëruese: Albanian Edition of the Healer Cat. Tagani, Iliriana Bisha, tr. (p. 1372)
—Matkakaverukset: Finnish Edition of Traveling Companions. Flores, Catty, illus. (p. 1425)
—Mellan Murarna: Swedish Edition of Between the Walls. Torstensson, Elisabeth, tr. (p. 1443)
—Menninkäisen Puutarha: Finnish Edition of the Gnome's Garden. Rautkallio, Outi, illus. (p. 1447)
—Mouse of the Opera. Korman, Susan, ed. (p. 1515)
—Mphaka Wamphamvu Zochiritsa: Chicheva Edition of the Healer Cat. Simbotah, Symon, tr. (p. 1517)
—Mphaka Wamphamvu Zochiritsa: Chicheva Edition of the Healer Cat. Symon Simbotah, Symon, tr. (p. 1517)
—Mr. Cannelloni's Circus. Korman, Susan, ed. (p. 1518)
—Musen På Operan: Swedish Edition of the Mouse of the Opera. Nikolowski-Bogomoloff, Angelika, tr. (p. 1528)
—Muurien Välissä: Finnish Edition of Between the Walls. Alemanno, Andrea, illus. (p. 1530)
—Nwa Mba Ogworia: Igbo Edition of the Healer Cat. Nwakpu, Ikechukwu John, tr. (p. 1632)
—Oopperan Hiiri: Finnish Edition of the Mouse of the Opera. Rautkallio, Outi, illus. (p. 1665)
—Osaat Lentää, Lintu Pieni: Finnish Edition of You Can Fly, Little Bird. Burda, Alexandra, illus. (p. 1673)
—Owl & the Shepherd Boy. Korman, Susan, ed. (p. 1688)
—Paka Tabibu: Swahili Edition of the Healer Cat. Njogu, Alphan, tr. (p. 1693)
—Parantajakissa: Finnish Edition of the Healer Cat. Bezak, Klaudia, illus. (p. 1699)
—Pearl, Our Butterfly. Korman, Susan, ed. (p. 1710)
—Pearl's Life. Korman, Susan, ed. (p. 1711)
—Perla, Vår Fjäril: Swedish Edition of Pearl, Our Butterfly. Angelika, Nikolowski-Bogomoloff, tr. (p. 1724)
—Perlas LIV: Swedish Edition of Pearl's Life. Angelika, Nikolowski-Bogomoloff, ed. (p. 1724)
—Polar Bears' Journey. Korman, Susan, ed. (p. 1769)
—Pöllö Ja Paimenpoika: Finnish Edition of the Owl & the Shepherd Boy. Flores, Catty, illus. (p. 1771)
—Pouvoirs de Céleste le Chat: French Edition of the Healer Cat. Gozen, Natacha, tr. (p. 1781)
—Räddad Ur Lågorna: Swedish Edition of Saved from the Flames. Torstensson, Elisabeth, tr. (p. 1833)
—Raspberry Red. Korman, Susan, ed. (p. 1842)
—Rävens Stad: Swedish Edition of the Fox's City. Nikolowski-Bogomoloff, Angelika, tr. (p. 1844)
—Reddet Fra Flammerne: Danish Edition of Saved from the Flames. Lundbeck, Merete, tr. (p. 1859)
—Reisgenoten: Dutch Edition of Traveling Companions. Van Eekelen, Mariken, tr. (p. 1862)
—Rejsekammerater: Danish Edition of Traveling Companions. Lundbeck, Merete, tr. (p. 1862)
—Reskamraterna: Swedish Edition of Traveling Companions. Torstensson, Elisabeth, tr. (p. 1869)
—Saga Flyttar: Swedish Edition of Stella & the Berry Bay. Nikolowski-Bogomoloff, Angelika, tr. (p. 1922)
—Saga Och Den Magiska Stenen: Swedish Edition of Stella & the Magic Stone. Nikolowski-Bogomoloff, Angelika, tr. (p. 1922)
—Sagas Taggiga Vän: Swedish Edition of Stella & Her Spiky Friend. Nikolowski-Bogomoloff, Angelika, tr. (p. 1922)
—Sang Kucing Penyembuh: Indonesian Edition of the Healer Cat. Anggarini, Dyah D., tr. (p. 1931)
—Sanni Ja Apteekin Salmiakki: Finnish Edition of Stella & Her Spiky Friend. Tamas, Emanuel, illus. (p. 1931)
—Sanni Ja Laatikkopäivät: Finnish Edition of Stella & the Berry Bay. Ahonen, Elina Johanna, illus. (p. 1931)
—Sanni Ja Taikakivi: Finnish Edition of Stella & the Magic Stone. Pelliccioni, Sanna, illus. (p. 1931)
—Sauvés des Flammes: French Edition of Saved from the Flames. Girval, Edith, tr. (p. 1937)
—Saved from the Flames. Korman, Susan, ed. (p. 1938)
—Scary Snakes. Korman, Susan, ed. (p. 1943)
—Seren y Gath Hud: Welsh Edition of the Healer Cat. Robinson, Evic, tr. (p. 1990)
—Shoemaker's Splendid Lamp. Korman, Susan, ed. (p. 2009)
—Sininen Lintu Muistelee: Finnish Edition of a Bluebird's Memories. Rautkallio, Outi, illus. (p. 2024)
—Sirkuskoirat Roope Ja Rops: Finnish Edition of Circus Dogs Roscoe & Rolly. Orazzini, Francesco, illus. (p. 2026)
—Skomakarens Sagolika Lampa: Swedish Edition of the Shoemaker's Splendid Lamp. Timonen Wahlstrom, Mai-Le, tr. (p. 2033)
—Stella & Her Spiky Friend. Korman, Susan, ed. (p. 2112)
—Stella & the Berry Bay. Korman, Susan, ed. (p. 2112)
—Stella & the Magic Stone. Korman, Susan, ed. (p. 2112)
—Suutarin Hieno Lamppu: Finnish Edition of the Shoemaker's Splendid Lamp. Styloy, Georgia, illus. (p. 2166)
—Tabib Mushuk: Uzbek Edition of the Healer Cat. Xushvaqov, Akmal, tr. (p. 2175)
—Terrific Teeth. Korman, Susan, ed. (p. 2207)
—Tervendaja Kass: Estonian Edition of the Healer Cat. Laansoo-Hamarik, Helen, tr. (p. 2208)
—Tervetuloa Kotiin, Helmi: Finnish Edition of Welcome Home, Pearl. Flores, Catty, illus. (p. 2208)
—Timo Taskurapu Ja Suuri Juhla: Finnish Edition of Colin the Crab Gets Married. Panchyshyn, Roksolana, illus. (p. 2247)
—Timo Taskurapu Rakastuu: Finnish Edition of Colin the Crab Falls in Love. Panchyshyn, Roksolana, illus. (p. 2247)
—Timo Taskuravun Aarre: Finnish Edition of Colin the Crab Finds a Treasure. Panchyshyn, Roksolana, illus. (p. 2247)
—Traveling Companions. Korman, Susan, ed. (p. 2280)
—Trollpojkens Trädgård: Swedish Edition of the Gnome's Garden. Nikolowski-Bogomoloff, Angelika, tr. (p. 2290)
—Tulesta Turvaan: Finnish Edition of Saved from the Flames. Flores, Catty, illus. (p. 2299)
—Ugglan Och Herdepojken: Swedish Edition of the Owl & the Shepherd Boy. Torstensson, Elisabeth, tr. (p. 2313)
—Uglen Og Gedehyrden: Danish Edition of the Owl & the Shepherd Boy. Lundbeck, Merete, tr. (p. 2313)
—Umelaphi Ikati: Zulu Edition of the Healer Cat. Ibilibo, Maybelle, tr. (p. 2316)
—Vadelmanpunainen: Finnish Edition of Raspberry Red. Styloy, Georgia, illus. (p. 2343)
—Vaggvisan I Dalen: Swedish Edition of Lullaby of the Valley. Torstensson, Elisabeth, tr. (p. 2343)
—Välkommen Hem, Perla: Swedish Edition of Welcome Home, Pearl. Angelika, Nikolowski-Bogomoloff, ed. (p. 2344)
—Villi Vauhti: Finnish Edition of the Wild Waves. Flores, Catty, illus. (p. 2359)
—Welcome Home, Pearl. Korman, Susan, ed. (p. 2397)
—Wild Waves. Korman, Susan, ed. (p. 2465)
—You Can Fly, Little Bird. Korman, Susan, ed. (p. 2526)
Perego, Jeanne, et al. Max & Benedict: A Bird's Eye View of the Pope's Daily Life. Casagrande, Donata Dal Molin, illus. (p. 1427)
Peregrine, Peter. Matilda Montfort, Vol. 1 Of 4: A Romantic Novel; in Four Volumes (Classic Reprint) (p. 1425)
—Matilda Montfort, Vol. 2 Of 4: A Romantic Novel (Classic Reprint) (p. 1425)
—Matilda Montfort, Vol. 3 Of 4: A Romantic Novel; in 4 Vol (Classic Reprint) (p. 1425)
Peregrinet, Pop. Told on the Way: Snappy Short Stories; Heard Aboard Trains Steamboats & in Hotel Lounges (Classic Reprint) (p. 2256)
Pereira, Diego Jourdan. Animal Antics Hidden Pictures. (p. 87)
—FLIP OUTS — Fairy Fun: Color Your Own Cartoon! (p. 749)
—Glow-In-the-Dark Fairy Princess Sticker Paper Doll. (p. 845)
—Glow-In-the-Dark Zombie Sticker Paper Doll. (p. 845)
—Learn to Draw Animals: How to Draw Like an Artist in 5 Easy Steps. (p. 1256)
—Learn to Draw Dinosaurs: How to Draw Like an Artist in 5 Easy Steps. (p. 1256)
—Pink Party Coloring Book. (p. 1746)
—Thumbs up! Thumbuddies Tattoos. (p. 2238)
Pereira, Diego Jourdan, illus. see Potter, Beatrix.
Pereira, Diego Jourdan, illus. see Sky Pony Press.
Pereira, Eliana, ed. see Egger, Daniel & Munoz, Lera.
Pereira, Eliana, ed. see Egger, Daniel.
Pereira, Jonathan. Lectures on Polarized Light: Delivered Before the Pharmaceutical Society of Great Britain; & in the Medical School of the London Hospital (Classic Reprint) (p. 1260)
Pereira, Kristin L., illus. see Massop, Kimberley.
Perelaer, Theophile Hubert. Baboe Dalima: Or the Opium Fiend (Classic Reprint) (p. 148)
Perelman, Helen. Bubble Gum Rescue. Waters, Erica-Jane, illus. (p. 288)
—Candy Fairies 3-Books-In-1! #2: Cool Mint; Magic Hearts; the Sugar Ball Waters, Erica-Jane, illus. (p. 322)
—Candy Fairies Sweet Collection: Chocolate Dreams; Rainbow Swirl; Caramel Moon; Cool Mint. Waters, Erica-Jane, illus. (p. 322)
—Candy Fairies Sweet-Tacular Collection Books 1-10: Chocolate Dreams; Rainbow Swirl; Caramel Moon; Cool Mint; Magic Hearts; the Sugar Ball; A Valentine's Surprise; Bubble Gum Rescue; Double Dip; Jelly Bean Jumble. Waters, Erica-Jane, illus. (p. 322)
—Caramel Moon. Waters, Erica-Jane, illus. (p. 327)
—Chocolate Challenge: Royal Sweets 5. Chin Mueller, Olivia, illus. (p. 380)
—Chocolate Dreams. Waters, Erica-Jane, illus. (p. 380)
—Chocolate Rose. Waters, Erica-Jane, illus. (p. 380)
—Coconut Clue. Waters, Erica-Jane, illus. (p. 411)
—Cool Mint. Waters, Erica-Jane, illus. (p. 449)
—Double Dip. Waters, Erica-Jane, illus. (p. 588)
—Frozen Treats. Waters, Erica-Jane, illus. (p. 796)
—Gooey Goblins: Halloween Special. Waters, Erica-Jane, illus. (p. 869)
—Jelly Bean Jumble. Waters, Erica-Jane, illus. (p. 1163)
—Magic Hearts Waters, Erica-Jane, illus. (p. 1377)
—Magic Hearts. Waters, Erica-Jane, illus. (p. 1377)
—Marshmallow Ghost: Royal Sweets 4. Chin Mueller, Olivia, illus. (p. 1409)
—Marshmallow Mystery. Waters, Erica-Jane, illus. (p. 1409)
—Mini Sweets. Waters, Erica-Jane, illus. (p. 1472)
—Minty Mess. Waters, Erica-Jane, illus. (p. 1473)
—Peppermint Princess: Super Special. Waters, Erica-Jane, illus. (p. 1720)
—Rainbow Swirl Waters, Erica-Jane, illus. (p. 1837)
—Rainbow Swirl. Waters, Erica-Jane, illus. (p. 1837)

—Rapunzel: A Day to Remember Studio IBOIX Staff, illus. (p. 1841)
—Rock Candy Treasure. Waters, Erica-Jane, illus. (p. 1894)
—Royal Rescue: Royal Sweets 1. Chin Mueller, Olivia, illus. (p. 1910)
—Royal Wedding: Super Special. Waters, Erica-Jane, illus. (p. 1910)
—Stolen Jewels: Royal Sweets 3. Chin Mueller, Olivia, illus. (p. 2120)
—Sugar Ball. Waters, Erica-Jane, illus. (p. 2147)
—Sugar Secrets: Royal Sweets 2. Chin Mueller, Olivia, illus. (p. 2147)
—Sweet Secrets. Waters, Erica-Jane, illus. (p. 2169)
—Taffy Trouble. Waters, Erica-Jane, illus. (p. 2175)
—Tiana: The Grand Opening. Studio IBOIX Staff, illus. (p. 2239)
—Valentine's Surprise Waters, Erica-Jane, illus. (p. 2344)
Perelman, S. J. Best of S. J. Perelman: With a Critical Introduction (Classic Reprint) (p. 207)
Perelman, Yakov. Amazing Experiments for Young Physicians. Willams, Brian, tr. (p. 64)
—Arithmetic for Fun. (p. 116)
—Entertaining Physics Problems. (p. 656)
—Entertaining Science Stories. (p. 656)
—Géométrie en Plein Air: Volume I. (p. 818)
—Geometry in the Open Air. (p. 818)
—Mechanics for Fun. (p. 1435)
—Physics at Every Step. (p. 1738)
Perelman-Bernstein, Helen. Feel the Noise! Tips & Tricks to Rockin' Camp. (p. 718)
Perepeczko, Jenny. Moses: The True Story of an Elephant Baby. (p. 1507)
Perera, Anna. Guantanamo Boy. (p. 901)
Perera, Hilda & Hilda, Perera. Pericopín. (p. 1723)
Perera, Jude. Beast. Perera, Vasana, illus. (p. 181)
Perera, Maria, illus. see Ware, Kate.
Perera, Oleene. Timmy Tangelo Goes Green. (p. 2247)
Perera, Rajni, illus. see Shraya, Vivek.
Perera, Vasana, illus. see Perera, Jude.
Peretti, Kim. Oodle Van Boodle & the Great Cake Adventure. (p. 1665)
Peretti, Paola. Distance Between Me & the Cherry Tree. Muir, Denise, tr. (p. 564)
Perez Aguilar, Graciela. Pequeño Dragón Aprende a Echar Fuego. (p. 1720)
Perez, Alfred, illus. see Dunn, Rebecca.
Pérez, Amada Irma. Mi Diario de Aquí Hasta Allá. Gonzalez, Maya Christina, illus. (p. 1455)
—Nana's Big Surprise. Gonzalez, Maya Christina, illus. (p. 1574)
Perez, Amada Irma, jt. auth. see Gonzalez, Maya Christina.
Perez, Ani. Zipporah's Farm. Wilson, Deborah, illus. (p. 2541)
Perez, Ashley Hope. Out of Darkness. (p. 1682)
—What Can't Wait. (p. 2407)
Perez, Bernard. First Three Years of Childhood. (p. 740)
Perez, Bernard & Christie, Alice. First Three Years of Childhood. (p. 740)
Perez, Bernard & Christie, Alice M. First Three Years of Childhood. (p. 740)
Pérez, Carmen, illus. see Bird, Benjamin.
Perez, Celia C. First Rule of Punk. (p. 739)
—Strange Birds: A Field Guide to Ruffling Feathers. (p. 2137)
Pérez, Daniel, illus. see Powell, Martin.
Pérez, Daniel, illus. see Shakespeare, William.
Perez de la Iglesia, Janina. Oro Salvaje. Uribe, Luisa, illus. (p. 1672)
Pérez Díaz, Enrique. Mysterious Stones. Ruiz, Alina, tr. (p. 1568)
Perez, Dorothy Thompson, illus. see Kitch, Anne E.
Perez Escrich, Enrique. Cura de Aldea: Drama en Tres Actos en Verso. (p. 485)
—Maestro de Hacer Comedias: Drama en Tres Actos; en Verso. (p. 1376)
Perez, Esther Ido, illus. see Yerushalmi, Miriam.
Perez, Esther Ito, illus. see Yerushalmi, Miriam.
Perez Gaviria, Lina Maria. Helado de Roca Lunar y Otras Ocurrencias. (p. 949)
Perez, George & Lim, Ron. Infinity Gauntlet: Deluxe Edition. (p. 1119)
—Infinity Gauntlet Marvel Select Edition. (p. 1119)
Perez, George, et al. Infinity by Starlin & Hickman Omnibus. (p. 1119)
—X-Men Epic Collection: Proteus. (p. 2515)
Perez, Isaac Loeb. Stories & Pictures (Classic Reprint) (p. 2122)
Pérez, Javier Serrano, illus. see Virgo, Seán.
Perez, Juan, tr. see Poe, Edgar Allan.
Perez, K. K. Tesla Legacy. (p. 2208)
Pérez, Karen H., tr. see Lataif, Nicole.
Perez, Kristina. Bright Raven Skies. (p. 281)
—Sweet Black Waves. (p. 2168)
—Wild Savage Stars: A Sweet Black Waves Novel. (p. 2464)
Perez, L. King. First Day in Grapes. Casilla, Robert, illus. (p. 736)
Pérez, Laura, illus. see Légère, Julie & Whyte, Elsa.
Perez, Lucia Angela, jt. auth. see Argueta, Jorge.
Pérez, Magdalena, illus. see José Ferrada, María.
Perez, Marlene. Comeback. (p. 428)
—Dead Is a Battlefield. (p. 517)
—Dead Is a Killer Tune. (p. 517)
—Dead Is a State of Mind. (p. 517)
—Dead Is Just a Dream. (p. 517)
—Dead Is Just a Rumor. (p. 517)
—Dead Is So Last Year. (p. 517)
Perez, Maureen T., illus. see Cesena, Denise.
Perez, Maureen T., jt. auth. see Cesena, Denise.
Perez, Melissa E. Adventures of Camron, Tiffany & Lydi. (p. 22)
Perez, Mike. Lionel Messi: the Ultimate Fan Book. (p. 1307)
Perez, Moni, illus. see Breakwell, Spike & Millar, Colin.
Pérez, Moni, illus. see Fakhouri, Shoua.
Perez, Moni, illus. see Kubuitsile, Lauri.
Pérez, Moni, illus. see Llewellyn, Claire.
Pérez, Moni, illus. see Pritchard, Gabby.
Pérez, Moni, illus. see Rickards, Lynne.
Pérez, Moni, illus. see Sagner, Sibel, et al.
Perez, Moni, illus. see Sagner, Sibel.
Pérez, Mònica, jt. auth. see Rey, H. A.
Perez Montero, Jose, illus. see Graaf, Anne De.
Perez, Nomar. It's Circle Time! Shapes. (p. 1144)
Perez, Nomar, illus. see Keefer, Mikal.
Perez, Nomar, illus. see Little Bee Books.
Perez, Pere. War of the Realms: Uncanny X-Men. (p. 2377)
Pérez, Ramón. Country of Wolves (p. 461)
Pérez, Ramón, illus. see Battle, Craig.
Perez, Ramon, illus. see Henson, Jim & Juhl, Jerry.
Perez, Ramon, jt. illus. see Medina, Paco.
Pérez, Ramón K., illus. see Gilroy, Henry.
Perez, Robert, illus. see Tilley, E. S.
Perez, Sara, illus. see Ikids Staff & Schimel, Lawrence.
Pérez, Sara Rojo, illus. see Ikids Staff.
Pérez, Sara Rojo, illus. see White, Mark & Aesop Enterprise Inc. Staff.
Pérez, Sara Rojo, illus. see White, Mark.
Perez, Sarah, jt. auth. see Callaway, Michael.
Perez, Sébastien. Genealogía de una bruja. (p. 814)
Perez Tomas Pastor, Jose. Introducción a Calc. Manual Visual de la Hoja de Cálculo de Open Office. (p. 1128)
Perez, Trisha B. Stage Fright. Rollins, Anthony, illus. (p. 2099)
Perez, Whitney Joan. Friendship. (p. 787)
Pérez-Cuadrado, Esther, illus. see Hawes, Alison.
Perez-Fessenden, Lourdes. Daddy & I. Perez-Fessenden, Lourdes, illus. (p. 494)
Pérez-Mercado, Mary Margaret. Splat! Torrey, Rich, illus. (p. 2084)
—¡Zas! Torrey, Richard L., illus. (p. 2538)
Perez-Moliere, Marnie, illus. see Leon, Georgina Lazaro.
Perez-Sauquillo, Vanesa. Cuentos con Beso para Las Buenas Noches / Bedtime Stories with Kisses. (p. 483)
Perez-Sauquillo, Vanesa, jt. auth. see Chbosky, Stephen.
Perez-Torres, Juliana, illus. see Gilbert, George.
Perfect, Gemma. Born to Rule. (p. 263)
—Kingmaker. (p. 1222)
—Seize the Crown. (p. 1985)
Perfect, Henry Theodore. Lady Beauclerc & Socialism (Classic Reprint) (p. 1236)
Perfit, Michael R., jt. auth. see Brown, Don.
Pergaud, Louis. Guerre des Boutons (Texte Integral) (p. 902)
—Tales of the Untamed: Dramas of the Animal World (Classic Reprint) (p. 2186)
Perham, Molly. Customize Your Clothes: Over 50 Simple, Fun Ideas to Transform Your Wardrobe & Accessories. Perham, Molly, ed. (p. 491)
Peri, Jacopo. Euridice: D'Ottavio Rinuccini Rappresentata Nello Sponsalitio Della Christianiss; Regina Di Francia, e Di Navarra (Classic Reprint) (p. 667)
—Euridice: Musiche in Stile Rappresentativo Trascritte in Notazione Moderna con Accompagnamento Di Basso Elaborato per Pianoforte (Classic Reprint) (p. 667)
Perica, illus. see Cinetto, Liliana.
Pericoli, Matteo. London for Children. (p. 1341)
Periers, Bonaventure des. Contes Ou les Nouvelles Recreations et Joyeux de VIS, de Bonaventure des Periers, Vol. 1 (Classic Reprint) (p. 445)
—Contes, Ou les Nouvelles Recréations et Joyeux Devis, Vol. 2 (Classic Reprint) (p. 445)
Perigaud, Ernest Louis Antoine. Expose de la Methode de Hansen Pour le Calcul des Perturbations Speciales des Petites Planetes (Classic Reprint) (p. 684)
Perihar, Amar Singh, jt. auth. see Dicker, Katie.
Perin, Pauline, illus. see Smith, Clyde R.
Perine, George Corbin. We're Coming, Bill, We're Coming, & Other War Poems (Classic Reprint) (p. 2400)
Peringer, Stephen Mercer, illus. see Spruill, Edward L. & Spruill, Sonya.
Perini, Mark, jt. auth. see Cross, Julie.
Perini, Mark & Cross, Julie. Halfway Perfect. (p. 911)
Perish, Patric. Aphids. (p. 105)
—Dragonflies. (p. 594)
—Earwigs. (p. 619)
—Survive an Earthquake. (p. 2164)
Perish, Patrick. Animal Trainer. (p. 92)
—Antelope Jackrabbits. (p. 102)
—Ants. (p. 103)
—Bark Scorpions. (p. 166)
—Bighorn Sheep. (p. 225)
—Bumblebees. (p. 297)
—Cockroaches. (p. 411)
—Collared Lizards. (p. 414)
—Crickets. (p. 474)
—Crystals. (p. 481)
—Desert Tortoises. (p. 532)
—Disgusting Animals. (p. 557)
—Disgusting Bodily Functions. (p. 557)
—Disgusting Bugs. (p. 557)
—Disgusting Foods. (p. 557)
—Disgusting Jobs. (p. 557)
—Disgusting Plants. (p. 558)
—Fennec Foxes. (p. 720)
—Gemstones. (p. 813)
—Grasshoppers. (p. 881)
—Maine. (p. 1383)
—Milkweed Bugs. (p. 1467)
—Mosquitoes. (p. 1507)
—Moths. (p. 1511)
—Roadrunners. (p. 1888)
—Sand Cats. (p. 1930)
—Sidewinders. (p. 2015)
—Skyscraper Builder. (p. 2034)
—Survive a Fire. (p. 2164)
—Survive a Flood. (p. 2164)
—Survive a Hurricane. (p. 2164)
—Survive a Plane Crash. (p. 2164)
—Survive a Tsunami. (p. 2164)
—Survive an Avalanche. (p. 2164)
—Survive on a Desert Island. (p. 2164)
—SWAT Team Member. (p. 2167)
—Termites. (p. 2207)
—Thorny Devils. (p. 2230)
—Walkingsticks. (p. 2372)
—Wasps. (p. 2382)
—What Makes It Rain? (p. 2418)
—Wilderness Rescue Pilot. (p. 2466)
Perisic, Zoran. Alien Called Freddy. (p. 46)
Perissinotto, Giada, illus. see Carbone, Courtney.
Perkens, Julia & Perkens, Anna. Colours with the Sham-Rocks. (p. 427)
—Counting with the Sham-Rocks. (p. 460)
—Seasons with the Sham-Rocks. (p. 1972)
Perkes, Alden. Santa Claus Book. (p. 1932)
Perkin, Ana. Pen-Leaves (Classic Reprint) (p. 1715)
Perkin, Rebecca. White Plains. Meehan, Martin, illus. (p. 2445)
Perkins, Al. Nose Book. Mathieu, Joe, illus. (p. 1622)
Perkins, Anne. Trailblazers in Politics (p. 2275)
Perkins, Annie. Pursuing Purity. (p. 1816)
Perkins, Bill, illus. see Abbott, Tony.
Perkins, C. E. Few Agonizing Spasms: Written Aboard the U. S. S. Enterprise During the Cruise of '95 (Classic Reprint) (p. 722)
Perkins, Chelsea, illus. see Yost, B. L.
Perkins, Chloe. Great American Story of Charlie Brown, Snoopy, & the Peanuts Gang! Burroughs, Scott, illus. (p. 883)
—Living in ... Around the World Collection: Living in ... Brazil; Living in ... China; Living in ... India; Living in ... Italy; Living in ... Mexico; Living in ... South Africa. Woolley, Tom, illus. (p. 1333)
—Living in ... Australia. Woolley, Tom, illus. (p. 1333)
—Living in ... China. Woolley, Tom, illus. (p. 1333)
—Living in ... India. Woolley, Tom, illus. (p. 1333)
—Living in ... Italy. Silva, Reg & Woolley, Tom, illus. (p. 1333)
—Living in ... Mexico. Woolley, Tom, illus. (p. 1333)
—Living in ... South Africa. Woolley, Tom, illus. (p. 1333)
—Living in ... South Korea. Woolley, Tom, illus. (p. 1333)
—Once upon a World Collection: Snow White; Cinderella; Rapunzel; the Princess & the Pea. (p. 1658)
—Princess & the Pea. Mirtalipova, Dinara, illus. (p. 1796)
—Rapunzel. Sreenivasan, Archana, illus. (p. 1841)
Perkins, Chloe & Silva, Reg. Living in ... Brazil. Woolley, Tom, illus. (p. 1333)
Perkins, Chris. No Name I Have. (p. 1614)
Perkins, Dan. Peter the Little Irish Seal. Sarkar, Pratima, illus. (p. 1730)
—Why Can't Grammy Remember Me? (p. 2455)
Perkins, Derrick. Farmer George & His Red Tractor. (p. 710)
Perkins, Edna Brush. White Heart of Mojave: An Adventure with the Outdoors of the Desert (Classic Reprint) (p. 2444)
Perkins, Edward C. Glimpse of the Heart of China (Classic Reprint) (p. 842)
Perkins, Eleanor Ellis. News from Notown (Classic Reprint) (p. 1600)
Perkins, Eli. Saratoga in 1901 (Classic Reprint) (p. 1935)
Perkins, Frederic B. Scrope, or the Lost Library: A Novel of New York & Hartford (Classic Reprint) (p. 1966)
—Scrope, or, the Lost Library: A Novel of New York & Hartford. (p. 1966)
Perkins, Frederic Beecher. My Three Conversations with Miss. Chester (Classic Reprint) (p. 1562)
Perkins, Frederick B. Devil-Puzzlers, & Other Studies (Classic Reprint) (p. 535)
Perkins, George. Pat Mcfree, the Irish Patentee: A Farce in One Act (Classic Reprint) (p. 1704)
Perkins Gilman, Charlotte. Crux: A Novel (Classic Reprint) (p. 480)
—Forerunner, Vol. 2: June, 1911 (Classic Reprint) (p. 765)
—What Diantha Did: A Novel (Classic Reprint) (p. 2407)
Perkins, Grant, illus. see McIntire, Travis.
Perkins, James R. Micro-Lab in Family Enrichment (Classic Reprint) (p. 1459)
Perkins, Jennifer. Theo's Magical Stone. (p. 2216)
Perkins, Justin, illus. see Jackson, Lajuana D.
Perkins, Karen, ed. see Botha, Maretha.
Perkins, Kassie. Where Is a Will, There Is a Way. (p. 2437)
Perkins, Kenneth B., jt. auth. see Hayes, Trudie L.
Perkins, Kevin. Little Blue Gnome. (p. 1312)
Perkins, Kevin John. Circlet. (p. 393)
Perkins, Laurie A. Beauregard the Fighting Fish. (p. 183)
—Doll Who Thought She Was Ugly. (p. 578)
Perkins, Lori L., illus. see Perkins, Myrna.
Perkins, Lucy Fitch. American Twins of 1812. (p. 74)
—Belgian Twins. (p. 195)
—Belgian Twins (Classic Reprint) (p. 195)
—Book of Joys: The Story of a New England Summer (Classic Reprint) (p. 259)
—Cave Twins (Classic Reprint) (p. 347)
—Dutch Twins. (p. 611)
—Dutch Twins (Classic Reprint) (p. 611)
—Eskimo Twins. (p. 662)
—Eskimo Twins (Classic Reprint) (p. 662)
—French Twins. (p. 784)
—French Twins (Classic Reprint) (p. 784)
—Irish Twins (Classic Reprint) (p. 1135)
—Japanese Twins. (p. 1160)
—Japanese Twins (Classic Reprint) (p. 1160)
—Mexican Twins (Classic Reprint) (p. 1454)
—Pioneer Twins (Classic Reprint) (p. 1748)
—Puritan Twins. (p. 1816)
—Puritan Twins (Classic Reprint) (p. 1816)
—Robin Hood: His Deeds & Adventures As Recounted in the Old English Ballads (Classic Reprint) (p. 1891)
—Scotch Twins. (p. 1962)
—Spartan Twins. (p. 2075)
—Spartan Twins (Classic Reprint) (p. 2075)
—Swiss Twins. (p. 2171)
—Swiss Twins (Classic Reprint) (p. 2171)
Perkins, Lucy Fitch & Broyles, Angela. American Twins of the Revolution. Broyles, Angela, ed. (p. 74)
Perkins, Lynne R. Criss Cross. (p. 475)
Perkins, Lynne Rae. As Easy As Falling off the Face of the Earth. (p. 124)
—Frank & Lucky Get Schooled. Perkins, Lynne Rae, illus. (p. 776)
—Nuts to You. Perkins, Lynne Rae, illus. (p. 1632)
—Secret Sisters of the Salty Sea. Perkins, Lynne Rae, illus. (p. 1979)
—Wintercake. Perkins, Lynne Rae, illus. (p. 2476)
Perkins, Lynne Rae, illus. see Codell, Esmé Raji.
Perkins, M. M. Greater Waterloo: A Love Story (Classic Reprint) (p. 891)
Perkins, Mair, illus. see Hainsworth, B. R.
Perkins, Mike. Iron Fist Vol. 1: The Trial of the Seven Masters. (p. 1135)
—Iron Fist Vol. 2: Sabertooth - Round 2. (p. 1135)
Perkins, Mike, illus. see Waid, Mark.
Perkins, Mike, et al. Thor: the Trial of Thor. (p. 2229)
Perkins, Miss Quinn. I Know When the Rainbow Comes. Perkins, Terrell D., illus. (p. 1067)
Perkins, Mitali. Bamboo People. (p. 163)
—Between Us & Abuela: A Family Story from the Border. Palacios, Sara, illus. (p. 210)
—Forward Me Back to You. (p. 770)
—Secret Keeper. (p. 1976)
—Tiger Boy. (p. 2241)
—Tiger Boy. Hogan, Jamie, illus. (p. 2241)
—You Bring the Distant Near. (p. 2525)
Perkins, Mitali, ed. Open Mic: Riffs on Life Between Cultures in Ten Voices. (p. 1665)
Perkins, Nancy, illus. see Greenaway, Kate.
Perkins, Nancy, illus. see Kerr, Terilyn.
Perkins, Papa. Oliver Doliver's Dinosaur Comes to Stay. (p. 1649)
Perkins, Peppermint. Familiar Letters of Peppermint Perkins (Classic Reprint) (p. 701)
Perkins, Polly P. Hedgerow Diaries. (p. 947)
Perkins, Raymond. Playtime Songs, Old & New: Arranged with Easy Accompaniments, Including Fourteen New Melodies (Classic Reprint) (p. 1761)
Perkins, Rodney R., illus. see VanDerTuuk-Perkins, Jennifer E.
Perkins, Roy D. Created Equal, but Not for Long: Dexter, Son of Marvin. (p. 469)
Perkins, Ruth, illus. see Young, Elizabeth L.
Perkins, Sarah, illus. see Robbins, Heather Roan.
Perkins, Sean. Adventures of MR Bread Head & the Disappearing Loaves. (p. 25)
Perkins, Stephanie. Anna & the French Kiss. (p. 97)
—Isla & the Happily Ever After. (p. 1138)
—Lola & the Boy Next Door. (p. 1340)
—My True Love Gave to Me: Twelve Holiday Stories. (p. 1563)
—Summer Days & Summer Nights: Twelve Love Stories. (p. 2149)
—There's Someone Inside Your House. (p. 2218)
Perkins, Stephanie, ed. Summer Days & Summer Nights: Twelve Summer Romances. (p. 2149)
Perkins, T. J. Art of the Ninja: Earth. Dumas, Ryan, illus. (p. 121)
—Four Little Witches Pinero, Eimi, illus. (p. 772)
Perkins, Terrell D., illus. see Perkins, Miss Quinn.
Perkins, Useni Eugene. Black Arts Movement. (p. 236)
—Hey Black Child. Collier, Bryan, illus. (p. 964)
Perkins, Wendy. Elephant. Longhi, Katya, illus. (p. 633)
—Japanese Spider Crabs. (p. 1160)
—Kindergarten Rich: Our Future Leaders. McGraw, Jinay, illus. (p. 1218)
—Penguin. (p. 1715)
—Sea Cucumbers. (p. 1967)
—Sea Dragons. (p. 1967)
—Star-Nosed Moles. (p. 2102)
Perkinson, Ellen. Muffin's Adventures As Told by Muffin: Muffin Goes to the Beach. (p. 1524)
—Muffin's New Home. (p. 1524)
Perkis, Andrea. Wright Brothers Make History! (p. 2511)
Perks, Anne-Marie, illus. see Horn, Sandra.
Perks, Joseph M. As Long As We Can Smile. Ojeda, Carlos, illus. (p. 124)
Perkyns, Dorothy. Bridget's Black '47. (p. 281)
Perl, Erica S. Aces Wild. (p. 10)
—All the Fun Winter Things #4. Chatterton, Chris, illus. (p. 54)
—All Three Stooges. (p. 55)
—Chicken Butt. Cole, Henry, illus. (p. 368)
—Chicken Butt's Back! Cole, Henry, illus. (p. 368)
—Ferocious Fluffity: A Mighty Bite-Y Class Pet. Cole, Henry, illus. (p. 721)
—Goatilocks & the Three Bears. Howard, Arthur, illus. (p. 849)
—Great Louweezie #1. Chatterton, Chris, illus. (p. 887)
—Happy Fell #3. Chatterton, Chris, illus. (p. 922)
—Lost & Found #2. Chatterton, Chris, illus. (p. 1352)
—Ninth Night of Hanukkah. Kober, Shahar, illus. (p. 1611)
—Penny & Clover, Follow That Ball! Martin, Leire, illus. (p. 1717)
—Penny & Clover, up & Over! Martin, Leire, illus. (p. 1717)
—Sharks! Slack, Michael, illus. (p. 2002)
—Totally Tardy Marty. Krosoczka, Jarrett J., illus. (p. 2267)
—Truth or Lie: Dinosaurs! (p. 2297)
—Truth or Lie: Presidents! (p. 2297)
—Truth or Lie: Dinosaurs! Slack, Michael, illus. (p. 2297)
—Truth or Lie - Sharks! Slack, Michael H., illus. (p. 2297)
—When Life Gives You O. J. (p. 2431)
Perl, Erica S. & Slack, Michael. Truth or Lie: Presidents! (p. 2297)
Perl, Lila. Genocide: Standby or Intervene? (p. 816)
—Immigration: This Land Is Whose Land? (p. 1101)
—Isabel's War. (p. 1138)
—Lilli's Quest. (p. 1301)
—Me & Fat Glenda. (p. 1432)
—Torture. (p. 2266)
Perl, Lila & Lazan, Marion Blumenthal. Four Perfect Pebbles: A True Story of the Holocaust (p. 772)
Perl, Lila & McCoy, Erin L. Genocide: When Is Intervention Necessary? (p. 816)
—Immigration: Welcome or Not? (p. 1101)
Perl, Sheri, jt. auth. see Corporate Contributor Staff.
Perla, Brian, illus. see Spergel, Heather.
Perla, Fabio, illus. see Ayachi, Janette.
Perlin, Don, et al. Defenders Epic Collection: the End of All Songs. (p. 525)
Perlman, Janet. Delicious Bug. Perlman, Janet, illus. (p. 526)

P

Perlman, Willa. Good Night, World. Fisher, Carolyn, illus. (p. 865)
Perlov, Rebecca Rosenberg. Rifka Takes a Bow Kawa, Cosei, illus. (p. 1879)
Perlzweig, Judith. Lamps from the Athenian Agora. (p. 1241)
Perman, LeAnn. My Name Was Bert. (p. 1557)
Permane, Terry, photos by see Hooke, R. Schuyler.
Perna, Debi, illus. see Tanaka, Shelley.
Pernaudet, Christophe & Chebret, Sébastien. Lobo Hace Huelga. (p. 1338)
Perner, Lars, ed. Scholars with Autism Achieving Dreams. (p. 1944)
Pernetz, Adriana. Gloria's Dream. Hudson, Elizabeth, illus. (p. 844)
—Once in a Forest. (p. 1657)
Pernice, Clare. Circus Girl. (p. 393)
—Real Mother Goose: Hardboiled Humpty Dumpty & More Scrambled Nursery Rhymes. (p. 1850)
Pernigotti, Chiara, tr. see Baccalario, P. D.
Pernigotti, Chiara, tr. see Baccalario, Pierdomenico & McGuinness, Nanette.
Pernigotti, Chiara, tr. see Baccalario, Pierdomenico.
Pernigotti, Chiara, tr. see Guerra, Elisa Puricelli.
Pernikoff, Doug. So What If Im a Bully. (p. 2050)
—So What If Im Adopted. (p. 2050)
—So What If My Parents Got Divorced. (p. 2050)
Pernisco, Atilio, illus. see Santillan, Suzanne.
Pernu, Dennis. Baseball. (p. 168)
—Basketball. (p. 170)
—Complete Guide to Sports. (p. 434)
—Football. (p. 761)
—Hockey. (p. 985)
Pero, Denis. My Little Handbook of Experiments: Sciences, Water & Light, Ecology. (p. 1553)
Pero, Denis & Auzou Publishing Staff. My Book of Animals: A Walk Through the National Parks. (p. 1534)
Pero, Kathleen S. Miss Molly Learns Responsibility. (p. 1479)
Perochon, Ernest. Nene, Vol. 1 (Classic Reprint) (p. 1587)
Perper, Talya. Steven Universe Orignal Graphic Novel: Ultimate Dough-Down: Ultimate Dough-Down. Omac, Meg, illus. (p. 2116)
Perrault, Charles. Barba Azul. (p. 165)
—Beauty & the Beast (Classic Reprint) (p. 185)
—Bedtime Stories: Little Red Riding Hood & Puss in Boots. Crane, Walter, illus. (p. 188)
—Bedtime Stories - the Sleeping Beauty & Cinderella. (p. 188)
—Belle Au Bois Dormant (Classic Reprint) (p. 197)
—Cinderella. Innocenti, Roberto, illus. (p. 391)
—Cinderella (Cenicienta) Fransoy, Monse, illus. (p. 392)
—Court of Oberon, or Temple of the Fairies: A Collection of Tales of Past Times (Classic Reprint) (p. 463)
—Fairy Tales of Charles Perrault: [Complete & Illustrated]. Mansion, J. E., tr. (p. 698)
—Fairy Tales of Charles Perrault (Classic Reprint) (p. 698)
—Gato con Botas y Otros Cuentos. (p. 812)
—Little Red Riding Hood. (p. 1326)
—Old-Time Stories. (p. 1648)
—Old-Time Stories (Classic Reprint) (p. 1648)
—OXFORD WORLD'S CLASSICS: THE COMPLETE FAIRY TALES. (p. 1689)
—Perrault's Fairy Tales. (p. 1724)
—Petit Chaperon Rouge. Goulevitch, Aure'lie, illus. (p. 1730)
—Popular Story of Blue Beard: Embellished with Neat Engravings (Classic Reprint) (p. 1777)
—Popular Story of Blue Beard (Classic Reprint) (p. 1777)
—Puss in Boots. Keraval, Gwen, illus. (p. 1817)
—Puss in Boots. Arthur, Malcolm, tr. from ENG. (p. 1817)
—Puss in Boots. Adams, Frank & Lawrence, C. H., illus. (p. 1817)
—Sleeping Beauty. Cowley, Joy, ed. (p. 2036)
—Sleeping Beauty of the Wood: An Entertaining Tale; to Which Is Added Paddy & the Bear, a True Story (Classic Reprint) (p. 2037)
—Story of Blue Beard (Classic Reprint) (p. 2129)
—Storyteller Book: Cinderella. Spenceley, Annabel, illus. (p. 2136)
—Tales of Mother Goose (Classic Reprint) (p. 2184)
—Tales of Passed Times (Classic Reprint) (p. 2185)
—Tales of Passed Times Written for Children (Classic Reprint) (p. 2185)
Perrault, Charles, jt. auth. see Christian Anderson, Hans.
Perrault, Charles, jt. auth. see Guillain, Charlotte.
Perrault, Charles, contrib. by. Little Mermaid. (p. 1321)
Perrault, Charles, et al. Greatest Fairy Tales. Rossi, Francesca, illus. (p. 891)
Perreault, Guillaume. Postman from Space. (p. 1780)
Perreault, Guillaume, illus. see Payette, Eveline.
Perreault, Guillaume, illus. see Sparrow, Kerry.
Perree, Leyland. Magic Custard Factory. McGhee, Stuart, illus. (p. 1377)
—¿Quién Es Quién En Brujilandia? (p. 1827)
Perret, Delphine. Bear Named Bjorn: Six Bear Stories. Perret, Delphine, illus. (p. 179)
—Pablo & His Chair. (p. 1690)
—Pedro & George. Perret, Delphine, illus. (p. 1712)
Perret, Delphine, illus. see Gutman, Colas.
Perret, Gaelle. Jour Grand-Pere M'a Donne un Ruisseau. (p. 1179)
Perrett, Lisa, illus. see Hunt, Sara R.
Perrett, Lisa, illus. see Innovative Kids Staff.
Perrett, Lisa, illus. see Rhatigan, Joe.
Perrett, Lisa, illus. see Walter Foster Jr. Creative Team.
Perrett, Lisa, illus. see Wax, Wendy.
Perretti, Angi. Identity of AngiArts: A Muse for Artistic Inspiration. (p. 1089)
Perreyve, Henri, jt. auth. see O'Meara, Kathleen.
Perri, David. Messy Larry. (p. 1452)
Perri, David J. Messy Larry. (p. 1452)
Perri, Jessica. Story of Rainbow Bear. Kushnareva, Julia, illus. (p. 2132)
Perricone, Mike. Big Bang. (p. 216)
Perrigo, James. Sheriff: A Modern Maine Story in Which Pride & Politics, Romance & Rum Are Curiously Intermingled (Classic Reprint) (p. 2006)
Perrigot, Susan, illus. see Evans, Christopher J.
Perril, Simon, ed. Salt Companion to John James. (p. 1925)
Perrin, Alice. Anglo-Indians (Classic Reprint) (p. 87)
—Free Solitude (Classic Reprint) (p. 782)
—Idolatry (Classic Reprint) (p. 1090)
—Star of India (Classic Reprint) (p. 2102)
—Stronger Claim (Classic Reprint) (p. 2142)
—Tales That Are Told. (p. 2186)
—Tales That Are Told (Classic Reprint) (p. 2186)
—Vow of Silence (Classic Reprint) (p. 2368)
—Waters of Destruction (Classic Reprint) (p. 2386)
—Woman in the Bazaar (Classic Reprint) (p. 2485)
Perrin, Bernadotte, jt. auth. see Homer.
Perrin, Christopher. Greek for Children, Primer A. (p. 892)
Perrin, Clotilde. At the Same Moment, Around the World. (p. 131)
—House of Madame M. Perrin, Clotilde, illus. (p. 1023)
—Inside the Villains. Perrin, Clotilde, illus. (p. 1124)
Perrin, Jean. Fables Amusantes: Avec une Table Generale et Particuliere des Mots, et de Leur Signification en Anglais, Selon l'Ordre des Fables (Classic Reprint) (p. 690)
Perrin, Jean Baptiste. Fables Amusantes: Avec une Table Generale et Particuliere des Mots et de Leur Signification en Anglais, Selon l'Ordre des Fables, Pour en Rendre la Traduction Plus Facile a l'Ecolier (Classic Reprint) (p. 690)
—Progressive French Reader (Perrin's Fables) Thoroughly Revised & Arranged to Be Used As a French Reader, Translator & Book of Composition & Conversation; with a General & Particular Index, to Render the Translation Easier to the Learner, Follow. (p. 1805)
—Selection of One Hundred of Perrin's Fables, Accompanied with a Key: Containing the Text, a Literal & a Free Translation, Arranged in Such a Manner As to Point Out the Difference Between the French & the English Idiom (Classic Reprint) (p. 1986)
—Selection of One Hundred of Perrin's Fables, Accompanied with a Key: Containing the Text, a Literal & a Free Translation, Arranged in Such a Manner As to Point Out the Difference Between the French & the English Idiom, Also, a Figured Pronunciation. (p. 1986)
—Selection of One Hundred of Perrin's Fables, Accompanied with a Key: Containing the Text, a Literal & a Free Translation, Arranged in Such a Manner As to Point Out the Difference Between the French & the English Idiom, Also a Figured Pronunciation O. (p. 1986)
Perrin, John. Fables Amusantes: Avec une Table Générale et Particulière des Mots et de Leur Signification en Anglois (Classic Reprint) (p. 690)
—Fables Amusantes: Avec une Table Generale et Particuliere des Mots et de Leur Signification en Anglais Selon l'Ordre des Fables, Pour en Rendre la Traduction Plus Facile a l'Ecolier (Classic Reprint) (p. 690)
—Fables Amusantes: Avec une Table Générale et Particulière des Mots et de Leur Signification en Anglais, Selon l'Ordre des Fables, Pour en Rendre la Traduction Plus Facile À l'Écolier (Classic Reprint) (p. 690)
—Fables Amusantes, Avec une Table Generale et Particuliere des Mots et de Leur Signification en Anglois: Selon l'Ordre des Fables, Pour en Rendre la Traduction Plus Facile a l'Ecolier (Classic Reprint) (p. 690)
—Selection of One Hundred of Perrin's Fables, Accompanied with a Key: Containing the Test, a Literal & a Free Translation, Arranged in Such a Manner As to Point Out the Difference Between the French & the English Idioms (Classic Reprint) (p. 1986)
—Selection of One Hundred of Perrin's Fables, Accompanied with a Key: Containing the Text, a Literal & a Free Translation, Arranged in Such a Manner As to Point Out the Difference Between the French & the English Idiom; Also Figured Pronunciation Of. (p. 1986)
Perrin, Leslie. Savannah from Alabama: Moved to Be a Friend. (p. 1937)
Perrin, Martine. What Do You See? Perrin, Martine, illus. (p. 2409)
Perrin, Tom J. Girl Who Travelled the World by Accident. (p. 837)
Perrin, Tom J. & Kish, Danielle. Boy Who Wears Red Trousers. (p. 271)
Perrine, Doug, photos by see Markle, Sandra.
Perrine, Jared. Era Chimera. Dishaw, Karen, illus. (p. 659)
Perrini, Angela, illus. see Bladen, Louise.
Perritano, John. 3D Printing. (p. 2547)
—Abraham Lincoln (Presidential Biographies) (p. 7)
—Agriculture (p. 36)
—American Maverick: The Story of John Mccain. (p. 73)
—Amityville. (p. 76)
—Apple. (p. 106)
—Australia. (p. 138)
—Battle of the Bots (p. 174)
—Bomb Squad Technician (p. 254)
—Border Security (p. 262)
—Brazil (p. 277)
—China (p. 377)
—Colonization & Settlement. (p. 418)
—Comet Catcher. (p. 429)
—Comet of Doom Laughead, Mike, illus. (p. 429)
—Construction Machines. (p. 443)
—Copper (p. 452)
—Desert Storm. (p. 532)
—Disgusting Stuff. (p. 558)
—Education, Poverty, & Inequality. (p. 626)
—Egyptian Prophecy. Laughead, Mike, illus. (p. 628)
—Fats & Cholesterol. (p. 715)
—Fault Lines. (p. 715)
—Fishing (p. 742)
—Flavorings, Colorings, & Preservatives. (p. 747)
—Food Safety. (p. 760)
—Football Numbers: Graphing Data. (p. 761)
—Football Numbers: Graphing Numbers. (p. 761)
—Forensics (p. 765)
—Freshwater Resources (p. 785)
—Germany (p. 822)
—Ghosts of Civil War Soldiers. (p. 829)
—Gnarly Sports Injuries (p. 845)
—Gnarly Sports Injuries. (p. 845)
—Going after Sparky! Pararescue Jumpers Bring Vietnam War Pilot Home (p. 854)
—Gold & Silver (p. 855)
—Hallucinogens: Ecstasy, LSD, & Ketamine Becker, Sara, ed. (p. 913)
—Health & Medicine van Dijk, Ruud, ed. (p. 943)
—Iron (p. 1135)
—Korean War. (p. 1231)
—Lewis & Clark Expedition. (p. 1282)
—Little Rock Nine. (p. 1327)
—Madness of Captain Cyclops (p. 1375)
—Making of the Modern World: 1945 to the Present: Culture & Customs in a Connected World (p. 1390)
—Making of the Modern World: 1945 to the Present: Migration & Refugees van Dijk, Ruud, ed. (p. 1390)
—Making of the Modern World: 1945 to the Present: Trade, Economic Life & Globalization van Dijk, Ruud, ed. (p. 1390)
—Marijuana & Synthetics Becker, Sara, ed. (p. 1405)
—Marine Resources (p. 1406)
—Medal of Honor. (p. 1435)
—Meltdown! Global Warming Puts the World on Thin Ice. (p. 1443)
—Morocco. (p. 1506)
—Most Disgusting Animals on the Planet (p. 1508)
—Most Disgusting Foods on the Planet (p. 1508)
—Most Disgusting Jobs on the Planet (p. 1508)
—Most Disgusting Places on the Planet (p. 1508)
—Mummies in the Library: Divide the Pages. (p. 1526)
—Opioids: Heroin, Oxycontin, & Painkillers Becker, Sara, ed. (p. 1667)
—Panama. (p. 1695)
—Performance-Enhancing Drugs: Steroids, Hormones, & Supplements Becker, Sara, ed. (p. 1723)
—Planes. (p. 1754)
—Reddit (p. 1859)
—Revolution in Communications. (p. 1873)
—Revolution in Transportation. (p. 1873)
—Salt (p. 1925)
—Saving Private Lynch! a Rescue Story from Operation Iraqi Freedom (p. 1938)
—Science & Technology van Dijk, Ruud, ed. (p. 1953)
—Science Beats Crime. (p. 1953)
—Science of Emotions. (p. 1957)
—Science of Movies (p. 1958)
—Seeing Halves: Symmetry in Our World. (p. 1984)
—Snickerblooms & the Age Bug Laughead, Mike, illus. (p. 2046)
—Space Machines. (p. 2071)
—Space Science (p. 2072)
—Spanish Missions. (p. 2074)
—Sports Science. (p. 2089)
—Starch & Other Carbohydrates. (p. 2105)
—Start the Game: Geometry in Sports. (p. 2107)
—Stem in Current Events: Transportation (p. 2113)
—Stimulants: Meth, Cocaine, & Amphetamines Becker, Sara, ed. (p. 2119)
—Storming the Somali Pirates! Navy Seals Save Hostages! (p. 2127)
—Sugar & Sweeteners. (p. 2147)
—SWAT Team (p. 2167)
—Terrorist Goes Down! Delta Forces in Syria Take Out an ISIS Leader (p. 2208)
—Toy Store Summer: Finding Area. (p. 2270)
—Transcontinental Railroad. (p. 2277)
—Ultimate Book of Dangerous Insects. (p. 2314)
—Ultimate Book of Dangerous Jobs. (p. 2314)
—Ultimate Book of Dangerous Sports & Activities. (p. 2314)
—Uranium (p. 2339)
—War & the Military (p. 2376)
—Warlock Stone (p. 2379)
—Wild Weather. (p. 2465)
—World War I. (p. 2505)
—Yosemite. (p. 2523)
Perritano, John, jt. auth. see ABDO Publishing Company Staff.
Perritano, John, jt. auth. see Crabtree Staff.
Perritano, Johnrau Dana M. Science of Movies. (p. 1958)
Perritt, Jordona, illus. see Johnson, Sandi.
Perro, Bryan. Amos Daragon #2: the Key of Braha. (p. 77)
Perroud, Benoit. On Ne Dit Pas... on Dit... . (p. 1653)
Perroud, Benoit, illus. see Laboucarie, Sandra.
Perrow, Angeli. Many Hands: A Penobscot Indian Story. Austin, Heather, illus. (p. 1400)
Perruchon, Jules. Chroniques de Zar'a yâ'eqôb et de Ba'eda Mâryâm, Rois d'Éthiopie de 1434 a 1478 (Texte Éthiopien et Traduction) Précédées d'une Introduction (Classic Reprint) (p. 389)
Perruzzi, Diane, illus. see Tong, Anthony.
Perry, Adam. Magicians of Elephant County. Perry, Adam, illus. (p. 1381)
—Mister Ray. (p. 1482)
Perry, Andrea. Bicklebys' Birdbath. Angaramo, Roberta, illus. (p. 215)
Perry, Anna C. Royer-Greaves Monthly, Vol. 51: 1980-1990 (Classic Reprint) (p. 1910)
Perry, Anne Gordon. Magnificent Moles of Mede Meadow. (p. 1382)
Perry, Aumi, illus. see Bean, Margo Cronbaugh.
Perry, Aumi Kauffman, illus. see Bean, Margo Cronbaugh.
Perry, Barbara. Moving Day. Brook, Autumn, illus. (p. 1516)
—Perfect Puddle. Brook, Autumn, illus. (p. 1722)
Perry, Bliss. Broughton House (Classic Reprint) (p. 286)
—Plated City (Classic Reprint) (p. 1758)
—Powers at Play (Classic Reprint) (p. 1783)
Perry, Brad Lee. Clumsy Claudia & the Gentle Forest Friends Perry, Diana Torri, illus. (p. 409)
Perry, Brenda. Taste Buddy. (p. 2192)
Perry, Brien. Education of Loosy Potts: Clean Your Room. Webb, Blair, illus. (p. 626)
—Education of Loosy Potts. (p. 626)
—Frog & Dog: Unlikely Friendships. Webb, Blair, illus. (p. 789)
—Frog & Dog - Unlikely Friendships. (p. 789)
Perry, Caroline. Bou. Parisot, Felicite, illus. (p. 265)
Perry, Celeste M. Queen of Chaos. (p. 1824)
Perry, Chrissie. Karate Kicks. (p. 1203)
—Last One in the Universe. (p. 1249)
—Lucky Jars & Broken Promises. Egmont, Hardie Grant, illus. (p. 1364)
—Private List for Camp Success. (p. 1802)
—Project Best Friend. (p. 1805)
—Project Best Friend. Kissi, Marta & Egmont, Hardie Grant, illus. (p. 1805)
—Truly Terrible Mistake. Egmont, Hardie Grant, illus. (p. 2295)
Perry, Chrissie, et al. Brilliant Besties (p. 282)
Perry, Curtis, illus. see Washington, Angel D.
Perry, Dakota. Vulture Itus (p. 2369)
Perry, Dale. Adventures of the Super Bunny Club. (p. 28)
Perry, Diana Torri, illus. see Perry, Brad Lee.
Perry, Douglas M. Boomer Likes to Point. (p. 261)
Perry, Edward Delavan. Monographs on Education in the United States, 6; the American University, Pp. 253-318. (p. 1494)
Perry, Edwin R. Syllabus, 1901 (Classic Reprint) (p. 2172)
Perry, Ellyse;Clark. Magic Feet. (p. 1377)
Perry, Ezra G. Trip Around Cape Cod: The South Shore & Historical Plymouth (Classic Reprint) (p. 2288)
—Trip Around Cape Cod: Nantucket, Marthas Vineyard, South Shore, & Historical Plymouth (Classic Reprint) (p. 2288)
Perry, Frances Foster. Their Hearts Desire (Classic Reprint) (p. 2215)
Perry, Frances Melville. Story of David Crockett: For Young Readers (Classic Reprint) (p. 2129)
Perry, Fred. Gold Digger Platinum (p. 855)
—Gold Digger - Platinum (p. 855)
—Grossery Games. (p. 898)
—Playing Dead. (p. 1760)
—Time Lincoln (p. 2244)
Perry, Fred, illus. see Shakespeare, William.
Perry, Fred & Dlin, Doug. Gold Digger Tech Manual. (p. 855)
Perry, George B. Slings & Arrows: Tales, Sketches & Verses, Grave & Gay (Classic Reprint) (p. 2038)
Perry, Geraldine S. Adventures of the Tinsel Tots. (p. 28)
Perry, Gina. Small. (p. 2039)
Perry, Gina, illus. see Bar-El, Dan.
Perry, Henry Ten Eyck, ed. see Congreve, William.
Perry, Isaac. Q Saves the Sun. Harrington, Shomari, illus. (p. 1821)
Perry, Jackie Hill. Jude - Teen Girls' Bible Study Book: Contending for the Faith in Today's Culture. (p. 1185)
Perry, Jennifer A., illus. see Szish, Jill Henry.
Perry, John. Book That Eats People. Fearing, Mark, illus. (p. 260)
—Story of Mitch. Kendall, Bryan, illus. (p. 2131)
Perry, John Jasiel, jt. auth. see Dafoe, Daniel.
Perry, John T. Mirror, Vol. 11: Waltham High School, Waltham, Mass. ; June 1916 (Classic Reprint) (p. 1475)
Perry, Jolene. All the Forever Things. (p. 54)
—Has to Be Love. (p. 936)
—Next Door Boys. (p. 1600)
—Stronger Than You Know. (p. 2142)
Perry, Jolene, jt. auth. see Desir, C.
Perry, Jolene, jt. auth. see Desir, Christa.
Perry, Joseph Franklin. Kennel Diseases: Their Symptoms, Nature, Causes, & Treatment (Classic Reprint) (p. 1209)
Perry, Kathy J. Feebs to the Rescue: Night of the Coon. Bruno, Elizabeth, ed. (p. 718)
—Feebs to the Rescue. Bruno, Elizabeth, ed. (p. 718)
Perry, Latashia M. Imagination Like Mine. (p. 1100)
Perry, Lauren. My Baby's First Love. Smith, Brittney, illus. (p. 1531)
Perry, Laurie. Kaycee's New School (p. 1207)
Perry, Lawrence. Prince or Chauffeur? A Story of Newport. (p. 1794)
—Prince or Chauffeur? A Story of Newport (Classic Reprint) (p. 1794)
Perry, Lee Ann, illus. see Freeman, Chip.
Perry, M. LaVora. History of the Civil Rights Movement. (p. 980)
—History of the Civil Rights Movement. Hill, Marc Lamont, ed. (p. 980)
Perry, Margie, illus. see Perrine, David L.
Perry, Mark. 'Post' Mark—Santa's Misfit Postman. (p. 1780)
Perry, Martine. Aritmetica Aritmetica: Resuelve el Problema de Cada Dibujo Coloreando Tus Respuestas. (p. 116)
Perry, Melanie Denise. Johnathan & Geneva the Adventures of Zeallionaire Kid's. Neal, Albert, ed. (p. 1174)
—Jonathan y Geneva Las Aventuras de Los Zeallionaire Kids. Neal, Albert, ed. (p. 1177)
Perry, Mia, tr. see Tada, Hiroshi.
Perry, Michael. Scavengers. (p. 1943)
Perry, Mike, illus. see Lamb, Sean.
Perry, Mike, illus. see Tea, Michelle.
Perry, Molly. Game. (p. 806)
Perry, Montanye. Motion Picture Story Magazine, Vol. 2: August 1911-January 1912 (Classic Reprint) (p. 1511)
Perry, Nicole. Resilient ME Gratitude Journal for Teens: Dream Big. (p. 1869)
Perry, Nicole P. & Lipp, Rebekah R. Let Your Light Shine: Kids Mini Gratitude Journal. (p. 1269)
Perry, Nora. Another Flock of Girls (Classic Reprint) (p. 100)
—Book of Love Stories (Classic Reprint) (p. 259)
—Flock of Girls & Boys. (p. 750)
—Flock of Girls & Boys (Classic Reprint) (p. 750)
—Flock of Girls, & Their Friends (Classic Reprint) (p. 750)
—Hope Benham: A Story for Girls (Classic Reprint) (p. 1001)
—New Songs & Ballads. (p. 1597)
—Rosebud Garden of Girls (Classic Reprint) (p. 1905)
—Three Little Daughters of the Revolution. (p. 2233)
—Three Little Daughters of the Revolution (Classic Reprint) (p. 2233)
—Tragedy of the Unexpected: And Other Stories (Classic Reprint) (p. 2274)
—Tragedy of the Unexpected. (p. 2274)
—Youngest Miss. Lorton, & Other Stories (Classic Reprint) (p. 2532)
Perry, Phil Franklin. Poems (Classic Reprint) (p. 1765)
Perry, Phyllis J. Missing Bones. (p. 1480)
—Pandas' Earthquake Escape Detwiler, Susan, illus. (p. 1696)
Perry, Phyllis Jean. Bold Women in Colorado History. (p. 254)

Perry, Phyllis Jean, jt. auth. see Gardner, Robert.
Perry, Rev Sue. Two in One: The Monday, Tuesday, Wednesday, Thursday, Friday, etc Folks! Everyone Must Make Decisions. (p. 2308)
Perry, Robert. Down at the Seaweed Cafe. Guzek, Greta, illus. (p. 590)
—Ferryboat Ride. Guzek, Greta, illus. (p. 721)
—My Vancouver Sketchbook. Guzek, Greta, illus. (p. 1563)
Perry, Salina. Adventures of Ellie & Blankie: Ellie Goes to India. (p. 23)
Perry, Sarah. If ... 25th Anniversary Edition. (p. 1090)
Perry, Sondra. Most Unusual Pet Ever, Henry Our Great Blue Heron & His Adventures 2nd Edition. Byer, Janice, illus. (p. 1508)
Perry Sr., Audie. Heroic Kids of the Inner Dimension (p. 962)
Perry, Stella George Stern. Angel of Christmas: A Vision of to-Day (Classic Reprint) (p. 85)
—Little Bronze Playfellows: A Phantasy for Children & Grown-Ups (Classic Reprint) (p. 1313)
—Melindy (Classic Reprint) (p. 1443)
Perry, Tally. Saving Sunny Stream, a Wormie Wormald Adventure. (p. 1939)
Perry, Thomas, jt. auth. see Deuker, Carl.
Perry, Tristan. Cinnamon Takes a Vacation: Furry Tails #2 (p. 392)
Perry, Trudy, illus. see Wiedmeyer, Nancy.
Perry, Valerie J. Trilby Learns a Lesson. (p. 2288)
Perry, W. A. American Game Fishes: Their Habits, Habitat, & Peculiarities; How, When, & Where to Angle for Them (Classic Reprint) (p. 71)
Perry, W. Thomas. Little Rossie (Classic Reprint) (p. 1327)
Perry, William. London Guide, & Stranger's Safeguard Against the Cheats, Swindlers, & Pickpockets That Abound Within the Bills of Mortality: Forming a Picture of London, As Regards Active Life; Collected from the Verbal Communications of William Perry, & Others. (p. 1341)
—Royal Standard English Dictionary: In Which the Words Are Not Only Rationally Divided into Syllables, Accurately Accented, Their Part of Speech Properly Distinguished, but Likewise, by a Key to This Work (Classic Reprint) (p. 1910)
—Trials of Ezra (Classic Reprint) (p. 2286)
Perry, William, jt. auth. see Johnson, Samuel.
Perryman, F. M. Pioneer Life in Illinois (Classic Reprint) (p. 1748)
Perryman, Grant N. Ama's Dream. (p. 62)
Perry-Warnes, Ned, illus. see Clare, Elisabeth.
Persad, Sabbithry. Operation: Reuse It! - Read Think Reuse. Campbell, Jenny, illus. (p. 1666)
Persano, Thomas. Ghana. (p. 826)
—Japan. (p. 1159)
Persano, Thomas & Orellana, Marjorie Faulstich. Israel. (p. 1140)
Perschbacher, Steve. God Goggles: Pride vs Humility. (p. 851)
Perse, Perse. Satires (Classic Reprint) (p. 1936)
—Traduction Nouvelle des Satyres de Perse et de Juvenal (Classic Reprint) (p. 2274)
Pershbacher, Gerald. Hero of Faith - C.F.W. Walther. (p. 961)
Persiani, Tony, illus. see Barton, Chris.
Persico, Zoe. Georgia's Terrific, Colorific Experiment. (p. 821)
Persico, Zoe, illus. see Acampora, Courtney & Fischer, Maggie.
Persico, Zoe, illus. see Clark, Karla.
Persico, Zoe, illus. see Crowe, Carmen.
Persico, Zoe, illus. see Dahl, Michael.
Persico, Zoe, illus. see Harrington, Claudia.
Persico, Zoe, illus. see Kilgore, Emily.
Persico, Zoe, illus. see May, Tallulah.
Persico, Zoe, illus. see Murray, Diana.
Persico, Zoe, illus. see Riding, Robin.
Persico, Zoe, illus. see Rue, Ginger.
Persico, Zoe, illus. see Sisler, Celeste & May, Tallulah.
Persico, Zoe, illus. see Swift, Ginger.
Persius, Persius. Satires de Perse et de Juvénal, Vol. 1 (Classic Reprint) (p. 1936)
—Traduction des Satires de Perse, et de Juvenal (Classic Reprint) (p. 2274)
Persky, Daniel. Spoken Hebrew: A Manual of Hebrew Conversations (Classic Reprint) (p. 2086)
Person, Elizabeth, illus. see Smith, Emma Bland.
Person, Michelle. Adventures of Kai & the Daddyman. (p. 24)
—Kai & the Daddyman. (p. 1201)
—Kai Gets Earrings. (p. 1201)
—Nathaniel English in Leaders of the Revolution. (p. 1577)
Person, Naomi, et al. Sow What? Hooper, Hadley & Stryk, Suzanne, illus. (p. 2070)
Person, Stephen. Army Night Stalkers in Action. (p. 118)
—Bubonic Plague: The Black Death! (p. 289)
—Collared Peccary: Cactus-Eater. (p. 414)
—Coral Reef: A Giant City under the Sea. (p. 453)
—Cougar: A Cat with Many Names. (p. 457)
—Devastated by a Volcano! (p. 535)
—Ghostly Alcatraz Island. (p. 829)
—Great Dane: Gentle Giant. (p. 885)
—Malaria: Super Killer! (p. 1391)
—Navy SEAL Team Six in Action. (p. 1583)
—Polar Bear: Shrinking Ice. (p. 1769)
—Roseate Spoonbill: Pretty in Pink. (p. 1905)
—Saving Animals after Tornadoes. (p. 1938)
—Saving Animals from Hurricanes. (p. 1938)
—Sled Dog: Powerful Miracle. (p. 2035)
—Struck by Lightning! (p. 2142)
—Voodoo in New Orleans. (p. 2367)
—Walrus: Tusk, Tusk. (p. 2373)
Person, Stephen & Salm, Rodney V. Coral Reef: A Giant City under the Sea. (p. 453)
Personal, Presenting. Last Cruise of the National: Or the People's Revenge (Classic Reprint) (p. 1247)
Personality, et al. Personality Matters. (p. 1725)
Persons Gilley, Janette. Sawyers Pond. (p. 1939)
Persons, Katelynn, jt. auth. see Colby, J. Z.
Persons, W. Scott. Dinosaurs of the Alberta Badlands. Csotonyi, Julius T., illus. (p. 551)
—Mega Rex: A Tyrannosaurus Named Scotty. Zaiken, Beth, illus. (p. 1441)
Pertierra, Daniel. Dragonslaying Maiden. (p. 596)
Pertile, Paula. Gingerbread Man. (p. 834)
Pertile, Paula, illus. see Wilson, Zachary.
Pertwee, Ernest. Scenes from Dickens: For Drawing-Room & Platform Acting (Classic Reprint) (p. 1943)
Pertwee, Roland. Men of Affairs. (p. 1446)
—Old Card (Classic Reprint) (p. 1644)
—Our Wonderful Selves (Classic Reprint) (p. 1681)
—Transactions of Lord Louis Lewis (Classic Reprint) (p. 2277)
Peru, Ruby. Bits of String Too Small to Save. (p. 235)
Perugini, Donna. Adventures of Amelia Airheart Butterfly. (p. 21)
—Do Angels Go Camping? (p. 570)
Perugini), Kate (. Comedy of Charles Dickens, Vol. 1: A Book of Chapters & Extracts Taken from the Writer's Novels (Classic Reprint) (p. 429)
Peruzzo, Nicolas. Safari Dreams. Peruzzo, Nicolas, illus. (p. 1921)
Pervanoglu, John. Dictionary of the English & Greek Languages: With a Preface, an Introduction on English Pronunciation, a Table of Irregular Verbs & a List of Abbreviations (Classic Reprint) (p. 542)
Pervinquiere, Leon. Études de Paléontologie Tunisienne, Vol. 1: Céphalopodes des Terrains Secondaires; Texte (Classic Reprint) (p. 666)
Pesca, Jodi. Angels Angels Everywhere. (p. 86)
Pesce, Angelique. Peas Are Green. (p. 1711)
Pesce, Dom. At the Kennel: Understanding Addition. (p. 131)
Peschke, M. Vacation Queen. Mourning, Tuesday, illus. (p. 2343)
Peschke, Marci. Art Queen. Mourning, Tuesday, illus. (p. 121)
—Blueberry Queen Mourning, Tuesday, illus. (p. 249)
—Cooking Queen. Mourning, Tuesday, illus. (p. 447)
—Cupcake Queen. Mourning, Tuesday, illus. (p. 485)
—Dancing Queen Mourning, Tuesday, illus. (p. 500)
—Drama Queen Mourning, Tuesday, illus. (p. 596)
—Fashion Queen. Mourning, Tuesday, illus. (p. 712)
—Fishing Queen. Mourning, Tuesday, illus. (p. 742)
—Football Queen Mourning, Tuesday, illus. (p. 761)
—Green Queen Mourning, Tuesday, illus. (p. 894)
—Gymnastics Queen. Mourning, Tuesday, illus. (p. 907)
—Hoop Queen Mourning, Tuesday, illus. (p. 1000)
—Kylie Jean Mourning, Tuesday, illus. (p. 1234)
—Kylie Jean Collection. Mourning, Tuesday, illus. (p. 1234)
—Party Queen Mourning, Tuesday, illus. (p. 1702)
—Pirate Queen. Mourning, Tuesday, illus. (p. 1750)
—Robot Queen. Mourning, Tuesday, illus. (p. 1892)
—Rodeo Queen Mourning, Tuesday, illus. (p. 1897)
—Singing Queen Mourning, Tuesday, illus. (p. 2024)
—Soccer Queen. Mourning, Tuesday, illus. (p. 2052)
—Spelling Queen Mourning, Tuesday, illus. (p. 2079)
—Summer Camp Queen Mourning, Tuesday, illus. (p. 2148)
—Vacation Queen. Mourning, Tuesday, illus. (p. 2343)
—Valentine Queen Mourning, Tuesday, illus. (p. 2344)
Peschke, Marci, jt. auth. see Green, Gail.
Peschke, Marci, jt. auth. see Meinking, Mary.
Peschke, Marci, jt. auth. see Ventura, Marne.
Pesenti, Antonia. Rhyme Flies. (p. 1875)
Pesenti, Antonia, illus. see Bell, Hilary.
Pesenti, Antonia, jt. auth. see Bell, Hilary.
Peshkoff, Alexei Maximovitch. Orloff Couple & Malva (Classic Reprint) (p. 1672)
Peskimo. Marvel Alphablock: The Marvel Cinematic Universe from a to Z. (p. 1412)
Peskimo, illus. see Abrams Appleseed.
Peskimo, illus. see Franceschelli, Christopher.
Peskimo, illus. see Lucasfilm LTD.
Peskimo, jt. auth. see Franceschelli, Christopher.
Peskowitz, Miriam. Code Like a Girl: Rad Tech Projects & Practical Tips. (p. 411)
Peskowitz, Miriam, jt. auth. see Buchanan, Andrea J.
Pesout, Christine. Earth, the Alphabet, & Me. Donaldson, Jennifer, illus. (p. 617)
Pessarrodona, Marina, illus. see O'Sullivan, Jill Korey.
Pessin-Whedbee, Brook. Who Are You? The Kid's Guide to Gender & Identity. Bardoff, Naomi, illus. (p. 2446)
Pessl, Marisha. Neverworld Wake. (p. 1591)
Pessoa, Karen. Cam's Sneakers. (p. 317)
Pestalozzi, Johann Heinrich. Leonard & Gertrude: A Popular Story, Written Originally in German; Translated into French, & Now Attempted in English (Classic Reprint) (p. 1267)
—Leonard & Gertrude: A Popular Story, Written Originally in German; Translated into French, & Now Attempted in English; with the Hope of Its Being Useful to All Classes of Society (Classic Reprint) (p. 1267)
—Leonard & Gertrude. (p. 1267)
Petach, Heidi. Daniel & the Lions. Dickson, Bill, illus. (p. 502)
Petechuk, David. Global Economy & the Environment (p. 843)
—Non-Continental: Alaska, Hawaii (p. 1618)
—PACs, Super PACs, & Fundraising. (p. 1691)
—Undead: Vampires, Zombies, & Other Strange Monsters. (p. 2320)
Petek-Markic, Zdenka. Birds. (p. 231)
Petelinsek, Kathleen. Crafting with Duct Tape: Even More Projects. Petelinsek, Kathleen, illus. (p. 466)
—Crafting with Tissue Paper. Petelinsek, Kathleen, illus. (p. 466)
—Learning to Make Books. Petelinsek, Kathleen, illus. (p. 1259)
—Learning to Sew. Petelinsek, Kathleen, illus. (p. 1259)
—Little Jack Horner. Petelinsek, Kathleen, illus. (p. 1319)
—Making Clay Bead Crafts. Petelinsek, Kathleen, illus. (p. 1388)
—Making Jewelry with Rubber Bands. Petelinsek, Kathleen, illus. (p. 1389)
—Making Sock Puppets. Petelinsek, Kathleen, illus. (p. 1390)
—Modeling Clay Creations. Petelinsek, Kathleen, illus. (p. 1486)
—Pipe Cleaner Crafts. Petelinsek, Kathleen, illus. (p. 1748)
Petelinsek, Kathleen, illus. see Alinas, Marv.
Petelinsek, Kathleen, illus. see Bailer, Darice.
Petelinsek, Kathleen, illus. see Berendes, Mary.
Petelinsek, Kathleen, illus. see Coleman, Kelly.
Petelinsek, Kathleen, illus. see Felix, Rebecca.
Petelinsek, Kathleen, illus. see Fontichiaro, Kristin & Truesdell, Ann.
Petelinsek, Kathleen, illus. see Fontichiaro, Kristin.
Petelinsek, Kathleen, illus. see Gregory, Josh.
Petelinsek, Kathleen, illus. see Harner, Jennifer L.
Petelinsek, Kathleen, illus. see Higgins, Nadia.
Petelinsek, Kathleen, illus. see Marsico, Katie.
Petelinsek, Kathleen, illus. see Matteson, Adrienne.
Petelinsek, Kathleen, illus. see McHugh, Jeff.
Petelinsek, Kathleen, illus. see Newman, Heather.
Petelinsek, Kathleen, illus. see Pearson, Yvonne.
Petelinsek, Kathleen, illus. see Rau, Dana Meachen.
Petelinsek, Kathleen, illus. see Reinke, Beth Bence.
Petelinsek, Kathleen, illus. see Simons, Lisa M. Bolt.
Petelinsek, Kathleen, illus. see Thornborough, Kathy.
Petelinsek, Kathleen, illus. see Truesdell, Ann & Fontichiaro, Kristin.
Petelinsek, Kathleen, illus. see Truesdell, Ann.
Petelinsek, Kathleen, illus. see Yomtov, Nel.
Petelinsek, Kathleen, illus. see Yomtov, Nelson.
Petelinsek, Kathleen, illus. see York, M. J.
Peten, Chantal, illus. see Ducatteau, Florence.
Peter, Andrea. Crime by Design. (p. 474)
Peter Carnavas, illus. see Williamson, John & Carnavas, Peter.
Peter, Dawn. Mark the Remarkable & Can't Say Can't. (p. 1407)
Peter, Mary T. Short Stories for Teens by Teens. (p. 2010)
Peter, Paul & Eagle, Kim. It's Raining, It's Pouring. Davenier, Christine & Gilbert, Rob, illus. (p. 1147)
Peter, Paul, et al. I'm in Love with a Big Blue Frog. Brunet, Joshua S., illus. (p. 1098)
Peter Pauper Press, Inc., creator. 100 Questions about Rocks & Minerals. (p. 2557)
Peter Pauper Press Inc, creator. ABC Animals. (p. 3)
Peter Pauper Press, Inc., creator. All the Birds in the World. (p. 53)
—Blank Comic Book (Stencil Included) (p. 243)
Peter Pauper Press Inc, creator. Brave, Strong, & Smart - That's Me! Coloring Book. (p. 276)
Peter Pauper Press, Inc., creator. Create Your Own Storybook. (p. 469)
—Dinos after Dark Shadow Book. (p. 548)
—Go to Bed, Sleepyhead! Bedtime Shadow Book. (p. 848)
—Good Night, Mommy Bedtime Shadow Book. (p. 864)
—Handwriting: Learn Cursive! (p. 916)
—Handwriting: Learn to Print! (p. 916)
—How I Trained My Dog in Ten Days. (p. 1032)
—I'm Learning My Colors! Board Book. (p. 1098)
—I'm Learning My First... (4-Book Set) (p. 1098)
—I'm Learning My First 101 Animals! Board Book. (p. 1098)
—I'm Learning My First 101 Words! Board Book. (p. 1098)
—I'm Learning My Numbers! Board Book. (p. 1098)
—Kids Unplugged Fashion Activity Book. (p. 1216)
—Learn Scissor Skills. (p. 1255)
Peter Pauper Press Inc, creator. Learn to Draw... 3D Illusions & More (Easy Step-By-Step Drawing Guide) (p. 1255)
Peter Pauper Press, Inc., creator. Learn to Draw... Animals! Easy Step-By-Step Drawing Guide. (p. 1256)
—Learn to Draw... Christmas! Easy Step-By-Step Drawing Guide. (p. 1256)
Peter Pauper Press Inc, creator. Learn to Draw... Cute Things (Easy Step-By-Step Drawing Guide) (p. 1256)
Peter Pauper Press, Inc., creator. Learn to Draw... Dinosaurs! Easy Step-By-Step Drawing Guide. (p. 1256)
—Learn to Draw... Faces! (p. 1256)
—Learn to Draw... Flower Garden! Easy Step-By-Step Drawing Guide. (p. 1256)
—Learn to Draw... Ocean Wonders! Easy Step-By-Step Drawing Guide. (p. 1256)
—Learn to Draw People! (p. 1256)
—Learn to Draw... Pets! (p. 1256)
—Learn to Draw... Princess Kingdom! Easy Step-By-Step Drawing Guide. (p. 1256)
—Learn to Draw... Things That Go! Easy Step-By-Step Drawing Guide. (p. 1257)
—Learn to Draw... Unicorns, Mermaids & More! (p. 1257)
Peter Pauper Press Inc, creator. Mood Flip Book. (p. 1500)
Peter Pauper Press, Inc., creator. My First Coloring Book: Animals. (p. 1543)
—My First Coloring Book: Numbers & Shapes. (p. 1543)
Peter Pauper Press Inc, creator. My First Opposites Board Book. (p. 1545)
—My First Shapes Board Book. (p. 1546)
—Practice Writing Pad (80 Sheets) (p. 1784)
Peter Pauper Press, Inc., creator. Rosie & Crayon. (p. 1906)
Peter Pauper Press Inc, creator. Scratch & Sketch America (Trace Along) (p. 1963)
—Scratch & Sketch Ballet (Trace Along) (p. 1963)
—Scratch & Sketch Dragons & Mythical Creatures (Trace Along) (p. 1963)
—Scratch & Sketch Extreme Cities (Trace Along) (p. 1963)
—Scratch & Sketch Fashion Show (Trace Along) (p. 1963)
—Scratch & Sketch Fine Art (Trace Along) (p. 1963)
Peter Pauper Press, Inc., creator. Scratch & Sketch Horses (Trace-Along) An Art Activity Book for Artistic Horse Lovers of All Ages. (p. 1963)
Peter Pauper Press Inc, creator. Scratch & Sketch Jurassic (Trace Along) (p. 1963)
—Scratch & Sketch Merry Christmas (Trace Along) (p. 1963)
Peter Pauper Press, Inc., creator. Scratch & Sketch National Parks (Trace-Along) An Art Activity Book for Artistic Rangers of All Ages. (p. 1963)
Peter Pauper Press Inc, creator. Scratch & Sketch Outer Space (Trace Along) (p. 1963)
—Scratch & Sketch Pirates (Trace Along) (p. 1963)
Peter Pauper Press, Inc., creator. Scratch & Sketch Take Flight (Trace-Along) An Art Activity Book for Artistic Aviators of All Ages. (p. 1963)
Peter Pauper Press Inc, creator. Scratch & Sketch Wild Safari (Trace Along) (p. 1963)
Peter Pauper Press, Inc., creator. Scratch & Sketch(tm) All about Me (Trace Along) (p. 1963)
—Scratch & Sketch(tm) Butterflies & Friends (Trace Along) (p. 1963)
—Scratch & Sketch(tm) Garden Fairies (Trace Along) (p. 1963)
—Scratch & Sketch(tm) Rain Forest (Trace Along) (p. 1963)
—Scratch & Sketch(tm) Sharks (Trace Along) (p. 1963)
—Scratch & Sketch(tm) under the Sea (Trace Along) (p. 1963)
—Scratch & Sketch(tm) Wild Cats (Trace Along) (p. 1963)
Peter Pauper Press Inc, creator. Seek & Find - Unicorns (Seek & Find) (p. 1984)
—Storybook Pad (40 Sheets) (p. 2136)
Peter Pauper Press, Inc., creator. Super Scratch & Sketch(tm) (Trace Along) (p. 2156)
—Teddy the Terrible. (p. 2198)
—Trace & Learn: Letters! (p. 2271)
—Trace & Learn: Numbers! (p. 2271)
—Trace & Learn: Sight Words! (p. 2271)
Peter Pauper Press Inc, creator. Unicorns Activity Book. (p. 2329)
—Unicorns Coloring Book. (p. 2329)
Peter Pauper Press, Inc., creator. Unicorn's Magical Day Bedtime Shadow Book. (p. 2329)
Peter Pauper Press Inc, creator. Where's the Narwhal? (Seek & Find) (p. 2441)
Peter Pauper Press Staff, et al. Vampires, Werewolves, Zombies: From the papers of Herr Doktor Max Sturm & Baron Ludwig Von Drang. Waldman, Bruce, illus. (p. 2346)
Peterfreund, Diana. Across a Star-Swept Sea. (p. 11)
—Ascendant. (p. 125)
—For Darkness Shows the Stars. (p. 762)
—In the Hall with the Knife: A Clue Mystery, Book One. (p. 1109)
—In the Study with the Wrench: A Clue Mystery, Book Two. (p. 1111)
—Omega City. (p. 1651)
—Omega City: Infinity Base. (p. 1651)
—Omega City: the Forbidden Fortress. (p. 1651)
—Rampant. (p. 1839)
Peter-Henderson, Jeannine, illus. see Peter, Joyce.
Peterkin, P. A. UFO Lands in USA! (X Books: Strange) Was Spacecraft Crash Covered Up? (p. 2313)
Peterman, Rosie L., et al. Divorce & Stepfamilies. (p. 566)
Peters, Adrea L. Becoming Truitt Skye: Book 1: the City on the Sea. (p. 187)
—Becoming Truitt Skye: Book One: the City on the Sea. (p. 187)
Peters, Andrew. Ravenwood. (p. 1844)
Peters, Andrew J. Banished Sons of Poseidon. (p. 164)
—Seventh Pleiade. (p. 1994)
Peters, Andy. Around the Universe in 80 Mazes. (p. 118)
—Maze Quest: Navigate the Mazes, Complete the Search & Find, Solve the Puzzle Fun. (p. 1430)
Peters, Andy, illus. see Giles, Sophie & Davis, Kate.
Peters, Anna. Friendly Rubbish Monsters. (p. 786)
Peters, Celeste A. Food. (p. 759)
—Food Q & A. (p. 760)
—Health. (p. 943)
—Health Q & A. (p. 943)
Peters, Charles. Girl's Own Outdoor Book: Containing Practical Help to Girls on Matters Relating to Outdoor Occupation & Recreation (Classic Reprint) (p. 839)
Peters, Chelsea N. Farzana's Journey: A Bangladesh Story of the Water, Land, & People. (p. 712)
Peters, Chris. Girls' Hockey (p. 838)
—Great Moments in Olympic Ice Hockey (p. 888)
—Hockey Season Ticket: The Ultimate Fan Guide. (p. 986)
—Hockey's New Wave: The Young Superstars Taking over the Game. (p. 986)
—New Home for Lolo: Moving into the Omaha Zoo's African Grasslands. (p. 1594)
—Stanley Cup Finals (p. 2101)
Peters, Daniel B., et al. Warrior Workbook: A Guide for Conquering Your Worry Monster. (p. 2379)
Peters, Danni. Testimony of Love. (p. 2209)
Peters, Darcy, illus. see Silcox, Beth Douglass.
Peters, Diane. Gaming: Before It Outplays You Shannon, Ben, illus. (p. 808)
—Gaming: Deal with It Before It Outplays You Shannon, Ben, illus. (p. 808)
—Girlness: Deal with It Body & Soul. Murray, Steven, illus. (p. 838)
—Privacy: Deal with It Like Nobody's Business Tankard, Jeremy, illus. (p. 1801)
—Procrastination: Deal with It All in Good Time Tankard, Jeremy, illus. (p. 1803)
Peters, Elisa. Earth. (p. 615)
—Earth: La Tierra. (p. 616)
—It's a Bird! (p. 1143)
—It's a Bird! Es un Ave! (p. 1143)
—It's a Bird! / ¡Es un Ave! (p. 1143)
—It's a Caterpillar! (p. 1143)
—It's a Caterpillar! Aes una Oruga! (p. 1143)
—It's a Caterpillar! / ¡Es una Oruga! (p. 1143)
—It's a Dragonfly! (p. 1143)
—It's a Dragonfly! Es una Libélula! (p. 1143)
—It's a Dragonfly! / ¡Es una Libélula! (p. 1143)
—It's a Sunflower! (p. 1143)
—It's a Sunflower! Es un Girasol! (p. 1143)
—It's a Sunflower! / ¡Es un Girasol! (p. 1143)
—It's an Apple Tree! (p. 1144)
—It's an Apple Tree! Es un Manzano! (p. 1144)
—It's an Apple Tree! / ¡Es un Manzano! (p. 1144)
—It's Snow! (p. 1147)
—It's Snow! La Nieve! (p. 1147)
—It's Snow! / ¡la Nieve! (p. 1147)
—Let's Ride the City Bus! (p. 1277)
—Let's Ride the Streetcar! (p. 1277)
—Let's Ride the Subway! (p. 1277)
—Let's Take the Ferry! (p. 1277)
—Let's Take the Train! (p. 1277)
—Malala Yousafzai: Pakistani Activist for Female Education. (p. 1391)
—Moon: La Luna. (p. 1501)
—Moon. (p. 1501)
—Outer Space: El Espacio Exterior. (p. 1684)

P

Petro-Roy, Jen. Good Enough: a Novel. (p. 862)
—You Are Enough: Your Guide to Body Image & Eating Disorder Recovery. (p. 2524)
Petrossi, Fabrizio. Disney Puppy Dog Pals: When Pugs Fly. (p. 563)
Petrossi, Fabrizio, illus. see Behling, Steve.
Petrossi, Fabrizio, illus. see Broderick, Kathy.
Petrossi, Fabrizio, illus. see Editors of PI Kids.
Petrossi, Fabrizio, illus. see Fischer, Maggie.
Petrossi, Fabrizio, illus. see Golden Books.
Petrossi, Fabrizio, illus. see Harmening, Derek.
Petrossi, Fabrizio, illus. see Huntley, Tex.
Petrossi, Fabrizio, illus. see James, Hollis.
Petrossi, Fabrizio, illus. see Matheis, Mickie.
Petrossi, Fabrizio, illus. see p i kids.
Petrossi, Fabrizio, illus. see PI Kids.
Petrossi, Fabrizio, illus. see Random House Disney Staff.
Petrossi, Fabrizio, illus. see Random House.
Petrossi, Fabrizio, illus. see Skwish, Emily.
Petrossi, Fabrizio, illus. see Tillworth, Mary.
Petrossi, Fabrizio, illus. see Vitale, Brooke.
Petrossi, Fabrizio, illus. see Wage, Erin Rose.
Petrossi, Fabrizio, illus. see Wagner, Veronica & P. I. Kids Staff.
Petrossi, Fabrizio, illus. see Wagner, Veronica.
Petrossi, Fabrizio, illus. see Ziegler-Sullivan, Ursula.
Petrossi, Fabrizio, jt. illus. see Moore, Harry.
Petrov, Anton, illus. see Kennedy, Pamela.
Petrov, Anton, illus. see Mackall, Dandi Daley.
Petrov, Anton, illus. see Schneider, Richard H.
Petrov, Vaughan, contrib. by. America Will Win Wwiii. (p. 70)
Petrova, Natalia. Twice Born in Russia: My Life Before & in the Revolution (Classic Reprint) (p. 2304)
Petrovic, Svetlana. Brown Bear, White Bear. Hardy, Vincent, illus. (p. 286)
Petrovich, Eduard, illus. see Caramagna, Joe.
Petrovich, Eduard, illus. see Cook, Katie.
Petrovskaya, Olga, ed. see AZ Books Staff.
Petrower, Scott, jt. auth. see Vitale, Brooke.
Petru, Suzin, illus. see Costanza, Francine.
Petruccio, Stephen, illus. see Halfmann, Janet.
Petruccio, Steven. At the Construction Site (en el Sitio de Construccion) Gongora, Oscar, tr. (p. 130)
Petruccio, Steven, illus. see Hillert, Margaret, et al.
Petruccio, Steven James. Air Force One Coloring Book. (p. 37)
—Alexander Hamilton Coloring Book. (p. 42)
—American Heroes Coloring Book. (p. 72)
—American Legends & Tall Tales. (p. 72)
—Apollo 11: First Men on the Moon Coloring Book. (p. 105)
—BOOST Trucks Coloring Book. (p. 262)
—Cars: Doodle, Design & Draw. (p. 334)
—Create Your Own Construction Truck Sticker Activity Book. (p. 469)
—Create Your Own Fire Truck. (p. 469)
—Design It! CARS. (p. 532)
—History of the Civil Rights Movement Coloring Book. (p. 980)
—History of the White House Coloring Book. (p. 981)
—Let's Build a House! Coloring Book. (p. 1270)
—Meet Ruth Bader Ginsburg Coloring Book. (p. 1439)
Petruccio, Steven James, illus. see Galvin, Laura Gates.
Petruccio, Steven James, illus. see Halfmann, Janet.
Petruccio, Steven James, illus. see Hernández, José M. & Ventura, Gabriela Baeza.
Petruccio, Steven James, illus. see Hillert, Margaret.
Petruccio, Steven James, illus. see Walker, Sally M.
Petruccio, Steven James, illus. see Zoehfeld, Kathleen Weidner.
Petruccio, Steven James, jt. auth. see Zoehfeld, Kathleen Weidner.
Petruccio, Steven James & Coloring Books Staff. Roadside Attractions Coloring Book: Weird & Wacky Landmarks from Across the USA! (p. 1889)
Petruccioli, Rita, illus. see Amson-Bradshaw, Georgia.
Petrucha, Stefan. Breaking Down Parker, Rick, illus. (p. 278)
—Hotel Transylvania Graphic Novel Vol. 2: My Little Monster-Sitter. Gladfelter, Allen & Zazo, illus. (p. 1007)
—Hotel Transylvania Graphic Novel Vol. 2: My Little Monster-Sitter. Gladfelter, Allen & Zazo, illus. (p. 1007)
—Manosaurs Vol. 1: Walk Like a Manosaur. Studios, Yellowhale, illus. (p. 1398)
—Prilla's Talent Magic Eye Studios Staff et al, illus. (p. 1792)
—Ripper. (p. 1885)
—Terrible Toys Henrique, Paulo, illus. (p. 2207)
Petrucha, Stefan & Kinney, Sarah. High School Musical Mystery II: The Lost Verse Murase, Sho, illus. (p. 969)
—Small Volcanoes. (p. 2040)
—Vampire Slayer Murase, Sho, illus. (p. 2346)
Petrucha, Stefan, et al. Papercutz Slices Boxed Set: Vol #1-3. (p. 1698)
Petruck, Rebecca. Boy Bites Bug. (p. 268)
—Steering Toward Normal. (p. 2112)
Petrulis, Sarah, illus. see Albright, Kendra S. & Gavigan, Karen W., eds.
Petrus, Hugo, illus. see Dumas, Alexandre & Thomas, Roy.
Petrus, Hugo, illus. see Dumas, Alexandre.
Petrus, Hugo, illus. see Van Lente, Fred.
Petrus, Junauda. Stars & the Blackness Between Them. (p. 2107)
Petrusek, Brett, illus. see Blair, Eric.
Petry, Ann. Harriet Tubman: Conductor on the Underground Railroad. (p. 933)
Petrzela, Natalia Mehlman. Classroom Wars: Language, Sex, & the Making of Modern Political Culture. (p. 401)
Pets Unchained. Big Dogs & Puppy Facts for Kids Dogs Book for Children Children's Dog Books. (p. 219)
—Bunny, Bunny, Bun-Bun - Caring for Rabbits Book for Kids Children's Rabbit Books. (p. 298)
—Giddy up Horsey! Yeehaw! Horses Book for Kids Children's Horse Books. (p. 831)
—Here Kitty! Kitty! Fun Facts Cats Book for Kids Children's Cat Books. (p. 958)
—Hey There Buddy! Labrador Retriever Kids Books Children's Dog Books. (p. 964)
—How to Train My Puppy! Puppy Care Book for Kids Children's Dog Books. (p. 1045)
—I Love My Doggie! Dog Care for Children Made Easy Children's Dog Books. (p. 1071)
—I Love My Puppy! Puppy Care for Kids Children's Dog Books. (p. 1072)
—My Pony Loves to Gallop! Horses Book for Children Children's Horse Books. (p. 1559)
—Officer Woof! Woof! Police Dogs Book for Kids Children's Dog Books. (p. 1640)
—Woof! Woof! Bark! Bark! German Shepherd Dog Book for Kids Children's Dog Books. (p. 2492)
Pett, Mark. Boy & the Airplane. Pett, Mark, illus. (p. 268)
—Girl & the Bicycle. Pett, Mark, illus. (p. 835)
—I'm Not Millie! (p. 1098)
—Lizard from the Park. Pett, Mark, illus. (p. 1336)
—This Is My Book! (p. 2225)
Pett, Mark, illus. see Jonker, Travis.
Pett, Mark & Rubinstein, Gary. Girl Who Never Made Mistakes. Pett, Mark, illus. (p. 837)
Pettapiece, Lauren, illus. see Butler, Megan Hewes & Odd Dot.
Pettengill, Lillian. Toilers of the Home: The Record of a College Woman's Experience As a Domestic Servant (Classic Reprint) (p. 2256)
Pettersen, Bev. Pony for Christmas: A Canadian Holiday Novella. (p. 1773)
Pettes, Helen. Mouse's Tail (Classic Reprint) (p. 1515)
Pettibone, Danielle. Back in Blue Moon. (p. 155)
—Once in Blue Moon. (p. 1657)
—Out of Blue Moon. (p. 1682)
—Twice in Blue Moon. (p. 2304)
Pettibone, James. Lodge Goat: Goat Rides, Butts & Goat Hairs, Gathered from the Lodge Rooms of Every Fraternal Order; More Than a Thousand Anecdotes, Incidents & Illustrations from the Humorous Side of Lodge Life (Classic Reprint) (p. 1339)
Pettiford, Rebecca. Angel Sharks. (p. 85)
—Año Nuevo Chino. (p. 100)
—Arctic Food Chains. (p. 112)
—Arctic Foxes. (p. 112)
—Arctic Hares. (p. 112)
—Basking Sharks. (p. 171)
—Big Rigs. (p. 222)
—Bridges. (p. 280)
—Bull Sharks. (p. 295)
—Capitolio. (p. 324)
—Chinese New Year. (p. 379)
—Christmas. (p. 383)
—Circulatory System. (p. 393)
—Coaches. (p. 409)
—Collared Lemmings. (p. 414)
—Composting. Fretland VanVoorst, Jenny, ed. (p. 436)
—Concert. Fretland VanVoorst, Jenny, ed. (p. 438)
—Concierto. (p. 438)
—Concrete Mixers. (p. 438)
—Crabs. (p. 465)
—Crossing Guards. (p. 478)
—Dams. (p. 499)
—Desert Food Chains. (p. 531)
—Día de Acción de Gracias. (p. 536)
—Día de Los Veteranos. (p. 537)
—Día de San Valentín. (p. 537)
—Digestive System. (p. 545)
—Diwali. (p. 566)
—Earth Movers. (p. 617)
—Easter. (p. 619)
—Electricity. (p. 631)
—Energy. (p. 650)
—Fall. (p. 699)
—Farm. Fretland VanVoorst, Jenny, ed. (p. 709)
—Fruits. Fretland VanVoorst, Jenny, ed. (p. 796)
—Garbage Collectors. (p. 808)
—Granja. (p. 880)
—Gravity. (p. 882)
—Great White Sharks. (p. 891)
—Halloween. (p. 911)
—Hammerhead Sharks. (p. 913)
—Hanukkah. (p. 919)
—Harp Seals. (p. 931)
—Harvesting. Fretland VanVoorst, Jenny, ed. (p. 936)
—Helicopters. (p. 950)
—Kwanzaa. (p. 1233)
—Lemon Sharks. (p. 1266)
—Mako Sharks. (p. 1390)
—Manatees. (p. 1396)
—Matter. (p. 1425)
—Muscular System. (p. 1528)
—Nervous System. (p. 1588)
—Nurse Sharks. (p. 1631)
—Ocean Food Chains. (p. 1635)
—Planting. Fretland VanVoorst, Jenny, ed. (p. 1757)
—Polar Bears. (p. 1769)
—Prairie Food Chains. (p. 1785)
—Puffer Fish. (p. 1811)
—Rain Forest Food Chains. (p. 1835)
—Reindeer. (p. 1862)
—Reporters. (p. 1866)
—Respiratory System. (p. 1869)
—Roller Coasters. (p. 1898)
—Sea Stars. (p. 1969)
—Seals. (p. 1970)
—Skeletal System. (p. 2030)
—Skyscrapers. (p. 2034)
—Snowplows. (p. 2049)
—Spring. (p. 2091)
—Stadiums. (p. 2099)
—State Capitol. Fretland VanVoorst, Jenny, ed. (p. 2108)
—Stingrays. (p. 2119)
—Summer. (p. 2148)
—Thanksgiving. (p. 2212)
—Tunnels. (p. 2299)
—Valentine's Day. (p. 2344)
—Vegetables. Fretland VanVoorst, Jenny, ed. (p. 2349)
—Veterans Day. (p. 2354)
—Wetland Food Chains. (p. 2403)
—Whale Sharks. (p. 2403)
—Winter. (p. 2475)
—Zamboni Ice Resurfacers. (p. 2538)
—Zoo. Fretland VanVoorst, Jenny, ed. (p. 2543)
—Zoológico. (p. 2543)
Pettiford, Rebecca, jt. auth. see Fretland VanVoorst, Jenny.
Pettinella, Amy. Lady Gaga. (p. 1237)
—Queen Latifah: Award-Winning Actress & Hip-Hop Activist. (p. 1823)
Pettingell, Karen. Nosy the Passover Lamb. Debra, Hoskins, illus. (p. 1622)
Pettingill, Charla, illus. see Puck.
Pettis, Olive G. Autobiography by Jesus of Nazareth: Being His Historical Life Given by Himself Through the Inspiration of the Scribe (Classic Reprint) (p. 140)
—Autobiography by Jesus of Nazareth. (p. 140)
Pettit, Kaylene & Pettit, Audrey. I Wonder... Kindy. (p. 1086)
Pettit, Lydia. Dixy's Dolphins. (p. 566)
Pettit, Mary S. Verses Stories & Translations (Classic Reprint) (p. 2352)
Pettit, Sydney G. Victoria College Annual: Year 1926-27 (Classic Reprint) (p. 2355)
Pettitt, Linda & Darrow, Sharon. Yafi's Family: An Ethiopian Boy's Journey of Love, Loss, & Adoption. Gilchrist, Jan Spivey, illus. (p. 2516)
Pettman, Kevin. ESports Superstars: Get the Lowdown on the World of Pro Gaming. (p. 663)
—Fortnite Battle Royale Pro Gamer Guide: Everything You Need to Get Victory Royale! (p. 769)
—Fortnite Ultimate Chapter 2 Guide. (p. 769)
—Fortnite Ultimate Winner's Guide. (p. 769)
—Guide to Britain & Ireland. (p. 903)
—Guide to Space. (p. 903)
—Infographic Guide to Football. (p. 1119)
—Paperscapes: the Spectacular Journey into Space: Turn This Book into an Out-Of-This-World Work of Art. (p. 1698)
—Soccer Number Crunch! (p. 2052)
—Space Number Crunch: The Figures, Facts, & Space Stats You Need to Know. (p. 2071)
—Space Number Crunch. (p. 2071)
—This Is Australia: An Illustrated Guide to an Extraordinary Country. (p. 2224)
—Ultimate Roblox Handbook: Packed Full of Pro Tricks, Tips & Secrets. (p. 2315)
Pettman, Kevin, contrib. by. Dinosaur Number Crunch. (p. 549)
Petty, Dev. Bear Must Go On. Todd, Brandon, illus. (p. 179)
—I Don't Want to Be a Frog. Boldt, Mike, illus. (p. 1064)
—I Don't Want to Be Big. Boldt, Mike, illus. (p. 1064)
—I Don't Want to Go to Sleep. Boldt, Mike, illus. (p. 1064)
—There's Nothing to Do! Boldt, Mike, illus. (p. 2218)
Petty, Devorah. Claymates. (p. 402)
Petty, Heather. Lock & Mori. (p. 1339)
—Mind Games. (p. 1469)
Petty, Heather W. Final Fall. (p. 727)
—Mind Games. (p. 1469)
Petty Hilger, Jen. Thisbe: Queen of Adventure. (p. 2227)
Petty, J. T. Clemency Pogue: Fairy Killer. Davis, Will, illus. (p. 403)
Petty, J. T., jt. auth. see Pope, Paul.
Petty, J. T. & Pope, Paul. Fall of the House of West. Rubín, David, illus. (p. 700)
Petty, Kate. Awesome Book of Tornadoes & Other Storms. Paiva, Johannah Gilman, ed. (p. 144)
—Great Grammar Book. Maizels, Jennie, illus. (p. 886)
—Gus Goes to School. (p. 906)
Petty, Kate, jt. auth. see Jeffrey, Gary.
Petty, William. Monster Truck Superstars: Top Trucks! Facts & Stats! Record Breakers! (p. 1497)
Petty, William Kevin, illus. see Bush, Emilie P.
Petz, Moritz. Day Everything Went Wrong. Jackowski, Amélie, illus. (p. 513)
Petz, Moritz & Jackowski, Amélie. Bad Mood. Jackowski, Amélie, illus. (p. 158)
Petzall, Guy. ULLAGAMI: Geometric Kirigami Pop-Ups. (p. 2314)
—Ullagami: Geometric Kirigami Pop-Ups. Vol. 1 (p. 2314)
Petzold, Dave. Seven Seas of Fleas. (p. 1994)
Pevear, Richard, tr. see Dumas, Alexandre.
Pevear, Ted F. & Pevear, Linda W. Date in the Junk Yard. (p. 509)
—Finding Little Feathers a Hub-A-Son. (p. 729)
Peverelly, Charles A. Book of American Pastimes: Containing a History of the Principal Base Ball, Cricket, Rowing, & Yachting Clubs of the United States (Classic Reprint) (p. 258)
Pevoto, Kimberly. Testing Me. (p. 2209)
Peyer, Tom, jt. auth. see Waid, Mark.
Peyer, Tom & Constant, Paul. Wrong Earth, Vol. 1. (p. 2514)
Peymani, Christine. Kitai's Journal. Katzenstein, Jason Adam, illus. (p. 1225)
Peyo. Aerosmurf. (p. 30)
—Baby Smurf. (p. 152)
—Madame Adolphine. (p. 1374)
—Purple Smurfs. (p. 1816)
—Return of the Smurfette. (p. 1871)
—Smurf Championship Games. (p. 2043)
—Smurflings. (p. 2043)
—Smurfs #14: The Baby Smurf. (p. 2043)
—Smurfs #24: the Smurf Reporter. (p. 2043)
—Smurfs #25: The Gambling Smurfs. (p. 2043)
—Smurfs #26: Smurf Salad. (p. 2043)
—Smurfs 3 In 1 #3: The Smurf Apprentice, the Astrosmurf, & the Smurfnapper. (p. 2043)
—Smurfs Anthology #2. (p. 2043)
—Smurfs Christmas. (p. 2043)
—Smurfs Village Behind the Wall #2: The Betrayal of SmurfBlossom. (p. 2043)
—Snow Giant. Peyo, illus. (p. 2047)
Peyo, illus. see Delporte, Yvan.
Peyo, jt. auth. see Delporte, Yvan.
Peyo & Delporte, Yvan. Return of the Smurfette. (p. 1871)
—Smurf Olympics (p. 2043)
—Smurf Soup. (p. 2043)
—Smurf vs. Smurf. (p. 2043)
Peyo, et al. Smurf Apprentice. (p. 2043)
—Smurfs & the Howlibird. (p. 2043)
Peypey. Rabbit Totem. (p. 1829)
Peyrat, Jerome, illus. see Aubineau, Francois.
Peyrols, Sylvaine. Body. Peyrols, Sylvaine, illus. (p. 253)
—Crocodile. Peyrols, Sylvaine, illus. (p. 477)
—Crocodiles. (p. 477)
—Dolphins. (p. 579)
—My First Discoveries - the Farm. (p. 1543)
Peyrols, Sylvaine, jt. auth. see Jeunesse, Gallimard.
Peyrols, Sylvaine, et al. Volcanoes. Stanley-Baker, Penelope, tr. (p. 2366)
Peyron Pichardo, Gabriela Rosario. Donde Van? (p. 581)
Peyton, Diane. Bright & Special Night. (p. 281)
—Mom, Why Is Sister Different? (p. 1490)
Peyton, J. Lewis. Tom Swindel: Or, the Adventures of a Boomer (Classic Reprint) (p. 2258)
Peyton, K. M. Minna's Quest IR. (p. 1473)
—No Turning Back IR. (p. 1615)
—Wild Lily. (p. 2464)
Peyton, Katherine, jt. auth. see Miller, Dean.
Peyton, Katherine & George, Enzo. World War II in Europe & North Africa: Preserving Democracy. (p. 2506)
—World War II in the Pacific: War with Japan. (p. 2506)
Peyton, Km. Far from Home. (p. 708)
Peyton, Veronica. Silo & the Rebel Raiders. (p. 2019)
Pez, illus. see Bornemann, Elsa.
Pez, illus. see Wolf, Ema.
Pez, Alberto. Tecitos de Lgrimas de Dragn. (p. 2198)
Pezet, A. Washington. Aristokia (Classic Reprint) (p. 116)
Pezz, tr. see Andersen, Hans Christian.
Pezzali, Walter, illus. see Guibert, Emmanuel & Sfar, Joann.
Pezzali, Walter, illus. see Guibert, Emmanuel.
Pezzi, Bryan. Arkansas: The Natural State. (p. 116)
—Arkansas. (p. 116)
—Craig Kielburger: Ma Vie. Karvonen, Tanjah, tr. from ENG. (p. 466)
—Craig Kielburger. (p. 466)
—David Suzuki: Ma Vie. Karvonen, Tanjah, tr. from ENG. (p. 511)
—David Suzuki. (p. 511)
—Emily Carr. (p. 642)
—Magical World of J. K. Rowling. (p. 1381)
—Massachusetts: The Bay State. (p. 1417)
—Massachusetts. (p. 1417)
—Terry Fox: Ma Vie. Karvonen, Tanjah, tr. from ENG. (p. 2208)
—Terry Fox. (p. 2208)
Pezzi, Bryan, jt. auth. see Durrie, Karen.
Pezzino, Martha, ed. see Rowles, Charles G., 3rd.
Pfaff, Ellen L. Talent Show. Baldwin, Cristal, illus. (p. 2180)
Pfaff, J. W. Ludewig Schmuddelig und der Zauberstock. (p. 1366)
Pfaff, Martina. Itchy's Itch. (p. 1142)
Pfannenstiel, Randall. Mr. B & Me. (p. 1517)
Pfau, Urd. Traumwald und Ihr Wolf. (p. 2279)
Pfeffer, Irwin, jt. auth. see Abraham, Henry.
Pfeffer, Nyomi & Pfeffer, Paul. American Adventure the Poodle Named Oodle. (p. 70)
—Introducing the Poodle Named Oodle. (p. 1129)
Pfeffer, Pierre. Grande, Fuerte y Sabio: el Elefante / Big, Strong & Smart Elephant. (p. 877)
Pfeffer, Rubin. Summer Supper. Austin, Mike, illus. (p. 2150)
Pfeffer, Susan Beth. Dead & the Gone. (p. 517)
—Life As We Knew It Collection. (p. 1290)
—Shade of the Moon. (p. 1996)
—This World We Live In (p. 2227)
Pfeffer, Wendy. Arctic Fox's Journey. Huff, Morgan, illus. (p. 112)
—From Seed to Pumpkin. Hale, James Graham, illus. (p. 793)
—From Tadpole to Frog. Keller, Holly, illus. (p. 793)
—Life in a Coral Reef. Jenkins, Steve, illus. (p. 1291)
—Light Is All Around Us. Meisel, Paul, illus. (p. 1298)
—Many Ways to Be A Soldier. (p. 1400)
—Shortest Day: Celebrating the Winter Solstice. Reisch, Jesse, illus. (p. 2011)
—Sounds All Around. Chernyshova, Anna, illus. (p. 2067)
—We Gather Together: Celebrating the Harvest Season. Bleck, Linda, illus. (p. 2390)
—What's It Like to Be a Fish? Keller, Holly, illus. (p. 2425)
Pfeffer, Wendy & American Museum of Natural History Staff. Wolf Pup, Level 1. (p. 2484)
—World of Sharks. (p. 2504)
Pfeffinger, Charla R., jt. auth. see Barchers, Suzanne I.
Pfeifenberger, Nina, illus. see Doskar, Julia.
Pfeifer, Marie. Mystery of the Missing Chocolate Chips. (p. 1570)
Pfeiffer, Chaviva Krohn. Making Hashem Proud: Stories of Kiddush Hashem in Everyday Life. Stern, Chani, illus. (p. 1389)
Pfeiffer, Emily. Flying Leaves from East & West (Classic Reprint) (p. 755)
—Rhyme of the Lady of the Rock: And How It Grew (Classic Reprint) (p. 1875)
Pfeiffer, Judith. We Didn't Know. (p. 2390)
Pfeiffer, Kathleen. Spartacus Sprout, Please Watch Out! (p. 2075)
Pfeiffer, Stephanie, illus. see Forest Service (U.S.), ed.
Pfeil, Cris. Eyes of the Arrow. (p. 689)
—Right Blood. (p. 1882)
—Shepherd's Rod. (p. 2006)
Pfeil, Helena a. Bill Perkins Proposin Day (Classic Reprint) (p. 226)
Pferdehirt, Julia. Blue Jenkins: Working for Workers. (p. 248)
Pfiffikus. 60 Minutes Makes an Hour - a Telling Time for Kids. (p. 2556)
—All in Good Time a Telling Time Book for Kids. (p. 52)
—Alphabet Activities Practice Book Toddler-Grade K - Ages 1 To 6. (p. 58)
—Amino Acids, Enzymes, Electrolytes, Glucose & More for Kids! Body Chemistry Edition - Children's Clinical Chemistry Books. (p. 75)
—Analog or Digital- a Telling Time Book for Kids. (p. 79)

—Comrades (Classic Reprint) (p. 437)
—Doctor Zay (Classic Reprint) (p. 574)
—Donald Marcy (Classic Reprint) (p. 581)
—Empty House: And Other Stories (Classic Reprint) (p. 645)
—Fourteen to One (Classic Reprint) (p. 773)
—Friends: A Duet. (p. 786)
—Friends: A Duet (Classic Reprint) (p. 786)
—Gates Ajar (Classic Reprint) (p. 811)
—Gates Between (Classic Reprint) (p. 811)
—Gypsy Breynton. (p. 907)
—Gypsy Breynton (Classic Reprint) (p. 907)
—Gypsy's Cousin Joy (Classic Reprint) (p. 907)
—Gypsy's Sowing & Reaping (Classic Reprint) (p. 907)
—Gypsy's Year at the Golden Crescent (Classic Reprint) (p. 907)
—Hedged (Classic Reprint) (p. 947)
—Jack the Fisherman (Classic Reprint) (p. 1153)
—Jonathan & David (Classic Reprint) (p. 1177)
—Loveliness: A Story. (p. 1362)
—Loveliness: A Story (Classic Reprint) (p. 1362)
—Madonna of the Tubs (Classic Reprint) (p. 1375)
—Men, Women, & Ghosts (Classic Reprint) (p. 1447)
—Oath of Allegiance: And Other Stories (Classic Reprint) (p. 1634)
—Old Maids, & Burglars in Paradise (Classic Reprint) (p. 1647)
—Old Maid's Paradise (Classic Reprint) (p. 1647)
—Sealed Orders (Classic Reprint) (p. 1970)
—Silent Partner (Classic Reprint) (p. 2017)
—Singular Life (Classic Reprint) (p. 2024)
—Story of Avis (Classic Reprint) (p. 2129)
—Successors of Mary the First (Classic Reprint) (p. 2146)
—Though Life Us Do Part (Classic Reprint) (p. 2230)
—Trixy (Classic Reprint) (p. 2290)
—Trotty's Wedding Tour, & Story-Book. (p. 2291)
—Trotty's Wedding Tour, & Story-Book (Classic Reprint) (p. 2291)
—Walled in a Novel (Classic Reprint) (p. 2373)
—Within the Gates (Classic Reprint) (p. 2482)
Phelps, Ethel Johnston. Hunter Maiden: Feminist Folktales from Around the World. Boynton, Suki, illus. (p. 1053)
Phelps, Ethel Johnston, ed. Kamala: Feminist Folktales from Around the World. Boynton, Suki, illus. (p. 1202)
—Sea Girl: Feminist Folktales from Around the World. Boynton, Suki, illus. (p. 1967)
—Tatterhood: Feminist Folktales from Around the World. Boynton, Suki, illus. (p. 2193)
Phelps, George Harrison. Six Stories (Classic Reprint) (p. 2029)
Phelps, Guy Fitch. Mountains of the Morning (Classic Reprint) (p. 1514)
Phelps, H. P. Menands: The Garden Suburb of Albany & Troy (Classic Reprint) (p. 1447)
Phelps, Inna. Somaya the Moroccan Goat. (p. 2058)
Phelps, Lavinia Howe. Dramatic Stories for Home & School Entertainment (Classic Reprint) (p. 597)
Phelps, Lincoln. Ida Norman, or Trials & Their Uses (Classic Reprint) (p. 1089)
Phelps, Margery. Halo's Glow. (p. 913)
Phelps, Michael & Abrahamson, Alan. How to Train with a T. Rex & Win 8 Gold Medals. Jenkins, Ward, illus. (p. 1045)
Phelps, Pauline. Cosy Corners: A Comedy in Four Acts (Classic Reprint) (p. 457)
—Jack's Brother's Sister: A Sketch in One Act (Classic Reprint) (p. 1153)
Phelps Ward, Elizabeth Stuart & Ward, Herbert D. Lost Hero. (p. 1353)
Phelps, William Lyon. Dash at the Pole (Classic Reprint) (p. 508)
—Selected Stories from Kipling (Classic Reprint) (p. 1986)
Phelps Williams, Janice. Still Her Spirit Sings: One Dog's Love, Lessons, Life & Legacy. (p. 2119)
Phen, Melissa. Elephant Shoes Are Hard to Find. (p. 634)
Phenix, Cora. Little Storm. (p. 1328)
Phethean, Ellen. Wall (p. 2372)
Phi, Bao. Different Pond. Bui, Thi, illus. (p. 545)
—My Footprints. Tran, Basia, illus. (p. 1547)
Phifer, Larry. World on a String. (p. 2504)
Phil, illus. see Pendziwol, Jean E.
Phil, Eun. Dreams of Flight: Aircraft. Kim, Ki-Hwan, illus. (p. 603)
Phil Mills Jr. Mud Between My Toes. (p. 1524)
Philadelphia, Clover Club. Anniversary Dinner of the Clover Club, Thursday, Jan. 19th, 1888 (Classic Reprint) (p. 100)
Philbin, Joanna. Daughters. (p. 509)
—Daughters Break the Rules. (p. 509)
—Daughters Take the Stage. (p. 510)
—Rules of Summer. (p. 1913)
Philbrick, Nathaniel. Ben's Revolution: Benjamin Russell & the Battle of Bunker Hill. Minor, Wendell, illus. (p. 201)
—In the Heart of the Sea (Young Readers Edition) The True Story of the Whaleship Essex. (p. 1109)
—Mayflower & the Pilgrims' New World. (p. 1430)
Philbrick, Rodman. Big Dark. (p. 219)
—Freak the Mighty. (p. 779)
—Mostly True Adventures of Homer P. Figg. (p. 1509)
—Who Killed Darius Drake? (p. 2448)
—Zane & the Hurricane: A Story of Katrina. (p. 2538)
Philbrick, Rodman & Harnett, Lynn. Final Nightmare. (p. 727)
—Haunting. (p. 939)
—Horror. (p. 1004)
Philbrick, W. R., jt. auth. see Philbrick, Rodman.
Philbrook, Harry B. Discussion of the Cause, Character & Operations of the Creator: What & Where Is God? (Classic Reprint) (p. 557)
Philbrook, Isabel. Stetson Oracle, Vol. 17: October 1928 (Classic Reprint) (p. 2116)
—Stetson Oracle, Vol. 17: January, 1929 (Classic Reprint) (p. 2116)
Philip, Aaron. This Kid Can Fly: It's about Ability (NOT Disability) (p. 2226)
Philip, Alexander. Essays Towards a Theory of Knowledge (Classic Reprint) (p. 663)
Philip, Alexander John. Dickens Dictionary: The Characters & Scenes of the Novels & Miscellaneous Works Alphabetically Arranged (Classic Reprint) (p. 541)
Philip, Bb. Mighty Maple. (p. 1463)
Philip, Claire. My First Book of Our World. (p. 1542)
—My First Book of Woodland Creatures. (p. 1543)
Philip, Claire, jt. auth. see Adams, Julia.
Philip, Claire, jt. auth. see De la Bédoyère, Camilla.
Philip, Claire, jt. auth. see Peebles, Alice.
Philip Dadd, illus. see Wodehouse, Pelham Grenville.
Philip, Deg, illus. see Marks, Ginger.
Philip, Herman. Above Her Station: The Story of a Young Woman's Life (Classic Reprint) (p. 7)
Philip, Neil. Folktales of America: Stockings of Buttermilk: Traditional Stories from the United States of America. Mair, Jacqueline, illus. (p. 757)
—Folktales of Mexico: Horse Hooves & Chicken Feet: Traditional Mexican Stories. Mair, Jacqueline, illus. (p. 757)
—Myths of the Vikings: Odin's Family & Other Tales of the Norse Gods. Foa, Maryclare, illus. (p. 1572)
Philip, Robert. Christian Experience: Or a Guide to the Perplexed (Classic Reprint) (p. 382)
Philip, Simon. I Don&'t Know What to Call My Cat. Bailey, Ella, illus. (p. 1064)
—I Really Want the Cake. Gaggiotti, Lucia, illus. (p. 1080)
—Todo Empezo Cuando Dije Si. (p. 2255)
—You Must Bring a Hat! Hindley, Kate, illus. (p. 2527)
Philip, Steele, jt. auth. see Steele, Philip.
Philipp, Lee. Token. (p. 2256)
Philipp, Lillie H. Piano Technique: Tone, Touch, Phrasing & Dynamics. (p. 1738)
Philippe, Ben. Field Guide to the North American Teenager. (p. 723)
Philippe, Dumont. Loi des Pyramides 2: L'H'ritage de Zac(la) (p. 1339)
—Loi des Pyramides. Chami Chikan(la) (p. 1339)
Philippe, Dupasquier, illus. see Gray, Nigel.
Philippe, Godard. Toile et Toi (Ne)(la) (p. 2256)
Philippe, Jean. Bibliotheque de Philosophie Contemporaine. les Anomalies Mentales Chez les Ecoliers. Etude Medico-Pedagogique Par les Docteurs. (p. 215)
Philipponneau, Olivier, illus. see Brière-Haquet, Alice.
Philippoussis, Silvana. I Am Me. (p. 1059)
Philipps, Colwyn Erasmus Arnold. Colwyn Erasmus Arnold Philipps, Captain, Royal Horse Guards: Elder Son of John Wynford Philipps 1st Baron St. Davids & 13th Baronet of Picton & Leonora His Wife; Born December 11, 1888, Killed in Action near Ypres, May 13, 1915 (Classic Reprint) (p. 427)
Philips, Austin. Fourth Man: An Original Comedy in One Act (Classic Reprint) (p. 773)
Philips, David Graham. Hungry Heart: A Novel (Classic Reprint) (p. 1052)
Philips, F. C. Burglar & the Judge: A Comedietta in One Act (Classic Reprint) (p. 299)
—Collections of British Authors, Vol. 255 Of 1: Tauchnits Edition; a Question of Colour (Classic Reprint) (p. 415)
—Dean & His Daughter, Vol. 1 (Classic Reprint) (p. 519)
—Dean & His Daughter, Vol. 2 of 3 (Classic Reprint) (p. 519)
—Jack & Three Jills: A Novel (Classic Reprint) (p. 1151)
—Lucky Young Woman, Vol. 3 Of 3: A Novel (Classic Reprint) (p. 1365)
—Mrs. Bouverie, Vol. 1 (Classic Reprint) (p. 1521)
—Mrs. Bouverie, Vol. 2 of 2 (Classic Reprint) (p. 1521)
—Question of Color (Classic Reprint) (p. 1826)
Philips, Fleur. Beautiful Girl: A Novel. (p. 184)
—Crumble. (p. 480)
Philips, Francis Charles. As in a Looking Glass (Classic Reprint) (p. 124)
—Lucky Young Woman. a Novel. (p. 1365)
—Lucky Young Woman a Novel, Vol. 1 of 3 (Classic Reprint) (p. 1365)
—Margaret Byng (Classic Reprint) (p. 1403)
—One Never Knows, Vol. 1 of 2 (Classic Reprint) (p. 1661)
Philips, Jeremy. Lost Eye of the Serpent. (p. 1353)
Philips, Karen, ed. My [Not-So] Perfect Life: A Fill-in-the-Blanks Journal. (p. 1558)
Philips, L. Perfect Ten. (p. 1723)
—Sometime after Midnight. (p. 2061)
Philips, Lyn D. Curiosity. Gadeselli, Natalie, illus. (p. 486)
Philips, Melville. Devil's Hat: A Sketch in Oil (Classic Reprint) (p. 536)
—Senator's Wife: Being a Tale of Washington Life (Classic Reprint) (p. 1988)
—Snap: A Novel (Classic Reprint) (p. 2045)
Philips, Mike, illus. see Johnson, Pete.
Philips, Mike, illus. see MacPhail, Catherine.
Philips, Page. Coast of Opportunity (Classic Reprint) (p. 410)
—Trail of the Waving Palm (Classic Reprint) (p. 2274)
Philips, Sean, illus. see Kirkman, Robert.
Philips, Tracy A. Did Someone You Love Die? (p. 543)
Philipson, Patricia, illus. see PI Kids.
Philipson, Sandra J. Ollie's Monsters & Other Stories. Campbell, Jenny, illus. (p. 1651)
Philleo, Calvin Wheller. Twice Married: A Story of Connecticut Life (Classic Reprint) (p. 2304)
Phillimore, Cecily Spencer. By an Unknown Disciple (Classic Reprint) (p. 305)
Phillip, Christopher. Love Is the Most Important Thing in the Universe. Lopez, Baldo Lazaro, illus. (p. 1360)
Phillip, Ortiz, illus. see Russell, Reba.
Phillipe, Monica. Danielle's Dance Class: Foundations for Multiplication. (p. 503)
Phillipe, Steve. When Cats Had No Tails. Edwards, Gina, illus. (p. 2429)
Phillipps, J. C. Wink: The Ninja Who Wanted to Be Noticed. (p. 2473)
Phillipps, L. March. With Rimington (Classic Reprint) (p. 2481)
Phillipps-Wolley, Clive. Gold, Gold, in Cariboo: A Story of Adventure in British Columbia (Classic Reprint) (p. 856)
—Gold, Gold, in Cariboo. (p. 856)
—Savage Svanetia, Vol. 1 of 2 (Classic Reprint) (p. 1937)
—Snap: A Legend of the Lone Mountain (Classic Reprint) (p. 2045)
—Sport in the Crimea & Caucasus (Classic Reprint) (p. 2087)
—Sportsman's Eden (Classic Reprint) (p. 2090)
Phillips, Adam. Fantastic Feats & Ridiculous Records. (p. 707)
Phillips Aka Professor Know-How, James. My Father's Workshop. (p. 1539)
Phillips, Alan, illus. see Cushing, Mims.
Phillips, Ann. Friends Are Everywhere: A Gift of Love. (p. 787)
Phillips, Athena Z. Carnie Vore Helps with Chores. Mills, Meredith E., illus. (p. 332)
—Herbie's Happy Birthday! Mills, Meredith E., illus. (p. 957)
Phillips, Barry. Cave Express. (p. 347)
Phillips, Bessie. G. H. S. Annual, 1907 (Classic Reprint) (p. 803)
Phillips, Beth Ann. Crystal Kingdom (p. 481)
Phillips, Bettine K. Aunt Dinah's Quilting Party (Classic Reprint) (p. 137)
Phillips, Betty Lou & Herndon, Roblyn. Night Before Christmas in New York Dickert, Sheryl, illus. (p. 1605)
—Night Before Christmas in Texas Dickert, Sheryl, illus. (p. 1605)
Phillips, Billy & Nissensen, Jenny. Once upon a Zombie: Book One: the Color of Fear. (p. 1658)
—Once upon a Zombie: Book Two: the Lord of the Curtain. (p. 1658)
Phillips, Bob. Best Ever Knock-Knock Jokes for Kids. Hawkins, ed. (p. 205)
—Super Duper Knock-Knock Jokes for Kids. (p. 2155)
Phillips, C. T. Maple Leaf: And Other Sketches (Classic Reprint) (p. 1401)
Phillips, Charles. Kings & Queens of Britain's Modern Age: From Hanover to Windsor - 1714-Today. (p. 1222)
Phillips, Charles & Kerrigan, Michael. Exploring the Life, Myth, & Art of the Slavic World. (p. 683)
Phillips, Charlotte. Kiss Me on This Cold December Night: Harperimpulse Contemporary Fiction (a Novella) (Do Not Disturb, Book 3) (p. 1224)
Phillips, Chelsea. Safety Is a Choice My Family Makes. (p. 1922)
Phillips, Clare. Emily & the Penny Adventure. (p. 642)
Phillips, Claude. Earlier Work of Titian. (p. 613)
Phillips, Clifton C. We Are Children of Eden. (p. 2389)
Phillips Cox, Audrey. Special Christmas Story: There Is No Place Like Home at Christmastime. (p. 2076)
Phillips, Craig. Adventures of Jack Scratch: The Quest for the Hiss-Paniola. Phillips, Craig, illus. (p. 24)
—Giants, Trolls, Witches, Beasts: Into the Deep, Dark Woods. (p. 831)
Phillips, Craig, illus. see Avasthi, Swati.
Phillips, Craig, illus. see Holub, Joan & Williams, Suzanne.
Phillips, Craig, illus. see Mason, Jane B. & Hines-Stephens, Sarah.
Phillips, Craig, illus. see Seven, John.
Phillips, Craig, illus. see Strasser, Todd.
Phillips, Craig, illus. see West, Tracey.
Phillips, Craig, illus. see Westerfeld, Scott.
Phillips, Craig, jt. auth. see Seven, John.
Phillips, Cynthia & Priwer, Shana. 101 Things You Didn't Know about Da Vinci: Inventions, Intrigue, & Unfinished Works. (p. 2558)
—Ancient Monuments. (p. 81)
—Bridges & Spans. (p. 280)
—Dams & Waterways. (p. 499)
—Frameworks: Bridges & Spans, Skyscrapers & High Rises, Dams & Waterways, Ancient Monuments, Modern Wonders (p. 775)
—Modern Wonders. (p. 1488)
—Skyscrapers & High Rises. (p. 2034)
Phillips, Dave. Americana Mazes. (p. 74)
—Ancient Treasure Mazes. (p. 82)
—Set Puzzles: Find Sets, Group Them, Fill the Grid. (p. 1993)
Phillips, Dave, illus. see Carlson, Caroline.
Phillips, Dave, illus. see Epstein, Adam Jay & Jacobson, Andrew.
Phillips, Dave & Regan, Lisa. Mind-Boggling Maze Games. Golina-Sagetelian, Irina & Fontabona, Virginia, illus. (p. 1469)
Phillips, Dave E. First Christmas. (p. 735)
Phillips, David Graham. Conflict: A Novel (Classic Reprint) (p. 439)
—Cost (Classic Reprint) (p. 457)
—Deluge (Classic Reprint) (p. 527)
—Fashionable Adventures of Joshua Craig: A Novel (Classic Reprint) (p. 712)
—Fortune Hunter (Classic Reprint) (p. 769)
—George Helm (Classic Reprint) (p. 819)
—Golden Fleece the American Adventures of a Fortune Hunting Earl (Classic Reprint) (p. 857)
—Husband's: Story a Novel (Classic Reprint) (p. 1055)
—Master-Rogue: The Confessions of a Croesus (Classic Reprint) (p. 1419)
—Old Wives for New: A Novel (Classic Reprint) (p. 1648)
—Plum Tree (Classic Reprint) (p. 1763)
—Second Generation (Classic Reprint) (p. 1973)
—Social Secretary (Classic Reprint) (p. 2053)
—Susan Lenox, Her Fall & Rise with a Portrait of the Author, Vol. 1 (Classic Reprint) (p. 2166)
—Susan Lenox, Vol. 2: Her Fall & Rise; with a Portrait of the Author (Classic Reprint) (p. 2166)
Phillips, Dawn, illus. see Kowalski, Bernard.
Phillips, Dee. Arctic Fox. (p. 112)
—Armadillo's Burrow. (p. 117)
—Atlas of My World. (p. 134)
—Baby's Day. (p. 153)
—Badger's Burrow. (p. 159)
—Big Zoo. (p. 224)
—Blast (p. 243)
—Burrowing Owl's Hideaway. (p. 300)
—Chipmunk's Hole. (p. 379)
—Collared Lemming. (p. 414)
—Colors. (p. 425)
—Dare (p. 504)
—Deadly Secret of Room 113. (p. 519)
—Desert Tortoise's Burrow. (p. 532)
—Doomed on Death Row. (p. 585)
—Dream of America (p. 602)
—Dream of America: The Story of an Immigrant. (p. 602)
—Dumped (p. 610)
—Eject (p. 630)
—Fight (p. 724)
—First Addition. (p. 735)
—First Words. (p. 740)
—Flying Lemur. (p. 755)
—Fox's Den. (p. 774)
—Friends? (p. 786)
—Fright at the Freemont Library. (p. 788)
—Ghostly Secret of Lakeside School. (p. 829)
—Gila Monster's Burrow. (p. 833)
—Gladiator. (p. 840)
—Goal (p. 849)
—Goodbye (p. 866)
—Green Tree Python. (p. 895)
—Grind (p. 897)
—Groundhog's Burrow. (p. 898)
—Harp Seal. (p. 931)
—Holocaust. (p. 989)
—I Want to Know about Dinosaurs. (p. 1085)
—Joyride (p. 1184)
—Kangaroo Rat's Burrow. (p. 1202)
—Koala. (p. 1230)
—Meerkat's Burrow. (p. 1438)
—Mirror (p. 1475)
—Nightmare in the Hidden Morgue. (p. 1608)
—Numbers. (p. 1630)
—Over the Top. (p. 1687)
—Pirate (p. 1749)
—Pirate: The Story of a Buccaneer. (p. 1749)
—Polar Bear. (p. 1769)
—Prairie Dog's Hideaway. (p. 1785)
—Rachel Carson: Environmental Pioneer. (p. 1832)
—Reindeer. (p. 1862)
—Resistance Fighter (p. 1869)
—Right Now! Sample Set (1 ea of 12 titles) (p. 1882)
—Runaway. (p. 1915)
—Samurai (p. 1929)
—Samurai: The Story of a Warrior. (p. 1929)
—Scout (p. 1962)
—Snowshoe Hare. (p. 2049)
—Spider Monkey. (p. 2080)
—Spotted Owl. (p. 2091)
—Tail Gunner. (p. 2176)
—Terror in the Underground Tunnel. (p. 2208)
—Titanic. (p. 2251)
—Trapped in the Abandoned Hospital. (p. 2279)
—Tree Frog. (p. 2284)
—Tree Kangaroo. (p. 2284)
—Vampire's Lair. (p. 2346)
—Vietnam (p. 2357)
—Vietnam: The Story of a Marine. (p. 2357)
—Viking (p. 2357)
—Viking: The Story of a Raider. (p. 2357)
—What Can I Be? (p. 2406)
—Who Can I Be? (p. 2446)
—Wombat's Burrow. (p. 2486)
—Woodpecker. (p. 2492)
—Yesterday's Voices Sample Set (1 ea of 6 titles) (p. 2521)
Phillips, Dee, jt. auth. see Gifford, Clive.
Phillips, Dee & Ticktock Media, Ltd. Staff. What Do Cats Do? (p. 2408)
—What Do Kangaroos Do? (p. 2408)
—What Do Monkeys Do? (p. 2408)
—What Do Rabbits Do? (p. 2408)
Phillips, Deette, illus. see Chaney, Denise.
Phillips, Deette, jt. illus. see Chaney, Denise.
Phillips, Denine. Through the Magic Shed: A Grand Adventure Lies Ahead! Burns, Theresa, illus. (p. 2237)
Phillips, Denine W. Through the Magic Shed: A Grand Adventure Lies Ahead! Burns, Theresa, illus. (p. 2237)
Phillips, Diane. Bobs the Dog. (p. 252)
Phillips, Dixie. Baby Jesus Is Missing. Snider, K. C., illus. (p. 151)
—Dragon Breath. (p. 593)
—One Noble Journey. Sponaugle, Kim, illus. (p. 1661)
—Whistling Dixie. Caponigro, Laureen, illus. (p. 2443)
Phillips, Dixie & Coles, Charlotte. Born in My Heart. Foster, Jack, illus. (p. 263)
Phillips, Dixie & Nolt, Rachel. Lonnie the Lawnmower. Foster, Jack, illus. (p. 1344)
Phillips, Dixie & Phillips, Sharon. Once upon an Empty Tomb. (p. 1658)
—Something to Crow About: A Children's Easter Musical. (p. 2061)
—Wonders with Wood: A Children's Easter Musical. (p. 2491)
Phillips, Dixie & Sharon. Tiny Homeless King: A Children's Christmas Musical. (p. 2249)
Phillips, Dixie & Sharon & Coles, Charlotte. Gardens: Children's Easter Musical. (p. 809)
Phillips, Dixie & Sharon, et al. Bethlehem's King Size Bed. (p. 208)
—Camiles Journey Master Playbook with Musical Scores. (p. 314)
Phillips, Dixie and Sharon, et al. Every Inch a King: A Children's Christmas Musical. (p. 670)
—Real Star of Bethlehem: A Children's Christmas Musical. (p. 1850)
Phillips, Dixie & Snider, K. C. Stilts the Stork. (p. 2119)
Phillips, Dorian. Rachel Carson: Environmental Pioneer. (p. 1832)
Phillips, Douglas, jt. auth. see Gritzner, Charles F.
Phillips, Douglas A. Human Rights. (p. 1050)
Phillips, E. C. Peeps into China: Or, the Missionary's Children (Classic Reprint) (p. 1714)
—Peeps into China Or: The Missionary's Children. (p. 1714)
Phillips, Edward Gideon. Diamonds from the Rough: Original Incidents & Stories (Classic Reprint) (p. 538)
Phillips, Elaine M. Horse Colouring Book. (p. 1004)
—I Am Having Twins Colouring Book. (p. 1058)
—Muscle Cars Colouring Book. (p. 1527)
—Vintage Trucks: Artistic Flair. (p. 2359)

Phillips, Ethel Calvert. Christmas Light (Classic Reprint) (p. 386)
—Story of Nancy Hanks (Classic Reprint) (p. 2131)
Phillips, F. Emily. Education of Antonia (Classic Reprint) (p. 626)
Phillips, Forbes. War & the Weird (Classic Reprint) (p. 2376)
Phillips, Fred. Christmas Choice. (p. 384)
—History Teacher: A Journey of Spiritual Transformation. (p. 981)
—History Teacher: Adventure in Estonia: Unearthing Divine Love. (p. 981)
Phillips, Gary R., illus. see Blessing, Charlotte.
Phillips, Gary R., illus. see Kramer, Jennifer Evans.
Phillips, Gavin. King Penguins on the Falkland Islands. (p. 1221)
Phillips, George Searle. Gypsies of the Danes' Dike: A Story of Hedge-Side Life in England, in the Year 1855 (Classic Reprint) (p. 907)
Phillips, George W. How to Produce Extracted Honey (Classic Reprint) (p. 1043)
Phillips, Georgina. Ouch! Extreme Feats of Human Endurance. (p. 1676)
Phillips, Gregory C. Cuentos Espeluznantes. (p. 483)
Phillips, H. Edwards. Inside a Stock Car. (p. 1122)
—On a Jet Ski. (p. 1652)
Phillips, Hamilton & Phillips, H. Edwards. Inside a Sprint Car. (p. 1122)
Phillips, Hannah. Here to Help: Bus Driver. (p. 958)
—Here to Help: Doctor. (p. 958)
Phillips, Heather. Cowardly Collie. (p. 464)
Phillips, Helen. Here Where the Sunbeams Are Green. (p. 958)
Phillips, Henry Wallace. Mascot of Sweet Briar Gulch (Classic Reprint) (p. 1417)
—Plain Mary Smith: A Romance of Red Saunders (Classic Reprint) (p. 1754)
—Red Saunders: His Adventures West & East. (p. 1858)
—Red Saunders: His Adventures West East (Classic Reprint) (p. 1858)
—Red Saunders' Pets & Other Critters. (p. 1858)
—Red Saunders Pets, & Other Critters (Classic Reprint) (p. 1858)
—Trolley Folly (Classic Reprint) (p. 2290)
Phillips, Hope Ann. Buddy's Play Date Day... (p. 290)
—Hoover's Day Out. (p. 1001)
Phillips, Hope Ann, illus. see Taylor, Myonna.
Phillips, Ian, illus. see McGillian, Jamie Kyle.
Phillips, J. L., illus. see Miles, Jeffrey A.
Phillips, Jacqui. Time to Shine: How to Help a Friend Who Is Being Bullied. Alonso, Marvin, illus. (p. 2245)
—Time to Shine: How to Help a Friend Who Is Being Bullied - Coloring Book: the Adventures of Stushy & Bello! Alonso, Marvin, illus. (p. 2245)
Phillips, Jamison, jt. auth. see Phillips, Patrick.
Phillips, Jane B., illus. see Haas, Carolyn B.
Phillips, Jennifer. Adorable Accessories: Paper Creations to Wear (p. 17)
—Girls Research! Amazing Tales of Female Scientists (p. 839)
—Picture Perfect! Glam Scarves, Belts, Hats, & Other Fashion Accessories for All Occassions. (p. 1740)
—Snappy Style: Paper Decoration Creations (p. 2045)
Phillips, Jessica. Zoom Along. (p. 2544)
—Zoom along at the Construction Site. (p. 2544)
Phillips, Jillian. What to Doodle? At the Aquarium. (p. 2421)
—What to Doodle? - Jr. Animals! (p. 2420)
—World Around Us! Hearing. (p. 2501)
—World Around Us! Seeing. (p. 2501)
Phillips, Jillian, illus. see Bockol, Leslie & Ikids Staff.
Phillips, Jillian, illus. see Ikids Staff.
Phillips, Jillian, illus. see Innovative Kids Staff.
Phillips, Jillian & Kurtz, John. Our Five Senses Coloring Book. (p. 1678)
Phillips, JoAnn, jt. auth. see Oaks, Kristen M.
Phillips, John Roberts. Story of My Life (Classic Reprint) (p. 2131)
Phillips, Justin. Kid Sherlock Volume 1. (p. 1213)
Phillips, Karen. Doodle Journal: My Life in Scribbles. (p. 584)
—Friendship Pixies: Charmed Little Dolls to Make & Share. (p. 788)
—My Fabulous Look Book: Fashion Drawing Made Easy. (p. 1538)
—Sticker Design Studio: Create Your Own Custom Stickers. (p. 2117)
—Straw Shooter Jets: Make Your Own Mini Air Force. Editors of Klutz, ed. (p. 2139)
—Truth about My Name: And What It Reveals about Me! (p. 2296)
—Write in White Doodle Journal: My Brilliant Scribbles. (p. 2512)
Phillips, Karen, ed. What about You? (p. 2404)
Phillips, Larissa. Cochise: Jefe apache (Cochise: Apache Chief) (p. 410)
—Cochise: Apache Chief / Cochise: Jefe Apache. (p. 410)
—Wild Bill Hickok: Legend of the Wild West. (p. 2462)
—Wild Bill Hickok: Legend of the American Wild West / Leyenda del oeste Americano. (p. 2462)
—Wild Bill Hickok: Leyenda del oeste americano (Wild Bill Hickok: Legend of the American Wild West) (p. 2462)
Phillips, Laverne, illus. see Mandelkorn, Carole.
Phillips, Lem. Illinois Magazine, Vol. 12: October, 1921 (Classic Reprint) (p. 1095)
Phillips, Liam & Plumm, Gabi. Mumble & Jumble & the Great Corpsicle Conundrum. (p. 1526)
Phillips, Linda. Librarian, the Firefighters, & the Arsonist. (p. 1284)
Phillips, Linda T., illus. see Bjornsen, Holly.
Phillips, Linda Vigen. Crazy. (p. 468)
Phillips, Logan. I Love You More. (p. 1079)
Phillips, Lorri. Ragamuffin Friends. (p. 1834)
Phillips, Louis. Late Night in the Rain Forest. Strozier, M. Stefan & Torres, Kyle, eds. (p. 1250)
Phillips, Lyn. Funky Fish 'n Friends: Dream Doodles. (p. 801)
—Handscapes: Dream Doodles. (p. 916)
—Ludicrous Lanza: Dream Doodles. (p. 1366)
Phillips, Marie. Memoirs of a Feline Heroine. (p. 1444)
Phillips, Marie Tello. Marie Tello Phillips' Book of Verses (Classic Reprint) (p. 1405)
Phillips, Mary Geisler. Anything Can Happen (Classic Reprint) (p. 104)
Phillips, Matt, illus. see Martin, Justin McCory.
Phillips, Matt, illus. see Meister, Cari.
Phillips, Matthew. Ingo Flamingo (p. 1120)
Phillips, Michael. Sword, the Garden, & the King. (p. 2171)
Phillips, Mike. Twelve Rebel Kings: The Legends of King Arthur: Merlin, Magic, & Dragons. (p. 2303)
Phillips, Mike, illus. see Bailey, Gerry & Law, Felicia.
Phillips, Mike, illus. see Kessler, Liz.
Phillips, Mike, illus. see MacPhail, Catherine.
Phillips, Mike, illus. see Mahy, Margaret.
Phillips, Mike, illus. see Nicholson, Mike.
Phillips, Mike, illus. see North, Laura.
Phillips, Mike, illus. see Oliver, Martin.
Phillips, Mike, illus. see Robinson, Tony.
Phillips, Mike, jt. auth. see Coleman, Michael.
Phillips, Mike, jt. auth. see Morgan, Michaela.
Phillips, Miriam. At the Recycling Center: Sharing & Reusing. (p. 131)
—How Can I Show Respect? Civic Virtues. (p. 1026)
—I Write Letters to Local Leaders: Taking Civic Action. (p. 1086)
—Polly the Pig's Problem: What's the Problem? (p. 1772)
—President for the Day! Digital Citizenship. (p. 1789)
—Princess Pippa Does Her Job: Getting It Done! (p. 1798)
—Suri Studies the Supreme Court: Understanding Government. (p. 2163)
—Willa the Witch Makes Magic: Checking Your Work. (p. 2468)
Phillips, Niki. Far Side of the Rainbow. (p. 709)
Phillips, Noah, illus. see Bikel, Theodore & Bikel, Aimee Ginsburg.
Phillips, Noell G. Ants That Were & Wish They Are (p. 104)
Phillips, Olivia, illus. see Stobie, Janet.
Phillips, Paul, jt. auth. see Donahue, Laurie.
Phillips, Phebe. Why Me? Positive Verse for Loss & Sadness: For Ages 3 & Up. Phillips, Phebe, illus. (p. 2458)
Phillips, Philip Lee. List of Geographical Atlases in the Library of Congress, Vol. 2: With Bibliographical Notes; Author List, Index (Classic Reprint) (p. 1308)
Phillips, Rachael, illus. see Ganeri, Anita.
Phillips, Raelene. Towpath to Truth: Finding Family on the Miami & Erie Canal. (p. 2270)
Phillips, Rebecca. Faking Perfect. (p. 699)
—Girl You Thought I Was. (p. 838)
—These Things I've Done. (p. 2219)
Phillips, Rebekah, illus. see Cameron, Kim M.
Phillips, Rebekah, illus. see Gibson, Catherine.
Phillips, Rebekah, illus. see Marie, Susan & Olive, Miss.
Phillips, Rebekah, illus. see Marie, Susan.
Phillips, Richard. Universal Preceptor: Being a General Grammar of Arts, Sciences, & Useful Knowledge (Classic Reprint) (p. 2332)
Phillips, Richard, jt. auth. see Comstock, John Lee.
Phillips, Richard Jones. Spectacles & Eyeglasses. (p. 2077)
Phillips, Robin. Who in the World Was the Acrobatic Empress? The Story of Theodora. (p. 2447)
Phillips, Rose. Color Me Gray. (p. 420)
—Cutting to the Chase. (p. 492)
—Minnie Gray, or Merit Rewarded (Classic Reprint) (p. 1473)
Phillips, Rosie. Beryl Maggott & the Bewitching Challenge. (p. 204)
Phillips, Ruby Ann. Dream Birthday Isik, Semur, illus. (p. 601)
—Fortune Cookie Fiasco. Isik, Semur, illus. (p. 769)
—Great & Powerful Isik, Semur, illus. (p. 883)
—Krystal Ball. (p. 1232)
—Pet Psychic. Isik, Semur, illus. (p. 1726)
Phillips, Samuel. Caleb Stukely, Vol. 1 of 3 (Classic Reprint) (p. 310)
Phillips, Sarah. First 100 Words. (p. 735)
—Flip, Flap, Match Noisy Farm. (p. 749)
Phillips, Sarah, jt. auth. see Bicknell, Joanna.
Phillips, Sean, illus. see Jones, Bruce.
Phillips, Semira A. Copyright, Mahaska (Classic Reprint) (p. 452)
Phillips, Sharon, jt. auth. see Phillips, Dixie.
Phillips, Sparkle. How to Meet the Man (or Woman) of your Dreams: Or at least, how I met Mine. (p. 1043)
Phillips, Susan Hensley. Dallas at the Fire Station: The Second Adventure of Dallas the Wonder Dog. (p. 498)
Phillips, Susan Hensley & Hensley, Rebecca R. Dallas the Wonder Dog: The First Adventure. (p. 498)
Phillips, Susan Hensley, et al. Dallas Doesn't Like Cats: The Third Adventure of Dallas the Wonder Dog. (p. 498)
Phillips, Sydni. Ewe Got Problems? (p. 675)
Phillips, Sylvia Marchant. Fables for the Frivolous: And Others (Classic Reprint) (p. 691)
Phillips, Terry M., jt. auth. see Friedlander, Mark P., Jr.
Phillips, Tom. Leicestershire Folk Tales for Children. (p. 1265)
Phillips, Tracy A. Losing Someone You Love: Dealing with Death & Dying. (p. 1352)
Phillips, Victoria. Why Is There a Raisin in My Meatloaf? (p. 2458)
Phillips, Waldorf H. By Jupiter!! A Satirical Operatic Burlesque, in Three Acts (Classic Reprint) (p. 305)
Phillips, Waldorf Henry. By Jupiter!! A Satirical Operatic Burlesque, in Three Acts (Classic Reprint) (p. 305)
Phillips, Walter Polk. My Debut in Journalism & Other Odd Happenings (Classic Reprint) (p. 1537)
—Oakum Pickings: A Collection of Stories, Sketches, & Paragraphs Contributed from Time to Time to the Telegraphic & General Press (Classic Reprint) (p. 1633)
Phillips, Walter S. Just about a Boy (Classic Reprint) (p. 1192)
Phillips, Watts. For a Woman's Sake: A Novel (Classic Reprint) (p. 762)
—Lost in London: A New & Original Drama, in Three Acts (Classic Reprint) (p. 1354)
—Wild Tribes of London (Classic Reprint) (p. 2465)
Phillips, Wendell Christopher. Diseases of the Ear, Nose & Throat: Medical & Surgical (Classic Reprint) (p. 557)
Phillips, William Barnet. Diamond Cross: A Tale of American Society (Classic Reprint) (p. 538)
Phillips, William Henry. Single Serpentine Course of the Moon Round the Sun & the Earth: Read at a Meeting of Members of the Society of Science, Letters & Art, of London (Classic Reprint) (p. 2024)
Phillips, Zack (Z J.). Water Cycle: Wyatt the Water Drop. Myers, Garrett, illus. (p. 2384)
Phillips-Duke, Barbara Jean, illus. see Scholastic, Inc. Staff & Barnes, Derrick.
Phillipson, Andrew, illus. see Speregen, Debra Newberger.
Phillipson, Patricia, illus. see Wage, Erin Rose.
Phillips-Poovey, Lisa. Lucy Wants to Go to School. (p. 1366)
Phillips-Wolley, Clive. Savage Svanetia, Vol. 2 of 2 (Classic Reprint) (p. 1937)
Phillott, D. C. Annotated English Translation of Urdu Roz-Marra, or Every-Day Urdu: The Text-Book for the Lower Standard Examination in Hindustani Examination (Classic Reprint) (p. 100)
Phillpotts, Eden. American Prisoner (Classic Reprint) (p. 73)
—Beacon (Classic Reprint) (p. 178)
—Brunel's Tower (Classic Reprint) (p. 287)
—Children of the Mist (Classic Reprint) (p. 372)
—Chronicles of St. Tid (Classic Reprint) (p. 389)
—Cornish Droll: A Novel (Classic Reprint) (p. 455)
—Cornish Droll. (p. 455)
—Curtain Raisers (Classic Reprint) (p. 490)
—Daniel Sweetland (Classic Reprint) (p. 503)
—Deal with the Devil (Classic Reprint) (p. 519)
—Demeter's Daughter (Classic Reprint) (p. 527)
—Doubloons (Classic Reprint) (p. 589)
—Down Dartmoor Way (Classic Reprint) (p. 590)
—Evander (Classic Reprint) (p. 668)
—Faith Tresilion (Classic Reprint) (p. 699)
—Fancy Free (Classic Reprint) (p. 705)
—Farm of the Dagger (Classic Reprint) (p. 710)
—Flint Heart: A Fairy Story (Classic Reprint) (p. 749)
—Folk Afield (Classic Reprint) (p. 757)
—Folly & Fresh Air (Classic Reprint) (p. 758)
—Forest on the Hill (Classic Reprint) (p. 766)
—Fun of the Fair (Classic Reprint) (p. 799)
—Good Red Earth (Classic Reprint) (p. 866)
—Green Alleys: A Comedy (Classic Reprint) (p. 893)
—Haven (Classic Reprint) (p. 940)
—Human Boy (Classic Reprint) (p. 1049)
—Human Boy Again (Classic Reprint) (p. 1049)
—Human Boy & the War (Classic Reprint) (p. 1049)
—In Sugar-Cane Land (Classic Reprint) (p. 1107)
—Joy of Youth (Classic Reprint) (p. 1184)
—Judge's Chair (Classic Reprint) (p. 1185)
—Knock at a Venture (Classic Reprint) (p. 1229)
—Loup-Garou! (Classic Reprint) (p. 1358)
—Lovers a Romance (Classic Reprint) (p. 1362)
—Lying Prophets: A Novel (Classic Reprint) (p. 1369)
—Lying Prophets. (p. 1369)
—Miser's Money (Classic Reprint) (p. 1477)
—Mother (Classic Reprint) (p. 1509)
—Mother of the Man (Classic Reprint) (p. 1510)
—My Laughing Philosopher (Classic Reprint) (p. 1551)
—Nursery: Banks of Colne (Classic Reprint) (p. 1631)
—Old Delabole (Classic Reprint) (p. 1645)
—Orphan Dinah (Classic Reprint) (p. 1672)
—Pan & the Twins (Classic Reprint) (p. 1695)
—Portreeve (Classic Reprint) (p. 1779)
—Red Redmaynes (Classic Reprint) (p. 1858)
—River (Classic Reprint) (p. 1887)
—Secret Woman (Classic Reprint) (p. 1979)
—Some Every-Day Folks: A Novel (Classic Reprint) (p. 2059)
—Some Every-Day Folks, Vol. 1 of 3 (Classic Reprint) (p. 2059)
—Sons of the Morning (Classic Reprint) (p. 2064)
—Spinners (Classic Reprint) (p. 2082)
—Statue: A Story of International Intrigue & Mystery (Classic Reprint) (p. 2109)
—Storm in a Teacup (Classic Reprint) (p. 2126)
—Striking Hours (Classic Reprint) (p. 2141)
—Thief of Virtue (Classic Reprint) (p. 2220)
—Three Brothers (Classic Reprint) (p. 2232)
—Told at 'the Plume' (Classic Reprint) (p. 2256)
—Transit of the Red Dragon & Other Tales (Classic Reprint) (p. 2278)
—Virgin in Judgment (Classic Reprint) (p. 2360)
—Whirlwind (Classic Reprint) (p. 2442)
—Widecombe Fair (Classic Reprint) (p. 2461)
Phillpotts, Mary Charlotte. Janet's Choice, Vol. 1 of 3 (Classic Reprint) (p. 1159)
Philogene, Melisa. Bailey's First Pair of Glasses. (p. 159)
Philomneste, G. P., jt. auth. see Peignot, Gabriel.
Philp, Nicola. Grain of Hope: A Picture Book about Refugees. Aldy, Aguirre, illus. (p. 875)
Philpot, Chelsey. Be Good Be Real Be Crazy. (p. 177)
—Even in Paradise. (p. 668)
Philpot, Graham, illus. see Morgan, Michaela.
Philpot, Graham, jt. auth. see Doyle, Malachy.
Philpott, Keith, illus. see Harvey, Tom, et al.
Phin, John. Dictionary of Practical Apiculture: Giving the Correct Meaning of Nearly Five Hundred Terms, According to the Usage of the Best Writers, Intended As a Guide to Uniformity of Expression Amongst Bee-Keepers, with Numerous Illustrations, Notes & Practica. (p. 542)
—How to Use the Microscope. (p. 1045)
—Practical Hints on the Selection & Use of the Microscope: Intended for Beginners (Classic Reprint) (p. 1784)
—Practical Hints on the Selection & Use of the Microscope. (p. 1784)
Phineas and Ferb. Phineas & Ferb Batter Up! (p. 1735)
Phinizy. Adventures of Pretzel Boy. Komilov, Onga, illus. (p. 27)
Phinn, Gervase. Who Am I? Ross, Tony, illus. (p. 2446)
Phinney, Patty McCoy. Makayla's Rainbow. (p. 1385)
Phippen, Amos R. Schoolmate, 1853, Vol. 3: A Monthly Reader for School & Home Instruction of Youth (Classic Reprint) (p. 1947)
Phipps, Catherine Wood, illus. see Desch, Sandra Lee.
Phipps, Harold Hp. Adventures of Tank & Pudge: Book 1 the Carnival. Ashby, Amy, ed. (p. 28)
Phipps, Kendra, ed. see Marsden, Mariah.
Phipps, Lisa. Facing the Lion. (p. 693)
—God's Great Idea. Brennan, Lisa, illus. (p. 853)
—Racing the Flame. (p. 1832)
Phipps, Liza & Thompson, Avril. History Showtime: Vikings. (p. 981)
Phipps, Michael, illus. see Dashner, James.
Phipps, Selwyn E. Magical Unicorn Society: a Brief History of Unicorns. Aitch et al, illus. (p. 1380)
—Magical Unicorn Society Official Handbook. Dardik, Helen et al, illus. (p. 1380)
Phipps, Shane. Carter Journals: Time Travels in Early U.S. History. (p. 335)
Phiri, Yemu. Mighty Girl's Journal. (p. 1462)
—Mighty Women of Africa. (p. 1464)
Phiz, illus. see Smedley, Frank E.
Phleger, Nansy. Li Chou & the Dragon's Promise. Phleger, Nansy, illus. (p. 1283)
—Sheila the Curious Sheep. (p. 2005)
Phoebe Morris, illus. see Hill, David.
Phoenix Books Staff. Disney(r) PIXAR CarsI Can Drive! (p. 562)
—Sofia the First Royal Picnic - Little Sound Book. (p. 2054)
—Thomas' Piano Book. (p. 2229)
Phoenix Books Staff, illus. see Publications International Ltd. Staff, ed.
Phoenix, Dark. Song of Death: Vocal Chronicles. (p. 2062)
Phoenix, ed. Little Gear Book Eric Carle. (p. 1317)
—Look & Find Toy Story 4. (p. 1345)
—Mickey's Christmas Songs with Keyboard. (p. 1459)
—My First Thomas & Friends - Get in Gear - Play-A-Sound. (p. 1546)
—Naughty or Nice? (p. 1582)
—Nickelodeon Paw Patrol, Bubble Guppies, & More! - Me Reader Electronic Reader & 8 Book Library - PI Kids (p. 1603)
—Race Ready! (p. 1831)
Phoenix, Gryffyn. Harbor Absolution. (p. 924)
Phoenix International Kids, creator. 24 Bk Carry Case My 1st Words. (p. 2554)
Phoenix International Publications, Inc. Trolls World Tour Look & Find. (p. 2290)
Phoenix International Staff. Baby Einstein: Little Piano Book. (p. 150)
—Disney Jr. Look & Find. (p. 560)
—Doc Mcstuffins the Doc Is in. (p. 573)
—Let's Go to the Doctor. (p. 1274)
—Princess Sofia. (p. 1799)
—Sesame at the Zoo Look & Find. (p. 1992)
—Thomas & Friends(r) - Thomas' Piano Book. (p. 2227)
—Thomas & Friends(tm)I Can Drive! (p. 2227)
—Thomas & the Telescope. (p. 2228)
—Write-and-Erase Look & Find(r) Disney: Packed with 'Find 'Ems & Picture Puzzles! Look, Circle, Wipe Clean, & Play Again! (p. 2512)
Phoenix, Jessica. My Art. (p. 1531)
—My Writing. (p. 1565)
Phoenix, John. Phoenixiana: Or, Sketches & Burlesques (Classic Reprint) (p. 1736)
Phoenix Learning Resources Staff, ed. Exploring Maps Volume 1. (p. 682)
—Guidebook to Better English: Level 1 Test Answer Key. (p. 904)
Phoenix, Leo. Lucy's Dream & the Sun Blokkers. (p. 1366)
Phoenix, P. J. Ifrait. (p. 1094)
Phoenix, Three. Daughter of the Sun. (p. 509)
Phommavanh, Oliver. Don't Follow Vee. (p. 583)
—Super Con-Nerd. (p. 2154)
Photodisc-Getty Staff, Images, photos by see McKay, Sindy.
Photographs, illus. see Machado, Antonio.
PHP Kenkyujo. Sekai o Kaeta Hito Ga Kodomo Datta Koro No Ohanashi. (p. 1985)
Phruapadit, Pimlada, illus. see Huff, Abby.
Phu, Esther. Summer Troubles (p. 2150)
Phumiruk, Dow. Mela & the Elephant. Chen, Ziyue, illus. (p. 1442)
Phumiruk, Dow, illus. see Baker, Mindy.
Phumiruk, Dow, illus. see Becker, Helaine.
Phumiruk, Dow, illus. see Harvey, Jeanne Walker.
Phumiruk, Dow, illus. see Hood, Susan & Somhiran, Pathana.
Phunny, U. R. Animal Jokes. (p. 90)
—Dinosaur Jokes. (p. 549)
Phuong, Minh. Stories for Young Children (Vol. 1 Of 3) (p. 2123)
Phuong, Thai My. Mario & the Aliens. (p. 1406)
Phuong, Thai My, illus. see Zanotti, Carolina.
Phyllarry (Rittmueller), Kathryn. Beauregart the Bear. (p. 183)
Phyllis, Archer. New Team Player. (p. 1597)
Phyllis Stella Jadosh. Well Then, You Must Be Lucky. (p. 2399)
PI Kids. Baby Einstein: Color & Carry. (p. 150)
—Baby Einstein: Music All Around. (p. 150)
—Baby Einstein. (p. 150)
—Baby Einstein: Rainbow of Color! (p. 150)
—Baby's First Year. (p. 154)
—Brain Games Kids: Toddler Time. Ackerman, Michele et al, illus. (p. 274)
—Disney: First Pet! (p. 558)
—Disney: First Loose Tooth! (p. 558)
—Disney: First Day of School! (p. 558)
—Disney: Alice Wants to Grow. Maruyama, Jerrod, illus. (p. 558)
—Disney: Mowgli's First Dance. Maruyama, Jerrod, illus. (p. 558)
—Disney: The Aristocats' Show. Maruyama, Jerrod, illus. (p. 558)
—Disney: Tinker Bell's Best Birthday Party. Maruyama, Jerrod, illus. (p. 558)
—Disney: Louie Likes Basketball: a Story about Sharing. Maruyama, Jerrod, illus. (p. 558)
—Disney. Philipson, Patricia et al, illus. (p. 558)
—Disney Baby: Tub Time! (p. 558)
—Disney Baby: Splishy Fishy! (p. 558)

P

—Disney Baby: Skidamarink-A-Doo, I Love You! (p. 558)
—Disney Baby: ABCs: Little First Look & Find Book & Puzzle. Disney Storybook Art Team, illus. (p. 558)
—Disney Frozen: Adventures on Ice. Mawhinney, Art & Disney Storybook Art Team, illus. (p. 559)
—Disney Frozen. (p. 559)
—Disney Frozen. Grupczynski, Kelly, illus. (p. 559)
—Disney Frozen 2: Olaf & Friends. Disney Storybook Art Team, illus. (p. 559)
—Disney Junior Mickey Mouse Clubhouse: Little First Look & Find Book & Puzzle. Disney Storybook Art Team & DiCicco, Sue, illus. (p. 560)
—Disney Junior Mickey Mouse Clubhouse: Let It Snow! Holiday Gift Set. DiCicco, Sue et al, illus. (p. 560)
—Disney Junior Puppy Dog Pals: Happy Howl-Oween! Disney Storybook Art Team, illus. (p. 560)
—Disney Junior Puppy Dog Pals: The Purr-Fect Toy. Disney Storybook Art Team, illus. (p. 560)
—Disney Junior Vampirina. Disney Storybook Artists, illus. (p. 560)
—Disney: Let's Play! First Look & Find. Disney Storybook Art Team & DiCicco Studios, illus. (p. 561)
pi kids. Disney Mickey Mouse Clubhouse: Songs to Go. Loter, Inc. & Disney Storybook Art Team, illus. (p. 561)
PI Kids. Disney Mickey Mouse Clubhouse. Disney Storybook Artists, illus. (p. 561)
—Disney Princess: Starlight Dreams. Disney Storybook Art Team, illus. (p. 562)
—Disney Princess: Talking Quiz Book. Disney Storybook Art Team, illus. (p. 562)
—Disney*Pixar: All Stars. (p. 564)
—Disney*Pixar: Talking Quiz Book. Disney Storybook Art Team, illus. (p. 564)
—DreamWorks Trolls: Write-And-Erase Look & Find. Mawhinney, Art, illus. (p. 603)
—DreamWorks Trolls. Mawhinney, Art, illus. (p. 603)
—Encyclopaedia Britannica Kids: Farm Animals. (p. 648)
—Jurassic World: Roll with the Dinosaurs. (p. 1192)
—Marvel: Heroes in Action. (p. 1411)
—Marvel: Sound Storybook Treasury. (p. 1411)
—Marvel. (p. 1411)
—Marvel Spider-Man: I'm Ready to Read. Legramandi, Francesco et al, illus. (p. 1412)
—My School Years. (p. 1560)
—Nickeldeon PAW Patrol: Little First Look & Find Book & Puzzle. Petrossi, Fabrizio, illus. (p. 1602)
—Nickelodeon. Santanach, Tino et al, illus. (p. 1602)
—Nickelodeon Butterbean's Cafe. Cespedes, Marcela, illus. (p. 1603)
—Nickelodeon PAW Patrol: 8-Book Set & Interactive Activity Pad. (p. 1603)
—Nickelodeon PAW Patrol: Pups at Play. Moore, Harry & Petrossi, Fabrizio, illus. (p. 1603)
—Nickelodeon PAW Patrol: Sweet Dreams, Pups! Moore, Harry & Petrossi, Fabrizio, illus. (p. 1603)
—Nickelodeon PAW Patrol: Ruff-Ruff Rescue Vehicles. Moore, Harry & MJ Illustrations, illus. (p. 1603)
—Nickelodeon PAW Patrol. Petrossi, Fabrizio, illus. (p. 1603)
—Nickelodeon PAW Patrol: Ready, Set, Snow! Holiday Gift Set. (p. 1603)
—Nickelodeon SpongeBob SquarePants: Look, Find, & Fun! (p. 1603)
—Peanuts: Christmas Is Here! Holiday Gift Set. Scott, Vicki, illus. (p. 1710)
—Peppa Pig. (p. 1719)
—Peppa Pig: Let's Pretend! (p. 1720)
—PJ Masks: Heroes on Halloween. (p. 1752)
—PJ Masks: I'm Ready to Read: Owlette. (p. 1752)
—Sesame Street: Busy Monsters. Berry, Bob et al, illus. (p. 1992)
—Thomas & Friends. (p. 2227)
—World of Eric Carle: Write-And-Erase Look & Find. (p. 2502)
PI Kids, adapted by. DreamWorks Trolls World Tour. (p. 603)
PI Kids & Grupczynski, Kelly. Disney Frozen: Little First Look & Find Book & Puzzle. (p. 559)
Pi, Susie & Pi, Vincent. Busy Toddler's a to Z. (p. 302)
Pia, illus. see Hope, Elizabeth.
Pia, illus. see Waung, Iris.
Piano, Maureen. My Adventure with Tidepools. (p. 1531)
Piantedosi, John J. Cat That Purred. Maglio-Macullar, Andrea, illus. (p. 342)
—Gospel for Children. Cioffi, Ben, illus. (p. 870)
Piatek, Doroth'e. Allumeur de Rves(!) (p. 57)
Piatkowska, Malgosia, illus. see Feek, Rory.
Piatt, Donn. Lone Grave of the Shenandoah, & Other Tales (Classic Reprint) (p. 1342)
—Poems & Plays (Classic Reprint) (p. 1765)
—Reverend Melancthon Poundex: A Novel (Classic Reprint) (p. 1873)
Piatt, Jennifer K. Happy Birthday, Daddy! (p. 920)
Piatt, Larry. Simple Bible Stories. (p. 2021)
Piatt, Louise Kirby. Bell Smith Abroad (Classic Reprint) (p. 196)
Piatt, S. M. B. Book about Baby: And Other Poems in Company, with Children (Classic Reprint) (p. 257)
Piatti, Celestino. Celestino Piatti's Animal ABC. (p. 350)
Piatti, Federico, illus. see Dahl, Michael.
Piazza, Carmelo & Buckley, James. Crazy for Science with Carmelo the Science Fellow. Geran, Chad, illus. (p. 469)
Piazza, Gail, illus. see Burton Robb, Diane.
Piazza, Gail, illus. see Robb, Diane Burton.
Piazzi, Giuseppe. Lezioni Elementari Di Astronomia, Vol. 1: Ad USO Del Real Osservatorio Di Palermo (Classic Reprint) (p. 1283)
Pica, Jane, illus. see Gilbert, Julie Kathleen.
Pica, Jane, illus. see Gomez, Sarah Hannah.
Pica, Jane, illus. see Putman Oakes, Cory.
Pica, Jane, illus. see Wage, Erin Rose.
Picano, Felice. Looking Glass Lives. (p. 1347)
—Lure. (p. 1369)
Picanyol, illus. see Matas, Toni.
Picard, Alice, illus. see Ogaki, Philippe, et al.
Picard, Charline, illus. see Pellegrini, Isabelle.
Picard, George H. Bishop's Niece (Classic Reprint) (p. 234)
—Old Boniface: A Novel (Classic Reprint) (p. 1644)
Picard, George Henry. Matter of Taste: A Novel (Classic Reprint) (p. 1426)
Picard, Marie-Julie, illus. see Allen, Lisa Christina.
Picard, Philippe Le. Nouvelle Fabrique des Excellens Traits de Verite: Livre Pour Inciter les Resveurs Tristes et Merancoliques a Vivre de Plaisir (Classic Reprint) (p. 1626)
Picard, Picard. Robert Helmont: Diary of a Recluse, 1870-1871 (Classic Reprint) (p. 1890)
Picard, Valérie. Invisible Garden Ferrer, Marianne, illus. (p. 1132)
Picasso, P, jt. auth. see Hodge, Susie.
Picasso, Pablo. Aves y Otros Animales de Pablo Picasso (Birds & Other Animals with Pablo Picasso) (Spanish Edition) (p. 143)
—Birds & Other Animals with Pablo Picasso. (p. 231)
Picasso, Pablo, jt. auth. see Penrose, Antony.
Picasso, Zelda. Baby Gardenia & Her Magic Glasses. (p. 150)
Picayo, Mario. Brown Pelicans. (p. 287)
—Fun, Fun, One Crab on the Run. Byer, Stacey, illus. (p. 799)
—Giraffe Hears the Drum. Alfonso, Anabel, illus. (p. 834)
—Sea Turtles of the Virgin Islands. (p. 1969)
Picayo, Mario & Picayo, Pablo. Four Wishes for Robbie. (p. 773)
Picayo, Mario, et al. Shark & the Parrotfish & Other Caribbean Fables. Ward, Cherise, illus. (p. 2001)
Picayo, Pablo, jt. illus. see Picayo, Mario.
Piccone, Marianna. Copernie the Bernie. (p. 451)
Piceno, Paul, illus. see Estrada, Jorge.
Piceno, Paul, jt. auth. see Laguarda, Elena.
Picerni, Paul. Being Five & Learning to Strive. (p. 194)
—Being Six & Blowing Out Candlesticks. (p. 195)
Picerni, Paul V. Being Eight Is Great. (p. 194)
—Being Four Is Never a Bore. (p. 194)
—Being Nine Seems Fine. (p. 194)
—Being Seven Is Not the Same As Being Eleven. (p. 195)
—Being Three Is the Best Age to Be. (p. 195)
—Being Two & Going to the Zoo. (p. 195)
Pich�, Chantal, illus. see Clark, Marilyn.
Pichard, Alexandra. Pen Pals. Pichard, Alexandra, illus. (p. 1715)
Piché, Chantal, illus. see Clark, Marilyn.
Pichel, Irving. Harvard Monthly, Vol. 57: Oct. , 1913, to Feb. , 1914 (Classic Reprint) (p. 936)
Pichelli, Sara. Marvel Monograph: the Art of Sara Pichelli. (p. 1412)
—Spider-Men II. (p. 2080)
Pichelli, Sara & Marquez, David. Avengers by Jason Aaron Vol. 2: World Tour. (p. 142)
Pichelli, Sara, et al. Fantastic Four by Dan Slott Vol. 1: Fourever. (p. 707)
—Miles Morales: Spider-Man. (p. 1465)
—Miles Morales: Ultimate Spider-Man Omnibus. (p. 1465)
Pichereau, A. P. Joel's Excursion: A Poem (Classic Reprint) (p. 1171)
Pichon. Carnet Blanc le Roi des Cinemas. (p. 332)
—Carnet Ligne le Roi des Cinemas. (p. 332)
Pichon, L. Absolutely Fantastic (At Some Things) Pichon, L., illus. (p. 9)
—Tom Gates: Extra Special Treats (Not) Pichon, L., illus. (p. 2257)
—Tom Gates: Genius Ideas (Mostly) Pichon, L., illus. (p. 2257)
—Tom Gates Is Absolutely Fantastic (at Some Things) Pichon, L., illus. (p. 2257)
—Tom Gates That's Me! (Books One, Two, Three) Pichon, L., illus. (p. 2257)
Pichon, Lauren. Messages from Maryam. (p. 1451)
Pichon, Liz. Brilliant World of Tom Gates: Read It & Go Ha! Ha! Ha! Pichon, Liz, illus. (p. 282)
—Everything's Amazing (Sort Of) Pichon, Liz, illus. (p. 674)
—Excellent Excuses (and Other Good Stuff) (p. 676)
—Tom Gates: Excellent Excuses (And Other Good Stuff) Pichon, Liz, illus. (p. 2257)
—TOM GATES: EXCUSAS PERFECTAS (Y OTRAS COSILLAS GENIALES) (p. 2257)
—TOM GATES: FESTIVAL DE GENIALIDADES (MÁS O MENOS) (p. 2257)
Pichon, Liz, illus. see Crompton, Richmal.
Pichon, Liz, illus. see Donaldson, Julia.
Pichon, Liz, illus. see Ellis, Gwen.
Pichon, Liz, illus. see Laird, Elizabeth.
Pichon, Liz, illus. see Mortimer, Rachael.
Pichora, Mark. Stargazing. (p. 2106)
Picini, Frank, illus. see Gifford, Clive.
Pick, Alice. Jamey's Promise (p. 1157)
Pick, William. Turf Register, & Sportsman & Breeder's Stud-Book, Vol. 1: Containing the Pedigrees & Performances of All the Horses, Mares, & Geldings That Have Appeared upon the British & Irish Turfs As Racers; Containing Pedigrees, Performances, &C. To 17. (p. 2299)
Pickard, Florie Willingham. Ides of March (Classic Reprint) (p. 1089)
Pickard, Gertrude Gould. Hove up by the Tide (Classic Reprint) (p. 1025)
Pickard, Kate E. R. Kidnapped & the Ransomed: Being the Personal Recollections of Peter Still & His Wife Vina, after Forty Years of Slavery (Classic Reprint) (p. 1213)
Pickard, Rhonda. Destiny Disc. (p. 534)
Pickard, William John. Spider Phaeton, & Other Stories (Classic Reprint) (p. 2081)
Pickell, James Ralph. Twenty-Four Days on a Troopship (Classic Reprint) (p. 2304)
Pickell, Sammy. Doxie. Everett, J. H., illus. (p. 591)
Picken, Andrew. Club-Book: Being the Original Tales, by James, Picken, Galt, Power, Jerdan, Gower, Moir, Cunningham, Hogg, Ritchie, &C (Classic Reprint) (p. 409)
—Club-Book, Vol. 3 Of 3: Being Original Tales, &C. by Various Authors (Classic Reprint) (p. 409)
—Dominie's Legacy, Vol. 2 of 3 (Classic Reprint) (p. 580)
—Traditionary Stories of Old Families & Legendary Illustrations of Family History, Vol. 1 Of 2: With Notes, Historical & Biographical (Classic Reprint) (p. 2274)
Picken, Lillian Hoxie. Crane First Reader (Classic Reprint) (p. 466)
—Crane Fourth Reader (Classic Reprint) (p. 466)
—Crane Second Reader (Classic Reprint) (p. 466)
—Crane Third Reader (Classic Reprint) (p. 466)
Pickenbach, Harry Edward. Deutschland Uber Ireland: And Other Poems (Classic Reprint) (p. 535)
Pickens, Charles E. Percy's Pet Pugusaur Pete, Bully Eradicator. (p. 1721)
Pickens, Macaeli, illus. see Redfield, Nadine.
Pickens, William. Vengeance of the Gods: And Three Other Stories of Real American Color Line Life (Classic Reprint) (p. 2350)
Pickering, Ellen. Cecil, the Orphan, Vol. 1: Or the Reward of Virtue; a Tale for the Young (Classic Reprint) (p. 348)
—Fright, Vol. 1 of 3 (Classic Reprint) (p. 788)
—Fright, Vol. 2 of 3 (Classic Reprint) (p. 788)
—Fright, Vol. 3 of 3 (Classic Reprint) (p. 788)
—Heiress, Vol. 1 Of 3: A Novel (Classic Reprint) (p. 949)
—Heiress, Vol. 2 Of 2: A Novel (Classic Reprint) (p. 949)
—Heiress, Vol. 2 Of 3: A Novel (Classic Reprint) (p. 949)
—Heiress, Vol. 3 Of 3: A Novel (Classic Reprint) (p. 949)
—Merchant's Daughter, Vol. 1 of 3 (Classic Reprint) (p. 1447)
—Nan Darrell, Vol. 1 Of 2: Or the Gipsy Mother (Classic Reprint) (p. 1573)
—Secret Foe: An Historical Novel (Classic Reprint) (p. 1975)
—Secret Foe, Vol. 1 Of 3: An Historical Novel (Classic Reprint) (p. 1975)
—Squire, Vol. 1 of 2 (Classic Reprint) (p. 2094)
—Squire, Vol. 1 of 3 (Classic Reprint) (p. 2094)
—Squire, Vol. 2 of 3 (Classic Reprint) (p. 2094)
—Who Shall Be Heir?, Vol. 2 of 3 (Classic Reprint) (p. 2449)
Pickering, Jeffrey. Adventures of Hair: Binks & the Magic Bowler. (p. 23)
Pickering, Jimmy. Skelly & Femur. Pickering, Jimmy, illus. (p. 2030)
Pickering, Jimmy, illus. see Jardine, Alan.
Pickering, Jimmy, illus. see Sage, Angie.
Pickering, Ken, jt. auth. see Sunderland, Margot.
Pickering, Kenneth, jt. auth. see Herzog, Michael.
Pickering, Kenneth, jt. auth. see Sugano, Douglas.
Pickering, Lynne. James & the Naughty Seagull. Pickering, Lynne, illus. (p. 1156)
Pickering, Miss Ellen. Secret Foe, Vol. 2 Of 3: An Historical Novel (Classic Reprint) (p. 1975)
—Who Shall Be Heir?, Vol. 1 of 3 (Classic Reprint) (p. 2449)
Pickering, Peggy. Four Seasons of Ted. (p. 772)
Pickering, Percival. Life Awry, Vol. 1 Of 3: A Novel (Classic Reprint) (p. 1290)
—Life Awry, Vol. 2 Of 3: A Novel (Classic Reprint) (p. 1290)
—Life Awry, Vol. 3 Of 3: A Novel (Classic Reprint) (p. 1290)
Pickering, Sidney. Key to Paradise (Classic Reprint) (p. 1211)
Pickering, Spencer. Memoirs of Anna Maria Wilhelmina Pickering, Vol. 1: Together with Extracts from the Journals of Her Father, John Spencer Stanhope, Describing His Travels on the Continent, & His Imprisonment under Napoleon (Classic Reprint) (p. 1444)
Pickering, William. Quadrupeds' PIC-Nic (Classic Reprint) (p. 1821)
Picket, Albert. Juvenile Mentor, or American School Class-Book No. 3: Being the Third Part of the Juvenile Spelling-Book, Containing Progressive Reading Lessons, in Prose & Verse, Adapted to the Comprehension of Youth (Classic Reprint) (p. 1200)
Pickett, Anola. Callahan Crossroads. (p. 312)
—Whisper Island. (p. 2442)
Pickett, Cheryl. Creation Inspirations: A New View of Your Neighborhood. (p. 470)
Pickett, Damon. Pot Belly Pee Wee. (p. 1780)
Pickett, George E. Heart of a Soldier; As Revealed in the Intimate Letters of Genl: George E. Pickett (Classic Reprint) (p. 945)
—Heart of a Soldier; As Revealed in the Intimate Letters of Genl. George E. Pickett. (p. 945)
Pickett, LaSalle Corbell. Bugles of Gettysburg (Classic Reprint) (p. 292)
—What Happened to Me (Classic Reprint) (p. 2411)
Pickett, Montgomery. Fourth Physician a Christmas Story (Classic Reprint) (p. 773)
Pickett, Natalie R. S e M P Ly 4 Girlz. (p. 1919)
Pickett, Prema. If You Only Knew. (p. 1093)
Pickford, John Aston. Week in the Yorkshire Dales - Scholar's Choice Edition. (p. 2396)
Pickford, Sue. When Angus Met Alvin. (p. 2429)
Pickford, Susan T. It's up to You, Griffin! Ramsey, Marcy Dunn, illus. (p. 1148)
Pickhardt Jr, Edward. Dusty the Dustball & Family: Their Adventure Begins. Sponaugle, Kim, illus. (p. 611)
Picking, Henry Forry, jt. auth. see Ward, Aaron.
Pickle, Amber D., illus. see Anderson, Richard Allen.
Pickle, Charley. Amy Price for President! (p. 77)
—What's the Matter with Jayden Jackson? (p. 2426)
Pickler, Debi, illus. see Fuhrmann, Paul.
Pickles, Catherine. Worzel Goes for a Walk! Will You Come, Too? Bourgonje, Chantal, illus. (p. 2509)
Picklesimer, Olivia. Health Care. Ferguson, Olivia, ed. (p. 943)
—Teen Sex. Ferguson, Olivia, ed. (p. 2199)
Picklesimer, Olivia, jt. auth. see Haugen, Hayley Mitchell.
Pickman, Richard. Anglo-American Colonization of Texas. (p. 86)
—Let's Volunteer! (p. 1278)
Pickman, Richard, jt. auth. see Mills, Nathan.
Pickrell, Karen & Ambrosio, Laura E. Buttons. Gledhill, Sarah, illus. (p. 304)
Pickron, Levi. Bart's Birthday: Includes Bart's Balloon. (p. 168)
Pickthall, M. L. C. Bridge a Story of the Great Lakes (Classic Reprint) (p. 280)
Pickthall, Marjorie L. C. Angels Shoes & Other Stories (Classic Reprint) (p. 86)
—Billy's Hero, or the Valley of Gold (Classic Reprint) (p. 227)
—Dick's Desertion; a Boy's Adventures in Canadian Forests: A Tale of the Early Settlement of Ontario (Classic Reprint) (p. 541)
—Little Hearts (Classic Reprint) (p. 1318)
—Worker in Sandalwood (Classic Reprint) (p. 2495)
Pickthall, Marmaduke. All Fools: Being the Story of Some Very Young Men & a Girl (Classic Reprint) (p. 51)
—As Others See Us (Classic Reprint) (p. 124)
—Children of the Nile (Classic Reprint) (p. 372)
—Enid: A Novel (Classic Reprint) (p. 655)
—House of Islam (Classic Reprint) (p. 1023)
—House of War (Classic Reprint) (p. 1023)
—Oriental Encounters: Palestine & Syria (1894-5-6) (Classic Reprint) (p. 1670)
—Sir Limpidus (Classic Reprint) (p. 2026)
—Tales from Five Chimneys (Classic Reprint) (p. 2182)
—Veiled Women (Classic Reprint) (p. 2349)
Pickthall, Marmaduke William. Myopes (Classic Reprint) (p. 1566)
—Valley of the Kings (Classic Reprint) (p. 2345)
Pickthall, Rudolf. Comic Kingdom: Napoleon, the Last Phase but Two (Classic Reprint) (p. 429)
Pico, Thom. Aster & the Accidental Magic. Karensac, illus. (p. 127)
Picolo, Gabriel, illus. see Garcia, Kami.
Picone, Emma Lee. My Blended Family. Harrel, Tina, illus. (p. 1533)
Picone, Linda. My Changing Body (p. 1535)
Picone, Veronica. Kate's First Face Paint: A Day at the Fair. (p. 1205)
Picot, Charles. Interesting Narrations in French: Consisting of Interesting Tales, Fables, & Ancedotes, Intended for Reading, Translation, & Particularly for Narration (Classic Reprint) (p. 1126)
Picou, Lin. Do I Have To... Reese, Bob, illus. (p. 570)
—Do I Have To ... Reese, Bob, illus. (p. 570)
—Pink Toys, Yes or No. (p. 1746)
—Who's Right. DuFalla, Anita, illus. (p. 2453)
Picou, Lin, jt. auth. see Karapetkova, Holly.
Picoult, Jodi & van Leer, Samantha. Between the Lines. (p. 210)
—Off the Page. Gilbert, Yvonne, illus. (p. 1640)
Picray, Michael E. Sun with Code. (p. 2151)
Picthall, Chez. Baby Animals. (p. 148)
—Baby Sees Boxed Set: Shapes. (p. 152)
—Bedtime. Hewett, Angela, illus. (p. 188)
—First Library. (p. 738)
—Flip Flaps Zoo. (p. 749)
—My Bike. Gunzi, Christiane, ed. (p. 1533)
—My Favourite Racers Sticker Book. Rayner, Katy, ed. (p. 1540)
—My Favourite Trucks Sticker Book. Rayner, Katy, ed. (p. 1540)
—On the Move. Gunzi, Christiane, ed. (p. 1655)
—Puppies. (p. 1814)
—Racers. Gunzi, Christiane, ed. (p. 1832)
—Ultimate Car Colouring Book. (p. 2314)
—Zoo Animals. (p. 2543)
Picthall, Chez & Award, Anna. Beach. (p. 178)
—Tell The Time Sticker Book. (p. 2202)
—Very First Book. (p. 2353)
Picthall, Chez & Gunzi. My Favourite Cars Sticker Book. Rayner, Katy, ed. (p. 1540)
Picthall, Chez & Gunzi, Christiane. Numbers. (p. 1630)
—Words. (p. 2494)
Picthall, Chez, creator. Flip Flap Colours: A Turn-the-Flap Book! (p. 749)
—Flip Flaps Shapes. (p. 749)
Picthall, Chez, des. Flowers. (p. 753)
—Hearts & Stars. (p. 946)
—Spots & Dots. (p. 2091)
Picton, Thomas, jt. auth. see Herbert, Henry William.
Picture Window Books Staff, jt. auth. see Firestone, Mary.
Picture Window Books Staff, jt. auth. see Meachen Rau, Dana.
Picture Window Books Staff, jt. auth. see Mortensen, Lori.
Picture Window Books Staff, jt. auth. see Owen, Ann.
Picture Window Books Staff, jt. auth. see Pearl, Norman.
Picture Window Books Staff, jt. auth. see Rosinsky, Natalie M.
Picture Window Books Staff, jt. auth. see Sherman, Josepha.
Picture Window Books Staff, jt. auth. see Stille, Darlene R.
Pictures, Eastin 16mm. List of Sound & Silent 16mm. Motion Pictures Available from Eastin 16mm. Pictures: Corrected to October 1, 1937 (Classic Reprint) (p. 1308)
Pictures, Warner Bros. Silhouettes of Stars, Players, & Directors of Warner Bros. Pictures, Inc (Classic Reprint) (p. 2018)
Pidcock-Reed, Heather. Environment. (p. 657)
—Immigration. (p. 1101)
Piddington, Lorraine. Aliens Who Loved Lemon Curd. Tee, Jacqueline, illus. (p. 47)
—Pete from Pluto & His Perfect Pies. (p. 1727)
Piddock, Charles. Cadillac Escalade ESV Platinum. (p. 308)
—Cold War. (p. 413)
—Creeps of the Deep: Explore the Ocean's Strangest Creatures. (p. 472)
—Earthquakes, Tsunamis, & Volcanoes: Set Of 10. Chiu, Andrew, illus. (p. 618)
—Earthquakes, Tsunamis, & Volcanoes: Prime Bridges Edition. Chiu, Andrew, illus. (p. 618)
—Earthquakes, Tsunamis, & Volcanoes: Bridges Edition, Set Of 10. Chiu, Andrew, illus. (p. 618)
—Ford Mustang. (p. 764)
—GMC Yukon Denali. (p. 845)
—Rachel Carson: A Voice for the Natural World. (p. 1832)
—Range Rover SV Autobiography LWB. (p. 1840)
—Ray Bradbury: Legendary Fantasy Writer. (p. 1844)
—Sound: Set Of 10. Carloni, Marco, illus. (p. 2067)
—Sound: Prime Bridges Edition. Carloni, Marco, illus. (p. 2067)
—Sound: Bridges Edition, Set Of 10. Carloni, Marco, illus. (p. 2067)
—Terremotos, Tsunamis y Volcanes. (p. 2207)
—Terremotos, Tsunamis y Volcanes - 6 Pack: Set of 6 Common Core Edition. (p. 2207)
Piddock, Charles & Keen, Jared. Future of Farming. (p. 803)
Piddock, Claire. All about Area. (p. 48)
—Decimals. (p. 523)
—Line, Bar, & Circle Graphs. (p. 1303)

P

Pike, Kenneth & Stewart, Isaac. Jacob's Journal of Doom: Confessions of an Almost-Deacon. (p. 1154)
Pike, Mary Hayden Green. Caste: A Story of Republican Equality (Classic Reprint) (p. 340)
Pike, Matt J. Apocalypse: Diary of a Survivor. Chant, Lisa, ed. (p. 105)
—Beath Becomes Her. Chant, Lisa, ed. (p. 182)
—Beath Defying. Chant, Lisa, ed. (p. 182)
—Creeping Beath. Chant, Lisa, ed. (p. 472)
—Life & Beath. Chant, Lisa, ed. (p. 1288)
—Scared to Beath. Chant, Lisa, ed. (p. 1941)
Pike, Oliver G. Bird Biographies: And Other Bird Sketches (Classic Reprint) (p. 230)
—In Bird-Land with Field-Glass & Camera (Classic Reprint) (p. 1104)
—Woodland, Field & Shore: Wild Nature Depicted with Pen & Camera (Classic Reprint) (p. 2491)
Pike, Oliver Gregory. Adventures in Bird-Land (Classic Reprint) (p. 20)
—Home Life in Bird-Land (Classic Reprint) (p. 996)
—Through Birdland Byways with Pen & Camera (Classic Reprint) (p. 2236)
—With the Birds on Hillside, Rock, & Dale (Classic Reprint) (p. 2481)
Pike, Olly. Prince & the Frog: A Story to Help Children Learn about Same-Sex Relationships. (p. 1793)
Pike, Tabitha R. Dragon Tears: The Legacy. (p. 594)
Pikiuris, M2r. Alma Extranjera. (p. 57)
Pikoj, Ed, illus. see Loewen, Mark.
Pil, et al. Frosty the Snowman. McGee, Warner, illus. (p. 795)
Pilcher, Sheron Jennings. Soapy Surprise. (p. 2051)
Pilcher, T. D. East Is East: Stories of Indian Life (Classic Reprint) (p. 619)
Pilegard, Virginia. Emperor's Army Tans, Adrian, illus. (p. 644)
Pileggi, Leah. Prisoner 88. (p. 1801)
Pileggi, Steve, illus. see Johnson, Spencer.
Pileggi, Steve, illus. see Tucker, Angel.
Pileggi, Steven, illus. see Monnar, Alexander.
Pilger, Seamus. Fart Squad. Gilpin, Stephen, illus. (p. 711)
—Fart Squad #2: Fartasaurus Rex. Gilpin, Stephen, illus. (p. 711)
—Fart Squad #3: Unidentified Farting Objects. Gilpin, Stephen, illus. (p. 711)
—Fart Squad #4: the Toilet Vortex. Gilpin, Stephen, illus. (p. 711)
—Fart Squad #5: Underpantsed! Gilpin, Stephen, illus. (p. 711)
—Fart Squad #6: Blast from the Past. Gilpin, Stephen, illus. (p. 711)
Pilgrim, A. W. J. Isley's Invite. Pocock, Joyce, ed. (p. 1140)
—Sid the Spider Who Lived in a Painting. Crownson, Jeff, ed. (p. 2014)
—Spot the Dog. Crownson, Jeff, ed. (p. 2090)
Pilgrim, A. W. J., illus. see Pocock, Joyce & Downey, Heidi, eds.
Pilgrim, A. W. J., illus. see Pocock, Joyce & Downie, Heidi, eds.
Pilgrim, Cheryl. Big & Little: A Story of Opposites. (p. 216)
Pilgrim, Cheryl, illus. see Preus, Margi.
Pilgrim, Cheryl, illus. see Vermillion, Patricia.
Pilgrim, Kingsley. Immortopia. (p. 1101)
Pilgrim, Thomas. Live Boys, or Charley & Nasho in Texas: A Narrative Relating to Two Boys of Fourteen, One a Texan, the Other a Mexican; Showing Their Life on the Great Texas Cattle Trail, & Their Adventures in the Indian Territory, Kansas, & Northern Texas. (p. 1332)
Pilgrim, Wil Corona, text. Spider-Man: Far from Home Prelude. (p. 2080)
Pilgrim, Will Corona & Di Vito, Andrea. Galaxy's Most Wanted. Villari, Laura, illus. (p. 805)
Pilgrim, Will Corona, text. Marvel's Black Panther Prelude. (p. 1413)
Pilkey, Dav. Adventures of Captain Underpants. (p. 22)
—Adventures of Captain Underpants. Pilkey, Dav, illus. (p. 22)
—Adventures of Ook & Gluk, Kung-Fu Cavemen from the Future. (p. 26)
—Adventures of Ook & Gluk, Kung-Fu Cavemen from the Future. Pilkey, Dav, illus. (p. 26)
—Adventures of Super Diaper Baby. (p. 28)
—Adventures of Super Diaper Baby. Pilkey, Dav, illus. (p. 28)
—Aventuras de Uuk y Gluk, Cavernícolas del Futuro y Maestros de Kung Fu. Pilkey, Dav, illus. (p. 142)
—Big, Bad Battle of the Bionic Booger Boy: The Night of the Nasty Nostril Nuggets. Pilkey, Dav, illus. (p. 216)
—Big Dog & Little Dog (Reader) (p. 219)
—Big Dog & Little Dog Getting in Trouble (Reader) (p. 219)
—Big Dog & Little Dog Going for a Walk (Reader) (p. 219)
—Brawl of the Wild. (p. 277)
—Brawl of the Wild. Pilkey, Dav, illus. (p. 277)
—Captain Underpants & the Attack of the Talking Toilets. Pilkey, Dav, illus. (p. 326)
—Captain Underpants & the Big, Bad Battle of the Bionic Booger Boy: The Revenge of the Ridiculous Robo-Boogers. Pilkey, Dav, illus. (p. 326)
—Captain Underpants & the Invasion of the Incredibly Naughty Cafeteria Ladies from Outer: And the Invasion of the Incredibly Naughty Cafeteria Ladies from Outer Space (and the Subsequent Assault of the Equally Evil Lunchroom Zombie Nerds) Pilkey, Dav, illus. (p. 326)
—Captain Underpants & the Perilous Plot of Professor Poopypants. (p. 326)
—Captain Underpants & the Revolting Revenge of the Radioactive Robo-Boxers. (p. 326)
—Captain Underpants & the Revolting Revenge of the Radioactive Robo-Boxers. Pilkey, Dav, illus. (p. 326)
—Captain Underpants & the Revolting Revenge of the Radioactive Robo-Boxers: Color Edition (Captain Underpants #10) Color Edition. Pilkey, Dav, illus. (p. 326)
—Captain Underpants & the Sensational Saga of Sir Stinks-a-Lot. Pilkey, Dav, illus. (p. 326)
—Captain Underpants & the Terrifying Return of Tippy Tinkletrousers. (p. 326)
—Captain Underpants & the Tyrannical Retaliation of the Turbo Toilet 2000. (p. 326)
—Captain Underpants & the Tyrannical Retaliation of the Turbo Toilet 2000. Pilkey, Dav, illus. (p. 326)
—Captain Underpants & the Wrath of the Wicked Wedgie Woman: Color Edition (Captain Underpants #5) Color Edition. Pilkey, Dav, illus. (p. 326)
—Captain Underpants Color Collection. Pilkey, Dav, illus. (p. 326)
—Dog Man. Pilkey, Dav, illus. (p. 576)
—Dog Man a Tale of Two Kitties. Pilkey, Dav, illus. (p. 576)
—Dog Man & Cat Kid. (p. 576)
—Dog Man & Cat Kid. Pilkey, Dav, illus. (p. 576)
—Dog Man - The Epic Collection. Pilkey, Dav, illus. (p. 576)
—Dog Man Unleashed. (p. 576)
—Dog Man Unleashed. Pilkey, Dav, illus. (p. 576)
—Dogzilla. Pilkey, Dav, illus. (p. 578)
—Dragón 1: un Amigo para Dragón: Un Libro de la Serie Acorn. Pilkey, Dav, illus. (p. 593)
—Dragon Gets By. (p. 593)
—Dragon's Fat Cat. (p. 595)
—Dumb Bunnies' Easter. Pilkey, Dav, illus. (p. 609)
—Dumb Bunnies Go to the Zoo. Pilkey, Dav, illus. (p. 609)
—For Whom the Ball Rolls. Pilkey, Dav, illus. (p. 764)
—Friend for Dragon. (p. 786)
—Friend for Dragon. Pilkey, Dav, illus. (p. 786)
—Gato Gordo de Dragón (Dragon's Fat Cat) Un Libro de la Serie Acorn. Pilkey, Dav, illus. (p. 812)
—God Bless the Gargoyles. (p. 851)
—Grime & Punishment. Pilkey, Dav, illus. (p. 896)
—Hallo-Wiener. Pilkey, Dav, illus. (p. 911)
—Historia de Dos Gatitos. Pilkey, Dav, illus. (p. 975)
—Hombre Perro. Pilkey, Dav, illus. (p. 995)
—Hombre Perro: la Pelea de la Selva. Pilkey, Dav, illus. (p. 995)
—Hombre Perro Se Desata. Pilkey, Dav, illus. (p. 995)
—Hombre Perro y Supergatito. Pilkey, Dav, illus. (p. 995)
—Invasion of the Potty Snatchers. (p. 1130)
—Invasion of the Potty Snatchers. Pilkey, Dav, illus. (p. 1130)
—Jurassic Jackrabbits from Jupiter. Santat, Dan, illus. (p. 1192)
—Lord of the Fleas. Pilkey, Dav, illus. (p. 1348)
—Mighty Robot vs. the Mecha-Monkeys from Mars. Santat, Dan, illus. (p. 1463)
—Mighty Robot vs. the Mutant Mosquitoes from Mercury. Santat, Dan, illus. (p. 1463)
—Mighty Robot vs. the Naughty Nightcrawlers from Neptune. Santat, Dan, illus. (p. 1463)
—Paperboy. (p. 1698)
—Paperboy. Pilkey, Dav, illus. (p. 1698)
—Perilous Plot of Professor Poopypants. Pilkey, Dav, illus. (p. 1723)
—Perrazo y Perrito Se Equivocan/Big Dog & Little Dog Making a Mistake (bilingual Reader) (p. 1724)
—Perrazo y Perrito Se Meten en Problemas/Big Dog & Little Dog Getting in Trouble (bilingual Reader) (p. 1724)
—Ricky Ricotta's Mighty Robot. (p. 1877)
—Ricky Ricotta's Mighty Robot. Santat, Dan, illus. (p. 1877)
—Ricky Ricotta's Mighty Robot vs. the Naughty Nightcrawlers from Neptune. Santat, Dan, illus. (p. 1877)
—Ricky Ricotta's Mighty Robot vs. the Unpleasant Penguins from Pluto. Santat, Dan, illus. (p. 1877)
—Ricky Ricotta's Mighty Robot vs. the Video Vultures from Venus. Santat, Dan, illus. (p. 1877)
—Super-Silly Sticker Studio. Klutz Editors, ed. (p. 2156)
—Tale of Two Kitties. (p. 2180)
—Tale of Two Kitties. Pilkey, Dav, illus. (p. 2180)
—Uranium Unicorns from Uranus. (p. 2339)
Pilkey, Dav, illus. see Blanco, Richard.
Pilkey, Dav, illus. see Garibaldi, Jose.
Pilkey, Dav, illus. see Johnson, Angela.
Pilkey, Dav & Beard, George. Adventures of Ook & Gluk, Kung-Fu Cavemen from the Future. (p. 26)
Pilkey, Dav & Garibaldi, Jose. Captain Underpants & the Wrath of the Wicked Wedgie Woman. Pilkey, Dav, illus. (p. 326)
Pilkington, Christopher. Birthday Box: Book 1. (p. 233)
—Birthday Box: Book 2. (p. 233)
—Birthday Box: Book 3. (p. 233)
Pilkington, John Carteret. Real Story of John Carteret Pilkington: Written by Himself (Classic Reprint) (p. 1850)
Pilkington, Laetitia. Memoirs of Mrs. Laetitia Pilkington, Wife to the REV. Mr. Matthew Pilkington: Written by Herself, Wherein Are Occasionally Interspersed, All Her Poems (Classic Reprint) (p. 1445)
—Memoirs of Mrs. Laetitia Pilkington, Wife to the REV. Mr. Matthew Pilkington, Vol. 2: Written by Herself, Wherein Are Occasionally Interspersed, Her Poems, with Variety of Secret Transactions, of Some Eminent Persons (Classic Reprint) (p. 1445)
—Memoirs of Mrs. lætitia Pilkington, Written by Herself: Wherein Are Occasionally Interspersed, Variety of Poems; As Also the Letters of Several Persons of Distinction; with the Conclusive Part of the Life of the Inimitable Dean Swift (Classic Reprint) (p. 1445)
Pilkington, Mary Hopkins. Rosina, Vol. 1 Of 5: A Novel (Classic Reprint) (p. 1906)
—Rosina, Vol. 2 Of 5: A Novel (Classic Reprint) (p. 1906)
—Rosina, Vol. 3 Of 5: A Novel (Classic Reprint) (p. 1906)
—Rosina, Vol. 4 Of 5: A Novel (Classic Reprint) (p. 1906)
—Rosina, Vol. 5 Of 5: A Novel (Classic Reprint) (p. 1906)
Pilkons, Alyssa. Confessions of a Teenage Lima Bean. (p. 439)
Pillay, Nalini. Haran Travels to London. (p. 924)
Pilling, Ann. Before I Go to Sleep: Bible Stories, Poems, & Prayers for Children. Denton, Kady MacDonald, illus. (p. 190)
—Black Harvest (Collins Modern Classics) (p. 238)
Pilling, Anne, ed. see Baxter, Tracey, et al.
Pilling, Anne, ed. see MacGregor, Fiona, et al.
Pilling, Anne, ed. see Morrison, Karen, et al.
Pilling, Anne, ed. see Paizee, Daphne, et al.
Pillo, Cary, illus. see Braver, Vanita.
Pillo, Cary, illus. see Hanford, Juliana.
Pillo, Cary, illus. see Harkrader, Lisa.
Pillo, Cary, illus. see Kilgore, Mary & Kilgore, Mitchell.
Pillo, Cary, illus. see May, Eleanor.
Pillo, Cary, illus. see Sileo, Frank J.
Pillo, Cary, illus. see Slade, Suzanne.
Pillot, édéric, illus. see Mrowiec, Katia.
Pilloton, Emily. Girls Garage: How to Use Any Tool, Tackle Any Project, & Build the World You Want to See (Teenage Trailblazers, STEM Building Projects for Girls) (p. 838)
Pillow, Ltd The Armadillo. Big 11+ Logic Puzzle Challenge. (p. 215)
Pillsbury, H. G. Figures Famed in Fiction, Drawn from the Original Sources (Classic Reprint) (p. 726)
Pillsbury, Hervey Gorham. Figures Famed in Fiction: Drawn from the Original Sources (Classic Reprint) (p. 726)
Pilo, Cary, illus. see Hall, Pamela.
Pilon, Frederick. Deaf Lover: A Farce, in Two Acts (Classic Reprint) (p. 519)
Pilon, Kilayla. Prophet's Daughter. (p. 1807)
Pilorget, Bruno, illus. see Massenot, Véronique.
Pilot Inc. Staff, illus. see Schaefer, Elizabeth.
Pilot Studio, illus. see Harper, Benjamin.
Pilot Studio, illus. see Lucasfilm Press.
Pilot Studio, illus. see Siglain, Michael.
Pilsworth, Graham, illus. see Grant, Vicki.
Pilsworth, Graham, illus. see Staunton, Ted.
Pilutti, Deb. Bear & Squirrel Are Friends ... Yes, Really! Pilutti, Deb, illus. (p. 179)
—Old Rock (Is Not Boring) Pilutti, Deb, illus. (p. 1648)
—Secrets of Ninja School. (p. 1980)
—Ten Rules of Being a Superhero. Pilutti, Deb, illus. (p. 2205)
Pilutti, Deb, illus. see Lehrhaupt, Adam.
Pilutti, Deb, illus. see Thoms, Susan Collins.
Pilz, M. H., illus. see Houran, Lori Haskins.
Pilz, M. H., illus. see May, Eleanor.
Pilz, M. H., illus. see Walker, Nan.
Pim, Herbert Moore. Unknown Immortals: In the Northern City of Success (Classic Reprint) (p. 2333)
Pimenta, Paula. Viviendo Mi Película 3: El Guion Inesperado de Fani. (p. 2364)
Pimental, Annette Bay & Lo, Rich. Mountain Chef: How One Man Lost His Groceries, Changed His Plans, & Helped Cook up the National Park Service. (p. 1513)
Pimentel, Alejandro, tr. see Rock, Lois.
Pimentel, Annette Bay. Do You Really Want to Meet a Pterosaur? Fabbri, Daniele, illus. (p. 572)
—Do You Really Want to Meet a Stegosaurus? Fabbri, Daniele, illus. (p. 572)
—Do You Really Want to Meet Allosaurus? Fabbri, Daniele, illus. (p. 572)
—Do You Really Want to Meet Ankylosaurus? Fabbri, Daniele, illus. (p. 572)
—Do You Really Want to Meet Iguanodon? Fabbri, Daniele, illus. (p. 572)
—Do You Really Want to Meet Tyrannosaurus Rex? Fabbri, Daniele, illus. (p. 572)
—Girl Running. Archer, Micha, illus. (p. 836)
—Mountain Chef. (p. 1513)
—My Brain. Alberini, Teresa, illus. (p. 1534)
—My Stomach. Alberini, Teresa, illus. (p. 1561)
Pimentel, Annette Bay & Lo, Rich. Mountain Chef: How One Man Lost His Groceries, Changed His Plans, & Helped Cook up the National Park Service. (p. 1513)
Pimentel Marcel. Al Final de la Fila. (p. 38)
Pimm, Nancy Roe. Jerrie Mock Story: The First Woman to Fly Solo Around the World. (p. 1164)
—Smoky, the Dog That Saved My Life: The Bill Wynne Story. (p. 2043)
Pina, Andrew. Baseball's Greatest Records (p. 169)
—Becoming a Pro Baseball Player. (p. 187)
—Career As a Border Patrol Agent. (p. 328)
—Story of African American Music. (p. 2129)
Pina, Andrew & Uschan, Michael. Serena Williams: Tennis Ace. (p. 1990)
Pina, Javier. Captain America: Steve Rogers Vol. 3: Empire Building. (p. 324)
Pina, Javier & Saiz, Jesus. Doctor Strange by Mark Waid Vol. 2: Remittance. (p. 573)
Pina, Leonor. Butterflies. (p. 303)
Pina Molina, Juan Ramon. Las Aventuras Del Profesor Thompson. (p. 1245)
Pinamonti, Donna Saccone. King Claude the Talking Dog. (p. 1220)
Pinard, Margaret. Dulci's Legacy. (p. 609)
Pinborough, Jan. Miss Moore Thought Otherwise: How Anne Carroll Moore Created Libraries for Children. Atwell, Debby, illus. (p. 1479)
Pinborough, Sarah. 13 Minutes: A Novel. (p. 2552)
Pinchard. Mystery & Confidence, Vol. 1 Of 3: A Tale (Classic Reprint) (p. 1568)
Pinchard, Elizabeth Sibthorpe. Blind Child, or Anecdotes of the Wyndham Family: Written for the Use of Young People (Classic Reprint) (p. 244)
—Blind Child, or Anecdotes of the Wyndham Family: Written for the Use of Young People, by a Lady (Classic Reprint) (p. 244)
—Dramatic Dialogues: For the Use of Young Persons (Classic Reprint) (p. 597)
—Family Affection: A Tale for Youth (Classic Reprint) (p. 702)
—Two Cousins: A Moral Story for the Use of Young Persons in Which Is Exemplified the Necessity of Moderation & Justice to the Attainment of Happiness (Classic Reprint) (p. 2307)
Pinchbeck, Neil. Rescue on the Road. (p. 1868)
Pinchot, Gifford. Bulletin No. 24: U. S. Department of Agriculture; a Primer of Forestry; Part I. - the Forest. (p. 296)
—Bulletin No. 24, Part II, U. S. Department of Agriculture. Bureau of Forestry. a Primer of Forestry. (p. 296)
—Bulletin No. 24, Part II. U. S. Department of Agriculture, Bureau of Forestry. a Primer of Forestry, Part II. - Practical Forestry. (p. 296)
—Bulletin No. 24. U. S. Department of Agriculture. Devision of Forestry. a Primer of Forestry. Part I. -The Forest. (p. 296)
—Bulletin No. 24. U. S. Department of Agriculture, Division of Forestry; a Primer of Forestry. Part I. - the Forest. (p. 296)
Pinckney, Esther R. In My Eyes You Are Beautiful. (p. 1106)
Pinckney, Julia. Am I Big Enough? A Fun Little Book on Manners Young, Timothy, illus. (p. 61)
Pinckney, Susanna Shulrick Hayne. Douglas: Tender & True (Classic Reprint) (p. 589)
Pincock, Amy. Quiet Book Patterns. (p. 1827)
Pincus, Greg. Homework Strike. (p. 998)
Pincus, Gregory K. 14 Fibs of Gregory K. (p. 2552)
—Homework Strike. (p. 998)
Pincus, Harriet, illus. see Sandburg, Carl.
Pincus, Harriet, illus. see Segal, Lore.
Pincus, Meeg. Miep & the Most Famous Diary: The Woman Who Rescued Anne Frank's Diary. Solano, Jordi, illus. (p. 1462)
—Senna Helps the Sea Lions: (and You Can, Too!) (p. 1988)
—Winged Wonders: Solving the Monarch Migration Mystery. Imamura, Yas, illus. (p. 2473)
Pindar, Heather. Beware the Mighty Bitey. Batori, Susan, illus. (p. 211)
—Froggy Day. Bakos, Barbara, illus. (p. 789)
—MOOsic Makers. Bakos, Barbara, illus. (p. 1503)
—Strictly No Crocs. Batori, Susan, illus. (p. 2141)
Pindar, Paul. London Legends, Vol. 1 of 2 (Classic Reprint) (p. 1341)
Pindar, Peter. Trial of Doctor John Wolcot: Otherwise Peter Pindar, Esq. for Criminal Conversation with the Wife of Mr. Knight, of the Royal Navy; Before the Right Hon. Lord Ellenborough, in the Court of King's Bench, Westminster; on June The 27th 1807. (p. 2286)
Pindar, Susan. Fireside Fairies, or Christmas at Aunt Elsie's (Classic Reprint) (p. 734)
Pinder, Andrew. Boys' Doodle Book: Amazing Picture to Complete & Create. (p. 272)
—Girls' Doodle Book: Amazing Pictures to Complete & Create. (p. 838)
—Icky, Sticky, Slimy Doodles: Gross, Full-Color Pictures to Complete & Create. (p. 1088)
—Journey Through Time Doodles. (p. 1182)
Pinder, Andrew, illus. see Collins, Tim.
Pinder, Andrew, illus. see Gifford, Clive.
Pinder, Andrew, illus. see Martin, Steve, et al.
Pinder, Andrew, illus. see Mitchell, Chris.
Pinder, Andrew, illus. see Oliver, Martin.
Pinder, Andrew, jt. auth. see Moore, Gareth.
Pinder, Eric. Cat in the Clouds. Walsh, Illustrated by T. B. R., illus. (p. 341)
—Counting Dinos. Bianda, Junissa, illus. (p. 460)
—How to Share with a Bear. Graegin, Stephanie, illus. (p. 1044)
—I'd Rather Be Riding My Bike. Cardinal, John, illus. (p. 1089)
—If All the Animals Came Inside. Brown, Marc, illus. (p. 1090)
—Perfect Pillow. Sheban, Chris, illus. (p. 1722)
Pindle, B. t. Miscellaneous Poems: Intended for the Amusement, If Not the Instruction of Those Who May Favor Them with Attention, When Time Is Not to Be Taken in the Estimate (Classic Reprint) (p. 1476)
Pindroh, Paula, illus. see Galvin, Laura Gates.
Pindroh, Paula, illus. see Parisi, Anthony.
Pine, Hank, illus. see Richmond, Jacob.
Pine, Macyle. Gift of a Lifetime: A Dog's Tale: Part One. (p. 832)
Pine, Margherita N., ed. see Howard, Becky L.
Pineau, Severine, tr. see Ward, John.
Pineda, Jon. Let's No One Get Hurt: A Novel. (p. 1276)
Pineda, Norman. Candle & a Key. (p. 321)
Pinede, Elaine. Duck Who Loved Raindrops. (p. 608)
Pinede, Nadine. Women in Film. (p. 2487)
Pinede, Nadine & Harris, Duchess. Sexism & Race. (p. 1995)
Pinelli, Amerigo, illus. see Brezenoff, Steve.
Pinelli, Amerigo, illus. see Collins, Ailynn.
Pinelli, Amerigo, illus. see Craver, Marcella Marino.
Pinelli, Amerigo, illus. see Farndon, John.
Pinelli, Amerigo, illus. see Jakubowski, Michele.
Pinelli, Amerigo, illus. see McKenzie, Precious.
Pinelli, Amerigo, illus. see Powling, Chris.
Pinelli, Amerigo, illus. see Rosen, Jonathan.
Pinelli, Amerigo, illus. see Terrell, Brandon.
Pinelli, Amerigo, illus. see Yomtov, Nelson.
Piner, Huston. Breaths We Take. (p. 279)
—Conjoined at the Soul. (p. 440)
—My Life As a Myth. (p. 1551)
Pinero, Arthur. Enchanted Cottage: A Fable, in Three Acts (Classic Reprint) (p. 647)
Pinero, Arthur W. Amazons: A Farcical Romance in Three Acts. (p. 67)
—Amazons: A Farcical Romance in Three Acts (Classic Reprint) (p. 67)
—Amazons. (p. 67)
—Letty: An Original Drama, in Four Acts & an Epilogue (Classic Reprint) (p. 1281)
—Thunderbolt: An Episode in the History of a Provincial Family, in Four Acts (Classic Reprint) (p. 2238)
—Times: A Comedy in Four Acts (Classic Reprint) (p. 2247)
—Times. (p. 2247)
Pinero, Arthur Wing. Dandy Dick: A Play in Three Acts (Classic Reprint) (p. 501)
—Hester's Mystery: A Comedy in One Act (Classic Reprint) (p. 963)
—Magistrate a Farce in Three Acts (Classic Reprint) (p. 1381)
—Playgoers: A Domestic Episode (Classic Reprint) (p. 1760)
—Profligate: A Play in Four Acts (Classic Reprint) (p. 1805)
—Schoolmistress: A Farce in Three Acts (Classic Reprint) (p. 1947)
—Schoolmistress. (p. 1947)
—Sweet Lavender: A Comedy in Three Acts (Classic Reprint) (p. 2169)
—Sweet Lavender. (p. 2169)
—Trelawny of the Wells: A Comedietta in Four Acts (Classic Reprint) (p. 2285)
—Trelawny of the Wells. (p. 2285)
Pinero, Eimi, illus. see Perkins, T. J.
Pinet, Hélène. Sculpture. Chabot, Jean-Philippe, illus. (p. 1966)
Pinette, Carol. Smiley Discovers Rain. McNeill, Sharlene, illus. (p. 2042)
—Smiley Goes to School. McNeill, Sharlene, illus. (p. 2042)
—Smiley's Birthday. McNeill, Sharlene, illus. (p. 2042)
—Smiley's Town. McNeill, Sharlene, illus. (p. 2042)

P

—Little Girl In: The Land of the Hiccups. (p. 1317)
Pipkin, Bonnie. Aftercare Instructions: A Novel. (p. 34)
Pippet, Gabriel, illus. see Salome, Mother Mary.
Pippet, Wilfrid, illus. see Du St Esprit, Sr Julie.
Pippin, Barbara, illus. see Guiffre, William A.
Pippin, Barbara, illus. see Guiffre, William.
Pippin, Jessica. Yo Estaba Muy Molesta: Lap Book. Poole, Helen, illus. (p. 2522)
—Yo Estaba Muy Molesta. Poole, Helen, illus. (p. 2522)
—Yo Puedo Ser Amable: Lap Book. Monés, Marc, illus. (p. 2522)
—Yo Puedo Ser Amable. Monés, Marc, illus. (p. 2522)
—¡Soy una Estrella! Oliver, Juan Bautista Juan, illus. (p. 2070)
—¡Soy una Estrella! Lap Book. Oliver, Juan Bautista Juan, illus. (p. 2070)
Pippin, Jessica & Newmark Learning, LLC. I Am a Star! Set Of 6. (p. 1057)
—I Am a Star! Lap Book with Teacher Guide. (p. 1057)
—I Can Be Kind: Set Of 6. (p. 1061)
—I Can Be Kind: Lap Book with Teacher Guide. (p. 1061)
—I Was So Mad: Set Of 6. (p. 1085)
—I Was So Mad: Lap Book with Teacher Guide. (p. 1085)
—Yo Estaba Muy Molesta: Set Of 6. (p. 2522)
—Yo Estaba Muy Molesta: Lap Book with Teacher Guide. (p. 2522)
—Yo Puedo Ser Amable: Set Of 6. (p. 2522)
—Yo Puedo Ser Amable: Lap Book with Teacher Guide. (p. 2522)
—¡Soy una Estrella! Set Of 6. (p. 2070)
—¡Soy una Estrella! Lap Book with Teacher Guide. (p. 2070)
Pippin-Mathur, Courtney. Dragons Rule, Princesses Drool! Pippin-Mathur, Courtney, illus. (p. 596)
—Maya Was Grumpy. (p. 1429)
—Maya Was Grumpy. Pippin-Mathur, Courtney, illus. (p. 1429)
Pippins, Andrea. Hey, Baby! A Baby's Day in Doodles. (p. 964)
Pippins, Andrea, illus. see Wilson, Jamia.
Pips, J. J. Extraordinary Journey of J. J. Pips. (p. 685)
Piquemal, Michel. Aïe ! J'Ai Mal ! Piccolophilo. Baas, Thomas, illus. (p. 36)
—C'Est À Moi ! Piccolophilo. Baas, Thomas, illus. (p. 353)
Piquet, Muriel. Tatou le Matou: Niveau 1 Livre de L'Eleve. (p. 2193)
—Tatou le Matou: Niveau 2 Guide Pedagogique. (p. 2193)
Piramal, Gita. Business Maharajas. (p. 301)
Pirc, Jerri J. Kate & Caboodle. Smith, Jane, illus. (p. 1204)
Pires, Curt. Fiction. (p. 722)
Piriano, Steven. Josh & Joey's Incredible Museum Adventure. (p. 1179)
Pirie, Lauren, illus. see Appleby, Danny.
Pirie, P. Kashmir: The Land of Streams & Solitudes. (p. 1204)
—Kashmir: The Land of Streams & Solitudes (Classic Reprint) (p. 1204)
Pirk, Wendy. Cats (p. 345)
—Dogs (p. 577)
—Farm Animals (p. 709)
Pirk, Wendy, jt. auth. see Einstein, Wendy.
Pirk, Wendy & Radford, Duane. Rodeo Roundup (p. 1897)
Pirk, Wendy & Super Explorers. Volcanoes (p. 2366)
Pirkis, C. L. At the Moment of Victory, Vol. 1 of 3 (Classic Reprint) (p. 131)
—Red Sister, Vol. 3 Of 3: A Story of Three Days & Three Months (Classic Reprint) (p. 1859)
Pirkis, Catherine Louisa. At the Moment of Victory, Vol. 3 of 3 (Classic Reprint) (p. 131)
—Red Sister, Vol. 1 Of 3: A Story of Three Days & Three Months (Classic Reprint) (p. 1859)
—Red Sister, Vol. 2 Of 3: A Story of Three Days & Three Months (Classic Reprint) (p. 1859)
Pirkola, Maksim & Pirkola, Phillip. Too Many Buddies: In My Room. (p. 2260)
Pirner, Connie White. Even Little Kids Get Diabetes. Westcott, Nadine Bernard, illus. (p. 668)
Pirnot, Dr Karen Hutchins & Pirnot, Karen Hutchins. Colors of Myself. Klanot, Sameon Clay, illus. (p. 426)
Pirnot, Karen Hutchins. Door in the Floor. Ross, Julie, illus. (p. 585)
—Rainbows Are the Best. Allen, Sandra Hutchins, illus. (p. 1837)
Pirnot, Karen Hutchins & Frey, Garret. Benny & the Butterfly: A Story about Feeling Different. (p. 200)
Piroddi, Chiara. Preschool Practice: A Collection of Skill-Building Activities. Baruzzi, Agnese, illus. (p. 1788)
Piroddi, Chiara & Baruzzi, Agnese. My First Book of Numbers. (p. 1542)
Pirola, Isabella. Steadfast. Tucker, Hilary, illus. (p. 2110)
Pirolli, Anna, illus. see Cali, Davide.
Pirolo, Antonella. Alicia Nel Belpaese. Flores, Hemerson Maury, illus. (p. 46)
Pirotta. Baby's First ABCs. (p. 154)
—Baby's First Animals. (p. 154)
—Baby's First Sea Creatures. (p. 154)
Pirotta, Saviour. Aesop's Fables. Johnson, Richard, illus. (p. 31)
—Around the World in 80 Tales. (p. 119)
—Big Book of Fairy Tales. (p. 217)
—Children's Stories from the Bible. Gilbert, Anne Yvonne & Andrew, Ian, illus. (p. 375)
—George & the Dragon: Band 13/Topaz (Collins Big Cat) Peluso, Martina, illus. (p. 818)
—Ghosts Who Danced: And Other Spooky Stories. Hess, Paul, illus. (p. 830)
—Puss in Boots. Newson, Karl, illus. (p. 1817)
—Snow Queen. Fleming, Lucy, illus. (p. 2048)
—Unicorn Prince. Ray, Jane, illus. (p. 2328)
Pirrone, Francesca. Bruno Has One Hundred Friends. (p. 288)
Pirscher, Johanna. Variations on an Old Theme (Classic Reprint) (p. 2348)
Pirz, Therese S. Kids Stuff French: Easy French Phrases for You & Your Kids. (p. 1216)
Pisapia, Blasco, illus. see Pavanello, Roberto.
Piskor, Ed. X-Men: Grand Design - X-Tinction. (p. 2515)
Pisos, Cecilia. Maquina de Hacer Tareas. (p. 1402)
Pisos, Cecilia Mabel. Esto Que Brilla en el Aire. (p. 665)
Pistinier, Caroline. Théo et le Lion. (p. 2212)
pistinier, caroline. Théo & the Lion. (p. 2215)
Pistoia, Sara. Counting. (p. 459)
—Fractions. (p. 775)
—Graphs. (p. 881)
—Measurement. (p. 1435)
—Measurements. (p. 1435)
—Money. (p. 1492)
—Patterns. (p. 1706)
—Shapes. (p. 2000)
—Time. (p. 2243)
Pistone, Nicholas. Art & Culture of Ancient Rome. (p. 120)
Pistone, Nicholas, et al. Art & Culture of Ancient Rome. (p. 120)
Pita, Charo. Thank You. Allepuz, Anuska, illus. (p. 2211)
Pitamic, Maja & Laidlaw, Jill. Modern Art Adventures: 36 Creative, Hands-On Projects Inspired by Artists from Monet to Banksy. (p. 1486)
—Three-Dimensional Art Adventures: 36 Creative, Artist-Inspired Projects in Sculpture, Ceramics, Textiles, & More. (p. 2232)
Pitamic, Maja & Laidlaw, Jill A. Fine Art Adventures: Over 35 Fun & Creative Art Projects Inspired by Classic Masterpieces from Around the World. (p. 730)
Pitcairn, Ansel, illus. see Bolden, Tonya.
Pitcher, Annabel. My Sister Lives on the Mantelpiece. (p. 1561)
—Yours Truly. (p. 2535)
Pitcher, Chelsea. S-Word. (p. 1919)
—This Lie Will Kill You. (p. 2226)
Pitcher, Jeff, jt. creator see Howlett, Bruce.
Pitchford, D. L. Stilettos & Stardust: A Gender-Swapped Cinderella Story. (p. 2119)
Pitchford, Dean. Big One-Oh. (p. 222)
—Captain Nobody. (p. 325)
Pitchford, Gareth. Quick Greek Myths. (p. 1827)
Pitcock, Tiffany. Just Friends. (p. 1193)
Pitilli, Thomas, illus. see de la Cruz, Melissa.
Pitkin, Walter B. Seeing America, Vol. 1: Farm & Field (Classic Reprint) (p. 1984)
—Seeing Our Country, Vol. 1 (Classic Reprint) (p. 1984)
Pitman, Benn. Phonographic Dictionary & Phrase Book (Classic Reprint) (p. 1736)
Pitman, Gayle E. Church for All. (p. 390)
—Church for All. Fournier, Laure, illus. (p. 390)
—Feminism from A to Z. (p. 720)
—Maddy. Passchier, Anne, illus. (p. 1374)
—Stonewall Riots: Coming Out in the Streets. (p. 2122)
—Story of Gilbert Baker & the Rainbow Flag. Clifton-Brown, Holly, illus. (p. 2130)
—This Day in June. Litten, Kristyna, illus. (p. 2224)
—When You Look Out the Window: How Phyllis Lyon & Del Martin Built a Community. Lyles, Christopher, illus. (p. 2434)
Pitman, Isaac. Selections from American Authors: Printed in the Advanced Style of Pitman's Shorthand (Classic Reprint) (p. 1986)
Pitman, James. Justice or Injustice? You Decide: True Life of Big Jim Pitman. (p. 1195)
Pitman, Marie J. European Breezes (Classic Reprint) (p. 667)
Pitman, Norman Hinsdale. Chinese Fairy Stories (Classic Reprint) (p. 378)
—Chinese Playmates, or the Boy Gleaners (Classic Reprint) (p. 379)
—Chinese Wonder Book: [Illustrated Edition]. T'Ang, Li Chu, illus. (p. 379)
—Chinese Wonder Book (Classic Reprint) (p. 379)
Pitman, Rich. Jimmy Threepwood & the Elixir of Light. (p. 1169)
—Jimmy Threepwood & the Veil of Darkness. (p. 1169)
Pitman, Sandra. 10 Busy Bumble Bees Sizemore, Carmen, illus. (p. 2549)
Pitman, William Dent. Quincunx Case (Classic Reprint) (p. 1828)
Pitner, Todd. Meet Zammy's New Friends: The Adventures of Zammy the Giant Sheepadoodle. Maria, Lisa, illus. (p. 1441)
Pitre, Louÿs. Feuille de Lune et la Tribu des Mots. Roy, Rejean, illus. (p. 721)
Pitre-Durocher, Sara, illus. see Scott, Mairghread.
Pitsk, Eva. Tale from the Water. (p. 2178)
Pitt, Anna. Leftover Pie: 101 Ways to Reduce Your Food Waste. (p. 1261)
Pitt, Chart. Spirit of the Light (Classic Reprint) (p. 2083)
Pitt, Christopher, jt. auth. see Vida, Marco Girolamo.
Pitt, Darrell. Broken Sun. (p. 285)
—Firebird Mystery. (p. 733)
—Lost Sword. (p. 1355)
—Monster Within. (p. 1497)
Pitt, Frances. Wild Creatures of Garden & Hedgerow (Classic Reprint) (p. 2463)
—Woodland Creatures: Being Some Wild Life Studies (Classic Reprint) (p. 2491)
Pitt, Marilyn. Back Seat Blues (FSTK ONLY) (p. 155)
—Cat Walk. (p. 342)
—Smelling Good. Bianchi, John, illus. (p. 2041)
—Smelling Good (FSTK ONLY) (p. 2041)
—What Are You Thinking? (p. 2406)
—Where the Birds Sit. (p. 2439)
Pitt, Marilyn, jt. auth. see Hileman, Jane.
Pitt, Marilyn & Hileman, Jane. I Like My Stuff. Bianchi, John, illus. (p. 1068)
—Let Me In. Bianchi, John, illus. (p. 1269)
—My Babies. (p. 1531)
—My Babies. Bianchi, John, illus. (p. 1531)
—Pretty Cat. (p. 1790)
—Pretty Cat. Bianchi, John, illus. (p. 1790)
—Storm. Bianchi, John, illus. (p. 2126)
—Up Here. Bianchi, John, illus. (p. 2337)
—Where Is My Boy? Bianchi, John, illus. (p. 2438)
—Where Is That Dog? Bianchi, John, illus. (p. 2438)
Pitt, Marilyn & Sanchez, Lucia M. Nevada: Snow Dog. Bianchi, John, illus. (p. 1589)
—Perro en Apuros: Let Me In. Bianchi, John, illus. (p. 1724)
Pitt, Marilyn & Sánchez, Lucía M. Solos en Casa. Bianchi, John, illus. (p. 2058)
Pitt, Marilyn & Sanchez, Lucia M. Tormenta: The Storm. Bianchi, John, illus. (p. 2265)
Pitt, Marilyn & Sánchez, Lucía M. ¡Arriba! Bianchi, John, illus. (p. 119)
Pitt, Marilyn, et al. Perro en Apuros: Let Me In. Bianchi, John & Taylor, Trace, illus. (p. 1724)
Pitt, Sarah. Peek a Boo! Farm. (p. 1712)
—Peek a Boo! Garden. (p. 1712)
—Peek a Boo! Ocean. (p. 1712)
—Peek a Boo! Zoo. (p. 1712)
Pitt, Sarah, illus. see David, Juliet.
Pitt, Sarah, illus. see Rainstorm Publishing.
Pitt, Sarah, illus. see Reader's Digest Staff.
Pitt, Sarah, illus. see Reasoner, Charles.
Pitt, Steve. Guyness: Deal with It Body & Soul. Murray, Steven, illus. (p. 906)
Pitt, Steve, jt. auth. see Slavens, Elaine.
Pittau, Francesco & Gervais, Bernadette. Open Ocean. (p. 1665)
Pittelli, Marilyn a. No, Go, & Tell! Ms. Clementine's Personal Safety Lesson. (p. 1613)
Pittenger, Jerry. Jesus Loves Me. (p. 1166)
Pittenger, Lemuel Arthur. Collection of Short Stories (Classic Reprint) (p. 415)
Pittman, Eddie. Red's Planet: Book 2: Friends & Foes. (p. 1860)
—Red's Planet. (p. 1860)
Pittman, Hannah Daviess. Belle of the Bluegrass Country: Studies in Black & White (Classic Reprint) (p. 197)
—Go Forth & Find (Classic Reprint) (p. 846)
Pittman, Helena Clare. Grain of Rice. (p. 875)
Pittman, Janet. Colourful Quilts for Playful Kids: 14 Colorful Projects with Dozens of Designs to Mix & Match. (p. 427)
Pittman, Natisha. You Are Beautiful: Every Child Is a Blessing. (p. 2524)
Pittman, Rickey E. Irish Alphabet (p. 1134)
Pittman, Samuel, II. Alligator Jazz Bailey, Sheila, illus. (p. 56)
Pittman, Seth. Raggy's Island. (p. 1834)
Pittman Steinkamp, Barbara. Little Blue Angel. (p. 1311)
Pittock, Prue, illus. see McKelvey, Katrina.
Pitts, Alena. Day Dreams & Movie Screens (p. 513)
Pitts, Alena & Pitts, Wynter. Shining Night (p. 2007)
Pitts, Byron. Be the One: Six True Stories of Teens Overcoming Hardship with Hope. (p. 178)
Pitts, Daphne. What Makes God Laugh. (p. 2418)
Pitts, John Linwood. Patois Poems of the Channel Islands: The Norman-French Text, Edited with Parallel English Translation, Historical Introduction, & Notes (Classic Reprint) (p. 1705)
Pitts, Kaitlyn, et al. Ansley's Big Bake Off (p. 101)
Pitts, M. R. Sketch the Cat Artistic Adventures: Vol 1 Shapes & Shading. (p. 2030)
Pitts, Marielle. Why Do You Have a Scar on Your Face? (p. 2457)
Pitts, Wynter. For Girls Like You: A Devotional for Tweens. Kerr, Kathleen, ed. (p. 762)
—For Girls Like You Coloring Book. (p. 762)
—God's Girl Says Yes: What God Can Do When We Follow Him. (p. 853)
—I Am Yours: Prayers for God's Girl. (p. 1060)
—You're God's Girl! Back-To-School Planner: *Organize Your Schoolwork & Activities *Dream about the Year Ahead *Discover God's Purpose for Your Life. (p. 2535)
Pitts, Wynter, jt. auth. see Pitts, Alena.
Pittsburgh, Carnegie Library Of. Annotated Catalogue of Books Used in the Home Libraries & Reading Clubs Conducted by the Children's Department: A Subject Arrangement with Author & Title Index (Classic Reprint) (p. 100)
—Catalogue of Books (Classic Reprint) (p. 342)
—Catalogue of Books in the Children's Department of the Carnegie Library of Pittsburgh (Classic Reprint) (p. 342)
—Catalogue of Books in the Children's Department of the Carnegie Library of Pittsburgh, Vol. 2 (Classic Reprint) (p. 342)
—Printed Catalogue Cards for Children's Book: An Announcement; Together with a List of 1, 053 Children's Books Agreed upon by the Cleveland Public Library & the Carnegie Library of Pittsburgh (Classic Reprint) (p. 1800)
Pitzer, Marjorie. Animal Fun for Everyone! Pitzer, Marjorie, photos by. (p. 89)
Pitzer, Marjorie W. I Like Berries, Do You? (p. 1067)
Pitzer, Suzanne, illus. see Grollman, Earl A.
Pitzorno, Bianca. House in the Tree. Parkin, Stephen, tr. (p. 1022)
Piu, Amandine, illus. see Escoffier, Michaël.
Piu, Amandine, illus. see Misslin, Sylvie.
Pivard, G., jt. auth. see Lemaresquier, D.
Pivard, Gilles. Where Is Turold. (p. 2438)
Piven, Hanoch. Let's Make Faces. Piven, Hanoch, illus. (p. 1275)
—My Best Friend Is As Sharp As a Pencil: & Other Funny Classroom Portraits. Piven, Hanoch, illus. (p. 1532)
—My Dog Is As Smelly As Dirty Socks: And Other Funny Family Portraits. Piven, Hanoch, illus. (p. 1537)
—My Dog Is As Smelly As Dirty Socks. (p. 1537)
—What Athletes Are Made Of. Piven, Hanoch, illus. (p. 2406)
—What Cats Are Made Of. Piven, Hanoch, illus. (p. 2407)
—What Presidents Are Made Of. (p. 2419)
—What Presidents Are Made Of. (p. 2419)
Piworski, Marcin, illus. see Abbott, Victoria.
Piworski, Marcin, illus. see Lamb, Jenny.
Piworski, Marcin, illus. see Rosen, Robert.
Piworski, Marcin, illus. see Wells, Robin.
Piwowarski, Marcin, illus. see Abbott, Victoria.
Piwowarski, Marcin, illus. see Cochran, Kate, et al.
Piwowarski, Marcin, illus. see Cottleston, B. D.
Piwowarski, Marcin, illus. see Davies, Rhona.
Piwowarski, Marcin, illus. see Gehl, Laura.
Piwowarski, Marcin, illus. see Godfrey, Jan.
Piwowarski, Marcin, illus. see Grudzina, Rebecca.
Piwowarski, Marcin, illus. see Hawes, Alison.
Piwowarski, Marcin, illus. see Hopgood, Sally.
Piwowarski, Marcin, illus. see Jacobs, Lily, et al.
Piwowarski, Marcin, illus. see James, Eric & Smallman, Steve.
Piwowarski, Marcin, illus. see James, Eric.
Piwowarski, Marcin, illus. see Ko, Hannah.
Piwowarski, Marcin, illus. see Koons, Linda.
Piwowarski, Marcin, illus. see Lamb, Jenny.
Piwowarski, Marcin, illus. see Lindeen, Mary.
Piwowarski, Marcin, illus. see Newman, Constance.
Piwowarski, Marcin, illus. see Parkes, Brenda.
Piwowarski, Marcin, illus. see Platten, Rachel.
Piwowarski, Marcin, illus. see Smith, Carrie.
Piwowarski, Marcin, illus. see Wells, Robin.
Pix, Henry. Miscellaneous Examples in Arithmetic. (p. 1476)
Pixar Animators, jt. auth. see Disney.
Pixar, told to. Monsters University Look & Find. (p. 1498)
—Monsters University Play a Sound. (p. 1498)
Pixel, Marcel. Monsters: 11 Paper Finger Puppets to Punch Out, Cut, Fold, & Glue, with 10 Scenes to Color—Plus Stickers! (p. 1497)
Pixel Mouse House LLC, illus. see Random House.
Pixel Mouse House, Pixel Mouse, illus. see Mitter, Matt.
Pixel Mouse House Staff, illus. see Golden Books & Chlebowski, Rachel.
Pixie, B. R. Just a Little Human. (p. 1192)
Pixley, Frank, jt. auth. see Read, Opie.
Pixley, Frank M. Argonaut, Vol. 2: January June, 1878 (Classic Reprint) (p. 114)
—Argonaut, Vol. 4: Saturday, January 4, 1879 Saturday, June 28, 1879 (Classic Reprint) (p. 114)
Pixley, Marcella. Freak. (p. 779)
—Ready to Fall. (p. 1848)
—Without Tess. (p. 2482)
Pixton, Amy. Indestructibles: All Year Round: A Book of Seasons. Búzio, Carolina, illus. (p. 1115)
—Indestructibles: Big & Little: A Book of Opposites. Búzio, Carolina, illus. (p. 1115)
—Indestructibles: Mary Had a Little Lamb. (p. 1115)
—Indestructibles: Things That Go! Chew Proof · Rip Proof · Nontoxic · 100% Washable (Book for Babies, Newborn Books, Vehicle Books, Safe to Chew) Lomp, Stephan, illus. (p. 1115)
Pixton, Amy, creator. Indestructibles: Humpty Dumpty. (p. 1115)
Pixton, Kaaren. Indestructibles Creep! Crawl! (p. 1115)
—Indestructibles Flutter! Fly! (p. 1115)
—Indestructibles: Jungle Rumble! (p. 1115)
—Indestructibles: Mama & Baby! (p. 1115)
—Indestructibles: Plip-Plop Pond! (p. 1115)
—Indestructibles Wiggle! March! (p. 1115)
Piyush Kumar. Myth: Prince Chandra & the Demon's War. (p. 1571)
Pizarro, Mireya. Wise Trees: This Book Is Filled with Colorful Hand Painted Trees. (p. 2478)
Pizer, Carol. Michael Jackson Saddleback Educational Publishing Staff, ed. (p. 1457)
—Witchcraft. (p. 2480)
Pizmoht, Natasa Gruden, illus. see Gaborova, Katarina.
Pizza, Miss Lisa. Ohh Ohhh, I Knew That! More Stories of Old Man Joe. (p. 1642)
Pizzelli, Anna, jt. auth. see Stilton, Geronimo.
Pizzelli, Anna, jt. auth. see Stilton, Thea.
Pizzigoni, Giuseppina, tr. see Verne, Jules.
Pizzo, Erika. Giving Farmer. Lewis, Josh, illus. (p. 840)
—Saving Farmer. Lewis, Josh, illus. (p. 1938)
Pizzoferrat, Deirdre. Very Hungry Cave Boy: Our Modern-Day Challenge with Kids & Their Brain. (p. 2353)
Pizzolante, Irene, illus. see duopress labs.
Pizzoli, Greg. 12 Days of Christmas. Pizzoli, Greg, illus. (p. 2551)
—Baloney & Friends. Pizzoli, Greg, illus. (p. 162)
—Tricky Vic: The Impossibly True Story of the Man Who Sold the Eiffel Tower. (p. 2288)
—Watermelon Seed. Pizzoli, Greg, illus. (p. 2386)
Pizzoli, Greg, illus. see Adams, Jennifer.
Pizzoli, Greg, illus. see Barnett, Mac.
Pizzoli, Greg, illus. see Brown, Margaret Wise.
Pizzoli, Greg, illus. see Dunlap, Cirocco.
Pizzoli, Greg, illus. see Krumwiede, Lana.
Pizzoli, Greg, illus. see Singer, Marilyn.
Pizzoli, Tamara. Tallulah the Tooth Fairy CEO. Fabiani, Federico, illus. (p. 2188)
PJ Masks. PJ Masks: PJ Masks vs the Baddies. (p. 1753)
—PJ Masks: Super Moon Mission Movie Theater & Storybook. (p. 1753)
PK Books Inc, prod. Adevtures of Captain Pickles. (p. 30)
Pla, Sally J. Someday Birds. McLaughlin, Julie, illus. (p. 2060)
—Stanley Will Probably Be Fine. Wolfhard, Steve, illus. (p. 2101)
Place, Francois. Last Giants. (p. 1247)
Place, Francois, illus. see De Fombelle, Timothée.
Place, Francois, illus. see Morpurgo, Michael.
Place, Frederick Robert. Blind Job: A Matter-Of-Fact Romance (Classic Reprint) (p. 244)
Place, Konohiki, illus. see Whyte, S. L.
Place, Robert M. Magic & Alchemy. (p. 1376)
Placides, Del S., illus. see Vogel-Placides, Joan Katherine.
Placido, D. C. Brim's Stone: The Journey to the Beginning. (p. 282)
Plafkin-Hurwitz, Marsha. Up 2 Snuff: Illustrated Book for Children. Plafkin-Hurwitz, Marsha, illus. (p. 2337)
Plage, Stella, illus. see Rissman, Rebecca.
Plagge, Anne. Marigold's Show & Tell. (p. 1405)
Plain, Ferguson. Eagle Feather - An Honour. Plain, Ferguson, illus. (p. 613)
Plain, Nancy. Light on the Prairie: Solomon D. Butcher, Photographer of Nebraska's Pioneer Days. (p. 1299)
Plain, Nancy, ed. see Custer, Elizabeth Bacon.
Plaisted, Caroline. 10 Things to Do Before You're 16. (p. 2550)
—Boy Talk. (p. 270)
—Girl Talk: Girl Talk: A Survival Guide to Growing Up. (p. 837)
Plaisted, Claire. Girlie & the War of the Wasps. (p. 838)
Plaja, Luisa. Write Your Own Blog. (p. 2512)

P

—Spectacle de la Nature, Ou Entretiens Sur les Particularites de l'Histoire Naturelle, Qui Ont Paru les Plus Propres a Rendre les Jeunes-Gens Curieux, et a Leur Former l'Esprit, Vol. 6: Contenant Ce Qui Regarde l'Homme en Societe (Classic Reprint) (p. 2077)
Pluche, Pluche. Spectacle de la Nature, Vol. 1: Or Nature Display'd, Being Discourses on Such Particulars of Natural History As Were Thought Most Proper to Excite the Curiosty, & from the Minds of Youth (Classic Reprint) (p. 2077)
Plucinski, Dee Chapman. Seeking String. (p. 1985)
Pluckrose, Henry. Capacity. (p. 323)
—Counting. (p. 459)
—Pattern. (p. 1706)
—Shape. (p. 2000)
—Size. (p. 2029)
—Time. (p. 2243)
—Weight. (p. 2396)
Pluckrose, Henry & Choos, Ramona G. Length. (p. 1266)
—Numbers. (p. 1630)
—Sorting. (p. 2066)
Pluff, Gary E. a-Z Basketball Book: What Every Player Needs to Know to Be Great at the Game! (p. 2)
Pluk, Jim. Parker & the Pear. (p. 1700)
Plum, Amy. After the End. (p. 34)
—Die for Me. (p. 543)
—Dreamfall. (p. 602)
—Neverwake. (p. 1591)
—Until I Die. (p. 2336)
—Until the Beginning. (p. 2336)
Plumb, Charles Sumner. Types & Breeds of Farm Animals (Classic Reprint) (p. 2310)
Plumb, Jennifer. Everything You Need to Know about Chicken Pox & Shingles. (p. 673)
Plumb, Kate. Where Have All the Trees Gone? (p. 2437)
Plumb, Sally. Pika's Tail: A Children's Story about Mountain Wildlife. Milligan, Sharlene, ed. (p. 1744)
Plume, Chris Big, illus. see Plume, Christopher Big.
Plume, Christopher Big. Legend of the Loons Necklace. Plume, Chris Big, illus. (p. 1262)
Plume, Icarus de. Island of Elcadar: A Pilgrimage to Novel-Land (Classic Reprint) (p. 1139)
Plume, Ilse, illus. see Langton, Jane.
Plume, Ilse, illus. see Sanford, Sally.
Plume, Ken, et al. There's a Zombie in My Treehouse! (p. 2218)
Plume, Porte. Trans-Atlantic Sketches, 1870 (Classic Reprint) (p. 2277)
Plumederat, Titi, tr. Bizarres, Bizarres, Ces Fromages ! (p. 235)
—Neige en Juillet, Moustaches Gelées ! (p. 1585)
—Noël Assourissant ! (p. 1617)
Plumeri Caterini, Mariella. Signora Delle Fiabe e Altre Fiabe. Caterini, Antonella, illus. (p. 2016)
Plumides, Damon & Boerke, Arthur Mark. Adventures of Caterwaul the Cat: Feline Pie. (p. 22)
Plumier, Lea. Story of Rhu the Fairy. Rambo, Angela, illus. (p. 2132)
Plumlee, Buddy, illus. see McClure, Brian D.
Plumley, Amie Petronis & Lisle, Andria. Sewing School (r): 21 Sewing Projects Kids Will Love to Make. (p. 1995)
—Sewing School (r) Box Set: Sewing School & Sewing School 2 (p. 1995)
—Sewing School (r) Fashion Design: Make Your Own Wardrobe with Mix-And-Match Projects Including Tops, Skirts & Shorts. (p. 1995)
—Sewing School (r) Quilts: 15 Projects Kids Will Love to Make; Stitch up a Patchwork Pet, Scrappy Journal, T-Shirt Quilt, & More. Burks, Justin Fox, photos by. (p. 1995)
Plummer, Annika. Apple Story. (p. 106)
Plummer, Annika G. Apple Story. (p. 106)
Plummer, Bill, III. Game America Plays: Celebrating 75 Years of the Amateur Softball Association (p. 806)
Plummer, Christy, illus. see Broulette, Natalie.
Plummer, J. G. Gift: Ja'marion. (p. 831)
Plummer, Mary Wright. Roy & Ray: In Mexico (Classic Reprint) (p. 1909)
—Roy & Ray in Canada (Classic Reprint) (p. 1909)
Plummer, Todd. I've Discovered Energy! (p. 1149)
—I've Discovered Force! (p. 1149)
—Superhero Science: Kapow! Comic Book Crime Fighters Put Physics to the Test. (p. 2160)
Plummer, Todd, jt. auth. see Mullins, Matt.
Plummer, Todd, et al. Superhero Science: Kapow! Comic Book Crime Fighters Put Physics to the Test. (p. 2160)
Plumridge, Marianne. If Dinosaurs Lived in My Town. Eggleton, Bob, illus. (p. 1090)
Plum-Ucci, Carol. Body of Christopher Creed. (p. 253)
—Fire Will Fall. (p. 733)
Plunk, Roger. God, Jesus & Reincarnation. (p. 851)
Plunket, Frederica. Here & There among the Alps. (p. 957)
—Here & There among the Alps (Classic Reprint) (p. 957)
Plunkett, Windyann. Fiddle Me a Riddle & Bring Me the Moon. Davidson, Mary, illus. (p. 722)
Plutarch. Anecdotes Selected from the Lives of Plutarch (Classic Reprint) (p. 85)
—Children's Plutarch (Plutarch's Lives Told in Simple Lanuage) with an Index Which Adapts the Stories to the Purpose of Moral Instruction (Classic Reprint) (p. 374)
Plutarch & White, Anne E. Plutarch Project Volume Five: Alexander & Timoleon. (p. 1763)
Plutarch, Frederick James, jt. auth. see Gould, Frederick James.
Pluth, Lisa Anderson. Haunting in Little River. (p. 939)
Plyler, Clint D. Night Night Hamlet. Boyce, Tami, illus. (p. 1606)
Plymak, John, illus. see Korman, Irv.
Plympton, A. G. Bud of Promise (Classic Reprint) (p. 290)
—Little Sister of Wilifred (Classic Reprint) (p. 1327)
Plympton, Almira George. Dear Daughter Dorothy (Classic Reprint) (p. 520)
—Glad Year Round: For Boys & Girls (Classic Reprint) (p. 840)
—Robin's Recruit (Classic Reprint) (p. 1891)
Pneuman, Angela. Lay It on My Heart. (p. 1253)
Po, Julia, illus. see Manor, Yael.
Poague, Walter S. Diary & Letters of a Marine Aviator (Classic Reprint) (p. 539)
Poate, Ernest M. Trouble at Pinelands: A Detective Story (Classic Reprint) (p. 2291)
Poblocki, Dan. Gathering. (p. 811)
—Ghost of Graylock. (p. 828)
—Haunting of Gabriel Ashe. (p. 939)
—Missing: Welcome to Your Nightmare... (p. 1480)
—Nightmarys. (p. 1608)
—No Way Out. (p. 1615)
—Stone Child. (p. 2121)
—You Can't Hide. (p. 2526)
Pobst, Sandy. Life of a Comet: Set Of 6. (p. 1293)
—Scientific Discovery in the Renaissance: Set Of 6. (p. 1959)
Pocha, Michael J. Thomas James & the Ringmaster. (p. 2228)
Poché, Calle y, et al. Sí, Sí Es Contigo / Yes, If It's with You. (p. 2014)
Pochik, Sonya L. Mr. Kryptonite & Ms. Boomerang. (p. 1519)
Pochini, Eugenio. Sangre Pirata. Renzi, Federico, tr. (p. 1931)
Pochocki, Ethel. Around the Year Once upon a Time Saints. Hatke, Ben, illus. (p. 119)
—Blessing of the Beasts. Moser, Barry, illus. (p. 244)
—Penny for a Hundred. (p. 1717)
—Rosebud & Red Flannel (p. 1905)
—Saints & Heroes. Owens, Mary Beth, illus. (p. 1924)
Pockell, Leslie, ed. 100 Great Poems for Boys. (p. 2557)
Pocket Press & Brittain, Kyle, eds. Pocket Guide to Alabama Criminal Laws. (p. 1764)
pocket.watch. Watch This Book! Inside the World of YouTube Stars Ryan ToysReview, HobbyKidsTV, JillianTubeHD, & EvanTubeHD. (p. 2383)
Pocock, Aaron, illus. see Blake-Wilson, Pamela.
Pocock, Aaron, illus. see Larson, Robert.
Pocock, Aaron, illus. see Tyrrell, Karen.
Pocock, Aaron, jt. auth. see Tyrrell, Karen.
Pocock, Guy N. Precis Writing for Beginners (Classic Reprint) (p. 1786)
Pocock, Joyce, ed. see Pilgrim, A. W. J.
Pocock, Joyce & Downey, Heidi, eds. Alfie's Holiday in Monaco. Pilgrim, A. W. J., illus. (p. 43)
Pocock, Joyce & Downie, Heidi, eds. Blue Knights Quest to America. Pilgrim, A. W. J., illus. (p. 248)
Pocock, Roger. Chariot of the Sun: A Fantasy (Classic Reprint) (p. 358)
—Cheerful Blackguard (Classic Reprint) (p. 364)
—Curly: A Tale of the Arizona Desert (Classic Reprint) (p. 488)
—Frontiersman (Classic Reprint) (p. 795)
—Man in the Open (Classic Reprint) (p. 1394)
—Sword & Dragon (Classic Reprint) (p. 2171)
Pocock, Roger S. Cheerful Blackguard (Classic Reprint) (p. 364)
Pocrass, Kate. Quotes & Questions: A Journal for Your Kid's Quotable Moments. (p. 1829)
Podd, Gloria. Royal Runt. (p. 1910)
Podesta, Lena, illus. see Marr, Melissa.
Podos, Rebecca. Like Water. (p. 1301)
—Mystery of Hollow Places. (p. 1569)
—Wise & the Wicked. (p. 2478)
Podrazik, Bud. Otto the Stout Was Afraid to Go Out. (p. 1676)
Podstawsk, Bożena, tr. see Pere, Tuula.
Podwal, Mark H., illus. see Witman, Melissa Buyer.
Poe. Poe's Road Trip to Ravens Gameday. (p. 1765)
Poe, E. Chat Noir et Autr Nouv. (p. 362)
—Double Assassinat Dans. (p. 588)
Poe, Edgar Allan. Cask of Amontillado: Fifteen of Edgar Allan Poe's Greatest Stories. (p. 339)
—Cask of Amontillado. (p. 339)
—Edgar Allan Poe's Tales of Death & Dementia. Grimly, Gris, illus. (p. 625)
—Gold Bug (Classic Reprint) (p. 855)
—Mystery Short Stories of Edgar Allan Poe. (p. 1571)
—Raven. Price, Ryan, illus. (p. 1843)
—Tales of Terror. Cambridge Experience Readers British English. Tales of Terror. Paperback. (p. 2185)
—Tales of the Grotesque & Arabesque. (p. 2186)
—Tell-Tale Heart & Other Stories. Grimly, Gris, illus. (p. 2202)
—Works of Edgar Allan Poe: In Five Volumes-Volume Two. (p. 2497)
—Works of Edgar Allan Poe: In Five Volumes-Volume Four. (p. 2497)
—Works of Edgar Allan Poe: In Five Volumes- Volumes Five. (p. 2497)
—Works of Edgar Allan Poe (Classic Reprint) (p. 2497)
—Works of Edgar Allan Poe (Volume I) (p. 2497)
—Works of Edgar Allan Poe (Volume II) (p. 2497)
—Works of Edgar Allan Poe (Volume III) (p. 2497)
—Works of Edgar Allan Poe, Vol. 5: With an Introduction & a Memoir (Classic Reprint) (p. 2497)
Poe, Edgar Allen. American Fiction (Classic Reprint) (p. 71)
—Bells (Classic Reprint) (p. 198)
—Edgar Allan Poe, Cuentos de Terror Contados para Niños. (p. 625)
—Gift: A Christmas & New Year's Present for 1842 (Classic Reprint) (p. 831)
—Raven: Includes Sound! (p. 1843)
—Stories for the Home Circle (Classic Reprint) (p. 2123)
—Stories of Edgar Allan Poe. McKowen, Scott, illus. (p. 2125)
—Tell-Tale Heart Package. Calero, Dennis, illus. (p. 2202)
—Works of Edgar Allan Poe, Including the Choicest of His Critical Essays (Classic Reprint) (p. 2497)
—Works of Edgar Allan Poe, Vol. 1: Tales (Classic Reprint) (p. 2497)
—Works of Edgar Allan Poe, Vol. 10: Miscellaneous (Classic Reprint) (p. 2497)
—Works of Edgar Allan Poe, Vol. 3 (Classic Reprint) (p. 2497)
—Works of Edgar Allan Poe, Vol. 4 Of 10: Newly Collected & Edited, with a Memoir, Critical Introductions & Notes (Classic Reprint) (p. 2497)
—Works of Edgar Allan Poe, Vol. 4 Of 10: Newly Collected & Edited, with a Memoir, Critical Introductions, & Notes (Classic Reprint) (p. 2497)
—Works of Edgar Allan Poe, Vol. 4 Of 5: Tales; Fantasy & Extravaganza; Humor (Classic Reprint) (p. 2497)
—Works of Edgar Allan Poe, Vol. 4 of 5 (Classic Reprint) (p. 2497)
—Works of Edgar Allan Poe, Vol. 6: Miscellaneous (Classic Reprint) (p. 2497)
—Works of Edgar Allan Poe, Vol. 6 of 10 (Classic Reprint) (p. 2497)
—Works of Edgar Allan Poe, Vol. 8 Of 10: Tales Humor (Classic Reprint) (p. 2497)
Poe, Edgar Allen, jt. auth. see Bowen, Carl.
Poe, Edgar Allen, jt. auth. see Harper, Benjamin.
Poe, Edgar Allen, jt. auth. see Manning, Matthew K.
Poe, Edgar Allen, jt. auth. see Tulien, Sean.
Poe, Edgar Allen & Harper, Benjamin. Tell-Tale Heart Calero, Dennis, illus. (p. 2202)
Poe, Gwen. Bingham the Bobcat. (p. 228)
Poe, Kristen. Healthy Heath & His Magic Fruits & Vegetables: A Book about Kids Nutrition, Kindness, & Celebrating Individuality. Cebu LL B, Vladimir, illus. (p. 944)
—Healthy Heather & Her Magic Fruits & Vegetables: : Take a Journey with Healthy Heather & Her Magic Fruits & Vegetables, a Book about Kids' Nutrition, Kindness, & Celebrating Individuality. (p. 944)
Poe, Mark. Danny & the Dreamweaver. DiSilvio, Rich, illus. (p. 504)
Poe, Mark Allen & Poe, Mark Andrew. Haunted Pizza. (p. 938)
Poe, Mark Andrew. Ending Easter. (p. 649)
—First Light (p. 738)
—Halloween Nightmares (p. 912)
—Harry & His Time Machine. (p. 934)
—Harry's Christmas Carol. (p. 935)
—Inkadink (p. 1120)
—Not Your Birthday Birthday. (p. 1624)
—Operation Big Top. (p. 1666)
—Scary Little Christmas (p. 1943)
—Scary Smart House. (p. 1943)
—Showdown on Nightingale Lane. (p. 2012)
—Snow Day (p. 2047)
—Spooky Socks. (p. 2087)
—Varita-Papel-O-Tijeras. (p. 2348)
—Wand-Paper-Scissors (p. 2374)
Poe, Mark Andrew & Kuhn, Suzanne Brooks. Shades & Shenanigans. (p. 1996)
Poe, Mark Andrew & Magnin, Joyce. Snowman (p. 2049)
Poe, Mark Andrew & Napier, Barry. Run Harry, Run. (p. 1914)
Poe, Marshall. House Divided. Purvis, Leland, illus. (p. 1022)
Poehlmann, Tristan. 12 Immigrants Who Made American Arts Great. (p. 2551)
—12 Immigrants Who Made American Technology Great. (p. 2551)
—Fossil Hunters. (p. 770)
—Stonewall Riots (the Fight for LGBT Rights) (p. 2122)
—Titanic Story. (p. 2251)
Poelman, Heidi. A Is for Abinadi: An Alphabet Book of Scripture Heroes. (p. 1)
—A Is for Abinadi (Activity Book) An Activity Book of Scripture Heroes. (p. 1)
—A Is for Adam: An Alphabet Book of Bible Heroes. (p. 1)
—Amazing Animals Who Changed the World. Kershner, Kyle, illus. (p. 64)
—Courageous People Who Changed the World. Kershner, Kyle, illus. (p. 462)
—I Can Love Like Jesus. (p. 1062)
—Inventors Who Changed the World. Kershner, Kyle, illus. (p. 1130)
—Jesus Worked Miracles. Pruett, Jason, illus. (p. 1167)
Poer, John Patrick Le. Modern Legionary (Classic Reprint) (p. 1487)
Poeschel, Ann. Helen of Troy (p. 949)
—Ireland. (p. 1134)
Poet, Jonny. Waddling to the Pond. Luchsinger, Linda, illus. (p. 2370)
Pogany, Elaine. Golden Cockerel: From the Original Russian Fairy Tale of Alexander Pushkin. Pogány, Willy, illus. (p. 857)
Pogany, Willy, illus. see Colum, Padraic.
Pogány, Willy, illus. see Edgar, M. G.
Pogány, Willy, illus. see Hawthorne, Nathaniel.
Pogány, Willy, illus. see Pogany, Elaine.
Pogány, Willy, jt. auth. see Colum, Padraic.
Poghosyan, Maya. Flying Island. (p. 755)
Pogioli, J. F. Lightbringer. (p. 1299)
Pogue, Carolyn. Gwen (p. 907)
Pogue, Jamie, illus. see Dougherty, Brandi.
Pogue, Kaye, ed. see Walker, Abbie Phillips.
Pogue, Pollough. British Columbia Magazine, Vol. 7: May, 1911 (Classic Reprint) (p. 283)
—British Columbia Magazine, Vol. 7: July, 1911 (Classic Reprint) (p. 283)
—British Columbia Magazine, Vol. 7: April, 1911 (Classic Reprint) (p. 283)
—British Columbia Magazine, Vol. 7: March, 1911 (Classic Reprint) (p. 283)
—British Columbia Magazine, Vol. 7: February, 1911 (Classic Reprint) (p. 283)
Pogue, Sarah, illus. see Leiloglou, Carolyn.
Poh, Jennie. Herbie's Big Adventure. Poh, Jennie, illus. (p. 957)
Poh, Jennie, illus. see Arnold, Marsha Diane.
Poh, Jennie, illus. see Berne, Emma Carlson.
Poh, Jennie, illus. see Davies, Becky.
Poh, Jennie, illus. see George, Joshua.
Poh, Jennie, illus. see Jones, Janey Louise.
Poh, Jennie, illus. see MacLeod, Jennifer Tzivia.
Poh, Jennie, illus. see Mawhinney, Lynnette.
Poh, Jennie, illus. see Orel, Brigita.
Poh, Jennie, illus. see Renauld, Laura.
Poh, Jennie, illus. see Woodhouse, Emma.
Pohl, Amelia J. Flint River. (p. 749)
—Ocmulgee River. (p. 1636)
—Savannah River. (p. 1937)
Pohl, Bl. Always Abbey: An Arthritis Story. (p. 61)
Pohl, David, illus. see Roberts, Willo Davis.
Pohl, Dora & Kremer, Kevin. Maggie's Christmas Miracle. Ely, Dave, illus. (p. 1376)
Pohl, Kathleen. Animales I See at the Zoo (p. 93)
—Animals I See at the Zoo/Animales Que Veo en el Zoológico (p. 94)
—Descubramos Países del Mundo (Looking at Countries) (p. 531)
—Looking at Countries (p. 1347)
Pohl, Laura. First 7. (p. 735)
—Last 8. (p. 1247)
Pohlemann, Terri. She Lives in the Stars. (p. 2004)
Pohlen, Jerome. Albert Einstein & Relativity for Kids: His Life & Ideas with 21 Activities & Thought Experiments. (p. 40)
—Apollo Missions for Kids: The People & Engineering Behind the Race to the Moon, with 21 Activities. (p. 106)
—Doodle Texas. Lemay, Violet, illus. (p. 584)
—Gay & Lesbian History for Kids: The Century-Long Struggle for LGBT Rights, with 21 Activities. (p. 812)
—Oddball Indiana: A Guide to 350 Really Strange Places. (p. 1637)
Pohlmann-Eden, Bernd. Secret of the Bounce-Back Mom. Hofer, Klaus C., tr. (p. 1977)
Pohlmeyer, Krista, jt. auth. see Random House.
Pohl-Weary, Emily. Not Your Ordinary Wolf Girl (p. 1624)
Pohrt, Tom, illus. see Durango, Julia.
Pohrt, Tom, illus. see George, Jean Craighead.
Pohrt, Tom, illus. see Pearce, Philippa.
Poillion, Mary. Tj Llama: It's Okay to Be Different. (p. 2252)
Poilpot, Theophile. Carnet Blanc Chemin de Fer D'Orleans. (p. 332)
—Carnet Ligne Chemin de Fer D'Orleans. (p. 332)
Poincare, Lucien. New Physics & Its Evolution. (p. 1596)
Poindexter, Stephanie. Octavious & His Busy Tentacles. (p. 1636)
Point Of Grace. Girls of Grace Journal. (p. 839)
Point, Susan A., contrib. by. People of the Land: Legends of the Four Host First Nations. (p. 1719)
Pointon, Matthew. Bathtime in Budapest. (p. 172)
—Peril in the Peak District. (p. 1723)
Poisson, Barbara Aoki. Ghana. Rotberg, Robert I., ed. (p. 826)
Poitier, Anton. Challenging Dot-To-Dot: 68 Timed Puzzles to Test Your Skill. Parchow, Marc et al, illus. (p. 354)
—Design & Doodle: a Book of Astonishing Invention: Amazing Things to Imagine, Draw, & Discover. (p. 532)
—Flippy Floppy Farm Animals. Touliatou, Sophia, illus. (p. 749)
—Flippy Floppy Jungle Animals. Touliatou, Sophia, illus. (p. 749)
—Flippy Floppy Ocean Animals. Touliatou, Sophia, illus. (p. 749)
—Once I Was a Cardboard Box... But Now I'm a Book about Polar Bears. Evans, Melvyn, illus. (p. 1657)
—Once I Was a Comic... But Now I'm a Book about Tigers. Evans, Melvyn, illus. (p. 1657)
Poivre, D'Arvor. Mysteres des Pirates - Freres de Sang, Freres D'Armes. (p. 1566)
Pokiak, James, jt. auth. see Willett, Mindy.
Pokiak, James, et al. Fiers d'Être Inuvialuits: Quviahuktunga Inuvialuugama (p. 723)
Pokoj, Ed, illus. see Loewen, Mark.
Pokorny, Susan. Ralphie Meets the Queen. (p. 1838)
Pol, Diego & Carballido, Jose Luis. Titanosaur. Gigena, Florencia, illus. (p. 2251)
Polacco, Patricia. a from Miss Keller. Polacco, Patricia, illus. (p. 1)
—Art of Miss Chew. Polacco, Patricia, illus. (p. 121)
—Because of Thursday. Polacco, Patricia, illus. (p. 186)
—Blessing Cup. Polacco, Patricia, illus. (p. 244)
—Bravest Man in the World. Polacco, Patricia, illus. (p. 277)
—Bully. Polacco, Patricia, illus. (p. 296)
—Bun Bun Button. Polacco, Patricia, illus. (p. 297)
—Butterfly (p. 303)
—Butterfly. (p. 303)
—Chicken Sunday. (p. 368)
—Clara & Davie. (p. 398)
—Fiona's Lace. Polacco, Patricia, illus. (p. 732)
—Gifts of the Heart. Polacco, Patricia, illus. (p. 832)
—Holes in the Sky. Polacco, Patricia, illus. (p. 987)
—In Our Mothers' House. Polacco, Patricia, illus. (p. 1106)
—January's Sparrow. Polacco, Patricia, illus. (p. 1159)
—Junkyard Wonders. Polacco, Patricia, illus. (p. 1191)
—Just in Time Abraham Lincoln. (p. 1193)
—Just in Time, Abraham Lincoln. Polacco, Patricia, illus. (p. 1193)
—Keeping Quilt: 25th Anniversary Edition. Polacco, Patricia, illus. (p. 1208)
—Lemonade Club. (p. 1266)
—Mermaid's Purse. Polacco, Patricia, illus. (p. 1449)
—Meteor! (p. 1452)
—Mr. Lincoln's Way. (p. 1519)
—Mr. Wayne's Masterpiece. Polacco, Patricia, illus. (p. 1521)
—Mrs. Katz & Tush. (p. 1522)
—My Rotten Redheaded Older Brother. (p. 1560)
—Picnic at Mudsock Meadow. (p. 1739)
—Remembering Vera. Polacco, Patricia, illus. (p. 1864)
—Thank You, Mr. Falker. Polacco, Patricia, illus. (p. 2211)
—Thunder Cake. (p. 2238)
—Tucky Jo & Little Heart. Polacco, Patricia, illus. (p. 2298)
Polacco, Patricia, illus. see Polacco, Ernest L.
Polack, Maria. Fiction Without Romance, Vol. 2 Of 2: Or the Locket-Watch (Classic Reprint) (p. 722)
Polak, J. E. R. Grammar & a Vocabulary of the Ipurina Language (Classic Reprint) (p. 875)
Polak, Monique. All In (p. 52)
—Bullies Rule (p. 296)
—Forensics Squad Unleashed (p. 765)
—Hate Mail (p. 937)
—I Am a Feminist: Claiming the F-Word in Turbulent Times (p. 1057)
—Junkyard Dog. (p. 1191)
—Leggings Revolt (p. 1264)
—Leggings Revolt. (p. 1264)
—Middle of Everywhere (p. 1460)
—Passover: Festival of Freedom (p. 1703)
—Passover Family (p. 1703)

—Planet Grief (p. 1755)
—Princess Angelica: Camp Catastrophe. Heinrichs, Jane, illus. (p. 1796)
—Princess Angelica, Camp Catastrophe Heinrichs, Jane, illus. (p. 1796)
—Princess Angelica, Junior Reporter. Heinrichs, Jane, illus. (p. 1796)
—Princess Angelica, Part-Time Lion Trainer Heinrichs, Jane, illus. (p. 1796)
—Pyro (p. 1819)
—Room for One More. (p. 1903)
—Straight Punch (p. 2136)
—Taste of Rain (p. 2192)
Polan, Alex. Capturing Cresselia: Unofficial Stories for Pokémon Collectors, #2. (p. 327)
—Catching the Jigglypuff Thief: PokéStop Stories, Book One. (p. 344)
—Catching the Jigglypuff Thief. (p. 344)
—Chasing Butterfree: Unofficial Adventures for Pokémon GO Players, Book Three. (p. 361)
—Chasing Butterfree. (p. 361)
—Cracking the Magikarp Code: Unofficial Adventures for Pokémon GO Players, Book Four. (p. 466)
—Cracking the Magikarp Code. (p. 466)
—Following Meowth's Footprints. (p. 758)
—Welcome to Camp Pikachu. (p. 2398)
Polan, Jason, illus. see Tea, Michelle.
Polanco, Amparo. Bosque Magico. (p. 263)
—Magical Forest. (p. 1380)
Poland, A., jt. auth. see Haaren, John H.
Poland, A. B., jt. auth. see Haaren, John H.
Poland, Carol A. & Poland, David W. Ratdog. Poland, James W., illus. (p. 1842)
Poland, James W., illus. see Poland, Carol A. & Poland, David W.
Poland, Pitch & Poland, Inglan. Lost & Found. Rose, Drew, illus. (p. 1352)
Polansky, Marisa. Hello My Name Is ... How Adorabilis Got His Name. (p. 951)
—If Keanu Were Your Boyfriend: The Man, the Myth, the WHOA! (p. 1092)
—Today I'm a Construction Worker. Lee, Maxine, illus. (p. 2254)
—Today I'm a Dancer. Lee, Maxine, illus. (p. 2255)
—Today I'm a Racecar Driver. Lee, Maxine, illus. (p. 2255)
—Today I'm a Veterinarian. Lee, Maxine, illus. (p. 2255)
Polanyi Levitt, Kari. De la Gran Transformacion a la Gran Financiarizacion. Sobre Karl Polanyi y Otros Ensayos. (p. 517)
Polark, Kelly. Rockabet: Classic Edition: Second Edition. (p. 1894)
—Rockabet: Classic Edition. Little, Kelli Ann, illus. (p. 1894)
Polat, Ercan, illus. see Gunes, Aysenur.
Polatin, Daria. Devil in Ohio. (p. 535)
Pole, Thomas. Anatomical Instructor: Or an Illustration of the Modern & Most Approved Methods of Preparing & Preserving the Different Parts of the Human Body & of Quadrupeds, by Injection, Corrosion, Maceration, Distention, Articulation, Modelling, Etc. (p. 79)
Poleahla, Anita. Celebrate My Hopi Name. James, Eric, illus. (p. 349)
Polen, Jeff. Greatest Sacrifice. (p. 892)
Polen, Teri. Gemini Connection. (p. 813)
—Sarah. (p. 1935)
—Subject A36. (p. 2145)
Polenova, Elena, illus. see Althaus, Frank.
Polette, Keith. Moon over the Mountain. (p. 1502)
—Moon over the Mountain. Russik, Michael, illus. (p. 1502)
—Moon over the Mountain/Luna Sobre la Montana. (p. 1502)
Polette, Nancy. N Is for Never Forget: POW-MIA a to Z. Dillon, Paul, illus. (p. 1572)
—Reading the Fifty States: Booktalks, Response Activities, & More (p. 1847)
—Spy with the Wooden Leg: The Story of Virginia Hall. (p. 2093)
Polette, Nancy J. Teaching Economic Concepts with Picture Books & Junior Novels (p. 2195)
Poletti, Frances & Yee, Kristina. Girl Who Ran: Bobbi Gibb, the First Woman to Run the Boston Marathon. Chapman, Susanna, illus. (p. 837)
Poletti, Marie-Laure. Grenadine: Niveau 1 Guide Pedagogique. (p. 895)
—Grenadine: Niveau 2 Guide Pedagogique. (p. 895)
Poletti, Marie-Laure & Himber, Céline. Adosphere: Niveau 1 Cahier d'Activites + CD-ROM. (p. 17)
—Adosphere 1 - Guide Pedagogique. (p. 17)
—Adosphere 1 - Livre du Professeur. (p. 17)
Poletti, Marie-Laure & Paccagnino. Grenadine: Niveau 2 Livre de L'Eleve. (p. 895)
Poletti, Marie-Laure, et al. Adosphere: Niveau 2 Livre du Professeur. (p. 17)
Polevoi, Petr, jt. auth. see Bain, R. Nisbet.
Poley, Lucy, illus. see O'Connor, Constance & Rojas, Natalia.
Polhamus, Bruce, illus. see Adams, Jesse.
Polhemus, Coleman, illus. see Nance, Andrew.
Poli, Giuseppe, illus. see Wallace, Adam.
Polidori, John William. Vampyre: A Tale. (p. 2347)
—Vampyre: A Tale (Classic Reprint) (p. 2347)
Polikoff, Barbara Garland. Her Mother's Secret. (p. 956)
Polina, Hrytskova, illus. see Given, Amanda.
Poling, Atarah L. Forbidden Secret: Shadows Behind Locked Doors. (p. 764)
Poling, Cathryne. Mommy Dots. (p. 1491)
Poling, Kyle, illus. see Aboff, Marcie & Lee, Sally.
Poling, Kyle, illus. see Aboff, Marcie.
Poling, Kyle, illus. see Boniface, William.
Poling, Kyle, illus. see Heos, Bridget.
Poling, Kyle, illus. see Johnson, J. Angelique.
Poling, Kyle, illus. see Karr, Lily.
Poling, Kyle, illus. see Lee, Sally.
Poling, Kyle, illus. see Oliver, Ilanit.
Poling, Kyle, illus. see Rustad, Martha E. H.
Polinko, Les, illus. see Karevold, Alison.
Polinsky, Paige. Indra Nooyi: CEO of PepsiCo. (p. 1117)
—Sara Seager: Planetary Scientist. (p. 1935)
—Sonia Sotomayor: Supreme Court Justice. (p. 2063)
Polinsky, Paige V. Alaskan Malamutes. (p. 40)
—American Girl Entrepreneur: Pleasant Rowland. (p. 71)
—Atlantis. (p. 133)
—Australian Cattle Dogs (p. 138)
—Basset Hounds. (p. 171)
—Beaver: Master Builder. (p. 185)
—Bermuda Triangle. (p. 203)
—Bluetick Coonhounds (p. 250)
—Bridges. (p. 280)
—Canals. (p. 321)
—Cavalier King Charles Spaniels. (p. 347)
—Chimpanzee: Brainy Beast. (p. 377)
—Chinese Shar-Peis (p. 379)
—Emperor Penguin: Sensational Survivor. (p. 644)
—ESP. (p. 662)
—Fortnite. (p. 769)
—Game on! (Set Of 6) (p. 807)
—Ghost Ships. (p. 828)
—Giant Centipede: Colossal Creeper of the Night. (p. 830)
—Giant Squid: Mysterious Monster of the Deep. (p. 831)
—Greater Swiss Mountain Dogs (p. 891)
—Humpback Whale: Marvelous Musician. (p. 1051)
—Indra Nooyi: CEO of PepsiCo. (p. 1117)
—Irish Wolfhounds. (p. 1135)
—Joanna Gaines. (p. 1170)
—Just Dance. (p. 1192)
—Madden NFL. (p. 1374)
—Make It Yourself! Coloring & Doodling. (p. 1386)
—Mario. (p. 1406)
—Mastiffs. (p. 1420)
—Minecraft. (p. 1470)
—Monopoly Mastermind: Charles B. Darrow. (p. 1494)
—Mr. Potato Head Inventor: George Lerner. (p. 1520)
—Pokémon. (p. 1768)
—Pokémon Designer: Satoshi Tajiri. (p. 1768)
—Protecting Backyard Animals. (p. 1808)
—Protecting Farm Animals. (p. 1808)
—Protecting Grassland Animals. (p. 1808)
—Rat Terriers (p. 1842)
—Rhinoceros Beetle: Heavyweight Champion. (p. 1874)
—Roads. (p. 1888)
—Rubik's Cube Creator: Erno Rubik. (p. 1911)
—Samoyeds (p. 1928)
—Sara Seager: Planetary Scientist. (p. 1935)
—Scottish Terriers. (p. 1962)
—Skyscrapers. (p. 2034)
—Sonia Sotomayor: Supreme Court Justice. (p. 2063)
—Spotted Hyena: Cackling Carnivore of the Savanna. (p. 2091)
—Super Senses. (p. 2156)
—Super Simple Experiments with Elements: Fun & Innovative Science Projects. (p. 2157)
—Super Simple Experiments with Forces: Fun & Innovative Science Projects. (p. 2157)
—Super Simple Experiments with Heat & Cold: Fun & Innovative Science Projects. (p. 2157)
—Super Simple Experiments with Light & Color: Fun & Innovative Science Projects. (p. 2157)
—Super Simple Experiments with Mass: Fun & Innovative Science Projects. (p. 2157)
—Super Strength. (p. 2158)
—Tunnels. (p. 2299)
—Wolverine: Powerful Predator. (p. 2484)
—Yo-Yo Maker: Pedro Flores. (p. 2523)
Polinsky, Paige V. & ABDO Publishing Company Staff. Animal Superstars (p. 92)
—Super Simple Science at Work: Set (p. 2157)
Polinsky, Paige V. & Craig, Diane. Super Simple Experiments with Electricity: Fun & Innovative Science Projects. (p. 2157)
Poliquin, Rachel. Beastly Puzzles: A Brain-Boggling Animal Guessing Game. Eggenschwiler, Byron, illus. (p. 182)
—Beavers. Frith, Nicholas John, illus. (p. 186)
—Moles. Frith, Nicholas John, illus. (p. 1489)
—Ostriches. Frith, Nicholas John, illus. (p. 1674)
Poliquin, Rachel & Frith, Nicholas John. Eels. (p. 627)
Polis, Gary A., illus. see Pringle, Laurence.
Polisar, Barry Louis. Curious Creatures: Animal Poems. Clark, David, illus. (p. 486)
—Something Fishy. Clark, David, illus. (p. 2060)
Polisar, Patti. Inside France's DGSE: The General Directorate for External Security. (p. 1123)
Polish, Jenn. Lunav. (p. 1368)
Polisner, Gae. In Sight of Stars: A Novel. (p. 1107)
—Jack Kerouac Is Dead to Me: A Novel. (p. 1152)
—Memory of Things: A Novel. (p. 1446)
—Memory of Things. (p. 1446)
—Pull of Gravity. (p. 1812)
—Summer of Letting Go. (p. 2149)
Polisner, Gae & Baskin, Nora Raleigh. Seven Clues to Home. (p. 1993)
Politakos, Pantelis, illus. see MacNeill, Lance J.
Politi, Leo. Emmet. (p. 644)
—Pedro: The Angel of Olvera Street. (p. 1712)
—Song of the Swallows. (p. 2063)
Politi, Leo, jt. auth. see Stalcup, Ann.
Politzer, Adam. Anatomical & Histological Dissection of the Human Ear: In the Normal & Diseased Condition (Classic Reprint) (p. 79)
—Lehrbuch der Ohrenheilkunde: Fur Praktische Arzte und Studierende (Classic Reprint) (p. 1265)
—Membrana Tympani in Health & Disease: Illustrated by Twenty-Four Chromo-Lithographs; Clinical Contributions to the Diagnosis & Treatment of Diseases of the Ear, with Supplement (Classic Reprint) (p. 1443)
Politzer, Adam & Stone, George. Anatomical & Histological Dissection of the Human Ear. (p. 79)
Politzer, Judy. Fractured Nursery Rhymes, Fairy Tales, & Potpourri. (p. 775)
Poliva, Oren. Help! There Is a Brain in My Head. (p. 953)
Polivka, Jef & Polivka, Rob. Dream of Flight: Alberto Santos-Dumont's Race Around the Eiffel Tower. Polivka, Rob, illus. (p. 602)
Polizzi, Michelle, illus. see Ortner, Nick & Taylor, Alison.
Polk, Burr H. Big American Caravan in Europe (Classic Reprint) (p. 215)
Polk, Douglas. Marie's Home (p. 1405)
Polk, Endie J. Gems: Selections from Literary Contributions to the Press (Classic Reprint) (p. 813)
Poll, Donn. Nathaniel & the Magic Apple. Nelson, Eric, ed. (p. 1577)
Poll, Max. Materials for German Prose Composition, Vol. 2: With Notes & Vocabulary; Narrative & Descriptive (Classic Reprint) (p. 1421)
Pollack, Gadi. Trakht Fun Frier: Herlikhe Mesholim Fun Di Gdoyle Ha-Doyres. (p. 2277)
Pollack, Jesse P. Acid King. (p. 11)
Pollack, Pam, jt. auth. see Belviso, Meg.
Pollack, Pam & Belviso, Meg. I Can't Sit Still! Living with ADHD. Fabrega, Marta, illus. (p. 1063)
—Who Was J. R. R. Tolkien? Moore, Jonathan & Harrison, Nancy, illus. (p. 2451)
—Who Was Joan of Arc? Thomson, Andrew, illus. (p. 2451)
—Who Was Lucille Ball? Copeland, Gregory, illus. (p. 2451)
—Who Was Nelson Mandela? Marchesi, Stephen, illus. (p. 2451)
—Who Was Steve Jobs? O'brien, John, illus. (p. 2452)
—Who Were the Three Stooges? (p. 2452)
—¡No Puedo Estar Quieto! Mi Vida con ADHD. Fabrega, Marta, illus. (p. 1614)
Pollack, Pam & Meg Belviso. Who Is George Lucas? (p. 2448)
Pollack, Pam & Who HQ. Who Was Nelson Mandela? Marchesi, Stephen, illus. (p. 2451)
Pollack, Pam, et al. Who Is Bono? Thomson, Andrew, illus. (p. 2447)
—Who Is J. K. Rowling? Marchesi, Stephen, illus. (p. 2448)
—Who Was Alexander Hamilton? Putra, Dede, illus. (p. 2450)
—Who Was Celia Cruz? Murray, Jake, illus. (p. 2450)
—Who Was Lewis Carroll? Qiu, Joseph J. M., illus. (p. 2451)
—Who Was Steve Jobs? O'Brien, John, illus. (p. 2452)
—Who Were the Three Stooges? Hammond, Ted, illus. (p. 2452)
Pollack, Pamela, jt. auth. see Belviso, Meg.
Pollack, Pamela & Belviso, Meg. Who Is J. K. Rowling? (p. 2448)
—Who Was Steve Jobs? (p. 2452)
Pollack, Pamela D. & Belviso, Meg. Who Was Alfred Hitchcock? (p. 2450)
—Who Was Charles Dickens? (p. 2450)
—Who Was Joan of Arc? (p. 2451)
—Who Was Susan B. Anthony? (p. 2452)
Pollack, Pamela D. & Meg Belviso. Who Was Lucille Ball? (p. 2451)
Pollack, Rachel. Fissure King: A Novel in Five Stories. (p. 742)
Pollak, Barbara, illus. see Blackstone, Margaret & Guest, Elissa Haden.
Pollak, Barbara, illus. see Friedman, Laurie.
Pollak, Dale. Velocity: From the Front Line to the Bottom Line. (p. 2350)
Pollak, Monika, illus. see Amenta, Charles A.
Pollak, Ora. He's Not Like Us! Ooli & Tooli When Life Is Unrooly. Benito, Lucia, illus. (p. 963)
—We're Lost! Ooli & Tooli When Life Is Unrooly. (p. 2400)
Pollakoff, Joseph. African Tale of the Enchanted Toy. (p. 33)
Pollan, Michael. Omnivore's Dilemma: Young Readers Edition. (p. 1652)
—Omnivore's Dilemma: The Secrets Behind What You Eat. (p. 1652)
—Omnivore's Dilemma for Kids. (p. 1652)
Polland, Madeleine. Fingal's Quest. (p. 730)
—Prince of the Double Axe. (p. 1794)
Pollard, Alfred W. Chaucer's Canterbury Tales: The Knight's Tale. (p. 363)
—Chaucer's Canterbury Tales: The Prologue (Classic Reprint) (p. 363)
—Chaucer's Canterbury Tales, Vol. 1 (Classic Reprint) (p. 363)
—Chaucer's Canterbury Tales, Vol. 2: Edited with Notes & Introduction (Classic Reprint) (p. 363)
—Romance of King Arthur & His Knights of the Round Table: Abridged from Malory's Morte d'Arthur (Classic Reprint) (p. 1900)
Pollard, Alfred W. 1859-1944, jt. auth. see Chaucer, Geoffrey.
Pollard, Alfred William. English Literature Chaucer (Classic Reprint) (p. 654)
Pollard, Brian, illus. see Meloche, Renee Taft.
Pollard, Bryan, illus. see Meloche, Renee Taft.
Pollard, Edward A. Black Diamonds: Gathered in the Darkey Homes of the South (Classic Reprint) (p. 237)
Pollard, Edward Alfred. Southern Spy; or Curiosities of Negro Slavery in the South: Letters from a Southerner to a Northern Friend (Classic Reprint) (p. 2069)
Pollard, Eliza F. Silver Hand: A Story of India in the Eighteenth Century (Classic Reprint) (p. 2019)
—White Dove of Amritzir a Romance of Anglo-Indian Life (Classic Reprint) (p. 2443)
Pollard, Hugh B. C. Busy Time in Mexico: An Unconventional Record of Mexican Incident. (p. 302)
—Busy Time in Mexico: An Unconventional Record of Mexican Incident (Classic Reprint) (p. 302)
Pollard, Josephine. Burden Lifted (Classic Reprint) (p. 299)
—Co Education (Classic Reprint) (p. 409)
—Decorative Sisters: A Modern Ballad (Classic Reprint) (p. 524)
—Gipsy's Adventures (Classic Reprint) (p. 834)
—God Made the World: A Collection of Bible Stories in Words, of Easy Reading for Little Children (Classic Reprint) (p. 852)
—God Made the World. (p. 852)
—Life of George Washington: In Words of One Syllable (Classic Reprint) (p. 1294)
—Winter Sports. (p. 2476)
Pollard, Josephine & Satterlee, Walter. Decorative Sisters. (p. 523)
Pollard, Levi Wilbur. Character, Juvenile & Other Poems (Classic Reprint) (p. 357)
Pollard, Percival. Cape of Storms: A Novel (Classic Reprint) (p. 323)
—Cape of Storms. (p. 323)
—Imitator: A Novel (Classic Reprint) (p. 1100)
—Lingo Dan: A Novel (Classic Reprint) (p. 1304)
Pollard, Rebecca S. Emma Bartlett, or Prejudice & Fanaticism (Classic Reprint) (p. 643)
—Pollard's: Synthetic Second Reader (Classic Reprint) (p. 1771)
—Pollard's Advanced Reader (Classic Reprint) (p. 1771)
—Pollard's Synthetic First Reader. (p. 1771)
—Pollard's Synthetic First Reader (Classic Reprint) (p. 1771)
—Pollard's Synthetic the Third Reader (Classic Reprint) (p. 1771)
Pollard, Rebecca Smith. First Book for Little Folks (Classic Reprint) (p. 735)
—Pollard's Synthetic Primer (Classic Reprint) (p. 1771)
Pollard, Simon. Genius of Bugs. (p. 815)
—Genius of Bugs. Rynhart, Kieran, illus. (p. 815)
—Why Is That Lake So Blue? A Children's Guide to New Zealand's Natural World. (p. 2458)
Pollard, Simon, photos by see Markle, Sandra.
Pollema-Cahill, Phyllis, jt. auth. see Reagan, Jean.
Pollen, George. Writings of George Pollen (Classic Reprint) (p. 2513)
Pollen, Samuel. Year I Didn't Eat. (p. 2519)
Pollert, Annette, jt. auth. see Smith, L. J.
Pollet, Aurelie. New York Day & Night. Bergier, Vincent, illus. (p. 1598)
Polley, Diane. Let's Go! Animal Tracks in the Snow! Hall, Marion, illus. (p. 1273)
Polley, Guy E. Poems: From Life (Classic Reprint) (p. 1765)
Polley, JoAnn. My Trip to Washington, D. C. Hanstick, Kevin, illus. (p. 1563)
Polley, JoAnn, jt. auth. see Polley, J. Patrick.
Polli, Elizabeth, tr. see Antigua, Kianny.
Pollinger, Gaye. Persnickety Witch of Fiddyment Creek. (p. 1725)
Pollinger, Gina, ed. see Shakespeare, William.
Pollock, Benjamin. Pollock's Juvenile Drama: The Blue Jackets, or Her Majesty's Service; a Farce, in One Act (Classic Reprint) (p. 1771)
Pollock, Beth. Next Step (p. 1600)
—Witch of Bloor Street (p. 2479)
Pollock, Channing. Little Gray Lady: A Play Without a Hero (Classic Reprint) (p. 1318)
Pollock, Francis. Jupiter Eight (Classic Reprint) (p. 1191)
Pollock, Hal. Meet the Brittles: In Monstermania. (p. 1439)
—Monster at the Bat. (p. 1495)
Pollock, J. A. Titus & Otis & the Arctic Adventure. (p. 2251)
Pollock, J. M. Unvarnished West: Ranching As I Found It (Classic Reprint) (p. 2337)
Pollock, Julius. Eunice, Vol. 1 Of 3: A Novel (Classic Reprint) (p. 667)
—Eunice, Vol. 2 Of 3: A Novel (Classic Reprint) (p. 667)
—Eunice, Vol. 3 Of 3: A Novel (Classic Reprint) (p. 667)
Pollock, Junia a. Ravelings of the Class of 1901 of Monmouth College (Classic Reprint) (p. 1843)
Pollock, Kristine, jt. auth. see Depalo, Madonna.
Pollock, Louise. Life & Adventures of Chanticleer, the Intelligent Rooster: An Interesting Story in Verse for Children (Classic Reprint) (p. 1288)
—National Kindergarten Manual: Containing Practical Model Lessons, Rules & Lectures for the Kinderarten & the Nursery, Stories, etc (Classic Reprint) (p. 1577)
Pollock, Malcolm & Hussey, Christopher. Abracadabra Woodwind - Abracadabra Flute Technique (Pupil's Book with CD) (p. 7)
Pollock, Sir Frederick, jt. auth. see Maitland, Frederic William.
Pollock, Tom. Conejo Blanco, Lobo Rojo. (p. 438)
—This Story Is a Lie. (p. 2227)
Pollock, Walter. Hot Bulb Oil Engines & Suitable Vessels (Classic Reprint) (p. 1006)
Pollock, Walter Herries. Hay Fever (Classic Reprint) (p. 941)
—Nine Men's Morrice: Stories Collected & Re-Collected (Classic Reprint) (p. 1609)
—Picture's Secret: A Story; to Which Is Added an Episode in the Life of Mr. Latimer (Classic Reprint) (p. 1741)
—Picture's Secret. (p. 1741)
Pollock/Shechinah Third Temple, Jerry. Divinely Inspired: Spiritual Awakening of a Soul. from Bipolar, Primal Therapy, Suicide & Science to God's Miracles. (p. 566)
—Messiah Interviews: Belonging to God. Beyond Miracles, Primal Therapy, Religion, Science, Bible History, Evolution, & Creation. (p. 1452)
Pollok, Robert, jt. auth. see Thomson, James.
Polly Jr., Jimmy Wayne, illus. see Hayes, Angela.
Polo Avendano, Samarys. Camaron Que Se Duerme. (p. 313)
Polo, Samarys. Kuchiklín Kuchiklán. (p. 1233)
Polon, Linda. Animal Curiosities. (p. 89)
Polonsky, Ami. Threads. (p. 2231)
Polseno, Jo, illus. see Lomask, Milton.
Polsky, Beanie, illus. see Cohen, Penny L.
Polsky, Milton E., jt. auth. see Berland, Howard.
Polsky, Sara. This Is How I Find Her. (p. 2224)
Polson, John. Monaco & Its Gaming Table (Classic Reprint) (p. 1492)
—Monaco & Its Gaming Tables (Classic Reprint) (p. 1492)
Polson, Kristen, illus. see Lester, Carol L.
Polson, Kristen, illus. see Lester, Carol.
Polson, Kristen, illus. see Lewis, Linda.
Polson, Steven, jt. auth. see Gipson, Fred.
Polt, Gabe. Robot Farm. (p. 1892)
Polt, Gabe, jt. auth. see Brooke, Samantha.
Poltarnees, Welleran. Hooray for Babies. (p. 1000)
Poltarnees, Welleran, compiled by. Big Book of Christmas. (p. 217)
polterink, illus. see Sturges, Lilah.
Poluchowicz, Krzysztof. Brooklyn ABC: A Scrapbook of Everyone's Favorite Borough. (p. 285)
Poluzz, Alessandroi, illus. see Jeffrey, Gary.
Poluzzi, Alessandro, illus. see Jeffrey, Gary.
Poluzzi, Alessandro, illus. see West, David.

P

Poluzzi, Allesandro, illus. see Jeffrey, Gary.
Polwart, Karine. Wee Bird Was Watching. Leiper, Kate, illus. (p. 2395)
Polyankakul, Polina, illus. see Best, Jessie L.
Polyansky, Nikita, illus. see Bloncourt, Nelson & Botero, Fernando.
Polyansky, Nikita, illus. see Bloncourt, Nelson.
Polydoros, Aden. Project Prometheus. (p. 1806)
Polydoros, Lori. Anacondas: On the Hunt. (p. 78)
—Awesome Video Game Competitions. (p. 145)
—BMX Greats. (p. 250)
—Crocodiles: On the Hunt. (p. 477)
—Dirt Bikes (p. 552)
—Drag Racing (p. 592)
—Fascinating Role-Playing Games. (p. 712)
—Grizzly Bears: Built for the Hunt. (p. 897)
—Indy Car Racing (p. 1118)
—Killer Animals: On the Hunt. (p. 1217)
—MMA Greats (p. 1484)
—Motocross Greats. (p. 1512)
—Motorcycle Racing (p. 1512)
—Piranhas: On the Hunt. (p. 1749)
—Skateboarding Greats. (p. 2030)
—Storytelling on Fabrics - Quilts, Tapestries, Story Cloths, & More: Set Of 6. (p. 2136)
—Strange but True Animals (p. 2137)
—Strange but True Sports (p. 2137)
—Top 10 Haunted Places (p. 2262)
—Top 10 Mythical Creatures (p. 2262)
—Top 10 UFO & Alien Mysteries (p. 2263)
—Wolves: On the Hunt. (p. 2485)
Polydoros, Lori & Adamson, Thomas K. Cool Competitions. (p. 448)
Polydoros, Lori & Benchmark Education Co., LLC. Storytelling on Fabrics: Quilts, Tapestries, Story Cloths, & More. (p. 2136)
Polydoros, Lori & Maurer, Tracy Nelson. Super Speed. (p. 2158)
Polydoros, Lori, et al. Predator Profiles. (p. 1786)
—Top 10 Unexplained. (p. 2263)
Polynkakul, Polina, illus. see Best, Jessie.
Pomaska, Anna. 3-D Coloring Book—My First Animal Mandalas. (p. 2547)
—3-D Coloring Book—My First Geometric Designs. (p. 2547)
—Anna Pomaska's Big Book of Puzzle Fun. (p. 97)
—BOOST Dinosaurs Coloring Book. (p. 262)
—Fun with Numbers. (p. 800)
—Mandalas Coloring Book. (p. 1396)
—My First Geometric Designs Coloring Book. (p. 1544)
—My First Mandalas - Animals. (p. 1544)
Pomaska, Anna & Coloring Books Staff. My First Mandalas - Nature. (p. 1544)
Pomaska, Anna & Newman-D'Amico, Fran. Crazy Crosswords Activity Book. (p. 469)
Pombo, Juan Manuel, tr. see Levine, Gail Carson.
Pombo, Luis G., illus. see Hernandez, Claudia.
Pombo, Mauricio, tr. see Papademetriou, Lisa.
Pomegranate, creator. Tunnel Calamity. (p. 2299)
Pomerantz, Charlotte. Piggy in the Puddle. Marshall, James, illus. (p. 1743)
Pomere, Jonas. Frequently Asked Questions about Self Mutilation & Cutting. (p. 784)
Pomerleau, Annie. At the Arcade: Understand Place Value. (p. 130)
Pomeroy, Annie J. Toadstool Tappers Tale. (p. 2254)
Pomeroy, Brick. Nonsense: Or Hits & Criticisms on the Follies of the Day (Classic Reprint) (p. 1618)
Pomeroy, Helen. New Swiss Family Robinson: Or Our Unknown Inheritance (Classic Reprint) (p. 1597)
Pomeroy, John. Scandinavian Ring, Vol. 1 Of 3: A Novel (Classic Reprint) (p. 1941)
Pomeroy, Mark M. Home Harmonies (Classic Reprint) (p. 996)
Pomeroy, Mark Mills. Brick-Dust: A Remedy for the Blues, & a Something for People to Talk about (Classic Reprint) (p. 280)
Pomeroy, Oren Day. Diagnosis & Treatment of Diseases of the Ear. (p. 537)
Pomeroy, Sarah B. & Kathirithamby, Jeyaraney. Maria Sibylla Merian: Artist, Scientist, Adventurer. (p. 1404)
Pomeroy, Shan, illus. see Silver, Karen.
Pommaux, Yvan. Oedipus: Trapped by Destiny: A TOON Graphic. (p. 1638)
—Orpheus in the Underworld. (p. 1673)
—Theseus & the Minotaur. (p. 2219)
Pommaux, Yvan, illus. see Ylla-Somers, Christophe.
Pommaux, Yvan & Kutner, Richard. Orpheus in the Underworld Pommaux, Yvan, illus. (p. 1673)
Pommier, Maurice. Grandpa's Workshop. Anderson, Brian, tr. from FRE. (p. 879)
Pompeï, Christine. Los Animales de la Sabana. (p. 1350)
Pompei, Maria Teresa, tr. see Dateno, Maria Grace.
Pompey, Dominique. I Am: The Abc's of Affirmations. (p. 1056)
Pomp'i, Christine. F'Es de L'Gende. (p. 721)
Pomplun, Tom, ed. see Henry, O., et al.
Pomplun, Tom, ed. see Irving, Washington, et al.
Pomplun, Tom, ed. see Lehman, John, et al.
Pomplun, Tom, ed. see London, Jack, et al.
Pomplun, Tom, ed. see London, Jack.
Pomplun, Tom, ed. see Smelcer, John E., et al.
Pomplun, Tom, ed. see Stoker, Bram.
Pomplun, Tom, ed. see Wilde, Oscar, et al.
Pomranz, Craig. Made by Raffi. Chamberlain, Margaret, illus. (p. 1374)
Pon, Cindy. Ruse. (p. 1916)
—Silver Phoenix: Beyond the Kingdom of Xia. (p. 2019)
—Silver Phoenix. (p. 2019)
—Want. (p. 2375)
Pona, Marta. Crazy Cat. (p. 468)
Ponce, Mari Luz, tr. see Brown, Ruth.
Ponce, Tina. Lost Eaglet. (p. 1353)
Pond, Frederick Eugene. Life & Adventures of Ned Buntline: With Ned Buntline's Anecdote of Frank Forester & Chapter of Angling Sketches (Classic Reprint) (p. 1288)
Pond, Paul. Jarhedz - the Jam Jar Busters. (p. 1160)
Ponder, A. J. Frankie Files. (p. 778)
Ponder, Rose O'Day. Clouds Big Time Out. (p. 408)
Ponder, S. E. G. Waters of Chastisement (Classic Reprint) (p. 2386)
Pong Wong, Lee. My Smelly Ass: Kids Funny Bedtime Story Picture Book. Montes, illus. (p. 1561)
Ponka, Katherine. Being a Toucan. (p. 194)
—Bird Watcher's Guide to Blue Jays. (p. 230)
—Carpenter Ants. (p. 333)
—Math on the Sun. (p. 1424)
Ponko, Cindy. Hugamasqueak. (p. 1048)
Ponnay, Brenda. Be Mine. Ponnay, Brenda, illus. (p. 177)
—Buhito Saca Sus Brios: (Little Hoo Gets the Wiggles Out) Ponnay, Brenda, illus. (p. 292)
—Buhito Saca Sus Bríos: (Little Hoo Gets the Wiggles Out) Ponnay, Brenda, illus. (p. 292)
—Code Come. Ponnay, Brenda, illus. (p. 411)
—Cody Barks. Ponnay, Brenda, illus. (p. 412)
—Cody Barks at Everyone. Ponnay, Brenda, illus. (p. 412)
—Cody Come Todo. Ponnay, Brenda, illus. (p. 412)
—Cody Eats. Ponnay, Brenda, illus. (p. 412)
—Cody Eats / Cody Come. Ponnay, Brenda, illus. (p. 412)
—Cody Eats Everything. Ponnay, Brenda, illus. (p. 412)
—Cody Eats Everything / Cody Come Todo. Ponnay, Brenda, illus. (p. 412)
—Cody Poops. Ponnay, Brenda, illus. (p. 412)
—Cody Poops Everywhere. Ponnay, Brenda, illus. (p. 412)
—Cody Sheds. Ponnay, Brenda, illus. (p. 412)
—Cody Sheds Everywhere. Ponnay, Brenda, illus. (p. 412)
—Colores: (Colors) Sandoval, Lenny, tr. (p. 422)
—Colors / Colores. Ponnay, Brenda, illus. (p. 426)
—Felices Pascuas Pequeño Buho: (Happy Easter, Little Hoo!) Ponnay, Brenda, illus. (p. 719)
—Feliz Navidad Buhito: (Merry Christmas, Little Hoo!) Ponnay, Brenda, illus. (p. 719)
—Good Night, Kitty Kitty! Ponnay, Brenda, illus. (p. 864)
—Happy Birthday, Little Hoo! Ponnay, Brenda, illus. (p. 920)
—Happy Birthday, Little Hoo! (¡Feliz Cumpleaños Pequeño Buho!) Ponnay, Brenda, illus. (p. 921)
—Happy Birthday Little Hoo / ¡feliz Cumpleaños Pequeño Buho! Ponnay, Brenda, illus. (p. 921)
—Happy Easter, Little Hoo! Ponnay, Brenda, illus. (p. 921)
—Happy Easter, Little Hoo! / Felices Pascuas Pequeño Buho! Ponnay, Brenda, illus. (p. 921)
—Hey, Kitty Kitty! Ponnay, Brenda, illus. (p. 964)
—It's Snot Fair: And Other Gross & Disgusting Jokes. Ponnay, Brenda, illus. (p. 1147)
—Kat Goes. Ponnay, Brenda, illus. (p. 1204)
—Kat Likes. Ponnay, Brenda, illus. (p. 1204)
—Kat Makes. Ponnay, Brenda, illus. (p. 1204)
—Kat Reads. Ponnay, Brenda, illus. (p. 1204)
—Kat Rides. (p. 1204)
—Kat Wears. Ponnay, Brenda, illus. (p. 1204)
—Knock Knock, Blub Blub! Fishy Underwater Jokes. Ponnay, Brenda, illus. (p. 1229)
—Knock Knock Boo Who? Ponnay, Brenda, illus. (p. 1229)
—Knock Knock, Lettuce In! And Other Funny Vegetable Jokes. Ponnay, Brenda, illus. (p. 1229)
—Little Hoo Gets the Wiggles Out. Ponnay, Brenda, illus. (p. 1318)
—Little Hoo Gets the Wiggles Out / Buhito Saca Sus Brios. Ponnay, Brenda, illus. (p. 1318)
—Little Hoo Goes Camping. Ponnay, Brenda, illus. (p. 1318)
—Little Hoo Goes to School. Ponnay, Brenda, illus. (p. 1318)
—Little Hoo Goes to School / el Pequeño Búho Va a la Escuela. Sandoval, Lenny, tr. (p. 1318)
—Little Hoo Goes to School / el Pequeño Búho Va a la Escuela. Ponnay, Brenda, illus. (p. 1318)
—Little Hoo Goes to the Beach. Ponnay, Brenda, illus. (p. 1318)
—Little Hoo Has the Flu. Ponnay, Brenda, illus. (p. 1318)
—Little Hoo Has the Flu / el Pequeño Búho Tiene Gripe. Ponnay, Brenda, illus. (p. 1318)
—Merry Christmas, Little Hoo! Ponnay, Brenda, illus. (p. 1450)
—Merry Christmas, Little Hoo! / Feliz Navidad Buhito. Sandoval, Lenny, tr. (p. 1450)
—Nat Can Code. Ponnay, Brenda, illus. (p. 1576)
—Nat Can Help. (p. 1576)
—Nat Plays Baseball. Ponnay, Brenda, illus. (p. 1576)
—Números Secretos Espías de la Agente Secreta Josephine. Ponnay, Brenda, illus. (p. 1630)
—Pequeño Búho Tiene Gripe. Ponnay, Brenda, illus. (p. 1720)
—Pequeño Búho Va a la Escuela: (Little Hoo Goes to School) Ponnay, Brenda, illus. (p. 1720)
—Pequeño Búho Va a la Escuela. Sandoval, Lenny, tr. (p. 1720)
—Pequeño Hoo Va a la Playa. Ponnay, Brenda, illus. (p. 1721)
—Secret Agent Josephine in Paris. Ponnay, Brenda, illus. (p. 1974)
—Secret Agent Josephine's Secret Spy Numbers (Números Secretos Espías de la Agente Secreta Josephine) Sandoval, Lenny, tr. (p. 1974)
—Time for Bed, Bunny (¡Hora de Dormir, Conejito!) Ponnay, Brenda, illus. (p. 2244)
—Time to Eat, Bunny! Ponnay, Brenda, illus. (p. 2245)
—Time to Eat, Bunny! / Hora de Comer, Conejito. Sandoval, Lenny, tr. (p. 2245)
—Time to Get Ready, Bunny! Ponnay, Brenda, illus. (p. 2245)
—Time to Get Ready, Bunny! / Es la Hora de Alistarse, Conejito. Sandoval, Lenny, tr. (p. 2245)
—Too School for Cool: And Other Smarty-Pants Jokes. (p. 2261)
—Who's Coming for Dinner, Little Hoo? Ponnay, Brenda, illus. (p. 2453)
—Who's There, Little Hoo? Ponnay, Brenda, illus. (p. 2454)
—¡Es la Hora de Alistarse, Conejito! Sandoval, Lenny, tr. (p. 660)
—¡Feliz Cumpleaños Pequeño Buho! Ponnay, Brenda, illus. (p. 719)
—¡feliz Cumpleaños Pequeño Buho! Ponnay, Brenda, illus. (p. 719)
—¡Hora de Comer, Conejito! (Time to Eat, Bunny!) Ponnay, Brenda, illus. (p. 1002)
—¡Hora de Dormir, Conejito! Ponnay, Brenda, illus. (p. 1002)
—¿quién Está Ahí, Pequeño Hoo? Ponnay, Brenda, illus. (p. 1827)
—¿quién Viene a Cenar, Pequeño Hoo? Ponnay, Brenda, illus. (p. 1827)
Ponnay, Brenda, illus. see Bickley, Chris.
Ponnay, Brenda, illus. see Lee, Calee M.
Ponnay, Brenda, illus. see Streza, Katrina.
Ponnay, Brenda, jt. auth. see Ponnay, Brenda.
Ponnay, Brenda & Ponnay, Brenda. Secret Agent Josephine in Paris. (p. 1974)
Ponomarov, Sergius, tr. see Chekov, Anton.
Pons, Adela, illus. see Galbraith, Kathryn O.
Pons, Bernadette, illus. see Buller, Jon & Schade, Susan.
Pons, Lele & De la Cruz, Melissa. Surviving High School: Do It for the Vine: A Novel. (p. 2165)
Ponsard, Christine, jt. auth. see Kieffer, Jean-Francois.
Ponsford, Sheila. Muffluppitts. (p. 1524)
Ponsonby, Emily. Clare Abbey, or the Trials of Youth, Vol. 1 of 2 (Classic Reprint) (p. 398)
—Mother's Trials (Classic Reprint) (p. 1510)
—Two Brothers, Vol. 3 of 3 (Classic Reprint) (p. 2307)
Ponsonby, Emily Charlotte Mary. Clare Abbey, or the Trials of Youth, Vol. 1 of 2 (Classic Reprint) (p. 398)
—Mary Lyndsay, Vol. 1 of 3 (Classic Reprint) (p. 1415)
—Mary Lyndsay, Vol. 2 of 3 (Classic Reprint) (p. 1415)
—Mother's Trials (Classic Reprint) (p. 1510)
—Pride & Irresolution: A New Series of the Discipline of Life (Classic Reprint) (p. 1791)
—Pride & Irresolution, Vol. 1 Of 3: A New Series of the Discipline of Life (Classic Reprint) (p. 1791)
—Two Brothers, Vol. 3 of 3 (Classic Reprint) (p. 2307)
Ponsor, Justin, illus. see Aaron, Jason.
Pont, Charles E., illus. see Leeming, Joseph.
Ponte, June. Fun & Simple Great Lakes State Crafts: Michigan, Ohio, Indiana, Illinois, Wisconsin, & Minnesota. (p. 798)
—Fun & Simple Pacific West State Crafts: California, Oregon, Washington, Alaska, & Hawaii. (p. 798)
—Fun & Simple Western State Crafts: Montana, Wyoming, Idaho, Utah, & Nevada. (p. 798)
Ponte, June, illus. see Hollow, Michele C.
Ponte, June, illus. see Miller, Heather.
Pontefract, Michelle. Grandma's Table. Cutler, Erin, illus. (p. 879)
—Zoe's Princess Pants. (p. 2541)
—Zoe's Princess Pants. Stammschroer, Danielle, illus. (p. 2541)
Ponter, Nick B. Connor Jackson & the Memory Thieves. (p. 441)
Ponthieu, Vismes Et De. Sporting Adventures of Charles Carrington, & Other Stories (Classic Reprint) (p. 2088)
Ponti, Claude. Adele in Sand Land: TOON Level 1. (p. 16)
—Chick & Chickie Play All Day! (p. 367)
—Chick & Chickie Play All Day! (p. 367)
—Chick & Chickie Play All Day! Ponti, Claude, illus. (p. 367)
—Hiznobyuti. Waters, Alyson, tr. (p. 982)
—My Valley. Waters, Alyson, tr. (p. 1563)
Ponti, Claude, illus. see Seyvos, Florence.
Ponti, James. Blue Moon. (p. 249)
—Camp Rock: Second Session #6: Sound Off! (p. 316)
—City Spies. (p. 395)
—Dark Days. (p. 506)
—Dead City. (p. 517)
—Framed! (p. 775)
—Framed! Crime-Fighting Collection: Framed!; Vanished!; Trapped! (p. 775)
—Trapped! (p. 2279)
—Vanished! (p. 2347)
Pontier-Carrels, Nicole. Don't Eat the Vegetables! (p. 582)
—Sammie's Strawberry. (p. 1928)
Pontis, Louis de. Memoirs of the Sieur de Pontis, Who Served in the Army Six & Fifty Years, under King Henry IV. , Lewis the XIII. , & Lewis the XIV: Containing Many Remarkable Passages Relating to the War, the Court, & the Government of Those Princes. (p. 1445)
Pontius, John M. Angels among Us: Millennial Quest Series, Book 2. (p. 86)
—Spirit of Fire: Millennial Quest Series, Book 1. (p. 2083)
Ponto, Joanna. Being a Good Citizen. (p. 193)
—Being Honest. (p. 194)
—Being Kind. (p. 194)
—Being Respectful. (p. 194)
—Columbus Day. (p. 427)
—Earth Day. (p. 616)
—Independence Day. (p. 1115)
—Mardi Gras. (p. 1403)
—St. Patrick's Day. (p. 2098)
—Thanksgiving. (p. 2212)
—Valentine's Day. (p. 2344)
—Veterans Day. (p. 2354)
Ponto, Joanna, jt. auth. see Gnojewski, Carol.
Ponto, Joanna & Boekhoff, P. M. Kids Love Space Crafts. (p. 1216)
Ponto, Joanna & Erlbach, Arlene. Christmas. (p. 383)
—Hanukkah. (p. 919)
Ponto, Joanna & Gabriel, Faith K. Kids Love Animal Crafts. (p. 1216)
Ponto, Joanna & Gnojewski, Carol. Day of the Dead. (p. 514)
—Kwanzaa. (p. 1233)
—Martin Luther King Jr. Day. (p. 1411)
—Ramadan. (p. 1839)
Ponto, Joanna & Hollow, Michele C. Kids Love Math Crafts. (p. 1216)
—Kids Love Sports Crafts. (p. 1216)
Ponto, Joanna & Leeper, Angela. Juneteenth. (p. 1189)
Ponto, Joanna & Mead, Wendy. Being Responsible. (p. 194)
Ponto, Joanna & Miller, Heather. Kids Love Art Crafts. (p. 1216)
Ponto, Joanna & Niven, Felicia Lowenstein. Kids Love Music Crafts. (p. 1216)
Ponto, Joanna & Parker-Rock, Michelle. Diwali. (p. 566)
Ponto, Joanna & Robinson, Fay. Halloween. (p. 912)
Ponto, Kristina. Fissy. (p. 742)
Ponton, Sharon. Shirley, Godfrey, & Mercy's Bedtime Story. (p. 2008)
Pontoppidan, Alain. My Encyclopedia of the Forest. (p. 1537)
Pont-Sainte-Maxence, Guernes de. Vie de Saint Thomas le Martyr: Poeme Historique du Xiie Siecle (1172-1174) (Classic Reprint) (p. 2356)
—Vie de Saint Thomas le Martyr: Poème Historique du Xiie Siècle (1172-1174) (Classic Reprint) (p. 2356)
Ponzi, Emiliano. Great New York Subway Map. (p. 888)
—Journey of the Penguin. (p. 1181)
Ponzio, Jean-Michel, illus. see Marazano, Richard.
Poo. Further Adventures of Goldilocks. (p. 802)
Poojara, Fiona. It's All about Family! (p. 1144)
Pooker, J. D. Ifs. (p. 1094)
Pool, Bettie Freshwater. Under Brazillian Skies (Classic Reprint) (p. 2321)
Pool, Eugene H. Heroic Women of the Art World. (p. 962)
Pool, John J. Woman's Influence in the East: As Shown in the Noble Lives of Past Queens & Princesses of India (Classic Reprint) (p. 2486)
Pool, Katy Rose. As the Shadow Rises. (p. 124)
—There Will Come a Darkness. (p. 2217)
Pool, Maria Louise. Against Human Nature: A Novel (Classic Reprint) (p. 34)
—Against Human Nature. (p. 34)
—Boss & Other Dogs (Classic Reprint) (p. 263)
—Dally (Classic Reprint) (p. 498)
—Friendship & Folly: A Novel (Classic Reprint) (p. 787)
—In a Dike Shanty (Classic Reprint) (p. 1103)
—In Buncombe County (Classic Reprint) (p. 1104)
—In the First Person a Novel (Classic Reprint) (p. 1108)
—Katharine North: A Novel (Classic Reprint) (p. 1205)
—Meloon Farm: A Novel (Classic Reprint) (p. 1443)
—Mere Folly (Classic Reprint) (p. 1448)
—Mrs. Keats Bradford a Novel (Classic Reprint) (p. 1522)
—Out of Step: A Novel (Classic Reprint) (p. 1682)
—Red-Bridge Neighborhood, a Novel: Illustrated by Clifford Carleton (Classic Reprint) (p. 1856)
—Roweny in Boston: A Novel (Classic Reprint) (p. 1909)
—Roweny in Boston. (p. 1909)
—Sand N Bushes (Classic Reprint) (p. 1930)
—Two Salomes: A Novel (Classic Reprint) (p. 2309)
—Two Salomes. (p. 2309)
—Vacation in a Buggy (Classic Reprint) (p. 2343)
Poole, Ann. Beach Friends. (p. 178)
—Field Friends. (p. 723)
Poole, Charles W. Chas. W. Poole's New Myriorama & Trips Abroad: Illustrated Vocally, Musically & Pictorially (Classic Reprint) (p. 361)
Poole, Diamond Catherine Cheyenne. Leslie the Old Hag Who Collected Souls. (p. 1268)
Poole, Ernest. Beggars' Gold (Classic Reprint) (p. 191)
—Harbor (Classic Reprint) (p. 924)
—His Family (Classic Reprint) (p. 974)
—His Second Wife (Classic Reprint) (p. 974)
—Millions (Classic Reprint) (p. 1468)
—Village: Russian Impressions (Classic Reprint) (p. 2358)
—Voice of the Street (Classic Reprint) (p. 2365)
Poole, Gabriella. Darke Academy 01: Secret Lives. (p. 507)
—Darke Academy 02: Blood Ties. (p. 507)
Poole, H. W. Abuse among Family & Friends. (p. 9)
—Alcohol & Tobacco Becker, Sara, ed. (p. 41)
—Alzheimer's Disease Walters, Anne S., ed. (p. 61)
—Anxiety Disorders Walters, Anne S., ed. (p. 104)
—Attention Deficit Hyperactivity Disorder Walters, Anne S., ed. (p. 135)
—Autism Spectrum Disorders Walters, Anne S., ed. (p. 139)
—Bipolar Disorder Walters, Anne S., ed. (p. 229)
—Coping with Sexual Violence & Harassment. (p. 451)
—Dealing with Dating & Romance. (p. 519)
—Depression Walters, Anne S., ed. (p. 530)
—Disability & Families (p. 553)
—Disruptive Behavior Disorders Walters, Anne S., ed. (p. 564)
—Drug & Alcohol Dependence Walters, Anne S., ed. (p. 606)
—Eating Disorders Walters, Anne S., ed. (p. 622)
—Foster Families (p. 771)
—Grizzly Bears. (p. 897)
—Homelessness & Families (p. 997)
—Immigrant Families (p. 1100)
—Incarceration & Families (p. 1112)
—LGBT Families (p. 1283)
—Military Families (p. 1466)
—Multigenerational Families (p. 1525)
—Multiracial Families (p. 1526)
—Obsessive-Compulsive Disorder Walters, Anne S., ed. (p. 1634)
—Over-The-Counter Drugs Becker, Sara, ed. (p. 1686)
—Post-Traumatic Stress Disorder Walters, Anne S., ed. (p. 1780)
—Prescription Drugs Becker, Sara, ed. (p. 1788)
—Preventing Sexual Assault & Harassment. (p. 1791)
—Schizophrenia Walters, Anne S., ed. (p. 1944)
—Single-Parent Families (p. 2024)
—Sleep Disorders Walters, Anne S., ed. (p. 2036)
—Teen Parents (p. 2199)
—Thai Family Table (p. 2211)
—Ultimate Book of Dangerous Animals. (p. 2314)
—Ultimate Book of Dangerous Places. (p. 2314)
Poole, Helen, illus. see Ashford, Rachel, et al.
Poole, Helen, illus. see Balsley, Tilda.
Poole, Helen, illus. see Bloomsbury USA.
Poole, Helen, illus. see Canetti, Yanitzia.
Poole, Helen, illus. see Daniel, Claire.
Poole, Helen, illus. see David, Juliet.
Poole, Helen, illus. see Garcia, Ellen.
Poole, Helen, illus. see Giachetti, Julia.
Poole, Helen, illus. see Greve, Meg.
Poole, Helen, illus. see Hord, Colleen.
Poole, Helen, illus. see Koons, Linda.
Poole, Helen, illus. see Linde, Barbara M.
Poole, Helen, illus. see Nunez, Jaclyn.
Poole, Helen, illus. see Parkes, Brenda.
Poole, Helen, illus. see Pippin, Jessica.
Poole, Helen, illus. see Richmond, Marianne, et al.
Poole, Helen, illus. see Schmauss, Judy Kentor.

Poole, Helen, illus. see Smith, Molly.
Poole, Helen, illus. see Sully, Katherine.
Poole, Hilary W. Anxieties & Fears in Daily Life. (p. 104)
—Cancer & Sickle Cell Disease. (p. 321)
—Catastrophes. (p. 343)
—Crime & Terrorism. (p. 474)
—Family Fears. (p. 702)
—Mexican Family Table (p. 1454)
—Military Families. (p. 1466)
—Nighttime Fears. (p. 1608)
—Phobias. (p. 1735)
—School Fears. (p. 1945)
—Separation Anxiety. (p. 1989)
—Symptoms & Treatments of Anxiety Disorders. (p. 2173)
—Ultimate Book of Dangerous Places. (p. 2314)
Poole, Hilary W. & Rich, Mari. Thai Family Table (p. 2211)
Poole, Hilary W. & Walters, Anne S. Medical Fears. (p. 1436)
—Social Fears. (p. 2053)
Poole, Hilary W. & Wood, H. P. Fakers: An Insider's Guide to Cons, Hoaxes, & Scams. Clark, David, illus. (p. 699)
Poole, J. Fables Calculated for the Amusement & Instruction of Youth: Originally Dedicated to a Young Prince, for Whose Improvement They Were Written Taken from the French (Classic Reprint) (p. 690)
Poole, John. Christmas Festivities: Tales, Sketches, & Characters, with Beauties of the Modern Drama (Classic Reprint) (p. 385)
—Intrigue: Or, Married Yesterday; a Comic Interlude, in One Act; As Performed at Theatre Royal, Drury Lane (Classic Reprint) (p. 1128)
—Little Pedlington & the Pedlingtonians (Classic Reprint) (p. 1324)
—Paul Pry's Delicate Attentions: And Other Tales (Classic Reprint) (p. 1707)
—Paul Pry's Journal of a Residence at Little Pedlington (Classic Reprint) (p. 1707)
—Phineas Quiddy: Or Sheer Industry (Classic Reprint) (p. 1735)
—Phineas Quiddy, Vol. 1 Of 3: Or Sheer Industry (Classic Reprint) (p. 1735)
—Scape-Goat: A Farce, in One Act (Classic Reprint) (p. 1941)
—Sketches & Recollections, Vol. 1 of 2 (Classic Reprint) (p. 2031)
—Year in an Hour, or the Cock of the Walk: A Farce in Two Acts; Performed at the Theatre Royal, Haymarket, on Thursday, June 17th, 1824 (Classic Reprint) (p. 2519)
Poole, Martina Franklin. Rudy Loves. (p. 1912)
Poole, Mary Jo, ed. see Thompson, Bruce E. R.
Poole, Othniel. Ellen Groovyeverything Happens: By Macchu True, As Told to Othniel Poole. (p. 637)
—Traquelero: A Quest for Happiness. (p. 2279)
Poole, Steven R., illus. see Reid, Christy.
Poole, Susie. All These Things: Based on 1 Corinthians 13:4-7. (p. 55)
—All These Things. (p. 55)
—Always near Me. (p. 61)
—Christmas Journey. Poole, Susie, illus. (p. 386)
—Time for Everything. (p. 2244)
—Whatever Is Lovely. (p. 2423)
Poole, Susie, illus. see Box, Su.
Poole, Susie, illus. see Hartman, Bob.
Poole, Susie, illus. see O'Connell, Rebecca.
Poole, Susie, jt. auth. see Hartman, Bob.
Poole, T. Deaf As a Post: A Farce, in One Act (Classic Reprint) (p. 519)
Poole, Tracy, illus. see Franklin, Cathy.
Pooler, Paige, illus. see Allen, Elise & Stanford, Halle.
Pooler, Paige, illus. see DeVillers, Julia.
Pooler, Paige, illus. see Dougherty, Brandi.
Pooley, Roger, ed. see Bunyan, John.
Poolos, Christine. American Flag. (p. 71)
—Deep-Sea Fishing. (p. 524)
—John Green (p. 1173)
—Truth about Pcp. (p. 2296)
—What Is an Object in the Sky? (p. 2414)
Poolos, J. Designing, Building, & Maintaining Websites. (p. 532)
—Mayflower: A Primary Source History of the Pilgrims' Journey to the New World. (p. 1430)
—Wild about ATVs/Vehículos todo Terreno. (p. 2462)
—Wild about Monster Trucks/Camionetas Gigantes. (p. 2462)
—Wild about Muscle Cars/Autos de Poder. (p. 2462)
Poolos, J., jt. auth. see Poolos, Jamie.
Poolos, Jamie. Designing, Building, & Maintaining Web Sites. (p. 532)
—Surfing & Wind Surfing. (p. 2163)
Poolos, Jamie, jt. auth. see Uhl, Xina M.
Poon, Anna, jt. auth. see Lonely Planet Kids.
Poon, Janice. Claire & the Water Wish. Poon, Janice, illus. (p. 397)
Poor, Agnes Blake. Boston Neighbours in Town & Out (Classic Reprint) (p. 264)
—Brothers & Strangers (Classic Reprint) (p. 286)
—Under Guiding Stars: A Massachusetts Story of the Century End (Classic Reprint) (p. 2321)
Poor, Barbara. Duck with Luck. (p. 608)
—Healthy Alphabet. (p. 943)
Poor, Barbara & Eichelberger, Elizabeth. Girl with the Curly Red Hair. (p. 837)
—Hawaii in the Sand. (p. 940)
—Holiday Story. (p. 988)
—My Trip to the Library. (p. 1563)
—Ooooooh It's Halloween. (p. 1665)
—You Are So Special. (p. 2524)
Poore, Ida Margaret Graves. Admiral's Wife in the Making, 1860 1903 (Classic Reprint) (p. 16)
Poore, Michael. Two Girls, a Clock, & a Crooked House: A Novel for Young People. (p. 2307)
Poortvliet, Rien, illus. see Haar, Jaap Ter & Mearns, Martha.
Poovey, Kim. Truer Words. (p. 2295)
Pop Art Properties Staff, illus. see Biskup, Agnieszka.
Pop Art Properties Staff, illus. see Bolte, Mari.
Pop Art Properties Staff, illus. see Enz, Tammy.
Pop Art Studios, illus. see Enz, Tammy.
Pop Art Studios Staff, illus. see Bethea, Nikole Brooks.
Pop Art Studios Staff, illus. see Enz, Tammy.
Popcak, Jacob, illus. see Hutto, Rebekah McLeod.
Popcak, Jacob H., illus. see Damiani, Philip J.
Pope, Alexander, jt. auth. see Homer, Homer.
Pope, Cheryl Lynn. Adventures of Princess Zari. Nyamor, Eric, illus. (p. 27)
Pope, Debra K. Adventures of Peanut: The Fox & the Crows. St Aubin, Mallari, illus. (p. 26)
Pope, Ellen Dittman. Friends with a Difference. Dixon, Carol, illus. (p. 787)
Pope, Elodie. In All Colors. Zarrin, Laura, illus. (p. 1104)
Pope Francis, Pope. Papa Francisco Dice... Boyd, Sheree, illus. (p. 1696)
—Pope Francis Says... Boyd, Sheree, illus. (p. 1776)
Pope, J. William. Tom Perkins: The Story of a Base Ball Player (Classic Reprint) (p. 2257)
Pope, Jessie. Three Jolly Huntsmen (Classic Reprint) (p. 2233)
Pope, Katrina. 12 Freedoms Gained. (p. 2551)
—Magic Wand. (p. 1379)
—Pretty Please with Sugar on Top. (p. 1790)
—Sit on the Pot I Think Not! (p. 2027)
—Where Does the Moon Sleep? (p. 2436)
Pope, Kevin, illus. see Hamilton, Martha & Weise, Mutch.
Pope, Kristen. Chimpanzees. (p. 377)
—Fennec Foxes. (p. 720)
—Salamanders. (p. 1924)
—What Is the Difference Between Clouds & Fog? (p. 2416)
Pope, Liz and Kate, illus. see Channing, Margot.
Pope, Liz and Kate, jt. auth. see Channing, Margot.
Pope, Liz & Pope, Kate. Itsy Bitsy Spider. (p. 1148)
—Row, Row, Row Your Boat. (p. 1908)
—Twinkle, Twinkle, Little Star. (p. 2305)
—Wheels on the Bus. (p. 2428)
Pope, Madeline. Rodney & Splodge Go to Topaz Town. (p. 1897)
Pope, Miller. ABC-Pirate-Coloring Book. (p. 4)
Pope, P. R. Queens of Antares: Volume 1 of the Bloodline Trilogy: Bloodline Returned: Bloodline Returned. (p. 1825)
Pope, Paul. Battling Boy. Pope, Paul, illus. (p. 175)
—Heavy Liquid. (p. 947)
—Sugary Shorts. (p. 2147)
—Year 100. (p. 2518)
Pope, Paul, jt. auth. see Petty, J. T.
Pope, Paul & Petty, J. T. Fall of the House of West. Rubín, David, illus. (p. 700)
—Rise of Aurora West. Rubín, David, illus. (p. 1885)
Pope, Paul & Renier, Aaron. Adventure Time: Sugary Shorts. Vol. 1 (p. 19)
Pope, Paul, et al. Adventure Time: Finn. Pearson, Luke, illus. (p. 19)
—Fall of the House of West. (p. 700)
Pope, Rex. British Economy Since 1914: A Study in Decline? (p. 283)
Pope, Richie, illus. see Biskup, Agnieszka & Collins, Terry.
Pope, Richie, illus. see Collins, Terry.
Pope, Robert, illus. see Busch, Robbie.
Pope, Robert, illus. see Cunningham, Scott.
Pope, Robert, illus. see Schulz, Charles M.
Pope, Robert, illus. see Schulz, Charles.
Pope, Robert, illus. see Schulz, Mark & Cooper, Jason.
Pope, Robert, illus. see Simmons, Alex.
Pope, Robert, jt. auth. see Kravitz, Darryl Taylor.
Pope, Robert, jt. auth. see Rozum, John.
Pope, Robert W., illus. see Schulz, Charles M. & Cooper, Jason.
Pope, W. C. Leisure Moments: A Collection of Short Writings on Various Subjects Presented in Prose & Rhyme (Classic Reprint) (p. 1266)
Popek, Emily. Copyright & Digital Ethics. (p. 452)
—Understanding the World of User-Generated Content. (p. 2326)
Popeo, Joanie, illus. see Hollenbeck, Kathleen M.
Popescu, Sinziana. Fuga Dariei Din Tinutul Pasarii Maiestre. (p. 797)
—Teatru Pentru Prichindei, Mari, Mici Si Mititei. (p. 2196)
—Theatre for Big, Small & Tiny Kids. Ursache, Daniela, tr. (p. 2215)
—Viaggio Di Vlad Nel Mondo-Di-La. Salone, Sara, tr. (p. 2354)
—Zborul Lui Petru Peste Taramul Balaurilor. (p. 2538)
Popeski, Fred. Oscar & Sarah. (p. 1673)
Popeson, Pamela, illus. see Weiss, Ellen.
Popham, Janet. Alligator Who Liked to Jump. (p. 56)
Popham, R. Brooks. Hither Thither (Classic Reprint) (p. 982)
Popham, William Lee. Yellowstone Park Romance: Description Being from the Author's Observation; Being Also a Lasting Souvenir & Convenient Guide for the Tourist (Classic Reprint) (p. 2521)
Popke, Suzanne L. Adventures of Tolei Mergen. (p. 29)
Popken, Dustin. Turq the Turtle: Land & Sea. (p. 2301)
Popko, Wendy, illus. see Williamson, Greg.
Popkp, Wendy, illus. see Williamson, Greg.
Poplak, Richard, ed. see Gilmore, Jason & Peterson, Paul.
Poplawska, Yolanda. Halifax Harbour 123 (BB) A Counting Book about Halifax Harbour (p. 911)
Popov, Nikolai. Great Shoe Parade. Popov, Nikolai, illus. (p. 889)
Popov, Nikolai, illus. see Springer, Jane, tr.
Popova, Maria & Bedrick, Claudia, eds. Velocity of Being: Letter to a Young Reader. (p. 2350)
Popovic, Lana. Blood Countess (a Lady Slayers Novel) (p. 245)
—Fierce Like a Firestorm. (p. 723)
—Wicked Like a Wildfire. (p. 2460)
Popovic, Pavle. Jugo Slav Stories: Translated from the Original & Edited with an Introduction (Classic Reprint) (p. 1186)
Popovich, Richard E., ed. see Beeson, Lea Ann.
Popovici, Danny, illus. see Churnin, Nancy.
Popp, K. Wendy, illus. see Bunting, Eve.
Popp, K. Wendy, illus. see Wood, Douglas.
Poppel, George. Battle of the Dinosaurs: An Antiwar Children's Fable. Bennett, Scott, illus. (p. 174)
—Planet of Trash: An Environmental Fable. Moyer, Barry, illus. (p. 1755)
Poppleton, G. New Elements of Conversation, in English & French: A Work Composed upon the Plan of That of Dr. Wanostrocht & John Perrin (Classic Reprint) (p. 1593)
Pops, Sandy. Pocketful of Animals. (p. 1764)
Popsicle, Lynnie & Odd Dot. Tiny World: Sculpting! Popsicle, Lynnie, illus. (p. 2250)
Popular Mechanics Press Editors, ed. Boy Scientist: 160 Extraordinary Experiments & Adventures. (p. 269)
PopularMMOs. PopularMMOs Presents a Hole New Activity Book: Mazes, Puzzles, Games, & More! Jones, Dani, illus. (p. 1777)
—PopularMMOs Presents a Hole New World. Jones, Dani, illus. (p. 1777)
—PopularMMOs Presents Enter the Mine. Jones, Dani, illus. (p. 1777)
Populoh, Valeska M., illus. see Cunningham, Steven C.
Popwell, Kelly. Farmer Roy's Big Beautiful Garden. (p. 711)
Popwell, Tammy L., illus. see Stroud, Jacob C.
Poquette, H. Alan. Maya's Magic: The Scourge of Gar. (p. 1429)
—Sebi's Great, Magical Train Ride Adventure. (p. 1973)
Porada, Henry. Inner Light. Michaels, Lisa J., illus. (p. 1121)
Porcella, Teresa. Night & Day. Fatus, Sophie, illus. (p. 1604)
—Wild Week. Queralt, Carmen, illus. (p. 2465)
Porcellato, Nives, illus. see Mason, Paul.
Porcellato, Nives, illus. see Whittaker, Helen.
Porcellino, John. Thoreau at Walden. Porcellino, John, illus. (p. 2230)
Porcellino, John, illus. see Gilmore, Jason & Peterson, Paul.
Porchat, Jean Jacques, tr. see Goethe, Johann Wolfgang von.
Porcheron, Tammy, illus. see Lewis, Carolyn.
Porchon, Paul. Nouveaux Elements de Geometrie: Rediges Conformement Aux Programmes du 27 Juillet 1905 des Lycees et Colleges (Classic Reprint) (p. 1625)
—Nouveaux el'ments de G'Om'trie: R'Dig's Conform'ment Aux Programmes du 27 Juillet 1905 des Lyc'es et Colleges (Classic Reprint) (p. 1625)
Pordd, Giulia, illus. see Cozzani, Federica.
Porena, Filippo. Scritti Di Geografia e Di Storia Della Geografia Concernenti L'Italia: Pubblicati in Onore Di Giuseppe Dalla Vedova (Classic Reprint) (p. 1966)
Porfiri, Maria. Native Girl. (p. 1578)
Porfirio, Guy. Jump! (p. 1188)
Porfirio, Guy, illus. see Bostrom, Kathleen Long.
Porfirio, Guy, illus. see Harvey, Gwen.
Porfirio, Guy, illus. see Levitin, Sonia.
Porfirio, Guy, illus. see Ottolenghi, Carol.
Porfirio, Karl. My Daddy's Heart Is Purple. (p. 1536)
Pornkerd, Vorrarit, illus. see Gilligan, Shannon.
Pornkerd, Vorrarit, illus. see Montgomery, R. A.
Porpora, Donnamarie. Grampa's Wings. (p. 876)
Porquet, Louis Fenwick De. Parisian Phraseology, or Choix de Phrases Diverses: Being a Collection of Sentences in Common Use, to Facilitate the Knowledge of the Formation of French Syntax (Classic Reprint) (p. 1700)
—Tesoretto Dello Scolare Italiano, or the Art of Translating Easy English into Italian at Sight: With a Complete English & Italian Lexicon of All the Words & Idioms Contained in the Work (Classic Reprint) (p. 2208)
—Tesoretto Dello Scolare Italiano, or the Art of Translating Easy English into Italian at Sight: With a Complete English & Italian Lexicon of All the Words & Idioms Contained in the Work; Being a New Method of Acquiring a Theoretical & Practical K. (p. 2208)
—Thesaurus Linguae Latinae, or the Art of Translating English into Latin at Sight: On the Plan of le Tresor (Classic Reprint) (p. 2218)
—Turning of English Idioms into French at Sight: Or, Sequel to Any Grammar Exercises (Classic Reprint) (p. 2300)
Porquet, Louis Philippe R. F. de. Tresor de l'Ecolier Francais, or Translating English into French at Sight (Classic Reprint) (p. 2285)
Porquet, Louis Philippe R. Fenwick De. Parisian Phraseology, or Choix de Phrases Diverses: Being a Collection of Sentences in Common Use, to Facilitate the Knowledge of the Formation of French Syntax, Intended for Those Who Are Desirous of Acquiring an Elegant & Correct Mode of Speaking The. (p. 1700)
—Tresor de l'Ecolier Francais, or the Art of Translating English into French at Sight (Classic Reprint) (p. 2285)
Porras, Carlos, tr. see Asimov, Isaac & Hantula, Richard.
Porras, Javier Fernando, illus. see Perrault, Charles.
Porras, Javier Fernando, illus. see Quiroga, Horacio.
Porrata, Mayra. Day Kyle Met Nuf. Rice, Kaleb & Deasey, Kevin, illus. (p. 513)
Porro, Guillermo F. Adventures of George & Reggie 2: King Orcan's Revenge. Barrera, Paige, ed. (p. 23)
Porro III, Guillermo F. Bloodminazue. (p. 246)
—Murdio. (p. 1527)
—Ringmaster of My Creative Imagination. (p. 1883)
Porsenna, Sandy. My first prayer Book. (p. 1545)
Port, Cynthia. Kibble Talk. Port, Cynthia, illus. (p. 1212)
Port, Moni. Bravo! Waechter, Philip, illus. (p. 277)
Port, Vanessa, illus. see Puffinton, Brick.
Porta, Carles. Band: Tales from the Hidden Valley: Tales from the Hidden Valley Book Three. (p. 163)
—Hello Mister Cold: Tales from the Valley, Book 2. (p. 951)
—Under the Water: Tales from the Hidden Valley: Tales from the Hidden Valley Book Four. (p. 2323)
Porta, Giambattista della. Natural Magick: In Twenty Books (Classic Reprint) (p. 1580)
—Natural Magick, by John Baptista Porta, a Neapolitane, in Twenty Books: Of the Causes of Wonderful Things, of the Generation of Animals, of the Production of New Plants, of Increasing Household-Stuff, of Changing Metals, of Counterfeiting Gold, of the Won. (p. 1580)
Portal, Alex. Applegates (p. 107)
Portch, Elizabeth, tr. see Jansson, Tove.
Portela, Francis, illus. see Van Lente, Fred.
Porter, A. M. Honor o'Hara, Vol. 1 Of 3: A Novel (Classic Reprint) (p. 999)
Porter, A. P. Minnesota. (p. 1473)
—Nebraska. (p. 1584)
Porter, Adele. Wild about Wisconsin Birds: For Bird Lovers of All Ages. (p. 2462)
Porter, Alan J. Cars: The Rookie. Carreres, Albert, illus. (p. 334)
—Cars: Route 66 Dash! Gladfelter, Allen, illus. (p. 334)
—Cars: Radiator Springs. Carreres, Albert, illus. (p. 334)
—Cars: Radiator Springs. Vol. 2 Carreres, Albert, illus. (p. 334)
—Cars: the Rookie. Carreres, Albert, illus. (p. 335)
—Joshua - the Polar Bear. He Can Foresee the Future & the Right Answers. (p. 1179)
—Rally Race. Magic Eye Studios, illus. (p. 1838)
Porter, Angela. Forever Inspired: Angela Porter's Tropical Rainforest Hidden Pictures. (p. 767)
Porter, Ann Emerson. Uncle Jerry's Letters to Young Mothers (Classic Reprint) (p. 2318)
Porter, Anna Maria. Coming Out, Vol. 1 Of 3: A Tale of the Nineteenth Century (Classic Reprint) (p. 430)
—Don Sebastian, or the House of Braganza: An Historical Romance; Four Volumes in Two (Classic Reprint) (p. 581)
—Don Sebastian, or the House of Braganza: An Historical Romance; Four Volumes in Two; Vol. I. & II (Classic Reprint) (p. 581)
—Don Sebastian, or the House of Braganza: An Historical Romance; Four Volumes in Two; Volume I. & II (Classic Reprint) (p. 581)
—Fast of St. Magdalen, Vol. 1 Of 3: A Romance (Classic Reprint) (p. 713)
—Fast of St. Magdalen, Vol. 2: A Romance (Classic Reprint) (p. 713)
—Honor o'Hara, Vol. 1 Of 2: A Novel (Classic Reprint) (p. 999)
—Hungarian Brothers (Classic Reprint) (p. 1052)
—Hungarian Brothers, Vol. 1 of 3 (Classic Reprint) (p. 1052)
—Knight of St. John, Vol. 1 Of 3: A Romance (Classic Reprint) (p. 1228)
—Knights of St. John, Vol. 2 Of 2: A Romance (Classic Reprint) (p. 1228)
—Village of Mariendorpt, Vol. 1 Of 4: A Tale (Classic Reprint) (p. 2358)
Porter, Augustus T. Danger We Survived. (p. 501)
Porter, B. C. Luck of Santa Claus: A Play for Young People (Classic Reprint) (p. 1364)
Porter, Bertha Currier. Village Postmistress: A Rural Comedy in Three Acts (Classic Reprint) (p. 2358)
—Voice of Authority: A Farce in Three Acts (Classic Reprint) (p. 2365)
Porter, Beverly J. One Amazing Night: A Christmas Story. Bower, Jan, illus. (p. 1658)
Porter, Bryan. Kit Dreamer & the Case of the Unlucky Lemur. (p. 1225)
Porter, Burton B. One of the People, His Own Story (Classic Reprint) (p. 1661)
Porter, C. Coping with Crohn's Disease & Ulcerative Colitis. (p. 451)
Porter, Cary, illus. see Brown, Tricia.
Porter, Charlotte. Clever Tales: Ludovic Halevy, Auguste Strindberg, Vsevolod Garshin, Villiers de l'Isle Adam, Alexander Kielland, Jakub Arbes (Classic Reprint) (p. 404)
—Poet Lore, Vol. 28: A Magazine of Letters; January-December, 1917 (Classic Reprint) (p. 1766)
—Poet Lore, Vol. 31: A Magazine of Letters; January-December, 1920 (Classic Reprint) (p. 1766)
Porter, Connie, jt. auth. see Bader, Bonnie.
Porter, David D. Arthur Merton: A Romance (Classic Reprint) (p. 122)
Porter, David Dixon. Allan Dare & Robert le Diable: A Romance (Classic Reprint) (p. 55)
Porter, David W., illus. see Yarrish, Karen Kern.
Porter, Diana. Beagle. (p. 178)
Porter, Duane. Charlie & the Chess Set. (p. 359)
Porter, Eleanor. Just David. (p. 1192)
—Pollyana. (p. 1772)
—Pollyanna. (p. 1772)
Porter, Eleanor H. Dawn (Classic Reprint) (p. 511)
—Just David. (p. 1192)
—Mary Marie (Classic Reprint) (p. 1415)
—Miss. Billy (Classic Reprint) (p. 1478)
—Miss. Billy's Decision (Classic Reprint) (p. 1478)
—Money, Love & Kate: Together with the Story of a Nickel (Classic Reprint) (p. 1492)
—Oh, Money! Money: A Novel (Classic Reprint) (p. 1642)
—Pollyana. (p. 1772)
—Pollyanna. (p. 1772)
—Pollyanna. Hindley, Kate, illus. (p. 1772)
—Pollyanna. McKowen, Scott, illus. (p. 1772)
—Pollyanna (100 Copy Limited Edition) (p. 1772)
—Pollyanna (1000 Copy Limited Edition) (p. 1772)
—Pollyanna (Classic Reprint) (p. 1772)
—Pollyanna Grows Up. (p. 1772)
—Pollyanna Grows up (Classic Reprint) (p. 1772)
—Road to Understanding (Classic Reprint) (p. 1888)
—Sister Sue (Classic Reprint) (p. 2027)
—Six Star Ranch (Classic Reprint) (p. 2029)
—Sunbridge Girls at Six Star Ranch. (p. 2152)
Porter, Eleanor H., jt. auth. see Olmstead, Kathleen.
Porter, Eleanor H., jt. auth. see Wardle, Sue.
Porter, Eleanor Hodgman. Across the Years (Classic Reprint) (p. 11)
—Cross Currents: The Story of Margaret (Classic Reprint) (p. 477)
—Just David (Classic Reprint) (p. 1192)
—Miss. Billy-Married (Classic Reprint) (p. 1478)
—Oh, Money! Money! A Novel (Classic Reprint) (p. 1642)
—Turn of the Tide: The Story of How Margaret Solved Her Problem (Classic Reprint) (p. 2300)
Porter, Elizabeth Crane. Mount Holyoke Book of Prose & Verse (Classic Reprint) (p. 1512)
Porter, Esther. Abby Wambach. (p. 3)
—Peeking under the City. Lozano, Andrés, illus. (p. 1713)
—Peeking under the Hood. Lozano, Andres & Lozano, Andrés, illus. (p. 1713)
—Scorpions (p. 1962)
—Serena Williams. (p. 1990)
—Sun Power: A Book about Renewable Energy (p. 2151)
—Termites (p. 2207)

P

—What's Sprouting in My Trash? A Book about Composting (p. 2426)

Porter, Esther, jt. auth. see Johnson, J. Angelique.

Porter, Esther & Kenney, Karen Latchana. What's Beneath. (p. 2423)

Porter, Gailyn. Gita Takes Wing. (p. 839)

Porter, Gary. Duffy: The Tale of a Terrier. (p. 609)

Porter, Grace Cleveland. Negro Folk Singing Games & Folk Games of the Habitants (Classic Reprint) (p. 1585)

Porter, Hank, illus. see Maris, Merrill de.

Porter, Harry. Dylan's Tale. Hedrick, Mandy, illus. (p. 612)

—Wolf. Stites, Theresa, illus. (p. 2483)

Porter, Henry. Two Angry Women of Abingdon (Classic Reprint) (p. 2306)

—Two Angry Women of Abington - Scholar's Choice Edition. (p. 2306)

Porter, Horace. Our Young Aeroplane Scouts in Germany: Winning the Iron Cross. (p. 1681)

—Our Young Aeroplane Scouts in Germany (Classic Reprint) (p. 1681)

—Subaltern's Share in the War: Home Letters of the Late George Weston Devenish, Lieut. R. an;, Attached R. F. C. ; with Introduction & Notes (Classic Reprint) (p. 2145)

Porter, Inman L. Little Bo. Darmawan, Iwan, illus. (p. 1312)

Porter, J. G. Zone Catalogue of 4050 Stars for the Epoch 1885: Observed with the Three-Inch Transit of the Cincinnati Observatory (Classic Reprint) (p. 2542)

Porter, James A. Prince of Anahuac: A Histori-Traditional Story Antedating the Aztec Empire (Classic Reprint) (p. 1794)

Porter, Jane. Coming Out, Vol. 2 Of 3: And the Field of the Forty Footsteps (Classic Reprint) (p. 430)

—Duke Christian of Luneburg, or Tradition from the Hartz, Vol. 3 (Classic Reprint) (p. 609)

—Duke Christian of Luneburg, or Tradition from the Hartz, Vol. 1 of 2 (Classic Reprint) (p. 609)

—Duke Christian of Luneburg, Vol. 2 Of 3: Or Tradition from the Hartz (Classic Reprint) (p. 609)

—Field of the Forty Footsteps: A Romance of the Seventeenth Century (Classic Reprint) (p. 723)

—Scottish Chiefs, Vol. 2: A Romance (Classic Reprint) (p. 1962)

—Scottish Chiefs, Vol. 2 Of 3: A Romance (Classic Reprint) (p. 1962)

—Sir Edward Seawards Narrative of His Shipwreck, & Consequent Discovery of Certain Islands in the Caribbean Sea, Vol. 2 Of 3: With a Detail of Many Extraordinary & Highly Interesting Events in His Life, from the Year 1733 to 1749 As Written in His Own. (p. 2025)

—Tales Round a Winter Hearth (Classic Reprint) (p. 2186)

—Thaddeus of Warsaw (Classic Reprint) (p. 2211)

—Thaddeus of Warsaw, Vol. 1 of 2 (Classic Reprint) (p. 2211)

—Thaddeus of Warsaw, Vol. 3: Four Volumes in Two (Classic Reprint) (p. 2211)

—Young Hearts, Vol. 1 Of 3: A Novel, by a Recluse (Classic Reprint) (p. 2531)

Porter, Jane, illus. see Stewart, Paul.

Porter, Janice Lee, illus. see Brill, Marlene Targ.

Porter, Janice Lee, illus. see Lowery, Linda & Keep, Richard.

Porter, Janice Lee, illus. see Lowery, Linda.

Porter, Janice Lee, illus. see Sutcliffe, Jane.

Porter, Janice Lee, illus. see Swain, Gwenyth.

Porter, Janice Lee, illus. see Walker, Sally M.

Porter, Janice Lee, illus. see Zemlicka, Shannon.

Porter, Janice Lee, jt. auth. see Lowery, Linda.

Porter, Jen. I Am Brave. Saunders, Katie, illus. (p. 1058)

—I Am Kind. Saunders, Katie, illus. (p. 1059)

—I Am Tidy. Saunders, Katie, illus. (p. 1060)

Porter, Jermain G. Catalogue of Proper Motion Stars (Classic Reprint) (p. 343)

Porter, John Addison. Sketches of Yale Life: Being Selections, Humorous & Descriptive, from the & Newspapers (Classic Reprint) (p. 2032)

Porter, John Hampden. Wild Beasts. (p. 2462)

Porter, John Thomas. System of Shorthand in Which the Vowels Are Expressed in the Consonant Stems by Making the Latter of Different Lengths. (p. 2174)

—System of Shorthand in Which the Vowels Are Expressed in the Consonant Stems by Making the Latter of Different Lengths (Classic Reprint) (p. 2174)

Porter, Karen White. Countdown to Navidad: A Family Christmas Across Borders. (p. 459)

Porter, Kevin Don. Missing. (p. 1480)

Porter, Lavinia Honeyman. By Ox Team to California: A Narrative of Crossing the Plains in 1860 (Classic Reprint) (p. 305)

Porter, Linn Boyd. Riverfall (Classic Reprint) (p. 1887)

Porter, Lynda C., illus. see Beasley, Jonathan & Porter, Rosanna I.

Porter, Mackenzie. In My Heart. Løvlie, Jenny, illus. (p. 1106)

Porter, Marisa Grace. Calisbury Christmas. Vanderstelt, Adrianna, illus. (p. 311)

Porter, Matthew. Calling All Animals. (p. 312)

—Flowers. (p. 753)

—Fox on the Loose! Porter, Matthew, illus. (p. 774)

—Monkey World ABC. (p. 1494)

—Tails Chasing Tails. (p. 2176)

Porter, Michael E., ed. see Sala-I-Martin, Xavier.

Porter, Michelle. Wesley Raccoon: The Old Man in the Houseboat. Mokrzycki, Olivia, illus. (p. 2401)

Porter, Mindy. Crumpled Feelings: A Lesson of Forgiveness. (p. 480)

Porter, Miss. Thaddeus of Warsaw (Classic Reprint) (p. 2211)

Porter, Miss Anna Maria. Fast of St. Magdalen, Vol. 3: A Romance (Classic Reprint) (p. 713)

—Hungarian Brothers, Vol. 2 of 3 (Classic Reprint) (p. 1052)

—Recluse of Norway, Vol. 1 of 4 (Classic Reprint) (p. 1853)

—Standard Novels, Vol. 11 Of 1: The Hungarian Brothers (Classic Reprint) (p. 2100)

Porter, Nick. Nicholas Flies. (p. 1602)

Porter, Noah. Science & Sentiment: With Other Papers Chiefly Philosophical (Classic Reprint) (p. 1953)

Porter, Phil. Two Plays for Young People: The Flying Machine; Smashed Eggs. (p. 2309)

Porter, Porter. Thaddeus of Warsaw (Classic Reprint) (p. 2211)

—Thaddeus of Warsaw, Vol. 1 of 2 (Classic Reprint) (p. 2211)

Porter, Rachel. Ally & Jordi's Adventure Through Florida. (p. 57)

Porter, Rebecca N. Girl from Four Corners a Romance of California to-Day (Classic Reprint) (p. 835)

Porter, Rose. Foundations, or Castles in the Air (Classic Reprint) (p. 771)

—My Son's Wife (Classic Reprint) (p. 1561)

—Summer Drift-Wood for the Winter Fire (Classic Reprint) (p. 2149)

Porter, Sarah. Alfred Dudley, or the Australian Settlers (Classic Reprint) (p. 43)

—Lost Voices. (p. 1356)

—Never-Contented Things: A Novel of Faerie. (p. 1589)

—Tentacle & Wing. (p. 2206)

—Twice Lost. (p. 2304)

Porter, Steve. Birds of Prey. (p. 232)

—Fairies. (p. 695)

—Mythical Beasts. (p. 1571)

—Sports Cars. (p. 2088)

Porter, Sue, illus. see Edwards, Pamela Duncan.

Porter, Suzie. Sailing. (p. 1923)

Porter, Tammy, illus. see Feather, Tami Flaming.

Porter, Tracey. Lark. (p. 1244)

Porter, William N. Miscellany of a Japanese Priest: Being a Translation of Tsure-Zure Gusa (Classic Reprint) (p. 1477)

Porter, William T. Big Bear of Arkansas: And Other Sketches, Illustrative of Characters & Incidents in the South & South-West (Classic Reprint) (p. 216)

Porter, William Townsend. Shock at the Front (Classic Reprint) (p. 2008)

Porter, William Trotter. Colonel Thorpe's Scenes in Arkansaw (Classic Reprint) (p. 418)

—Quarter Race in Kentucky: And Other Sketches, Illustrative of Scenes, Characters, & Incidents, Throughout the Universal Yankee Nation (Classic Reprint) (p. 1822)

Porter Zasada, Marc. Alice Through the Looking Glass - a Children's Play. (p. 45)

Porterfield, Jason. Aliens at Home: Studying Extreme Environment Species to Learn about Extraterrestrial Life (p. 47)

—Angry Birds & Rovio Entertainment (p. 87)

—Annie Oakley: Wild West Sharpshooter. (p. 100)

—Annie Oakley: Wild West Sharpshooter / Tiradora del Lejano Oeste. (p. 100)

—Annie Oakley: Tiradora del Lejano Oeste (Annie Oakley: Wild West Sharpshooter) (p. 100)

—Baseball in the American League Central Division. (p. 168)

—Baseball in the National League East Division. (p. 169)

—Basketball in the ACC (Atlantic Coast Conference) (p. 171)

—Basketball in the Big East Conference. (p. 171)

—Becoming a Quality Assurance Engineer. (p. 187)

—Benefits of Spaceflight & Space Exploration. (p. 199)

—Bowfishing. (p. 266)

—Calvin Hill & Grant Hill: One Family's Legacy in Football & Basketball. (p. 313)

—Careers in Undercover Gang Investigation. (p. 330)

—Chile: A Primary Source Cultural Guide. (p. 376)

—Conducting Basic & Advanced Searches. (p. 438)

—Cristiano Ronaldo: Soccer Champion. (p. 475)

—Election of Barack Obama: Race & Politics in America. (p. 631)

—Engineering Solutions for Earthquakes (p. 652)

—Fab Lab Creating with Milling Machines. (p. 690)

—File Sharing: Rights & Risks. (p. 726)

—Frederick Douglass: Abolitionist & Fighter for Equality. (p. 781)

—Homestead Act Of 1862: A Primary Source History of the Settlement of the American Heartland in the Late 19th Century. (p. 998)

—How a Depression Works. (p. 1025)

—How Lyndon B. Johnson Fought the Vietnam War. (p. 1033)

—Julian Assange & Wikileaks. (p. 1187)

—Jump-Starting a Career in Radiology. (p. 1188)

—Kurt Busch: NASCAR Driver. (p. 1233)

—Law & Personal Health: Your Legal Rights. (p. 1253)

—Lincoln-Douglas Senatorial Debates Of 1858: A Primary Source Investigation. (p. 1303)

—Major League Baseball: The Great Steroid Scandals. (p. 1385)

—Marco Polo. (p. 1403)

—Maria Sharapova: Tennis Grand Slam Champion. (p. 1404)

—Montana: Past & Present. (p. 1499)

—Niklas Zennstrom & Skype. (p. 1609)

—Problems & Progress in American Politics: The Growth of the Democratic Party in the Late 1800s. (p. 1803)

—Robots, Cyborgs, & Androids. (p. 1893)

—Robots, Jobs, & You (p. 1893)

—Separation of Church & State: Interpreting the Constitution. (p. 1989)

—Stephen Curry: NBA Sharpshooter. (p. 2115)

—Third Amendment: Upholding the Right to Privacy. (p. 2222)

—Third Amendment: The Right to Privacy in the Home. (p. 2222)

—Tim Berners-Lee (p. 2243)

—Virginia: Past & Present. (p. 2360)

—What Is the Executive Branch? (p. 2416)

—What You Need to Know about Mortgages (p. 2423)

—White & Black Hat Hackers. (p. 2443)

—Your Career in the Army. (p. 2533)

Porterfield, Jason, jt. auth. see Crayton, Lisa A.

Porterfield, Jason, jt. auth. see Sebree, Chet'la.

Porterfield, Katie. Homestead a to Z. (p. 998)

—Sewanee Night Before Christmas. (p. 1995)

Porterfield, Scott, illus. see Lee, Karin.

Portes, Andrea. Anatomía de una Inadaptada: Anatomy of a Misfit (Spanish Edition) (p. 79)

—Anatomy of a Misfit. (p. 79)

—Fall of Butterflies. (p. 700)

—Henry & Eva & the Castle on the Cliff. (p. 954)

—Henry & Eva & the Famous People Ghosts. (p. 954)

—Liberty: The Spy Who (Kind of) Liked Me. (p. 1283)

—Liberty: the Spy Who (Kind of) Liked Me. (p. 1284)

Porteus, Tim. East Lothian Folk Tales for Children. (p. 619)

Portice, Michelle. Kit & Kaboodle Go Camping. Mortimer, Mitch, illus. (p. 1225)

—Kit & Kaboodle Take the Train. Mortimer, Mitch, illus. (p. 1225)

Portier-Tock, Charlotte, illus. see Aspden, K. L.

Portillo, Josie, illus. see Grant, Holly.

Portis, Antoinette. Best Frints at Skrool. Portis, Antoinette, illus. (p. 206)

—Best Frints in the Whole Universe. (p. 206)

—Froodle. Portis, Antoinette, illus. (p. 795)

—Hey, Water! (p. 964)

—Kindergarten Diary. Portis, Antoinette, illus. (p. 1218)

—New Green Day. (p. 1594)

—Not a Box Board Book. Portis, Antoinette, illus. (p. 1622)

—Now. (p. 1627)

—Princess Super Kitty. Portis, Antoinette, illus. (p. 1799)

—Wait. (p. 2370)

Portis, Michael. Pinky Got Out! Richmond, Lori, illus. (p. 1747)

Portman, Frank. Andromeda Klein. (p. 84)

Portman, Lionel. Three Asses in Bolivia (Classic Reprint) (p. 2231)

Portman, Michael. Are There Other Earths? (p. 112)

—Are UFOs Real? (p. 113)

—Blinding Blizzards. (p. 244)

—Chargers. (p. 358)

—Chevelles. (p. 367)

—Could an Asteroid Harm Earth? (p. 458)

—Could We Live on Other Planets? (p. 458)

—Deadly Floods. (p. 518)

—Destructive Hurricanes. (p. 534)

—Drew Brees. (p. 604)

—Fighter Jets. (p. 725)

—Gorillas in Danger. (p. 870)

—Is There Life on Mars? (p. 1137)

—Marine Corps. (p. 1405)

—Mustangs. (p. 1530)

—Pandas in Danger. (p. 1696)

—Sea Turtles in Danger. (p. 1969)

—Tasmanian Devils in Danger. (p. 2192)

—Tigers in Danger. (p. 2242)

—Torinos. (p. 2265)

—Whales in Danger. (p. 2404)

—What Is an Eclipse? (p. 2414)

—Where Did the Moon Come From? (p. 2436)

—Why Do Astronauts Wear Spacesuits? (p. 2455)

—Why Isn't Pluto a Planet? (p. 2458)

Portmann, Rosemarie, ed. see Verlag, Don Bosco Medien.

Portner, Mayer. Soil (Classic Reprint) (p. 2055)

Portnoy, Amy, illus. see Becker, Bonny.

Portnoy, Mindy Avra. Tale of Two Seders. Cis, Valeria, illus. (p. 2180)

Portolano, Cristina, illus. see Farndon, John.

Portolos Nam, Goldie. Ralston Rams. (p. 1838)

Portor, Laura Spencer. Adventures in Indigence & Other Essays (Classic Reprint) (p. 20)

—Genevieve a Story of French School Days (Classic Reprint) (p. 815)

—Story of Little Angels (Classic Reprint) (p. 2131)

Portus, Sam. Fascism: Radical Nationalism (p. 712)

Portwood, Andrew, illus. see Givens, Terryl L.

Posada, Jorge. Play Ball! ón, Raúl, illus. (p. 1759)

—Sí, Puedes. Colón, Raúl, illus. (p. 2014)

Posada, Mia. Guess What Is Growing Insi. (p. 903)

—Summer Green to Autumn Gold: Uncovering Leaves' Hidden Colors. Posada, Mia, illus. (p. 2149)

—Who Was Here? Discovering Wild Animal Tracks. Posada, Mia, illus. (p. 2451)

Posada, Mia, illus. see Glaser, Linda.

Posada, Mia, illus. see Hirsch, Rebecca E.

Posada, Mia, jt. auth. see Kerrod, Robin.

Posen, Mick, illus. see Costain, Meredith.

Posesorski, Sherie & Second Story Press Staff. Old Photographs (p. 1647)

Posey, Dick. Just Common Folks (Classic Reprint) (p. 1192)

Posey, S. A. M. Last Station Master: A Boy, a Terroist, a Secret, & Trouble. (p. 1249)

Posey, Sandra Mizumoto. Rabbits with Stars in their Eyes. (p. 1830)

Posey, Sarah, illus. see Parker, Joanne.

Poskitt, Kjartan. Agatha Parrot & the Heart of Mud. Hargis, Wes, illus. (p. 35)

—Agatha Parrot & the Odd Street School Ghost. Hargis, Wes, illus. (p. 35)

—Codes: How to Make Them & Break Them! Baker, Ian, illus. (p. 412)

—Escape from Hotel Infinity (Numbers) Tayal, Amit & Nagar, Sachin, illus. (p. 661)

—Harry Houdini (the First Names Series) Ford, Geraint, illus. (p. 934)

Poskitt, Kjartan & Casey, Catherine. Attack on Circuit City (Statistics) Wolski, Igor & Godbey, Cory, illus. (p. 135)

Poskitt, Kjartan & Litton, Jonathan. Island of Tomorrow (Geometry) Wolski, Igor & Ledoyen, Sam, illus. (p. 1140)

—Lost in the Fourth Dimension (Measurement) Wolski, Igor & Ledoyen, Sam, illus. (p. 1354)

Posner, Fran, jt. auth. see Posner-Sanchez, Andrea.

Posner, Richard. Goodnight Cinderella. (p. 867)

—Sparrows Flight. (p. 2075)

—Sweet Pain. (p. 2169)

Posner-Sanchez, Andrea. Abby (Sesame Street Friends) (p. 3)

—Always a Princess (Disney Princess) Disney Storybook Artists Staff, illus. (p. 61)

—Ariel Is My Babysitter (Disney Princess) Cortes, Mario et al, illus. (p. 115)

—Ariel's Dolphin Adventure - Snow White's New Friend Random House Disney Staff, illus. (p. 115)

—As Big As a Whale (Disney Junior: Doc Mcstuffins) RH Disney Staff, illus. (p. 124)

—Bath Time with Ariel (Disney Princess) DiCicco, Sue, illus. (p. 172)

—Big Bird (Sesame Street Friends) (p. 216)

—Boomer Gets His Bounce Back (Disney Junior: Doc Mcstuffins) RH Disney Staff, illus. (p. 261)

—Bubble-Rific! RH Disney Staff, illus. (p. 289)

—Bunny Magic! (Disney Junior: Sofia the First) RH Disney Staff, illus. (p. 298)

—Christmas ABCs: a Golden Alphabet Book. (p. 383)

—Christmas Party. Random House Disney Staff, illus. (p. 386)

—Christmas Peeps (Peeps) Random House, illus. (p. 386)

—Cookie (Sesame Street Friends) (p. 446)

—Count (Sesame Street Friends) Random House, illus. (p. 458)

—Cuddly Princess Pals. Random House Disney Staff, illus. (p. 482)

—Dinosaurs A to Z. Golden Books Staff et al, illus. (p. 550)

—Doc Is the Best Medicine! (Disney Junior: Doc Mcstuffins) Wall, Mike, illus. (p. 572)

—Dog Days. (p. 575)

—Elmo (Sesame Street Friends) (p. 639)

—Elmo's Lucky Day (Sesame Street) Mathieu, Joe, illus. (p. 639)

—Fang-Tastic! (Disney Junior: Henry Hugglemonster) Laguna, Fabio & Gallego, James, illus. (p. 706)

—Follow That Hippo! (Disney Junior: the Lion Guard) Cortes, Mario & Colletti, Marco, illus. (p. 757)

—Frozen Christmas (Disney Frozen) Random House Disney Staff, illus. (p. 795)

—Good Night, Princess! (Disney Princess) Legramandi, Francesco & Matta, Gabriella, illus. (p. 865)

—Grover (Sesame Street Friends) Random House, illus. (p. 899)

—Happy Peeps-Oween! Massironi, Daniela, illus. (p. 923)

—Hello, Olaf! (p. 951)

—Hugglefish (Disney Junior: Henry Hugglemonster) Laguna, Fabio & Gallego, James, illus. (p. 1048)

—I Am a Princess (Disney Princess) Matta, Gabriella & Legramandi, Francesco, illus. (p. 1057)

—I Am Ariel (Disney Princess) RH Disney Staff & Batson, Alan, illus. (p. 1058)

—Knight in Sticky Armor (Disney Junior: Doc Mcstuffins) Random House Disney Staff, illus. (p. 1228)

—Let Your Peepsonality Shine! (Peeps) Random House, illus. (p. 1269)

—Little Princess. Alvarez, Lorena, illus. (p. 1325)

—Meet Maui. (p. 1438)

—Meet Maui. Disney Storybook Art Team, illus. (p. 1438)

—Miles from Tomorrowland (Disney Junior: Miles from Tomorrowland) RH Disney Staff, illus. (p. 1465)

—Monsters in a Box (Disney/Pixar Monsters University) Random House Disney Staff, illus. (p. 1498)

—Oaken's Invention. Random House Disney, illus. (p. 1633)

—Olaf's Frozen Adventure (Disney Frozen) Chou, Joey, illus. (p. 1644)

—Olaf's Frozen Adventure Little Golden Book (Disney Frozen) Chou, Joey, illus. (p. 1644)

—Oscar (Sesame Street Friends) Random House, illus. (p. 1673)

—Palace Pets Ultimate Handbook (Disney Princess: Palace Pets) Random House Disney Staff, illus. (p. 1694)

—Peep on a Perch (Peeps) Random House, illus. (p. 1713)

—Peeps at School. Massironi, Daniela, illus. (p. 1714)

—Perfect Tea Party (Disney Junior: Sofia the First) Random House Disney Staff, illus. (p. 1723)

—Pirate Games. Random House Disney Staff, illus. (p. 1750)

—Pixie Puzzles, Games, & More! Christy, Jana, illus. (p. 1752)

—Quiet Time with Belle (Disney Princess) DiCicco, Sue, illus. (p. 1828)

—Royal Easter. (p. 1909)

—Royal Easter (Disney Princess) RH Disney Staff et al, illus. (p. 1909)

—Royal Pet Problem. RH Disney Staff, illus. (p. 1910)

—Royal Wedding Album (Disney Princess) RH Disney Staff, illus. (p. 1910)

—S Is for School! (Sesame Street) A Lift-The-Flap Board Book. Brannon, Tom, illus. (p. 1919)

—Shadow Play! Random House Disney Staff, illus. (p. 1997)

—Shake Your Tail Feathers (Disney Junior: Doc Mcstuffins) Random House Disney Staff, illus. (p. 1998)

—Shop with Minnie (Disney Junior: Mickey Mouse Clubhouse) RH Disney, illus. (p. 2009)

—Skipping Day (Disney Junior: Jake & the Neverland Pirates) Random House Disney Staff, illus. (p. 2033)

—Sleepy Time with Aurora (Disney Princess) RH Disney Staff & DiCicco, Sue, illus. (p. 2037)

—Sofia the First Little Golden Book Favorites (Disney Junior: Sofia the First) Lee, Grace & Disney Storybook Artists, illus. (p. 2054)

—Sofia the Second (Disney Junior: Sofia the First) RH Disney Staff, illus. (p. 2054)

—Sofia's Royal World (Disney Junior: Sofia the First) Lee, Grace & Disney Storybook Artists Staff, illus. (p. 2054)

—Sweetest Easter (Peeps) Massironi, Daniela, illus. (p. 2169)

—Teacup to the Rescue! (Disney Princess: Palace Pets) RH Disney Staff & DiCicco, Sue, illus. (p. 2195)

—Three Royal Birthdays! (Disney Princess) Legramandi, Francesco & Matta, Gabriella, illus. (p. 2235)

—Time to Fly! (Disney Junior: Sheriff Callie's Wild West) Fruchter, Jason, illus. (p. 2245)

—Toby the Cowsitter (Disney Junior: Sheriff Callie's Wild West) RH Disney Staff & Fruchter, Jason, illus. (p. 2254)

—Two Princesses & a Baby (Disney Junior: Sofia the First) RH Disney Staff & Studio IBOIX Staff, illus. (p. 2309)

—Wish upon a Star (Disney Princess) Random House Disney Staff, illus. (p. 2478)

Posner-Sanchez, Andrea, jt. auth. see Golden Books.

Posner-Sanchez, Andrea, jt. auth. see Jordan, Apple.

Posner-Sanchez, Andrea, jt. auth. see Random House Editors.

Posner-Sanchez, Andrea, jt. auth. see Random House Staff.

Posner-Sanchez, Andrea, jt. auth. see Random House.

Posner-Sanchez, Andrea, jt. auth. see RH Disney Staff.

Posner-Sanchez, Andrea, jt. auth. see Saxon, Victoria.

Posner-Sanchez, Andrea, jt. illus. see Cohee, Ron.

Posner-Sanchez, Andrea & Hitchcock, Laura. Moana Little Golden Book (Disney Moana) RH Disney Staff & Sastrawinata-Lemay, Griselda, illus. (p. 1485)

Posner-Sanchez, Andrea & Julius, Jessica. Oaken's Invention (Disney Frozen) Random House Disney Staff, illus. (p. 1633)
Posner-Sanchez, Andrea & Posner, Fran. Night Before Peepsmas. Mora, Julissa, illus. (p. 1605)
Posner-Sanchez, Andrea & Random House Staff. Snowman Surprise (Disney Junior: Doc Mcstuffins) Golden Books Staff, illus. (p. 2049)
Posner-Sanchez, Andrea & Spaziante, Patrick. Don't Pat This Cat! (p. 583)
Posner-Sanchez, Andrea & Weinberg, Jennifer Liberts. Bow-Bot Robot (Disney Junior: Minnie's Bow Toons) RH Disney Staff, illus. (p. 265)
Posnock, Michael A. Adventures of Wilbur the Wave. (p. 29)
Post, C. C. Driven from Sea to Sea: Or Just a Campin (Classic Reprint) (p. 605)
—Ten Years a Cowboy (Classic Reprint) (p. 2205)
Post, Charles Clement. Ten Years a Cowboy (Classic Reprint) (p. 2205)
Post, Christian Frederick. Second Journal of Christian Frederick Post: On a Message from the Governor of Pensilvania to the Indians on the Ohio (Classic Reprint) (p. 1973)
Post, Edward. Archive, Vol. 50: October 1936 (Classic Reprint) (p. 111)
Post, Emily. By Motor to the Golden Gate (Classic Reprint) (p. 305)
—Eagle's Feather (Classic Reprint) (p. 613)
—Flight of a Moth (Classic Reprint) (p. 748)
—Title Market (Classic Reprint) (p. 2251)
Post, Grace. Three Dogs Go Walking. Mogyorosi, Nicole, illus. (p. 2232)
Post, Howard, jt. auth. see Emerson, Scott.
Post, John D. United States Reader: Containing a Variety of Exercises in Reading, Punctuation, Figures of Speech, Spelling, &C., for the Use of Schools (Classic Reprint) (p. 2332)
POST, L. E. E., illus. see Post, Lee.
Post, Mae Celeste. Loitering in Oregon (Classic Reprint) (p. 1340)
Post, Martin. Riverton Minister (Classic Reprint) (p. 1888)
Post, Mary A. Poverty Hollow: A True Story (Classic Reprint) (p. 1782)
Post, Melville Davisson. Dwellers in the Hills (Classic Reprint) (p. 611)
—Gilded Chair: A Novel (Classic Reprint) (p. 833)
—Man of Last Resort: Or the Clients of Randolph Mason (Classic Reprint) (p. 1394)
—Mountain School-Teacher (Classic Reprint) (p. 1514)
—Sleuth of St. James's Square (Classic Reprint) (p. 2038)
Post, Sarah E. Psychical Experiences: A Diary of 1891 (Classic Reprint) (p. 1809)
Post, Van Zo. Diana Ardway (Classic Reprint) (p. 538)
Post, Waldron Kintzing. Harvard Stories: Sketches of the Undergraduate (Classic Reprint) (p. 936)
—Smith Brunt a Story of the Old Navy (Classic Reprint) (p. 2042)
Postert, Petra. I Need All of It. Rassmus, Jens, illus. (p. 1079)
Postgate, Daniel. Love Stinks. (p. 1361)
—Rumpled Stilton Skin. (p. 1914)
Postgate, Daniel, illus. see Bird, Shelia May.
Postgate, Daniel, illus. see Oliver, Martin.
Postgate, Daniel, jt. auth. see Poskitt, Kjartan.
Postgate, Daniel, tr. see Oliver, Martin.
Postigo Cubo, Virgilio. Nico, el Pequeño Detective. (p. 1604)
—Nico, the Little Detective. (p. 1604)
Postlethwa. Modern Biology: Non-Consumable Lab Material Kit Grades 9-12. (p. 1486)
Poston, Ashley. Bookish & the Beast. (p. 260)
—Geekerella: A Fangirl Fairy Tale. (p. 813)
—Heart of Iron. (p. 945)
—Princess & the Fangirl. (p. 1795)
—Soul of Stars. (p. 2066)
Posuka, Demizu. Promised Neverland (Volume 1 Of 16) (p. 1806)
Pota, Giovanni, illus. see Bethea, Nikole Brooks, et al.
Pota, Giovanni, illus. see Bethea, Nikole Brooks.
Pota, Giovanni, illus. see Biskup, Agnieszka.
Pota, Giovanni, illus. see Yomtov, Nel.
Potach, Steven G., ed. see Culen, Konstantin.
Potapenko, Olga, ed. see AZ Books Staff.
Potarazu, Sreedhar. Get off the Dime: The Secret of Changing Who Pays for Your Health Care. (p. 824)
Potard, Céline. Monsters: A Magic Lens Hunt for Creatures of Myth, Legend, Fairy Tale, & Fiction. Ledesma, Sophie, illus. (p. 1497)
Poteet, Jen. Night under the Circus Tent. (p. 1608)
Potes, Marisa. Efecto Elefante. (p. 627)
Potey Mollina, José Luis. pergamino de Zenit y el descubrimiento de los sellos Divinos. (p. 1723)
Poth, Karen. Listen up, Larry (p. 1308)
—Mess Detectives & the Case of the Lost Temper (p. 1451)
—Sheerluck Holmes & the Case of the Missing Friend (p. 2005)
Poth, Karen, jt. auth. see Zondervan Staff.
Potma, Johan. Monster in My House. (p. 1496)
Potocar, Lisa Y. Sweet Glory. (p. 2168)
—Train to Glory. (p. 2275)
Potoma, Alison. Smith Family Secret: Book 1. Reul, Sarah Lynne, illus. (p. 2042)
Potter, Alice, illus. see Puffinton, Brick.
Potter, Alice, illus. see West, Tracey.
Potter, Alicia. Miss Hazeltine's Home for Shy & Fearful Cats. Sif, Birgitta, illus. (p. 1478)
—Mrs. Harkness & the Panda. Sweet, Melissa, illus. (p. 1522)
Potter, Anne & DeNize, Anne. Recycled Window. (p. 1855)
Potter, Beatrix. All about Peter. (p. 50)
—Beatrix Potter's Beloved Tales: Includes the Tale of Tom Kitten, the Tale of Jemima Puddle-Duck, the Tale of Mr. Jeremy Fisher, the Tailor of Gloucester, & the Tale of Squirrel Nutkin. (p. 183)
—Beatrix Potter's Picture Books. (p. 183)
—Cecily Parsley's Nursery Rhymes. Potter, Beatrix, illus. (p. 348)
—Cecily Parsley's Nursery Rhymes (Classic Reprint) (p. 348)
—Christmas Wish: A Peter Rabbit Tale. Taylor, Eleanor, illus. (p. 387)
—Classic Tale of Benjamin Bunny Oversized Padded Board Book. Santore, Charles, illus. (p. 400)
—Classic Tale of Mr. Jeremy Fisher: The Classic Edition. Santore, Charles, illus. (p. 400)
—Classic Tale of Peter Rabbit: A Little Apple Classic. Santore, Charles, illus. (p. 400)
—Classic Tale of Peter Rabbit Board Book: The Classic Edition. Santore, Charles, illus. (p. 400)
—Classic Tale of Peter Rabbit Hardcover: And Other Cherished Stories (the Classic Edition) Santore, Charles, illus. (p. 400)
—Classic Tale of Peter Rabbit Oversized Padded Board Book: The Classic Edition. Santore, Charles, illus. (p. 400)
—Classic Tale of Peter Rabbit Touch-And-Feel Board Book: The Classic Edition. Santore, Charles, illus. (p. 401)
—Classic Tale of the Flopsy Bunnies: The Classic Edition. Santore, Charles, illus. (p. 401)
—Classic Tale of the Flopsy Bunnies Oversized Padded Board Book. Santore, Charles, illus. (p. 401)
—Classics to Color: the Tale of Peter Rabbit. Pereira, Diego Jourdan, illus. (p. 401)
—Complete Tales of Beatrix Potter's Peter Rabbit: Contains the Tale of Peter Rabbit, the Tale of Benjamin Bunny, the Tale of Mr. Tod, & the Tale of the Flopsy Bunnies. (p. 435)
—Cuento Clásico de Pedrito, el Conejo Travieso: A Little Apple Classic (Spanish Edition of Classic Tale of Peter Rabbit) Santore, Charles, illus. (p. 483)
—Good Night, Peter: A Peter Rabbit Tale. (p. 865)
—Great Big Treasury of Beatrix Potter. (p. 884)
—Happy Birthday! A Peter Rabbit Tale. (p. 920)
—Hello, Peter! (p. 951)
—Hikayatul Arnabi Budayr. (p. 970)
—Histoire de Pierre Lapin. Potter, Beatrix, illus. (p. 975)
—Histoire de Pierre Lapin (Classic Reprint) (p. 975)
—Historia de Peter Rabbit. Albert, Virginia, illus. (p. 975)
—I Love You, Daddy. (p. 1078)
—I Love You, Mommy. (p. 1079)
—Jeremy Fisher Rocks Out. (p. 1164)
—Love from Peter Rabbit. (p. 1359)
—Painting & Drawing Book: With Tale of Peter Rabbit (Classic Reprint) (p. 1693)
—Peter Follows His Nose: A Scratch-And-Sniff Book. (p. 1728)
—Peter Hops Aboard: A Peter Rabbit Tale. (p. 1728)
—Peter Rabbit. (p. 1729)
—Peter Rabbit 123: A Counting Book. (p. 1729)
—Peter Rabbit 5-Minute Stories. (p. 1729)
—Peter Rabbit & the Pumpkin Patch. Palmer, Ruth, illus. (p. 1729)
—Peter Rabbit Baby Book. (p. 1729)
—Peter Rabbit Baby Cards for Milestone Moments: 30 Cards for Your Little Bunny. (p. 1729)
—Peter Rabbit Classic Tales Mini Gift Set: The Classic Collection. Santore, Charles, illus. (p. 1729)
—Peter Rabbit Deluxe Plush Gift Set: The Classic Edition Board Book + Plush Stuffed Animal Toy Rabbit Gift Set. Santore, Charles, illus. (p. 1729)
—Peter Rabbit Finger Puppet Book. (p. 1729)
—Peter Rabbit: Happy Birthday! (p. 1729)
—Peter Rabbit, I Love You. (p. 1729)
—Peter Rabbit Plush Gift Set: The Classic Edition Board Book + Plush Stuffed Animal Toy Rabbit Gift Set. Santore, Charles, illus. (p. 1729)
—Pumpkin for Peter: A Peter Rabbit Tale. (p. 1812)
—Red Riding Hood. Oxenbury, Helen, illus. (p. 1858)
—Roly-Poly Pudding (Classic Reprint) (p. 1899)
—Spring Surprise: A Peter Rabbit Tale. (p. 2092)
—Story of a Fierce Bad Rabbit. Potter, Beatrix, illus. (p. 2128)
—Story of Miss Moppet. Potter, Beatrix, illus. (p. 2131)
—Story of Peter Rabbit. McCue, Lisa, illus. (p. 2132)
—Tailor of Gloucester. (p. 2176)
—Tailor of Gloucester (Classic Reprint) (p. 2176)
—Tale of Benjamin Bunny. (p. 2178)
—Tale of Benjamin Bunny. Rasmussen, Wendy, illus. (p. 2178)
—Tale of Benjamin Bunny (Classic Reprint) (p. 2178)
—Tale of Ginger & Pickles. Potter, Beatrix, illus. (p. 2179)
—Tale of Jemima Puddle-Duck. (p. 2179)
—Tale of Johnny Town-Mouse. (p. 2179)
—Tale of Kitty in Boots. Blake, Quentin, illus. (p. 2179)
—Tale of Mr. Jeremy Fisher. Potter, Beatrix, illus. (p. 2179)
—Tale of Mr. Jeremy Fisher (Classic Reprint) (p. 2179)
—Tale of Mr. Tod. (p. 2179)
—Tale of Mrs. Tiggy-Winkle. (p. 2179)
—Tale of Mrs. Tittlemouse. (p. 2179)
—Tale of Mrs. Tittlemouse. Beatrix, Potter, illus. (p. 2179)
—Tale of Mrs. Tittlemouse. Rasmussen, Wendy, illus. (p. 2179)
—Tale of Peter Rabbit: A Sound Story Book. (p. 2179)
—Tale of Peter Rabbit. (p. 2179)
—Tale of Peter Rabbit. McPhail, David, illus. (p. 2179)
—Tale of Peter Rabbit. Beatrix, Potter, illus. (p. 2179)
—Tale of Peter Rabbit (100 Copy Limited Edition) (p. 2179)
—Tale of Peter Rabbit (Classic Reprint) (p. 2179)
—Tale of Peter Rabbit & Other Stories: The Beatrix Potter Collection. (p. 2179)
—Tale of Peter Rabbit Holiday Edition. (p. 2179)
—Tale of Pigling Bland. (p. 2179)
—Tale of Squirrel Nutkin. (p. 2179)
—Tale of Squirrel Nutkin. Beatrix, Potter, illus. (p. 2179)
—Tale of Squirrel Nutkin. Rasmussen, Wendy, illus. (p. 2179)
—Tale of Squirrel Nutkin (1000 Copy Limited Edition) (p. 2179)
—Tale of Squirrel Nutkin (Classic Reprint) (p. 2179)
—Tale of the Flopsy Bunnies. (p. 2180)
—Tale of the Flopsy Bunnies. Rasmussen, Wendy, illus. (p. 2180)
—Tale of the Pie & the Patty Pan. (p. 2180)
—Tale of Timmy Tiptoes. (p. 2180)
—Tale of Timmy Tiptoes (Classic Reprint) (p. 2180)
—Tale of Tom Kitten. (p. 2180)
—Tale of Tom Kitten. Beatrix, Potter, illus. (p. 2180)
—Tale of Tom Kitten (Classic Reprint) (p. 2180)
—Tale of Two Bad Mice. Potter, Beatrix, illus. (p. 2180)
—Tale of Two Bad Mice (Classic Reprint) (p. 2180)
—Tickle, Tickle, Peter! (p. 2240)
—Two Beatrix Potter Plays. (p. 2307)
—What Can You See Peter? A Peter Rabbit Lift-The-Flap Book. (p. 2407)
—Where Is Peter Rabbit? A Lift-The-Flap Book. (p. 2438)
Potter, Beatrix, jt. auth. see Barker, Cicely Mary.
Potter, Beatrix & Aesop, Aesop. Tale of Johnny Town-Mouse. Rasmussen, Wendy, illus. (p. 2179)
Potter, Beatrix & Warne, Frederick. Story of the Movie. (p. 2134)
Potter, Becky Ann. Have You Been to Independence Hall? (p. 939)
Potter, Bethany. Power of the People: The Story of the U. S. Presidential Election of 2016 & How & Why It Made History. (p. 1782)
Potter, Cheryl. Broken Circle: Student Workbook. (p. 284)
Potter, Christina. Hudson & Rodney: Go to New York. (p. 1047)
—Pepe Aprende a Correr de Nuevo: Una Conmovedora Historia Real. (p. 1719)
—Pepe Learns to Run Again: An Inspirational True Story. (p. 1719)
Potter, Christine. Gracie's Time. (p. 874)
—In Her Own Time. (p. 1105)
—What Time Is It There? (p. 2420)
Potter, Dave. Storm Clouds over Mountain View Middle School. (p. 2126)
Potter, David. Accidental Honeymoon (Classic Reprint) (p. 10)
—I Fasten a Bracelet (Classic Reprint) (p. 1064)
—Left Behinds: Abe Lincoln & the Selfie That Saved the Union. (p. 1261)
—Left Behinds: the IPhone That Saved George Washington. (p. 1261)
—Streak (Classic Reprint) (p. 2139)
Potter, Dawn. Isobel's Tree. (p. 1140)
Potter, Deirdre. Frogs in the Cistern. (p. 790)
Potter, Dorothea. Wellspring Farm: Book 2. (p. 2400)
Potter, Dorothy. Under the Eagle: Three Plays with a Prologue & Epilogue (Classic Reprint) (p. 2321)
Potter, Eliza. Hairdresser's Experience: In High Life (Classic Reprint) (p. 910)
Potter, Elizabeth Gray. Lure of San Francisco: A Romance amid Old Landmarks (Classic Reprint) (p. 1369)
Potter, Elizabeth M., jt. auth. see Potter, Beatrix.
Potter, Ellen. Big Foot & Little Foot (p. 220)
—Bog Beast (Big Foot & Little Foot #4) Sala, Felicita, illus. (p. 253)
—Going Places. Leng, Qin, illus. (p. 855)
—Humming Room. (p. 1050)
—Kneebone Boy. (p. 1227)
—Monster Detector (p. 1495)
—Monster Detector (Big Foot & Little Foot #2) Sala, Felicita, illus. (p. 1495)
—Monster Detector (Big Foot & Little Foot #2) Sala, Felicita, illus. (p. 1495)
—Olivia Kidney Secret Beneath City. (p. 1650)
—Otis Dooda: Downright Dangerous. Heatley, David, illus. (p. 1675)
—Piper Green & the Fairy Tree: Pie Girl. Leng, Qin, illus. (p. 1748)
—Piper Green & the Fairy Tree: Going Places. Leng, Qin, illus. (p. 1748)
—Piper Green & the Fairy Tree: Going Places (1 CD Set) Leng, Qin, illus. (p. 1748)
—Piper Green & the Fairy Tree. Leng, Qin, illus. (p. 1748)
—Piper Green & the Fairy Tree: Pie Girl (1 CD Set) Leng, Qin, illus. (p. 1749)
—Piper Green & the Fairy Tree: Pie Girl (1 Paperback/1 CD Set) Leng, Qin, illus. (p. 1749)
—Piper Green & the Fairy Tree: Going Places. Leng, Qin, illus. (p. 1749)
—Piper Green & the Fairy Tree: Pie Girl. Leng, Qin, illus. (p. 1749)
—Piper Green And The Fairy Tree Too Much Good Luck. Leng, Qin, illus. (p. 1749)
—Pish Posh. (p. 1751)
—Slob. (p. 2038)
—Squatchicorns (p. 2094)
—Squatchicorns (Big Foot & Little Foot #3) Sala, Felicita, illus. (p. 2094)
Potter, Ellen & Mazer, Anne. Spilling Ink: a Young Writer's Handbook. Phelan, Matt, illus. (p. 2082)
Potter, Ellen & Sala, Felicita. Big Foot & Little Foot (Book #1) (p. 220)
Potter, F. Scarlett. Melcomb Manor: A Family Chronicle; Arranged from the Papers of Richard Brent, Esq., Sometime of Melcomb (Classic Reprint) (p. 1442)
Potter, Frank Hunter. Marriage for Love (Classic Reprint) (p. 1408)
Potter, Giselle. Tell Me What to Dream About. Potter, Giselle, illus. (p. 2202)
—This Is My Dollhouse. Potter, Giselle, illus. (p. 2225)
—Year I Didn't Go to School. Potter, Giselle, illus. (p. 2519)
Potter, Giselle, illus. see Best, Cari.
Potter, Giselle, illus. see Davis, Jacky.
Potter, Giselle, illus. see Guglielmo, Amy & Tourville, Jacqueline.
Potter, Giselle, illus. see Hopkinson, Deborah.
Potter, Giselle, illus. see Manna, Anthony & Mitakidou, Christodoula.
Potter, Giselle, illus. see Manna, Anthony L. & Mitakidou, Christodoula.
Potter, Giselle, illus. see McKissack, Patricia C.
Potter, Giselle, illus. see Osborne, Mary Pope.
Potter, Giselle, illus. see Schotter, Roni.
Potter, H. L. D. Manual of Reading: In Four Parts; Orthophony, Class Methods, Gesture, & Elocution; Designed for Teachers & Students (Classic Reprint) (p. 1399)
Potter, Heather, illus. see Murphy, Sally.
Potter, Heather, illus. see Wolfer, Dianne.
Potter, Jean. Science in Seconds for Kids. (p. 1955)
—Science in Seconds with Toys. (p. 1955)
Potter, Jean, jt. auth. see Kohl, MaryAnn F.
Potter, Jennifer M., illus. see Hosford, Kate.
Potter, Jennifer M., illus. see Smith, Emma Bland.
Potter, Joe. My First Odd One Out: Over 50 Fantastic Puzzles. (p. 1545)
—My First Spot the Difference: Over 50 Fantastic Puzzles. Virgili, Marta Costa, illus. (p. 1546)
Potter, Joe & Golding, Elizabeth. My First Unicorn Dot-To-Dot: Over 50 Fantastic Puzzles. Buckingham, Faye, illus. (p. 1546)
Potter, John E. Potter's American Monthly 1878: An Illustrated Magazine of History, Literature, Science & Art; Vols. 10 & 11 (Classic Reprint) (p. 1781)
Potter, Jonathan. Crabs on the Beach. (p. 465)
—We're Going Turkey Hunting. (p. 2400)
—Why Do We Celebrate Independence Day? (p. 2457)
Potter, Katherine, illus. see Schulz, Kathy.
Potter, Kay. I Hate Fairies! the Adventures of Katie James. (p. 1065)
Potter, Margaret. Fire of Spring (Classic Reprint) (p. 732)
Potter, Margaret Horton. Uncanonized a Romance of English Monachism (Classic Reprint) (p. 2317)
Potter, Mark. Onesimus, the Prince & the Slave. (p. 1663)
Potter, Mary Knight. Councils of Croesus (Classic Reprint) (p. 458)
Potter, Melisande, illus. see Castaldo, Nancy F.
Potter, Melody, illus. see Fraser, Amy.
Potter, Miriam Clark. Pinafore Pocket Story Book (Classic Reprint) (p. 1745)
Potter, Molly. Que Sucede Dentro de Mi Cabeza? Jennings, Sarah, illus. (p. 1823)
—What's Worrying You? Jennings, Sarah, illus. (p. 2427)
Potter, Olave. Weeds: A Story of Women Shifting for Themselves (Classic Reprint) (p. 2396)
Potter, Patrick. Ask Me, Ask Me, Ask Me: Random Questions for Awesome Conversations. (p. 126)
—Ellie's Amazing Outfits. Smith, Haley Rachel, illus. (p. 638)
Potter, Rubee. Gramma's Rocks. (p. 876)
Potter, Ryan. Perennial (p. 1721)
Potter, Samuel Otway Lewis. Compend of Visceral Anatomy: Especially Adapted to the Use of Medical Students (Classic Reprint) (p. 433)
Potter, Sandra Dawn, jt. auth. see Kshir, Donna M.
Potter, Shira. Monster at Recess: A Book about Teasing, Bullying & Building Friendships. (p. 1495)
Potter, T. Chalmers. Bee-Keeping for Sedentary Folk, or for Professional People: The Clergyman, the Lawyer, the Doctor, the Teacher & All Others Whose Duties in Life Render It Necessary for Them to Be Mostly Indoors but Who Feel the Need of Some Suitable Recreation in the O. (p. 189)
—Queenie: The Autobiography of an Italian Queen Bee (Classic Reprint) (p. 1824)
Potter, Thomas Rossell. History & Antiquities of Charnwood Forest: With an Appendix on the Geology, Botany & Ornithology of the District (Classic Reprint) (p. 976)
Potter, Tina & Dietrich, Kenny. Secrets in the Forest. (p. 1980)
Potter, Tony, jt. compiled by see Crosbie, Duncan.
Potter, Tracy. Charlie the Chimp's Day Out. (p. 360)
Potter, V. M. To Europe on a Stretcher (Classic Reprint) (p. 2252)
Potter, William. By the Shore. Calle, Juan, illus. (p. 306)
—Creepy Mazes. Trinidad, Leo, illus. (p. 473)
—Dangerous Mazes. Trinidad, Leo, illus. (p. 502)
—Desert Animals. Calle, Juan, illus. (p. 531)
—Dinosaur Activity Book. (p. 548)
—Epic Adventures Calle, Juan, illus. (p. 657)
—Fact-Packed Animal Activity Book. Coleman, Stephanie Fizer, illus. (p. 694)
—Fact-Packed Dinosaur Activity Book. Coleman, Stephanie Fizer, illus. (p. 694)
—Fantastic Monsters Calle, Juan, illus. (p. 707)
—Forest Animals. Calle, Juan, illus. (p. 765)
—Gothic Horror Calle, Juan, illus. (p. 872)
—Grassland Animals. Calle, Juan, illus. (p. 881)
—Heroes of History & Myth Calle, Juan, illus. (p. 962)
—How to Create Fantasy Art. Calle, Juan, illus. (p. 1039)
—Jungle Animals. Calle, Juan, illus. (p. 1189)
—Moon Explorer's Model Book: Includes 2 Fantastic Models. Deo, Laura, illus. (p. 1501)
—Open Waters. Calle, Juan, illus. (p. 1666)
—Over the Reef. Calle, Juan, illus. (p. 1686)
—Scary Mazes. Trinidad, Leo, illus. (p. 1943)
—Space Creativity Book. (p. 2071)
—Steampunk World Calle, Juan, illus. (p. 2111)
—Super Cute Drawing Book: Step-By-step Kawaii Creatures! Emelyanova, Tanya, illus. (p. 2154)
—Urban Magic Calle, Juan, illus. (p. 2339)
—Weird Mazes. Trinidad, Leo, illus. (p. 2397)
—Whales, Sharks, & Dolphins. Calle, Juan, illus. (p. 2404)
—Whizz Kidz: Brain Puzzles. Scott, Matthew, illus. (p. 2446)
—Whizz Kidz: Number Puzzles. Scott, Matthew, illus. (p. 2446)
Potter, William, jt. auth. see Butterfield, Moira.
Potter, William, jt. auth. see Calle, Juan.
Potter, William, jt. auth. see Trinidad, Leo.
Potter, William, jt. auth. see Virr, Paul.
Potters, Rebecca. Happy Halloween! (Kindi Kids) (p. 922)
Potthast, Edward, jt. auth. see Stuart, Ruth McEnery.
Pottinger, Henry. Blue & Green, or the Gift of God, Vol. 1 Of 3: A Romance of Old Constantinople (Classic Reprint) (p. 248)
—Blue & Green or, the Gift of God, Vol. 3 Of 3: A Romance of Old Constantinople (Classic Reprint) (p. 248)
Pottle, Emery Bemsley. Late Mr. Rollins & Other College Farces (Classic Reprint) (p. 1250)
Pottle, Frederick Albert. Stretchers: The Story of a Hospital Unit on the Western Front (Classic Reprint) (p. 2141)
Pottle, Robert, jt. auth. see Lansky, Bruce.
Pottorf, Patricia D. Hebee, the Quibber. (p. 947)
Potts Dawson, Eileen, illus. see Wagner, Jay.
Potts, Edward L. Bright Side: With History of My Life (Classic Reprint) (p. 281)
Potts, Francesca. All about Allergies. (p. 48)
—All about Broken Bones. (p. 48)
—All about Colds. (p. 49)
—All about Cuts & Bruises. (p. 49)
—All about Ear Infections. (p. 49)
—All about Sore Throats. (p. 50)
—Left Brain, Right Brain: Facts, Trivia, & Quizzes. (p. 1261)

P

—What's Your Personality? Facts, Trivia, & Quizzes. (p. 2427)
Potts, Henry. Circuit Companions (Classic Reprint) (p. 393)
Potts, Molly. Falling Moon. (p. 701)
Potts, Nikki. Frog Moves Out of the Rain Forest. Lenoir, Maarten, illus. (p. 789)
—Goat Moves Out of the Barnyard. Lenoir, Maarten, illus. (p. 849)
—Habitat Hunter. Lenoir, Maarten, illus. (p. 908)
—It Disappears! Magical Animals That Hide in Plain Sight. (p. 1141)
—It Glows! Magical Animals That Give off Light. (p. 1141)
—It Transforms! Magical Animals That Change Before Your Eyes. (p. 1142)
—It's Still Alive! Magical Animals That Regrow Parts. (p. 1147)
—Magical Animals. (p. 1379)
—Meerkat Moves Out of the Desert. Lenoir, Maarten, illus. (p. 1437)
—My First Guide to Fast Vehicles. (p. 1544)
—Owl Moves Out of the Forest. Lenoir, Maarten, illus. (p. 1689)
—Penguin Moves Out of the Antarctic. Lenoir, Maarten, illus. (p. 1716)
—Shark Moves Out of the Ocean. Lenoir, Maarten, illus. (p. 2002)
—Totally Amazing Facts about Cats. (p. 2266)
Potts, Nikki, jt. auth. see Wedel, Mathew J.
Potts, Pk. Little Girl Named Sad. Roehrig, Nancy, ed. (p. 1317)
Potts, Steve. American Alligators (p. 70)
—American Bison (p. 70)
—Armadillos (p. 117)
—Iroquois. (p. 1136)
Potts, Steve, et al. North American Animals. (p. 1620)
Potts, Sue. Get Fit with Video Workouts. (p. 823)
Potts, William. Under My Pillow. (p. 2321)
Potvvin, K. Potwin. What Girls Can Do: Not to Be Ministered unto but to Minister (Classic Reprint) (p. 2410)
Pötzsch, Oliver & Pötzsch, Oliver. Sword of Power. McGill, Jaime, tr. (p. 2171)
Pouatcha, Pearly. Die Geheimnisvolle Blume. Schroer, P., tr. (p. 543)
—Fleur Mystique. Fedor, Ashley, ed. (p. 748)
Pouchain, Martin. Fete des Fous. (p. 721)
Pouchet, Félix-Archimède. Zoologie Classique, Ou Histoire Naturelle du Regne Animal, Vol. 2: Contenant les Animaux Invertebres (Classic Reprint) (p. 2543)
Pouchet, G. & Guillaume, J. Societe de l'Histoire de la Revolution Francaise; les Sciences Pendant la Terreur; d'Apres les Documents du Temps et les Piecel des Archives Nationales. (p. 2053)
Poulakidas, Georgene. Civil War. (p. 396)
Poulin, Andree. Best Time. Beha, Philippe, illus. (p. 208)
—Magic Clothesline. Arbona, Marion, illus. (p. 1377)
—Monkey in the Mud. Eudes-Pascal, Elisabeth, illus. (p. 1493)
Poulin, Andrée. That's Not Hockey! Girard, Félix, illus. (p. 2213)
—Worst Time. Beha, Philippe, illus. (p. 2509)
Poulin, Ashley, jt. auth. see Feierabend, John M.
Poulin, Bernard A. Hold My Hand: A Father & Son Book. Bercier, Dominic, illus. (p. 987)
Pouliot, Pamela Davis. Xola Lola's Journey from Mexico to Vermont. (p. 2516)
Poulsen, David A. Last Sam's Cage. (p. 1249)
—Numbers. (p. 1630)
—Old Man. (p. 1647)
—Shivers & Shakes. (p. 2008)
Poulsen, E. D. Journey for Sol. (p. 1181)
Poulsson, Emilie. Finger Plays for Nursery & Kindergarten. Bridgman, L. T., illus. (p. 731)
—Finger Plays for Nursery & Kindergarten (Classic Reprint) (p. 731)
—In the Child's World: Morning Talks & Stories for Kindergartens, Primary Schools & Homes (Classic Reprint) (p. 1108)
—In the Child's World. (p. 1108)
—Kindergarten Review, 1900-1901, Vol. 11 (Classic Reprint) (p. 1218)
—Runaway Donkey, & Other Rhymes for Children (Classic Reprint) (p. 1915)
—Top-Of-the-World: Stories for Boys & Girls (Classic Reprint) (p. 2263)
—What Happened to Inger Johanne: As Told by Herself (Classic Reprint) (p. 2411)
Poulsson, Laura E. Lisbeth Longfrock: Translated from the Norwegian of Hans Aanrud (Classic Reprint) (p. 1308)
Poulter, David. Morris & Mini Minor & Friends: A Day at the Seaside. (p. 1506)
Poulter, John. Discoveries of John Poulter, Alias Baxter: Who Was Apprehended for Robbing Dr. Hancock of Salisbury, on Clarken down, near Bath; & Thereupon Discovered a Most Numerous Gang of Villains, Many of Which Have Been Already Taken (Classic Reprint) (p. 555)
Poulton, Emma E. Transforming. (p. 2277)
Poulton, Mark, jt. auth. see Marz, Ron.
Pound, Blake. Deer Hunting. (p. 525)
—Duck Hunting. (p. 608)
—Fly Fishing. (p. 754)
—Pheasant Hunting. (p. 1733)
Pound, Brinkley Burks. When Eva Hollers. Kiszla, Paula Ingram & Kiszla, B. Matthew, illus. (p. 2430)
Pound, Louise. Blends, Their Relation to English Word Formation (Classic Reprint) (p. 243)
Pound, Sandra R. Keaton's Carrots. Watson, Emily Grace, illus. (p. 1207)
Pounder, Sibéal. Bad Mermaids Make Waves. Cockcroft, Jason, illus. (p. 158)
—Witch Switch. Anderson, Laura Ellen, illus. (p. 2480)
—Witch Wars. Anderson, Laura Ellen, illus. (p. 2480)
Pounders, Louis. Frank, an Architect's Dog. (p. 776)
Pountney, Beth, jt. auth. see Bicknell, Joanna.
Poupard, illus. see Beka.
Pouriseth, Phal, illus. see pierSath, Chath.
Pourquie, Bernadette & Gambini, Cécile. Strange Trees: And the Stories Behind Them. Broad, Yolanda Stern, tr. (p. 2138)
Pousette, Kelly. Do Not Rake Your Garden in a Party Dress. (p. 570)
Pousette, Kelly, illus. see Bar-el, Dan.
Pousette, Kelly, illus. see Dyer, Nick.
Pousette, Kelly, illus. see Van, Muon Thi.
Pouson, Mel, ed. see Bailey, Diane.
Pouson, Mel, ed. see Gardner, Jane.
Pouson, Mel, ed. see Jane Gardner.
Pouson, Mel, ed. see Rich, Mari.
Poux, Jennifer. Amazing Women in Sports: Issue #5. (p. 67)
—Chloe X Halle: Issue #2. (p. 380)
—Jonas Brothers: Issue #4. (p. 1177)
Pova, Rosie J. If I Weren't with You. (p. 1091)
Povenmire, Dan, illus. see O'Ryan, Ellie.
Povey, Andrea, illus. see Kane, Gillian.
Povey, Jeff. Delete. (p. 526)
—Shift. (p. 2007)
Pow, Tom. Sixteen String Jack & the Garden of Adventure. Andrew, Ian, illus. (p. 2029)
Powell, Angela. Alicia's Blended Family. Gillen, Rosemarie, illus. (p. 46)
Powell, Anthony. Afternoon Men: A Novel (Classic Reprint) (p. 34)
—Our Cat Hogan - Could He Be Part Dog? Stodden, Lindsay, illus. (p. 1677)
Powell, Anton, jt. auth. see Steele, Philip.
Powell, B. D. William Mcfadden & the Puzzle Organ 2nd Edition. (p. 2468)
Powell, Baden. General & Elementary View of the Undulatory Theory: As Applied to the Dispersion of Light, & Some Other Subjects, Including the Substance of Several Papers, Printed in the Philosophical Transactions, & Other Journals (Classic Reprint) (p. 814)
—General & Elementary View of the Undulatory Theory, As Applied to the Dispersion of Light, & Some Other Subjects. (p. 814)
—General & Elementary View of the Undulatory Theory As Applied to the Dispersion of Light - Scholar's Choice Edition. (p. 814)
Powell, Carmen. Matthew & the Magic Goat. (p. 1426)
Powell, Charles. Poets in the Nursery (Classic Reprint) (p. 1767)
Powell, Christine. Bootsie's Underground Adventure. (p. 262)
Powell, Claire, illus. see Berkman, Pam & Hearst, Dorothy.
Powell, Claire, illus. see Sperring, Mark.
Powell, Consie. Peregrine's Sky. Powell, Consie, illus. (p. 1721)
Powell, Consie, illus. see Bevis, Mary.
Powell, Consie, illus. see Jones, Jennifer Berry.
Powell, Consie, illus. see Kurtz, Kevin.
Powell, Consie, illus. see Miche, Mary.
Powell, Consie, illus. see Miché, Mary.
Powell, Consie, illus. see Radcliffe, Robin.
Powell, Consie, illus. see Ross, Michael Elsohn.
Powell, Cortney Faye. Melowy Vol. 1: The Test of Magic. Jampole, Ryan, illus. (p. 1443)
—Melowy Vol. 2: The Fashion Club of Colors. Jampole, Ryan, illus. (p. 1443)
—Melowy Vol. 3: Time to Fly. Jampole, Ryan, illus. (p. 1443)
Powell, Cortney Faye, jt. auth. see Star, Danielle.
Powell, Daniel M. King Grrr-egory & the Angel. (p. 1220)
Powell, Dawn. Locusts Have No King (Classic Reprint) (p. 1339)
—Whither (Classic Reprint) (p. 2445)
Powell, Debbie. Trucks. Powell, Debbie, illus. (p. 2293)
Powell, Debbie, illus. see Big Picture Press.
Powell, Dimity. At the End of Holyrood Lane. Johnston, Nicky, illus. (p. 130)
—Fix-It Man. Johnston, Nicky, illus. (p. 745)
Powell, Doug, jt. auth. see Parker, Amy.
Powell, E. Sandy. Washington. (p. 2381)
Powell, Elizabeth. Math at the Game. (p. 1421)
—Math at the Zoo. (p. 1421)
Powell, Eric. Hillbilly. (p. 972)
Powell, Eric, illus. see Twain, Mark, pseud.
Powell, Eric, et al. Spook House 2. Marsh, Tracy, ed. (p. 2086)
Powell, F. York. Old Stories from British History (Classic Reprint) (p. 1648)
Powell, Frances. by-Ways of Braithe (Classic Reprint) (p. 306)
—House on the Hudson (Classic Reprint) (p. 1023)
—Old Maid's Vengeance (Classic Reprint) (p. 1647)
—Old Mr. Davenant's Money (Classic Reprint) (p. 1647)
—Prisoner of Ornith Farm (Classic Reprint) (p. 1801)
Powell, G. H. Animal Episodes & Studies in Sensation. (p. 89)
—Animal Episodes & Studies in Sensation (Classic Reprint) (p. 89)
Powell, Gary Allison. In That Land There Are Giants. Johnston, Jillian S., illus. (p. 1107)
Powell, Gregg E. Goobadabers. Lea, Corinne, illus. (p. 861)
Powell, Huw. Lost Sword: A Spacejackers Novel. (p. 1355)
—Pirate King. (p. 1750)
—Spacejackers. (p. 2073)
Powell, Ida Adaline. Driftwood (Classic Reprint) (p. 604)
Powell, James. House of Fear: Attack of the Killer Snowmen & Other Stories. Morales, Jethro & Jensen, Josh, illus. (p. 1023)
Powell, James, illus. see Tingwald, Jady Ann.
Powell, James, illus. see Tingwald, July Ann.
Powell, Janet. St. Louis Zoo. (p. 2097)
Powell, Jennifer. Colors of Mackinac Island. Powell, Jennifer, photos by. (p. 426)
Powell, Jenny. Putting on a Play: Stop Bullying Me! (p. 1818)
Powell, Jessica Ernst, tr. see Iturralde, Edna.
Powell, Jillian. Aztecs. (p. 146)
—China. (p. 377)
—Discover Through Craft: China & the Shang Dynasty. (p. 555)
—Discover Through Craft: the Maya. (p. 555)
—Egypt. (p. 628)
—Egyptians. (p. 629)
—Explaining Cystic Fibrosis. (p. 679)
—First World War: Band 11 Lime/Band 16 Sapphire (Collins Big Cat Progress) (p. 740)
—Greeks. (p. 893)
—Hattie the Dancing Hippo. Dodson, Emma, illus. (p. 937)
—India. (p. 1115)
—My New Babysitter. (p. 1557)
—My New Friend. (p. 1558)
—My New Sister. (p. 1558)
—My New Stepdad. (p. 1558)
—Oh, Jet! (p. 1641)
—Olympic Heroes: Band 05/Green (Collins Big Cat) (p. 1651)
—Projects with Rainforests. (p. 1806)
—Projects with Weather & Seasons. (p. 1806)
—Romans. (p. 1901)
—Vikings. (p. 2357)
—War Art: Band 10 White/Band 17 Diamond (Collins Big Cat Progress) (p. 2376)
Powell, Jillian & Buckingham, Matt. Middle Ages. (p. 1460)
Powell, Jillian & O'Shea, Clare. Cooking with Cereals & Grains. (p. 447)
Powell, Kelley. Merit Birds. (p. 1448)
Powell, Kelly. Songs from the Deep. (p. 2063)
Powell, Laura. Burn Mark. (p. 299)
—Witch Fire. (p. 2479)
Powell, Luciana Navarro. My Dad Is the Best Playground. (p. 1536)
Powell, Luciana Navarro, illus. see Bryant, Megan E.
Powell, Luciana Navarro, illus. see Christie, Tory.
Powell, Luciana Navarro, illus. see Dealey, Erin.
Powell, Luciana Navarro, illus. see Paul, Miranda.
Powell, Luciana Navarro, illus. see Rosa-Mendoza, Gladys.
Powell, Luciana Navarro, illus. see Schwartz, Betty & Seresin, Lynn.
Powell, Marc & Neal, David. How to Draw Action Manga. (p. 1039)
—How to Draw Cute Manga. (p. 1040)
—How to Draw Dramatic Manga. (p. 1040)
—How to Draw Fantasy Manga. (p. 1040)
—How to Draw Manga Adventure. (p. 1041)
—How to Draw Manga Mecha. (p. 1041)
Powell, Margaret E., jt. auth. see Messner, Kate.
Powell, Marie. Asking Questions about Video Games. (p. 126)
—Asking Questions about Violence in Popular Culture. (p. 126)
—Dan Can! Cartwright, Amy, illus. (p. 499)
—Explore with Ferdinand Magellan. (p. 680)
—Explore with Jacques Cartier. (p. 680)
—Go to Bed, Ted! Cartwright, Amy, illus. (p. 848)
—Map Trap. Cartwright, Amy, illus. (p. 1401)
—Native Nations of the Arctic & Subarctic. (p. 1578)
—Stop, Pop! Cartwright, Amy, illus. (p. 2122)
—Stop Right There: A Book about Periods. (p. 2122)
—Take a Pause, Paul: A Book about Commas. Lewis, Anthony, illus. (p. 2176)
—This Is Exciting! A Book about Exclamation Points. (p. 2224)
—Traditional Stories of the Arctic & Subarctic Nations. (p. 2273)
—Traditional Stories of the Plains Nations. (p. 2273)
—Unsolved! (p. 2335)
—We're Going to the Smiths' House: A Book about Apostrophes. (p. 2400)
—What Good Is a U? (p. 2411)
—What Good Is a Y? (p. 2411)
—What Good Is an A? (p. 2411)
—What Good Is an E? (p. 2411)
—What Good Is an I? (p. 2411)
—What Good Is an O? (p. 2411)
—What Is That? A Book about Question Marks. Lewis, Anthony, illus. (p. 2416)
—When, Jen? Cartwright, Amy, illus. (p. 2431)
—Win, Min! By Marie Powell: Illustrated by Amy Cartwright. Cartwright, Amy, illus. (p. 2470)
Powell, Marie, jt. auth. see Heos, Bridget.
Powell, Marie, jt. auth. see Norton, Jeff.
Powell, Martin. Fog of Fear (p. 756)
—Private Eye Princess & the Emerald Pea: A Graphic Novel. Cano, Fernando, illus. (p. 1801)
—Rapunzel vs. Frankenstein: A Graphic Novel. Lozano, Omar, illus. (p. 1842)
—Seven Voyages of Sinbad Pérez, Daniel et al, illus. (p. 1994)
—Seven Voyages of Sinbad. Pérez, Daniel et al, illus. (p. 1994)
Powell, Martin A. Fog of Fear. (p. 756)
—Stolen Superpowers (p. 2120)
Powell, Martin A., et al. Stolen Superpowers. (p. 2121)
Powell, Martin & Rayo, Alberto. Far Out Fairy Tales. Lozano, Omar, illus. (p. 708)
Powell, Mary. Cherry Violet: A Tale of the Great Plague (Classic Reprint) (p. 366)
—Poplar House Academy, Vol. 1 of 2 (Classic Reprint) (p. 1776)
—Tasso & Leonora (Classic Reprint) (p. 2192)
—Year Nine: A Tale of the Tyrol (Classic Reprint) (p. 2519)
Powell, Maud Macrory. City of Grit & Gold. (p. 395)
Powell, Melissa. Tongue Twister Competition. (p. 2260)
Powell, Mia, illus. see Gianferrari, Maria.
Powell, Michael. Do My Ears Ever Stop Growing? And 70 Other Questions That Keep You Awake at Night. (p. 570)
Powell, Nate, illus. see Castellucci, Cecil.
Powell, Nate, illus. see Lewis, John & Aydin, Andrew.
Powell, Nathan, illus. see Riordan, Rick & Venditti, Robert.
Powell, Patricia Hruby. Josephine: The Dazzling Life of Josephine Baker. Robinson, Christian, illus. (p. 1179)
—Lift As You Climb: The Story of Ella Baker. Christie, R. Gregory, illus. (p. 1297)
—Loving vs. Virginia: A Documentary Novel of the Landmark Civil Rights Case. Strickland, Shadra, illus. (p. 1362)
Powell, R. A. Odd Socks. (p. 1637)
Powell, Rich, illus. see Highlights for Children Editorial Staff.
Powell, Richard & Powell, Richard. If You See a Cow. Martin Larranaga, Ana, illus. (p. 1093)
—If You See a Tiger. Martin Larranaga, Ana, illus. (p. 1093)
Powell, Robert. Princess & the Lion Tamer. (p. 1796)
Powell, Robert, et al. Aani & the Tree Huggers. Moore, Nancy & Springhouse Publishing Company Staff, eds. (p. 2)
Powell, Sammy. Arrowheads, Inc. Finethy, Buddy, illus. (p. 119)
—Fox Tree. (p. 774)
—Little John's Secret. Finethy, Buddy, illus. (p. 1319)
Powell, Sarah Deanna & Hazel, Tony. Budleigh & Rexford. (p. 290)
—Princess Porcelaina. (p. 1799)
Powell Smith, Brendan. Baby Moses: The Brick Bible for Kids. (p. 151)
—Daniel in the Lions' Den: The Brick Bible for Kids. (p. 503)
—Jonah & the Whale: The Brick Bible for Kids. (p. 1177)
Powell Sr., Liam Patrick. 1-2-3 Under-Dog! (p. 2545)
Powell, Sydney Walter. Noah's Ark: A Novel (Classic Reprint) (p. 1616)
Powell, Tiger. Gummy Bear. (p. 905)
—Obamabear: Hail to the Chief. (p. 1634)
—Smiley Riley & the Golden Gate Warriors. (p. 2042)
Powell, Vicky Lyn & Powell Jr, Joseph Leroy. Crabapple Tree Series: Wilber's Story. (p. 465)
Powell, Walter. How to Draw the Life & Times of Andrew Johnson. (p. 1041)
Powell, Walter L. Benedict Arnold: Revolutionary War Hero & Traitor. (p. 199)
Powell, William F. Perspective. (p. 1725)
Powell-Tuck, Maudie. Last Stop on the Reindeer Express. Mountford, Karl James, illus. (p. 1249)
—Messy Book. Smythe, Richard, illus. (p. 1452)
—Pirates Aren't Afraid of the Dark! Edgson, Alison, illus. (p. 1750)
—Pumpkin Party! Guile, Gill, illus. (p. 1813)
—Space Train. Mountford, Karl James, illus. (p. 2072)
—Very Merry Christmas. Guile, Gill, illus. (p. 2353)
Powelson, Jannifer. Rachel & Sammy Learn about Trees. (p. 1832)
Power, Alice, illus. see Delaney, Majella.
Power, Bob. Dodge Vipers. (p. 574)
—Ferraris. (p. 721)
—Lamborghinis. (p. 1240)
—Maseratis. (p. 1417)
Power, Bob & Roza, Greg. Sports Tips, Techniques, & Strategies: An Insider's Guide to Paintball (p. 2089)
Power, Effie. First Selection of Five Hundred Children's Books by the Michigan State (Classic Reprint) (p. 739)
Power, Effie L. List of Books for Girls (Classic Reprint) (p. 1308)
—Lists of Stories & Programs for Story Hours (Classic Reprint) (p. 1309)
Power, Eileen, jt. auth. see Power, Rhoda.
Power, Elle, illus. see Larson, Hope & Ball, Jackie.
Power, Elle, illus. see Rivera, Lilliam.
Power, Eloise. Apple Tree Inside of Me. (p. 107)
Power, Frank. Letters from Khartoum: Written During the Siege. (p. 1279)
—Letters from Khartoum: Written During the Siege (Classic Reprint) (p. 1279)
Power, J. Tracey. Stonewall Jackson: Hero of the Confederacy. (p. 2122)
Power, Laura. Air-Born. (p. 37)
Power, Marguerite A. Keepsake, 1851 (Classic Reprint) (p. 1208)
—Nelly Carew, Vol. 1 of 2 (Classic Reprint) (p. 1586)
—Nelly Carew, Vol. 2 of 2 (Classic Reprint) (p. 1586)
—Sweethearts & Wives, Vol. 1 of 3 (Classic Reprint) (p. 2169)
Power, Michael. Zoo. (p. 2543)
Power, Molly. Up & down with Lena Larocha. Carter, Barbara, illus. (p. 2337)
Power, Nicholas D. Paudie's Magical Adventures. (p. 1706)
Power, P. B. One Moss-Rose. (p. 1661)
Power, Philip Bennett. Oiled Feather (Classic Reprint) (p. 1643)
Power, Rhoda. Under the Bolshevik Reign of Terror. (p. 2321)
—Under the Bolshevik Reign of Terror (Classic Reprint) (p. 2321)
Power, Rhoda & Power, Eileen. Boys & Girls of History. (p. 272)
Power, Rory. Burn Our Bodies Down. (p. 299)
—Burn Our Bodies down 9-Copy Floor Display (p. 299)
—Burn Our Bodies down Indie Signed 9-Copy Floor Display (p. 300)
—Wilder Girls. (p. 2466)
Power, S. D. Art of Good Manners, or Children's Etiquette (Classic Reprint) (p. 121)
Power, Teresa. ABCs of Yoga for Kids. Rietz, Kathleen, illus. (p. 5)
Power, Teresa Anne. ABCs of Yoga for Kids 56 Learning Cards. Rietz, Kathleen, illus. (p. 5)
—ABECE de Yoga para Ninos. Rietz, Kathleen, illus. (p. 5)
Power, Tyrone. Impressions of America, Vol. 1 Of 2: During the Years 1833, 1834, & 1835 (Classic Reprint) (p. 1102)
Powers, Alfred. Marooned in Crater Lake: Stories of the Skyline Trail, the Umpqua Trail, & the Old Oregon Trail. (p. 1408)
—Marooned in Crater Lake: Stories of the Skyline Trail, the Umpqua Trail, & the Old Oregon Trail (Classic Reprint) (p. 1408)
Powers, Carol Hoyt. Isle of Whims (Classic Reprint) (p. 1140)
Powers, David M. F. Schmetterling Ohne Flügel. Vail, Sue, tr. (p. 1944)
Powers, Elaine A. Don't Call Me Turtle. Thorpe, Nicholas, illus. (p. 582)
Powers, Ella M. Silver-Burdett Readers: First Book (Classic Reprint) (p. 2019)
—Silver-Burdett Readers: Third Book (Classic Reprint) (p. 2019)
Powers, Ella Marie. Silver-Burdett Readers, Vol. 2 (Classic Reprint) (p. 2019)
—Stories of Famous Pictures (Classic Reprint) (p. 2125)
Powers, Elvira J. Hospital Pencillings: Being a Diary While in Jefferson General Hospital, Jeffersonville, Ind., & Others at Nashville, Tennessee, As Matron & Visitor (Classic Reprint) (p. 1006)
—Hospital Pencillings. (p. 1006)
Powers, Gayvin. Iona Fay: An Irish Fairy Tale. (p. 1133)
—Iona Fay & the Fire Keepers: A Modern Fairy Tale Adventure. (p. 1133)
Powers, Gretchen Ellen, illus. see Warner, Gertrude Chandler.
Powers, Helen. Tattoos & Tiramisu. (p. 2193)
Powers, J. L. Amina. (p. 75)
—Colors of the Wind: The Story of Blind Artist & Champion Runner George Mendoza. Mendoza, George, illus. (p. 426)

P

—Good Night, Zombie. Bruno, Iacopo, illus. (p. 865)
—Home Sweet Horror. (p. 997)
—Home Sweet Horror. Bruno, Iacopo, illus. (p. 997)
—I Scream, You Scream! Bruno, Iacopo, illus. (p. 1081)
—Jigsaw Jones: the Case from Outer Space. (p. 1168)
—Jigsaw Jones: the Case of the Bear Scare. (p. 1168)
—Jigsaw Jones: the Case of the Best Pet Ever. (p. 1168)
—Jigsaw Jones: the Case of the Bicycle Bandit. (p. 1168)
—Jigsaw Jones: the Case of the Buried Treasure. (p. 1168)
—Jigsaw Jones: the Case of the Disappearing Dinosaur. (p. 1168)
—Jigsaw Jones: the Case of the Glow-In-the-Dark Ghost. (p. 1168)
—Jigsaw Jones: the Case of the Hat Burglar. Alley, R. W., illus. (p. 1168)
—Jigsaw Jones: the Case of the Haunted Scarecrow. (p. 1168)
—Jigsaw Jones: the Case of the Vanishing Painting. (p. 1168)
—Nightmareland. Bruno, Iacopo, illus. (p. 1608)
—Pirate's Guide to First Grade. (p. 1751)
—Pirate's Guide to First Grade. Ruth, Greg, illus. (p. 1751)
—Worst Mascot Ever. (p. 2509)
Preller, James, jt. auth. see Barbo, Maria S.
Preller, James, jt. auth. see Kovacs, Deborah.
Prelutsky, Jack. Carnival of the Animals. GrandPre, Mary, illus. (p. 332)
—Good Sports: Rhymes about Running, Jumping, Throwing, & More. Raschka, Chris, illus. (p. 866)
—It's Christmas! (p. 1144)
—It's Christmas! Hafner, Marylin, illus. (p. 1144)
—It's Raining Pigs & Noodles. Stevenson, James, illus. (p. 1147)
—It's Valentine's Day! (p. 1148)
—It's Valentine's Day. Hafner, Marylin, illus. (p. 1148)
—I've Lost My Hippopotamus. Urbanovic, Jackie, illus. (p. 1149)
—New Kid on the Block. Stevenson, James, illus. (p. 1595)
—Silver Moon: Lullabies & Cradle Songs. Ishida, Jui, illus. (p. 2019)
—Something Big Has Been Here. Stevenson, James, illus. (p. 2060)
—Stardines Swim High Across the Sky: And Other Poems. Berger, Carin, illus. (p. 2106)
—There's No Place Like School: Classroom Poems. Manning, Jane, illus. (p. 2218)
Preminger, Tanya. Sean Goes to Barcelona: A Children's Book about Soccer & Goals. Cudignotto, Elettra, illus. (p. 1970)
Premise Entertainment, illus. see Disney Book Group.
Premise Entertainment, illus. see Disney Books.
Premise Entertainment, illus. see Weeks, Kermit.
Premo Steele, Cassie. Resisters. Alley, Amy, illus. (p. 1869)
Premonville, Marie de & Volpari, Daniela. Cleopatra: Queen of the Nile. (p. 403)
Prénat, Sophie. Ultimate Spotlight: Trains. Schleef, Vinciane, illus. (p. 2315)
Prendergast, G. S. Cold Falling White. (p. 413)
—Zero Repeat Forever. (p. 2540)
Prendergast, Gabrielle. Audacious (p. 136)
—Capricious (p. 324)
—Frail Days (p. 775)
—If Pluto Was a Pea. Gerlings, Rebecca, illus. (p. 1092)
—Pandas on the Eastside (p. 1696)
—Pinch Me (p. 1745)
Prendergast, Gabrielle S. Cero Se Repite Siempre. (p. 353)
Prendergast, Kate. Dog on a Digger. Prendergast, Kate, illus. (p. 576)
—Sleep: How Nature Gets Its Rest. Prendergast, Kate, illus. (p. 2036)
Prendergast, R. L. Baby, Please Go to Sleep. Macibórski, Charmaine, illus. (p. 152)
Prendergast, Thomas. Mastery Series: Latin (Classic Reprint) (p. 1420)
—Mastery Series: French (Classic Reprint) (p. 1420)
Prentice, Amy. Towser Dog's Story (Classic Reprint) (p. 2270)
Prentice, Andrew. Amelia Earhart (the First Names Series) Smith, Mike, illus. (p. 69)
—Ghost & Bone. (p. 827)
—Write Your Own Sci-Fi & Fantasy Stories IR. (p. 2512)
Prentice, Emmett & Kalan. Dudley & the Forest Monster. (p. 609)
Prentice Hall Dictionary Editors. Middle Grades Math - Course 2: Tools for Success. (p. 1460)
Prentice Hall Directories Staff. Middle Grades Math - Course 1: Tools for Success. (p. 1460)
Prentice, Hiram Buck. Our Homage to the Past: An Historical Address Delivered at Founder's Day Celebration of Illinois Woman's College, Jacksonville, Illinois, October 13, 1910 (Classic Reprint) (p. 1678)
Prentice, Justin & Prentice, Jeff. It Can Be Scary When You Move. (p. 1141)
Prentice, May Humphrey. Children's Library (Classic Reprint) (p. 374)
Prentice, Priscilla, illus. see Robertson, Rachel.
Prentice-Hall Staff. Prentice Hall - Explorations & Applications: A Pre-Algebra Approach, 1999. (p. 1787)
Prenting, Ruth. I Spy ABC: Totally Crazy Letters. Ancutici, Manuela, photos by. (p. 1082)
Prentiss. How Sorrow Was Changed into Sympathy: Words of Cheer for Mothers, Bereft of Little Children (Classic Reprint) (p. 1035)
Prentiss, C. W. Polydactylism in Man & the Domestic Animals, with Especial Reference to Digital Variations in Swine (Classic Reprint) (p. 1772)
Prentiss, E. Aunt Jane's Hero (Classic Reprint) (p. 137)
—Avis Benson: Or, Mine & Thine; with Other Sketches (Classic Reprint) (p. 143)
—Little Lou's Sayings & Doings (Classic Reprint) (p. 1321)
—Little Susy's Little Servants (Classic Reprint) (p. 1328)
—Pemaquid a Story of Old Times in New England (Classic Reprint) (p. 1714)
Prentiss, Elizabeth. Aunt Jane's Hero. (p. 137)
—Flower of the Family: A Book for Girls (Classic Reprint) (p. 752)
—Fred, & Maria, & Me (Classic Reprint) (p. 780)
—Home at Greylock (Classic Reprint) (p. 995)
—Little Susy's Six Birthdays. (p. 1328)
—Little Susy's Six Birthdays (Classic Reprint) (p. 1328)
—Little Susy's Six Teachers (Classic Reprint) (p. 1328)
—Little Susy's Six Teachers - Scholar's Choice Edition. (p. 1328)
—Six Little Princesses & What They Turned Into: And Other Fairy Tales (Classic Reprint) (p. 2028)
—Stepping Heavenward. (p. 2115)
—Stepping Heavenward (Classic Reprint) (p. 2115)
Prentiss, Janet. Just Plain Peter (Classic Reprint) (p. 1194)
Prentzas. Democratic Republic of Congo. (p. 528)
—It's Cool to Learn about Countries: Iran. (p. 1144)
—It's Cool to Learn about Countries: Democratic Republic of Congo. (p. 1144)
Prentzas, G. S. Arkansas (Revised Edition) (p. 116)
—Brooklyn Bridge. (p. 285)
—Cuban Revolution. (p. 482)
—Emancipation Proclamation. (p. 640)
—Georgia. (p. 820)
—Law & Your Family: Your Legal Rights (p. 1253)
—Lost at Sea. (p. 1352)
—Marshall Plan. (p. 1409)
—Roanoke. (p. 1889)
—Smart Strategies for Paying for College. (p. 2041)
—Wyoming (Revised Edition) (p. 2515)
Prentzas, G. S., jt. text see Wilker, Josh.
Prentzas, G. S. (Scott). Truth about Inhalants. (p. 2296)
Prentzas, Scott. Gps. (p. 873)
—Radar Guns. (p. 1833)
Presbrey, Eugene Wiley. New England Folks: A Love Story (Classic Reprint) (p. 1593)
Presbury, B. F. Mustee, or Love & Liberty (Classic Reprint) (p. 1530)
Prescott, Anne M. Hawaii (Classic Reprint) (p. 940)
—Makapala-By-the-Sea, Vol. 1: Hawaii (Classic Reprint) (p. 1385)
Prescott, Augusta. Stairway on the Wall (Classic Reprint) (p. 2099)
Prescott, B. B. Aurona (p. 137)
Prescott, Brian. Chloe Knows Her Alphabet. (p. 380)
—Chloe Saves Christmas. (p. 380)
—Chloe the Campervan Goes on Holiday. (p. 380)
Prescott, Clara, illus. see Tonn, Jessica.
Prescott, Deborah Lee. Cane Di Nome Mitzvah: A Dog Named Mitzvah. (p. 322)
—Mazeltov, Mitzvah! (p. 1431)
—Mitzvah Gets Scared. (p. 1484)
—Mitzvah le Chien: Une Histoire Tres Vraie. (p. 1484)
Prescott, Deborah Lee & Felman, Ellen. Perro Llamado Mitzvah: A Dog Named Mitzvah. (p. 1724)
Prescott, Della R. Day in a Colonial Home (Classic Reprint) (p. 513)
Prescott, E. Livingston. Apotheosis of Mr. Tyrawley (Classic Reprint) (p. 106)
Prescott, Folami, jt. auth. see Kunjufu, Jawanza.
Prescott, Harriet Elizabeth. Amber Gods: And Other Stories (Classic Reprint) (p. 67)
—Azarian: An Episode (Classic Reprint) (p. 145)
Prescott, Katharine, tr. see de Balzac, Honore.
Preshous, Jody L. Who Flung Dung? (p. 2447)
Presley, Daniel & Polders, Claire. Whale in Paris. McGuire, Erin, illus. (p. 2403)
Presley, Elvis. Elvis Presley's Love Me Tender. Graegin, Stephanie, illus. (p. 640)
—Elvis Presley's Quiéreme con Ternura. Graegin, Stephanie, illus. (p. 640)
Presley, Loren John, illus. see Tucker, Michael P.
Presnall, Judith Janda. Yukon: Sled Dog Elliot, Mark, illus. (p. 2536)
Press, Applesauce. 3-D Disgusting Doodles Book & Kit: Where Your Gross-Out Imagination Jumps off the Page! (p. 2547)
Press, Bothwell. Naughty Madge & Other Old-Fashioned Children's Stories. (p. 1582)
Press, Cider Mill. Marshmallow Launcher: Ready, Aim, Fire-Here Come the Marshmallows! (p. 1409)
Press, Cider Mill, ed. What's Missing: Look & Look & Look-Can You Find What's Missing? (p. 2425)
Press, David P. Abraham Lincoln: The Great Emancipator. (p. 7)
Press, Disney Lucasfilm, illus. see Berne, Emma Carlson.
Press, Gazzapper. Marvelous Comic Creator: Blank Comic Book for Kids (150 Pages) (p. 1413)
Press, Gorham, jt. auth. see Sturgis, Granville Forbes.
Press, Hidden Helm. World of Wild Dogs. (p. 2504)
Press, Ignatius, et al. Our Life in the Church: 8 Grade Activity Book, Revised. (p. 1679)
Press, Indomita. What Doesn't Kill You: An Anthology of YA Short Fiction. (p. 2410)
Press, J. Abra-Ca-Doodle! (p. 7)
—Doodles of Sam Dibble. (p. 584)
—Double Trouble #2 Kline, Michael, illus. (p. 589)
Press, J. P. Welcome to Arabic with Sesame Street (r). (p. 2398)
—Welcome to French with Sesame Street (r). (p. 2398)
—Welcome to German with Sesame Street (r). (p. 2398)
—Welcome to Hebrew with Sesame Street (r). (p. 2398)
—Welcome to Mandarin Chinese with Sesame Street (r). (p. 2398)
—Welcome to Mandarin with Sesame Street (r). (p. 2398)
—Welcome to Spanish with Sesame Street (r). (p. 2398)
Press, Jenny, illus. see Barrie, J. M.
Press, Jenny, illus. see Baxter, Nicola.
Press, Jenny, illus. see Young, Lesley.
Press, John. Return of the Purple Paw. (p. 1871)
Press, Judy. Bubbe's Got the Beat Hall, Mary, illus. (p. 288)
—Case of the Missing Kiddush Cup. (p. 337)
—Pinky Bloom & the Case of the Missing Kiddush Cup. Waters, Erica-Jane, illus. (p. 1747)
Press, Little Bear. My Big Red Coloring Book Vol. 1: Over 100 Big Pages of Family Activity! Coloring, Abcs, 123s, Characters, Puzzles, Mazes, Shapes, Letters + Numbers for Boys, Girls, Toddlers & Even Adults! Age 3+ (p. 1533)
Press, Lucasfilm, illus. see Ausu, Meredith & Hopps, Kevin.
Press, Lucasfilm, illus. see Heddle, Jennifer & Kinberg, Simon.
Press, Lucasfilm, illus. see Schaefer, Elizabeth & Murray, Charles.
Press, Lucasfilm, illus. see Siglain, Michael, et al.
Press, Magdalene. Addition Facts Colouring Book 1-12: The Easy Way to Learn the Addition Tables. (p. 15)
—First 100 Instant Words Colouring Book: For Reading, Writing & Spelling Fluency. (p. 734)
—Multiplication Facts Colouring Book 1-12: The Easy Way to Learn the Times Tables. (p. 1525)
—Subtraction Facts Colouring Book 12-1: The Easy Way to Learn the Subtraction Tables. (p. 2146)
Press, Marvel, illus. see West, Alexandra.
Press, Minerva. Biography of a Spaniel: To Which Is Annexed the Idiot; a Tale (Classic Reprint) (p. 229)
—Enchanter, or Wonderful Story Teller: In Which Is Contained a Series of Adventures, Curious, Surprising, & Uncommon; Calculated to Amuse, Instruct, & Improve Younger Minds (Classic Reprint) (p. 647)
—Fairiest: Or Surprising & Entertaining Adventures of the Aerial Beings (Classic Reprint) (p. 696)
—My Bird & My Dog: A Tale for Youth (Classic Reprint) (p. 1533)
PRESS, Modern Curriculum. Long Vowels (p. 1343)
Press, Muriel A. C. Laxdaela Saga: Translated from the Icelandic (Classic Reprint) (p. 1253)
Press, Muriel A. C., tr. see Anonymous.
Press, Odhams. Picturegoer, 1936, Vol. 6: The Screen's Most Popular Magazine (Classic Reprint) (p. 1741)
—Picturegoer, Vol. 3: January, 1922 (Classic Reprint) (p. 1741)
—Pictures & the Picturegoer: The Screen Magazine; Vol. 9-10; January-December, 1925 (Classic Reprint) (p. 1741)
—Pictures & the Picturegoer, Vol. 5: The Screen Magazine; January, 1923 (Classic Reprint) (p. 1741)
Press, Ozo. Naughty or Nice Journal: 90-Day. (p. 1582)
Press, Piccadilly Fountain. Piccadilly Fountain Press Beg to Announce That They Started the Publication of the Lombard Street Edition of the Novels of Charles Dickens: By the Issue on October 15 of Pickwick (to Be Completed in 20 Fortnightly Parts) Parts I to IV Are Now Ready. (p. 1738)
Press, Pikachu. Catch Pikachu! DELUXE Look & Listen Set. (p. 343)
—Guide to Pokemon Legends. (p. 903)
—Pokemon Felties: How to Make 16 of Your Favorite Pokemon. (p. 1768)
—Super Pokemon Pop-Up: Black Kyurem. (p. 2156)
Press, Shadow Books. This Vampire Bites! Touch My Journal & You'll See. (p. 2227)
Press, Stuyvesant. Tree of Knowledge: A Document (Classic Reprint) (p. 2284)
Press, Sydney Eastern Daily. Broad Norfolk: Being a Series of Articles & Letters Reprinted from the Eastern Daily Press (Classic Reprint) (p. 284)
Press, University. Copious Greek-English Vocabulary: Compiled from the Best Authorities (Classic Reprint) (p. 451)
Press, Vail-Ballou. After Three Years: The Story of the Application of an Old Principle in Platemaking & Its Adaptation to Book Printing (Classic Reprint) (p. 34)
Press, Waterford, jt. auth. see Kavanagh, James.
Pressberg, Dava. Harold the Hamster. (p. 931)
—How Leaves Work. (p. 1033)
—Life of Frederick Douglass. (p. 1294)
—Producers, Consumers, & Decomposers. (p. 1804)
—Teacher's Tools. (p. 2195)
—Vipers. (p. 2360)
Pressel, Diane. Simba's Adventures in the Wide World. (p. 2020)
Pressens', E. de. Ninette (Classic Reprint) (p. 1610)
Pressens', Elise de. Journ'e de Petit Jean (Classic Reprint) (p. 1180)
Pressense, E. De. Ninette (Classic Reprint) (p. 1610)
—White House at St. Real: A Story for School-Boys (Classic Reprint) (p. 2444)
Pressense, Elise De. Journee de Petit Jean (Classic Reprint) (p. 1181)
Pressey, Park. Vocational Reader (Classic Reprint) (p. 2364)
Pressland, Arthur John, jt. auth. see Kerschensteiner, Georg.
Pressler, Dave, illus. see Berger, Samantha & Brockenbrough, Martha.
Pressley, A. T. Kicked Out of the North Pole. (p. 1212)
Prest, Thomas Peckett. Newgate: A Romance (Classic Reprint) (p. 1600)
—Vice & Its Victim: Or Phoebe, the Peasant's Daughter, a Romantic Tale of Real Life (Classic Reprint) (p. 2355)
Prestel. Botticelli: Coloring Book (p. 264)
Prestel, ed. see Roeder, Annette.
Prestel, ed. Coloring Book: Turner. (p. 422)
—Coloring Book: Great Artists. (p. 422)
Prestel Publishing. Antoni Gaudí: Create Your Own City Sticker Book. (p. 103)
—Colouring Book Antoni Gaudi. (p. 427)
—Roy Lichtenstein: Coloring Book. (p. 1909)
Presti, Lori, jt. auth. see Daronco, Mickey.
Preston, Anna. Glory & the Dream (Classic Reprint) (p. 844)
—Record of a Silent Life (Classic Reprint) (p. 1854)
Preston, Archie, illus. see Spinelli, Eileen.
Preston, Carole, illus. see Littlewood, Graham.
Preston Chushcoff, Jennifer. Blaze of Dragons & Other Fairytale Families. (p. 243)
—Flurry: A Mini Snowflakes Pop-Up Book. Yeretskaya, Yevgeniya, illus. (p. 753)
Preston, Effa E. Dolls on Dress Parade (Classic Reprint) (p. 579)
—In a Toy Shop: A Christmas Play for Small Children (Classic Reprint) (p. 1103)
—Party in Mother Goose Land: An One-Act Play for Primary Children (Classic Reprint) (p. 1702)
—Strike in Santa Land: A Play in One Act (Classic Reprint) (p. 2141)
Preston, Giza. Oscar: Dogs Have Dreams Too. (p. 1673)
Preston, Graham, illus. see Clark, Paul.
Preston, Harriet Waters. Aspendale (Classic Reprint) (p. 126)
—Is That All? (Classic Reprint) (p. 1137)
Preston, Ian. Princess & the Fowl One. Wood, Laura, illus. (p. 1795)
—Relly, Ogi Ogi & the Secret of Dragon's Teeth Cave. Wood, Laura, illus. (p. 1863)
Preston, J. S. Gaboon Stories (Classic Reprint) (p. 804)
Preston, Jack. Finding His Balance: Or the Bank Clerk Who Came Back (Classic Reprint) (p. 729)
—Screen Star (Classic Reprint) (p. 1964)
Preston, James, photos by see Smith, Loretta.
Preston, Janice. Bellie Bear Bart the Little Dog with the Big Heart. (p. 198)
Preston, John. Pleasures of the World: A Religious Comedy in Three Acts (Classic Reprint) (p. 1762)
—Truants: A Comedy in One Act, for Church Purposes (Classic Reprint) (p. 2292)
Preston, L. M. Explorer X: Beta. (p. 680)
—Pack. (p. 1691)
—Pack - Retribution: Retribution. (p. 1691)
Preston, Laura. Aldeane: A Novel (Classic Reprint) (p. 41)
—Boy's Trip Across the Plains. (p. 273)
—Boy's Trip Across the Plains (Classic Reprint) (p. 273)
Preston, Lizzie. I Heart Mermaids. (p. 1066)
Preston, Lizzie, illus. see Huff, Abby.
Preston, Lizzie, et al. I Heart Christmas. (p. 1066)
—I Heart Cute Unicorns. (p. 1066)
Preston, Lyman. Stories for the Whole Family, Young & Old, Male & Female (Classic Reprint) (p. 2123)
Preston, Margaret (Junkin). Handful of Monographs: Continental & English (Classic Reprint) (p. 915)
—Silverwood: A Book of Memories (Classic Reprint) (p. 2020)
Preston, Margaret J. Aunt Dorothy: An Old Virginia Plantation Story (Classic Reprint) (p. 137)
Preston, Natasha. Anónimo. (p. 100)
—Awake. (p. 143)
—Cabin. (p. 307)
—Cellar. (p. 350)
—Lost. (p. 1352)
—Natasha Preston Collection. (p. 1576)
—Noche en Que Todo Cambió. (p. 1617)
—Twin. (p. 2305)
—You Will Be Mine. (p. 2528)
Preston, Penny. Controlling the Blood. (p. 446)
Preston, Sara. Hicks at College: A Comedy in Three Acts (Classic Reprint) (p. 965)
Preston, Sydney H. On Common Ground (Classic Reprint) (p. 1652)
Preston, Sydney Herman. Abandoned Farmer (Classic Reprint) (p. 3)
Preston, Thorne & Langston, Moore. #Justachicken Coloring Book. (p. 1194)
Preston, Wendy. Sydney for Kids: The Choice Guide to over 400 Fun Activities in & Around Sydney. (p. 2172)
Preston-Gannon, Frann. By the Light of the Moon. Preston-Gannon, Frann, illus. (p. 306)
—Dandylion Summer. Preston-Gannon, Frann, illus. (p. 501)
—Dave's Cave. Preston-Gannon, Frann, illus. (p. 510)
—Dave's Rock. Preston-Gannon, Frann, illus. (p. 510)
—Deep Deep Sea. (p. 524)
—Dinosaur Farm. (p. 549)
—Hot Dog, Cold Dog. (p. 1006)
—How to Lose a Lemur. (p. 1042)
—Journey Home. (p. 1181)
—My World: A Book of First Words. (p. 1565)
—Pepper & Poe. (p. 1720)
—Pepper y Poe. (p. 1720)
—Sloth Slept On. (p. 2039)
—What a Hoot! (p. 2404)
Preston-Gannon, Frann, illus. see Bernstrom, Daniel.
Preston-Gannon, Frann, illus. see Crow, Nosy.
Preston-Gannon, Frann, illus. see Pace, Anne Marie.
Preston-Gannon, Frann, illus. see Scanlon, Liz Garton.
Preston-Gannon, Frann, illus. see Schaefer, Lola M. & Schaefer, Adam.
Preston-Paroski, Amanda. Uni-Giraffe. (p. 2327)
Preszler, June, et al. Expert Pet Care. (p. 679)
Preto, Antonella. Mimosa Tree. (p. 1469)
Pretor, Alfred. My Pretty Jane, or Judy & I (Classic Reprint) (p. 1559)
—Ronald & I or Studies from Life (Classic Reprint) (p. 1901)
Pretreger, Lidija. Pick-a-WooWoo - Angel Steps: Love You, Miss You Rose, Carolyn Maree, illus. (p. 1738)
Pretty, Dave. Sandlands. (p. 1931)
Pretty, Jen. Darkness Sleeping: Origins of Morgana le Fay. (p. 508)
Preuitt, Sheela. 20-Minute (or Less) Animation Hacks. (p. 2553)
—20-Minute (or Less) Digital Storytelling Hacks. (p. 2553)
—20-Minute (or Less) Filter Hacks. (p. 2553)
—20-Minute (or Less) Meme Hacks. (p. 2553)
—Mission HTML. (p. 1481)
—Mission JavaScript. (p. 1481)
—Mission Python. (p. 1481)
—Mission Ruby. (p. 1481)
Preumayr, Josefina, illus. see Rebel Girls.
Preus, Margi. Bamboo Sword. (p. 163)
—Enchantment Lake: A Northwoods Mystery. (p. 647)
—Heart of a Samurai (p. 945)
—Heart of a Samurai. (p. 945)
—Littlest Voyageur. Pilgrim, Cheryl, illus. (p. 1332)
—Shadow on the Mountain. (p. 1997)
—Storm's Coming! Geister, David, illus. (p. 2127)
—West of the Moon. (p. 2402)
Preuss, Sarah Louise, illus. see Diggle, David Mark.
Preusser, Heather. Symphony of Cowbells. Ewen, Eileen Ryan, illus. (p. 2173)
Preussler, Otfried. Krabat & the Sorcerer's Mill. Bell, Anthea, tr. from GER. (p. 1231)
—Little Water-Sprite. Bell, Anthea, tr. from GER. (p. 1329)
—Little Witch. Bell, Anthea, tr. (p. 1329)
—Robber Hotzenplotz. Bell, Anthea, tr. (p. 1889)
Prevec, Rose Anne, illus. see Hammond, Charmaine.
Prevedel, Brenda. Nick Gets Moving. Gulley, Robin R., ed. (p. 1602)

Prevention Magazine Editors, ed. see Ellis, Rosemary & Fittante, Ann.
Preveza, Amy, illus. see Hallinan, Annie.
Previn, Alicia L. Strange Disappearance of Walter Tortoise. Previn, Alicia L., illus. (p. 2137)
Previn, Stacey. If Snowflakes Tasted Like Fruitcake. (p. 1092)
Previn, Stacey, illus. see Donahue, Jill Lynn.
Prévost, Abbé. Dean of Coleraine, Vol. 3 Of 3: A Moral History Founded on the Memoirs of an Illustrious Family in Ireland (Classic Reprint) (p. 519)
Prevost, Alphonse, jt. auth. see Daudet, Alphonse.
Prevost, Antoine Francois. Dean of Coleraine, Vol. 2 Of 3: A Moral History; Founded on the Memoirs of an Illustrious Family in Ireland (Classic Reprint) (p. 519)
Prevost, E. W. Supplement to the Glossary of the Dialect of Cumberland. (p. 2162)
—Supplement to the Glossary of the Dialect of Cumberland (Classic Reprint) (p. 2162)
Prevost, Guillaume. Gate of Days (p. 811)
Prévost, Guillaume & Rodarmor, William. Circle of Gold: The Book of Time III. (p. 392)
Prevost, Katherine. Margaret Worthington: Or Holding Forth the Word of Life (Classic Reprint) (p. 1403)
Prevost, Marcel. Benoit Castain (Classic Reprint) (p. 201)
—Frederique (Classic Reprint) (p. 782)
Prevost, Mikela. Let's Have a Dog Party. (p. 1274)
Prevost, Mikela, illus. see Hyde, Heidi Smith.
Prevost, Mikela, illus. see Ludwig, Trudy.
Prevost, Prevost. Life & Entertaining Adventures of Mr. Cleveland, Natural Son of Oliver Cromwell, Vol. 2: Giving a Particular Account of His Unhappiness in Love, Marriage, Friendship, &C. & His Great Sufferings in Europe & America (Classic Reprint) (p. 1289)
—Story of Manon Lescaut & of the Chevalier des Grieux (Classic Reprint) (p. 2131)
Prewett, Maggie, illus. see Corpus, Terrizita.
Prewett, Maggie, illus. see Saffioti, Trina.
Prewitt, Emma Young. Karlene Hoy, or in Need of a Guide & Guard (Classic Reprint) (p. 1203)
Preza, Bruno Gonzalez, illus. see Lazaro, Georgina.
Prezio, Victor, illus. see Furman, A. L., ed.
Preziosi, Lisa. Ice Maiden's Tale. (p. 1088)
Prezioso, Alexander. Birdie in the Desert. (p. 231)
—Charlie the Goose. (p. 360)
Prezioso, Bree Ann. Chain Hat. (p. 353)
Prezoto, Vanessa, illus. see Betto.
Price. Mister Magnificent. (p. 1482)
Price, A. Wilful Young Woman, Vol. 1 of 3 (Classic Reprint) (p. 2467)
—Wilful Young Woman, Vol. 2 (Classic Reprint) (p. 2467)
Price, A. T. G. Simplicity (Classic Reprint) (p. 2022)
Price, Alice. Wilful Young Woman, Vol. 3 of 3 (Classic Reprint) (p. 2467)
Price, Allison W. A. Dragons & the Words of Knowledge. (p. 595)
Price, Andy, illus. see Anderson, Ted & Cook, Katie.
Price, Andy, illus. see Anderson, Ted, et al.
Price, Andy, illus. see Anderson, Ted.
Price, Andy, illus. see Cook, Katie.
Price, Andy, illus. see Whitley, Jeremy.
Price, Andy, illus. see Zahler, Thom, et al.
Price, Anne. Raptors of North America: A Coloring Book of Eagles, Hawks, Falcons, & Owls. (p. 1841)
Price, Caleb, illus. see Hughes, Annette.
Price, Christine, illus. see Mitchell, Lucy Sprague.
Price, Colin. Story-Writing-Coding. Price-Mohr, Ruth, illus. (p. 2136)
Price, Dana Lynn. G Is for Gorilla. (p. 804)
Price, Danielle Marie. Anxious Ellie. (p. 104)
Price, Dann. Wesley the Weasel Can't Stop His Sneezel. (p. 2401)
Price, David J. Tom & Emily's Incredible Adventure to the World of the Gossamerians. (p. 2256)
Price, Denise. Buddy & His Colorado Adventure. (p. 290)
Price, Denise D. Freedom Trail Pop up Book of Boston. (p. 783)
Price, Edith Ballinger. Blue Magic (Classic Reprint) (p. 249)
—Fortune of the Indies (Classic Reprint) (p. 769)
—Happy Venture (Classic Reprint) (p. 924)
Price, Edward G. Zambezi Allies. (p. 2538)
Price, Eleanor C. Gerald, Vol. 1 of 3 (Classic Reprint) (p. 821)
—Gerald, Vol. 3 of 3 (Classic Reprint) (p. 821)
—Queen's Man: A Romance of the Wars, of the Roses (Classic Reprint) (p. 1825)
—Red Towers, Vol. 1 of 3 (Classic Reprint) (p. 1859)
Price, Eleanor Catherine. Angelot: A Story of the First Empire (Classic Reprint) (p. 86)
Price, Elizabeth. Frederica Dennison Spinster (Classic Reprint) (p. 781)
—Meadow Farm Talent Show. (p. 1434)
Price, Ella Perry. Cry Heard (Classic Reprint) (p. 480)
Price, Ellen Ann. Gladly's Magic. (p. 839)
Price, Emma. Another Girl Calls My Dad Daddy. (p. 101)
Price, Emma, ed. Portia's Incdedible Journey. (p. 1779)
Price, Fiona. Ivory Tower. (p. 1149)
Price, Guy, illus. see Casey, Karen.
Price, Guy J., illus. see Parsons, Julie.
Price, Hattie Longstreet, illus. see Curtis, Alice.
Price, Ian, jt. auth. see Pogue, Carolyn.
Price, Isaac. Direct Method of Teaching English to Foreigners, Vol. 1 (Classic Reprint) (p. 552)
Price, Jacob. Buyers' Manual & Business Guide: Being a Description of the Leading Business Houses, Manufactories, Inventions, etc; of the Pacific Coast, Together with Copious & Readable Selections, Chiefly from California Writers (Classic Reprint) (p. 304)
Price, Jacqueline D. Jason's Journey. (p. 1161)
Price, Jane. Underworld: Exploring the Secret World Beneath Your Feet Hancock, James Gulliver, illus. (p. 2326)
Price, Joann, ed. see Herndon, Ajaye & de Vance, Glynis W.
Price Jr, Wilmer. Happy Josh. (p. 923)
Price, Julius M. My Bohemian Days in London (Classic Reprint) (p. 1534)
—My Bohemian Days in Paris (Classic Reprint) (p. 1534)
—On the Path of Adventure (Classic Reprint) (p. 1655)
Price, Justine. Class Mural: Reason with Shapes & Their Attributes. (p. 399)
—Dreams of a Puppy. (p. 603)
Price, Karen. Connor Mcdavid: Hockey Superstar. (p. 441)
—Nathan MacKinnon: Hockey Superstar. (p. 1577)
—Olympic Records. (p. 1651)
—Red Gerard. (p. 1857)
Price, Karlene. Spellbook of Notes, Magic & Music. (p. 2079)
Price, Kathy. Mardi Gras Almost Didn't Come This Year. Williams, Carl Joseph, illus. (p. 1403)
Price, Kevin. Kumakana: A Gronups Tale. (p. 1233)
Price, Kevin, ed. see The Born Storytellers.
Price, Kevin, ed. Fields of Wheat: And other Romance Stories. (p. 723)
—Ice Castles: A Born Storytellers Collection of Teen Fiction & Romance. (p. 1087)
—Mystery of Love: A Born Storyteller Collection of Mystery Adventure & Science Fiction Stories. (p. 1569)
Price, Lillian L. Lads & Lassies of Other Days (Classic Reprint) (p. 1236)
Price, Lillian Louise. Wandering Heroes (Classic Reprint) (p. 2375)
Price, Lissa. Starters. (p. 2107)
Price, Lucien. Immortal Youth: A Study in the Will to Create (Classic Reprint) (p. 1101)
Price, M. J. Skin I'm In. (p. 2032)
Price, M. J. Momot. Grandma & Grandpa Are Retiring. (p. 877)
Price, Mara & Ventura, Gabriela Baeza. Grandma's Chocolate/El Chocolate de Abuelita. Fields, Lisa, illus. (p. 878)
Price, Margaret Barnes. Daddy's Widow: A Long Island Story (Classic Reprint) (p. 495)
Price, Margaret Evans. Child's Book of Myths. (p. 375)
—Hansel & Gretel (Classic Reprint) (p. 919)
Price, Margaret Evans, illus. see Dover, et al.
Price, Margaret Evans, illus. see Grimm, Jacob & Grimm, Wilhelm K.
Price, Margaret Evans, illus. see Moore, Clement C.
Price, Margaret Evans, illus. see Moore, Clement Clarke.
Price, Margaret Evans & Wadsworth, Wallace C. Once upon a Time Tales: With Read & Listen MP3 Download. Bates, Katharine Lee, ed. (p. 1658)
Price, Marilyn. Grandma's Cookies. (p. 878)
Price, Mathew. Cachorro. Goldman, Judy, tr. (p. 307)
—Gatito. Goldman, Judy, tr. (p. 811)
—Pollito. Goldman, Judy, tr. (p. 1771)
Price, Matt. Mystery of the Ancient Anchor. Ettinger, Doris, illus. (p. 1569)
Price, Michael. Captain Noah's Zoo. (p. 325)
Price, Mina, illus. see Christie, Tory.
Price, Mina, illus. see Taddonio, Lea.
Price, Mina, illus. see Zahler, Diane.
Price, Nick. Wonderful Wizard of Oz. (p. 2490)
Price, Nick, illus. see Bearn, Emily.
Price, Nick, illus. see Blane, Francisco.
Price, Nick, illus. see Jeffries, Katherine.
Price, Nick, illus. see Morgan, Michaela.
Price, Nigel. Cambridge IGCSE India Studies. (p. 313)
Price, Novella. Grammy, Where Are You Going? (p. 876)
Price, Pamela S. Cool Baking (p. 447)
—Cool Cakes & Cupcakes: Easy Recipes for Kids to Bake. (p. 447)
—Cool Cookies & Bars: Easy Recipes for Kids to Bake. (p. 448)
—Cool Holiday Treats: Easy Recipes for Kids to Bake. (p. 449)
—Cool Pet Treats: Easy Recipes for Kids to Bake. (p. 449)
—Cool Pies & Tarts: Easy Recipes for Kids to Bake. (p. 449)
—Cool Quick Breads: Easy Recipes for Kids to Bake. (p. 450)
Price, Planaria & West, Helen Reichmann. Claiming My Place: a True Story of Defiance, Deception, & Coming of Age in the Shadow of the Holocaust. (p. 397)
Price, Rebecca, illus. see Holliday, Bobby.
Price, Reynolds. Perfect Friend. (p. 1722)
Price, Robin. Threadneedle 01. McGrory, Paul, illus. (p. 2231)
Price, Roger. Dinosaur Mad Libs. (p. 549)
Price, Roger & Mad Libs Staff. Give Me Liberty or Give Me Mad Libs. (p. 840)
—I Love Seattle Mad Libs. (p. 1072)
Price, Roger & Stern, Leonard. Ad Lib Mad Libs. (p. 13)
—Easter Eggstravaganza Mad Libs. (p. 620)
—Gobble Gobble Mad Libs. (p. 849)
—Grand Slam Mad Libs. (p. 877)
—Happily Ever Mad Libs. (p. 919)
—Holly, Jolly Mad Libs. (p. 988)
—Mad about Animals Mad Libs. (p. 1373)
—Mad Libs Forever. (p. 1373)
—Rock 'n' Roll Mad Libs. (p. 1894)
—Spy Mad Libs. (p. 2093)
—Wizard of Oz Mad Libs. (p. 2483)
Price, Roger & Stern, Leonard, creators. Hanukkah Mad Libs (p. 919)
—Mr. Men Little Miss Mad Libs. (p. 1519)
—Ninjas Mad Libs. (p. 1610)
—Penguin Classics Mad Libs. (p. 1716)
—Totally Pink Mad Libs. (p. 2267)
—Undead Mad Libs. (p. 2320)
Price, Ronnalda, ed. see Martin, Paige.
Price, Ryan, illus. see Poe, Edgar Allan.
Price, Sean. Hannibal of Carthage (p. 918)
—Modern Spies. (p. 1487)
—Unsolved Crime Mysteries. (p. 2335)
—Water Pollution. (p. 2385)
Price, Sean, jt. auth. see Price, Sean Stewart.
Price, Sean, et al, contrib. by. Passengers of the Titanic: Traveling on an Ill-Fated Ship (p. 1703)
Price, Sean Stewart. Adolf Hitler. (p. 16)
—Amazing Military Robots (p. 65)
—Amazing Military Robots. (p. 65)
—Kids' Guide to Pro Wrestling (p. 1215)
—Modern Spies (p. 1487)
—Pirates: Truth & Rumors Doty, Eldon, illus. (p. 1750)
—Sports. Doty, Eldon, illus. (p. 2088)
—U. S. Presidents: Truth & Rumors. Doty, Eldon, illus. (p. 2312)
—Vanished! Magic Tricks & Great Escapes (p. 2347)
—World War II Spies (p. 2506)
—World's Deadliest Animals. (p. 2507)
Price, Sean Stewart & DiConsiglio, John. News Never Stops (p. 1600)
Price, Sean Stewart & Price, Sean. Attila the Hun: Leader of the Barbarian Hordes. (p. 135)
—Cixi: Evil Empress of China? (p. 397)
—Henry VIII: Royal Beheader. (p. 955)
Price, Sean Stewart, et al. Unsolved Mystery Files. (p. 2335)
—World Record Breakers. (p. 2504)
Price, Shannon. Thousand Fires. (p. 2231)
Price, Sidney. What's a Belly Button Good For? (p. 2423)
Price, Stern, jt. auth. see Jones, Karl.
Price Stern Sloan & Hargreaves, Adam. Dr. First. Hargreaves, Adam, illus. (p. 591)
—Dr. Twelfth. Hargreaves, Adam, illus. (p. 592)
Price, Stern, Sloan Publishing Staff & Merrell, Billy. Bob's Burgers Mad Libs. (p. 252)
Price, Susan. Ghost Song. (p. 828)
—How the Bear Lost His Tail. Ogilvie, Sara, illus. (p. 1035)
Price, T. Buchanan. Snap: The Ox-Train Era; Early Troubles of Border Trade (Classic Reprint) (p. 2045)
Price, Timothy. Leon the Left Sock. (p. 1267)
—Shelby & Carter & the Great Trolley Heist. (p. 2005)
—Shelby the Shopping Trolley. (p. 2005)
Price, Tyvon. Adopted by the Streets. (p. 17)
Price-Brown, J. In the Van, or the Builders (Classic Reprint) (p. 1111)
Price-Brown, Price-Brown. In the Van: Or the Builders (Classic Reprint) (p. 1111)
Price-Groff, Claire & Kaplan, Elizabeth. Illinois. (p. 1095)
Price-Groff, Claire, et al. Illinois. (p. 1095)
Priceman, Marjorie. How to Make a Cherry Pie & See the U. S. A. (p. 1043)
—How to Make a Cherry Pie & See the U. S. A. Priceman, Marjorie, illus. (p. 1043)
Priceman, Marjorie, illus. see Andrews, Julie & Hamilton, Emma Walton.
Priceman, Marjorie, illus. see Griffin, Kitty.
Priceman, Marjorie, illus. see Lee Stone, Tanya.
Priceman, Marjorie, illus. see Manzano, Sonia.
Priceman, Marjorie, illus. see Rusch, Elizabeth.
Priceman, Marjorie, illus. see Singer, Marilyn.
Priceman, Marjorie, illus. see Spinelli, Eileen.
Priceman, Marjorie, illus. see Winter, Jonah.
Price-Mohr, R. M. Miss Lovelace's Code Rebooted. (p. 1479)
—Miss Lovelace's Unexplained Code. (p. 1479)
Price-Mohr, Ruth, illus. see Price, Colin.
Price-Wright, Heather. Life in Numbers: Choose Your Career (Level 5) (p. 1292)
—Mexican Rule of California. (p. 1454)
Prichard, Andrew. Blockbuster Bible: Filming the Bible Story for 9-11 Year Olds. (p. 245)
Prichard, Helen M. Friends & Foes in the Transkei: An Englishwoman's Experiences During the Cape Frontier War of 1877-8 (Classic Reprint) (p. 786)
Prichard, Hesketh. November Joe: Detective of the Woods. (p. 1627)
—November Joe: Detective of the Woods (Classic Reprint) (p. 1627)
Prichard, K. S. Pioneers (Classic Reprint) (p. 1748)
Prichard, Katharine Susannah. Black Opal (Classic Reprint) (p. 238)
Prichard, Sarah J. Old Stone Chimney (Classic Reprint) (p. 1648)
—Only Woman in the Town: And Other Tales of the American Revolution (Classic Reprint) (p. 1664)
Prichard, Sarah Johnson. Shawnie Wade (Classic Reprint) (p. 2004)
Priddis, C. Michael, illus. see Daybell, Chad G.
Priddy, Al. Through the Mill: The Life of a Mill-Boy (Classic Reprint) (p. 2237)
—Through the School: The Experiences of a Mill Boy in Securing an Education (Classic Reprint) (p. 2237)
Priddy Books. Abre y Cierra. Animales (Libro con Ventanas) (p. 8)
—Quita y Pon. Animales. (p. 1828)
—Quita y Pon. Colores. (p. 1828)
—Quita y Pon. la Casa. (p. 1828)
Priddy Books, Priddy. Alphaprints: Easter 123 Mini: Mini Version. (p. 59)
Priddy Books Staff. I Want to Be a Builder & Firefighter (p. 1084)
Priddy Books Staff & Priddy, Roger. My Big Animal Book. (p. 1532)
Priddy, Brenda. Mason Jar Scientist: 30 Jarring STEAM-Based Projects. (p. 1417)
Priddy, Roger. 1000 Activities. (p. 2560)
—1000 Animal Stickers. (p. 2560)
—12 Days of Christmas: A Lift-The-tab Book. (p. 2551)
—ABC Touch & Feel : P is for Puppy. (p. 4)
—Adam & Eve: Baby's First Bible. (p. 14)
—Alphaprints: 123. (p. 59)
—Alphaprints: ABC. (p. 59)
—Alphaprints: Alphababies. (p. 59)
—Alphaprints: Animal Opposites. (p. 59)
—Alphaprints: Boo! Touch & Feel. (p. 59)
—Alphaprints: Colors. (p. 59)
—Alphaprints: Create Your Own: A Sticker & Doodle Activity Book. (p. 59)
—Alphaprints: Curious Cat & Other Fluffy Friends. (p. 59)
—Alphaprints: Dinoshapes. (p. 59)
—Alphaprints Dot to Dot Activity Book. (p. 59)
—Alphaprints: Easter 123. (p. 59)
—Alphaprints First Words. (p. 59)
—Alphaprints First Words Matching Set. (p. 59)
—Alphaprints Fun in the Sun! (p. 59)
—Alphaprints: Gobble Gobble. (p. 59)
—Alphaprints: Happy Dog & Other Furry Friends. (p. 59)
—Alphaprints: Ho, Ho, Ho! A Touch-And-Feel Book. (p. 59)
—Alphaprints: Hungry Hippo & Other Safari Animals. (p. 59)
—Alphaprints: Magical Creatures. (p. 59)
—Alphaprints: Quirky Bird & Other Feathered Friends. (p. 59)
—Alphaprints: Rocky Raccoon & Other Woodland Friends. (p. 59)
—Alphaprints Sea Life. (p. 59)
—Alphaprints: Silly Squid & Other Fishy Friends. (p. 59)
—Alphaprints: Sweet Heart: A Touch-And-Feel Book. (p. 59)
—Alphaprints: Trace, Write, & Learn 123. (p. 60)
—Alphaprints: Tweet! Tweet! A Touch-And-Feel Book. (p. 60)
—Alphaprints: Wipe Clean Workbook ABC. (p. 60)
—Animal Buddies: Cow. (p. 88)
—Animal Buddies: Monkey. (p. 88)
—Awesome Activities: Bug Bites: With Glow-In-the-Dark Bugs Plus Fun Stickers. (p. 144)
—Baby Can Do: Bedtime Baby: Touch & Feel. (p. 149)
—Baby Can Do: Peekaboo Baby: With a Fun Mirror Surprise. Munday, Natalie, ed. (p. 149)
—Baby Shaker Teethers Animals. (p. 152)
—Baby Touch & Feel: Hugs. (p. 153)
—Baby Touch & Feel: Little Penguin. (p. 153)
—Baby's First Sound Book: Farm: A Sound Book. (p. 154)
—Baby's First Sound Book: Zoo: A Sound Book. (p. 154)
—Baby's First Treasure Hunt. (p. 154)
—Bright Baby: Happy Thanksgiving. (p. 281)
—Bright Baby Lift-The-Tab: Words. (p. 281)
—Bright Baby Touch & Feel Easter. (p. 281)
—Bright Baby Touch & Feel Fall. (p. 281)
—Bright Baby Touch & Feel Hanukkah. (p. 281)
—Bright Baby Touch & Feel Hugs & Kisses. (p. 281)
—Bright Baby Touch & Feel Merry Christmas. (p. 281)
—Bright Baby Words/Palabras: English-Spanish. (p. 281)
—Bunny & Friends Touch & Feel. (p. 298)
—Busca y Encuentra: en el Parque. Campabadal, Monica, tr. (p. 300)
—Busca y Encuentra: en Mi Casa. Campabadal, Monica, tr. (p. 300)
—Busy Babies Colors. (p. 301)
—Busy Babies Farm Animals. (p. 301)
—Busy Babies Words. (p. 301)
—Busy Babies Zoo Animals. (p. 301)
—Calendar Fun: Countdown to Christmas. (p. 310)
—Carry-Along Tab Book: My Easter Basket. (p. 334)
—Changing Picture Book: Chirp, Chirp. (p. 356)
—Changing Picture Book: Christmas Surprise. (p. 356)
—Chunky Pack: Baby Animals Chunky Set (3 Titles) Pets, Farm, & Wild Animals. (p. 390)
—Chunky Pack: Christmas. (p. 390)
—Chunky Pack: Easter. (p. 390)
—Chunky Pack: Halloween. (p. 390)
—Chunky Pack: Valentine. (p. 390)
—Chunky Set: Play Tractor. (p. 390)
—Chunky Set: Play Train. (p. 390)
—Clever Bots: Busy Bots. (p. 404)
—Color & Activity Books Dinosaur: With over 60 Stickers, Pictures to Color, Puzzle Fun & More! (p. 419)
—Color Me: Farm. (p. 420)
—Color Me: Trucks. (p. 420)
—Counting Collection: Counting Dinosaurs. (p. 460)
—Dinosaur ABC: Board Book. (p. 548)
—Dinosaur Galore! A Changing Picture Book. (p. 549)
—Dot to Dot for Tiny Tots. (p. 588)
—Dot to Dot for Tiny Tots Wipe Clean Activity Book. (p. 588)
—Duckling & Friends Touch & Feel. (p. 608)
—Early Learning Fun: Match It! Includes Wipe-Clean Pen. (p. 614)
—Easter Croc: Full of Pop-Up Surprises! (p. 619)
—Fancy Pants: Turn the Wheel to Find My Pants. (p. 706)
—First 100 Animals. (p. 734)
—First 100 Animals Lift-The-Flap: Over 50 Fun Flaps to Lift & Learn. (p. 734)
—First 100 Animals Padded (large) (p. 734)
—First 100 Christmas Words. (p. 734)
—First 100: First 100 Bible Words Padded. (p. 734)
—First 100 : First Book of Colors Padded. (p. 734)
—First 100 Lift the Flap Farm Words. (p. 734)
—First 100 Lift the Flap Numbers: Over 50 Fun Flaps to Lift & Learn. (p. 734)
—First 100 Lift-The-Flap Bilingual First Words. (p. 734)
—First 100 Numbers. (p. 734)
—First 100 Padded: First Farm Words. (p. 734)
—First 100 Padded: Numbers Colors Shapes. (p. 734)
—First 100 Stickers: Animals: Over 500 Stickers. (p. 734)
—First 100 Stickers: First Numbers, Colors, Shapes. (p. 734)
—First 100 Stickers: Trucks & Things That Go: Sticker Book. (p. 734)
—First 100 Stickers: Words: Over 500 Stickers. (p. 734)
—First 100 Trucks: And Things That Go. (p. 735)
—First 100 Trucks & Things That Go Lift-The-Flap: Over 50 Fun Flaps to Lift & Learn. (p. 735)
—First 100 Words. (p. 735)
—First 100 Words Lift-The-Flap: Over 35 Fun Flaps to Lift & Learn. (p. 735)
—First 100 Words Padded (large) (p. 735)
—First Learning Numbers Play Set. (p. 738)
—First Learning Play Set: Farm. (p. 738)
—First Learning Play Set: Things That Go. (p. 738)
—First Songs Library: Over 50 Songs! Includes 3 Books with a CD. (p. 739)
—Fluffy Chick & Friends. (p. 753)
—Forest Friends: a Lift-And-learn Book. (p. 766)
—Funny Faces: Easter Parade. (p. 801)
—Funny Faces Halloween Jack. (p. 801)
—Funny Faces Santa Claus. (p. 801)
—Funny Faces: Vampire Pets. (p. 801)
—Funny Friends: Barnyard Bottoms: A Silly Seek-And-find Book! (p. 801)
—Fuzzy Bee & Friends. (p. 803)
—Gira y Aprende. Animales Bebés. (p. 834)
—Gira y Aprende. en la Granja. (p. 834)
—Giraffe Is Lost: An Animal Search-And-find Book. (p. 834)
—Great Turkey Race: With a Roaring Engine Sound. (p. 890)
—Happy St. Patrick's Day. (p. 923)
—Hello Baby: Animals: A High-Contrast Board Book. (p. 950)
—Hello Baby: Baby Grip: A High Contrast Book. (p. 950)
—Hello Baby: Faces: A High-Contrast Board Book. (p. 950)
—Hello Baby: Words: A High-Contrast Board Book. (p. 950)

P

—Hora de Comer. Campabadal, Monica, tr. (p. 1002)
—Hora de Jugar. Campabadal, Monica, tr. (p. 1002)
—How to Draw: Includes Wipe-Clean Pen. (p. 1039)
—Kitten & Friends Touch & Feel. (p. 1225)
—Let's Pretend Builders Tool Kit: With Book & Press-Out Pieces. (p. 1277)
—Let's Pretend Chef's Kitchen. (p. 1277)
—Let's Pretend Princess Party Set: With Book & Press-Out Pieces. (p. 1277)
—Let's Pretend Race Driver Set: With Book & Press-Out Pieces. (p. 1277)
—Lift the Flap: Fairy Tales. (p. 1297)
—Lift the Flap: Nursery Rhymes. (p. 1297)
—Lift the Tab: Christmas. (p. 1297)
—Lift-The-Flap Tab: Colors, Numbers, Shapes. (p. 1297)
—Lift-The-Flap Tab: Farm. (p. 1297)
—Lift-The-Flap Tab: First 50 Words. (p. 1297)
—Lift-The-Flap Tab: on the Go. (p. 1297)
—Lift-The-Flap Tab: Santa's Workshop. (p. 1297)
—Lift-The-Flap Tab: Spooky House. (p. 1297)
—Lift-The-Flap Tab: Trucks. (p. 1297)
—Lift-The-tab: I Love You. (p. 1297)
—Little Friends: All You Need Is Love: A Lift the Flaps Book. (p. 1317)
—Little Friends: Barnyard Fun! A Lift-The-Flap Book. (p. 1317)
—Little Friends: Big Adventure: With 10 Busy Sounds. (p. 1317)
—Little Friends: Big & Small: A Book about Opposites. (p. 1317)
—Little Friends: Home for Christmas: A Lift-The-Flap Book. (p. 1317)
—Little Friends: Home Sweet Home: A Lift-The-Flap Book. (p. 1317)
—Little Friends: Let's Play: With Four Magical Sounds. (p. 1317)
—Little Friends: Little Monkey: A Hide-And-Seek Book with a Felt Friend. (p. 1317)
—Little Friends: Sleepy Time. (p. 1317)
—Little Friends Sound Book: Colors. (p. 1317)
—Little Friends Sound Book: Numbers. (p. 1317)
—Little Friends: Splish Splash. (p. 1317)
—Little Friends: Trick or Treat: A Lift-The-flap Book. (p. 1317)
—Look Closer: Around the Farm. (p. 1345)
—Look Closer: under the Ocean. (p. 1345)
—Maze Book: Follow Me. (p. 1430)
—Maze Book: Follow Me Around the World. (p. 1430)
—Maze Book: Follow Me Fairy Tales. (p. 1430)
—Maze Book: Follow Me Halloween. (p. 1430)
—Maze Book: Follow Me Santa. (p. 1430)
—Maze Book: Follow My Heart. (p. 1430)
—Maze Book: Follow the Bunny. (p. 1430)
—Mi Libro Desplegable de Animales. (p. 1455)
—Mi Libro Desplegable de Dinosaurios. (p. 1455)
—Mini Tab Books: Farm. (p. 1472)
—Mini Tab Books: Numbers. (p. 1472)
—Mini Tab Books: Trucks & Things That Go. (p. 1472)
—Mini Tab Books: Words. (p. 1472)
—Mini Tab: Christmas. (p. 1472)
—Mini Tab: Easter. (p. 1472)
—Mini Tab: I Love You. (p. 1472)
—Mini Tab: Rudolph the Red-Nosed Reindeer. (p. 1472)
—Mix & Match: Christmas. (p. 1484)
—Mix & Match: Halloween. (p. 1484)
—Mo Chéad Foclóir. Ó' Murchadha, Niall, tr. (p. 1485)
—My Big Animal Book. (p. 1532)
—My Big Dinosaur Book. (p. 1532)
—My Big Seek-And-Find Book: With Wipe-Clean Pen! (p. 1533)
—My Big Train Book. (p. 1533)
—My Big Truck Book. (p. 1533)
—My Big Word Book (casebound) (p. 1533)
—My First Alphabet Jigsaw Set. (p. 1540)
—My First Alphabet Touch & Feel. (p. 1540)
—My First Numbers Domino Set (p. 1545)
—My First Places: My First Farm. (p. 1545)
—My First Places: My First Town: A Flap Book. (p. 1545)
—My First Play & Learn: Grocery Store: A Fun Early Learning Book with Reusable Play Pieces. (p. 1545)
—My First Wipe Clean: Pen Control. (p. 1546)
—My First Words Matching Game & Book Set: Three Games & a Book (p. 1547)
—My Fun Flap Book: My Fun Farm Trip. (p. 1548)
—My Fun School Bus Lift-The-flap. (p. 1548)
—My Giant Fold-Out Book of Animals. (p. 1548)
—My Giant Seek-And-Find Activity Book: More Than 200 Activities: Match It, Puzzles, Searches, Dot-To-Dot, Coloring, Mazes, & More! (p. 1548)
—My Little Book of Animals. (p. 1552)
—My Little Book of Trucks & Things That Go. (p. 1552)
—My Little Book of Words. (p. 1552)
—My Little World: How Do You Feel? A Book about Emotions. (p. 1554)
—My Little World: Let's Poop! A Turn-The-Wheel Book for Potty Training. (p. 1554)
—My Little World: Watch Me Grow. (p. 1554)
—My Super Duper Drawing Activity Book: With over 200 Stickers. (p. 1562)
—My World: A Hand-Drawn Book with 350 Words to Learn, Things to Count, Lots to Find. (p. 1565)
—Night Night Farm. (p. 1606)
—Noisy Fire Truck Sound Book. (p. 1617)
—Noisy Tractor Sound Book. (p. 1618)
—Nursery Rhymes: Book & Toy Gift Set. (p. 1631)
—Nursery Rhymes Touch & Feel. (p. 1631)
—On the Move: Drive Me! (p. 1655)
—Picture Fit: a Flurry of Snowflakes. (p. 1740)
—Picture Fit Board Books: a Caboodle of Cuddles. (p. 1740)
—Picture Fit Board Books: a Mischief of Monsters. (p. 1740)
—Picture Fit Board Books: a Parade of Animals: A Clever Counting Book. (p. 1740)
—Picture Fit Board Books: a Parade of Animals (Large) A Counting Book. (p. 1740)
—Picture Fit Board Books: a Stampede of Dinosaurs: An Opposites Book. (p. 1740)
—Picture Fit Board Books: a Stampede of Dinosaurs (Large) An Opposites Book. (p. 1740)
—Picture Fit Board Books: a Toy Box of Shapes: A Touch-And-learn Alphaprints Book. (p. 1740)
—Picture Fit Board Books: a Traffic Jam of Trucks: A Clever Colors Book. (p. 1740)
—Picture Fit Board Books: a Traffic Jam of Trucks (Large) A Colors Book. (p. 1740)
—Picture Play: Playtime. (p. 1740)
—Pivot Book: Move It! (p. 1752)
—Play & Learn 123: First 100 Words, with Novelties on Every Page. (p. 1758)
—Play & Learn ABC: First 100 Words, with Novelties on Every Page. (p. 1758)
—Play & Learn: Colors: First 100 Words, with Lots of Fun Novelties. (p. 1758)
—Playtown: A Lift-The-Flap Book. (p. 1761)
—Playtown: Airport (revised Edition) A Lift-The-Flap Book. (p. 1761)
—Playtown Chunky Pack: Construction. (p. 1761)
—Playtown: Construction: A-Lift-The-Flap-Book. (p. 1761)
—Playtown: Emergency: A Lift-The-Flap Book. (p. 1761)
—Pop & Play: Pop, Flip, Cook. (p. 1775)
—Pop-Up Dinosaurs: A Pop-Up Book to Get Your Jaws Into. (p. 1775)
—Pop-Up Surprise Haunted House: A Seriously Spooky Pop-Up Book. (p. 1775)
—Preschool Color & Activity Book. (p. 1788)
—Priddy Baby Lift-The-flap: Baby's Day. (p. 1791)
—Priddy Baby Lift-The-flap: Bedtime. Bermingham, Alice-May, ed. (p. 1791)
—Priddy Baby Lift-The-flap: Color. (p. 1791)
—Priddy Baby Lift-The-flap: Farm. (p. 1791)
—Priddy Learning: My First 1000 Words: A Photographic Catalog of Baby's First Words. (p. 1791)
—Priddy Learning: My First Clock Book. (p. 1791)
—Priddy Learning: My First Wipe Clean Starting School: A Fun Early Learning Book. (p. 1791)
—Priddy Learning: My First Wipe Clean Words: A Fun Early Learning Book. (p. 1791)
—Pull the Tab: Colors. (p. 1812)
—Pull the Tab: Trucks. (p. 1812)
—Puppy & Friends Touch & Feel. (p. 1814)
—Puzzle & Play: Alphabet Train: A Press-Out Puzzle Book! (p. 1818)
—Puzzle & Play: Color Bus: A Press-Out Puzzle Book! (p. 1818)
—Puzzle Play Set: ALPHABET: Three Chunky Books & a Giant Jigsaw Puzzle! (p. 1818)
—Puzzle Play Set: MY PLAY FARM: Three Chunky Books & a Giant Jigsaw Puzzle! (p. 1818)
—Puzzle Play Set: PLAYTOWN: Three Chunky Books & a Giant Jigsaw Puzzle! Set (p. 1818)
—Red Car, Green Car: A Changing Colors Book. (p. 1856)
—Rudolph the Red-Nosed Reindeer Lift-The-Tab. (p. 1912)
—Santa Street Chunky Set: Santa's Workshop, Snowflake House, Gingerbread House. (p. 1933)
—Search & Find: Santa's Gifts: A Novelty Book. (p. 1970)
—See, Touch, Feel: A First Sensory Book. (p. 1982)
—See, Touch, Feel: ABC. (p. 1982)
—See, Touch, Feel: Christmas. (p. 1982)
—See, Touch, Feel: Create: A Creative Play Book. (p. 1982)
—See, Touch, Feel: Halloween. (p. 1982)
—See, Touch, Feel: Roar: A First Sensory Book. (p. 1982)
—See, Touch, Feel: Spring. (p. 1982)
—See Touch Feel: Thanksgiving. (p. 1982)
—Shiny Shapes: Easter Surprise. (p. 2007)
—Shiny Shapes: Hooray for Thanksgiving! (p. 2007)
—Shiny Shapes: Love You Always. (p. 2007)
—Shiny Shapes: My Christmas Star. (p. 2007)
—Shiny Shapes: the Pumpkin Patch. (p. 2007)
—Simple First Words Let's Say Our Colors. (p. 2021)
—Simple First Words Let's Talk. (p. 2021)
—Sing-Along Songs with CD. (p. 2023)
—Slide & Find Easter. (p. 2038)
—Slide & Find Spooky. (p. 2038)
—Smart Kids Dinosaurs: With More Than 30 Stickers. (p. 2040)
—Smart Kids: Predators: The World's Deadliest Hunters. (p. 2040)
—Smart Kids Reptiles & Amphibians: With More Than 30 Stickers. (p. 2040)
—Smart Kids Sharks: With More Than 30 Stickers. (p. 2040)
—Smart Kids Space: With More Than 30 Stickers. (p. 2040)
—Smart Kids: Space: For Kids Who Really Love Space! (p. 2040)
—Sneak-A-Peek: Colors. (p. 2045)
—Spooky Bus: With a Creepy Halloween Sound. (p. 2086)
—Spooky Street. (p. 2087)
—Squishy Turtle Cloth Book. (p. 2095)
—Stick & Play: My Busy Barn. (p. 2117)
—Sticker Activity Animals. (p. 2117)
—Sticker Activity Numbers. (p. 2117)
—Sticker Doodle Boo! Things That Go Boo! with over 200 Stickers. (p. 2117)
—Sticker Doodle Do. (p. 2117)
—Sticker Doodle I Love You: Awesome Things to Do, with over 200 Stickers. (p. 2117)
—Sticker Doodle You. (p. 2117)
—Sticker Early Learning: Colors. (p. 2118)
—Sticker Early Learning: Numbers. (p. 2118)
—Sticker Friends: Bear: 300 Reusable Stickers. (p. 2118)
—Sticker Friends: Bunny. (p. 2118)
—Sticker Friends: Chick: 300 Reusable Stickers. (p. 2118)
—Sticker Friends: Christmas: Over 300 Reusable Stickers. (p. 2118)
—Sticker Friends: Farm. (p. 2118)
—Sticker Friends: Halloween: 300 Reusable Stickers. (p. 2118)
—Sticker Friends: Kitten: 300 Reusable Stickers. (p. 2118)
—Sticker Friends: Love Bug. (p. 2118)
—Sticker Friends: Puppy: 300 Reusable Stickers. (p. 2118)
—Stickerpedia: Packed with Fascinating Facts, Absorbing Activities & over 8000 Stickers! (p. 2118)
—Sun. (p. 2150)
—Super Dinky Doodles: With over 100 Stickers & Lots of Fun Surprises! (p. 2154)
—Tiny Tots Fun Book: Stickers, Coloring, & Stencils! with Multi-Colored Pen. (p. 2250)
—Toddler Town: City. (p. 2255)
—Toddler Town: Zoo. (p. 2255)
—Treasure Hunt: on the Farm: A Fold-Out Book. (p. 2281)
—Treasure Hunt: Treasure Hunt for Kids. (p. 2282)
—Turn the Wheel: Odd Jobs. (p. 2300)
—Turn the Wheel: Spooky Pants. (p. 2300)
—We Are a Family (Small Format) (p. 2388)
—What's in My House? A Slide & Find Book. (p. 2424)
—What's in My Truck? A Slide & Find Book. (p. 2424)
—What's in the Box? A Spooky Search-And-find. (p. 2424)
—What's on My Farm? A Slide-And-find Book with Flaps. (p. 2425)
—Where Does Pig Live? A Barnyard Search-And-find Book. (p. 2436)
—Wiggle & the Whale (an Alphaprints Picture Book) A Book of Funny Friends. (p. 2461)
—Wipe Clean Activities: Road Trip. (p. 2476)
—Wipe Clean Activities: Spooky Halloween. (p. 2476)
—Wipe Clean Activities: under the Sea: With Fin-Tastic Stickers! (p. 2476)
—Wipe Clean Activities: Unicorn Magic: With Fantastical Stickers! (p. 2476)
—Wipe Clean Activities: Vacation Time. (p. 2476)
—Wipe Clean: Bilingual Workbook Ready for School. (p. 2477)
—Wipe Clean: Early Learning Workbook. (p. 2477)
—Wipe Clean: First Words. (p. 2477)
—Wipe Clean: Giant Activity Workbook. (p. 2477)
—Wipe Clean: Pen Control. (p. 2477)
—Wipe Clean: Starting School. (p. 2477)
—Wipe Clean: Starting School Workbook. (p. 2477)
—Wipe Clean Workbook: 10 Minute Reading, Writing, & Math (enclosed Spiral Binding) Ages 6-7; with Pen. (p. 2477)
—Wipe Clean Workbook: Cursive Handwriting. (p. 2477)
—Wipe Clean Workbook Lowercase Alphabet. (p. 2477)
—Wipe Clean Workbook: Lowercase Alphabet (enclosed Spiral Binding) Ages 3-6; with Pen & Flash Cards. (p. 2477)
—Wipe Clean Workbook: My First Letters & Numbers: Ages 3+; with Pen. (p. 2477)
—Wipe Clean Workbook: Number Skills (enclosed Spiral Binding) (p. 2477)
—Wipe Clean Workbook Numbers 1-20. (p. 2477)
—Wipe Clean Workbook: Sight Words (enclosed Spiral Binding) (p. 2477)
—Wipe Clean Workbook: Starting Spelling: An Introduction to Spelling with 48 Pages of Practical Exercises to Do Many Times Over. (p. 2477)
—Wipe Clean Workbook: Times Tables (enclosed Spiral Binding) (p. 2477)
—Wipe Clean Workbook Tracing & Pen Control. (p. 2477)
—Wipe Clean Workbook: Uppercase Alphabet (enclosed Spiral Binding) (p. 2477)
Priddy, Roger, jt. auth. see Priddy Books Staff.
Priddy, Roger, adapted by. Baby Bear, Baby Bear, What Do You See? Cloth Book. (p. 149)
Pride, Dana. My Friend Is Deaf. Brown, Jahla, illus. (p. 1547)
Pride, Dana L. So How Is That a Bully? (p. 2050)
Pride, H. Hammond. Golden Rod: April, 1909 (Classic Reprint) (p. 858)
—Golden-Rod: January 1909 (Classic Reprint) (p. 858)
Prideaux, William Francis. Mother Goose's Melody: A Facsimile Reproduction of the Earliest Known Edition; with an Introduction & Notes (Classic Reprint) (p. 1509)
Pridemore, Lola. Other Girls: A Young Adult Paranormal Novel About a Witch, a Ghost & a Mystery. (p. 1674)
Pridmore, Chris. Last Child of Leif. (p. 1247)
Priebe, Gigi. Adventures of Henry Whiskers. Duncan, Daniel, illus. (p. 24)
—Long Way Home. Duncan, Daniel, illus. (p. 1343)
Priebe, Ken. Gnomes of the Cheese Forest & Other Poems. (p. 845)
—Let There Be Owls Everywhere: Another Book of Poems. (p. 1269)
Priebe, Trisha & Jenkins, Jerry B. Glass Castle. (p. 841)
—Paper Boat. (p. 1697)
—Ruby Moon. (p. 1911)
Priebe, Val. Basketball Breakdown. (p. 171)
—Five Fouls & You're Out! Santillan, Jorge H., illus. (p. 743)
—I Don't Want to Live on the Tennis Court Santillan, Jorge H., illus. (p. 1064)
—I Only Surf Online Santillan, Jorge H., illus. (p. 1080)
—It's Hard to Dribble with Your Feet Santillan, Jorge H., illus. (p. 1145)
Priebisch, Karin. Marchen - eine Brucke Zwischen Zwei Welten. (p. 1402)
Priemaza, Anna. Fan the Fame. (p. 705)
—Kat & Meg Conquer the World. (p. 1204)
Pries, Terra. Secrets of Wonderland: The Queen Returns. (p. 1981)
Priess, Brett. Go, Percy, Go! van de Beek, Mariella, illus. (p. 848)
Priest, Cherie. Agony House. O'Connor, Tara, illus. (p. 35)
—I Am Princess X. Ciesemier, Kali, illus. (p. 1059)
Priest, Christopher & Texeira, Mark. Marvel Knights Black Panther by Priest & Texeira: the Client. (p. 1412)
Priest, Elizabeth. Changeling's Choice: Book II of the Troutespond Series. (p. 356)
—Concrete Faery: Book I of the Troutespond Series. (p. 438)
—Midsummer Dance: Book III of the Troutespond Series. (p. 1462)
Priest, Iris Aspinall, illus. see Webster, Jean.
Priest, Josiah. Wonders of Nature & Providence, Displayed: Compiled from Authentic Sources, Both Ancient & Modern, Being an Account of Various & Strange Phenomena Existing in Nature, of Travels, Adventures, Singular Providences, &c (Classic Reprint) (p. 2490)
Priest, Mary E. Recitations Dialogues, Vol. 2: For Special Days in the Sunday School (Classic Reprint) (p. 1853)
Priest, Robert. Paper Sword. (p. 1697)
—Rosa Rose. Krygsman, Joan, illus. (p. 1904)
—Second Kiss: Spell Crossed. (p. 1973)
Priester, Jen. God Likes Me. (p. 851)
—Secret Closet. (p. 1975)
Priester, Jennifer. Mortal Realm Witch: The Magical Adventures of Dww2. Priester, Jennifer, illus. (p. 1507)
Priesti, Lori, jt. auth. see Daronco, Mickey.
Priestley, Alice, illus. see Gilmore, Rachna.
Priestley, Alice, illus. see Setterington, Ken.
Priestley, Alice, jt. auth. see Gilmore, Rachna.
Priestley, Chris. Curse of the Werewolf Boy. (p. 489)
—Dead Men Stood Together. (p. 518)
—Through Dead Eyes. (p. 2236)
—Treasure of the Golden Skull. (p. 2282)
Prieto, Anita C. Little Louisiana. Knorr, Laura, illus. (p. 1321)
Prieto, Iliana. Juicio a Tres Brujas. (p. 1186)
—Nina y el Rey Dragon. (p. 1609)
Prieto, Rafaela. Myvera's Love of Sunshine. (p. 1572)
Prieu, Remi & Vives, Melanie. Escape Game Adventure: the Mad Hacker: The Mad Hacker Gunto, El, illus. (p. 661)
Prigent, Andree, illus. see Paranuzzi, Fred.
Priggins, Author of Peter. Parish Clerk, Vol. 3 of 3 (Classic Reprint) (p. 1700)
Prigioniero, Lily. De las cuevas a los Lienzos. (p. 517)
—From Caves to Canvas & de las cuevas a los Lienzos: 6 English, 6 Spanish Adaptations Hanner, Albert, illus. (p. 791)
Prigmore, Shane, illus. see Ganz-Schmitt, Sue.
Prigmore, Shane, illus. see Scieszka, Jon.
Prignano, Barbara. Angelo: The Underappreciated Ant. (p. 86)
—How Bunnies Got Their Cottontails. (p. 1026)
—Tiny Tomato & His Terrific Manners. Kalpart, illus. (p. 2250)
Prijatel, Patricia. How Did the Pirate Get onto the Mountain? (p. 1027)
Prima Games. Pokémon Hoenn Region Field Guide. (p. 1768)
—Pokémon Sinnoh Region Field Guide. (p. 1768)
Prima Games Staff. Pokemon Activity Book. (p. 1768)
Primavera, Elise. Auntie Claus & the Key to Christmas. (p. 137)
—Auntie Claus Gift Edition. Primavera, Elise, illus. (p. 137)
—Auntie Claus, Home for the Holidays. Primavera, Elise, illus. (p. 137)
—I'm a Baked Potato! Medina, Juana, illus. (p. 1097)
—Libby of High Hopes. (p. 1283)
—Libby of High Hopes. Primavera, Elise, illus. (p. 1283)
—Louise the Big Cheese: Divine Diva. Goode, Diane, illus. (p. 1357)
—Louise the Big Cheese & the Back-To-School Smarty-Pants. Goode, Diane, illus. (p. 1357)
—Louise the Big Cheese & the La-Di-Da Shoes. Goode, Diane, illus. (p. 1358)
—Louise the Big Cheese & the Ooh-la-La Charm School. Goode, Diane, illus. (p. 1358)
—Making Mistakes on Purpose. (p. 1389)
—Marigold Star. Primavera, Elise, illus. (p. 1405)
—Ms. Rapscott's Girls. (p. 1523)
—Project Blue Ribbon. Primavera, Elise, illus. (p. 1805)
Prime, Anne, tr. see Adbage, Emma.
Prime, Annie, tr. see Adbage, Lisen.
Prime, Samuel Irenaeus. Letters from Switzerland (Classic Reprint) (p. 1280)
—Travels in Europe & the East, Vol. 1 Of 2: A Year in England, Scotland, Ireland, Wales, France, Belgium, Holland, Germany, Austria, Italy, Greece, Turkey, Syria, Palestine, & Egypt (Classic Reprint) (p. 2281)
—Under the Trees (Classic Reprint) (p. 2323)
—Walking with God: The Life Hid with Christ (Classic Reprint) (p. 2372)
Prime, W. C. Along New England Roads (Classic Reprint) (p. 58)
—Among the Northern Hills (Classic Reprint) (p. 76)
—I Go a-Fishing (Classic Reprint) (p. 1065)
—I Go a-Fishing - Scholar's Choice Edition. (p. 1065)
Prime, William Cowper. Later Years (Classic Reprint) (p. 1250)
Primeau, Chuck, illus. see Easton, Marilyn.
Primeau, Chuck, illus. see Steele, Michael Anthony.
Primeros, Pasos. Actividades Didacticas para Ninos: Juegos y Actividades para Ninos de Entre 3 a 5 Anos de Edad. (p. 12)
Primiano, Jay, jt. auth. see Rocco, John.
Primmasone, Bruce, illus. see Hasan, K. A.
Primogenita, Primogenita. Recollections of Childhood: Or, Sally, the Faithful Nurse (Classic Reprint) (p. 1854)
Primrose, Alison. Non-Verbal Reasoning, Age 9-11. (p. 1618)
—Verbal Reasoning, Age 10-12. (p. 2351)
Prince, Amy, tr. see Ehlert, Lois.
Prince, Andrea, illus. see Morgan, Emily.
Prince, April Jones. 101 Dinosaurs: And Other Prehistoric Reptiles. Kolar, Bob, illus. (p. 2558)
—Dive In! Berg, Michelle, illus. (p. 565)
—Goldenlocks & the Three Pirates. Salerno, Steven, illus. (p. 860)
—Snowy Race. Davenier, Christine, illus. (p. 2049)
—Who Was Frederick Douglass? (p. 2450)
—¿Qué Hacen las Ruedas Todo el Día? Laroche, Giles, illus. (p. 1822)
Prince, April Jones & Who HQ. Who Was Frederick Douglass? Squier, Robert, illus. (p. 2450)
Prince, Brian, illus. see Jonell, Bob.
Prince, Cheryl. Belle's Wild Journey. (p. 198)
Prince, Edward. Wake up, England! Being the Amazing Story of John Bull - Socialist. (p. 2371)
—Wake up, England! Being the Amazing Story of John Bull Socialist (Classic Reprint) (p. 2371)
Prince, George. Tamar (Classic Reprint) (p. 2188)
Prince, Gregory L. Runkus Black: Starting Something. (p. 1915)
Prince, Helen Choate. At the Sign of the Silver Crescent (Classic Reprint) (p. 131)
—Story of Christine Rochefort (Classic Reprint) (p. 2129)
Prince, Jack. Master's Chef. (p. 1419)
Prince, Jennifer S. Life & Times of Asheville's Thomas Wolfe. (p. 1289)
Prince, John T. Arithmetic by Grades for Inductive Teaching, Drilling & Testing, Book Number One. (p. 116)

—Stop Zits & Acne! Explaining Where They Come from - How to Stop Them - Hygiene for Kids - Children's Disease Books. (p. 2122)
—Summer Fun Activities to Help Me Be Smart Before I Go to Kindergarten - Children's Early Learning Books. (p. 2149)
—T-Rex (Tyrannosaurus Rex)! Fun Facts about the T-Rex - Dinosaurs for Children & Kids Edition - Children's Biological Science of Dinosaurs Books. (p. 2174)
—Triceratops (Three Horned Face)! Fun Facts about the Triceratops - Dinosaurs for Children & Kids Edition - Children's Biological Science of Dinosaurs Books. (p. 2287)
—Velociraptor (Raptors)! Fun Facts about the Velociraptor - Dinosaurs for Children & Kids Edition - Children's Biological Science of Dinosaurs Books. (p. 2349)
—Vitamins! - What Foods Give You Which Vitamins - Healthy Eating for Kids - Children's Diet & Nutrition Books. (p. 2363)
—What My Body Needs to Grow! a Kid's First Book All about Nutrition - Healthy Eating for Kids - Children's Diet & Nutrition Books. (p. 2419)
—Whiskers to Tails! All about Lions (Big Cats Wildlife) - Children's Biological Science of Cats, Lions & Tigers Books. (p. 2442)
—Whiskers to Tails! All about Tigers (Big Cats Wildlife) - Children's Biological Science of Cats, Lions & Tigers Books. (p. 2442)
—Zinc! Foods That Give You Daily Zinc - Healthy Eating for Kids - Children's Diet & Nutrition Books. (p. 2540)
Prodigy Wizard Books. Addition Games for Second Graders Math Essentials Children's Arithmetic Books. (p. 15)
—Addition Grade 1 Math Essentials Children's Arithmetic Books. (p. 15)
—Alphabet Writing Practice Workbook Preschool Edition. (p. 59)
—Counting Basics Workbook 1st Grade. (p. 459)
—Cursive Handwriting Book: Children's Reading & Writing Education Books. (p. 489)
—Cursive Handwriting Workbook Grade 6: Children's Reading & Writing Education Books. (p. 490)
—First Words Books for Toddlers: Children's Reading & Writing Education Books. (p. 740)
—First Words Picture Book: Children's Reading & Writing Education Books. (p. 740)
—Fractions 4th Grade Math Essentials: Children's Fraction Books. (p. 775)
—Fractions Books for Kids Math Essentials: Children's Fraction Books. (p. 775)
—Fractions Children's Book Math Essentials: Children's Fraction Books. (p. 775)
—Fractions for 3rd Grade Math Essentials: Children's Fraction Books. (p. 775)
—Fractions for 5th Graders Math Essentials: Children's Fraction Books. (p. 775)
—Handwriting Practice for Teens: Children's Reading & Writing Education Books. (p. 916)
—Learn to Read Workbook Kindergarten Edition. (p. 1257)
—Multiplication Division Workbook Math Essentials Children's Arithmetic Books. (p. 1525)
—Multiplication Games for 3rd Graders Math Essentials Children's Arithmetic Books. (p. 1525)
—Multiplication Grade 3 Math Essentials Children's Arithmetic Books. (p. 1525)
—Multiplication Workbook Math Essentials Children's Arithmetic Books. (p. 1525)
—Penny Wise & Pound Smarts! - Counting Money Learning Activity Book: Children's Money & Saving Reference. (p. 1717)
—Phonics for 1st Grade: Children's Reading & Writing Education Books. (p. 1736)
—Phonics for 2nd Grade: Children's Reading & Writing Education Books. (p. 1736)
—Phonics for Grade 2: Children's Reading & Writing Education Books. (p. 1736)
—Phonics for Kindergarten Grade K Home Workbook: Children's Reading & Writing Education Books. (p. 1736)
—Phonics for Reading Level 2: Children's Reading & Writing Education Books. (p. 1736)
—Phonics for Toddlers: Children's Reading & Writing Education Books. (p. 1736)
—Piggy Bank & the Clock - Time & Money Book: Children's Money & Saving Reference. (p. 1743)
—Printing Practice 1st Grade: Children's Reading & Writing Education Books. (p. 1800)
—Ratios & Proportions Math Essentials: Children's Fraction Books. (p. 1843)
—Ratios Made Simple Math Essentials: Children's Fraction Books. (p. 1843)
—Ratios Math Book Children's Fraction Books. (p. 1843)
—Subtraction Kindergarten Math Essentials Children's Arithmetic Books. (p. 2146)
—Teach Kids to Count Money! - Counting Money Learning: Children's Money & Saving Reference. (p. 2194)
—Trace Your Letters Workbook Tracing Edition. (p. 2272)
—Write-And-Learn Sight Word Practice Pages Reading & Phonics Teaching Materials. (p. 2512)
Prodor, Bob, illus. see Davidge, James.
Productions, Donkey Ollie. Tales of Donkey Ollie. (p. 2184)
Productions, Georgia. Amazingly Disorganised Help Dictionary. (p. 67)
Proenneke, Richard. More Readings from One Man's Wilderness: The Journals of Richard L. Proenneke, 1974-1980 (Classic Reprint) (p. 1505)
Proenneke, Richard L. More Readings from One Man's Wilderness: The Journals of Richard L. Proenneke, 1974-1980 (Classic Reprint) (p. 1505)
Profeit, R. A. Under Lochnagar (Classic Reprint) (p. 2321)
Professor, Baby. 1st Grade Geography: Continents of the World. (p. 2546)
—Match This & Match That! Matching Game Kids Edition Activity Books for Kids 5-7. (p. 1420)
—Mexico for Kids: People, Places & Cultures - Children Explore the World Books. (p. 1454)
Professor Beaver. Ancient China's Inventions, Technology & Engineering - Ancient History Book for Kids Characteristics of Early Societies. (p. 80)
—Evolution of Humans According to Uncle Charles - Understanding Life Systems - Growth & Changes in Animals. (p. 675)
—Just Keep Swimming - Underwater Volcanoes, Trenches & Ridges - Geography for Kids Patterns in the Physical Environment. (p. 1193)
—Leto's Hidden Twins: Artemis & Apollo - Mythology Book for Kids Greek & Roman Past & Present Societies. (p. 1269)
—Mecca, Baghdad, Cordoba & More - the Major Cities of Islamic Rule - History Book for Kids Past & Present Societies. (p. 1435)
—Science & Inventions of the Islamic Golden Age - Religion & Science Characteristics of Early Societies Grade 4. (p. 1953)
—Umayyad, Abbasid & Ottoman Caliphates - Islamic Empire: Characteristics of Early Societies Grade 4. (p. 2316)
—United States Civics - Bill of Rights for Kids 1787 - 2016 Incl Amendments Social, Economic & Political Context (Us Precontact) (p. 2331)
—What's Inside the Forbidden City? Ancient History Book for Kids Past & Present Societies. (p. 2425)
—World's Most Useful Animals - Horses, Cows, Chickens & More - Animal Books 2nd Grade Physical Features & Communities. (p. 2507)
Proffitt, Kim. Coco the Little Red Bird: Massy Returns. (p. 411)
Profiri, Charline. Guess Who's in the Desert. Swan, Susan, illus. (p. 903)
—He's Your Daddy: Ducklings, Joeys, Kits, & More Gabriel, Andrea, illus. (p. 963)
—Rain, Rain, Stay Today: Southwestern Nursery Rhymes. Watson, Laura, illus. (p. 1835)
Profitt, Hannah, illus. see Smith, Crystal.
Profugus, Fato. White Olive: And Other Romances of the Riviera (Classic Reprint) (p. 2444)
Progiante, J. M. Blua Son_o en Antverpeno. (p. 247)
—Malbeno de Tarumo Kaj Nurana. (p. 1391)
Program, Indiana University Digital Libr. Woman's Strategy: Or the First Time I Saw Her, a Novel (Classic Reprint) (p. 2486)
Prohl, Hedwig. Where Is Heaven? (Classic Reprint) (p. 2437)
Prohosky, Eva, jt. auth. see Forehand, Terri.
Proimos, James. 12 Things to Do Before You Crash & Burn. (p. 2551)
—Complete Adventures of Johnny Mutton. (p. 434)
—Mac & Cheese: A Friendship Story That Celebrates Being Different. Proimos, James, illus. (p. 1371)
—Todd's TV. Proimos, James, illus. (p. 2255)
—Waddle! Waddle! Proimos, James, illus. (p. 2370)
Proimos, James, illus. see Collins, Suzanne.
Proimos, James, III & Proimos, James, Jr. Apocalypse Bow Wow. Proimos, James, III & Proimos, James, Jr., illus. (p. 105)
Proimos, James, Jr. Apocalypse Meow Meow. Proimos, James, Jr., illus. (p. 105)
—Knuckle & Potty Destroy Happy World. Proimos, James, Jr., illus. (p. 1230)
Proimos, James, Jr., jt. auth. see Proimos, James, III.
Project Firefly, illus. see Weeks, Kermit.
Project, Louisiana Writers'. Gumbo YA-YA: A Collection of Louisiana Folk Tales (Classic Reprint) (p. 905)
—Gumbo YA-YA (Classic Reprint) (p. 905)
Project, Making Of America. Century Illustrated Monthly Magazine, Vol. 83: November 1911 to April 1912 (Classic Reprint) (p. 352)
—Century, Vol. 75: Illustrated Monthly Magazine; November, 1907, to April, 1908 (Classic Reprint) (p. 352)
—Century, Vol. 81: Illustrated Monthly Magazine; November, 1910, to April, 1911 (Classic Reprint) (p. 352)
—Littell's Living Age, Vol. 107: October, November, December, 1870 (Classic Reprint) (p. 1309)
—Littell's Living Age, Vol. 130: July, August, September, 1876 (Classic Reprint) (p. 1310)
—Littell's Living Age, Vol. 188: January, February, March, 1891 (Classic Reprint) (p. 1310)
—Littell's Living Age, Vol. 51: From the Beginning, Vol. 166; July, August, September, 1885 (Classic Reprint) (p. 1310)
—Putnam's Magazine, Vol. 3: Original Papers on Literature, Science, Art, & National Interests; January-June, 1869 (Classic Reprint) (p. 1818)
—Putnam's Monthly, 1856, Vol. 7: A Magazine of Literature, Science, & Art (Classic Reprint) (p. 1818)
—Putnam's Monthly Magazine of American Literature, Science, & Art, Vol. 7: January to July, 1856 (Classic Reprint) (p. 1818)
—Putnam's Monthly Magazine of American Literature, Science, & Art, Vol. 4: July to December 1854 (Classic Reprint) (p. 1818)
—Putnam's Monthly Magazine of American Literature, Science, & Art, Vol. 8: July to January, 1857 (Classic Reprint) (p. 1818)
—Putnam's Monthly, Vol. 10: Magazine of American Literature, Science & Art; July-September, 1857 (Classic Reprint) (p. 1818)
—Scribner's Magazine, Vol. 4: July-December, 1888 (Classic Reprint) (p. 1965)
—Which, the Right, or the Left? (Classic Reprint) (p. 2441)
Projetos, Fenix, ed. see Lobato, Monteiro.
Prokofyev, Dmitry, tr. see Curtiss, Dominique.
Prokop, Ginny. Little People Angel Book. (p. 1324)
Prokopowicz, Linda. Rocky the Reading Dog. (p. 1896)
Prokos, Anna. Blades of Green: Adventures in Backyard Habitats. Blake, Mike, illus. (p. 242)
—Don't Blow Your Top! A Look Inside Volcanoes. Selivanova, Elena, illus. (p. 582)
—Elephants. (p. 634)
—Ice Queen: Exploring Icebergs & Glaciers. Tablason, Jamie, illus. (p. 1088)
—No Bones about It: Discovering Dinosaurs. Kendall, Gideon, illus. (p. 1612)
—Seed Power: Discovering How Plants Grow. Clegg, Dave, illus. (p. 1982)
—Star Light, Star Bright: Exploring Our Solar System. Clegg, Dave, illus. (p. 2102)
Prokos, Anna & Voege, Debra. Half-Pipe Homonyms. Angle, Scott, illus. (p. 911)
—Slap Shot Synonyms & Antonyms. (p. 2035)
—Track Star Sentences. (p. 2272)
Prole, Helen, illus. see David, Juliet & Ayliffe, Alex.
Prole, Helen, illus. see David, Juliet.
Prom, Shirley, illus. see Rendall, Jaydine.
Propes, Chrysti Carol. I Am. Bostrom, Laura, illus. (p. 1056)
—I Am Here. Bostrom, Laura, illus. (p. 1058)
Prophete, Evanda. Dress for Grandma. (p. 604)
ProPio, tr. see Hernandez, Mario.
Propst, Milam McGraw. Further Adventures of Ociee Nash. (p. 802)
Prose, Francine. Bullyville. (p. 297)
—Rhino, Rhino, Sweet Potato. Armstrong, Matthew S., illus. (p. 1874)
—Touch. (p. 2267)
—Turning. (p. 2300)
Prosek, James. Bird, Butterfly, Eel. (p. 230)
—Day My Mother Left. Prosek, James, illus. (p. 513)
Prosmitsky, Jenya, illus. see Cleary, Brian P.
Prosper, John. Gold-Killer a Mystery of the New Underworld (Classic Reprint) (p. 856)
Prosser. Fables for the Young Folks (Classic Reprint) (p. 691)
Prosser, Charonne. Cambridge IGCSE(tm) Spanish Workbook (Collins Cambridge IGCSE(tm)) (p. 313)
Prosser, Sue, illus. see Elson, Clare.
Prosterman, Daniel, jt. auth. see Bryant, Megan E.
Prostko, Andrea. Strike One! (p. 2141)
Prothero, Tiffany. Let's Go Green! An Earth-Friendly Coloring Book. (p. 1273)
Prothero, Tiffany, illus. see Brezenoff, Steve.
Prothero, Tiffany, illus. see Dahl, Michael.
Prothero-Lewis, Helen. Hooks of Steel, Vol. 1 of 3 (Classic Reprint) (p. 1000)
—Hooks of Steel, Vol. 3 (Classic Reprint) (p. 1000)
—Thraldom (Classic Reprint) (p. 2231)
Protopapas, Athanassios. Lemon & Lime Library: An Articulation Screen & Resource Pack. Pack (p. 1266)
Prottsman, Kiki. Coding with Anna & Elsa: A Frozen Guide to Blockly. (p. 412)
—Coding with Anna & Elsa: A Frozen Guide to Blockly. Disney Storybook Artists, Disney Storybook, illus. (p. 412)
—My First Coding Book. (p. 1543)
Prottsman, Kiki, jt. auth. see Dorling Kindersley Publishing Staff.
Proud, Amy. Izzy the Very Bad Burglar. (p. 1150)
Proud, Amy, illus. see Booth, Anne.
Proud, Amy, illus. see Koontz, Robin Michal.
Proudfit, Benjamin. Bayley. (p. 176)
—Benjamin Franklin. (p. 200)
—Brock Lesnar. (p. 284)
—Building the White House. (p. 295)
—Daniel Bryan. (p. 502)
—Let's Go to a Birthday Party! (p. 1273)
—Let's Go to a Carnival (p. 1273)
—Let's Go to a Cookout! (p. 1273)
—Let's Go to a Halloween Party! (p. 1273)
—Let's Go to a Parade! (p. 1273)
—Let's Go to the Fair! (p. 1274)
—Miz. (p. 1484)
—Oregon Trail. (p. 1670)
—Pacific Coast Highway. (p. 1691)
—Roman Reigns. (p. 1899)
—Seahorses (p. 1969)
—Seals (p. 1970)
—Walruses (p. 2373)
—Why Do Ice Cubes Float? (p. 2456)
—Why Does Food Go Bad? (p. 2457)
—Writing Book Reports. (p. 2513)
—Writing Letters. (p. 2513)
—Writing Opinion Papers. (p. 2513)
—Writing Poems. (p. 2513)
—Writing Research Papers. (p. 2513)
Proudfoot, Andrea Hofer. Child's Christ-Tales, Vol. 3 (Classic Reprint) (p. 375)
Proudfoot, Dean, jt. auth. see Holt, Sharon.
Proudfoot, Kenneth. Home Depot Manifesto! Positive Suggestions to Boost the Future of Retailing! (p. 996)
Proulx, Denis, illus. see Esparza-Vela, Mary.
Proulx, Denis, illus. see Loccisano, Rina Fuda.
Proulx, Denis, illus. see Averette, Sonya M.
Proulx, Denis, illus. see Gould, Terry.
Proulx, Denis, illus. see M a.
Proulx, Denis, illus. see Milot, Carryanne.
Proulx, Denis, illus. see Novinsky, J. L.
Proulx, Denis, illus. see Stephens, Heather.
Proulx, Denis, illus. see Worthen, Rashawn.
Prout, Chessy & Abelson, Jenn. I Have the Right To: A High School Survivor's Story of Sexual Assault, Justice, & Hope. (p. 1066)
Prout, Louise, illus. see Bursztynski, Sue.
Proutsos, Steve. Daddy's Little Princess. (p. 495)
Prouty, Olive Higgins. Bobbie, General Manager: A Novel (Classic Reprint) (p. 252)
—Fifth Wheel: A Novel (Classic Reprint) (p. 724)
—Fifth Wheel. (p. 724)
—Good Sports (Classic Reprint) (p. 866)
—Star in the Window: A Novel (Classic Reprint) (p. 2102)
Provata-Carlone, Mika, tr. see Seyvos, Florence.
Provata-Carlone, Mika, tr. see Szac, Murielle.
Provencal, Amy. Allison the Alligator. (p. 56)
Provencher, Annematie, illus. see Finneron, Karyn A.
Provencher, Devon. God: A Theological Primer Series. Provencher, Jessica, illus. (p. 850)
—Gospel: A Theological Primer Series. Provencher, Jessica, illus. (p. 870)
—Jesus: A Theological Primer Series. Provencher, Jessica, illus. (p. 1165)
Provencher, Jessica, illus. see Provencher, Devon.
Provencio, Marta. Christmas Dragon. (p. 385)
Provensen, Alice. Glorious Flight: Across the Channel with Louis Bleriot. (p. 844)
—Master Swordsman & the Magic Doorway: Two Legends from Ancient China. Provensen, Alice, illus. (p. 1419)
—Murphy in the City. Provensen, Alice, illus. (p. 1527)
Provensen, Alice, illus. see Brown, Margaret Wise.
Provensen, Alice, illus. see Jackson, Kathryn.
Provensen, Alice, illus. see Werner Watson, Jane.
Provensen, Alice & Provensen, Martin. Golden Mother Goose. (p. 858)
Provensen, Martin, illus. see Brown, Margaret Wise.
Provensen, Martin, illus. see Jackson, Kathryn.
Provensen, Martin, illus. see Werner Watson, Jane.
Provensen, Martin, jt. auth. see Provensen, Alice.
Provoost, Anne. Falling 20th Anniversary Edition. Nieuwenhuizen, John, tr. (p. 701)
Provost, Maxime. My Austrian Love: The History of the Adventures of an English Composer in Vienna, Written in the Trenches by Himself (Classic Reprint) (p. 1531)
Prows, Jackie, illus. see Pardew, David.
Prowse, Jean. P. N. S. Anecho, 1940-1 (Classic Reprint) (p. 1690)
Prozeller, Ellen Lucey. 32 Days: A Story of Faith & Courage. (p. 2555)
Prude, Alfred Marion. Benton Battle Field (Classic Reprint) (p. 201)
Prudhomme, Donna. PROCESSbook: A Goal Planning Workbook Designed to Help Middle School Students Set Goals & Increase Their Confidence. (p. 1803)
Prue, Kyle. Ashes: Book III of the Feud Trilogy. (p. 125)
—Flames: Book II of the Feud Trilogy. (p. 746)
—Sparks: Book I of the Feud Trilogy. (p. 2075)
Prue, Nancy C. Friends & Adventures. (p. 786)
Pruessen, Linda. Saving Eyesight: Adventures of Seva Around the World. (p. 1938)
Pruett, Jason. Seek & Find: Book of Mormon Stories (Board Book) (p. 1984)
—Seek & Find Book of Mormon Stories. (p. 1984)
—So You Want to See the World? (p. 2051)
Pruett, Jason, illus. see Poelman, Heidi.
Pruett, Joe. Black Eyed Kids Volume 2. Marts, Mike, ed. (p. 238)
Pruett, Joe, ed. see Ennis, Garth.
Pruett, Joe, ed. see Gaiman, Neil, et al.
Pruett, Joe, ed. see Starlin, Jim.
Pruett, Joshua. DreamWorks Dragons: Adventures with Dragons: A Pop-Up History. (p. 603)
Pruett, Joshua, jt. auth. see Peterson, Scott.
Pruett, Mary. Color the Western Birds: Discover the Great Outdoors. (p. 421)
Pruett, Nichole Lee. My Best Friend. Rowton, Caitlin, illus. (p. 1532)
Pruitt, Dudley. Haverfordian: Volumes XLII-XLIII; May, 1922-May, 1924 (Classic Reprint) (p. 940)
Pruitt, Gwendolyn, illus. see Ross, Jill.
Pruitt, H. A. Anelthalien (p. 85)
Pruitt, Kat. Si Si the Circus Cat. Griffner, Rebecca, illus. (p. 2014)
Pruitt, Keith. These Amazing Animals. (p. 2218)
Pruitt, Priscilla. Billy the Bully: Choose Love. (p. 227)
Prune, Nat. College Chaps (Classic Reprint) (p. 415)
—Wedding Bells: And Other Sketches (Classic Reprint) (p. 2395)
Prunier, James. Elephants. (p. 634)
—My First Discoveries -Dinosaurs. (p. 1543)
—Trains. Grant, Donald & Prunier, James, illus. (p. 2276)
Prunier, James & Matthews, Sarah. Dinosaurs. Prunier, James & Galeron, Henri, illus. (p. 550)
Prus, Jennifer. Toddler's Abc of Blessings. McIlhany, illus. (p. 2255)
Pruyn, Mary. Grandmamma's Letters from Japan (Classic Reprint) (p. 878)
Pruzansky, Binyomin. Stories for a Child's Heart. Katz, Tova, illus. (p. 2123)
Pry, Peter. Peter Pry's Puppet Show, Vol. 2 (Classic Reprint) (p. 1729)
Pry, Rebecca, illus. see Novak, Margaret.
Pryce, Adam, illus. see Jones, Cath.
Pryce, Adam, illus. see O'Neill, Juliana.
Pryce, Adam, illus. see Rodriguez, Stephanie.
Pryce, Adam, illus. see Streza, Nancy.
Pryce, D. Hugh. Goddesses Three, Vol. 1 Of 2: A Novel (Classic Reprint) (p. 852)
Pryce, Richard. Christopher (Classic Reprint) (p. 388)
—David Penstephen (Classic Reprint) (p. 511)
—Elementary Jane (Classic Reprint) (p. 632)
—Statue in the Wood (Classic Reprint) (p. 2109)
—Successor: A Novel (Classic Reprint) (p. 2146)
—Time & the Woman: A Story of the Early Nineties (Classic Reprint) (p. 2243)
—Visit: A Play in One Act (Classic Reprint) (p. 2362)
—Winifred Mount, Vol. 1 Of 2: A Novel (Classic Reprint) (p. 2473)
Pryce, Sasha. Labby's Adventures. (p. 1235)
Pryce, Trevor. Amphibians' End (a Kulipari Novel #3) Greene, Sanford, illus. (p. 77)
Pryce, Trevor & Naftali, Joel. Rainbow Serpent: A Kulipari Novel. Greene, Sanford, illus. (p. 1836)
Pryce, Trevor & Ziebart, David A. Foster Broussard: Demons of the Gold Rush. (p. 771)
Pryce, William. Archaeologia Cornu-Britannica; or, an Essay to Preserve the Ancient Cornish Language; Containing the Rudiments of That Dialect, in a Cornish Grammar & Cornish-English Vocabulary. (p. 110)
—Archaeologia Cornu-Britannica, or an Essay to Preserve the Ancient Cornish Language: Containing the Rudiments of That Dialect, in a Cornish Grammar & Cornish-English Vocabulary (Classic Reprint) (p. 110)
Pryde, Anthony. Jenny Essenden (Classic Reprint) (p. 1164)
—Ordeal of Honor (Classic Reprint) (p. 1669)
Pryde, David. Queer Folk of Fife: Tales from the Kingdom (Classic Reprint) (p. 1825)
—Queer Folk of Fife. (p. 1825)
Prydz, Alvide. Heart of the Northern Sea (Classic Reprint) (p. 945)
Prydz, Alvilde. Sanpriel: The Promised Land (Classic Reprint) (p. 1931)

P

—Early Learning: My First Library. (p. 614)
—Electronic Time for Learning: Music. (p. 632)
—Electronic Time for Learning: States. (p. 632)
—Electronic Time for Learning: The Human Body. (p. 632)
—Elmo & Friends. (p. 638)
—Elmo Goes to the Doctor. (p. 638)
—Elmo's Neighborhood Lights & Music Treasury. (p. 639)
—Enchanted Forest. (p. 647)
—Eric Carle Counting Write & Erase Sound. (p. 659)
—Eric Carle Little Pop-Up Song Book. (p. 659)
—Explore with Elmo Magnifying Glass Sound Book. (p. 680)
—Fairy Tales. Goodell, Jon & Clar, David Austin, illus. (p. 697)
—Finding Nemo: A Party for Nemo. (p. 730)
—Finding Nemo: Let's Go to School. (p. 730)
—Finding Nemo: Hide & Seek: Book & Plush. (p. 730)
—Finding Nemo - Let's Go to School. (p. 730)
—Fire Truck: (Play-a-Sound Book) (p. 733)
—First Look & Find Hello Kitty. (p. 738)
—First Look & Find Little Elf. (p. 738)
—First Words (Listen & Learn Sound Book) (p. 740)
—Friendship Songs. (p. 788)
—Full Moon Monster Madness (Look & Find) (p. 797)
—Fun to Color. (p. 800)
—Fun to Draw. (p. 800)
—Good Night, Little Bear: A Sleepy Time Tale. (p. 864)
—Goof's Adventure. (p. 869)
—Grandma Loves You: Stories to Share. (p. 878)
—Green Lantern Large Play a Sound. (p. 894)
—Gross (Look & Find) (p. 898)
—Halloween Is Coming! (p. 912)
—Happy Baby. (p. 920)
—Hello Kitty: Hello Songs: Play-A-Sound Digital Music Player Book. (p. 951)
—Hello Kitty I Love to Play Piano. (p. 951)
—Hello Kitty: My Friend Hello Kitty: Play-A-Sound Book & Cuddly Hello Kitty. (p. 951)
—Hello Kitty Sweet Songs: Play-A-Sound. (p. 951)
—Hello Kitty(r); Hello Kitty's Guitar. (p. 951)
—Holiday Easter Play a Song Disney Bunnies. (p. 987)
—I Can Be a Princess: Picture Book. (p. 1061)
—I Can Read! (p. 1063)
—I Love You. (p. 1078)
—If You're Happy & You Know It! (p. 1093)
—Interactive Play a Sound Thomas the Tank. (p. 1125)
—It's Riddle Time! (p. 1147)
—Itsy Bitsy Spider. (p. 1148)
—Jake & the Neverland Pirates. (p. 1155)
—Jake & the Neverland Pirates: What Do You See? Pop up Book & Flashlight Set. (p. 1155)
—Jesus Loves Me. (p. 1166)
—Kindergarten Boot Camp. (p. 1218)
—Let's Have a Race, Surprises, Little Engines. (p. 1274)
—Let's Learn to Read! (p. 1274)
—Lights & Music Treasury. (p. 1300)
—Lights & Music Treasury 10Led Spa Disney Classics. (p. 1300)
—Lights, Music, & Me! Love Sparkles. (p. 1300)
—Little Carry Case Spa Cars 8 Bks. (p. 1313)
—Little Sound the Princess & the Frog. (p. 1328)
—Look & Find: Myths & Heroes. (p. 1344)
—Look & Find: Disney Princess: Magical Moments. (p. 1344)
—Look & Find Activity Pad Mickey Mouse. (p. 1344)
—Look & Find - Animals. (p. 1344)
—Look & Find - Captain America: The First Avenger. (p. 1344)
—Look & Find - Cars (p. 1344)
—Look & Find: Disney Pixar Cars. (p. 1344)
—Look & Find: Disney Princess: Winter Dreams. (p. 1344)
—Look & Find Elmo. (p. 1344)
—Look & Find Green Lantern. (p. 1344)
—Look & Find - My First Look & Find Barney. (p. 1344)
—Look & Find: Nickelodeon: Teenage Mutant Ninja Turtles. (p. 1344)
—Look & Find - Noah's Arc & Other Bible Stories. (p. 1344)
—Look & Find: Snoopy. (p. 1345)
—Look & Find Wolverine & X Men. (p. 1345)
—Marvel: Spider-Man: Spectacular Spider Powers! (p. 1412)
—Mater Saves the Day. (p. 1421)
—Mejores Amigos. (p. 1442)
—Mickey & Friends Look & Find Extreme. (p. 1459)
—Mickey Mouse 10 Song Sound. (p. 1459)
—Mickey Mouse Clubhouse: Count To 10. (p. 1459)
—Mickey Mouse Clubhouse: Play Day Songs. (p. 1459)
—Mickey Mouse Clubhouse: Hot Dog! Sing Along! (p. 1459)
—Mickey Mouse Clubhouse: Ask a Silly Question. (p. 1459)
—Mickey Mouse Clubhouse: Lights on, Lights Off! (p. 1459)
—Mickey Mouse Clubhouse: Telling Time with Mickey. (p. 1459)
—Mickey Mouse Clubhouse: Mickey's Silly Shadow Book. (p. 1459)
—Mickey Mouse Clubhouse: Mickey & Friends (Look & Find) (p. 1459)
—Mickey Mouse Clubhouse: Doctor Kit Book & Mickey Plush. (p. 1459)
—Mickey Mouse Clubhouse: Las canciones de piano de Mickey. (p. 1459)
—Mickey Mouse Clubhouse. (p. 1459)
—Mickey Mouse Clubhouse (book Block) (p. 1459)
—Mickey Mouse Clubhouse: Colors: Sing & Learn. (p. 1459)
—Mickey Mouse Clubhouse: Sing-along Christmas Songs: Holiday Play-a-Song Book. (p. 1459)
—Mickey Mouse Clubhouse Super Look & Find Activity Pad with Stickers. (p. 1459)
—Mickey Mouse Clubhouse, What's Different? (p. 1459)
—Mickey Mouse Clubhouse - Who's Not Sleepy? (p. 1459)
—Mickey's Adventure. (p. 1459)
—Mickey's Clubhouse Drum Song Sound. (p. 1459)
—Mickey's Piano Songs Play & Learn. (p. 1459)
—Minnie Mouse: Pretty Piano Play-Along: Piano Book. (p. 1473)
—Minnie Mouse: Surprise, Surprise! Play-A-Sound Book. (p. 1473)
—Monsters Can Share. (p. 1497)
—Move to the Music. (p. 1516)
—My 1st Libraries Disney Classics. (p. 1530)
—My Alphabet Book. (p. 1531)
—My Colors Book. (p. 1535)
—My First Book Block - First Words. (p. 1542)
—My First Book Block Set Animals. (p. 1542)
—My First Book Block Set Disey Princess. (p. 1542)
—My First Look & Find - Chuggington. (p. 1544)
—My First Look & Find Winnie The Pooh. (p. 1544)
—My First Phonics Dictionary. (p. 1545)
—My First Story Reader Dora the Explorer. (p. 1546)
—My First U.S. Map Puzzle. (p. 1546)
—My First Wipe-off: A to Z Animals Dictionary. (p. 1546)
—My Little Prayer Book. (p. 1554)
—My Little Treasury Cuddle up Stories. (p. 1554)
—My Little Treasury: First Prayers & Blessings. (p. 1554)
—My Little Treasury My First Bible Stories. (p. 1554)
—My Numbers Book. (p. 1558)
—My Shapes Book. (p. 1560)
—Nickelodeon Dora the Explorer: When I Grow Up. (p. 1603)
—Nickelodeon Dora the Explorer: Follow the Music. (p. 1603)
—Nickelodeon Dora the Explorer: Let's Go! (Musical Treasury) (p. 1603)
—Nickelodeon Dora the Explorer: Choo, Choo, Let's Go! (p. 1603)
—Nickelodeon Dora the Explorer: Cook with Dora: Abuela's Birthday Fiesta. (p. 1603)
—Nickelodeon Dora the Explorer: Follow the Music: Piano Book. (p. 1603)
—Nickelodeon Dora the Explorer Little Piano Book. (p. 1603)
—Nickelodeon(tm) Spongebob Squarepants: Look & Find(r). (p. 1603)
—Night Before Christmas Giant Look & Find. (p. 1605)
—Numbers (Listen & Learn Sound Book) (p. 1630)
—Numbers Learning Board. (p. 1630)
—Old MacDonald Had a Farm. (p. 1646)
—On Sesame Street. (p. 1653)
—Once upon a Potty Sound Book for Boys. (p. 1657)
—Once upon a Time. (p. 1658)
—Out & About. (p. 1682)
—Padded Treasury 160 Spa Sesame Street. (p. 1691)
—Phineas & Ferb Time for Fun Play-A-Sound. (p. 1735)
—Planes 2 Look & Find. (p. 1754)
—Planes up, up & Away! (p. 1755)
—Play a Sound 10 Stories Winnie the Pooh. (p. 1758)
—Play & Learn Piano Dora. (p. 1759)
—Play & Learn Piano Elmo. (p. 1759)
—Play-a-Puzzle Book: Halloween. (p. 1758)
—Play-a-Puzzle trade; Book: Alphabet. (p. 1758)
—Please & Thank You. (p. 1762)
—PNO BK Spa Disney Princess. (p. 1763)
—Pooh's Pop-up Stories. (p. 1774)
—Pooh's Pop-up Stories 2. (p. 1774)
—Popping up on Sesame Street. (p. 1776)
—Potty Time for Monsters. (p. 1781)
—Potty Time with Big Sister Dora. (p. 1781)
—Potty Time with Elmo. (p. 1781)
—Potty Time with Tiger: Boy. (p. 1781)
—Potty Time with Tiger: Girl. (p. 1781)
—Preschool Reading & Math Activities. (p. 1788)
—Princess & the Frog. (p. 1796)
—Princess Magic. (p. 1798)
—Princess Songs Play & Learn. (p. 1799)
—Pub Time Sports Trivia. (p. 1810)
—Race Car. (p. 1830)
—Race Day. (p. 1831)
—Rainbow Kittens A Colorful Tale. (p. 1836)
—Read to Me Grandma (Keepsake Story Collection) (p. 1845)
—Really Useful Engines. (p. 1851)
—Record a Song Old Mac Donald. (p. 1854)
—Record A Story: My Grandma Is Special. (p. 1854)
—Record a Story: My Grandpa Is Special. (p. 1854)
—Record a Story: 'Twas the Night Before Christmas. (p. 1854)
—Record a Story Elmo'S Bedtime Wish. (p. 1854)
—Record a Story with Thomas & Friends: Good Night, Little Engine. (p. 1854)
—Record Story Goldilocks 3 Bears. (p. 1854)
—Record Story Little Red Riding Hood. (p. 1854)
—Record Story Three Little Pigs. (p. 1854)
—Record Story Ugly Duckling. (p. 1854)
—Record-A-Memory School Years. (p. 1854)
—Right on Time Rescues. (p. 1882)
—Ring-a-Ling! A Friend Is Here. (p. 1883)
—Ring-A-Ling Day! (p. 1883)
—Rock & Roll with Elmo. (p. 1894)
—Rockin' on the Railway. (p. 1895)
—Rudolph the Red-Nosed Reindeer: Little Pop-Up Song Book. (p. 1912)
—Rudolph the Red-Nosed Reindeer (Book & Plush) (p. 1912)
—Rudolph the Red-Nosed Reindeer (Look & Find) (p. 1912)
—Rudolph the Red-Nosed Reindeer(r): A Flashlight Adventure Sound Book. (p. 1912)
—Scooby Doo: Spooky Shadows: Flashlight Adventure Sound Book. (p. 1961)
—Sesame I Can Do It. (p. 1992)
—Sesame Play a Sound Stero. (p. 1992)
—Sesame St Let's Go to School First Look & Find. (p. 1992)
—Sesame Street: Potty Time Songs. (p. 1992)
—Sesame Street: Good Night Stories. (p. 1992)
—Sesame Street: Merry Christmas, Elmo! (p. 1992)
—Sesame Street: The Itsy Bitsy Spider. (p. 1992)
—Sesame Street: My First Book of Firsts. (p. 1992)
—Sesame Street: Monsters in the Bathroom. (p. 1992)
—Sesame Street: Trick or Treat with Elmo. (p. 1992)
—Sesame Street: Potty Time with Elmo (Look & Find) (p. 1992)
—Sesame Street: Elmo's Potty Book (First Look & Find) (p. 1992)
—Sesame Street: Merry Christmas, Elmo! (Book & Plush) (p. 1992)
—Sesame Street: Potty Time Songs. Berry, Bob et al, illus. (p. 1992)
—Sesame Street: Sing with Elmo, Let's Sing! & Wake up, Elmo! (p. 1992)
—Sesame Street (Musical Treasury) (p. 1992)
—Sesame Street, Ding Dong, Elmo's Here! (p. 1992)
—Sesame Street: Find a Friend: A Busy Box Book. (p. 1992)
—Sesame Street Happy Birthday to You. (p. 1992)
—Sesame Street Picture Puzzle. (p. 1992)
—Sesame Street: Sing & Play Guitar Songs. (p. 1992)
—Sesame Street(r) Elmo's Valentine. (p. 1992)
—Sesame Street(r) Happy Easter, Elmo! (p. 1992)
—Sesame Street(r) Listen & Learn in Your Neighborhood. (p. 1992)
—Sesame Street(r) Where Is Elmo's Friend? Play-A-Sound(r) Lift-a-Flap Sound Book. (p. 1993)
—Sesame Write & Erase Board Book. (p. 1993)
—Shapes Wipe off Learning Board. (p. 2000)
—Sing-Along Songs. (p. 2023)
—Sketch This: Hundreds of Ways to Express Yourself! (p. 2030)
—Sleepy Baby. (p. 2037)
—Smurfs Large Play a Sound. (p. 2043)
—Sofia the First - Sofia's Royal Day: Includes 6 Punch-Out Play Pieces. Phoenix Books Staff, illus. (p. 2054)
—Soft! Furry! Bumpy! A Touch, Hear, & Learn with Elmo Book. (p. 2054)
—Solar System Puzzle. (p. 2056)
—Spider Sense Spider-Man: Super Villain Showdown. (p. 2081)
—SpongeBob Squarepants (Little Look & Find) (p. 2086)
—Spongebob Squarepants Sea Mail. (p. 2086)
—Starry Sky Songs. (p. 2106)
—Staying Smart in Summer: Entering 1st Grade. (p. 2110)
—Staying Smart in Summer: Entering 2nd Grade. (p. 2110)
—Staying Smart in Summer: Entering Kindergarten. (p. 2110)
—Steering Wheel Spa Cars. (p. 2112)
—Stories to Grow on Spa Disney Classics. (p. 2126)
—Stories to Grow on Spa Mickey Mouse Clubhous. (p. 2126)
—Story Reader Me Reader & Disney 8-Book Library. (p. 2135)
—Sunny Sing-Along Songs. (p. 2153)
—Sunshine Doodle Book. Designs, Dena, illus. (p. 2153)
—Super Fun Sticker Activities: More Than 1,000 Stickers! (p. 2155)
—Surprise for Belle. (p. 2163)
—Teenage Mutant Ninja Turtles(tm) Dojo: A Flashlight Adventure Sound Book. (p. 2200)
—Teenage Ninja Turtles: Skateboard Heroes! (p. 2200)
—Things That Go Board Book. (p. 2221)
—Thomas & Friends: Sodor Snapshots. (p. 2227)
—Thomas & Friends: Engine Roll Call. (p. 2227)
—Thomas & Friends: Let's Go, Thomas! (p. 2227)
—Thomas & Friends: Sing-Along Songs. (p. 2227)
—Thomas & Friends: Lights, Music & Me! (p. 2227)
—Thomas & Friends: A Busy Day on Sodor. (p. 2227)
—Thomas & Friends: Play-a-Tune Puzzle Book. (p. 2227)
—Thomas & Friends: Ding! Dong! A Visit from Thomas. (p. 2227)
—Thomas & Friends: Super Look & Find Activity Pad with Stickers. (p. 2227)
—Thomas & Friends Super Look & Find Activity Pad. (p. 2227)
—Thomas & Friends(tm) Super Look & Find(r) Activity Pad: Spot the Find 'ems, Find the Differences! Giant Play Scene! More Than 50 Stickers! (p. 2227)
—Thomas Celebration Pop Up Sound. (p. 2228)
—Thomas Great to be Engine Little Sound. (p. 2228)
—Thomas, Railway Race Day Little Lift & Listen. (p. 2229)
—Thomas Songs Play & Learn. (p. 2229)
—Thomas the Tank Good Morning Engines. (p. 2229)
—Tinker Bell: Talent Shines Through. (p. 2248)
—Tinker Bell: Songs from Pixie Hollow. (p. 2248)
—Tinker Bell. (p. 2248)
—Tinker Bell (Book & Plush) (p. 2248)
—Tinker Bell -Tink's Magical Day. (p. 2248)
—Tinkerbell. (p. 2248)
—Touch & Hear Adventure. (p. 2268)
—Toy Story 3: New Friends. (p. 2270)
—Toys to the Rescue. (p. 2271)
—Tractor. (p. 2272)
—Trains. (p. 2276)
—Treasure Hunt. (p. 2281)
—Up & down! Play-a-Sound Book & Huggable Kai-lan. (p. 2337)
—Vampires & Other Scary Creatures(Look & Find) (p. 2346)
—Very Busy Day for Sodor: (Stereo Play-a-Sound) (p. 2352)
—Video Play a Sound Dora. (p. 2356)
—What Do You See? (p. 2409)
—What's Different. (p. 2423)
—What's Different? (p. 2423)
—What's Different Finding Nemo. (p. 2423)
—Whats That Sound? (p. 2426)
—Where in the World. (p. 2437)
—Who's Not Sleepy? (p. 2453)
—Winnie the Pooh: I Love You Winnie the Pooh. (p. 2474)
—Winnie the Pooh: Super Look & Find Activity Pad. (p. 2474)
—Winnie the Pooh: Sing along with Pooh (Little Pop-up Songbook) (p. 2474)
—Winnie the Pooh: Super Look & Find Activity Pad with Stickers. (p. 2474)
—Winnie the Pooh (Find-A-Friend Book) (p. 2474)
—Winnie the Pooh Drum Sound. (p. 2474)
—Winnie the Pooh Large Look & Find Activity Pad. (p. 2474)
—Winnie The Pooh Large Play A Sound. (p. 2474)
—World of Eric Carle - Baby Animals. (p. 2502)
—World of Eric Carle - Baby's First Animal Treasury: Plays Music While You Read! (p. 2502)
—World of Eric Carle: Merry Christmas: Play-A-Sound Book. (p. 2502)
—World of Eric Carle(tm) Hear Bear Roar. (p. 2502)
—Write-And-Erase Look & Find(r) Disney Minnie: Packed with 'find 'ems & Picture Puzzles! Look, Circle, Wipe Clean, & Play Again! (p. 2512)
—Write-And-Erase Look & Find(r) Disney(r) Sofia the First: More Than 100 Find 'ems! Find & Corcle 'em. Wipe Clean & Play Again! (p. 2512)
—Writing Skills Wipe off Leaning Board. (p. 2513)
—Xylophone Dora. (p. 2516)
—Yesterday & Today: Chevrolet. (p. 2521)
—Zoom! (p. 2544)

Publications International Ltd. Staff, et al. Yesterday & Today Nashville. (p. 2521)

Publisher, La Luz Books & Reyes, Maria de la Luz. ¿cómo Voy a Hablar con Abuela? Illustrations, Blueberry, illus. (p. 433)

Publisher, Saure, ed. see Gutierrez, Pello.

Publisher, Saure, ed. see Lopetegi, Jose a.

Publisher, Saure, ed. see Martinez De Antonana, Gonzalo.

Publishers, Chelsea House, jt. auth. see Winter, William West.

Publishers, Chelsea House, creator. Animal Behavior Set, 6-Volumes. (p. 88)
—Building America: Then & Now Set, 8-Volumes. (p. 294)
—Costume & Fashion Source Books, 8-Volumes. (p. 457)
—Leaders of the Civil War Era Set, 10-Volumes. (p. 1254)
—Restless Earth Set, 6-Volumes. (p. 1870)

Publishing, Arcturus. Animal Drawing, Doodling & Coloring. (p. 89)
—Color by Numbers Animals. (p. 419)
—Complete Guide to Drawing Comics. (p. 434)
—Jungle. (p. 1189)
—Knock Knock! Who's There? 500 Hilarious Jokes for Kids. (p. 1229)
—Really Cool Craft Book. (p. 1851)

Publishing, Autumn. I Want to Color BIG Pictures. (p. 1085)

Publishing, Baobab, illus. see Autrey, Matasha Elaine.

Publishing, Baobab, illus. see Brandon III, Fred Lee.

Publishing, Baobab, illus. see Coley, Regina E.

Publishing, Baobab, illus. see Goldsmith-Tate, Shayla.

Publishing, Baobab, illus. see Kelvonia, India.

Publishing, Baobab, illus. see Nixon, Tiffany.

Publishing, Berean. My Pony Planner. (p. 1559)

Publishing, Berlitz. Berlitz English Flash Cards. (p. 203)
—Berlitz Phrase Book & Dictionary Dutch (Bilingual Dictionary) (p. 203)

Publishing, Chouette. Caillou, My First ABC: The Alphabet Soup. Brignaud, Pierre, illus. (p. 309)

Publishing, Chouette & Paradis, Anne. Caillou, Sweet Dreams: Nightlight Book. Dupuis, Karina et al, illus. (p. 309)

Publishing Co, Learn with Colour. Learn with Color Routine & Time with ABC's Coloring Book: Whilst Coloring Learn about Clocks & Telling the Time, Daily School Routine & Practice the Alphabet, Early Years Learning with Color for Toddlers & Preschoolers. (p. 1257)
—Learn with Colour Routine & Time with ABC's Colouring Book: Whilst Coloring Learn about Clocks & Telling the Time, Daily School Routine & Practice the Alphabet, Early Years Learning with Color for Toddlers & Preschoolers. (p. 1257)

Publishing, Crimson Cloak, contrib. by. Santa's Little Helpers. (p. 1933)

Publishing, Gameplay. Amazing World of Slime Coloring Book: 25 Popular Slimes - Fishbowl Slime, Butter Slime, Unicorn Slime, Fluffy Slime, Popcorn Slime & More! (p. 67)
—Animals Coloring Book for Kids & Toddlers: 50 Different Animals Including Farm Animals, Jungle Animals, Woodland Animals & Sea Animals (Jumbo Activity Book for Kids Ages 2-4, 4-8, Boys & Girls, Fun Early Learning) (p. 94)
—Feliz Pascua - Libro de Matemáticas para Colorear: Arte con Píxeles para niños: Problemas con Sumas, Restas, Multiplicaciones y Divisiones (Ejercicios de Matemáticas para Primaria) (p. 719)
—Stampy Cat Maths: Problems for Elementary School. (p. 2100)

Publishing, Gameplay & Coloring Books, Kids. Winter Wonderland Color by Number for Kids: Christmas & Winter Themed Coloring Activity Book. (p. 2476)

Publishing, Gameplay & Library, Math Coloring. Animals Math Coloring Book: Addition & Subtraction Practice, Grades 1-2 (Pixel Art for Kids) (p. 95)
—Animals Math Coloring Book: Multiplication & Division Practice, Grades 3-4 (Pixel Art for Kids) (p. 95)
—Merry Christmas Math Coloring Book: Pixel Art for Kids: Addition, Subtraction, Multiplication & Division Practice Problems (Christmas Activity Books for Kids) (p. 1450)
—Spooky Math Coloring Book: Addition, Subtraction, Multiplication & Division Practice Problems (Halloween Activity Books for Kids) (p. 2087)

Publishing, Gameplay & Series, Color by Number. Animals Color by Number for Kids: 50 Animals Including Farm Animals, Jungle Animals, Woodland Animals & Sea Animals (Jumbo Coloring Activity Book for Kids Ages 4-8, Boys & Girls, Fun Early Learning) (p. 94)

Publishing, Hatchback. Rockin' Rams Stories. (p. 1895)

Publishing Inc, Make It Happen. Blank Comic Book for Girls: Activity Sketchbook with Professional & Unique Layouts. (p. 243)
—My Comic Book: Rookie Series 001. (p. 1535)
—Rap Journal: Rapper Notebook for Writing Lyrics, Rhymes & Ideas. (p. 1841)
—Rap Journal: Rapper Notebook for Writing Lyrics & Composing Rap Music. (p. 1841)

Publishing, Jake Stories, illus. see Labelle, Charles J.

Publishing, Jake Stories, illus. see Labelle, Charles.

Publishing, Jake Stories, jt. auth. see Labelle, Charles J.

Publishing, Magic Journal, jt. auth. see Journals, Summer Smith.

Publishing, Mginternet. Birds of Number 10. (p. 232)

Publishing, S. a. Boxer & Brandon: English Greek. (p. 267)
—Boxer & Brandon: Chinese Edition. (p. 267)
—Boxer & Brandon: Greek Language Children's Book. (p. 267)
—Boxer & Brandon: Korean Language Children's Book. (p. 267)
—Boxer & Brandon: Chinese English Bilingual Edition. (p. 267)
—Boxer & Brandon: English Chinese Bilingual Edition. (p. 267)
—Boxer & Brandon: Russian English Bilingual Edition. (p. 267)
—Boxer & Brandon: Tagalog English Bilingual Edition. (p. 267)
—Boxer & Brandon: English Korean Bilingual Children's Books. (p. 267)
—Boxer & Brandon (English Arabic Children's Book) Arabic Kids Book. (p. 267)
—Boxer & Brandon (English Hungarian Children's Book) Hungarian Kids Book. (p. 267)

P

—Book of Dust: the Secret Commonwealth (Book of Dust, Volume 2) (p. 258)
—Brujula Dorada. (p. 287)
—Catalejo Lacado. (p. 342)
—Daga. (p. 495)
—Der goldene Kompass. (p. 530)
—Epouvantail et Son Valet. (p. 659)
—Firework-Maker's Daughter. (p. 734)
—Golden Compass Graphic Novel, Complete Edition. (p. 857)
—His Dark Materials: The Golden Compass, the Subtle Knife, the Amber Spyglass. (p. 974)
—His Dark Materials: Once upon a Time in the North. Lawrence, John, illus. (p. 974)
—His Dark Materials: the Golden Compass (HBO Tie-In Edition) (p. 974)
—Libro de la Oscuridad. (p. 1286)
—Libro de la Oscuridad I. la Bella Salvaje. (p. 1286)
—Libro de la Oscuridad II. la Comunidad Secreta. (p. 1286)
—Ruby in the Smoke. (p. 1911)
—Scarecrow & His Servant. (p. 1941)
—Two Crafty Criminals! And How They Were Captured by the Daring Detectives of the New Cut Gang. (p. 2307)
Pulman, Felicity. Ring Through Time. (p. 1883)
—Rue for Repentance. (p. 1912)
Pulman, G. P. R. Rustic Sketches: Being Rhymes on Angling & Other Subjects Illustrative of Rural Life, &C. , in the Dialect of the Best of England; with Notes & a Glossary (Classic Reprint) (p. 1917)
Pulsar Studios Staff, illus. see Maddox, Jake.
Pulsifer, Janice. Do Not Be Afraid. (p. 570)
Pulsifer, Tristan, jt. auth. see Johnson, Jacquelyn Elnor.
Pulsifer, Tristan & Johnson, Jacquelyn Elnor. I Want a Bearded Dragon. (p. 1084)
—I Want a Kitten or a Cat. (p. 1084)
—I Want a Leopard Gecko: Book 1. (p. 1084)
—I Want a Leopard Gecko. (p. 1084)
—I Want a Puppy or a Dog. (p. 1084)
Pulszky, Theresa. Tales & Traditions of Hungary (Classic Reprint) (p. 2181)
Pulver, Harry, Jr., illus. see Rooney, Melissa.
Pulver, Mary Brecht. Spring Lady (Classic Reprint) (p. 2092)
Pulver, Robin. Case of the Incapacitated Capitals. Reed, Lynn Rowe, illus. (p. 337)
—Happy Endings: A Story about Suffixes. (p. 922)
—Happy Endings: A Story about Suffixes. Reed, Lynn Rowe, illus. (p. 922)
—Nouns & Verbs Have a Field Day. Reed, Lynn Rowe, illus. (p. 1625)
—Persuading Miss Doover. Sisson, Stephanie Roth, illus. (p. 1725)
—Punctuation Takes a Vacation. Reed, Lynn Rowe, illus. (p. 1814)
—Silent Letters Loud & Clear. Reed, Lynn Rowe, illus. (p. 2017)
Pulvers, Roger, tr. see Corporation (NHK), Japan Broadcasting.
Pumphrey, Jerome & Pumphrey, Jarrett. Old Truck. (p. 1648)
Pumphrey, Margaret B. Stories of the Pilgrims. (p. 2125)
—Stories of the Pilgrims (Classic Reprint) (p. 2125)
Puncel, María, tr. see Minarik, Else Holmelund.
Punch, Punch. London Medical Student, & Curiosities of Medical Experience (Classic Reprint) (p. 1341)
—Mrs. Caudle's Curtain Lectures (Classic Reprint) (p. 1521)
Punches, Piper. Brave Hearts: The Lavender Fairies. (p. 276)
Pung, Alice. Lucy & Linh. (p. 1365)
—Marly & the Goat Masciullo, Lucia, illus. (p. 1408)
—Marly's Business. Masciullo, Lucia, illus. (p. 1408)
Pung, Alice & Masciullo, Lucia. Marly Walks on the Moon. (p. 1408)
Punkinhead, Tatie. Plungermania! (p. 1763)
Punnett, Yvonne, ed. see Punnett, Dick.
Punniyamurthi, Kavitha. Lucy's Purple Pullover. Punniyamurthi, Kavitha, illus. (p. 1366)
Punset, Ana. Best Friends Forever: Primer año en el Internado / Best Friends Forever: First Year at Boarding School. (p. 206)
Punshon, Ernest Robertson. Bittermeads Mystery (Classic Reprint) (p. 235)
—Constance West (Classic Reprint) (p. 443)
Punter, R. Pirate Adventures. (p. 1749)
Punter, Russell. Chilly Little Penguin. (p. 377)
—Clásicos en Cómic Usborne Drácula(Dracula) (p. 399)
—Cow Takes a Bow. Blunt, Fred, illus. (p. 464)
—Danny & the Dragon. (p. 504)
—Easter Story. (p. 620)
—Encyclopedia of Planet Earth: Internet-Linked. Harvey, Gil, illus. (p. 648)
—Flamingo Plays Bingo. (p. 746)
—Hyena Ballerina IR. (p. 1056)
—Kitty Kat Kitty Kat Rome. (p. 1226)
—Kitty Kat Kitty Kat Washington DC. (p. 1226)
—Kitty Kat, Kitty Kat Where Have You Been - London. (p. 1226)
—Kitty Kat, Kitty Kat Where Have You Been - New York. (p. 1226)
—Kitty Kat, Kitty Kat Where Have You Been - Paris. (p. 1226)
—Llamas in Pajamas. (p. 1337)
—Odyssey. (p. 1638)
—Pirate Stories for Little Children. (p. 1750)
—Poodle Draws Doodles. (p. 1773)
—Scaredy Cat. (p. 1941)
—Sherlock Holmes: The Hound of the Baskervilles. (p. 2006)
—There Was a Crooked Man. Semple, David, illus. (p. 2217)
—Three Musketeers. (p. 2234)
—Underpants for Ants. Blunt, Fred, illus. (p. 2324)
Punter, Russell & MacKinnon, Mairi. Snail Brings the Mail. Blunt, Fred, illus. (p. 2044)
Punter, Russell, retold by. Illustrated Stories from the Greek Myths. (p. 1096)
Puoti, Basilio. Avviamento All'arte Dello Scrivere: O Prime Esercitazioni Di Comporre in Italiano per I Giovaneti (Classic Reprint) (p. 143)
Puppel, Douglas. Hero Named Mark. Verrill, William, illus. (p. 961)
Purcell, Gordon, illus. see Adamson, Thomas K.
Purcell, Gordon, illus. see Burgan, Michael & Hoena, Blake A.
Purcell, Gordon, illus. see Burgan, Michael.
Purcell, Gordon, illus. see Doeden, Matt.
Purcell, Gordon, illus. see Fandel, Jennifer.
Purcell, Gordon, illus. see Fontes, Justine & Fontes, Ron.
Purcell, Gordon, illus. see Fontes, Ron & Fontes, Justine.
Purcell, Gordon, illus. see Fontes, Ron.
Purcell, Kim. This Is Not a Love Letter. (p. 2225)
—Trafficked. (p. 2274)
Purcell, Mark C. & Murphy, Jason R. Mindfulness for Teen Anger: A Workbook to Overcome Anger & Aggression Using MBSR & DBT Skills. (p. 1470)
Purcell, Rebecca. Cat Can Fly. (p. 341)
—Zip, the World's Greatest Robot. (p. 2541)
Purcell, Stuart. Aviary on Queen Street. (p. 143)
—Heartblazer: Children's Underground Fantasy Novel for 9-12 Year Olds. (p. 946)
—Pocketful of Stories. (p. 1764)
Purcell, Susan. Animals. (p. 93)
—Letters. (p. 1279)
—Numbers. (p. 1630)
—Three Little Pigs. (p. 2233)
—Words. (p. 2494)
Purcell, W. L. Words & Illustrations: Special Cartoons (Classic Reprint) (p. 2494)
Purchase, Brendan, illus. see Hibbitts, Mark.
Purchase, Commission on War Supplies. Royal Commission Concerning Purchase of War Supplies & Sale of Small Arms Ammunition, Vol. 1: Evidence (Classic Reprint) (p. 1909)
Purchase, Elizabeth. Charlie Meets Santa. Larina, Lida, illus. (p. 360)
—Warm for Winter. Foltz-Gray, Matthew, illus. (p. 2379)
Purdie, Kate. Personal Hygiene. (p. 1725)
—Sunshine & Drought. (p. 2153)
Purdie, Kathryn. Bone Crier's Moon. (p. 255)
—Burning Glass. (p. 300)
—Crystal Blade. (p. 481)
—Frozen Reign. (p. 796)
Purdon, K. F. Folk of Furry Farm, the Romance of an Irish Village (Classic Reprint) (p. 757)
Purdon, Katherine Frances. Candle & Crib (Classic Reprint) (p. 321)
—Dinny of the Doorstep (Classic Reprint) (p. 547)
Purdy, Charles McMorris. Old Academy (Classic Reprint) (p. 1644)
Purdy, Elizabeth, jt. auth. see Books, Golson.
Purdy, Elizabeth Rholetter. Celebrating Women in American History. (p. 350)
Purdy, Jill. James Madison, the U. S. Constitution: Set Of 12. (p. 1157)
—James Madison, the U. S. Constitution. (p. 1157)
Purdy, Rebekah L. Summer Marked. (p. 2149)
—Winter People. (p. 2476)
Puren, Barbara-Anne. Family Just Like Mine. (p. 702)
Purenins, Stef, jt. auth. see Graley, Sarah.
Puri, Devi. Making Tools in the Wild (p. 1390)
—Plants That Hide. (p. 1757)
—Recycling, Reusing, & Conserving. (p. 1855)
—Seeds, Bulbs, & Sprouts. (p. 1983)
—Sydney Works at the School Store. (p. 2172)
Puri, Pooja. Jungle. (p. 1189)
Purkiss, Cathy. Flat on Top. (p. 747)
Purkiss, Keith. Very Clumsy Elf. (p. 2353)
Purkiss, Sue. Jack Fortune: And the Search for the Hidden Valley. (p. 1152)
—Life & Times of William Shakespeare: Band 18/Pearl. (p. 1290)
Purnama, Adif. Dinosaurs Doing Things: 25 Pictures of Dinosaurs That Are Fun & Easy for Kids to Color. (p. 551)
—Dinosaurs Doing Things, Volume 2: 25 More Pictures of Dinosaurs That Are Fun & Easy for Kids to Color. (p. 551)
Purnawan, Jeff, illus. see Wallace, Danielle.
Purnell, Brontez. Nightlife of Jacuzzi Gaskett. Peterson, Elise R., illus. (p. 1608)
Purnell, Gerald, illus. see Anderson, Richard.
Purnell, Gerald, illus. see Burgess, Gloria J. McEwen.
Purnell, Teresa, illus. see Lamond, Peter.
Purpus, Daphne Ashling. Fox, the Stag, & the Dragon. (p. 774)
Pursell, Olivia. When Grandma Goes to Heaven. (p. 2430)
Pursh, Frederick. Flora Americæ Septentrionalis, or a Systematic Arrangement & Description of the Plants of North America, Vol. 1 Of 2: Containing, Besides What Have Been Described by Preceding Authors, Many New & Rare Species, Collected During Twelve Years' Travel An. (p. 750)
Purslow, Frances. Descriptive Paragraphs. (p. 531)
—Expository Paragraphs. (p. 684)
—Narrative Paragraphs. (p. 1575)
—Persuasive Paragraphs. (p. 1725)
—Precipitation. (p. 1786)
—Rugby. (p. 1912)
—Water Cycle. (p. 2384)
Purslow, Neil. Minnesota: The North Star State. (p. 1473)
—Minnesota. (p. 1473)
—R.L. Stine. (p. 1888)
—Spooky World of R.L. Stine. (p. 2087)
Purtill, C. Leigh. FaceSpace Face-Off! (p. 693)
—In Your Face. (p. 1112)
Purtle, Louise. Potato Pie Pirate. Guiza, Victor, illus. (p. 1781)
Purton, Michael. Show Me How: I Can Make Music. (p. 2012)
Purves, Dale. You & Your Brain: A Neuroscientist Explains the Brain to His 10 Year Old Grandson. (p. 2524)
Purvis, Kaneta. Planter: Pot of Dirt. (p. 1757)
—Shae & Lee's Lemonade Stand. (p. 1998)
Purvis, Leland, illus. see Jablonski, Carla.
Purvis, Leland, illus. see Poe, Marshall.
Puschkin, Alexander L. M. Captain's Daughter (Classic Reprint) (p. 326)
Pushies, Fred J., jt. auth. see Aronin, Miriam.
Pushies, Fred J., jt. auth. see Lunis, Natalie.
Pushies, Fred J., jt. auth. see Markovics, Joyce L.
Pushies, Fred J., jt. auth. see Rudolph, Jessica.
Pushies, Fred J., jt. auth. see Sandler, Michael.
Pushkareva, Natalia & Levin, Eve. Women in Russian History: From the Tenth to the Twentieth Century. (p. 2487)
Pushker, Gloria Teles & Tarman, Mel. Toby Belfer Learns about Heroes & Martyrs Henriquez, Emile, illus. (p. 2254)
Pushkin, Alexander. Eugene Oneguine: A Romance of Russian Life in Verse. (p. 667)
—Marie: A Story of Russian Love (Classic Reprint) (p. 1404)
—Skazki Pushkina - Fairy Tales. Bilibin, Ivan, illus. (p. 2030)
Pushkin, Alexander, jt. auth. see Borrow, George Henry.
Pushkin, Alexander & Borrow, George Henry. Targum. (p. 2191)
Pushkin, Alexksandr Sergeevich. Daughter of the Commandant. (p. 509)
Puskarich, Michelle, illus. see Hill, Lisa.
Put, Klaartje van der, illus. see Chronicle Books Staff & Image Books Staff.
Put, Klaartje van der, illus. see Chronicle Books Staff & ImageBooks Staff.
Put, Klaartje van der, illus. see Image Books Staff & Chronicle Books Staff.
Put, Klaartje van der, illus. see ImageBooks Staff & Chronicle Books (Firm) Staff.
Put, Klaartje van der, illus. see ImageBooks Staff & Chronicle Books Staff.
Put Me In The Story & Sully, Katherine. Abigail Santa's Secret Elf. Seal, Julia, illus. (p. 5)
—Addison Santa's Secret Elf. Seal, Julia, illus. (p. 15)
—Aiden Santa's Secret Elf. Seal, Julia, illus. (p. 36)
—Alexander Santa's Secret Elf. Seal, Julia, illus. (p. 42)
—Allison Santa's Secret Elf. Seal, Julia, illus. (p. 56)
—Amelia Santa's Secret Elf. Seal, Julia, illus. (p. 69)
—Andrew Santa's Secret Elf. Seal, Julia, illus. (p. 84)
—Anthony Santa's Secret Elf. Seal, Julia, illus. (p. 102)
—Aria Santa's Secret Elf. Seal, Julia, illus. (p. 115)
—Aubrey Santa's Secret Elf. Seal, Julia, illus. (p. 135)
—Ava Santa's Secret Elf. Seal, Julia, illus. (p. 141)
—Avery Santa's Secret Elf. Seal, Julia, illus. (p. 143)
—Benjamin Santa's Secret Elf. Seal, Julia, illus. (p. 200)
—Brooklyn Santa's Secret Elf. Seal, Julia, illus. (p. 285)
—Camila Santa's Secret Elf. Seal, Julia, illus. (p. 314)
—Carter Santa's Secret Elf. Seal, Julia, illus. (p. 335)
—Charlotte Santa's Secret Elf. Seal, Julia, illus. (p. 361)
—Chloe Santa's Secret Elf. Seal, Julia, illus. (p. 380)
—Christopher Santa's Secret Elf. Seal, Julia, illus. (p. 388)
—Daniel Santa's Secret Elf. Seal, Julia, illus. (p. 503)
—David Santa's Secret Elf. Seal, Julia, illus. (p. 511)
—Dylan Santa's Secret Elf. Seal, Julia, illus. (p. 612)
—Elijah Santa's Secret Elf. Seal, Julia, illus. (p. 635)
—Elizabeth Santa's Secret Elf. Seal, Julia, illus. (p. 636)
—Ella Santa's Secret Elf. Seal, Julia, illus. (p. 637)
—Emily Santa's Secret Elf. Seal, Julia, illus. (p. 642)
—Emma Santa's Secret Elf. Seal, Julia, illus. (p. 643)
—Ethan Santa's Secret Elf. Seal, Julia, illus. (p. 666)
—Evelyn Santa's Secret Elf. Seal, Julia, illus. (p. 668)
—Gabriel Santa's Secret Elf. Seal, Julia, illus. (p. 804)
—Grace Santa's Secret Elf. Seal, Julia, illus. (p. 873)
—Hannah Santa's Secret Elf. Seal, Julia, illus. (p. 918)
—Harper Santa's Secret Elf. Seal, Julia, illus. (p. 931)
—Henry Santa's Secret Elf. Seal, Julia, illus. (p. 955)
—I Am Santa's Secret Elf. Seal, Julia, illus. (p. 1059)
—Isaac Santa's Secret Elf. Seal, Julia, illus. (p. 1138)
—Isabella Santa's Secret Elf. Seal, Julia, illus. (p. 1138)
—Jackson Santa's Secret Elf. Seal, Julia, illus. (p. 1154)
—Jacob Santa's Secret Elf. Seal, Julia, illus. (p. 1154)
—James Santa's Secret Elf. Seal, Julia, illus. (p. 1157)
—Jaxon Santa's Secret Elf. Seal, Julia, illus. (p. 1161)
—Jayden Santa's Secret Elf. Seal, Julia, illus. (p. 1161)
—John Santa's Secret Elf. Seal, Julia, illus. (p. 1174)
—Joseph Santa's Secret Elf. Seal, Julia, illus. (p. 1178)
—Joshua Santa's Secret Elf. Seal, Julia, illus. (p. 1179)
—Layla Santa's Secret Elf. Seal, Julia, illus. (p. 1253)
—Leah Santa's Secret Elf. Seal, Julia, illus. (p. 1255)
—Liam Santa's Secret Elf. Seal, Julia, illus. (p. 1283)
—Lillian Santa's Secret Elf. Seal, Julia, illus. (p. 1301)
—Logan Santa's Secret Elf. Seal, Julia, illus. (p. 1339)
—Lucas Santa's Secret Elf. Seal, Julia, illus. (p. 1363)
—Madison Santa's Secret Elf. Seal, Julia, illus. (p. 1375)
—Mason Santa's Secret Elf. Seal, Julia, illus. (p. 1417)
—Matthew Santa's Secret Elf. Seal, Julia, illus. (p. 1426)
—Mia Santa's Secret Elf. Seal, Julia, illus. (p. 1456)
—Michael Santa's Secret Elf. Seal, Julia, illus. (p. 1458)
—My Granddaughter Is Santa's Secret Elf. Seal, Julia, illus. (p. 1548)
—My Grandson Is Santa's Secret Elf. Seal, Julia, illus. (p. 1549)
—My Nephew Is Santa's Secret Elf. Seal, Julia, illus. (p. 1557)
—My Niece Is Santa's Secret Elf. Seal, Julia, illus. (p. 1558)
—Natalie Santa's Secret Elf. Seal, Julia, illus. (p. 1576)
—Noah Santa's Secret Elf. Seal, Julia, illus. (p. 1616)
—Oliver Santa's Secret Elf. Seal, Julia, illus. (p. 1650)
—Olivia Santa's Secret Elf. Seal, Julia, illus. (p. 1650)
—Samuel Santa's Secret Elf. Seal, Julia, illus. (p. 1929)
—Savannah Santa's Secret Elf. Seal, Julia, illus. (p. 1937)
—Scarlett Santa's Secret Elf. Seal, Julia, illus. (p. 1942)
—Sebastian Santa's Secret Elf. Seal, Julia, illus. (p. 1973)
—Sophia Santa's Secret Elf. Seal, Julia, illus. (p. 2064)
—Victoria Santa's Secret Elf. Seal, Julia, illus. (p. 2355)
—William Santa's Secret Elf. Seal, Julia, illus. (p. 2468)
—Zoey Santa's Secret Elf. Seal, Julia, illus. (p. 2541)
Puterbaugh, Alivia. He Calls Me His Dandelion. (p. 941)
Putlitz, Gustav Heinrich Gans. What the Wood Whispers to Itself (Classic Reprint) (p. 2420)
Putman Oakes, Cory. Second-Best Haunted Hotel on Mercer Street. Pica, Jane, illus. (p. 1973)
Putman-Maggiotto. Adventures of Sasha Boo: The Block Party. (p. 27)
Putnam, Allen. Natty, a Spirit: His Portrait & His Life (Classic Reprint) (p. 1579)
Putnam, Edward Everett. Reward of Patient Love: And Flowers from the Garden of Thought (Classic Reprint) (p. 1874)
Putnam, Eleanor. Bob's Breaking in (Classic Reprint) (p. 252)
—Old Salem (Classic Reprint) (p. 1648)
—Woodland Wooing (Classic Reprint) (p. 2492)
Putnam, Elizabeth Cabot. On Duty & Off: Letters of Elizabeth Cabot Putnam (Classic Reprint) (p. 1652)
Putnam, Frederic Ward. University of California Publications in American Archaeology & Ethnology, 1907-1910, Vol. 6 (Classic Reprint) (p. 2333)
Putnam, Frederic Ward, jt. auth. see Packard, Alpheus Spring.
Putnam, George Haven. Little Gingerbread Man (Classic Reprint) (p. 1317)
Putnam, George I. In Blue Uniform: An Army Novel (Classic Reprint) (p. 1104)
—On the Offensive: An Army Story (Classic Reprint) (p. 1655)
Putnam, George Palmer. In the Oregon Country: Out-Doors in Oregon, Washington, & California, Together with Some Legendary Lore, & Glimpses of the Modern West in the Making (Classic Reprint) (p. 1110)
—Smiting of the Rock: A Tale of Oregon (Classic Reprint) (p. 2042)
Putnam, Harriet. Life of Abraham Lincoln for Young People: Told in Words of One Syllable. (p. 1293)
—Life of Abraham Lincoln for Young People: Told in Words of One Syllable (Classic Reprint) (p. 1293)
Putnam, Israel. Daniel Everton, Volunteer-Regular: A Romance of the Philippines (Classic Reprint) (p. 502)
—Shavetail (Classic Reprint) (p. 2003)
Putnam, J. Wesley. Hidden Things (Classic Reprint) (p. 966)
Putnam, James. DK Eyewitness Books: Mummy: Discover the Secrets of Mummies from the Early Embalming, to Bodies Preserved In. (p. 567)
Putnam, Jeff. Tsunami! Deadly Wall of Water. (p. 2298)
Putnam, Jeff, jt. auth. see Miller, Reagan.
Putnam, Mabel. Alex Goodwin's Deed (Classic Reprint) (p. 42)
Putnam, Marian Cabot. Memoir of Frances Cabot Putnam: A Family Chronicle (Classic Reprint) (p. 1443)
Putnam, Mary Lowell. Fifteen Days: An Extract from Edward Colvil's Journal (Classic Reprint) (p. 724)
Putnam, Nina Wilcox. Believe You Me (Classic Reprint) (p. 196)
—Esmeralda: Or Every Little Bit Helps (Classic Reprint) (p. 662)
—Impossible Boy (Classic Reprint) (p. 1102)
—In Search of Arcady (Classic Reprint) (p. 1107)
—Inner Voice (Classic Reprint) (p. 1121)
—It Pays to Smile (Classic Reprint) (p. 1141)
—Laughter Limited (Classic Reprint) (p. 1252)
—Orthodoxy (Classic Reprint) (p. 1673)
—West Broadway (Classic Reprint) (p. 2401)
—When the Highbrow Joined the Outfit (Classic Reprint) (p. 2433)
Putnam, Richelle & Aycock, John. Inspiring Life of Eudora Welty. (p. 1125)
Putnam, Samuel. Analytical Reader: Containing Lessons in Simultaneous Reading & Defining, with Spelling from the Same (Classic Reprint) (p. 79)
Putnam, Samuel P. Golden Throne: A Romance (Classic Reprint) (p. 859)
Putnam, Say. Little Freddie Feeding His Soul (Classic Reprint) (p. 1317)
Putnam, Shirley. Tipyn o'Bob, Vol. 6: November, 1908 (Classic Reprint) (p. 2251)
Putnum, Frederic Ward, jt. auth. see Packard, Alpheus Spring.
Putra, Dede, illus. see Alexander, Heather & Who HQ.
Putra, Dede, illus. see Anderson, Kirsten & Who HQ.
Putra, Dede, illus. see Bailey, Diane & Who HQ.
Putra, Dede, illus. see Edgers, Geoff & Hempel, Carlene.
Putra, Dede, illus. see Fabiny, Sarah & Who HQ.
Putra, Dede, illus. see Holub, Joan & Who HQ.
Putra, Dede, illus. see Hopkinson, Deborah & Who HQ.
Putra, Dede, illus. see Kramer, Barbara & Who HQ.
Putra, Dede, illus. see Labrecque, Ellen.
Putra, Dede, illus. see Manzanero, Paula K. & Who HQ.
Putra, Dede, illus. see McDonough, Yona Z. & Who HQ.
Putra, Dede, illus. see Medina, Nico & Who HQ.
Putra, Dede, illus. see Pascal, Janet B. & Who HQ.
Putra, Dede, illus. see Pollack, Pam, et al.
Putra, Dede, illus. see Rau, Dana Meachen & Who HQ.
Putra, Dede, illus. see Spinner, Stephanie & Who HQ.
Putra, Dede, illus. see Stine, Megan & Who HQ.
Putra, Dede, jt. auth. see Medina, Nico.
Putra, Lio, illus. see Lance, B. E.
Putra, Lio, jt. auth. see Smith, Damon L.
Putri, Maria. Scratchie: A Touch-And-Feel Cat-Venture. Putri, Maria, illus. (p. 1963)
Putri, Putut, illus. see Palavics, Sue.
Putsman, Helen, photos by see Evans, Cheryl & Smith, Lucy.
Puttapipat, Niroot. Nutcracker. Puttapipat, Niroot, illus. (p. 1632)
Puttapipat, Niroot, illus. see Pierpont, James Lord.
Puttenham, George. Arte of English Poesie: June 1589 (Classic Reprint) (p. 122)
Puttkammer, Kyle. Hero Cats: Midnight over Stellar City Volume 2. (p. 961)
—Hero Cats of Skyworld a New Realm: Volume 6. (p. 961)
—Hero Cats of Stellar City: New Visions. Vol. 5 (p. 961)
—Hero Cats of Stellar City: Year One Hardcover. (p. 961)
—Hero Cats: Season Finale Volume 7. (p. 961)
Puttock, Simon. Folette et Gribouille Lunettes. (p. 757)
—Mouse's First Night at Moonlight School. Pye, Ali, illus. (p. 1515)
—Thing. Egneus, Daniel, illus. (p. 2220)
Putumayo Kids Staff, creator. African Sticker Collection. (p. 33)
—Europe Sticker Collection. (p. 667)
—Latin America Sticker Coll. (p. 1250)
Puvilland, Alex, illus. see Westerfeld, Scott.
Puybaret, Eric. Coffret des Masques. (p. 413)
—Echasses Rouges. (p. 622)
—Echasses Rouges (Pg 70) (p. 622)
Puybaret, Éric. Interior Castle: A Boy's Journey into the Depths of His Heart. (p. 1126)
—Los islotes de Pedestal: Viaje al país de los magos. (p. 1351)

Q

Quartz, Jane & Quartz, Oliver. How Much Are We Alike? (p. 1034)
Quasar, Gian. Hell Ship. (p. 950)
Quasha, J. How to Draw Alabama's Sights & Symbols. (p. 1039)
—How to Draw Alaska's Sights & Symbols. (p. 1039)
Quasha, Jennifer. Birth & Growth of a Nation: Hands-on Projects about Symbols of American Liberty. (p. 233)
—Covered Wagons: Hands-on Projects about America's Westward Expansion. (p. 464)
—Gold Rush: Hands-on Projects about Mining the Riches of California. (p. 856)
—How to Draw Arizona's Sights & Symbols. (p. 1039)
—How to Draw Arkansas's Sights & Symbols. (p. 1039)
—How to Draw California's Sights & Symbols. (p. 1040)
—How to Draw Colorado's Sights & Symbols. (p. 1040)
—How to Draw Connecticut's Sights & Symbols. (p. 1040)
—How to Draw Delaware's Sights & Symbols. (p. 1040)
—How to Draw Florida's Sights & Symbols. (p. 1040)
—How to Draw Georgia's Sights & Symbols. (p. 1040)
—How to Draw Hawaii's Sights & Symbols. (p. 1040)
—How to Draw Idaho's Sights & Symbols. (p. 1040)
—Jamestown: Hands-on Projects about One of America's First Communities. (p. 1157)
—Robert Rogers: Rogers' Rangers, & the French & Indian War. (p. 1890)
Quashie, Safiya. Soccer Lesson. (p. 2052)
Quast, Michael. Adventure Jungle. (p. 18)
Quatrelles, Quatrelles. Days of Chivalry, or the Legend of Croquemitaine (Classic Reprint) (p. 515)
Quatro, Sheila. Dolla the Lamb Goes on a Picnic. (p. 578)
Quattlebaum, Mary. Jo MacDonald Had a Garden. Bryant, Laura J., illus. (p. 1169)
—Jo MacDonald Hiked in the Woods. Bryant, Laura J., illus. (p. 1169)
—Jo MacDonald Saw a Pond. Bryant, Laura J., illus. (p. 1169)
—Mighty Mole & Super Soil. Wallace, Chad, illus. (p. 1463)
—NGR Hedgehogs (L1) (p. 1601)
Quattro, Jacquelyn. There's a Mouse at My House! There's a Bug on My Rug! (p. 2218)
Quaw, M. M. Love Affair in Wonderland (Classic Reprint) (p. 1358)
Quaw, Mignon. Peppy Program for Men (Classic Reprint) (p. 1720)
—Progressive Agricultural Programs (Classic Reprint) (p. 1805)
Quay, Emma. Not a Cloud in the Sky. (p. 1622)
—Rudie Nudie. (p. 1912)
—Scarlett, Starlet. (p. 1942)
—Shrieking Violet. (p. 2013)
Quay, Emma, illus. see D'Ath, Justin.
Quay, Emma, illus. see Daddo, Andrew.
Quay, John Paul de. Colourama? Pop up the Past. (p. 427)
Quay, John Paul de, illus. see Oxlade, Chris & Farndon, John.
Quayle, Ruth. Battle of the Blighty Bling. Heyman, Eric, illus. (p. 174)
—Race to Hornswaggle Rock. Davenport, Philip, illus. (p. 1831)
—That Bear Can't Babysit. Friend, Alison, illus. (p. 2212)
Quayle, Susan. Mouse & the Storm. Muldoon, Melissa, illus. (p. 1514)
—Mouse's Best Day Ever: Children's Reflexology to Soothe Sore Teeth & Tums. Muldoon, Melissa, illus. (p. 1515)
Quayle, Virginia. Gifts of Christmas. (p. 832)
—Whattknotts' Halloween. (p. 2427)
Quebodeaux, Vernice, jt. auth. see Martin, Tamara.
Queen, Ben. Bear. Todd-Stanton, Joe, illus. (p. 179)
Queen, Dana, illus. see Castleton, Chaffee.
Queen, Jaccara & Huff, Libby, creators. I: The Passions, Struggles, & World of the IGeneration. (p. 1056)
Queen, Kindness. Kitty Kitty Rescues Mr. Gator. Dennis, Jeannette, illus. (p. 1226)
Queen, Kindness & Dennis, Jeannette. Kitty Kitty Rescues Mr. Gator. (p. 1226)
Queen, R. Darkchylde: The Ariel Chylde Saga. (p. 507)
Queen, The Maroon. Zahra & the Magic of the Glorious Sun. (p. 2538)
Queenston, Rory. Rachel Carson: Saving the Environment. (p. 1832)
Quek, Lynette, jt. auth. see Sheehan, Patricia.
Quekett, John. Practical Treatise on the Use of the Microscope: Including the Different Methods of Preparing Examining Animal, Vegetable, & Mineral Structures (Classic Reprint) (p. 1784)
Quenstedt, Friedrich August. Sonst und Jetzt: Populäre Vorträge Über Geologie (Classic Reprint) (p. 2064)
Quentin, Blake, jt. auth. see Yeoman, John.
Quentin, Zara. Airwoman: Book 1. (p. 38)
Queralt, Carmen, illus. see Porcella, Teresa.
Querido, I. Toil of Men (Classic Reprint) (p. 2256)
Querin, Pamela, illus. see Lewis, Beverly.
Querin, Pamela, jt. auth. see Lewis, Beverly.
Quesada, Joe. Marvel Art of Joe Quesada - Expanded Edition. (p. 1412)
—Marvel Portfolio: Joe Quesada. (p. 1412)
Quesada, Joe, et al. X-Factor Epic Collection: X-Aminations. (p. 2515)
Quesnel, Alain. Dioses y Heroes de la Antigua Grecia. (p. 552)
—Pharaons et Dieux de l'Egypte Ancienne. Ruffieux, Jean-Marie & Chagnaud, Y., illus. (p. 1733)
Quest, Suzanne, jt. auth. see Smith, Carol.
Questell, Jaime. By a Charm & a Curse. (p. 305)
Questmarc Publishing, creator. Chat Pack for Kids: Creative Questions to Ignite the Imagination. (p. 362)
Queux, Le. Golden Face: A Great Crook Romance (Classic Reprint) (p. 857)
—This House to Let (Classic Reprint) (p. 2224)
Queux, William Le. As We Forgive Them (Classic Reprint) (p. 125)
—Bomb-Makers: Being Some Curious Records Concerning the Craft & Cunning of Thedore Drost, an Enemy Alien in London, Together with Certain Revelations Regarding His Daughter Ells (Classic Reprint) (p. 254)
—Closed Book: Concerning the Secret of the Borgias (Classic Reprint) (p. 407)
—Count's Chauffeur (Classic Reprint) (p. 461)
—Her Royal Highness: A Romance of the Chancelleries of Europe (Classic Reprint) (p. 956)
—House of Whispers (Classic Reprint) (p. 1023)
—Hunchback of Westminster (Classic Reprint) (p. 1051)
—Minister of Evil: The Secret History of Rasputin's Betrayal of Russia. (p. 1472)
—Mysterious 3 (Classic Reprint) (p. 1567)
—Mystery of the Green Ray (Classic Reprint) (p. 1570)
—Number 70, Berlin: A Story of Britain's Peril (Classic Reprint) (p. 1629)
—Scribes & Pharisees: A Story of Literary London (Classic Reprint) (p. 1965)
—Spies of the Kaiser: Plotting the Downfall of England (Classic Reprint) (p. 2082)
—Stolen Statesman: Being the Story of a Hushed-Up Mystery (Classic Reprint) (p. 2120)
—Treasure of Israel (Classic Reprint) (p. 2282)
—Woman's Debt (Classic Reprint) (p. 2486)
—Zeppelin Destroyer: Being Some Chapters of Secret History (Classic Reprint) (p. 2539)
Quevedo, Enrique, illus. see Aparici, Irene.
Quevedo, Enrique, illus. see Nuno, Fran.
Quevedo, Francisco de. Visions of Dom Francisco de Quevedo Villegas, Knight of the Order of St. James (Classic Reprint) (p. 2362)
—Works of Don Francisco de Quevedo, Vol. 1 Of 3: Containing the Author's Life; the Visions (Classic Reprint) (p. 2497)
—Works of Don Francisco de Quevedo, Vol. 2 Of 3: Containing, Curious History of the Night Adventurer; the Life of Paul the Spanish Sharper, Book I (Classic Reprint) (p. 2497)
—Works of Don Francisco de Quevedo, Vol. 2 Of 3: Translated from the Spanish; Containing, Curious History of the Night Adventurer; the Life of Paul the Spanish Sharper, Book I (Classic Reprint) (p. 2497)
—Works of Don Francisco de Quevedo, Vol. 3 Of 3: The Life of Paul the Spanish Sharper Book II; Fortune in Her Wits; Proclamation by Old Father Time; a Treatise of All Things Whatsoever, Past, Present, & to Come; Letters on Several Occasions. (p. 2497)
—Works of Don Francisco de Quevedo, Vol. 3 Of 3: Containing the Life of Paul the Spanish Sharper Book Fortune in Her Wits; Proclamation by Old Father Time; a Treatise of All Things Whatsoever; Past, Present, & to Come. Letters on Several Occasions. (p. 2497)
—Works of Don Francisco de Quevedo, Vol. 3 Of 3: Translated from Spanish; Containing, the Life of Paul the Spanish Sharper, Book III; Fortune in Her Wits; Proclamation by Old Father Time; a Treatise of All Things Whatsoever, Past, Present, & to Come; (p. 2497)
Quevedo-Villegas, Francisco De. Pablo de Segovia, the Spanish Sharper (Classic Reprint) (p. 1690)
Queyrat, Frédéric. Imagination et Ses Varietes Chez L'Enfant: Etude de Psychologie Experimentale Appliquee a l'Education Intellectuelle (Classic Reprint) (p. 1100)
Quezada, José Luis. Cities of Texas. (p. 394)
—Geography of Texas. (p. 817)
Quezadas, Juan Carlos. Oki: Tripulante de Terremotos. (p. 1643)
Qui, Joseph. Baby King - Arch Books. (p. 151)
Quiambao, Maria Eloisa C. It's Nighttime. Quiambao, Nikolai C., illus. (p. 1146)
Quiambao, Nikolai C., illus. see Quiambao, Maria Eloisa C.
Quick, Anita. Alfred the Great. (p. 43)
Quick, Bo & Quick, Stacia. Moon Rise: A Tucker Family Adventure. (p. 1502)
Quick, Gunner. Itty Bitty Tree Frogs (p. 1149)
Quick, Herbert. Aladdin Co: A Romance of Yankee Magic (Classic Reprint) (p. 39)
—Broken Lance (Classic Reprint) (p. 284)
—Brown Mouse (Classic Reprint) (p. 287)
—Double Trouble, or Every Hero His Own Villain (Classic Reprint) (p. 589)
—Fairview Idea: A Story of the New Rural Life (Classic Reprint) (p. 696)
—In the Fairyland of America: A Tale of the Pukwudjies (Classic Reprint) (p. 1108)
—Vandemark's Folly (Classic Reprint) (p. 2347)
—Virginia of the Air Lanes (Classic Reprint) (p. 2361)
—Yellowstone Nights (Classic Reprint) (p. 2521)
Quick, Jack B. Unicorn Poop Joke Book. (p. 2328)
Quick, Jonathan. Gulliver Joe (Classic Reprint) (p. 905)
Quick, Matthew. All Together Now. (p. 55)
—Boy21. (p. 271)
—Every Exquisite Thing. (p. 670)
—Forgive Me, Leonard Peacock. (p. 768)
—Sorta Like a Rock Star. (p. 2066)
Quickel, Kelly. Scripture Cat: The Word Is Where It's at for This Cat. (p. 1966)
—Scripture Cat: The Word Is Where It's at for This Cat, Featuring Paws for Reflection Bible Study. (p. 1966)
Quiding, Charlotte Bremer, jt. auth. see Bremer, Fredrika.
Quien, George. Reminiscences of the Service & Experience of Lieut. George Quien of Company K, Twenty-Third Regiment, Conn. Vols (Classic Reprint) (p. 1865)
Quigg, Lemuel Ely. Tin-Types Taken in the Streets of New York: A Series of Stories & Sketches Portraying Many Singular Phases of Metropolitan Life (Classic Reprint) (p. 2248)
Quigley, Andrea. What on Earth?: Bees. Morgan, Paulina, illus. (p. 2419)
Quigley, Chris. Josie the Christmas Saving Cat. (p. 1179)
Quigley, E. M. How to Teach Beginners to Read: Thought Method (Classic Reprint) (p. 1044)
Quigley, Margery Closey. Index to Kindergarten Songs Including Singing Games & Folk Songs (Classic Reprint) (p. 1115)
Quigley, Michael. Monkey's Riddle. (p. 1494)
Quihuis, Albert. Search for the Lost Art of Making Tortillas. (p. 1971)
Quijano, Jonathan. Make Your Movie. (p. 1387)
—Make Your Own Action Thriller (p. 1387)
—Make Your Own Comedy (p. 1387)
—Make Your Own Horror Movie (p. 1387)
—Make Your Own Sci-Fi Flick (p. 1387)
Quijas, Evelyn, illus. see Baker, Georgette L.
Quiles, Moses. Diez Pasos para Pacar el Boogie. Quiles q's Imaginative Design, Moses, illus. (p. 544)
—Ten Steps on Getting the Boogieman Out of Our Room: Diez Pasos para Sacar el Boogie. Quiles, Moses, illus. (p. 2205)
Quiles q's Imaginative Design, Moses, illus. see Quiles, Moses.
Quill, Charlie. History of the Blues. (p. 980)
—Michelangelo: His Life & Art. (p. 1458)
Quill, Penumbra. My Little Pony: Ponyville Mysteries: Cursed Crusaders. (p. 1554)
—My Little Pony: Ponyville Mysteries: Journey to the Livewood. (p. 1554)
—My Little Pony: Ponyville Mysteries: Peryton Panic. (p. 1554)
—My Little Pony: Ponyville Mysteries: Riddle of the Rusty Horseshoe. (p. 1554)
—My Little Pony: Ponyville Mysteries: Tail of the Timberwolf. (p. 1554)
—My Little Pony: Ponyville Mysteries: the Cutie Mark Chronicles Volume 1. (p. 1554)
Quillan, Penny. Changing up Christmas. (p. 356)
—Rabbit Knight & the Wolf: An Easter Tale. (p. 1829)
Quillen, Carl. Dragon Girl Myra. (p. 593)
Quillen, Robert. Path Wharton Found (Classic Reprint) (p. 1704)
Quiller-Couch, A. T. Hetty Wesley (Classic Reprint) (p. 963)
—Major Vigoureux (Classic Reprint) (p. 1385)
—Mayor of Troy (Classic Reprint) (p. 1430)
—Sir John Constantine: Memoirs of His Adventures at Home & Abroad & Particularly in the Island of Corsica: Beginning with the Year 1756 (Classic Reprint) (p. 2025)
—True Tilda (Classic Reprint) (p. 2295)
—Two Sides of the Face: Midwinter Tales (Classic Reprint) (p. 2309)
—Westcotes (Classic Reprint) (p. 2402)
—White Wolf & Other Fireside Tales (Classic Reprint) (p. 2445)
Quiller-Couch, A. Thomas. Laird's Luck, & Other Fireside Tales (Classic Reprint) (p. 1240)
Quiller-Couch, Arthur. Beauty & the Beast. Domínguez, Ángel, illus. (p. 185)
—Brother Copas (Classic Reprint) (p. 286)
—Foe-Farrell (Classic Reprint) (p. 756)
—Historical Tales from Shakespeare (Yesterday's Classics) (p. 976)
—Mayor of Troy (Classic Reprint) (p. 1430)
—News from the Duchy (Classic Reprint) (p. 1600)
—Sleeping Beauty, & Other Fairy Tales: From the Old French (Classic Reprint) (p. 2036)
Quiller-Couch, Arthur Thomas. Corporal Sam, & Other Stories (Classic Reprint) (p. 456)
—Dead Man's Rock: A Romance. (p. 518)
—Delectable Duchy: Stories, Studies, & Sketches (Classic Reprint) (p. 526)
—Delectable Duchy. (p. 526)
—Golden Pomp. (p. 858)
—Lady Good-For-Nothing (Classic Reprint) (p. 1237)
—Laird's Luck: And Other Fireside Tales (Classic Reprint) (p. 1240)
—Naughts & Crosses. (p. 1582)
—Nicky-Nan, Reservist (Classic Reprint) (p. 1604)
—Pilgrims' Way: A Little Scrip of Good Counsel for Travellers (Classic Reprint) (p. 1745)
—Shakespeare's Christmas: And Other Stories (Classic Reprint) (p. 1999)
—Ship of Stars (Classic Reprint) (p. 2008)
—Twelve Dancing Princesses & Other Fairy Tales. Nielsen, Kay, illus. (p. 2303)
—Warwickshire Avon (Classic Reprint) (p. 2381)
—Westcotes (Classic Reprint) (p. 2402)
Quiller-Couch, Arthur Thomas & Q. Naughts & Crosses. (p. 1582)
Quiller-Couch, Mabel. Treasure Book of Children's Verse (Classic Reprint) (p. 2281)
Quiller-Couch, Sir Arthur Thomas. Shining Ferry (Classic Reprint) (p. 2007)
Quillinan, Dorothy Wordsworth. Journal of a Few Months' Residence in Portugal, Vol. 2 Of 2: And Glimpses of the South of Spain (Classic Reprint) (p. 1180)
Quillinan, Edward. Conspirators: Or the Romance of Military Life (Classic Reprint) (p. 443)
Quimby, Alden Walker. Valley Forge: A Tale (Classic Reprint) (p. 2344)
Quin, Michael J. Nourmahal, an Oriental Romance, Vol. 1 of 3 (Classic Reprint) (p. 1625)
Quin, Mike. More Dangerous Thoughts (Classic Reprint) (p. 1504)
—On the Drumhead: A Selection from the Writing of Mike Quin; a Memorial Volume; Edited, with a Biographical Sketch (Classic Reprint) (p. 1654)
Quinby, Michelle. Connecting the 21st Century to the Past: What Makes America America, 2000-The Present. (p. 441)
—Connecting the 21st Century to the Past: What Makes America America, 2000-The Present. Rakove, Jack N., ed. (p. 441)
—How America Became America: Wars at Home (1812/1820) (p. 1025)
—Wars at Home: America Forms an Identity (1812-1820) (p. 2381)
—Wars at Home: America Forms an Identity (1812-1820) Rakove, Jack N., ed. (p. 2381)
Quinby, Moses. Mysteries of Bee-Keeping Explained. (p. 1566)
Quince, Lia. Abby & Jules. (p. 3)
Quincey, Thomas de. Walladmor, Vol. 1 of 2 (Classic Reprint) (p. 2373)
Quincey, Thomas de, see de Quincey, Thomas.
Quincy, Edmund. Haunted Adjutant, & Other Stories. (p. 937)
—Haunted Adjutant, & Other Stories (Classic Reprint) (p. 937)
—Wensley, & Other Stories (Classic Reprint) (p. 2400)
Quindlen, Kelly. Late to the Party. (p. 1250)
Quin-Harkin, Janet. Toe Shoe Trouble. (p. 2256)
Quinlan, David. Tim Horton: Portrait of an Extraordinary Canadian (p. 2243)
Quinlan, Don. Rick Hansen: Larger Than Life (p. 1877)
—Rick Hansen: A Larger Than Life Biography (p. 1877)
Quinlan, Evelyn. Spirit Asleep (Classic Reprint) (p. 2082)
Quinlan, Julia. Different Kinds of Maps. (p. 545)
Quinlan, Julia J. Alfa Romeo. (p. 43)
—Aston Martin. (p. 127)
—Audi. (p. 136)
—Collect & Analyze Data. (p. 414)
—Corvette. (p. 456)
—Different Kinds of Maps. (p. 545)
—Dingoes. (p. 547)
—Everything You Need to Know about Voting Rights & Voter Disenfranchisement. (p. 674)
—Ferrari. (p. 721)
—GPS & Computer Maps. (p. 873)
—Hinduism. (p. 972)
—Honey Badgers. (p. 999)
—How to Draw a Map. (p. 1039)
—Hyenas. (p. 1056)
—Jaguar. (p. 1155)
—Keys, Legends, & Symbols in Maps. (p. 1212)
—Lamborghini. (p. 1240)
—Latitude, Longitude, & Direction. (p. 1251)
—Lotus. (p. 1356)
—Maserati. (p. 1417)
—Mercedes. (p. 1447)
—Mustang. (p. 1530)
—Plate Tectonics. (p. 1758)
—Scale & Distance in Maps. (p. 1941)
—Tasmanian Devils. (p. 2192)
—What Are Sea Invertebrates? (p. 2406)
—What Is the Tundra? (p. 2417)
—Wild Boars. (p. 2463)
—Wolverines. (p. 2484)
Quinlan, Julia J. & Furgang, Adam. Truth Behind Snack Foods. (p. 2297)
—Truth Behind Soft Drinks. (p. 2297)
Quinlan, Julia J. & Johanson, Paula. Truth Behind Factory Foods. (p. 2297)
Quinlan, Julia J. & Watson, Stephanie. Truth Behind Manufactured Meats. (p. 2297)
Quinlan Labelle, Patooti, et al. Diary of Patooti the Pig. (p. 540)
Quinlan, Nola, jt. auth. see Barker, Lori.
Quinlan, Susan E. Case of the Monkeys That Fell from the Trees: And Other Mysteries in Tropical Nature. (p. 338)
—Puffins. (p. 1811)
Quinlivan, Ada. Blake the Baker: Develop Understanding of Fractions & Numbers. (p. 242)
—Choctaw (p. 380)
—Mealtime. (p. 1434)
—Opossums. (p. 1667)
Quinlivan, Ana. Hummingbirds: World's Fastest Wings. (p. 1050)
Quinlivan, Kelly. Science Museum Time! Work with Time (p. 1957)
Quinn, Amy. Gaming with Bloxels. (p. 808)
—Making Electric Jewelry. (p. 1388)
—Making Slime. (p. 1390)
Quinn, Arthur Hobson. Pennsylvania Stories (Classic Reprint) (p. 1717)
Quinn, Barbara & Isler, Claudia. Understanding Your Right to Vote. (p. 2326)
Quinn, Courtney, illus. see Dyan, Penelope.
Quinn, David. Go to Sleep, Little Creep. Spires, Ashley, illus. (p. 849)
Quinn, Drake. Lost in Yellowstone: The Extraordinary True Adventure Story of Truman Everts & His Courage, Endurance & Survival in the Wilderness. (p. 1354)
Quinn, Gloria W. Lemon Water. (p. 1266)
Quinn, Jason. Beautiful Game - Survival. Sharma, Lalit Kumar, illus. (p. 184)
Quinn, Jordan. Bard & the Beast. McPhillips, Robert, illus. (p. 166)
—Den of Wolves. McPhillips, Robert, illus. (p. 528)
—False Fairy. (p. 701)
—False Fairy. McPhillips, Robert, illus. (p. 701)
—Ghost in the Castle. McPhillips, Robert, illus. (p. 827)
—Kingdom of Wrenly 3 Books In 1! The Lost Stone; the Scarlet Dragon; Sea Monster! McPhillips, Robert, illus. (p. 1222)
—Kingdom of Wrenly Collection #3: The Bard & the Beast; the Pegasus Quest; the False Fairy; the Sorcerer's Shadow. McPhillips, Robert, illus. (p. 1222)
—Let the Games Begin! McPhillips, Robert, illus. (p. 1269)
—Lost Stone. (p. 1355)
—Lost Stone. McPhillips, Robert, illus. (p. 1355)
—Pegasus Quest. McPhillips, Robert, illus. (p. 1714)
—Scarlet Dragon. (p. 1942)
—Scarlet Dragon. McPhillips, Robert, illus. (p. 1942)
—Sea Monster! McPhillips, Robert, illus. (p. 1967)
—Secret World of Mermaids. McPhillips, Robert, illus. (p. 1979)
—Sorcerer's Shadow. McPhillips, Robert, illus. (p. 2065)
—Thirteenth Knight. McPhillips, Robert, illus. (p. 2223)
—Witch's Curse. McPhillips, Robert, illus. (p. 2480)
Quinn, K. A. S. Queen Alone. (p. 1823)
Quinn, Kate Karyus. Another Little Piece. (p. 101)
—Down with the Shine. (p. 591)
Quinn, Kate Karyus & Lunetta, Demitria. Anti/Hero. Gil, Maca, illus. (p. 103)
Quinn, Katherine, illus. see Gallo, Ana.
Quinn, Laura. Monkey Blue. (p. 1493)
—What on Earth Is under My Bed? McHugh, Kevin, illus. (p. 2419)
Quinn, Lauren D. Fruits. (p. 796)
—Heredity. (p. 958)
Quinn, Lin. Best Mud Pie. Rooney, Ronnie, illus. (p. 207)
Quinn, Patricia O. Attention, Girls! A Guide to Learn All about Your AD/HD. Pearce, Carl, illus. (p. 135)
Quinn, Patricia O. & Maitland, Theresa E. Laurie. On Your Own: A College Readiness Guide for Teens with ADHD/LD. Ische, Bryan, illus. (p. 1656)

R

—Big Snowman, Little Snowman (Disney Frozen) RH Disney, illus. (p. 223)
—Chasing Rainbows. Ruiz, Aristides & Mathieu, Joe, illus. (p. 362)
—Chocolate Voyage. Aikins, Dave, illus. (p. 380)
—Cooking with the Grinch. (p. 447)
—Cooking with the Grinch (Dr. Seuss) Brannon, Tom, illus. (p. 447)
—Frozen. (p. 795)
—Halloween Fun for Everyone! (Dr. Seuss/Cat in the Hat) Brannon, Tom, illus. (p. 912)
—Have No Fear! Halloween Is Here! (Dr. Seuss/the Cat in the Hat Knows a Lot About. Brannon, Tom, illus. (p. 939)
—High? Low? Where Did It Go? All about Animal Camouflage. Ruiz, Aristides, illus. (p. 968)
—High? Low? Where Did It Go? All about Animal Camouflage. Ruiz, Aristides & Mathieu, Joe, illus. (p. 968)
—Hooray for Hair! (Dr. Seuss/Cat in the Hat) Brannon, Tom, illus. (p. 1001)
—How to Help the Earth-By the Lorax. (p. 1042)
—How to Help the Earth-By the Lorax. Ruiz, Aristides et al, illus. (p. 1042)
—Huff & Puff. Guile, Gill, illus. (p. 1047)
—Huff & Puff & the New Train. Guile, Gill, illus. (p. 1047)
—Huff & Puff Have Too Much Stuff! Guile, Gill, illus. (p. 1047)
—I Am Cindy-Lou Who. (p. 1058)
—I Am Sam-I-Am. Brannon, Tom, illus. (p. 1059)
—I Love You, Grandma! Hitch, David, illus. (p. 1078)
—If I Ran the Dog Show: All about Dogs. Ruiz, Aristides & Mathieu, Joe, illus. (p. 1091)
—King Cecil the Sea Horse (Dr. Seuss/Cat in the Hat) Moroney, Christopher, illus. (p. 1220)
—Look for the Lorax. (p. 1345)
—Look for the Lorax (Dr. Seuss) (p. 1345)
—Love You, Hug You, Read to You! Endersby, Frank, illus. (p. 1361)
—Miles & Miles of Reptiles: All about Reptiles. Ruiz, Aristides & Mathieu, Joe, illus. (p. 1465)
—Night Lights. (p. 1606)
—Night Lights (Dr. Seuss/Cat in the Hat) Ruiz, Aristides & Mathieu, Joe, illus. (p. 1606)
—Oh, Baby, the Places You'll Go! Seuss, illus. (p. 1641)
—Oh, the Things You Can Do That Are Good for You! All about Staying Healthy. Ruiz, Aristides, illus. (p. 1642)
—On the First Day of First Grade. Jennings, Sarah, illus. (p. 1654)
—On the First Day of Kindergarten. Hughes, Laura, illus. (p. 1654)
—On the First Day of Summer Vacation. Jennings, Sarah, illus. (p. 1654)
—Out of Sight till Tonight! All about Nocturnal Animals. (p. 1682)
—Planet Name Game. (p. 1755)
—Reindeer's First Christmas / New Friends for Christmas. (p. 1862)
—Tale about Tails (Dr. Seuss/the Cat in the Hat Knows a Lot about That!) Brannon, Tom, illus. (p. 2178)
—Tree Doctor. (p. 2284)
—Trick-or-Treat!/Aye-Aye! Ruiz, Aristides & Mathieu, Joe, illus. (p. 2287)
—What Cat Is That? All about Cats. Ruiz, Aristides & Mathieu, Joe, illus. (p. 2407)
—Who Hatches the Egg? All about Eggs. Ruiz, Aristides & Mathieu, Joe, illus. (p. 2447)
—Why Oh Why Are Deserts Dry? All about Deserts. Ruiz, Aristides & Mathieu, Joe, illus. (p. 2458)
—Wings & Paws & Fins & Claws. Ruiz, Aristides, illus. (p. 2473)
—¡Te Amo, Te Abrazo, Leo Contigo!/Love You, Hug You, Read to You! Endersby, Frank, illus. (p. 2194)
Rabe, Tish, ed. see Galvin, Laura Gates.
Rabe, Tish, jt. auth. see RH Disney Staff.
Rabe, Tish, jt. auth. see Worth, Bonnie.
Rabei, Carolina. Crunch! Rabei, Carolina, illus. (p. 480)
Rabei, Carolina, illus. see de la Mare, Walter.
Rabei, Caroline, illus. see de la Mare, Walter.
Rabelais. Gargantua et Pantagruel+cd Nouveaute. (p. 810)
Rabelais, François. First Edition of the Fourth Book of the Heroic Deeds & Sayings of the Noble Pantagruel (Classic Reprint) (p. 736)
—Fourth Book of the Heroic Deeds & Sayings of the Good Pantagruel: His Voyages & Wonders (Classic Reprint) (p. 773)
—Life of Gargantua & the Heroic Deeds of Pantagruel: From the French of Rabelais (Classic Reprint) (p. 1294)
Rabelais, Francois. Oeuvres de Maitre François Rabelais, Vol. 2: Publiées Sous le Titre de Faits et Dits du Géant Gargantua et de Son Fils Pantagruel, Avec la Prognostication Pantagrueline, l'Épître du Limosin, la Crème Philosophale, Deux Épîtres À Deux Vieilles De. (p. 1639)
Rabelais, François. Pantagruel, King of the Dipsodes: With His Heroic Acts & Prowesses (Classic Reprint) (p. 1696)
—Sequel to Pantagruel: Being Books III, IV, & V of Rabelais Gargantua (Classic Reprint) (p. 1989)
—Works of Francis Rabelais, Vol. 1: Translated from the French (Classic Reprint) (p. 2497)
—Works of Francis Rabelais, Vol. 4 Of 4: Translated from the French, with Explanatory Notes (Classic Reprint) (p. 2497)
—Works of Francois Rabelais, Vol. 5 (Classic Reprint) (p. 2497)
—Works of Mr. Francis Rabelais, Doctor in Physick, Vol. 2 Of 2: Containing Five Books of the Lives, Heroick Deeds Saying of Gargantua & His Sonne Pantagruel (Classic Reprint) (p. 2499)
Rabelais, Francois & Smith, W. F. (William Francis). First Edition of the Fourth Book of the Heroic Deeds & Sayings of the Noble Pantagruel. (p. 736)
Raben, Molly. Explore North Korea: 12 Key Facts. (p. 680)
Rabenhorst, C. t. New Pocket-Dictionary of the German & English Languages: In Two Parts; I. English & German, II. German & English (Classic Reprint) (p. 1596)
Raber, James Briggs. Scott the Shot: Helping Children Understand the Main Reason for Receiving Shots. Duman, Crystal, ed. (p. 1962)
Rabey, Louise, illus. see Lacey, Susan.
Rabideau, Jennifer L. Dust Bunnies under My Bed. (p. 611)
—Spiders in the Attic. (p. 2081)
Rabideau, Lacy. Picture Book of the Mass: Illustrated by the Masters. (p. 1740)
Rabiger, Joanna. Daily Prison Life (p. 496)
—Government Intelligence Agencies Gomez, Manny, ed. (p. 873)
Rabin, Shri, jt. auth. see Pelletier, Cynthia L.
Rabinowitz, Alan. Boy & a Jaguar. Chien, Cátia, illus. (p. 268)
Rabinowitz, H. Gleaner: June, 1924 (Classic Reprint) (p. 841)
—Gleaner: April, 1924 (Classic Reprint) (p. 841)
—Gleaner: January, 1925 (Classic Reprint) (p. 841)
—Gleaner: September 1924 (Classic Reprint) (p. 841)
Rabjohn, R. H. & Wilson, John. Soldier's Sketchbook: The Illustrated First World War Diary of R.H. Rabjohn. (p. 2057)
Rabley, Stephen. Red Rock/Roca Roja. Rabley, Stephen & Ursell, Martin, illus. (p. 1858)
Rabon, Elaine Hearn, illus. see Dolson, Carol Bland.
Rabon, Elaine Hearn, illus. see Thrasher, Grady.
Rabone, S. Vocabulary of the Tonga Language: Arranged in an Alphabetical to Which Is Annexed a List of Idiomatical Phrases (Classic Reprint) (p. 2364)
Rabou, John. Sheep Out of Water. Van, Annelies, illus. (p. 2005)
Rabou, John, illus. see Dowley, Tim & Bewley, Robert.
Rabstejnek, Bette. Very Impatient & Pesky Puppy. (p. 2353)
Raby, Charlotte. Collins Big Cat Phonics for Letters & Sounds - Pat It: Band 01A/Pink A Blake, Beccy, illus. (p. 416)
—Collins Big Cat Phonics for Letters & Sounds - Pit Pat: Band 01A/Pink A (p. 416)
—Collins Big Cat Phonics for Letters & Sounds - the Dragon King's Daughter: Band 07/Turquoise Fusi, Alessandra, illus. (p. 417)
Raby, Charlotte & Guille-Marrett, Emily. Collins Big Cat Phonics for Letters & Sounds - I Spy Fairytales: Band 00/Lilac. Partington, Deborah, illus. (p. 416)
Raby, Meg & Pallmer, Elisa. My Brother Otto (p. 1534)
Racanelli, Marie. Albino Animals. (p. 41)
—Animal Mimics. (p. 90)
—Animals with Armor. (p. 96)
—Animals with Pockets. (p. 96)
—Camouflaged Creatures. (p. 315)
—Crazy Nature (p. 469)
—Underground Animals. (p. 2323)
Racaniello, P. Emilia & Emma Say Please. (p. 642)
—Emilia & Emma Say Sorry. (p. 642)
—Emilia & Emma Say Thank You. (p. 642)
—Marcella & the Magic Hat. (p. 1402)
—Stella Asks What. (p. 2112)
—Stella Asks When. (p. 2112)
—Stella Asks Where. (p. 2113)
—Stella Asks Who. (p. 2113)
—Stella Asks Why. (p. 2113)
Race, Esma. Enchanted World of Bracken Lea. Greaves, Martin, illus. (p. 647)
Race, Esma & Greaves, Martin. Enchanted World of Bracken Lea. (p. 647)
Race, Martha. Rummage: An One-Act Comedy with Musical Numbers (Classic Reprint) (p. 1914)
Racehorse for Young Readers. Awesome STEM Science Experiments: More Than 50 Practical STEM Projects for the Whole Family. (p. 145)
—Learn to Draw People: How to Draw Like an Artist in 5 Easy Steps. (p. 1256)
—My First 1000 Words: With 1000 Colorful Pictures! (p. 1540)
Racehorse for Young Readers & The Brothers Grimm. Grimm's Fairy Tales. Cramer, Rie, illus. (p. 896)
Racehorse Publishing, jt. auth. see Grahame, Kenneth.
Racehorse Publishing, jt. auth. see Twain, Mark, pseud.
Rache, Elmer, illus. see Garis, Howard R.
Rachel, Drapkin, illus. see Joseph, Costa & Christopher, Romero.
Rachel, Rachel. All about the College Boys: A Book of Many Tales, Advice & Warning (Classic Reprint) (p. 50)
Rachmuhl, Françoise. Mortals & Immortals of Greek Myth. (p. 1507)
Rachov, Y. [the Old Man's Mitten]. (p. 2214)
Racine, Patrice. Quest of the Last Dodo Bird. (p. 1826)
Racine, Sheryl, jt. auth. see Wagner, Kathi.
Racine, Victoria, illus. see Lopez, Christopher P.
Rackham, Arthur. Land of Enchantment (Classic Reprint) (p. 1241)
—Mother Goose: The Old Nursery Rhymes; Illustrated (Classic Reprint) (p. 1509)
Rackham, Arthur, illus. see (aesop), Esope.
Rackham, Arthur, illus. see Aesop, Aesop.
Rackham, Arthur, illus. see Andersen, Hans Christian.
Rackham, Arthur, illus. see Andersen, Hans.
Rackham, Arthur, illus. see Barrie, J. M.
Rackham, Arthur, illus. see Bianco, Margery Williams.
Rackham, Arthur, illus. see Grahame, Kenneth.
Rackham, Arthur, illus. see Grimm, Jacob & Grimm, Wilhelm.
Rackham, Arthur, illus. see Grimm, Jacob.
Rackham, Arthur, illus. see Moore, Clement C.
Rackham, Arthur, illus. see Nesbit, E.
Rackham, Arthur, illus. see Solnit, Rebecca.
Rackham, Arthur, illus. see Stephens, James.
Rackham, Arthur, jt. auth. see Barrie, J. M.
Rackham, Arthur, jt. auth. see Kipling, Rudyard.
Rackham, Arthur, jt. auth. see Stephens, James.
Rackham, Arthur, jt. auth. see Swift, Jonathan.
Rackham, Arthur, tr. see Grahame, Kenneth.
Rackham, Jennifer. Dash of Belladonna. (p. 508)
Rackham, Jennifer, illus. see Johnson, Mike.
Rackhan, Arthur, illus. see Stephens, James.
Racklyeft, Jess, illus. see McCartney, Tania.
Racklyeft, Jess, jt. auth. see McCartney, Tania.
Racknor & Morrow. Wordszart. (p. 2495)
Rackstraw, E. C. Make-Believe: A Comedietta (Classic Reprint) (p. 1386)
Ractliffe, Justin. Dads: A Field Guide. Glassby, Cathie, illus. (p. 495)
Racz, Michael, illus. see Mann, Elizabeth.
Raczka, Bob. Beware! Day, Larry, illus. (p. 211)
—Guyku: A Year of Haiku for Boys. Reynolds, Peter H., illus. (p. 906)
—Speaking of Art: Colorful Quotes by Famous Painters. (p. 2076)
—Summer Wonders. Stead, Judy, illus. (p. 2150)
—Wet Cement: A Mix of Concrete Poems. (p. 2403)
—Who Loves the Fall? (p. 2449)
Raczka, Bob & Reynolds, Peter H. Guyku: A Year of Haiku for Boys. Reynolds, Peter H., illus. (p. 906)
Raczka, Robert. Fall Mixed Up. Cameron, Chad, illus. (p. 700)
—Joy in Mudville. Dibley, Glin, illus. (p. 1184)
—Name That Style: All about Isms in Art. (p. 1573)
—Niko Draws a Feeling. Shin, Simone, illus. (p. 1609)
Radabah, Caleen. Road Leads Somewhere. (p. 1888)
Radaviciute, Diana, illus. see Blanco, Alberto.
Radcliff, Ann. Mysteries of Udolpho, a Romance, Vol. 1 Of 3: Interspersed with Some Pieces of Poetry (Classic Reprint) (p. 1567)
Radcliffe, Alexander. Ovid Travestie: A Burlesque upon Ovid's Epistles (Classic Reprint) (p. 1688)
—Ovid Travestie. (p. 1688)
—Works of Capt. Alex. Radcliffe. (p. 2496)
—Works of Capt. Alex; Radcliffe in One Volume: Viz; Ovids Travestie, or a Burlesque upon Ovids Epistles; Likewise His Ramble, an Anti-Heroick Poem, with Several Miscellanies (Classic Reprint) (p. 2496)
Radcliffe, Ann. Mysteries of Udolpho, Vol. 1 Of 4: A Romance; Interspersed with Some Pieces of Poetry (Classic Reprint) (p. 1567)
—Mysteries of Udolpho, Vol. 4 Of 4: A Romance, Interspersed with Some Pieces of Poetry (Classic Reprint) (p. 1567)
Radcliffe, Ann Ward. Castles of Athlin & Dunbayne: A Highland Story (Classic Reprint) (p. 340)
—Mysteries of Udolpho, Vol. 1 Of 4: A Romance; Interspersed with Some Pieces of Poetry (Classic Reprint) (p. 1567)
—Mysteries of Udolpho, Vol. 4 Of 4: A Romance, Interspersed with Some Pieces of Poetry (Classic Reprint) (p. 1567)
—Posthumous Works of Anne Radcliffe, Vol. 1 of 4 (Classic Reprint) (p. 1780)
—Romance of the Forest, Vol. 1 Of 3: Interspersed with Some Pieces of Poetry; the Third Edition (Classic Reprint) (p. 1900)
Radcliffe, Robin. Canoeman Joe. Powell, Consie, illus. (p. 322)
Radcliffe, Thomas, illus. see Weakland, Mark.
Radcliffe, Tj. Cedar Island Dreams. Farmer, Hilary, illus. (p. 348)
Radcliffe-Rogers, Barbara & Seavey, Lura Rogers. Dominican Republic. (p. 580)
Radclyffe, jt. ed. see Lynch, Katherine E.
Raddon, Anna. After Migaadiwin. (p. 33)
Radecki, Barbara. Messenger 93. (p. 1451)
Radecliffe, Noel. Wheel Within Wheel, Vol. 3 of 3 (Classic Reprint) (p. 2427)
Radecliffe, Noell. Wheel Within Wheel, Vol. 1 of 3 (Classic Reprint) (p. 2427)
Rademacher, Andreas Gunther. Biggi, Luke und das Grimolino. (p. 225)
Rademacher, Nana. Estuvimos Aquí / We Were Here. (p. 665)
Radencich, Michael, illus. see Nirgiotis, Nicholas.
Rader, Laura. Twelve Days of Christmas in California. (p. 2303)
—Twelve Days of Christmas in California. Rader, Laura, illus. (p. 2303)
Rader, Laura, illus. see Mayr, Diane.
Rader, Laura, illus. see Ziefert, Harriet.
Rader, Mark. Baby Einstein: Amazing Animals. (p. 150)
Rader, Victoria. Spotty the Colt. (p. 2091)
Rades, Corina & Rades, Dennis. Dolores Found a New Family. (p. 579)
Radeva, Milena, illus. see Nathaniel, Ally.
Radeva, Milena, illus. see Pere, Tuula.
Radeva, Sabina. Charles Darwin's on the Origin of Species. (p. 358)
Radford, Dave. Gray Flowers. Dickison, Forrest, illus. (p. 882)
Radford, Dollie. Songs for Somebody (Classic Reprint) (p. 2063)
Radford, Duane, jt. auth. see Pirk, Wendy.
Radford, Heather. Asquinn Twins: Frontier Life. Oakley, Darlene, ed. (p. 126)
Radford, James & Wooders, Dave. Adventures on the Queen Mary: ... tales of a Teenage Crew Member! (p. 29)
Radford, Karen, illus. see Bailey, Gerry.
Radford, Karen, illus. see Ganeri, Anita.
Radford, Megan. Canada Doodles Cook, Peter, illus. (p. 320)
Radford, Nick, illus. see Stosuy, Brandon.
Radford, Sarah. How to Make Friends & Stay Friends: (and Other Helpful Hints) (p. 1043)
Radford, Tracey. Brian the Lion Goes into Space. (p. 279)
Radhakrishnan, Santhya S., illus. see Hobbs, J. T.
Radice, Teresa. Violette Around the World, Vol. 1: My Head in the Clouds! Turconi, Stefano, illus. (p. 2360)
—Violette Around the World, Vol. 2: a New World Symphony! Turconi, Stefano, illus. (p. 2360)
Radice, Teresa, jt. auth. see Disney.
Radin, Edwin. Gersham & the Golem. (p. 823)
Radin, Paul. Autobiography of a Winnebago Indian (Classic Reprint) (p. 140)
—Culture of the Winnebago: As Described by Themselves (Classic Reprint) (p. 484)
—Semi-Historical Account of the War of the Winnebago & Foxes (Classic Reprint) (p. 1987)
—Some Myths & Tales of the Ojibwa of Southeastern Ontario (Classic Reprint) (p. 2059)
Radivoeva, Svetla. Malina's Jam: Walt Disney Animation Studios Artist Showcase. Radivoeva, Svetla, illus. (p. 1392)
Radjou, Anna Nazaretz, illus. see Trooboff, Rhoda.
Radka, Sara, illus. see Ronan, Amanda.
Radley, Barbara H. Welcome Home Bella. (p. 2397)
Radley, Gail. Centipedes. (p. 351)
—Facebook. (p. 693)
—Kyle Jeffries, Pilgrim. Burns, Taurus, illus. (p. 1234)
—Los Ciempiés. (p. 1350)
—Los Milpiés. (p. 1351)
—Millipedes. (p. 1468)
—Understanding Islam. (p. 2325)
—US Marine Corps. (p. 2340)
Radley, Gail, jt. auth. see Harris, Duchess.
Radley, Gail & Harris, Duchess. Sexism at Work. (p. 1995)
Radley, L. F. Change. (p. 355)
—Easy Peasy: When You Know. (p. 621)
Radley, Laura D. Apprenticeships (p. 107)
Radley, S. F. Magic. (p. 1376)
Radman, David. Peek & Boo Are Looking for You. Shuler, Douglas, illus. (p. 1713)
Radnedge, Aidan Keir. 50 Things You Should Know about: Soccer. (p. 2556)
Radnor, Leona. Photoplay Writer (Classic Reprint) (p. 1737)
Radomski, Kassandra. Apollo 13 Mission: Core Events of a Crisis in Space (p. 106)
—Battle for a New Nation: Causes & Effects of the Revolutionary War. (p. 173)
—Mr. Madison's War: Causes & Effects of the War of 1812. (p. 1519)
—People & Places of the Midwest. (p. 1718)
—Secrets of Mars. (p. 1980)
—Secrets of Saturn. (p. 1980)
Radomski, Kassandra, et al. United States by Region. (p. 2330)
Radomski, Kassandra Kathleen. So You Want to Be a U. S. Representative. (p. 2051)
—So You Want to Be a U. S. Senator. (p. 2051)
Radtke, Becky. Going Green! Activity Book. (p. 854)
—Keep the Scene Green! Earth-Friendly Activities. (p. 1207)
Radtke, Becky, illus. see Lucey, Marcia T., ed.
Radtke, Becky J. All about Marvelous Me! A Draw & Write Journal. (p. 49)
—BOOST Keep the Scene Green! Earth-Friendly Activities. (p. 262)
—Christmas Color by Number. (p. 384)
—Draw It! Animals. (p. 598)
—Draw It! Princesses, Mermaids & Fairies. (p. 598)
—Draw It! Sea Life. (p. 598)
—Four Seasons of Fun Activity Book. (p. 772)
—Halloween Color by Number. (p. 912)
—Hooray for the USA! Activity Book. (p. 1001)
—Magical Mermaids Activity Book. (p. 1380)
—Princess Activity Book. (p. 1795)
—SPARK Theme Park Maze Craze. (p. 2075)
—Super Rides & Water Slides Mazes. (p. 2156)
—Unicorns Awesome Activity Book. (p. 2329)
Radtke, Becky J., illus. see Gould, Judith S. & Gould, Evan Jay.
Radtke, Roger, illus. see Jerome, Kate B.
Radu, Michael. Islam in Europe. (p. 1139)
Radunsky, Vladimir, illus. see Berne, Jennifer.
Radunsky, Vladimir, illus. see Raschka, Chris.
Radunsky, Vladimir, illus. see Twain, Mark, pseud.
Radunsky, Vladimir, jt. auth. see Raschka, Chris.
Radwan, Hassan. Haupmann Diamond. (p. 939)
—Rashid & the Missing Body. (p. 1842)
Rady, Michael. Quest for Neveragain. (p. 1825)
Radzinski, Kandy. Where to Sleep. (p. 2440)
—Where to Sleep. Radzinski, Kandy, illus. (p. 2440)
Radzinski, Kandy, illus. see Schonberg, Marcia.
Radzinski, Kandy, illus. see Scillian, Devin.
Radziwill, Princess Catherine. Disillusions of a Crown Princess: Being the Story of the Courtship & Married Life of Cecile, Ex-Crown Princess of Germany (Classic Reprint) (p. 558)
Rae, Adelyn. Amazing Tales of the Portal Pen. (p. 66)
Rae, Alison. Oil, Plastics, & Power. (p. 1643)
—Trees & Timber Products. (p. 2284)
Rae, Andrew, illus. see Ingram, Catherine.
Rae, Andrew, illus. see Regan, Lisa.
Rae, Angela. All of Us. (p. 53)
Rae, Catalina. Small Price to Pay. Legan, Christian, ed. (p. 2040)
—Vanishing Point. Legan, Christian, ed. (p. 2347)
Rae, Cheryl. Portals to Xandria: What's So Special about Dragon Poop? (p. 1779)
Rae, Ebony. Calliope Crow. (p. 312)
—Calliope Crow Christmas. (p. 312)
Rae, Elspeth & Rae, Rowena. Duck in a Sock: Four Phonics Stories. Gutierrez, Elisa, illus. (p. 608)
—Meg & Greg: a Duck in a Sock. Gutierrez, Elisa, illus. (p. 1441)
—Meg & Greg: Frank & the Skunk. Gutiérrez, Elisa, illus. (p. 1441)
Rae, Gwynned. Mary in America. Vulliamy, Clara, illus. (p. 1415)
—Mary in London. Vulliamy, Clara, illus. (p. 1415)
Rae, Herbert. Maple Leaves in Flanders Fields. (p. 1401)
—Maple Leaves in Flanders Fields (Classic Reprint) (p. 1401)
Rae, John, illus. see Larned, W. T. & La Fontaine, Jean de.
Rae, John & Carroll, Lewis. New Adventures of Alice: A Sequel to Lewis Carroll's Wonderland. (p. 1591)
Rae, Johnelle. Perfect's Overrated. (p. 1723)
Rae, Kimberly. Buying Samir. (p. 304)
—Capturing Jasmina. (p. 327)
—Seeking Mother. (p. 1985)
Rae, Kristin. Wish You Were Italian: An If Only Novel. (p. 2479)
—Wish You Were Italian. (p. 2479)
Rae, Linda. Angel & the Piper. (p. 85)
Rae, Milne. Bottle in the Smoke a Tale of Anglo-Indian Life (Classic Reprint) (p. 265)
—Morag: A Tale of the Highlands of Scotland (Classic Reprint) (p. 1503)
—Morag. (p. 1503)
—Rinaultrie (Classic Reprint) (p. 1883)
Rae, Navah. Job for Comet. (p. 1170)

Rae, Philippa. Count the Sheep to Sleep. Röhr, Stéphanie, illus. (p. 458)
—Wilma's Magic Hat. James, Ashleigh, illus. (p. 2470)
Rae, Rowena. Cacti. (p. 307)
—Chemical World: Science in Our Daily Lives. (p. 365)
—Land Use. (p. 1242)
—Rachel Carson & Ecology for Kids: Her Life & Ideas, with 21 Activities & Experiments. (p. 1832)
—Southern Ocean. (p. 2069)
Rae, Teydon. Kami Koala Goes to the Zoo. (p. 1202)
Rae, Thelma. Pioneer Families. (p. 1748)
Raeside, Adrian. Rainbow Bridge: A Visit to Pet Paradise. (p. 1836)
Raf, Mindy. Symptoms of My Insanity. (p. 2173)
Rafail, Dyllan. Super Senses. (p. 2156)
Rafanan, Patrick, illus. see Kleinman, Emily & Mudpuppy.
Rafanan, Patrick, illus. see Mudpuppy & Alpert, Yelena Moroz.
Raff, Anna, illus. see Adler, David A.
Raff, Anna, illus. see Flake, Sharon G.
Raff, Anna, illus. see Harper, Charise Mericle.
Raff, Anna, illus. see Lewis, J. Patrick.
Raff, Anna, illus. see Pryor, Katherine.
Raff, Anna, illus. see Wolf, Allan.
Raff, Anna, jt. auth. see Larsen, Mylisa.
Raff, Steffani. Ravenous Gown: And 14 More Tales about Real Beauty. (p. 1844)
Raffa, Edwina & Rigsby, Annelle. Escape to the Everglades (p. 662)
Raffaella, Dowling. Make Your Own Finger Puppets! Tips & Techniques for Fabulous Fun. (p. 1387)
Raffaella, Ligi, illus. see Davidson, Susanna & Stowell, Louie.
Raffaelli, Sean & Dreske, Erin. Dogs Don't Have Pockets. Konecny, John, illus. (p. 577)
Raffalovich, George. Deuce & All (Classic Reprint) (p. 535)
—Planetary Journeys & Earthly Sketches (Classic Reprint) (p. 1755)
Raffa-Mulligan, Teena. Mad Dad for Sale. (p. 1373)
—Seven Day Dragon. (p. 1993)
—Solo Dan. Langfield, Kym, illus. (p. 2057)
—When the Moon Is a Smile. Caloutti, Amy, illus. (p. 2433)
—Who Dresses God? ... for God's house Is this world we share & God Is in it Everywhere. Rooke, Veronica, illus. (p. 2447)
Raffensperger. Eagle Tree. (p. 613)
Rafferty, John P. Biomes & Ecosystems. (p. 229)
—Britannica Guide to Predators & Prey (p. 283)
—Carnivores: Meat-Eating Mammals. (p. 332)
—Climate & Climate Change. (p. 405)
—Conservation & Ecology. (p. 442)
—Deserts & Steppes. (p. 532)
—Forests & Grasslands. (p. 767)
—Grazers. (p. 883)
—Lakes & Wetlands. (p. 1240)
—Living Earth (p. 1333)
—Meat Eaters: Raptors, Sharks, & Crocodiles. (p. 1435)
—Oceans & Oceanography. (p. 1636)
—Primates. (p. 1793)
—Rats, Bats, & Xenarthrans. (p. 1843)
—Reptiles & Amphibians. (p. 1867)
—Rivers & Streams. (p. 1887)
—Rocks. (p. 1896)
Rafferty, John P., ed. Carnivores: Meat-Eating Mammals. (p. 332)
—Primates. (p. 1793)
—Rats, Bats, & Xenarthrans. (p. 1843)
Rafferty, Kavel, illus. see Telesmanic, Shayna.
Rafferty, Michael, jt. auth. see Bryan, Dick.
Raffety, Sarah Jane. Picture Gospel for Children of All Ages. (p. 1740)
Raffi. Raffi Songs to Read Boxed Set: Baby Beluga; Wheels on the Bus; down by the Bay (p. 1834)
—Shake My Sillies Out. Lam, Maple, illus. (p. 1998)
Raffin, Deborah. Mitzi's World: Seek & Discover More Than 150 Details in 15 Works of Folk Art. Scott, Jane Wooster, illus. (p. 1484)
Raffit, Eliot. Lucky the Golden Elephant. (p. 1365)
Rafi, Natasha. Jinni on the Roof: A Ramadan Story. Channa, Abdul Malik, illus. (p. 1169)
Rafter, Chez. Otto the Otter's Muddy Puddle. Frongia, Daniela, illus. (p. 1676)
Rafter, Dan. Gearz: Superficial #2. (p. 812)
Rafter, J. Savindroog, or the Queen of the Jungle, Vol. 2 of 3 (Classic Reprint) (p. 1938)
Rafter, Michael. Percy Blake, or the Young Rifleman, Vol. 2 of 3 (Classic Reprint) (p. 1721)
—Rifleman: Or Adventures of Percy Blake (Classic Reprint) (p. 1879)
Rafter, Pauline Frost. City & Town: A Third Reader (Classic Reprint) (p. 394)
—City & Town: A Fourth Reader (Classic Reprint) (p. 394)
Rafter, Rafter. Percy Blake, or the Young Rifleman, Vol. 1 of 3 (Classic Reprint) (p. 1721)
—Percy Blake, Vol. 3 Of 3: Or, the Young Rifleman (Classic Reprint) (p. 1721)
Raftery, Anthony. Arain Ata Leagta AR an Reactuire, or Songs Ascribed to Raftery: Being the Fifth Chapter of the Songs of Connacht Now for the First Time Collected, Edited & Translated (Classic Reprint) (p. 109)
Raga, Silvia, illus. see Gurney, Stella.
Raga, Silvia, illus. see Harrison, Paul.
Raga, Silvia, illus. see Hibbert, Clare.
Raga, Silvia, illus. see Oliver, Jane.
Raga, Silvia, illus. see Turpin, Nick.
Raga, Sylvia, illus. see Hibbert, Clare.
Ragache, Gilles. Los Vikingos Heroes de Los Mares. (p. 1351)
Ragan, Jewel Coochie. Lost & Found. Ragan, Jewel Coochie, illus. (p. 1352)
Ragan, Lyn. Berc's Inner Voice. (p. 202)
—Berc's Inner Voice. Meyer, Alison, illus. (p. 202)
Ragan, Sean Michael. Popular Science Inventor's Manual. (p. 1777)
Ragel-Dial, Tasha. Say What?, a Photo Book of Inspirational Bible Verses for Kids - Featuring the Photography of Tasha Ragel-Dial. Ragel-Dial, Tasha, photos by. (p. 1940)
Ragg, Alban E. Blue Jay, Vol. 1: July, 1904 (Classic Reprint) (p. 248)
Ragg-Kirkby, Helena, jt. auth. see Hub, Ulrich.
Raghbeer, Anjali. Jar of Sound: Bhil Art. Kundu, Kunal, illus. (p. 1160)
—Rescue by Design: Madhubani Art. Modak, Tejas, illus. (p. 1868)
Ragheb, Masa. Mandy in the Clouds. (p. 1397)
Raglin, Tim, illus. see Brown, Marcy & Haley, Dennis.
Raglin, Tim, illus. see Brown, Marcy, et al.
Raglin, Tim, illus. see Hartman, Bob.
Raglin, Tim, illus. see Kipling, Rudyard.
Raglin, Tim, illus. see McKay, Sindy.
Ragogna, Danielle, illus. see Mathis, Mandi C.
Ragoowansi, Rohan. All for a Handful of Dreams. (p. 52)
Ragozin, Zenaide A. Little Russian Masterpieces: Chosen & Translated from the Original Russian (Classic Reprint) (p. 1327)
—Little Russian Masterpieces. (p. 1327)
—Little Russian Masterpieces, Vol. 4 Of 9: Chosen & Translated from the Original Russian (Classic Reprint) (p. 1327)
Ragsdale, Brenda, illus. see Deanes-Henley, Amy.
Ragsdale, Brenda, illus. see Fondren, Johnny.
Ragsdale, Brenda, illus. see McCain, Don.
Ragsdale, Brenda, illus. see Neely-Dorsey, Patricia.
Ragsdale, Linda. Alphabetter. Hogan, Martina, illus. (p. 59)
—Brain Storm. Molina, Claudio, illus. (p. 275)
—How I Did It. Syed, Anoosha, illus. (p. 1032)
—Not Opposites. Mohanamani, Imodraj, illus. (p. 1623)
—Peace Dragon. Furlotti, Marco, illus. (p. 1709)
—Positively Purple. Brooks, P. S., illus. (p. 1779)
—This Raindrop: Has a Billion Stories to Tell. Bassani, Srimalie, illus. (p. 2226)
—Words. Mohanamani, Imodraj, illus. (p. 2494)
Ragsdale, Lulah. Miss. Dulcie from Dixie (Classic Reprint) (p. 1478)
—Next-Besters (Classic Reprint) (p. 1600)
Ragsdale, Quineka. Demarcus Jones & the Solar Calendar V. Harris Jr, Alvin, illus. (p. 527)
Ragsdale, Susan & Saylor, Ann. Brain Boosters for Groups in Jar: Brain-Enhancing Games to Get Teens Moving & Connecting. (p. 274)
—Imagination Boosters in a Jar: What-If Scenarios to Spark Creativity, Self-Discovery, Relationship Building, & Fun. (p. 1100)
Rahal, Eliot. Midnight Vista. Marts, Mike, ed. (p. 1461)
Raham, Gary, illus. see Biederman, Judy McPherson.
Rahel, Mandula. Csipkehoka: Es Mas Verses Mesek. (p. 481)
Rahim, Rahimah. Trunk. (p. 2295)
Rahim, Yasmeen. Hassan & Aneesa Celebrate Eid. Burgess, Omar, illus. (p. 936)
—Hassan & Aneesa Go to Masjid. Burgess, Omar, illus. (p. 936)
—Hassan & Aneesa Love Ramadan. Burgess, Omar, illus. (p. 936)
—Hassan & Aneesah Go to Madrasa. Burgess, Omar, illus. (p. 936)
Rahimi, Ilgar, illus. see Mastiri, Maryam.
Rahimi, Joey, jt. auth. see G. de la Parra, John.
Rahir, Renee. Eagle. Animals in the Wild. (p. 613)
Rahm, Frank H. Reminiscences of His Capture & Escape from Prison & Adventures Within the Federal Lines (Classic Reprint) (p. 1865)
Rahm, Ida. Miss. Nancy (Classic Reprint) (p. 1479)
Rahmandust, Mustafá. Bazi Ba Angusht Ha. Ladan, Halla, illus. (p. 176)
Rahwan, Dunia. Barefoot Books Incredible Animals. Formica, Paola, illus. (p. 166)
Rai, Bali. Read on - Kiss of Death. (p. 1845)
Rai, Rachel, illus. see Vest, Terri L.
Raible, Alton, illus. see Snyder, Zilpha Keatley.
Raichert, Lance. Treasury of Values for Children. (p. 2283)
Raicht, Mike & Smith, Brian. Tree Mail. (p. 2284)
Raidt, Gerda, illus. see Holtei, Christa & Woofter, Susi.
Raij, Emily. Chefs. (p. 364)
—Climate Change & You: How Climate Change Affects Your Life. (p. 405)
—Doctors. (p. 574)
—Donate Money. (p. 581)
—Earn Money. (p. 615)
—Farmers. (p. 711)
—Ghosts of the Rich & Famous. (p. 829)
—Kids Can Help. (p. 1214)
—Kids Can Help Animals. (p. 1214)
—Kids Can Help Fight Poverty. (p. 1214)
—Kids Can Help Kids. (p. 1214)
—Kids Can Help the Environment. (p. 1214)
—Librarians. (p. 1284)
—Meteorologists. (p. 1453)
—Most Haunted Places in the United States. (p. 1508)
—Most Haunted Places in the World. (p. 1508)
—My Digestive System: A 4D Book. (p. 1537)
—Rey Mysterio. (p. 1874)
—Spooked! (p. 2086)
—Spooked Pack A. (p. 2086)
—Tracking Ghosts. (p. 2272)
—Wide World of Weather: Weather & Climate Around the World. (p. 2461)
Raij, Emily, jt. auth. see Labrecque, Ellen.
Raij, Emily, jt. auth. see Meinking, Mary.
Raij, Emily & Reina, Mary. Earn It, Save It, Spend It! (p. 615)
Raikow, R. B. Where Is My Home? (p. 2438)
Raiku, Makoto. Animal Land 10. (p. 90)
—Animal Land 7. (p. 90)
—Animal Land 8. (p. 90)
—Animal Land 9. (p. 90)
Railey, Julia Houston. Show down (Classic Reprint) (p. 2012)
Railey, Shawna. Messy Life of Blue. (p. 1452)
Railsback, Lisa. Betti on the High Wire. (p. 209)
Railton, Fanny, illus. see Lindsay, Maud.
Raimbault, Christophe, illus. see De Mullenheim, Sophie.
Raimond, C. E. Open Question: A Tale of Two Temperaments (Classic Reprint) (p. 1665)
Raimondo, Sharon. Martus & the Cave. (p. 1411)
Raimundo, Joana, illus. see Nabais, Rita.
Rain, Derrick. Albert Einstein (p. 40)
Rain, Mandy. Rock 'n' Roll. (p. 1894)
—Spring Fling. (p. 2092)
Raina, Arushi. When Morning Comes (p. 2432)
Rainbird, Becky. Taking Notes. (p. 2178)
Rainbolt, Jo Ann Sayman. Mountain Journey (p. 1513)
Rainbow. 44 Cats: Cats Rock! Rainbow, illus. (p. 2555)
—44 Cats: Meet the Cats. Rainbow, illus. (p. 2555)
RainboWindow. Leviticus, I Love You. RainboWindow, illus. (p. 1282)
Raine, Allen. All in a Month: And Other Stories (Classic Reprint) (p. 52)
—Neither Storehouse nor Barn (Classic Reprint) (p. 1586)
—On the Wings of the Wind (Classic Reprint) (p. 1656)
—Torn Sails: A Tale of a Welsh Village (Classic Reprint) (p. 2265)
—Welsh Singer: A Novel (Classic Reprint) (p. 2400)
Raine, Dahye. Unusual Quinns. (p. 2337)
Raine, Eliza. Olympus Academy: The Jinxed Journey. (p. 1651)
—Olympus Academy: The Titan's Treasure. (p. 1651)
—Skies of Olympus: Books One, Two & Three. (p. 2032)
—Storms of Olympus: Books Seven, Eight & Nine. (p. 2127)
—Tides of Olympus: Books Four, Five & Six. (p. 2240)
Raine, James Watt. Public Speaking: For Normal & Academy Students (Classic Reprint) (p. 1810)
Raine, Kai. These Lies That Live Between Us. (p. 2219)
Raine, Liza. Your Feet. (p. 2533)
—Your Hands. (p. 2533)
Raine, William Mac Leod. Fighting Edge (Classic Reprint) (p. 725)
Raine, William MacLeod. Big-Town Round-Up. (p. 223)
—Big-Town Round-Up (Classic Reprint) (p. 223)
—Bonanza: A Story of the Gold Trail (Classic Reprint) (p. 255)
—Brand Blotters (Classic Reprint) (p. 275)
—Bucky O'Connor: A Tale of the Unfenced Border (Classic Reprint) (p. 289)
—Crooked Trails & Straight (Classic Reprint) (p. 477)
—Daughter of the Dons: A Story of New Mexico Today. (p. 509)
—Daughter of the Dons: A Story of New Mexico to-Day (Classic Reprint) (p. 509)
—Gunsight Pass: How Oil Came to the Cattle Country & Brought the New West (Classic Reprint) (p. 905)
—Gunsight Pass. (p. 905)
—Highgrader (Classic Reprint) (p. 970)
—Iron Heart (Classic Reprint) (p. 1135)
—Man Four-Square (Classic Reprint) (p. 1394)
—Man-Size (Classic Reprint) (p. 1395)
—Mavericks (Classic Reprint) (p. 1426)
—Oh, You Tex (Classic Reprint) (p. 1642)
—Ridgway of Montana: (Story of to-Day, in Which the Hero Is Also the Villain) (p. 1878)
—Ridgway of Montana: A Story of Today, in Which the Hero Is Also the Villain (Classic Reprint) (p. 1878)
—Sheriff's Son (Classic Reprint) (p. 2006)
—Steve Yeager (Classic Reprint) (p. 2116)
—Tangled Trails: A Western Detective Story. (p. 2190)
—Tangled Trails: A Western Detective Story (Classic Reprint) (p. 2190)
—Texas Ranger (Classic Reprint) (p. 2209)
—TEXAS RANGER (Wild West Adventure) (p. 2209)
—Troubled Waters (Classic Reprint) (p. 2292)
—Vision Splendid: A Story of to-Day (Classic Reprint) (p. 2362)
—Vision Splendid. (p. 2362)
—Wyoming a Story of Outdoor West. (p. 2515)
—Wyoming a Story of the Outdoor West (Classic Reprint) (p. 2515)
—Yukon Trail: A Tale of the North. (p. 2536)
—Yukon Trail: A Tale of the North (Classic Reprint) (p. 2536)
Rainer, Art. Great Lemonade Stand Standoff (the Secret Slide Money Club, Book 1) (p. 887)
—Mad Cash Dash (the Secret Slide Money Club, Book 2) (p. 1373)
—Trouble at the Toy Store (the Secret Slide Money Club, Book 3) (p. 2291)
Raines, Jennifer. Laughs for Porcupine (p. 1252)
Raines, Shirley. Birds: Discovering North American Species. Hart, Curt, photos by. (p. 231)
—Butterflies: Exploring the Life Cycle. Hart, Curt, photos by. (p. 303)
Rainey, Barbara. What God Wants for Christmas. Walker, John, illus. (p. 2410)
Rainey, Evelyn. Daisy & the Three Shoes. (p. 497)
Rainey, Jamarion. ADHD & Me. (p. 16)
Rainey, Merrill, illus. see Loewen, Nancy.
Rainey, Merrill & Odd Dot. Color, Cut, Create Play Sets: Dinosaur World. Rainey, Merrill, illus. (p. 420)
—Color, Cut, Create Play Sets: Horse Ranch. Rainey, Merrill, illus. (p. 420)
Rainey, P. L. Abby Sue, Where Are You? (p. 3)
Rainey, Rich. Vampire Life (p. 2346)
Rainey, Stephen Mark. Ameri-Scares West Virginia: Lair of the Mothman. (p. 69)
—Elizabeth Massie's Ameri-Scares Michigan: The Dragon of Lake Superior. (p. 636)
Rainey, Thomas Claiborne. Along the Old Trail, Vol. 1: Pioneer Sketches of Arrow Rock & Vicinity (Classic Reprint) (p. 58)
Rainey, William, jt. auth. see Molesworth.
Rainey-Bell, Charlene D. Awkward the Duck & His Musical Adventure. (p. 145)
Rainfield, Cheryl. Scars. (p. 1942)
—Stained. (p. 2099)
Rainford, Peta. Isabella's Adventures in Numberland. (p. 1138)
—Jacob Starke Loves the Dark. (p. 1154)
—Milly's Marvellous Mistakes. (p. 1468)
—Niggle. (p. 1604)
Rainier, S. T., jt. auth. see Page, J.
Rainier, S.T., jt. auth. see Page, J.
Rainis, Kenneth G. Cell & Microbe Science Fair Projects. (p. 350)
Rainmaker Entertainment, illus. see Man-Kong, Mary.
Rainmaker Entertainment Staff, illus. see Man-Kong, Mary.
Rains, C. J., jt. auth. see Delarosa, Mila.
Rains, Charlotte J. Ladybug! Ladybug! (p. 1239)
—Meagan's Wish. Macvean, Alexandra H., illus. (p. 1434)
Rains, Deborah. Sebastian Rae. (p. 1973)
Rains, Deborah Jane. 2011's New Year with Cuddles & Snuggles. (p. 2561)
—Cuddles & Snuggles. (p. 482)
—Racing with Randy. (p. 1832)
—Spooky Happy Halloween with Cuddles & Snuggles. (p. 2087)
—St Patrick's Day with Cuddles & Snuggles. (p. 2098)
Rains, Doug. You Can Call Me Al. (p. 2525)
Rains, Fanny L. By Land & Ocean, or the Journal & Letters of a Young Girl Who Went to South Australia with a Lady Friend, Then Alone to Victoria, New Zealand, Sydney, Singapore, China, Japan, & Across the Continent of America Home (Classic Reprint) (p. 305)
Rains, Rob, ed. see Castle, George.
Rains, Rob, ed. see Noble, Marty.
Rainsford, Blair, jt. auth. see Mattern, Joanne.
Rainstorm Publishing. Peek-A-Boo Farm. Pitt, Sarah, illus. (p. 1712)
Rainstorm Publishing, ed. Alphabet. Hills, Laila, illus. (p. 58)
—Alphabet. Abbott, Simon, illus. (p. 58)
—Alphabet. Bradley, Jennie, illus. (p. 58)
—Animal Colors. Jarzabek, Ela, illus. (p. 88)
—Animal Numbers. Jarzabek, Ela, illus. (p. 90)
—Animals. Hills, Laila, illus. (p. 93)
—Animals. Abbott, Simon, illus. (p. 93)
—Bedtime Prayers. Whitlow, Stephen, illus. (p. 188)
—Colors. Doyle, Lizzy, illus. (p. 425)
—Colors. Hills, Laila, illus. (p. 426)
—Dinosaur Shapes. Hill, Laila, illus. (p. 549)
—Farm. Antonini, Gabriel, illus. (p. 709)
—Farmyard ABC. Hills, Laila, illus. (p. 711)
—Garden. Antonini, Gabriele, illus. (p. 808)
—In the Wild. Boetger, Nikki, illus. (p. 1111)
—Jungle. Antonini, Gabriel, illus. (p. 1189)
—Jungle 123. Hills, Laila, illus. (p. 1189)
—Monster Colors. Hills, Laila, illus. (p. 1495)
—Numbers. Doyle, Lizzy, illus. (p. 1630)
—Numbers. Hills, Laila, illus. (p. 1630)
—Numbers. Abbott, Simon, illus. (p. 1630)
—Numbers. Bradley, Jennie, illus. (p. 1630)
—Ocean. Antonini, Gabriel, illus. (p. 1635)
—Old MacDonald. Antonini, Gabriel, illus. (p. 1646)
—Peek a Boo Halloween. Boetger, Nikki, illus. (p. 1712)
—Peek-A-Boo Animals. Hills, Laila, illus. (p. 1712)
—Peek-A-Boo Colors. Hills, Laila, illus. (p. 1712)
—Peek-A-Boo Numbers. Hills, Laila, illus. (p. 1712)
—Peek-A-Boo Words. Hills, Laila, illus. (p. 1712)
—Planes, Trains, & Animobiles. Doyle, Lizzy, illus. (p. 1755)
—Ten Little Monkey's. Antonini, Gabriel, illus. (p. 2204)
—There Was an Old Lady Who Swallowed a Fly. Antonini, Gabriel, illus. (p. 2217)
—Time for Christmas. Massironi, Daniela, illus. (p. 2244)
—Time for Easter. Massironi, Daniela, illus. (p. 2244)
—Time for Halloween. Massironi, Daniela, illus. (p. 2244)
—Vehicles. Hills, Laila, illus. (p. 2349)
—Wheels on the Bus. Antonini, Gabriel, illus. (p. 2428)
—Words. Hills, Laila, illus. (p. 2494)
—Words. Abbott, Simon, illus. (p. 2494)
Rainville, Roxanne, illus. see Boyle, Jacqueline & Lupone Stonis, Susan.
Rainville, Roxanne, illus. see Mueller, Jenna.
Rainwater, Matt J., illus. see Tobin, Paul.
Rainwater, Matthew J., illus. see Tobin, Paul.
Raish, Jason, illus. see Baptiste, Tracey.
Raish, Jason, illus. see Gregory, Josh.
Raisinghani, Jaya. Sweet Child of Mine. (p. 2168)
Raisman, Aly. Fierce: How Competing for Myself Changed Everything. (p. 723)
Raisman, Aly & Lawrence, Blythe. Fierce: How Competing for Myself Changed Everything. (p. 723)
Raisner Glass, Beth. Blue-Ribbon Dad. Moore, Margie, illus. (p. 249)
Raiten-D'Antonio, Toni, jt. auth. see Williams, Margery.
Raivitch, David. Ashrej: Path of Hope. (p. 125)
Raiya, M. Owl. (p. 1688)
Raiz, James, illus. see Sarracini, Chris & Furman, Simon.
Raizk, Leyla Marie, illus. see Raizk, Mary Ann.
Raj, Sandesh. Village School. (p. 2358)
Raja, Sheela, jt. auth. see Lohmann, Raychelle Cassada.
Raja, Sheena. I Heart Art. (p. 1066)
Rajab, Ahmed, tr. see Umar, Mohammed.
Rajak, Juliette, illus. see McWood, Allison.
Rajan, Lisa. Tara Binns: Big Idea Engineer: Band 14/Ruby (Collins Big Cat) (p. 2191)
—Tara Binns: Double-Quick Doctor: Band 13/Topaz (Collins Big Cat) (p. 2191)
—Tara Binns: High-Flying Pilot: Band 12/Copper (Collins Big Cat) (p. 2191)
Rajan, Y. S., jt. auth. see Kalam, Abdul A.P.J.
Rajawat, Hema. Polly & Her Magical Hat. (p. 1771)
Rajberti, Giovanni. Sul Gatto: Cenni Fisiologico-Morali (Classic Reprint) (p. 2148)
Rajcak, Hélène, illus. see Alzial, Sylvain, et al.
Rajcak, Hélène, illus. see Laverdunt, Damien.
Rajczak, Kristen. 20 Fun Facts about Pioneer Women. (p. 2553)
—20 Fun Facts about Stars. (p. 2553)
—20 Fun Facts about the Great Pyramid (p. 2553)
—20 Fun Facts about Women in Ancient Egypt. (p. 2553)
—20 Fun Facts about Women in Ancient Greece & Rome. (p. 2553)
—Be a Meteorologist. (p. 176)
—Climate Zones. (p. 405)
—Climbing Mount Everest. (p. 405)
—Comets. (p. 429)
—Commas & Colons with Your Class. (p. 430)
—Complete Sentences with Your Family. (p. 435)

R

—Conjunctions with Your Friends. (p. 440)
—Creative Cocoa Recipes. (p. 470)
—Delicious Dairy Recipes. (p. 527)
—Demi Lovato. (p. 528)
—Donner Party. (p. 582)
—Famous Graveyards. (p. 703)
—Fantastic Fruit Recipes. (p. 707)
—Freaky Stories about Our Bodies. (p. 780)
—German Shepherds. (p. 822)
—Great Danes. (p. 885)
—Great Grain Recipes. (p. 886)
—How Snakes & Other Animals Taste the Air. (p. 1035)
—I'm Allergic to Bees. (p. 1097)
—Instagram & Kevin Systrom & Mike Krieger (p. 1125)
—Irish Wolfhounds. (p. 1135)
—Jaden Smith. (p. 1154)
—Jellyfish (p. 1163)
—Justin Bieber. (p. 1195)
—Latitude & Longitude. (p. 1251)
—Laura Ingalls Wilder in Her Own Words. (p. 1252)
—Life As a Pioneer. (p. 1290)
—Life in the American Colonies. (p. 1292)
—Life on a Wagon Train. (p. 1295)
—Lightning. (p. 1299)
—Mayflower Compact. (p. 1430)
—Mujeres en Los Negocios (Women in Business) (p. 1525)
—Nelson Mandela. (p. 1587)
—Northern Lights. (p. 1621)
—Perfect Pasta Recipes. (p. 1722)
—Pulling Dogs. (p. 1812)
—Racing the Iditarod. (p. 1832)
—Rainbows. (p. 1837)
—Renaissance Fairs (p. 1865)
—Rescue Dogs. (p. 1868)
—Sequential Words with Your Pets. (p. 1990)
—Shooting Stars. (p. 2009)
—Skateboarding. (p. 2029)
—Subjects & Verbs with Your Neighbors. (p. 2145)
—Terrifying Tornadoes. (p. 2207)
—Thoroughbreds. (p. 2230)
—Transition Words with Your Team. (p. 2278)
—Types of Maps. (p. 2310)
—Very Tasty Vegetable Recipes. (p. 2354)
—Watch Apple Trees Grow. (p. 2382)
—Watch Corn Grow. (p. 2382)
—Watch Grass Grow. (p. 2382)
—Watch Grass Grow / ¡Mira cómo crece el Césped! (p. 2382)
—Watch Tulips Grow. (p. 2383)
—Watch Tulips Grow / ¡Mira cómo crecen los Tulipanes! (p. 2383)
—Women in Business. (p. 2487)
Rajczak, Kristin. Civil Rights Movement in Texas. (p. 396)
Rajczak, Michael. Amber. (p. 67)
—Attack of the Stink Bugs. (p. 135)
—Attack of the Zebra Mussels. (p. 135)
—Be a Citizen Scientist! (p. 176)
—Becoming President. (p. 187)
—Before Andrew Jackson Was President. (p. 190)
—Before Franklin D. Roosevelt Was President. (p. 190)
—Before Thomas Jefferson Was President. (p. 191)
—Deadly Droughts. (p. 518)
—Haunted! The White House. (p. 937)
—Haunted! Gettysburg. (p. 937)
—Haunted! the White House. (p. 938)
—How Did the Liberty Bell Get Its Crack?— & Other FAQs about American History. (p. 1027)
—Life on the Mayflower (p. 1295)
—Maps Throughout American History (p. 1401)
—Meet the President. (p. 1440)
—Meet the President's Cabinet. (p. 1440)
—Muhammad Ali (p. 1524)
—Sea Urchins. (p. 1969)
—Texas Geography. (p. 2209)
—Transcontinental Railroad (p. 2277)
—Underground Railroad (p. 2323)
—Visiting the Great Lakes. (p. 2363)
Rajczak Nelson, Kristen. All about Christmas Angels (p. 48)
—All about Christmas Carols. (p. 48)
—All about Christmas Trees (p. 48)
—All about Elves (p. 49)
—All about Reindeer (p. 50)
—All about Santa. (p. 50)
—All about the North Pole (p. 50)
—All about the Three Kings (p. 50)
—Amphibians. (p. 77)
—Andrew Carnegie & the Steel Industry. (p. 83)
—Bruno Mars: Singer & Songwriter. (p. 288)
—China Anne McClain: Actress, Singer, & Songwriter. (p. 378)
—Ed Sheeran: Singer-Songwriter. (p. 624)
—Fangtooth Fish. (p. 706)
—Gareth's Guide to Writing a Best Seller. (p. 810)
—How Do People Vote? (p. 1029)
—How Do You Gain Time When You Fly West? And Other FAQS about Time & Travel. (p. 1029)
—How Oil Is Formed. (p. 1034)
—Inside the Civil Rights Movement. (p. 1123)
—Jefferson Davis: Leader of the Confederacy. (p. 1163)
—Mammals. (p. 1393)
—Maya Angelou: African American Poet. (p. 1429)
—Mayflower Compact. (p. 1430)
—Melania Trump: First Lady of the United States. (p. 1442)
—More Freaky Stories about Our Bodies. (p. 1504)
—Sequential Words with Your Pets. (p. 1990)
—Serena Williams: Tennis Star. (p. 1990)
—U.S. Constitution. (p. 2340)
—What Are Igneous Rocks? (p. 2405)
—What Are Metamorphic Rocks? (p. 2405)
—What Are Minerals? (p. 2405)
—What Is Voting? (p. 2417)
—Who Can Vote? (p. 2446)
—Who Do People Vote For? (p. 2447)
—Why Should People Vote? (p. 2459)
Rajendra Nargundkar & Romi Sainy. Digital Marketing: Cases from India. (p. 546)
Rajendra, Vijeya & Rajendra, Sundran. Australia. (p. 138)
Rajendra, Vijeya, et al. Iran. (p. 1133)
Rajendran, Sowmya. Boy Who Asked Why: The Story of Bhimrao Ambedkar. Gade, Satwik, illus. (p. 270)
Rajic, Alex. Alefbet Illuminated. Rajic, Alex, illus. (p. 41)
Rajiv Arora. Impact Your Destiny: 21 Real Life Destiny Encounters Prakaash Kriya - Reinventing Lives. (p. 1101)
Rajoria, Swati. Baby's First Numbers. (p. 154)
—Baby's First Words. (p. 154)
—Friendship Story Book Collection 3 Stories. (p. 788)
—Wonderful Story Book Collection 3 Stories. (p. 2490)
Raju, P. V. Ramaswami. Indian Fables. (p. 1116)
—Indian Fables (Classic Reprint) (p. 1116)
—Tales of the Sixty Mandarins (Classic Reprint) (p. 2186)
Rajvanshi, Ayush, illus. see D'souza, Nadine.
Rake, Jody S. Adélie Penguins. (p. 16)
—Earth. (p. 615)
—Emperor Penguins. (p. 644)
—Faceless, Spineless, & Brainless Ocean Animals. (p. 693)
—Gentoo Penguins. (p. 817)
—Jellyfish. (p. 1163)
—King Penguins. (p. 1221)
—Kings of the Oceans. (p. 1223)
—Kings of the Rivers. (p. 1223)
—Little Penguins. (p. 1324)
—Mars. (p. 1409)
—Mercury. (p. 1448)
—Oceanic Whitetip Sharks: A 4D Book. (p. 1636)
—Penguins! (p. 1716)
—Rockhopper Penguins. (p. 1895)
—Sand Tiger Sharks: A 4D Book. (p. 1930)
—Sea Dragons. (p. 1967)
—Sea Urchins. (p. 1969)
—Thresher Sharks: A 4D Book. (p. 2236)
—Venus. (p. 2351)
—What Is Force? (p. 2415)
—What Is Sound? (p. 2416)
Rake, Jody S., jt. auth. see Foxe, Steve.
Rake, Jody Sullivan. Beluga Whales up Close [Scholastic]. (p. 198)
—Bloodsuckers of the Animal World. (p. 246)
—Blue Whales up Close [Scholastic]. (p. 249)
—Bottlenose Dolphin up Close [Scholastic]. (p. 265)
—Carcass Chewers of the Animal World. (p. 327)
—Disgusting Creature Diets. (p. 557)
—Endangered Oceans: Investigating Oceans in Crisis. (p. 649)
—Garbage Gorgers of the Animal World. (p. 808)
—Gross Me Out. (p. 898)
—Hippos: In the Wild. (p. 973)
—Hyenas: On the Hunt (p. 1056)
—Killer Whales up Close [Scholastic]. (p. 1217)
—Leatherback Sea Turtles (p. 1259)
—Meerkats. (p. 1437)
—Meerkats, Moles, & Voles: Animals of the Underground. (p. 1438)
—Mudskippers & Other Extreme Fish Adaptations (p. 1524)
—Orcas (p. 1669)
—Polar Bears: On the Hunt (p. 1769)
—Poop & Puke Eaters of the Animal World. (p. 1774)
—Pumas: On the Hunt. (p. 1812)
—Pythons. (p. 1819)
—Roots, Bulbs, & Bacteria: Growths of the Underground. (p. 1903)
—Sea Anemones. (p. 1966)
—Sea Cucumbers. (p. 1967)
—Soil, Silt, & Sand: Layers of the Underground. (p. 2055)
—Speed, Strength, & Stealth: Animal Weapons & Defenses. (p. 2078)
—Spines, Horns, & Armor: Animal Weapons & Defenses. (p. 2082)
—Star-Nosed Moles & Other Extreme Mammal Adaptations (p. 2102)
—Underground Safari. (p. 2324)
—Why Bed Bugs Bite & Other Gross Facts about Bugs. (p. 2455)
—Why Feet Smell & Other Gross Facts about Your Body (p. 2457)
—Why Rabbits Eat Poop & Other Gross Facts about Pets (p. 2458)
—Why Vampire Bats Suck Blood & Other Gross Facts about Animals (p. 2459)
Rake, Jody Sullivan, jt. auth. see Iyer, Rani.
Rake, Jody Sullivan, jt. auth. see Riehecky, Janet.
Rake, Jody Sullivan, et al. Extreme Adaptations (p. 686)
Rake, Matthew. Creatures of the Rain Forest. Mendez, Simon, illus. (p. 472)
—Creepy, Crawly Creatures. Mendez, Simon, illus. (p. 473)
—If Prehistoric Beasts Were Alive Today. Mendez, Simon, illus. (p. 1092)
—Prehistoric Ancestors of Modern Animals. Mendez, Simon, illus. (p. 1787)
—Prehistoric Giants. Mendez, Simon, illus. (p. 1787)
—Prehistoric Predators. Mendez, Simon, illus. (p. 1787)
—Prehistoric Sea Beasts. Mendez, Simon, illus. (p. 1787)
—Real Life Monsters: Amazing Monster-Like Animals of the Rainforest, Desert. Mendez, Simon, illus. (p. 1849)
—Rise of Mammals. Minister, Peter, illus. (p. 1885)
—Scaly, Slippery Creatures. Mendez, Simon, illus. (p. 1941)
Rakhi Kapoor. Expecting Daddy Delivers: Be the Man Your Partner & Your Baby Adore. (p. 677)
Rakos, Lynnda. Let's Color Together — Princesses, Mermaids & Fairies. (p. 1270)
—Let's Color Together — Robots. (p. 1270)
Rakos, Lynnda, et al. Princesses, Mermaids & Fairies Coloring Book. (p. 1800)
Rakove, Jack N., ed. see LaClair, Teresa.
Rakove, Jack N., ed. see Quinby, Michelle.
Rakove, Jack N., ed. see Sharp, Constance.
Rakove, Jack N., ed. see South, Victor.
Rakove, Jack N., ed. see Windsor, Wesley.
Rakra Rinpoche, Tethong Thubten Choedhar. Life of Buddha in Colloquial Tibetan. Shingza Rinpoche, Choekyi Gyaltsen, ed. (p. 1294)
Rakuraku, Maraea, tr. see Johnson, Mike.
Ralaivao, Zafimamy Gabriella, tr. see Pere, Tuula.
Raleigh, Albert Sidney. Philosophia Hermetica; a Course of Ten Lessons, Being an Introduction to the Philosophy of Alchemy. (p. 1735)
Raleigh, Cecil. Belle of Cairo: A New & Original Musical Play (Classic Reprint) (p. 197)
—Sins of Society: A Novel (Classic Reprint) (p. 2025)
Raleigh, Michael H. Ted & Jimmy (p. 2198)
Raleigh, Walter. Laughter from a Cloud (Classic Reprint) (p. 1252)
Raley, Gary. Grandpa's Bear Story. (p. 879)
Raley, Harold. Prodigal. (p. 1803)
Raliver, Jo. Rodney the Rather Rare Rainbowsaurus. (p. 1897)
Ralles, H. J. Looking Out My Window. (p. 1347)
Ralli, Constantine. Strange Story of Falconer Thring (Classic Reprint) (p. 2138)
Rallis, Chris, illus. see Batten, Mary.
Rallis, Chris, illus. see Sollinger, Emily.
Rallison, Janette. Just One Wish. (p. 1194)
—My Fair Godmother. (p. 1538)
—My Unfair Godmother. (p. 1563)
—Wrong Side of Magic. (p. 2514)
Ralls, Ken. Henrietta Hippo Learns to Dance. McQuitty, LaVonia Corbin, illus. (p. 954)
Ralls, Whitney. My Little Pony: Equestria Girls: Make Your Own Magic: Starswirl Do-Over. (p. 1553)
Ralph, Brian. Cave In. (p. 347)
—Reggie-12. (p. 1861)
Ralph, Julian. Angel in a Web (Classic Reprint) (p. 85)
—Millionairess (Classic Reprint) (p. 1468)
—People We Pass: Stories of Life among the Masses of New York City (Classic Reprint) (p. 1719)
—People We Pass. (p. 1719)
—Prince of Georgia & Other Tales (Classic Reprint) (p. 1794)
Ralph, Julian E. That Dutchman, or the German Barber's Humorous Sketches (Classic Reprint) (p. 2212)
Ralph, Karin, illus. see Ryan, Mike.
Ralph Lewis, Brenda. Untold History of the Kings & Queens of England. (p. 2336)
—Untold History of the Kings & Queens of Europe. (p. 2336)
Ralph, Rachel. Jeremy Steadfast Told a Lie. Burt, Emily, illus. (p. 1164)
—Real Story of Jack & the Beanstalk. (p. 1850)
Ralphs, Matt. Fire Witch: Fire Girl 2. (p. 733)
—Season of the Witch: A Spellbinding History of Witches & Other Magical Folk. Tamarit, Núria, illus. (p. 1972)
—Space Jump: Band 11 Lime/Band 17 Diamond (Collins Big Cat Progress) (p. 2071)
Ralphson, G. Harvey. Boy Scout Electricians: Or the Hidden Dynamo (Classic Reprint) (p. 269)
—Boy Scouts Beyond the Arctic Circle: Or, the Lost Expedition. (p. 269)
—Boy Scouts Beyond the Arctic Circle: Or the Lost Expedition (Classic Reprint) (p. 269)
—Boy Scouts in a Motor Boat: Or Adventures on the Columbia River (Classic Reprint) (p. 269)
—Boy Scouts in a Submarine: Or Searching an Ocean Floor (Classic Reprint) (p. 269)
—Boy Scouts in a Submarine. (p. 269)
—Boy Scouts in an Airship: The Warning from the Sky. (p. 269)
—Boy Scouts in Mexico: On Guard with Uncle Sam. (p. 269)
—Boy Scouts in Southern Waters. (p. 269)
—Boy Scouts in the North Sea. (p. 269)
—Boy Scouts in the Philippines: The Key to the Treaty Box. (p. 269)
—Boy Scouts in the Philippines: Or the Key to the Treaty Box (Classic Reprint) (p. 269)
—Boy Scouts Mysterious Signal or Perils of the Black Bear Patrol. (p. 269)
—Boy Scouts on Hudson Bay: The Disappearing Fleet. (p. 270)
—Boy Scouts on Motorcycles with the Flying Squadron. (p. 270)
Ralphson, George Harvey. Boy Scout Camera Club: Or, the Confession of a Photograph. (p. 269)
—Boy Scouts in Belgium, or under Fire in Flanders (Classic Reprint) (p. 269)
—Boy Scouts in Mexico: Or, on Guard with Uncle Sam. (p. 269)
—Boy Scouts on Motorcycles: With the Flying Squadron. (p. 270)
Ralston, Carole. Light in the Forest. (p. 1298)
Ralston, W. R. S. Liza: A Nest of Nobles (Classic Reprint) (p. 1336)
Ralston-Gray, Cheryl. Good Day, Bad Day. (p. 862)
Raluca, Cristina Cirti, illus. see Hall, Tara.
Ram, Praba & Preuitt, Sheela. Thukpa for All. Ranade, Shilpa, illus. (p. 2238)
Ram, Sangana. Nalladhor Mattram. Mahesh, Chitra, ed. (p. 1573)
Rama, Sue, illus. see Codell, Esmé Raji.
Rama, Sue, illus. see Harley, Diana.
Rama, Sue, illus. see Miller, Heather Lynne.
Rama, Sue, illus. see Park, Linda Sue & Durango, Julia.
Ramachandran, Ganesh, photos by see Steele, Mariah.
Ramadan, Danny. Salma the Syrian Chef. Bron, Anna, illus. (p. 1925)
Ramadan, Emma, tr. see Marnier, Richard.
Ramadier, Cedric. Attention Aux Ogres ! Devaux, Clement, illus. (p. 135)
Ramadier, Cédric. Shhh! This Book Is Sleeping. Bourgeau, Vincent, illus. (p. 2007)
Ramalho, Rosa. Mary Our Mother Col Bk (5pk) Coutinho, Ivan, illus. (p. 1415)
Raman, Prinja. Hacia Los Confines Del Universo. (p. 908)
Ramanan, Nitya. Pineapple Cavities. (p. 1745)
Ramanathan, Khavin. Odyssey Through Morgatonia. (p. 1638)
Ramanathan, Priya. Mustache Man. Gupta, Garima, illus. (p. 1530)
Ramanathan, Vidya. Sanskritan Me Samskrtam Mahyam: Rochte Delights. (p. 1931)
Ramani, Madhvi. Nina & the Kung-Fu Adventure. (p. 1609)
—Nina & the Travelling Spice Shed. (p. 1609)
Ramasubbu, Krish. Spirit of the Unborn. (p. 2083)
Ramathas, Ann. Dog Called Cat. (p. 575)
Ramberg, J. J. Startup Club. (p. 2108)
Ramble, R. A. Rassi. (p. 1842)
Rambo, Angela, illus. see Plumier, Lea.
Rambo, Jini. Archive, Vol. 78: November, 1965 (Classic Reprint) (p. 111)
Rambo, Pamela, jt. auth. see Vaughan, Brian K.
Ramdas, Jeevaraja, illus. see Petrilli, Laura.
Rame, Louisa De La. Bimbi: Stories for Children (Classic Reprint) (p. 228)
—Dog of Flanders: A Christmas Story (Classic Reprint) (p. 576)
—Moufflou: And Other Stories (Classic Reprint) (p. 1512)
—Nurnberg Stove (Classic Reprint) (p. 1631)
Rame, Louise De La. Dog of Flanders, the Nürnberg Stove & Other Stories. (p. 576)
—Moufflon: The Dog of Florence (Classic Reprint) (p. 1512)
Rame, Maria Louise. Beatrice Boville: And Other Stories (Classic Reprint) (p. 183)
—Dog of Flanders & the Nurnberg Stove (Classic Reprint) (p. 576)
—House-Party; Don Gesualdo; & a Rainy June (Classic Reprint) (p. 1024)
—Moths (Classic Reprint) (p. 1511)
—Moths, Vol. 2 Of 3: A Novel (Classic Reprint) (p. 1511)
—Puck, and, in Maremma, Vol. 9 (Classic Reprint) (p. 1810)
—Signa: A Story (Classic Reprint) (p. 2016)
—Signa, Vol. 1 Of 3: A Story (Classic Reprint) (p. 2016)
—Signa, Vol. 2 Of 3: A Story (Classic Reprint) (p. 2016)
—Two Offenders (Classic Reprint) (p. 2308)
Rameck, Hunt, et al. We Beat the Street: How a Friendship Pact Led to Success. (p. 2389)
Ramée, Lisa Moore. Good Kind of Trouble. (p. 863)
Ramee, Lisa Moore. Something to Say. (p. 2061)
Ramee, Louise De La, see de la Ramée, Louise.
Ramen, Fred. Albucasis (Abu al-Qasim Al-Zahrawi) Renowned Muslim Surgeon of the Tenth Century. (p. 41)
—Hermann Goring: Hitler's Second-in-Command. (p. 959)
—Hernán Cortés: The Conquest of Mexico & the Aztec Empire. (p. 959)
—Influenza. (p. 1119)
—Jerry West. (p. 1164)
—Sleeping Sickness & Other Parasitic Tropical Diseases. (p. 2037)
—Tuberculosis. (p. 2298)
Ramen, Fred, jt. auth. see Campbell, Forest G.
Ramey, Albina. Maya in the Nimbus Valley. (p. 1429)
Ramey, Stacie. Homecoming. (p. 997)
—It's My Life. (p. 1146)
—Secrets We Bury. (p. 1981)
—Sister Pact. (p. 2027)
Rami, Maya. Who Is Buddha? (p. 2447)
Ramirez, Alma, tr. see Driscoll, Laura.
Ramirez, Alma B., tr. see James, Anne.
Ramírez, Ana, illus. see de la Peña, Matt.
Ramírez, Claudia. Ladrona de la Luna. (p. 1236)
Ramirez, D. a. & Ramirez, D. A. Kingdom of Glass. (p. 1222)
Ramirez, Elizandro de los Angeles, illus. see Batres, Ethel.
Ramirez Gallo, Ricardo, illus. see Roach, Vicki.
Ramírez González, Ana, illus. see Agell, Charlotte.
Ramirez, Gracie D. Ella's Great American Adventure. (p. 637)
Ramirez, Herman, illus. see Torres, Eliseo & Sawyer, Timothy L.
Ramirez, Iz. Bob the Lizard Swope, Brenda, illus. (p. 252)
Ramirez, James. Carmencita, the Pearl of Seville (Classic Reprint) (p. 332)
Ramirez, Jose, illus. see Cumpiano, Ina.
Ramirez, Jose, illus. see Mahin, Michael.
Ramirez, Jose, illus. see Villaseñor, Victor.
Ramirez, Jose, jt. auth. see Cumpiano, Ina.
Ramirez, Juanan & Schiti, Valerio. Iron Man: the Ultron Agenda: The Ultron Agenda. (p. 1135)
Ramirez, Ken. You, Me, Naideen & a Bee. (p. 2527)
Ramirez, Lasean. Jamal's Wagon. (p. 1156)
—Push & Pull. (p. 1817)
Ramirez, Leonardo. Ice Orphan of Ganymede. (p. 1088)
—Orb of Terra. (p. 1669)
—Secret of the Great Red Spot. (p. 1977)
Ramirez, Orlando L., illus. see Marin, Cheech.
Ramirez, Samuel, illus. see Sanchez, Juanita L.
Ramirez, Stephanie, illus. see Cicierega, Emmy.
Ramirez, Stephanie, illus. see Houghton, Shane & Renzetti, Rob.
Ramirez-Christensen, Esperanza. My First Book of Haiku Poetry: A Picture, a Poem, a Dream. Gallup, Tracy, illus. (p. 1542)
Ramljak, Marijan. Are You My Friend? (p. 113)
—Are You My Mommy? (p. 113)
—Where Do I Live? (p. 2436)
—Where Is My Daddy? (p. 2438)
Ramljak, Marijan, illus. see McElroy, Jean.
Ramlogan, Nitya, illus. see Guerrero, Elsie.
Ramnanan, Hana. How the Little Star Made It Home. (p. 1036)
Ramon, Andy, illus. see Staat, Virginia Parker.
Ramon, El Primo, illus. see Bensson, Michelle.
Ramón, El Primo, illus. see Maurer, Tracy Nelson.
Ramon, Velma J. What Will I Be Today? (p. 2422)
Ramon, Yrgane, illus. see Cazenove, Christophe & Richez, Herve.
Ramondelli, Livio, illus. see Metzen, Chris, et al.
Ramondetta, Christine. Marvelous Mister Moon. Cain, Allison, illus. (p. 1413)
Ramos, Amy Jones, illus. see Martin, Brenda Darnley.
Ramos, Beatriz Helena, illus. see Rosenberg, Pam.
Ramos, Belen. Way to Fairyleland: Commemorative Edition. (p. 2387)
Ramos, Bethany. Lions Can't Eat Spaghetti. Morrow, Nicole, illus. (p. 1307)
Ramos, Dania. Who's Ju? (p. 2453)
Ramos, Felizardo Duke. Sock City Dinky's Arrival. (p. 2054)
Ramos, Felizardoduke. Sock City Super Stretch. (p. 2054)
Ramos, Humberto. Amazing Spider-Man by Nick Spencer Vol. 2: Friends & Foes. (p. 66)
—Champions: Because the World Still Needs Heroes. (p. 355)
—Champions Vol. 2: The Freelancer Lifestyle. (p. 355)

—Marvel Monograph: the Art of Humberto Ramos - Spider-Man. (p. 1412)
Ramos, Jose, illus. see Sanderson, Jeannette & Benchmark Education Co., LLC.
Ramos, Jose, illus. see Sanderson, Jeannette.
Ramos, Jose, illus. see Schiller, Pamela Byrne.
Ramos, Jose, illus. see Swain, Cynthia & Benchmark Education Co., LLC.
Ramos, Jose, illus. see Swain, Cynthia.
Ramos, Luis. Chronicles of Moses. (p. 389)
—Jesus a Real Life Super Hero. (p. 1165)
—Jose y Su Historia. (p. 1178)
—Joseph & His Brothers. (p. 1178)
—Las Cronicas de Moises. (p. 1245)
Ramos, Mario. I Am So Clever. Ramos, Mario, illus. (p. 1060)
—I Am So Handsome. (p. 1060)
—I Am So Strong. (p. 1060)
Ramos, Odalys Q. Allow Me to Introduce Myself. Graham, Michael, illus. (p. 57)
Ramos, Ramona J. Summer with Kaitlyn & Lexi. (p. 2150)
Ramos Revillas, Antonio. Dama de la Selva. (p. 499)
Ramoutar, Tagore. Arabellafella's First Reading Book. (p. 108)
—Brownie the Monkey Visits the Zoo. Cline, Ian, photos by. (p. 287)
—Eric Boyle the Crocodile Chooses a New Car. (p. 659)
—I Love Birds! (p. 1069)
—Trains, Engines & Locomotives: I Love Trains. (p. 2276)
Ramphal, Vic. Bonny Malt: Prince of Swan. (p. 256)
—Dancing in a Cake Cathedral. (p. 500)
Rampley, Leigh, illus. see Huffman, Jared.
Rampley, Leigh, illus. see Schlimpert, Sherrill.
Ramsaroop, Yuvraj. Miracle on the Train Track. (p. 1474)
Ramsay. Summer in Spain (Classic Reprint) (p. 2149)
Ramsay, Allan, jt. auth. see Adler, Cyrus.
Ramsay, Connie. Pugs Are People, Too. Eves, Mickey, illus. (p. 1812)
Ramsay, David. History of the American Revolution Cohen, Lester H., ed. (p. 980)
Ramsay, Gwen. Vox Fluminis, 1936 (Classic Reprint) (p. 2368)
Ramsay, Jana & Ramsay, Nicole. Comedy. (p. 429)
Ramsay, John Martin, compiled by. Dog Tales: Some Are Tall & Some Are True but All Pay Humorous Tribute to Man's Best Friend. (p. 576)
Ramsay, M. S. Lydia, illus. see Denny, M. S. Ange.
Ramsay, Mark. Good Neighbors' Cheese Feast: A Cheesy Mouse Tale of Subtraction with Regrouping. Robinson, Susan G., illus. (p. 863)
—Good Neighbors Store an Award: A Cheesy Mouse Tale of Addition with Regrouping. Robinson, Susan G., illus. (p. 863)
Ramsay, Nicole. Comedy. (p. 429)
Ramsay, Rina. Straw (Classic Reprint) (p. 2139)
—Way of a Woman: A Novel (Classic Reprint) (p. 2387)
Ramsay, Robert L. Short Stories of America: Edited with an Introductory Essay, Course Outline, & Reading Lists (Classic Reprint) (p. 2010)
Ramsay, Thea. Lucy. (p. 1365)
Ramsay, W. M. Everyday Life in Turkey (Classic Reprint) (p. 672)
Ramsay-Laye, Elizabeth. Social Life & Manners in Australia: Being the Notes of Eight Years Experience (Classic Reprint) (p. 2053)
Ramsden, Charles T., jt. auth. see Barbour, Thomas.
Ramsden, Guendolen. Smile Within a Tear: And Other Fairy Stories (Classic Reprint) (p. 2042)
Ramsden, Melvyn. Rescuing Spelling. (p. 1868)
Ramsdin-Firth, Bernice. Return to Lolibran & the Witch's Lair: Black & White Version. Ramsdin-Firth, Bernice & Shandler, Georgette, illus. (p. 1871)
Ramsey, Calvin Alexander, jt. auth. see Stroud, Bettye.
Ramsey, Calvin Alexander & Stroud, Bettye. Belle, the Last Mule at Gee's Bend: A Civil Right's Story. (p. 197)
Ramsey, Cecelia, tr. see Aladjidi, Virginia.
Ramsey, Edward Bannerman. Reminiscences of Scottish Life & Character. (p. 1865)
Ramsey, Grace. Bugs. (p. 292)
—Haunted Hotels. (p. 938)
—Haunted Objects. (p. 938)
Ramsey, Jo. Ball Caps & Khakis. (p. 161)
—Blue Jeans & Sweatshirts. (p. 248)
—Dolphins in the Mud. (p. 580)
—High Heels & Lipstick. (p. 968)
—Jet Black. (p. 1167)
—Midnight Chat. (p. 1461)
—Nail Polish & Feathers. (p. 1573)
—Opening Up. (p. 1666)
—Shoulder Pads & Flannel. (p. 2011)
—Time of Darkness. (p. 2245)
—Where No One Knows. (p. 2439)
—Work Boots & Tees. (p. 2495)
Ramsey, K. D. 's Magical March in the Mall Looking for Christmas. (p. 1919)
Ramsey, L. A., illus. see Morton, William A.
Ramsey, L. W. Siren, Vol. 3: September, 1913 (Classic Reprint) (p. 2026)
Ramsey, Marathon Montrose. Progressive Exercises in Spanish Prose Composition: With Notes & a Vocabulary (Classic Reprint) (p. 1805)
Ramsey, Marcy, illus. see Naylor, Phyllis Reynolds.
Ramsey, Marcy Dunn. Rosie's Posies Ramsey, Marcy Dunn, illus. (p. 1906)
Ramsey, Marcy Dunn, illus. see Bunting, Elaine & D'Amario, Patricia.
Ramsey, Marcy Dunn, illus. see Cummings, Priscilla.
Ramsey, Marcy Dunn, illus. see Curtis, Jennifer Keats.
Ramsey, Marcy Dunn, illus. see Jensen, Ann.
Ramsey, Marcy Dunn, illus. see McVicker, Mary.
Ramsey, Marcy Dunn, illus. see Meacham, Margaret.
Ramsey, Marcy Dunn, illus. see Pickford, Susan T.
Ramsey, Sherry D. Planet Fleep: A Science Twins Adventure. (p. 1755)
—Seventh Crow. (p. 1994)
Ramsey, Torren. Ojibwe. (p. 1643)
Ramsnips, Tunder. Hardly Boys. (p. 930)
Ramstad, Ralph L., illus. see Schott, Jane A.
Ramstein, Anne-Margot, illus. see Arégui, Matthias, et al.
Ramstein, Anne-Margot & Arégui, Matthias. Inside Outside. Ramstein, Anne-Margot & Arégui, Matthias, illus. (p. 1123)
Ramtri, Rocco. 50 States, by a Seven-Year-Old. Lanot, Harvey, illus. (p. 2555)
Ramuz, C.F. Reign of the Evil One (Classic Reprint) (p. 1862)
Ran, Dana Meachen, jt. auth. see Gordon, Sharon.
Ran, Gila. Lemonheads, the Crown of Wisdom. (p. 1266)
Ran Lee, Hye, illus. see Burnett, Frances Hodgson.
Rana, Raj & Cushing, Ian. Language Change. (p. 1243)
Ranade, Shilpa, illus. see Ram, Praba & Preuitt, Sheela.
Ranade, Soumitra. Tak-Tak! Suleman, Shilo Shiv, illus. (p. 2176)
Rance, Alex. Tiger's Roar. McG, Shane, illus. (p. 2242)
Ranchetti, Sebastiano, illus. see Ottina, Laura.
Rancour, Thom. Legend of the Hartwick Pines. Russell, Tom, illus. (p. 1262)
Rand, Ann. Listen! Listen! Rand, Paul, illus. (p. 1308)
—What Can I Be? King, Ingrid Fiksdahl, illus. (p. 2406)
Rand, Betseygail & Rand, Colleen. Big Bunny. Rand, Colleen, illus. (p. 218)
Rand, Casey. DNA & Heredity (p. 569)
—Food (p. 759)
—Forces & Motion. (p. 764)
—George Washington Oxford Bible Staff, illus. (p. 819)
—Giant Morays & Other Extraordinary Eels (p. 830)
—Graphing Sports (p. 881)
—Producing Vegetables (p. 1804)
—Temperature (p. 2202)
—Time (p. 2243)
Rand, Edward A. All Aboard for Sunrise Lands: A Trip Through California Across the Pacific to Japan, China, & Australia (Classic Reprint) (p. 48)
—Behind Manhattan Gables: A Story of New Amsterdam 1663-1664 (Classic Reprint) (p. 192)
—Candle in the Sea, or, Winter at Seal's Head. (p. 321)
—Candle in the Sea, or Winter at Seal's Head (Classic Reprint) (p. 321)
—Drummer-Boy of the Rappahannock: Or Taking Sides (Classic Reprint) (p. 606)
—Knight That Smote the Dragon, or the Young People's Gough (Classic Reprint) (p. 1228)
—Mill at Sandy Creek (Classic Reprint) (p. 1467)
—Sailor-Boy Bob (Classic Reprint) (p. 1923)
Rand, Edward Augustus. All Aboard for the Lakes & Mountains: A Trip to Picturesque Localities in the United States (Classic Reprint) (p. 48)
Rand, Edward Sprague. Traditionary Stories: Extant among the Tapoia Indians Inhabiting the Valley of the Middle Amazon in Northern Brazil (Classic Reprint) (p. 2274)
Rand, Emily. Dog Day. (p. 575)
—House Full of Stuff. (p. 1022)
—In the Darkness of the Night. (p. 1108)
—Little Fish. (p. 1316)
Rand, Frank Prentice. John Epps (Classic Reprint) (p. 1172)
Rand, Johnathan. Amer Ch Double Thrillers. (p. 69)
—American Chillers #26 Oklahoma Outbreak. (p. 71)
—American Chillers #27 Kentucky Komodo Dragons. (p. 71)
—American Chillers #28 Curse of the Connecticut Coyotes. (p. 71)
—American Chillers #29 Oregon Oceanauts. (p. 71)
—Freddie Fernortner #11: Tadpole Trouble. (p. 781)
Rand, Mary Abbot. Holly & Mistletoe (Classic Reprint) (p. 988)
—Home Spun Yarns (Classic Reprint) (p. 997)
Rand McNally. Are We There Yet? Awty. (p. 113)
—Kids' Illustrated World Map Folded. (p. 1215)
—Kids' Road Atlas: Kra. (p. 1216)
—Map It! Jr Landforms Boardbook. (p. 1400)
—Map It! Jr Waterways Boardbook. (p. 1400)
—Signature United States Wall Map (Folded) (p. 2016)
Rand McNally, creator. Coast-To-Coast Games. (p. 410)
—Kids' Backseat Travel Kit. (p. 1214)
Rand, Paul, illus. see Rand, Ann.
Rand, Silas Tertius. Dictionary of the Language of the Micmac Indians: Who Reside in Nova Scotia, New Brunswick, Prince Edward Island, Cape Breton & Newfoundland (Classic Reprint) (p. 542)
—Dictionary of the Language of the Micmac Indians. (p. 542)
Rand, Ted, illus. see Archambault, John & Martin, Bill, Jr.
Rand, Ted, illus. see Moore, Clement C.
Rand, Ted, illus. see Prelutsky, Jack.
Rand, Ted, illus. see Tunnell, Michael O.
Rand, Ted & Moore, Clement C. Night Before Christmas. (p. 1605)
Rand, Tracy, illus. see Westendorf, Sandra.
Randall, Alex. Little Yellow Riding Hood. (p. 1330)
—Rhyming Book. (p. 1875)
—Tickle the Monster. (p. 2240)
Randall, Alice. Diary of B. B. Bright, Possible Princess. (p. 540)
Randall, Alice & Randall Williams, Caroline. Diary of B. B. Bright, Possible Princess. Strickland, Shadra, illus. (p. 540)
Randall, Angel. Snow Angels. (p. 2047)
Randall, Annie G. State Normal Magazine, Vol. 7: October, 1902 June, 1903 (Classic Reprint) (p. 2109)
—State Normal Magazine, Vol. 8: December, 1903 (Classic Reprint) (p. 2109)
Randall, Barbara. Jacob Daddy. Randall, Barbara & Newman, J. Heidi, eds. (p. 1154)
Randall, Barbie. Overworked Shoes. (p. 1688)
Randall, Charles E. Uncle Sam's Forest Rangers: August 18, 1939 (Classic Reprint) (p. 2319)
—Uncle Sam's Forest Rangers: October 8, 1942 (Classic Reprint) (p. 2319)
—Uncle Sam's Forest Rangers: January 28, 1943 (Classic Reprint) (p. 2319)
—Uncle Sam's Forest Rangers: December 10, 1942 (Classic Reprint) (p. 2319)
—Uncle Sam's Forest Rangers: Episode No. 23; June 16, 1932 (Classic Reprint) (p. 2319)
—Uncle Sam's Forest Rangers: Episode No. 34; June 30, 1932 (Classic Reprint) (p. 2319)
—Uncle Sam's Forest Rangers: Episode No. 352; August 25, 1939 (Classic Reprint) (p. 2319)
—Uncle Sam's Forest Rangers: Episode No. 36; October 20, 1932 (Classic Reprint) (p. 2319)
—Uncle Sam's Forest Rangers: October 6, 1939; Episode No. 358 (Classic Reprint) (p. 2319)
—Uncle Sam's Forest Rangers, Vol. 1: A Radio Drama Serial Presented by the National Broadcasting Company with the Cooperation of the United States Forest Service; Episodes 1 to 45, 1932 (Classic Reprint) (p. 2319)
—Uncle Sams Forest Rangers, Vol. 14: April 7, 1932 (Classic Reprint) (p. 2319)
—Uncle Sam's Forest Rangers, Vol. 18: May 5, 1932 (Classic Reprint) (p. 2319)
—Uncle Sam's Forest Rangers, Vol. 27: July 28, 1932 (Classic Reprint) (p. 2319)
—Uncle Sam's Forest Rangers, Vol. 29: August 11, 1932 (Classic Reprint) (p. 2319)
—Uncle Sam's Forest Rangers, Vol. 3: January 21, 1932 (Classic Reprint) (p. 2319)
—Uncle Sam's Forest Rangers, Vol. 30: August 18, 1932 (Classic Reprint) (p. 2319)
—Uncle Sam's Forest Rangers, Vol. 300: July 8, 1938 (Classic Reprint) (p. 2319)
—Uncle Sam's Forest Rangers, Vol. 301: July 22, 1938 (Classic Reprint) (p. 2319)
—Uncle Sam's Forest Rangers, Vol. 31: August 25, 1932 (Classic Reprint) (p. 2319)
—Uncle Sam's Forest Rangers, Vol. 34: September 15, 1932 (Classic Reprint) (p. 2319)
—Uncle Sam's Forest Rangers, Vol. 343: June 21, 1939 (Classic Reprint) (p. 2319)
—Uncle Sam's Forest Rangers, Vol. 346: July 14 1939 (Classic Reprint) (p. 2319)
—Uncle Sam's Forest Rangers, Vol. 366: December 22, 1939 (Classic Reprint) (p. 2319)
—Uncle Sam's Forest Rangers, Vol. 38: November 3, 1932 (Classic Reprint) (p. 2319)
—Uncle Sam's Forest Rangers, Vol. 416: December 24, 1940 (Classic Reprint) (p. 2319)
—Uncle Sam's Forest Rangers, Vol. 42: December 8, 1932 (Classic Reprint) (p. 2319)
—Uncle Sam's Forest Rangers, Vol. 45: December 29, 1932 (Classic Reprint) (p. 2319)
—Uncle Sam's Forest Rangers, Vol. 487: May 22, 1942 (Classic Reprint) (p. 2319)
—Uncle Sam's Forest Rangers, Vol. 489: June 5, 1942 (Classic Reprint) (p. 2319)
—Uncle Sam's Forest Rangers, Vol. 490: June 12, 1942 (Classic Reprint) (p. 2319)
—Uncle Sams Forest Rangers, Vol. 503: September 11, 1942 (Classic Reprint) (p. 2319)
—Uncle Sams Forest Rangers, Vol. 504: September 18, 1942 (Classic Reprint) (p. 2319)
—Uncle Sam's Forest Rangers, Vol. 508: October 15, 1942 (Classic Reprint) (p. 2319)
—Uncle Sam's Forest Rangers, Vol. 513: November 19, 1942 (Classic Reprint) (p. 2319)
—Uncle Sam's Forest Rangers, Vol. 521: February 4, 1943 (Classic Reprint) (p. 2319)
—Uncle Sam's Forest Rangers, Vol. 522: February 11, 1943 (Classic Reprint) (p. 2319)
—Uncle Sam's Forest Rangers, Vol. 524: March 4, 1943 (Classic Reprint) (p. 2319)
—Uncle Sam's Forest Rangers, Vol. 526: March 16, 1943 (Classic Reprint) (p. 2319)
—Uncle Sam's Forest Rangers, Vol. 527: March 25, 1943 (Classic Reprint) (p. 2319)
—Uncle Sam's Forest Rangers, Vol. 9: March 3, 1932 (Classic Reprint) (p. 2319)
Randall, Chuck. Curley's Wish Comes True. (p. 488)
Randall, Craig. Haunted Inn on the Hill. (p. 938)
Randall, David. Clovermead: In the Shadow of the Bear. (p. 408)
Randall, David J. Christianity: Is It True? Answering Questions Through Real Lives. (p. 382)
—Messages from Grandad: Encouragement for a Young Christian. (p. 1451)
Randall, Emma. Book of Love. Randall, Emma, illus. (p. 259)
—Over the River & Through the Wood. (p. 1686)
—Twelve Days of Christmas. (p. 2303)
Randall, Emma, illus. see Burroughs, Caleb.
Randall, Emma, illus. see Fliess, Sue.
Randall, F. J. Bermondsey Twin (Classic Reprint) (p. 203)
—Love & the Ironmonger (Classic Reprint) (p. 1359)
Randall, Frederick John. Love & the Ironmonger (Classic Reprint) (p. 1359)
Randall, Henry. Bobcats: Linces Rojos. (p. 252)
—Bobcats. (p. 252)
—Cheetahs: Guepardos. (p. 364)
—Cheetahs. (p. 364)
—Cougars. (p. 457)
—Cougars / Pumas. (p. 457)
—Lynxes: Linces. (p. 1370)
—Lynxes. (p. 1370)
—Ocelots: Ocelotes. (p. 1636)
—Ocelots. (p. 1636)
—Wildcats: Gatos Monteses. (p. 2465)
—Wildcats. (p. 2465)
Randall, Homer. Army Boys in France, or from Training Camp to Trenches (Classic Reprint) (p. 118)
—Army Boys in the French Trenches: Or Hand to Hand Fighting with the Enemy (Classic Reprint) (p. 118)
—Army Boys on the Firing Line: Or, Holding Back the German Drive. (p. 118)
Randall, Isabelle. Lady's Ranche Life in Montana (Classic Reprint) (p. 1239)
Randall, Jesseca. Christopher Columbus: Navigated by God - A Historical Children's Novel about One of the Most Important Figures of the Age of Exploration. (p. 388)
Randall, Joanne M. Adventures of Largo & Shelby. McIntosh, Jason D., illus. (p. 25)
Randall, Joaqun. Lurucha. (p. 1369)
Randall, Jory. My Day at the Beach. (p. 1536)
—My Day at the Farm. (p. 1536)
—My Day at the Park. (p. 1536)
—My Day in the City. (p. 1537)
—My Day in the Forest. (p. 1537)
—My Day in the Mountains. (p. 1537)
Randall, Julia Davenport. Blessing Esau: Experiments in High School English-Teaching (Classic Reprint) (p. 244)
Randall, Julieann T. Jade's Journey. Ada, Carol, illus. (p. 1154)
Randall, Lee Brandt, illus. see St. Pierre, Todd-Michael & Aesop, Aesop.
Randall, Lee Brandt, illus. see St. Pierre, Todd-Michael.
Randall, M. Canadian Reader: Designed for the Use of Schools & Families (Classic Reprint) (p. 321)
Randall, Marilyn. Best of Best Friends. (p. 207)
—Elmer the Christmas Elf. (p. 638)
—Hard Nut to Crack. (p. 929)
—Inside Out. (p. 1123)
Randall, Marisa. Geographic Features of New York City. (p. 817)
Randall, Rick. Adventures of Rick & Jack. (p. 27)
Randall, Ron, illus. see Jolley, Dan.
Randall, Ron, illus. see Limke, Jeff.
Randall, Ron, illus. see Storrie, Paul D.
Randall, Ronne. Before I Go to Sleep. Kerins, Tony, illus. (p. 190)
—Birth. (p. 233)
—Children's Stories from Myths & Legends: Classic Tales from Around the World. Howells, Graham, illus. (p. 375)
—Hanukkah Sweets & Treats. (p. 919)
—Journey of Life: Birth. (p. 1181)
—Jungle Jeep. Cottage Door Press & Parragon Books, eds. (p. 1190)
—Little Red Hen. (p. 1326)
—Marriage. (p. 1408)
—Moment Like This: A Story of Love Between Parent & Child. Scott, Peter, illus. (p. 1490)
—One More Hug: Wish upon a Star for Sweet Dreams in This Cozy, Cuddly Story. Khushi, Suzanne, illus. (p. 1661)
—Thanksgiving Sweets & Treats. (p. 2212)
—Tractor Trouble. Cottage Door Press & Parragon Books, eds. (p. 2273)
—Where Food Comes From. (p. 2437)
Randall, Ronne & Orme, Helen. Healthy Eating: The Best Start in Science. (p. 943)
Randall, Susan M. Summer Things: A Sensible View. (p. 2150)
Randall, Thomas. Waking: A Winter of Ghosts. (p. 2371)
Randall, Vienna. I Am Braver Than... (p. 1058)
Randall Williams, Caroline, jt. auth. see Randall, Alice.
Randall, Winifred J. As I Remember (Classic Reprint) (p. 124)
Randall, Wyatt William, jt. auth. see Remsen, Ira.
Randazzo, Tony, illus. see Ikids Staff.
Randell, Beverley. Rigby PM Platinum Collection: Individual Student Edition Yellow (Levels 6-8) Baby Bear Goes Fishing. (p. 1880)
Randell, Beverley, jt. auth. see Smith.
Randell, Esther, ed. see Whaler, Norman.
Randerath, Jeanette & Winterhager, Randerath -. ¡vuela, Yoa, Vuela! (p. 2368)
Randisi, Jodie. My Thoughts Exactly: By Darcy Diggins, Middle School Biospychologist. (p. 1562)
Randle, Kristen D. Only Alien on the Planet. (p. 1664)
Randle, Lalah Ruth. My Mountain Tops: The Romance of a Journey Across the Canadian Rockies. (p. 1557)
—My Mountain Tops: The Romance of a Journey Across the Canadian Rockies (Classic Reprint) (p. 1557)
Randle-Bustamonte, Ra'Quann. Decided We Fall. (p. 523)
Randles, Slim. Ol' Jimmy Dollar. Montoya, Jerry, illus. (p. 1644)
Randles, Slim & Montoya, Jerry. Ol' Jimmy Dollar. (p. 1644)
Randleson, Sara A., jt. auth. see Kinton, Ada Florence.
Rando, Caterina. You Can Think Differently. (p. 2526)
Rando, Licia. Warmest Place of All. Jewett, Anne, illus. (p. 2379)
Randol, Susan. I Before e (Except after C) Easy, Cool Ways to Remember Facts. (p. 1060)
Randolph. Iris, Vol. 1 of 3 (Classic Reprint) (p. 1134)
—Iris, Vol. 2 of 3 (Classic Reprint) (p. 1134)
—Little Pansy, Vol. 1 of 3 (Classic Reprint) (p. 1324)
—Little Pansy, Vol. 2 of 3 (Classic Reprint) (p. 1324)
—Reseda, Vol. 1 of 3 (Classic Reprint) (p. 1869)
—Wild Hyacinth: A Novel (Classic Reprint) (p. 2463)
—Woodroffe, Vol. 1 of 3 (Classic Reprint) (p. 2492)
—Woodroffe, Vol. 2 of 3 (Classic Reprint) (p. 2492)
—Woodroffe, Vol. 3 of 3 (Classic Reprint) (p. 2492)
Randolph, Agnes D. Meta Wallace, or the Seen & Unseen: A Tale (Classic Reprint) (p. 1452)
Randolph, Althea. Bouquet of Rhymes for Children (Classic Reprint) (p. 265)
Randolph, Anson D. F. One Hour a Week (Classic Reprint) (p. 1660)
Randolph, Connie. Emblem Brightly Shines with Casper Joe. (p. 641)
Randolph, Grace. Muppet Peter Pan. Mebberson, Amy, illus. (p. 1527)
Randolph, Grace, jt. auth. see Ghiglione, Marco.
Randolph, Grace & Barks, Carl. Muppet Peter Pan. Mebberson, Amy, illus. (p. 1527)
Randolph, Grace, et al. Fraggle Rock: Tails & Tales. Beedle, Tim, ed. (p. 775)
Randolph, Innes. Poems. (p. 1765)
Randolph, J. Thornton. Cabin & Parlor: Or, Slaves & Masters (Classic Reprint) (p. 307)
Randolph, Jennifer & Benchmark Education Co. Staff. Women of the Civil War. (p. 2487)
Randolph, Joane. Light in My World. (p. 1298)
Randolph, Joanne. All about a Day/Los Días. (p. 48)
—All about an Hour/Las Horas. (p. 48)
—All about the Months/Los Meses. (p. 50)
—All about the Seasons. (p. 50)
—All about the Seasons/Las Estaciones. (p. 50)
—Ambulances/Ambulancias. (p. 68)
—Angel of Goliad: Francisca Alvarez & the Texas War for Independence. (p. 85)
—Bella: A Butterfly's Story. (p. 196)

R

—Black Widow Spiders (p. 240)
—Bulldozers. (p. 296)
—Call of Liberty: Marquis de Lafayette & the American Revolution. (p. 311)
—Classroom Pets (p. 401)
—Coastguard Boats/Lanchas Guardacostas. (p. 410)
—Concrete Mixers. (p. 438)
—Crab Spiders (p. 465)
—Earth Movers (p. 617)
—Electricity in My World/la electricidad en mi Mundo. (p. 631)
—Emergency Helicopters/Helicopteros de Emergencia. (p. 641)
—Family of Ducks. (p. 702)
—Fire Trucks/Camiones de Bomberos. (p. 733)
—Frankie: A Frog's Story. (p. 778)
—Gases in My World/Los gases en mi Mundo. (p. 811)
—Gears in My World/Engranajes en mi Mundo. (p. 812)
—Greenley: A Tree's Story. (p. 895)
—Home for Sue. (p. 996)
—Inclined Planes in My World/Planos inclinados en mi Mundo. (p. 1113)
—Jumping Spiders (p. 1189)
—Let's Draw a Bird with Shapes. (p. 1271)
—Let's Draw a Bird with Shapes/Vamos a dibujar un ave usando Figuras. (p. 1271)
—Let's Draw a Butterfly with Circles. (p. 1271)
—Let's Draw a Butterfly with Circles / Vamos a dibujar una mariposa usando Círculos. (p. 1271)
—Let's Draw a Dinosaur with Shapes. (p. 1271)
—Let's Draw a Dinosaur with Shapes/Vamos a dibujar un dinasaurio usando Figuras. (p. 1271)
—Let's Draw a Horse with Rectangles. (p. 1271)
—Let's Draw a Horse with Rectangles / Vamos a dibujar un caballo usando Rectángulos. (p. 1271)
—Let's Draw a Truck with Shapes. (p. 1271)
—Let's Draw a Truck with Shapes/Vamos a dibujar un camión usando Figuras. (p. 1271)
—Let's Draw a Turtle with Half Circles/ Vamos a dibujar una tortuga usando medios Círculos. (p. 1271)
—Levers in My World/Palancas en mi Mundo. (p. 1282)
—Light in My World/la luz en mi Mundo. (p. 1298)
—Liquids in My World/Los líquidos en mi Mundo. (p. 1308)
—Math Exploration: Using Math to Learn about the Continents Set. (p. 1422)
—My Friend the Box Turtle. (p. 1548)
—My Friend the Ferret. (p. 1548)
—My Friend the Hermit Crab. (p. 1548)
—My Friend the Iguana. (p. 1548)
—My Friend the Miniature Horse. (p. 1548)
—My Friend the Potbellied Pig. (p. 1548)
—Number Crunch Your Way Around Africa. (p. 1629)
—Number Crunch Your Way Around Asia. (p. 1629)
—Number Crunch Your Way Around Australia. (p. 1629)
—Orb-Weaver Spiders (p. 1669)
—Police Cars/Patrullas. (p. 1770)
—Pony Ride. (p. 1773)
—Pulleys in My World/Poleas en mi Mundo. (p. 1812)
—Road Machines (p. 1888)
—Road Milling Machines. (p. 1888)
—Road Pavers. (p. 1888)
—Road Rollers. (p. 1888)
—Road Scrapers. (p. 1888)
—Rock for Mom. (p. 1894)
—Rose: A Flower's Story. (p. 1904)
—Sharks: Hunters of the Deep (p. 2002)
—Slide at School. (p. 2038)
—Snowplows. (p. 2049)
—Solids in My World/Los sólidos en mi Mundo. (p. 2057)
—Sounds in My World/Los sonidos en mi Mundo. (p. 2067)
—Stormy: A Storm Cloud's Story. (p. 2127)
—Tarantulas (p. 2191)
—Tow Trucks/Gruas. (p. 2269)
—Wedges in My World/Cunas en mi Mundo. (p. 2395)
—What Are the Elements of Weather? (p. 2406)
—What I Look Like When I am Confused / Cómo me veo cuando estoy Confundido. (p. 2412)
—What I Look Like When I am Sad / Cómo me veo cuando estoy Triste. (p. 2412)
—Wheel Loaders. (p. 2427)
—Wheels & Axels in My World/Ejes y ruedas en mi Mundo. (p. 2428)
—Whose Back Is This? (p. 2454)
—Whose Back Is This? De Quién Es Esta Espalda? (p. 2454)
—Whose Back Is This? / ¿de quién es esta Espalda? (p. 2454)
—Whose Eyes Are These? (p. 2454)
—Whose Eyes Are These? De Quién Son Estos Ojos? (p. 2454)
—Whose Eyes Are These? / ¿de quién son estos Ojos? (p. 2454)
—Whose Nose Is This? (p. 2454)
—Whose Nose Is This? De Quién Es Esta Nariz? (p. 2454)
—Whose Nose Is This? / ¿de quién es esta Nariz? (p. 2454)
—Whose Teeth Are These? (p. 2454)
—Whose Teeth Are These? De Quién Son Estos Dientes? (p. 2454)
—Whose Teeth Are These? / ¿de quién son estos Dientes? (p. 2454)
—Whose Toes Are Those? (p. 2454)
—Whose Toes Are Those? De Quién Son Estas Patas? (p. 2454)
—Whose Toes Are Those? / ¿de quién son estas Patas? (p. 2454)
—Whose Tongue Is This? (p. 2454)
—Whose Tongue Is This? De Quién Es Esta Lengua? (p. 2454)
—Whose Tongue Is This? / ¿de quién es esta Lengua? (p. 2454)
—Wolf Spiders (p. 2484)
Randolph, Joanne, contrib. by. Myths & Legends of Ancient Egypt & Africa. (p. 1571)
—Myths & Legends of Ancient Greece & Rome. (p. 1571)
Randolph, Joanne, ed. Abolitionists Join the Fight. (p. 6)
—African American Artists & Writers. (p. 32)
—African American Explorers & Adventurers. (p. 32)
—African American Inventors & Scientists. (p. 32)
—African American Musicians & Entertainers. (p. 32)
—African American Politicians & Civil Rights Activists. (p. 32)
—Air Pressure Driving the Weather! (p. 37)
—Battle at Gettysburg. (p. 173)
—Cavalry in the Civil War. (p. 347)
—Celtic Myths & Legends. (p. 351)
—Early American Legends & Folktales. (p. 613)
—Extreme Weather Ahead! (p. 687)
—Eyes Have It. (p. 689)
—From Slaves to Soldiers. (p. 793)
—Growth & Aging. (p. 900)
—Hurricane Warning! (p. 1054)
—Jet Stream Steering the Winds! (p. 1167)
—Living & Working in Ancient China. (p. 1333)
—Living & Working in Ancient Greece. (p. 1333)
—Living & Working in Ancient Mesopotamia. (p. 1333)
—Living & Working in Ancient Rome. (p. 1333)
—Living & Working in the Pre-Columbian Americas. (p. 1333)
—Microbes: The Good, the Bad, & the Ugly. (p. 1459)
—Mr. Lincoln. (p. 1519)
—Mythology & Legends Around the World. (p. 1571)
—Myths & Legends of Ancient Egypt & Africa. (p. 1571)
—Myths & Legends of Ancient Greece & Rome. (p. 1571)
—Myths & Legends of India. (p. 1571)
—Myths & Legends of the First Peoples of the Americas. (p. 1571)
—Myths & Legends of the Middle East. (p. 1571)
—Norse Myths & Legends. (p. 1620)
—Northern Lights Sighting! (p. 1622)
—Pioneering African Americans. (p. 1748)
—Poems about Animals. (p. 1765)
—Poems about Autumn. (p. 1765)
—Poems about Nature. (p. 1765)
—Poems about Spring. (p. 1765)
—Poems about Summer. (p. 1765)
—Poems about Weather. (p. 1765)
—Poems about Winter. (p. 1765)
—Pump It Up: The Heart & Blood. (p. 1812)
—Reconstructing America. (p. 1854)
—Slave States, Free States, & the Missouri Compromise. (p. 2035)
—Taste & Digestion. (p. 2192)
—Tornado Alert! (p. 2265)
—Understanding the Brain. (p. 2325)
Randolph, John Carroll. Patriotic Songs. (p. 1705)
Randolph, Khary, illus. see Thompson, Robbie.
Randolph, Khary & Silas, Thony. Mosaic Vol. 2: Down Below. (p. 1507)
Randolph, Leah R. Safe Place for Justin. (p. 1922)
Randolph, Robert. Ben the Flying Cat Sappington, Ray, illus. (p. 199)
Randolph, Ryan. Alexander Hamilton's Economic Plan: Solving Problems in America's New Economy. (p. 42)
—Bank Robber's End: The Death of Jesse James. (p. 164)
—Betsy Ross: The American Flag, & Life in a Young America. (p. 209)
—How to Spend Smart. (p. 1044)
—Karts. (p. 1204)
—Marbury V. Madison: The New Supreme Court Gets More Powers. (p. 1402)
Randolph, Ryan P. Benjamin Franklin: Inventor, Writer, & Patriot. (p. 200)
—How to Earn Money. (p. 1042)
—How to Make a Budget. (p. 1043)
—How to Manage Risk. (p. 1043)
—How to Save & Invest. (p. 1044)
—How to Spend Smart. (p. 1044)
—How to Use Credit. (p. 1045)
—New Research Techniques: Getting the Most Out of Search Engine Tools. (p. 1597)
—Price You Pay: A Look at Supply & Demand. (p. 1791)
—Robotics. (p. 1892)
Random, B. Alienship. (p. 47)
—Ridership. (p. 1878)
Random House. 1 2 3 Blaze! (Blaze & the Monster Machines) Pixel Mouse House LLC, illus. (p. 2545)
—1, 2, 3, Tea! (Shimmer & Shine) Cespedes-Alicea, Marcela, illus. (p. 2545)
—12 Engines of Christmas (Thomas & Friends) (p. 2551)
—Abraca-Genie! Random House & Aikins, Dave, illus. (p. 7)
—Adventure Bay Treasury (PAW Patrol) Random House, illus. (p. 18)
—Adventure Story Collection (Nickelodeon) Random House, illus. (p. 19)
—All about the Troll. Random House, illus. (p. 50)
—Barbie 5-Minute Stories: the Sister Collection (Barbie) (p. 165)
—Barbie Dreamtopia Step into Reading (Barbie) (p. 165)
—Barbie Star Light Adventure. (p. 166)
—Barbie Summer 2016 Chapter Book (Barbie) (p. 166)
—Barbie Summer 2016 Movie Pictureback (Barbie) (p. 166)
—Barbie You Can Be 5-Minute Stories (Barbie) (p. 166)
—Best Sisters Ever!(Barbie) (p. 207)
—Beware of Bebop & Rocksteady! (Teenage Mutant Ninja Turtles) Spaziante, Patrick, illus. (p. 211)
—Big Book of Engines (Thomas & Friends) Random House, illus. (p. 217)
—Big Egg Rescue! (Top Wing) Aikins, Dave, illus. (p. 220)
—Big Fish, Little Fish: a Book of Opposites (Bubble Guppies) Random House, illus. (p. 220)
—Bigfoot's Spring Break (Teenage Mutant Ninja Turtles) Spaziante, Patrick, illus. (p. 224)
—Birthday Wish (Barbie Dreamtopia) (p. 234)
—Blazing Shapes! (Blaze & the Monster Machines) Dynamo Limited, illus. (p. 243)
—Blue's Winter Day! (Blue's Clue & You) Aikins, Dave, illus. (p. 250)
—Box Full of Wishes (Shimmer & Shine) 4 Board Books. Random House, illus. (p. 266)
—Chase Is on the Case! (Paw Patrol) Petrossi, Fabrizio, illus. (p. 361)
—Chase's Super Sniffer! Random House, illus. (p. 361)
—Christmas Adventures! (Nickelodeon) Random House, illus. (p. 383)
—Christmas Elf Countdown! Wohnoutka, Mike, illus. (p. 385)
—Christmas Friends Forever! (Sunny Day) Legramandi, Francesco & Matta, Gabriella, illus. (p. 385)
—Christmas Heroes! (DC Justice League) Random House, illus. (p. 385)
—Christmas Heroes! (PAW Patrol) Random House, illus. (p. 385)
—Color Day Party! Laguna, Fabio & Batson, Alan, illus. (p. 420)
—Color Magic (Shimmer & Shine) Random House, illus. (p. 420)
—Colorful Christmas!/Snow Day! (Frosty the Snowman) Random House, illus. (p. 422)
—Corn & Peg Step into Reading (Corn & Peg) Random House, illus. (p. 454)
—Count on the Easter Pups! (PAW Patrol) MJ Illustrations, illus. (p. 458)
—Count with Blue! (Blue's Clues & You) Aikins, Dave, illus. (p. 459)
—Country Style! (Sunny Day) Random House, illus. (p. 461)
—DC Super Friends 5-Minute Story Collection (DC Super Friends) Random House, illus. (p. 516)
—Dinos & Discoveries/Emily Saves the World (p. 548)
—Do-Gooders Unite! (Corn & Peg) Random House, illus. (p. 570)
—Dora Goes to School/Dora Va a la Escuela (Dora the Explorer) MJ Illustrations, illus. (p. 585)
—Dora's Farm Rescue! (Dora the Explorer) Random House, illus. (p. 586)
—Dr. Seuss Beginner Fun Activity Book: 5 Books in 1: Opposites & Differences; Rhyming Words; Letter Sounds; Easy Addition; Counting Beyond 100. (p. 592)
—DreamWorks: the Official Coloring Book. Random House, illus. (p. 603)
—Driving Force! (Blaze & the Monster Machines) Garcia, Segundo, illus. (p. 605)
—Duke's Tale. Random House, illus. (p. 609)
—Easter 1, 2, 3! (Butterbean's Cafe) Legramandi, Francesco & Matta, Gabriella, illus. (p. 619)
—Elmo's 123. (p. 639)
—Elmo's ABC Song (Sesame Street) (p. 639)
—Elmo's World: Dancing! (Sesame Street) Random House, illus. (p. 639)
—Elmo's World: Music! (Sesame Street) Random House, illus. (p. 639)
—Engine Surprises (Thomas & Friends) (p. 651)
—Epic Turtle Tales (Teenage Mutant Ninja Turtles) Random House, illus. (p. 658)
—Everything That Glitters Is Guy! Laguna, Fabio, illus. (p. 673)
—Fabulous Friends! (Shimmer & Shine) Random House, illus. (p. 692)
—Fairy Friends (Butterbean's Café) Random House, illus. (p. 696)
—Fairytale Collection (Barbie) (p. 698)
—Farm Alarm! (Team Umizoomi) Fruchter, Jason, illus. (p. 709)
—Fearsome Footprints/Thomas the Brave (Thomas & Friends) Stubbs, Tommy, illus. (p. 717)
—Feel the Power (Blaze & the Monster Machines) Hechtenkopf, Omar, illus. (p. 718)
—Five Classic Golden Book Tales. (p. 743)
—Five Fin-Tastic Stories (Bubble Guppies) Random House, illus. (p. 743)
—Five Playtime Tales (Nick, Jr.) Random House, illus. (p. 745)
—Five Puptacular Tales! (PAW Patrol) (p. 745)
—Five Tank Engine Tales (Thomas & Friends) Courtney, Richard, illus. (p. 745)
—Five Undersea Stories (SpongeBob SquarePants) Random House, illus. (p. 745)
—Flip the Lid! (Teenage Mutant Ninja Turtles: Half-Shell Heroes) Spaziante, Patrick, illus. (p. 749)
—Follow That Egg! (Team Umizoomi) Aikins, David, illus. (p. 757)
—Follow Your Nose! a Scratch-And-Sniff Adventure (Nella the Princess Knight) Random House, illus. (p. 758)
—Frosty's First Christmas (Frosty the Snowman) Cucca, Vincenzo & Hao, Katrina Mae, illus. (p. 795)
—Gold Rush Pups! (PAW Patrol) MJ Illustrations, illus. (p. 856)
—GoldieBlox Chapter Book #2 (GoldieBlox) Random House et al, illus. (p. 860)
—Good Night, Adventure Bay! (PAW Patrol) Random House, illus. (p. 863)
—Great Cake Race. (p. 884)
—Great Cake Race (Barbie Dreamhouse Adventures) (p. 884)
—Great Island Adventure. (p. 887)
—Grumpy America: a Paper Doll Book (Grumpy Cat) MJ Illustrations, illus. (p. 900)
—Halloween 1, 2, 3! (Top Wing) Doescher, Erik, illus. (p. 912)
—Halloween Adventures! (Nickelodeon) Random House, illus. (p. 912)
—Halloween Heroes! (Paw Patrol) Random House, illus. (p. 912)
—Halloween Surprise! (Butterbean's Cafe) Cespedes-Alicea, Marcela, illus. (p. 912)
—Happy Holidays, Blaze! (Blaze & the Monster Machines) Random House, illus. (p. 922)
—Happy Howl-O-ween! (Barbie) (p. 923)
—Happy, Sad, Mad, & Glad! (Thomas & Friends) Spaziante, Patrick, illus. (p. 923)
—Happy Troll-O-ween! Random House, illus. (p. 924)
—Hatastrophe (Disney Muppet Babies) Disney Storybook Artists, illus. (p. 936)
—Haunted House Party! (Bubble Guppies) MJ Illustrations, illus. (p. 938)
—Heart of a Ninja (Teenage Mutant Ninja Turtles) Random House, illus. (p. 945)
—Hello, Friends! (Blue's Clues & You) Random House, illus. (p. 950)
—Henry in the Dark (Thomas & Friends) (p. 955)
—Here Comes Frosty! (Frosty the Snowman) Random House, illus. (p. 958)
—Here Comes Peter Cottontail. Random House, illus. (p. 958)
—Hero in You! DC SuperHero Girls: My Amazing Adventure Journal. Random House, illus. (p. 961)
—Hero Story Collection (DC Super Friends) (p. 961)
—Hide-And-Go-Swim! (Bubble Guppies) MJ Illustrations, illus. (p. 967)
—High-Flying Skye (PAW Patrol) MJ Illustrations, illus. (p. 968)
—Holiday Helpers! (PAW Patrol) Random House, illus. (p. 987)
—Holiday Treats! (Butterbean's Café) Garcia, Brianna, illus. (p. 988)
—Hooray for Dads! (SpongeBob SquarePants) Random House, illus. (p. 1000)
—How to Be a Cat/How to Be a Dog (the Secret Life of Pets 2) Random House, illus. (p. 1037)
—Hug Day! (DreamWorks Trolls) Random House, illus. (p. 1048)
—I Love Engines! (Thomas & Friends) Marshmallow Creative, illus. (p. 1069)
—I Love King Dad! (p. 1069)
—I Love King Dad! (Nella the Princess Knight) Myers, Nneka, illus. (p. 1069)
—I Love My Mami! (Dora the Explorer) Aikins, Dave, illus. (p. 1071)
—I Love Queen Mom! (Nella the Princess Knight) Random House & Myers, Nneka, illus. (p. 1072)
—Ice Team (Paw Patrol) Jackson, Mike, illus. (p. 1088)
—If I Had Your Vote—By the Cat in the Hat. Brannon, Tom, illus. (p. 1091)
—It's a SpongeBob Christmas! (SpongeBob SquarePants) Random House, illus. (p. 1143)
—It's All about Me! (p. 1144)
—It's Spring! (DreamWorks Trolls) Random House, illus. (p. 1147)
—Jingle Pups (PAW Patrol) Random House, illus. (p. 1169)
—Jingle Smells!: a Scratch-And-Sniff Adventure (PAW Patrol) Random House, illus. (p. 1169)
—Jurassic Park: the Deluxe Novelization (Jurassic Park) Random House, illus. (p. 1192)
—Justice Collection. Random House, illus. (p. 1194)
—Lend a Helping Paw (PAW Patrol) Jackson, Mike, illus. (p. 1266)
—Let's Find Adventure! (Paw Patrol) Jackson, Mike, illus. (p. 1272)
—Let's Pick Apples! (Barbie) Dynamo Limited, illus. (p. 1276)
—Let's Visit the Doctor (PAW Patrol) Lovett, Nate, illus. (p. 1278)
—Little Red Rescue Box (PAW Patrol) 4 Board Books. Random House, illus. (p. 1326)
—Loose Tooth (Barbie) (p. 1348)
—Lorax Deluxe Doodle Book. (p. 1348)
—Love Is Everywhere! (Sunny Day) Random House, illus. (p. 1360)
—Love the Fur You're in (Sesame Street) (p. 1361)
—Magical Mermaids! (Shimmer & Shine) Aikins, Dave, illus. (p. 1380)
—Magical Pet Friends! (Shimmer & Shine) Random House, illus. (p. 1380)
—Make It Sparkle! (Shimmer & Shine) Random House, illus. (p. 1386)
—Meet Rusty Rivets! (Rusty Rivets) Cassity, Donald, illus. (p. 1439)
—Meet Shimmer & Shine! (Shimmer & Shine) Cardona, Jose Maria, illus. (p. 1439)
—Meet the Machines! (Blaze & the Monster Machines) 4 Board Books. Random House, illus. (p. 1440)
—Meet the Pets. Random House, illus. (p. 1440)
—Mermaid Park Mystery (Barbie) Random House, illus. (p. 1449)
—Merry Christmas, Shimmer & Shine! (Shimmer & Shine) Random House, illus. (p. 1450)
—Minecraft Official Animals Sticker Book (Minecraft) Random House, illus. (p. 1471)
—Mission PAW (PAW Patrol) Lovett, Nate, illus. (p. 1481)
—Monster Machine Treasury (Blaze & the Monster Machines) Random House, illus. (p. 1496)
—Monster Machines on the Go! (Blaze & the Monster Machines) 4 Board Books. Random House, illus. (p. 1496)
—Mulan & the Dragon Race/a Song for Cinderella (Disney Princess) Random House, illus. (p. 1525)
—Mutant Files (Teenage Mutant Ninja Turtles) Random House, illus. (p. 1530)
—My Blue Railway Book Box (Thomas Friends) (p. 1534)
—My First Pet (Barbie) (p. 1545)
—My First Songs (Sesame Street) Brannon, Tom, illus. (p. 1546)
—My First Thomas & Friends ABC Book (Thomas & Friends) (p. 1546)
—My Little Super Hero Word Book (DC Justice League) Random House, illus. (p. 1554)
—My Thomas Potty Book (Thomas & Friends) (p. 1562)
—Nella the Princess Knight Board Book (Nella the Princess Knight) Random House, illus. (p. 1586)
—Nickelodeon 5-Minute Christmas Stories (Nickelodeon) Random House, illus. (p. 1603)
—Nickelodeon 5-Minute Girl-Power Stories (Nickelodeon) Random House, illus. (p. 1603)
—Nickelodeon Bedtime Treasury (Nickelodeon) Random House, illus. (p. 1603)
—Nickelodeon Pictureback Collection (Nickelodeon) Random House, illus. (p. 1603)
—Ninja Dad! (Teenage Mutant Ninja Turtles) Johnson, Shane, illus. (p. 1610)
—Ninjas on Ice! (Teenage Mutant Ninja Turtles) Spaziante, Patrick, illus. (p. 1610)
—One Paw-Some Christmas: a Magnetic Play Book (PAW Patrol) Random House, illus. (p. 1661)
—Open the Barn Door... Santoro, Christopher, illus. (p. 1665)
—Patrol Pals (Paw Patrol) Random House, illus. (p. 1706)
—PAW Patrol 5-Minute Stories Collection (PAW Patrol) Random House, illus. (p. 1708)
—PAW Patrol Big Lift-And-Look Board Book (PAW Patrol) Moore, Harry, illus. (p. 1708)
—PAW Patrol Deluxe Step into Reading (PAW Patrol) Random House, illus. (p. 1708)
—PAW Patrol on the Roll! (PAW Patrol) Random House, illus. (p. 1708)
—Paw Patrol Treasury (PAW Patrol) Random House, illus. (p. 1708)
—Pawsome Puppy Adventures! Random House, illus. (p. 1708)

R

—Team Numbers (Paw Patrol) Random House Staff, illus. (p. 2196)
—Time for School! (Bubble Guppies) Random House Staff, illus. (p. 2244)
—UmiCar's Big Race (Team Umizoomi) Random House Staff & Aikins, David, illus. (p. 2316)
—You're Fired! (p. 2535)
Random House Staff, illus. see Awdry, W. & Berrios, Frank.
Random House Staff, illus. see Awdry, Wilbert V.
Random House Staff, illus. see Awdry, Wilbert V. & Wrecks, Billy.
Random House Staff, illus. see Eberly, Chelsea.
Random House Staff, illus. see Golden Books & Chlebowski, Rachel.
Random House Staff, illus. see James, Hollis.
Random House Staff, illus. see Man-Kong, Mary & Inches, Alison.
Random House Staff, illus. see Man-Kong, Mary, et al.
Random House Staff, illus. see Man-Kong, Mary.
Random House Staff, illus. see Scarry, Richard.
Random House Staff, illus. see Teitelbaum, Michael.
Random House Staff, illus. see Tillworth, Mary.
Random House Staff, illus. see Webster, Christy.
Random House Staff, illus. see Wrecks, Billy.
Random House Staff, jt. auth. see Berrios, Frank.
Random House Staff, jt. auth. see Chlebowski, Rachel.
Random House Staff, jt. auth. see Golden Books Staff.
Random House Staff, jt. auth. see Golden Books.
Random House Staff, jt. auth. see Posner-Sanchez, Andrea.
Random House Staff, jt. auth. see Random House Editors.
Random House Staff, jt. auth. see Seiss, Ellie.
Random House Staff, jt. auth. see Shealy, Dennis R.
Random House Staff, jt. auth. see Webster, Christy.
Random House Staff & Carbone, Courtney. Danger - Dinosaurs! Random House Staff, illus. (p. 501)
Random House Staff & Disney Editors. Five Tales from the Road. (p. 745)
Random House Staff & Holtz, Thomas R. T. Rex: Hunter or Scavenger? (Jurassic World) Random House Staff, illus. (p. 2174)
Random House Staff & Posner-Sanchez, Andrea. Dog Days. Random House Staff, illus. (p. 575)
Random House Staff & Roper, Robert. Dora Goes to the Doctor/Dora Goes to the Dentist (Dora the Explorer) Random House Staff, illus. (p. 585)
Random House Staff & Webster, Christy. Robot Rampage! (Teenage Mutant Ninja Turtles) Random House Staff & Spaziante, Patrick, illus. (p. 1892)
Random House Staff & Wilson, Sarah. Moms Are the Best! (SpongeBob SquarePants) Random House Staff, illus. (p. 1491)
Random, Roderick. Expedition of Humphry Clinker, Vol. 2 (Classic Reprint) (p. 677)
Randoplh, Grace, illus. see Ghiglione, Marco & Randolph, Grace.
Rands, William Brighty. Lilliput Levee: Poems of Childhood, Child-Fancy, & Child-Like Moods (Classic Reprint) (p. 1301)
—Shoemakers' Village, Vol. 1 of 2 (Classic Reprint) (p. 2009)
Rane, Walter, illus. see Tripp, Valerie.
Raney, Ken. It's Probably Good Dinosaurs Are Extinct. (p. 1147)
Raney, Renee Simmons. Hairy, Scary, but Mostly Merry Fairies! Curing Nature Deficiency Through Folklore, Imagination, & Creative Activities. Crowe, Carolyn Walker, illus. (p. 910)
Raney, Tom, illus. see Jurgens, Dan, et al.
Ranga, Katherine. Jesus Loves Me: A Bedtime Prayer. Ang, Selvi, illus. (p. 1166)
Rangan, Nalini. Hinduism. (p. 972)
Ranganathan, Murali. Govind Narayan's Mumbai: An Urban Biography From 1863 (p. 873)
Range, Ellen. Take Note! Taking & Organizing Notes. (p. 2177)
Rangel, Aralie. Giraffe That Ate the Moon: Babl Children's Books in Chinese & English. Kwong, Alvina, illus. (p. 834)
—Giraffe That Ate the Moon / Ang Dyirap Na Kinain Ang Buwan: Babl Children's Books in Tagalog & English. (p. 834)
Rangel, Fernando, illus. see Mann, Elizabeth.
Rangel, Rawderson, illus. see Rinker, Gary W.
Ranger, Robin. Up in the Garret (Classic Reprint) (p. 2338)
Rangner, Mike K., illus. see Ward, Jennifer.
Ranjalkar, Shreyans. My Sunny British Days - Stories for Children by a Child. (p. 1562)
Rank, A. Lady Of. Glanville Family, Vol. 1 of 3 (Classic Reprint) (p. 841)
Rank, Young Lady Of. Jack Daw at Home (Classic Reprint) (p. 1152)
Rankie, Barbara. Addition Unplugged (p. 15)
—Subtraction Unplugged (p. 2146)
Rankin, Arthur a. Gunboat Boys; or Harry & Artie among the Guerillas, Vol. 3: August 1, 1896 (Classic Reprint) (p. 905)
Rankin, Bruce H., illus. see Ivanoff, George.
Rankin, Carroll Watson. Adopting of Rosa Marie: A Sequel to Dandelion Cottage. (p. 17)
—Castaways of Pete's Patch: A Sequel to the Adopting of Rosa Marie. (p. 339)
—Cinder Pond (Classic Reprint) (p. 391)
—Dandelion Cottage (Classic Reprint) (p. 500)
Rankin, Cindy. Under the Ashes. (p. 2321)
Rankin, Emma Lydia. Stoneman's Raid: A North Carolina Woman's Experience in the Civil War (Classic Reprint) (p. 2121)
Rankin, H. L. Chaya & the Spider Gem. White, Siobhán, illus. (p. 363)
Rankin, Heather & Rankin, Heather. All It Takes Is One Friend. (p. 52)
Rankin, Hollie. House That Wouldn¿t Fall Down. (p. 1024)
—When the Sun Fell Out of the Sky. (p. 2433)
Rankin, Joan. Goldilocks & the Three Rhinos: A South African Retelling. (p. 860)
—Goldilocks & the Three Rhinos. (p. 860)
Rankin, Joan, illus. see Capucilli, Alyssa Satin.
Rankin, Joan, illus. see Hartmann, Wendy.
Rankin, Joan, illus. see Hatton, Jenny.
Rankin, Joan, illus. see Ruddell, Deborah.
Rankin, Joan, illus. see Stewart, Dianne.
Rankin, Joan, illus. see Wilson, Karma.
Rankin, Joan E., illus. see Capucilli, Alyssa Satin.
Rankin, Joan E., illus. see Ruddell, Deborah.
Rankin, Krystina Renae. What Did God Make? (p. 2408)
Rankin, Laura. My Turn! Rankin, Laura, illus. (p. 1563)
—Ruthie & the (Not So) Very Busy Day. Rankin, Laura, illus. (p. 1918)
Rankin, Laura, illus. see Gibson, Ginger Foglesong.
Rankin, Laura, illus. see McCall Smith, Alexander.
Rankin, Laura, illus. see Shore, Diane Z.
Rankin, Laura, illus. see Underwood, Deborah K.
Rankin, Mary Everett. Course for Beginners, in Religious Education: With Lessons for One Year for Children Five Years of Age (Classic Reprint) (p. 462)
Rankin, Reginald. Subaltern's Letters to His Wife (Classic Reprint) (p. 2145)
Rankin, Renee. Miss Lantz & Sadey: First in the Series of Little Sunshines Life Journey. (p. 1479)
Rankin, Robert H. Belles Lettres, 1935, Vol. 1: An Annual Anthology of Student Writing (Classic Reprint) (p. 197)
Rankine, H., illus. see Croucher, Vicki.
Rankine, William John Macquorn. Manual of the Steam Engine & Other Prime Movers (Classic Reprint) (p. 1399)
Rankova, Silviya. How Olly Met His New Family: Children & Their Pets. (p. 1034)
Rankovic, Ana, illus. see Herda, Kylie.
Ranlett, Louis Felix. Let's Go! The Story of A. S. No. 2448602 (Classic Reprint) (p. 1273)
Ranney, David James. Dave Ranney, or Thirty Years on the Bowery: An Autobiography (Classic Reprint) (p. 510)
Rannow, Vicki. What Shall I Believe? (p. 2419)
Ranola-Collier, Jean. Living Water. (p. 1334)
Ranous, Dora Knowlton Thompson. Diary of a Daly Debutante 1910: Being Passages from the Journal of a Member (Classic Reprint) (p. 539)
Ranslem, Scot. Trouble with Bubbles. (p. 2292)
Ransom, Candice. Amanda Panda & the Bigger, Better Birthday. Grove, Christine, illus. (p. 61)
—Amanda Panda Quits Kindergarten. Grove, Christine, illus. (p. 61)
—Apple Picking Day! Meza, Erika, illus. (p. 106)
—Big Rigs on the Move. (p. 222)
—Bones in the White House: Thomas Jefferson's Mammoth. Christoph, Jamey, illus. (p. 255)
—Chocolate Chip Cookies. (p. 380)
—Cross-Pollination. (p. 478)
—Dance Team. (p. 500)
—Day of the Black Blizzard. Harden, Laurie, illus. (p. 514)
—Eerie Haunted Houses. (p. 627)
—French Fries. (p. 784)
—Garden Day! (p. 809)
—Garden Day! Meza, Erika, illus. (p. 809)
—George Washington. (p. 819)
—George Washington & the Story of the U. S. Constitution. Reeves, Jeni, illus. (p. 820)
—How Aircraft Carriers Work. (p. 1025)
—How Fighter Jets Work. (p. 1031)
—James Madison. (p. 1157)
—Jazz Dance. (p. 1162)
—Legendary Bigfoot. (p. 1263)
—Let's Explore the Five Senses. (p. 1272)
—Let's Explore the Sense of Smell. (p. 1272)
—Life-Saving Adventure of Sam Deal, Shipwreck Rescuer. (p. 1295)
—Monster Trucks. (p. 1497)
—Mysterious Loch Ness Monster. (p. 1567)
—Night of the Hurricane's Fury. Tong, Paul, illus. (p. 1607)
—Parts of a Flower. (p. 1701)
—Rebel Mckenzie. (p. 1852)
—Snow Day! (p. 2047)
—Snow Day! Meza, Erika, illus. (p. 2047)
—Stock Cars. (p. 2120)
—Thomas Jefferson. (p. 2228)
—Tools & Treasures of Ancient China. (p. 2261)
—Tooth Fairy's Night. (p. 2262)
—Twelve Days of Christmas in Washington, D. C. Hollander, Sarah, illus. (p. 2303)
—What Was the Continental Congress? And Other Questions about the Declaration of Independence. (p. 2421)
—What's Great about Indiana? (p. 2424)
—Who Wrote the U. S. Constitution? And Other Questions about the Constitutional Convention of 1787. (p. 2452)
—Why Did English Settlers Come to Virginia? And Other Questions about the Jamestown Settlement. (p. 2455)
Ransom, Candice F. How Aircraft Carriers Work. (p. 1025)
—How Fighter Jets Work. (p. 1031)
—Let's Explore the Five Senses. (p. 1272)
—Let's Explore the Sense of Smell. (p. 1272)
—Mysterious Loch Ness Monster. (p. 1567)
—Pembroke Welsh Corgis. (p. 1714)
Ransom, Fletcher C. My Policies in Jungleland (Classic Reprint) (p. 1559)
Ransom, Jeanie Franz. Big Red & the Little Bitty Wolf: A Tale about Bullies. Zivoin, Jennifer, illus. (p. 222)
—Cowboy Car. Nedelcu, Ovi, illus. (p. 464)
—Crown Affair. Axelsen, Stephen, illus. (p. 479)
—There's a Cat in Our Class! A Tale about Getting Along. Langdo, Bryan, illus. (p. 2217)
—What Really Happened to Humpty? Axelsen, Stephen, illus. (p. 2419)
Ransom, L. M. Tilt. (p. 2243)
Ransom, Marty. Our Father, Our Soldier, Our Hero. (p. 1678)
Ransom, Nick. Instant Bible Dramas: Easy Skits for Elementary Kids. (p. 1125)
Ransom, R. Assembled Alphabet, or Acceptance of a's Invitation: Concluding with a Glee for Three Voices; Being a Sequel to the Invited Alphabet (Classic Reprint) (p. 127)
Ransom, Rochelle. Truth Trippers. (p. 2297)
Ransome, Arthur. Aladdin & His Wonderful Lamp in Rhyme (Classic Reprint) (p. 39)
—Bohemia in London (Classic Reprint) (p. 254)
—Favorite Russian Fairy Tales. Galkin, Simon, illus. (p. 716)
—Hoofmarks of the Faun (Classic Reprint) (p. 1000)
—Old Peter's Russian Tales (Classic Reprint) (p. 1647)
—Old Peter's Russian Tales - Scholar's Choice Edition. (p. 1647)
—Russian Fairy Tales: Illustrated 18 Short Fairy Tales for Children. Zvorykin, Boris, illus. (p. 1917)
—Soldier & Death: A Russian Folk Tale Told in English (Classic Reprint) (p. 2056)
—Swallowdale. Ransome, Arthur, illus. (p. 2167)
—Swallows & Amazons. (p. 2167)
—We Didn't Mean to Go to Sea. (p. 2390)
Ransome, Galya. Russia in Our World. (p. 1917)
Ransome, Galya, jt. auth. see Bowden, Rob.
Ransome, James, illus. see Alexander, Jessica & Shore, Diane Z.
Ransome, James, illus. see Cline-Ransome, Lesa.
Ransome, James, illus. see Hopkinson, Deborah.
Ransome, James, illus. see Howard, Elizabeth Fitzgerald.
Ransome, James, illus. see McMorrow, T. E.
Ransome, James, illus. see Mitchell, Margaree King.
Ransome, James, illus. see Shore, Diane Z. & Alexander, Jessica.
Ransome, James, illus. see Turner, Ann.
Ransome, James, illus. see Woodson, Jacqueline.
Ransome, James E. Bell Rang. Ransome, James E., illus. (p. 196)
—New Red Bike! (p. 1597)
Ransome, James E., illus. see Bandy, Michael S. & Stein, Eric.
Ransome, James E., illus. see Bowen, Fred.
Ransome, James E., illus. see Bunting, Eve.
Ransome, James E., illus. see Cline-Ransome, Lesa.
Ransome, James E., illus. see Hopkinson, Deborah.
Ransome, James E., illus. see Johnson, James Weldon.
Ransome, James E., illus. see Jordan, Deloris.
Ransome, James E., illus. see Matteson, George & Ursone, Adele.
Ransome, James E., illus. see Nolen, Jerdine.
Ransome, James E., illus. see Thomson, Sarah L.
Ransome, James E., illus. see Weatherford, Carole Boston.
Ransome, James E., illus. see Wolff, Ferida.
Ransome, Jessie. Story of the Siege Hospital in Peking, & Diary of Events from May to August, 1900 (Classic Reprint) (p. 2134)
Ranson, Claire, jt. auth. see Webb, Sarah.
Ranson, Erin. Fuzzy Farm. Green, Barry, illus. (p. 803)
—Fuzzy Ocean. Green, Barry, illus. (p. 803)
—Pequena Osa y Sus Amigos. (p. 1720)
—Ten Little Bears. Atkins, Alison, illus. (p. 2204)
Ranson, Kim, illus. see Marie, Susan.
Ranson, Walker, jt. auth. see Selfors, Suzanne.
Ransone, Rob, ed. see Leder, Barbara Turner.
Ranucci, Claudia, illus. see Achor, Shawn & Blankson, Amy.
Ranucci, Claudia, illus. see Crowe, Caroline.
Ranucci, Claudia, illus. see Escrivá, Victoria Pérez.
Ranucci, Claudia, illus. see Fliess, Sue.
Ranucci, Claudia, illus. see Freedman, Claire.
Ranucci, Claudia, illus. see Rosen Schwartz, Corey & Call, Kirsti.
Rao, Anuradha. One Earth: People of Color Protecting Our Planet. (p. 1659)
Rao, Joe. Cool Story Behind Snow. Downey, Dagney, illus. (p. 450)
—Looking Up! The Science of Stargazing. Borgions, Mark, illus. (p. 1347)
Rao, Lisa, jt. auth. see Ciminera, Siobhan.
Rao, N. Rajasekhar, tr. see Pere, Tuula.
Rao, Rohitash, illus. see Nelson, Peter.
Rao, Sandhya. My Mother's Sari. Sabnani, Nina, illus. (p. 1557)
Rao, Shruthi. 20 Indians Who Changed the World. (p. 2553)
Raoul, Louis Vincent. Trois Satiriques Latins, Vol. 2: Perse et Horace (Classic Reprint) (p. 2290)
Rap, John. Woman in the Mirror: Halloween in the Machine. Asmorot, Dodot, illus. (p. 2485)
—Woman in the Mirror. Asmorot, Dodot, illus. (p. 2485)
Rapaport, Giles, jt. auth. see Levy, Didier.
Raper, Eleanor. Little Girl Lost: A Tale for Little Girls (Classic Reprint) (p. 1317)
Rapetti, Louis Nicolas. Li Livres de Jostice et de Plet: Publie Pour la Premiere Fois d'Apres le Manuscrit Unique de la Bibliotheque Nationale (Classic Reprint) (p. 1283)
—Li Livres de Jostice et de Plet: Publié Pour la Première Fois d'Après le Manuscrit Unique de la Bibliothèque Nationale (Classic Reprint) (p. 1283)
Raphael, Antoine Archange. Marcel, le Jeune Esprit Positif, Livre2. (p. 1402)
Raphael, John N. Pictures of Paris Some Parisians (Classic Reprint) (p. 1741)
Raphael, Solli. Limelight. (p. 1302)
Raphael, Taffy E., jt. auth. see Au, Kathryn.
Raphaelson, Sampson M. Siren, Vol. 6 (Classic Reprint) (p. 2026)
Rapha'lle, Frier. Vibrations. (p. 2355)
Rapine, Dawn. Federal Forces: Careers As Federal Agents Set. (p. 717)
Rapkin, Mickey. It's Not a Bed, It's a Time Machine. Martinez, Teresa, illus. (p. 1146)
—It's Not a School Bus, It's a Pirate Ship. Martinez, Teresa, illus. (p. 1146)
Rapkins, Linna. Light of Glory: Children's Stories on the Early Days of the Unification Church. Rapkins, Linnna, ed. (p. 1298)
Rapkins, Linnna, ed. see Rapkins, Linna.
Rapoport, Rebecca & Yoder, J. A. Game of Nim & Graph Theory: Fun, Hands-On Activities for Learning Math. (p. 807)
—Geometry & Topology: Fun, Hands-On Activities for Learning Math. (p. 818)
—Little Learning Labs: Math Games for Kids: 25+ Fun, Hands-On Activities for Learning with Shapes, Puzzles, & Games. (p. 1320)
—Maps Curves & Fractals: Fun, Hands-On Activities for Learning with Coloring Maps, Stitching Curves, & Fantastic Fractals. (p. 1401)
—Math Games Lab for Kids: 24 Fun, Hands-On Activities for Learning with Shapes, Puzzles, & Games. (p. 1423)
—Tangrams & Puzzles: Fun, Hands-On Activities for Learning Math. (p. 2190)
Rapoport, Sandra E. Queen & the Spymaster: A Novel Based on the Story of Esther. (p. 1823)
Raposo, Joe. Sing. (p. 2023)
—Sing. Lichtenheld, Tom, illus. (p. 2023)
—Sunny Day: a Celebration of the Sesame Street Theme Song. (p. 2152)
Raposo Trueman, Aria. Magic Through the Mirror. (p. 1379)
Rapp, Adam. Children & the Wolves. Ering, Timothy Basil, illus. (p. 371)
—Decelerate Blue. (p. 523)
—Fum. (p. 798)
—Punkzilla. (p. 1814)
Rapp, Doris Gaines. Shyloe & the Mayor. (p. 2013)
—Tucker Mcbride. (p. 2298)
Rapp, Julie, et al. Diggory's First Adventure. (p. 546)
Rapp, Valerie. Protecting Earth's Air Quality. (p. 1808)
Rappa, Francesca. Melody West & the Cherry Blossom: The Adventurous Melody West Series Book Five. (p. 1443)
Rappaport, Carrie, et al. Best Sense for Safety. (p. 207)
Rappaport, Doreen. 42 Is Not Just a Number: The Odyssey of Jackie Robinson, American Hero. (p. 2555)
—Abe's Honest Words: The Life of Abraham Lincoln. Nelson, Kadir, illus. (p. 5)
—Abe's Honest Words. Nelson, Kadir, illus. (p. 5)
—Beyond Courage: The Untold Story of Jewish Resistance During the Holocaust. (p. 211)
—Beyond Courage. (p. 211)
—Eleanor, Quiet No More. Kelley, Gary, illus. (p. 630)
—Elizabeth Started All the Trouble. Faulkner, Matt, illus. (p. 636)
—Frederick's Journey: the Life of Frederick Douglass. Ladd, London, illus. (p. 782)
—Helen's Big World: The Life of Helen Keller. Tavares, Matt, illus. (p. 949)
—Jack's Path of Courage: The Life of John F. Kennedy. Tavares, Matt, illus. (p. 1153)
—John's Secret Dreams: The Life of John Lennon. Collier, Bryan, illus. (p. 1175)
—Lady Liberty: A Biography. Tavares, Matt, illus. (p. 1237)
—Ruth Objects: The Life of Ruth Bader Ginsburg. Velasquez, Eric, illus. (p. 1918)
—To Dare Mighty Things: The Life of Theodore Roosevelt. Payne, C. F., illus. (p. 2252)
Rappoport, Bernice. Community of Washington, D. C. Set Of 6. (p. 432)
—Habitats of Africa: Set Of 6. (p. 908)
Rappoport, Bernice & Benchmark Education Company, LLC Staff. Comunidad de Washington, D. C. Set of 6 Common Core Edition. (p. 437)
—Los Hábitats De África: Set of 6 Common Core Edition. (p. 1350)
Rappoport, Ken. Baseball's Top 10 Home Run Hitters. (p. 169)
—Baseball's Top 10 Pitchers. (p. 169)
—Basketball's Top 10 Slam Dunkers. (p. 171)
—Biggest Upsets in Sports (p. 225)
—Dale Earnhardt, Jr: A Car Racer Who Cares. (p. 498)
—David Wright: A Baseball Star Who Cares. (p. 511)
—Derek Jeter: Champion Baseball Star. (p. 530)
—Ladies First: Women Athletes Who Made a Difference (p. 1236)
—Michigan Wolverines (p. 1459)
—Peyton Manning: Champion Football Star. (p. 1732)
—Richard Sherman. (p. 1877)
—Russell Wilson. (p. 1917)
—Texas a & M Aggies (p. 2209)
—Tim Tebow: A Football Star Who Cares. (p. 2243)
Rapson, Helen. Reggie Did It! (p. 1861)
Rarus, Pat. Careers in E-Commerce. (p. 329)
—Careers in Info Tech. (p. 330)
—LGBT Rights Movement. (p. 1283)
—Skilled Jobs in Engineering. (p. 2032)
—Skilled Jobs in Technology. (p. 2032)
Rasberry, Beverly. Place to Get Well. (p. 1753)
Rasch, Heidi M., illus. see Eastman, Charles Alexander.
Raschka, Chris. Ball for Daisy. (p. 161)
—Ball for Daisy. Raschka, Chris, illus. (p. 161)
—Buggy Bug. (p. 292)
—Clammy Clam. (p. 397)
—Crabby Crab. (p. 465)
—Daisy Gets Lost. Raschka, Chris, illus. (p. 497)
—Doggy Dog. (p. 577)
—Doorman's Repose. (p. 585)
—Everyone Can Learn to Ride a Bicycle. Raschka, Chris, illus. (p. 672)
—Foot in the Mouth: Poems to Speak, Sing, & Shout. (p. 761)
—Hip Hop Dog. Radunsky, Vladimir, illus. (p. 973)
—Little Black Crow. (p. 1311)
—Magic Flute. Raschka, Chris, illus. (p. 1377)
—Mama Baby. Raschka, Chris, illus. (p. 1392)
—Moosey Moose. (p. 1503)
—Mother Goose of Pudding Lane. Radunsky, Vladimir, illus. (p. 1509)
—New Shoes. Raschka, Chris, illus. (p. 1597)
—New York Is English, Chattanooga Is Creek. Raschka, Chris, illus. (p. 1599)
—Paul Writes (a Letter) (p. 1707)
—Saint Spotting. (p. 1924)
—Side by Side: A Celebration of Dads. (p. 2014)
—Whaley Whale. (p. 2404)
—Yo! Yes? (p. 2522)
Raschka, Chris, illus. see Bell, Marvin.
Raschka, Chris, illus. see Bitterman, Albert.
Raschka, Chris, illus. see Brown, Margaret Wise.
Raschka, Chris, illus. see Creech, Sharon.
Raschka, Chris, illus. see Fogliano, Julie.
Raschka, Chris, illus. see Harris, Robie H.
Raschka, Chris, illus. see Hooks, Bell.

R

—Europe (p. 667)
—Everything You Need to Know about Free Speech. (p. 673)
—Extreme Movie Stunts (p. 687)
—Faith. (p. 698)
—Female Serial Killers. (p. 720)
—Getting Paid to Manage Social Media. (p. 826)
—Getting Paid to Work in 3D. (p. 826)
—Getting the Most Out of Makerspaces to Build Unmanned Aerial Vehicles. (p. 826)
—Getting the Most Out of Makerspaces to Explore Arduino & Electronics. (p. 826)
—Getting to Know Hackety Hack. (p. 826)
—Getting to Know Java. (p. 826)
—Healing. (p. 943)
—Historical Serial Killers. (p. 976)
—How George W. Bush Fought the Wars in Iraq & Afghanistan. (p. 1031)
—Inheritance & Variation of Traits. (p. 1120)
—Jamie Oliver. (p. 1157)
—Mexican-American War. (p. 1453)
—Miguel Cabrera: Triple Crown Winner. (p. 1464)
—Modern-Day Serial Killers. (p. 1486)
—Music in Theater. (p. 1529)
—Mysterious Places. (p. 1568)
—Near East (p. 1584)
—Personality. (p. 1725)
—Powering up a Career in Internet Security. (p. 1783)
—Protecting the Environment Through Service Learning (p. 1808)
—Rachael Ray. (p. 1832)
—Senses. (p. 1989)
—Sidney Crosby. (p. 2015)
—Social Network-Powered Investing & Saving Opportunities. (p. 2053)
—Solving Real World Problems with Chemical Engineering (p. 2058)
—Strengthening Public Speaking Skills. (p. 2140)
—Thomas Paine: Author of Common Sense. (p. 2229)
—Using Computer Science in Health Care Careers. (p. 2341)
—Virtual Reality (p. 2361)
—Washington's Farewell Address. (p. 2382)
—Working As a Hairstylist in Your Community. (p. 2495)
Rauf, Don, jt. auth. see Fireside, Harvey.
Rauf, Don & Bryan, Bethany. Hair & Makeup in Theater. (p. 910)
Rauf, Don & Cawthorne, Nigel. World's Worst Acts of Brutality. (p. 2508)
Rauf, Don & Vescia, Monique. Actor. (p. 13)
—Choose Your Own Career Adventure at NASA. (p. 381)
—Choose Your Own Career Adventure on a Cruise Ship. (p. 381)
—Choose Your Own Career Adventure on Broadway. (p. 381)
—Fashion Designer. (p. 712)
—Hollywood. (p. 988)
—Virtual Apprentice (p. 2361)
—Virtual Apprentice: Oceanographer. (p. 2361)
—Virtual Apprentice: Cartoon Animator. (p. 2361)
Rauf, Don & Williams, Judith. Forensic Science Specialists: Making Sense of Crime Scene Evidence. (p. 765)
Rauf, Don, et al. Are You Depressed? (p. 113)
—Choose Your Own Career Adventure in the Military. (p. 381)
—What You Can Do about Breast Cancer. (p. 2422)
—What You Can Do about Food Poisoning. (p. 2422)
Rauff, James. Am I Obsolete? (p. 61)
Raugewitz, Chad. Lightning Boy. (p. 1300)
Raughley, Sarah. Fate of Flames. (p. 714)
—Legacy of Light. (p. 1261)
—Siege of Shadows. (p. 2015)
Rauh, Michael Peter. Divine Inspirations in 2019 - the Year of Dreams. (p. 566)
Rauker, Lucy. Awesome Animal Trivia. (p. 144)
Raul, Gonzalez, illus. see Camper, Cathy.
Raúl, III. ¡Vamos! Let's Go to the Market. (p. 2345)
Raúl, III, illus. see Boie, Kirsten.
Raúl, III, illus. see Camper, Cathy.
Raum, Elizabeth. Abraham Lincoln (p. 7)
—Abraham Lincoln Oxford Bible Staff, illus. (p. 7)
—At Battle in the Revolutionary War: An Interactive Battlefield Adventure. (p. 129)
—Aztec Empire: An Interactive History Adventure (p. 146)
—Bearded Dragons. (p. 180)
—Bears Make Dens. Romina Martí, illus. (p. 180)
—Bears Make Dens. Marti, Romina, illus. (p. 180)
—Beavers Build Lodges. Romina Martí, illus. (p. 186)
—Beavers Build Lodges. Marti, Romina, illus. (p. 186)
—Bees Build Beehives. Romina Martí, illus. (p. 189)
—Bees Build Beehives. Marti, Romina, illus. (p. 189)
—Big, Bold, Adventurous Life of Lavinia Warren. (p. 217)
—Birds Build Nests. Romina Martí, illus. (p. 232)
—Birds Build Nests. Marti, Romina, illus. (p. 232)
—Black Widow Spiders. (p. 240)
—Blizzard! (p. 245)
—Blue-Ringed Octopuses. (p. 249)
—Boston Massacre: An Interactive History Adventure. (p. 264)
—Box Jellyfish. (p. 266)
—Bryce Harper. (p. 288)
—California Gold Rush: An Interactive History Adventure. (p. 310)
—Cam Newton. (p. 313)
—Can You Survive Storm Chasing? An Interactive Survival Adventure (p. 319)
—Carli Lloyd. (p. 331)
—Cedric & the Dragon. Crittenden, Nina Victor, illus. (p. 348)
—Chameleons. (p. 355)
—Chloe Kim. (p. 380)
—Christmas Crossroads. (p. 385)
—Cold, Hard Facts about Science & Medicine in Colonial America (p. 413)
—Costa Rica (p. 457)
—Crossroads among the Gentiles. (p. 478)
—Crossroads in Galilee. (p. 478)
—Cutting a Path: Daniel Boone & the Cumberland Gap. (p. 491)
—Declaration of Independence (p. 523)
—Dreadful, Smelly Colonies: The Disgusting Details about Life in Colonial Amer. (p. 600)
—Dreadful, Smelly Colonies: The Disgusting Details about Life in Colonial America (p. 600)
—Earthquake! (p. 617)
—Easter Island. (p. 620)
—Egyptian Pyramids. (p. 628)
—Expanding a Nation: Causes & Effects of the Louisiana Purchase (p. 677)
—Exploring the New Hampshire Colony. (p. 683)
—Flood! (p. 750)
—Fossil Fuels & Biofuels. (p. 770)
—Geckos. (p. 813)
—Gila Monsters. (p. 833)
—Great Wall of China. (p. 890)
—Green Iguanas. (p. 894)
—Guide Dogs. (p. 903)
—Haiti (p. 910)
—Harriet Tubman. (p. 933)
—Helping Others (p. 953)
—Homes: From Caves to Eco-Pods. (p. 998)
—Hurricane! (p. 1054)
—I Know Someone with ADHD (p. 1067)
—I Know Someone with HIV/AIDS (p. 1067)
—J. J. Watt. (p. 1150)
—K-9 Police Dogs. (p. 1201)
—Komodo Dragons. (p. 1231)
—Las Abejas y Sus Colmenas (Bees Build Beehives) Romina Martí, illus. (p. 1245)
—Lebron James. (p. 1260)
—Let's Think about the Power of Advertising (p. 1278)
—Los Castores y Sus Madrigueras. Martí, Romina, illus. (p. 1350)
—Los Castores y Sus Madrigueras (Beavers Build Lodges) Romina Martí, illus. (p. 1350)
—Los Orangutanes y Sus Nidos (Orangutans Build Tree Nests) Romina Martí, illus. (p. 1351)
—Los Osos y Sus Guaridas (Bears Make Dens) Romina Martí, illus. (p. 1351)
—Los Pájaros y Sus Nidos (Birds Build Nests) Romina Martí, illus. (p. 1351)
—Machu Picchu. (p. 1372)
—Malala Yousafzai. (p. 1391)
—Marie Curie. (p. 1405)
—Maya Moore. (p. 1429)
—Mayflower Compact (p. 1430)
—North Korea (p. 1621)
—Orangutans Build Tree Nests. Romina Martí, illus. (p. 1668)
—Orangutans Build Tree Nests. Marti, Romina, illus. (p. 1668)
—Orphan Trains: An Interactive History Adventure (p. 1672)
—Pledge of Allegiance in Translation: What It Really Means. (p. 1762)
—Poison Dart Frogs. (p. 1767)
—Potato Clocks & Solar Cars: Renewable & Nonrenewable Energy. (p. 1780)
—Pro Sports Biographies: Bryce Harper. (p. 1802)
—Pro Sports Biographies: Cam Newton. (p. 1802)
—Pro Sports Biographies: Carli Lloyd. (p. 1802)
—Pro Sports Biographies: Chloe Kim. (p. 1802)
—Pro Sports Biographies: Serena Williams. (p. 1802)
—Rabbits Dig Burrows. (p. 1830)
—Rabbits Dig Burrows. Romina Martí, illus. (p. 1830)
—Relationships Whiz: Facts & Figures about Families, Friends, & Feelings. (p. 1862)
—Resisting British Rule: An Interactive American Revolution Adventure. (p. 1869)
—Revolutionary War: An Interactive History Adventure. (p. 1874)
—Revolutionary War Timeline (p. 1874)
—Ruby Bridges. (p. 1911)
—Sally Ride. (p. 1925)
—Scoop on Clothes, Homes, & Daily Life in Colonial America. (p. 1961)
—Scorpions. (p. 1962)
—Serena Williams. (p. 1990)
—Social Media Savvy: Facts & Figures about Selfies, Smartphones, & Standing Out. (p. 2053)
—Song & Dance: A Journey Through Musical Theater. (p. 2062)
—South Korea (p. 2069)
—Spies of the American Revolution: An Interactive Espionage Adventure. (p. 2081)
—Star Spangled Banner in Translation: What It Really Means. (p. 2103)
—Stealing Nazi Secrets in World War II: An Interactive Espionage Adventure. (p. 2110)
—Stephen Curry. (p. 2115)
—Stingrays. (p. 2119)
—Stonefish. (p. 2121)
—Stonehenge. (p. 2121)
—Surviving Floods (p. 2165)
—Surviving Hurricanes (p. 2165)
—Surviving Tornadoes (p. 2165)
—Susan B. Anthony. (p. 2166)
—Taipans. (p. 2176)
—Taj Mahal. (p. 2176)
—Tenth Amendment: States' Rights. (p. 2206)
—Tornado! (p. 2265)
—Transportation: From Walking to High Speed Rail. (p. 2278)
—True Stories of the Revolutionary War. Kinsella, Pat, illus. (p. 2295)
—Twenty-First Century Shakespeare. (p. 2304)
—U. S. Marines by the Numbers (p. 2312)
—What Did the Aztecs Do for Me? (p. 2408)
—What Did the Vikings Do for Me? (p. 2408)
—Wildfire! (p. 2466)
—Wind Energy. (p. 2471)
—Work: From Plows to Robots. (p. 2495)
—World War II: An Interactive History Adventure (p. 2505)
—World War II Naval Forces (p. 2506)
—World War II Naval Forces: An Interactive History Adventure. (p. 2506)
—World War II Timeline (p. 2506)
Raum, Elizabeth, jt. auth. see Braun, Eric Mark.
Raum, Elizabeth, jt. auth. see Burgan, Michael.
Raum, Elizabeth & Burgan, Michael. Revolutionary War Experience: An Interactive History Adventure. (p. 1874)
Raum, Elizabeth & Collins, Terry. You Choose: Historical Eras. (p. 2527)
Raum, Elizabeth & Doak, Robin S. Exploring the Maryland Colony. (p. 683)
Raum, Elizabeth, et al. Cause & Effect (p. 346)
—Let's Think About (p. 1278)
—Life in the American Colonies. (p. 1292)
—Stories of War. (p. 2126)
—True War Stories: Personal Accounts of History's Greatest Conflicts. Kinsella, Pat et al, illus. (p. 2295)
—World War II Soldiers' Experience. (p. 2506)
Raun, Robert L. Tales of the Clam Club: Turtle Soup. (p. 2185)
Rausch, David. Major League Baseball. (p. 1385)
—Major League Soccer. (p. 1385)
—National Basketball Association. (p. 1577)
—National Football League. (p. 1577)
—National Hockey League. (p. 1577)
—United States Tennis Association. (p. 2332)
Rausch, Jessi. She Shines Bright. (p. 2004)
Rauscher, Amariah, illus. see Greenawalt, Kelly.
Raushenbush, John. Mike Mulligan: The Magic Eagle of Yellowstone. (p. 1464)
Rauss, Ron. Can I Just Take a Nap? Shepperson, Rob, illus. (p. 317)
Rautenberg, Karen Rita. Ballerina Detective & the Missing Jeweled Tiara. (p. 161)
Rautkallio, Outi, illus. see Pere, Tuula.
Rau-Tobin, Joanna. Ted E. Bear the Labradoodle. Rau, Dinah M., illus. (p. 2198)
Ravage, M. E. American in the Making: The Life Story of an Immigrant. (p. 72)
—American in the Making: The Life Story of an Immigrant (Classic Reprint) (p. 72)
Ravaglia, Paola, illus. see Davies, Gill.
Ravanelli, Terry, illus. see Gosselin, Kim.
Ravasi, Gianfranco. Abraham: Father of Our Faith. (p. 7)
Rave, Arte, illus. see Roger, Rachel & Lineberry, Joe.
Ravel, Edeet. Boy Is Not a Bird (p. 269)
—Held. (p. 949)
Raven, Abuelo. Bode & Porter Save the Lakota Herd: A Short Story by Abuelo Raven. (p. 253)
Raven, Gloria. Jackie Jamis: Jumping in the Hay! Raven, Gloria, illus. (p. 1153)
Raven, J. E. Smidgeons & the Glugs. (p. 2041)
—Smidgeons & the Glugs II: The Rescue. Russo, Erin, illus. (p. 2041)
Raven, Margot Theis. Rags Hero Dog of WWI: A True Story. Brown, Petra, illus. (p. 1834)
Raven, Nicky. Robin Hood: The Classic Adventure Tale. Gilbert, Anne Yvonne, illus. (p. 1891)
Raven, Nil. Two Years in Wall Street, or Why Was I Born? Consisting of Riches, Jokes, & Disappointments (Classic Reprint) (p. 2310)
Raven, Peter H. Raven, Biology, 2017, 11e (AP Edition) Student Print Bundle (Student Edition with AP Focus Review Guide) (p. 1843)
Ravenel, Florence Leftwich. Vie Seint Edmund le Rei: An Anglo-Norman Poem of the Twelfth Century by Denis Piramus (Classic Reprint) (p. 2356)
Raven-Hill, L. Our Battalion: Being Some Slight Impressions of His Majesty's Auxiliary Forces, in Camp & Elsewhere (Classic Reprint) (p. 1676)
Ravenhill, Mark. Plays for Young People: Citizenship; Scenes from Family Life; Totally over You. (p. 1761)
Ravenscraft, Stephen, jt. auth. see Goodall, Jane.
Raventos, Miriam. Yoga Storytime: Breathe - Stretch - Be Calm Giron, Maria, illus. (p. 2523)
Ravera, Giuseppe. My Ballet Bag. Pagnoni, Roberta et al, illus. (p. 1531)
Ravilious, Kate. Power: Ethical Debates about Resources & the Environment. (p. 1782)
Ravishankar, Anushka. Rumor. Kini, Kanyika, illus. (p. 1914)
Ravishankar, Sumona Bagchi. Jungle Trails: Stories for Little Wild Ones. (p. 1190)
Raw, Victoria Frances. Ferocious Feral Felines. (p. 721)
Rawal, Ishita, illus. see Crofoot, Nancy.
Rawal, Sucheta. Beato Goes to Brazil. (p. 183)
—Beato Goes to Indonesia. (p. 183)
—Beato Goes to Japan. (p. 183)
Rawandzi, Kardason. Little Blue Dinosaur. (p. 1312)
—Little Blue Dinosaur. Ferraz, Mayhara, illus. (p. 1312)
Rawat, Tania, illus. see Crofoot, Nancy.
Rawitz, Bernhard. Lehrbuch der Mikroskopischen Technik (Classic Reprint) (p. 1265)
Rawl, Paige. Positiva. (p. 1779)
Rawl, Paige, et al. Positive: A Memoir. (p. 1779)
Rawlence, Guy. Highwayman (Classic Reprint) (p. 970)
Rawlings, Charles. Olla Podrida (Classic Reprint) (p. 1650)
Rawlings, Louise, illus. see Rock, Lois.
Rawlings, Marjorie Kinnan. Secret River. Dillon, Leo & Dillon, Diane, illus. (p. 1978)
—Yearling. Wyeth, N. C., illus. (p. 2519)
Rawlings, Stacey. My Heart Is a House. Rawlings, Stacey and Monterio, illus. (p. 1549)
Rawlings, Stacey and Monterio, illus. see Rawlings, Stacey.
Rawlins, Abi & Frizzell, Catherine. Is It OK to Ask Questions about Autism? (p. 1137)
Rawlins, Donna, jt. auth. see Wild, Margaret.
Rawlinson, James H. Through St. Dunstan's to Light (Classic Reprint) (p. 2237)
Rawlinson, Julia. Fletcher & the Falling Leaves. (p. 748)
—Fletcher & the Snowflake Christmas. Beeke, Tiphanie, illus. (p. 748)
—Fletcher & the Springtime Blossoms. (p. 748)
—Fletcher & the Springtime Blossoms. Beeke, Tiphanie, illus. (p. 748)
—Fletcher & the Summer Show. Beeke, Tiphanie, illus. (p. 748)
—Sweet Dreaming. Wong, Nicole, illus. (p. 2168)
Rawls, Linnea V. Chlo-Jo's Friends Around the World. Veres, Csongor, illus. (p. 379)
Rawls, Nicholas. Elephant of Frimley. (p. 634)
Rawls, Wilson. Where the Red Fern Grows. (p. 2439)
Rawlyk, George, jt. auth. see Downie, Mary Alice.
Rawnsley, H. D. By Fell & Dale at the English Lakes by the Rev. H. d (Classic Reprint) (p. 305)
—Chapters at the English Lakes (Classic Reprint) (p. 357)
—Flower-Time in the Oberland (Classic Reprint) (p. 752)
—Lake Country Sketches (Classic Reprint) (p. 1240)
—Life & Nature at the English Lakes. (p. 1289)
—Life & Nature at the English Lakes (Classic Reprint) (p. 1289)
—Nation's Heritage (Classic Reprint) (p. 1578)
—Past & Present at the English Lakes (Classic Reprint) (p. 1703)
—Round the Lake Country (Classic Reprint) (p. 1908)
Rawnsley, Willingham Franklin. Early Days at Uppingham under Edward Thring (Classic Reprint) (p. 614)
Rawson, Abel M. Junior Partners (Classic Reprint) (p. 1191)
—Seraltha (Classic Reprint) (p. 1990)
Rawson, Christopher, jt. auth. see Wilkes, Angela.
Rawson, Donald. Crimson & Gray, Vol. 11: Published Quarterly by the Students of the Mary E. Wells High School; November, 1927 (Classic Reprint) (p. 475)
Rawson, Katherine. Abigail Breslin. (p. 5)
—Brenda Song. (p. 279)
—Daniel Radcliffe. (p. 503)
—Jonas Brothers. (p. 1177)
—Taylor Swift. (p. 2193)
—Vanessa Hudgens. (p. 2347)
Rawson, Maud Stepney. Tales of Rye Town (Classic Reprint) (p. 2185)
Rawson, Stepney. Lady of the Regency (Classic Reprint) (p. 1238)
Ray, Anna Chapin. Ackroyd of the Faculty (Classic Reprint) (p. 11)
—Brentons (Classic Reprint) (p. 279)
—Day: Her Year in New York (Classic Reprint) (p. 512)
—Dick: A Story for Boys & Girls (Classic Reprint) (p. 540)
—Each Life Unfulfilled (Classic Reprint) (p. 613)
—Half a Dozen Girls (Classic Reprint) (p. 910)
—Hearts & Creeds (Classic Reprint) (p. 946)
—In Blue Creek Canon (Classic Reprint) (p. 1104)
—Janet: Her Winter in Quebec (Classic Reprint) (p. 1158)
—Janet at Odds (Classic Reprint) (p. 1158)
—Margaret Davis, Tutor (Classic Reprint) (p. 1403)
—Nathalie's Sister: The Last of the Mcalister Records (Classic Reprint) (p. 1576)
—On Board the Beatic (Classic Reprint) (p. 1652)
—On the Firing Line a Romance of South Africa (Classic Reprint) (p. 1654)
—Over the Quicksands (Classic Reprint) (p. 1686)
—Phebe, Her Profession: A Sequel to Tedd, Her Book (Classic Reprint) (p. 1733)
—Sheba (Classic Reprint) (p. 2004)
—Sidney: Her Summer on the St. Lawrence (Classic Reprint) (p. 2015)
—Teddy, Her Book (Classic Reprint) (p. 2198)
—Teddy Her Daughter: A Sequel to Teddy: Her Book (Classic Reprint) (p. 2198)
—Ursula's Freshman (Classic Reprint) (p. 2340)
—Woman with a Purpose (Classic Reprint) (p. 2486)
Ray, Caitlin. Revenge (p. 1872)
Ray, Charles. Hollywood Shorts: Compiled from Incidents in the Everyday Life of Men & Women Who Entertain in Pictures (Classic Reprint) (p. 989)
Ray, Christie Jones. Baby Mouse with Rosebud & Sugarlump. (p. 151)
—Eliza at Rose Water Cottage. (p. 636)
Ray, Christie Jones, jt. auth. see Ray, Christie Jones.
Ray, Christie Jones & Ray, Christie Jones. Eliz. (p. 636)
—Eliza & a Cottage Door. (p. 636)
—Eliza Celebrates a Royal Wedding. (p. 636)
—Eliza Has a Cousin. (p. 636)
—Eliza Will Not Be Afraid. (p. 636)
—Fox Family of Franklin. (p. 774)
—Goat's Milk & Gardening. (p. 849)
—Pick-A-Pick-a-Pumpkin. (p. 1738)
Ray, Clarence E. Tracy, the Bandit: Or the Romantic Life & Crimes of a Twentieth Century Desperado (Classic Reprint) (p. 2273)
Ray, Crystol T. Grumpy the Clown. (p. 901)
Ray, Dale Marie. Moody Mae. Ray, Dale Marie & Ray, Joli, illus. (p. 1500)
Ray, Deborah Kogan. Impossible Voyage of Kon-Tiki. Ray, Deborah Kogan, illus. (p. 1102)
Ray, Deborah Kogan, illus. see Cummings, E. E.
Ray, Delia. Finding Fortune. (p. 729)
—Ghost Girl: A Blue Ridge Mountain Story. (p. 827)
—Here Lies Linc. (p. 958)
Ray, Francine & Bay, Francine. Stories of the Blessed Sacrament. (p. 2125)
Ray, Frederick Augustus. Maid of the Mohawk (Classic Reprint) (p. 1383)
Ray, George R. Kasba (White Partridge) A Story of Hudson Bay (Classic Reprint) (p. 1204)
Ray, George Raymond. Kasba (White Partridge) A Story of Hudson Bay (Classic Reprint) (p. 1204)
Ray, Gracie. Falling Slowly. (p. 701)
Ray II, McSellin. Unveiled. (p. 2337)
Ray, J. Hamilton. Squirrels on Skis. Lemaître, Pascal, illus. (p. 2095)
Ray, Jane. Cinderella. Ray, Jane, illus. (p. 391)
—Classic Fairy Tales: Candlewick Illustrated Classic. (p. 400)
—Hansel et Gretel. (p. 919)
—Twelve Days of Christmas. (p. 2303)
Ray, Jane, illus. see Davies, Nicola.
Ray, Jane, illus. see Ellinas, Georghia.
Ray, Jane, illus. see Hofmeyr, Dianne.
Ray, Jane, illus. see Pirotta, Saviour.
Ray, Jane, illus. see Steven, Kenneth.
Ray, Jane, jt. auth. see Joslin, Mary.
Ray, John. Complete Collection of English Proverbs: Also, the Most Celebrated Proverbs of the Scotch, Italian, French, Spanish, & Other Languages (Classic Reprint) (p. 434)
Ray, John, jt. auth. see Bohn, Henry George.
Ray, Joli, illus. see Ray, Dale Marie.
Ray, Joseph. Ray's New Primary Arithmetic for Young Learners (Classic Reprint) (p. 1844)

—Course of True Love Never Did Run Smooth, and, Singleheart & Doubleface: A Matter-Of-Fact Romance (Classic Reprint) (p. 462)
—Cream: By Charles Reade Contains Jack of All Trades, a Matter-Of-Fact Romance, & the Autobiography of a Thief (Classic Reprint) (p. 469)
—Foul Play: A Novel (Classic Reprint) (p. 771)
—Foul Play, Vol. 1 of 2 (Classic Reprint) (p. 771)
—Foul Play, Vol. 2 of 2 (Classic Reprint) (p. 771)
—Foul Play, Vol. 3 of 3 (Classic Reprint) (p. 771)
—Good Fight: And Other Tales (Classic Reprint) (p. 862)
—Good Fight (Classic Reprint) (p. 862)
—Good Stories (Classic Reprint) (p. 866)
—Good Stories; Good Stories of Man & Other Animals; Readiania (Classic Reprint) (p. 866)
—Griffith Gaunt: Or Jealousy (Classic Reprint) (p. 896)
—Griffith Gaunt, or Jealousy (Classic Reprint) (p. 896)
—Griffith Gaunt, Vol. 1 Of 3: Or Jealously (Classic Reprint) (p. 896)
—Griffith Gaunt, Vol. 3 Of 3: Or Jealousy (Classic Reprint) (p. 896)
—Hard Cash: A Matter-Of-Fact Romance (Classic Reprint) (p. 929)
—Hard Cash, a Matter-Of-Fact Romance, Vol. 2: Singleheart & Doubleface, and, Good Stories of Man & Other Animals (Classic Reprint) (p. 929)
—Hard Cash, Vol. 1: A Matter-Of-Fact Romance (Classic Reprint) (p. 929)
—Hard Cash, Vol. 1 Of 3: A Matter-Of-Fact Romance (Classic Reprint) (p. 929)
—Hard Cash, Vol. 2 of 3 (Classic Reprint) (p. 929)
—Hard Cash, Vol. 3 of 3 (Classic Reprint) (p. 929)
—It Is Never to Late to Mend (Classic Reprint) (p. 1141)
—It Is Never Too Late to Mend. (p. 1141)
—It Is Never Too Late to Mend (Classic Reprint) (p. 1141)
—It Is Never Too Late to Mend, Vol. 1 Of 2: A Matter of Fact Romance (Classic Reprint) (p. 1141)
—Jilt: A Novel (Classic Reprint) (p. 1168)
—Jilt & Other Stories (Classic Reprint) (p. 1168)
—Jilt, &C: Good Stories of Man & Other Animals (Classic Reprint) (p. 1168)
—Love Me Little Love Me Long (Classic Reprint) (p. 1360)
—Love Me Little, Love Me Long, Vol. 2 of 2 (Classic Reprint) (p. 1360)
—Peg Woffington: A Novel (Classic Reprint) (p. 1714)
—Peg Woffington. (p. 1714)
—Peg Woffington & Christie Johnstone (Classic Reprint) (p. 1714)
—Peg Woffington, Christie Johnstone, & Other Stories. (p. 1714)
—Peg Woffington, Christie Johnstone, & Other Stories (Classic Reprint) (p. 1714)
—Peg Woffington, Christie Johnstone, etc. , & a Simpleton (Classic Reprint) (p. 1714)
—Peg Woffington; the Knightsbridge Mystery; the Kindly Jest; an Old Bachelor's Adventure; a Stroke of Business; What Has Become of Lord Camelford's Body? (Classic Reprint) (p. 1714)
—Perilous Secret (Classic Reprint) (p. 1723)
—Perilous Secret, Vol. 1 of 2 (Classic Reprint) (p. 1723)
—Put Yourself in His Place. (p. 1817)
—Put Yourself in His Place (Classic Reprint) (p. 1817)
—Put Yourself in His Place, Vol. 1 (Classic Reprint) (p. 1817)
—Put Yourself in His Place, Vol. 1 of 3 (Classic Reprint) (p. 1817)
—Put Yourself in His Place, Vol. 2: The Wandering Heir (Classic Reprint) (p. 1817)
—Put Yourself in His Place, Vol. 2 (Classic Reprint) (p. 1818)
—Put Yourself in His Place, Vol. 2 of 3 (Classic Reprint) (p. 1818)
—Simpleton: A Story of the Day (Classic Reprint) (p. 2022)
—Simpleton. (p. 2022)
—Simpleton, and, White Lies (Classic Reprint) (p. 2022)
—Singleheart & Doubleface: A Matter-Of-Fact Romance (Classic Reprint) (p. 2024)
—Singleheart & Doubleface. (p. 2024)
—Terrible Temptation: A Story of to-Day, Pp. 1-167. (p. 2207)
—Terrible Temptation: A Story of to-Day (Classic Reprint) (p. 2207)
—Terrible Temptation: A Story of the Day (Classic Reprint) (p. 2207)
—Terrible Temptation (Classic Reprint) (p. 2207)
—Terrible Temptation, Vol. 1 Of 3: A Story of the Day (Classic Reprint) (p. 2207)
—Trade Malice, a Personal Narrative: And the Wandering Heir, a Matter of Fact Romance (Classic Reprint) (p. 2273)
—Trade Malice, a Personal Narrative. (p. 2273)
—Wandering Heir; the Autobiography of a Thief; Jack of All Trades (Classic Reprint) (p. 2375)
—White Elephant: A Story (Classic Reprint) (p. 2443)
—White Lies: A Novel (Classic Reprint) (p. 2444)
—White Lies. (p. 2444)
—White Lies, Vol. 1 Of 3: A Story (Classic Reprint) (p. 2444)
—White Lies, Vol. 3: A Story (Classic Reprint) (p. 2444)
—Woman Hater, Vol. 1 of 2 (Classic Reprint) (p. 2485)
—Woman Hater, Vol. 2 of 2 (Classic Reprint) (p. 2485)
—Woman-Hater: A Novel (Classic Reprint) (p. 2485)
—Woman-Hater. (p. 2485)
—Woman-Hater, Vol. 1 of 3 (Classic Reprint) (p. 2485)
—Woman-Hater, Vol. 2 of 3 (Classic Reprint) (p. 2485)
—Woman-Hater, Vol. 3 of 3 (Classic Reprint) (p. 2485)
—Works of Charles Reade, Vol. 2: Illustrated with One Hundred & Twelve Full-Page Wood Engravings, Hard Cash, Love Me Little, Love Me Long (Classic Reprint) (p. 2497)
—Works of Charles Reade, Vol. 4: Illustrated with One Hundred & Twelve Full-Page Wood Engravings; Foul Play (Classic Reprint) (p. 2497)
—Works of Charles Reade, Vol. 6 Of 9: Illustrated with One Hundred & Twelve Full-Page Wood Engravings; White Lies, a Perilous Secret (Classic Reprint) (p. 2497)
—Works of Charles Reade, Vol. 7: A New Edition in Nine Volumes, Illustrated with One Hundred & Twelve Full-Page Wood Engravings; a Woman-Hater Griffith Gaunt; or, Jealousy (Classic Reprint) (p. 2497)

Reade, Clara. Cheetahs. (p. 364)
—Hippos. (p. 973)
—Intuicin: El Sexto Sentido / Intuition: the Sixth Sense De La Vega, Eida, ed. (p. 1129)
—Intuition: The Sixth Sense (p. 1129)
—Lions. (p. 1307)
—Meerkats. (p. 1437)
—Olfato / Smell De La Vega, Eida, ed. (p. 1649)
—Smell (p. 2041)
—Warthogs. (p. 2381)
—Zebras. (p. 2539)
Reade, Compton. Mr. Sillifant Suckoothumb, & Other Oxford Yarns (Classic Reprint) (p. 1520)
—Rose & Rue, Vol. 1 Of 3: A Novel (Classic Reprint) (p. 1904)
—Rose & Rue, Vol. 2 Of 3: A Novel (Classic Reprint) (p. 1904)
—Rose & Rue, Vol. 3 Of 3: A Novel (Classic Reprint) (p. 1904)
Reade, O. K. Little Girl & Her Shadow. (p. 1317)
Reade, Simon. Private Peaceful. (p. 1802)
Reade, William. Outcast (Classic Reprint) (p. 1684)
Reade, Winwood. African Sketch-Book, Vol. 2 Of 2: With Maps & Illustrations (Classic Reprint) (p. 33)
Reader, Jack. Los Tambores de Mi Hermana (My Sister's Drums) de la Vega, Eida, tr. (p. 1351)
—Los Tambores de Mi Hermana / My Sister's Drums. de la Vega, Eida, tr. (p. 1351)
—My Sister's Drums. (p. 1561)
—Separation of Powers: The Importance of Checks & Balances. (p. 1989)
—Story Behind Groundhog Day (p. 2127)
—Trip to the Farmers' Market. (p. 2289)
—Working on the Farm. (p. 2496)
Readers, Canadian Catholic. First Read, Vol. 1: Approved by the Education Department for Use in the Roman Catholic Separate Schools of Ontario (Classic Reprint) (p. 739)
Reader's Digest Editors. Talking Puzzles Sounds on the Farm. (p. 2187)
Reader's Digest, Reader's, ed. Reader's Digest Fun Jokes for Funny Kids. (p. 1846)
—Reader's Digest Fun Jokes for Funny Kids Vol. 2. (p. 1846)
Reader's Digest Staff. Dora the Explorer My Favorite Story. (p. 586)
—Mickey Mouse Clubhouse Gift Set. (p. 1459)
—Sesame Street Gift Set. (p. 1992)
—Tractor Trouble Drive Through Storybook. Pitt, Sarah, illus. (p. 2273)
Reader's Digest Staff & Disney Storybook Artists Staff. Rapunzel's Dream Walmart Edition Storybook with Musical Hairbrush. (p. 1842)
Readey, Marijo. Totally, Unabashedly Incomplete Book about Bugs: Black & White Edition. (p. 2267)
Reading & Writing Workbook Team. English & Language Arts Grade 1 Workbook: First Grade Reading Comprehension & Writing Ela Book. (p. 653)
—English & Language Arts Grade 2 Workbook: Ela 2nd Grade Reading Comprehension & Writing Book. (p. 653)
Reading, Joseph H. Ogowe Band: A Narrative of African Travel (Classic Reprint) (p. 1641)
Reading, Joseph H. (Joseph Hankinson). Ogowe Band. (p. 1641)
Reading, Smart. Oregon Reads Aloud: A Collection of 25 Children's Stories by Oregon Authors & Illustrators. (p. 1670)
Ready, Anna. Mississippi. (p. 1482)
Ready, Dee. Dentists Help (p. 529)
—Doctors Help (p. 574)
—Farmers Help (p. 711)
—Firefighters Help (p. 734)
—Librarians Help (p. 1284)
—Nurses Help (p. 1631)
—Our Community Helpers. (p. 1677)
—Police Officers Help (p. 1770)
—Veterinarians Help (p. 2354)
Ready, Tricia. M Is for Mongolia. Sandro, Turburam, illus. (p. 1370)
Reagan, Jean. Como Cuidar de Tu Mama. (p. 432)
—Como Sorprender a Tu Papa. (p. 433)
—How to Babysit a Grandma. (p. 1037)
—How to Babysit a Grandma. Wildish, Lee, illus. (p. 1037)
—How to Babysit a Grandma & a Grandpa Boxed Set (p. 1037)
—How to Catch Santa. Wildish, Lee, illus. (p. 1038)
—How to Get Your Teacher Ready. Wildish, Lee, illus. (p. 1042)
—How to Raise a Mom. Wildish, Lee, illus. (p. 1043)
—How to Read to a Grandma or Grandpa. Wildish, Lee, illus. (p. 1043)
—How to Scare a Ghost. Wildish, Lee, illus. (p. 1044)
—How to Surprise a Dad. Wildish, Lee, illus. (p. 1044)
Reagan, Jean & Pollema-Cahill, Phyllis. Always My Brother (p. 61)
Reagan, Jean & Wildish, Lee. Como Cuidar a Tu Abuela. (p. 432)
—How to Raise a Mom. (p. 1043)
—How to Scare a Ghost. (p. 1044)
Reagan, Jerkwenton. Soldier Island. (p. 2056)
Reagan, Laura Lyles. How to Raise Respectful Parents: Better Communication for Teen & Parent Relationships. (p. 1043)
Reagan, Liz. Another Way Out. (p. 101)
Reagan, Marianne & Reagan, John. It's Okay to Be Me. (p. 1147)
Reagan, Mike, illus. see Lerangis, Peter.
Reagan, Nancy. First Thanksgiving. (p. 740)
—Who's at Home? (p. 2453)
Reagan, Naomi. Butterflies & Moths: Represent & Interpret Data. (p. 303)
Reagan, Susan, illus. see Arnold, Marsha Diane.
Reagan, Susan, illus. see DePrisco, Dorothea.
Reagan, Susan, illus. see Dotlich, Rebecca Kai.
Reagan, Susan, illus. see Elkins, Stephen.
Reagan, Susan, illus. see Zebrowska, Emilia.
Reagan, Susan Joy, illus. see Carlson, Melody.
Reagan, Susan Joy, illus. see Elkins, Stephen.
Real Sports Network, Real Sports. Kevin Durant. (p. 1210)
Reality, Romance and. Francesca Carrara, Vol. 1 of 3 (Classic Reprint) (p. 776)

Really Big Coloring Books. Ted Cruz to the Future - Comic Coloring Activity Book. (p. 2198)
Ream, Jacquie. Bully Dogs. (p. 296)
Ream, Robaire, illus. see Matejovsky, Char.
Reaman, George Elmore. English for New-Canadians (Classic Reprint) (p. 653)
Reaney, G. S. Romance of an Emergency (Classic Reprint) (p. 1900)
Reaoch, Barbara. Jesus Christmas: Explore God's Amazing Plan for Christmas. (p. 1166)
Rearden, Don, jt. auth. see Settie, Jimmy.
Reardon, Anne Edith. Story of Autumn. (p. 2129)
Reardon, Jasmine. Little Miss Shopper. (p. 1322)
Reardon, Kenneth. Arguenot, Vol. 8: November, 1927 (Classic Reprint) (p. 115)
Reardon, Lecia. My Paperback Book. (p. 1558)
Rearick, Ben. Better Lunch Line. (p. 209)
Reasoner, Charles. Animal Friends on the Farm. Pitt, Sarah, illus. (p. 89)
—Animals in the Jungle. Pitt, Sarah, illus. (p. 95)
—Bear Hugs. (p. 179)
—Brrrr! (p. 287)
—Bug Babies. Devaney, Adam, illus. (p. 291)
—Color Crunch! (p. 420)
—Colors in the Garden. Pitt, Sarah, illus. (p. 426)
—Day Around Town. (p. 512)
—Day at School. (p. 512)
—Day at the Farm. (p. 512)
—Desert Tails. Nelson, Judy, illus. (p. 532)
—Dinosaur Babies. Devaney, Adam, illus. (p. 548)
—Dinosaurs. (p. 550)
—Dinosaurs. Doherty, Paula, illus. (p. 550)
—Fan-Tab-U-Lus: Dinosaurs. Devaney, Adam, illus. (p. 705)
—Fan-Tab-U-Lus: Jungle Animals. Devaney, Adam, illus. (p. 705)
—Farm. (p. 709)
—Farm Animals. Doherty, Paula, illus. (p. 709)
—Farm Babies. Devaney, Adam, illus. (p. 710)
—First Words at the Park. Pitt, Sarah, illus. (p. 740)
—Hey, Diddle, Diddle Le Ray, Marina, illus. (p. 964)
—Hickory, Dickory, Dock. Le Ray, Marina, illus. (p. 965)
—Honey Bunny. (p. 999)
—I'm Just a Crab. (p. 1098)
—I'm Just a Little Cow. Orkrania, Alexia, illus. (p. 1098)
—Insects. Doherty, Paula, illus. (p. 1122)
—Inside Jolly Rodger's Pirate Ship. (p. 1123)
—Inside Old MacDonald's Barn. (p. 1123)
—Itsy Bitsy Spider Le Ray, Marina, illus. (p. 1148)
—Jack & Jill Le Ray, Marina, illus. (p. 1151)
—Jungle. Devaney, Adam, illus. (p. 1189)
—Jungle Animals. Doherty, Paula, illus. (p. 1189)
—Jungle Babies. Devaney, Adam & Doherty, Paula, illus. (p. 1189)
—Little Bo Peep Le Ray, Marina, illus. (p. 1312)
—Number Munch! (p. 1629)
—Numbers under the Sea. Pitt, Sarah, illus. (p. 1630)
—Ocean Tails. Nelson, Judy, illus. (p. 1636)
—Ooink! (p. 1665)
—Peep! Peep! (p. 1713)
—Puppy Love. (p. 1815)
—Reptiles. (p. 1867)
—Shapes at the Beach. Pitt, Sarah, illus. (p. 2000)
—Shapes for Lunch! (p. 2000)
—Twinkle, Twinkle, Little Star Le Ray, Marina, illus. (p. 2305)
—Whooo? (p. 2453)
Reasoner, Charles, illus. see Beall, Pamela Conn & Nipp, Susan Hagen.
Reasoner, Charles, illus. see Cooke, Brandy.
Reasoner, Charles, illus. see Lee, Howard.
Reasoner, Charles, illus. see Thompson, Kate.
Reasoner, John, illus. see Cooke, Brandy.
Reasor, Mick, illus. see Meltzer Kleinhenz, Sydnie.
Reasor, Mick, illus. see Meltzer-Kleinhenz, Sydnie.
Reasor, Teresa J. Willy C. Sparks. (p. 2470)
Reaveley, Trevor, illus. see Bailey, Gerry.
Reaveley, Trevor, illus. see Nussbaum, Ben.
Reaveley, Trevor, jt. auth. see Bailey, Gerry.
Reavely, Trever, illus. see Bentley, Dawn.
Reavely, Trevor, illus. see Bentley, Dawn.
Reavely, Trevor, illus. see Nussbaum, Ben.
Reaves, Daniel, illus. see Hawes, Dorothy.
Reaves, Michael, jt. auth. see Gaiman, Neil.
Reaves, William P., jt. auth. see Rydberg, Viktor.
Reavis, Vicky 'A' Blevins. Night Before Christmas. (p. 1605)
Reba, Russell. Courage the Hawk: Overcoming Fear. (p. 462)
Rebate Sánchez, Carlos. PATIO EN EL CENTRO DEL UNIVERSO. (p. 1705)
Rebaud, Robert & Gallin-Rebaud, Sarah. Dr. Sarah Veterinaire des Insectes. (p. 592)
Rebboah, Julie. Magic Words: Discovering the Adventure of Reading. (p. 1379)
Rebec, Ariel. Bellashelly. (p. 197)
Rebecca, Amy. Healthy Habits: The Rainbow Food. (p. 944)
Rebecca, Rebecca. Tramps in New York (Classic Reprint) (p. 2277)
—Turtle Who Did His Best. (p. 2301)
Rebecca, Rivard, illus. see Zolty, Meredith.
Rebecca, Spencer, illus. see Cameron, Kim.
Rebecca, Stead. When You Reach Me. (p. 2434)
Rebek, Lillie. Home of the Dragon: A Tonquinese Idyll, Told in Seven Chapters (Classic Reprint) (p. 996)
—Home of the Dragon. (p. 996)
Rebel Girls. Alicia Alonso Takes the Stage. Preumayr, Josefina, illus. (p. 46)
—Dr. Wangari Maathai Plants a Forest. Mello, Eugenia, illus. (p. 592)
—Junko Tabei Masters the Mountains. Galbany, Montse, illus. (p. 1191)
Rebele-Henry, Brynne. Orpheus Girl. (p. 1673)
Rebelka, Jakub, illus. see Tierney, Josh.
Rebello, Gleeson & Harisiades, Jamie. Darebone's Big Break. (p. 505)
—Darebone's Big Break (Hardcover) (p. 505)
Rebello, Lauren. Emily & Max: The Hide & Seek Potato. (p. 642)

Reber, Deborah. Doable: The Girls' Guide to Accomplishing Just about Anything. (p. 572)
Reber, Deborah & Goode, Caroline. Love, Love, Love: Language of Love; Cupidity. (p. 1360)
Reber, Kelseyleigh. If I Fall: The Circle & Cross: Book One. (p. 1091)
Rebman, Nick. Animals (Library Bound Set Of 10) (p. 95)
—Animals (Paperback Set Of 10) (p. 95)
—Baseball. (p. 168)
—Basketball. (p. 170)
—Butterflies. (p. 303)
—Cats. (p. 345)
—Cuando Crezca (When I Grow Up) When I Grow Up. (p. 481)
—Dance. (p. 499)
—Desiertos (Deserts) Deserts. (p. 532)
—Dogs. (p. 577)
—Dolphins. (p. 579)
—Eagles. (p. 613)
—Eyewitness to the Treaty of Versailles. (p. 689)
—Football. (p. 761)
—Gymnastics. (p. 907)
—Hockey. (p. 985)
—Horses. (p. 1005)
—Lacrosse. (p. 1235)
—Las Enfermeras (Nurses) Nurses. (p. 1245)
—Lions. (p. 1307)
—Los Bomberos (Firefighters) Firefighters. (p. 1350)
—Los Dentistas (Dentists) Dentists. (p. 1350)
—Los Policías (Police Officers) Police Officers. (p. 1351)
—Mexican-American War. (p. 1453)
—Monkeys. (p. 1494)
—Montañas (Mountains) Mountains. (p. 1499)
—Océanos (Oceans) Oceans. (p. 1636)
—Pandas. (p. 1695)
—Ríos (Rivers) Rivers. (p. 1884)
—Sharks. (p. 2002)
—Soccer. (p. 2051)
—Sports (Library Bound Set Of 10) (p. 2089)
—Sports (Paperback Set Of 10) (p. 2089)
—Swimming. (p. 2170)
—Visita a Mi Escuela (a Visit to My School) A Visit to My School. (p. 2362)
—We Take Care of Pets. (p. 2392)
—What Comes First? A Book about Sequences. (p. 2407)
—What Goes Together? A Book about Opposites. (p. 2410)
—What Is Biggest? A Book about Sizes. (p. 2414)
—What Is on Top? A Book about Positions. (p. 2415)
—Which Is the Circle? A Book about Shapes. (p. 2441)
—Which One Is Not Like the Others? A Book about Differences. (p. 2441)
—Who Is Happy? A Book about Emotions. (p. 2448)
—Who Is Wearing Blue? A Book about Colors. (p. 2448)
—Wrestling. (p. 2511)
—¿Qué Hay en Mi Vecindad? (What Is in My Neighborhood?) What Is in My Neighborhood? (p. 1822)
—¿Quién Está en Mi Comunidad? (Who Is in My Community?) Who Is in My Community? (p. 1827)
Rebman, Renée C. Anatomy of an Earthquake (p. 79)
Rebman, Renee C. Are You Doing Risky Things? Cutting, Bingeing, Snorting, & Other Dangers. (p. 113)
Rebman, Renee C. & Barrett, Tracy. Cats. (p. 345)
—Cows. (p. 464)
—How Do Tornadoes Form? (p. 1029)
—Rats. (p. 1843)
—Vultures. (p. 2369)
Rebmann, Chad & Nicholas, Matt. Relics of Youth Volume 1. Wassel, Adrian F. & Booher, David M., eds. (p. 1863)
Rebora, Cecilia, illus. see Achor, Shawn & Blankson, Amy.
Rebora, Cecilia, illus. see Casale, Karen.
Rebora, Cecilia, illus. see Gadot, A. S.
Reboucas, Thalita. Hada Me Vino a Visitar. (p. 909)
Rebscher, Susanne. Julio César. Schleper, Frank, tr. from GER. (p. 1187)
—Where's the Architect: From Pyramids to Skyscrapers. an Architecture Look & Find Book. Von Sperber, Annabelle, illus. (p. 2440)
Rebus, Anna. PiedsNoirs: Les Autochtones du Canada. Karvonen, Tanjah, tr. from ENG. (p. 1742)
Rebus, Anna & Kissock, Heather. Blackfoot. (p. 240)
Recall. Drownin University a Fresh Year. (p. 606)
Recaman, Bernardo. Jugar con Mas Numeros. (p. 1186)
Recasens, Elena, tr. see Vail, Rachel.
Recast, Margot. Luna de Vainilla. (p. 1368)
Recchioni, Robert. Orphans: The Beginning. Vol. 1 (p. 1672)
Rech, Lindsay Faith. It Started with a Dare. (p. 1142)
Recheis, Käthe. Lisa y el Gato Sin Nombre. (p. 1308)
Rechenberg, Mary Koeberl. Barney Big Ears: Learns a Lesson about Friendship. (p. 167)
—How Do I Know God Loves Me? Buchheit, Barbie, illus. (p. 1028)
Recher, Andrew, illus. see Stewart, Melissa.
Recher, Andrew, illus. see Vogel, Julia.
Rechin, Kevin. Guess Again! 1,001 Rib-Tickling Riddles from Highlights. (p. 902)
Rechin, Kevin, illus. see Coyle, Carmela Lavigna.
Rechin, Kevin, illus. see Winter, Max.
Rechlin. Dino Babies! (p. 547)
Rechlin, Ted. Build Your Own Giant Robots Super Sticker Book. (p. 293)
—ComicQuest TIME TRAVEL TROUBLE. (p. 430)
—Howl: A New Look at the Big Bad Wolf. (p. 1047)
—Superheroes! (p. 2160)
—Superheroes Stained Glass Coloring Book. (p. 2160)
—What to Doodle? Manga! (p. 2421)
Rechlin, Ted & Coloring Books Staff. Build a Poster Coloring Book—Robots & Wreckage. (p. 293)
Rechlin, Ted & Paper Dolls. Robot Battle Paper Action Figures. (p. 1892)
Rechlin, Ted & Stickers. Mecha Robot Stickers. (p. 1435)
Rechner, Amy. Afghanistan. (p. 31)
—Astronaut. (p. 128)
—Baseball Player. (p. 169)
—Cuba. (p. 482)

Reed, Leslie. Netop, Vol. 7: December, 1926 (Classic Reprint) (p. 1589)
Reed, Linda Davis, illus. see Snavlin, Joyce Burgess.
Reed, Lisa, illus. see Bostrom, Kathleen Long.
Reed, Lisa, illus. see Jeffress, Robert.
Reed, Lisa, illus. see Kennedy, Pamela & Brady, Anne Kennedy.
Reed, Lisa, illus. see Kennedy, Pamela.
Reed, Lisa, illus. see Moredock, Rebekah.
Reed, Lisa, illus. see Thomas, M. J.
Reed, Lisa, illus. see Traditional.
Reed, Lisa, illus. see VeggieTales.
Reed, Liz & Reed, Jimmy. Sweet Competition. Reed, Liz & Reed, Jimmy, illus. (p. 2168)
—Sweet Success. Reed, Liz & Reed, Jimmy, illus. (p. 2169)
Reed, Lucas Albert. My Garden Neighbors: True Stories of Nature's Children (Classic Reprint) (p. 1548)
Reed, Lynn Rowe. Bear's Big Breakfast. Helquist, Brett, illus. (p. 180)
—Benny Shark Goes to Friend School. Montijo, Rhode, illus. (p. 200)
—Fireman Fred. (p. 734)
—Fireman Fred. Reed, Lynn Rowe, illus. (p. 734)
—Shark Kiss, Octopus Hug. Cornell, Kevin, illus. (p. 2002)
Reed, Lynn Rowe, illus. see Pulver, Robin.
Reed, M. K. Americus. Hill, Jonathan, illus. (p. 75)
—Dinosaurs: Fossils & Feathers. Flood, Joe, illus. (p. 550)
—Science Comics: Dinosaurs: Fossils & Feathers. Flood, Joe, illus. (p. 1954)
—Science Comics: Wild Weather: Storms, Meteorology, & Climate. Hill, Jonathan, illus. (p. 1954)
Reed, M. K. & Smith, Brian "Smitty". Castoffs Vol. 2: Into the Wastelands. Yates, Wyeth, illus. (p. 340)
—Castoffs Vol. 3: Rise of the Machines. Yates, Wyeth, illus. (p. 340)
Reed, Margery Verner. Under-Currents (Classic Reprint) (p. 2321)
Reed, Melody. Goo Disaster (p. 861)
—Major Eights 1: Battle of the Bands. Pépin, Émilie, illus. (p. 1385)
—Major Eights 2: Scarlet's Big Break. Pépin, Émilie, illus. (p. 1385)
—Major Eights 3: the Goo Disaster! Pépin, Émilie, illus. (p. 1385)
—Major Eights 4: Starstruck. Pépin, Émilie, illus. (p. 1385)
—Major Eights 5: the New Bandmate. Pépin, Émilie, illus. (p. 1385)
—New Bandmate (p. 1591)
—Starstruck (p. 2107)
Reed, Michael. Amazing Vegetables. (p. 66)
—Bongo Beats News. (p. 256)
—Hey Dude. (p. 964)
—Magnificent Dancing Circle Snails. Calendar Snails! (p. 1382)
—Our Insect Helpers: Hunters & Pollinators. (p. 1678)
—Why the World Needs Fungi? a Coloring Book. (p. 2459)
Reed, Mike, illus. see Clements, Andrew.
Reed, Mike, illus. see Kilgras, Heidi.
Reed, Mike, illus. see Myers, Tim & Myers, Tim J.
Reed, Mike, illus. see Nolan, Lucy.
Reed, Mike, illus. see Sauer, Tammi.
Reed, Mike, illus. see Williams-Garcia, Rita.
Reed, Mvrtle. Lavender & Old Lace (Classic Reprint) (p. 1253)
Reed, Myra G. Jinks & Betty (Classic Reprint) (p. 1169)
Reed, Myrtle. At the Sign of the Jack o' Lantern (Classic Reprint) (p. 131)
—Book of Clever Beasts: Studies in Unnatural History (Classic Reprint) (p. 258)
—Flower of the Dusk (Classic Reprint) (p. 752)
—Lavender & Old Lace (Classic Reprint) (p. 1253)
—Master of the Vineyard (Classic Reprint) (p. 1418)
—Master's Violin (Classic Reprint) (p. 1420)
—Old Rose & Silver (Classic Reprint) (p. 1648)
—Shadow of Victory a Romance of Fort Dearborn (Classic Reprint) (p. 1997)
—Spinner in the Sun (Classic Reprint) (p. 2082)
—Threads of Grey & Gold (Classic Reprint) (p. 2231)
—Weaver of Dreams (Classic Reprint) (p. 2394)
—White Shield: Stories (Classic Reprint) (p. 2445)
Reed, Nan Terrell. Prose & Poems (Classic Reprint) (p. 1807)
Reed, Nathan, illus. see Brisenden, Rhys.
Reed, Nathan, illus. see Friel, Maeve.
Reed, Nathan, illus. see McAllister, Angela.
Reed, Nathan, illus. see Mitchell, Kita.
Reed, Nathan, illus. see Tsang, Katie & Tsang, Kevin.
Reed, Nathan, jt. auth. see Emmett, Jonathan.
Reed, Nathan, jt. auth. see Sykes, Julie.
Reed, Neil, illus. see Shone, Rob.
Reed, Philip, illus. see Parkin, Jessica.
Reed, Phillip, illus. see Parkin, Jessica.
Reed, Rebecca Harrison, illus. see Plourde, Lynn.
Reed, Rebecca Perley. Story of Our Forbears (Classic Reprint) (p. 2132)
Reed, Riley. Squirrelia. (p. 2095)
Reed, Robert. Naturetopolis. (p. 1582)
Reed, Sam. Fair to Hope. (p. 695)
Reed, Sarah A. Romance of Arlington House (Classic Reprint) (p. 1900)
Reed, Stephen, illus. see Lewman, David.
Reed, Susan. Up, up, Up! Oldfield, Rachel, illus. (p. 2338)
Reed, Susan, illus. see McDonald, Jill.
Reed, Susan, illus. see Mehrabi, Jacqueline.
Reed, Susan, illus. see Oldfield, Rachel.
Reed, Susan Kent. Beatrice the Hip-Hop Bee. (p. 183)
Reed, Susannah, et al. Guess What! American English Level 2 Student's Book. (p. 902)
Reed, Talbot Baines. Roger Ingleton- Minor. (p. 1897)
—Willoughby Captains (Classic Reprint) (p. 2469)
Reed, Thomas Benton. Private in Gray (Classic Reprint) (p. 1801)
Reed, Troy. Across the Border. (p. 11)
Reed, Verbena. Bird-Nest: Boarding House (Classic Reprint) (p. 230)
Reed, Verner Z. Adobeland Stories (Classic Reprint) (p. 16)
Reeder, A. P. Around the Golden Deep: A Romance of the Sierras (Classic Reprint) (p. 118)
Reeder, Amy & Montclare, Brandon. BFF #5: Know How. Bustos, Natacha & Bonvillain, Tamra, illus. (p. 212)
—Eureka! Bustos, Natacha & Bonvillain, Tamra, illus. (p. 667)
—'Nuff Said. Bustos, Natacha & Bonvillain, Tamra, illus. (p. 1629)
—Old Dogs & New Tricks. Bustos, Natacha & Bonvillain, Tamra, illus. (p. 1645)
—Out of the Frying Pan... Bustos, Natacha & Bonvillain, Tamra, illus. (p. 1683)
—Repeat after Me. Bustos, Natacha & Bonvillain, Tamra, illus. (p. 1866)
Reeder, Eric. Charleston. (p. 359)
—Farming Dogs. (p. 711)
—Minority Soldiers Fighting in the American Revolution. (p. 1473)
—Sinkholes. (p. 2024)
Reeder, Jayci, illus. see Driscoll, Stephanie.
Reeder, Marilou. Daring Prince Dashing. West, Karl, illus. (p. 505)
—Willow the Armadillo. Mottram, Dave, illus. (p. 2469)
Reeder, Marty. How to Become a Pirate Hunter. (p. 1038)
Reeder, R. Chris. Changeling's Daughter. (p. 356)
Reedpen, Peregrine. Our Town, or Rough Sketches of Character, Manners, &C, Vol. 2 of 2 (Classic Reprint) (p. 1681)
—Our Town, Vol. 1 Of 2: Or, Rough Sketches of Character, Manners, &C (Classic Reprint) (p. 1681)
Reeds, Alice. Echoes. (p. 623)
Reed-Tichenor, Susan. Christmas Snowflake. (p. 386)
Reedy, E. L. & Wade, A. M. Upon Broken Wings. (p. 2338)
Reedy, Trent. Burning Nation. (p. 300)
—Divided We Fall. (p. 566)
—Divided We Fall (Divided We Fall Trilogy, Book 1) (p. 566)
—Gamer Army. (p. 807)
—Last Full Measure. (p. 1247)
—Words in the Dust. (p. 2494)
Reef, Catherine. Arthur Miller. (p. 122)
—Brontë Sisters: The Brief Lives of Charlotte, Emily, & Anne. (p. 285)
—Florence Nightingale: The Courageous Life of the Legendary Nurse. (p. 751)
—Frida & Diego: Art, Love, Life. (p. 785)
—Leonard Bernstein & American Music. (p. 1267)
—Life of Paul Laurence Dunbar: Portrait of a Poet. (p. 1295)
—Mary Shelley: The Strange True Tale of Frankenstein's Creator. (p. 1416)
—Noah Webster: Man of Many Words. (p. 1616)
—Poetry Came in Search of Me: The Story of Pablo Neruda. (p. 1767)
—Sarah Bernhardt: The Divine & Dazzling Life of the World's First Superstar. (p. 1935)
—Victoria: Portrait of a Queen. (p. 2355)
Reeg, Cynthia. From the Grave. (p. 793)
—Hamster Holidays: Noun & Adjective Adventures. Grady, Kit, illus. (p. 914)
—Into the Shadowlands. (p. 1128)
Reehorst, Jane. Guided Meditations for Children. (p. 904)
Reekles, Beth. Kissing Booth. (p. 1224)
Reely, Mary Katharine. Daily Bread: A Window to the South; the Lean Years, One-Act Plays (Classic Reprint) (p. 495)
—Early Ohios & Rhode Islands Reds: A Comedy in One Act (Classic Reprint) (p. 615)
Rees, Abraham. Cyclopædia, or Universal Dictionary of Arts, Science & Literature, Vol. 8 of 39 (Classic Reprint) (p. 493)
Rees, Alfred W. Creatures of the Night: A Book of Wild Life in Western Britain (Classic Reprint) (p. 472)
Rees, Alfred Wellesley. Heron of Castle Creek: And Other Sketches of Bird Life (Classic Reprint) (p. 963)
Rees, Arthur J. Moon Rock (Classic Reprint) (p. 1502)
Rees, Bob. Civil War (p. 396)
Rees, Brennan. Nuit des Demons. (p. 1629)
Rees Brennan, Sarah. Demon's Covenant. (p. 528)
—Season of the Witch (Chilling Adventures of Sabrina: Netflix Tie-In Novel) (p. 1972)
—Untold (the Lynburn Legacy Book 2) (p. 2336)
Rees Brennan, Sarah, et al. Shadowhunters Short Story Paperback Collection: The Bane Chronicles; Tales from the Shadowhunter Academy; Ghosts of the Shadow Market. (p. 1997)
Rees, Celia. Sovay. (p. 2070)
—Tear Jar: Band 18/Pearl (Collins Big Cat) (p. 2196)
—This Is Not Forgiveness. (p. 2225)
Rees, Christine. Broken Rivalry. (p. 285)
—Hidden Legacy. (p. 966)
Rees, Claude A. Chun Ti-Kung: His Life & Adventures. a Novel. (p. 390)
—Chun Ti-Kung: His Life & Adventures; a Novel (Classic Reprint) (p. 390)
Rees, Douglas. Buttercup the Bigfoot. Munoz, Isabel, illus. (p. 303)
—Elektra's Adventures in Tragedy. (p. 632)
—Jeannette Claus Saves Christmas. Latyk, Olivier, illus. (p. 1162)
—Tyrannosaurus Rex vs. Edna the Very First Chicken. (p. 2311)
—Uncle Pirate to the Rescue. Auth, Tony, illus. (p. 2318)
—Vampire High. (p. 2346)
Rees, Ennis. Lions & Lobsters & Foxes & Frogs: Fables from Aesop. Gorey, Edward, illus. (p. 1307)
Rees, Guy Parker. Tom & Millie: Whizzy Busy People. (p. 2257)
Rees, Gwyneth. Rani's Sea Spell: a Rani Book 2. (p. 1841)
—Shell Princess: a Rani Book 3. (p. 2005)
—Something Secret. (p. 2060)
Rees, James. Mysteries of City Life, or Stray Leaves from the World's Book: Being a Series of Tales, Sketches, Incidents, & Scenes Founded upon the Notes of a Home Missionary (Classic Reprint) (p. 1566)
Rees, L. L. We Four: Where We Went & What We Saw in Europe (Classic Reprint) (p. 2390)
Rees, Leighton J. Denzil the Hard-Nosed Reindeer. (p. 529)
Rees, Lexi. Book Dragon Club. (p. 257)
—Creative Writing Skills: Over 70 Fun Activities for Children. (p. 471)
—Eternal Seas. (p. 665)
—Laboratorio Di Scrittura Creativa. (p. 1235)
Rees, Mary, illus. see Oram, Hiawyn.
Rees, Peter. Why Do Crocodiles Snap? Level 3 Factbook. (p. 2456)
—Why Do Raindrops Fall? Level 3 Factbook. (p. 2456)
—Why Do Swings Swing? Level 4 Factbook. (p. 2457)
—Why Does Water Freeze? Level 3 Factbook. (p. 2457)
Rees, Rob. Backyard Cookbook. (p. 156)
Rees, Robbins. God in My World! (p. 851)
Rees, Robert. Owen Tanat: A Story of Welsh Life (Classic Reprint) (p. 1688)
Rees, Rosemary. Lake of Enchantment (Classic Reprint) (p. 1240)
—Sing a Song of Sydney: A Novel (Classic Reprint) (p. 2023)
—Wild, Wild Heart (Classic Reprint) (p. 2465)
Reese, Albert Moore. Introduction to Vertebrate Embryology: Based on the Study of the Frog & the Chick (Classic Reprint) (p. 1129)
Reese, Annie Eloise. What Was That? A Story of Intrigue & Fascination for Young Children. (p. 2421)
Reese, Bob, illus. see Karapetkova, Holly & Picou, Lin.
Reese, Bob, illus. see Karapetkova, Holly & Robins, Maureen.
Reese, Bob, illus. see Moreta, Gladys & Picou, Lin.
Reese, Bob, illus. see Picou, Lin.
Reese, Bob, illus. see Robbins, Maureen & Steinkraus, Kyla.
Reese, Bob, illus. see Robbins, Maureen.
Reese, Bob, illus. see Steinkraus, Kyla.
Reese, Brandon. Cave Dada. (p. 347)
—Draw Me Healthy! Reese, Brandon, illus. (p. 598)
—Oothar the Blue. (p. 1665)
Reese, Brandon, illus. see Charlesworth, Liza.
Reese, Brandon, illus. see Flash Kids Editors, ed.
Reese, Brandon, illus. see Okee Dokee Brothers Staff.
Reese, Jeff, photos by see Feeney, Stephanie & Moravcik, Eva.
Reese, Jenn. Above World. (p. 7)
—Game of Fox & Squirrels. (p. 807)
—Horizon. (p. 1003)
—Mirage. (p. 1475)
Reese, Jon. Critical World Issues: Drugs (p. 476)
Reese, Jonathan, illus. see Taylor, Trace, et al.
Reese, Lulu T. Winnowing: Drama in Five Acts (Classic Reprint) (p. 2474)
Reese Martin, Faith. Ghost Train to Freedom: An Adventure on the Underground Railroad. Sachs, Barry, illus. (p. 828)
Reese, Mary. Bio 1023 Plants & Humans: Note-Taking Manual. (p. 228)
Reese, Nia Mya. Bully at School: A Bully's Perspective. (p. 296)
—Sore Loser: (don't Be One!) G, D., illus. (p. 2065)
—Sore Loser (Don't Be One!) Coloring Book. G, D., illus. (p. 2065)
Reese, Rick, illus. see Markel, Michelle.
Reese, Sarah Simons. Little Poem Book (Classic Reprint) (p. 1324)
Reese, Shalonda. Barton Street Kids: Meet the Ellies. (p. 168)
Reese, Steven, tr. see Manzano, Roberto.
Reese, Tanna. How Rocko's Escape Turned to an Adventure. (p. 1035)
Reeser, Anna Mae. Ruby & Ralph Take a Chance. Fox, Carolyn a, illus. (p. 1911)
Rees-Jones, Paul. Silly Animal World! (p. 2018)
Reeve, Arthur B. Constance Dunlap (Classic Reprint) (p. 443)
—Guy Garrick (Classic Reprint) (p. 906)
—Romance of Elaine (Classic Reprint) (p. 1900)
Reeve, Clara. Fatherless Fanny, or a Young Lady's First Entrance into Life: Being the Memoirs of a Little Mendicant & Her Benefactors (Classic Reprint) (p. 714)
—Memoirs of Sir Roger de Clarendon, the Natural Son of Edward, Prince of Wales, Commonly Called the Black Prince: With Anecdotes of Many Other Eminent Persons of the Fourteenth Century (Classic Reprint) (p. 1445)
—Memoirs of Sir Roger de Clarendon, the Natural Son of Edward, Prince of Wales, Commonly Called the Black Prince, Vol. 1 Of 3: With Anecdotes of Many Other Eminent Persons of the Fourteenth Century (Classic Reprint) (p. 1445)
—Old English Baron: A Gothic Story (Classic Reprint) (p. 1645)
—School for Widows, Vol. 1 Of 3: A Novel (Classic Reprint) (p. 1946)
—Two Mentors: A Modern Story (Classic Reprint) (p. 2308)
Reeve, Elizabeth. Sassy: the short stories of being a service Dog. (p. 1936)
Reeve, Elizabeth, jt. auth. see Verdick, Elizabeth.
Reeve, J. Stanley. Rhubarb: The Diary of a Gentleman's Hunter (Classic Reprint) (p. 1875)
Reeve, Kirk. Sun Father, Corn Mother: A Novel. (p. 2151)
Reeve, Penny. God Made Something Beautiful. (p. 852)
—God Made Something Clever. (p. 852)
—God Made Something Strong. (p. 852)
Reeve, Philip. Black Light Express. (p. 238)
—Cakes in Space. McIntyre, Sarah, illus. (p. 309)
—Carnival in a Fix. McIntyre, Sarah, illus. (p. 332)
—Darkling Plain. (p. 507)
—Fever Crumb (p. 722)
—Goblins. (p. 850)
—Here Lies Arthur. (p. 958)
—Infernal Devices. (p. 1118)
—Machinations Infernales. (p. 1372)
—Mortal Engines. (p. 1507)
—Night Flights: A Mortal Engines Collection. McQue, Ian, illus. (p. 1605)
—No Such Thing As Dragons. (p. 1615)
—Oliver & the Sea Monkeys. McIntyre, Sarah, illus. (p. 1649)
—Oliver & the Seawigs. McIntyre, Sarah, illus. (p. 1649)
—Predator's Gold. (p. 1787)
—Pugs of the Frozen North. McIntyre, Sarah, illus. (p. 1812)
—Railhead. (p. 1835)
—Station Zero. (p. 2109)
—Web of Air Seife, Emily, ed. (p. 2395)
Reeve, Philip, illus. see d'Lacey, Chris.
Reeve, Philip, jt. auth. see Poskitt, Kjartan.
Reeve, Rosie. To Grandma, with Love. (p. 2252)
Reeve, Rosie, illus. see Oram, Hiawyn.
Reeve, Rosie, illus. see Symes, Ruth Louise.
Reeve, Sophia. Mysterious Wanderer, Vol. 1 Of 3: A Novel (Classic Reprint) (p. 1568)
Reeve, Terry. Nora & the Black Dog of Bungay. (p. 1619)
Reeve, Tony, illus. see Oliver, Martin.
Reeve, Tony, tr. see Oliver, Martin.
Reeve, Wybert. Not So Bad after All: An Original Comedy in Three Acts (Classic Reprint) (p. 1623)
—Romance of Reality, or Tales from a Wanderer's Diary (Classic Reprint) (p. 1900)
Reeves, Alice. Carlos the Chameleon: A Story to Help Empower Children to Be Themselves. Kirk, Phoebe, illus. (p. 332)
—Molly the Mole: A Story to Help Children Build Self-Esteem. Kirk, Phoebe, illus. (p. 1489)
—Vincent the Vixen: A Story to Help Children Learn about Gender Identity. Kirk, Phoebe, illus. (p. 2359)
Reeves, Arthur M. Lad & Lass: A Story of Life in Iceland; Translated from the Icelandic (Classic Reprint) (p. 1235)
—Lad & Lass: A Story of Life in Iceland. Translated from the Icelandic of Jon Pordarson Thoroddsen. (p. 1236)
Reeves, Arthur Middleton. Lad & Lass: A Story of Life in Iceland; Translated from the Icelandic (Classic Reprint) (p. 1235)
Reeves, Daniel. Sisters of the Forest. (p. 2027)
Reeves, Daniel M. Fairy Tale of the Wishing Well. (p. 697)
Reeves, Dia. Bleeding Violet. (p. 243)
—Slice of Cherry. (p. 2038)
Reeves, Diane Lindsey. Architecture & Construction. (p. 111)
—Find Your Future in Science. (p. 728)
—Find Your Future in Technology. (p. 728)
—Food & Natural Resources. (p. 759)
—Get a Job at the Grocery Store. (p. 823)
—Get a Job at the Shoping Mall. (p. 823)
—Glamorous Jobs. (p. 841)
—Goofy Jobs. (p. 869)
—Gross Jobs. (p. 898)
—Gutsy Jobs. (p. 906)
—Health Sciences. (p. 943)
—Information Technology. (p. 1119)
—Law & Public Safety. (p. 1253)
—Making Choices at Home. (p. 1388)
—Making Choices at School. (p. 1388)
—Making Choices for My Healthy Body. (p. 1388)
—Making Choices in My Community. (p. 1388)
—Making Choices on My Team. (p. 1388)
—Making Choices with Friends. (p. 1388)
—Manufacturing. (p. 1399)
—Stem. (p. 2113)
—Transportation. (p. 2278)
—Way Out Work Set, 6-Volumes. (p. 2387)
Reeves, Diane Lindsey & Gunzenhauser, Kelly. Career Ideas for Teens in Marketing. (p. 328)
Reeves, Diane Lindsey & Karlitz, Gail. Information Technology. (p. 1119)
Reeves, Diane Lindsey & Kelley, K. C. Choose Your Own Career Adventure at the Olympics. (p. 381)
—Choose Your Own Career Adventure at the Super Bowl. (p. 381)
Reeves, Diane Lindsey & White, Kelly. Choose Your Own Career Adventure at the White House. (p. 381)
Reeves, Eira. Jesus & Me Every Day Book 1 (p. 1165)
—Would You Like to Know Jesus? Jefferson, Graham, illus. (p. 2510)
Reeves, Eira, illus. see Dowley, Tim & Jefferson, Graham.
Reeves, Eira, illus. see Dowley, Tim, et al.
Reeves, Eira, illus. see Dowley, Tim.
Reeves, Eira, jt. auth. see Dowley, Tim.
Reeves Gibbons, Maria. What about Us? (p. 2404)
Reeves, Jeni, illus. see Brown, Susan Taylor.
Reeves, Jeni, illus. see Douglass, Susan L.
Reeves, Jeni, illus. see Fishman, Cathy Goldberg.
Reeves, Jeni, illus. see Krensky, Stephen.
Reeves, Jeni, illus. see Patrick, Jean L. S.
Reeves, Jeni, illus. see Ransom, Candice.
Reeves, Jeni, illus. see Zemlicka, Shannon.
Reeves, Jordan & Reeves, Jen Lee. Born Just Right. (p. 263)
Reeves, Marian C. L. Pilot Fortune (Classic Reprint) (p. 1745)
Reeves, Marian Calhoun Legare. Ingemisco (Classic Reprint) (p. 1119)
Reeves, Pamela. United We Stand, a Story about Two Bullies. LaGrange, Tiffany, illus. (p. 2332)
Reeves, Patrick, jt. auth. see Madlener, Michael.
Reeves, Pauline, illus. see Fehr, Daniel.
Reeves, Pauline, illus. see Steele, Michael Anthony.
Reeves, Ruth, illus. see Cooper, Paul Fenimore.
Reeves, Tara McClary, jt. auth. see Jenkins, Amanda.
Reeves, Thomas. I Had a Cat. (p. 1065)
Reeves, William P., jt. auth. see Rydberg, Viktor.
Reference, Brown. Exploring the World of Reptiles & Amphibians, 6-Volume Set (p. 684)
Reflections Notebooks & Journals. I Can Be a Writer Children's Creative Journal. (p. 1061)
—Universal Notes Book: Journal & Planner Edition. (p. 2332)
Regalia Stankey, Linda. Saying Good-Bye. (p. 1940)
Regan, Anne, ed. see Ames, Arbour, et al.
Regan, Anne, ed. First Time for Everything. (p. 740)
—Harmonious Hearts. (p. 931)
—Harmonious Hearts 2015. (p. 931)
—Harmonious Hearts 2016: Stories from the Young Author Challenge. (p. 931)
Regan, Dana, illus. see Berry, Joy.
Regan, Dana, illus. see Ellis, Gwen.
Regan, Dana, illus. see Grant, Jim & Grant, Caleb.
Regan, Dana, illus. see Harkrader, Lisa.
Regan, Dana, illus. see Hillert, Margaret & Collodi, Carlo.
Regan, Dana, illus. see Hillert, Margaret, et al.
Regan, Dana, illus. see Hillert, Margaret.
Regan, Dana, illus. see Hillman, Emilee.
Regan, Dana, illus. see Hillman, Emilie.
Regan, Dana, illus. see Hoena, Blake.
Regan, Dana, illus. see Kennedy, Nancy B.
Regan, Dana, illus. see Kesselring, Susan.

Regan, Dana, illus. see McKissack, Patricia C. & McKissack, Fredrick L.
Regan, Dana, illus. see Moncure, Jane Belk.
Regan, Dana, illus. see Rosa-Mendoza, Gladys.
Regan, Dana, illus. see Silverman, Buffy.
Regan, Dana, illus. see StJohn, Amanda.
Regan, Dana, illus. see Warner, Sally.
Regan, Dian. Dragon Stone Curtis, Stacy, illus. (p. 594)
—Snow Blew Inn. Cushman, Doug, illus. (p. 2047)
—Space Boy & the Snow Monster. Neubecker, Robert, illus. (p. 2071)
Regan, Dian Curtis. Space Boy & His Dog. Neubecker, Robert, illus. (p. 2071)
—Space Boy & the Space Pirate. Neubecker, Robert, illus. (p. 2071)
Regan Gregson, Susan. Cyber Literacy: Evaluating the Reliability of Data. (p. 492)
Regan, John. Emigrant's Guide: To the Western States of America; or, Backwoods & Prairies (Classic Reprint) (p. 641)
Regan, Laura, illus. see Fredericks, Anthony D.
Regan, Laura, illus. see Marzollo, Jean.
Regan, Lisa. Animal Riddles. (p. 91)
—Awesome Women Activity Book. Wright, Louise, illus. (p. 145)
—Ballet Dancer. (p. 162)
—Biology Is Wild. (p. 229)
—Brain Boosters: Math Puzzles. (p. 274)
—Brain Boosters: Memory Puzzles. Wood, Steven, illus. (p. 274)
—Broadway Star. (p. 284)
—Bugs. Roberts, Steve, illus. (p. 292)
—Chemistry Is Explosive. (p. 365)
—Circus Performer. (p. 393)
—Cool Kid's Field Guide to Space. Bull, Peter, illus. (p. 449)
—Cool Kid's Field Guide to Weather. Hutchinson, Tim, illus. (p. 449)
—Crazy Critters Joke Book (p. 469)
—Dippy Dinosaur Joke Book (p. 552)
—Don't Be Sad, Sam: It's Ok. (p. 582)
—Don't Get Angry, Annie: Stay Calm. (p. 583)
—Farm Animals. Thompson, Kim, illus. (p. 709)
—Farmyard Riddles. (p. 711)
—Flashlight Explorers: Animals at Night. (p. 747)
—Fluttering Fairies Activity Fun. (p. 753)
—Funniest Joke Book Ever. (p. 801)
—Glow down Deep: Amazing Creatures That Light Up. (p. 845)
—Haunted Hotel: Solve Its Mysteries! (p. 938)
—Hilarious Jokes for Kids: 3 Books Packed with Jokes, Wisecracks, & Riddles (p. 971)
—Horses. Jackson, Ian, illus. (p. 1005)
—Human Body Is Awesome: 101 Incredible Things Every Kid Should Know. (p. 1049)
—Inca Adventure: A Quest of Questions! (p. 1112)
—Knock Knock Joke Book (p. 1229)
—Kooky Kitchen Joke Book (p. 1231)
—Let's Explore the Dinosaur World: Includes a Slot-Together 3-D Model! Jefferys, Rhys, illus. (p. 1272)
—Lunchtime Riddles. (p. 1369)
—Magician. (p. 1381)
—Mind-Blowing Math. Jefferys, Rhys, illus. (p. 1469)
—Monster Laughs Joke Book (p. 1496)
—Monster Puzzles. (p. 1497)
—Movie Star. (p. 1516)
—My Crazy Inventions Sketchbook: 50 Awesome Drawing Activities for Young Inventors. Rae, Andrew, illus. (p. 1536)
—Nature at Night. (p. 1580)
—No Hitting, Henry: Don't Hurt. (p. 1613)
—Physics Is Out of This World. (p. 1738)
—Planet Earth Is Awesome. (p. 1755)
—Pop Star. (p. 1775)
—Puzzle Ponies Activity Fun. (p. 1818)
—Ridiculous Riddles Joke Book (p. 1878)
—Supercharged Science. Jefferys, Rhys, illus. (p. 2159)
—Super-Cute Baby Animals Activity Book. Loman, Sam, illus. (p. 2154)
—Super-Cute Kittens & Puppies Activity Book. Loman, Sam, illus. (p. 2154)
—Treasure Hunt: Find the Fortune! (p. 2281)
—Underwater Riddles. (p. 2326)
—Wait Your Turn, Tilly: Be Patient. (p. 2370)
—Whizz Kidz: Mazes. (p. 2446)
Regan, Lisa, illus. see Elliot, Rachel.
Regan, Lisa, jt. auth. see Enright, Amanda.
Regan, Lisa, jt. auth. see Loman, Sam.
Regan, Lisa, jt. auth. see Phillips, Dave.
Regan, Lisa & Harman, Alice. Space Is Awesome: 101 Incredible Things Every Kid Should Know. (p. 2071)
—Technology Is Awesome! 101 Incredible Things Every Kid Should Know. (p. 2197)
Regan, Lisa & Webb, Trudi. Caveman Capers Activity Fun. Green, Barry, illus. (p. 347)
—Magical Fairies Activity Fun. Green, Barry, illus. (p. 1380)
—Pirates Ahoy! Activity Fun. Green, Barry, illus. (p. 1750)
—Playful Ponies Activity Fun. Green, Barry, illus. (p. 1760)
Regan, Lisa Regan & Chiacchiera, Moreno. Puzzle Quest. (p. 1818)
Regan, Michael. Bad Days in Science & Invention. (p. 157)
—Bringing Back Our Tundra. (p. 282)
—Cost of College. (p. 457)
—Gardner Museum Heist. (p. 809)
—George Washington & the American Presidency. (p. 820)
—Great Chicago Fire: A Cause-And-Effect Investigation. (p. 884)
—Samsung. (p. 1928)
—Understanding Sikhism. (p. 2325)
—Vladimir Putin: President of Russia. (p. 2364)
Regan, Michael, jt. auth. see Higgins, Melissa.
Regan, Patricia. Little Christmas Tree: Open & Stand up the Tree! (p. 1314)
—Musical Christmas Tree. (p. 1529)
Regan, Patrick. Marvelous Monsters Talent Show. Bonson, Tom, illus. (p. 1413)
—Nutcracker. Kuricheva, Natasha, illus. (p. 1632)
Regan, Peter. Riverside: Exit Point. (p. 1887)
Regas, Ricard & Cañagueral, Albert. Secrets of Ancient Ritual Sites: The Citadel of Machu Picchu & Stonehenge. (p. 1980)
Rege Jr., Rob. Weaver Festival Phenomenon. (p. 2394)
Regensburg, Jill. Runaway Dandelion: Adventures in Sustainability. (p. 1915)
Reger, Rob. Emily & the Strangers Volume 2: Breaking the Record Farris, Cat, illus. (p. 642)
—Emily the Strange Volume 3: the 13th Hour. (p. 642)
Reger, Rob & Gruner, Jessica. Emily the Strange: Dark Times. Reger, Rob & Parker, Buzz, illus. (p. 642)
—Emily the Strange: Piece of Mind. Reger, Rob & Parker, Buzz, illus. (p. 642)
—Emily the Strange: Stranger & Stranger. Reger, Rob & Parker, Buzz, illus. (p. 642)
Regholec, C. A. T. Elephant That Forgot to Remember. (p. 634)
Regier, Melanie B., illus. see Cook, Mindy.
Regin, Andrew. Guardians: Volume 1. (p. 901)
Reginelli, Nina. Geraldine's Rainy Day. (p. 821)
Region, United States. Geographical And. Contributions to North American Ethnology, Vol. 3 (Classic Reprint) (p. 445)
Regis, Natalie. Genetically Modified Crops & Food. (p. 815)
—NASCAR & Its Greatest Drivers (p. 1576)
Regis, Natalie, jt. auth. see Chiu, David.
Regis, Natalie & Chiu, David. Insider's Guide to Wrestling (p. 1124)
Register, F. M. Caswell News, Vol. 1: March, 1936 (Classic Reprint) (p. 341)
Register, J. R., illus. see Simpon, Tj.
Regnaud, Paul. Chariot de Terre Cuite (Mricchakatika), Vol. 2: Drame Sanscrit Attribue Au Roi Cudraka, Traduit et Annote des Scolies Inedites de Lalla Dikshita (Classic Reprint) (p. 358)
Regnier, Guylaine, illus. see Ferre, Gil.
Regordosa, Adria. Dustrats: Or, the Adventures of Sir Muffin Muffinsson. (p. 611)
Regwan, Sol. Dylan & His Magical Robot. (p. 612)
—Dylan & His Magical Robot Dyslexic Edition: Dyslexic Font. (p. 612)
—Dylan & His Magical Robot Dyslexic Font. (p. 612)
—Geraldine & the Most Spectacular Science Project Muzzio, Denise, illus. (p. 821)
—Geraldine & the Space Bees. Muzzio, Denise, illus. (p. 821)
Reh, Rusalka. Pizzicato: The Abduction of the Magic Violin Wilson, David Henry, tr. (p. 1752)
—Secret of the Water Knight Derbyshire, Katy, tr. (p. 1978)
Rehahn, Manuela. Die Robinos - Sockenmonster: Oder Wie Kommen Die Locher in Die Strumpfe! (p. 544)
—Die Traurige Prinzessin. Rehahn, Manuela, illus. (p. 544)
—Fynn und der Kleine Drache: 2. Auflage... (p. 803)
—Robino ABC: Lernen Mit Den Sockenmonstern... (p. 1891)
Rehak, Jay. Sideline (Book One) (p. 2015)
Rehak, Jay C. Sideline Ink: (book Two) Motyashok, Iryna, illus. (p. 2015)
Rehak, Jay Carl. Sideline: Book One. (p. 2015)
Rehan, M., illus. see Bermudez, Jenna & Bermudez, Jasia.
Rehatsek, Edward. Amusing Stories: Translated from the Persian (Classic Reprint) (p. 77)
Rehberg, Emily. Thunder Is Not Scary. Craig, Branden Chapin & Chapin, Jimmy, illus. (p. 2238)
Reher, Matt. All about Beetles. (p. 48)
—All about Butterflies. (p. 48)
—All about Spiders. (p. 50)
—All Bees Have Jobs. (p. 51)
—Animals & Tools. (p. 94)
—Animals & Tools (FSTK) (p. 94)
—Animals Sleep in Lots of Ways (FSTK) (p. 95)
—Are You a Fish? (Big Book) (p. 113)
—Are You in My Family? (Big Book) (p. 113)
—Beetles Are Built Like Tanks. (p. 190)
—Blue Whale Babies. (p. 249)
—Book of Beetles. (p. 258)
—Book of Flies. (p. 258)
—Book of Sharks. (p. 259)
—Butterflies or Moths. (p. 303)
—Can You See the Beetle? (p. 319)
—Come in Here, Crocs! (p. 428)
—Could a Tiger Be My Pet? (p. 458)
—Dan Gets a Call. (p. 499)
—Dan Gets a Call (FSTK) (p. 499)
—Dan Gets a Cat. (p. 499)
—Dan Gets a Cat (FSTK) (p. 499)
—Desert Bugs. (p. 531)
—Farmers Like Barn Owls. (p. 711)
—Fish Eggs. (p. 741)
—Frogs & Toads. (p. 790)
—Frogs & Toads (Big Book) (p. 790)
—Grand Scam. (p. 877)
—Grand Scam, The (FSTK) (p. 877)
—Grasshoppers on the Go. (p. 881)
—Grasshoppers Sing. (p. 881)
—Hippos Eat. (p. 973)
—Hippos Eat (B & N) (p. 973)
—Hurricane Survival Guide. (p. 1054)
—I Grow Up. (p. 1065)
—Ladybug Babies. (p. 1238)
—Let's Quit (FSTK) (p. 1277)
—Life of a Mosquito. (p. 1293)
—Life on the Blue Planet. (p. 1295)
—Mosquito Moms. (p. 1507)
—My Pet Snake. (p. 1559)
—Orcas: The Wolves of the Seas. (p. 1669)
—Orcas Have to Eat. (p. 1669)
—Orcas Have to Eat (B & N) (p. 1669)
—Penguin Gets Away. (p. 1716)
—Savanna Teeth. (p. 1937)
—Sending a Letter. (p. 1988)
—She Wants to Be Queen. (p. 2004)
—Slam Bam Sam. (p. 2034)
—Slam Bam Sam (FSTK) (p. 2034)
—Some Animals Play Tricks. (p. 2058)
—Some Animals Play Tricks (FSTK) (p. 2058)
—Spiders Don't Suck Blood. (p. 2081)
—Sunflowers Grow (FSTK ONLY) (p. 2152)
—Swamp Bugs. (p. 2167)
—That's Fast! (p. 2213)
—Throwback: A Look at Sports (FSTK ONLY) (p. 2237)
—What Bug Is That? (p. 2406)
—What's So Good about Matt? (p. 2425)
—What's So Good about Matt? (FSTK) (p. 2425)
—When the Wolves Came Back. (p. 2433)
—When the Wolves Came Back (FSTK ONLY) (p. 2433)
—Who Can I Call? (p. 2446)
—Wolf Babies Eat. (p. 2483)
—Wolves Eat. (p. 2485)
—Wolves Eat (B & N) (p. 2485)
Reher, Matt, jt. auth. see Córdova, Alina Karam.
Reher, Matt, jt. auth. see Sánchez, Lucía M.
Reher, Matt & Taylor Fonzone. Top 10 Most Disgusting Facts about the Human Body. (p. 2262)
—Top 10 Most Disgusting Facts about the Human Body (FSTK ONLY) (p. 2262)
Rehman, Mina. Dead Girl Haunting. (p. 517)
Reiach, Margaret Amy, illus. see Kalman, Bobbie.
Reiach, Margaret Amy, illus. see MacAulay, Kelley & Kalman, Bobbie.
Reibeling, Brandon, illus. see Dahl, Michael & Moore, Mark.
Reibeling, Brandon, illus. see Loewen, Nancy.
Reibstein, Mark. Wabi Sabi. (p. 2369)
—Yugen. Young, Ed, illus. (p. 2536)
Reich, Austin. Adventures of the Lions in the Most Magical Place on Earth. Reich, Tyler, illus. (p. 28)
—Adventures of the Rabbits in the Magic Kingdom. Reich, Tyler, illus. (p. 28)
—Adventures of the Squirrels in Epcot. Reich, Tyler, illus. (p. 28)
Reich, Dale. Graham's Shiny Things. (p. 875)
—Noah's Neighbor. (p. 1616)
Reich, jennifer. When Miss Bluebird Died. (p. 2432)
Reich, Jonathan, illus. see Brennan, Matt.
Reich, Kass. Hamsters Holding Hands (p. 914)
—Hamsters on the Go (p. 914)
—This Little Hamster (p. 2226)
—Up Hamster, down Hamster (p. 2337)
Reich, Kass, illus. see Alary, Laura.
Reich, Kass, illus. see Bailey, Linda.
Reich, Kass, illus. see Hampson, Sarah.
Reich, Kass, illus. see Humphrey, Anna.
Reich, Kass, illus. see Messier, Mireille.
Reich, Kelly. If a Cat Could Talk. (p. 1090)
Reich, Kimberly. Adeline Armadillo & the Armor of God: The Bejeweled Belt of Truth. (p. 16)
—Glenda the Gardner & the Parable of the Sower. (p. 842)
—Heartwarming Happenings of Hildy Hi-Faloot: Kindling Kindness. (p. 946)
—Olivia the Ostrich Takes a Leap of Faith. (p. 1650)
Reich, Kimberly & Esposito, valentina. Awesome Antics of Ana-Laya: No Use Crying over Spilt Glue. (p. 144)
Reich, Robert E. Harry MacFly's the Old Mill Adventure. Reich, Robert E., illus. (p. 934)
Reich, Susanna. Minette's Feast: The Delicious Story of Julia Child & Her Cat. Bates, Amy, illus. (p. 1471)
—Stand up & Sing! Pete Seeger, Folk Music, & the Path to Justice. Gustavson, Adam, illus. (p. 2100)
Reich, Tina. Ella's Big Catch. Sukmanindya, Windha, illus. (p. 637)
—How Popo Got His Name. Hwan, Diandra, illus. (p. 1034)
Reich, Tyler, illus. see Reich, Austin.
Reichard, Susan E. Who on Earth Is Sylvia Earle? Undersea Explorer of the Ocean. (p. 2449)
Reichardt, Marisa. Bajo el Agua. (p. 159)
Reichel London, Rachel R. Time Capsule Diary. (p. 2244)
Reichel, Tammi, tr. see Röder, Marlene.
Reichel, Tammi, tr. see Schrocke, Kathrin.
Reichert, Adam L. Bigfoot's First Haircut. (p. 224)
Reichert, Amy. Take Your Mama to Work Today. Boiger, Alexandra, illus. (p. 2177)
Reichert, Paul. Lemonade Ripple: A Sweet Story of Kindness & Charity. (p. 1266)
Reicherter, Daryn. Cambodian Dancer: Sophany's Gift of Hope. Penh, Bophal, tr. (p. 313)
Reichl London, Rachel R. Time Capsule Diary. (p. 2244)
Reichman, Beverley. Cindi the Teenie Chiweenie. (p. 392)
—Kevin Can. Reichman, Debbie, illus. (p. 1210)
—Kevin Is a Smart Cookie. Burran, Debbie, illus. (p. 1210)
Reichman, Debbie, illus. see Reichman, Beverley.
Reichs, Brendan. Chrysalis. (p. 389)
—Genesis. (p. 814)
—Nemesis. (p. 1587)
Reichs, Brendan, jt. auth. see Condie, Ally.
Reichs, Brendan, jt. auth. see Reichs, Kathy.
Reichs, Kathy. Code. (p. 411)
—Virals (p. 2360)
—Virals. (p. 2360)
Reichs, Kathy & Reichs, Brendan. Code. (p. 411)
—Seizure. (p. 1985)
—Trace Evidence. (p. 2271)
—Virals. (p. 2360)
Reid, Adam, et al. Tiny Chef: And Da Mishing Weshipee Boook. (p. 2248)
Reid, Agnes Just. Letters of Long Ago (Classic Reprint) (p. 1280)
Reid, Aimee. Mama's Day with Little Gray. (p. 1393)
—You Are My Friend: The Story of Mister Rogers & His Neighborhood. Phelan, Matt, illus. (p. 2524)
Reid, Alastair. Ounce, Dice, Trice. Shahn, Ben, illus. (p. 1676)
—Supposing. Gill, Bob, illus. (p. 2162)
Reid, Andrea. Growing up with Autism. (p. 900)
Reid Banks, Lynne & Stephenson, Omri. Polly & Jake. (p. 1771)
—Spice Rack. (p. 2080)
Reid, Barbara. Picture a Tree. Reid, Barbara, illus. (p. 1739)
—Picture the Sky. (p. 1741)
Reid, Barbara, illus. see Moore, Clement C.
Reid, Bertha Westbrook. Wallace Reid: His Life Story (Classic Reprint) (p. 2373)
Reid, C. L. Crazy for Apples. (p. 469)
—Emma Every Day. (p. 643)
—Going on a Field Trip. (p. 854)
—Party Problems. (p. 1702)
—Tap Dance Troubles. (p. 2191)
Reid, Camilla. Lulu & the Noisy Baby. Busby, Ailie, illus. (p. 1367)
—Lulu Loves Colours. Busby, Ailie, illus. (p. 1367)
—Lulu Loves Numbers. Busby, Ailie, illus. (p. 1367)
—Lulu Loves Shapes. Busby, Ailie, illus. (p. 1367)
—Peekaboo: Apple. Arrhenius, Ingela P., illus. (p. 1713)
—Peekaboo: Farm. Arrhenius, Ingela P., illus. (p. 1713)
Reid, Charles. Ghost of Heroes Past. (p. 828)
Reid, Charles G. Ug. (p. 2313)
Reid, Christian. After Many Days: A Novel (Classic Reprint) (p. 33)
—After Many Days. (p. 33)
—Comedy of Elopement (Classic Reprint) (p. 429)
—Daughter of Bohemia: A Novel (Classic Reprint) (p. 509)
—Fairy Gold (Classic Reprint) (p. 696)
—Heart of Steel: A Novel (Classic Reprint) (p. 945)
—Land of the Sun: Vistas Mexicanas (Classic Reprint) (p. 1242)
—Little Maid of Arcady (Classic Reprint) (p. 1321)
—Lost Lode: And Stella's Discipline (Classic Reprint) (p. 1355)
—Man of the Family: A Novel (Classic Reprint) (p. 1395)
—Man of the Family. (p. 1395)
—Morton House: A Novel (Classic Reprint) (p. 1507)
—Morton House. (p. 1507)
—Nina's Atonement: A Novel (Classic Reprint) (p. 1609)
—Princess Nadine (Classic Reprint) (p. 1798)
—Question of Honor: A Novel (Classic Reprint) (p. 1826)
—Secret Bequest (Classic Reprint) (p. 1975)
—Series: A Bummer Idyl (Classic Reprint) (p. 1991)
—Under the Southern Cross: A War Drama in Four Acts (Classic Reprint) (p. 2323)
—Valerie Aylmer: A Novel (Classic Reprint) (p. 2344)
Reid, Christy. Simon the Guide Dog. Poole, Steven R., illus. (p. 2020)
Reid, David. Honorable Fido Lincoln, Judge Teaches Property Law. (p. 999)
Reid, Dee. Monster Max's BIG Breakfast: Have Fun with Numbers. (p. 1496)
—Monster Megan's BIG Clean Up: Have Fun with Shapes. (p. 1496)
—Monster Molly's BIG Day Out: Have Fun with Opposites. (p. 1496)
—Monster Mo's BIG Party: Have Fun with Colors. (p. 1496)
Reid, Demetra. Alice's ABC's: Version 2. Deffenbaugh, Dena, illus. (p. 46)
Reid, Donalda & Second Story Press Staff. Way It Is (p. 2387)
Reid, E. W. Robin Hood Reader: Authorized for Use in the Public Schools of British Columbia (Classic Reprint) (p. 1891)
Reid, Edith Gittings. Florence Nightingale a Drama (Classic Reprint) (p. 751)
Reid, Emily. Space Claymation. (p. 2071)
—Sports Claymation. (p. 2088)
—Underwater Claymation. (p. 2326)
Reid, Eric. Chequered Leaves from Siam (Classic Reprint) (p. 365)
—Spears of Deliverance: A Tale of White Men & Brown Women in Siam (Classic Reprint) (p. 2076)
Reid, F. J. Midwinter Child. (p. 1462)
Reid, Fiona, illus. see Alden, Peter C.
Reid, Forrest. At the Door of the Gate (Classic Reprint) (p. 130)
—Following Darkness (Classic Reprint) (p. 758)
—Garden God: A Tale of Two Boys (Classic Reprint) (p. 809)
—Gentle Lover: A Comedy of Middle Age (Classic Reprint) (p. 816)
—Pender among the Residents (Classic Reprint) (p. 1715)
—Pirates of the Spring (Classic Reprint) (p. 1751)
—Spring Song (Classic Reprint) (p. 2092)
Reid, Gavin & Guise, Jennie. Dyslexia Assessment. (p. 612)
Reid, George, jt. auth. see Smiles, Samuel.
Reid, Gillian, illus. see Van Ness, Jonathan.
Reid, Grace Stuart. Americans in Exile: From the Pictures & Papers of Paul Duane, Ex-Officer of the United States Army (Classic Reprint) (p. 75)
Reid, Hugo. Elements of Astronomy: Adapted for Use in Schools & Private Study (Classic Reprint) (p. 633)
Reid, Hunter. At the Carnival! Hinton, Stephanie, illus. (p. 130)
—Beach Day! Hinton, Stephanie, illus. (p. 178)
—Bright Lights Bright City. (p. 281)
—Bright Lights, Bright City. Hinton, Stephanie, illus. (p. 281)
—In the Garden. Chiu, Alex, illus. (p. 1109)
—In the Rainforest. Chiu, Alex, illus. (p. 1110)
—Let's Have a Picnic! Hinton, Stephanie, illus. (p. 1274)
—Mighty Dinos. Chiu, Alex, illus. (p. 1462)
—Noisy Robots. Chiu, Alex, illus. (p. 1618)
—Sweetest Treats. Hinton, Stephanie, illus. (p. 2169)
—Vroom! Zoom! Chiu, Alex, illus. (p. 2368)
Reid, Isabelle. Serafina Moon. (p. 1990)
Reid, James. Across the Sea (p. 11)
—Dinosaur House (p. 549)
—Edward the Explorer (p. 627)
—Nuisance, Vol. 8: Annual Number; May, 1916 (Classic Reprint) (p. 1629)
—Ready, Set, Go! (p. 1848)
—This Is My Story by Frederick G. Frog (p. 2225)
—Your Guide to Superheroes (p. 2533)
Reid, James E. Movie Classic, Vol. 10: March, 1936 (Classic Reprint) (p. 1516)
—Movie Classic, Vol. 9: September 1935 (Classic Reprint) (p. 1516)
Reid, Janet. Granny Rags. (p. 880)
Reid, John. Chronicle of Small Beer (Classic Reprint) (p. 388)
—Ghost, the Cat & the King. (p. 828)
Reid, John G. People & Josh Wilson. (p. 1718)
Reid, John T. Art Rambles in the Highlands & Islands of Scotland (Classic Reprint) (p. 121)

R

Reid, Julia. Alex & the Magical Flying Coat. Grafe, Amanda, illus. (p. 42)
Reid, Kamilla. Miist. (p. 1464)
Reid, Kimberly. Perfect Liars. (p. 1722)
—Prettyboy Must Die. (p. 1791)
—Sweet 16 to Life. (p. 2168)
Reid, Kimm. Chasm of Acheron. (p. 362)
—It's OK to Cry. Tilma, Taralee, illus. (p. 1146)
—Mist over Leviathan. (p. 1482)
—One for All. (p. 1659)
—Perfidy of Labyrinth. (p. 1723)
—Veiled Sun Blood Moon. (p. 2349)
—War of the Firmament. (p. 2376)
Reid, Kylie Renee. KK Cooks Guacamole. Reid, Tierra Destiny, ed. (p. 1227)
—KK Loves Gymnastics. Reid, Tierra Destiny, ed. (p. 1227)
Reid, Laurence. Motion Picture, 1940-1941, Vol. 60 (Classic Reprint) (p. 1511)
—Motion Picture Classic, Vol. 27: July, 1928 (Classic Reprint) (p. 1511)
—Motion Picture Classic, Vol. 28: January, 1929 (Classic Reprint) (p. 1511)
—Motion Picture Classic, Vol. 31: July, 1930 (Classic Reprint) (p. 1511)
—Motion Picture, Vol. 42: August 1931-January 1932 (Classic Reprint) (p. 1511)
—Motion Picture, Vol. 44: August, 1932 (Classic Reprint) (p. 1511)
—Motion Picture, Vol. 45: February, 1933 (Classic Reprint) (p. 1511)
—Motion Picture, Vol. 46: August, 1933 (Classic Reprint) (p. 1511)
—Motion Picture, Vol. 47: February, 1934 (Classic Reprint) (p. 1511)
—Motion Picture, Vol. 48: The Original Film Magazine Edited in Hollywood & New York; August 1934-January 1935 (Classic Reprint) (p. 1511)
—Motion Picture, Vol. 53: February, 1937 (Classic Reprint) (p. 1511)
—Motion Picture, Vol. 54: Combined with Movie Classic; August, 1937 (Classic Reprint) (p. 1511)
—Motion Picture, Vol. 56: Incorporating Movie Classic; August, 1938 (Classic Reprint) (p. 1511)
—Motion Picture, Vol. 57: A Fawcett Publication; February, 1939 (Classic Reprint) (p. 1511)
—Motion Picture, Vol. 59: February, 1940 (Classic Reprint) (p. 1511)
—Motion Picture, Vol. 61: Incorporating Movie Classic; February-July 1941 (Classic Reprint) (p. 1511)
—Movie Classic: September, 1931 (Classic Reprint) (p. 1516)
—Movie Classic, Vol. 2: The Tabloid Magazine of the Screen; April, 1932 (Classic Reprint) (p. 1516)
—Movie Classic, Vol. 3: The Tabloid Magazine of the Screen; September, 1932-February, 1933 (Classic Reprint) (p. 1516)
—Movie Classic, Vol. 5: January-July, 1934 (Classic Reprint) (p. 1516)
—Movie Classic, Vol. 7: September, 1934 (Classic Reprint) (p. 1516)
Reid, Mayne. Andrew Deverel, Vol. 2 Of 2: The History of an Adventurer in New Guinea (Classic Reprint) (p. 83)
—Boy Hunters of the Mississippi (Classic Reprint) (p. 268)
—Bush-Boys: Or the History & Adventures of a Cape Farmer & His Family in the Wild Karoos of Southern Africa (Classic Reprint) (p. 301)
—Castaways. (p. 339)
—Child Wife (Classic Reprint) (p. 370)
—Child Wife, Vol. 1 Of 3: A Tale of the Two Worlds (Classic Reprint) (p. 370)
—Child Wife, Vol. 2 Of 3: A Tale of the Two Worlds (Classic Reprint) (p. 370)
—Child Wife, Vol. 3 Of 3: A Tale of the Two Worlds (Classic Reprint) (p. 370)
—Death Shot. (p. 521)
—Death Shot, Vol. 1 Of 3: A Romance of Forest & Prairie (Classic Reprint) (p. 521)
—Death-Shot: A Story Retold (Classic Reprint) (p. 521)
—Desert Home: Or the Adventures of a Lost Family in the Wilderness (Classic Reprint) (p. 531)
—Flag of Distress: A Story of the South Sea - Scholar's Choice Edition. (p. 745)
—Flag of Distress. (p. 745)
—Forest Exiles: Or, the Perils of a Peruvian Family amid, the Wilds of the Amazon (Classic Reprint) (p. 766)
—Forest Exiles. (p. 766)
—Free Lance. (p. 782)
—Free Lances: A Romance of the Mexican Valley (Classic Reprint) (p. 782)
—Free Lances. (p. 782)
—Gaspar, the Gaucho: A Tale of the Gran Chaco (Classic Reprint) (p. 811)
—Lost Lenore: Or the Adventures of a Rolling Stone (Classic Reprint) (p. 1354)
—Lost Lenore, or the Adventures of a Rolling Stone, Vol. 2 of 3 (Classic Reprint) (p. 1354)
—Maroon: A Novel (Classic Reprint) (p. 1408)
—Maroon. (p. 1408)
—Maroon, Vol. 1 of 3 (Classic Reprint) (p. 1408)
—Maroon, Vol. 2 of 3 (Classic Reprint) (p. 1408)
—No Quarter (Classic Reprint) (p. 1614)
—No Quarter!, Vol. 1 (Classic Reprint) (p. 1614)
—No Quarter!, Vol. 2 (Classic Reprint) (p. 1614)
—No Quarter!, Vol. 3 (Classic Reprint) (p. 1614)
—Scalp Hunters. (p. 1941)
—Scalp Hunters, Vol. 1 Of 3: Or Romantic Adventures in Northern Mexico (Classic Reprint) (p. 1941)
—Scalp-Hunters: Or, Romantic Adventures in Northern Mexico (Classic Reprint) (p. 1941)
—Stories about Animals (Classic Reprint) (p. 2122)
—White Gauntlet: A Novel (Classic Reprint) (p. 2444)
—White Gauntlet. (p. 2444)
—Young Voyageurs: Or the Boy Hunters in the North (Classic Reprint) (p. 2532)
Reid, Mayne, et al. Forest Exiles. (p. 766)
Reid, Megan. Althea Gibson: the Story of Tennis' Fleet-Of-Foot Girl. Freeman, Laura, illus. (p. 60)
Reid, Michael, et al. Laugh-Along Nursery Rhymes. (p. 1251)
Reid, Mick, illus. see Braun, Eric.
Reid, Mick, illus. see Clay, Kathryn & Vonne, Mira.
Reid, Mick, illus. see Dale, Jenny & Rowe, Michael.
Reid, Mick, illus. see Dale, Jenny.
Reid, Mick, illus. see Gerver, Jane E.
Reid, Mick, illus. see Troupe, Thomas Kingsley.
Reid, Pamela Carrington. Little One. Tolman, Tom, illus. (p. 1323)
Reid, Raziel. Followers. (p. 758)
—When Everything Feels Like the Movies. (p. 2430)
Reid, Rob. Comin' down to Storytime. Bernard Westcott, Nadine, illus. (p. 430)
—Wave Goodbye Williams, Lorraine, illus. (p. 2386)
Reid, Robin L. Rhyming Ricky Rutherford. Lipp, Tony, illus. (p. 1875)
Reid, Roger. Time. (p. 2243)
Reid, Savil Grey, jt. auth. see Oates, Eugene William.
Reid, Scott, jt. ed. see Greenhaven Press Staff.
Reid, Siuna A. Reptiles Are Cool- Understanding My Tortoise. Lodge, Vivienne E., ed. (p. 1867)
Reid, Siuna Ann. Reptiles Are Cool- Understanding My Lizard. Lodge, Vivienne E., ed. (p. 1867)
Reid, Stef. Against the Odds: Band 18/Pearl (Collins Big Cat) Bannister, Philip, illus. (p. 34)
Reid, Stephanie. Feelings (p. 718)
—Feelings. (p. 718)
—My Body (p. 1534)
—My Body. (p. 1534)
—My Country (p. 1536)
—School (p. 1945)
—School. (p. 1945)
—Space (p. 2070)
—Space. (p. 2070)
—Time (p. 2243)
—Time. (p. 2243)
Reid, Stephanie, jt. auth. see Aucoin, Lee.
Reid, Struan. Astronauts Sticker Book IR. (p. 128)
—See Inside Bridges, Towers & Tunnels IR. (p. 1981)
—Stained Glass Coloring. (p. 2099)
—Victorian Patterns to Color. (p. 2355)
Reid, Struan, jt. auth. see Harvey, Gill.
Reid, Struan & Stowell, Louie. My First Pirate Book. Allen, Peter, illus. (p. 1545)
Reid, Stuart. Gorgeous George & His Stupid Stinky Stories: New! Pender, John, illus. (p. 870)
—Gorgeous George & the Jumbo Jobby Juicer: 2017 Edition. Pender, John, illus. (p. 870)
—Gorgeous George & the Timewarp Trouser Trumpets. Pender, John, illus. (p. 870)
—Gorgeous George & the Unidentified Unsinkable Underpants Part 1: 2017 Edition. Pender, John, illus. (p. 870)
—Gorgeous George & the Zigzag Zit-Faced Zombies: New 2017 Edition. Pender, John, illus. (p. 870)
—Grandpa Jock & the Incredible Iron-Bru-Man Incident. Pender, John, illus. (p. 879)
Reid, Sue. Spotlight on Russia: Band 18/Pearl (Collins Big Cat) (p. 2091)
Reid, Sylvia. Funny Tale of Cameron & the Boxes. (p. 801)
Reid, Sylvia C. Dream Match. (p. 602)
Reid, Thomas. Inquiry into the Human Mind: On the Principles of Common Sense (Classic Reprint) (p. 1121)
Reid, Thomas Wilson. Gabrielle Stuart, or the Flower of Greenan, Vol. 1 Of 2: A Scottish Romance (Classic Reprint) (p. 804)
Reid, Tierra Destiny, ed. see Houston, Terence.
Reid, Tierra Destiny, ed. see Reid, Kylie Renee.
Reid, Vince, illus. see McGann, Erika.
Reid, William. Children's Praise Book. (p. 374)
Reida, Sarah S. Monsterville: a Lissa Black Production. (p. 1498)
Reide, Mackenzie. Adventurers the Mask of the Troll. (p. 19)
—Adventurers Troll Creek. (p. 19)
Reidenbaugh, Tara S. Corgi Miracle: A True Story. (p. 454)
Reider, Katja, jt. auth. see Clever Publishing.
Reid-Girardot, Marion. Steve of the Bar-G Ranch a Thrilling Story of Life, on the Plains of Colorado (Classic Reprint) (p. 2116)
Reidy, Jean. All Through My Town. Timmers, Leo, illus. (p. 55)
—Busy Builders, Busy Week! Timmers, Leo, illus. (p. 302)
—Pup 681: A Sea Otter Rescue Story. Crowley, Ashley, illus. (p. 1814)
—Too Princessy! Leloup, Geneviève, illus. (p. 2261)
—Truman. Cummins, Lucy Ruth, illus. (p. 2295)
—When the Snow Is Deeper Than My Boots Are Tall. Chou, Joey, illus. (p. 2433)
Reif, Cheryl. Sonics on Tour: The Respiratory System. Noé, illus. (p. 2064)
Reifel, Nola. Adventures in Grandma's Wyoming Garden. (p. 20)
Reiff, Chris, illus. see Wallace, Daniel.
Reiff, Rachel Haugrud. Sandra Cisneros. (p. 1931)
Reiff, Raychel Haugrud. Aldous Huxley: Brave New World. (p. 41)
—Sandra Cisneros. (p. 1931)
—William Golding. (p. 2468)
Reifsnyder, Scotty, illus. see Murray, David.
Reigel, Connie. Don't Cry, Little Spruce. (p. 582)
Reigns, Marie. Adventures of Cat & Jude. (p. 22)
Reihs, Linda. Adventures of Maddy Morphis. (p. 25)
Reil-Berry, Stacie. Stop! Growing. (p. 2122)
Reiley, Darren. Whisper. (p. 2442)
Reilly, Carmel. Boy at the Park. Reynolds, Pat, illus. (p. 268)
—Comets, Asteroids, & Meteoroids. (p. 429)
—Earth's Atmosphere. (p. 618)
REILLY, Carmel. Making Headlines Fast Lane Purple Fiction (p. 1389)
Reilly, Carmel. Moon. (p. 1501)
—Planets. (p. 1756)
—Rigby PM Stars Bridge Books: Individual Student Edition Gold Junior Superstars. (p. 1880)
—Stars. (p. 2106)
—Sun. (p. 2151)
Reilly, Emily. Saving Ivy. (p. 1938)
Reilly, Frank. Walt Disney's Treasury of Classic Tales, Vol. 3. Ushler, John, illus. (p. 2374)
Reilly, Heather. Melody's Marvelous Mixture. (p. 1443)
Reilly, Hope. Ghost Horse at Cove House: A Book about the Strength of Friendship. (p. 827)
Reilly, James M. Veldt, the Lion Hunter: A Comic Opera Whirl (Classic Reprint) (p. 2349)
Reilly, K. J. Words We Don't Say. (p. 2495)
Reilly, Kathleen M. Cities: Discover How They Work. Casteel, Tom, illus. (p. 394)
—Explore Life Cycles! 25 Great Projects, Activities, Experiments. Stone, Bryan, illus. (p. 679)
—Explore Soil! With 25 Great Projects. Stone, Bryan, illus. (p. 680)
—Explore Solids & Liquids! With 25 Great Projects. Stone, Bryan, illus. (p. 680)
—Food - 25 Amazing Projects: Investigate the History & Science of What We Eat. Carbaugh, Samuel, illus. (p. 759)
—Food - 25 Amazing Projects: Investigate the History & Science of What We Eat. Carbaugh, Samuel & Rizvi, Farah, illus. (p. 759)
—Human Body: Get under the Skin with Science Activities for Kids. Cornell, Alexis, illus. (p. 1049)
—Natural Disasters: Investigate Earth's Most Destructive Forces with 25 Projects. Casteel, Tom, illus. (p. 1579)
—Planet Earth: Finding Balance on the Blue Marble with Environmental Science Activities for Kids. Casteel, Tom, illus. (p. 1755)
Reilly, Kathleen M. & Takacs-Moore, Mary. Energy: 25 Projects Investigate Why We Need Power & How We Get It. Takacs-Moore, Mary, illus. (p. 650)
Reilly, Kevin. Dams & Levees (p. 499)
—Ports (p. 1779)
—Tunnels (p. 2299)
—Waste Management (p. 2382)
—Zoom in on Tunnels. (p. 2544)
Reilly, Kristin & Morris, Pamela. Gift of Love. (p. 832)
Reilly, Mary-Jo, et al. Mexico. (p. 1454)
Reilly, Michelle, illus. see Larsen, Donna R.
Reilly, Pamela. My Day at the Zoo. (p. 1536)
Reilly, Peter J. Hanging with the Hangers. Erickson, Donna J., ed. (p. 917)
Reimer, Jackie. No Thanks, but I'd Love to Dance! Choosing to Live Smoke Free. Reimer, Jackie, illus. (p. 1615)
Reimer, Susan. Embers. (p. 641)
Reimers, Johannes. Unto the Heights of Simplicity (Classic Reprint) (p. 2336)
Reimes, Philippe De. Romance of Blonde of Oxford & Jehan of Dammartin. (p. 1900)
—Romance of Blonde of Oxford & Jehan of Dammartin (Classic Reprint) (p. 1900)
Reimiller, Diane. Brayden & Ryan's Summer Vacation. Jastrzebski, Brandy, illus. (p. 277)
Reimiller, Diane L. Duck Named Quackers Jastrzebski, Brandy, illus. (p. 608)
Reimold, O. S. Industrial Studies & Exercises. (p. 1118)
—Philippine Education Series: Industrial Studies & Exercises. (p. 1734)
Rein, Mary, ed. Budding Gardener. (p. 290)
Reina, Andres. Amigo de Dios: Un Libro Ilustrado para niños Que Desean Estar Más Cerca de Dios. (p. 75)
Reina, Mary. Earn Money. (p. 615)
—Learn about Money. (p. 1255)
—Make Money Choices. (p. 1386)
—Money & You. (p. 1492)
—Save Money. (p. 1937)
—Science of a Hurricane. (p. 1957)
—Spend Money. (p. 2079)
—Tour of Your Respiratory System Jones, Chris B., illus. (p. 2269)
Reina, Mary, jt. auth. see Raij, Emily.
Reinagel, Brady. Larry Fitzgerald: Pro Bowl Receiver. (p. 1245)
Reinbold, Cobe. Dangerous Past. (p. 502)
Reinbold, Otto. Die Nase in Ihrer Physiognomischen Bedeutung (Classic Reprint) (p. 544)
Reinders, Veronica. Adventures at Angels Rest: Maggie Feathers. (p. 19)
Reiner, Carl. Tell Me A Scary Story... but Not Too Scary. (p. 2201)
—Tell Me a Silly Story. Bennett, James, illus. (p. 2201)
—Tell Me Another Scary Story... but Not Too Scary! Bennett, James & Bennett, Carl A., illus. (p. 2201)
Reinert, Dba Cristina D. Vaughn's Adventures. (p. 2348)
Reinert, Linda M. Talking Is Hard for Me! Encouraging Communication in Children with Speech-Language Difficulties. Lynch, Emily S., illus. (p. 2187)
Reinford, Luanne, illus. see Witmer, Edith.
Reingold, Adam. Beaver's Lodge: Building with Leftovers. (p. 186)
—Beaver's Lodge. (p. 186)
—Leveled by an Earthquake! (p. 1281)
—Smallpox: Is It Over? (p. 2040)
Reingold, Alan, illus. see Glasthal, Jacqueline B.
Reinhard, Sarah. Bienvenido, Nino Jesus: Reflexiones de Adviento y Navidad para la Familia. (p. 215)
Reinhard, Thilo, tr. see Torvund, Helge & Johnsen, Mari Kanstad.
Reinhardt, Dana. Et' o J'Ai Appris Voler(!) (p. 665)
—How to Build a House. (p. 1038)
—Odessa Again. (p. 1638)
—Summer I Learned to Fly. (p. 2149)
—Tell Us Something True. (p. 2202)
—Things a Brother Knows. (p. 2220)
Reinhardt, Dirk. Niños del Tren: La Bestia y el Sueño Imposible. (p. 1611)
Reinhardt, Jennifer Black. Blue Ethel. (p. 248)
Reinhardt, Jennifer Black, illus. see Applegate, Katherine.
Reinhardt, Jennifer Black, illus. see McGinty, Alice B.
Reinhardt, Jennifer Black, illus. see Park, Linda Sue.
Reinhardt, Jennifer Black, illus. see Slade, Suzanne.
Reinhardt, Jennifer Black, illus. see Vaught, Susan.
Reinhardt, Liz. Rebels Like Us. (p. 1852)
Reinhart, Larry, illus. see Blankenship, Paula.
Reinhart, Larry, illus. see McKay, Sindy.
Reinhart, Larry, illus. see Ross, Dev & Canetti, Yanitzia.
Reinhart, Larry, illus. see Ross, Dev.
Reinhart, Matthew. Disney*Pixar: A Pop-Up Celebration. Reinhart, Matthew, illus. (p. 564)
—My Little Pony: the Castles of Equestria: An Enchanted My Little Pony Pop-Up Book. (p. 1554)
—Pop-Up Book of Nursery Rhymes: A Classic Collectible Pop-Up. Reinhart, Matthew, illus. (p. 1775)
Reinhart, Matthew, illus. see Palatini, Margie.
Reinhart, Matthew & Sabuda, Robert. Gods & Heroes. Reinhart, Matthew & Sabuda, Robert, illus. (p. 853)
Reinhart, Robin. Fierce Freshwater Fish: Measure Lengths in Standard Units. (p. 723)
Reinhart, Ruth. Literary Supplement of Wellesley College News, Vol. 3: November 26, 1925 (Classic Reprint) (p. 1309)
Reinke, Beth. Backhoes Dig! (p. 156)
—Concrete Mixers Stir! (p. 438)
—Cranes Lift! (p. 467)
Reinke, Beth Bence. Bulldozers Push! (p. 296)
—Carla's Cloud Catastrophe. Nielson, Ginger, illus. (p. 331)
—Dump Trucks Haul! (p. 610)
—Fire Trucks on the Go. (p. 733)
—Following Special Diets. (p. 758)
—Front Loaders Scoop! (p. 795)
—Frozen March of Emperor Penguins. (p. 795)
—Garbage Trucks on the Go. (p. 808)
—Grains Group. (p. 875)
—Healthy Eating Habits. (p. 943)
—Healthy Foods Around the World. (p. 943)
—Healthy Snacks. (p. 944)
—Helicopters on the Go. (p. 950)
—Measuring Time with a Clock. Petelinsek, Kathleen, illus. (p. 1435)
—Measuring Volume. Petelinsek, Kathleen, illus. (p. 1435)
—Measuring Weight. Petelinsek, Kathleen, illus. (p. 1435)
—Nutrition Basics (p. 1632)
—Race Cars on the Go. (p. 1831)
—School Buses on the Go. (p. 1945)
—Sugars & Fats. (p. 2147)
—Superfast Stock Car Racing. (p. 2159)
—Tractors on the Go. (p. 2273)
—Where Did the Caterpillar Go? (p. 2435)
—Why Do Leaves Change Color? (p. 2456)
—Why We Eat Dairy. (p. 2459)
—Why We Eat Fruits. (p. 2459)
—Why We Eat Grains. (p. 2459)
—Why We Eat Protein. (p. 2459)
—Why We Eat Vegetables. (p. 2459)
Reinke, Beth Bence, contrib. by. BEAGLES. (p. 178)
Reinke, Vicki. Barney Goes to the Horse Show. (p. 167)
Reinkens, Brynn. How Has the #MeToo Movement Changed Society? (p. 1031)
Reino, Jessica. Food Allergies: The Ultimate Teen Guide (p. 759)
Reinsch, Paul. Young Citizen's Reader: How Government Works - Elections State & Federal, the Public Sector, & the Law of the US Constitution. (p. 2530)
—Young Citizen's Reader. (p. 2530)
Reintgen, Scott. Nyxia. (p. 1632)
—Nyxia Liberada. (p. 1632)
—Nyxia Sublevada. (p. 1632)
—Nyxia Unleashed. (p. 1632)
—Nyxia Uprising. (p. 1632)
—Saving Fable. (p. 1938)
—Talespinners: Saving Fable. (p. 2187)
Reintjes, Susan B. Through the Fairy Door. Sparling, Bren M., illus. (p. 2237)
Reis, Don. Colossal Bottomless Depths of Blubbo. (p. 426)
—Glorious Effervescence of Blubbo. (p. 844)
Reis, Erica, illus. see Armand, Villavert, et al.
Reis, Lauren, illus. see Hoyle, Alice.
Reis, Rod. New Mutants by Jonathan Hickman Vol. 1. (p. 1596)
—Winter Soldier: Second Chances. (p. 2476)
Reis, Rod, jt. illus. see Quinones, Joe.
Reis, Ronald A. Christopher Columbus & the Age of Exploration for Kids: With 21 Activities. (p. 388)
—Easter Island. (p. 620)
—Empire State Building. (p. 645)
—Great Depression & the New Deal: America's Economy in Crisis. (p. 885)
—Henry Ford for Kids: His Life & Ideas, with 21 Activities. (p. 955)
—Mickey Mantle. (p. 1459)
—New York City Subway System. (p. 1598)
—US Congress for Kids: Over 200 Years of Lawmaking, Deal-Breaking, & Compromising, with 21 Activities. (p. 2340)
—Valentino. (p. 2344)
Reis, Tatiane Gusmao. Mais Que Um Sonho. (p. 1384)
Reisberg, Esther. Big Book of Amazing Animals. (p. 217)
—Big Book of Sea Creatures. (p. 218)
Reisberg, Mira, illus. see Ata, Te, et al.
Reisberg, Mira, illus. see Ata, Te.
Reisberg, Mira, illus. see Corpi, Lucha & National Geographic Learning Staff.
Reisberg, Mira, illus. see Flor Ada, Alma & Zubizarreta, Rosalma, trs.
Reisberg, Mira, illus. see Rohmer, Harriet.
Reisch, J. A. Mi Primera Biblia. Rimmington, Natasha, illus. (p. 1456)
Reisch, Jesse, illus. see Fredericks, Anthony D.
Reisch, Jesse, illus. see Pfeffer, Wendy.
Reisch, Jesse, illus. see Stevenson, Robert Louis.
Reisch, Jesse, illus. see Todd, Traci N.
Reisch, Jessie, illus. see Elkins, Stephen.
Reisender, Reisender. My Grandfather's Old Coat: A Political Allegory (Classic Reprint) (p. 1548)
Reisfeld, Randi. CC (Cape Cod) (p. 348)
—Industrial Revolution: Set Of 6. (p. 1117)
—Industrial Revolution: Bridges Edition. Canas, Alex, illus. (p. 1117)

—Industrial Revolution: Bridges Edition Set of 6 with Common Core Indicators. Canas, Alex, illus. (p. 1117)
—No Strings Attached: CC (Cape Cod); Partiers Preferred. (p. 1615)
—Roaring 20s & the Great Depression: Set Of 6. (p. 1889)
—Roaring 20s & the Great Depression: Bridges Edition. Ginerva, Dante, illus. (p. 1889)
—Roaring 20s & the Great Depression: Bridges Edition Set of 6 with Common Core Indicators. Ginerva, Dante, illus. (p. 1889)
—This Is the Sound: The Best of Alternative Rock. (p. 2225)
—Trouble with Trix (Winx Club) Golden Books, illus. (p. 2292)
—Welcome to Alfea Golden Books, illus. (p. 2398)
Reisfeld, Randi & Jackie Robb. Causes of the American Revolution: Set Of 6. (p. 347)
—Causes of the American Revolution: Bridges Edition. Freeman, Gary, illus. (p. 347)
—Causes of the American Revolution: Bridges Edition Set of 6 with Common Core Indicators. Freeman, Gary, illus. (p. 347)
—Faces of the American Revolution: Set Of 6. (p. 693)
—Faces of the American Revolution: Bridges Edition. Freeman, Gary, illus. (p. 693)
—Faces of the American Revolution: Bridges Edition Set of 6 with Common Core Indicators. Freeman, Gary, illus. (p. 693)
Reisman, Michael. Simon Bloom, the Gravity Keeper. (p. 2020)
Reisner, Molly. Dora & the Unicorn King (Dora the Explorer) Aikins, David, illus. (p. 585)
—Dora's Birthday Surprise! Aikins, David, illus. (p. 586)
—Dora's Princess Party. Aikins, Dave, illus. (p. 586)
—Frozen 2 Mad Libs Junior. (p. 795)
—Halloween Hoedown! (p. 912)
—Halloween Hoedown! (Dora the Explorer) Aikins, David, illus. (p. 912)
—Hatchimals Mad Libs Junior. (p. 936)
—I Love My Pet! Mad Libs Junior. (p. 1072)
—Trolls Mad Libs. (p. 2290)
Reisner, Molly & Davies, Dorien. Baby Shower Mad Libs. (p. 152)
Reiss, Johanna. Upstairs Room. (p. 2339)
Reiss, John J. Numbers. Reiss, John J., illus. (p. 1630)
—Shapes. Reiss, John J., illus. (p. 2000)
Reiss, Kathryn. Bundle of Trouble: A Rebecca Mystery. Giovine, Sergio, illus. (p. 297)
—Message in a Bottle: A Julie Mystery. (p. 1451)
—Riddle of the Prairie Bride. (p. 1878)
—Strange Case of Baby H. (p. 2137)
—Tangled Web: A Julie Mystery. Tibbles, Jean-Paul, illus. (p. 2190)
Reiss, Mike. Santa's Eleven Months Off Montgomery, Michael G., illus. (p. 1933)
—Santa's Eleven Months Off. (p. 1933)
—Turtle & Tortoise Are Not Friends. Spires, Ashley, illus. (p. 2301)
Reiss, Mike, jt. auth. see Reiss, Mike.
Reiss, William, illus. see Banks, Steven & Hillenburg, Stephen.
Reiss, William, illus. see Banks, Steven.
Reitemeier, Lou. Jack & Me & His Little G. G. A Halloween Romance. Vanvonderen, Sue, ed. (p. 1151)
Reitenour, Nick, illus. see Block, Jan.
Reiter, Chris, jt. auth. see Katirgis, Jane.
Reiter, Chris, jt. auth. see Warhol, Tom.
Reiter, David P. Bringing down the Wall. Babajanyan, Sona, illus. (p. 282)
—Die Mauer Zu Fall Bringen. Beer, Michele, tr. from ENG. (p. 544)
—Greenhouse Effect. Dunk, Sarah, illus. (p. 895)
—Las Armas de Fuego. Rosales-Martinez, Guadalupe, tr. from ENG. (p. 1245)
Reiter, David P. & Bevin, Shane. Tiger Takes the Big Apple. (p. 2241)
Reiter, Harriet G. Boyhood of Lincoln (Classic Reprint) (p. 271)
Reiter, Xee, illus. see Yang, Kao Kalia.
Reith, Sharon L. Infestation! Roaches, Bedbugs, Ants, & Other Insect Invaders (p. 1118)
Reitmann, Kathleen. Cattle. (p. 346)
Reitmeyer, Andrea & Clever Publishing. Sydney the Seal Saves the Sea: Protect the Planet Together. (p. 2172)
Reitmeyer, Hans. What People Eat. (p. 2419)
Reitmeyer, Shannon. Proud Inchworm. Reitmeyer, Shannon, illus. (p. 1808)
Reitsma, Mara & Shy, Elo. Adventures of Cali the Cat, Cali's Missing Human. (p. 22)
Reizenstein, Elmer L. On Trial: The Story of a Woman at Bay (Classic Reprint) (p. 1656)
Reizer, Edwina & Licata, Rosemarie. Magic Mountain. (p. 1378)
Rejino, Mona. Just for Kids: HLSPL Composer Showcase NFMC 2014-2016 Selection Elementary Level. (p. 1193)
Reju, Sarah. God Is Better Than Princesses. (p. 851)
—God Is Better Than Trucks: A-Z. (p. 851)
Reker, Martin, ed. see Shein, Erik Daniel.
Reker, Martin, jt. auth. see Shein, Erik Daniel.
Relf, Adam, illus. see Clarke, Catriona.
Relf, Patricia. Magic School Plants Seeds. (p. 1378)
Relf, Terrie Leigh, ed. Planting the Seeds: Young Writers Drabble Contest. (p. 1757)
Relic, Mark. Markus. (p. 1407)
Relihan, Bernard. Netop, Vol. 10: May, 1930 (Classic Reprint) (p. 1589)
—Netop, Vol. 10: November, 1929 (Classic Reprint) (p. 1589)
Rella, Concetta Rose & Couri, Megan. Windsong. (p. 2472)
Reller, Marcia Mattingly, illus. see Watson, Donn, ed.
Relyea, Alison, illus. see Grossnickle, Mary.
Relyea, C. M., illus. see Jackson, Gabrielle E.
Relyea, C. M., jt. auth. see Barbour, Ralph Henry.
Relyea, C. M., jt. auth. see Little, Frances.
Relyea, C. M., jt. auth. see Webster, Jean.
Relyea, Charles M., illus. see Mathewson, Christy.
Relyea, Gregg F. Parent/Teacher Manual for Trouble at the Watering Hole Children's Book. (p. 1699)
Relyea, Gregg F. & Weiss, Josh N. Bullied No More! The Continuing Adventures of Emo & Chickie. (p. 296)
Relyea, Gregg F. & Weiss, Joshua N. Phony Friends, Besties Again: The Continuing Adventures of Emo & Chickie. (p. 1736)
rem, illus. see Schreiber, Ellen.
Remarque, Erich Maria. All Quiet on the Western Front. Wimperis, Sarah, illus. (p. 53)
Reme, Caroline. Jasmine Hates Wash Hair Days! (p. 1160)
Remenar, Kristen. Groundhog's Dilemma. Faulkner, Matt, illus. (p. 898)
Remender, Rick. Corps! (p. 456)
—Fear Agent Library Edition Volume 2. Thorpe, Patrick, ed. (p. 716)
Remender, Rick, et al. Fractured Fables. (p. 775)
Remesz, Natasza, illus. see Coleman, Valerie.
Remey, Grace Anne. Lion's Pride: A Tail of Deployment. Remey, Grace Anne, illus. (p. 1307)
Remick, Carrie. Written in the Stars. (p. 2514)
Remick, Martha. Millicent Halford: A Tale of the Dark Days of Kentucky in the Year 1861 (Classic Reprint) (p. 1467)
—Millicent Halford. (p. 1467)
Remien, Robert. Outback Bob: And the 20-Foot Purple Ape. Budd, Jordan, illus. (p. 1683)
Remigius, Baker John. Old & New Style Fixed Dates Calendars & the Principles & Results of Emendations; a Paper Read - Scholar's Choice Edition. (p. 1644)
Reminger, Kay. Finding the Way Home. (p. 730)
Remington, Frederic. Crooked Trails. (p. 477)
—John Ermine of the Yellowstone (Classic Reprint) (p. 1172)
—Men with the Bark on (Classic Reprint) (p. 1446)
—Pony Tracks (Classic Reprint) (p. 1773)
—Sundown Leflare (Classic Reprint) (p. 2152)
Remington, Frederic, jt. auth. see Longfellow, Henry.
Remington, Laurel. Cake & Confessions. (p. 309)
—Secrets & Scones. (p. 1979)
Remington, Mary E. Extracts from the Journals of Miss. M. E. Remington, Missionary of the Welcome Hall Mission, New Haven, Conn (Classic Reprint) (p. 685)
Reminick, Gerald. Ollie Otter's Special Gift: A Story from Quiet Pond. Quintero, michelle, illus. (p. 1650)
Remkiewicz, Frank. Gus Gets Scared. (p. 906)
—Gus Grows a Plant. (p. 906)
—Gus Loses a Tooth. (p. 906)
—Gus Makes a Friend. (p. 906)
—Gus Makes a Gift. (p. 906)
Remkiewicz, Frank, illus. see Kline, Suzy.
Remkiewicz, Frank, illus. see Lewis, J. Patrick.
Remkiewicz, Frank, illus. see London, Jonathan & Wells, Rosemary.
Remkiewicz, Frank, illus. see London, Jonathan.
Remkiewicz, Frank, illus. see Martin, David Lozell.
Remkiewicz, Frank, illus. see Michalak, Jamie.
Remkiewicz, Frank, illus. see Murphy, Stuart J.
Remkiewicz, Frank, illus. see Riggs Vetter, Jennifer.
Remkiewicz, Frank, jt. auth. see London, Jonathan.
Remmel, Victoria. Bipolar Bear: A Resource to Talk about Mental Health (p. 229)
Remois, Leon Le. Histoire Merveilleuse et Effroyable Arrivee en Normandie En 1470: Dont la Copie Fidele (Classic Reprint) (p. 975)
Remolina, Tere. Leyendas de Todo Mexico: Leyendas Que Perduran en la Memoria de Cada Habitante. (p. 1282)
Remolina, Tere, et al. Leyendas de Todo Mexico. (p. 1282)
Rempel, Alliana. One. (p. 1658)
Rempel, Billi-Jo, illus. see Beere, Lisa.
Rempel, J. D. Marigold & the Snoring King. (p. 1405)
Remphry, Martin. Pirates Are Stealing Our Cows. Remphry, Martin, illus. (p. 1750)
Remphry, Martin, illus. see Fischel, Emma.
Remphry, Martin, illus. see Martin, Steve.
Remphry, Martin, illus. see North, Laura.
Rempt, Fione. Rico the Brave Sock Monkey. (p. 1877)
Remsburg, Rebecca. Night, Night, Knight (p. 1606)
Remsen, Ira. Chemical Experiments: Prepared to Accompany Remsen's Introduction to the Study of Chemistry (Classic Reprint) (p. 365)
—Laboratory Manual: Containing Directions for a Course of Experiments in General Chemistry, Systematically Arranged to Accompany the Author's Elements of Chemistry (Classic Reprint) (p. 1235)
Remus, Marc. Gallery of Wonders. (p. 806)
—Golden Maple Tree. (p. 858)
—Uprising: Books for Kids: a Magical Children's Fantasy Series. (p. 2339)
Remussi, Diego. Leyendas de Los Incas, Mayas y Aztecas Contada para Niños. (p. 1282)
—Leyendas Mapuches Contadas para Niños. (p. 1282)
Remy, Jean S. Lives of the Presidents: Told in Words of One Syllable (Classic Reprint) (p. 1332)
Ren, Amber, illus. see Smith, Danna.
Ren, Amber, illus. see Willems, Mo.
Ren, et al. Investigating Why Leaves Change Their Color. (p. 1131)
Ren, Rongrong. Chinese Folk Tales. (p. 378)
Ren, Rongrong, ed. Chinese Folk Tales: Volume 2. (p. 378)
Renae, Cameo. Hidden Wings. (p. 966)
Renae, Rissa. Grimms & Garms. (p. 896)
Renan, Ernest. De l'Origine du Langage - Scholar's Choice Edition. (p. 517)
Renard, Jules. Poil de Carotte. (p. 1767)
Renard, Maurice. New Bodies for Old (Classic Reprint) (p. 1591)
Renart, Jean. Lai de l'Ombre (Classic Reprint) (p. 1239)
Renaud, Anne. Bloom of Friendship: The Story of the Canadian Tulip Festival (p. 247)
—Boy Who Invented the Popsicle: The Cool Science Behind Frank Epperson's Famous Frozen Treat. Pavlovi?, Milan, illus. (p. 271)
—Fania's Heart Rudnicki, Richard, illus. (p. 706)
—Into the Mist: The Story of the Empress of Ireland. (p. 1128)
—Mr. Crum's Potato Predicament. Sala, Felicita, illus. (p. 1518)
—Pier 21: Stories from near & Far (p. 1742)
—True Tale of a Giantess: The Story of Anna Swan. Lafrance, Marie, illus. (p. 2295)
Renaud, Joanne, illus. see Coleman, Wim & Perrin, Pat.
Renaud, Marguerite, jt. auth. see Parker, Emma.
Renaud, Paul. Tarot. (p. 2192)
Renauld, Laura. Fred's Big Feelings: The Life & Legacy of Mister Rogers. Barrager, Brigette, illus. (p. 782)
—Porcupine's Pie Poh, Jennie, illus. (p. 1778)
Renaut, Jean. Lai D'Ignaures: En Vers, du Xiie Siecle (Classic Reprint) (p. 1239)
Renberg, Dalia Hardof. King Solomon & the Bee. Heller, Ruth, illus. (p. 1221)
Rencoukos, Lindsey. Adventures of Princess Penelope. (p. 27)
Rendall, Jaydine. High Plains Heroes: Josiah. (p. 968)
—High Plains Heroes: Laughing Wolf. (p. 968)
—High Plains Heroes: Josiah. Prom, Shirley, illus. (p. 968)
Rendeiro, Charlene, illus. see Hopkins, Lee Bennett.
Rendell, Joanne, jt. auth. see Brody, Jessica.
Render, Willian. Sketches, Instructive & Entertaining, in English, German, & French: Containing Historical Tales, Heroic Actions, Anecdotes, Recreations in Natural History, Statistical Information, &C (Classic Reprint) (p. 2031)
Rendina, Donna Rae. Golden Leaf. Bronowski, Karen Kmetz, illus. (p. 858)
Rendle, Frank. Victoria College Annual: Year 1927-1928 (Classic Reprint) (p. 2355)
Rendle, Steve. Extreme Cars: Speed, Power, Torque & More! (p. 686)
Rendon, Amalia, illus. see Beighton, Matt.
Rendon, Daniel, illus. see Lobdell, Scott.
Rendon, Joel, illus. see Navarrete, Federico.
Rendon, Leah, ed. see Dzidrums, Christine.
Rendon, Leah, jt. auth. see Dzidrums, Christine.
Rendu, Victor. Animaux de la France (Classic Reprint) (p. 96)
Rene, Anastacia. Herman Gets a Haircut. (p. 959)
René, Ellen. Investigating How Flowers Grow. (p. 1131)
—Investigating Spiders & Their Webs. (p. 1131)
—Investigating Volcanic Eruptions. (p. 1131)
—Investigating Why Animals Shed Their Skin. (p. 1131)
—Investigating Why It Rains. (p. 1131)
—Investigating Why Leaves Change Their Color. (p. 1131)
Rene, Michelle. Manufactured Witches. (p. 1399)
Rene, Perez, illus. see Heller, Andrew.
René, Richard. Edge of Mysterion: Another Tale of Mysterion. (p. 625)
Rene, Sharon. Mixed Bag of God's Grace. (p. 1484)
Renee, Ashley, illus. see Bembry, Shanylah.
Renee, Ashley, illus. see Clark, Johanna.
Renee, Ashley, illus. see Williams, Iris M.
Renee, Chantell. Undaunted. (p. 2320)
Renee, Duke. Volcanic Rose. (p. 2366)
Renee, Haley, illus. see Pants, S'Mar T.
Renee, Lindsey. What Kind of Fairy Is Merry Berry? (p. 2418)
Renehan, Patrick, jt. auth. see Penne, Barbra.
Renek, Nava. Venice Is for Cats. (p. 2350)
Renert, Gerry. Nathan Saves Summer. Bradshaw, Carrie Anne, illus. (p. 1577)
—Nathan Saves Summer/Nathan Rescata el Verano. Bradshaw, Carrie Anne, illus. (p. 1577)
Renfrey, G. S. Golden Sands of Isalan: Book 2 - Chrysalis. (p. 859)
Renfro, Ed, illus. see Sansevere-Dreher, Diane.
Renfroe, Ann. Living Ice Cream Guys. Wilson, Alonza S., illus. (p. 1333)
Renfroe, Emma, illus. see Lancaster, Camille.
Renfroe, Leisa, illus. see Trechsel, Kelli.
Renfrow, Lisa. Breaking Point. (p. 278)
Rengel, Marian. Pakistan: A Primary Source Cultural Guide. (p. 1694)
Renger, Nikolai, illus. see Herget, Gundi & Garlid, Ann.
Renier, Aaron. Unsinkable Walker Bean. Renier, Aaron, illus. (p. 2335)
—Unsinkable Walker Bean & the Knights of the Waxing Moon. (p. 2335)
Renier, Aaron, illus. see Eggers, Dave.
Renier, Aaron, illus. see Morris, Gerald.
Renier, Aaron, illus. see Pinkwater, Daniel M.
Renier, Aaron, jt. auth. see Pope, Paul.
Reninger, Anthony. Ella. (p. 637)
Renn, Diana. Tokyo Heist. (p. 2256)
Renne, Philip K., illus. see O'Hearn, Michael.
Renne, Rachel, illus. see Owen, Sarah.
Renner, Barbara. Lonnie the Loon Finds His Home. Kinney, Davina, illus. (p. 1344)
—Lonnie the Loon Flies South for the Winter. Kinney, Davina, illus. (p. 1344)
—Lonnie the Loon Learns to Call. (p. 1344)
—Quincy the Quail & the Mysterious Egg. Wells, Amanda M., illus. (p. 1828)
—Quincy the Quail Leads His Family on an Adventure. Wells, Amanda M., illus. (p. 1828)
—Spring! Time to Build a Nest, a Story about Trumpeter Swans. Goldner, Rita, illus. (p. 2092)
Renner, Benjamin. Big Bad Fox. (p. 216)
Renner, C. J., et al. Soccer Longshot Maese, Fares, illus. (p. 2052)
—Soccer Longshot Maese, Fares & Aburto, Jesus, illus. (p. 2052)
Renner, Ellen. Castle of Shadows. (p. 340)
Renner, Jodie. Childhood Regained: Canadian Teachers' Guide. (p. 370)
Renner, Jodie, et al. Childhood Regained: American Schools Edition. (p. 370)
—Childhood Regained: Canadian Schools Edition. (p. 370)
—Childhood Regained: Student Edition, Grades 4 To 6. (p. 370)
Renner, Kate, illus. see Bentley, Hope A. C.
Renner, Oliver. Uberall Gleich. (p. 2313)
Rennert, Laura Joy. Emma, the Extra Ordinary Princess. Florian, Melanie, illus. (p. 643)
—Royal Princess Academy: Dragon Dreams. Florian, Melanie, illus. (p. 1910)
Renneville, Madame de. Charles & Eugenia (Classic Reprint) (p. 358)
Rennie, Cliff. Goal Behind the Curtain. (p. 849)
—Offside in Ecuatina. (p. 1641)
Rennie, Henri 'Renoir'. For the Young & Old Souls. (p. 764)
Rennie, James. Alphabet of Scientific Chemistry, for the Use of Beginners (Classic Reprint) (p. 59)
—Architecture of Birds: With Engravings (Classic Reprint) (p. 111)
Rennie, Susan. 12 Days O Yule Land, Matthew, illus. (p. 2551)
—Oxford Roald Dahl Dictionary: From Aardvark to Zozimus, a Real Dictionary of Everyday & Extra-Usual Words. (p. 1689)
Rennie, Susan, tr. see Kerr, Judith.
Rennison, Louise. Angus, Thongs & Full-Frontal Snogging. (p. 87)
—Are These My Basoomas I See Before Me? (p. 112)
—Are These My Basoomas I See Before Me? Final Confessions of Georgia Nicolson. (p. 112)
—Midsummer Tights Dream. (p. 1462)
—Stop in the Name of Pants! (p. 2122)
—Taming of the Tights. (p. 2189)
—Withering Tights. (p. 2482)
Rennocks, Sam. Under the Sea ABC. (p. 2322)
Rennocks, Sam, illus. see Hayes, Susan.
Rennolds, Harney. Out of the Ashes: A Possible Solution to the Social Problem of Divorce (Classic Reprint) (p. 1682)
Reno, Stephanie, illus. see Wilson, Beth S.
Reno, University of Nevada. Artemisia, Vol. 102: Spring, 2008 (Classic Reprint) (p. 122)
Renon, Delphine, illus. see Andriamirado, Natacha.
Renon, Delphine, jt. auth. see Andriamirado, Natacha.
Renouf, Michael, illus. see Cattanach, Ann.
Renshaw, Brian. Lonely Little Mesa. (p. 1342)
Rensink, Jessy, illus. see MacLeod, Angus.
Rensselaer, Schuyler Van. Many Children (Classic Reprint) (p. 1400)
—One Man Who Was Content; Mary; the Lustigs; Corinna's Fiammetta (Classic Reprint) (p. 1660)
Renta, Kathryn, illus. see Bab Bonde, Jessica.
Renthrope, Damon, illus. see Wendel, Gretchen Schomer & Schomer, Adam Anthony.
Renton, Lesley. Cat Between Two Worlds. (p. 341)
Rentta, Sharon, illus. see Nolan, Tina.
Renuka, Singh (Ed). Boundless As the Sky. (p. 265)
Renwick, Jessica. Bow of Anarchy. (p. 266)
—Guitar of Mayhem. (p. 904)
Renwick, Thomas. Narrative of the Case of Miss. Margaret Mcavoy: With an Account of Some Optical Experiments Connected with It (Classic Reprint) (p. 1575)
Renz, Ulrich. Cygnes Sauvages - de Wilde Zwanen (Français - Néerlandais). d'Après un Conte de Fées de Hans Christian Andersen: Livre Bilingue Pour Enfants À Partir de 4-6 Ans, Avec Livre Audio MP3 À Télécharger. Kleimaker, Christa, tr. (p. 493)
—Cygnes Sauvages - Die Wilden Schwäne (Français - Allemand). d'Après un Conte de Fées de Hans Christian Andersen: Livre Bilingue Pour Enfants À Partir de 4-6 Ans, Avec Livre Audio MP3 À Télécharger. Andler, Martin, tr. (p. 493)
—Cygnes Sauvages - I Cigni Selvatici (Français - Italien). d'Après un Conte de Fées de Hans Christian Andersen: Livre Bilingue Pour Enfants À Partir de 4-6 Ans, Avec Livre Audio MP3 À Télécharger. Galeati, Clara, tr. (p. 493)
—Cygnes Sauvages - the Wild Swans (Français - Anglais). d'Après un Conte de Fées de Hans Christian Andersen: Livre Bilingue Pour Enfants À Partir de 4-6 Ans, Avec Livre Audio MP3 À Télécharger. Andler, Martin, tr. (p. 493)
—De Vilda Svanarna - Khoo'hâye Wahshee (Svenska - Persiska, Farsi, Dari). Efter en Saga AV Hans Christian Andersen: Tvåspråkig Barnbok Med Ljudbok SOM Mp3-Nedladdning, Från 4-6 År. Thordsen, Narona, tr. (p. 517)
—Die Wilden Schwäne - Albajae Albary (Deutsch - Arabisch). Nach Einem Märchen Von Hans Christian Andersen: Zweisprachiges Kinderbuch Mit MP3 Hörbuch Zum Herunterladen, AB 4-6 Jahren. Othman, Inana, tr. (p. 544)
—Die Wilden Schwäne - de Vilda Svanarna (Deutsch - Schwedisch). Nach Einem Märchen Von Hans Christian Andersen: Zweisprachiges Kinderbuch Mit MP3 Hörbuch Zum Herunterladen, AB 4-6 Jahren. Thordsen, Narona, tr. (p. 544)
—Die Wilden Schwäne - Khoo'hâye Wahshee (Deutsch - Persisch, Farsi, Dari). Nach Einem Märchen Von Hans Christian Andersen: Zweisprachiges Kinderbuch Mit MP3 Hörbuch Zum Herunterladen, AB 4-6 Jahren. (p. 544)
—Die Wilden Schwäne - the Wild Swans (Deutsch - Englisch). Nach Einem Märchen Von Hans Christian Andersen: Zweisprachiges Kinderbuch Mit MP3 Hörbuch Zum Herunterladen, AB 4-6 Jahren. Savill, Pete, tr. (p. 544)
—Die Wilden Schwäne - Villijoutsenet (Deutsch - Finnisch). Nach Einem Märchen Von Hans Christian Andersen: Zweisprachiges Kinderbuch Mit MP3 Hörbuch Zum Herunterladen, AB 4-6 Jahren. Konttinen, Janika Tuulia, tr. (p. 544)
—Dorme Bem, Lobinho - Que Duermas Bien, Pequeno Lobo. Livro Infantil Bilingue (Portugues - Espanhol) (p. 586)
—Dormi Bene, Piccolo Lupo - Priyatnykh Snov, Malen'kiy Volchyonok (Italiano - Russo) Libro per Bambini Bilingue Da 2-4 Anni, con Audiolibro MP3 Da Scaricare. Haase, Margherita, tr. (p. 586)
—Dormi Bene, Piccolo Lupo - Schlaf Gut, Kleiner Wolf (Italiano - Tedesco) Libro per Bambini Bilingue Da 2-4 Anni, con Audiolibro MP3 Da Scaricare. Haase, Margherita, tr. (p. 586)
—Dors Bien, Petit Loup - Dormi Bene, Piccolo Lupo (Français - Italien) Livre Bilingue Pour Enfants À Partir de 2-4 Ans, Avec Livre Audio MP3 À Télécharger. Lottiger, Celeste, tr. (p. 587)
—Dors Bien, Petit Loup - Nam Jayyidan Ayyuha Adh-Dhaib As-Sagir (Français - Arabe) Livre Bilingue Pour Enfants À Partir de 2-4 Ans, Avec Livre Audio MP3 À Télécharger. Bouyssery, Abdelaaziz, tr. (p. 587)
—Dors Bien, Petit Loup - Que Duermas Bien, Pequeño Lobo (Français - Espagnol) Livre Bilingue Pour Enfants À Partir de 2-4 Ans, Avec Livre Audio MP3 À Télécharger. Landmesser, Anneli, tr. (p. 587)

R

—Dors Bien, Petit Loup - Shpii Dobshe, Mawi Vilku (Français - Polonais) Livre Bilingue Pour Enfants À Partir de 2-4 Ans, Avec Livre Audio MP3 À Télécharger. Lottigier, Celeste, tr. (p. 587)
—My Most Beautiful Dream - Minun Kaikista Kaunein Uneni (English - Finnish) Bilingual Children's Picture Book, with Audiobook for Download. Konttinen, Janika, tr. (p. 1556)
—My Most Beautiful Dream - Moj Najljepsi San (English - Croatian) Bilingual Children's Picture Book, with Audiobook for Download. Agnew, Sefa, tr. (p. 1556)
—My Most Beautiful Dream - Ndoto Yangu Nzuri Sana Kuliko Zote (English - Swahili) Bilingual Children's Picture Book, with Audiobook for Download. Saito, Yumiko, tr. (p. 1556)
—My Most Beautiful Dream - Visul Meu Cel Mai Frumos (English - Romanian) Bilingual Children's Picture Book, with Audiobook for Download. Roiban, Bianca, tr. (p. 1556)
—Nam Jayyidan Ayyuha Adh-Dhaib As-Sagir - Sleep Tight, Little Wolf (Arabic - English) Bilingual Children's Book with MP3 Audiobook for Download, Age 2-4 & Up. Boussayer, Abdelaaziz, tr. (p. 1573)
—Schlaf Gut, Kleiner Wolf - Dors Bien, Petit Loup (Deutsch - Französisch) Zweisprachiges Kinderbuch Mit MP3 Hörbuch Zum Herunterladen, AB 2-4 Jahren. Lottigier, Celeste, tr. (p. 1944)
—Schlaf Gut, Kleiner Wolf - Nam Jayyidan Ayyuha Adh-Dhaib As-Sagir (Deutsch - Arabisch) Zweisprachiges Kinderbuch Mit MP3 Hörbuch Zum Herunterladen, AB 2-4 Jahren. (p. 1944)
—Schlaf Gut, Kleiner Wolf - Nuku Hyvin, Pieni Susi (Deutsch - Finnisch) Zweisprachiges Kinderbuch Mit MP3 Hörbuch Zum Herunterladen, AB 2-4 Jahren. Hach, Virpi, tr. (p. 1944)
—Schlaf Gut, Kleiner Wolf - Priyatnykh Snov, Malen'kiy Volchyonok (Deutsch - Russisch) Zweisprachiges Kinderbuch Mit MP3 Hörbuch Zum Herunterladen, AB 2-4 Jahren. Hordiyenko, Svetlana, tr. (p. 1944)
—Schlaf Gut, Kleiner Wolf - Ràhat Bekhàb, Gorge Kutshak (Deutsch - Persisch, Farsi, Dari) Zweisprachiges Kinderbuch Mit MP3 Hörbuch Zum Herunterladen, AB 2-4 Jahren. (p. 1944)
—Schlaf Gut, Kleiner Wolf - Sleep Tight, Little Wolf (Deutsch - Englisch) Zweisprachiges Kinderbuch Mit MP3 Hörbuch Zum Herunterladen, AB 2-4 Jahren. (p. 1944)
—Sleep Tight, Little Wolf (Arabic Edition) A Bedtime Story for Sleepy (and Not So Sleepy) Children. Brinkmann, Barbara, illus. (p. 2036)
—Sleep Tight, Little Wolf (French Edition) Brinkmann, Barbara, illus. (p. 2036)
—Sleep Tight, Little Wolf (Italian Edition) A Bedtime Story for Sleepy (and Not So Sleepy) Children. Brinkmann, Barbara, illus. (p. 2036)
—Sleep Tight, Little Wolf - Dors Bien, Petit Loup (English - French) Bilingual Children's Book with MP3 Audiobook for Download, Age 2-4 & Up. Savill, Pete, tr. (p. 2036)
—Sleep Tight, Little Wolf - Que Duermas Bien, Pequeño Lobo (English - Spanish) Bilingual Children's Book with MP3 Audiobook for Download, Age 2 & Up. Landmesser, Anneli, tr. (p. 2036)
—Sleep Tight, Little Wolf - Schlaf Gut, Kleiner Wolf (English - German) Bilingual Children's Book with MP3 Audiobook for Download, Age 2-4 & Up. Savill, Pete, tr. (p. 2036)
—Sleep Tight, Little Wolf - Slaap Lekker, Kleine Wolf (English - Dutch) Bilingual Children's Book with MP3 Audiobook for Download, Age 2-4 & Up. Van Den Berg, Jonathan, tr. (p. 2036)
—Sleep Tight, Little Wolf - Sov Gott, Lilla Vargen (English - Swedish) Bilingual Children's Book with MP3 Audiobook for Download, Age 2-4 & Up. Thordsen, Narona, tr. (p. 2036)
—Sov Gott, Lilla Vargen - Dormi Bene, Piccolo Lupo. Tvaspråkig Bambok (Svenska - Italienska). (p. 2069)
—Sov Gott, Lilla Vargen - Jal Ja, Kkoma Neugdaeya. Tvaspråkig Bambok (Svenska - Koreanska). (p. 2069)
—Sov Gott, Lilla Vargen - Que Duermas Bien, Pequeño Lobo (Svenska - Spanska) Tvåspråkig Barnbok Med Ljudbok SOM Mp3-Nedladdning, Från 2-4 År. Bienzle Arruda, Katrin, tr. (p. 2069)
—Sov Gott, Lilla Vargen - Sleep Tight, Little Wolf (Svenska - Engelska) Tvåspråkig Barnbok Med Ljudbok SOM Mp3-Nedladdning, Från 2-4 År. Thordsen, Narona, tr. (p. 2069)
—Wild Swans - Albajae Albary (English - Arabic). Based on a Fairy Tale by Hans Christian Andersen: Bilingual Children's Book with MP3 Audiobook for Download, Age 4-6 & Up. Othman, Inana, tr. (p. 2464)
—Wild Swans - de Vilda Svanarna (English - Swedish). Based on a Fairy Tale by Hans Christian Andersen: Bilingual Children's Book with MP3 Audiobook for Download, Age 4-6 & Up. Thordsen, Narona, tr. (p. 2464)
—Wild Swans - Khoo'hàye Wahshee (English - Persian, Farsi, Dari). Based on a Fairy Tale by Hans Christian Andersen: Bilingual Children's Book with MP3 Audiobook for Download, Age 4-6 & Up. Mortezai, Jahan, tr. (p. 2465)
—Wild Swans - les Cygnes Sauvages (English - French). Based on a Fairy Tale by Hans Christian Andersen: Bilingual Children's Book with MP3 Audiobook for Download, Age 4-6 & Up. Andler, Martin, tr. (p. 2465)
—Wild Swans - Los Cisnes Salvajes (English - Spanish). Based on a Fairy Tale by Hans Christian Andersen: Bilingual Children's Book with MP3 Audiobook for Download, Age 4-6 & Up. Canedo, Marcos, tr. (p. 2465)
Renzetti, Rob. Onward: Quests of Yore. Disney Storybook Art Team et al, illus. (p. 1664)
Renzetti, Rob & Hirsch, Alex. Gravity Falls: Journal 3. Gonsalves, Andy et al, illus. (p. 882)
Renzetti, Rob & Vine, Rachel. DuckTales: Solving Mysteries & Rewriting History! Foley, Niki, illus. (p. 608)
Renzi, Federico, tr. see Pochini, Eugenio.
Renzi, Pam. Global Christmas. (p. 843)
Renzoni, Mark, photos by see Renzoni, Phil.
Renzoni, Phil. Baby Who Started a Revolution. Parise, Anna Maria, ed. (p. 153)
Reonegro, Antonio, jt. auth. see Coy, John.
Repetto, Gary. Afraid of the Dark. (p. 31)
Repetto, Laurie, illus. see Thomas, Charlene.
Repino, Robert. Spark & the League of Ursus: A Novel. (p. 2074)
Repka, Janice. Clueless Girl's Guide to Being a Genius. (p. 409)
Repka, Janice, jt. auth. see Rosensweig, Jay B.
Repkin, Mark. Mommy Breastfeeds My Baby Brother/ Mama Amamanta A Mi Hermanito. Moneysmith, David, illus. (p. 1490)
Replogle, Charles. Among the Indians of Alaska (Classic Reprint) (p. 76)
Reppel, Phyllis, illus. see Martinez, Elsie & Stelly, Colette.
Reppen, Ellisiv. Chess: Be the King! Hartberg, Flu, illus. (p. 366)
Reppion, John, jt. auth. see Moore, Leah.
Repplier, Agnes. Cat: Being a Record of the Endearments & Invectives Lavished by Many Writers upon an Animal Much Loved & Much Abhorred (Classic Reprint) (p. 341)
—Fireside Sphinx (Classic Reprint) (p. 734)
—In Our Convent Days - Scholar's Choice Edition. (p. 1106)
Repplier, Banning. Shipbuilder, 1935, Vol. 5 (Classic Reprint) (p. 2008)
Requien, Esprit. Catalogue des Coquilles de l'Ile de Corse, 1848 (Classic Reprint) (p. 342)
Requier, A. J. Great Quackqua; or Brothers of the Shadow: A Burlesque Operetta; in Two Acts (Classic Reprint) (p. 888)
Requier, Augustus Julian. Old Sanctuary: A Romance of the Ashley (Classic Reprint) (p. 1648)
Rere The Storyteller. I Am a Wish. (p. 1057)
Resau, Laura. Estrella en el Bosque (Star in the Forest) (p. 665)
—Indigo Notebook. (p. 1117)
—Lightning Queen. (p. 1300)
—Ruby Notebook. (p. 1911)
—Star in the Forest. (p. 2102)
—Tree of Dreams. (p. 2284)
Resberg, Kathy. Kimberly's Cats & Dogs Foundation Farm. (p. 1218)
Rescek, Sanja. Easter Bunny's Helpers. (p. 619)
Rescek, Sanja, illus. see Bradshaw, Sarah.
Rescek, Sanja, illus. see Burton, Jeffrey & Tornow, Chani.
Rescek, Sanja, illus. see Burton, Jeffrey.
Rescek, Sanja, illus. see Fronis, Aly.
Rescek, Sanja, illus. see Fry, Sonali.
Rescek, Sanja, illus. see Piper, Sophie.
Rescek, Sanja, illus. see Rock, Lois.
Rescek, Sanja, illus. see Schulz, Kathy.
Rescek, Sanja, illus. see Sequoia Children's Publishing.
Rescek, Sanja, illus. see Slater, Teddy.
Rescek, Sanja, illus. see Tiger Tales.
Rescek, Sanja, illus. see Wing, Scarlett.
Rescek, Sanja, jt. illus. see Slater, Teddy.
Resch, Elyse. Intuitive Eating Workbook for Teens: A Non-Diet, Body Positive Approach to Building a Healthy Relationship with Food. (p. 1129)
Reschofsky, Jean, illus. see Goff-Tuttle, Marie Jaume.
Research, American Society For Psychical. Proceedings of the American Society for Psychical Research, Vol. 5: Section B of the American Institute for Scientific Research (Classic Reprint) (p. 1803)
—Proceedings of the American Society for Psychical Research, Vol. 12: Section B of the American Institute for Scientific Research (Classic Reprint) (p. 1803)
—Proceedings of the American Society for Psychical Research, 1912, Vol. 6: Section B of the American Institute for Scientific Research (Classic Reprint) (p. 1803)
—Proceedings of the American Society for Psychical Research, 1909, Vol. 3: Section B of the American Institute for Scientific Research; Parts I-II (Classic Reprint) (p. 1803)
—Proceedings of the American Society for Psychical Research, 1907, Vol. 1: Section B of the American Institute for Scientific Research; Parts I-III (Classic Reprint) (p. 1803)
Research & Education Association Editors, illus. see Loeb, Jeph & Sale, Tim.
Resh, Jr Mike. Cardinal Connection: A Cardinal Is Near. Kernen, Steven, illus. (p. 328)
Resh, Mike. Dneirf. (p. 570)
Resh, Mike Jr. Cardinal Connection: A Cardinal Is Near. Kernen, Steven, illus. (p. 328)
Resman, Michael. Lllana Ageiraü. Cayetano, Eldred Roy, tr. (p. 1301)
—Oh God, Where Are You? Fahy, Emer, illus. (p. 1641)
—Villagers. Senelwa, Fred, tr. (p. 2358)
Resnick, Eugene V. AP US History: With 2 Practice Tests. (p. 105)
—AP US History Premium: With 5 Practice Tests. (p. 105)
Resnick, Eugene V., et al. Regents Exams & Answers: U. S. History & Government 2020. (p. 1861)
Resnick, Jacqueline, text. Splat the Cat: Twice the Mice. (p. 2084)
Resnicoff, Stan. BIG Parade: New York. (p. 222)
—BIG Parade: Los Angeles. (p. 222)
—BIG Parade: San Francisco. (p. 222)
—Stanley, the Seal of Approval. (p. 2101)
—Tom, the Talking Toilet. (p. 2258)
—Who'll Do the Moo? (p. 2453)
Resor, Joy. Designed to Shine! Read Aloud Rhymes for Any Size Heart. Connell, Lauren, illus. (p. 532)
Respicio, Mae. House That Lou Built. (p. 1024)
Respofford, A. Library of Wit & Humor, Vol. 1: Prose & Poetry Selected from the Literature of All Times & Nations (Classic Reprint) (p. 1285)
Respress-Churchwell, Gloria & Freeman, Laura. Follow Chester! A College Football Team Fights Racism & Makes History. (p. 757)
Ressich, John. Oddly Enough (Classic Reprint) (p. 1637)
Restelli, Grazia, illus. see Krebs, Laurie.
Restivo, Andrea E. Arabella & the Perilous Pantheon. (p. 108)
Restrepo, Andres, illus. see Friedman, Geddy & Hernandez, Michael, eds.
Restrepo, Bettina. Illegal. (p. 1095)
—Moose & Magpie Rogers, Sherry, illus. (p. 1503)
Restrepo, Bettina & Rogers, Sherry. Moose & Magpie (p. 1503)
Retnani, Mehdi, tr. from ARA. Alya & the Three Cats. Fidawi, Maya, illus. (p. 61)
Retnyw, Werdna. Odds & Ends, Pictures of Town, & Mirth & Metre (Classic Reprint) (p. 1638)
Rettenmund, Tamara, illus. see Charlip, Remy.
Rettore. Duck & Friends: A Soft & Fuzzy Book Just for Baby! (p. 607)
—Elephant & Friends. (p. 633)
—Farm. (p. 709)
—Forest. (p. 765)
—Giraffe & Friends. (p. 834)
—Jungle. (p. 1189)
—Nighty Night Bear. (p. 1608)
—Penguin & Friends: A Soft & Fuzzy Book Just for Baby! (p. 1715)
—Sea: A Soft Book & Mirror for Baby! (p. 1966)
Retwick, Roy, illus. see Wood, Greg V.
Retwick, Roy, illus. see Wood, Greg V. & Benchmark Education Co.
Retz, Zac, illus. see Lefebvre, Jason.
Retzlaff, Shay, illus. see Shafer, Patty.
Reuben, Borgen, photos by see Learn As You Grow.
Reul, Robin. My Kind of Crazy. (p. 1550)
Reul, Sarah Lynne. Allie All Along. (p. 56)
—Breaking News. Reul, Sarah Lynne, illus. (p. 278)
—Farm the Farm: A Lift-The-Flap Book. Reul, Sarah Lynne, illus. (p. 710)
—Nerp! (p. 1588)
—Pet the Pets: A Lift-The-Flap Book. Reul, Sarah Lynne, illus. (p. 1726)
Reul, Sarah Lynne, illus. see Potoma, Alison.
Reusser, Kayleen. Celebrities Giving Back: A Guide to Giving Back. (p. 350)
—Day by Day with Taylor Swift. (p. 513)
—Hades. (p. 909)
—Hephaestus. (p. 956)
—Hermes. (p. 959)
—Leona Lewis. (p. 1267)
—Recipe & Craft Guide to Indonesia. (p. 1853)
—Selena Gomez. (p. 1986)
Reusswig, William, illus. see Lowery, Lawrence F.
Reuter, Fritz. In the Year 13: A Tale of Mecklenburg (Classic Reprint) (p. 1112)
—Old Story of My Farming Days: UT Mine Stromtid, Volume II - Scholar's Choice Edition. (p. 1648)
—Old Story of My Farming Days: UT Mine Stromtid, Volume III - Scholar's Choice Edition. (p. 1648)
—Old Story of My Farming Days (UT Mine Stromtid); in Three Volumes, Vol. I. (p. 1648)
—Old Story of My Farming Days, Vol. 1 Of 3: UT Mine Stromtid (Classic Reprint) (p. 1648)
—Seed-Time & Harvest: A Novel (Classic Reprint) (p. 1983)
Reuter Hapgood, Harriet. How to Be Luminous. (p. 1037)
—Raiz Cuadrada Del Verano. (p. 1838)
Reuter, William L. King Can Do No Wrong (Classic Reprint) (p. 1220)
Reuterstrand, Siri. Ellis Goes to the Doctor. Wik, Jenny, illus. (p. 638)
—Ellis Is Scared of the Dark. Wik, Jenny, illus. (p. 638)
Reuther, Marco. Klara Plotzky und der Elfenvampir. (p. 1227)
Reva, Maria, tr. see McMaster, Juliet & Cote, Patricia.
Revah, Noemie. Mister Horizontal & Miss Vertical. Zagnoli, Olimpia, illus. (p. 1482)
Revah, Patricia, illus. see Blanco, Alberto.
Revell, Cindy, illus. see Roberts, Jillian.
Revell, Cindy, illus. see StJohn, Amanda.
Revell, Cindy, illus. see Waldman, Debby & Feutl, Rita.
Revell, Cindy, illus. see Waldman, Debby.
Revell, Cindy, illus. see West, Tracey.
Revell, Genevieve and Kerrin & Revell, Kerrin. Sillyverse. (p. 2019)
Revell, Sharon. Gracie Youngblood. Revell, Sharon, illus. (p. 874)
Revell, Sharon, illus. see Brown, Sharon Lee.
Revell, Sharon, illus. see Criser, Starla K.
Revell, Sharon, illus. see Criser, Starla.
Revelle, Rick. Algonquin Spring: An Algonquin Quest Novel. (p. 44)
—Algonquin Sunset: An Algonquin Quest Novel. (p. 44)
—I Am Algonquin: An Algonquin Quest Novel. (p. 1057)
Revelman, P. Adventures of Tiny Tinsel Tinker the Third. (p. 29)
Revels, Robert, illus. see Shah, Idries.
Reveno, Katie. Synchro Sisters Forever: Mermaid Dreams. Szecsi, Susan, illus. (p. 2173)
Revenson, Jody. Candy Bonanza. (p. 322)
—Fantastic Beasts: the Crimes of Grindelwald: Movie Magic. (p. 707)
—Harry Potter: Diagon Alley: a Movie Scrapbook. (p. 935)
—Harry Potter: Hogwarts: a Movie Scrapbook. (p. 935)
—J. K. Rowling's Wizarding World: the Dark Arts: a Movie Scrapbook. (p. 1150)
—Movie Magic: Extraordinary People & Fascinating Places. (p. 1516)
Revenson, Jody & Burton, Bonnie. J. K. Rowling's Wizarding World: Movie Magic Volume Three: Amazing Artifacts. (p. 1150)
Revere, M. P. Bride's Hero (Classic Reprint) (p. 280)
Revere, Paul & Longfellow, Henry. Paul Revere's Ride. (p. 1707)
Reville, Frederick Douglas. Rebellion: A Story of the Red River Uprising (Classic Reprint) (p. 1852)
Reville, Jane. Ravens of Time Go Underground with Harriet Tubman. (p. 1844)
Revilo, Oliver. Our First Squeezin', or Harry May & Sally June, or the Old Way of Courtin' (Classic Reprint) (p. 1678)
Revis, Beth. Across the Universe (p. 11)
—Across the Universe. (p. 11)
—Ahsoka & Padmé. Pinto, Valentina, illus. (p. 36)
—Bid My Soul Farewell. (p. 215)
—Give the Dark My Love. (p. 840)
—Million Suns: An Across the Universe Novel. (p. 1468)
—Million Suns. (p. 1468)
—Shades of Earth. (p. 1996)
—Star Wars Rebel Rising. (p. 2104)
Revoil, Benedict Henry. Shooting & Fishing in the Rivers, Prairies, & Backwoods of North America, Vol. 1 of 2 (Classic Reprint) (p. 2009)
Revoir, Joyce, illus. see Foust, Cindy G.
Revoy, Antoine. Animus. (p. 96)
Revoy, Antoine, illus. see San Souci, Robert D.
Revoy, Antoine, illus. see Shecter, Vicky Alvear.
Rew, Barbara, jt. auth. see Freland, Cindy.
Rew, Jen, illus. see Hunter, Alex.
ReWalt, Nancy E. Aerial: A Spider's Tale. Cranford, Darren, illus. (p. 30)
—Aerial: A Trip to Remember. Cranford, Darren, illus. (p. 30)
Rewalt, Nancy E. Aerial Meets Farmer Fedamore. Cranford, Darren, illus. (p. 30)
—Lost & Found: Goldilocks & the Three Bears Revisited. Cranford, Darren, illus. (p. 1352)
Rewse, Katie, illus. see Charles, Beth.
Rex, Adam. Champions of Breakfast. (p. 355)
—Cold Cereal (p. 413)
—Fat Vampire: A Never Coming of Age Story. (p. 713)
—Frankenstein Makes a Sandwich. (p. 778)
—Frankenstein Takes the Cake. (p. 778)
—Nothing Rhymes with Orange. (p. 1625)
—Pluto Gets the Call. Keller, Laurie, illus. (p. 1763)
—Star Wars Are You Scared, Darth Vader? Rex, Adam, illus. (p. 2104)
—True Meaning of Smekday Rex, Adam, illus. (p. 2294)
—True Meaning of Smekday. (p. 2294)
—Unstoppable: (Family Read-Aloud Book, Silly Book about Cooperation) Park, Laura, illus. (p. 2335)
—Why? Keane, Claire, illus. (p. 2454)
—Xo, Ox: A Love Story. Campbell, Scott, illus. (p. 2516)
Rex, Adam, illus. see Barnett, Mac, et al.
Rex, Adam, illus. see Barnett, Mac.
Rex, Adam, illus. see Daywalt, Drew.
Rex, Adam, illus. see Gaiman, Neil.
Rex, Adam, illus. see Kelly, Katy.
Rex, Adam, jt. auth. see Messner, Kate.
Rex, Adam & Robinson, Christian. School's First Day of School. (p. 1947)
Rex, Deloney, illus. see Hoskins, Maria.
Rex, Katy & Genolet, Andres. Sweet Valley High. (p. 2169)
Rex, Michael. Backpack Aquarium: Icky Ricky #6. (p. 156)
—Birthday Party of Dread. Rex, Michael, illus. (p. 233)
—Brooms Are for Flying! (p. 285)
—Eat Pete. Rex, Michael, illus. (p. 621)
—Egg of Misery: Fangbone, Third Grade Barbarian. Rex, Michael, illus. (p. 628)
—Egg of Misery. (p. 628)
—End of the World Rex, Michael, illus. (p. 649)
—Facts vs. Opinions vs. Robots. Rex, Michael, illus. (p. 694)
—Fangbone! Third-Grade Barbarian. (p. 706)
—Fangbone! Third-Grade Barbarian. Rex, Michael, illus. (p. 706)
—Goodnight Goon: a Petrifying Parody. Rex, Michael, illus. (p. 867)
—Hole to China. (p. 987)
—Icky Ricky #2: the End of the World. Rex, Michael, illus. (p. 1088)
—Icky Ricky #3: the Dead Disco Raccoon. Rex, Michael, illus. (p. 1088)
—Pals. (p. 1694)
—Runaway Mummy: A Petrifying Parody. (p. 1915)
—Runaway Mummy: a Petrifying Parody. (p. 1915)
—Third-Grade Barbarian. (p. 2222)
—Toilet Paper Mummy. Rex, Michael, illus. (p. 2256)
—Two-Dollar Dirt Shirt. (p. 2307)
Rex, Michael, illus. see Branley, Franklyn M.
Rex, Michael, illus. see Bunting, Eve.
Rex, Michael, illus. see Friend, David.
Rex, Michael, illus. see Murphy, Stuart J.
Rex, Michael, jt. auth. see Friend, David.
Rex, Michael, jt. auth. see Murphy, Stuart J.
Rexing, Debbie. Writing Traits... My Perilous Journey, & I'm Only A 3rd Grader! (p. 2513)
Rey and others, Rey and. Great Big Dinosaur Treasury. (p. 884)
Rey, Carol. Iris Wall, Cracker Cowgirl Lux, Eldon, illus. (p. 1134)
Rey, H. A. Apple Harvest: Curious about Harvest Time. (p. 106)
—Around Town (p. 119)
—Awake-Asleep Cloth Book & Door Hanger. (p. 143)
—Builds a Tree House. (p. 295)
—Builds an Igloo. (p. 295)
—Busy Days with Curious George. (p. 302)
—C Is for Curious. (p. 306)
—Car Wash. (p. 327)
—Christmas Countdown. (p. 385)
—Curious about Christmas. (p. 486)
—Curious Baby Counting. (p. 486)
—Curious Baby Everyday Shapes Puzzle Book: A Puzzle Play Book. (p. 486)
—Curious George (Set Of 8) (p. 487)
—Curious George: a Halloween Boo Fest. (p. 486)
—Curious George & the Dump Truck. (p. 486)
—Curious George & the Ice Cream Surprise. (p. 486)
—Curious George & the Puppies (with Bonus Stickers & Audio) (p. 486)
—Curious George & the Sleepover. (p. 486)
—Curious George & the Summer Games. (p. 486)
—Curious George Apple Harvest. (p. 487)
—Curious George at the Baseball Game (Jorge el Curioso en el Partido de Beisbol) (p. 487)
—Curious George at the Park. Meyer, Emily, ed. (p. 487)
—Curious George Boxcar Derby (CGTV 8x8) (p. 487)
—Curious George Builds a Tree House (CGTV Reader) (p. 487)
—Curious George Classic Collection. (p. 487)
—Curious George Colors Eggs. (p. 487)
—Curious George Curious about Fall (tabbed Board Book) (p. 487)
—Curious George Curious about Learning Boxed Set. (p. 487)

Reynolds, Henry Robert. Notes of the Christian Life: A Selection of Sermons Preached (Classic Reprint) (p. 1624)
Reynolds, Hunter. Hunting with Great White Sharks. (p. 1054)
Reynolds, J. H. Monsterstreet: The Boy Who Cried Werewolf. (p. 1498)
—Monsterstreet #2: the Halloweeners. (p. 1498)
—Monsterstreet #3: Carnevil. (p. 1498)
—Monsterstreet #4: Camp of No Return. (p. 1498)
Reynolds, Jan. Cycle of Rice, Cycle of Life: A Story of Sustainable Farming. Reynolds, Jan, photos by. (p. 492)
—Only the Mountains Do Not Move: A Maasai Story of Culture & Conservation Reynolds, Jan, photos by. (p. 1664)
Reynolds, Jason. As Brave As You. (p. 124)
—Boy in the Black Suit. (p. 269)
—For Every One. (p. 762)
—Ghost (p. 827)
—Ghost. (p. 827)
—Jason Reynolds's Track Series: Ghost; Patina; Sunny; Lu. (p. 1161)
—Jason Reynolds's Track Series Paperback Collection: Ghost; Patina; Sunny; Lu. (p. 1161)
—Long Way Down. (p. 1343)
—Look Both Ways: A Tale Told in Ten Blocks. Nabaum, Alexander, illus. (p. 1345)
—Lu (p. 1363)
—Lu. (p. 1363)
—Miles Morales. (p. 1465)
—Miles Morales: Spider-Man. (p. 1465)
—Miles Morales: Spider-Man. Nelson, Kadir, illus. (p. 1465)
—Patina (p. 1705)
—Patina. (p. 1705)
—Sunny (p. 2152)
—Sunny. (p. 2152)
—When I Was the Greatest. (p. 2431)
Reynolds, Jason, jt. auth. see Petry, Ann.
Reynolds, Jason & Brendan Kiely. All American Boys. (p. 51)
Reynolds, Jason & Griffin, Jason. My Name Is Jason. Mine Too: Our Story. Our Way. (p. 1557)
—My Name Is Jason. Mine Too: Our Story. Our Way. Griffin, Jason, illus. (p. 1557)
Reynolds, Jason & Kendi, Ibram X. Stamped: Racism, Antiracism, & You: A Remix of the National Book Award-Winning Stamped from the Beginning. (p. 2100)
Reynolds, Jason & Kiely, Brendan. All American Boys. (p. 51)
—Chicos Típicamente Americanos. (p. 369)
Reynolds, Jason, et al. Hope Nation: YA Authors Share Personal Moments of Inspiration. Brock, Rose, ed. (p. 1002)
Reynolds, Jean, ed. see InkThinkTank.
Reynolds, Jeff, jt. auth. see Reynolds, Jeff E.
Reynolds, Jennifer Lea. Cat Who Loved the Moon. (p. 342)
Reynolds, Joey. Girl with the Dinosaur Tooth. Ebensperger, Michael, illus. (p. 837)
Reynolds, John. Cambridge Checkpoint English Workbook 2. (p. 313)
—Robyn Hood: Outlaw Princess. (p. 1893)
Reynolds, John Hamilton. Benjamin the Waggoner: A Ryghte Merrie & Conceitede Tale in Verse; a Fragment (Classic Reprint) (p. 200)
Reynolds, Joseph William. Mystery of Miracles: A Scientific & Philosophical Investigation (Classic Reprint) (p. 1569)
Reynolds, Joshua a. Treasure on the Southern Moor. (p. 2282)
—Williams House. (p. 2469)
Reynolds, Justin A. Opposite of Always. (p. 1667)
Reynolds, K. A. Land of Yesterday. (p. 1242)
—Spinner of Dreams. (p. 2082)
Reynolds, Katharine. Green Valley (Classic Reprint) (p. 895)
Reynolds, Lori. My Name Is Mac. Cardwell, Brett, illus. (p. 1557)
Reynolds, Lucy Brown. Drops of Spray, from Southern Seas (Classic Reprint) (p. 605)
Reynolds, Luke. Bedtime Blast-Off! Yamada, Mike, illus. (p. 188)
—Fantastic Failures: True Stories of People Who Changed the World by Falling down First. (p. 707)
—If My Love Were a Fire Truck: A Daddy's Love Song. Mack, Jeff, illus. (p. 1092)
—If My Love Were a Fire Truck. Mack, Jeff, Illus. (p. 1092)
Reynolds, Luke, jt. auth. see Montijo, Rhode.
Reynolds, Luke, ed. Break These Rules: 35 YA Authors on Speaking up, Standing Out, & Being Yourself. (p. 278)
Reynolds, Madeline. Illusions. (p. 1096)
Reynolds, Marty. Soldier of Grace. (p. 2056)
Reynolds, Mattie. Sharing with Others: An Introduction to Financial Literacy. (p. 2001)
—Super-Smart Shopping: An Introduction to Financial Literacy. (p. 2158)
Reynolds May. Billy & the Day Before Yesterday. (p. 227)
Reynolds, Michael. Engine-Driving Life: Or Stirring Adventures & Incidents in the Lives of Locomotive Engine-Drivers (Classic Reprint) (p. 651)
Reynolds, Michael, tr. River. (p. 1887)
Reynolds, Mike. How to Analyze the Films of Spike Lee (p. 1036)
Reynolds, Minnie J. Crayon Clue (Classic Reprint) (p. 468)
Reynolds, Osborne. On an Inversion of Ideas As to the Structure of the Universe. (p. 1652)
Reynolds, Pat, illus. see Reilly, Carmel.
Reynolds, Paul. Sydney & Simon: to the Moon! Reynolds, Peter H., illus. (p. 2172)
Reynolds, Paul A. Going Green! Reynolds, Paul A. & Reynolds, Peter H., illus. (p. 854)
Reynolds, Paul A., jt. auth. see Reynolds, Peter.
Reynolds, Paul A. & Reynolds, Peter H. Going Places. Reynolds, Peter H., illus. (p. 855)
Reynolds, Peter. Ish. (p. 1138)
—Word Collector. (p. 2493)
Reynolds, Peter, illus. see Potter, Ellen.
Reynolds, Peter & Reynolds, Paul A. Full Steam Ahead! (p. 797)
Reynolds, Peter H. Be You! Reynolds, Peter H., illus. (p. 178)
—Best Kid in the World: A SugarLoaf Book. Reynolds, Peter H., illus. (p. 206)
—Big Screen Books: For Big Fans of Story Sharing: the Dot Download: the Dot - Download. (p. 222)
—Coleccionista de Palabras. (p. 413)
—Dot: Make Your Mark Kit. Reynolds, Peter H., illus. (p. 587)
—Happy Dreamer. (p. 921)
—I'm Here. Reynolds, Peter H., illus. (p. 1098)
—Make Your Mark Gallery: a Coloring Book-Ish. Reynolds, Peter H., illus. (p. 1387)
—North Star. Reynolds, Peter H., illus. (p. 1621)
—Peter Reynolds Creatrilogy Box Set (Dot, Ish, Sky Color) (p. 1729)
—Playing from the Heart. Reynolds, Peter H., illus. (p. 1760)
—Rose's Garden. Reynolds, Peter H., illus. (p. 1906)
—Say Something! Reynolds, Peter H., illus. (p. 1940)
—Sky Color. Reynolds, Peter H., illus. (p. 2033)
—Smallest Gift of Christmas. Reynolds, Peter H., illus. (p. 2040)
—¡Di algo! (Say Something!) Reynolds, Peter H., illus. (p. 536)
Reynolds, Peter H., illus. see Brallier, Jess M.
Reynolds, Peter H., illus. see FableVision.
Reynolds, Peter H., illus. see Mcdonald, Megan & Michalak, Jamie.
Reynolds, Peter H., illus. see Mcdonald, Megan.
Reynolds, Peter H., illus. see McDonald, Megan.
Reynolds, Peter H., illus. see Mcdonald, Megan.
Reynolds, Peter H., illus. see McDonald, Megan.
Reynolds, Peter H., illus. see Mcdonald, Megan.
Reynolds, Peter H., illus. see McDonald, Megan.
Reynolds, Peter H., illus. see Mcdonald, Megan.
Reynolds, Peter H., illus. see McDonald, Megan.
Reynolds, Peter H., illus. see Mcdonald, Megan.
Reynolds, Peter H., illus. see McDonald, Megan.
Reynolds, Peter H., illus. see Mcdonald, Megan.
Reynolds, Peter H., illus. see McDonald, Megan.
Reynolds, Peter H., illus. see Mcdonald, Megan.
Reynolds, Peter H., illus. see McDonald, Megan.
Reynolds, Peter H., illus. see Mcdonald, Megan.
Reynolds, Peter H., illus. see McDonald, Megan.
Reynolds, Peter H., illus. see Mcdonald, Megan.
Reynolds, Peter H., illus. see McDonald, Megan.
Reynolds, Peter H., illus. see Mcdonald, Megan.
Reynolds, Peter H., illus. see McDonald, Megan.
Reynolds, Peter H., illus. see Mcdonald, Megan.
Reynolds, Peter H., illus. see McDonald, Megan.
Reynolds, Peter H., illus. see Mcdonald, Megan.
Reynolds, Peter H., illus. see McDonald, Megan.
Reynolds, Peter H., illus. see Mcdonald, Megan.
Reynolds, Peter H., illus. see McDonald, Megan.
Reynolds, Peter H., illus. see Mcdonald, Megan.
Reynolds, Peter H., illus. see McDonald, Megan.
Reynolds, Peter H., illus. see Mcdonald, Megan.
Reynolds, Peter H., illus. see McDonald, Megan.
Reynolds, Peter H., illus. see Mcdonald, Megan.
Reynolds, Peter H., illus. see McDonald, Megan.
Reynolds, Peter H., illus. see Mcdonald, Megan.
Reynolds, Peter H., illus. see McGhee, Alison.
Reynolds, Peter H., illus. see Mcghee, Alison.
Reynolds, Peter H., illus. see McGhee, Alison.
Reynolds, Peter H., illus. see Mcghee, Alison.
Reynolds, Peter H., illus. see New York Hall of Science, The.
Reynolds, Peter H., illus. see O'Brien, Thomas C.
Reynolds, Peter H., illus. see Raczka, Bob.
Reynolds, Peter H., illus. see Reynolds, Paul A.
Reynolds, Peter H., illus. see Reynolds, Paul.
Reynolds, Peter H., illus. see Robinson, Michelle.
Reynolds, Peter H., illus. see Rosenthal, Amy Krouse.
Reynolds, Peter H., illus. see Stearns, Peggy Healy.
Reynolds, Peter H., illus. see Verde, Susan & Badiel, Georgie.
Reynolds, Peter H., illus. see Verde, Susan.
Reynolds, Peter H., jt. auth. see Mcdonald, Megan.
Reynolds, Peter H., jt. auth. see Raczka, Bob.
Reynolds, Peter H., jt. auth. see Reynolds, Paul A.
Reynolds, Quentin. Amazing Mr. Doolittle: A Biography of Lieutenant General James H. Doolittle (Classic Reprint) (p. 66)
Reynolds, Robert. Rabbit's Tale: A Tale for Children. (p. 1830)
—Trouble's Garden. (p. 2292)
Reynolds, Robert R. Wanderlust (Classic Reprint) (p. 2375)
Reynolds, Ruth, jt. auth. see Ryan, Margaret.
Reynolds, Shauna LaVoy. Poetree. Maydani, Shahrzad, illus. (p. 1767)
Reynolds, Shaye. I Am an American Citizen. (p. 1057)
—In Search of Tiger Sharks (p. 1107)
—Life Cycle of a Chicken. (p. 1290)
—Rattlesnakes. (p. 1843)
—Volcanoes. (p. 2366)
Reynolds, Stephen. Holy Mountain: A Satire on Tendencies (Classic Reprint) (p. 995)
—How 'Twas: Short Stories & Small Travels (Classic Reprint) (p. 1046)
Reynolds, Sue, jt. auth. see Neiman, Tommy.
Reynolds, Thomas E. Shadows, Vol. 33: Literary Magazine of the Creighton University; October, 1931 (Classic Reprint) (p. 1998)
Reynolds, Thomas F. Shadows, Vol. 22: Spring 1931 (Classic Reprint) (p. 1998)
—Shadows, Vol. 22: Literary Magazine of the Creighton University; February, 1931 (Classic Reprint) (p. 1998)
—Shadows, Vol. 23: Literary Magazine of the Creighton University; Christmas 1931 (Classic Reprint) (p. 1998)
Reynolds, Toby. Animals of the World. (p. 95)
—Continents of the World. (p. 445)
—I Can Draw Cars & Trucks. Sanford, Grace, illus. (p. 1062)
—I Can Draw People. Sanford, Grace, illus. (p. 1062)
—I Can Draw Pets. Sanford, Grace, illus. (p. 1062)
—I Can Draw Wild Animals. Sanford, Grace, illus. (p. 1062)
—Mini Artist: Set 2. (p. 1471)
—Papercraft. (p. 1698)
—Printing. (p. 1800)
Reynolds, Toby & Calver, Paul. Aviation. (p. 143)
—Birds of Prey. (p. 232)
—Explorers & Pioneers. (p. 680)
—Fearless Women: Courageous Females Who Refused to Be Denied. (p. 717)
—Global Warming. (p. 844)
—Incredible Successes. (p. 1114)
—Machines. (p. 1372)
—Ocean Life. (p. 1635)
—Rocks, Crystals, & Gems. (p. 1896)
—Unsung Heroes: Fearless Men & Women Who Changed the World. (p. 2336)
Reynolds, W. D. Miss. Martha Brownlow, or the Heroine of Tennessee: A Truthful & Graphic Account of the Many Perils & Privations Endured by Miss. Martha Brownlow (Classic Reprint) (p. 1479)
Reynolds, Warren, jt. auth. see Williams, Heather DiLorenzo.
Reynolds, Wendy A. & Hayes, Amy. Turning Apples into Applesauce. (p. 2300)
Reynolds, William Hampton. Our Brother's Child: And Other Stories (Classic Reprint) (p. 1676)
Reynoldson, Fiona. Geothermal Energy & Bioenergy. (p. 821)
Reynoso, David, et al. Fun Math Problem Solving for Elementary School Volume 2. (p. 799)
Reynoso, David, et al, eds. Math Challenge I-B Counting & Probability. (p. 1421)
—Math Challenge I-B Number Theory. (p. 1421)
Reynoso, Michelle. En: A Girl Energy-Bending Between Worlds. (p. 646)
—Light of the Dying. (p. 1298)
Reza, Fawzia. Mary & Her New Friends. (p. 1414)
Rezaei, Heidi, illus. see Rezaei, Heidi P.
Rezaei, Heidi P. Come Count with Happy Campers! Ghaderi, Simin & Rezaei, Heidi, illus. (p. 428)
Rezaei, Sara. Niki's Adventure in the Mysterious Forest. (p. 1608)
Reznicek, Curtis, illus. see Witt, Janice.
Reznikoff, Charles. Chatterton, the Black Death, & Meriwether Lewis, Three Plays by Charles Reznikoff (Classic Reprint) (p. 362)
RH Disney. Aladdin Deluxe Step into Reading (Disney Aladdin) RH Disney, illus. (p. 39)
—Anna, Elsa, & Friends (Disney Frozen 2) Disney Storybook Art Team, Disney Storybook, illus. (p. 97)
—Aurora's Story (Disney Princess) Disney Storybook Art Team, Disney Storybook, illus. (p. 138)
—Baby, You're Super! (Disney/Pixar the Incredibles 2) RH Disney, illus. (p. 153)
—Back on Track (Disney/Pixar Cars 3) RH Disney, illus. (p. 155)
—Behold! the Majestic Unicorn (and Other Not-So-Magical Beings) (Disney/Pixar Onward) Disney Storybook Art Team, Disney Storybook, illus. (p. 193)
—Belle's Story Collection (Disney Beauty & the Beast) RH Disney, illus. (p. 198)
—Beware the Kakamora! (Disney Moana) RH Disney, illus. (p. 211)
—Big Hero 6 (Disney Big Hero 6) RH Disney, illus. (p. 220)
—Coco Little Golden Book (Disney/Pixar Coco) The Disney Storybook Art Team, illus. (p. 411)
—Day with Dad (Disney/Pixar Onward) Disney Storybook Art Team, Disney Storybook, illus. (p. 515)
—Disney: Nine Classic Tales (Disney Mixed Property) (p. 561)
—Doc Mcstuffins Little Golden Book Library (Disney Junior: Doc Mcstuffins) As Big As a Whale; Snowman Surprise; Bubble-Rific!; Boomer Gets His Bounce Back; a Knight in Sticky Armor (p. 572)
—Ducky & Bunny Help Out! (Disney/Pixar Toy Story 4) Disney Storybook Art Team, Disney Storybook, illus. (p. 608)
—Five Classic Tales (Disney Classics) (p. 743)
—Five Enchanting Tales (Disney Princess) (p. 743)
—Frozen Big Golden Book (Disney Frozen) RH Disney, illus. (p. 795)
—Frozen Story Collection (Disney Frozen) RH Disney, illus. (p. 796)
—Game Time! RH Disney, illus. (p. 807)
—Home for a Princess: a Peek Inside 9 Disney Princess Castles (Disney Princess) RH Disney, illus. (p. 996)
—Inside Out Big Golden Book (Disney/Pixar Inside Out) RH Disney, illus. (p. 1123)
—Moana Big Golden Book (Disney Moana) RH Disney, illus. (p. 1485)
—Moana Little Golden Board Book (Disney Princess) Disney Storybook Art Team, Disney Storybook, illus. (p. 1485)
—Monsters, Inc. Little Golden Book (Disney/Pixar Monsters, Inc.) RH Disney, illus. (p. 1498)
—Mulan's Happy Panda (Disney Princess: Palace Pets) RH Disney, illus. (p. 1525)
—Mulan's Perfect Present/Jasmine's New Friends (Disney Princess) RH Disney, illus. (p. 1525)
—Nine Disney Princess Tales (Disney Princess) RH Disney, illus. (p. 1609)
—Oh, Brother! (Disney/Pixar Onward) RH Disney, illus. (p. 1641)
—Olaf Loves to Read! (Disney Frozen 2) RH Disney, illus. (p. 1644)
—Olaf's Little Library (Disney Frozen) 4 Board Books. Disney Storybook Art Team, Disney Storybook, illus. (p. 1644)
—Onward Deluxe Step into Reading #1 (Disney/Pixar Onward) Disney Storybook Art Team, Disney Storybook, illus. (p. 1664)
—Princess & the Frog Little Golden Book (Disney Princess & the Frog) RH Disney, illus. (p. 1796)
—Pua & Heihei (Disney Moana) RH Disney, illus. (p. 1810)
—Quest for the Heart (Disney Moana) RH Disney, illus. (p. 1826)
—Ralph Breaks the Internet. RH Disney, illus. (p. 1838)
—Rapunzel's Perfect Pony (Disney Princess: Palace Pets) RH Disney, illus. (p. 1842)
—Shapes, Colors, Counting & More! (Disney/Pixar Cars) RH Disney, illus. (p. 2000)
—Show-and-Tell. The Disney Storybook Art Team, illus. (p. 2012)
—Toy Story 4 Movie Storybook (Disney/Pixar Toy Story 4) RH Disney, illus. (p. 2270)
—Walt Disney's Alice in Wonderland Little Golden Board Book (Disney Classic) Disney Storybook Art Team, Disney Storybook, illus. (p. 2374)
—Walt Disney's Cinderella Little Golden Board Book (Disney Classic) Disney Storybook Art Team, Disney Storybook, illus. (p. 2374)
—Walt Disney's Pinocchio Little Golden Board Book (Disney Classic) Dempster, Al, illus. (p. 2374)
—Wreck-It Ralph 2 Deluxe Hardcover Junior Novelization (Disney Wreck-It Ralph 2) RH Disney, illus. (p. 2511)
—Wreck-It Ralph Little Golden Book (Disney Wreck-It Ralph) RH Disney, illus. (p. 2511)
—Zom-Azing Posters, Facts, & More! (Disney Zombies) RH Disney, illus. (p. 2541)
RH Disney, illus. see Berrios, Frank.
RH Disney, illus. see Depken, Kristen L.
RH Disney, illus. see Finnegan, Delphine.
RH Disney, illus. see Francis, Suzanne.
RH Disney, illus. see Green, Rico.
RH Disney, illus. see Homberg, Ruth.
RH Disney, illus. see Jordan, Apple.
RH Disney, illus. see Katschke, Judy.
RH Disney, illus. see Lagonegro, Melissa.
RH Disney, illus. see Man-Kong, Mary.
RH Disney, illus. see McCullough, Kathy.
RH Disney, illus. see Memling, Carl.
RH Disney, illus. see Posner-Sanchez, Andrea.
RH Disney, illus. see Rabe, Tish.
RH Disney, illus. see Saxon, Victoria.
RH Disney, illus. see Soderberg, Erin.
RH Disney, illus. see Thorpe, Kiki.
RH Disney, illus. see Tillworth, Mary.
RH Disney, illus. see Weinberg, Jennifer Liberts.
RH Disney, illus. see Werner, Jane.
RH Disney & Higginson, Sheila Sweeny. Adventures of Violet & Dash: Friend or Foe? (Disney/Pixar the Incredibles 2) RH Disney et al, illus. (p. 29)
RH Disney & McCullough, Kathy. Jasmine's Quest for the Stardust Sapphire (Disney Aladdin) RH Disney & Dale-Scott, Lindsay, illus. (p. 1160)
RH Disney Staff. Amazing Ariel! (Disney Princess) RH Disney Staff, illus. (p. 64)
—Anna's Icy Adventure. RH Disney Staff, illus. (p. 98)
—Ariel's Royal Wedding/Aurora's Royal Wedding (Disney Princess) RH Disney Staff, illus. (p. 115)
—Aurora Plays the Part. Disney Storybook Artists, illus. (p. 138)
—Back on Track. RH Disney Staff, illus. (p. 155)
—Belle - Discovery. RH Disney Staff, illus. (p. 197)
—Belle's Friendship Invention/Tiana's Friendship Fix-Up (Disney Princess) RH Disney Staff, illus. (p. 197)
—Cake-Tillion (Disney Palace Pets: Whisker Haven Tales) RH Disney Staff, illus. (p. 309)
—Can You Find Dory? RH Disney Staff, illus. (p. 318)
—Cars 2 Little Golden Book (Disney/Pixar Cars 2) RH Disney Staff, illus. (p. 334)
—Cars 3 Big Golden Book (Disney/Pixar Cars 3) RH Disney Staff, illus. (p. 334)
—Cars 3 Deluxe Junior Novelization (Disney/Pixar Cars 3) RH Disney Staff, illus. (p. 334)
—Cars 3 Junior Novelization (Disney/Pixar Cars 3) RH Disney Staff, illus. (p. 334)
—Cars 3 Pictureback with Tattoos (Disney/Pixar Cars 3) RH Disney Staff, illus. (p. 334)
—Cinderella's Best Creations/Snow White & the Three Giants (Disney Princess) RH Disney Staff, illus. (p. 392)
—Coco Deluxe Hardcover Junior Novelization (Disney/Pixar Coco) RH Disney Staff, illus. (p. 411)
—Coco Deluxe Step into Reading with Cardstock (Disney/Pixar Coco) RH Disney Staff, illus. (p. 411)
—Coco Deluxe Step into Reading with Stickers (Disney/Pixar Coco) RH Disney Staff, illus. (p. 411)
—Coco Junior Novelization (Disney/Pixar Coco) RH Disney Staff, illus. (p. 411)
—Critterzen Clue Contest (Disney Palace Pets: Whisker Haven Tales) RH Disney Staff, illus. (p. 476)
—Disney Princess Beginnings: Aurora Plays the Part. Disney Storybook Artists, illus. (p. 562)
—Disney Princess Beginnings: Ariel Makes Waves (Disney Princess) RH Disney Staff, illus. (p. 562)
—Disney Princess Heart Strong #2 (Disney Princess) RH Disney Staff, illus. (p. 563)
—Dory's Sea of Wonders. RH Disney Staff, illus. (p. 587)
—Dory's Story. RH Disney Staff, illus. (p. 587)
—Driven to Win! RH Disney Staff, illus. (p. 605)
—Fairy's Fire. RH Disney Staff, illus. (p. 698)
—Family Mystery (Disney/Pixar Coco) RH Disney Staff, illus. (p. 702)
—Finding Dory. RH Disney Staff, illus. (p. 729)
—Finding Dory Big Golden Book (Disney/Pixar Finding Dory) RH Disney Staff, illus. (p. 729)
—Finding Dory Deluxe Step into Reading (Disney/Pixar Finding Dory) RH Disney Staff, illus. (p. 729)
—Finding Dory Little Golden Book (Disney/Pixar Finding Dory) RH Disney Staff, illus. (p. 729)
—Finding Dory Padded Board Book (Disney/Pixar Finding Dory) RH Disney Staff, illus. (p. 729)
—Finding Dory Pictureback with Stickers (Disney/Pixar Finding Dory) RH Disney Staff, illus. (p. 729)
—Finding Dory: the Deluxe Junior Novelization (Disney/Pixar Finding Dory) RH Disney Staff, illus. (p. 729)
—Flounder Loves Ariel (Disney Princess) RH Disney Staff, illus. (p. 752)
—Frozen Holiday Special Big Golden Book (Disney Frozen) Disney Storybook Art Team, illus. (p. 795)
—Frozen Holiday Special Deluxe Junior Novelization (Disney Frozen) RH Disney Staff, illus. (p. 795)
—Frozen Monster (Disney Frozen) RH Disney Staff, illus. (p. 795)
—Furry, Fluffy & Fabulous! (Disney Princess: Palace Pets) Disney Storybook Artists Staff, illus. (p. 802)
—Good Dinosaur Junior Novelization (Disney/Pixar the Good Dinosaur) RH Disney Staff, illus. (p. 862)

R

—William & Kate: The Prince & Princess. (p. 2468)
Riboli, Renzo. Favole Di Fagiolino Scoreggino. (p. 715)
Ribot, Theodule. Essai Sur les Passions (Classic Reprint) (p. 663)
Ribot, Theodule Armand. Essai Sur les Passions (Classic Reprint) (p. 663)
Ribowsky, Helene & Zlotowitz, Rachel. Search Is On! Can You Find the Ten Pieces of Chametz? Black, Elisheva, illus. (p. 1971)
Ric, Glenn. World Without: A Land in Peril. (p. 2506)
—World Without Part 3: Rise of the Fras. Morre, Elisabeth, ed. (p. 2506)
Ricahrdson, Brittany, illus. see Ricahrdson, Larry.
Ricahrdson, Larry. Metal Mike. Ricahrdson, Brittany, illus. (p. 1452)
Ricard, Anouk. Anna & Froga: Completely Bubu. (p. 97)
—Anna & Froga: Fore! Fore! Dascher, Helge, tr. (p. 97)
—Anna & Froga: I Dunno, What Do You Want to Do? I Dunno, What Do You Want to Do? Dascher, Helge, tr. (p. 97)
—Anna & Froga: Wanna Gumball? Wanna Gumball? Dascher, Helge, tr. (p. 97)
Ricard, Antoine. Fontaine (Classic Reprint) (p. 759)
Ricard, Matthieu & Gruhl, Jason. Our Animal Neighbors: Compassion for Every Furry, Slimy, Prickly Creature on Earth. Hall, Becca, illus. (p. 1676)
Ricardicus, illus. see Sayalero, Myriam.
Ricceri, David, illus. see Schwartz, Barry L. & Levine, Mark H.
Ricchi, Brenda. Grandchildren's Bible Journeys - the Creation Story. (p. 877)
—Grandchildren's Bible Journey-the Big Fall. (p. 877)
Ricchio, Mike. In Spite of It All: According to Mikey Volume 1. (p. 1107)
Ricchiuti, Paul B. Hi, Kids! 7-In-1 Stories by Paul Ricchiuti. (p. 964)
—Runaway World. (p. 1915)
—Stepladder Junction & Other Stories. (p. 2115)
—Treasure on Spyglass Hill. (p. 2282)
Ricci, Aida. Memories from the Enchanted City of Rome, Italy. (p. 1446)
Ricci, Andrés, illus. see Riley, Zach.
Ricci, Andres Martinez, illus. see Higgins, Nadia.
Ricci, Andrés Martínez, illus. see Slade, Suzanne.
Ricci, Andres Martinez, jt. auth. see Higgins, Nadia.
Ricci, Caitlin. Battle Born. (p. 173)
—Crush. (p. 480)
—Head above Water. (p. 942)
—Weathering the Storm. (p. 2394)
Ricci, Caitlin, jt. auth. see Burns, A. M.
Ricci, Caitlin & Burns, A. M. Shifting Tides. (p. 2007)
Ricci, Caitlin, et al. Three Times the Charm. (p. 2235)
Ricci, Christine. I Love My Abuela! Miller, Victoria, illus. (p. 1070)
—Nella's Unicorn Rescue. Random House & Sorrentino, Alessandra, illus. (p. 1586)
Ricci, Victor H. Ups & Downs in Canada (Classic Reprint) (p. 2339)
Ricciardi, Charles. Night the Bullies Were Bullied! Ricciardi, Charles, illus. (p. 1607)
Riccio, Christine. Again, but Better: A Novel. (p. 34)
Riccio, Frank, illus. see Myers, Bill.
Riccio, Vincent. All the Way Down: The Violent Underworld of Street Gangs (Classic Reprint) (p. 54)
Ricciuti, Edward R. Federal Bureau of Investigation. (p. 717)
—¿Qué Hay Dentro? (p. 1822)
Ricciuti, Edward R., jt. auth. see Gordon, Sharon.
Rice, Adrienne. How Many? (p. 1033)
Rice, Alfred Ernest. Oregon Girl: A Tale of American Life, in the New West (Classic Reprint) (p. 1670)
Rice, Alice Caldwell Hegan. Romance of Billy-Goat Hill. (p. 1900)
—Romance of Billy-Goat Hill (Classic Reprint) (p. 1900)
Rice, Alice Hegan. Calvary Alley (Classic Reprint) (p. 312)
—Honorable Percival (Classic Reprint) (p. 1000)
—Miss. Mink's Soldier: And Other Stories (Classic Reprint) (p. 1479)
—Mr. Opp (Classic Reprint) (p. 1519)
—Quin (Classic Reprint) (p. 1828)
—Sandy (Classic Reprint) (p. 1931)
Rice, Arthur L. Village Photographer (Classic Reprint) (p. 2358)
Rice, Ashley. Girls Rule: A Very Special Book Created Especially for Girls. (p. 839)
—Girls Rule: A very special book created especially for girls — UPDATED EDITION — (p. 839)
—Make Your Dreams Come True: A Girl's Guide to Always Believing in Yourself. (p. 1387)
—You Are a Girl Who Totally Rocks: Always Be True to You! (p. 2524)
Rice, Bill. Survival! Desert (p. 2164)
—Survival! Jungle (p. 2164)
Rice, Bill & Rice, William, 5th. Survival! Ocean (p. 2164)
Rice, Caroleann. Ladybug & the Bully Frog. Berton, Charles, illus. (p. 1238)
Rice, Christie, illus. see Umpherville, Tina.
Rice, Christina. Fluttershy & Iron Will. Garbowska, Agnes & Uyetake, Neil, illus. (p. 753)
—Granny & the Flim Flam Brothers. Fleecs, Tony et al, illus. (p. 880)
—My Little Pony: Ponyville Mysteries. Garbowska, Agnes, illus. (p. 1554)
Rice, Christina, jt. auth. see Anderson, Ted.
Rice, Christina, jt. auth. see Whitley, Jeremy.
Rice, Christina & Anderson, Ted. My Little Pony Omnibus Volume 4. Garbowska, Agnes et al, illus. (p. 1554)
Rice, Christina & Whitley, Jeremy. My Little Pony: Friendship Is Magic Volume 19. Coller, Casey W. et al, illus. (p. 1553)
Rice, Christina & Zahler, Thom. My Little Pony: Friends Forever Volume 9 Garbowska, Agnes et al, illus. (p. 1553)
—My Little Pony: Friendship Is Magic Volume 13 Garbowska, Agnes et al, illus. (p. 1553)
—My Little Pony Omnibus Volume 5. Garbowska, Agnes et al, illus. (p. 1554)
Rice, Clay. Ants 'N' Uncles. (p. 103)
—Lonely Shadow. (p. 1342)
—Mama, Let's Make a Moon. (p. 1392)
—Stick. (p. 2117)
Rice, Condoleezza. Condoleezza Rice: A Memoir of My Extraordinary, Ordinary Family & Me. (p. 438)
Rice, Courtney, jt. auth. see Redford, Marjorie.
Rice, D. M. Visit to a Car Factory (p. 2362)
—Visit to a Farm (p. 2362)
Rice, Daniel. Pugs. (p. 1812)
Rice, David & Garcia, Mike D. Heart-Shaped Cookies. (p. 945)
Rice, David L. Lifetimes. Maydak, Michael S., illus. (p. 1297)
Rice, David L., jt. auth. see Anthony, Joseph.
Rice, David L. & Calvert, Trudy L. Do Animals Have Feelings Too? (p. 570)
Rice, Dona. 20th Century Superstar: Disney. (p. 2554)
—Aventuras de Viaje: Figuras Bidimensionales. (p. 142)
—Colas. (p. 413)
—Crazy Creatures: Deep Ocean. (p. 468)
—Fútbol Bandera: Resta. (p. 802)
—Gérmenes: Suma y Resta. (p. 822)
—Gran Barrera de Coral: Valor Posicional. (p. 876)
—Historia Del Correo: Datos. (p. 975)
—Historia Del Helado. (p. 975)
—King's Cross: Partición de Figuras. (p. 1222)
—Look Out Below! (p. 1346)
—Mohandas Gandhi (p. 1488)
—Roberto Clemente (p. 1891)
—Saving the World: The Chocolate Pilot. (p. 1939)
—Serengueti. (p. 1990)
—Sombreros. (p. 2058)
—What Kind of Weather? (p. 2418)
—Zapatos. (p. 2538)
—¡Al Bate! Historia Del Béisbol. (p. 38)
—¿Qué Tipo de Tiempo? (p. 1823)
Rice, Dona, jt. auth. see Housel, Debra J.
Rice, Dona, jt. auth. see Rice, William.
Rice, Dona & Austin, Elizabeth. Cooling Off. (p. 451)
—Making Music. (p. 1389)
—Staying Warm. (p. 2110)
Rice, Dona & Montgomery, Anne. Helping Injured Animals. (p. 953)
—Raising Silkworms. (p. 1838)
Rice, Dona & Otterman, Joseph. Powered by the Sun. (p. 1783)
—Seeing More Stars. (p. 1984)
—Studying Snowflakes. (p. 2144)
Rice, Dona & Wilder, Nellie. Making Water Safe. (p. 1390)
—Solving Problems as the Zoo. (p. 2058)
Rice, Dona Herweck. Agua. (p. 36)
—Alexander Hamilton's New York City (Alexander Hamilton) (p. 42)
—Alice in the Garden of Flowers (Science) (p. 45)
—All in the Family (p. 52)
—Always Growing. (p. 61)
—Amazing Animals: Tails. (p. 63)
—America Then & Now. (p. 70)
—American Heroes. (p. 72)
—American Through & Through (p. 74)
—American Through & Through Lap Book (p. 74)
—America's Eagle (Foundations) (p. 75)
—Animal Eyes (p. 89)
—Animal Mothers & Babies (p. 90)
—Art & Culture. (p. 120)
—Art of Shadow Puppets. (p. 121)
—Aventuras de Viaje: Suma Hasta 100. (p. 142)
—Bad Guys & Gals of the Ancient World (p. 157)
—Bad Guys & Gals of the High Seas (p. 157)
—Bad Guys & Gals on the High Seas (p. 157)
—Banff National Park Area. (p. 163)
—Batter Up! History of Baseball (p. 173)
—Batter Up! History of Baseball (p. 173)
—Bee's Life (p. 190)
—Being Like Butterflies. (p. 194)
—Best You: Calm Down (Level 1) (p. 208)
—Best You: Making Things Right (Level 2) (p. 208)
—Big & Little (p. 216)
—Big Kid School (p. 221)
—Biography of J. K. Rowling, (Grade 8) (p. 229)
—Buen Trabajo. (p. 290)
—Building Sandcastles. (p. 294)
—Butterfly's Life (p. 304)
—Casas Alrededor Del Mundo. (p. 336)
—Circus Fun (Grade 1) (p. 393)
—Color-Changing Cephalopods. (p. 420)
—Colores. (p. 422)
—Colors (p. 426)
—Comer Bien. (p. 429)
—Communicate! Animal Talk. (p. 431)
—Communicate! How You Say It. (p. 431)
—Communicate! Pop Song Lyrics (Level 3) (p. 431)
—Communicate! Tongue Twisters (Level 2) (p. 431)
—Cómo Crecen las Plantas. (p. 432)
—Cosas con Alas. (p. 456)
—Creative Machines. (p. 471)
—Culture of Calendars. (p. 484)
—Day & Night: Time (p. 512)
—Day & Night. (p. 512)
—Deception: Real or Fake News? (p. 523)
—Delicious & Nutritious (p. 526)
—Designing National Parks. (p. 533)
—Dónde Ir. (p. 581)
—Eating Right (p. 622)
—En Movimiento. (p. 646)
—Engineering Marvels: The Eiffel Tower: Measurement (Grade 4) (p. 652)
—Environment: A World of Change (p. 657)
—Esta Soy Yo. (p. 664)
—Estados Unidos Entonces y Ahora. (p. 664)
—Fantastic Kids: Theater Kids (Level 1) (p. 707)
—Fantastic Kids: Malala Yousafzai (Level 5) (p. 707)
—Figuras. (p. 726)
—First Fire. (p. 736)
—Folding Paper. (p. 757)
—Frog's Life (p. 790)
—Game Changers: A Biography of J. K. Rowling. (p. 807)
—Going Buggy! (p. 854)
—Good Work. (p. 866)
—Grand Old Flag (Foundations) (p. 877)
—Grande y Pequeño. (p. 877)
—Growing Up (p. 899)
—Growth & Change (p. 900)
—Hatching a Chick. (p. 936)
—Here Comes the Sun (p. 958)
—Héroes Estadounidenses. (p. 961)
—History of Ice Cream. (p. 978)
—History of Listening to Music: Displaying Data. (p. 978)
—History of Mail. (p. 978)
—Hit It! - History of Tools (p. 982)
—Homes Around the World (p. 998)
—How Plants Grow (p. 1034)
—I Can (p. 1061)
—I Can Be Anything (p. 1061)
—I Have Music. (p. 1066)
—I Wear My Feelings. (p. 1085)
—Interdependence of Living Things (p. 1126)
—Into Space. (p. 1128)
—Jackie Robinson: Hometown Hero. (p. 1153)
—Jimmy Carter: For the People. (p. 1168)
—Juliette Gordon Low: The First Girl Scout. (p. 1187)
—Keeping Fit with Sports (p. 1208)
—Kids Around the World (p. 1214)
—Land (p. 1241)
—Laura Ingalls Wilder: Pioneer Woman (America in The 1800s) (p. 1252)
—Legacy: The Names Behind the Brands. (p. 1261)
—Let's Camp! (Grade 1) (p. 1270)
—Like Them (Grade 1) (p. 1301)
—Living in Sunlight Extremes. (p. 1333)
—Lo Mejor de Ti: Calmarse. (p. 1338)
—Lugares del Mundo. (p. 1366)
—Madres Animales y Sus Crías. (p. 1375)
—Making a Mummy. (p. 1388)
—Making Crayons. (p. 1388)
—Mantenerse en Forma con Deportes. (p. 1398)
—Manteneerse Sano. (p. 1398)
—Maps & Globes. (p. 1401)
—Marvelous Me: My Face. (p. 1413)
—Marvelous Me: My Feet. (p. 1413)
—Marvelous Me: My Hands. (p. 1413)
—Mi Gran Familia. (p. 1455)
—Money Matters: A Classroom Economy: Adding & Subtracting Decimals (Grade 5) (p. 1493)
—Mountain of Presidents (Foundations) (p. 1514)
—Mountain Travel (Grade 1) (p. 1514)
—My Big Family (p. 1532)
—Navigating at Sea (Grade 3) (p. 1582)
—Niños Alrededor del Mundo. (p. 1611)
—Ojos de Animales. (p. 1643)
—On the Go (p. 1654)
—Organic Farming. (p. 1670)
—Our Neighborhood. (p. 1679)
—Physical Feats & Failures (p. 1737)
—Piecing Art Together. (p. 1742)
—Places Around the World (p. 1753)
—Places to Go (p. 1753)
—Please Don't Feed the Animals. (p. 1762)
—Pollination (p. 1771)
—Predict It! (p. 1787)
—Puedo Hacer Cualquier Cosa. (p. 1811)
—Raising Babies: What Animal Parents Do (p. 1838)
—Science Detectives (p. 1954)
—Sea Life (p. 1967)
—Shapes (p. 2000)
—Showdown: Real or Pretend. (p. 2012)
—Showdown: The Fight for Space (Level 5) (p. 2012)
—Siempre Crece. (p. 2015)
—Soccer or Basketball (Grade 1) (p. 2052)
—Sort It! (p. 2066)
—Soy Maravilloso. (p. 2070)
—Spectacular Sports: Flag Football: Subtraction (Grade 1) (p. 2078)
—Staying Healthy (p. 2110)
—Stepping into Louisa May Alcott's World. (p. 2115)
—Stepping into Louisa May Alcott's World (Grade 7) (p. 2115)
—Store Map (Grade 1) (p. 2122)
—Teedie: The Boy Who Would Be President. (p. 2198)
—Terreno. (p. 2207)
—Things with Wings (p. 2221)
—This Is Me (p. 2225)
—Tiempo. (p. 2240)
—Too Much Trash! (p. 2261)
—Trabajadores. (p. 2271)
—Traits for Survival (p. 2276)
—Travel Adventures: Camping. (p. 2279)
—Travel Adventures: The Serengeti. (p. 2279)
—Travel Adventures: The Everglades: Addition Within 100 (Grade 2) (p. 2279)
—Travel Adventures: Carlsbad Caverns: Identifying Arithmetic Patterns (Grade 3) (p. 2279)
—Travel Adventures: Yosemite: Perimeter & Area (Grade 4) (p. 2280)
—Two Artists. (p. 2307)
—Unsolved! History's Mysteries (p. 2335)
—USA Las Matematicas. (p. 2341)
—USA Las Matemáticas - Descríbelo. (p. 2341)
—Use Math: Compare It. (p. 2341)
—Use Your Math Mind: Group It. (p. 2341)
—Use Your Math Mind: Describe It. (p. 2341)
—Vida de una Abeja. (p. 2356)
—Vida de una Mariposa. (p. 2356)
—Vida de Una Rana. (p. 2356)
—Vida Marina. (p. 2356)
—Water (p. 2384)
—Water Bodies (p. 2384)
—We Are Here. (p. 2389)
—Weather (p. 2394)
—What a Scientist Sees. (p. 2404)
—What Animal Parents Do (p. 2404)
—What the Evidence Shows. (p. 2420)
—What Toys Can Do. (p. 2421)
—Workers (p. 2495)
—Yo Sé. (p. 2522)
—You Are There! London 1666. (p. 2525)
—You Are There! Pearl Harbor, December 7, 1941. (p. 2525)
—Your World: Germs. (p. 2534)
—Your World: : Shoes. (p. 2535)
—¡Comunicate! El Habla Animal. (p. 437)
—¡Comunícate! Cómo lo Dices. (p. 437)
—¡Locos por Insectos y Arañas! (p. 1339)
Rice, Dona Herweck & Coan, Sharon. Special Me. (p. 2077)
Rice, Dona Herweck & Petersen, Casey Null. School Around the World (p. 1945)
Rice, Dona Herweck & Thompson, Chad. Old Mother Hubbard. (p. 1647)
Rice, Dona Herweck, et al. All about Me. (p. 49)
—Let's Explore Earth & Space Science, Grades 4-5. (p. 1272)
Rice, Dona Herwick. John Henry (p. 1173)
—Paul Bunyan (p. 1707)
Rice, Dona Herwick, jt. auth. see Housel, Debra J.
Rice, Dona Herwick & Bradley, Kathleen. Chief Joseph & the Nez Perce (p. 369)
—Lewis & Clark (p. 1282)
—Molly Pitcher (p. 1489)
Rice, Dona Herwick & Housel, Debra. Civil War Hero of Marye's Heights (p. 397)
Rice, Dona Herwick & Isecke, Harriet. Child Labor & the Industrial Revolution (p. 369)
—Civil Rights: Freedom Riders (p. 396)
—Remember the Alamo (p. 1864)
Rice, Dona Herwick & Shannon, Catherine. Narcissa Whitman & the Westward Movement (p. 1575)
Rice, Dona Herwick & Sugarman, Dorothy Alexander. Women's Suffrage (p. 2488)
—World War II: Battle of Normandy (p. 2505)
Rice, Donna. Magic is Me. Rice, Doug, illus. (p. 1377)
Rice, Donna Herweck. I Can Be Anything. (p. 1061)
Rice, Doug, illus. see Rice, Donna.
Rice, Earle. Billie Holiday. (p. 226)
—Biosecurity: Preventing Biological Warfare. (p. 229)
—Careers in the US Army. (p. 330)
—Causes of the Mexican-American War. (p. 347)
—Causes of the Vietnam War. (p. 347)
—Charlie Parker. (p. 360)
—FDR & the New Deal. (p. 716)
—Life & Times of Attila the Hun. (p. 1289)
—Life & Times of Clovis. (p. 1289)
—Life & Times of Eleanor of Aquitaine. (p. 1289)
—Missiles: Self-Guided Explosives. (p. 1480)
—Rockets & Satellites: Surveillance from Space. (p. 1895)
—Vietnam War Musteen, Jason R., ed. (p. 2357)
Rice, Earle & Camelo, Wilson. Careers in the US Air Force. (p. 330)
Rice, Earle, Jr. Battle of Marathon. (p. 174)
—Haunted Battlefields Little BigHorn: Little BigHorn. (p. 937)
—Haunted Battlefields Verdun: Verdun. (p. 937)
—How Franklin D. Roosevelt Fought World War II. (p. 1031)
Rice, Elizabeth. Genetic Engineering. (p. 815)
Rice, Frances, jt. auth. see Rice, Wallace.
Rice, Harry E. Eve & the Evangelist: A Romance of A. D. 2108 (Classic Reprint) (p. 668)
Rice, Howard. Step into the Desert (p. 2114)
—Step into the Forest (p. 2114)
—Step into the Rainforest (p. 2114)
Rice, Inez & Bobri, Vladimir. March Wind. (p. 1402)
Rice, James. Gaston Joins the Circus (p. 811)
—Gaston(r) Joins the Circus (p. 811)
Rice, James, illus. see Blazek, Sarah Kirwan.
Rice, James, illus. see Davis, David.
Rice, James, illus. see Layne, Steven.
Rice, James, illus. see McWilliams, Amanda & Moore, Clement C.
Rice, James, jt. auth. see Besant, Sir.
Rice, James, jt. auth. see Besant, Walter.
Rice, Joseph Mayer. Rational Spelling Book, Vol. 1 (Classic Reprint) (p. 1843)
Rice Jr., Earle. Al Qaeda. (p. 38)
—Evolution of Government & Politics in China. (p. 675)
—Evolution of Government & Politics in North & South Korea. (p. 675)
—Ganges River. (p. 808)
—Hezbollah. (p. 964)
—Islamic State. (p. 1139)
—Muslim Brotherhood. (p. 1529)
—Orion Spacecraft. (p. 1672)
—Tigris/Euphrates River. (p. 2242)
—Virginia Class Submarines. (p. 2361)
—Yangtze River. (p. 2517)
Rice, K. McDowell. Dr. Hardhack's Prescription: A Play for Children in Four Acts (Classic Reprint) (p. 591)
—Good King Wenceslas: A Christmas Play for Children, in Two Acts (Classic Reprint) (p. 863)
—Mrs. Bagg's Bargain Day: A Comedy in Two Acts (Classic Reprint) (p. 1521)
Rice, Kaleb, illus. see Porrata, Mayra.
Rice, Karen. Forbidden Sneeze. (p. 764)
Rice, Katelyn. American Indians of the West: Battling the Elements. (p. 72)
—Florida in the Early 20th Century: Boom & Bust. (p. 751)
—Great Leap Westward. (p. 887)
—Savannah: Hostess City of the South. (p. 1937)
—Settling & Unsettling the West (America in The 1800s) (p. 1993)
—Spanish-American War. (p. 2073)
Rice, Katelyn, jt. auth. see Kuligowski, Stephanie.
Rice, Katelyn & Kuligowski, Stephanie. Dangerous Catch! Deep Sea Fishers (p. 501)
Rice, Katharine McDowell. Good As Gold: A Comedy in Four Acts (Classic Reprint) (p. 861)
Rice, Lisa A., jt. auth. see Feldhahn, Shaunti.
Rice, Louise. New Blood: A Story of the Folks That Make America (Classic Reprint) (p. 1591)
Rice, Luanne. Beautiful Lost. (p. 184)
—Pretend She's Here. (p. 1790)
—Secret Language of Sisters. (p. 1976)
Rice, M. L. Melody of Light. (p. 1443)

R

—Five Mice in a Mouse-Trap: By the Man in the Moon. (p. 744)
—Five Mice in a Mouse-Trap: By the Man in the Moon; Done in the Vernacular, from the Lunacular (Classic Reprint) (p. 744)
—Five Minute Stories (Classic Reprint) (p. 744)
—Florence Nightingale the Angel of the Crimea: A Story for Young People (Classic Reprint) (p. 751)
—Geoffrey Strong (Classic Reprint) (p. 817)
—Golden Windows: A Book of Fables for Young & Old (Classic Reprint) (p. 859)
—Golden-Breasted Kootoo: And Other Stories. (p. 856)
—Golden-Breasted Kootoo (Classic Reprint) (p. 856)
—Grand-Mother: The Story of a Life That Never Was Lived (Classic Reprint) (p. 877)
—Hildegarde's Harvest. (p. 971)
—Hildegarde's Harvest (Classic Reprint) (p. 971)
—Hildegarde's Holiday: A Sequel to Queen Hildegarde (Classic Reprint) (p. 971)
—Hildegarde's Holiday a Story for Girls. (p. 971)
—Hildegarde's Home. (p. 971)
—Hildegarde's Home (Classic Reprint) (p. 971)
—Hildegarde's Neighbors. (p. 971)
—Hildegarde's Neighbors (Classic Reprint) (p. 971)
—Hurdy-Gurdy (Classic Reprint) (p. 1054)
—In Blessed Cyrus (Classic Reprint) (p. 1104)
—In My Nursery (Classic Reprint) (p. 1106)
—Isla Heron. (p. 1139)
—Isla Heron (Classic Reprint) (p. 1139)
—Jim of Hellas or in Durance Vile: Bethesda Pool (Classic Reprint) (p. 1168)
—Joan of Arc (Classic Reprint) (p. 1170)
—Laura Bridgman: The Story of an Opened Door (Classic Reprint) (p. 1252)
—Love & Rocks (Classic Reprint) (p. 1359)
—Margaret Montfort. (p. 1403)
—Margaret Montfort (Classic Reprint) (p. 1403)
—Marie (Classic Reprint) (p. 1405)
—Merryweathers. (p. 1450)
—Miss. Jimmy (Classic Reprint) (p. 1478)
—Narcissa or the Road to Rome: In Verona (Classic Reprint) (p. 1575)
—Nautilus (Classic Reprint) (p. 1582)
—Peggy. (p. 1714)
—Peggy (Classic Reprint) (p. 1714)
—Pig Brother, & Other Fables & Stories: A Supplementary Reader for the Fourth School Year (Classic Reprint) (p. 1743)
—Pippin: A Wandering Flame (Classic Reprint) (p. 1749)
—Queen Hildegarde: A Story for Girls (Classic Reprint) (p. 1823)
—Quicksilver Sue (Classic Reprint) (p. 1827)
—Rita. (p. 1886)
—Rita (Classic Reprint) (p. 1886)
—Rosin the Beau. (p. 1906)
—Stepping Westward (Classic Reprint) (p. 2115)
—Three Margarets. (p. 2234)
—Three Margarets (Classic Reprint) (p. 2234)
—Three Minute Stories. (p. 2234)
—Toto's Merry Winter. (p. 2267)
—Toto's Merry Winter (Classic Reprint) (p. 2267)
—When I Was Your Age. (p. 2431)
—When I Was Your Age (Classic Reprint) (p. 2431)
Richards, Laura Elizabeth. Four Feet, Two Feet, & No Feet: Or, Furry & Feathery Pets, & How They Live (Classic Reprint) (p. 772)
—Green Satin Gown (Classic Reprint) (p. 894)
—Mrs. Tree (Classic Reprint) (p. 1523)
—Mrs. Tree's Will (Classic Reprint) (p. 1523)
—Piccolo (Classic Reprint) (p. 1738)
—Rosin the Beau: A Sequel to Melody & Marie (Classic Reprint) (p. 1906)
—Snow-White; or, the House in the Wood (Classic Reprint) (p. 2048)
—Some Say: Neighbours in Cyrus (Classic Reprint) (p. 2059)
—Three Minute Stories (Classic Reprint) (p. 2234)
—Two Noble Lives: Samuel Gridley Howe, Julia Ward Howe (Classic Reprint) (p. 2308)
—Wooing of Calvin Parks (Classic Reprint) (p. 2492)
Richards, Laura Elizabeth Howe. Joyous Story of Toto (Classic Reprint) (p. 1184)
—Melody (Classic Reprint) (p. 1443)
—Queen Hildegarde. (p. 1823)
—Up to Calvin's (Classic Reprint) (p. 2338)
Richards, Lawrence O. Gospel of Mark (p. 871)
—NIrV Adventure Bible for Early Readers, Hardcover, Full Color Interior, Lion (p. 1611)
—NIV Adventure Bible, Leather Soft, Zebra Print, Full Color Interior (p. 1611)
—NIV Adventure Bible, Leathersoft, Gray, Full Color Interior (p. 1611)
Richards, Lawrence O., jt. auth. see Jim, Madsen.
Richards, Lawrence O. & Zondervan Staff. King James Version Kids Study Bible (p. 1220)
Richards, Lela Horn. Caroline's Career (Classic Reprint) (p. 333)
—Only Henrietta (Classic Reprint) (p. 1664)
—Then Came Caroline (Classic Reprint) (p. 2215)
Richards, Linda L. Death Was in the Blood. (p. 522)
Richards, Lisa. Family Short Stories Book. (p. 703)
—Family Stories: A Collection of Short Stories by Lisa Richards (p. 703)
Richards, Lucas, illus. see Morrison-Andrews, Sharalyn.
Richards, Lucy, illus. see Donaldson, Julia.
Richards, Lucy, jt. auth. see Donaldson, Julia.
Richards, Lucy, jt. auth. see Morpurgo, Michael.
Richards, Lynne. Fearless Four: Braced for Battle. Semple, Dave, illus. (p. 717)
Richards, Lysander Salmon. Breaking Up: Or the Birth, Development & Death of the Earth & Its Satellite in Story (Classic Reprint) (p. 278)
Richards, M. A. Out of Darkness. (p. 1682)
Richards, M. & Creese, S. Carry Me Rough N Tough - Emergency. (p. 334)
—Carry Me Rough N Tough - Trucks. (p. 334)
Richards, Marian Edwards. Zandrie (Classic Reprint) (p. 2538)
Richards, Mark & Creese, Sarah. Diggers & Dumpers. (p. 546)
Richards, Mark, et al. Tractors. (p. 2273)
Richards, Markita. Good Vibes Start Here: A JOURNAL for Tween & Teen GIRLS with a VISION & a PLAN. (p. 866)
—Pretty Melanin Me! Coloring & Activity Book. (p. 1790)
Richards, Markita & Richards, Jadon. Striving for Progress Not Perfection: A Journal for Tween & Teen Boys with a Vision & a Plan. (p. 2141)
Richards, Marlee. Johnstown Flood: Core Events of Deadly Disaster (p. 1175)
Richards, Marlee, jt. auth. see Brill, Marlene Targ.
Richards, Mary. Modern Art Journal. (p. 1486)
—Splat! The Most Exciting Artists of All Time. (p. 2084)
Richards, Maureen. Good Witches in Stitches: Book 1. (p. 866)
Richards, Mike. Hallucinations or Reality. (p. 913)
Richards, Natalie D. Five Total Strangers. (p. 745)
—Gone Too Far. (p. 861)
—My Secret to Tell. (p. 1560)
—One Was Lost. (p. 1663)
—Six Months Later. (p. 2028)
—We All Fall Down. (p. 2388)
—What You Hide. (p. 2422)
Richards, Patti. All about Social Networking. (p. 50)
—Apollo Missions. (p. 106)
—Space Shuttle Missions. (p. 2072)
Richards, R. C. Railroad Accidents, Their Cause & Prevention; Pp. 1-109. (p. 1835)
Richards, R. J. Carl Goes to Mouse World. (p. 331)
Richards, Rosalind. Northern Countryside (Classic Reprint) (p. 1621)
Richards, Sarah C. Easy Primer (Classic Reprint) (p. 621)
Richards, Steve. Hooray for Hexagons. Richards, Steve & Farnsworth, Lauren, illus. (p. 1001)
Richards, Sue, jt. auth. see Richards, Lawrence O.
Richards, T. Addison. Romance of American Landscape (Classic Reprint) (p. 1900)
Richards, Tanya, illus. see Paulin, Chrita.
Richards, Teresa. Topaz Reign. (p. 2264)
—Windfall App. (p. 2472)
Richards, Theodora, illus. see Richards, Keith.
Richards, Theodore. Scotty Kid: The Life Story of Brother Tommy (Classic Reprint) (p. 1962)
Richards, Tobe A. Piano Chords for Kids... & Big Kids Too! (p. 1738)
Richards, Tobe A., jt. auth. see Eriksson, Nancy.
Richards, Virginia Helen, illus. see Dateno, Maria Grace.
Richards, Virginia Helen, illus. see Halpin, D. Thomas.
Richards, Virginia Helen, illus. see Jenkins, Diana R.
Richards, Virginia Helen, illus. see MacDonald, Maryann.
Richards, Virginia Helen, jt. auth. see Halpin, D. Thomas.
Richards, Virginia Helen & Halpin, D. Thomas. Blessed Miguel Pro. (p. 244)
Richards, William C. Harry's Vacation: Or, Philosophy at Home (Classic Reprint) (p. 935)
Richards, William Carey. School Fellow, 1854, Vol. 6: A Magazine for Boys & Girls (Classic Reprint) (p. 1945)
Richardson, Abby Sage. Stories from Old English Poetry (Classic Reprint) (p. 2124)
Richardson, Adele D. Freight Trains in Action (p. 783)
—Owls (p. 1689)
Richardson, Adele D., jt. auth. see Haffmann, Janet.
Richardson, Adele D., et al. Birds. (p. 231)
Richardson, Arleta. Across the Border. (p. 11)
—Prairie Homestead. (p. 1785)
—Whistle-Stop West. (p. 2443)
Richardson, Benjamin Ward. On Alcohol: A Course of Six Cantor Lectures Delivered Before the Society of Arts (Classic Reprint) (p. 1652)
—On Alcohol. (p. 1652)
Richardson, Benjamin Ward & Royal Scottish Society of Arts. On Alcohol. (p. 1652)
Richardson, Betsy. Carnival (p. 332)
—Christmas & Hanukkah (p. 383)
—Easter, Passover & Festivals of Hope (p. 620)
—Halloween & Remembrances of the Dead (p. 912)
—Independence Days (p. 1115)
—Lent, Yom Kippur & Days of Repentance (p. 1266)
—Marking the Religious New Year (p. 1407)
—Ramadan (p. 1839)
—Ringing in the Western & Chinese New Year. (p. 1883)
—Thanksgiving & Other Festivals of the Harvest (p. 2212)
Richardson, Bill. Alphabet Thief Bikadoroff, Roxanna, illus. (p. 59)
—Bunny Band Bikadoroff, Roxanna, illus. (p. 298)
—Promise Basket Kolesar, Slavka, illus. (p. 1806)
Richardson, Bridgett, jt. auth. see Lamb, Esther.
Richardson, Carol Patricia. Eight Acres & a Cow. (p. 629)
Richardson, Cathie, illus. see Eismann, Sheila F. & Putz, Ali F.
Richardson, Charles. New Dictionary of the English Language, Vol. 2: L to Z (Classic Reprint) (p. 1592)
—Tales of a Warrior: Sanguine but Not Sanguinary for Old-Time People (Classic Reprint) (p. 2183)
Richardson, Charles F. End of the Beginning (Classic Reprint) (p. 648)
Richardson, D. L. Feedback. (p. 718)
Richardson, D. N. Girdle Round the Earth: Home Letters from Foreign Lands (Classic Reprint) (p. 835)
Richardson, Deborra. Treasures at the Museum. (p. 2282)
Richardson, Donna. Birds Being Birds. (p. 232)
Richardson, Dorothy. Long Day: The Story of a New York Working Girl (Classic Reprint) (p. 1342)
Richardson, Dorothy M. Backwater (Classic Reprint) (p. 156)
—Honeycomb (Classic Reprint) (p. 999)
—Interim (Classic Reprint) (p. 1126)
—Pointed Roofs (Classic Reprint) (p. 1767)
—Tunnel (Classic Reprint) (p. 2299)
Richardson, E. E. Black Bones. (p. 237)
—Curse Box. (p. 488)
Richardson Ed D, Donna Castle. Little Lilly Ladybug. (p. 1320)
—Teeny Tiny Tadpole: Kids Literature. (p. 2200)
Richardson, Erik. Alexander the Great. (p. 43)
—Applying Functions to Everyday Life. (p. 107)
—NATO, the Warsaw Pact, & the Iron Curtain. (p. 1579)
—Vaccination. (p. 2343)
Richardson, Erik & Chow-Miller, Ian. Integrated Robotics. (p. 1125)
Richardson, Faye. Car Accident. (p. 327)
Richardson, Frank Howard. For Girls Only: The Doctor Discusses the Mysteries of Womanhood (Classic Reprint) (p. 762)
Richardson, Frederick. Book of Drawings (Classic Reprint) (p. 258)
—Great Children's Stories. (p. 884)
Richardson, Frederick, illus. see Faulkner, Georgene.
Richardson, Frederick, illus. see Grover, Eulalie Osgood.
Richardson, Frederick, illus. see Thorne-Thomsen, Gudrun.
Richardson, Frederick, illus. see Treadwell, Harriette Taylor & Free, Margaret.
Richardson, G. Machu Picchu. (p. 1372)
Richardson, George. Nativity of Our Lord Jesus Christ: From the Meditations of Anne Catherine Emmerich (Classic Reprint) (p. 1579)
Richardson, George Forrest. Neighborhood Letters (Classic Reprint) (p. 1585)
Richardson, Gillian. 10 Plants That Shook the World. Rosen, Kim, illus. (p. 2550)
—10 Routes That Crossed the World. Rosen, Kim, illus. (p. 2550)
—10 Ships That Rocked the World. Rosen, Kim, illus. (p. 2550)
—Ecosystems. (p. 624)
—Ecosystems QandA. (p. 624)
—Kaboom! Explosions of All Kinds. (p. 1201)
—Mountain Extremes. (p. 1513)
Richardson, Gillian & Kissock, Heather. Machu Picchu. (p. 1372)
Richardson, H. D. Dogs: Their Origin & Varieties; Directions As to Their General Management, & Simple Instructions As to Their Treatment under Disease (Classic Reprint) (p. 577)
—Hive & the Honey-Bee: With Plain Directions for Obtaining a Considerable Annual Income from This Branch of Rural Economy; to Which Is Added, an Account of the Diseases of Bees, with Their Remedies (Classic Reprint) (p. 982)
Richardson, H. H. Johnson's Primer (Classic Reprint) (p. 1175)
Richardson, Hazel. Trade & Commerce in the Ancient World. Crabtree Publishing Staff, ed. (p. 2273)
Richardson, Hazel, jt. auth. see Miller, Reagan.
Richardson, Henrietta H. Johnson's First Reader (Classic Reprint) (p. 1175)
—Johnson's Second Reader: Illustrated (Classic Reprint) (p. 1175)
Richardson, Henry Handel. Getting of Wisdom (Classic Reprint) (p. 825)
—Maurice Guest (Classic Reprint) (p. 1426)
Richardson, Jade. Hue of You. (p. 1047)
Richardson, Jael Ealey. Stone Thrower: A Daughter's Lessons, a Father's Life James, Matt, illus. (p. 2121)
Richardson, James D. Compilation of the Messages & Papers of the Presidents: Abraham Lincoln; Volume 6; PT. 1. (p. 433)
—Compilation of the Messages & Papers of the Presidents: James Knox Polk; Volume 4; PT. 3. (p. 433)
Richardson, James Hugh. Spring Street: A Story of Los Angeles (Classic Reprint) (p. 2092)
Richardson, Jan. Guided Reading Teacher's Companion: Prompts, Discussion Starters & Teaching Points. (p. 904)
—Next Step Forward in Guided Reading: An Assess-Decide-Guide Framework for Supporting Every Reader. (p. 1600)
—Next Step Guided Reading in Action Grades K-2 Revised Edition. (p. 1600)
Richardson, Jan & Dufresne, Michéle. Next Step Forward in Word Study & Phonics. (p. 1600)
Richardson, Jan & Lewis, Ellen. Next Step Forward in Reading Intervention: The RISE Framework. (p. 1600)
Richardson, Jeffery. Wormwood Adventures New Friends. (p. 2508)
Richardson, Jill. Hobbits, You, & the Spiritual World of Middle-Earth. (p. 985)
Richardson, John. Wau-Nan-Gee, or the Massacre at Chicago: A Romance of the American Revolution (Classic Reprint) (p. 2386)
Richardson Jr, Robert E. 7 Biblical Responses to Bullying: Taking Your Kids from Victim to Victor. (p. 2548)
Richardson, Justin & Parnell, Peter. Christian, the Hugging Lion. Bates, Amy June, illus. (p. 382)
Richardson, Kae, illus. see Beere, Lisa.
Richardson, Kara, illus. see Dundy, Melanie Richardson.
Richardson, Kim, jt. auth. see Meissner, David.
Richardson, Kimberly Stanton. Gus Learns to Fly: Self-Defense Is Self-Discovery. Crowley, Adam A., photos by. (p. 906)
Richardson, Kyle. Beast Heart. (p. 181)
Richardson, Larry. Metal Mike. (p. 1452)
Richardson, Leander. Dark City: Or Customs of the Cockneys (Classic Reprint) (p. 506)
Richardson, Lilith. TORO Special Edition Paperback. (p. 2265)
Richardson, Lin Douglas. Meaning of Me. (p. 1434)
Richardson, Linda Marie. Rabbit Full of Hugs & Kisses. (p. 1829)
Richardson, Lucile. Victoire, 1919, Vol. 12: The High School Annual (Classic Reprint) (p. 2355)
Richardson, Markayla, illus. see Hall, Richard.
Richardson, Merrick Abner. Eight Days Out (Classic Reprint) (p. 629)
—Looking Back: An Autobiography (Classic Reprint) (p. 1347)
Richardson, Mike. Return of the Gremlins. (p. 1871)
Richardson, Mike, illus. see Snyder, Susan E.
Richardson, Mike & Chadwick, Paul. Best Wishes. (p. 208)
Richardson, Millie. Words Have Feelings Too. (p. 2494)
Richardson, Nikki. Beautiful Lie (p. 184)
Richardson, Norval. Cave Woman (Classic Reprint) (p. 347)
—Lead of Honour (Classic Reprint) (p. 1254)
Richardson, Owen, illus. see Colfer, Eoin.
Richardson, Owen, illus. see Hughes, Devon.
Richardson, Owen, illus. see Hunter, Erin.
Richardson, Owen, illus. see Jackson, Erik Forrest & Leroux, Gaston.
Richardson, Paul. Taylah's Got Talent. (p. 2193)
Richardson, Penny, illus. see Larocque, Donna-Lee.
Richardson, Peter, illus. see Jeffrey, Gary.
Richardson, Robert Earl, jt. auth. see Forbes, Stephen Alfred.
Richardson, Robert Lorne. Colin of the Ninth Concession: A Tale of Scottish Pioneer Life in Eastern Ontario (Classic Reprint) (p. 414)
—Colin of the Ninth Concession a Tale of Scottish Pioneer Life in Eastern Ontario (Classic Reprint) (p. 414)
Richardson, S. Lee. Backyard Series Volume Two: The Baby Bear Scare Story. (p. 157)
Richardson, Samuel. Clarissa Harlowe, Vol. 6 Of 9: Or the History of a Young Lady (Classic Reprint) (p. 398)
—Clarissa, or the History of a Young Lady, Vol. 1 Of 4: Comprehending the Most Important Concerns of Private Life, & Particularly Shewing the Distresses That May Attend the Misconduct Both of Parents & Children, in Relation to Marriage. (p. 398)
—Clarissa; or the History of a Young Lady, Vol. 3 Of 8: Comprehending the Most Important Concerns of Private Life; & Particularly Shewing the Distresses That May Attend the Misconduct Both of Parents & Children, in Relation to Marriage. (p. 398)
—Clarissa, or the History of a Young Lady, Vol. 4 Of 4: Comprehending the Most Important Concerns of Private Life; & Particularly Shewing the Distresses That May Attend the Misconduct Both of Parents & Children, in Relation to Marriage. (p. 399)
—Clarissa; or the History of a Young Lady, Vol. 5 Of 8: Comprehending the Most Important Concerns of Private Life; & Particularly Shewing the Distresses That May Attend the Misconduct Both of Parents & Children, in Relation to Marriage. (p. 399)
—Clarissa, Vol. 2: A Novel (Classic Reprint) (p. 399)
—History of Clarisa Harlowe, Vol. 4 Of 8: In a Series of Letters (Classic Reprint) (p. 977)
—History of Clarissa Harlowe, Vol. 3 Of 8: In a Series of Letters (Classic Reprint) (p. 977)
—History of Sir Charles Grandison, in a Series of Letters: In Seven Volumes, Vols. 1-4 (Classic Reprint) (p. 979)
—Novelist's Magazine, Vol. 14: Containing the First, Second, Third, & Fourth Volumes, of Clarissa (Classic Reprint) (p. 1626)
—Pamela, or Virtue Rewarded: In a Series of Familiar Letters from a Beautiful Young Damsel to Her Parents; in Four Volumes (Classic Reprint) (p. 1694)
—Pamela, or Virtue Rewarded: In a Series of Familiar Letters from a Beautiful Young Damsel to Her Parents; Published in Order to Cultivate Principles of Virtue & Religion in the Minds of the Youth of Both Sexes (Classic Reprint) (p. 1694)
—Pamela, or Virtue Rewarded: In a Series of Familiar Letters from a Beautiful Young Damsel to Her Parents; Published in Order to Cultivate the Principles of Virtue & Religion in the Minds of the Youth of Both Sexes; a Narrative Which Has Its Foundation I. (p. 1694)
—Pamela or Virtue Rewarded (Classic Reprint) (p. 1694)
—Pamela, or Virtue Rewarded; in a Series of Letters, from a Beautiful Young Damsel to Her Parents: Designed to Inculcate the Principles of Virtue & Religion in the Youth of Both Sexes (Classic Reprint) (p. 1694)
—Pamela, or Virtue Rewarded, Vol. 1 of 4 (Classic Reprint) (p. 1695)
Richardson, Sandra Lee. Backyard Series: Volume One (p. 157)
Richardson, Sarah. Art in a Box. (p. 121)
—Make Your Mark: The Drawing Book for Children. (p. 1387)
Richardson, Sharde. Watched. (p. 2383)
Richardson, Steve. Lavender Blue: & the Faeries of Galtee Wood. (p. 1253)
—Paisley Rabbit & the Treehouse Contest. (p. 1693)
Richardson, Tanya Carroll. Zen Teen: 40 Ways to Stay Calm When Life Gets Stressful. (p. 2539)
Richardson, Teresa Eden. English Girl in Tokyo (Classic Reprint) (p. 653)
Richardson, Tiffanya. Trinity Jones: The Queen of the GhettoA Fictional Poetic Memoir (p. 2288)
Richardson, Timariay A. Billy Bean & the Chocolate Dragon. (p. 227)
Richardson, Tobias Gibson. Elements of Human Anatomy: General, Descriptive, & Practical (Classic Reprint) (p. 633)
Richardson, Tracy. Field. (p. 722)
—Indian Summer. (p. 1116)
Richardson, Travis. Lost in Clover. (p. 1354)
Richardson, Warren. Dr. Zell & the Princess Charlotte: An Autobiographical Relation of Adventures in the Life of a Distinguished Modern Necromancer, Seer & Theosophist (Classic Reprint) (p. 592)
Richardson-Jones, Tessa, illus. see Stowell, Gordon.
Richardson-Jones, Tessa, illus. see Umansky, Kaye.
Richards-Quinteros, Robin. Witch & the Crow. (p. 2479)
Richards-Ross, Sanya. Right on Track: Run, Race, Believe (p. 1882)
—Run with Me: The Story of a U. S. Olympic Champion (p. 1914)
Richberg, Donald. In the Dark (Classic Reprint) (p. 1108)
Richburg, Justin, illus. see Farrington, Catinia.
Richburg, Sheila. Story of Panhandle Pete Part One. (p. 2132)
Richel, Patricia. Patsy the Seagull Visits Ellis Island. (p. 1706)
Richelet, Pierre. Dictionnaire de la Langue Francoise, Ancienne et Moderne, Vol. 1: A-D (Classic Reprint) (p. 542)
—Dictionnaire de la Langue Francoise, Ancienne et Moderne, Vol. 2: E-O (Classic Reprint) (p. 542)
—Dictionnaire de la Langue Françoise, Ancienne et Moderne, Vol. 3: P-Z (Classic Reprint) (p. 542)

—Dictionnaire de la Langue Franoise, Ancienne et Moderne, Vol. 1: A-D (Classic Reprint) (p. 542)
—Dictionnaire de la Langue Franoise, Ancienne et Moderne, Vol. 2: E-O (Classic Reprint) (p. 542)
—Dictionnaire François, Contenant les Mots et les Choses, Plusieurs Nouvelles Remarques Sur la Langue Françoise: Ses Expressions Propres, Figurées et Burlesques, la Prononciation des Mots les Plus Difficiles, le Genre des Noms, le Régime des Verbes. (p. 542)
—Nouveau Dictionnaire Francois, Vol. 1: Contenant Generalement Tous les Mots, les Matieres, et Plusieurs Nouvelles Remarques Sur la Langue Francoise (Classic Reprint) (p. 1625)
—Nouveau Dictionnaire François, Vol. 1: Contenant Généralement Tous les Mots, les Matières, et Plusieurs Nouvelles Remarques Sur la Langue Françoise (Classic Reprint) (p. 1625)
Richemont, Enid. Big Purple Wonderbook. Waldek, Kelly, illus. (p. 222)
—Brownilocks & the Three Bowls of Cornflakes. (p. 287)
—Night of the Were-Boy. (p. 1607)
—Princess Frog. Bernstein, Galia, illus. (p. 1797)
Richens, Carol & Smith, Lori. Lori's Summer Fun with Tamara! (p. 1349)
Richepin, Jacques. Cadet-Roussel: Comédie en Trois Actes, en Vers (Classic Reprint) (p. 308)
Richert, Catherine. Animal Rescue: Represent & Solve Problems Involving Addition. (p. 91)
Richert, Scott P. Bill Bryson. (p. 226)
—King Lear. (p. 1220)
Riches Hall, Sara, illus. see Bell, Michael J.
Riches, M. E. Comet Club. (p. 429)
Richetti, John J., ed. see Dafoe, Daniel.
Richey, Beth & Wood, Paula. When a Grown-Up You Love Hurts You. (p. 2429)
Richey, Rachel, ed. see Kelly, Fred.
Richez, Herve, jt. auth. see Cazenove, Christophe.
Richie, Laura. Advent Storybook: 25 Bible Stories Showing Why Jesus Came. Dale, Ian, illus. (p. 18)
—Easter Storybook: 40 Bible Stories Showing Who Jesus Is. Dale, Ian, illus. (p. 620)
Richie, Morgan W. Sensitive Pirate. Richie, Morgan W., illus. (p. 1989)
Richle, Urs. I Love You Thiiiiiis Much! - Illustrated by Johan Walder. Walder, Johan, illus. (p. 1079)
Richle, Urs & Axelrad, Monica. Lia & the Peas - or What Is Cancer? (p. 1283)
Richler, Mordecai. Jacob Two-Two & the Dinosaur. Petricic, Dusan, illus. (p. 1154)
—Jacob Two-Two Meets the Hooded Fang. Petricic, Dusan, illus. (p. 1154)
—Jacob Two-Two's First Spy Case. Petricic, Dusan, illus. (p. 1154)
—Stick Your Neck Out (Classic Reprint) (p. 2117)
Richman, Julia. Good Citizenship (Classic Reprint) (p. 862)
Richman, Julia & Beckerling, Celeste. Huddle of Hippos. (p. 1047)
Richman, Karyn. Land Where All Things Become Beautiful. (p. 1242)
Richman, Kim. Bedlam in Grandma Green's Garden. (p. 188)
Richman, Sarah. Cheat. (p. 363)
—Family Ties. (p. 703)
Richmond, A. B. Nemesis of Chautauqua Lake: Or Circumstantial Evidence (Classic Reprint) (p. 1587)
Richmond, Allen. First Twenty Years of My Life (Classic Reprint) (p. 740)
Richmond, Amanda and Logan. Mommy & Me, a to Z Alphabet Book. (p. 1490)
Richmond, Ben. Baby Panda Chews Bamboo. (p. 152)
Richmond, Ben, jt. auth. see American Museum of Natural History.
Richmond, Benjamin. What Are the Three Branches of the Government? And Other Questions about the U. S. Constitution. (p. 2406)
—Where Do Garbage Trucks Go? (p. 2436)
—Why Is the Sea Salty? And Other Questions about the Ocean. Azhderian, Cecelia, illus. (p. 2458)
Richmond, Blair. Last Mile: The Lithia Trilogy, Book 3. (p. 1248)
—Out of Breath: The Lithia Trilogy, Book 1. (p. 1682)
Richmond, Caroline Tung. Darkest Hour. (p. 507)
—Live in Infamy: What If the Axis Powers Had Won World War II. (p. 1332)
—Only Thing to Fear. (p. 1664)
Richmond, Caroline Tung, ed. see Chapman, Elsie, et al.
Richmond, Celia. Egypt, Greece, & Rome (Classic Reprint) (p. 628)
—Richmond: Second Reader (Classic Reprint) (p. 1877)
Richmond, Grace Louise Smith. Indifference of Juliet (Classic Reprint) (p. 1117)
—Round the Corner in Gay Street (Classic Reprint) (p. 1908)
Richmond, Grace S. Bells of St. John's (Classic Reprint) (p. 198)
—Brown Study (Classic Reprint) (p. 287)
—Foursquare (Classic Reprint) (p. 773)
—Listening Post (Classic Reprint) (p. 1308)
—Mrs. Red Pepper (Classic Reprint) (p. 1523)
—On Christmas Day in the Morning (Classic Reprint) (p. 1652)
—Red & Black (Classic Reprint) (p. 1856)
—Red of the Redfields (Classic Reprint) (p. 1858)
—Red Pepper Burns (Classic Reprint) (p. 1858)
—Red Pepper's Patients: With an Account of Anne Linton's Case in Particular. (p. 1858)
—Red Pepper's Patients: With an Account of Anne Linton's Case in Particular (Classic Reprint) (p. 1858)
—Second Violin (Classic Reprint) (p. 1974)
—Strawberry Acres (Classic Reprint) (p. 2139)
—Under the Country Sky (Classic Reprint) (p. 2321)
—Whistling Mother (Classic Reprint) (p. 2443)
—With Juliet in England (Classic Reprint) (p. 2481)
Richmond, Grace Smith. Brotherly House (Classic Reprint) (p. 286)
—Brown Study (Classic Reprint) (p. 287)
—On Christmas Day in the Evening (Classic Reprint) (p. 1652)
—Red Pepper Returns (Classic Reprint) (p. 1858)
—Twenty-Fourth of June: Midsummer's Day (Classic Reprint) (p. 2304)
—Under the Christmas Stars (Classic Reprint) (p. 2321)
Richmond, Jacob. Polly Perfect & the Tragic Fart. Pine, Hank, illus. (p. 1772)
Richmond, Kip, illus. see Kenny, Eileen.
Richmond, Legh. Dairyman's Daughter: An Authentic Narrative, Abridged (Classic Reprint) (p. 497)
Richmond, Lori. Bunny'S Staycation. (p. 298)
—Pax & Blue. Richmond, Lori, illus. (p. 1708)
Richmond, Lori, illus. see Dempsey, Kristy.
Richmond, Lori, illus. see Kubart, Tim.
Richmond, Lori, illus. see Martin, David.
Richmond, Lori, illus. see Portis, Michael.
Richmond, Marianne. Be Brave Little One. (p. 177)
—Bedtime Blessings. (p. 188)
—Big Boys Go Potty. Richmond, Marianne, illus. (p. 218)
—Big Girls Go Potty. Richmond, Marianne, illus. (p. 220)
—Friendly Floppy Fishie, What Do Wish For? (p. 786)
—Grandma Loves Me! (p. 878)
—Grandma's Love. (p. 878)
—Grandpa Loves Me! (p. 879)
—Hooray for You! (p. 1001)
—I Believe in You. (p. 1060)
—I Love You All Ways. Kolanovic, Dubravka, illus. (p. 1078)
—I Love You So. (p. 1079)
—I Love You So... (p. 1079)
—I Promise You. (p. 1080)
—If I Could Keep You Little. (p. 1091)
—If I Could Keep You Little... (p. 1091)
—Night Night Book. Richmond, Marianne, illus. (p. 1606)
—Oh, the Things My Mom Will Do. (p. 1642)
—You Are My Heart. (p. 2524)
—You Are My Kiss Goodnight. (p. 2524)
—You Are My Merry. (p. 2524)
—You're a Big Brother. (p. 2535)
—You're a Big Sister. (p. 2535)
Richmond, Marianne, et al. Minnesota Books for Kids Gift Set. Poole, Helen & Dunn, Robert, illus. (p. 1473)
Richmond, Peter. Game for Life: John Madden. (p. 807)
Richmond, Phyllis. Student's Pen, Vol. 6: June, 1925 (Classic Reprint) (p. 2143)
Richmond, Susan Edwards. Bird Count Coleman, Stephanie Fizer, illus. (p. 230)
Richmond, Wren. Apache. (p. 105)
Richoll, Stephanie, illus. see DeLong, Lucianne.
Richtel, Matt. Runaway Booger. Wildish, Lee, illus. (p. 1915)
Richter, A. Boats that Float: Learning the OA Sound. (p. 251)
—By the Ocean: Learning the Long O Sound. (p. 306)
Richter, Abigail. Deadly Mosquitoes. (p. 519)
Richter, Allen. America's Oldest Colony: The Story of St. Augustine. (p. 75)
Richter, Cheryl R., photos by see Taus-Bolstad, Stacy.
Richter, Cindy. Pete's Big Paws - Hardcover. Peters, Rob, illus. (p. 1730)
Richter, Debra A. Hamster on the Run. LiveLearn, Robert, illus. (p. 914)
—Hamster on the Run, Let's Play in the Snow. LiveLearn, Robert, illus. (p. 914)
—Two Frogs & the Lost Wedding Band. (p. 2307)
Richter, Georg Friedrich. G. Frid. Richteri de Natalibus Fulminum Tractatus Physicus: Accedit Appendix Qua Litterae et Observationes Quaedam Huc Pertinentes Maffei, Lionii, Pagliarini, Aliorumque Continentur (Classic Reprint) (p. 803)
Richter, Jean Paul Friederich. Flower, Fruit & Thorn Pieces, or the Married Life, Death, & Wedding of the Advocate of the Poor, Firmian Stanislaus Siebenkas, Vol. 1 of 2 (Classic Reprint) (p. 752)
Richter, Jean Paul Friedrich. Flower, Fruit, & Thorn Pieces: Or, the Wedded Life, Death, & Marriage of Firmian Stanislaus Siebenkaes, Parish Advocate in the Burgh of Kuhschnappel, a Genuine Thorn Piece (Classic Reprint) (p. 752)
—Flower, Fruit, & Thorn Pieces, or the Married Life, Death, & Wedding of the Advocate of the Poor, Firmian Stanislaus Siebenkas, Vol. 1 of 2 (Classic Reprint) (p. 752)
—Flower, Fruit & Thorn Pieces, Vol. 2 Of 2: Or the Married Life, Death, & Wedding of the Advocate of the Poor (Classic Reprint) (p. 752)
—Hesperus, Vol. 1 Of 2: Or Forty-Five Dog-Post-Days, a Biography (Classic Reprint) (p. 963)
Richter, Joanne. Iran: The Culture. (p. 1133)
—Iran - The Culture. (p. 1133)
Richter, Joanne, jt. auth. see Fast, April.
Richter, Jutta. Beyond the Station Lies the Sea. Brailovsky, Anna, tr. (p. 212)
Richter, Ludwig. Mother Goose from Germany (Classic Reprint) (p. 1509)
Richter, Murray. Lucky Rocks. (p. 1365)
Richter, Rudolf. LaFontaine et Lamotte (Classic Reprint) (p. 1239)
Richter, Sandy. Life of Florence Nightingale. (p. 1294)
Richter, Virginia Rose. Taken: A Willow Lane Mystery, #4. (p. 2177)
Richter, W. D., jt. auth. see Rauch, Earl Mac.
Richwould, Mary. South Sea Fortune, or the Chaplain Advanced to the Saddle, Vol. 1: Containing the Genuine Private Memoirs of a Worthy Family in Gloucestershire, from the Fatal Year 1720, to the Year 1748 (Classic Reprint) (p. 2069)
Rickard, Kris A. & Bial, Raymond. People & Culture of the Arapaho. (p. 1718)
—People & Culture of the Blackfeet. (p. 1718)
Rickard, Scarlett, illus. see Henderson, Neil G.
Rickard, Victor. Cathy Rossiter (Classic Reprint) (p. 345)
—Fire of Green Boughs (Classic Reprint) (p. 732)
—Fool's Errand (Classic Reprint) (p. 761)
—House of Courage (Classic Reprint) (p. 1022)
—Light above the Cross Roads (Classic Reprint) (p. 1298)
Rickards, Clifford. Prison Chaplain on Dartmoor (Classic Reprint) (p. 1801)
Rickards, Lynne. All about Honey Green Band. (p. 49)
—Baking Bread: Green Band. (p. 160)
—Big City Yellow Band. Roberts, Ley Honor, illus. (p. 219)
—Collins Big Cat Phonics for Letters & Sounds - Noisy Neesha: Band 06/Orange Jennings, Sarah, illus. (p. 416)
—Four Clever Brothers 1 Pathfinders. Bernstein, Galia, illus. (p. 772)
—Games Pink a Band. (p. 807)
—Harris the Hero Grant, Gabby, illus. (p. 933)
—Hide & Seek Green Band. Pérez, Moni, illus. (p. 967)
—Houses & Homes. Red Band. (p. 1024)
—I Can Help Pink a Band. (p. 1062)
—My Dad Is a Builder Pink B Band. Hustache, Timothy, illus. (p. 1536)
—My First Train Trip. Honor Roberts, Ley, illus. (p. 1546)
—Omar Can Help Red Band. Pérez, Moni, illus. (p. 1651)
—Pink! (p. 1746)
—Playgrounds Yellow Band. (p. 1760)
—Rowan the Red Squirrel Mitchell, Jon, illus. (p. 1909)
—Skye the Puffling: A Wee Puffin Board Book Mitchell, Jon, illus. (p. 2034)
—Skye the Puffling: A Baby Puffin's Adventure Mitchell, Jon, illus. (p. 2034)
—Willow the Wildcat Harris-Jones, Kirsteen, illus. (p. 2469)
—You & Me 2 Wayfarers. Brecon, Connah & Painter, Andrew, illus. (p. 2524)
Rickards, Lynne & Roberts, Ley Honor. Diego Fandango Yellow Band. Rogers, Alan, illus. (p. 544)
Ricken LeRoux, Patricia. Dog Collar: Issue 1. (p. 575)
Ricker, Everett W. Notes on the Birds of Hull, Massachusetts. (p. 1624)
—Notes on the Birds of Hull, Massachusetts (Classic Reprint) (p. 1624)
Ricker, Jeffrey. Unwanted. (p. 2337)
Ricker, Sarah B. In the Sixties (Classic Reprint) (p. 1111)
Rickert, Edith. Folly (Classic Reprint) (p. 758)
—Golden Hawk (Classic Reprint) (p. 857)
—Reaper (Classic Reprint) (p. 1851)
Rickert, Edith, jt. auth. see Furnivall, Frederick James.
Rickert, Marie. Cindy Finds a Home. (p. 392)
Rickerty, Simon. Crayon: A Colorful Tale about Friendship. Rickerty, Simon, illus. (p. 468)
—Peanut: A Nutty Tale about Sharing. Rickerty, Simon, illus. (p. 1709)
Rickerty, Simon, illus. see Bently, Peter.
Rickerty, Simon, illus. see Bonwill, Ann.
Rickerty, Simon, illus. see Brownlow, Michael.
Rickerty, Simon, illus. see Brownlow, Mike.
Rickerty, Simon, illus. see Lewis, Jill.
Rickett, Arthur. Mimes & Rhymes (Classic Reprint) (p. 1468)
Rickett, Sally. Minky the Shoebox Monkey - a Little Monkey with a Long Way to Go. (p. 1472)
Ricketts, Charles S. Dial, 1896 (Classic Reprint) (p. 537)
Ricketts, Mark Scott, illus. see Plourde, Lynn.
Rickham, Elethia, tr. see Sherlock, Philip.
Ricks, Christopher, ed. see Milton, John.
Ricks, Patricia J. Treasured: A Higher Realms Novel. (p. 2282)
Ricks, Sam, illus. see Adler, David A.
Ricks, Sam, illus. see Apple, Sam.
Ricks, Sam, illus. see Barrows, Annie.
Ricks, Sam, illus. see Brallier, Max & Chabert, Jack.
Ricks, Sam, illus. see Chabert, Jack.
Ricks, Sam, illus. see Dougherty, John.
Ricks, Sam, illus. see Hopper, Ada.
Ricks, Sam, jt. auth. see Adler, David A.
Rico, Fernando Ruiz. Cuentos para Ser Escuchados. (p. 483)
Rico, Gaby, illus. see Lima, Rossy E. & Padilla, Gerald a.
Rico, J. D. Dagger Mountain. (p. 495)
Ridd, Madeleine. Millie's Brilliant Birthday Plan. (p. 1468)
Riddel, Leisha, illus. see Smith, Kiwi & Lustgarten, Kurt.
Riddell. Earl's Promise, Vol. 2 Of 3: A Novel (Classic Reprint) (p. 613)
—Frank Sinclair's Wife, Vol. 1 Of 3: And Other Stories (Classic Reprint) (p. 777)
—Mortomley's Estate, Vol. 1 Of 3: A Novel (Classic Reprint) (p. 1507)
Riddell, Charlotte. Earl's Promise, Vol. 1 Of 3: A Novel (Classic Reprint) (p. 613)
—Phemie Keller, Vol. 1 Of 3: A Novel (Classic Reprint) (p. 1733)
Riddell, Chris. Chris Riddell's Doodle-A-Day. (p. 382)
—Emperor of Absurdia. (p. 644)
—Goth Girl & the Fete Worse Than Death. (p. 872)
—Goth Girl & the Ghost of a Mouse. (p. 872)
—Goth Girl & the Sinister Symphony. (p. 872)
—Goth Girl & the Wuthering Fright. (p. 872)
—Great Big Cuddle: Poems for the Very Young. (p. 884)
—Mr Underbed. Riddell, Chris, illus. (p. 1521)
—My Little Book of Big Freedoms. (p. 1552)
—Ottoline & the Purple Fox: Book 4. (p. 1676)
—Poems to Live Your Life By. Riddell, Chris, illus. (p. 1765)
—Travels with My Sketchbook. (p. 2281)
—Wendel & the Robots. (p. 2400)
—Wendel's Workshop. (p. 2400)
Riddell, Chris, illus. see Dorfman, Ariel.
Riddell, Chris, illus. see Gaiman, Neil.
Riddell, Chris, illus. see McGough, Roger.
Riddell, Chris, illus. see Platt, Richard.
Riddell, Chris, illus. see Rosen, Michael.
Riddell, Chris, illus. see Stewart, Paul & Stewart, Paul.
Riddell, Chris, illus. see Stewart, Paul.
Riddell, Chris, illus. see Swift, Jonathan.
Riddell, Chris, jt. auth. see Cave, Kathryn.
Riddell, Chris, jt. auth. see Stewart, Paul.
Riddell, Chris & Carroll, Lewis. Hunting of the Snark. Riddell, Chris, illus. (p. 1053)
Riddell, Chris & Stewart, Paul. Edge Chronicles: Freeglader. (p. 625)
—Edge Chronicles: the Curse of the Gloamglozer. (p. 625)
Riddell, H. Above Suspicion: A Novel (Classic Reprint) (p. 7)
—Berna Boyle, Vol. 1 Of 3: A Love Story of the Country down (Classic Reprint) (p. 204)
—Frank Sinclair's Wife, & Other Stories, Vol. 3 of 3 (Classic Reprint) (p. 777)
Riddell, J. H. Austin Friars (Classic Reprint) (p. 138)
—Austin Friars, Vol. 1 Of 3: A Novel (Classic Reprint) (p. 138)
—Berna Boyle: A Love Story of the County down (Classic Reprint) (p. 204)
—Berna Boyle, Vol. 2 Of 3: A Love Story of the County down (Classic Reprint) (p. 204)
—Berna Boyle, Vol. 3 Of 3: A Love Story of the County down (Classic Reprint) (p. 204)
—City & Suburb: A Novel (Classic Reprint) (p. 394)
—Daisies & Buttercups, Vol. 1 Of 3: A Novel (Classic Reprint) (p. 497)
—Did He Deserve It? (Classic Reprint) (p. 542)
—Earl's Promise: A Novel (Classic Reprint) (p. 613)
—Earl's Promise. (p. 613)
—Earl's Promise, Vol. 3 Of 3: A Novel (Classic Reprint) (p. 613)
—Far above Rubies, Vol. 1 Of 3: A Novel (Classic Reprint) (p. 708)
—Frank Sinclair's Wife, Vol. 2 Of 3: And Other Stories (Classic Reprint) (p. 777)
—Government Official, Vol. 1 Of 3: A Novel (Classic Reprint) (p. 873)
—Head of the Firm, Vol. 1 Of 3: A Novel (Classic Reprint) (p. 942)
—Home, Sweet Home: A Novel (Classic Reprint) (p. 997)
—Home, Sweet Home. (p. 997)
—Home, Sweet Home, Vol. 1 Of 3: A Novel (Classic Reprint) (p. 997)
—Joy after Sorrow: A Novel (Classic Reprint) (p. 1184)
—Life's Assize (Classic Reprint) (p. 1296)
—Mitre Court, Vol. 1 Of 3: A Tale of the Great City (Classic Reprint) (p. 1483)
—Mitre Court, Vol. 2 Of 3: A Tale of the Great City (Classic Reprint) (p. 1483)
—Mitre Court, Vol. 3 Of 3: A Tale of the Great City (Classic Reprint) (p. 1484)
—Mortomley's Estate: A Novel (Classic Reprint) (p. 1507)
—Mortomley's Estate, Vol. 3 Of 3: A Novel (Classic Reprint) (p. 1507)
—My First Love & My Last Love: A Novel (Classic Reprint) (p. 1544)
—My First Love & My Last Love. a Novel. (p. 1544)
—Phemie Keller (Classic Reprint) (p. 1733)
—Race for Wealth: A Novel (Classic Reprint) (p. 1831)
—Race for Wealth. (p. 1831)
—Race for Wealth, Vol. 1 Of 3: A Novel (Classic Reprint) (p. 1831)
—Senior Partner, Vol. 1 Of 3: A Novel (Classic Reprint) (p. 1988)
—Struggle for Fame, Vol. 1 Of 3: A Novel (Classic Reprint) (p. 2142)
—Susan Drummond: A Novel (Classic Reprint) (p. 2166)
—Susan Drummond. (p. 2166)
—Susan Drummond, Vol. 1 Of 3: A Novel (Classic Reprint) (p. 2166)
Riddell, Joseph H. Race for Wealth, Vol. 1 Of 2: A Novel (Classic Reprint) (p. 1831)
Riddell, Shona. Tale of the Anzac Tortoise. Gauldie, Matt, illus. (p. 2180)
Ridder, Araceli. Suit for Stanley. (p. 2148)
Riddle, A. G. Bart Ridgeley: A Story of Northern Ohio (Classic Reprint) (p. 168)
—Portrait: A Romance of the Cuyahoga Valley (Classic Reprint) (p. 1779)
—Romance of the Capital (Classic Reprint) (p. 1900)
—Tory's Daughter: A Romance of the North-West (Classic Reprint) (p. 2266)
—Tory's Daughter. (p. 2266)
Riddle, A. G. (Albert Gallatin). Bart Ridgeley. (p. 168)
Riddle, Albert Gallatin. Castle Gregory: A Story of the Western Reserve Woods in the Olden Times. (p. 340)
—Castle Gregory: A Story of the Western Reserve Woods in the Olden Times (Classic Reprint) (p. 340)
Riddle, George. George Riddle's Readings (Classic Reprint) (p. 819)
Riddle, John. Marco Polo: 13th Century Italian Trader. (p. 1403)
—Robert F. Scott: British Explorer of the South Pole. (p. 1890)
Riddle, John & Simons, Rae. Firefighter. Riggs, Ernestine G. & Gholar, Cheryl, eds. (p. 733)
—Veterinarian. (p. 2354)
Riddle, Mark. Margarash. Miller, Tim, illus. (p. 1403)
Riddle, Peter H. No Room: A Read-Aloud Story of Christmas. Hustins, Shelley, illus. (p. 1614)
—Painted Ponies of Partequineus & the Summer of the Kittens: Two Novels for Young Readers. (p. 1693)
Riddle, Tohby. Milo: A Moving Story. (p. 1468)
Riddle, Tohby, illus. see Dubosarsky, Ursula.
Riddle, Waide. Red River County from Short Story to Screenplay: From Short Story to Screenplay. (p. 1858)
Riddle, Waide Aaron. Chocolate Man A Children's Horror Tale. Aragon Art Studio, illus. (p. 380)
Riddle, William. Cherished Memories of Old Lancaster-Town & Shire (Classic Reprint) (p. 365)
—Nicholas Comenius: Or Ye Pennsylvania Schoolmaster of Ye Olden Time (Classic Reprint) (p. 1602)
Riddolls, Tom. Sally Ride: The First American Woman in Space. (p. 1925)
—Tigers. (p. 2242)
Riddolls, Tom, jt. auth. see Wearing, Judy.
Riddolls, Tom & Wearing, Judy. Hillary Clinton. (p. 971)
—Tiger Woods. (p. 2241)
—Zac Efron. (p. 2537)
Rideal, Charles F. Some People We Meet: Being Bits of Everyday Character & Piquant Pictures of Persons (Classic Reprint) (p. 2059)
Rideau, J. & Asso, B. Falklands War. Chauvin, D. & Uderzo, M., illus. (p. 699)
Rideing, William H. Boyhood of Famous Authors (Classic Reprint) (p. 271)
—How Tyson Came Home: A Story of England & America (Classic Reprint) (p. 1046)
—In the Land of Lorna Doone: And Other Pleasurable Excursions in England (Classic Reprint) (p. 1109)
—Stray Moments with Thackeray: His Humor, Satire, & Characters; Being Selections from His Writings, Prefaced with a Few Biographical Notes (Classic Reprint) (p. 2139)

R

Ridenour, Melissa Harker. Scary Ghosts & Playful Ghosts: Children's Tales of Fright & Delight. (p. 1942)
—What Would You Do? A Kid's Guide to Staying Safe in a World of Strangers. Fehling, Leslie, illus. (p. 2422)
Rideout, Flora. Mona Nantow (p. 1492)
Rideout, Henry Milner. Admiral's Light (Classic Reprint) (p. 16)
—Beached Keels (Classic Reprint) (p. 178)
—Dragon's Blood (Classic Reprint) (p. 595)
—Far Cry (Classic Reprint) (p. 708)
—Fern Seed (Classic Reprint) (p. 720)
—Key of the Fields & Boldero (Classic Reprint) (p. 1211)
—Siamese Cat (Classic Reprint) (p. 2014)
—Tin Cowrie Dass: A Story (Classic Reprint) (p. 2247)
—Twisted Foot (Classic Reprint) (p. 2306)
—William Jones: Indian, Cowboy, American Scholar, & Anthropologist in the Field (Classic Reprint) (p. 2468)
—Winter Bell (Classic Reprint) (p. 2475)
Rideout, J. B. Camping Out in California (Classic Reprint) (p. 316)
—Six Years on the Border: Or, Sketches of Frontier Life (Classic Reprint) (p. 2029)
—Six Years on the Border. (p. 2029)
Rideout, Kenneth & Wolf, Jonathan. AP Physics 2 with Online Tests. (p. 104)
Rider, Catherine. Kiss Me in New York. (p. 1224)
—Kiss Me in Paris. (p. 1224)
Rider, Debbie. Makaela Mouse, Where Are You? (p. 1385)
—What's That Smell in Josh's Room? (p. 2426)
Rider, Taira, tr. see Carmi, Tali.
Ridge, Jacqueline. Adventures of Scrappy the Cat. (p. 27)
Ridge, Jennifer. Between Worlds. (p. 210)
Ridge, Judith. Book That Made Me: A Collection of 32 Personal Stories. (p. 260)
Ridge, Judith, ed. Book That Made Me: A Collection of 32 Personal Stories. (p. 260)
Ridge, Rachel Anne. Flash the Donkey Makes New Friends. Ridge, Rachel Anne, illus. (p. 746)
Ridge, Sally, jt. auth. see Hildebrand, Jens.
Ridge, W. Pett. Amazing Years (Classic Reprint) (p. 67)
—Erb (Classic Reprint) (p. 659)
—Lost Property: The Story of Maggie Cannon (Classic Reprint) (p. 1355)
—Mixed Grill (Classic Reprint) (p. 1484)
—Name of Garland (Classic Reprint) (p. 1573)
—Second Opportunity of Mr. Staplehurst (Classic Reprint) (p. 1974)
—Son of the State (Classic Reprint) (p. 2062)
—Splendid Brother (Classic Reprint) (p. 2085)
—Table d'Hote (Classic Reprint) (p. 2175)
—Wickhamses (Classic Reprint) (p. 2460)
Ridge, William Pett. Breaker of Laws (Classic Reprint) (p. 278)
—Madame Prince (Classic Reprint) (p. 1374)
—Mrs. Galers Business (Classic Reprint) (p. 1522)
—Next Door Neighbours (Classic Reprint) (p. 1600)
Ridge, Yolanda. Crispr: A Powerful Way to Change DNA. Boersma, Alex, illus. (p. 475)
—Road Block (p. 1888)
Ridgely, Newton. By Law of Might: Of the Campaign in Sunset; a Romance of the Real Wall Street (Classic Reprint) (p. 305)
Ridges, David J. Book of Mormon Made Easier for Teens Set. (p. 259)
—Book of Mormon Made Easier for Teens Vol 1. (p. 259)
Ridgeway, Algernon. Westover's Ward, Vol. 1 of 3 (Classic Reprint) (p. 2402)
Ridgeway, Nicola. How to Draw a Fashion Model Using Grids for Beginners (Grid Drawing for Kids) Use Grids & Learn How to Draw Fashion Girls & Fashion Model Figures, with Realistic Fashion Dresses Step by Step. (p. 1039)
—Libro de Pintar para niños de 4 Años (Búhos 2) (p. 1286)
—Livre de Coloriage Simple Pour les Tous Petits (Emoticônes 1) Ce Livre Contient 40 Pages à Colorier Avec des Lignes Très épaisses. Ce Livre Aidera les Jeunes Enfants à développer le Contrôle du Stylo et à Exercer Leurs Compétences en Motrices Fines. (p. 1336)
—Livre de Coloriage Simple Pour les Tous Petits (Selfies Animaux) Ce Livre Contient 40 Pages à Colorier Avec des Lignes Très épaisses. Ce Livre Aidera les Jeunes Enfants à développer le Contrôle du Stylo et à Exercer Leurs Compétences en Motrices Fines. (p. 1336)
—Livres Pour les Enfants de 4 Ans (Dinosaures) (p. 1336)
Ridgeway, Nicola, jt. auth. see Manning, James.
Ridgeway, Nicola & Manning, James. Art & Craft for Preschool (Cut & Paste Emoji Eggs - Volume 2) This Book Has 20 Full Colour Puzzle Worksheets. This Book Comes with 6 Downloadable PDF Books. (p. 120)
—Art & Craft Ideas for Kids (Cut & Paste Emoji Eggs) This Book Has 20 Full Colour Puzzle Worksheets. This Book Comes with 6 Downloadable PDF Books. (p. 120)
—Arts & Crafts for Kids (Cut & Paste Buildings - Volume 2) This Book Has 20 Full Colour Worksheets. This Book Comes with 6 Downloadable Kindergarten PDF Workbooks. (p. 124)
—Ausmalen Von Buchseiten Für Kinder (Malbücher Für 4-Jährige) - Feen: Dieses Buch Bietet 40 Seiten in Farbe. Dieses Buch Soll Kleinen Kindern Helfen, Die Kontrolle über Den Stift Zu Entwickeln und Ihre Feinmotorik Zu Trainieren. (p. 138)
—Ballerina Coloring Pages (Coloring Pages for Kids) This Book Has 40 Ballerina Coloring Pages for Children Four & over. Comes with 6 Bonus PDF Coloring Books. (p. 161)
—Bücher Für Vierjährige (Malbücher Für 4-Jährige) - Piraten: Dieses Buch Bietet 40 Seiten in Farbe. Dieses Buch Soll Kleinen Kindern Helfen, Die Kontrolle über Den Stift Zu Entwickeln und Ihre Feinmotorik Zu Trainieren. (p. 289)
—Bücher Für Vierjährige (Malbücher Für 4-Jährige) - Prinzessinnen und Prinzen: Dieses Buch Bietet 40 Seiten in Farbe. Dieses Buch Soll Kleinen Kindern Helfen, Die Kontrolle über Den Stift Zu Entwickeln und Ihre Feinmotorik Zu Trainieren. (p. 289)
—Color Cut & Paste Worksheets for Kindergarten (Cars) This Book Has 36 Color Cut & Paste Worksheets. This Book Comes with 6 Downloadable PDF Color Cut & Glue Workbooks. (p. 420)
—Color Cut & Paste Worksheets for Kindergarten (Faces) This Book Has 40 Color Cut & Paste Worksheets. This Book Comes with 6 Downloadable PDF Color Cut & Glue Workbooks. (p. 420)
—Color Cut & Paste Worksheets for Kindergarten (Dinosaurs) (p. 420)
—Color Cut & Paste Worksheets for Kindergarten (Emoji Eggs) This Book Has 40 Color Cut & Paste Worksheets. This Book Comes with 6 Downloadable PDF Color Cut & Glue Workbooks. (p. 420)
—Coloring Book for 4 Year Olds (Dogs) This Book Has 38 Coloring Pages. This Book Will Assist Young Children to Develop Pen Control & to Exercise Their Fine Motor Skills. (p. 423)
—Coloring Book for 4 Year Olds (Easter Eggs 2) This Book Has 40 Coloring Pages. This Book Will Assist Young Children to Develop Pen Control & to Exercise Their Fine Motor Skills. (p. 423)
—Coloring Book for 4 Year Olds (Emoji 2) This Book Has 40 Coloring Pages. This Book Will Assist Young Children to Develop Pen Control & to Exercise Their Fine Motor Skills. (p. 423)
—Coloring Book for 4 Year Olds (Gingerbread Houses 1) This Book Has 40 Coloring Pages. This Book Will Assist Young Children to Develop Pen Control & to Exercise Their Fine Motor Skills. (p. 423)
—Coloring Book for 4 Year Olds (Owls 1) This Book Has 40 Coloring Pages. This Book Will Assist Young Children to Develop Pen Control & to Exercise Their Fine Motor Skills. (p. 423)
—Coloring Books for Kids (Buildings) This Book Has 40 Coloring Pages with Several Levels of Difficulty. (p. 425)
—Coloring Pages for 4 Year Olds (Dinosaurs) (p. 425)
—Coloring Pages for 4 Year Olds (Planes) This Book Has 40 Coloring Pages. This Book Will Assist Young Children to Develop Pen Control & to Exercise Their Fine Motor Skills. (p. 425)
—Coloring Pages for 4 Year Olds (Superheroes & Villains) This Book Has 40 Coloring Pages. This Book Will Assist Young Children to Develop Pen Control & to Exercise Their Fine Motor Skills. (p. 425)
—Construction Paper Crafts (Cut & Paste Buildings) This Book Has 20 Full Colour Worksheets. This Book Comes with 6 Downloadable Kindergarten PDF Workbooks. (p. 443)
—Construction Paper Crafts (Cut & Paste Superheroes & Villains Puzzles) This Book Has 20 Full Colour Puzzle Worksheets. This Book Comes with 6 Downloadable PDF Books. (p. 443)
—Cut & Glue Worksheets (Flowers) This Book Has 20 Full Colour Worksheets. This Book Comes with 6 Downloadable Kindergarten PDF Workbooks. (p. 491)
—Cut & Glue Worksheets (Owls) This Book Has 20 Full Colour Worksheets. This Book Comes with 6 Downloadable Kindergarten PDF Workbooks. (p. 491)
—Cut & Glue Worksheets - Volume 2 (Flowers) This Book Has 20 Full Colour Worksheets. This Book Comes with 6 Downloadable Kindergarten PDF Workbooks. (p. 491)
—Cut & Paste Worksheets - Dinosaurs. (p. 491)
—Cut & Paste Worksheets for Kindergarten (Faces) This Book Has 20 Full Colour Worksheets. This Book Comes with 6 Downloadable Kindergarten PDF Workbooks. (p. 491)
—Cut & Paste Worksheets for Kindergarten - Volume 2 (Faces) This Book Has 20 Full Colour Worksheets. This Book Comes with 6 Downloadable Kindergarten PDF Workbooks. (p. 491)
—Cut & Paste Worksheets - Volume 2 (Dinosaurs) (p. 491)
—Einfärben Dicker Linien (Malbuch Für Kinder) - Superhelden. (p. 629)
—Este Libro Ayudará a Los niños Pequeños a Desarrollar el Control de la Pluma y Ejercitar Sus Habilidades Motoras Finas. (p. 664)
—Este Libro Contiene 40 láminas para Colorear con líneas Extra Gruesas. Este Libro Ayudará a Los niños Muy Pequeños a Desarrollar el Control Del lápiz y Ejercitar Sus Habilidades Motoras Finas. (p. 664)
—Fairy Coloring Pages (Coloring Pages for Kids) This Book Has 40 Fairy Coloring Pages for Children Four & over. Comes with 6 Bonus PDF Coloring Books. (p. 696)
—Fashion Coloring Book for 4 to 9 Year Olds: This Fashion Coloring Book, Has 39 Illustrated Fashion Models Wearing Their Own Fashion Designs. These Fashion Coloring Book Pages Will Make an Excellent Fashion Coloring Book Gift for Girls. Plus 6 Coloring Boo. (p. 712)
—Fichas de Trazar y Colorear (Animales Haciéndose un Selfie) Este Libro Ayudará a Los niños Pequeños a Desarrollar el Control de la Pluma y Ejercitar Sus Habilidades Motoras Finas. (p. 722)
—Fichas de Trazar y Colorear (Búhos 2) Este Libro Ayudará a Los niños Pequeños a Desarrollar el Control de la Pluma y Ejercitar Sus Habilidades Motoras Finas. (p. 722)
—Fichas de Trazar y Colorear (Casas de Jengibre 1) Este Libro Ayudará a Los niños Pequeños a Desarrollar el Control de la Pluma y Ejercitar Sus Habilidades Motoras Finas. (p. 722)
—Fichas de Trazar y Colorear (Emojis 2) Este Libro Ayudará a Los niños Pequeños a Desarrollar el Control de la Pluma y Ejercitar Sus Habilidades Motoras Finas. (p. 722)
—Fichas de Trazar y Colorear (Huevos de Pascua 1) Este Libro Ayudará a Los niños Pequeños a Desarrollar el Control de la Pluma y Ejercitar Sus Habilidades Motoras Finas. (p. 722)
—Fichas de Trazar y Colorear (Muñecos y Casas de Jengibre) Este Libro Ayudará a Los niños Pequeños a Desarrollar el Control de la Pluma y Ejercitar Sus Habilidades Motoras Finas. (p. 722)
—Fiches de Travail Avec Images à Reproduire Grâce Aux Pointillés et à Colorier (Clowns) (p. 722)
—Fiches de Travail Avec Images à Reproduire Grâce Aux Pointillés et à Colorier (Emoticônes) Ce Livre Aidera les Jeunes Enfants à développer le Contrôle du Stylo et à Exercer Leurs Compétences en Motrices Fines. (p. 722)
—Fiches de Travail Avec Images à Reproduire Grâce Aux Pointillés et à Colorier (Chouettes 2) Ce Livre Aidera les Jeunes Enfants à développer le Contrôle du Stylo et à Exercer Leurs Compétences en Motrices Fines. (p. 722)
—Fiches de Travail Avec Images à Reproduire Grâce Aux Pointillés et à Colorier (Animaux Mignons) Ce Livre Aidera les Jeunes Enfants à développer le Contrôle du Stylo et à Exercer Leurs Compétences en Motrices Fines. (p. 722)
—Fiches de Travail Avec Images à Reproduire Grâce Aux Pointillés et à Colorier (Maisons en Pain D'épice) Ce Livre Aidera les Jeunes Enfants à développer le Contrôle du Stylo et à Exercer Leurs Compétences en Motrices Fines. (p. 722)
—Fiches de Travail Avec Images à Reproduire Grâce Aux Pointillés et à Colorier (Maisons en Pain Dépice 1) Ce Livre Aidera les Jeunes Enfants à développer le Contrôle du Stylo et à Exercer Leurs Compétences en Motrices Fines. (p. 722)
—Fiches de Travail Avec Images à Reproduire Grâce Aux Pointillés et à Colorier (des Animaux Qui Prennent des Selfies) Ce Livre Aidera les Jeunes Enfants à développer le Contrôle du Stylo et à Exercer Leurs Compétences en Motrices Fines. (p. 722)
—Fiches de Travail de Traçage Sur Pointillés (Ballerines) (p. 722)
—Fogli Da Tracciare e Da Colorare (Animale-Selfie) Questo Libro è Stato Progettato per Aiutare I Bambini a Sviluppare il Controllo Sulla Penna e Ad Allenare le Loro Capacità Motorie. (p. 756)
—Fogli Da Tracciare e Da Colorare (Emoji 2) Questo Libro è Stato Progettato per Aiutare I Bambini a Sviluppare il Controllo Sulla Penna e Ad Allenare le Loro Capacità Motorie. (p. 756)
—Fogli Da Tracciare e Da Colorare (Emojis 3) (p. 756)
—Fogli Da Tracciare e Da Colorare (Gufi 1) Questo Libro è Stato Progettato per Aiutare I Bambini a Sviluppare il Controllo Sulla Penna e Ad Allenare le Loro Capacità Motorie. (p. 756)
—Fogli Da Tracciare e Da Colorare (Orsacchiotti 1) (p. 756)
—Fogli Di Lavoro Dei Tracciati e Dei Colori (Gufi 2) Questo Libro è Stato Progettato per Aiutare I Bambini a Sviluppare il Controllo Sulla Penna e Ad Allenare le Loro Capacità Motorie. (p. 756)
—Fogli Di Lavoro Dei Tracciati e Dei Colori (Omini Di Pan Di Zenzero e Case 1) Questo Libro è Stato Progettato per Aiutare I Bambini a Sviluppare il Controllo Sulla Penna e Ad Allenare le Loro Capacità Motorie. (p. 756)
—Four Year Old Coloring Book (Emoji Eggs) This Book Has 40 Coloring Pages. This Book Comes with 6 Bonus PDF Books & Will Assist Young Children to Develop Pen Control & to Exercise Their Fine Motor Skills. (p. 773)
—Graffiti (Ausmalen Von Buchseiten Für Kinder) Dieses Buch Bietet 40 Seiten in Farbe. (p. 875)
—Graffiti Coloring Pages for Kids (Coloring Pages for Kids) (p. 875)
—How to Draw a Clown Using Grids for Beginners - Grid Drawing for Kids. (p. 1039)
—How to Draw a Fairy Using Grids for Beginners - Grid Drawing for Kids: This Book Teaches Kids How to Draw Using Grids. This Book Contains 40 Illustrations & 40 Grids to Practice With. (p. 1039)
—How to Draw a House (Grid Drawing for Beginners) This Book Teaches Kids How to Draw Using Grids. This Book Contains 40 Illustrations & 40 Grids to Practice With. (p. 1039)
—How to Draw a Pirate Using Grids for Beginners - Grid Drawing for Kids. (p. 1039)
—How to Draw a Princess & a Prince Using Grids for Beginners (Grid Drawing for Kids) This Book Teaches Kids How to Draw Using Grids. This Book Contains 40 Illustrations & 40 Grids to Practice With. (p. 1039)
—How to Draw Animals Taking Selfies Using Grids for Beginners: Grid Drawing for Kids. (p. 1039)
—How to Draw Comic Superheroes Using Grids for Beginners (Grid Drawing for Kids) This Book Teaches Kids How to Draw Using Grids. This Book Contains 40 Illustrations & 40 Grids to Practice With. (p. 1040)
—How to Draw Dinosaurs Using Grids for Beginners (Grid Drawing for Kids) (p. 1040)
—Libro Da Colorare per I Bambini Di 4 Anni (Animale - Selfie) Questo Libro Offre 40 Pagine a Colori. Questo Libro è Stato Progettato per Aiutare I Bambini a Sviluppare il Controllo Sulla Penna e Ad Allenare le Loro Capacità Motorie. (p. 1285)
—Libro Da Colorare per I Bambini Di 4 Anni (Animali Carini) Questo Libro Offre 40 Pagine a Colori. Questo Libro è Stato Progettato per Aiutare I Bambini a Sviluppare il Controllo Sulla Penna e Ad Allenare le Loro Capacità Motorie. (p. 1286)
—Libro Da Colorare per I Bambini Di 4 Anni (Case Di Pan Di Zenzero 1) (p. 1286)
—Libro Da Colorare per I Bambini Di 4 Anni (Emoji 2) Questo Libro Offre 40 Pagine a Colori. Questo Libro è Stato Progettato per Aiutare I Bambini a Sviluppare il Controllo Sulla Penna e Ad Allenare le Loro Capacità Motorie. (p. 1286)
—Libro Da Colorare per I Bambini Di 4 Anni (Gufo 2) Questo Libro Offre 40 Pagine a Colori. Questo Libro è Stato Progettato per Aiutare I Bambini a Sviluppare il Controllo Sulla Penna e Ad Allenare le Loro Capacità Motorie. (p. 1286)
—Libro Da Colorare per I Bambini Di 4 Anni (Omini Di Pan Di Zenzero e Case) Questo Libro Offre 40 Pagine a Colori. Questo Libro è Stato Progettato per Aiutare I Bambini a Sviluppare il Controllo Sulla Penna e Ad Allenare le Loro Capacità Motorie. (p. 1286)
—Libro Da Colorare per I Bambini Di 4 Anni (Orsacchiotti 1) (p. 1286)
—Libro Da Colorare per I Bambini Di 4 Anni (Uovo Di Pasqua 3) Questo Libro Offre 40 Pagine a Colori. Questo Libro è Stato Progettato per Aiutare I Bambini a Sviluppare il Controllo Sulla Penna e Ad Allenare le Loro Capacità Motorie. (p. 1286)
—Libro de Colorear Sencillo para niños de Preescolar (Búho 2) Este Libro Contiene 40 láminas para Colorear con líneas Extra Gruesas. Este Libro Ayudará a Los niños Muy Pequeños a Desarrollar el Control Del lápiz y Ejercitar Sus Habilidades Motoras Finas. (p. 1286)
—Libro de Colorear Sencillo para niños de Preescolar (Ositos 2) Este Libro Contiene 40 láminas para Colorear con líneas Extra Gruesas. Este Libro Ayudará a Los niños Muy Pequeños a Desarrollar el Control Del lápiz y Ejercitar Sus Habilidades Motoras Finas. (p. 1286)
—Libro de Colorear Sencillo para niños de Preescol (Emoticonos 2) Este Libro Contiene 40 láminas para Colorear con líneas Extra Gruesas. Este Libro Ayudará a Los niños Muy Pequeños a Desarrollar el Control Del lápiz y Ejercitar Sus Habilidades Motoras Fin. (p. 1286)
—Libro de Colorear Sencillo para niños de Preescolar (Emoticonos 1) Este Libro Contiene 40 láminas para Colorear con líneas Extra Gruesas. Este Libro Ayudará a Los niños Muy Pequeños a Desarrollar el Control Del lápiz y Ejercitar Sus Habilidades Motoras F. (p. 1286)
—Libro de Colorear Sencillo para niños de Preescolar (Lindos Animalitos) Este Libro Contiene 40 láminas para Colorear con líneas Extra Gruesas. Este Libro Ayudará a Los niños Muy Pequeños a Desarrollar el Control Del lápiz y Ejercitar Sus Habilidades Moto. (p. 1286)
—Libro de Colorear Sencillo para niños de Preescolar (Huevos de Pascua 1) Este Libro Contiene 40 láminas para Colorear con líneas Extra Gruesas. Este Libro Ayudará a Los niños Muy Pequeños a Desarrollar el Control Del lápiz y Ejercitar Sus Habilidades Mot. (p. 1286)
—Libro de Colorear Sencillo para niños de Preescolar (Muñecos de Jengibre 1) Este Libro Contiene 40 láminas para Colorear con líneas Extra Gruesas. Este Libro Ayudará a Los niños Muy Pequeños a Desarrollar el Control Del lápiz y Ejercitar Sus Habilidades. (p. 1286)
—Libro de Pintar para niños de 4 años (Animales Haciéndose Selfies) Este Libro Contiene 40 láminas para Colorear. Este Libro Ayudará a Los niños Pequeños a Desarrollar el Control de la Pluma y Ejercitar Sus Habilidades Motoras Finas. (p. 1286)
—Libro de Pintar para niños de 4 Años (Búhos 1) Este Libro Contiene 40 láminas para Colorear. Este Libro Ayudará a Los niños Pequeños a Desarrollar el Control de la Pluma y Ejercitar Sus Habilidades Motoras Finas. (p. 1286)
—Libro de Pintar para niños de 4 Años (Casas de Jengibre 1) Este Libro Contiene 40 láminas para Colorear. Este Libro Ayudará a Los niños Pequeños a Desarrollar el Control de la Pluma y Ejercitar Sus Habilidades Motoras Finas. (p. 1286)
—Libro de Pintar para niños de 4 Años (Emoticonos 2) (p. 1286)
—Libro de Pintar para niños de 4 Años (Emoticonos 3) Este Libro Contiene 40 láminas para Colorear con líneas Extra Gruesas. Este Libro Ayudará a Los niños Muy Pequeños a Desarrollar el Control Del lápiz y Ejercitar Sus Habilidades Motoras Finas. (p. 1286)
—Libro de Pintar para niños de 4 años (Huevos de Pascua 3) Este Libro Contiene 40 láminas para Colorear. Este Libro Ayudará a Los niños Pequeños a Desarrollar el Control de la Pluma y Ejercitar Sus Habilidades Motoras Finas. (p. 1286)
—Libro de Pintar para niños de 4 años (Huevos de Pascua 2) Este Libro Contiene 40 láminas para Colorear con líneas Extra Gruesas. Este Libro Ayudará a Los niños Muy Pequeños a Desarrollar el Control Del lápiz y Ejercitar Sus Habilidades Motoras Finas. (p. 1286)
—Libro de Pintar para niños de 4 años (Lindos Animalitos) (p. 1287)
—Libro de Pintar para niños de 4 años (Muñecos y Casas de Jengibre) Este Libro Contiene 40 láminas para Colorear. Este Libro Ayudará a Los niños Pequeños a Desarrollar el Control de la Pluma y Ejercitar Sus Habilidades Motoras Finas. (p. 1287)
—Libro de Pintar para niños de 4 Años (Ositos 1) Este Libro Contiene 40 láminas para Colorear. Este Libro Ayudará a Los niños Pequeños a Desarrollar el Control de la Pluma y Ejercitar Sus Habilidades Motoras Finas. (p. 1287)
—Livre de Coloriage Pour Enfants (Immeubles) (p. 1336)
—Livre de Coloriage Pour Enfants (Sirènes) (p. 1336)
—Livre de Coloriage Pour les Enfants de 4 Ans (Animaux Mignons) Ce Livre Contient 40 Pages à Colorier. Ce Livre Aidera les Jeunes Enfants à développer le Contrôle du Stylo et à Exercer Leurs Compétences en Motrices Fines. (p. 1336)
—Livre de Coloriage Pour les Enfants de 4 Ans (Chouettes 1) (p. 1336)
—Livre de Coloriage Pour les Enfants de 4 Ans (Chouettes 2) Ce Livre Contient 40 Pages à Colorier. Ce Livre Aidera les Jeunes Enfants à développer le Contrôle du Stylo et à Exercer Leurs Compétences en Motrices Fines. (p. 1336)
—Livre de Coloriage Pour les Enfants de 4 Ans (Maisons en Pain Dépice 1) Ce Livre Contient 40 Pages à Colorier. Ce Livre Aidera les Jeunes Enfants à développer le Contrôle du Stylo et à Exercer Leurs Compétences en Motrices Fines. (p. 1336)
—Livre de Coloriage Pour les Enfants de 4 Ans (Nounours 2) (p. 1336)
—Livre de Coloriage Pour les Enfants de 4 Ans (OEufs de Pâques 2) Ce Livre Contient 40 Pages à Colorier. Ce Livre Aidera les Jeunes Enfants à développer le Contrôle du Stylo et à Exercer Leurs Compétences en Motrices Fines. (p. 1336)
—Livre de Coloriage Simple Pour les Tous Petits (Chouettes 2) Ce Livre Contient 40 Pages à Colorier Avec des Lignes Très épaisses. Ce Livre Aidera les Jeunes Enfants à développer le Contrôle du Stylo et à Exercer Leurs Compétences en Motrices Fines. (p. 1336)
—Livres Pour les Enfants de 4 Ans (Oeufs émoticônes) (p. 1336)
—Malbuch Für 4-Jährige (Tier Selfies) Dieses Buch Bietet 40 Seiten in Farbe. Dieses Buch Soll Kleinen Kindern Helfen, Die Kontrolle über Den Stift Zu Entwickeln und Ihre Feinmotorik Zu Trainieren. (p. 1391)
—Nachzeichnen und Ausmalblätter (Emoji 2) Dieses Buch Bietet 40 Nachzeichnen und Ausmalblätter. Dieses Buch Soll Kleinen Kindern Helfen, Die Kontrolle über Den Stift Zu Entwickeln und Ihre Feinmotorik Zu Trainieren. (p. 1572)

—Nachzeichnen und Ausmalblätter (Lebkuchenhäuser 1) Dieses Buch Bietet 40 Nachzeichnen und Ausmalblätter. Dieses Buch Soll Kleinen Kindern Helfen, Die Kontrolle über Den Stift Zu Entwickeln und Ihre Feinmotorik Zu Trainieren. (p. 1572)

—Nachzeichnen und Ausmalblätter (Lebkuchenmänner Und -Häuser 1) Dieses Buch Bietet 40 Nachzeichnen und Ausmalblätter. Dieses Buch Soll Kleinen Kindern Helfen, Die Kontrolle über Den Stift Zu Entwickeln und Ihre Feinmotorik Zu Trainieren. (p. 1572)

—Nachzeichnen und Ausmalblätter (Osterrei 1) Dieses Buch Bietet 40 Nachzeichnen und Ausmalblätter. Dieses Buch Soll Kleinen Kindern Helfen, Die Kontrolle über Den Stift Zu Entwickeln und Ihre Feinmotorik Zu Trainieren. (p. 1572)

—Nachzeichnen und Ausmalblätter (Teddybären 1) Dieses Buch Bietet 40 Nachzeichnen und Ausmalblätter. Dieses Buch Soll Kleinen Kindern Helfen, Die Kontrolle über Den Stift Zu Entwickeln und Ihre Feinmotorik Zu Trainieren. (p. 1572)

—Nachzeichnen und Ausmalblätter (Teddybären 2) Dieses Buch Soll Kleinen Kindern Helfen, Die Kontrolle über Den Stift Zu Entwickeln und Ihre Feinmotorik Zu Trainieren. (p. 1572)

—Pages à Colorier Pour Enfants (Graffiti) (p. 1692)

—Pages de Ballerines à Colorier (Pages à Colorier Pour Enfants) (p. 1692)

—Pages de Clowns à Colorier (Pages à Colorier Pour Enfants) (p. 1692)

—Pages de Fées à Colorier (Pages à Colorier Pour Enfants) (p. 1692)

—Pages de Pirates à Colorier (Pages à Colorier Pour Enfants) (p. 1692)

—Pages de Princesses à Colorier (Pages à Colorier Pour Enfants) (p. 1692)

—Preschool Cut & Paste Worksheets Volume 2 - (Easter Eggs) This Book Has 20 Full Colour Worksheets. This Book Comes with 6 Downloadable Kindergarten PDF Workbooks. (p. 1788)

—Princess Coloring Pages (Coloring Pages for 4 Year Olds) This Book Has 40 Coloring Pages. This Book Will Assist Young Children to Develop Pen Control & to Exercise Their Fine Motor Skills. (p. 1797)

—Questo Libro Offre 40 Pagine a Colori con Linee Extra Spesse. Questo Libro è Stato Progettato per Aiutare I Bambini a Sviluppare il Controllo Sulla Penna e Ad Allenare le Loro Capacità Motorie. (p. 1826)

—Simple Toddler Coloring Book (Castles) This Book Has 40 Coloring Pages with Extra Thick Lines. This Book Will Assist Young Children to Develop Pen Control & to Exercise Their Fine Motor Skills. (p. 2022)

—Simple Toddler Coloring Book (Dogs) This Book Has 38 Coloring Pages with Extra Thick Lines. This Book Will Assist Young Children to Develop Pen Control & to Exercise Their Fine Motor Skills. (p. 2022)

—Simple Toddler Coloring Book (Easter Eggs 1) This Book Has 40 Coloring Pages with Extra Thick Lines. This Book Will Assist Young Children to Develop Pen Control & to Exercise Their Fine Motor Skills. (p. 2022)

—Simple Toddler Coloring Book (Emojis 1) This Book Has 40 Coloring Pages with Extra Thick Lines. This Book Will Assist Young Children to Develop Pen Control & to Exercise Their Fine Motor Skills. (p. 2022)

—Simple Toddler Coloring Book (Gingerbread Men 1) This Book Has 40 Coloring Pages with Extra Thick Lines. This Book Will Assist Young Children to Develop Pen Control & to Exercise Their Fine Motor Skills. (p. 2022)

—Simple Toddler Coloring Book (Planes) This Book Has 40 Coloring Pages with Extra Thick Lines. This Book Will Assist Young Children to Develop Pen Control & to Exercise Their Fine Motor Skills. (p. 2022)

—Trace & Color Worksheets (Castles) This Book Has 40 Trace & Color Worksheets. This Book Will Assist Young Children to Develop Pen Control & to Exercise Their Fine Motor Skills. (p. 2271)

—Trace & Color Worksheets (Cats) This Book Has 40 Trace & Color Worksheets. This Book Will Assist Young Children to Develop Pen Control & to Exercise Their Fine Motor Skills. (p. 2271)

—Trace & Color Worksheets (Cute Animals) This Book Has 40 Trace & Color Worksheets. This Book Will Assist Young Children to Develop Pen Control & to Exercise Their Fine Motor Skills. (p. 2271)

—Trace & Color Worksheets (Dogs) This Book Has 38 Trace & Color Worksheets. This Book Will Assist Young Children to Develop Pen Control & to Exercise Their Fine Motor Skills. (p. 2271)

—Trace & Color Worksheets (Easter Eggs 1) This Book Has 40 Trace & Color Worksheets. This Book Will Assist Young Children to Develop Pen Control & to Exercise Their Fine Motor Skills. (p. 2271)

—Trace & Color Worksheets (Gingerbread Houses 1) This Book Has 40 Trace & Color Worksheets. This Book Will Assist Young Children to Develop Pen Control & to Exercise Their Fine Motor Skills. (p. 2271)

—Trace & Color Worksheets (Gingerbread Men & Houses) (p. 2271)

—Trace & Color Worksheets (Owls 1) (p. 2271)

—Trace & Color Worksheets (Owls 2) This Book Has 40 Trace & Color Worksheets. This Book Will Assist Young Children to Develop Pen Control & to Exercise Their Fine Motor Skills. (p. 2271)

—Trace & Color Worksheets (Teddies 1) This Book Has 40 Trace & Color Worksheets. This Book Will Assist Young Children to Develop Pen Control & to Exercise Their Fine Motor Skills. (p. 2271)

—Tracing Sheets (Emoji Eggs) This Book Has 40 Tracing Worksheets. This Book Will Assist Young Children to Develop Pen Control & to Exercise Their Fine Motor Skills. (p. 2272)

—Tracing Worksheets (Dinosaurs) (p. 2272)

—Tracing Worksheets (Fairies) This Book Has 40 Tracing Worksheets. This Book Will Assist Young Children to Develop Pen Control & to Exercise Their Fine Motor Skills. (p. 2272)

—Tracing Worksheets (Fashion Models) This Book Has 40 Tracing Worksheets. This Book Will Assist Young Children to Develop Pen Control & to Exercise Their Fine Motor Skills. (p. 2272)

—Tracing Worksheets (Heroes & Villains) This Book Has 40 Tracing Worksheets. This Book Will Assist Young Children to Develop Pen Control & to Exercise Their Fine Motor Skills. (p. 2272)

—Tracing Worksheets (Princes & Princesses) This Book Has 40 Tracing Worksheets. This Book Will Assist Young Children to Develop Pen Control & to Exercise Their Fine Motor Skills. (p. 2272)

—Tracing Worksheets - Pirates. (p. 2272)

Ridgeway, Ridgeway. Early Recollections of James Whitcomb Riley (Classic Reprint) (p. 615)

Ridgeway, William. Report of the Proceedings in Cases of High Treason, at a Court of Oyer & Terminer, Vol. 1 Of 2: Held at the New Sessions House, under a Special Commission, in the Months of August, September, & October, 1803 (Classic Reprint) (p. 1866)

—Report of the Proceedings in Cases of High Treason, at a Court of Oyer & Terminer, Vol. 2 Of 2: Held in the New Sessions House, under a Special Commission, in the Months of August, September, & October, 1803 (Classic Reprint) (p. 1866)

Ridgrway, Algernon. Westover's Ward, Vol. 3 of 3 (Classic Reprint) (p. 2402)

Ridgway, Christine E. Skytown. (p. 2034)

Ridgway, Robert. Birds of North & Middle America: A Descriptive Catalogue of the Higher Groups, Genera, Species, & Subspecies of Birds Known to Occur in North America, from the Arctic Lands to the Isthmus of Panama, the West Indies & Other Islands of the Caribb. (p. 232)

Ridgway, Robert & Friedmann, Herbert. Birds of North & Middle America: A Descriptive Catalog of the Higher Groups, Genera, Species, & Subspecies of Birds Known to Occur in North America, from the Arctic Lands to the Isthmus of Panama, the West Indies & Other Islands of the Caribbea. (p. 232)

Ridgway, Sam H., jt. auth. see Goldish, Meish.

Ridgway, Tom. Mad Cow Disease: Bovine Spongiform Encephalopathy. (p. 1373)

—Smallpox. (p. 2040)

Ridgway, Tony. All Animal Lives Matter. Ridgway, Tony, illus. (p. 51)

—Cat Tails. (p. 342)

—Songs of the Wild. (p. 2063)

Riding, Robin. Mermaids Fast Asleep. Persico, Zoe, illus. (p. 1449)

Ridley, Alice, illus. see Emina, Peter.

Ridley, Annie E. Backward Glance: The Story of John Ridley, a Pioneer (Classic Reprint) (p. 156)

Ridley, Frances. Stunt Pros. (p. 2145)

Ridley, Frances J. Special Effects. (p. 2076)

Ridley, James. Tales of the Genii, or the Delightful Lessons of Horam, the Son of Asmar, Vol. 2: Faithfully Translated from the Persian Manuscript; & Compared with the French & Spanish Editions Published at Paris & Madrid (Classic Reprint) (p. 2185)

Ridley, Kimberley. Extreme Survivors: Animals That Time Forgot (p. 687)

Ridley, Kimberly. Secret Bay Raye, Rebekah, illus. (p. 1974)

—Secret Pool Raye, Rebekah, illus. (p. 1978)

Ridley, Kimberly & Raye, Rebekah. Secret Bay (p. 1975)

Ridley, R. W. Banshee Worm King. (p. 164)

Ridley, Sarah. Beans to Chocolate. (p. 179)

—Bee to Honey. (p. 189)

—Blossom to Apple. (p. 247)

—In the Home. (p. 1109)

—Life in Ancient Egypt. (p. 1292)

—Life in Ancient Greece. (p. 1292)

—Life in Roman Times. (p. 1292)

—Life in Viking Times. (p. 1293)

—Martin Luther King: ...And the Fight for Equality. (p. 1410)

—Remembering the Fallen of the First World War. (p. 1864)

—Seeds to Bread. (p. 1984)

—Suffragettes & the Fight for the Vote. (p. 2147)

—Super Scientists: David Attenborough. (p. 2156)

—Tell Me What You Remember: Clothes. (p. 2202)

—Tell Me What You Remember: Family Life. (p. 2202)

—Tell Me What You Remember: Food. (p. 2202)

—Tell Me What You Remember: Pastimes & Toys. (p. 2202)

—Tell Me What You Remember: School. (p. 2202)

—Tell Me What You Remember: Sport. (p. 2202)

—Winston Churchill: ...And World War II. (p. 2474)

Ridley, Sarah, jt. auth. see Barraclough, Sue.

Ridolfi, Isabella, jt. auth. see Mills, Nathan.

Ridout, Cefn. DK Readers L2: Marvel's Ultimate Villains. (p. 568)

—Ultimate Villains. (p. 2316)

Ridout, Cefn, jt. auth. see Dorling Kindersley Publishing Staff.

Ridpath, Karla. Grandma Kardi & the Story Tree: A Tale of Make Believe. (p. 878)

Ridsdale, Knowles. Gate of Fulfillment (Classic Reprint) (p. 811)

Rie, Jannie. Community Food Tree. (p. 432)

Riebel, Tiffany a. Calico & Patch: Just Like Me & Big Adventure. (p. 310)

Riechmann, Annie & Smith, Dawn Suzette. Whatever the Weather: Science Experiments & Art Activities for No Matter What the Day Brings. (p. 2423)

Rieder, Floor, illus. see Schutten, Jan Paul.

Riedle, Tamera. Anteater That Would Not Burp. (p. 101)

—Night Balloon. (p. 1604)

—Ode to a Little Plant. (p. 1638)

—Pip Pip Hooray! a Celebration of Bat Names. (p. 1748)

Riedler, Amelia, ed. see Clark, M. H.

Riedler, Amelia, ed. see Yamada, Shale.

Riega, Maria, tr. see Gordon, Michael.

Riegelman, Rianna. Red Roger to the Rescue. Schorr, Bill, illus. (p. 1858)

Riegelman, Rianna & Accord Publishing Staff. Safari: A Build & Play Story. Chandler, Shannon, illus. (p. 1921)

Riehecky, Janet. Camouflage & Mimicry: Animal Weapons & Defenses. (p. 315)

—Carnotaurus & Other Odd Meat-Eaters: The Need-To-Know Facts. Hughes, Jon, illus. (p. 332)

—Cobras: On the Hunt. (p. 410)

—Great White Sharks: On the Hunt. (p. 891)

—Iguanodon & Other Bird-Footed Dinosaurs: The Need-To-Know Facts. Hughes, Jon, illus. (p. 1094)

—Insects. (p. 1122)

—Killer Whales: On the Hunt. (p. 1217)

—Komodo Dragons [Scholastic]: On the Hunt. (p. 1231)

—Megalodon [Scholastic]. (p. 1442)

—Orangutans (p. 1668)

—Poisons & Venom: Animal Weapons & Defenses. (p. 1768)

—Reptiles. (p. 1867)

—Slime, Poop, & Other Wacky Animal Defenses. (p. 2038)

—Teeth, Claws, & Jaws: Animal Weapons & Defenses. (p. 2201)

—Triceratops (p. 2287)

—Velociraptor (p. 2349)

Riehecky, Janet, jt. auth. see Crewe, Sabrina.

Riehecky, Janet & Rake, Jody Sullivan. Animal Weapons & Defenses. (p. 92)

Riehecky, Janet, et al. Endangered & Threatened Animals. (p. 649)

Riehle, Mary Ann McCabe. Is for Airplane: An Aviation Alphabet. Craig, David, illus. (p. 1136)

—Little Kid's Table. Uhles, Mary, illus. (p. 1320)

—M Is for Mom: A Child's Alphabet. Ellison, Chris, illus. (p. 1370)

Riel, Jörn & Chodzin, Sherab. Raiders: The Inuk Quartet. Vol. 2 Cann, Helen, illus. (p. 1835)

Riel, Jorn, et al. Snowstorm. Cann, Helen, illus. (p. 2049)

Rieley, Daniel, illus. see Farrer, Maria.

Rieley, Daniel, illus. see Mosca, Julia Finley.

Rieley, Daniel, illus. see Parachini, Jodie.

Rieley, Daniel, illus. see Tamura, Marikka.

Riely, Nan. Creighton Quarterly Shadows, Vol. 27: April, 1936 (Classic Reprint) (p. 473)

Riera, Lucas. Extinct: An Illustrated Exploration of Animals That Have Disappeared. (p. 685)

Ries, Alex, illus. see Becker, Helaine.

Ries, Ariel Slamet. Witchy. (p. 2480)

Ries, Lori. Aggie Gets Lost. Dormer, Frank W., illus. (p. 35)

—Aggie the Brave. Dormer, Frank W., illus. (p. 35)

—Good Dog, Aggie. Dormer, Frank W., illus. (p. 862)

Ries, Lori, et al. Tita y Ben: Tres Cuentos. Dormer, Frank W., illus. (p. 2251)

Riesbeck, Emily. It's Your Funeral. Kramer, Ellen, illus. (p. 1148)

Rieser, Karen. Cat with Three Tales. (p. 342)

Riess, Natalie. Space Battle Lunchtime Vol. 1: Lights, Camera, Snacktion. (p. 2070)

—Space Battle Lunchtime Vol. 2: A Recipe for Disaster. Vol. 2 (p. 2070)

Riess, Natalie & Goetter, Sara. Dungeon Critters. (p. 610)

Riette, Susanne, illus. see Conroe, Lindy.

Rietz, Kathleen. ABCs of Yoga for Kids: A Book of Coloring. (p. 5)

Rietz, Kathleen, illus. see Berkes, Marianne.

Rietz, Kathleen, illus. see Halfmann, Janet.

Rietz, Kathleen, illus. see North, Sherry.

Rietz, Kathleen, illus. see Pattison, Darcy.

Rietz, Kathleen, illus. see Power, Teresa Anne.

Rietz, Kathleen, illus. see Power, Teresa.

Rieux, Jean de Serre de. Dons des Enfans de Latone: La Musique et la Chase du Cerf (Classic Reprint) (p. 582)

—Dons des Enfans de Latone: La Musique et la Chasse du Cerf, Poëmes dédiés Au Roy (Classic Reprint) (p. 582)

Rife, Douglas M. & Capaldi, Gina. American Revolution. Lyall, Dennis, illus. (p. 73)

—Letters for Freedom: the Civil War. Lyall, Dennis, illus. (p. 1279)

Riffe, Ruth. Survival Guide for the Teenage Life. Smith, Geoff & Aretha, David, eds. (p. 2164)

Riffle, Rich. Buzzby Bee. (p. 305)

Riffle, Sherry L. Wide Eyed Bry. (p. 2460)

Rifkin, L. Nine Lives of Romeo Crumb: Life Seven. (p. 1609)

—Nine Lives of Romeo Crumb: Life 6. Hartman, Kurt, illus. (p. 1609)

Rifkin, L. (Lauren). Nine Lives of Romeo Crumb: Life Two. (p. 1609)

—Nine Lives of Romeo Crumb: Life Three. (p. 1609)

—Nine Lives of Romeo Crumb: Life Five. Hartman, Kurt, illus. (p. 1609)

Rifkin, Lauren I. Nine Lives of Romeo Crumb: Life Eight. (p. 1609)

Rifkin, Sherri & Bennett, Olivia. Allegra Biscotti Collection. (p. 55)

Rigano, Giovanni, illus. see Colfer, Eoin & Donkin, Andrew.

Rigano, Giovanni, illus. see Ehrbar, Gregory.

Rigaud, Debbie. Perfect Shot. (p. 1723)

—Truly Madly Royally. (p. 2295)

Rigaud, Louis & Boisrobert, Anouck. That's My Hat! (p. 2213)

Rigaudie, Mylène, illus. see Benoit-Renard, Anne.

Rigaudie, Mylène, illus. see Husar, Jaco & Husar, Stephane.

Rigaudie, Mylene, illus. see Isern, Susanna.

RIGBY. Growing Nation: Fifth Grade Class Collection Books. (p. 899)

—Now We Live in the USA! Third Grade Big Books. (p. 1628)

Rigby. On Our Way to English: Student Edition Grade 3 2014. (p. 1653)

—On Our Way to English: Student Activity Book Grade 3. (p. 1653)

—Rigby Flying Colors: Custom Bookroom Package Grade 1 Prince George County. (p. 1879)

—Rigby Intervention by Design: Ibd Ext Tote Grades K-2. (p. 1879)

—Rigby Literacy: Student Reader Bookroom Package Grade 1 (Level 5) Uh-Oh! (p. 1879)

—Rigby Literacy: Student Reader Bookroom Package Grade 1 (Level 10) Vroom! (p. 1879)

—Rigby Literacy: Student Reader Bookroom Package Grade K (Level 5) up & Down. (p. 1879)

—Rigby Literacy: Student Reader Bookroom Package Grade K (Level 3) I Like Dogs. (p. 1879)

—Rigby Literacy: The Student Reader Bookroom Package Grade 1 (Level 4) New Hat. (p. 1879)

—Rigby Literacy: The Student Reader Bookroom Package Grade 3 (Level 18) Ice Man. (p. 1879)

—Rigby Literacy: Student Reader Bookroom Package Grade K (Level 5) Elephant Walk. (p. 1879)

—Rigby Literacy: Student Reader Bookroom Package Grade K (Level 5) Super Shopping. (p. 1879)

—Rigby Literacy: The Student Reader Bookroom Package Grade 2 (Level 11) Toy Tooth. (p. 1879)

—Rigby Literacy: Student Reader Bookroom Package Grade K (Level 4) Curly Is Hungry. (p. 1879)

—Rigby Literacy: The Student Reader Bookroom Package Grade 3 (Level 18) First Fire. (p. 1879)

—Rigby Literacy: Student Reader Bookroom Package Grade 3 (Level 18) Mammoth Mistake. (p. 1879)

—Rigby Literacy: The Student Reader Bookroom Package Grade 1 (Level 7) Lion's Dinner. (p. 1879)

—Rigby Literacy: Student Reader Bookroom Package Grade 3 (Level 19) Woodcutter & Bear. (p. 1879)

—Rigby Literacy: Student Reader Bookroom Package Grade 3 (Level 19) Space Station Orion. (p. 1879)

—Rigby Literacy: Student Reader Bookroom Package Grade 3 (Level 17) Ready, Steady, Rhyme. (p. 1879)

—Rigby Literacy: Student Reader Bookroom Package Grade 1 (Level 7) Everyone Says Sh-H-H-H! (p. 1879)

—Rigby Literacy by Design: Big Book Grade 1 Schools Then & Now. (p. 1879)

—Rigby Literacy by Design: Big Book Grade K a Picture Dictionary of Mammals. (p. 1879)

—Rigby Literacy by Design: Comprehension & Progress Monitoring Bundle Grade 1. (p. 1879)

—Rigby Literacy by Design: Leveled Reading Instructional Bundle Level a Grade K. (p. 1879)

—Rigby Literacy by Design: Leveled Reading Instructional Bundle Level AA Grade K. (p. 1879)

—Rigby Literacy by Design: Leveled Reading Instructional Bundle Level R Grade 4. (p. 1880)

—Rigby Literacy by Design South Carolina: Bridge Card Package Grade 3. (p. 1880)

—Rigby Literacy by Design South Carolina: Teacher Edition Pack Grade 1. (p. 1880)

—Rigby Literacy by Design South Carolina: Teacher Edition Package Grade K. (p. 1880)

—Rigby Literacy by Design South Carolina: Test Prep Student Edition Grade 1. (p. 1880)

—Rigby Mainsails: Teacher's Guide on Level Red 2003. (p. 1880)

—Rigby Mainsails: Teacher's Guide Intervention Red 2004. (p. 1880)

—Rigby Mainsails: Leveled Reader Bookroom Package Blue Comets. (p. 1880)

—Rigby on Our Way to English: Take-Home Phonics Stories Grade 3. (p. 1880)

RIGBY. Rigby on Our Way to English: Leveled Reader Grade 2 (Level I) Desert Clowns. (p. 1880)

Rigby. Rigby on Our Way to English Texas: Progress Tests Grade 2. (p. 1880)

—Rigby on Our Way to English Texas: Student Workbook Grade 3. (p. 1880)

—Rigby on Our Way to English Texas: Student Worktext Grade 1. (p. 1880)

—Rigby on Our Way to English Texas: Student Edition Grade 3 2012. (p. 1880)

—Rigby on Our Way to English Texas: Teacher Edition Set Grade 1 2012. (p. 1880)

—Rigby on Our Way to English Texas: Student Edition & Workbook Package Grade 3 2012. (p. 1880)

—Rigby PM: PM Ultra Benchmark 60 Add-To Pack. (p. 1880)

—Rigby PM: McLass: Reading 3D PM Add-To Pack Grades K-4. (p. 1880)

—Rigby PM: Leveled Reader Emerald Level 25 Making Art with Light. (p. 1880)

—Rigby PM Plus Extension: Leveled Reader Bookroom Package Emerald (Levels 25-26) the Puppet Show. (p. 1880)

—Rigby PM Stars Bridge Books: Individual Student Edition Gold Clean-Up Day. (p. 1880)

—Rigby PM Stars Bridge Books: Individual Student Edition Gold Rosie Moves In. (p. 1880)

—Rigby PM Stars Bridge Books: Individual Student Edition Orange the Flying Tree. (p. 1880)

—Rigby PM Stars Bridge Books: Individual Student Edition Orange Chicken Surprise. (p. 1880)

—Rigby PM Stars Bridge Books: Individual Student Edition Gold after the High Tide. (p. 1880)

—Rigby PM Stars Bridge Books: Individual Student Edition Purple Hassan's New Friend. (p. 1880)

—Rigby PM Stars Bridge Books: Individual Student Edition Turquoise Wide-Mouthed Frog. (p. 1880)

—Rigby PM Stars Bridge Books: Individual Student Edition Purple Treasure in the Attic. (p. 1880)

—Rigby PM Stars Bridge Books: Individual Student Edition Purple Pickles & the Very Large Fly. (p. 1880)

—Rigby Reading Mainsails: On/below Leveled Reader Grades 5-8. (p. 1880)

—Rigby Reading Mainsails: On/below Leveled Reader Grades 5-8 Epidemic! (p. 1880)

—Rigby Reading Mainsails: On/below Leveled Reader Grades 5-8 Design It! (p. 1880)

—Rigby Reading Mainsails: On/below Leveled Reader Grades 5-8 Into the Cold. (p. 1880)

—Rigby Reading Mainsails: On/below Leveled Reader Grades 5-8 for or Against. (p. 1880)

—Rigby Reading Mainsails: On/below Leveled Reader Grades 5-8 Caught on Camera. (p. 1880)

—Rigby Reading Mainsails: On/below Leveled Reader Grades 5-8 Forensics in Fire. (p. 1880)

—Rigby Reading Mainsails: On/below Leveled Reader Grades 5-8 Air Traffic Control. (p. 1880)

R

—Rigby Reading Mainsails: On/below Leveled Reader Grades 5-8 Grandpa's Mumbling House. (p. 1880)
—Rigby Reading Mainsails: On/below Leveled Reader Grades 5-8 Glaciers: Landscape Carvers. (p. 1880)
—Rigby Reading Mainsails: On/below Leveled Reader Grades 5-8 More Helpful Hints for Boring Moments. (p. 1880)
—Rigby Reading Mainsails: On/below Leveled Reader Grades 6-8 Avatar. (p. 1881)
—Rigby Reading Mainsails: On/below Leveled Reader Grades 6-8 Koevasi. (p. 1881)
—Rigby Reading Mainsails: On/below Leveled Reader Grades 5-8 the Fall. (p. 1881)
—Rigby Reading Mainsails: On/below Leveled Reader Grades 6-8 Game Over. (p. 1881)
—Rigby Reading Mainsails: On/below Leveled Reader Grades 5-8 Space Junk. (p. 1881)
—Rigby Reading Mainsails: On/below Leveled Reader Grades 5-8 Wait & Hope. (p. 1881)
—Rigby Reading Mainsails: On/below Leveled Reader Grades 6-8 Blood Diamonds. (p. 1881)
—Rigby Reading Mainsails: On/below Leveled Reader Grades 6-8 Hunger & Excess. (p. 1881)
—Rigby Reading Mainsails: On/below Leveled Reader Grades 5-8 Super Structures. (p. 1881)
—Rigby Reading Mainsails: On/below Leveled Reader Grades 6-8 Facing Jesse James. (p. 1881)
—Rigby Reading Mainsails: On/below Leveled Reader Grades 6-8 Design It ? Edition 2. (p. 1881)
—Rigby Reading Mainsails: On/below Leveled Reader Grades 6-8 the Complete Survival Guide. (p. 1881)
—Rigby Reading Mainsails: On/below Leveled Reader Grades 5-8 the Biggest Girl in the World. (p. 1881)
—Rigby Reading Sails: Teacher Resource Book Gold Grade 4. (p. 1881)
—Rigby Reading Sails: Advanced Fluency Silver Level Add To. (p. 1881)
—Rigby Reading Sails: Fluency Gold Level Set 2 Add to Pack. (p. 1881)
—Rigby Reading Sails: Teacher Resource Book Orange Grade 2. (p. 1881)
—Rigby Reading Sails: Advanced Fluency Emerald Level Add To. (p. 1881)
—Rigby Reading Sails: Fluency Purple Level Set 2 Add to Pack. (p. 1881)
—Rigby Reading Sails: Gold Non Fiction Add to Pack Extension. (p. 1881)
—Rigby Reading Sails: Teacher Resource Book Silver Grades 4-5. (p. 1881)
—Rigby Reading Sails: Orange Non Fiction Add to Pack Extension. (p. 1881)
—Rigby Reading Sails: Purple Non Fiction Add to Pack Extension. (p. 1881)
—Rigby Reading Sails: Teacher Resource Book Emerald Grades 4-5. (p. 1881)
—Rigby Reading Sails: Leveled Reader Orange Grade 2 Book 1: Charlie. (p. 1881)
—Rigby Reading Sails: Leveled Reader Purple Grade 3 Book 2: Fossils. (p. 1881)
—Rigby Reading Sails: Leveled Reader Orange Grade 2 Book 6: Mr. Bean. (p. 1881)
—Rigby Reading Sails: Leveled Reader Purple Grade 3 Book 3: Slow Joe. (p. 1881)
—Rigby Reading Sails: Advanced Fluency Silver Level Non Fiction Add To. (p. 1881)
—Rigby Reading Sails: Launching Fluency Orange Level Set 3 Add to Pack. (p. 1881)
—Rigby Reading Sails: Advanced Fluency Emerald Level Non Fiction Add To. (p. 1881)
—Rigby Reading Sails: Leveled Reader Purple Grade 3 Book 9: Banana Cake. (p. 1881)
—Rigby Reading Sails: Leveled Reader Orange Grade 2 Book 10: Sea Turtles. (p. 1881)
—Rigby Reading Sails: Leveled Reader Purple Grade 3 Book 7: Stop That Pup! (p. 1881)
—Rigby Reading Sails: Leveled Reader Purple Grade 3 Book 5: Just This Once. (p. 1881)
—Rigby Reading Sails: Leveled Reader Orange Grade 2 Book 5: Long Hairy Legs. (p. 1881)
—Rigby Reading Sails: Leveled Reader Purple Grade 3 Book 10: Codes & Ciphers. (p. 1881)
—Rigby Reading Sails: Leveled Reader Orange Grade 2 Book 4: My Donkey Can Read. (p. 1881)
—Rosie Demands the Bill. (p. 1906)
RIGBY. Under the Canopy: Fourth Grade Class Collection Books. (p. 2321)
Rigby. When Day Turned to Night. (p. 2429)
Rigby, Amanda, illus. see Mathew, Laura.
Rigby, Deborah, illus. see Baxter, Nicola.
Rigby, Deborah, illus. see Mahy, Margaret.
Rigby, Deborah, illus. see Scott, Janine.
Rigby, Ed & Dooley, Angela. Mouse of the Match. (p. 1515)
Rigby Education Staff. Animals Say... (p. 95)
—Discovery World Yel Sizes. (p. 557)
Rigby Education Staff, jt. auth. see Brasch, Nicolas.
Rigby, Grayson. Expedition to the Galapagos Islands. (p. 677)
Rigby, Liz. Keep Your Heart. (p. 1207)
Rigby, Robert. Goal - Glory Days. (p. 849)
Rigby, Robert & Cámara, Noemí. Gol II: Viviendo el Sueño. (p. 855)
Rigg, Annie & Woram, Catherine. Fun Christmas Crafts to Make & Bake: Over 60 Festive Projects to Make with Your Kids. (p. 798)
Rigg, Diana. Teach a Child to READ in... 3 Simple Steps. Walter, Deborah, illus. (p. 2194)
Riggan, Brittany E., illus. see Buck, Ginger K.
Riggin, Lisa. Abigail & the Lost Purse. Calvert-Weyant, Linda, illus. (p. 5)
Riggins, David C. Fatherless. (p. 714)
Riggins, T. K. Next Level Hot. (p. 1600)
Riggle, Charlotte. Saint Nicholas Day Snow. Hughes, R. J., illus. (p. 1923)
Riggle, Karen. How Pumpkin Became a Pie. (p. 1034)
Riggs, Alice Shepard. Shepard of Aintab (Classic Reprint) (p. 2005)
Riggs, Arthur Stanley. With Three Armies: On & Behind the Western Front (Classic Reprint) (p. 2482)
Riggs, Carol. Body Institute. (p. 253)
—Lying Planet. (p. 1369)
Riggs, Eleanor. Stories from Lands of Sunshine (Classic Reprint) (p. 2124)
Riggs, Ernestine G., ed. see Bonnice, Sherry.
Riggs, Ernestine G., ed. see Brinkerhoff, Shirley.
Riggs, Ernestine G., ed. see Intosh, Kenneth Mc & McIntosh, Kenneth.
Riggs, Ernestine G., ed. see Libal, Joyce & Simons, Rae.
Riggs, Ernestine G., ed. see Libal, Joyce.
Riggs, Ernestine G., ed. see Riddle, John & Simons, Rae.
Riggs, Ernestine G., ed. see Sanna, Ellyn.
Riggs, Ernestine G., ed. see Simons, Rae & Gommer, Viola Ruelke.
Riggs, Ernestine G., ed. see Vitale, Ann.
Riggs, James Gilbert, jt. auth. see Goldsmith, Oliver.
Riggs, Jenna, illus. see Rizzi, Kathleen.
Riggs, Jenna, jt. auth. see Berner, Beth E.
Riggs, Jenny Oates. Remember This. Auth, Dennis, illus. (p. 1864)
Riggs, Jon & Evanoff, Corrine R. Little Blue Planet. Nazar, Alexandria, illus. (p. 1312)
Riggs, Jonny. Frank Has the Sniffles. Bristow, Ian C., illus. (p. 777)
Riggs, Kate. Across the Universe: Asteroids. (p. 11)
—Across the Universe: Comets. (p. 11)
—Across the Universe: Galaxies. (p. 11)
—Across the Universe: Moons. (p. 11)
—Across the Universe: Planets. (p. 11)
—Adjectives. (p. 16)
—Adverbs. (p. 30)
—Alligators. (p. 56)
—Amazing Animals: Whales. (p. 63)
—Amazing Animals: Bats. (p. 63)
—Amazing Animals: Beavers. (p. 63)
—Amazing Animals: Bighorn Sheep. (p. 63)
—Amazing Animals: Brown Bears. (p. 63)
—Amazing Animals: Camels. (p. 63)
—Amazing Animals: Cheetahs. (p. 63)
—Amazing Animals - Cheetahs. (p. 63)
—Amazing Animals: Cougars. (p. 63)
—Amazing Animals - Dolphins. (p. 63)
—Amazing Animals: Eagles. (p. 63)
—Amazing Animals: Elephants. (p. 63)
—Amazing Animals - Elephants. (p. 63)
—Amazing Animals: Falcons. (p. 63)
—Amazing Animals: Flamingos. (p. 63)
—Amazing Animals: Geckos. (p. 63)
—Amazing Animals: Gorillas. (p. 63)
—Amazing Animals: Hawks. (p. 63)
—Amazing Animals: Hummingbirds. (p. 63)
—Amazing Animals: Killer Whales. (p. 63)
—Amazing Animals: Leopards. (p. 63)
—Amazing Animals: Moose. (p. 64)
—Amazing Animals: Raccoons. (p. 64)
—Amazing Animals: Sea Lions. (p. 64)
—Amazing Animals: Sea Turtles. (p. 64)
—Amazing Animals: Storks. (p. 64)
—Amazing Animals: Tortoises. (p. 64)
—Amazing Animals: Vultures. (p. 64)
—Amazing Animals: Whales. (p. 64)
—Amazing Animals: Wild Horses. (p. 64)
—Amazing Animals - Wolves. (p. 63)
—Amazing Animals: Wolves. (p. 64)
—Amazing Animals: Woodpeckers. (p. 64)
—Amazing Animals: Zebras. (p. 64)
—Ambulances. (p. 67)
—Antelopes. (p. 102)
—Apatosaurus. (p. 105)
—Arctic Tundra. (p. 112)
—Armadillos. (p. 117)
—Armored Vehicles. (p. 117)
—Autonomous Vehicles. (p. 140)
—Baby Bears. (p. 149)
—Baby Dolphins. (p. 150)
—Baby Elephants. (p. 150)
—Baby Foxes. (p. 150)
—Baby Giraffes. (p. 150)
—Baby Gorillas. (p. 150)
—Baby Kangaroos. (p. 151)
—Baby Koalas. (p. 151)
—Baby Lions. (p. 151)
—Baby Monkeys. (p. 151)
—Baby Pandas. (p. 152)
—Baby Penguins. (p. 152)
—Baby Seals. (p. 152)
—Baby Tigers. (p. 153)
—Bats. (p. 173)
—Battleships. (p. 175)
—Beagles. (p. 178)
—Beavers. (p. 186)
—Bee. (p. 189)
—Brown Bears. (p. 286)
—Bulldogs. (p. 296)
—Bullet Trains. (p. 296)
—Butterfly. (p. 303)
—Camels. (p. 314)
—Cheetahs. (p. 364)
—Chimpanzees. (p. 377)
—Chipmunks. (p. 379)
—Colons & Semicolons. (p. 419)
—Colors of Nature. Paolo, Domeniconi, illus. (p. 426)
—Computer Science. (p. 437)
—Cougars. (p. 457)
—Counting on Birds. van der Linde, Jori, illus. (p. 460)
—Crowds of Creatures. Fiammetta, Dogi, illus. (p. 479)
—Deserts. (p. 532)
—Dig It! Kubinyi, Laszlo, illus. (p. 545)
—Dolphins. (p. 579)
—Drones. (p. 605)
—Ducks. (p. 608)
—Eagles. (p. 613)
—Easter Island. (p. 620)
—Egyptian Pyramids. (p. 628)
—Eiffel Tower. (p. 629)
—Elephants. (p. 634)
—Empire State Building. (p. 645)
—Enchanted Castles. (p. 646)
—End of the Cold War. (p. 648)
—Escorpion Fv101. (p. 662)
—Fairy Godmothers. (p. 696)
—Falcons. (p. 699)
—Fire Trucks. (p. 733)
—Flamingos. (p. 746)
—Food for Life: Arctic Tundra. (p. 759)
—Food for Life: Deserts. (p. 759)
—Food for Life: Mountains. (p. 759)
—Food for Life: Oceans. (p. 759)
—Food for Life: Prairies. (p. 759)
—Food for Life: Rainforests. (p. 760)
—Foxes. (p. 774)
—Freight Trains. (p. 783)
—French Revolution: Days of Change. (p. 784)
—French Revolution. (p. 784)
—FV101 Scorpion (tank) (p. 803)
—Fv101 Scorpion / Kate Riggs. (p. 803)
—Geckos. (p. 813)
—Giraffes. (p. 834)
—Gladiators. (p. 840)
—Golden Gate Bridge. (p. 857)
—Gorillas. (p. 870)
—Grammar Basics: Adjectives. (p. 875)
—Grammar Basics: Adverbs. (p. 875)
—Grammar Basics: Nouns. (p. 875)
—Grammar Basics: Verbs. (p. 875)
—Great Recession. (p. 888)
—Great Wall of China. (p. 890)
—Great Warriors: Gladiators. (p. 891)
—Great Warriors: Knights. (p. 891)
—Great Warriors: Pirates. (p. 891)
—Great Warriors: Samurai. (p. 891)
—Grow with Me: Bee. (p. 899)
—Grow with Me: Butterfly. (p. 899)
—Grow with Me: Frog. (p. 899)
—Grow with Me: Ladybug. (p. 899)
—Grow with Me: Sunflower. (p. 899)
—Grow with Me: Tomato. (p. 899)
—Hawks. (p. 940)
—Helicopters. (p. 950)
—Hippopotamuses. (p. 973)
—How Fast Can You Go? Williams, Nate, illus. (p. 1031)
—Hummingbirds. (p. 1050)
—In the Garden. Felix, Monique, illus. (p. 1109)
—Indy Cars. (p. 1118)
—Jets. (p. 1167)
—Kangaroos. (p. 1202)
—Killer Whales. (p. 1217)
—Knights. (p. 1228)
—Ladybug. (p. 1238)
—Las Ardillas Listadas. (p. 1245)
—Leopards. (p. 1268)
—Let's Go Outside. Felix, Monique, illus. (p. 1273)
—Light Rails. (p. 1299)
—Lions. (p. 1307)
—Los Patos. (p. 1351)
—Machu Picchu. (p. 1372)
—Magical Creatures. (p. 1380)
—Making Music: Drums. (p. 1389)
—Making Music: Flute. (p. 1389)
—Making Music: Guitar. (p. 1389)
—Making Music: Piano. (p. 1389)
—Making Music: Trumpet. (p. 1389)
—Making Music: Violin. (p. 1389)
—Manatees. (p. 1396)
—Mice. (p. 1457)
—Moles. (p. 1489)
—Monkeys. (p. 1494)
—Monorails. (p. 1495)
—Moons. (p. 1503)
—Moose. (p. 1503)
—Mount Rushmore. (p. 1513)
—Mountains. (p. 1514)
—NASA X-43 a (unmanned Aircraft) (p. 1576)
—NASA X-43a. (p. 1576)
—Neptune. (p. 1587)
—New Horizons. (p. 1594)
—New Horizons (space Probe) (p. 1594)
—Nouns. (p. 1625)
—Nuevos Horizontes. (p. 1629)
—Oceans. (p. 1636)
—Octopuses. (p. 1637)
—On the Farm. Dogi, Fiammetta, illus. (p. 1654)
—Ostriches. (p. 1674)
—Pandas. (p. 1695)
—Passenger Trains. (p. 1703)
—Penguins. (p. 1716)
—Pirates. (p. 1750)
—Planets. (p. 1756)
—Polar Bears. (p. 1769)
—Prairies. (p. 1785)
—Princes & Princesses. (p. 1795)
—Pterodactyls. (p. 1810)
—Pugs. (p. 1812)
—Quotation Marks & Apostrophes. (p. 1829)
—Raccoons. (p. 1830)
—Rainforests. (p. 1837)
—Release of Nelson Mandela. (p. 1863)
—Rescue Boats. (p. 1868)
—Robins. (p. 1891)
—Robots. (p. 1893)
—Samurai. (p. 1929)
—Saturn. (p. 1936)
—Sea Lions. (p. 1967)
—Sea Turtles. (p. 1969)
—Seed Needs Sun. Dogi, Fiammetta, illus. (p. 1982)
—Seedlings: Bullet Trains. (p. 1983)
—Seedlings: Camels. (p. 1983)
—Seedlings: Cheetahs. (p. 1983)
—Seedlings: Chickens. (p. 1983)
—Seedlings: Clownfish. (p. 1983)
—Seedlings: Coral Reefs. (p. 1983)
—Seedlings: Cows. (p. 1983)
—Seedlings: Dolphins. (p. 1983)
—Seedlings: Eagles. (p. 1983)
—Seedlings: Elephants. (p. 1983)
—Seedlings: Geckos. (p. 1983)
—Seedlings: Giraffes. (p. 1983)
—Seedlings: Goats. (p. 1983)
—Seedlings: Gorillas. (p. 1983)
—Seedlings: Indy Cars. (p. 1983)
—Seedlings: Jets. (p. 1983)
—Seedlings: Killer Whales. (p. 1983)
—Seedlings: Koalas. (p. 1983)
—Seedlings: Lions. (p. 1983)
—Seedlings: Monkeys. (p. 1983)
—Seedlings: Motorcycles. (p. 1983)
—Seedlings: Nurses. (p. 1983)
—Seedlings: Octopuses. (p. 1983)
—Seedlings: Pandas. (p. 1983)
—Seedlings: Penguins. (p. 1983)
—Seedlings: Pickup Trucks. (p. 1983)
—Seedlings: Polar Bears. (p. 1983)
—Seedlings: Sea Lions. (p. 1983)
—Seedlings: Sharks. (p. 1983)
—Seedlings: Snakes. (p. 1983)
—Seedlings: Speedboats. (p. 1983)
—Seedlings: Stock Cars. (p. 1983)
—Seedlings: Tanker Trucks. (p. 1983)
—Seedlings: Teachers. (p. 1983)
—Seedlings: Tigers. (p. 1983)
—Seedlings: Tow Trucks. (p. 1983)
—Seedlings: Veterinarians. (p. 1983)
—Seedlings: Whales. (p. 1983)
—Seedlings: Wild Horses. (p. 1983)
—Seedlings: Wolves. (p. 1983)
—Seedlings: Zebras. (p. 1983)
—Shapes All Around. Devernay, Laëtitia, illus. (p. 2000)
—Sharks. (p. 2002)
—Snakes. (p. 2044)
—Sounds of the Forest. Dogi, Fiammetta, illus. (p. 2067)
—Speedboats. (p. 2078)
—Spells & Potions. (p. 2079)
—Sr-71 Blackbird. (p. 2095)
—SR-71 Blackbird (plane) (p. 2095)
—Stegosaurus. (p. 2112)
—Stock Cars. (p. 2120)
—Stonehenge. (p. 2121)
—Storks. (p. 2126)
—Suez Canal. (p. 2147)
—Sun. (p. 2151)
—Sunflower. (p. 2152)
—Taj Mahal. (p. 2176)
—That's Creepy! Dogi, Fiammetta, illus. (p. 2213)
—Tigers. (p. 2242)
—To the Rescue! Williams, Nate, illus. (p. 2253)
—Tomato. (p. 2258)
—Tortoises. (p. 2266)
—Triceratops. (p. 2287)
—Tyrannosaurus Rex. (p. 2311)
—Under the Sea. Tom, Leonard, illus. (p. 2322)
—Velociraptor. (p. 2349)
—Verbs. (p. 2351)
—Vultures. (p. 2369)
—Whales. (p. 2403)
—What Is Cubism? (p. 2415)
—What Is Gothic Art? (p. 2415)
—What Is Impressionism? (p. 2415)
—What Is Modernism? (p. 2415)
—What Is Realism? (p. 2416)
—What Is Romanticism? (p. 2416)
—When Dinosaurs Lived: Apatosaurus. (p. 2429)
—When Dinosaurs Lived: Velociraptor. (p. 2429)
—Wicked Stepmothers. (p. 2460)
—Wild Backyard. Dogi, Fiammetta, illus. (p. 2462)
—Wild Horses. (p. 2463)
—Wolves. (p. 2485)
—Woodpeckers. (p. 2492)
—Zebras. (p. 2539)
Riggs, Kate & Sheban, Chris. Beyond the Stars. (p. 212)
Riggs, Mary L. Dragon Forge the Ballad of Beighn. (p. 593)
Riggs, Philip a. Little Heartbroken Angel. (p. 1318)
Riggs, Ransom. Conference of the Birds. (p. 438)
—Hollow City: The Second Novel of Miss Peregrine's Peculiar Children. (p. 988)
—Hollow City. Riggs, Ransom, illus. (p. 988)
—Hollow City: the Graphic Novel: The Second Novel of Miss Peregrine's Peculiar Children. (p. 988)
—Library of Souls: The Third Novel of Miss Peregrine's Peculiar Children. (p. 1285)
—Library of Souls. (p. 1285)
—Map of Days: Miss. Peregrine's Peculiar Children. (p. 1400)
—Map of Days. (p. 1400)
—Mapa de Los días. el Hogar de Miss Peregrine / a Map of Days. (p. 1401)
—Miss Peregrine's Home for Peculiar Children. (p. 1479)
—Miss Peregrine's Journal for Peculiar Children. (p. 1479)
—Miss Peregrine's Peculiar Children Boxed Set (p. 1479)
—Penguin Teen Unboxed: Peregrine (p. 1716)
—Tales of the Peculiar. Davidson, Andrew, illus. (p. 2186)
Riggs, Ransom, et al. Miss Peregrine's Home for Peculiar Children. (p. 1479)
Riggs, Sandy. Habitats of Australia: Set Of 6. (p. 908)
—Three Ancient Communities: Set Of 6. (p. 2231)
Riggs, Shannon. Not in Room 204: Breaking the Silence of Abuse. Zollars, Jaime, illus. (p. 1623)
Riggs, Thomas, jt. ed. see Greenhaven Press Editors.
Riggs, Thomas, ed. Are Players' Unions Good for Professional Sports Leagues? (p. 112)
—Book Banning. (p. 257)
—Democracy in the Poetry of Walt Whitman. (p. 528)
Riggs Vetter, Jennifer. Down by the Station. Remkiewicz, Frank, illus. (p. 590)
Right, Emma. Keeper of Reign. (p. 1208)

R

—Man in Lower Ten (Classic Reprint) (p. 1394)
—Mary Roberts Rinehart's Romance Book: K; the Amazing Interlude; the Street of Seven Stars (Classic Reprint) (p. 1416)
—Poor Wise Man (Classic Reprint) (p. 1775)
—Street of Seven Stars (Classic Reprint) (p. 2140)
—Tenting To-Night: A Chronicle of Sport & Adventure in Glacier Park & the Cascade Mountains (Classic Reprint) (p. 2206)
—Through Glacier Park, Seeing America First with Howard Eaton (Classic Reprint) (p. 2236)
—Tish: The Chronicle of Her Escapades & Excursions. (p. 2251)
—Tish: The Chronicle of Her Escapades & Excursions (Classic Reprint) (p. 2251)
—Tish: The Adventures & Mystery Cases of Letitia Carberry, Tish: the Chronicle of Her Escapades & Excursions & More Tish. (p. 2251)
—Twenty-Three & a Half Hours Leave (Classic Reprint) (p. 2304)
—When a Man Marries (Classic Reprint) (p. 2429)
—Where There's a Will (Classic Reprint) (p. 2440)
Rinehart, Susie Caldwell. Eliza & Dragonfly. (p. 636)
—Eliza & the Dragonfly. Hovemann, Anisa Claire, illus. (p. 636)
Riner, Dax. Pelé. (p. 1714)
Riney-Kehrberg, Pamela. Always Plenty to Do: Growing up on a Farm in the Long Ago. (p. 61)
Ring, Barbara. $100, 000 Club Paper; a Play for Club Women: One-Act Comedy (Classic Reprint) (p. 2556)
Ring, Jamie. Frankfortvilles Strange Challenge. (p. 778)
Ring, Jeremy. Your Newest, Bestest Friend. (p. 2534)
Ring, Phyllis Edgerly. Jamila Does Not Want a Bat in Her House. Hosack, Leona, illus. (p. 1157)
Ring, Susan. Earth. (p. 615)
—Election Connection: the Official Nickelodeon Guide to Electing the President (Nickelodeon) Random House, illus. (p. 631)
—Elok. (p. 639)
—Herbie. (p. 957)
—Honeybees: An Amazing Insect Discovery BK. (p. 999)
—Pete's Surprise. (p. 1730)
—Polar Bear Babies. McCue, Lisa, illus. (p. 1769)
—Where Should Turtle Be? Klein, Laurie Allen, illus. (p. 2439)
Ring, Susan, jt. auth. see Dorling Kindersley Publishing Staff.
Ring, Susan, jt. auth. see Scollon, Bill.
Ring, Susan & Gillespie. Cat. (p. 341)
Ring, Susan & Gillespie, Katie. Cat. (p. 341)
Ring, Susan & Roumanis, Alexis. Dwarf Planets. (p. 611)
—Earth. (p. 615)
—Jupiter. (p. 1191)
—Mercury. (p. 1448)
—Neptune. (p. 1587)
—Saturn. (p. 1936)
—Uranus. (p. 2339)
—Venus. (p. 2351)
Ringgold, Faith. Harlem Renaissance Party. Ringgold, Faith, illus. (p. 930)
—Henry Ossawa Tanner: His Boyhood Dream Comes True. Ringgold, Faith, illus. (p. 955)
—My Grandmother's Story Quilt. (p. 1548)
—Tar Beach. (p. 2191)
—We Came to America. (p. 2390)
Ringgold, Faith, illus. see Brooks, Gwendolyn.
Ringley, Patrick & Brown, Anne Corbett. Adventures of the Nutters, the Tree Highway. Cotton, Sue Lynn, illus. (p. 28)
Ringli, Andrea, illus. see Lyon, Rachel.
Ringling, Alfred. Life Story of the Ringling Brothers Illustrated: Humorous Incidents, Thrilling Trials, Many Hardships, & Ups & Downs, Telling How the Boys Built a Circus, & Showing the True Road to Success (Classic Reprint) (p. 1296)
Ringo, Mary Lou. That's Not Fair. (p. 2213)
Ringsmuth, Katherine J. At Work in the Wrangells: a Photographic History, 1895-1966: A Photographic History, 1895-1966. National Park Service (U.S.), ed. (p. 131)
Ringstad, Arnold. Allosaurus. (p. 57)
—Biking. (p. 225)
—Bizarre Origins of Kangaroo Court & Other Idioms. McGeehan, Dan, illus. (p. 235)
—Bobcats. (p. 252)
—Building of the Golden Gate Bridge. (p. 294)
—Building of the Hoover Dam. (p. 294)
—Cheetahs. (p. 364)
—Coelophysis. (p. 412)
—Compelling Histories of Long Arm of the Law & Other Idioms. McGeehan, Dan, illus. (p. 433)
—Constellation Scorpius: The Story of the Scorpion. Morrow, J. T., illus. (p. 443)
—Constellation Taurus: The Story of the Bull. Morrow, J. T., illus. (p. 443)
—Cougars. (p. 457)
—Cycle of Photosynthesis. (p. 492)
—Dinosaur Myths, Busted! (p. 549)
—Diplodocus. (p. 552)
—Garbage Collector. (p. 808)
—How Do Engineers Reuse Rockets? (p. 1028)
—Hunting. (p. 1053)
—Jaguars. (p. 1155)
—Kayaking. (p. 1207)
—Leopards. (p. 1268)
—Lions. (p. 1307)
—Medical Myths, Busted! (p. 1436)
—NASA Takes Photography into Space. (p. 1576)
—Over-the-Top Histories of Chew the Scenery & Other Idioms. McGeehan, Dan, illus. (p. 1687)
—Plant Life Cycle. (p. 1756)
—Portable Toilet Cleaner. (p. 1778)
—Puffins & Penguins. (p. 1811)
—Science of Solar Energy. (p. 1958)
—Sewer Inspector. (p. 1995)
—Shocking Stories Behind Lightning in a Bottle & Other Idioms. McGeehan, Dan, illus. (p. 2008)
—Thrilling Sources of Push the Envelope & Other Idioms. McGeehan, Dan, illus. (p. 2236)
—Tigers. (p. 2242)
—Totally Amazing Facts about Reptiles. (p. 2266)
—True Stories of Animal Antics. (p. 2294)
—True Stories of Animal Friends. (p. 2294)
—True Stories of Animal Oddities. (p. 2294)
—True Stories of Animal Tricks & Talents. (p. 2294)
—Unbelievable Origins of Snake Oil & Other Idioms. McGeehan, Dan, illus. (p. 2317)
—Velociraptor. (p. 2349)
—What's Inside a Clock? (p. 2425)
—What's Inside a Computer Mouse? (p. 2425)
—What's Inside a Digital Camera? (p. 2425)
—What's Inside a Drone? (p. 2425)
—What's Inside a DVD Player? (p. 2425)
—What's Inside a Keyboard? (p. 2425)
—What's Inside a Radio? (p. 2425)
—What's Inside a Remote Control? (p. 2425)
—What's Inside a Remote-Controlled Car? (p. 2425)
—What's Inside a Toaster? (p. 2425)
—What's Inside a VCR? (p. 2425)
—What's Inside Headphones? (p. 2425)
Ringstad, Arnold, jt. auth. see Jd, Duchess Harris.
Ringstad, Arnold, jt. auth. see Kallio, Jamie.
Ringstad, Arnold, jt. auth. see Nelson, Penelope.
Ringstad, Arnold, jt. auth. see Smibert, Angie.
Ringstad, Arnold, jt. auth. see Ventura, Marne.
Ringtved, Glenn. Cry, Heart, but Never Break. Moulthrop, Robert, tr. (p. 480)
Ringwald, Whitaker. Secret Box. (p. 1975)
—Secret Cipher. (p. 1975)
—Secret Fire. (p. 1975)
Rininger, Alyce. Ka-Boom. Lucas, Diane, illus. (p. 1201)
Rink, Donna M. Alpha Buddies Land. (p. 58)
Rinka, Kelci, illus. see Rich, Heidi Wilke.
Rinker, Gary W. Very Best Toy. Rangel, Rawderson, illus. (p. 2352)
Rinker, Jess. Dare Sisters. (p. 504)
Rinker, Jessica. Lost on the Titanic (Out of Time Book 1) Stancliffe, Bethany, illus. (p. 1355)
Rinker, Jessica M. Gloria Takes a Stand: How Gloria Steinem Listened, Wrote, & Changed the World. Peoples-Riley, Daria, illus. (p. 844)
Rinker, Sherri Duskey. 12 Sleighs of Christmas. Parker, Jake, illus. (p. 2551)
—Big Machines: The Story of Virginia Lee Burton. Rocco, John, illus. (p. 221)
—Buenas Noches, Construccion. Buenas Noches, Diversion. Lázaro, Georgina & Mlawer, Teresa, trs. (p. 290)
—Celebrate You! Kang, A. N., illus. (p. 349)
—Cement Mixer's ABC: Goodnight, Goodnight, Construction Site (Alphabet Book for Kids, Board Books for Toddlers, Preschool Concept Book) Long, Ethan, illus. (p. 351)
—Construction Site on Christmas Night. Ford, A. G., illus. (p. 443)
—Excavator's 123: Goodnight, Goodnight, Construction Site (Counting Books for Kids, Learning to Count Books, Goodnight Book) Long, Ethan, illus. (p. 676)
—Goodnight, Goodnight, Construction Site: Glow in the Dark Edition. Lichtenheld, Tom, illus. (p. 867)
—Goodnight, Goodnight, Construction Site. Lichtenheld, Tom, illus. (p. 867)
—Goodnight, Goodnight Construction Site (Hardcover Books for Toddlers, Preschool Books for Kids) Lichtenheld, Tom, illus. (p. 867)
—Goodnight Goodnight Construction Site Sound Book: (Construction Books for Kids, Books with Sound for Toddlers, Children's Truck Books, Read Aloud Books) Lichtenheld, Tom, illus. (p. 867)
—How to Put an Octopus to Bed: (Going to Bed Book, Read-Aloud Bedtime Book for Kids) Schwarz, Viviane, illus. (p. 1043)
—Let's Go! Lichtenheld, Tom, illus. (p. 1273)
—Mighty, Mighty Construction Site. (p. 1463)
—Mighty, Mighty Construction Site. Lichtenheld, Tom, illus. (p. 1463)
—Mighty, Mighty Construction Site Sound Book. Lichtenheld, Tom, illus. (p. 1463)
—Revver the Speedway Squirrel. Willan, Alex, illus. (p. 1874)
—Silly Wonderful You. McDonnell, Patrick, illus. (p. 2019)
—Steam Train, Dream Train. Lichtenheld, Tom, illus. (p. 2110)
—Steam Train, Dream Train Colors. Lichtenheld, Tom, illus. (p. 2111)
—Steam Train, Dream Train Counting. Lichtenheld, Tom, illus. (p. 2111)
—Steam Train, Dream Train Sound Book. Lichtenheld, Tom, illus. (p. 2111)
—Three Cheers for Kid McGear! Ford, A. G., illus. (p. 2232)
—Tiny & the Big Dig. Myers, Matt, illus. (p. 2248)
Rinker, Sherri Duskey & Lichtenheld, Tom. Bulldozer's Shapes: Goodnight, Goodnight, Construction Site. Long, Ethan, illus. (p. 296)
—Dump Truck's Colors: Goodnight, Goodnight, Construction Site. Long, Ethan, illus. (p. 610)
—Goodnight, Goodnight, Construction Site. (p. 867)
—Steam Train, Dream Train. (p. 2110)
Rinker, Sherri Duskey, et al. Crane Truck's Opposites. (p. 466)
Rinpoché, Yongey Mingyur & Hayden, Torey. Ziji: The Puppy Who Learned to Meditate. Larrison, Charity, illus. (p. 2540)
Rioja, Alberto Jimenez, tr. see Cronin, Doreen.
Rioja, Alberto Jimenez, tr. see Ganeri, Anita, et al.
Rioja, Alberto Jimenez, tr. see Harris, Robie H.
Rioja, Alberto Jimenez, tr. see Joseph, Lynn.
Rioja, Alberto Jimenez, tr. see Silverstein, Shel.
Rioja, Alberto Jimenez, tr. see Tibo, Gilles.
Rion, Hanna. Smiling Road (Classic Reprint) (p. 2042)
Riordan, James, jt. auth. see Myers, Bill.
Riordan, James, jt. auth. see Tolstoy, Leo.
Riordan, Kathleen B. Lost Christmas Ornament. (p. 1353)
Riordan, Rick. 39 Clues: The Sword Thief. (p. 2555)
—39 Clues Book 1: The Maze of Bones. (p. 2555)
—9 from the Nine Worlds (Magnus Chase & the Gods of Asgard) (p. 2549)
—Battle of the Labyrinth. (p. 174)
—Burning Maze. (p. 300)
—Burning Maze. Rocco, John, illus. (p. 300)
—Burning Maze (Trials of Apollo, Book Three) (p. 300)
—Dark Prophecy. Rocco, John, illus. (p. 506)
—Dark Prophecy (the Trials of Apollo, Book Two) (p. 506)
—Demigods & Magicians: Percy & Annabeth Meet the Kanes. (p. 528)
—For Magnus Chase: Hotel Valhalla Guide to the Norse Worlds (an Official Rick Riordan Companion Book) Your Introduction to Deities, Mythical Beings, & Fantastic Creatures. (p. 763)
—From Percy Jackson: Camp Half-Blood Confidential (an Official Rick Riordan Companion Book) Your Real Guide to the Demigod Training Camp. (p. 792)
—From the Kane Chronicles Brooklyn House Magician's Manual (an Official Rick Riordan Companion Book) Your Guide to Egyptian Gods & Creatures, Glyphs & Spells, & More. (p. 794)
—Hammer of Thor. (p. 913)
—Heroes of Olympus, Book Five the Blood of Olympus (new Cover) (p. 962)
—Heroes of Olympus, Book Five the Blood of Olympus (Heroes of Olympus, the, Book Five) (p. 962)
—Heroes of Olympus, Book Four the House of Hades. (p. 962)
—Heroes of Olympus, Book One the Lost Hero. (p. 962)
—Heroes of Olympus, Book One the Lost Hero (Heroes of Olympus, the, Book One) (p. 962)
—Heroes of Olympus, Book One the Lost Hero (new Cover) (p. 962)
—Heroes of Olympus - Book Three the Mark of Athena. (p. 962)
—Heroes of Olympus, Book Three the Mark of Athena (new Cover) (p. 962)
—Heroes of Olympus, Book Two the Son of Neptune. (p. 962)
—Heroes of Olympus, Book Two the Son of Neptune (Heroes of Olympus, the, Book Two) (p. 962)
—Heroes of Olympus, Book Two the Son of Neptune (new Cover) (p. 962)
—Heroes of Olympus Books 1-5 Prepack. (p. 962)
—Heroes of Olympus Paperback Boxed Set (10th Anniversary Edition) (p. 962)
—Heroes of Olympus, the, Book Five the Blood of Olympus. (p. 962)
—Heroes of Olympus the Demigod Diaries (the Heroes of Olympus, Book 2) (p. 962)
—Hidden Oracle. (p. 966)
—Hidden Oracle (Trials of Apollo, Book One) (p. 966)
—House of Hades. (p. 1023)
—House of Hades (Heroes of Olympus, the, Book Four: the House of Hades) (p. 1023)
—House of Hades (the Heroes of Olympus, Book Four (new Cover) (p. 1023)
—Kane Chronicles, Book One: the Red Pyramid. (p. 1202)
—Kane Chronicles, Book Three the Serpent's Shadow (p. 1202)
—Kane Chronicles, Book Three the Serpent's Shadow (new Cover) Griffin, Matt, illus. (p. 1202)
—Kane Chronicles, Book Two the Throne of Fire (p. 1202)
—Kane Chronicles, the, Book One the Red Pyramid (the Kane Chronicles, Book One) Griffin, Matt, illus. (p. 1202)
—Kane Chronicles, the, Book Two the Throne of Fire (Kane Chronicles, the, Book Two) Griffin, Matt, illus. (p. 1202)
—Kane Chronicles, the Paperback Box Set (the Kane Chronicles Box Set with Graphic Novel Sampler) Griffin, Matt, illus. (p. 1202)
—Lost Hero. (p. 1353)
—Magnus Chase & the Gods of Asgard. (p. 1382)
—Magnus Chase & the Gods of Asgard, Book 1 the Sword of Summer. (p. 1382)
—Magnus Chase & the Gods of Asgard Book 1 the Sword of Summer (Magnus Chase & the Gods of Asgard Book 1) (p. 1382)
—Magnus Chase & the Gods of Asgard, Book 2 the Hammer of Thor. (p. 1382)
—Magnus Chase & the Gods of Asgard, Book 3 the Ship of the Dead. (p. 1382)
—Magnus Chase & the Gods of Asgard, Book 3 the Ship of the Dead (Magnus Chase & the Gods of Asgard, Book 3) (p. 1382)
—Magnus Chase & the Gods of Asgard Hardcover Boxed Set. (p. 1382)
—Magnus Chase Coloring Book (a Magnus Chase Book) Robinson, Keith, illus. (p. 1382)
—Magos y Semidioses Percy Jackson Se une a Los Kane/ Demigods & Magicians: Percy & Annabeth Meet the Kanes. (p. 1382)
—Mark of Athena. (p. 1407)
—Percy Jackson & the Olympians (p. 1721)
—Percy Jackson & the Olympians. (p. 1721)
—Percy Jackson & the Olympians, Book Five the Last Olympian (Percy Jackson & the Olympians, Book Five) (p. 1721)
—Percy Jackson & the Olympians, Book Four the Battle of the Labyrinth (Percy Jackson & the Olympians, Book Four) (p. 1721)
—Percy Jackson & the Olympians the Lightning Thief Illustrated Edition. Rocco, John, illus. (p. 1721)
—Percy Jackson & the Olympians the Ultimate Guide (Percy Jackson & the Olympians) (p. 1721)
—Percy Jackson Demigod Collection. (p. 1721)
—Percy Jackson T03 le Sort du Titan (Ed 2010) (p. 1721)
—Percy Jackson T05 - le Dernier Olympien. (p. 1721)
—Percy Jackson T4 la Bataille du Labyrinthe. (p. 1721)
—Percy Jackson: the Demigod Files. (p. 1721)
—Percy Jackson y Los Heroes Griegos / Percy Jackson's Greek Heroes. (p. 1721)
—Percy Jackson's Greek Gods. (p. 1721)
—Percy Jackson's Greek Gods. Rocco, John, illus. (p. 1721)
—Percy Jackson's Greek Heroes. (p. 1721)
—Percy Jackson's Greek Heroes. Rocco, John, illus. (p. 1721)
—Read Riordan. (p. 1845)
—Red Pyramid. (p. 1858)
—Sea of Monsters. (p. 1968)
—Serpent's Shadow. (p. 1991)
—Ship of the Dead. (p. 2008)
—Sombra de la Serpiente: Las Cronicas de Kane, III. (p. 2058)
—Son of Neptune. (p. 2062)
—Sword of Summer. (p. 2171)
—Throne of Fire. (p. 2236)
—Titan's Curse. (p. 2251)
—Trials of Apollo 3-Book Paperback Boxed Set. (p. 2286)
—Trials of Apollo Book One the Hidden Oracle. (p. 2286)
—Trials of Apollo Camp Jupiter Classified (an Official Rick Riordan Companion Book) A Probatio's Journal. (p. 2286)
—Tyrant's Tomb (the Trials of Apollo, Book Four, Special Limited Edition) Rocco, John, illus. (p. 2311)
—Tyrant's Tomb (the Trials of Apollo, Book Four) (p. 2311)
—ÚLTIMO HÉROE DEL OLIMPO: PERCY JACKSON Y LOS DIOSES DEL OLIMPO V. (p. 2316)
Riordan, Rick, jt. auth. see Venditti, Robert.
Riordan, Rick & Collar, Orpheus. Kane Chronicles - Book One Red Pyramid: the Graphic Novel Collar, Orpheus, illus. (p. 1202)
—Kane Chronicles, Book Three the Serpent's Shadow: the Graphic Novel. Collar, Orpheus, illus. (p. 1202)
—Kane Chronicles, the, Book One the Red Pyramid: the Graphic Novel (Kane Chronicles, the, Book One) Collar, Orpheus, illus. (p. 1202)
—Serpent's Shadow. (p. 1991)
Riordan, Rick & Scholastic, Inc. Staff. Black Book of Buried Secrets. (p. 237)
Riordan, Rick & Venditti, Robert. Heroes of Olympus, Book One the Lost Hero: the Graphic Novel (Heroes of Olympus, Book One) Powell, Nathan, illus. (p. 962)
—Heroes of Olympus, Book Two, the Son of Neptune: the Graphic Novel. Dodé, Antoine & Collar, Orpheus, illus. (p. 962)
—Percy Jackson & the Olympians Sea of Monsters, the: the Graphic Novel. Futaki, Attila & Gaspar, Tamas, illus. (p. 1721)
—Percy Jackson & the Olympians the Battle of the Labyrinth: the Graphic Novel (Percy Jackson & the Olympians) Collar, Orpheus & Dodé, Antoine, illus. (p. 1721)
—Percy Jackson & the Olympians the Last Olympian: the Graphic Novel. Collar, Orpheus & Dodé, Antoine, illus. (p. 1721)
—Percy Jackson & the Olympians the Lightning Thief: the Graphic Novel. Futaki, Attila & Villarrubia, Jose, illus. (p. 1721)
—Percy Jackson & the Olympians the Titan's Curse: the Graphic Novel. Futaki, Attila & Guilhaumond, Gregory, illus. (p. 1721)
—Titan's Curse. (p. 2251)
Riordan, Rick, ed. Demigods & Monsters: Your Favorite Authors on Rick Riordan's Percy Jackson & the Olympians Series. (p. 528)
Riordan, Rick, et al. Vespers Rising. (p. 2354)
Riordan, Timothy B. Prince of Quacks: The Notorious Life of Dr. Francis Tumblety, Charlatan & Jack the Ripper Suspect (p. 1794)
Rios, Daniela, illus. see B, Maggie.
Ríos, Esmeralda, illus. see Llamas Camacho, Edith.
Ríos, Esmeralda, illus. see Mariano Leyva, José.
Rios, Janet. Millas Hacia la Libertad. (p. 1467)
Rios, Julia & Krasnostein, Alisa, eds. Year's Best YA Speculative Fiction 2015. (p. 2519)
Rios, Margarita, tr. see Rios, Yuri M.
Rios, Michael. Sudoku Puzzles for Clever Kids. (p. 2147)
Rios, Seth, illus. see Cannon, Barney.
Rios, Yuri M. Kingdom of Ice. Rios, Margarita, tr. (p. 1222)
Riou, jt. auth. see Verne, Jules.
Riou, Edouard, jt. auth. see Enault, Louis.
Riou, Gaston. Diary of a French Private: War Imprisonment 1914 1915 (Classic Reprint) (p. 539)
Rioux, Jacqueline. Why Dragons Cannot Go Shopping. Mar, Sandra, illus. (p. 2457)
Rioux, Jo, illus. see Anderson, M. T.
Rioux, Jo-Anne, illus. see Labatt, Mary.
Ripa, Cesare. Iconologia: Or, Moral Emblems (Classic Reprint) (p. 1088)
—Iconologia: Overo Descrittione Di Diverse Imagini Cauate Dall'antichita, et Di Propria Inuentione (Classic Reprint) (p. 1088)
Ripa, Matteo. Memoirs of Father Ripa: During Thirteen Years' Residence at the Court of Peking in the Service of the Emperor of China; with an Account of the Foundation of the College for the Education of Young Chinese at Naples (Classic Reprint) (p. 1444)
Ripes, Laura. Spaghetti-Slurping Sewer Serpent Zenz, Aaron, illus. (p. 2073)
Riphagen, Loes. Animals Home Alone. (p. 94)
Ripken, Cal, Jr. Hothead. (p. 1007)
Ripken Jr., Cal. Cal Ripken Jr. 's All-Stars Super-Sized Slugger. Cowherd, Kevin, illus. (p. 309)
—Closer. (p. 407)
—Out at Home. (p. 1682)
Ripley, Abida. Finding Family. (p. 729)
—Karate Monster. (p. 1203)
—Linah's Helpers: A Multicultural Story. (p. 1303)
—Paper Tiger P. (p. 1697)
—Rainbow Tea. (p. 1837)
Ripley, Catherine. How? The Most Awesome Question & Answer Book about Nature, Animals, People, Places—And You! Ritchie, Scot, illus. (p. 1025)
—Why? The Best Ever Question & Answer Book about Nature, Science & the World Around You. Ritchie, Scot, illus. (p. 2454)
Ripley, Eliza. Social Life in Old New Orleans: Being Recollections of My Girlhood (Classic Reprint) (p. 2053)
Ripley, Ellen. Erosion. (p. 660)
—What Are Rules & Laws? (p. 2405)
Ripley, Ellen, jt. auth. see Mills, Nathan.
Ripley Entertainment. All Consuming. (p. 51)
—Amazing Earth. (p. 64)
—Beyond Belief. (p. 211)
—Beyond Understanding. (p. 212)
—Life in the Fast Lane. (p. 1292)
—Off the Wall. (p. 1640)
—Taking Life to Extremes. (p. 2178)
—Totally Obsessed. (p. 2267)

—Werewolves (p. 2401)
—What Is a Family? (p. 2413)
—What Would You Do? (p. 2422)
—What's Great about Connecticut? (p. 2423)
—What's Great about New Hampshire? (p. 2424)
—Women in Fashion (p. 2487)
—Women in War (p. 2487)
—World War I: Why They Fought. (p. 2505)
—Yoga for You. (p. 2523)
—Yoga for Your Mind & Body: A Teenage Practice for a Healthy, Balanced Life. (p. 2523)
—You're Hired! Business Basics Every Babysitter Needs to Know (p. 2535)
Rissman, Rebecca, jt. auth. see Burgan, Michael.
Rissman, Rebecca, jt. auth. see Harris, Nancy.
Rissman, Rebecca, jt. auth. see Higgins, Melissa.
Rissman, Rebecca, jt. auth. see Jones, Jen.
Rissman, Rebecca, jt. auth. see Mortensen, Lori.
Rissman, Rebecca & Boone, Mary. Beauty Hacks. (p. 185)
Rissman, Rebecca & Smith, Sian. Caring for Your Teeth (p. 331)
—Eating Well (p. 622)
—Getting Exercise (p. 825)
—Keeping Clean (p. 1208)
—Staying Safe in the Sun (p. 2110)
Rissman, Rebecca, et al. Amazing Animal Architects. (p. 63)
Risso, Lidia Leticia. Ensamblar. (p. 656)
—Huellas. (p. 1047)
Ristaino, Andy. Escape from Dullsville. (p. 661)
Ristau, Kate. Clockbreakers. (p. 406)
—Shadow Girl. (p. 1996)
Ristord, Emmanuel, illus. see Hedelin, Pascale.
Ristow, Trevor, illus. see Ehrenhaft, Daniel.
Ristuccia, Michelle a. Charlie Cat Does Not Like Halloween. (p. 359)
Riswold, Gilbert, illus. see Noyes, Alfred.
Rita, Albert. Bravo! Brio: A Holiday Adventure-Fantasy. (p. 277)
Rita, Author of. Confidences (Classic Reprint) (p. 439)
Rita, Rita. Corinna, Vol. 3: A Study (Classic Reprint) (p. 454)
—Darby & Joan (Classic Reprint) (p. 504)
—Diana of the Ephesians: A Novel (Classic Reprint) (p. 538)
—Good Mrs. Hypocrite: A Study in Self-Righteousness (Classic Reprint) (p. 863)
—Grey Life: A Romance of Modern Bath (Classic Reprint) (p. 896)
—Husband of Importance (Classic Reprint) (p. 1055)
—Jill's Journal: A Novel (Classic Reprint) (p. 1168)
—Laird o Cockpen (Classic Reprint) (p. 1240)
—Laird o' Cockpen, Vol. 1 Of 3: A Novel (Classic Reprint) (p. 1240)
—Laird o Cockpen, Vol. 2: A Novel (Classic Reprint) (p. 1240)
—Man in Possession (Classic Reprint) (p. 1394)
—Master Wilberforce: The Study of a Boy (Classic Reprint) (p. 1419)
—Miss. Kate: Or, Confessions of a Caretaker (Classic Reprint) (p. 1479)
—My Lady Coquette, Vol. 1 Of 3: A Novel (Classic Reprint) (p. 1551)
—Peg, the Rake (Classic Reprint) (p. 1714)
—Pointing Finger (Classic Reprint) (p. 1767)
—Souls: A Comedy of Intentions (Classic Reprint) (p. 2066)
Ritch, Catherine. Zipper Finds a Job. Trexler, Jennifer Suther, illus. (p. 2541)
Ritcher, Paul O. Siren, Vol. 21: September, 1930 (Classic Reprint) (p. 2026)
Ritchey, Jessica, illus. see Stiller, Catrina.
Ritchey, Kate. Goofy's Sledding Contest. (p. 869)
—Huey, Dewey, & Louie's Rainy Day. (p. 1047)
—Perfect Picnic. (p. 1722)
Ritchey, Kate & Bader, Bonnie. Lion, Tiger, & Bear, Level 4. (p. 1306)
Ritchie, Alison. C'Est Pas Bientot Fini les Mou. (p. 353)
—Me & My Grandma! Edgson, Alison, illus. (p. 1433)
—Me & My Grandpa! (p. 1433)
—Tortoise & the Hare. Noj, Nahta, illus. (p. 2266)
Ritchie, Anna Cora. Mimic Life, or Before & Behind the Curtain: A Series of Narratives (Classic Reprint) (p. 1469)
—Twin Roses: A Narrative (Classic Reprint) (p. 2305)
Ritchie, Anne Thackeray. Blackstick Papers (Classic Reprint) (p. 240)
—Chapters from Some Unwritten Memoirs. (p. 357)
—Chapters from Some Unwritten Memoirs (Classic Reprint) (p. 357)
—Jack the Giant-Killer (Classic Reprint) (p. 1153)
—Miss. Angel, and, Fulham Lawn (Classic Reprint) (p. 1478)
—Mrs. Dymond, Vol. 1 of 2 (Classic Reprint) (p. 1522)
—Story of Elizabeth: With Other Tales & Sketches (Classic Reprint) (p. 2130)
—Toilers & Spinsters: And Other Essays (Classic Reprint) (p. 2256)
—Village on the Cliff (Classic Reprint) (p. 2358)
Ritchie, Archibald Tucker. Dynamical Theory of the Formation of the Earth, Vol. 2 (Classic Reprint) (p. 612)
Ritchie, Brendan. Beyond Carousel. (p. 211)
—Carousel. (p. 333)
Ritchie, David, jt. auth. see Gates, Alexander E.
Ritchie, Edward Wilson. Roll Call (Classic Reprint) (p. 1898)
Ritchie, Garrett, et al. Beep! Navigating Through ADHD. (p. 189)
Ritchie, J. Ewing. Night Side of London (Classic Reprint) (p. 1607)
Ritchie, Kate. I Just Couldn't Wait to Meet You. Somerville, Hannah, illus. (p. 1066)
Ritchie, Krista & Ritchie, Becca. Last Hope: A Raging Ones Novel. (p. 1248)
—Raging Ones. (p. 1834)
Ritchie, Leitch. Game of Life (Classic Reprint) (p. 807)
—Travelling Sketches on the Rhine, & in Belgium & Holland: With Twenty-Six Beautifully Finished Engravings, from Drawings by Clarkson Stanfield, Esq. (Classic Reprint) (p. 2280)
Ritchie, Lily Munsell. Chicken Little Jane. (p. 368)
Ritchie, Mary, ed. see Dunning, Rebecca.
Ritchie, Miss Thackeray. From an Island: A Story & Some Essays (Classic Reprint) (p. 790)
Ritchie, Paymaneh. Hello, My Name Is Oliver. (p. 951)
Ritchie, Ritchie. From Friend to Friend: With a Portrait (Classic Reprint) (p. 791)
Ritchie, Robert Welles. Dust of the Desert (Classic Reprint) (p. 611)
—Trails to Two Moons (Classic Reprint) (p. 2275)
Ritchie, Scot. Everything Kids' More Puzzles Book: From Mazes to Hidden Pictures - & Hours of Fun in Between. (p. 673)
—Federica (p. 717)
—Follow That Bee! A First Book of Bees in the City. Ritchie, Scot, illus. (p. 757)
—Follow That Map! A First Book of Mapping Skills. Ritchie, Scot, illus. (p. 757)
—Join the No-Plastic Challenge! A First Book of Reducing Waste. Ritchie, Scot, illus. (p. 1175)
—Lilliana & the Frogs. (p. 1301)
—Look at That Building! A First Book of Structures. Ritchie, Scot, illus. (p. 1345)
—Look Where We Live! A First Book of Community Building. Ritchie, Scot, illus. (p. 1346)
—My House Is Alive! The Weird & Wonderful Sounds Your House Makes. (p. 1550)
—Owen at the Park (p. 1688)
—P'ésk'a & the First Salmon Ceremony (p. 1726)
—See How We Move! A First Book of Health & Well-Being. Ritchie, Scot, illus. (p. 1981)
—See What We Eat! A First Book of Healthy Eating. Ritchie, Scot, illus. (p. 1982)
Ritchie, Scot, illus. see Graves, Harmon.
Ritchie, Scot, illus. see Heidbreder, Robert.
Ritchie, Scot, illus. see Moser, Elise.
Ritchie, Scot, illus. see Ripley, Catherine.
Riti, Marsha, illus. see Barkley, Callie.
Riti, Marsha, illus. see Brokamp, Elizabeth.
Ritland, Mike, et al. Navy SEAL Dogs: My Tale of Training Canines for Combat. (p. 1583)
Ritner, Amelia. Puppy Who Wasn't. Leidemer, Adam, illus. (p. 1815)
Ritorto, Kristina. I Am a Survivor. (p. 1057)
Rits, Susan Katherine. Pirates of Bair Island. (p. 1751)
Ritson, Amanda. Where Has My Mother Gone? (p. 2437)
Ritson, Joseph. Fairy Tales, Legends & Romances Illustrating Shakespeare & Other Early English Writers: To Which Are Prefixed Two Preliminary Dissertations I. on Pigmies, II. on Fairies (Classic Reprint) (p. 698)
—Gammer Gurton's Garland, or the Nursery Parnassus: A Choice Collection of Pretty Songs & Verses for the Amusement of All Little Good Children Who Can Neither Read nor Run (Classic Reprint) (p. 808)
—Now First Collected; to Which Are Prefixed Two Dissertations: 1. Two on Pygmies, 2. Fairies (Classic Reprint) (p. 1627)
—Robin Hood: A Collection of the Popular Poems, Songs, & Ballads, Relative to That Celebrated English Outlaw (Classic Reprint) (p. 1891)
—Robin Hood: A Collection of All the Ancient Poems, Songs & Ballads, Now Extant, Relative to That Celebrated English Outlaw (Classic Reprint) (p. 1891)
—Robin Hood: A Collection of All the Ancient Poems, Songs, & Ballads, Now Extant Relative to That Celebrated English Outlaw. to Which Are Prefixed Historical Anecdotes of His Life, Vol. II. (p. 1891)
—Robin Hood: A Collection of All the Ancient Poems, Songs, & Ballads, Now Extant, Relative to That Celebrated English Outlaw; to Which Are Prefixed Historical Anecdotes of His Life (Classic Reprint) (p. 1891)
—Robin Hood: A Collection of All the Ancient Poems, Songs, & Ballads, Now Extant Relative to That Celebrated English Outlaw. to Which Are Prefixed Historical Anecdotes of His Life, in Two Volumes, Vol. I. [London-1832]. (p. 1891)
—Robin Hood, Vol. 1: A Collection of All the Ancient Poems, Songs, & Ballads, Now Extant Relative to That Celebrated English Outlaw (Classic Reprint) (p. 1891)
—Robin Hood, Vol. 1: Collection of All the Ancient Poems, Songs, & Ballads, Now Extant Relative to That Celebrated English Outlaw, to Which Are Prefixed Historical Anecdotes of His Life (Classic Reprint) (p. 1891)
—Select Collection English Songs, Vol. 3 Of 3: With Their Original Airs; & a Historical Essay on the Origin & Progress of National Song (Classic Reprint) (p. 1985)
—Select Collection English Songs, with Their Original Airs, Vol. 2 Of 3: And a Historical Essay on the Origin & Progress of National Song (Classic Reprint) (p. 1985)
—Select Collection of English Songs. (p. 1985)
—Select Collection of English Songs, Vol. 3 of 3 (Classic Reprint) (p. 1985)
—Select Collection of English Songs, with Their Original Airs, Vol. 1 Of 3: And a Historical Essay on the Origin & Progress of National Song (Classic Reprint) (p. 1985)
Ritson, Joseph, et al. Fairy Tales, Legends & Romances. (p. 698)
Ritt, Allye M. Taking the Ice: Khalli's Big Test. (p. 2178)
Rittenberg, Max. Every Man His Price (Classic Reprint) (p. 670)
—Swirling Waters (Classic Reprint) (p. 2170)
Rittenhouse, Ralph, ed. see Donahue, Laurie.
Rittenhouse, Ralph, jt. auth. see Donahue, Laurie.
Rittenhouse, Rufus. Boyhood Life in Iowa: Forty Years Ago, As Found in the Memoirs of Rufus Rittenhouse (Classic Reprint) (p. 271)
Ritter, Adam, illus. see Hsu, Stacey W.
Ritter, Christie R. Mother Teresa: Humanitarian & Advocate for the Poor (p. 1510)
Ritter, Christie Rose. Obesity. (p. 1634)
—South Africa (p. 2068)
Ritter, Elizabeth. Guitarra de Mi Hermano (My Brother's Guitar) de la Vega, Eida, tr. (p. 904)
—Guitarra de Mi Hermano / My Brother's Guitar. de la Vega, Eida, tr. (p. 904)
—My Brother's Guitar. (p. 1535)
Ritter, Elizabeth A. Happy Valentine's Day! (p. 924)
Ritter, John P. Book of Mock Trials: Containing Fourteen Original Plays, Representing Humorous Court-Room Scenes, Adapted to the Limits of the Parlor, & Arranged for Public or Private Performances (Classic Reprint) (p. 259)
—Crossroads of Destiny (Classic Reprint) (p. 478)
Ritter, Maria. Adventures of Wilhelm, a Rat's Tale. (p. 29)
Ritter, William. Beastly Bones: A Jackaby Novel. (p. 182)
—Beastly Bones. (p. 182)
—Dire King: A Jackaby Novel. (p. 552)
—Ghostly Echoes: A Jackaby Novel. (p. 829)
—Jackaby. (p. 1153)
—Oddmire, Book 1: Changeling. (p. 1638)
Ritterhouse, Jennifer. Discovering the South: One Man's Travels Through a Changing America in The 1930s. (p. 556)
Rittershaus, Adeline. Die Neuisländischen Volksmärchen: Gesammelte Geschichten Von Elfen, Trollen und Gespenstern (Vollständige Ausgabe) (p. 544)
Rittman, Dede. Color Grady with Glasses. (p. 420)
—Grady Gets Glasses. (p. 875)
Rittmueller, Jeanne, illus. see Haave, Meghan.
Ritz, C. Tiger's World: Growing Up. (p. 2242)
Ritz, Karen, illus. see Bunting, Eve.
Ritz, Karen, illus. see Pearson, Yvonne.
Ritz, Karen, illus. see Ransom, Candice.
Ritz, Karen, illus. see Wetterer, Margaret K.
Ritz, Lee F. Sun & the Wind. Hale, Randy, illus. (p. 2151)
Ritzmann, Christine. These Are the Things That I Found in Your Fur. (p. 2218)
Ritzmann, Mary B., illus. see Riachi, Ghassan Diab & Mitchell, Anna B.
RIUS. Atlas para niñas y niños / Atlas for Girls & Boys. (p. 134)
Riva Palacio, Mariana. Incas. Sánchez, Diego Francisco, illus. (p. 1112)
Riva Palacio Obon, Martha. Orfeo. (p. 1670)
Riva, Peter. Kidnapped on Safari: A Thriller. (p. 1213)
Rivadeneira, Caryn. Grit & Grace Betz, Katy, illus. (p. 897)
—Gritty & Graceful: 15 Inspiring Women of the Bible Soekamo, Sonya Abby, illus. (p. 897)
—It's Not Fair! A Book about Having Enough Muñoz, Isabel, illus. (p. 1146)
—Mine! A Counting Book about Sharing Gulliver, Amanda, illus. (p. 1470)
—Noodle Helps Gabriel Say Goodbye. Alpaugh, Priscilla, illus. (p. 1618)
—Penny Helps Portia Face Her Fears. Alpaugh, Priscilla, illus. (p. 1717)
—Robot Helps Max & Lily Deal with Bullies. Alpaugh, Priscilla, illus. (p. 1892)
—Sparky Helps Mary Make Friends. Alpaugh, Priscilla, illus. (p. 2075)
—Wrong Shoes: A Book about Money & Self-Esteem Ross, Graham, illus. (p. 2514)
Rivadeneira, Caryn Dahlstrand. Story of Noah's Ark: A Spark Bible Story. Grosshauser, Peter, illus. (p. 2132)
Rivard, Émilie & Rivard, Émilie. Really & Truly. Delisle, Anne-Claire, illus. (p. 1851)
Rivard, Erin. Agattu: The Alaskan Caribou. (p. 35)
Rivard, Joanna. Tiny Truths Wonder & Wisdom: Everyday Reminders from Psalms & Proverbs (p. 2250)
Rivard, Joanna & Penner, Tim. Tiny Truths Illustrated Bible (p. 2250)
Rivard, Rebecca, illus. see Zolty, Meredith.
Rivas, Joe, et al. Special Needs. (p. 2077)
Rivas, Miguel Díaz, illus. see FGTeeV.
Rivas, Miguel Díaz, illus. see Oxtra, Cristina.
Rivas, Spelile. Cucuy Stole My Cascarones / el Coco Me Robó Los Cascarones. Baeza Ventura, Gabriela, tr. (p. 482)
Rivas, Spelile & Plascencia, Amira. No Time for Monsters/No Hay Tiempo para Monstruos. Cervantes, Valeria, illus. (p. 1615)
Rivas, Victor, illus. see Andersen, Hans & Stone Arch Books Staff.
Rivas, Victor, illus. see Lyons, Jayne.
Rivas, Victor, illus. see Meister, Cari.
Rivas, Victor, illus. see Miedoso, Andres.
Rivas, Victor, illus. see Peabody, Erin.
Rivas, Victor, illus. see Schwartz, Alvin.
Rivas, Victor, illus. see Stone Arch Books Staff.
Rivens, Beverly. Who's Playing Who. (p. 2453)
River, Felipe, tr. see Espada, Carlos.
River Lake Press. Osprey Summer. (p. 1674)
Rivera, Addy, illus. see Platt, Christine.
Rivera, Alane & Rivera, Raymundo. Rocks, Jeans, & Busy Machines: An Engineering Kids Storybook. (p. 1896)
Rivera, Alba Marina, illus. see Saki.
Rivera, Alex. Bronxshapes. Rivera, Alex, illus. (p. 285)
—Bronxtones. Rivera, Alex, illus. (p. 285)
Rivera, Andrea. Air. (p. 37)
—Airplanes. (p. 37)
—Boats. (p. 251)
—Cars. (p. 334)
—Cloth. (p. 407)
—Clouds. (p. 408)
—Conservation. (p. 442)
—Deserts. (p. 532)
—Droughts. (p. 606)
—Earthquakes. (p. 617)
—Forests. (p. 767)
—Fossils. (p. 770)
—Gems. (p. 813)
—Glass. (p. 841)
—Grasslands. (p. 881)
—Gravity. (p. 882)
—Hurricanes. (p. 1054)
—Inclined Planes. (p. 1113)
—Lakes & Rivers. (p. 1240)
—Levers. (p. 1282)
—Light. (p. 1298)
—Living & Nonliving. (p. 1333)
—Metal. (p. 1452)
—Minerals. (p. 1471)
—Moon. (p. 1501)
—Motion. (p. 1511)
—Motorcycles. (p. 1512)
—Mountains. (p. 1514)
—Oceans. (p. 1636)
—Ores. (p. 1670)
—Paper. (p. 1697)
—Plants. (p. 1757)
—Plastic. (p. 1758)
—Pulleys. (p. 1812)
—Rain. (p. 1835)
—Recycling. (p. 1855)
—Rocks. (p. 1896)
—Screws. (p. 1965)
—Snow. (p. 2046)
—Soils. (p. 2055)
—Solar Power. (p. 2055)
—Sound. (p. 2067)
—Sun. (p. 2151)
—Thunder & Lightning. (p. 2238)
—Tornadoes. (p. 2265)
—Trains. (p. 2276)
—Trucks. (p. 2293)
—Tsunamis. (p. 2298)
—Water. (p. 2384)
—Wedges. (p. 2395)
—Wheels & Axles. (p. 2428)
—Wildfires. (p. 2466)
—Wind Power. (p. 2471)
—Wood. (p. 2491)
Rivera, Ann. Baby Alpaca's Adventure. Brizzi, Liz, illus. (p. 148)
Rivera Carbajal, Adriana, illus. see Moran Gama, Claudia Elena.
Rivera, Carlos. Technology Brings Us Together - 6 Pack: Set of 6 with Teacher Materials Common Core Edition. (p. 2197)
Rivera, Dee Dee. In the Beginning. (p. 1107)
Rivera, Dee Dee & Clark, F. M. Little Pine. (p. 1324)
Rivera, Dewey. I Did Not Get First Place. (p. 1064)
Rivera, Diego, illus. see Marín, Guadalupe Rivera.
Rivera, Felipe. Entrevistando un Gigante. (p. 657)
Rivera, Fernando. Changdinho. (p. 355)
Rivera, Gabby. Juliet Takes a Breath. (p. 1187)
Rivera, Hanae, illus. see Justice, William E.
Rivera, Lilliam. Dealing in Dreams. (p. 519)
—Education of Margot Sanchez. (p. 626)
—Goldie Vance: the Hotel Whodunit. Power, Elle, illus. (p. 860)
—Never Look Back. (p. 1590)
Rivera, Lorna A. Bailey Becomes a Therapy Dog. Matthews, Amanda L., illus. (p. 159)
Rivera, Marc. Life Can Be a Piece of Cake! (p. 1290)
Rivera, Mariano. Closer: Young Readers Edition. (p. 407)
Rivera, Matthew, illus. see Britain, Lory.
Rivera, Matthew, illus. see Cattie, Becky & Luebbe, Tara.
Rivera, Matthew, illus. see Chen, Eva.
Rivera, Matthew, illus. see Gates, Mariam.
Rivera, Paolo Manuel. Spider-Man: One Moment in Time. (p. 2080)
Rivera, Rafael, et al. Baseball on Mars/Béisbol en Marte. Rivera, Rafael et al, illus. (p. 169)
Rivera, Raquel. Show Mode (p. 2012)
—Tuk & the Whale Gerber, Mary Jane, illus. (p. 2299)
Rivera, Roberta, illus. see Krapp, JoAnn Vergona.
Rivera, Ryan. A Is for Atlanta. (p. 1)
Rivera, Sheila, jt. auth. see Howard, Melanie A.
Rivera Sonda, Addy, illus. see Alessandri, Alexandra.
Rivera-Ashford, Aaron. Ralph Wrecks This Book! (p. 1838)
Rivera-Ashford, Roni Capin. My Tata's Remedies - Los Remedios de Mi Tata. Castro L., Antonio, illus. (p. 1562)
Rivera-Lassen, Carmen Leonor. No estás. (p. 1612)
—Qué crees? Astacio, Mrinall Álvarez, illus. (p. 1822)
River-Jedd, Ridgley. Figureheads of Petty Port. (p. 726)
Rivero, Marcos Almada, illus. see Esperon, Maria Garcia.
Rivero, Marcos Almada, illus. see Gundersheimer (Mister G), Ben.
Rivero Weber, Paulina. Zooetica: Una Mirada Filosofica a Los Animales. (p. 2543)
Rivers, Dean. Conundrums, Riddles & Puzzles: Containing One Thousand of the Latest & Best Conundrums, Gathered from Every Conceivable Source, & Comprising Many That Are Entirely New & Original (Classic Reprint) (p. 446)
—Full of Fun: Comprising Conundrums, Talks, Jokes (Classic Reprint) (p. 797)
Rivers, Doug E. Banjora: The Bat That Couldn't Fly. (p. 164)
Rivers, George R. R. Captain Shays: A Populist of 1786 (Classic Reprint) (p. 326)
—Count's Snuff-Box: A Romance of Washington & Buzzard's Bay During the War of Bay (Classic Reprint) (p. 461)
Rivers, George Robert Russell. Governor's Garden: A Relation of Some Passages in the Life of His Excellency Thomas Hutchinson, Sometime Captain-General & Governor-In-Chief of His Majesty's Province of Massachusetts Bay (Classic Reprint) (p. 873)
Rivers, Karen. All That Was. (p. 53)
—Encyclopedia of Me. (p. 648)
—Finding Ruby Starling. (p. 730)
—Girl in the Well Is Me. (p. 836)
—Love, Ish. (p. 1360)
—Naked Mole Rat Saves the World. (p. 1573)
—Possibility of Whales. (p. 1780)
—What Is Real (p. 2416)
—You Are the Everything. (p. 2525)
Rivers, Lawrence. Coretta Scott King (p. 454)
Rivers, Mary. Mr. Marshmallow. (p. 1519)
Rivers, Olivia. Tone Deaf. (p. 2260)
Rivers, P. S. Who Is Santa Claus? (p. 2448)
Rivers, Phoebe. Ghost Town (p. 828)
—Ghost Town. (p. 828)
—Giving up the Ghost (p. 840)
—Giving up the Ghost. (p. 840)
—Haunted Memories (p. 938)
—Haunted Memories. (p. 938)
—Kindred Spirits. (p. 1219)
—Mischief Night. (p. 1477)

R

Bone, Prevented or Cured by Balancing the Foot (Classic Reprint) (p. 761)
Roberge, Tracy. Jacob & Alec Explore Shenzhen's Windows of the World. (p. 1154)
—Jacob & Alec Move to Hong Kong. (p. 1154)
Roberson, Carra, ed. see Alexander, Cory.
Roberson, Emily. Lifestyles of Gods & Monsters. (p. 1297)
Roberson, Jennifer. Jesus Shows Love Inside & Out. (p. 1166)
Roberson, Karen L. If I Take My Horse to School. Boyce, Tami, illus. (p. 1091)
Roberson, Karla, jt. auth. see Scholastic, Inc. Staff.
Roberson, Melondy. Adriann Takes a Stand. Offord, Roszella, illus. (p. 17)
Roberston, Alison. Rigby Reading Sails: Leveled Reader Emerald Grades 4-5 Book 11: Flower Power. (p. 1881)
—Rigby Reading Sails: Leveled Reader Emerald Grades 4-5 Book 4: Mind Your Manners. (p. 1881)
Robert, Belt & Harte, Lawrence. Sales Representative Agreements: How to Get Better Company/Rep Relationships, Increase Sales, & Reduce Conflicts. (p. 1924)
Robert, Bruno, illus. see Feek, Rory.
Robert, Bruno, illus. see Fusek Peters, Andrew.
Robert, Bruno, illus. see Shaw, Stephanie.
Robert, Bulla Clyde. Chalk Box Kid. (p. 354)
Robert, Bulla Clyde & Bulla. Shoeshine Girl. (p. 2009)
Robert, Bulla Clyde & Clyde, Bulla. Lion to Guard Us. (p. 1306)
Robert, Cormier. Chocolate War. (p. 380)
Robert, E. Methode de Langue Anglaise, Vol. 1 (Classic Reprint) (p. 1453)
Robert, Kraus. Leo the Late Bloomer. (p. 1267)
Robert, LeyHonor, illus. see Hawes, Alison.
Robert, Lipsyte. Contender. (p. 444)
Robert, Louis de. Eternal Enigma: A Romance in the Life of Yvette Guilbert (Classic Reprint) (p. 665)
Robert, Lytle. Mr. Blair's Labyrinth. Gayle, Vandercook, illus. (p. 1517)
Robert, Margaret B. Mademoiselle Mori, Vol. 2 Of 2: A Tale of Modern Rome (Classic Reprint) (p. 1375)
Robert, Nadine. Bruno, the Standing Cat. Jullien, Jean, illus. (p. 288)
—Elsie. Kastelic, Maja, illus. (p. 639)
—Joseph Fipps. Godbout, Genevieve, illus. (p. 1178)
—Toshi's Little Treasures. Aki, Aki, illus. (p. 2266)
Robert, Na'ima B. Going to Mecca. Cavallini, Valentina, illus. (p. 855)
—Mabrook! a World of Muslim Weddings. Adl, Shirin, illus. (p. 1371)
—Ramadan Moon. Adl, Shirin, illus. (p. 1839)
Robert, Nolan. What Are Natural Resources? (p. 2405)
Robert, Peters. Da Goodie Monsta. Robert, Peters, illus. (p. 494)
Robert, Robert Lee. My First Ubie the Ubinator Coloring Book: Alphabet Wonders. Mathis, Shawn, illus. (p. 1540)
Robert Ross, Editor, ed. see Wilde, Oscar.
Robert, Sion. Shadows from the Past. (p. 1998)
Robert, Yannick, illus. see Goodhart, Pippa.
Robert, Yannick, illus. see Husar, Stephane.
Robert, Yannick, illus. see Page, Nick & Page, Claire.
Robert, Yannick, jt. auth. see Cali, Davide.
Robert-Dumas, Charles. Grandmother's Fairy Tales (Classic Reprint) (p. 879)
Robert-Houdin, Jean-Eugène. Memoirs of Robert-Houdin, Ambassador, Author, & Conjuror, Vol. 1 of 2 (Classic Reprint) (p. 1445)
Roberti, Alessandra, illus. see Milbourne, Anna.
Roberti, Alessandra, jt. auth. see Milbourne, Anna.
Roberto, Anna, ed. see Mewburn, Kyle.
Roberto, Nelsa. Illegally Blonde. (p. 1095)
Roberton, Fiona. Tale of Two Beasts. (p. 2180)
Roberts. Delmore, or Modern Friendship, Vol. 1 Of 3: A Novel (Classic Reprint) (p. 527)
—Duty: A Novel, Vol. 2 of 3 (Classic Reprint) (p. 611)
—Duty: A Novel, Vol. 3 of 3 (Classic Reprint) (p. 611)
Roberts (Tomfoolery), Tomos. Great Realization. Nomoco, illus. (p. 888)
Roberts, Abigail B. Using a Thermometer. (p. 2341)
—Using Lenses. (p. 2341)
—Using Measuring Cups. (p. 2342)
Roberts, Alice Jane, illus. see Roberts, Trixie.
Roberts, Alice Jane, illus. see Woodcock, Jane.
Roberts, Angela. Barbie Loves Ballet. Wolcott, Karen, illus. (p. 165)
—Ponies! (p. 1773)
Roberts, Barbara. Adventures of Phoebe Flower: Stories of a Girl with ADHD. (p. 26)
Roberts, Barbara Carroll. Nikki on the Line. (p. 1609)
Roberts, Becca. Tornadoes. (p. 2265)
Roberts, Becky. Grannie B the Wise Old Owl. (p. 880)
Roberts, Bethany. Easter Mice! (p. 620)
—Valentine Mice! (p. 2344)
—Valentine Mice! Cushman, Doug, illus. (p. 2344)
—Valentine Mice! Board Book. Cushman, Doug, illus. (p. 2344)
Roberts, Casey, tr. see Hotte, Sylvain.
Roberts, Cecil. Adrift in America: Or Work & Adventure in the States (Classic Reprint) (p. 17)
—Goose Fair: A Novel (Classic Reprint) (p. 869)
—Sails of Sunset: A Novel (Classic Reprint) (p. 1923)
Roberts, Ceri. Refugees & Migrants. Kai, Hanane, illus. (p. 1861)
Roberts, Chalmers. Tales from Blackwood: Being the Most Famous Series of Stories Ever (Classic Reprint) (p. 2182)
Roberts, Charles. Manual of Anthropometry, or a Guide to the Physical Examination & Measurement of the Human Body: Containing a Systematic Table of Measurements, an Anthropometrical Chart or Register, & Instructions for Making Measurements on an Uniform Plan. (p. 1399)
Roberts, Charles G. D. Around the Camp-Fire (Classic Reprint) (p. 118)
—Backwoodsmen (Classic Reprint) (p. 156)
—Balkan Prince (Classic Reprint) (p. 161)
—By the Marshes of Minas (Classic Reprint) (p. 306)
—Children of the Wild (Classic Reprint) (p. 372)
—Earth's Enigmas (Classic Reprint) (p. 618)
—Feet of the Furtive (Classic Reprint) (p. 719)
—Forge in the Forest: Being the Narrative of the Acadian Ranger, Jean de Mer, Seigneur de Briart; & How He Crossed the Black ABBE; & of His Adventures in a Strange Fellowship (Classic Reprint) (p. 767)
—Heart of the Ancient Wood (Classic Reprint) (p. 945)
—Heart That Knows (Classic Reprint) (p. 945)
—Hoof & Claw (Classic Reprint) (p. 1000)
—Jim: The Story of a Backwoods Police Dog (Classic Reprint) (p. 1168)
—King of the Mamozekel: Illustrated by Charles Livingston Bull (Classic Reprint) (p. 1221)
—Kings in Exile (Classic Reprint) (p. 1223)
—Kings Treasuries of Literature (Classic Reprint) (p. 1223)
—Ledge on Bald Face (Classic Reprint) (p. 1260)
—More Kindred of the Wild (Classic Reprint) (p. 1505)
—Neighbors Unknown (Classic Reprint) (p. 1586)
—Raid from Beausejour & How the Carter Boys Lifted the Mortgage: Two Stories of Acadie (Classic Reprint) (p. 1834)
—Secret Trails (Classic Reprint) (p. 1979)
—Sister to Evangeline: Being the Story of Yvonne de Lamourie, & How She Went into Exile with the Villagers of Grand Pre (Classic Reprint) (p. 2027)
Roberts, Charles George Douglas. Barbara Ladd (Classic Reprint) (p. 165)
—Feet of the Furtive (Classic Reprint) (p. 719)
—House in the Water: A Book of Animal Stories (Classic Reprint) (p. 1022)
—House Party: An Account of Stories Told at a Gathering of Famous American Authors (Classic Reprint) (p. 1024)
—In the Deep of the Snow (Classic Reprint) (p. 1108)
—In the Morning of Time (Classic Reprint) (p. 1110)
—Kindred of the Wild: A Book of Animal Life (Classic Reprint) (p. 1219)
—Red Fox: The Story of His Adventurous Career in the Ringwaak Wilds & of His Final Triumph over the Enemies of His Kind (Classic Reprint) (p. 1857)
—Red Oxen of Bonval (Classic Reprint) (p. 1858)
—Watchers of the Trails: A Book of Animal Life (Classic Reprint) (p. 2383)
Roberts, Charles Humphrey. Down the o-Hi-O (Classic Reprint) (p. 590)
Roberts, Charlotte, illus. see Lynas, Peter.
Roberts, Chloe Garcia, tr. see Decur.
Roberts, Christa. Guinness World Records: Incredible Animals: Amazing Animals & Their Awesome Feats! (p. 904)
—Guinness World Records: Amazing Body Records! 100 Mind-Blowing Body Records from Around the World! (p. 904)
—Guinness World Records: Awesome Entertainers! (p. 904)
—Guinness World Records: Incredible Animals! (p. 904)
—Living the Dream. (p. 1334)
—Rio 2. (p. 1883)
Roberts, Cokie. Founding Mothers: Remembering the Ladies. Goode, Diane, illus. (p. 771)
Roberts, Cokie, jt. auth. see Bolden, Tonya.
Roberts, Constance. Sigil in Shadow. (p. 2016)
Roberts, D. W. Pep Squad Mysteries Book 1: Cavern in the Hills. (p. 1719)
—Pep Squad Mysteries Book 2:the Haunting of Townsand Hall. (p. 1719)
—Pep Squad Mysteries Book 4: Prediction of Danger. (p. 1719)
Roberts, Daniel. Adventures of Tumbleweed Smith. (p. 29)
—Boy & Dinosaur. (p. 268)
—Douglas Diggly Super Spy. (p. 589)
—Esmeralda's Picnic. (p. 662)
—Funny Jokes for Young Folks. (p. 801)
—Harrison & His Dinosaur Robot & the Little Sister. (p. 933)
—Harrison & His Dinosaur Robot Visit the Doctor. (p. 933)
—Harrison, Hadley & Their Dinosaur Robots. (p. 934)
—I Will Not Chew Gum in School. (p. 1085)
—Itchy Twitchy Nose. (p. 1142)
—It's the Biggest Booger in the World! (p. 1147)
—Lennon the Penguin Moves to the Beach. (p. 1266)
—Little Bugs' Bedtime. (p. 1313)
—Little Girl & the Unicorn. (p. 1317)
—Mildred the Scary Cow. (p. 1465)
—Monsters at Work. (p. 1497)
—Mouse with Superpowers. (p. 1515)
—My Brother Is a Brat. (p. 1534)
—Penguin's Vacation. (p. 1716)
—Sneaky Pie Bandits. (p. 2045)
—Trip Through Outer Space. (p. 2288)
—Wake up Book. (p. 2371)
Roberts, David. On a Night Like No Other. (p. 1652)
—Suffragette. Roberts, David, illus. (p. 2147)
Roberts, David, illus. see Ardagh, Philip.
Roberts, David, illus. see Beaty, Andrea.
Roberts, David, illus. see Bently, Peter.
Roberts, David, illus. see Clary, Julian.
Roberts, David, illus. see Compestine, Ying.
Roberts, David, illus. see Crimi, Carolyn.
Roberts, David, illus. see Crompton, Richmal.
Roberts, David, illus. see Donaldson, Julia.
Roberts, David, illus. see Fleischman, Paul.
Roberts, David, illus. see Gardner, Sally.
Roberts, David, illus. see Grahame, Kenneth.
Roberts, David, illus. see Lloyd-Jones, Sally.
Roberts, David, illus. see MacDonald, Alan.
Roberts, David, illus. see Macdonald, Alan.
Roberts, David, illus. see MacDonald, Alan.
Roberts, David, illus. see Priestley, Chris.
Roberts, David, illus. see Roberts, Lynn.
Roberts, David, illus. see Robinson, Michelle.
Roberts, David, illus. see Rosenthal, Amy Krouse.
Roberts, David, jt. auth. see MacDonald, Alan.
Roberts, Dean, et al. Complete English for Cambridge Lower Secondary. (p. 434)
Roberts, Deborah. Mr Otagiri's Promise. Ju-Young Im, Joy & Da-Young Im, Linda, illus. (p. 1519)
Roberts, Dw. Pep Squad Mysteries #19: Chaos Before the Costume Party. (p. 1719)
—Pep Squad Mysteries Book: Mystery in the Lions' Maze. (p. 1719)
—Pep Squad Mysteries Book: Trouble on Avalance Mountain. (p. 1719)
—Pep Squad Mysteries Book 18: Secret of the Magician's Trick. (p. 1719)
—Pep Squad Mysteries Book 20: Riddle of the Red Rock. (p. 1719)
—Pep Squad Mysteries Book 21: Ruse of the Ruthless Rustlers. (p. 1719)
—Pep Squad Mysteries Book 22: Terror in the Ghost Town. (p. 1719)
—Pep Squad Mysteries Book 7: The Deadly Doll. (p. 1719)
—Pep Squad Mysteries Book 8: Shock of the Scarecrow. (p. 1719)
Roberts, E. Alan. Noah & His Ark. (p. 1615)
Roberts, Edith Adelaide. Epidermal Cells of Roots: A Dissertation Submitted to the Faculty of the Ogden Graduate School, of Science in Candidacy for the Degree of Doctor of Philosophy (Department of Botany) (Classic Reprint) (p. 658)
Roberts, Edwards, jt. auth. see Jackson, Helen Hunt.
Roberts, Elbridge Gerry. Naval Engagement: A Marine Narrative of Love & War. (p. 1582)
—Naval Engagement: A Marine Narrative of Love & War (Classic Reprint) (p. 1582)
Roberts, Elizabeth Madox. Under the Tree (Classic Reprint) (p. 2323)
Roberts, Ellen Jane. Disastrous Dillon. (p. 553)
Roberts, Emily. Express Yourself: A Teen Girl's Guide to Speaking up & Being Who You Are. (p. 684)
Roberts, Erin. Child Who Never Was: A Bronnie Browne Mystery. (p. 370)
Roberts, Esylit Nest, jt. auth. see Paulsen, Gary.
Roberts, Evelyn. How to Be Wired for Career Success. (p. 1038)
Roberts, F. C. Historical Incidents: What Our Women in the War Did & Suffered (Classic Reprint) (p. 976)
Roberts, Florence. Fifteen Years with the Outcast (Classic Reprint) (p. 724)
Roberts, G. E. Theodore. Captain Love; the History of a Most Romantic Event in the Life of an English Gentleman During the Reign of His Majesty George the First (Classic Reprint) (p. 325)
—Flying Plover: His Stories, Told Him by Squat-By-the-Fire (Classic Reprint) (p. 755)
Roberts, Gaylia, illus. see Bishop, Rhonda.
Roberts, George. Roberts' Semi-Monthly Magazine for Town & Country, Vol. 13: July 15, 1841 (Classic Reprint) (p. 1891)
Roberts, H. Chalmers. Tales from Blackwood: Being the Most Famous Series of Stories Ever Published, Especially Selected from That Celebrated English Publication (Classic Reprint) (p. 2182)
—Tales from Blackwood: Being the Most Famous Series of Stories Ever Published, Especially Selected from That Celebrated English Publication. Series II, Vol. I. (p. 2182)
—Tales from Blackwood: Being the Most Famous Series of Stories Ever Published, Especially Selected from That Celebrated English Publication. Series II, Vol. VI. (p. 2182)
—Tales from Blackwood, Vol. 1: Being the Most Famous Series of Stories Ever Published, Especially Selected from That Celebrated English Publication (Classic Reprint) (p. 2182)
—Tales from Blackwood, Vol. 7: Being the Most Famous Series of Stories Ever Published Especially Selected from That Celebrated English Publication (Classic Reprint) (p. 2182)
Roberts, H. Donald. Adventures of Shuster: The Very Special Rooster. Gelhardt, Rob, illus. (p. 27)
Roberts, H. L. 23: 27. (p. 2554)
Roberts, Heather H. Raven & the Forest Angels. (p. 1843)
Roberts, In Pursuit of the Curious Bangle J. In Pursuit of the Curious Bangle. (p. 1106)
Roberts, J. P., illus. see Gnap, Jean.
Roberts, J. P., illus. see Lisbona, Margie Taylor.
Roberts, James. Face of the King (Classic Reprint) (p. 693)
—Starcadia Quest: Heart of a Star. Mazzara, Aurelio, illus. (p. 2105)
Roberts, James, et al. Transformers: IDW Collection Phase Two Volume 3 Milne, Alex & Salgado, Jimbo, illus. (p. 2277)
Roberts, Jenny. Barron's First Grammar, Punctuation & Spelling Dictionary: Includes Flashcards Plus Online Games & Worksheets. (p. 167)
Roberts, Jeremy. Beatles: Music Revolutionaries. (p. 182)
—Chinese Mythology A to Z, Second Edition. (p. 378)
—Drugs & Dieting. (p. 606)
—Japanese Mythology A to Z, Second Edition. (p. 1160)
Roberts, Jeremy, illus. see Sazaklis, John.
Roberts, Jeremy, jt. auth. see Ellis, Catherine.
Roberts, Jeremy, jt. auth. see Lowery, Zoe.
Roberts, Jeremy, jt. auth. see Roscoe, Kelly.
Roberts, Jeremy & Marion, V. Kenneth. Mind Games. (p. 1469)
Roberts, Jessie (Alexander). Jessie Alexander's Platform Sketches: Original & Adapted (Classic Reprint) (p. 1165)
Roberts, Jeyn. Dark Inside. (p. 506)
—Rage Within. (p. 1834)
—When They Fade. (p. 2434)
Roberts, Jillian. Just Enough Series Bundle. Revell, Cindy, illus. (p. 1193)
—On Our Nature Walk: Our First Talk about Our Impact on the Environment. Heinrichs, Jane, illus. (p. 1653)
—On the Internet: Our First Talk about Online Safety Heinrichs, Jane, illus. (p. 1655)
—On the News: Our First Talk about Tragedy Heinrichs, Jane, illus. (p. 1655)
—On the Playground: Our First Talk about Prejudice Heinrichs, Jane, illus. (p. 1655)
—Under Our Clothes: Our First Talk about Our Bodies Heinrichs, Jane, illus. (p. 2321)
—What Happens When a Loved One Dies? Our First Talk about Death Revell, Cindy, illus. (p. 2411)
—Where Do Babies Come From? Our First Talk about Birth Revell, Cindy, illus. (p. 2436)
—Why Do Families Change? Revell, Cindy, illus. (p. 2456)
Roberts, Jillian & Casap, Jaime. On Our Street: Our First Talk about Poverty Heinrichs, Jane, illus. (p. 1653)
Roberts, Joel, illus. see Williams Jr., Floyd.
Roberts, Johanna, illus. see Cummings, Elizabeth Mary.
Roberts, John Bingham. Compend of Anatomy: For Use in the Dissecting Room, & in Preparing for Examinations (Classic Reprint) (p. 433)
Roberts, Josh. Witches of Willow Cove. (p. 2480)
Roberts, Joshua, illus. see Bowles, Sharon.
Roberts, Jp, illus. see Brooks, Karen a.
Roberts, Jp, illus. see Imbs, Nancy Schnoebelen.
Roberts, Jp, illus. see Moon, Debi.
Roberts, Jp, illus. see Stevenson, Lorie.
Roberts, Jp, illus. see Van Jaarsveld, Gemay.
Roberts, Justin. Smallest Girl in the Smallest Grade. Robinson, Christian, illus. (p. 2040)
Roberts, Karen-Ann, illus. see Byrne, Jeffrey Roy.
Roberts, Katherine. Unicorns & Magical Horses: A Spellbinding Ride Through Classic Tales of Wonder. (p. 2329)
Roberts, Kathryn. Net Neutrality. (p. 1588)
—Reproductive Rights (p. 1867)
Roberts, Kathryn, ed. Campaign Finance. (p. 316)
—Clean Energy. (p. 402)
—Global Health (p. 843)
—Internet Journalism & Fake News. (p. 1127)
—Violence Against Women. (p. 2359)
Roberts, Kathy. Way of the Bear: A Story the Whole Family Colors. Collins, Dawn, illus. (p. 2387)
—We All Have Wings: A Story the Whole Family Colors. Collins, Dawn, illus. (p. 2388)
Roberts, Kay. Forever Evergreen. Sponaugle, Kim, illus. (p. 767)
Roberts, Kayla. Frederick Douglass: Freedom Fighter. (p. 781)
Roberts, Kelly Hughes. Road to Chianti. (p. 1888)
Roberts, Kenneth Lewis. Sun Hunting (Classic Reprint) (p. 2151)
Roberts, Kevin D. New Home on Crotty Island. (p. 1594)
Roberts, Laura. Careers If You Like Music. (p. 329)
—Careers in Digital Media. (p. 329)
—Careers in Gaming. (p. 329)
—Little I's Butterflies. Cole, Cindy, ed. (p. 1321)
Roberts, Laura Peyton. Green. (p. 893)
Roberts, Leonie. My Colorful Chameleon: A Fun Rhyming Story about a Silly Pet. Byrne, Mike, illus. (p. 1535)
Roberts, Lewis Niles. Story of Nedda, an Italian Reservist's Wife (Classic Reprint) (p. 2131)
Roberts, Ley Honor, illus. see Clarke, Zoë.
Roberts, Ley Honor, illus. see Rickards, Lynne.
Roberts, Ley Honor, jt. auth. see Rickards, Lynne.
Roberts, Lisa Brown. Bookworm Crush. (p. 261)
—How (Not) to Fall in Love. (p. 1034)
—Playing the Player. (p. 1760)
—Resisting the Rebel. (p. 1869)
Roberts, Lynn. Cinderella: an Art Deco Fairy Tale. (p. 392)
—Little Red: a Fizzingly Funny Fairy Tale. Roberts, David, illus. (p. 1325)
—Rapunzel: a Groovy 1970's Fairy Tale. (p. 1841)
—Sleeping Beauty. (p. 2036)
—Sleeping Beauty: a Mid-Century Fairy Tale. Roberts, David, illus. (p. 2036)
Roberts, Marc, jt. auth. see Roberts, P. J.
Roberts, Margaret. Bride Picotee (Classic Reprint) (p. 280)
—Child of the Revolution: A Novel (Classic Reprint) (p. 370)
—Child of the Revolution (Classic Reprint) (p. 370)
—Denise, Vol. 1 (Classic Reprint) (p. 528)
—Denise, Vol. 2 (Classic Reprint) (p. 528)
—In the Olden Time, Vol. 1 of 2 (Classic Reprint) (p. 1110)
—Mademoiselle Mori: A Tale of Modern Rome. (p. 1375)
—Mademoiselle Mori: A Tale of Modern Rome (Classic Reprint) (p. 1375)
—Mademoiselle Mori. (p. 1375)
—Mademoiselle Mori, Vol. 1: A Tale of Modern Rome, in Two Volumes (Classic Reprint) (p. 1375)
—On the Edge of the Storm (Classic Reprint) (p. 1654)
—Tempest Tossed: The Story of Seejungfer (Classic Reprint) (p. 2203)
—Women of the Last Days of Old France (Classic Reprint) (p. 2487)
Roberts, Margaret Wade. Duty, Vol. 1 Of 3: A Novel (Classic Reprint) (p. 611)
Roberts, Marilyn. Journalist's Journey: Harold Norwood Hubbard. (p. 1180)
Roberts, Mary Jo, illus. see Boyd, William T.
Roberts, Mary Sue, photos by see Crow, Marilee.
Roberts, MarySue, photos by see Crow, Marilee.
Roberts, MarySue, photos by see Reeg, Cynthia.
Roberts, Maureen. Spirit of Ganesh: Slum Kids of Calcutta. (p. 2083)
Roberts, Megan, illus. see Glassco, Jill Watson.
Roberts, Michael. Dealing the Cards: A Savannah Girl Novel. (p. 519)
—Jungle ABC. (p. 1189)
—Nightwaster. (p. 1608)
Roberts, Michael Anthony. Savannah Girl: Street Smart. (p. 1937)
Roberts, Miranda, illus. see Meyer, Linda.
Roberts, Morley. Colossus: A Story of to-Day (Classic Reprint) (p. 427)
—Idlers (Classic Reprint) (p. 1090)
—In Low Relief, Vol. 1 Of 2: A Bohemian Transcript (Classic Reprint) (p. 1106)
—In Low Relief, Vol. 2: A Bohemian Transcript (Classic Reprint) (p. 1106)
—Lady Penelope (Classic Reprint) (p. 1238)
—Painted Rock: Tales & Narratives of Painted, Rock, South Panhandle, Texas, Told, by Charlie Baker, Late of That City, & Also of Snyder, Scurry County (Classic Reprint) (p. 1693)

R

Robins, E. P. Disillusion or the Story of Amedee's Youth (Classic Reprint) (p. 558)
Robins, Edward. Chasing an Iron Horse or a Boy's Adventures in the Civil War (Classic Reprint) (p. 361)
Robins, Eleanor. Art Show Mystery (p. 121)
—Aztec Ring Mystery (p. 146)
—Back-Up Quarterback (p. 156)
—Be Fair (p. 177)
—Best Week Ever (p. 208)
—Boy of Their Dreams (p. 269)
—Break All Rules (p. 277)
—Broken Promise (p. 285)
—Don't Blame Me 2011 (p. 582)
—Don't Get Caught (p. 583)
—Double-Cross (p. 588)
—Drama Club Mystery (p. 596)
—Easy Pass (p. 621)
—Easy Way (p. 621)
—Fastest Runner (p. 713)
—Field Trip Mystery (p. 723)
—Friend or Foe? (p. 786)
—It Does Matter (p. 1141)
—It Is Not a Date (p. 1141)
—Just Be Yourself (p. 1192)
—Last Time (p. 1249)
—Library Book Mystery (p. 1284)
—Lucky Falcon Mystery (p. 1364)
—Missing Test Mystery (p. 1481)
—No Exceptions (p. 1612)
—No Limits (p. 1613)
—One Date Too Many (p. 1659)
—One More Chance (p. 1661)
—Pay Back (p. 1708)
—Right Kind of Win (p. 1882)
—Secret Admirer Mystery (p. 1974)
—Secret Message (p. 1977)
—Someone to Count (p. 2060)
—Time to Move On (p. 2245)
—Too Late (p. 2260)
—Trust Me (p. 2296)
—Very Good Year (p. 2353)
—Where Is Mr. Zane? (p. 2438)
—Worst Year Ever (p. 2509)
—Wrong Way (p. 2514)
Robins, Elizabeth. Come & Find Me (Classic Reprint) (p. 428)
—Convert (Classic Reprint) (p. 446)
—Dark Lantern: A Story with a Prologue (Classic Reprint) (p. 506)
—Magnetic North (Classic Reprint) (p. 1381)
—Messenger (Classic Reprint) (p. 1451)
—My Little Sister (Classic Reprint) (p. 1554)
—Under the Southern Cross (Classic Reprint) (p. 2323)
Robins, G. m. Ides of March, Vol. 1 of 3 (Classic Reprint) (p. 1089)
Robins, Gertrude. Loving As We Do, & Other Plays (Classic Reprint) (p. 1362)
Robins, Helen Josephine. Scholars & the Children: A Christmas Play (Classic Reprint) (p. 1944)
Robins, Jim, illus. see West, David.
Robins, Jim, jt. auth. see Cox, Robert.
Robins, Maria. Alice in Wonderland: Based on the Original Story by Lewis Carroll. (p. 45)
Robins, Maureen. Habitat for Bats. (p. 908)
—One Land, Many Cultures. (p. 1660)
—Snakes in Third Grade! (p. 2044)
Robins, Maureen, jt. auth. see Karapetkova, Holly.
Robins, Maureen, jt. auth. see Steinkraus, Kyla.
Robins, Maureen Picard. One Land, Many Cultures. (p. 1660)
—What Are the Us Regions? (p. 2406)
Robins, Navi, illus. see Clark, Donita J.
Robins, Sally Nelson. Gloucester: One of the First Chapters of the Commonwealth of Virginia (Classic Reprint) (p. 845)
—Man's Reach (Classic Reprint) (p. 1398)
—Scuffles (Classic Reprint) (p. 1966)
Robins, Sandy. For the Love of Cats: An A-to-Z Primer for Cat Lovers of All Ages. Anderson, Mark, illus. (p. 763)
Robins, Tudor. After Lucas. (p. 33)
—Faults. Smith, Hilary, ed. (p. 715)
—Join Up. Smith, Hilary, ed. (p. 1175)
—Objects in Mirror. (p. 1634)
—Six-Month Horse. (p. 2028)
Robins, W., jt. auth. see Smith, S.
Robins, Wesley, illus. see Brown, Carron.
Robins, Wesley, illus. see Claybourne, Anna.
Robins, Wesley, illus. see Green, Jen.
Robins, Wesley & Hodge, Susie. Great Art in 30 Seconds: 30 Awesome Art Topics for Curious Kids. (p. 883)
Robinson, A. M. Vampire Crush. (p. 2346)
Robinson, A. Mary F. Arden: A Novel, Vol. 1 of 2 (Classic Reprint) (p. 112)
—Emily Bronte (Classic Reprint) (p. 642)
Robinson, Alan. M Star Prince & Princess. (p. 1370)
Robinson, Alan James, illus. see Dunphy, Madeleine.
Robinson, Albert. Account of Some Recent Improvements in the System of Navigating the Ganges by Iron Steam Vessels (Classic Reprint) (p. 10)
Robinson, Amy. First King of England in a Dress. (p. 737)
Robinson, Andrew, illus. see Unwin, Mike.
Robinson, Andrew R., jt. auth. see Caramagna, Joe.
Robinson, Andrew R. & Caramagna, Joe. Take the Milanoand Run Animation, Marvel, illus. (p. 2177)
Robinson, Anitha. Broken Dreams. (p. 284)
—Broken Promises. (p. 285)
—Broken Worlds. (p. 285)
Robinson, Aquila. Septic Zombie - a Short Story. (p. 1989)
Robinson, Asher Cheyenne. Willie the Wren. (p. 2469)
Robinson, Ashley Victoria & Inman, Jason. Science! the Elements of Dark Energy. Beiko, Samantha, ed. (p. 1959)
Robinson, Aunya N. Irish the Fairy Baby - Hardcover. Robinson, Aunya N., illus. (p. 1135)
Robinson, Barbara. Best Christmas Pageant Ever. (p. 205)
—Best Christmas Pageant Ever (picture Book Edition) Cornell, Laura, illus. (p. 205)
Robinson, Barbara J., illus. see Blotnick, Elihu.
Robinson, Beatriz M. Magnificent Journey of Roopert the Scribe & the Great Princess Paasha. Papson, Kylie, illus. (p. 1382)
Robinson, Ben & Reily, Marcus. Star Trek Designing Starships Volume 2: Voyager & Beyond. (p. 2103)
Robinson, Benjamin. Dolores, a Tale of Disappointment & Distress: Compiled, Arranged & Edited from the Journal, Letters & Other Mss; of Roland Verson, Esq. ; & from Contributions by & Conversations with the Vernon Family, of Rushbrook, in Carolina (Classic Reprint) (p. 579)
Robinson, Beth. Safe Family Coloring Book. (p. 1922)
—Safe Touch Book. Green, Noel, illus. (p. 1922)
—Where Will I Grow Up? Green, Noel, illus. (p. 2440)
Robinson, Bill, illus. see David, Erica.
Robinson, Bill, illus. see Katschke, Judy.
Robinson, Bonita. Little Seed That Could. (p. 1327)
Robinson, Breanna. Be Gone, Fear. (p. 177)
Robinson, Bud. Sunshine & Smiles (Classic Reprint) (p. 2153)
Robinson, C. Clough. Dialect of Leeds & Its Neighbourhood, Illustrated by Conversations & Tales of Common Life, Etc: To Which Are Added a Copious Glossary, Notices on the Various Antiquities, Manners, & Customs, & General Folk-Lore of the District. (p. 537)
Robinson, Camila. Best Thanksgiving Ever! - 6 Pack: Set of 6 with Teacher Materials Common Core Edition. (p. 208)
Robinson, Candace & Delgadillo, Gerardo. Bacon Pie. (p. 157)
Robinson, Casey W. Iver & Ellsworth. Larson, Melissa, illus. (p. 1149)
Robinson, Celia Myrover. Rowena's Happy Summer (Classic Reprint) (p. 1909)
Robinson, Charles, illus. see Buchwald, Emilie.
Robinson, Charles, illus. see Burnett, Frances Hodgson.
Robinson, Charles, illus. see Field, Eugene.
Robinson, Charles, illus. see Jerrold, Walter, ed.
Robinson, Charles, illus. see Jerrold, Walter.
Robinson, Charles, illus. see Stevenson, Robert Louis.
Robinson, Charles, illus. see Wilde, Oscar.
Robinson, Charles, jt. auth. see Jerrold, Walter.
Robinson, Charles, jt. auth. see Wilde, Oscar.
Robinson, Charles Henry. Longhead: The Story of the First Fire (Classic Reprint) (p. 1344)
Robinson, Charles Mulford. Rochester Ways (Classic Reprint) (p. 1894)
—Third Ward Traits (Classic Reprint) (p. 2223)
Robinson, Chris, ed. see Henson, Jim & Juhl, Jerry.
Robinson, Christian. Another. Robinson, Christian, illus. (p. 100)
—You Matter. Robinson, Christian, illus. (p. 2527)
Robinson, Christian, illus. see Ashman, Linda.
Robinson, Christian, illus. see Barnett, Mac.
Robinson, Christian, illus. see Brown, Margaret Wise.
Robinson, Christian, illus. see de la Peña, Matt.
Robinson, Christian, illus. see DiPucchio, Kelly.
Robinson, Christian, illus. see Fogliano, Julie.
Robinson, Christian, illus. see Powell, Patricia Hruby.
Robinson, Christian, illus. see Roberts, Justin.
Robinson, Christian, illus. see Rylant, Cynthia.
Robinson, Christian, illus. see Watson, Renée.
Robinson, Christian, jt. auth. see Rex, Adam.
Robinson, Christine. It Was Us. (p. 1142)
Robinson, Chuck. Critical World Issues: Racism (p. 476)
Robinson, Cindy. Baby Baobab. Robinson, Cindy, illus. (p. 149)
Robinson, Cindy, et al. Disney Princess. (p. 562)
Robinson, Corabel E. Framingham State Normal School Class of 1916 (Classic Reprint) (p. 775)
Robinson, Craig & Mansbach, Adam. Jake the Fake Goes for Laughs. Knight, Keith, illus. (p. 1156)
—Jake the Fake Keeps His Cool. Knight, Keith, illus. (p. 1156)
—Jake the Fake Keeps It Real. Knight, Keith, illus. (p. 1156)
Robinson, David. David Robinson: the Mushroom Picker. (p. 511)
—My Little Man. (p. 1553)
Robinson, Deanna. Amber the Crystal Fairy. (p. 67)
Robinson, Diane Mae. Dragon Grammar Book: Grammar for Kids, Dragons, & the Whole Kingdom. Breadcrumbs, Ink, illus. (p. 593)
—Dragon Grammar Book: Grammar for Kids, Dragons, & the Whole Kingdom. Ink, Breadcrumbs, illus. (p. 593)
—Sir Princess Petra: The Pen Pieyu Adventures. (p. 2026)
—Sir Princess Petra: The Pen Pieyu Adventures. Kickingbird, Samantha, illus. (p. 2026)
—Sir Princess Petra Coloring Book. (p. 2026)
—Sir Princess Petra's Mission: The Pen Pieyu Adventures. (p. 2026)
—Sir Princess Petra's Mission: The Pen Pieyu Adventures. Bermundo, Michael, illus. (p. 2026)
—Sir Princess Petra's Talent: The Pen Pieyu Adventures. Kickingbird, Samantha, illus. (p. 2026)
—Sir Princess Petra's Talent: Book 2 in the International Award-Winning Children's Fantasy Series. (p. 2026)
Robinson, Don, illus. see Calma, Jocelyn.
Robinson, Don, illus. see Crowe, Ellie.
Robinson, Don, illus. see Gillespie, Jane.
Robinson, Don, illus. see Paikai, Tammy.
Robinson Dunne, Kate. Ludlow Lost. (p. 1366)
Robinson, E. A. Gun-Bearer: A War Novel (Classic Reprint) (p. 905)
Robinson, E. Kay. Country Day by Day (Classic Reprint) (p. 461)
—My Nature Notebook (Classic Reprint) (p. 1557)
Robinson Ed. D., Shannon R. Adventures of Katie Koala: Oops! My Momma Is Lost! Swope, Brenda, illus. (p. 24)
Robinson, Edith. Captain of the School (Classic Reprint) (p. 326)
—Little Daughter of Liberty (Classic Reprint) (p. 1315)
—Loyal Little Maid (Classic Reprint) (p. 1363)
—Penhallow Tales (Classic Reprint) (p. 1716)
Robinson, Edward Jewitt. Tales & Poems of South India. (p. 2181)
—Tales & Poems South India: From the Tamil (Classic Reprint) (p. 2181)
Robinson, Edwin Arlington. Avon's Harvest (Classic Reprint) (p. 143)
—Captain Craig: A Book of Poems (Classic Reprint) (p. 325)
—King Jasper: A Poem (Classic Reprint) (p. 1220)
—Matthias at the Door (Classic Reprint) (p. 1426)
—Porcupine: A Drama in Three Acts (Classic Reprint) (p. 1778)
—Three Taverns: A Book of Poems. (p. 2235)
—Three Taverns: A Book of Poems (Classic Reprint) (p. 2235)
Robinson, Edwin Meade. Enter Jerry (Classic Reprint) (p. 656)
Robinson, Eliot H. Maid of Mirabelle: A Romance of Lorraine (Classic Reprint) (p. 1383)
—Man Proposes: Or the Romace of John Alden Shaw (Classic Reprint) (p. 1395)
—Smiles a Rose of the Cumberlands (Classic Reprint) (p. 2042)
—Smiling Pass: Being a Further Account of the Career of Smiles; a Rose of the Cumberlands (Classic Reprint) (p. 2042)
Robinson, Eliza Serena. Consequence. (p. 442)
Robinson, Emma. Armourer's Daughter, or the Border Riders, Vol. 1 Of 3: A Novel (Classic Reprint) (p. 117)
—Dorothy Firebrace, or the Armourer's Daughter of Birmingham, Vol. 1 of 3 (Classic Reprint) (p. 586)
—Dorothy Firebrace, Vol. 2 Of 3: Or the Armourer's Daughter of Birmingham (Classic Reprint) (p. 587)
—Whitefriars, or the Days of Charles the Second (Classic Reprint) (p. 2445)
—Whitefriars, or the Days of Charles the Second, Vol. 1 Of 2: An Historical Romance (Classic Reprint) (p. 2445)
—Whitehall, or the Days of Charles I, Vol. 1: An Historical Romance (Classic Reprint) (p. 2445)
—Whitehall, or the Days of Charles I, Vol. 2 (Classic Reprint) (p. 2445)
Robinson, Emma A. Stories of Bible Victories: From the Old Testament (Classic Reprint) (p. 2124)
Robinson, Erin, illus. see Messner, Kate & Powell, Margaret E.
Robinson, Erin K., illus. see Hudson, Cheryl.
Robinson, Everton. Child's Guide to Wisdom. (p. 376)
Robinson, Evic, tr. see Pere, Tuula.
Robinson, F. A. Mastered Men: With an Introduction (Classic Reprint) (p. 1419)
—Mastered Men. (p. 1419)
Robinson, F. Mabel. Woman of the World: An Every-Day Story (Classic Reprint) (p. 2485)
Robinson, F. W. As Long As She Lived, Vol. 2 of 3 (Classic Reprint) (p. 124)
—Bridge of Glass, Vol. 2 of 3 (Classic Reprint) (p. 280)
—Coward Conscience, Vol. 1 of 3 (Classic Reprint) (p. 464)
—Her Face Was Her Fortune, Vol. 1 of 3 (Classic Reprint) (p. 956)
—In Bad Hands & Other Tales, Vol. 3 of 3 (Classic Reprint) (p. 1104)
—In Bad Hands, Vol. 1 Of 3: And Other Tales (Classic Reprint) (p. 1104)
—In Bad Hands, Vol. 2 Of 3: And Other Tales (Classic Reprint) (p. 1104)
—Little Kate Kirby, Vol. 1 of 3 (Classic Reprint) (p. 1320)
—Man She Cared for, Vol. 1 of 3 (Classic Reprint) (p. 1395)
—Owen, a Waif, Vol. 2 of 3 (Classic Reprint) (p. 1688)
—Romance of a Back Street, Vol. 25 (Classic Reprint) (p. 1899)
—Slaves of the Ring, Vol. 1 Of 3: Or Before & after (Classic Reprint) (p. 2035)
—Wrayford's Ward, & Other Tales, Vol. 1 of 3 (Classic Reprint) (p. 2511)
Robinson, Fay. Baked Potatoes. (p. 160)
—Bear's Icicles. (p. 180)
—Celebrating Chinese New Year. (p. 349)
—Chinese New Year. (p. 379)
—Fun Halloween Crafts. (p. 799)
—Into the Rain Forest. Lopez, Paul, illus. (p. 1128)
—It's 6 P. M. (p. 1143)
—Plants in Different Habitats. (p. 1757)
—Sand Dunes. (p. 1930)
Robinson, Fay, jt. auth. see Ponto, Joanna.
Robinson, Fay, jt. auth. see Schafer, Susan.
Robinson, Fay, retold by. Fire Keeper. (p. 732)
Robinson, Fiona. 3-2-3 Detective Agency: The Disappearance of Dave Warthog. (p. 2546)
—Ada's Ideas: The Story of Ada Lovelace, the World's First Computer Programmer. (p. 14)
—Bluest of Blues: Anna Atkins & the First Book of Photographs. (p. 250)
—Las Ideas de ADA. (p. 1246)
—Whale Shines: An Artistic Tail. (p. 2403)
—What Animals Really Like. (p. 2404)
Robinson, Frances Mabel. Plan of Campaign: A Story of the Fortune of War (Classic Reprint) (p. 1754)
Robinson, Frederick W. Anne Judge, Spinster, Vol. 1 of 3 (Classic Reprint) (p. 98)
Robinson, Frederick William. As Long As She Lived, Vol. 1 of 3 (Classic Reprint) (p. 124)
—Christie's Faith (Classic Reprint) (p. 383)
—Mattie: A Stray (Classic Reprint) (p. 1426)
—Memoirs of Jane Cameron, Vol. 1 Of 2: Female Convict (Classic Reprint) (p. 1444)
—No Man's Friend, Vol. 1 of 3 (Classic Reprint) (p. 1613)
—Owen, Vol. 1 Of 3: A Waif (Classic Reprint) (p. 1688)
—Poor Zeph! (Classic Reprint) (p. 1775)
—Slaves of the Ring (Classic Reprint) (p. 2035)
—Slaves of the Ring, or Before & after, Vol. 2 of 3 (Classic Reprint) (p. 2035)
—Woodleigh, Vol. 1 of 3 (Classic Reprint) (p. 2492)
—Woodleigh, Vol. 2 of 3 (Classic Reprint) (p. 2492)
Robinson, G. C. Grandma Bubbles. (p. 878)
Robinson, G. P. Debt (Classic Reprint) (p. 522)
Robinson, Garrett, ed. see Bolger, Z. C.
Robinson, Gary. Billy Buckhorn ABNORMAL. (p. 227)
—Danny Blackgoat, Rugged Road to Freedom. (p. 504)
—Lands of Our Ancestors. (p. 1243)
—Little Brother of War. (p. 1313)
—Native American Twelve Days of Christmas. Hummingbird, Jesse T., illus. (p. 1578)
—Paranormal: A Billy Buckhorn Supernatural Adventure. (p. 1699)
—Supranormal. (p. 2162)
—Thunder on the Plains. (p. 2238)
—Tribal Journey. (p. 2286)
Robinson, Gordon, illus. see Carroll, Lewis, pseud.
Robinson, Gwen G. Jensen Case. (p. 1164)
Robinson, Hamline Elijah. Ancestor Hunting: Some Account of a Week Spent in Windham County, Vermont, During the Month of June, 1901 (Classic Reprint) (p. 79)
Robinson, Harry Perry. Life Story of a Black Bear (Classic Reprint) (p. 1296)
—Men Born Equal: A Novel (Classic Reprint) (p. 1446)
—Men Born Equal. (p. 1446)
Robinson, Hazel M. Original Two Bits: A Farce in Two Acts (Classic Reprint) (p. 1671)
Robinson, Heath, illus. see Andersen, Hans.
Robinson, Helen, ed. see Carlson, Glenn E.
Robinson, Hilary. Beauty & the Pea. Sanfilippo, Simona, illus. (p. 185)
—Christmas Fairy Tale Mix-Up. Smith, Jim, illus. (p. 385)
—Cinderella & the Beanstalk. Sanfilippo, Simona, illus. (p. 392)
—Croc Shock! Gordon, Mike, illus. (p. 476)
—Elves & the Emperor. Sanfilippo, Simona, illus. (p. 640)
—Goldilocks & the Wolf. Sanfilippo, Simona, illus. (p. 860)
—Hansel, Gretel, & the Ugly Duckling. Sanfilippo, Simona, illus. (p. 919)
—Must Know Stories: Level 2: the Frog Prince. (p. 1530)
—Over the Moon! Abbott, Jane, illus. (p. 1686)
—Over the Moon. Abbott, Jane, illus. (p. 1686)
—Rapunzel & the Billy Goats. Sanfilippo, Simona, illus. (p. 1841)
—Snow White & the Enormous Turnip. Sanfilippo, Simona, illus. (p. 2048)
—Spooky Fairy Tale Mix-Up: Hundreds of Flip-Flap Stories. Smith, Jim, illus. (p. 2087)
—Ted's Party Bus. (p. 2198)
—Ted's Party Bus. Sharp, Melanie, illus. (p. 2198)
—Three Pigs & a Gingerbread Man. Sanfilippo, Simona, illus. (p. 2234)
Robinson, Hilary & Catling, Andy. Aladdin & the Lamp. (p. 39)
Robinson, Hilda & Kunkel, Jeff. Didn't We Have Fun! Robinson, Hilda, illus. (p. 543)
Robinson, Horatio N. Key to the Progressive Practical Arithmetic: Including Analyses of the Miscellaneous Examples in the Progressive Intellectual Arithmetic: for Teachers Only. (p. 1212)
Robinson, Horatio Nelson. Elementary Treatise on Algebra: Designed As First Lessons in That Science (Classic Reprint) (p. 632)
—Key to Robinson's New Elementary Algebra: For Teachers & Private Learners (Classic Reprint) (p. 1211)
Robinson, J. B. Serpent of Sugar Creek Colony: A Temperance Narrative of Pioneer Life in Ohio (Classic Reprint) (p. 1991)
Robinson, J. H. Lone Star: Or, the Texas Bravo; a Tale of the Southwest (Classic Reprint) (p. 1342)
—Silver-Knife, or the Hunters of the Rocky Mountains: An Autobiography (Classic Reprint) (p. 2019)
Robinson, J. P. Kay. With Botha's Army: With Introductory Letter by General Botha (Classic Reprint) (p. 2481)
Robinson, J. R. Spiffy Kids!! Storybook of Feelings Collection. (p. 2082)
Robinson, James, illus. see Mountney, Ross.
Robinson, Janet. Courageous James & the Sneezy Dragon. (p. 462)
Robinson, Janie. Preston, the Not-So-Perfect-Pig. Snider, K. C., illus. (p. 1790)
Robinson, Jayme, illus. see Sapre, Reshme.
Robinson, Jeleasa. Why Hasn't the Tooth Fairy Been? (p. 2458)
Robinson, Jeleasa M. My Mum Says I'm a Wriggle Worm. Robinson, Jeleasa M., illus. (p. 1557)
Robinson, Jennifer. Isabella's Shoes. (p. 1138)
Robinson, Jeremy. Last Hunter: Ascent. (p. 1248)
Robinson, Jessie B., jt. auth. see Eisenberg, Azriel.
Robinson, Jill & Bekoff, Marc. Saving Moon Bears. Frankenhuyzen, Gijsbert van, illus. (p. 1938)
Robinson, Jimmie. Make the Grade. (p. 1387)
Robinson, Jo, illus. see Reyes, Cynthia.
Robinson, Jo, illus. see Reyes-Grange, Lauren & Reyes, Cynthia.
Robinson, Joan G. Teddy Robinson Meets Father Christmas & Other Stories. (p. 2198)
Robinson, Joanna J. Greece. (p. 892)
—Guatemala. (p. 902)
—Italy. (p. 1142)
—Mexico. (p. 1454)
Robinson, Joanna Jarc. Andrew & Allen Learn about Adverbs. Boyer, Robin, illus. (p. 83)
—Phillip & Penny Learn about Pronouns. Hu, Caroline, illus. (p. 1734)
Robinson, John Hovey. Life & Adventures of Wm. Harvard Stinchfield, or the Wanderings of a Traveling Merchant: An Owre True Tale, of the Gaming Table & Bowl (Classic Reprint) (p. 1288)
Robinson, Joseph Barlow. Owd Sammy Twitcher's Visit Tu't Gret Exibishun e Darby (Classic Reprint) (p. 1688)
Robinson Jr, E. B. Nemest & His Toolbox: Self-Awareness. Williams, Iris M., ed. (p. 1588)
Robinson Jr, Fred. Tragedy Brings Togetherness. (p. 2274)
Robinson, Julia Marie. Race, Religion, & the Pulpit: Rev. Robert L. Bradby & the Making of Urban Detroit. (p. 1831)
Robinson, Julie. Seasons in Our Garden. Lindsay, Pattie, illus. (p. 1972)
Robinson, Kate. Lewis & Clark: Exploring the American West. (p. 1282)
Robinson, Kathleen Marie. Magic Doorknob (p. 1377)
Robinson, Keith. Chamber of Ghosts. (p. 354)
—Valley of Monsters. (p. 2345)
Robinson, Keith, illus. see Hoge, Robert.
Robinson, Keith, illus. see Riordan, Rick.
Robinson, Kelley. Naming: Book One of the Magic of Io Series. Curtiss, Melody, illus. (p. 1573)

—Mission to Moon Farm (Secrets of Bearhaven #2) (p. 1481)
—Secrets of Bearhaven. Dearsley, Ross, illus. (p. 1980)
Rocha, Lorraine, illus. see Deenihan, Jamie L. B.
Rocha, Lorraine, illus. see Nogales, Jill.
Rocha, Lucas. Where We Go from Here. Helena, Larissa, tr. (p. 2440)
Rocha, Ruth. Lines, Squiggles, Letters, Words. Matoso, Madalena, illus. (p. 1304)
Roche, Art. Art for Kids: Comic Strips - Create Your Own Comic Strips from Start to Finish. (p. 121)
—Art for Kids: Cartooning: The Only Cartooning Book You'll Ever Need to Be the Artist You've Always Wanted to Be. (p. 121)
—Knights of Boo'Gar. (p. 1228)
Roche, Arthur Somers. Day of Faith (Classic Reprint) (p. 513)
—More Honorable Man (Classic Reprint) (p. 1505)
—Plunder (Classic Reprint) (p. 1763)
—Slander (Classic Reprint) (p. 2035)
—Uneasy Street (Classic Reprint) (p. 2327)
Roche, Camille, tr. see Stein, Carol.
Roche, Camille, tr. Tea Party Trouble / Problème de Thé (English-French) (Disney Fancy Nancy) Disney Storybook Art Team, illus. (p. 2194)
Roche, Denis, illus. see Evans, Lezlie.
Roche, Harriet A. On Trek in the Transvaal: Or over Berg & Veldt in South Africa (Classic Reprint) (p. 1656)
Roche, Jackie. Derby Ram. (p. 530)
Roche, Jackie, illus. see Kullab, Samya.
Roche, Maite. Beautiful Story of Jesus. Roche, Maite, illus. (p. 184)
—Bible for Little Ones. (p. 213)
Roche, Maïte. Christmas! (p. 383)
Roche, Maite. First Noel. Roche, Maite, illus. (p. 738)
—Gospel for Little Ones. (p. 870)
Roche, Maïte. Hail Mary. (p. 909)
Roche, Maite. My First Bedtime Prayers. (p. 1540)
—My First Pictures of Easter. (p. 1545)
—My First Pictures of Jesus. (p. 1545)
Roche, Maïte. My First Prayers for the Whole Year. (p. 1545)
—My Picture Book of the Bible. (p. 1559)
—My Picture Book of the Catholic Faith. Roche, Maïte, illus. (p. 1559)
—Our Father. (p. 1678)
Roche, Maria Regina. Nocturnal Visit, Vol. 3: A Tale (Classic Reprint) (p. 1617)
Roche, May. Jokiest Joking Bathroom Joke Book Ever Written ... No Joke! 1,001 Hilarious Potty Jokes to Make You Laugh While You Go. Brack, Amanda, illus. (p. 1176)
Roche, Mazo De la. Explorers of the Dawn (Classic Reprint) (p. 681)
Roche, Patricia Jo. I Am More Than a Name. (p. 1059)
Roche, Regina Maria. Bridal of Dunamore, Vol. 2 Of 3: And Lost & Won, Two Tales (Classic Reprint) (p. 280)
—Bridal of Dunamore, Vol. 3: And Lost & Won (Classic Reprint) (p. 280)
—Children of the Abbey: A Tale (Classic Reprint) (p. 371)
—Children of the Abbey (Classic Reprint) (p. 371)
—Contrast, Vol. 1 of 3 (Classic Reprint) (p. 445)
—Discarded Son, or Haunt of the Banditti, Vol. 2 Of 5: A Tale (Classic Reprint) (p. 553)
—Discarded Son; or, Haunt of the Banditti, Vol. 4 Of 5: A Tale (Classic Reprint) (p. 553)
—Monastery of St. Columb, or, the Atonement, Vol. 2 Of 2: A Novel (Classic Reprint) (p. 1492)
—Munster Cottage Boy, Vol. 1 Of 4: A Tale in Four Volumes (Classic Reprint) (p. 1527)
—Munster Cottage Boy, Vol. 2 Of 4: A Tale (Classic Reprint) (p. 1527)
—Tradition of the Castle, or Scenes in the Emerald Isle, Vol. 3 of 4 (Classic Reprint) (p. 2273)
—Tradition of the Castle, Vol. 1 Of 4: Or, Scenes in the Emerald Isle (Classic Reprint) (p. 2273)
—Trecothick Bower, or the Lady of the West Country, Vol. 1 Of 2: A Tale (Classic Reprint) (p. 2283)
Roche, Sophie von La. Sophie in London 1786: Being the Diary of Sophie V. la Roche; Translated from the German with an Introductory Essay (Classic Reprint) (p. 2065)
Roche, Sue, illus. see Howell, Simon & Howell, Anita.
Rochea, Vanessa. Kamlyn's Journal (p. 1202)
Rocheleau, Paul, photos by see Thorne-Thomsen, Kathleen.
Rochelin, Ghyslaine. Coconut Tree. Bertoni, Oliver, illus. (p. 411)
Rochelle, Maria. Jasmine at Work. Linsdell, Jo, illus. (p. 1160)
—Jasmine at Work (Coloring Book) Linsdell, Jo, illus. (p. 1160)
—Jasmine's Got Talent! Linsdell, Jo, illus. (p. 1160)
Rochelle, Warren. Called. (p. 312)
Rochester, Boys & Girls Clubs of. N Is for New York: Written by Kids for Kids. (p. 1572)
Rochester, Karen. Be Brave. Chadwick, Kat, illus. (p. 177)
Rochon, Isaiah. One of Many in the Universe. (p. 1661)
Rochon, Ken. Kenny's Favorite Things. Battle, Ryan, illus. (p. 1209)
Rocio Bonilla, Oriol Malet. Max y los superhéroes. (p. 1428)
Rocío, Martínez Pérez, jt. auth. see Martínez, Rocío.
Rock, Brian. Détective Déductif: (the Deductive Detective in French) Troff, Sophie, tr. (p. 534)
—Detective Deductivo Rogers, Sherry, illus. (p. 534)
—Tyler Files #1: Smarty Pants! (p. 2310)
—Tyler Files #2: Hollow Weenie. (p. 2310)
—Tyler Files #3: My Nose Is Running! (p. 2310)
—With All My Heart. Banta, Susan, illus. (p. 2481)
Rock, Brian & Rogers, Sherry. Detective Deductivo Rogers, Sherry, illus. (p. 534)
Rock, J. K. Camp Forget-Me-Not. (p. 315)
—Camp Payback. (p. 316)
Rock, Jonathan. Out of Bounds Bk. 1 (p. 1682)
—Search & Rescue: 'For Anyone Thinking of Becoming a Scout, Go for It, Come & Join the Big Adventure' (p. 1970)
—White Water (p. 2445)
Rock, Joseph Francis Charles. Indigenous Trees of the Hawaiian Islands - Scholar's Choice Edition. (p. 1117)
Rock, Julianne. You Are... (p. 2524)
Rock, Lois. Bible & Me. Massari, Alida, illus. (p. 213)
—Biblia y Yo / the Bible & Me. Massari, Alida, illus. (p. 214)
—Canoeing & Kayaking. (p. 322)
—Easter Story - Pack 10. (p. 620)
—Gift for Baby's Dedication Rescek, Sanja, illus. (p. 832)
—Good Samaritan & Other Parables of Jesus. Allsopp, Sophie, illus. (p. 866)
—In the Beginning: Bible Stories for Little Hands Bolam, Emily, illus. (p. 1107)
—Jesus Is Born: A Spot-the-Difference Jigsaw Book Bolam, Emily, illus. (p. 1166)
—Journey into the Bible. Rowland, Andrew, illus. (p. 1181)
—Lion Bible to Keep for Ever. Allsopp, Sophie, illus. (p. 1305)
—Lion Book of Prayers to Keep for Ever. Allsopp, Sophie, illus. (p. 1306)
—Lion First Book of Parables Vagnozzi, Barbara, illus. (p. 1306)
—Little Life of Jesus - To Read & Treasure. Langton, Roger W., illus. (p. 1320)
—Look Inside Bible Times. Lewis, Anthony, illus. (p. 1346)
—Look Inside Nativity Coloji, Livia, illus. (p. 1346)
—Look Inside Noah's Ark. Coloji, Livia, illus. (p. 1346)
—Look Inside the Time of Jesus. Orlandi, Lorenzo, illus. (p. 1346)
—Lost Sheep: A Spot-the-Difference Jigsaw Book Bolam, Emily, illus. (p. 1355)
—Mi Primer Libro de Historias de la Biblia (My First Book of Bible Stories) Vagnozzi, Barbara, illus. (p. 1455)
—Mi Primera Historia de Jonas y la Ballena (My Very First Story Jonah & the Whale) (p. 1456)
—Mi Primera Historia de la Navidad (My Very First Christmas Story) (p. 1456)
—Mi Primera Historia de No y el Arca (My Very First Noah & the Ark) (p. 1456)
—My Very First Bible & Prayers Ayliffe, Alex, illus. (p. 1564)
—My Very First Bible Stories Bumper Sticker Book Ayliffe, Alex, illus. (p. 1564)
—My Very First Nativity Story. Ayliffe, Alex, illus. (p. 1564)
—Noah's Ark: A Spot-the-Difference Jigsaw Book Bolam, Emily, illus. (p. 1616)
—Noah's Ark. Allsopp, Sophie, illus. (p. 1616)
—On That Christmas Night. Jay, Alison, illus. (p. 1653)
—Prayers & Verses for Your First Holy Communion. Jay, Alison, illus. (p. 1785)
—Tiny Tots Bible. Widdowson, Kay, illus. (p. 2250)
—Tiny Tots Easter Widdowson, Kay, illus. (p. 2250)
—Viaje Por la Biblia. Pimentel, Alejandro, tr. (p. 2355)
Rock, Lois, jt. auth. see Williamson, Karen.
Rock, Meghan. Rachel Carson: Marine Biologist & Winner of the National Book Award. (p. 1832)
—String Theory. (p. 2141)
Rock 'n Learn. Alphabet Al's ABC Book of Words & Rhymes. (p. 58)
—Animals Point & Name with 44 Rhymes. (p. 95)
Rock, 'N Learn. Colors, Shapes & Counting: A Point & Name Book of Rhymes. (p. 426)
Rock 'n Learn. Letter Sounds: Silly Sentences - Early Phonics Skills. (p. 1278)
Rock 'N Learn, creator. Addition & Subtraction Rap. (p. 15)
Rock, Nic. How to Get on the Naughty List. Wu, Helen, illus. (p. 1042)
Rock, Nora. Fly Away (p. 754)
Rock, Peter. Klickitat. (p. 1227)
—My Abandonment. (p. 1530)
Rock Spring Elementary. Roadrunner Writing Rocks! (p. 1888)
Rock, Zack. Good Story. Rock, Zack, illus. (p. 866)
—Homer Henry Hudson's Curio Museum. (p. 997)
Rockefeller, Harry. I Wish Sons Came with Instructions (p. 1086)
Rockefeller, John Davison. Random Reminiscences of Men & Events. (p. 1840)
Rockefeller, Matt, illus. see Doctorow, Cory.
Rockefeller, Matt, illus. see Eaton, Jason Carter.
Rockefeller, Matt, illus. see Heos, Bridget.
Rockefeller, Matt, illus. see Siegel, Mark & Siegel, Alexis.
Rockefeller, Matt, illus. see Vago, Mike.
Rockett, Kinsey M. Prisoner of War. (p. 1801)
—Trial at the Ridge. (p. 2285)
Rockett, Paul. Francisco Goya (p. 776)
—History of Britain in 12... Assorted Animals. (p. 977)
—History of Britain in 12... Bites of Food. (p. 977)
—History of Britain in 12... Feats of Engineering. (p. 977)
—Leonardo Da Vinci (p. 1267)
—Mapping Africa. (p. 1401)
—Mapping Asia. (p. 1401)
—Mapping Australia & Oceania, & Antarctica. (p. 1401)
—Mapping Europe. (p. 1401)
—Mapping North America. (p. 1401)
—Mapping South America. (p. 1401)
—Pieter Bruegel (p. 1743)
Rockfield, Darryl, illus. see Beeson, Lea Ann.
Rocklein, Constance. What's Wrong with a Selfie? (p. 2427)
Rockliff, Mara. Anything but Ordinary Addie: The True Story of Adelaide Herrmann, Queen of Magic. Bruno, Iacopo, illus. (p. 104)
—Around America to Win the Vote: Two Suffragists, a Kitten, & 10,000 Miles. Hooper, Hadley, illus. (p. 118)
—Billie Jean! How Tennis Star Billie Jean King Changed Women's Sports. Baddeley, Elizabeth, illus. (p. 226)
—Born to Swing: Lil Hardin Armstrong's Life in Jazz. Wood, Michele, illus. (p. 263)
—Chik Chak Shabbat. Brooker, Kyrsten, illus. (p. 369)
—Doctor Esperanto & the Language of Hope. Dzierzawska, Zosia, illus. (p. 573)
—Get Real: What Kind of World Are YOU Buying? (p. 824)
—Gingerbread for Liberty! How a German Baker Helped Win the American Revolution. Kirsch, Vincent X., illus. (p. 834)
—Grudge Keeper Wheeler, Eliza, illus. (p. 900)
—Lights! Camera! Alice! The Thrilling True Adventures of the First Woman Filmmaker. Ciraolo, Simona, illus. (p. 1300)
—Me & Momma & Big John. Low, William, illus. (p. 1432)
—Mesmerized: How Ben Franklin Solved a Mystery That Baffled All of France. Bruno, Iacopo, illus. (p. 1451)
—Next to an Ant. Constantin, Pascale, illus. (p. 1600)
Rocklin, Joanne. Five Lives of Our Cat Zook. (p. 744)
—Fleabrain Loves Franny. (p. 747)
—Good Guys, Bad Guys. Carpenter, Nancy, illus. (p. 862)
—I Say Shehechiyanu. Filipina, Monika, illus. (p. 1081)
—Love, Penelope. Knisley, Lucy, illus. (p. 1361)
—One Day & One Amazing Morning on Orange Street. (p. 1659)
Rockoff, Lisa & Weiner, Arlene. Hilda Ma Tilda - Where's Finn? A Beautiful Illustrated Story Book for Children. Chakraborty, Pradip, illus. (p. 971)
Rockwell, Anne. Apples & Pumpkins. Rockwell, Lizzy, illus. (p. 107)
—At the Beach. Rockwell, Harlow, illus. (p. 130)
—At the Beach. Rockwell, Harlow & Rockwell, Lizzy, illus. (p. 130)
—At the Supermarket. Rockwell, Anne, illus. (p. 131)
—Big George: How a Shy Boy Became President Washington. Phelan, Matt, illus. (p. 220)
—Big George: How a Shy Boy Became President Washington. Trueman, Matthew & Phelan, Matt, illus. (p. 220)
—Bugs Are Insects. (p. 292)
—Bugs Are Insects. Jenkins, Steve, illus. (p. 292)
—First Day of School. Rockwell, Lizzy, illus. (p. 736)
—First Snowfall. (p. 739)
—First Snowfall. Rockwell, Lizzy, illus. (p. 739)
—Hey, Charleston! The True Story of the Jenkins Orphanage Band. Bootman, Colin, illus. (p. 964)
—Hiking Day. Rockwell, Lizzy, illus. (p. 971)
—Let's Go to the Hardware Store. (p. 1274)
—Library Day. (p. 1284)
—Library Day. Rockwell, Lizzy, illus. (p. 1284)
—My Spring Robin. Rockwell, Harlow, illus. (p. 1561)
—One Bean. (p. 1658)
—Presidents' Day. Rockwell, Lizzy, illus. (p. 1789)
—Spy Called James: The True Story of James Lafayette, Revolutionary War Double Agent. Cooper, Floyd, illus. (p. 2093)
—St. Patrick's Day. Rockwell, Lizzy, illus. (p. 2098)
—What's So Bad about Gasoline? Fossil Fuels & What They Do. Meisel, Paul, illus. (p. 2425)
—Zoo Day. Rockwell, Lizzy, illus. (p. 2543)
Rockwell, Carey. Danger in Deep Space. (p. 501)
—Treachery in Outer Space. (p. 2281)
Rockwell, Donna. Seeing Stars! One Boy's Quest for the Stars of the Sea. (p. 1984)
Rockwell, Ethel Theodora. Freeport Pageant of the Black Hawk Country (Classic Reprint) (p. 783)
Rockwell, Eve. Make Your Own Christmas Cards. (p. 1387)
Rockwell, Frederick Frye. Key to the Land: What a City Man Did with a Small Farm (Classic Reprint) (p. 1212)
Rockwell, Harlow, illus. see Rockwell, Anne.
Rockwell, Harlow, jt. auth. see Rockwell, Anne.
Rockwell, Joanna, illus. see Souliere, Lisa.
Rockwell, Lizzy. Bird Is a Bird. (p. 230)
—Bird Is a Bird. Rockwell, Lizzy, illus. (p. 230)
—Busy Body Book: A Kid's Guide to Fitness. (p. 302)
—Good Enough to Eat: A Kid's Guide to Food & Nutrition. Rockwell, Lizzy, illus. (p. 862)
—How Do You Feel? (p. 1029)
—Mammal Is an Animal. (p. 1393)
—Plants Feed Me. (p. 1757)
—Plants Feed Me. Rockwell, Lizzy, illus. (p. 1757)
Rockwell, Lizzy, illus. see Hulme, Joy N.
Rockwell, Lizzy, illus. see Jenkins, Priscilla Belz.
Rockwell, Lizzy, illus. see Rockwell, Anne.
Rockwell, Lizzy & Fowler, Allan. What's the Weather? (p. 2426)
Rockwell, Norman, illus. see Public Domain, Public.
Rockwell, Reese. Small Things (Classic Reprint) (p. 2040)
Rockwood, Caroline Washburn. East Florida Romance (Classic Reprint) (p. 619)
Rockwood, Leigh. Allosaurus. (p. 57)
—Ancient Egyptian Culture. (p. 80)
—Ancient Egyptian Daily Life. (p. 80)
—Ancient Egyptian Economy. (p. 80)
—Ancient Egyptian Geography. (p. 80)
—Ancient Egyptian Government. (p. 80)
—Ancient Egyptian Technology. (p. 81)
—Ankylosaurus. (p. 96)
—Brachiosaurus. (p. 274)
—Chimpanzees Are Smart! (p. 377)
—Creepy Crawlies (p. 472)
—Diplodocus. (p. 552)
—Dogs Are Smart! (p. 577)
—Dolphins Are Smart! (p. 580)
—Flies & Maggots Are Gross! (p. 748)
—Hadrosaurus. (p. 909)
—Horses Are Smart! (p. 1005)
—Iguanodon. (p. 1094)
—Parrots Are Smart! (p. 1701)
—Pigs Are Smart! (p. 1744)
—Plesiosaurus. (p. 1762)
—Pteranodon. (p. 1809)
—Slugs Are Gross! (p. 2039)
—Stegosaurus. (p. 2112)
—T. Rex. (p. 2174)
—Tell Me the Difference Between a Bee & a Wasp. (p. 2202)
—Tell Me the Difference Between a Frog & a Toad. (p. 2202)
—Tell Me the Difference Between a Porcupine & a Hedgehog. (p. 2202)
—Tell Me the Difference Between a Rabbit & a Hare. (p. 2202)
—Tell Me the Difference Between a Seal & a Sea Lion. (p. 2202)
—Tell Me the Difference Between an Alligator & a Crocodile. (p. 2202)
—Triceratops. (p. 2287)
—V Ancient Egyptian Geography. (p. 2343)
—Velociraptor. (p. 2349)
Rockwood, Leigh, jt. auth. see Clark, Willow.
Rockwood, Roy. Dave Dashaway & His Hydroplane. (p. 510)
—Jack North's Treasure Hunt: Daring Adventures in South America. (p. 1152)
—Jack North's Treasure Hunt: Or Daring Adventures in South America (Classic Reprint) (p. 1152)
—Lost on the Moon: Or in Quest of the Field of Diamonds (Classic Reprint) (p. 1355)
—Through the Air to the North Pole: Or, the Wonderful Cruise of the Electric Monarch. (p. 2237)
—Under the Ocean to the South Pole: The Strange Cruise of the Submarine Wonder. (p. 2322)
—Under the Ocean to the South Pole: Or, the Strange Cruise of the Submarine Wonder. (p. 2322)
—Under the Ocean to the South Pole. (p. 2322)
—Wizard of the Sea: A Trip under the Ocean. (p. 2483)
Rockworth, Janice. Juelz Santana. (p. 1186)
—Nas. (p. 1576)
—Wu-Tang Clan. (p. 2514)
Rocky, Kati. To Pieces. (p. 2253)
Rocus, Kathy. Shandy & Orion: Two Happy Guinea Pigs. Moss, Jennifer & Moss, Jessica, illus. (p. 1999)
Rod and Staff Publishers, Inc Staff, contrib. by. My Little Bird Book. (p. 1552)
Rod and Staff Publishers Staff, contrib. by. My Little Flower Book. (p. 1552)
Rodaah, Rahma. Muhiima's Quest. (p. 1525)
Rodale, Maya. Lady Miss Penny Goes to Lunch. Flint, Gillian, illus. (p. 1237)
Rodanas, Kristina, illus. see London, Jonathan.
Rodari, Gianni. Cuentos Escritos a Maquina. Estrada, Ixchel, illus. (p. 483)
—Libro de Los Porques, el. Animales. (p. 1286)
—Libro de Los Porques, el. Cielo y Tierra. (p. 1286)
—Telephone Tales. Shugaar, Anthony, tr. (p. 2201)
—Y 7. Facchini, Vittoria, illus. (p. 2516)
Rodari, Gianni & Molly, Francesco. Jugar con el Baston. (p. 1186)
Rodd, Ralph. Secret of the Flames (Classic Reprint) (p. 1977)
Rodda, Emily. Best-Kept Secret. (p. 206)
—Deltora Quest 1. Niwano, Makoto, illus. (p. 527)
—Deltora Quest 2. Niwano, Makoto, illus. (p. 527)
—Deltora Quest 3. Niwano, Makoto, illus. (p. 527)
—Deltora Quest 4. Niwano, Makoto, illus. (p. 527)
—Deltora Quest 5. Niwano, Makoto, illus. (p. 527)
—Deltora Quest 6. Niwano, Makoto, illus. (p. 527)
—Deltora Quest 7. Niwano, Makoto, illus. (p. 527)
—Deltora Quest 8. Niwano, Makoto, illus. (p. 527)
—Deltora Quest 9. Niwano, Makoto, illus. (p. 527)
—Fairy Realm #1: the Charm Bracelet Bk. 1. Vitale, Raoul, illus. (p. 697)
—Fairy Realm #2: the Flower Fairies. Vitale, Raoul, illus. (p. 697)
—Golden Door. (p. 857)
—Hungry Isle: Star of Deltora. (p. 1052)
—Hungry Isle. (p. 1052)
—Pigs Might Fly. (p. 1744)
—Shadows of the Master. (p. 1998)
—Silver Door. (p. 2019)
—Something Special. (p. 2060)
—Third Door. (p. 2222)
—Towers of Illica: Star of Deltora. (p. 2269)
—Towers of Illica. (p. 2269)
—Two Moons: Star of Deltora. (p. 2308)
—Two Moons. (p. 2308)
—Wizard of Rondo. (p. 2483)
Roddam, George. Life & Art of Paul Gauguin. Harasymowicz, Slawa, illus. (p. 1288)
—Life & Art of Vincent Van Gogh. Harasymowicz, Sawa, illus. (p. 1288)
Roddick, Melissa. Time for Gym Class: Count to Tell the Number of Objects. (p. 2244)
Roddy, Lee. D. J. Dillon Adventure Series Set 1. (p. 494)
—Ladd Family Adventure Novels Set One (p. 1236)
Roddy-Worsham, Clara. Bear Baby & New Baby Forever. (p. 179)
—Bear Baby Goes Fishing. (p. 179)
—Bear Baby's Birthday Gift. (p. 179)
Rode, Linda & Moodie, Fiona. In the Never-Ever Wood. (p. 1110)
Rode, Linda, et al. I, a Living Arrow. (p. 1056)
Rode, Maureen. Day with Little Duke. Kinstle Nocera, Suzanne, illus. (p. 515)
Rodeheaver, Homer. Song Stories of the Sawdust Trail (Classic Reprint) (p. 2063)
Rodeheaver, Margaret. Porkington Hamm. (p. 1778)
Rodeheaver, Margaret M. Haunted Holiday: A Christmas Cookie Ghost Story. (p. 938)
Rodemann, Otros. Llamado y Misin de la Iglesia. Humildad, Integridad, Sencillez, Unidad: The Call & Mission of the Church. (p. 1337)
Rodenberg, Julius. Island of the Saints: A Pilgrimage Through Ireland (Classic Reprint) (p. 1140)
Röder, Marlene. In the River Darkness. (p. 1110)
—In the River Darkness. Reichel, Tammi, tr. (p. 1110)
Roderick, Christina. No Peanuts for Pete. (p. 1614)
Roderick, Cindy. Henry the Hound Knocks Grandma Down. (p. 955)
Roderick, Julian. Felix Jones & the Treasure of the Typhon. (p. 719)
Roderick, Stacey. Birds from Head to Tail. Moriya, Kwanchai, illus. (p. 232)
—Bugs from Head to Tail. Moriya, Kwanchai, illus. (p. 292)
—Dinosaurs from Head to Tail. Moriya, Kwanchai, illus. (p. 551)
—Ocean Animals from Head to Tail. Moriya, Kwanchai, illus. (p. 1635)
Rodger, Anne-Marie. Sports Jokes, Riddles, & Games. (p. 2089)
Rodger, Ellen. Ancient Egypt Inside Out. (p. 80)
—Ancient Mesopotamia Inside Out. (p. 81)
—Arctic Research Journal. (p. 112)
—Bloodsucking Lice & Fleas. (p. 246)
—Fetal Alcohol Spectrum Disorder. (p. 721)
—Great Lakes Research Journal. (p. 887)
—Hoping for a Home after Myanmar. (p. 1002)
—How Does the Canadian Government Work? (p. 1030)
—Is There a Future for Fossil Fuels? (p. 1137)
—Jazz Jennings: Voice for LGBTQ Youth. (p. 1162)
—Mississippi River Research Journal. (p. 1482)
—Monster & Creepy-Crawly Jokes, Riddles, & Games. (p. 1495)
—My New Home after Iraq. (p. 1558)

Roe, E. P. Barriers Burned Away (Classic Reprint) (p. 167)
—Day of Fate (Classic Reprint) (p. 513)
—Driven Back to Eden (Classic Reprint) (p. 605)
—From Jest to Earnest (Classic Reprint) (p. 792)
—He Fell in Love with His Wife (Classic Reprint) (p. 941)
—His Sombre Rivals, Vol. 13 (Classic Reprint) (p. 974)
Roe, E. R. Brought to Bay (Classic Reprint) (p. 286)
—Gray & the Blue: A Story Founded on Incidents Connected with the War for the Union (Classic Reprint) (p. 882)
Roe, Eden. Garden of Words. (p. 809)
Roe, Edward P. Taken Alive & Other Stories: With an Autobiography (Classic Reprint) (p. 2177)
Roe, Edward Payson. Hornet's Nest: A Story of Love & War (Classic Reprint) (p. 1003)
—Knight of the Nineteenth Century (Classic Reprint) (p. 1228)
—Miss. Lou, and, Driven Back to Eden: Illustrated (Classic Reprint) (p. 1479)
—Nature's Serial Story, Vol. 1 (Classic Reprint) (p. 1582)
—Near to Nature's Heart (Classic Reprint) (p. 1584)
—Original Belle, Vol. 6 (Classic Reprint) (p. 1671)
—Unexpected Result, & Other Stories (Classic Reprint) (p. 2327)
—What Can She Do? (Classic Reprint) (p. 2407)
—Works of E. P. Roe (Classic Reprint) (p. 2497)
—Young Girl's Wooing (Classic Reprint) (p. 2531)
Roe, Frances M.A. Army Letters from an Officer's Wife 1871-1888 (Classic Reprint) (p. 118)
Roe, Gary. Difference Maker: Overcoming Adversity & Turning Pain into Purpose, Every Day (Teen Edition) (p. 544)
—Difference Maker: Overcoming Adversity & Turning Pain into Purpose, Every Day (Adult Edition) (p. 544)
—Living on the Edge: How to Fight & Win the Battle for Your Mind & Heart. (p. 1333)
—Living on the Edge: How to Fight & Win the Battle for Your Mind & Heart (Teen Edition) (p. 1333)
Roe, Mary Abigail. Long Search (Classic Reprint) (p. 1343)
Roe, Mechal Renee. Cool Cuts. (p. 448)
—Happy Hair. (p. 922)
Roe, Mechal Renee, illus. see Harris, Kamala.
Roe, Monika, illus. see Florence, Debbi Michiko.
Roe, Monika, illus. see Wallach, Marlene.
Roe, Robin. List of Cages. (p. 1308)
Roe, Vingie E. Tharon of Lost Valley (Classic Reprint) (p. 2212)
—Val of Paradise (Classic Reprint) (p. 2343)
Roe, Vingie Eve. Heart of Night Wind: A Story of the Great North West (Classic Reprint) (p. 945)
Roebuck, M. F. C. Nyitso a Novel of West Africa (Classic Reprint) (p. 1632)
Roeder, Annette. 13 Buildings Children Should Know. (p. 2552)
—Art Coloring Book. (p. 120)
—Coloring Book Miro. (p. 424)
—Leonardo Da Vinci: Coloring Book. (p. 1267)
—Vincent Van Gogh. Prestel, ed. (p. 2359)
Roeder, Hans Albert. Beitrag Zur Kenntniss des Terrain a Chailles und Seiner Zweischaler in der Umgegend Von Pfirt Im Ober-Elsass: Inaugural-Dissertation der Mathematischen und Naturwissenschaftlichen Facultat der Kaiser-Wilhelms-Universitat Strassburg Zur Erlangung der Doc. (p. 195)
Roeder, Vanessa. Box Turtle. (p. 266)
—Lucy & the String. Roeder, Vanessa, illus. (p. 1365)
Roeder, Virginia M., illus. see Chrismer, Melanie.
Roefaro, Maryann. Snippets from the Inside-Out by Millie the Dog. (p. 2046)
Roegiers, Charles B. Rufus Rides a Catfish: (and Other Fables from the Farmstead) Patterson, Priscilla, illus. (p. 1912)
Roegiers, Maud. Princesse Qui P'Te(la) (p. 1799)
—Take the Time: Mindfulness for Kids. (p. 2177)
Roehl, Tessa. Aurora Plays the Part (p. 138)
—Disney Before the Story: Mulan's Secret Plan. Disney Storybook Art Team & Shimabukuro, Denise, illus. (p. 559)
—Disney Princess Beginnings: Tiana's Best Surprise (Disney Princess) RH Disney Staff, illus. (p. 562)
—Tiana's Best Surpris (p. 2239)
—Tiana's Best Surprise. (p. 2239)
Roehl, Tessa, jt. auth. see RH Disney Staff.
Roehler, Yvonne Fetig, illus. see Washburn, Sandi.
Roehrig, Artemis. Creepy, Crawly Tattoo Bugs: 60 Temporary Tattoos That Teach. Ditner, Jillian, illus. (p. 473)
—Roaring, Rumbling Tattoo Dinosaurs: 50 Temporary Tattoos That Teach. Gregory, Aaron John, illus. (p. 1889)
—Super, Strong Tattoo Sharks: 50 Temporary Tattoos That Teach. Gregory, Aaron John, illus. (p. 2158)
Roehrig, Artemis, jt. auth. see Demas, Corinne.
Roehrig, Caleb. Death Prefers Blondes. (p. 521)
—Fell of Dark. (p. 719)
—Last Seen Leaving. (p. 1249)
—White Rabbit. (p. 2445)
Roehrig, Catharine, jt. auth. see Metropolitan Museum of Art Staff.
Roehrig, Nancy, ed. see Potts, Pk.
Roemer, Heidi Bee. Peekity Boo - What You Can Do! Wohnoutka, Mike, illus. (p. 1713)
Roemer, Heidi Bee, ed. see Hoyte, Carol-Ann.
Roemer, Jean. Polyglot Reader, & Guide for Translation: Consisting of a Series of English Extracts, with Their Translation into French, German, Spanish, & Italian; the Several Parts Designed to Serve As Mutual Keys (Classic Reprint) (p. 1772)
Roemhildt, Mark. Gladiators. (p. 840)
—Jack Swagger. (p. 1152)
Roemisch, Matt. Ask Someone Grumpy to Read You This Book. Mansker, Jennifer, ed. (p. 126)
—Purple Polka-Dotted Peanut Butter Eater. Szanyi, Joshua, illus. (p. 1816)
Roe-Pimm, Nancy. Colo's Story. (p. 426)
Roeser, Matt. Oh No, Astro! Woodard, Brad, illus. (p. 1642)
Roessel, David & Rampersad, Arnold, eds. Poetry for Young People: Langston Hughes. Andrews, Benny, illus. (p. 1767)
Roesser, Blanche. Fast Fact Multiplication. (p. 713)
—Fast Fact Subtraction. (p. 713)
—Story of Leo the Lion. (p. 2131)
—Story of Pegasus. (p. 2132)
—Story of Perseus. (p. 2132)
Roesser, Marie. Dust Bowl (p. 610)
—Exploring the Aquarium. (p. 683)
—Exploring the Forest. (p. 683)
—Exploring the Pond. (p. 683)
—Middle Ages (p. 1460)
—Spanish-American War (p. 2073)
—What Makes Lightning & Thunder? (p. 2418)
—Why Do Leaves Change Colors? (p. 2456)
—Why Does the Moon Change Shape? (p. 2457)
Roettiger, Laura. Aliana Reaches for the Moon. Boroff, Ariel, illus. (p. 44)
Roetzheim, William, ed. Modern Nursery Rhymes. (p. 1487)
Rofé, Jennifer, jt. auth. see Peterson, Mary.
Roff, Don. Holiday Magic. (p. 987)
Roff, Jason T. Careers in E-Commerce: Software Development. (p. 329)
Roff, Kimberly A., jt. auth. see Roff, Jason T.
Roffe, Michael, illus. see Wilkinson-Latham, Christopher.
Roffey, Chris. Building BIG Apps, Level 3. (p. 294)
—Coding Club Python: Interactive Adventures Level 2. (p. 412)
—Python, Level 2: Next Steps. (p. 1819)
Roffler, Crystal H., ed. see Wilson, Jd.
Roffler, Ethan, illus. see Wilson, Jd.
Rogala, Judy. Dog Days of Christmas. Stroede, Paul, illus. (p. 575)
Rogalski, Mark. Make Me a Monster. (p. 1386)
Rogan, Bernie. Creatures of the Sea: Can You Guess Me. (p. 472)
Rogé. French Fry King. Rogé, illus. (p. 784)
Rogasky, Barbara. Rapunzel. Hyman, Trina Schart, illus. (p. 1841)
Rogé. Haiti My Country (p. 910)
Roge. Mingan My Village (p. 1471)
Roge, illus. see Chartrand, Lili.
Rogé, illus. see Lapointe, Stéphanie.
Roge, Adolphe. Golden Calf: A Play in Four Acts (Classic Reprint) (p. 857)
Roger, Fernandes, illus. see McNutt, Nan.
Roger, Hoffman, illus. see Hoffman, Nancy.
Roger, Jacques Francois. Fables Sénégalaises Recueillies de l'Ouolof, et Mises en Vers Français: Avec des Notes Destinées a Faire Connaître la Sénégambie, Son Climat, Ses Principales Productions, la Civilisation et les Moeurs des Habitans (Classic Reprint) (p. 691)
Roger, Marie-Sabine. Of Course They Do! Boys & Girls Can Do Anything. Sol, Anne, photos by. (p. 1639)
Roger, Noëlle. Victim's Return (Classic Reprint) (p. 2355)
Roger, Rachel & Lineberry, Joe. Graphing the Mystery. Rave, Arte, illus. (p. 881)
Rogers, Alan, illus. see Eeles, Alex.
Rogers, Alan, illus. see French, Vivian.
Rogers, Alan, illus. see Gates, Susan.
Rogers, Alan, illus. see Rickards, Lynne & Roberts, Ley Honor.
Rogers, Albert R. Story of Beautiful Jim Key: The Most Wonderful Horse in All the World (Classic Reprint) (p. 2129)
Rogers, Amanda. My Favorite Things of Fall. (p. 1539)
Rogers, Amy B. American Communities: We Live in a Suburb (p. 71)
—Caribou of the Tundra. (p. 330)
—Do Kids Need Recess? (p. 570)
—Girls Play Basketball. (p. 839)
—Girls Play Softball. (p. 839)
—I Learn from My Brother & Sister. (p. 1067)
—Incredible Emeralds. (p. 1113)
—Moose (p. 1503)
—Orion. (p. 1672)
—Que Hacen Los Bomberos? / What Do Firefighters Do? (p. 1822)
—Que Hacen Los Doctores? / What Do Doctors Do? (p. 1822)
—Recipes of the Civil War. (p. 1853)
—Should Boys & Girls Go to Separate Schools? (p. 2011)
—Should Girls Play Sports with Boys? (p. 2011)
—Soccer: Science at Your Feet. (p. 2052)
—We Live in a City (p. 2391)
—What Are Human Rights? (p. 2405)
—What Are Student Rights? (p. 2406)
—What Do Doctors Do? (p. 2408)
—What Do Firefighters Do? (p. 2408)
—What's Racism? (p. 2425)
Rogers, Amy B. & Davenport, John. American Revolution: Fighting for Independence. (p. 73)
Rogers, Andrea L. Mary & the Trail of Tears: A Cherokee Removal Survival Story. Forsyth, Matt, illus. (p. 1414)
Rogers, Andy. Puppy Brothers Adventures with Forest Friends - Children's Picture Book for Ages 3 To 8. (p. 1815)
—Who's Who of Pro Football: A Guide to the Game's Greatest Players. (p. 2454)
Rogers, Andy, et al. Who's Who of Pro Sports. (p. 2454)
Rogers, Anna A. Peace & the Vices (Classic Reprint) (p. 1709)
Rogers, Austin Flint. Introduction to the Study of Minerals: A Combined Text-Book & Pocket Manual (Classic Reprint) (p. 1129)
—Introduction to the Study of Minerals & Rocks: A Combined Text-Book & Pocket Manual (Classic Reprint) (p. 1129)
Rogers, Benjamin, illus. see Rogers, Hunter W.
Rogers, Bernadette. Sunflower Adventures. (p. 2152)
Rogers, Betty Lou. ABC's for Teens, & What They Mean. (p. 4)
—Acquiring the Human Skills of Thinking, Saying, Doing. (p. 11)
—Bossy Susie Saucy! (p. 264)
—Capricious Caleb O'Connor. (p. 324)
—Chris Earns His MBA in Manners, Behavior, Attitude. (p. 382)
—God & Country. (p. 850)
—History, Love It & Learn or Hate It & Harm. (p. 977)
—Human Dilemma of the Young. (p. 1049)
—Jealousy. (p. 1162)
—Kate Earns Her MBA-1. (p. 1204)
—Loves Flowers Hates Weeds. (p. 1362)
—Parables Jesus's Timely Tales. (p. 1698)
—So, You Think We Shouldn't Have Dropped the Bomb ? (p. 2051)
—Teens, Consider All Circumstances & Consequences! (p. 2200)
—Ten Commandments. (p. 2203)
—USA, Democracy, the American Way. (p. 2341)
Rogers, Blessing. Gabby & Ralph Meet Their New Teacher. (p. 804)
Rogers, Bud, et al. Truth Revealed Padilla, Ariel, illus. (p. 2297)
Rogers, Charles Gordon. Government Clerks: A Book of Ballads (Classic Reprint) (p. 872)
Rogers, Charlotte Boardman. Mistress of Many Moods (Classic Reprint) (p. 1483)
Rogers, Danielle. Detective Red & the Case of the Baby Caterpillar. (p. 534)
Rogers, Darrin D. Ari Bella's Ferret. (p. 115)
Rogers, David, illus. see Adams, Jesse.
Rogers, Debbie. Princess Annabelle. Williams, Rachel, illus. (p. 1796)
Rogers, Derek G. Monstrous Myths & Fabulous Fables. (p. 1498)
Rogers, Diana. Critters of Grassy Green Plains: Got to Get the Critters Counted. (p. 476)
Rogers, Don. Adventures of Shawn & Jeremy. (p. 27)
—Adventures of Shawn & Jeremy with Sister Nicole & the Hot Air Balloon: Volume Two. (p. 27)
Rogers, Eleanor. Purrcy's Discovery. (p. 1816)
Rogers, Emma Winner. Journal of a Country Woman (Classic Reprint) (p. 1180)
Rogers, Ethel. Sebago-Wohelo Camp Fire Girls (Classic Reprint) (p. 1973)
Rogers, Frances. Mr. Brady's Camera Boy (Classic Reprint) (p. 1518)
Rogers, Frances, jt. auth. see Bosher, Kate Langley.
Rogers, Frances, jt. auth. see Stratton-Porter, Gene.
Rogers, Frances Louise. Pylgrym Cronycles (Classic Reprint) (p. 1819)
Rogers, Fred. Beautiful Day in the Neighborhood: The Poetry of Mister Rogers. Flowers, Luke, illus. (p. 184)
—It's You I Like: A Mister Rogers Poetry Book. Flowers, Luke, illus. (p. 1148)
—Mister Rogers' Neighborhood: Henrietta Meets Someone New. Golden Books, illus. (p. 1482)
—Mister Rogers Neighborhood LGB 6-Copy Clip Strip Fall 2019 (p. 1482)
—Won't You Be My Neighbor? A Mister Rogers Poetry Book. Flowers, Luke, illus. (p. 2491)
Rogers, Frederick. Seven Deadly Sins - Scholar's Choice Edition. (p. 1993)
Rogers, Grace McLeod. Joan at Halfway (Classic Reprint) (p. 1169)
Rogers, Gregory, illus. see Davis, Tony.
Rogers, Gregory, illus. see Gwynne, Phillip.
Rogers, Gregory, illus. see Watts, Frances.
Rogers, Hal. Cherry Pickers. (p. 366)
—Tractors. (p. 2273)
Rogers, Hunter W. Diadem: The Adventures of Hans & Feetz. Rogers, Benjamin, illus. (p. 537)
Rogers, Jacqueline. Goblin Moon. Rogers, Jacqueline, illus. (p. 849)
Rogers, Jacqueline, illus. see Adams, Alison.
Rogers, Jacqueline, illus. see Bush, Laura & Hager, Jenna Bush.
Rogers, Jacqueline, illus. see Cleary, Beverly.
Rogers, Jacqueline, illus. see Drummond, Ree.
Rogers, Jacqueline, illus. see Gilman, Grace.
Rogers, Jacqueline, illus. see Karr, Lily.
Rogers, Jacqueline, illus. see Mayer, Kirsten.
Rogers, Jacqueline, illus. see Peterson, John & Slater, Teddy.
Rogers, Jacqueline, illus. see Salisbury, Graham.
Rogers, Jacqueline, illus. see San Souci, Robert D.
Rogers, Jacqueline, illus. see Siy, Alexandra.
Rogers, Jacqueline, illus. see Smith, Carrie.
Rogers, Jacqueline, illus. see Wallace, Bill.
Rogers, Jacqueline, illus. see Washington, Donna L. & Washington, Donna.
Rogers, Jacqueline, tr. see Dumas, Alexandre.
Rogers, Jahshua. Dash on the Run! Rogers, Jahshua, illus. (p. 508)
Rogers, James Grafton. Goldenrod Lode: A Frontier Drama in Verse (Classic Reprint) (p. 860)
Rogers, James S. Our Regiment: A Military Drama Compiled from Incidents in the War of the Rebellion, & Respectfully Dedicated to the Grand Army of the Republic (Classic Reprint) (p. 1680)
Rogers, Jane & Benchmark Education Co., LLC Staff. Best Nest. (p. 207)
—Get Well, Red Hen! (p. 825)
Rogers, Jane, et al. Get Well, Red Hen! - Big Bus - a Sled Club: BuildUp Unit 2 Lap Book. Anderson, Nicola & Greenhead, Bill, illus. (p. 825)
Rogers, Jean. Goodbye, My Island. Munoz, Rie, illus. (p. 866)
Rogers, Jennifer. While the Stars Are at Play. (p. 2442)
Rogers, Jesse & Rogers, Seaweed. It Started with a Pumpkin Seed. (p. 1142)
Rogers, John R. Looking Forward: Or the Story of an American Farm (Classic Reprint) (p. 1347)
Rogers, Jon. Bear at the Fair. (p. 179)
Rogers, Jonathan. Charlatan's Boy: A Novel. (p. 358)
Rogers, Jr Kenneth. Chronicles of the Last Liturian - Book Two: Love & Fear. (p. 389)
Rogers, Julia Ellen. Shell Book: A Popular Guide to a Knowledge of the Families of Living Mollusks, & an Aid to the Identification of Shells Native & Foreign (Classic Reprint) (p. 2005)
Rogers, Juniata. Arctic Ocean. (p. 112)
—Atlantic Ocean. (p. 133)
—Foggy. (p. 756)
—Icy. (p. 1089)
—Indian Ocean. (p. 1116)
—Pacific Ocean. (p. 1691)
—Southern Ocean. (p. 2069)
—Sunny. (p. 2152)
—Windy. (p. 2472)
Rogers, Kara. Battling & Managing Disease. (p. 175)
—Cloning. (p. 406)
—Engineering Solutions for Epidemics & Pandemics (p. 652)
—Genetic Engineering. (p. 815)
—Health & Disease in Society (p. 943)
—Infectious Diseases. (p. 1118)
—Medicine & Healers Through History. (p. 1436)
—Substance Use & Abuse. (p. 2146)
Rogers, Kara, ed. 100 Most Influential Scientists of All Time. (p. 2557)
—Endocrine System. (p. 650)
—New Thinking about Genetics. (p. 1597)
Rogers, Kate. Air Marshals (p. 37)
—Exploring the Sun. (p. 683)
—Girls Play Lacrosse. (p. 839)
—I Can Count To 10! Number Names & Count Sequence. (p. 1061)
—Mechanics (p. 1435)
—Police Officers on the Job. (p. 1770)
—Robert Fulton Invents the Steamboat. (p. 1890)
—What's Gun Control? (p. 2424)
—Zodiac Killer: Terror in California. (p. 2541)
Rogers, Katie & Higgins-Smith, Mark. How Feather Frog Feels. (p. 1031)
Rogers, Kelly. Buyer Beware Peterschmidt, Betsy, illus. (p. 304)
—House Sitters Peterschmidt, Betsy, illus. (p. 1024)
—Key Peterschmidt, Betsy, illus. (p. 1210)
—Starving Ghost: An Up2U Mystery Adventure. Glenn, Ebony, illus. (p. 2108)
—Study Group. Peterschmidt, Betsy, illus. (p. 2144)
Rogers, Kelly & ABDO Publishing Company Staff. Rm. 201 Peterschmidt, Betsy, illus. (p. 1888)
Rogers, Kenneth, Jr. Chronicles of the Last Liturian: Book Three, Infinite Truths & Impossible Lies. (p. 389)
Rogers, Kirsteen. Christmas Coloring Book. (p. 384)
—Christmas Patterns Coloring Book. (p. 386)
—First Illustrated Math Dictionary IR. (p. 737)
—Haunted House Sticker Book. (p. 938)
—Illustrated Elementary Science Dictionary IR. (p. 1096)
—Monsters Sticker Book. (p. 1498)
—Mummies & Pyramids: Internet-Linked. (p. 1526)
—Spooky Coloring Book. (p. 2086)
Rogers, Kirsteen, ed. see Clarke, Phillip & Khan, Sarah.
Rogers, Kirsteen, ed. see Dalby, Elizabeth.
Rogers, Kirsteen, ed. see Marks, Anthony.
Rogers, Kirsteen, jt. auth. see Howell, Laura.
Rogers, Kirsteen & Everall, Nayera. Patterns Coloring Book. (p. 1706)
Rogers, Kirsteen & Large, Tori. Illustrated Elementary Math Dictionary. (p. 1096)
Rogers, Kirsteen, et al. Usborne Science Encyclopedia: Internet-Linked. Bhachu, Verinder, illus. (p. 2341)
Rogers, Lauren. Skyler & the Se. Sexton, Jessa, ed. (p. 2034)
Rogers, Leeann. Ms Tulper Is Her Name. (p. 1523)
Rogers, Lela E. Ginger Rogers & the Riddle of the Scarlet Cloak: An Original Story Featuring Ginger Rogers, Famous Motion-Picture Star, As the Heroine (Classic Reprint) (p. 833)
Rogers, Leslie E. It Is Me. Wilhelm, Doris L., illus. (p. 1141)
Rogers, Lillian Emily, jt. auth. see Wohlfarth, Julia Helen.
Rogers, Linda Lee. When Grandma Comes to Play. (p. 2430)
Rogers, Lisa. 16 Words: William Carlos Williams & the Red Wheelbarrow. Groenink, Chuck, illus. (p. 2552)
—Hound Won't Go. Ishihara, Meg, illus. (p. 1021)
Rogers, Lisa Waller. Remember the Alamo! The Runaway Scrape Diary of Belle Wood, Austin's Colony 1835-1836. (p. 1864)
Rogers, Logan, illus. see Linder, Todd.
Rogers, Madalyn V., illus. see Liner, Robin.
Rogers, Marcus. Through the Fire to Be on Fire. (p. 2237)
Rogers, Marshall, et al. Marvel Masterworks: Doctor Strange Vol. 9. (p. 1412)
Rogers, Mary Hulbert. Children of the Night (Classic Reprint) (p. 372)
Rogers, Melissa, illus. see Waters, Galadriel, ed.
Rogers, Michelle Elizabeth. Adventures of Brutus & Baby: A Haunted Halloween. Collier, Kevin Scott, illus. (p. 22)
Rogers, Naomi. Amazing Tree House. (p. 66)
Rogers, Nikki. Beautiful Girl Like You. Rogers, Nikki, illus. (p. 184)
—Hero Like You. Rogers, Nikki, illus. (p. 961)
Rogers, Paul. What Will the Weather Be Like Today? Kazuko, illus. (p. 2422)
Rogers, Paul, illus. see Dylan, Bob.
Rogers, Paul, illus. see Marsalis, Wynton.
Rogers, Peter, illus. see Farrell, Tom.
Rogers, Rachel. Surprised by Subtraction. (p. 2163)
Rogers, Rachel & Lineberry, Joe. Salvados Por la Suma. Swofford, Morgan, illus. (p. 1926)
—Saved by Addition. Swofford, Morgan, illus. (p. 1938)
—Surprised by Subtraction. Swofford, Morgan, illus. (p. 2163)
Rogers, Ralph. Pierian 1916: Being the Year Book of the Richmond High School (Classic Reprint) (p. 1742)
Rogers, Ramona. Buck & Penny. (p. 289)
Rogers, Robert Cameron. Old Dorset: Chronicles of a New York Country-Side. (p. 1645)
—Old Dorset: Chronicles of a New York Country-Side (Classic Reprint) (p. 1645)
Rogers, Robert L. Tom Johnson (Classic Reprint) (p. 2257)
Rogers, Roy. Best of Alex Toth & John Buscema Roy Rogers Comics. Herman, Daniel, ed. (p. 207)
Rogers, Sara B. Ezra Hardman, M. an;, of Wayback College: And Other Stories (Classic Reprint) (p. 689)
Rogers Seavey, Lura. Switzerland. (p. 2171)
Rogers, Seth. Life in a Cube. (p. 1291)
—Maestros: Tiempo. (p. 1376)
—On the Job: Teachers: Time (Grade 1) (p. 1655)
Rogers, Shannon, jt. auth. see Batterson, Jason.
Rogers, Sherry, illus. see Allen, Nancy Kelly.
Rogers, Sherry, illus. see Cole, Carol A.

—Classic Corvettes (p. 400)
—Classic GTOs (p. 400)
—Matemáticas con Mascotas / Math with Pets. de la Vega, Eida, tr. (p. 1421)
—Matemáticas en el Parque / Math at the Park. de la Vega, Eida, tr. (p. 1421)
Romaine, Garret. Cool Crystal Creations: Exploring the Wonders of the Earth with Single Strand & Crystal Clusters. (p. 448)
—Geology Lab for Kids: 52 Projects to Explore Rocks, Gems, Geodes, Crystals, Fossils, & Other Wonders of the Earth's Surface. (p. 818)
—Little Learning Labs: Geology for Kids: 26 Projects to Explore Rocks, Gems, Geodes, Crystals, Fossils, & Other Wonders of the Earth's Surface; Activities for STEAM Learners. (p. 1320)
—Rocking Out with Rocks: Exploring the Wonders of Ingenious, Sedimentary, & Metamorphic Rocks. (p. 1895)
—Solar System, Space Rocks, & Beyond: Exploring the Wonders of Space Particles & Meteorites. (p. 2056)
—Understanding the Earth: Exploring the Wonders of the Earth's Surface & Its Amazing Geological Events. (p. 2325)
Romaine, Robert Dexter. New Age of Gold: Or the Life & Adventures of Robert Dexter Romaine (Classic Reprint) (p. 1591)
Romaine, William. Treatise upon the Walk of Faith, Vol. 1 of 2 (Classic Reprint) (p. 2283)
Roman, Celso. Arbol de Los Tucanes. (p. 109)
—Gusanito Investigador. (p. 906)
—Trébol Mágico de Las Tres R. (p. 2283)
Roman, Dave. Astronaut Academy: Re-Entry. Roman, Dave, illus. (p. 128)
—Teen Boat! The Race for Boatlantis. Green, John, illus. (p. 2198)
—Zero Gravity. Roman, Dave, illus. (p. 2539)
Roman, Dave, illus. see Hernández, Gabriel, et al.
Roman, Dave, illus. see Stine, R. L.
Roman, Edward. My Busy Year. (p. 1535)
Roman, Elisabeth. Ciel Racont' Aux Enfants(le. (p. 390)
Roman, Gabriel, illus. see Baumann, J. L.
Roman, Gemma, illus. see Du Mesnil, Sabine.
Roman, Jose M. Protectors of the Old World: Jurassic Fighters. (p. 1808)
—Valor Raptor: And the Protectors of the Old World. (p. 2345)
Roman, Lisa. Boots. Steckler, Megan, illus. (p. 262)
Roman, Nora. Using a Ruler. (p. 2341)
—Using a Scale. (p. 2341)
—Using Magnets. (p. 2341)
Roman Saint-Pierre, Erika. Hoppa's Big Move. Newman, J. Heidi, ed. (p. 1002)
Roman, T. J. Where the Sidewalk Begins. (p. 2439)
Roman, Teresa. Legacy. (p. 1261)
Romana, Emilia. Wolfheart 2. (p. 2484)
Roman-Crofts, Denisia. Adventures of Monkey See Monkey Doo. (p. 25)
Romanek, Trudee. Government & Law in the Early Islamic World. (p. 872)
—Great Ideas of the Renaissance. (p. 887)
—Life in a Commercial City. (p. 1291)
—Raising the Stakes (p. 1838)
—Science, Medicine, & Math in the Early Islamic World. (p. 1957)
—Splash It Swimming. (p. 2084)
Romanenko, Vasilisa, illus. see Mermelstein, Yael.
Romanenko, Vitaliy, illus. see Mermelstein, Yael.
Romanes, Ethel. Story of an English Sister (Ethel Georgina Romanes-Sister Etheldred) (Classic Reprint) (p. 2129)
Romanes, George John. Animal Intelligence. (p. 90)
—Mind & Motion & Monism. (p. 1469)
Romanet, Caroline, illus. see Graham, Ian.
Romanet, Caroline, illus. see Longstaff, Abie.
Romanet, Caroline, illus. see Parker, Steve.
Romanet, Caroline, illus. see Samson, Lucretia.
Romanini, Davide, illus. see Fadda, Liana.
Romano, Amy. Historical Atlas of the United Arab Emirates. (p. 976)
—Historical Atlas of the United States & Its Territories. (p. 976)
Romano, Amy & Baum, Margaux. Germ Warfare. (p. 821)
Romano, Ann Marie. Before You Sleep: A Bedtime Book of Gratitude. Hobai, Ioana, illus. (p. 191)
Romano, John L. & Hage, Sally M., eds. Best Practices in Prevention. (p. 207)
Romano, Louis. Zip Code. (p. 2541)
Romano, Michael. My Max Score AP U. S. History: Maximize Your Score in Less Time. (p. 1555)
Romano, Michael J., et al. Regents Exams & Answers: Global History & Geography 2020. (p. 1861)
Romano, Tom. Watcher in the Lighthouse. (p. 2383)
Romano-Dwyer, Lisa. Boys of Milverton Book Series: New Beginnings. (p. 273)
Romanoff, Zan. Grace & the Fever. (p. 873)
—Song to Take the World Apart. (p. 2063)
Romanstine-Hall, Alice. Sunglass Island. (p. 2152)
Roman-Stumpff, Bianca, illus. see Kontis, Alethea.
Roman-Stumpff, Bianca, jt. auth. see Kontis, Alethea.
Romasco-Moore, Maria. Some Kind of Animal. (p. 2059)
Romatif, Alexia. Los Animales de la Granja. (p. 1350)
—Los Animales Del Bosque. (p. 1350)
—Los Animales Del Mar. (p. 1350)
Romay, Alexis, tr. see Bates, Amy June & Bates, Juniper.
Romay, Alexis, tr. see Capucilli, Alyssa Satin.
Romay, Alexis, tr. see Carle, Eric.
Romay, Alexis, tr. see Engle, Margarita.
Romay, Alexis, tr. see Gibbs, Stuart.
Romay, Alexis, tr. see Tabby, Abigail.
Romay, Alexis, tr. see Verde, Susan.
Romberger, James, illus. see Lansdale, John L., et al.
Rombough, John, illus. see Highway, Tomson.
Rome, Ami Margolin, jt. auth. see Margolin, Phillip.
Rome, Jacqueline Thomas. Do I Have to Clean My Room? (p. 570)
—Do I Have to Clean My Room? Brown, Lillie Wyatt, illus. (p. 570)
—Do I Have to Go to Church Today? Thomas, Pamela L., illus. (p. 570)
Rome, Jamie & Curry, Paul. Oops! the Fish Died. Spencer, Tim, illus. (p. 1665)
Rome, Jane S. Teaching God's Children an Amazing Adventure. (p. 2195)
Romens, Dan, illus. see McIntyre, Lpc.
Romeo, Angelina, et al. Gooda & Goda. (p. 866)
Romeo, Emily. Veront: Los Cobradores de Vidas. (p. 2352)
—Veront: Los Secretos de la Muerte. (p. 2352)
Romeo, Robyn. Zoe & Zac - When the Crow Came to Chat. (p. 2541)
Romer, Alejandra Barba, illus. see Pedersen, Karoline Pahus.
Romer, Mabel. Peke's Pilgrimage (Classic Reprint) (p. 1714)
Romer, Ruth, jt. auth. see Kramer, Alan.
Romer, Valerie, illus. see Gedall, Gary Edward.
Romer, Valerie, jt. auth. see Gedall, Gary Edward.
Romero, Alejandra Barba, illus. see Pedersen, Karoline Pahus.
Romero, Benito, tr. see Barrie, J. M.
Romero, Bernardita. Mummy, What's in Your Tummy? Romero, Bernardita, illus. (p. 1526)
Romero, Danitza, illus. see Guay, Tia.
Romero, Gina, illus. see Altieri, Marion.
Romero Gutiérrez, Astrid. Cuentos de Angeles Para Ninos. (p. 483)
Romero, Jordan. No Summit Out of Sight: The True Story of the Youngest Person to Climb the Seven Summits. (p. 1615)
Romero, Jordan, et al. Boy Who Conquered Everest: The Jordan Romero Story. (p. 270)
Romero, José Rubén. Mexicas: Los Indígenas de Mesoamérica II. Flores, Olvier, illus. (p. 1454)
Romero, Kyle & Padron, Maria Lorena. Herbert Hoover Junior Ranger Activity Book. National Park Service Staff & Herbert Hoover National Historic Site (U.S), eds. (p. 957)
Romero, Leonardo. Hawkeye: Kate Bishop Vol. 3: Family Reunion. (p. 940)
Romero, Leonardo & Walsh, Michael. Hawkeye: Private Eye. (p. 940)
Romero, Libby. Albert Einstein. (p. 40)
—Animal Architects. (p. 88)
—Animals That Change Color. (p. 95)
—DK Life Stories Amelia Earhart. (p. 568)
—DK Life Stories: Helen Keller. Ager, Charlotte, illus. (p. 568)
—DK Life Stories: Jane Goodall. Ager, Charlotte, illus. (p. 568)
—Ibn Al-Haytham. (p. 1087)
—Mayflower: The Perilous Voyage That Changed the World. (p. 1430)
—NGR Ibn Al-Haytham (L3) The Man Who Discovered How We See. (p. 1601)
—Skyscrapers. (p. 2034)
—What Is an Archaeologist? (p. 2414)
Romero, Martha Elena. Luisol y Las Pesadillas. (p. 1366)
Romero, Naomi, illus. see Turner, Marie B.
Romero, R. M. Dollmaker of Krakow. (p. 579)
Romero, Soledad. Depeche Mode: The Unauthorized Biography. López del Hierro, Fernando, illus. (p. 529)
—Metallica: The Unauthorized Biography. Navas, David, illus. (p. 1452)
—Queen: The Unauthorized Biography. Castelló, Laura, illus. (p. 1823)
Romero-Anderson, Emerita. Milagro of the Spanish Bean Pot. Pijoan, Randall, illus. (p. 1465)
Romero-Robinette, Joella. Allie & Bailey Show: Meet Our Family. (p. 56)
Romeu, Antoni. Mi Primer Quijote. (p. 1456)
Romina Marti, illus. see Raum, Elizabeth.
Romines, Garrett & Miko, Christopher. Unofficial Holy Bible for Minecrafters: A Children's Guide to the Old & New Testament. (p. 2334)
Romita, John. Marvel Visionaries: John Romita Sr. (p. 1413)
Romita, John, illus. see Pak, Greg.
Romita, John & Lieber, Larry. Spectacular Spider-Man: Io, This Monster. (p. 2077)
Romita, John & Romita, John, Jr. Daredevil: The Man Without Fear. (p. 505)
—Marvel Visionaries: John Romita Jr. (p. 1413)
Romita, John, et al. Hulk: World War Hulk Omnibus. (p. 1048)
—Thor: Heroes Return Omnibus. (p. 2229)
—X-Force Epic Collection: X-Cutioner's Song. (p. 2515)
—X-Men Milestones: Mutant Massacre. (p. 2515)
Romita, John, Jr., illus. see Nocenti, Ann.
Romita, John, Jr., illus. see Straczynski, J. Michael.
Romita, John, Jr., jt. illus. see Romita, John.
Romita, Tom. Grumpy Dad Shovels Snow. Guarracino, Nick, illus. (p. 901)
Romito, Dee. BFF Bucket List. (p. 212)
—Birthday Castle: Fort Builders Inc. 1. Kissi, Marta, illus. (p. 233)
—Happy Tails Lodge: Fort Builders Inc. 2. Kissi, Marta, illus. (p. 924)
—No Place Like Home. (p. 1614)
—Pies from Nowhere: How Georgia Gilmore Sustained the Montgomery Bus Boycott. Freeman, Laura, illus. (p. 1742)
—Postcards from Venice. (p. 1780)
Romkey, Shawna. Easterly. (p. 620)
Romo, Adriana, illus. see Newman, Lesléa.
Romo, Brandyn. Rustlings of an Old Tree. (p. 1917)
Romo, Michelle Sachiko. Frankie's Magical Day: A First Book of Whimsical Words. (p. 778)
Romolino, Kimberly. Day at Sea. (p. 512)
Rompella, Natalie. Cookie Cutters & Sled Runners. (p. 446)
—Experiments in Light & Sound with Toys & Everyday Stuff. (p. 678)
—Experiments in Material & Matter with Toys & Everyday Stuff. (p. 678)
—Obsessive-Compulsive Disorder: The Ultimate Teen Guide. (p. 1634)
—World Never Sleeps Schwartz, Carol, illus. (p. 2502)
Rompella, Natalie, jt. auth. see Sohn, Emily.
Romphf, Joshua. Code a Minecraft Mod in JavaScript Step by Step (p. 411)
Romspert, George W. Western Echo: A Description of the Western States & Territories of the United States, As Gathered in a Tour by Wagon (Classic Reprint) (p. 2402)
Romulo, Liana. Filipino Celebrations: A Treasury of Feasts & Festivals. Dandan-Albano, Corazon, illus. (p. 726)
—Filipino Children's Favorite Stories: Fables, Myths & Fairy Tales. De Leon, Joanne, illus. (p. 726)
—My First Book of Tagalog Words: An ABC Rhyming Book of Filipino Language & Culture. Laurel, Jaime, illus. (p. 1543)
Ron. De Dheeks en Dhoorns. (p. 516)
Ron, Berry. Daddy Do You Love Me. (p. 495)
—Mommy Do You Love Me. (p. 1491)
Ronald, Robrahn, illus. see Bodenstein, Dan.
Ronaldo, Denise. Lost City Spotted from Space! (X Books: Strange) Is an Ancient Land under the Sand? (p. 1353)
Ronalds, Francis. Catalogue of Books & Papers Relating to Electricity, Magnetism, the Electric Telegraph, &C: Including the Ronald's Library (Classic Reprint) (p. 342)
Ronan, Amanda. Decision. Radka, Sara, illus. (p. 523)
—Discovery. Radka, Sara, illus. (p. 556)
—Experiment. Radka, Sara, illus. (p. 678)
—Fight. Radka, Sara, illus. (p. 724)
—Master Plan. Radka, Sara, illus. (p. 1419)
—Switch. Radka, Sara, illus. (p. 2171)
Ronchi, Ermes. Hail Mary. (p. 909)
Rondeau, Amanda, jt. auth. see ABDO Publishing Company Staff.
Rondeau, Amanda, jt. auth. see Scheunemann, Pam.
Rondeau, Amanda, jt. auth. see Tuminelly, Nancy.
Rondelli, Geminiano. Urania, Custode Del Tempo: Varie Considerazioni (Classic Reprint) (p. 2339)
Rondina, Catherine. Carey Price: How a First Nations Kid Became a Superstar Goaltender. (p. 330)
—Don't Touch That Toad & Other Strange Things Adults Tell You. Sylvester, Kevin, illus. (p. 584)
—Gossip: Before Word Gets Around Workman, Dan, illus. (p. 872)
—Lying: Deal with It Straight Up Workman, Dan, illus. (p. 1369)
—P. K. Subban: Fighting Racism to Become a Hockey Superstar & Role Model for Athletes of Colour. (p. 1690)
—Rudeness: Deal with It If You Please Workman, Dan, illus. (p. 1912)
Rondo, Glenn, illus. see Perdue II, D.
Ronertchambers, Ronertchambers. Chambers's Journal of Popular Literature, Science & Arts, 1888, Vol. 5 (Classic Reprint) (p. 354)
Rong, Chua Chang. Journey for a Better Future: Colniezy Rong. (p. 1181)
Rong, Yap Kun, illus. see Dahl, Michael.
Rong, Yu, illus. see Bright, Rachel.
Rong, Yu, illus. see Dowson, Nick.
Rong, Yu, illus. see Wenxuan, Cao.
Rongner, Bridget, ed. see Merline, Sharlene.
Roni, Emi & Qayyum, Aleeza, eds. Ink Movement's Mississauga Youth Anthology Volume VI. (p. 1120)
Ronne, Susan. Webster the Spelling Dog. (p. 2395)
Ronney, Ronnie, illus. see Moncure, Jane Belk.
Ronney, Ronnie, illus. see Petersen, Christine.
ronnybas, illus. see Sorenson, Margo.
Ronquillo, Nadia, illus. see Manning, Campbell.
Ronsley, Jill, ed. see Whyte, S. L.
Ronstant, Paul, illus. see Griffin, Paul.
Rood, Brian, illus. see Dawson, Delilah.
Rood, Brian, illus. see Disney Book Group.
Rood, Brian, illus. see Heddle, Jennifer.
Rood, Brian, illus. see Hilton, Dave, et al.
Rood, Brian, illus. see Patrick, Ella.
Rood, Brian, illus. see Schaefer, Elizabeth.
Rood, Brian, illus. see Siglain, Michael.
Rood, Brian, illus. see Thornton, Randy.
Rood, Henry Edward. Company Doctor: An American Story (Classic Reprint) (p. 433)
Roode, Daniel. Little Bea. Roode, Daniel, illus. (p. 1311)
—Little Bea & the Snowy Day. Roode, Daniel, illus. (p. 1311)
Roode, Daniel, illus. see Ainsworth, Kimberly.
Roode, Daniel, illus. see Beaumont, Karen.
Roode, Daniel, illus. see Birdsong, Minnie.
Roode, Daniel, illus. see Holub, Joan.
Roode, Daniel, illus. see Surratt, Tereasa & Charlton-Perrin, Donna.
Roode, Laura, illus. see Burton, Jeffrey.
Roof, Katharine Metcalf. Stranger at the Hearth (Classic Reprint) (p. 2138)
Rook, Clarence. London Side-Lights (Classic Reprint) (p. 1341)
Rook, E. C. Young People's Speaker: Designed for Young People of Twelve Years; Containing Selections in Both Prose & Verse for Every Season & Every Occasion (Classic Reprint) (p. 2532)
Rook, Emma Cecilia. Child's Own Speaker: Composed of Recitations, Dialogues, Motion Songs & Tableaux for Children of Six Years (Classic Reprint) (p. 376)
—Young Folks' Entertainments: Comprising Many New & Novel Motion Songs, Charades, Pantomimes, Tableaux, Concert Recitations Drills, etc;, for Home & School Entertainment (Classic Reprint) (p. 2531)
Rook, Lizzie J. Tiny Tot's Speaker: Designed for the Wee Ones (Classic Reprint) (p. 2250)
Rook, William G. Canadian Home Journal, Vol. 15: July, 1918 (Classic Reprint) (p. 320)
Rooke, Margaret. You Can Change the World! Everyday Teen Heroes Making a Difference Everywhere. (p. 2525)
Rooke, Thom. Germ's Journey Trimmer, Tony, illus. (p. 822)
Rooke, Veronica, illus. see Mulligan, Monique.
Rooke, Veronica, illus. see Raffa-Mulligan, Teena.
Rooker, Angie. Enchanted Sacred Garden: Dragon. (p. 647)
Rooker, William Velpeau. Weatherbeaten Man: A Tale of American Patriotism (Classic Reprint) (p. 2394)
Rooks, Jo. Box of Butterflies. (p. 266)
—Doug's Dung. (p. 589)
—Hector. (p. 947)
—Layla's Luck. (p. 1253)
—Lucy's Light. (p. 1366)
—Sophie's Shell. (p. 2065)
Rookstool, Yakiri. Christmas Star. (p. 387)
Roome, Anne Ross. Global Economy. (p. 843)
Roome, Anne Ross, jt. auth. see Roome, Hugh.
Roome, Anne Ross & Mattern, Joanne. Cesar Chavez. (p. 353)
Roome, Hugh. Bald Eagles. (p. 160)
—Franklin D. Roosevelt: American Hero. (p. 778)
—Franklin D. Roosevelt. (p. 778)
—Lions: Kings of the Grasslands. (p. 1307)
—Lions. (p. 1307)
—Martin Luther King Jr. (p. 1410)
—Polar Bears. (p. 1769)
—Turkey. (p. 2299)
Roome, Hugh & Roome, Anne Ross. Global Economy. (p. 843)
Rooney, Ann. Amazing Mysteries: Messages from Beyond. (p. 66)
Rooney, Anne. 50 Amazing Things Kids Need to Know about Math. (p. 2555)
—50s & 60s. (p. 2556)
—Aerospace Engineering & the Principles of Flight. (p. 30)
—Agricultural Engineering & Feeding the Future. (p. 36)
—Alan Turing & His Binary Computer Code. (p. 39)
—Albert Einstein & His Theory of Relativity. (p. 40)
—Alexander Fleming & the Discovery of Penicillin. (p. 42)
—Astronomers in Action. (p. 129)
—Audio Engineering & the Science of Soundwaves. (p. 136)
—Biologists in Action. (p. 229)
—Build a City. (p. 292)
—Build a Theme Park. (p. 293)
—Creative & Media Careers. (p. 470)
—Creatures from the Past: Band 17/Diamond (Collins Big Cat) (p. 471)
—Dealing with Drugs. (p. 519)
—Drugs on the Street. (p. 606)
—Earthquake: Perspectives on Earthquake Disasters (p. 617)
—Entomologists in Action. (p. 656)
—Extreme Machines: The Fastest, Weirdest, Strongest Machines on Earth! (p. 686)
—Genetic Engineering & Developments in Biotechnology. (p. 815)
—Health & Medicine: The Impact of Science & Technology. (p. 943)
—History of Medicine. (p. 978)
—History of Psychology. (p. 979)
—Infectious Diseases. (p. 1118)
—Internet Safety. (p. 1127)
—James Watson & Francis Crick & the Discovery of Dna. (p. 1157)
—Jonas Salk & the First Polio Vaccine. (p. 1177)
—Kidnaps. (p. 1213)
—Math in 30 Seconds. (p. 1423)
—Math Journey Through Planet Earth. (p. 1424)
—Math Journey Through Space. (p. 1424)
—Math Journey Through the Animal Kingdom. (p. 1424)
—Math Journey Through the Human Body. (p. 1424)
—Mega Machine Record Breakers. (p. 1441)
—Micro Facts! 500 Fantastic Facts about Your Body. (p. 1459)
—Minecraft STEM Challenge - Build a City: A Step-by-Step Guide Packed with STEM Facts. (p. 1471)
—Minecraft STEM Challenge - Build a Theme Park: A Step-By-step Guide Packed with STEM Facts. (p. 1471)
—Muffin. Julian, Sean, illus. (p. 1524)
—Optical Engineering & the Science of Light. (p. 1667)
—Race Hate. (p. 1831)
—Rachel Carson. Lundie, Isobel, illus. (p. 1832)
—Reducing the Carbon Footprint. (p. 1860)
—Responding to Emergencies (p. 1869)
—Science of Seafaring: The Float-Tastic Facts about Ships. Affonso, Alexandre & Beach, Bryan, illus. (p. 1958)
—Secret Services. (p. 1979)
—Space Record Breakers. (p. 2072)
—Strange Places. (p. 2138)
—UFOs & Aliens. (p. 2313)
—Women in Science - Rachel Carson. Lundie, Isobel, illus. (p. 2487)
—World after Super-Plague. (p. 2501)
—You Wouldn't Want to Live Without Antibiotics. Antram, David, illus. (p. 2529)
—You Wouldn't Want to Live Without Gravity! Bergin, Mark, illus. (p. 2529)
—You Wouldn't Want to Live Without Math! Bergin, Mark, illus. (p. 2529)
—You Wouldn't Want to Live Without Simple Machines! Bergin, Mark, illus. (p. 2529)
—You Wouldn't Want to Live Without the Internet! (p. 2529)
—You Wouldn't Want to Live Without the Internet! Bergin, Mark, illus. (p. 2529)
—You Wouldn't Want to Live Without Vaccinations! Antram, David, illus. (p. 2529)
Rooney, Anne, jt. auth. see Crabtree Staff.
Rooney, Anne, jt. auth. see Hibbert, Clare.
Rooney, Anne, jt. auth. see Lonely Planet Kids.
Rooney, Anne & Lonely Planet Kids. Dinosaur Atlas Gilleard, James, illus. (p. 548)
Rooney, Anne & Savery, Annabel. Creative & Media Careers. (p. 470)
Rooney, Anne & Wilson, Joe. Pirates: Dead Men's Tales. (p. 1750)
Rooney, C. J., illus. see Pahls, Stevie Kay.
Rooney, Christina. Saila & Betty (English) Hinch, Ali, illus. (p. 1923)
Rooney, Claire. Color of Dust. (p. 420)
Rooney, Colin. Weak Made Strong: Enduring Tragedy & the Battles As a Fatherless Man (p. 2393)
Rooney, Ellen, illus. see Chaffee, Kim.
Rooney, Ellen, illus. see Singh, Rina.
Rooney, Melissa. Eddie the Electron Moves Out. Pulver, Harry, Jr., illus. (p. 624)
Rooney, Melissa B. Fate of the Frog. (p. 714)
Rooney, Rachel. My Life As a Goldfish: And Other Poems. (p. 1551)
—Problem with Problems. Hicks, Zehra, illus. (p. 1803)
—Sleeping Beauty: Band 12/Copper (Collins Big Cat) (p. 2037)
Rooney, Ronnie. Thanksgiving Recipes Rooney, Ronnie, illus. (p. 2212)

R

Rose, Gary J. Hitting Rock Bottom: New Beginnings for at-Risk Youth. (p. 982)
Rose, Giada, illus. see Cropsey, Melinda M.
Rose, Hayley. Do's & Don'ts. (p. 587)
Rose, Heidi, illus. see Stihler, Cherie B.
Rose, Hilda, illus. see Barber, Jill.
Rose, Hilda, illus. see Chalker Browne, Susan.
Rose, Hilda, illus. see Fitch, Sheree.
Rose, Hilda, illus. see Sullivan-Fraser, Deannie.
Rose, Hugh James. Untrodden Spain & Her Black Country. (p. 2336)
—Untrodden Spain, & Her Black Country, Vol. 1 Of 2: Being Sketches of the Life & Character, of the Spaniard of the Interior (Classic Reprint) (p. 2336)
Rose, Imogen. Initiation: Japanese Language Edition. Galeano, Tomomi, tr. (p. 1120)
Rose, J. B., jt. auth. see Tharp, Jason.
Rose, J. B. & Tharp, Jason. School Tail Tharp, Jason, illus. (p. 1947)
Rose, J. M. Dillon & the Dark Elves. (p. 546)
Rose, January. Groovy Groovy Land: Where Every Girl Is a Princess. (p. 898)
Rose, Jennie. Noonistan. (p. 1619)
Rose, Jennifer. It's Not a Perfect World but I'll Take It: 50 Life Lessons for Teens Like Me - Who Are Kind of (You Know) Autistic. (p. 1146)
Rose, Jenny. Dream It, Believe It, Manatee Patty. (p. 601)
Rose, Jeremy. Dog's Divorce. (p. 577)
—Rookie the Rucksack. (p. 1903)
Rose, Jessica, illus. see Baird, Kade.
Rose, Judith Robbins. Look Both Ways in the Barrio Blanco. (p. 1345)
Rose, Julianna, illus. see KaBOOM!.
Rose, Katherine. Annie Oakley. (p. 100)
Rose, Kim, jt. auth. see Allen-Conn, B. J.
Rose, Larkin. No Leavin' Love. (p. 1613)
Rose, Lila. Senseless Attraction. (p. 1989)
Rose, Lilliana. Flower Predictions. (p. 752)
Rose, Lily, et al. Phillipines. (p. 1734)
Rose, Lisa. Circle Needs a Ball Gown. (p. 392)
Rose, Lucy, illus. see Hoare, Ben.
Rose, Lucy, illus. see Lonely Planet Kids & Rooney, Anne.
Rose, Malcolm. Water Cycle. Sims, Sean, illus. (p. 2384)
Rose, Marilyn C. Kylie Gets a Cochlear Implant. (p. 1234)
Rose, Marisa. There's an Alien in Mommy's Belly. (p. 2218)
Rose, Martha Mary. Pretty Kitty of the House. (p. 1790)
Rose, Martin, jt. auth. see Huser, Glen.
Rose, Mary. Doctor, Doctor. Wright, Craig, ed. (p. 573)
—Dolphin Readers Starter. My Family. International Edition. Wright, Craig, ed. (p. 579)
—Little Helpers. Wright, Craig, ed. (p. 1318)
Rose, Matilda. When You Adopt a ... Starwhal. Budgen, Tim, illus. (p. 2434)
Rose, Matt. Streak of Yellow (Classic Reprint) (p. 2139)
Rose, Melanie, illus. see Browning, Kurt.
Rose, Melanie, illus. see Edwards, Pamela Duncan.
Rose, Melanie, illus. see Herzog, Brad.
Rose, Melanie, illus. see Napier, Matt.
Rose, Melanie, illus. see Scillian, Devin.
Rose, Melanie, illus. see Smith, Marie & Smith, Roland.
Rose, Melanie, illus. see Ulmer, Michael.
Rose, Melanie, illus. see Ulmer, Mike & Ulmer, Michael.
Rose, Melanie, jt. auth. see Napier, Matt.
Rose, Micky, illus. see Smith, Geof.
Rose, Mollie, illus. see Vidaurri, S. M.
Rose, Nana. Butterscotch Princess. (p. 304)
Rose, Nancy. Merry Christmas, Squirrels! (p. 1450)
—Secret Life of Squirrels. (p. 1977)
—Secret Life of Squirrels: a Love Story. (p. 1977)
—Secret Life of Squirrels: Back to School! (p. 1977)
Rose, Naomi C. Tashi & the Tibetan Flower Cure. (p. 2192)
—Where Snow Leopard Prowls: Wild Animals of Tibet. Rose, Naomi C., illus. (p. 2439)
Rose, Naomi C., ed. see Grady, Joanne.
Rose Newey, Kathryn. Animals in the Forest: The Day Terrible Things Came. (p. 95)
Rose, Patti Renee. Himalia Gets a Dog. (p. 972)
Rose, Paula. Heartbroken Father: 10-Year-Old Gracie & the Save a Soul Prayer Team. (p. 946)
Rose, R. M. & Leuzinger, Shannon. Guardians or Demons. (p. 902)
Rose, Rachel. Indonesia. (p. 1117)
Rose, Rebecca. Finding Technicolour. (p. 730)
Rose, Robin. Brave Little Red: Sound Book Wood Module with Handle. Cottage Door Press, ed. (p. 276)
—Happy Little Elephant: Sound Book Wood Module with Handle. Cottage Door Press, ed. (p. 923)
—Love You, Little 'Potamus: Early Bird Sound. Cottage Door Press, ed. (p. 1361)
—New Little Puppy: Sound Book Wood Module with Handle. Cottage Door Press, ed. (p. 1595)
—Sweet Little Unicorn: Sound Book Wood Module with Handle. Cottage Door Press, ed. (p. 2169)
Rose, Roxanna. Desires: A Legacy Novel. (p. 533)
—Malevolence: A Legacy Novel. (p. 1392)
Rose, S. J. Plant Agriculture Education: 2012 Edition. (p. 1756)
Rose Salih, Sara. Tales of a Sevie. (p. 2183)
Rose, Sandra. My Mom Has Wheels. Talbott, Sherri, illus. (p. 1555)
Rose, Silvia, illus. see Harold, Jay.
Rose Simms, Susan. Mount Rushmore. (p. 1513)
—Statue of Liberty. (p. 2109)
—US Flag. (p. 2340)
Rose, Simon. Agricultural Drones. (p. 36)
—Air Force. (p. 37)
—Air Force Special Operations. (p. 37)
—Amazing Volcanoes Around the World. (p. 66)
—American Revolutionary War. (p. 74)
—Andromeda: The Myth & Science. (p. 84)
—Animal Caretaker. (p. 88)
—Army. (p. 117)
—Army Rangers. (p. 118)
—Aung San Suu Kyi. (p. 136)
—Belugas. (p. 198)
—Black Dawn. (p. 237)
—Blood: All about the Cardiovascular System. (p. 245)
—Bones: All about the Skeletal System. (p. 255)
—Brain: All about the Nervous System. (p. 274)
—Canada's Olympic Torch. (p. 320)
—Cardiovascular System. (p. 328)
—Circulatory System. (p. 393)
—Civil War. (p. 396)
—Coast Guard. (p. 410)
—Colosseum. (p. 427)
—Coral Reefs. (p. 453)
—Cygnus the Swan: The Myth & Science. (p. 493)
—Delta Force. (p. 527)
—Digestive System. (p. 545)
—Doomsday Mask (p. 585)
—Drones. (p. 605)
—Estuaries. (p. 665)
—Evaluating Arguments about Food. (p. 668)
—Evaluating Arguments about Technology. (p. 668)
—Evaluating Arguments about the Environment. (p. 668)
—Family Groups. (p. 702)
—First Settlers: 1492-1607. (p. 739)
—Fisher. (p. 741)
—Flambeau Olympique: Les Emblèmes Canadiens. McMann, Julie, tr. from ENG. (p. 746)
—Globes. (p. 844)
—Green Berets. (p. 893)
—Hercules: The Myth & Science. (p. 957)
—House of Representatives. (p. 1023)
—Into the Web. (p. 1128)
—Loonies: Canadian Icons. (p. 1348)
—Loonies: Les Emblèmes Canadiens. McMann, Julie, tr. from ENG. (p. 1348)
—Lungs: All about the Respiratory System. (p. 1369)
—Marine Corps. (p. 1405)
—Marine Corps Special Operations. (p. 1405)
—Mechanic. (p. 1435)
—Meteors. (p. 1453)
—Mexican-American War. (p. 1453)
—Muscles: All about the Muscular System. (p. 1528)
—Muscular System. (p. 1528)
—Navy. (p. 1582)
—Navy SEALs. (p. 1583)
—Nelson Mandela. (p. 1587)
—Nervous System. (p. 1588)
—Office of the President. (p. 1640)
—One World Trade Center. (p. 1663)
—Oriental Pearl. (p. 1670)
—Orion: The Myth & Science. (p. 1672)
—Parallel Destiny: A Flashback Novel. (p. 1699)
—Pegasus: The Myth & Science. (p. 1714)
—Physical Maps. (p. 1737)
—Plumber. (p. 1763)
—Polar Ice Caps. (p. 1770)
—Polar Regions. (p. 1770)
—Resource Conservation. (p. 1869)
—Respiratory System. (p. 1869)
—Sea Urchins. (p. 1969)
—Senate. (p. 1988)
—Shadowzone. (p. 1998)
—Sheikh Zayed Al Nahyan Grand Mosque. (p. 2005)
—Skeletal System. (p. 2030)
—Sources of Light. (p. 2068)
—Sphere of Septimus (p. 2080)
—Split History of World War II: A Perspectives Flip Book (p. 2085)
—Sri Harmandir Sahib. (p. 2095)
—Stomach: All about the Digestive System. (p. 2121)
—Supreme Court. (p. 2162)
—Taxidermist. (p. 2193)
—Ticks. (p. 2240)
—Time Camera (p. 2244)
—Twisted Fate: A Flashback Novel. (p. 2306)
—Underground Transportation Systems. (p. 2324)
—Ursa Major: The Myth & Science. (p. 2340)
—Vietnam War: 1954-1975. (p. 2357)
—War of 1812. (p. 2376)
—What Is Light? (p. 2415)
—World War II: 1939-1945. (p. 2505)
—Zapotecs. (p. 2538)
Rose, Simon, jt. auth. see McDowell, Pamela.
Rose, Simon & McDowell, Pamela. Sea Urchins. (p. 1969)
Rose, Simon, et al. Drones. (p. 605)
Rose, Susanna Van, see Van Rose, Susanna.
Rose, Tammy Marie. Majik the Black Unicorn (p. 1385)
—Munchkin. (p. 1526)
Rose, Tara. Tinker Mice. (p. 2248)
Rose, Tiffany. M Is for Melanin: A Celebration of the Black Child. (p. 1370)
Rose Wage, Erin. Disney Baby: Winnie the Pooh. (p. 559)
—Nickelodeon PAW Patrol: Ding Dong, It's the PAW Patrol! (p. 1603)
—Nickelodeon: PAW Patrol. (p. 1603)
Rose, Whitney. Woo Hoo, the Growing You'll Do. (p. 2491)
Rose, William G. Stories of the Stage (Classic Reprint) (p. 2125)
Rose, William Ganson. Ginger Cure (Classic Reprint) (p. 833)
—Rousing of Parkside (Classic Reprint) (p. 1908)
Rose, William Stewart. Court & Parliament of Beasts: Freely Translated from the Animali Parlanti of Giambattista Casti; a Poem in Seven Cantos (Classic Reprint) (p. 462)
—Orlando Innamorato: Translated into Prose from the Italian of Francesco Berni & Interspersed with Extracts in the Same Stanza As the Original (Classic Reprint) (p. 1672)
Roseberg, Anders. Priscilla & the Sandman. Parajes, Danilo, illus. (p. 1801)
Roseboro', Viola. Old Ways & New Stories (Classic Reprint) (p. 1648)
Roseborough, Elizabeth. Blue Sharks (p. 249)
—Bull Sharks (p. 296)
—Freshwater Sharks (p. 785)
—Great White Sharks. (p. 891)
—Mako Sharks (p. 1390)
—Rays (p. 1844)
—Thresher Sharks (p. 2236)
—Tiger Sharks (p. 2241)
—Women's Soccer on the Rise (p. 2488)
Rosebrough, Ellen. Dora's Chilly Day. (p. 586)
—Dora's Chilly Day (Dora the Explorer) Mcgee, Warner & MJ Illustrations Staff, illus. (p. 586)
Rosegger, Peter. Earth & the Fullness Thereof: A Romance of Modern Styria (Classic Reprint) (p. 616)
—Forest Farm: Tales of the Austrian Tyrol. (p. 766)
—Forest Farm: Tales of the Austrian Tyrol (Classic Reprint) (p. 766)
—Forest Schoolmaster (Classic Reprint) (p. 766)
—God Seeker: A Tale of Old Styria (Classic Reprint) (p. 852)
—I. N. R. I: A Prisoner's Story of the Cross. (p. 1079)
—I. N. R. I: A Prisoner's Story of the Cross (Classic Reprint) (p. 1079)
Rose-Innes, Cosmo. With Paget's Horse to the Front (Classic Reprint) (p. 2481)
Roselius, J. Chris. Danica Patrick: Racing to History. (p. 502)
—Houston Astros (p. 1024)
—Houston Rockets (p. 1025)
—Magic Johnson: Basketball Star & Entrepreneur (p. 1377)
—Michigan State Spartans (p. 1459)
—Richard Petty: The King of Racing. (p. 1876)
—San Antonio Spurs (p. 1929)
—Superfast Drag Racing. (p. 2159)
—Superfast Rally Car Racing. (p. 2159)
—Surviving School: Managing School & Career Paths (p. 2165)
—Texas Longhorns (p. 2209)
Rosell, Joel Franz. Concierto No. 7 para Viol-N y Brujas. (p. 438)
—Tito y el Misterioso Amicus. (p. 2251)
Roselli, Stephanie, ed. Budding Scientist. (p. 290)
ROSELLO, Jarod. Red Panda & Moon Bear. (p. 1858)
Roseman-Mendoza, Natalie. Maritza's Garden Path. (p. 1406)
Rosemary, Sutcliff. Black Ships Before Troy: The Story of the Iliad. (p. 239)
Rosemary Wells. McDuff & the Baby. Rusan Jeffers, illus. (p. 1432)
Rosemary, Wells, jt. auth. see Wells, Rosemary.
Rosen, A. J. Entwined. (p. 657)
Rosen, Aaron. Journey Through Art: A Global Art Adventure. Dalzell, Lucy, illus. (p. 1181)
Rosen, Aaron & Watts, Riley. Where's Your Creativity? Maijala, Marika, illus. (p. 2441)
Rosen, Anne, illus. see Adams, David J.
Rosen, Anne, illus. see Gamble, Adam & Jasper, Mark.
Rosen, Anne, illus. see Gamble, Adam & Mackey, Bill.
Rosen, Anne, illus. see Gamble, Adam.
Rosen, Anne, illus. see Jasper, Mark.
Rosen, Anne, illus. see Vrba, Christina.
Rosen, Chaya & Braverman, Rivkie. Our New Special Baby. (p. 1679)
Rosen Classroom, creator. Map Activities for Primary Sources of Immigration & Migration in America: Reproducible Blackline Masters. (p. 1400)
Rosen, Daniel. Batallas de la Guerra Civil. (p. 172)
—Batallas de la Guerra Civil - 6 Pack: Set of 6 Common Core Edition. (p. 172)
—Battles of the Civil War: Set of 6: Antietam. (p. 175)
—Battles of the Civil War - 6 Pack: Set of 6 with Common Core Teacher Materials. (p. 175)
—Battles of the Civil War - 6 Pack: Set of 6 Bridges Edition with Common Core Teacher Materials. (p. 175)
—Dred Scott & the Supreme Court: Set Of 6. (p. 603)
—Economic Systems - 6 Pack: Set of 6 with Common Core Teacher Materials. (p. 624)
—Economic Systems - 6 Pack: Set of 6 Bridges Edition with Common Core Teacher Materials. (p. 624)
—Sistemas Economicos. (p. 2027)
—Sistemas Economicos - 6 Pack: Set of 6 Common Core Edition. (p. 2027)
Rosen, Devora. Mystery in Spain. (p. 1569)
Rosen, Emma. Lily the Limpet Gets Lost. Blackery, Evgeniia, illus. (p. 1302)
Rosen, Erwin. In the Foreign Legion (Classic Reprint) (p. 1109)
Rosen, Jonathan. From Sunset till Sunrise: Devin Dexter #2. (p. 793)
—Night of the Living Cuddle Bunnies: Devin Dexter #1. (p. 1607)
—Night of the Living Cuddle Bunnies. (p. 1607)
—Rockefeller Caper. Pinelli, Amerigo, illus. (p. 1895)
—Why Do Animals Go There? (p. 2455)
—Why Do Animals Live There? (p. 2455)
Rosen, Karen. Great Moments in Olympic Swimming & Diving (p. 888)
—Great Moments in Olympic Track & Field (p. 888)
Rosen, Kim, illus. see Peters, Marilee.
Rosen, Kim, illus. see Richardson, Gillian.
Rosen, Kymberlee S. Do You Have Better Manners Than the Monkeys at the Zoo? (p. 571)
Rosen, L. C. Camp. (p. 315)
—Jack of Hearts (and Other Parts) (p. 1152)
Rosen, Lev Ac. Memory Wall. (p. 1446)
Rosen, Lucy. Batman Phonics Fun! Farley, Rick et al, illus. (p. 172)
—Blast Off! (p. 243)
—Despicable Me 2: Meet the Minions. (p. 533)
—Friends & Foes. Gordon, Steven E. & Gordon, Eric A., illus. (p. 786)
—I Am Bane. Cohn, Scott, illus. (p. 1058)
—Justice League: Meet the Justice League. Gordon, Eric A. & Gordon, Steven E., illus. (p. 1195)
—Long Live King Bob! (p. 1343)
—Meet the Justice League. (p. 1440)
—Minions: Who's the Boss? (p. 1472)
—Minions: Dracula's Last Birthday. (p. 1472)
—My Little Pony: Meet Princess Twilight Sparkle. (p. 1553)
—Paranorman: Meet the Ghosts. (p. 1699)
—Parasite City. Gordon, Steven E. & Gordon, Eric A., illus. (p. 1699)
—Planet 51. (p. 1755)
—Superman's Superpowers. Tong, Andie, illus. (p. 2160)
Rosen, Lucy, et al. Squeakquel: Meet the 'Munks. (p. 2094)
Rosen, Lucy, text. Despicable Me: My Dad the Super Villain. (p. 533)
Rosen, M. S. Jessica. Miss Little Bea Sharp. Martinez, David R., illus. (p. 1479)
Rosen, Marvin. Becca in Cyberland (p. 186)
Rosen, Michael. Aesop's Fables Hackiyan, Talleen, illus. (p. 31)
—Bah! Humbug! Ross, Tony, illus. (p. 159)
—Bananas in My Ears: A Collection of Nonsense Stories, Poems, Riddles, & Rhymes. Blake, Quentin, illus. (p. 163)
—Barking for Bagels. Ross, Tony, illus. (p. 166)
—Bilal's Brilliant Bee. Ross, Tony, illus. (p. 225)
—Bob the Bursting Bear. Ross, Tony, illus. (p. 252)
—Bus Is for Us. Tyler, Gillian, illus. (p. 300)
—Centrally Heated Knickers. (p. 352)
—Fantastic Mr. Dahl. Blake, Quentin, illus. (p. 707)
—Giggly Wiggly: Playtime Rhymes. Riddell, Chris, illus. (p. 833)
—Hampstead the Hamster. Ross, Tony, illus. (p. 913)
—Happy Harry's Cafe. Holland, Richard, illus. (p. 922)
—Send for a Superhero! McEwen, Katharine, illus. (p. 1988)
—Tiny Little Fly. Waldron, Kevin, illus. (p. 2249)
—Uncle Gobb & the Dread Shed. Layton, Neal, illus. (p. 2318)
—Vamos a Cazar un Oso. (p. 2345)
—Were Going on a Bear Hunt. (p. 2400)
—We're Going on a Bear Hunt: Sound Book. Oxenbury, Helen, illus. (p. 2400)
—We're Going on a Bear Hunt: 30th Anniversary Edition. Oxenbury, Helen, illus. (p. 2400)
—We're Going on a Bear Hunt: Anniversary Edition of a Modern Classic. Oxenbury, Helen, illus. (p. 2400)
—We're Going on a Bear Hunt. Oxenbury, Helen, illus. (p. 2400)
—We're Going on a Bear Hunt: Changing Picture Book. Oxenbury, Helen, illus. (p. 2400)
—We're Going on a Bear Hunt: Snow Globe Edition. Oxenbury, Helen, illus. (p. 2400)
—We're Going on a Bear Hunt Sound Book. Oxenbury, Helen, illus. (p. 2400)
—What Is Poetry?: the Essential Guide to Reading & Writing Poems. Calder, Jill, illus. (p. 2416)
—What's So Special about Dickens? Nayler, Sarah, illus. (p. 2425)
—What's So Special about Shakespeare? Nayler, Sarah, illus. (p. 2425)
—You Wait till I'm Older Than You! (p. 2528)
Rosen, Michael & Layton, Neal. Uncle Gobb & the Green Heads. (p. 2318)
Rosen, Michael & Young, Annemarie. What Is Humanism? How Do You Live Without a God? & Other Big Questions for Kids. (p. 2415)
Rosen, Michael, ed. Classic Poetry: Candlewick Illustrated Classic. Howard, Paul, illus. (p. 400)
Rosen, Michael J. Ben of All Trades: the Most Inventive Boyhood of Benjamin Franklin. Tavares, Matt, illus. (p. 199)
—Bonding with Your Dog. (p. 255)
—Chanukah Lights. Sabuda, Robert, illus. (p. 357)
—Fishing Gear. (p. 742)
—Forever Flowers. Danowski, Sonja, illus. (p. 767)
—Fresh Fish. (p. 784)
—Girls vs. Guys: Surprising Differences Between the Sexes. (p. 839)
—Gone Fishing. (p. 861)
—Greatest Table. Stadtlander, Becca, illus. (p. 892)
—Handling Your Dog. (p. 915)
—Horse's Haiku. Fellows, Stan, illus. (p. 1005)
—Hound Dog's Haiku: And Other Poems for Dog Lovers. Azarian, Mary, illus. (p. 1021)
—In the Quiet, Noisy Woods. Won, Annie, illus. (p. 1110)
—Listening to Your Dog. (p. 1309)
—Maine Coon's Haiku: And Other Poems for Cat Lovers. White, Lee, illus. (p. 1384)
—Million Stories of Marco Polo. (p. 1468)
—Mind-Boggling Numbers. Patton, Julia, illus. (p. 1469)
—Outrageous Animal Adaptations: From Big-Eared Bats to Frill-Necked Lizards. (p. 1685)
—Perfect Spot. (p. 1723)
—Place Hacking: Venturing off Limits. (p. 1753)
—Reel Time: Fishing Gear. (p. 1860)
—Reel Time: Fresh Fish. (p. 1860)
—Reel Time: Gone Fishing. (p. 1860)
—Reel Time: Tackling the Box. (p. 1860)
—Reel Time: Take the Bait. (p. 1860)
—Reel Time: the Perfect Spot. (p. 1860)
—Sailing the Unknown: Around the World with Captain Cook. Pritelli, Maria Cristina, illus. (p. 1923)
—Sailing the Unknown. Pritelli, Maria Cristina, illus. (p. 1923)
—School for Pompey Walker. (p. 1946)
—Sensing Like Your Dog. (p. 1989)
—Speaking to Your Dog. (p. 2076)
—Tackling the Box. (p. 2175)
—Take the Bait. (p. 2177)
—Treating Your Dog. (p. 2283)
Rosen, Michael J. & Carlson, Daniel. Just My Type: Understanding Personality Profiles. (p. 1194)
Rosen, Michael J. & Kaboom! Staff. Let's Build a Playground. Kelson, Ellen & Cecil, Jennifer, illus. (p. 1270)
Rosen, Michael J. & Kassoy, Ben. Crazy Buildings. Jones, Doug, illus. (p. 468)
Rosen, Michael J., ed. Workers' Tales: Socialist Fairy Tales, Fables, & Allegories from Great Britain. (p. 2495)
Rosen Publishing Group. Get Outdoors (p. 824)
Rosen Publishing Staff. African American Quartet (p. 32)
—All about the Author: Set 3 (p. 50)
—American History Arts & Crafts (p. 72)
—Animal Cannibals (p. 88)
—Artists Through the Ages: Set 2 (p. 123)
—Best Job Ever (p. 206)
—Brain Games (p. 274)
—Britannica Beginner Bios (p. 282)
—Britannica Common Core Library: Set 2 (p. 282)
—Britannica Guide to Cell Biology (p. 283)
—Checkered Flag (p. 363)
—Conspiracies & Cover-Ups (p. 442)

—Core Language Skills: Set 2 (p. 454)
—Core Skills: Set 2 (p. 454)
—Creating Comics (p. 470)
—Digital & Information Literacy: Set 8 (p. 546)
—Drawing Is Awesome! (p. 599)
—Excellent Science Experiments (p. 676)
—Exploring Ancient Civilizations (p. 681)
—Exploring Food Chains & Food Webs (p. 681)
—Farmyard Friends (p. 711)
—Fitness for the Mind & Body (p. 742)
—Giants on the Road (p. 831)
—Glow-In-the-Dark Animals (p. 845)
—Greatest Records in Sports (p. 892)
—Guide for Curious Minds: Set 2 (p. 903)
—Heroes & Legends (p. 961)
—Holiday Origami: Set 2 (p. 987)
—How Kids Lived (p. 1033)
—Infomax Common Core Math Readers: Levels I - L (p. 1119)
—Infomax Common Core Math Readers: Levels I - O (p. 1119)
—Inside Special Forces: Set 2 (p. 1123)
—Inside Sports: Set 2 (p. 1123)
—Internet Biographies: Set 3 (p. 1127)
—Invaders from Earth (p. 1130)
—Know Your Rights (p. 1230)
—Let's Find Out! the Human Body (p. 1272)
—Let's Find Out! Weather (p. 1272)
—Let's Talk about It (p. 1278)
—Living Fossils (p. 1333)
—Media Literacy (p. 1436)
—Objects in Space (p. 1634)
—Original Thinkers (p. 1671)
—Remarkable Lgbtq Lives (p. 1863)
—Right Degree for Me (p. 1882)
—Save the Animals (p. 1937)
—Scatalog: A Kid's Field Guide to Animal Poop: Set 2 (p. 1943)
—Scientific Breakthroughs (p. 1959)
—Scientist's Guide to Physics: Set 2 (p. 1959)
—Service Learning for Teens (p. 1991)
—Sports Tips, Techniques, & Strategies: Set 2 (p. 2089)
—Spotlight on Space Science (p. 2091)
—Story of Math: Core Principles of Mathematics (p. 2131)
—Teen Life 411: Set 2 (p. 2199)
—Understanding the Paranormal (p. 2325)
—Wild Side (p. 2464)
Rosen, Rachel & Benchmark Education Co., LLC Staff. Rob, Ron, & I. (p. 1889)
—Sit, Sit, Sit. (p. 2027)
Rosen, Rachel, et al. Sit, Sit, Sit - I Can Fit! - I Am Pat: StartUp Unit 3 Lap Book. (p. 2027)
Rosen, Robert. Ants Everywhere! de Polonia, Nina, illus. (p. 103)
—Bad Rex! Fiorentino, Chiara, illus. (p. 158)
—Dinosaur Museum. Bassani, Srimalie, illus. (p. 549)
—Dust Everywhere. Fiorentino, Chiara, illus. (p. 611)
—Family Photo. De Polonia, Nina, illus. (p. 702)
—Family Photo. de Polonia, Nina, illus. (p. 702)
—Hungry for Worms. Curzon, Brett, illus. (p. 1052)
—It's Too Noisy! Piworski, Marcin, illus. (p. 1148)
—My Favorite Sport. De Polonia, Nina, illus. (p. 1539)
—My Favorite Sport. de Polonia, Nina, illus. (p. 1539)
—Not Yet! Grott, Isabella, illus. (p. 1624)
—Our Snowy Day. Curzon, Brett, illus. (p. 1680)
—Wally & Molly Go to the Beach. Bassani, Srimalie, illus. (p. 2373)
—Where Is My Eraser? Piworski, Marcin, illus. (p. 2438)
Rosen, Roger, ed. see Mahoney, Ellen Voelckers.
Rosen Schwartz, Corey & Call, Kirsti. Mootilda's Bad Mood. Ranucci, Claudia, illus. (p. 1503)
Rosen, Steven & Steventon, John. History of Rock. (p. 979)
Rosen, Suri. Playing with Matches. (p. 1761)
Rosen, Suri, jt. auth. see Miller, Reagan.
Rosenbaum, Andria Warmflash. Big Sister, Little Monster. Fotheringham, Edwin, illus. (p. 223)
—Frozen 2: Anna, Elsa, & the Secret River. Shimabukuro, Denise & Naggi, Elena, illus. (p. 795)
—Hand in Hand. Shleifer, Maya, illus. (p. 914)
Rosenbaum, Andria Warmflash & Gill, Deirdre. Trains Don't Sleep. Rosenbaum, Andria Warmflash & Gill, Deirdre, illus. (p. 2276)
Rosenbaum, Elizabeth, photos by see Trooboff, Rhoda.
Rosenbaum, Jonathan. Adorable Beastling. (p. 17)
Rosenbaum, Nathan. Songs & Symphonies. (p. 2063)
Rosenbaum, Thane. Stranger Within Sarah Stein. (p. 2138)
Rosenberg, Aaron. 42 - The Official Movie Novel. (p. 2555)
—Blackout: Danger in the Dark. (p. 240)
—Cryptologists: Life Making & Breaking Codes. (p. 480)
—Flood: Race Against Time. (p. 750)
—Height of the Storm: A Mutants & Masterminds Novel. (p. 948)
—Kick Scooters: Techniques & Tricks. (p. 1212)
—Mountain Biking: Techniques & Tricks. (p. 1513)
—Taig Khris: In-Line Skating Superstar. (p. 2176)
—World War II. (p. 2505)
Rosenberg, Aaron, jt. auth. see Vale, Jenna.
Rosenberg, Aaron & Michalski, Peter. Advanced Skateboarding. (p. 18)
Rosenberg, Amye. Melly's Menorah. (p. 1443)
—Surprise in the Mail! Salanitro, Robert, illus. (p. 2163)
Rosenberg, Carol Killman. Ignatius: A Long Story about a Small Rock. Rosenberg, Carol Killman, illus. (p. 1094)
Rosenberg, concept. Reach Your Goal. (p. 1845)
Rosenberg, David. Zany at the Zoo. (p. 2538)
Rosenberg, Faigy & Weiss, Esti. Hot! Hot! Hot! David, Racheli, illus. (p. 1006)
Rosenberg, Gary, et al. Jon & Jayne's Guide to Getting Through School. (p. 1176)
Rosenberg, Harvey. Zoey's Web World. Brito, Carlos, illus. (p. 2541)
Rosenberg, James N. Return to Mutton (Classic Reprint) (p. 1871)
Rosenberg, Kenneth. STEAM Jobs in Game Development. (p. 2110)
Rosenberg, Liz. House of Dreams: The Life of L. M. Montgomery. Morstad, Julie, illus. (p. 1023)
—House of Dreams: the Life of L. M. Montgomery. Morstad, Julie, illus. (p. 1023)
—What James Said. Myers, Matthew, illus. (p. 2417)
Rosenberg, Madelyn. Canary in the Coal Mine. (p. 321)
—Cyclops of Central Park. Tentler-Krylov, Victoria, illus. (p. 493)
—Happy Birthday, Tree! A Tu B'Shevat Story. Christy, Jana, illus. (p. 921)
—How to Behave at a Dog Show. Ross, Heather, illus. (p. 1038)
—How to Behave at a Tea Party. Ross, Heather, illus. (p. 1038)
—Nanny X. (p. 1574)
—Schmutzy Family. Meisel, Paul, illus. (p. 1944)
Rosenberg, Madelyn, jt. auth. see Shang, Wendy Wan-Long.
Rosenberg, Madelyn & Crockett, Mary. Dream Boy. (p. 601)
Rosenberg, Madelyn & Shang, Wendy Wan-Long. This Is Just a Test: A Novel. (p. 2224)
Rosenberg, Madelyne. Take Care. Gregori, Giuliana, illus. (p. 2177)
Rosenberg, Mary, jt. auth. see Kunze, Susan.
Rosenberg, Matthew. Rocket Raccoon: Grounded. (p. 1895)
Rosenberg, Meira. Indiana Bamboo: A Novel. (p. 1116)
Rosenberg, Michael. Chilly Goes to Australia. (p. 377)
—Chilly Goes to Hong Kong & China: Another Chilly the Toy Polar Bear Adventure. (p. 377)
—Chilly Goes to Peru. (p. 377)
—Fabulous Fanshaws. Kalpart, illus. (p. 692)
—Fabulous Fanshaws Book Two: The Return to Lendorth. Kalpart, illus. (p. 692)
—Little Lost Tune: More Adventures from Bendalot. (p. 1321)
Rosenberg, Moshe. Morality for Muggles: Ethics in the Bible & the World of Harry Potter. (p. 1504)
Rosenberg, Natascha, illus. see Harris, Robie H.
Rosenberg, Natascha, illus. see Harris, Robie.
Rosenberg, Natascha, illus. see Sanchez Vegara, Maria Isabel.
Rosenberg, Natascha, illus. see Seltzer, Eric.
Rosenberg, Natascha & Kempter, Christa. When Mama Can't Sleep. (p. 2432)
Rosenberg, Pam. Baseball Jokes. Ostrom, Bob, illus. (p. 169)
—Bug Jokes. Ostrom, Bob, illus. (p. 291)
—Cave Crawlers (p. 347)
—Dinosaur Jokes. Ostrom, Bob, illus. (p. 549)
—Gross-Out Jokes. Ostrom, Bob, illus. (p. 898)
—How Did That Get to My Table? Cereal. (p. 1027)
—How Did That Get to My Table? Ice Cream. (p. 1027)
—How Did That Get to My Table? Orange Juice. (p. 1027)
—How Did That Get to My Table? Peanut Butter. (p. 1027)
—Monster Jokes. Ostrom, Bob, illus. (p. 1496)
—School Jokes. Ostrom, Bob, illus. (p. 1946)
—Tongue Twisters. Ostrom, Bob, illus. (p. 2260)
—Volcano Explorers (p. 2366)
—Waterfall Watchers (p. 2385)
Rosenberg, Rachelle, illus. see Houser, Jody.
Rosenberg, Rachelle, illus. see Lambert, Nancy.
Rosenberg, Rachelle, illus. see Thompson, Robbie.
Rosenberg, Rachelle, illus. see Wong, Clarissa.
Rosenberg, Rachelle, illus. see Wyatt, Chris.
Rosenberg, Rachelle, jt. illus. see Lim, Ronald.
Rosenberg, Sydell. H Is for Haiku: A Treasury of Haiku from a to Z. Chalabi, Sawsan, illus. (p. 907)
Rosenberg, Tziporah. Round & Round the Jewish Year: Elul-Tishrei. Vol. 1 Beifus, Ruth, illus. (p. 1907)
Rosenberry, Vera, illus. see Guthrie, Woody.
Rosenberry, Vera, illus. see Jane, Pamela.
Rosenberry, Vera, illus. see McDonald, Megan.
Rosenberry, Vera, illus. see Shepard, Aaron.
Rosenblatt, Darcey. Lost Boys. (p. 1352)
Rosenblatt, Judy, photos by see Wells, Leah.
Rosenblatt, Lynn. Monarch Magic! Butterfly Activities & Nature Discoveries. (p. 1492)
Rosenblatt, Lynn M. Monarch Buddies: Munch-A-Bunch of Milkweed! (p. 1492)
—Woolly Bear the Banded Caterpillar: Life Cycle, Friends & Adventures. (p. 2493)
Rosenblatt, Naomi, illus. see Wells, Leah.
Rosenbloom, Evey. Let Yourself Sparkle. (p. 1269)
—You Were Born to Be You. (p. 2528)
Rosenblum, Cameron Kelly. Stepping off Place. (p. 2115)
Rosenblum, Gregg. City 1. (p. 394)
—Fugitive X. (p. 797)
—Revolution 19. (p. 1873)
Rosenbusch, Harry. Microscopical Physiography of the Rock-Making Minerals. (p. 1460)
Rosencreutz, Christian. Hermetick Romance, or the Chymical Wedding (Classic Reprint) (p. 959)
Rosendale, Diana. Pet Tales Featuring Chester, Lady & Mipi. (p. 1726)
Rosendo, Joseph, ed. see Dorling Kindersley Publishing Staff.
Rosendorf, Mark. Witches of Vegas. (p. 2480)
Rosener, Geo M. College Days: A College Comedy in Three Acts, Set in Rural Relief (Classic Reprint) (p. 415)
Rosener, George M. Sleepy Hollow: A Romance of the Revolution in Three Acts (Classic Reprint) (p. 2037)
—When Ann Acted (Classic Reprint) (p. 2429)
Rosenfeld, D. L., ed. see Altein, Chani.
Rosenfeld, D. L., ed. see Fajnland, Leibel.
Rosenfeld, D. L., ed. see Hodakov, Levi.
Rosenfeld, D. L., ed. see Levy, Leah.
Rosenfeld, D. L., ed. see Lieberman, Naomi.
Rosenfeld, D. L., ed. see Weber, Rivka Doba.
Rosenfeld, Dina. Chanukah Story for Night Number Three. (p. 357)
—It's Called Kibud Av Va'Eim: A Story about Honoring Parents. Ebert, Len, illus. (p. 1144)
—Yossi & Laibel Learn to Help. Nodel, Norman, illus. (p. 2524)
Rosenfeld, Dina, ed. see Benenfeld, Rikki.
Rosenfeld, Dina, ed. see Heald, Robin.
Rosenfeld, Dina, ed. see Mermelstein, Yael.
Rosenfeld, Sydney. Children of Destiny: A Play in Four Acts (Classic Reprint) (p. 371)
Rosenfield, Hutchings and. Hutchings' Illustrated California Magazine, Vol. 5: July, 1860, to June, 1861 (Classic Reprint) (p. 1055)
Rosengarten, Frank H. Eight Journeys Abroad (Classic Reprint) (p. 629)
Rosengarten, Philipp G., jt. auth. see Stuermer, Christoph B.
Rosenhain, Walter. Westminster Series. Glass Manufacture. (p. 2402)
Rosenhan, Tiffany. Girl from Nowhere. (p. 835)
Rosenkranz, Karl. Die Poesie und Ihre Geschichte: Eine Entwicklung der Poetischen Ideale der Völker (Classic Reprint) (p. 544)
Rosenow, Ty. Historical Adventures of Thomas Balfour. (p. 976)
Rosenstand. Moral of the Story: an Introduction to Ethics. (p. 1503)
Rosenstein, Jerry. Christmas Tree That Nobody Wanted. (p. 387)
Rosenstiehl, Agnès. Silly Lilly & the Four Seasons Rosenstiehl, Agnès, illus. (p. 2018)
Rosenstiehl, Agnes. Silly Lilly in What Will I Be Today? (p. 2018)
Rosenstiehl, Agnès. Silly Lilly in What Will I Be Today? Rosenstiehl, Agnès, illus. (p. 2018)
Rosenstock, Barb. Ben Franklin's Big Splash: The Mostly True Story of His First Invention. Schindler, S. D., illus. (p. 198)
—Blue Grass Boy: The Story of Bill Monroe, Father of Bluegrass Music. Fotheringham, Edwin, illus. (p. 248)
—Camping Trip That Changed America: Theodore Roosevelt, John Muir, & Our National Parks. Gerstein, Mordecai, illus. (p. 316)
—Dorothea's Eyes: Dorothea Lange Photographs the Truth. Dubois, Gerard, illus. (p. 586)
—Fight of the Century: Alice Paul Battles Woodrow Wilson for the Vote. Green, Sarah, illus. (p. 725)
—Leave It to Abigail! The Revolutionary Life of Abigail Adams. Baddeley, Elizabeth, illus. (p. 1259)
—Littlest Mountain. Hall, Melanie, illus. (p. 1331)
—Noisy Paint Box: The Colors & Sounds of Kandinsky's Abstract Art. GrandPré, Mary, illus. (p. 1617)
—Otis & Will Discover the Deep: The Record-Setting Dive of the Bathysphere. Roy, Katherine, illus. (p. 1675)
—Prairie Boy: Frank Lloyd Wright Turns the Heartland into a Home. Neal, Christopher Silas, illus. (p. 1784)
—Secret Kingdom: Nek Chand, a Changing India, & a Hidden World of Art. Nivola, Claire A., illus. (p. 1976)
—Streak: How Joe Dimaggio Became America's Hero. Widener, Terry, illus. (p. 2139)
—Thomas Jefferson Builds a Library. O'Brien, John, illus. (p. 2228)
—Through the Window: Views of Marc Chagall's Life & Art. GrandPré, Mary, illus. (p. 2237)
—Vincent Can't Sleep: Van Gogh Paints the Night Sky. GrandPré, Mary, illus. (p. 2359)
—Yogi: The Life, Loves, & Language of Baseball Legend Yogi Berra. Widener, Terry, illus. (p. 2523)
Rosenstock, Gabriel. I Met a Man from Artikelly: Verse for the Young & Young at Heart. Staunton, Mathew, illus. (p. 1079)
Rosenstock, Gabriel, tr. see Staunton, Aoife.
Rosensweig, Jay B. & Repka, Janice. Stupendous Dodgeball Fiasco. Dibley, Glin, illus. (p. 2145)
Rosenthal, Amy K. Little Oink. (p. 1323)
Rosenthal, Amy Krouse. Al Pha's Bet. Durand, Delphine, illus. (p. 38)
—Awake Beautiful Child. Lam, Gracia, illus. (p. 143)
—Bedtime for Mommy. Pham, Leuyen, illus. (p. 188)
—Choo-Choo School. Yamada, Mike, illus. (p. 381)
—Chopsticks. Magoon, Scott, illus. (p. 381)
—Cookies Board Book: Bite-Size Life Lessons. Dyer, Jane, illus. (p. 446)
—Don't Blink! Roberts, David, illus. (p. 582)
—Duck! Rabbit! (p. 608)
—Duck! Rabbit! Lichtenheld, Tom, illus. (p. 608)
—Duck! Rabbit! (Bunny Books, Read Aloud Family Books, Books for Young Children) (p. 608)
—Exclamation Mark. Lichtenheld, Tom, illus. (p. 676)
—Friendshape. Lichtenheld, Tom, illus. (p. 787)
—I Wish You More (Encouragement Gifts for Kids, Uplifting Books for Graduation) Lichtenheld, Tom, illus. (p. 1086)
—Little Books Boxed Set Featuring Little Pea Little Hoot Little Oink: (Baby Board Books, Nursery Rhymes, Children's Book Sets, Nursery Books) Corace, Jen, illus. (p. 1312)
—Little Hoot. Corace, Jen, illus. (p. 1318)
—Little Miss, Big Sis. Reynolds, Peter H., illus. (p. 1322)
—Little Miss, Big Sis Board Book. Reynolds, Peter H., illus. (p. 1322)
—Little Oink. Corace, Jen, illus. (p. 1323)
—Little Pea. Corace, Jen, illus. (p. 1324)
—Moo Moo, I Love You. Lichtenheld, Tom, illus. (p. 1500)
—One Smart Cookie: Bite-Size Lessons for the School Years & Beyond. Dyer, Jane & Dyer, Brooke, illus. (p. 1662)
—Plant a Kiss. Reynolds, Peter H., illus. (p. 1756)
—Plant a Kiss Board Book. Reynolds, Peter H., illus. (p. 1756)
—Spoon. Magoon, Scott, illus. (p. 2087)
—Sugar Cookies: Sweet Little Lessons on Love. Dyer, Jane & Dyer, Brooke, illus. (p. 2147)
—That's Me Loving You. White, Teagan, illus. (p. 2213)
—This Plus That: Life's Little Equations. Corace, Jen, illus. (p. 2226)
—Uni the Unicorn. Barrager, Brigette, illus. (p. 2327)
—Uni the Unicorn & the Dream Come True. Barrager, Brigette, illus. (p. 2327)
—Uni the Unicorn Uni's First Sleepover. Barrager, Brigette, illus. (p. 2327)
—Uni's First Sleepover. (p. 2329)
—Uni's Land of Unicorns Board Book Boxed Set: Uni the Unicorn; Uni the Unicorn & the Dream Come True. Barrager, Brigette, illus. (p. 2329)
—Valentine for Uni the Unicorn. (p. 2344)
—Wonder Book. Schmid, Paul, illus. (p. 2488)
—Wumbers. (p. 2514)
—Yes Day! Lichtenheld, Tom, illus. (p. 2521)
Rosenthal, Amy Krouse, jt. auth. see Chlebowski, Rachel.
Rosenthal, Amy Krouse & Lichtenheld, Tom. Exclamation Mark. (p. 676)
Rosenthal, Amy Krouse & Redmond, Lea. On the Spot: Countless Funny Stories. te Loo, Sanne, illus. (p. 1656)
Rosenthal, Amy Krouse & Rosenthal, Paris. Dear Girl, A Celebration of Wonderful, Smart, Beautiful You! Hatam, Holly, illus. (p. 520)
Rosenthal, Amy Krouse, narrated by. Spoon. (p. 2087)
Rosenthal, Beth, jt. ed. see Greenhaven Press Editors.
Rosenthal, Beth, ed. Atheism. (p. 132)
—Gay Parenting. (p. 812)
Rosenthal, Betsy R. Looking for Me: In This Great Big Family. (p. 1347)
—Porcupine's Picnic: Who Eats What? Capizzi, Giusi, illus. (p. 1778)
Rosenthal, Cathy M. Lucky Tale of Two Dogs. Warrick, Jessica, illus. (p. 1365)
Rosenthal, Christina, illus. see Darnall, Lyn.
Rosenthal, Cynthia. Day in Mexico. (p. 513)
—Matt Does Math at the Ball Game. (p. 1425)
Rosenthal, Eileen. Bobo the Sailor Man! Rosenthal, Marc, illus. (p. 252)
—I Must Have Bobo! Rosenthal, Marc, illus. (p. 1079)
—I'll Save You Bobo! Rosenthal, Marc, illus. (p. 1095)
Rosenthal, Haskell And Judith. Flutter the Butterfly with the Dull Brown Wings. (p. 753)
Rosenthal, Jason B., jt. auth. see Rosenthal, Paris.
Rosenthal, Marc. 1 Robot Lost His Head: a Robot Counting Book. (p. 2546)
—Big Bot, Small Bot: A Book of Robot Opposites. (p. 218)
Rosenthal, Marc, illus. see Appelt, Kathi.
Rosenthal, Marc, illus. see Lennon, John & McCartney, Paul.
Rosenthal, Marc, illus. see McGhee, Alison.
Rosenthal, Marc, illus. see Rosenthal, Eileen.
Rosenthal, Marc, illus. see Verdick, Elizabeth.
Rosenthal, Marc, illus. see Zimmerman, Andrea & Clemesha, David.
Rosenthal, Michele Marie. Frog & the Tadpole's Great Swamp Adventure (p. 789)
Rosenthal, Paris. Dear Baby, A Love Letter to Little Ones. Hatam, Holly, illus. (p. 520)
Rosenthal, Paris, jt. auth. see Rosenthal, Amy Krouse.
Rosenthal, Paris & Rosenthal, Jason B. Dear Boy, A Celebration of Cool, Clever, Compassionate You! Hatam, Holly, illus. (p. 520)
Rosenthal, Robin, illus. see Armitage, Duane & McQuerry, Maureen.
Rosenthal, Robin, illus. see Snyder, Gabi.
Rosenthal, S. L. Mama, Where Do Our Butterflies Go in the Winter? (p. 1392)
Rosenthal, Sally. Matzo Frogs. Sheldon, David, illus. (p. 1426)
Rosenthaler, Leopold. Grundzüge der Chemischen Pflanzenuntersuchung (Classic Reprint) (p. 901)
Rosenwasser, Rena, ed. see Kitrilakis, Thalia.
Rosenwasser, Robert, illus. see Kitrilakis, Thalia.
Rosenzweig, Zeb. Duckrt: Mystery at the Museum. (p. 608)
—Duckrt Escapes from Jail. (p. 608)
Roser, Nancy, jt. see deRuberts, Barbara.
Rosero, Evelio José. Teresita Cantaba / Teresita Used to Sing (Torre de Papel Naranja) Spanish Edition. (p. 2206)
Roset, Conrad, illus. see Sanchez Vegara, Maria Isabel.
Rosewald, Mary. Tara's Telescope. (p. 2191)
Rosewarne, Graeme, illus. see Madgwick, Wendy.
Rosewarne, Graham, illus. see Johnson, Jinny.
Rosewarne, Graham, illus. see Parker, Steve.
Rosewater, Kit. Shelly Struggles to Shine (the Derby Daredevils Book #2) Escabasse, Sophie, illus. (p. 2005)
Rosewater, Kit & Escabasse, Sophie. Derby Daredevils: Kenzie Kickstarts a Team: (the Derby Daredevils Book #1) (p. 530)
Roshell, Starshine, jt. auth. see Gigliotti, Jim.
Roshell, Starshine, jt. auth. see Merwin, E.
Rosher, Harold. With the Flying Squadron: Being the War Letters of the Late Harold Rosher to His Family (Classic Reprint) (p. 2482)
Rosier, Maggie. Aliens. (p. 47)
—Dinosaurs. (p. 550)
—Robots. (p. 1893)
—Sharks. (p. 2002)
Rosier, Paul C., jt. auth. see Bonvillain, Nancy.
Rosier, Paul C. & Crompton, Samuel Willard. Cheyenne. (p. 367)
Rosin, Lindsey. Cherry. (p. 366)
Rosing, Norbert. Polar Bears. (p. 1769)
Rosinski, illus. see Hamme, Van.
Rosinski, illus. see Van Hamme, Jean.
Rosinski, Adolf, illus. see Van Hamme, Jean.
Rosinski, Grzegorz, illus. see Dufaux, Jean.
Rosinski, Grzegorz, illus. see Van Hamme, Jean.
Rosinski, Grzegorz, illus. see van Hamme, Jean.
Rosinski, Grzegorz, illus. see Van Hamme, Jean.
Rosinsky, Lisa. Inevitable & Only. (p. 1118)
Rosinsky, Lisa, jt. auth. see Lévy, Didier.
Rosinsky, Natalie M. Ancient China (p. 80)
Roske, Melissa. Kat Greene Comes Clean. (p. 1204)
Roski, Gayle G., illus. see Olivas, John D.
Roski, Gayle Garner, illus. see Olivas, John D.
Roski, Gayle Garner, illus. see Smith, Icy.
Roski, Gayle Garner, illus. see Smith, Michael.
Roski, Gayle Garner, jt. auth. see Smith, Michael.
Roskies, David G., jt. auth. see Roskies, Diane K.
Roskifte, Kristin. Animal Beauty. (p. 88)
—Everybody Counts: A Counting Story from 1 to 7. 5 Billion. (p. 671)
Roskinski, Grzegorz, illus. see Van Hamme, Jean.
Roskos, Evan. Dr. Bird's Advice for Sad Poets. (p. 591)
Rosli, Shazana, illus. see Taib, Saadah.
Rosling, George. Four: Friends for Life. (p. 771)
—Four - Book Three - Celebrations. (p. 771)
—Four - Book Two - Teamwork. (p. 771)
Roslund, Samantha. Join Forces: Teaming up Online. (p. 1175)
Roslund, Samantha & Fontichiaro, Kristin. Maker Faire. (p. 1387)
Roslund, Samantha & Rodgers, Emily Puckett. Makerspaces. (p. 1388)

R

Roslyn, Jacquelyn, illus. see Ureel, Jessica & Jacobs, Jessica.
Rosman, Jessica. Kindy Kitchen. Lodge, Nettie, illus. (p. 1219)
Rosmer, Anna Alice Chapin Engelbert Hump. Konigskinder the Royal Children a Fairy Tale Founded on the Fairy Opera (Classic Reprint) (p. 1231)
Rosner, Ernest. John Herkner (Classic Reprint) (p. 1173)
Rosner, Gillian, tr. see Amaury.
Rosner, Gillian, tr. see Weil, Sylvie.
Rosner, Karl. King (Classic Reprint) (p. 1220)
Rosny Aine, J. -H. Guerre du Feu. (p. 902)
Roso, Thomas. Italian Novelists, Vol. 3 Of 4: Selected from the Most Approved Authors in That Language; from the Earliest Period down to the Close of the Eighteenth Century; Arranged in an Historical & Chronological Series; Second Edition (Classic Reprint) (p. 1142)
Rosoff, Meg. Good Dog, Mctavish. Easton, Grace, illus. (p. 862)
—It's a Moose! Ercolini, David, illus. (p. 1143)
—McTavish Goes Wild. Easton, Grace, illus. (p. 1432)
—Picture Me Gone. (p. 1740)
—There Is No Dog. (p. 2216)
Rosoff, Meg, jt. auth. see Peet, Mal.
Ross. Balance of Comfort, or the Old Maid & Married Woman, Vol. 1 Of 3: A Novel (Classic Reprint) (p. 160)
—Legend of the Grand Gordons (Classic Reprint) (p. 1262)
—Violet Keith: An Autobiography (Classic Reprint) (p. 2360)
—Violet Keith. (p. 2360)
Ross, illus. see Alton, Kevin & Alton, Britta.
Ross, Albert. Black Adonis (Classic Reprint) (p. 236)
—Garston Bigamy (Classic Reprint) (p. 810)
—His Private Character (Classic Reprint) (p. 974)
—Love Gone Astray (Classic Reprint) (p. 1359)
—Moulding a Maiden (Classic Reprint) (p. 1512)
—Original Sinner (Classic Reprint) (p. 1671)
—Out of Wedlock (Classic Reprint) (p. 1683)
—Speaking of Ellen (Classic Reprint) (p. 2076)
—Sugar Princess (Classic Reprint) (p. 2147)
—Their Marriage Bond (Classic Reprint) (p. 2215)
—Thou Shalt Not (New Series) (Classic Reprint) (p. 2230)
—Young Miss. Giddy (Classic Reprint) (p. 2531)
Ross, Aleksandra. Don't Call the Wolf. (p. 582)
Ross, Alex. Marvels 25th Anniversary Hardcover Edition. (p. 1413)
—Marvels Monster-Sized Edition. (p. 1413)
—Marvels Postcard Book. (p. 1413)
Ross, Alex, illus. see Busiek, Kurt.
Ross, Alex & Krueger, Jim. Earth X. (p. 617)
Ross, Alex, et al. Absolute Kingdom Come. (p. 9)
Ross, Alexander Milton. Birds of Canada: With Descriptions of Their Plumage, Habits, Food, Song, Nests, Eggs, Times of Arrival & Departure (Classic Reprint) (p. 232)
—Birds of Canada. (p. 232)
Ross, Allison J., jt. auth. see Harrison, Scott.
Ross, Andrew J., illus. see Jones, Karl.
Ross, Andrew J., illus. see Schonfeld, Sara.
Ross, Anna. Knock, Knock! Who's There? (Sesame Street) A Lift-The-Flap Board Book. Mathieu, Joe, illus. (p. 1229)
Ross, Ashley. Jacob's Wings. (p. 1154)
Ross, Barbara & Beatty, Nicholas. Goops Circus: A Whimsical Telling of Do-Good Tales. Camille, Diana, illus. (p. 869)
Ross, Barnaby. Tragedy of Y: A Drury Lane Mystery (Classic Reprint) (p. 2274)
Ross, Bob, illus. see Pearlman, Robb.
Ross, Brad. Hocus Pocus Al I Mi Choo. Arnold, Michael, illus. (p. 986)
Ross, C., illus. see Dorison, Xavier & Nury, Fabian.
Ross, Charles H. Book of Cats: A Chit-Chat Chronicle of Feline Facts & Fancies, Legendary, Lyrical, Medical, Mirthful & Miscellaneous (Classic Reprint) (p. 258)
—Book of Cats. (p. 258)
Ross, Charles Henry. Penny Wedding: A Romance of Love & War, Wasted Affections, Empty Physic Bottles, & Unpaid School Bills (Classic Reprint) (p. 1717)
Ross, Chas H. Judy, or the London Serio-Comic Journal, 1877, Vol. 21 (Classic Reprint) (p. 1186)
Ross, Christine, illus. see Holden, Pam.
Ross, Christopher, jt. auth. see Ross, Michael.
Ross, Chrystal, illus. see Ecclesiastes, Anthony.
Ross, Chudney. Lone Bean. (p. 1342)
Ross, Clinton. Meddling Hussy: Being Fourteen Tales Retold (Classic Reprint) (p. 1436)
—Meddling Hussy. (p. 1436)
—Scarlet Coat (Classic Reprint) (p. 1942)
—Trooper of the Empress (Classic Reprint) (p. 2291)
—Zuleka: Being the History of an Adventure in the Life of an American Gentleman, with Some Account of the Recent Disturbances in Dorola (Classic Reprint) (p. 2545)
Ross, D. Victoria. Thank You Father God for Christmas. (p. 2211)
—Thank You Father God for Heaven. (p. 2211)
Ross, Daisy. Peter's Pets. (p. 1730)
Ross, Dalton. Top Teams Ever: Football, Baseball, Basketball, & Hockey Winners. (p. 2264)
Ross, Daniel Vaughn, illus. see Petrucha, Stefan, et al.
Ross, Dave. Star Wars Legends Epic Collection: Legacy Vol. 3. (p. 2104)
Ross, Dave, et al. Excalibur Epic Collection: Girl's School from Heck. (p. 676)
Ross, David. World's Most Powerful Battleships. (p. 2507)
—World's Most Powerful Submarines. (p. 2507)
Ross, Dev. We Both Read Bilingual Edition-Frank & the Tiger/Sapi y el Globo. Reinhart, Larry, illus. (p. 2389)
—We Both Read Bilingual Edition-Frank & the Tiger/Sapi y el Tigre. Canetti, Yanitzia, tr. from ENG. (p. 2389)
—We Both Read-Frank & the Tiger. Reinhart, Larry, illus. (p. 2389)
—We Both Read-Oh No! We're Doing a Show! Johnson, Meredith, illus. (p. 2390)
—We Both Read-Soccer! Wenzel, David, illus. (p. 2390)
Ross, Dev & Canetti, Yanitzia. Frank & the Balloon: Sapi y el Globo. Reinhart, Larry, illus. (p. 776)
Ross, Donald. Scribble Squad in the Weird Weird West. (p. 1965)
Ross, Edward Halford. Reduction of Domestic Mosquitos: Instructions for the Use of Municipalities, Town Councils, Health Officers, Sanitary Inspectors Residents in Warm Climates (Classic Reprint) (p. 1860)
Ross, Elizabeth. Belle Epoque. (p. 197)
Ross, Ellen Edith Alice. Wreck of the White Bear, East Indiaman (Classic Reprint) (p. 2511)
Ross, Emily. Half in Love with Death. (p. 911)
Ross, Fiona. Chilly Milly Moo. (p. 377)
Ross, Frank Elmore, jt. auth. see Newcomb, Simon.
Ross, Gary. Bartholomew Biddle & the Very Big Wind. Myers, Matthew, illus. (p. 168)
Ross, Graham. Bible-Story Doodles: Favorite Scenes to Complete & Create. (p. 214)
Ross, Graham, illus. see Brouwer, Sigmund.
Ross, Graham, illus. see Hopper, Ada.
Ross, Graham, illus. see Rivadeneira, Caryn.
Ross, Graham, illus. see Sharpe, Luke.
Ross, Graham T., illus. see Skene, Pat.
Ross, Heather, illus. see Calmenson, Stephanie & Cole, Joanna.
Ross, Heather, illus. see DiPucchio, Kelly.
Ross, Heather, illus. see Messner, Kate.
Ross, Heather, illus. see Murray, Diana.
Ross, Heather, illus. see Rosenberg, Madelyn.
Ross, Heather, illus. see Springstubb, Tricia.
Ross, Hendry Durie. From Far Dakota: And Otherwhere (Classic Reprint) (p. 791)
Ross, Henry M. Her Blind Folly (Classic Reprint) (p. 956)
Ross, Isabel. Farm. Cunliffe, Ian, illus. (p. 709)
Ross, Isabel Otter-Barry. My First Wild Activity Book. Lebrun, Maxime, illus. (p. 1546)
Ross, James. Fabulae Aesopi Selectae, or Select Fables of Aesop: With an English Translation As Literal As Possible (Classic Reprint) (p. 692)
Ross, Janet. Early Days Recalled (Classic Reprint) (p. 614)
—Fourth Generation (Classic Reprint) (p. 773)
Ross, Jay. Bungalow 29. Klimko, Andrew, illus. (p. 297)
Ross, Jeanne. Rock Riddles. (p. 1894)
Ross, Jeff. Above All Else (p. 6)
—At Ease (p. 129)
—Coming Clean (p. 430)
—Dawn Patrol (p. 512)
—Drop (p. 605)
—Easy Street. (p. 621)
—Set You Free (p. 1993)
—Shark. (p. 2001)
—Shutout (p. 2013)
—Up North (p. 2338)
Ross, Jerry L. & Gunderson, Susan G. Becoming a Spacewalker: My Journey to the Stars. (p. 187)
Ross, Jesse Paul & Puzzling Sports Institute Staff. Slapshot Hockey Quizbook: 50 Fun Games Brought to You by the Puzzling Sports Institute. (p. 2035)
Ross, Jill. Blake Family Vacation. Pruitt, Gwendolyn, illus. (p. 242)
—Real Nitty-Gritty. Pruitt, Gwendolyn, illus. (p. 1850)
—What's the Matter, Mr. Ticklebritches? Pruitt, Gwendolyn, illus. (p. 2426)
Ross, Joel. Beast & Crown. (p. 181)
—Beast & Crown #2: the Ice Witch. (p. 181)
—Fog Diver. (p. 756)
—Lost Compass. (p. 1353)
Ross, John. Corean Primer: Being Lessons in Corean on All Ordinary Subjects, Transliterated on the Principles of the Mandarin Primer, by the Same Author (Classic Reprint) (p. 454)
Ross, John Wilson. Tacitus & Bracciolini: The Annals Forged in the Xvth Century. (p. 2175)
Ross, Julie, illus. see Pimot, Karen Hutchins.
Ross, Katharine. Twinkle, Twinkle, Little Bug. Cooke, Tom & Brannon, Tom, illus. (p. 2305)
Ross, Kathy. Beautiful Beads. Bosch, Nicole in den, illus. (p. 183)
—Beautiful Beads. In Den Bosch, Nicole, illus. (p. 183)
—Creative Kitchen Crafts. Bosch, Nicole in den, illus. (p. 471)
—Creative Kitchen Crafts. In Den Bosch, Nicole, illus. (p. 471)
—Earth-Friendly Crafts: Clever Ways to Reuse Everyday Items. Malépart, Céline, illus. (p. 616)
—Jazzy Jewelry, Pretty Purses, & More! Bosch, Nicole in den, illus. (p. 1162)
—One-of-a-Kind Stamps & Crafts. Bosch, Nicole, illus. (p. 1661)
—One-of-a-Kind Stamps & Crafts. Bosch, Nicole in den, illus. (p. 1661)
Ross Kennedy, illus. see Lihou, Gavin.
Ross, Lanette. Charlie the Cat. (p. 360)
Ross, Laura. Hand Puppets: How to Make & Use Them. (p. 914)
Ross, Leanne R., illus. see Schmal, Mary I.
Ross, Liesl. Bonnie B-One's Supersonic Move. Buchanan, Alexander "lex", illus. (p. 256)
Ross, Lillian E. Argonauts (Classic Reprint) (p. 114)
Ross, Linda B., adapted by. Tom Sawyer: Read Aloud Classics Edition Big Book. (p. 2257)
Ross, Lucy M. Changelings (Classic Reprint) (p. 356)
Ross, Luke. Star Wars: Darth Maul. (p. 2104)
—Star Wars: the Force Awakens Adaptation. (p. 2105)
Ross, Luke, illus. see Wendig, Chuck.
Ross, Luke & Smith, Cory. Star Wars: Age of Republic. (p. 2104)
Ross, M., illus. see Gordon, Elizabeth.
Ross, M. T., illus. see Gordon, Elizabeth.
Ross, M. T., illus. see Kirkwood, Edith Brown.
Ross, Malcolm. Climber in New Zealand (Classic Reprint) (p. 405)
Ross, Mandy & Ladybird Books Staff. Chicken Licken. (p. 368)
—Little Red Riding Hood. (p. 1326)
Ross, Marilyn. Dark Shadows the Complete Paperback Library Reprint Volume 6: Barnabas Collins. (p. 507)
—Dark Shadows the Complete Paperback Library Reprint Volume 5: The Curse of Collinwood. (p. 507)
—Dark Shadows the Complete Paperback Library Reprint Volume 4: The Mystery of Collinwood. (p. 507)
—Dark Shadows the Complete Paperback Library Reprint Volume 3: Strangers at Collins House. (p. 507)
—Dark Shadows the Complete Paperback Library Reprint Volume 1: Dark Shadows. Herman, Eileen Sabrina, ed. (p. 507)
Ross, Marlene. Adventures of Donny the Doorknob. Hallam, Colleen and Peggy, illus. (p. 23)
Ross, Marrianne & Ross, Marianne. Bible Detectives - Samuel. (p. 213)
Ross, Martín. Beggars on Horseback: A Riding Tour in North Wales (Classic Reprint) (p. 191)
—Beggars on Horseback. (p. 191)
Ross, Martín, jt. auth. see Somerville, Edith Oe.
Ross, Martín & Somerville, Edith. Beggars on Horseback. (p. 191)
Ross, Martín & Somerville, Edith None. Beggars on Horseback. (p. 191)
Ross, Marylin. Dark Shadows the Complete Paperback Library Reprint Volume 8: The Demon of Barnabas Collins. (p. 507)
—Dark Shadows the Complete Paperback Library Reprint Volume 7: The Secret of Barnabas Collins. (p. 507)
Ross, Matthew. Woppaglove's Picnic. (p. 2493)
Ross, Melanie H., jt. auth. see Willis, Jeanne.
Ross, Melanie H. & Willis, Jeanne. Mayfly Day. Ross, Tony, illus. (p. 1430)
Ross, Melissa. Angels Watching over Us. (p. 86)
—Today I Am a Penguin. Ross, Melissa, illus. (p. 2254)
Ross, Melissa, illus. see Arbo, Barbara.
Ross, Melissa, illus. see Brewer, Leanna Jayne.
Ross, Melissa, illus. see Brewer, Leanna.
Ross, Michael. Across the Great Divide: Book 1 the Clouds of War (p. 11)
Ross, Michael & Johnson, Greg. 10 Reasons to Stay Christian in High School: A Guide to Staying Sane When Everyone Else Has Jumped off the Deep End. (p. 2550)
Ross, Michael & Ross, Christopher. Finding Faith in a Minecrafty World: 80 a-To-Z (Kid Only) Survival Secrets [an Unofficial Guide]. Skinner, ed. (p. 729)
—Kid's Game Plan for Great Choices: An All-Sports Devotional. (p. 1215)
Ross, Michael Elsohn. Plantology: 30 Activities & Observations for Exploring the World of Plants. (p. 1757)
—She Takes a Stand: 16 Fearless Activists Who Have Changed the World. (p. 2004)
Ross, Michelle. Tekatu Learns Obedience. Kolpak, Nadiia, illus. (p. 2201)
Ross, Neil M., jt. auth. see Mackenzie, Carine.
Ross, Nick. Fishing. (p. 742)
Ross, P. T. Yeoman's Letters (Classic Reprint) (p. 2521)
Ross, Patrick. Oliver: The Great Escape. Burcham, David, illus. (p. 1649)
Ross, Paul. Rodney the Chimney Sweep & Jemima Four Foot: Twitch's New Home & Mystery at the Manor. (p. 1897)
Ross, Peg, ed. see Buckey, Sarah Masters.
Ross, Philip. My First Book of Bible Prayers. (p. 1542)
Ross, Rebecca. Queen's Resistance. (p. 1825)
—Queen's Rising. (p. 1825)
—Rebelion de la Reina. (p. 1852)
—Resistencia de la Reina. (p. 1869)
—Sisters of Sword & Song. (p. 2027)
Ross, Robert Baldwin, jt. auth. see Wilde, Oscar.
Ross, Robert L. Booster, Vol. 25: June, 1921 (Classic Reprint) (p. 262)
Ross, Ronald. Mosquito Brigades & How to Organise Them (Classic Reprint) (p. 1507)
Ross, Samuel B., jt. auth. see Ross, Samuel B., Jr.
Ross, Samuel B., Jr. & Ross, Samuel B. Extraordinary Spirit of Green Chimneys: Connecting Children & Animals to Create Hope. (p. 685)
Ross, Sarah C. E., jt. auth. see Acheson, James.
Ross, Sherry. Return of the Vinetropes. (p. 1871)
Ross, Sonny. Duck Gets a Job. Ross, Sonny, illus. (p. 608)
Ross, Stewart. Henry VIII: Guilty or Innocent? (p. 955)
—Hiroshima. (p. 973)
—Into the Unknown: How Great Explorers Found Their Way by Land, Sea, & Air. Biesty, Stephen, illus. (p. 1128)
—Seaside Holidays. (p. 1972)
—Sport Technology. (p. 2088)
Ross, Stewart & Lonely Planet Kids. Unfolding Journeys Amazon Adventure Sparks, Jenni, illus. (p. 2327)
—Unfolding Journeys - Following the Great Wall Ngai, Victo, illus. (p. 2327)
—Unfolding Journeys Rocky Mountain Explorer Davidson, Annie, illus. (p. 2327)
—Unfolding Journeys - Wonders of Egypt Starkoff, Vanina, illus. (p. 2327)
Ross, Stewart & Woodward, Joe. Pearl Harbor. (p. 1710)
Ross, Susan. Kiki & Jacques. (p. 1216)
Ross, Susan L. Searching for Lottie. (p. 1971)
Ross, Susan R. Drat That Cat! Amatori, Stephanie, illus. (p. 597)
Ross, Suzanne. BOOST Rain Forest Activity Book. (p. 262)
—Nature Mazes. (p. 1581)
Ross, Suzy, illus. see Steer, Joanne.
Ross, Sylvia. Blue Jay Girl. (p. 248)
Ross, Tara K. Fade to White. (p. 694)
Ross, Timothy & Whitt, Shannon. Clever Costumes. (p. 404)
Ross, Tony. Anty-War Story. Ross, Tony, illus. (p. 104)
—Don't Do That! Ross, Tony, illus. (p. 582)
—Goldilocks & the Three Bears. (p. 861)
—Henry V, a Midsummer's Night Dream, the Merchant of Venice, Hamlet. (p. 955)
—I Didn't Do It! Ross, Tony, illus. (p. 1064)
—I Don't Want to Go to the Hospital! Ross, Tony, illus. (p. 1064)
—I Don't Want to Wash My Hands! Ross, Tony, illus. (p. 1064)
—I Feel Sick! Ross, Tony, illus. (p. 1065)
—I Want a Bedtime Story! Ross, Tony, illus. (p. 1084)
—I Want a Bunny! (p. 1084)
—I Want a Friend! Ross, Tony, illus. (p. 1084)
—I Want a Sister! Ross, Tony, illus. (p. 1084)
—I Want My Dad! Ross, Tony, illus. (p. 1084)
—I Want My Dinner! (p. 1084)
—I Want My Dummy! (p. 1084)
—I Want My Light On! Ross, Tony, illus. (p. 1084)
—I Want My Potty! (p. 1084)
—I Want My Tooth! (p. 1084)
—I Want Snow! Ross, Tony, illus. (p. 1084)
—I Want to Do It Myself! Ross, Tony, illus. (p. 1085)
—I Want to Go Home! Ross, Tony, illus. (p. 1085)
—I Want to Win! Ross, Tony, illus. (p. 1085)
—Jack & the Beanstalk. (p. 1151)
—Little Princess Dress Up! Sticker Activity Book. (p. 1325)
—My Favourite Fairy Tales. Ross, Tony, illus. (p. 1540)
—Nights Before Christmas: 24 Classic Christmas Stories to Read Aloud. (p. 1608)
—Nights Before Christmas. (p. 1608)
—Our Kid. Ross, Tony, illus. (p. 1678)
—Rita's Rhino. Ross, Tony, illus. (p. 1886)
—Shakespeare Stories: Much Ado about Nothing, the Taming of the Shrew, Macbeth, Romeo & Juliet. (p. 1999)
—Silly Mr Wolf. (p. 2018)
—Super Dooper Jezebel. Ross, Tony, illus. (p. 2154)
—Uridu an Afuz! Salim, Adunis, illus. (p. 2340)
—Uridu an Utfu Al-Dawl! Salim, Adunis, illus. (p. 2340)
Ross, Tony, illus. see Ahlberg, Allan.
Ross, Tony, illus. see Banks, Lynne Reid.
Ross, Tony, illus. see Boyd, Colin.
Ross, Tony, illus. see Bradman, Tony.
Ross, Tony, illus. see Burchett, Jan & Vogler, Sara.
Ross, Tony, illus. see Carroll, Lewis, pseud.
Ross, Tony, illus. see Danziger, Paula, et al.
Ross, Tony, illus. see Danziger, Paula.
Ross, Tony, illus. see Demers, Dominique.
Ross, Tony, illus. see Finney, Wendy.
Ross, Tony, illus. see Grindley, Sally.
Ross, Tony, illus. see Lindgren, Astrid.
Ross, Tony, illus. see Matthews, Andrew.
Ross, Tony, illus. see McCaughrean, Geraldine.
Ross, Tony, illus. see McKay, Hilary.
Ross, Tony, illus. see Mitchelhill, Barbara.
Ross, Tony, illus. see Phinn, Gervase.
Ross, Tony, illus. see Rosen, Michael.
Ross, Tony, illus. see Ross, Melanie H. & Willis, Jeanne.
Ross, Tony, illus. see Simon, Francesca.
Ross, Tony, illus. see Skidmore, Steve & Barlow, Steve.
Ross, Tony, illus. see Waddell, Martin.
Ross, Tony, illus. see Walliams, David.
Ross, Tony, illus. see Whybrow, Ian.
Ross, Tony, illus. see Willis, Jeanne.
Ross, Tony, jt. auth. see Blacker, Terence.
Ross, Tony, jt. auth. see Carroll, Lewis, pseud.
Ross, Tony, jt. auth. see Delafosse, Claude.
Ross, Tony, jt. auth. see Ross, Tony.
Ross, Tony, jt. auth. see Whybrow, Ian.
Ross, Tony, jt. auth. see Willis, Jeanne.
Ross, Tony & Ross, Tony. Goldilocks & the Three Bears. (p. 860)
Ross, Tracey. My Book of Feelings: A Book to Help Children with Attachment Difficulties, Learning or Developmental Disabilities Understand Their Emotions. Salaman, Rosy, illus. (p. 1534)
Ross, Valerie. Knowing Jesus Means Knowing Peace. (p. 1230)
Ross, Warren. Red Boots & Assorted Things. Usova, Victoria, illus. (p. 1856)
Ross Williamson, Hugh. Young People's Book of Saints: Sixty-Three Saints of the Western Church from the First to the Twentieth Century. Connelly, Sheila, illus. (p. 2532)
Rossa, Paloma. Mindful Moments at Bedtime: Tall Trade Format. Cottage Door Press, ed. (p. 1470)
—Star Signs for Little Astrologers. Cottage Door Press, ed. (p. 2103)
Rossel, Seymour. Holocaust: An End to Innocence. (p. 989)
Rossell, Judith. Oliver. Rossell, Judith, illus. (p. 1649)
—Play with Your Plate! (a Mix-And-Match Play Book) (p. 1760)
—Wakestone Hall (Stella Montgomery, Book 3) (p. 2371)
—Withering-By-Sea. Rossell, Judith, illus. (p. 2482)
—Wormwood Mire. Rossell, Judith, illus. (p. 2508)
Rossell, Judith, illus. see Brian, Janeen.
Rossell, Judith, illus. see Holmes, Janet A.
Rossell, Judith, illus. see Kerr, Eleanor.
Rossell, Judith, illus. see Stills, Caroline.
Rossell, Judith, jt. auth. see Simons, Moya.
Rossendale, Helen. Tales from Pinocchio. (p. 2182)
Rosser, William Henry, jt. auth. see White, James.
Rossetti, Carol, illus. see Sanders, Jessica.
Rossetti, Christina. Blooming Beneath the Sun. Bryan, Ashley, illus. (p. 247)
—Maude: Prose Verse (Classic Reprint) (p. 1426)
—Speaking Likenesses (Classic Reprint) (p. 2076)
Rossetti, Christina Georgina. Commonplace, & Other Short Stories (Classic Reprint) (p. 431)
Rossetti-Shustak, Bernadette. I Love You Through & Through: Board Book & Plush. Church, Caroline Jayne, illus. (p. 1079)
—I Love You Through & Through (Te Quiero, Yo Te Quiero) Church, Caroline Jayne, illus. (p. 1079)
—I Love You Through & Through at Christmas, Too! Church, Caroline Jayne, illus. (p. 1079)
—I Love You Through & Through at Christmas, Too! / ¡En Navidad También Te Quiero! Church, Caroline Jayne, illus. (p. 1079)
Ross-Hudson, Reba. Spotless. (p. 2090)
Rossi, Ann. Native Americans of the Southwest: Set Of 6. (p. 1578)
—Southeast: Set Of 6. (p. 2069)
Rossi, Ann, jt. auth. see National Geographic Learning, National Geographic Learning.
Rossi, Ann & Benchmark Education Company, LLC Staff. Sureste: Set of 6 Common Core Edition. (p. 2162)
Rossi, Christian, illus. see Dorison, Xavier & Nury, Fabien.
Rossi, Francesca. Little Mermaid. (p. 1321)
Rossi, Francesca, illus. see Perrault, Charles, et al.
Rossi, Francesca, illus. see Stevenson, Robert Louis.
Rossi, Francesca, illus. see Swift, Jonathan.
Rossi, Francesca, illus. see Verne, Jules.

R

Roujon, Jacques. Battles Bivouacs: A French Soldier's Note-Book (Classic Reprint) (p. 175)
Roulaine, Katherine. Chang & Olan. (p. 355)
-Roulet, Mary F. Nixon. Spaniard at Home (Classic Reprint) (p. 2073)
Roulier, Logan K. Mouthful of Words. (p. 1515)
Roulston, Alyssa. Ruby Goes Camping. (p. 1911)
Roumanis, A. r., ed. see Martin, Dayna.
Roumanis, A. r., jt. auth. see Martin, Dayna.
Roumanis, Alexis. Africa. (p. 32)
—Antarctica. (p. 101)
—Asia. (p. 126)
—Australia. (p. 138)
—Baboons. (p. 148)
—Blue Marlin. (p. 249)
—Coral Reefs. (p. 453)
—Deserts. (p. 532)
—Dwarf Planets. (p. 611)
—Earth. (p. 615)
—Europe. (p. 667)
—Exploring Continents: Asia. (p. 681)
—Exploring Continents: Europe. (p. 681)
—Exploring Continents: Australia. (p. 681)
—Exploring Continents: South America. (p. 681)
—Giant Octopus. (p. 830)
—Grasslands. (p. 881)
—I Am a Komodo Dragon. (p. 1057)
—I Am a Red Panda. (p. 1057)
—I Am a Sloth. (p. 1057)
—I Am a Tasmanian Devil. (p. 1057)
—I Am a Warthog. (p. 1057)
—Jupiter. (p. 1191)
—Mars. (p. 1409)
—Mercury. (p. 1448)
—Mountains. (p. 1514)
—Neptune. (p. 1587)
—North America. (p. 1620)
—Oceans. (p. 1636)
—Rainforests. (p. 1837)
—Saturn. (p. 1936)
—South America. (p. 2068)
—Sun. (p. 2151)
—Uranus. (p. 2339)
—Venus. (p. 2351)
—What Is COVID-19? (Engaging Readers, Level 1) (p. 2415)
Roumanis, Alexis, jt. auth. see Carr, Aaron.
Roumanis, Alexis, jt. auth. see Ring, Susan.
Roumer, Edwidge B. Hopeful Heart. (p. 1002)
Roumiguière, Cécile. Nasia's Dream. Rea, Simone, illus. (p. 1576)
Rouncville, Bibi. Gimbels & Gooseberries. (p. 833)
—Sea Bugs & Moose Eggs. (p. 1967)
—Trouble at Binka Bridge. (p. 2291)
Round, Graham, illus. see Bryant-Mole, Karen & Tyler, Jenny.
Round, Graham, illus. see Bryant-Mole, Karen.
Round, Suzanne. Dragonfire Crystal. (p. 594)
Round, William Marshall Fitts. Achsah: A New England Life-Study (Classic Reprint) (p. 11)
Rounds, Charles Ralph. Wisconsin in Story & Song: Selections from the Prose & Poetry of Badger State Writers (Classic Reprint) (p. 2477)
Rounds, Erin. Charlotte's Bones: The Beluga Whale in a Farmer's Field Carver, Allison, illus. (p. 361)
—Where's Winter. Stevens, Tammie, ed. (p. 2441)
Rounds, Glen. Whitey's Sunday Horse (Classic Reprint) (p. 2445)
Rounds, Harriet. Magic Stairway (p. 1379)
Roundtree, Abigail. Pathway to Statehood: The Territory of Colorado Joins the Union (p. 1705)
Roundtree, La' Motta. Curse Within. (p. 489)
Roundy, William Noble. Uncle Sam's Visit to the U. S. Senate (Classic Reprint) (p. 2319)
—Visit of Apollo: This Bit of a S a Tale of the Times, Depicted in Simple & Readable Ryhmes (Classic Reprint) (p. 2362)
Rountree, Elizabeth. State Normal Magazine, Vol. 22: May, 1918 (Classic Reprint) (p. 2108)
—State Normal Magazine, Vol. 22: April, 1918 (Classic Reprint) (p. 2108)
—State Normal Magazine, Vol. 22: January, 1918 (Classic Reprint) (p. 2108)
—State Normal Magazine, Vol. 22: October, 1917 (Classic Reprint) (p. 2108)
—State Normal Magazine, Vol. 22: December, 1917 (Classic Reprint) (p. 2108)
—State Normal Magazine, Vol. 22: February, 1918 (Classic Reprint) (p. 2108)
—State Normal Magazine, Vol. 22: November, 1917 (Classic Reprint) (p. 2108)
Rountree, Harry, illus. see Carroll, Lewis, pseud.
Rountree, Roshni. Beautiful Hair. (p. 184)
Roupnel, Gaston. Nono, Love & the Soil (Classic Reprint) (p. 1618)
Rourke, Brigid. Tools of Science. (p. 2261)
Rourke Educational Media, creator. History of America. (p. 977)
Rourke Publishing Staff, ed. see Cooper, Jason.
Rourke Publishing Staff, ed. see Greve, Tom.
Rourke Publishing Staff, ed. see Ohare, Ted.
Rourke, Thomas. Thunder below (Classic Reprint) (p. 2238)
Rous, Sheri, ed. see Callella, Trisha.
Rous, Sheri, ed. see Cernek, Kim & Shiotsu, Vicky.
Rous, Sheri, ed. see Shiotsu, Vicky.
Rousay II, Richard A. Choose the Right 'Walk with Alma' (p. 381)
—Choose the Right! Walk with Ruth. (p. 381)
Rouse, Adelaide L. Annice Wynkoop, Artist: The Perseverance of a Country Girl (Classic Reprint) (p. 99)
Rouse, Adelaide Louise. Under My Own Roof (Classic Reprint) (p. 2321)
Rouse, Andy, photos by see Schindel, John.
Rouse, Bonna, illus. see Crossingham, John.
Rouse, Bonna, illus. see Kalman, Bobbie.
Rouse, Bonna, jt. auth. see Crossingham, John.
Rouse, Geoff. Kiss Before Morning. (p. 1224)
Rouse, Lidany, compiled by. Children's Letters to Their Hero. (p. 374)
Rouse, Mark, illus. see Gow, Iain.
Rouse, Shelley. Sweet Briar Magazine, Vol. 12: November, 1920 (Classic Reprint) (p. 2168)
Rouse, W. H. D. Giant Crab & Other Tales from Old Indi. (p. 830)
—Giant Crab, & Other Tales from Old India (Classic Reprint) (p. 830)
—Perse Playbooks, Vol. 4: No; 4. First-Fruits of the Play Method in Prose (Classic Reprint) (p. 1724)
—Tales from the Isles of Greece: Being Sketches of Modern Greek Peasant Life Translated from the Greek of Argyris Ephtaliotis (Classic Reprint) (p. 2183)
—Talking Thrush: And Other Tales from India (Classic Reprint) (p. 2187)
Rouse, W. H. D., jt. auth. see Crooke, William.
Rouse, W. H. D., ed. Giant Crab & Other Tales from Old Indi. (p. 830)
Rouse, Walt. Adventures of Clever Kitty. Bowker, Margie, illus. (p. 22)
Rouse, William Henry Denham. Arabian Nights: Edited with an Introduction (Classic Reprint) (p. 108)
Roush, April, illus. see Hapka, Cathy, pseud.
Roush, Sigel. Swamps: A Record of Pioneer Days in the Middle West (Classic Reprint) (p. 2167)
Rouss, Shannan, jt. auth. see Rouss, Sylvia A.
Rouss, Sylvia. Hanukkah Fable of Little Dreidel & Silver Menorah. Derby, T. L., illus. (p. 919)
—Holiday for Ari Ant. (p. 987)
—Touch of Chanukah: A Touch & Feel Book. Becker, Boruch, illus. (p. 2268)
Rouss, Sylvia A. Circle of Smiles: A Story about Beit Issie Shapiro, Israel's Leading Organization in the Field of Disability. (p. 393)
—Holiday for Ari Ant Kahn, Katherine, illus. (p. 987)
—Sammy Spider's First Bar Mitzvah. Kahn, Katherine Janus, illus. (p. 1928)
—Sammy Spider's First Book of Jewish Holidays Kahn, Katherine Janus, illus. (p. 1928)
—Sammy Spider's First Day of School. Kahn, Katherine Janus, illus. (p. 1928)
—Sammy Spider's First Mitzvah. Kahn, Katherine Janus, illus. (p. 1928)
—Sammy Spider's First Simchat Torah Kahn, Katherine Janus, illus. (p. 1928)
—Sammy Spider's First Yom Kippur. Kahn, Katherine Janus, illus. (p. 1928)
—Sammy Spider's Hanukkah Colors Kahn, Katherine Janus, illus. (p. 1928)
—Sammy Spider's New Friend Kahn, Katherine Janus, illus. (p. 1928)
—Sammy Spider's New Friend. Kahn, Katherine, illus. (p. 1928)
—Sammy Spider's Passover Shapes. Kahn, Katherine Janus, illus. (p. 1928)
—Yosef's Dream Blumenfeld, Tamar, illus. (p. 2523)
Rouss, Sylvia A. & Rouss, Shannan. Watermelon in the Sukkah. Iosa, Ann, illus. (p. 2386)
Rouss, Sylvia A. & Turndorf, Genene Levy. Sammy Spider's First Taste of Hanukkah: A Cookbook. Kahn, Katherine Janus, illus. (p. 1928)
Rouss, Sylviaa01. Littlest Pair Hannon, Holly, illus. (p. 1331)
Rousseau, Craig, illus. see Caramagna, Joe.
Rousseau, Craig, illus. see McCool, Ben.
Rousseau, Craig, illus. see Stewart, Michael, et al.
Rousseau, Craig, illus. see Thomas, Rich.
Rousseau, Craig, illus. see Tobin, Paul & Gray, Scott.
Rousseau, Élise. Chevaux Racont's(les) (p. 367)
Rousseau, Henri, jt. auth. see Markel, Michelle.
Rousseau, Jean-Jacques. Confessions of J. J. Rousseau, Vol. 1: With the Reveries of the Solitary Walker (Classic Reprint) (p. 439)
Rousseau, Stefan. Afrique Racont'e Aux Enfants(l') (p. 33)
Rousseau, Stephanie. Princesses (Make It Now!) Press-Out & Play. (p. 1800)
Rousseau, Victor. Big Muskeg (Classic Reprint) (p. 221)
Rousseff, Minnie, illus. see Gilbert, Paul.
Rousseff, Minnie H., illus. see Gilbert, Paul T.
Roussel, A. Legendes Morales de L'Inde: Empruntees Au Bhagavata Purana et Au Mahabharata, Traduites du Sanscrit (Classic Reprint) (p. 1263)
Rousselow, Jeff. Bury the Dead. (p. 300)
Roussey, Christine. My Funny Bunny. (p. 1548)
—My Lazy Cat. (p. 1551)
—My Stinky Dog. (p. 1561)
Roussey, Christine, illus. see Witek, Jo.
Roussin, Simon. Forever Young: the Boy Who Couldn't Die: A TOON Graphic. (p. 767)
Roussos, Eleni. Marvel: Heroes vs. Villains. (p. 1412)
—Marvel Spider-Man: into the Spider-Verse Movie Theater Storybook. (p. 1412)
—Moviemaking Magic of Marvel Studios: Heroes & Villains. (p. 1516)
—Spider-Man: Homecoming - the Art of the Movie. (p. 2080)
Roussos, Eleni, text. Marvel's Captain Marvel: the Art of the Movie. (p. 1413)
—Spider-Man: Far from Home - the Art of the Movie. (p. 2080)
Roussos, J. C. Gift for Santa. (p. 832)
Routledge, Robert. Science in Sport Made Philosophy in Earnest: Being an Attempt to Illustrate Some Elementary Principles of Physical Knowledge by Means of Toys & Pastimes (Classic Reprint) (p. 1955)
Rouviere, Henrietta. Old Irish Baronet, or Manners of My Country, Vol. 1 Of 3: A Novel (Classic Reprint) (p. 1646)
Roux, Alphonse A. Louise Necker, at Ten Years of Age, or the Authoress of Corinne: An Historical & Moral Comedy, in One Act (Classic Reprint) (p. 1357)
Roux, Augustin. Traité de la Culture et de la Plantation des Arbres a Ouvrer: Avec la Manière d'Exploiter, de débiter et d'Enchantillonner les Bois, Suivant les Differens Usages Ausquels Ils Sont Propres Pour les Besoins de la Vie (Classic Reprint) (p. 2276)
Roux, Hugues Le. Acrobats & Mountebanks (Classic Reprint) (p. 11)
—On the Field of Honor: Au Champ d'Honneur (Classic Reprint) (p. 1654)
Roux, Madeleine. Asylum. (p. 129)
—Asylum Novellas: The Scarlets, the Bone Artists, the Warden. (p. 129)
—Catacomb. (p. 342)
—Corte de Las Sombras. (p. 456)
—Court of Shadows. (p. 463)
—Court of Shadows. Compiet, Iris, illus. (p. 463)
—Escape Del Asylum. (p. 661)
—Escape from Asylum. (p. 661)
—House of Furies. Compiet, Iris, illus. (p. 1023)
—Mansion de Las Furias. (p. 1398)
—Sanctum. (p. 1930)
—Tomb of Ancients. (p. 2258)
—Tomb of Ancients. Compiet, Iris, illus. (p. 2258)
Roux, Philibert-Joseph Le. Dictionaire Comique, Satyrique, Critique, Burlesque, Libre et Proverbial: Avec une Explication Tre's-Fide'le de Toutes les Maniéres de Parler Burlesques, Comiques, Libres, Satyriques, Critiques et Proverbiales, Qui Peuvent Se Rencontrer Dans les Meilleur. (p. 541)
—Dictionnaire Comique, Satyrique, Critique, Burlesque, Libre et Proverbial: Avec une Explication Tres-Fidele de Toutes les Manieres de Parler Burlesques, Comiques, Libres, Satyriques, Critiques et Proverbiales, Qui Peuvent Se Rencontter Dans les Meilleurs. (p. 542)
Roux, Stéphane, illus. see Millici, Nate, et al.
Roux, Stéphane, illus. see Siglain, Michael.
Roux, Stéphane, jt. auth. see Heddle, Jennifer.
Roux, Sylvie. Petit Clin d'Oeil des Anges. (p. 1730)
Roux, Tony-George. Carnet Blanc Sport D'Hiver. (p. 332)
—Carnet Ligne Sport D'Hiver. (p. 332)
Rouzzo, David J. Adventures of Black Kitty. (p. 22)
—What's Inside My Birthday Gift? (p. 2425)
—What's Inside My Christmas Gift? (p. 2425)
Rover, Winnie. Neptune at the Golden Horn (Classic Reprint) (p. 1587)
Rovere, Amy. And Still They Bloom: A Family's Journey of Loss & Healing. Spector, Joel, illus. (p. 83)
Rovère, Maxime. Docteur Jekyll et Mister Hyde. (p. 573)
Rovira, Francesc, illus. see Maria Machado, Ana.
Rovira, Pere. Busca los animales del zoo. (p. 300)
Row, Caroline Bigelow Le. Duxberry Doings: A New England Story (Classic Reprint) (p. 611)
Row, Jan, illus. see Martin, Darrin Todd.
Row, Jan, jt. auth. see Martin, Darrin Todd.
Row, Richard, illus. see Stuchner, Joan Betty.
Row, Robert Keable, jt. auth. see Robbins, Carolyn M.
Rowan, Arthur Blennerhassett. Gleanings after Grand Tour-Ists (Classic Reprint) (p. 842)
Rowan, Charles A. I Like to Love. (p. 1068)
Rowan, Ellis. Flower-Hunter in Queensland & New Zealand (Classic Reprint) (p. 752)
Rowan, Hope. Ten Days in the North Woods: A Kids' Hiking Guide to the Katahdin Region. Fitch, Jada, illus. (p. 2204)
Rowan, Isabelle. Furborn. (p. 802)
Rowan, Jennifer L. Afghanistan. (p. 31)
—Causes of the Civil War. (p. 347)
—Mexico. (p. 1454)
—Russia. (p. 1917)
—United Kingdom. (p. 2330)
Rowan, Karen. Isabela Captura un Congo. Seely, Contee & López, Pablo Ortega, eds. (p. 1138)
Rowan, Richard Wilmer. Modern Spies Tell Their Stories: Personal Narratives of Many Exploits in Secret Service (Classic Reprint) (p. 1487)
Rowan Roberts, Ida. Framed by Who? (p. 775)
—Striking Resemblance. (p. 2141)
Rowan, Ron, jt. auth. see Johnson, D. C.
Rowand, Phyllis. It Is Night. Dronzek, Laura, illus. (p. 1141)
Rowbotham, Genna. Bella & the Tooth Fairy. (p. 196)
Rowcroft, Albert E. Philip Darrell, a Romance of English Home Life, Vol. 2 of 3 (Classic Reprint) (p. 1734)
—Philip Darrell, Vol. 1 Of 3: A Romance; of English Home Life (Classic Reprint) (p. 1734)
Rowcroft, Charles. Fanny: The Little Milliner (Classic Reprint) (p. 706)
—Man Without a Profession, Vol. 1 of 3 (Classic Reprint) (p. 1396)
—Tales of the Colonies: Or, the Adventures of an Emigrant (Classic Reprint) (p. 2185)
—Tales of the Colonies, or the Adventures of an Emigrant, Vol. 2 of 3 (Classic Reprint) (p. 2185)
—Tales of the Colonies, Vol. 1 Of 3: Or, the Adventures of an Emigrant (Classic Reprint) (p. 2185)
Rowe, Alan, illus. see Heddle, Becca.
Rowe, Amanda. If There Never Was a You. Skomorokhova, Olga, illus. (p. 1092)
Rowe, Andrew. Love Me for Who I Am. (p. 1360)
Rowe, Anne Burgess. Newest Angel. (p. 1600)
Rowe, Brooke. Building a Lava Lamp. Bane, Jeff, illus. (p. 294)
—Building a Volcano. Bane, Jeff, illus. (p. 294)
—Creating Rain. Bane, Jeff, illus. (p. 470)
—Floating a Paper Clip. Bane, Jeff, illus. (p. 750)
—Making a Telephone. Bane, Jeff, illus. (p. 1388)
—Playing Musical Bottles. Bane, Jeff, illus. (p. 1760)
—Playing with Solar Heat. Bane, Jeff, illus. (p. 1761)
—Shining a Penny. Bane, Jeff, illus. (p. 2007)
—What City Should You Live In? (p. 2407)
—What Club Should You Try? (p. 2407)
—What Color Is Your Aura? (p. 2407)
—What Creature Are You Most Like? (p. 2407)
—What Decade Do You Belong In? (p. 2407)
—What Kind of Friend Are You? (p. 2418)
—What Kind of Royalty Are You? (p. 2418)
—What Kind of Spender Are You? (p. 2418)
—What Kind of Sports Pro Are You? (p. 2418)
—What Monster Are You Most Like? (p. 2419)
—What Pet Should You Get? (p. 2419)
—What TV Show Should You Be On? (p. 2421)
—What's Your Dream Job? (p. 2427)
—What's Your Perfect Vacation? (p. 2427)
—What's Your Spirit Animal? (p. 2427)
—What's Your Superpower? (p. 2427)
Rowe, Caroline. Secret Life of Bears. (p. 1976)
Rowe, Chelsea H. Ebenezer Has a Word for Everything Dormer, Frank, illus. (p. 622)
Rowe, Chistopher, jt. auth. see Bond, Gwenda.
Rowe, Clarence, jt. auth. see Raine, William MacLeod.
Rowe, Colin, illus. see St John Thomas, Gareth.
Rowe, Dana. Pavo Explores the Solar System. (p. 1708)
Rowe, Eleanor. Night Before - Easter. (p. 1604)
Rowe, Eva McKenzie & Hodge, Darren. Harrison Bean. (p. 933)
Rowe, Harlan P. House of Unfulfilled Desire (Classic Reprint) (p. 1023)
Rowe, Harriet, illus. see Hodgson, Karen J.
Rowe, Helen. Fun with Pets: A Pop-Up Book. (p. 800)
Rowe, Helen, illus. see Lobo, Julia & Bunting, Rose.
Rowe, Helen, illus. see Lobo, Julia.
Rowe, Henrietta G. Maid of Bar Harbor (Classic Reprint) (p. 1383)
Rowe, Henrietta Gould. Re-Told Tales of the Hills & Shores of Maine (Classic Reprint) (p. 1844)
Rowe, Illustrator Colin, jt. auth. see St John Thomas, Gareth.
Rowe, Janet. Aliera Wants to Be a Monkey. Neal, Amee S., illus. (p. 47)
Rowe, Jeanette. First 1, 2, 3. (p. 734)
—First Words. (p. 740)
Rowe, Jeannette. Rex the Tyrannosaurus. (p. 1874)
—Tip the Triceratops. (p. 2250)
Rowe, Jeffrey. Gravity Falls: Dipper & Mabel & the Curse of the Time Pirates' Treasure! A Select Your Own Choose-Venture! Cicierega, Emmy, illus. (p. 882)
Rowe, John. Little Stories for Little People. (p. 1328)
Rowe, John, ed. see Kipling, Rudyard.
Rowe, John, illus. see Harris, Annaka.
Rowe, John, illus. see Kipling, Rudyard & Landolf, Diane Wright.
Rowe, Kelsey. Vax-Force. Iannaco, Nick, illus. (p. 2348)
Rowe, L. S., illus. see Draper, C. F.
Rowe, Michael, jt. auth. see Dale, Jenny.
Rowe, Michael Langham, illus. see Batten, Mary.
Rowe, Michael Langham, illus. see Dubowski, Cathy East & Dubowski, Mark.
Rowe, Richard. Life in the London Streets, or Struggles for Daily Bread (Classic Reprint) (p. 1292)
—Passages from the Diary of an Early Methodist. (p. 1702)
—Passages from the Diary of an Early Methodist (Classic Reprint) (p. 1702)
Rowe, T. Atlantean Focus. (p. 132)
Rowe, Thereza. Hearts. (p. 946)
—In the Woods. (p. 1112)
—Mister Pip. (p. 1482)
—Sticker, Shape, Create: A Sticker Art Activity Book. (p. 2118)
Rowe, Thereza & Biebow, Natascha. Stay, Benson! (p. 2109)
Rowe, W. W. Eedoo. (p. 627)
—Eedoo 2: Invaders from Blore. (p. 627)
—Eedoo Book III: Friends from Lollia. (p. 627)
—Fantazimals (Paperback) (p. 708)
—Jerry's Madness. (p. 1164)
—Jerry's Magnificence. (p. 1164)
—Jerry's Mastery. (p. 1164)
—Jerry's Mystery. (p. 1164)
—My Aunt. (p. 1531)
—Wand Goes Wild. (p. 2374)
—Wizard's Wayward Wand. (p. 2483)
Rowe, W. W. & Filius, Charles A. Things Alive! & Other Freaky Secrets. (p. 2220)
Rowe, William. Amazing, Awesome Whadda-Ya-Wanna-Be Book. (p. 64)
—Laurie, Foggy, & Silk. (p. 1252)
—Sparrow's Arrows. (p. 2075)
—Zoomy Elephant. (p. 2544)
Rowell, A. S. Silver Bullet, or the Young Relic Hunters of the Palmetto State: A Story of Today (Classic Reprint) (p. 2019)
Rowell, Adelaide C. Hail the Conquering Hero: A Comedy in Three Acts (Classic Reprint) (p. 909)
Rowell, Duchess Harris: Rebecca. History of Criminal Law. (p. 977)
Rowell, Kimberley. Townie Spider. (p. 2270)
Rowell, Lori E. Hortis the Tortoise. (p. 1005)
Rowell, Rainbow. Carry On: A Novel. (p. 334)
—Carry On. (p. 334)
—Eleanor & Park: Exclusive Special Edition. (p. 630)
—Eleanor & Park. (p. 630)
—Eleanor & Park / Eleanor & Park. (p. 630)
—Fangirl: A Novel. (p. 706)
—Fangirl. (p. 706)
—Fangirl (Spanish Edition) (p. 706)
—Pumpkinheads. Hicks, Faith Erin, illus. (p. 1813)
—Pumpkinheads (Spanish Edition) (p. 1813)
—Rainbow Rowell. (p. 1836)
—Runaways by Rainbow Rowell Vol. 4: But You Can't Hide. Genolet, Andres, illus. (p. 1915)
—Runaways by Rainbow Rowell Vol. 5: Canon Fodder. Genolet, Andres, illus. (p. 1915)
—Wayward Son. (p. 2388)
Rowell, Rebecca. 12 Most Amazing American Cities. (p. 2551)
—12 Most Amazing American Inventions. (p. 2551)
—12 Most Amazing American Natural Wonders. (p. 2551)
—Ancient India (p. 81)
—Building Rockets. (p. 294)
—Building Stadiums. (p. 295)
—Charles Lindbergh: Groundbreaking Aviator (p. 358)
—Emmanuel Macron: President of France. (p. 643)
—Energy & Waves Through Infographics. Sciuto, Alex, illus. (p. 650)
—Forces & Motion Through Infographics. Dean, Venitia, illus. (p. 764)
—Iraq (p. 1133)
—John F. Kennedy's Presidency. (p. 1172)
—Louisiana Purchase (p. 1358)
—Natural Gas. (p. 1579)

—Calendar Mysteries #11: November Night. Gurney, John Steven, illus. (p. 310)
—Calendar Mysteries #5: May Magic. Gurney, John Steven, illus. (p. 310)
—Calendar Mysteries #6: June Jam. Gurney, John Steven, illus. (p. 310)
—Calendar Mysteries #8: August Acrobat. Gurney, John Steven, illus. (p. 310)
—Calendar Mysteries #9: September Sneakers. Gurney, John Steven, illus. (p. 310)
—Capital Mysteries #12: the Ghost at Camp David. Bush, Timothy, illus. (p. 323)
—Capital Mysteries #14: Turkey Trouble on the National Mall. Bush, Timothy, illus. (p. 323)
—Castle Crime. (p. 340)
—Colossal Fossil. (p. 426)
—Ghost at Camp David. (p. 827)
—Grand Canyon Grab (p. 876)
—Grand Canyon Grab. Gurney, John Steven, illus. (p. 876)
—January Joker. Gurney, John Steven, illus. (p. 1159)
—July Jitters: Calendar Mysteries #7. Gurney, John Steven, illus. (p. 1188)
—July Jitters. (p. 1188)
—June Jam Gurney, John Steven, illus. (p. 1189)
—June Jam. (p. 1189)
—March Mischief: Calendar Mysteries #3. Gurney, John Steven, illus. (p. 1402)
—March Mischief. (p. 1402)
—October Ogre. (p. 1636)
—Secret at Jefferson's Mansion. Bush, Timothy, illus. (p. 1974)
—September Sneakers. (p. 1989)
—Sleepy Hollow Sleepover. (p. 2037)
—to Z Mysteries: Collection #1 Gurney, John Steven, illus. (p. 2254)
—to Z Mysteries Super Edition #10: Colossal Fossil. Gurney, John Steven, illus. (p. 2254)
—to Z Mysteries Super Edition #12: Space Shuttle Scam. Gurney, John Steven, illus. (p. 2254)
—to Z Mysteries Super Edition #4: Sleepy Hollow Sleepover. Gurney, John Steven, illus. (p. 2254)
—to Z Mysteries Super Edition #5: the New Year Dragon Dilemma. Gurney, John Steven, illus. (p. 2254)
—to Z Mysteries Super Edition #8: Secret Admirer. Gurney, John Steven, illus. (p. 2254)
—Trapped on the D. C. Train! Capital Mysteries #13. Bush, Timothy, illus. (p. 2279)
Roy, Ronald. Capital Mysteries #14: Turkey Trouble on the National Mall Bush, Timothy, illus. (p. 323)
—December Dog. (p. 523)
—New Year's Eve Thieves. (p. 1598)
—New Year's Eve Thieves. Gurney, John Steven, illus. (p. 1598)
—November Night. (p. 1627)
—Turkey Trouble on the National Mall. (p. 2300)
Roy, Simon, jt. auth. see Graham, Brandon.
Roy, Suman, illus. see Dewar, Andrew.
Roy, Susan. Mysteries in the Sky. (p. 1566)
Roy, Tamba. Gift for Anansi. (p. 832)
Roy, Wendy. Kelly Confident Shows You Why... It's POWERFUL to be a GIRL! It's POWERFUL to be a GIRL! (p. 1209)
Royal, Andre. Hippo-Critic: A Tale of Epic Proportions. Royal Jr, Andre, illus. (p. 973)
royal, bria, illus. see Kaba, Mariame.
Royal British Columbia Museum Staff, photos by see Swanson, Diane.
Royal Horticultural Society. Under Your Feet... Soil, Sand & Everything Underground. Tang, Wenjia, illus. (p. 2323)
Royal Jr, Andre, illus. see Royal, Andre.
Royal Observatory, Greenwich, Greenwich, jt. auth. see Collins Maps.
Royal Scottish Society of Arts, jt. auth. see Richardson, Benjamin Ward.
Royalist, A. Loyalist's Daughter, Vol. 2 Of 4: A Novel or Tale of the Revolution (Classic Reprint) (p. 1363)
Royalist, Royalist. Loyalist's Daughter, or Tale of the Revolution, Vol. 3 of 4 (Classic Reprint) (p. 1363)
Royall, Anne. Mrs. Royall's Southern Tour, or Second Series of the Black Book, Vol. 2: In Three or More Volumes (Classic Reprint) (p. 1523)
—Tennessean: A Novel, Founded on Facts (Classic Reprint) (p. 2205)
Roybal, Laura. Blood Brothers. (p. 245)
Royce, Brenda Scott. Date. (p. 509)
—One Wordy Bird. Madden, Colleen, illus. (p. 1663)
—Smithsonian Reader Level 3: Sharks! (p. 2042)
Royce, Brenda Scott, et al. Smithsonian Readers: Amazing Animals Level 2. (p. 2042)
Royce, Ellie. Auntie Uncle: Drag Queen Hero. Chambers, Hannah, illus. (p. 137)
Royce, Josiah. Feud of Oakfield Creek: A Novel of California Life (Classic Reprint) (p. 721)
Royce, Ralph, jt. auth. see Knight, Clayton.
Royce, Ron. At the Butterfly Conservatory: Represent & Interpret Data (p. 130)
Royce, Topher. Nez Perce. (p. 1601)
Royder, Mike, illus. see Roper, Uncle Hardy.
Roydhouse, Sally. Find & Seek New York. (p. 727)
—Find & Seek Singapore. (p. 727)
Roydhouse, Sandy. Oceans of the World. (p. 1636)
Roydon, Michael, illus. see Smith, Marie & Smith, Roland.
Royer, April C. One Magic. (p. 1660)
Royer, Ashley. Remember to Forget. (p. 1864)
—Remember to Forget: From Wattpad Sensation @_smilelikeniall (p. 1864)
Royer, Franchon. Padre Pro: Mexican Hero. (p. 1692)
Royer, Karen L., illus. see Royer, Karen.
Roy-Laber, Cheryl. Final Level: Animalized. (p. 727)
Royle, Edwin Milton. Peace & Quiet: A Novel (Classic Reprint) (p. 1709)
—Silent Call (Classic Reprint) (p. 2017)
Royle, Robert. Tracts Consisting of Observations about the Saltness of the Sea: An Account of a Statical Hygroscope & Its Uses; Together with an Appendix about the Force of the Air's Moisture; a Fragment about the Natural & Preternatural State of Bodies. (p. 2273)
Royo, Luis, illus. see Martin, George R. R.
Royse, Maria, illus. see Kucharik, Elena & Goodings, Christina.
Royse, Suzanna L. Maria & the Magic of the Rainbow. (p. 1404)
Royster, Gloria Jean & Dobreva, Iana. Go! in the Snow. (p. 846)
Royster, Ka-Sandra. Cough Syrup in Mommy's Hair. (p. 458)
Royston, Angela. Adapted to Survive (p. 14)
—Adapted to Survive: Animals That Climb (p. 14)
—Adapted to Survive: Animals That Dig (p. 14)
—Adapted to Survive: Animals That Hunt (p. 14)
—All about Forces. (p. 49)
—All about Magnetism. (p. 49)
—All about Sound. (p. 50)
—Allergies. (p. 56)
—Alligator. (p. 56)
—Amphibians. (p. 77)
—Ancient Greek Adventure. (p. 81)
—Animal Classification. (p. 88)
—Animal Classifications. (p. 88)
—Asthma. (p. 127)
—Astronauts Working in Space. (p. 128)
—Ballet (p. 162)
—Ballroom (p. 162)
—Bean's Life. (p. 179)
—Birds. (p. 231)
—Bones & Muscles. (p. 255)
—Colds, the Flu, & Other Infections. (p. 413)
—Cuts, Bruises, & Breaks. (p. 491)
—Diary of A... (p. 539)
—Diary of a Ballerina. (p. 539)
—Diary of a Circus Performer (p. 539)
—Diary of a Dog Walker (p. 539)
—Diary of a Pilot (p. 539)
—Diet. (p. 544)
—Disappearing Wildlife. (p. 553)
—Discover & Share: Planet Earth. (p. 554)
—Discover & Share: Space. (p. 554)
—DK Readers L1: Truck Trouble. (p. 568)
—Electricity. (p. 631)
—Experiments with a Flashlight. (p. 678)
—Experiments with a Lemon. (p. 678)
—Experiments with a Ruler. (p. 678)
—Experiments with Water. (p. 679)
—Explaining Asthma. (p. 679)
—Explaining Down's Syndrome. (p. 679)
—Fighting Smallpox. (p. 725)
—Fire Fighter! (p. 732)
—Fish. (p. 741)
—Food Chains & Webs (p. 759)
—Forces: Pushes & Pulls. (p. 764)
—Forces & Motion (p. 764)
—Grassland Food Chains (p. 881)
—Gun Crimes. (p. 905)
—Head Lice. (p. 942)
—Henry Ford & the Assembly Line (p. 955)
—Heroes of Medicine & Their Discoveries. (p. 962)
—Homes That Move. (p. 998)
—Homicide. (p. 998)
—Hoping for Peace in the Middle East. (p. 1002)
—Hostile Homes: Extreme Habitats. (p. 1006)
—How to Survive in the Desert. (p. 1044)
—How to Survive in the Rain Forest. (p. 1044)
—Hurricanes! (p. 1054)
—Inventors Who Changed the World. (p. 1130)
—Invertebrates. (p. 1131)
—Life Cycles. (p. 1291)
—Light & Dark. (p. 1298)
—Love to Dance. (p. 1361)
—Mammals. (p. 1393)
—Mountain Food Chains (p. 1513)
—Ocean Explorer! (p. 1635)
—Ocean Food Chains (p. 1635)
—Ocean It's My Home! (p. 1635)
—Ocean - It's My Home! (p. 1635)
—Oceans. (p. 1636)
—Polar Bears & Their Homes. (p. 1769)
—Race That Bike! Forces in Vehicles. (p. 1831)
—Race to Survive Climate Change. (p. 1831)
—Rain Forest Food Chains (p. 1835)
—Read Me! Love to Dance: Ballroom. (p. 1845)
—Reptiles. (p. 1867)
—River Food Chains (p. 1887)
—Robert Fulton & the Steamboat (p. 1890)
—Salmón (p. 1925)
—Save the Giant Panda (p. 1937)
—Save the Gorilla (p. 1937)
—Save the Tiger (p. 1938)
—Science of Heat. (p. 1957)
—Science of Hurricanes. (p. 1958)
—Science of Volcanoes. (p. 1958)
—Science vs. Crime. (p. 1959)
—Science vs. Natural Disasters. (p. 1959)
—Senses. (p. 1989)
—Shark: Killer King of the Ocean. (p. 2001)
—Shark. (p. 2001)
—Sir Isaac Newton: Overlord of Gravity. (p. 2025)
—Sound & Hearing. (p. 2067)
—Space. (p. 2070)
—Space Blog. (p. 2070)
—Storms! (p. 2127)
—Tadpole Story. (p. 2175)
—Tap (p. 2191)
—Tooth Decay. (p. 2262)
—Truck Trouble. (p. 2292)
—Using Electricity. (p. 2341)
—What Do You Know about Plants? (p. 2409)
—What Happens If We Overfish the Oceans? (p. 2411)
—What Happens When an Ice Cap Melts? (p. 2411)
—Why Do I Brush My Teeth? (p. 2456)
—Why Do I Run? (p. 2456)
—Why Do I Sleep? (p. 2456)
—Why Do I Wash My Hands? (p. 2456)
—Why We Need Proteins. (p. 2459)
—Why We Need Water & Fiber. (p. 2459)
—Win That Sprint! Forces in Sport. (p. 2470)
—Wolf. (p. 2483)
Royston, Angela & Hawksley, Gerald. My Big Book of the World. Hawksley, Gerald, illus. (p. 1532)
Royther, Chris. Zippy's Christmas Tree. (p. 2541)
Roytman, Arkady. Adventures of King Arthur Coloring Book. (p. 24)
—Build-a-Window Halloween Stained Glass Coloring Book. (p. 293)
—Fairy Princess. (p. 697)
—Fantasy Warriors Stained Glass Coloring Book. (p. 708)
—GOAL! the Hockey Coloring Book. (p. 849)
—Greek & Roman Gods Stained Glass Coloring Book. (p. 892)
—How to Draw Sharks. (p. 1041)
—Knights & Dragons. (p. 1228)
—Maneki Neko Lucky Cat Coloring Book. (p. 1397)
—Martial Arts Coloring Book. (p. 1410)
—Secret Agent Sticker Activity. (p. 1974)
—Soccer Coloring Book. (p. 2052)
—Things That Go Dot-To-Dot Fun: Count from 1 To 101! (p. 2221)
—Treasures of King Tut's Tomb Stained Glass Coloring Book. (p. 2283)
—Wild Animals Dot-to-Dot Fun! Count from 1 to 101. (p. 2462)
—World of Dragons Coloring Book. (p. 2502)
Roytman, Arkady, jt. auth. see Dutton, Michael.
Roytman, Arkady & Coloring Books Staff. Outer Space. (p. 1684)
Roytman, Arkady & Paper Dolls for Grownups Staff. Glow-in-the-Dark Ghouls Paper Action Figures. (p. 845)
Roytman, Arkady, et al. Build a 3-D Poster Coloring Book — Outer Space. (p. 292)
—Build a Poster Coloring Book—Atlantis. (p. 293)
—Build a Poster Coloring Book—Space. (p. 293)
Roza, Autumn & Roza, Greg. Miranda Cosgrove. (p. 1475)
Roza, G. Lots of Leaves: Learning the L Sound. (p. 1356)
—On Flat Land: Learning the FL Sound. (p. 1652)
Roza, Greg. America's First Highway. (p. 75)
—Arctic Ecosystem. (p. 112)
—Armed And Dangerous (p. 117)
—Bacteria up Close. (p. 157)
—Beastly Beetles. (p. 182)
—Beavers. (p. 186)
—Beneath Earth's Surface. (p. 199)
—Bill & Melinda Gates. (p. 226)
—Bizarre Life Cycle of a Cicada. (p. 235)
—Bo Diddley: Rock-And-Roll All-Star. (p. 250)
—Bromine. (p. 285)
—Calcium. (p. 309)
—Career as a Carpenter. (p. 328)
—Careers in the Coast Guard's Search & Rescue Units. (p. 330)
—Chomp! The Great White Shark & Other Animals That Bite. (p. 381)
—Choosing a Career in the Military. (p. 381)
—Chromium. (p. 388)
—Colony of New York. (p. 419)
—Colony of Rhode Island. (p. 419)
—Comets & Asteroids: Space Rocks. (p. 429)
—Dale Earnhardt Jr: NASCAR Driver. (p. 498)
—Deadly Bacteria. (p. 518)
—Deadly Black Widows. (p. 518)
—Deadly Pufferfish. (p. 519)
—Decomposers. (p. 523)
—Disaster Relief Workers. (p. 553)
—Drawing Dracula. (p. 599)
—Drawing Frankenstein. (p. 599)
—Drawing Godzilla. (p. 599)
—Drawing King Kong. (p. 599)
—Early Explorers of Texas. (p. 614)
—Eighth Amendment: Preventing Cruel & Unusual Punishment. (p. 629)
—Exploring Rocks & Minerals. (p. 682)
—Freaky Flies. (p. 780)
—Frequently Asked Questions about Driving & the Law. (p. 784)
—Frequently Asked Questions about Emergency Lifesaving Techniques. (p. 784)
—Game of Chess: Applying Strategies from Simple to Complex Problems. (p. 807)
—Getting the Most Out of Makerspaces to Make Musical Instruments. (p. 826)
—Great Lakes. (p. 887)
—Gross Things on Buses, Trains, & Planes. (p. 898)
—Gross Things under Your Feet. (p. 898)
—Guide My Pen: The Poems of Phillis Wheatley. (p. 903)
—Halogen Elements. (p. 913)
—Harley-Davidson: An All-American Legend. (p. 930)
—Heads or Tails? Exploring Probability Through Games. (p. 942)
—Henry Ford: Pioneer of Modern Industry. (p. 955)
—Hockey. (p. 985)
—Hoover Dam: Applying Problem-Solving Strategies. (p. 1001)
—How Are Stars Born? (p. 1026)
—How Do Aqueducts Work? (p. 1028)
—How Do Sewers Work? (p. 1029)
—Hubble Space Telescope: Understanding & Representing Numbers up to 1 Billion. (p. 1047)
—Immigration & Migration. (p. 1101)
—Incredible Story of Aircraft Carriers. (p. 1114)
—Inside an Ant Colony. (p. 1122)
—Jellyfish. (p. 1163)
—Judo (p. 1185)
—Kevin Harvick: NASCAR Driver. (p. 1210)
—Landfills: Habitat Havoc. (p. 1242)
—Landfills. (p. 1242)
—Listen Up: Knowing When & When Not to Speak. (p. 1308)
—Looking at Differences Between Living & Nonliving Things with Graphic Organizers. (p. 1347)
—Mapping Antarctica. (p. 1401)
—Mi Primer Paseo a la Ciudad / My First Trip to a City (p. 1455)
—Mi Primer Paseo a la Playa / My First Trip to the Beach (p. 1455)
—Mi Primera Visita a la Biblioteca / My First Trip to the Library (p. 1456)
—Missouri: Past & Present. (p. 1482)
—Murder of Crows. (p. 1527)
—Murder of Crows / una Bandada de Cuervos. (p. 1527)
—Muscular System. (p. 1528)
—My First Trip to a City (p. 1546)
—My First Trip to a Farm (p. 1546)
—My First Trip to the Beach (p. 1546)
—My First Trip to the Library (p. 1546)
—Mysterious Mantises. (p. 1567)
—Neptune: The Stormy Planet. (p. 1587)
—Nevada: Past & Present. (p. 1589)
—Olympic Math: Working with Percentages & Decimals. (p. 1651)
—Optical Artist: Exploring Patterns & Symmetry. (p. 1667)
—Oregon: Past & Present. (p. 1670)
—Ossuaries & Charnel Houses. (p. 1674)
—OutKast. (p. 1685)
—Phew! The Skunk & Other Stinky Animals. (p. 1733)
—Pluto: The Dwarf Planet. (p. 1763)
—Poison! The Spitting Cobra & Other Venomous Animals. (p. 1767)
—Poke! The Sea Urchin & Other Animals with Spikes. (p. 1768)
—Powerful Earthquakes. (p. 1783)
—Repulsive Roaches. (p. 1868)
—RobotRiot! (p. 1893)
—Sidney Crosby. (p. 2015)
—Skeletal System. (p. 2030)
—Sting! The Scorpion & Other Animals That Sting. (p. 2119)
—Strange Spiders. (p. 2138)
—Tasmanian Devil vs. Hyena. (p. 2192)
—Texas Cities: Then & Now. (p. 2209)
—Thomas Alva Edison (p. 2227)
—Titanium (p. 2251)
—Tundra: Life in a Frozen Landscape. (p. 2299)
—Wedges. (p. 2395)
—Weird Walking Sticks. (p. 2397)
—Westward Expansion. (p. 2402)
—What Happens When I Throw Up? (p. 2412)
—What Is a Black Hole? (p. 2413)
—What Is Fiction? (p. 2415)
—Where We Play Sports: Measuring the Perimeters of Polygons. (p. 2440)
—Why People Work. (p. 2458)
—Your Neighbor the Alley Cat. (p. 2534)
—Your Neighbor the Coyote. (p. 2534)
—Your Neighbor the Mouse. (p. 2534)
—Your Neighbor the Pigeon. (p. 2534)
—Your Neighbor the Raccoon. (p. 2534)
—Your Neighbor the Squirrel. (p. 2534)
—Zap! The Electric Eel & Other Electric Animals. (p. 2538)
—Zirconium. (p. 2541)
Roza, Greg, jt. auth. see Mills, Nathan.
Roza, Greg, jt. auth. see Power, Bob.
Roza, Greg, jt. auth. see Thompson, Elissa.
Roza, Greg & Burdick, Mason. Soccer. (p. 2051)
Rozanski, Johnathan Enter. Growing Around: Party Panic. Molony, Meghan, illus. (p. 899)
Rozant, Ina. Actress's Pilgrimage (Classic Reprint) (p. 13)
Rozarena, P., tr. see Lechermeier, Philippe.
Rozarena, P., tr. see Patricelli, Leslie.
Rozas, Alfredo Rodríguez. Catastrofe Del 16 de Agosto de 1906 en la Republica de Chile (Classic Reprint) (p. 343)
Rozelaar, Angie. Great Pumpkin Contest. Rozelaar, Angie, illus. (p. 888)
Rozelaar, Angie, illus. see Jamieson, Tom & Demidova, Olga.
Rozelaar, Angie, illus. see Mudpuppy.
Rozelaar, Angie, illus. see Prasadam-Halls, Smriti.
Rozelaar, Angie, illus. see Sauer, Tammi.
Rozen, R. Dan un Gad in Milhomeh Afn Oytser. Krishevski, E., illus. (p. 499)
—In Trit Fun Di Farkhapte Kinder. Krishevski, E., illus. (p. 1112)
Rozett, Louise. Ice Queen: Catherine the Great Seizes Power in Russia. (p. 1088)
Rozevskis, Diana. Crystal Waters & on to North America. (p. 481)
—Crystal Waters It Began in Europe. (p. 481)
Rozier, Dana. Natural Hawai'i: An Inquisitive Kid's Guide. (p. 1579)
Rozier, Lucy Margaret. Jackrabbit Mccabe & the Electric Telegraph. Espinosa, Leo, illus. (p. 1153)
Rozier, Titus. Cha Cha's Big Race. (p. 353)
Rozier, Vince. God's Fruit in Me. Liang, Mindy, illus. (p. 853)
Rozinski, Bob, photos by see Jackson, Donna M.
Rozler, Lora. Freshly Baked Pie. (p. 785)
—Lucky Me Dolby, Jan, illus. (p. 1365)
Rozman Clark, Tea & Mueller, Rachel Lauren, eds. Immigration Stories from a Fargo High School: Green Card Youth Voices. (p. 1101)
—Immigration Stories from a Minneapolis High School: Green Card Youth Voices. (p. 1101)
—Immigration Stories from a St. Paul High School: Green Card Youth Voices. (p. 1101)
Rozman Clark, Tea, et al, eds. Immigration Stories from an Atlanta High School: Green Card Youth Voices. (p. 1101)
Rozum, Fred & Gross, Scott. Scooby-Doo & Those Meddling Kids (p. 1960)
Rozum, John. Scooby-Doo in Yankee Doodle Danger Laguna, Fabio, illus. (p. 1961)
Rozum, John & Laguna, Fabio. Scooby-Doo in Fright Ride (p. 1961)
Rozum, John & Pope, Robert. Scooby-Doo & the Monster of a Thousand Faces! (p. 1960)
Rozumowicz, Sue. Gabby's Gumball Garden. Ellsworth, Jayden, illus. (p. 804)
—Three Royal Moons. Ellsworth, Jayden, illus. (p. 2235)
Ru, Mic, illus. see Bruneau, Laura & Timmons, Beverly.
Ruano, Alfonso, illus. see Amado, Elisa.
Ruano, Alfonso, illus. see Argueta, Jorge.
Ruano, Kelsy C., illus. see Ruano, Tony.

R

Rudolph, Shaina & Royer, Danielle. All My Stripes: A Story for Children with Autism. Zivoin, Jennifer, illus. (p. 53)
Rudolph, Stefanie, illus. see Levy, Shira, et al.
Rudrabhatla, Ayati. Tom & Lilly's Planet Munch Adventures. (p. 2257)
Rudwin, Maximilian J. Devil Stories: An Anthology. (p. 535)
—Devil Stories: An Anthology (Classic Reprint) (p. 535)
Rudy, Maggie. City Mouse, Country Mouse. (p. 395)
—I Wish I Had a Pet. Rudy, Maggie, illus. (p. 1086)
—Sootypaws: a Cinderella Story. Rudy, Maggie, illus. (p. 2064)
Rudy, Maggie & Abrams, Pam. House That Mouse Built. Wolf, Bruce, photos by. (p. 1024)
Rudy, Marco, illus. see Denton, Shannon Eric.
Rudyard Kipling. Illustrated Kipling Classics (p. 1096)
Rue, Ginger. Aleca Zamm Fools Them All. (p. 41)
—Aleca Zamm Is a Wonder. Persico, Zoe, illus. (p. 41)
—Aleca Zamm Is Ahead of Her Time. (p. 41)
—Aleca Zamm Travels Through Time. (p. 41)
—Aleca Zamm Wonder-Ful Collection: Aleca Zamm Is a Wonder; Aleca Zamm Is Ahead of Her Time; Aleca Zamm Fools Them All; Aleca Zamm Travels Through Time. (p. 41)
—Hard Rock. (p. 929)
—Rock 'n' Roll Rebel. (p. 1894)
Rue, Leonard Lee. Alligators & Crocodiles. (p. 56)
—Elephants (p. 634)
—Wolves (p. 2485)
—Wolves - PB: A Portrait of the Animal World. (p. 2485)
Rue, Nancy. So Not Okay (p. 2050)
—Sorry I'm Not Sorry: An Honest Look at Bullying from the Bully (p. 2066)
—You Can't Sit with Us - Mean Girl Makeover (p. 2526)
Rue, Nancy N. Boyfriends, Burritos & an Ocean of Trouble (p. 271)
—Everything You Need to Know about Peer Mediation. (p. 674)
—Lucy Doesn't Wear Pink (p. 1366)
—Lucy Finds Her Way (p. 1366)
—Lucy Out of Bounds (p. 1366)
—Lucy's Perfect Summer (p. 1366)
—Motorcycles, Sushi & One Strange Book (p. 1512)
—Niv, Ultimate Bible for Girls, Leathersoft, Teal (p. 1612)
—Sophie Steps Up (p. 2065)
—Sophie's Drama (p. 2065)
—Sophie's Friendship Fiasco. (p. 2065)
Rue, Nancy N., jt. auth. see Carlson, Melody.
Rue, Nancy N., et al. Beauty of Believing: 365 Devotions That Will Change Your Life (p. 185)
Ruebush, McKenna. Enter a Glossy Web. Zollars, Jaime, illus. (p. 656)
Rueda, Claudia. Bunny Overboard. (p. 298)
—Bunny Slopes. (p. 298)
—Hungry Bunny. (p. 1052)
—No Amado, Elisa, tr. (p. 1612)
Rueda, Claudia, illus. see Flor Ada, Alma.
Rueda, Claudia, illus. see Underwood, Deborah.
Rueda, Flores. Directo Al Coraz?n. (p. 552)
Rueda, Marty. Emma Stone. (p. 643)
Rue-Hughes, Teresha. Sungi Bear Cool Boys: We Got This! (p. 2152)
—Sungi Bear Cute Girls: We Got This! (p. 2152)
Ruel, Adeline. Big Bear Can't Fall Asleep. Ruel, Adeline, illus. (p. 216)
Ruell, L J, illus. see Patrick, B. & Schotz, Leo D.
Ruelle, Karen, illus. see Ruelle, Karen Gray.
Ruelle, Karen Gray. Grand Mosque of Paris: A Story of How Muslims Rescued Jews During the Holocaust. DeSaix, Deborah Durland, illus. (p. 877)
—Peter's War: A Boy's True Story of Survival in World War II Europe. Durland DeSaix, Deborah, illus. (p. 1730)
Ruelle, Karen Gray & Desaix, Deborah Durland. Grand Mosque of Paris: A Story of How Muslims Rescued Jews During the Holocaust. (p. 877)
Ruelos, Joanne, jt. auth. see Reyes, Gabrielle.
Ruete, Emilie. Memoirs of an Arabian Princess (Classic Reprint) (p. 1444)
Ruete, Emily. Memoirs of an Arabian Princess: An Autobiography (Classic Reprint) (p. 1444)
Rufener, Brenda. Since We Last Spoke. (p. 2023)
—Where I Live. (p. 2437)
Ruff, Gloria B., jt. auth. see Camarena, Cathy.
Ruff, Jerry & Saint Mary's Press Staff. Ben & Allie's Bible Adventures: New Testament. Johnson, Jill, illus. (p. 198)
—Ben & Allie's Bible Adventures: Old Testament Set. Johnson, Jill, illus. (p. 198)
Ruff, Jim, illus. see Ruff, Zeata P.
Ruff, Kimberly & Sheets, Leslie. Brave Just Like Me. (p. 276)
Ruff, Kimberly & Venturi-Pickett, Stacy. Brave Just Like Me. Sheets, Leslie, illus. (p. 276)
Ruff, Tia. There Was Once a Young Ranger Who Swallowed the Sun. (p. 2217)
Ruff, Veronica. Protectors: The Beginning. (p. 1808)
—Protectors. (p. 1808)
Ruff, Zeata. Gumdrop Tree. (p. 905)
Ruff, Zeata P. Gumdrop Tree. Ruff, Zeata P. & Ruff, Jim, illus. (p. 905)
Ruffenach, Jessie, ed. see Powell, Patricia Hruby.
Ruffenach, Jessie E., ed. see Flood, Nancy Bo.
Ruffenach, Jessie Eve, ed. see Yazzie, Seraphine G.
Ruffet, Shoeburn. Shoeburn & the Ill-Fitting Necklace. (p. 2009)
Ruffieux, Jean-Marie, illus. see Quesnel, Alain.
Ruffin, Fran. Cats. (p. 345)
—Whales / Ballenas. (p. 2404)
Ruffin, Frances E. Annie Oakley. (p. 100)
—Clara Barton. (p. 398)
—Creating a City Park: Dividing Three-Digit Numbers by One-Digit Numbers Without Remainders. (p. 469)
—Creating a City Park: Dividing Three-digit Numbers by One-digit Numbers Without Remainders. (p. 469)
—Martin Luther King & the March on Washington. (p. 1410)
—Molly Pitcher. (p. 1489)
—Polycystic Ovary Syndrome. (p. 1772)
—Sally Hemings. (p. 1925)
—Sojourner Truth: Early Abolitionist. (p. 2055)
—Unsinkable Molly Brown. (p. 2335)
Ruffin, Frances E., jt. auth. see Brown, Jonatha A.
Ruffin, Frances E. & Melville, Wilma. Military Dogs. (p. 1466)
Ruffini, Giovanni. Dear Experience: A Tale (Classic Reprint) (p. 520)
—Lorenzo Benoni: Or Passages in the Life of an Italian (Classic Reprint) (p. 1349)
—Lorenzo Benoni, or Passages in the Life of an Italian (Classic Reprint) (p. 1349)
Ruffini, John. Carlino: And Other Stories (Classic Reprint) (p. 331)
—Doctor Antonio (Classic Reprint) (p. 573)
—Quiet Nook in the Jura (Classic Reprint) (p. 1828)
Ruffle, Mark, illus. see Llewellyn, Claire.
Ruffle, Mark, illus. see Naish, Darren.
Ruffle, Mark, illus. see Walker, Richard.
Ruffner, Peter & Hillstrom, Kevin. Worker's Unite! The American Labor Movement. (p. 2495)
Ruffo, J.I. HOMELESS: LEYENDAS DE LA INJUSTICIA SOCIAL. (p. 997)
Ruffolo, Rob, illus. see Roe, David & Reader's Digest Editors.
Rufus, Quintus Curtius. Quinte Curce de la Vie et des Actions d'Alexandre le Grand, Vol. 1 (Classic Reprint) (p. 1828)
—Quinte-Curce, de la Vie d'Alexandre, Vol. 2: Avec les Supplémens (Classic Reprint) (p. 1828)
Rufus, Rob. Vinyl Underground. (p. 2359)
Rugari, Anne. Just Like Me! A Book about a Girl with a Rare Disease. (p. 1193)
Rugg, Jim, illus. see Seagle, Steven T.
Rugg, Jim, illus. see Whedon, Zack & Horse, Dark.
Rugg, Jim & Maruca, Brian. Street Angel Gang. (p. 2140)
—Street Angel: Superhero for a Day. (p. 2140)
Ruggeri, Agnes C. Day & a Night (Classic Reprint) (p. 512)
Ruggeri, Alida, illus. see Greve, Meg.
Ruggieri, J. G. Weather Changes, Mountains Move, & Islands Disappear. (p. 2394)
Ruggieri, Linda. Amazing Animals: Critter Camp: Division (Grade 3) (p. 63)
Ruggiero, Adriane, jt. auth. see Sebree, Chet'la.
Ruggles, John. Recollections of a Lucknow Veteran, 1845-1876 (Classic Reprint) (p. 1853)
Ruggles, William Nelson. Out of the Ozarks (Classic Reprint) (p. 1683)
Ruha, Rob, tr. see Tipene, Tim.
Ruhl, Arthur. Antwerp to Gallipoli: A Year of War on Many Fronys & Behind Them (Classic Reprint) (p. 104)
—Antwerp to Gallipoli: A Year of War on Many Fronts, & Behind Them (Classic Reprint) (p. 104)
—Second Nights: People & Ideas of the Theatre to-Day (Classic Reprint) (p. 1973)
—White Nights: And Other Russian Impressions (Classic Reprint) (p. 2444)
—White Nights, & Other Russian Impressions (Classic Reprint) (p. 2444)
Ruhl, Greg, illus. see Tanaka, Shelley.
Ruin Mist Publications Staff, jt. auth. see Stanek, Robert, pseud.
Ruivo, Antonia. Uma Traca Chamada Esperanca. (p. 2316)
Ruiz, Alfonso, illus. see Gonzalez, Jorge & Collodi, Carlo.
Ruiz, Alfonso, illus. see Gunderson, Jessica & Gonzalez, Jorge.
Ruiz, Alfonso, illus. see Gunderson, Jessica.
Ruiz, Alfonso, illus. see Hoena, Blake A. & Gonzalez, Jorge.
Ruiz, Alfonso, illus. see Stoker, Bram.
Ruiz, Alina, tr. see Pérez Díaz, Enrique.
Ruiz, Angeles, illus. see Lepon, Shoshana.
Ruiz, Aristides, illus. see Golden Books Staff.
Ruiz, Aristides, illus. see Golden Books.
Ruiz, Aristides, illus. see Rabe, Tish.
Ruiz, Aristides, illus. see Worth, Bonnie.
Ruíz, Carlos, tr. see Blackaby, Susan & Jones, Christianne C.
Ruíz, Carlos, tr. see Blackaby, Susan.
Ruíz, Carlos, tr. see Jones, Christianne C.
Ruíz, Carlos, tr. see Meachen Rau, Dana.
Ruiz, Cecilia. Gift from Abuela. Ruiz, Cecilia, illus. (p. 832)
Ruiz, Derek, ed. see Fitzpatrick, Becca.
Ruiz, Felix, illus. see Hopeless, Dennis.
Ruiz, Fernando, jt. auth. see Parent, Dan.
Ruiz, Fernando & Esquivel, Eric. Animal Jam. (p. 90)
Ruiz, Frances. Fairy Bond: Book Two of the Key to Embralia. (p. 696)
Ruiz, Javier. Sword of the Emperor: The Riders. (p. 2171)
Ruiz, Joe, illus. see Barton, Sarah & Wilkins, Ray.
Ruiz Johnson, Mariana. Colibri Chante et Danse: Chansons et Comptines Latino-Américaines. (p. 413)
—Hummingbird Sings & Dances: Latin American Lullabies & Nursery Rhymes. (p. 1050)
Ruiz Johnson, Mariana, illus. see Silver, Skye.
Ruiz, Jose. Immigration to North America: Mexican Immigrants Anderson, Stuart, ed. (p. 1101)
Ruiz, José. Mexican Immigrants. (p. 1454)
Ruiz, Joy Hwang, illus. see Underwood, Deborah.
Ruiz, Juan. Libro de Buen Amor: Texte du Xive Siècle, Publié Pour la Première Fois Avec les leçon des Trois Manuscrits Connus (Classic Reprint) (p. 1286)
Ruiz, Margarita. Gallina de Los Huevos de Oro. (p. 806)
—Porquerizo. (p. 1778)
—Rapunzel. (p. 1841)
Ruiz, Nacho, ed. Aves: Colorea la Naturaleza. (p. 143)
—Mamíferos: Colorea la Naturaleza. (p. 1393)
Ruiz Parra, Emiliano. Los Hijos de la Ira. (p. 1350)
Ruiz, Pedro, illus. see Ruiz, Clarisa & Reyes, Yolanda.
Ruiz, Rachel. Martin Luther King, Jr: Graphic Biographies. Dunn, Fiona W. & Skeate, Sarah, illus. (p. 1411)
—Recess Bully. May, Steve, illus. (p. 1853)
—Runaway Robot. May, Steve, illus. (p. 1915)
—Superhero Harry (p. 2159)
—Superhero Project. May, Steve, illus. (p. 2160)
—When Hillary Rodham Clinton Played Ice Hockey. Doneva, Steliyana, illus. (p. 2430)
—When Penny Met POTUS. Manwill, Melissa A., illus. (p. 2432)
—When Rosa Parks Went Fishing. Fedele, Chiara, illus. (p. 2432)
—Wild Field Trip. May, Steve, illus. (p. 2463)
Ruiz Rico, Fernando & Rubio S. Tales to Find a Cure. (p. 2186)
Ruiz, Roser, tr. see Curato, Mike.
Ruiz, Rosie, illus. see Costa, Gigi.
Ruiz, Ruth Ann. Coping with the Death of a Brother or Sister. (p. 451)
Ruiz, Tracy. You Are My Beloved. (p. 2524)
Ruiz Zafón, Carlos. Marina. (p. 1405)
Ruiz-Flores, Lupe. Alicia's Fruity Drinks / Las Aguas Frescas de Alicia. Baeza Ventura, Gabriela, tr. from ENG. (p. 46)
—Battle of the Snow Cones/La Guerra de las Raspas. (p. 174)
—Lupita's First Dance / el Primer Baile de Lupita. Baeza Ventura, Gabriela, tr. (p. 1369)
Ruiz-Flores, Lupe & Rosales-Yeomans, Natalia. Let's Salsa. Rosales-Yeomans, Natalia, tr. (p. 1277)
Ruiz-Gutierrez, Marisela, tr. see Grant, Irma.
Ruland, Christine. Along Freedom's Rails. (p. 58)
Ruland, Wilhelm. Legends of the Rhine (Classic Reprint) (p. 1264)
Rule, Heather. All about Women's College Gymnastics. (p. 51)
—College Basketball Underdog Stories. (p. 415)
—Olympic Games Upsets. (p. 1651)
—Sports' Greatest Turnarounds. (p. 2089)
—Ultimate NASCAR Road Trip. (p. 2315)
—Wayne Gretzky & the Edmonton Oilers. (p. 2388)
—Women in Sports Media. (p. 2487)
—Women in the Olympics. (p. 2487)
Rule, Rebecca. Iciest, Diciest, Scariest Sled Ride Ever! Thermes, Jennifer, illus. (p. 1088)
—N Is for New Hampshire. Snyder, Scott, photos by. (p. 1572)
Ruley, Garrett. Hollin. (p. 988)
Rullmann, John D. Bob Greenfellow's Sketches (Classic Reprint) (p. 251)
Rumbam, Stella. Deeper & Deeper (Tetun Edition) - Nani Iha Tasi. Fedorava, Marianna, illus. (p. 525)
Rumbaugh, Melinda. Somebunny Loves You! (p. 2060)
Rumble, Chris. My Dad Is Coming to Career Day but Hopefully the Earth Will Be Destroyed. (p. 1536)
Rumble, Simon, illus. see Jackson, Kyle.
Rumbolt, Paula Ikuutaq. Origin of Day & Night Lishchenko, Lenny, illus. (p. 1671)
Rumbough, George P. C. From Dust to Ashes: A Romance of the Confederacy (Classic Reprint) (p. 791)
Rumford, James. Beo-Bunny. (p. 201)
—Rain School. (p. 1836)
Rumikuu, illus. see Ng, Kaye.
Rumiz, Susanna, illus. see Allen, Kathy.
Rumiz, Susanna, illus. see Hayes, Susan.
Rumiz, Susanna, illus. see Litton, Jonathan.
Rumjhum SenGupta. About the Bee, the Butterfly & a Bunny! Learning Through Stories. (p. 6)
Rumley, Shawn, et al. RJ's Creepy Tales: Camp Toxic. (p. 1888)
Rummel, Verna. I Can Too (p. 1063)
Rummelhart, Don. Mjolnir: A Story about Ultimate. (p. 1484)
Rumsch, BreAnn. Abraham Lincoln. (p. 7)
—Arabian Horses (p. 108)
—Bill Clinton. (p. 226)
—Clydesdale Horses (p. 409)
—Franklin Pierce. (p. 779)
—George W. Bush. (p. 819)
—Good Sports Don't Give Up. Petrik, Mike, illus. (p. 866)
—Good Sports Use Teamwork. Petrik, Mike, illus. (p. 866)
—Good Sports, Win or Lose. Petrik, Mike, illus. (p. 866)
—Grover Cleveland. (p. 899)
—Herbert Hoover. (p. 957)
—James K. Polk. (p. 1157)
—Martin Van Buren. (p. 1411)
—Money Matters (p. 1493)
—Palomino Horses (p. 1694)
—Pinto Horses (p. 1747)
—Rutherford B. Hayes. (p. 1918)
—Saving & Investing (p. 1938)
—Shetland Ponies (p. 2006)
—Thoroughbred Horses (p. 2230)
—Ulysses S. Grant. (p. 2316)
—William Taft. (p. 2468)
—Woodrow Wilson. (p. 2492)
Rumsch, BreAnn & Mallman, Mark. Good Sports Play Fair. Petrik, Mike, illus. (p. 866)
Rumsey, Frances. My Very Own Organic Cookbook: Bananas. (p. 1564)
—My Very Own Organic Cookbook: Potatoes. (p. 1564)
—My Very Own Organic Cookbook: The Teen, Book 1. (p. 1564)
Runberg, Sylivain. Orbital 2: Ruptures. Saincatin, Jerome, tr. (p. 1669)
Runberg, Sylvain. Orbital: Scars. Vol. 1 Saincatin, Jerome, tr. (p. 1669)
—Orbital 3: Nomads Pellé, Serge, illus. (p. 1669)
—Orbital Vol. 5: Justice. Pelle, Serge, illus. (p. 1669)
Runbury, Selina. Glory, Glory, Glory: And Other Narratives (Classic Reprint) (p. 844)
Runciman, James. Romance of the Coast (Classic Reprint) (p. 1900)
Rundell, Katherine. Cartwheeling in Thunderstorms. (p. 335)
—Cartwheeling in Thunderstorms. Castrillón, Melissa & Castrillón, Melissa, illus. (p. 335)
—Explorer. (p. 680)
—Good Thieves. (p. 866)
—Into the Jungle: Stories for Mowgli. Williams, Kristjana S., illus. (p. 1128)
—One Christmas Wish. Sutton, Emily, illus. (p. 1659)
—Rooftoppers. (p. 1902)
—Rooftoppers. Fan, Terry, illus. (p. 1902)
—Wolf Wilder. (p. 2484)
Rundell, Katherine, ed. Book of Hopes: Words & Pictures to Comfort, Inspire & Entertain. (p. 258)
Rundle, Elizabeth. Two Vocations: Or, the Sisters of Mercy at Home, a Tale (Classic Reprint) (p. 2309)
Rundman, Dawn. Spark Rotation Leader Guide: David. (p. 2074)
—Spark Rotation Leader Guide: A Storm. (p. 2074)
—Spark Rotation Leader Guide: Creation. (p. 2074)
—Spark Rotation Leader Guide: Four Friends. (p. 2074)
—Spark Rotation Leader Guide: Ten Men Healed. (p. 2074)
—Spark Rotation Leader Guide: Doubting Thomas. (p. 2074)
—Spark Rotation Leader Guide: Isaac & Rebekah. (p. 2074)
—Spark Rotation Leader Guide: Wedding at Cana. (p. 2074)
—Spark Rotation Leader Guide: Banquet with Simon. (p. 2074)
—Spark Rotation Leader Guide: Daniel & the Lions. (p. 2074)
—Spark Rotation Leader Guide: Fruit of the Spirit. (p. 2074)
—Spark Rotation Leader Guide Hannah & Samuel. (p. 2074)
—Spark Rotation Leader Guide Holy Week & Easter. (p. 2074)
—Spark Rotation Leader Guide House on the Rock. (p. 2074)
—Spark Rotation Leader Guide Jesus Is Born. (p. 2074)
—Spark Rotation Leader Guide Jonah & the Big Fish. (p. 2074)
—Spark Rotation Leader Guide Love Is. (p. 2074)
—Spark Rotation Leader Guide Lydia. (p. 2074)
—Spark Rotation Leader Guide Palm Sunday to Easter Sunday. (p. 2074)
—Spark Rotation Leader Guide Ruth. (p. 2074)
—Spark Rotation Leader Guide the Battle of Jericho. (p. 2074)
—Spark Rotation Leader Guide the Burning Bush. (p. 2074)
—Spark Rotation Leader Guide the Lord Is My Shepherd. (p. 2074)
—Spark Rotation Leader Guide the Lost Sheep & Lost Coin. (p. 2074)
—Spark Rotation Leader Guide the Plagues. (p. 2074)
—Spark Rotation Leader Guide the Sower. (p. 2074)
—Spark Rotation Leader Guide Wandering in the Wilderness. (p. 2074)
Runham, Isobel, illus. see Cockrill, Kathryn.
Runholt, Susan. Mystery of the Third Lucretia. (p. 1570)
Runkel, William M. Wontus: The Corps of Observation (Classic Reprint) (p. 2491)
Runkle, Bertha. Truth about Tolna (Classic Reprint) (p. 2296)
Runkle, Toni & Webb, Stephen. Glitter Girl. (p. 843)
Runnells, Patricia, illus. see DePrisco, Dorothea.
Runnells, Treesha, illus. see DePrisco, Dorothea.
Runnells, Treesha, illus. see O'Brien, Melanie.
Runnentrom, Bengt-Arne, illus. see Zak, Monica.
Runnerstrom, Bengt-Arne, illus. see Zak, Monica.
Running, Danny. Matilda the Brave: Oh How Time Flies. (p. 1425)
—Matilda the Brave-A Visit from Her Cousins. (p. 1425)
—Matilda the Brave- a Visit from Her Cousins. (p. 1425)
—Matilda the Brave-Be Brave. (p. 1425)
—Matilda the Brave-First Year of Travels. (p. 1425)
—Matilda the Brave-Parts of the Body. (p. 1425)
Running Press. Baby Bowie: A Book about Adjectives. Pintachan, illus. (p. 149)
—Baby Elvis: A Book about Opposites. Pintachan, illus. (p. 150)
—Baby KISS: A Book about Colors. Pintachan, illus. (p. 151)
—Berenstain Bears Light-Up Tree House. (p. 202)
—Elf on the Shelf: Magnet Set & Christmas Countdown Calendar. (p. 635)
—Fantastic Beasts & Where to Find Them: Newt Scamander's Case: With Sound. (p. 707)
—Goodnight, Constellations. McAlister, Rachel, illus. (p. 867)
—Little Prince: Light-Up Rose & Illustrated Book. (p. 1325)
—My Cat Book: A Keepsake Journal for My Pet. Lowery, Mike, illus. (p. 1535)
—My Dog Book: A Keepsake Journal for My Pet. Lowery, Mike, illus. (p. 1537)
—My Emoji Journal: Express Yourself with Your Favorite Emoji. (p. 1537)
—New Big Book of U. S. Presidents 2016 Edition. (p. 1591)
—Story of David & Goliath. Dardik, Helen, illus. (p. 2129)
Running Press, ed. CreARTivity: Chunky Chalk. (p. 469)
—CreARTivity: Paint, Print, & Roll. (p. 469)
—Frozen: Melting Olaf the Snowman Kit. (p. 795)
—Peanuts Finger Puppet Theater: Starring Charlie Brown & Snoopy! (p. 1710)
—Posters to Color: Oceans. (p. 1780)
—Posters to Color: Space. (p. 1780)
—Scratch & Stencil: Ponies. (p. 1963)
—Scratch & Stencil: Wintery White. (p. 1963)
Running Press, Running. My First Horoscope. McAlister, Rachel, illus. (p. 1544)
Runstedler, Nancy. Beautiful Goodbye. (p. 184)
—Pay It Forward Kids: Small Acts, Big Change (p. 1708)
Runton, Andy. Owly & Wormy, Bright Lights & Starry Nights. Runton, Andy, illus. (p. 1689)
—Owly & Wormy, Friends All Aflutter! Runton, Andy, illus. (p. 1689)
Runyan, Arthur Lester. I Want a Woman with a Soul: And Other Poems (Classic Reprint) (p. 1084)
Runyan, Brandy. Year of You: Journal of My Child. (p. 2519)
Runyen, Elizabeth. Watch Me Draw Disney's Mickey Mouse Clubhouse. (p. 2383)
Runyon, Anne Marshall. Longneedle. (p. 1344)
Ruocco, L. A. Nothing: Literal Nothing Lite(r)ªL TM Volume 0 (0pages) There Is No End As There Is No Beginning to This Book, Nothing Between U & I on the Keyboard -La Ru(c)&co. Enterprises 2014 * (p. 1624)
Ruocco, Paul, illus. see Amarone, Morgan.
Ruoff, Ian, illus. see Saucier, Michelle Ann.
Ruotolo, Flavia. From Morning to Night. (p. 792)
Rupchand, Vanessa. Mindful Me. (p. 1470)
Rupert Baus, Abby. Violet & Beaumont. (p. 2359)
Rupert, C. L. Tittle Tattle (Classic Reprint) (p. 2251)
Rupert, Chris, illus. see Bledsoe, Michele.
Rupert, Mad. Regular Show Vol. 10. Howell, Laura, illus. (p. 1862)
Rupert, Mad, illus. see Ostertag, Molly Knox, et al.
Rupke, Rachel. Tuktu's Birthday (Inuktitut/English) Hinch, Ali, illus. (p. 2299)
Ruplin, Lois L., illus. see Ruplin, Ferdinand A.
Rupp, Cecelia, ed. How to Be #1 Kid at Table Manners: Activity Book. (p. 1037)

R

—Journey to Lake Taupo & Australian & New Zealand Tales & Sketches (Classic Reprint) (p. 1182)
Russell, Rachel R. Dork Diaries: Tales from a Not-So-Fabulous Life (Hc) (p. 586)
—Dork Diaries: Tales from a Not-So-Popular Party Girl. (p. 586)
—Dork Diaries 3: Tales from a Not-So-Talented Pop Star (Hc) (p. 586)
—Dork Diaries 6: Tales from a Not-So-Happy Heartbreaker. (p. 586)
—Dork Diaries 7: Tales from a Not-So-Glam TV Star. (p. 586)
Russell, Rachel Renée. Desastroso Max Crumbly: Que Asco de Dia. (p. 530)
Russell, Rachel Renee. Desastroso Max Crumbly #2: Caos Escolar. (p. 530)
Russell, Rachel Renée. Dork Diaries Russell, Rachel Renée, illus. (p. 586)
—Dork Diaries Set Russell, Rachel Renée, illus. (p. 586)
Russell, Rachel Renee. Dork Diaries: Tales from a Not-So-Fabulous Life. (p. 586)
Russell, Rachel Renée. Dork Diaries 11: Tales from a Not-So-Friendly Frenemy. Russell, Rachel Renée, illus. (p. 586)
—Dork Diaries 12: Tales from a Not-So-Secret Crush Catastrophe. Russell, Rachel Renée, illus. (p. 586)
—Dork Diaries 13: Tales from a Not-So-Happy Birthday. Russell, Rachel Renée, illus. (p. 586)
—Dork Diaries 14: Tales from a Not-So-Best Friend Forever. Russell, Rachel Renée, illus. (p. 586)
—Dork Diaries 2: Tales from a Not-So-Popular Party Girl. Russell, Rachel Renée, illus. (p. 586)
—Dork Diaries 4: Tales from a Not-So-Graceful Ice Princess. Russell, Rachel Renée, illus. (p. 586)
—Dork Diaries 6: Tales from a Not-So-Happy Heartbreaker. Russell, Rachel Renée, illus. (p. 586)
—Dork Diaries 9: Tales from a Not-So-Dorky Drama Queen. Russell, Rachel Renée, illus. (p. 586)
—Dork Diaries Books 10-12: Dork Diaries 10; Dork Diaries 11; Dork Diaries 12. Russell, Rachel Renée, illus. (p. 586)
—Dork Diaries Books 1-10 (Plus 3 1/2 & OMG!) Dork Diaries 1; Dork Diaries 2; Dork Diaries 3; Dork Diaries 3 1/2; Dork Diaries 4; Dork Diaries 5; Dork Diaries 6; Dork Diaries OMG!; Dork Diaries 7; Dork Diaries 8; Dork Diaries 9; Dork Diaries 10. Russell, Rachel Renée, illus. (p. 586)
—Dork Diaries Friendship Box. Russell, Rachel Renée, illus. (p. 586)
—How to Dork Your Diary. (p. 1039)
—How to Dork Your Diary. Russell, Rachel Renée, illus. (p. 1039)
—Locker Hero. Russell, Rachel Renée, illus. (p. 1339)
—Misadventures of Max Crumbly 2: Middle School Mayhem. Russell, Rachel Renée, illus. (p. 1476)
—Misadventures of Max Crumbly 3: Masters of Mischief. Russell, Rachel Renée, illus. (p. 1476)
—Misadventures of Max Crumbly Collection: The Misadventures of Max Crumbly 1; the Misadventures of Max Crumbly 2; the Misadventures of Max Crumbly 3. Russell, Rachel Renée, illus. (p. 1476)
—OMG!:All about Me Diary! Russell, Rachel Renée, illus. (p. 1652)
—Tales from a Not-So-Dorky Drama Queen (p. 2181)
—Tales from a Not-So-Dorky Drama Queen. (p. 2181)
—Tales from a Not-So-Fabulous Life. (p. 2181)
—Tales from a Not-So-Fabulous Life. Russell, Rachel Renée, illus. (p. 2181)
—Tales from a Not-So-Glam TV Star. (p. 2182)
—Tales from a Not-So-Glam TV Star. Russell, Rachel Renée, illus. (p. 2182)
—Tales from a Not-So-Happily Ever After. (p. 2182)
Russell, Rachel Renee. Tales from a Not-So-Happy Birthday. (p. 2182)
Russell, Rachel Renée. Tales from a Not-So-Perfect Pet Sitter. Russell, Rachel Renée, illus. (p. 2182)
—Tales from a Not-So-Smart Miss Know-It-All. Russell, Rachel Renée, illus. (p. 2182)
—Tales from a Not-So-Talented Pop Star. Russell, Rachel Renée, illus. (p. 2182)
Russell, Rachel Renee, illus. see Russell, Rachel Renée.
Russell, Rachel Renée, et al. Tales from a Not-So-Friendly Frenemy. (p. 2181)
—Tales from a Not-So-Popular Party Girl. (p. 2182)
Russell, Randy. Dead Rules. (p. 518)
Russell, Raymond. Asleep & Awake (Classic Reprint) (p. 126)
Russell, Reba. Barkley the Bear Belongs: Overcoming an Orphan Heart. Ortiz, Phillip, illus. (p. 166)
—Courage the Hawk: Overcoming Fear. Phillip, Ortiz, illus. (p. 462)
Russell, Rita. Logan's Little Bug. (p. 1339)
—Logan's Many Hats. (p. 1339)
Russell, Robert Howard. Delft Cat, & Other Stories (Classic Reprint) (p. 526)
Russell, Rocky. Tico. (p. 2240)
Russell, Romina. Black Moon. (p. 238)
—Estrella Errante. (p. 665)
—Luna Negra. (p. 1368)
—Ofiucus Asciende. (p. 1641)
—Thirteen Rising. (p. 2223)
—Zodiac. (p. 2541)
Russell, Romina & Loftin, Nikki. Wandering Star. (p. 2375)
Russell, Ruth. Lake Front (Classic Reprint) (p. 1240)
Russell, Shane. Phloomp! (p. 1735)
Russell, Sharman Apt. Teresa of the New World. (p. 2206)
Russell, Stormy Corrin. Elimination. (p. 635)
—Liberation. (p. 1283)
Russell, Susan. Jar Full of Angel Feathers. (p. 1160)
Russell, T. Baron. Borlase & Son: A Novel (Classic Reprint) (p. 263)
Russell, Tamlyn. Lilly Grace's Conversation: Monday Is Getting It Done Day. Eberle, Lis, illus. (p. 1302)
Russell, Thomas Herbert. Stories of Boy Scouts & Girls' Open Air Clubs: Modern Methods of Character Building; a Manual of Work & Recreation in Which Many Valuable Lessons Are Taught That Prepare Boys & Girls for Future Usefulness (Classic Reprint) (p. 2124)
Russell, Tom, illus. see Rancour, Thom.
Russell, Tyler, jt. auth. see Kingsbury, Karen.
Russell, W. Clark. Alone on a Wide Wide Sea, Vol. 1 of 3 (Classic Reprint) (p. 58)
—Convict Ship, Vol. 1 of 3 (Classic Reprint) (p. 446)
—Golden Hope, Vol. 3 Of 3: A Romance of the Deep (Classic Reprint) (p. 857)
—Is He the Man? (Classic Reprint) (p. 1136)
—Jack's Courtship, Vol. 1 Of 3: A Sailor's Yarn of Love & Shipwreck (Classic Reprint) (p. 1153)
—What Cheer! (Classic Reprint) (p. 2407)
Russell, Walter. Age of Innocence (Classic Reprint) (p. 35)
—Bending of the Twig (Classic Reprint) (p. 199)
Russell, Waterman Spaulding Chapman. Iceland Horseback Tours in Saga Land (Classic Reprint) (p. 1088)
Russell, Wendy Thomas & Goodman, Sarah. MEdia. (p. 1436)
Russell, William. Primary Reader: A Selection of Easy Reading Lessons, with Introductory Exercises in Articulation, for Young Children (Classic Reprint) (p. 1792)
Russell, William Clark. Abandoned (Classic Reprint) (p. 2)
—Alone on a Wide Wide Sea, Vol. 3 of 3 (Classic Reprint) (p. 58)
—Deceased Wife's Sister & My Beautiful Neighbour. (p. 522)
—Deceased Wife's Sister, & My Beautiful Neighbour. In Three Volumes. Vol. III. (p. 522)
—Deceased Wife's Sister, & My Beautiful Neighbour, Vol. 3 of 3 (Classic Reprint) (p. 522)
—Frozen Pirate. (p. 796)
—Jack's Courtship, Vol. 2 Of 3: A Sailor's Yarn of Love & Shipwreck (Classic Reprint) (p. 1153)
—Jilted! or, My Uncle's Scheme: A Novel, in Three Volumes, Vol. I. (p. 1168)
—Jilted! or My Uncle's Scheme, Vol. 2: A Novel (Classic Reprint) (p. 1168)
—Jilted, Vol. 3 Of 3: Or, My Uncle's Scheme; a Novel, in Three Vols (Classic Reprint) (p. 1168)
—John Holdsworth Chief Mate (Classic Reprint) (p. 1173)
—Mate of the Good Ship York: Or the Ship's Adventure (Classic Reprint) (p. 1420)
—Romance of a Midshipman (Classic Reprint) (p. 1900)
—Romance of a Transport (Classic Reprint) (p. 1900)
—Tale of Two Tunnels: A Romance of the Western Waters (Classic Reprint) (p. 2180)
—Tale of Two Tunnels. (p. 2180)
—Wrong Side Out (Classic Reprint) (p. 2514)
Russell, William Howard. Adventures of Doctor Brady (Classic Reprint) (p. 23)
—Adventures of Doctor Brady, Vol. 1 of 3 (Classic Reprint) (p. 23)
—My Diary in India, Vol. 2 Of 2: In the Year 1858-9 (Classic Reprint) (p. 1537)
Russell, Willy. Our Day Out: Improving Standards in English Through Drama at Key Stage 3 & GCSE. Gunton, Mark, ed. (p. 1677)
Russell-Brown, Katheryn. Little Melba & Her Big Trombone Morrison, Frank, illus. (p. 1321)
—Voice Named Aretha. Freeman, Laura, illus. (p. 2365)
Russell-Gilmer, Phyllis A. Where Do Crickets Go When Winter Comes? Jones, Chamira, illus. (p. 2436)
Russell-Roberts, Juliet. Great Mystery. (p. 888)
—Pixikins. (p. 1752)
Russett, Bruce, ed. see Docalavich, Heather.
Russett, Bruce, ed. see Nelson, Sheila.
Russett, Bruce, ed. see Smith, Roger.
Russett, Bruce, ed. see Walker, Ida.
Russett, Bruce M. Triangulating Peace (Classic Reprint) (p. 2286)
Russik, Michael, illus. see Polette, Keith.
Russita, Tanja, illus. see Arrechea, Raquel.
Russita, Tanja, illus. see Martin, Wilkie J.
Russo, Angela B. Beautiful. (p. 183)
Russo, Blythe, illus. see Adhikary, Anita B.
Russo, Blythe, illus. see Venable, Colleen Af & Odd Dot.
Russo, Brian. Yoga Bunny. Russo, Brian, illus. (p. 2523)
Russo, Brian, illus. see Hamill, Laura & Cramer, Jolene.
Russo, David Anson. Around the World: The Great Treasure Hunt. Russo, David Anson, illus. (p. 118)
—Great Treasure Hunt. Russo, David Anson, illus. (p. 890)
Russo, Erin. Angus Parker, Circus Tiger. Russo, Erin, illus. (p. 87)
Russo, Erin, illus. see Raven, J. E.
Russo, Frank M. Sleigh. Cittadino, Kyle & Cittadino, Kristen, illus. (p. 2038)
Russo, Gina & Benchmark Education Co., LLC Staff. Big Job. (p. 221)
Russo, Kristen J. Surprising Facts about Being a Marine. (p. 2164)
—Surprising Facts about Being a Navy Sailor. (p. 2164)
—Surprising Facts about Being an Air Force Airman. (p. 2164)
—Surprising Facts about Being an Army Soldier. (p. 2164)
—What You Didn't Know about U. S. Military Life. (p. 2422)
Russo, Kristin J. Animal Facts or Fibs. (p. 89)
—Facts or Fibs? (p. 694)
—Human Body Facts or Fibs. (p. 1049)
—Space Facts or Fibs. (p. 2071)
—Survival Facts or Fibs. (p. 2164)
—Surviving in Space. (p. 2165)
—Surviving the Cave. (p. 2165)
—Surviving the Ice. (p. 2165)
—Surviving the Storm. (p. 2165)
Russo, Mallory Kate. Hotel Christmas. (p. 1007)
Russo, Maria Octavia, illus. see Wiley, Jennie.
Russo, Marisabina. Bunnies Are Not in Their Beds. (p. 298)
—Bunnies Are Not in Their Beds. Russo, Marisabina, illus. (p. 298)
—I Will Come Back for You. (p. 1085)
—Little Bird Takes a Bath. Russo, Marisabina, illus. (p. 1311)
—Peter Is Just a Baby. (p. 1728)
Russo, Mary. Grandma Loves Pillows. (p. 878)
Russo, Meredith. Birthday: A Novel. (p. 233)
—Birthday. (p. 233)
—If I Was Your Girl. (p. 1091)
Russo, Michael, jt. auth. see Brehm, Mike.
Russo, Monica. Birdology: 30 Activities & Observations for Exploring the World of Birds. (p. 231)
—Treecology: 30 Activities & Observations for Exploring the World of Trees & Forests. (p. 2284)
Russo, Steve. Bible Promise Book(r) for Teens: Timeless Answers for Tough Questions. (p. 213)
Russo, Steve, jt. auth. see Phillips, Bob.
Russom, Brandon. Balthazar Bunny & the Quest for Slicey, Slicey, Cut, Cut. (p. 162)
Russon, Anne E., photos by see Smith, Dale.
Russon, Penni. Endsister. (p. 650)
Rust, Graham, illus. see Burnett, Frances Hodgson.
Rust, Kari. House at the End of the Road. (p. 1022)
—Tricky. (p. 2287)
Rust, Margaret. Queen of the Fishes: An Adaptation in English of a Fairy Tale of Valois (Classic Reprint) (p. 1824)
Rust, Ned. Patrick Griffin's First Birthday on Ith. (p. 1705)
Rust, Ned, jt. auth. see Patterson, James.
Rust, Rachel. All Kinds of Bad. (p. 52)
—Girl Scorned. (p. 836)
—Or the Girl Dies. (p. 1668)
—Watched Girl. (p. 2383)
Rustad, Martha. Michael Makes Friends at School. Becker, Paula, illus. (p. 1457)
—Sam Visits the School Library. Golden, Jess, illus. (p. 1926)
—Tanya Takes the School Bus. Becker, Paula, illus. (p. 2190)
Rustad, Martha E. Dolphins [Scholastic]. (p. 580)
—Foxes & Their Dens [Scholastic]. (p. 774)
—Hojas en Otoño. (p. 986)
—Personas en Otoño. (p. 1725)
—Rays [Scholastic]. (p. 1844)
—Sea Turtles [Scholastic]. (p. 1969)
—Space. (p. 2070)
Rustad, Martha E., jt. auth. see Rustad, Martha E. H.
Rustad, Martha E. H. 100 Snowflakes: A Winter Counting Book. (p. 2557)
—100 Snowflakes: a Winter Counting Book. (p. 2557)
—Across the Country 18, 19, 20: A Transportation Counting to 20 Book. (p. 11)
—Across the Country 18, 19, 20: a Transportation Counting to 20 Book. (p. 11)
—Algunos Niños Tienen Autismo. (p. 44)
—All about Animals in Winter. (p. 48)
—All about Christmas. (p. 48)
—All about Spring. (p. 50)
—Amazing Sights of the Sky. (p. 66)
—Animal Camouflage in the Desert [Scholastic]. (p. 88)
—Animal Camouflage in the Snow [Scholastic]. (p. 88)
—Animales en Invierno/Animals in Winter (p. 93)
—Animals in Fall: Preparing for Winter. Enright, Amanda, illus. (p. 94)
—Animals in Spring. (p. 94)
—Animals Working Together (p. 96)
—Ants & Aphids Work Together. (p. 103)
—Astronaut's Life. (p. 128)
—Baby Animals & Their Homes. (p. 148)
—Baby Animals in Burrows. (p. 148)
—Baby Animals in Dens. (p. 148)
—Baby Animals in Nests. (p. 148)
—Baby Animals in Pouches. (p. 148)
—Baby Duck Story (p. 150)
—Baby Penguin Story (p. 152)
—Baby Polar Bear Story. (p. 152)
—Baby Sea Otter Story. (p. 152)
—Baby Seal Story. (p. 152)
—Beagles. (p. 178)
—Becoming an Astronaut. (p. 187)
—Birthdays in Many Cultures. (p. 234)
—Black Holes. (p. 238)
—Boxers. (p. 267)
—Bulldogs. (p. 296)
—Bullfrogs. (p. 296)
—Can We Ring the Liberty Bell? Poling, Kyle, illus. (p. 317)
—Can You Sing the Star-Spangled Banner ? Poling, Kyle, illus. (p. 319)
—Chicks 2, 4, 6: A Baby Animals Counting by Twos Book. (p. 369)
—Chicks 2, 4, 6: a Baby Animals Counting by Twos Book. (p. 369)
—Clown Fish & Sea Anemones Work Together (p. 408)
—Colorful Foods. (p. 422)
—Constellations. (p. 443)
—Diversión con Animales en Otoño. Enright, Amanda, illus. (p. 565)
—Diversión con Calabazas en Otoño (Fall Pumpkin Fun) Enright, Amanda, illus. (p. 565)
—Diversión con Las Hojas de Otoño. Enright, Amanda, illus. (p. 565)
—Diversión con Manzanas en Otoño. Enright, Amanda, illus. (p. 565)
—Diversión en el Clima de Otoño. Enright, Amanda, illus. (p. 565)
—Do Trees Get Hungry? Noticing Plant & Animal Traits. Moran, Mike, illus. (p. 571)
—Does the Sun Sleep? Noticing Sun, Moon, & Star Patterns. Conger, Holli, illus. (p. 575)
—Dogs (p. 577)
—Down the Field 10, 20, 30: A Football Counting by Tens Book. (p. 590)
—Down the Field 10, 20, 30: a Football Counting by Tens Book. (p. 590)
—Driest Places on Earth. (p. 604)
—Earth. (p. 615)
—Eclipses. (p. 623)
—En el Espacio. (p. 646)
—Estrellas. (p. 665)
—Exploring Space. (p. 682)
—Fall Animal Fun. Enright, Amanda, illus. (p. 700)
—Fall Apple Fun. Enright, Amanda, illus. (p. 700)
—Fall Apples: Crisp & Juicy. Enright, Amanda, illus. (p. 700)
—Fall Harvest Fun. Enright, Amanda, illus. (p. 700)
—Fall Harvests: Bringing in Food. Enright, Amanda, illus. (p. 700)
—Fall Leaves: Colorful & Crunchy. Enright, Amanda, illus. (p. 700)
—Fall Leaves Fun. Enright, Amanda, illus. (p. 700)
—Fall Pumpkin Fun. Enright, Amanda, illus. (p. 700)
—Fall Pumpkins: Orange & Plump. Enright, Amanda, illus. (p. 700)
—Fall Weather: Cooler Temperatures. Enright, Amanda, illus. (p. 700)
—Fall Weather Fun. Enright, Amanda, illus. (p. 700)
—Foxes. (p. 774)
—German Shepherds. (p. 822)
—Great Leaders & Thinkers of Ancient Greece (p. 887)
—Green Foods. (p. 894)
—Healthy Me. (p. 944)
—Hearing. (p. 944)
—Highest Places on Earth. (p. 969)
—Historia de un Pato Bebé) Strictly Spanish Translation Services Staff, tr. (p. 150)
—How Books Are Made (p. 1026)
—Hurricanes (p. 1054)
—I Can Reduce Waste. (p. 1063)
—I Care for My Teeth. (p. 1063)
—I Eat Well. (p. 1064)
—I Stay Active. (p. 1083)
—Inclined Planes. (p. 1113)
—Is a Bald Eagle Really Bald? Conger, Holli, illus. (p. 1136)
—Labrador Retrievers. (p. 1235)
—Language Arts (p. 1243)
—Learning about Ads. (p. 1257)
—Learning about Fact & Opinion. (p. 1257)
—Learning about Folktales, Fables, & Fairy Tales (p. 1257)
—Learning about Media Literacy. (p. 1257)
—Learning about Nonfiction (p. 1257)
—Learning about Privacy. (p. 1257)
—Let's Go to the Library (p. 1274)
—Levers. (p. 1282)
—Life in Space. (p. 1292)
—Lowest Places on Earth. (p. 1363)
—Luna/the Moon. (p. 1368)
—Magnificent Moths. (p. 1382)
—Measuring Distance. (p. 1435)
—Measuring Length. (p. 1435)
—Measuring Temperature. (p. 1435)
—Measuring Time. (p. 1435)
—Measuring Volume. (p. 1435)
—Measuring Weight. (p. 1435)
—Mice. (p. 1457)
—Milky Way. (p. 1467)
—Moon. (p. 1501)
—Moon [Scholastic]: Revised Edition. (p. 1502)
—Moray Eels & Cleaner Shrimp Work Together. (p. 1504)
—My Body (p. 1534)
—My Body Systems. (p. 1534)
—My Circulatory System: A 4D Book. (p. 1535)
—My Nervous System: A 4D Book. (p. 1557)
—My Respiratory System: A 4D Book. (p. 1560)
—My Skeletal System: A 4D Book. (p. 1561)
—NASA (p. 1576)
—Northern Lights. (p. 1621)
—On a Safari 5, 10, 15: A Counting by Fives Book. (p. 1652)
—On a Safari 5, 10, 15: a Counting by Fives Book. (p. 1652)
—One More Bug: An Insect Addition Book. (p. 1661)
—Orange Foods. (p. 1668)
—Owls. (p. 1689)
—Parts of a Book (p. 1701)
—People in Spring (p. 1718)
—Planetas. (p. 1755)
—Planets. (p. 1756)
—Planets [Scholastic]. (p. 1756)
—Plants in Spring (p. 1757)
—Poodles. (p. 1774)
—Pulleys. (p. 1812)
—Raccoons. (p. 1830)
—Rainbows. (p. 1837)
—Reading Is Everywhere (p. 1847)
—Red Foods. (p. 1857)
—Saint Bernards. (p. 1923)
—Saltwater Stumper: A Zoo Animal Mystery (p. 1925)
—Scottish Terriers. (p. 1962)
—Screws. (p. 1965)
—Seeing. (p. 1984)
—Sharks [Scholastic]. (p. 2003)
—Shooting Stars. (p. 2009)
—Simple Machines. (p. 2022)
—Smelling. (p. 2041)
—Snakes (p. 2044)
—Sol/the Sun (p. 2058)
—Space (p. 2070)
—Space Stations (p. 2072)
—Space Travel. (p. 2072)
—Space Vehicles. (p. 2072)
—Stars [Scholastic]. (p. 2107)
—Stunning Spiders. (p. 2145)
—Sun. (p. 2151)
—Sun [Scholastic]. (p. 2151)
—Tanya Takes the School Bus. Becker, Paula J., illus. (p. 2190)
—Tasting. (p. 2192)
—Today Is a Cold Day. (p. 2255)
—Today Is a Hot Day. (p. 2255)
—Today Is a Rainy Day. (p. 2255)
—Today Is a Snowy Day. (p. 2255)
—Today Is a Sunny Day. (p. 2255)
—Today Is a Windy Day. (p. 2255)
—Touching. (p. 2268)
—Transportation in Many Cultures. (p. 2278)
—Water (p. 2384)
—Weather in Spring (p. 2394)
—Wedges. (p. 2395)
—Wettest Places on Earth (p. 2403)
—What Is Inside the Lincoln Memorial? Poling, Kyle, illus. (p. 2415)
—What Is It Made Of? Noticing Types of Materials. Schneider, Christine M., illus. (p. 2415)
—What Is the Weather Today? (p. 2417)
—What's in a Cave? (p. 2424)
—What's in a Pond? (p. 2424)
—What's in a Tree? (p. 2424)
—What's in There? (p. 2424)

—Wheels & Axles. (p. 2428)
—When Will It Rain? Noticing Weather Patterns. Conger, Holli, illus. (p. 2434)
—Why Are There Stripes on the American Flag? Poling, Kyle, illus. (p. 2455)
—Why Is the Statue of Liberty Green? Conger, Holli, illus. (p. 2458)
—Wonderful World of Reading. (p. 2490)
—Working in Space. (p. 2496)
—World's Longest Snake & Other Animal Records. (p. 2507)
—Yellow Foods. (p. 2520)
—Zebras & Oxpeckers Work Together. (p. 2539)
Rustad, Martha E. H., jt. auth. see Gray-Wilburn, Renée.
Rustad, Martha E. H., jt. auth. see Peterson, Megan Cooley.
Rustad, Martha E. H., jt. auth. see Sweeney, Alyse.
Rustad, Martha E. H., jt. auth. see Wittrock, Jeni.
Rustad, Martha E. H. & Becerra-Cárdenas, José. Diversión con la Cosecha de Otoño. Enright, Amanda, illus. (p. 565)
Rustad, Martha E. H. & Clay, Kathryn. Celebrate Winter. (p. 349)
Rustad, Martha E. H. & Hiti, Samuel. Babylonians: Life in Ancient Babylon. (p. 153)
Rustad, Martha E. H. & Kalz, Jill. Droughts: Be Aware & Prepare (p. 606)
—Tornadoes: Be Aware & Prepare (p. 2265)
Rustad, Martha E. H. & Morey, Allan. Awesome Asian Animals. (p. 144)
Rustad, Martha E.H. Beagles. (p. 178)
—Boxers. (p. 267)
—Bulldogs. (p. 296)
—German Shepherds. (p. 822)
—Labrador Retrievers. (p. 1235)
—Poodles. (p. 1774)
—Saint Bernards. (p. 1923)
—Scottish Terriers. (p. 1962)
Rustad, Martha Elizabeth Hillman. All Kinds of Families. (p. 52)
—Capybaras. (p. 327)
—Care for Your Body. (p. 328)
—Care for Your Teeth. (p. 328)
—Community Questions. (p. 432)
—Dung Beetles. (p. 610)
—Families Share Values. (p. 702)
—Families Then & Now. (p. 702)
—Families Work Together. (p. 702)
—Family Celebrations. (p. 702)
—Family Traditions. (p. 703)
—How Can People Help Communities? (p. 1026)
—Limit Screen Time. (p. 1303)
—Manatees. (p. 1396)
—Mob of Meerkats. (p. 1485)
—Pack of Wolves. (p. 1691)
—President of the United States. (p. 1789)
—Pythons. (p. 1819)
—Rest Your Body. (p. 1870)
—Serving on a Jury. (p. 1992)
—State Governor. (p. 2108)
—U. S. Senate. (p. 2312)
—What Makes a Community? (p. 2418)
—What Makes a Family. (p. 2418)
—What Makes a Family? (p. 2418)
—Who Are Community Leaders? (p. 2446)
—Why Do Communities Need Rules? (p. 2456)
Rustad, Martha Elizabeth Hillman, jt. auth. see Kortuem, Amy.
Rustad, Martha Elizabeth Hillman & Schuh, Mari. Health & My Body. (p. 943)
Rustad, Marthe E. H. Bats. (p. 173)
Rustgi, Jennifer. Moon of My Own White, Ashley, illus. (p. 1502)
Rusticus, Rusticus. Recitations (Classic Reprint) (p. 1853)
Rusu, Meredith. Ashyln's Fall Fiesta. (p. 125)
—Big Island Race (Clifford) Oxley, Jennifer, illus. (p. 221)
—Big Red School. (p. 222)
—Big Red School. Simard, Remy, illus. (p. 222)
—Brother/Sister Squad (p. 286)
—Charmer Girls Rock! (p. 361)
—Christmas Cookie Thief. (p. 385)
—Dinosaur Danger! (p. 548)
—Dinosaur Disaster! (p. 548)
—Disney Princess Sleeping Beauty Read-Along Storybook & CD. (p. 563)
—Doctors to the Rescue. (p. 574)
—Doctors to the Rescue. Eone, illus. (p. 574)
—Egg-Stra Special Easter. Bricking, Jennifer, illus. (p. 628)
—Emmet Gets Tough. (p. 644)
—George & Harolds Epic Comix Collection: Epic Tales of Captain Underpants (p. 818)
—Horrifyingly Haunted Hack-A-Ween (the Epic Tales of Captain Underpants TV: Comic Reader) (p. 1004)
—Incredibles 2: Sweet Dreams, Jack-Jack. Gurihiru, illus. (p. 1114)
—It's Pool Time! (p. 1147)
—It's Pool Time! Simard, Remy, illus. (p. 1147)
—Jornada Escolar de Peppa Peppa's School Day. Eone, illus. (p. 1178)
—Kendall's Snow Fort. (p. 1209)
—Learning to Share. (p. 1259)
—Learning to Share (Peppa Pig) EOne, illus. (p. 1259)
—Legend of the Brown Ninja. (p. 1262)
—Mighty Girl! (Scholastic Reader, Level 2: WellieWishers by American Girl) (p. 1462)
—New Ninja. (p. 1596)
—Owen to the Rescue. (p. 1688)
—Owen's Guide to Survival. (p. 1688)
—Peppa Goes Apple Picking. (p. 1719)
—Peppa Goes Apple Picking. Eone, illus. (p. 1719)
—Peppa Pig: Hide-And-Seek: Scratch Magic. EOne, illus. (p. 1720)
—Peppa Visits the Aquarium (Peppa Pig) (p. 1720)
—Peppa's School Day. (p. 1720)
—Peppa's School Day. Eone, illus. (p. 1720)
—Piece of Cake. (p. 1742)
—Pikmi to Be Your Valentine. (p. 1744)
—Play Time for Peppa & George (Peppa Pig) Eone, illus. (p. 1759)
—Police Pursuit! (p. 1770)
—Pony Surprise. (p. 1773)
—Pumpkin Contest. Eone, illus. (p. 1812)
—Python's Revenge. (p. 1819)
—Pythor's Revenge. (p. 1819)
—Robin's Guide to Being Cool(Er) (p. 1891)
—School for Crooks. (p. 1945)
—School Play. (p. 1946)
—Sky Police! (p. 2034)
—Spooky Sleepover (Clifford the Big Red Dog Storybook) (p. 2087)
—Star Wars Rebels Ezra's Wookiee Rescue. (p. 2105)
—Star Wars Rebels: the Inquisitor's Trap. (p. 2105)
—Story of Clifford. (p. 2129)
—Sun down, Monsters Up! (p. 2151)
—Sunny Day Scavenger Hunt. (p. 2152)
—UglyDolls: a Perfectly Imperfect Guide to Life. (p. 2314)
—Unicorn Treasure Hunt. Bricking, Jennifer, illus. (p. 2329)
—Yo-Kai Are Real! (p. 2522)
—Yo-Kai Watch. Scholastic, Illus. (p. 2522)
—¡Compartir Es Genial! Eone, illus. (p. 433)
Rusu, Meredith, jt. auth. see Disney Press Staff.
Rusu, Meredith, jt. auth. see Scholastic.
Rusu, Meredith, jt. auth. see Whitehill, Simcha.
Rusu, Meredith, adapted by. Yo-Kai Are Real! (p. 2522)
Ruta, Angelo, illus. see Ferguson, Sinclair B.
Ruta, Angelo, illus. see Piper, Sophie.
Ruta, Angelo, illus. see Sims, Lesley.
Ruta, Angelo, illus. see Skevington, Andrea.
Rutchik, Gregory Alan. Stella Do It: A Young Adult Story about Independence. (p. 2113)
Ruter, P. S. Reminiscences of a Virginia Physician (Classic Reprint) (p. 1865)
—Reminiscences of a Virginia Physician, Vol. 1 of 2 (Classic Reprint) (p. 1865)
Rutgers, Lispenard. On & off the Saddle: Characteristic Sights & Scenes from the Great Northwest to the Antilles (Classic Reprint) (p. 1652)
Ruth and Mark. Max the Cool Doodle. (p. 1428)
Ruth, Clarence. Colors de la Runway (p. 426)
Ruth, Greg. Coming Home. Ruth, Greg, illus. (p. 430)
—Lost Boy. (p. 1352)
Ruth, Greg, illus. see Avi.
Ruth, Greg, illus. see Golden, Christopher & Lebbon, Tim.
Ruth, Greg, illus. see Mack, Tracy & Citrin, Michael.
Ruth, Greg, illus. see Messner, Kate.
Ruth, Greg, illus. see Obama, Barack.
Ruth, Greg, illus. see Preller, James.
Ruth, Greg, illus. see Wood, Douglas.
Ruth, Krauss & Krauss. Carrot Seed. (p. 334)
Ruth, Madison. Blood Dreamer: Obleignia Chronicles. (p. 246)
—Winter of Lost Dreamers: Obleignia Chronicles. (p. 2475)
Ruth, Peggy Joyce. My Own Psalm 91 Book: German. (p. 1558)
—My Own Psalm 91 Book: Russian. (p. 1558)
—My Own Psalm 91 Book: Ukrainian. (p. 1558)
—My Own Psalm 91 Book: Vietnamese English. (p. 1558)
—My Own Psalm 92 Book: Simplified Chinese-English. (p. 1558)
Ruth, Tamara, jt. auth. see Ruth, E. G.
Ruthann, Keulen, illus. see Baker, Elizabeth D.
Rutherfoord, Peggy. African Voices: An Anthology of Native African Writing (Classic Reprint) (p. 33)
Rutherford, Alexa, illus. see Bromilow, Mary.
Rutherford, Alexa, illus. see Kiehm, Eve Begley.
Rutherford, Alexander. Bffs (Best Friends Forever) the First in the Alex's Dreams Trilogy. (p. 212)
Rutherford, Clarice. Dog Is a Dog: And That's Why He's So Special. (p. 576)
Rutherford, Jill. Tama the Extraordinary Cat: The True Story of the Cat Who Saved a Railway Company & Became a Goddess. a Story for Children & People Who Love Cats. Crowe, Louise, illus. (p. 2188)
Rutherford, John. Charlie Chatterton: A Montreal Story; with Canadian & Other Poems (Classic Reprint) (p. 359)
Rutherford, Kris. Batting Ninth. (p. 173)
Rutherford, Kristina. Level the Playing Field: The Past, Present, & Future of Women's Pro Sports. (p. 1281)
Rutherford, Lucy. Demi Lovato & Selena Gomez: The Complete Unofficial Story of the BFFs. (p. 528)
Rutherford, Mara. Crown of Coral & Pearl. (p. 479)
Rutherford, Mark. Catharine Furze (Classic Reprint) (p. 344)
—Catharine Furze, Vol. 1 of 2 (Classic Reprint) (p. 344)
—Clara Hopgood (Classic Reprint) (p. 398)
—Miriam's Schooling & Other Papers (Classic Reprint) (p. 1475)
—More Pages from a Journal: With Other Papers (Classic Reprint) (p. 1505)
—Pages from a Journal with Other Papers. (p. 1692)
—Revolution in Tanner's Lane (Classic Reprint) (p. 1873)
Rutherford, Meg, illus. see Stimson, Joan.
Rutherford, Peter. Giant Fun-to-Find Puzzles Busy Animals: Search for Pictures in Eight Exciting Scenes. (p. 830)
—Let's Look on the Move. Spong, Clive, illus. (p. 1275)
—Noah's Ark. (p. 1616)
Rutherford, Peter, illus. see Crosbie, Duncan.
Rutherford, Peter, illus. see Ford, James Evelyn & Salariya, David.
Rutherford, Robynn. This Little Dragon. James, Katie, illus. (p. 2226)
Rutherford, Sherene. Robin Sparrow & Porcupine Pete's Adventure. (p. 1891)
Rutherford, Susan. Adentures of Walter Pigeon. (p. 16)
—Adventures of Walter Pigeon. (p. 29)
Rutherford, Terry. If Creation Could Talk, What Would It Say? (p. 1090)
Rutherford, William G. Story of Garfield: Farm-Boy, Soldier, & President. (p. 2130)
Ruth-Killgore, Chanacee. Alphabet Soup. (p. 59)
Ruth-Sommer, Hermann. Alte Musikinstrumente: Ein Leitfaden Fur Sammler (Classic Reprint) (p. 60)
Rutkin, David. Nothing but the Truth. (p. 1624)
Rutkoski, Marie. Cabinet of Wonders: The Kronos Chronicles: Book I. (p. 307)
—Celestial Globe. (p. 350)
—Chronique de Kronos - le Cabinet des Merveilles. (p. 389)
—Globe Celeste T2-Les Nouvelles Aventures de Petra Kronos. (p. 844)
—Jewel of the Kalderash: The Kronos Chronicles: Book III. (p. 1167)
—Midnight Lie. (p. 1461)
—Shadow Society. (p. 1997)
—Winner's Curse. (p. 2473)
Rutkowski, Chris A. I Saw It Too! Real UFO Sightings. (p. 1080)
Rutland, Elijah, illus. see Manning, Justin & Waugh, Simone.
Rutland, J. Chilly Da Vinci. (p. 377)
—I Love You No Matter What: A Prince Chirpio Story (p. 1079)
Rutledge, A. B. Miles Away from You. (p. 1465)
Rutledge, Archibald. Old Plantation Days (Classic Reprint) (p. 1648)
Rutledge, Brooke Kodish. Rainbow Shines Through Clara. (p. 1836)
Rutledge, Clint. Dare to Be Different. Kemp, Dory, illus. (p. 504)
Rutledge, Johnny. Grant's Sports Adventures: Math & Football. (p. 880)
Rutledge, Kara. Jaro & Frog. (p. 1160)
Rutledge, Lauren, illus. see Olson, Lisa Gammon.
Rutledge, Stanley a. Pen Pictures from the Trenches (Classic Reprint) (p. 1715)
Rutledge, Susan. Ty the Turtle in the Land of the Can'ts. Mahardhika, Stevie, illus. (p. 2310)
Rutley, Erika L. Adventures in Pup-A-Dupping. (p. 20)
Rutley, Frank. Study of Rocks: An Elementary Text-Book of Petrology - Scholar's Choice Edition. (p. 2144)
—Study of Rocks. (p. 2144)
Rutman, Meredyth & Rutman, Rhett. Couch Potato Classroom. (p. 457)
Rutt, Preston. Tortoise vs. Hare: The Rematch. Redlich, Ben, illus. (p. 2266)
Ruttan, Molly. Stray. Ruttan, Molly, illus. (p. 2139)
Ruttan, Molly, illus. see Rayner, Abigail.
Rutten, Nicole, illus. see Conan, Sally Anne.
Rutten, Nicole, illus. see Hill, Susanna Leonard.
Rutter, Frank. Path to Paris: The Rambling Record of a Riverside Promenade (Classic Reprint) (p. 1704)
Rutter, Owen. Song of Tiadatha (Classic Reprint) (p. 2063)
Ruttimann, Johann Jakob, jt. auth. see Thackeray, William Makepeace.
Ruttle, Kate, jt. auth. see Budgell, Gill.
Rutylo, Iryna, illus. see Leigh, A. J.
Rutzebeck, Hjalmar. Alaska Man's Luck: A Romance of Fact. (p. 40)
—Alaska Man's Luck: A Romance of Fact (Classic Reprint) (p. 40)
Ruurs, Margriet. Amazing Animals: The Remarkable Things That Creatures Do. Hancock, W. Allan, illus. (p. 63)
—Birthdays Around the World. Barron, Ashley, illus. (p. 234)
—Bus to the Badlands Dávila, Claudia, illus. (p. 300)
—Bus to the Badlands. Dávila, Claudia, illus. (p. 300)
—Elephant Keeper: Caring for Orphaned Elephants in Zambia. Covo, Pedro, illus. (p. 634)
—Families Around the World. Gordon, Jessica Rae, illus. (p. 701)
—Ghost of the Mill House Dávila, Claudia, illus. (p. 828)
—Mountain Alphabet. Kiss, Andrew, illus. (p. 1513)
—My School in the Rain Forest: How Children Attend School Around the World. (p. 1560)
—Robert Bateman: the Boy Who Painted Nature (p. 1890)
—School Days Around the World. Feagan, Alice, illus. (p. 1945)
Ruz Velasco, David. Mil Kilos de Aire. (p. 1465)
RUZICKA, Carol, illus. see Baker, Bill.
Ruzicka, Carol, illus. see Norton, John.
Ruzicka, Delores F., illus. see Zachmeyer, Mary L.
Ruzicka, Oldrich. How Things Are Made. Hetmerová, Alexandra, illus. (p. 1036)
Ruzima, Keza. Girl Power: The Adventures of a Teenage Circle. (p. 836)
Ruzycki, Dan Dan. Adventures of Pillow Head: The Fallen Star. Hunter, Robbie Chase, illus. (p. 26)
Ruzzier, Sergio. Fox & Chick: The Party & Other Stories. (p. 773)
—Fox & Chick: the Party: And Other Stories. (p. 773)
—Fox & Chick: the Quiet Boat Ride & Other Stories (Early Chapter for Kids, Books about Friendship, Preschool Picture Books) (p. 773)
—Good Boy. Ruzzier, Sergio, illus. (p. 861)
—Two Mice. (p. 2308)
Ruzzier, Sergio, illus. see Bunting, Eve.
Ruzzier, Sergio, illus. see Cohen, Caron Lee.
Ruzzier, Sergio, illus. see Heide, Florence Parry & Van Clief, Sylvia Worth.
Ruzzier, Sergio, illus. see Heide, Florence Parry.
Ruzzier, Sergio, illus. see Hesterman, Katie.
Ruzzier, Sergio, illus. see Krauss, Ruth.
Ruzzier, Sergio, illus. see Robinson, Michelle.
Ruzzier, Sergio, illus. see Yorinks, Arthur.
RV 1960 Staff. Biblia Tu Andar Diario. (p. 214)
Ryall, Jeanette. Clay Art. (p. 402)
—Food Art. (p. 759)
—Junk Art. (p. 1191)
—Nature Art. (p. 1580)
—Paper Art. (p. 1697)
—Sand Art. (p. 1930)
Ryals, J. V. Yankee Doodle Dixie; or Love the Light of Life (Classic Reprint) (p. 2517)
Ryals, Katherine. Storytime Stickers: Baby Animals at Play. Berlin, Rose Mary, illus. (p. 2136)
Ryals, Lexi. Christmas with Kate & Mim-Mim. (p. 388)
—More Jammin' with the Jonas Brothers: An Unauthorized Biography. (p. 1505)
—Teeny Tiny Animals. (p. 2200)
—When I Grow Up: Taylor Swift. (p. 2431)
Ryan, A. K. Know God, Know Peace: Devotional Artistic Photography (p. 1229)
Ryan, Aidan M. Power of Java. (p. 1782)
—Recognizing Bias. (p. 1853)
Ryan, Amy Kathleen. Vibes. (p. 2355)
—Zen & Xander Undone. (p. 2539)
Ryan, Ann Marie. Best Gift. Denis, Florencia, illus. (p. 206)
Ryan, Bernard. Secret Service. (p. 1979)
Ryan, Candace. Zoo Zoom! Pamintuan, Macky, illus. (p. 2543)
Ryan, Carrie. Dark & Hollow Places. (p. 505)
—Dead-Tossed Waves. (p. 518)
—Divide & Conquer. (p. 565)
—Forest of Hands & Teeth. (p. 766)
Ryan, Carrie & Davis, John Parke. City of Thirst. (p. 395)
—Iron Tide Rising. (p. 1136)
—Map to Everywhere. (p. 1401)
—Shadows of the Lost Sun. (p. 1998)
Ryan, Carrie, ed. Foretold: 14 Tales of Prophecy & Prediction. (p. 767)
Ryan, Cecil. Method of Acquiring an Understanding of the Character & Relationship Problems of Older Boys (Classic Reprint) (p. 1453)
Ryan, Cheryl, jt. auth. see Harshman, Marc.
Ryan, Christopher. Moon & the Mouse. Tillson, Linda L., illus. (p. 1501)
Ryan, Darlene. Cuts Like a Knife (p. 491)
—Five Minutes More (p. 744)
—Pieces of Me (p. 1742)
Ryan, Emma. Surprising Swimmers. (p. 2164)
Ryan, Eoin, illus. see Webb, Mary & Ni Laoghaire, Ide.
Ryan, Evelyn. Guinea Pigs Are Not Pigs! (p. 904)
Ryan, Feliceta Brophy. Key to English (Classic Reprint) (p. 1211)
Ryan, G. William. Little Donkey: A Palm Sunday/Easter Story for All Ages. (p. 1315)
Ryan, Gregory & Ryan, Elizabeth. ABC's of Thomas Merton: A Monk at the Heart of the World. (p. 5)
Ryan, Hannah, illus. see English, Rose.
Ryan, Hope. Geek & His Artist. (p. 813)
Ryan, Hugh. Hunt. (p. 1052)
—Spy Academy: Mission Twinpossible. (p. 2093)
Ryan, James. Elementary Treatise on Algebra, Theoretical & Practical: Adapted to the Instruction of Youth in Schools & Colleges (Classic Reprint) (p. 632)
Ryan, Janice, illus. see Puckett, Diane.
Ryan, Jeanne. Nerve. (p. 1588)
Ryan, Justin. 101 Secrets from a Pokemon Master. (p. 2558)
Ryan, Karlene Kay. Genevieve & the Moon. Johnson, Meredith, illus. (p. 815)
—Genevieve Goes to School. Johnson, Meredith, illus. (p. 815)
Ryan, Kate Moira. Expeditioner's Club: Rio Roosevelt. Vol. 1 (p. 677)
Ryan, Marah Ellis. Bondwoman (Classic Reprint) (p. 255)
—Flower of France: A Story of Old Louisiana (Classic Reprint) (p. 752)
—For the Soul of Rafael: With Many Illustrations from Photographs Taken Expressly for This Book (Classic Reprint) (p. 763)
—House of the Dawn (Classic Reprint) (p. 1023)
—In Love's Domains: A Trilogy (Classic Reprint) (p. 1106)
—Merze: The Story of an Actress (Classic Reprint) (p. 1451)
—Miss. Moccasins (Classic Reprint) (p. 1479)
—My Quaker Maid (Classic Reprint) (p. 1559)
—Pagan of the Alleghanies (Classic Reprint) (p. 1692)
—Squaw Elouise (Classic Reprint) (p. 2094)
—That Girl Montana (Classic Reprint) (p. 2212)
—Told in the Hills: A Novel (Classic Reprint) (p. 2256)
—Treasure Trail a Romance of the Land of Gold & Sunshine (Classic Reprint) (p. 2282)
—Woman of the Twilight, the Story of a Story (Classic Reprint) (p. 2485)
Ryan, Margaret. Collins Big Cat Phonics for Letters & Sounds - in the Frog Bog: Band 03/Yellow Capriotti, Benedetta, illus. (p. 416)
—Littlest Dragon. Smith, Jamie, illus. (p. 1331)
—Littlest Dragon Gets the Giggles. Smith, Jamie, illus. (p. 1331)
—Littlest Dragon Goes for Goal. Smith, Jamie, illus. (p. 1331)
Ryan, Mary C. Aiden Pike: Step Right Up! DeSantis, Mike, illus. (p. 36)
—Bus from Outer Space. (p. 300)
Ryan, Matthew. Box. (p. 266)
—Move. (p. 1515)
Ryan, Matthew & Cherwin, Roy. Open up & Take a Look at Grandpa Roy's Children's Book. (p. 1666)
Ryan, Michael, illus. see David, Peter.
Ryan, Mike. Amazing Football: Stars, Stats & Facts. (p. 65)
—Football Stars. (p. 762)
Ryan, Nancy. Bookworm & His New Book. (p. 261)
Ryan, Nellie. Designer Doodles. (p. 532)
—Doodles Dancing: Graceful & Gorgeous Pictures to Create & Complete. (p. 584)
—Dream House Doodles. (p. 601)
—Fabulous Fashion. Ryan, Nellie, illus. (p. 692)
Ryan, Nellie, jt. illus. see Davies, Hannah.
Ryan, Nellie, et al. Girls' World of Doodles: Over 100 Pictures to Complete & Create. (p. 839)
—Gorgeous Doodles: Pretty, Full-Color Pictures to Create & Complete. (p. 870)
Ryan, Pam Muñoz. Dreamer. (p. 602)
—Dreamer. Sís, Peter, illus. (p. 602)
—Dreamer. Sís, Peter & Sís, Peter, illus. (p. 602)
—Echo. (p. 623)
—Eco. (p. 623)
—Esperanza Rising. (p. 662)
—Hello Ocean. Astrella, Mark, illus. (p. 951)
—Soñador. Sís, Peter, illus. (p. 2062)
—Tony Baloney: Pen Pal. Fotheringham, Ed, illus. (p. 2260)
—Tony Baloney: Buddy Trouble. Fotheringham, Ed, illus. (p. 2260)
—Tony Baloney: School Rules. Fotheringham, Edwin, illus. (p. 2260)
—Tony Baloney. Fotheringham, Edwin, illus. (p. 2260)
—Tony Baloney Yo Ho Ho, Halloween! Fotheringham, Edwin, illus. (p. 2260)

R

—Yo Ho Ho, Halloween! Fotheringham, Ed, illus. (p. 2522)
Ryan, Pam Muñoz & McInerney, Kathleen. Paint the Wind. (p. 1693)
Ryan, Pat. Car Racing Greats. (p. 327)
—Iowa. (p. 1133)
Ryan, Pat & Hoena, Blake. Kansas. (p. 1203)
Ryan, Patrick. In Mike We Trust. (p. 1106)
Ryan, Patrick, jt. auth. see Mayhew, James.
Ryan, Paul, et al. Iron Man Epic Collection: War Machine. (p. 1135)
Ryan, Peter. Online Bullying. (p. 1663)
Ryan, Peter K. Black Ops & Other Special Missions of the U. S. Air Force Combat Control Team. (p. 238)
—Careers in Electronic Publishing. (p. 329)
—How the Gold Standard Works. (p. 1035)
—Powering up a Career in Robotics. (p. 1783)
—Social Networking. (p. 2053)
Ryan, Phillip. Freight Trains. (p. 783)
—Monorails. (p. 1495)
—Passenger Trains. (p. 1703)
—Steam-Powered Trains. (p. 2110)
—Streetcars. (p. 2140)
—Subways. (p. 2146)
Ryan, R. F. Enos, or the Last of the Modocs: A Melodrama, in Two Acts (Classic Reprint) (p. 655)
Ryan, Regina Sara, jt. auth. see April, Elyse.
Ryan, Rob. Invisible Kingdom. (p. 1132)
Ryan, Rob, illus. see Duffy, Carol Ann.
Ryan, Rob, jt. auth. see Duffy, Carol Ann.
Ryan, Ruth. In the Swamp, Oh Yeah, in the Swamp. Seahorse, Risa, illus. (p. 1111)
Ryan, Sara. Bad Houses. Hahn, Sierra, ed. (p. 158)
Ryan, Sean. Spain in Our World. (p. 2073)
Ryan, Sean, jt. auth. see Cadenhead, MacKenzie.
Ryan, Sean, et al. Spider-Man: Spider-Sense of Adventure. Pennino, Mario del et al, illus. (p. 2080)
Ryan, Susannah, illus. see Maestro, Betsy.
Ryan, Todd. Arizona Cardinals. (p. 116)
—Carolina Panthers. (p. 333)
—Dallas Cowboys. (p. 498)
—Houston Texans. (p. 1025)
—Las Vegas Raiders. (p. 1246)
—Michigan Wolverines. (p. 1459)
—Minnesota Vikings. (p. 1473)
—New York Jets. (p. 1599)
—Oklahoma Sooners. (p. 1644)
—Seattle Seahawks. (p. 1973)
—Tennessee Volunteers. (p. 2206)
Ryan, Tom. Big Time (p. 223)
—Giant Man from a Tiny Town: A Story of Angus MacAskill Hoyt, Christopher, illus. (p. 830)
—I Hope You're Listening. (p. 1066)
—Keep This to Yourself. (p. 1207)
—Pop Quiz (p. 1775)
—Tag Along (p. 2176)
—Totally Unrelated (p. 2267)
Ryan, Trish & Weber, Penny. What Do You See? a Child's Perspective on Life. (p. 2409)
Ryan, Valerie J. Lucinda's Wormy Journey. (p. 1364)
Ryan-Herndon, Lisa L. Wild Amazon. (p. 2462)
Ryan-Herndon, Lisa L., jt. auth. see Scholastic Australia Staff.
Ryan-Lush, Geraldine. Gravel Pit Kids. (p. 882)
—Law-Breaking Adventures of Teacher Tabitha: 978-0-9947339-6-2. (p. 1253)
Ryans, Bianca. Eclipse. (p. 623)
—Wally's Wish. (p. 2373)
Ryback, Carol. Lost City. (p. 1353)
Ryback, Carol, jt. auth. see Blashfield, Jean F.
Ryback, Carol, jt. auth. see Stille, Darlene R.
Rybak, B. E. Potcakes. Burch, Ellen, illus. (p. 1781)
Rybka, Teagan & Rybka, Sam. Twinning It: Dance, Acro, YouTube & Living Life to the Fullest. (p. 2305)
Rybolt, Leah M., jt. auth. see Rybolt, Thomas R.
Rybolt, Thomas R. Chemistry in Your Everyday Life (p. 365)
—Soda Pop Science Fair Projects. (p. 2054)
Rybolt, Thomas R. & Mebane, Robert C. Environmental Science Fair Projects, Revised & Expanded Using the Scientific Method. LaBaff, Tom & LaBaff, Stephanie, illus. (p. 657)
Rybolt, Thomas R. & Rybolt, Leah M. Smelly Science Fair Projects. (p. 2041)
Ryce, John. Oath in Heaven: An Early Victorian Romance (Classic Reprint) (p. 1634)
Ryce, Kenesha. Vio's Violin: We Imagine Music Series. (p. 2360)
Ryce, Mark. Mrs. Drummond's Vocation (Classic Reprint) (p. 1522)
Ryckman, Tatiana. Alexander Hamilton: The First Secretary of Treasury & an Author of the Federalist Papers. (p. 42)
—Investigating Matter Through Modeling (p. 1131)
—Panama Canal. (p. 1695)
Ryckman, Tatiana & Bial, Raymond. People & Culture of the Mandan. (p. 1718)
Ryckman, Tatiana & Jones, Edith. Othello. (p. 1674)
Ryckman, Tatiana, et al. Texas (p. 2209)
Rycroft, Nina, illus. see French, Jackie.
Rycroft, Nina, illus. see Harris, Stephen.
Rycroft, Nina, illus. see Wild, Margaret.
Rydaker, Ewa. Lucia Morning in Sweden. Lewis, Anne Gillespie, ed. (p. 1363)
Rydberg, Viktor. Singoalla: A Mediaeval Legend (Classic Reprint) (p. 2024)
Ryden, Linda. Henry Is Kind: A Story of Mindfulness Malone, Shearry, illus. (p. 955)
—Rosie's Brain. Ryden, Linda, illus. (p. 1906)
Ryder, Abigail L., illus. see English, Rose.
Ryder, Annie H. New Every Morning: A Year Book for Girls (Classic Reprint) (p. 1593)
Ryder, Chloe. Best Friends Forever! (p. 206)
—Princess Ponies 1: a Magical Friend. (p. 1798)
—Princess Ponies 10: the Pumpkin Ghost. (p. 1798)
—Princess Ponies 11: Season's Galloping. (p. 1798)
—Princess Ponies 2: a Dream Come True. (p. 1798)
—Princess Ponies 3: the Special Secret. (p. 1798)
—Princess Ponies 4: a Unicorn Adventure! (p. 1798)
—Princess Ponies 5: an Amazing Rescue. (p. 1798)
—Princess Ponies 7: a Special Surprise. (p. 1798)
—Princess Ponies 8: a Singing Star. (p. 1798)
—Princess Ponies 9: the Lucky Horseshoe. (p. 1798)
—Valentine's Adventure! (p. 2344)
Ryder, Grizzly. Woodside Reminiscence (Classic Reprint) (p. 2492)
Ryder, Joanne. Bear of My Heart. Moore, Margie, illus. (p. 179)
—My Father's Hands. Graham, Mark, illus. (p. 1538)
—Night Flight. Schwartz, Amy, illus. (p. 1605)
—Panda Kindergarten. (p. 1695)
—Panda Kindergarten. Feng, Katherine, illus. (p. 1695)
—Panda Kindergarten. Feng, Katherine, photos by. (p. 1695)
—Where Butterflies Grow. Cherry, Lynne, illus. (p. 2435)
—Won't You Be My Kissaroo? (p. 2491)
—Won't You Be My Kissaroo? (padded Board Book) Sweet, Melissa, illus. (p. 2491)
Ryder, Joanne, jt. auth. see Yep, Laurence.
Ryder, Michael Todd. Twins. (p. 2306)
Ryder, Robert O. Young Lady Across the Way (Classic Reprint) (p. 2531)
Ryder, Ronald Peter. Sleeping with Lazarus. (p. 2037)
Ryding, Paul, illus. see Chambers, Veronica.
Ryding, Paul, jt. auth. see Chambers, Veronica.
Rye, Edgar. Quirt & the Spur: Vanishing Shadows of the Texas Frontier (Classic Reprint) (p. 1828)
Ryee, William De. Truth Unadorned: A Romance of Realism (Classic Reprint) (p. 2297)
Ryerson, Egerton. Story of My Life Being Reminiscences of Sixty Years' Public Service in Canada. (p. 2131)
Ryerson, Richard A., jt. ed. see Fremont-Barnes, Gregory.
Rygier-Nalkowska, Sofja. Kobiety (Women) A Novel of Polish Life (Classic Reprint) (p. 1230)
Ryherd, Saundra. Adventures of Sparky (p. 28)
Rykaczewski, Erazm. Dokladny Slownik Polsko-Angielski I Angielsko-Polski: Czerpany Z Najlepszych Zrodel Krajowych I Obcych (Classic Reprint) (p. 578)
Ryken, Philip Graham. Ecclesiastes (Redesign) Why Everything Matters. (p. 622)
Rylance, Ulrike. Emma in Buttonland. Morby, Connie Stradling, tr. (p. 643)
Rylander, Chris. Codename Zero. (p. 412)
—Countdown Zero. (p. 459)
—Crisis Zero. (p. 475)
—Curse of Greg. (p. 488)
—Fourth Stall. (p. 773)
—Fourth Stall Part II (p. 773)
—Fourth Stall Part III. (p. 773)
—Legend of Greg. (p. 1262)
—Rise of Greg. (p. 1885)
Rylands, Warren, jt. auth. see Gilles, Renae.
Rylands, Warren, jt. auth. see Williams, Heather DiLorenzo.
Rylant, Cynthia. All in a Day. McClure, Nikki, illus. (p. 52)
—Annie & Snowball & the Book Bugs Club. (p. 99)
—Annie & Snowball & the Book Bugs Club. Stevenson, Suçie & Stevenson, Suçie, illus. (p. 99)
—Annie & Snowball & the Cozy Nest. Stevenson, Suçie, illus. (p. 99)
—Annie & Snowball & the Cozy Nest. Stevenson, Suçie & Stevenson, Suçie, illus. (p. 99)
—Annie & Snowball & the Grandmother Night. (p. 99)
—Annie & Snowball & the Grandmother Night. Stevenson, Suçie & Stevenson, Suçie, illus. (p. 99)
—Annie & Snowball & the Magical House. Stevenson, Suçie, illus. (p. 99)
—Annie & Snowball & the Magical House. Stevenson, Suçie & Stevenson, Suçie, illus. (p. 99)
—Annie & Snowball & the Shining Star. Stevenson, Suçie, illus. (p. 99)
—Annie & Snowball & the Shining Star. Stevenson, Suçie & Stevenson, Suçie, illus. (p. 99)
—Annie & Snowball & the Teacup Club. Stevenson, Suçie & Stevenson, Suçie, illus. (p. 99)
—Annie & Snowball & the Thankful Friends. (p. 99)
—Annie & Snowball & the Thankful Friends. Stevenson, Suçie, illus. (p. 99)
—Annie & Snowball & the Wedding Day. (p. 99)
—Annie & Snowball & the Wedding Day. Stevenson, Suçie, illus. (p. 99)
—Annie & Snowball Collector's Set 2 Stevenson, Suçie, illus. (p. 99)
—Bear. McDaniels, Preston, illus. (p. 179)
—Beautiful Stories of Life: Six Greek Myths, Retold. Ellis, Carson, illus. (p. 184)
—Beauty & the Beast. Park, Meg, illus. (p. 185)
—Brownie & Pearl Get Dolled Up. Biggs, Brian, illus. (p. 287)
—Brownie & Pearl Go for a Spin. Biggs, Brian, illus. (p. 287)
—Brownie & Pearl Grab a Bite. Biggs, Brian, illus. (p. 287)
—Brownie & Pearl Hit the Hay. Biggs, Brian, illus. (p. 287)
—Brownie & Pearl Make Good. Biggs, Brian, illus. (p. 287)
—Brownie & Pearl Ready-to-Read Collection: Brownie & Pearl Step Out; Brownie & Pearl Get Dolled Up; Brownie & Pearl Grab a Bite; Brownie & Pearl See the Sights; Brownie & Pearl Go for a Spin; Brownie & Pearl Hit the Hay. Biggs, Brian, illus. (p. 287)
—Brownie & Pearl See the Sights. Biggs, Brian, illus. (p. 287)
—Brownie & Pearl Step Out. Biggs, Brian, illus. (p. 287)
—Brownie & Pearl Take a Dip. Biggs, Brian, illus. (p. 287)
—Cobble Street Cousins Complete Collection: In Aunt Lucy's Kitchen; a Little Shopping; Special Gifts; Some Good News; Summer Party; Wedding Flowers. Halperin, Wendy Anderson, illus. (p. 410)
—Creation. Rylant, Cynthia, illus. (p. 470)
—Ecclesiastes: To Everything There Is a Season. Rylant, Cynthia, illus. (p. 622)
—Everyday House. Rylant, Cynthia, illus. (p. 671)
—Everyday Town. Rylant, Cynthia, illus. (p. 672)
—God Got a Dog. Frazee, Marla, illus. (p. 851)
—Gooseberry Park & the Master Plan. Howard, Arthur, illus. (p. 869)
—Henny, Penny, Lenny, Denny, & Mike. Austin, Mike, illus. (p. 954)
—Henry & Mudge Ready-To-Read Value Pack: Henry & Mudge; Henry & Mudge & Annie's Good Move; Henry & Mudge in the Green Time; Henry & Mudge & the Forever Sea; Henry & Mudge in Puddle Trouble; Henry & Mudge & the Happy Cat. Stevenson, Suçie & Stevenson, Suçie, illus. (p. 954)
—Henry & Mudge Ready-To-Read Value Pack #2: Henry & Mudge & the Long Weekend; Henry & Mudge & the Bedtime Thumps; Henry & Mudge & the Big Sleepover; Henry & Mudge & the Funny Lunch; Henry & Mudge & the Great Grandpas; Henry & Mudge & the Tall Tree House. Stevenson, Suçie, illus. (p. 954)
—Henry & Mudge the Complete Collection: Henry & Mudge; Henry & Mudge in Puddle Trouble; Henry & Mudge & the Bedtime Thumps; Henry & Mudge in the Green Time; Henry & Mudge & the Happy Cat; Henry & Mudge Get the Cold Shivers; Henry & Mudge under the Yellow Moon, Etc. Stevenson, Suçie, illus. (p. 954)
—Herbert's First Halloween. Henry, Steven, illus. (p. 957)
—In November. Kastner, Jill, illus. (p. 1106)
—Life. Wenzel, Brendan, illus. (p. 1287)
—Lighthouse Family Collection: The Storm; the Whale; the Eagle; the Turtle; the Octopus; the Otter; the Sea Lion; the Bear. McDaniels, Preston, illus. (p. 1299)
—Lighthouse Family Paperback Collection: The Storm; the Whale; the Eagle; the Turtle; the Octopus; the Otter; the Sea Lion; the Bear. McDaniels, Preston, illus. (p. 1299)
—Little Penguins. Robinson, Christian, illus. (p. 1324)
—Motor Mouse. Howard, Arthur, illus. (p. 1512)
—Motor Mouse Delivers. Howard, Arthur, illus. (p. 1512)
—Mr. Putter & Tabby Clear the Decks. Howard, Arthur, illus. (p. 1520)
—Mr. Putter & Tabby Dance the Dance. (p. 1520)
—Mr. Putter & Tabby Drop the Ball. (p. 1520)
—Mr. Putter & Tabby Drop the Ball. Howard, Arthur, illus. (p. 1520)
—Mr. Putter & Tabby Hit the Slope. Howard, Arthur, illus. (p. 1520)
—Mr. Putter & Tabby Ring the Bell. Howard, Arthur, illus. (p. 1520)
—Mr. Putter & Tabby Run the Race. Howard, Arthur, illus. (p. 1520)
—Mr. Putter & Tabby Smell the Roses. Howard, Arthur, illus. (p. 1520)
—Mr. Putter & Tabby Turn the Page. (p. 1520)
—Mr. Putter & Tabby Turn the Page. Howard, Arthur, illus. (p. 1520)
—Nativity. Rylant, Cynthia, illus. (p. 1579)
—Night in the Country. Szilagyi, Mary, illus. (p. 1606)
—Old Woman Who Named Things. Brown, Kathryn, illus. (p. 1648)
—Otter. McDaniels, Preston, illus. (p. 1675)
—Poppleton. (p. 1776)
—Poppleton. Teague, Mark, illus. (p. 1776)
—Poppleton & Friends. (p. 1776)
—Poppleton Every Day. (p. 1776)
—Poppleton in Spring. Teague, Mark, illus. (p. 1776)
—Rosetown. (p. 1906)
—Scarecrow. Stringer, Lauren, illus. (p. 1941)
—Sea Lion. McDaniels, Preston, illus. (p. 1967)
—Sleeping Beauty. McGuire, Erin, illus. (p. 2036)
—Tormenta. (p. 2265)
—Van Gogh Café. (p. 2347)
—We Love You, Rosie! Davick, Linda, illus. (p. 2391)
Rylant, Cynthia, jt. auth. see Lobel, Arnold.
Rylant, Cynthia & Howard, Arthur. Mr. Putter & Tabby Dance the Dance. Howard, Arthur, illus. (p. 1520)
Ryle, John Charles. Living or Dead? A Series of Some Truths (Classic Reprint) (p. 1334)
—No More Crying: An Address to Children (Classic Reprint) (p. 1613)
Ryles, Briony & Hall, Derek. Ages of Steam & Electricity. (p. 35)
—Early 20th Century. (p. 613)
—Medieval Period & the Renaissance. (p. 1437)
—Modern World. (p. 1488)
—Prehistory & the Classical Period. (p. 1787)
—Scientific Revolution. (p. 1959)
Ryley, Ann. Fanny Fitz-York, Vol. 1 Of 3: Heiress of Tremorne (Classic Reprint) (p. 706)
Ryley, David, illus. see Kovacs, Victoria.
Ryley, Madeleine Lucette. American Citizen (Classic Reprint) (p. 71)
Ryley, S. W. Itinerant in Scotland, Vol. 3 of 3 (Classic Reprint) (p. 1142)
—Itinerant, in Scotland, Vol. 7 (Classic Reprint) (p. 1142)
—Itinerant, or Memoirs of an Actor, Vol. 1 (Classic Reprint) (p. 1142)
—Itinerant, or Memoirs of an Actor, Vol. 1 of 2 (Classic Reprint) (p. 1142)
—Itinerant, or Memoirs of an Actor, Vol. 2: Part II (Classic Reprint) (p. 1143)
—Itinerant, Vol. 1 Of 3: Or, Memoirs of an Actor (Classic Reprint) (p. 1143)
—Itinerant, Vol. 2 Of 3: Or Memoirs of an Actor (Classic Reprint) (p. 1143)
—Itinerant, Vol. 4: Or Memoirs of an Actor (Classic Reprint) (p. 1143)
—Itinerant, Vol. 5: Or Memoirs of an Actor (Classic Reprint) (p. 1143)
—Itinerant, Vol. 6: Or Memoirs of an Actor (Classic Reprint) (p. 1143)
Ryley, Samuel William. Itinerant, in Scotland, Vol. 7 (Classic Reprint) (p. 1142)
—Itinerant, or Memoirs of an Actor, Vol. 3: Part 2 (Classic Reprint) (p. 1143)
—Itinerant, or Memoirs of an Actor, Vol. 3 of 3 (Classic Reprint) (p. 1143)
Rymar, Yurko, illus. see Waugh, Mat.
Rymenants, Stef, illus. see Colting, Fredrik & Medina, Melissa.
Rymer, Dawn. Chum! A Bear Story. (p. 390)
Rymer, James Malcolm. String of Pearls, or the Barber of Fleet Street: A Domestic Romance (Classic Reprint) (p. 2141)
Rymer, Thomas a. Link, Vol. 10: July 1952 (Classic Reprint) (p. 1304)
—Link, Vol. 10: May, 1952 (Classic Reprint) (p. 1304)
—Link, Vol. 10: April 1952 (Classic Reprint) (p. 1304)
—Link, Vol. 10: June, 1952 (Classic Reprint) (p. 1304)
—Link, Vol. 10: March 1952 (Classic Reprint) (p. 1304)
—Link, Vol. 10: October 1952 (Classic Reprint) (p. 1304)
—Link, Vol. 10: February, 1952 (Classic Reprint) (p. 1304)
—Link, Vol. 10: November, 1952 (Classic Reprint) (p. 1304)
—Link, Vol. 10: September 1952 (Classic Reprint) (p. 1304)
—Link, Vol. 8: October-November, 1950 (Classic Reprint) (p. 1305)
—Link, Vol. 8: December 1950 January 1951 (Classic Reprint) (p. 1305)
—Link, Vol. 9: April-May, 1951 (Classic Reprint) (p. 1305)
—Link, Vol. 9: February March, 1951 (Classic Reprint) (p. 1305)
—Link, Vol. 9: August-September, 1951 (Classic Reprint) (p. 1305)
—Th Link, Vol. 11: February, 1953 (Classic Reprint) (p. 2210)
Ryn, Aude van, illus. see Pappworth, Sara.
Ryn Katryn Digital Arts, illus. see Barr, Stephanie.
Rynd, Evelyne Elsye. Mrs. Green (Classic Reprint) (p. 1522)
Ryndak, Rob. Alligator or Crocodile? (p. 56)
—Bats. (p. 173)
—Crocodiles. (p. 477)
—Dolphin or Porpoise? (p. 579)
—Frog or Toad? (p. 789)
—Jungle Animals. (p. 1189)
—Leopard or Jaguar? (p. 1267)
—Monkeys. (p. 1494)
—Parrots. (p. 1701)
—Sloths. (p. 2039)
—Toucans. (p. 2267)
—Turtle or Tortoise? (p. 2301)
Rynders, Dawn, jt. auth. see Wallingford, Stephanie.
Rynhart, Kieran, illus. see Lloyd, Helen.
Rynhart, Kieran, illus. see Pollard, Simon.
Ryniak, Christopher, illus. see Amato, Mary.
Ryon, Loriel. Into the Tall, Tall Grass. (p. 1128)
Rypdal, Olla, ed. see Lippert, Audbjorg Gjerde.
Ryser, Nicolas, illus. see Richard, Laurent.
Ryski, Dawid. My Four Seasons. (p. 1547)
—What Do Grown-Ups Do All Day? (p. 2408)
Ryski, Dawid, illus. see Napier, Lauren.
Ryskind, Morrie. Home Movie Scenario Book: With Twenty New Plots for the Amateur Producer (Classic Reprint) (p. 996)
Rzasa, Jennifer, illus. see Bolte, Mari.
Rzeczkowski, Frank & Rosier, Paul C. Lakota Sioux. (p. 1240)

S

S, ., ed. see Dickens, Charles.
S, A. L. Gretchen's Gift: Or, a Noble Sacrifice; an Original Tale (Classic Reprint) (p. 896)
S B, Alexander. My Heart to Give. (p. 1549)
S Ball, R. Great Astronomers. (p. 883)
S Brumbaugh, Cindy. Tea with Benny & the Honeybee. (p. 2194)
S, C. Leaves from a Diary in Lower Bengal (Classic Reprint) (p. 1259)
S, C. W. Every-Day Life: A Play (Classic Reprint) (p. 670)
S, Charles Reginald. Your Uncle Lew: A Natural-Born American; a Novel (Classic Reprint) (p. 2534)
S, Corinne. Pawns of Liberty: A Story of Fighting Yesterdays in the Balkans (Classic Reprint) (p. 1708)
S, E. A. B. Virginia Dare: A Romance of the Sixteenth Century (Classic Reprint) (p. 2361)
S, E. W. Children's Hour (Classic Reprint) (p. 374)
S. Fox, Culpeo. Fox & the Crow. (p. 774)
S G, Louise, jt. auth. see Goulet, L. S.
S Hatti, Kalyankumar. Making Great Leaders Happen: Shaping Leaders of Tomorrow. (p. 1389)
S. I. International, jt. auth. see Brooke, Samantha.
S. I. International, jt. auth. see Olsen, Leigh.
S. I. International Staff, jt. auth. see Gallo, Tina.
S, J. Sentimental Calendar: Being Twelve Funny Stories (Classic Reprint) (p. 1989)
S, J. L. P. Chevalier Errant: Pour Supplément du Zopire François (Classic Reprint) (p. 367)
S, Karen. Itty Bitty Christmas. (p. 1149)
S, L. M. Country Landlords, Vol. 3 of 3 (Classic Reprint) (p. 461)
S, M. De. Esculapédie: Poëme Divisé en Huit Chants (Classic Reprint) (p. 662)
S MacHaffie, Dale. Whale's Tails. (p. 2404)
S, Maria. Mommy, Can I Eat This? (p. 1491)
S Nowicki, Karen. Itty Bitty & the Lion Day. (p. 1148)
S., Samantha. Before the Internet. (p. 191)
S Santa Rosa, Nereide. Childhood of Walter Elias Disney. Barreto, Andre, illus. (p. 370)
S, Sarah. Under the Pear Tree, or Little Crosses (Classic Reprint) (p. 2322)
S. Surges, Carol. Food Chains (p. 759)
S, Vera, illus. see N, Naila.
S Violette, Palumbo, illus. see Mishriky, Mireille.
S, W. Tommy & Jack: Their Wit, Fun & High Spirits; Amusing Stories by or about Our Soldiers & Sailors (Classic Reprint) (p. 2259)
S Wadile, Gaurav. Forgotten Past. (p. 768)
S Woodrum, Linda. Dragonpuss Apple Mcgee. (p. 595)
S Xerxeas, Hannah. Mute Silence. (p. 1530)
Sa Bu. Hanna Himbeere. (p. 918)
Sa, Rachel. Lewton Experiment (p. 1282)
Saa, Pitu, illus. see Fink, Nadia.
Saab, Julie. Little Lola. Gothard, David, illus. (p. 1321)
—Little Lola Saves the Show. Gothard, David, illus. (p. 1321)
Saaf, Donald. ABC Animal Orchestra. (p. 3)

S

Sadler, Sonia Lynn, illus. see Johnson, Jen Cullerton.
Sadler, Sonia Lynn, illus. see Patrick, Denise Lewis.
Sadlier, Anna T. Lost Jewel of the Mortimers (Classic Reprint) (p. 1354)
—Talisman (Classic Reprint) (p. 2187)
—Ubaldo & Irene, Vol. 1: A Historical Romance; from the Italian of Antonio Bresciani, S. J (Classic Reprint) (p. 2313)
—Wayward Winifred (Classic Reprint) (p. 2388)
Sadlier, Anna Theresa. Phileas Fox, Attorney (Classic Reprint) (p. 1734)
—Red Inn of Saint Lyphar (Classic Reprint) (p. 1857)
Sadlier, Cheryl. In the Beginning. (p. 1107)
—Who Is God. (p. 2448)
Sadlier, J. Blakes & Flanagans: A Tale, Illustrative of Irish in the United States (Classic Reprint) (p. 242)
—Heiress of Kilorgan: Or Evenings with the Old Geraldines (Classic Reprint) (p. 949)
—Hermit of the Rock: A Tale of Cashel (Classic Reprint) (p. 959)
—Hermit of the Rock. (p. 959)
—Knout: A Tale of Poland (Classic Reprint) (p. 1229)
—Maureen Dhu, the Admiral's Daughter: A Tale of the Claddagh of Galway (Classic Reprint) (p. 1426)
—New Lights; or Life in Galway: A Tale (Classic Reprint) (p. 1595)
—Old House by the Boyne, or Recollections of an Irish Borough (Classic Reprint) (p. 1646)
—Vendetta: And Other Tales (Classic Reprint) (p. 2350)
Sadlier, J. S. Willy Burke: Or the Irish Orphan in America (Classic Reprint) (p. 2470)
Sadlier, James a. Sadlier's Catholic Second Reader: Containing Complete Course in Articulation; Exercises in Spelling & Pronunciation; Choice Readings, & Review Questions (Classic Reprint) (p. 1921)
Sadlier, Rosemary. Kids Book of Black Canadian History. Wang, Qijun, illus. (p. 1214)
Sadowsky, Lulu. Sweet Briar Inside Out (Classic Reprint) (p. 2168)
Sadr, Ayeshe, illus. see Krishna, McArthur.
Sadu, Itah. Greetings, Leroy Delinois, Alix, illus. (p. 895)
Sadurní, Pep Molist. reina de la noche. (p. 1862)
Saedi Bocci, Goali. Social Media Workbook for Teens: Skills to Help You Balance Screen Time, Manage Stress, & Take Charge of Your Life. (p. 2053)
Saedi, Sara. Americanized: Rebel Without a Green Card. (p. 74)
Saedi, Sara, contrib. by. Americanized: Rebel Without a Green Card. (p. 74)
Saeed, Aisha. Amal Unbound. (p. 61)
—Bilal Cooks Daal. Syed, Anoosha, illus. (p. 225)
—Diana & the Island of No Return. (p. 538)
—Written in the Stars. (p. 2514)
Saeed, Aisha, jt. auth. see Albertalli, Becky.
Saeed, Aisha, jt. ed. see Ali, S. K.
Saelig, S. M., illus. see Osborne, Mary Pope.
Saemann, Kara, illus. see Trotta, Lee.
Sáenz, Benjamin Alire. Aristotle & Dante Discover the Secrets of the Universe. (p. 116)
—Inexplicable Logic of My Life. (p. 1118)
Saenz, Benjamin Alire. Last Night I Sang to the Monster. (p. 1248)
—Perfect Season for Dreaming (Un Tiempo Perfecto para Soñar) Andrade Valencia, Esau, illus. (p. 1722)
—Perrita Que le Encantaban las Tortillas. Garcia, illus. (p. 1724)
Sáenz, Benjamin Alire, jt. auth. see Sáenz, Benjamin Alire.
Sáenz, Benjamin Alire & Sáenz, Benjamin Alire. Aristotle & Dante Discover the Secrets of the Universe. (p. 116)
—He Forgot to Say Goodbye. (p. 941)
Sáenz, Miguel, tr. see Ende, Michael.
Saervold, Ola Johann. Erling a Tale from the Land of the Midnight-Sun (Classic Reprint) (p. 660)
Sáez Castan, Javier. Venganza de Edison (Bolsillo) (p. 2350)
Saez, Sofia, illus. see Freire De Matos, Isabel.
Safar, Lina, illus. see Barberi, Gladys.
Safar, Lina, illus. see Maillis, Nicole.
Safar, Lina, illus. see Shein, Erik Daniel & Reker, Martin.
Safar, Lina, illus. see Shein, Erik Daniel.
Safayiniya, Mahdiyah, illus. see Mastiri, Maryam.
Safeblade, Evelyn. White Birch. (p. 2443)
Saffioti, Trina. Old Frangipani Tree at Flying Fish Point. Prewett, Maggie, illus. (p. 1645)
Safford, Mary J. New Journal of Marie Bashkirtseff: From Childhood to Girlhood (Classic Reprint) (p. 1594)
Safford, Mary J., jt. auth. see Ebers, Georg.
Safford, Mary Joanna, jt. auth. see Ebers, Georg.
Safi, Aminah Mae. Not the Girls You're Looking For. (p. 1623)
—Tell Me How You Really Feel. (p. 2201)
Safieh, Charlotte. Cry for the Ocean. Piper, Tamara, illus. (p. 480)
Safier, David. 28 Days: a Novel of Resistance in the Warsaw Ghetto. (p. 2554)
Safina, Carl. Beyond Words: What Elephants & Whales Think & Feel (a Young Reader's Adaptation) Safina, Carl, illus. (p. 212)
—Beyond Words: What Wolves & Dogs Think & Feel (a Young Reader's Adaptation) Safina, Carl, illus. (p. 212)
Safirstein, Julie. Night & Day: A Big Book of Opposites. (p. 1604)
Safra, M. Di Geshikhte Fun Kriyes Yam Suf: Mitgelebt Loyt Di Hayntige Velt. Hanan, Yaakov, illus. (p. 536)
Safran, Claire. TV Radio Mirror, Vol. 58: July, 1962 (Classic Reprint) (p. 2302)
Safran, Sheri. All Kinds of Festivals. Fuller, Rachel, illus. (p. 52)
—All Kinds of People. Damon, Emma, illus. (p. 52)
—Bully. Tipping, Naomi, illus. (p. 296)
—Let's Dress! Fuller, Rachel, illus. (p. 1271)
Safro, Jill, ed. see Sweeny, Sheila.
Safroni-Middleton, A. Sailor & Beachcomber, Confessions of a Life at Sea, in Australia, & amid the Islands of the Pacific (Classic Reprint) (p. 1923)
—Vagabond's Odyssey: Being Further Reminiscences of a Wandering Sailor-Troubadour in Many Lands (Classic Reprint) (p. 2343)
Säfström, Maja. Animals of a Bygone Era: An Illustrated Compendium. (p. 95)
Saft, Lauren. Those Girls. (p. 2230)
Safwat, Adham. Red Sea Escape: Caesarion Lives! (p. 1858)
Sagar, Lindsey. Story of Country. (p. 2129)
Sagar, Lindsey, illus. see Copper, Jenny.
Sagar, Lindsey, illus. see Editors of Caterpillar Books.
Sagar, Lindsey, illus. see Marx, Jonny.
Sagara, Sou & Okomeken. Hentai Prince & the Stony Cat. (p. 956)
Sagard, Gabriel. Dictionaire de la Langue Huronne: Necessaire a Ceux Qui N'Ont l'Intelligence d'Icelle, et Ont a Traiter Avec les Sauvages du Pays (Classic Reprint) (p. 541)
Sagasti, Miriam, illus. see Metzger, Steve.
Sagata, Bruce. Ride with My Dad. Rus, Marta, illus. (p. 1878)
Sagata, Bruce & Estrada, Jomar. I Can See a Cuscus. (p. 1063)
Sage, ed. see Ballantyne, Sonya.
Sage, A. N. Kartega. (p. 1204)
Sage, Agnes Carr. Boys & Girls of the White House (Classic Reprint) (p. 272)
—Little Colonial Dame: A Story of Old Manhattan Island (Classic Reprint) (p. 1314)
—Two Girls of Old New Jersey: A School-Girl Story of '76 (Classic Reprint) (p. 2307)
Sage, Alain René Le. Adventures of Gil Blas of Santillane, Vol. 1 Of 4: A New Translation (Classic Reprint) (p. 23)
—Adventures of Gil Blas of Santillane, Vol. 4 of 4 (Classic Reprint) (p. 23)
—Adventures of Robert Chevalier, Call'd de Beauchene, Captain of a Privateer in New-France, Vol. 1 of 2 (Classic Reprint) (p. 27)
Sage, Alain Rene Le. Devil upon Crutches in England, or Night Scenes in London, Vol. 1: A Satirical Work (Classic Reprint) (p. 535)
—Devil upon Crutches, Vol. 1 Of 2: From the Diable Boiteux of Mr. le Sage, a New Translation; to Which Are Now First Added, Asmodeus's Crutches, a Critical Letter upon the Work, & Dialogues Between Two Chimneys of Madrid (Classic Reprint) (p. 535)
—History of Vanillo Gonzales, Surnamed the Merry Batchelor, Vol. 1 of 2 (Classic Reprint) (p. 981)
Sage, Alain René Le. Life & Adventures of Guzman d'Alfarache, or the Spanish Rogue, Vol. 3 of 3 (Classic Reprint) (p. 1288)
Sage, Alexis N. AetherBlood. (p. 31)
—Aetherblood. (p. 31)
—AetherBorn. (p. 31)
—AetherQueen. (p. 31)
—Aetherqueen. (p. 31)
Sage, Alison. Going on a Plane Purple Band. (p. 854)
Sage, Angie. Araminta Spookie 4: Vampire Brat. Pickering, Jimmy, illus. (p. 109)
—Araminta Spookie 5: Ghostsitters. Pickering, Jimmy, illus. (p. 109)
—Darke (p. 507)
—Darke. Zug, Mark, illus. (p. 507)
—Enchanter's Child, Book One: Twilight Hauntings. (p. 647)
—Fyre. (p. 803)
—Fyre. Zug, Mark, illus. (p. 803)
—Gargoyle Hall: An Araminta Spookie Adventure. (p. 810)
—Magyk Book. (p. 1382)
—Maximillian Fly. (p. 1428)
—Pathfinder. (p. 1704)
—Queste. Zug, Mark, illus. (p. 1826)
—Rise of the Dragons. (p. 1885)
—Septimus Heap, Book Five: Syren. Zug, Mark, illus. (p. 1989)
—Septimus Heap, Book Six: Darke. Zug, Mark, illus. (p. 1989)
—Septimus Heap: the Magykal Papers. Zug, Mark, illus. (p. 1989)
—Skeleton Island. (p. 2030)
—Todhunter Moon: Sandrider. Zug, Mark, illus. (p. 2255)
—TodHunter Moon, Book One: PathFinder. Zug, Mark, illus. (p. 2255)
—TodHunter Moon, Book Three: StarChaser. Zug, Mark, illus. (p. 2255)
—TodHunter Moon, Book Two: SandRider. Zug, Mark, illus. (p. 2255)
Sage, Colin. Level up Level 5 Student's Book. (p. 1281)
Sage, David. Adzul, the Heirs of the Medallion Book 1. (p. 30)
—Lita. (p. 1309)
Sage, Erica. Jacked Up. (p. 1153)
Sage, James. Old Misery. Ayto, Russell, illus. (p. 1647)
Sage, Molly, illus. see Gilpin, Rebecca.
Sage, Molly, illus. see Gulliver, Amanda & Turnbull, Stephanie.
Sage, Trina, illus. see Krohn, Kathryn T.
Sage, William. By Right Divine (Classic Reprint) (p. 305)
—Claybornes: A Romance of the Civil War (Classic Reprint) (p. 402)
—District Attorney (Classic Reprint) (p. 565)
—Frenchy: The Story of a Gentleman (Classic Reprint) (p. 784)
—Robert Tournay: A Romance of the French Revolution (Classic Reprint) (p. 1890)
Sagendorph, Jean. Starry Night, Hold Me Tight. Siebold, Kim, illus. (p. 2106)
Sager, Ed & Frye, Mike. Bootlegger's Lady: Tribulations of a Pioneer Woman. (p. 262)
Sager, Ryan K. World's Greatest Chocolate-Covered Pork Chops. (p. 2507)
Sagerman, Evan. Giraffe Rescue Company. Chou, Joey, illus. (p. 834)
Sagert, John. Second Blight War. (p. 1973)
Saggar, Gaytri. Three Dreaming Trees. (p. 2232)
Saghafi, Majid, tr. see Akbarpour, Ahmad.
Saghy, Christopher, illus. see Wilson, Judith Vt.
Sagner, Sibel. Show & Tell Day Blue Band. Perez, Moni, illus. (p. 2012)
Sagner, Sibel, et al. Day at the Museum Blue Band. Pérez, Moni, illus. (p. 512)
Sagramola, Giulia, illus. see Rich, KaeLyn.
Saha, Ayan, illus. see Lewis, Latoya.
Saha, Sujata, illus. see Fox, Julie G.
Saha, Tulika. 'Kosho & Sid on the Rainbow' (p. 1231)
Sahai, Supriya, illus. see Lim, Annalees.
Saheed, Julian, et al. Storyteller's Chest. (p. 2136)
Sahgal, Lara & Axelrod, Toby. Hans & Sophie Scholl (p. 918)
Sahgal, Lara & Levy, Janey. Primary Source Investigation of the Erie Canal. (p. 1792)
Sahin, Yusuf Kerem. Yusuf Around the World: Mission Istanbul. (p. 2537)
Sahm, Jina Marion. There's a Cat Flying Around My House! (p. 2217)
Saia, Jordan, illus. see Coulthurst, Audrey.
Saia, Stephanie. Hunting with Crocodiles. (p. 1054)
Saichann, Alberto, illus. see Lagonegro, Melissa.
Said. Seven Voyages of Sinbad the Sailor. Rashin, illus. (p. 1994)
Said, S. F. Phoenix. McKean, Dave, illus. (p. 1735)
Saidens, Amy, jt. auth. see Burnham, Niki.
Saidian, Siyavush. Brady vs. Brees vs. Rodgers vs. Montana (p. 274)
—Careers for People Who Love Comics, Animation, & Manga (p. 329)
—Careers for People Who Love Crafting (p. 329)
—Careers for People Who Love the Great Outdoors (p. 329)
—Great Depression: Worldwide Economic Crisis. (p. 885)
—Transatlantic Slave Trade: Slavery Comes to the New World. (p. 2277)
—Ways to Make Money Working with Animals (p. 2388)
—Ways to Make Money Working with Your Hands (p. 2388)
—What Is Basketball? (p. 2414)
—What Is Football? (p. 2415)
Saikia, Mayur. Anansi & His Children. (p. 79)
Saillard, Gustave. Essai Sur la Fable en France Au Dix-Huitieme Siecle (Classic Reprint) (p. 663)
—Florian, Sa Vie, Son Oeuvre (Classic Reprint) (p. 751)
Saillard, Remi. Funny Machines for George the Sheep: A Children's Book Inspired by Leonardo Da Vinci. (p. 801)
Sailor, Old. Greenwich Hospital: A Series of Naval Sketches, Descriptive of the Life of a Man-Of-War's Man (Classic Reprint) (p. 895)
—Hamilton King: Or, the Smuggler & the Dwarf (Classic Reprint) (p. 913)
—Hamilton King, Vol. 1 Of 3: Or, the Smuggler & the Dwarf (Classic Reprint) (p. 913)
—Topsail-Sheet Blocks, or the Naval Foundling, Vol. 2 of 3 (Classic Reprint) (p. 2264)
Sailor, Peter. Ronnie & the Big Red Apple. (p. 1902)
Saincantin, Jerome, tr. see Dorison, Xavier.
Saincantin, Jerome, tr. see Gilson.
Saincantin, Jerome, tr. see Tome.
Saincantin, Jerome, tr. see Runberg, Sylvain.
Saincatin, Jerome, tr. see Runberg, Sylvain.
Saincilus, Larimer, illus. see Jeune, Marie Carole.
Saint James, Synthia, illus. see Nikola-lisa, W. & Nikola-lisa, W.
Saint Louis, Ahha Studios, illus. see Stotz, Allyn M.
Saint Mary's Press, Saint Mary's. Discover the Saints. (p. 555)
Saint Mary's Press, Saint Mary's, ed. Catholic Children's Bible, Revised (hardcover) (p. 345)
Saint Mary's Press Staff. Catholic Children's Bible Coloring Book: Read It! Live It! Love It! Color It! (p. 345)
—Catholic Children's Bible, Revised (paperback) (p. 345)
Saint Mary's Press Staff, ed. Biblia Católica para Niños. (p. 214)
Saint, Mimi. Bride's Price. Wendt, Yohanna, illus. (p. 280)
Saint Rain, Justice. Animals Building Character: An Activities Book to Color. Gordon-Lucas, Bonnie, illus. (p. 94)
Saint-Amour, Catiana. Ours Qui Rendait Visite. (p. 1681)
Saint-Denis, Louis-Etienne. Napoleon from the Tuileries to St. Helena: Personal Recollections of the Emperor's Second Nameluke & Valet Louis Etienne St. Denis (Known As Ali) (Classic Reprint) (p. 1575)
Saint-Dizier, Marie. Abejas, Hormigas, Termitas Insectos Que Viven en Familia / Bees, Ants, Termites: Insects That Live in Families. Jarrie, Martin, illus. (p. 5)
Sainte Croix, Judith. Everything You Need to Know about Meditation. (p. 674)
Saint-Ellen, Tarah-Lynn. Claim Your Crown: Walking in Confidence & Worth As a Daughter of the King. (p. 397)
Sainte-Marie, Buffy. Hey Little Rockabye: A Lullaby for Pet Adoption. Hodson, Ben, illus. (p. 964)
Sainte-Palaye, J. -B De La Curne De. Dictionnaire Historique de l'Ancien Langage François, Ou Glossaire de la Langue Françoise Depuis Son Origine Jusqu'au Siècle de Louis XIV, Vol. 7: H-Myt (Classic Reprint) (p. 542)
—Dictionnaire Historique de l'Ancien Langage François, Ou Glossaire de la Langue Françoise Depuis Son Origine Jusqu'au Siècle de Louis XIV, Vol. 4: Contenant Signification Primitive et Secondaire des Vieux Mots, Vieux Mots Employés Dans les Chants Des. (p. 542)
—Dictionnaire Historique de l'Ancien Langage François, Ou Glossaire de la Langue Françoise Depuis Son Origine Jusqu'au Siècle de Louis XIV, Vol. 3: Contenant, Signification Primitive et Secondaire des Vieux Mots, Vieux Mots Employés Dans les Chants Des. (p. 542)
—Dictionnaire Historique de l'Ancien Langage Francois, Ou Glossaire de la Langue Francoise, Depuis Son Origine Jusqu'au Siecle de Louis XIV, Vol. 5: Signification Primitive et Secondaire des Vieux Mots; Vieux Mots Employes Dans les Chants des Trouveres. (p. 542)
Saint-Exupery, Antoine. Petit Prince. (p. 1730)
Saint-Exupèry, Antoine de. Little Prince. (p. 1325)
Saint-Exupery, Antoine De. Little Prince. Adreani, Manuela, illus. (p. 1325)
Saint-Exupéry, Antoine de. principito (edición con las acuarelas originales del autor) (p. 1800)
—Principito / the Little Prince. (p. 1800)
Saint-exupery, Antoine De. Principito / the Little Prince. (p. 1800)
Saint-Exupery, Antoine De, see De Saint-Exupéry, Antoine.
Saint-Exupery, Antoine De, see Potter, Elizabeth M. & De Saint-Exupéry, Antoine.
Saint-Hilaire, Etienne Geoffroy. Cours de l'Histoire Naturelle des Mammifères: Partie Comprenant Quelques Vues Préliminaires de Philosophie Naturelle, et l'Histoire des Singes, des Makis, des Chauve-Souris et de la Taupe (Classic Reprint) (p. 462)
Saintine, Joseph Xavier. Solitary of Juan Fernandez: The Real Robinson Crusoe. (p. 2057)
Saintine, Joseph Xavier Boniface. Picciola (Classic Reprint) (p. 1738)
Saintine, X. B. Woman's Whims, or the Female Barometer: Translated from the French (Classic Reprint) (p. 2486)
Saintine, Xavier B. Picciola: From the French (Classic Reprint) (p. 1738)
—Woman's Whims, or the Female Barometer: Translated from the French (Classic Reprint) (p. 2486)
Saint-Jean, Idola. Recitations Enfantines (Classic Reprint) (p. 1853)
—Récitations Enfantines (Classic Reprint) (p. 1853)
Saint-Onge, Danielle, jt. auth. see Szpirglas, Jeff.
Saint-Pathus, Guillaume De. Miracles de Saint Louis (Classic Reprint) (p. 1474)
Saint-Pierre, Bernadin de. Paul & Virginia (Classic Reprint) (p. 1707)
Saint-Pierre, Bernardin. Paul & Virginia (Classic Reprint) (p. 1707)
Saint-Pierre, Bernardin de. History of the Adventures, Love, & Constancy, of Paul & Virginia (Classic Reprint) (p. 980)
—Paul & Virginia: An Indian Tale (Classic Reprint) (p. 1707)
—Paul & Virginia (Classic Reprint) (p. 1707)
—Paul & Virginia, and, Elizabeth, or the Exiles of Siberia, a Tale, Founded on Facts (Classic Reprint) (p. 1707)
Saint-Pierre, Jacques-Bernardin-Henri de. Paul & Virginia: Translated from the French (Classic Reprint) (p. 1707)
Saints, C. of Jesus Christ of Latter-Day. Te Karere, Vol. 28: Hanuere 17, 1934 (Classic Reprint) (p. 2194)
Saints, Church Of Jesus Christ Of Latter. Moral Stories for Little Folks: For Sunday Schools, Primary Associations & Home Teaching (Classic Reprint) (p. 1503)
Saint-Saens, Camille. Javotte: Ballet en 1 Acte et 3 Tableaux (Classic Reprint) (p. 1161)
Saintsbury, George. Fielding (Classic Reprint) (p. 723)
—Honore de Balzac, Vol. 2 (Classic Reprint) (p. 1000)
—Novels, Tales & Letters of Prosper Merimee: A Chronicle of the Reign of Charles IX (Classic Reprint) (p. 1627)
—Novels, Tales & Letters of Prosper Merimee, Vol. 1 Of 8: Last Stories & Translations (Classic Reprint) (p. 1627)
—Political Verse. (p. 1771)
Saintsbury, George, jt. auth. see de Balzac, Honore.
Saintsbury, George, jt. auth. see Peacock, Thomas Love.
Saintsbury, George, jt. auth. see Sterne, Laurence.
Saintsbury, George, jt. auth. see Thackeray, William Makepeace.
Sainz-Yaksic, Larisa & Schweppenheiser, Bob. Looking for Love. (p. 1347)
Saito, Diogo, illus. see Lucasfilm Press.
Saito, Diogo, illus. see Peterson, Scott & Ferrari, Alessandro.
Saito, Diogo, illus. see Peterson, Scott.
Saito, Diogo, illus. see Siglain, Michael.
Saito, Ioe, illus. see McCarthy, Ralph F.
Saito, Masamitsu, illus. see Kaneko, Yuki.
Saito, Masamitsu, illus. see Konagaya, Kiyomi.
Saito, Ryusuke. Jiu Er's Star. (p. 1169)
Saito, Shiuichiro. Loyal Ronins, an Historical Romance, Translated from the Japanese (Classic Reprint) (p. 1363)
Saito, Taeko. Kiss the Frog. (p. 1224)
Saito, Yumiko, tr. see Renz, Ulrich.
Saiz, Charolette a. Apomia. (p. 106)
Saiz, Jesus. Doctor Strange by Mark Waid Vol. 1: Across the Universe. (p. 573)
—Doctor Strange by Mark Waid Vol. 4: The Choice. (p. 573)
Saiz, Jesus, jt. illus. see Pina, Javier.
Saiz, Jesus, et al. Avengers: Standoff. (p. 142)
Sajnani, Rhea. Winkle: Volume 1. (p. 2473)
Sajnani, Surya. Color Me: Who's in the Rain Forest? Sajnani, Surya, illus. (p. 420)
—Friendly Faces in the Forest (2020 Edition) Baby's First Soft Book. Sajnani, Surya, illus. (p. 786)
—Friendly Faces in the Wild (2020 Edition) Baby's First Soft Book. Sajnani, Surya, illus. (p. 786)
—Friendly Faces on the Farm (2020 Edition) Baby's First Soft Book. Sajnani, Surya, illus. (p. 786)
—Good Night You, Good Night Me: A Soft Bedtime Book with Mirrors. Sajnani, Surya, illus. (p. 865)
—Moo, Cluck, Baa! the Farm Animals Are Hungry: A Press & Listen Sound Book. Sajnani, Surya, illus. (p. 1500)
—Pitter Patter Penguin (2020 Edition) Baby's First Soft Book - Crinkly Feet! (p. 1751)
—Tiptoe Tiger (2020 Edition) Baby's First Soft Book - Crinkly Paws! (p. 2250)
—Wee Gallery Friendly Faces: Forest. (p. 2395)
Sakade, Florence. Folktales from Japan: Fables, Myths & Fairy Tales for Children. Hayashi, Yoshio, illus. (p. 757)
—Japanese Children's Favorite Stories. Kurosaki, Yoshisuke, illus. (p. 1159)
—Kintaro's Adventures & Other Japanese Children's Stories. Hayashi, Yoshio, illus. (p. 1223)
—Little One-Inch & Other Japanese Children's Favorite Stories. Kurosaki, Yoshisuke, illus. (p. 1323)
—More Japanese Children's Favorite Stories. Hayashi, Yoshio, illus. (p. 1505)
—Urashima Taro & Other Japanese Children's Favorite Stories. Hayashi, Yoshio, illus. (p. 2339)
Sakai, Komako. Emily's Balloon. (p. 642)
—Snow Day. (p. 2047)
Sakai, Komako, illus. see Aman, Kimiko.
Sakai, Komako, illus. see Kato, Yukiko.
Sakai, Komako, illus. see Nakawaki, Hatsue.
Sakai, Komako, creator. Velveteen Rabbit. (p. 2350)
Sakai, Stan. Adventures of Nilson Groundthumper & Hermy. Wright, Brendan, ed. (p. 26)
—Usagi Yojimbo Saga Volume 3 Ltd. Ed. Sakai, Stan, illus. (p. 2341)
Sakamoto, Miki, illus. see Bullard, Lisa.
Sakamoto, Miki, illus. see Gainer, Cindy.
Sakamoto, Miki, illus. see Metzger, Steve.
Sakamoto, Miki, illus. see Zobel Nolan, Allia.
Sakamoto, Miki, illus. see Zobel-Nolan, Allia.

S

Sakamoto, Naoko & Kamo. How to Draw Almost Everything for Kids. (p. 1039)
Sakamoto-Sims, Serene, illus. see Medina, K.
Sakanakun. Gensundai Suizokukan. Matsuzawa, Yoji, photos by. (p. 816)
Sakany, Lois. Canada: A Primary Source Cultural Guide. (p. 319)
—Cell Regulation: Understanding How Cell Functions, Growth, & Division Are Regulated. (p. 350)
Sakas Shropshire, Karla. Who Ghost There? Random House, illus. (p. 2447)
—Who Ghost There? (the Loud House) Random House, illus. (p. 2447)
Saker -Parsons, Helen. Searching for Cecil. (p. 1971)
Saker, Ronald E., ed. see Fleet, Saker &.
Sakhavarz, Nazy, illus. see Brass, Alice.
Saki. Gabriel-Ernest & Other Tales. Blake, Quentin, illus. (p. 804)
Saki, Saki. Chronicles of Clovis (Classic Reprint) (p. 389)
—Reginald (Classic Reprint) (p. 1861)
—Reginald in Russia: And Other Sketches (Classic Reprint) (p. 1861)
Sakmar-Sullivan, Eva M. Kangaroo's Out of This World Restaurant Sakmar-Sullivan, Eva M., illus. (p. 1202)
—Silly Looking Thing (p. 2018)
—Willie the Taxi Cat (p. 2469)
Sakowski, Nadeen. Adventures of Bailey Wiggins. (p. 21)
Sakprayoonpong, Worachet Boon, illus. see Friedlander, Mark P., Jr.
Saks, Dan. Families Belong. Smart, Brooke, illus. (p. 701)
Saksena, Salini. Anthony Horowitz. (p. 102)
Sakshi, Mangal, illus. see Tucci, Lizelle Marpa.
Saksie, Judy, contrib. by. Seed Song. (p. 1983)
Sakti, Galih, illus. see Grant, Rick S.
Sakurai, Gamon. Ajin, Volume 12: Demi-Human. (p. 38)
Sakurai, Susumu. Exciting Adventure World of Numbers. (p. 676)
Sakurazaka, Hiroshi. All You Need Is Kill 1. (p. 55)
Sakya, Kalden D. Life of the Great Mahasiddha Virupa. (p. 1295)
Sala, Felicita. What's Cooking at 10 Garden Street? Recipes for Kids from Around the World. (p. 2423)
Sala, Felicita, illus. see Fulton, Lynn.
Sala, Felicita, illus. see Giardino, Alexandria.
Sala, Felicita, illus. see Lehrhaupt, Adam.
Sala, Felicita, illus. see Mattiangeli, Susanna.
Sala, Felicita, illus. see Potter, Ellen.
Sala, Felicita, illus. see Renaud, Anne.
Sala, Felicita, illus. see Valdez, Patricia.
Sala, Felicita, jt. auth. see Potter, Ellen.
Sala, George Augustus. After Breakfast, or Pictures Done with a Quill, Vol. 1 of 2 (Classic Reprint) (p. 33)
—After Breakfast, Vol. 2 Of 2: Or Pictures Done with a Quill (Classic Reprint) (p. 33)
—Baddington Peerage, Vol. 1 Of 3: Who Won, & Who Wore It, a Story of the Best & the Worst Society (Classic Reprint) (p. 158)
—Breakfast in Bed: Or Philosophy Between the Sheets (Classic Reprint) (p. 278)
—Breakfast in Bed: Or, Philosophy Between the Sheets. a Series of Indigestible Discourses, Pp. 1-273. (p. 278)
—Breakfast in Bed. (p. 278)
—Captain Dangerous. (p. 325)
—Dutch Pictures: With Some Sketches in the Flemish Manner (Classic Reprint) (p. 611)
—Dutch Pictures: With Some Sketches in the Flemish Manner; & Pictures Done with a Quill (Classic Reprint) (p. 611)
—From Waterloo to the Peninsula, Vol. 1 Of 2: Four Months Hard Labor in Belgium, Holland, Germany, & Spain (Classic Reprint) (p. 794)
—From Waterloo to the Peninsula, Vol. 2 Of 2: Four Months Hard Labour in Belgium, Holland, Germany, & Spain (Classic Reprint) (p. 794)
—Gaslight & Daylight: With Some London Scenes They Shine upon (Classic Reprint) (p. 811)
—Journey Due North: Being Notes of a Residence in Russia (Classic Reprint) (p. 1181)
—Lady Chesterfield's Letters to Her Daughter (Classic Reprint) (p. 1236)
—Looking at Life, or Thoughts & Things (Classic Reprint) (p. 1347)
—Make Your Game; or, the Adventures of the Stout Gentleman. (p. 1387)
—Make Your Game, or the Adventures of the Stout Gentleman, the Slim Gentleman, & the Man with the Iron Chest: A Narrative of the Rhine & Thereabouts (Classic Reprint) (p. 1387)
—Papers Humorous & Pathetic: Being Selections from the Works of George Augustus Sala; Revised & Abridged by the Author for Public Reading (Classic Reprint) (p. 1698)
—Paris Herself Again in 1878-9 (Classic Reprint) (p. 1700)
—Paris Herself Again, Vol. 2 Of 2: In 1878-9 (Classic Reprint) (p. 1700)
—Quite Alone, Vol. 1 of 3 (Classic Reprint) (p. 1828)
—Quite Alone, Vol. 2 of 3 (Classic Reprint) (p. 1828)
—Quite Alone, Vol. 3 of 3 (Classic Reprint) (p. 1828)
—Sala's Journal, Vol. 1: A Weekly Magazine for All; from April 30 to December 31, 1892 (Classic Reprint) (p. 1924)
—Seven Sons of Mammon: A Story (Classic Reprint) (p. 1994)
—Seven Sons of Mammon, Vol. 1 Of 3: A Story (Classic Reprint) (p. 1994)
—Strange Adventures of Captain Dangerous: Who Was a Soldier, a Pirate, a Merchant, a Spy, a Slave among the Moors, a Bashaw in the Service of the Great Turk, & Died at Last in His Own House in Hanover Square; a Narrative in Plain English. (p. 2137)
—Strange Adventures of Captain Dangerous. (p. 2137)
—Strange Adventures of Captain Dangerous, Vol. 1 Of 3: Who Was a Soldier, a Sailor, a Merchant, a Spy, a Slave among the Moors, a Bashaw in the Service of the Grand Turk, & Died at Last in His Own House in Hanover Square; a Narrative in Old-Fashioned. (p. 2137)
—Strange Adventures of Captain Dangerous, Vol. 2 Of 3: Who Was a Soldier, a Sailor, a Merchant, a Spy, a Slave among the Moors, a Bashaw in the Service of the Grand Turk, & Died at Last in HS Own House in Hanover Square; a Narrative in Old-Fashioned. (p. 2137)
—Temple Bar, Vol. 43: A London Magazine for Town & Country Readers; December, 1874 to April, 1875 (Classic Reprint) (p. 2203)
—Temple Bar, Vol. 85: With Which Is Incorporated Bentley's Miscellany, a London Magazine, for Town & Country Readers; January to April 1889 (Classic Reprint) (p. 2203)
—Temple Bar, Vol. 95: May to August 1892 (Classic Reprint) (p. 2203)
—Temple Bar, Vol. 99: September to December 1893 (Classic Reprint) (p. 2203)
—Twice Round the Clock, or the Hours of the Day & Night in London (Classic Reprint) (p. 2304)
—Two Prima Donnas (Classic Reprint) (p. 2309)
—Under the Sun: Essays Mainly Written in Hot Countries (Classic Reprint) (p. 2323)
—Under the Sun. (p. 2323)
—William Hogarth: Painter, Engraver, & Philosopher; Essays on the Man, the Work, & the Time (Classic Reprint) (p. 2468)
Sala, Laurenne. You Made Me a Dad. Malbrough, Mike, illus. (p. 2527)
—You Made Me a Mother. Glasser, Robin Preiss, illus. (p. 2527)
Sala, Richard. Hidden. (p. 965)
Sala, Sharon. Lunatic Detective. (p. 1368)
—Lunatic Revenge. (p. 1368)
—Lunatic Times Two. (p. 1368)
—My Lunatic Life. (p. 1555)
Salaam, Yusef, jt. auth. see Zoboi, Ibi.
Salaberria, Leire, illus. see Barrie, J. M.
Salaberria, Leire, illus. see Kaiser, Lisbeth.
Salaberria, Leire, illus. see Ngozi Adichie, Chimamanda.
Salaberria, Leire, jt. auth. see Kaiser, Lisbeth.
Salad, Grandma. How the Mockingbird Found His Tune. McNamara-Gordon, Sallie, illus. (p. 1036)
Salaka, Michael. Animals in Hiding. (p. 94)
—Islands & Archipelagos. (p. 1140)
—Why Do We Have to Listen to People We Disagree With? (p. 2457)
Salam, Palwasha Bazger. Stranger's Farewell: English-Pashto Edition. Lafrance, Marie, illus. (p. 2139)
—Wisdom of Ahmad Shah: English-Pashto Edition. Delmar, Natasha, illus. (p. 2477)
Salaman, Rosy, illus. see Ross, Tracey.
Salaman, Rosy, illus. see Tozer, Sarah.
Salamoff, Paul J. Presidential Pets: The History of the Pets in the White House. Davis, Darren G., ed. (p. 1789)
Salamone, Jenna, illus. see Gagliardi, Alyssa.
Salane, Jeffrey. Haunting of Hounds Hollow. (p. 939)
—Justice. (p. 1194)
—Lawless. (p. 1253)
—Lego Movie. Kiernan, Kenny, illus. (p. 1265)
—Mayhem. (p. 1430)
Salanitro, Robert, illus. see Benhamu, Margaret.
Salanitro, Robert, illus. see Rosenberg, Amye.
Salapek, Timothy. - the Legend of Boyne Mountain - (p. 2214)
Salariya, Daivid, jt. auth. see Macdonald, Fiona.
Salariya, David. Ancient Greek Myths. (p. 81)
Salariya, David, jt. auth. see Cook, Peter.
Salariya, David, jt. auth. see Ford, Michael.
Salariya, David, jt. auth. see Graham, Ian.
Salariya, David, jt. auth. see Hepplewhite, Peter.
Salariya, David, jt. auth. see Macdonald, Fiona.
Salariya, David, jt. auth. see Matthews, Rupert.
Salariya, David, jt. auth. see Morley, Jacqueline.
Salariya, David, jt. auth. see Pipe, Jim.
Salariya, David, creator. Scary Creatures (p. 1942)
Salariya, ed. Book of Ancient Egyptian Mummies - Groan! Antram, David, illus. (p. 258)
—Book of Pirates - Arrr! Antram, David, illus. (p. 259)
—Dinosaurs. Antram, David, illus. (p. 550)
—Unsinkable Titanic - Look Out! Antram, David, illus. (p. 2335)
Salas, Laura. Leaf Can Be ... (Millbrook Picture Books) (p. 1254)
Salas, Laura Purdie. And Then There Were Eight: Poems about Space. (p. 83)
—Are You Living? A Song about Living & Nonliving Things Garofoli, Viviana, illus. (p. 113)
—BookSpeak! Poems About Books. Bisaillon, Josée, illus. (p. 261)
—C Is for Cake! A Birthday Alphabet (p. 306)
—Catch Your Breath: Writing Poignant Poetry. (p. 344)
—Clover Kitty Goes to Kittygarten. Nakata, Hiroe, illus. (p. 408)
—Colors of Fall. (p. 426)
—Colors of Insects. (p. 426)
—Colors of Sports (p. 426)
—Colors of the Ocean (p. 426)
—Colors of the Ocean. (p. 426)
—Colors of Weather. (p. 426)
—Eight Great Planets! A Song about the Planets De Giorgi, Sergio, illus. (p. 629)
—Home on the Earth: A Song about Earth's Layers Garofoli, Viviana, illus. (p. 996)
—How to Make a Rainbow: A Crayola Color Story. (p. 1043)
—How to Make a Rainbow: A Crayola (r) Color Story. (p. 1043)
—If You Were the Moon. Kim, Jaime, illus. (p. 1093)
—In the Middle of the Night: Poems from a Wide-Awake House. Matteson, Angela, illus. (p. 1109)
—J Is for Jingle Bells: A Christmas Alphabet (p. 1150)
—Leaf Can Be ... Dabija, Violeta, illus. (p. 1254)
—Meet My Family! Animal Babies & Their Families. Coleman, Stephanie Fizer, illus. (p. 1438)
—Picture Yourself Writing Poetry: Using Photos to Inspire Writing. (p. 1741)
—Rock Can Be ... Dabija, Violeta, illus. (p. 1894)
—S Is for Score! A Sports Alphabet (p. 1919)
—Secrets of the Loon. Dayton, Charles, photos by. (p. 1981)
—Snack, Snooze, Skedaddle: How Animals Get Ready for Winter. Gévry, Claudine, illus. (p. 2044)
—Snowman - Cold = Puddle: Spring Equations. Archer, Micha, illus. (p. 2049)
—Water Can Be ... Dabija, Violeta, illus. (p. 2384)
—Wild World of Animal. (p. 2465)
—Y Is for Yak: A Zoo Alphabet (p. 2516)
Salas, Laura Purdie & Nichols, Cheyenne. Sad Is... (p. 1920)
—Scared Is... (p. 1941)
—Scared Is ... (p. 1941)
Salas, Laura Purdie & Weakland, Mark. Bubbles Float, Bubbles Pop (p. 289)
Salas, Nadia, illus. see Frazier, Duewa.
Salas, Robert. Inside the UFO Archives. (p. 1124)
Salati, Doug, illus. see dePaola, Tomie.
Salati, Giorgio. Brina the Cat #1: If the Gang of the Feline Sun. Cornia, Christian, illus. (p. 282)
—Disney: Where's Donald? Bagnoli, Gabriele & Bovo, Beatrice, illus. (p. 558)
—Disney Hamlet, Starring Donald Duck (Graphic Novel) De Lorenzi, Paolo, illus. (p. 560)
Salati, Giorgio & Cornia, Christian. Brina the Cat #2: City Cat. (p. 282)
Salatin, Joel & Salatin, Rachel. Patrick's Great Grass Adventure with Greg the Grass Farmer. (p. 1705)
Salaysay, Cynthia. Private Lessons. (p. 1801)
Salazar, Aida. Moon Within. (p. 1502)
Salazar, Amanda S. R., illus. see Ondersma, Erin.
Salazar, Carrie, illus. see Harris-Wyrick, Wayne.
Salazar, Carrie, illus. see Smith, Emma Bland.
Salazar, Carrie, illus. see Zabel, Vivian.
Salazar, Edgar. Uncanny X-Men: Superior Vol. 4: IvX. (p. 2317)
Salazar, Edgar, illus. see Houser, Jody.
Salazar, Edgar & Sandoval, Gerardo. Venom & X-Men: Poison-X. (p. 2350)
Salazar, Gloria. Ballena Roja Que Se Trago una Danta Blanca. (p. 161)
Salazar, J. C. Of Dreams & Thorns. (p. 1639)
Salazar, Julia. Spanish Words on the Road (p. 2074)
Salazar, Lisa Marie. My New Red Boots. (p. 1558)
Salazar, Madelyn & Welsh, Faith. If the Slipper Fits. (p. 1092)
Salazar Nelson, Stephany. Lovely Amelia Travels. Baron, Michelle, illus. (p. 1362)
Salazar, Ramon. Planeta Magico. (p. 1755)
Salazar, Sam. Jordin Sparks. (p. 1178)
—One Direction. (p. 1659)
Salazar, Sam & Kennon, Michou. Jordin Sparks. (p. 1178)
Salazar, Sydney. Being a Bullfrog (p. 193)
—Spanish Words at School (p. 2074)
Salazar, Vivian, illus. see Bass, William E.
Salazar, Vivian Rose, illus. see Bass, William E.
Salcedo Barrero, Juliana, illus. see Castilla, Julia Mercedes.
Salcedo, Erica, illus. see Clarkson, Steph.
Salcedo, Erica, illus. see Foote, Kristen.
Salcedo, Erica, illus. see James, Greg & Smith, Chris.
Salcedo, Erica, illus. see Ondaatje, Griffin.
Salcedo, Erica, illus. see Sanchez Vegara, Maria Isabel.
Salcedo, Erica, illus. see Wilhelm, Hans.
Saldana, Carmen, illus. see Caston, Jane.
Saldana, Carmen, illus. see Hegarty, Patricia.
Saldaña, Carmen, illus. see Kregenow, Julia.
Saldaña, Carmen, illus. see Loney, Andrea J.
Saldana, Carmen, illus. see McCleary, Stacey.
Saldana, Carmen, illus. see Schaub, Michelle.
Saldaña, Jr. Good Long Way. (p. 863)
Saldana, Michael a. Real Stories the Life & Adventures of Wally by Golly! The Goodest, Smartest, & Prettiest Doggy in the Whole World! He Is! (p. 1850)
Saldana, Rene. Case of Pen Gone Missing/El Caso de la Pluma Perdida. Villarroel, Carolina, tr. from ENG. (p. 336)
—Dale, Dale, Dale / Hit It, Hit It, Hit It: Una Fiesta de Numeros / a Fiesta of Numbers. Flores, Carolyn Dee, illus. (p. 498)
Saldaña, René. Dancing with the Devil & Other Tales from Beyond / Bailando con el Diablo y Otros Cuentos del Más Allá. Baeza Ventura, Gabriela, tr. from ENG. (p. 500)
—Lemon Tree Caper: A Mickey Rangel Mystery / la Intriga del limonero: Colección Mickey Rangel, detective Privado. Rosales-Yeomans, Natalia, tr. from ENG. (p. 1266)
—Mystery of the Mischievous Marker / el Misterio Del Malvado Marcador: A Mickey Rangel Mystery / Colección Mickey Rangel, Detective Privado. Villarroel, Carolina, tr. from ENG. (p. 1570)
Saldana, Rene, Jr. Mystery Bigger Than Big / un Misterio Mas Grande Que Grandisimo: A Mickey Rangel Mystery / Colección Mickey Rangel, Detective Privado. (p. 1568)
Saldana, Zoe. Filming Stop-Motion Animation. (p. 726)
Salde, Caroline. 65+ Tips on What to Do As Retired: - Tips for Young Retirees: Inspiration for a Happy Free Life. (p. 2556)
Saldin, Erin. Dead Enders. (p. 517)
—Girls of No Return. (p. 839)
Saldivar, Jose A. Adventures of Oskar: Oskar's New School. Nilsson, Janet Busbey, ed. (p. 26)
Sale, Antoine De La. Quinze Joyes de Mariage: Texte de l'Édition Princeps du Xve Siècle (Classic Reprint) (p. 1828)
—Quinze Joyes de Mariage: Texte de l'Edition Princeps de Vxe Siecle; Premiere Reimpression (Classic Reprint) (p. 1828)
—Quinze Joyes de Mariage (Classic Reprint) (p. 1828)
Sale, Graham, illus. see Boritzer, Etan.
Sale, Tim. MARVEL KNIGHTS: Jeph Loeb & Tim Sale: Yellow, Blue, Gray & White Omnibus. (p. 1412)
Sale, Tim, illus. see Loeb, Jeph.
Sale, Tim, jt. auth. see Loeb, Jeph.
Salem, Eman, illus. see Munshey, Sana.
Salem, I., jt. auth. see Wigden, Susan.
Salem, Iosi, illus. see Fridman, Sashi.
Salem, Maru, illus. see Zapple, Elias.
Salem Press Editors. All Quiet on the Western Front. Murdoch, Brian, ed. (p. 53)
—Canterbury Tales, by Geoffrey Chaucer. Lynch, Jack, ed. (p. 323)
—Red Badge of Courage, by Stephen Crane. Link, Eric Carl, ed. (p. 1856)
—Slaughterhouse-Five. Mustazza, Leonard, ed. (p. 2035)
—Sun Also Rises. Newlin, Keith, ed. (p. 2151)
Salem Press Editors, ed. see Johnson, Rafer.
Salemi, Lucia, illus. see Meyer, Jane.
Salerni, Dianne K. Caged Graves. (p. 308)
—Eighth Day. McClellan, David, illus. (p. 629)
—Eleanor, Alice, & the Roosevelt Ghosts. (p. 630)
—Inquisitor's Mark. (p. 1121)
—Morrigan's Curse. (p. 1506)
—We Hear the Dead. (p. 2391)
Salerno, Anthony Vincent. Little Al, the Angel. Gillen, Rosemarie, illus. (p. 1310)
Salerno, Joe, illus. see Winton, Alais.
Salerno, Steven. Wild Child. (p. 2463)
Salerno, Steven, illus. see Biebow, Natascha.
Salerno, Steven, illus. see Brown, Margaret Wise.
Salerno, Steven, illus. see Elya, Susan Middleton.
Salerno, Steven, illus. see Fern, Tracey.
Salerno, Steven, illus. see Fliess, Sue.
Salerno, Steven, illus. see Franco, Betsy.
Salerno, Steven, illus. see Freeman, Martha.
Salerno, Steven, illus. see Kraft, Betsy Harvey.
Salerno, Steven, illus. see Orgill, Roxane.
Salerno, Steven, illus. see Prince, April Jones.
Salerno, Steven, illus. see Sanders, Rob.
Salerno, Steven, illus. see Stone, Tanya Lee.
Salerno, Steven, illus. see Vernick, Audrey.
Salerno, Steven, jt. auth. see Franco, Betsy.
Salerno, Steven, tr. see Orgill, Roxane.
Sales, Amanda. Mike Pence: Vice President of the United States. (p. 1464)
Sales, Leila. Esta Noche Las Calles Son Nuestras. (p. 664)
—If You Don't Have Anything Nice to Say. (p. 1092)
—Last Kids on Earth Mad Libs. (p. 1248)
—Mostly Good Girls. (p. 1509)
—Once Was a Time: An Alliteration Adventure. (p. 1658)
—Past Perfect. (p. 1703)
—This Song Will Save Your Life: A Novel. (p. 2227)
—Tonight the Streets Are Ours: A Novel. (p. 2260)
Saley, Met L. Realm of the Retailer: The Retail Lumber Trade, Its Difficulties & Successes, Its Humor & Philosophy, Its Theory & Practice, with Practical Yard Ideas (Classic Reprint) (p. 1851)
Salg, Bert, illus. see Edwards, Leo.
Salg, Bert, illus. see Heyliger, William.
Salgado. Nuevas Canciones Infantiles. (p. 1629)
Salgado, Adela, tr. see Blankenship, J. B.
Salgado, Diego C. Men Who Wrecked. (p. 1446)
Salgado, Jimbo, illus. see Roberts, James, et al.
Salgado, Laura J. Mission: Achor Valley. (p. 1481)
Salgado, Vanessa E. Day at the National Museum of Dance. (p. 512)
Salgari, Emilio. Captain Tempesta. Lorenzutti, Nico, tr. (p. 326)
—Sandokán. (p. 1931)
—Tesoro de Los Incas. (p. 2208)
Salgari, Emilio, jt. auth. see Salgari, Emilio.
Salicrup, Jim & Gladir, George. Three Stooges Graphic Novels #1: Bed Bugged (p. 2235)
Salicrup, Jim, et al. My Name Is Orange - Secret Agent Orange! Parker, Rick, illus. (p. 1557)
Salim, Adisa. Adventures of Loc & Platt. (p. 25)
Salim, Adunis, illus. see Ross, Tony.
Salinas, Alex, illus. see Martin, Bob.
Salinas, Erika, illus. see Whitman, David L.
Salinas, Eva. Inventaron los Latinoamericanos: Innovaciones Asombrosas. (p. 1130)
—Inventarons los Latinamericanos: Innovaciones Asombrosas. (p. 1130)
—Latin Americans Thought of It: Amazing Innovations. (p. 1250)
Salinas, Jerson. Las Cronicas Del Sortilegio. (p. 1245)
Salinas, Veronica. Voyage Eirheim, Jeanne, tr. (p. 2368)
Salinas-Diaz, Vanesa. Chico Bear's Big Texas Adventure. (p. 369)
Salinger, J. D. Catcher in the Rye. (p. 344)
Salino, Carolina. Why I Am Not a Princess. Salino, Carolina, illus. (p. 2458)
Salisbury, Graham. Banjo. (p. 164)
—Calvin Coconut: Man Trip. Rogers, Jacqueline, illus. (p. 312)
—Calvin Coconut: The Zippy Fix. Rogers, Jacqueline, illus. (p. 312)
—Calvin Coconut #9: Extra Famous. Rogers, Jacqueline, illus. (p. 312)
—Calvin Coconut: Dog Heaven. Rogers, Jacqueline, illus. (p. 312)
—Calvin Coconut: Man Trip. Rogers, Jacqueline, illus. (p. 312)
—Calvin Coconut: Rocket Ride. Rogers, Jacqueline, illus. (p. 312)
—Calvin Coconut: the Zippy Fix. (p. 312)
—Calvin Coconut: Zoo Breath. Rogers, Jacqueline, illus. (p. 312)
—Dog Heaven. Rogers, Jacqueline, illus. (p. 576)
—Hero of Hawaii. Rogers, Jacqueline, illus. (p. 961)
—Hunt for the Bamboo Rat. (p. 1052)
—Kung Fooey. Rogers, Jacqueline, illus. (p. 1233)
—Night of the Howling Dogs. (p. 1607)
—Trouble Magnet. Rogers, Jacqueline, illus. (p. 2291)
—Under the Blood-Red Sun. (p. 2321)
Salisbury, Jesse. Glossary of Words: Used in South-East Worcestershire (Classic Reprint) (p. 845)
—Glossary of Words & Phrases Used in S. E. Worcestershire: Together with Some of the Sayings, Customs, Superstitions, Charms, &C. , Common in That District (Classic Reprint) (p. 845)
—Glossary of Words & Phrases Used in S. E. Worcestershire, Together with Some of the Sayings, Customs, Superstitions, Charms, &C. Common in That District. (p. 845)
—Words & Phrases Used in S. E. Worcestershire: Together with Some of the Sayings, Customs, Superstitions, Charms, &C. Common in That District (Classic Reprint) (p. 2494)
Salisbury, Linda. Earthquake Surprise: A Bailey Fish Adventure. Tornatore, Carol, illus. (p. 617)
—Sword & the Broom: The Exceptional Career & Accomplishments of John Mercer Langston. (p. 2171)
Salisbury, Linda G. Mudd Saves the Earth: Booger Glue, Cow Diapers & Other Good Ideas. (p. 1524)

—Trouble in Contrary Woods: A Bailey Fish Adventure. Tomatore, Carol, illus. (p. 2291)
Salisbury, Mark. Walt Disney's Alice in Wonderland: an Illustrated Journey Through Time. (p. 2374)
Salisbury, Melinda. Scarecrow Queen. (p. 1941)
—Sin Eater's Daughter. (p. 2023)
Salisbury, Rollin D., jt. auth. see Chamberlin, Thomas Chrowder.
Saliwa-Mogale, Ncebakazi Faith, tr. see Umar, Mohammed.
Salkey, Andrew. Drought. (p. 605)
—Earthquake. (p. 617)
—Hurricane (p. 1054)
—Riot (p. 1884)
Salle, Ludovic, illus. see George, Sam.
Sallengre, Albert Henrik De. Histoire de Pierre de Montmaur, Professeur Royal en Langue Grecque Dans l'Université de Paris, Vol. 1 (Classic Reprint) (p. 975)
—Histoire de Pierre de Montmaur, Vol. 2: Professeur Royal en Langue Grecque Dans l'Universite de Paris (Classic Reprint) (p. 975)
Salley, Coleen. Epossumondas Plays Possum. Stevens, Janet, illus. (p. 659)
Sallis, Melanie. Chewing Gum Cindy. (p. 367)
Sallows, Lee C. F. Geometric Magic Squares: A Challenging New Twist Using Colored Shapes Instead of Numbers. (p. 818)
Salm, Arthur. Anyway: A Story about Me with 138 Footnotes, 27 Exaggerations, & 1 Plate of Spaghetti. (p. 104)
—Anyway* *a Story about Me with 138 Footnotes, 27 Exaggerations, & 1 Plate of Spaghetti. (p. 104)
Salm, Rodney V., jt. auth. see Person, Stephen.
Salmansohn, Pete & Kress, Stephen W. Giving Back to the Earth: Teacher's Guide to Project Puffin & Other Seabird Studies. Gagliardo, Lucy, illus. (p. 840)
Salmaso, Darryl. Twitch & Fidget Go to Ottawa. (p. 2306)
—Twitch & Fidget Go to Town. (p. 2306)
Salmeron, Carmelo, jt. auth. see Narváez, Concha López.
Salmeron, Carmelo & Lopez Narvaez, Concha. Tinka. (p. 2248)
Salmerón Carmelo, et al. Leyenda del Viajero Que No Podía Detenerse. (p. 1282)
Salmieri, Daniel. Bear & Wolf. (p. 179)
—Osa y Lobo. (p. 1673)
Salmieri, Daniel, illus. see Pennypacker, Sara.
Salmieri, Daniel, illus. see Rubin, Adam.
Salmieri, Daniel, jt. auth. see Rubin, Adam.
Salmon, David. Longmans' Junior School Composition (Classic Reprint) (p. 1344)
Salmon, Jeremy Alan. Round & Round. (p. 1907)
Salmon, Mica G., ed. see Crow Salmon, Caroline.
Salmon, Mica G., illus. see Crow Salmon, Caroline.
Salmon, Nina. Nola & the Sprickle. (p. 1618)
Salmon, Sheryl. Adventures of Kaptain Kristian. (p. 24)
Salmon, Steven. Very New Day. (p. 2353)
Salmon, William. Aristotle's Master-Piece, or the Secrets of Nature Displayed in the Generation of Man: Complete in Three Parts; to Which Is Added, a Treasure of Health, or the Family Physician (Classic Reprint) (p. 116)
Salmond, Jared, illus. see Weimer, Brandon.
Salmone, Anthony. Arabic English Dictionary on a New System, Vol. 2 Of 2: English Index (Classic Reprint) (p. 109)
Salmone, Habib Anthony. Arabic English Dictionary on a New System, Vol. 2 Of 2: English Index (Classic Reprint) (p. 109)
Salmons, Tony, et al. Dakota North: Design for Dying. (p. 498)
Salom, Andrée. Flow, Flow, Flow. Salom, Ivette, illus. (p. 752)
Salom, Andree. When the Anger Ogre Visits. Salom, Ivette, illus. (p. 2433)
Salom, Ivette, illus. see Marlowe, Sara.
Salom, Ivette, illus. see Salom, Andree.
Salom, Ivette, illus. see Salom, Andrée.
Salom, Susie. Kyle Finds Her Way. (p. 1234)
Salome, Chloelia. Reborn: A Novelette. (p. 1852)
Salome, Mary. Saints & Festivals: A Cycle of the Year for Young People (Classic Reprint) (p. 1924)
Salome, Mother Mary. Saints & Festivals: A Cycle of the Year for Young People. Pippet, Gabriel, illus. (p. 1924)
Salomo, Xavier, illus. see Marti, Mertixell.
Salomon, Bob & Young, Rick. Beyond the Laces. (p. 212)
Salomon, David. Baby Panda Goes Wild! (p. 152)
—Penguins! (p. 1716)
Salomon, Jill. Be. (p. 176)
Salomon, Peter Adam. All Those Broken Angels. (p. 55)
Salomons, Elizabeth. 1900: Canadian Decades. (p. 2561)
Salon, David. Three Sisters. (p. 2235)
Salone, Sara, tr. see Popescu, Sinziana.
Salonen, Roxane Beauclair. Twelve Days of Christmas in North Dakota. Golden, Jess, illus. (p. 2303)
—Twelve Days of Christmas in North Dakota. Golden, Jessica, illus. (p. 2303)
Salote, Ana. Oy Yew. (p. 1690)
Salqueiro, Adolfo. Carlos Gonzalez. (p. 331)
Salsbury, Rebecca. Liberty: The Giant Killer (Classic Reprint) (p. 1283)
Salsi, Lynn. Jack & the Giants. Young, James, illus. (p. 1151)
Salt, Henry Stephens, jt. auth. see Thoreau, Henry.
Salt, Rachel. Plastic Problem. (p. 1758)
Salt, Zelda. 20 Fun Facts about the Respiratory System. (p. 2553)
—Be a Geneticist. (p. 176)
—Be a Marine Biologist. (p. 176)
—Be a Microbiologist. (p. 176)
—Be an Aerospace Engineer. (p. 176)
Salten, Felix. Bambi: A Life in the Woods. Chambers, Whittaker, tr. (p. 163)
—Bambi: A Life in the Woods. Cowdrey, Richard, illus. (p. 163)
—Bambi. (p. 163)
—Bambi's Children: The Story of a Forest Family. Tilley, R. Sudgen, ed. (p. 163)
—Djibi. Levin, Raya, tr. (p. 567)
—Forest World. Greenburger, Sanford Jerome & Milton, Paul R., trs. (p. 766)
—Hound of Florence. Paterson, Huntley, tr. (p. 1021)
—Perri. Mussey, Barrows, tr. (p. 1724)
—Renni the Rescuer. Kaufman, Kenneth C., tr. (p. 1866)
Salter. Holt Mcdougal Eastern World Indiana: Student Edition Grades 6-8 2010. (p. 991)
—Holt Mcdougal Eastern World Indiana: Student One-Stop CD-ROM Grades 6-8 2010. (p. 991)
—Holt Mcdougal Western World Indiana: Student One-Stop CD-ROM Grades 6-8 2010. (p. 994)
—Holt Mcdougal World Regions: Student One-Stop (Set of 25) Grades 6-8 Introduction to Geography 2009. (p. 994)
—Holt Mcdougal World Regions: Interactive Online Edition with Student One-Stop 6 Year Grades 6-8 Intro to Geography 2009. (p. 994)
Salter, Amy Jo, ed. see Larocque, Donna-Lee.
Salter, Charlotte. Bone Snatcher. (p. 255)
—Where the Woods End. (p. 2440)
Salter, Christopher L. & Whiteford, Gary T. China. (p. 377)
Salter, Edward. Boy, the Pebble & the Dolphins. (p. 270)
Salter, Edward, illus. see Salter, Sean.
Salter, John William 1820-1869, jt. auth. see Huxley, Thomas Henry.
Salter, Kay. Fourteenth Summer: So begins the search for a suitable Bride. Noe, Amy, ed. (p. 773)
—Thirteenth Summer: More fun & adventure on the Carolina Coast. Noe, Amy, ed. (p. 2223)
—Twelfth Summer: Coming of age in a time of War. Noe, Amy, ed. (p. 2302)
Salter, Mary J. Lost Receipt: Or Frustrated Designs (Classic Reprint) (p. 1355)
Salter, Michelle Lewis. Kitty Who Found His Meeooww. Stone, Jonny, illus. (p. 1226)
Salter, Olive Mary. Martha & Mary (Classic Reprint) (p. 1410)
Salter, Peter King. Whitepatch a Romance for Quiet People, Vol. 3 of 3 (Classic Reprint) (p. 2445)
Salter, Safaya, illus. see Kipling, Rudyard.
Salter, Sean. Boy & the Pebble. Salter, Edward, illus. (p. 268)
Salter, Sydney. My Big Nose & Other Natural Disasters. (p. 1533)
—Swoon at Your Own Risk. (p. 2171)
Salter, Wanda, jt. auth. see Robertson, Carolyn.
Salters, S. a. I Wanna Go to Heaven Too. (p. 1084)
Salthouse, Betty. Animal Adventures at Rainbow Cottage. Frankland, Martha, illus. (p. 87)
—Cuckoo Call. (p. 482)
—Fossil Hunters. (p. 770)
—Parrot Talk. (p. 1701)
Salti, Kim. Riley's Imagination Super Highway - Adventures in Dreamworld. (p. 1883)
Saltonstall, Frances A. F. Butlers: A Play in Two Acts (Classic Reprint) (p. 303)
Saltoun, Lord. Scraps, Vol. 1 Of 2: Or Scenes, Tales, & Anecdotes from Memories of My Earlier Days (Classic Reprint) (p. 1963)
Saltus, Edgar. Daughters of the Rich (Classic Reprint) (p. 510)
—Enthralled: A Story of International Life Setting Forth the Curious Circumstances Concerning Lord Cloden & Oswald Quain (Classic Reprint) (p. 656)
—Ghost Girl (Classic Reprint) (p. 827)
—Mary Magdalen: A Chronicle (Classic Reprint) (p. 1415)
—Monster (Classic Reprint) (p. 1495)
—Mr. Incoul's Misadventure: A Novel (Classic Reprint) (p. 1518)
—Mr. Incoul's Misadventure. (p. 1518)
—Pace That Kills: A Chronicle (Classic Reprint) (p. 1691)
—Paliser Case (Classic Reprint) (p. 1694)
—Perfume of Eros: A Fifth Avenue Incident (Classic Reprint) (p. 1723)
—Tales Before Supper from Théophile Gautier & Prosper Merimée: Told in English by Myndart Verelst (Classic Reprint) (p. 2181)
—Transient Guest & Other Episodes (Classic Reprint) (p. 2278)
—Truth about Tristrem Varick: A Novel (Classic Reprint) (p. 2296)
—Vanity Square a Story of Fifth Avenue Life (Classic Reprint) (p. 2347)
Saltus, Francis. Flasks & Flagons. (p. 747)
—Witch of en-Dor & Other Poems (Classic Reprint) (p. 2479)
Saltykov, Mikhail Y. Family of Noblemen (Classic Reprint) (p. 702)
Saltz, Gail. Amazing You ! (p. 67)
—Changing You! A Guide to Body Changes & Sexuality. Cravath, Lynne Avril, illus. (p. 356)
Saltzberg, Barney. Abraza Este Libro (Hug This Book!) (Spanish Edition) (p. 8)
—Andrew Drew & Drew. (p. 83)
—Beautiful Oops! (p. 184)
—Chengdu Can Do. Saltzberg, Barney, illus. (p. 365)
—Chengdu Could Not Would Not Fall Asleep. Saltzberg, Barney, illus. (p. 365)
—Cornelius P. Mud, Are You Ready for Baby? Saltzberg, Barney, illus. (p. 454)
—Crazy Hair Day (p. 469)
—Crazy Hair Day. Saltzberg, Barney, illus. (p. 469)
—Dog & Rabbit: A Story in Three Parts. Saltzberg, Barney, illus. (p. 575)
—Enough Is Enough! Saltzberg, Barney, illus. (p. 655)
—Hug This Book! (p. 1048)
—Hug This Book! Benaglia, Fred, illus. (p. 1048)
—Inside This Book: (are Three Books). (p. 1124)
—My Book of Beautiful Oops! A Scribble It, Smear It, Fold It, Tear It Journal for Young Artists. (p. 1534)
—One of These Is Not Like the Others. (p. 1661)
—Redbird: Colors, Colors, Everywhere! (p. 1859)
—Star of the Week. Saltzberg, Barney, illus. (p. 2102)
—Tea with Grandpa. Saltzberg, Barney, illus. (p. 2194)
—Twinkle, Twinkle, ABC: A Mixed-Up, Mashed-up Melody. Benaglia, Fred, illus. (p. 2305)
—Would You Rather Be a Princess or a Dragon? (p. 2510)
Saltzman, Amy. Still Quiet Place for Teens: Simple Mindfulness Practices to Ease Stress & Difficult Emotions. (p. 2119)
Salute, Dom. Bugricks. (p. 292)
Salva, Edwin. Tatler, Vol. 12: June, 1933 (Classic Reprint) (p. 2192)
Salvador, António, illus. see Carvalho, Sérgio Luís de.
Salvador, Paula Louise. Trygg the Dinosaur. (p. 2297)
Salvaggio, Tony, jt. auth. see Henderson, Jason.
Salvaje, Pablo. Animalkind. (p. 93)
Salvati, Urbano. Anthology of a Childhood Dream. (p. 102)
—Legend of the Wishing Pearl. Evangelista, Galina, illus. (p. 1263)
—Number Jungle. Evangelista, Galina, illus. (p. 1629)
—Terra Porkorum: The Planet of the Pigs. Darby, Hope, illus. (p. 2207)
Salvatore, R. A. Demon Spirit. (p. 528)
—Legacy. (p. 1261)
Salvatore, R. A., et al. Worlds of Dungeons & Dragons (p. 2507)
Salvatorelli, Angelo Michael. Tired Man in a Tired Town. (p. 2251)
Salvatus, Mark, illus. see Olizon-Chikiamco, Norma.
Salvidge, Guy. Yellowcake Summer. (p. 2521)
Salvin, Osbert & Frederick Ducane Godman. Biologia Centrali-Americana: Aves (Volume II) (p. 229)
Salvo, Roberto Di, illus. see West, Alexandra.
Salway, Lance, tr. see Lieshout, Ted van.
Salway, Norma. My Maine School Bus Driver. Salway, Norma, illus. (p. 1555)
Salwey, Kenny. Muskrat for Supper: Exploring the Natural World with the Last River Rat. (p. 1529)
Salyer, Adam Ernest, illus. see Salyer, Jennifer Marie.
Salyer, Hannah. Packs: Strength in Numbers. (p. 1691)
Salyer, Jennifer Marie. My Shadow. Salyer, Adam Ernest, illus. (p. 1560)
Salyer, Martha Young. Oft Told Tales Retold (Classic Reprint) (p. 1641)
Salzano, Tammi. All the Love in the World. Fleming, Lucy, illus. (p. 54)
—I Love You Just the Way You Are. Grey, Ada, illus. (p. 1079)
—Kill Order. (p. 1217)
—One Little Blueberry. Whelan, Kat, illus. (p. 1660)
—One Snowy Day. Wood, Hannah, illus. (p. 1662)
—One Sunny Day. (p. 1662)
—One Sunny Day. Wood, Hannah, illus. (p. 1662)
—One Windy Day. Wood, Hannah, illus. (p. 1663)
—Truck Party. Wood, Hannah, illus. (p. 2292)
Salzano, Tammi, jt. auth. see Dakota, Heather.
Salzano, Tammi, jt. auth. see Schwartz, Heather E.
Salzano, Tammi J. Night Sky. Myers, Lawrence E., illus. (p. 1607)
—Rocks, Minerals, & Gemstones. Jankowski, Daniel, illus. (p. 1896)
Salzano, Tammi J., et al. Animal Friends. (p. 89)
Salzberg, Helen, illus. see Falzon, Adrienne.
Salzler, Laurie. Day Cagney Lost Her Wag. Starner, Lynn, illus. (p. 513)
Salzman, Jeremiah. Day of the Sandwich. Smith, Stephan, illus. (p. 514)
—Mike's Adventure Packs: England. Smith, Stephan, illus. (p. 1464)
Salzmann, Ann. Kids Do Grown Up. (p. 1214)
—Rainbow Rhymes. (p. 1836)
Salzmann, Christian G. Elements of Morality, for the Use of Children: With an Introductory Address to Parents; Translated from the German (Classic Reprint) (p. 633)
Salzmann, Christian Gotthilf. Elements of Morality: For the Use of Young Persons (Classic Reprint) (p. 633)
Salzmann, Mary Elizabeth. Aircraft (p. 37)
—Amazing Inventions (p. 65)
—Astronauts (p. 128)
—Automobile (p. 140)
—Baby Alligators (p. 148)
—Baby Eagles (p. 150)
—Baby Goats (p. 150)
—Baby Gorillas (p. 150)
—Baby Polar Bears (p. 152)
—Baby Tigers (p. 153)
—Baseball by the Numbers (p. 168)
—Basketball by the Numbers (p. 171)
—Bats, Sticks & Rackets (p. 173)
—Benjamin Franklin (p. 200)
—Biggest, Baddest Book of Flight (p. 224)
—Brush Your Teeth! Healthy Dental Habits. (p. 288)
—Camera (p. 314)
—Dentist's Tools (p. 529)
—Doctor's Tools (p. 574)
—Eat Your Vegetables! Healthy Eating Habits. (p. 622)
—Farm Babies. (p. 710)
—Fluttering Butterflies (p. 753)
—Food. (p. 759)
—Football by the Numbers (p. 761)
—Forest Babies. (p. 765)
—It's A! (p. 1143)
—It's F! (p. 1145)
—It's I! (p. 1145)
—It's J! (p. 1145)
—It's P! (p. 1147)
—It's U! (p. 1148)
—It's W! (p. 1148)
—It's Z! (p. 1148)
—Jungle Babies. (p. 1189)
—Know Your Numbers: Toys. (p. 1229)
—Know Your Numbers: Nature. (p. 1229)
—Know Your Numbers: Animals. (p. 1229)
—Michael Faraday (p. 1457)
—Money for Clothes (p. 1492)
—Money for Entertainment (p. 1492)
—Money for Food (p. 1492)
—Money for Hobbies (p. 1492)
—Money for School (p. 1492)
—Money for Toys (p. 1492)
—Ocean Babies. (p. 1635)
—Out of This World (p. 1683)
—Phonograph (p. 1736)
—Polar Babies. (p. 1769)
—Rachel's Home on Bear Mountain: A Story about Connecticut. Doucet, Bob, illus. (p. 1832)
—Run! Jump! Play! Healthy Active Habits. (p. 1914)
—Shoes, Boots & Cleats (p. 2009)
—Sleep All Night! Healthy Sleeping Habits. (p. 2036)
—Super Saint Bernards Doucet, Bob, illus. (p. 2156)
—Take a Bath! (p. 2176)
—Telegraph (p. 2201)
—Telephone (p. 2201)
—Veterinarian's Tools (p. 2354)
—Wear a Helmet! (p. 2393)
—What in the World Is a Clarinet? (p. 2413)
—What in the World Is a Drum? (p. 2413)
—What in the World Is a Flute? (p. 2413)
—What in the World Is a Guitar? (p. 2413)
—What in the World Is an Ounce? CD & Book. (p. 2413)
—Zoo Babies. (p. 2543)
Salzmann, Mary Elizabeth, jt. auth. see ABDO Publishing Company Staff.
Salzscheider. Pandora: A Novel (Classic Reprint) (p. 1696)
Sam, Dan & Sam, Dan. Buenos días, Avril (Good Morning, April - Spanish Edition) ¡Estás en Delhi! (You're in Delhi) (p. 291)
Sam, Kurutsi Dan'azumi. Big Photograph of Sir Ahmadu Bello: And Other Short Stories for Children & Young Adults. (p. 222)
Sam Lam, Chris, illus. see Keoghan, Angela.
Samai, Nadjat. Mako le Petit Machin ! Mais Qui Est-il ? (p. 1390)
Samanci, Özge. Dare to Disappoint: Growing up in Turkey. (p. 505)
Samanich, John G., jt. auth. see Powell, Jillian.
Samaniego, César. Great Book of Explorers: With Augmented Realty. (p. 884)
Samaniego, César, illus. see Johnston, KT.
Samaniego, Félix M. Fábulas de Samaniego. (p. 692)
Samaniego, Felix María. Fabulas en Verso Castellano: Para el USO Del Real Seminario Bascongado (Classic Reprint) (p. 692)
Samant, Parikshit Nagesh, ed. March to Opulence: A Special Assortment of Classics, Biographies, Histories, Speeches, & More, for the Makers of a Bright Tomorrow. (p. 1402)
Samantha Des Jardins. Sticky the Elf. (p. 2119)
Samantha Manon. Mystery of the Sun Sapphire. (p. 1570)
Samantha May Cerney, illus. see Oldenburg, Richard.
Samantha, Weiland. Learning English with Tasha & Benji: Volume Two. Kumar, Ambadi, illus. (p. 1258)
Samargedlis, Michelle, illus. see Peterson, Linda L.
Samaroo, Krishna a. Nowherians. (p. 1628)
Samarow, Gregor. For Sceptre & Crown, Vol. 1 Of 2: A Romance of the Present Time (Classic Reprint) (p. 763)
Samartze, Iris & Verne, Jules. 20,000 Leagues under the Sea, or, Nemo, Nautilus & Other Mysteries of the Deep. (p. 2562)
—Around the World in Eighty Days: Or, A Fortune Made of Experiences. (p. 119)
Samartzi, Iris & Verne, Jules. From the Earth to the Moon: Or A Cannon for Peace. (p. 793)
Samatova-Foley, Elmira, jt. auth. see Foley, Mike.
Sambourne, Linley, illus. see Kingsley, Charles.
Sambrook, Hana, jt. auth. see Fitzgerald, F. Scott.
Sames, Sandra, ed. see Burke, Jacquie.
SAMi. Let's Learn Colors & Shapes. (p. 1274)
SAMi Staff. Look, Baby! (p. 1345)
Samiuddin, Shahrezad, jt. auth. see Sheehan, Sean.
Sammarco, Teresa "T". What If Book. Curley, Carol, illus. (p. 2413)
Sammis, Fred R. Radio & Television Mirror, Vol. 15: January, 1941 (Classic Reprint) (p. 1833)
—Radio & Television Mirror, Vol. 16: July-December, 1941 (Classic Reprint) (p. 1833)
—Radio & Television Mirror, Vol. 32: July, 1949 (Classic Reprint) (p. 1833)
—Radio Mirror, 1936-1937, Vol. 7 (Classic Reprint) (p. 1833)
—Radio Mirror, Vol. 11: November, 1938 (Classic Reprint) (p. 1833)
—Radio Mirror, Vol. 12: May-October 1939 (Classic Reprint) (p. 1833)
—Radio Mirror, Vol. 20: July, 1943 (Classic Reprint) (p. 1833)
—Radio Mirror, Vol. 23: The Magazine of Radio Romances; January 1945 (Classic Reprint) (p. 1833)
—Radio Mirror, Vol. 6: May, 1936 (Classic Reprint) (p. 1833)
—Radio Mirror, Vol. 8: May 1937 (Classic Reprint) (p. 1833)
—Radio Mirror, Vol. 9: November, 1937 (Classic Reprint) (p. 1833)
—Radio Romances, Vol. 24: July-December, 1945 (Classic Reprint) (p. 1833)
—Radio Television Mirror, Vol. 36: July, 1951 (Classic Reprint) (p. 1833)
—Radio-TV Mirror, Vol. 37: January-June, 1952 (Classic Reprint) (p. 1833)
—Radio-TV Mirror, Vol. 38: July, 1952 (Classic Reprint) (p. 1833)
—Radio-TV Mirror, Vol. 41: January, 1954 (Classic Reprint) (p. 1833)
Sammix, Fred R. Radio Mirror, Vol. 28: July-December, 1947 (Classic Reprint) (p. 1833)
Sammon, G. D. Wolf Boy. (p. 2483)
Sammons, Deborah K. Huck the Bull Rider. (p. 1047)
—Tutu Christmas. (p. 2302)
Sammons, Sandra. Henry Flagler, Builder of Florida. (p. 955)
—Marjorie Kinnan Rawlings & the Florida Crackers (p. 1407)
—Marjory Stoneman Douglas & the Florida Everglades (p. 1407)
Sammons, Sandra Wallus. Marjorie Kinnan Rawlings & the Florida Crackers (p. 1407)
—Three Marjories: Marjory Stoneman Douglas, Marjorie Kinnan Rawlings, Marjorie Harris Carr & Their Contributions to Florida. (p. 2234)
—Zora Neale Hurston: Wrapped in Rainbows. (p. 2544)
Sammons, Teresa. Aldon the Sloth. Navas, Tamera, illus. (p. 41)
Samms, Olivia. Sketchy. (p. 2032)
Sammurtok, Nadia. In My Anaana's Amautik. Lishchenko, Lenny, illus. (p. 1106)
—Owl & the Two Rabbits. Cutler, Marcus, illus. (p. 1688)
—Siuluk: The Last Tuniq Nix, Rob, illus. (p. 2028)
—What Can Ataata Fix? (Inuktitut/English) Pedersen, Emma, illus. (p. 2406)

—Cocodrilos Del Nilo. (p. 411)
—Guinea (Spanish) (p. 904)
—Lluvia. (p. 1338)
—Madagascar (English) (p. 1373)
Sánchez, Lucía M. & Warren, Heather. ¿Oso Pardo U Oso Negro? (ENIL FSTK ONLY) (p. 1674)
Sánchez, Lucía M. & Washington, Joi. Básquetbol. (p. 171)
Sánchez, Lucía M., et al. Así Cazan Los Osos Polares. (p. 125)
—Comer Se Ha Dicho (ENIL FSTK ONLY) (p. 429)
Sanchez, Mamen. Emmanuel Kelly: Dream Big! Brokenbrow, Jon, tr. (p. 643)
—Emmanuel Kelly: ¡Sueña a lo grande! Celej, Zuzanna, illus. (p. 643)
Sanchez, Maria, illus. see Lazaro, Georgina.
Sanchez, Micah. Natural Resource Depletion. (p. 1580)
Sanchez, Michael. Natural History Collector: Hunt, Discover, Learn! Expert Tips on How to Care for & Display Your Collections & Turn Your Room into a Cabinet of Curiosities. (p. 1579)
Sanchez, Miguel R., illus. see Gogerly, Liz.
Sanchez, Nellie Van de Grift. Life of Mrs. Robert Louis Stevenson (Classic Reprint) (p. 1294)
Sanchez Quesada, Ana Yaheli. Fábulas Del Universo. (p. 692)
Sanchez, Ricardo. Spotlight Soccer Waryanto, Ian, illus. (p. 2091)
Sanchez, Ricardo, jt. auth. see Wolfram, Amy.
Sanchez S., Jimena, illus. see Simonson, Louise.
Sanchez, Samuel. Loco Amor. (p. 1339)
—Loco Amor (en Espa?ol) (p. 1339)
Sanchez, Sara, illus. see Ashman, Linda.
Sanchez, Sara, illus. see Burlison, Tom.
Sanchez, Sara, illus. see de Anda, Diane.
Sanchez, Sara, illus. see Stevenson, Robert Louis.
Sanchez, Sara, illus. see Zur Muehlen, Nersel.
Sanchez, Sergio Garcia, illus. see Spiegelman, Nadja.
Sanchez, Shayla. Rainbow Pals. Pasek, Joanna, illus. (p. 1836)
Sánchez, Sonia. Here I Am. (p. 958)
Sánchez, Sonia, illus. see Adelman, Hallee.
Sánchez, Sonia, illus. see Florian, Douglas.
Sánchez, Sonia, illus. see Kim, Patti.
Sanchez, Sonia, illus. see Lamba, Marie & Lamba, Baldev.
Sánchez, Sonia, illus. see Maier, Brenda.
Sánchez, Sonia, illus. see Mantchev, Lisa.
Sánchez, Sonia, illus. see Medina, Meg.
Sánchez, Sonia, illus. see Tarcov, Susan.
Sánchez, Sonia, tr. see Jordan-Lake, Joy.
Sanchez, Sr., illus. see Falligant, Erin & Higgins, Nadia.
Sánchez, Sr., illus. see Falligant, Erin.
Sanchez, Sr., illus. see Higgins, Nadia, et al.
Sánchez, Sr., illus. see Higgins, Nadia.
Sanchez, Sr., illus. see Hoena, Blake.
Sanchez, Sr., illus. see Stockland, Patricia M.
Sanchez, Story by Jimmy Sanchez Art by. Babycito to the Rescue Babycito Al Rescate. (p. 153)
Sanchez Vegara, Maria Isabel. Amelia Earhart. MARIADIAMANTES, illus. (p. 69)
—Anne Frank. Dorosheva, Sveta, illus. (p. 98)
—Aretha Franklin. Blackwell, Amy, illus. (p. 114)
—Astrid Lindgren. Hunter, Linzie, illus. (p. 128)
—Audrey Hepburn. Arrazola, Amaia, illus. (p. 136)
—Billie Jean King. Sofroniou, Miranda, illus. (p. 226)
—Bob Dylan. Roset, Conrad, illus. (p. 251)
—Bruce Lee. Bustos, Miguel, illus. (p. 287)
—Coco Chanel. Albero, Ana, illus. (p. 411)
—David Attenborough. Noh, Mikyo, illus. (p. 511)
—Dolly Parton. Solak, Daria, illus. (p. 579)
—Ella Fitzgerald. Alca, Bàrbara, illus. (p. 637)
—Elton John. Beer, Sophie, illus. (p. 640)
—Evonne Goolagong Cawley. (p. 675)
—Frida Kahlo Doll & Book Set: For the Littlest Dreamers. Eng, Gee Fan, illus. (p. 785)
—Georgia O'Keeffe. Salcedo, Erica, illus. (p. 821)
—Harriet Tubman: My First Harriet Tubman. Aguado, Pili, illus. (p. 933)
—Jean-Michel Basquiat. (p. 1162)
—Jesse Owens. Jansen, Anna Katharina, illus. (p. 1165)
—Little Me, Big Dreams Journal: Draw, Write & Color This Journal. (p. 1321)
—Little People, Big Dreams: Music Stars: 3 Books from the Best-Selling Series! Ella Fitzgerald - Dolly Parton - Josephine Baker. (p. 1324)
—Maria Montessori: My First Maria Montessori. (p. 1404)
—Mother Teresa: My First Mother Teresa. Rosenberg, Natascha, illus. (p. 1510)
—Mother Teresa. Rosenberg, Natascha, illus. (p. 1510)
—Stephen Hawking. Hunt, Matt, illus. (p. 2115)
—Steve Jobs. Lewis, Aura, illus. (p. 2116)
—Vivienne Westwood: My First Vivienne Westwood. Callaghan, Laura, illus. (p. 2364)
—Wilma Rudolph: My First Wilma Rudolph. Flower, Amelia, illus. (p. 2470)
—Wilma Rudolph. Flower, Amelia, illus. (p. 2470)
Sanchez Vegara, Maria Isabel & Alca, Bàrbara. Ella Fitzgerald: My First Ella Fitzgerald. (p. 637)
Sanchez Vegara, Maria Isabel & Arrayas, Albert. Mahatma Gandhi: My First Mahatma Gandhi. (p. 1382)
Sanchez Vegara, Maria Isabel & Brosmind. Muhammad Ali: My First Muhammad Ali. (p. 1525)
Sanchez Vegara, Maria Isabel & Eng, Gee Fan. Frida Kahlo: My First Frida Kahlo. (p. 785)
Sanchez Vegara, Maria Isabel & Hunter, Linzie. Astrid Lindgren. (p. 128)
Sanchez Vegara, Maria Isabel & Solak, Daria. Dolly Parton: My First Dolly Parton. (p. 579)
Sanchez Vegara, Maria Isabel & Sorlet, Agathe. Josephine Baker: My First Josephine Baker. (p. 1179)
—Josephine Baker. (p. 1179)
Sanchez Vegara, Maria Isabel, concept. Little People, BIG DREAMS Learning Cards: 40 Fascinating Fact Cards. (p. 1324)
—Little People, BIG DREAMS Matching Game: Put Your Brain to the Test with All the Girls of the Little People, BIG DREAMS Series! (p. 1324)
Sanchez, Victoria M. Pilar's Worries. Golden, Jess, illus. (p. 1744)
Sanchez, Yoss, illus. see Kyle, Tracey.
Sanchez-Gomez, Eva, illus. see Fletcher, Graham.
Sánchez-Korrol, Virginia. Feminist & Abolitionist: The Story of Emilia Casanova. (p. 720)
—Surprise for Teresita / una Sorpresa para Teresita. Flores, Carolyn Dee, illus. (p. 2163)
Sancton, Sylvaine. Some Birds ... Sancton, Sylvaine, photos by. (p. 2058)
Sand, Dolores, tr. see Florence, Melanie.
Sand, George. Bagpipers (Classic Reprint) (p. 159)
—Consuelo: A Novel (Classic Reprint) (p. 444)
—Consuelo, Vol. 1 of 2 (Classic Reprint) (p. 444)
—Consuelo, Vol. 2 of 2 (Classic Reprint) (p. 444)
—Consuelo, Vol. 3 (Classic Reprint) (p. 444)
—Consuelo, Vol. 4 Of 4: Translated from the French (Classic Reprint) (p. 444)
—Fadette (Classic Reprint) (p. 694)
—Fanchon the Cricket (Classic Reprint) (p. 705)
—Francois the Waif (Classic Reprint) (p. 776)
—Handsome Lawrence: A Sequel to a Rolling Stone (Classic Reprint) (p. 916)
—Handsome Lawrence. (p. 916)
—Master Mosaic-Workers (Classic Reprint) (p. 1418)
—Mauprat (Classic Reprint) (p. 1426)
—Miller of Angibault (Classic Reprint) (p. 1467)
—Monsieur Sylvestre (Classic Reprint) (p. 1495)
—Nanon (Classic Reprint) (p. 1574)
—Novels, Vol. 10: Les Beaux, and, Messieurs de Bois-Dore, Vol. II (Classic Reprint) (p. 1627)
—Novels, Vol. 3 of 3 (Classic Reprint) (p. 1627)
—Petite Fadette. (p. 1731)
—Piccinino, Vol. 1 (Classic Reprint) (p. 1738)
—Rolling Stone (Classic Reprint) (p. 1898)
—Rolling Stone, and, Handsome Laurence (Classic Reprint) (p. 1898)
—Snow Man: A Novel (Classic Reprint) (p. 2047)
—Snow Man, Vol. 2 (Classic Reprint) (p. 2047)
—Teverino: A Romance (Classic Reprint) (p. 2209)
—Teverino. (p. 2209)
—What Flowers Say: And Other Stories. Erskine Hirko, Holly, tr. (p. 2410)
S�ez, Sof�a, illus. see Freire De Matos, Isabel.
Sandall, Ellie. Copycat Bear! Sandall, Ellie, illus. (p. 452)
—Daisy Plays Hide-and-Seek. Sandall, Ellie, illus. (p. 498)
—Everybunny Count! Sandall, Ellie, illus. (p. 671)
—Everybunny Dance! (p. 671)
—Everybunny Dream! Sandall, Ellie, illus. (p. 671)
Sandalow, Brian. Jose Altuve: Baseball Superstar. (p. 1178)
Sandars, Virginia. Life's Devotion, Vol. 1 of 3 (Classic Reprint) (p. 1296)
Sandberg, Jack. Ruby the Hummingbird. (p. 1911)
Sandberg, Tj. Stranger & Saint Private Eyes: The Case of the Missing Christmas Star. (p. 2138)
Sandberg, Winter. Private Display of Affection. (p. 1801)
—Private Display of Affection [Library Edition]. (p. 1801)
Sandblom, Shelley. Polka Pigs & Other Bedtime Stories. (p. 1771)
Sandburg, Carl. Abe Lincoln Grows Up. Daugherty, James, illus. (p. 5)
—Poetry for Kids: Carl Sandburg. Benzel, Kathryn, ed. (p. 1767)
—Rootabaga Stories. (p. 1903)
—Rootabaga Stories (Classic Reprint) (p. 1903)
—Slabs of the Sunburnt West (Classic Reprint) (p. 2034)
—Smoke & Steel, and, Slabs of the Sunburnt West (Classic Reprint) (p. 2043)
—Wedding Procession of the Rag Doll & the Broom Handle & Who Was in It. Pincus, Harriet, illus. (p. 2395)
Sandeen, Del. Coping with Racial Profiling (p. 451)
—Maya Angelou: Writer & Activist (p. 1429)
—Thomas Jefferson & Sally Hemings. (p. 2228)
Sandel, Peter. Rimrock: The Illumination Stone. (p. 1883)
Sandelin, Karen. Baby Jake's Birthday: Learn 9 Ways to Spell the Long a Sound. Letheby, Lavinia, illus. (p. 151)
—Dance of the Fancy Pants Ants: Learn to Spell the Short a Sound. (p. 500)
—My Best Friend Fred: Learn 6 Ways to Spell the Short e Sound. (p. 1532)
—Poppy's Top Shop: Learn 4 Ways to Spell the Short o Sound. (p. 1776)
—Three Free Wishes: Learn 12 Ways to Spell the Long e Sound. (p. 2233)
Sandelin, Karen & Letheby, Lavinia. Diamonds in the Sky: Learn 11 Ways to Spell the Long I Sound. (p. 538)
—Joanna Goanna: Learn 9 Ways to Spell the Long o Sound. (p. 1170)
Sandelin, Karen & Williams, Amber. Ewes in the Queue: Learn 10 Ways to Spell the Long U Sound. (p. 675)
—Itchy Witch: Learn 5 Ways to Spell the Short I Sound. (p. 1142)
Sandelin, Karen L. Stuck in the Mud: Learn 6 Ways to Spell the Short U Sound. Letheby, Lavinia, illus. (p. 2143)
Sander, Ellie. What I Do When I'm Not with You: Teacher Occupation. (p. 2412)
Sander, Harold. Larry (Classic Reprint) (p. 1244)
Sander, L. C., jt. auth. see Nyerup, Rasmus.
Sander, Sonia. 3, 2, 1, Liftoff! (p. 2546)
—Big-Top Scooby-Doo! Movie Reader. (p. 223)
—Calling All Cars! (p. 312)
—Chill Out, Scooby-Doo! Duendes Del Sur Staff, illus. (p. 377)
—Fire Truck to the Rescue! (p. 733)
—Help Is on the Way! (p. 952)
—LEGO City Reader Collection: LEGO City Emergency. (p. 1264)
—Play Ball, Pikachu! (p. 1759)
—Ready for Takeoff! (p. 1847)
—Scooby-Doo & the Battle of the Snowboarders Alcadia, S. N. C., illus. (p. 1960)
—Scooby-Doo & the Big Catch Alcadia, S. N. C., illus. (p. 1960)
—Scooby-Doo & the Chocolate Phantom (p. 1960)
—Scooby-Doo & the International Express. (p. 1960)
—Scooby-Doo in Food Fight! (p. 1961)
—Scooby-Doo in Keepaway Camp Gross, Scott, illus. (p. 1961)
—Scooby-Doo in Raging River Adventure Alcadia, S. N. C., illus. (p. 1961)
—Scooby-Doo in Shiver Me Timbers (p. 1961)
—Scooby-Doo Steals the Dog Show Alcadia, S. N. C., illus. (p. 1961)
—Smash That Trash! Shannon, David et al, illus. (p. 2041)
—Trainer's Notebook (Pokémon) (p. 2275)
—Werewolf Watch. (p. 2401)
—Witching Hour. (p. 2480)
Sander, Sonia & May, Kyla. Pug Blasts Off. May, Kyla, illus. (p. 1811)
Sanders. Matthew Dale, Farmer (Classic Reprint) (p. 1426)
Sanders, Alexandrea & Sanders, Brittney. Crushin' It. (p. 480)
Sanders, Allan, illus. see Martin, Ruth.
Sanders, Allan, illus. see Wood, A. J.
Sanders, Alvin Howard. Black Swans: And Other Friends Indoors & Out (Classic Reprint) (p. 239)
—In Winter Quarters: From Dumbiedykes to Town & Back Again (Classic Reprint) (p. 1112)
—New Walks in Old Ways (Classic Reprint) (p. 1597)
—Road to Dumbiedykes: Some Rambling Thoughts of One Who Found It (Classic Reprint) (p. 1888)
Sanders, Angela. 100 Days: The Glory Experiment. (p. 2556)
Sanders, Belinda M. Moon Has Phases. (p. 1501)
Sanders, Bernie. Bernie Sanders's Guide to Political Revolution. (p. 204)
Sanders, Brian, illus. see Jenkins, Martin.
Sanders, Brooke. Who Can I Trust? The Barricaded City. (p. 2446)
Sanders, Charles W. Sanders' Union Speaker: Containing a Great Variety of Exercises for Declamation, Both in Prose & Verse (Classic Reprint) (p. 1931)
—School Reader: Containing Progressive Lessons in Reading, Exercises in Articulation & Inflection, Definitions, &C (Classic Reprint) (p. 1946)
—School Reader, Vol. 2: Containing Easy Progressive Lessons in Reading & Spelling (Classic Reprint) (p. 1946)
Sanders, Charles Walton. Sanders' High School Reader: Embracing a Comprehensive Course of Instruction in the Principles of Rhetorical Reading; with a Choice Collection of Exercises in Reading, Both in Prose & Poetry; for the Use of the Higher Classes in Schools of Every Grade. (p. 1930)
—Sanders' Test-Speller: Designed for the Use of the Higher Classes in Schools, & for Teachers' Institutes (Classic Reprint) (p. 1930)
—Sanders' Union Pictorial Primer: Introductory to the Union Readers (Classic Reprint) (p. 1930)
—Sanders' Union Reader, Number One: For Primary Schools & Families (Classic Reprint) (p. 1930)
—Sanders' Union Reader, Vol. 2: For Primary Schools & Families (Classic Reprint) (p. 1930)
—Sanders' Union Speller: Being a Clear & Complete Exhibition of English Orthography & Orthoepy, on the Basis of the New Illustrated Edition of Webster's Great American Dictionary (Classic Reprint) (p. 1931)
Sanders, Dori. Clover. (p. 408)
Sanders, Doug. Idaho. (p. 1089)
—Missouri. (p. 1482)
—Nebraska. (p. 1584)
—North Dakota. (p. 1621)
—Oklahoma. (p. 1643)
—Superstorm Sandy. (p. 2162)
Sanders, Doug & Bjorklund, Ruth. North Dakota. (p. 1621)
Sanders, Doug & Boehme, Gerry. Missouri. (p. 1482)
Sanders, Doug & Gorman, Jacqueline Laks. Idaho. (p. 1089)
Sanders, Doug & Herrington, Lisa M. Utah. (p. 2342)
Sanders, Doug & Horn, Geoffrey M. Oklahoma. (p. 1643)
Sanders, Doug & Schauer, Pete. Nebraska. (p. 1584)
Sanders, Doug, et al. Idaho. (p. 1089)
—Utah. (p. 2342)
Sanders, Ella Frances. Eating the Sun: Small Musings on a Vast Universe. (p. 622)
Sanders, Gaye Lynn. Chameleon Girl Again. (p. 355)
Sanders, Helen Fitzgerald. Little Mother America (Classic Reprint) (p. 1323)
Sanders, Jane. Seashore Stroll (p. 1972)
—Woodland Wonder (p. 2492)
Sanders, Jayneen. ABC of Body Safety & Consent: Teach Children about Body Safety, Consent, Safe/unsafe Touch, Private Parts, Body Boundaries & Respect. Dawson, Courtney, illus. (p. 4)
—Algunos Secretos Nunca Deben Guardarse. Smith, Craig, illus. (p. 44)
—I'm Calm: A Book to Help Kids Overcome Anxiety & Stressful Situations. Zamazing, Cherie, illus. (p. 1098)
—My Body! What I Say Goes! Teach Children about Body Safety, Safe & Unsafe Touch, Private Parts, Consent, Respect, Secrets & Surprises. Hancock, Anna, illus. (p. 1534)
—No Difference Between Us: Teach Children about Gender Equality, Respectful Relationships, Feelings, Choice, Self-Esteem, Empathy, Tolerance. Gulliver, Amanda, illus. (p. 1612)
—No Means No! Teaching Personal Boundaries, Consent; Empowering Children by Respecting Their Choices & Right to Say 'no!' Zamazing, Cherie, illus. (p. 1613)
—Pearl Fairweather Pirate Captain: Teaching Children Gender Equality, Respect, Empowerment, Diversity, Leadership, Recognising Bullying. Danson, Lesley, illus. (p. 1710)
—Resilience: A Book to Encourage Resilience, Persistence & to Help Children Bounce Back from Challenges & Adversity. Cardoso, Sofia, illus. (p. 1869)
—Some Secrets Should Never Be Kept: Protect Children from Unsafe Touch by Teaching Them to Always Speak Up. (p. 2059)
—Talking about Feelings: A Book to Assist Adults in Helping Children Unpack, Understand & Manage Their Feelings & Emotions. Zamazing, Cherie, illus. (p. 2187)
—You, Me & Empathy: Teaching Children about Empathy, Feelings, Kindness, Compassion, Tolerance & Recognising Bullying Behaviours. Cardoso, Sofia, illus. (p. 2527)
Sanders, Jessica. Love Your Body: Your Body Can Do Amazing Things... Rossetti, Carol, illus. (p. 1361)
Sanders, Joe Sutliff, tr. see Shakespeare, William.
Sanders, Jon, jt. auth. see Simpson, Mike.
Sanders, Konnilaree Walker. Legend of Little Bigfoot's Ice Cream Cone. Sanders, Konnilaree Walker, illus. (p. 1262)
—Pete & the Night Time Shadows. Sanders, Konnilaree Walker, illus. (p. 1727)
Sanders, Leslie. Joyous Life. Sanders, Michelle, illus. (p. 1184)
Sanders, Martin B., jt. auth. see Xavier, Imbeus.
Sanders, Michael J. Preteen Challenges: Hurdling to Your Success. (p. 1790)
Sanders, Michelle, illus. see Sanders, Leslie.
Sanders, Moira. Gastro Blast: Make Tasty Treats & Learn Great Science: Comics, Quizzes & Questions Answered! Get Ready to Make Science Delicious! (p. 811)
Sanders, Mt. Monty & Friends African Adventure: The Mission to Save Kaluwa. Saunders, Zoe, illus. (p. 1500)
—Monty & the Land of the Dinodogs. Saunders, Zoe, illus. (p. 1500)
—Monty & the Ocean Rescue: A Plastic Disaster. Saunders, Zoe, illus. (p. 1500)
—Monty & the Slobbernosserus. Sharp, Rebecca, illus. (p. 1500)
Sanders, Nancy I. America's Black Founders: Revolutionary Heroes & Early Leaders with 21 Activities. (p. 75)
—Apostle Paul (p. 106)
—Bible Explorer's Guide: 1,000 Amazing Facts & Photos (p. 213)
—Bible Favorites. Wood, Hannah, illus. (p. 213)
—Frederick Douglass for Kids: His Life & Times, with 21 Activities. (p. 782)
—Guía de Exploradores de la Biblia: 1000 Datos y Fotos Fascinantes (p. 903)
—Jane Austen for Kids: Her Life, Writings, & World, with 21 Activities. (p. 1158)
—Jesus (p. 1165)
—King David (p. 1220)
—Mary (p. 1414)
—Very Oldest Pear Tree. Imamura, Yasmin, illus. (p. 2353)
Sanders, Nancy I., jt. auth. see Hering, Marianne.
Sanders, Nancy I., jt. auth. see Sanders, Jeff.
Sanders, Rick, illus. see Solomita, Cindy.
Sanders, Rob. Ball & Balloon. Yoon, Helen, illus. (p. 161)
—Bling Blaine: Throw Glitter, Not Shade. Rizzo, Letizia, illus. (p. 244)
—Fighting Infantryman: The Story of Albert D. J. Cashier, Transgender Civil War Soldier. Ali, Nabi, illus. (p. 725)
—Mayor Pete: The Story of Pete Buttigieg. Hastings, Levi, illus. (p. 1430)
—Peaceful Fights for Equal Rights. Schorr, Jared Andrew, illus. (p. 1709)
—Pride: the Story of Harvey Milk & the Rainbow Flag. Salerno, Steven, illus. (p. 1792)
—Rodzilla. Santat, Dan, illus. (p. 1897)
—Ruby Rose, Big Bravos. Ohi, Debbie Ridpath, illus. (p. 1911)
—Ruby Rose: off to School She Goes. Ohi, Debbie Ridpath, illus. (p. 1911)
—Stonewall: a Building. an Uprising. a Revolution. Christoph, Jamey, illus. (p. 2122)
Sanders, Russell J. All You Need Is Love. (p. 55)
—Book of Ethan. (p. 258)
—Colors. (p. 426)
—Special Effect. (p. 2076)
—Titanic Summer. (p. 2251)
—You Can't Tell by Looking. (p. 2526)
Sanders, Sammy. Bryce's Bike Race: Add Within 20. (p. 288)
Sanders, Sandy. Ms. Goozenpopa's Crazy Alphabet Show & Tell. (p. 1523)
Sanders, Scott & d'Errico, Camilla. Camilla d'Errico's Burn. d'Errico, Camilla, illus. (p. 314)
Sanders, Scott Russell. Crawdad Creek. (p. 467)
—Floating House. Cogancherry, Helen, illus. (p. 750)
—Meeting Trees. (p. 1441)
Sanders, Shelly. Rachel's Promise (p. 1832)
Sanders, Steven, et al. Uncanny X-Men by Kieron Gillen: the Complete Collection Vol. 1. (p. 2317)
Sanders, Sue. Tell Me the Story about... . the Hebrew Boys. (p. 2202)
Sanders, T. H. My Japanese Year (Classic Reprint) (p. 1550)
Sanders, Ted. Box & the Dragonfly. Bruno, Iacopo, illus. (p. 266)
—Keepers #2: the Harp & the Ravenvine. Bruno, Iacopo, illus. (p. 1208)
—Keepers #3: the Portal & the Veil. Bruno, Iacopo, illus. (p. 1208)
—Keepers #4: the Starlit Loom. Bruno, Iacopo, illus. (p. 1208)
—Keepers: the Box & the Dragonfly. Bruno, Iacopo, illus. (p. 1208)
Sanders, Thomas E. Opening Exercises for Schools (Classic Reprint) (p. 1666)
Sanders, William H. Vocabulary of the Umbundu Language: Comprising Umbundu-English & English-Umbundu; Lists of Three Thousand Words Used by the Inhabitants of Bailundu & Bihe, & Other Countries of West Central Africa (Classic Reprint) (p. 2364)
Sanders-Blackman, Jacqueline. Perceptive Pj & the Making of a Mathlete - Easy Reader Edition. (p. 1721)
—Smart Sarah & the Magic of Science. (p. 2040)
Sanders-Clarke, Alan. Smugglers of Mousehole: Book 1. (p. 2043)
—Smugglers of Mousehole: Book 2: the Cave of Secrets. (p. 2043)
—Smugglers of Mousehole: Book 3: the Race to la Morna. (p. 2043)
—Smugglers of Mousehole: Book 4: the Search for the Crystal Skulls. (p. 2043)

Sandersen, Sarah. Kindergarten Letters, Words & Sentences Writing Workbook: Kindergarten Homeschool Curriculum Scholastic Workbook to Boost Writing, Reading & Phonics (Trace Letters ABC Print Handwriting Book, Pre K & Kids Ages 3-5) (p. 1218)
Sanderson, Ana, ed. see MacGregor, Helen.
Sanderson, Brandon. Alcatraz Contra Los Bibliotecarios / Alcatraz vs. the Evil Librarians. (p. 41)
—Alcatraz Versus the Scrivener's Bones. (p. 41)
—Alcatraz vs. the Evil Librarians. Lazo, Hayley, illus. (p. 41)
—Calamity. (p. 309)
—Calamity (Spanish Edition) (p. 309)
—Estelar / Starsight. (p. 664)
—Firefight. (p. 733)
—Hero of Ages: A Mistborn Novel (p. 961)
—Knights of Crystallia: Alcatraz vs. the Evil Librarians. (p. 1228)
—Las Lentes Fragmentadas / Alcatraz Versus the Shattered Lens. (p. 1246)
—Reckoners Series Boxed Set (p. 1853)
—Rithmatist. (p. 1886)
—Rithmatist. McSweeney, Ben, illus. (p. 1886)
—Scrivener's Bones: Alcatraz vs. the Evil Librarians. (p. 1966)
—Shattered Lens: Alcatraz vs. the Evil Librarians. (p. 2003)
—Skyward. (p. 2034)
—Starsight. (p. 2107)
—Steelheart. (p. 2112)
Sanderson, Brooke. Some Experiences Afloat & Ashore: Being Notes of a Trip to England in the Summer of 1904, with an Incidental Reference to Dr. Rutherford (Classic Reprint) (p. 2059)
Sanderson, Camilla. John Sanderson the First: Or, a Pioneer Preacher at Home. (p. 1174)
—John Sanderson the First: Or, a Pioneer Preacher at Home (Classic Reprint) (p. 1174)
Sanderson, Caroline. Jane Austen: Novelist. (p. 1158)
Sanderson, Elizabeth. Circle of the Year (Classic Reprint) (p. 393)
Sanderson, G. P. Thirteen Years among the Wild Beasts of India: Their Haunts & Habits from Personal Observations; with an Account of the Modes & Capturing & Taming Elephants (Classic Reprint) (p. 2223)
—Thirteen Years among the Wild Beasts of India. (p. 2223)
Sanderson, Geoff. What Color Is It? (p. 2407)
Sanderson, Isabel. Story of Stumper. (p. 2132)
Sanderson, James Gardner. Cornell Stories (Classic Reprint) (p. 454)
Sanderson, Jeannette. Echo & Narcissus: Set Of 6. Ramos, Jose, illus. (p. 623)
—Martin Luther King Jr. , Letter from Birmingham Jail: Set Of 12. (p. 1411)
—Martin Luther King Jr. , Letter from Birmingham Jail. (p. 1411)
—Walt Whitman, o Captain! My Captain! (p. 2374)
—Walt Whitman, o Captain! My Captain! Set Of 12. (p. 2374)
Sanderson, Jeannette & Benchmark Education Co., LLC. Echo & Narcissus. Ramos, Jose, illus. (p. 623)
Sanderson, Jessica B., illus. see Symington, Martha M.
Sanderson, John. American in Paris, Vol. 1 of 2 (Classic Reprint) (p. 72)
Sanderson, Lyle Ward. Chickadee-Dee & His Friends (Classic Reprint) (p. 368)
Sanderson, Ruth. Crystal Mountain. Sanderson, Ruth, illus. (p. 481)
—Enchanted Wood. Sanderson, Ruth, illus. (p. 647)
—Golden Mare, the Firebird, & the Magic Ring. (p. 858)
—Nativity. (p. 1579)
—Papa Gatto: An Italian Fairy Tale. Sanderson, Ruth, illus. (p. 1696)
—Rose Red & Snow White. Sanderson, Ruth, illus. (p. 1905)
—Snow Princess. Sanderson, Ruth, illus. (p. 2047)
Sanderson, Ruth, illus. see Doty, Jean Slaughter.
Sanderson, Ruth, illus. see Hapka, Catherine, pseud & Hapka, Cathy.
Sanderson, Ruth, illus. see Hapka, Catherine, pseud.
Sanderson, Ruth, illus. see Hart, Alison.
Sanderson, Ruth, illus. see Hermes, Patricia.
Sanderson, Ruth, illus. see Kendall, Jane F.
Sanderson, Ruth, illus. see Klimo, Kate.
Sanderson, Ruth, illus. see Sanderson, Whitney.
Sanderson, Ruth, illus. see Yolen, Jane.
Sanderson, Sarah. Trace Letters: Alphabet Handwriting Practice Workbook for Kids: ABC Print Handwriting Book & Preschool Writing Workbook with Sight Words for Pre K, Kindergarten & Kids Ages 3-5. (p. 2271)
Sanderson, Sean, illus. see Scand, Sandra.
Sanderson, Whitney. Boston Tea Party Sparks Revolution. (p. 264)
—Calvino: Horse Diaries #14. Sanderson, Ruth, illus. (p. 313)
—Darcy. (p. 504)
—Darcy. Sanderson, Ruth, illus. (p. 504)
—Ferrari 488 GTB. (p. 721)
—Heart Song: Book 1. Tejido, Jomike, illus. (p. 945)
—Heartsong's Missing Foal: Book 1. Tejido, Jomike, illus. (p. 946)
—Horse Diaries #15: Lily. Sanderson, Ruth, illus. (p. 1004)
—Horse Diaries #5: Golden Sun. Sanderson, Ruth, illus. (p. 1004)
—Intro to Dressage. (p. 1128)
—Intro to Eventing. (p. 1128)
—Intro to Horse Racing. (p. 1128)
—Lily: Horse Diaries #15. Sanderson, Ruth, illus. (p. 1302)
—Living with ADHD. (p. 1334)
—Penny Sanderson, Ruth, illus. (p. 1717)
—Red Key: Book 4. Tejido, Jomike, illus. (p. 1857)
—September 11 Attacks Transform America. (p. 1989)
—Stolen Magic: Book 3. Tejido, Jomike, illus. (p. 2120)
—Unicorn Uncovered: Book 2. Tejido, Jomike, illus. (p. 2329)
—Unicorns of the Secret Stable (Set Of 4) Tejido, Jomike, illus. (p. 2329)
Sanders-Wells, Linda. Maggie's Monkeys. Carter, Abby, illus. (p. 1376)
Sandes, Flora. English Woman-Sergeant in the Serbian Army (Classic Reprint) (p. 655)
Sandes, John. Call of the Southern Cross: A Romance of Australia (Classic Reprint) (p. 311)
—Designing Fate (Classic Reprint) (p. 532)
Sand-Eveland, Cyndi. Tinfoil Sky. (p. 2248)
Sandford, Barbara, illus. see Anderson, P. G.
Sandford, Grace, illus. see Louise, Kate.
Sandford, Grace, illus. see Mann, Greyson.
Sandford, Grace, illus. see Weber, Jen Funk.
Sandford, John, illus. see Maddox, Marjorie.
Sandford, John, illus. see Tucker, Kathy.
Sandford, John, pseud & Cook, Michele. Outrage. (p. 1685)
—Rampage. (p. 1839)
—Uncaged. (p. 2317)
—Uncaged (the Singular Menace, 1) (p. 2317)
Sandford, Terri. Missing Nursery Rhymes. (p. 1480)
Sandford-Hall, Isla. Challenge Everything: the Extinction Rebellion Youth Guide to Saving ThePlanet. (p. 354)
Sandham, Elizabeth. Adopted Daughter: A Tale for Young Persons (Classic Reprint) (p. 17)
—Adventures of Poor Puss: In Two Parts (Classic Reprint) (p. 27)
—Deaf & Dumb (Classic Reprint) (p. 519)
—Friendship: A Tale (Classic Reprint) (p. 787)
—Grandfather, or the Christmas Holidays: A Tale (Classic Reprint) (p. 877)
—History of William Selwyn (Classic Reprint) (p. 981)
—Lucilla, or the Reconciliation, Vol. 1 of 2 (Classic Reprint) (p. 1363)
—Perambulations of a Bee & a Butterfly: In Which Are Delineated Those Smaller Traits of Character Which Escape the Observation of Larger Spectators (Classic Reprint) (p. 1721)
—Providential Care: A Tale, Founded on Facts (Classic Reprint) (p. 1808)
—School-Fellows: A Moral Tale, for Young Ladies (Classic Reprint) (p. 1945)
—Twin Sisters: A Tale for Youth (Classic Reprint) (p. 2305)
—Ursula, or the Insufficiency of Human Attainments (Classic Reprint) (p. 2340)
Sandham, Henry, illus. see Burnett, Frances Hodgson.
Sandham, Henry, jt. auth. see Poe, Edgar Allen.
Sandheim, May, illus. see Jacob, Violet.
Sandhu, Navjit. Nayan's Family Fruit Salad. Santos, Anthony Erazo, illus. (p. 1583)
Sandhu, Param, illus. see Trotman, Rita.
Sandiford, Ted, illus. see Bousquet, Anthea.
Sandiford, Ted M., illus. see Henry, Arnold.
Sandin, Joan, tr. see Björk, Christina.
Sandison, Lois E. Tipyn o'Bob, Vol. 13: September 28, 1915 (Classic Reprint) (p. 2251)
Sandland, Amanda. Ukaliq & Kalla Look for Bugs (English) (p. 2314)
—Ukaliq & Kalla's Hunting Tools (English) (p. 2314)
Sandland, Amanda, illus. see Aglukark, David & Aglukark, Dorothy.
Sandland, Amanda, illus. see Aglukark, Susan.
Sandland, Amanda, illus. see Akulukjuk, Roselynn.
Sandland, Amanda, illus. see Bailey, Jenna.
Sandland, Amanda, illus. see Hale, Jessie.
Sandland, Amanda, illus. see Inhabit Education.
Sandland, Amanda, illus. see Main, Heather.
Sandland, Amanda, illus. see Mallory, Carolyn & Mallory, Carolyn.
Sandland, Amanda, illus. see Vsetula, Maren.
Sandler, Karen. Awakening: Tankborn #2. (p. 143)
—Awakening. (p. 143)
—Rebellion (p. 1852)
Sandler, Martin W. 1919 the Year That Changed America. (p. 2561)
—Apollo 8: The Mission That Changed Everything. (p. 106)
—Civil War. (p. 396)
—Dust Bowl Through the Lens: How Photography Revealed & Helped Remedy a National Disaster. (p. 611)
—How the Beatles Changed the World. (p. 1035)
—Immigrants. (p. 1100)
—Impossible Rescue: The True Story of an Amazing Arctic Adventure. (p. 1102)
—Imprisoned: The Betrayal of Japanese Americans During World War II. (p. 1102)
—Inventors. (p. 1130)
—Iron Rails, Iron Men, & the Race to Link the Nation: The Story of the Transcontinental Railroad. (p. 1135)
—Race Through the Skies: The Week the World Learned to Fly. (p. 1831)
—What Was America's Deadliest War? And Other Questions about the Civil War. Hunt, Robert, illus. (p. 2421)
—Why Did the Whole World Go to War? And Other Questions about... World War II. Barrett, Robert, illus. (p. 2455)
—Whydah: A Pirate Ship Feared, Wrecked, & Found. (p. 2460)
—Whydah: a Pirate Ship Feared, Wrecked, & Found. (p. 2460)
Sandler, Martin W., et al. Contemporary Art: World Currents. (p. 444)
Sandler, Michael. Aaron Rodgers & the Green Bay Packers: Super Bowl XLV. (p. 2)
—Adrian Peterson. (p. 17)
—Ben Roethlisberger. (p. 199)
—Brett Favre. (p. 279)
—Brian Urlacher. (p. 279)
—Catastrophic Storms: Set Of 6. (p. 343)
—Cool Snowboarders. (p. 450)
—Daring BMXers. (p. 505)
—Donovan Mcnabb. (p. 582)
—Drew Brees & the New Orleans Saints. (p. 604)
—Dynamic Drag Racers. (p. 612)
—Electrifying Eco Race Cars. (p. 632)
—Eli Manning & the New York Giants: Super Bowl Xlvi. (p. 635)
—Explorers of the Americas: Set Of 6. (p. 680)
—Fast Rides (p. 713)
—Gnarly Skateboarders. (p. 845)
—Hot Hot Rods. (p. 1006)
—Jet-Powered Speed. (p. 1167)
—Joe Flacco & the Baltimore Ravens: Super Bowl XLVII. (p. 1171)
—John Cena. (p. 1172)
—Ladainian Tomlinson. (p. 1236)
—Larry Fitzgerald. (p. 1245)
—LeBron James: I Love Challenges! (p. 1260)
—Malcolm Smith & the Seattle Seahawks: Super Bowl XLVIII. (p. 1391)
—Mark Sanchez. (p. 1407)
—Matt Hasselbeck. (p. 1425)
—Mighty MotoXers. (p. 1463)
—Most Spectacular Quarterbacks. (p. 1508)
—Peyton Manning. (p. 1732)
—Pro Football's Dream Teams. (p. 1802)
—Pro Football's Stars of the Defense. (p. 1802)
—Rally Car Dudes. (p. 1838)
—Rock. (p. 1894)
—Stupendous Sports Stadiums. (p. 2145)
—Super Surfers. (p. 2158)
—Tim Tebow. (p. 2243)
—Tony Gonzalez. (p. 2260)
—Tony Romo. (p. 2260)
—Troy Polamalu. (p. 2292)
Sandler, Michael & Benchmark Education Company, LLC Staff. Tormentas Catastróficas: Set of 6 Common Core Edition. (p. 2265)
Sandler, Michael & Cohen, Eric. Randy Orton. (p. 1840)
—Triple H. (p. 2289)
Sandler, Michael & McNessor, Mike. Electrifying Eco-Race Cars. (p. 632)
Sandler, Michael & Pushies, Fred J. Today's Marine Heroes. (p. 2255)
Sandler, Michael & Zegers, Charlie. Amar'e Stoudemire. (p. 62)
—Derrick Rose. (p. 530)
—Dwyane Wade. (p. 611)
—Kevin Durant. (p. 1210)
Sandler, Vladik, illus. see Shaked, S.
Sandmann, Alexa L., jt. see Baxter, Kathleen.
Sandner, Lionel. What Is Electromagnetism? (p. 2415)
Sandor, Steven. Called Up. (p. 312)
—Easy Out. (p. 621)
—Stick Pick. (p. 2117)
—Trolled. (p. 2290)
Sandoval, Ana Valay, jt. auth. see Valay, Ana Patricia.
Sandoval, Gerardo, illus. see Bowen, Carl & Fuentes, Benny.
Sandoval, Gerardo, illus. see Bunn, Cullen & Chapman, Clay.
Sandoval, Gerardo, illus. see Ciencin, Scott & Fuentes, Benny.
Sandoval, Gerardo, illus. see Fein, Eric & Fuentes, Benny.
Sandoval, Gerardo, illus. see Fuentes, Benny & Hoena, Blake A.
Sandoval, Gerardo, illus. see Hoena, Blake A. & Fuentes, Benny.
Sandoval, Gerardo, illus. see Marvel Comics.
Sandoval, Gerardo, illus. see Stevens, Eric & Fuentes, Benny.
Sandoval, Gerardo, illus. see Terrell, Brandon & Fuentes, Benny.
Sandoval, Gerardo, illus. see Yomtov, Nel & Fuentes, Benny.
Sandoval, Gerardo, illus. see Yomtov, Nel, et al.
Sandoval, Gerardo, jt. auth. see Andersen, Hans.
Sandoval, Gerardo, jt. illus. see Salazar, Edgar.
Sandoval, Gustavo. Owls & Owlets. (p. 1689)
Sandoval, Jaime Alfonso. Campamento Miedo / Camp Fear. (p. 316)
—Doce Sustos y un Perico / Twelve Scares & a Parakeet. (p. 573)
—Los Fantasmas de Fernando. (p. 1350)
—Padres Padrísimos, S. A. (p. 1692)
Sandoval, John. Witches of Ruidoso. (p. 2480)
Sandoval, Lenny, tr. see Foster, Stephen.
Sandoval, Lenny, tr. see Lee, Calee M.
Sandoval, Lenny, tr. see Ponnay, Brenda.
Sandoval, Lenny, tr. see Streza, Katrina.
Sandoval, Lenny, tr. see Streza, Nancy.
Sandoval, Lynda. Father Knows Best. (p. 714)
Sandoval, Maria Calderon. In December. (p. 1104)
Sandoval, Rafa, illus. see Van Lente, Fred.
Sandoval, Tony. Windy Day. (p. 2472)
Sandoval, Tony, illus. see Kennedy Johnson, Phillip.
Sandoval, Tony, illus. see Nitz, Jai.
Sandoz, Matt, illus. see Howard, Assuanta.
Sandquist, Tanya. Trevor the Turkey Gets Clean. (p. 2285)
Sandrine, Beau. 24 Comptines en Attendant le P're No'l. (p. 2554)
—Aie ! (p. 36)
—Aventure de Super-Poilu. (p. 142)
—Aventures Megachouettes de Mademoiselle Chacha. Episode 1: La Robe Froufrous(les) (p. 142)
—Aventures Megachouettes de Mademoiselle Chacha. Episode 2: Chacha Se Cherche un Papa(les) (p. 142)
—Hippopotin(l') (p. 973)
—Ma Maman Est Comme A. (p. 1371)
—Ma Mamie Est Comme Cl. (p. 1371)
Sandro, Turburam, illus. see Ready, Tricia.
Sandrock, Sherry. Lemon & a Pea. (p. 1266)
Sands, Crystal. Women & Feminism Today. (p. 2486)
Sands, Emily. Egyptology Coloring Book. (p. 629)
Sands, Harold. Dashing Sally Duel, & Other Stories (Classic Reprint) (p. 508)
Sands, Kathryn N. Billy's Big Adventure. (p. 227)
Sands, Kevin. Assassin's Curse. (p. 127)
—Blackthorn Key. (p. 240)
—Blackthorn Key Cryptic Collection Books 1-4: The Blackthorn Key; Mark of the Plague; the Assassin's Curse; Call of the Wraith. (p. 240)
—Call of the Wraith. (p. 312)
—Mark of the Plague. (p. 1407)
—Señal de la Plaga. (p. 1988)
Sands, Robert Charles. Writings of Robert C. Sands, in Prose & Verse, Vol. 2 Of 2: With a Memoir of the Author (Classic Reprint) (p. 2514)
Sandstrom, Karen, illus. see Holbrook, Sara E.
Sandu, Anca. Churchill's Tale of Tails Sandu, Anca, illus. (p. 390)
Sandu, Anca, illus. see Schnitzlein, Danny.
Sandu, Anca, illus. see Slyke, Rebecca van.
Sandusky, Thomas & Hill, Kathy. Peter the Poison Dart Frog, Stories of the Rainforest. Johnson, Gretchen, illus. (p. 1730)
—Spidy the Spider Monkey. Johnson, Gretchen, illus. (p. 2081)
Sandvik, Lin-Marita. Bjornen Tor Blir Meisterbakar. Sandvik, Lin-Marita, photos by. (p. 236)
—Bjornen Tor Blir Mesterbaker. Sandvik, Lin-Marita, photos by. (p. 236)
—Bjørnen Tor Drar På øglejakt: (serie, 7 Bøker) (p. 236)
—Bjornen Tor Feirar Jul. Sandvik, Lin-Marita, photos by. (p. 236)
—Bjornen Tor Feirer Jul. Sandvik, Lin-Marita, photos by. (p. 236)
—Bjørnen Tor Fer På øglejakt: (serie, 7 Bøker) (p. 236)
—Bjornen Tor Finn Vikingskatten. Sandvik, Lin-Marita, photos by. (p. 236)
—Bjornen Tor Gjer ein Dagsferie. (p. 236)
—Bjornen Tor Gjor en Dagsferie. (p. 236)
—Bjornen Tor Lagar Ei Gulrot. (p. 236)
—Bjornen Tor Lager en Gulrot. (p. 236)
—Bjornen Tor Reddar ein Venn. (p. 236)
—Bjornen Tor Redder en Venn. (p. 236)
—Tor the Bear Becomes an Expert Baker. (p. 2264)
—Tor the Bear Becomes an Expert Baker. Sandvik, Lin-Marita, photos by. (p. 2264)
—Tor the Bear Celebrates Christmas. Sandvik, Lin-Marita, photos by. (p. 2264)
—Tor the Bear Makes a Carrot: (7 Book Series) (p. 2264)
—Tor the Bear Makes a Carrot. (p. 2264)
—Tor the Bear Rescues a Friend. Sandvik, Lin-Marita, photos by. (p. 2264)
—Tor the Bear Takes a Daycation: (7 Book Series) (p. 2264)
—Tor the Bear Takes a Daycation. (p. 2264)
Sandvold, Lynnette Brent. Genetics. (p. 815)
—Revolution in Construction. (p. 1873)
Sandwick, Richard L. How to Study & What to Study. (p. 1044)
—How to Study & What to Study (Classic Reprint) (p. 1044)
Sandwick, Richard Lanning. High School Word Book. (p. 969)
Sandy Creek (Firm) Staff, contrib. by. Brick by Brick 123. (p. 280)
—Discover Dinosaurs: Prehistoric Beast, Fossils, & Fun Facts! (p. 554)
—Let's Learn Shapes. (p. 1274)
—Liners & Merchant Ships. (p. 1304)
—Medical Chart. (p. 1436)
—My First Book of Ocean Creatures: Learn about Jellyfish, Sharks, Deep Sea Creatures, & More with Fun Facts! (p. 1542)
—My First Book of Pets: Learn about Dogs, Cats, Lizards, & More with Fun Facts! (p. 1543)
—My First Book of Sharks: Learn about Great Whites, Hammerheads, Goblin Sharks, & More with Fun Facts! (p. 1543)
—My First Book of Wild Animals: Learn about Zebras, Elephants, Pandas, & More with Fun Facts! (p. 1543)
—Our Solar System & Beyond: Planets, Stars, Space Travel & Fun Facts! (p. 1680)
Sandy Flett, illus. see Barkla, Charlotte.
Sandy, J. P., illus. see Cleary, Brian P.
Sandy, John, illus. see Cleary, Brian P.
Sandys, Miles. Michael Carmichael: A Story of Love & Mystery (Classic Reprint) (p. 1457)
Sandys, Oliver. Ginger-Jar (Classic Reprint) (p. 833)
—Pleasure Garden (Classic Reprint) (p. 1762)
Sandys, William. Christmas Carols, Ancient & Modern; Including the Most Popular in the West of England, & the Airs to Which They Are Sung: Also Specimens of French Provincial Carols, with an Introduction & Notes (Classic Reprint) (p. 384)
—Christmas Carols, Ancient & Modern, Including the Most Popular in the West of England, & the Airs to Which They Are Sung; Also Specimens of French Provincial Carols. with an Introduction & Notes, etc. - Scholar's Choice Edition. (p. 384)
Sane, Justin. Heart of a Corpse; an Undead Engagement Part One. Sane, Justin, illus. (p. 944)
Sanfelippo, Ana, illus. see Andres, Jose Carlos.
Sanfelippo, Ana, illus. see Kaiser, Lisbeth.
Sanfilippo, Simona. Rapunzel. (p. 1841)
Sanfilippo, Simona, illus. see Box, Su.
Sanfilippo, Simona, illus. see Fliess, Sue.
Sanfilippo, Simona, illus. see Robinson, Hilary.
Sanfilippo, Simona, illus. see Wilding, Valerie.
Sanfilippo, Terry. Land of Plaid. Sanfilippo, Terry, illus. (p. 1242)
Sanford. Today's Teen. (p. 2255)
Sanford, Amelia. Advertising Girls: A Masque of Very Fly Leaves in Two Scenes (Classic Reprint) (p. 30)
Sanford, Brandon, ed. see Hughes, James W.
Sanford, Carlton Elisha. Letters, Essays, & Biographical Sketches (Classic Reprint) (p. 1279)
Sanford, D. P. Frisk & His Flock (Classic Reprint) (p. 788)
Sanford, Ezekiel. Humours of Eutopia, Vol. 2 Of 2: A Tale of Colonial Times (Classic Reprint) (p. 1051)
Sanford, Fernando. Some Observations upon the Conductivity of a Copper Wire in Various Dielectrics. (p. 2059)
—Some Observations upon the Conductivity of a Copper Wire in Various Dielectrics (Classic Reprint) (p. 2059)
Sanford, Frederick R. Bursting of a Boom (Classic Reprint) (p. 300)
Sanford, Grace, illus. see Reynolds, Toby.
Sanford, J. E. His One Tune, & a Few Others (Classic Reprint) (p. 974)
Sanford, M. M. Visit to el-Fay-Gno-Land (Classic Reprint) (p. 2362)
Sanford, Mabel Adelina. Joseph's City Beautiful: A Story of Old Nauvoo on the Mississippi (Classic Reprint) (p. 1179)
Sanford, Mary Bourchier. Romance of a Jesuit Mission: A Historical Novel (Classic Reprint) (p. 1900)
Sanford, Sally. Henry & the Huckleberries: A Visit with Mr. Thoreau at Walden Pond. Plume, Ilse, illus. (p. 954)

S

Sanford, Timothy L. Tengo que Ser Perfecto: (y otras herejias de la casa Pastoral) Rdm, tr. from ENG. (p. 2205)
Sanford, William. Margo's Pen (p. 1404)
Sanford, William R. Apache Chief Geronimo. (p. 105)
—Comanche Chief Quanah Parker. (p. 427)
—Hunkpapa Lakota Chief Sitting Bull. (p. 1052)
—Nez Percé Chief Joseph. (p. 1601)
—Oglala Lakota Chief Red Cloud. (p. 1641)
—Oglala Sioux Chief Crazy Horse. (p. 1641)
—Seminole Chief Osceola. (p. 1988)
Sanford, William R., jt. auth. see Green, Carl R.
Sanford, William R., jt. auth. see Sanford, Carl R.
Sanford, William R. & Green, Carl R. Bill Pickett: Courageous African-American Cowboy. (p. 226)
—Brigham Young: Courageous Mormon Leader. (p. 281)
—Buffalo Bill Cody: Courageous Wild West Showman. (p. 291)
—Calamity Jane: Courageous Wild West Woman. (p. 309)
—Daniel Boone: Courageous Frontiersman. (p. 502)
—Davy Crockett: Courageous Hero of the Alamo. (p. 511)
—John C. Frémont: Courageous Pathfinder of the Wild West. (p. 1172)
—Kit Carson: Courageous Mountain Man. (p. 1225)
—Richard King: Courageous Texas Cattleman. (p. 1876)
—Sacagawea: Courageous American Indian Guide. (p. 1920)
—Sam Houston: Courageous Texas Hero. (p. 1926)
—Zebulon Pike: Courageous Rocky Mountain Explorer. (p. 2539)
Sanger, George P. Fifth Report of the Class Secretary of the Class of 1874 of Harvard College. June, 1884 - June 1889. (p. 724)
Sanger, William Cary. When Hearts Are Young: And Other Stories (Classic Reprint) (p. 2430)
Sangha, Mandy. Where's Nanni? (p. 2440)
Sangha Mitra, Ms Janice. Golden Bear: The Story of a Flowering Heart. Sangha Mitra, Ms Janice, illus. (p. 856)
SanGiacomo, Scott, illus. see Duke, Nell K., et al.
SanGiacomo, Scott, illus. see Lentini, Rochelle, et al.
Sang-Kwen, Lee. Pato Que Voló Al Cielo. Jung Woo, Nam, illus. (p. 1705)
Sangngg, illus. see Twede, Shane K.
Sangree, Allen. Jinx: Stories of the Diamond (Classic Reprint) (p. 1169)
Sangster, Alan, jt. auth. see Wood, Frank.
Sangster, Caitlin. Dead Moon Rising. (p. 518)
—Last Star Burning. (p. 1249)
—Shatter the Suns. (p. 2003)
Sangster, Margaret E. Art of Home-Making: In City & Country in Mansion & Cottage (Classic Reprint) (p. 121)
—Eleanor Lee: A Novel (Classic Reprint) (p. 630)
—Friends O'Mine: A Book of Poems & Stories (Classic Reprint) (p. 787)
—Janet Ward: A Daughter of the Manse (Classic Reprint) (p. 1159)
—My Garden of Hearts: A Collection of the Best Short Stories & Essays Written During a Long Literary Lifetime (Classic Reprint) (p. 1548)
Sangster, Margaret Elizabeth. Holiday Stories for Young People. (p. 988)
—Home Life Made Beautiful: In Story, Song, Sketch & Picture (Classic Reprint) (p. 996)
—Island of Faith (Classic Reprint) (p. 1139)
—Mother Book (Classic Reprint) (p. 1509)
Sangster, Margaret Elizabeth Munson. Good Manners for All Occasions: A Practical Manual (Classic Reprint) (p. 863)
—Happy School Days (Classic Reprint) (p. 923)
—Twilight Tales: Twenty-Four Stories of Love & Romance from Real Life (Classic Reprint) (p. 2305)
Sangster, Rena Urania Nott. Power of GC, a Romance of London, England: In Seven Chapters (Classic Reprint) (p. 1782)
Sanguedolce, Patty & Cowne, Chris. In the Belly of an Elephant. (p. 1108)
Sanie, Michael. 7 Berceuses a Quatre Petites Mains. (p. 2548)
Sanjeev, Sanyal. Incredible History of the Indian Ocean. (p. 1113)
Sankaranarayanan, Ayswarya, illus. see Subramaniam, Manasi.
Sankey, Rachel Ellen. Darkest Before Dawn. (p. 507)
Sanmiguel, Rosario, tr. see Bertrand, Diane Gonzales.
Sanna, Alessandro. Castle of Books. (p. 340)
—Pinocchio: The Origin Story. (p. 1747)
Sanna, E. J. Heroin & Other Opioids: Poppies' Perilous Children. Henningfield, Jack E., ed. (p. 963)
—Lloyd Banks. (p. 1338)
—Marijuana: Mind-Altering Weed. (p. 1405)
—Marijuana: Mind-Altering Weed. Henningfield, Jack E., ed. (p. 1405)
Sanna, Ellyn. Big Portions, Big Problems. Garcia, Victor, ed. (p. 222)
—Childcare Worker. Riggs, Ernestine G. & Gholar, Cheryl, eds. (p. 370)
—Gallup Guides for Youth Facing Persistent Prejudice Muslims. (p. 806)
—Homeland Security Officer. Riggs, Ernestine G. & Gholar, Cheryl, eds. (p. 997)
—Mexican Facts & Figures. (p. 1454)
—Mexico: Facts & Figures. (p. 1454)
—Native North American Indians. (p. 1579)
—Nature's Wrath: Surviving Natural Disasters. (p. 1582)
—People with Mental & Physical Challenges. (p. 1719)
—Special Education Teacher. Riggs, Ernestine G. & Gholar, Cheryl, eds. (p. 2076)
—Those Who Remain: What It Means to Be a Survivor. (p. 2230)
Sanna, Ellyn, jt. auth. see Seba, Jaime.
Sanna, Emily. Gay Believers: Homosexuality & Religion. (p. 812)
—How Does Air Pollution Affect Your Health? (p. 1030)
—Pop Monsters: The Modern-Day Craze for Vampires & Werewolves. (p. 1775)
Sanna, Francesca. Journey. (p. 1181)
—Me & My Fear. (p. 1433)
—Viaje. (p. 2354)
Sanna, Gabriel. Baseball & Softball. (p. 168)
Sanna, Guillermo. Bullseye: the Colombian Connection. (p. 296)
Sanna, Guillermo, jt. illus. see Blake, Nelson.
Sanna, Jeanine & Indovino, Shaina C. Austria. Bruton, John, ed. (p. 139)
—France. Bruton, John, ed. (p. 776)
Sanna, Jeanine & Indovino, Shaina Carmel. Austria. (p. 139)
—France. (p. 776)
Sanna, Lindsey. Game. (p. 806)
Sanne, Don, illus. see Coons, Susan Anderson.
Sanne, Kat. Pepa, BonBon & Nita ?Celebrate Cinco de Mayo? (p. 1719)
—Pepa, BonBon & Nita Celebrate the Fourth of July. (p. 1719)
—Pepa, BonBon & Nita Feed the Birds. (p. 1719)
—Pepa, BonBon & Nita Rockin the House. (p. 1719)
Sanne, Thea Marie, ed. see Bjelland, Hildegunn.
Sanne, Thea Marie, ed. Ninjana: Det Store Skredet. Bjelland, Hildegunn, tr. (p. 1610)
Sanrio. Happy St. Patrick's Day, Hello Kitty. (p. 923)
—Hello Kitty Goes to Camp. (p. 951)
Sanrio & Kabushiki, Kaisha. Day of Thanks. (p. 514)
Sanrio Company. Let's Play with Sanrio's Characters. (p. 1277)
Sans Auteur. Alphabet Illustré Fleurs Trente Gravures. (p. 59)
—De la Peche de la Sardine et des Industries Qui S'y Rattachent, Par un Pecheur. (p. 517)
—Manuel des Jeunes Gens Ou Sciences, Arts et Récréations Qui Leur Conviennent. (p. 1399)
Sans, Claparo, illus. see Varnell, Brandon.
Sanschagrin, Joceline. Caillou: The Broken Castle. Brignaud, Pierre, illus. (p. 308)
—Caillou - A Day at the Farm. Brignaud, Pierre, illus. (p. 308)
—Caillou at the Doctor. Brignaud, Pierre, illus. (p. 308)
—Caillou: It's Mine! Brignaud, Pierre, illus. (p. 309)
—Caillou, Potty Time. Brignaud, Pierre, illus. (p. 309)
Sansevere-Dreher, Diane. Explorers Who Got Lost. Renfro, Ed, illus. (p. 681)
Sansevero, Tony, illus. see Cockrum, James L.
Sansevero, Tony, illus. see Morris, Kimberly & Burke, Kathleen.
Sansevero, Tony, illus. see Wermund, Jerry.
Sansó, Bárbara, illus. see Rincón, Gilda.
Sansom, Fiona, illus. see Claybourne, Anna.
Sansom, Fiona, illus. see Elgin, Kathy.
Sansom, Fiona, illus. see McFadden, Deanna.
Sansom, Fiona, illus. see Morris, Neil.
Sansom, Fiona, jt. auth. see Bingham, Jane.
Sansom, Mary J. Holiday Trip to Canada (Classic Reprint) (p. 988)
Sanson, A. J. Navigation Atmospherique: Explications Complementaires Sur le Systeme, Physique, Mecanique, Pterophore, Dynamique et Trigonometrique de Sanson Pere et Fils, Precedees de l'Aeronautique des Dames, Lettre en Prose et en Verse Libres, Suivis de L' (p. 1582)
Sanson, Rachel. Tails from History Collection: A Raccoon at the White House; a Parrot in the Painting; a Puppy for Helen Keller; the Cat Who Ruled the Town; a Sea Otter to the Rescue; a Pony with Her Writer. (p. 2176)
Sanson, Rachel, illus. see Dougherty, Rachel.
Sanson, Rachel, illus. see Feldman, Thea.
Sanson, Rachel, illus. see Nakamura, May.
Sansone, V. K. Carpenter & His Wife. (p. 333)
—Daunting Quest for Quincy & Quigley. (p. 510)
—Heavenly Hannah's Little Black Hat. (p. 947)
—Katie Bear & Friends (Book One) (p. 1205)
—Katie Bear & Friends (Book Three) (p. 1205)
—Pandora's Incredible Journey. (p. 1696)
—Strange Day at the Zoo. (p. 2137)
—Tweens Book of Shorts. (p. 2302)
—WANTED: Children for Toys. (p. 2375)
Sansum, Cyril a. Apocalypse Was a Long Time Ago: The Holy Bible Rediscovered by Young People in a Future World. (p. 105)
Sansum, Vicki, jt. auth. see Enderle, Dotti.
Sant, Sharon. Runners. (p. 1915)
Santa Ana, Antonio. Los Ojos Del Perro Siberiano. (p. 1351)
Santa, Carlos Piedra. Animales Mensajeros. (p. 93)
Santa, Carlos Piedra, illus. see Zea, Amilcar.
Santa, et al. Where Elves Come From. (p. 2437)
Santa Maria, Christa, des. Zoo Animal Crafts (p. 2543)
Santacroce, John P. Nine Thousand Miles to Adventure: The Story of an American Boy in the Philippines. (p. 1610)
—Running Across the Moon. (p. 1915)
Santacruz, Juan, illus. see Benjamin, Paul.
Santacruz, Juan, illus. see Parker, Jeff.
Santamaria, Jenni & Ross Keyes, Joan. Oxford Picture Dictionary Content Area for Kids English Dictionary. (p. 1689)
Santamaria, Jenni Currie, et al. Oxford Picture Dictionary Content Areas for Kids. (p. 1689)
Santana, Breanna. Biblical ABC's for You & Me. (p. 214)
—Lizzy the Lonely. (p. 1337)
Santana, Elaina. Tania: Volume 1 (p. 2190)
Santana, Erin. Spud Jr. Saves the Golden Gate Bridge. (p. 2093)
Santana, Eva. Soy un Cerdito. (p. 2070)
Santana, Francesca. Incredible Adventure. (p. 1113)
Santana, Gabriela. Mitologia Mexicana para Ninos. (p. 1483)
Santana, Gabriela de los Angeles. Cuentos de Titanes para Ninos. (p. 483)
Santana, Pavlina, tr. see Pere, Tuula.
Santana, Rachel. Who's Older? Understand & Apply Properties of Operations. (p. 2453)
Santana, Sara. Awakened. (p. 143)
Santana, Sara Elizabeth. Sanctuary. (p. 1930)
Santana, Sr. Stella. We Are the People of This World: Book One. Bear, Andrea, illus. (p. 2389)
Santana, Victor, tr. see Xist Publishing.
Santana-Banks, Kelly. Dinosaur Adventure: A Field Trip to Remember. Dutta, Dipali, illus. (p. 548)
Santanach, Tino, illus. see Beakman, Onk.
Santanach, Tino, illus. see Jackson, Kristen L.
Santanach, Tino, illus. see PI Kids.
Santat, Dan. Adventures of Beekle: the Unimaginary Friend. (p. 21)
—After the Fall (How Humpty Dumpty Got Back up Again) Santat, Dan, illus. (p. 34)
—Are We There Yet? (p. 113)
—Mighty Robot vs. the Stupid Stinkbugs from Saturn. (p. 1463)
—Sidekicks. Santat, Dan, illus. (p. 2015)
—Stupid Stinkbugs from Saturn. (p. 2145)
—Xiao Bai Zhao Peng You (2015 Nian Kai Di Ke Jin Jiang Zuo Pin) (Simplified Chinese) (p. 2516)
Santat, Dan, illus. see Angleberger, Tom.
Santat, Dan, illus. see Barnett, Mac.
Santat, Dan, illus. see Beasley, Kate.
Santat, Dan, illus. see Beaty, Andrea.
Santat, Dan, illus. see Berger, Samantha.
Santat, Dan, illus. see Bird, Betsy.
Santat, Dan, illus. see Choldenko, Gennifer.
Santat, Dan, illus. see Diesen, Deborah.
Santat, Dan, illus. see Elya, Susan Middleton.
Santat, Dan, illus. see Gidwitz, Adam.
Santat, Dan, illus. see Going, K. L.
Santat, Dan, illus. see Gutman, Dan.
Santat, Dan, illus. see Isaacs, Anne.
Santat, Dan, illus. see Lê, Minh.
Santat, Dan, illus. see Marsoli, Lisa Ann.
Santat, Dan, illus. see Pilkey, Dav.
Santat, Dan, illus. see Piper, Watty.
Santat, Dan, illus. see Reynolds, Aaron.
Santat, Dan, illus. see Sanders, Rob.
Santat, Dan, illus. see Sauer, Tammi.
Santat, Dan, illus. see Schwartz, Corey Rosen & Gomez, Rebecca J.
Santat, Dan, illus. see Schwartz, Corey Rosen.
Santat, Dan, illus. see Scieszka, Jon, et al.
Santat, Dan, illus. see Selfors, Suzanne.
Santat, Dan, illus. see Spratt, R. A.
Santat, Dan, illus. see Taccone, Jorma.
Santat, Dan, illus. see Yee, Lisa.
Santat, Dan, illus. see Zappa, Ahmet.
Santat, Dan & Willems, Mo. Cookie Fiasco (Elephant & Piggie Like Reading!) Santat, Dan & Willems, Mo, illus. (p. 446)
—Harold & Hog Pretend for Real! (Elephant & Piggie Like Reading!) (p. 931)
Santella, Andrew. French & Indian War. (p. 783)
—Kentucky. (p. 1209)
—Plains Indians (p. 1754)
Santella, Thomas & Triggle, David J. Hallucinogens. (p. 913)
Santerre, S. Psychologie du Nombre et des Opérations Élémentaires de l'Arithmétique: La Genèse des Premières Notions de l'Arithmétique, Notions de Suite, de Nombre, de Somme et de Différence, Roduit et Quotient (Classic Reprint) (p. 1809)
Santiago, Chiori. Home to Medicine Mountain. (p. 997)
—Home to Medicine Mountain. Lowry, Judith, illus. (p. 997)
Santiago, Fabi. Tiger in a Tutu. (p. 2241)
Santiago, Kayley. Rebuilding Arcadia. (p. 1853)
Santiago McNeill, Lisa, illus. see Brown, William.
Santiago, Rose Mary, illus. see Shah, Idries.
Santiago, Rose Mary, tr. see Shah, Idries.
Santiago, Ruth E. Gabrielle's Violin. McInerny, Judi, illus. (p. 804)
Santiago, Shelly. Fairies of Tythian. (p. 696)
Santiago, Weberson, illus. see Elia, Stella.
Santillan, Jorge, illus. see Eason, Sarah.
Santillan, Jorge, illus. see Schwaeber, Barbie Heit.
Santillan, Jorge, jt. auth. see Jones, Richard.
Santillan, Jorge & British Broadcasting Company Staff. When's the Doctor? (p. 2435)
Santillan, Jorge & Eason, Sarah. Drawing Dinosaurs. (p. 599)
—Drawing Dragons. (p. 599)
—Drawing Fairies, Mermaids, & Unicorns. (p. 599)
—Drawing Knights & Castles. (p. 599)
—Drawing Pirates & Pirate Ships. (p. 599)
Santillan, Jorge H. Sports Illustrated Kids Victory School Superstars (p. 2089)
Santillan, Jorge H., illus. see Gassman, Julie A.
Santillan, Jorge H., illus. see Gunderson, Jessica.
Santillan, Jorge H., illus. see Kreie, Chris.
Santillan, Jorge H., illus. see LeBoutillier, Nate.
Santillan, Jorge H., illus. see Nickel, Scott.
Santillan, Jorge H., illus. see Priebe, Val.
Santillan, Jorge H., illus. see Yasuda, Anita.
Santillan, Mariano, illus. see Edison, Richard E.
Santillan, Suzanne. Grandma's Pear Tree. Pernisco, Atilio, illus. (p. 878)
Santillanes, Alexander Vidal, illus. see Mara, Nichole.
Santilli, Shirley. Trouble in Treeville. Santilli Wolfinger, Lorrie, illus. (p. 2291)
Santilli Wolfinger, Lorrie, illus. see Santilli, Shirley.
Santillian, Beatriz & Aird, Hamish. Pericles: Athenian Statesman & Patron of the Arts. (p. 1723)
Santillian, Beatriz & Morgan, Julian. Hadrian: Emperor of Rome. (p. 909)
Santillian, Beatriz & Morris, Ian Macgregor. Leonidas I: Warrior King of Sparta. (p. 1267)
Santillian, Beatriz & Randall, Bernard. Alexander the Great: Macedonian King & Conqueror. (p. 43)
—Solon: Athenian Statesman & Poet. (p. 2058)
Santillian, Beatriz & Thomas, Susanna. Ahmose I: Pharaoh of the 18th Dynasty. (p. 36)
—Ramses II: The Most Powerful Pharaoh of Ancient Egypt. (p. 1839)
—Snefru: Pharaoh of the 4th Dynasty. (p. 2046)
Santini, Antonio. Inclinationum Appendix Seù to Geometriæ Pleroma (Classic Reprint) (p. 1113)
Santini, Bertrand. Yark. Gapaillard, Laurent, illus. (p. 2518)
Santini, Debrah L., illus. see Santucci, Barbara.
Santini, Donna. Cooper Goes to the Vet: Golden Retriever. (p. 451)
Santini, Philip. Harvey's Adventures. Chambers, Z., illus. (p. 936)
Santitoro, Theresa, illus. see Isler, Linda Germano.
Santo, Nicole Miyuki. Kids' Book of Hand Lettering: 20 Lessons & Projects to Decorate Your World. (p. 1214)
Santolouco, Mateus, illus. see Denton, Shannon Eric.
Santolouco, Mateus, illus. see Waltz, Tom & Eastman, Kevin B.
Santolouco, Mateus, illus. see Waltz, Tom & Eastman, Kevin.
Santomauro, Fabio, illus. see Elvgren, Jennifer.
Santomauro, Josie. ASD Zoo of Kalamazoo. (p. 125)
—You Are Special Too: A Book for Brothers & Sisters of Children Diagnosed with Asperger Syndrome. Marino, Carla, illus. (p. 2524)
—Your Special Friend: A Book for Peers of Children Diagnosed with Asperger Syndrome. Marino, Carla, illus. (p. 2534)
Santomenna, Marco D., jt. auth. see Santomenna, Joan E.
Santomero, Angela C. Baby Is Here! (p. 151)
—Big Brother Daniel. Fruchter, Jason, illus. (p. 218)
—Daniel & the Nutcracker. Fruchter, Jason, illus. (p. 502)
—Daniel Goes to the Carnival. (p. 502)
—Daniel Has an Allergy. (p. 503)
—Daniel's First Sleepover. (p. 503)
—Goodnight, Daniel Tiger. (p. 867)
—Goodnight, Daniel Tiger. Style Guide Staff, illus. (p. 867)
—Happy Halloween, Daniel Tiger! A Lift-The-Flap Book. Fruchter, Jason, illus. (p. 922)
—Merry Christmas, Daniel Tiger! A Lift-The-Flap Book. Fruchter, Jason, illus. (p. 1450)
Santomero, Angela C., adapted by. You Are Special, Daniel Tiger! (p. 2524)
Santopolo, Jill. All That Glitters. (p. 53)
—Bad News Nails. (p. 158)
—Bling It On! (p. 244)
—Fashion Disaster. (p. 712)
—Fashion Disaster. Mingus, Cathi, illus. (p. 712)
—Glam Opening! Mingus, Cathi, illus. (p. 841)
—Nina, the Pinta, & the Vanishing Treasure (p. 1609)
—Picture-Perfect Mess. (p. 1740)
—Purple Nails & Puppy Tails. (p. 1816)
—Sparkle Spa 4-Books-In-1! All That Glitters; Purple Nails & Puppy Tails; Makeover Magic; True Colors. (p. 2075)
—Sparkle Spa Spa-Tacular: All That Glitters; Purple Nails & Puppy Tails; Makeover Magic; True Colors; Bad News Nails; a Picture-Perfect Mess; Bling It On!; Wedding Bell Blues; Fashion Disaster; Glam Opening! (p. 2075)
—True Colors. (p. 2294)
—Wedding Bell Blues. (p. 2395)
Santora, Bud, illus. see Wooten, Arthur.
Santore, Charles. Aesop's Fables: The Classic Edition. (p. 31)
—Aesop's Fables: A Little Apple Classic. (p. 31)
—Illustrated Treasury of Classic Children's Stories. (p. 1096)
—Silk Princess: The Classic Edition. Santore, Charles, illus. (p. 2018)
—Snow White: A Little Apple Classic. (p. 2048)
—Stowaway on Noah's Ark: The Classic Edition. Santore, Charles, illus. (p. 2136)
—Stowaway on Noah's Ark Board Book: The Classic Edition. Santore, Charles, illus. (p. 2136)
—Stowaway on Noah's Ark Oversized Padded Board Book: The Classic Edition. Santore, Charles, illus. (p. 2136)
—Timeless Tales Mini Gift Set: Big Stories for Little Hands. (p. 2246)
—William the Curious: Knight of the Water Lilies. (p. 2469)
—William the Curious: Knight of the Water Lilies: The Classic Edition. Santore, Charles, illus. (p. 2469)
—Wizard of Oz Coloring Book: The Classic Edition. (p. 2483)
Santore, Charles, illus. see Aesop.
Santore, Charles, illus. see Andersen, Hans.
Santore, Charles, illus. see Baum, L. Frank.
Santore, Charles, illus. see Brothers Grimm, Brothers.
Santore, Charles, illus. see Carroll, Lewis, pseud.
Santore, Charles, illus. see Longfellow, Henry Wadsworth.
Santore, Charles, illus. see Longfellow, Henry.
Santore, Charles, illus. see Moore, Clement C.
Santore, Charles, illus. see Moore, Clement.
Santore, Charles, illus. see Potter, Beatrix.
Santore, Charles, illus. see Williams Bianco, Margery.
Santore, Charles, illus. see Williams, Margery.
Santore, Marcia. Craft Artists: A Practical Career Guide (p. 466)
—Fine Artists: A Practical Career Guide (p. 730)
—Good King Wenceslas: A Beloved Carol Retold in Pictures for Today's Families of All Faiths & Backgrounds. (p. 863)
—Plumbers: A Practical Career Guide (p. 1763)
Santorelli, Mildred. Adventures of Grandma Mimi & Her Boys. (p. 23)
Santoro. My Secret Place. Santoro, illus. (p. 1560)
Santoro, illus. see Santoro Licensing.
Santoro, Christopher. It's Haunted! (p. 1145)
—It's My State! - Group 6. (p. 1146)
—It's My State Group 8 (p. 1146)
—Open Santa's Door. (p. 1665)
—Open the Church Door. (p. 1665)
—Open the Preschool Door. (p. 1665)
Santoro, Christopher, illus. see Altman, Linda Jacobs.
Santoro, Christopher, illus. see Baker, Ken.
Santoro, Christopher, illus. see Bjorklund, Ruth.
Santoro, Christopher, illus. see Burgan, Michael.
Santoro, Christopher, illus. see Evans, Nate & Brown, Stephanie Gwyn.
Santoro, Christopher, illus. see Gaines, Ann Graham.
Santoro, Christopher, illus. see Haney, Johannah.
Santoro, Christopher, illus. see Hart, Joyce.
Santoro, Christopher, illus. see Hicks, Terry Allan.
Santoro, Christopher, illus. see King, David C.
Santoro, Christopher, illus. see Knudsen, Michelle.
Santoro, Christopher, illus. see Milton, Joyce.
Santoro, Christopher, illus. see Petreycik, Rick.
Santoro, Christopher, illus. see Random House.
Santoro, Christopher, illus. see Sanders, Doug.
Santoro, Christopher, jt. auth. see Random House.
Santoro Licensing. Once upon a Gorjuss Time: Six Classic Tales to Dream By. Santoro, illus. (p. 1657)
Santoro, Lucio & Santoro, Meera. Wild Oceans: A Pop-Up Book with Revolutionary Technology. (p. 2464)
Santoro, Scott. Candy Cane Lane. Santoro, Scott, illus. (p. 322)
—Which Way to Witch School? Santoro, Scott, illus. (p. 2441)
Santos, Adriana, illus. see Newman, Tracy.

Sartoris, Adelaide. Past Hours, Vol. 1 of 2 (Classic Reprint) (p. 1703)
—Past Hours, Vol. 2 of 2 (Classic Reprint) (p. 1703)
Sartorius, Evohn. Bobbie, His Family & Dog Bingo (p. 252)
Sarver, Charles. Country Boy (Classic Reprint) (p. 461)
Sarvis, Barbara Hageman. Long Journey. (p. 1343)
Sarwari, Zohra. Inheritance: A Journey to China (Book 1) (p. 1120)
—Inheritance: A Journey to Africa (Book 4) (p. 1120)
Sasa, Fungisayi. Search for the Perfect Head. (p. 1971)
Sasaki, Chris, illus. see Ledyard, Stephanie.
Sasaki, Chris, illus. see Leung, Julie.
Sasaki, Ellen Joy, illus. see Bateman, Teresa.
Sasaki, Masahiro & DiCicco, Sue. Complete Story of Sadako Sasaki. (p. 435)
Sasano, David. Oh Yuck! I Sat on a Duck! Ruble, Eugene, illus. (p. 1642)
Sasek, M. This Is Munich: A Children's Classic. (p. 2225)
Sasek, Miroslav. This Is America: A National Treasury. (p. 2224)
—This Is Australia. (p. 2224)
—This Is Greece. (p. 2224)
—This Is the Way to the Moon. (p. 2225)
—This Is the World: A Global Treasury. (p. 2225)
—This Is Washington, D. C. (p. 2225)
Sasheva, Iva, illus. see Isaacs, Sally Senzell.
Sasheva, Iva, illus. see Isaacs, Sally.
Sashida, Kazu. Hiroshima's Life Water. (p. 974)
Sasiain, Leire, illus. see Newton, Jay.
Sasic, Natasha, illus. see Banks, Steven.
Sasky, Jazmin, illus. see Gilman, Michelle.
Sasley, Brent. Cold War in the Middle East, 1950-1991. (p. 413)
Sass, Adam. Surrender Your Sons. (p. 2164)
Sasscer, Abby. Sophie's Stuff. Cayless, Sophie, illus. (p. 2065)
Sasse, Lena. Sayuri. (p. 1941)
Sassi, Kelly. Best Teen Writing of North Dakota 2018. (p. 208)
Sassi, Laura. Amor Es Bondadoso Chaperon, Lison, illus. (p. 76)
—Diva Delores & the Opera House Mouse. Gerlings, Rebecca, illus. (p. 565)
—Goodnight, Ark Chapman, Jane, illus. (p. 867)
—Goodnight, Manger Chapman, Jane, illus. (p. 867)
—Love Is Kind Chaperon, Lison, illus. (p. 1360)
—Love Is Kind Bonnet, Rosalinde, illus. (p. 1360)
Sassin, Eva, illus. see Crow, Melinda Melton.
Sassin, Eva, illus. see Ives, Rob.
Sassin, Eva, illus. see Mason, Paul.
Sassin, Eva, illus. see Oxlade, Chris.
Sassin, Eva, jt. auth. see Crow, Melinda Melton.
Sasso, Sandy Eisenberg. Butterflies under Our Hats. Rothenberg, Joani Keller, illus. (p. 303)
—I Am God's Paintbrush. Compton, Annette, illus. (p. 1058)
—Regina Jonas: The Girl Who Persisted. Lucas, Margeaux, illus. (p. 1861)
—Shema in the Mezuzah: Listening to Each Other. Rothenberg, Joani Keller, illus. (p. 2005)
—Story of And: The Little Word That Changed the World. Rothenberg, Joani Keller, illus. (p. 2129)
—When God Gave Us Words. Zoellis, Darcy Day, illus. (p. 2430)
Sassoli De Bianchi, Massimiliano. What weighs more: 1 kg of iron or 1 kg of Feathers? (p. 2422)
Sassone, Richard. Galangous. Sassone, Richard, illus. (p. 805)
Sassouni, Maral, illus. see Kramer, Jackie Azúa.
Sastrawinata-Lemay, Griselda. Blue Spot: Walt Disney Animation Studios Artist Showcase. Sastrawinata-Lemay, Griselda, illus. (p. 249)
Sastrawinata-Lemay, Griselda, illus. see Fejeran, Tony.
Sastrawinata-Lemay, Griselda, illus. see Francis, Suzanne.
Sastrawinata-Lemay, Griselda, illus. see Posner-Sanchez, Andrea & Hitchcock, Laura.
Sastre, Elvira. Aquella Orilla Nuestra / That Shore of Ours. (p. 108)
Satcher, Mike. Out of the Flock. (p. 1682)
Satenstein, Diane & Ross, Dave "Persue". Origins of Bunny Kitty: A Tale for All Ages. (p. 1672)
Sater, Steven. Alice by Heart. (p. 44)
Sateren, Shelley Swanson. Fearless Freddie. Melmon, Deborah, illus. (p. 717)
—Growling Gracie. Melmon, Deborah, illus. (p. 900)
—Homesick Herbie. Melmon, Deborah, illus. (p. 998)
—Lunchroom Fight. Sullivan, Mary, illus. (p. 1369)
—Max & Zoe. Sullivan, Mary, illus. (p. 1427)
—Max & Zoe at Recess Sullivan, Mary, illus. (p. 1427)
—Max & Zoe at School Sullivan, Mary, illus. (p. 1427)
—Max & Zoe at Soccer Practice Sullivan, Mary, illus. (p. 1427)
—Max & Zoe at the Dentist Sullivan, Mary, illus. (p. 1427)
—Max & Zoe at the Doctor Sullivan, Mary, illus. (p. 1427)
—Max & Zoe at the Library Sullivan, Mary, illus. (p. 1427)
—Max & Zoe Celebrate Mother's Day Sullivan, Mary, illus. (p. 1427)
—Max & Zoe: the Lunchroom Fight Sullivan, Mary, illus. (p. 1427)
—Max & Zoe: the Science Fair Sullivan, Mary, illus. (p. 1427)
—Max & Zoe: the Very Best Art Project Sullivan, Mary, illus. (p. 1427)
—Max & Zoe: Too Many Tricks Sullivan, Mary, illus. (p. 1427)
—Mudball Molly. Melmon, Deborah, illus. (p. 1524)
—School Concert. Sullivan, Mary, illus. (p. 1945)
—Science Fair. Sullivan, Mary, illus. (p. 1954)
—Too Many Tricks. Sullivan, Mary, illus. (p. 2261)
—Very Best Art Project. Sullivan, Mary, illus. (p. 2352)
Sath, Keosha. Just Like You. (p. 1193)
Sati, Suruchi, illus. see Lake, Angie.
Sato, Anna & Sato, Eriko. My First Japanese Kanji Book: Learning Kanji the Fun & Easy Way! Sato, Anna & Sato, Eriko, illus. (p. 1544)
Sato, Hannah. My Family's Journey. (p. 1538)
Sato, Koichi. Infinite Coloring Dazzling Designs. (p. 1118)
Sato, Maki. Animals Brag about Their Bottoms. Bergstrom, Brian, tr. (p. 94)
Sato, Masahiko. Talpidae Buses. (p. 2188)
Sato, Miki, illus. see Del Rizzo, Suzanne.
Sato, Shozo. Ikebana: Create Beautiful Flower Arrangements with This Traditional Japanese Art. (p. 1094)
Sato, Take, jt. auth. see Ozaki, Yei Theodora.
Sato, Tsutomu. Irregular at Magic High School, Vol. 4 (light Novel) Nine School Competition Arc, Part II. (p. 1136)
—Irregular at Magic High School, Vol. 5 (light Novel) Summer Vacation Arc +1. (p. 1136)
—Irregular at Magic High School, Vol. 6 (light Novel) Yokohama Disturbance Arc, Part I. (p. 1136)
Sato, Yuki, illus. see Ando, Yuma.
Satoru, Noda. Golden Kamuy (Volume 1 Of 19) (p. 858)
Satoshi, Yamamoto, illus. see Kusaka, Hidenori.
Satou, Kiyouko. Let's Make It Fun! Piggy Bank. (p. 1275)
Satow, Ernest. Kuaiwa Hen, Twenty-Five Exercises: In the Yedo Colloquial, for the Use of Students, with Notes (Classic Reprint) (p. 1233)
Satterfield, April. Leah Bug & Her Flying Friends. Guthrie, Lewis, illus. (p. 1255)
Satterfield, Jacob, illus. see Otter.
Satterfield, Mary & Satterfield, Nathaniel. Leaping Lady: A Tall Tale from Mary & Nathaniel Satterfield. (p. 1255)
Satterlee, Anna E. Found: A Young Nobleman: a Play in Two Acts Three Scenes (Classic Reprint) (p. 771)
—Wonder Girl: A Tourist Tale of California (Classic Reprint) (p. 2488)
Satterlee, Walter, jt. auth. see Pollard, Josephine.
Satterthwaite, Molly, illus. see Spencer, Bevin Rolfs.
Sattgast, L. J. Rhyme Bible Storybook Cleyet-Merle, Laurence, illus. (p. 1875)
—Rhyme Bible Storybook for Little Ones Cleyet-Merle, Laurence, illus. (p. 1875)
Satthianadhan, S. Kamala: A Story of Hindu Life (Classic Reprint) (p. 1202)
Sattin, Samuel. Bezkamp. Hickman, Jen, illus. (p. 212)
—Glint Book One: The Cloud Raiders. McGinty, Ian, illus. (p. 843)
Sattler, David, jt. auth. see Sattler, Jennifer.
Sattler, Jennifer. Bully. Sattler, Jennifer, illus. (p. 296)
—Chick 'n' Pug. (p. 367)
—Chick 'n' Pug Christmas. (p. 367)
—Chick 'n' Pug Meet the Dude. (p. 367)
—Chick 'n' Pug: the Love Pug. (p. 367)
—Dirty Birdies. Sattler, Jennifer, illus. (p. 552)
—Dollop & Mrs. Fabulous. (p. 579)
—Frankie the Blankie. (p. 778)
—Go to Sheep. Shum, Benson, illus. (p. 848)
—Hide 'n' Sheep. Shum, Benson, illus. (p. 967)
—My Friend Moe. (p. 1547)
—One Red Sock. Sattler, Jennifer, illus. (p. 1662)
—Pig Kahuna. (p. 1743)
—Pig Kahuna Pirates! (p. 1743)
—Sylvie: The Colorful Flamingo. (p. 2173)
—Sylvie. (p. 2173)
—Who's Hatching? (p. 2453)
—Who's That Pig? (p. 2453)
Sattler, Jennifer & Sattler, David. Jungle Gym. Sattler, Jennifer, illus. (p. 1190)
Satyajit, Ray. Aventures de Goopy et Bagha, Autres Histoires du Bengale(les) (p. 142)
Satz, Mario. Camino. Kono, Yara, illus. (p. 314)
—Pluma. Beitia, Maria, illus. (p. 1763)
Sauber, Robert, illus. see Mayberry, Lynn M.
Sauceda, Vickie. Doobie Kind & Mean Gene. (p. 584)
Saucerman, Linda. Carbon. (p. 327)
—Hydrogen. (p. 1055)
—Ozzy Osbourne & Kelly Osbourne. (p. 1690)
Saucier, Aldric J. Gotcha, Katchya. (p. 872)
Saudo, Coralie. My Dad at the Zoo. Di Giacomo, Kris, illus. (p. 1536)
—My Dad Is Big & Strong, But... A Bedtime Story. Di Giacomo, Kris, illus. (p. 1536)
Sauer, Abe. Goodnight Loon. Davauer, Nathaniel, illus. (p. 867)
Sauer, Drake & Sauer, Katheryn. Betsy the Brachiosaurus. (p. 209)
Sauer, Richard, illus. see Wallace, K. K.
Sauer, Tammi. But the Bear Came Back. Taylor, Dan, illus. (p. 303)
—Caring for Your Lion. Cummings, Troy, illus. (p. 331)
—Chicken Dance. Santat, Dan, illus. (p. 368)
—Cowboy Camp. Reed, Mike, illus. (p. 464)
—Go Fish! Waring, Zoe, illus. (p. 846)
—I Love Cake! Starring Rabbit, Porcupine, & Moose. Rozelaar, Angie, illus. (p. 1069)
—Knock Knock. Francis, Guy, illus. (p. 1229)
—Little Chicken. Taylor, Dan, illus. (p. 1313)
—Making a Friend. Friend, Alison, illus. (p. 1388)
—Mary Had a Little Glam. Brantley Newton, Vanessa, illus. (p. 1415)
—Mary Had a Little Glam. Brantley-Newton, Vanessa, illus. (p. 1415)
—Me Want Pet! Shea, Bob, illus. (p. 1433)
—Mostly Monsterly. Magoon, Scott, illus. (p. 1509)
—Mr. Duck Means Business. Mack, Jeff, illus. (p. 1518)
—Nugget & Fang: Race Around the Reef. Slack, Michael, illus. (p. 1629)
—Nugget & Fang: Friends Forever—Or Snack Time? Slack, Michael, illus. (p. 1629)
—Nugget & Fang: Friends Forever - Or Snack Time? Slack, Michael, illus. (p. 1629)
—Nugget & Fang. (p. 1629)
—Nugget & Fang (lap Board Book) Friends Forever—Or Snack Time? Slack, Michael, illus. (p. 1629)
—Nugget & Fang Go to School. Slack, Michael, illus. (p. 1629)
—Oh, Nuts! Krall, Dan, illus. (p. 1642)
—Princess in Training. Berger, Joe, illus. (p. 1797)
—Quiet Wyatt. Howard, Arthur, illus. (p. 1828)
—Roar! Starin, Liz, illus. (p. 1889)
—Truck, Truck, Goose! Waring, Zoe, illus. (p. 2292)
—Truck, Truck, Goose! Board Book. Waring, Zoe, illus. (p. 2292)
—Twelve Days of Christmas in Oklahoma. Hutto, Victoria, illus. (p. 2303)
—Wordy Birdy. Mottram, Dave, illus. (p. 2495)
—Wordy Birdy 4-Copy L-Card (p. 2495)
—Wordy Birdy Meets Mr. Cougarpants. Mottram, Dave, illus. (p. 2495)
—Your Alien. Fujita, Goro, illus. (p. 2532)
—Your Alien Returns. Fujita, Goro, illus. (p. 2532)
Sauerhofer, Ulrike. I Spy 123: Totally Crazy Numbers. Ancutici, Manuela, photos by. (p. 1082)
Sauerstein, Paul. Uber Lydgate's Aesopubersetzung: Inaugural-Dissertation Zur Erlangung der Philosophischen Doctorwurde an der Universitat Leipzig (Classic Reprint) (p. 2313)
Sauerwein, Wilhelm, tr. see Scott, Walter.
Saujani, Reshma. Girls Who Code: Learn to Code & Change the World. (p. 839)
Saul, George Brandon. Age of Yeats: The Golden Age of Irish Literature (Classic Reprint) (p. 35)
Saul, Laya. My Friend Is Jewish. (p. 1547)
—Recipe & Craft Guide to Israel. (p. 1853)
—Ways to Help after a Natural Disaster: A Guide to Giving Back. (p. 2388)
—Ways to Help Disadvantaged Youth: A Guide to Giving Back. (p. 2388)
—We Visit Israel. (p. 2392)
Saul, Robert A. All about Children. (p. 48)
—All about Children. Rens, Jan Yalich, illus. (p. 48)
Saules, Tony de, jt. auth. see Arnold, Nick.
Saulite, Anita. Secret Money Diary of Chloe Appleseed: My Gotta Have It Pair of Shoes. (p. 1977)
Saulles, Tony De, see Arnold, Nick & De Saulles, Tony.
Saulles, Tony De, see De Saulles, Tony.
Sauls, Lynn B. Gabriel Goes to Washington: Through Big Brown Eyes; the Adventures of Gabriel the Poodle. Sauls, Lynn B., illus. (p. 804)
Sault, Alicia Dianne. Fairest Fairies. (p. 695)
Sault, R. O. Captain Waters, & Bill His Bo'son a Tale of the Ocean & the Farm (Classic Reprint) (p. 326)
Sault, Richard, jt. auth. see Leybourn, William.
Saumande, Juliette. In Search of Happiness. Weller, Andrew, tr. from FRE. (p. 1107)
—My Little Album of Dublin: An English & Irish Word Book. Krüse, Tarsila, illus. (p. 1552)
Saumande, Juliette, et al. No Me da Miedo! 10 Historias Escalofriantes. (p. 1613)
Saumell, Marina, illus. see Tsavaris-Lecourezos, Demetra.
Saumell, Marina, illus. see Womick, Chip.
Saumery, Lambert De. Devil Turn'd Hermit: Or the Adventures of Astaroth Banish'd from Hell, a Satirical Romance (Classic Reprint) (p. 535)
Saumier, Chantelle. Vinnie! Star of the Show. (p. 2359)
—Vinnie! the Hurricane. (p. 2359)
Saumya Gupta & Saransh Goswami. Engineer Se Insaan Tak. (p. 651)
Saunders, Alexander. Magical Tale of Hillary & Harold Greenwood. (p. 1380)
Saunders, Alfred H. Moving Picture World, Vol. 1: June 1, 1907 (Classic Reprint) (p. 1517)
—Moving Picture World, Vol. 1: September 1907 (Classic Reprint) (p. 1517)
—Moving Picture World, Vol. 1: November 2, 1907 (Classic Reprint) (p. 1517)
—Moving Picture World, Vol. 2: April 4, 1908 (Classic Reprint) (p. 1517)
—Moving Picture World, Vol. 2: March 7, 1908 (Classic Reprint) (p. 1517)
Saunders, Alfred M. Moving Picture World, Vol. 2: January 11, 1908 (Classic Reprint) (p. 1517)
Saunders, Amy. When God Made the World. (p. 2430)
Saunders, Ashley & Saunders, Leslie. Rule of Many. (p. 1913)
—Rule of One. (p. 1913)
Saunders, Brianna. Magic Marble. (p. 1378)
Saunders, Catherine. Amazing Powers. (p. 66)
—Are Ewoks Scared of Stormtroopers? (p. 112)
—DK Readers L2: LEGO Friends: Let's Go Riding! (p. 568)
—DK Readers L3: LEGO Friends: Summer Adventures. (p. 568)
—DK Readers L3: Star Wars: the Legendary Yoda: Discover the Secret of Yoda's Life! (p. 568)
—DK Readers L4: LEGO NINJAGO: Team Ninja. (p. 569)
—Grammy Gets Treed. Shupe, Kyla, illus. (p. 876)
—Jedi & the Force. (p. 1162)
—Legendary Yoda. (p. 1263)
—LEGO(r) FRIENDS Character Encyclopedia: The Ultimate Guide to the Girls & Their World. (p. 1264)
—Story of Darth Vader. (p. 2129)
—Team Ninja. (p. 2196)
Saunders, Catherine, jt. auth. see Casey, Joe.
Saunders, Catherine & DK. Marvel Amazing Powers. (p. 1412)
—Marvel Amazing Powers [RD3]. (p. 1412)
Saunders, Charles Francis. California Padres & Their Missions (Classic Reprint) (p. 311)
—Under the Sky in California (Classic Reprint) (p. 2323)
Saunders, Chris. Wish. Saunders, Chris, illus. (p. 2478)
Saunders, Chris, illus. see Warren, Rick.
Saunders, Claire, et al. Power Book: What Is It, Who Has It & Why? Joelle Avelino, Joelle, illus. (p. 1782)
Saunders, Craig. What Is the Theory of Plate Tectonics? (p. 2417)
Saunders, Darren. Alternative Christmas Tree. (p. 60)
Saunders, Duncan. Smuggler's Apprentice. (p. 2043)
Saunders, Eric. Boost Your IQ: Maximize the Power of Your Brain. (p. 262)
Saunders, Gary L. My Life with Trees: A Sylvan Journey. (p. 1552)
Saunders, George. Fox 8: A Story. Cardinal, Chelsea, illus. (p. 773)
—Very Persistent Gappers of Frip. Smith, Lane, illus. (p. 2353)
Saunders, Gr. Cluckenstein: The Halloween Chicken. (p. 409)
Saunders, Harry M. Teenagers on an Adventure: Journey of Two Boys & a Girl. (p. 2200)
Saunders, Jami Lynn. Feral: Book I of the Werecat Saga. (p. 720)
—Rabid: Book II of the Werecat Saga. (p. 1830)
Saunders, John. Abel Drake's Wife (Classic Reprint) (p. 5)
—Israel Mort, Overman, Vol. 1 Of 3: A Story of the Mine (Classic Reprint) (p. 1141)
—Martin Pole, Vol. 1 of 2 (Classic Reprint) (p. 1411)
—Martin Pole, Vol. 2 of 2 (Classic Reprint) (p. 1411)
—One Against the World; or Reuben's War, Vol. 2 Of 3: A Novel (Classic Reprint) (p. 1658)
—One Against the World, Vol. 1 Of 3: Or Reuben's War (Classic Reprint) (p. 1658)
Saunders, Karen. Suzy P. Forever Me. (p. 2167)
Saunders, Kate. Beswitched. (p. 208)
—Curse of the Chocolate Phoenix. (p. 489)
—Five Children on the Western Front. (p. 743)
—Land of Neverendings. (p. 1241)
—Land of Neverendings. (p. 1242)
—Little Secret. Carman, William, illus. (p. 1327)
—Magicalamity. (p. 1381)
—Whizz Pop Chocolate Shop. (p. 2446)
Saunders, Kate & Nesbit, E. Five Children on the Western Front. (p. 743)
Saunders, Katherine. High Mills (Classic Reprint) (p. 968)
—High Mills, Vol. 1 of 3 (Classic Reprint) (p. 968)
Saunders, Katie. Color Fun! (an Abacus Book) (p. 420)
—Let's Learn Opposites. (p. 1274)
—Little Reindeer. (p. 1327)
—Olive the Alien. (p. 1649)
Saunders, Katie, illus. see Bicknell, Joanna & Page, Nick.
Saunders, Katie, illus. see Birdsong, Minnie.
Saunders, Katie, illus. see Bullard, Lisa.
Saunders, Katie, illus. see Page, Nick & Page, Claire.
Saunders, Katie, illus. see Porter, Jen.
Saunders, Lisa & Weber, Penny. From Stars to Stable: Includes Interactive Talking Points with Children. (p. 793)
-**Saunders, Margaret Baillie.** Black Sheep Chapel (Classic Reprint) (p. 239)
Saunders, Margaret Baillie. Litany Lane: A Novel (Classic Reprint) (p. 1309)
Saunders, Marshall. Beautiful Joe: An Autobiography of a Dog. (p. 184)
—Beautiful Joe: An Autobiography (Classic Reprint) (p. 184)
—Beautiful Joe. (p. 184)
—Beautiful Joe's Paradise, or the Island of Brotherly Love: A Sequel to 'Beautiful Joe' (Classic Reprint) (p. 184)
—Bonnie Prince Fetlar: The Story of a Pony & His Friend (Classic Reprint) (p. 256)
—Boy, the Wandering Dog: Adventures of a Fox-Terrier (Classic Reprint) (p. 270)
—Daisy (Classic Reprint) (p. 497)
—Deficient Saints: A Tale of Maine (Classic Reprint) (p. 525)
—For His Country, and, Grandmother & the Crow (Classic Reprint) (p. 762)
—For the Other Boy's Sake, & Other Stories (Classic Reprint) (p. 763)
—Girl from Vermont: The Story of a Vacation School Teacher (Classic Reprint) (p. 835)
—Golden Dicky the Story of a Canary, & His Friends (Classic Reprint) (p. 857)
—Her Sailor: A Love Story (Classic Reprint) (p. 956)
—House of Armour (Classic Reprint) (p. 1022)
—Jimmy Gold-Coast, or the Story of a Monkey & His Friends (Classic Reprint) (p. 1168)
—King of the Park (Classic Reprint) (p. 1221)
—My Pets: Real Happenings in My Aviary (Classic Reprint) (p. 1559)
—Princess Sukey: The Story of a Pigeon, & Her Human Friends (Classic Reprint) (p. 1799)
—Pussy Black-Face, or the Story of a Kitten & Her Friends: A Book for Boys & Girls, Illustrated by Diantha Home Marlowe (Classic Reprint) (p. 1817)
—Rose a Charlitte: An Acadien Romance (Classic Reprint) (p. 1904)
—Story of the Gravelys: A Tale for Girls (Classic Reprint) (p. 2133)
—Tilda Jane, an Orphan in Search of a Home: A Story for Boys & Girls (Classic Reprint) (p. 2242)
Saunders, Mary Ann. Maria Bartlett, or the Advantages of Application: Embracing Remarks on the Education & Manners of Females (Classic Reprint) (p. 1404)
Saunders, Matt, illus. see Kassner, Heather.
Saunders, Merriam. My Whirling, Twirling Motor. Lyon, Tammie, illus. (p. 1565)
Saunders, Mike. Inside Coding. (p. 1122)
Saunders, Mike, illus. see Dicker, Katie.
Saunders, Mike, illus. see Dickler, Katie.
Saunders, Nigel, jt. auth. see Solway, Andrew.
Saunders, Rachael, illus. see Doran, Sally.
Saunders, Rachael & Cole, Lon. We Love the Farm: Two Books in One! (p. 2391)
Saunders, Rachel, illus. see Brown, Carron.
Saunders, Ripley D. Colonel Todhunter of Missouri (Classic Reprint) (p. 418)
Saunders, Ripley Dunlap. John Kenadie: Being the Story of His Perplexing Inheritance (Classic Reprint) (p. 1173)
Saunders, Rob. Dragon River. Martin, Gillian, illus. (p. 594)
Saunders, Sara. Swirly. Pierce, Matthew, illus. (p. 2171)
Saunders, Suzie. Haze the Happy Helper. (p. 941)
Saunders, Tom. I Want to Go to the Moon. Nugent, Cynthia, illus. (p. 1085)
Saunders, Vivien. Adventures of Annika. Muckle, Christine, illus. (p. 21)
Saunders, William Duncan. Fifteen Years Old: Being Letters, Notes & Manuscripts Left Behind by William Duncan Saunders, & Picked up by His Friends G. C. R. & A. W (Classic Reprint) (p. 724)
Saunders, Zina, illus. see Banks, Steven.
Saunders, Zina, illus. see Beechen, Adam.
Saunders, Zina, illus. see Beinstein, Phoebe.
Saunders, Zina, illus. see Inches, Alison.
Saunders, Zina, illus. see Ricci, Christine.
Saunders, Zoe, illus. see Appleby, Linda.
Saunders, Zoe, illus. see Sanders, Mt.
Saunderson, Chris, illus. see Jeffs, Stephanie.
Saunderson, Chris, illus. see Lane, Leena.
Saunders-Smith, Gail. Animal Robots (p. 91)
—Apple Trees. (p. 107)
—Frogs. (p. 790)

S

Sawin, James M. Souvenir Book Providence Teachers' Bazaar: Infantry Hall November 25-26-27-28-29-30, 1901 (Classic Reprint) (p. 2069)
Sawler, Sarah. 100 Things You Don't Know about Atlantic Canada (for Kids) (p. 2557)
Sawtelle, M. P. Heroine Of '49: A Story of the Pacific Coast. (p. 963)
—Heroine Of '49: A Story of the Pacific Coast (Classic Reprint) (p. 963)
Sawvel, Gennai, illus. see Huston-Holm, Patty & McFerin, Kathy.
Sawvel, Gennai, illus. see Huston-Holm, Patty.
Sawyer, Amy. Chicago Bears. (p. 367)
Sawyer, Ava. Fossils. (p. 770)
—Human Environmental Impact: How We Affect Earth. (p. 1049)
—Humans & Earth's Atmosphere: What's in the Air? (p. 1050)
—Humans & Other Life on Earth: Sharing the Planet. (p. 1050)
—Humans & Our Planet. (p. 1050)
—Humans & the Hydrosphere: Protecting Earth's Water Sources. (p. 1050)
—Igneous Rocks. (p. 1094)
—Metamorphic Rocks. (p. 1452)
—Rocks. (p. 1896)
—Sedimentary Rocks. (p. 1981)
Sawyer, Caroline M. Ladies' Repository, 1863, Vol. 3: An Universalist Monthly Magazine (Classic Reprint) (p. 1236)
—Merchant's Widow: And Other Tales (Classic Reprint) (p. 1447)
Sawyer, Cate. Umbilical Family: Start a Loving Conversation about Adoption, Egg Donation, Step-Parenting, Same Sex Parenting, & More. Avellis, Adriana, illus. (p. 2316)
Sawyer, Darren, photos by see Rayner, Matthew.
Sawyer, Don. Where the Rivers Meet (p. 2439)
Sawyer, Edith A. Mary Cameron: A Romance of Fisherman's Island. (p. 1414)
—Mary Cameron: A Romance of Fisherman's Island (Classic Reprint) (p. 1414)
Sawyer, Horace M. Life of a Hobo Barber (Classic Reprint) (p. 1293)
Sawyer, J. Clark. Los Cometas Helados: A Veces Tienen Colas. (p. 1350)
—Nuestra Luna: El Objeto MÁS Brillante Del Cielo Nocturno. (p. 1629)
—Our Moon: Brightest Object in the Night Sky. (p. 1679)
—PlutÓN: No Es un Planeta. (p. 1763)
Sawyer, J. Clark, jt. auth. see Glaser, Chaya.
Sawyer, J. Scott. Broccoli Bush. Bozeman, Gary, illus. (p. 284)
Sawyer, Jacqueline. Little Racer Big Heart. (p. 1325)
Sawyer, Kem Knapp. Amazing Underground Railroad: Stories in American History. (p. 66)
—Amazing Underground Railroad. (p. 66)
—Grace Akallo & the Pursuit of Justice for Child Soldiers. (p. 873)
—Harriet Tubman. (p. 933)
—Mohandas Gandhi. (p. 1488)
Sawyer, Kim. Trial with No Exit. (p. 2286)
Sawyer, Kim Vogel. Katy's Debate (p. 1206)
—Katy's Decision (p. 1206)
—Katy's Homecoming (p. 1206)
—Katy's New World (p. 1206)
Sawyer Lee, Hannah Farnham. Contrast: Or, Modes of Education. (p. 445)
Sawyer, Moses H. Lieutenant Colborn, or the Disinherited (Classic Reprint) (p. 1287)
Sawyer, Muriel, tr. see Dupuis, Jenny Kay & Kacer, Kathy.
Sawyer, Nettie Alice. Little Kingdom First Reader (Classic Reprint) (p. 1320)
Sawyer, Odessa, illus. see Bracken, Beth & Fraser, Kay.
Sawyer, Odessa, illus. see Dembar Greene, Jacqueline.
Sawyer, Peter, illus. see Miller, Karen.
Sawyer, Ruth. Doctor Danny (Classic Reprint) (p. 573)
—Herself, Himself Myself: A Romance (Classic Reprint) (p. 963)
—Journey Cake, Ho! (p. 1181)
—Leerie (Classic Reprint) (p. 1261)
—Primrose Ring (Classic Reprint) (p. 1793)
—Seven Miles to Arden (Classic Reprint) (p. 1993)
—Silver Sixpence (Classic Reprint) (p. 2020)
—This Way to Christmas (Classic Reprint) (p. 2227)
Sawyer, Sarah. Denny Hamlin: NASCAR Driver. (p. 529)
—Florida: Past & Present. (p. 751)
Sawyer, T. J. Flower Basket: A Tale for Youth (Classic Reprint) (p. 752)
Sawyer, Timothy L., jt. auth. see Torres, Eliseo.
Sawyer, Walter Leon. Local Habitation (Classic Reprint) (p. 1338)
—Outland Journey (Classic Reprint) (p. 1685)
Sawyer-Aitch, Anne. Nalah & the Pink Tiger. Sawyer-Aitch, Anne, illus. (p. 1573)
Sax, Aline. War Within These Walls. (p. 2377)
Sax, Anita. One Step at a Time. Jasuna, Aija, illus. (p. 1662)
—Oscar & the Zoo. Jasuna, Aija, illus. (p. 1673)
Sax, Sarah, illus. see Doyle, Bill.
Saxby, Argyll. Taming of the Rancher: A Story of Western Canada (Classic Reprint) (p. 2189)
Saxby, Claire. Big Red Kangaroo. Byrne, Graham, illus. (p. 222)
—Dingo. Harricks, Tannya, illus. (p. 547)
—Emu. Byrne, Graham, illus. (p. 645)
—Koala. Vivas, Julie, illus. (p. 1230)
—Meet the ANZACs. Berry, Max, illus. (p. 1439)
—Meet Weary Dunlop. Lord, Jeremy, illus. (p. 1441)
—Meet... Weary Dunlop. Lord, Jeremy, illus. (p. 1441)
—Seadog. Jellett, Tom, illus. (p. 1969)
Saxby, Jessie Margaret. Rock-Bound: A Story of the Shetland Isles (Classic Reprint) (p. 1894)
Saxe, John G. Clever Stories of Many Nations. (p. 404)
—Clever Stories of Many Nations (Classic Reprint) (p. 404)
Saxe, John Godfrey. Masquerade & Other Poems (Classic Reprint) (p. 1417)
Saxelby, Anne, illus. see Saxelby, Pam.
Saxelby Melville Wintle, Henry. Ignorant Learned: Researches after the Long Lost Mysteries of Free-Masonry - Scholar's Choice Edition. (p. 1094)
Saxelby, Pam. Great Grace Escape. Saxelby, Anne, illus. (p. 886)
—Josie the Great. (p. 1179)
Saxena, Shalini. Bird Watcher's Guide to Goldfinches. (p. 230)
—Legend of King Arthur. (p. 1262)
—Legend of Sleepy Hollow. (p. 1262)
—Nero: Ruthless Roman Emperor. (p. 1588)
—Paul Revere Didn't Say "The British Are Coming!" Exposing Myths about the American Revolution. (p. 1707)
—Saving the Endangered Gray Wolf (p. 1939)
—Volleyball & Its Greatest Players (p. 2367)
Saxena, Shalini, ed. see Barrington, Richard.
Saxena, Shalini, ed. see Ray, Michael.
Saxena, Shalini, ed. Dictatorship, Fascism, & Totalitarianism. (p. 541)
—History of Marines Around the World (p. 978)
—Top 101 Artists (p. 2263)
Saxon, Charles D. Modern Screen, Vol. 42: January-November, 1951 (Classic Reprint) (p. 1487)
—Modern Screen, Vol. 48: December, 1953 (Classic Reprint) (p. 1487)
—Modern Screen, Vol. 49: America's Greatest Movie Magazine; December, 1954-December, 1955 (Classic Reprint) (p. 1487)
—Modern Screen, Vol. 50: January, 1956 (Classic Reprint) (p. 1487)
Saxon, Elizabeth Lyle. Southern Woman's War Time Reminiscences (Classic Reprint) (p. 2069)
Saxon, Harold. Under the King's Bastion: A Romance of Quebec, Comprising Many True & Interesting Historical Sketches & Descriptions of the Customs & Habits of the People of Quebec, Ancient & Modern (Classic Reprint) (p. 2322)
Saxon, John. Handbook for County Social Services Boards. (p. 915)
Saxon, Lucy. Almost King. (p. 57)
—Take Back the Skies. (p. 2176)
Saxon Publishers. Saxon Math 1: Parcc Test Preparation Student Workbook. (p. 1939)
—Saxon Math 1 California: Student Worksheet 8pk. (p. 1939)
—Saxon Math 1 California: Student Material Consumable 8pk. (p. 1939)
—Saxon Math 1 Oklahoma: Teacher Material Kit. (p. 1939)
—Saxon Math 1 Tennessee: Sov Bundle Grade 1. (p. 1939)
—Saxon Math 2: Parcc Test Preparation Student Workbook. (p. 1939)
—Saxon Math 2 California: Student Worksheet 8pk. (p. 1939)
—Saxon Math 2 California: Student Material Consumable 8pk. (p. 1939)
—Saxon Math 2 Florida: 32 Student Kit 2010. (p. 1940)
—Saxon Math 2 Tennessee: Sov Bundle. (p. 1940)
—Saxon Math 3: Parcc Test Preparation Student Workbook. (p. 1940)
—Saxon Math 3 Florida: Test Prep Teachbook. (p. 1940)
—Saxon Math 3 Indiana: Test Prep Teachbook. (p. 1940)
—Saxon Math 3 Oklahoma: Test Prep Teachbook. (p. 1940)
—Saxon Math 4 Florida: Test Prep Teachbook. (p. 1940)
—Saxon Math 4 Oklahoma: Test Prep Teachbook. (p. 1940)
—Saxon Math 5 Florida: Test Prep Teachbook. (p. 1940)
—Saxon Math 5 Indiana: Test Prep Teachbook. (p. 1940)
—Saxon Math 5 Oklahoma: Test Prep Teachbook. (p. 1940)
—Saxon Math 6 West Virginia: Test Prep Workbook. (p. 1940)
—Saxon Math 7 West Virginia: Test Prep Workbook. (p. 1940)
—Saxon Math Algebra 1 Tennessee: Teacher Edition Bundle 2010. (p. 1940)
—Saxon Math Algebra 2 Tennessee: Teacher Edition Bundle 2010. (p. 1940)
—Saxon Math Course 1 Tennessee: Teacher's Manual Bundle 2010. (p. 1940)
—Saxon Math Course 2 Florida: Test Prep Handbook Grade 7. (p. 1940)
—Saxon Math Course 2 Tennessee: Teacher's Manual Bundle 2010. (p. 1940)
—Saxon Math Course 3 Tennessee: Teacher's Manual Bundle 2010. (p. 1940)
—Saxon Math Florida: Test Prep Teachbook. (p. 1940)
—Saxon Math Geometry Tennessee: Teacher Edition Bundle 2010. (p. 1940)
—Saxon Math Intermediate 3: Parcc Test Preparation Student Workbook. (p. 1940)
—Saxon Math Intermediate 3 Tennessee: Sov Bundle Grade 3. (p. 1940)
—Saxon Math Intermediate 3 Tennessee: Teacher Materials Bundle 2010. (p. 1940)
—Saxon Math Intermediate 3 West Virginia: Test Prep Workbook. (p. 1940)
—Saxon Math Intermediate 4: Teacher Bundle 2012. (p. 1940)
—Saxon Math Intermediate 4 Tennessee: Teacher's Manual Bundle 2010. (p. 1940)
—Saxon Math K: Parcc Test Preparation Student Workbook. (p. 1940)
—Saxon Math K California: Student Worksheet 8pk. (p. 1940)
—Saxon Math K California: Student Material Consumable 8pk. (p. 1940)
—Saxon Math K Tennessee: Teacher Materials Bundle 2010. (p. 1940)
—Saxon Math West Virginia: Test Prep Workbook. (p. 1940)
—Saxon Physics: Classroom Package Adaptation. (p. 1940)
Saxon, Vickie. Be Mindful, Donald! A Mickey & Friends Story. Disney Storybook Artists, illus. (p. 177)
—Be Mindful, Donald! A Mickey & Friends Story. Disney Storybook Artists, Disney Storybook, illus. (p. 177)
—Just Like Me? A Frozen Story. Disney Storybook Artists, illus. (p. 1193)
—Just Like Me? A Frozen Story. Disney Storybook Artists, Disney Storybook, illus. (p. 1193)
Saxon, Victoria. Anna & Elsa's Secret Playtime (Disney Frozen) RH Disney Staff, illus. (p. 97)
—Big Trouble in Little Rodentia. (p. 223)
—Cars 3 Little Golden Book (Disney/Pixar Cars 3) Wu, Vivien, illus. (p. 334)
—Colors of Caring. (p. 426)
—Disney Junior Fancy Nancy: Nancy Takes the Case. Disney Storybook Art Team, Disney Storybook, illus. (p. 560)
—Disney Junior Fancy Nancy: Shoe la La! (p. 560)
—Disney Junior Fancy Nancy: Toodle-Oo, Miss Moo. (p. 560)
—Disney Princess the Essential Guide, New Edition. (p. 563)
—Frozen (Disney Frozen) Lee, Grace & Cagol, Andrea, illus. (p. 795)
—Here to Cheer! A Sticker & Activity Book. (p. 958)
—Neon Beach Party. (p. 1587)
—Olaf Waits for Spring. (p. 1644)
—Olaf Waits for Spring (Disney Frozen) RH Disney, illus. (p. 1644)
—Ready to Play! (p. 1848)
—Ready to Play! (Disney Infinity) RH Disney Staff & Doescher, Erik, illus. (p. 1848)
—Shoe-La-la. (p. 2009)
—Toodle-Oo, Miss Moo. (p. 2261)
—Walking the Bob (Disney Junior Puppy Dog Pals) Sefati, Maryam, illus. (p. 2372)
Saxon, Victoria, jt. auth. see Disney.
Saxon, Victoria & Posner-Sanchez, Andrea. Belle Is My Babysitter (Disney Princess) Laguna, Fabio & Andreu, Meritxell, illus. (p. 197)
Saxon, Victoria & RH Disney Staff. Frozen Fever. RH Disney Staff, illus. (p. 795)
Saxton, Anna. Scott Kelly: Astronaut Twin Who Spent a Year in Space. (p. 1962)
Saxton, Evelyn. Droll Stories of Isthmian Life (Classic Reprint) (p. 605)
Saxton, Hope I. Digger, the Service Dog. (p. 545)
Saxton, Jo. Snail Trail: In Search of a Modern Masterpiece. (p. 2044)
Saxton, Patricia. Book of Fairies. Saxton, Patricia, illus. (p. 258)
Say, Allen. Drawing from Memory. (p. 599)
—Drawing from Memory. Say, Allen, illus. (p. 599)
—Favorite Daughter. (p. 715)
—Favorite Daughter. Say, Allen, illus. (p. 715)
—Grandfather's Journey. (p. 877)
—Inker's Shadow. (p. 1120)
—Sign Painter. (p. 2016)
—Silent Days, Silent Dreams. Say, Allen, illus. (p. 2017)
—Tea with Milk. Say, Allen, illus. (p. 2194)
—Tree of Cranes. Say, Allen, illus. (p. 2284)
Say, Thomas. Complete Writings of Thomas Say, on the Conchology of the United States (Classic Reprint) (p. 436)
—Complete Writings of Thomas Say on the Entomology of North America, Vol. 1 (Classic Reprint) (p. 436)
Sayalero, Myriam. Cuentos para niñas Sin Miedo / Stories for Fearless Girls. Ricardicus & Lopez, Ricard, illus. (p. 483)
—Folktales for Fearless Girls: The Stories We Were Never Told. Torrent, Dani, illus. (p. 757)
Saybrook, Emily L. Sabrina Hackett (Classic Reprint) (p. 1920)
Sayce, Conrad Harvey. Golden Buckles, Vol. 8 (Classic Reprint) (p. 856)
Sayed, Joud. Vorada: And the Attack of the Scientist. (p. 2367)
Sayegh, Rob, illus. see Berry-Byrd, Holly.
Sayeh Stone. Shaped Animals. (p. 2000)
Sayekti, Sri, illus. see Davis Jr, Christopher.
Sayer, Ann Marie Mulhearn, jt. auth. see Slobodkina, Esphyr.
Sayer, Blair, illus. see Haley, Patty.
Sayer, Chloe. Incan Empire. (p. 1112)
Sayer, Geoff, jt. auth. see Marshall, David.
Sayer, Karen, jt. auth. see Hardy, Thomas.
Sayer, Marjorie. Girl Mechanic of Wanzhou. (p. 836)
Sayer, Melissa & Naik, Anita. Too Fat? Too Thin? The Healthy Eating Handbook. (p. 2260)
Sayer, Reimunt, jt. auth. see Optic, Oliver, pseud.
Sayers, Louisa Sarah. Henry Acton, Vol. 1: And Other Tales (Classic Reprint) (p. 954)
Sayers, Rachel, illus. see Heeney, Bronwyn.
Sayle, Stephen. Cam & Zara the Travel Bugs. (p. 313)
Sayler, H. L. Terrible Teddy & Peaceful Bill or the Quest of the Treasure Box (Classic Reprint) (p. 2207)
Sayler, Harry Lincoln. Boy Scouts of the Air at Greenwood School (Classic Reprint) (p. 270)
Sayler, Mary Harwell. Prescription Pain Relievers. (p. 1788)
Sayler, Sali Ann. Little Bird Told Me That Love Is a Verb. (p. 1311)
Sayles, Elizabeth, illus. see Bauer, Marion Dane.
Sayles, Elizabeth, illus. see Corey, Shana.
Sayles, Elizabeth, illus. see Krilanovich, Nadia.
Sayles, Elizabeth, illus. see Mora, Pat.
Sayles, Elizabeth, illus. see Wood, Douglas.
Saylor, Emma R. Last Mile-Stone (Classic Reprint) (p. 1248)
Saylor, Sarah. Adventure with the Doxies. (p. 19)
Saylor-Marchant, Linda. Hip Hop into Reading Series: It's easy to read & rap/read & rap like the President. (p. 973)
Saynor, Jill. Clarence the Coffee Bean. (p. 398)
Sayre, April Pulley. Being Frog. Sayre, April Pulley, illus. (p. 194)
—Best in Snow. (p. 206)
—Bloom Boom! Sayre, April Pulley, photos by. (p. 247)
—Cityscape: Where Science & Art Meet. Sayre, April Pulley, illus. (p. 396)
—Did You Burp? How to Ask Questions (or Not!) Hernandez, Leeza, illus. (p. 543)
—Eat Like a Bear. Jenkins, Steve, illus. (p. 621)
—Exploring Earth's Biomes (p. 681)
—Feel the Fog. Sayre, April Pulley, photos by. (p. 718)
—Full of Fall. (p. 797)
—Go, Go, Grapes! A Fruit Chant. Sayre, April Pulley, photos by. (p. 846)
—Here Come the Humpbacks! Hogan, Jamie, illus. (p. 957)
—If You're Hoppy. Urbanovic, Jackie, illus. (p. 1093)
—Let's Go Nuts! Seeds We Eat. Sayre, April Pulley, illus. (p. 1273)
—Like a Lizard. Laberis, Stephanie, illus. (p. 1300)
—Meet the Howlers! Miller, Woody, illus. (p. 1440)
—Rah, Rah, Radishes! A Vegetable Chant. Sayre, April Pulley, photos by. (p. 1834)
—Rah, Rah, Radishes! Classroom Edition. Sayre, April Pulley, photos by. (p. 1834)
—Raindrops Roll. Sayre, April Pulley, photos by. (p. 1837)
—Seagulls Soar. Bogdanska, Kasia, illus. (p. 1969)
—Slowest Book Ever. Murphy, Kelly, illus. (p. 2039)
—Squirrels Leap, Squirrels Sleep. Jenkins, Steve, illus. (p. 2095)
—Thank You, Earth: A Love Letter to Our Planet. Sayre, April Pulley, illus. (p. 2211)
—Turtle, Turtle, Watch Out! Patterson, Annie, illus. (p. 2301)
—Warbler Wave. Sayre, April Pulley, photos by. (p. 2377)
—Woodpecker Wham! Jenkins, Steve, illus. (p. 2492)
Sayre, Jeff, jt. auth. see Sayre, April Pulley.
Sayre, Jeff & Sayre, April Pulley. One Is a Snail, Ten Is a Crab Big Book: A Counting by Feet Book. Cecil, Randy, illus. (p. 1660)
Sayre, Jill K. Fairies of Turtle Creek. (p. 696)
Sayre, Joel. Hizzoner the Mayor: A Novel (Classic Reprint) (p. 982)
Sayre, Justin. Mean. (p. 1434)
—Pretty. (p. 1790)
Sayre, Michael, illus. see Brill, Marlene Targ.
Sayre, Michael S., illus. see Parker, Joan Goldstein.
Sayre, Theodore Burt. Son of Carleycroft: A Dramatic Romance (Classic Reprint) (p. 2061)
—Tom Moore: An Unhistorical Romance, Founded on Certain Happenings in the Life of Ireland's Greatest Poet (Classic Reprint) (p. 2257)
—Two Summer Girls & I. (p. 2309)
—Two Summer Girls & I (Classic Reprint) (p. 2309)
Sayres, Brianna Caplan. Night Night, Curiosity. O'Rourke, Ryan, illus. (p. 1606)
—Tiara Saurus Rex. Boldt, Mike, illus. (p. 2239)
—Where Do Diggers Celebrate Christmas? Slade, Christian, illus. (p. 2436)
—Where Do Diggers Sleep at Night? Slade, Christian, illus. (p. 2436)
—Where Do Diggers, Trains, & Planes Sleep at Night? Board Book Boxed Set Slade, Christian, illus. (p. 2436)
—Where Do Jet Planes Sleep at Night? Slade, Christian, illus. (p. 2436)
—Where Do Speedboats Sleep at Night? Slade, Christian, illus. (p. 2436)
—Where Do Steam Trains Sleep at Night? Slade, Christian, illus. (p. 2436)
Sayyah, Ryan. Tilt for Vesh-Rai'han. (p. 2243)
Sazaklis, Athena Maria. Captain Marvel Little Golden Book (Marvel) Gaylord, Penelope R., illus. (p. 325)
Sazaklis, John. Barnyard Brainwash Baltazar, Art, illus. (p. 167)
—Batman: An Origin Story. Baltazar, Art & Vecchio, Luciano, illus. (p. 172)
—Batman Classic: The Batman Reusable Sticker Book. (p. 172)
—Batman Classic: Gotham's Villains Unleashed! Mada Design Staff, illus. (p. 172)
—Batman Classic: Dawn of the Dynamic Duo. Gordon, Eric A. & Gordon, Steven E., illus. (p. 172)
—Battle in Metropolis. (p. 174)
—Battle on the Moon (Marvel Avengers) Gaylord, Penelope R., illus. (p. 175)
—Biggest Little Hero Baltazar, Art, illus. (p. 225)
—Billy Burger, Model Citizen. Robinson, Lee, illus. (p. 227)
—Campfire Vampire. Fabicka, Patrycja, illus. (p. 316)
—Candy Store Caper Baltazar, Art, illus. (p. 322)
—Clayface Returns. Beavers, Ethen, illus. (p. 402)
—Dangers of Dog Walking. Robinson, Lee, illus. (p. 502)
—Day of Doom. (p. 513)
—Deep-Sea Duel Baltazar, Art, illus. (p. 524)
—Design & Draw. (p. 532)
—Fate of Krypton. Roberts, Jeremy, illus. (p. 714)
—Ferret Fiasco. Robinson, Lee, illus. (p. 721)
—Ghostbusters (Ghostbusters) Batson, Alan, illus. (p. 828)
—Ghostbusters/Ghostbusters 2016 Big Golden Book. Golden Books & Batson, Alan, illus. (p. 828)
—Ghosts of Griffin Rock. (p. 829)
—Goat on a Boat Bradley, Jessica, illus. (p. 849)
—Guardians of the Galaxy (Marvel: Guardians of the Galaxy) Borkowski, Michael & Atiyeh, Michael, illus. (p. 902)
—Hopping Hero Baltazar, Art, illus. (p. 1002)
—I Am She-Ra! (She-Ra) Clester, Shane, illus. (p. 1059)
—I Am Simba (Disney the Lion King) Batson, Alan, illus. (p. 1060)
—I Am the Flash. (p. 1060)
—I Am the Genie (Disney Aladdin) Batson, Alan, illus. (p. 1060)
—Incredibles (Disney/Pixar the Incredibles) Clark, Don, illus. (p. 1114)
—Jumping for Junk Food. Robinson, Lee, illus. (p. 1188)
—Land Before Prime. (p. 1241)
—Lazarus Plan. Beavers, Ethen, illus. (p. 1254)
—Man of Steel. (p. 1395)
—Mystery of the Maze Monster Neely, Scott, illus. (p. 1570)
—Night of the Digging Dog. (p. 1607)
—Optimus Prime Versus Predaking. (p. 1667)
—Recess Is Ruined. Robinson, Lee, illus. (p. 1853)
—Return of the Dinobot. (p. 1871)
—Rocket to the Rescue! Atiyeh, Michael & Borkowski, Michael, illus. (p. 1895)
—Royal Rodent Rescue Baltazar, Art, illus. (p. 1910)
—Salamander Smackdown. Baltazar, Art, illus. (p. 1924)
—Slime Time! Fabicka, Patrycja, illus. (p. 2038)
—Superman: Escape from the Phantom Zone. Gordon, Steven E., illus. (p. 2160)
—Superman Saves Smallville. Roberts, Jeremy, illus. (p. 2160)
—Superman vs. Bizarro Vecchio, Luciano, illus. (p. 2160)
—Super-Villain Smackdown! Beavers, Ethen, illus. (p. 2159)
—Swamp Creature Teacher. Fabicka, Patrycja, illus. (p. 2167)
—Swamp Thing vs the Zombie Pets Baltazar, Art, illus. (p. 2167)
—Thunder Strike. Spaziante, Patrick, illus. (p. 2238)
—Thunder Strike! (Marvel: Thor) Spaziante, Patrick, illus. (p. 2238)
—Who You Gonna Call? Golden Books, illus. (p. 2452)
—Wonder Woman: An Origin Story. Baltazar, Art & Vecchio, Luciano, illus. (p. 2489)
—You Choose Stories: Batman. Beavers, Ethen, illus. (p. 2527)
Sazaklis, John, illus. see McVeigh, Mark W.
Sazaklis, John, illus. see Teitelbaum, Michael.
Sazaklis, John, jt. auth. see Manning, Matthew K.

Sazaklis, John & Farley, John. Attack of the Toyman. (p. 135)
Sazaklis, John & Foxe, Steve. Drift's Samurai Showdown. (p. 604)
Sazaklis, John & Merkel, Joe F. Day of the Undead. Tong, Andie, illus. (p. 514)
Sazaklis, John & Vancata, Brad. Superman: Day of Doom. Smith, Andy, illus. (p. 2160)
Sazaklis, John, retold by. Marvel Ultimate Spider-Man: Spider-Man & His Amazing Friends. (p. 1413)
Sbandelli, Angela, illus. see Scheel, Morgan Lee.
Sburelin, Glenda. Ogres & Giants: With Augmented Reality. (p. 1641)
Scadden, Kathryn, illus. see Nolan, Nancy.
Scaglia, Beatriz, jt. auth. see Hawthorne, Nathaniel.
Scaife, Roger Livingston. Confessions of a Debutante (Classic Reprint) (p. 439)
Scala, Vincent. Beep Beep Goes the Bus Driver (p. 189)
Scalawag: (A Kathy Dubetz Production). Unicorns in the Mist: Books One & Two. (p. 2329)
Scales, Jocelyn. Crystal Goes Back to Camp. (p. 481)
Scales, Paul. Nancy Bo & Ergonwold's Nest. (p. 1574)
Scales, Simon, illus. see Spurr, Elizabeth.
Scales, Simon, jt. auth. see Millett, Peter.
Scaletta, Kurtis. Jinxed! Wight, Eric, illus. (p. 1169)
—Lukezilla Beats the Game. Sossella, David, illus. (p. 1367)
—Mudville. (p. 1524)
—Rooting for Rafael Rosales. (p. 1903)
—Tanglewood Terror. (p. 2190)
—Topps League Story: Book Three: Zip It! Wight, Eric, illus. (p. 2264)
—Topps League Story: Book Six: Batter Up! Beavers, Ethen, illus. (p. 2264)
—Trailblazers: Jackie Robinson: Breaking Barriers in Baseball. (p. 2275)
Scalf, Chris, illus. see Bailey, Gerry.
Scalf, Chris, illus. see Nussbaum, Ben & McIntosh, G. B.
Scalf, Chris, illus. see Nussbaum, Ben.
Scalf, Christopher, illus. see Nussbaum, Ben.
Scalia, Johnna, illus. see Houser, Sue.
Scaliger, Joseph. Scaligerana, Thuana, Perroniana, Pithoeana, et Colomesiana, Vol. 2: Ou Remarques Historiques, Critiques, Morales, et Littéraires (Classic Reprint) (p. 1941)
—Scaligerana, Thuana, Perroniana, Pithoeana, et Colomesiana, Ou Remarques Historiques, Critiques, Morales, et Littéraires, Vol. 1 (Classic Reprint) (p. 1941)
Scaling, Sam T. Marv the Moose Is on the Loose. Stanley, Susan, illus. (p. 1411)
Scalisi, Patrick. Key to the Universe. (p. 1212)
Scally, Robert. Jeff Bezos: Founder of Amazon & the Kindle. (p. 1162)
Scamander, Newt, jt. auth. see Rowling, J. K.
Scand, Sandra. Time for Bed Little Red. Sanderson, Sean, illus. (p. 2244)
Scandanavia Publishing House. Héroes - Biblias de Rompecabezas. (p. 961)
—Historias Favoritos - Biblias de Rompecabezas. (p. 975)
—MIS Primeras Historias - Biblias de Rompecabezas. (p. 1476)
Scandella, Alessandra, illus. see Capriolo, Paola.
Scandiffio, Laura. Digging Deep: How Science Unearths Puzzles from the Past. (p. 546)
—Fight to Learn: The Struggle to Go to School. (p. 725)
—People Who Said No: Courage Against Oppression. (p. 1719)
Scandinavia Publishing House Staff, ed. see Alex, Ben.
Scandinavia Publishing House Staff, ed. see Garwin, Elaine & Youd, Pauline.
Scandinavia Publishing, prod. Children's Bible - CEV. (p. 372)
Scandlin, Horace Winthrop. Wicked John Goode (Classic Reprint) (p. 2460)
Scandrett, William Christopher. Adventures of Old Swifton Road: Lee's Incredible Journey. (p. 26)
Scanlan, Lawrence. Big Red Horse: The Story of Secretariat & the Loyal Groom Who Loved Him. (p. 222)
Scanlan, Nelle M. Boudoir Mirrors of Washington: Anonymous (Classic Reprint) (p. 265)
Scanland, Earle. Physicians, Their Patients, Pills, Paregoric & Poisons (Classic Reprint) (p. 1738)
Scanland, John Milton. Life of Pat F. Garrett & the Taming of the Border Outlaw: A History of the Gun Men & Outlaws, & a Life-Story of the Greatest Sheriff of the Old Southwest (Classic Reprint) (p. 1295)
Scanlin, Dorothy. Sun Shines down on Bendsville. (p. 2151)
Scanlon, Garrett K. Just Say No Because Every Story Needs a Hero: Includes a Promise Agreement to Earn Added Rewards for Saying No to Binge Drinking, Drug Use, & Smoking in High School. (p. 1194)
Scanlon, Liz Garton. All the World. Frazee, Marla, illus. (p. 54)
—Another Way to Climb a Tree. (p. 101)
—Great Good Summer. (p. 886)
—Happy Birthday, Bunny! Graegin, Stephanie, illus. (p. 920)
—In the Canyon. Wolff, Ashley, illus. (p. 1108)
—Kate, Who Tamed the Wind. White, Lee, illus. (p. 1204)
—Noodle & Lou. Howard, Arthur, illus. (p. 1618)
—One Dark Bird. Preston-Gannon, Frann, illus. (p. 1659)
—Thank You, Garden. Shin, Simone, illus. (p. 2211)
Scanlon, Liz Garton & Vernick, Audrey. Five Minutes: (That's a Lot of Time) (No, It's Not) (Yes, It Is) Tallec, Olivier, illus. (p. 744)
Scanlon, Michael. How We Met! Little Airplane Productions Staff, illus. (p. 1046)
Scanlon, Michael, illus. see McDoogle, Farrah.
Scanlon, Michael, illus. see Seiss, Ellie.
Scantlebury, Elizabeth Ellis. Homes of the World's Babies: Illustrated with Paper Cuttings in Silhouette (Classic Reprint) (p. 998)
Scarace, Caroly. Dragons. (p. 595)
Scarborough, Dorothy. Famous Modern Ghost Stories (Classic Reprint) (p. 704)
—From a Southern Porch (Classic Reprint) (p. 790)
—Humorous Ghost Stories (Classic Reprint) (p. 1050)
—On the Trail of Negro Folk-Songs (Classic Reprint) (p. 1656)
Scarborough, George. Lure (Classic Reprint) (p. 1369)
Scarborough, Ginger. Dave the Dragonfly. Ware, Chelsey, illus. (p. 510)
Scarborough, Kate. Wasp Builds a Nest. Camm, Martin, illus. (p. 2382)
Scarborough, Kate, jt. auth. see Brush, Jim.
Scarborough, R. A. Starblade: The Beginning (p. 2105)
Scarborough, Rob, illus. see Arvidson, Douglas.
Scarborough, Sheryl. To Catch a Killer: A Novel. (p. 2252)
—To Right the Wrongs. (p. 2253)
Scarborough, Sheryl & Canetti, Yanitzia. About Bugs: Acerca de Los Insectos. (p. 6)
Scarbrough, Mary Hertz. African American Writers & Journalists. (p. 32)
—African American Writers & Journalists. Hill, Marc Lamont, ed. (p. 32)
—Heroes of the American Revolution. (p. 962)
—Presidential Politics by the Numbers. (p. 1789)
Scardina, Tom, illus. see England, Don.
Scardoni, Bianca. Inception. (p. 1112)
—Iniquitous. (p. 1120)
—Invidious. (p. 1132)
Scarfe, David. Wild Book: Outdoor Activities to Unleash Your Inner Child. (p. 2463)
Scargill, William Pitt. Atherton, a Tale of the Last Century, Vol. 3 of 3 (Classic Reprint) (p. 132)
—Blue-Stocking Hall, Vol. 1 of 2 (Classic Reprint) (p. 249)
—Rank & Talent, Vol. 1 Of 3: A Novel (Classic Reprint) (p. 1841)
—Tales of My Time, Vol. 1 of 3 (Classic Reprint) (p. 2184)
—Tales of My Time, Vol. 3 (Classic Reprint) (p. 2184)
Scarlet, Janina. Dark Agents: Violet & the Trial of Trauma. Alvendia, Vince, illus. (p. 505)
—Superhero Therapy: Mindfulness Skills to Help Teens & Young Adults Deal with Anxiety, Depression, & Trauma. Alves, Wellinton, illus. (p. 2160)
Scarlet, Patrick. Clowns Courage: Undergraduate Rubrics in Part from the Magazine of the University (Classic Reprint) (p. 408)
Scarlet, Tyler, illus. see Walker, Landry Quinn.
Scarpa, Daniel, illus. see Courtauld, Sarah.
Scarpa, Romano, illus. see Castellan, Andrea, et al.
Scarpa, Romano, et al. Mickey Mouse Donald Duck: The Pirates of Tabasco Bay/Duck Avenger Strikes Again (p. 1459)
—Uncle Scrooge: Tyrant of the Tides. (p. 2319)
—Uncle Scrooge: the Bodacious Butterfly Trail. (p. 2319)
Scarpati, Kevin. Minnesota Vikings. (p. 1473)
Scarpetta, Yasmina. Corazon de Oso. (p. 453)
Scarron, Paul. Comic Romance of Monsieur Scarron, Vol. 1 of 2 (Classic Reprint) (p. 429)
—Comical Romance, Vol. 2 Of 2: And Other Tales (Classic Reprint) (p. 430)
—French Belles-Letters: From 1640 to 1870 (Classic Reprint) (p. 783)
—Whole Comical Works of Mons. Scarron, Vol. 1 Of 2: Containing His Comical Romance of a Company of Stage-Players, in Three Parts Complete (Classic Reprint) (p. 2452)
—Whole Comical Works of Mons. Scarron, Vol. 2: Containing Avarice Chastis'd, or the Miser Punish'd; the Useless Precaution; the Hypocrites; the Innocent Adultery; the Generous Lover; His Select Letters, Characters, &C (Classic Reprint) (p. 2452)
Scarrow, Alex. Plague Land. (p. 1754)
—Plague Land: No Escape. (p. 1754)
—Plague Land: Reborn. (p. 1754)
Scarrow, Alex & Bale, Tim. TimeRiders (p. 2247)
Scarrow, Kristine. 11th Hour. (p. 2550)
—Gamer's Guide to Getting the Girl. (p. 807)
—Throwaway Girl. (p. 2237)
Scarry, Huck. All about Anne (p. 48)
Scarry, Huck, jt. auth. see Scarry, Richard.
Scarry, Janet. Land of Whodunnit. (p. 1242)
Scarry, Patricia. Richard Scarry's Just for Fun. Scarry, Richard, illus. (p. 1877)
—Richard Scarry's the Country Mouse & the City Mouse. Scarry, Richard, illus. (p. 1877)
Scarry, Patsy. Bebe Lapin Deviendra Grand. (p. 186)
—Bunny Book. Scarry, Richard, illus. (p. 298)
—Richard Scarry's Good Night, Little Bear. Scarry, Richard, illus. (p. 1877)
—Richard Scarry's the Bunny Book. Scarry, Richard, illus. (p. 1877)
—Surprise D'Oscar. (p. 2163)
Scarry, Patsy, et al. Richard Scarry's Best Little Golden Books Ever! Scarry, Richard, illus. (p. 1876)
Scarry, Richard. Best Little Board Book Ever. Random House Staff, illus. (p. 206)
—Best Lowly Worm Book Ever! (p. 206)
—Boats. Scarry, Richard, illus. (p. 251)
—Egg in the Hole. Golden Books Staff, illus. (p. 628)
—Grand Livre des Transports. (p. 876)
—Planes. Scarry, Richard, illus. (p. 1754)
—Richard Scarry Mr. Paint Pig's ABC's. Random House Staff, illus. (p. 1876)
—Richard Scarry Stocking Stuffers 6-Copy Clip Strip Fall 2019 (p. 1876)
—Richard Scarry's Best Bunny Book Ever! Scarry, Richard, illus. (p. 1876)
—Richard Scarry's Best Little Word Book Ever! (p. 1876)
—Richard Scarry's Best Little Word Book Ever! Scarry, Richard, illus. (p. 1876)
—Richard Scarry's Best Nursery Tales Ever. (p. 1876)
—Richard Scarry's Books on the Go: 4 Board Books. (p. 1876)
—Richard Scarry's Box Full of Bunnies: The Bunny Book; I Am a Bunny; Just for Fun; Naughty Bunny; Polite Elephant (p. 1876)
—Richard Scarry's Bunnies. Scarry, Richard, illus. (p. 1876)
—Richard Scarry's Busy Busy Airport. (p. 1876)
—Richard Scarry's Busy Busy Boxed Set: Busy Busy Airport; Busy Busy Cars & Trucks; Busy Busy Construction Site; Busy Busy Farm. (p. 1876)
—Richard Scarry's Busy Busy Cars & Trucks. (p. 1876)
—Richard Scarry's Busy Busy Construction Site. (p. 1876)
—Richard Scarry's Busy Busy Farm. (p. 1876)
—Richard Scarry's Busy, Busy World. Scarry, Richard, illus. (p. 1876)
—Richard Scarry's Busytown Seek & Find! Scarry, Richard, illus. (p. 1876)
—Richard Scarry's Cars. (p. 1876)
—Richard Scarry's Cars & Trucks. Scarry, Richard, illus. (p. 1876)
—Richard Scarry's Cars & Trucks & Things That Go: Read Together Edition. (p. 1876)
—Richard Scarry's Christmas Mice. Scarry, Richard, illus. (p. 1877)
—Richard Scarry's Funniest Storybook Ever! (p. 1877)
—Richard Scarry's Good Night, Little Bear. (p. 1877)
—Richard Scarry's Just Right Word Book! Scarry, Richard, illus. (p. 1877)
—Richard Scarry's Lowly Worm Word Book. Scarry, Richard, illus. (p. 1877)
—Richard Scarry's Naughty Bunny. (p. 1877)
—Richard Scarry's Nicky Goes to the Doctor. (p. 1877)
—Richard Scarry's Pig Will & Pig Won't. Scarry, Richard, illus. (p. 1877)
—Richard Scarry's Polite Elephant. Scarry, Richard, illus. (p. 1877)
—Richard Scarry's Postman Pig & His Busy Neighbors. (p. 1877)
—Richard Scarry's Postman Pig & His Busy Neighbors. Scarry, Richard, illus. (p. 1877)
—Richard Scarry's Rabbit & His Friends. (p. 1877)
—Richard Scarry's the Adventures of Lowly Worm & Other Stories. (p. 1877)
—Richard Scarry's the Animals of Farmer Jones. (p. 1877)
—Richard Scarry's the Night Before the Night Before Christmas! Scarry, Richard, illus. (p. 1877)
—Richard Scarry's the Rooster Struts. (p. 1877)
—Richard Scarry's Vrooming, Zooming Stories. (p. 1877)
—Richard Scarry's What Do People Do All Day? (p. 1877)
—Scarry Busy Week - Four in One Bind-Up. (p. 1942)
—Trucks. (p. 2293)
Scarry, Richard, illus. see Daly, Kathleen N.
Scarry, Richard, illus. see Golden Books Staff.
Scarry, Richard, illus. see Jackson, Kathryn & Jackson, Byron.
Scarry, Richard, illus. see Jackson, Kathryn.
Scarry, Richard, illus. see Nolte, Nancy.
Scarry, Richard, illus. see Risom, Ole.
Scarry, Richard, illus. see Scarry, Patricia.
Scarry, Richard, illus. see Scarry, Patsy, et al.
Scarry, Richard, illus. see Scarry, Patsy.
Scarry, Richard, jt. auth. see Scarry, Huck.
Scarry, Richard & Golden Books Staff. Richard Scarry's Nicky Goes to the Doctor. (p. 1877)
Scarry, Richard, et al. Richard Scarry's Best Box of Little Golden Books Ever! 12 Little Golden Books. (p. 1876)
Scarsella, Vincent L. Escape from the Psi Academy. (p. 661)
—Return to the Psi Academy. (p. 1871)
Scartazzini, Giovanni Andrea. A. Scartazzini Conversation-Book in English & Italian: A. Scartazzini Novissimo Manuale Di Conversazione, Inglese e Italiano (Classic Reprint) (p. 2)
Scates, Douglas E. Tamarack, Vol. 8: January 1917 (Classic Reprint) (p. 2188)
—Tamarack, Vol. 8: October, 1916 (Classic Reprint) (p. 2188)
—Tamarack, Vol. 8: December, 1916 (Classic Reprint) (p. 2188)
Scattergood, Augusta. Glory Be. (p. 844)
—Making Friends with Billy Wong. (p. 1389)
—Way to Stay in Destiny. (p. 2387)
Scavuzzo, Wendy. Tornado Alert! (p. 2265)
Scebold, Clyde C. Jackson (Aka Pops) III. Adventuresome Kittens. (p. 30)
Scelsa, Kate. Fans of the Impossible Life. (p. 706)
Scepanski, Jennifer. Tale of Little Sprout. (p. 2179)
Sceptre, Michael J. Pied Piper: Love & Redemption. (p. 1742)
Schaaf, Fred. Seeing the Sky: 100 Projects, Activities & Explorations in Astronomy. Myers, Doug, illus. (p. 1984)
Schaal, Patty. Nighttide on a Vineyard Farm. Datz, Margot, illus. (p. 1608)
Schab, Lisa M. Cool, Calm, & Confident: A Workbook to Help Kids Learn Assertiveness Skills. (p. 447)
—Put Your Feelings Here: A Creative DBT Journal for Teens with Intense Emotions. (p. 1817)
—Put Your Worries Here: A Creative Journal for Teens with Anxiety. (p. 1817)
—Self-Esteem for Teens: Six Principles for Creating the Life You Want. (p. 1987)
—Self-Esteem Habit for Teens: 50 Simple Ways to Build Your Confidence Every Day. (p. 1987)
—Self-Esteem Workbook for Teens: Activities to Help You Build Confidence & Achieve Your Goals. (p. 1987)
Schaberg, Jan Eberle. Winnie's Farm. Jendrysik, Barbara L., illus. (p. 2474)
Schabert, Kyrill, tr. see Winterfeld, Henry.
Schabram, Dennis W. Sugar & Me (p. 2147)
Schach, David. Comanche Warriors. (p. 427)
—Loch Ness Monster. (p. 1338)
—Sea Monsters. (p. 1968)
Schacher, Tracey, illus. see Powell, Joyce.
Schachner, Judy. Class Action. (p. 399)
—Dewey Bob. Schachner, Judy, illus. (p. 536)
—Great Bean Caper. (p. 884)
—Sarabella's Thinking Cap. (p. 1935)
—Skippyjon Jones. (p. 2033)
—Skippyjon Jones Cirque de Ole. (p. 2033)
—Skippyjon Jones, Class Action. (p. 2033)
—Skippyjon Jones in Mummy Trouble. (p. 2033)
—Skippyjon Jones in the Doghouse. (p. 2033)
—Skippyjon Jones, Lost in Spice. (p. 2033)
—Skippyjon Jones, Lost in Spice. Schachner, Judy, illus. (p. 2033)
—Skippyjon Jones Presto-Change-O. (p. 2033)
—Skippyjon Jones Snow What. (p. 2033)
—Stretchy Mchandsome. Schachner, Judy, illus. (p. 2141)
—Up, up, & Away! (p. 2338)
Schachte, Kylie. You're Next. (p. 2535)
Schachter, Esty. Pickled Watermelon. (p. 1739)
—Pickled Watermelon. Orbe, Alex, illus. (p. 1739)
Schacker, Jennifer, jt. ed. see Jones, Christine A.
Schad, Leanne. Lia Saves the Sea. (p. 1283)
Schade, Susan. Riff Raff Sails the High Cheese. Kennedy, Anne, illus. (p. 1879)
—Riff Raff the Mouse Pirate. Kennedy, Anne, illus. (p. 1879)
—Simon's Dream. Buller, Jon, illus. (p. 2021)
Schader, Karen, ed. see Bryant, John E.
Schader, Karen, ed. see Huebner, Dawn.
Schader, Kim, et al. Loom Band It: 60 Rubberband Projects for the Budding Loomineer. (p. 1348)
Schader Lee, Susan, jt. auth. see Sterling Children's, Sterling.
Schaefer, A. R. Spotlight on Asia (p. 2091)
Schaefer, Adam, jt. auth. see Crewe, Sabrina.
Schaefer, Adam, jt. auth. see Schaefer, Lola M.
Schaefer, Adam R., jt. auth. see Schaefer, A. R.
Schaefer, Carole Lexa. Children's Garden: Growing Food in the City. Morgan, Pierr, illus. (p. 374)
—Ciao, Baby! in the Park. Tobia, Lauren, illus. (p. 390)
—Ciao, Baby! Ready for a Ride. Tobia, Lauren, illus. (p. 390)
—Made by Hand: a Crafts Sampler. Stadtlander, Becca, illus. (p. 1374)
—Monkey & Elephant: Candlewick Sparks. Bernstein, Galia, illus. (p. 1493)
—Monkey & Elephant & a Secret Birthday Surprise. Bernstein, Galia, illus. (p. 1493)
—Monkey & Elephant & the Babysitting Adventure. Bernstein, Galia, illus. (p. 1493)
—Monkey & Elephant Get Better. Bernstein, Galia, illus. (p. 1493)
—Monkey & Elephant Go Gadding. Bernstein, Galia, illus. (p. 1493)
Schaefer, Elizabeth. Ballet Lesson. (p. 162)
—Ballet Lessons. (p. 162)
—Force Awakens: Episode VII. White, Dave, illus. (p. 764)
—Force Awakens. White, David A., illus. (p. 764)
—I Am Mr. Spock. Beavers, Ethen, illus. (p. 1059)
—Lección de Ballet. (p. 1260)
—Rey Meets BB-8. (p. 1874)
—Rey's Story. (p. 1874)
—Solo - Star Wars. Random House & Pilot Inc. Staff, illus. (p. 2057)
—Star Wars the Force Awakens Storybook. (p. 2105)
—Star Wars: the Last Jedi (Star Wars) Batson, Alan, illus. (p. 2105)
—Star Wars: the Last Jedi Movie Storybook. Rood, Brian, illus. (p. 2105)
—We Are the Resistance (Star Wars) Batson, Alan, illus. (p. 2389)
—World of Reading Star Wars the Force Awakens: Rey Meets BB-8: Level 1. Rood, Brian, illus. (p. 2504)
Schaefer, Elizabeth & Hopps, Kevin. Hera's Phantom Flight. (p. 957)
Schaefer, Elizabeth & Murray, Charles. Star Wars Rebels: Kanan's Jedi Training. Press, Lucasfilm, illus. (p. 2105)
Schaefer, Jack. Old Ramon. West, Harold E., illus. (p. 1648)
—Shane. (p. 1999)
—Stubby Pringle's Christmas. Bjorklund, Lorence, illus. (p. 2143)
Schaefer, Laura. Littler Women: A Modern Retelling. (p. 1330)
—Secret Ingredient. Rim, Sujean, illus. (p. 1976)
—Teashop Girls. Rim, Sujean, illus. (p. 2196)
Schaefer, Laura Scott. Snout vs. Snowman: The Crumbles Chronicles: Tails of a Nervous Dog. (p. 2046)
Schaefer, Laura, suppl. Littler Women. (p. 1330)
Schaefer, Lola. Bot Battles. (p. 264)
—Easter Surprises. McCue, Lisa, illus. (p. 620)
—Flying Robots. (p. 755)
—Human-Like Robots. (p. 1049)
—One Special Day: A Story for Big Brothers & Sisters. Meserve, Jessica, illus. (p. 1662)
—Please Pass the Manners! Mealtime Tips for Everyone. Lewis, Kellie, illus. (p. 1762)
—Robots on the Job. (p. 1893)
Schaefer, Lola M. Airplanes in Action. (p. 37)
—Alexander Graham Bell. (p. 42)
—Algunos Niños Son Sordos. (p. 44)
—Arrowhawk: A True Survival Story. Swiatkowska, Gabi, illus. (p. 119)
—Arrowhawk. Swiatkowska, Gabi, illus. (p. 119)
—Bear & the Star. Andersen, Bethanne, illus. (p. 179)
—Boo Who? A Foldout Halloween Adventure. Frost, Michael, photos by. (p. 256)
—Bot Battles. (p. 264)
—Carta para Mi Amigo: Set Of 6. (p. 335)
—Cotton Plant to Cotton Shirt. (p. 457)
—Cotton Plant to Cotton Shirt & de una planta a una camisa de Algodón: 6 English, 6 Spanish Adaptations (p. 457)
—De una Planta a una Camisa de Algodón: Set Of 6. (p. 517)
—Erosión: Set Of 6. (p. 660)
—Frankie Stein Atteberry, Kevan, illus. (p. 778)
—Frankie Stein Starts School. (p. 778)
—Frankie Stein Starts School. Atteberry, Kevan, illus. (p. 778)
—Happy Halloween, Mittens. Hartung, Susan Kathleen, illus. (p. 922)
—Hidden Dangers: Seek & Find 13 of the World's Deadliest Animals. Armstrong, Tymn, illus. (p. 965)
—How Did This City Grow? (p. 1027)
—Las Máquinas Simples: Set Of 6. (p. 1246)
—Letter to a Friend. (p. 1278)
—Letter to a Friend & una carta para mi Amigo: 6 English, 6 Spanish Adaptations (p. 1279)
—Lifetime: The Amazing Numbers in Animal Lives. Neal, Christopher Silas, illus. (p. 1297)
—Mi Corazón: Set Of 6. (p. 1454)
—Mi Cuerpo: Set Of 6. (p. 1454)
—Mittens at School. (p. 1484)
—Mittens at School. Hartung, Susan Kathleen, illus. (p. 1484)
—Mittens, Where Is Max? Hartung, Susan Kathleen, illus. (p. 1484)
—My Body & Mi Cuerpo: 6 English, 6 Spanish Adaptations (p. 1534)
—One Special Day: A Story for Big Brothers & Sisters. Meserve, Jessica, illus. (p. 1662)

S

—Run for Your Life! Predators & Prey on the African Savanna. Meisel, Paul, illus. (p. 1914)
—Sea Stars [Scholastic]. (p. 1969)
—Semitrucks in Action (p. 1988)
—Simple Machines & Las máquinas Simples: 6 English, 6 Spanish Adaptations (p. 2022)
—Some Kids Are Blind: A 4D Book. (p. 2059)
—Some Kids Are Deaf: A 4D Book. (p. 2059)
—Some Kids Use Wheelchairs: A 4D Book. (p. 2059)
—Some Kids Wear Leg Braces: A 4D Book. (p. 2059)
—Somos Iguales: Set Of 6. (p. 2061)
—Tow Trucks in Action. (p. 2269)
—Understanding Differences. (p. 2324)
—We are All Alike. (p. 2388)
—Welcome Home And ¡Bienvenidos! 6 English, 6 Spanish Adaptations (p. 2397)
—What Is Matter? (p. 2415)
—What Is Matter? & ¿Qué es la Materia? 6 English, 6 Spanish Adaptations (p. 2415)
—What's That, Mittens? Hartung, Susan Kathleen, illus. (p. 2426)
—Who Makes the Rules? (p. 2449)
—Who Makes the Rules? & ¿Quién hace las Reglas? 6 English, 6 Spanish Adaptations (p. 2449)
—Your Heart. (p. 2534)
—¡Bienvenidos! Set Of 6. (p. 215)
—¿Como Crecio Esta Ciudad? Set Of 6. (p. 432)
—¿Qué Es la Materia? Set Of 6. (p. 1822)
—¿Quién Hace Las Reglas? Set Of 6. (p. 1827)
Schaefer, Lola M. & Schaefer, Adam. Because of an Acorn: (Nature Autumn Books for Children, Picture Books about Acorn Trees) Preston-Gannon, Frann, illus. (p. 186)
Schaefer, Nikki. Potty Train. Schaefer, Nikki, illus. (p. 1781)
Schaefer, Susi. Cat Ladies. Schaefer, Susi, illus. (p. 341)
Schaefer, Susi, illus. see Fischer, Kristen.
Schaefer, Valorie. Care & Keeping of You: The Body Book for Younger Girls. Vol. 1 (p. 328)
—Care & Keeping of You 1: The Body Book for Younger Girls. (p. 328)
Schaeffer, Brittany. Freddy Frog & the Bully. (p. 781)
Schaeffer, Evelyn Schuyler. Isabel Stirling (Classic Reprint) (p. 1138)
Schaeffer, Julia. Midwest States: Set Of 6. (p. 1462)
Schaeffer, L. M. Sketches of Travels in South America, Mexico & California (Classic Reprint) (p. 2032)
Schaeffer, Mary F. Cycle of Work in the Kindergarten & Primary School, Vol. 1 (Classic Reprint) (p. 492)
Schaeffer, Rebecca. Not Even Bones. (p. 1623)
—Only Ashes Remain. (p. 1664)
—When Villains Rise. (p. 2434)
Schaentzler, Adrienne Anifant. Tickle Daggers. (p. 2240)
Schaerer, Kathrin, illus. see Pauli, Lorenz.
Schafbuch, Michael, illus. see Kernahan, Maria.
Schafer, Albert. Illusionology: The Secret Science of Magic. Wyatt, David & Pinfold, Levi, illus. (p. 1096)
Schafer, Ann, illus. see Lembke, Linda.
Schafer, Georg E., ed. see Loffler (Text), Doris & Hassert (Illustrationen), Anna Beatrix.
Schafer, Halina. Who Found Who? (p. 2447)
Schafer, Halina J. Fiona & the Extra-Special Invisible Gifts. (p. 732)
Schafer, Hermann. Uber Die Pariser Hss. 1451 und 22555 der Huon de Bordeaux-Sage: Beziehung der HS. 1451 Zur Chanson de Croissant; Die Chanson de Huon et Callisse; Die Chanson de Huon, Roi de Feerie (Classic Reprint) (p. 2313)
Schafer, Holden J., illus. see Steininger-Moore, Cheryl A.
Schafer, Rick, photos by see King, William.
Schafer, Steve. Border. (p. 262)
Schafer, Susan. Capybaras. (p. 327)
—Chinese Giant Salamanders. (p. 378)
—DNA & Genes. (p. 569)
—Heredity. (p. 958)
—Invasive Mammals. (p. 1130)
—Invasive Reptiles & Amphibians. (p. 1130)
—Saltwater Crocodiles. (p. 1925)
Schafer, Susan & Meredith, Susan Markowitz. Lions. (p. 1307)
Schafer, Susan & Robinson, Fay. Tigers. (p. 2242)
Schaffer, Alvina S. Tiki. (p. 2242)
Schaffer, Andrea, jt. auth. see Stilton, Geronimo.
Schaffer, Andrea, jt. auth. see Stilton, Thea.
Schaffer, Andrea, tr. see Stilton, Thea.
Schaffer, Julia & Benchmark Education Company, LLC Staff. Los Estados Del Medio Oeste: Set of 6 Common Core Edition. (p. 1350)
Schaffer, Mary Towsend Sharples. Old Indian Trails: Incidents of Camp & Trail Life, Covering Two Years' Exploration Through the Rocky Mountains of Canada (Classic Reprint) (p. 1646)
Schaffer, Nancy. Guard the Fort. (p. 901)
Schaffter, Ehren. Through the Curtain. (p. 2237)
Schafrath, Ty, illus. see Bender, Elaine.
Schafrath, Ty, illus. see McCullough, Myrina D.
Schaick, George van. Girl at Big Loon Post (Classic Reprint) (p. 835)
—Son of the Otter (Classic Reprint) (p. 2062)
—Sweetapple Cove (Classic Reprint) (p. 2169)
Schalk, Anita. Lost Sheep. (p. 1355)
Schalkwijk, Bob, photos by see Burgess, Don.
Schallert, Ann. Message for Woman: The Teenage Girl. (p. 1451)
Schallmayer, Wilhelm. Beiträge Zu Einer Nationalbiologie: Nebst Einer Kritik der Methodologischen Einwände und Einem Anhang Über Wissenschaftliches Kritikerwesen (Classic Reprint) (p. 195)
Schallmo, Carolyn, illus. see Lamb, Jim.
Schalter, Ty. Can Certain Religions Be Outlawed? (p. 317)
—Gymnastics for Fun & Fitness (p. 907)
—Soccer for Fun & Fitness (p. 2052)
Schamber, Kimberly, illus. see Wahl, Jan.
Schami, Rafik. Storyteller of Damacus. Knorr, Peter, illus. (p. 2136)
Schamp, Tom. 1, 2, 3, Count with Me! (p. 2545)
—It's a Great, Big Colorful World. (p. 1143)
Schanilec, Gaylord, illus. see Coy, John.
Schank, Amanda, illus. see Scholastic & West, Tracey.
Schank, Amanda, illus. see West, Tracey.
Schantz, Becky. How to Grow a Hippo! Mitchell, Anne, illus. (p. 1042)
Schantz, Sarah Elizabeth. Fig. (p. 724)
Schanzer, Rosalyn. Witches: The Absolutely True Tale of Disaster in Salem. (p. 2480)
Schanzer, Rosalyn, illus. see Lauber, Patricia.
Schanzer, Rosalyn, jt. auth. see Eisenberg, Ann.
Schapira, Leah & Dwek, Victoria. Kids Cooking Made Easy. Lailah, Daniel, photos by. (p. 1214)
Schappert, Kim. Getting Through Cancer One Step at a Time. (p. 826)
Scharer, Kathrin. It Was Like This, No Like This. (p. 1142)
Schärer, Kathrin, illus. see Pauli, Lorenz.
Scharer, Niko. Emily's House Fitzgerald, Joanne, illus. (p. 642)
Scharer, Patricia. Responsive Literacy: A Comprehensive Framework. (p. 1870)
Scharper, Philip. Santa Claus Was Once a Kid Too / German Edition: Babl Children's Books in German & English. Hannon, Tara, illus. (p. 1932)
—Santa Claus Was Once a Kid Too / Ong Gia Santa Claus Cung Da Tung la Mot Cau Be: Babl Children's Books in Vietnamese & English. (p. 1932)
—Santa Claus Was Once a Kid Too / Si Santa Claus Ay Minsan Din Na Naging Bata: Babl Children's Books in Tagalog & English. (p. 1932)
Scharschmidt, Sherry, illus. see Hacohen, Dean.
Scharschmidt, Sherry, jt. auth. see Hacohen, Dean.
Schartup, Adam, illus. see Aryal, Naren.
Schartup, Adam, illus. see Milani, Joan.
Schartup, Adam, illus. see Warner, Roxie & Warner, Christian.
Schary, Dore. Case History of a Movie (Classic Reprint) (p. 336)
Schatz, Dennis. Inside Out T. Rex: Explore the World's Most Famous Dinosaur! (p. 1123)
—Uncover a T. Rex. Bonadonna, Davide & Keitzmueller, Christian, illus. (p. 2320)
Schatz, Dennis & Fraknoi, Andrew. Solar Science: Exploring Sunspots, Seasons, Eclipses, & More. (p. 2056)
Schatz, Kate. Rad American Women A-Z: Rebels, Trailblazers, & Visionaries Who Shaped Our History ... & Our Future! Klein Stahl, Miriam, illus. (p. 1833)
Schatz, Kate & Stahl, Miriam Klein. Rad Women Worldwide: Artists & Athletes, Pirates & Punks, & Other Revolutionaries Who Shaped History. (p. 1833)
Schatz, Letta. So Many Henrys (p. 2050)
Schaub, Karl Rudolf, jt. auth. see Goldsmith, Oliver.
Schaub, Michelle. Finding Treasure: A Collection of Collections. Saldana, Carmen, illus. (p. 730)
—Fresh-Picked Poetry: A Day at the Farmers' Market. Huntington, Amy, illus. (p. 785)
—This or That Sports Debate: A Rip-Roaring Game of Either/or Questions. (p. 2226)
—Vehicles of World War I (p. 2349)
Schaue, Pete. Charter Schools & School Vouchers. (p. 361)
Schauer, Clifford. Suzy & the Bug. (p. 2166)
Schauer, Donald D. Careers in Trucking. (p. 330)
Schauer, Loretta, illus. see Brown, Margaret Wise.
Schauer, Loretta, illus. see Clark, Jane.
Schauer, Loretta, illus. see Knapman, Timothy.
Schauer, Loretta, illus. see Tiger Tales.
Schauer, M. RIP, M. D. Vosburg, M., illus. (p. 1884)
Schauer, Pete. General Contractor. (p. 814)
—Politicians on Social Media. (p. 1771)
—Russell Wilson: Super Bowl Sensation. (p. 1917)
Schauer, Pete, jt. auth. see Idzikowski, Lisa.
Schauer, Pete, jt. auth. see Sanders, Doug.
Schauer, Pete, ed. Homelessness & Street Crime. (p. 997)
—Police Training & Excessive Force. (p. 1770)
Schauer, Peter J. People Behind Cult Murders. (p. 1718)
—Russell Wilson: Super Bowl Sensation. (p. 1917)
—What You Need to Know about Violent Crimes, Felonies, & the Law (p. 2423)
Schauer, Peter J., ed. AIDS & Other Killer Viruses & Pandemics. (p. 36)
—Big Pharma & Drug Pricing. (p. 222)
Schauffler, Adolph Frederick. Memories of a Happy Boyhood: Long Ago, & Far Away (Classic Reprint) (p. 1446)
Schauffler, Rachel Capen. Goodly Fellowship (Classic Reprint) (p. 867)
Schauffler, Robert Haven. Fiddler's Luck: The Gay Adventures of a Musical Amateur. (p. 722)
—Fiddler's Luck: The Gay Adventures of a Musical Amateur (Classic Reprint) (p. 722)
—Romantic America (Classic Reprint) (p. 1901)
—Thanksgiving: Its Origin, Celebration & Significance As Related in Prose & Verse (Classic Reprint) (p. 2212)
—Where Speech Ends: A Music Maker's Romance (Classic Reprint) (p. 2439)
Schaumberg, Deborah. Tombs. (p. 2259)
Schautz, Irmela, illus. see Koller, Kathrin.
Schear, Niza P. My Pixie Dixie. (p. 1559)
Schechter, Lynn R. My Big Fat Secret: How Jenna Takes Control of Her Emotions & Eating. Chin, Jason, illus. (p. 1532)
Scheck, Isabel. Emilie the Little Elephant. (p. 642)
Scheckel, Larry. Can People Just Burst into Flames? Answers to 170 Other Such Questions. (p. 317)
—I Always Wondered about That: 101 Questions & Answers about Science & Other Stuff. (p. 1056)
—I Just Keep Wondering: 121 Questions & Answers about Science & Other Stuff. (p. 1066)
—I Wondered about That Too: 111 Questions & Answers about Science & Other Stuff. (p. 1086)
Schecter, Barbara. Real Live Monsters: Level 2. Braginetz, Donna, illus. (p. 1849)
Schecter, Deborah. Nursery Rhymes: Adorable Art Projects with Easy Directions & Rebus Support That Build Beginning Reading Skills. (p. 1631)
Schecter, Ellen. Boy Who Cried Wolf! Chalk, Gary, illus. (p. 270)
Scheel, Morgan Lee. Fabulous Glitter Girl. Sbandelli, Angela, illus. (p. 692)
Scheer, Jacqueline. Sticksville. Sturm, Adrienne, illus. (p. 2118)
Scheer, Julian. Rain Makes Applesauce (Restored Edition) Bileck, Marvin, illus. (p. 1835)
Scheerger, Sarah. Operation Frog Effect. (p. 1666)
Scheerger, Sarah Lynn. Are You Still There. (p. 113)
—Mitzvah Pizza. Melmon, Deborah, illus. (p. 1484)
—Opposite of Love. (p. 1667)
Scheff, Marc, illus. see Gill, Shelley.
Scheff, Matt. Aaron Rodgers (p. 2)
—Aircraft Carriers: A 4D Book. (p. 37)
—Alex Morgan: Soccer Star. (p. 42)
—Aly Raisman. (p. 61)
—Amazing Human Feats of Distance. (p. 65)
—Amazing Human Feats of Engineering. (p. 65)
—Amazing NFL Stories: 12 Highlights from NFL History. (p. 66)
—Andrew Luck (p. 84)
—ATVs (p. 135)
—Best Extreme Sports Stars of All Time (p. 206)
—Best NFL Quarterbacks of All Time (p. 207)
—Best NFL Running Backs of All Time (p. 207)
—Brock Lesnar. (p. 284)
—Carson Wentz: Football Star. (p. 335)
—Classic NFL Games: 12 Thrillers from NFL History. (p. 400)
—Dak Prescott: Football Star. (p. 498)
—Derek Carr: Football Star. (p. 530)
—Destroyers: A 4D Book. (p. 534)
—Dirt Bikes (p. 552)
—Dolph Ziggler. (p. 579)
—Drones: A 4D Book. (p. 605)
—Eli Manning: Football Superstar (p. 635)
—Excelling in Football. (p. 676)
—Fighter Planes: A 4D Book. (p. 725)
—Gordie Howe. (p. 869)
—Hovercraft (p. 1025)
—Humvees: A 4D Book. (p. 1051)
—Incredible Baseball Records. (p. 1113)
—Incredible Football Records. (p. 1113)
—Indy Cars (p. 1118)
—J. J. Watt. (p. 1150)
—James Harden: Basketball Star. (p. 1157)
—Jamie Bestwick (p. 1157)
—Jeff Gordon (p. 1162)
—Jets (p. 1167)
—Katie Ledecky. (p. 1205)
—Kelly Slater (p. 1209)
—Kyle Busch (p. 1234)
—Lyn-Z Adams Hawkins Pastrana (p. 1370)
—Maya Moore. (p. 1429)
—Michael Phelps. (p. 1458)
—Mighty Military Machines. (p. 1463)
—Naomi Osaka. (p. 1574)
—NBA & WNBA Finals: Basketball's Biggest Playoffs. (p. 1583)
—Olympic Stars (Set) (p. 1651)
—Peyton Manning (p. 1732)
—Pro Basketball Finals. (p. 1802)
—Pro Wrestling's Greatest (Set) (p. 1802)
—Pro Wrestling's Greatest Faces. (p. 1802)
—Pro Wrestling's Greatest Matches. (p. 1802)
—Pro Wrestling's Greatest Rivalries. (p. 1802)
—Pro Wrestling's Greatest Secrets Exposed. (p. 1802)
—Russell Wilson (p. 1917)
—Shaun White (p. 2003)
—Simone Biles. (p. 2021)
—Simone Manuel. (p. 2021)
—Skydiving. (p. 2034)
—Snowmobiles (p. 2049)
—Speed Machines (p. 2078)
—Speedboats (p. 2078)
—Stanley Cup Finals: Hockey's Greatest Tournament. (p. 2101)
—Summer Olympics: World's Best Athletic Competition. (p. 2150)
—Super Bowl: Football's Game of the Year. (p. 2154)
—Superbikes (p. 2159)
—Surfing. (p. 2163)
—Tanks: A 4D Book. (p. 2190)
—Tom Brady: Football Superstar (p. 2257)
—Tom Brady: Football Superstar. (p. 2257)
—Tony Hawk (p. 2260)
—Tony Stewart (p. 2260)
—Torah Bright (p. 2264)
—Usain Bolt. (p. 2341)
—World Cup: Soccer's Greatest Tournament. (p. 2501)
—World Series: Baseball's Fall Classic. (p. 2504)
Scheff, Matt, jt. auth. see ABDO Publishing Company Staff.
Scheff, Matt, jt. auth. see Ervin, Phil.
Scheff, Matt, jt. auth. see Gordon, Nick.
Scheff, Matt, jt. auth. see Mason, Tyler.
Scheff, Matt & Campbell, Dave. Minnesota Vikings (p. 1473)
Scheff, Matt & Kortemeier, Todd. San Diego Chargers (p. 1929)
Scheffel, Joseph V von. Ekkehard, Vol. 1: A Tale of the Tenth Century (Classic Reprint) (p. 630)
Scheffel, Joseph Viktor. Ekkehard, Vol. 2 Of 2: A Tale of the Tenth Century (Classic Reprint) (p. 630)
Scheffel, Joseph Viktor von. Ekkehard, Vol. 1 Of 2: A Tale of the Tenth Century (Classic Reprint) (p. 630)
Scheffler, Axel. Axel Scheffler Rhyming Stories Book 1: Pip the Dog & Freddy the Frog. (p. 145)
—Axel Scheffler the Noisy Farm Book. (p. 145)
—Mother Goose's Action Rhymes (p. 1509)
—Noisy Farm. (p. 1617)
—On the Farm. (p. 1654)
—Pip & Posy: The New Friend. (p. 1748)
Scheffler, Axel, illus. see Crow, Nosy.
Scheffler, Axel, illus. see Donaldson, Julia & Robertson, James.
Scheffler, Axel, illus. see Donaldson, Julia.
Scheffler, Axel, illus. see Henry Wilson, David.
Scheffler, Axel, illus. see Morgan, Gaby.
Scheffler, Axel, illus. see Nosy Crow Staff.
Scheffler, Axel, illus. see Nosy Crow.
Scheffler, Axel, illus. see Oborne, Martine.
Scheffler, Axel, illus. see Whybrow, Ian.
Scheffler, Axel & Nosy Crow Staff. Pip & Posy: the Snowy Day. Scheffler, Axel, illus. (p. 1748)
Scheibe, Adam, illus. see English, Wesley.
Scheibe, Nancy, illus. see Strauss, Kevin.
Scheibel, Johann Ephraim, jt. auth. see Scheffelt, Michael.
Scheiber, Jennifer & Swain, Cynthia. Seasons - 6 Pack: Set of 6 with Teacher Materials Common Core Edition. (p. 1972)
Scheider, Sarah. Invisible Izzy Takes the Stage. (p. 1132)
Scheiding, Marcia L., illus. see Sundberg, Angela M., et al.
Scheidl, Gerda Marie. Little Gardener. Watts, Bernadette, illus. (p. 1317)
Scheidt, Dave. Wrapped up Vol. 1. McMahon, Scoot, illus. (p. 2510)
—Wrapped up Vol. 2. McMahon, Scoot, illus. (p. 2510)
Scheie, Jesse. Kisses to Heaven Scheie, Jesse, illus. (p. 1224)
Scheier, Leah. Rules of Rain. (p. 1913)
—Your Voice Is All I Hear. (p. 2534)
Scheinberg, Shepsil, illus. see Lazewnik, Libby.
Scheiner, A., illus. see Hoffmann, E. T. A.
Scheiner, Julius. Die Spectralanalyse der Gestirne (Classic Reprint) (p. 544)
Schell, Amanda. Finding a Home. (p. 729)
Schell, J. R. Legion: An Army of One. (p. 1264)
—Legion: Rise of the Black Hand. (p. 1264)
Schell, Liisa & Schell, Spencer. Oh, to Be a Knight. (p. 1642)
Schell, Stanley. Girl Impersonations (Classic Reprint) (p. 835)
—Monologues (Classic Reprint) (p. 1494)
—Werner's Readings & Recitations, Vol. 31: Hallowe'en Festivities (Classic Reprint) (p. 2401)
—Werner's Readings & Recitations, Vol. 40: Thanksgiving Celebrations (Classic Reprint) (p. 2401)
—Werner's Readings & Recitations, Vol. 56: Dramatic Selections (Classic Reprint) (p. 2401)
Schell, Wilhelm. Theorie der Bewegung und der Kräfte, Vol. 2: Ein Lehrbuch der Theoretischen Mechanik; 3. Theorie der Kräfte U. Ihrer Aequivalenz (Dynamik Im Weiteren Sinne Einschl. Statik); 4. Theorie der Durch Kräfte Erzeugten Bewegung (Kinetik Od. Dynamik Im Engeren. (p. 2216)
Schellekens, Willem. UK & Piep: The Magic of a Tree & the Strength of Gnomes. Schellekens, Willem, illus. (p. 2314)
Schellen, Heinrich & Estes, Dana. Spectrum Analysis Explained. (p. 2078)
Schellenberg, B. a. Prince among Dragons. Schellenberg, Emma Grace, ed. (p. 1793)
Schellenberg, Emma Grace, ed. see Schellenberg, B. a.
Scheller, Debbie. Field Guide to Mermaids of the Great Lakes. (p. 723)
Scheltema, Ruth. Tales from Logs: Flight Logs Tell True Adventures of Missionary Pilots. (p. 2182)
Schem, Lida C. Hyphen, Vol. 1 (Classic Reprint) (p. 1056)
Schembri, Pamela, jt. auth. see Catalanotto, Peter.
Schembri, Xenia. Brave Little Bear: Too Big Not to Share. McGregor, Jody, illus. (p. 276)
Schemerhorn, Bobbi. Mechanical Dragons: Air. (p. 1435)
—Mechanical Dragons: Earth. (p. 1435)
—Mechanical Dragons: Spirit. (p. 1435)
—Mechanical Dragons: Reunion. (p. 1435)
—Mechanical Dragons: Fire&water. (p. 1435)
—Mechanical Dragons: Fire & Water. (p. 1435)
Schemery, Beau. 7th of London. (p. 2549)
—7th of Victoria. (p. 2549)
—Last Blade. (p. 1247)
—Unlikely Hero. (p. 2333)
—Unlikely Hero [Library Edition]. (p. 2333)
Schenck, Carl Alwin. Art of the Second Growth; or, American Sylviculture. (p. 121)
Schenck, Ella Syfers. Little Pine Cone. Laween, illus. (p. 1324)
Schenck, Eunice Morgan. Tipyn o'Bob, Vol. 4: November, 1906 (Classic Reprint) (p. 2251)
Schenck, J. W. Rescued Child (Classic Reprint) (p. 1868)
Schenck, Linda, jt. auth. see Thor, Annika.
Schenck, Linda, tr. see Thor, Annika.
Schenk, Margareta. Fifth Door. Verlag, Kelebek, ed. (p. 724)
Schenkel, Daniel, jt. auth. see Furness, William Henry.
Schenkel, Katie. Alice, Secret Agent of Wonderland: A Graphic Novel. Cano, Fernando, illus. (p. 45)
—My Slime Is Alive! Calle, Juan, illus. (p. 1561)
Schenker, Hilary, illus. see House, Silas & Vaswani, Neela.
Schenker, Sybille, illus. see Grimm, Jacob.
Schenkman, Richard. Girl from Atlantis. Braga, Humberto, illus. (p. 835)
Schenkofsky, Henry. Summer with the Union Men (Classic Reprint) (p. 2150)
Scheppler, Bill. Al-Biruni: Master Astronomer & Muslim Scholar of the Eleventh Century. (p. 38)
—Guantánamo Bay & Military Tribunals: The Detention & Trial of Suspected Terrorists. (p. 901)
—Iraqi Insurgents: Resisting America's Nation-Building in Iraq. (p. 1133)
—Iron Man Triathlon. (p. 1135)
Scher, Jon. Top 10 Hockey Heroes. (p. 2262)
Scher, Paula. Brownstone. (p. 287)
Scherber, Diana, illus. see Scherrer, Maura L.
Scherberger, Patrick, illus. see David, Erica.
Scherberger, Patrick, illus. see Lee, Stan.
Scherberger, Patrick, illus. see McKeever, Sean & Lee, Stan.
Scherberger, Patrick, illus. see McKeever, Sean.
Scherberger, Patrick, illus. see Parker, Jeff & Lee, Stan.
Scherberger, Patrick, illus. see Tobin, Paul.
Scherck, P. S. Prym & the Magic Sun Necklace. (p. 1809)
Scherer, Donovan Harold. Fear & Sunshine. Scherer, Donovan Harold, illus. (p. 716)
Scherer, Glenn & Fletcher, Marty. Who on Earth Is Aldo Leopold? Father of Wildlife Ecology. (p. 2449)
—Who on Earth Is Rachel Carson? Mother of the Environmental Movement. (p. 2449)
Scherer, Glenn & Library. True Mountain Rescue Stories. (p. 2294)
Scherer, Lauri S. Social Protest. Gillard, Arthur, ed. (p. 2053)

Schlunke, Eva. Little Worm's Big Question (p. 1330)
Schmal, Mary I. Moon Glow & Twisted Brew: Book Two. (p. 1501)
—Wandering Pirate Ship. (p. 2375)
—Wandering Pirate Ship. Ross, Leanne R., illus. (p. 2375)
Schmalle- Scharber, Geri. Dragon's Tail. (p. 596)
Schmalzer, Sigrid. Moth & Wasp, Soil & Ocean: Remembering Chinese Scientist Pu Zhelong's Work for Sustainable Farming. Chan, Melanie Linden, illus. (p. 1509)
Schmatz, Pat. Bluefish. (p. 250)
—Key to Every Thing. (p. 1211)
—Lizard Radio. (p. 1336)
Schmaus, Marcia L. Adventures of Snooper. (p. 28)
Schmauss, Judy Kentor. Animal Faces. Kelly, Brett, ed. (p. 89)
—Animal Family. (p. 89)
—Arañita. Filella, Luis, illus. (p. 109)
—Arañita - 6 Pack. (p. 109)
—Arcoiris. (p. 111)
—Arcoiris - 6 Pack. (p. 111)
—Camina Conmigo. (p. 314)
—Camina Conmigo - 6 Pack. (p. 314)
—Caminata. Filella, Luis, illus. (p. 314)
—Caminata - 6 Pack. (p. 314)
—Caras de Animales. (p. 327)
—Caras de Animales - 6 Pack. (p. 327)
—Carros de Juguete. (p. 334)
—Carros de Juguete - 6 Pack. (p. 334)
—Casa. (p. 336)
—Casa - 6 Pack. (p. 336)
—Cena. (p. 351)
—Cena - 6 Pack. (p. 351)
—Circles & Squares. Koons, Linda, ed. (p. 393)
—Círculos y Cuadrados. (p. 393)
—Círculos y Cuadrados - 6 Pack. (p. 393)
—Cloudy Days. Kelly, Brett, ed. (p. 408)
—Contar Gatos. Czernichowska, illus. (p. 444)
—Contar Gatos - 6 Pack. (p. 444)
—Desfile. Rocchi, Elisa, illus. (p. 532)
—Desfile - 6 Pack. (p. 532)
—Días Nublados. (p. 540)
—Días Nublados - 6 Pack. (p. 540)
—Diversión en la Granja. (p. 565)
—Diversión en la Granja - 6 Pack. (p. 565)
—Do This with Me. Koons, Linda, ed. (p. 571)
—Doctor. (p. 573)
—Doctora. McMahon, Bob, illus. (p. 574)
—Doctora - 6 Pack. (p. 574)
—Él Viene Conmigo - 6 Pack. (p. 630)
—Empujar y Halar. (p. 645)
—Empujar y Halar - 6 Pack. (p. 645)
—Estación de Bomberos. (p. 664)
—Estación de Bomberos - 6 Pack. (p. 664)
—Flowers. Pulley, Kelly, illus. (p. 753)
—Fresh Market. Kelly, Brett, ed. (p. 785)
—Fruit on a Stick. Chatterton, Chris, illus. (p. 796)
—Fruit Surprise. Kelly, Brett, ed. (p. 796)
—Frutas en un Pincho. Chatterton, Chris, illus. (p. 796)
—Frutas en un Pincho - 6 Pack. (p. 796)
—Fun on the Farm. Kelly, Brett, ed. (p. 799)
—He Comes with Me. (p. 941)
—Hogar. Park, Sun, illus. (p. 986)
—Hogar - 6 Pack. (p. 986)
—House. Koons, Linda, ed. (p. 1022)
—I Am the Sky. Solis, Fermin, illus. (p. 1060)
—I Can Go. Kelly, Brett, ed. (p. 1062)
—I Can Hear It! Rocchi, Elisa, illus. (p. 1062)
—I Have a Family. (p. 1065)
—I Like You. Koons, Linda, ed. (p. 1068)
—Las Familias de Los Animales. (p. 1245)
—Las Familias de Los Animales - 6 Pack. (p. 1245)
—Las Flores. Pulley, Kelly, illus. (p. 1245)
—Las Flores - 6 Pack. (p. 1245)
—Las Gotas de Agua. Bautista, Juan & Oliver, Juan, illus. (p. 1246)
—Las Gotas de Agua - 6 Pack. (p. 1246)
—Las Nubes. Bisacco, Stefania, illus. (p. 1246)
—Las Nubes - 6 Pack. (p. 1246)
—Las Plantas. (p. 1246)
—Las Plantas - 6 Pack. (p. 1246)
—Las Señales. (p. 1246)
—Las Señales - 6 Pack. (p. 1246)
—Little & Big. (p. 1310)
—Los Arboles. (p. 1350)
—Los árboles - 6 Pack. (p. 1350)
—Me Caes Bien. (p. 1433)
—Me Caes Bien - 6 Pack. (p. 1433)
—Mercado de Productos Frescos. (p. 1447)
—Mercado de Productos Frescos - 6 Pack. (p. 1447)
—Mi Ensalada. Poole, Helen, illus. (p. 1455)
—Mi Ensalada - 6 Pack. (p. 1455)
—Mi Gatito. Palacios, Sarah, illus. (p. 1455)
—Mi Gatito - 6 Pack. (p. 1455)
—Mi Gráfico. Filella, Luis, illus. (p. 1455)
—Mi Gráfico - 6 Pack. (p. 1455)
—Mi Perro Pequeño. (p. 1455)
—Mi Perro Pequeño - 6 Pack. (p. 1455)
—Mira Como Voy! Lopez, Ayesha, illus. (p. 1474)
—Mira Mi Jardin. Filella, Luis, illus. (p. 1474)
—Mira Mi Jardín - 6 Pack. (p. 1474)
—MIS Esquís. Lopez, Ayesha, illus. (p. 1476)
—Mis Esquís - 6 Pack. (p. 1476)
—MIS Tomates. (p. 1476)
—Mis Tomates - 6 Pack. (p. 1476)
—My Garden. Fililla, Luis, illus. (p. 1548)
—My Little Cat. Palacios, Sarah, illus. (p. 1552)
—My Little Dog. Kelly, Brett, ed. (p. 1552)
—My Salad. (p. 1560)
—My Skis. Lopez, Ayesha, illus. (p. 1561)
—Nosotros Podemos Comer. (p. 1622)
—Nosotros Podemos Comer - 6 Pack. (p. 1622)
—Parade. Rocchi, Elisa, illus. (p. 1698)
—Parade Feathers. Berchtold, Lauren Marie, illus. (p. 1698)
—Pequeno y Grande. (p. 1721)
—Pequeño y Grande - 6 Pack. (p. 1721)
—Pizza. (p. 1752)
—Pizza. Koons, Linda, ed. (p. 1752)
—Pizza - 6 Pack. (p. 1752)
—Plumas para Desfilar. Berchtold, Lauren Marie, illus. (p. 1763)
—Plumas para Desfilar - 6 Pack. (p. 1763)
—Ponte Esto. (p. 1773)
—Ponte Esto - 6 Pack. (p. 1773)
—Put This On. Kelly, Brett, ed. (p. 1817)
—Que Es? (p. 1822)
—Rainbow. Kelly, Brett, ed. (p. 1836)
—Raindrops. Bautista Juan Oliver, Juan, illus. (p. 1837)
—Short & Tall. Koons, Linda, ed. (p. 2010)
—Sorpresa con Las Frutas. (p. 2065)
—Sorpresa con Las Frutas - 6 Pack. (p. 2065)
—Spider. Filella, Luis, illus. (p. 2080)
—Storm. (p. 2126)
—Subir la Colina. Flowers, Luke, illus. (p. 2145)
—Subir la Colina - 6 Pack. (p. 2145)
—Tabla Del Tiempo. (p. 2175)
—Tabla Del Tiempo - 6 Pack. (p. 2175)
—Ten Cuidado. (p. 2203)
—Ten Cuidado - 6 Pack. (p. 2203)
—This Plant. (p. 2226)
—Tiempo. Oliver, Juan Bautista Juan, illus. (p. 2240)
—Tiempo - 6 Pack. (p. 2240)
—Tormenta. Atkinson, Cale, illus. (p. 2265)
—Tormenta - 6 Pack. (p. 2265)
—Toy Cars. Koons, Linda, ed. (p. 2270)
—Trees. Kelly, Brett, ed. (p. 2284)
—Up a Big Hill. Flowers, Luke, illus. (p. 2337)
—Viene Conmigo. Innerebner, Jessika von, illus. (p. 2356)
—Walk. Filella, Luis, illus. (p. 2371)
—Walk with Me. Kelly, Brett, ed. (p. 2372)
—Watch Me Go. Lopez, Ayesha, illus. (p. 2383)
—We Can Eat. (p. 2390)
—Weather Chart. Kelly, Brett, ed. (p. 2394)
—What Is It? Kelly, Brett, ed. (p. 2415)
—Yo Puedo Flotar. (p. 2522)
—Yo Puedo Flotar - 6 Pack. (p. 2522)
—Yo Puedo Ir. (p. 2522)
—Yo Puedo Ir - 6 Pack. (p. 2522)
—Yo Puedo Oirlos! Rocchi, Elisa, illus. (p. 2522)
—Yo Puedo Oler. (p. 2522)
—Yo Puedo Oler - 6 Pack. (p. 2522)
—Yo Se Dibujar. Solis, Fermin, illus. (p. 2522)
—Yo Soy el Cielo. Solis, Fermin, illus. (p. 2522)
—Yo Soy el Cielo - 6 Pack. (p. 2522)
—Yo Tengo una Familia. (p. 2522)
—Yo Tengo una Familia - 6 Pack. (p. 2522)
—¡a Jugar con la Pelota! (p. 1)
—¡a Jugar con la Pelota! - 6 Pack. (p. 1)
—¡Mira Como Voy! - 6 Pack. (p. 1474)
—¡Yo Puedo oírlos! - 6 Pack. (p. 2522)
—¿Qué Es? - 6 Pack. (p. 1822)
Schmauss, Judy Kentor, jt. auth. see Sohn, Emily.
Schmauss, Judy Kentor & Newmark Learning, LLC. Animal Faces: Set Of 6. (p. 89)
—Animal Family: Set Of 6. (p. 89)
—Circles & Squares: Set Of 6. (p. 393)
—Clouds: Set Of 6. (p. 408)
—Cloudy Days: Set Of 6. (p. 408)
—Counting Cats: Set Of 6. (p. 460)
—Dinner: Set Of 6. (p. 547)
—Do This with Me: Set Of 6. (p. 571)
—Doctor: Set Of 6. (p. 573)
—Fire Station: Set Of 6. (p. 733)
—Flowers: Set Of 6. (p. 753)
—Fresh Market: Set Of 6. (p. 785)
—Fruit on a Stick: Set Of 6. (p. 796)
—Fruit Surprise: Set Of 6. (p. 796)
—Fun on the Farm: Set Of 6. (p. 799)
—He Comes with Me: Set Of 6. (p. 941)
—Home: Set Of 6. (p. 995)
—House: Set Of 6. (p. 1022)
—I Am the Sky: Set Of 6. (p. 1060)
—I Can Float: Set Of 6. (p. 1062)
—I Can Go: Set Of 6. (p. 1062)
—I Can Hear It! Set Of 6. (p. 1062)
—I Can Smell: Set Of 6. (p. 1063)
—I Have a Family: Set Of 6. (p. 1065)
—I Like You: Set Of 6. (p. 1068)
—Little & Big: Set Of 6. (p. 1310)
—My Garden: Set Of 6. (p. 1548)
—My Graph: Set Of 6. (p. 1549)
—My Little Cat: Set Of 6. (p. 1552)
—My Little Dog: Set Of 6. (p. 1552)
—My Salad: Set Of 6. (p. 1560)
—My Skis: Set Of 6. (p. 1561)
—My Tomatoes: Set Of 6. (p. 1562)
—Parade: Set Of 6. (p. 1698)
—Parade Feathers: Set Of 6. (p. 1698)
—Pizza: Set Of 6. (p. 1752)
—Play Ball! Set Of 6. (p. 1759)
—Push & Pull: Set Of 6. (p. 1817)
—Put This On: Set Of 6. (p. 1817)
—Rainbow: Set Of 6. (p. 1836)
—Raindrops: Set Of 6. (p. 1837)
—Short & Tall: Set Of 6. (p. 2010)
—Signs: Set Of 6. (p. 2016)
—Spider: Set Of 6. (p. 2080)
—Storm: Set Of 6. (p. 2126)
—This Plant: Set Of 6. (p. 2226)
—Toy Cars: Set Of 6. (p. 2270)
—Trees: Set Of 6. (p. 2284)
—Up a Big Hill: Set Of 6. (p. 2337)
—Walk: Set Of 6. (p. 2371)
—Walk with Me: Set Of 6. (p. 2372)
—Watch Me Go: Set Of 6. (p. 2383)
—We Can Eat: Set Of 6. (p. 2390)
—Weather: Set Of 6. (p. 2394)
—Weather Chart: Set Of 6. (p. 2394)
—What Is It? (p. 2415)
Schmeidler, Daniel, illus. see J, Thais Sherell.
Schmeil, Otto. Text-Book of Zoology: Treated from a Biological Standpoint (Classic Reprint) (p. 2210)
Schmelz, Ingeborg. Spatzenjunge Flori. (p. 2075)
Schmerhorn, Rick. Immigration to North America: Undocumented Immigration & Homeland Security Anderson, Stuart, ed. (p. 1101)
Schmermund, Elizabeth. Architecture: Cool Women Who Design Structures. Chandhok, Lena, illus. (p. 111)
—Breaking down Tasks: Using Decomposition. (p. 278)
—Code Breakers & Spies of the War on Terror. (p. 411)
—Combining Tasks: Using Composition. (p. 428)
—Confronting Disinformation. (p. 440)
—Do Women Have Equal Rights? (p. 571)
—Explore Skyscrapers! With 25 Great Projects. Crosier, Mike, illus. (p. 680)
—Following Instructions: Using Control. (p. 758)
—Minority Soldiers Fighting in the Vietnam War. (p. 1473)
—New Frontiers in Astronomy. (p. 1593)
—Reading & Interpreting the Works of Harper Lee. (p. 1846)
—Telescopes, Probes, Spacecraft, & the Future of Space Exploration. (p. 2201)
—Women in Technology. (p. 2487)
Schmermund, Elizabeth, jt. auth. see Edwards, Judith.
Schmermund, Elizabeth & Bjorklund, Ruth. Massachusetts. (p. 1417)
Schmermund, Elizabeth & McGowan, Tom. Maximilien Robespierre & the French Revolution. (p. 1428)
Schmermund, Elizabeth & Miller, Caitlyn. Dealing with Sexual Harassment (p. 519)
Schmermund, Elizabeth & Robeson, Dale. Twelfth Night. (p. 2302)
Schmermund, Elizabeth & Tan, Chung Lee. Finland. (p. 731)
Schmermund, Elizabeth, contrib. by. Breaking down Tasks: Using Decomposition. (p. 278)
—Combining Tasks: Using Composition. (p. 428)
Schmermund, Elizabeth, ed. Campus Sexual Violence. (p. 317)
—Civil Disobedience. (p. 396)
—Domestic Terrorism. (p. 580)
—Identity Politics. (p. 1089)
—Immigration Bans. (p. 1101)
Schmermund, Elizabeth, et al. Massachusetts. (p. 1417)
Schmickl, Angela. Matador Who Ran Away from the Spider. Greenfelder, Jill & Rosado, Veronica, illus. (p. 1420)
Schmid, Christoph Von. Basket of Flowers; or Piety & Truth Triumphant: A Tale for the Young (Classic Reprint) (p. 170)
—Canary Bird (Classic Reprint) (p. 321)
—Carrier Pigeon (Classic Reprint) (p. 334)
—Christmas Eve, or the Story of Poor Anthony (Classic Reprint) (p. 385)
—How Henry Von Eichenfels Came to the Knowledge of God (Classic Reprint) (p. 1031)
—Water Pitcher (Classic Reprint) (p. 2385)
Schmid, Christopher. Flower Basket: From the German (Classic Reprint) (p. 752)
Schmid, Christopher Von. Pet Lamb, & Other Tales: Translated from the German (Classic Reprint) (p. 1726)
Schmid, Corinne. Ziggy Learns His ABCs. (p. 2540)
Schmid, Debi, illus. see Hedegaard, Lise.
Schmid, Eleonore. Santa Claus & the Dormouse. (p. 1932)
Schmid, Emma. Hey Diddle Diddle. (p. 964)
Schmid, Herman. Chancellor of the Tyrol, Vol. 2 (Classic Reprint) (p. 355)
—Habermeister: A Tale of the Bavarian Mountains (Classic Reprint) (p. 908)
Schmid, Katie Kelley. Nat Turner & Slave Life on a Southern Plantation. (p. 1576)
Schmid, Lisa. Ollie Oxley & the Ghost: The Search for Lost Gold. (p. 1650)
Schmid, Paul. Hugs from Pearl. Schmid, Paul, illus. (p. 1048)
—Little Bear Dreams. (p. 1311)
—Perfectly Percy. Schmid, Paul, illus. (p. 1723)
—Pet for Petunia. (p. 1726)
—Pet for Petunia. Schmid, Paul, illus. (p. 1726)
—Petunia Goes Wild. Schmid, Paul, illus. (p. 1732)
Schmid, Paul, illus. see Colman, Michelle Sinclair.
Schmid, Paul, illus. see Rosenthal, Amy Krouse.
Schmid, Paul, illus. see Thompson, Laurie Ann.
Schmid, Susan Maupin. Ghost of a Chance. Marlin, Lissy, illus. (p. 828)
—If the Magic Fits. (p. 1092)
—Starlight Slippers. Marlin, Lissy, illus. (p. 2106)
Schmidt, Alejandra, tr. see Fleming, Candace.
Schmidt, Alex & Schmidt, Steve. Our Federal Constitution, Our Missouri Constitution. Schmidt, Dennis, ed. (p. 1678)
—Our Federal Constitution, Our Wisconsin Constitution. Schmidt, Dennis, ed. (p. 1678)
Schmidt, Alex J. & Schmidt, Steven L. Our Federal Constitution, Our Michigan Constitution. Schmidt, Dennis, ed. (p. 1678)
Schmidt, Amy. Back to Dog-Gone School. Schmidt, Ron, illus. (p. 155)
—Dog-Gone School. Schmidt, Ron, photos by. (p. 576)
Schmidt, Andy. This Is Black Panther. (p. 2224)
Schmidt, Andy & Barr, Mike W. Star Trek Motion Picture Trilogy. Chee, (IL, illus. (p. 2103)
Schmidt, Anita, illus. see DeYoung, Andrew.
Schmidt, Anthony, illus. see Craddock, Petra.
Schmidt, Bryan Thomas. Abraham Lincoln Dinosaur Hunter. (p. 7)
Schmidt, Bryan Thomas, ed. see Pedersen, David J.
Schmidt, Caleb, illus. see Paulding, Steve.
Schmidt, Calie. Drummer Boy. Pace, Alycia, illus. (p. 606)
—Ransom. (p. 1841)
Schmidt, Carol. Butterfly Fairies Stained Glass Coloring Book. (p. 304)
—Creative Haven Kaleidoscope Designs Stained Glass Coloring Book. (p. 470)
—Creative Haven Patchwork Quilt Designs Coloring Book. (p. 471)
—Witches Stained Glass Coloring Book. (p. 2480)
Schmidt, Carol & Coloring Books Staff. Japanese Stencil Designs Stained Glass Coloring Book. (p. 1160)
Schmidt, Carter, illus. see Paulding, Steve.
Schmidt, Deborah, illus. see Risch, Scott.
Schmidt, Debra. Careers in Sports & Fitness. (p. 330)
Schmidt, Dennis, ed. see Schmidt, Alex & Schmidt, Steve.
Schmidt, Dennis, ed. see Schmidt, Alex J. & Schmidt, Steven L.
Schmidt, Dennis, illus. see Schmidt, Alex & Schmidt, Steve.
Schmidt, Dennis, illus. see Schmidt, Alex J. & Schmidt, Steven L.
Schmidt, Dennis & Schmidt, Esther, photos by. Baby Wild Animals (p. 153)
Schmidt, Elton. Colorado's Changing Cities: Then & Now (p. 422)
Schmidt, Erica, illus. see Koons, Linda.
Schmidt, Erica Lyn, illus. see Craddock, Petra.
Schmidt, Erica Lyn, illus. see McGowan, Chris.
Schmidt, Gary D. Anson's Way. (p. 101)
—Lizzie Bright & the Buckminster Boy. (p. 1336)
—Martin de Porres: The Rose in the Desert. Diaz, David, illus. (p. 1410)
—Okay for Now. (p. 1643)
—Orbiting Jupiter. (p. 1669)
—Pay Attention, Carter Jones. (p. 1708)
—So Tall Within: Sojourner Truth's Long Walk Toward Freedom. Minter, Daniel, illus. (p. 2050)
—Straw into Gold. (p. 2139)
—Trouble. (p. 2291)
—Wednesday Wars. (p. 2395)
—What Came from the Stars. (p. 2406)
Schmidt, Gary D. & Stickney, Elizabeth. Almost Time. Karas, G. Brian, illus. (p. 57)
Schmidt, Gary D., ed. Poetry for Young People: Robert Frost. Sorensen, Henri, illus. (p. 1767)
Schmidt, Gisela B. 20 Frühlingsgeschichten Für Groß und Klein. (p. 2553)
Schmidt, Hans. Jona: Eine Untersuchung Zur Vergleichenden Religionsgeschichte (Classic Reprint) (p. 1176)
Schmidt, Immanuel. Dictionary of the English & German Languages for Home & School, Vol. 2 Of 2: In Two Parts, with Special Reference to Dr. Felix Flugel's Universal English-German & German-English Dictionary; German-English (Classic Reprint) (p. 542)
Schmidt, J. Marc, illus. see Franks, Jason.
Schmidt, Jacqueline. Patchwork Goes under Cover. (p. 1704)
Schmidt, Jacqueline, illus. see Greiner, Gail.
Schmidt, Jenelle Leanne. 'Twas an Evening in Bethlehem. Klein, Sierra, illus. (p. 2302)
Schmidt, Jessica, jt. auth. see Schmidt, Julie.
Schmidt, Jonathon, ed. see Yolen, Jane.
Schmidt, Julie. My Piggy Bank: Number Names & Count Sequence. (p. 1559)
Schmidt, Julie & Schmidt, Jessica. My Piggy Bank: Number Names & Count Sequence. (p. 1559)
Schmidt, Karenlee, illus. see Paxton, Tom.
Schmidt, Katen, illus. see Nolen, Jerdine.
Schmidt, Kimberly K. Henry's Discovery. Marina, Saumell, illus. (p. 956)
Schmidt, Kimmy. Legends of Greemulax. (p. 1263)
Schmidt, Kristina Edelkamp. Miss Flavia & the Cookie Cottage. Cologne, Starla, illus. (p. 1478)
Schmidt, Laura Stewart. Until Proven Innocent. (p. 2336)
Schmidt, M., illus. see Jackson, S. & Raymond, A.
Schmidt, M., et al. Shadow & Friends European Vacation. (p. 1996)
Schmidt, Maegan. Us Constitution & Bill of Rights (p. 2340)
—US Constitution & Bill of Rights. (p. 2340)
Schmidt, Maria T. Fire Trucks. (p. 733)
Schmidt, Mary. Curly White Bear. (p. 488)
Schmidt, Mary L., et al. Shadow & Friends Ocean Adventure. (p. 1996)
—Suzy Has a Secret. (p. 2167)
Schmidt, Matthew P. City & the Dungeon: And Those Who Dwell & Delve Within. (p. 394)
Schmidt, Max, et al. Hijos de la Selva: La Fotografiá Etnográfica de Max Schmidt = Sons of the Forest: The Ethnographic Photography of Max Schmidt. (p. 970)
Schmidt, Mel Mae. Die Geschichte Vom Muckelpuckchen. (p. 543)
—Velourion & Lavinia. (p. 2350)
Schmidt, Mollie. Children of Courage. (p. 371)
—It Happened in Maine. Wood, Madeline, illus. (p. 1141)
Schmidt, Nolan. Lanelle & the Elementary School Lock-In. (p. 1243)
—Lanelle & the Ghost of Davidson Elementary. (p. 1243)
—Smushed, Soggy Sandwiches. (p. 2043)
Schmidt, Rebecca C. Weird Things That Happen When Someone You Love Dies: A Book of Lists. (p. 2397)
Schmidt, Rebecca L. Movie Magic. (p. 1516)
—Power of the Fortrex. (p. 1782)
Schmidt, Ron, illus. see Schmidt, Amy.
Schmidt, Ron, photos by see Schmidt, Amy.
Schmidt, Shawntay. Invincible Me. Du Pont, Brittany, illus. (p. 1132)
Schmidt, Stanley F. Life of Fred Calculus Expanded Edition. (p. 1294)
—Life of Fred—Edgewood. (p. 1294)
—Life of Fred—Farming. (p. 1294)
Schmidt, Steven L., jt. auth. see Schmidt, Alex J.
Schmidt, Tiffany. Bookish Boyfriends. (p. 261)
—Boy Next Story: A Bookish Boyfriends Novel. (p. 269)
—Break Me Like a Promise: Once upon a Crime Family. (p. 277)
—Bright Before Sunrise. (p. 281)
—Talk Nerdy to Me: A Bookish Boyfriends Novel. (p. 2187)
Schmidt, Troy. Bible Trivia, Jokes, & Fun Facts for Kids. (p. 214)
—Donkey & Jesus. Jones, Cory, illus. (p. 581)
—Donkey Tells His Side of the Story: Hey God, I'm Sorry to Be Stubborn, but I Just Don't Like Anyone Riding on My Back! Jones, Cory, illus. (p. 581)
—Frog & the Plagues. Jones, Cory, illus. (p. 789)
—Lion & Daniel. Jones, Cory, illus. (p. 1305)
—Lion Tells His Side of the Story: Hey God, I'm Starving in This Den So Why Won't You Let Me Eat This Guy Named Daniel?! Jones, Cory, illus. (p. 1306)

—Raven & Noah's Ark. Jones, Cory, illus. (p. 1843)
—Whale & Jonah. Jones, Cory, illus. (p. 2403)
Schmidt, Troy, jt. auth. see Lucado, Max.
Schmidt-Kyanka, Anita. Sapsucker Blues: The Story of an Endearing Family of Great Blue Herons. (p. 1934)
Schmit, Paul. Prinz Patrick Oder Wenn der Dritte Weltkrieg Naht. (p. 1801)
Schmitt, Adam P. Speechless. (p. 2078)
Schmitt, Conrad. Asi Se Dice 2009, Level 1A. (p. 125)
—¡Así Se Dice! (p. 125)
Schmitt, Gary. R. O. Dents in the School. (p. 1829)
Schmitt, Gladys. Alexandra (Classic Reprint) (p. 43)
Schmitt, Louis J., illus. see Landry, Cornell P.
Schmitt, Petra Maria. Why Is the Banana Crooked ? (p. 2458)
Schmitt, Rebecca. Doll Book. (p. 578)
Schmitt, Robin. Bible Gems to Remember Devotions for Kids: 52 Devotions with Easy Bible Memory in 5 Words or Less (p. 213)
—Bible Gems to Remember Illustrated Bible: 52 Stories with Easy Bible Memory in 5 Words or Less (p. 213)
Schmitt, Sarah J. It's a Wonderful Death. (p. 1144)
Schmitt, Sheri. Aventures Avec Peanut. (p. 142)
—Avventure con Peanut (Italian) (p. 143)
Schmitz, Cecile & Mouchet, Klutt. Father Damien Hawaii's Saint. (p. 714)
Schmitz, James H. Other Likeness. (p. 1674)
Schmitz, L. Dora. Buchholz Family. Stinde, Julius, ed. (p. 289)
Schmitz, L. Dora, jt. auth. see Stinde, Julius.
Schmitz, Mark. Manga Boys Coloring Book. (p. 1397)
—Manga Paper Dolls. (p. 1397)
Schmitz, Sheri. Hedgies Rainbow of Lessons. (p. 948)
Schmitz, Tamara, illus. see Friedman, Laurie.
Schmitz, Tamara, illus. see Tangvald, Christine Harder.
Schmitzer, Jeanne Cannella, jt. auth. see Appelt, Kathi.
Schmolze, Ian, illus. see Larner, Eric.
Schmudde, Erik. Disney/Pixar Toy Story Movie Theater. (p. 564)
Schmutz, Janine, et al, texts. What Is Art? 27 Questions 27 Answers. (p. 2414)
Schnabel, Louis. Voegele's Marriage & Other Tales. (p. 2364)
—Voegele's Marriage & Other Tales (Classic Reprint) (p. 2364)
Schnall, Emily, illus. see Everin, Gretchen.
Schnapps, Charles H. Archag, the Little Armenian (Classic Reprint) (p. 110)
Schneck, Marcus. Kittens. (p. 1226)
—Puppies. (p. 1814)
Schneck, Marcus & Caravan, Jill. Cats. (p. 345)
—Dogs. (p. 577)
Schneder, Anna Margaret. O Mura San, with a Glimpse of the Country in Which She Lived (Classic Reprint) (p. 1633)
Schnee, Silke. Prince Noah & the School Pirates. Sistig, Heike, illus. (p. 1794)
—Prince Who Was Just Himself. Sistig, Heike, illus. (p. 1795)
Schneeberger, Anne. Bubble's Cuddles. (p. 289)
Schnee-Bosch, Penny. Mommy Always Comes Back. Bosch, David, illus. (p. 1490)
Schneid, Elisabeth, ed. see Verlag, Don Bosco Medien.
Schneid, Frances E., illus. see Storper, Barbara.
Schneider, Anne. Ballerino. (p. 161)
Schneider, Antonie. Snow for Everyone! Chang, Pei-Yu, illus. (p. 2047)
Schneider, Barbara Hoss, illus. see Dalpra-Berman, Gina.
Schneider, Camillo Karl. Illustriertes Handbuch der Laubholzkunde, Vol. 1: Charakteristik der in Mitteleuropa Heimischen und Im Freien Angepflanzten Angiospermen Gehölz-Arten und Formen Mit Ausschluss der Bambuseen und Kakteen (Classic Reprint) (p. 1097)
Schneider, Christa. Light It! Creations That Glow, Shine, & Blink. (p. 1298)
—Make It Yourself! Comics & Graphic Novels. (p. 1386)
—Move It! Projects You Can Drive, Fly, & Roll. (p. 1515)
Schneider, Christine M., illus. see Bullard, Lisa.
Schneider, Christine M., illus. see Harrast, Tracy L.
Schneider, Christine M., illus. see Rustad, Martha E. H.
Schneider, Claude, illus. see Jeffers, Dawn.
Schneider, David. Dillan Mcmillan, Please Eat Your Peas. Shelly, Jeff, Sr., illus. (p. 546)
Schneider, Dianna. Rocky Ford Stories: Sleepytime at Rocky Ford. (p. 1896)
Schneider, Emma & Holland, Rebecca. Jacob & His Out of the Ordinary Playground. (p. 1154)
Schneider, Erin L. Summer of Sloane. (p. 2149)
Schneider, Ingrid E., jt. ed. see Allison, Maria T.
Schneider, Josh. Bedtime Monsters. (p. 188)
—Everybody Sleeps (but Not Fred) (p. 671)
—Kid Amazing vs. the Blob. (p. 1212)
—Meanest Birthday Girl. (p. 1434)
—Princess Sparkle-Heart Gets a Makeover. (p. 1799)
—Tales for Very Picky Eaters. Schneider, Josh, illus. (p. 2181)
—Ultrabot's First Playdate. (p. 2316)
Schneider, Karl Ernst. Musikalische Lied in Geschichtlicher Entwickelung: Übersichtlich und Gemeinfaßlich Dargestellt (Classic Reprint) (p. 1529)
Schneider, Katy, illus. see Charest, Emily MacLachlan & MacLachlan, Patricia.
Schneider, Leighanne, illus. see Achurch, Holly.
Schneider, Marine. I Am Life. (p. 1059)
Schneider, Marine, illus. see Helland Larsen, Elisabeth.
Schneider, Marnie. Football Freddie & Fumble the Dog: Gameday in Atlanta. (p. 761)
—Football Freddie & Fumble the Dog: Gameday in Pittsburgh. (p. 761)
Schneider, Rex, illus. see Burk, Rachelle.
Schneider, Rex, illus. see Carroll, Lewis, pseud.
Schneider, Rex, tr. see Carroll, Lewis, pseud.
Schneider, Richard H. Why Christmas Trees Aren't Perfect. (p. 2455)
Schneider, Robyn. Beginning of Everything. (p. 192)
—Extraordinary Means. (p. 685)
—Invisible Ghosts. (p. 1132)
—You Don't Live Here. (p. 2527)
Schneider, S., illus. see Roosevelt, Wyn.
Schneider, Seri, jt. auth. see Clark, Michael.
Schneider, Tina. Ninja Boy's Secret. (p. 1610)
Schnell, David. Night Before Baseball at the Park by the Bay. Pamintuan, Macky, illus. (p. 1604)
Schnell, Gwendolyn a. Mary Rose & Me: Learn Bible Truths Together. (p. 1416)
Schnell, Lisa. Bees Buzz. (p. 189)
—Water All Around. (p. 2384)
—Where Does It Come From? (p. 2436)
Schnell, Lisa K. Human Body Systems. (p. 1049)
—Leaves Fall. (p. 1259)
Schnell, Selynn. Backpack Jungle. (p. 156)
Schnetzler, Pattie. Ten Little Dinosaurs. Harris, Jim, illus. (p. 2204)
Schnick, Bernice. Confident Carly. Tenenbaum, Linda, illus. (p. 439)
Schnittkind, Henry T. Best College Short Stories, 1917-18 (Classic Reprint) (p. 205)
Schnitzlein, Danny. Gnu & Shrew. Sandu, Anca, illus. (p. 845)
—Monster Who Ate My Peas Faulkner, Matt, illus. (p. 1497)
Schnitzler, Arthur. Casanova's Homecoming (Classic Reprint) (p. 336)
—Gallant Cassian: A Puppet-Play in One Act (Classic Reprint) (p. 806)
—Playing with Love, and, the Prologue to Anatol (Classic Reprint) (p. 1761)
—Road to the Open (Classic Reprint) (p. 1888)
—Viennese Idylls (Classic Reprint) (p. 2356)
Schnobrich, Emily. Delaware. (p. 526)
—New York. (p. 1598)
Schnoor, Joel F. Aunt Ruth: The Queen of English & Her Reign of Error. (p. 137)
—Aunt Ruth Grammar Drills for Excellence I: A Workbook Companion to I Laid an Egg on Aunt Ruth's Head. (p. 137)
—Aunt Ruth Grammar Drills for Excellence I Answer Key: A Workbook Companion to I Laid an Egg on Aunt Ruth's Head. (p. 137)
—Aunt Ruth Grammar Drills for Excellence II: A Workbook Companion to Aunt Ruth: the Queen of English & Her Reign of Error. (p. 137)
—Aunt Ruth Grammar Drills for Excellence II Answer Key: A Workbook Companion to Aunt Ruth: the Queen of English & Her Reign of Error. (p. 137)
Schnoor, T. H. Turtle & the Hair. (p. 2301)
Schnur, Dawn. Bailey's Tree House Adventures. (p. 159)
Schnur, Susan. Tashlich at Turtle Rock. Schnur-Fishman, Anna & Steele-Morgan, Alexandra, illus. (p. 2192)
Schnur, Susan & Schnur-Fishman, Anna. Tashlich at Turtle Rock Steele-Morgan, Alex, illus. (p. 2192)
Schnur-Fishman, Anna, illus. see Schnur, Susan.
Schnur-Fishman, Anna, jt. auth. see Schnur, Susan.
Schnurr, Douglas. Nativity: A Children's Book. (p. 1579)
Schnurr, Rosina G. Eraser Cookies. Marsden, Suzanne, illus. (p. 659)
Schobergh, Andrea, ed. see Bey Non Assumpst for Bobby Bosco Faust.
Schoberle, Cecile. Day Lights, Night Lights. (p. 513)
—Morning Sounds, Evening Sounds. (p. 1506)
Schobert, H. Picked up in the Streets: A Romance (Classic Reprint) (p. 1739)
Schoch, William. Introduction to Geometry: A Manual of Exercises for Beginners (Classic Reprint) (p. 1129)
Schock, Georg. Hearts Contending: A Novel (Classic Reprint) (p. 946)
Schoebinger, Chris, jt. auth. see Beck, Glenn.
Schoeder, Alan. In Daddy's Arms I Am Tall: African Americans Celebrating Fathers. Steptoe, Javaka, illus. (p. 1104)
Schoeller, Jen. Biggest, Baddest Book of Sea Creatures (p. 224)
—Biggest, Baddest Book of Space (p. 224)
Schoen, Clint. Pooch Chronicles. Missey, Erica, illus. (p. 1773)
Schoen, Robin. Grandmother's Guest: The Blue Lady of Wilton. Hoar, Gail, illus. (p. 879)
Schoenberg, Jane. Baby Hustle: An Interactive Book with Wiggles & Giggles! Conrad, Liz, illus. (p. 151)
Schoenbohm, Ann. Rising above Shephersdsville. (p. 1886)
Schoenbrun, Diana, illus. see Grant, Adam & Grant, Allison Sweet.
Schoenbrun, Diana, illus. see Vernick, Audrey.
Schoene, Kerstin. Todos Los Animales Creeeecen! (p. 2256)
Schoene, Kerstin & Gunetsreiner, Nina. Milo Is Not a Dog Today. (p. 1468)
Schoenherr, Ian. Read It, Don't Eat It! Schoenherr, Ian, illus. (p. 1845)
Schoenherr, Ian, illus. see Cashore, Kristin.
Schoenherr, Ian, illus. see Jacques, Brian.
Schoenherr, Ian, illus. see MacKnight, Wendy McLeod.
Schoenherr, Ian, illus. see Meloy, Maile.
Schoenherr, John, illus. see Craighead George, Jean.
Schoenherr, John, illus. see George, Jean Craighead.
Schoening, Dan. Green Lantern (p. 894)
Schoening, Dan, illus. see Acampora, Michael V.
Schoening, Dan, illus. see Acampora, Michael Vincent.
Schoening, Dan, illus. see Bright, J. E.
Schoening, Dan, illus. see Burnham, Erik & Waltz, Tom.
Schoening, Dan, illus. see Burnham, Erik.
Schoening, Dan, illus. see Carbone, Courtney.
Schoening, Dan, illus. see Crawford, Philip & Crawford, Philip Charles.
Schoening, Dan, illus. see Dahl, Michael.
Schoening, Dan, illus. see Hoena, B. A.
Schoening, Dan, illus. see Hoena, Blake A.
Schoening, Dan, illus. see Hoena, Blake A. & Hoena, B. A.
Schoening, Dan, illus. see Kupperberg, Paul.
Schoening, Dan, illus. see Mason, Jane B.
Schoening, Dan, illus. see Simonson, Louise.
Schoening, Dan, illus. see Sonneborn, Scott.
Schoening, Dan, illus. see Steele, Michael A.
Schoening, Dan, illus. see Stephens, Sarah Hines & Hines-Stephens, Sarah.
Schoening, Dan, illus. see Stephens, Sarah Hines.
Schoening, Dan, illus. see Sutton, Laurie S.
Schoening, Dan, illus. see Tulien, Sean, et al.
Schoening, Dan, illus. see Wrecks, Billy.
Schoeningh, Debby. Little Raindrop. Brown, Margaret, illus. (p. 1325)
Schoen-Smith, Sieglinde, illus. see von Olfers, Sibylle.
Schoettler, Joan. Good Fortune in a Wrapping Cloth. Lanan, Jessica, illus. (p. 862)
—Ruth Asawa: A Sculpting Life Van Wagoner, Traci, illus. (p. 1918)
Schoffman, Stuart, tr. see Yehoshua, A. B. & Dostoevsky, Fyodor.
Schoffstall, John. Half-Witch: A Novel. (p. 911)
Schofield, Angela, illus. see Nourigat, Paul.
Schofield, Charles. Sketch Book: Prose & Poetry (Classic Reprint) (p. 2030)
—Sketch Book. (p. 2030)
Schofield, Christina Diane, illus. see Gunn, Robin Jones.
Schofield, Jayne. Peep & Find: Dragons. (p. 1713)
—Peep & Find: in the Jungle. (p. 1713)
—Peep & Find: under the Ocean. (p. 1713)
—Peep & Find: Unicorns. (p. 1713)
Schofield, Jayne, illus. see Weerasekera, Becky.
Schofield, Jo & Danks, Fiona. Den Book. (p. 528)
Schofield, Mary Mercer. Guidon, Vol. 3: Oct;-Nov;, 1906 (Classic Reprint) (p. 904)
Schofield, Vicki. Ben & Marty: A Forest Day. Schofield, Vicki, illus. (p. 198)
—Ben & Marty: An Eggomatic Day. Schofield, Vicki, illus. (p. 198)
—Ben & Marty: A Rainy Day Parade. Schofield, Vicki, illus. (p. 198)
—Marty Moves In. (p. 1411)
—Travelling Sock Snacker. (p. 2280)
Schofield-Farmer, Twila, illus. see Entinger, Chad.
Schofield-Morrison, Connie. I Got the Christmas Spirit. Morrison, Frank, illus. (p. 1065)
—I Got the Rhythm. Morrison, Frank, illus. (p. 1065)
—I Got the School Spirit. Morrison, Frank, illus. (p. 1065)
Scholars, Hjcs. ABC Kids. (p. 4)
—African American History: For Kids, by Kids. (p. 32)
—Greatest Kids Ever! (p. 891)
—Henry Johnson & the Harlem Hellfighters. (p. 955)
Scholastic. 0-20 Numbers Set Bulletin Board. (p. 2545)
—100 Task Cards in a Box: Informational Text. (p. 2557)
—100 Task Cards in a Box: Literary Text. (p. 2557)
—1-2-3 Draw! (p. 2545)
—123 Pre-K Workbook. (p. 2559)
—5 Big & Busy Trucks (Scholastic Early Learners) (p. 2547)
—50 First Words Flashcards. (p. 2555)
—ABC 123 Write & Wipe Flip Book: Scholastic Early Learners. (p. 3)
—ABC Pre-K Workbook. (p. 4)
—Active Listening Bulletin Board. (p. 12)
—Adventure Collection (p. 18)
—Alola Chapter Book. (p. 57)
—Alone Together. (p. 58)
—Alphabet. (p. 58)
—Amazing Animals: Kindergarden A-D Reader Box Set. (p. 63)
—Amazing Animals Big & Small: A First Book of Opposites. (p. 63)
—An Adjective Is... a Word That Describes a Noun. (p. 78)
—Animal Antics: First Grade Reader Box Set. (p. 87)
—Another Way to Say... (p. 101)
—Armadillos (Wild Life LOL!) (p. 117)
—Baby Singing: 30 Steps to Help Your Baby Communicate. (p. 152)
—Back in Action! (p. 155)
—Bedtime for Baby Shark. (p. 188)
—Behavior Clip Chart. (p. 192)
—Black Bears (Wild Life LOL!) (p. 237)
—Black Bears (Wild Life LOL!) (p. 237)
—Blue Waves. (p. 249)
—Brain-Focused Strategies for Learning-And Living Grade 6-8. (p. 274)
—Brain-Focused Strategies for Learning-And Living Grades 3-5. (p. 274)
—Build This City! (p. 293)
—Bulletin Board: Kindness Is a Gift. (p. 296)
—Bulletin Board: Our Feelings. (p. 296)
—Calendar. (p. 310)
—Can You Find Colors? (p. 318)
—Character Traits: How Characters Feel & Behave. (p. 358)
—Circle Brights Scalloped Trimmer. (p. 392)
—Class Birthday Graph Bulletin Board. (p. 399)
—Classroom Awards Postcards. (p. 401)
—Color Your Classroom Accents. (p. 421)
—Color Your Classroom Birthdays Chart. (p. 421)
—Color Your Classroom Name Plates. (p. 421)
—Color Your Classroom Welcome Chart. (p. 421)
—Colors & Shapes in Photos Bulletin Board. (p. 426)
—Colors in the Cold. (p. 426)
—Compound Words. (p. 436)
—Conversation Starters: Bulletin Board. (p. 446)
—Counting. (p. 459)
—Counting Machines. (p. 460)
—Counting to 100. (p. 460)
—D Is for Duck (Scholastic Early Learners) (p. 494)
—Day of the Departed (LEGO Ninjago: Reader) (p. 514)
—Dino's Busy Book (Scholastic Early Learners) (p. 548)
—Dinosaur Makers (Scholastic Early Learners) (p. 549)
—Dream-Along Nursery Rhymes. (p. 601)
—Early Learning: Ready to Read. (p. 614)
—Early Learning Sticker Workbook. (p. 614)
—Easter Surprise (Peppa Pig) EOne, illus. (p. 620)
—Election Activity Kit, Revised Edition. (p. 631)
—En un Pesebre Lejano (Away in a Manager) (p. 646)
—Esports the Ultimate Guide. (p. 663)
—Farm Animals Jigsaw Puzzle (Scholastic Early Learners) (p. 709)
—Farm Tails (Scholastic Early Learners) (p. 710)
—Festival of Mud! (p. 721)
—First 100 Animals. (p. 734)
—First 100 Things That Go. (p. 735)
—First 100 Words. (p. 735)
—First Sorting. (p. 739)
—First Tracing & Mazes. (p. 740)
—Flash Cards: Addition 0 - 12. (p. 746)
—Flash Cards: Alphabet. (p. 746)
—Flash Cards: Colors & Shapes. (p. 746)
—Flash Cards: Multiplication 0 - 12. (p. 746)
—Flash Cards: Numbers 0 - 100. (p. 746)
—Flash Cards: Sight Words. (p. 746)
—Flashcards - 50 Sight Words. (p. 747)
—Fun at the Fair: a Sticker Storybook (Peppa Pig) EOne, illus. (p. 798)
—Fun with Friends. (p. 800)
—Funny Furry Tales! (p. 801)
—George Catches a Cold. EOne, illus. (p. 818)
—Get Ready for Pre-K Write & Wipe Practice. (p. 824)
—Giant Pandas (Wild Life LOL!) (p. 831)
—Giant Workbook: Get Ready for Pre-K. (p. 831)
—Growth Mindset: Bulletin Board. (p. 900)
—Handwriting. (p. 916)
—Harry Potter: Magical Artifacts Coloring Book. (p. 935)
—Harry Potter: Magical Creatures Postcard Coloring Book. (p. 935)
—Harry Potter Magical Places & Characters Coloring Book. (p. 935)
—Harry Potter Magical Places & Characters Postcard Coloring Book. (p. 935)
—Harry Potter Magical Places & Characters Poster Coloring Book. (p. 935)
—Harry Potter Postcard Coloring Book. (p. 935)
—Harry Potter Poster Coloring Book. (p. 935)
—Harry Potter - The Coloring Book. (p. 934)
—Hello Summer Postcards. (p. 952)
—Homophones. (p. 998)
—Hot Dog, Cold Dog. (p. 1006)
—Hundred Chart Anchor Chart. (p. 1051)
—I Count Vehicles. (p. 1064)
—I Love You, Baby Shark. (p. 1078)
—Imathematicas Al Maximo! Guia de Implementacion: Medicion, Geometria, Datos y Probabilidad y Algebra. (p. 1100)
—Incentive Chart. (p. 1112)
—Inspirational African American Quotes Poster (p. 1124)
—Inspirational Quotes Poster Set. (p. 1124)
—Is That a Caterpillar? (p. 1137)
—Is Your Smile Like a Crocodile's? (p. 1138)
—It Is Time For... (p. 1141)
—Johto Handbook. (p. 1175)
—Kindergarten. (p. 1218)
—Kindergarten Mix & Match Silly Sentences (Scholastic Early Learners) (p. 1218)
—Kindergarten Wipe-Clean Workbook. (p. 1219)
—Kindness Postcards. (p. 1219)
—Knees & Toes. (p. 1227)
—Language Arts (6-Chart Set): Anchor Chart. (p. 1243)
—Learn to Write. (p. 1257)
—Learning Mats: Long Vowels. (p. 1258)
—Learning Mats: Match, Trace & Write Numbers. (p. 1258)
—Learning Mats: Match, Trace & Write the Alphabet. (p. 1258)
—Learning Mats: Short Vowels. (p. 1258)
—Learning Mats: Word Families. (p. 1258)
—Learning Puzzles: Addition & Subtraction. (p. 1258)
—Learning Puzzles: Beginning Sounds. (p. 1258)
—Learning Puzzles: Classifying. (p. 1258)
—Learning Puzzles: Numbers. (p. 1258)
—Learning Puzzles: Rhyming. (p. 1258)
—Learning Puzzles: Vowel Sounds. (p. 1258)
—Let's Get Cooking! (p. 1273)
—Let's Go, Construction Trucks! (p. 1273)
—Let's Go! Jigsaw Puzzle (Scholastic Early Learners) (p. 1273)
—Let's Go, Rescue Trucks! (p. 1273)
—Letter Links (Scholastic Early Learners) (p. 1278)
—Letter Sounds. (p. 1278)
—Library Labels Accents. (p. 1284)
—Lift the Flap: First 100 Words. (p. 1297)
—Lift the Flap: Look Who's Talking! (p. 1297)
—Little Plane Learns to Write. (p. 1324)
—Little Skill Seekers: Alphabet. (p. 1328)
—Little Skill Seekers: Alphabet Connect the Dots. (p. 1328)
—Little Skill Seekers: Basic Concepts. (p. 1328)
—Little Skill Seekers: Beginning Sounds. (p. 1328)
—Little Skill Seekers: Colors & Shapes. (p. 1328)
—Little Skill Seekers: Early Math. (p. 1328)
—Little Skill Seekers: Handwriting Practice. (p. 1328)
—Little Skill Seekers: Pre-K Math Practice. (p. 1328)
—Little Skill Seekers: Sight Words. (p. 1328)
—Little Skill Seekers: Sorting & Matching. (p. 1328)
—Look at Me! (p. 1345)
—Look Who's Mooing! Lift the Flap. (p. 1346)
—Maker Genius: 50+ Home Science Experiments. (p. 1387)
—Map Skills for Today: Grade 1. (p. 1401)
—Matematicas Al Maximo Cuaderno de Practica 1a. (p. 1420)
—Matematicas Al Maximo Cuaderno de Practica 2. (p. 1420)
—Matematicas Al Maximo Cuaderno de Practica 6. (p. 1421)
—Matematicas Al Maximo Guia Del Profesor 1a. (p. 1421)
—Matematicas Al Maximo Guia Del Profesor 2. (p. 1421)
—Matematicas Al Maximo Kindergarten Guia Del Profesor A. (p. 1421)
—Matematicas Al Maximo Kindergarten Texto Del Estudiante A. (p. 1421)
—Matematicas Al Maximo Texto Del Estudiante 1a. (p. 1421)
—Mindup Curriculum - Grades Prek-2: Brain-Focused Strategies for Learning-And Living. (p. 1470)
—Missing Easter Bunny. (p. 1480)
—More Sight Words Bulletin Board. (p. 1505)
—My Favorite Color Is... (p. 1539)
—My First Book of Colors. (p. 1542)
—My First Learning Library (p. 1544)
—My Learning Library. (p. 1551)
—My Mommy. (p. 1556)
—News Leveled Informational Texts, Grade 3: High-Interest at Three Lexile Levels with Comprehension Questions. (p. 1600)
—News Leveled Informational Texts, Grade 4: High-Interest Passages at Three Lexile Levels with Comprehension Questions. (p. 1600)
—Night Creatures: A Lift-the-Flap Book. EOne, illus. (p. 1605)
—Noisy Touch & Lift Farm. (p. 1618)
—Noisy Touch & Lift Truck. (p. 1618)

S

—Nouns. (p. 1625)
—Opposites. (p. 1667)
—Our Birthdays! (p. 1676)
—Our Government: Bulletin Board. (p. 1678)
—Our Photo Alphabet Bulletin Board. (p. 1680)
—Our United States Bulletin Board. (p. 1681)
—Peek a Who: Do You Purr, Too? (p. 1713)
—Peek-a-Boo Baby! (p. 1712)
—Peek-a-Who? Are You My Mom? (p. 1713)
—Peppa & Pals. EOne, illus. (p. 1719)
—Peppa Goes to the Zoo. EOne, illus. (p. 1719)
—Peppa Phonics Boxed Set. (p. 1719)
—Peppa Plays Soccer (Peppa Pig: 8x8) EOne, illus. (p. 1720)
—Peppa's Busy Day Magnet Book (Peppa Pig) EOne, illus. (p. 1720)
—Peppa's Christmas Wish. (p. 1720)
—Peppa's Easter Egg Hunt. EOne, illus. (p. 1720)
—Peppa's First Colors (Peppa Pig) Eone, illus. (p. 1720)
—Phonics. (p. 1736)
—Pokémon Coloring Adventures. (p. 1768)
—Pr1me Mathematics Kindergarten Teacher's Guide A. (p. 1783)
—Pre-K. (p. 1786)
—Preschool Basic Skills: Fine-Motor & Scissor Skills. (p. 1788)
—Prime Mathematics Coursebook 6b. (p. 1793)
—Prime Mathematics Practice Book 1b. (p. 1793)
—Prime Mathematics Teacher's Guide 1a. (p. 1793)
—Rhymes. (p. 1875)
—Schedule. (p. 1944)
—Scholastic Book of World Records 2019. (p. 1944)
—Scholastic Pocket Dictionary. (p. 1945)
—Scholastic Pocket Dictionary of Synonyms, Antonyms & Homonyms. (p. 1945)
—Scholastic Success with Addition & Subtraction Grade 1. (p. 1945)
—Scholastic Success with Addition & Subtraction Grade 2. (p. 1945)
—Scholastic Success with Addition, Subtraction, Multiplication & Division Grade 4. (p. 1945)
—Scholastic Success with Fractions & Decimals. (p. 1945)
—Shake Look Touch (Scholastic Early Learners) (p. 1998)
—Shapes. (p. 2000)
—Shapes at Home. (p. 2000)
—Shapes in the Sky. (p. 2000)
—Shopping Game (Scholastic Early Learners) (p. 2009)
—Sight Words. (p. 2016)
—Sight Words: Bulletin Board. (p. 2016)
—Sing with Me ABC (Scholastic Early Learners) (p. 2023)
—Slide & Find ABC Animals. (p. 2038)
—Solucion de Problemas Matematicos: El Metodo Del Modelo de Barras. (p. 2058)
—Squeak-A-Boo (Scholastic Early Learners) (p. 2094)
—Stats & Facts on over 150 Brand-New Pokémon! Scholastic, illus. (p. 2109)
—STEM Gears Scalloped Trimmer. (p. 2113)
—Storybook Collection. (p. 2136)
—Synonyms & Antonyms. (p. 2173)
—Tape It Up! Birthdays Mini Bulletin Board. (p. 2191)
—Tape It Up! Class Expectations Chart. (p. 2191)
—Tape It Up! Class Jobs Bulletin Board. (p. 2191)
—Tape It Up! Name Plates. (p. 2191)
—Tape It Up! Welcome Bulletin Board. (p. 2191)
—Teacher Kindness Planner. (p. 2195)
—Tooth Fairy. (p. 2262)
—Touch & Feel 123. (p. 2267)
—Touch & Feel ABC (Scholastic Early Learners) (p. 2267)
—Touch & Feel ABC: Scholastic Early Learners (Touch & Feel) (p. 2267)
—Touch & Feel Baby Animals. (p. 2267)
—Touch & Feel Farm. (p. 2267)
—Touch & Feel Winter. (p. 2268)
—Touch, Slide, & Lift Busy Farm (Scholastic Early Learners) (p. 2268)
—Trace, Lift, & Learn ABC (Scholastic Early Learners) (p. 2272)
—Trace, Play, & Learn: ABC 123 (Scholastic Early Learners) (p. 2272)
—Tracing. (p. 2272)
—Turn to Learn Watch Me Grow!: a Book of Life Cycles (Scholastic Early Learners) (p. 2300)
—Twinkle, Twinkle Time for Bed. (p. 2305)
—Unique Unicorn: Bulletin Board. (p. 2329)
—Verbs. (p. 2351)
—Very First Phonics Pre-K Wipe-Clean Workbook: (p. 2353)
—We Are Engineers! Bulletin Board. (p. 2389)
—Welcome to Our Class! (p. 2398)
—Welcome to Our Class! Chart. (p. 2398)
—What Is Red? (p. 2416)
—What Is Yellow? (p. 2417)
—Wheels on the Truck Go 'Round & 'Round. (p. 2428)
—White Waves. (p. 2445)
—Who Is in Your Family? (p. 2448)
—Wipe Clean Workbooks - Pen Control (Scholastic Early Learners) (p. 2477)
—Wipe-Clean Practice in ABCs, 123s, Colors & Shapes, Grade Pre-K. (p. 2477)
—Wipe-Clean Summer Activity Book: Get Ready for Pre-K (Scholastic Early Learners) (p. 2477)
—Wipe-Clean Summer Book: Pre-K. (p. 2477)
—Wipe-Clean Workbook, Grade 1. (p. 2477)
—Wipe-Clean Workbooks: Sight Words (Scholastic Early Learners) (p. 2477)
—Woof! (p. 2492)
—Word Families. (p. 2493)
—Word Families: Bulletin Board. (p. 2493)
—Words We Know - English-Spanish. (p. 2495)
—World of Ninjago. (p. 2503)
—World of the Hunger Games: The Official Coloring Book. (p. 2504)
—Write & Wipe ABC 123. (p. 2512)
—Write & Wipe Early Math 123. (p. 2512)
—Write & Wipe Get Ready for Pre-K. (p. 2512)
Scholastic, illus. see Barbo, Maria S.
Scholastic, illus. see Brooke, Samantha.
Scholastic, illus. see Dewin, Howie & Dewin, Howard.
Scholastic, illus. see Easton, Marilyn.
Scholastic, illus. see Howard, Kate.
Scholastic, illus. see Landers, Ace.
Scholastic, illus. see Margles, Samantha.
Scholastic, illus. see Rusu, Meredith.
Scholastic, jt. auth. see Cawthon, Scott.
Scholastic, jt. auth. see Charlesworth, Liza.
Scholastic, jt. auth. see Scholastic.
Scholastic / LeapFrog, jt. auth. see Kirk, David.
Scholastic / LeapFrog, jt. auth. see Marzollo, Jean.
Scholastic & Howard, Kate. Junior Novel. (p. 1191)
—Welcome to Apocalypseburg. (p. 2398)
Scholastic & Imagine Publishing Staff. Game On! 2017: All the Best Games - Awesome Facts & Coolest Secrets. (p. 807)
Scholastic & Rusu, Meredith. Emmet Gets Tough. (p. 644)
Scholastic & Tracosas, L. J. White House Winners: What You Don't Know about the Presidents. Lynch, Josh, illus. (p. 2444)
Scholastic & West, Tracey. Island of Magical Creatures Schank, Amanda & Häggman-Sund, Hedvig, illus. (p. 1139)
Scholastic & Winters, Terra. Overwatch. (p. 1688)
Scholastic Australia Staff & Ryan-Herndon, Lisa L. Who Lives in the Forest? (p. 2449)
Scholastic Book Editors, jt. auth. see Klutz Editors.
Scholastic Canada Ltd. Staff, jt. auth. see Charlesworth, Liza.
Scholastic Canada Ltd. Staff, jt. auth. see Fleming, Maria.
Scholastic Early Learners, Scholastic Early. 1st Letters & Phonics. (p. 2546)
—ABC. (p. 3)
—Math Practice. (p. 1424)
—My World Get Ready for Pre-K Workbook. (p. 1565)
—Pre-K. (p. 1786)
—Ready for Reading. (p. 1847)
—Sorting & Matching. (p. 2066)
—Sorting for Stem. (p. 2066)
—Tracing & Mazes. (p. 2272)
—Writing & Spelling. (p. 2513)
Scholastic Early Learners Staff. My First Book of Shapes; Mi Primer Libro de Figuras. (p. 1543)
—Oraciones Divertidas. (p. 1668)
Scholastic Early Learners Staff, jt. auth. see Scholastic, Inc. Staff.
Scholastic Editors. Bedtime for Peppa. (p. 188)
—Classic Collector's Handbook: An Official Guide to the First 151 Pokemon. (p. 400)
—Day of the Departed. (p. 514)
—George Catches a Cold. (p. 818)
—Peppa Plays Soccer. (p. 1720)
—Peppa's Halloween Party. (p. 1720)
—Pokemon Deluxe Essential Handbook. (p. 1768)
—Primera Fiesta de Pijamas de Peppa (Peppa's First Sleepover) (p. 1793)
—Princess Leia. (p. 1798)
—Quest for the Crystal. (p. 1826)
—Rescue Mission. (p. 1868)
—Scholastic Almanac for Kids 2016. (p. 1944)
—Space Justice! (p. 2071)
Scholastic Editors, jt. auth. see Steele, Michael Anthony.
Scholastic Editors & Fry, Jason. Darth Vader. (p. 508)
Scholastic Editors & Howard, Kate. Return of the Djinn. (p. 1871)
Scholastic Editors & Marsham, Liz. Harley Quinn: Wild Card. (p. 930)
Scholastic Editors & Wiltshire, Alex. Minecraft: Blockopedia. (p. 1470)
Scholastic Editors, ed. Last Laugh! (p. 1248)
Scholastic, et al. Welcome to Chef Club! (p. 2398)
Scholastic Inc. Daily Word Ladders: Content Areas, Grades 4-6. (p. 497)
—Little Skill Seekers: Kindergarten Workbook. (p. 1328)
—Little Skill Seekers: Pre-K Workbook. (p. 1328)
—Little Skill Seekers: Preschool Workbook. (p. 1328)
—Peppa's Windy Fall Day. (p. 1720)
—Phoenix Colossal Comics Collection. (p. 1736)
Scholastic, Inc. Pug Blasts Off (p. 1811)
—Pug's Snow Day (p. 1812)
Scholastic Inc. Spellbinding Guide to the Films of the Wizarding World (Fantastic Beasts: the Crimes of Grindelwald) (p. 2079)
Scholastic Inc. (US) Staff, contrib. by. All about Me/ Todo Sobre Mí. (p. 49)
—My Favorite Food/ Mi Comida Favorita. (p. 1539)
Scholastic Inc, contrib. by. Halloween Wipe-Clean Activity Book. (p. 912)
—My Favorite Food. (p. 1539)
Scholastic Inc., Staff. All about Me. (p. 49)
Scholastic, Inc. Staff. All Around Me. (p. 51)
—All Around Me/a Mi Alrededor. (p. 51)
—Amazing Animals/ Animales Increíbles. (p. 63)
Scholastic Inc Staff. Away in a Manger. (p. 144)
Scholastic, Inc. Staff. Best Friends (Peppa Pig) Eone, illus. (p. 206)
—Cantaba la Rana. Sebastián, Soledad, illus. (p. 322)
—Carry & Learn Numbers. Ward, Sarah G., illus. (p. 334)
Scholastic Inc. Staff. Class Trip. (p. 400)
Scholastic, Inc. Staff. Dentist Trip. (p. 529)
—Dentist Trip (Peppa Pig) (p. 529)
—Dogs 101. (p. 577)
—Dolphin Rescue. (p. 579)
Scholastic Inc., Staff. Dream-Along Nursery Rhymes. Huliska-Beith, Laura et al, illus. (p. 601)
Scholastic, Inc. Staff. Ever after High: Yearbook. (p. 669)
Scholastic Inc, Staff. Flash Cards Set - 50 Spanish-English First Words. (p. 746)
Scholastic, Inc. Staff. Friends Forever. (p. 787)
—Girls' Life Guide to Being the Most Amazing You. Bokram, Karen, ed. (p. 838)
Scholastic Inc, Staff. Go! Field Guide: Rocks & Minerals. (p. 846)
Scholastic Inc., Staff. Go! Field Guide: Sharks. (p. 846)
Scholastic, Inc. Staff. Good Night, Peppa (Peppa Pig) (p. 865)
Scholastic Inc, Staff. Harry Potter - Magical Creatures Coloring Book. (p. 934)
Scholastic Inc Staff. Haunted Halloween: Movie Novel. (p. 937)
Scholastic, Inc. Staff. Hunger Games Official Illustrated Movie Companion. (p. 1052)
Scholastic Inc, Staff. Jesus Loves Me. (p. 1166)
—Jesús Me Ama / Jesus Loves Me. (p. 1166)
Scholastic, Inc. Staff. Jumbo Book of Kindergarten Fun. (p. 1188)
Scholastic Inc, Staff. Jumbo Book of Pre-K Fun. (p. 1188)
—Learning Mats: Alphabet. (p. 1258)
—Learning Mats: Numbers & Counting. (p. 1258)
—Learning Mats: Patterns. (p. 1258)
—Learning Mats: Sight Words. (p. 1258)
—Magical Yearbook. (p. 1381)
—Map Skills for Today: Grade 4. (p. 1401)
—Next Step Guided Reading in Action Grades 3 & up Revised Edition. (p. 1600)
Scholastic, Inc. Staff. Peppa Goes Swimming. (p. 1719)
—Peppa's Chalk ABCs. (p. 1720)
—Peppa's First Pet. (p. 1720)
—Peppa's Windy Fall Day. (p. 1720)
Scholastic Inc, Staff. Phoenix Colossal Comics Collection (p. 1736)
—Phoenix Colossal Comics Collection #1. (p. 1736)
Scholastic Inc Staff. Pikmi to Be Your Valentine! (p. 1744)
Scholastic, Inc. Staff. Plan Your Destiny: A Spellbinding School Planner. (p. 1754)
—Pokemon: Kalos Region Handbook. (p. 1768)
—Pokemon: Kalos Region Handbook. (p. 1768)
Scholastic Inc, Staff. Pokémon School Challenge. (p. 1768)
Scholastic Inc Staff. Pups Save a Pinata. (p. 1815)
Scholastic, Inc. Staff. Ready for Takeoff! (p. 1847)
Scholastic Inc Staff. Riverdale High Student Handbook. (p. 1887)
—Royal Makeover. (p. 1910)
Scholastic Inc., Staff. Scholastic Children's Dictionary (2019) (p. 1944)
Scholastic Inc, Staff. Scholastic Nonfiction Book Collection, Grade 3. (p. 1945)
Scholastic, Inc. Staff. Scooby-Doo: Frankencreepy Movie Reader. (p. 1960)
—Space Justice! (p. 2071)
—Spy vs. Spy. (p. 2093)
—Super Sinnoh. (p. 2158)
Scholastic Inc, Staff. Superscience Mysteries Kit. (p. 2161)
Scholastic, Inc. Staff. Vowel Sounds. (p. 2368)
Scholastic Inc, Staff. What Is Blue? (p. 2414)
Scholastic, Inc. Staff, ed. see Beech, Linda Ward, et al.
Scholastic, Inc. Staff, ed. see Beech, Linda, et al.
Scholastic, Inc. Staff, ed. see Heinst, Marie.
Scholastic, Inc. Staff, ed. see Landers, Ace & Cartwheel Editors.
Scholastic, Inc. Staff, illus. see Holmes, Anna.
Scholastic, Inc. Staff, illus. see Landers, Ace.
Scholastic, Inc. Staff, illus. see Stine, R. L.
Scholastic, Inc. Staff, illus. see Stine, R. L. & Ferguson, Jo Ann.
Scholastic, Inc. Staff, jt. auth. see Bridwell, Norman.
Scholastic, Inc. Staff, jt. auth. see Carman, Patrick.
Scholastic, Inc. Staff, jt. auth. see Charlesworth, Liza.
Scholastic, Inc. Staff, jt. auth. see Fisher-Wright, Blanche.
Scholastic, Inc. Staff, jt. auth. see London, C. Alexander.
Scholastic, Inc. Staff, jt. auth. see Riordan, Rick.
Scholastic, Inc. Staff, jt. auth. see Rowling, J. K.
Scholastic, Inc. Staff, jt. auth. see Slater, Teddy.
Scholastic, Inc. Staff, jt. auth. see Warhola, James.
Scholastic, Inc. Staff, jt. auth. see Windham, Ryder.
Scholastic, Inc. Staff, jt. contrib. by see Childrens Press Staff.
Scholastic, Inc. Staff, jt. contrib. by see Franklin Watts.
Scholastic, Inc. Staff, jt. contrib. by see Piney Grove Elementary School (Kernsville, N.C.) Staff.
Scholastic, Inc. Staff, jt. contrib. by see Tangerine Press Staff.
Scholastic, Inc. Staff & Beech, Linda Ward. 180 Essential Vocabulary Words: Independent Learning Packets That Help Students Learn the Most Important Words They Need to Succeed in School. (p. 2559)
—180 Essential Vocabulary Words for 6th Grade: Independent Learning Packets That Help Students Learn the Most Important Words They Need to Succeed in School. (p. 2559)
Scholastic, Inc. Staff & Brooks, Riley. Edward or Jacob? Quick Quizzes for Fans of the Twilight Saga. (p. 627)
Scholastic, Inc. Staff & Farshtey, Greg. Challenge of Mata Nui. (p. 354)
—Lego Ninjago. (p. 1265)
Scholastic, Inc. Staff & Howard, Kate. Road Chip. (p. 1888)
Scholastic, Inc. Staff & Kaplan, Arie. Official Stormtrooper Training Manual. (p. 1641)
Scholastic, Inc. Staff & Kogge, Michael. Cross Fire. (p. 477)
Scholastic, Inc. Staff & La Bretesche, Genevieve de. Scholastic First Picture Dictionary. Manzanero, Paula, ed. (p. 1944)
Scholastic, Inc. Staff & Ladybird Books Staff. Peppa's First Sleepover. (p. 1720)
Scholastic, Inc. Staff & Malone, Sydney. For Me & U! Fun for BFFs. (p. 763)
Scholastic, Inc. Staff & Marsham, Liz. Movie Flip Book. (p. 1516)
Scholastic, Inc. Staff & Scholastic Early Learners Staff. Lift the Flap: Look Who's Talking! (p. 1297)
—Noisy Touch & Lift Farm. (p. 1618)
—Noisy Touch & Lift Truck. (p. 1618)
Scholastic, Inc. Staff & Silver, Ivy. Time for a Picnic. (p. 2244)
Scholastic, Inc. Staff & Stine, R. L. Write Your Fright. (p. 2512)
Scholastic, Inc. Staff & Watson, Jude. Doublecross - Mission Titanic (p. 589)
Scholastic, Inc. Staff & Weisman, Greg. Traveler. Didier, Samwise, illus. (p. 2280)
Scholastic, Inc. Staff & West, Tracey. Snake Attack! (p. 2044)
Scholastic, Inc. Staff & Wheeler, Alex. Hostage. (p. 1006)
Scholastic, Inc. Staff & Windham, Ryder. Fire Ring Race (p. 733)
Scholastic, Inc. Staff, contrib. by. 1, 2, 3. (p. 2545)
—ABC. (p. 3)
—Baby Animals. (p. 148)
—Bedtime for Rainforest Babies. (p. 188)
Scholastic Inc, Staff, contrib. by. Book of World Records 2018: World Records, Trending Topics, & Viral Moments. (p. 260)
Scholastic, Inc. Staff, contrib. by. Can You Say Please? (p. 318)
—Color with Clifford the Big Red Dog. (p. 421)
—Contemporary Cursive Grades 2-4. (p. 444)
—Counting 1 to 10. (p. 459)
—Counting 1 To 20. (p. 459)
—Day at Charm School. (p. 512)
Scholastic Inc, Staff, contrib. by. Harry Potter Magical Artifacts Poster Coloring Book. (p. 935)
Scholastic, Inc. Staff, contrib. by. Hot Wheels: The Collector's Handbook. (p. 1007)
—I Am Bigger Than... (p. 1058)
—Is It Hot Enough for You? Global Warming Heats Up. (p. 1137)
Scholastic Inc Staff, contrib. by. Lego DC Comics Super Heroes Reader Collection: To the Rescue! (p. 1264)
Scholastic, Inc. Staff, contrib. by. LEGO Friends: Meet the Friends. (p. 1264)
—Let's Go to the Firehouse. (p. 1274)
—Let's Go to the Library. (p. 1274)
—Look Inside. (p. 1346)
—Magellan Heist (p. 1376)
—Peppa's Storytime Box. (p. 1720)
—Population 1.3 Billion: China Becomes a Super Superpower. (p. 1777)
—Red Pepper, Yellow Squash: A Book of Colors. (p. 1858)
—Red Truck, Yellow Bus: A Book of Colors. (p. 1859)
—Rocks & Minerals. (p. 1896)
—Scholastic Success with Addition & Subtraction. (p. 1945)
—Seasons. (p. 1972)
—Shopkins Shoppies Poster Book. (p. 2009)
—Story of Peppa Pig. (p. 2132)
—Traditional Manuscript Grades K-1. (p. 2273)
—Trucks Around the City. (p. 2293)
—What Happens Next? Caterpillar to Butterfly. (p. 2411)
—What Happens Next? Seed to Plant. (p. 2411)
—What Is the Weather Today? (p. 2417)
—World of Harry Potter: Harry Potter Poster Book. (p. 2503)
Scholastic, Inc. Staff, ed. Class Trip. (p. 400)
—Save the Day. (p. 1937)
Scholastic Library Publishing. Ancient World. (p. 82)
—Cornerstones of Freedom. (p. 454)
—Cornerstones of Freedom, Third Series. (p. 454)
—Enchantment of the World. (p. 647)
—Nature's Children. (p. 1581)
—Rookie Read: About Safety. (p. 1902)
—Rookie Read: About Community. (p. 1902)
—Rookie Read: About Geography—Continents. (p. 1902)
—Rookie Read-about(r) Dinosaurs. (p. 1902)
—Rookie Read-about(r) Sports. (p. 1902)
—Rookie Ready to Learn (p. 1902)
—Rookie Ready to Learn Español. (p. 1903)
—Three Little Kittens Get Dressed. (p. 2233)
—True Book—Civics. (p. 2294)
—True Book—Earth Science. (p. 2294)
—True Book-Experiments. (p. 2293)
—True Book—Information Literacy. (p. 2294)
—True Book-Physical Science. (p. 2293)
—True Book-the Civil War. (p. 2293)
—True Book-the Thirteen Colonies. (p. 2293)
—True Book-the U. S. Regions. (p. 2293)
—War in Iraq: From the Front Lines to the Home Front. (p. 2376)
Scholastic Library Publishing Staff, contrib. by. Scholastic Nonfiction Book Collection, Grade 1. (p. 1944)
—Scholastic Nonfiction Book Collection, Grade 2. (p. 1945)
Scholastic Publishing. Around the World with Peppa. (p. 119)
Scholastic Staff. Lost Egg. (p. 1353)
Scholastic Staff, jt. auth. see Selznick, Brian.
Scholastic Teacher Resources. Little Skill Seekers: Word Searches. (p. 1328)
Scholastic Teacher Resources Staff. 100 Words for Kids to Read in First Grade. (p. 2558)
—100 Words for Kids to Read in Kindergarten. (p. 2558)
—Christmas Wipe-Clean Activity Book. (p. 387)
—Early Learning: Ready to Learn. (p. 614)
—Little Skill Seekers: Mazes. (p. 1328)
—Little Skill Seekers: Numbers & Counting. (p. 1328)
—Spring Wipe-Clean Activity Book. (p. 2092)
Scholastic Teacher Resources Staff, jt. auth. see Charlesworth, Liza.
Scholastic Teacher's Friend. File Organizer (Black) Pocket Chart. (p. 726)
Scholastic Teaching Resources, Scholastic Teaching. Alphabet Phonics, Numbers, Counting, Handwriting Between Grades Pre K & K. (p. 59)
Scholastic Teaching Resources Staff. Kindergarten Basic Skills: Alphabet & Fine-Motor Skills. (p. 1218)
—Let's Find Out: My Rebus Readers Multiple-Copy Set: Box 2. (p. 1272)
—Map Skills for Today: Grade 3. (p. 1401)
—My Rebus Readers. (p. 1559)
—Weekly Reader: Summer Express (Between Grades 1 & 2) (p. 2396)
Scholastic Teaching Resources Staff, contrib. by. Jumbo Book of Fun for Kids. (p. 1188)
Scholdeners. Cursive Handwriting Workbook: 2-In-1 Book Set for Kids (Cursive for Beginners / Cursive Writing Practice Book) (p. 490)
—Cursive Handwriting Workbook for Kids: 3-In-1 Writing Practice Book to Master Letters, Words & Sentences. (p. 490)
—Cursive Handwriting Workbook for Teens: Cursive Writing Practice Workbook for Teens, Tweens & Young Adults

S

—Messenger, Vol. 2: May, 1906 (Classic Reprint) (p. 1451)
—Messenger, Vol. 2: March, 1906 (Classic Reprint) (p. 1451)
—Messenger, Vol. 5: April, 1909 (Classic Reprint) (p. 1452)
—Messenger, Vol. 5: October, 1908 (Classic Reprint) (p. 1452)
—Messenger, Vol. 5: December, 1908 (Classic Reprint) (p. 1452)
—Messenger, Vol. 5: February, 1909 (Classic Reprint) (p. 1452)
—Messenger, Vol. 6: May, 1910 (Classic Reprint) (p. 1452)
—Messenger, Vol. 6: April, 1910 (Classic Reprint) (p. 1452)
—Messenger, Vol. 6: September, 1909 (Classic Reprint) (p. 1452)
—Messenger, Vol. 7: October, 1910 (Classic Reprint) (p. 1452)
—Messenger, Vol. 8: October, 1911 (Classic Reprint) (p. 1452)
School, Duxbury High. Partridge: June 1941 (Classic Reprint) (p. 1701)
—Partridge: June, 1938 (Classic Reprint) (p. 1701)
—Partridge: Commencement Issue; June 1940 (Classic Reprint) (p. 1701)
—Partridge, 1935 (Classic Reprint) (p. 1701)
—Partridge, 1942 (Classic Reprint) (p. 1701)
—Partridge, Vol. 10: June 14, 1933 (Classic Reprint) (p. 1701)
School, East Bridgewater High. Student's Pen, Vol. 1: June, 1920 (Classic Reprint) (p. 2143)
—Student's Pen, Vol. 11: June 1932 (Classic Reprint) (p. 2143)
—Student's Pen, Vol. 19: June, 1939 (Classic Reprint) (p. 2143)
—Student's Pen, Vol. 21: Graduation Issue; June, 1941 (Classic Reprint) (p. 2143)
—Student's Pen, Vol. 23: June, 1943 (Classic Reprint) (p. 2143)
—Student's Pen, Vol. 9: June, 1930 (Classic Reprint) (p. 2143)
School, East High. Quill, Vol. 24: June, 1929 (Classic Reprint) (p. 1828)
—Quill, Vol. 27: June, 1931 (Classic Reprint) (p. 1828)
School, East Technical High. June Bug, 1913 (Classic Reprint) (p. 1189)
School, Edward F. Searles High. Class Book, 1930 (Classic Reprint) (p. 399)
—Class Book, 1931 (Classic Reprint) (p. 399)
—Class Book, 1938 (Classic Reprint) (p. 399)
—Class Book, 1939 (Classic Reprint) (p. 399)
—Class Book, 1940 (Classic Reprint) (p. 399)
—Class Book, 1941, Edward F. Searles High School, Methuen, Massachusetts (Classic Reprint) (p. 399)
—Class Book, 1942 (Classic Reprint) (p. 399)
—Class Book, 1944 (Classic Reprint) (p. 399)
School, Elizabeth City High. Spotlight, 1921 (Classic Reprint) (p. 2090)
—Spotlight, 1922 (Classic Reprint) (p. 2090)
—Spotlight, 1923 (Classic Reprint) (p. 2090)
—Spotlight, 1929, Vol. 9 (Classic Reprint) (p. 2090)
—Spotlight, 1931, Vol. 11 (Classic Reprint) (p. 2090)
—Spotlight, 1943 (Classic Reprint) (p. 2090)
School, Elmhurst High. Anlibrum, 1934, Vol. 2 (Classic Reprint) (p. 97)
School, Elwood High. Crescent, 1919 (Classic Reprint) (p. 473)
School, Emmerich Manual High. Senior Booster: June 1923 (Classic Reprint) (p. 1988)
—Senior Booster: June 1926 (Classic Reprint) (p. 1988)
—Senior Booster: January, 1931 (Classic Reprint) (p. 1988)
—Senior Booster, 1924 (Classic Reprint) (p. 1988)
—Senior Booster, 1941 (Classic Reprint) (p. 1988)
—Senior Booster, Vol. 28: January, 1923 (Classic Reprint) (p. 1988)
School, Emmerich Manual Training High. Booster, Vol. 21: June, 1919 (Classic Reprint) (p. 262)
—Booster, Vol. 22: January 1920 (Classic Reprint) (p. 262)
—Senior Booster: June 1920 (Classic Reprint) (p. 1988)
—Senior Booster: June 1929 (Classic Reprint) (p. 1988)
—Senior Booster: June, 1928 (Classic Reprint) (p. 1988)
—Senior Booster: January 1929 (Classic Reprint) (p. 1988)
—Senior Booster, Vol. 34: January, 1926 (Classic Reprint) (p. 1988)
School, English High. English High School Record, Vol. 49: January 1934 (Classic Reprint) (p. 653)
—English High School Record, Vol. 51: April 1936 (Classic Reprint) (p. 653)
—English High School Record, Vol. 51: December 1935 (Classic Reprint) (p. 653)
—English High School Record, Vol. 51: January, 1936 (Classic Reprint) (p. 653)
—English High School Record, Vol. 52: November, 1931 (Classic Reprint) (p. 653)
—Record, Vol. 56: April 1941 (Classic Reprint) (p. 1854)
School, Fairmont State Normal. Mound: Number of Normal Bulletin; June, 1919 (Classic Reprint) (p. 1512)
—Mound, 1909 (Classic Reprint) (p. 1512)
—Mound, 1910 (Classic Reprint) (p. 1512)
—Mound, 1911 (Classic Reprint) (p. 1512)
—Mound, 1912 (Classic Reprint) (p. 1512)
—Mound, 1914 (Classic Reprint) (p. 1512)
—Mound, 1915 (Classic Reprint) (p. 1512)
—Mound, 1918, Vol. 11 (Classic Reprint) (p. 1512)
—Mound, 1921, Vol. 13 (Classic Reprint) (p. 1512)
School, Farm and Trades. Thompson's Island Beacon, Vol. 15: May, 1911 April, 1912 (Classic Reprint) (p. 2229)
—Thompson's Island Beacon, Vol. 19: May, 1915 (Classic Reprint) (p. 2229)
—Thompson's Island Beacon, Vol. 24: May, 1920 (Classic Reprint) (p. 2229)
—Thompson's Island Beacon, Vol. 28: May, 1924 (Classic Reprint) (p. 2229)
—Thompson's Island Beacon, Vol. 36: May, 1932 (Classic Reprint) (p. 2229)
—Thompson's Island Beacon, Vol. 45: January 1942 (Classic Reprint) (p. 2229)
—Thompson's Island Beacon, Vol. 50: May, 1946 (Classic Reprint) (p. 2229)
School, Farmington High. Olive & Gold: April 1913 (Classic Reprint) (p. 1649)
School, Farmville State Female Normal. Around the Year with Our Class: Class of 1911 (Classic Reprint) (p. 119)
—Guidon, Vol. 1: February, 1905 (Classic Reprint) (p. 904)
—Guidon, Vol. 3: Jan; Feb;, 1907 (Classic Reprint) (p. 904)
—Guidon, Vol. 4: May June, 1908 (Classic Reprint) (p. 904)
—Guidon, Vol. 4: October November, 1907 (Classic Reprint) (p. 904)
—Guidon, Vol. 5: May June 1909 (Classic Reprint) (p. 904)
—Guidon, Vol. 5: March-April, 1909 (Classic Reprint) (p. 904)
—Senior Class Book, 1910 (Classic Reprint) (p. 1988)
—Virginian, 1901 (Classic Reprint) (p. 2361)
—Virginian, 1903 (Classic Reprint) (p. 2361)
School, Farmville State Normal. Focus: January, 1914 (Classic Reprint) (p. 755)
—Focus, Vol. 1: April, 1911 (Classic Reprint) (p. 756)
—Focus, Vol. 1: January, 1912 (Classic Reprint) (p. 756)
—Focus, Vol. 1: October, 1911 (Classic Reprint) (p. 756)
—Focus, Vol. 2: May, 1912 (Classic Reprint) (p. 756)
—Focus, Vol. 2: March, 1912 (Classic Reprint) (p. 756)
—Focus, Vol. 2: February, 1912 (Classic Reprint) (p. 756)
—Focus, Vol. 3: May, 1913 (Classic Reprint) (p. 756)
—Focus, Vol. 3: April, 1913 (Classic Reprint) (p. 756)
—Focus, Vol. 3: December, 1913 (Classic Reprint) (p. 756)
—Focus, Vol. 3: November, 1913 (Classic Reprint) (p. 756)
—Focus, Vol. 3: Alumnae Number, June 1913 (Classic Reprint) (p. 756)
—Focus, Vol. 4: January, 1915 (Classic Reprint) (p. 756)
—Focus, Vol. 4: December, 1914 (Classic Reprint) (p. 756)
—Focus, Vol. 4: February, 1914 (Classic Reprint) (p. 756)
—Focus, Vol. 4: November, 1914 (Classic Reprint) (p. 756)
—Focus, Vol. 5: May, 1915 (Classic Reprint) (p. 756)
—Focus, Vol. 5: March, 1915 (Classic Reprint) (p. 756)
—Focus, Vol. 5: January, 1916 (Classic Reprint) (p. 756)
—Focus, Vol. 5: November-December, 1915 (Classic Reprint) (p. 756)
—Focus, Vol. 5: Alumnae Number; September, 1915 (Classic Reprint) (p. 756)
—Focus, Vol. 6: April, 1916 (Classic Reprint) (p. 756)
—Focus, Vol. 6: January, 1917 (Classic Reprint) (p. 756)
—Focus, Vol. 6: December, 1916 (Classic Reprint) (p. 756)
—Focus, Vol. 7: October, 1917 (Classic Reprint) (p. 756)
—Focus, Vol. 7: November, 1917 (Classic Reprint) (p. 756)
—Focus, Vol. 8: June, 1918 (Classic Reprint) (p. 756)
—Focus, Vol. 9: March, 1919 (Classic Reprint) (p. 756)
—Focus, Vol. 9: October-November, 1919 (Classic Reprint) (p. 756)
School, Findlay Senior High. Blue & Gold 1919: The Year Book of Findlay High School, a Record of the Various Activities of the School Year (Classic Reprint) (p. 248)
—Blue & Gold 1920: The Year Book of Findlay High School; a Record of the Various Activities of the School Year (Classic Reprint) (p. 248)
—Blue & Gold, Vol. 19: May 1, 1922 (Classic Reprint) (p. 248)
—Blue & Gold, Vol. 20: May 1, 1923 (Classic Reprint) (p. 248)
School, Fisher. Semma, 1944 (Classic Reprint) (p. 1988)
School, Fitchburg High. 1905 Class Book (Classic Reprint) (p. 2561)
—1918 Class Book: Capre Diem (Classic Reprint) (p. 2561)
—1922 Class Book (Classic Reprint) (p. 2561)
—1926 Class Book (Classic Reprint) (p. 2561)
—Black & Orange, 1915 (Classic Reprint) (p. 236)
—Boulder, 1929 (Classic Reprint) (p. 265)
—Boulder, 1937 (Classic Reprint) (p. 265)
—Boulder, 1938 (Classic Reprint) (p. 265)
—Class Book, '09 (Classic Reprint) (p. 399)
—Class Book, 1919 (Classic Reprint) (p. 399)
—Class Book, 1924 (Classic Reprint) (p. 399)
—Class Book, 1927 (Classic Reprint) (p. 399)
—Class Book, 1928 (Classic Reprint) (p. 399)
—Class Book of 1907 (Classic Reprint) (p. 399)
—Class Book of 1910 (Classic Reprint) (p. 399)
—Class Book of 1913 (Classic Reprint) (p. 399)
—F. H. S. Class Book, 1923 (Classic Reprint) (p. 689)
—Green & Gold, 1914, Vol. 1 (Classic Reprint) (p. 893)
School, Fitchburg Normal. Saxifrage, 1924, Vol. 3 (Classic Reprint) (p. 1939)
School, Fitchburg State Normal. Saxifrage of the Class of Nineteen Twenty-Five, Vol. 4 (Classic Reprint) (p. 1939)
School, Fort Wayne High. Caldron Annual, 1919 (Classic Reprint) (p. 309)
—Caldron, Vol. 8: June, 1911 (Classic Reprint) (p. 309)
—Eniauton of 1900 (Classic Reprint) (p. 655)
—Eniauton of '97 (Classic Reprint) (p. 655)
—Vadette of '98 (Classic Reprint) (p. 2343)
—Vedette, 1898 (Classic Reprint) (p. 2348)
—Vedette, 1899 (Classic Reprint) (p. 2348)
School, Fort Wayne Manual Training. Caldron, 1917 (Classic Reprint) (p. 309)
School, Fourth District Agricultural. Premier, 1923, Vol. 1 (Classic Reprint) (p. 1787)
School, Framingham Normal. Dial, 1923 (Classic Reprint) (p. 537)
—Senior Quill: June, 1909 (Classic Reprint) (p. 1988)
School, Framingham State Normal. Dial, 1919 (Classic Reprint) (p. 537)
—Dial, 1930 (Classic Reprint) (p. 537)
School, Francis W. Parker. Francis W. Parker School Studies in Education, Vol. 8 (Classic Reprint) (p. 776)
School, Fulton. Fulton, 1922 (Classic Reprint) (p. 797)
School, Gainesville High. Alachuan, 1913, Vol. 1 (Classic Reprint) (p. 39)
—Alachuan, 1923, Vol. 6 (Classic Reprint) (p. 39)
School, Goldsboro High. Our Memory Book, 1925 (Classic Reprint) (p. 1679)
—Tarpitur, 1921 (Classic Reprint) (p. 2192)
—Tarpitur, 1922 (Classic Reprint) (p. 2192)
—Tarpitur, 1923 (Classic Reprint) (p. 2192)
School, Goshen High. Crimson: Class of Nineteen Twenty-One (Classic Reprint) (p. 474)
—Crimson: March 1915 (Classic Reprint) (p. 475)
—Crimson: October 1914 (Classic Reprint) (p. 475)
—Crimson, 1914 (Classic Reprint) (p. 475)
—Crimson, Vol. 12: February, 1918 (Classic Reprint) (p. 475)
—Crimson, Vol. 6: October, 1911 (Classic Reprint) (p. 475)
School, Grafton High. Spotlight, 1940 (Classic Reprint) (p. 2090)
School, Great Falls High. Fourteenth Annual Roundup: June, 1921 (Classic Reprint) (p. 773)
—Roundup, 1917, Vol. 10 (Classic Reprint) (p. 1908)
—Round-Up, Vol. 7: January, 1914 (Classic Reprint) (p. 1908)
School, Greenfield High. Camaraderie, 1913 (Classic Reprint) (p. 313)
—Camaraderie 1916: The Annual of the Senior Class of Greenfield High School (Classic Reprint) (p. 313)
School, Greensboro High. Annual, 1909 (Classic Reprint) (p. 100)
—Sage: May 1920 (Classic Reprint) (p. 1922)
School, Greenville High. Chief (Classic Reprint) (p. 369)
—Chief, Vol. 12: May, 1922 (Classic Reprint) (p. 369)
—Chief, Vol. 13: May, 1923 (Classic Reprint) (p. 369)
—Chief, Vol. 8: May, 1918 (Classic Reprint) (p. 369)
—G. H. S. Chief, Vol. 4: May, 1914 (Classic Reprint) (p. 803)
—Tau, 1918 (Classic Reprint) (p. 2193)
—Tau, 1921 (Classic Reprint) (p. 2193)
School, Hagerstown High. Epitome, 1922, Vol. 4: The Year Book of Hagerstown High School (Classic Reprint) (p. 659)
School, Harrisonburg State Normal. Schoolma'am, 1911, Vol. 2 (Classic Reprint) (p. 1947)
—Schoolma'am, 1919, Vol. 10 (Classic Reprint) (p. 1947)
School, Hickory High. Hickory Log, 1921 (Classic Reprint) (p. 965)
—Hickory Log, 1924 (Classic Reprint) (p. 965)
—Hickory Log, 1933 (Classic Reprint) (p. 965)
—Hickory Log, 1934, Vol. 12 (Classic Reprint) (p. 965)
School, Hicksville High. Hixonian, 1921, Vol. 6 (Classic Reprint) (p. 982)
School, Highlands. Summit, 1941 (Classic Reprint) (p. 2150)
School, Holland High. Boomerang 1921: Annual (Classic Reprint) (p. 261)
School, Holly High. Tell Tale, 1940 (Classic Reprint) (p. 2202)
School, Houston Heights High. Pennant, 1923 (Classic Reprint) (p. 1717)
School, Howe High. Howe-Ite, 1942 (Classic Reprint) (p. 1046)
School, Huntington High. Modulus: Twelfth Annual of Senior Class, 1923 (Classic Reprint) (p. 1488)
—Modulus, 1916 (Classic Reprint) (p. 1488)
—Modulus, 1918 (Classic Reprint) (p. 1488)
—Modulus, 1919 (Classic Reprint) (p. 1488)
—Modulus, 1920, Vol. 9 (Classic Reprint) (p. 1488)
—Modulus, 1933, Vol. 22 (Classic Reprint) (p. 1488)
School, Indiana State Normal. Instano, 1914, Vol. 3 (Classic Reprint) (p. 1125)
—Instano, 1922, Vol. 11 (Classic Reprint) (p. 1125)
—Instano, 1923, Vol. 12 (Classic Reprint) (p. 1125)
—Instano, 1925, Vol. 14 (Classic Reprint) (p. 1125)
—Instano, 1926, Vol. 15 (Classic Reprint) (p. 1125)
—Orient 1919: First Yearbook (Classic Reprint) (p. 1670)
School, Joliet Township High. Jollier, 1907 (Classic Reprint) (p. 1176)
—Jollier, 1910 (Classic Reprint) (p. 1176)
—Jths Memory Book, 1917 (Classic Reprint) (p. 1184)
School, Jonathan Dayton High. Regionalogue, 1942 (Classic Reprint) (p. 1861)
School, Kendallville High. Kay Aitch Ess, 1923, Vol. 11 (Classic Reprint) (p. 1207)
School, Kirklin High. Kay, 1923 (Classic Reprint) (p. 1207)
School, Kokomo High. Sargasso (Classic Reprint) (p. 1935)
—Sargasso, 1916 (Classic Reprint) (p. 1935)
—Sargasso, 1921 (Classic Reprint) (p. 1935)
School, Lake View Hospital Training. Annual, 1921 (Classic Reprint) (p. 100)
School, Lakeview Medical Center Nursing. Paragon 1981 (Classic Reprint) (p. 1699)
School, Lancaster High. Debris, Vol. 1: June, 1909 (Classic Reprint) (p. 522)
School, Lansing High. Oracle, 1899 (Classic Reprint) (p. 1668)
—Oracle, 1906, Vol. 15 (Classic Reprint) (p. 1668)
—Oracle, 1921, Vol. 31 (Classic Reprint) (p. 1668)
School, Lenoir High. Timber Tints, 1927, Vol. 2: A Year Book (Classic Reprint) (p. 2243)
School, Lewis and Clark High. Tiger: June, 1920 (Classic Reprint) (p. 2241)
—Tiger: June, 1921 (Classic Reprint) (p. 2241)
—Tiger: Class of January 1923 (Classic Reprint) (p. 2241)
—Tiger, 1921 (Classic Reprint) (p. 2241)
—Tiger, 1929 (Classic Reprint) (p. 2241)
—Tiger, 1938 (Classic Reprint) (p. 2241)
School, Lexington High. Crystal, 1934, Vol. 9 (Classic Reprint) (p. 481)
—Crystal, 1935, Vol. 10 (Classic Reprint) (p. 481)
—Crystal, 1938, Vol. 13 (Classic Reprint) (p. 481)
—Crystal, 1943, Vol. 17: World War II, Edition 2 (Classic Reprint) (p. 481)
School, Liberty High. Cardinal & Gold, 1912 (Classic Reprint) (p. 328)
—Liberty Bell, 1913 (Classic Reprint) (p. 1284)
—Liberty Bell, 1915 (Classic Reprint) (p. 1284)
—Lux, 1914 (Classic Reprint) (p. 1369)
—Ye Liberty, Vol. 7: May, 1911 (Classic Reprint) (p. 2518)
School, Liberty Union High. Broadcaster, Vol. 1: June 12, 1925 (Classic Reprint) (p. 284)
—Broadcaster, Vol. 1: Oct; 17, 1924 (Classic Reprint) (p. 284)
—Broadcaster, Vol. 2: January 15, 1926 (Classic Reprint) (p. 284)
—Liberty Lion, 1939 (Classic Reprint) (p. 1284)
—Liberty Union High School Yearbook, 1909 (Classic Reprint) (p. 1284)
School, Lick-Wilmerding. 1995 Lick Wilmerding (Classic Reprint) (p. 2561)
—L. W. Tiger, 1952 (Classic Reprint) (p. 1234)
—Lick-Wilmerding, 1990 (Classic Reprint) (p. 1287)
—Lick-Wilmerding School, 2009 (Classic Reprint) (p. 1287)
—Lw-Tiger, 1951 (Classic Reprint) (p. 1369)
—Tiger: June 1996 (Classic Reprint) (p. 2241)
—Tiger: June, 1998 (Classic Reprint) (p. 2241)
—Tiger, 1979 (Classic Reprint) (p. 2241)
—Tiger, 1992 (Classic Reprint) (p. 2241)
—Tiger, 1994 (Classic Reprint) (p. 2241)
—Tiger, 1999 (Classic Reprint) (p. 2241)
—Tigers, 1988 (Classic Reprint) (p. 2242)
School, Lick-Wilmerding High. Lick-Wilmerding High School, 1991 (Classic Reprint) (p. 1287)
—Tiger, 1983 (Classic Reprint) (p. 2241)
School, Lincoln High. Railsplitter: January 1924 (Classic Reprint) (p. 1835)
School, Lincolnton High. 1924 Pine Burr (Classic Reprint) (p. 2561)
—Pine Burr, 1922 (Classic Reprint) (p. 1745)
—Pine Burr, 1923 (Classic Reprint) (p. 1745)
—Pine Burr, 1927, Vol. 6 (Classic Reprint) (p. 1745)
School, London Normal. Spectrum, 1935 (Classic Reprint) (p. 2078)
—Spectrum, 1939 (Classic Reprint) (p. 2078)
—Year Book of Class of 1932-1933 (Classic Reprint) (p. 2518)
School, Los Angeles Normal. Children's Literature (Classic Reprint) (p. 374)
School, Los Angeles State Normal. Exponent: Summer, 1910 (Classic Reprint) (p. 684)
—Exponent, 1907, Vol. 1 (Classic Reprint) (p. 684)
—Exponent, 1909 (Classic Reprint) (p. 684)
—Exponent, 1912 (Classic Reprint) (p. 684)
—Exponent, 1917, Vol. 23 (Classic Reprint) (p. 684)
—Normal Exponent: Winter, '01 (Classic Reprint) (p. 1619)
—Normal Exponent: January, 1903 (Classic Reprint) (p. 1619)
—Normal Exponent (Classic Reprint) (p. 1619)
—Normal Exponent, 1900 (Classic Reprint) (p. 1619)
—Normal Exponent, 1901, Vol. 13 (Classic Reprint) (p. 1619)
—Normal Exponent, Vol. 14: Summer, 1902 (Classic Reprint) (p. 1619)
School, Louisiana State Normal. Potpourri, 1911 (Classic Reprint) (p. 1781)
—Potpourri, 1912 (Classic Reprint) (p. 1781)
—Potpourri, 1914 (Classic Reprint) (p. 1781)
School, Ludington High. Oriole, 1915 (Classic Reprint) (p. 1672)
School, Macon High. Oipi, 1912, Vol. 4 (Classic Reprint) (p. 1643)
School, Mansfield High. Annual, 1922, Vol. 15 (Classic Reprint) (p. 100)
—High School Annual, 1918, Vol. 11 (Classic Reprint) (p. 968)
—M. H. S. Annual, 1915, Vol. 8 (Classic Reprint) (p. 1370)
—Mansfield High School Annual, 1923, Vol. 16 (Classic Reprint) (p. 1398)
—Mhs Annual, 1916 (Classic Reprint) (p. 1454)
—Oracle, 1907, Vol. 1 (Classic Reprint) (p. 1668)
School, Mansfield State Normal. Carontawan, 1918 (Classic Reprint) (p. 333)
—Carontawan, Alias the Little Town on the Hill, 1920 (Classic Reprint) (p. 333)
School, Manual Training High. Booster, Vol. 12: June, 1915 (Classic Reprint) (p. 262)
—Manual Training High School Annual: May, 1900 (Classic Reprint) (p. 1399)
—Manual Training High School Annual: June, 1904 (Classic Reprint) (p. 1399)
—Senior Booster: June 1927 (Classic Reprint) (p. 1988)
—Senior Booster: June, 1930 (Classic Reprint) (p. 1988)
School, Marion High. Cactus, 1922, Vol. 4 (Classic Reprint) (p. 307)
School, Marple Newtown High. Memories: A Record of the Class of 1937, Marple-Newtown High School (Classic Reprint) (p. 1445)
—Memories, 1992 (Classic Reprint) (p. 1445)
—Tatler, 1933 (Classic Reprint) (p. 2192)
School, Marple Newtown Senior High. Carpe Diem, Seize the Day, 1997 (Classic Reprint) (p. 333)
—Memories, 1986 (Classic Reprint) (p. 1445)
—Memories, 1995 (Classic Reprint) (p. 1445)
—MN Memories, 2004-2005 (Classic Reprint) (p. 1485)
School, Mary E. Wells High. Crimson & Gray: November 1929 (Classic Reprint) (p. 475)
—Crimson & Gray: November 1930 (Classic Reprint) (p. 475)
—Crimson & Gray, 1937-1938, Vol. 21 (Classic Reprint) (p. 475)
—Crimson & Gray, Vol. 17: November, 1933 (Classic Reprint) (p. 475)
—Crimson & Gray, Vol. 26: December 1943 (Classic Reprint) (p. 475)
—Crimson & Gray, Vol. 3: December, 1919 (Classic Reprint) (p. 475)
—Crimson & Gray, Vol. 5: 1921-1923 (Classic Reprint) (p. 475)
School, Maryland State Normal. Tower Light, Vol. 1: October, 1927 (Classic Reprint) (p. 2269)
—Tower Light, Vol. 2: October, 1928 (Classic Reprint) (p. 2269)
—Tower Light, Vol. 3: October, 1929; Travel Number (Classic Reprint) (p. 2269)
—Tower Light, Vol. 4: October, 1930-June, 1931 (Classic Reprint) (p. 2269)
—Tower Light, Vol. 5: October, 1931 (Classic Reprint) (p. 2269)
—Tower Light, Vol. 6: October, 1932-June, 1933 (Classic Reprint) (p. 2269)
—Tower Light, Vol. 7: October, 1933-June, 1934 (Classic Reprint) (p. 2269)
—Tower Light, Vol. 8: October, 1934 (Classic Reprint) (p. 2269)
School, Massachusetts Fitchburg High. 1925 Class Book (Classic Reprint) (p. 2561)
School, Massachusetts State Normal. Normal Offering, 1921, Vol. 23 (Classic Reprint) (p. 1619)
School Mathematics Project. SMP Interact for Key Stage 3 Mathematics: Projectable PDFs for the T (Support) tier. (p. 2043)
School, Maynard High. Columbiad 1916: Christmas Number (Classic Reprint) (p. 427)
—Screech Owl: June, 1933 (Classic Reprint) (p. 1964)
—Screech Owl: June, 1937 (Classic Reprint) (p. 1964)
—Screech Owl: June, 1938 (Classic Reprint) (p. 1964)
—Screech Owl: June, 1939 (Classic Reprint) (p. 1964)
—Screech Owl: June, 1941 (Classic Reprint) (p. 1964)
—Screech Owl: June, 1942 (Classic Reprint) (p. 1964)
—Screech Owl: April, 1931 (Classic Reprint) (p. 1964)
—Screech Owl: March, 1930 (Classic Reprint) (p. 1964)
—Screech Owl, 1934 (Classic Reprint) (p. 1964)
—Screech Owl, 1940 (Classic Reprint) (p. 1964)
School, Meadow High. Tuscarora, Vol. 1 (Classic Reprint) (p. 2301)

S

School, Talmudical Academy High. Elchanite: June, 1934 (Classic Reprint) (p. 630)
—Elchanite: June, 1938 (Classic Reprint) (p. 630)
—Elchanite: June, 1939 (Classic Reprint) (p. 630)
—Elchanite: June, 1942 (Classic Reprint) (p. 630)
School, Tarboro High. Spy Glass, 1929, Vol. 1 (Classic Reprint) (p. 2093)
—Tar Bucket, 1934 (Classic Reprint) (p. 2191)
—Tar-Bo-Rah, 1921-1922 (Classic Reprint) (p. 2191)
School, Technical High. Arsenal Cannon, Vol. 9: June 8, 1917 (Classic Reprint) (p. 120)
School, Thompson's Island Farm. Thompson's Island Beacon, Vol. 9: May, 1905 April, 1906 (Classic Reprint) (p. 2229)
School, Thompson's Island Farm and Trade. Thompson's Island Beacon, Vol. 12: May, 1908-April, 1909 (Classic Reprint) (p. 2229)
—Thompson's Island Beacon, Vol. 25: May, 1921 (Classic Reprint) (p. 2229)
—Thompson's Island Beacon, Vol. 56: May 1952 April 1953 (Classic Reprint) (p. 2229)
School, Three Rivers High. Reflector, 1916 (Classic Reprint) (p. 1860)
—Reflector, 1918 (Classic Reprint) (p. 1860)
—Reflector, 1920 (Classic Reprint) (p. 1860)
—Reflector, 1921 (Classic Reprint) (p. 1860)
School, Tipton High. Tiptonian, 1908, Vol. 10 (Classic Reprint) (p. 2250)
—Tiptonian, 1909, Vol. 11: The Year Book of the Tipton High School (Classic Reprint) (p. 2250)
—Tiptonian, 1910, Vol. 12: The Year Book of the Tipton High School (Classic Reprint) (p. 2250)
—Tiptonian, 1911, Vol. 13 (Classic Reprint) (p. 2250)
—Tiptonian, 1913, Vol. 15: Being a Review of the High School Activities During the Past Year (Classic Reprint) (p. 2250)
School, Toledo Central High. Almanac, Vol. 16: Published by the Annual Board of the Toledo Central High School, 1914 (Classic Reprint) (p. 57)
School, Trinity College. Trinity College School Record, Vol. 32: March 1st, 1929 (Classic Reprint) (p. 2288)
School, Tubman High. Maids & a Man, 1921, Vol. 2 (Classic Reprint) (p. 1383)
—Maids & a Man, 1923, Vol. 4 (Classic Reprint) (p. 1383)
—Maids & a Man, 1924, Vol. 5 (Classic Reprint) (p. 1383)
—Maids & a Man, 1926 (Classic Reprint) (p. 1383)
—Maids & a Man, 1927 (Classic Reprint) (p. 1383)
—Maids & a Man, 1928 (Classic Reprint) (p. 1383)
—Maids & a Man, 1930 (Classic Reprint) (p. 1383)
—Maids & a Man, 1934 (Classic Reprint) (p. 1383)
—Senior, 1929 (Classic Reprint) (p. 1988)
—Senior Year-Book, 1944 (Classic Reprint) (p. 1988)
School, Turner Falls High. Echo, Vol. 14: Christmas, 1917 (Classic Reprint) (p. 623)
School, Turners Falls High. Echo, Vol. 14: June 1918 (Classic Reprint) (p. 623)
—Netop, Vol. 1: February, 1920 (Classic Reprint) (p. 1589)
—Netop, Vol. 11: March, 1931 (Classic Reprint) (p. 1589)
—Netop, Vol. 16: June 1933 (Classic Reprint) (p. 1589)
—Netop, Vol. 2: June, 1922 (Classic Reprint) (p. 1589)
—Netop, Vol. 4: May, 1924 (Classic Reprint) (p. 1589)
—Netop, Vol. 4: February, 1924 (Classic Reprint) (p. 1589)
—Netop, Vol. 5: February, 1925 (Classic Reprint) (p. 1589)
—Netop, Vol. 6: June, 1926 (Classic Reprint) (p. 1589)
—Netop, Vol. 6: November 1925 (Classic Reprint) (p. 1589)
—Netop, Vol. 7: March 1927 (Classic Reprint) (p. 1589)
—Netop, Vol. 7: November 1926 (Classic Reprint) (p. 1589)
School, Union High. Hoosier, 1923, Vol. 2 (Classic Reprint) (p. 1001)
School, University High. Clarion: Class of 1931 (Classic Reprint) (p. 398)
—U & I in 1946, Vol. 25: June 1946 (Classic Reprint) (p. 2311)
—U & I, Vol. 9: June, 1930 (Classic Reprint) (p. 2311)
—Uni, 84-85 (Classic Reprint) (p. 2327)
—University High School, 1994-1995 (Classic Reprint) (p. 2333)
—You & I, 1986-1987 (Classic Reprint) (p. 2524)
School, University of Illinois High. U & I University High School Annual, Vol. 13: Published by the Senior Class, University of Illinois High School Library; June 1934 (Classic Reprint) (p. 2311)
—Uni High Yearbook, 1990 (Classic Reprint) (p. 2327)
School, University of Illinoisat High. U & I University High School Manual, Vol. 7: June, 1928 (Classic Reprint) (p. 2311)
School, Valparaiso High. Valenian, 1919, Vol. 3 (Classic Reprint) (p. 2344)
—Valenian, 1921 (Classic Reprint) (p. 2344)
—Valenian, 1923 (Classic Reprint) (p. 2344)
—Valparaiso High School Annual, 1907 (Classic Reprint) (p. 2345)
—Valparaiso High School Annual & Alumni Edition, 1910 (Classic Reprint) (p. 2345)
—Vee Aich Ess, 1916 (Classic Reprint) (p. 2348)
School, Van Wert High. Excalibur, 1923, Vol. 5 (Classic Reprint) (p. 676)
School, Vera High. Echo: Senior Number, 1922-1923 (Classic Reprint) (p. 623)
—Echo, Vol. 6: June 1920 (Classic Reprint) (p. 623)
—Echo, Vol. 7: June, 1921 (Classic Reprint) (p. 623)
School, Victoria High. Camosun, 1920, Vol. 12 (Classic Reprint) (p. 315)
—Camosun, 1942, Vol. 34 (Classic Reprint) (p. 315)
—Camosun, Vol. 1: June 1909 (Classic Reprint) (p. 315)
—Camosun, Vol. 13: March, 1921 (Classic Reprint) (p. 315)
—Camosun, Vol. 13: December, 1920 (Classic Reprint) (p. 315)
—Camosun, Vol. 16: June, 1924 (Classic Reprint) (p. 315)
—Camosun, Vol. 22: Year 1929-1930 (Classic Reprint) (p. 315)
—Camosun, Vol. 6: April, 1914 (Classic Reprint) (p. 315)
School, Victoria Provincial Normal. Anecho, 1928-1929 (Classic Reprint) (p. 85)
—Anecho of the Provincial Normal School, Victoria, for 1926-1927 (Classic Reprint) (p. 85)
—Normal School Annual, 1924 (Classic Reprint) (p. 1619)
School, Virginia High. Virginian, 1926 (Classic Reprint) (p. 2361)
—Virginian, 1938 (Classic Reprint) (p. 2361)
School, Wabash High. Sycamore, 1914 (Classic Reprint) (p. 2172)
School, Wakefield High. Debater, 1923 (Classic Reprint) (p. 522)
—Debater, Vol. 3: June, 1915 (Classic Reprint) (p. 522)
—W. H. S. Debater, Vol. 1: December, 1912 (Classic Reprint) (p. 2369)
—W. H. S. Debater, Vol. 4: April, 1916 (Classic Reprint) (p. 2369)
—Wakefield High School Debater: May, 1931 (Classic Reprint) (p. 2371)
School, Walnut Grove High. Annuary, 1915, Vol. 1 (Classic Reprint) (p. 100)
School, Waltham High. Mirror: Graduation Number, 1928 (Classic Reprint) (p. 1475)
—Mirror, 1929 (Classic Reprint) (p. 1475)
School, Wapakoneta High. 1912 Retrospect, Vol. 5 (Classic Reprint) (p. 2561)
School, Ward-Belmont. Chimes, Vol. 1: December, 1936 (Classic Reprint) (p. 377)
—Milestones, 1914 (Classic Reprint) (p. 1465)
—Milestones, 1917 (Classic Reprint) (p. 1465)
—Milestones, 1918 (Classic Reprint) (p. 1465)
—Milestones, 1924 (Classic Reprint) (p. 1465)
—Milestones, 1928 (Classic Reprint) (p. 1465)
School, Washington-Lee High. Blue & Gray, 1992, Vol. 65 (Classic Reprint) (p. 248)
—Blue & Gray, 1993, Vol. 66 (Classic Reprint) (p. 248)
—Life in General, 2004 (Classic Reprint) (p. 1292)
—Penman, Vol. 7: Fall, 1953 (Classic Reprint) (p. 1717)
School, Waterloo High. Rosebud, 1914 (Classic Reprint) (p. 1905)
—Rosebud, 1917 (Classic Reprint) (p. 1905)
—Rosebud 1918: Being the Seventh Annual Published by the Waterloo High School (Classic Reprint) (p. 1905)
—Rosebud, 1923, Vol. 12 (Classic Reprint) (p. 1905)
School, Wayland High. Broadcaster: January, 1944 (Classic Reprint) (p. 284)
School, Weaver High. Class Book of 1925 a (Classic Reprint) (p. 399)
—Class Book of 1925 B (Classic Reprint) (p. 399)
—Class Book of 1926a (Classic Reprint) (p. 399)
—Class Book of 1926b (Classic Reprint) (p. 399)
—Portal, 1940 (Classic Reprint) (p. 1778)
—Portal, 1942 (Classic Reprint) (p. 1779)
School, Wendell High. Echoes of 1936 (Classic Reprint) (p. 623)
School, Wentworth High. Golden Leaves, 1938 (Classic Reprint) (p. 858)
School, West Chester State Normal. 1920 Serpentine: The Blue & the Gray (Classic Reprint) (p. 2561)
—Serpentine, 1911 (Classic Reprint) (p. 1991)
—Serpentine, 1912 (Classic Reprint) (p. 1991)
—Serpentine, 1913 (Classic Reprint) (p. 1991)
—Serpentine, 1917 (Classic Reprint) (p. 1991)
—Serpentine, 1918 (Classic Reprint) (p. 1991)
—Serpentine 1921: The Brown & the Gold (Classic Reprint) (p. 1991)
—Serpentine, 1922, Vol. 11: The Black & the Gold (Classic Reprint) (p. 1991)
—Serpentine, 1924, Vol. 13 (Classic Reprint) (p. 1991)
—Serpentine, 1926, Vol. 15 (Classic Reprint) (p. 1991)
—Serpentine, 1927, Vol. 16 (Classic Reprint) (p. 1991)
—Serpentine, Vol. 14: June 1925 (Classic Reprint) (p. 1991)
School, West High. Occident, Vol. 13: June 1923 (Classic Reprint) (p. 1635)
School, West Side High. Legenda, 1922 (Classic Reprint) (p. 1263)
School, Western Illinois State Normal. Sequel, 1916, Vol. 13 (Classic Reprint) (p. 1989)
School, Westfield Normal. Tekoa: June, 1923 (Classic Reprint) (p. 2201)
School, Westfield State Normal. Tekoa: Senior Yearbook, 1926 (Classic Reprint) (p. 2201)
School, Westminster. Fascinating History of Astronomy. (p. 712)
—Fascinating World of Geography. (p. 712)
School, Weymouth High. Nugget, 1914 (Classic Reprint) (p. 1629)
—Reflector, 1930 (Classic Reprint) (p. 1860)
—Reflector, 1931 (Classic Reprint) (p. 1860)
—Reflector, Vol. 10: February Issue, 1932 (Classic Reprint) (p. 1860)
—Reflector, Vol. 9: Number Two, Christmas Issue 1930 (Classic Reprint) (p. 1860)
School, Williamsburg High. Tattler, 1924 (Classic Reprint) (p. 2193)
—Tattler, 1926 (Classic Reprint) (p. 2193)
—Tattler, 1928 (Classic Reprint) (p. 2193)
—Tattler, 1929 (Classic Reprint) (p. 2193)
—Tattler, 1931 (Classic Reprint) (p. 2193)
—Tattler, 1932 (Classic Reprint) (p. 2193)
—Tattler, 1934 (Classic Reprint) (p. 2193)
—Tattler, 1936 (Classic Reprint) (p. 2193)
School, Wilmington High. Class Book of 1940 (Classic Reprint) (p. 399)
—Wilmington Alpha: Commencement, 1929 (Classic Reprint) (p. 2470)
School, Winamac High. Totem: Commencement Number, 1910 (Classic Reprint) (p. 2267)
—Totem 1911: Commencement Number (Classic Reprint) (p. 2267)
—Totem, 1914 (Classic Reprint) (p. 2267)
School, Winchester High. Melting Pot, 1923 (Classic Reprint) (p. 1443)
School, Winimac High. Totem, 1915 (Classic Reprint) (p. 2267)
—Totem, 1920 (Classic Reprint) (p. 2267)
School, Winston City High. Black & Gold: May 19, 1911 (Classic Reprint) (p. 236)
—Black & Gold, Vol. 1: April, 1911 (Classic Reprint) (p. 236)
—Black & Gold, Vol. 1: November, 1910 (Classic Reprint) (p. 236)
—Black & Gold, Vol. 15: December, 1925 (Classic Reprint) (p. 236)
—Black & Gold, Vol. 2: December, 1911 (Classic Reprint) (p. 236)
—Black & Gold, Vol. 2: November, 1911 (Classic Reprint) (p. 236)
—Black & Gold, Vol. 2: The Senior Class Number; May, 1912 (Classic Reprint) (p. 236)
—Black & Gold, Vol. 3: March, 1913 (Classic Reprint) (p. 236)
—Black & Gold, Vol. 3: December, 1912 (Classic Reprint) (p. 236)
—Black & Gold, Vol. 3: November, 1912 (Classic Reprint) (p. 236)
School, Winston-Salem City High. Black & Gold, Vol. 4: May, 1914 (Classic Reprint) (p. 236)
—Black & Gold, Vol. 4: March, 1914 (Classic Reprint) (p. 236)
—Black & Gold, Vol. 4: November, 1913 (Classic Reprint) (p. 236)
—Black & Gold, Vol. 5: May, 1915 (Classic Reprint) (p. 236)
—Black & Gold, Vol. 5: November, 1914 (Classic Reprint) (p. 236)
—Black & Gold, Vol. 6: May, 1916 (Classic Reprint) (p. 236)
—Black & Gold, Vol. 7: December, 1916 (Classic Reprint) (p. 236)
—Black & Gold, Vol. 7: November, 1916 (Classic Reprint) (p. 236)
—Black & Gold, Vol. 8: April, 1918 (Classic Reprint) (p. 236)
—Black & Gold, Vol. 8: December, 1917 (Classic Reprint) (p. 236)
—Black & Gold, Vol. 8: Published Quarterly by the Upper Classes of the Winston-Salem City High School; July, 1918 (Classic Reprint) (p. 236)
—Black & Gold, Vol. 9: June 1919 (Classic Reprint) (p. 236)
—Black & Gold, Vol. 9: November, 1919 (Classic Reprint) (p. 236)
School, Yeshiva University High. Elchanite, 1928 (Classic Reprint) (p. 630)
School Zone, compiled by. Bible Themed Readiness. (p. 214)
—Early Math. (p. 615)
—Early Reading. (p. 615)
—Readiness. (p. 1846)
—Trim the Tree 123. (p. 2288)
School Zone, ed. Get Ready for First Grade 1 Ages 6-7. (p. 824)
—Get Ready for Kindergarten K Ages 5-6. (p. 824)
—Get Ready for Preschool P Ages 3-5. (p. 824)
—Jolly Color by Number. (p. 1176)
—Jolly Dot to Dots. (p. 1176)
—Jolly Hidden Pictures. (p. 1176)
—Jolly Mazes. (p. 1176)
—Math Basics 2. (p. 1421)
—Math Basics 3. (p. 1421)
—Math Readiness. (p. 1424)
School Zone Publishing. Bible Alphabet Fun. (p. 213)
School Zone Publishing, ed. Bible Dot to Dots 1-25. (p. 213)
—Bible Hidden Pictures. (p. 213)
—Bible Mazes. (p. 213)
—Discover the Zoo. (p. 555)
—Explore the City. (p. 680)
—Preschool. (p. 1788)
—Travel the World. (p. 2280)
School Zone Saff, ed. Big Codes, Puzzles & More: Activity Book. (p. 219)
School Zone Staff. Big Hidden Pictures & More. (p. 220)
—Big Mazes & More. (p. 221)
—My First Dot-To-Dots. (p. 1544)
—My First Hidden Pictures. (p. 1544)
—My First Mazes. (p. 1545)
—My First Smart Art Alphabet. (p. 1546)
School, Zone Staff, ed. Alphabet Writing & Drawing Tablet Ages 3-7. (p. 59)
School Zone Staff, ed. Big Dot to Dots & More. (p. 219)
—Big Math 1-2. (p. 221)
—Big Spelling 1-3. (p. 223)
—Big Third Grade. (p. 223)
School, Zone Staff, ed. Cursive Writing & Drawing Tablet Ages 7-Up. (p. 490)
—Fun & Games First Grade Ages 6-7. (p. 798)
—Fun & Games Kindergarten Ages 5-6. (p. 798)
—Numbers Writing & Drawing Tablet Ages 3-7. (p. 1630)
Schoolcraft, Henry R. Myth Hiawatha: And Other Oral Legends, Mythologic & Allegoric, of the North American Indians (Classic Reprint) (p. 1571)
Schoolcraft, Henry Rowe. Algic Researches, Vol. 2 Of 2: Comprising Inquiries Respecting the Mental Characteristics of the North American Indians, First Series, Indian Tales & Legends (Classic Reprint) (p. 44)
—Indian Fairy Book: From the Original Legends (Classic Reprint) (p. 1116)
Schools, Arsenal Technical. Arsenal Cannon: June 1928 (Classic Reprint) (p. 120)
—Arsenal Cannon: June, 1918 (Classic Reprint) (p. 120)
—Arsenal Cannon: June, 1919 (Classic Reprint) (p. 120)
—Arsenal Cannon: June, 1927 (Classic Reprint) (p. 120)
—Arsenal Cannon: June, 1940 (Classic Reprint) (p. 120)
—Arsenal Cannon: January 1922 (Classic Reprint) (p. 120)
—Arsenal Cannon: January, 1920 (Classic Reprint) (p. 120)
—Arsenal Cannon: January, 1926 (Classic Reprint) (p. 120)
—Arsenal Cannon: January, 1929 (Classic Reprint) (p. 120)
—Arsenal Cannon: Powder Magazine; January, 1918 (Classic Reprint) (p. 120)
—Arsenal Cannon, 1942, Vol. 59 (Classic Reprint) (p. 120)
—Arsenal Cannon, Vol. 35: June, 1930 (Classic Reprint) (p. 120)
—Arsenal Cannon, Vol. 37: June 1931 (Classic Reprint) (p. 120)
—Arsenal Cannon, Vol. 39: Semi-Annual Magazine; June, 1932 (Classic Reprint) (p. 120)
—Arsenal Cannon, Vol. 41: June, 1933 (Classic Reprint) (p. 120)
—Arsenal Cannon, Vol. 47: June, 1936 (Classic Reprint) (p. 120)
—Arsenal Cannon, Vol. 51: June, 1938 (Classic Reprint) (p. 120)
—Arsenal Cannon, Vol. 54: January, 1940 (Classic Reprint) (p. 120)
—Arsenal Cannon, Vol. 57: June, 1941 (Classic Reprint) (p. 120)
Schools, Boston Public. Community of Writers: District a, Boston Public Schools, June 1988 (Classic Reprint) (p. 432)
Schools, Deans of Girls in Chicago High. Manners & Conduct in School & Out (Classic Reprint) (p. 1397)
Schools, Indianapolis Arsenal Technical. Arsenal Cannon, Vol. 23: June, 1924 (Classic Reprint) (p. 120)
Schools, Lick Wilmerding and Lux. L. W. I Life: December, 1920 (Classic Reprint) (p. 1234)
—L. W. L. Life: June, 1921 (Classic Reprint) (p. 1234)
—L. W. L. Life: December, 1922 (Classic Reprint) (p. 1234)
—L. W. L. Life, Vol. 1: October, 1915 (Classic Reprint) (p. 1234)
—L. W. L. Life, Vol. 1: December, 1915 (Classic Reprint) (p. 1234)
—L. W. L. Life, Vol. 1: Lick Wilmerding Lux Commencement; June, 1916 (Classic Reprint) (p. 1234)
—L. -W. -L. Life, Vol. 14: Supplement; October 1916 (Classic Reprint) (p. 1234)
—L. W. L. Life, Vol. 23: June, 1937 (Classic Reprint) (p. 1234)
—L. W. L. Life, Vol. 24: May, 1939 (Classic Reprint) (p. 1234)
—L. W. L. Life, Vol. 24: A Publication Produced by the Students of Lick Wilmerding Lux; June, 1938 (Classic Reprint) (p. 1234)
—Lwl Life, Vol. 1: March, 1916 (Classic Reprint) (p. 1369)
—I-W-L Life, Vol. 8: Lick, Wilmerding, Lux; Commencement June, 1922 (Classic Reprint) (p. 1234)
—L-W-L Life, Vol. 9: June, 1923 (Classic Reprint) (p. 1234)
Schoolwide, compiled by. Elephant & Piggie: Favorite Characters & Series Grades K-1. (p. 633)
Schoombee, Cherese. Frilly Lilly. (p. 788)
Schoon, Christian. Under Nameless Stars. (p. 2321)
Schoon, Kelly. Oh Where Oh Where Can You Be? (p. 1642)
Schoonen-Van Schooten, Silvia. Top! De Kracht Van Voelen en Denken, Hand in Hand! (p. 2262)
Schoonmaker, Christina, illus. see Farrow, Nancy L.
Schoonmaker, Edwin Davies. Americans (Classic Reprint) (p. 75)
Schoonmaker, Elizabeth. Square Cat. Schoonmaker, Elizabeth, illus. (p. 2094)
Schoonmaker, Frances. Black Alabaster Box. (p. 236)
—Last Crystal. (p. 1247)
Schoonmaker, Frances, ed. Poetry for Young People: Henry Wadsworth Longfellow. Wallace, Chad, illus. (p. 1767)
Schoonmaker, Gail. Big Picture Bible Crafts: 101 Simple & Amazing Crafts to Help Teach Children the Bible. (p. 222)
Schoonmaker, Gail, illus. see Piper, Noël.
Schoonover, Brent, illus. see Olson, Nathan & Glaser, Jason.
Schoonover, Brent, illus. see Trumbauer, Lisa.
Schoonover-Egolf, Jean. Molly Mcbride & the Party Invitation. (p. 1489)
—Molly Mcbride & the Plaid Jumper. (p. 1489)
Schoon-Tanis, Joel, illus. see Cornou, Maria Eugenia & Witvliet, John D.
Schorer, Mark. State of Mind: Thirty-Two Stories (Classic Reprint) (p. 2109)
Schories, Pat. Biscuit & the Big Parade! (p. 234)
—Biscuit Flies a Kite. (p. 234)
—Biscuit Visits the Farm. (p. 234)
—Pie for Chuck. (p. 1742)
—Squeak the Mouse Likes His House. (p. 2094)
Schories, Pat, illus. see Capucilli, Alyssa Satin.
Schorr, Bill, illus. see Riegelman, Rianna.
Schorr, Bill & Smith, Ralph. Tucker Grizzwell&'s Worst Week Ever. (p. 2298)
—Tucker Grizzwell's Worst Week Ever. (p. 2298)
Schorr, Jared, illus. see Lisberg, Anneke & Joosse, Barbara.
Schorr, Jared Andrew, illus. see Sanders, Rob.
Schorr, Loretta. Attacked (p. 135)
Schorr, Melissa. Identity Crisis. (p. 1089)
Schorr, Rachel. What a Golem. (p. 2404)
Schorr, Titus. Asra Is from India (p. 126)
—Backyard Fun (p. 157)
—Ben Is Good at Spelling (p. 199)
—Big Change (p. 219)
—Building a Home for Chick (p. 294)
—Doing Homework with Dad (p. 578)
—Earth Day (p. 616)
—Field Trip Day (p. 723)
—Food Fair (p. 759)
—Gift (p. 831)
—Lia's Big Job (p. 1283)
—Matzo Mystery (p. 1426)
—May's Horse (p. 1430)
—Mrs. Gupta's Sari (p. 1522)
—My Dad Is in the Army Overseas (p. 1536)
—My Mother Is a Pilot (p. 1556)
—My New Family (p. 1558)
—My New Room, My New Brothers (p. 1558)
—My Robot (p. 1560)
—My Special Desk (p. 1561)
—Our Town Is 100 Years Old (p. 1681)
—Package (p. 1691)
—Places in Our Classroom (p. 1753)
—Playground Adventure (p. 1760)
—Secret Santa (p. 1978)
—Spelling Bee (p. 2079)
—Star Watch (p. 2105)
—Stars & Stripes (p. 2107)
—Symbols of America (p. 2173)
—Tony's Tree (p. 2260)
—Tricky Fox (p. 2287)
—Truck Parade (p. 2292)
—We Celebrate Christmas (p. 2390)
—We Celebrate Passover (p. 2390)
—Wings (p. 2473)
Schossow, Peter. Where Is Grandma? Schossow, Peter, illus. (p. 2437)

S

—Raccoons. (p. 1830)
—Ragdoll Cats. (p. 1834)
—Raising a Bag of Toys: Pulley vs. Inclined Plane. (p. 1838)
—Ramadan. (p. 1839)
—Regal Tangs. (p. 1861)
—Robins. (p. 1891)
—Salamanders. (p. 1924)
—Sea Horses. (p. 1967)
—Sea Stars. (p. 1969)
—Sea Turtles. (p. 1969)
—Search & Rescue Dogs (p. 1970)
—Sharks. (p. 2002)
—Siamese Cats. (p. 2014)
—Snakes. (p. 2044)
—Snowboarding. (p. 2048)
—Soccer. (p. 2051)
—Soil Basics (p. 2055)
—Sphynx Cats. (p. 2080)
—Spring. (p. 2091)
—Squirrels. (p. 2095)
—Stars of Stock Car Racing (p. 2107)
—Stephen Curry. (p. 2115)
—Stingrays. (p. 2119)
—Sugars & Fats (p. 2147)
—Summer. (p. 2148)
—Supersmart Dog. (p. 2161)
—Supersmart Dolphin. (p. 2161)
—Supersmart Elephant. (p. 2161)
—Supersmart Octopus. (p. 2161)
—Supersmart Orangutan. (p. 2161)
—Supersmart Parrot. (p. 2161)
—Tang Fish. (p. 2189)
—Tornadoes. (p. 2265)
—Tornadoes [Scholastic]. (p. 2265)
—Tractor Race. (p. 2273)
—Tsunamis. (p. 2298)
—Tsunamis [Scholastic]. (p. 2298)
—Turtles. (p. 2301)
—U. S. House of Representatives (p. 2312)
—U. S. Presidency (p. 2312)
—U. S. Senate (p. 2312)
—Uso del Hilo Dental. (p. 2342)
—Vegetables on Myplate (p. 2349)
—Verano. (p. 2351)
—Volcanoes. (p. 2366)
—Volleyball. (p. 2367)
—Waterfalls (p. 2385)
—We All Have Value: A Story of Respect. Byrne, Mike, illus. (p. 2388)
—Whales. (p. 2403)
—Where Does Light Come From? (p. 2436)
—Why Is Light Important? (p. 2458)
—Winter. (p. 2475)
—Yes I Can! A Story of Grit. Byrne, Mike, illus. (p. 2521)
—¡Muévete! Strictly Spanish LLC. Staff, tr. (p. 1524)
Schuh, Mari C. & Lopez, Giessi. Colores del Otoño Crayola. (p. 422)
—Colores del Verano Crayola. (p. 422)
—Libro de Contar de Crayola. (p. 1286)
—Libro de Formas de Crayola. (p. 1286)
—Libro de Patrones de Crayola. (p. 1286)
Schulbaum, Michael, illus. see Singh, Rajinder.
Schulberg, Budd. Some Faces in the Crowd (Classic Reprint) (p. 2059)
Schuler, Carrie, illus. see Blackaby, Susan & Cicciarelli, Joellyn.
Schuler, Christoph. Kiki. Eisenring, Rahel Nicole, illus. (p. 1216)
Schuler, Dorothy. Wings. (p. 2473)
Schuler, Harold H. Fort Sisseton. (p. 769)
Schuler, Ivan, jt. auth. see Wattles, Willard Austin.
Schuler, Kimberly B. I Will Remember You: My Catholic Guide Through Grief. (p. 1085)
Schuler, Susan, tr. see Stoker, Bram.
Schulkers, Robert. Gray Ghost: A Seckatary Hawkins Mystery. (p. 882)
—Stoner's Boy: A Seckatary Hawkins Mystery. (p. 2121)
Schulkers, Robert Franc. Red Runners (Classic Reprint) (p. 1858)
Schull, Jodie A., jt. auth. see Nagle, Jeanne.
Schuller, Leo Sarkadi. Within Four Walls Children at Play: Two Plays (Classic Reprint) (p. 2482)
Schulman, Beth. Cardboard Castle. (p. 328)
Schulman, Janet. 10 Easter Egg Hunters: A Holiday Counting Book. Davick, Linda, illus. (p. 2549)
—10 Easter Egg Hunters. (p. 2549)
—10 Trick-or-Treaters: A Halloween Counting Book. Davick, Linda, illus. (p. 2550)
—10 Trim-the-Tree'ers. Davick, Linda, illus. (p. 2550)
—10 Valentine Friends. Davick, Linda, illus. (p. 2550)
Schulman, L. B. Stolen Secrets. (p. 2120)
Schult, Sherry. Adventures of Didi & Mr Taco. Banks, Sandra, illus. (p. 23)
Schulte, Mary. Dover Demon. (p. 590)
—Helen Griener: Cofounder of iRobot Corporation. (p. 949)
Schulte, Mary E. Final Four: All about College Basketball's Biggest Event. (p. 727)
—Synchronized Skating. (p. 2173)
Schultheis, Jonathan. Princess with the Broken Heart. (p. 1799)
Schultz, Barbara, illus. see Gunderson, Jessica Sarah.
Schultz, Doreen. Days of Noah. (p. 515)
Schultz, Erica. Silver Spurs of Oz: A Graphic Novel. Lozano, Omar, illus. (p. 2020)
Schultz, Ernest. Serpentine, 1914 (Classic Reprint) (p. 1991)
Schultz, Hope Erica. Sinister Regent. (p. 2024)
Schultz, James Willard. Apauk, Caller of Buffalo (Classic Reprint) (p. 105)
—Bird Woman (Sacajawea) the Guide of Lewis & Clark: Her Own Story Now First Given to the World. (p. 231)
—Bird Woman (Sacajawea) the Guide of Lewis & Clark: Her Own Story Now First Given to the World (Classic Reprint) (p. 231)
—Blackfeet Tales of Glacier National Park (Classic Reprint) (p. 240)
—Lone Bull's Mistake: A Lodge Pole Chief Story (Classic Reprint) (p. 1342)
—My Life As an Indian: The Story of a Red Woman & a White Man in the Lodges of the Blackfeet (Classic Reprint) (p. 1551)
—On the Warpath (Classic Reprint) (p. 1656)
—Sinopah: The Indian Boy (Classic Reprint) (p. 2025)
—With the Indians in the Rockies (Classic Reprint) (p. 2482)
Schultz, Jeanne. Colette (Classic Reprint) (p. 413)
—Story of Collette: From the French of la Neuvaine de Collette (Classic Reprint) (p. 2129)
Schultz, Jeff. Explore American History (p. 679)
Schultz, Jolene, illus. see Slade, Suzanne.
Schultz, Leslie & Braulick, J. J. M. And Sometimes Y. Newman, Heather, illus. (p. 83)
Schultz, Michael, illus. see Fort, Gary W.
Schultz, Mitchel E. & Grob, Bernard. Grob's Basic Electronics. (p. 897)
Schultz Nicholson, Lorna. Bent Not Broken: Madeline & Justin (p. 201)
—Big Air (p. 215)
—Fighting for Gold: The Story of Canada's Sledge Hockey Paralympic Gold. (p. 725)
—Superhero Ninja Wrestling Star. (p. 2160)
—Winning Gold: Canada's Incredible 2002 Olympic Victory in Women's Hockey (p. 2474)
Schultz Nicholson, Lorna, jt. auth. see Nicholson, Lorna Schultz.
Schultz, Paul, illus. see McDonald, Lisa.
Schultz, R. M. Eve of the Pharaoh: Historical Adventure & Mystery. (p. 668)
—Night of Devoured Souls. (p. 1607)
—Unearthing the Dawn. (p. 2327)
Schultz, Walter A., jt. auth. see Schulz, Walter A.
Schultz, Walter-Alexandre. Origami Dinosaurs. (p. 1671)
Schultze, Arthur. Plane Geometry. (p. 1754)
Schultze, Gwendolyn. Dog That's Not a Poodle. Cameron, Ed, illus. (p. 576)
Schulz, Andrea. North Carolina. (p. 1620)
Schulz, August. Die Geschichte der Kultivierten Getreide, Vol. 1 (Classic Reprint) (p. 543)
Schulz, Barbara, illus. see Biskup, Agnieszka Józefina.
Schulz, Barbara, illus. see Biskup, Agnieszka.
Schulz, Barbara, illus. see Burgan, Michael & Hoena, Blake A.
Schulz, Barbara, illus. see Burgan, Michael.
Schulz, Barbara, illus. see Collins, Terry.
Schulz, Barbara, illus. see Fontes, Justine & Fontes, Ron.
Schulz, Barbara, illus. see Fontes, Ron.
Schulz, Barbara, illus. see Gunderson, Jessica Sarah.
Schulz, Barbara, illus. see Krohn, Katherine.
Schulz, Barbara, illus. see Sohn, Emily Beth.
Schulz, Barbara, illus. see Sohn, Emily.
Schulz, Barbara, illus. see Storrie, Paul D.
Schulz, Barbara, jt. illus. see Seeley, Tim.
Schulz, Charles. Snoopy: Cowabunga! (p. 2046)
—Snoopy's Thanksgiving. (p. 2046)
—You Got a Rock, Charlie Brown! Pope, Robert, illus. (p. 2527)
Schulz, Charles, illus. see Lundell, Margo.
Schulz, Charles, illus. see Verr, Harry Coe.
Schulz, Charles M. All Tied Up (p. 55)
—Batter up, Charlie Brown! (p. 173)
—Be a Good Sport, Charlie Brown! Scott, Vicki, illus. (p. 176)
—Be Thankful, Be Giving. Jeralds, Scott, illus. (p. 177)
—Charlie Brown: POW!: a Peanuts Collection. (p. 359)
—Charlie Brown: Here We Go Again: a Peanuts Collection. (p. 359)
—Charlie Brown: All Tied up (PEANUTS AMP Series Book 13) (p. 359)
—Charlie Brown & Friends: A Peanuts Collection. (p. 359)
—Charlie Brown Christmas: The Making of a Tradition. (p. 359)
—Charlie Brown Christmas: Deluxe Edition. Scott, Vicki, illus. (p. 359)
—Charlie Brown Christmas: Pop-Up Edition. Scott, Vicki, illus. (p. 359)
—Charlie Brown Christmas: with Sound & Music. (p. 359)
—Charlie Brown Christmas Wrapping Paper Activity Book. (p. 359)
—Charlie Brown Thanksgiving. Jeralds, Scott, illus. (p. 359)
—Christmas Is Here! Pope, Robert, illus. (p. 386)
—Friends Make Everything Better! Snoopy & Woodstock's Great Adventure; Woodstock's Sunny Day; Nice to Meet You, Franklin!; Be a Good Sport, Charlie Brown!; Snoopy's Snow Day! (p. 787)
—Gobble up, Snoopy! Jeralds, Scott, illus. (p. 849)
—Good Grief! Charlie Brown Doodles: Create & Complete Pictures with the Peanuts Gang. (p. 862)
—Happy Halloween, Charlie Brown! Pope, Robert, illus. (p. 922)
—Happy Thanksgiving, Snoopy! Jeralds, Scott, illus. (p. 924)
—Happy Valentine's Day, Charlie Brown! Jeralds, Scott, illus. (p. 924)
—Here Comes the Easter Beagle! Pope, Robert, illus. (p. 958)
—I'm Not Your Sweet Babboo! (p. 1099)
—It's Hockey Time, Franklin! Jeralds, Scott, illus. (p. 1145)
—It's the Easter Beagle, Charlie Brown. Scott, Vicki, illus. (p. 1147)
—It's the Easter Beagle, Charlie Brown: with Sound & Music. (p. 1147)
—It's the Great Pumpkin, Charlie Brown: Deluxe Edition. Scott, Vicki, illus. (p. 1147)
—It's the Great Pumpkin, Charlie Brown: with Sound & Music. (p. 1147)
—Let's Go to the Library! Pope, Robert, illus. (p. 1274)
—Lucy: Speak Out! (p. 1365)
—Lucy: Speak Out!: a Peanuts Collection. (p. 1365)
—Lucy - Speak Out! (p. 1365)
—Merry Christmas, Charlie Brown! Pope, Robert, illus. (p. 1450)
—Nice to Meet You, Franklin! Pope, Robert, illus. (p. 1602)
—No Rest for the Easter Beagle. Jeralds, Scott, illus. (p. 1614)
—Peanuts 5-Minute Stories. (p. 1710)
—Peanuts: Be Active. (p. 1710)
—Peanuts: Be Friends. (p. 1710)
—Peanuts: Be Joyful: Peanuts Wisdom to Carry You Through. (p. 1710)
—Peanuts: Be Thankful. (p. 1710)
—Peanuts: Be Unique. (p. 1710)
—Peanuts Holiday Box Set. (p. 1710)
—Peanuts Ready-To-Read Value Pack: Time for School, Charlie Brown; Make a Trade, Charlie Brown!; Lucy Knows Best; Linus Gets Glasses; Snoopy & Woodstock; Snoopy, First Beagle on the Moon! (p. 1710)
—Peanuts: the Gang's All Here! (p. 1710)
—Read with the Peanuts Gang: Time for School, Charlie Brown; Make a Trade, Charlie Brown!; Peppermint Patty Goes to Camp; Lucy Knows Best; Linus Gets Glasses; Snoopy & Woodstock. (p. 1845)
—Shoot for the Moon, Snoopy! Scott, Vicki, illus. (p. 2009)
—Snoopy: What's Wrong with Dog Lips? (p. 2046)
—Snoopy: Cowabunga!: a Peanuts Collection. (p. 2046)
—Snoopy: Boogie down!: a Peanuts Collection. (p. 2046)
—Snoopy: What's Wrong with Dog Lips?: a Peanuts Collection. (p. 2046)
—Snoopy & Woodstock: Best Friends Forever! Pope, Robert, illus. (p. 2046)
—Snoopy: Boogie down! (PEANUTS AMP Series Book 11) A PEANUTS Collection. (p. 2046)
—Snoopy Came to Play. Scott, Vicki, illus. (p. 2046)
—Snoopy: First Beagle in Space (PEANUTS AMP Series Book 14) A PEANUTS Collection. (p. 2046)
—Snoopy, First Beagle on the Moon! Pope, Robert, illus. (p. 2046)
—Snoopy Goes to School. Pope, Robert, illus. (p. 2046)
—Snoopy to the Rescue: A Peanuts Collection. (p. 2046)
—Snoopy to the Rescue. (p. 2046)
—Snoopy's Christmas Surprise. Scott, Vicki, illus. (p. 2046)
—Snoopy's Snow Day! Pope, Robert, illus. (p. 2046)
—Super Box of Snoopy. (p. 2154)
—Valentine for Linus! Jeralds, Scott, illus. (p. 2344)
—Waiting for the Great Pumpkin. (p. 2370)
—Woodstock's First Flight! Jeralds, Scott, illus. (p. 2492)
—Woodstock's Sunny Day. Scott, Vicki, illus. (p. 2492)
—You Got a Rock, Charlie Brown! Pope, Robert, illus. (p. 2527)
—You're a Big Brother, Charlie Brown! Jeralds, Scott, illus. (p. 2535)
Schulz, Charles M., illus. see Skwish, Emily.
Schulz, Charles M., jt. auth. see Pastis, Stephan.
Schulz, Charles M. & Barton, Elizabeth Dennis. Be Kind, Be Brave, Be You! Jeralds, Scott, illus. (p. 177)
Schulz, Charles M. & Cooper, Jason. Charles M. Schulz' Snoopy. Scott, Vicki & Braddock, Paige, illus. (p. 358)
—Peanuts Original Graphic Novel: Snoopy: a Beagle of Mars. Pope, Robert W., illus. (p. 1710)
—Peanuts Vol. 10. Braddock, Paige & Scott, Vicki, illus. (p. 1710)
Schulz, Charles M. & Gallo, Tina. Who's Your Valentine, Charlie Brown? Scott, Vicki, illus. (p. 2454)
Schulz, Charles M. & Houghton, Shane. Peanuts Braddock, Paige, illus. (p. 1710)
Schulz, Charles M. & Mendelson, Lee. It's the Great Pumpkin: The Making of a Television Classic. (p. 1147)
Schulz, Charles M. & Nakamura, May. My First 100 Peanuts Words. Scott, Vicki, illus. (p. 1540)
Schulz, Charles M. & Scott, Vicki. It's Tokyo, Charlie Brown! Braddock, Paige, illus. (p. 1148)
Schulz, Charles M., creator. Charles M. Schulz's Linus. (p. 358)
—Peanuts: Be Brave: Peanuts Wisdom to Carry You Through. (p. 1710)
—Peanuts: Be Kind: Peanuts Wisdom to Carry You Through. (p. 1710)
—Peanuts: Be Yourself! (p. 1710)
—Peanuts: Snoopy Loves to Doodle: Create & Complete Pictures with the Peanuts Gang. (p. 1710)
—Peanuts: You Can Be Anything! (p. 1710)
—Snoopy & Woodstock: Best Friends. (p. 2046)
Schulz, Christian Dahl. Professional Sports Organizations. (p. 1804)
Schulz, Elizabeth. Montezuma II. (p. 1499)
—Respect for Rules & Laws. (p. 1869)
Schulz, Heidi. Hook's Revenge. (p. 1000)
—Hook's Revenge. Hendrix, John, illus. (p. 1000)
—Hook's Revenge, Book 2: the Pirate Code. Hendrix, John, illus. (p. 1000)
Schulz, Heidi & Robertson, Chris. Giraffes Ruin Everything. (p. 834)
Schulz, Janet, illus. see Schulz, Walter A.
Schulz, Kathy. Always Be Safe. (p. 61)
—I Do Not Want To. Rescek, Sanja, illus. (p. 1064)
—I Need a Little Help. Iosa, Ann, illus. (p. 1079)
—Necesito una Ayudita. Iosa, Ann, illus. (p. 1584)
Schulz, Mark & Cooper, Jason. Race for Your Life, Charlie Brown! Pope, Robert, illus. (p. 1831)
Schulz, Monte. This Side of Jordan. (p. 2227)
Schulz, Walter A. Johnny Moore & the Wright Brothers' Flying Machine. Bowles, Doug, illus. (p. 1175)
Schulz, Walter A. & Schultz, Walter A. Johnny Moore & the Wright Brothers' Flying Machine. Bowles, Doug, illus. (p. 1175)
Schulze, Bianca. 101 Books to Read Before You Grow Up: The Must-Read Book List for Kids. (p. 2558)
—101 Books to Read Before You Grow Up. (p. 2558)
Schulze, Bianca & Clever Publishing. Don't Wake the Dragon: An Interactive Bedtime Story! Hardy, Samara, illus. (p. 584)
Schulze, Kris. We Are the Same. (p. 2389)
—Welcome to Beansville. (p. 2398)
Schulze, Marc-Alexander. Child Is Born: The Nativity Story. (p. 369)
Schumacher, Bev. Critters (Chinese/English) (p. 476)
—Dress Up (Chinese/English) (p. 604)
—Patterns (Chinese/English) (p. 1706)
—What Color Is It? (Chinese/English) (p. 2407)
—Where Will You Find Me? (Chinese/English) (p. 2440)
Schumacher, Bruno. Contesse d'Anjou, Altfranzösischer Roman Aus Dem Jahre 1316; I. Teil: Inaugural-Dissertation (Classic Reprint) (p. 445)
Schumacher, Cassandra. Code Breakers & Spies of the American Revolution. (p. 411)
—Cornelius Vanderbilt: Railroad Tycoon (p. 454)
—True Teen Stories from Afghanistan & Pakistan: Surviving the Taliban. (p. 2295)
—Work, Exchange, & Technology in the United States. (p. 2495)
Schumacher, Cassandra, jt. auth. see Gascoigne, Ingrid.
Schumacher, Cassandra, et al. Rhode Island (p. 1875)
Schumacher, Henry. Fair Enchantress: A Romance of Lady Hamilton's Early Years (Classic Reprint) (p. 695)
Schumacher, Julie. Black Box. (p. 237)
—Unbearable Book Club for Unsinkable Girls. (p. 2317)
Schumacher, Philip, tr. see Knecht, F. J.
Schumacher, Thomas. How Does the Show Go on the Frozen Edition: An Introduction to the Theater. (p. 1030)
Schuman, Michael. Bob Dylan. (p. 251)
—Charles Schulz. (p. 359)
—Halle Berry: A Biography of an Oscar-Winning Actress. (p. 911)
—Led Zeppelin. (p. 1260)
—Margaret Cho: Comedian, Actress, & Activist. (p. 1403)
—Will Smith: A Biography of Rapper Turned Movie Star. (p. 2467)
—Will Smith a Biography of a Rapper Turned Movie Star. (p. 2467)
Schuman, Michael A. Adam Sandler: Celebrity with Heart. (p. 14)
—Alexander Graham Bell: Scientist & Inventor. (p. 42)
—Angelina Jolie: Celebrity with Heart. (p. 86)
—Beyonc: A Biography of a Legendary Singer. (p. 211)
—Emma! Amazing Actress Emma Stone. (p. 642)
—Halle Berry: A Biography of an Oscar-Winning Actress. (p. 911)
—Led Zeppelin: Legendary Rock Band. (p. 1260)
—Life of Martin Luther King, Jr: Leader for Civil Rights. (p. 1294)
—Maya & Aztec Mythology Rocks! Bock, William Sauts, illus. (p. 1429)
—Rihanna: Music Megastar. (p. 1882)
—Robert Pattinson: Shining Star. (p. 1890)
—Scarlett Johansson: Hollywood Superstar. (p. 1942)
—Tina Fey: TV Comedy Superstar. (p. 2248)
—Will Smith: A Biography of a Rapper Turned Movie Star. (p. 2467)
Schuman, Michael A., jt. auth. see Schuman, Michael.
Schuman, Michael A. & Schraff, Anne E. Martin Luther King Jr: Fighting for Civil Rights. (p. 1411)
Schuman, Michael A., et al. Delaware. (p. 526)
Schuman, Michael & Schuman, Michael A. Write Science Fiction in 5 Simple Steps. (p. 2512)
Schumann, Marc. Ha Jin. (p. 908)
Schumerth, Cynthia. I Am Horton. (p. 1058)
Schuna, Ramona, illus. see Brown, Elizabeth.
Schunemann, Ryan, illus. see Bush, Randall B.
Schuon, Catherine & Fitzgerald, Michael Oren, eds. King James Christmas: Biblical Selections with Illustrations from Around the World (p. 1220)
Schupack, Sara. Indira Gandhi. (p. 1117)
—Merchant of Venice. (p. 1447)
Schuppe, Erich. Die Chanson Garin de Monglene Nach Den Hss. Prl, Vol. 1: Inaugural-Dissertation (Classic Reprint) (p. 543)
Schuppert, David, illus. see Kudlinski, Kathleen V.
Schur, Maxine Rose. Brave with Beauty: A Story of Afghanistan. Dewitt-Grush, Patricia et al, illus. (p. 276)
—There's a Babirusa in My Bathtub: Fact & Fancy about Curious Creatures. Maydak, Michael, illus. (p. 2217)
—There's a Babirusa in My Bathtub: Fact & Fancy about Curious Creatures Maydak, Michael S., illus. (p. 2217)
—Word Dancer. (p. 2493)
Schurch, Maylan. Sword of Denis Anwyck. (p. 2171)
Schuren, Shannon. Virtue of Sin. (p. 2361)
Schurr, Cathleen. Shy Little Kitten Book & Vinyl Record. Tenggren, Gustaf, illus. (p. 2013)
Schurr, Cathleen, jt. auth. see Depken, Kristen L.
Schuss, Dale R. Pathetica: A 1980's Memoir. (p. 1704)
Schuster, Claud. Peaks & Pleasant Pastures (Classic Reprint) (p. 1709)
Schuster, Otto John. Treasures of Mayville (Classic Reprint) (p. 2283)
Schusterman, Michelle. Friends, Fugues, & Fortune Cookies. Kote, Genevieve, illus. (p. 787)
—Graveyard Slot. (p. 882)
—Spell & Spindle. (p. 2078)
—Spotlight on Coding Club! #4. (p. 2091)
—Theater of Forever & Ever. (p. 2215)
Schute, Diane & Marshall, Gail. Long Trip. (p. 1343)
Schutten, Jan Paul. Mystery of Life: How Nothing Became Everything. Watkinson, Laura, tr. from DUT. (p. 1569)
Schutz, Samantha. I Don't Want to Be Crazy. (p. 1064)
Schutzer, Dena, illus. see England, Linda.
Schuurmans, Hilde, illus. see Dessers, Rik.
Schuyler Brenckle, Gretchen. Cat Named Denali, Book Two: Arlington! (p. 341)
Schuyler, George S. Black No More: Being an Account of the Strange & Wonderful Workings of Science in the Land of the Free, A. D. 1933-1940. (p. 238)
Schuyler, William. Under Pontius Pilate: Being a Part of the Correspondence Between Caius Claudius Proculus in Judea & Lucius Domitius Ahenobarbus at Athens in the Years 28 & 29 A. d (Classic Reprint) (p. 2321)
Schwab, Alicia, illus. see Johnson, Katharine.
Schwab, V. E. near Witch. (p. 1584)
Schwab, Victoria. Archived. (p. 111)
—Cancion Salvaje. (p. 321)
—City of Ghosts. (p. 395)
—Ciudad de Los Fantasmas. (p. 396)
—Dark Vault: Unlock the Archive. (p. 507)
—Dueto Oscuro. (p. 609)
—Everyday Angel: Three Novels. (p. 671)
—Los túneles de huesos. (p. 1351)
—New Beginnings. (p. 1591)
—Our Dark Duet. (p. 1677)
—This Savage Song. (p. 2226)

—This Savage Song. (p. 2227)
Schwabach, Karen. Hope Chest. (p. 1001)
—Storm Before Atlanta. (p. 2126)
Schwabacher, Martin. Minnesota. (p. 1473)
—West Virginia. (p. 2402)
Schwabacher, Martin & Mortensen, Lori. Elephants. (p. 634)
Schwabacher, Martin & Otfinoski, Steven. Puerto Rico. (p. 1811)
Schwacber, Barbie Heit. Alphabet of Earth. Vitsky, Sally, illus. (p. 59)
Schwaeber, Barbie. Alphabet of Earth. Vitsky, Sally, illus. (p. 59)
Schwaeber, Barbie, jt. auth. see Cohan, George M.
Schwaeber, Barbie H., ed. see Galvin, Laura Gates & Studio Mouse Staff.
Schwaeber, Barbie Heit. Alphabet of Bears. Nelson, Will et al, illus. (p. 59)
—Alphabet of Dance. Ward, Damian, illus. (p. 59)
—Alphabet of Dance. Wood, Damian, illus. (p. 59)
—Alphabet of Dinosaurs. Buchs, Thomas et al, illus. (p. 59)
—Alphabet of Insects. Buchs, Thomas, illus. (p. 59)
—Alphabet of Music. Clark, Debbie, illus. (p. 59)
—Alphabet of Music. Santillan, Jorge & Clark, Debbie, illus. (p. 59)
Schwaeber, Barbie Heit, ed. see Bentley, Dawn.
Schwaeber, Barbie Heit, ed. see Galvin, Laura Gates.
Schwaeber, Barbie Heit, ed. see Gates Galvin, Laura.
Schwaeber, Barbie Heit, ed. see Soundprints Staff.
Schwake, Susan. 3D Art Lab for Kids: 32 Hands-On Adventures in Sculpture & Mixed Media - Including Fun Projects Using Clay, Plaster, Cardboard, Paper, Fiber Beads & More! (p. 2547)
—Art Camp: 52 Art Projects for Kids to Explore. (p. 120)
—Art for All Seasons. (p. 121)
—Art Lab for Kids: 52 Creative Adventures in Drawing, Painting, Printmaking, Paper, & Mixed Media-For Budding Artists of All Ages. (p. 121)
—Art Lab for Kids: Express Yourself: 52 Creative Adventures to Find Your Voice Through Drawing, Painting, Mixed Media, & Sculpture. (p. 121)
—Little Learning Labs: Art for Little Kids: 26 Playful Projects for Preschoolers; Activities for STEAM Learners. (p. 1320)
Schwalb, Suzanne. Things That Glow Bedtime Shadow Book. (p. 2220)
Schwalbe, Linda. Ida & the World Beyond Mount Kaiserzipf. Wilson, David Henry, tr. (p. 1089)
Schwandt, Mary. Story of Mary Schwandt: Her Captivity During the Sioux Outbreak, 1862 (Classic Reprint) (p. 2131)
Schwann, Duncan. Book of a Bachelor (Classic Reprint) (p. 258)
Schwartz, Alexandra Cassel. Daniel Loves Playtime! (p. 503)
—Mom Tiger's New Job. (p. 1490)
Schwartz, Alexandra Cassel, prologue by. Daniel Goes to the Dentist. (p. 502)
Schwartz, Alexandra Cassel, summ. Helpers in Your Neighborhood. (p. 953)
Schwartz, Allan A., jt. auth. see Edson, Ann.
Schwartz, Alvin. Gold & Silver, Silver & Gold: Tales of Hidden Treasure. Christiana, David, illus. (p. 855)
—Historias de Miedo para Contar en la Oscuridad 1. Helquist, Brett, illus. (p. 975)
—In a Dark, Dark Room & Other Scary Stories: Reillustrated Edition. Rivas, Victor, illus. (p. 1103)
—Más Historias de Miedo para Contar en la Oscuridad. Helquist, Brett, illus. (p. 1416)
—More Scary Stories to Tell in the Dark. (p. 1505)
—More Scary Stories to Tell in the Dark. Helquist, Brett, illus. (p. 1505)
—More Scary Stories to Tell in the Dark. Gammell, Stephen, illus. (p. 1505)
—More Scary Stories to Tell in the Dark Movie Tie-In Edition. Gammell, Stephen, illus. (p. 1505)
—Scary Stories 3: More Tales to Chill Your Bones. (p. 1943)
—Scary Stories 3: More Tales to Chill Your Bones. Helquist, Brett, illus. (p. 1943)
—Scary Stories 3: More Tales to Chill Your Bones. Gammell, Stephen, illus. (p. 1943)
—Scary Stories 3 Movie Tie-In Edition: More Tales to Chill Your Bones. Gammell, Stephen, illus. (p. 1943)
—Scary Stories 3-Book Box Set Movie Tie-In Edition: Scary Stories to Tell in the Dark, More Scary Stories to Tell in the Dark, Scary Stories 3. Gammell, Stephen, illus. (p. 1943)
—Scary Stories Box Set: Complete Collection with Brett Helquist Art Helquist, Brett, illus. (p. 1943)
—Scary Stories Paperback Box Set: The Complete 3-Book Collection with Classic Art by Stephen Gammell. Gammell, Stephen, illus. (p. 1943)
—Scary Stories to Tell in the Dark. (p. 1943)
—Scary Stories to Tell in the Dark. Helquist, Brett, illus. (p. 1943)
—Scary Stories to Tell in the Dark Movie Tie-In Edition. Gammell, Stephen, illus. (p. 1943)
—Scary Stories to Tell in the Dark: Three Books to Chill Your Bones: All 3 Scary Stories Books with the Original Art! Gammell, Stephen, illus. (p. 1943)
—Superman: The Atomic Age Superman, 1953-1956 Boring, Wayne, illus. (p. 2160)
Schwartz, Alvin & Helquist, Brett. Serie Historias de Miedo para Contar en la Oscuridad: (Paquete 3 Volúmenes) (p. 1991)
Schwartz, Amy. 100 Things I Love to Do with You. (p. 2557)
—100 Things That Make Me Happy. (p. 2557)
—13 Stories about Harris. (p. 2552)
—Boys Team. Schwartz, Amy, illus. (p. 273)
—Busy Babies. Schwartz, Amy, illus. (p. 301)
—Glorious Day. Schwartz, Amy, illus. (p. 844)
—I Can't Wait! Schwartz, Amy, illus. (p. 1063)
—Oma & Bobo. (p. 1651)
—Things That Make Me Happy. (p. 2221)
—What James Likes Best. Schwartz, Amy, illus. (p. 2417)
Schwartz, Amy, illus. see Feder, Jane.
Schwartz, Amy, illus. see Ryder, Joanne.
Schwartz, Anna L. Okie the Wonder Dog. Dumm, Brian Caleb, illus. (p. 1643)
Schwartz, Anna L., et al. Brother Bobcat & His Journey to Health: The Right Diet Helps Control Diabetes. Bedoni, Lillian, illus. (p. 286)
Schwartz, Barry L. Adam's Animals. Doneva, Stellyana, illus. (p. 14)
Schwartz, Barry L. & Levine, Mark H. Judaism's Great Debates. Klossner, John & Ricceri, David, illus. (p. 1185)
Schwartz, Bennett L. Khadim & the Wanderers. (p. 1212)
Schwartz, Betty & Seresin, Lynn. Puppies, Puppies, Everywhere! A Back-And-Forth Opposites Book. Powell, Luciana Navarro, illus. (p. 1814)
Schwartz, Betty Ann. One to Ten... & Back Again. Shakir, Susie, illus. (p. 1662)
Schwartz, Betty Ann & Seresin, Lynn. My Barnyard! A Read & Play Book! Bendall-Brunello, John, illus. (p. 1531)
—Run, Run Piglet. Ng, Neiko, illus. (p. 1914)
Schwartz, Carol. Old Mother Hubbard. Schwartz, Carol, illus. (p. 1647)
Schwartz, Carol, illus. see Edwards, Roberta.
Schwartz, Carol, illus. see Hillert, Margaret & Collodi, Carlo.
Schwartz, Carol, illus. see Hillert, Margaret.
Schwartz, Carol, illus. see Hulme, Joy N.
Schwartz, Carol, illus. see Pierce, Terry & Hanson, Scott T.
Schwartz, Carol, illus. see Rompella, Natalie.
Schwartz, Carol, illus. see Slade, Suzanne.
Schwartz, Carol, illus. see Stewart, Melissa.
Schwartz, Corey Rosen. Ninja Red Riding Hood. Santat, Dan, illus. (p. 1610)
—Three Ninja Pigs. Santat, Dan, illus. (p. 2234)
—Twinderella, a Fractioned Fairy Tale. Marcero, Deborah, illus. (p. 2305)
Schwartz, Corey Rosen & Coulton, Beth. Goldi Rocks & the Three Bears. Wragg, Nate, illus. (p. 860)
Schwartz, Corey Rosen & Gomez, Rebecca J. Hensel & Gretel, Ninja Chicks. Santat, Dan, illus. (p. 956)
—What about Moose? Yamaguchi, Keika, illus. (p. 2404)
Schwartz, Corey Rosen, et al. Two Tough Trucks. Leung, Hilary, illus. (p. 2309)
Schwartz, Dana. And We're Off. (p. 83)
Schwartz, David & Schwartz, David M. Q Is for Quark: A Science Alphabet Book. Doner, Kim, illus. (p. 1821)
Schwartz, David M. & Schy, Yael. Where in the Wild? Camouflaged Creatures Concealed... & Revealed. Kuhn, Dwight, photos by. (p. 2437)
Schwartz, Ella. Can You Crack the Code? A Fascinating History of Ciphers & Cryptography. Williams, Lily, illus. (p. 318)
—Make This! (p. 1387)
Schwartz, Ellen. Avalanche Dance. (p. 141)
—Case of the Missing Deed. (p. 337)
—Cellular. (p. 351)
—Heart of a Champion. (p. 944)
—Princess Dolls Ando, Mariko, illus. (p. 1797)
Schwartz, Friedrich Leberecht Wilhelm. Ursprung der Mythologie: Dargelegt an Griechischer und Deutscher Sage (Classic Reprint) (p. 2340)
Schwartz, Gary. King of Average. (p. 1220)
Schwartz, Heather. French Revolution: Terror & Triumph (p. 784)
—Lizzie Johnson: Texan Cowgirl (p. 1336)
—Lizzie Johnson: Vaquera Texana. (p. 1336)
—Marie Antoinette: The Controversial Queen of France (p. 1405)
—Outside the Box: New Ideas! (Level 2) (p. 1685)
—Sports for All: The Impact of Title IX (Level 5) (p. 2089)
—Unsung Heroes: Risk Takers (Level 8) (p. 2336)
—War, Cattle, & Cowboys: Texas as a Young State (p. 2376)
Schwartz, Heather E. Alexander Hamilton: The Story of a Statesman. (p. 42)
—American Indians of the East: Woodland People. (p. 72)
—Ariana Grande: Music Superstar. (p. 115)
—Astronaut Ellen Ochoa. (p. 128)
—Athena: Greek Goddess of Wisdom & War. (p. 132)
—Balance Beam: Tips, Rules, & Legendary Stars. (p. 160)
—Bank Wisely. (p. 164)
—Basics of Game Design. (p. 170)
—Beyoncé: The Queen of Pop. (p. 211)
—Carli Lloyd: Soccer Star. (p. 331)
—Causes of the Civil War: A House Divided. (p. 347)
—Civil Rights Act of 1964: A Primary Source Exploration of the Landmark Legislation. (p. 396)
—Code-Breaker & Mathematician Alan Turing. (p. 411)
—Conteo: Las Estaciones. (p. 444)
—Cookie Monster's Foodie Truck: A Sesame Street (r) Celebration of Food. (p. 446)
—Cool Engineering Activities for Girls (p. 448)
—Counting: The Seasons. (p. 459)
—Crazy Creatures: Amazing Amazon. (p. 468)
—Cyberbullying (p. 492)
—Early Explorers. (p. 614)
—Floor Exercise: Tips, Rules, & Legendary Stars. (p. 750)
—Florida's Government: Power, Purpose, & People. (p. 751)
—Foul, Filthy American Frontier: The Disgusting Details about the Journey Out West. (p. 771)
—Freedom Riders: A Primary Source Exploration of the Struggle for Racial Justice (p. 783)
—Gangsters, Bootleggers, & Bandits. (p. 808)
—Girls Rebel! Amazing Tales of Women Who Broke the Mold (p. 839)
—Growth of Florida: Pioneers & Technological Advances. (p. 900)
—Gymnastics. (p. 907)
—History of Gaming. (p. 978)
—Hora de la Verdad: Grupos de Animales. (p. 1002)
—Incredible Science Trivia: Fun Facts & Quizzes. (p. 1114)
—Incredible Tech Trivia: Fun Facts & Quizzes. (p. 1114)
—John Mccain: The Courage of Conviction. (p. 1173)
—JoJo Siwa: Fan Favorite. (p. 1175)
—Kylie Jenner: Makeup Mogul. (p. 1234)
—Lin-Manuel Miranda: Revolutionary Playwright, Composer, & Actor. (p. 1303)
—Lion King Quizzes: Hakuna Matat. (p. 1306)
—Lion King Quizzes: Hakuna Matata. (p. 1306)
—Locked up for Freedom: Civil Rights Protesters at the Leesburg Stockade. (p. 1339)
—Make Good Choices: Your Guide to Making Healthy Decisions. (p. 1386)
—Make It: Unusual Art. (p. 1386)
—Malala Yousafzai: Heroic Education Activist. (p. 1391)
—Manualidades: Arte Inusual. (p. 1399)
—March on Washington: A Primary Source Exploration of the Pivotal Protest (p. 1402)
—Marjorie Kinnan Rawlings: Writing in Rural Florida. (p. 1406)
—Mary McLeod Bethune: Education & Equality. (p. 1415)
—Michelle Obama: Political Icon. (p. 1458)
—Mimicking Nature. (p. 1469)
—Miranda Cosgrove. (p. 1475)
—Misty Copeland: Principal Ballerina. (p. 1483)
—Morkie: A Cross Between a Maltese & a Yorkshire Terrier (p. 1506)
—NASA Astronomer Nancy Grace Roman. (p. 1576)
—NASA Mathematician Katherine Johnson. (p. 1576)
—Origami: Dividing Fractions. (p. 1670)
—Our Leaders in Government. (p. 1679)
—Outlaws, Gunslingers, & Thieves. (p. 1685)
—Pairs Skating. (p. 1693)
—Pocahontas: Her Life & Legend. (p. 1764)
—Safe Social Networking (p. 1922)
—Save Wisely. (p. 1938)
—Science Educator & Advocate Bill Nye. (p. 1954)
—Science of a Race Car: Reactions in Action. (p. 1957)
—Seeking Freedom: Causes & Effects of the Flight of the Nez Perce. (p. 1984)
—Selena Gomez. (p. 1986)
—Showdown: Animal Homes. (p. 2012)
—Simone Manuel: Swimming Star. (p. 2021)
—Singles Skating. (p. 2024)
—Spend Wisely. (p. 2079)
—Staying Dry. (p. 2110)
—Steal the Scene: Writing Amazing Drama. (p. 2110)
—Stress Less: Your Guide to Managing Stress. (p. 2140)
—Taylor Swift. (p. 2193)
—Taylor Swift: Superstar Singer & Songwriter. (p. 2194)
—Theodore Roosevelt's Presidency. (p. 2216)
—Tomochichi: A Chief & a Friend. (p. 2259)
—Top Ice Hockey Tips. (p. 2263)
—Top Volleyball Tips. (p. 2264)
—Tracking a Storm. (p. 2272)
—Unofficial Guide to Minecraft Construction. (p. 2334)
—Unofficial Guide to Minecraft Mining & Farming. (p. 2334)
—Video Games Save the World. (p. 2356)
—War of 1812: By the Dawn's Early Light. (p. 2376)
—World of Angry Birds. (p. 2502)
—World of Minecraft. (p. 2503)
—Wreck-It Ralph Quizzes: When the Game Is over, the Fun Begins. (p. 2511)
Schwartz, Heather E., jt. auth. see Boothroyd, Jennifer.
Schwartz, Heather E., jt. auth. see Greenhaven Press Editors.
Schwartz, Heather E., jt. auth. see Mauleon, Daniel.
Schwartz, Heather E., jt. auth. see Mortensen, Lori.
Schwartz, Heather E. & Maurer, Tracy Nelson. Gymnastics. (p. 907)
Schwartz, Heather E. & Meinking, Mary. Star Biographies. (p. 2102)
Schwartz, Heather E. & Salzano, Tammi. Around the World: An Amazing World. (p. 118)
Schwartz, Heather E., et al. Figure Skating. (p. 726)
—Star Biographies. (p. 2102)
Schwartz, Joanne. City Alphabet Beam, Matt, illus. (p. 394)
—Fight On! Cape Breton Coal Miners,1900-1925 (p. 725)
—Old Woman Kazemi, Nahid, illus. (p. 1648)
—Pinny in Fall Malenfant, Isabelle, illus. (p. 1747)
—Pinny in Summer Malenfant, Isabelle, illus. (p. 1747)
—Pueblo Frente Al Mar. (p. 1810)
—Town Is by the Sea Smith, Sydney, illus. (p. 2270)
Schwartz, Julia A. Elinor's College Career, Vol. 1 of 4 (Classic Reprint) (p. 635)
Schwartz, Julia Augusta. Five Little Strangers: And How They Came to Live in America (Classic Reprint) (p. 744)
—Vassar Studies (Classic Reprint) (p. 2348)
—Wilderness Babies (Classic Reprint) (p. 2466)
—Wonderful Little Lives (Classic Reprint) (p. 2489)
Schwartz, Kacey, illus. see Chace, Rebecca.
Schwartz, Katherine, ed. see Yedwab, Paul Michael.
Schwartz, Kristi. Divorced Together: For teh Sake of the Children. (p. 566)
Schwartz, Lynne Sharon, tr. see Gandolfi, Silvana.
Schwartz, Marcia. Lobo & the Rabbit Stew. Campbell, Brent, illus. (p. 1338)
—Lobo & the Rabbit Stew/El Lobo y el Caldo de Conejo. Campbell, Brent, illus. (p. 1338)
Schwartz, Marianne. Ventura's Vacation Adventure. (p. 2350)
Schwartz, Marie Sophie. Two Family Mothers (Classic Reprint) (p. 2307)
Schwartz, R. A. Legacy Commencement. (p. 1261)
Schwartz, Richard Evan. Gallery of the Infinite. (p. 806)
—Life on the Infinite Farm. (p. 1295)
—You Can Count on Monsters: The First 100 Numbers & Their Characters. (p. 2525)
Schwartz, Roslyn. Mole Sisters & the Blue Egg. (p. 1488)
—Mole Sisters & the Question. (p. 1488)
—Mole Sisters & the Rainy Day. (p. 1488)
—Mole Sisters & the Wavy Wheat. (p. 1488)
Schwartz, Roy. Darkness in Lee's Closet & the Others Waiting There. (p. 508)
Schwartz, Sara Leah. Let's Use Them Right: Social Skills for My Hands, Feet, & Mouth. David, Racheli, illus. (p. 1278)
Schwartz, Sheila. Lies Will Take You Somewhere. (p. 1287)
Schwartz, Tina P. Bass Fishing. (p. 171)
—Deep-Sea Fishing. (p. 524)
—Depression: The Ultimate Teen (p. 530)
—Depression: The Ultimate Teen Guide (p. 530)
—Fly-Fishing. (p. 754)
—Freshwater Fishing. (p. 785)
—Ice Fishing. (p. 1087)
—Salmon Fishing. (p. 1925)
—Writing & Publishing: The Ultimate Teen Guide. (p. 2513)
Schwartz, Tom. Spaceship Earth: A Beginning Without End. (p. 2073)
Schwartz, Tom W. Handsome Brothers. (p. 916)
Schwartz, Tom W. & Schwartz, Wendy. Definite Probability: A Tale of a Boy Named Probably Who Discovers Himself Undoubtably. (p. 525)
Schwartz, Travis. Balloon Time. (p. 162)
Schwartz, Virginia Frances. Among the Fallen. (p. 76)
—Nutz! Leist, Christina, illus. (p. 1632)
Schwartz, Wendy, jt. auth. see Schwartz, Tom W.
Schwartze, Hermann. Pathologische Anatomie des Ohres (Classic Reprint) (p. 1704)
Schwartzenberger, Tina. Don Cherry. (p. 580)
Schwartzenberger, Tina, ed. see Lomberg, Michelle.
Schwartzkopf, Jere. Playtime on the Clothesline. (p. 1761)
Schwartzkopf, Jere, illus. see Kizer, Amelia.
Schwarz, Alan. Baseball All-Stars: Today's Greatest Players. (p. 168)
Schwarz, Philip, ed. see Burgan, Michael.
Schwarz, Philip, ed. see Kachur, Matthew.
Schwarz, Philip, ed. see Worth, Richard.
Schwarz, S. L. Treasure at Lure Lake. (p. 2281)
Schwarz, Venessa Bellido. Medical Technology. (p. 1436)
Schwarz, Viviane. Animals with Tiny Cat. Schwarz, Viviane, illus. (p. 96)
—Counting with Tiny Cat. Schwarz, Viviane, illus. (p. 460)
—How to Be on the Moon. Schwarz, Viviane, illus. (p. 1037)
—How to Find Gold. Schwarz, Viviane, illus. (p. 1042)
—Is There a Dog in This Book? Schwarz, Viviane, illus. (p. 1137)
Schwarz, Viviane, illus. see Conlon, Dom.
Schwarz, Viviane, illus. see Deacon, Alexis.
Schwarz, Viviane, illus. see Rinker, Sherri Duskey.
Schwarzbauer, Heike, tr. see Ende, Michael.
Schwarzenegger, Katherine. Maverick & Me. Harris, Phyllis, illus. (p. 1426)
Schwarzkopf, Giselle. Olivia. (p. 1650)
Schwarzkopf, Tom. Secrets of Dynamite Point (p. 1980)
Schwebel, Sara L., ed. see O'Dell, Scott.
Schwegler, Stephanie. Lotta Von Abinosia: Und Die Palindrafen. (p. 1356)
—Lotta Von Abinosia: Im Reich der Nichtmagier. (p. 1356)
Schweigel, Max. Esclarmonde, Clarisse et Florent, Yde et Olive: Drei Fortsetzungen der Chanson Von Huon de Bordeaux, Nach der Einzigen Turiner Handschrift Zum Erstenmal Veroeffentlicht (Classic Reprint) (p. 662)
Schweikert, Harry C. French Short Stories Edited for School Use (Classic Reprint) (p. 784)
Schweikert, Harry Christian. Russian Short Stories (Classic Reprint) (p. 1917)
Schweitzer, Albert. J. S. Bach Newman, Ernest, tr. from GER. (p. 1151)
Schweitzer, Jeffrey. Mundane Ghost. Schweitzer, Jeffrey, illus. (p. 1526)
Schweitzer, Karen. Cocker Spaniel. (p. 411)
—Dachshund. (p. 494)
—Making the Band. (p. 1390)
—Real World. (p. 1850)
—Shaun White. (p. 2003)
Schweitzer, Megan, ed. see Noble, Josh.
Schweitzer, Patty, illus. see Wolcott, P. A.
Schweizer, Chris. Creeps: Book 2: the Trolls Will Feast! (p. 472)
—Creeps: Book 1: Night of the Frankenfrogs. (p. 472)
—Creeps: Book 3 the Attack of the Jack-O-Lanterns. (p. 472)
—Crogan Adventures: Catfoot's Vengeance. (p. 477)
—Crogan Adventures. (p. 477)
—Curse of the Attack-O-Lanterns. (p. 489)
—History Comics: the Roanoke Colony: America's First Mystery. (p. 977)
—Maker Comics: Fix a Car! (p. 1387)
—Tricky Coyote Tales. Thomas, Chad, illus. (p. 2287)
—Tricky Fox Tales. Paroline, Shelli & Paroline, Michelle, illus. (p. 2287)
—Tricky Monkey Tales. Thomas, Chad, illus. (p. 2288)
—Tricky Rabbit Tales. Giallongo, Zack, illus. (p. 2288)
—Tricky Raven Tales. Witt, David, illus. (p. 2288)
—Tricky Spider Tales. Huddleston, Courtney, illus. (p. 2288)
Schwemm, Diane. Year I Turned Sixteen: Rose, Daisy, Laurel, Lily. (p. 2519)
Schweninger, Ann, illus. see Van Leeuwen, Jean.
Schweppe, Deirdre. Migrating Animals: Use Place Value Understanding & Properties of Operations to Add & Subtract. (p. 1464)
Schweppe, Scott C. General Wolf & Sergeant Wilcox: A Scottales Book. Pauley, Christopher D., ed. (p. 814)
Schwer, M. J. Questioning Quinn. (p. 1826)
Schwieder, Dorothy, et al. Iowa Past to Present: The People & the Prairie. (p. 1133)
Schwieger, Ruby Jane. Murder at Emerson's. (p. 1527)
Schwind, Beverly Lahote. Patches & Her Backpack Adventures. (p. 1704)
Schwinn, Aleaha. What Happens When I Yawn? (p. 2412)
Schwinn, Ruth E. Henry & Dale. Flores, Justin, illus. (p. 954)
Schy, Yael & Schwartz, David. What in the Wild? Mysteries of Nature Concealed... And Revealed. Kuhn, Dwight, photos by. (p. 2413)
Sciandra, Michael E., contrib. by. MODERN NERD'S GUIDE TO: LARPING. (p. 1487)
Sciandra, Mike. Cybercrime: Using Computers As Weapons. (p. 492)
—Modern Nerd's Guide to LARPing. (p. 1487)
Sciarrino, Stephanie. Multiplication at the Marina: Multiply Within 100. (p. 1525)
Sciarrone, Claudio, illus. see Bazaldua, Charles.
Sciarrone, Claudio, illus. see Carbone, Courtney.
Sciarrone, Claudio, illus. see Ferrari, Alessandro.
Sciarrone, Claudio, illus. see Golden Books.
Scibilia, Jade Zora. Solar Panels: Harnessing the Power of the Sun. (p. 2055)
Scidmore, Eliza R. As the Hague Ordains: Journal of a Russian Prisoner's Wife in Japan (Classic Reprint) (p. 124)
Science & Voege, Debra. Energy Today (p. 651)

Science, Manchester Institute of Arts an. Nature Study, Vol. 4: 1903 1904 (Classic Reprint) (p. 1581)

Science Museum, The. Super-Intelligent, High-Tech Robot Book. (p. 2155)

Science, Punk. Punk Science: Intergalactic Supermassive Space Book (p. 1814)

Sciences, Society of Arts and. O. Henry Memorial Award Prize Stories Of 1921: Chosen by the Society of Arts & Sciences (Classic Reprint) (p. 1633)

Scientific American Staff. 21st Century Robotics. (p. 2554)

—Beyond Extreme Physics. (p. 211)

—Endangered Earth. (p. 649)

—Extreme Engineering. (p. 686)

—Extreme Physics. (p. 687)

—Fighting Infectious Diseases. (p. 725)

—Future of the Web. (p. 803)

—Mysteries of the Milky Way. (p. 1567)

—Nanotech Revolution. (p. 1574)

—Tackling Cancer. (p. 2175)

Scieszka, Jon. All-Purpose SPHDZ Boxed Set: SPHDZ Book #1!; SPHDZ Book #2!; SPHDZ Book #3!; SPHDZ 4 Life! Prigmore, Shane, illus. (p. 53)

—AstroNuts Mission One: the Plant Planet. Weinberg, Steven, illus. (p. 129)

—Dizzy Izzy. Gordon, David et al, illus. (p. 567)

—Dizzy Izzy. Shannon, David et al, illus. (p. 567)

—Frank Einstein & the Antimatter Motor. (p. 777)

—Frank Einstein & the Antimatter Motor. Biggs, Brian, illus. (p. 777)

—Frank Einstein & the Antimatter Motor (Frank Einstein Series #1) Book One. Biggs, Brian, illus. (p. 777)

—Frank Einstein & the Bio-Action Gizmo (Frank Einstein Series #5) Book Five. Biggs, Brian, illus. (p. 777)

—Frank Einstein & the BrainTurbo. Biggs, Brian, illus. (p. 777)

—Frank Einstein & the BrainTurbo (Frank Einstein Series #3) Biggs, Brian, illus. (p. 777)

—Frank Einstein & the BrainTurbo (Frank Einstein Series #3) Book Three. Biggs, Brian, illus. (p. 777)

—Frank Einstein & the Electro-Finger. Biggs, Brian, illus. (p. 777)

—Frank Einstein & the Electro-Finger (Frank Einstein Series #2) Book Two. Biggs, Brian, illus. (p. 777)

—Frank Einstein & the EvoBlaster Belt (Frank Einstein Series #4) Book Four. Biggs, Brian, illus. (p. 777)

—Frank Einstein & the Space-Time Zipper (Frank Einstein Series #6) Biggs, Brian, illus. (p. 777)

—Frank Einstein & the Space-Time Zipper (Frank Einstein Series #6) Book Six. Biggs, Brian, illus. (p. 777)

—Frog Prince. Johnson, Steve, illus. (p. 789)

—Great Truck Rescue. Shannon, David et al, illus. (p. 890)

—Guys Read: Thriller. Helquist, Brett, illus. (p. 907)

—Jon Scieszka's Trucktown Garage, Design, illus. (p. 1176)

—Kat's Maps. Long, Loren et al, illus. (p. 1206)

—Kat's Maps. Shannon, David et al, illus. (p. 1206)

—Kat's Mystery Gift. Gordon, David et al, illus. (p. 1206)

—Kat's Mystery Gift. Shannon, David et al, illus. (p. 1206)

—Math Curse. Smith, Lane, illus. (p. 1422)

—Melvin's Valentine. Shannon, David et al, illus. (p. 1443)

—Race from a to Z Gordon, David et al, illus. (p. 1831)

—Robot Zot! Shannon, David, illus. (p. 1892)

—Smash! Crash! (p. 2041)

—SPHDZ 4 Life! Prigmore, Shane, illus. (p. 2080)

—SPHDZ Book #1! Prigmore, Shane, illus. (p. 2080)

—SPHDZ Book #2! Prigmore, Shane, illus. (p. 2080)

—SPHDZ Book #3! Prigmore, Shane, illus. (p. 2080)

—Spooky Tire. Shannon, David et al, illus. (p. 2087)

—Truckery Rhymes. (p. 2292)

—Truckery Rhymes. Shannon, David et al, illus. (p. 2292)

—Trucks Line Up. Gordon, David et al, illus. (p. 2293)

—Trucks Line Up. Shannon, David et al, illus. (p. 2293)

—Trucksgiving. Shannon, David et al, illus. (p. 2293)

—True Story of the 3 Little Pigs. Smith, Lane, illus. (p. 2295)

—True Story of the 3 Little Pigs / la Verdadera Historiade Los TresCerditos. (p. 2295)

—True Story of the Three Little Pigs 25th Anniversary Edition. Smith, Lane, illus. (p. 2295)

—Uh-Oh, Max. Shannon, David et al, illus. (p. 2314)

—Welcome to Trucktown! Shannon, David et al, illus. (p. 2399)

Scieszka, Jon, ed. see Angleberger, Tom, et al.

Scieszka, Jon, ed. see Brown, Dustin.

Scieszka, Jon, jt. narrated by see Willems, Mo.

Scieszka, Jon & Barnett, Mac. Battle Bunny. Myers, Matthew, illus. (p. 173)

Scieszka, Jon & Biggs, Brian. Frank Einstein & the Electro-Finger (Frank Einstein Series #2) Book Two. (p. 777)

Scieszka, Jon & Brian Biggs. Frank Einstein & the Electro-Finger. (p. 777)

Scieszka, Jon & Christopher Healy. Heroes & Villains. (p. 961)

Scieszka, Jon & Gidwitz, Adam. Terrifying Tales. (p. 2207)

Scieszka, Jon, et al. Guys Read: Funny Business. (p. 907)

—Guys Read: Terrifying Tales. Grimly, Gris, illus. (p. 907)

—Guys Read: the Sports Pages. Santat, Dan, illus. (p. 907)

—Guys Read: True Stories. (p. 907)

Scillian, Corey, jt. auth. see Scillian, Devin.

Scillian, Devin. D Is for down Under: An Australia Alphabet. (p. 494)

—D Is for down Under: An Australia Alphabet. Cook, Geoff, illus. (p. 494)

—Johnny Kaw: A Tall Tale. Sneed, Brad, illus. (p. 1175)

—Memoirs of a Goldfish. Bowers, Tim, illus. (p. 1444)

—Memoirs of a Hamster. Bowers, Tim, illus. (p. 1444)

—Memoirs of a Parrot. Bowers, Tim, illus. (p. 1444)

—Memoirs of an Elf. Bowers, Tim, illus. (p. 1444)

—Missile Toe: A Very Confused Christmas. Kelley, Marty, illus. (p. 1480)

Scillian, Devin & Scillian, Corey. One Kansas Farmer: A Kansas Number Book. Bowles, Doug, illus. (p. 1660)

Scillian, Devin & Young, Judy. Westward Journeys. Ellison, Chris et al, illus. (p. 2403)

—Westward Journeys. Ettinger, Bill Farnsworth et al, illus. (p. 2403)

Scioli, Tom, text. Fantastic Four: Grand Design. (p. 707)

Scirri, Kaitlin. Andrew Carnegie: Industrialist & Philanthropist. (p. 83)

—How Facebook Changed the World. (p. 1031)

—Misty Copeland: Ballet Dancer (p. 1483)

—Ruth Bader Ginsburg: Supreme Court Justice (p. 1918)

—Science of Controlling Electricity & Weather. (p. 1957)

—Science of Invisibility & X-Ray Vision. (p. 1958)

—Thomas Edison (p. 2228)

Scissors, Scissors. Ha! Ha! Ha: A Volume of Humorous & Satirical Sketches, Selected from the Leading Journals of the Day (Classic Reprint) (p. 908)

Sciuto, Alex, illus. see Higgins, Nadia.

Sciuto, Alex, illus. see Rowell, Rebecca.

Sclater, William Lutley. List of the Batrachia in the Indian Museum (Classic Reprint) (p. 1308)

Scneider, Marnie. Football Freddie & Fumble the Dog: Gameday in Philadelphia. (p. 761)

Scobie, Andrea. Colortimebooks Fashion Beauty Puzzle Book. (p. 426)

Scobie, Andrea, illus. see Waldman, Alan/A.

Scobie, Jennifer Jayne. If Only Nathan Knew - Version A. (p. 1092)

—Jellyfish Jellyfish. (p. 1163)

—Kendrick in the Land of the Giant Kangaroos. (p. 1209)

—Zoey Searches for Zero. (p. 2541)

Scobie, Lorna, illus. see Davies, Nicola.

Scobie, Lorna, illus. see Prasadam-Halls, Smriti.

Scoffham, Stephen, jt. auth. see Collins Maps.

Scoffham, Stephen & Bridge, Colin. Change. (p. 355)

—Collins Primary Geography Pupil Book 1 And 2 (p. 417)

—Investigation (p. 1131)

—Movement (p. 1516)

—Primary Geography. (p. 1792)

Scoffham, Stephen & Collins Kids, Collins. UK in Maps (Collins Primary Atlases) (p. 2314)

—World in Maps (Collins Primary Atlases) (p. 2502)

Scofield, Anna Bishop. Insights & Heresies Pertaining to the Evolution of the Soul. (p. 1124)

Scofield, Charles J. Subtle Adversary: A Tale of Callitso County (Classic Reprint) (p. 2146)

Scofield, Chris. Shark Curtain. (p. 2001)

Scoggins, Adam. Mr. Stinky's Adventures. (p. 1521)

Scoggins, Jocelyn, illus. see Achilles, Carole.

Scolari, Silvano, illus. see Berrios, Frank.

Scolero, Elizabeth, illus. see Grapes, Elizabeth.

Scoles, Jessica, illus. see Martin, Merci & Bishop, Wanda.

Scollard, Clinton. Boy's Book of Rhyme (Classic Reprint) (p. 272)

—Cloistering of Ursula: Being Certain Chapters from the Memoirs of Andrea, Marquis of Uccelli, & Count of Castelpulchio, Done into English (Classic Reprint) (p. 406)

—Count Falcon of the Eyrie: A Narrative Wherein Are Set Forth the Adventures Ventures Guido Orrabelli Del Falchi During a Certain Autumn of His Career (Classic Reprint) (p. 458)

—Hills of Song. (p. 972)

—Knight of the Highway (Classic Reprint) (p. 1228)

—Man-At-Arms: A Romance of the Days of Gian Galeazzo Visconti, the Great Viper (Classic Reprint) (p. 1394)

—Man-At-arms. (p. 1394)

—Under Summer Skies (Classic Reprint) (p. 2321)

—Vicar of the Marches (Classic Reprint) (p. 2355)

Scollard, Clinton, jt. auth. see Sherman, Frank Dempster.

Scollen, C. My Big Book for Boys. (p. 1532)

—My Big Book for Girls. (p. 1532)

—My Giant Sticker Stencil. (p. 1548)

Scollen, Chris. 1000 Stickers Sweet Treats. (p. 2560)

Scollon, Bill. Beware the Kakamora! (p. 211)

—Disney Puppy Dog Pals. Disney Storybook Art Team, illus. (p. 563)

—Facing Your Fears: A Toy Story Tale. (p. 693)

—Good Dinosaur Little Golden Book (Disney/Pixar the Good Dinosaur) Rocco, Michaelangelo, illus. (p. 862)

—Kung Fu Panda. Golden Books, illus. (p. 1233)

—Miles from Tomorrowland: Who Stole the Stellosphere? (p. 1465)

—Minnie: Case of the Missing Sparkle-Izer. Loter Inc. Staff, illus. (p. 1473)

—Moana Guide Book (Disney Moana) Random House Disney Staff, illus. (p. 1485)

—Training of the Broom. (p. 2275)

—Walt Disney: Drawn from Imagination. Disney Book Group & Brown, Adrienne, illus. (p. 2373)

—Walt Disney: Drawn from Imagination. (p. 2374)

—Wreck-It Ralph 2 Movie Storybook (Disney Wreck-It Ralph 2) Disney Storybook Artists Staff, illus. (p. 2511)

Scollon, Bill, jt. auth. see Random House Disney Staff.

Scollon, Bill, jt. auth. see RH Disney Staff.

Scollon, Bill, adapted by. Disney Elena of Avalor: Princesa Al Rescate. (p. 559)

—Zootopia. (p. 2544)

Scollon, Bill & Disney Book Group. Minnie Be My Sparkly Valentine. Disney Storybook Art Team, illus. (p. 1473)

Scollon, Bill & Disney Books. Minnie Easter Bonnet Parade: Includes Stickers. Disney Storybook Art Team, illus. (p. 1473)

Scollon, Bill & Johnson, Greg. Miles from Tomorrowland: Who Stole the Stellosphere? Team, Disney Storybook Art, illus. (p. 1465)

Scollon, Bill & Nee, Chris. Engine Nine, Feelin' Fine! (p. 651)

Scollon, Bill & Rabb, Michael. Doc Mcstuffins: Starry, Starry Night. Studio, Character Building & Team, Disney Storybook Art, illus. (p. 572)

Scollon, Bill & Redeker, Kent. Doc Mcstuffins: Brave Dragon. Studio, Character Building & Team, Disney Storybook Art, illus. (p. 572)

—Henry Hugglemonster: The Huggleball Game. Entertainment, Premise, illus. (p. 955)

Scollon, Bill & Ring, Susan. Mickey Mouse Clubhouse: Minnie's Summer Vacation. Loter, Inc., illus. (p. 1459)

Scollon, Bill & Scollon, Devra Newberger. Transformers Recycle It! (p. 2277)

Scollon, Bill & Tyrrell, Colm. Henry Hugglemonster: Snow Day. Entertainment, Premise, illus. (p. 955)

Scollon, Bill & Valentine, Ed. Doc Mcstuffins: Peaches Pie, Take a Bath! Studio, Character Building & Team, Disney Storybook Art, illus. (p. 573)

Scollon, Bill, et al. Sofia's Princess Adventures. (p. 2054)

Scollon, Devra Newberger, jt. auth. see Scollon, Bill.

Scollon, William. Case of the Missing Sparkle-Izer. (p. 338)

—Doc Mcstuffins: Brave Dragon. (p. 572)

—Doc Mcstuffins: Starry, Starry Night. (p. 572)

—Jake & the Never Land Pirates: Pirate Campout. (p. 1155)

—Minnie: Be My Sparkly Valentine. (p. 1473)

Sconce, Harvey J. Romance of Everfarm (Classic Reprint) (p. 1900)

Scoon, Saska. Miss Rosie's Academy of Dance: Annie Twinkle-Toes' First Week. (p. 1480)

Scoot, et al. Sami the Samurai Squirrel: Welcome to Woodbriar. (p. 1927)

Scoppettone, Carolyn Cory. Hold This Alpaugh, Priscilla, illus. (p. 987)

Scoppettone, Sandra. Happy Endings Are All Alike. (p. 922)

Scorer, John G. Scorer's Successful Selections & Principles of Voice & Action: A Treatise on the Science & Art of Elocution, with a Collection of Tested & Approved Selections for Recitation on All Occasions; Including the Choicest Gems of Elocution & Oratory Fr. (p. 1961)

Scoresby, Natassia a, illus. see Hough, William E.

Scorey, John, illus. see Mayes, Susan.

Scorza, Nick. People of the Lake. (p. 1719)

Scot, P. G. Personal Narrative of the Escape from Nowgong to Banda & Nagode (Classic Reprint) (p. 1725)

Scotford, Groenewald & Scotford, Tina. Bush Buffet in the Land of Kachoo. (p. 301)

—Mighty Elephant in the Land of Kachoo: The Land of Kachoo Series. Groenewald, Frans, illus. (p. 1462)

Scotford, Tina. Saving the Rhino in the Land of Kachoo: The Land of Kachoo Series. Groenewald, Frans, illus. (p. 1939)

Scotland, Church Of. Life & Work, Vol. 1: A Parish Magazine; January to December, 1879 (Classic Reprint) (p. 1290)

Scott, A. L. S. Horace the Seal. (p. 1003)

—Pint-Size the Perro & the Little White Lie. (p. 1747)

Scott, Adam M. Aliens Don't Like Cheese. (p. 47)

Scott, Angela, jt. auth. see Scott, Jonathan.

Scott, Angela, photos by see Scott, Jonathan.

Scott, Ann, ed. see Murdin, Lesley.

Scott, Ann, illus. see Seyderhelm, Amanda.

Scott, Ashley, illus. see Colodny, Lisa & Colodny, Samantha.

Scott, Ayneka. Butterfly Guide. (p. 304)

Scott Bailey, Arthur. Sleepy Time Tales - the Tale of Benny Badger. (p. 2037)

—Sleepy Time Tales - the Tale of Cuffy Bear. (p. 2037)

—Sleepy Time Tales - the Tale of Dickie Deer Mouse. (p. 2037)

—Sleepy Time Tales - the Tale of Ferdinand Frog. (p. 2037)

—Sleepy Time Tales - the Tale of Frisky Squirrel. (p. 2037)

—Sleepy Time Tales - the Tale of Grandfather Mole. (p. 2037)

—Sleepy Time Tales - the Tale of Grumpy Weasel. (p. 2037)

—Sleepy Time Tales - the Tale of Master Meadow Mouse. (p. 2037)

—Sleepy Time Tales - the Tale of Nimble Deer. (p. 2037)

Scott, Benjamin. Progress of Locomotion: Being Two Lectures on the Advances Made in Artificial Locomotion in Great Britain. Pp. 5-80. (p. 1805)

—Progress of Locomotion: Being Two Lectures on the Advances Made in Artificial Locomotion in Great Britain (Classic Reprint) (p. 1805)

Scott, Betty. Wellesley Magazine, Vol. 6: November 1897 (Classic Reprint) (p. 2399)

—Wellesley Magazine, Vol. 6: February 19, 1898 (Classic Reprint) (p. 2399)

Scott, Bob, illus. see Pastis, Stephan & Schulz, Charles M.

Scott, Brandon James. Big Pet Story. (p. 222)

—Pancake Express. (p. 1695)

Scott, Brandon James, illus. see Stinson, Kathy.

Scott, Briana Corr. She Dreams of Sable Island: A Paper Doll Book (p. 2004)

Scott, C. A. Dawson. Treasure Trove (Classic Reprint) (p. 2282)

Scott, C. Kay. Blind Mice (Classic Reprint) (p. 244)

Scott, Caitlin. Treasure Hunting: Looking for Lost Riches. (p. 2282)

Scott, Carey. Magic & Mystery. (p. 1376)

Scott, Carrie Emma. Popular Books for Boys & Girls: A Graded List with Annotations (Classic Reprint) (p. 1777)

Scott, Cassandra. Boys & Girls Are Created2Produce. (p. 272)

Scott, Cavan. Attack of the Necron. (p. 134)

—Claws of the Genestealer. (p. 402)

—Escape: Prelude. Cummins, Lucy Ruth & Buisán, David, illus. (p. 661)

—Han & Chewie Adventure (p. 914)

—Heist #3. Cummins, Lucy Ruth & Buisán, David, illus. (p. 949)

—Journey to Star Wars: the Rise of Skywalker a Finn & Poe Adventure. Charretier, Elsa, illus. (p. 1182)

—Luke & Leia Adventure (p. 1366)

—Machine of Doom. (p. 1372)

—Penguins of Madagascar Volume 4. Ferreyra, Lucas, illus. (p. 1716)

—Secrets of the Tau. (p. 1981)

—Snare #1. Cummins, Lucy Ruth & Buisán, David, illus. (p. 2045)

—Star Wars: A Luke & Leia Adventure. Charretier, Elsa, illus. (p. 2103)

—Star Wars a Luke & Leia Adventure: A Choose Your Destiny Chapter Book. Charretier, Elsa, illus. (p. 2103)

—Star Wars Adventures #1: Better the Devil You Know, Part 1. Charm, Derek et al, illus. (p. 2103)

—Star Wars Adventures in Wild Space the Cold: Book 5. (p. 2103)

—Star Wars Adventures in Wild Space the Snare: Book 1. (p. 2103)

—Star Wars Adventures: Return to Vader's Castle. Francavilla, Francesco et al, illus. (p. 2104)

—Star Wars Adventures: Tales from Vader's Castle. Charm, Derek et al, illus. (p. 2104)

—Star Wars an Obi-Wan & Anakin Adventure: A Choose Your Destiny Chapter Book. Charretier, Elsa, illus. (p. 2104)

—Star Wars: Choose Your Destiny (Book 1) a Han & Chewie Adventure. Charretier, Elsa, illus. (p. 2104)

—Tales from Vader's Castle. (p. 2183)

—War of the Orks. (p. 2376)

Scott, Cavan, jt. auth. see Huddleston, Tom.

Scott, Cavan, jt. auth. see Walker, Landry Q.

Scott, Cavan & Flynn, Ian. Star Wars Adventures Vol. 9: Fight the Empire! Charm, Derek et al, illus. (p. 2104)

Scott, Cavan & Matthews, Alex. Penguins Collection 2. Ferrerya, Lucas, illus. (p. 1716)

Scott, Cavan & Snider, Brandon T. Skylanders Universe: The Complete Collection. (p. 2034)

Scott, Cavan & Walker, Landry Q. Star Wars Adventures Vol. 1: Heroes of the Galaxy Charm, Derek et al, illus. (p. 2104)

Scott, Cavan, comment. Finn & Poe Adventures. (p. 731)

—Obi-Wan & Anakin Adventure. (p. 1634)

Scott, Cavan, et al. Doctor Who: the Missy Chronicles. (p. 574)

—Penguins of Madagascar: Operation Heist. Vol. 2 Bartolini, Egle, illus. (p. 1716)

—Star Wars Adventures #2: Better the Devil You Know, Part 2. Charretier, Elsa et al, illus. (p. 2103)

—Star Wars Adventures Vol. 4: Smuggler's Blues. Charm, Derek, illus. (p. 2104)

Scott, Celicia. Dangerous Depressants & Sedatives. Borus, Joshua, ed. (p. 501)

—Doping: Human Growth Hormone, Steroids, & Other Performance-Enhancing Drugs. Borus, Joshua, ed. (p. 585)

—Energy Drinks, Coffee, Soda, & Pills. Borus, Joshua, ed. (p. 650)

—Facebook(Tm) How Mark Zuckerberg Connected More Than a Billion Friends. (p. 693)

—Hard Drugs: Cocaine, LSD, PCP, & Heroin. Borus, Joshua, ed. (p. 929)

—My Daily Diet: Proteins. Prock, Lisa Albers, ed. (p. 1536)

—My Daily Diet: Vegetables. Prock, Lisa Albers, ed. (p. 1536)

—New Drugs: Bath Salts, Spice, Salvia, & Designer Drugs. Borus, Joshua, ed. (p. 1592)

—Sports & Fitness. Hart, Diane H., ed. (p. 2088)

—Twitter: How Jack Dorsey Changed the Way We Communicate. (p. 2306)

—Weight Lifting & Strength Building. Hart, Diane H., ed. (p. 2396)

—YouTube: How Steve Chen Changed the Way We Watch Videos. (p. 2536)

Scott, Ceylan. On a Scale of One to Ten. (p. 1652)

Scott, Charles A. Haunted Man: A Dramatization in Three Acts of Chas; Dickens' Charistmas Story of the Same Title (Classic Reprint) (p. 938)

Scott, Charles Augustus. Great Expectations: A Drama in Five Acts; Dramatized from Dicken's Popular Work of the Same Name (Classic Reprint) (p. 886)

—Old Scrooge: A Christmas Carol in Five Staves, Dramatized from Charles Dickens' Celebrated Christmas Story (Classic Reprint) (p. 1648)

Scott, Chris. Unseen. (p. 2335)

Scott, Chris Fornell, jt. auth. see Miller, John.

Scott, Christopher L., illus. see Pendleton, Claudette M.

Scott, Clark C., jt. auth. see Bennett, Doraine.

Scott, Clarke C., jt. auth. see Donohue, Moira Rose.

Scott, Clement. Among the Apple Orchards (Classic Reprint) (p. 76)

—Drawing-Room Plays & Parlour Pantomimes (Classic Reprint) (p. 600)

—Ellen Terry (Classic Reprint) (p. 637)

—Green Room Stories (Classic Reprint) (p. 894)

—Old Days in Bohemian London (Recollections of Clement Scott) (Classic Reprint) (p. 1645)

—Wheel of Life: A Few Memories & Recollections (de Omnibus Rebus) (p. 2427)

—Wheel of Life: A Few Memories & Recollections de Omnibus Rebus (Classic Reprint) (p. 2427)

Scott, Clement W. Round about the Islands, or Sunny Spots near Home (Classic Reprint) (p. 1907)

—Stage Door: Stories by Those Who Enter It (Classic Reprint) (p. 2099)

Scott, Colin. Children's Secret Diary. (p. 375)

—Speedy Kids Coloring Book. (p. 2078)

Scott Curtis, Joan. Numerada. (p. 1630)

Scott, D. P. Christmas Elf. Hayward, Roy, illus. (p. 385)

Scott, Damion, illus. see Casey, Joe.

Scott, Damion, illus. see Jenkins, Paul.

Scott, Dan. Big Buildings of the Ancient World. (p. 218)

Scott, Danny. Calum's Big Break Morentorn, Alice A., illus. (p. 312)

—Calum's Cup Final Morentorn, Alice A., illus. (p. 312)

—Calum's Hard Knock Morentorn, Alice A., illus. (p. 312)

—Calum's New Boots Morentorn, Alice A., illus. (p. 312)

—Calum's New Team Morentorn, Alice A., illus. (p. 312)

—Calum's Tough Match Morentorn, Alice A., illus. (p. 312)

Scott, David Clement. Cyclopaedic Dictionary of the Mang'anja Language Spoken in British Central Africa (Classic Reprint) (p. 493)

Scott, Debora. Mission to Save Goodness Garden. Nancy, Elizabeth, illus. (p. 1481)

Scott, Dee Mary. Adventures of Charles & Camilla Chinchilla. (p. 22)

Scott, Dixon. Stratford-On-Avon with Leamington & Warwick (Classic Reprint) (p. 2139)

Scott, Drew & Scott, Jonathan. Builder Brothers: Better Together. Smith, Kim, illus. (p. 293)

—Builder Brothers: Big Plans. Smith, Kim, illus. (p. 293)

Scott, Duncan Campbell. In the Village of Viger (Classic Reprint) (p. 1111)

Scott, E., illus. see Lee, G.

Scott, Earnestine E. Little Mike's Family: A Novel for Second & Third Graders. (p. 1322)

Scott Edgar, illus. see Beck, Adrian.

Scott, Edna Lyman. Story Telling: What to Tell & How, to Tell It (Classic Reprint) (p. 2135)

Scott, Elaine. Buried Alive! How 33 Miners Survived 69 Days Deep under the Chilean Desert. (p. 299)

—Our Moon: New Discoveries about Earth's Closest Companion. (p. 1679)

—Space, Stars, & the Beginning of Time: What the Hubble Telescope Saw. (p. 2072)

—To Pluto & Beyond. (p. 2253)

Scott, Elizabeth. Between Here & Forever. (p. 210)

—Love You Hate You Miss You. (p. 1361)

—Miracle. (p. 1474)

—Something, Maybe. (p. 2060)

—Stealing Heaven. (p. 2110)

—Unwritten Rule. (p. 2337)

Scott, Ellen. Avocado Stickers. (p. 143)

—Design Your Own Sugar Skull Sticker Activity Book. (p. 532)

—Design Your Own Teddy Bears Sticker Activity Book. (p. 532)

—Glitter Flamingos Stickers. (p. 843)

—Glitter Llama Stickers. (p. 843)

—Glitter Pineapples Stickers. (p. 843)

—Silly Sloths Stickers. (p. 2018)

—T-Shirt Talk Stickers. (p. 2174)

Scott Enakevwe, Linda. One Drunk in the Family Is Enough: The Adventures of Lily Sutton # 2. (p. 1659)

Scott, Eric. Day the Rainbow Ended. (p. 514)

—Great Fairytale Robbery. (p. 886)

—Island of Lost Dolls. (p. 1139)

—Santa & the Cyberspace Plot. (p. 1931)

Scott, Ernest. Life of Captain Matthew Flinders. (p. 1294)

Scott, Eva I. Great Adventure (Classic Reprint) (p. 883)

Scott, Evelyn. Narcissus (Classic Reprint) (p. 1575)

—Narrow House (Classic Reprint) (p. 1575)

Scott, Firth. Rider of Waroona (Classic Reprint) (p. 1878)

Scott, Florence E. Through the Yellowstone with Paul & Peggy (Classic Reprint) (p. 2237)

Scott, Francina. Romance of a Trained Nurse (Classic Reprint) (p. 1900)

Scott, Frank J. Tom Oreo or Littlebee's Mine: A Play in Four Acts (Classic Reprint) (p. 2257)

Scott, Frederick George. Elton Hazlewood: A Memoir, by His Friend Henry Vane (Classic Reprint) (p. 640)

—Great War As I Saw It. (p. 890)

—Great War As I Saw It (Classic Reprint) (p. 890)

Scott, G. Firth. Colonial Born: A Tale of the Queensland Bush (Classic Reprint) (p. 418)

Scott, Galvin, illus. see Linn, Susie.

Scott, Gavin, illus. see Fodor, Cecile Olesen.

Scott, Gavin, illus. see Fodor, Cecilie.

Scott, Gavin, illus. see Freedman, Claire.

Scott, Gavin, illus. see Linn, Susie.

Scott, Gavin, illus. see Pedersen, Karoline Pahus.

Scott, Gavin, illus. see Simon, Mary Manz.

Scott, Gavin, jt. auth. see Freedman, Claire.

Scott, George Gordon. Clumber Chase; or Love's Riddle Solved by a Royal Sphinx, Vol. 1 Of 3: A Tale of the Restoration (Classic Reprint) (p. 409)

Scott, Gertrude Fisher. Jean Cabot at Ashton (Classic Reprint) (p. 1162)

Scott, Gillian. C. J. 's Mystical Adventure: The Magic Beyond the Mist. (p. 306)

Scott, Gini Graham. Sandy the Seagull & the Bird Patrol. (p. 1931)

—Sandy the Seagull, the Surfers & the Kites. Korolev, Nick, illus. (p. 1931)

Scott, Greg, illus. see Cosby, Andrew & Nelson, Michael Alan.

Scott, Greg, jt. illus. see Larroca, Salvador.

Scott, Gwen. Blackberry Junction. Baker, David, illus. (p. 240)

—Dog That Wore Glasses. (p. 576)

—In Between the Cracks: The Search for Zar. (p. 1104)

Scott, H. Percy. Seeing Canada & the South (Classic Reprint) (p. 1984)

Scott, Harriet. Hen-Pecked Husband, Vol. 1 Of 3: A Novel (Classic Reprint) (p. 954)

—Hen-Pecked Husband, Vol. 2: A Novel (Classic Reprint) (p. 954)

—Henrietta: A Novel (Classic Reprint) (p. 954)

—Henrietta. (p. 954)

Scott, Helenus. Adventures of a Rupee: Wherein Are Interspersed Various Anecdotes Asiatic & European (Classic Reprint) (p. 21)

—Adventures of a Rupee. (p. 21)

Scott, Henry. Legionaries: A Story of the Great Raid (Classic Reprint) (p. 1264)

Scott, Honoria. Amatory Tales of Spain, France, Switzerland, & the Mediterranean, Vol. 2 Of 4: Containing the Fair Andalusian, Rosolia of Palermo, & the Maltese Portrait; Interspersed with Pieces of Original Poetry (Classic Reprint) (p. 62)

Scott, Hugh Stowell. Suspense (Classic Reprint) (p. 2166)

—Works of Henry Seton Merriman, Vol. 11: The Vultures (Classic Reprint) (p. 2498)

Scott, Hugh Stowell, jt. auth. see Merriman, Henry Seton.

Scott, J. Frank. Uplift, 1950, Vol. 38: A Monthly Journal (Classic Reprint) (p. 2338)

—Uplift, 1951, Vol. 39: A Monthly Journal (Classic Reprint) (p. 2338)

—Uplift, Vol. 37: January 1949 (Classic Reprint) (p. 2338)

Scott, Jacqueline C. Ms. Carolyn: The Principal. (p. 1523)

Scott, James W. Jack Hardin's Rendering of the Arabian Nights: Being a New Translation in up-To-Date English; with Wise Comments, Explanations, by This Eminent Linguist (Classic Reprint) (p. 1152)

Scott, Jane Wooster, illus. see Raffin, Deborah.

Scott, Janine. Café Cosmos. Wood, Hannah, illus. (p. 308)

—Growing a Plant. (p. 899)

—Living in Hong Kong: Set Of 6. (p. 1333)

—Mars Mouse. Wood, Hannah, illus. (p. 1409)

—Noisy Parrot. Rigby, Deborah, illus. (p. 1618)

—Ocean of Animals (p. 1635)

—Rain Forest Life (p. 1835)

Scott, Jay & Scott, Liz. Alex & the Amazing Lemonade Stand. (p. 42)

Scott, Jeffery Warren. Calling Card of the King. (p. 312)

Scott, Jennifer, illus. see Harney Jr., Robert.

Scott, Jenny. Book 1: Vision of Gold. Yong, Billy, illus. (p. 257)

—Book 2: Vision of Flames. Yong, Billy, illus. (p. 257)

—Book 3: Vision of a Star. Yong, Billy, illus. (p. 257)

—Book 4: Vision of Pearls. Yong, Billy, illus. (p. 257)

—Clairvoyant Claire (Set) Yong, Billy, illus. (p. 397)

Scott, Jeremy. Strings. (p. 2141)

Scott, Jerry. Zits: Chillax Borgman, Jim, illus. (p. 2541)

—Zits: Shredded. Borgman, Jim, illus. (p. 2541)

Scott, Jerry & Borgman, Jim. Extra Cheesy Zits: A Zits Treasury. (p. 685)

—Extra Cheesy Zits. (p. 685)

Scott, Joanna, illus. see Barr, Dicky.

Scott, Joanna I. Stanley the Moose: Book One of the Woodsie Tails Series. (p. 2101)

Scott, John. London Magazine, Vol. 4: July to December, 1921 (Classic Reprint) (p. 1341)

Scott, John, illus. see Fox, Stephanie.

Scott, John L., jt. auth. see Sarkees-Wircenski, Michelle.

Scott, John Loughran, jt. auth. see Bulfinch, Thomas.

Scott, John Reed. Beatrix of Clare (Classic Reprint) (p. 183)

—Colonel of the Red Huzzars (Classic Reprint) (p. 418)

—First Hurdle, & Others (Classic Reprint) (p. 737)

—Impostor: A Tale of Old Annapolis (Classic Reprint) (p. 1102)

—Last Try (Classic Reprint) (p. 1250)

—Princess Dehra (Classic Reprint) (p. 1797)

—Red Emerald (Classic Reprint) (p. 1856)

—Unforgiving Offender (Classic Reprint) (p. 2327)

—Woman in Question (Classic Reprint) (p. 2485)

Scott, Jonathan. Arabian Nights Entertainments, Carefully Revised & Occasionally Corrected from the Arabic, Vol. 3 Of 6: To Which Is Added, a Selection of New Tales (Classic Reprint) (p. 109)

—Arabian Nights Entertainments, Carefully Revised, & Occasionally Corrected from the Arabic, Vol. 6 Of 6: To Which Is Added, a Selection of New Tales, Now First Translated from the Arabic Originals; Also, an Introduction & Notes, Illustrative of Th. (p. 109)

—Arabian Nights Entertainments, Vol. 1 Of 6: Carefully Revised, & Occasionally Corrected from the Arabic; to Which Is Added, a Selection of New Tales, Now First Translated from the Arabic Originals; Also, an Introduction & Notes, Illustrative of Th. (p. 109)

—Arabian Nights Entertainments, Vol. 2 Of 6: Carefully Revised, & Occasionally Corrected from the Arabic; to Which Is Added, a Selection of New Tales, Now First Translated from the Arabic Originals (Classic Reprint) (p. 109)

—Arabian Nights Entertainments, Vol. 3 Of 4: With an Introduction, Illustrative of the Religion, Manners, & Customer of the Mohammedans (Classic Reprint) (p. 109)

—Arabian Nights Entertainments, Vol. 4 Of 6: Carefully Revised, & Occasionally Corrected from the Arabic; to Which Is Added, a Selection of New Tales, Also, an Introduction & Notes, Illustrative of the Religion, Manners & Customs, of the Mahummed. (p. 109)

—Tigers of Ranthambore. Scott, Angela, photos by. (p. 2242)

Scott, Jonathan and Angela. Honey & Toto: the Story of a Cheetah Family 1 Pathfinders. (p. 999)

Scott, Jonathan & Scott, Angela. Great Migration White Band. (p. 887)

—Scarface: the Real Lion King Gold Band. (p. 1942)

Scott, Jordan. I Talk Like a River. Smith, Sydney, illus. (p. 1083)

—I Talk Like a River 4-Copy L-Card (p. 1083)

Scott Jr, Charlie N. Sam's Sleigh Shop. (p. 1928)

Scott, Julia H. Blind Widow: And Her Family (Classic Reprint) (p. 244)

Scott, Julie, illus. see Ward, Jennifer.

Scott, Karen, jt. auth. see Smith, Kathryn.

Scott, Kate. Collins Big Cat Phonics for Letters & Sounds - How the Ear Can Hear: Band 03/Yellow (p. 416)

—Spies in Disguise: Boy in a Tutu. (p. 2081)

Scott, Katie. Animalium Coloring Book. Scott, Katie, illus. (p. 93)

Scott, Katie, illus. see Big Picture Press, Big Picture.

Scott, Katie, illus. see Broom, Jenny.

Scott, Katie, illus. see Davidson, Susanna.

Scott, Katie, illus. see Willis, Kathy.

Scott, Keith. Bear Man. Hill, Steve, illus. (p. 179)

Scott, Kenlynn Dorothy. Monster Tails: A Green-Eyed Boy Named Harvey. Klassen, Jon, illus. (p. 1497)

Scott, Kevin John. Frederik Sandwich & the Earthquake That Couldn't Possibly Be. (p. 782)

—Frederik Sandwich & the Mayor Who Lost Her Marbles. (p. 782)

Scott, Kieran. He's So Not Worth It. (p. 963)

—Only Everything. (p. 1664)

—She's So Dead to Us. (p. 2006)

—Something True. (p. 2061)

—This Is So Not Happening. (p. 2225)

Scott, Kieran, see Brian, Kate, pseud.

Scott, Kiernan, jt. auth. see Scott, Kieran.

Scott, Kimberley. Wipe-Clean First Math. (p. 2477)

—Wipe-Clean First Words. (p. 2477)

Scott, Kimberley, illus. see Gallo, Tina.

Scott, Kimberley, illus. see Greenwell, Jessica.

Scott, Kimberley, illus. see Hemming, Alice.

Scott, Kimberley, illus. see MacLaine, James.

Scott, Kimberley, illus. see McKay, Hilary.

Scott, Kimberly, illus. see Claybourne, Anna.

Scott, Korey, illus. see Gordon, Jon.

Scott, Korey, illus. see Hansen, Amy S.

Scott, Korey, illus. see Hansen, Amy S. & Olien, Rebecca.

Scott, Korey, illus. see Wright, Mary H. & Frontiera, Deborah K.

Scott, Lady. Amazing Marriage, Vol. 1 (Classic Reprint) (p. 65)

—Skeleton in the Cupboard, Vol. 1 of 2 (Classic Reprint) (p. 2030)

Scott, Laura Platas. Life in the US Special Operations Forces. (p. 1293)

Scott, Laurence W. Mooted Question, & Other Rhymes, Vol. 1 (Classic Reprint) (p. 1503)

Scott, Laurie, jt. auth. see Dick, William.

Scott, Leader. Nook in the Apennines, or a Summer Beneath the Chestnuts (Classic Reprint) (p. 1619)

Scott, Leonard. Early Reminiscences: A Poem, Recounting Incidents Occurring in the Youth of the Author, & Describing Country Life in the Province of New Brunswick, Forty Years Ago (Classic Reprint) (p. 615)

Scott, Leroy. Daughter of Two Worlds: A Novel of New York Life (Classic Reprint) (p. 509)

—No. 13 Washington Square. (p. 1612)

—No; 13 Washington Square (Classic Reprint) (p. 1612)

—Partners of the Night (Classic Reprint) (p. 1701)

—Shears of Destiny (Classic Reprint) (p. 2004)

—To Him That Hath (Classic Reprint) (p. 2252)

—Walking Delegate (Classic Reprint) (p. 2372)

Scott, Libby & Westcott, Rebecca. Can You See Me? (p. 319)

Scott, Lindsay. My Little Book of Bible Stories. (p. 1552)

Scott, Lisa. My Cousin's House. (p. 1536)

Scott, Lisa Ann. All That Glitters. Burns, Heather, illus. (p. 53)

—Back on the Map. (p. 155)

—Call Plays Fair. (p. 310)

—Cascadia Saves the Day. (p. 336)

—Dreams That Sparkle Burns, Heather, illus. (p. 603)

—Dreams That Sparkle (Enchanted Pony Academy #4) (p. 603)

—Fairies Forever. (p. 695)

—Lana Swims North. (p. 1241)

—Let It Glow Burns, Heather, illus. (p. 1269)

—Let It Glow (Enchanted Pony Academy #3) (p. 1269)

—Nixie Makes Waves. (p. 1612)

—Perfectly Popular. (p. 1723)

—School of Charm. (p. 1946)

—Too Many Cats! (p. 2260)

—Treasure Trap. (p. 2282)

—Wings That Shine Burns, Heather, illus. (p. 2473)

Scott, Lisa Ann, jt. auth. see Meadows, Daisy.

Scott, Liz, jt. auth. see Scott, Jay.

Scott, Logan. Rangers of Unity. (p. 1841)

Scott, Lucy. Busy Busy! Scott, Lucy, illus. (p. 302)

Scott, Lucy P. Grandmother's Book of Verses for Her Grandchildren (Classic Reprint) (p. 879)

Scott, Luke. Through a Crystal Doorknob. (p. 2236)

Scott, Mairghread. City on the Other Side. (p. 395)

—Robots & Drones. (p. 1893)

—Science Comics: Robots & Drones: Past, Present, & Future. Chabot, Jacob, illus. (p. 1954)

—Transformers: Windblade - Distant Stars. Howell, Corin & Pitre-Durocher, Sara, illus. (p. 2277)

Scott, Mairghread, jt. auth. see Caramagna, Joe.

Scott, Mairghread, jt. auth. see Johnson, Mike.

Scott, Marc. Beginner's Projects in Coding. Marston, Mick, illus. (p. 192)

Scott, Marc, illus. see McKay, Sindy.

Scott, Margaret. Jimmy Gets a Pet Passport. (p. 1168)

—Medieval Clothing & Costumes: Displaying Wealth & Class in Medieval Times. (p. 1436)

Scott, Marilyn. Lightening Bug's Message of Love. (p. 1299)

Scott, Marlo, illus. see Alves-Malcolm, Greta.

Scott, Martin J. Boy Knight. (p. 269)

Scott, Martin Jerome. Mother Machree: A Novel (Classic Reprint) (p. 1510)

Scott, MaryJo, et al. Corduroy's Colors. (p. 453)

—Corduroy's Seasons. (p. 453)

Scott, Mathew. Lots to Spot: Ocean. (p. 1356)

Scott, Matt. Big Scoop of Something. (p. 222)

—Did You Laugh When You Stubbed Your Toe? (p. 543)

—Have You Ever Watched What Your World Does? (p. 939)

—Where Do You Want to Go? (p. 2436)

Scott, Matthew. Autobiography of Matthew Scott, Jumbo's Keeper: Formerly of the Zoological Society's Gardens, London, & Receiver of Sir Edwin Landseer Medal in 1866; Also Jumbo's Biography, by the Same Author (Classic Reprint) (p. 140)

—Autobiography of Matthew Scott, Jumbo's Keeper. (p. 140)

—Brain Boosters: Sudoku Puzzles. (p. 274)

—Whizz Kidz: Super Word Search. (p. 2446)

Scott, Matthew, illus. see Potter, William.

Scott, Matthew A. Cyril Squirrel & the Wonderfully Worrisome Task. (p. 493)

Scott, Meg Bolton. Calamity's Christmas. (p. 309)

Scott, Melanie. Marvel Ultimate Quiz Book: Are You a Marvel Expert? (p. 1413)

Scott, Melanie, ed. see Barbieri, Robert P.

Scott, Melanie, jt. auth. see Barbieri, Robert P.

Scott, Melanie, jt. auth. see Dorling Kindersley Publishing Staff.

Scott, Melanie, jt. auth. see Marsham, Liz.

Scott, Melanie & DK. DC Comics Ultimate Character Guide, New Edition. (p. 516)

Scott, Melody S. Elijah & Moses. (p. 635)

Scott, Michael. Alchemyst: The Secrets of the Immortal Nicholas Flamel. (p. 41)

—Alchemyst. (p. 41)

—Enchantress. (p. 647)

—HECHICERA. (p. 947)

—Necromancer. (p. 1584)

—Necromancer the Secrets of the Immortal Nicholas Flamel. (p. 1584)

—Sorceress. (p. 2065)

—Sorceress the Secrets of the Immortal Nicholas Flamel. (p. 2065)

—Tom Cringle's Log. (p. 2257)

—Warlock. (p. 2379)

—Warlock the Secrets of the Immortal Nicholas Flamel. (p. 2379)

Scott, Michele. Dark Harmony: A Vivienne Taylor Horse Lover's Mystery (p. 506)

—Perfect Harmony: A Vivienne Taylor Horse Lover's Mystery (p. 1722)

—Silent Harmony (p. 2017)

Scott, Michelle. I'm Different. (p. 1098)

Scott, Mindi. Freefall. (p. 783)

—Live Through This. (p. 1332)

Scott, Molly. Broken Bones Are No Fun, but Broken Bones Won't Stop My Play! Baker, David, illus. (p. 284)

Scott, Natalie. Wheels Make it Work. (p. 2428)

Scott, O. W. Gilead Guards: A Story of War-Times in a New England Town (Classic Reprint) (p. 833)

Scott, P. E. S. Kathleen Mavourneen: An Australian Tale (Classic Reprint) (p. 1205)

Scott, Patricia, et al. Music Express - Music Express Early Years Foundation Stage: Complete Music Scheme for Early Years Foundation Stage - Second Edition (p. 1528)

Scott, Patricia Ethel Stonehouse). Years of Forgetting (Classic Reprint) (p. 2520)

Scott, Patrick. Big Beasts. (p. 216)

Scott, Peter, illus. see Clarke, Phillip.

Scott, Peter, illus. see Frith, Alex.

Scott, Peter, illus. see Greenwell, Jessica.

Scott, Peter, illus. see Khan, Sarah.

Scott, Peter, illus. see Randall, Ronne.

Scott, Peter, illus. see Rogers, Kirsteen.

Scott, Peter, illus. see Tatchell, Judy & Rogers, Kirsteen.

Scott, Peter, illus. see Turnbull, Stephanie.

Scott, Peter & Scott, Jane. Soil the Seapony. (p. 2057)

Scott, Peter David, illus. see Kahn, Sarah.

Scott, Phil. Nicknames. (p. 1604)

Scott, Robbin Joanna. Ducky's Real Life Adventures. (p. 608)

Scott, Robert Henry. Elementary Meteorology. (p. 632)

Scott, Ron. Latte's Counting Book (p. 1251)

Scott, Rose G. Tenth Life. (p. 2206)

Scott, Russell & Petrone Miller, Patti. Endangered Species Series, Elephants. Fiorillo, Gabriella, illus. (p. 649)

Scott, Sabrina & Scott, Brigett. What's That in Mom's Belly? (p. 2426)

Scott, Sandra Elaine. Home: Casa. Mills, Jasmine, illus. (p. 995)

—Magical Day Activity Book. Mills, Jasmine, illus. (p. 1380)

Scott, Sarah. Description of Millenium Hall, & the Country Adjacent: Together with the Characters of the Inhabitants, & Such Historical Anecdotes & Reflections, As May Excite in the Reader Proper Sentiments of Humanity, & Lead the Mind to the Love of Virtue. (p. 531)

Scott, Sarah Chamberlin, illus. see Green, Holly G.

Scott Scott Gatty, Alfred. Aunt Judy's Song-Book for Children - Scholar's Choice Edition. (p. 137)

Scott, Shannon. Only a Boy Named David. Lucas, Nya a, illus. (p. 1664)

Scott, Sir Walter. Fortunes of Nigel, Vol. 2 of 2 (Classic Reprint) (p. 770)

—Lady of the Lake. (p. 1238)

—Waverley: Or 't Is Sixty Years since (Classic Reprint) (p. 2386)

—Waverley. (p. 2386)

Scott, Stanley. Tales of Bohemia, Taverns, & the Underworld: Stories & Sketches of People Famous, Infamous, & Obscure (Classic Reprint) (p. 2183)

Scott, Steph & Akers, Katie. Let's Go Outside. (p. 1273)

—Rainy Day Kids Adventure Book: Outdoor Games & Activities for the Wind, Rain & Snow. (p. 1837)

Scott, Stephanie. Buckle Up: A Children's Imaginary Journey about Self-Control. Barinova, Olga, illus. (p. 289)

Scott, Stephen K. World According to Professor Petey. Scott, Stephen K. & Holbrook, Jef, illus. (p. 2501)

Scott, Steve, illus. see Parker, Jeff.

Scott, Susan, illus. see Cohen-Spence, Susan.

Scott, Susan, illus. see O'Connell, Isabel.

Scott, Sutton Selwyn. Mobilians: Or Talks about the South (Classic Reprint) (p. 1485)

—Southbooke (Classic Reprint) (p. 2069)

Scott, Sybil. Rough & Smooth, Vol. 1 Of 3: A Novel (Classic Reprint) (p. 1907)

Scott, Taira. Mommy, Mommy Why Am I So Different? (p. 1491)

Scott, Tay. One Ravenwood Halloween. Kearney, Mary Lowie, illus. (p. 1662)

—One Ravenwood Winter. Kearney, Mary Lowie, illus. (p. 1662)

Scott, Temple. Novels of the Sisters Bronte (Classic Reprint) (p. 1627)

—Silver Age: And Other Dramatic Memories (Classic Reprint) (p. 2019)

—Wisdom of Dickens (Classic Reprint) (p. 2477)

Scott, Temple, jt. auth. see Stevenson, Robert Louis.

Scott, Thomas Jefferson. Missionary Life among the Villages in India (Classic Reprint) (p. 1481)

Scott, Val. Wolves Are Sleeping Sheep. (p. 2485)

Scott, Vicki, illus. see Cooper, Jason.

Scott, Vicki, illus. see Pl Kids.

Scott, Vicki, illus. see Schulz, Charles M.

Scott, Vicki, illus. see Schulz, Charles M. & Cooper, Jason.

Scott, Vicki, illus. see Schulz, Charles M. & Gallo, Tina.

Scott, Vicki, illus. see Schulz, Charles M. & Nakamura, May.

Scott, Vicki, jt. auth. see Schulz, Charles M.

Scott, Vicki & Koth, Mona. Animals. Cottage Door Press, ed. (p. 93)

—Faces. Cottage Door Press, ed. (p. 693)

—Feelings. Cottage Door Press, ed. (p. 718)

—Love. Cottage Door Press, ed. (p. 1358)

Scott, Victoria. Hear the Wolves. (p. 944)

—Liberator. (p. 1283)

—Titans. (p. 2251)

—Violet Grenade. (p. 2360)

—We Told Six Lies. (p. 2392)

Scott, W. J. Scott's Monthly Magazine, Vol. 6: July, 1868 (Classic Reprint) (p. 1962)

Scott, Walter. Abbot: Being the Sequel of the Monastery (Classic Reprint) (p. 3)

—Abbot, Vol. 1 (Classic Reprint) (p. 3)

—Abbot, Vol. 1 Of 3: Being the Sequel of the Monastery (Classic Reprint) (p. 3)

—Abbot, Vol. 2 (Classic Reprint) (p. 3)

—Abbot, Vol. 2 of 3 (Classic Reprint) (p. 3)

—Abbot, Vol. 3 of 3 (Classic Reprint) (p. 3)

—Antiquary, Vol. 1 (Classic Reprint) (p. 103)

—Bride of Lammermoor (Classic Reprint) (p. 280)

—Bride of Lammermoor & Keepsake Stories & Chronicle of Canongate (Classic Reprint) (p. 280)

—Castle Dangerous, Appendix, Etc: Early Poems & the Lay of the Last Minstrel (Classic Reprint) (p. 340)

Scroggins, Jimmy. Three Circles - Teen Bible Study Book: Gospel Conversations for Life. (p. 2232)
—Three Circles - Teen Bible Study Leader Kit: Gospel Conversations for Life. (p. 2232)
Scroggs, Kirk. Secret Spiral of Swamp Kid. Scroggs, Kirk, illus. (p. 1979)
Scrope, George Poulett. Geology & Extinct Volcanos of Central France (Classic Reprint) (p. 818)
Scruggs, Jacquelene. Let's Begin: Activity Book. (p. 1270)
Scruggs, Kathy, tr. see Johnson, Kelly.
Scrutator, Scrutator. Lord Fitzwarine, Vol. 3 of 3 (Classic Reprint) (p. 1348)
—Squire of Beechwood, Vol. 1 Of 3: A True Tale (Classic Reprint) (p. 2094)
Scruton, Ben, illus. see Gifford, Clive.
Scruton, Clive, illus. see Goldish, Meish.
Scruton, Clive, illus. see Gray, Keith.
Scudamore, Angelika. Happy Birthday to You! (p. 921)
—Little Puppy's Busy Day. (p. 1325)
—Noah's Ark Animal ABCs (p. 1616)
Scudamore, Angelika, illus. see Ditchburn, Suzannah.
Scudamore, Angelika, illus. see Garnett, Jaye.
Scudamore, Angelika, illus. see Huff, Abby.
Scudamore, Angelika, illus. see Simon, Mary Manz.
Scudamore, Angelika, illus. see Soban Biniashvili, Freidele Galya.
Scudamore, Angelika, illus. see Stauffer, Lisa Lowe.
Scudamore, Angelika, illus. see Tafuni, Gabriele & Casey, Catherine.
Scudamore, Angelika, illus. see Wage, Erin Rose.
Scudamore, Beverly. Pure Fake (p. 1815)
Scudder, A. M. Attractive Truths in Lesson & Story (Classic Reprint) (p. 135)
Scudder, H. E. Dwellers in Five-Sisters Court (Classic Reprint) (p. 611)
Scudder, Horace E. Book of Legends (Classic Reprint) (p. 259)
—English Bodley Family (Classic Reprint) (p. 653)
—English Bodley Family, & the Viking Bodleys (Classic Reprint) (p. 653)
—Fables & Folk Stories (Classic Reprint) (p. 690)
—Mr. Bodley Abroad, and, the Bodley Grandchildren & Their Journey in Holland (Classic Reprint) (p. 1518)
Scudder, Horace Elisha. American Prose: Hawthorne; Irving; Longfellow Whittier; Holmes; Lowell; Thoreau; Emerson (Classic Reprint) (p. 73)
—American Prose. (p. 73)
—American Prose; (p. 73)
—Bodley Grandchildren: And Their Journey in Holland (Classic Reprint) (p. 253)
—Bodleys Afoot (Classic Reprint) (p. 253)
—Bodleys on Wheels (Classic Reprint) (p. 253)
—Bodleys on Wheels & the Bodleys Afoot (Classic Reprint) (p. 253)
—Bodleys Telling Stories (Classic Reprint) (p. 253)
—Book of Folk Stories (Classic Reprint) (p. 258)
—Childhood in Literature & Art, with Some Observations on Literature for Children: A Study - Scholar's Choice Edition. (p. 370)
—Childhood in Literature & Art with Some Observations on Literature for Children - Scholar's Choice Edition. (p. 370)
—Children's Book: A Collection of the Best & Most Famous Stories & Poems in the English Language (Classic Reprint) (p. 372)
—Doings of the Bodley Family: In Town & Country (Classic Reprint) (p. 578)
—Doings of the Bodley Family in Town & Country. (p. 578)
—Mr. Bodley Abroad (Classic Reprint) (p. 1518)
—Riverside Literature Series; Verse & Prose for Beginners in Reading: Selected from English & American Literature. (p. 1887)
—Riverside Magazine for Young People, 1870, Vol. 4: An Illustrated Monthly (Classic Reprint) (p. 1888)
—Stories from My Attic (Classic Reprint) (p. 2124)
—Verse & Prose for Beginners in Reading, Vol. 1 Of 2: Selected from English & American Literature (Classic Reprint) (p. 2352)
—Viking Bodleys: An Excursion into Norway & Denmark (Classic Reprint) (p. 2357)
Scudder, Horace Elisha & And Others. American Prose. (p. 73)
Scudder, Joseph. Captain Waltham: A Tale of Southern India (Classic Reprint) (p. 326)
Scudder, Robert a. My Experience in the World War (Classic Reprint) (p. 1538)
Scudder, Samuel Hubbard. Butterflies: Their Structure, Changes & Life-Histories, with Special Reference to American Forms; Being an Application of the Doctrine of Descent to the Study of Butterflies; with an Appendix of Practical Instructions (Classic Reprint) (p. 303)
—Butterflies of the Eastern United States & Canada, Vol. 2: With Special Reference to New England; Lycaenidae, Papilionidae, Hesperidae (Classic Reprint) (p. 303)
Scudder, Vida Dutton. Listener in Babel: Being a Series of Imaginary Conversations Held (Classic Reprint) (p. 1308)
—Listener in Babel: Being a Series of Imaginary Conversations Held at the Close of the Last Century (Classic Reprint) (p. 1308)
Scuderi, Lucia. Si Oigo. Turrion, Celia, tr. (p. 2014)
—Si Sabe A. Turrion, Celia, tr. (p. 2014)
—Si Toco. Turrion, Celia, tr. (p. 2014)
Scudery, Madeleine de. Conversations Morales de l'Esperance, l'Envie, la Paresse, la Tyrannie de l'Usage, la Colere, l'Incertitude, Vol. 1 (Classic Reprint) (p. 446)
Scuh, Mari. Collies. (p. 416)
Scull, Elaine, illus. see Buck, Pearl S.
Scull, Marie-Louise, illus. see MacDonald, Margaret.
Scully, B. E. Tower of Together. (p. 2269)
Scully, W.C. White Hecatomb: And Other Stories (Classic Reprint) (p. 2444)
Scully, William Charles. Between Sun & Sand: A Tale of an African Desert (Classic Reprint) (p. 210)
—By Veldt & Kopje (Classic Reprint) (p. 306)
—Reminiscences of a South African Pioneer. (p. 1865)
—Reminiscences of a South African Pioneer (1st Series Wanderjahre) (Classic Reprint) (p. 1865)
Scupoli, Lorenzo. Spiritual Combat. (p. 2084)
Scurlark, Robin Law. T Is for Texas Tech. (p. 2174)
Scutts, Julian. What Makes Life Worth Living, Poetry, Children & Animals. (p. 2418)
Scythe, Adam, illus. see Rayne, C. M.
Sdralevich, Teresa. Poster Power: Great Posters & How to Make Them. (p. 1780)
Sea, Fanny P. Nursery, Vol. 1: A Magazine for Youngest Readers (Classic Reprint) (p. 1631)
Seabag-Montefiore, Mary. Secret Garden. (p. 1975)
Seabaugh, Jan, illus. see Shookuhi, Aminjon.
Seabolt, Carolyn. Oliver's Travels. (p. 1650)
Seaborn, Julia. Pippin the Poodle Dog. (p. 1749)
Seabra, Carla. Little Girl Monster Who Only Wore Tutus. (p. 1317)
Seabrook, Heather. Lego Chima - Heroes' Quest. (p. 1264)
Seabrook, Lochlainn. Honest Jeff & Dishonest Abe: A Southern Children's Guide to the Civil War. (p. 998)
—Quotable Nathan Bedford Forrest: Selections from the Writings & Speeches of the Confederacy's Most Brilliant Cavalryman. (p. 1829)
—Saddle, Sword, & Gun: A Biography of Nathan Bedford Forrest for Teens. (p. 1921)
Seabrooke, Brenda. Boy Who Saved the Town Burns, Howard M., illus. (p. 271)
—Chester Town Tea Party Smith, Nancy C., illus. (p. 366)
Seabrooks, Lydia, illus. see Young, Elizabeth.
Seachrest, Effie. Story Land: Outlines for the Child Life Composition Pictures (Classic Reprint) (p. 2128)
Seader, Karen. Be Everything You Can Be: Book 2. Lynn, Valerie, illus. (p. 177)
—In Your Heart Lives a Rainbow: Book 1. Lynn, Valerie, illus. (p. 1112)
—Ride the Rainbow: Book 3. Lynn, Valerie, illus. (p. 1878)
Seado, Sarah. Houses of Lorian Hollow: The Soundtrack to Your Scream. (p. 1024)
Seafield, Frank. Literature & Curiosities of Dreams, Vol. 1 Of 2: A Commonplace Book of Speculations Concerning the Mystery of Dreams & Visions, Records of Curious & Well-Authenticated Dreams, & Notes on the Various Modes of Interpretation Adopted in Ancient A. (p. 1309)
Seager, Charlotte. My [Secret] YouTube Life. (p. 1560)
Seager, Chloe. Dating Disasters of Emma Nash. (p. 509)
Seager, Patsy, illus. see Larter, Maureen.
Seagle, Steven T. Camp Midnight. (p. 315)
—Camp Midnight vs. Camp Daybright. (p. 315)
Seagram, Giles. Bushmen All: A Romance of the Never-Never (Classic Reprint) (p. 301)
Seagrave, Sadie Fuller. Saints' Rest (Classic Reprint) (p. 1924)
Seagraves, Erin, jt. auth. see Martínez, Clarissa G.
Seagraves, Erin & Baker, Heather. My Neighbors & Their Simple Machines. (p. 1557)
Seagraves, Sabrina. Dancer. (p. 500)
Seagull, Robert. Adventure to Septumus Sevusere & the Magic Glowing Rings. (p. 19)
—Mindbender's Revenge Book One. (p. 1470)
Seah, Audrey, et al. Vietnam. (p. 2357)
Seah, Elliott. Elliott's Guide to Dinosaurs. (p. 638)
Seahorn, Tara. Hold Me, Mold Me, Bold Me. (p. 987)
—Lost & Found. (p. 1352)
Seahorse, Risa, illus. see Ryan, Ruth.
Seal, Caitlin. Trinity of Bones. (p. 2288)
—Twice Dead. (p. 2304)
Seal, Daisy, selected by. Cute Animals US: Color by Numbers. (p. 491)
—Exotic Birds US: Color by Numbers. (p. 677)
Seal, Glenda. Birth of Billy Bird. (p. 233)
Seal, Julia. Farmyard Words. (p. 711)
—Jungle 123. (p. 1189)
—Sketchbook. (p. 2030)
Seal, Julia, illus. see Atkins, Jill.
Seal, Julia, illus. see Bucknell, Kate.
Seal, Julia, illus. see Dale, Elizabeth.
Seal, Julia, illus. see Gifford, Kathie Lee.
Seal, Julia, illus. see Joyce, Melanie.
Seal, Julia, illus. see Put Me In The Story & Sully, Katherine.
Seal, Kerry. Five Silly Pumpkins: A Pop-up Halloween Book. Smith, Jane, illus. (p. 745)
Seal, Vickie Di-Ann. Edgar Tells the Truth. (p. 625)
Seale, Emma S. Jingles of a Happy Mother Goose (Classic Reprint) (p. 1169)
Seale, Stephen E., ed. see Lockwood, Ingersoll.
Sealey, Edmund J. Toast. (p. 2254)
Sealey, John. Magic Wishbone. (p. 1379)
Sealey, Katrina. Angry, Angry Angus. (p. 87)
Sealey, M. A. Ed Lindsay. Raising Girls' Voices: Guiding Girls to Listen, Trust, Share, & Use Their Voices. (p. 1838)
Sealey, Philip. Sorcerer's Tome. (p. 2065)
Sealock, Rick, illus. see Schnetzler, Pattie L.
Seals, A. B. Rockford: A Romance (Classic Reprint) (p. 1895)
—Rockford. (p. 1895)
Sealsfield, Charles. Cabin Book: Or, National Characteristics (Classic Reprint) (p. 307)
—Rambleton: A Romance of Fashionable Life in New-York During the Great Speculation of 1836 (Classic Reprint) (p. 1839)
—Tokeah, Vol. 2 Of 2: Or, the White Rose (Classic Reprint) (p. 2256)
Sealy, T. H. Porcelain Tower, or Nine Stories of China (Classic Reprint) (p. 1778)
Seaman, Annalie. Build! a Knight's Castle: Paper Toy Archaeology. (p. 293)
Seaman, Augusta Huiell. Boarded-Up House. (p. 251)
—Sapphire Signet (Classic Reprint) (p. 1934)
—Slipper Point Mystery (Classic Reprint) (p. 2038)
Seaman, Elizabeth Cochran. Six Months in Mexico (Classic Reprint) (p. 2028)
Seaman, Jim & Vitalich, Vivienne. Where Does the Trombone Go? the Sex Ed Questions You Won't Believe Kids Ask (and Answered by Their Teachers) (p. 2436)
Seaman, Kathleen. Annycole (p. 100)
Seaman, Lucy. Mr Mouse Morgan. Swope, Brenda, illus. (p. 1519)
Seaman, Owen. Borrowed Plumes (Classic Reprint) (p. 263)
—Oedipus the Wreck, or to Trace the Knave (Classic Reprint) (p. 1638)
—Punch, Vol. 144: January-June, 1913 (Classic Reprint) (p. 1813)
—Punch, Vol. 150: January-June, 1916 (Classic Reprint) (p. 1813)
—Punch, Vol. 152: January-June, 1917 (Classic Reprint) (p. 1813)
—Punch, Vol. 154: January-June, 1918 (Classic Reprint) (p. 1813)
—Punch's Twenty Almanacks, 1842-1861 (Classic Reprint) (p. 1814)
Seamon, Hollis. Somebody up There Hates You: A Novel. (p. 2060)
Seamus. Company of the Flaming Sword: Buried Treasure. (p. 433)
Sean Lee. Longwold. (p. 1344)
Sean Ryan, jt. auth. see Cadenhead, MacKenzie.
Searchfield, Emilie. Heiress of Wyvern Court. (p. 949)
Searcy, Amanda. I'll Find You. (p. 1095)
—Truth Beneath the Lies. (p. 2297)
—Watch You Burn. (p. 2383)
Searing, A. E. P. Land of Rip Van Winkle: A Tour Through the Romantic Parts of the Catskills; Its Legends & Traditions (Classic Reprint) (p. 1242)
Searl, Duncan. Beagle: A Howling Good Time. (p. 178)
—Cairn Terrier: Hero of Oz. (p. 309)
Searle, E. W. With a Policeman in South Africa, or Three Years in the Natal Mounted Police: A True Narrative (Classic Reprint) (p. 2481)
Searle, January. Leaves from Sherwood Forest (Classic Reprint) (p. 1259)
Searle, Katharine. Three War Sketches: Her Story, the March of Truth, Hatred Sketches Her Story the March of Truth (Classic Reprint) (p. 2235)
—Two Plays: Roderick's Career, Game (Classic Reprint) (p. 2309)
Searle, Margaret Cassie. Bad Debts: A Drama in One Act (Classic Reprint) (p. 157)
Searles, Jean Randolph. Further Annals of the Girl in the Slumber-Boots (Classic Reprint) (p. 802)
Searles, William Henry. Field Engineering: A Handbook of the Theory & Practice of Railway Surveying, Location, & Construction (Classic Reprint) (p. 723)
Sears, Anna Wentworth. Two on a Tour in South America (Classic Reprint) (p. 2309)
Sears, Baldwin. Circle in the Square: The Story of a New Battle on Old Fields (Classic Reprint) (p. 392)
Sears, Bart, illus. see Marz, Ron.
Sears, Ben. House of the Black Spot. (p. 1023)
—Ideal Copy. (p. 1089)
Sears, Brenda L. Boonday & the Covfefee Tree: The Answer or the Problem. (p. 261)
Sears, Cynthia A. Dragon Lord: The Fairy Princess Chronicles - Book 2. (p. 594)
—Dragon's Eye. (p. 595)
—Fairy Queen: The Fairy Princess Chronicles - Book 5. (p. 697)
—Secret of the Fae: The Fairy Princess Chronicles - Book 7. (p. 1977)
Sears, Edmund H. Pictures of the Olden Time: As Shown in the Fortunes of a Family of the Pilgrims (Classic Reprint) (p. 1741)
Sears, Edmund Hamilton. Son of the Prefect: A Story of the Reign of Tiberius (Classic Reprint) (p. 2062)
Sears, Elizabeth. Film Fun: January, 1917 (Classic Reprint) (p. 726)
Sears, Gale. Missing Christmas Treasure. Johnson, Meredith, illus. (p. 1480)
Sears, George Washington. Woodcraft & Camping. (p. 2491)
Sears, Hamblen. Box of Matches (Classic Reprint) (p. 266)
Sears, Herbert Mason. Journal of a Canteen Worker (Classic Reprint) (p. 1180)
Sears, John Van Der Zee. My Friends at Brook Farm. (p. 1548)
—My Friends at Brook Farm (Classic Reprint) (p. 1548)
Sears, Joseph Hamblen. None but the Brave (Classic Reprint) (p. 1618)
Sears, Kathleen. Weather 101: From Doppler Radar & Long-Range Forecasts to the Polar Vortex & Climate Change, Everything You Need to Know about the Study of Weather. (p. 2394)
Searson, J. W. Studies in Reading (Classic Reprint) (p. 2144)
Seaton, Bryan, ed. see Middleton, Gayle & Dwonch, Dave.
Seaton, Bryan, ed. see Zag, Jeremy, et al.
Seaton, Kit, illus. see Bardugo, Leigh.
Seaton, Sierra, illus. see Ferguson, Tina L.
Seaton, William. Life Lessons for Mike. Sadeghi, Mina, illus. (p. 1293)
Seatsfield, Seatsfield. Life in the New World: Or Sketches of American Society (Classic Reprint) (p. 1293)
Seatter, Pamela, illus. see Douglass Thom, Kara.
Seatter, Pamela, illus. see Skwish, Emily.
Seattle Public Library Foundation, Seattle Public & Somali Family Task Force, Somali Family, compiled by. Baro Af-Soomaali. (p. 167)
—Baro Tirinta Af Soomaaliga: Learn to Count in Somali. (p. 167)
Seaver, C. H. American Boys' Book of Electricity. (p. 70)
Seaver, Edwin P. Franklin Primary Arithmetic. (p. 779)
Seaver, H. L. Latin School Register, Vol. 15: October, 1895 (Classic Reprint) (p. 1250)
—Latin School Register, Vol. 15: February, 1896 (Classic Reprint) (p. 1250)
Seaver, Robert, jt. auth. see Cowper, William.
Seaverns, Fanny P. Nursery, 1869, Vol. 5: A Monthly Magazine for Youngest Readers (Classic Reprint) (p. 1631)
—Nursery, 1877, Vol. 21: A Monthly Magazine for Youngest Readers (Classic Reprint) (p. 1631)
—Nursery, Vol. 11: A Monthly Magazine for Youngest Readers (Classic Reprint) (p. 1631)
—Nursery, Vol. 13: A Monthly Magazine for Youngest Readers (Classic Reprint) (p. 1631)
—Nursery, Vol. 14: A Monthly Magazine for Youngest Readers (Classic Reprint) (p. 1631)
—Nursery, Vol. 3: A Magazine for Youngest Readers (Classic Reprint) (p. 1631)
Seavey, Lura Rogers. Czech Republic: Enchantment of the World. (p. 493)
—Ethiopia. (p. 666)
—Nigeria. (p. 1604)
Seavy, Tom. Dom Quick Jota (Classic Reprint) (p. 580)
Seaward, Edward. Sir Edward Seaward's Narrative of His Shipwreck, & Consequent Discovery of Certain Islands in the Caribbean Sea, Vol. 1 Of 3: With a Detail of Many Extraordinary & Highly Interesting Events in His Life, from the Year 1733 to 1749, As Written in His Ow. (p. 2025)
Seawell, Molly Elliot. Betty at Fort Blizzard (Classic Reprint) (p. 209)
—Betty's Virginia Christmas (Classic Reprint) (p. 210)
—Children of Destiny (Classic Reprint) (p. 371)
—Franceska (Classic Reprint) (p. 776)
—Great Scoop (Classic Reprint) (p. 889)
—History of the Lady Betty Stair: A Novel (Classic Reprint) (p. 980)
—Lively Adventures of Gavin Hamilton. (p. 1332)
—Lively Adventures of Gavin Hamilton (Classic Reprint) (p. 1332)
—Maid Marion, & Other Stories (Classic Reprint) (p. 1383)
—Strange, Sad Comedy (Classic Reprint) (p. 2138)
—Throckmorton: A Novel (Classic Reprint) (p. 2236)
—Throckmorton. (p. 2236)
—Victory (Classic Reprint) (p. 2356)
Seaworthy, Gregory. Nag's Head, or Two Months among the Bankers: A Story of Sea-Shore Life & Manners (Classic Reprint) (p. 1572)
Seaworthy, Oscar. Port Side Pirates Puzzle. Harter, Debbie, illus. (p. 1778)
Seaworthy, Oscar & Collins, Mark. Port Side Pirates! Harter, Debbie, illus. (p. 1778)
Seay, Dave, illus. see Counce, Betty.
Seba, Jaime. Being Gay, Staying Healthy. (p. 194)
—Coming Out: Telling Family & Friends. (p. 430)
—Ellen DeGeneres: From Comedy Club to Talk Show. (p. 637)
—Gallup Guides for Youth Facing Persistent Prejudice: Blacks. (p. 806)
—Gallup Guides for Youth Facing Persistent Prejudice. (p. 806)
—Gallup Guides for Youth Facing Persistent Prejudice - The LGBT Community. (p. 806)
—Gay & Lesbian Role Models. (p. 812)
—Gay Characters in Theatre, Movies, & Television: New Roles, New Attitudes. (p. 812)
—Gay Issues & Politics: Marriage, the Military, & Work Place Discrimination. (p. 812)
—Gay People of Color: Facing Prejudices, Forging Identities. (p. 812)
—Gays & Mental Health: Fighting Depression, Saying No to Suicide. (p. 812)
—Homosexuality Around the World: Safe Havens, Cultural Challenges. (p. 998)
Seba, Jaime A. Feeling Wrong in Your Own Body: Understanding What It Means to Be Transgender. (p. 718)
—Gay & Lesbian Role Models. (p. 812)
—Gay Issues & Politics: Marriage, the Military, & Work Place Discrimination. (p. 812)
—Smashing the Stereotypes: What Does It Mean to Be Gay, Lesbian, Bisexual, or Transgender? (p. 2041)
Seba, Jaime & Sanna, Ellyn. Gallup Guides for Youth Facing Persistent Prejudice. (p. 806)
Sebag-Montefiore, Mary, ed. Tale of Two Cities: Internet-Referenced. Ablett, Barry, illus. (p. 2180)
Sebastian, illus. see Cabanillas, Laura Sabin.
Sebastian Bolden, E. Tabansi & the Golden Touch. (p. 2174)
Sebastian, Eleonore, illus. see Fadden, Chelsea.
Sebastian, Emily. Armadillos. (p. 117)
—Badgers. (p. 159)
—Chipmunks. (p. 379)
—Colonial & Postcolonial Experience in Latin America & the Caribbean. (p. 418)
—Foxes. (p. 774)
—Moles. (p. 1489)
—Mongooses. (p. 1493)
—My Brothers & Sisters: MIS Hermanos. (p. 1535)
—My Brothers & Sisters. (p. 1535)
—My Cousins: MIS Primos. (p. 1536)
—My Cousins. (p. 1536)
—My Dad. (p. 1536)
—My Dad(Mi Papá) (p. 1536)
—Technology of the Medieval & Early Modern Worlds (p. 2197)
Sebastian, Emily, ed. Culture of Russia. (p. 484)
—Geography of Russia. (p. 817)
Sebastian, Laura. Ash Princess. (p. 125)
—Dama de Humo / Lady Smoke. (p. 499)
—Ember Queen. (p. 641)
—Lady Smoke. (p. 1238)
—Princesa de Cenizas / Ash Princes. (p. 1795)
Sebastian Quigley, Sebastian, illus. see Harris, Nicholas.
Sebastián, Soledad, illus. see Scholastic, Inc. Staff.
Sebastian, Teresa L. & Harrell, Angel R. Kootie Kids & the Attack of the Poot Troop. (p. 1231)
Sebe, Masayuki. 100 Animals on Parade! Sebe, Masayuki, illus. (p. 2556)
—100 Hungry Monkeys! (p. 2557)
—100 Hungry Monkeys! Sebe, Masayuki, illus. (p. 2557)
—Let's Count To 100! Sebe, Masayuki, illus. (p. 1271)
Sebela, Christopher. Crowded Volume 2. (p. 479)
Sebestyen, Adam. Characters of Letterworld. Sebestyen, Adam, illus. (p. 358)
Sebhatu, Temnete, ed. Best Teen Writing of 2008. (p. 208)
Sebra, Richard. It's Chinese New Year! (p. 1144)
—It's Christmas! (p. 1144)
—It's Cinco de Mayo! (p. 1144)
—It's Diwali! (p. 1144)
—It's Easter! (p. 1145)
—It's Halloween! (p. 1145)

S

Segret, Alexia. Voile Magique. (p. 2365)
Seguin, Karen C. Christmas Story. (p. 387)
Seguin, Lisbeth Gooch. Rural England: Loiterings along the Lanes, the Common-Sides, & the Meadow-Paths, with Peeps into the Halls, Farms, & Cottages (Classic Reprint) (p. 1916)
Seguin, Marilyn. No Ordinary Lives: Four 19th Century Teenage Diaries. (p. 1614)
—Young & Courageous: American Girls Who Made History. (p. 2530)
Seguin-Magee, Luke, illus. see Gallo, Tina.
Séguin-Magee, Luke, illus. see Morey, Allan.
Séguin-Magee, Luke, illus. see Nawrocki, Mike.
Séguin-Magee, Luke, illus. see Peale, Jonathan.
Segundo, Sondra Simone & Segundo, Sondra Simone. Killer Whale Eyes. (p. 1217)
Segur, Comtes. Auberge de l Ange Gard. (p. 135)
—Bon Petit Diable. (p. 255)
—Memoires d un Ane. (p. 1444)
—Petite Fill Mode Segur. (p. 1731)
—Vacances Segur. (p. 2343)
Segur, Comtesse De. Petites Filles Modeles. (p. 1731)
Segur, Comtesse De, see De Segur, Comtesse.
Segur, De. Bons Enfants (Classic Reprint) (p. 256)
—Little Saint of Nine Years: A Biographical Notice (Classic Reprint) (p. 1327)
Segur, Louis Gaston De. Wonders of Lourdes (Classic Reprint) (p. 2490)
Segur, Mme La Comtesse De. Malheurs de Sophie (Classic Reprint) (p. 1392)
Segur, Sophie. Old French Fairy Tales. (p. 1645)
—Old French Fairy Tales (Classic Reprint) (p. 1645)
—Petites Filles Modeles. (p. 1731)
—Petites Filles Modeles (Classic Reprint) (p. 1731)
Segur, Sophie Comtesse De. Malheurs de Sophie (Classic Reprint) (p. 1392)
Segura, Alex. Star Wars Poe Dameron: Free Fall. (p. 2104)
Segura, Jovan Carl, illus. see Muncaster, Sandie.
Segura, Judith. Valija de Cuentos Familiares. Gallo, Valeria, illus. (p. 2344)
Segura, Samuel. Metal. (p. 1452)
Sehgal, Kabir & Sehgal, Surishtha. Bucket of Blessings. Tsong, Jing Jing, illus. (p. 289)
—P Is for Poppadoms! An Indian Alphabet Book. Ito, Hazel, illus. (p. 1690)
—Thread of Love. Hoang, Zara Gonzalez, illus. (p. 2231)
—Wheels on the Tuk Tuk. Golden, Jess, illus. (p. 2428)
Sehgal, Surishtha & Sehgal, Kabir. Festival of Colors. Harrison, Vashti, illus. (p. 721)
Sehler, Mark, illus. see Smith, Annette.
Sehlin, Gunhild. Mary's Little Donkey Muller, Helene, illus. (p. 1416)
—Mary's Little Donkey: And the Escape to Egypt Latham, Hugh, tr. (p. 1416)
Sehr, V. Kaci. Elephant Who Believes in Santa Claus. (p. 634)
—Unicorn in Disguise. (p. 2328)
Seib, Anke & Cameron, Emma. Out of This Place. (p. 1683)
Seibel, Monique, illus. see Adler, Pamela.
Seibert, August. Trip to Germany During Wartime, by a Medical Free-Lance (Classic Reprint) (p. 2289)
Seibert, Elizabeth A. Bro Code. (p. 284)
Seibert, Mary Frances. Zulma: A Story of the Old South (Classic Reprint) (p. 2545)
Seibert, Monica L. I Am Lily, Hear Me Roar. (p. 1059)
Seibido, Shuppan. Collection of Trains. (p. 415)
Seibold, J. Otto. Lost Sloth. (p. 1355)
Seibold, J. Otto, illus. see Sierra, Judy.
Seibold, Thomas K. 12 Joys of Christmas. McCulley Seibold, Sheri, illus. (p. 2551)
Seid, Christina. Saturdays in Chinatown. (p. 1936)
Seidel, Charleen. Tale of Tails: A Grand Animal Anthology. Cannon, Lane, illus. (p. 2180)
—Tale of Tails: A Grand Animal Anthology. Lane, Cannon, illus. (p. 2180)
Seidel, Jeff. Alabama Crimson Tide (p. 39)
—Chelsea FC. (p. 365)
—College Football Underdog Stories. (p. 415)
—Georgia Bulldogs. (p. 820)
—Pro Baseball Upsets. (p. 1802)
—South Carolina Gamecocks. (p. 2068)
—Ultimate College Basketball Road Trip. (p. 2314)
—Virginia Tech Hokies. (p. 2361)
Seidelman, Michael. Everyone Dies in the Garden of Syn. (p. 672)
—No One Dies in the Garden of Syn. (p. 1614)
Seiden, Art, illus. see Berg, Jean Horton & dePaola, Tomie.
Seiden, Art, illus. see Brown, Margaret Wise.
Seiden, Art, illus. see Grosset and Dunlap Staff & dePaola, Tomie.
Seidenberg, Mark & Milky, D. J. Kung Fu Klutz & Karate Cool (p. 1233)
Seiders, Marian, illus. see Ali, Anila & Gottlieb, Karen.
Seidler, R. M. Key to Time. (p. 1212)
Seidler, Tor. Chien a New York. (p. 369)
—Firstborn. Sheban, Chris, illus. (p. 740)
—Oh, Rats! Evans, Gabriel, illus. (p. 1642)
Seidlitz, Lauri. 1990: Canadian Decades. (p. 2561)
—Legacy of World War II. (p. 1261)
Seidlitz, Serge, illus. see Lerner, Jarrett.
Seidman, Amy. Adventures of Bebop Bunny. (p. 21)
Seidman, David. What If I'm an Atheist? A Teen's Guide to Exploring a Life Without Religion. (p. 2413)
Seidman, David, jt. auth. see January, Brendan.
Seidman, Richard. Secret of Ebbets Field. (p. 1977)
Seif, Daniel. April Gets Adopted! The Story of April, & How She Finds Her Forever Home. All of April's Adventures Begin Here! Seif, Diana, ed. (p. 108)
Seif, Diana, ed. see Seif, Daniel.
Seif Simpson, Martha. What NOT to Give Your Mom on Mother's Day Christy, Jana, illus. (p. 2419)
Seife, Emily, ed. see Reeve, Philip.
Seiferling, Dena, illus. see Becker, Helaine.
Seifert, Brandon. Witch Doctor Volume 2: Mal Practice TP: Mal Practice TP. (p. 2479)
Seifert, Sheila, jt. auth. see Hering, Marianne.
Seifert, Sheila & Brack, Chris. Poison at the Pump. (p. 1767)
—Swept into the Sea. (p. 2169)
Seifert, Theresa. Sandy Rose. (p. 1931)
Seigel, Jonathan & Rother, Beverly S. Myrtle the Turtle & Popeye the Mouse: Learning about Our Solar System. (p. 1566)
Seigel, Rachel. California & Other Western Wildfires. (p. 310)
—Debate about Playing Video Games. (p. 522)
—Debate about School Uniforms. (p. 522)
—Ed Sheeran. (p. 624)
—Vampires. (p. 2346)
Seigel , Rachel. Vampires. (p. 2346)
Seigerman, David. Becky Sauerbrunn. (p. 187)
—Tamba Hali. (p. 2189)
Seigle, Marilyn. Mouse Caper. Penley, Maegan, illus. (p. 1514)
Seigneur, Francoise. Panique Au Parc. (p. 1696)
—Petites Graines de la Tendresse. (p. 1731)
—Petites Graines de L'Amour. (p. 1731)
—Rêverie. (p. 1873)
—Rose et le Jardinier. Tsubomi No Yume, illus. (p. 1905)
Seiler, Carl. Handbook of the Diagnosis & Treatment of Diseases of the Throat, Nose, & Naso-Pharynx (Classic Reprint) (p. 915)
Seiler, George P. Smokeville's Social: A Minstrel Show in Two Parts (Classic Reprint) (p. 2043)
Seim, Donna Marie. Hurricane Mia: A Caribbean Adventure. Spellman, Susan, illus. (p. 1054)
Seinor, Karen. Human Body. (p. 1049)
Seiple, Samantha. Byrd & Igloo: A Polar Adventure. (p. 306)
—Death on the River of Doubt: Theodore Roosevelt's Amazon Adventure. (p. 521)
—Death on the River of Doubt: Theodore Roosevelt's Amazon Adventure. (p. 521)
—Lincoln's Spymaster: Allan Pinkerton, America's First Private Eye. (p. 1303)
—Lincoln's Spymaster: Allan Pinkerton, America's First Private Eye. (p. 1303)
—Nazi Saboteurs: Hitler's Secret Attack on America. (p. 1583)
Seiple, Susan K. What's a Witch to Do? (p. 2423)
Seiple, Todd, jt. auth. see Seiple, Samantha.
Seiss, Ellie. Best Friends: A Chock-a-Block Book. Scanlon, Michael, illus. (p. 206)
—Dora's Princess Pals. (p. 586)
Seiss, Ellie & Random House Staff. Dora & the Unicorn King. (p. 585)
Seither, Marci. Miss Marci Goes to Ireland. (p. 1479)
SEITOUSHA. I Love Japan: An English-Japanese Picture Book. (p. 1069)
Seitz, Don Carlos. Elba & Elsewhere (Classic Reprint) (p. 630)
—Farm Voices (Classic Reprint) (p. 710)
—Whistler Stories (Classic Reprint) (p. 2443)
Seitz, J. B. Freddy the Flea. (p. 781)
Seitz, Melissa. Stewie Meets New Friends. Accrocco, Anthony, illus. (p. 2117)
Seiver, Julia A. B. Birkwood: A Novel (Classic Reprint) (p. 233)
Seivwright, Leonard, illus. see Landy, Adrienne.
Seixas, Ana, illus. see Flint, Katy.
Seixas, Ana, illus. see Gifford, Clive.
Sejanus, Sejanus. Littledale, Vol. 1 (Classic Reprint) (p. 1330)
—Littledale, Vol. 2 of 3 (Classic Reprint) (p. 1330)
—Littledale, Vol. 3 of 3 (Classic Reprint) (p. 1330)
Sejour, Achille Pierre Dionis Du. Essai Sur les Comètes en Général, et Particulièrement Sur Celles Qui Peuvent Approcher de l'Orbite de la Terre (Classic Reprint) (p. 663)
Sejung, Kim. D'Bardeur Rouge(le) (p. 516)
Sekai, Sakura. Hi ! Taxi. (p. 964)
Sekaz, Jennah, illus. see Toney, Toni.
Seki, Sunny. Last Kappa of Old Japan: A Magical Journey of Two Friends. Seki, Sunny, illus. (p. 1248)
—Yuko-Chan & the Daruma Doll: The Adventures of a Blind Japanese Girl Who Saves Her Village. (p. 2536)
Seki, Sunny, illus. see Moon, Josephine.
Sekiya, Seiku. Earthquake Investigation Committee Catalogue of Japanese Earthquakes (Classic Reprint) (p. 617)
Sekoto, Gerard. Short & Billy Boy: A Tale of Two Naughty Dogs. (p. 2010)
Sekowsky, Mike, illus. see Fox, Gardner & DC Comics Staff.
Sekula, John, illus. see Villabona, Nancy Sue.
Sekulic, Britt, illus. see Payne, Ed & Johnson, Vail.
Selak, Joy H. Ceegee's Gift. (p. 348)
Selber, Danielle. Pope Francis Bobblehead. (p. 1776)
Selbert, Kathryn. War Dogs. Selbert, Kathryn, illus. (p. 2376)
—Ye Cannae Shove Yer Granny off a Bus: A Favourite Scottish Rhyme with Moving Parts (p. 2518)
Selbert, Kathryn, illus. see Colombe, Rose.
Selbert, Kathryn, illus. see Dismondy, Maria.
Selbert, Kathryn, illus. see Golden, Lucy.
Selbert, Kathryn, illus. see Jinks, Jenny.
Selbert, Kathryn, illus. see Marx, Jonny.
Selbert, Kathryn, illus. see Puffinton, Brick.
Selbert, Kathryn, illus. see Swift, Ginger.
Selbert, Kathryn, illus. see Williamson, Karen.
Selbherr, C. Charlie & Molly Coloring & Word Search Book for Kids: Dog Coloring Book for Ages 5 & up. (Us Version) Kahn, M., illus. (p. 359)
—Charlie Makes a Friend: Join in Charlie's Adventures As He Searches for a Playmate. Book 2 from 'the Charlie & Molly Book Collection'. Bedtime Story, Rhyming Books, Picture Books, Dog Books. Kahn, M., illus. (p. 360)
—Coloring & Word Search Book for Kids: Book 1 - Coloring Book for Ages 5 & up. (Us Version) Kahn, M., illus. (p. 422)
—My Mate Molly & My Chum Charlie: Children's Book Introducing Two Dog Friends & Their Family, Bedtime Story, Rhyming Books, Picture Books, Book 1. Kahn, M., illus. (p. 1555)
—What Makes My Dad Special? Nugraha, illus. (p. 2418)
Selbrede, C. M. Valley Chronicles: Quest. (p. 2344)
Selby, Ashley, illus. see VonFeder, Rosa.
Selby, Charles. Boots at the Swan: A Farce in One Act (Classic Reprint) (p. 262)
—Phantom Breakfast! A Farce in One Act (Classic Reprint) (p. 1732)
—Young Mother: A Comic Drama in One Act (Classic Reprint) (p. 2531)
Selby, Clarence J. Echoes from the Rainbow City (Classic Reprint) (p. 623)
Selby, Joel, illus. see VonFeder, Rosa.
Selby, Shannon, illus. see Coffey, Joe.
Selby, Thomas G. Chinaman: In His Own Stories (Classic Reprint) (p. 378)
Selden, Catharine. English Nun, or the Sorrows of Edward & Louisa: A Novel (Classic Reprint) (p. 654)
Selden, G. C. Dartmouth Sketches: Selected from the Undergraduate Publications of Dartmouth College (Classic Reprint) (p. 508)
Selden, George. Harry Kitten & Tucker Mouse / Chester Cricket's Pigeon Ride: Two Books in One. Williams, Garth, illus. (p. 934)
—Tucker's Countryside. Williams, Garth, illus. (p. 2298)
Selden, Samuel, ed. see Shakespeare, William.
Seleccion. Declamador Universal. (p. 523)
Selene, Lyra. Amber & Dusk. (p. 67)
Seles, Monica. Love Match. (p. 1360)
Seles, Monica & LaRosa, James. Academy: Game On (p. 9)
—Game On. (p. 807)
Self, David. Saint Paul Cockcroft, Jason, illus. (p. 1923)
Self, H. I. M. Tramp's Scraps (Classic Reprint) (p. 2277)
Self, Jeffery. Drag Teen. (p. 592)
—Very, Very Bad Thing. (p. 2354)
Self, Margaret Cabell. Treasury of Horse Stories (Classic Reprint) (p. 2283)
Self, Tammy. Love of a Bright Star. (p. 1360)
Selfors, Suzanne. Coffeehouse Angel. (p. 412)
—Fairy Swarm. Santat, Dan, illus. (p. 697)
—Fortune's Magic Farm. (p. 770)
—Lonely Lake Monster. Santat, Dan, illus. (p. 1342)
—Order of the Unicorn. Santat, Dan, illus. (p. 1669)
—Sasquatch Escape. Santat, Dan, illus. (p. 1936)
—Semi-Charming Kind of Life. (p. 1987)
—Smells Like Dog. (p. 2041)
—Smells Like Pirates. (p. 2041)
—Smells Like Treasure. (p. 2041)
—Spirit Riding Free: Lucky & the Mustangs of Miradero. (p. 2083)
—Spirit Riding Free: the Adventure Begins. (p. 2083)
—To Catch a Mermaid. (p. 2252)
—Wedgie & Gizmo. Fisinger, Barbara, illus. (p. 2395)
—Wedgie & Gizmo vs. the Great Outdoors. Fisinger, Barbara, illus. (p. 2395)
—Wedgie & Gizmo vs. the Toof. Fisinger, Barbara, illus. (p. 2395)
—Wish upon a Sleepover. (p. 2478)
Selfors, Suzanne & Ranson, Walker. Braver: A Wombat's Tale. (p. 277)
Selig, Josh. Ride the Potato Train. (p. 1878)
—Ride the Potato Train. Gibbons, Cassandra, illus. (p. 1878)
—Small Potatoes Go Camping. Gibbons, Cassandra, illus. (p. 2040)
Selig, William P. Bedtime Stories. (p. 188)
Seligman, James. Adventures of Willow Downunder. (p. 29)
—Bailey the Siamese Cat & the Nasty Mean Dragon. (p. 159)
Seligman, V. J. Macedonian Musings (Classic Reprint) (p. 1372)
Selincourt, Hugh De. Boy's Marriage (Classic Reprint) (p. 272)
—Fair House (Classic Reprint) (p. 695)
—Nine Tales (Classic Reprint) (p. 1609)
—Soldier of Life (Classic Reprint) (p. 2056)
—Way Things Happen (Classic Reprint) (p. 2387)
Selinsky. Billy Boggle & the Color Changing Fruit. (p. 227)
Selinsky, Jen. Animals & Me - a to Z. (p. 93)
—Billy Boggle & the Color Changing Fruit. (p. 227)
—Billy Boggle & the Color Changing Fruit Coloring Book. (p. 227)
—Bunny's Song. (p. 298)
—Fun with Shapes. (p. 800)
—Me & Daddy. (p. 1432)
—Our Beloved Ashley. (p. 1676)
—So Many Things We Want to Be! (p. 2050)
—Walnut the Squirrel. (p. 2373)
—Year Family. (p. 2518)
—You Are You! (p. 2525)
—You Are You. (p. 2525)
Selivanova, Elena, illus. see Dale, Katie.
Selivanova, Elena, illus. see Hillert, Margaret.
Selivanova, Elena, illus. see Nellist, Glenys.
Selivanova, Elena, illus. see Prokos, Anna.
Selke, Ilona. Ravi Apni Kalpana Ka Prayog Karna Seektha Hai: Hamari Dhimaag Aur Hamari Kalpana Ki Chipi Huyi Shakti Ke Rahasyo Ko Uchahar Karti Ek Kahani. (p. 1844)
Sell, Chad. Cardboard Kingdom. (p. 328)
—Doodleville. (p. 585)
—Doodleville/Cardboard Kingdom Indie 9-Copy Pre-Pack (p. 585)
Sell, Tina. Mrs. Jones, Rascal & Me. (p. 1522)
Sellar, Gordon. True Makers of Canada: The Narrative of Gordon Sellar, Who Emigrated to Canada in 1825 (Classic Reprint) (p. 2294)
Sellar, Robert. Gleaner Tales (Classic Reprint) (p. 841)
—Hemlock: A Tale of the War 1812 (Classic Reprint) (p. 954)
—Morven (Classic Reprint) (p. 1507)
—Summer of Sorrow, Abner's Device & Other Stories (Classic Reprint) (p. 2149)
Sellaro, Brendan. Space Santa Holiday Hero. (p. 2072)
Sellaro, Brendan, illus. see Hamilton, Lily & Myers, Barbara.
Sellars, Willie. Dipnetting with Dad. Easthope, Kevin, illus. (p. 552)
Selleck, Kristen. Finn & Wolfie Save the Universe (Except for Cleveland) (p. 731)
Selleck, Richelle. Little Red Riding Hood. Myer, Ed, illus. (p. 1326)
Sellen, Sandi. Splendiddly Fazztabulous Grandmas. Maltman Dinwoodie, Heather, illus. (p. 2085)
Sellers, Carolyn, jt. auth. see Sandrey, Alexander.
Sellers, Charles. Subtracting with Seals. (p. 2146)
—Tales from the Lands of Nuts & Grapes: Spanish & Portuguese Folklore (Classic Reprint) (p. 2183)
—Tales from the Lands of Nuts & Grapes. (p. 2183)
Sellers, Elizabeth Jaudon. From 18 To 20: A Novel (Classic Reprint) (p. 790)
—From 18 To 20. (p. 790)
Sellers, Luke. Know the Game: Complete Skills: Cricket. (p. 1229)
Sellers, Martha. Story of a Life (Classic Reprint) (p. 2128)
Sellers, Ronnie. ABCs of Trucks, Boats Planes, & Trains. Rowland, Andy, illus. (p. 5)
—Bellybutton Fuzz & Other Poems to Ponder. (p. 198)
—If Christmas Were a Poem. Ackley, Peggy Jo, illus. (p. 1090)
Sellier, Marie. Renoir's Colors. (p. 1866)
—What the Rat Told Me. Louis, Catherine, illus. (p. 2420)
Sellner, Joelle. Punky Brewster: Punky Power. Vamos, Lesley, illus. (p. 1814)
Sellon, Gertrude. Man's Boot, & Other Tales; or, Fabulous Truths - Scholar's Choice Edition. (p. 1398)
Sells, Miss Claire M. Rabbits & Their Night-Time Habits: (the Amusing Adventures of Missy & Mr. Bun) (p. 1830)
Sells, S. E. Princess Chrysalline, or the Maiden Who Couldn't Laugh (Classic Reprint) (p. 1796)
Selmes, Caroline, illus. see Turner, Tracey.
Selous, Edmund. Beautiful Birds (Classic Reprint) (p. 183)
—Bird Life Glimpses (Classic Reprint) (p. 230)
—Bird Watcher in the Shetlands: With Some Notes on Seals & Digressions (Classic Reprint) (p. 230)
—Bird Watching (Classic Reprint) (p. 231)
—Tommy Smith at the Zoo (Yesterday's Classics) (p. 2259)
—Tommy Smith's Animals. Ord, G. W., illus. (p. 2259)
—Tommy Smith's Animals (Classic Reprint) (p. 2259)
Selover, Arthur, illus. see Linkowski, Tami Leli.
Selover, Lisa, illus. see Linkowski, Tami Leli.
Selph, Fannie Eoline. Texas, or the Broken Link in the Chain of Family Honors: A Romance of the Civil War (Classic Reprint) (p. 2209)
Seltin, Donald M. Life's Hidden Panacea. (p. 1297)
Seltzer, Adele Szold, jt. auth. see Bonsels, Waldemar.
Seltzer, Adele Szold, jt. auth. see Tillier, Claude.
Seltzer, Charles Alden. Beau Rand (Classic Reprint) (p. 183)
—Boss of the Lazy y (Classic Reprint) (p. 263)
—Firebrand Trevison, Vol. 5 (Classic Reprint) (p. 733)
—Ranchman, Vol. 5 (Classic Reprint) (p. 1840)
—Range Boss (Classic Reprint) (p. 1840)
—Square Deal Sanderson (Classic Reprint) (p. 2094)
—Sunset Trail Omnibus: Containing Two Complete Novels; the Ranchman; Square Deal Sanderson (Classic Reprint) (p. 2153)
—Trail Horde, Vol. 5 (Classic Reprint) (p. 2274)
—Vengeance of Jefferson Gawne (Classic Reprint) (p. 2350)
—West (Classic Reprint) (p. 2401)
Seltzer, Eric. Arf! Buzz! Cluck! A Rather Noisy Alphabet. Creighton-Pester, David, illus. (p. 114)
—Bake, Mice, Bake! (p. 160)
—Bake, Mice, Bake! Rosenberg, Natascha, illus. (p. 160)
—Knight Owls: Ready-To-Read Pre-Level 1. Disbury, Tom, illus. (p. 1228)
—Knight Owls. (p. 1228)
—Long Dog. (p. 1343)
—Long Dog (Scholastic Reader, Level 1) (p. 1343)
—Party Pigs! (p. 1702)
—Party Pigs! Disbury, Tom, illus. (p. 1702)
—Sea Sheep. Disbury, Tom, illus. (p. 1968)
—Space Cows. (p. 2071)
—Space Cows. Disbury, Tom, illus. (p. 2071)
Seltzer, Eric & Hall, Kirsten. Dog on His Bus. Braun, Sébastien, illus. (p. 576)
Seltzer, Jerry, illus. see Abbott, Rosalind.
Seltzer, Jerry, illus. see Collins, Charles.
Seltzer, Jerry Joe. There Are Fairies in My Tub. Seltzer, Jerry Joe, illus. (p. 2216)
Seltzer, Jerry Joe, illus. see Abbott, Roz.
Seltzer, Sara Leah. Day Full of Mitzvos. Katz, Avi, illus. (p. 513)
Seltzer, Thomas. Best Russian Short Stories (Classic Reprint) (p. 207)
Seluk, Nick. Brain Is Kind of a Big Deal. Seluk, Nick, illus. (p. 275)
—Sun Is Kind of a Big Deal. Seluk, Nick, illus. (p. 2151)
Selvan, Jennifer. Jenlania: Jennifer's Little World. (p. 1163)
Selvaraj, Sasha Emma. Muir Magic! Colonna, Morgan, illus. (p. 1525)
Selwyn, A. Tales of the Vicarage (Classic Reprint) (p. 2186)
Selwyn, Edgar. When Danny Came Marching Home a Farce in One Act (Classic Reprint) (p. 2429)
Selwyn, Josephine. How Can I Get Fit? (p. 1026)
—How Do I Move? (p. 1028)
—How Do You Measure Rain & Wind? (p. 1030)
—What Do Plants Need? (p. 2408)
—What Holidays Do You Have? (p. 2412)
—When Does Water Turn into Ice? (p. 2430)
—Who Uses This Machine? (p. 2450)
Selwyn, Toby, ed. see Harris, Chaz.
Selyov, Trebor E., ed. see Fox, Lee White.
Selzer, Adam. I Kissed a Zombie, & I Liked It. (p. 1067)
—Smart Aleck's Guide to American History. (p. 2040)
Selzer, Anita. I Am Sasha. (p. 1059)
Selznick, Brian. Baby Monkey, Private Eye. (p. 151)
—Boy of a Thousand Faces. Selznick, Brian, illus. (p. 269)
—Marvels. (p. 1413)
—Marvels. Selznick, Brian, illus. (p. 1413)
—Wonderstruck. Selznick, Brian, illus. (p. 2491)
Selznick, Brian, illus. see Clements, Andrew.
Selznick, Brian, illus. see Kerley, Barbara.
Selznick, Brian, illus. see Levithan, David.
Selznick, Brian, illus. see Martin, Ann M.
Selznick, Brian, illus. see Martin, Ann M. & Godwin, Laura.
Selznick, Brian, illus. see Rowling, J. K.
Selznick, Brian, illus. see Ryan, Pam Muñoz.
Selznick, Brian, illus. see Seidler, Tor.
Selznick, Brian & Scholastic Staff. Wonderstruck Movie Scrapbook. (p. 2491)

—Christmas Tree. (p. 387)
—Color Me Crocodile: 3D Puzzle & Book. (p. 420)
—Color Me Giraffe: 3D Puzzle & Book. (p. 420)
—Color Me Owl Desk Set: 3D Puzzle & Book. (p. 420)
—Color Me Playhouse: 3D Puzzle & Book. (p. 420)
—Cozy Cottage: My First Dollhouse 3D Puzzle & Book. (p. 465)
—Crocodile: Wildlife 3D Puzzle & Books. (p. 477)
—Curious Kitten. (p. 488)
—Dinosaurs: My First Little Seek & Find. (p. 550)
—Doodle Journal Book. (p. 584)
—Fluffy Chick. (p. 753)
—Get Excited about Preschool. (p. 823)
—Get Ready, Santa! (p. 824)
—Giraffe: Wildlife 3D Puzzle & Books. (p. 834)
—Goldilocks & the Three Bears. (p. 860)
—Good Night, Little Bear. (p. 864)
—Grandma Loves You. (p. 878)
—I Love You. (p. 1078)
—If You're Happy & You Know It. (p. 1093)
—Jonah & the Whale. (p. 1177)
—Kangaroo: Wildlife 3D Puzzle & Books. (p. 1202)
—Kittens: Seek & Find. Rescek, Sanja, illus. (p. 1226)
—Let's Play ABC Bingo! (p. 1276)
—Little Drummer Boy. (p. 1315)
—Little Elf. (p. 1316)
—Little Lamb. (p. 1320)
—Little Red Riding Hood. (p. 1326)
—Me & My Life. (p. 1433)
—Mega Doodle: Seek & Find. (p. 1441)
—Merry Christmas. (p. 1449)
—My Amazing Animals Activity Book. (p. 1531)
—My Awesome Sports Activity Book. (p. 1531)
—My Fabulous Activity Book. (p. 1538)
—My First 1000 Words: Active Minds Reference Series. (p. 1540)
—My First 1000 Words: Softcover Active Minds Reference Series. (p. 1540)
—My First Book of Animals: Active Minds Reference Series. (p. 1542)
—My First Book of Animals: Softcover Active Minds Reference Series. (p. 1542)
—My First Dictionary: Active Minds Reference Series. (p. 1543)
—My First Firehouse: 3D Puzzle & Book. (p. 1544)
—My Little Book of Animal Adventures. (p. 1552)
—My Little Book of Manners. (p. 1552)
—My Super Puzzle Book. (p. 1562)
—My Super Winter Activity Book. (p. 1562)
—My Ultimate Activity Book. (p. 1563)
—National Geographic Space Exploration: 3D Puzzle & Book. (p. 1577)
—National Geographic Undersea: 3D Puzzle & Book. (p. 1577)
—Night Before Christmas. (p. 1605)
—On the Farm: My First Little Seek & Find. (p. 1654)
—Plesiosaurus: 3D Puzzle & Book. (p. 1762)
—Plesiosaurus Activity Book. (p. 1762)
—Puppies: Seek & Find. Byrne, Mike, illus. (p. 1814)
—Rose Retreat: My First Dollhouse 3D Puzzle & Book. (p. 1905)
—Sloth: Wildlife 3D Puzzle & Book. (p. 2038)
—Snowman's Snow Day. (p. 2049)
—Snowy Owl Family. (p. 2049)
—Stegosaurus: 3D Puzzle & Book. (p. 2112)
—Stegosaurus Activity Book. (p. 2112)
—Stupendous Travel. (p. 2145)
—Super Activity Book. (p. 2154)
—T. Rex: 3D Puzzle & Book. (p. 2174)
—Things That Go. (p. 2221)
—Three Little Pigs. (p. 2233)
—Tiny Puppies. (p. 2249)
—Tiny Tiger. (p. 2250)
—Triceratops: 3D Puzzle & Book. (p. 2287)
—Triceratops Activity Book. (p. 2287)
—Twelve Days of Christmas. (p. 2303)
—Twinkle, Twinkle, Little Star. (p. 2305)
—Tyrannosaurus Activity Book. (p. 2311)
—Ugly Duckling. (p. 2313)
—Under the Sea: My First Little Seek & Find. (p. 2322)
—Wheels on the Bus. (p. 2428)
—You Can Go Potty! (p. 2526)
—Zebra: Wildlife 3D Puzzle & Books. (p. 2538)
Serafin, Serafin. Malvaloca: A Drama in Three Acts (Suggested by an Andalusian Song) (Classic Reprint) (p. 1392)
Serafini, Frank. Looking Closely Through the Forest Serafini, Frank, illus. (p. 1347)
Serani, Deborah. Sometimes When I'm Sad. Teis, Kyra, illus. (p. 2061)
Serao, Matilde. Ballet Dancer & on Guard (Classic Reprint) (p. 162)
—Conquest of Rome (Classic Reprint) (p. 442)
—Conquest of Rome (la Conquista Di Roma) (Classic Reprint) (p. 442)
—Fantasy (Classic Reprint) (p. 708)
—In the Country of Jesus (Classic Reprint) (p. 1108)
—Land of Cockayne (Classic Reprint) (p. 1241)
—Land of Cockayne, Vol. 1: Translated from the Italian; a Frontispiece & a Biographical Sketch (Classic Reprint) (p. 1241)
—Sterminator Vesevo (Vesuvius the Great Exterminator) Diary of the Eruption of April 1906 (Classic Reprint) (p. 2116)
Seraphine, Rainey Leigh. Aristotle the Rebel. (p. 116)
—Bonny Bilby. (p. 256)
—Greta's Dilemma. (p. 895)
—Pappinbarra Flood. (p. 1698)
—This Is Evie Hope. (p. 2224)
—Voracious Vocabulary & Sumptuous Synonyms. (p. 2367)
Seraphini, Temisa. Secret Lives of Unicorns. Robin, Sophie, illus. (p. 1977)
Seraydarian, Prescott, jt. auth. see Sedita, Francesco.
Serbanescu, Luminita, illus. see Clackdoyle, Carolyn.
Serdna, Uncle. Bert the Penguin's: I Know I've Seen That Cat Before. (p. 204)
Sereda, Maja, illus. see Gumede, William.
Seredy, Kate. Chestry Oak. (p. 366)
Seredy, Kate, illus. see Bianco, Margery Williams.
Serena Geddes, illus. see Murrell, Belinda.
Sereno, Paul C., jt. auth. see Lunis, Natalie.
Sereno, Paul C. & Lunis, Natalie. Supercroc: Paul Sereno's Dinosaur Eater. (p. 2159)
Seresin, Lynn, jt. auth. see Schwartz, Betty Ann.
Seresin, Lynn & Schwartz, Betty Ann. Hop, Hop Bunny. Ng, Neiko, illus. (p. 1001)
Seret, Bernard. Little Book of Knowledge: Sharks. Sole, Julien, illus. (p. 1312)
Sergeant, Adeline. Chase: A Tale of the Southern States (Classic Reprint) (p. 361)
—Chase: A Tale of the Southern States, from the French of Jules Lermina (Classic Reprint) (p. 361)
—Cynthia's Ideal (Classic Reprint) (p. 493)
—Daunay's Tower: A Novel (Classic Reprint) (p. 510)
—Deadly Foe: A Romance of the Northern Seas. (p. 518)
—Deadly Foe: A Romance of the Northern Seas (Classic Reprint) (p. 518)
—Failure of Sibyl Fletcher: A Novel (Classic Reprint) (p. 695)
—In Vallombrosa: A Sequence (Classic Reprint) (p. 1112)
—Mistress of Quest a Novel (Classic Reprint) (p. 1483)
—My Lady's Diamonds (Classic Reprint) (p. 1551)
—Nellie Maturin's Victory (Classic Reprint) (p. 1586)
—Open Foe, Vol. 1 Of 3: A Romance (Classic Reprint) (p. 1665)
—Reparation: A Novel (Classic Reprint) (p. 1866)
—Roy's Repentance (Classic Reprint) (p. 1910)
—Seventy Times Seven, Vol. 1 Of 3: A Novel (Classic Reprint) (p. 1995)
—Under False Pretences: A Novel (Classic Reprint) (p. 2321)
Sergeant, Adeline & Lermina, Jules. Chase. (p. 361)
Sergeant, Elizabeth Shepley. French Perspectives (Classic Reprint) (p. 784)
—Shadow-Shapes: The Journal of a Wounded Woman, October 1918-May 1919 (Classic Reprint) (p. 1997)
Sergeant, Grandma. Adventures of the Five Forest Fairies: Stories from Inside My Head. (p. 28)
Sergeant, Katharine. Tipyn o'Bob, Vol. 11: November 1, 1913 (Classic Reprint) (p. 2251)
Sergeeva, Mary, illus. see Everett, Forrest.
Sergeeva, Masha, illus. see Uzorova, Olga & Nefedova, Elena.
Serger, Peter a. I'm a Boy. (p. 1097)
—Tiffie. (p. 2240)
Sergeyeva, Marina. Nikki & Nick Are Great Friends to Pick. Sergeyeva, Marina, illus. (p. 1608)
Sergi, Rossella. Deep Scar, Vol. 01. (p. 524)
—Deep Scar, Vol. 02. (p. 524)
Sergiacomi, Jessica E. & Covert, Jacquelyn D. Skunk Who Lost His Stink. Kenyon, Richard J., illus. (p. 2033)
Serhant, Emilia Bechrakis. To the Moon & Back for You. Keller, E. G., illus. (p. 2253)
Series, Color by Number, jt. auth. see Publishing, Gameplay.
Series, Michelle Lynch, jt. auth. see Sánchez, Lucía M.
Serino, Robert. Adventures of Pea-Shooter: Into the Forbidden Forest. Lally, Cory, illus. (p. 26)
Serl, Elmer Willis. Swaying Tree Tops (Classic Reprint) (p. 2167)
Serl, Emma. In Fableland (Classic Reprint) (p. 1104)
—In the Animal World (Classic Reprint) (p. 1107)
—Work-A-Day Doings (Classic Reprint) (p. 2495)
—Work-A-Day Doings on the Farm. (p. 2495)
—Work-A-Day Doings on the Farm (Classic Reprint) (p. 2495)
Serl, Emma, et al. Work-A-Day Doings. (p. 2495)
Serle, Hildegarde, tr. see Dabos, Christelle.
Serle, Rebecca. Edge of Falling. (p. 625)
—Famous in Love. (p. 704)
—Truly Madly Famously. (p. 2295)
—When You Were Mine. (p. 2434)
Serle, Thomas James. Players, or the Stage of Life, Vol. 2 of 3 (Classic Reprint) (p. 1760)
Serlin, David, jt. auth. see Selznick, Brian.
Serlin, Wm J. Gleaner, Vol. 2: April, 1902 (Classic Reprint) (p. 841)
Serling, Rod & Kneece, Mark. Odyssey of Flight 33. Timmons, Johnny & Grabe, Robert, illus. (p. 1638)
Serman, Gina L., ed. see Fast, Suellen M.
Sermon, Rhonda. Midnight Society. (p. 1461)
Serna-Vara, Ana. NUESTRO BEBÉ. (p. 1629)
Seroney, Kibny'aanko Arap. Cheebtabuut, Blue Berries & the Monsters Den. (p. 363)
Seroya, Tea, illus. see Coffelt, Soraya.
Seroya, Tea, illus. see Downie, David.
Serpa, Dylon J. Moosey's Adventures: The Way Home. (p. 1503)
Serpentelli, John, illus. see Kelso, Susan.
Serra, Adolfo. Caperucita Roja. (p. 323)
—Different Story. (p. 545)
Serra Huerta, Luis, tr. see Meyer, Kai.
Serra, Sebastia, illus. see Compestine, Ying Chang.
Serra, Sebastia, illus. see Garcia, Cristina.
Serra, Sebastia, illus. see Gregory, Josh.
Serra, Sebastià, illus. see Kudlinski, Kathleen V.
Serra, Sebastiá, illus. see Lyall, Casey.
Serra, Sebastia, illus. see Sacre, Antonio.
Serra, Sebastià, illus. see Vamos, Samantha R.
Serra, Sebastiá, illus. see Yates, Philip.
Serrano Burgos, Pilar. Reto. (p. 1870)
Serrano, Francisco. Malinche: The Princess Who Helped Cortés Conquer the Aztec Empire Ourious, Susan, tr. (p. 1392)
—Our Lady of Guadalupe Davalos, Felipe, 1st, illus. (p. 1678)
Serrano, Javier, illus. see Sierra I. Fabra, Jordi & Sierra i Fabra, Jordi.
Serrano, Javier, tr. see Sierra I. Fabra, Jordi & Sierra i Fabra, Jordi.
Serrano, Kristina M. Sole Voices (p. 2057)
Serrano, Mary Jane Christie, jt. auth. see Breton, Jules.
Serrano, Pablo, illus. see Serrano, Francisco.
Serrano, Pepe. Cómo Envolver un Regalo en 10 Pasos. (p. 432)
Serrano, Pilar. Hoy No Juegas. Canizales, illus. (p. 1047)
—Today You Can't Play. Canizales, illus. (p. 2255)
Serrano, Shea. Bun B's Rapper Coloring & Activity Book. (p. 297)
Serrano, Tina. Catfish Caper. (p. 344)
—Urban Scavenger Hunt (p. 2339)
Serrao, Vanessa Monica. Rudy the Beagle. (p. 1912)
Serrato, M., ed. see Alva, Kristian.
Serrato, Moises, jt. auth. see Alva, Kristian.
Serre, Celinka. Stardust Destinies I: Variate Facing. Gilks, Marg, ed. (p. 2106)
Serres, Alain. I Have the Right to Be a Child Mixter, Helen, tr. (p. 1066)
Sertori, J. M. Early Kings of England: Band 14/Ruby (Collins Big Cat) (p. 614)
Sertori, Trisha. Dairy Foods. (p. 497)
—Fats & Oils. (p. 715)
—Fruits, Vegetables, & Legumes. (p. 796)
—Grains, Bread, Cereal & Pasta. (p. 875)
—Meats, Fish, Eggs, Nuts, & Beans. (p. 1435)
—Vitamins & Minerals. (p. 2363)
Sertrew, Saul. Splendid Misery: A Farce, in One Act (Classic Reprint) (p. 2085)
Servant, J. C. Adventures of Lottie & Layla. (p. 25)
Servello, Joe, illus. see Kotzwinkle, William.
Server, David & Lanzing, Jackson. Penguins of Madagascar (p. 1716)
Server, Lee. Lions (p. 1307)
—Lions - Pb: A Portrait of the Animal World. (p. 1307)
—Tigers (p. 2242)
—Tigers - Pb: A Portrait of the Animal World. (p. 2242)
Service, National Board For Historical. War Readings (Classic Reprint) (p. 2377)
Service, National Park. Grant-Kohs Ranch: Junior Rancher Booklet (Classic Reprint) (p. 880)
—Sleeping Bear Dunes National Lakeshore: Junior Ranger Workbook (Classic Reprint) (p. 2036)
Service, Pamela F. #4 Alien Encounter. Gorman, Mike, illus. (p. 2547)
—#5 Alien Contact. Gorman, Mike, illus. (p. 2547)
—Alien Contact Gorman, Mike, illus. (p. 46)
—Alien Encounter. Gorman, Mike, illus. (p. 46)
—Alien Envoy. Gorman, Mike, illus. (p. 46)
—Alien Expedition. (p. 47)
—Camp Alien. (p. 315)
—Escape from Planet Yastol. Gorman, Mike, illus. (p. 661)
—My Cousin, the Alien. (p. 1536)
—Not-So-Perfect Planet. Gorman, Mike, illus. (p. 1623)
—Stinker's Return. (p. 2119)
—Wizards of Wyrd World. Gorman, Mike, illus. (p. 2483)
Service, Private (W A. A. C.) on Active. Letters of Thomasina Atkins (Classic Reprint) (p. 1281)
Service, Robert W. Poisoned Paradise: A Romance of Monte Carlo (Classic Reprint) (p. 1768)
—Pretender: A Story of the Latin Quarter (Classic Reprint) (p. 1790)
—Trail Of 98: A Northland Romance (Classic Reprint) (p. 2274)
Service, Sisters of. Field at Home: January 1944 (Classic Reprint) (p. 723)
—Field at Home: January, 1941 (Classic Reprint) (p. 723)
—Field at Home: January, 1942 (Classic Reprint) (p. 723)
—Field at Home: January, 1943 (Classic Reprint) (p. 723)
Service, U. S. Dep of Agriculture Radio. Autobiographies of Bugs & Rodents: Feb. 1, 1927 (Classic Reprint) (p. 139)
Service, U. S. Dept of Agriculture Radi. Young Folks' Program: April 6, 1928 (Classic Reprint) (p. 2531)
Service, United States. Forest. Kenai Lake Ycc: Chugach National Forest; January 1979 (Classic Reprint) (p. 1209)
—Uncle Sam's Forest Rangers: No. 506; October 2, 1942 (Classic Reprint) (p. 2319)
—Uncle Sam's Forest Rangers: No. 361; October 27, 1939 (Classic Reprint) (p. 2319)
—Uncle Sam's Forest Rangers: No. 367; December 29, 1939 (Classic Reprint) (p. 2319)
—Uncle Sam's Forest Rangers: Episode 40; November 17, 1932 (Classic Reprint) (p. 2319)
—Uncle Sam's Forest Rangers: Episode No. 523; February 1943 (Classic Reprint) (p. 2319)
Service, United States National Cinema. National Cinema Service Presents the 1942-1943 Film Rental Library Catalog (Classic Reprint) (p. 1577)
Services, Christian Editing, ed. see Henry Jr, Nelson K.
Serviss, Garrett Putman. Astronomy with the Naked Eye: A New Geography of the Heavens - Scholar's Choice Edition. (p. 129)
—Pleasures of the Telescope: An Illustrated Guide for Amateur Astronomers & a Popular Description o - Scholar's Choice Edition. (p. 1762)
Servos, Launcelot Cressy. Practical Instruction in Golf. (p. 1784)
Serwaa, Maame. Perfect As I Am. Forkuo, Fleance, illus. (p. 1722)
Serwacki, Kevin & Pallace, Chris. Joey & Johnny, the Ninjas: Epic Fail. Serwacki, Kevin & Pallace, Chris, illus. (p. 1171)
—Joey & Johnny, the Ninjas: Get Mooned. Serwacki, Kevin & Pallace, Chris, illus. (p. 1171)
Sesa, jt. auth. see Beck, Lynn G.
Sesame Street. People in Your Neighborhood. (p. 1718)
—Sesame Street: 1 2 3 Count with Elmo! A Look, Lift, & Learn Book. (p. 1992)
—Sesame Street Elmo's Musical Hugs. (p. 1992)
—Sesame Street Music Player Storybook: Collector's Edition. (p. 1992)
Sesame Street Staff, creator. Sesame Street: Elmo & Me! Boxed Set. (p. 1992)
—Sesame Street: Early Learning Boxed Set. (p. 1992)
—Sesame Street: My First Manners Boxed Set. (p. 1992)
Sesame Street Workshop Staff. Shalom Sesame DVD Set (p. 1999)
Sesame Workshop. Get Well Soon! (p. 825)
—Heroes Wear Masks: Elmo's Super School Adventure. (p. 962)
—Love: From Sesame Street. (p. 1358)
—Sesame Street Big Book of ABCs And 123s. (p. 1992)
—Sesame Street Big Book of Elmo: A Treasury of Stories. (p. 1992)
—Sesame Street Christmas Treasury. (p. 1992)
—Sesame Street I Can Do It! A Treasury of Stories. (p. 1992)
—Sweet Dreams: A Goodnight Lullaby. Nelson, Marybeth, illus. (p. 2168)
Sesame Workshop, illus. see Brooke, Susan Rich.
Sesame Workshop, jt. auth. see Alexander, Kwame.
Sesame Workshop & Guendelsberger, Erin. Cookies for Elmo. (p. 446)
Sesame Workshop & Hill, Susanna Leonard. Dream: With Sesame Street. Nelson, Marybeth, illus. (p. 600)
Sesame Workshop & Manning, Craig. Big Bird's Big Bad Day: A Story about Turning Frowns Upside Down. (p. 216)
—Family: On Sesame Street. (p. 702)
Sesame Workshop, Sesame. Sesame Street: a Very Elmo Christmas. (p. 1992)
Sesame Workshop Staff. All Tucked in on Sesame Street! (p. 55)
—Great Easter Race! (p. 885)
—Happy Birthday! A Birthday Party Book. (p. 920)
—Happy Halloween! (p. 922)
—I Am a Friend. (p. 1057)
—I Like School. (p. 1068)
—I Love You Just Like This! (p. 1078)
—Just One You! (p. 1194)
—Kindness Makes the World Go Round. (p. 1219)
—Let's Make a Friend! (p. 1275)
—Love: From Sesame Street. Kwiat, Ernie, illus. (p. 1358)
—Messy Alphabet Book! (p. 1452)
—Messy Alphabet Book! An ABC Book! (p. 1452)
—Off to School! (p. 1640)
—Sesame Play-N-Learn 123S. (p. 1992)
—Sesame Play-N-Learn Dot to Dots. (p. 1992)
—Sesame Play-N-Learn Mazes. (p. 1992)
—Shalom Sesame Set. (p. 1999)
—Toddler Time Explore Animals with Elmo. (p. 2255)
—Toddler Time Explore Seasons with Cookie Monster. (p. 2255)
—Twas the Night Before Christmas on Sesame Street. (p. 2302)
—'Twas the Night Before Christmas on Sesame Street! (p. 2302)
—You Can Do It! A Little Book about the Big Power of Perseverance. (p. 2525)
Sesame Workshop Staff & McQuillan, Susan. Sesame Street Let's Cook! (p. 1992)
Sesame Workshop Staff, ed. ABC Sesame Street Flash Cards. (p. 4)
—My First Library Sesame Street: 12 Board Books. Berry, Bob et al, illus. (p. 1544)
—Pets Elmos World Flash Cards. (p. 1731)
—Your Body Elmos World Flash Cards. (p. 2533)
Sesen, Cihan. Stop the Rain, Issue #1. (p. 2122)
Sesera, Susan. Fuzzy Bear: Where Are You? (p. 803)
Sesma, C. Basic ESL Workbook: Level 1 (p. 169)
—Basic ESL Workbook: Level 2 (p. 169)
—Basic ESL Workbook: Level 3 (p. 169)
Sesselberg, Martha F. In Amazon Land: Adaptations from Brazilian Writers, with Original Selections (Classic Reprint) (p. 1104)
Sester, Richard, jt. auth. see Bowling, Joyce E.
Setbon, Jessica, tr. see Feder, Yael.
Setchell, William A. Laboratory Practice for Beginners in Botany. (p. 1235)
—Laboratory Practice for Beginners in Botany (Classic Reprint) (p. 1235)
Setford, Steve & Woodcock, Jon. DK Workbooks: Coding in Scratch: Games Workbook: Create Your Own Fun & Easy Computer Games. (p. 569)
—DK Workbooks: Coding in Scratch: Projects Workbook: Make Cool Art, Interactive Images, & Zany Music. (p. 569)
Seth, illus. see Snicket, Lemony, pseud.
Seth, jt. auth. see Snicket, Lemony, pseud.
Seth, jt. auth. see Stanley, John.
Seth, Shantum. Siddhartha Gautama: The Life of the Buddha - Based on Original Sources. Mukherjee, Aniruddha, illus. (p. 2014)
Seth, Shaun. Economics: The Study of Production, Distribution, & Consumption (p. 624)
—Key Figures of the Korean War. (p. 1211)
Seth, Shaun, ed. Key Figures of the Korean War. (p. 1211)
Setlers, A. Descendent of One of the Fir. Old Times in West Tennessee: Reminiscences Semi-Historic of Pioneer Life & the Early Emigrant Settlers in the Big Hatchie Country (Classic Reprint) (p. 1648)
Setliff, Carolyn C. Christmas Carols for Kids: 10 Elementary Piano Solos with Optional Accompaniment. (p. 384)
Seto, Janice. Coloring Book Walking for Clean Water: Pukatawagan on the Move. (p. 424)
—Walking for Clean Water: Pukatawagan on the Move: in Cree & English. Caribou, Ralph, tr. (p. 2372)
Seton, Ernest Thompson. Animal Heroes: Being the Histories of a Cat, a Dog, a Pigeon, a Lynx, Two Wolves a Reindeer & in Elucidation of the Same over 200 Drawings (Classic Reprint) (p. 90)
—Animal Heroes. (p. 90)
—Arctic Prairies: Being the Account of a Voyage to the Region North of Aylemer Lake. (p. 112)
—Arctic Prairies: A Canoe-Journey of 2,000 Miles in Search of the Caribou; Being the Account of a Voyage to the Region North of Aylemer Lake. (p. 112)
—Bannertail: The Story of a Graysquirrel. (p. 164)
—Bannertail - the Story of a Gray Squirrel. (p. 164)
—Biography of a Silver-Fox, or Domino Reynard of Goldur Town: With over 100 Drawings (Classic Reprint) (p. 229)
—Boy Scouts of America - a Handbook of Woodcraft, Scouting, & Life-Craft - with Which Is Incorporated by Arrangement General Sir Robert Baden-Powell's Scouting for Boys. (p. 269)
—Forester's Manual: Or the Forest Trees of Eastern North America (Classic Reprint) (p. 767)
—Johnny Bear, & Other Stories from Lives of the Hunted. (p. 1174)
—Krag & Johnny Bear with Pictures (Classic Reprint) (p. 1231)
—Lives of the Hunted: Containing a True Account of the Doings of Five Quadrupeds Three Birds, and, in

—Children's History of the Society of Friends: Chiefly Compiled from Sewell's History (Classic Reprint) (p. 374)
Sewell. Children of Summerbrook: Scenes of Village Life, Described in Simple Verse (Classic Reprint) (p. 371)
—Our Father's Care: A Ballad (Classic Reprint) (p. 1678)
Sewell, A. Black Beauty: The Autobiography of a Horse, Pp. 1-249. (p. 237)
Sewell, Amy & Ogilvie, Heather. She's Out There! Essays by 35 Young Women Who Aspire to Lead the Nation - The Next Generation of Presidential Candidates. Ripps, Robert A., photos by. (p. 2006)
Sewell, Anna. Anna Sewell's Black Beauty: We Call Them Dumb Animals, & So They Are, for They Cannot Tell Us How They Feel, but They Do Not Suffer Less Because They Have No Words. (p. 97)
—Black Beauty: The Autobiography of a Horse. (p. 237)
—Black Beauty: The Autobiography of a Horse (Classic Reprint) (p. 237)
—Black Beauty. (p. 237)
—Black Beauty. Brown, Ruth, illus. (p. 237)
—Black Beauty. Aldin, Cecil, illus. (p. 237)
—Black Beauty. Birmingham, Christian, illus. (p. 237)
—Black Beauty (100 Copy Limited Edition) (p. 237)
—Black Beauty (1000 Copy Limited Edition) (p. 237)
—Black Beauty (Illustrated) Classic of World Literature. (p. 237)
—Black Beauty, in Words of One Syllable: An Adaptation for the Little Folks of Anna Sewell's Autobiography of a Horse (Classic Reprint) (p. 237)
—Black Beauty, Young Folks' Edition - Abridged with Original Illustrations. (p. 237)
—Classic Starts(r): Black Beauty. Corvino, Lucy, illus. (p. 400)
Sewell, Anna, jt. auth. see Brown, Ruth.
Sewell, Anna & Ladybird Books Staff. Black Beauty. Matyjaszek, Kasia, illus. (p. 237)
Sewell, Byron W. Alix's Adventures in Wonderland: Lewis Carroll's Nightmare. (p. 48)
—Snarkmaster: A Destiny in Eight Fits. a Tale Inspired by Lewis Carroll's the Hunting of the Snark. Sewell, Byron W., illus. (p. 2045)
Sewell, Byron W. & Carroll, Lewis. Ålpok's Adventures in Goatland. (p. 57)
Sewell, Byron W. & Everson, Michael. Alice's Bad Hair Day in Wonderland: A Tangled Tale. (p. 46)
Sewell, Cornelius V. V. Gentleman in Waiting (Classic Reprint) (p. 816)
Sewell, Debbie. Stella & Stanley. (p. 2112)
Sewell, E. M. Dictation Exercises (Classic Reprint) (p. 541)
—Experience of Life (Classic Reprint) (p. 678)
Sewell, Earl. Lesson Learned. (p. 1268)
—Maya's Choice. (p. 1429)
—Way Too Much Drama. (p. 2387)
Sewell, Earl, et al. Boyfriend Shopping: Shopping for My Boyfriend My Only Wish All I Want for Christmas Is You. (p. 271)
Sewell, Elisabeth. Bible Activity Book. (p. 213)
Sewell, Elizabeth. Sketches: Three Tales: I. Walter Lorimer; II. the Emblems of Life; III. the Lost Inheritance (Classic Reprint) (p. 2031)
Sewell, Elizabeth M. Amy Herbert (Classic Reprint) (p. 77)
—Cleve Hall (Classic Reprint) (p. 404)
Sewell, Elizabeth Missing. After Life: Sequel to 'the Journal of a Home Life' (Classic Reprint) (p. 33)
—Amy Herbert, Vol. 1 of 2 (Classic Reprint) (p. 77)
—Cleve Hall, Vol. 1 of 2 (Classic Reprint) (p. 404)
—Cleve Hall, Vol. 2 of 2 (Classic Reprint) (p. 404)
—Earl's Daughter (Classic Reprint) (p. 613)
—Earl's Daughter, Vol. 1 (Classic Reprint) (p. 613)
—Glimpse of the World (Classic Reprint) (p. 842)
—Home Life: A Journal (Classic Reprint) (p. 996)
—Journal Kept During a Summer Tour, for the Children of a Village School, Vol. 1 Of 3: From Ostend to the Lake of Constance (Classic Reprint) (p. 1180)
—Katharine Ashton, Vol. 1 of 2 (Classic Reprint) (p. 1205)
—Land Without the Sabbath: A Grandmother's Tale (Classic Reprint) (p. 1242)
—Laneton Parsonage: A Tale (Classic Reprint) (p. 1243)
—Laneton Parsonage: A Tale for Children (Classic Reprint) (p. 1243)
—Laneton Parsonage, Vol. 3: A Tale (Classic Reprint) (p. 1243)
—Margaret Percival, Vol. 1 of 2 (Classic Reprint) (p. 1403)
—Uncle Peter's Fairy Tale for the Nineteenth Century (Classic Reprint) (p. 2318)
—Ursula a Tale of Country Life (Classic Reprint) (p. 2340)
Sewell, Helen. Ming & Mehitable (Classic Reprint) (p. 1471)
Sewell, Helen, illus. see Coatsworth, Elizabeth.
Sewell, Helen, jt. auth. see Coatsworth, Elizabeth.
Sewell, James Witt. Classical Grammar. (p. 401)
Sewell, Matt. Atlas of Amazing Birds: (fun, Colorful Watercolor Paintings of Birds from Around the World with Unusual Facts, Ages 5-10, Perfect Gift for Young Birders & Naturalists) (p. 133)
—Big Bird Spot. (p. 216)
—Colorful World of Dinosaurs (watercolor Illustrations & Fun Facts about 46 Dinosaurs) (p. 422)
—Dinosaurs & Other Prehistoric Creatures. (p. 550)
Sewell, Sue. Poppy the Three-Legged Puppy. (p. 1776)
Sewell, Terry. Battle of the Reds & the Greys. (p. 174)
Sewell, W. Amy Herbert, Vol. 2 of 2 (Classic Reprint) (p. 77)
Sewell, William. Hawkstone a Tale of & for England in 184, Vol. 2 of 2 (Classic Reprint) (p. 941)
—Hawkstone, Vol. 1 Of 2: A Tale of & for England in 1845 (Classic Reprint) (p. 941)
—Ursula a Tale of Country Life, Vol. 1 of 2 (Classic Reprint) (p. 2340)
Sewer, Anecia. Why Transfer Day, Anyway. (p. 2459)
Sexaur, Donald. Kramer Makes David Smile. (p. 1231)
Sexson, Julie. I Can Make a Difference! A sweet Story of Giving. (p. 1062)
Sexton, Anne, jt. auth. see Kumin, Maxine.
Sexton, Bernard. Gray Wolf Stories: Indian Mystery Tales of Coyote, Animals & Men (Classic Reprint) (p. 883)
Sexton, Bethany. Big Dog, Little Dog, Fish. Briggs Johnson, Chloe, illus. (p. 219)
Sexton, Brenda. Have a Silly Easter! (p. 939)
—You Can Draw Fairies & Princesses Sexton, Brenda, illus. (p. 2525)
—You Can Draw Pets Sexton, Brenda, illus. (p. 2525)
Sexton, Brenda, illus. see Charlesworth, Liza & Scholastic, Inc. Staff.
Sexton, Brenda, illus. see Fleming, Maria.
Sexton, Brenda, jt. auth. see Bruning, Matt.
Sexton, Brenda, jt. auth. see Cerato, Mattia.
Sexton, Brenda & Sloan, Price Stern. Have a Crazy Christmas! Sexton, Brenda, illus. (p. 939)
Sexton, Brenton, illus. see Simeon, S. & Golden Books Staff.
Sexton, Colleen. African Elephant. (p. 32)
—Anacondas. (p. 78)
—Angelfish. (p. 86)
—Astronauts. (p. 128)
—Australia. (p. 138)
—Barracudas. (p. 167)
—Bengal Tiger. (p. 199)
—Blastoff! Readers - Oceans Alive (p. 243)
—Boa Constrictors. (p. 251)
—Box Jellyfish. (p. 266)
—Brazil. (p. 277)
—Canada. (p. 319)
—Caring for Your Horse. (p. 331)
—Caring for Your Parakeet. (p. 331)
—Caring for Your Rabbit. (p. 331)
—Caring for Your Turtle. (p. 331)
—Cobras. (p. 410)
—Copperheads. (p. 452)
—Coral Reefs. (p. 453)
—Coral Snakes. (p. 453)
—Cottonmouths. (p. 457)
—Cuttlefish. (p. 492)
—Frogfish. (p. 789)
—Glaciers. (p. 840)
—Ireland. (p. 1134)
—Japan. (p. 1159)
—Life Cycle of a Bee. (p. 1290)
—Life Cycle of a Butterfly. (p. 1290)
—Life Cycle of a Cat. (p. 1290)
—Life Cycle of a Chicken. (p. 1290)
—Life Cycle of a Cow. (p. 1290)
—Life Cycle of a Dog. (p. 1290)
—Life Cycle of a Frog. (p. 1291)
—Life Cycle of a Ladybug. (p. 1291)
—Life Cycle of a Penguin. (p. 1291)
—Life Cycle of a Salmon. (p. 1291)
—Life Cycle of a Sea Horse. (p. 1291)
—Life Cycle of a Turtle. (p. 1291)
—Lionfish. (p. 1307)
—Mambas. (p. 1393)
—Manta Rays. (p. 1398)
—Mexico. (p. 1454)
—Moon. (p. 1501)
—Ponds. (p. 1773)
—Puffins. (p. 1811)
—Pythons. (p. 1819)
—Rat Snakes. (p. 1842)
—Rattlesnakes. (p. 1843)
—Saltwater Crocodile. (p. 1925)
—Sea Snakes. (p. 1968)
—Shrimp. (p. 2013)
—Sidewinders. (p. 2015)
—Solar System. (p. 2056)
—Space Stations. (p. 2072)
—Sponges. (p. 2086)
—Sun. (p. 2151)
—Sweden. (p. 2168)
—Swordfish. (p. 2171)
—Tide Pools. (p. 2240)
—Tundra. (p. 2299)
—Uranus. (p. 2339)
—Venus. (p. 2351)
Sexton, Colleen, jt. auth. see Lindeen, Mary.
Sexton, Colleen A. Japan. (p. 1159)
Sexton, Colleen & Bartell, Jim. India. (p. 1115)
—Russia. (p. 1917)
Sexton, Colleen & Grack, Rachel. France. (p. 776)
—Spain. (p. 2073)
Sexton, Colleen & Simmons, Walter. China. (p. 377)
—Cuba. (p. 482)
—Egypt. (p. 628)
—England. (p. 652)
—Germany. (p. 822)
—Israel. (p. 1140)
—Italy. (p. 1142)
—Thailand. (p. 2211)
—Vietnam. (p. 2357)
Sexton, Ella M. Stories of California (Classic Reprint) (p. 2124)
Sexton, Ethelyn. Busy Day in Bangville: A Comedy in One Act Playing Thirty Minutes (Classic Reprint) (p. 302)
—Miss. Burnett Puts One Over: An One-Act Play for Six Girls (Classic Reprint) (p. 1478)
Sexton, Jessa, ed. see Rogers, Lauren.
Sexton, Jessa R. Mobert's Irish Experience. Sexton, Jessa R., photos by. (p. 1485)
—Saturday. (p. 1936)
Sexton, Jessa R., ed. see Cutrer, Elisabeth.
Sexton, Jessa R., ed. see Robertson, Robbin Davis.
Sexton, Jessa R. & Hilliard, K. Mark. ABCs of Storytelling for Young Writers. (p. 5)
Sexton, Jessa R., ed. Fruitful Faith: A Devotional Study Written by Teens for Teens. (p. 796)
Sexton, Jessa Rose. Eldy & Ohi. Miele, Brianna, illus. (p. 630)
—Rose-Pie. Morozova, Anastasia, illus. (p. 1905)
Sexton, Jessa Rose, ed. see Hilliard, Charles E.
Sexton, Laura, illus. see Koppers, Kristen.
Sexton, Ralph. Ralph Sexton Story: From the Mountains Came the Light; the Trials, Triumphs, & Good Times of a Mountain Preacher (Classic Reprint) (p. 1838)
Sexton, Richard, photos by see Delehanty, Randolph.
Sexton, Samuel. Deafness & Discharge from the Ear: The Modern Treatment for the Radical Cure of Deafness, Otorrhoea, Noises in the Head, Vertigo, & Distress in the Ear (Classic Reprint) (p. 519)
Sexton, Shirley. Fairy with an Attitude. (p. 698)
Seybold, Celisa. Keys to Adventure. (p. 1212)
—Keys to Adventure Take Flight. (p. 1212)
Seydel, Andrea. Positivity One Day at a Time: 365 Inspirations to Help Develop a Growth Mindset, Positivity, & Strength. (p. 1779)
Seydel, Andrea D. Finding Happy. (p. 729)
Seyderhelm, Amanda. Isaac & the Red Jumper. Scott, Ann, illus. (p. 1138)
Seydou, Garba B. One Man Army. (p. 1660)
Seyers, Nay. Reybot Hearts Popcorn. (p. 1874)
Seyfert, Ella Maie. Little Amish Schoolhouse (Classic Reprint) (p. 1310)
Seyffert, Oskar. Toys (Classic Reprint) (p. 2271)
Seyforth, Edward L. Horribly Frightening Deception (p. 1003)
Seymour, Beatrice Kean. Intrusion (Classic Reprint) (p. 1129)
—Invisible Tides (Classic Reprint) (p. 1132)
Seymour, Chas W. Home, Sweet Home (Classic Reprint) (p. 997)
Seymour, Eleonora. Christmas Book. (p. 384)
—Learn to Count. (p. 1255)
Seymour, F. Grace. Good Time Primer (Classic Reprint) (p. 866)
Seymour, George Lucas. Sunday: 1885; Reading for Young & Old; with Upwards of Two Hundred & Fifty Original Illustrations (Classic Reprint) (p. 2152)
Seymour, Jeff. Nadya Skylung & the Cloudship Rescue. Helquist, Brett, illus. (p. 1572)
Seymour, John D. True Irish Ghost Stories. (p. 2294)
—True Irish Ghost Stories (Classic Reprint) (p. 2294)
Seymour, Mary Sue. Friends in a Storm. Flynn, Samantha, illus. (p. 787)
Seymour, Marysue. Where Will We Fly. Spadaccini, Cheryl, illus. (p. 2440)
Seymour, Michaela. Shasta. (p. 2003)
—Why Do We Celebrate Martin Luther King Jr. Day? (p. 2457)
Seymour, Richard Arthur. Pioneering in the Pampas; or, the First Four Years of a Settler's Experience in the la Plata Camps. (p. 1748)
—Pioneering in the Pampas, or the First Four Years of a Settler's Experience in the la Plata Camps (Classic Reprint) (p. 1748)
Seymour, Robert. Library of Fiction, Vol. 1: Or Family Story-Teller; Consisting of Original Tales, Essays, & Sketches of Characters (Classic Reprint) (p. 1285)
Seymour, Silas. Review of the Theory of Narrow Gauges As Applied to Main Trunk Lines of Railway. (p. 1873)
—Review of the Theory of Narrow Gauges As Applied to Main Trunk Lines of Railway (Classic Reprint) (p. 1873)
Seymour, Simon. Wolves. (p. 2485)
Seymour, Walter. Ups & Downs of a Wandering Life (Classic Reprint) (p. 2339)
Seyvos, Florence. Pockety: The Tortoise Who Lived As She Pleased. Provata-Carlone, Mika, tr. (p. 1764)
Sezgin, Orhan. Adventures of Little Selim. (p. 25)
Sfar, Joan, jt. auth. see De Saint-Exupéry, Antoine.
Sfar, Joann. Pequeño Vampiro y la Sociedad Protectora de Perros. (p. 1721)
Sfar, Joann, illus. see De Saint-Exupéry, Antoine.
Sfar, Joann, illus. see Guibert, Emmanuel.
Sfar, Joann, jt. auth. see Guibert, Emmanuel.
Sferazza, Jeff. Communication Around the World. (p. 431)
—Cooking Around the World. (p. 446)
—Holidays Around the World. (p. 988)
Sfetcu, Nicolae, tr. see Leung, Chow & Davis, Mary Hayes.
Sfetsios-Conover, Debra, illus. see Cronin, Doreen.
Sfichi-Hortopan, Sfiki Sviki. Mops, Chops, Pooches, & Pigs: Gertrude & Gunter: Orphans in the Storm. (p. 1503)
Sforza, Lucia, illus. see Nam, Jeong-hee & Cowley, Joy.
Sg, Matthew, jt. auth. see Gonzalez, Maya Christina.
Sg, Matthew, jt. auth. see Gonzalez, Maya.
Sgariata, Margherita, illus. see Francaviglia, Riccardo.
Sgouros, Yorgos. First Christmas (p. 735)
Sgouros, Yorgos, illus. see James, Bethan.
Shaabneh, Nevien. Mohamed Salah: Get to Know the Soccer Superstar. (p. 1488)
Shabazz, Aminah, illus. see Shabazz-Ugwumba, Sarah.
Shabazz, Ilyasah. Malcolm Little: The Boy Who Grew up to Become Malcolm X. Ford, A. G., illus. (p. 1391)
Shabazz, Ilyasah & Magoon, Kekla. X: A Novel. (p. 2515)
—X: a Novel. (p. 2515)
Shabazz, Ilyasah, et al. Betty Before X. (p. 209)
Shabazz-Ugwumba, Sarah. Arielle's Two Grand. Wag Publishing, ed. (p. 115)
—Kwanzaa Family. Gulley, Robin, ed. (p. 1233)
—Modern Medicine. Wag Publishing, ed. (p. 1487)
—So Many Books. Wag Publishing, ed. (p. 2050)
Shackelford, David, illus. see Henderson, Richard.
Shackelford, Ethel. Jumping-Off Place (Classic Reprint) (p. 1189)
—Life of Me (Classic Reprint) (p. 1294)
Shackelford, Otis M. Lillian Simmons: Or the Conflict of Sections (Classic Reprint) (p. 1301)
Shackell, John, illus. see Mayes, Susan.
Shackell, William. Parlour Portfolio, or Post-Chaise Companion, Vol. 1 Of 2: Being a Selection of the Most Amusing & Interesting Articles & Anecdotes That Have Appeared in the Magazines, Newspapers, & Other Daily & Periodical Journals, from the Year 1700, to The. (p. 1700)
Shacklefoote, Allehue. Feats & Defeats of an Arkansaw Showman (Classic Reprint) (p. 717)
Shackleford, Maudie. Upside-Down Tale. (p. 2339)
Shackleton, Caroline. Avalanche! High Intermediate Book with Online Access (p. 141)
—Deep Blue: Discovering the Sea Intermediate Book with Online Access. (p. 524)
—Down to Earth Intermediate Book with Online Access. (p. 590)
—Get Smart: Our Amazing Brain Intermediate Book with Online Access. (p. 825)
—Lift off: Exploring the Universe High Intermediate Book with Online Access. (p. 1297)
—Money Tree: the Business of Organics High Intermediate Book with Online Access (p. 1493)
—Poison: Medicine, Murder, & Mystery High Intermediate Book with Online Access. (p. 1768)
—Robots: the Next Generation? High Intermediate Book with Online Access. (p. 1893)
—Trapped! The Aron Ralston Story High Intermediate Book with Online Access. (p. 2279)
Shackleton, Ernest. South: Ernest Shackelton. Pierse, Maurice, illus. (p. 2068)
—South: The Story of Shackleton's Last Expedition, 1914-1917. (p. 2068)
Shackleton, Kath, ed. Survivors of the Holocaust: True Stories of Six Extraordinary Children. Whittingham, Zane, illus. (p. 2165)
Shackleton, Robert. Many Waters: A Story of New York (Classic Reprint) (p. 1400)
—Toomey & Others (Classic Reprint) (p. 2262)
—Touring Great Britain (Classic Reprint) (p. 2269)
—Unvisited Places of Old Europe (Classic Reprint) (p. 2337)
ShackletonCaroline. SKIN UPPER INTERMEDIATE BOOK WITH ONLINE ACCESS. (p. 2032)
—UP IN THE AIR: OUR FIGHT AGAINST GRAVITY INTERMEDIATE BOOK WITH ONLINE ACCESS. (p. 2337)
—WHEEL LOW INTERMEDIATE BOOK WITH ONLINE ACCESS. (p. 2427)
Shacter, Sara. Just So Willow. Laberis, Stephanie, illus. (p. 1194)
Shaddix, M. K. Aisling's Summer Diary. (p. 38)
Shade, Jeff. Unusual Education. (p. 2337)
Shade-Fletcher, Peggi Sue. One Brave White Rabbit & Those Three Little Pigs. (p. 1659)
Shadow, Ben. Echoes of a Belle: Or, a Voice from the Past (Classic Reprint) (p. 623)
Shadravan, Sara. Louis & Lola. (p. 1357)
Shadrick, Crystal Star. My Name Was Fear. Stone, Karen, ed. (p. 1557)
Shae, Jordan. Handy Measuring: Measure Lengths. (p. 917)
Shaeffer, Adam. Little Leaf. Qualls, Turbo, illus. (p. 1320)
Shafer, Barbara. Baby Tigers. (p. 153)
Shafer, Bobbie J. Curse of the Black Rose. (p. 489)
—Dance of the Scorpion. (p. 500)
—Quest for the Sorcerer's Staff. (p. 1826)
—Secrets of Willow Grove. (p. 1981)
Shafer, Cameron. Barent Creighton: A Romance (Classic Reprint) (p. 166)
Shafer, Donald Cameron. Stories of an Old Dutch Town: In Verse (Classic Reprint) (p. 2124)
Shafer, Patty. Annie the Texas Ranch Dog - Danger at Lost Maples. Retzlaff, Shay, illus. (p. 100)
—Annie the Texas Ranch Dog - Injured Hero. Retzlaff, Shay, illus. (p. 100)
—Annie the Texas Ranch Dog - New Life in Utopia. Retzlaff, Shay, illus. (p. 100)
Shafer, Sara Andrew. Day Before Yesterday (Classic Reprint) (p. 512)
Shafer, Viola. Child's Heart. (p. 376)
Shaffer, Christy. Fairies Around the World. (p. 695)
—Glow-In-the-Dark Snowflakes Stickers. (p. 845)
—Glow-In-the-Dark Tattoos Snowflakes. (p. 845)
Shaffer, Eric, illus. see Baker, Georgette.
Shaffer, Grant, illus. see Cumming, Alan.
Shaffer, Grant, illus. see Margulies, Julianna & Margulies, Paul.
Shaffer, Jan. Summoning Stone Book Two: Vision Caster. (p. 2150)
Shaffer, Jennifer. I Want to Play! (p. 1085)
Shaffer, Jody Jensen. Bearded Dragons (p. 180)
—Benjamin Banneker: Self-Made Man. (p. 200)
—Black-Footed Ferrets. (p. 238)
—Bread. (p. 277)
—Bread Before the Store. McGeehan, Dan, illus. (p. 277)
—Chip off the Old Block. Miyares, Daniel, illus. (p. 379)
—City & Country. (p. 394)
—Coach Floats: The Sound of OA. (p. 409)
—Grizzly Bear (p. 897)
—Grizzly Bear Paperback. (p. 897)
—It's a Field Trip, Busy Bus! Messer, Claire, illus. (p. 1143)
—It's Your First Day of School, Busy Bus! Messer, Claire, illus. (p. 1148)
—Jean Can Teach: The Sound of EA. (p. 1162)
—Lea Michele. (p. 1254)
—Let's Play! The Sound of AY. (p. 1276)
—My Heart. Alberini, Teresa, illus. (p. 1549)
—My Lungs. Alberini, Teresa, illus. (p. 1555)
—My Muscles. Alberini, Teresa, illus. (p. 1557)
—Ninja Warriors. (p. 1610)
—Prudence the Part-Time Cow. Laberis, Stephanie, illus. (p. 1809)
—Sitting Bull: Eagles Cannot Be Crows. (p. 2028)
—Spies & Pies: The Sound of IE. (p. 2081)
—Taylor Lautner. (p. 2193)
—Three Bees: The Sound of EE. (p. 2232)
—Trail: The Sound of AI. (p. 2274)
—Vampires & Light Gervasio, illus. (p. 2346)
—What's Your Story, Sequoyah? (p. 2427)
—You Can Too! Success after Failure (Level 5) (p. 2526)
Shaffer, Lindsay. 4x4 Trucks. (p. 2547)
—ATVs. (p. 135)
—Australian Cattle Dogs. (p. 138)
—Bearded Vultures. (p. 180)
—Bichons Frises. (p. 215)
—Brittanys. (p. 284)
—Brown Bears. (p. 286)
—Games Around the World. (p. 807)
—Greyhounds. (p. 896)
—Motocross Cycles. (p. 1512)
—Mountain Goats. (p. 1513)
—Mountain Lions. (p. 1513)
—Pikas. (p. 1744)
—Snow Leopards. (p. 2047)
—Transportation Around the World. (p. 2278)
Shaffer, Paul, illus. see Kinney Gaventa, Sarah & Davila, Mary.

S

Shang, Wendy Wan-Long, jt. auth. see Rosenberg, Madelyn.
Shang, Wendy Wan-Long & Rosenberg, Madelyn. This Is Just a Test. (p. 2224)
Shange, Ntozake. Coretta Scott. Nelson, Kadir, illus. (p. 454)
—Float Like a Butterfly. Rodriguez, Edel, illus. (p. 750)
—Freedom's a-Callin Me. Brown, Rod, illus. (p. 783)
—We Troubled the Waters. Brown, Rod, illus. (p. 2392)
Shank, Bob, jt. auth. see Kshir, Donna M.
Shank, Diane S. Minnow Kisses. Bailey, Terri L., illus. (p. 1473)
Shank, Don. Smokestack Jack with Boomer & Zoomer. (p. 2043)
Shank, Marilyn Sue. Child of the Mountains. (p. 370)
Shankar, Kiara & Shankar, Vinay. Primrose's Curse COLORING & ACTIVITY BOOK. (p. 1793)
—Primrose's Curse COLORING & ACTIVITY BOOK (COLOR EDITION) (p. 1793)
Shanker, Myrna Gelman. Lazar, the Good Deed Dog. Robinson, Linda, illus. (p. 1254)
Shanker, Tarun & Zekas, Kelly. These Vicious Masks. (p. 2219)
Shankland, Ora. Jug O'Fun: 708 Choice Scraps for after Dinner Speakers (Classic Reprint) (p. 1186)
Shankle, Melanie. Fearless Faith: 100 Devotions for Girls (p. 717)
—Piper & Mabel: Two Very Wild but Very Good Dogs Watkins, Laura, illus. (p. 1748)
Shankles, Rachel. Triple S Farm Adventures: Hawkie's in Trouble. (p. 2289)
—Triple S Farm Adventures: Hootie to the Rescue. (p. 2289)
Shankman, Adam & Sullivan, Laura L. Girl about Town: A Lulu Kelly Mystery. (p. 835)
—Murder among the Stars: A Lulu Kelly Mystery. (p. 1527)
—Murder among the Stars. (p. 1527)
Shankman, Ed. Bourbon Street Band Is Back. O'Neill, Dave, illus. (p. 265)
—Champ & Me by the Maple Tree: A Vermont Tale. O'Neill, Dave, illus. (p. 355)
—Cods of Cape Cod. O'Neill, Dave, illus. (p. 412)
—I Went to the Party in Kalamazoo. Frank, Dave, illus. (p. 1085)
—Monkey See, Zebra Do: A Zoo Party. O'Neill, Dave, illus. (p. 1494)
—My Grandma Lives in Florida. O'Neill, Dave, illus. (p. 1548)
—Where's the Bathroom? O'Neill, Dave, illus. (p. 2440)
—Whimsical Washington Night: The Adventures of a DC Duo. O'Neill, Dave, illus. (p. 2442)
Shanly, Stephen. Adventure Steve in the Atlantic (for 8-13 Year Olds) Dusan, Lakicevic, illus. (p. 19)
Shann, Melissa, ed. see Denchukwu, Nkem.
Shanna & Silva. Count on Me [4]. (p. 458)
—Make It Rain [4]. (p. 1386)
—Right Crew [4]. (p. 1882)
Shannacappo, Neal, illus. see Jonnie, Brianna.
Shannon, Ben, illus. see Mototsune, Kat.
Shannon, Ben, illus. see Paniaq, Herve.
Shannon, Ben, illus. see Peters, Diane.
Shannon, Ben, illus. see Slavens, Elaine.
Shannon, Ben, illus. see Staunton, Ted.
Shannon, C. Hazelwood. Pageant, 1896 (Classic Reprint) (p. 1692)
Shannon, Catherine, jt. auth. see Rice, Dona Herwick.
Shannon, Charles H. Dial, 1889 (Classic Reprint) (p. 537)
Shannon, Chelsey. Chelsey: My True Story of Murder, Loss, & Starting Over. (p. 365)
Shannon, David. Bad Case of Stripes. (p. 157)
—Bizzy Mizz Lizzie. (p. 236)
—Bizzy Mizz Lizzie. Shannon, David, illus. (p. 236)
—Bugs in My Hair! Shannon, David, illus. (p. 292)
—David Va a la Escuela. Shannon, David, illus. (p. 511)
—Duck on a Bike. (p. 608)
—Duck on a Tractor. (p. 608)
—Duck on a Tractor. Shannon, David, illus. (p. 608)
—Duck on Bike. (p. 608)
—Grow up, David! Shannon, David, illus. (p. 899)
—It's Christmas, David! Shannon, David, illus. (p. 1144)
—Jangles: A Big Fish Story. Shannon, David, illus. (p. 1159)
—Mr. Nogginbody & the Childish Child. (p. 1519)
—Mr. Nogginbody Gets a Hammer. (p. 1519)
—No, David! Shannon, David, illus. (p. 1612)
—Pato en Tractor (Duck on a Tractor) (p. 1705)
—Rain Came Down. (p. 1835)
—Uh-Oh, David! A David Sticker Book. Shannon, David, illus. (p. 2314)
—¡Crece Ya, David! Shannon, David, illus. (p. 472)
—¡No, David! Shannon, David, illus. (p. 1612)
Shannon, David, illus. see Auerbach, Annie.
Shannon, David, illus. see Bergen, Lara.
Shannon, David, illus. see Harper, Benjamin.
Shannon, David, illus. see Johnson, Bruce Bailey.
Shannon, David, illus. see Long, Melinda.
Shannon, David, illus. see Martin, Rafe.
Shannon, David, illus. see Mason, Tom & Danko, Dan.
Shannon, David, illus. see Mason, Tom, et al.
Shannon, David, illus. see McKown, Hunter.
Shannon, David, illus. see Parker, Sydney.
Shannon, David, illus. see Robertson, Robbie.
Shannon, David, illus. see Sander, Sonia.
Shannon, David, illus. see Scieszka, Jon.
Shannon, David, illus. see Teitelbaum, Michael.
Shannon, David, illus. see Testa, Maggie.
Shannon, Dianne. Lost Dreams. (p. 1353)
Shannon, Doug, illus. see Shannon, Jennifer.
Shannon, Drew, illus. see Eamer, Claire.
Shannon, Drew, illus. see Lloyd Kyi, Tanya.
Shannon, Drew, illus. see Page, Nathan.
Shannon, Edward N. Giuseppino: An Occidental Story (Classic Reprint) (p. 839)
Shannon, George. One Family. Gomez, Blanca, illus. (p. 1659)
—Turkey Tot. Mann, Jennifer K., illus. (p. 2300)
—Very Witchy Spelling Bee. Fearing, Mark, illus. (p. 2354)
Shannon, George & Paschkis, Julie. Who Put the Cookies in the Cookie Jar? (p. 2449)
Shannon, Jennifer. Anxiety Survival Guide for Teens: CBT Skills to Overcome Fear, Worry, & Panic. Shannon, Doug, illus. (p. 104)
Shannon, Julia H. Take Me to the Farm: Stand Here Stories. (p. 2177)
Shannon, Marilyn, jt. auth. see Wile, Jay L.
Shannon, Molly. Tilly the Trickster. Hoyt, Ard, illus. (p. 2243)
Shannon, R. J. Rita Rain & the Shadow Apprentice: Book 1. (p. 1886)
Shannon, Sandra G., ed. August Wilson's Pittsburgh Cycle: Critical Perspectives on the Plays (p. 136)
Shannon Strand, Courtney. Ella's Umbrella. Lounsbury, Jennica, illus. (p. 637)
Shannon, Terry Miller. Barnyard Rumble. (p. 167)
—Boy & the Eagle. (p. 268)
—Families Have Stories to Tell. (p. 701)
—Family Baseball Star. (p. 702)
—Forces That Shape Earth. (p. 764)
—George & the Cherry Tree. (p. 818)
—Good Sports. (p. 866)
—Key to City Maps. (p. 1211)
—Leela's Treasure. Smillie, Natalie, illus. (p. 1261)
—Mall Map Saves the Day. (p. 1392)
—Maps & More Maps. (p. 1401)
—New Hampshire. (p. 1594)
—Oregon. (p. 1669)
—Paul's Big Dig. (p. 1708)
—Play Ball! (p. 1759)
—Reindeer Holiday. (p. 1862)
Shannon, Terry Miller, jt. auth. see Blackwood, Gary L.
Shannon-Riddle, Deidre. Peeka's Perseverance. (p. 1713)
Shanower, Eric. Adventures in Oz (p. 20)
—Giant Garden of Oz. (p. 830)
—Marvelous Land of Oz Horwitz, Michael, ed. (p. 1413)
—Marvelous Land of Oz: Vol. 1 Young, Skottie, illus. (p. 1413)
—Return to Slumberland. Rodriguez, Gabriel, illus. (p. 1871)
—Wonderful Wizard of Oz Young, Skottie, illus. (p. 2490)
—Wonderful Wizard of Oz. Young, Skottie, illus. (p. 2490)
—Wonderful Wizard of Oz: Vol. 1 (p. 2490)
—Wonderful Wizard of Oz: Vol. 3 Young, Skottie, illus. (p. 2490)
Shanower, Eric, illus. see Einhorn, Edward.
Shanower, Eric & Baum, L. Frank. Marvelous Land of Oz: Adapted from the Novel by L. Frank Baum. Young, Skottie, illus. (p. 1413)
—Wonderful Wizard of Oz Young, Skottie, illus. (p. 2490)
Shanté, Angela. Noisy Classroom. Hawkins, Alison, illus. (p. 1617)
Shantz-Hilkes, Chloe. Hooked: When Addiction Hits Home. (p. 1000)
Shao, M. E. Continuity: Coalescence. (p. 445)
ShaoLan, et al. Chineasy for Children: Learn 100 Words. (p. 378)
Shapera, Paul M. Iran's Religious Leaders. (p. 1133)
Shapiro, Alla, illus. see Lopatina, Irina.
Shapiro, Anna Ratner. Red Ruth: The Birth of Universal Brotherhood (Classic Reprint) (p. 1858)
Shapiro, Arnold. Mice Squeak, We Speak. (p. 1457)
Shapiro, Deborah & Daniel, Lea. Letters from the Sea. Shapiro, Deborah & Daniel, Alan, illus. (p. 1280)
Shapiro, Esmé. Ooko. (p. 1665)
Shapiro, Esmé, illus. see Maclear, Kyo.
Shapiro, Esmé, illus. see McNamara, Margaret.
Shapiro, Gary, jt. auth. see Medina, Sylvia M.
Shapiro, Gordon & Crafts, Gregory. Super Sidekick: The Musical. (p. 2156)
Shapiro, J. H. Magic Trash: A Story of Tyree Guyton & His Art. Brantley-Newton, Vanessa, illus. (p. 1379)
Shapiro, Lawrence E. ADHD Workbook for Kids: Helping Children Gain Self-Confidence, Social Skills, & Self-Control. (p. 16)
Shapiro, Lindy. Moon Mangoes. Peterson, Kathleen, illus. (p. 1502)
Shapiro, Marc. Fame: Selena Gomez. Davis, Darren G., ed. (p. 701)
—Stephenie Meyer: The Unauthorized Biography of the Creator of the Twilight Saga. (p. 2115)
Shapiro, Michelle, illus. see Jules, Jacqueline.
Shapiro, Michelle, illus. see Kroll, Steven.
Shapiro, Neil, illus. see Dresner, Hal.
Shapiro, Ouisie, jt. auth. see Florio, John.
Shapiro, Pepper, illus. see Meyer, Kim Shapiro.
Shapiro, Rob. Book of Sam. (p. 259)
Shapiro, Rose. Where's Andrew? (p. 2440)
Shapiro, Sara. What Do You See? A Book about the Seasons. (p. 2409)
Shapiro, Simon. Faster, Higher, Smarter: Bright Ideas That Transformed Sports. (p. 713)
—It's a Feudal, Feudal World: A Different Medieval History. Kinnaird, Ross, illus. (p. 1143)
Shapiro, Susan G., ed. see Caratsev, Serghei I., et al.
Shapiro-Hurt, Sandy. Sylvia Rose & the Cherry Tree Yan, Xindi, illus. (p. 2173)
shapouri, naiyer. Sweet Dreams Buggy. (p. 2168)
Shapur, Fredun. Round & Round & Square. (p. 1907)
Shapur, Fredun, illus. see Shapur, Mira.
Shapur, Mira. Singer & the Paint. Shapur, Fredun, illus. (p. 2024)
Sharafeddine, Fatima. Amazing Discoveries of Ibn Sina Ali, Intelaq, illus. (p. 64)
—Servant (p. 1991)
—Servant. (p. 1991)
Sharber, Kate Trimble. Amazing Grace: Who Proves That Virtue Has Its Silver Lining (Classic Reprint) (p. 65)
—Annals of Ann (Classic Reprint) (p. 98)
—At the Age of Eve (Classic Reprint) (p. 130)
Sharboneau, Shanalee. My Daddy Loves Me: I'm His Little Girl. (p. 1536)
Shardlow, Billy. Santa Saves the Day. (p. 1933)
Share, Laura F. Life of a Spiritualist Medium: A Most Interesting Autobiography Abounding with Strange & Marvelous Psychic Phenomena Illustrating Clairvoyance, Clairaudience, Clairsentience, Healing by Spirit Power, Prophecy, & the Rescue of Spirits in Darkness, (p. 1293)
Sharenow, Robert. Berlin Boxing Club. (p. 203)
—Girl in the Torch. (p. 836)
—My Mother the Cheerleader. (p. 1556)
Sharer, Avigail. Here, There, Everywhere: Kids' True Stories about Finding Hashem in Their Lives. (p. 958)
Sharer, John. Ants Don't Talk, Do They? Mazhar, Jay, illus. (p. 103)
Shargel, Leon. Rainbow Tree. (p. 1837)
—Reuben & the Rainbow Tree. (p. 1872)
Sharief, Shereen. My First Quran with Pictures: Juz' Amma Part 1. Aljudai, Abdullah Ibn Yusuf, ed. (p. 1545)
Sharif, Medeia. Bestest. Ramadan. Ever. (p. 208)
—Girl Without a Face. (p. 837)
Sharif, Meghan. Poverty & Economic Inequality. (p. 1782)
—Why Do Wolf Spiders Make Burrows? And Other Odd Arachnid Adaptations. (p. 2457)
Sharif, Meghan, jt. auth. see Linde, Barbara M.
Sharif-Harris, Hamidah S. Oh Havana! (p. 1641)
—Story of Little Buzz & the Magic Book. (p. 2131)
Sharipovas, Alesja, ed. see AZ Books Staff.
Sharkawy, Azza. Observe It! (p. 1634)
—Predict It! (p. 1787)
—Question It! (p. 1826)
—Share It! (p. 2001)
Sharkey, Alex. Classic Bikes (p. 400)
—Classic Cars (p. 400)
Sharkey, Niamh, illus. see Doyle, Malachy.
Sharkey, Niamh, illus. see Lupton, Hugh.
Sharkey, Niamh, illus. see Walker, Richard.
Sharkey, Niamh, jt. auth. see Doyle, Malachy.
Sharkey, Paulette Bochnig. Doll for Grandma: A Story about Alzheimer's Disease. Woo, Samantha, illus. (p. 578)
Sharkey-Brumund, Mariah McIntyre. Omnipotent. (p. 1652)
Sharma, Aditya. Champs of Devgarh. (p. 355)
Sharma, Ishika, illus. see Gorrell, Sarah Walker.
Sharma, Kavita. Healthy Happy Me: Easy-Peasy Guide to Awesome Health. (p. 944)
Sharma, Lalit Kumar. Daredevil by Chip Zdarsky Vol. 2: No Devils, Only God. (p. 505)
Sharma, Lalit Kumar, illus. see Bechko, Corinna.
Sharma, Lalit Kumar, illus. see Cowsill, Alan.
Sharma, Lalit Kumar, illus. see Deshpande, Sanjay.
Sharma, Lalit Kumar, illus. see Helfand, Lewis.
Sharma, Lalit Kumar, illus. see Quinn, Jason.
Sharma, Natasha. Princess Easy Pleasy. Kuriyan, Priya, illus. (p. 1797)
Sharma, Nick. Shalu, Diwali: The Festival of Lights. (p. 1999)
—Shalu, Holi: The Festival of Colors. (p. 1999)
Sharma, Nisha. My So-Called Bollywood Life. (p. 1561)
Sharma, Rachna. Weirdo. (p. 2397)
Sharma, Radha. Life of Jorja Bear. (p. 1294)
Sharma, Rajinder. Life Post- 1939. (p. 1295)
Sharma, Sejal. Proper Grown-Up. (p. 1807)
Sharma, Shivan. Castle, Dragons & a Cricket Ball. (p. 340)
Sharma, Vishwamitra. Inspire Yourself. (p. 1124)
—World Famous Indians. (p. 2501)
Sharmaine, Gail. Through the Bush. (p. 2237)
Sharman, Annie. Martyrs' Isle, or Madagascar: The Country, the People, & the Missions (Classic Reprint) (p. 1411)
Sharmat, Andrew & Sharmat, Marjorie Weinman. Nate the Great & the Missing Birthday Snake. Wheeler, Jody, illus. (p. 1576)
Sharmat, Marjorie Weinman & Sharmat, Andrew. Nate the Great & the Wandering Word. Wheeler, Jody, illus. (p. 1576)
Sharmat, Marjorie Weinman & Sharmat, Mitchell. Nate the Great & the Hungry Book Club. Wheeler, Jody, illus. (p. 1576)
—Nate the Great, Where Are You? Wheeler, Jody, illus. (p. 1576)
Sharmat, Mitchell. Berkley, the Terrible Sleeper. Kurilla, Renée, illus. (p. 203)
—Gregory, the Terrible Eater. Dewey, Ariane & Aruego, Jose, illus. (p. 895)
Sharon, Amma. Gnome's Winter Solstice Tale: Would You Unquestionably Rather Be Yourself? (p. 845)
—Snappy the Curious Woodland Gnome: What Else Is Possible? (p. 2045)
Sharon, Creech. Love That Dog. (p. 1361)
Sharon, Parker G., illus. see Ellis, Juanita B.
Sharon, Santoni. Night in the Refuge - une Nuit Au Refuge. (p. 1606)
Sharon, Shinn. Shattered Warrior. (p. 2003)
Sharp, Alice, illus. see Harrast, Tracy.
Sharp, Anne, jt. illus. see Denchfield, Nick.
Sharp, Anne Wallace. Ice Hockey. (p. 1088)
—Women Civil Rights Leaders. (p. 2486)
Sharp, Anne Wallace, ed. Freedom Rides. (p. 783)
Sharp, Anthea. Elfhame. (p. 635)
—Hawthorne: A Dark Elf Fantasy. (p. 941)
—Star Compass. (p. 2102)
Sharp, Cara. Wandalyns. (p. 2374)
Sharp, Cathy. Boy with the Latch Key (Halfpenny Orphans, Book 4) (p. 271)
Sharp, Cato Ensor. Stories of the Angels (Classic Reprint) (p. 2125)
Sharp, Cecil J. Sword Dances of Northern England: Songs & Dance Airs (Classic Reprint) (p. 2171)
Sharp, Cecil James. English Folk-Chanteys: With Pianoforte Accompaniment, Introduction & Notes (Classic Reprint) (p. 653)
—Folk-Songs of English Origin Collected in the Appalachian Mountains (Classic Reprint) (p. 757)
Sharp, Cheryl, illus. see Worley, Ashley.
Sharp, Chris, illus. see Barry, Ron & Fitzgerald, Paula.
Sharp, Chris, illus. see Berry, Ron & Mead, David.
Sharp, Chris, illus. see Berry, Ron.
Sharp, Chris, illus. see Kempf, Joe & Pescarino, Cathy.
Sharp, Chris, illus. see Lashbrook, Marilyn.
Sharp, Chris, illus. see Mead, David & Berry, Ron.
Sharp, Chris, illus. see Mead, David.
Sharp, Chris, illus. see Smart Kidz, ed.
Sharp, Chris, illus. see Weimer, Heidi R.
Sharp, Chris, illus. see Weimer, Heidi.
Sharp, Chris, jt. auth. see Berry, Ron.
Sharp, Colby, ed. Creativity Project: An Awesometastic Story Collection. (p. 471)
Sharp, Constance. America Is Born, 1770-1800. (p. 70)
—America Is Born, 1770-1800. Rakove, Jack N., ed. (p. 70)
—Beyond Our Shores: America Extends Its Reach,1890-1899. (p. 212)
—Beyond Our Shores: America Extends Its Reach,1890-1899. Rakove, Jack N., ed. (p. 212)
—Beyond Our Shores (1890/1899) (p. 212)
—Thomas Jefferson & the Growing United States (1800-1811) (p. 2228)
—Thomas Jefferson & the Growing United States (1800-1811) Rakove, Jack N., ed. (p. 2228)
Sharp, Craig, illus. see Bishop, Michele.
Sharp, Dallas Lore. Beyond the Pasture Bars (Classic Reprint) (p. 212)
—Face of the Fields (Classic Reprint) (p. 693)
—Fall of the Year (Classic Reprint) (p. 700)
—Hills of Hingham (Classic Reprint) (p. 972)
—Lay of the Land (Classic Reprint) (p. 1253)
—Lay of the Land (Yesterday's Classics) Horsfall, Robert Bruce, illus. (p. 1253)
—Roof & Meadow (Classic Reprint) (p. 1902)
—Spring of the Year (Classic Reprint) (p. 2092)
—Spring of the Year (Yesterday's Classics) (p. 2092)
—Summer (Classic Reprint) (p. 2149)
—Summer (Yesterday's Classics) Horsfall, Robert Bruce, illus. (p. 2150)
—Watcher in the Woods (Classic Reprint) (p. 2383)
—Where Rolls the Oregon (Classic Reprint) (p. 2439)
—Whole Year Round (Classic Reprint) (p. 2453)
—Wild Life near Home (Classic Reprint) (p. 2464)
—Winter (Classic Reprint) (p. 2475)
—Winter (Yesterday's Classics) (p. 2476)
Sharp, Dan, illus. see Mancini, Lee Ann.
Sharp, Daryon. Journey to the Enchanted Forest with Little Jimmy. (p. 1182)
Sharp, Euan. Diggedy Dozer in Ned at Night. (p. 545)
Sharp, Evelyn. At the Relton Arms (Classic Reprint) (p. 131)
—Making of a Prig (Classic Reprint) (p. 1389)
—Other Side of the Sun: Fairy Stories (Classic Reprint) (p. 1675)
—Rebel Women (Classic Reprint) (p. 1852)
—Story of the Weathercock (Classic Reprint) (p. 2135)
—Youngest Girl in the School (Classic Reprint) (p. 2532)
Sharp, Gene, illus. see Greene, Carol.
Sharp, Gene, illus. see Matthias, Catherine.
Sharp, Gene, jt. auth. see Matthias, Catherine.
Sharp, Hilda M. Pawn in Pawn (Classic Reprint) (p. 1708)
—Stars in Their Courses (Classic Reprint) (p. 2107)
Sharp, J. L. Persephia. (p. 1724)
Sharp, Jennifer. I Love the Way You Giggle. Greaves, Naomi, illus. (p. 1072)
—I'm Just Little. Greaves, Naomi, illus. (p. 1098)
—Imagine. Greaves, Naomi, illus. (p. 1100)
—Imagine. Naomi, Greaves, illus. (p. 1100)
Sharp, Joshua. Marot & Walter's Almanack, for the Year of Our Lord 1826: Being the Second after Bissextile, or Leap Year, & the 50th & 51st, of American Independence (Classic Reprint) (p. 1408)
Sharp, Karen. Under Alex's Bed: Young Boys Amazing Journey. (p. 2321)
Sharp, Katharine. Jocelyn West a Tale of the Grand Canon (Classic Reprint) (p. 1170)
Sharp, Katharine Dooris. Summer in a Bog (Classic Reprint) (p. 2149)
Sharp, Katie. Soil. (p. 2055)
Sharp, Katie, jt. auth. see Sohn, Emily.
Sharp, Katie John. Smokeless Tobacco: Not a Safe Alternative. (p. 2043)
Sharp, Katie John, jt. auth. see Sohn, Emily.
Sharp, Lani. Has Anyone Seen the Creature? (p. 936)
Sharp, Laura. Key Prince. (p. 1211)
Sharp, Linda, illus. see Hrdlitschka, Shelley & Schidlo, Rae.
SHARP Literacy, compiled by. Banking on Your Future: A Blueprint for Entrepreneurial, Technical & Trade Careers. (p. 164)
—Growing up Strong: Healthy Children can Change the World. (p. 900)
Sharp, Lydia. Whenever I'm with You. (p. 2435)
Sharp, Margery. Rescuers. Williams, Garth, illus. (p. 1868)
Sharp, Mary, ed. see Brenner, Vida.
Sharp, Melanie, illus. see De Marco, Clare.
Sharp, Melanie, illus. see Robinson, Hilary.
Sharp, Michael. Captain Tristan Am I. Van Tine, Laura, illus. (p. 326)
Sharp, N. L. Flower Girl / the Ring Bear. Hantula, Timothy James, illus. (p. 752)
Sharp, Pam, illus. see Nicksich, Karen Marie.
Sharp, Paul. Pablo el Lanzador. Sharp, Paul, illus. (p. 1690)
—Paul the Pitcher. (p. 1707)
—Paul the Pitcher. Sharp, Paul, illus. (p. 1707)
Sharp, Paul, illus. see Bardina, Patricia & Burgess, Joanne.
Sharp, Paul, illus. see Greene, Carol.
Sharp, Paul, illus. see Hapka, Cathy, pseud.
Sharp, Paul, illus. see Harrast, Tracy.
Sharp, R. Farquharson, tr. see Ibsen, Henrik.
Sharp, Rachel, illus. see Morris, A. R.
Sharp, Rebecca, illus. see Sanders, Mt.
Sharp, Sharon. Planet Chaos (p. 1755)
Sharp, Thelma. Saturday Appaloosa Graham, Georgia, illus. (p. 1936)
Sharp, Todd, illus. see Edgar, Robert.
Sharp, Todd, illus. see Mosher, Jennifer.
Sharp, William. Gypsy Christ, & Other Tales (Classic Reprint) (p. 907)
—Madge o' the Pool: The Gypsy Christ & Other Tales (Classic Reprint) (p. 1375)
—Silence Farm (Classic Reprint) (p. 2017)
—Sport of Chance, Vol. 1 of 3 (Classic Reprint) (p. 2087)
—Wives in Exile: A Comedy in Romance (Classic Reprint) (p. 2482)
—Wives in Exile. (p. 2482)

S

Shaw, Natalie, adapted by. Doozers Build a Birdhouse. (p. 585)
—Doozers Stick with It. (p. 585)
—Dragon Heroes. (p. 593)
—Meet PJ Robot! (p. 1439)
—Operation Easter Egg. (p. 1666)
—Operation Glitter Hero. (p. 1666)
—Pumpkin Guts Versus the Vampires. (p. 1812)
—Race to the Moon! (p. 1831)
—Space Mall. (p. 2071)
—Two Teen Vampires! (p. 2309)
—Welcome to Drac's Castle! (p. 2398)
Shaw, Natalie, comment. Doozers Make a Rainbow. (p. 585)
Shaw, Peter, illus. see Wild, Margaret.
Shaw Ph D, Aaron. Sully P. Snooferpoot's Amazing New Christmas Pot. Diamond, Lane, ed. (p. 2148)
—Sully P. Snooferpoot's Amazing New Dayswitcher. Diamond, Lane, ed. (p. 2148)
Shaw, Rebecca. Elisha's Great Mission. (p. 636)
Shaw, Sadie. Mosses from a Rolling Stone (Classic Reprint) (p. 1508)
Shaw, Sandra Anne. Mary's Gift. Rosales, Mary, tr. (p. 1416)
Shaw, Sandy. Adventures of Dilly Dog: Dilly at the Lakes. (p. 23)
Shaw, Sarah, illus. see Chand, Emlyn.
Shaw, Scott. Shrek - Living Green (p. 2013)
Shaw, Solomon Benjamin. Touching Incidents & Remarkable Answers to Prayer: As Related by John B. Gough, Bishop Bowman, LL. D. , Mrs. Mary Grant Cramer, James H. Potts, D. D. , Mathew Hale Smith, John Wesley, T. de Witt Talmage, D. D. , George Muller, & Many Others. (p. 2268)
Shaw, Sonny, illus. see Adams, Bill.
Shaw, Stan, illus. see Wilde, Oscar, et al.
Shaw, Stanley. Siren of the Snows (Classic Reprint) (p. 2026)
Shaw, Stephanie. Bedtime in the Meadow. Watkins, Laura, illus. (p. 188)
—By the Light of the Moon. Harry, Rebecca, illus. (p. 306)
—Cookie for Santa. Robert, Bruno, illus. (p. 446)
—Lullaby Farm. Harry, Rebecca, illus. (p. 1367)
—Moo la La! Cow Goes Shopping. (p. 1500)
—Piece by Piece. Daigneault, Sylvie, illus. (p. 1742)
—Schnitzel: A Cautionary Tale for Lazy Louts. Barry, Kevin, illus. (p. 1944)
—Under the Sleepy Stars. Harry, Rebecca, illus. (p. 2323)
Shaw, Susan. One of the Survivors. (p. 1661)
—Tunnel Vision. (p. 2299)
Shaw, Thomas. Study of Breeds in America: Cattle, Sheep & Swine (Classic Reprint) (p. 2144)
Shaw, Thomas B. Heretic, Vol. 2 Of 3: Or, the German Stranger, an Historical Romance of the Court of Russia in the Fifteenth Century (Classic Reprint) (p. 959)
Shaw, Tina. Rigby Reading Sails: Leveled Reader Emerald Grades 4-5 Book 3: the Fishing Trip. (p. 1881)
—Rigby Reading Sails: Leveled Reader Emerald Grades 4-5 Book 12: the Walking Stick. (p. 1881)
Shaw, Tucker. Anxious Hearts. (p. 104)
—Oh Yeah, Audrey! (p. 1642)
Shaw, W. Frank. Preacher's Promptuary of Anecdote: Stories, New & Old, Arranged, Indexed, & Classified, for the Use of Preachers, Teachers & Catechists (Classic Reprint) (p. 1786)
Shaw, William Francis. Juvenal, Persius, Martial, & Catullus: An Experiment in Translation (Classic Reprint) (p. 1195)
Shaw, Yvonne, illus. see Shaw, Laura.
Shawell, Julia. Radio Mirror, Vol. 3: November, 1934 (Classic Reprint) (p. 1833)
Shaw-Fullilove, Maggie. Who Was Responsible? (Classic Reprint) (p. 2451)
Shawmeker, Harvey. Tales from a Boy's Fancy: A Volume of Stories & Poems (Classic Reprint) (p. 2181)
Shawn, Robinson P. B. Jerry the Squirrel: Volume One. (p. 1164)
Shaw-Peterson, Kimberly, illus. see Ruprecht, Jennifer L.
Shaw-Russell, Susan. Animal ABC. (p. 87)
—Build Your Own Breakfast Sticker Activity Book. (p. 293)
—Build Your Own Burger Sticker Activity Book. (p. 293)
—Cool Cupcakes Coloring Book. (p. 448)
—Coral Reef Fish Friends Sticker Activity Book. (p. 453)
—Create Your Own Aliens Sticker Activity Book. (p. 469)
—Day with the Dinosaurs Sticker Activity Book. (p. 515)
—Deep Sea Diner Sticker Activity Book. (p. 524)
—Make Your Own Bookmark Sticker Activity Book: Monsters, Robots & More! (p. 1387)
—Make Your Own Bookmark Sticker Activity Book: Princesses, Mermaids & More! (p. 1387)
—Moustache Sticker Activity Book. (p. 1515)
—Robots Activity Book. (p. 1893)
—Seek, Sketch & Color — Alphabet. (p. 1984)
—Seek, Sketch & Color — Animals. (p. 1984)
—Smiley Robot Tattoos. (p. 2042)
—Snow White Activity Book. (p. 2048)
—Spark - Amazing Animals Coloring Book. (p. 2074)
—Three Bears Activity Book. (p. 2231)
—Under the Sea Party Sticker Activity Book. (p. 2322)
Shaw-Russell, Susan & Activity Books Staff. Bee Cool! Sticker Activity Book. (p. 189)
—Build Your Own Cupcake Sticker Activity Book. (p. 293)
—Tortoise & the Hare. (p. 2266)
Shaw-Russell, Susan, et al. Animals on Parade Find & Color. (p. 95)
Shaw-Sloane, T. J. Gnomic Sunbeams (Classic Reprint) (p. 845)
Shaw-Smith, Emma, illus. see Gershator, David & Gershator, Phillis.
Shawyer, Jo. Legend of the Paymaster's Gold. (p. 1262)
Shay, Frank. Contemporary One-Act Plays Of 1921: American (Classic Reprint) (p. 444)
—Treasury of Plays for Men (Classic Reprint) (p. 2283)
—Treasury of Plays for Women (Classic Reprint) (p. 2283)
Shay, Kenley. Marsha Mellow Goes Missing: An Unofficial Story for Shopkins Collectors. (p. 1409)
—Prommy Meets Her Match: An Unofficial Story for Shopkins Collectors. (p. 1806)
Shay, Marissa. Pinch Hitter. (p. 1745)
Shay, Mary Bernard. Friend for Bobby. (p. 786)
Shay, Michael K. Flash in Time: A Novel. (p. 746)
Shay, Rori. Elected. (p. 630)
—Suspected. (p. 2166)
Shayan, Mohammad, illus. see Whaler, Norman.
Shayibi, Sundus, illus. see Ata-Allah, Salma.
Shayibi, Sundus, illus. see Tahir, Samar.
Shayla, Raquel, ed. see Benkendorf, Lynne.
Shchedrin, N. E. Golloviev Family (Classic Reprint) (p. 861)
She, Kai-Yu. Mr. Doom. (p. 1518)
She, Liu, illus. see Ma, Zheng & Li, Zheng.
Shea, Abigail. Victoria Justice. (p. 2355)
—Wolves in Danger. (p. 2485)
Shea, Adele. Wolves in Danger. (p. 2485)
Shea, Betty. Animals of the Desert: Adapting to Survive. (p. 95)
Shea, Bob. Ballet Cat What's Your Favorite Favorite? Shea, Bob, illus. (p. 162)
—Buddy & the Bunnies in: Don't Play with Your Food! (p. 290)
—Cheetah Can't Lose. Shea, Bob, illus. (p. 364)
—Crash, Splash, or Moo! (p. 467)
—Dinosaur vs. School. Shea, Bob, illus. (p. 549)
—Dinosaur vs. the Library. Shea, Bob, illus. (p. 549)
—Dinosaur vs. the Potty. Shea, Bob, illus. (p. 549)
—I'm a Shark. Shea, Bob, illus. (p. 1097)
—Kid Sheriff & the Terrible Toads. Smith, Lane, illus. (p. 1213)
—Oh, Daddy! Shea, Bob, illus. (p. 1641)
—Race You to Bed. Shea, Bob, illus. (p. 1831)
—Unicorn Is Maybe Not So Great after All. Shea, Bob, illus. (p. 2328)
—Unicorn Thinks He's Pretty Great. Shea, Bob, illus. (p. 2328)
—Who Wet My Pants? OHora, Zachariah, illus. (p. 2452)
Shea, Bob, illus. see Caswell, Deanna.
Shea, Bob, illus. see Colleen, Marcie.
Shea, Bob, illus. see DiPucchio, Kelly.
Shea, Bob, illus. see Harper, Charise Mericle.
Shea, Bob, illus. see John, Jory.
Shea, Bob, illus. see Sauer, Tammi.
Shea, Bobby Kennedy. Patterns with Pandas. (p. 1706)
Shea, Bobby Kennedy & Kennedy Shea, Bobby. Patterns with Pandas. (p. 1706)
Shea, C. O. Conductors & Insulators. (p. 438)
Shea, Cait. Shadow Jumper: The Quest. (p. 1996)
Shea, Christopher Ambrose. Diary of a Bachelor (Classic Reprint) (p. 539)
Shea, Cornelius. Look Out for Paint: A Farce Comedy in Three Acts (Classic Reprint) (p. 1346)
Shea, Denise, illus. see Bridges, Sarah.
Shea, Denise, illus. see Dahl, Michael.
Shea, Denise, illus. see Meachen Rau, Dana.
Shea, Eileen. Shep & the Momma Mongoose. (p. 2005)
Shea, Hannah. Hannah's Faith & Grace. (p. 918)
Shea, Jerry. Where Does the Recycling Go? (p. 2436)
Shea, John. Canticle: Biblical Songs Illuminated. Mullan, G. E., illus. (p. 323)
—Combating Computer Viruses. (p. 428)
—Declaration of Independence. (p. 523)
—If I Wasn't Me. (p. 1091)
—Outsiders. (p. 1685)
—Respiratory System. (p. 1869)
Shea, John & Harmon, Michael B. Kid from Southie. (p. 1213)
Shea, John & Shea, John M. Declaration of Independence. (p. 523)
Shea, John M. Digestive System. (p. 545)
—DNA up Close. (p. 570)
—Eleanor Roosevelt in Her Own Words. (p. 630)
—Franklin D. Roosevelt in His Own Words. (p. 779)
—Gross Things about Your Body. (p. 898)
—Heroes of the US Coast Guard. (p. 962)
—Self-Injury & Cutting: Stopping the Pain. (p. 1987)
—Syracuse Basketball. (p. 2174)
—Thomas Jefferson in His Own Words (p. 2228)
—Tuskegee Airmen. (p. 2301)
—Viruses up Close. (p. 2361)
—Vlad the Impaler. (p. 2364)
Shea, John M., jt. auth. see Shea, John.
Shea, Kevin. H Is for Hockey: A NHL Alumni Alphabet. Dewar, Ken, illus. (p. 907)
—H Is for Hockey. (p. 907)
—H Is for Hockey: An NHL Alumni Alphabet. Dewar, Ken, illus. (p. 908)
Shea, Kevin Pearce. Snoop Dogg. (p. 2046)
Shea, Lisa, text. Meet the Black Widow. (p. 1439)
Shea, Louis, illus. see Mitchell, Laine.
Shea, Margaret. Gals They Left Behind (Classic Reprint) (p. 806)
Shea, Mary Molly. Being a Manatee (p. 193)
—Being a Manatee. (p. 193)
—Foods of India. (p. 760)
—Giraffes. (p. 834)
—Intimidating Elephants. (p. 1127)
—Lions. (p. 1307)
—Making Line Graphs. (p. 1389)
—Massive Moose. (p. 1418)
—Menacing Chimpanzees. (p. 1447)
—Taylor Swift. (p. 2193)
—Wildebeests. (p. 2466)
Shea, Mary Molly, contrib. by. Poisonous Slow Lorises. (p. 1768)
'Shea, Michael Vincent O. Every-Day Speller, Vol. 1: Grades One & Two (Classic Reprint) (p. 670)
Shea, Molly. Alicia Keys. (p. 46)
—Black Eyed Peas. (p. 238)
Shea, Nicole. American Revolution. (p. 73)
—Animals & Climate Change. (p. 93)
—Be an Astronomer. (p. 176)
—Creepy Amphibians. (p. 472)
—Creepy Birds. (p. 472)
—Creepy Bugs. (p. 472)
—Creepy Mammals. (p. 473)
—Creepy Sea Creatures. (p. 473)
—Elizabeth Cady Stanton in Her Own Words. (p. 636)
—Frederick Douglass in His Own Words (p. 782)
—Poaching & Illegal Trade. (p. 1763)
Shea, Pegi Deitz. Liberty Rising: The Story of the Statue of Liberty. Zahares, Wade, illus. (p. 1284)
—Noah Webster: Weaver of Words. Vachula, Monica, illus. (p. 1616)
Shea, Robert Kennedy. Hunting. (p. 1053)
Shea, Steve, ed. see Tamayo, Alex.
Shea, Steve, ed. see Vinson, Haley.
Shea, Tess & Pohlen, Jerome. San Francisco Baby: A Local Baby Book. Lemay, Violet, illus. (p. 1929)
Shea, Therese. 20 Fun Facts about Hippos. (p. 2553)
—20 Fun Facts about Spiders. (p. 2553)
—20 Fun Facts about the US Constitution. (p. 2553)
—African Burial Ground. (p. 32)
—Africanized Honeybee vs. Army Ant. (p. 33)
—All about Bicycles. (p. 48)
—America's Electoral College: Choosing the President Comparing & Analyzing Charts, Graphs, & Tables. (p. 75)
—Anthropologists at Work. (p. 102)
—Arctic Hares. (p. 112)
—Around the Globe: Where Are Your Ancestors From? (p. 118)
—Attack of the Bullfrogs. (p. 134)
—Avoiding Online Hoaxes. (p. 143)
—Becoming a Pro Basketball Player. (p. 187)
—Before Teddy Roosevelt Was President. (p. 190)
—Bigfoot Trail. (p. 224)
—Biosphere 2: Solving Word Problems. (p. 229)
—Bird Watcher's Guide to Cardinals. (p. 230)
—Bizarre Life Cycle of an Octopus. (p. 235)
—Black Ops & Other Special Missions of the U. S. Army Green Berets. (p. 238)
—Bloodsucking Vampire Bats. (p. 246)
—Bobcats in the Dark. (p. 252)
—Boston Massacre (p. 264)
—Brad Paisley. (p. 274)
—Britannica Beginner BIOS: Set 2. (p. 282)
—Career As a Secret Service Agent. (p. 328)
—CC Sabathia. (p. 348)
—Climbing Mount Everest: Understanding Commutative, Associative & Distributive Properties. (p. 405)
—Colorado's Trailblazers: Pioneers in Science, Technology, & Engineering (p. 422)
—Cornelius Vanderbilt & the Railroad Industry. (p. 454)
—Creepy Reptiles. (p. 473)
—Crocodiles (p. 477)
—Crypts & Tombs. (p. 481)
—Dead Sea. (p. 518)
—Dementia. (p. 527)
—Discovering Egyptian Dynasties. (p. 555)
—Discovering STEM at the Zoo. (p. 556)
—Do Cows Have Two Stomachs? And Other FAQs about Animals. (p. 570)
—Droughts & Heat Waves. (p. 606)
—Emma Stone: Actress. (p. 643)
—Fables, Myths, & Legends. (p. 691)
—Foods of China. (p. 760)
—Freaky Weather Stories. (p. 780)
—Gareth's Guide to Building a Robot. (p. 810)
—Gareth's Guide to Building a Space Probe. (p. 810)
—Getting to Know Lego Mindstorms. (p. 826)
—Ghosts Subtract! (p. 830)
—Godzilla. (p. 854)
—Gold (p. 855)
—Grizzly Bears. (p. 897)
—Hammerhead Sharks. (p. 913)
—Harvesting Equipment (p. 936)
—Haunted! the Queen Mary. (p. 938)
—Heat in Action. (p. 946)
—History of the Chesapeake Bay. (p. 980)
—How a Skyscraper Is Built. (p. 1025)
—How Do I Use an Atlas? (p. 1028)
—How Do Reservoirs Work? (p. 1029)
—How Dolphins & Other Animals Use Sonar. (p. 1030)
—Immigration to America: Identifying Different Points of View about an Issue. (p. 1101)
—Investigating UFOs & Aliens (p. 1131)
—John Lee Hooker: King of the Blues. (p. 1173)
—Kate DiCamillo: Newbery Medal-Winning Author. (p. 1204)
—Kendrick Lamar: Storyteller of Compton (p. 1209)
—Kendrick Lamar: Becoming the Voice of Compton (p. 1209)
—Ladybugs up Close (p. 1239)
—Land & Climate of Latin America. (p. 1241)
—Lions. (p. 1307)
—Louisiana Purchase. (p. 1358)
—Lupita Nyong'o: Oscar-Winning Actress (p. 1369)
—Meet the House of Representatives. (p. 1440)
—Mummies Multiply! (p. 1526)
—Mummies of Ancient Egypt. (p. 1526)
—Overfishing. (p. 1687)
—Planting Equipment (p. 1757)
—Pufferfish. (p. 1811)
—Racing Horses. (p. 1832)
—Reading Map Keys. (p. 1847)
—Real-Life Monsters? (p. 1849)
—Really Strange Reptiles. (p. 1851)
—Robotics Club: Teaming up to Build Robots. (p. 1893)
—Rock & Ice Climbing. (p. 1894)
—Rosa Parks (p. 1904)
—Saving the Endangered American Bald Eagle (p. 1939)
—Scorpions. (p. 1962)
—Sharon Draper: Author. (p. 2003)
—Silver (p. 2019)
—Sinking of the Titanic. (p. 2024)
—Sixth Amendment: The Rights of the Accused in Criminal Cases. (p. 2029)
—Solving Real World Problems with Mechanical Engineering (p. 2058)
—Statue of Liberty Wasn't Made to Welcome Immigrants: Exposing Myths about U.S. Landmarks. (p. 2109)
—Stephen Curry: Basketball's MVP. (p. 2115)
—Steve Jobs & Apple. (p. 2116)
—This Book Can Poison! (p. 2223)
—Toby Keith. (p. 2254)
—Top 10 Secrets for Managing Credit Cards & Paying Bills Successfully. (p. 2263)
—United States Constitution. (p. 2331)
—Usher. (p. 2341)
—Using Your Bones. (p. 2342)
—Using Your Lungs (p. 2342)
—Vampires Divide! (p. 2346)
—Watch Peas Grow. (p. 2383)
—Watch Peas Grow / ¡Mira cómo crecen los Guisantes! (p. 2383)
—Watch Pine Trees Grow. (p. 2383)
—Watch Pine Trees Grow / ¡Mira cómo crecen los Pinos! (p. 2383)
—We Need Spiders. (p. 2392)
—Werewolves Do Word Problems! (p. 2401)
—What Are Community Rules & Laws? (p. 2405)
—What Are Crustaceans? (p. 2405)
—What If I Need Stitches? (p. 2413)
—What Is Animal Migration? (p. 2414)
—When Blizzards Blow. (p. 2429)
—When Tornadoes Touch Down. (p. 2434)
—Why Do Lobsters Eat Each Other? And Other Odd Crustacean Adaptations. (p. 2456)
—Witches Add! (p. 2480)
—Zendaya: Actress & Singer. (p. 2539)
—Zombies Read Graphs! (p. 2542)
—Zoom in on the Liberty Bell. (p. 2544)
Shea, Therese & Harasymiw, Therese. Transcontinental Railroad: Connecting the Nation. (p. 2277)
Shea, Therese & Nardo, Don. Civil War: A Nation Divided. (p. 396)
Shea, Therese & Shea, Therese M. Inside the Labor Movement. (p. 1123)
Shea, Therese M. 20 Fun Facts about Bullfrogs (p. 2553)
—Aboard USS Constitution (p. 6)
—Alexander Hamilton: Founding Father & Treasury Secretary. (p. 42)
—Before Ronald Reagan Was President. (p. 190)
—Daily Life Then & Now. (p. 496)
—Is a Turtle a Good Pet for Me? (p. 1136)
—Louisiana Purchase & the Lewis & Clark Expedition. (p. 1358)
—Rocked by Earthquakes. (p. 1895)
—Was Dr. Frankenstein Real? (p. 2381)
Shea, Therese M., jt. auth. see Shea, Therese.
Sheafer, Silvia Anne. Life of Aretha Franklin: Queen of Soul. (p. 1294)
Sheaffer, C. H. Soccer Heart: A Story & Guide for the Friendly Contender. (p. 2052)
Sheahan, Michael. Roof Top Hop. (p. 1902)
Shealy, Dennis. I'm a Monster Truck. Staake, Bob, illus. (p. 1097)
—I'm a Truck. (p. 1097)
—Joker's Joyride - Built for Speed. Random House Editors, illus. (p. 1176)
Shealy, Dennis & Miryam. Favorites: I'm a Truck/The Happy Man & His Dump Truck/I'm a Monster Truck. Staake, Bob et al, illus. (p. 716)
Shealy, Dennis R. I Am Captain Snowball! (p. 1058)
—I Am Captain Snowball! (the Secret Life of Pets 2) Borkowski, Michael, illus. (p. 1058)
—I'm a Bulldozer. (p. 1097)
—I'm a Monster Truck. Staake, Bob, illus. (p. 1097)
—I'm a Snowplow. Staake, Bob, illus. (p. 1097)
—I'm a T. Rex! Biggs, Brian, illus. (p. 1097)
—I'm a Truck LGB 6-Copy Clip Strip Fall 2019 (p. 1097)
—My Little Golden Book about Dinosaurs. Laberis, Steph, illus. (p. 1552)
—My Little Golden Book about Weather. (p. 1553)
—Noisy Garage. (p. 1617)
—Park Is Open (Jurassic World) Random House, illus. (p. 1700)
—Riddle Me This! (DC Super Friends) Random House, illus. (p. 1878)
—Solar System. Johnson, Richard, illus. (p. 2056)
—T. Rex Trouble! (DC Super Friends) DeCarlo, Mike et al, illus. (p. 2174)
Shealy, Dennis R., jt. auth. see Golden Books Staff.
Shealy, Dennis R., des. Queen of Cats! (p. 1824)
Shear, Dani. Foodie Club. Weinstein, Holly, illus. (p. 760)
Shear, Sylvester R. Baldwin Speller (Classic Reprint) (p. 161)
Shearar, James. Prinkle & His Friends, Vol. 2 Of 3: A Novel (Classic Reprint) (p. 1800)
Sheard, Virna. By the Queen's Grace a Novel (Classic Reprint) (p. 306)
—Golden Apple Tree (Classic Reprint) (p. 856)
Shearer, Alex. Cloud Hunters. (p. 407)
—Great Blue Yonder. (p. 884)
—Message to the Sea. (p. 1451)
—Sky Run. (p. 2034)
Shearer, Amelia. God Made Seasons. Marlin, Kathryn, illus. (p. 852)
—God's Armor for Me. Burroughs, Scott, illus. (p. 853)
Shearer, Cynthia & Washington, George. Handwriting by George 28-55: Rules of Civility & Decent Behaviour in Company & Conversation: Rules 28-53 to Draw & Write (p. 916)
Shearer, Deborah, jt. auth. see Vogt, Gregory.
Shearer, Florence. Cara's Carrot Cake. (p. 327)
—Magic Mermaid. (p. 1378)
Shearer, James. Prinkle & His Friends, Vol. 1 Of 3: A Novel (Classic Reprint) (p. 1800)
Shearham, Victoria. How about a Dinosaur? (p. 1025)
Shearham, Victoria, illus. see Fine, Esther Sokolov & Head, Jim.
Shearin, Hubert Gibson. Syllabus of Kentucky Folk-Songs (Classic Reprint) (p. 2172)
Shearon, Lillian Nicholson. Little Mixer (Classic Reprint) (p. 1322)
Shearring, Maisie Paradise. I'm Actually Really Grown up Now. (p. 1097)
Shearring, Maisie Paradise, illus. see Beauvais, Clémentine.
Shearwater, Cate. Going for Gold. (p. 854)
Shearwater, Cate, jt. auth. see Bruton, Catherine.
Sheban, Chris, illus. see Bateman, Teresa.
Sheban, Chris, illus. see Bernheimer, Kate.

S

Shelley, John, illus. see Sutcliffe, Jane.
Shelley, Mary. Falkner: A Novel (Classic Reprint) (p. 699)
—Fortunes of Perkin Warbeck: A Romance (Classic Reprint) (p. 770)
—Frankenstein. (p. 777)
—Frankenstein. Gelev, Penko, illus. (p. 777)
—Frankenstein: The Graphic Novel. (p. 778)
—Frankenstein Williams, Anthony, illus. (p. 778)
—Frankenstein Fisher, Eric Scott, illus. (p. 778)
—Frankenstein. (p. 778)
—Frankenstein. Dominguez, Oscar, illus. (p. 778)
—Frankenstein (Classic Reprint) (p. 778)
—Frankenstien. (p. 778)
—Gris Grimly's Frankenstein. Grimly, Gris, illus. (p. 897)
—Ladybird Classics - Frankenstein. (p. 1238)
—Last Man. (p. 1248)
—Lodore, Vol. 3 of 3 (Classic Reprint) (p. 1339)
—Tales & Stories: Now First Collected (Classic Reprint) (p. 2181)
Shelley, Mary, jt. auth. see Shelley, Mary.
Shelley, Mary & Broseta, Teresa. Frankenstein. (p. 778)
Shelley, Mary & MacDonald, Fiona. Frankenstein. (p. 778)
Shelley, Mary & Shelley, Mary. Frankenstein. (p. 778)
Shelley, Mary Wollstonecraft. Frankenstein. (p. 778)
Shelley, Mortimer M. Blobson's Dire Mishaps in a Barn Storming Company (Classic Reprint) (p. 245)
Shelley, Rex. Japan. (p. 1159)
Shelley, T. C. Monster Who Wasn't. (p. 1497)
Shellie, Shamari G., illus. see Czerwinski, Lynn.
Shellito, Coy N. Sequelle, 1917 (Classic Reprint) (p. 1989)
Shellley, Mary & Villanueva, Lilia. Frankenstein. Buque Letras. (p. 778)
Shelly, Jeff. How to Draw Dinosaurs: Step-By-step Instructions for 20 Prehistoric Creatures. (p. 1040)
—Learn to Draw Cars & Trucks. (p. 1256)
—Learn to Draw Dinosaurs. (p. 1256)
Shelly, Jeff, illus. see Bateman, Teresa.
Shelly, Jeff, illus. see Pearson, Mary E.
Shelly, Jeff, jt. auth. see Pearson, Mary E.
Shelly, Jeff, jt. illus. see Fisher, Diana.
Shelly, Jeff, Sr., illus. see Schneider, David.
Shelly, Mary W., jt. auth. see Stoker, Bram.
Shelnutt, Charlene, illus. see Doxey, Carol E.
Shelton, A., jt. auth. see Brown, Bruce.
Shelton, Albert L. Pioneering in Tibet (Classic Reprint) (p. 1748)
Shelton, Angela. Tilda Pinkerton's Magical Hats. (p. 2242)
—Tilda Pinkerton's Magical Hats. Murray, James, illus. (p. 2242)
Shelton, C. D. Kid's Guide to Being a Winner Workbook. (p. 1215)
Shelton, C. H., jt. auth. see Shelton, C. H.
Shelton, C. H. & Shelton, C. H. Kid's Guide to Being a Winner. Gillespie, Greg G., illus. (p. 1215)
Shelton, C. M. Cosmic Chaos. (p. 456)
Shelton, Carolyn & Chappell, Colin. Odessa Chronicles: A Collection of Stories for Children of All Ages. (p. 1638)
Shelton, Connie. Trophy Wife Exchange: Heist Ladies Caper Mysteries, Book 2. (p. 2291)
Shelton, Crystal G. Theodore's Rings. (p. 2216)
Shelton, Dave. Boy & a Bear in a Boat. (p. 268)
—Thirteen Chairs. (p. 2223)
Shelton, David. David Slays the Dragon. (p. 511)
Shelton, Donna. Lost in Time. (p. 1354)
Shelton, F. W. Salander & the Dragon: A Romance of Hartz Prison (Classic Reprint) (p. 1924)
—Up the River (Classic Reprint) (p. 2338)
Shelton, Flora Beal. Sunshine & Shadow on the Tibetan Border (Classic Reprint) (p. 2153)
Shelton, Frederick William. Crystalline, or the Heiress of Fall down Castle: A Romance (Classic Reprint) (p. 481)
—Peeps from a Belfry (Classic Reprint) (p. 1714)
Shelton, Jane De Forest. Salt-Box House: Eighteenth Century Life in a New England Hill Town. [1900]. (p. 1925)
—Salt-Box House: Eighteenth Century Life in a New England Hill Town (Classic Reprint) (p. 1925)
Shelton, Josh. Hey Tree, What Should I Be? Pullenza, Sam, illus. (p. 964)
—Imagine a World. Pullenza, Sam, illus. (p. 1100)
Shelton, Karen. Famous Americans: Ready-to-Go Units That Include Mini-Books, Read-Aloud Plays, Graphic Organizers, & Writing Activities That Teach about 12 Important Americans. (p. 703)
Shelton, Mason Bradford. Rocky Mountain Adventures (Classic Reprint) (p. 1896)
Shelton, Paula Young. Child of the Civil Rights Movement. ón, Raul, illus. (p. 370)
Shelton, Sam. My Haunted School Year. (p. 1549)
—My Haunted Summer. (p. 1549)
—Nyght Lyght Presents: Tales So Scary, You Will Sleep with a Light On. (p. 1632)
Shelton, Sherry, jt. auth. see Burgo, Ann.
Shelton, Tiffany. College Cookbook: Healthy, Budget-Friendly Recipes for Every Student Gain Energy While Enjoying Delicious Meals. (p. 415)
Shelton, Trent. Straight up: Honest, Unfiltered, As-Real-As-I-Can-Put-It Advice for Life's Biggest Challenges (p. 2136)
Shelton, William Henry. Last Three Soldiers (Classic Reprint) (p. 1249)
—Man Without a Memory: And Other Stories (Classic Reprint) (p. 1396)
Shelton-MacKenzie, Adelheid. Aureola, or the Black Sheep: A Story of German Social Life (Classic Reprint) (p. 137)
Shems, Ed, illus. see Joven, C. C.
Shem-Tov, Tami & Sandbank, Rachella. Concert in the Sand. Ofer, Avi, illus. (p. 438)
—Queen in Jerusalem. Ofer, Avi, illus. (p. 1823)
Shen, Fuke. Computer Science Footprints Change the World Science Series(chinese Edition) (p. 437)
Shen, Kristy & Leung, Bryce. Little Miss Evil. (p. 1322)
Shen, Prudence. Nothing Can Possibly Go Wrong. Hicks, Faith Erin, illus. (p. 1625)
Shen, Roddie. Whoever's Heard of a Hibernating Pig? (p. 2452)
Shen, Tkin. Rambles of the Emperor Ching Tih in Këang Nan, Vol. 1 Of 2: A Chinese Tale (Classic Reprint) (p. 1839)
Shen, Zhizhong. Footprint Agronomy Change the World Science Series(chinese Edition) (p. 762)
Shendrik, Svetlana, illus. see Clever Publishing.
Shene, Paula. Mandy - The Alpha Dog: The Chronicles of the K-9 Boys & Girls on Locus Street. Shene, Prescott, illus. (p. 1397)
Shene, Prescott, illus. see Shene, Paula.
Sheneman, Drew. Don't Eat That. (p. 582)
—Nope. (p. 1619)
Sheng, Ann, illus. see Alary, Laura.
Shenhav, Haya. Mitz Petel , Hebrew edition. (p. 1484)
Shenk, David. Dilogoentreunmusulmnyuncristiano: A Muslim & a Christian in Dialogue. (p. 547)
Shenoi, Krishna Bala, illus. see Benjamin, A. H.
Shenoi, Krishna Bala, illus. see Shekhar, Hansda Sowvendra.
Shenton, Edward, illus. see Moody, Ralph.
Shepard, Aaron. Adventures of Mouse Deer: Favorite Tales of Southeast Asia. Gamble, Kim, illus. (p. 25)
—Baker's Dozen: A Saint Nicholas Tale. Edelson, Wendy, illus. (p. 160)
—Baker's Dozen: A Saint Nicholas Tale, with Bonus Cookie Recipe for St. Nicholas Christmas Cookies. (p. 160)
—Baker's Dozen: A Saint Nicholas Tale, with Bonus Cookie Recipe & Pattern for St. Nicholas Christmas Cookies (Special Edition) Edelson, Wendy, illus. (p. 160)
—Baker's Dozen: A Saint Nicholas Tale, with Bonus Cookie Recipe & Pattern for St. Nicholas Christmas Cookies (25th Anniversary Edition) Edelson, Wendy, illus. (p. 160)
—Christmas Truce: A Story of World War 1. (p. 387)
—Christmas Truce: A Story of World War 1. Edelson, Wendy, illus. (p. 387)
—King o' the Cats. Sorra, Kristin, illus. (p. 1220)
—Lady White Snake: A Tale from Chinese Opera: Bilingual - Traditional Chinese & English. Chen, Isabella, tr. (p. 1238)
—Lady White Snake: A Tale from Chinese Opera: Bilingual - Simplified Chinese & English. Zhang, Song Nan, illus. (p. 1238)
—Man Who Sang to Ghosts: A Japanese Legend, Retold from the Story of Hoichi & Based on the Tale of the Heike. (p. 1395)
—Princess of India: An Ancient Tale (30th Anniversary Edition) Rosenberry, Vera, illus. (p. 1798)
—Quackling: A Feathered Fairy Tale. Edelson, Wendy, illus. (p. 1821)
—Quackling: A Very Loud Fairy Tale. Edelson, Wendy, illus. (p. 1821)
—Sea King's Daughter: A Russian Legend. (p. 1967)
—Sea King's Daughter: A Russian Legend. Spirin, Gennady, illus. (p. 1967)
—Skeeter & the Weasels. Watson, Anne L., illus. (p. 2030)
—Swan Knight: A Medieval Legend, Retold from Wagner's Lohengrin. (p. 2167)
Shepard, Ashleigh. Adventures of Young Shep: Young Shep Saves the Game. (p. 29)
Shepard, Charles O. Christmas Stories for My Sister's Children: Personal Reminiscences of a Not Uneventful Life (Classic Reprint) (p. 387)
Shepard, Ernest H., illus. see Ellison, Virginia H.
Shepard, Ernest H., illus. see Grahame, Kenneth & Williams, Nicholas.
Shepard, Ernest H., illus. see Grahame, Kenneth.
Shepard, Ernest H., illus. see Milne, A. A.
Shepard, George Llewellyn. Class Book 1920: Ad Summum (Classic Reprint) (p. 399)
Shepard, H. Fern. Pictures That Hang on Memory's Wall (Classic Reprint) (p. 1741)
Shepard, Joe. Growing 360. (p. 899)
Shepard, Mary, illus. see Travers, P. L.
Shepard, Mary, jt. auth. see Travers, P. L.
Shepard, Morgan. Observations of Jay (a Dog) And Other Stories (Classic Reprint) (p. 1634)
—Wags: Philosophy of a Peaceful Pup (Classic Reprint) (p. 2370)
Shepard, Ray Anthony. Now or Never! Fifty-Fourth Massachusetts Infantry's War to End Slavery. (p. 1628)
Shepard, Sara. Ali's Pretty Little Lies. (p. 47)
—Amateurs. (p. 62)
—Burned. (p. 300)
—Deadly. (p. 518)
—Follow Me. (p. 757)
—Good Girls. (p. 862)
—Hide & Seek. (p. 967)
—Killer. (p. 1217)
—Las Chicas Buenas / the Good Girls. (p. 1245)
—Las Chicas Perfectas / the Perfectionists. (p. 1245)
—Last Seen. (p. 1249)
—Lying Game. (p. 1369)
—Lying Game #2: Never Have I Ever. (p. 1369)
—Lying Game #3: Two Truths & a Lie. (p. 1369)
—Lying Game #4: Hide & Seek. (p. 1369)
—Lying Game #6: Seven Minutes in Heaven. (p. 1369)
—Perfectionists. (p. 1723)
—Perfectionists TV Tie-In Edition. (p. 1723)
—Pretty Little Liars #10: Ruthless. (p. 1790)
—Pretty Little Liars #12: Burned. (p. 1790)
—Pretty Little Liars #13: Crushed. (p. 1790)
—Pretty Little Liars #15: Toxic. (p. 1790)
—Pretty Little Liars #2: Flawless TV Tie-In Edition. (p. 1790)
—Pretty Little Liars: Ali's Pretty Little Lies. (p. 1790)
—Pretty Little Liars Bind-Up #1: Pretty Little Liars & Flawless. (p. 1790)
—Pretty Little Liars Bind-Up #2: Perfect & Unbelievable. (p. 1790)
—Pretty Little Liars Box Set: Books 1 To 4 (p. 1790)
—Pretty Little Liars: Pretty Little Secrets. (p. 1790)
—Pretty Little Liars TV Tie-In Edition. (p. 1790)
—Ruthless. (p. 1918)
—Stunning. (p. 2145)
—Twisted. (p. 2306)
Shepard, Shepherd. Mirrors: Penned Influences Vol One. (p. 1476)
Shepard, William. Illustrated Our Young Folks' Josephus: The Antiquities of the Jews, the Jewish Wars. (p. 1096)
Shepardson, Lucia. Butterfly Trees (Classic Reprint) (p. 304)
Shephard, Colin, jt. auth. see Rees, Rosemary.
Shephard, Dave, illus. see Biskup, Agnieska.
Shephard, Dave, illus. see Fields, Jan.
Shephard, David, illus. see Hoena, B. A.
Shephard, David, illus. see Hoena, Blake.
Shephard, David, illus. see Webb, Christina & Lonely Planet Kids.
Shephard, G. S. Before the Rummage Sale: An Entertainment in One Act (Classic Reprint) (p. 191)
—When Ma Took Office: A Comedy in One Act (Classic Reprint) (p. 2432)
Shepherd, Ambrose. Men in the Making. (p. 1446)
Shepherd, Andy. Boy Who Grew Dragons. (p. 271)
Shepherd, Angela. Through the Lens #1: Ava's Big Surprise. (p. 2237)
Shepherd, Anita. Easter Rabbit's Magic. (p. 620)
—Santa Genie. (p. 1932)
—Scareboo's Halloween Trick. (p. 1941)
Shepherd, Audrey. Morgana the Recession Witch. (p. 1506)
Shepherd, C. K. Across America by Motor-Cycle (Classic Reprint) (p. 11)
Shepherd, David & Plummer, William K. We Were There at the Driving of the Golden Spike. (p. 2393)
Shepherd, Deborah. Thread Through Time. (p. 2231)
Shepherd, Donna J. Ava's Secret Tea Party. Sinclair, Bella, illus. (p. 141)
—Bradybug. Grady, Kit, illus. (p. 274)
—Dotty's Topsy Tale. Collier, Kevin Scott, illus. (p. 588)
—Sully's Topsy Tale. Collier, Kevin Scott, illus. (p. 2148)
Shepherd, Donna J. & Foster, Jack. Where Is Salami. (p. 2438)
Shepherd, Dorothea Alice. How Two Girls Tried Farming: Originally Published in the Atlantic Monthly for February, 1875; Here Given with Amplifications & Additions (Classic Reprint) (p. 1046)
Shepherd, Ettrick. Tales & Sketches, Vol. 4: Including the Browne of Bodsbeck, Winter Evening Tales, Sheperd's Calendar, &C. , &C (Classic Reprint) (p. 2181)
—Tales & Sketches, Vol. 6 (Classic Reprint) (p. 2181)
Shepherd, Gail. True History of Lyndie B. Hawkins. (p. 2294)
Shepherd, J. A. Old Hendrik's Tales - 13 South African Folk Tales. (p. 1646)
Shepherd, Jacqui. Aggi the Ant: Little Stories, Big Lessons. (p. 35)
—Bongi the Beetle: Little Stories, Big Lessons. (p. 256)
—Cale the Crab: Little Stories, Big Lessons. (p. 309)
—Cobus the Cockroach: Little Stories, Big Lessons. (p. 410)
—Dabi the Dolphin: Little Stories, Big Lessons. (p. 494)
—Dis-Cow-Very: Fun with Words, Valuable Lessons. (p. 552)
—Eddie Gets a Fright! Little Stories, Big Lessons. (p. 624)
—Elroy the Eel: Little Stories, Big Lessons. (p. 639)
—Enor-Mouse: Fun with Words, Valuable Lessons. (p. 655)
—Fatima the Fly: Little Stories, Big Lessons. (p. 715)
—Fear-Foal: Fun with Words, Valuable Lessons. (p. 716)
—Finny the Fish: Little Stories, Big Lessons. (p. 731)
—For-Goat-Ten: Fun with Words, Valuable Lessons. (p. 762)
—G-Lamb-Orous: Fun with Words, Valuable Lessons. (p. 804)
—Gonzo the Grasshopper: Little Stories, Big Lessons. (p. 861)
—Hap-Pig-Ness: Fun with Words, Valuable Lessons. (p. 919)
—Hope-Frog-Ly: Fun with Words, Valuable Lessons. (p. 1002)
—Imag-Hen-Ation: Fun with Words, Valuable Lessons. (p. 1099)
—Invisi-Bull: Fun with Words, Valuable Lessons. (p. 1132)
—Jojo's Journey: Little Stories, Big Lessons. (p. 1176)
—Lala the Ladybug: Little Stories, Big Lessons. (p. 1240)
—Little Grey Horse Who Loved to Run: Little Stories, Big Lessons. (p. 1318)
—Mindi the Moth: Little Stories, Big Lessons. (p. 1470)
—Monkey Who Wanted to Be Different: Little Stories, Big Lessons. (p. 1494)
—Ozzy the Octopus: Little Stories, Big Lessons. (p. 1690)
—Patti the Prawn: Little Stories, Big Lessons. (p. 1706)
—Pinky Breaks the Rules: Little Stories, Big Lessons. (p. 1747)
—Proud Old Owl: Little Stories, Big Lessons. (p. 1808)
—Rabbit & the Fox: Little Stories, Big Lessons. (p. 1829)
—Ruby Right: Little Stories, Big Lessons. (p. 1911)
—Safina the Shark: Little Stories, Big Lessons. (p. 1922)
—Sam the Spider: Little Stories, Big Lessons. (p. 1926)
—Solomon the Snail: Little Stories, Big Lessons. (p. 2058)
—Suzy the Seal: Little Stories, Big Lessons. (p. 2167)
—Tagu the Turtle: Little Stories, Big Lessons. (p. 2176)
—Un-Hap-Puppy: Fun with Words, Valuable Lessons. (p. 2317)
—Unkind Buffalo: Little Stories, Big Lessons. (p. 2333)
—Wadi the Whale: Little Stories, Big Lessons. (p. 2370)
—Wally Gets a Tummy Ache! Little Stories, Big Lessons. (p. 2373)
—Webster the Worm: Little Stories, Big Lessons. (p. 2395)
Shepherd, Jessica. Grandma. (p. 877)
Shepherd, Joanne. What I Look Like When I am Scared / Cómo me veo cuando estoy Asustado. (p. 2412)
—What I Look Like When I am Surprised / Cómo me veo cuando estoy Sorprendido. (p. 2412)
Shepherd, Jodie. Barack Obama: Groundbreaking President. (p. 164)
—Black-And-White Animals. (p. 236)
—Crayola Comparing Sizes. (p. 468)
—Crayola Opposites Book. (p. 468)
—Crayola Sorting Book. (p. 468)
—Crayola Spring Colors. (p. 468)
—Crayola Winter Colors. (p. 468)
—Day with Doctors. (p. 515)
—Day with Firefighters. (p. 515)
—Day with Librarians. (p. 515)
—Day with Mail Carriers. (p. 515)
—Day with Paramedics. (p. 515)
—Day with Police Officers. (p. 515)
—Days of the Week. (p. 515)
—Flamingos. (p. 746)
—Grand Teton National Park. (p. 877)
—Grover's Eight Nights of Light (Sesame Street) Mathieu, Joe, illus. (p. 899)
—Hillary Clinton. (p. 971)
—It's a Good Thing There Are Earthworms. (p. 1143)
—It's Passover, Grover! (Sesame Street) Mathieu, Joe, illus. (p. 1147)
—Jane Goodall. (p. 1158)
—Joshua Tree. (p. 1179)
—Joshua Tree National Park. (p. 1179)
—Journey to the Sun. Becker, Paula J., illus. (p. 1183)
—K Is for Kindness (Sesame Street) Brannon, Tom, illus. (p. 1201)
—Kindness & Generosity: It Starts with Me! (p. 1219)
—Libro de Opuestos de Crayola. (p. 1286)
—Mae Jemison. (p. 1375)
—Maurice Sendak: King of the Wild Things. (p. 1426)
—Optimism: Sunny-Side Up! (p. 1667)
—Perseverance: I Have Grit! (p. 1724)
—Porpoises. (p. 1778)
—Presidents of the United States of America. (p. 1789)
—Serena Williams: A Champion on & off the Court. (p. 1990)
—Sweet Christmas on Sesame Street (Sesame Street) A Scratch & Sniff Story. Brannon, Tom, illus. (p. 2168)
—To the Moon! Byrne, Mike, illus. (p. 2253)
—To the Sun! Becker, Paula J., illus. (p. 2253)
—Where Can That Silly Monkey Be? Your Turn, My Turn Reader. Haefele, Steve, illus. (p. 2435)
—Zion National Park. (p. 2541)
Shepherd, Jodie, jt. auth. see Artifact Group, The.
Shepherd, Jodie, jt. auth. see Kimmelman, Leslie.
Shepherd, Jodie & Lopez, Giessi. Colores de la Primavera Crayola. (p. 422)
—Colores del Invierno Crayola. (p. 422)
—Libro de Clasificar de Crayola. (p. 1286)
—Libro de Comparar Tamaños de Crayola. (p. 1286)
Shepherd, Juanita. Eye of the Dawn. (p. 688)
Shepherd, Kat. Babysitting Nightmares: the Phantom Hour. Vieira, Rayanne, illus. (p. 155)
—Babysitting Nightmares: the Shadow Hand. Vieira, Rayanne, illus. (p. 155)
—Babysitting Nightmares: the Twilight Curse. Vieira, Rayanne, illus. (p. 155)
—Babysitting Nightmares: the Vampire Doll. (p. 155)
—Gemini Mysteries: the North Star (the Gemini Mysteries Book 1) (p. 813)
Shepherd, Keith D., illus. see LaFaye, A.
Shepherd, Mariah. Can You Find Me? (p. 318)
Shepherd, Megan. Cage. (p. 308)
—Gauntlet. (p. 812)
—Grim Lovelies. (p. 896)
—Grim Lovelies. Encantos Siniestros. (p. 896)
—Her Dark Curiosity. (p. 956)
—Hunt. (p. 1052)
—Madman's Daughter. (p. 1375)
—Midnight Beauties. (p. 1461)
—Secret Horses of Briar Hill. (p. 1976)
Shepherd, Sheri Rose. God, Where Are You? (p. 852)
—Hero's Prayer. (p. 963)
—Lord's ArmyThe Lord's Army. (p. 1349)
—Princess Prayer. (p. 1799)
Shepherd, William A., jt. auth. see Conn, Herbert William.
Shepherd, William G. Scar That Tripled: A True Story of the Great War (Classic Reprint) (p. 1941)
Sheppard, Alfred Tresidder. Quest of Ledgar Dunstan (Classic Reprint) (p. 1826)
—Rise of Ledgar Dunstan (Classic Reprint) (p. 1885)
—Running Horse Inn (Classic Reprint) (p. 1916)
Sheppard, Bonnie, jt. auth. see Harper, Suzanne.
Sheppard, Christopher James. Vampire's Dentist. (p. 2346)
Sheppard, Edmund Ernest. Bad Man's Sweetheart (Classic Reprint) (p. 158)
Sheppard, Elizabeth. Charles Auchester, Vol. 1 of 2 (Classic Reprint) (p. 358)
—Charles Auchester, Vol. 2 (Classic Reprint) (p. 358)
Sheppard, Elizabeth Sara. Charles Auchester: A Memorial (Classic Reprint) (p. 358)
—Counterparts: Or the Cross of Love (Classic Reprint) (p. 459)
—Counterparts, or the Cross of Love, Vol. 1 of 3 (Classic Reprint) (p. 459)
—Counterparts, Vol. 3 Of 3: Or the Cross of Love (Classic Reprint) (p. 459)
—Little Willie (Classic Reprint) (p. 1329)
—Rumor (Classic Reprint) (p. 1914)
—Rumour, Vol. 1 of 3 (Classic Reprint) (p. 1914)
—Rumour, Vol. 2 of 3 (Classic Reprint) (p. 1914)
Sheppard, Holden. Invisible Boys. (p. 1132)
Sheppard, John. Narrative of All the Robberies, Escapes, &C. of John Sheppard: Giving an Exact Description of the Manner of His Wonderful Escape from the Castle in Newgate, & of the Methods He Took Afterward for His Security (Classic Reprint) (p. 1575)
Sheppard, Keith. In the Kingdom of the Fair-Eyes. (p. 1109)
—Welcome to the Crazyverse: A Collection of Comic Poems about Famous People in History. (p. 2398)
—Wonderland Revisited & the Games Alice Played There. (p. 2490)
Sheppard, Kristen. Big Race Old. Martineau, Philip James, illus. (p. 222)
Sheppard, Markette. My Rainy Day Rocket Ship. Palmer, Charly, illus. (p. 1559)
—What Is Light? Johnson, Cathy Ann, illus. (p. 2415)
Sheppard, Nathan. Saratoga Chips & Carlsbad Wafers: The Pursuit of Happiness & Health at the Two Great Mineral Water Resorts of America & Europe (Classic Reprint) (p. 1935)
Sheppard, Si. Heroes & Legends: Set 2. (p. 961)
—Heroes of the Trojan War. (p. 962)
Sheppard, Vivien, illus. see Wills, Michael E.
Sheppard, W. L. Oddities in Southern Life & Character (Classic Reprint) (p. 1637)
Sheppard, William Henry. Presbyterian Pioneers in Congo (Classic Reprint) (p. 1788)
Sheppard, Wm. L. Detailed Minutiae of Soldier Life in the Army of Northern Virginia, 1861-1865 (Classic Reprint) (p. 534)
Shepperson, Claude A., illus. see Smith Wiggin, Kate Douglas.

S

—Experiment in Altruism (Classic Reprint) (p. 678)
—Henry Worthington: Idealist (Classic Reprint) (p. 956)
—Princess Pourquoi (Classic Reprint) (p. 1799)
—Puritan Bohemia (Classic Reprint) (p. 1815)
—Worn Doorstep (Classic Reprint) (p. 2508)
Sherwood, Margaret Pollock. Daphne, an Autumn Pastoral (Classic Reprint) (p. 504)
Sherwood, Mary (Neal). Jack: From the French of Alphonse Daudet, Author of Sidonie, Robert Helmont, etc (Classic Reprint) (p. 1151)
Sherwood, Mary Elizabeth Wilson. Sarcasm of Destiny, or Nina's Experience: A Novel (Classic Reprint) (p. 1935)
Sherwood, Mary Martha. Fairchild Family (Classic Reprint) (p. 695)
—Governess, or the Young Female Academy (Classic Reprint) (p. 872)
—Hedge of Thorns (Classic Reprint) (p. 947)
—History of the Fairchild Family, or the Child's Manual, Vol. 1: Being a Collection of Stories, Calculated to Show the Importance & Effects of a Religious Education (Classic Reprint) (p. 980)
—Indian Chief (Classic Reprint) (p. 1116)
—Juliana Oakley: A Tale (Classic Reprint) (p. 1187)
—Katharine Seward (Classic Reprint) (p. 1205)
—Lady of the Manor, Vol. 4 Of 4: Being a Series of Conversations on the Subject of Confirmation, Intended for the Use of the Middle & Higher Ranks of Young Females (Classic Reprint) (p. 1238)
—Lily of the Valley (Classic Reprint) (p. 1302)
—Mrs. Sherwood's Juvenile Library - Scholar's Choice Edition. (p. 1523)
—Well-Timed Dream, and, Katharine Seward: Interspersed with Other Pieces (Classic Reprint) (p. 2399)
—Works of Mrs. Sherwood, Vol. 1 (Classic Reprint) (p. 2499)
—Works of Mrs. Sherwood, Vol. 14: Being the Only Uniform Edition Ever Published in the United States (Classic Reprint) (p. 2499)
—Works of Mrs. Sherwood, Vol. 2: Being the Only Uniform Edition Ever Published in the United States (Classic Reprint) (p. 2499)
Sherwood, Mary Martha Butt Henry. Little Henry & His Bearer Boosey (Classic Reprint) (p. 1318)
Sherwood, Robert E. There Shall Be No Night (Classic Reprint) (p. 2216)
Sherwood, S. J. Denounced: Book 1 a Grey Sun. (p. 529)
Sherwood, Sj. Denounced: Book 3 Creaking Dawn. (p. 529)
—Denounced: Book 2 Shifting Horizons. (p. 529)
Sherwood-Sitts, Herm. Fox & Farmer Beeching. (p. 774)
—Secret of Cypress Swamp. (p. 1977)
Shestakova, Anna, ed. see AZ Books Staff.
Sheth, Kashmira. Boys Without Names. (p. 273)
—Feast of Peas. Ebbeler, Jeffrey, illus. (p. 717)
—Keeping Corner. (p. 1208)
—Nina Soni, Former Best Friend. Kocsmiersky, Jenn, illus. (p. 1609)
—Nina Soni, Sister Fixer. Kocsmiersky, Jenn, illus. (p. 1609)
—Sona & the Wedding Game Jaeggi, Yoshiko, illus. (p. 2062)
—Tiger in My Soup Ebbeler, Jeffrey, illus. (p. 2241)
Sheth, Sheetal. Always Anjali. (p. 61)
Shetland, J. J. Cat on Sean's Balcony. (p. 342)
Shetley, Susanna. Jolt Felt Around the World. (p. 1176)
Shetterly, Margot Lee. Hidden Figures: The True Story of Four Black Women & the Space Race. Freeman, Laura, illus. (p. 965)
—Hidden Figures. (p. 965)
—Hidden Figures Young Readers' Edition. (p. 965)
Shetterly, Susan Hand. Swimming Home Raye, Rebekah, illus. (p. 2170)
Shetty, Lakshmi, illus. see Shetty, Lalitha A.
Shetty, Lalitha A. Tales of Toy World. Shetty, Lakshmi, illus. (p. 2186)
Shetty, Suresh. Invisible Universe. (p. 1132)
Shevah, Emma. Dara Palmer's Major Drama. (p. 504)
—Dream on, Amber. Crawford-White, Helen, illus. (p. 602)
—Lexie's Little Lie. (p. 1282)
Shew, E. L. If Men Were Wise (Classic Reprint) (p. 1092)
—If Men Were Wise, Vol. 2 of 3 (Classic Reprint) (p. 1092)
—If Men Were Wise, Vol. 3 Of 3: A Novel (Classic Reprint) (p. 1092)
Shew, Joel. Water-Cure Manual: A Popular Work, Embracing Descriptions of the Various Modes of Bathing, the Hygienic & Curative Effects of Air, Exercise, Clothing, Occupation, Diet, Water-Drinking, &C (Classic Reprint) (p. 2384)
Shewan-Friend, Hannah. Inky Babble. Shewan-Friend, Hannah, illus. (p. 1120)
Shi, Ellen, illus. see Demas, Corinne & Roehrig, Artemis.
Shi, Ellen, illus. see Hopkins, Lee Bennett.
Shi, Ellen, illus. see Yolen, Jane.
Shi, Nai-An. Water Margin. (p. 2385)
Shi, Qian. Weaver. Shi, Qian, illus. (p. 2394)
Shi, Shannon. English. (p. 652)
Shi, Xianqin. Buddies: Secrets of Our Heart, Nervous System & Muscles. (p. 290)
Shi, Yixin. Four Wishes (Includes 1 CD) (p. 773)
Shibamoto, Thores, illus. see Suzukaze, Ryo.
Shibley, Fred Warner. Bundle of Yarns (Classic Reprint) (p. 297)
—Garden at the Winkle Woods in the Wilderness (Classic Reprint) (p. 809)
Shibutani, Alex, et al. Kudo Kids: the Mystery of the Masked Medalist. Ma Van As, Yaoyao, illus. (p. 1233)
Shichtman, Sandra H. Michael Bloomberg. (p. 1457)
—Sonia Sotomayor. (p. 2063)
Shichtman, Sandra H. & Indenbaum, Dorothy. Joy of Creation: The Story of Clara Schumann. (p. 1184)
Shickle, Ian, illus. see Cameron, Kristy.
Shickman, Allan Richard. Dael & the Painted People. (p. 495)
—Zan-Gah & the Beautiful Country. (p. 2538)
Shiefman, Vicky. Who Has Wiggle-Waggle Toes? Chessa, Francesca, illus. (p. 2447)
Shiei, illus. see Roberts, Rachel.
Shiel, M. P. Last Miracle (Classic Reprint) (p. 1248)
—Unto the Third Generation (Classic Reprint) (p. 2336)
—White Wedding (Classic Reprint) (p. 2445)
Shiel, Matthew Phipps. Children of the Wind (Classic Reprint) (p. 372)
—Lost Viol (Classic Reprint) (p. 1356)
—Weird o' It (Classic Reprint) (p. 2397)
Shiela, Alejandro, illus. see Melissa, Berg.
Shield, Guy, jt. auth. see Parker, Danny.
Shield, Rocsanne. Save Magic City. (p. 1937)
Shield, William. Poor Soldier: A Comic Opera (Classic Reprint) (p. 1774)
Shields, Amy. Little Kids First Big Book of Why. (p. 1320)
—NG Chapters: Best Friends Forever: And More True Stories of Animal Friendships. (p. 1601)
—Trains (1 Hardcover/1 CD) (p. 2276)
—Trains (1 Paperback/1 CD) (p. 2276)
Shields, Breeana. Poison's Cage. (p. 1768)
—Poison's Kiss. (p. 1768)
Shields, Carol Diggory. Baby's Got the Blues. Tobia, Lauren, illus. (p. 154)
—Wombat Walkabout. Blackall, Sophie, illus. (p. 2486)
Shields, Charles J. Argentina Henderson, James D., ed. (p. 114)
—Belize Henderson, James D., ed. (p. 196)
—Belize. (p. 196)
—Brazil Henderson, James D., ed. (p. 277)
—Central America: Facts & Figures. (p. 351)
—Central America: Facts & Figures Henderson, James D., ed. (p. 351)
—Central America Today (p. 351)
—Chile Henderson, James D., ed. (p. 376)
—Costa Rica Henderson, James D., ed. (p. 457)
—Costa Rica. (p. 457)
—Guatemala Henderson, James D., ed. (p. 902)
—Guatemala. (p. 902)
—Honduras Henderson, James D., ed. (p. 998)
—Honduras. (p. 998)
—Nicaragua Henderson, James D., ed. (p. 1602)
—Nicaragua. (p. 1602)
—Panama Henderson, James D., ed. (p. 1695)
—Panama. (p. 1695)
—Peru Henderson, James D., ed. (p. 1725)
—Salvador Henderson, James D., ed. (p. 1926)
—Salvador. (p. 1926)
—Uruguay Henderson, James D., ed. (p. 2340)
—Venezuela Henderson, James D., ed. (p. 2350)
Shields, Chris, illus. see Watt, Fiona.
Shields, Gertrude M. Caste Three (Classic Reprint) (p. 340)
Shields, Gillian. Elephantantrum! Johnson-Isaacs, Cally, illus. (p. 634)
—Eternal. (p. 665)
—Immortal. (p. 1101)
—Library Lily. Chessa, Francesca, illus. (p. 1284)
—Littlest Bunny. Lovsin, Polona, illus. (p. 1330)
—When the World Is Full of Friends. Currey, Anna, illus. (p. 2434)
—When the World Is Ready for Bed (padded Board) Currey, Anna, illus. (p. 2434)
—When the World Was Waiting for You. Currey, Anna, illus. (p. 2434)
Shields, Jessika & Shields, Robert. Don't Feed the Monster. (p. 582)
Shields, Kathleen. Constellation Crimes. (p. 443)
Shields, Kathleen J. Ally Cat, a Tale of Survival. (p. 57)
—Constellation Crimes. (p. 443)
—Dandy Lion, a Legend of Love & Loss. (p. 501)
—Ghost Dogs: Seeing Is Believing. (p. 827)
—Hamilton Troll Cookbook: Easy to Make Recipes for Children. Bryant, Carol W. & Klug, Leigh A., illus. (p. 913)
—Hamilton Troll Meets Chatterton Squirrel. Klug, Leigh A. & Bryant, Carol W., illus. (p. 913)
—Hamilton Troll Meets Dinosaurs. Klug, Leigh A. & Bryant, Carol W., illus. (p. 913)
—Hamilton Troll Meets Elwood Woodpecker. Klug, Leigh A. & Bryant, Carol W., illus. (p. 913)
—Hamilton Troll Meets Skeeter Skunk. Klug, Leigh A. & Bryant, Carol W., illus. (p. 913)
—Hamilton Troll Meets Whitaker Owl. Klug, Leigh A. & Bryant, Carol W., illus. (p. 913)
Shields, Stephanie. Star Princess & the Kitchen Witch. (p. 2102)
Shields, Sue, illus. see Jenkins, Martin.
Shields, Sue, illus. see Ross, Stewart.
Shields, Susan, illus. see Ross, Stewart.
Shields, T. D. Into Light. (p. 1128)
—Into Shadow. (p. 1128)
Shields, Vicki. Mooshka the Bear. (p. 1503)
Shiell, Mike, illus. see Adderson, Caroline.
Shiell, Mike, illus. see Kay, Edward.
Shiell, Trevor. Pete's Journey. (p. 1730)
Shiels, Tony "Doc". Monstrum! a Wizard's Tale. (p. 1498)
Shifler, Ann. Lone, Lone Cloud. Birky, Rachael, illus. (p. 1342)
Shiga, Jason. Meanwhile: Pick Any Path. 3,856 Story Possibilities. (p. 1434)
Shigarova, Julia, jt. auth. see Clever Publishing.
Shigarova, Julia & Clever Publishing. Cool Things to Do: Puzzles, Mazes & More. (p. 450)
—Max the Rabbit Builds a Snowman: Includes a Clever Puzzle. (p. 1428)
—Max the Rabbit Digs a Hole: Includes a Clever Puzzle. (p. 1428)
—Max the Rabbit Learns to Swim: Includes a Clever Puzzle. (p. 1428)
—Max the Rabbit Plays Hide & Seek: Includes a Clever Puzzle. (p. 1428)
—Rainy Day Doodles: More Than 100 Pages for Drawing, Coloring, & Creating. (p. 1837)
Shigemi, Shiukichi. Japanese Boy (Classic Reprint) (p. 1159)
Shigeta, Sayaka. Ryori o Sitewa Ikenai Nabe. (p. 1919)
Shih, Jamie, tr. see Yamamura, Yuko.
Shih, Seiko, ed. see Yamamura, Yuko.
Shihata, Ahmed S. Birth of a Champion. (p. 233)
Shiina, You, illus. see Kazuki, Miya.
Shikarpur, Deepak & Bhawat, Adv Vaishali. Cybercrimes Technology's Menace of the 21st Century. (p. 492)
Shillaber, B. p. Ike Partington: Or, the Adventures of a Human Boy & His Friends (Classic Reprint) (p. 1094)
—Knitting-Work a Web of Many Textures (Classic Reprint) (p. 1229)
—Life & Sayings of Mrs. Partington: And Others of the Family (Classic Reprint) (p. 1289)
—Partingtonian Patchwork, Blifkins the Martyr (Classic Reprint) (p. 1701)
Shillaber, Benjamin Penhallow. Double-Runner Club: Or the Lively Boys of Rivertown (Classic Reprint) (p. 589)
Shilling, Brian C. Wee Box. (p. 2395)
Shillinglaw, Bruce, illus. see Zoehfeld, Kathleen Weidner.
Shiloh, Ramon, illus. see Hausman, Gerald.
Shiloh, Ramon, illus. see Houser, Sue.
Shilson, S. Assassin of Shadows. (p. 127)
Shimabukuro, Denise, illus. see Ferrari, Alessandro.
Shimabukuro, Denise, illus. see Newberger Speregen, Devra.
Shimabukuro, Denise, illus. see Roehl, Tessa.
Shimabukuro, Denise, illus. see Rosenbaum, Andria Warmflash.
Shimabukuro, Denise, illus. see Speregen, Debra Newberger.
Shimada, Tatsuo. Wonder Move: Wonder of Human Body. (p. 2489)
Shimatsuka, Eri. Zen Scratch Art: Scandinavian Design. (p. 2539)
Shimazaki, Masao. Iya to Yuyo: SEI Boryoku Gyakutai ni Awanai 'Say No!' (p. 1150)
Shimin, Symeon, illus. see Hamilton, Virginia.
Shimizu, Michio. Ding Dong. McLaughlin, Sako, tr. (p. 547)
Shimizu, Yuko, illus. see Bouwman, H. M.
Shimizu, Yuko, illus. see Moss, Marissa.
Shimizu, Yuko, illus. see Uehashi, Nahoko & Hirano, Cathy.
Shimizu, Yuko, illus. see Uehashi, Nahoko.
Shimizu, Yuko, illus. see Wilde, Oscar.
Shimmen, Cathy, illus. see Milbourne, Anna.
Shimmen, Cathy, illus. see Page, Nick & Page, Claire.
Shimmerwing, Talula. Best Kind of Fairy. (p. 206)
Shimone, MacKie, illus. see Chelsea, Smith Lee.
Shimose Poe, Mayumi. Alice on the Island: A Pearl Harbor Survival Story. Trunfio, Alessia & Forsyth, Matt, illus. (p. 45)
Shin, Ami. Mice in the City: London. (p. 1457)
—Mice in the City: New York. (p. 1457)
Shin, Ami & Harris, Jamie. Mice in the City: Around the World. (p. 1457)
Shin, Bo Reum. Planting Beans. (p. 1757)
Shin, Hae Won. My Summer. (p. 1562)
Shin, HaYoung, illus. see Gunderson, Jessica.
Shin, Hye-eun & Cowley, Joy. Warli People. Jeong, Su-bi, illus. (p. 2379)
Shin, Janet Jaywan, tr. see Lee, T. S.
Shin, Ji-Soo, illus. see Kim, Young-Ah.
Shin, Monte. Mirror Play. Shin, Monte, illus. (p. 1475)
Shin, Seon-Woong. What a Beautiful World! The Earth's Layers. Choi, Eun-yeong, illus. (p. 2404)
Shin, Simone, illus. see Banks, Kate.
Shin, Simone, illus. see Best, Cari.
Shin, Simone, illus. see Doering, Amanda F. & Higgins, Melissa.
Shin, Simone, illus. see Doering, Amanda.
Shin, Simone, illus. see Going, K. L.
Shin, Simone, illus. see Higgins, Melissa.
Shin, Simone, illus. see Humphreys, Jessica Dee & Ambrose, Rona.
Shin, Simone, illus. see Isabella, Jude.
Shin, Simone, illus. see Pierce, Terry.
Shin, Simone, illus. see Raczka, Robert.
Shin, Simone, illus. see Scanlon, Liz Garton.
Shin, Sun Yung. Cooper's Lesson. Cogan, Kim, illus. (p. 451)
Shin, Sun-Mi. Hanbok, My Fairy Friends, My Child. (p. 914)
Shin, Yujin. My Magical Dragon. (p. 1555)
—My Magical Mermaid. (p. 1555)
—My Magical Unicorn. (p. 1555)
Shinaberry, Jr Ted H. Pirates, Eye Gougers, & Native American Rings. (p. 1751)
Shinabery, Michael Ray. Legendary Locals of Alamogordo. (p. 1263)
Shindle, Janet. Nana's Magic Swing. (p. 1574)
Shine, illus. see Santucci, Barbara.
Shine, Andrea, illus. see Brisson, Pat.
Shine, Andrea, illus. see Quattlebaum, Mary.
Shine, Andrea, illus. see Santucci, Barbara.
Shine, Joe. Bobby Sky: Boy Band or Die. (p. 252)
—I Become Shadow. (p. 1060)
Shine, M. Gifford. Little Journeys into the Invisible: A Woman's Actual Experiences in the Fourth Dimension (Classic Reprint) (p. 1319)
Shingle, Jude, illus. see Moodey, Mary.
Shingoose, Nahanni. Powwow Summer. (p. 1783)
Shingu, Fumiaki, jt. auth. see Ono, Mari.
Shingu, Susumu. Traveling Butterflies. (p. 2280)
—Wandering Whale Sharks. (p. 2375)
Shingza Rinpoche, Choekyi Gyaltsen, ed. see Rakra Rinpoche, Tethong Thubten Choedhar.
Shinick, Kevin. Journey to Star Wars: the Rise of Skywalker Force Collector. Foti, Tony, illus. (p. 1182)
Shinjo, Shelly, illus. see Elliott, Zetta & Terasaki, Stanley Todd.
Shinjo, Shelly, illus. see Terasaki, Stanley Todd.
Shinkai, Makoto. 5 Centimeters per Second Novel: One More Side. (p. 2548)
—Your Name. , Vol. 2 (manga) (p. 2534)
Shinkai, Makoto & Kanoh, Arata. Your Name. Another Side:Earthbound (light Novel) (p. 2534)
Shinkewski, Sarah, illus. see McTaggart, Keven & McTaggart, Nathan.
Shinn, George W. Stories for the Happy Days of Christmas Time (Classic Reprint) (p. 2123)
Shinn, Milicent Washburn. Biography of a Baby (Classic Reprint) (p. 229)
—Notes on the Development of a Child (Classic Reprint) (p. 1624)
Shinno, Stephanie. Syler & the Sandpaper Towel. Douglas, Vannick, illus. (p. 2172)
Shinoda, Anna. Learning Not to Drown. (p. 1258)
Shinomiya, Brian. Queen of Cordova: Dark Isles Book 2. (p. 1824)
Shinsuke, Yoshitake. Can You See? Still Can't See? (p. 318)
Shinzi, Katoh. Tian Kong Xiao Xiong. (p. 2239)
Shiotsu, Vicky. Build-A-Skill Instant Books: Synonyms & Antonyms. (p. 293)
Shioya, Sakae. When I Was a Boy in Japan (Classic Reprint) (p. 2431)
—When I Was a Boy in Japan - Scholar's Choice Edition. (p. 2431)
Ship, Penman. Cursive Workbook - 1. Practice Letters - 2. Form Words - 3. Transcribe Bible Verses: Learn Cursive & Scripture Passages - Trace, Memorize, & Write Freehand - Handwriting Practice Pages - Reproducible Writing Worksheets (Kids, Teens, & Adults) (p. 490)
—Tracing: Letters, Numbers, Shapes, & Logic - Unicorn Edition: Preschoolers & Kids Ages 3-5 - Handwriting & Counting Workbook. (p. 2272)
—Tracing: Motor Vehicle Edition (Ages 3-5) 100+ Pages: Letters, Numbers, Shapes, & Logic - Cars, Trucks, Planes & Things That Go. (p. 2272)
Shipe, Becky, illus. see Nettleton, Pamela Hill.
Shipe, Rebecca. My Daddy Is a Leukemia Super Hero. (p. 1536)
Shiplee, Albert E. Bird's Eye View of Life. (p. 232)
Shiplett, Danaye. Paint My World with Colors. (p. 1693)
Shipley, Jocelyn. Impossible. (p. 1102)
—Impossible. (p. 1102)
—Stranded. (p. 2137)
Shipley, Jocelyn, jt. auth. see Loughead, Deb.
Shipley, Josh, illus. see Cangelose, Andrew.
Shipley, Matthew, illus. see Littlejohn, James.
Shipley, Matthew, jt. auth. see Littlejohn, James.
Shipley, Sharon. Danforth the Dragon. (p. 501)
Shipley, Space. Extraordinary Sam. (p. 685)
Shiply, Lyn, jt. auth. see Ballard, John E.
Shipman, Dorothy Middlebrook. Jolly Hallowe'en Book (Classic Reprint) (p. 1176)
Shipman, Josie, illus. see Kruse, Donald W.
Shipman, Justina A. Don't Be Chicken with Type 1 Diabetes. (p. 582)
Shipman, Louis Evan. Guards of the Guards: Or the Fortunes of War (Classic Reprint) (p. 902)
Shipman, Nell. Under the Crescent (Classic Reprint) (p. 2321)
Shipman, Talitha, illus. see Amstutz, Lisa.
Shipman, Talitha, illus. see Coy, John.
Shipman, Talitha, illus. see Koffsky, Ann D.
Shipman, Talitha, illus. see Viau, Nancy.
Shipp, Catherine Elisabeth. 12 Great Tips on Writing a Speech. (p. 2551)
—12 Great Tips on Writing Fiction. (p. 2551)
Shipp, D. M. My Book of Little Poems That Gave Me a Fright! (p. 1534)
Shipp, Frederick. Sassamon 1927: Yearbook (Classic Reprint) (p. 1936)
Shipp, John. Memoirs of the Extraordinary Military Career of John Shipp. (p. 1445)
—Memoirs of the Extraordinary Military Career of John Shipp, Late a Lieutenant in His Majesty's 87th Regiment, Vol. 2 (Classic Reprint) (p. 1445)
Shipp, Josh. Teen's Guide to World Domination: Advice on Life, Liberty, & the Pursuit of Awesomeness. (p. 2200)
Shipp, Shawn and Eric. Mirabelle. (p. 1474)
Shippen, Lauren. Infinite Noise: A Bright Sessions Novel. (p. 1118)
—Neon Darkness. (p. 1587)
Shippey, Lee. Personal Glimpses of Famous Folks: And Other Selections from the Lee Side o'L. a (Classic Reprint) (p. 1725)
Shipton, Bernard. Camosun, Vol. 25: June, 1933 (Classic Reprint) (p. 315)
Shipton, Clarence J. Money Against Money: A Play on High Finance (Classic Reprint) (p. 1492)
Shipton, H. Hugo. College Boy Bill: A Picture of Student Life in the Rushing Season; (Classic Reprint) (p. 415)
Shipton, Helen. Alston Crucis, Vol. 1 of 3 (Classic Reprint) (p. 60)
Shipton, Rosemary. 1960: Canadian Decades. (p. 2561)
Shipton, Vicky. New York. (p. 1598)
Shira, Arielle, illus. see Angues, Lisa.
Shirai, Shiro. Wall-E. (p. 2373)
Shiraishi, Ashima. How to Solve a Problem: The Rise (and Falls) of a Rock-Climbing Champion. Xiao, Yao, illus. (p. 1044)
Shirazi, J. M., jt. auth. see Gorky, Maksim.
Shirazi, Shaista. AQA GCSE (9-1) Biology Grade 6/7 Booster Workbook. (p. 108)
Shire, Eliza. Jax L. Jones & the Pesky I Problem. (p. 1161)
Shireen, Nadia. Billy & the Beast. (p. 227)
—PlayShapes: Emperor Penguin. (p. 1761)
—PlayShapes: Seal. (p. 1761)
—Yeti & the Bird. Shireen, Nadia, illus. (p. 2521)
Shirer, Priscilla. Radiant: His Light, Your Life for Teen Girls & Young Women. (p. 1833)
—Unseen: the Prince Warriors 365 Devotional. (p. 2335)
Shirer, Priscilla & Detwiler, Gina. Prince Warriors. (p. 1795)
—Prince Warriors & the Swords of Rhema. (p. 1795)
—Prince Warriors Deluxe Box Set. (p. 1795)
—Winter War. (p. 2476)
Shirk, Linda, illus. see Gerber, Mary Lichty.
Shirk, Linda, illus. see Martin, Elaine S. Bowman.
Shirk, Linda, illus. see Miller, Mary R.
Shirley, Alice. Gentle Lion & the Little Owlet. (p. 816)
Shirley, Cailey, ed. see Shirley, Cindy L.
Shirley, Cailey, ed. see Shirley, Cindy.
Shirley, Cindy. Kitty Ballou's Sanctuary Zoo. Shirley, Cailey, ed. (p. 1226)
Shirley, Cindy L. Kitty Ballou's Sanctuary Zoo: Color Illustration Edition. Shirley, Cailey, ed. (p. 1226)
Shirley, David & Hart, Joyce. Alabama. (p. 38)
—North Carolina. (p. 1620)
Shirley, Debra. Best Friend on Wheels. (p. 206)

S

—Riddle Diddle Rainforest. Bauer, Stephanie, illus. (p. 1878)
—Riddle Diddle Safari. Bauer, Stephanie, illus. (p. 1878)
Shore, Diane Z. & Fairbanks, Jessica Alexander. Just My Style. Canby, Kelly, illus. (p. 1194)
Shore, Elayne. Candy Girl. (p. 322)
Shore, Emily. Aquarium. (p. 108)
—Aviary. (p. 143)
—Garden. (p. 808)
—Journal of Emily Shore (Classic Reprint) (p. 1180)
—Temple. (p. 2203)
—Temple Twins. (p. 2203)
Shore, Henry N. Old Foye Days, Vol. 2: An Authentic Account of the Exploits of the Smugglers in & Around the Port of Fowey (Classic Reprint) (p. 1645)
Shore, Jim. Magic in the Attic: a Button & Squeaky Adventure. (p. 1377)
Shore, Lewis Erle, jt. auth. see Foster, Michael.
Shore, Lisa G. Mother Nature's Kiss. (p. 1510)
Shore, Paul. Bobsleigh Jellybeans. (p. 253)
Shore, Viola Brothers. Heritage: And Other Stories (Classic Reprint) (p. 959)
Shore, W. Teignmouth. Pest (Classic Reprint) (p. 1726)
Shoreline Publishing Group, jt. auth. see Buckley Jr., James.
Shores, Erika L. All about Beagles (p. 48)
—All about Chihuahuas (p. 48)
—All about Rottweilers (p. 50)
—Amelia Earhart. (p. 69)
—Apples. (p. 107)
—Celebrate Fall. (p. 348)
—Deadliest Animals on Earth. (p. 518)
—Deadliest Bugs on Earth. (p. 518)
—Harvest Time. (p. 936)
—How Food Gets from Farms to Store Shelves. (p. 1031)
—How Garbage Gets from Trash Cans to Landfills. (p. 1031)
—How to Make Bubbles: A 4D Book. (p. 1043)
—How to Make Bubbles. (p. 1043)
—Lakes: A 4D Book. (p. 1240)
—Leaves. (p. 1259)
—More Funny Knock-Knock Jokes (p. 1504)
—Mountain Lions (p. 1513)
—Oceans: A 4D Book. (p. 1636)
—Pet Dogs up Close. (p. 1726)
—Ponds: A 4D Book. (p. 1773)
—Pumpkins. (p. 1813)
—Rivers: A 4D Book. (p. 1887)
—Sam Walton (p. 1926)
—Silly Classroom Jokes (p. 2018)
—Snow Leopards (p. 2047)
Shores, Erika L., jt. auth. see Clay, Kathryn.
Shores, Erika L., jt. auth. see Shores, Lori.
Shores, Erika L., jt. auth. see Winter, Judy A.
Shores, Erika L. & Peterson, Megan Cooley. Here to There. (p. 958)
Shores, Erika L., et al. Business Leaders (p. 301)
Shores, Ken. Donkey Christmas. (p. 581)
—I Spent Christmas with Jesus. (p. 1082)
Shores, Lori. Cómo Hacer Slime. (p. 432)
—Cómo Hacer un Cohete Efervescente. (p. 432)
—Cómo Hacer un Globo con Olor Misterioso. Translations.com Staff, tr. (p. 432)
—Hands-On Science Fun. (p. 916)
—How to Build a Fizzy Rocket: A 4D Book. (p. 1038)
—How to Build a Fizzy Rocket. (p. 1038)
—How to Build a Tornado in a Bottle (p. 1038)
—How to Build a Tornado in a Bottle: A 4D Book. (p. 1038)
—How to Build Flipsticks. (p. 1038)
—How to Make a Liquid Rainbow (p. 1043)
—How to Make a Liquid Rainbow: A 4D Book. (p. 1043)
—How to Make a Mystery Smell Balloon: A 4D Book. (p. 1043)
—How to Make a Mystery Smell Balloon. (p. 1043)
—How to Make Slime: A 4D Book. (p. 1043)
—How to Make Slime. (p. 1043)
Shores, Lori & Capstone Press Staff. Hands-On Science Fun (p. 916)
Shores, Lori & Shores, Erika L. Hands-On Science Fun. (p. 916)
Shorey, John. Beautiful Book for Little Children (Classic Reprint) (p. 183)
Shorey, John L. Beautiful Book for Little Children. (p. 183)
—Nursery, 1874, Vol. 15: A Monthly Magazine for Youngest Readers (Classic Reprint) (p. 1631)
—Nursery, Vol. 19: A Monthly Magazine for Youngest Readers (Classic Reprint) (p. 1631)
Shorrock, Claire, illus. see Dealey, Erin.
Shorrock, Claire & Tebbs, Victoria. Magnus. (p. 1382)
Short, David H. Shawn: The Adventures of an Irish Immigrant to the US in the Late 19C. (p. 2003)
Short, Elizabeth, tr. see Johnson, Sandi.
Short, Gregory T., illus. see Weathers, Regina Lorick.
Short, J. Rodney. Barnibee, la Abejita Asombrosa. Inglish, Nick, illus. (p. 167)
Short, Jacob. Colorado Situation, or Maria & Her Husband in Politics & Society (Classic Reprint) (p. 422)
Short, John L. Fun for Doctors & Their Patients: Fifty Authentic Ghost Stories by Fifty Experienced Physicians (Classic Reprint) (p. 799)
Short, Kasey, illus. see Elmore, Amber.
Short, Marion. Blossoming of Mary Anne: A Play in Four Acts (Classic Reprint) (p. 247)
—Lights of Happyland: An One Act Play (Classic Reprint) (p. 1300)
—Miss. Somebody Else: A Comedy in Four Acts (Classic Reprint) (p. 1480)
Short M.S., Jeff. Kid's World (p. 1216)
Short, Robbie, illus. see Ehrmantraut, Brenda.
Short, Robbie, illus. see Weiss, Bobbi & Weiss, David.
Short, Robert Louis, jt. auth. see Wells, Webster.
Short, Robyn & Williams, Nanon McKewn. Peace People. Bailey, Lindsey, illus. (p. 1709)
Short, Thomas. New Observations, Natural, Moral, Civil, Political & Medical on City, Town, & Country Bills of Mortality: To Which Are Added, Large & Clear Abstracts of the Best Authors Who Have Wrote on That Subject; with an Appendix on the Weather & Meteors. (p. 1596)
Shortall, Katherine. y Girl in France (Classic Reprint) (p. 2516)
Shortall, Leonard, illus. see Holl, Adelaide.
Shortall, Leonard, illus. see Sobol, Donald J.
Shortall, Leonard W., illus. see Sobol, Donald J.
Shortcut, Daisy. Our Show: A Humorous Account of the International Exposition, in Honor of the Centennial Anniversary of American Independence, from Inception to Completion (Classic Reprint) (p. 1680)
Shortelle, Dennis, jt. auth. see Gardner, Robert.
Shorter, Clement King. Immortal Memories. (p. 1101)
Shorter, Dora Sigerson. Country-House Party (Classic Reprint) (p. 461)
—Father Confessor: Stories of Death & Danger (Classic Reprint) (p. 714)
Shortfellow, Harry Wandsworth. Song of Drop o' Wather (Classic Reprint) (p. 2062)
Shortfellow, Tom. Mary Kale, or Big Thunder! Chief of the Anti-Renters (Classic Reprint) (p. 1415)
Shortfield, Luke. Western Merchant (p. 2402)
Shorthouse, J. H. Little Schoolmaster Mark, Vol. 2: A Spiritual Romance (Classic Reprint) (p. 1327)
—Sir Percival, Vol. 11: A Story of the Fast & of the Present (Classic Reprint) (p. 2026)
Shorthouse, Joseph Henry. Little Schoolmaster Mark: A Spiritual Romance (Classic Reprint) (p. 1327)
—Little Schoolmaster Mark. (p. 1327)
Shortle, Stacy & Mooney, Dean J. M. Train Ride to Grandma's (with NO Chocolate Donut!) Wulfing, Amy J., illus. (p. 2275)
Shortley, Michele, illus. see Krensky, Stephen.
Shortt, Yvonne. New York City Public School Goes Green. (p. 1598)
Shortte, Moashella. Mirror. (p. 1475)
Shortz, Will. Will Shortz Presents Math Masters Sudoku: 150 Puzzles for Clever Kids: Sudoku for Kids Volume 1. (p. 2467)
Shoshan, Beth. Mess Monsters at Christmas. (p. 1451)
Shotland, Julia Eliza. Restdale (Classic Reprint) (p. 1870)
Shotwell, Sheila Solomon. Gone Before Spring. (p. 861)
Shotz, Jennifer Li. Brave. (p. 276)
—Chestnut. (p. 366)
—Hero. (p. 959)
—Hero: Hurricane Rescue. (p. 961)
—Hero: Rescue Mission. (p. 961)
—Hurricane Rescue. (p. 1054)
—Max: Best Friend. Hero. Marine. (p. 1427)
—Scout: National Hero. (p. 1962)
—Scout: Firefighter. (p. 1963)
—Scout: National Hero. (p. 1963)
—Scout: Storm Dog. (p. 1963)
—Star. (p. 2101)
Shoudy, Emma. My Lord, the Count: A Society Drama (Classic Reprint) (p. 1554)
Shoulders, Debbie, jt. auth. see Shoulders, Michael.
Shoulders, Debbie & Shoulders, Michael. G Is for Gladiators: An Ancient Rome Alphabet. Juhasz, Victor, illus. (p. 804)
—T Is for Titanic: A Titanic Alphabet. van Frankenhuyzen, Gijsbert, illus. (p. 2174)
Shoulders, Michael. Cicada. (p. 390)
—Crossing the Dead Line: Stephen's Journey Through the Civil War. (p. 478)
—D Is for Dump Truck: A Construction Alphabet. Culotta, Kent, illus. (p. 494)
—Goodnight Baby Bear. Weidner, Teri, illus. (p. 867)
—Katydid. (p. 1206)
—Little Tennessee. (p. 1329)
Shoulders, Michael & Shoulders, Debbie. M Is for Money: An Economics Alphabet. Kelley, Marty, illus. (p. 1370)
Shouoto, Aya. He's My Only Vampire, Vol. 10. (p. 963)
—He's My Only Vampire, Vol. 4. (p. 963)
Shoup, John A., III. History of Syria (p. 980)
Shoup, Kate. American Culture & Society. (p. 71)
—Billie Jean King: The Battle of the Sexes & Title IX. (p. 226)
—California Gold Rush. (p. 310)
—Coding Careers in Internet Security (p. 412)
—Coding Careers in the Military (p. 412)
—Corruption in Politics (p. 456)
—Danica Patrick: Breaking Speed Barriers. (p. 502)
—Dealing with School Shootings (p. 519)
—Egypt. (p. 628)
—Fiebre del Oro. Green, Christina, tr. (p. 722)
—Freedom Riders: Civil Rights Activists Fighting Segregation. (p. 783)
—From New Amsterdam to New York: Dutch Settlement of America. (p. 792)
—Gold Rush. (p. 856)
—India. (p. 1115)
—Israel-Palestine Border Conflict. (p. 1141)
—Lady Liberty. Antal, Lara & Gennari, Joel, illus. (p. 1237)
—Life As a Navajo Code Talker in World War II. (p. 1290)
—Life As a Passenger on the Titanic. (p. 1290)
—Life As a Soldier in the Civil War. (p. 1290)
—Life As an Engineer on the First Railroads in America. (p. 1290)
—Lionel Messi: Legendary Soccer Player (p. 1306)
—My Country 'Tis of Thee. (p. 1536)
—Nazi Propaganda: Jews in Hitler's Germany. (p. 1583)
—Pakistan. (p. 1694)
—Paris Saint-Germain FC (p. 1700)
—Particle Physics. (p. 1701)
—Partition of India. (p. 1701)
—Quantum Mechanics. (p. 1822)
—Real Madrid (p. 1849)
—Rohypnol. (p. 1897)
—Rosie the Riveter: A Cultural Icon. Landsberg, Bryan, illus. (p. 1906)
—South Africa. (p. 2068)
—Standing in an Ambassador's Shoes. (p. 2101)
—Standing in the Secretary of Homeland Security's Shoes. (p. 2101)
—Technology of Ancient Greece. (p. 2197)
—Texas & the Mexican War. (p. 2209)
Shoup, Kate, jt. auth. see Madison, Amelia.
Shoup, Kate & Spence, Kelly. Ellen DeGeneres: Television Comedian & Gay Rights Activist. (p. 637)
Shouse, Eric. Good Shepherd. (p. 866)
Shovan, Laura. Last Fifth Grade of Emerson Elementary. (p. 1247)
—Takedown. (p. 2177)
Shovan, Laura, jt. auth. see Faruqi, Saadia.
Shove, Rhiannon. Burn after Writing Teen. New Edition. (p. 299)
Show What You Know Publishing. Swyk on Staar Math Gr 4, Parent/Teacher Edition: Preparation for the State of Texas Assessments of Academic Readiness. (p. 2172)
—Swyk on Staar Math Gr 4, Student Workbook: Preparation for the State of Texas Assessments of Academic Readiness. (p. 2172)
—Swyk on Staar Reading Gr 5, Parent/Teacher Edition: Preparation for the State of Texas Assessments of Academic Readiness. (p. 2172)
—Swyk on Staar Reading Gr 5, Student Workbook: Preparation for the State of Texas Assessments of Academic Readiness. (p. 2172)
—Swyk on Staar Reading/Math Gr 3, Parent/Teacher Edition: Preparation for the State of Texas Assessments of Academic Readiness. (p. 2172)
—Swyk on Staar Reading/Math Gr 3, Student Workbook: Preparation for the State of Texas Assessments of Academic Readiness. (p. 2172)
—Swyk on Staar Reading/Writing Gr 4, Parent/Teacher Edition: Preparation for the State of Texas Assessments of Academic Readiness. (p. 2172)
—Swyk on Staar Reading/Writing Gr 4, Student Workbook: Preparation for the State of Texas Assessments of Academic Readiness. (p. 2172)
—Swyk on Staar Science Gr 5, Parent/Teacher Edition: Preparation for the State of Texas Assessments of Academic Readiness. (p. 2172)
—Swyk on Staar Science Gr 5, Student Workbook: Preparation for the State of Texas Assessments of Academic Readiness. (p. 2172)
—Swyk on Staar Social Studies Gr 8, Parent/Teacher Edition: Preparation for the State of Texas Assessments of Academic Readiness. (p. 2172)
—Swyk on Staar Social Studies Gr 8, Student Workbook: Preparation for the State of Texas Assessments of Academic Readiness. (p. 2172)
Showalter, Elaine, ed. see Alcott, Louisa May.
Showalter, Gena. Alice in Zombieland. (p. 45)
—Everlife. (p. 670)
—Evil Queen. (p. 674)
—Firstlife. (p. 740)
—Glass Queen. (p. 841)
—Intertwined. (p. 1127)
—Lifeblood. (p. 1296)
—Mad Zombie Party. (p. 1373)
—Oh My Goth. (p. 1642)
—Queen of Zombie Hearts. (p. 1824)
—Through the Zombie Glass. (p. 2237)
—Twisted. (p. 2306)
—Unraveled. (p. 2335)
Showalter, Kristin, illus. see Olsen, S. R.
Showerman, Grant. Country Chronicle (Classic Reprint) (p. 461)
Showers, Paul. Where Does the Garbage Go? (p. 2436)
—Where Does the Garbage Go? Chewning, Randy, illus. (p. 2436)
Shrader, Dana. Tony Talks in Tongues. (p. 2260)
Shragg, Karen, jt. auth. see Landstrom, Lee Ann.
Shragg, Karen I. Lucy's Hero: Remembering Paul Wellstone. Klotz, Bryan, illus. (p. 1366)
Shragg, Karen I., jt. auth. see Landstrom, Lee Ann.
Shraya, Vivek. Boy & the Bindi. Perera, Rajni, illus. (p. 268)
Shreder, Etienne, illus. see Van Hamme, Jean.
Shreeve, Elizabeth. Oliver at the Window. McDonald, Candice Hartsough, illus. (p. 1649)
Shrek & Shaw!, Scott. Shrek. (p. 2013)
Shrestha, Sudesha, illus. see McKiver, Debbie.
Shrestha, Sudesha, illus. see Moore, Kate.
Shreve, Steve. Adventures of Benny (p. 21)
—Adventures of Charlie: Bigfoot or the Value of a Smelly Friend. Shreve, Steve, illus. (p. 22)
—Bogey Man: Or a Good Argument for Not Picking Your Nose. Shreve, Steve, illus. (p. 254)
—Monkey Island: Or the Advantage of Opposable Thumbs. Shreve, Steve, illus. (p. 1493)
—Mummy: Or Another Great Use for Toilet Paper. (p. 1526)
—Pirates: Or the Truth about Life on the High Seas. Shreve, Steve, illus. (p. 1750)
—Stan & the Toilet Monster. Shreve, Steve, illus. (p. 2100)
Shreve, Susan. Search for Baby Ruby. (p. 1971)
Shreve, Thomas Hopkins. Drayton: A Story of American Life (Classic Reprint) (p. 600)
Shrimpton, Nicholas, ed. see Trollope, Anthony.
Shrivasav, Ankur. Kabaggi Pe Zindagi: Jaha Shabdo Ko Panaah Mil Jaati Hai. (p. 1201)
Shriver, John S. To My Adopted Nevvy (Classic Reprint) (p. 2253)
Shroades, John, illus. see Klimo, Kate.
Shroades, John / W., illus. see Lowell, Susan.
Shrock, F. H. Honto, the Red Man's Daughter (Classic Reprint) (p. 1000)
Shrock, Joseph Earl, jt. auth. see Livingston, Leon Ray.
Shroder, John F., et al. Afghanistan. (p. 31)
Shroff, Vaishali. Adventures of Padma & a Blue Dinosaur. (p. 26)
Shroom, Rahima, illus. see Odg, Fuse.
Shrubshall & Free. Around the Pind in 80 Days: A Musical for Children. (p. 118)
Shrubsole, W. Christian Memoirs, or a Review of the Present State of Religion in England: In the Form of a New Pilgrimage to the Heavenly Jerusalem; Containing, by Way of Allegorical Narrative, a Great Variety of Dialogues on the Most Interesting Subjects, Adventures O. (p. 382)
Shrum, Brianna. How to Make Out. (p. 1043)
—Never Never. (p. 1590)
Shrum, Brianna R. Art of French Kissing. (p. 121)
—How to Make Out. (p. 1043)
—Kissing Ezra Holtz (and Other Things I Did for Science) (p. 1225)
Shrum, Jessica. Squeak & Jumbo: The Problem Solving Pair. (p. 2094)
Shryer, Donna & Dawson, Stephen. Body Fuel: A Guide to Good Nutrition. (p. 253)
Shryer, Donna & Forschmiedt, Jodi. Peak Performance: Sports Nutrition. (p. 1709)
Shu, Li, tr. see Kurtz, Kevin.
Shua, Ana Mar-A. Las Cosas Que Odio y Otras Exageraciones: Things I Hate & Other Exaggerations. (p. 1245)
Shub, Elizabeth, tr. see Singer, Isaac Bashevis.
Shubael, Shubael. Dark Strain (Classic Reprint) (p. 507)
Shubin, Jon, illus. see Shubin, Masha.
Shubin, Masha. Bad Hare Day: A Shubin Cousins Adventure. Shubin, Trinity, illus. (p. 158)
—Camp Caper: A Shubin Cousins Adventure. Hayes, Kathy & Hayes, David, illus. (p. 315)
—Fairytale Fracas: A Shubin Cousins Adventure. Shubin, Jon, illus. (p. 698)
Shubin, Trinity, illus. see Shubin, Masha.
Shuckard, William Edward, jt. auth. see Swainson, William.
Shuckburgh, Emily & Chambers, Catherine. Polar Scientist: The Coolest Jobs on the Planet HL Studios Staff, illus. (p. 1770)
Shue, Alan. Grant the Ant: And Zeater the Sneaky Anteater. Wilson, Elisa & Shue, Linda Nicole, illus. (p. 880)
Shue, Linda Nicole, illus. see Shue, Alan.
Shuemann, Bettina. 13 Women Artists Children Should Know. (p. 2552)
Shuey, Lillian. David of Juniper Gulch: A Story of the Placer Regions of California (Classic Reprint) (p. 511)
Shuey, Lillian Hinman. Don Luis Wife: A Romance of the West Indies, from Her Letters, & the Manuscripts of the Padre, the Doctor Caccavelli, Marc, Aurele Curate of Semana (Classic Reprint) (p. 581)
—Don Luis' Wife. (p. 581)
Shufelberger, Amanda, jt. auth. see Livingston, Mary A.
Shufelberger, Amanda & Livingston, Mary A. Buddy, the Wayward Wolverine. Livingston, Tim, illus. (p. 290)
Shuffle, Rube. Yellowstone Letters (Classic Reprint) (p. 2521)
Shugaar, Anthony, tr. see Rodari, Gianni.
Shugert, Fanny Alricks. Little Lady Bertha (Classic Reprint) (p. 1320)
Shuh, Mari. Adrian Peterson. (p. 17)
Shuizhu & Gunji. Sword Master Vol. 1: War of the Ancients. (p. 2171)
Shuker, Denis. Attack at Shark Bay: A Riwaka Gang Adventure. (p. 134)
—Rescue on Mount Hopeless: A Riwaka Gang Adventure. (p. 1868)
—Trapped on Devil's Peak: A Riwaka Gang Adventure. (p. 2279)
Shuker, Denis W. Escape from Deadman's Gully: A Riwaka Gang Adventure. (p. 661)
Shukla, Nikesh. Boxer. (p. 267)
Shukla, Rajesh Kumar. Kya Hai Muskil, Jab Kuchh Nahi Tera. (p. 1234)
Shukla, Umesh. Love You Back Grandma. Balogh, Andras, illus. (p. 1361)
Shuky. Knights Club: the Alliance of Dragons: The Comic Book You Can Play. Waltch & Novy, illus. (p. 1228)
—Knights Club: the Bands of Bravery: The Comic Book You Can Play. Waltch & Novy, illus. (p. 1228)
—Knights Club: the Buried City: The Comic Book You Can Play. Waltch & Novy, illus. (p. 1228)
—Knights Club: the Message of Destiny: The Comic Book You Can Play. Novy & Waltch, illus. (p. 1228)
Shuler, Douglas, illus. see Radman, David.
Shuler, Marjorie. For Rent - One Pedestal. (p. 763)
—For Rent-One Pedestal (Classic Reprint) (p. 763)
Shuler, Nancy. Nick the Basset Hound. (p. 1602)
Shulevitz, Uri. Dusk. Shulevitz, Uri, illus. (p. 610)
—How I Learned Geography. (p. 1032)
—Snow Shulevitz, Uri, illus. (p. 2046)
—Snow. (p. 2046)
—Snow Storytime Set. Shulevitz, Uri, illus. (p. 2048)
—Treasure. (p. 2281)
Shulimson, Sarene. Lights Out Shabbat Ebbeler, Jeffrey, illus. (p. 1300)
Shull, Megan. Bounce. (p. 265)
—Swap. (p. 2167)
Shulman, Dee. Polly Price's Totally Secret Diary: Mum in Love. (p. 1772)
Shulman, Holly. Dolley Madison: Her Life, Letters, & Legacy. (p. 578)
Shulman, Mark. Abraham Lincoln: Defender of the Union! Martin, Tom, illus. (p. 7)
—Alexander Hamilton: the Fighting Founding Father! Tindall, Kelly, illus. (p. 42)
—All You Need Is a Pencil: the Totally Sick Sick-Day Activity Book. (p. 55)
—All You Need Is a Pencil: the Wild & Crazy Summer Fun Activity Book. (p. 55)
—Benjamin Franklin: Inventor of the Nation! Tindall, Kelly, illus. (p. 200)
—Gorilla Garage Nguyen, Vincent, illus. (p. 870)
—I Voted: Making a Choice Makes a Difference. Bloch, Serge, illus. (p. 1083)
—Mom & Dad Are Palindromes. (p. 1490)
—Susan B. Anthony: Champion for Voting Rights! Tindall, Kelly, illus. (p. 2166)
—Walt Disney: the Magical Innovator! Frampton, Otis, illus. (p. 2374)
Shulman, Mark, jt. auth. see De La Hoya, Oscar.
Shulman, Naomi. Be Kind: You Can Make the World a Happier Place! 125 Kind Things to Say & Do. Pan, Hsinping, illus. (p. 177)
Shulman, Neil. Corporate Kid. (p. 456)
Shulman, Polly. Grimm Legacy. (p. 896)
—Poe Estate. (p. 1765)
Shulman, Stephanie J. Nose Pickers. (p. 1622)

Siegel, Mark, illus. see Siegel, Siena Cherson.
Siegel, Mark, illus. see Simon, Tanya & Simon, Richard.
Siegel, Mark, illus. see Wheeler, Lisa.
Siegel, Mark & Siegel, Alexis. 5 Worlds Book 1: the Sand Warrior. Bouma, Xanthe et al, illus. (p. 2548)
—5 Worlds Book 2: the Cobalt Prince Bk. 2. Rockefeller, Matt et al, illus. (p. 2548)
—5 Worlds Book 3: the Red Maze. Bouma, Xanthe et al, illus. (p. 2548)
—Red Maze. Bouma, Xanthe et al, illus. (p. 1857)
—Sand Warrior. Bouma, Xanthe et al, illus. (p. 1930)
Siegel, Marlys. Adventures of ... What's Your Name? (p. 20)
Siegel, Melanie, illus. see Ingalls, Ann.
Siegel, Randy. One Proud Penny. Bloch, Serge, illus. (p. 1661)
Siegel, Rebecca. Mayflower: The Ship That Started a Nation. Lauritano, Michael & Love, Mike, illus. (p. 1430)
—Rivers & Streams! With 25 Science Projects for Kids. Casteel, Tom, illus. (p. 1887)
Siegel, Siena Cherson. To Dance: Special Edition. Siegel, Mark, illus. (p. 2252)
Siegel, William, illus. see McNeely, Marian Hurd.
Siegemund-Broka, Austin & Wibberley, Emily. Always Never Yours. (p. 61)
—Por Siempre Jamás. (p. 1778)
Siegert, Mia. Jerkbait. (p. 1164)
Siegle, David K. Doc & the Princess. (p. 572)
Siegler, Karelyn, illus. see White, Amy.
Sieling, Peter. Growing up on a Farm: Responsibilities & Issues. (p. 900)
Siemasz, Greg. Hockey (p. 985)
Siemens, Charles William. On the Conservation of Solar Energy: A Collection of Papers & Discussions (Classic Reprint) (p. 1654)
Siemens, Jared. Bison. (p. 234)
—Blue. (p. 247)
—Centipedes. (p. 351)
—Chefs. (p. 364)
—Chickens. (p. 368)
—City. (p. 394)
—Construction Worker. (p. 444)
—Dentists. (p. 529)
—Doctors. (p. 574)
—Dragonflies. (p. 595)
—Ducks. (p. 608)
—Farmer. (p. 710)
—Fennec Fox. (p. 720)
—Ferret. (p. 721)
—Firefighters. (p. 733)
—Frog. (p. 789)
—Goats. (p. 849)
—Goliath Beetles. (p. 861)
—Grasshoppers. (p. 881)
—Green. (p. 893)
—Guinea Pig. (p. 904)
—Hedgehog. (p. 947)
—Horses. (p. 1005)
—How Water Shapes the Earth. (p. 1046)
—I am a Lobster. (p. 1057)
—Iguana. (p. 1094)
—Librarians. (p. 1284)
—Mosquitoes. (p. 1507)
—Octopus. (p. 1637)
—Pigs. (p. 1744)
—Police Officers. (p. 1770)
—Ponies. (p. 1773)
—Potbellied Pig. (p. 1781)
—Purple. (p. 1816)
—Scorpions. (p. 1962)
—Sheep. (p. 2004)
—Teachers. (p. 2195)
—Turkeys. (p. 2300)
—Veterinarians. (p. 2354)
—Yellow. (p. 2520)
Siemens, Jared, jt. auth. see Carr, Aaron.
Siemens, Jared, jt. auth. see Cuthbert, Megan.
Siemens, Jared, jt. auth. see Rodriguez, Cindy.
Siemens, Jared, jt. auth. see Wendel, S. E.
Siemens, Jared & Willis, John. Organisms. (p. 1670)
Siemens, Mary, tr. see Football, Virginia & Mantla, Rosa.
Siemens, Wendy, illus. see Damirchelli, Majid.
Siemensma, Hanneke, illus. see van der Hammen, Gijs.
Siems, Annika, illus. see Dreyer, Wolfgang.
Siena, Bernardino Da. Novellette Ed Esempi Morali Di S. Bernardino Da Siena (Classic Reprint) (p. 1626)
Siena, H. H. Princess Montesquiou Montlu. There's Rosemary (Classic Reprint) (p. 2218)
Siena, San Bernardino Da. Novellette, Esempi Morali e Apologhi (Classic Reprint) (p. 1626)
Sienkewicz, Thomas J., ed. see Salem Press Editors.
Sienkiewicz, Bill, illus. see Dreamworks, et al.
Sienkiewicz, Henry. On the Sunny Shore (Classic Reprint) (p. 1656)
Sienkiewicz, Henryk. After Bread: A Story of Polish Emigrant Life to America (Classic Reprint) (p. 33)
—Children of the Soil (Classic Reprint) (p. 372)
—Deluge; an Historical Novel of Poland, Sweden, & Russia, Vol. 2 Of 2: A Sequel to with Fire & Sword (Classic Reprint) (p. 527)
—Deluge, Vol. 1 Of 2: An Historical Novel of Poland, Sweden, & Russia, a Sequel to with Fire & Sword (Classic Reprint) (p. 527)
—For Daily Bread: And Other Stories (Classic Reprint) (p. 762)
—Hania (Classic Reprint) (p. 917)
—Her Tragic Fate (Classic Reprint) (p. 956)
—In Desert & Wilderness (Classic Reprint) (p. 1104)
—In Vain (Classic Reprint) (p. 1112)
—Irony of Life: The Polanetzki Family (Classic Reprint) (p. 1136)
—Knights of the Cross: An Historical Romance (Classic Reprint) (p. 1228)
—Knights of the Cross, or Krzyzacy: Historical Romance (Classic Reprint) (p. 1228)
—Knights of the Cross, Vol. 1 of 2 (Classic Reprint) (p. 1228)
—Let Us Follow Him: And Other Stories (Classic Reprint) (p. 1269)
—Lillian Morris & Other Stories. (p. 1301)
—New Soldier, or Nature & Life (Classic Reprint) (p. 1597)
—On the Bright Shore (Classic Reprint) (p. 1653)
—On the Field of Glory an Historical Novel, of the Time of King John Sobieski (Classic Reprint) (p. 1654)
—Pan Michael: An Historical Novel (Classic Reprint) (p. 1695)
—Pan Michael: An Historical Novel of Poland, the Ukraine, & Turkey, a Sequel to with Fire & Sword & the Deluge (Classic Reprint) (p. 1695)
—Sielanka: An Idyll (Classic Reprint) (p. 2015)
—Sielanka: A Forest Picture, & Other Stories (Classic Reprint) (p. 2015)
—Through the Desert (Classic Reprint) (p. 2237)
—Whirlpools; a Novel of Modern Poland: Translated from the Polish by Max a Drezmal (Classic Reprint) (p. 2442)
—With Fire & Sword: A Tale of the Past (Classic Reprint) (p. 2481)
—With Fire & Sword: An Historical Novel of Poland & Russia (Classic Reprint) (p. 2481)
—Yanko: The Musician & Other Stories (Classic Reprint) (p. 2517)
Sienkiewicz, Henryk & Binion, Samuel Augustus. Knights of the Cross. (p. 1228)
Sienna, Piero Da. Bella Camilla: Poemetto (Classic Reprint) (p. 197)
Sieroszewski, Vaclaw. Flight from Siberia (Classic Reprint) (p. 748)
Sierra, Alejandro Guichot Y. Ciencia de la Mitología: El Gran Mito Ctónico-Solar (Classic Reprint) (p. 391)
Sierra, Donn. Candin Book 2: The Visitors. (p. 321)
Sierra, Gabby & Mulicakova, Katarina. From Mexico & Slovakia - Memoirs of Two Immigrants' Journeys to the United States. (p. 792)
Sierra, Holly, illus. see Sweet, J. H.
Sierra, Holly, illus. see Sweet, J. H., et al.
Sierra i Fabra, Jordi. Lo Demas Es Silencio. (p. 1338)
Sierra I Fabra, Jordi. Sala de Conflictos. (p. 1924)
Sierra, Juan Ramon, illus. see Nino, Jairo Anibal.
Sierra, Judy. Ballyhoo Bay. Anderson, Derek, illus. (p. 162)
—Everyone Counts. Brown, Marc, illus. (p. 672)
—Great Dictionary Caper. Comstock, Eric, illus. (p. 885)
—Make Way for Readers. Karas, G. Brian, illus. (p. 1387)
—Mind Your Manners, B. B. Wolf. (p. 1470)
—Mind Your Manners, B. B. Wolf. Seibold, J. Otto, illus. (p. 1470)
—Never Kick a Ghost & Other Silly Chillers. Constantin, Pascale, illus. (p. 1590)
—Sleepy Little Alphabet: A Bedtime Story from Alphabet Town. Sweet, Melissa, illus. (p. 2037)
—Suppose You Meet a Dinosaur: A First Book of Manners. (p. 2162)
—Suppose You Meet a Dinosaur: a First Book of Manners. Bowers, Tim, illus. (p. 2162)
—Tell the Truth, B. B. Wolf. Seibold, J. Otto, illus. (p. 2202)
—Thelonius Monster's Sky-High Fly Pie. (p. 2215)
—We Love Our School! Davick, Linda, illus. (p. 2391)
—We Love Our School! A Read-Together Rebus Story. Davick, Linda, illus. (p. 2391)
Sierra, JulieAnn. Legacy & the Dark Prince (p. 1261)
Sierra-Feldman, Sam, jt. auth. see Feldman, Enrique C.
Sierrai Fabra, Jordi. (estupenda) Historia de Dragones y Princesas (mss o Menos) (p. 665)
Siers, Sophie. Gift Horse. (p. 832)
Sieveking, I. Giberne. Autumn Impressions of the Gironde (Classic Reprint) (p. 140)
Sieveking, Lance De G. Dressing Gowns & Glue (Classic Reprint) (p. 604)
Sieveking, Laura. Amelia Chamelia & the Birthday Party. Bermudez, Alyssa, illus. (p. 69)
—Amelia Chamelia & the Gelato Surprise. Bermudez, Alyssa, illus. (p. 69)
—Amelia Chamelia & the School Play: Amelia Chamelia 3. Bermudez, Alyssa, illus. (p. 69)
—Royal Academy of Sport for Girls: Leap of Faith. (p. 1909)
Sievers, Jen. Just Breathe: A Mindfulness Adventure. (p. 1192)
Sievers, Lee, illus. see Follett, Ross C.
Sievert, Claus, illus. see Tolstoy, Leo & Riordan, James.
Sievert, Terri. Forecasting Weather (p. 765)
—Unsolved Mystery of the Loch Ness Monster. (p. 2335)
—Unsolved Mystery of UFOs. (p. 2335)
Sievert, Tim, illus. see Johnson, Hal.
Siewart, Pauline. Look What I Can Do! (p. 1346)
—Look What I Can Make! (p. 1346)
—Look What I Can Play! (p. 1346)
—See What I Can Do! (p. 1982)
—See What I Can Make! (p. 1982)
—See What I Can Play! (p. 1982)
Siewart, Pauline, illus. see Baxter, Nicola.
Siewers, Carl, jt. auth. see Tromholt, Sophus.
Siewert, Pauline, illus. see David, Juliet.
Siewert, Pauline, illus. see Jones, Susan.
Siewert, Pauline, illus. see Knudson, Tara.
Siewert, Pauline, illus. see Pierpont, James Lord.
Siewert, Pauline, jt. auth. see Baxter, Nicola.
Sif, Birgitta. Frances Dean Who Loved to Dance & Dance. Sif, Birgitta, illus. (p. 776)
—Oliver. Sif, Birgitta, illus. (p. 1649)
—Swish & Squeak's Noisy Day. (p. 2171)
—Where My Feet Go. (p. 2439)
Sif, Birgitta, illus. see Bergman, Mara.
Sif, Birgitta, illus. see Lucas, Angie.
Sif, Birgitta, illus. see Oram, Hiawyn.
Sif, Birgitta, illus. see Potter, Alicia.
Sigafoose, Richard, jt. auth. see Sigafoose, Dick.
Sigafus, Kim. Nowhere to Hide. (p. 1628)
Sigafus, Kim & Ernst, Lyle. Native Writers-Voices of Power (p. 1579)
Siganakis, Pandora. Lexie's Wish. (p. 1282)
Siggins, Gerard. Atlantis United: Sports Academy Book 1. (p. 133)
—Rugby Flyer: Haunting History, Thrilling Tries. (p. 1912)
—Rugby Heroes. (p. 1913)
—Rugby Rebel. (p. 1913)
—Rugby Redzone: Sports Academy Book 2. (p. 1913)
—Rugby Runner: Ancient Roots, Modern Boots. (p. 1913)
—Rugby Warrior: Back in School. Back in Sport. Back in Time. (p. 1913)
Siggs, Sarah. Mud Boy: A Story about Bullying. Crosby, Amy, illus. (p. 1524)
Siglain, Michael. Breakout! Marvel Artist Staff, illus. (p. 278)
—Escape from Darth Vader. Roux, Stéphane, illus. (p. 661)
—Finn & Rey Escape! (p. 731)
—First Order Villains. (p. 738)
—Han & Chewie Return! (p. 914)
—Journey to Star Wars: the Last Jedi the Power of the Force. Rood, Brian, illus. (p. 1182)
—Journey to Star Wars: the Rise of Skywalker First Order Villains (Level 2 Reader) Saito, Diogo & Aime, Luigi, illus. (p. 1182)
—Journey to Star Wars: the Rise of Skywalker Resistance Heroes (Level 2 Reader) Saito, Diogo & Aime, Luigi, illus. (p. 1182)
—Power of the Force. (p. 1782)
—Rescue from Jabba's Palace. (p. 1868)
—Resistance Heroes. (p. 1869)
—Star Wars: Trapped in the Death Star! Studio, Pilot, illus. (p. 2105)
—Trapped in the Death Star! (p. 2279)
—Use the Force! Roux, Stéphane, illus. (p. 2341)
—World of Reading Star Wars Use the Force! Level 2. Pilot Studio, illus. (p. 2504)
Siglain, Michael, adapted by. Zeb to the Rescue. (p. 2538)
Siglain, Michael, et al. Star Wars Rebels: Zeb to the Rescue. Press, Lucasfilm, illus. (p. 2105)
Sigle, Maria L. Redletter. (p. 1859)
Sigler, Scott. Alight. (p. 47)
—Alive. (p. 48)
—Alone. (p. 57)
—Starter (p. 2107)
Sigman, Margie. Problem with Meli (p. 1803)
Sigmon, Ray. Huntington Beach State Park: Visitor's Guide (Classic Reprint) (p. 1054)
Sigmon-Heck, Christina. Birthday Wish. (p. 234)
—Smile for Only You! (p. 2041)
Signe Morrison, Susan, ed. see Wehlen Morrison, Joan.
Signer, Dan. More Lunch Lines: Tear-Out Riddles for Lunchtime Giggles (Lunch Jokes for Kids, Notes for Kids' Lunch Boxes with Silly Kid Jokes) James, Steve, illus. (p. 1505)
Signor, Florence R. Plays for School Days: Twenty-One Selected Plays That Have Been Used Successfully in the Schoolroom, for Pupils of Intermediate & Grammar Grades (Classic Reprint) (p. 1761)
Signor, Priscilla M. Adventures of Hooch & Mile-A-Minute-Freebee. Buehrle, Jacquelyn, illus. (p. 24)
Signor Sr., S. Ernest. Book of David: Volume One. (p. 258)
—Book of Esther. (p. 258)
—Book of Ruth. (p. 259)
Sigourney, L. H. Child's Book: The Consisting of Original Articles, in Prose & Poetry (Classic Reprint) (p. 375)
—Lucy Howard's Journal (Classic Reprint) (p. 1366)
Sigourney, Lydia H. Ladies' Companion, Vol. 19: And Literary Expositor; a Monthly Magazine Embracing Every Department of Literature; Embellished with Original Engravings, & Music Arranged for the Piano Forte, Harp & Guitar (Classic Reprint) (p. 1236)
Sigourney, Lydia Howard. Boy's & Girl's Illustrated Olio (Classic Reprint) (p. 272)
Sigrid, Martinez. Bonjour Bebe Dauphin. (p. 256)
Sigsawa, Keiichi, jt. auth. see Kawahara, Reki.
Sigurdsson, Rev. Rupert. Lifetime of Pets (p. 1297)
Sigurjonsson, Johann. Modern Icelandic Plays, VI of the Hills: The Hraun Farm (Classic Reprint) (p. 1487)
Sihler, K. Elizabeth. Against Odds: A Personal Narrative of Life in Horse Heaven (Classic Reprint) (p. 34)
Siino, Frances. Superhero. (p. 2159)
Siivola, Liz. Little Mouse Finds a New Home. DuPont, Brittany, illus. (p. 1323)
Sijercic, Hedina. Unusual Family: A Romani Folktale. Greven, Doris, illus. (p. 2337)
Sikdar, Anushka. Isles of Mist. (p. 1140)
—Tiger & Lily: A Collection of Thoughts. (p. 2241)
Sikes, Jan. Flutter Your Wings. Evans, Nancy, illus. (p. 753)
Sikes, Mary Montague. Artful Animal Alphabet. (p. 122)
Sikkens, Crystal. Bar Graphs. (p. 164)
—Dam Holds Back. (p. 499)
—Day & Night. (p. 512)
—Dome Stays Strong. (p. 580)
—Four Seasons. (p. 772)
—From Seed to Pumpkin. (p. 793)
—Life Cycle of a Rabbit. (p. 1291)
—Picture Graphs. (p. 1740)
—Road Connects Places. (p. 1888)
—Tunnel Runs Through. (p. 2299)
Sikora, Frank & Batcheler, Michelle. Frank M. Johnson, Jr: Courageous Judge. (p. 777)
Sikorskaia, Margarita, illus. see Dalton, Angela.
Sikorskaia, Margarita, illus. see Schrenk, Lorenz.
Sikorskaia, Margarita, illus. see Shaw, Nancy Jo.
Sikoryak, Bob, illus. see Sturm, James.
Siku, illus. see Anderson, Jeff & Thomas, Richard.
Sil, Avijit, illus. see Winzenried, Chandra.
Silas, Thony, illus. see Higgins, Kyle.
Silate, Jennifer. Betsy Ross: Creator of the American Flag. (p. 209)
—Betsy Ross: Creator of the American Flag / Creadora de la bandera Estadounidense. (p. 209)
—Betsy Ross: Creadora de la bandera estadounidense (Betsy Ross: Creator of the American Flag) (p. 209)
—Calhoun-Randolph Debate on the Eve of the War Of 1812: A Primary Source Investigation. (p. 310)
—Last Stand: The Final Military Campaign of General George Armstrong Custer. (p. 1249)
—Little Sure Shot: Annie Oakley & Buffalo Bill's Wild West Show. (p. 1328)
—Seeing the Future: The Final Vision of Sitting Bull. (p. 1984)
—Statue of Liberty. (p. 2109)
—Your Mayor: Local Government in Action. (p. 2534)
Silber, Jere. Color the Sky. (p. 421)
—Tree Story Coloring Book. (p. 2284)
Silberberg, Alan. Awesome, Almost 100% True Adventures of Matt & Craz. Silberberg, Alan, illus. (p. 144)
—Meet the Latkes. (p. 1440)
—Milo: Sticky Notes & Brain Freeze. Silberberg, Alan, illus. (p. 1468)
Silberg, Francis Barry. Story of Chanukah. Levy, Pamela R., illus. (p. 2129)
—Story of Passover. Britt, Stephanie McFetridge, illus. (p. 2132)
Silberg, Jackie, jt. auth. see Schiller, Pam.
Silberman, Dani. Three Monkey Brothers. (p. 2234)
Silberrad, U. L. Petronilla Heroven (Classic Reprint) (p. 1731)
Silberrad, Una L. Good Comrade (Classic Reprint) (p. 862)
Silberrad, Una Lucy. Curayl (Classic Reprint) (p. 485)
—Desire (Classic Reprint) (p. 533)
—Keren of Lowbole (Classic Reprint) (p. 1210)
—Lady of Dreams (Classic Reprint) (p. 1237)
—Second Book of Tobiah (Classic Reprint) (p. 1973)
Silberschlag, Eisig. Poet Lore, Vol. 45: World Literature & the Drama; Summer-Autumn, 1939 (Classic Reprint) (p. 1766)
Silbert, Jack. Honest Abe's Funny Money Book. (p. 998)
Silbert, Jack, jt. auth. see D'Agnese, Joseph.
Silbert, Ken, illus. see Lawrence, Anne Michelle.
Silcox, Beth Douglass. Little Rumely Man. Peters, Darcy, illus. (p. 1327)
Silcox, Diane. Light to Keep. Moates, Carol Meetze, illus. (p. 1299)
Silen, Andrea. NGR Rainforests (L2) (p. 1601)
Silen, Yenan. Tierra de Valientes. (p. 2240)
Sileo, Frank J. Bee Calm: The Buzz on Yoga. Keay, Claire, illus. (p. 189)
—Bee Heartful: Spreading Loving-Kindness. Keay, Claire, illus. (p. 189)
—Bee Still: An Invitation to Meditation. Keay, Claire, illus. (p. 189)
—Did You Hear? A Story about Gossip. Zivoin, Jennifer, illus. (p. 543)
—Don't Put Yourself down in Circus Town: A Story about Self-Confidence. Cornelison, Sue, illus. (p. 583)
—Sally Sore Loser: A Story about Winning & Losing. Pillo, Cary, illus. (p. 1925)
—World of Pausabilities: An Exercise in Mindfulness. Zivoin, Jennifer, illus. (p. 2503)
Silin-Palmer, Pamela, illus. see Loehr, Mallory.
Silivanch, Annalise. Career as a Teacher. (p. 328)
—Making the Right College Choice: Technical, 2 Year, 4 Year. (p. 1390)
—Rebuilding America's Infrastructure. (p. 1852)
Sill, Cathryn. About Amphibians: A Guide for Children Sill, John, illus. (p. 6)
—About Amphibians / Sobre Los Anfibios: A Guide for Children / una Guía para Niños Sill, John, illus. (p. 6)
—About Birds: A Guide for Children Sill, John, illus. (p. 6)
—About Birds / Sobre Los Pájaros: A Guide for Children / una Guía para Niños Sill, John, illus. (p. 6)
—About Fish: A Guide for Children Sill, John, illus. (p. 6)
—About Fish / Sobre Los Peces: A Guide for Children / una Guía para Niños Sill, John, illus. (p. 6)
—About Habitats: Deserts. Sill, John, illus. (p. 6)
—About Habitats: Forests Sill, John, illus. (p. 6)
—About Habitats: Grasslands Sill, John, illus. (p. 6)
—About Habitats: Mountains Sill, John & Sill, John, illus. (p. 6)
—About Habitats: Oceans Sill, John, illus. (p. 6)
—About Habitats: Polar Regions Sill, John, illus. (p. 6)
—About Habitats: Rivers & Streams Sill, John, illus. (p. 6)
—About Habitats: Seashores Sill, John, illus. (p. 6)
—About Hummingbirds: A Guide for Children Sill, John, illus. (p. 6)
—About Hummingbirds. Sill, John, illus. (p. 6)
—About Insects. (p. 6)
—About Insects / Sobre Los Insectos: A Guide for Children / una Guía para Niños Sill, John, illus. (p. 6)
—About Mammals: A Guide for Children Sill, John, illus. (p. 6)
—About Marine Mammals: A Guide for Children Sill, John, illus. (p. 6)
—About Parrots: A Guide for Children Sill, John, illus. (p. 6)
—About Penguins: A Guide for Children Sill, John, illus. (p. 6)
—About Raptors: A Guide for Children Sill, John, illus. (p. 6)
—About Reptiles / Sobre Los Reptiles: A Guide for Children / una Guía para Niños Sill, John, illus. (p. 6)
—About Seabirds: A Guide for Children. Sill, John, illus. (p. 6)
—About Woodpeckers: A Guide for Children. Sill, John, illus. (p. 6)
—Curious about Birds. Sill, John, illus. (p. 486)
—Sobre Los Insectos: Una Guía para Niños. Sill, John, illus. (p. 2051)
—Sobre Los Mamíferos: Una Guía para Niños. Sill, John, illus. (p. 2051)
—Sobre Los Pájaros: Una Guía para Niños Sill, John, illus. (p. 2051)
—Sobre Los Peces: Una Guía para Niños. Sill, John, illus. (p. 2051)
Sill, Cathryn, jt. auth. see Sill, Cathryn P.
Sill, Cathryn P. About Birds: A Guide for Children. Sill, John, illus. (p. 6)
—About Penguins: A Guide for Children Sill, John, illus. (p. 6)
Sill, Cathryn P., illus. see Torre, Cristina de la.
Sill, E. r. Mozart: A Biographical Romance (Classic Reprint) (p. 1517)
Sill, John, illus. see Alden, Peter C. & Peterson, Roger Tory.
Sill, John, illus. see Sill, Cathryn P.
Sill, John, illus. see Sill, Cathryn P. & Sill, Cathryn.
Sill, John, illus. see Sill, Cathryn.
Sill, John, illus. see Torre, Cristina de la.
Sill, Lisa. Stem: Lasers: Measuring Length (Grade 2) (p. 2113)
Sill, Lisa M. CTIM - Láseres: Medición de la Longitud. (p. 481)
Sillani, Febe, illus. see Malerba, Giulia.
Sillars-Powell, Tessa. Super Squishies, Slime, & Putty: 40 Insane Recipes! (p. 2158)

S

Sim, David, illus. see SteveSongs Staff.
Sim, Robert J., illus. see Patch, Edith M.
Sim, Stephanie. Copycat. (p. 452)
Sim, Tara. Chainbreaker. (p. 353)
—Firestarter. (p. 734)
—Scavenge the Stars. (p. 1943)
—Timekeeper. (p. 2246)
Sima, Jessie. Harriet Gets Carried Away. Sima, Jessie, illus. (p. 933)
—Love, Z. Sima, Jessie, illus. (p. 1361)
—Not Quite Narwhal. Sima, Jessie, illus. (p. 1623)
—Spencer's New Pet. Sima, Jessie, illus. (p. 2079)
Sima, Jessie, illus. see Trimmer, Christian.
Simandan, Voicu Mihnea. Ironman. A Play. (p. 1136)
Simanu-Klutz, Luafata, tr. see Carroll, Lewis, pseud.
Simard, Donna. Shhh! It's a Surprise! Hidden Treasures on the West Coast. (p. 2006)
—Shhh! It's a Surprise: Off to Nunavut. (p. 2007)
—Tommy's Feet. (p. 2259)
Simard, Rémy. Gustave Tanaka, Shelley, tr. (p. 906)
—Simone: Even More Monstrous! (p. 2021)
Simard, Remy, illus. see Hall, Kirsten.
Simard, Remy, illus. see Jones, Christianne C.
Simard, Remy, illus. see Korb, Rena B. & Weinhaus, Anthony J.
Simard, Remy, illus. see Meister, Cari.
Simard, Remy, illus. see Mortensen, Lori.
Simard, Remy, illus. see Murphy, Stuart J.
Simard, Remy, illus. see Richards, Kitty.
Simard, Remy, illus. see Rosa-Mendoza, Gladys.
Simard, Remy, illus. see Rusu, Meredith.
Simard, Tim. Haunted Hikes of Vermont. (p. 938)
Simas, Richard. Mystery of the Portuguese Waltzes Clarke, Caroline, illus. (p. 1570)
Simbotah, Symon, tr. see Pere, Tuula.
Sime, J. G. Our Little Life: A Novel of Today (Classic Reprint) (p. 1679)
Sime, William. Haco the Dreamer, Vol. 1 Of 2: A Tale of Scotch University Life (Classic Reprint) (p. 909)
Simeon, Stephen Louis. Daniele Cortis: A Novel Translated from the Italian of Antonio Fogazzaro (Classic Reprint) (p. 503)
Simeon, Stephen Louis & Fogazzaro, Antonio. Daniele Cortis. (p. 503)
Simes, Wyno, tr. see Umar, Mohammed & Greene, Soukaina Lalla.
Simes, Wyno, tr. see Umar, Mohammed.
Simhaee, Rebeka. Avi's Choice: A Story about Bikur Cholim-Visiting the Sick. Hechter, Janice, illus. (p. 143)
—Sara Finds A Mitzva. Leverton, Yossi, ed. (p. 1935)
Simhananda, B. Jyoti for Kids: A Meditative Technique of Purification by the Light. (p. 1201)
Similien, Peri. Vestige: Peace No More. (p. 2354)
Siminovich, Lorena. Alex & Lulu: Two of a Kind. Siminovich, Lorena, illus. (p. 42)
—Alex et Lulu -Bravo L'Artiste. (p. 42)
—I Like Toys. Siminovich, Lorena, illus. (p. 1068)
—My Favorite Things Flash Cards. (p. 1539)
—You Are My Baby - Farm. (p. 2524)
—You Are My Baby: Garden. (p. 2524)
—You Are My Baby: Meadow: (Baby First Boards Books for Easter, Bunny Books, Whale Ocean Books) (p. 2524)
—You Are My Baby: Ocean. (p. 2524)
—You Are My Baby - Safari. (p. 2524)
—You Are My Baby: Woodland. (p. 2524)
Siminovich, Lorena, illus. see Gillingham, Sara.
Siminovitch, Lorena. Alex et Lulu -Amies Comme Chien et Chat. (p. 42)
Simkins, Aron. Dream Big: The Journey of the Jazz Bear. (p. 601)
Simkins, Ed, jt. auth. see Richards, Jon.
Simkins, J. Dean. Ants & the Children of the Garden: Relating the Habits of the Black Harvester Ant & Giving Considerable Information about Ants in General (Classic Reprint) (p. 103)
Simko, Joe. Sweet Rot: The Purple Meltdown Book 3 Simko, Joe, illus. (p. 2169)
—Sweet Rot, Book 2: Raiders of the Lost Art (p. 2169)
Simko, Joe, illus. see Consiglio, Joe.
Simko, Joe, illus. see Stine, R. L. & The Topps Company.
Simko, Joe, illus. see Stine, R.I.
Simler, Isabelle. Blue Hour. (p. 248)
—My Wild Cat. (p. 1565)
—Web. (p. 2395)
Simler, Isabelle, illus. see Ardizzone, Sarah.
Simmans, Sean, illus. see Wells, H. G.
Simmers, George. Animals Like Reading! (p. 95)
Simmonds, Brian, illus. see Wolfer, Dianne.
Simmonds, Florence. New Book of Martyrs: From the French of Georges Duhamel (Classic Reprint) (p. 1591)
Simmonds, Frank H., illus. see Caudle, P. L.
Simmonds, Irene. Our Trip to Europe (Classic Reprint) (p. 1681)
Simmonds, Jane. Cocker Spaniel. (p. 411)
Simmonds, Janet. Perky Emigrates: The Adventures of Perky the Tortoise. Koster, Sonja, illus. (p. 1724)
Simmonds, Peter Lund. Animal Products: Their Preparation, Commercial Uses, & Value (Classic Reprint) (p. 91)
—Animal Products; (p. 91)
Simmonds, Posy. Baker Cat. Simmonds, Posy, illus. (p. 160)
—Fred. (p. 780)
—Lulu & the Chocolate Wedding. (p. 1367)
—Lulu & the Flying Babies. (p. 1367)
Simmonds-Hurn, Zak, illus. see Furman, Simon & Ferreyra, Lucas.
Simmons, Alex. Scooby-Doo in Dead & Let Spy Pope, Robert, illus. (p. 1960)
Simmons, Allan H., ed. see Conrad, Joseph.
Simmons, Anthea. Best, Best Baby! (p. 205)
—I'm Big Now! Birkett, Georgie, illus. (p. 1098)
—Lightning Mary. (p. 1300)
Simmons, Beth E., jt. auth. see Cerullo, Mary M.
Simmons, Bethany, illus. see Osborne, Erin.
Simmons, Cari & Alexander, Heather. Picture Perfect #1: Bending over Backwards. (p. 1740)
Simmons, Cari & Burns, Laura J. Picture Perfect #5: All Together Now. Mingus, Cathi, illus. (p. 1740)
Simmons, Cari & Douglas, Lola. Picture Perfect #2: You First. (p. 1740)
Simmons, Cari & Metz, Melinda. Picture Perfect #4: Between Us. (p. 1740)
Simmons, Cari & Zulkey, Claire. Picture Perfect #3: Best Frenemies. (p. 1740)
Simmons, Clara Ann. Sauncey & Mr. King's Gallery Geer, Charles, illus. (p. 1937)
Simmons, Edward. From Seven to Seventy: Memoires of a Painter & a Yankee (Classic Reprint) (p. 793)
Simmons, Elly, illus. see Herrera, Juan Felipe.
Simmons, Grace. Miss Grace & Winifred. (p. 1478)
Simmons, Harry P. Under the Kerosene Lamp: Being the Prairie Pioneer's Primer (Classic Reprint) (p. 2322)
Simmons, Herbert. Corner Boy: A Novel (Classic Reprint) (p. 454)
Simmons, J. A. Hannah's First Airplane Ride. (p. 918)
Simmons, J. B. Blue Tower. (p. 249)
Simmons, Jane. Beryl: a Pig's Tale. (p. 204)
—Ebb & Flo & the Baby Seal. Simmons, Jane, illus. (p. 622)
—Ebb & Flo & the Greedy Gulls. (p. 622)
Simmons, Joann. Azazel. (p. 145)
Simmons, JoAnne. How God Grows a Girl of Grace: A Devotional. (p. 1031)
Simmons, Joy. I Can't Wait to Be on TV! (p. 1063)
Simmons Jr, Frank. Monkey That Had No Tree to Climb: A Story for Children. (p. 1494)
Simmons, Judy, illus. see Elick, Celeste Kaufhold.
Simmons, K. Clash of Time: Book 1: the Missing Piece. (p. 399)
Simmons, Kelly. I Was a Foster Failure. (p. 1085)
Simmons, Kevin. Boy Who Called 911. (p. 270)
Simmons, Kristen. Article 5. (p. 123)
—Articulo 5. (p. 123)
—Deceivers. (p. 522)
—Glass Arrow. (p. 841)
—Pacifica. (p. 1691)
—Scammed. (p. 1941)
Simmons, Kristen, jt. auth. see Raasch, Sara.
Simmons, L. B. We, the Wildflowers. (p. 2392)
Simmons, Laura and Roshonda. Alex & Her Clubhouse Friends. Azevedo, Lafayette, illus. (p. 42)
Simmons, Lisa. Bo Goes to Hawaii. Briggs, Alice, illus. (p. 250)
—Sadie Sees Paris. Briggs, Alice a, illus. (p. 1921)
Simmons, Lisa Hendrix. Kip Macallister Adventures: Bodyguard. (p. 1223)
—Kip Macallister Adventures: Close Cover. (p. 1224)
Simmons, Lynn. Bo & the Christmas Bandit Lyne, Alison, illus. (p. 250)
Simmons, Marc, illus. see Westheimer, Ruth K. & Lehu, Pierre A.
Simmons, Mark, illus. see Bolte, Mari.
Simmons, Mark, illus. see Wilkins, Ebony Joy.
Simmons, Mark, illus. see Yomtov, Nelson.
Simmons, Matt J. Jackie Robinson: Breaking the Color Line in Baseball. (p. 1153)
Simmons, Maude E. Geraldine's Treachery: A Play in Five Acts (Classic Reprint) (p. 821)
Simmons, Mervin C. Three Times & Out (Classic Reprint) (p. 2235)
Simmons, Nataly, illus. see Ciofalo, J. F.
Simmons, Nataly, illus. see Cutelli, Nick.
Simmons, R., illus. see J Douglas.
Simmons, Randy. Basic Training: A Manual for Teens. (p. 170)
Simmons, Robert, illus. see Hancock, Susan G.
Simmons, Roshonda & Simmons, Laura. Day Out with Mom: A Day Out with Mom. Centineo, Ornella, illus. (p. 514)
Simmons, Russell, illus. see Mayer, Nicole & Mayer, Ryan.
Simmons, Sean. Together We Make a Family. (p. 2256)
Simmons, Sheila. My Alabama Notebook. (p. 1531)
Simmons, Steven J. & Moore, Cyd. Alice & Greta: A Tale of Two Witches. (p. 44)
Simmons, Walter. Cambodia. (p. 313)
—Colombia. (p. 417)
—Czech Republic. (p. 493)
—Dominican Republic. (p. 580)
—Egypt. (p. 628)
—Iran. (p. 1133)
—Morocco. (p. 1506)
—Pakistan. (p. 1694)
—Poland. (p. 1769)
—Salvador. (p. 1926)
—Vietnam. (p. 2357)
Simmons, Walter, jt. auth. see Sexton, Colleen.
Simmons, Walter E., jt. auth. see Tukey, Greenleaf S.
Simmons-Jacobi, Allison. Dear God... Love Booger. (p. 520)
Simms, Albert Clint. My Values & Morales Treasury. (p. 1563)
Simms, Florence May. Étoffe du Pays: Lower St. Lawrence Sketches (Classic Reprint) (p. 666)
Simms, Genevieve, illus. see Cotter, Charis.
Simms, Genevieve, illus. see Uegaki, Chieri.
Simms, Jennifer. Teens & Distracting Driving. (p. 2200)
Simms, Jennifer, jt. auth. see Harris, Duchess.
Simms, Laura. Stories to Nourish the Hearts of Our Children. Krizmanic, Tatjana, illus. (p. 2126)
Simms, Susan Rose. Mount Rushmore. (p. 1513)
—Statue of Liberty. (p. 2109)
—US Flag. (p. 2340)
Simms, W. Gillmore. Guy Rivers, the Outlaw: A Tale of Georgia (Classic Reprint) (p. 906)
SIMMs, W. Gilmore. Eutaw: A Sequel to the Forayers, or the Raid of the Dog-Days; a Tale of the Revolution (Classic Reprint) (p. 668)
—Partisan: A Romance of the Revolution (Classic Reprint) (p. 1701)
—Southward Ho! A Spell of Sunshine (Classic Reprint) (p. 2069)
—Woodcraft, or Hawks about the Dovecote: A Story of the South at the Close of the Revolution (Classic Reprint) (p. 2491)
Simms, William Gilmore. As Good As a Comedy, or the Tennesseean's Story (Classic Reprint) (p. 124)
—Border Beagles: A Tale of Mississippi (Classic Reprint) (p. 262)
—Border Beagles. (p. 262)
—Carl Werner, an Imaginative Story, Vol. 1 Of 2: With Other Tales of Imagination (Classic Reprint) (p. 331)
—Carl Werner, an Imaginative Story; with Other Tales of Imagination; Vol. II. (p. 331)
—Cassique of Kiawah: A Colonial Romance (Classic Reprint) (p. 339)
—Charlemont; or the Pride of the Village: A Tale of Kentucky (Classic Reprint) (p. 358)
—Confession, or the Blind Heart: A Domestic Story (Classic Reprint) (p. 439)
—Forayers: Or the Raid of the Dog-Days (Classic Reprint) (p. 764)
—Golden Christmas: A Chronicle of St. John's, Berkeley; Compiled from the Notes of a Briefless Barrister (Classic Reprint) (p. 857)
—Guy Rivers, Vol. 1 Of 2: A Tale of Georgia (Classic Reprint) (p. 906)
—Helen Halsey, or the Swamp State of Conelachita: A Tale of the Borders (Classic Reprint) (p. 949)
—Katharine Walton, or the Rebel of Dorchester (Classic Reprint) (p. 1205)
—Life in America, or the Wigwam & the Cabin (Classic Reprint) (p. 1292)
—Maroon: A Legend of the Caribbees, & Other Tales (Classic Reprint) (p. 1408)
—Mellichampe a Legend of the Santee (Classic Reprint) (p. 1443)
—Partisan: A Romance of the Revolution (Classic Reprint) (p. 1701)
—Partisan, Vol. 1 Of 2: A Tale of the Revolution (Classic Reprint) (p. 1701)
—Partisan, Vol. 2 Of 2: A Tale of the Revolution (Classic Reprint) (p. 1701)
—Richard Hurdis: Tale of Alabama (Classic Reprint) (p. 1876)
—Richard Hurdis. (p. 1876)
—Richard Hurdis, or the Avenger of Blood, Vol. 2 Of 2: Tale of Alabama (Classic Reprint) (p. 1876)
—Woodcraft or Hawks about the Dovecote; a Story of the South at the Close of the Revolution (Classic Reprint) (p. 2491)
—Yemassee: A Romance of Carolina (Classic Reprint) (p. 2521)
—Yemassee. (p. 2521)
Simner, Janni Lee. Bones of Faerie. (p. 256)
—Faerie After. (p. 694)
—Faerie Winter (p. 694)
Simó, Roger, illus. see Ohlin, Nancy.
Simon, A. Christopher, illus. see Loye, David.
Simon, A. Christopher, jt. auth. see Loye, David.
Simon Abbott. 100 Questions about Oceans. (p. 2557)
Simon Abbott & Abbott, Simon. 100 Questions about... Sharks. (p. 2557)
Simon, Alyssa & Romano, Amy. How Cells Divide, Reproduce, & Specialize (p. 1027)
Simon, Amy. Can I Go Too? (p. 317)
Simon, Amy Price. Can I Go Too? (p. 317)
Simon and Schuster. Lady Midnight. (p. 1237)
Simon and Schuster & Chu, Wesley. Red Scrolls of Magic. (p. 1858)
Simon and Schuster & Nielsen, Cliff. Queen of Air & Darkness. (p. 1824)
Simon & Schuster UK. Holiday Ha Ha Ha! (p. 987)
—Silhouette Theatre - Sleeping Beauty. (p. 2018)
Simon and Schuster UK Staff. Colour in 5 SOS! (p. 427)
—Colour in One Direction! (p. 427)
—Ultimate Boy Band Pack! (p. 2314)
Simon and Schuster/LeapFrog Staff, jt. auth. see Cronin, Doreen.
Simon and Schuster/LeapFrog Staff, jt. auth. see Falconer, Ian.
Simon, Annette. Robot Zombie Frankenstein! Simon, Annette, illus. (p. 1892)
Simon, Arlyne. Abby Invents Unbreakable Crayons. Necsulescu, Diana, illus. (p. 3)
Simon, Chad-Michael. Yellowstone: The Bears of Caldera. (p. 2521)
Simon, Charnan. Dance Team. (p. 500)
—Earth. (p. 615)
—Luna the Wake-Up Cat. Huang, Benrei, illus. (p. 1368)
—Mars. (p. 1409)
—Plan B. (p. 1754)
—Pumpkin Fever. Bryan-Hunt, Jan, illus. (p. 1812)
—Shattered Star. (p. 2003)
—Super Cool Science Experiments: Compounds & Mixtures. (p. 2154)
—Wolves. (p. 2485)
Simon, Charnan, jt. auth. see Kazunas, Ariel.
Simon, Charnan & Kazunas, Ariel. Killer Whales. (p. 1217)
—Super Cool Science Experiments: Water. (p. 2154)
Simon, Charnan & Kazunis, Ariel. Experiment with Water. (p. 678)
Simon, Coco. Alexis: The Icing on the Cupcake. (p. 43)
—Alexis & the Missing Ingredient. (p. 43)
—Alexis & the Perfect Recipe. (p. 43)
—Alexis Cool As a Cupcake. (p. 43)
—Alexis Cool as a Cupcake. (p. 43)
—Alexis Cupcake Crush. (p. 43)
—Alexis Gets Frosted. (p. 43)
—Alexis the Icing on the Cupcake. (p. 43)
—Alexis's Cupcake Cupid. (p. 43)
—Alexis's Half-Baked Idea. Bishop, Tracy, illus. (p. 43)
—Banana Splits. (p. 163)
—Cracks in the Cone. (p. 466)
—Cupcake Diaries 3 Books In 1! #4: Mias Boiling Point; Emma, Smile & Say Cupcake!; Alexis Gets Frosted. (p. 485)
—Cupcake Diaries Collection: Katie & the Cupcake Cure; Mia in the Mix; Emma on Thin Icing; Alexis & the Perfect Recipe. (p. 485)
—Donut for Your Thoughts. (p. 584)
—Emma: Lights! Camera! Cupcakes! (p. 643)
—Emma: Sugar & Spice & Everything Nice. (p. 643)
—Emma All Stirred Up! (p. 643)
—Emma Catwalks & Cupcakes! (p. 643)
—Emma: Lights! Camera! Cupcakes! (p. 643)
—Emma on Thin Icing. (p. 643)
—Emma Raining Cats & Dogs... & Cupcakes! (p. 643)
—Emma Raining Cats & Dogs ... & Cupcakes! (p. 643)
—Emma, Smile & Say Cupcake! (p. 643)
—Emma Sugar & Spice & Everything Nice. (p. 643)
—Emma's Not-So-Sweet Dilemma. (p. 644)
—Family Recipe. (p. 703)
—Hole in the Middle. (p. 987)
—Ice Cream Queen. (p. 1087)
—Ice Cream Sandwiched. (p. 1087)
—Katie: Just Desserts. (p. 1205)
—Katie & the Cupcake Cure. (p. 1205)
—Katie & the Cupcake War. (p. 1205)
—Katie, Batter Up! (p. 1205)
—Katie Cupcakes & Wedding Bells. (p. 1205)
—Katie Just Desserts. (p. 1205)
—Katie Sprinkled Secrets. (p. 1205)
—Katie Sprinkles & Surprises. (p. 1205)
—Katie Starting from Scratch. (p. 1205)
—Katie's New Recipe. (p. 1206)
—Mia: A Matter of Taste. (p. 1456)
—Mia: Fashion Plates & Cupcakes. (p. 1456)
—Mia a Matter of Taste. (p. 1456)
—Mia Fashion Plates & Cupcakes. (p. 1456)
—Mia in the Mix. (p. 1456)
—MIA Measures Up. (p. 1456)
—Mia Measures Up. (p. 1456)
—Mia the Way the Cupcake Crumbles. (p. 1456)
—Mia's Baker's Dozen (p. 1457)
—Mia's Baker's Dozen. (p. 1457)
—Mia's Boiling Point. (p. 1457)
—Mia's Recipe for Disaster. (p. 1457)
—Purr-Fect Scoop. (p. 1816)
—Rocky Road Ahead. (p. 1896)
—So Jelly! (p. 2050)
—Sprinkle of Friendship. (p. 2093)
—Sprinkle Sundays Collection: Sunday Sundaes; Cracks in the Cone; the Purr-Fect Scoop; Ice Cream Sandwiched. (p. 2093)
—Sprinkles Before Sweethearts. (p. 2093)
—Sugar, Spice, & Sprinkles. (p. 2147)
—Sunday Sundaes. (p. 2152)
—Too Many Toppings! (p. 2261)
Simon, Coco & West, Tracey. MIA, the Way the Cupcake Crumbles. (p. 1456)
Simon Dietz, Suzanne. Germans Coming to America — Johnnie's Adventures: A Bilingual Book. Fetzner, Anika, tr. (p. 822)
Simon, Eddy. Pelé: The King of Soccer. Brascaglia, Vincent, illus. (p. 1714)
Simon, Elizabeth. Iguana. (p. 1094)
—Making of Lillian. (p. 1390)
—Rat. (p. 1842)
—Tyler Adams & the Adventures of Bravura: the First Quest. (p. 2310)
Simon, Emma & Streissguth, Thomas. Raoul Wallenberg (p. 1841)
Simon, Eric M., illus. see Kaufmann, Helen L.
Simon, Francesca. Goat Cafe. Broadley, Leo, illus. (p. 849)
—Hack & Whack. Cotterill, Charlotte, illus. (p. 908)
—Higgledy Piggledy the Hen Who Loved to Dance. Moseng, Elisabeth, illus. (p. 968)
—Horrid Henry Ross, Tony, illus. (p. 1003)
—Horrid Henry. (p. 1003)
—Horrid Henry. Ross, Tony, illus. (p. 1003)
—Horrid Henry & the Abominable Snowman Ross, Tony, illus. (p. 1004)
—Horrid Henry & the Abominable Snowman. (p. 1004)
—Horrid Henry & the Abominable Snowman. Ross, Tony, illus. (p. 1004)
—Horrid Henry & the Mummy's Curse. (p. 1004)
—Horrid Henry & the Mummy's Curse. Ross, Tony, illus. (p. 1004)
—Horrid Henry & the Scary Sitter Ross, Tony, illus. (p. 1004)
—Horrid Henry & the Scary Sitter. Ross, Tony, illus. (p. 1004)
—Horrid Henry & the Soccer Fiend. (p. 1004)
—Horrid Henry & the Zombie Vampire. Ross, Tony, illus. (p. 1004)
—Horrid Henry Annual 2020. Ross, Tony, illus. (p. 1004)
—Horrid Henry: Horrid Henry's Gold Medal Games: Colouring, Puzzles & Activities. (p. 1004)
—Horrid Henry Robs the Bank. Ross, Tony, illus. (p. 1004)
—Horrid Henry Rocks Ross, Tony, illus. (p. 1004)
—Horrid Henry Rocks. Ross, Tony, illus. (p. 1004)
—Horrid Henry's Christmas. Ross, Tony, illus. (p. 1004)
—Horrid Henry's Haunted House. (p. 1004)
—Horrid Henry's Joke Book. Ross, Tony, illus. (p. 1004)
—Mega-Mean Time Machine Ross, Tony, illus. (p. 1441)
—Mega-Mean Time Machine. (p. 1441)
—Mega-Mean Time Machine. Ross, Tony, illus. (p. 1441)
—Monster Movie. Ross, Tony, illus. (p. 1496)
—Monstrous Child. (p. 1498)
—Stinkbomb. (p. 2119)
—Stinkbomb. Ross, Tony, illus. (p. 2119)
—Tricks the Tooth Fairy Ross, Tony, illus. (p. 2287)
—Tricks the Tooth Fairy. (p. 2287)
—Tricks the Tooth Fairy. Ross, Tony, illus. (p. 2287)
—Underpants. (p. 2324)
—Underpants. Ross, Tony, illus. (p. 2324)
—Wakes the Dead Ross, Tony, illus. (p. 2371)
—Wakes the Dead. Ross, Tony, illus. (p. 2371)
Simon, Gus. Squanto Was Helpful. (p. 2094)
Simon, J. F. Spezialist M. A. F. II: Kampf Für Die Unsterblichkeit. (p. 2079)
Simon, Jamie Rae. Adventures of Gracie: Gracie Comes Home. (p. 23)
Simon, Jenne. Andrea's New Horse. (p. 83)
—Ballet Recital. (p. 162)
—Day at Charm School. (p. 512)
—Double Trouble. (p. 589)

—Essential Character Guide. (p. 663)
—Friend to Trust. Gómez, Ana, illus. (p. 786)
—Hatchimals CollEGGtibles: the Official CollEGGtor's Guide. (p. 936)
—Lalaloopsy: Chasing Rainbows. (p. 1240)
—Lalaloopsy: Easter Eggs-Travaganza. Hill, Prescott, illus. (p. 1240)
—Lalaloopsy: School Day! Hill, Prescott, illus. (p. 1240)
—Lalaloopsy: the Ballet Recital. Hill, Prescott, illus. (p. 1240)
—Let's Pick Apples. Hill, Prescott, illus. (p. 1276)
—Loves. (p. 1362)
—Magic Charm Chase. (p. 1377)
—Meet the Little Charmers (Little Charmers) (p. 1440)
—Monster Mash: A Halloween Story. (p. 1496)
—Monster Mash. (p. 1496)
—Ready to Be Responsible. Nowowiejska, Kasia, illus. (p. 1848)
—Roar of Respect. Nowowiejska, Kasia, illus. (p. 1889)
—Snow Day!, Level 2. Hill, Prescott, illus. (p. 2047)
—Sparkle Bunny Day! (Little Charmers: 8x8) (p. 2075)
—Tell the Time! Hino, Sachiho, illus. (p. 2202)
—Ultimate Handbook (Shopkins: Shoppies) (p. 2315)
—Winter Adventure. (p. 2475)
Simon, Jenne, adapted by. Magic Charm Chase. (p. 1377)
Simon, Jessica. Guess What? I Still Love You. (p. 902)
Simon, John Oliver, tr. see Luján, Jorge.
Simon, Karen, tr. see Payette, Eveline.
Simon, Kristen Koerner. Jack's Knack: Book Three of the Blue Forest Series: Book Three of the Blue Forest Series. (p. 1153)
Simon, Laurent, illus. see Cauchy, Véronique.
Simon, Leslie. Wish You Were Here: An Essential Guide to Your Favorite Music Scenes—From Punk to Indie & Everything in Between. (p. 2478)
Simon, Linda. Pug on Wheels. (p. 1811)
Simon, Lionel. Guardián de Rak: I. Rafael y el Péndulo. (p. 901)
Simon, Margaret. Blessen. (p. 244)
—Sunshine: A Blessen Novel. (p. 2153)
Simon, Margaret Gibson. Bayou Song. Cantrell, Anna, illus. (p. 176)
Simon, Mary Manz. Countdown to Christmas Hartley, Brian, illus. (p. 459)
—Family Time Bible Anaya, Fátima, illus. (p. 703)
—First Feelings (padded Cover) Twelve Stories for Toddlers. Stott, Dorothy, illus. (p. 736)
—First Virtues (padded Cover) 12 Stories for Toddlers. (p. 740)
—Hear Me Read Bible. (p. 944)
—My Christmas Story Tree Scott, Gavin, illus. (p. 1535)
—My Easter Basket (die-Cut) The True Story of Easter. Scudamore, Angelika, illus. (p. 1537)
—My March to the Manger: A Celebration of Jesus' Birth. Scudamore, Angelika, illus. (p. 1555)
—My Picnic Basket: And How God Is Always Near. Fenimore, Kristina, illus. (p. 1559)
—Pumpkin Gospel (die-Cut) A Story of a New Start with God. Scudamore, Angelika, illus. (p. 1812)
—With Love, from Me to You Ice, Corinna, illus. (p. 2481)
Simon, Mary Manz, see Manz Simon, Mary.
Simon, Nadine. Flickers of True Destiny. (p. 748)
—Treasured Dream. (p. 2282)
Simon, Norma. All Families Are Special. Flavin, Teresa, illus. (p. 51)
—All Kinds of Families. Brannen, Sarah S., illus. (p. 52)
Simon, Philip, ed. see Brancatelli, Joe, et al.
Simon, Philip, ed. see Hogan, Peter.
Simon, Philip, ed. see Melo, Filipe.
Simon, Philip, ed. Art of Plants vs. Zombies: A Visual Book. (p. 121)
Simon, Rainer, illus. see Kuehn, Birgit S.
Simon, Rainer, illus. see Kuehn, Birgit.
Simon, Rj. Ruby Lane. (p. 1911)
Simon, Samantha. Clinical & Medical Laboratory Scientists. (p. 406)
—Emts & Paramedics. (p. 645)
—Nurses. (p. 1631)
—Orthotists & Prosthetists. (p. 1673)
—Physician Assistants. (p. 1737)
—Speech Pathologists & Audiologists. (p. 2078)
Simon, Scott. Sunnyside Plaza. (p. 2153)
Simon, Seymour. Big Cats: Revised Edition. (p. 219)
—Big Cats. (p. 219)
—Butterflies. (p. 303)
—Cats. (p. 345)
—Coral Reefs. (p. 453)
—Deadly Ants. Downey, William, illus. (p. 518)
—Destination: Mars. (p. 533)
—Destination: Mars: Revised Edition. (p. 533)
—Destination: Moon. (p. 533)
—Dogs. (p. 577)
—Dolphins. (p. 579)
—Elephants. (p. 634)
—Exoplanets. (p. 677)
—Extreme Earth Records. (p. 686)
—Frogs. (p. 790)
—Ghosts. (p. 829)
—Global Warming. (p. 844)
—Guts: Revised Edition. (p. 906)
—Horses: Revised Edition. (p. 1005)
—How to Talk to Your Computer. Lowery, Mike, illus. (p. 1044)
—Hurricanes. (p. 1054)
—Icebergs & Glaciers: Revised Edition. (p. 1088)
—Insects. (p. 1122)
—Our Solar System: Revised Edition. (p. 1680)
—Penguins. (p. 1716)
—Poisonous Snakes. Downey, William, illus. (p. 1768)
—Rocks & Minerals. (p. 1896)
—Science Dictionary. (p. 1954)
—Sea Creatures. (p. 1967)
—Secret Clocks: Time Senses of Living Things. Brett, Jan, illus. (p. 1975)
—Seymour Simon's Silly Riddles & Jokes Coloring Book. Kendrick, D., illus. (p. 1995)
—Strange Mysteries from Around the World. (p. 2138)
—Sun: Revised Edition. (p. 2151)
—Sun. (p. 2151)
—Tornadoes: Revised Edition. (p. 2265)
—Tropical Rainforests. (p. 2291)
—Vampire Bats: Extreme Animals. (p. 2345)
—Water. (p. 2384)
—Why Do Kittens Do That? Real Things Kids Love to Know. (p. 2456)
—Wildfires. (p. 2466)
—Wolves. (p. 2485)
Simon, St, tr. see Hoffmann, E. T. A.
Simon, Steven, jt. auth. see Benjamin, Daniel.
Simon, Susan, illus. see Rouss, Sylvia A.
Simon, T. R. Cursed Ground. (p. 489)
—Zora & Me: the Cursed Ground. (p. 2544)
Simon, T. R., jt. auth. see Bond, Victoria.
Simon, Tanya & Simon, Richard. Oskar & the Eight Blessings. Siegel, Mark, illus. (p. 1673)
Simon, Theodore, jt. auth. see Binet, Alfred.
Simon, Ute, illus. see Burnett, Frances Hodgson.
Simon, Ute, illus. see Dickens, Charles.
Simon, Ute, illus. see Gamble, Adam & Jasper, Mark.
Simon, Ute, illus. see Norwich, Grace.
Simon, Ute, illus. see Pyle, Howard.
Simon, Ute, illus. see Stoker, Bram.
Simonds, Arthur Beaman. American Song: A Collection of Representative American Poems, with Analytical & Critical Studies of the Writers (Classic Reprint) (p. 74)
—American Song. (p. 74)
Simonds, Kevin. Tomb of Father Time. (p. 2258)
Simonds, William, jt. auth. see Aimwell, Walter.
Simonds, William Edward. George Fitch: A Memorial (Classic Reprint) (p. 819)
—Introduction to the Study of English Fiction. (p. 1129)
—Introduction to the Study of English Fiction (Classic Reprint) (p. 1129)
Simone, Francina. Smash It! (p. 2041)
Simone, Jacquelyn. Ciara. (p. 390)
—How Do AIDS & Politics Connect? (p. 1027)
—Nutrition & Politics. (p. 1632)
—Outkast. (p. 1685)
Simone, Julia. Halo Cat. Simone, Julia, illus. (p. 913)
Simone, Maisie. Cake! (p. 309)
Simone, Ni-Ni. Dear Yvette. (p. 521)
—No Boyz Allowed. (p. 1612)
—Teenage Love Affair. (p. 2199)
—True Story. (p. 2295)
Simone, Ni-Ni & Abrams, Amir. Get Ready for War. (p. 824)
—Heels, Heartache & Headlines. (p. 948)
—Lights, Love & Lip Gloss. (p. 1300)
—Put Your Diamonds Up. (p. 1817)
Simone, Ni-Ni & London, Kelli. Break-Up Diaries. (p. 278)
Simone, Val Edward. Dragons, Dragons, Dragons: A Trilogy. (p. 595)
—Proton Gator & Friends Coloring Book. McGill, Joshua, illus. (p. 1808)
Simoneau, D. K. Santa's (Zany, Wacky, Just Not Right!) Night Before Christmas. (p. 1934)
Simonet, Andrew. Wilder. (p. 2466)
Simonet, Brad. Did You Know ... (p. 543)
—Ily ... Daddy. (p. 1097)
Simonet, Evan. Jake & the Sailing Tree. (p. 1155)
Simonin, Martial. Sur l'Orbite de (108) Hecube: These (Classic Reprint) (p. 2162)
Simonis, Magdalena. Drip's Big Journey. (p. 604)
Simons, Alan L. Incredible Adventures of Captain Cameron MacDuddyfunk in Cuggermuggerland. Boggelen-Heutink, Ellen van, illus. (p. 1113)
Simons, Anna. 21st-Century Challenges of Command: A View from the Field. (p. 2554)
Simons, Barbara Brooks. Citizenship in Ancient Times - 6 Pack: Set of 6 with Common Core Teacher Materials. (p. 394)
—Citizenship in Ancient Times - 6 Pack: Set of 6 Bridges Edition with Common Core Teacher Materials. (p. 394)
—Daily Life in Medieval Times - 6 Pack: Set of 6 with Common Core Teacher Materials. (p. 496)
—Daily Life in Medieval Times - 6 Pack: Set of 6 Bridges Edition with Common Core Teacher Materials. (p. 496)
—Escape to Freedom the Underground Railroad: Set Of 6. (p. 662)
—Minerals & Rocks - 6 Pack: Set of 6 with Common Core Teacher Materials. (p. 1471)
—Minerals & Rocks - 6 Pack: Set of 6 Bridges Edition with Common Core Teacher Materials. (p. 1471)
Simons, Brad. Birthday Present from Another Dimension. (p. 233)
Simons, D. M. Keep Her Safe. (p. 1207)
Simons, Kate. Medieval Wanders & Wonders: Understanding Northern Spain & the Camino de Santiago. (p. 1437)
Simons, Lisa M. B. Amazing Animal Stunts. (p. 63)
—Jacqueline Woodson. Byers, Michael, illus. (p. 1154)
—Jerry Pinkney. Byers, Michael, illus. (p. 1164)
Simons, Lisa M. Bolt. Airmen of the U. S. Air Force [Scholastic]. (p. 37)
—Back to Pass: A Choose Your Path Football Book. (p. 155)
—Beastly Firepower: Military Weapons & Tactics Inspired by Animals. (p. 182)
—Beastly Robots & Drones: Military Technology Inspired by Animals. (p. 182)
—Benjamin Banneker: Self-Educated Scientist. (p. 200)
—Cinquain Poems. Petelinsek, Kathleen, illus. (p. 392)
—Daily Life in Ancient Greece (p. 496)
—First Olympics of Ancient Greece (p. 738)
—Haikus. Petelinsek, Kathleen, illus. (p. 909)
—Henry Ford: A 4D Book. (p. 955)
—How to Read a Map. (p. 1043)
—How to Read a Nonfiction Book. (p. 1043)
—Jacqueline Woodson. Byers, Michael, illus. (p. 1154)
—Kadir Nelson. Byers, Michael, illus. (p. 1201)
—Madam C. J. Walker: Inventor & Businesswoman. (p. 1374)
—Marie Curie: Physicist & Chemist. (p. 1405)
—Nikki Grimes. Byers, Michael, illus. (p. 1608)
—Rachel Carson: A 4D Book. (p. 1832)
—Rev up Your Writing in Letters & E-Mails. Gallagher-Cole, Mernie, illus. (p. 1872)
—Rev up Your Writing in Opinion Pieces. Gallagher-Cole, Mernie, illus. (p. 1872)
—Rhyming Poems. Petelinsek, Kathleen, illus. (p. 1875)
—Soldiers of the U. S. Army [Scholastic]. (p. 2057)
—Special Ops Mission Timelines. (p. 2077)
—Transportation Long Ago & Today (p. 2278)
—U. S. Air Force by the Numbers (p. 2311)
—U. S. Army by the Numbers (p. 2311)
—U. S. Army Green Beret Missions: A Timeline. (p. 2311)
—U. S. Army Ranger Missions: A Timeline. (p. 2311)
—U. S. Marine Raider Missions: A Timeline. (p. 2312)
—U. S. Navy SEAL Missions: A Timeline. (p. 2312)
—U. S. WASP: Trailblazing Women Pilots of World War II. (p. 2311)
—Unusual & Awesome Jobs Using Math: Stunt Coordinator, Cryptologist, & More. (p. 2336)
—Women in Combat: Bringing the Fight to the Front Lines. (p. 2487)
—Your Favorite Authors. Byers, Michael, illus. (p. 2533)
Simons, Lisa M. Bolt, jt. auth. see Hofer, Charles C.
Simons, Lisa M. Bolt, et al. Long Ago & Today (p. 1342)
—Military by the Numbers (p. 1466)
—U. S. Military by the Numbers (p. 2312)
Simons, Marijke. Flying Squirrel Stowaways: From Halifax to Boston (p. 755)
Simons, Marijke, illus. see Coates, Jan.
Simons, Moya. Hello God. Coutts, Lisa, illus. (p. 951)
Simons, Moya & Rossell, Judith. My Amazing Poo Plant. (p. 1531)
Simons, Paullina. I Love My Baby Because... Thomas, Cassia, illus. (p. 1070)
—Poppet Gets Two Big Brothers. (p. 1776)
Simons, Rae. Adoptive Parents. (p. 17)
—All about Money: The History, Culture, & Meaning of Modern Finance. (p. 49)
—At Home in Your Body: Care for the Shape You're In. (p. 129)
—Bigger Isn't Always Better: Choosing Your Portions. (p. 224)
—Blended Families. (p. 243)
—Business Math. (p. 301)
—Caring for Wild Animals. (p. 331)
—Does Television Make You Fat? Lifestyle & Obesity. (p. 575)
—Ellen Degeneres. (p. 637)
—Entrepreneurship. (p. 657)
—Fashion Math. (p. 712)
—Grandparents Raising Kids. (p. 879)
—Guide to Teaching Young Adults about Money. (p. 903)
—Healthy Skin. McDonnell, Mary Ann & Forman, Sara, eds. (p. 944)
—How Do AIDS & Poverty Connect? (p. 1027)
—How Do AIDS & Poverty Connect? (p. 1028)
—How Does the Environment Affect You? (p. 1030)
—I Eat When I'm Sad: Food & Feelings. (p. 1064)
—Kid's Guide to AIDS & HIV. (p. 1215)
—Kid's Guide to Allergies. (p. 1215)
—Kid's Guide to Asthma. (p. 1215)
—Kid's Guide to Bugs & How They Can Make You Sick. (p. 1215)
—Kid's Guide to Cancer. (p. 1215)
—Kid's Guide to Diabetes. (p. 1215)
—Kid's Guide to Immunizations. (p. 1215)
—Kid's Guide to Malnutrition. (p. 1215)
—Kid's Guide to Pollution & How It Can Make You Sick. (p. 1215)
—Kid's Guide to Viruses & Bacteria. (p. 1215)
—Money & Relationships. (p. 1492)
—Nutrition & Poverty. (p. 1632)
—Single Parents. (p. 2024)
—Spending Money. (p. 2079)
—Sports Math. (p. 2089)
—Sustainable Lifestyles in a Changing Economy. (p. 2166)
—Teen Parents. (p. 2199)
—Texas Hold'em: The Learning Curve of Life. (p. 2209)
—Too Many Sunday Dinners: Family & Diet. (p. 2261)
Simons, Rae, jt. auth. see Libal, Joyce.
Simons, Rae, jt. auth. see Riddle, John.
Simons, Rae, jt. auth. see Stewart, Sheila.
Simons, Rae & Gommer, Viola Ruelke. Nurse. Riggs, Ernestine G. & Gholar, Cheryl, eds. (p. 1631)
Simons, Rae & Indovino, Shaina C. Spain. Bruton, John, ed. (p. 2073)
Simons, Rae & Indovino, Shaina Carmel. Luxembourg. (p. 1369)
—Spain. (p. 2073)
—United Kingdom. (p. 2330)
—United Kingdom. Bruton, John, ed. (p. 2330)
Simons, Sally, illus. see Walker, Colin.
Simons, Sarah Emma. Better English, Vol. 2 Of 3: For Speaking & Writing (Classic Reprint) (p. 209)
Simons, Val. What Else Could Cheeper Do? (p. 2410)
Simonsen Brown, Janet. Why Did God Make Bubbles? Excuse Me, Sir, but You Are Sitting on My Mother. (p. 2455)
Simonsen, Craig. Fountaineville. (p. 771)
Simonson, Bill. Hungry Homeless Dog. Simonson, Bill, illus. (p. 1052)
—Itt 'N' Ott's Pizza Journey. (p. 1148)
Simonson, Curtis. Parables of a Pastor's Kid. (p. 1698)
Simonson, Lona Marie. Grandma Lucy Feeds the Birds Herges, Connie, illus. (p. 878)
Simonson, Louise. Ares' Underworld Army. Vecchio, Luciano, illus. (p. 114)
—Beauty & the Dreaded Sea Beast: A Graphic Novel. Frampton, Otis, illus. (p. 185)
—Bizarro Is Born! Doescher, Erik, illus. (p. 235)
—Blancanieves y Los Siete Robots: Una Novela Gráfica. Sanchez S., Jimena, illus. (p. 242)
—Death of Baldur. Garcia, Eduardo, illus. (p. 521)
—Drama en la Secundaria. Cho, Sumin, illus. (p. 596)
—Giganta's Colossal Double-Cross. Vecchio, Luciano, illus. (p. 832)
—Gran Chisme. Cho, Sumin, illus. (p. 876)
—Harley Quinn's Crazy Creeper Caper. Vecchio, Luciano, illus. (p. 930)
—Joker & Harley Quinn's Justice League Jailhouse. Levins, Tim, illus. (p. 1176)
—Las Malvadas de la Escuela Secundaria. Cho, Sumin, illus. (p. 1246)
—Lex Luthor's Power Grab! Vecchio, Luciano, illus. (p. 1282)
—Monster Magic. Schoening, Dan, illus. (p. 1496)
—Runaround Rumor. Cho, Sumin, illus. (p. 1914)
—Snow White & the Seven Robots. Sanchez, Jimena, illus. (p. 2048)
Simonson, Louise & Mason, Jane B. Junior High Drama Cho, Sumin, illus. (p. 1191)
Simonson, Louise, et al. Far Out Fairy Tales. Frampton, Otis et al, illus. (p. 708)
—Marvel Vault of Heroes: Thor. Cliquet, Ronan, illus. (p. 1413)
Simonson, Michael. You Are Brilliant. (p. 2524)
Simonson, Walt, et al. Star Wars Legends: Forever Crimson. (p. 2104)
Simonson, Walt, text. Thor by Walt Simonson Omnibus. (p. 2229)
—Thor by Walt Simonson Vol. 1. (p. 2229)
Simont, Marc, illus. see Krauss, Ruth.
Simont, Marc, illus. see Lord, Bette Bao.
Simont, Marc, illus. see Thurber, James.
Simont, Marc, illus. see Udry, Janice May.
Simonton, Tom, illus. see Furr, L. David.
Simonton, Tom, illus. see Hood, Douglas.
Simpkins, Jonas. Reveries of a Woodsawyer; or, Sum Slicings of Cord-Wood: Being Serio-Comic Views of Life As It Is, As Taken from the Top of a Saw-Buck (Classic Reprint) (p. 1873)
Simple, Author of Peter. Poacher (Classic Reprint) (p. 1763)
Simplyharmony. My Sister Would Make a Good President. Coleman, Joan, illus. (p. 1561)
Simpon, Tj. Tiny Paul the Tarantula Takes a Walk Register, J. R., illus. (p. 2249)
Simpson, Adam, illus. see Howard, Annabel.
Simpson, Agnes. Here a Little & There a Little (Classic Reprint) (p. 957)
Simpson, B. G. Bailey's Road. (p. 159)
—Winds of Time: Oracles of the Great-Gulf-Book One. (p. 2472)
Simpson, C. E. Eighth Grade Witch. Utomo, Gabhor, illus. (p. 629)
Simpson, C. H. Life in the Far West: Or a Detective's Thrilling Adventures among the Indians & Outlaws of Montana (Classic Reprint) (p. 1292)
Simpson, C. M, jt. auth. see Anderle, Michael.
Simpson, Caroll. First Beaver (p. 735)
—First Mosquito (p. 738)
Simpson, Carolyn. Coping with Post-Traumatic Stress Disorder (PTSD) Dealing with Tragedy. (p. 451)
Simpson, Charles. Life in the Mines; or Crime Avenged: Including Thrilling Adventures among Miners & Outlaws (Classic Reprint) (p. 1292)
—Yankee's Adventures in South Africa (Classic Reprint) (p. 2517)
Simpson, Clare. My Heaven Book. (p. 1549)
—Why Do We Have to Be So Quiet in Church? And 12 Other Questions Kids Have. Harker, Kay, illus. (p. 2457)
Simpson, Dana. Amiga Muy Especial / Phoebe & Her Unicorn. (p. 75)
—Camping with Unicorns (Phoebe & Her Unicorn Series Book 11) Another Phoebe & Her Unicorn Adventure. (p. 316)
—Heavenly Nostrils Chronicle. (p. 947)
—Magic Storm. (p. 1379)
—Magical Adventures of Phoebe & Her Unicorn. (p. 1379)
—Ozy & Millie. (p. 1690)
—Phoebe & Her Unicorn: A Heavenly Nostrils Chronicle. (p. 1735)
—Phoebe & Her Unicorn Book 12. (p. 1735)
—Phoebe & Her Unicorn in the Magic Storm. (p. 1735)
—Phoebe & Her Unicorn in Unicorn Theater: Phoebe & Her Unicorn Series Book 8. (p. 1735)
—Phoebe & Her Unicorn Theater (p. 1735)
—Rainy Day Unicorn Fun: Phoebe & Her Unicorn. (p. 1837)
—Rainy Day Unicorn Fun: A Phoebe & Her Unicorn Activity Book. (p. 1837)
—Razzle Dazzle Unicorn (p. 1844)
—Razzle Dazzle Unicorn: Another Phoebe & Her Unicorn Adventure. (p. 1844)
—Shimmering Box of Unicorn Sparkles. (p. 2007)
—Today I'll Be a Unicorn. (p. 2254)
—Unicorn Bowling (p. 2328)
—Unicorn Bowling: Another Phoebe & Her Unicorn Adventure. (p. 2328)
—Unicorn Crossing (p. 2328)
—Unicorn Crossing: Another Phoebe & Her Unicorn Adventure. (p. 2328)
—Unicorn Crossing. (p. 2328)
—Unicorn of Many Hats: Another Phoebe & Her Unicorn Adventure. (p. 2328)
—Unicorn of Many Hats (Phoebe & Her Unicorn Series Book 7) (p. 2328)
—Unicorn on a Roll: Another Heavenly Nostrils Chronicle. (p. 2328)
—Unicorn on a Roll. (p. 2328)
—Unicorn Theater (p. 2328)
—Unicorn vs. Goblins: Another Phoebe & Her Unicorn Adventure. (p. 2329)
—Unicorn Whisperer (p. 2329)
—Unicorn Whisperer: Another Phoebe & Her Unicorn Adventure. (p. 2329)
—Unicorn Whisperer (Phoebe & Her Unicorn Series Book 10) Another Phoebe & Her Unicorn Adventure. (p. 2329)
Simpson, Dana, illus. see Verdi, Jessica & Lyons, Maddox.
Simpson, Deb. Pink Place Paperback. (p. 1746)
Simpson, Don, et al. Crazy. (p. 468)
Simpson, Drew & Davis, Rory. Bubble Bursters of Bathville. (p. 288)
Simpson, Duncan. Helda of Lohgard. (p. 949)
Simpson, Dwain, jt. auth. see Simpson, Carolyn.
Simpson, Evangeline Mars. Marplot Cupid: With Illustrations (Classic Reprint) (p. 1408)
Simpson, Evelyn Blantyre. Robert Louis Stevenson Originals (Classic Reprint) (p. 1890)
Simpson, Finn, illus. see Harrington, Jenna.
Simpson, Geoffrey. Reynard's Dream. (p. 1874)

S

—Three Hares: Bloodline. (p. 2233)
Simpson, Howard. Through Loona's Door: A Tammy & Owen Adventure with Carter G. Woodson. (p. 2236)
Simpson, Howard, illus. see Foster, William H.
Simpson, Howard, illus. see Hudson, Cheryl Willis.
Simpson, Howard, illus. see Hudson, Katura J.
Simpson, J. M. Faithful Margaret: A Novel (Classic Reprint) (p. 699)
Simpson, James Young. Cat-Stane, Edinburghshire: Is It Not the Tombstone of the Grandfather of Hengist & Horsa? (Classic Reprint) (p. 342)
Simpson, Jemma. Corie & Torie. (p. 454)
Simpson, Joe & Bembibre, Cecilia. Tocando el Vacío. (p. 2254)
Simpson, John. Condor One. (p. 438)
Simpson, John Thomas. Hidden Treasure: The Story of a Chore Boy, Who Made the Old Farm Pay (Classic Reprint) (p. 966)
Simpson, Josephine. Old Mother Earth: Her Highways & by-Ways (Classic Reprint) (p. 1647)
Simpson, Kara, illus. see Redford, Ali.
Simpson, Kate. Finding Granny: We Never Really Lose the People We Love ... Jones, Gwynneth, illus. (p. 729)
Simpson, Kathleen. Geography of Africa: Set Of 6. (p. 817)
—Geography of Africa: Bridges Edition. Aloisi, Giuliano, illus. (p. 817)
—Geography of Africa: Bridges Edition Set of 6 with Common Core Indicators. Aloisi, Giuliano, illus. (p. 817)
—Geography of Asia & Australia: Set Of 6. (p. 817)
—Geography of Asia & Australia: Bridges Edition. Aloisi, Giuliano, illus. (p. 817)
—Geography of Asia & Australia: Bridges Edition Set of 6 with Common Core Indicators. Aloisi, Giuliano, illus. (p. 817)
—Geography of Europe: Set Of 6. (p. 817)
—Geography of Europe: Bridges Edition. Aloisi, Giuliano, illus. (p. 817)
—Geography of Europe: Bridges Edition Set of 6 with Common Core Indicators. Aloisi, Giuliano, illus. (p. 817)
—Geography of Mexico: Set Of 6. (p. 817)
—Geography of the Americas: Set Of 6. (p. 817)
—Geography of the Americas: Bridges Edition. Aloisi, Giuliano, illus. (p. 817)
—Geography of the Americas: Bridges Edition Set of 6 with Common Core Indicators. Aloisi, Giuliano, illus. (p. 817)
—Naturaleza de la Vida. (p. 1580)
—Naturaleza de la Vida - 6 Pack: Set of 6 Common Core Edition. (p. 1580)
—Nature of Life: Set Of 10. Greenhead, Bill, illus. (p. 1581)
—Nature of Life: Prime Bridges Edition. Greenhead, Bill, illus. (p. 1581)
—Nature of Life: Bridges Edition, Set Of 10. Greenhead, Bill, illus. (p. 1581)
—Physical & Human Geography: Set Of 6. (p. 1737)
—Physical & Human Geography: Bridges Edition. Aloisi, Giuliano, illus. (p. 1737)
—Physical & Human Geography: Bridges Edition Set of 6 with Common Core Indicators. Aloisi, Giuliano, illus. (p. 1737)
—Women in the Renaissance: Set Of 6. (p. 2487)
Simpson, L. M., illus. see Daulby, Joan.
Simpson, Logan. Princess Misty & the Drought. (p. 1798)
Simpson, Louie. My Mom Votes! (p. 1556)
Simpson, Lupe. Chronicles of Pillowcase. Heras, Ruth, illus. (p. 389)
Simpson, Maria. Brother G. M. Rose (Classic Reprint) (p. 286)
—Roseville Seminary: A Temperance Story (Classic Reprint) (p. 1906)
—Roseville Seminary. (p. 1906)
Simpson, Marilyn Bohlen, ed. see Simpson, Jeffrey L.
Simpson, Martha Seif. Dreidel That Wouldn't Spin: A Toyshop Tale of Hanukkah Bernhard, Durga Yael, illus. (p. 603)
—Esther's Gragger: A Toyshop Tale of Purim (p. 665)
Simpson, Mary, illus. see Merrill, Yvonne Y.
Simpson, Michelle, illus. see Axel, Meaghan.
Simpson, Michelle, illus. see Danneberg, Julie.
Simpson, Michelle, illus. see Fandel, Jennifer Lee.
Simpson, Michelle, illus. see Fatehali, Shaista Kaba.
Simpson, Michelle, illus. see Latham, Donna.
Simpson, Michelle, illus. see Slater, David Michael.
Simpson, Mike. Exceptional Wilmot Grundy. (p. 676)
Simpson, Mike & Sanders, Jon. Traveler. (p. 2280)
Simpson, Monica. 123 at the Zoo. (p. 2559)
—ABCs at School. (p. 4)
—ABCs with Animals. (p. 5)
Simpson, N. J. Not So Random. (p. 1623)
Simpson, Phillip. All about Tigers: A Description Text (p. 50)
—Big Cats Head to Head: A Compare & Contrast Text (p. 219)
—How Can We Save the Cheetah? A Problem & Solution Text (p. 1026)
—Life Cycle of a Leopard: A Sequence & Order Text (p. 1291)
—Lion Habitats under Threat: A Cause & Effect Text (p. 1306)
—Marine Biomes Around the World. (p. 1405)
—Tundra Biomes Around the World. (p. 2299)
Simpson, Rob, illus. see Meenaghan, M. S. Margaret.
Simpson, Robert. Bite of Benin: Where Many Go in but Few Come Out (Classic Reprint) (p. 235)
Simpson, Selwyn G. Thomas Edward Brown, the Manx Poet: An Appreciation. (p. 2228)
—Thomas Edward Brown, the Manx Poet: An Appreciation (Classic Reprint) (p. 2228)
Simpson, Selwyn G. & Wilson, J. M. Thomas Edward Brown, the Manx Poet; an Appreciation. (p. 2228)
Simpson, Shari. SleepWakers, Book #1 Sam Saves the Night. (p. 2037)
Simpson, Steve. Farmer in the Dell. (p. 710)
Simpson, Steve, illus. see Galan, Alvaro.
Simpson, Steve, illus. see Jones, Karl.
Simpson, Thomas. Elements of Geometry: With Their Application to the Mensuration of Superficies & Solids, to the Determination of the Maxima & Minima of Geometrical Quantities, & to the Construction of a Great Variety of Geometrical Problems (Classic Reprint) (p. 633)
—Essays on Several Curious & Useful Subjects, in Speculative & Mix'd Mathematicks: Illustrated by a Variety of Examples (Classic Reprint) (p. 663)
Simpson, Tynicka, illus. see West, Melissa.
Simpson, Violet A. Bonnet Conspirators: A Story of 1815 (Classic Reprint) (p. 256)
Simpson-Urrutia, Julia Juwairiah. Burning Boats: The Birth of Muslim Spain. (p. 300)
Sims, Agnes, illus. see Travers, P. L.
Sims, Blanche, illus. see Alberto, Daisy.
Sims, Blanche, illus. see Charney, Steve.
Sims, Blanche, illus. see Driscoll, Laura.
Sims, Blanche, illus. see Dussling, Jennifer.
Sims, Blanche, illus. see Giff, Patricia Reilly.
Sims, Blanche, illus. see Jackson, Ellen.
Sims, Blanche, illus. see Knudsen, Michelle.
Sims, Blanche, illus. see May, Eleanor.
Sims, Blanche, illus. see McGillian, Jamie Kyle.
Sims, Blanche, illus. see Walker, Nan.
Sims, Brianna. Marissa the Mermaid: Counting by the Sea. (p. 1406)
—Marissa the Mermaid: Counting by the Sea. Amy, Rodriguez, illus. (p. 1406)
Sims, Bryan, illus. see Lovitt, Charles.
Sims, C. Bailey. Candlewax. (p. 322)
Sims, Chris & Bowers, Chad. Down Set Fight. Kowalchuk, Scott, illus. (p. 590)
—Infinity Countdown: Darkhawk. (p. 1119)
Sims, David, illus. see Davison, Roz & Laird, Elizabeth.
Sims, Diondra. Death of the Hybrid King. (p. 521)
Sims, Geo R. Two London Fairies (Classic Reprint) (p. 2308)
Sims, George. Legend of Willie Smalls. (p. 1263)
Sims, George R. Dagonet Abroad (Classic Reprint) (p. 495)
—How the Poor Live, and, Horrible London (Classic Reprint) (p. 1036)
—Living London, Vol. 1: Its Work & Its Play, Its Humour & Its Pathos, Its Sights & Its Scenes; Section II (Classic Reprint) (p. 1333)
—Living London, Vol. 2: Its Work & Its Play, Its Humour & Its Pathos, Its Sights & Its Scenes; Section I (Classic Reprint) (p. 1333)
—Tinkletop's Crime (Classic Reprint) (p. 2248)
Sims, George Robert. Coachman's Club, or Tales Told Out of School (Classic Reprint) (p. 409)
—Lifeboat, & Other Poems (Classic Reprint) (p. 1296)
—Living London, Vol. 1: Its Work & Its Play, Its Humour & Its Pathos, Its Sights & Its Scenes (Classic Reprint) (p. 1333)
—Without the Limelight: Theatrical Life As It Is (Classic Reprint) (p. 2482)
Sims, Guy A., jt. auth. see Myers, Walter Dean.
Sims, Guy A. & Myers, Walter Dean. Monster: a Graphic Novel. Anyabwile, Dawud, illus. (p. 1495)
Sims, Harold "Catman". Kevin Tames the Bullies. (p. 1210)
—Kevin Tells the Story of Catman2. (p. 1210)
Sims, Janet G. Cristy & Her Amazing Friends. (p. 475)
Sims, Janice. Grandma's Basket. Storr, Nicola, illus. (p. 878)
Sims, John Earl. Nocatula, 1930 (Classic Reprint) (p. 1617)
Sims, Kendrick. Bully. (p. 296)
—Lazar & Jingles & Bunson in Holiday Gifts. (p. 1254)
—Mirrors in Strange Places. (p. 1476)
Sims, L., jt. auth. see Dickens, Charles.
Sims, L., jt. auth. see Edom, H.
Sims, L., jt. auth. see Millard, A.
Sims, Lesley. Anne of Green Gables. (p. 99)
—Delightful Illustrated Stories (was Illustrated Stories for Girls) (p. 527)
—Goat in a Boat. (p. 849)
—Historias Ilustradas de Aventuras(Illust Adventure Stories) (p. 975)
—How Zebras Got Their Stripes. (p. 1046)
—Illustrated Classics Action & Adventure Stories for Young Readers. (p. 1096)
—Illustrated Classics Enchanting Stories for Young Readers. (p. 1096)
—Illustrated Classics for Children. (p. 1096)
—Illustrated Classics for Girls. Mason, Conrad, illus. (p. 1096)
—Lizard in a Blizzard. (p. 1336)
—Magical Stories for Little Children. (p. 1380)
—Seal at the Wheel. (p. 1970)
—Spider in a Glider. (p. 2080)
—Tales for Little Children. (p. 2181)
Sims, Lesley, ed. see Dickins, Rosie & Pratt, Leonie.
Sims, Lesley, jt. auth. see Dickens, Charles.
Sims, Lesley, jt. auth. see Dickins, Rosie.
Sims, Lesley, jt. auth. see Sims, Lesley.
Sims, Lesley & Sims, Lesley. Stories from Around the World for Children. (p. 2123)
Sims, Lesley, ed. Illustrated Adventure Stories. (p. 1096)
—Illustrated Animal Stories. Mason, Conrad, illus. (p. 1096)
Sims, Leslie B., jt. auth. see Firth, Rachel.
Sims, Mamie Hunt. Negro Mystic Lore (Classic Reprint) (p. 1585)
Sims, Michael. Fungus Witch. (p. 801)
Sims, Nat. Peekaboo Barn. Tabor, Nathan, illus. (p. 1713)
—Peekaboo Barn / ¿Quién Está en el Granero? Tabor, Nathan, illus. (p. 1713)
Sims, Renita. Bubblegum Boy. Martin, Oshane, illus. (p. 289)
Sims, Rudine. Bishop Daniel A. Payne: Great Black Leader. (p. 234)
Sims, Sean, illus. see Green, Dan.
Sims, Sean, illus. see Harper, Kathryn.
Sims, Sean, illus. see Rose, Malcolm.
Sims, Stephanie, ed. see Gunning, Mark.
Sims, Steve. Drawing Dungeon Creatures. (p. 599)
—Drawing Heroic Warriors. (p. 599)
Simson, Dana, illus. see Dunlap, Julie.
Simson, James. Gipsies: As Illustrated by John Bunyan, Mrs. Carlyle, & Others. & Do Snakes Swallow Their Young? (p. 834)
—Gipsies: As Illustrated by John Bunyan, Mrs. Carlyle, & Others; & Do Snakes Swallow Their Young? (Classic Reprint) (p. 834)
—Reminiscences of Childhood at Inverkeithing: Or Life at a Lazaretto (Classic Reprint) (p. 1865)
Simukka, Salla. As Red As Blood. Witesman, Owen Frederick, tr. (p. 124)
Simukka, Salla & Witesman, Owen. As White As Snow. (p. 125)
—Sisterland. (p. 2027)
Simwenyi, Robbinson Namasaka. Death, the Only Gift (p. 521)
—Young Detectives. (p. 2530)
Sinatra, Amanda. Hollow. (p. 988)
Sinatsch, Nancy & Quackenbush, N. Jane. Amazing Grace Newton & the Missing Noodle. (p. 65)
Sinclair, Albert Thomas. American Gypsies (Classic Reprint) (p. 72)
—American-Romani Vocabulary (Classic Reprint) (p. 74)
Sinclair, Alex, illus. see Azzarello, Brian & Loeb, Jeph.
Sinclair, Alison. Lightborn. (p. 1299)
Sinclair, Angie, ed. see Herzog, Joyce.
Sinclair, April E. Flu. (p. 753)
Sinclair, Bella, illus. see O'Connor, Jane.
Sinclair, Bella, illus. see Shepherd, Donna J.
Sinclair, Bertrand W. Big Timber, a Story of the Northwest: With Frontpiece by Douglas Duer (Classic Reprint) (p. 223)
—Land of Frozen Suns: A Novel (Classic Reprint) (p. 1241)
—North of Fifty-Three (Classic Reprint) (p. 1621)
—Poor Man's Rock (Classic Reprint) (p. 1774)
—Raw Gold: A Novel (Classic Reprint) (p. 1844)
—Raw Gold. (p. 1844)
Sinclair, Catherine. Cross Purposes a Novel, Vol. 2 of 3 (Classic Reprint) (p. 478)
—Cross Purposes, Vol. 1 Of 3: A Novel (Classic Reprint) (p. 478)
—Hill & Valley, or Hours in England & Wales (Classic Reprint) (p. 971)
—Holiday House: A Series of Tales; Dedicated to Lady Diana Boyle (Classic Reprint) (p. 987)
—Holiday House. (p. 987)
—London Homes: Including the Murder Hole; the Drowning Dragoon; the Priest & the Curate; Lady Mary Pierrepoint;& Frank Vansittart (Classic Reprint) (p. 1341)
—Modern Accomplishments, or the March of Intellect (Classic Reprint) (p. 1486)
—Modern Flirtations: A Novel (Classic Reprint) (p. 1486)
—Modern Flirtations, Vol. 1 Of 3: Or, a Month at Harrowgate (Classic Reprint) (p. 1486)
—Modern Society: Or the March of Intellect, the Conclusion of Modern Accomplishments (Classic Reprint) (p. 1487)
—Scotland & the Scotch: Or the Western Circuit, Dedicated to the Highland Society (Classic Reprint) (p. 1962)
Sinclair, Dan, ed. see Herzog, Joyce.
Sinclair, Donna. Family Story Bible Colouring Book. (p. 703)
Sinclair, Drew, illus. see Isherwood, Mark.
Sinclair, Drew, illus. see Morgan, Rebecca.
Sinclair, Ellery. Christie's Choice (Classic Reprint) (p. 383)
Sinclair, Francis. Where the Sun Sets: Memories from Other Years & Lands (Classic Reprint) (p. 2439)
Sinclair, Gardine. Keira at Stageschool. (p. 1208)
—Mystery at Stageschool. (p. 1568)
—Stageschool by the Sea. (p. 2099)
Sinclair, Isabel. From Gray to Gold. (p. 791)
Sinclair, James. Instructions for Collecting & Preserving Valuable Lepidoptera for Scientific Purposes (Classic Reprint) (p. 1125)
Sinclair, Jeff, illus. see Gardner, Martin.
Sinclair, John. Scenes & Stories of the North of Scotland (Classic Reprint) (p. 1943)
Sinclair, Julie L. & Beevor, Lucy. Invention of the Airplane. (p. 1130)
Sinclair, Loretta Lea. Prizin of Zin. (p. 1802)
Sinclair, May'. Anne Severn & the Fieldings (Classic Reprint) (p. 99)
—Audrey Craven (Classic Reprint) (p. 136)
—Belfry (Classic Reprint) (p. 195)
—Combined Maze (Classic Reprint) (p. 428)
—Creators a Comedy (Classic Reprint) (p. 471)
—Divine Fire. (p. 566)
—Divine Fire (Classic Reprint) (p. 566)
—Immortal Moment: The Story of Kitty Tailleur (Classic Reprint) (p. 1101)
—Journal of Impressions in Belgium, 1915 (Classic Reprint) (p. 1180)
—Judgment of Eve (Classic Reprint) (p. 1185)
—Mary Olivier: A Life. (p. 1415)
—Mary Olivier: A Life (Classic Reprint) (p. 1415)
—Mr. Waddington of Wyck (Classic Reprint) (p. 1521)
—Rector of Wyck (Classic Reprint) (p. 1855)
—Return of the Prodigal (Classic Reprint) (p. 1871)
—Romantic (Classic Reprint) (p. 1901)
—Superseded (Classic Reprint) (p. 2161)
—Three Sisters (Classic Reprint) (p. 2235)
—Tree of Heaven. (p. 2284)
—Tree of Heaven (Classic Reprint) (p. 2284)
—Two Sides of a Question (Classic Reprint) (p. 2309)
—Tysons: Mr. & Mrs. Nevill Tyson. (p. 2311)
—Tysons: Mr. & Mrs. Nevill Tyson (Classic Reprint) (p. 2311)
Sinclair, Mehded Maryam. Miraculous Happenings in the Year of the Elephant. (p. 1474)
—Trust of Treasures. Desira, Angela, illus. (p. 2296)
—When Wings Expand. (p. 2434)
Sinclair, Pembroke. Dealing with Devils. (p. 519)
—Humanity's Hope. (p. 1050)
Sinclair, Upton. Captain of Industry Being the Story of a Civilized Man (Classic Reprint) (p. 326)
—Damaged Goods the Great Play les Avaries by Brieux (Classic Reprint) (p. 499)
—Jungle (Classic Reprint) (p. 1190)
—King Coal: A Novel (Classic Reprint) (p. 1220)
—King Midas: A Romance (Classic Reprint) (p. 1220)
—Love's Pilgrimage: A Novel (Classic Reprint) (p. 1362)
—Metropolis (Classic Reprint) (p. 1453)
—Oil! A Novel (Classic Reprint) (p. 1643)
—Pot Boiler: A Comedy in Four Acts. (p. 1780)
—Pot Boiler: A Comedy in Four Acts (Classic Reprint) (p. 1780)
—Prince Hagen: A Phantasy (Classic Reprint) (p. 1794)
—Samuel the Seeker (Classic Reprint) (p. 1929)
—Spy (Classic Reprint) (p. 2093)
—They Call Me Carpenter: A Tale of the Second Coming. (p. 2219)
—They Call Me Carpenter: A Tale of the Second Coming (Classic Reprint) (p. 2219)
—They Call Me Carpenter. (p. 2219)
—Wet Parade (Classic Reprint) (p. 2403)
Sinclair, Valerie, jt. auth. see Evans, D. L.
Sinclair, William. Scottish Life & Humor (Classic Reprint) (p. 1962)
Sindelar, Joseph C. Father Thrift & His Animal Friends (Classic Reprint) (p. 714)
Sindelar, Joseph Charles. Closing Day Entertainments (Classic Reprint) (p. 407)
—Washington Day Entertainments: Recitations, Plays, Dialogues, Drills, Tableaux, Pantomimes, Quotations, Songs, Tributes, Stories, Facts (Classic Reprint) (p. 2381)
Sindell, Martin. Satisfied at Last (Classic Reprint) (p. 1936)
Sinel, Natasha. Fix. (p. 745)
—Soulstruck: A Novel. (p. 2066)
—Soulstruck. (p. 2066)
Sinfield, Irene. Julia & her Bears on Holiday. (p. 1186)
Singer, Agathe. Anywhere, Anytime Art: Gouache: An Artist's Guide to Painting with Gouache on the Go! (p. 104)
Singer, Alexis. Alexis: My True Story of Internet Sex with a Married Man. (p. 43)
Singer, Allison. Ghostly Tales of Charleston. (p. 829)
—What Does the President Do? (p. 2410)
Singer, Allison, ed. see Kaye, Megan.
Singer, Allison & Kempster-Barry, Rachel. This Book Is about You. (p. 2224)
Singer, Beth & Benchmark Education Co., LLC Staff. Red Bird Chirps. (p. 1856)
—We Can Fix It! (p. 2390)
Singer, Daniel J. Big Game Fields of America, North & South: Illustrated from Photographs by the Author & Three Drawings by Charles Livingston Bull (Classic Reprint) (p. 220)
Singer, David. Concurso Por la Princesa Mas Linda Del Mundo: El Barco Mas Grande y Mas Lindo Del Mundo. (p. 438)
—Contest for the Most Beautiful Princess in the World: The Biggest & Most Beautiful Boat in the World. (p. 445)
—Yisrael Sheli/My Israel: People & Places. (p. 2522)
Singer, Isaac Bashevis. Parakeet Named Dreidel. Berkson, Suzanne Raphael, illus. (p. 1699)
—Why Noah Chose the Dove. (p. 2458)
—Why Noah Chose the Dove. Shub, Elizabeth, tr. from ENG. (p. 2458)
Singer, Isidore, jt. auth. see Francke, Kuno.
Singer, Jane, jt. auth. see Wright, John D.
Singer, Jane E. Meat. (p. 1435)
—Rice. (p. 1876)
—Soybeans. (p. 2070)
—Wheat. (p. 2427)
Singer, Marilyn. Bird Singing, Bird Winging. Semple, Lucy, illus. (p. 230)
—Caterpillars. (p. 344)
—Echo Echo: Reverso Poems about Greek Myths. Masse, Josée, illus. (p. 623)
—Float, Flutter. (p. 750)
—Float, Flutter. Durst, Kathryn, illus. (p. 750)
—Follow Follow: A Book of Reverso Poems. Masse, Josée, illus. (p. 757)
—Follow the Recipe: Poems about Imagination, Celebration, & Cake. Priceman, Marjorie, illus. (p. 758)
—Full Moon Is Rising. (p. 797)
—Full Moon Is Rising, a (1 Paperback/1 CD) (p. 797)
—Fun with Animals Friendship Box. Zaidi, Nadeem, illus. (p. 800)
—Gulp, Gobble: Ready-To-Read Pre-Level 1. Durst, Kathryn, illus. (p. 905)
—Gulp, Gobble. (p. 905)
—Hair! Animal Fur, Wool, & More. Colombet, Julie, illus. (p. 910)
—Have You Heard about Lady Bird? Poems about Our First Ladies. Carpenter, Nancy, illus. (p. 939)
—I'm the Big One Now! Poems about Growing Up. Christy, Jana, illus. (p. 1099)
—Mirror Mirror: A Book of Reverso Poems. Masse, Josée, illus. (p. 1475)
—Miss Muffet, or What Came After. Litchfield, David, illus. (p. 1479)
—On the Same Day in March. (p. 1655)
—Rutherford B. , Who Was He? Poems about Our Presidents. Hendrix, John, illus. (p. 1918)
—Stick Is an Excellent Thing: Poems Celebrating Outdoor Play. Pham, Leuyen, illus. (p. 2117)
—Strange Place to Call Home: The World's Most Dangerous Habitats & the Animals That Call Them Home. Young, Ed, illus. (p. 2138)
—Tallulah's Ice Skates. Boiger, Alexandra, illus. (p. 2188)
—Tallulah's Nutcracker. Boiger, Alexandra, illus. (p. 2188)
—Tallulah's Solo. Boiger, Alexandra, illus. (p. 2188)
—Tallulah's Tap Shoes. Boiger, Alexandra, illus. (p. 2188)
—Tallulah's Toe Shoes. Boiger, Alexandra, illus. (p. 2188)
—Tallulah's Tutu. Boiger, Alexandra, illus. (p. 2188)
—What Is Your Dog Doing? Habbley, Kathleen, illus. (p. 2417)
—What's a Banana? Pizzoli, Greg, illus. (p. 2423)
—What's an Apple? Pizzoli, Greg, illus. (p. 2423)
Singer, Marilyn & Cairns, Julia. Full Moon Is Rising. (p. 797)
Singer, Neal. Wonders of Nuclear Fusion: Creating an Ultimate Energy Source. (p. 2490)
Singh, Aditi Wardhan. How Our Skin Sparkles: A Growth Mindset Children's Book for Global Citizens about Acceptance. (p. 1034)
Singh, Amulya. Jules, the Lightning Bug. Lutz, Patrick & Neal, Lindsay, illus. (p. 1186)
Singh, Asavari. How to Draw the Craziest, Creepiest Characters James, Martin et al, illus. (p. 1041)
—How to Draw the Fastest, Coolest Cars James, Martin et al, illus. (p. 1041)
—How to Draw the Most Exciting, Awesome Manga James, Martin et al, illus. (p. 1041)
Singh, Deanna. I Am a Boy of Color. Nsorma, Ammar, illus. (p. 1057)
—I Am a Girl of Color. (p. 1057)
Singh, Jason. Teen Aged. (p. 2198)

S

—Demons Unfolding. (p. 528)
Skakandi, Viktoria, illus. see Weber, Vicky.
Skalla, Nancy. Grandma's Telos Boxes of Wishes. (p. 879)
Skalla, Werner, tr. see Renz, Ulrich.
Skamble, Skimble. Fairy Tales, Vol. 1 (Classic Reprint) (p. 698)
Skancke, Jennifer. Addicted to Opioids. (p. 15)
Skancke, Jennifer L., jt. ed. see Friedman, Lauri S.
Skardarasy, Doreen L., illus. see Hereford, L. F.
Skead, Robert A. & Skead, Robert J. Patriots, Redcoats & Spies (p. 1706)
Skead, Robert & Simmel, Mike. Mighty Mike Bounces Back: A Boy's Life with Epilepsy. (p. 1463)
Skead, Robert J. Submarines, Secrets & a Daring Rescue (p. 2145)
Skead, Robert J., jt. auth. see Skead, Robert A.
Skeat, Walter. Nine Specimens of English Dialects: Edited from Various Sources (Classic Reprint) (p. 1609)
Skeat, Walter W. Chaucer: The Minor Poems (Classic Reprint) (p. 362)
—Complete Works of Geoffrey Chaucer (Classic Reprint) (p. 435)
—Glossaries of Words Used in Swaledale, Cleveland, Kent, Surrey, Oxford, Warwickshire, & Whitby (Classic Reprint) (p. 844)
—Lancelot of the Laik: A Scottish Metrical Romance, (about 1490-1500 A. D.) (Classic Reprint) (p. 1241)
—Lancelot of the Laik. (p. 1241)
—Nine Specimens of English Dialects, & Two Collections of Derbicisms (Classic Reprint) (p. 1609)
Skeat, Walter W., jt. auth. see Fitzherbert, Master.
Skeat, Walter William. Lancelot of the Laik: A Scottish Metrical Romance, (about 1490-1500 A. D.) (Classic Reprint) (p. 1241)
—Tale of Gamelyn (Classic Reprint) (p. 2179)
Skeat, Walter William, jt. auth. see Chaucer, Geoffrey.
Skeate, Sarah, illus. see Ruiz, Rachel.
Skeen, Michelle, et al. Communication Skills for Teens: How to Listen, Express, & Connect for Success. (p. 431)
—Just as You Are: A Teen's Guide to Self-Acceptance & Lasting Self-Esteem. (p. 1192)
Skeens, Matthew, illus. see Firestone, Mary, et al.
Skeens, Matthew, illus. see Firestone, Mary.
Skeens, Matthew, illus. see Mortensen, Lori.
Skeens, Matthew, illus. see Pearl, Norman.
Skeens, Matthew, illus. see Seuling, Barbara.
Skeens, Matthew, illus. see Suen, Anastasia.
Skeens, Matthew, illus. see Troupe, Thomas Kingsley.
Skeers, Linda. Dinosaur Lady. Alvarez Miguens, Marta, illus. (p. 549)
—Impossible Patriotism Project. (p. 1102)
—Women Who Dared: 52 Fearless Daredevils, Adventurers, & Rebels. Gosling, Livi, illus. (p. 2488)
Skeesuck, Justin, illus. see Gray, Patrick.
Skeffington, Francis Sheehy. Prodigal Daughter: A Comedy in One Act (Classic Reprint) (p. 1803)
Skeffington, Miranda. My Little Pony: Best Gift Ever. (p. 1553)
—My Little Pony: Friendship Is Magic: Collectible Poster Book. (p. 1553)
—My Little Pony: Mini Pony Collector's Guide with Exclusive Figure. (p. 1554)
Skehan, Krista, illus. see Spieker, Diana.
Skelley, Billie Holladay. Hugh Armstrong Robinson: The Story of Flying Lucky 13, an Aviation Pioneer. (p. 1048)
Skelley, James. Beaverton's Dilemma: A Leopold the Lawmux Adventure. (p. 186)
Skelley, Jen, illus. see Mudpuppy.
Skelley, Paula, jt. auth. see Loewen, Nancy.
Skelton, J. R., illus. see Marshall, H. E.
Skelton, J. Wallace. Transphobia: Deal with It & Be a Gender Transcender. Johnson, Nick, illus. (p. 2278)
Skelton, John. Band of Acadians. (p. 163)
—Summers & Winters at Balmawhapple, Vol. 1: A Second Series of Ihe Table-Talk of Shirley (Classic Reprint) (p. 2150)
—Thalatta! or the Great Commoner: A Political Romance (Classic Reprint) (p. 2211)
Skelton, Matthew. Story of Cirrus Flux. (p. 2129)
Skene, Felicia. Hidden Depths (Classic Reprint) (p. 965)
—Hidden Depths, Vol. 1 (Classic Reprint) (p. 965)
—Hidden Depths, Vol. 2: 'Veritas Est Major Charitas' (Classic Reprint) (p. 965)
—Wayfaring Sketches among the Greeks & Turks, & on the Shores of the Danube: By a Seven Years' Resident in Greece (Classic Reprint) (p. 2387)
Skene, Rona. American Girl: Discover Science. (p. 71)
—LEGO Amazing Vehicles. (p. 1264)
—LEGO Amazing Vehicles (Library Edition) (p. 1264)
—LEGO Animal Atlas: Discover the Animals of the World. (p. 1264)
—LEGO Animal Atlas (Library Edition) Discover the Animals of the World. (p. 1264)
—LEGO Epic History: Includes Four Exclusive LEGO Mini Models. (p. 1264)
—LEGO Epic History. (p. 1264)
Skene, Todd & Aulakh, Amneet. N Is for Nutrition: Rhymes by the Alphabet. Crossley, Kezzia, illus. (p. 1572)
Skerl, Peter, jt. auth. see Kraljic, Helena.
Skerry, Brian, photos by see Lawler, Janet.
Skerry, Brian, photos by see Mallory, Kenneth.
Sketchley, Arthur. Brown Papers (Classic Reprint) (p. 287)
—Mrs. Brown on the Tichborne Case (Classic Reprint) (p. 1521)
—Mrs. Brown on Women's Rights (Classic Reprint) (p. 1521)
—Mrs. Brown Series (Classic Reprint) (p. 1521)
—Mrs. Brown's Visit to the Paris Exhibition (Classic Reprint) (p. 1521)
—Mrs. Brown's Visits to Paris (Classic Reprint) (p. 1521)
Sketchwell, Barnaby. London Characters, or Fashions & Customs of the Present Century, Vol. 1 of 2 (Classic Reprint) (p. 1340)
—London Characters, Vol. 1: Or, Anecdotes, Fashions, & Customs, of the Present Century (Classic Reprint) (p. 1340)
Sketch_kids_inc. My Secret Scribblings & Sketches! Drawing Pad & Sketch Book for Boys & Girls (Kids Sketchbook) (p. 1560)
Skevington, Andrea. Bible Story Retold in Twelve Chapters. Skevington, Andrea, illus. (p. 214)
—Little Christmas Tree Hussey, Lorna, illus. (p. 1314)
—Little Christmas Tree. Hussey, Lorna, illus. (p. 1314)
—Prayers & Verses Through the Bible. Skevington, Andrea, illus. (p. 1785)
Skewes, John. Chicago ABC: a Larry Gets Lost Book. (p. 367)
—Larry Loves Boston! A Larry Gets Lost Book. (p. 1245)
—Larry Loves Chicago! A Larry Gets Lost Book. Skewes, John, illus. (p. 1245)
—Larry Loves New York City! Skewes, John, illus. (p. 1245)
—Larry Loves Portland! Skewes, John, illus. (p. 1245)
—Larry Loves San Diego! A Larry Gets Lost Book. (p. 1245)
—Larry Loves San Francisco! Skewes, John, illus. (p. 1245)
—Larry Loves Washington, DC! (p. 1245)
—New York City ABC: a Larry Gets Lost Book. (p. 1598)
—Portland ABC. (p. 1779)
—San Francisco ABC: a Larry Gets Lost Book. (p. 1929)
—Seattle ABC a Larry Gets Lost Book. (p. 1972)
Skewes, John, illus. see Holtzen, Mark.
Skewes, John, jt. auth. see Mullin, Michael.
Skewes, John & Fox, Andrew. Larry Gets Lost in Prehistoric Times: From Dinosaurs to the Stone Age. Skewes, John, illus. (p. 1245)
—Larry Gets Lost in Washington, DC. Skewes, John, illus. (p. 1245)
Skewes, John & Mullin, Michael. Larry Gets Lost in Alaska. Skewes, John, illus. (p. 1245)
—Larry Gets Lost in Boston. Skewes, John, illus. (p. 1245)
—Larry Gets Lost in Chicago. Skewes, John, illus. (p. 1245)
—Larry Gets Lost in New York City. Skewes, John, illus. (p. 1245)
—Larry Gets Lost in Philadelphia. Skewes, John, illus. (p. 1245)
—Larry Gets Lost in Portland. Skewes, John, illus. (p. 1245)
Skewes, John & Ode, Eric. Elliott the Otter: The Totally Untrue Story of Elliott Bay. Skewes, John, illus. (p. 638)
—Larry Gets Lost in San Diego. (p. 1245)
—Larry Gets Lost in Seattle: 10th Anniversary Edition. (p. 1245)
—Larry Gets Lost under the Sea. Skewes, John, illus. (p. 1245)
Skewes, John, et al. Larry Gets Lost in Los Angeles. Skewes, John, illus. (p. 1245)
—Larry Gets Lost in San Francisco. Skewes, John, illus. (p. 1245)
—Larry Gets Lost in Texas. Skewes, John, illus. (p. 1245)
Ski, Jenn, illus. see Ikids Staff.
Skiba, Sabina. Temple of Syan. (p. 2203)
Skidmore, Donna, illus. see Summer, Sunny W.
Skidmore, Lauren. Fairest Poison. (p. 695)
—What Is Lost. (p. 2415)
Skidmore, Marlene. In Trouble Again! (p. 1112)
Skidmore, Steve & Barlow, Steve. EDGE: I HERO: Monster Hunter: Vampire. Davidson, Paul, illus. (p. 625)
—Lost Diary of Erik Bloodaxe, Viking Warrior. (p. 1353)
—Lost Diary of Shakespeare's Ghostwriter. (p. 1353)
Skiles, Janet. Color & Count. (p. 419)
—Crafts Around the House. (p. 466)
—Happy Birthday! Stickers. (p. 921)
—Happy Birthday! Tattoos. (p. 921)
—Just Ducky! Stickers. (p. 1192)
—Silly Sea Animals Tattoos. (p. 2018)
Skiles, Janet, illus. see Cecchini, Marie E.
Skiles, Janet & Coloring Books Staff. How to Care for Your Cat: A Color & Learn Guide for Kids. (p. 1038)
Skillen, Roy. Three Wise Men. (p. 2235)
Skillern, Ross Hall. Catarrhal & Suppurative Diseases of the Accessory Sinuses of the Nose (Classic Reprint) (p. 343)
Skillicorn, Helen. Friendship Crafts. (p. 787)
—Spooky Crafts. (p. 2086)
Skillicorn, Mike. Death of a Wallaby: The Wobbly Wallaby II. (p. 521)
—Way Home: The Wobbly Wallaby III. (p. 2387)
Skillicorn, Phillipa, et al. Primary Science. (p. 1792)
Skillin, Joseph. Once upon a Time People Were Kind. (p. 1658)
Skilling, Marie. Powers of Benjamin Frank. (p. 1783)
Skillman, John B. Skillman's New-York Police Reports: Illustrated with Engravings; Written in 1828-29 (Classic Reprint) (p. 2032)
Skilton, Sarah. High & Dry. (p. 968)
Skinas, John. Pictures of God: A Child's Guide to Understanding Icons. (p. 1741)
Skinas, John Kosmas. From God to You: The Icon's Journey to Your Heart. (p. 791)
Skindzier, Jon, jt. auth. see C.Laird, Elizabeth.
Skindzier, Jon, jt. auth. see Helmer, Jay.
Skinner, ed. see Arthur, Kay & Arndt, Janna.
Skinner, ed. see Bob Gresh.
Skinner, ed. see DeStefano, Anthony.
Skinner, ed. see Dungy, Tony & Dungy, Lauren.
Skinner, ed. see Dunham, Wendy.
Skinner, ed. see Emmerson, Janice & Harvest House Publishers Staff.
Skinner, ed. see Emmerson, Janice.
Skinner, ed. see George, Elizabeth.
Skinner, ed. see George, Jim & George, Elizabeth.
Skinner, ed. see George, Jim.
Skinner, ed. see Gresh, Dannah.
Skinner, ed. see Harvest House Publishers & Harvest House Publishers Staff.
Skinner, ed. see Harvest House Publishers Staff.
Skinner, ed. see Hitchen, Danielle.
Skinner, ed. see Kluck, Ted.
Skinner, ed. see Merritt, James.
Skinner, ed. see Omartian, Stormie.
Skinner, ed. see Ross, Michael & Ross, Christopher.
Skinner, ed. see Rothschild, Jennifer.
Skinner, ed. see Silverthorne, Sandy.
Skinner, ed. see Spier Weaver, Rachel & Haggard, Anna.
Skinner, ed. see TerKeurst, Lysa & TerKeurst, Hope.
Skinner, ed. see Workman Publishing Co., Inc. Staff.
Skinner, Ada M. Dramatic Stories for Reading & Acting (Classic Reprint) (p. 597)
—Emerald Story Book: Stories & Legends of Spring, Nature & Easter (Classic Reprint) (p. 641)
—Garnet Story Book: Tales of Cheer Both Old & New (Classic Reprint) (p. 810)
—Little Folks' Christmas Stories & Plays (Classic Reprint) (p. 1316)
—Pearl Story Book: Stories & Legends of Winter, Christmas, & New Year's Day (Classic Reprint) (p. 1710)
—Topaz Story Book: Stories & Legends of Autumn, Hallowe'en, & Thanksgiving (Classic Reprint) (p. 2264)
Skinner, Ada M., jt. auth. see Dickinson, Asa Don.
Skinner, Ada Maria. Turquoise Story Book: Stories & Legends of Summer & Nature (Classic Reprint) (p. 2301)
Skinner, Althea G., ed. see DeStefano, Anthony.
Skinner, Althea G., ed. see Silverthorne, Sandy.
Skinner, Anna. Maths Outside & in for the Early Years Foundation Stage (p. 1425)
Skinner, Charles M. Myths & Legends of Our Own Land. (p. 1571)
—Myths & Legends of Our Own Land, Vol. 1 (Classic Reprint) (p. 1571)
—Nature in a City Yard: Some Rambling Dissertations Thereupon (Classic Reprint) (p. 1580)
—With Feet to the Earth (Classic Reprint) (p. 2481)
Skinner, Charles Montgomery. Do-Nothing Days (Classic Reprint) (p. 570)
Skinner, Christine Way. Jesus Invites Me to the Feast: My First Eucharist Journal. (p. 1166)
Skinner, Constance Lindsay. Good-Morning, Rosamond (Classic Reprint) (p. 863)
Skinner, Cornelia Otis. Dithers & Jitters (Classic Reprint) (p. 565)
Skinner, Daphne. Albert Keeps Score. (p. 40)
—Albert Keeps Score. Melmon, Deborah, illus. (p. 40)
—Right Place for Albert: One-To-One Correspondence. Melmon, Deborah, illus. (p. 1882)
—Right Place for Albert. Melmon, Deborah, illus. (p. 1882)
Skinner, Dawn. Can't Help but Love Those Babies. West, Matthew M., illus. (p. 322)
—My Family, My Home. West, Matthew, illus. (p. 1538)
—Unforgettable Night at the Movies. West, Matthew M., illus. (p. 2327)
Skinner, E. W. Diary of St. Blair. (p. 540)
—St. Blair: Sybille's Reign. (p. 2096)
—St. Blair: Children of the Night. (p. 2096)
Skinner, ed. Bible Infographics for Kids: Giants, Ninja Skills, a Talking Donkey, & What's the Deal with the Tabernacle? (p. 213)
Skinner, Eleanor L. Merry Tales (Classic Reprint) (p. 1450)
Skinner, Eleanor Louise. Children's Plays (Classic Reprint) (p. 374)
—Nursery Tales from Many Lands (Classic Reprint) (p. 1631)
Skinner, Harriet Pearl. Boys Who Became Famous Men: Stories of the Childhood of Poets, Artists, & Musicians (Classic Reprint) (p. 273)
Skinner, Henrietta Dana. Espiritu Santo: A Novel (Classic Reprint) (p. 662)
—Faith Brandon: A Novel (Classic Reprint) (p. 698)
—Heart & Soul: A Novel (Classic Reprint) (p. 944)
Skinner, Hubert Marshall. Schoolmaster in Comedy & Satire: Arranged & Edited for the Special Use of Teachers' Reading Circles & Round Tables (Classic Reprint) (p. 1947)
—Schoolmaster in Comedy & Satire: Arranged & Edited for the Special Use of Teachers' Reading Circles & Round Tables; a Companion Volume to the Schoolmaster in Literature (Classic Reprint) (p. 1947)
Skinner, J. After the Storm, Vol. 1: Or, Jonathan & His Neighbours in 1865-6 (Classic Reprint) (p. 34)
Skinner, J. E. Hilary. After the Storm, Vol. 2 Of 2: Or, Jonathan & His Neighbours in 1865-6 (Classic Reprint) (p. 34)
Skinner, J. L. Little Incidents of the Battle of Lexington, Mo (Classic Reprint) (p. 1319)
Skinner, James. Done & Dusted. (p. 581)
Skinner, James W. T., illus. see Dee.
Skinner, Kerry L., ed. see Harned, Bert.
Skinner, Lynn. Eugene the Mouse at the Big Farmhouse: The Contentment of a Creative Mouse. Davis, Pharis, illus. (p. 667)
Skinner, Lynn C. Alex Is Mr. Jolly. Dohm, Ingrid, illus. (p. 42)
—Anytime Is Party Time for Eugene the Mouse: The Wisdom of a Creative Mouse. Dohm, Ingrid, illus. (p. 104)
—Happy Birthday Dolly. Dohm, Ingrid, illus. (p. 920)
—How Does Your Garden Grow: God's Master Plan. (p. 1030)
Skinner, Matthew James & Wells, Travis. Milo & the Lost Colors. (p. 1468)
Skinner, Meg, illus. see Sevaru, Molly.
Skinner, Meg, illus. see Takuna, John Fred.
Skinner, Paige. Good Girl the Pup. (p. 862)
Skinner, Richard. Diary of a Junior Detective/ Ben Baxter's Private Diary. (p. 539)
Skinner, Robert. Penman, 1963-64, Vol. 17 (Classic Reprint) (p. 1716)
Skinner, Russell Scott, illus. see Bashford, Helen.
Skinner, Sharon. Rocket Shoes. Jenkins, Ward, illus. (p. 1895)
Skinner, Vicky. All Our Worst Ideas. (p. 53)
—How to Breathe Underwater. (p. 1038)
—We Are the Ghosts. (p. 2389)
Skinner, W. H. Lessons in English: Based upon Principles of Literary Interpretation, a Manual for Teachers of All Grades, with Lessons for Pupils of the First & Second Grades (Classic Reprint) (p. 1269)
Skinner, William. That Loon o Baxter's: A Tale of Scottish Fisher Life (Classic Reprint) (p. 2213)
Skinner-Vance, Lcsw Mary. Rescue Dogs: The Early Years How Ruff Beginnings Become Happy Tails. (p. 1868)
Skipp, Hui, illus. see Baker, Kate.
Skipp, Hui, illus. see Scribens, Sunny.
Skipper, John C. Frank Robinson: A Baseball Biography (p. 777)
Skipworth, Kelly. Twelve Ordinary Men. (p. 2303)
Skipworth, Kelly & Fernández, Cecilia. Los doce disipulos (The Twelve Ordinary Men) (p. 1350)
Skipworth, Mark. Illinois Chronicles: The Story of the State of Illinois - from Its Birth to the Present Day. (p. 1095)
—Texas Chronicles: The History of Texas from Earliest Times to the Present Day. (p. 2209)
Skipworth, Patrick, jt. auth. see Lloyd, Christopher.
Skivington, Peter. Nose Nibbling Monster. Hussain, Zara, illus. (p. 1622)
Sklansky, Amy E. My Rainbow Surprise. Dunn, Anna, illus. (p. 1559)
—Sweet Hearts. Dunn, Anna, illus. (p. 2168)
—You Are My Little Pumpkin Pie. (p. 2524)
Sklar, Andy, illus. see Kidd, Ronald.
Sklar, Peggy A. Sister Thea Bowman: Do You Hear Me, Church? (p. 2027)
Sklar, Tanya. Islamic-Jewish Relations Before 1947. (p. 1139)
Sklovsky, Max. Dynasty: A Novel of Chicago's Industrial Evolution (Classic Reprint) (p. 612)
Skocz, Anita Joyce. Kite Tale. (p. 1225)
Skofield, James. Bear & Bird. Thermes, Jennifer, illus. (p. 179)
—Detective Dinosaur Undercover. Alley, R. W., illus. (p. 534)
Skog, Jason. Kurt Angle: From Olympian to Wrestling Machine (p. 1233)
—NHL: History & Heroes: the Story of the Chicago Blackhawks. (p. 1601)
—Taking the Shot. (p. 2178)
Skog, Jason & Kalz, Jill. Displaying the Shot. (p. 564)
Skogen, J. M. Dallas Mavericks. (p. 498)
—Memphis Grizzlies. (p. 1446)
—Oklahoma City Thunder. (p. 1643)
—Portland Trail Blazers. (p. 1779)
—Utah Jazz. (p. 2342)
—Washington Wizards. (p. 2382)
Skogen, J. M., jt. auth. see Skogen, J. m.
Skogen, J. m. & Skogen, J. M. Memphis Grizzlies. (p. 1446)
Skogen, Jennifer. Burning. (p. 300)
—Burning #1 (p. 300)
—Distant Deep #5. (p. 564)
—Forests of the Night #2. (p. 767)
—Shattered. (p. 2003)
—Sinews of Thy Heart #4. (p. 2023)
—Tyger, Tyger #6. (p. 2310)
—What Dread Hand #3. (p. 2410)
Skogen, Jenny. Film. (p. 726)
Skomorokhova, Olga, illus. see Mireles, Ashley Marie.
Skomorokhova, Olga, illus. see Rowe, Amanda.
Skon, Sandy, illus. see Lamb.
Skorackiji, Olga, ed. see Fitzgerald, Josephine.
Skordy, Anne Marie. Start with Your Heart. Collier, Kevin, illus. (p. 2107)
Skorlinski, Cynthia. My Little Erica. (p. 1552)
Skorpen, Neal, illus. see Klug, Kirsten.
Skou, Nick, illus. see Jordan, Claire.
Skougaard, Shari. Grumpy Goo, I Love You. (p. 901)
Skovran, Victoria, illus. see Rissman, Rebecca.
Skovron, Jon. Man Made Boy. (p. 1394)
—Misfit. (p. 1477)
—Struts & Frets. (p. 2142)
Skoyles, Anna. On My Back Paws: A Lonely Dog, a Magic Spell & a Friendship to Be Saved! (p. 1653)
—Wishes. (p. 2479)
Skrbina, Daniel William. Knight to Remember: Gulliver's Journey Continues (p. 1228)
Skrbina, Janet. River in the City. (p. 1887)
Skrepnick, Michael, illus. see Bakker, Robert T.
Skrepnick, Michael W., illus. see Williams, Judith.
Skrepnick, Michael William, illus. see Bakker, Robert T.
Skrine, John Huntley. Uppingham by the Sea: A Narrative of the Year at Borth (Classic Reprint) (p. 2339)
Skrine, Mary Jessie Hammond. Bedesman 4 (Classic Reprint) (p. 188)
Skroback Hennessey, Gail. Fashion Rules! A Closer Look at Clothing in the Middle Ages. Sabin, Tracy, illus. (p. 712)
—Mrs. Paddington & the Silver Mousetraps: A Hair-Raising History of Women's Hairstyles in 18th-Century London. Cox, Steve, illus. (p. 1522)
Skromovas, Andrea. Gifts You Cannot Buy: An Empowering Children's Book about Values & Gratitude. Skromovas, Andrea, illus. (p. 832)
Skrutskie, Emily. Abyss Surrounds Us. (p. 9)
—Edge of the Abyss. (p. 625)
—Hullmetal Girls. (p. 1048)
Skrypuch, Marsha Forchuk. Adrift at Sea: A Vietnamese Boy's Story of Survival. Deines, Brian, illus. (p. 17)
—Best Gifts MacKay, Elly, illus. (p. 206)
—Dance of the Banished (p. 500)
—Last Airlift: A Vietnamese Orphan's Rescue from War. (p. 1247)
—Making Bombs for Hitler. (p. 1388)
—One Step at a Time: A Vietnamese Child Finds Her Way. (p. 1662)
—Sky of Bombs, Sky of Stars: A Vietnamese War Orphan Finds Home. (p. 2033)
—Stolen Girl. (p. 2120)
—War Below. (p. 2376)
Skulski, Jenny. Gerbil Escapes! (p. 821)
Skulski, Monica Fitch, jt. auth. see Kulig, Ann.
Skurzynski, Gloria. Afterwar. (p. 34)
—Good-Bye, Billy Radish. (p. 861)
—This Is Rocket Science: True Stories of the Risk-Taking Scientists Who Figure Out Ways to Explore Beyond Earth. (p. 2225)
Skuse, C. J. Pretty Bad Things. (p. 1790)
—Rockoholic. (p. 1895)
Skuta, Matt. Bee with the Backward Stripes. (p. 189)
Skuy, David. Band of Merry Kids (p. 163)
—Starting Eleven. (p. 2108)
—Striker. (p. 2141)
Skwara, Maike Lena. Diogo the Little Dinosaur. Barr, Bailey, illus. (p. 551)
Skwish, Emily. Baby Einstein: Here We Go! (p. 150)
—Baby Einstein: First Look & Find Book & Blocks. (p. 150)
—Baby Einstein: Busy World. Shutterstock.com, photos by. (p. 150)

S

Slater, Veronica D. Cerf-Volant de Mon Père. Migliore, Valentina, illus. (p. 353)
—My Father's Kite. Migliore, Valentina, illus. (p. 1538)
Slater, Veronica D., jt. auth. see Migliore, Valentina.
Slater-Milligan, Joey. Psy. (p. 1809)
Slaton, Donna F. Ben Beagle Plays. (p. 198)
Slattery, Kathryn. 365 Bible Answers for Curious Kids: An If I Could Ask God Anything Devotional (p. 2560)
—Dear God, I Have a Question: Honest Answers to Kids' Questions about Faith (p. 520)
—If I Could Ask God Anything: Awesome Bible Answers for Curious Kids (p. 1091)
Slattery, Margaret. Costly Star (Classic Reprint) (p. 457)
—Girl & Her Religion. (p. 835)
—New Paths Through Old Palestine (Classic Reprint) (p. 1596)
Slaughenhaupt, Grace. Castle Gold. (p. 340)
Slaughter, Frances Elizabeth, jt. auth. see Southey, Rosamond.
Slaughter, Gertrude. Shakespeare & the Heart of a Child (Classic Reprint) (p. 1998)
Slaughter, Michael R. Big Heart: A Story of a Girl & Her Horse. Mangis Sink, Theresa, illus. (p. 220)
Slaughter, Tom, illus. see Jocelyn, Marthe.
Slauson, Harold Whiting. First Aid to the Car or Highway Hints & Helps: Guide to Road-Side Repairs & Improvised Replacements. (p. 735)
Slavens, Elaine. Arguing: Word by Word Murray, Steven, illus. (p. 115)
—Bullying: Deal with It Before Push Comes to Shove. Kerrigan, Brooke, illus. (p. 297)
—Fighting: Without Coming to Blows Murray, Steven, illus. (p. 725)
—Peer Pressure: Deal with It Without Losing Your Cool Shannon, Ben, illus. (p. 1714)
Slavens, Elaine & James Lorimer and Company Ltd. Staff. Fighting: Without Coming to Blows Murray, Steven, illus. (p. 725)
Slavens, Elaine & Pitt, Steve. Teasing: Before the Joke's on You Geoffroi, Remie, illus. (p. 2196)
Slavicek, Louise Chipley. Anne Hutchinson. (p. 98)
—Boer War. (p. 253)
—Establishment of the State of Israel. (p. 664)
—I. M. Pei. (p. 1079)
—Jane Addams. (p. 1157)
—Paul Robeson. (p. 1707)
—Salem Witch Trial: Hysteria in Colonial America. (p. 1924)
Slavici, Ioan. Lucky Mill (Classic Reprint) (p. 1365)
Slavin, Bill. Big Top Otto. Slavin, Bill, illus. (p. 223)
—Who Broke the Teapot?! (p. 2446)
Slavin, Bill, illus. see Ashby, Ruth.
Slavin, Bill, illus. see Bailey, Linda.
Slavin, Bill, illus. see Beiser, Tim.
Slavin, Bill, illus. see Bourgeois, Paulette.
Slavin, Bill, illus. see Drake, Jane & Love, Ann.
Slavin, Bill, illus. see Fyvie, Erica.
Slavin, Bill, illus. see Heidbreder, Robert.
Slavin, Bill, illus. see Jackson, Ellen B.
Slavin, Bill, illus. see Kulling, Monica.
Slavin, Bill, illus. see Levy, Janice.
Slavin, Bill, illus. see Love, Ann & Drake, Jane.
Slavin, Bill, illus. see Moore, Christopher.
Slavin, Bill, illus. see Nicolson, Cynthia Pratt & Bourgeois, Paulette.
Slavin, Bill, illus. see Owens, Ann-Maureen & Yealland, Jane.
Slavin, Bill, illus. see Sheldrick Ross, Catherine.
Slavin, Bill, illus. see Spinelli, Eileen.
Slavin, Bill, illus. see Staunton, Ted & Staunton, Will.
Slavin, Bill, illus. see Staunton, Ted.
Slavin, Bill, illus. see Whitehouse, Howard.
Slavin, Bill, illus. see Zimelman, Nathan.
Slavin, Bill, jt. auth. see Bourgeois, Paulette.
Slavin, Bill, jt. auth. see Kulling, Monica.
Slavin, David. Odd Gods: the Oddyssey. Lane, Adam J. B., illus. (p. 1637)
Slavin, David & Weitzman, Daniel. Odd Gods. Lane, Adam J. B., illus. (p. 1637)
Slavin, John Mark. My Friend Dad. (p. 1547)
Slavit, Norma. Elephant Who Had Allergies. (p. 634)
—Pork Buns & High-Fives. (p. 1778)
Slayback-Carper, Minnette. Dance of Death: And Other Stories (Classic Reprint) (p. 500)
—Dance of Death. (p. 500)
Slayton, Fran Cannon. Snowball Moon. Bishop, Tracy, illus. (p. 2048)
Sleath, Frederick. Sniper Jackson (Classic Reprint) (p. 2046)
Sleath, Lara. For Her Sister. (p. 762)
Sleator, William. Phantom Limb. (p. 1732)
—Test. (p. 2208)
Sledge, Shronda. Sky & I. (p. 2033)
Slee, Natasha. Design Line: History of Women's Fashion. Mander, Sanna, illus. (p. 532)
—Style Guide: Fashion from Head to Toe. Stadtlander, Becca, illus. (p. 2145)
—Style Guide - Fashion from Head to Toe: 35 Prints to Colour. Stadtlander, Becca, illus. (p. 2145)
Sleeman, Matthew. Follow Jesus with Peter: His Letter in 25 Readings. (p. 757)
—Meet Jesus in Mark. (p. 1438)
Sleeper, M. Two Sicilies: Sketches & Stories of Their Scenery, Customs, History, Painters, etc (Classic Reprint) (p. 2309)
Sleeper, M. G. Sweden & Norway: Sketches & Stories of Their Scenery, Customs, History, Legends, etc (Classic Reprint) (p. 2168)
Sleeper, Martha G. (Quincy). Pictures from the History of Spain (Classic Reprint) (p. 1741)
Sleeper-Smith, Susan. Indigenous Prosperity & American Conquest: Indian Women of the Ohio River Valley, 1690-1792. (p. 1117)
Sleeping Bear Editor, ed. Diary of an American Kid. (p. 540)
Sleeping Bear Press. Diary of a Canadian Kid. Moore, Cyd, illus. (p. 539)
—Diary of a Pennsylvania Kid. (p. 539)
—Little Dance. Benoit, Renné, illus. (p. 1315)
Slegers, Liesbet. Archeologists & What They Do. (p. 110)
—Child in the Manger. (p. 369)
—Doctors & What They Do. (p. 574)
—Funny Tails. (p. 801)
—Happy Easter! (p. 921)
—Happy Halloween! (p. 922)
—I Am Going to Bed. (p. 1058)
—Move! (p. 1515)
—My Daddy & Me. (p. 1536)
—My Mommy & Me. (p. 1556)
—Nacho. Turrion, Celia, tr. (p. 1572)
—Puppy for Kevin. (p. 1815)
—Surprise! (p. 2163)
—Veterinarians & What They Do. (p. 2354)
Sleigh, Barbara. Carbonel & Calidor: Being the Further Adventures of a Royal Cat. Front, Charles, illus. (p. 327)
—Kingdom of Carbonel. Kennedy, Richard, illus. (p. 1222)
Sleight, A. J. Transport Adventure. (p. 2278)
Sleight, Mary B. House at Crague, or Her Own Way (Classic Reprint) (p. 1022)
Sleight, Mary Breck. Island Heroine: The Story of a Daughter of the Revolution (Classic Reprint) (p. 1139)
Sleightholm, Heather. Snow on Martinmas. Sleightholm, Heather, illus. (p. 2047)
Sleightholme, Julie. Making of Mabel. (p. 1390)
Sleiman, Dina L. Chivalrous. (p. 379)
—Courageous. (p. 462)
—Dauntless. (p. 510)
Sleith III, Eric. You & Me = We. (p. 2524)
Slemmer, Boyd. Journey. (p. 1181)
Slemons, Josiah Morris. Prospective Mother: A Handbook for Women During Pregnancy. (p. 1807)
Slenzak, Miller. I Can Be a Chef. (p. 1061)
—I Can Be a Pilot. (p. 1061)
—I Can Be a Soccer Player. (p. 1061)
Slepian, Curtis. Digging up Dinosaurs. (p. 546)
—Hamilton vs. Jefferson (Alexander Hamilton) (p. 913)
—You Are There! Ancient China 305 BC. (p. 2525)
—You Are There! Ancient China 305 BC. (p. 2525)
—You Are There! Gettysburg, July 1. 3 1863. (p. 2525)
Slettnes, Elisabeth, illus. see Hendren, Trista.
Sleva, Michael, illus. see Wechsler, Kimberly.
Slezak, Roy E. Marsha the Manatee. (p. 1409)
Slick, Jonathan. High Life in New York (Classic Reprint) (p. 968)
—High Life in New York City (Classic Reprint) (p. 968)
Slick, Sam. Season-Ticket (Classic Reprint) (p. 1972)
Slick, Samuel, jt. auth. see Haliburton, Thomas.
Slier, Debby. Babies, Babies (p. 147)
—Babies on the Go! (p. 147)
—Cradle Me (p. 466)
—Loving Me (p. 1362)
Slike, Janet. Take a Closer Look at Your Eyes. (p. 2176)
—Take a Closer Look at Your Heart. (p. 2176)
Slim Goodbody Corp. What's on Myplate? A Guide to Good Nutrition. (p. 2425)
Slim Goodbody Corp., creator. What's on Myplate? A Guide to Good Nutrition. (p. 2425)
Sliney, Will. Ben Reilly: Scarlet Spider Vol. 3: Slingers Return. (p. 199)
—Ben Reilly: Scarlet Spider Vol. 5: Deal with the Devil. (p. 199)
—Spider-Man 2099 Vol. 6: Apocalypse Soon. (p. 2080)
—Star Wars: Galaxy's Edge. (p. 2104)
—Star Wars: the Rise of Kylo Ren. (p. 2105)
Slingerland, Janet. 12 Biggest Breakthroughs in Sports Technology. (p. 2550)
—12 Epic Animal Adventures. (p. 2551)
—12 Epic Races. (p. 2551)
—12 Immigrants Who Made American Sports Great. (p. 2551)
—Coding 1, 2, 3. (p. 412)
—Construction Vehicles. (p. 443)
—Engineering the Eiffel Tower. (p. 652)
—Explore Atoms & Molecules! With 25 Great Projects. Aucoin, Matt, illus. (p. 679)
—History's Forgotten War Stories. (p. 981)
—Hombres Lobo y Estados de la Materia. Mosquito, Angel, illus. (p. 995)
—Military Vehicles. (p. 1467)
—Rescue Vehicles. (p. 1868)
—Secret Lives of Plants! Kemarskaya, Oksana, illus. (p. 1977)
—Sports Science & Technology in the Real World. (p. 2089)
—Superfast Motorcycle Racing. (p. 2159)
—Video Game Coding. (p. 2356)
—Werewolves & States of Matter Mosquito, Angel, illus. (p. 2401)
—What Causes a Rainbow? (p. 2407)
—What Makes the Sky Blue? (p. 2418)
—Wi-Fi. (p. 2460)
Slingerland, Janet & Patrick Weidman. Engineering the Eiffel Tower. (p. 652)
Slingsby, Cecil. Norway, the Northern Playground: Sketches of Climbing & Mountain Exploration in Norway Between 1872 & 1903 (Classic Reprint) (p. 1622)
Slingsby, Henry. My Grandmother's Guests & Their Tales (Classic Reprint) (p. 1548)
—My Grandmother's Guests & Their Tales, Vol. 1 of 2 (Classic Reprint) (p. 1548)
Slingsby, Miki, photos by see Erickson, Paul.
Slinkard, Doreen. Wicky Wacky Farm Stories: Peppi Goes to China. (p. 2460)
Slivensky, Katie. Countdown Conspiracy. (p. 459)
—Seismic Seven. (p. 1985)
Slivers, Ash. Land of the O-O: Facts, Figures, Fables, & Fancies (Classic Reprint) (p. 1242)
—Land of the O-O. (p. 1242)
Sliwerski, Jessica Reid. Cancer Hates Kisses. Song, Mika, illus. (p. 321)
Sloan, Andy. Opinions about Ocean Health: Set Of 6. (p. 1666)
Sloan, Andy & Benchmark Education Co., LLC. Opinions about Ocean Health. (p. 1666)
Sloan, Annie L. Carolinians an Old-Fashioned Love Story of Stirring Times in the Early Colony of Carolina (Classic Reprint) (p. 333)
Sloan, Brian. Tale of Two Summers. (p. 2180)
Sloan, Carolyn. Welcome to Jazz: A Swing-Along Celebration of America's Music, Featuring When the Saints Go Marching In. Gibson, Jessica, illus. (p. 2398)
Sloan, Christopher. Mummies: Dried, Tanned, Sealed, Drained, Frozen, Embalmed, Stuffed, Wrapped, & Smoked... & We're Dead Serious. (p. 1526)
Sloan, Claire. Then You Can See the Sky. (p. 2215)
Sloan, Dave U. Fogy Days & Now, or the World Has Changed (Classic Reprint) (p. 756)
Sloan, Gregory C. My Life with the Stars. (p. 1552)
Sloan, Holly Goldberg. Contar de 7 En 7. (p. 444)
—Counting by 7s. (p. 459)
—Counting By 7s. (p. 460)
—Counting by 7s. (p. 460)
—Pequeña. (p. 1720)
—Short. (p. 2010)
—To Night Owl from Dogfish. (p. 2253)
—To Night Owl from Dogfish 8-Copy SIGNED FD W/ GWP Keychains (p. 2253)
Sloan, Holly Goldberg & Wolitzer, Meg. To Night Owl from Dogfish. (p. 2253)
Sloan, Jaclyn, illus. see Allen, Karen Mutchler.
Sloan, Katharine E. New Sloan Readers: Containing a Complete Course in Phonics. First Reader. (p. 1597)
—New Sloan Readers: Containing a Complete Course in Phonics; Second Reader. (p. 1597)
—New Sloan Readers: Containing a Complete Course in Phonics; Primer (Classic Reprint) (p. 1597)
—New Sloan Readers: Containing a Complete Course in Phonics Second Reader (Classic Reprint) (p. 1597)
—Primary Readers: Containing a Complete Course in Phonics, First Book. (p. 1792)
—Primary Readers, Vol. 2: Containing a Complete Course in Phonics (Classic Reprint) (p. 1792)
Sloan, Katharine Emily. New Sloan Readers: Containing a Complete Course in Phonics; First Reader (Classic Reprint) (p. 1597)
—Primary Readers, Vol. 1: Containing a Complete Course in Phonics (Classic Reprint) (p. 1792)
Sloan, Letarsha. Learning the Alphabet with Jesus. (p. 1258)
Sloan, Lillie. Winifred Rose Armstrong: It Happened. (p. 2473)
Sloan, Mba Claudia & Wilson, Mfa. Ginger Dog or Ginger Bear? La Perrita Ginger o la Osa Ginger? (p. 833)
Sloan, Michael, illus. see Lane, Andy.
Sloan, Michael, illus. see Tompkins, Michael A. & Martinez, Katherine A.
Sloan, Michelle. Baby Deer Rescue (Animal Adventure Club 1) George, Hannah, illus. (p. 149)
—Baby Otter Rescue (Animal Adventure Club 2) George, Hannah, illus. (p. 151)
—Greyfriars Bobby: a Puppy's Tale Bia, Elena, illus. (p. 896)
Sloan, Milo. Jazz It Up. Kris, illus. (p. 1162)
Sloan, Monty, photos by see Hillert, Margaret.
Sloan, Nicole. Mama Needs a Minute. (p. 1392)
Sloan, Peter, illus. see Carroll, Lewis, pseud.
Sloan, Price Stern, jt. auth. see Sexton, Brenda.
Sloan, Price Stern & Mad Libs Staff. Doctor Who Mad Libs. (p. 574)
—Mad Libs Mania. (p. 1373)
Sloan, Price Stern, et al. Flip, Sip, or Mad Libs. (p. 749)
Sloan, S. a. Season of the Demon. (p. 1972)
Sloan, William. Of Bees & Bats of Crocodiles & Cats. (p. 1639)
Sloane, A. D. Twelve Realms. (p. 2303)
Sloane, Julia M. Smiling Hill-Top & Other California Sketches (Classic Reprint) (p. 2042)
Sloane, T. O'Conor. Rapid Arithmetic: Quick & Special Methods in Arithmetical Calculation Together with a Collection of Puzzles & Curiosities of Numbers; Pp. 5-184. (p. 1841)
Sloat, Teri. Pablo in the Snow. Bonnet, Rosalinde, illus. (p. 1690)
—Zip! Zoom! on a Broom. Bonnet, Rosalinde, illus. (p. 2541)
Sloat, Teri, illus. see Winslow, Barbara.
Slobodchikoff, Michael O. Building Hegemonic Order Russia's Way: Order, Stability, & Predictability in the Post-Soviet Space. (p. 294)
Slobodian, Michael. And Away They Went: A Saskatchewan Adventure. (p. 82)
Slobodkin, Louis & Slobodkin, Florence. Too Many Mittens / a Good Place to Hide / the Little Mermaid Who Could Not Sing. (p. 2261)
Slobodkina, E., jt. auth. see Slobodkina, Esphyr.
Slobodkina, Esphyr. Caps for Sale: A Tale of a Peddler, Some Monkeys & Their Monkey Business. Slobodkina, Esphyr, illus. (p. 324)
—Caps for Sale Board Book: A Tale of a Peddler, Some Monkeys & Their Monkey Business. Slobodkina, Esphyr, illus. (p. 324)
Slobodkina, Esphyr & Sayer, Ann Marie Mulhearn. Caps for Sale & the Mindful Monkeys. Slobodkina, Esphyr, illus. (p. 324)
—More Caps for Sale: Another Tale of Mischievous Monkeys. Slobodkina, Esphyr, illus. (p. 1504)
—More Caps for Sale: Another Tale of Mischievous Monkeys Board Book. Slobodkina, Esphyr, illus. (p. 1504)
Slobodkina, Esphyr & Slobodkina, E. Caps for Sale. (p. 324)
Slocombe, Megan. Trip to Italy. (p. 2289)
Slocum, James. Shadow of War. (p. 1997)
Slomski, Genevieve T. Living with Cancer (p. 1334)
Slonecker, Chris, jt. auth. see Slonecker, William T.
Slonim, David. I Loathe You. (p. 1068)
—I Loathe You. Slonim, David, illus. (p. 1068)
Slonim, David, illus. see Bell-Rehwoldt, Sheri.
Slonim, David, illus. see Collins, Pat Lowery.
Slonim, David, illus. see Newman, Lesléa & Newman, Lesléa.
Slonim, David, illus. see Noullet, Georgette.
Slonim, David, illus. see Pearson, Susan.
Slonim, David, illus. see Spinelli, Eileen.
Slonim, David, illus. see Sturgis, Brenda Reeves.
Slonim, David, illus. see Vestergaard, Hope.
Slonim, David, illus. see Wallace, Bill & Wallace, Carol.
Slonim, David, illus. see Yacowitz, Caryn.
Sloop, Hoyt O. Uplift, 1909, Vol. 51 (Classic Reprint) (p. 2338)
—Uplift, Vol. 48: January, 1960 (Classic Reprint) (p. 2338)
—Uplift, Vol. 49: January, 1961 (Classic Reprint) (p. 2338)
—Uplift, Vol. 50: January 1962 (Classic Reprint) (p. 2338)
—Uplift, Vol. 52: January, 1964 (Classic Reprint) (p. 2338)
Sloper, Gilly. Fairies of Jenny's Field. (p. 695)
Slosberg, Susie. This Morning Maxwelton Got up on the Wrong Side. Pacifico, Phyllis, illus. (p. 2226)
Sloss, Robert Thompson. Book of the Automobile: A Practical Volume Devoted to the History Construction, Use & Care of Motor Cars & to the Subject of Motoring in America (Classic Reprint) (p. 260)
Slosson, Annie Trumbull. Aunt Abby's Neighbors (Classic Reprint) (p. 136)
—Aunt Liefy (Classic Reprint) (p. 137)
—Dissatisfied Soul, & a Prophetic Romancer (Classic Reprint) (p. 564)
—Dumb Foxglove: And Other Stories (Classic Reprint) (p. 609)
—Fishin Jimmy (Classic Reprint) (p. 742)
—Heresy of Mehetabel Clark (Classic Reprint) (p. 959)
—Seven Dreamers (Classic Reprint) (p. 1993)
—Simples from the Master's Garden (Classic Reprint) (p. 2022)
—Story-Tell Lib (Classic Reprint) (p. 2135)
—White Christopher (Classic Reprint) (p. 2443)
Slote, Alfred. Hang Tough, Paul Mather. (p. 917)
—Jake. (p. 1155)
Sloth, Ryan. Iowa State Cyclones Football a to Z. (p. 1133)
—Iowa State Fair a to Z. (p. 1133)
Slotsve, Kaoru, tr. see Womack, Rowena.
Slott, Dan. Fantastic Four by Dan Slott Vol. 5: Point of Origin. (p. 707)
Slott, Dan, et al. Phantasm Strikes! Burchett, Rick, illus. (p. 1732)
Slotta, Karen. Case of the Missing Carp. (p. 337)
Slovenski, Peter, jt. auth. see Beaulieu, Michael.
Slover, R. D. Oliver Logan & the Witness Tree. (p. 1649)
Slow, Edward. Wiltshire Moonraker's Edition of West Countrie Rhymes (Classic Reprint) (p. 2470)
Slowinski, Seniha. Rocky Rocks & the Colourful Socks. Roberts, Nick, illus. (p. 1896)
Sloyer, Elliot. Safety Pin: Summer Camp Stories. Guiza, Victor, illus. (p. 1922)
Sloyer, Sarah. Dumpling Cats Coloring Book with Stickers. (p. 610)
Slubby & Hobo. Elixirs of Life & Death. (p. 636)
Sluiter, Vicky. Oliver's Moving Day. (p. 1650)
Slusar, Julia, ed. see AZ Books Staff.
Slutsky, Adam & Croce, Pat. Plunder ARC. (p. 1763)
Sluyterman van Langeweyde, Ira, illus. see Hosch, Amanda.
Sly, Costard. Sayings & Doings at the Tremont House, Vol. 2: In the Year 1832 (Classic Reprint) (p. 1940)
Sly, Stacey. What Should I Eat? Gentry, Susana, photos by. (p. 2420)
Sly, William James. World Stories Retold for Modern Boys & Girls (Classic Reprint) (p. 2505)
Slyke, Lucille Van. Little Miss. by-The-Day (Classic Reprint) (p. 1322)
Slyke, Rebecca van. Lana Lynn Howls at the Moon Sandu, Anca, illus. (p. 1241)
Slyke, Rebecca Van, see Van Slyke, Rebecca.
Smalbach, Richard, ed. Capitalism. (p. 324)
Smale, Denise L. Santa I Moved! (p. 1932)
—What If the Sun Didn't Rise. Smale, Denise L. & Blowars, Ryan, illus. (p. 2413)
Smale, H. Serio-Comico-(Canino)-Polyglottos (Classic Reprint) (p. 1991)
Smale, Holly. Geek Girl. (p. 813)
—Geek Girl: Model Misfit. (p. 813)
—Geek Girl: Picture Perfect. (p. 813)
Small, A. K. Bright Burning Stars. (p. 281)
Small, Adrienne H. If You Ask a Scientist a Question. Blair, Tim, illus. (p. 1092)
Small, Albion W. Meaning of Social Science. (p. 1434)
Small, Brian C. Wake up Ponte Vedra. Nielson, Ginger a, illus. (p. 2371)
Small, Cathleen. 20 Great Career-Building Activities Using Facebook. (p. 2553)
—American Life & Communication from the Telephone to Twitter. (p. 72)
—Barbara Mcclintock: Cytogeneticist & Discoverer of Mobile Genetic Elements. (p. 165)
—Baseball. (p. 168)
—Basketball. (p. 170)
—Becoming a U. S. Citizen. (p. 187)
—Bessie Coleman: First African American & Native American Pilot. (p. 205)
—Carpenter. (p. 333)
—Chelsea Clinton: Democratic Campaigner & Advocate. (p. 365)
—Chelsea Manning: Intelligence Analyst. (p. 365)
—Claudette Colvin: Civil Rights Activist (p. 401)
—Cloning. (p. 406)
—Code Breakers & Spies of World War II. (p. 411)
—Collapse of Communism & the Break up of the Soviet Union. (p. 414)
—Colonial Interactions with Native Americans. (p. 418)
—Crossing the Border. (p. 478)
—Deportation. (p. 529)
—Fab Lab Creating with Vinyl Cutters. (p. 690)
—Football. (p. 761)
—Frankenstein's Monster. (p. 778)
—History of Immigration. (p. 978)
—Hockey. (p. 985)
—How Plants Grow. (p. 1034)
—How to Start an Online Business. (p. 1044)
—Immigrants of Extraordinary Ability. (p. 1101)
—Interracial Marriage: Loving V. Virginia. (p. 1127)
—Lacrosse. (p. 1235)
—Legend of Sleepy Hollow: The Headless Horseman. Antal, Lara, illus. (p. 1262)
—Make the Most of Facebook & Other Social Media. (p. 1387)
—Manchester United FC (p. 1396)
—Melinda Gates: Philanthropist & Education Advocate. (p. 1443)

Full bibliographic information is available on the Title Index page number referenced in parentheses at the end of each entry

—Mike Lupica. (p. 1464)
—Mummies. (p. 1526)
—Organ Transplants. (p. 1670)
—Partition of Ireland. (p. 1701)
—Science of Mind Control & Telepathy. (p. 1958)
—Soccer. (p. 2051)
—Spelling & Vocabulary. (p. 2079)
—Strategic Inventions of the Korean War. (p. 2139)
—Strategic Inventions of the Vietnam War. (p. 2139)
—Surveillance & Your Right to Privacy. (p. 2164)
—U. S. Borders. (p. 2312)
—Undocumented Immigrants. (p. 2326)
—Using VR in Medicine (p. 2342)
—What Are Hardware & Software? (p. 2405)
—Who Are Conservatives & What Do They Believe In? (p. 2446)
—Wind, Waves, & the Sun: The Rise of Alternative Energy. (p. 2471)
Small, Cathleen, contrib. by. Colonial Interactions with Native Americans. (p. 418)
Small, Charlie. Daredevil Desperados of Destiny. (p. 505)
—Piratas de la Isla Perfidia. Isern, Carol, tr. (p. 1749)
Small, David. Imogene Comes Back! (p. 1101)
—Imogene's Antlers. (p. 1101)
Small, David, illus. see Appelt, Kathi.
Small, David, illus. see Armstrong, Jennifer.
Small, David, illus. see Ashman, Linda.
Small, David, illus. see Broach, Elise.
Small, David, illus. see Buzzeo, Toni.
Small, David, illus. see Cronin, Doreen.
Small, David, illus. see Durand, Hallie.
Small, David, illus. see Henson, Heather.
Small, David, illus. see Hoban, Russell.
Small, David, illus. see Howland, Naomi.
Small, David, illus. see Kennedy, Edward M.
Small, David, illus. see Sandburg, Carl.
Small, David, illus. see St. George, Judith.
Small, David, illus. see Stewart, Sarah.
Small, David, illus. see Weeks, Sarah.
Small, Divannah. From Abandoned to Above. (p. 790)
Small, Evelyn Robin, jt. ed. see Curtis, Chasity L.
Small, Jan, illus. see Dicello, Bob.
Small, Jessi Leigh, illus. see David, Joan Mitchell.
Small, Lily. Bailey the Bunny. (p. 159)
—Bella the Bunny: Fairy Animals of Misty Wood. (p. 197)
—Chloe the Kitten: Fairy Animals of Misty Wood. (p. 380)
—Daisy the Deer: Fairy Animals of Misty Wood. (p. 498)
—Hailey the Hedgehog. (p. 909)
—Kylie the Kitten. (p. 1234)
—Mia the Mouse: Fairy Animals of Misty Wood. (p. 1456)
—Paddy the Puppy. (p. 1692)
—Paige the Pony. (p. 1692)
—Penny the Puppy (p. 1717)
—Penny the Puppy: Fairy Animals of Misty Wood. (p. 1717)
—Penny the Puppy. (p. 1717)
—Poppy the Pony: Fairy Animals of Misty Wood. (p. 1776)
—Poppy the Pony. (p. 1776)
—Poppy the Pony & Hailey the Hedgehog Bindup: Fairy Animals of Misty Wood. (p. 1776)
Small, Martin. Meet MR Love & Mrs You & Their Wonderful Planet. Davies, Joe, illus. (p. 1438)
Small, Pat. Muffin-Pan Baby. (p. 1524)
Small, Rachel, ed. see Hinchcliffe, Christopher.
Small, Rachel, jt. auth. see Kissock, Heather.
Small, Shannon, illus. see Dixon, Nasheema S.
Small, Steve, illus. see Prasadam-Halls, Smriti.
Small, Vanessa. Mystery at Pleasant Park. Small, Vanessa, illus. (p. 1568)
Small World Creations. Baby Animals. (p. 148)
—Chalkboard Christmas. (p. 354)
—Farm Animals. (p. 709)
—In the Garden. (p. 1109)
—Woodland Animals. (p. 2491)
small world creations, Laura-Anne. Click, Click! Magic Pictures Change Color in Water! Robjohns, Laura-Anne, illus. (p. 404)
small world creations ltd. Blubb, Blubb! (p. 247)
—Splish Splash. (p. 2085)
Small World Creations Ltd. Zippy Wheels: Diggers. (p. 2541)
—Zippy Wheels: Dump Trucks. (p. 2541)
—Zippy Wheels: Firetrucks. (p. 2541)
—Zippy Wheels: Tractors. (p. 2541)
Small World Creations, Small World. Busy Bee's Garden! Haines, Emma, illus. (p. 302)
—Glub, Glub! Magic Pictures Change Color in Water! Robjohns, Laura-Anne, illus. (p. 845)
Small World Creations Staff. Ladybug's Pond. (p. 1239)
Small, Wylie J. Great Prune Caper. (p. 888)
Smalley, Carol. Exploring Earth's Biomes. (p. 681)
—Green Changes You Can Make Around the House. (p. 893)
—Project Guide to Fishes & Amphibians. (p. 1806)
—Project Guide to Sponges, Worms, & Mollusks. (p. 1806)
Smalley, Carol Parenzan. Care for a Pet Hamster. (p. 328)
Smalley, Jack. Movie Classic, Vol. 11: September, 1936 (Classic Reprint) (p. 1516)
Smalley, Ruth Ann. Sheila Says We're Weird Emery, Jennifer, illus. (p. 2005)
Smallman, Michelle. Adventures of the Traveling Glasses. Gonzalez, Julian, illus. (p. 28)
—Aventures d'une Paire de Lunettes en Voyage. Gonzalez, Julian, illus. (p. 142)
Smallman, Steve. Cock-A-Doodle-Poo! Weiser, Florence, illus. (p. 410)
—Friend for Bear. Pedler, Caroline, illus. (p. 786)
—I'm Not Grumpy! (p. 1098)
—Nativity: Step by Step with Steve Smallman. (p. 1579)
—Noah & the Animals: Step-by-Step with Steve Smallman. (p. 1615)
—Not-So-Brave Penguin: A Story about Overcoming Fears. Smallman, Steve, illus. (p. 1623)
—Poo in the Zoo. Grey, Ada, illus. (p. 1773)
—Santa Is Coming to Alabama. Dunn, Robert, illus. (p. 1932)
—Santa Is Coming to Alaska. Dunn, Robert, illus. (p. 1932)
—Santa Is Coming to Arkansas. Dunn, Robert, illus. (p. 1932)
—Santa Is Coming to Boston. Dunn, Robert, illus. (p. 1932)
—Santa Is Coming to Buffalo. Dunn, Robert, illus. (p. 1932)
—Santa Is Coming to Calgary. Dunn, Robert, illus. (p. 1932)
—Santa Is Coming to California. Dunn, Robert, illus. (p. 1932)
—Santa Is Coming to Canada. Dunn, Robert, illus. (p. 1932)
—Santa Is Coming to Colorado. Dunn, Robert, illus. (p. 1932)
—Santa Is Coming to Connecticut. Dunn, Robert, illus. (p. 1932)
—Santa Is Coming to Dallas. Dunn, Robert, illus. (p. 1932)
—Santa Is Coming to Delaware. Dunn, Robert, illus. (p. 1932)
—Santa Is Coming to Edmonton. Dunn, Robert, illus. (p. 1932)
—Santa Is Coming to Florida. Dunn, Robert, illus. (p. 1932)
—Santa Is Coming to Georgia. Dunn, Robert, illus. (p. 1932)
—Santa Is Coming to Hawaii. Dunn, Robert, illus. (p. 1932)
—Santa Is Coming to Idaho. Dunn, Robert, illus. (p. 1932)
—Santa Is Coming to Illinois. Dunn, Robert, illus. (p. 1932)
—Santa Is Coming to Indiana. Dunn, Robert, illus. (p. 1932)
—Santa Is Coming to Iowa. Dunn, Robert, illus. (p. 1932)
—Santa Is Coming to Kansas. Dunn, Robert, illus. (p. 1932)
—Santa Is Coming to Kansas City. Dunn, Robert, illus. (p. 1932)
—Santa Is Coming to Kentucky. Dunn, Robert, illus. (p. 1932)
—Santa Is Coming to Louisiana. Dunn, Robert, illus. (p. 1932)
—Santa Is Coming to Maine. Dunn, Robert, illus. (p. 1932)
—Santa Is Coming to Maryland. Dunn, Robert, illus. (p. 1932)
—Santa Is Coming to Massachusetts. Dunn, Robert, illus. (p. 1932)
—Santa Is Coming to Minnesota. Dunn, Robert, illus. (p. 1932)
—Santa Is Coming to Mississippi. Dunn, Robert, illus. (p. 1932)
—Santa Is Coming to Montana. Dunn, Robert, illus. (p. 1932)
—Santa Is Coming to Nashville. Dunn, Robert, illus. (p. 1932)
—Santa Is Coming to Nebraska. Dunn, Robert, illus. (p. 1932)
—Santa Is Coming to Nevada. Dunn, Robert, illus. (p. 1932)
—Santa Is Coming to New Hampshire. Dunn, Robert, illus. (p. 1932)
—Santa Is Coming to New Jersey. Dunn, Robert, illus. (p. 1932)
—Santa Is Coming to Newfoundland. Dunn, Robert, illus. (p. 1932)
—Santa Is Coming to North Carolina. Dunn, Robert, illus. (p. 1932)
—Santa Is Coming to Nova Scotia. Dunn, Robert, illus. (p. 1932)
—Santa Is Coming to Ohio. Dunn, Robert, illus. (p. 1932)
—Santa Is Coming to Oklahoma. Dunn, Robert, illus. (p. 1932)
—Santa Is Coming to Oregon. Dunn, Robert, illus. (p. 1932)
—Santa Is Coming to Pennsylvania. Dunn, Robert, illus. (p. 1932)
—Santa Is Coming to Pittsburgh. Dunn, Robert, illus. (p. 1932)
—Santa Is Coming to Portland. Dunn, Robert, illus. (p. 1932)
—Santa Is Coming to Rhode Island. Dunn, Robert, illus. (p. 1932)
—Santa Is Coming to San Diego. Dunn, Robert, illus. (p. 1932)
—Santa Is Coming to San Francisco. Dunn, Robert, illus. (p. 1932)
—Santa Is Coming to South Carolina. Dunn, Robert, illus. (p. 1932)
—Santa Is Coming to South Dakota. Dunn, Robert, illus. (p. 1932)
—Santa Is Coming to Tennessee. Dunn, Robert, illus. (p. 1932)
—Santa Is Coming to Texas. Dunn, Robert, illus. (p. 1932)
—Santa Is Coming to Toronto. Dunn, Robert, illus. (p. 1932)
—Santa Is Coming to Utah. Dunn, Robert, illus. (p. 1932)
—Santa Is Coming to Vancouver. Dunn, Robert, illus. (p. 1932)
—Santa Is Coming to Vermont. Dunn, Robert, illus. (p. 1932)
—Santa Is Coming to Virginia. Dunn, Robert, illus. (p. 1932)
—Santa Is Coming to Washington. Dunn, Robert, illus. (p. 1932)
—Santa Is Coming to Washington, D. C. Dunn, Robert, illus. (p. 1932)
—Santa Is Coming to West Virginia. Dunn, Robert, illus. (p. 1933)
—Santa Is Coming to Wisconsin. Dunn, Robert, illus. (p. 1933)
—Santa Is Coming to Wyoming. Dunn, Robert, illus. (p. 1933)
—Very Greedy Bee. Tickle, Jack, illus. (p. 2353)
—Wolves Who Came for Dinner. (p. 2485)
—Wolves Who Came for Dinner. Driedemy, Joelle, illus. (p. 2485)
Smallman, Steve, illus. see David, Juliet.
Smallman, Steve, illus. see Ellis, Gwen.
Smallman, Steve, jt. auth. see James, Eric.
Smallman, Steve, et al. My First Santa&'s Coming to Michigan. Dunn, Robert, illus. (p. 1545)
—My First Santa&'s Coming to Minnesota. Dunn, Robert, illus. (p. 1545)
—My First Santa&'s Coming to New Jersey. Dunn, Robert, illus. (p. 1545)
—My First Santa&'s Coming to Ohio. Dunn, Robert, illus. (p. 1545)
—My First Santa&'s Coming to Texas. Dunn, Robert, illus. (p. 1545)
—My First Santa's Coming to My House. Dunn, Robert, illus. (p. 1545)
Smalls, David, illus. see Stewart, Sarah.
Smalls, Irene. My Nana & Me. Johnson, Cathy Ann, illus. (p. 1557)
Smalls, June. Celtic Gods, Heroes, & Mythology. (p. 351)
—We Need Prairie Dogs. (p. 2392)
Smallshot, Jasper. Squibs & Crackers: Serious, Comical & Tender (Classic Reprint) (p. 2094)
Smallwood, Edward. Czar, Vol. 1 Of 3: Ivan Vassilivitch, the Terrible (Classic Reprint) (p. 493)
—Czar, Vol. 3 Of 3: Ivan Vassilivitch, the Terrible (Classic Reprint) (p. 493)
—Manuella, the Executioner's Daughter, Vol. 1 Of 3: A Story of Madrid (Classic Reprint) (p. 1399)
Smallwood, John, jt. auth. see Hareas, John.
Smallwood, John, jt. auth. see Ladewski, Paul.
Smallwood, Richelle. Be Brave. (p. 177)
—Small Frye: Alexandra's Giant Dreams. (p. 2039)
Smallwood, Saily & Jones, Bryony. Circle. Fox, Rebecca, illus. (p. 392)
—Rectangle. Fox, Rebecca, illus. (p. 1855)
—Square. Fox, Rebecca, illus. (p. 2094)
—Triangle. Fox, Rebecca, illus. (p. 2286)
Smart, Andy. Bob'n Joe Book One: Lunch Time. Smart, Andy, illus. (p. 252)
Smart, Andy, illus. see Brown, Adam.
Smart, Andy, jt. auth. see Brown, Adam.
Smart Apple Media Staff, jt. auth. see MacDonald, Margaret.
Smart Apple Media Staff, jt. auth. see Selwyn, Josephine.
Smart, Brooke, illus. see Saks, Dan.
Smart, Chiquila. I Want to Be a Rainbow. (p. 1084)
Smart Ed D, Jacqueline Yvonne. What Makes a Bully? (p. 2418)
Smart, Ed D. Jacqueline Yvonne. What Makes a Bully? (p. 2418)
Smart, Hawley. At Fault, Vol. 1 Of 3: A Novel (Classic Reprint) (p. 129)
—Beatrice & Benedick: A Romance of the Crimea (Classic Reprint) (p. 183)
—Beatrice & Benedick, Vol. 1: A Romance of the Crimea (Classic Reprint) (p. 183)
—Beatrice & Benedick, Vol. 2 Of 2: A Romance of the Crimea (Classic Reprint) (p. 183)
—Bitter Is the Rind, Vol. 1 of 3 (Classic Reprint) (p. 235)
—Bound to Win, Vol. 1 Of 3: A Tale of the Turf (Classic Reprint) (p. 265)
—Bound to Win, Vol. 2 Of 3: A Tale of the Turf (Classic Reprint) (p. 265)
—Bound to Win, Vol. 3 Of 3: A Tale of the Turf (Classic Reprint) (p. 265)
—Breezie Langton: A Story of 'Fifty-Two to 'Fifty-Five' (Classic Reprint) (p. 279)
—Breezie Langton, Vol. 1 Of 3: A Story of Fifty-Two to Fifty-Five (Classic Reprint) (p. 279)
—Broken Bonds, Vol. 1 of 3 (Classic Reprint) (p. 284)
—Broken Bonds, Vol. 2 of 3 (Classic Reprint) (p. 284)
—Broken Bonds, Vol. 3 of 3 (Classic Reprint) (p. 284)
—Cecile, Vol. 1 Of 3: Or Modern Idolaters (Classic Reprint) (p. 348)
—Cecile, Vol. 2 Of 3: Or, Modern Idolaters (Classic Reprint) (p. 348)
—Courtship in Seventeen Hundred & Twenty & in Eighteen Hundred & Sixty: Romances of Two Centuries (Classic Reprint) (p. 463)
—Courtship in Seventeen Hundred & Twenty, Vol. 1 Of 2: In Eighteen Hundred & Sixty (Classic Reprint) (p. 463)
—Courtship, Vol. 2 Of 2: In Seventeen Hundred & Twenty, in Eighteen Hundred & Sixty (Classic Reprint) (p. 463)
—False Cards (Classic Reprint) (p. 701)
—False Start, Vol. 1 Of 3: A Novel (Classic Reprint) (p. 701)
—False Start, Vol. 2: A Novel (Classic Reprint) (p. 701)
—False Start, Vol. 3 Of 3: A Novel (Classic Reprint) (p. 701)
—From Post to Finis, Vol. 3 Of 3: A Novel (Classic Reprint) (p. 793)
—From Post to Finish, Vol. 1 Of 3: A Novel (Classic Reprint) (p. 793)
—Great Tontine: A Novel (Classic Reprint) (p. 890)
—Hard Lines: A Novel (Classic Reprint) (p. 929)
—Hard Lines. (p. 929)
—Hard Lines, Vol. 1 Of 3: A Novel (Classic Reprint) (p. 929)
—Hard Lines, Vol. 2 Of 3: A Novel (Classic Reprint) (p. 929)
—Hard Lines, Vol. 3 Of 3: A Novel (Classic Reprint) (p. 929)
—Long Odds, Vol. 1 Of 3: A Novel (Classic Reprint) (p. 1343)
—Long Odds, Vol. 2 Of 3: A Novel (Classic Reprint) (p. 1343)
—Long Odds, Vol. 3 Of 3: A Novel (Classic Reprint) (p. 1343)
—Master of Rathkelly, Vol. 2 Of 2: A Novel (Classic Reprint) (p. 1418)
—Modern Idolaters, Vol. 3 of 3 (Classic Reprint) (p. 1487)
—Plunger: A Turf Tragedy of Five-And-Twenty Years Ago (Classic Reprint) (p. 1763)
—Race for a Wife: A Novel (Classic Reprint) (p. 1831)
—Racing Rubber: A Novel (Classic Reprint) (p. 1832)
—Racing Rubber. (p. 1832)
—Saddle & Sabre: A Novel (Classic Reprint) (p. 1921)
—Saddle & Sabre, Vol. 1 Of 3: A Novel (Classic Reprint) (p. 1921)
—Sunshine & Snow, Vol. 1 Of 3: A Novel (Classic Reprint) (p. 2153)
—Sunshine & Snow, Vol. 2: A Novel (Classic Reprint) (p. 2153)
—Tie & Trick: A Melodramatic Story (Classic Reprint) (p. 2240)
—Tie & Trick. (p. 2240)
—Tie & Trick, Vol. 3 Of 3: A Melodramatic Story (Classic Reprint) (p. 2240)
—Without Love or Licence: A Tale of South Devon (Classic Reprint) (p. 2482)
—Without Love or Licence. (p. 2482)
—Without Love or Licence a Tale of South Devon, Vol. 1 of 3 (Classic Reprint) (p. 2482)
Smart, Jamie. Bunny vs. Monkey. Smart, Jamie, illus. (p. 298)
—Bunny vs. Monkey Book 3. (p. 298)
—Bunny vs. Monkey: Book Three. (p. 298)
—Where's the Doctor? (p. 2440)
Smart, Karen a. Shattered but Sheltered: The Aftermath of Childhood Sexual Assault. (p. 2003)
Smart Kids Publishing Staff, ed. see Berry, Ron.
Smart Kidz, ed. see Berry, Ron.
Smart Kidz, ed. see Mead, David.
Smart Kidz, ed. see Weimer, Heidi R.
Smart Kidz, creator. 123s of How I Love You. (p. 2559)
—ABC's of How I Love You: You're My Alphabet of Love! (p. 4)
—I'm a Little Teapot. (p. 1097)
—It's Potty Time for Boys. (p. 1147)
—Itsy Bitsy Spider. (p. 1148)
—Jesus Loves Me! (p. 1166)
—Jesus Loves the Little Children. (p. 1166)
—Jingle Bells. (p. 1169)
—This Is the Way We Take a Bath. (p. 2225)
—This Little Piggy Went to Market. (p. 2226)
Smart Kidz, ed. It's Potty Time for Girls. Sharp, Chris, illus. (p. 1147)
—It's Potty Time for Girls. Sharp, Chris & Currant, Gary, illus. (p. 1147)
Smart Kidz Media. Love Bug: Sad. (p. 1359)
Smart Kidz Media, creator. O Christmas Tree! (p. 1633)
—Silent Night. (p. 2017)
—Up on the Housetop! (p. 2338)
Smart Kidz Media Studios Staff, ed. It's Bedtime! (p. 1144)
Smart, Kyle, illus. see Nickel, Scott & Evanier, Mark.
Smarter Activity Books. Absolute Best Way to Find It... Hidden Pictures to Find Activity Book for Adults. (p. 9)
—Awesome Doodles to Color, Coloring Book. (p. 144)
—Be a Leader! a Maze Activity Book. (p. 176)
—Behind the Scenes at a Symphony Coloring Book. (p. 193)
—Best Designs to Color: Bushy Tailed Animals, a Coloring Book. (p. 205)
—Beware of the Dead End! a Challenging Maze Activity Book. (p. 211)
—Big Eyes in the Sea: A Coloring Book. (p. 220)
—Blaze a New Trail! a Great Maze Activity Book. (p. 243)
—Blowdryers, Bouffants & Brushes Coloring Book. (p. 247)
—Butterfly Designs to Color & Relax, a Coloring Book. (p. 304)
—Cathedral of Light Stained Glass Coloring Book. (p. 344)
—Classic Accessories: Coloring Vintage Ornaments. (p. 400)
—Color the Tension Away: An Adult Mandala Coloring Book. (p. 421)
—Color Victorian Ladies: A Coloring Book. (p. 421)
—Coloring & Loving It - Adults Coloring Books Super Fun - Vol 1. (p. 422)
—Coloring Fashion Designs, a Coloring Book. (p. 425)
—Coloring for Your Spiritual Side: Sacred Mandala Coloring Book. (p. 425)
—Coloring Mandalas, Relax by Coloring Coloring Book. (p. 425)
—Complex Coloring Fun for Adults - Volume 1. (p. 436)
—Create Balance: An Adult Mandala Coloring Book. (p. 469)
—Creating Art: Jumbo Coloring Book for Adults. (p. 470)
—Creative Snow People: Snow Zombies & More Coloring Book. (p. 471)
—Cultures That Designed Totem Poles Coloring Book. (p. 485)
—Doodle the Ancient World. (p. 584)
—Easy Mandalas for Relaxation Coloring Book. (p. 620)
—Entertaining Entanglements! Adult Maze Activity Book. (p. 656)
—Eternity of Love, Happiness, & Dreams Come True Coloring Book. (p. 666)
—Extreme Coloring: A Mother & Child Coloring Book. (p. 686)
—Extreme Elephant Mandalas to Color Coloring Book. (p. 686)
—Fly Away! Beautiful Birds Coloring Book Edition. (p. 754)
—Great Adventures in the World of Nature Coloring Book. (p. 883)
—Green Sand Beaches of the Big Island Coloring Book. (p. 894)
—Harrowing Tales of Magic Gone Wrong Coloring Book. (p. 934)
—Honu the Hawaiian Sea Turtle Coloring Book. (p. 1000)
—It's the Art I Love! Coloring Book. (p. 1147)
—Journey Whales Take: The Exciting Coloring Book. (p. 1183)
—Let's Escape the Maze! Maze Activity Book. (p. 1271)
—Looking for Love: An Adult Activity Book of Hidden Pictures. (p. 1347)
—Lost Art: A Hidden Pictures Book for Adults. (p. 1352)
—Lost but Not Forgotten. the Ultimate Search & Find Activity Book. (p. 1353)
—Lost in a Box of Chocolates! Valentine's Day Hidden Picture Activity Book. (p. 1354)
—Lost in Space: An Activity Book for Adults with Hidden Pictures. (p. 1354)
—Lounging by the Poolside Activity Book. (p. 1358)
—Love Is in the Air: Seek & Find Activity Book. (p. 1360)
—Manga Dissected: Steps to Improving Your Drawing Prowess Activity Book. (p. 1397)
—Marvelous Mazes! a Challenging Adult Activity Book. (p. 1413)
—Mastering the Art of Manga! a How to Draw Activity Book. (p. 1419)
—Mazes for Adults - Mind Busters - Twist & Turn Activity Book. (p. 1431)
—Mischievous Fairies & Their Tricks Coloring Book. (p. 1477)
—Oodles of Hilarious Doodles! Oodles of Coloring Designs Coloring Book. (p. 1665)
—Orchids at Home & in the Wild Coloring Book. (p. 1669)
—Paintings, Sculptures & Other Artwork Coloring Book. (p. 1693)
—Popular Doll Fashions by Decade Coloring Book. (p. 1777)
—Popular Jack-O-Lantern Brain Designs Coloring Book. (p. 1777)
—Popular Motorcycle Helmet Designs Coloring Book. (p. 1777)
—Popular Theater & Play Masks Coloring Book. (p. 1777)
—Popular Volkswagen Beetle Designs Coloring Book. (p. 1777)
—Pots & Vases for Fancy Flowers Coloring Book. (p. 1781)
—Practice Mindfulness with Mandalas: An Adult Coloring Book. (p. 1784)
—Put It Together! the Jigsaw Puzzle Coloring Book. (p. 1817)
—Relax into the Circles Coloring Book. (p. 1862)
—Simple & Easy Mandalas Coloring Book. (p. 2021)
—Simple Coloring: A Butterfly Ornament Coloring Book. (p. 2021)
—Stress Relief Through Coloring. (p. 2141)
—Super Sleuth Amazing Maze Challenge Adult Activity Book. (p. 2158)
—Supreme Maze Collection: Kids Activity Book. (p. 2162)
—Swinging 70s Hippie Hair Coloring Book. (p. 2170)
—Think Green! St. Patrick's Day Coloring Book. (p. 2221)
—Toasters & Microwaves: Modern Kitchen Coloring Book. (p. 2254)
—Top Modern Motorcycle Designs Coloring Book. (p. 2263)
—Top Papier Mache Mask Designs Coloring Book. (p. 2263)
—Top Prom Corsage Choices Coloring Book. (p. 2263)
—Top Winter Traditions Coloring Book. (p. 2264)
—Totem Pole Animals & Other Symbols Coloring Book. (p. 2267)
—Totem Pole Designs by Region Coloring Book. (p. 2267)
—Totem Pole Peoples & Their Art Coloring Book. (p. 2267)
—Tranquil & Calm Surroundings Coloring Book. (p. 2277)
—Two Heartbreakers in Love Coloring Book. (p. 2308)
—Types of Totem Poles Coloring Book. (p. 2310)
—What YA Look'n at! Cross Eyed Coloring Book. (p. 2422)
—Where Is It? Hidden Picture to Find Activities for Adults. (p. 2437)

—Where Is It? the Absolute Best Hidden Picture to Find Activities for Adults. (p. 2437)
—Where Is It? the Very Best Hidden Picture to Find Activities for Adults. (p. 2438)
—Where to Run? the Ultimate Maze Challenge Activity Book. (p. 2440)
—Where'd It Go? Hidden Pictures to Find Activities for Adults. (p. 2440)
—Which Way Do I Go? a Maze Activity Book. (p. 2441)
—Wild Pack Animals Coloring Book. (p. 2464)
—Winding, Wandering Webs! a Challenging & Fun Adult Level Maze Activity Book. (p. 2472)
—Woo-Hootie-Too! Wacky Whistlers Coloring Book. (p. 2491)
—Yoshi! Anime Artist How to Drawing & Activity Book. (p. 2523)
—Zen Doodle Monsters Coloring Book. (p. 2539)
Smarter Activity Books for Kids. #1 Children's Dot to Dot Puzzle Book. (p. 2546)
—2 Cute Baby Angels with Wings Coloring Book. (p. 2546)
—3-In-1 Learning Activity Book for Kids. (p. 2547)
—Absolute Best Connecting the Dots for Young Children. (p. 9)
—Absolute Best Cut Out Activity Book for Kids. (p. 9)
—Absolute Best Cut Out Activity Book for Kids Activity Book. (p. 9)
—Absolute Best Dot to Dot for Children. (p. 9)
—Absolute Best Hidden Pictures to Find Activity Book for Kids: Where Is It? Activity Book. (p. 9)
—Absolute Best How to Draw Activity Book for Kids Activity Book. (p. 9)
—Absolute Drawing Basics for Kids Activity Book. (p. 9)
—Activities That Make Kids Smile Mazes Edition. (p. 13)
—Activity Adventure Book for Kids Activity Book. (p. 13)
—Activity Alley! Kids Activity Book. (p. 13)
—Activity Central! Kids Activity Book. (p. 13)
—Adorable Babies: Babysitting Fun Coloring & Puzzle Book. (p. 17)
—Advanced Kid's Maze Activity Book. (p. 18)
—Adventures in Coloring: Big Eyed Sea Creatures Coloring Book. (p. 20)
—Adventures in Thinking! Kids Challenge Mega Awesome Activity Book. (p. 20)
—African Dancing & You Coloring Book. (p. 32)
—All Fun Activities for Kids Coloring Book. (p. 52)
—All Kids Cut, Color & Create Activity Book. (p. 52)
—All Shades of Green! Tree Shapes Coloring Book. (p. 53)
—Alphabet Expert's Connect the Dots Activity Book. (p. 59)
—Amazing Artist's How to Draw Activity Book. (p. 64)
—Amazing Baby Birds to Color Coloring Book. (p. 64)
—Amazing Book of Mazes: Kids Activity Book. (p. 64)
—Amazing Maze Collection: Kids Activity Book. (p. 65)
—Amazing World of Drawing! How to Draw Activity Book. (p. 67)
—American Women Role Models Coloring Book. (p. 74)
—Animal Dot to Dot Activity Book. (p. 89)
—Animals Have Shadows, Too! an Activity Book. (p. 94)
—Animals in the Wild Coloring Book. (p. 95)
—Antibodies & More: Immune System Coloring Book. (p. 102)
—Are You Gonna Wear That? Clothes Dot to Dot. (p. 113)
—Art of Animals: A Children's Coloring Book. (p. 121)
—Art Sleuth in Action! Connect the Dots Activity Book. (p. 122)
—Artist's Guide: How to Draw Activity Book. (p. 123)
—Artsy & Cute Animals Coloring Book. (p. 124)
—Attack of the Thunder Lizards! Super Dinosaur Coloring Book. (p. 135)
—Baby Birds Coloring Book & Journal Coloring Book. (p. 149)
—Barns to Bars: Buildings with One Purpose Coloring Book. (p. 167)
—Basketball Dreams: A Sports Coloring Book. (p. 171)
—Be an Artist! a Dot to Dot Activity Book. (p. 176)
—Beautiful Shapes: A Great Dot to Dot Activity Book. (p. 184)
—Beep Beep: Gadget Coloring Book. (p. 189)
—Beginner's Guide to Drawing: How to Draw for Beginners. (p. 192)
—Beginning Artist: Connect the Dots Activity Book. (p. 192)
—Bicycles, Buses & Green Transportation a Coloring Book. (p. 215)
—Big & Beautiful: Vehicles Coloring Book. (p. 216)
—Big Beak Bird Feathers Coloring Book. (p. 216)
—Big Mazes Across the Pages! Kids Maze Activity Book. (p. 221)
—Bird & Fowl Coloringbook. (p. 230)
—Birds of Every Shade Coloring Book. (p. 232)
—Birds That Will Make You Laugh Coloring Book. (p. 232)
—Black Cats That Scare the Pants off of You. (p. 237)
—Blooming Flowers, Falling Leaves, & Flowing Waters Coloring Book. (p. 247)
—Boom! Crash! Drawing Comics in Easy Steps Activity Book. (p. 261)
—Boredom Crusher for Boys Activity Book. (p. 262)
—Boys' Clubhouse: No Girls Allowed Activity Book. (p. 272)
—Brain-Bending Mazes! Kids Maze Activity Book. (p. 274)
—Brass Instruments Are Fab! a Coloring Book. (p. 276)
—Bright Skies & Beautiful Country Coloring Book. (p. 281)
—Building up to Colors: A Construction Based Coloring Book. (p. 295)
—Bunnies, Ducks, & Other Barnyard Cuties! My Adorable Farm Animal Coloring Book. (p. 298)
—Butterflies & Caterpillars! a Maze Activity Book. (p. 303)
—Butterfly Ornaments for Kids, a Coloring Book. (p. 304)
—By Menorah Light: A Hanukkah Coloring Book. (p. 305)
—Camping Is Fun! a Maze Activity Book. (p. 316)
—Can You Find These Things? Seek & Find Activity Book. (p. 318)
—Can You See Invisible Art? Connect the Dots Activity Book. (p. 318)
—Can You See the Picture? a Dot to Dot Activity Book. (p. 319)
—Can You See What I See? — Hidden Pictures. (p. 319)
—Car Trip Fun! Boys' Activity Book. (p. 327)
—Car Trip Play Time! Fun & Quiet Children's Activity Book. (p. 327)
—Careers in Water Sports Coloring Book. (p. 330)
—Caring for Mothers & Grandmothers Coloring Book. (p. 331)
—Castles, Knights & Dragons Coloring Book. (p. 340)
—Cat Stepped in the Pumpkin Pie Coloring Book. (p. 342)
—Cattle Round-Up: Working the Farm Coloring Book. (p. 346)
—Caves, Mines & Other Dwarven Places Coloring Book. (p. 347)
—Characters from the Ninja Kids Movie Coloring Book. (p. 358)
—Chicks, Ducklings & Other Baby Birds Coloring Book. (p. 369)
—Children's Creative Escape: Fun Activity Book. (p. 373)
—Chock Full of Mazes! Mega Maze Book. (p. 380)
—Choo Choo! the Trains Coloring Book. (p. 381)
—Christmas Bells Are Ringing! Happy Holidays Coloring Book. (p. 383)
—Christmas Is Coming Soon! My Maze Activity Book. (p. 386)
—Christmas Is Here So Let's Color a Christmas Coloring Book. (p. 386)
—Chubby the Owl & Her Friends Coloring Book. (p. 389)
—Clowning All Around Town Coloring Book. (p. 408)
—Color a Christmas Dream Coloring Book. (p. 419)
—Color a Picture Pattern Children's Coloring Book. (p. 419)
—Color Angel Ornaments: Vintage Ornaments Coloring Book. (p. 419)
—Color Between the Lines! Color Fun Coloring Book. (p. 419)
—Color Magical Pictures Childrens' Coloring Book. (p. 420)
—Color Me a Rainbow of Colors! Childrens' Coloring Book. (p. 420)
—Color Me Red, Color Me Green, Color Me Coloring Book. (p. 420)
—Color the Animals ABCs Coloring Book. (p. 421)
—Color the Christmas Spirit Coloring Book. (p. 421)
—Color the Circus with Us Coloring Book. (p. 421)
—Color Your Favorite Animals Coloring Book. (p. 421)
—Colorful Candy: A Candy Coloring Book. (p. 422)
—Coloring Animal Designs, a Coloring Book. (p. 422)
—Coloring Oodles of Doodles Childrens' Coloring Book. (p. 425)
—Coloring with Laughter & Giggles All Day Long Coloring Book. (p. 425)
—Coloring Your Imagination! Color Designs into Pictures Coloring Book. (p. 425)
—Common Household & Garden Beetles Coloring Book. (p. 431)
—Common Northeastern American Wild Animals Coloring Book. (p. 431)
—Connect the Camouflaged Clues! Dot to Dot Activity Book. (p. 440)
—Connect the Clues! Dot to Dot Activity Book. (p. 440)
—Connect the Dots: Nice 'n' Easy Dot to Dot Activity Book. (p. 440)
—Connect the Dots & Crack the Code! Dot to Dot Activity Book. (p. 441)
—Connect the Dots & Create a Picture Activity Book. (p. 441)
—Connect the Dots! Connect the Dots Activity Book. (p. 441)
—Connect the Dots, Mazes & Opposites Activity Book for Kids. (p. 441)
—Connecting Dots from a to Z - Connect the Dots Activity Book. (p. 441)
—Cool Cars Coloring Book. (p. 448)
—Corals & Sea Stars Coloring Book. (p. 453)
—Cows & Bulls: In the Fence Coloring Book. (p. 464)
—Crazy Chameleons! Reptile Fun Coloring Book. (p. 468)
—Crazy Critters Scary Dinosaur Coloring Book. (p. 469)
—Crazy Critters! Silly Animal Coloring Book. (p. 469)
—Crazy Cut Outs! Cut Outs Activity Book. (p. 469)
—Crazy Kids Numbered Dot to Dot Picture Activity Book. (p. 469)
—Create a Rainbow of Colors Coloring Book. (p. 469)
—Create Magic Designs Childrens' Coloring Book. (p. 469)
—Creative Imaginations Magical Color Fun Coloring Book. (p. 471)
—Crests & Symbols of Medieval Knights Coloring Book. (p. 474)
—Cut Outs & Opposites Activity Book for Kids. (p. 491)
—Cute As a Button - an Animal Faces Coloring Book. (p. 491)
—Cute Guardian Angels with Halos Coloring Book. (p. 491)
—Cute Hoots! Owlets in the Wild Coloring Book. (p. 491)
—Danger! All the Construction Coloring You Could Want Coloring Book. (p. 501)
—Decorate Your Dream Room Coloring Book. (p. 523)
—Deluge of Terror Coloring Book. (p. 527)
—Diving for Pretty Pearls! Coloring Book. (p. 566)
—Do You Want to Be a Princess? Princess Activity Book. (p. 572)
—Do You Want to Dance? Coloring Book. (p. 572)
—Dog Activity Book for Kids, Activity Book. (p. 575)
—Don't Be Lost! Find Your Way Back Home Activity Book. (p. 582)
—Dot 2 Dot for Kids Activity Book. (p. 587)
—Dot to Dot: Fun for the Whole Family. (p. 587)
—Dot to Dot: A Journey to Completeness. (p. 587)
—Dotted Wonderland! a Connect the Dots Activity Book. (p. 588)
—Drawing Shapes Inside Shapes Inside Shapes Activity Book. (p. 600)
—Dreams Come True: A Fairies Coloring Book. (p. 603)
—Dressing Dandies & Darlings Coloring Book. (p. 604)
—Educational Activities for Kids Activity Book. (p. 626)
—Encourage Mind Use Kids Activity Book. (p. 648)
—Entertain & Train Your Brain! a Fun-Filled, Challenging Activity Book for Kids. (p. 656)
—Entertaining & Educational Kids Activity Book. (p. 656)
—Every Day a New Challenge! Activity Book for Kids. (p. 670)
—Everyday Physics: Science Is All Around You Coloring Book. (p. 672)
—Everyone Can Add, Subtract, Multiple & Divide Activity Book. (p. 672)
—Evolution of Organisms Coloring Book. (p. 675)
—Extreme Activity Book for Kids Coloring Book Edition. (p. 686)
—Extreme Coloring: Mischief, a Coloring Book. (p. 686)
—Extreme Coloring: Big Eyed Sea Creatures Coloring Book. (p. 686)
—Extreme Coloring Book Adventure: Cartoon Butterflies, a Coloring Book. (p. 686)
—Extreme Coloring Doodles Coloring Book. (p. 686)
—Extreme Connect the Dots for Kids Activity Book. (p. 686)
—Extreme Spot the Difference for Boys & Girls Activity Book. (p. 687)
—Extreme Spot the Difference for Boys Only Activity Book. (p. 687)
—Family Fun Night Kids Activity Book. (p. 702)
—Family's First Thanksgiving Together Coloring Book. (p. 703)
—Fantastic & Challenging Kids Activity Book. (p. 706)
—Fascinating Activities for Kids Coloring Book Edition. (p. 712)
—Feathers of All Types & Sizes Coloring Book. (p. 717)
—Fins & Fishy Fun Coloring Book. (p. 731)
—First Class Transportation Services Coloring Book. (p. 736)
—Flying Around the Moon Coloring Book. (p. 754)
—For Educators & Kids Activity Book. (p. 762)
—For the Love of Activities Kids' Coloring Book Edition. (p. 763)
—For the Love of Kids Activity Book. (p. 763)
—For the Love of Whales & Blubber Coloring Book. (p. 763)
—From Cocoon to Butterfly: An Insect Coloring Book. (p. 791)
—From Water to Land: Tiny Amphibians Coloring Book. (p. 794)
—Fruits & Vegetables a-Z Coloring Book. (p. 796)
—Fruity Adventures! Featuring Vegetables Coloring Book. (p. 796)
—Fun Activities for Kids Coloring Book Edition. (p. 798)
—Fun & Engaging Kids Activity Book. (p. 798)
—Fun & Light Kids Activity Book. (p. 798)
—Fun & More Kids Activity Book. (p. 798)
—Fun, Fantastic Favorites! Activity Book for Kids. (p. 799)
—Fun for Me from a to Z! Super Fun Activity Book. (p. 799)
—Fun, Fun Fun! Super Activity Book for Kids. (p. 799)
—Fun in the Sun: Visiting the Beach Coloring Book Edition. (p. 799)
—Fun Stuff for Kids Activity & Coloring Book Edition. (p. 800)
—Fun-Filled Games & Adventures Super Activity Book for Kids. (p. 799)
—Game of Strategies & Other Activities. (p. 807)
—Games, Word Searches, & Puzzles, Oh My! Super Fun Activity Book for Kids. (p. 808)
—Get Moving! Sports & Exercise Coloring Book Edition. (p. 824)
—Get off the Computer Kids Activity Book. (p. 824)
—Giant Book of Activities for Kids Coloring Book Edition. (p. 830)
—Girl Power! Female Super Hero Coloring Book Edition. (p. 836)
—Girl Scout Word Search Activity Book. (p. 836)
—Gorilla Who Ate Too Many Bananas Coloring Book. (p. 870)
—Growing in God's Word Super Church Coloring Book. (p. 899)
—Hammer or Screwdriver: A Tool Coloring Book. (p. 913)
—Hanging by a Spider's Thread Coloring Book. (p. 917)
—Happily Ever After: A Fairies Coloring Book. (p. 919)
—Happy Students! a Friendly Coloring Book. (p. 923)
—Happy Turtle Squad Coloring Book. (p. 924)
—Have Fun Today with Trash Coloring Book. (p. 939)
—Helpful Helicopters Touching down Coloring Book. (p. 953)
—Hero's Greatest Fear Coloring Book. (p. 963)
—Hidden Pictures & Scissor Skills Activity Book for Kids. (p. 966)
—High Altitude Cruising: Airplane Coloring Book. (p. 968)
—Hint of Magic & Mice: A Fairies Coloring Book. (p. 972)
—Holly, Jolly Holiday Fun Christmas Coloring Book. (p. 988)
—Hooting in a Tree: Birds of Flight Coloring Book. (p. 1001)
—It's My Birthday! a Maze Activity Book. (p. 1146)
—I've Got Maze Mania! Kids Activity Book. (p. 1149)
—Jet Setters! Airplanes & Flying Machines Dot to Dot. (p. 1167)
—Journey to the Secrets: Hidden Picture Activity Book. (p. 1183)
—Jumping Spider Tea Party Coloring Book. (p. 1189)
—Jungle Animals to Color Coloring Book. (p. 1189)
—Just for Boys! Fun Activity Book. (p. 1193)
—Just Unicorns Coloring Book. (p. 1194)
—Kids! Have Fun with This Mazes Activity Book. (p. 1215)
—Kids Maze Craze: A Maze Activity Book. (p. 1216)
—Kids Quest! Hidden Picture Activity Book. (p. 1216)
—King Arthur & His Knights Coloring Book. (p. 1220)
—Knot a-Gain! Ropes & Twisted Things Connect the Dots. (p. 1229)
—Know Your Planet: Land & Water Coloring Book. (p. 1229)
—Large & in Charge! Colossal Collection of Dinosaurs Coloring Book. (p. 1244)
—Learn How to Draw! Activity Book. (p. 1255)
—Learn New Skills by Doing Mazes Activity Book. (p. 1255)
—Learn Something New! Learn to Draw Activity Book. (p. 1255)
—Learn to Draw Something New Activity Book. (p. 1257)
—Learn Your ABC's with Mazes Activity Book. (p. 1257)
—Learn Your Lines! Connect the Dots Activity Book. (p. 1257)
—Learning How to Draw! Activity Book. (p. 1258)
—Learning to Draw Can Be Easy & Rewarding Learn to Draw Activity Book. (p. 1258)
—Learning to Draw Like the Pros! How to Draw Activity Book. (p. 1258)
—Legendary Beasts! the Diverse Dinosaur Activity Book. (p. 1263)
—Let's Be Active! an Excercise Coloring Book. (p. 1270)
—Let's Build a Snow Man Maze Activity Book. (p. 1270)
—Let's Draw! How to Draw Activity Book. (p. 1271)
—Let's Draw, Kids! Connect All the Dots Activity Book. (p. 1271)
—Let's Find the Escape! Kids Maze Activity Book. (p. 1273)
—Let's Find Treasures in the Woods Activity Book. (p. 1273)
—Let's Go to the Ocean! a Maze Activity Book. (p. 1274)
—Let's Have Fun at the Zoo: A Maze Activity Book. (p. 1274)
—Let's Match! Fun Memory Game Activity Book Featuring Horses. (p. 1275)
—Let's Play 'I Spy' Maze Activity Book. (p. 1276)
—Life As a Wolf Coloring Book. (p. 1290)
—Life in Nine Panels - a How to Draw Comics Activity Book. (p. 1292)
—Look! I'm Drawing! How to Draw Activity Book. (p. 1346)
—Looking for Differences! a Spot the Difference Activity Book. (p. 1347)
—Looking for Pictures! a Hidden Search Activity Book. (p. 1347)
—Looking for the Perfect Pet: A Hidden Picture Activity Book. (p. 1347)
—Lost! a Mesmerizing Maze Adventure Activity Book. (p. 1352)
—Lost in the Dark & Twisty Woods Maze Activity Book. (p. 1354)
—Lovely Lines & Crazy Curves Connect the Dots Activities. (p. 1362)
—Magical Matches! Puzzles & Activities for Kids Activity Book. (p. 1380)
—Make a Match! Puzzles for Kids Activity Book. (p. 1385)
—Make a Mess with Trash Coloring Books. (p. 1385)
—Make It Like Michelangelo: How to Draw Book. (p. 1386)
—Manga: A How to Draw Activity Book. (p. 1397)
—Manga How To: Step-By-Step to Drawing Anime Activity Book. (p. 1397)
—Man's Best Friend: Coloring Household Pets. (p. 1398)
—Many Landscapes of the USA Coloring Book. (p. 1400)
—Marvelous Mazes Activity Book. (p. 1413)
—Marvelous Moths Insect Coloring Book. (p. 1413)
—Massive Maze Mania! a Fun Adventure Awaits Kids Activity Book. (p. 1418)
—Master Maze Runner! Boost Kindergarten Brain Power with Maze Activities. (p. 1418)
—Master Miyamoto Musashi's Two-Handed Coloring Book. (p. 1418)
—Match & Color Activity Book for Boys Activity Book. (p. 1420)
—Match & Learn! an Educational Activity Book. (p. 1420)
—Match & Learn for Preschoolers: A Matching Activity Book. (p. 1420)
—Match Math: A Fun, Educational Activity Book. (p. 1420)
—Match the Flag with the Country Activity Book. (p. 1420)
—Match the Magic Alphabet Shapes Matching Game Activity Book. (p. 1420)
—Match the Wine with the Food Activity Book. (p. 1420)
—Match with Me: A Matching Activity Book. (p. 1420)
—Matching, Dot to Dot & Hidden Pictures Activity Book for Kids. (p. 1420)
—Matching Game for 2 Year Old. (p. 1420)
—Matching Game for 3 Year Old. (p. 1420)
—Matching Game for 4 Year Old. (p. 1420)
—Matching Game for 4 Year Olds. (p. 1420)
—Matching Game for Kids. (p. 1420)
—Matching Game for Preschoolers. (p. 1420)
—Matching Game for Toddlers. (p. 1420)
—Matching Game Preschool Edition. (p. 1420)
—Matching Games for 2 Year Olds. (p. 1420)
—Mazes 4th Grade Workbook for Kids. (p. 1431)
—Mazes Age 6 - Super Fun Activity Book. (p. 1431)
—Mazes & Coloring Book - Double the Fun Activity Book. (p. 1431)
—Mazes & Connect the Dots Activity Book for Kids. (p. 1431)
—Mazes & Dot to Dots - Super Fun Activity Book. (p. 1431)
—Mazes & Puzzles for Kids - Super Fun Activity Book. (p. 1431)
—Mazes Book for Kids - into the Labyrinth Activity Book. (p. 1431)
—Mazes Books for Children - Super Fun Brain Training Activity Book. (p. 1431)
—Mazes for Children - Super Fun Activity Book. (p. 1431)
—Mazes for Kids Age 5 - Super Fun Activity Book. (p. 1431)
—Mazes for Kids Age 7 - Super Fun Activity Book. (p. 1431)
—Mazes for Kids Age 8 - Super Fun Activity Book. (p. 1431)
—Mazes for Preschoolers - Super Fun Activity Book. (p. 1431)
—Mazes for Teens - Super Fun Activity Book. (p. 1431)
—Mazes for Toddlers - Super Fun Activity Book. (p. 1431)
—Mazes from Around the World: Kids Activity Book. (p. 1431)
—Mazes Kindergarten - Edition: Tiny Tots Maze Fun. (p. 1431)
—Mazes Things That Go - Planes, Trains, Cars & Trucks. (p. 1431)
—Mazes Workbook for Children - Grade 4 Edition. (p. 1431)
—Mazes Workbook for Kids - Ages 4 & Up. (p. 1431)
—Mermaids, Sailors & Pirates Coloring Book. (p. 1449)
—Milking the Cow: A Day in the Barn Coloring Book. (p. 1467)
—Mountains Made by God's Hands Coloring Book. (p. 1514)
—My First Body Part Coloring Book. (p. 1542)
—My First Shapes & Sizes ABC Coloring Book. (p. 1546)
—My Jungle Animal Alphabet Coloring Book. (p. 1550)
—Mystery Pictures: A Guessing Game of Dot to Dots. (p. 1570)
—Not So Scary Monsters Coloring Book. (p. 1623)
—Ocean Mysteries! Weird Marine Life Coloring Book. (p. 1635)
—Oh! How I Love Rainbows Coloring Book. (p. 1641)
—One, Two, Three Strikes You're Out! a Baseball Coloring Book. (p. 1663)
—Original Farm Favorites Coloring Book. (p. 1671)
—Our Favorite Candy Easter Bunnies & Candy Easter Eggs Coloring Book. (p. 1678)
—Our Savior Rose Again on Easter Sunday! Coloring Book. (p. 1680)
—Outdoor Diving Locations Around the World Coloring Book. (p. 1684)
—Outer Space: Count & Color the Planets Coloring Book. (p. 1684)
—Outrageously Preposterous Coloring Entertainment for All! Positively Fun Coloring Book. (p. 1685)
—Pail & Shovel! the Beach Toys Coloring Book. (p. 1692)
—Paws, Claws & Hooves! Pretty Pets Coloring Book. (p. 1708)
—Peppermint Pages, a Candy Coloring Book. (p. 1720)
—Physicists at Work: Coloring Book. (p. 1738)
—Places Where Dressing up Is Required Coloring Book. (p. 1753)
—Play Ball! Games Using Balls Coloring Book. (p. 1759)
—Play Sports with Me! Coloring Book. (p. 1759)
—Playing in Parks with Mom Coloring Book. (p. 1760)
—Playtime Fun Color Me Coloring Book. (p. 1761)
—Popular European Bus Trips Coloring Book. (p. 1777)
—Porpoises Are Our Friends Coloring Book. (p. 1778)
—Prancing in the Pasture! Pretty Ponies Coloring Book. (p. 1785)
—Preschool Activity Books Matching Edition. (p. 1788)
—Preschool Activity Workbook Mazes & More. (p. 1788)
—Press Here to Cook Coloring Book. (p. 1790)
—Pretty Swimsuits for Summer Coloring Book. (p. 1791)

Smith, A. g. & Smith, A. G. White House Cut & Assemble. (p. 2444)
Smith, Abbie Nora. Bobtail Dixie (Classic Reprint) (p. 253)
Smith, Abby. Pettikin. (p. 1731)
Smith, Abby, illus. see Toombs, Tom.
Smith, Adah E. Kathie's Peculiar Views (Classic Reprint) (p. 1205)
Smith, Adam. At the End of Your Tether. Glass, V. V., illus. (p. 130)
Smith, Adam I. P. Abraham Lincoln. (p. 7)
—Stormy Present: Conservatism & the Problem of Slavery in Northern Politics, 1846-1865. (p. 2127)
Smith, Adelaide Pugh. Child Dialect Verse (Classic Reprint) (p. 369)
Smith, Adolphe. Woman of Mind, Vol. 2 Of 3: A Novel (Classic Reprint) (p. 2485)
Smith, Adrienne. Clavius: The Hapless Tooth Fairy. (p. 402)
Smith, Agnes Smith Lewis Agnes. Eastern Pilgrims: The Travels of Three Ladies (Classic Reprint) (p. 620)
Smith, Ahmara, illus. see Maison, Corey.
Smith, Aimee & Johnston, Deon. My Hometown Is the Best Place to Visit. (p. 1550)
Smith, Al. Koala & Bunny: Instilling Protective Behaviours In Children. (p. 1230)
Smith, Alastair, jt. auth. see Le Rolland, L.
Smith, Alastair, jt. auth. see Miles, Lisa.
Smith, Albert. Adventures of Mr. Ledbury & His Friend Jack Johnson (Classic Reprint) (p. 25)
—Adventures of Mr. Ledbury & His Friend Jack Johnson, Vol. 1 of 3 (Classic Reprint) (p. 25)
—Bentley's Miscellany, 1859, Vol. 46 (Classic Reprint) (p. 201)
—Comic Almanack: An Ephemeris in Jest & Earnest, Containing Merry Tales, Humorous Poetry, Quips, & Oddities; First Series, 1835-1843 (Classic Reprint) (p. 429)
—Comic Tales & Sketches (Classic Reprint) (p. 429)
—English Hotel Nuisance (Classic Reprint) (p. 653)
—Fortunes of the Cattergood Family, Vol. 1 of 3 (Classic Reprint) (p. 770)
—Fortunes of the Scattergood Family, Vol. 2 of 3 (Classic Reprint) (p. 770)
—Gavarni in London: Sketches of Life & Character; with Illustrative Essays by Popular Writers (Classic Reprint) (p. 812)
—London Medical Student (Classic Reprint) (p. 1341)
—Month at Constantinople (Classic Reprint) (p. 1499)
—Natural History of the Gent (Classic Reprint) (p. 1579)
—Pottleton Legacy: A Story of Town & Country Life (Classic Reprint) (p. 1781)
—Story of Mont Blanc (Classic Reprint) (p. 2131)
—Struggles & Adventures of Christopher Tadpole (Classic Reprint) (p. 2142)
—To China & Back 1859: Being a Diary Kept, Out & Home (Classic Reprint) (p. 2252)
—Wassail-Bowl, Vol. 1 of 2 (Classic Reprint) (p. 2382)
—Wassail-Bowl, Vol. 2 of 2 (Classic Reprint) (p. 2382)
—Wild Oats & Dead Leaves (Classic Reprint) (p. 2464)
Smith, Albert, jt. auth. see Leech, John.
Smith, Albert W. Giant & Other Nonsense Verse (Classic Reprint) (p. 830)
Smith, Alene L., jt. auth. see Smith, George Bundy.
Smith, Alex. Home. Smith, Alex, illus. (p. 995)
Smith, Alex T. Claude at the Beach Smith, Alex T., illus. (p. 401)
—Claude at the Circus Smith, Alex T., illus. (p. 401)
—Claude in the City Smith, Alex T., illus. (p. 401)
—Claude in the Country Smith, Alex T., illus. (p. 401)
—Claude in the Spotlight Smith, Alex T., illus. (p. 401)
—Claude on the Big Screen Smith, Alex T., illus. (p. 401)
—Claude on the Slopes Smith, Alex T., illus. (p. 401)
—How Winston Delivered Christmas. (p. 1046)
—Little Red & the Very Hungry Lion. Smith, Alex T., illus. (p. 1326)
—Mr. Penguin & the Catastrophic Cruise. Smith, Alex T., illus. (p. 1520)
—Mr. Penguin & the Fortress of Secrets. Smith, Alex T., illus. (p. 1520)
—Mr. Penguin & the Lost Treasure Smith, Alex T., illus. (p. 1520)
—Santa Claude. (p. 1932)
Smith, Alex T., illus. see Adams, Richard.
Smith, Alex T., illus. see Almond, David.
Smith, Alex T., illus. see Cottringer, Anne.
Smith, Alex T., illus. see Kemp, Anna.
Smith, Alex T., illus. see McAllister, Angela.
Smith, Alexander. Alfred Hagart's Household, Vol. 1 of 2 (Classic Reprint) (p. 43)
—Summer in Skye (Classic Reprint) (p. 2149)
—Summer in Skye, Vol. 1 of 2 (Classic Reprint) (p. 2149)
—Summer in Skye, Vol. 2 (Classic Reprint) (p. 2149)
Smith, Alexander Gordon. Death Sentence: Escape from Furnace 3. (p. 521)
—Death Sentence. (p. 521)
—Devil's Engine: Hellfighters. (p. 536)
—Devil's Engine: Hellwalkers: (Book 3) (p. 536)
—Devil's Engine: Hellwalkers. (p. 536)
—Execution: Escape from Furnace 5. (p. 676)
—Fugitives: Escape from Furnace 4. (p. 797)
—Fugitives. (p. 797)
—Fury. (p. 802)
—Hellfighters. (p. 950)
—Hellraisers. (p. 952)
—Lockdown: Escape from Furnace 1. (p. 1339)
—Solar System: A Breathtaking Tour of the Universe & How It Works with More Than 300 Incredible Photographs & Illustrations. (p. 2056)
—Solar System. (p. 2056)
—Solitary: Escape from Furnace 2. (p. 2057)
Smith, Alexandra. Yancy Yellowhammer. (p. 2517)
Smith, Ali. Story of Antigone. Paoletti, Laura, illus. (p. 2129)
Smith, Ali, jt. auth. see Howson, Imogen.
Smith, Ali, jt. auth. see Wallach, Tommy.
Smith, Alice Prescott. Legatee (Classic Reprint) (p. 1261)
—Off the Highway (Classic Reprint) (p. 1640)
Smith, Alice Weston. Alice Weston Smith, 1868-1908: Letters to Her Friends & Selections from Her Note-Books (Classic Reprint) (p. 46)
Smith, Allie, illus. see DiTerlizzi, Angela.
Smith, Allie, illus. see Diterlizzi, Angela.
Smith, Allie, illus. see Sector, Emma.
Smith, Amber. Last to Let Go. (p. 1249)
—Something Like Gravity. (p. 2060)
—Way I Used to Be. (p. 2387)
—Way I Used to Be. Twomey, Kevin, photos by. (p. 2387)
Smith, Amber & Nolting, Mia. Something Like Gravity. (p. 2060)
Smith, Andrea. Mi Plan D. (p. 1455)
Smith, Andrea Neile. Who Aiden Was. (p. 2446)
Smith, Andrea P. Casey Jones. (p. 339)
—Daniel Boone. (p. 502)
—Davy Crockett. (p. 511)
—Day in the Life of Colonial Silversmith Paul Revere. (p. 513)
—First Thanksgiving. (p. 740)
—Jim Bowie. (p. 1168)
—Johnny Appleseed. (p. 1174)
—Journey of the Mayflower. (p. 1181)
—Mystery of Roanoke, the Lost Colony. (p. 1569)
—Paul Bunyan. (p. 1707)
—Pocahontas & John Smith. (p. 1764)
—Salem Witch Trials. (p. 1924)
Smith, Andrew. 100 Sideways Miles. (p. 2557)
—Alex Crow. (p. 42)
—Exile from Eden: Or, after the Hole. Smith, Andrew, illus. (p. 677)
—Ghost Medicine. (p. 827)
—Grasshopper Jungle. (p. 881)
—In the Path of Falling Objects. (p. 1110)
—Passenger. (p. 1703)
—Rabbit & Robot. (p. 1829)
—Size of the Truth. (p. 2029)
—Stand-Off. Bosma, Sam, illus. (p. 2100)
—Winger. (p. 2473)
—Winger. Bosma, Sam, illus. (p. 2473)
Smith, Andy, illus. see Lemke, Donald.
Smith, Andy, illus. see Sazaklis, John & Vancata, Brad.
Smith, Andy J., illus. see Nickel, Scott.
Smith, Angela Burnette. Pawsible Moments. (p. 1708)
Smith, Angie. For Such a Time As This: Stories of Women from the Bible, Retold for Girls. Brookshire, Breezy, illus. (p. 763)
Smith, Anna Marion. Mother Goose & What Happened Next (Classic Reprint) (p. 1509)
Smith, Anne, illus. see Candlewick Press Staff.
Smith, Anne, illus. see Robb, Don.
Smith, Anne, illus. see Smith, John D. H.
Smith, Annette. Saturday Morning Soccer. Holt, Richard, illus. (p. 1936)
Smith, Annette L. Last Day at Center Ridge School (Classic Reprint) (p. 1247)
Smith, Annie Laura. Neil Armstrong: First Man on the Moon. Gierhart, Steve, ed. (p. 1586)
—Sally Ride: America's First Woman Astronaut. Gierhart, Steve, ed. (p. 1925)
Smith, April. Loving Grace. (p. 1362)
Smith, Arlene. My Two Moms. (p. 1563)
Smith, Art. Art Smith's Story 1915: The Autobiography of the Boy Aviator Which Appeared As a Serial in the Bulletin (Classic Reprint) (p. 122)
Smith, Arthur. Doin's o' Jim o' Doads: Sketches of Lancashire Life (Classic Reprint) (p. 578)
Smith, Arthur Cosslett. Monk & the Dancer (Classic Reprint) (p. 1493)
—Turquoise Cup & the Desert (Classic Reprint) (p. 2301)
Smith, Arthur D. Howden. Fighting the Turk in the Balkans: An American's Adventures with the Macedonian Revolutionists (Classic Reprint) (p. 726)
—Grey Maiden, the Story of a Sword Through the Ages (Classic Reprint) (p. 896)
Smith, Arthur Douglas Howden. Commodore Vanderbilt: An Epic of American Achievement (Classic Reprint) (p. 430)
Smith, Asa. Smith's Illustrated Astronomy: Designed for the Use of the Public or Common Schools in the United States; Illustrated with Numerous Original Diagrams (Classic Reprint) (p. 2042)
Smith, Ashley, illus. see Holzer, Angela.
Smith, Aubrey. How to Build a Robot (With Your Dad) 20 Easy-to-Build Robotic Projects. (p. 1038)
Smith, Austin, illus. see Nabors, Wayne.
Smith, B. Beaver & the Muskrat. Koensgen, Joseph, illus. (p. 185)
Smith, B. M. Evan & Cassie Go on a Train Meet Smith, Mandy M., illus. (p. 668)
—My Very Own Picnic Basket: An Evan & Cassie Adventure. (p. 1564)
Smith, B. R. Adventures of Zuma: The Tale of the Tail. (p. 29)
Smith, Barbara. Lost Diary Secrets. (p. 1353)
Smith, Barbara A. Otis Paul & Harry the Hairy Echidna. (p. 1675)
Smith, Barbara Maxine. God Loves You & You Love Yourself -To God You Are Special. (p. 851)
Smith, Barry, illus. see Redmond, Diane.
Smith, Ben. How Are Oceans & Lakes Alike? (p. 1025)
—What Makes the Air Dirty? (p. 2418)
—Where Can You Find Hard & Soft Things? (p. 2435)
—Where Do Big Cats Live? (p. 2436)
—Who Listens to the Weather Forecast? (p. 2448)
—Why Do We Celebrate? (p. 2457)
—Why Does This Float? (p. 2457)
Smith, Ben Bailey. Bear Moves. Akyuz, Sav, illus. (p. 179)
—I Am Bear. Akyüz, Sav, illus. (p. 1058)
Smith, Benjamin. Graven Vengeance: Overlord Warriors. (p. 882)
Smith, Benjamin Eric, jt. auth. see Ramrattan Smith, Sherry.
Smith, Bernice, illus. see Essrow, Wende.
Smith, Bertha Whitridge. Only a Dog: A Story of the Great War (Classic Reprint) (p. 1664)
—Traveller's Tales: Told in Letters from Belgium, Germany, England, Scotland, France, & Spain (Classic Reprint) (p. 2280)
Smith, Bertram. Caravan Days (Classic Reprint) (p. 327)
—Days of Discovery (Classic Reprint) (p. 515)
—Running Wild (Classic Reprint) (p. 1916)
Smith, Bill. Joe Smith His Waxworks (Classic Reprint) (p. 1171)
Smith, Bill D. Freshwater or Salt Water? (p. 785)
Smith, Bill D. & Machajewski, Sarah. Freshwater or Salt Water? (p. 785)
Smith, Bill O. Chickadees At Night. Murphy, Charles R., illus. (p. 368)
Smith, Brady & Thiessen, Tiffani. You're Missing It! Smith, Brady, illus. (p. 2535)
Smith, Brandon D. To God Alone - Teen Bible Study: 5 Core Beliefs of the Reformation. (p. 2252)
Smith, Bree. Handcuffs, Wishes, & Misinterpreted Kisses. (p. 915)
—What She Couldn't Say. (p. 2419)
Smith, Brenda, illus. see Sister Flowers.
Smith, Brendan Powell. Assassination! The Brick Chronicle of Attempts on the Lives of Twelve US Presidents. (p. 127)
—Assassination! The Brick Chronicle Presents Attempts on the Lives of Twelve US Presidents. (p. 127)
—Brick Bible for Kids Box Set: The Complete Set. (p. 280)
—Christmas Story: The Brick Bible for Kids. (p. 387)
—Complete Brick Bible for Kids: Six Classic Bible Stories. (p. 434)
—Easter Story. (p. 620)
—Jonah & the Whale: The Brick Bible for Kids. (p. 1177)
—Joseph & the Colorful Coat: The Brick Bible for Kids. (p. 1178)
—Miracles of Jesus: The Brick Bible for Kids. (p. 1474)
—Noah's Ark: The Brick Bible for Kids. (p. 1616)
Smith, Brennan. Survivors. (p. 2165)
Smith, Brent. Daddy's Wish. Duffy, Spencer, illus. (p. 495)
Smith Bresciani, Cathleen & Eldredge, Richard. Sassafrass Jones & the Search for a Forever Home. (p. 1936)
Smith, Brett. Stephen Curry: Basketball MVP. (p. 2115)
Smith, Brian. Intrepid EscapeGoat: Curse of the Buddha's Tooth. Conkling, Jon & DeVito, Michael A., eds. (p. 1128)
Smith, Brian, illus. see Steinberg, D. J.
Smith, Brian, jt. auth. see Lucado, Max.
Smith, Brian, Brian. Memory. (p. 1446)
Smith, Brian "Smitty". Pea, Bee, & Jay #1: Stuck Together. (p. 1709)
—Pea, Bee, & Jay #2: Wannabees. (p. 1709)
Smith, Briony May. Margaret's Unicorn. (p. 1403)
Smith, Briony May, illus. see Faber, Polly.
Smith, Briony May, illus. see Robinson, Michelle.
Smith, Briony May, illus. see Willis, Jeanne.
Smith, Brittney, illus. see Perry, Lauren.
Smith, Bron, illus. see Myers, R. E.
Smith, Brooke. Brinley Discovers Santa: A Bold Introduction to the Meaning Behind Santa Claus. Myers, Robbie, illus. (p. 282)
—Keeper of Wild Words: (Nature for Kids, Exploring Nature with Children) Kloepper, Madeline, illus. (p. 1208)
—Mango Tree. Gomes, Tania, illus. (p. 1397)
—Mimi & Maty to the Rescue! Book 1: Roger the Rat Is on the Loose! Arnold, Alli, illus. (p. 1468)
—Mimi & Maty to the Rescue!: Roger the Rat Is on the Loose! Bk. 1 Arnold, Alli, illus. (p. 1469)
—Mimi & Maty to the Rescue! Book 3: C. C. the Parakeet Flies the Coop! Arnold, Alli, illus. (p. 1469)
—Mimi & Maty to the Rescue! Book 2: Sadie the Sheep Disappears Without a Peep! Arnold, Alli, illus. (p. 1469)
—Paint Little Girl. (p. 1693)
—Tortoise & the Flair. Gomes, Tania, illus. (p. 2266)
Smith, Bruce. Poppies in Bloom (p. 1776)
Smith, Bryan. How Did You Miss That? A Story Teaching Self-Monitoring. Griffin, Lisa M., illus. (p. 1027)
—If Winning Isn't Everything, Why Do I Hate to Lose? Martin, Brian, illus. (p. 1092)
—I'll Never Get All of That Done! A Story about Planning & Prioritizing. Griffin, Lisa, illus. (p. 1095)
—Is There an App for That? Wish, Katia, illus. (p. 1137)
—Mindset Matters. Griffin, Lisa, illus. (p. 1470)
—Of Course It's a Big Deal. (p. 1639)
—What Were You Thinking? Learning to Control Your Impulses. Griffin, Lisa, illus. (p. 2422)
Smith, Bryan, jt. auth. see Smith, Paula.
Smith, C. Alphonso. Smith-McMurry Language Series: First Book (Classic Reprint) (p. 2042)
—Smith-McMurry Language Series: Second Book (Classic Reprint) (p. 2042)
Smith, C. G. Furley. Quixote, the Weaver, Vol. 1 of 3 (Classic Reprint) (p. 1829)
Smith, C. Michelle. Skeeter Sneeter Doodlebop. Foreman, A., illus. (p. 2030)
—Skeeter Uses Manners. Foreman, A., illus. (p. 2030)
Smith, C. S. From Slavery to Citizenship: And, from the Cotton Fields to Grasshopper Plains (Classic Reprint) (p. 793)
Smith, Caighlan. Children of Daedala. (p. 371)
—Children of Icarus. (p. 371)
Smith, Cameron. Adventures of Rocky Lizard. (p. 27)
Smith, Candace. Bathtime Dance. (p. 172)
—Someday... (p. 2060)
Smith, Carol. Tales of Wonder Woods. (p. 2186)
Smith, Carol & Quest, Suzanne. Dr Daphne & Nurse Moira Stories. (p. 591)
Smith, Caroline. Writing & Developing Social Stories. (p. 2513)
Smith, Caroline F. Story of a Child: Translated from the French of Pierre Loti (Classic Reprint) (p. 2128)
Smith, Carrie. Baby Animals: Lap Book. (p. 148)
—Bird Homes: Lap Book. (p. 230)
—Boy Who Cried Wolf: Classic Tales Edition. Kelley, Gerald, illus. (p. 270)
—Chicken Little: Classic Tales Series. Harpster, Steve, illus. (p. 368)
—Cinderella: Classic Tales Edition. Greenhead, Bill, illus. (p. 391)
—Counting Insects: Lap Book. (p. 460)
—Crow & the Pitcher: Classic Tales Series. Greenhead, Bill, illus. (p. 478)
—Enormous Turnip: Classic Tales Edition. Rogers, Jacqueline, illus. (p. 655)
—Finding Shapes: Lap Book. (p. 730)
—Giant Turnip: Lap Book Edition. Piwowarski, Marcin, illus. (p. 831)
—Giant Turnip: Small Book Edition. Piwowarski, Marcin, illus. (p. 831)
—Goldilocks & the Three Bears: Classic Tales Edition. Greenhead, Bill, illus. (p. 860)
—Human Emotions & Las emociones Humanas: 6 English, 6 Spanish Adaptations Hanner, Albert, illus. (p. 1049)
—Jumping Monkeys. Harpster, Steve, illus. (p. 1188)
—Jumping Monkeys: Lap Book Edition. Daubney, Kate, illus. (p. 1189)
—Jumping Monkeys: Small Book Edition. Daubney, Kate, illus. (p. 1189)
—Las emociones Humanas. Hanner, Albert, illus. (p. 1245)
—Lion & the Rabbit: Classic Tales Edition. Greenhead, Bill, illus. (p. 1305)
—Little Bo Peep. Abbott, Jason, illus. (p. 1312)
—Little Red Hen: Classic Tales Series. Palmer, James, illus. (p. 1326)
—Little Red Riding Hood: Classic Tales Edition. Kelley, Gerald, illus. (p. 1326)
—Mary's Lamb Goes to School: Lap Book Edition. Corbalán, Begoña, illus. (p. 1416)
—Mary's Lamb Goes to School: Small Book Edition. Corbalán, Begoña, illus. (p. 1416)
—Princess & the Pea: Classic Tales Edition. Harpster, Steve, illus. (p. 1796)
—Stone Soup: Lap Book Edition. Ebbeler, Jeff, illus. (p. 2121)
—Stone Soup: Small Book Edition. Ebbeler, Jeff, illus. (p. 2121)
—Stone Soup: Classic Tales Edition. Rogers, Jacqueline, illus. (p. 2121)
—Tortoise & Hare Run a Race: Lap Book Edition. Berchtold, Lauren, illus. (p. 2266)
—Tortoise & Hare Run a Race: Small Book Edition. Berchtold, Lauren, illus. (p. 2266)
—Ugly Duckling: Classic Tales Edition. Rogers, Jacqueline, illus. (p. 2313)
—We See with Our Eyes: Lap Book. (p. 2392)
—Where Are Bo Peep's Sheep? Abbott, Jason, illus. (p. 2435)
Smith, Carrie, jt. auth. see Jones, Tammy.
Smith, Carrie, concept. Baby Animals Whiteboard CD. (p. 148)
—Bird Homes Whiteboard CD. (p. 230)
—Counting Insects Whiteboard CD. (p. 460)
—Finding Shapes Whiteboard CD. (p. 730)
—Jumping Monkeys Whiteboard CD. (p. 1189)
—We See with Our Eyes Whiteboard CD. (p. 2392)
—Where Are Bo Peep's Sheep? Whiteboard CD. (p. 2435)
Smith, Carrie J. Teacher's Manual to Accompany Easy Road to Reading (Classic Reprint) (p. 2195)
Smith, Carrie Josephine. Easy Road to Reading: Primer (Classic Reprint) (p. 621)
—Easy Road to Reading: Third Reader (Classic Reprint) (p. 621)
—Easy Road to Reading Second Reader (Classic Reprint) (p. 621)
Smith, Carter. Diamond at the Door. (p. 538)
Smith, Carter, jt. ed. see Nash, Gary B.
Smith, Cat, illus. see Thomassie, Tynia.
Smith, Cat Bowman, illus. see Gardiner, John Reynolds.
Smith, Cat Bowman, illus. see Levitin, Sonia.
Smith, Cat Bowman, illus. see Thomas, Peggy.
Smith, Cat Bowman, illus. see Thomassie, Tynia.
Smith, Catharine Bowman, illus. see Gardiner, John Reynolds.
Smith, Catherine. Parakeet. (p. 1699)
Smith, Cathy. Cheri: A Not So Standard Poodle! (p. 365)
Smith, Cecilia. I Like! (p. 1067)
—Mole Gets Sick. (p. 1488)
—Winter Time. (p. 2476)
Smith, Charles. Elementary Treatise on Conic Sections (Classic Reprint) (p. 632)
—Out at First. (p. 1682)
Smith, Charles A. Among the Lilies & Elsewhere, with Jesus: Pleasant Talks with the Young on Passages of Scripture (Classic Reprint) (p. 76)
Smith, Charles Adam. Inlets & Outlets: Familiar Talks about the Five Senses (Classic Reprint) (p. 1120)
Smith, Charles Alphonso. O. Henry: A Biography (Classic Reprint) (p. 1633)
—O. Henry: William Sidney Porter (Classic Reprint) (p. 1633)
Smith, Charles Augustus. Steam Using: Or Steam Engine Practice (Classic Reprint) (p. 2111)
Smith, Charles H., see Arp, Bill, pseud.
Smith, Charles Hatch. George Melville: An American Novel (Classic Reprint) (p. 819)
Smith, Charles John. Synonyms Discriminated: A Dictionary of Synonymous Words in the English Language, Illustrated with Quotations from Standard Writers (Classic Reprint) (p. 2173)
—Synonyms Discriminated: A Complete Catalogue of Synonymous Words in the English Language, with Descriptions of Their Various Shades of Meaning, & Illustrations of Their Usages & Specialities (Classic Reprint) (p. 2173)
Smith, Charles Manby. Curiosities of London Life, or Phases, Physiological & Social, of the Great Metropolis (Classic Reprint) (p. 486)
—Little World of London, or Pictures in Little of London Life (Classic Reprint) (p. 1330)
Smith, Charles R. What Makes Us Strong. (p. 2418)
Smith, Charles R., jt. ed. see Aronson, Marc.
Smith, Charles R., Jr. 28 Days: Moments in Black History That Changed the World. Evans, Shane W., illus. (p. 2554)
—Black Jack: The Ballad of Jack Johnson. Evans, Shane W., illus. (p. 238)
—Brick by Brick. (p. 280)
—Brick by Brick. Cooper, Floyd, illus. (p. 280)
—Brown Sugar Babies. Smith, Charles R., Jr., illus. (p. 287)

—Cornhill Magazine, Vol. 14: January to June, 1903 (Classic Reprint) (p. 455)
—Cornhill Magazine, Vol. 24: July to December, 1871 (Classic Reprint) (p. 455)
—Cornhill Magazine, Vol. 4: July to December, 1861 (Classic Reprint) (p. 455)
—Cornhill Magazine, Vol. 8: January to June 1900 (Classic Reprint) (p. 455)
Smith, George Bundy & Smith, Alene L. You Decide! Applying the Bill of Rights to Real Cases. (p. 2527)
—You Decide! Instruction/Answer Guide: Applying the Bill of Rights to Real Cases. (p. 2527)
Smith, George Gilman. Boy in Gray: A Story of the War (Classic Reprint) (p. 268)
—Boy in Gray. (p. 268)
Smith, George Murray. Cornhill Magazine, Vol. 22: January to June, 1894 (Classic Reprint) (p. 455)
Smith, George Washington. Smileys: A Tale of Hardwoodlands (Classic Reprint) (p. 2042)
Smith, Gertrude. Arabella & Araminta (Classic Reprint) (p. 108)
Smith, Gloria. Annie Elf & Bo Bo Robin. (p. 100)
—Annie Elf & Flippy Butterfly. (p. 100)
—Annie Elf Meets Mitty Mouse. Smith, Claire, illus. (p. 100)
Smith, Gordon Arthur. Crown of Life (Classic Reprint) (p. 479)
—Pagan (Classic Reprint) (p. 1692)
—There Goes the Groom (Classic Reprint) (p. 2216)
Smith, Grace E. Arrow-Maker's Daughter: A Camp Fire Play; Adapted from Longfellow's Poem of Hiawatha (Classic Reprint) (p. 119)
Smith, Graham. Sideways Man: Imagine If You Kept Seeing Someone Around Your Neighbourhood but Only Ever Saw Him Sideways! Smith, Graham, illus. (p. 2015)
Smith, Graham, illus. see Dale, Jay.
Smith, Greg & Tanner, Michael. Out of the Woods Lehner, Zach, illus. (p. 1683)
Smith, Greg Leitich. Borrowed Time. (p. 263)
—Chronal Engine. Henry, Blake, illus. (p. 388)
—Ninjas, Piranhas, & Galileo. (p. 1610)
Smith, Gwendoline. Book of Knowing: Know How You Think, Change How You Feel. (p. 259)
Smith, H. Sutton. Yakusu, the Very Heart of Africa: Being Some Account of the Protestant Mission at Stanley Falls, Upper Congo (Classic Reprint) (p. 2517)
Smith, Haley Rachel, illus. see Potter, Patrick.
Smith, Hannah. Christian's Secret of a Happy Life. (p. 383)
Smith, Hannah Whitall. Christian's Secret to a Happy Life. (p. 383)
Smith, Harriet Gaylord. Papers & Verses (Classic Reprint) (p. 1698)
Smith, Harriet Lummis. Agatha's Aunt (Classic Reprint) (p. 35)
—Other People's Business: The Romantic Career of the Practical Miss Dale. (p. 1674)
—Other People's Business: The Romantic Career of the Practical Miss. Dale (Classic Reprint) (p. 1674)
—Peggy Raymond's Success: Or, the Girls of Friendly Terrace (Classic Reprint) (p. 1714)
—Peggy Raymond's Way: Or, Blossom Time at Friendly Terrace (Classic Reprint) (p. 1714)
—Pollyanna of the Orange Blossoms (Classic Reprint) (p. 1772)
Smith, Harry B. Robin Hood: A Comic Opera in Three Acts (Classic Reprint) (p. 1891)
Smith, Harry James. Amédée's Son (Classic Reprint) (p. 68)
—Cape Breton Tales (Classic Reprint) (p. 323)
—Enchanted Ground: An Episode in the Life of a Young Man (Classic Reprint) (p. 647)
—Little Teacher: A Comedy in Four Acts (Classic Reprint) (p. 1329)
Smith, Harry Worcester, jt. auth. see Forester, Frank.
Smith, Heath. Mr. Gilmore's Glasses. (p. 1518)
Smith, Heather. Agony of Bun O'Keefe. (p. 35)
—Angus All Aglow. (p. 87)
—Barry Squires, Full Tilt. (p. 168)
—Baygirl (p. 175)
—Chicken Girl. (p. 368)
—Idée Pour Papi Kerrigan, Brooke, illus. (p. 1089)
—Phone Booth in Mr. Hirota's Garden Wada, Rachel, illus. (p. 1736)
—Plan for Pops Kerrigan, Brooke, illus. (p. 1754)
Smith, Heidi, illus. see Gardner, Kate.
Smith, Heidi, illus. see Gruener, Nina.
Smith, Helen. Day with Oaky & Other Stories for Small Children. (p. 515)
Smith, Helen, illus. see Baxter, Nicola.
Smith, Helen, illus. see St. John, Patricia.
Smith, Henry. Life & Adventures of Henry Smith, the Celebrated Razor Strop Man: Embracing a Complete Collection of His Original Songs, Queer Speeches, Humorous Letters, & Odd, Droll, Strange & Whimsical, Savings, Now Published for the First Time. (p. 1288)
Smith, Henry, illus. see Denson, Calvin.
Smith, Henry, illus. see Wainewright, Max.
Smith, Henry Justin. Deadlines (Classic Reprint) (p. 518)
—Other Side of the Wall (Classic Reprint) (p. 1675)
—Other Side, of the Wall (Classic Reprint) (p. 1675)
Smith, Herbert. Golden Rod, 1916, Vol. 25 (Classic Reprint) (p. 858)
—Golden-Rod, Vol. 25: December, 1915 (Classic Reprint) (p. 858)
—Golden-Rod, Vol. 26: April, 1916 (Classic Reprint) (p. 858)
—Golden-Rod, Vol. 26: February, 1916 (Classic Reprint) (p. 858)
—Golden-Rod, Vol. 26: June, 1916 (Classic Reprint) (p. 859)
—Golden-Rod, Vol. 26: March, 1916 (Classic Reprint) (p. 859)
Smith, Hilary. Panda Pediatrician: The 100th Day of School. (p. 1695)
Smith, Hilary, ed. see Robins, Tudor.
Smith, Hilary T. Sense of the Infinite. (p. 1989)
Smith, Hillary T. Welcome to the Jungle, Revised Edition: Facing Bipolar Without Freaking Out. (p. 2398)
Smith, Holly C. Tyler the Monkey & Andy the Mouse. (p. 2310)
Smith, Hope Anita. Keeping the Night Watch. Lewis, E. B., illus. (p. 1208)
—Way a Door Closes. Evans, Shane W., illus. (p. 2387)
Smith, Horace. Adam Brown, the Merchant, Vol. 3 of 3 (Classic Reprint) (p. 14)
—Adam Brown, Vol. 1 Of 3: The Merchant (Classic Reprint) (p. 14)
—Adam Brown, Vol. 2 Of 3: The Merchant (Classic Reprint) (p. 14)
—Brambletye House, or Cavaliers & Roundheads (Classic Reprint) (p. 275)
—Brambletye House, Vol. 1 Of 3: Or Cavaliers & Roundheads; a Novel (Classic Reprint) (p. 275)
—Gaieties & Gravities, Vol. 2 Of 3: A Series of Essays, Comic Tales, & Fugitive Vagaries, Now First Collected (Classic Reprint) (p. 805)
—Gaieties & Gravities, Vol. 3 Of 3: A Series of Essays, Comic Tales, & Fugitive Vagaries (Classic Reprint) (p. 805)
—Interludes: Being Two Essays, a Farce, & Some Verses (Classic Reprint) (p. 1126)
—Interludes (Third Series) Being Two Essays, a Ghost Story, & Some Verses (Classic Reprint) (p. 1126)
—Jane Lomax, or a Mother's Crime, Vol. 1 of 3 (Classic Reprint) (p. 1158)
—Jane Lomax, Vol. 2 Of 3: Or a Mother's Crime (Classic Reprint) (p. 1158)
—Midsummer Medley for 1830, Vol. 2 Of 2: A Series of Comic Tales, Sketches, & Fugitive Vagaries, in Prose & Verse (Classic Reprint) (p. 1462)
—Midsummer Medley, Vol. 1 Of 2: A Series of Comic Tales in Prose & Verse (Classic Reprint) (p. 1462)
—Moneyed Man, Vol. 1 Of 2: Or the Lesson of a Life (Classic Reprint) (p. 1493)
—New Forest, Vol. 1 Of 2: A Novel (Classic Reprint) (p. 1593)
—New Forest, Vol. 2 Of 3: A Novel (Classic Reprint) (p. 1593)
—New Forest, Vol. 3 Of 3: A Novel (Classic Reprint) (p. 1593)
—Reuben Apsley, Vol. 1 of 3 (Classic Reprint) (p. 1872)
—Tales of the Early Ages, Vol. 1 of 2 (Classic Reprint) (p. 2185)
—Tor Hill, Vol. 1 of 3 (Classic Reprint) (p. 2264)
—Tor Hill, Vol. 2 of 2 (Classic Reprint) (p. 2264)
—Zillah a Tale of the Holy City, Vol. 2 of 4 (Classic Reprint) (p. 2540)
—Zillah, Vol. 2 Of 3: A Tale of the Holy City (Classic Reprint) (p. 2540)
Smith, Hostetter And. Hostetter's Illustrated United States Almanac 1873: For Merchants, Mechanics, Miners, Farmers, Planters, & General Family Use; Carefully Calculated for Such Meridians & Latitudes As Are Best Suited for an Universal Calendar for the United States. (p. 1006)
—Hostetter's Illustrated United States Almanac 1878: For Merchants, Mechanics, Miners, Farmers, Planters, & General Family Use (Classic Reprint) (p. 1006)
Smith, Hubert. Tent Life with English Gipsies in Norway (Classic Reprint) (p. 2206)
Smith, Huhana, illus. see Tipene, Tim.
Smith, I. Gregory. Chief Ancient Philosophies: The Ethics of Aristotle. (p. 369)
—Chief Ancient Philosophies; the Ethics of Aristotle. (p. 369)
Smith, Ian. MR Stratfold's School for Monsters. (p. 1521)
Smith, Ian, illus. see Charlesworth, Liza.
Smith, Ian, illus. see Prasadam-Halls, Smriti & Halls, Smriti.
Smith, Ian & Julian, Sean. Rooster's Alarm. Smith, Ian, illus. (p. 1903)
Smith, Icy. Daddy, My Favorite Guy. (p. 495)
—Half Spoon of Rice: A Survival Story of the Cambodian Holocaust. Nhem, Sopaul, illus. (p. 911)
—Mystery of the Giant Mask of Sanxingdui. Roski, Gayle Garner, illus. (p. 1570)
—Three Years & Eight Months. Kindert, Jennifer C., illus. (p. 2236)
Smith, Isaac. Rabbit & Maow's Visit to Grandpa's House. (p. 1829)
Smith, Ivy. Roxie & the Deer. (p. 1909)
—Roxie y Los Ciervos. Maney, Melissa, illus. (p. 1909)
—Stickers VIP. (p. 2118)
—Stickers VIP. Maney, Melissa, illus. (p. 2118)
—Sully's New Home. (p. 2148)
Smith, J. a. x. Half-Way (Classic Reprint) (p. 911)
Smith, J. Albert. Goosey Green. (p. 869)
Smith, J. C. Sarah Colleen. (p. 1935)
Smith, J. K. Juvenile Lessons: Or the Child's First Reading Book (Classic Reprint) (p. 1200)
Smith, J. L. Blue & Purple Egg. Baker, David, illus. (p. 248)
Smith, J. Q. Humorous Sketches & Addresses (Classic Reprint) (p. 1051)
Smith, J. Thorne. Biltmore Oswald 1918: The Diary of a Hapless Recruit (Classic Reprint) (p. 227)
—Out o' Luck: Biltmore Oswald Very Much at Sea (Classic Reprint) (p. 1682)
Smith, J. W. Economic Democracy Pbk: A Grand Strategy for World Peace & Prosperity, 2nd Edition. (p. 624)
Smith, Jabez Burritt. High Joe, or the Logger's Story (Classic Reprint) (p. 968)
Smith, Jacquelyn. Pitty the City Kitty; Tokyo. Smith, Jacquelyn & Kalafatis, John, illus. (p. 1752)
Smith, Jacqui, illus. see Lincoln, James.
Smith, Jalisa Rose. In His Absence I Can Still Feel His Presence: (English with a Spanish Version Inside) Illustrations, Blueberry, illus. (p. 1105)
Smith, James. Booandik Tribe of South Australian Aborigines: A Sketch of Their Habits, Customs, Legends, & Language (Classic Reprint) (p. 256)
—Comic Miscellanies in Prose & Verse, Vol. 2 Of 2: With a Selection from His Correspondence, & Memoirs of His Life (Classic Reprint) (p. 429)
—Memoirs, Letters, & Comic Miscellanies, in Prose & Verse, of the Late James Smith, Vol. 1 of 2 (Classic Reprint) (p. 1444)
—Memoirs, Letters, & Comic Miscellanies, Vol. 1 Of 2: In Prose & Verse (Classic Reprint) (p. 1444)
—Quadrature & Geometry of the Circle Demonstrated (Classic Reprint) (p. 1821)
Smith, James Cosslett. Judas Iscariot: Read Before the Witenagemote on Good Friday Night, 1891 (Classic Reprint) (p. 1185)
Smith, James H., jt. auth. see Chadsey, Charles E.
Smith, James Harvey. Tales from Mcclure's: Humor (Classic Reprint) (p. 2182)
Smith, James Henery. Maudelle: A Novel Founded on Facts Gathered from Living Witnesses (Classic Reprint) (p. 1426)
Smith, James J. Mikey's Monster. (p. 1465)
Smith, James J. & James, Hollis. Mikey's Monster (Teenage Mutant Ninja Turtles) Spaziante, Patrick, illus. (p. 1465)
Smith, James Otis. Black Heroes of the Wild West: Featuring Stagecoach Mary, Bass Reeves, & Bob Lemmons. (p. 238)
Smith, Jamie, illus. see Barbo, Maria S. & Preller, James.
Smith, Jamie, illus. see Goodings, Christina.
Smith, Jamie, illus. see K J Bullock.
Smith, Jamie, illus. see Orloff, Karen Kaufman.
Smith, Jamie, illus. see Preller, James.
Smith, Jamie, illus. see Ryan, Margaret.
Smith, Jamie, illus. see Slater, Teddy.
Smith, Jan. Encyclopaedia Britannica: Animals All Around. (p. 648)
Smith, Jan, illus. see David, Juliet.
Smith, Jan, illus. see Holub, Joan.
Smith, Jan, illus. see Stanley, Malaika Rose.
Smith, Jan, illus. see Van-Pottelsberghe, Louise.
Smith, Jane. Hello, New House. Smith, Jane, illus. (p. 951)
—It's Easter, Chloe Zoe! Smith, Jane, illus. (p. 1145)
—It's Halloween, Chloe Zoe! Smith, Jane, illus. (p. 1145)
—It's Thanksgiving, Chloe Zoe! Smith, Jane, illus. (p. 1147)
—It's the First Day of Kindergarten, Chloe Zoe! Smith, Jane, illus. (p. 1147)
—It's the First Day of Preschool, Chloe Zoe! Smith, Jane, illus. (p. 1147)
—It's Valentine's Day, Chloe Zoe! Smith, Jane, illus. (p. 1148)
Smith, Jane, illus. see Pirc, Jerri J.
Smith, Jane, illus. see Seal, Kerry.
Smith, Jane Mary. Journal of the Lady Beatrix Graham (Classic Reprint) (p. 1180)
Smith, Jared, ed. see Crowther, Calvin.
Smith, Jason W. To Master the Boundless Sea: The U. S. Navy, the Marine Environment, & the Cartography of Empire. (p. 2253)
Smith, Jay. Adventures of Chewy the Chihuahua & Her Sidekick Cupcake. Morrison, Stacey, illus. (p. 22)
Smith, Jean Mitchell. Sunshine-Shadder (Classic Reprint) (p. 2153)
Smith, Jean Rogers. Hyacinth from Limbo: And Other Stories (Classic Reprint) (p. 1055)
Smith, Jeff. Bone. Smith, Jeff, illus. (p. 255)
—BONE Adventures. (p. 255)
—Bone Adventures. (p. 255)
—Bone Handbook. (p. 255)
—Crown of Horns. Smith, Jeff, illus. (p. 479)
—Graphix Collection Smith, Jeff, illus. (p. 881)
—Little Mouse Gets Ready. (p. 1323)
—Little Mouse Gets Ready, Level 1. (p. 1323)
—Old Man's Cave. Smith, Jeff, illus. (p. 1647)
—Rose. Vess, Charles, illus. (p. 1904)
—Smiley's Dream Book: From the Creator of BONE. (p. 2042)
—William Clark: Explorer & Diplomat. (p. 2468)
Smith, Jeff, illus. see Lester, Sharon.
Smith, Jeff, illus. see Sniegoski, Tom.
Smith, Jeff, jt. auth. see Sniegoski, Tom.
Smith, Jeff & Sniegoski, Tom. Tall Tales. Smith, Jeff, illus. (p. 2188)
Smith, Jen. Blakefields Mansion. (p. 242)
Smith, Jen, illus. see Kent, Alex.
Smith, Jennifer, illus. see Smith, Scott P.
Smith, Jennifer E. Field Notes on Love. (p. 723)
—Hello, Goodbye, & Everything in Between. (p. 951)
—Statistical Probability of Love at First Sight. (p. 2109)
—Storm Makers. Helquist, Brett, illus. (p. 2126)
—This Is What Happy Looks Like. (p. 2225)
—Windfall. (p. 2472)
Smith, Jennifer W. Orchard Birds. (p. 1669)
Smith, Jeremy. Why Why Why... Did Pirates Bury Their Treasure? (p. 2459)
Smith, Jessie Carney & Wynn, Linda T. Freedom Facts & Firsts: 400 Years of the African American Civil Rights Experience. (p. 782)
Smith, Jessie R. Four True Stories of Life & Adventure (Classic Reprint) (p. 773)
—Story of Washington (Classic Reprint) (p. 2135)
Smith, Jessie Willcox. Dickens's Children: Ten Drawings (Classic Reprint) (p. 541)
—Little Mother Goose: With Numerous Illustrations in Full Color & Black & White (Classic Reprint) (p. 1323)
Smith, Jessie Willcox, illus. see Coussens, Penrhyn W.
Smith, Jessie Willcox, illus. see Crothers, Samuel McChord.
Smith, Jessie Willcox, illus. see Moore, Clement C.
Smith, Jessie Willcox, jt. auth. see Burnett, Frances Hodgson.
Smith, Jessie Willcox, jt. auth. see MacDonald, George.
Smith, Jessie Willcox, jt. auth. see Moore, Clement Clarke.
Smith, Jessie Willcox, jt. auth. see Stevenson, Robert Louis.
Smith, Jessie Willcox & Wells, Carolyn. Seven Ages of Childhood. (p. 1993)
Smith, Jill & Diller, Howard. Consonant Primer II. (p. 442)
Smith, Jim. Barry Loser & the Case of the Crumpled Carton. (p. 168)
—Barry Loser & the Holiday of Doom. (p. 168)
—Barry Loser & the Trouble with Pets. (p. 168)
—Barry Loser Is the Best at Football NOT! (p. 168)
—Barry Loser's Book of Keel Stuff. (p. 168)
—Barry Loser's Christmas Joke Book. (p. 168)
—Future Ratboy & the Attack of the Killer Robot Grannies. (p. 803)
—Future Ratboy & the Quest for the Missing Thingy. (p. 803)
—I Am So over Being a Loser. (p. 1060)
—I Am Sort of a Loser. (p. 1060)
Smith, Jim, illus. see Blackburn, Katie.
Smith, Jim, illus. see Robinson, Hilary.
Smith, Jim & Loser, Barry. I Am Still Not a Loser. (p. 1060)
Smith, Jim W. W., illus. see Loxton, Daniel.
Smith, Jimmie. Jonas Little Donkey, Big Job. (p. 1177)
Smith, Jodene. Day the Crayons Quit. (p. 514)
Smith, Jodene Lynn & Garbani, Tony. Oats, Peas, Beans, & Barley Grow. (p. 1634)
Smith, Jodene Lynn & Reid, Stephanie. Animales. (p. 92)
—Animals. (p. 93)
—Plantas. (p. 1756)
—Plants. (p. 1757)
Smith, Jodene Lynn & Rice, Dona. Animal Homes (p. 90)
—Hogares de los Animales. (p. 986)
—Si Fuera un Árbol. (p. 2013)
Smith, Jodene Lynn & Rice, Dona Herweck. Animal Homes. (p. 90)
—Hogares de los Animales. (p. 986)
—If I Were a Tree. (p. 1091)
—Si Fuera un Árbol. (p. 2013)
Smith, Jodene Lynn & Thompson, Chad. Baa, Baa, Black Sheep. (p. 147)
—Beh, Beh, Borreguito Negro. (p. 192)
Smith, Jodie D. History of the Chisum War, or Life of Ike Fridge: Stirring Events of Cowboy Life on the Frontier (Classic Reprint) (p. 980)
Smith, John. Confessions of a Housekeeper (Classic Reprint) (p. 439)
—Fairy Book: Illustrated with Eighty One Cuts by Adams (Classic Reprint) (p. 696)
—General View of the Agriculture of the County of Argyle: With Observations on the Means of Its Improvement, Drawn up for the Consideration of the Board of Agriculture & Internal Improvement (Classic Reprint) (p. 814)
—Platonic Affections (Classic Reprint) (p. 1758)
—Sketches of Cantabs (Classic Reprint) (p. 2031)
—Tiger the Mule. Smith, D. W., illus. (p. 2241)
Smith, John A. Letters from Europe to the Children: Uncle John upon His Travels (Classic Reprint) (p. 1279)
Smith, John B. Explanation of Terms Used in Entomology. (p. 679)
—Explanation of Terms Used in Entomology - Scholar's Choice Edition. (p. 679)
Smith, John Bernhard. Role of Insects in the Forest: From the Annual Report of the State Geologist of New Jersey for 1899 (Classic Reprint) (p. 1898)
Smith, John Bernhardt. Report on the Mosquito Investigation: November 29th, 1902 (Classic Reprint) (p. 1866)
Smith, John D. H. Whale Whisperers Smith, Anne, illus. (p. 2403)
Smith, John G. Adventures of Eugene. (p. 23)
Smith, John Leonard. Merchant of Mount Vernon (Classic Reprint) (p. 1447)
Smith, John Moyr. Tales of Old Thule (Classic Reprint) (p. 2185)
Smith, John Russell. Catalogue of an Unique Collection of Ancient English Broadside Ballads Printed Entirely in the Black Letter (Classic Reprint) (p. 342)
Smith, John Talbot. Art of Disappearing (Classic Reprint) (p. 121)
—Saranac a Story of Lake Champlain (Classic Reprint) (p. 1935)
—Woman of Culture: A Canadian Romance (Classic Reprint) (p. 2485)
Smith, John Thomas. Nollekens & His Times, Vol. 1 Of 2: Comprehending a Life of That Celebrated Sculptor; & Memoirs of Several Contemporary Artists, from the Time of Roubiliac, Hogarth, & Reynolds, to That of Fuseli, Flaxman, & Blake (Classic Reprint) (p. 1618)
Smith, Jonathan. Struggling with Social Media. (p. 2142)
—White Hat Hacking. (p. 2444)
Smith, Jordan. Deception: Reality TV. (p. 523)
Smith, Jos. A., illus. see Bardoe, Cheryl.
Smith, Jos. A., illus. see Fleischman, Sid.
Smith, Joseph. Clear & Comprehensive View of the Being, Nature, & Attributes of God: Formed Not Only upon the Divine Authority of the Holy Scriptures, but the Solid Reasonings & Testimonies of the Best Authors, Both Heathen & Christian, Which Have Writ upon Th. (p. 402)
—Juvenile Instructor, Vol. 42: July 5, 1907 (Classic Reprint) (p. 1198)
Smith, Joseph F. Heroines of Mormondom (Classic Reprint) (p. 963)
—Improvement Era, Vol. 19: December, 1915 (Classic Reprint) (p. 1103)
—Improvement Era, Vol. 19: February, 1916 (Classic Reprint) (p. 1103)
—Juvenile Instructor, Vol. 37: Designed for the Advancement of the Young; October 1, 1902 (Classic Reprint) (p. 1195)
—Juvenile Instructor, 1906, Vol. 41: An Illustrated Semi-Monthly Magazine, Designed Expressly for the Education & Elevation of the Young (Classic Reprint) (p. 1195)
—Juvenile Instructor, 1916, Vol. 51: An Illustrated Monthly Magazine, Designed Expressly for the Education & Elevation of the Young (Classic Reprint) (p. 1195)
—Juvenile Instructor, Vol. 37: July 1, 1902 (Classic Reprint) (p. 1198)
—Juvenile Instructor, Vol. 37: Designed for the Advancement of the Young; June 1, 1902 (Classic Reprint) (p. 1198)
—Juvenile Instructor, Vol. 37: Designed for the Advancement of the Young; August 1, 1902 (Classic Reprint) (p. 1198)
—Juvenile Instructor, Vol. 37: Designed for the Advancement of the Young; December 1, 1902 (Classic Reprint) (p. 1198)
—Juvenile Instructor, Vol. 37: Organ of the Deseret Sunday School Union; February 15, 1902 (Classic Reprint) (p. 1198)
—Juvenile Instructor, Vol. 38: March 15, 1903 (Classic Reprint) (p. 1198)
—Juvenile Instructor, Vol. 38: January 1, 1903 (Classic Reprint) (p. 1198)
—Juvenile Instructor, Vol. 38: December 1, 1903 (Classic Reprint) (p. 1198)
—Juvenile Instructor, Vol. 38: February 1, 1903 (Classic Reprint) (p. 1198)
—Juvenile Instructor, Vol. 38: November 1, 1903 (Classic Reprint) (p. 1198)

—Gorillas: Beasts of the Wild. (p. 870)
—Grizzly Bears: Fierce Hunters. (p. 897)
—Hippos: Huge & Hungry. (p. 973)
Smith, Lucy Sackett. Elephants: From Trunk to Tail. (p. 634)
—Mighty Mammals (p. 1463)
—Tigers: Prowling Predators. (p. 2242)
Smith, Lynley. Acorn Adventures. (p. 11)
—Greenstone Mystery. (p. 895)
Smith, M. A., jt. auth. see Smith, M. a.
Smith, M. a. & Smith, M. A. Boy & His Wizard. Freeland, Devon & Contreras-Freeland, Gina, illus. (p. 268)
Smith, M. E. Love & Liking, Vol. 2 Of 3: A Novel (Classic Reprint) (p. 1359)
Smith, M. Jane. First Fry Bread: A Gitxsan Story. Wheeler, Jordan, ed. (p. 737)
Smith, Mabell S. C. Ethel Morton & the Christmas Ship. (p. 666)
—Ethel Morton at Chautauqua. (p. 666)
—Ethel Morton at Rose House. (p. 666)
—Ethel Morton's Enterprise. (p. 666)
—Ethel Morton's Holidays. (p. 666)
Smith, Mabell Shippie Clarke. Ethel Morton at Rose House (Classic Reprint) (p. 666)
Smith, Madge S. Alberta & the Others: A Truthful Story of Western Canada (Classic Reprint) (p. 40)
Smith, Maggie. And I Have You: A Book of Mothers & Babies. (p. 82)
—One Naked Baby. (p. 1661)
Smith, Maggie, illus. see Berry, Joy.
Smith, Maggie, illus. see George, Kristine O'Connell.
Smith, Maggie, illus. see Markes, Julie.
Smith, Maggie, illus. see Park, Linda Sue.
Smith, Maggie, illus. see Roosa, Karen.
Smith, Mandy M., illus. see Smith, B. M.
Smith, Maralyn. Halloween Is Here Tonight. (p. 912)
—Roller Rabbit. (p. 1898)
—Santa Is on His Way Tonight. (p. 1933)
Smith, Marcelle, illus. see Smith, Leone.
Smith, Margaret Bayard. Winter in Washington, or Memoirs of the Seymour Family, Vol. 1 of 2 (Classic Reprint) (p. 2475)
Smith, Marie, jt. auth. see Smith, Roland.
Smith, Marie & Smith, Roland. T Is for a Time. Graef, Renee, illus. (p. 2174)
Smith, Mark. Land of Fences. (p. 1241)
—Road to Winter. (p. 1888)
—Wilder Country. (p. 2466)
Smith, Mark David. Caravaggio: Signed in Blood (p. 327)
Smith, Marna J. Playing Safe with Preston. (p. 1760)
Smith, Martin. In-Line Skating. (p. 1105)
Smith, Martina. Historia de la Creacion: Un Relato de la Biblia Chispita. Grosshauser, Peter & Temple, Ed, illus. (p. 975)
—Historia de la Navidad: Un Relato de la Biblia Chispita. Grosshauser, Peter & Temple, Ed, illus. (p. 975)
—Story of Christmas: A Spark Bible Story Grosshauser, Peter, illus. (p. 2129)
—Story of Easter: A Spark Bible Story Grosshauser, Peter, illus. (p. 2130)
—Story of King David: A Spark Bible Story. Grosshauser, Peter, illus. (p. 2131)
Smith, Mary. Cranberry Cove Stories (Classic Reprint) (p. 466)
Smith, Mary Claire, illus. see Petty, Kate.
Smith, Mary Elizabeth, illus. see Shell, S. E.
Smith, Mary Emily Estella. Eskimo Stories (Classic Reprint) (p. 662)
Smith, Mary L. Ramblings of Clyde Frog & Jasmine. Bermejo, Hilbert, illus. (p. 1839)
Smith, Mary Lou. Celebrate Easter. (p. 348)
—Celebrate Halloween. (p. 348)
—Celebrate Saint Patrick's Day. (p. 349)
—I See Squares. (p. 1082)
—I See Triangles. (p. 1082)
Smith, Mary P. Wells. Browns (Classic Reprint) (p. 287)
Smith, Mary Prudence Wells. Their Canoe Trip (Classic Reprint) (p. 2215)
Smith, Mary Stuart. From Virginia to Georgia: A Tribute in Song (Classic Reprint) (p. 794)
—Lang Syne or the Wards of Mount Vernon: A Tale of the Revolutionary Era (Classic Reprint) (p. 1243)
Smith, Mary-Lou. I See Stars. (p. 1082)
Smith, Matt. Barbarian Lord. Smith, Matt, illus. (p. 165)
Smith, Matt, illus. see Derico, Laura Ring.
Smith, Matt, illus. see Schreiber, Joe.
Smith, Matthew, illus. see Marz, Ron.
Smith, Matthew Clark. Lighter Than Air: Sophie Blanchard, the First Woman Pilot. Tavares, Matt, illus. (p. 1299)
—Lighter Than Air: Sophie Blanchard, the First Woman Pilot: Candlewick Biographies. Tavares, Matt, illus. (p. 1299)
Smith, Matthew Dow, jt. auth. see Tipton, Denton J.
Smith, Matthew Ross. Lizzy Legend. (p. 1337)
Smith, Mattie Sampson. Miss. Claire's Pupils (Classic Reprint) (p. 1478)
Smith, Maude Summer. Busy Christmas Fairies: A Short Operetta for Kindergarten or First Grade Children (Classic Reprint) (p. 302)
Smith, Maudie. All the King's Tights (Early Reader) (p. 54)
—Opal Moonbaby & the Best Friend Project (book 1) (p. 1665)
Smith, Maureen Theresa. Your Moontime Magic: A Girl's Guide to Getting Your Period & Loving Your Body. (p. 2534)
Smith, Maurice. Uncle Charles & Me! (p. 2318)
Smith, Mavis, illus. see McMullan, Kate.
Smith, Maximilian. History of Juneteenth. (p. 978)
—Story of Cinco de Mayo. (p. 2129)
—What Is Groundhog Day? (p. 2415)
Smith, Maxwell. Fruit Magazine, Vol. 4: Scientific Farmer & Canadian Citizen; January, 1912 (Classic Reprint) (p. 796)
—Fruit Magazine, Vol. 4: Scientific Farmer & Canadian Citizen; December, 1911 (Classic Reprint) (p. 796)
—Fruit Magazine, Vol. 5: Scientific Farmer & Canadian Citizen; July, 1912 (Classic Reprint) (p. 796)
—Fruit Magazine, Vol. 5: Scientific Farmer & Canadian Citizen; September, 1912 (Classic Reprint) (p. 796)
Smith, Melanie. Detention Gang: Day of the Dead. (p. 535)
—Twist in the Branch. (p. 2306)
Smith, Melissa Cheesman, jt. auth. see Rasinski, Timothy V.
Smith Meyer, Ruth. Tyson's Sad Bad Day. (p. 2311)
Smith, Michael. It Starts with a Raindrop: Comienza con una Gota de Lluvia. Goley, Jonathon & Alvarenga, Angela, illus. (p. 1142)
—My Ducky Buddy. Oliva, Octavio, illus. (p. 1537)
—My Ducky Buddy/Mi Amigo el Pato. Oliva, Octavio, illus. (p. 1537)
—Relativity. Oliva, Octavio, illus. (p. 1862)
—Shackleton - the Boss: The Remarkable Adventures of Ernest Shackleton. Brady, Annie, illus. (p. 1996)
—Thomas the T. Rex: The Journey of a Young Dinosaur to Los Angeles. Roski, Gayle Garner, illus. (p. 2229)
Smith, Michael & Aguiler, Manny. Smile: B una Sonrisa. Aguiler, Manny, illus. (p. 2041)
Smith, Michael & Oliva, Octavio. Grasshopper Buddy. Oliva, Octavio, illus. (p. 881)
—Relativity: Relatividad. Oliva, Octavio, illus. (p. 1862)
Smith, Michael & Roski, Gayle Garner. Thomas the T. Rex: The Journey of a Young Dinosaur to Los Angeles. Roski, Gayle Garner, illus. (p. 2229)
Smith, Michael & Wang, Emily. My Ducky Buddy. Oliva, Octavio, illus. (p. 1537)
Smith, Michael W. Let's Get Ready for Bed (p. 1273)
Smith, Michael W. & Nawrocki, Mike. Let's Get Ready for Bed (p. 1273)
—Merry Christmas, Nighty Night (p. 1450)
—Nighty Night & Good Night (p. 1608)
—Nighty Night & Good Night Gift Set (p. 1608)
Smith, Michael W., Jr., jt. auth. see Goodman, Susan E.
Smith, Michelle. Play On. (p. 1759)
Smith, Michelle, illus. see Morrissey, Melissa.
Smith, Mike. Hundred Decker Bus. (p. 1051)
Smith, Mike, illus. see Prentice, Andrew.
Smith, Mike, illus. see Williamson, Lisa.
Smith, Mildred M. Louie the Blue Frog. (p. 1357)
Smith, Milton. Swan Quarter. (p. 2167)
Smith, Minna Caroline. Joy of Captain Ribot: Authorized Translation from the Original A. Palacio Valdes (Classic Reprint) (p. 1184)
Smith, Minnie. Is It Just? (Classic Reprint) (p. 1137)
Smith, Miranda. What's Inside? McLelland, Kate, illus. (p. 2424)
Smith, Miranda, jt. auth. see Callery, Sean.
Smith, Miss Diane Pearl. Princess S Magickal Christmas. (p. 1799)
Smith, Misty. Adventures of Lucky Harry Truckee the Desert Tortoise. (p. 25)
—Green Cheese & Chocolate. (p. 893)
—Slight & Might & the World of Thoughts: A Fairytale for All. (p. 2038)
Smith, Molly. Border Breakdown: The Fall of the Berlin Wall. (p. 262)
—Border Breakdown: The Fall of the Berlin Wall. Opie, David, illus. (p. 262)
—día Que Me Sentí Triste: Lap Book. Poole, Helen, illus. (p. 537)
—día Que Me Sentí Triste. Poole, Helen, illus. (p. 537)
—Don't Worry, Mason. Poole, Helen, illus. (p. 584)
—Don't Worry, Mason Lap Book. Poole, Helen, illus. (p. 584)
—No Te Preocupes, Mateo: Lap Book. Poole, Helen, illus. (p. 1615)
—No Te Preocupes, Mateo. Poole, Helen, illus. (p. 1615)
—Paciencia, María: Lap Book. Patton, Julia, illus. (p. 1691)
—Paciencia, María. Patton, Julia, illus. (p. 1691)
—Roly-Poly Pillbugs. (p. 1899)
—Sé Honesta, Julia: Lap Book. Monés, Marc, illus. (p. 1966)
—Sé Honesta, Julia. Monés, Marc, illus. (p. 1966)
—Yo Puedo Seguir Las Reglas: Lap Book. Patton, Julia, illus. (p. 2522)
—Yo Puedo Seguir Las Reglas. Patton, Julia, illus. (p. 2522)
Smith, Molly & Newmark Learning, LLC. Be Honest, Jess: Set Of 6. (p. 177)
—Be Honest, Jess: Lap Book with Teacher Guide. (p. 177)
—Be Patient, Maddie: Set Of 6. (p. 177)
—Be Patient, Maddie: Lap Book with Teacher Guide. (p. 177)
—Day I Felt Sad: Set Of 6. (p. 513)
—Day I Felt Sad: Lap Book with Teacher Guide. (p. 513)
—día Que Me Sentí Triste: Set Of 6. (p. 537)
—día Que Me Sentí Triste: Lap Book with Teacher Guide. (p. 537)
—Don't Worry, Mason: Set Of 6. (p. 584)
—Don't Worry, Mason: Lap Book with Teacher Guide. (p. 584)
—I Can Follow the Rules: Set Of 6. (p. 1062)
—I Can Follow the Rules: Lap Book with Teacher Guide. (p. 1062)
—No Te Preocupes, Mateo: Set Of 6. (p. 1615)
—No Te Preocupes, Mateo: Lap Book with Teacher Guide. (p. 1615)
—Paciencia, María: Set Of 6. (p. 1691)
—Paciencia, María: Lap Book with Teacher Guide. (p. 1691)
—Sé Honesta, Julia: Set Of 6. (p. 1966)
—Sé Honesta, Julia: Lap Book with Teacher Guide. (p. 1966)
—Yo Puedo Seguir Las Reglas: Set Of 6. (p. 2522)
—Yo Puedo Seguir Las Reglas: Lap Book with Teacher Guide. (p. 2522)
Smith, Molly & NRDC. NRDC Simple Steps for Kids Activity Book. Carpenter, Tad, illus. (p. 1628)
Smith, Nancy. Christmas Duck. (p. 385)
—Fed by Ravens. (p. 717)
—Whale of a Tale. (p. 2403)
Smith, Nancy C., illus. see Seabrooke, Brenda.
Smith, Natalie. Habitat Protection. (p. 908)
Smith, Neil. Jason & the Argonauts (p. 1160)
—Robin Hood (p. 1891)
Smith, Nellie J. Stories & Poems (Classic Reprint) (p. 2122)
Smith, Nellie May. Mother's Reply: A Pamphlet for Mothers (Classic Reprint) (p. 1510)
Smith, Nerissia. Prince de'Mario's Adventure Dartes, Staci, illus. (p. 1794)
Smith, Nicole, ed. see Instructables.com.
Smith, Nigel. Industrial Revolution. (p. 1117)
—Nathalia Buttface & the Embarrassing Camp Catastrophe (Nathalia Buttface) (p. 1576)
—Nathalia Buttface & the Most Embarrassing Dad in the World (Nathalia Buttface) (p. 1576)
—Nathalia Buttface & the Most Embarrassing Five Minutes of Fame Ever (Nathalia Buttface) (p. 1576)
—Nathalia Buttface & the Most Epically Embarrassing Trip Ever (Nathalia Buttface) (p. 1576)
—Nathalia Buttface & the Totally Embarrassing Bridesmaid Disaster (Nathalia Buttface) (p. 1576)
Smith, Niki. BTS Army Handbook. (p. 288)
—Deep & Dark Blue. (p. 524)
Smith, Nikki. Five Little Speckled Frogs Activity Guide. (p. 744)
Smith, Nikki Shannon. Amazing Life of Azaleah Lane. Lobo, Mari, illus. (p. 65)
—Ann Fights for Freedom: An Underground Railroad Survival Story. Trunfio, Alessia, illus. (p. 97)
—Charlotte Spies for Justice: A Civil War Survival Story. Trunfio, Alessia, illus. (p. 361)
—Dramatic Life of Azaleah Lane. Felix, Gloria, illus. (p. 597)
—Little Christmas Elf. Mitchell, Susan, illus. (p. 1314)
—Noelle at Sea: A Titanic Survival Story. Trunfio, Alessia & Forsyth, Matt, illus. (p. 1617)
—Sarah Journeys West: An Oregon Trail Survival Story. Trunfio, Alessia, illus. (p. 1935)
—Star Like Jesse Owens. (p. 2102)
—Treasure Hunt. (p. 2281)
Smith, Nikkolas. Golden Girls of Rio. (p. 857)
Smith, Nikkolas, illus. see Walters, Meg.
Smith, Noah. Big Book of Super Hero Bedtime Stories. (p. 218)
Smith, Nora A., jt. auth. see Wiggin, Kate Douglas.
Smith, Nora Archibald. Plays, Pantomimes & Tableaux for Children (Classic Reprint) (p. 1761)
—Under the Cactus Flag a Story of Life in Mexico (Classic Reprint) (p. 2321)
Smith, Nora Archibald, jt. auth. see Wiggin, Kate Douglas Smith.
Smith, Nora Archibald, jt. auth. see Wiggin, Kate Douglas.
Smith, Nora Archibald, jt. ed. see Wiggin, Kate Douglas.
Smith, Nora Del. Cave (a Comedy in Three Acts), and, the Woman's Masquerade (a Comedy in One Act) (Classic Reprint) (p. 347)
Smith, O. G. Picture-Play Weekly, Vol. 1: April 10 to October 2, 1915 (Classic Reprint) (p. 1740)
Smith, Ora. Christmas Story of Light. Smith, Ora, illus. (p. 387)
Smith, Ormond G. Picture-Play Magazine, Vol. 12: March-August 1920 (Classic Reprint) (p. 1740)
Smith, Owen, illus. see Armstrong, Jennifer.
Smith, P. Athene, illus. see Cooper, John E. & Cooper, Margaret.
Smith, P. Athene, tr. see Cooper, John E. & Cooper, Margaret.
Smith, Paige. 12 Immigrants Who Made the American Military Great. (p. 2551)
Smith, Patricia. Leafy Sea Dragons. Mitten, Luana K., ed. (p. 1254)
Smith, Patrick D. Land Remembered: the Graphic Novel Frattino, Andre, illus. (p. 1242)
Smith, Paul. Come & Count with Us. Tee, Jacqueline, illus. (p. 428)
—Little Lost Egg. Smith, Steven, illus. (p. 1321)
Smith, Paula. Attention-Deficit & Other Behavior Disorders. (p. 135)
—Autism & Other Pervasive Developmental Disorders. (p. 139)
—Be the Change for the Environment. (p. 177)
—Be the Change in the World. (p. 177)
—Be the Change in Your Community. (p. 178)
—Be the Change in Your School. (p. 178)
—Birthdays in Different Places. (p. 234)
—Clothing in Different Places. (p. 407)
—Depression & Other Mood Disorders. (p. 530)
—Earthquakes, Eruptions, & Other Events That Change Earth. (p. 618)
—Foods in Different Places. (p. 760)
—Homes in Different Places. (p. 998)
—How Do Wind & Water Change Earth? (p. 1029)
—Measure It! (p. 1434)
—Model It! (p. 1486)
—Phobias & Other Anxiety Disorders. (p. 1735)
—Plan & Investigate It! (p. 1754)
—Protecting Earth's Surface. (p. 1808)
—Prove It! (p. 1808)
—Schizophrenia & Other Psychotic Disorders. (p. 1944)
—Schools in Different Places. (p. 1947)
—Transportation in Different Places. (p. 2278)
—Understanding Metaphors. (p. 2325)
—Understanding Personification. (p. 2325)
—Understanding Similes. (p. 2325)
Smith, Paula & Colozza Cocca, Lisa. Calendar Math. (p. 310)
—Time Word Problems. (p. 2246)
Smith, Paula & Kopp, Megan. Be the Change in Your Community. (p. 178)
Smith, Paula & Mason, Helen. Length Word Problems. (p. 1266)
—Word Problems: Mass & Volume. (p. 2493)
Smith, Peggy B., jt. auth. see Ryder, Verdene.
Smith, Peter. Language Exercises for First, Second & Third Book Pupils (Classic Reprint) (p. 1243)
—Monsieur Albert Rides to Glory. Graham, Bob, illus. (p. 1495)
Smith, Phil, illus. see Lowery, Lawrence F.
Smith, Pieter Ernst. Donkey Is Not Stupid, a Donkey Can Think. Shirley-Smith, Sanette, illus. (p. 581)
Smith, Poca T. Margoleen (Classic Reprint) (p. 1404)
Smith, Pohla, jt. auth. see Cantwell, Lois.
Smith, R. B. Hugging to Music: A Story from Life (Classic Reprint) (p. 1048)
—Hugging to Music. (p. 1048)
Smith, R. Bosworth. Bird Life & Bird Lore (Classic Reprint) (p. 230)
Smith, R. Cadwallader. Nature's Nurseries (Yesterday's Classics) (p. 1582)
Smith, R. M. Peep in the Deep - Sea Creature Counting Book: Sea Creature Counting Book. (p. 1713)
Smith, Raissa B., illus. see Smith, Brenda J.
Smith, Ralph W., jt. auth. see Seagle, Edward E., Jr.
Smith, Raymond R. Righteous Ray-Ray Has a Bad Day. (p. 1882)
—Righteous Ray-Ray Has a Bad Day Beginning Readers Edition. Davis, Alan, illus. (p. 1882)
Smith, Reneka. Amazing Grace. (p. 65)
Smith, Rich. Alabama (p. 38)
—Arkansas (p. 116)
—Bill of Rights (p. 226)
—California (p. 310)
—Georgia (p. 820)
—Illinois (p. 1095)
—Indiana (p. 1116)
—Kentucky (p. 1209)
—Louisiana (p. 1358)
—Massachusetts (p. 1417)
—Mississippi (p. 1482)
—Oklahoma (p. 1643)
—Oregon (p. 1669)
Smith, Richard. Cheeky Monkey. (p. 363)
Smith, Richard B. & Bernard, Felix. Walking in a Winter Wonderland: Based on the Song by Felix Bernard & Richard B. Smith. Hopgood, Tim, illus. (p. 2372)
—Walking in a Winter Wonderland. Hopgood, Tim, illus. (p. 2372)
Smith, Richard G., illus. see Murphy, Emily.
Smith, Richard Gordon. Ancient Tales & Folklore of Japan (Classic Reprint) (p. 82)
Smith, Richard Mcallister. Confederate Primer (Classic Reprint) (p. 438)
—Confederate Spelling Book, with Reading Lessons for the Young: Adapted to the Use of Schools or for Private Instruction (Classic Reprint) (p. 438)
Smith, Rita & Baish, Vanessa. Self-Image & Eating Disorders. (p. 1987)
Smith, Robert. Angel Finds the Way. (p. 85)
Smith, Roberta, illus. see Cameron, Ann.
Smith, Robin W. If You Got It a Truck Brought It: For We the People. Smith, Robin W., illus. (p. 1092)
Smith, Robin Wayne. If You Got It, a Truck Brought It. Smith, Robin Wayne, illus. (p. 1092)
Smith, Rod. Michael Collins: The Big Fellow. (p. 1457)
—Pádraig Pearse & the Easter Rising 1916. Dillon, Derry, illus. (p. 1692)
Smith, Roger. History of Punishment & Imprisonment. (p. 979)
—Human Rights & Protecting Individuals Russett, Bruce, ed. (p. 1050)
—Humanitarian Relief & Lending a Hand Russett, Bruce, ed. (p. 1050)
—Political Prisoners. (p. 1771)
—Rural Teens on the Move: Cars, Motorcycles, & off-Road Vehicles. (p. 1916)
—Treatment of Prisoners & Prison Conditions. (p. 2283)
Smith, Roger & McIntosh, Martha. Juveniles Growing up in Prison. (p. 1200)
Smith, Roger B. Adventures of Xavier Winfield & His Pal Oggie, EPISODE ONE: The Great Camping Adventure. (p. 29)
Smith, Roland. Ascent: A Peak Marcello Adventure. (p. 125)
—Ascent. (p. 125)
—Beneath. (p. 199)
—Chupacabra. (p. 390)
—Descent. (p. 531)
—Edge. (p. 625)
—Elephant Run. (p. 634)
—Kitty Hawk. (p. 1226)
—Mutation. (p. 1530)
—Shatterproof. (p. 2003)
—Storm Runners. (p. 2127)
—Surge. (p. 2163)
—Tentacles. (p. 2206)
—White House. (p. 2444)
—White House. (p. 2444)
Smith, Roland, jt. auth. see Spradlin, Michael P.
Smith, Roland, jt. auth. see Spradlin, Michael.
Smith, Roland & Smith, Marie. S Is for Smithsonian: America's Museum Alphabet. Frankenhuyzen, Gijsbert van, illus. (p. 1919)
Smith, Roland & Spradlin, Michael P. Alamo. (p. 39)
—Windy City (p. 2472)
Smith, Ronald L. Black Panther: The Young Prince. (p. 239)
—Black Panther the Young Prince. (p. 239)
—Edge. (p. 625)
—Gloom Town. (p. 844)
—Hoodoo. (p. 1000)
—Mesmerist. (p. 1451)
—Owls Have Come to Take Us Away. (p. 1689)
Smith, Rosemarie. Meet the Bubblechomps - & the Bubblechomps Go Skiing. (p. 1439)
Smith, Rosemary. Lizard Tales: Lizzie Walks on the Wild Side. (p. 1336)
—Lizzie Goes to Tea. (p. 1336)
—Three Wishes for Maddy. (p. 2235)
—Woody Gets Dunked. (p. 2492)
Smith, Rosie. My Mom's the Best. Whatley, Bruce, illus. (p. 1556)
Smith, Rosie & Whatley, Bruce. Danny Da Vinci: the Secret of the Mona Lisa. (p. 504)
Smith, Rowland. Greek Romances of Heliodorus, Longus, & Achilles Tatius: Comprising the Ethiopics; or Adventures of Theagenes & Chariclea; the Pastoral Amours of Daphnis & Chloe; & the Loves of Clitopho & Leucippe (Classic Reprint) (p. 893)
Smith, Roy. Louphole Forest Tells Its Tale of Enchantment. Magpie, ed. (p. 1358)
Smith, Rupert. Poets of World War I (p. 1767)
Smith, Russell D. Wild White Woods: Or a Winter Camp on the Canada Line (Classic Reprint) (p. 2465)
Smith, Ruth-Mary, illus. see Navolio, Kara.
Smith, S. Hey Silly Cat! Dont Tease the Dog! (p. 964)
Smith, S. & Robins, W. Airport Sticker Book. (p. 38)
Smith, S. Theyre. Old Cronies: A Comedietta in One Act, for Two Male Characters (Classic Reprint) (p. 1645)
Smith, Sam. Around the World Mazes. (p. 119)
—Flags Book & Jigsaw Puzzle. (p. 746)

Smithsonian Institution Dept of Entomo, jt. creator see Entomological Society of Washington.
Smithsonian Institution, ed. Dinosaurs & More! Write-with-Me Alphabet. (p. 550)
—Insects A to Z. (p. 1122)
—Oh Where, Oh Where Has My Little Dog Gone? (p. 1642)
Smithsonian Institution Staff, jt. auth. see Galvin, Laura Gates.
Smithsonian Institution Staff, jt. auth. see Halfmann, Janet.
Smithsonian Institution Staff, jt. auth. see Hammerslough, Jane.
Smithsonian Institution Staff, jt. auth. see Zoehfeld, Kathleen Weidner.
Smithsonian Institution Staff, contrib. by. Destined for Space: Our Story of Exploration (p. 534)
Smithsonian Kids, photos by see Murphy, Patricia J.
Smithsonian Kids, photos by see Wing, Scarlett & Cottage Door Press.
Smithsonian Kids, photos by see Wing, Scarlett.
Smithwick, John. All-Star Players (p. 53)
—Meet Lebron James: Basketball's King James. (p. 1438)
—Meet Peyton Manning: Football's Top Quarterback. (p. 1439)
Smithwick, John W. Drift. (p. 604)
Smithwick, Julie. I Love Seeds. Fritz Perry, Marie, illus. (p. 1072)
Smithwick, Noah. Facsimile Reproduction of the Evolution of a State: Or Recollections of Old Texas Days (Classic Reprint) (p. 693)
Smithyman, Kathryn, jt. auth. see Kalman, Bobbie.
Smith-Young, Lucinda. Seven Seals: A Sinner's Dream; Conversion; Daniel in the Lion's Den; Meditation; Distance of Falling; Vision of the Judgement; Vision of after the Judgement (Classic Reprint) (p. 1994)
Smittenaar, H. G., tr. see Jer, Baant.
Smolik, Jane Petrlik. Currents. (p. 488)
Smolin, Lori A. & Grosvenor, Mary B. Nutrition & Eating Disorders. (p. 1632)
Smolin, Michael, illus. see Stone, Jon.
Smoljan, Marina, illus. see Brooks, D. K.
Smolka, Bo. Baltimore Ravens (p. 162)
—Baseball (p. 168)
—Florida Marlins. (p. 751)
—Girls Play to Win Lacrosse. (p. 839)
—Inside MLB (p. 1123)
—Jackie Robinson Breaks the Color Barrier (p. 1153)
—Miami Marlins (p. 1456)
—Negro Leagues' Integration Era. (p. 1585)
—Story of the Negro Leagues. (p. 2134)
—Washington Redskins (p. 2382)
Smollett, T. Adventures of Telemachus, Vol. 1: The Son of Ulysses (Classic Reprint) (p. 28)
Smollett, Tobias. Adventures of Sir Launcelot Greaves (Classic Reprint) (p. 28)
—Miscellaneous Works of Tobias Smollett, M. d, Vol. 3: With Memoirs of His Life & Writings; Containing the Adventures of Peregrine Pickle, Part II. & Plays & Poems (Classic Reprint) (p. 1477)
—Miscellaneous Works of Tobias Smollett, M. d, Vol. 1 Of 6: With Memoirs of His Life & Writings; Containing the Adventures of Roderick Random (Classic Reprint) (p. 1477)
—Miscellaneous Works of Tobias Smollett, M. d, Vol. 5 Of 6: With Memoirs of His Life & Writings; Containing the Adventures of Sir Launcelot Greaves, & Travels Through France & Italy (Classic Reprint) (p. 1477)
Smollett, Tobias George. Adventures of Ferdinand Count Fathom: In Two Volumes (Classic Reprint) (p. 23)
—Adventures of Peregrine Pickle, Vol. 1 Of 4: In Which Are Included, Memoirs of a Lady of Quality (Classic Reprint) (p. 26)
—Adventures of Peregrine Pickle, Vol. 1 of 4 (Classic Reprint) (p. 26)
—Adventures of Roderick Random: In Two Volumes (Classic Reprint) (p. 27)
—Adventures of Roderick Random (Classic Reprint) (p. 27)
—Adventures of Roderick Random, Vol. 3 of 3 (Classic Reprint) (p. 27)
—Adventures of Sir Launcelot Greaves: And the Adventures of an Atom (Classic Reprint) (p. 28)
—Adventures of Sir Launcelot Greaves (Classic Reprint) (p. 28)
—Expedition of Humphry Clinker (Classic Reprint) (p. 677)
—Expedition of Humphry Clinker, Vol. 1 of 2 (Classic Reprint) (p. 677)
—Miscellaneous Works of Tobias Smollett: Complete in One Volume, with Memoir of the Author (Classic Reprint) (p. 1477)
—Miscellaneous Works of Tobias Smollett M. d, Vol. 3: With Memoirs of His Life & Writings; Containing, the Adventures of Peregrine Pickle, Part II. , & Plays & Poems (Classic Reprint) (p. 1477)
—Miscellaneous Works of Tobias Smollett, M. d, Vol. 3: With Memoirs of His Life & Writings; Containing the Adventures of Peregrine Pickle, Part II. & Plays & Poems (Classic Reprint) (p. 1477)
—Miscellaneous Works of Tobias Smollett, M. d, Vol. 1 Of 6: With Memoirs of His Life & Writings; Containing the Life of Smollett, & the Adventures of Roderick Random (Classic Reprint) (p. 1477)
—Miscellaneous Works of Tobias Smollett, M. d, Vol. 6 Of 6: With Memoirs of His Life & Writings; Containing the Expedition of Humphry Clinker, and, the Adventures of an Atom (Classic Reprint) (p. 1477)
—Miscellaneous Works of Tobias Smollett, M. d, Vol. 5 Of 6: With Memoirs of His Life & Writings; Containing the Adventures of Sir Launcelot Greaves, & Travels Through France & Italy (Classic Reprint) (p. 1477)
—Miscellaneous Works of Tobias Smollett, M. d, Vol. 4 Of 6: With Memoirs of His Life & Writings; Containing the Adventure of Ferdinand Count Fathom, & an Account of the Expedition Against Carthagena (Classic Reprint) (p. 1477)
—Miscellaneous Works of Tobias Smollett, M. d, Vol. 4 Of 6: With Memoirs of His Life & Writings by Robert Anderson M. D. ; Containing the Adventures of Ferdinand Count Fathom; an Account of the Expedition Against Carthagena (Classic Reprint) (p. 1477)
—Miscellaneous Works of Tobias Smollett, Vol. 4 Of 5: To Which Is Prefixed, Memoirs of His Life & Writings (Classic Reprint) (p. 1477)
—Select Works of Tobias Smollett, Vol. 1 Of 2: Containing the Adventures of Peregrine Pickle, & the Adventures of Ferdinand Count Fathom (Classic Reprint) (p. 1986)
—Select Works of Tobias Smollett, Vol. 2 Of 2: Containing the Adventures of Roderick Random; the Adventures of Sir Launcelot Greaves; the Expedition of Humphry Clinker; the History & Adventures of an Atom; & Poems (Classic Reprint) (p. 1986)
—Works of Tobias Smollet, Vol. 1 (Classic Reprint) (p. 2500)
—Works of Tobias Smollett: With a Memoir of His Life & Writings (Classic Reprint) (p. 2500)
—Works of Tobias Smollett. (p. 2500)
—Works of Tobias Smollett, Carefully Selected & Edited from the Best Authorities: With Numerous Original Historical Notes & a Life of the Author (Classic Reprint) (p. 2500)
—Works of Tobias Smollett, Vol. 10 Of 12: The Adventures of Sir Launcelot Greaves (Classic Reprint) (p. 2500)
—Works of Tobias Smollett, Vol. 12: Miscellanies (Classic Reprint) (p. 2500)
—Works of Tobias Smollett, Vol. 2: With an Introduction (Classic Reprint) (p. 2500)
—Works of Tobias Smollett, Vol. 2: With an Introduction by W. E. Henley (Classic Reprint) (p. 2500)
—Works of Tobias Smollett, Vol. 2: Roderick Random, Part III, & Sir Launcelot Greaves (Classic Reprint) (p. 2500)
—Works of Tobias Smollett, Vol. 3: The Adventures of Peregrine Pickle (Classic Reprint) (p. 2500)
Smollin, Michael, illus. see Cerf, Roseanne.
Smollin, Michael, illus. see Stone, Jon & Albee, Sarah.
Smollin, Michael, illus. see Stone, Jon.
Smoot, Madeline, ed. Monsters Hiding in Your Closet. (p. 1498)
—Perilous Princesses. (p. 1723)
Smouha, C. K. Sock Story. Marton, Eleonora, illus. (p. 2054)
Smouse, Phil. Bible Storybook for Girls. (p. 214)
Smucker, Anna. No Star Nights. Johnson, Steve & Fancher, Lou, illus. (p. 1615)
Smucker, Anna Egan. Brother Giovanni's Little Reward. Hall, Amanda, illus. (p. 286)
—Golden Delcious: A Cinderella Apple Story. Kemly, Kathleen, illus. (p. 857)
Smucker, Anna Egan, jt. auth. see Harshman, Marc.
Smucker, Emily. Emily: My True Story of Chronic Illness & Missing Out on Life. (p. 642)
Smucker, Samuel Mosheim. Yankee Slave Driver, or the Black & White Rivals (Classic Reprint) (p. 2517)
Smucker, Shawn. Edge of over There. (p. 625)
Smundak, Katharina. Truth Behind GMOs. (p. 2297)
Smy, Pmc. Jeremy & the Magic Shelf. (p. 1164)
Smyer, Lori. Journey Through Galaxies (p. 1181)
Smykowski, Sarah. Most Powerful Words about Civil Rights (p. 1508)
Smyles, Jg. Bunny Bunda's First Adventure. (p. 298)
Smylie, Adolphe E. Marines: And Other War Verse (Classic Reprint) (p. 1406)
Smyth, Bethinna & Winkelmann, Rachele. Sleepy Monk. (p. 2037)
Smyth, Christy M. Danny & Debbie Dove Talk to God. (p. 503)
Smyth, Ciara. Falling in Love Montage. (p. 701)
Smyth, Ethel. Impressions That Remained, Vol. 1 Of 2: Memoirs; Part I. the Smyth Family Robinson to 1877); Part II. Germany & Two Winters in Italy (1877 to 1880) (Classic Reprint) (p. 1102)
—Impressions That Remained, Vol. 2 Of 2: Memoirs; Part II (Continued), Germany & Two Winters in Italy, (1880 to 1885); Part III, in the Desert, (1885 to 1891) (Classic Reprint) (p. 1102)
Smyth, Fiona, illus. see Silverberg, Cory.
Smyth, George Hutchinson. Little Bessie (Classic Reprint) (p. 1311)
Smyth, Iain, illus. see Ratnett, Michael.
Smyth, J. Paterson. Boys & Girls Life of Christ (Yesterday's Classics) (p. 272)
Smyth, Jimmy. Causeway Coast. (p. 347)
—Fairy Princess. (p. 697)
—Leprechaun. Ozzy, illus. (p. 1268)
—Lost Fairy. (p. 1353)
—Magic Garden. (p. 1377)
—Titanic the Untold Story. (p. 2251)
Smyth, Lindley. True Stories about Children of All Nations: True Stories of Boys & Girls in Every Land; Their Sports & Games & How They Live (Classic Reprint) (p. 2294)
Smyth, Marie, jt. auth. see Trotsky, Rebecca.
Smyth, Whitney, ed. see McHugh, Jessica.
Smythe, Albert Ernest Stafford. Mrs. Lothbury's Gospel (Classic Reprint) (p. 1522)
Smythe, E. Louise. Primary Reader: Old-Time Stories, Fairy Tales & Myths, Retold by Children. (p. 1792)
Smythe, Emma Louise. Primary Reader: Old-Time Stories, Fairy Tales & Myths, Retold by Children (Classic Reprint) (p. 1792)
—Reynard the Fox (Classic Reprint) (p. 1874)
Smythe, James P. Rescuing the Czar: Two Authentic Diaries Arranged & Translated. (p. 1868)
—Rescuing the Czar: Two Authentic Diaries Arranged & Translated (Classic Reprint) (p. 1868)
Smythe, Katie. Our Class Goldfish. (p. 1677)
—Robins Lay Eggs. (p. 1891)
—Squirrel Gets Ready. (p. 2095)
—Summer Picnic. (p. 2150)
Smythe, Richard, illus. see Blackburn, Katie.
Smythe, Richard, illus. see Jenkins, Martin.
Smythe, Richard, illus. see McCanna, Tim.
Smythe, Richard, illus. see Ng, Yvonne.
Smythe, Richard, illus. see Parachini, Jodie.
Smythe, Richard, illus. see Powell-Tuck, Maudie.
Smythe, Richard, jt. auth. see Stansbie, Stephanie.
Smythe, Theresa. Chester's Colorful Easter Eggs. Smythe, Theresa, illus. (p. 366)
Smythies, Gordon. Acquitted, Vol. 1 Of 3: A Novel (Classic Reprint) (p. 11)
—Acquitted, Vol. 2 Of 3: A Novel (Classic Reprint) (p. 11)
—Acquitted, Vol. 3 Of 3: A Novel (Classic Reprint) (p. 11)
—Breach of Promise, Vol. 1 Of 3: A Novel (Classic Reprint) (p. 277)
—Daily Governess, or Self-Dependence, Vol. 1 of 3 (Classic Reprint) (p. 496)
—Matchmaker, Vol. 3 Of 3: A Novel (Classic Reprint) (p. 1420)
—Warning to Wives, or the Platonic Lover, Vol. 1 Of 3: A Novel (Classic Reprint) (p. 2379)
Smythies, Harriet M. G. Bride Elect, Vol. 2 Of 3: A Novel (Classic Reprint) (p. 280)
Smythies, Smythies. Lover's Quarrel, or the County Ball, Vol. 1 of 3 (Classic Reprint) (p. 1362)
Snader, Gregory, illus. see Krone, Thelma Smith.
Snadowsky, Daria. Anatomy of a Single Girl. (p. 79)
Snair, Iona, jt. auth. see Huff, Tim.
Snaith, Andy, photos by see Bicknell, Joanna & Page, Nick.
Snaith, Andy, photos by see Gordon, Bob.
Snaith, Andy, photos by see Phillips, Sarah.
Snaith, J. C. Araminta (Classic Reprint) (p. 109)
—Broke of Covenden (Classic Reprint) (p. 284)
—Henry Northcote (Classic Reprint) (p. 955)
—Mistress Dorothy Marvin: Being Excerpta from the Memoirs of Sir Edward Armstrong, Baronet, of Copeland Hall, in the County of Somerset (Classic Reprint) (p. 1483)
—Mrs. Fitz (Classic Reprint) (p. 1522)
—Sailor (Classic Reprint) (p. 1923)
—Van Roon (Classic Reprint) (p. 2347)
—William Jordan Junior (Classic Reprint) (p. 2468)
Snaith, John Collis. Araminta (Classic Reprint) (p. 109)
—Lady Barbarity: A Romantic Comedy (Classic Reprint) (p. 1236)
—Principal Girl (Classic Reprint) (p. 1800)
Snaith, Simone. Between the Water & the Woods. Kipin, Sara, illus. (p. 210)
Snaith, Tai. You Might Find Yourself. (p. 2527)
Snape, Charles & Snape, Juliet. Brain Busters: Games, Puzzles & More! (p. 274)
—Mind Twisters: Games, Puzzles & More! (p. 1469)
Snape, Emily. Alphabet of Hugs. (p. 59)
—Flight: Invent Your Own Mix-and-Match Vehicles! Alexander, Rilla, illus. (p. 748)
—Hey! Look at You... in the Jungle. (p. 964)
—Hey! Look at You... on the Move. (p. 964)
—Motor Mix: Emergency. Alexander, Rilla, illus. (p. 1512)
—Old MacDonald Had a Baby. Steele, K-Fai, illus. (p. 1646)
Snape, Jenny, illus. see Robertson, J. Jean.
Snape, Jessica. Three Little Monsters & the Ghost of Wisdom Woods. Mills, Jasmine, illus. (p. 2233)
—Three Little Monsters In: Gruesome Gets a Toothache. Mills, Jasmine, illus. (p. 2233)
Snapp, Gwendolyn. Girl Who Called the North Wind. (p. 837)
Snashall, Sarah. Oxford International Primary English Student Anthology 2. (p. 1689)
—Spelling Skills. (p. 2079)
Snavely, Debbie, ed. see Laders, Mary E.
Snavlin, Joyce Burgess. Adirondack ABCs. Reed, Linda Davis, illus. (p. 16)
Snawder, Lynn. Happy Magical Dreams. (p. 923)
Snead, Anna. Bird That Sang the Prettiest Song. (p. 230)
Sneath, E. Hershey. Doing Right: A Course in Character Building (Classic Reprint) (p. 578)
—Golden Key Book: A School Reader (Classic Reprint) (p. 858)
—Golden Ladder Book: A School Reader (Classic Reprint) (p. 858)
—Golden Path Book: A School Reader (Classic Reprint) (p. 858)
—Golden Rule Series: The Golden Door Book; a School Reader (Classic Reprint) (p. 859)
—Golden Word Book: A School Reader (Classic Reprint) (p. 859)
Sneath, Eli Hershey. Golden Deed Book: A School Reader (Classic Reprint) (p. 857)
Snedden, Genevra Sisson. Docas: The Indian Boy of Santa Clara (Classic Reprint) (p. 573)
Snedden, Robert. Adaptation & Survival (p. 14)
—Air Force. (p. 37)
—Ancient China. (p. 80)
—Ancient Egypt. (p. 80)
—Ancient Greece. (p. 81)
—Ancient Rome. (p. 82)
—Atlantis & Other Lost Worlds. (p. 133)
—Aztec, Inca & Maya. (p. 146)
—Aztec, Inca, & Maya. (p. 146)
—Castles & Fortresses. (p. 340)
—Chemical Engineering & Chain Reactions. (p. 365)
—Emotion & Your Brain. (p. 644)
—Exploring Space. (p. 682)
—Fungi. (p. 801)
—How Do Scientists Explore Space? (p. 1029)
—How Does a Waterfall Become Electricity? (p. 1030)
—Mary Anning: Fossil Hunter. (p. 1414)
—Materials Engineering & Exploring Properties. (p. 1421)
—Medical Technology. (p. 1436)
—Medieval World. (p. 1437)
—Navy. (p. 1582)
—Nutrition: From Birth to Old Age (p. 1632)
—Railroads. (p. 1835)
—Roads. (p. 1888)
—Robotics in Space. (p. 1893)
—Robotics in the Military. (p. 1893)
—Scientists Behind Living Things (p. 1959)
—Scientists Behind the Environment (p. 1959)
—Sleep, Dreams, & Your Brain. (p. 2036)
—Stephen Hawking: Master of the Cosmos. (p. 2115)
—Understanding Food & Digestion. (p. 2324)
—Understanding Muscles & the Skeleton. (p. 2325)
—Understanding the Brain & the Nervous System. (p. 2325)
—Variation in Living Things (p. 2348)
Snedden, Robert, jt. auth. see Crabtree Staff.
Snedden, Robert, jt. auth. see Graf, Mike.
Snedding, Robert, jt. auth. see Parker, Steve.
Snedding, Robert, et al. Brief Illustrated History. (p. 281)
Sneddon, Bradley. Alexander Fleming (p. 42)
—Benjamin Franklin (p. 200)
—Charles Darwin (p. 358)
Snedegar, Eugenia. Ellie Goes Potty (p. 638)
Snedeker, Caroline Dale. Spartan (Classic Reprint) (p. 2075)
—Theras: The Story of an Athenian Boy (Classic Reprint) (p. 2216)
Snedeker, Erin. Littlest Elf: Marvin Mcgee & the Candle of Fate. Drotleff, David J., illus. (p. 1331)
Snedeker, Florence Watters. Family Canoe Trip (Classic Reprint) (p. 702)
Snedeker, Gus. Apple a Day: Folk Proverbs & Riddles. (p. 106)
—Apple a Day: Folk Proverbs & Riddles. Jabbour, Alan, ed. (p. 106)
—Campfire Songs, Ballads, & Lullabies: Folk Music. (p. 316)
—Campfire Songs, Ballads, & Lullabies: Folk Music. Jabbour, Alan, ed. (p. 316)
—Celebrations Throughout the Year: Holiday Folklore. (p. 350)
—Celebrations Throughout the Year: Holiday Folklore. Jabbour, Alan, ed. (p. 350)
—Heroes, Fools, & Ghosts: Folk Tales & Legends. (p. 961)
—Heroes, Fools, & Ghosts: Folk Tales & Legends. Jabbour, Alan, ed. (p. 961)
—Quilts, Rag Dolls, & Rocking Chairs: Folk Arts & Crafts. (p. 1828)
—Quilts, Rag Dolls, & Rocking Chairs: Folk Arts & Crafts. Jabbour, Alan, ed. (p. 1828)
—Tell Me a Story: Family Folklore. (p. 2201)
—Tell Me a Story: Family Folklore. Jabbour, Alan, ed. (p. 2201)
Snedeker, Joseph. Everything KIDS' Weather Book: From Tornadoes to Snowstorms, Puzzles, Games, & Facts That Make Weather for Kids Fun! (p. 673)
Sneed, Brad, illus. see Andersen, Hans Christian.
Sneed, Brad, illus. see Bunting, Eve.
Sneed, Brad, illus. see Clark, Stacy.
Sneed, Brad, illus. see Krensky, Stephen.
Sneed, Brad, illus. see Morris, Carla.
Sneed, Brad, illus. see Scillian, Devin.
Sneed, Brad, illus. see Walton, Rick.
Sneed, Dani. Man Who Invented the Ferris Wheel: The Genius of George Ferris. (p. 1395)
Sneed, Dani, jt. auth. see Fisher, Doris.
Sneed, Erinn. Black Crayon: Coloring & Activity Book. (p. 237)
—Black Crayon It's All about You: Coloring & Activity Book. (p. 237)
—Vegan I Am: Coloring Book, with Recipes, Activities & Resource Guide. (p. 2348)
Sneed, Jerelyn, contrib. by. Just Be Me. (p. 1192)
Sneed, Patty, illus. see Kuhns, Jennifer.
Sneeringer, Jessica, ed. Frostfire Worlds: November 2019. (p. 795)
—Frostfire Worlds May 2019. (p. 795)
Sneideman, Josh & Twamley, Erin. Climate Change: The Science Behind Melting Glaciers & Warming Oceans with Hands-On Science Activities. Cornell, Alexis, illus. (p. 405)
Sneideman, Joshua & Twamley, Erin. Renewable Energy: Discover the Fuel of the Future. Brinesh, Heather Jane, illus. (p. 1866)
Sneider, Cary I. Jake & the Quake. (p. 1155)
Sneider, Cary I., photos by see Gould, Alan.
Sneider, Jonathan, illus. see Boyle, Keri Claiborne.
Sneider, Marian, jt. auth. see Vander Zee, Ruth.
Snel, Eline. Sitting Still Like a Frog Activity Book: 75 Mindfulness Games for Kids. Boutavant, Marc, illus. (p. 2028)
Snelbaker, Carmela. Thank You for Your Service, Sheep! (p. 2211)
Snell, Alexis, illus. see Acioli, Socorro.
Snell, Frederick John. Customs of Old England. (p. 491)
Snell, Gordon. King of Quizzical Island. McKee, David, illus. (p. 1220)
Snell, Roy J. Blue Envelope. (p. 248)
—Crimson Flash (Classic Reprint) (p. 475)
—Curlie Carson Listens In. (p. 488)
—Little White Fox, & His Arctic Friends (Classic Reprint) (p. 1329)
—Lost in the Air. (p. 1354)
—Triple Spies. (p. 2289)
Snellenberger, Earl & Snellenberger, Bonita. Noah's Ark Pre-School Activity Book. Snellenberger, Earl & Snellenberger, Bonita, illus. (p. 1616)
Sneller, Jennifer L. Cooper & Kat. (p. 451)
Snellgrove, Chris. Bruno Mars (p. 288)
—Drake (p. 596)
Snelling, Patricia. Louis's Garden Party. (p. 1358)
Snerling, Tina, illus. see McCartney, Tania.
Snerling, Tina, jt. auth. see McCartney, Tania.
Sneve, Virginia Driving Hawk. Standing Bear of the Ponca. (p. 2100)
Sneyers, Joachim, illus. see Leyssens, Jan.
Snezhana, Ivinskaya, ed. see AZ Books Staff.
Snicket, Lemony, pseud. 13 Words. Kalman, Maira, illus. (p. 2552)
—All the Wrong Questions: Question 1: Also Published As Who Could That Be at This Hour? Seth, illus. (p. 54)
—Bad Mood & the Stick. (p. 158)
—Bad Mood & the Stick. Forsythe, Matthew, illus. (p. 158)
—Composer Is Dead. Ellis, Carson, illus. (p. 436)
—Dark. Klassen, Jon, illus. (p. 505)
—File under: 13 Suspicious Incidents. Seth, illus. (p. 726)
—Goldfish Ghost. Brown, Lisa, illus. (p. 860)
—Poison for Breakfast. (p. 1768)
—Read Something Else: Collected & Dubious Wit & Wisdom of Lemony Snicket. (p. 1845)
—Series of Unfortunate Events #1: the Bad Beginning Netflix Tie-In. Helquist, Brett, illus. (p. 1991)
—Series of Unfortunate Events #10: the Slippery Slope Netflix Tie-In. Helquist, Brett & Kupperman, Michael, illus. (p. 1991)
—Series of Unfortunate Events #11: the Grim Grotto Netflix Tie-In. Helquist, Brett & Kupperman, Michael, illus. (p. 1991)

—Series of Unfortunate Events #12: the Penultimate Peril Netflix Tie-In. Helquist, Brett & Kupperman, Michael, illus. (p. 1991)
—Series of Unfortunate Events #13: the End Netflix Tie-In. Helquist, Brett & Kupperman, Michael, illus. (p. 1991)
—Series of Unfortunate Events #1-4 Netflix Tie-In Box Set. Helquist, Brett, illus. (p. 1991)
—Series of Unfortunate Events #3: the Wide Window Netflix Tie-In. Helquist, Brett & Kupperman, Michael, illus. (p. 1991)
—Series of Unfortunate Events #4: the Miserable Mill Netflix Tie-In. Helquist, Brett & Kupperman, Michael, illus. (p. 1991)
—Series of Unfortunate Events #5: the Austere Academy, Netflix Tie-In. Helquist, Brett & Kupperman, Michael, illus. (p. 1991)
—Series of Unfortunate Events #9: the Carnivorous Carnival Netflix Tie-In. Helquist, Brett & Kupperman, Michael, illus. (p. 1991)
—Shouldn't You Be in School? Seth, illus. (p. 2011)
—Swarm of Bees. Alexander, Rilla, illus. (p. 2167)
—When Did You See Her Last? Seth, illus. (p. 2429)
—Who Could That Be at This Hour? Seth, illus. (p. 2446)
—Who Could That Be at This Hour? Also Published As All the Wrong Questions: Question 1. Seth, illus. (p. 2447)
Snicket, Lemony, pseud & Seth. Who Could That Be at This Hour? (p. 2446)
Snider, Brandon T. Amazo & the Planetary Reboot. Levins, Tim, illus. (p. 67)
—Attack of the Movie Monsters. (p. 134)
—Bane Drain. Lozano, Omar & Brizuela, Dario, illus. (p. 163)
—Battle for Wakanda. (p. 174)
—Bizarro & the Doppelgängers of Doom. Levins, Tim, illus. (p. 235)
—Black Panther: The Battle for Wakanda. Studios, Caravan, illus. (p. 239)
—Black Panther: the Battle for Wakanda. Marvel Press Artist, illus. (p. 239)
—Cheetah Unleashed. Vecchio, Luciano, illus. (p. 364)
—Circe's Dark Reign. Vecchio, Luciano, illus. (p. 392)
—Dangerous Rescue. (p. 502)
—Doctor Strange: Mystery of the Dark Magic. (p. 573)
—Doctor Strange: Mystery of the Dark Magic. Pham, Khoi et al, illus. (p. 573)
—Double Trouble. Lozano, Omar, illus. (p. 589)
—Gamora's Galactic Showdown: Starring Gamora. Qualano, Pasquale & Sotomayor, Chris, illus. (p. 808)
—Gorilla Grodd & the Primate Protocol Levins, Tim, illus. (p. 870)
—Grow up, Ant-Man! Von Innerebner, Jessika, illus. (p. 899)
—Guardians of the Galaxy: Gamora's Galactic Showdown! (p. 901)
—Guardians of the Galaxy Doodles. Montalvo-Lagos, Tomás, illus. (p. 901)
—Guardians of the Galaxy: Gamora's Galactic Showdown. Marvel Press Artist, illus. (p. 902)
—Guardians of the Galaxy: Gamora's Galactic Showdown. Qualano, Pascale & Sotomayor, Chris, illus. (p. 902)
—Hanazuki: Book of Treasures: The Official Guide. (p. 914)
—How to Be Annoying: A Joke Book. (p. 1037)
—LOL: a Keepsake Journal of Hilarious Q&As. (p. 1340)
—Meet Quickshadow. (p. 1439)
—My Little Pony: the Elements of Harmony Vol. II. (p. 1554)
—My Little Pony: the Wonderbolts Academy Handbook. (p. 1554)
—Rain of Fear! Brizuela, Dario, illus. (p. 1835)
—Rick & Morty Mad Libs Joke Book. (p. 1877)
—Spider-Man Doodles. Montalvo-Lagos, Tomás, illus. (p. 2080)
—Star Wars Droids Mad Libs. (p. 2104)
—Starro & the Cyberspore. Levins, Tim & Lokus, Rex, illus. (p. 2106)
—This or That? (p. 2226)
—This or That? 2. (p. 2226)
—Tricks & Treats! Brizuela, Dario, illus. (p. 2287)
—What Would Captain Kirk Do? Intergalactic Wisdom from the Captain of the U. S. S. Enterprise. (p. 2422)
—What Would Captain Picard Do? Captain's Orders from the U. S. S. Enterprise. (p. 2422)
—Wonder Woman Mad Libs. (p. 2489)
—Wonder Woman the Amazing Amazon. Vecchio, Luciano, illus. (p. 2489)
—Write It Out! Hundreds of Writing Prompts to Inspire Creative Thinking. (p. 2512)
Snider, Brandon T., jt. auth. see Clark, Kent.
Snider, Brandon T., jt. auth. see Scott, Cavan.
Snider, Brandon T., adapted by. Ghost in the Machine. (p. 827)
—Meet Quickshadow. (p. 1439)
Snider, Brandon T. & Sutton, Laurie S. Amazing Adventures of Batman! (p. 62)
Snider, Brandon T., et al. Justice League. Levins, Tim, illus. (p. 1195)
Snider, Dee. We're Not Gonna Take It: A Children's Picture Book. McCartney, Margaret, illus. (p. 2400)
Snider, Denton Jaques. Freeburgers: A Novel (Classic Reprint) (p. 782)
—Walk in Hellas: Or the Old in the New (Classic Reprint) (p. 2371)
Snider, Grant. What Color Is Night? (p. 2407)
—What Sound Is Morning? (p. 2420)
Snider, Grant, illus. see Cain, Susan, et al.
Snider, Jackie, illus. see Cifuentes, Carolina, ed.
Snider, Jackie, illus. see Cifuentes, Carolina.
Snider, Jackie, illus. see Rosa-Mendoza, Gladys.
Snider, Jesse Blaze. Muppet Snow White. Paroline, Shelli, illus. (p. 1527)
—Return of Buzz Lightyear Watson, Nathan, illus. (p. 1870)
—Return of Buzz Lightyear Vol. 2. Watson, Nathan, illus. (p. 1871)
—Toy Story: Toy Overboard. Watson, Nathan, illus. (p. 2270)
—Toy Story: Some Assembly Required. Watson, Nathan, illus. (p. 2270)
Snider, K. C., illus. see Calvani, Mayra.
Snider, K. C., illus. see Crow, Marilee.
Snider, K. C., illus. see Finke, Margot.
Snider, K. C., illus. see Glover, Emma M.
Snider, K. C., illus. see Kelso, Mary Jean.
Snider, K. C., illus. see Luce, Catherine.
Snider, K. C., illus. see McNamee, Kevin.
Snider, K. C., illus. see Phillips, Dixie.
Snider, K. C., illus. see Reece, Colleen L. & DeMarco, Julie Reece.
Snider, K. C., illus. see Robinson, Janie.
Snider, K. C., illus. see Samuels, Jack.
Snider, K. C., illus. see Stephenson, Susan.
Snider, K. C., jt. auth. see Crow, Marilee.
Snider, K. C., jt. auth. see Kelso, Mary Jean.
Snider, K. C., jt. auth. see Phillips, Dixie.
Snider, Kc. Silence. Snider, Kc, illus. (p. 2017)
Snider, Kc, illus. see Barker, Susan.
Snider, Kc, illus. see Berger, Susan J.
Snider, Kc, illus. see Dubbeld, Janene a.
Snider, Kc, illus. see Gibson, Jacob & Phillips, Dixie.
Snider, Kc, illus. see Glover, Emma M.
Snider, Kc, illus. see Hunter, Christopher.
Snider, Kc, illus. see Kelso, Mary Jean.
Snider, Kc, illus. see McDine, Donna M.
Snider, Kc, illus. see Nott, Michelle.
Snider, Sharon, illus. see Dunlap, Sonya.
Sniegoski, Thomas E. Fallen 1: The Fallen & Leviathan (p. 700)
—Fallen 2: Aerie & Reckoning. (p. 700)
—Fallen 3: End of Days. Vol. 3 (p. 700)
—Fallen 4: Forsaken. (p. 700)
—Fallen 5: Armageddon. (p. 700)
—Monstrous. (p. 1498)
—Savage. (p. 1937)
—Specter Rising. (p. 2078)
Sniegoski, Thomas E., jt. auth. see Golden, Christopher.
Sniegoski, Thomas E. & Golden, Christopher. Battle for Arcanum. (p. 173)
—Dragon Secrets. (p. 594)
—Ghostfire. (p. 829)
—Magic Zero. (p. 1379)
Sniegoski, Tom. Monstrous. (p. 1498)
—Quest for the Spark. (p. 1826)
—Quest for the Spark. Smith, Jeff, illus. (p. 1826)
Sniegoski, Tom, jt. auth. see Smith, Jeff.
Sniegoski, Tom & Smith, Jeff. Tall Tales. Smith, Jeff, illus. (p. 2188)
Snitbhan, Nuanprang. Kindness Cards for Kids: 52 Ways to Make Every Day a Little Better. (p. 1219)
Snitkin, Harvey R. Practicing for Young Musicians: You Are Your Own Teacher. (p. 1784)
Snitsellaar, Nicole. Maya's Tree: Story Book. (p. 1429)
Snively, Gloria. Explore the Rocky Shore with Sam & Crystal Gillmore, Karen, illus. (p. 680)
—Explore the Wild Coast with Sam & Crystal Gillmore, Karen, illus. (p. 680)
—High Tide, Low Tide: A Shoreline Activity Book. Gillmore, Karen, illus. (p. 969)
Snively, Susan, ed. see Dickinson, Emily.
Snoddy, Gillian, ed. see Hex, Kathleen.
Snodgrass, Lady Cecily. Really Rotten Princess. Lester, Mike, illus. (p. 1851)
—Really Rotten Princess & the Awful, Icky Election. Lester, Mike, illus. (p. 1851)
—Really Rotten Princess & the Cupcake Catastrophe. Lester, Mike, illus. (p. 1851)
Snook, Lee Owen. House Across the Way (Classic Reprint) (p. 1022)
Snook, Marygrace. Hannah's Dancing Bear. (p. 918)
Snorradottir, Asthildur Bj. Raphael: The Angel Who Decided to Visit Earth. Bjarnason, Bjarni Thor, illus. (p. 1841)
Snortum, Marty, photos by see Beery, Barbara.
Snow, A. E. Bellamy Rising. (p. 197)
—Meadow Perkins, Trusty Sidekick. (p. 1434)
Snow, Abby. Resubmerged. (p. 1870)
Snow, Alan. How Dinosaurs Really Work! Snow, Alan, illus. (p. 1027)
—How Kids Really Work. Snow, Alan, illus. (p. 1033)
—Speed Birds. (p. 2078)
—Worse Things Happen at Sea! A Tale of Pirates, Poison, & Monsters. Snow, Alan, illus. (p. 2509)
Snow, Alan, illus. see Bowvayne.
Snow, Alan, illus. see Murray, Andrew.
Snow, Bradlee. Jack the Cat: An Angel's Tale. (p. 1153)
Snow, Carleena. Generous Jennifer: Sharing Is Contagious. Borowski, Maripat, illus. (p. 814)
Snow, Carol. Last Place on Earth. (p. 1249)
—Snap. (p. 2045)
—Switch. (p. 2171)
Snow, D. C. Champ Bailey. (p. 355)
Snow, Eliza R. Story of Jesus. (p. 2130)
Snow, Ella. Sunshine Challed: A Wonderful Little Book for Little Children, Big Children, & Parents (Classic Reprint) (p. 2153)
Snow, Francis Haffkine. Red Flowers (Classic Reprint) (p. 1857)
Snow, Ivy, jt. auth. see Bloomsbury.
Snow, Jess. Outreach Services for Teens: A Starter Guide. (p. 1685)
Snow, Jess X., illus. see Cho, Tina.
Snow, Kate. Kindergarten Math with Confidence Bundle. (p. 1218)
—Kindergarten Math with Confidence Instructor Guide. (p. 1218)
Snow, Kate, et al. Division Facts That Stick: Help Your Child Master the Division Facts for Good in Just Ten Weeks. (p. 566)
—Multiplication Facts That Stick: Help Your Child Master the Multiplication Facts for Good in Just Ten Weeks. (p. 1525)
Snow, Kel. Rockton: A Story of Spring-Time Recreations (Classic Reprint) (p. 1896)
Snow, Kevin. Ronda Rousey: Conquering New Ground. (p. 1902)
Snow, Louis Franklin, jt. auth. see Stevenson, Robert Louis.
Snow, Maya. Blade's Edge. (p. 242)
—Sisters of the Sword 2: Chasing the Secret. (p. 2027)
Snow, Pegeen. Eat Your Peas, Louise! Venezia, Mike, illus. (p. 622)
Snow, Peggy. Explore Canada: 12 Key Facts. (p. 679)
—Explore Cuba: 12 Key Facts. (p. 679)
—Explore Greece: 12 Key Facts. (p. 679)
Snow, RuthAnne. When the Truth Unravels. (p. 2433)
Snow, Sarah, illus. see Formento, Alison.
Snow, Scott, illus. see Kimmel, E. Cody.
Snow, Scott, illus. see Kimmel, Elizabeth Cody.
Snow, Stephanie, illus. see Everin, Gretchen.
Snow, Susie. Old Cookie Jar. Motz, Mike, illus. (p. 1645)
Snow, Virginia Brimhall. Fall Walk (p. 700)
—Spring Walk (p. 2092)
—Summer Walk (p. 2150)
—Winter Walk (p. 2476)
Snow, Wesley. Tree's Life. (p. 2284)
Snow, William Leonard. High School Prize Speaker (Classic Reprint) (p. 969)
Snowden, Gary. Hank & Kale Visit the Aquarium. Smith, William E., illus. (p. 917)
—Lost Treasure of Hawkins Cave. Pierce Clark, Donna, illus. (p. 1356)
Snowden, Keighley. Barbara West (Classic Reprint) (p. 165)
—Princess Joyce (Classic Reprint) (p. 1797)
—Tales of the Yorkshire Wolds (Classic Reprint) (p. 2186)
Snowden, William W. Ladies' Companion, 1838, Vol. 9: A Monthly Magazine, Embracing Every Department of Literature (Classic Reprint) (p. 1236)
—Ladies' Companion, 1840, Vol. 14: A Monthly Magazine Embracing Every Department of Literature, Embellished with Original Engravings, & Music, Arranged for the Piano Forte, Harp & Guitar (Classic Reprint) (p. 1236)
Snowden-Fine, Lily. Why Do Dogs Sniff Butts? Curious Questions about Your Favorite Pets. (p. 2456)
Snowden-Fine, Lily & Crumpton, Nick. Why Do Cats Meow? Curious Questions about Your Favorite Pets. (p. 2456)
Snowdon, Ellie, illus. see Peters, Helen.
Snowe, Jaqueline. Best Player. (p. 207)
—Challenge Accepted. (p. 354)
—Game Changer. (p. 806)
—No Easy Catch. (p. 1612)
Snowe, Olivia. Beauty & the Basement Lamoreaux, Michelle, illus. (p. 184)
—Cassie & the Woolf Lamoreaux, Michelle, illus. (p. 339)
—Dandelion & the Witch Lamoreaux, Michelle, illus. (p. 500)
—Girl & the Seven Thieves Lamoreaux, Michelle, illus. (p. 835)
—Glass Voice Lamoreaux, Michelle, illus. (p. 841)
—Hansen & Gracie Lamoreaux, Michelle, illus. (p. 919)
—Home in the Sky Lamoreaux, Michelle, illus. (p. 996)
—Sealed-Up House Lamoreaux, Michelle, illus. (p. 1970)
Snowman, Daniel. Giuseppe Verdi: Composer. (p. 839)
Snowman, Scott M., jt. auth. see Snowman, Tracy L.
Snozek, Lee Anne. Simply Square Designs. (p. 2023)
—Terrific Triangles. (p. 2207)
Snozek, Lee Anne & Coloring Books for Adults. Outrageous Octagons. (p. 1685)
Snyder, Adeline. Hunting with Mountain Lions (p. 1054)
Snyder, Amberley Lana. Walk Ride Rodeo: A Story about Amberley Snyder. Krekk, Gabriel, illus. (p. 2372)
Snyder, Barb, ed. see Harris, Janice L. & Lisech, Howard.
Snyder, Barb, ed. see Harris, Janice L., et al.
Snyder, Bernadette McCarver. 110 Fun Facts about God's Creation: Is It Animal, Vegetable, or Mineral? (p. 2559)
Snyder, Betsy. I Can Dream. (p. 1062)
—I Can Explore. (p. 1062)
Snyder, Betsy, illus. see Bergen, Lara.
Snyder, Betsy E. Bulldozer. (p. 296)
—Fire Engine. (p. 732)
—Haiku Night. (p. 909)
—Have You Ever Tickled a Tiger? (p. 939)
—I Can Dance. (p. 1061)
—I Can Play. (p. 1063)
—I Haiku You. (p. 1065)
—Lily's Potty. (p. 1302)
—Sweet Dreams Lullaby. (p. 2168)
—Train. (p. 2275)
Snyder, Betsy E., illus. see Cleary, Brian P.
Snyder, Betsy E., illus. see Fliess, Sue.
Snyder, Carrie. Jammie Day! Kerrigan, Brooke, illus. (p. 1157)
Snyder, Casey. Adventures of Food. (p. 23)
—Miss Fit the Dog & the Football Eating Tree. (p. 1478)
—Miss Fit the Dog Saves Christmas. (p. 1478)
Snyder, Charity S. Poetry of Adoption: My Struggle to Be Triumphant. (p. 1767)
Snyder, Charles M. Flaw in the Sapphire (Classic Reprint) (p. 747)
—Runaway Robinson (Classic Reprint) (p. 1915)
Snyder, Charles McCoy. Flaw in the Sapphire (Classic Reprint) (p. 747)
Snyder, Deborah. Choice. (p. 380)
—Chosen. (p. 381)
Snyder, Gabi. Two Dogs on a Trike. Rosenthal, Robin, illus. (p. 2307)
Snyder, Gail. Angry Girl? Girls Dealing with Feelings. (p. 87)
—Brooke Knows Best. (p. 285)
—Careers If You Like Helping People. (p. 329)
—Careers If You Like Science. (p. 329)
—David Cook. (p. 511)
—Growing up in Canada. (p. 900)
—Jealous Girl? Girls Dealing with Feelings. (p. 1162)
—Kelly Clarkson. (p. 1209)
—Kids & Obesity. (p. 1214)
—Lonely Girl? Girls Dealing with Feelings. (p. 1342)
—Seth Mcfarlane Family Guy: Family Guy. (p. 1993)
—Sudan. (p. 2146)
—Teen Guide to Starting a Business. (p. 2199)
—Teens & Alcohol. Developed in Association with the Gallup Organization Staff, ed. (p. 2200)
Snyder, Gail, jt. auth. see Marcovitz, Hal.
Snyder, Harold E., illus. see Curtis, Alice Turner.
Snyder, Ili, illus. see Snyder, Max.
Snyder, J. M. Journey to Venus (p. 1183)
Snyder, Jane. Days of the Week: Learning Ordinal Numbers. (p. 515)
Snyder, Jill. Same but Different. (p. 1927)
Snyder, Joe, illus. see Helsel, Sandra.
Snyder, Joel, illus. see Lamm, C. Drew.
Snyder, Joel, illus. see Petrie, Catherine.
Snyder, Joel, illus. see Rottmann, Erik.
Snyder, Joel, illus. see Walker, Sally M.
Snyder, Joel, illus. see Zoehfeld, Kathleen Weidner.
Snyder, John. Lost Angel: A Christmas Dream. (p. 1352)
—Lost Angel: A Christmas Dream (Classic Reprint) (p. 1352)
Snyder, John K., III, jt. auth. see Conrad, Joseph.
Snyder, Karen. Camp Charlie, the Adventures of Grandma Lipstick. LaGrange, Tiffany, illus. (p. 315)
—Mona Lisa's Makeover. LaGrange, Tiffany, illus. (p. 1492)
—Safari Smooches. LaGrange, Tiffany, illus. (p. 1921)
Snyder, Kari, illus. see Donovan, Patricia.
Snyder, Laurel. Any Which Wall. Pham, Leuyen, illus. (p. 104)
—Baxter, the Pig Who Wanted to Be Kosher. (p. 175)
—Baxter, the Pig Who Wanted to Be Kosher. Goldin, David, illus. (p. 175)
—Bigger Than a Bread Box. (p. 224)
—Camp Wonderful Wild Whitt, Carlynn, illus. (p. 316)
—Charlie & Mouse. Hughes, Emily, illus. (p. 359)
—Charlie & Mouse & Grumpy. Hughes, Emily, illus. (p. 359)
—Charlie & Mouse Even Better Hughes, Emily, illus. (p. 359)
—Charlie & Mouse Even Better: Book 3. Hughes, Emily, illus. (p. 359)
—Charlie & Mouse Outdoors: Book 4 (Classic Children's Book, Beginning Chapter Book, Illustrated Books for Children) Hughes, Emily, illus. (p. 359)
—Forever Garden. Cotterill, Samantha, illus. (p. 767)
—Hungry Jim. (p. 1052)
—King of Too Many Things. Damant, Aurore, illus. (p. 1221)
—My Jasper June. (p. 1550)
—Orphan Island. (p. 1672)
—Penny Dreadful. Halpin, Abigail, illus. (p. 1717)
—Seven Stories Up. (p. 1994)
—Swan: The Life & Dance of Anna Pavlova. Morstad, Julie, illus. (p. 2167)
—Up & down the Scratchy Mountains. Dorman, Brandon & Call, Greg, illus. (p. 2337)
Snyder, Lydia. Rhinos in Danger. (p. 1875)
Snyder, Marcia Penfield. Eight Lands in Eight Weeks: A Package of Diary Letters to Beloved Stay-At-Homes (Classic Reprint) (p. 629)
Snyder, Maria V. Dawn Study. (p. 512)
—Navigating the Stars. (p. 1582)
—Storm Watcher. (p. 2127)
Snyder, Maria V., et al. Spirited. (p. 2083)
Snyder, Max. King with No Kingdom. Snyder, Max & Snyder, Ili, illus. (p. 1221)
Snyder, Peter Etril, illus. see Forler, Nan.
Snyder, Phil L., ed. see Becker, Carl L.
Snyder, R. Bradley & Engelsgjerd, Marc. What Every Child Needs to Know about Cancer. (p. 2410)
Snyder, R. Bradley, et al. What Every Child Needs to Know about Elvis Presley. (p. 2410)
Snyder, Robert. Brewster Messenger of God. (p. 279)
—Tale from the Smoky Mountains: The Tree That Loved. (p. 2178)
Snyder, Ronda, illus. see Milliner, Donna L.
Snyder, Sandy. There's Only One I in Charlie. Ferrenburg, Susie, illus. (p. 2218)
Snyder, Scott. AD after Death. (p. 13)
—Zero Year - Dark City (p. 2540)
Snyder, Scott, photos by see Rule, Rebecca.
Snyder, Sharon J. Zeus Comes Home. (p. 2540)
Snyder, Stacy T. My Name Is Sugar. Johnson, Anne M., illus. (p. 1557)
—Sugar Shack. Johnson, Anne M., illus. (p. 2147)
Snyder, Susan E. Grandma's Crazy Chickens. Richardson, Mike, illus. (p. 878)
—Mouse Who Came to Lunch. Cotton, Sue Lynn, illus. (p. 1515)
Snyder, Ted. Neverland Rascals: To Neverland. Espinosa, Sharon, ed. (p. 1590)
Snyder, Will P. Billie Boy & I: And Other Child Verse for Adult Readers (Classic Reprint) (p. 226)
Snyder, Zilpha Keatley. Black & Blue Magic. (p. 236)
—Egypt Game. (p. 628)
—Egypt Game. Raible, Alton, illus. (p. 628)
—Headless Cupid. Raible, Alton, illus. (p. 942)
—William S. & the Great Escape. (p. 2468)
—William's Midsummer Dreams. (p. 2469)
—Witches of Worm. (p. 2480)
—Witches of Worm. Raible, Alton, illus. (p. 2480)
Snyders, Natalie & Stuckey, Kevin. Articulation Quick Take along Mini-Book: Ta120. (p. 123)
Snyders, Natalie, et al. Vocabulary Quick Take along Mini-Book: Ta230. (p. 2364)
Snyman, Kristy. My Rainbow of Energy. (p. 1559)
—Rainbow Within. (p. 1837)
So, Hyeon. Río de Piedras de Lava Rojas y Calientes / a River of Red, Hot Lava Stones. Min, Eun-Jeong, illus. (p. 1883)
So, Meilo. Read a Rhyme, Write a Rhyme. (p. 1845)
So, Meilo, illus. see Coombs, Kate.
So, Meilo, illus. see Cousteau, Philippe & Hopkinson, Deborah.
So, Meilo, illus. see Gibson, Amy.
So, Meilo, illus. see Hopkinson, Deborah.
So, Meilo, illus. see London, Jonathan.
So, Meilo, illus. see Look, Lenore.
So, Meilo, illus. see McLaughlin, Lauren.
So, Meilo, illus. see Miles, Liz.
So, Meilo, illus. see Mora, Pat & Domínguez, Adriana.
So, Meilo, illus. see Mora, Pat, et al.
So, Meilo, illus. see Mora, Pat.
So, Meilo, illus. see O Flatharta, Antoine.
So, Meilo, illus. see Thong, Roseanne Greenfield.
So, Meilo, illus. see Wenxuan, Cao.
So, Million. Count on Me: An Adaptation of Three Little Pigs. (p. 458)
Soane, George. Falls of Clyde: A Melo-Drama in Two Acts (Classic Reprint) (p. 701)
—Frolics of Puck, Vol. 1 of 2 (Classic Reprint) (p. 790)

S

—New Curiosities of Literature, & Book of the Months, Vol. 2 of 2 (Classic Reprint) (p. 1592)
—Specimens of German Romance, Selected & Translated from Various Authors, Vol. 2 of 3 (Classic Reprint) (p. 2077)
—Specimens of German Romance, Vol. 1 of 3 (Classic Reprint) (p. 2077)
Soanes, Zeb. Gaspard the Fox. Mayhew, James, illus. (p. 811)
—Gaspard the Fox Postcard Pack. Mayhew, James, illus. (p. 811)
Soares, Dimas. Ellie & Her 2 Boys. (p. 637)
Soares, Paul, jt. auth. see Milton, Stephanie.
Soares, Sue, ed. Fire & Chaos: Book 3 of the Traveler's League. Lamoureux, Hampton & Faul, Tara, illus. (p. 732)
Soares, Valérie. Lily & Kayden's 1969 Woodstock Adventure. Tzekov, Jack, illus. (p. 1302)
Soban Biniashvili, Freidele Galya. I Love Matzah Scudamore, Angelika, illus. (p. 1070)
—There Is a Reason Why. Zimmer, Glenn, illus. (p. 2216)
Sobat, Gail Sidonie. Chance to Dance for You. (p. 355)
Sobb, Evi I. & Distasi, Danise C. Love Like Louie: An Adventure of a Girl & a Lost Dog. (p. 1360)
Sobel, Bernard. Three Plays (Classic Reprint) (p. 2234)
Sobel, Daniel. Narrowing the Attainment Gap: a Handbook for Schools. (p. 1575)
Sobel, David S. What's the Catch: How to Avoid Getting Hooked & Manipulated. Jackson, Jeff, illus. (p. 2426)
Sobel, Deane. Philip the Sea Lion. (p. 1734)
Sobel, Gerrie. Jacob & His Magical Flying Bears. Torres, Dottie, illus. (p. 1154)
—Jacob & His Magical Flying Bears, a Halloween Story. Torres, Dottie, illus. (p. 1154)
Sobel J. D., Syl, jt. auth. see Sobel, Syl.
Sobel, June. B Is for Bulldozer (lap Board Book) A Construction ABC. Iwai, Melissa, illus. (p. 146)
—Goodnight Train (lap Board Book) Huliska-Beith, Laura, illus. (p. 868)
—Goodnight Train Rolls On! Huliska-Beith, Laura, illus. (p. 868)
—Santa & the Goodnight Train. Huliska-Beith, Laura, illus. (p. 1931)
—Tow Truck Joe. Corrigan, Patrick, illus. (p. 2269)
—Trick-Or-Treat with Tow Truck Joe. Corrigan, Patrick, illus. (p. 2287)
Sobel, June & Huliska-Beith, Laura. Goodnight Train Rolls on! (board Book) (p. 868)
Sobel, June & Iwai, Melissa. B Is for Bulldozer: A Construction ABC. Iwai, Melissa, illus. (p. 146)
Sobel, Sheila. Color Blind. (p. 419)
Sobel, Syl. U. S. Constitution & You. (p. 2312)
Sobersides, Timothy. Letter from Timothy Sobersides, Extinguisher-Maker, at Wolverhampton, to Jonathan Blast, Bellows-Maker, at Birmingham (Classic Reprint) (p. 1278)
Sobey, Ed. Build Your Own Robot Science Fair Project. (p. 293)
—Electrical Engineering: Learn It, Try It! (p. 631)
—Motorboat Book: Build & Launch 20 Jet Boats, Paddle-Wheelers, Electric Submarines & More. (p. 1512)
—Robotics Engineering: Learn It, Try It! (p. 1893)
Sobey, Ed, ed. Electric Motor Experiments. (p. 631)
—Radio-Controlled Car Experiments. (p. 1833)
—Robot Experiments. (p. 1892)
—Solar Cell & Renewable Energy Experiments. (p. 2055)
Sobey, Glen. War Blog. (p. 2376)
Sobha, Geeta. Green Technology: Earth-friendly Innovations. (p. 895)
Sobieski, Aniela, illus. see Young, Chuck.
Sobiloff, Imelda Rose. Martina Ballerina. (p. 1411)
Sobol, Donald J. Encyclopedia Brown Shortall, Leonard, illus. (p. 648)
—Encyclopedia Brown & His Best Cases Ever. (p. 648)
—Encyclopedia Brown & the Case of the Dead Eagles Shortall, Leonard, illus. (p. 648)
—Encyclopedia Brown & the Case of the Midnight Visitor Brandi, Lillian & Shortall, Leonard, illus. (p. 648)
—Encyclopedia Brown & the Case of the Secret Pitch Shortall, Leonard, illus. (p. 648)
—Encyclopedia Brown & the Case of the Secret UFOs. (p. 648)
—Encyclopedia Brown & the Case of the Soccer Scheme. Bernadin, James, illus. (p. 648)
—Encyclopedia Brown Boy Detective. (p. 648)
—Encyclopedia Brown, Boy Detective Shortall, Leonard, illus. (p. 648)
—Encyclopedia Brown, Boy Detective. Shortall, Leonard W., illus. (p. 648)
—Encyclopedia Brown Finds the Clues Shortall, Leonard, illus. (p. 648)
—Encyclopedia Brown Gets His Man Shortall, Leonard, illus. (p. 648)
—Encyclopedia Brown Gets His Man. Shortall, Leonard W., illus. (p. 648)
—Encyclopedia Brown Keeps the Peace Shortall, Leonard, illus. (p. 648)
—Encyclopedia Brown Lends a Hand Shortall, Leonard, illus. (p. 648)
—Encyclopedia Brown Saves the Day Shortall, Leonard, illus. (p. 648)
—Encyclopedia Brown Solves Them All Shortall, Leonard, illus. (p. 648)
—Encyclopedia Brown, Super Sleuth. (p. 648)
—Encyclopedia Brown Takes the Case Shortall, Leonard, illus. (p. 648)
—Encyclopedia Brown Tracks Them Down Shortall, Leonard, illus. (p. 648)
Sobol, John. Born Derby, Cindy, illus. (p. 263)
—Friend or Foe? Tolstikova, Dasha, illus. (p. 786)
Sobol, Richard. Breakfast in the Rainforest: A Visit with Mountain Gorillas. Sobol, Richard, photos by. (p. 278)
—Growing Peace: A Story of Farming, Music, & Religious Harmony (p. 899)
—Story of Silk: From Worm Spit to Woven Scarves. Sobol, Richard, illus. (p. 2132)
Sobol, Richard, illus. see Hudson, Cheryl Willis.
Sobotta, Johannes. Atlas & Textbook of Human Anatomy - Scholar's Choice Edition. (p. 133)
—Atlas & Text-Book of Human Anatomy, Vol. 1: Bones, Ligaments, Joints, & Muscles (Classic Reprint) (p. 133)
—Atlas & Text-Book of Human Anatomy, Vol. 2: The Viscera, Including the Heart (Classic Reprint) (p. 133)
—Atlas & Text-Book of Human Anatomy, Vol. 3: Vascular System, Lymphatic System, Nervous System & Sense Organs (Classic Reprint) (p. 133)
Sobran, Joseph. Henry IV, Part 1. (p. 955)
—Twelfth Night. (p. 2302)
Sobrino, Javier. Finch. Brokenbrow, Jon, tr. (p. 727)
—Night Sounds Amado, Elisa, tr. (p. 1607)
—Ojos de Lobo. Müllerová, Lucie, illus. (p. 1643)
—Pinzón. Delicado, Federico, illus. (p. 1747)
—¡Tachán, Tachán! Müllerová, Lucie, illus. (p. 2175)
Sobrino, Ray. Ralphie the Roach. (p. 1838)
SoccerGrlProbs. SoccerGrlProbs Presents: the Ladyballer's Guide to Life. (p. 2052)
Socha, Piotr. Bees: A Honeyed History. (p. 189)
Socha, Piotr & Grajkowski, Wojciech. Trees: A Rooted History. (p. 2284)
Sochard, Fred, illus. see Alix, Cecile.
Sochor, Lesia, illus. see Love, Pamela.
Societies, Astrotekton and Philaretian. Oak Leaves, 1920, Vol. 17: Edited & Published by the Astrotekton & Philaretian Societies, Meredith College, Raleigh, North Carolina (Classic Reprint) (p. 1633)
Societies, Estherian and Lanier Literary. Sororian, Vol. 2 (Classic Reprint) (p. 2065)
—Sororian, Vol. 3 (Classic Reprint) (p. 2065)
Societies, Lanier and Estherian Literary. Sororian, 1917, Vol. 4 (Classic Reprint) (p. 2065)
Society, American Camellia. Nomenclatural Cross-Reference List (Classic Reprint) (p. 1618)
Society, American Humane Education. Strike at Shane's: A Prize Story of Indiana (Classic Reprint) (p. 2141)
Society, American Nature. Nature-Study Review, Vol. 16 (Classic Reprint) (p. 1581)
Society, American Nature Study. Nature-Study Review, Vol. 1: Devoted to All Phases of Nature-Study in Elementary Schools; January, 1905 (Classic Reprint) (p. 1581)
—Nature-Study Review, Vol. 13: January, 1917 (Classic Reprint) (p. 1581)
—Nature-Study Review, Vol. 18: Devoted to Elementary Science in the Official Organ of the American Nature-Study Society, January-February, 1922 (Classic Reprint) (p. 1581)
Society, American Reform Tract And Book. Aunt Sally: The Cross the Way to Freedom (Classic Reprint) (p. 137)
Society, American Tract. Cowslip Gatherers (Classic Reprint) (p. 465)
—Grace's Visit: A Tale for the Young (Classic Reprint) (p. 873)
—History of Ann Lively & Her Bible (Classic Reprint) (p. 977)
—History of Jenny Hickling: An Authentic Narrative (Classic Reprint) (p. 978)
—History of Thomas Frankland (Classic Reprint) (p. 981)
—Home Stories, for Boys & Girls (Classic Reprint) (p. 997)
—Journey (Classic Reprint) (p. 1181)
—Little Willie: A True Story (Classic Reprint) (p. 1329)
—Maple Hill, or Aunt Lucy's Stories (Classic Reprint) (p. 1401)
—Mary Jones: And Other Books for Children (Classic Reprint) (p. 1415)
—Memoir of Mary Lothrop: Who Died in Boston, March 18, 1831, Aged Six Years & Three Months (Classic Reprint) (p. 1443)
—Narratives of Eliza Cunningham: Dinah Doudney; & the Children of the Forest (Classic Reprint) (p. 1575)
—Stories for the Little Ones: Nos, 1, 2, 3, 4 (Classic Reprint) (p. 2123)
—Tom Steady: A Pretty History for Good Children (Classic Reprint) (p. 2258)
—Travellers' Wonders (Classic Reprint) (p. 2280)
Society, Animals Cruelty Prevention. Our Animal Friends, Vol. 22: An Illustrated Monthly Magazine; September 1894-August 1895 (Classic Reprint) (p. 1676)
Society, Bodleian. Classic Tales by Famous Authors: Containing Complete Selections from the World's Best Authors with Prefatory Biographical & Synoptical Notes (Classic Reprint) (p. 401)
Society, Boston Sunday School. Mother's True Stories (Classic Reprint) (p. 1510)
Society, Catholic Publication. Alba's Dream, & Other Stories: Original & Translated (Classic Reprint) (p. 40)
Society, Christian Tract. Young Disciples (Classic Reprint) (p. 2530)
Society, Church Missionary. Round World, & They That Dwell Therein, Vol. 3: 1903, (Being the Sixty-First Volume from the Beginning) (Classic Reprint) (p. 1908)
Society, Delphian. World's Progress: With Illustrative Texts from Masterpieces of Egyptian, Hebrew, Greek, Latin, Modern European & American Literature (Classic Reprint) (p. 2508)
—World's Progress: With Illustrative Texts from Master-Pieces of Egyptian, Hebrew, Greek, Latin, Modern European & American Literature (Classic Reprint) (p. 2508)
Society, Dublin. Instructions for Managing Bees (Classic Reprint) (p. 1125)
Society, Early English Text. Three Kings' Sons (Englisht from the French), Vol. 1: The Text (Classic Reprint) (p. 2233)
Society, Ebell. Ebell: A Journal of Literature & Current Events; May (Classic Reprint) (p. 622)
Society, Enfield Historical. Enfield Echo, Vol. 14: June, 1926 (Classic Reprint) (p. 651)
Society, English Dialect. Glossaries of Lincolnshire & Sussex Words (Classic Reprint) (p. 844)
—Glossaries of Lincolnshire & Sussex Words, Vol. 6 (Classic Reprint) (p. 844)
Society, Estherian Literary. Sororian, Vol. 1 (Classic Reprint) (p. 2065)
Society for Promoting Christian Knowledge. Mary & Charlie: Or, Every Day Faults (Classic Reprint) (p. 1414)
Society, Great Britain Religious Tract. Death-Beds (Classic Reprint) (p. 521)
—Motherless Bairns, & Who Sheltered Them (Classic Reprint) (p. 1510)
Society, Great Britain Royal Geographica. Journal of a Trip to Iceland: By a Fellow of the Royal Geographical Society (Classic Reprint) (p. 1180)
Society, Illinois Humane. Humane Advocate, Vol. 2: April 1907 (Classic Reprint) (p. 1050)
Society, India, jt. auth. see Tagore, Rabindranath.
Society, International Bibliophile. Bibliophile Library of Literature, Art & Rare Manuscripts, Vol. 2: History, Biography, Science, Poetry, Drama, Travel, Adventure, Fiction, & Rare & Little-Known Literature from the Archives of the Great Libraries of the World (Classic Reprint) (p. 215)
—Bibliophile Library of Literature, Art & Rare Manuscripts, Vol. 24 Of 30: History, Biography, Science, Poetry, Drama, Travel, Adventure, Fiction, & Rare & Little-Known Literature from the Archives of the Great Libraries of the World; a Record Of. (p. 215)
Society, Jaffna Book. First Lessons in English & Tamul: Designed to Assist Tamul Youth in the Study of the English Language, Part I. (p. 738)
—First Lessons in English & Tamul, Vol. 1: Designed to Assist Tamul Youth in the Study of the English Language (Classic Reprint) (p. 738)
—Phrase Book, or Idiomatic Exercises in English & Tamil: Designed to Assist Tamil Youths in the Study of the English Language (Classic Reprint) (p. 1737)
—Phrase Book, or Idiomatic Exercises in English & Tamil: Arranged under Several Heads, with an Index; Designed to Assist Tamil Youth in the Study of the English Language (Classic Reprint) (p. 1737)
Society, Juno. REV. John Smith Died-And Went to Jupiter Via Hell (Classic Reprint) (p. 1872)
Society, Leeds Mechanics' Institution an. Royal Bazaar Gazette: May 27-30, 1868 (Classic Reprint) (p. 1909)
Society, London. Brilliant Tales of London Society (Classic Reprint) (p. 282)
Society, London Missionary. Words & Sentences in Malagasy, English, & French, Vol. 1 (Classic Reprint) (p. 2494)
Society, London Religious Tract. Book about Animals (Classic Reprint) (p. 257)
—Botanical Ladder for the Young (Classic Reprint) (p. 264)
—Girl's Week-Day Book, 1836 (Classic Reprint) (p. 839)
Society, Los Angeles Ebell. Ebell, Vol. 2: A Journal of Literature & Current Events (Classic Reprint) (p. 622)
Society, Massachusetts Sabbath School. Golden Rule: A Dialogue Between Little Grace & Her Mother (Classic Reprint) (p. 859)
—Memoir of Hannah B. Cook: Who Died in Campton, N. H. , December 7, 1831, Aged Seven Years (Classic Reprint) (p. 1443)
—String of Pearls for Little Children: Written for the Massachusetts Sabbath School Society, & Approved by the Committee of Publication (Classic Reprint) (p. 2141)
Society, National Audubon. Audubon Magazine, Vol. 1: Published in the Interests of the Audubon Society for the Protection of Birds; February, 1887, to January, 1888 (Classic Reprint) (p. 136)
—Bird Lore, 1899, Vol. 1: An Illustrated Bi-Monthly Magazine Devoted to the Study & Protection of Birds (Classic Reprint) (p. 230)
Society, New York University. Boys' & Girls' Bookshelf: I. Index, II. Reading & Study Courses, III. Graded & Classified Index; a Guide to the Bookshelf's Use & Enjoyment by Young Readers (Classic Reprint) (p. 272)
Society, Pennsylvania-German. Proceedings & Addresses at Fiftieth Anniversary, Lancaster, Pa. , October 17, 1941, Vol. 50 (Classic Reprint) (p. 1803)
—Proceedings & Addresses at Lancaster, October 9, 1925, Vol. 36 (Classic Reprint) (p. 1803)
Society, Percy. Early English Poetry, Ballads, & Popular Literature of the Middle Ages, Vol. 6: Edited from Original Manuscripts & Scarce Publications (Classic Reprint) (p. 614)
—Early English Poetry, Ballads, & Popular Literature of the Middle Ages, Vol. 12: Edited from Original Manuscripts & Scarce Publications (Classic Reprint) (p. 614)
—Early English Poetry, Ballads, Vol. 11: And Popular Literature of the Middle Ages (Classic Reprint) (p. 614)
—Early English Poetry, Ballads, Vol. 17: And Popular Literature of the Middle Ages; Edited from Original Manuscripts & Scarce Publications (Classic Reprint) (p. 614)
Society, Percy, jt. auth. see Halliwell-Phillipps, James Orchard.
Society, Philobiblon. Miscellanies of the Philobiblon Society, Vol. 11 (Classic Reprint) (p. 1477)
—Miscellanies of the Philobiblon Society, Vol. 5 (Classic Reprint) (p. 1477)
Society, Promoting Christian Knowledge. Earth's Many Voices (Classic Reprint) (p. 618)
Society, Protestant Episcopal Tract. Mother's Trials & Triumphs (Classic Reprint) (p. 1510)
—Tracts for Missionary Use, Vol. 5 (Classic Reprint) (p. 2273)
Society, Religious Tract. Beer Shop (Classic Reprint) (p. 189)
—Cornish Fishermen's Watch-Night: And Other Stories (Classic Reprint) (p. 455)
—Folly of Fortune Telling (Classic Reprint) (p. 758)
—Little Ann, or Familiar Conversations upon Interesting Subjects: Between a Child & Her Parents (Classic Reprint) (p. 1310)
—Love Sweetens Truth; or How Caleb Conquered (Classic Reprint) (p. 1361)
—Maurice Guildford: Or the Trials of a Small Boy (Classic Reprint) (p. 1426)
—Old Roger Bond (Classic Reprint) (p. 1648)
—Sunday at Home 1884: A Family Magazine for Sabbath Reading (Classic Reprint) (p. 2152)
—Sweet Story of Old (Classic Reprint) (p. 2169)
Society, Religious Tract and Book. English Instructor (Classic Reprint) (p. 654)
Society, South Carolina Tract. Railway Guide (Classic Reprint) (p. 1835)
Society, Southern Historical Publication. South in the Building of the Nation, Vol. 8 of 12 (Classic Reprint) (p. 2069)
Society, The Religious Tract. Rose-Bud: A Christian Gift to the Young. (p. 1905)
Society, Topsfield Historical. Historical Collections of the Topsfield Historical Society, 1896, Vol. 2 (Classic Reprint) (p. 976)
—Historical Collections of the Topsfield Historical Society, 1906, Vol. 11 (Classic Reprint) (p. 976)
Society, Unitarian. Catalogue of Unitarian Sabbath School Library, March, 1869 (Classic Reprint) (p. 343)
Society, University. Boys' & Girls' Bookshelf, Vol. 9: Children's Book of Fact & Fancy (Part I) (Classic Reprint) (p. 272)
—Home Kindergarten Manual: A Handbook of the Education & Character-Training of Little Children for Parents & Teachers (Classic Reprint) (p. 996)
Society, Winnetka Congregational Church. Good Recipes (Classic Reprint) (p. 865)
Socin, Adolf, jt. auth. see Heyne, Moriz.
Sockabasin, Allen & Raye, Rebekah. Thanks to the Animals (p. 2211)
Socolovsky, Gisela. LOS COLORES. (p. 1350)
Sodagar, D. D. Adam & Eve. (p. 14)
—Adam, Eve & the Forbidden Tree. (p. 14)
—Squirlette's Friends Move Out! (p. 2094)
Sodano, Meg, illus. see Farber, Katy.
Sodano, Meg, illus. see Talbert, Cj.
Sodaro, Craig. Blazing Hot Rods: By Craig Sodaro. (p. 243)
—Civil War Spies (p. 397)
—Dangerous, Disastrous, Unusual History of War (p. 501)
—U. S. Marines Special Operations Regiment: The Missions. (p. 2312)
Sodaro, Craig, jt. auth. see Raatma, Lucia.
Sodaro, Craig, et al. Dream Cars. (p. 601)
Sode, Modupe. Beyond Outstanding: Using the Principles of Daniel to Live Your Best God-Given Life. (p. 212)
Soderberg, Dan. Edie Medium. (p. 626)
Soderberg, Dan & Soderberg, Greyson. Ascensor Jones - Encuentro con Los Hermanos Wright. (p. 125)
Soderberg Downing, Erin, jt. auth. see Soderberg, Erin.
Soderberg, Erin. Best in Class: Puppy Pirates Super Special #2. (p. 206)
—Daring Dreamers Club #1: Milla Takes Charge (Disney: Daring Dreamers Club) RH Disney & Syed, Anoosha, illus. (p. 505)
—Dinosaur Dig Sur, Duendes Del, illus. (p. 548)
—Lost at Sea. Cox, Russ, illus. (p. 1352)
—Piper Cooks up a Plan. Syed, Anoosha, illus. (p. 1748)
—Pug vs. Pug: May the Best Pup Win! (p. 1811)
—Puppy Pirates #1: Stowaway! (p. 1815)
—Puppy Pirates #2: X Marks the Spot. (p. 1815)
—Puppy Pirates #4: Sea Sick. (p. 1815)
—Puppy Pirates #5: Search for the Sea Monster. (p. 1815)
—Puppy Pirates: Set Sail for Adventure (Books 1-4) (p. 1815)
—Puppy Pirates Super Special #1 Ghost Ship. (p. 1815)
—Puppy Pirates Super Special #2: Best in Class. (p. 1815)
—Quirks & the Freaky Field Trip. Jack, Colin, illus. (p. 1828)
—Quirks & the Quirkalicious Birthday. Light, Kelly, illus. (p. 1828)
—Quirks in Circus Quirkus. (p. 1828)
—Race to the North Pole. (p. 1831)
—Scooby-Doo & the Dinosaur Ghost Sur, Duendes del, illus. (p. 1960)
—Scooby-Doo & the Mystery at the Park Sur, Duendes del, illus. (p. 1960)
Soderberg, Erin & Soderberg Downing, Erin. Puppy Pirates #6: Pug vs. Pug. (p. 1815)
Soderberg, Erin & Wasserman, Robin. Stowaway! (p. 2136)
Soderberg, Greyson, jt. auth. see Soderberg, Dan.
Soderberg, Kimberly, illus. see Ekster, Carol Gordon.
Sodkte, Matthias. Habra Moscardones con Gusto a Zanahorias? (p. 908)
Sodré, Julie, illus. see Grimm, Sandra.
Soekarno, Sonya Abby, illus. see Rivadeneira, Caryn.
Soekoe, Minette. Huffy & Puffy. (p. 1047)
Soelver, Anita, illus. see Stemp, Patrick S.
Soemple, Soemple. A. B. C. Capers: A Playlet in One Scene for Twenty-Eight Children, Fourteen Boys & Fourteen Girls (Classic Reprint) (p. 1)
Soentpiet, Chris, illus. see Farris, Christine King.
Soentpiet, Chris, illus. see Laminack, Lester L.
Soentpiet, Chris & Hale, Christy. Amazing Places. (p. 66)
Soentpiet, Chris K., illus. see Bunting, Eve.
Soentpiet, Chris K., illus. see Hopkins, Lee Bennett, ed.
Soentpiet, Chris K., illus. see Hopkins, Lee Bennett.
Soentpiet, Chris K., illus. see Laminack, Lester L.
Soentpiet, Chris K., illus. see Raven, Margot Theis.
Soentpiet, Chris K. & Hale, Christy. Amazing Places. (p. 66)
Soentpiet, Chris K., et al. Molly Bannaky. (p. 1489)
Soes, Mimi. My Bug Buddy. (p. 1535)
Soetoro-Ng, Maya. Escalera a la Luna. Morales, Yuyi, illus. (p. 661)
—Ladder to the Moon. Morales, Yuyi, illus. (p. 1236)
—Ladder to the Moon with CD. Morales, Yuyi, illus. (p. 1236)
Soffe, Caroline Dawn. Billy Barnet & the House of Fern: An Environmental Story. (p. 227)
—Bluebell Wood. (p. 249)
—Burrows of Trother. (p. 300)
Soffer, Allison Sarnoff. Apple Days: A Rosh Hashanah Story McMahon, Bob, illus. (p. 106)
Soffer, Gilad. Duck's Vacation. (p. 608)
Soffer, Ruth. Birds in Flight Coloring Book. (p. 232)
—BOOST Arctic & Antarctic Life Coloring Book. (p. 262)
—BOOST North American Desert Life Coloring Book. (p. 262)
—Cats Stained Glass Coloring Book. (p. 346)
—Creative Haven in Full Bloom Coloring Book. (p. 470)
—Dogs Stained Glass Coloring Book. (p. 578)
—Glitter Tattoos Flowers & Birds. (p. 843)
—Swampland Plants & Animals Coloring Book. (p. 2167)
Soffer, Ruth & Coloring Books Staff. Beautiful Birds in Mated Pairs Stained Glass Coloring Book. (p. 183)
Soffritti, Donald, illus. see Enna, Bruno.
Soffritti, Donald, illus. see Parent, Nancy.
Sofilas, Mark, illus. see Graham, Mark.

Sofilas, Mark, illus. see Husar, Stephane.
Sofka, Amy E., jt. auth. see Justice, Laura M.
Sofranac, Rodo. Polly & the Peanut Pull. (p. 1771)
Sofroniou, Miranda, illus. see Sanchez Vegara, Maria Isabel.
Sogabe, Aki, illus. see Lachenmeyer, Nathaniel.
Sogorb, Lluís. Golondrina No Hace Primavera: Reflexiones para Amantes de la Naturaleza... Incluida la Humana. (p. 861)
Sohmer, Ryan. Gutters (p. 906)
—Least I Could Do Beginnings Volume 1: Look at Me: Look at Me. (p. 1259)
Sohn, Amy & Le Pape, Orna. Brooklyn Bailey, the Missing Dog. VanderPloeg, Libby, illus. (p. 285)
Sohn, Emily. Adventures in Sound with Max Axiom Super Scientist: An Augmented Reading Science Experience. Martin, Cynthia, illus. (p. 20)
—Adventures in Sound with Max Axiom Super Scientist: 4D an Augmented Reading Science Experience. Martin, Cynthia, illus. (p. 20)
—Astro the Alien Learns about Friendship Aón, Carlos, illus. (p. 128)
—Astro the Alien Learns about Honesty Aón, Carlos, illus. (p. 128)
—Astro the Alien Learns about Patience Aón, Carlos, illus. (p. 128)
—Astro the Alien Learns about the Dodo. Aón, Carlos, illus. (p. 128)
—Astro the Alien Learns about the Golden Toad. Aón, Carlos, illus. (p. 128)
—Astro the Alien Learns about the Passenger Pigeon. Aón, Carlos, illus. (p. 128)
—Astro the Alien Learns about the Tasmanian Tiger. Aón, Carlos, illus. (p. 128)
—Astro the Alien Learns about the Woolly Mammoth. Aón, Carlos, illus. (p. 128)
—Astro the Alien Learns about T-Rex. Aón, Carlos, illus. (p. 128)
—Astro the Alien Visits Desert Animals. (p. 128)
—Astro the Alien Visits Farm Animals. (p. 128)
—Astro the Alien Visits Ocean Animals. (p. 128)
—Crash Course in Forces & Motion with Max Axiom Super Scientist: An Augmented Reading Science Experience. Erwin, Steve, illus. (p. 467)
—Crash Course in Forces & Motion with Max Axiom Super Scientist: 4D an Augmented Reading Science Experience. Erwin, Steve, illus. (p. 467)
—Crash Course in Forces & Motion with Max Axiom, Super Scientist. Erwin, Steve, illus. (p. 467)
—Earth Materials. (p. 617)
—Environments. (p. 657)
—Experiments in Earth Science & Weather with Toys & Everyday Stuff. (p. 678)
—Experiments in Forces & Motion with Toys & Everyday Stuff. (p. 678)
—Food & Nutrition. (p. 759)
—Journey Through the Digestive System with Max Axiom, Super Scientist Martin, Cynthia & Schulz, Barbara, illus. (p. 1182)
—Levers & Pulleys. (p. 1282)
—Living Systems. (p. 1334)
—Magnetism & Electricity. (p. 1381)
—Matter & Energy. (p. 1425)
—Measurement. (p. 1435)
—Mixtures & Solutions. (p. 1484)
—Models & Designs. (p. 1486)
—Paper from Wood. (p. 1697)
—Patterns & Textures. (p. 1706)
—Skateboarding: How It Works. (p. 2029)
—Solids & Liquids. (p. 2057)
—Sound. (p. 2067)
—Structures of Life. (p. 2142)
—Variables & Experiments. (p. 2348)
Sohn, Emily & Ash Sullivan, Erin. New Plants: Seeds in the Soil Patch. (p. 1596)
—Weather & the Water Cycle: Will it Rain? (p. 2394)
Sohn, Emily & Bair, Diane. Food & Nutrition: Eating to Win. (p. 759)
—Pebbles, Sand, & Silt. (p. 1711)
Sohn, Emily & Brennan, Joseph. Balance & Motion: Toying with Gravity. (p. 160)
—Magnetism & Electricity: The Broken Toy Car. (p. 1381)
—Mixtures & Solutions: The Sugar in the Tea. (p. 1484)
Sohn, Emily & Brennan, Joseph K. Balance & Motion. (p. 160)
Sohn, Emily & Fellows, Fred. Levers & Pulleys: Lift Anything! (p. 1282)
Sohn, Emily & Fellows, Frederick. Variables & Experiments: Getting Across the River. (p. 2348)
Sohn, Emily & Foster, Barbara J. Animal Needs. (p. 90)
Sohn, Emily & Gendler, Joel. Solids & Liquids: Who Messed up My Sand? (p. 2057)
Sohn, Emily & Hansen, Anya. Models & Designs: It's a Roller Coaster Ride! (p. 1486)
Sohn, Emily & Harter, Adam. Landforms: The Ever-changing Earth. (p. 1242)
—Landforms. (p. 1242)
—Sun, Moon, & Stars: A Cosmic Case. (p. 2151)
—Sun, Moon, & Stars. (p. 2151)
Sohn, Emily & Kentor Schmauss, Judy. Air & Weather: Where'd My Hat Go? (p. 37)
—Structures of Life: What Is this Fossil? (p. 2142)
Sohn, Emily & Klobuchar, Lisa. Fabric: It's Got You Covered! (p. 692)
—Fabric. (p. 692)
Sohn, Emily & Linde, Barbara. Environments: Beetles in the Garden. (p. 657)
Sohn, Emily & Ohlenroth, Pat. Solar Energy. (p. 2055)
Sohn, Emily & Ohlenroth, Patricia. Living Systems: Life's Inside Story. (p. 1334)
—Solar Energy: Saving the School Budget. (p. 2055)
Sohn, Emily & Rompella, Natalie. Fun Science. (p. 800)
Sohn, Emily & Rothbardt, Karen. Insects: Which One Doesn't Belong? (p. 1122)
—Insects. (p. 1122)
—Trees: Worlds Within Leaves. (p. 2284)
—Trees. (p. 2284)
Sohn, Emily & Rothbardt, Karen J. Insects: Which One Doesn't Belong? (p. 1122)
Sohn, Emily & Schmauss, Judy Kentor. Air & Weather. (p. 37)
Sohn, Emily & Sharp, Katie. Human Body: Train it Right. (p. 1049)
—Measurement: The Measured Mystery. (p. 1435)
Sohn, Emily & Sharp, Katie John. Human Body. (p. 1049)
Sohn, Emily & Sullivan, Erin Ash. New Plants. (p. 1596)
—Weather & the Water Cycle. (p. 2394)
Sohn, Emily & Townsend, Laura. Animal Needs: Who's New at the Zoo? (p. 90)
—Patterns & Textures: Who Took the Pets? (p. 1706)
—Water: Watch It Change. (p. 2384)
—Water. (p. 2384)
Sohn, Emily & Tsang, Nina. Matter & Energy: Finding the Power. (p. 1425)
Sohn, Emily & Wright, Pam. Earth Materials: The Mystery Rocks. (p. 617)
—Paper from Wood: Dollhouse Decisions. (p. 1697)
—Sound: Music to Your Ears. (p. 2067)
Sohn, Emily Beth. Illuminating World of Light with Max Axiom, Super Scientist: 4D an Augmented Reading Science Experience. Derington, Nick, illus. (p. 1096)
—Journey Through the Digestive System with Max Axiom, Super Scientist: 4D an Augmented Reading Science Experience. Martin, Cynthia & Schulz, Barbara, illus. (p. 1182)
—National Woman's Party Fight for Suffrage. (p. 1578)
Sohn, Ruth H. Crossing Cairo: A Jewish Woman's Encounter with Egypt. (p. 478)
Soileau, Hodges, illus. see Warner, Gertrude Chandler.
Soisson, Chelsea. Tate's Wayward Voyage. (p. 2192)
Sojdr, Martin, illus. see Bartikova, Petra.
Sojo, Cecila I. Everything Kids' Learning Spanish Book: Exercises & Puzzles to Help You Learn Espanol. (p. 673)
Sojos, Catalina. Ecuador. Bladimir, Trejo, illus. (p. 624)
—Ecuador. Trejo, Bladimir, illus. (p. 624)
Sokol, Bill, illus. see Hicks, Clifford B.
Sokol, Dawn DeVries. Doodle Diary: Art Journaling for Girls (p. 584)
—Doodle Journeys: A Fill-In Journal for Everyday Explorers. (p. 584)
—Doodle Sketchbook: Art Journaling for Boys (p. 584)
—Here, Kitty Kitty (p. 958)
—Kennel Club (p. 1209)
Sokol, Leslie & Fox, Marci G. Think Confident, Be Confident Workbook for Teens: Activities to Create Unshakable Self-Confidence & Reach Your Goals. (p. 2221)
Sokol, Ron. Retrieval. (p. 1870)
Sokolava, Valerie, illus. see McFadden, Deanna.
Sokolava, Valerie, illus. see Olmstead, Kathleen, et al.
Sokolova, Valerie, illus. see Bowman, Crystal.
Sokolova, Valerie, illus. see Spinner, Stephanie.
Sokolov-Mikitov, I. S. Russkii Les: Roman. Bastrykin, Viktor, illus. (p. 1917)
Sol & K'naan. When I Get Older: The Story Behind Wavin' Flag. Gutierrez, Rudy, illus. (p. 2430)
Sol, Anne, photos by see Roger, Marie-Sabine.
Sol90 Editorial Staff. Visual Guide to Birds. (p. 2363)
—Visual Guide to Fish & Amphibians. (p. 2363)
—Visual Guide to Invertebrates. (p. 2363)
—Visual Guide to Plants, Algae, & Fungi. (p. 2363)
—Visual Guide to Reptiles & Dinosaurs. (p. 2363)
Sola, Lawrence H. Jeremy's Adventures: Miracle on Main Street. (p. 1164)
Sola, Sola. American Girl: And Her Four Years in a Boys' College (Classic Reprint) (p. 71)
Solacolu, Théodore. Influence de Quelques Aliments Minéraux Sur les Fonctions et la Structure des Végétaux: Thèse (Classic Reprint) (p. 1119)
Solages, Mahalia. What Morning Is This? (p. 2419)
Solaim, Lamis S. Silent Nightingale. (p. 2017)
Solak, Daria, illus. see Sanchez Vegara, Maria Isabel.
Solak, Daria, jt. auth. see Sanchez Vegara, Maria Isabel.
Solana, Maria T., tr. see French, Vivian.
Solana, Sister. My Heart Song. Mbd, Dion, illus. (p. 1549)
Solanine. Prince Bari Volume 3. (p. 1794)
—Prince Bari Volume 4. (p. 1794)
Solano, Jordi, illus. see Lang, Heather.
Solano, Jordi, illus. see McShane, Marianne.
Solano, Jordi, illus. see Pincus, Meeg.
Solano, Jordi, illus. see Sheehy, Shawn.
Solano, Jordi, illus. see Young, Judy.
Solari, Kylee, illus. see Pelleschi, Andrea.
Solari, María J., jt. auth. see Kipling, Rudyard.
Solaro, Amy. Fantastic Features of Peculiar Creatures. (p. 707)
Solberg, Elin. Det Ensamma Huset (Hjärtebyserien) (p. 534)
—Lonely House. (p. 1342)
Solbert, Ronni, illus. see Merrill, Jean.
Soldene, Emily. My Theatrical & Musical Recollections. (p. 1562)
—My Theatrical & Musical Recollections (Classic Reprint) (p. 1562)
Soldier, Ayesha. Click Start 1 Primary: Computer Science for Schools. (p. 404)
—Click Start 2 Primary: Computer Science for Schools. (p. 404)
Solé, Francisco, illus. see Ruiz, Celia & Stevenson, Robert Louis.
Solé, Francisco, tr. see Ruiz, Celia & Stevenson, Robert Louis.
Sole, Julien, illus. see Seret, Bernard.
Solecki, Kristen, illus. see Students of the 826 Valencia writing programs, Students of the 826 Valencia writing.
Soleil. Gentle Haven of Rhymes & Verses. (p. 816)
Soleiman, Serg, illus. see Strange, Jason.
Solenne and Thomas, illus. see de Mullenheim, Sophie.
Solenova, Kate, illus. see Gordon, Lisa.
Soler, Jaume & Conangla, Maria Mercè. Emotional Explorers: A Creative Approach to Managing Emotions (p. 644)
Soler, Sara, illus. see Tobin, Paul.
Soles, Connie McGhee. Meo: The Pharaoh of Cats. (p. 1447)
—Meo: The Pharaoh of Cats Coloring Book. (p. 1447)
Soles, Henry, ed. NEW Children of Color Holy Bible Hardcover Edition. Carter, Fred et al, illus. (p. 1592)
Soley, Liesel. Can You Be an Artist? Soley, Liesel, illus. (p. 318)
Solga, Kim, jt. auth. see Kohl, MaryAnn F.
Solger, Reinhold, jt. auth. see Roemer, Jean.
Solheim, James. Only Alex Addleston in All These Mountains. Ebbeler, Jeffrey, illus. (p. 1664)
Soli, Tina, illus. see Bringsvaerd, Tor Age.
Soliday, Michael. Keltian's Warriors: The Final Gift - Book Three of the Keltian Trilogy. (p. 1209)
—Keltian's Warriors: Keltian's Warriors: the Final Gift - Book Three of the Keltian Trilogy. (p. 1209)
Solimene, Laura, ed. see Stowe, Harriet Beecher.
Solimine, John. Does Frankenstein Get Hungry? Solimine, John, illus. (p. 575)
Soling, Cevin. Boris the Dog. Kille, Steve, illus. (p. 263)
Solino, Ali. Alligator, Bayou, Crawfish. Huber, Candice, ed. (p. 56)
Solinski, J. E. Meet Charlie. (p. 1438)
Solis, Fermin. Eek! Yikes! Boo! (p. 627)
Solis, Fermin, illus. see Schmauss, Judy Kentor.
Solis, Fermin, illus. see Townsend, John.
Solís, Fermín, illus. see Walden, Libby.
Solis, Fermin, illus. see Young, Dawn.
Solis, Laurie. Freda's Little Red Huset. Solis, Natalia & Solis, Tatiana, eds. (p. 780)
Solis, Natalia, ed. see Solis, Laurie.
Solis, Octavio. Santos & Santos. (p. 1934)
Solis, Tatiana, ed. see Solis, Laurie.
Solitaire, Solitaire. Streaks of Squatter Life, & Far-West Scenes, Vol. 1: A Series of Humorous Sketches Descriptive of Incidents & Character in the Wild West, to Which Are Added Other Miscellaneous Pieces (Classic Reprint) (p. 2139)
Soliz, Adela. Bullying. (p. 297)
Soliz-Daramola, Mary. Pelumi!!!... & the Shiny Stones. (p. 1714)
Soll, Karen. Coldest Places on the Planet. (p. 413)
—Extreme Earth. (p. 686)
—Highest Places on the Planet. (p. 969)
—Hottest Places on the Planet. (p. 1007)
—Lowest Places on the Planet. (p. 1363)
Solle, J. Stephenson Du. Letters from Europe (Classic Reprint) (p. 1279)
Sollers, Jim, illus. see Bloxam, Frances.
Sollers, Jim, illus. see Plourde, Lynn.
Sollinger, Emily. Dare to Repair! (p. 505)
—Dinotrux to the Rescue! (p. 551)
—Owls: Birds of the Night. Rallis, Chris, illus. (p. 1689)
—Tale of Gulliver. (p. 2179)
—Thirsty Day in the Crater. (p. 2223)
—This Is Our World: A Story about Taking Care of the Earth. Brown, Jo, illus. (p. 2225)
Sollinger, Emily, adapted by. Can We Build It? Yes We Can! (p. 317)
—Dinotrux to the Rescue! (p. 551)
—Lofty & the Giraffe. (p. 1339)
Sollish, Ari. Touch of Passover - French (Pessa'h Sur le Bout des Doigts) (p. 2268)
Sollitt, G. Elanette. Sweet Briar Magazine, Vol. 9: November, 1917 (Classic Reprint) (p. 2168)
Solly, Gloria, jt. illus. see Cruzan, Patricia.
Solly, Gloria D., illus. see Cruzan, Patricia.
Solly, Henry. James Woodford, Carpenter & Chartist, Vol. 2 of 2 (Classic Reprint) (p. 1157)
—James Woodford, Vol. 1 Of 2: Carpenter & Chartist (Classic Reprint) (p. 1157)
—Lady Stella & Her Lover, Vol. 3 (Classic Reprint) (p. 1238)
Solner Heimer, Patricia. Li'l Earth. Solner Heimer, Patricia, illus. (p. 1301)
Solnit, Rebecca. Cinderella Liberator. Rackham, Arthur, illus. (p. 392)
Solo, Hope. Hope Solo: My Story Young Readers' Edition. (p. 1002)
Solod, Margo. Coyote Summer: A Summerhood Island Book. (p. 465)
Solodar, Marisol. Bailey's Band: Develop Understanding of Fractions & Numbers (p. 159)
Sologub, Fedor. Sweet-Scented Name: And Other Fairy Tales, Fables & Stories (Classic Reprint) (p. 2169)
Sologub, Feodor. Created Legend (Classic Reprint) (p. 469)
—Little Demon (Classic Reprint) (p. 1315)
—Old House: And Other Tales (Classic Reprint) (p. 1646)
Soloman, Debra. I Have Autism. (p. 1066)
Solomita, Cindy. Adventures of Callie the Curious Cat. Sanders, Rick, illus. (p. 22)
Solomon, Andrew. Far from the Tree: Young Adult Edition—How Children & Their Parents Learn to Accept One Another ... Our Differences Unite Us. (p. 708)
Solomon, Barbara. Girl Who Wanted to Become a Princess. (p. 837)
—Princess Kamala & the Dogon Oracle. (p. 1797)
Solomon, Beth. Habu & the Lost Zebra. Baykovska, Ira, illus. (p. 908)
Solomon, Dane, jt. auth. see Wolny, Philip.
Solomon, Debra, illus. see Wollard, Kathy.
Solomon, Debra, jt. auth. see Wollard, Kathy.
Solomon, Diane & Carey, Mark. Ravenstone: The Secret of Ninham Mountain. (p. 1844)
Solomon, Diane L. & Carey, Mark. Ravenstone: The Secret of Ninham Mountain. (p. 1844)
Solomon, Harry. Day Silver Snowed. Solomon, Harry, illus. (p. 514)
Solomon, Heather, illus. see Wheeler, Lisa.
Solomon, Heather M., illus. see Coombs, Kate.
Solomon, Heather M., illus. see Del Negro, Janice M.
Solomon, Heather M., illus. see Weeks, Sarah.
Solomon, Ivan, jt. auth. see Groberman, Micah.
Solomon, Jane. Dictionary of Difficult Words: With More Than 400 Perplexing Words to Test Your Wits! Lockhart, Louise, illus. (p. 541)
Solomon, Jef. Right in My Own Neighborhood. (p. 1882)
Solomon, Kerita, illus. see Shivers, Ellen C.
Solomon, Martha. Christmas in Da Hood. (p. 385)
Solomon, Matt & Pauls, Chris. Giant Smugglers. (p. 831)
Solomon, Rachel Lynn. Our Year of Maybe. (p. 1681)
—You'll Miss Me When I'm Gone. (p. 2529)
Solomon, Raymond J. Gleaner: November, 1944 (Classic Reprint) (p. 841)
Solomon, Ron, jt. auth. see Solomon, Iris L.
Solomon, Sharon. Cathy Williams, Buffalo Soldier Lorenzetti, Doreen, illus. (p. 345)
—Lewis Tewanima: Born to Run Fields, Lisa, illus. (p. 1282)
—Walk With Grandpa/Un Paseo con el Abuelo. Del Risco, Eida, tr. (p. 2372)
Solomon, Sharon K. Ride High with the Wave. (p. 1878)
—Walk with Grandpa. Barcita, Pamela, illus. (p. 2372)
Solomon, Sharon K., jt. auth. see Bridy, Dan.
Solomon Sr, Carl. Do Animals Believe in God? (p. 570)
—Jacob's Backyard Safari. (p. 1154)
Solomon, Steven. Homophobia: Deal with It & Turn Prejudice into Pride Johnson, Nick, illus. (p. 998)
Solomons, David. Doctor Who: the Secret in Vault 13. (p. 574)
—My Brother Is a Superhero. (p. 1534)
—My Gym Teacher Is an Alien Overlord. (p. 1549)
Solomons, Shani. Twinigma. (p. 2305)
Solon, Juan Carlos & Chronicle Books Staff. Alphabit: An ABC Quest in 8-Bit - Follow the Quest, Find the Hidden Pictures, & Bring Back the Treasure! Press Start. (p. 59)
Solórzano Garcia, Gerardo. One Eagle's Journey to Glory. (p. 1659)
Solotareff, Gregoire. Dictionary of Witches. (p. 542)
—Wolfy. Solotareff, Gregoire, illus. (p. 2484)
—You Big & Me Small. (p. 2525)
Solounias, Basil, tr. see Zaidan, Jurji.
Solovyov, Vladimir. Seven Soviet Plays (Classic Reprint) (p. 1994)
Soloy, Lauren. When Emily Was Small. (p. 2430)
Solsness, Lars Porsenna. Utgard: Embodying Sundary Notes of a Wanderjahr on Hyperborean Shores (Classic Reprint) (p. 2342)
Soltaire, Delores. Baby Animals Are Born. (p. 148)
Soltera, Maria. Lady's Ride Across Spanish Honduras. (p. 1239)
—Lady's Ride Across Spanish Honduras (Classic Reprint) (p. 1239)
Soltesz, C. C. Bebe & the Blue Macaw. (p. 186)
Soltis, Sue. Nothing Like a Puffin. Kolar, Bob, illus. (p. 1625)
—Stars Just up the Street. Davenier, Christine, illus. (p. 2107)
Solutions (P) Ltd, Matrix Media, illus. see Jensen, Fredrich William.
Solutions Ltd, Matrix Media, illus. see Dunn, Lynn.
Solvet, P. -Louis. Etudes Sur la Fontaine Louis, Ou Notes et Excursions Litteraires Sur Ses Fables: Precedees de Son Eloge Inedit (Classic Reprint) (p. 666)
—ÉTudes Sur la Fontaine Louis, Ou Notes et Excursions Littéraires Sur Ses Fables: PRéCédées de Son ÉLoge Inédit (Classic Reprint) (p. 666)
Solway, Andrew. Aircraft (p. 37)
—Buildings & Structures (p. 295)
—Cadenas y Redes Alimentarias. (p. 308)
—Chemistry. (p. 365)
—Civil Engineering & the Science of Structures. (p. 396)
—Classifying Mammals. (p. 401)
—Climate Change. (p. 405)
—Communication: The Impact of Science & Technology. (p. 431)
—Energy & Matter. (p. 650)
—Food & Digestion. (p. 759)
—Food Chains & Webs (p. 759)
—From Crashing Waves to Music Download: An Energy Journey Through the World of Sound. (p. 791)
—From Sunlight to Blockbuster Movies: An Energy Journey Through the World of Light. (p. 793)
—Genetics. (p. 815)
—Graphing Immigration (p. 881)
—Graphing War & Conflict (p. 881)
—Growing. (p. 899)
—Heart & Lungs. (p. 944)
—Human Body: Investigating an Unexplained Death. Stayte, James, illus. (p. 1049)
—Jupiter & the Outer Planets (p. 1191)
—Resources. (p. 1869)
—Science of a Loaf of Bread: The Science of Changing Properties. (p. 1957)
—Scientists Behind Earth's Processes (p. 1959)
—Scientists Behind Energy (p. 1959)
—Secrets of Animal Life Cycles. (p. 1980)
—Secrets of Flight. (p. 1980)
—Secrets of Habitats. (p. 1980)
—Secrets of Heat & Cold. (p. 1980)
—Secrets of Pollution & Conservation. (p. 1980)
—Transportation (p. 2278)
—Universe. (p. 2332)
—Waste Disposal. (p. 2382)
—Why Is There Life on Earth? (p. 2458)
Solway, Andrew, jt. auth. see Crabtree Staff.
Solway, Andrew & Graham, Ian. Energy Journeys. (p. 651)
—Energy Transfers. (p. 651)
Solway, Jeff, illus. see Vernon, Steve.
Soma, Kohei. Bu Neng Diu de Bao Bei (Simplified Chinese) (p. 288)
Somà, Marco, illus. see Call, Davide.
Somà, Marco, illus. see Isern Iñigo, Susanna.
Soma, Marco, illus. see Isern, Susanna.
Somaiah, B. Ranjan, illus. see Somaiah, Rosemarie.
Somaiah, Ranjan, illus. see Somaiah, Rosemarie.
Somaiah, Ranjan, jt. auth. see Somaiah, Rosemarie.
Somaiah, Rosemarie. Indian Children's Favorite Stories: Fables, Myths & Fairy Tales. Somaiah, Ranjan & Somaiah, B. Ranjan, illus. (p. 1116)
Soman, David. How to Two. (p. 1045)
—Monster Next Door. (p. 1496)

S

—Three Bears in a Boat. Soman, David, illus. (p. 2231)
Soman, David, illus. see Davis, Jacky.
Soman, David, illus. see Heller, Maryellen.
Soman, David, jt. auth. see Davis, Jacky.
Soman, David & Davis, Jacky. Little Box of Ladybug Girl Soman, David, illus. (p. 1312)
—Play All Day with Ladybug Girl. Soman, David, illus. (p. 1758)
—Who Can Play? (p. 2446)
Somers, Ian. Secret Gift. (p. 1975)
Somers, J. J. Jim's Western Gems (Classic Reprint) (p. 1169)
Somers, Robert. Martyr of Glencree, Vol. 1 Of 3: A Romance Too True (Classic Reprint) (p. 1411)
Somerset, Helen. Adventures of Mrs. Colonel Somerset in Caffraria, During the War (Classic Reprint) (p. 25)
Somerset, Lady Henry. Under the Arch (Classic Reprint) (p. 2321)
Somervill, Barbara. Actor. (p. 13)
—Commercial Fisher. (p. 430)
—Dental Hygienist. (p. 529)
—Ethiopia. (p. 666)
—Fire Ant. (p. 732)
—Florida Panther. (p. 751)
—Food Scientist. (p. 760)
—Green General Contractor. (p. 894)
—Grizzly Bear. (p. 897)
—Japan. (p. 1159)
—Marine Biologist. (p. 1405)
—Mexico. (p. 1454)
—Monitor Lizard. (p. 1493)
—Musician. (p. 1529)
—Python. (p. 1819)
—Small Indian Mongoose. (p. 2039)
Somervill, Barbara A. Alabama. (p. 38)
—Ancient Maya. (p. 81)
—Animal Cells & Life Processes (p. 88)
—Arizona. (p. 116)
—Arizona (Revised Edition) (p. 116)
—Australia & Oceania. (p. 138)
—Colorado. (p. 421)
—Distance, Area, & Volume (p. 564)
—Elizabeth Blackwell: America's First Female Doctor. (p. 636)
—Empire of the Aztecs. (p. 645)
—Empire of the Incas, Revised Edition. (p. 645)
—Glaciers. (p. 840)
—Graphing Health & Disease (p. 881)
—Graphing Natural Disasters (p. 881)
—Hong Kong. (p. 999)
—Hurricanes. (p. 1054)
—Iran. (p. 1133)
—Japan. (p. 1159)
—Mass & Weight (p. 1417)
—Mississippi. (p. 1482)
—New York. (p. 1598)
—Niger. (p. 1604)
—Pennsylvania (Revised Edition) (p. 1717)
—Plains & Plateaus. (p. 1754)
—Plant Cells & Life Processes (p. 1756)
—Producing Fish (p. 1804)
—Producing Grains (p. 1804)
—Real World Data (p. 1850)
—South Carolina. (p. 2068)
—South Carolina (Revised Edition) (p. 2068)
—South Korea. (p. 2069)
—Spain. (p. 2073)
—Speed & Acceleration (p. 2078)
—Story Behind Coal (p. 2127)
—Story Behind Glass (p. 2127)
—Story Behind Maps (p. 2127)
—Story Behind Paper (p. 2127)
—Story Behind Rubber (p. 2127)
—Taiwan. (p. 2176)
—Tennessee. (p. 2206)
—Texas. (p. 2209)
—Texas (Revised Edition) (p. 2209)
—United Arab Emirates. (p. 2329)
—West. (p. 2401)
Somervill, Barbara A., jt. auth. see Gray, Susan H.
Somervill, Barbara A. & Capstone Press Staff. Measure It! (p. 1434)
Somervill, Barbara A., et al. True Stories. (p. 2294)
Somervill, Barbara & Gray, Susan H. Wild Boar. (p. 2463)
Somerville, Charles. Shriek: A Satirical Burlesque (Classic Reprint) (p. 2013)
Somerville, Charles C. E Is for Egypt. Somerville, Charles C., illus. (p. 612)
Somerville, Charles C., jt. auth. see Elliott, Ned.
Somerville, E. Enthusiast (Classic Reprint) (p. 656)
—Grand Filly (Classic Reprint) (p. 876)
—Holy Island (Classic Reprint) (p. 995)
—Nineteenth-Century Miracle (Classic Reprint) (p. 1610)
—Philippa's Fox-Hunt (Classic Reprint) (p. 1734)
—Some Experiences of an Irish R. M (Classic Reprint) (p. 2059)
—Story of the Discontented Little Elephant: Told in Pictures & Rhyme (Classic Reprint) (p. 2133)
—Through Connemara in a Governess Cart. (p. 2236)
—Through Connemara in a Governess Cart (Classic Reprint) (p. 2236)
—Waters of Strife (Classic Reprint) (p. 2386)
Somerville, E. Ce. Dan Russel the Fox: An Episode in the Life of Miss. Rowan (Classic Reprint) (p. 499)
Somerville, E. OE. All on the Irish Shore: Irish Sketches. (p. 53)
—All on the Irish Shore: Irish Sketches (Classic Reprint) (p. 53)
—Badminton Magazine, December 1898: Some Experiences of an Irish R. M (Classic Reprint) (p. 159)
—Badminton Magazine, October 1898: Some Experiences of an Irish R. M. ; No; I Great-Uncle Mccarthy (Classic Reprint) (p. 159)
—Further Experiences of an Irish R. M (Classic Reprint) (p. 802)
—Grand Filly (Classic Reprint) (p. 876)
—In the Vine Country (Classic Reprint) (p. 1111)
—Irish Cousin (Classic Reprint) (p. 1134)
—Irish Memories (Classic Reprint) (p. 1134)
—Mount Music (Classic Reprint) (p. 1512)
—Naboth's Vineyard: A Novel (Classic Reprint) (p. 1572)
—Real Charlotte (Classic Reprint) (p. 1849)
—Real Charlotte, Vol. 1 of 3 (Classic Reprint) (p. 1849)
—Silver Fox (Classic Reprint) (p. 2019)
—Some Experiences of an Irish R. M (Classic Reprint) (p. 2059)
—Some Irish Yesterdays (Classic Reprint) (p. 2059)
—Story of the Discontented Little Elephant: Told in Pictures & Rhyme (Classic Reprint) (p. 2133)
—Stray-Aways (Classic Reprint) (p. 2139)
—Waters of Strife (Classic Reprint) (p. 2386)
Somerville, Edith. In Mr. Knox's Country (Classic Reprint) (p. 1106)
—Lisheen Races, Second-Hand (Classic Reprint) (p. 1308)
—Policy of the Closed Door (Classic Reprint) (p. 1770)
—Some Experiences of an Irish R. M: No; II. Trinket's Colt (Classic Reprint) (p. 2059)
—Some Experiences of an Irish R. M, Vol. 7: A Misdeal (Classic Reprint) (p. 2059)
Somerville, Edith, jt. auth. see Ross, Martin.
Somerville, Edith None, jt. auth. see Ross, Martin.
Somerville, Edith Oe. Badminton Magazine, July 1899: Some Experiences of an Irish R. M. ; No; X. , the House of Fahy (Classic Reprint) (p. 159)
—In Mr. Knox's Country (Classic Reprint) (p. 1106)
—Lisheen Races, Second-Hand (Classic Reprint) (p. 1308)
—Policy of the Closed Door (Classic Reprint) (p. 1770)
—Some Experiences of an Irish R. M, Vol. 7: A Misdeal (Classic Reprint) (p. 2059)
Somerville, Elizabeth. Choice Tales: For the Improvement of Youth of Both Sexes (Classic Reprint) (p. 380)
—History of Little Charles: And His Friend Frank Wilful (Classic Reprint) (p. 978)
—Village Maid, or Dame Burton's Moral Stories for the Instruction & Amusement of Youth to Which Are Added, Plain Tales (Classic Reprint) (p. 2358)
Somerville, Hannah, illus. see Ritchie, Kate.
Somerville, Henry. Racer of Illinois (Classic Reprint) (p. 1832)
Somerville, Louisa. Alphabet & First Words, Ages 6-7. Tulip, Jenny, illus. (p. 58)
—Phonics, Ages 6-7. Tulip, Jenny, illus. (p. 1736)
—Times Tables, Ages 6-7. Tulip, Jenny, illus. (p. 2247)
Somerville, Mary. On Molecular & Microscopic Science. (p. 1653)
—On Molecular & Microscopic Science, Vol. 1 of 2 (Classic Reprint) (p. 1653)
Somina, Yulia, illus. see Wigglesworth, Laura.
Somina, Yuliya, illus. see Dapre, Alan.
Somis, Ignazio. True & Particular Account: Of the Most Surprising Preservation, & Happy Deliverance, of Three Women Who Were Buried, Thirty-Seven Day's, in the Ruins of a Stable, by a Heavy Fall of Snow, from the Mountains, at the Village of Bergemoletto, in Italy; (p. 2293)
Sommariva, Jon, illus. see Beatty, Scott.
Sommariva, Jon, illus. see Jackson Miller, John, et al.
Sommariva, Jon, illus. see Manning, Matthew K.
Sommer, Carl. Androcles & the Lion. Martinez, Jorge, illus. (p. 84)
—Ant & the Grasshopper. Noé, Ignacio, illus. (p. 101)
—Boy Who Cried Wolf. Bogdan, Enache, illus. (p. 270)
—Can You Help Me Find My Smile? Me Puedes Ayudar a Encontrar Mi Sonrisa? Budwine, Greg, illus. (p. 318)
—Chicken Little. Mercado, Jorge, illus. (p. 368)
—Country Mouse & the City Mouse. Noe, Ignacio, illus. (p. 461)
—Dare to Dream! Martinez, Jorge et al, illus. (p. 505)
—Dare to Dream! ¡Atrévete a Soñar! Martínez, Jorge et al, illus. (p. 505)
—Donkey, Fox, & the Lion. Noé, Ignacio, illus. (p. 581)
—Dream. Martínez, Jorge et al, illus. (p. 600)
—Dream (Sueña) Martínez, Jorge et al, illus. (p. 602)
—Eagle & the Chickens. Noé, illus. (p. 613)
—Emperor & the Seed. Martinez, Jorge, illus. (p. 644)
—Emperor's New Clothes. Noe, Ignacio, illus. (p. 645)
—Fast Forward. Budwine, Greg, illus. (p. 713)
—Fast Forward(Avance Acelarado) Budwine, Greg, illus. (p. 713)
—Great Deception. Noé, illus. (p. 885)
—Great Deception(El Gran Engaño) Noé, illus. (p. 885)
—Great Royal Race. Westbrook, Dick, illus. (p. 889)
—Great Royal Race(La Gran Carrera Real) Westbrook, Dick, illus. (p. 889)
—Hopeless to Hopeful. Vignolo, Enrique, illus. (p. 1002)
—I Am a Lion! Budwine, Greg, illus. (p. 1057)
—I Am a Lion!(Yo Soy un León!) Budwine, Greg, illus. (p. 1057)
—If Only I Were- James, Kennon, illus. (p. 1092)
—If Only I Were...(Si Yo Fuese...) James, Kennon, illus. (p. 1092)
—It's Not Fair!(No Es Justo) ! Budwine, Greg, illus. (p. 1146)
—King of the Pond. Budwine, Greg, illus. (p. 1221)
—King of the Pond(El Rey Del Estanque) Budwine, Greg, illus. (p. 1221)
—Light Your Candle. James, Kennon, illus. (p. 1299)
—Light Your Candle(Enciende Tu Vela) James, Kennon, illus. (p. 1299)
—Lion & the Mouse. Mercado, Jorge, illus. (p. 1305)
—Lion & the Three Bulls. Mercado, Jorge, illus. (p. 1305)
—Little Red Hen. Noe, Ignacio, illus. (p. 1326)
—Little Red Riding Hood. Noe, Ignacio, illus. (p. 1326)
—Little Red Train. James, Kennon, illus. (p. 1326)
—Little Red Train(El Trenecito Rojo) James, Kennon, illus. (p. 1326)
—Lost & Found. Budwine, Greg, illus. (p. 1352)
—Lost & Found(Perdida y Encontrada) Budwine, Greg, illus. (p. 1352)
—Mayor for a Day: Alcalde Por un Dia. Westbrook, Dick, illus. (p. 1430)
—Mayor for a Day. Westbrook, Dick, illus. (p. 1430)
—Miller, His Son & Their Donkey. Denman, Michael, illus. (p. 1467)
—Miserable Millie(La Pobrecita Mili) Vignolo, Enrique, illus. (p. 1477)
—No Longer a Dilly Dally. James, Kennon, illus. (p. 1613)
—No Longer a Dilly Dally(iNunca Mas a Troche y Moche) James, Kennon, illus. (p. 1613)
—No One Will Ever Know. Budwine, Greg, illus. (p. 1614)
—No One Will Ever Know(Nadie Se Va a Enterar) Westbrook, Dick, illus. (p. 1614)
—Noise! Noise! Noise!(Ruido! Ruido! Ruido!) James, Kennon, illus. (p. 1617)
—Proud Rooster & Little Hen. Budwine, Greg, illus. (p. 1808)
—Proud Rooster & Little Hen(Gallito Orgulloso y Gallinita) Budwine, Greg, illus. (p. 1808)
—Race. Budwine, Greg, illus. (p. 1830)
—Race(La Carrera) Budwine, Greg, illus. (p. 1831)
—Racing Fools. Budwine, Greg, illus. (p. 1832)
—Rebel. Vignolo, Enrique, illus. (p. 1852)
—Rebel(El Rebelde) Vignolo, Enrique, illus. (p. 1852)
—Revolt. Budwine, Greg, illus. (p. 1873)
—Revolt(La Revuelta) Budwine, Greg, illus. (p. 1873)
—Richest Poor Kid. Martinez, Jorge, illus. (p. 1877)
—Roar. Budwine, Greg, illus. (p. 1889)
—Roar(El Rugido) Budwine, Greg, illus. (p. 1889)
—Runaway(La Escapada) Vignolo, Enrique, illus. (p. 1915)
—Sly Fox & the Chicks. James, Kennon, illus. (p. 2039)
—Sly Fox & the Chicks(El Zorro Astuto y los Pollitos) James, Kennon, illus. (p. 2039)
—Spike the Rebel!(pua, el Rebelde!) Vignolo, Enrique, illus. (p. 2082)
—Stone Soup. Denman, Michael, illus. (p. 2121)
—Three Little Pigs. Budwine, Greg, illus. (p. 2233)
—Three Little Pigs(Los Tres Cerditos) Budwine, Greg & Vignolo, Enrique, illus. (p. 2234)
—Tied up in Knots(Enredados) Budwine, Greg, illus. (p. 2240)
—Time Remote! Budwine, Greg, illus. (p. 2245)
—Time Remote!(El Control Del Tiempo!) Budwine, Greg, illus. (p. 2245)
—Tortoise & the Hare. Vignolo, Enrique, illus. (p. 2266)
—Town Musicians of Bremen. Denman, Michael L., illus. (p. 2270)
—Ugly Caterpillar. Budwine, Greg, illus. (p. 2313)
—Ugly Caterpillar(La Oruga Fea) Budwine, Greg, illus. (p. 2313)
—Ugly Princess. Martinez, Jorge, illus. (p. 2314)
—You Move You Lose. James, Kennon, illus. (p. 2527)
—You Move You Lose(El Que Se Mueva, Pierde) James, Kennon, illus. (p. 2527)
—Your Job Is Easy(Tu Trabajo Es Facil) James, Kennon, illus. (p. 2534)
Sommer, Carl & Aesop, Aesop. Divide to Conquer. Mercado, Jorge, illus. (p. 565)
—Divide to Conquer(Divide y Venceras) Mercado, Jorge, illus. (p. 565)
—Silent Scream. Bogdan, Enache, illus. (p. 2017)
—Silent Scream(El Grito Silencioso) Bogdan, Enache, illus. (p. 2017)
—Tiny Giant. Mercado, Jorge, illus. (p. 2249)
—Tiny Giant(La Gigante Pequeña) Mercado, Jorge, illus. (p. 2249)
Sommer, Cindy. Salvando Las Flores de Camelia Klein, Laurie Allen, illus. (p. 1926)
—Saving Kate's Flowers Klein, Laurie Allen, illus. (p. 1938)
Sommer, E. Van. Lionel Franklin's Victory: A Tale (Classic Reprint) (p. 1306)
Sommer, Heinrich Oskar. Vulgate Version of the Arthurian Romances, Vol. 7: Supplement: le Livre d'Artus, with Glossary (Classic Reprint) (p. 2369)
Sommer, K. J. Shattered New Start. (p. 2003)
Sommer, Nathan. Angelfish. (p. 86)
—Audi R8 Spyder. (p. 136)
—BMW M4. (p. 250)
—Cocker Spaniels. (p. 411)
—Eagles. (p. 613)
—Eels. (p. 627)
—Falcons. (p. 699)
—Golden Eagle vs. Great Horned Owl. (p. 857)
—Hawks. (p. 940)
—Jaguar F-Type. (p. 1155)
—Kites. (p. 1225)
—Komodo Dragon vs. Orangutan. (p. 1231)
—Mars. (p. 1409)
—Mercury. (p. 1448)
—Moon. (p. 1501)
—Neptune. (p. 1587)
—Newfoundlands. (p. 1600)
—Nissan GT-R. (p. 1611)
—Owls. (p. 1689)
—Pluto & the Dwarf Planets. (p. 1763)
—Saint Bernards. (p. 1923)
—Sea Otters. (p. 1968)
—Siberian Tiger vs. Brown Bear. (p. 2014)
—Squids. (p. 2094)
—Uranus. (p. 2339)
—Vultures. (p. 2369)
—West Highland White Terriers. (p. 2401)
—Wolf Pack vs. Moose. (p. 2484)
Sommer, Shelley. Hammerin' Hank Greenberg: Baseball Pioneer. (p. 913)
Sommers, Annie. College Athletics: Steroids & Supplement Abuse. (p. 415)
Sommers, Annie Leah. Frequently Asked Questions about Foster Care. (p. 784)
—Great National Soccer Teams. (p. 888)
Sommers, Annie Leah, jt. auth. see Sommers, Michael A.
Sommers, Audrey. Mickey the Monarch. Mattie, Dugan, ed. (p. 1459)
Sommers, Cecil. Temporary Heroes (Classic Reprint) (p. 2203)
Sommers, Elena. Mary of Philiphia & Her Seven Children. (p. 1415)
Sommers, Jackie Lea. Truest. (p. 2295)
Sommers, Michael. Basketball in the Big 12 Conference. (p. 171)
—Cocaine. (p. 410)
—Ehud Olmert: Prime Minister of Israel. (p. 629)
—Football in the Big 12. (p. 761)
—NFL: Steroids & Human Growth Hormone. (p. 1601)
—Silicon. (p. 2018)
—Tsunami: True Stories of Survival. (p. 2298)
—Vermont: Past & Present. (p. 2352)
—Wildlife Photographers: Life Through a Lens. (p. 2466)
Sommers, Michael A. Antarctic Melting: The Disappearing Antarctic Ice Cap. (p. 101)
Sommers, Michael A., jt. auth. see Cross, Nathaniel.
Sommers, Michael A., jt. auth. see Orr, Tamra.
Sommers, Michael A., jt. auth. see Thompson, Elissa.
Sommers, Michael A., jt. auth. see Winters, Adam.
Sommers, Michael A., jt. auth. see Zahensky, Kenneth.
Sommers, Nora. Houdini the Rabbit: In 'Cause Mommas Don't Lie. (p. 1007)
Sommersby, Jennifer. Sleight. (p. 2038)
Sommerset, Mark. Baa Baa Smart Sheep. Sommerset, Rowan, illus. (p. 147)
—I Love Lemonade. Sommerset, Rowan, illus. (p. 1070)
Sommerset, Rowan, illus. see Sommerset, Mark.
Sommerville, Edith. Some Experiences of an Irish R. M (Classic Reprint) (p. 2059)
Sommerville, Edith Oe. Some Experiences of an Irish R. M (Classic Reprint) (p. 2059)
Sommerville, Hannah, illus. see Allen, Emma.
Somna, Institut. Anidodos. (p. 87)
—Hypnododos. (p. 1056)
—Mon Dodo Turquoise. (p. 1491)
—Neige. (p. 1585)
—Sable. (p. 1919)
Somova, Masha, illus. see Halverson, Kristen.
Somoza, Ramon. niña Perdida. (p. 1609)
—Rescate en el Infierno. (p. 1868)
Somper, Justin. Allies & Assassins. (p. 56)
—Black Heart. (p. 238)
—Blood Captain. (p. 245)
—Dead Deep. (p. 517)
—Empire of Night. (p. 645)
—Immortal War. (p. 1101)
Somtow, S. P. Forgetting Places. (p. 768)
—Stone Buddha's Tears. (p. 2121)
—Wizard's Apprentice. (p. 2483)
Son, Dean And. Sick Robin Redbreast & His Kind Nurse Jenny Wren (Classic Reprint) (p. 2014)
Son, Eugene. Spider-Verse #4. Caramagna, Joe, illus. (p. 2081)
Son, Eugene, jt. auth. see Caramagna, Joe.
Son, John. Asia. (p. 126)
—If You Were a Kid on the Mayflower. Zanni, Roger, illus. (p. 1093)
—Relaxation & Yoga. (p. 1862)
Son, Thomas G. Newman and. American Bee Journal, Vol. 23: January 5, 1887 (Classic Reprint) (p. 70)
Son, William Warwick and. Boy's Own Paper, Vol. 7: March, 1885 (Classic Reprint) (p. 273)
Sonda, Addy Rivera, illus. see Penney, Shannon.
Sonder, Ben. Legacy of Norman Rockwell (p. 1261)
—Parrots: A Portrait of the Animal World. (p. 1701)
—Parrots. (p. 1701)
—Parrots - Pb: A Portrait of the Animal World. (p. 1701)
Sonderegger, Ueli. Magic Hat: The Adventures of the Little Hippie-Witch, Volume 1. (p. 1377)
—O Chapéu Mágico: As Aventuras Da Bruxinha Hippie, Volume 1. Lisboa, Leo Bryan, tr. (p. 1633)
Sondereker, Kierra, ed. Drawing Chibi: Learn How to Draw Kawaii People, Animals, & Other Utterly Cute Stuff. Art, Tessa Creative, illus. (p. 599)
Sonenshine, Randi. Nest That Wren Built. Hunter, Anne, illus. (p. 1588)
Sones, Sonya. Opposite of Innocent. (p. 1667)
—Saving Red. (p. 1938)
—Sonya Sones Collection: One of Those Hideous Books Where the Mother Dies; What My Mother Doesn't Know; What My Girlfriend Doesn't Know. (p. 2064)
—Stop Pretending: What Happened When My Big Sister Went Crazy. (p. 2122)
—To Be Perfectly Honest: A Novel Based on an Untrue Story. (p. 2252)
—What My Girlfriend Doesn't Know. (p. 2419)
Song, Amira. Horse Lovers Forever. (p. 1004)
Song, Christina, illus. see Palermo, Sharon Gibson.
Song, Danielle, illus. see Payne, Jody.
Song, Dosu. Comic Maple Story Math Thief 41. (p. 429)
Song, E., illus. see Song, Robyn.
Song, Jeong-Hwa, illus. see Lee, Mi-Ae.
Song, Kori, illus. see O'Callaghan, Joanne.
Song, Mihee, tr. My First Korean Dictionary. (p. 1544)
Song, Mika. Picnic with Oliver. Song, Mika, illus. (p. 1739)
—Tea with Oliver. Song, Mika, illus. (p. 2194)
Song, Mika, illus. see Bailey, Jenn.
Song, Mika, illus. see Derby, Sally.
Song, Mika, illus. see Gale, Heather.
Song, Mika, illus. see Rissi, Anica Mrose.
Song, Mika, illus. see Sliwerski, Jessica Reid.
Song, Miss Anna R. Tripawd Toffee: Adventures of a 3 - Legged Cat. Ledger, Craig, illus. (p. 2289)
Song, Sok. Everyday Origami: A Foldable Fashion Guide. Song, Sok, illus. (p. 672)
—Fashion Origami. Song, Sok, illus. (p. 712)
—Origami Accessories: A Foldable Fashion Guide. Song, Sok, illus. (p. 1670)
—Origami Chic: A Guide to Foldable Fashion. Song, Sok, illus. (p. 1671)
—Origami Outfits: A Foldable Fashion Guide. Song, Sok, illus. (p. 1671)
Song, Sonya Annita. I Want an Ostrich: Coloring Book. Fallahee, Kate, illus. (p. 1084)
—My Teacher Dad. Fallahee, Kate, illus. (p. 1562)
Song, United States Archive of Folk. Check-List of Recorded Songs in the English Language in the Archive of American Folk Song to July 1940: Alphabetical List with Geographical Index (Classic Reprint) (p. 363)
Songer, Steve, illus. see Parry, Jay A.
Song-i, Yoon. Saint Teresa of Avila, God's Troublemaker. (p. 1924)
Songs, Steve, illus. see Engel, Christiane.
Songs, Steve, jt. auth. see Dobbins, Jan.
Songs, Steve, jt. auth. see Engel, Christiane.

S

Soudée, Guirec. Hen Who Sailed Around the World: A True Story. (p. 954)
Souder, Edmund A. Leaves from the Battle-Field of Gettysburg: A Series of Letters from a Field Hospital; & National Poems (Classic Reprint) (p. 1259)
Souder, Patricia. Blindness & Vision Impairment. Albers, Lisa et al, eds. (p. 244)
Souders, J. A. Revelations: A Novel. (p. 1872)
Souders, Taryn. Coop Knows the Scoop. (p. 451)
—Dead Opossums: Are Fair Game. (p. 518)
—Dead Possums Are Fair Game. (p. 518)
—How to (Almost) Ruin Your Summer. (p. 1036)
—Whole-Y Cow! Fractions Are Fun. Mai-Wyss, Tatjana, illus. (p. 2453)
Soufie, Regani. Dodue la Petite Souris(la) (p. 575)
—Margot et le Bain D'Hector. (p. 1404)
—Sorci're(la) (p. 2065)
Souhami, Jessica. Gerald the Lion. (p. 821)
Souhila. Château Arc-En-Ciel. Editions La Liseuse, Junior, ed. (p. 362)
—Foret Magique. La Liseuse, Editions, ed. (p. 767)
—forèt Magique. Editions La Liseuse, Junior, ed. (p. 767)
—Noël de Sam. Editions La Liseuse Junior, ed. (p. 1617)
Soul, Books with. Baby Sharks Are Real: Story Notebook: Spark Creativity for Boys & Girls. a Fun Baby Shark Adventure. : Story Notebook Series: Write Your First Book. (p. 152)
—Journal for My Future: Possibilities: Anything Is Possible—If You Believe. (p. 1180)
—Unicorns Are Real: Story Notebook: for Kids Grades 3-6: a Fun Unicorn Adventure Activity Gift for Girls & Boys. (p. 2329)
Soule, Caroline A. Home Life: Or a Peep Across the Threshold (Classic Reprint) (p. 996)
Soule, Caroline Augusta. Pet of the Settlement: A Story of Prairie-Land (Classic Reprint) (p. 1726)
Soule, Charles. Black Squadron: Volume 1. Noto, Phil, illus. (p. 239)
—Black Squadron: Volume 2. Noto, Phil, illus. (p. 239)
—Black Squadron: Volume 3. Noto, Phil, illus. (p. 239)
—Curse Words Volume 5. (p. 489)
—Devil's Devil. (p. 536)
—Hole Damned World. (p. 987)
—Lockdown: Volume 1. Noto, Phil, illus. (p. 1339)
—Lockdown: Volume 2. Noto, Phil, illus. (p. 1339)
—Lockdown: Volume 3. Noto, Phil, illus. (p. 1339)
Soule, Jean Conder. Never Tease a Weasel. Booth, George, illus. (p. 1590)
Soule, Richard. Dictionary of English Synonymes & Synonymous or Parallel Expressions: Designed As a Practical Guide to Aptness & Variety of Phraseology (Classic Reprint) (p. 541)
—Dictionary of English Synonymes & Synonymous or Parallel Expressions. (p. 541)
—Dictionary of English Synonymes & Synonymous or Parallel Expressions, Designed As a Practical Guide to Aptness & Variety of Phraseology. (p. 541)
Souleiman, Serg, illus. see Dahl, Michael.
Soulie, Laurence. Where Is My Sock? (p. 2438)
Soulier, Daniel, illus. see Berocay, Roy.
Souliere, Lisa. Toasters Are Easy, School Not So Much. Rockwell, Joanna, illus. (p. 2254)
Soullie, Prosper. Fontaine et Ses Devanciers: Ou Histoire de l'Apologue Jusqu'a la Fontaine Inclusivement (Classic Reprint) (p. 759)
Soumagnac, Virginie, illus. see Monari, Manuela.
So-Un, Kim. Korean Children's Favorite Stories: Fables, Myths & Fairy Tales. Kyoung-Sim, Jeong, illus. (p. 1231)
—Three Korean Fairy Tales: Beloved Stories & Legends Retold for Children. Kyoung-Sim, Jeong, illus. (p. 2233)
Soundar, Chitra. Farmer Falgu Goes Kite Flying. Nair, Kanika, illus. (p. 710)
—Mangoes, Mischief, & Tales of Friendship: Stories from India. Krishnaswamy, Uma, illus. (p. 1397)
—Shubh Diwali! Chua, Charlene, illus. (p. 2013)
—You're Safe with Me. Mistry, Poonam, illus. (p. 2535)
—You're Snug with Me. Mistry, Poonam, illus. (p. 2535)
—You're Strong with Me. Mistry, Poonam, illus. (p. 2535)
Soundararajan, Chitra. Let's Look at India. (p. 1275)
—Let's Look at the United Kingdom. (p. 1275)
Soundararajan, Chitra, jt. auth. see Meinking, Mary.
Soundprints. Grizzly Bear Cub's First Fish: Wilderness Adventures. (p. 897)
—Panda Cub in the Bamboo Forest: Wilderness Adventures. (p. 1695)
—Polar Bear Cub & Mommy: Wilderness Adventures. (p. 1769)
—Prickly Porcupine: Wilderness Adventures. (p. 1791)
Soundprints, creator. Flamingo Grows Up. (p. 746)
—New Baby Giraffe. (p. 1591)
—Orang Utan's Playtime. (p. 1668)
—Panda's Busy Day. (p. 1696)
—Rhinoceros's Bathtime. (p. 1875)
—Tiger Cub See-and-Do. (p. 2241)
Soundprints Editorial Staff, jt. auth. see Galvin, Laura Gates.
Soundprints Staff. Elephant & Mommy. (p. 633)
Soundprints Staff, ed. see Studio Mouse Staff.
Soundprints Staff, jt. auth. see Odierno, Lisa.
Soundprints Staff & Galvin, Laura Gates. First Look at Aircraft. (p. 738)
Soup, Cuthbert. Whole Nother Story. Timmins, Jeffrey Stewart, illus. (p. 2453)
Sourcebooks. Love Is Love Is Love Is Love. (p. 1360)
—To the Best Mom Ever! (p. 2253)
—Twisted. (p. 2306)
Sourcebooks & Hart, Phyllis F. Find the Farter. Laughead, Mike, illus. (p. 728)
Sourcebooks & Juliano, Larissa. How to Build a Leprechaun Trap. (p. 1038)
Sourcebooks & Silverman, Laura. Girl Out of Water. (p. 836)
Sourcebooks, Inc Staff. Baby's First Mother Goose Treasury. (p. 154)
Sourcebooks Inc., Staff. To the Best Dad Ever! (p. 2253)
Sourcebooks Jabberwocky & McCurdie, Trevor. Dolphin's Wish: How You Can Help Make a Difference & Save Our Oceans. Battistel, Cinzia, illus. (p. 580)
Sourdais, Clèmentine. Inventive Animals: My Nature Sticker Activity Book. (p. 1130)
Sourdais, Cl'mentine. Mes Animaux du Monde. (p. 1451)
Soury, G'Rard. Dauphins(les) (p. 510)
Sousa, Agusti, illus. see Berchtig, Frauke.
Sousa, John Philip. Pipetown Sandy (Classic Reprint) (p. 1749)
—Transit of Venus (Classic Reprint) (p. 2278)
Sousa, Mauricio de. Monica Adventures #1: Who Can Afford the Price of Friendship Today? (p. 1493)
—Monica Adventures #2: We Fought Each Other As Kids... Now We're in Love?! Zazo, illus. (p. 1493)
—Monica Adventures #3: Who's Saying Nasty Things about Me... Online?! (p. 1493)
—Monica Adventures #4: Should I Say Yes... to Nick Nope? (p. 1493)
—We Fought Each Other As Kids... Now We're in Love?! Zazo, illus. (p. 2390)
—Who Can Afford the Price of Friendship Today? (p. 2446)
Sousa, Yolanda De. Mamá adivina. (p. 1392)
Soussana, Nathalie. Songs in the Shade of the Cashew & Coconut Trees: Lullabies & Nursery Rhymes from West Africa & the Caribbean. Gueyfier, Judith, illus. (p. 2063)
Soussana, Nathalie, et al. Songs from the Garden of Eden: Jewish Lullabies & Nursery Rhymes. Alemagna, Beatrice, illus. (p. 2063)
Soutar, Andrew. Honor of His House (Classic Reprint) (p. 999)
Soutar, D. G. Australian Golfer. (p. 138)
Souter, Elaine. Snowy's Adventures: Color Me Book. (p. 2050)
—Snowy's Adventures. (p. 2050)
Souter, Gerry, jt. auth. see Kiland, Taylor Baldwin.
Souter, Gerry & Souter, Janet. War in Afghanistan & Iraq: The Daily Life of the Men & Women Serving in Afghanistan & Iraq. Carlton Books Staff, ed. (p. 2376)
South, Coleman & Newsome, Joel. Jordan. (p. 1177)
South, Coleman, et al. Syria: Cultures of the World. (p. 2174)
South, Colon. Out West, or, from London to Salt Lake City & Back. (p. 1683)
—Out West, or from London to Salt Lake City & Back (Classic Reprint) (p. 1683)
South, Eudora Lindsay. Luther in Rome: Or, Corradina, the Last of the Hohenstaufen; a Religio-Historical Romance (Classic Reprint) (p. 1369)
—Wayside Notes & Fireside Thoughts (Classic Reprint) (p. 2388)
South, Mark. Moonbow. (p. 1502)
South, Robert. Smithy: A Drama (Classic Reprint) (p. 2042)
South, Tanya. Deflowered Garden (p. 526)
South, Victor. America in the 20th Century (1913-1999) (p. 70)
—America in the 20th Century (1913-1999) Rakove, Jack N., ed. (p. 70)
—Connecting the 21st Century to the Past (2000-The Present) (p. 441)
—Remember the Alamo: Americans Fight for Texas, 1820-1845. (p. 1864)
—Remember the Alamo: Americans Fight for Texas, 1820-1845. Rakove, Jack N., ed. (p. 1864)
—Remember the Alamo (1820-1845) (p. 1864)
—Shifting Role: America & the World, 1900-1912. (p. 2007)
—Shifting Role: America & the World, 1900-1912. Rakove, Jack N., ed. (p. 2007)
—Shifting Role (1900/1912) (p. 2007)
Southall, Ed & Pantaloni, Vincent. Geometry Snacks, Ages 8-18: Geometrical Figures Designed to Challenge, Confuse & Enlighten. (p. 818)
Southall, Ivan. Hills End. (p. 972)
Southall, James Powell Cocke. Principles & Methods of Geometrical Optics: Especially As Applied to the Theory of Optical Instruments (Classic Reprint) (p. 1800)
Southall, John. Treatise of Buggs: Shewing When & How They Were First Brought into England; How They Are Brought into & Infect Houses; Their Nature, Several Foods, Times & Manner of Spawning & Propagating in This Climate (Classic Reprint) (p. 2283)
Southall, Margo. Ready-To-Go Differentiated Literacy Centers: Grade 1: Engaging Centers Designed to Help Every Student Meet the Common Core. (p. 1848)
Southard, E. e. Latin School Register, Vol. 12: April 1893 (Classic Reprint) (p. 1250)
Southcote, Tansor. By River & by Sea: An Australian Story (Classic Reprint) (p. 305)
Southerland, Clay. Aggies, 1930, Vol. 4: Magazine of the Fourth District A. & M. School (Classic Reprint) (p. 35)
Southerland, Shane. Fiercely? Friendly? Jungle Tiger Tail. (p. 723)
Southerland, Taylor, illus. see Halpert, Ben.
Southern Lion Books, ed. see McCain, Charles.
Southern Living Editors. Southern Cookie Book. (p. 2069)
Southern Research Station (U.S.), ed. see Waldrop, Thomas A. & Goodrick, Scott L.
Southers, Sherri C., et al. Hudson & the Sea Monster. (p. 1047)
Southey, Caroline. Chapters on Churchyards (Classic Reprint) (p. 357)
Southey, Caroline Bowles. Birth-Day: A Poem - Scholar's Choice Edition. (p. 233)
—Birth-Day: A Poem, in Three Parts; to Which Are Added, Occasional Verses (Classic Reprint) (p. 233)
—Chapters on Churchyards, Vol. 1 of 2 (Classic Reprint) (p. 357)
—Early Called: The Stoic, & the Lansbys of Lansby Hall (Classic Reprint) (p. 614)
Southey, Robert. Goldilocks & the Three Bears. (p. 860)
—Journal of a Tour: In the Netherlands in the Autumn of 1815 (Classic Reprint) (p. 1180)
—Letters from England, Vol. 2 Of 3: By Don Manuel Alvarez Espriella (Classic Reprint) (p. 1279)
—Letters Written During a Journey in Spain & a Short Residence, Vol. 2 Of 2: In Portugal (Classic Reprint) (p. 1281)
—Letters Written During a Journey in Spain, & a Short Residence in Portugal, Vol. 1 of 2 (Classic Reprint) (p. 1281)
—Letters Written During a Journey in Spain, Vol. 1 Of 2: And a Short Residence in Portugal (Classic Reprint) (p. 1281)
—Letters Written During a Short Residence in Spain & Portugal. (p. 1281)
—Letters Written During a Short Residence in Spain & Portugal (Classic Reprint) (p. 1281)
Southey, Robert, jt. auth. see Bunyan, John.
Southey, Rosamond. Storm & Sunshine in South Africa (Classic Reprint) (p. 2126)
Southey, Tanya. Ollie & the Starchaser. (p. 1650)
Southgate, Anna & Li, Yishan. Drawing Manga Faces & Bodies. (p. 599)
—Drawing Manga Mecha, Weapons, & Wheels. (p. 599)
—Drawing Manga Men. (p. 599)
—Drawing Manga Women. (p. 599)
Southgate, Anna & Sparrow, Keith. Drawing Manga Boys. (p. 599)
—Drawing Manga Expressions & Poses. (p. 599)
—Drawing Manga Weapons, Vehicles, & Accessories. (p. 599)
Southgate, Vera. Three Little Pigs. (p. 2233)
Southgate, Vera & Ladybird Books Staff. Beauty & the Beast. (p. 185)
Southon, Josephine. Color Me: Trucks. Keylock, Andy, illus. (p. 420)
—I Heart Butterflies. (p. 1066)
Southorn, Michael, illus. see Newman, Elaine.
Southwell, David. Unsolved Political Mysteries. (p. 2335)
Southworth, Dorothy Eliza Nevitte. Hidden Hand (Classic Reprint) (p. 965)
Southworth, E. D. E. N. Bride's Fate: The Sequel to the Changed Brides (Classic Reprint) (p. 280)
—Changed Brides (Classic Reprint) (p. 356)
—Cruel As the Grave (Classic Reprint) (p. 479)
—Curse of Clifton: Or, the Widowed Bride (Classic Reprint) (p. 488)
—Fair Play: A Novel (Classic Reprint) (p. 695)
—Fatal Secret: And Other Stories (Classic Reprint) (p. 713)
—Haunted Homestead: A Novel (Classic Reprint) (p. 938)
—Hidden Hand (Classic Reprint) (p. 965)
—How He Won Her: A Sequel to Fair Play (Classic Reprint) (p. 1031)
—India: The Pearl of Pearl River (Classic Reprint) (p. 1116)
—Ishmael: Or, in the Depths (Classic Reprint) (p. 1138)
—Ishmael, or in the Depths (Classic Reprint) (p. 1138)
—Lilith: A Novel (Classic Reprint) (p. 1301)
—Love's Bitterest Cup: A Sequel to Her Mother's Secret (Classic Reprint) (p. 1362)
—Miriam, the Avenger: Or the Missing Bride (Classic Reprint) (p. 1475)
—Mother-In-Law: Or, the Isle of Rays a Tale (Classic Reprint) (p. 1510)
—Mother-In-Law, or Married in Haste (Classic Reprint) (p. 1510)
—Noble Lord: The Sequel to the Lost Heir of Linlithgow (Classic Reprint) (p. 1616)
—Popular Books: In Handsome Cloth Binding (Classic Reprint) (p. 1777)
—Popular Books (Classic Reprint) (p. 1777)
—Prince of Darkness: A Romance of the Blue Ridge (Classic Reprint) (p. 1794)
—Self-Raised or from the Depths (Classic Reprint) (p. 1987)
—Shannondale (Classic Reprint) (p. 1999)
—Sybil Brotherton: A Novel (Classic Reprint) (p. 2172)
—Test of Love: Being Third & Last Part of the Trail of the Serpent (Classic Reprint) (p. 2208)
—Tortured Heart: Being of the Trail of the Serpent (Classic Reprint) (p. 2266)
—Tried for Her Life: A Novel (Classic Reprint) (p. 2288)
—Two Sisters (Classic Reprint) (p. 2309)
—Unloved Wife: A Novel (Classic Reprint) (p. 2333)
—Victor's Triumph: The Sequel to a Beautiful Fiend (Classic Reprint) (p. 2356)
—Vivia, or the Secret of Power (Classic Reprint) (p. 2364)
—When Shadows Die: A Sequel to Love's Bitterest Cup (Classic Reprint) (p. 2433)
—Why Did He Wed Her? A Novel (Classic Reprint) (p. 2455)
—Widow's Son: Or Left Alone (Classic Reprint) (p. 2461)
—Wife's Victory: And Other Nouvellettes (Classic Reprint) (p. 2461)
Southworth, E. Dorothy Eliza Nevitt. Discarded Daughter: Or the Children of the Isle (Classic Reprint) (p. 553)
Southworth, Emma D. E. N. Fatal Secret: And Other Stories (Classic Reprint) (p. 714)
Southworth, Emma Dorothy Eliza Nevitte. Lilith. (p. 1301)
Southworth, Gertrude Van Duyn. Builders of Our Country, Book I (Yesterday's Classics) (p. 294)
—Builders of Our Country, Book II (Yesterday's Classics) (p. 294)
Southworth, Gordon, jt. auth. see Scott, Fred.
Southworth, May Elizabeth. Great Small Cat, & Others: Seven Tales (Classic Reprint) (p. 889)
Southworth, Roma. Kiddo Mementos: Children's Tales for the Young at Heart. (p. 1213)
Southworth, Rs. Lost Heir (Classic Reprint) (p. 1353)
Southworth, S. A. Hester Strong's Life Work: Or, the Mystery Solved (Classic Reprint) (p. 963)
—Inebriate's Hut: Or the First Fruits of the Maine Law (Classic Reprint) (p. 1118)
Souva, Jacob, illus. see Bright, Paul.
Souva, Jacob, illus. see Lasley, Matthew.
Souva, Jacob, illus. see Lee, Britney Winn.
Souva, Jacob, illus. see Prochovnic, Dawn Babb.
Souvestre, Emile. Attic Philosopher: Un Philosophe Sous les Toits (Classic Reprint) (p. 135)
—Attic Philosopher in Paris: Or, a Peep at the World from a Garre; Being the Journal of a Happy Man (Classic Reprint) (p. 135)
—Attic Philosopher in Paris, or a Peep at the World from a Garret: The Journal of a Happy Man (Classic Reprint) (p. 135)
—Attic Philosopher in Paris, or a Peep at the World from a Garret: Being the Journal of a Happy Man (Classic Reprint) (p. 135)
—Brittany & la Vendee: Tales & Sketches; with a Notice of the Life & Literary Character of Emile Souvestre (Classic Reprint) (p. 284)
—Leaves from a Family Journal (Classic Reprint) (p. 1259)
—Pleasures of Old Age: From the French of Emile Souvestre (Classic Reprint) (p. 1762)
—Popular Legends of Brittany: An English Version of Souvestre's Foyer Breton, from a German (Classic Reprint) (p. 1777)
Souza, Cláudia. Princess to the Rescue Ammirati, Christelle & Second Story Press Staff, illus. (p. 1799)
Souza, Jared, illus. see Everin, Gretchen.
Souza, Kathleen. June Moon. (p. 1189)
Souza, Pete. Dream Big Dreams: Photographs from Barack Obama's Inspiring & Historic Presidency (Young Readers) (p. 601)
Sovak, Jan. 3-D Coloring Book—Dangerous Animals. (p. 2546)
—3-D Coloring Book—Dinosaurs. (p. 2546)
—Build a Giant Poster Coloring Book—Under the Sea. (p. 292)
—Deadly Creatures Coloring Book. (p. 518)
—Deadly Insects & Arachnids. (p. 518)
—Dinosaurs! Coloring Book. (p. 551)
—Dinosaurs of the Cretaceous Era. (p. 551)
—Dinosaurs of the Triassic Era. (p. 551)
—Endangered Animals. (p. 649)
—Fairy World. (p. 698)
—Learning about Spiders: With 12 Stickers. (p. 1258)
—Let's Explore! Dinosaurs Sticker Coloring Book: With 30 Stickers! (p. 1271)
—Let's Explore! Sea Animals. (p. 1272)
—Lost in the Amazon: Hidden Pictures. (p. 1354)
—Manatees Coloring Book. (p. 1396)
—Mega Dinosaurs Coloring Book. (p. 1441)
Sovak, Jan & Coloring Books Staff. Build a Poster Coloring Book—Dinosaurs. (p. 293)
Sovak, Jan, et al. Build a 3-D Poster Coloring Book — Fairies. (p. 292)
Sovak, Jean-Marc Superville, illus. see Chibbaro, Julie.
Soveral, Helio Do. Neguinho e Juracy: Cenas Domesticas de Um Casal Incompreensivel (Classic Reprint) (p. 1585)
Sovereign, Danielle. Explore Iran: 12 Key Facts. (p. 679)
Sovern, Megan Jean. Meaning of Maggie. (p. 1434)
Sowa, Marzena. That Night, a Monster. (p. 2213)
Sowards, Ben. Asleep on the Hay: A Dust Bowl Christmas. Sowards, Ben, illus. (p. 126)
Sowards, Ben, illus. see Skye, Obert.
Sowards, Ben, illus. see Wright, Jason F.
Sowden, Emily. Trapped in Silver. (p. 2279)
Sowder, Joseph, jt. told to see Sowder, G. Wesley.
Sowell, Naomi. Mission of Freedom. (p. 1481)
Sower, Christopher. Nutzliche Anweisung Oder Beyhulfe VOR Die Teutschen Um Englisch Zu Lernen: Wie Es VOR Neu-Ankommende und Andere Im Land Gebohrne Land-Und Handwercks-Leute, Welche der Englischen Sprache Erfahrne und Geubte Schulmeister und Preceptores Ermangelen, (p. 1632)
Sowerby, Dale. Adventures of Baggy & Paxton: Trouble in Dawlish Warren. (p. 21)
—Adventures of Baggy & Paxton: The Search for Baggy & Psycho. (p. 21)
—Adventures of Baggy & Paxton: The Strange Egg of Eagleton Sands. (p. 21)
Sowerby, George Brettingham, jt. auth. see Kingsley, Charles.
Sowerby, Githa. Rutherford & Son: A Play in Three Acts (Classic Reprint) (p. 1918)
Sowerby, Githa & Sowerby, Millicent. Cinderella. (p. 391)
Sowerby, John G. At Home (Classic Reprint) (p. 129)
Sowerby, Malcolm, illus. see Wyeth, Tony.
Sowerby, Millicent, jt. illus. see Sowerby, Githa.
Sowles, Joann I. Martin. Darkness (the Brookehaven Vampires Series #2) The Brookehaven Vampires. (p. 508)
—Tainted Blood (the Brookehaven Vampires #3): The Brookehaven Vampires. Vol. 3 (p. 2176)
Soye, Alison, illus. see Clayton, Coo.
Soye, Alison, jt. auth. see Clayton, Coo.
Soyer, Alexis. Soyer's Culinary Campaign: Being Historical Reminiscences of the Late War (Classic Reprint) (p. 2070)
Sozapato, illus. see Williams, Ricardo.
Spaceheater, Dreamstime Com, illus. see Cubbinz, Zenaida.
Spach, Édouard, jt. auth. see Buffon, Georges-Louis Leclerc.
Spachner, Karen D., illus. see Jackson, Kimberly.
Spack, Gary. Cat Burglars. (p. 341)
Spack, Gary J. Snack Machine. (p. 2044)
Spackman, Jeff, illus. see Hubbell, Patricia.
Spadaccini, Cheryl, illus. see Seymour, Marysue.
Spades, Evelyn. Adventures of Becki the Chicken: Series 1. (p. 21)
Spady, Angela & Thomas Nelson Publishing Staff. Channing O'Banning & the Rainforest Rescue (p. 356)
—Channing o'Banning & the Turquoise Trail (p. 356)
Spady, Angie. Catie Conrad: Faith, Friendship & Fashion Disasters. Everidge, Channing, illus. (p. 345)
Spafford, Suzy. Witzy's Fall Collection. (p. 2482)
Spafford, Suzy, illus. see Petersen-Fleming, Judy & Spafford, Judy.
Spafford-Fitz, Karen. Push Back. (p. 1817)
—Saving Grad. (p. 1938)
—Taking the Lead. (p. 2178)
Spagnol, Hannah, illus. see Spagnol, Noreen.
Spagnol, Noreen. Life with Daddy... & His Boyfriend. Spagnol, Hannah & Spagnol, Tayleigh, illus. (p. 1296)
—Life with Mommy... & Her Girlfriend. (p. 1296)
Spagnol, Tayleigh, illus. see Spagnol, Noreen.
Spagnoli, Cathy. Nine-In-One:Grr! Grr! Horn, Nancy, illus. (p. 1609)
Spagnoli, John. Sunflower Story. (p. 2152)
Spaight, Anne J. Big Rigs on the Go. (p. 222)

S

Spearman, Frank H. Close of the Day (Classic Reprint) (p. 407)
—Daughter of a Magnate (Classic Reprint) (p. 509)
—Doctor Bryson: A Novel (Classic Reprint) (p. 573)
—Held for Orders: Stories of Railroad Life (Classic Reprint) (p. 949)
—Laramie: Holds the Range (Classic Reprint) (p. 1244)
—Merrilie Dawes (Classic Reprint) (p. 1449)
—Mountain Divide (Classic Reprint) (p. 1513)
—Nan of Music Mountain (Classic Reprint) (p. 1573)
—Robert Kimberly (Classic Reprint) (p. 1890)
—Whispering Smith (Classic Reprint) (p. 2442)
Spearman, Frank Hamilton. Nerve of Foley, & Other Railroad Stories (Classic Reprint) (p. 1588)
Spearman, Terry, illus. see Spearman, David.
Spears, Anthony, et al. Chef Junior: A Real Food Guide to Learning How to Cook—By Kids for Kids. (p. 364)
Spears, Ashley E., illus. see Forester, MaMa Eagle.
Spears, Ashley E., illus. see Shams, K.
Spears, Ashley E., illus. see Stover, Anne Long.
Spears, Jr. Derek's Dilemm. (p. 530)
Spears Kallus, Heather. Thank You, Hurricane Harvey. (p. 2211)
Spears, Raymond S. Diamond Tolls (Classic Reprint) (p. 538)
Spears, Rick, illus. see Halls, Kelly Milner.
Spears, Rick. C., illus. see Halls, Kelly Milner.
Specht, Jessica, illus. see Michaels, Joanna.
Speck, F. G. Myths & Folk-Lore of the Timiskaming Algonquin & Timagami Ojibwa (Classic Reprint) (p. 1571)
Speck, John Rhodes. How I Got My Education: With a Few Remarks on I'm Slightly in Love As I Pass on (Classic Reprint) (p. 1032)
—How I Got My Education. (p. 1032)
Speck, Katie & De Tagyos, Paul Rátz. Maybelle & the Haunted Cupcake. (p. 1430)
Specksgoor, Meg. I Am Water (p. 1060)
Speckter, Otto. One Hundred Picture Fables. (p. 1660)
Specter, Baron. All in a Night's Work Kneupper, Setch, illus. (p. 52)
—Chasing Whales Aboard the Charles W. Morgan Evans, Dustin, illus. (p. 362)
—Dodging Danger on the Dartmouth Evans, Dustin, illus. (p. 575)
—Drama at Dungeon Rock: #6 Evans, Dustin, illus. (p. 596)
—Ghostly Whispers: Book 10. Boyden, Robin, illus. (p. 829)
—Ghosts of Pheasant Hill: Book 7. Boyden, Robin, illus. (p. 829)
—Graveyard Diaries Set 2 (Set) Boyden, Robin, illus. (p. 882)
—Hobgoblins Just Wanna Have Fun: Book 8. Boyden, Robin, illus. (p. 985)
—How Not to Be Killed by a Zombie Kneupper, Setch, illus. (p. 1034)
—Lighthouse of Terror Evans, Dustin, illus. (p. 1299)
—Spooky Short Sands Shipwreck: #4 Evans, Dustin, illus. (p. 2087)
—Star Island Spirits: #5 Evans, Dustin, illus. (p. 2102)
—To Werewolf or Not to Werewolf Kneupper, Setch, illus. (p. 2254)
—Vampires Are Not Your Friends Kneupper, Setch, illus. (p. 2346)
—Zombies Revisited: Book 9. Boyden, Robin, illus. (p. 2542)
Spector, Annette M., jt. auth. see Greenberg, David E.
Spector, Baron. Approaching the Undead Kneupper, Setch, illus. (p. 107)
—Tracking Your Nightmare Kneupper, Setch, illus. (p. 2272)
Spector, Joel, illus. see Gillooly, Eileen, ed.
Spector, Joel, illus. see Rovere, Amy.
Spector, Todd. How to Pee: Potty Training for Girls. Chung, Arree, illus. (p. 1043)
—How to Pee: Potty Training for Boys: Potty Training for Boys. Chung, Arree, illus. (p. 1043)
Spector-Steinmetz, Wendy. Rock Fairy. (p. 1894)
Spee, Gitte, illus. see Nilsson, Ulf.
Speechley, Greta. Arts & Crafts for Myths & Tales. (p. 124)
—Backyard Crafts. (p. 156)
—Bead Crafts. (p. 178)
—Birthday Crafts. (p. 233)
—Valentine Crafts. (p. 2344)
—World Crafts. (p. 2501)
Speechley, Michael. All New Must Have Orange 430. (p. 53)
—Gift. (p. 831)
Speechmark. Early Objects: Colorcards. (p. 615)
—Familiar Verbs: In Context. (p. 701)
—How Are They Feeling? (p. 1026)
—How's Teddy? (p. 1047)
—Prepositions: Colorcards. (p. 1787)
—Sequences: 6 & 8-Step for Children. (p. 1990)
—Sport & Leisure. (p. 2087)
—Who, What, When, Where Colorcards. (p. 2452)
Speechmark Publishing Limited Staff, jt. auth. see Franklin, Ian.
Speechmark Staff, jt. auth. see Franklin, Ian.
Speed, J. a. Messenger, Vol. 4: May, 1908 (Classic Reprint) (p. 1452)
—Messenger, Vol. 4: June, 1908 (Classic Reprint) (p. 1452)
—Messenger, Vol. 4: March, 1908 (Classic Reprint) (p. 1452)
—Messenger, Vol. 4: Published Monthly During the School Year by the Students of Durham High School, N. C. ; April 1908 (Classic Reprint) (p. 1452)
Speed, Nell. Molly Brown's Orchard Home. (p. 1489)
—Molly Brown's Orchard Home (Classic Reprint) (p. 1489)
—Molly Brown's Sophomore Days (Classic Reprint) (p. 1489)
Speed Shaskan, Trisha. Itty Bitty Witch. Yan, Xindi, illus. (p. 1149)
Speed Shaskan, Trisha Sue. De Veras, ¡Cenicienta Es Bien Pesada! El Cuento de Cenicienta Contado Por la Madrastra Malvada. Guerlais, Gerald Claude, illus. (p. 517)
—Honestamente, ¡Caperucita Roja Era Muy Vanidosa! El Cuento de Caperucita Roja Contado Por el Lobo. Guerlais, Gerald Claude, illus. (p. 998)
Speedy, Cornelia. My Wanderings in the Soudan, Vol. 1 of 2 (Classic Reprint) (p. 1564)
Speedy, Cornelia Mary. My Wanderings in the Soudan, Vol. 2 of 2 (Classic Reprint) (p. 1564)
Speedy Kids. 1, 2,3 Count! Counting Puzzles for Kids - Activity Book Grade 2. (p. 2545)
—1,2,3... Can You Color Me? Coloring Book Numbers. (p. 2559)
—50 Word Wheel Puzzles to Solve: Activity Book 5th Grade. (p. 2556)
—Activity Book 1st Grade. Picture Reading Storytelling. Logic & Creativity Boosters: Fairytale Coloring & Fantasy Dot to Dots. Kids Activity Books Ages 4-8. (p. 13)
—Activity Book for Kids. 1,2,3,4... Do You Want More? Easy to Difficult Color by Number on the Go. 100+ Pages of Multi-Themed Coloring for Stress Relief. (p. 13)
—Activity Book for Kids 4-5. Letters, Numbers, Fruits & Shapes. Building the Foundation of Early Learning One Concept at a Time. Includes Coloring & Connect the Dots Exercises. (p. 13)
—Activity Book Grade 2. My Little Girl Knows Fairytales & More. Full Page Fantasy Coloring & Other Puzzles to Enjoy. Coloring Activity Book Age 7-9. (p. 13)
—Activity Book - Hidden Pictures Edition. (p. 13)
—Activity Books for Ages 6-10. These Little Piggies Met the Fairies. Read & Do Exercises for Boys & Girls. Coloring, Storytelling, Connecting Dots & Color by Number. (p. 13)
—Activity Books for Kids Ages 4-8. Coloring, How to Draw & Dot to Dot Exercises of Healthy Eats. Hours of Satisfying Mental Meals for Kids to Digest Solo or with Friends. (p. 13)
—Add Fraction Activity Book for Kids: Math Workbook for Kids. (p. 14)
—Advanced Grid by Grid Exercises for Young Artists: Drawing Book for Kids. (p. 18)
—Affenwahnsinn Malbuch (German Edition) (p. 31)
—Animal Coloring for the Advanced Colorists - Full Page Coloring Book. (p. 88)
—Art du Mandala Facile: Designs Pour Coloristes (French Edition) (p. 120)
—Astronaut Does a Moon Walk Dance! Coloring & Activity Book for Kids. (p. 128)
—Bastelbuch Kinder: Malbuch Für Kinder (German Edition) (p. 171)
—Bastelbuch Pferde: Malbuch Für Kinder (German Edition) (p. 171)
—Bastelbuch Schmuck: Malbuch Für Kinder (German Edition) (p. 171)
—Bastelbuch Vögel: Malbuch Für Kinder (German Edition) (p. 171)
—Berufstätige Malbuch (German Edition) (p. 204)
—Big Drawing Book of Animals: Drawing Book for Children. (p. 219)
—Biologie-Malbuch Ausgabe Menschliche Anatomie (German Edition) (p. 229)
—Blumengarten-Malbuch (German Edition) (p. 250)
—Blumenornamente: Malbuch (German Edition) (p. 250)
—Bonfire Night: Everything Camping Coloring Book for Children. (p. 256)
—Book of Farm Animals. Easy & Educational Activity Book of Farm Animals & More. More Than 100 Exercises of Coloring, Color by Number & Drawing. (p. 258)
—Boost Your Spelling Skills with Word Scrambles! Word Activity Book for Kids. (p. 262)
—Botanik-Malbuch Ausgabe Pflanzen und Blumen (German Edition) (p. 264)
—Busse, Lastwagen und Traktoren Malbuch (German Edition) (p. 301)
—Busy Book of Pumpkins & Halloween - Halloween Activity Book for Kids. (p. 302)
—C Comme Colorier ! Livre de Coloriage Pour Enfants (French Edition) (p. 306)
—Cahier de Coloriage Art Therapie (French Edition) (p. 308)
—Can You Say Boo! Halloween Coloring Book Children's Halloween Books. (p. 318)
—Can You See Where They Are? Hidden Pictures Book: Four Seasons Edition. (p. 319)
—Can You See Where They're at? Hidden Pictures Book: Farm Animals Edition. (p. 319)
—Catch That Easter Bunny! Easter Coloring Book Children's Easter Books. (p. 344)
—Célébrez la Vie ! Journal de Gratitude (French Edition) (p. 350)
—Challenging Dot to Dot Puzzles for Kids. (p. 354)
—Challenging Sudoku Puzzles for Elementary Students. (p. 354)
—Chemie-Malbuch (German Edition) (p. 365)
—Children Activity Books. How to Draw the Symbols of Celebrations Around the World. Bonus Pages Include Coloring & Color by Number Xmas Edition. Merry Activity Book for Kids of All Ages. (p. 371)
—Children's Books Age 5-6. Cats & Dogs Are Best of Friends. Rewarding Coloring & Dot to Dot Children's Books Age 5-6. Lessons on Numbers & Colors Included! (p. 373)
—Chinese New Year Festival - Chinese New Year Coloring Book Children's Chinese New Year Books. (p. 379)
—Christi Geburt Malbuch Bibelausgabe (German Edition) (p. 382)
—Christmas Cheer - Christmas Coloring Books for Kids Children's Christmas Books. (p. 384)
—Christmas Cut Out for Little Boys & Girls - Activity Book Age 8. (p. 385)
—Christmas Trees Are the Best! Christmas Coloring Books Children's Christmas Books. (p. 387)
—Christmas-Inspired Hidden Pictures Activity Book for Kids. (p. 386)
—Churches Can Be Fun Too! Mazes, Matching & Dot to Dot Activity Book for Kids. (p. 390)
—Collection of the Best Children's Games: A Vocabulary Activity Book for Kids. (p. 415)
—Color by Math! Activity Coloring Book for Kids. (p. 419)
—Color by Number: Under the Waves Edition Activity Book for 2nd Grade. (p. 419)
—Color by Number for Kids. Wild Animals Activity Book for Older Kids with Land & Sea Creatures to Identify. Challenging Mental Boosters for Better Focus at School. (p. 419)
—Color by Number! Super Fun Edition for Kids. (p. 419)
—Color by Sum: Times & New Years Edition - Activity Book Age 10. (p. 420)
—Color It in! Basic Skills Drills - Activity Book for Kids Ages 4-5. (p. 420)
—Color Me Right! a-Follow-The-Instructions Coloring Book for Girls. (p. 420)
—Coloriage Amusant de Robots et de Chiens Pour Enfant (Edition Grand Format) 100 (French Edition) (p. 422)
—Coloriage Amusant de Robots et de Dinosaures (Super Grand Livre) 100 (French Edition) (p. 422)
—Coloriage de Robots -Livres d'Éveil Pour Enfants (French Edition) (p. 422)
—Colorie-Moi ! Livre de Coloriage Pour Enfants (French Edition) (p. 422)
—Coloring & Activity for Kids. a Special Speedy Book of All Things That Go. 100+ Pages of Coloring & Activity Book for Older Kids with Big How to Draw Pictures. (p. 422)
—Coloring Book Fruits. Prek Fruit Coloring & Activity Book with Flowers & Vegetables. Tummy-Licious Natural Produce for Coloring, Drawing & Identification. (p. 424)
—Coloring Book of Animals. on-The-Go Coloring Book of Happy Animals. Colors & Animals Do It Anywhere Knowledge Booster. (p. 424)
—Colorions des Cupcakes - Livre de Coloriage Pour Enfants (French Edition) (p. 425)
—Comme Animaux ! Grand Livre de Coloriage d'Animaux (French Edition) (p. 430)
—Connect the Dots Books. a Sensational Learning Tool for Struggling Math Learners. Random Themed Numberific Activity Book for Improved Number Sense. (p. 441)
—Connect the Dots for Kids. Friendly Neighbors: Getting to Know Your Community Helpers with Labeled Coloring Exercises for Better Information Retention. (p. 441)
—Copy That Grid! Guided Drawing Book for All Ages. (p. 452)
—Count off! Learning More about Numbers: Activity Book Kindergarten. (p. 458)
—Countdown to Christmas! 60 Days to the Holiday Coloring Book 8 Year Old. (p. 459)
—Crazy Maze for Days! Mazes Book for 8 Year Old. (p. 469)
—Cross the Odd Ones! Odd One Out Activity Book for Children. (p. 478)
—Dauphins: Livre de Coloriage (French Edition) (p. 510)
—Delightful Menorah Lights - Hanukkah Coloring Books for Kids Children's Jewish Holiday Books. (p. 527)
—Delights of Hanukkah - Hanukkah Coloring Books for Kids Children's Jewish Holiday Books. (p. 527)
—Delphine: Malbuch 2 (German Edition) (p. 527)
—Dents de la Mer ! Livre de Coloriage de Requins (French Edition) (p. 529)
—Design-Malbuch Mandala (German Edition) (p. 532)
—Dessin Rapide: Livre de Coloriage de Cowboys (French Edition) (p. 533)
—Die Augen Haben's in Sich! Malbuch Mit Großäugigen Tieren (German Edition) (p. 543)
—Dinosaurier-Malbuch 2 (German Edition) (p. 550)
—Dot to Dot Books for Kids Ages 4-8. Connect the Dots Exercises of All the Animals & Insects of the World. Dot Activity Book for Boys & Girls. (p. 588)
—Dots, Dots & More Dots! Dot to Dot Puzzle Book. (p. 588)
—Dotto! Fun Animals Dot to Dot Puzzles for Kids. (p. 588)
—Down Flew a Black Bird to Peck on Me! Bird-Inspired Coloring & Activity Book for Kids. (p. 590)
—Drachen: Malbuch 2 (German Edition) (p. 592)
—Dragons: Livre de Coloriage (French Edition) (p. 595)
—Dragons Go a-Dancing! Chinese New Year Activity Books for Kids Age 5-6. (p. 595)
—Drapeaux de Toutes les Nations: Super Grand Livre de Coloriage Pour Enfants (French Edition) (p. 597)
—Drapeaux du Monde: Coloriage Amusant (French Edition) (p. 597)
—Drapeaux du Monde Entier: Coloriage Amusant de Super Drapeaux (French Edition) (p. 597)
—Draw Me Some Clothes on! Weather-Themed Drawing Book for Kids. (p. 598)
—Drawing Book Exercises for Kids Aged 6-8. (p. 599)
—Drawing Exercises for Your Future Picasso: Drawing Book for Boys. (p. 599)
—Drawing Inspirations from Every Season: Drawing Book for Beginners. (p. 599)
—Drawing Pictures Grid by Grid: Drawing Book for Beginners. (p. 599)
—Dream Catcher Coloring Book for Extreme Fun. (p. 601)
—Dschungeltiere Malbuch (German Edition) (p. 607)
—Dschungel-Tiere-Malbuch Für Kinder (German Edition) (p. 607)
—Easy Mazes for Hard-To-Please Players: Activity Book Elementary. (p. 621)
—Easy-Peasy! Mazes Book for Children Ages 3-5. (p. 621)
—Educational Activity Book. the Everything Kids Do Activity Book of Colors, Dots & Numbers for Children Ages 6-8. Consistent Practice for Comfortable School Learning. (p. 626)
—Edutaining Mazes for 5 - 7 Year Olds. (p. 626)
—Einhorn-Malbuch (German Edition) (p. 629)
—Elephants! Coloring Designs for Kids. (p. 634)
—En Garde! Chivalrous Duels Coloring Book. (p. 646)
—Enchanted Garden: Relaxing Coloring Book for Adults. (p. 647)
—Entertaining Drawing Exercises for Princesses: Drawing Book for Girls. (p. 656)
—Erntedankfest-Malbuch (German Edition) (p. 660)
—Eulen-Malbuch Für Kinder (German Edition) (p. 667)
—Eureka! I Found It - Seek & Find Activity Book for Kids. (p. 667)
—Extreme Dot to Dot Activity Book for Kids. (p. 686)
—F Steht Für Farbe! Malbuch Für Kinder (German Edition) (p. 690)
—Fantastique: Livre de Coloriage (French Edition) (p. 707)
—Fantasy Color Book. Enchanted Fairies, Unicorns & Mermaids to Color. Includes Color by Number Templates. Activity Book for Princesses & Older Kids. (p. 708)
—Farm Activity Book for Kids. Little Activity Book of Coloring & Connect the Dots. Basic Skills for Early Learning Foundation, Identifying Farm Animals & Numbers for Kindergarten to Grade 1. (p. 709)
—Farm Animals: Coloring & Activity Book. (p. 709)
—Fashion Drawing Games: Drawing Book for Girls. (p. 712)
—Fées: Livre de Coloriage (French Edition) (p. 718)
—Ferien in Den USA Malbuch (German Edition) (p. 720)
—Feuerwehrmann Malbuch (German Edition) (p. 721)
—Feuerwehrmänner: Malbuch (German Edition) (p. 721)
—Find It! Hidden Picture Activity Book. (p. 728)
—Finde Den Unterschied, Labyrinthe und Punkt-Zu-Punkt-Aktivitätenbuch (German Edition) (p. 728)
—Firecrackers Are So Loud! Chinese New Year Coloring Book Children's Chinese New Year Books. (p. 733)
—Flaggen Aller Länder: Jumbo-Malbuch Für Kinder (German Edition) (p. 746)
—Flaggen der Welt: Ausmalspaß (German Edition) (p. 746)
—Flaggen Rund Um Die Welt: Toller Spaß Mit Ausmalen Von Flaggen (German Edition) (p. 746)
—Flaggen-Malbuch: Farben Rund Um Die Welt (German Edition) (p. 746)
—Fleurs: Livre de Coloriage (French Edition) (p. 748)
—Flower Power: The 80's Coloring Book for Kids. (p. 752)
—Fly, Flying, Flew: Coloring Book Birds Edition. (p. 754)
—Food Junkie's Guide: A Grid by Grid Drawing Book for Children. (p. 760)
—Freitagabend: Halloween-Malbuch (German Edition) (p. 783)
—Fruit & Flower Baskets for Free! a Coloring & Activity Book for Kids. (p. 796)
—Geschäftige Roboter Malbuch (German Edition) (p. 823)
—Gobble Gobble! Thanksgiving Coloring Books Children's Thanksgiving Books. (p. 849)
—Gotcha! Jaws Shark Coloring Book for Kids. (p. 872)
—Grand Livre de Coloriage de Jouets Pour Garçons (French Edition) (p. 876)
—Grandma's 90th Birthday: A Coloring Book for Boys & Girls. (p. 878)
—Grid Copy Puzzles: Christmas Edition: Drawing Book for Kids. (p. 896)
—Grid Copy Puzzles: Thanksgiving Edition: Drawing Book for Kids. (p. 896)
—Grid Copy Puzzles: Valentine's Day Edition: Drawing Book for Kids. (p. 896)
—Guck-Guck und Lustige Tiere Malbuch (German Edition) (p. 902)
—Haiwoche Malbuch (German Edition) (p. 910)
—Halloween Coloring Book. Monsters from the Other Realm. Scary Halloween Color & Connect the Dots for Kids & Adults. No Fuss Skills-Based Exercise Book for Sharing. (p. 912)
—Hanukkah Matata: Religious Activity Book for 7 Year Old Girl. (p. 919)
—Hanukkah with the Family: A Coloring Book for Kids & Adults. (p. 919)
—Happy Birthday Jesus! Christmas Coloring Book for 4 Year Old. (p. 920)
—Happy Chinese New Year - Chinese New Year Coloring Book Children's Chinese New Year Books. (p. 921)
—Happy Easter to All: Easter Coloring Books for Kids Children's Easter Books. (p. 921)
—Happy Hanukkah - Hanukkah Coloring Books for Kids Children's Jewish Holiday Books. (p. 922)
—Happy Happy Halloween - Halloween Coloring Book Children's Halloween Books. (p. 922)
—Happy New Year! Coloring Book for Kids. (p. 923)
—Happy Thanksgiving! Thanksgiving Coloring Books Children's Thanksgiving Books. (p. 924)
—Haunted House - Halloween Coloring Book for Kids Children's Halloween Books. (p. 938)
—He Is Risen! Easter Coloring Book Children's Easter Books. (p. 941)
—Herr Polizist Malbuch (German Edition) (p. 963)
—Hey Rick, Draw Me Quick! a Complete-The-Image Drawing Book for Kids. (p. 964)
—Hey There Turkey! Thanksgiving Coloring Books Children's Thanksgiving Books. (p. 964)
—Hidden Pictures Activity Book for 9 Year Old Boys. (p. 966)
—Homme de L'Espace: Livre de Coloriage de l'Espace (French Edition) (p. 998)
—How Many Can You Find? Counting Puzzles for Kids - Activity Book Grade 2. (p. 1033)
—How to Draw for Kids. More Than 100 Pages of How to Draw Animals with Step-By-Step Instructions. Creative Exercises for Little Hands with Big Imaginations (Drawing Books Age 8-12) (p. 1040)
—How to Survive a Zombie Invasion: Mazes for Kids. (p. 1044)
—Huge Vocab Is Oh-So-Fab! Word Scrabble Activity Book 8 Year Old. (p. 1048)
—Hunt for Easter Eggs - Easter Coloring Books for Kids Children's Easter Books. (p. 1052)
—I Hear Reindeers on the Rooftop! Coloring Book Christmas. (p. 1066)
—I Love Dots! Simple Dot to Dot Book for Kids. (p. 1069)
—Ich Liebe Babys: Kinder-Malbuch (German Edition) (p. 1088)
—Ich Liebe Es Cupcakes Zu Backen Malbuch (German Edition) (p. 1088)
—Ich Liebe Sport Malbuch (German Edition) (p. 1088)
—Ich Liebe Wrestling-Masken Malbuch (German Edition) (p. 1088)
—Ich Sehe Dich: Malbuch Mit Tieren (German Edition) (p. 1088)
—Im Inneren Deines Gehirns Malbuch (German Edition) (p. 1098)
—In der Küche Malbuch Für Mädchen (Alter 10) (German Edition) (p. 1104)
—In Meiner Küche Malbuch (German Edition) (p. 1106)
—In the Wild! Coloring Book of the Animal Kingdom. (p. 1111)
—Indianerstämme Totempfähle Malbuch (German Edition) (p. 1117)
—Interesting Coloring & Activity Books for Little Girls to Have. (p. 1126)
—Interesting Puzzles for Young Kids to Do: Activity Book for Children. (p. 1126)
—Its an Amazing World! Dot to Dot for Kids. (p. 1144)
—It's in the Petal! Daisy Game for Young Word Geniuses - Activity Book Volume 1. (p. 1145)
—It's My Birthday! a Party Themed Activity Book for Kids. (p. 1146)

—Only Girls Know the Way: Mazes & Coloring Activity Books for Girls Bundle (p. 1664)
—Pink Educational Bundle: Mazes & More Bundled Activity Book for Girls 4 Years Old & Up (p. 1746)
—See It to Solve It: Easy to Intermediate Coloring Activity Books Bundle Senses Special (p. 1982)
—See Me Roll & Go: Things That Go Coloring Activity Books for Kids Bundle (p. 1982)
—Spooky Geeky Halloween: Themed Bundle Coloring Books Kids (p. 2087)
—Thank Book: Journal Inspiration. (p. 2211)
—Thought Keeper: Journal Your Way. (p. 2230)
—What a Combo! Mazes & Hidden Object Books for Kids Age 8-10 Bundle (p. 2404)
—Writer's Notebook: Journal 400 Pages. (p. 2512)
—XieXie, China! Chinese New Year Festival Coloring Kids Activity Books Ages 5-8 Bundle (p. 2516)
—You Could Use a Break: Mazes & Word Games for Kids: Grade 2 Bundle (p. 2527)
—You Got This, Princess! Fashion Activity Books for Girls Bundle (p. 2527)
—You Should Focus Better: Bundled Hidden Object & Mazes Activity Books for Kids Age 10 (p. 2528)
Speedy Publishing LLC. 101 Hidden Pictures to Find Activities for Adults. (p. 2558)
—101 Very Challenging Connect the Dots for Adults. (p. 2558)
—101 Very Challenging Dot to Dot for Kids. (p. 2558)
—ABC Coloring Book. (p. 3)
—Adult Activity Book: Dot to Dots. (p. 17)
—Advanced Coloring Book. (p. 17)
—Adventures in Coloring: A Mandalas Coloring Book. (p. 20)
—Adventures in Extreme Coloring: A Mischief Coloring Book. (p. 20)
—Airplane Coloring Book. (p. 37)
—Alex's Big Adventure. (p. 43)
—Amazing Doodles to Color, Coloring Book. (p. 64)
—American Girl Coloring Book. (p. 71)
—Anatomy: Coloring Book for Kids- Awesome Fun. (p. 79)
—Art: Coloring Book for Kids- Awesome Fun. (p. 120)
—Art Coloring Book. (p. 120)
—Autobuses y Camiones Libro de niños para Colorear (Spanish Edition) (p. 140)
—Baby-Malbücher (German Edition) (p. 151)
—Bajo el Mar Libro de niños para Colorear (Spanish Edition) (p. 159)
—Bambole: Libro Da Colorare (Italian Edition) (p. 163)
—Barking up the Wrong Tree: An Adult Activity Book of Hidden Pictures. (p. 166)
—Bart's Bad Day. (p. 168)
—Bastelbuch Drachen (German Edition) (p. 171)
—Bastelbuch Eulen (German Edition) (p. 171)
—Bastelbuch Fur Kinder (German Edition) (p. 171)
—Bastelbuch Geburtstag: Malbuch Für Kinder (German Edition) (p. 171)
—Bastelbuch Hochzeitseinladungen (German Edition) (p. 171)
—Bastelbuch Kleinkinder: Malbuch Für Kinder (German Edition) (p. 171)
—Bastelbuch Mädchen (German Edition) (p. 171)
—Bastelbuch Ostern: Malbuch Für Kinder (German Edition) (p. 171)
—Bastelbuch Piraten: Malbuch Für Kinder (German Edition) (p. 171)
—Bastelbuch Roboter: Malbuch Für Kinder (German Edition) (p. 171)
—Bastelbuch Vorschule: Malbuch Für Kinder (German Edition) (p. 171)
—Be Very Afraid! Masks Coloring Book. (p. 178)
—Beautiful Princess Coloring Book. (p. 184)
—Bekleidungs Malbuch (German Edition) (p. 195)
—Big Squares & Little Triangles! Shapes Books for Preschoolers. (p. 223)
—Birds: Coloring Book for Kids- Awesome Fun. (p. 231)
—Birds: Coloring Book for Children- Awesome Fun. (p. 231)
—Blumen: Malbuch 2 (German Edition) (p. 250)
—Blumen: Malbuch Für Kinder (German Edition) (p. 250)
—Blumenmädchen: Malbuch Für Kinder (German Edition) (p. 250)
—Blumen-Ornamente: Malbuch Für Kinder (German Edition) (p. 250)
—Bombero y Los Bomberos: Libro de niños para Colorear (Spanish Edition) (p. 254)
—Botany Coloring Book (Plants & Flowers Edition) (p. 264)
—Brave Knights & Scary Dragons Coloring Book. (p. 276)
—Buses, Trucks & Tractors Coloring Book. (p. 301)
—Bus- und Lkw-Malbuch Für Kinder (German Edition) (p. 300)
—Busy Robots Coloring Book. (p. 302)
—Busy Working People Coloring Book. (p. 302)
—Caballeros y Dragones Libro de niños para Colorear (Spanish Edition) (p. 307)
—Cahier de Coloriage Animaux (French Edition) (p. 308)
—Cahier de Coloriage Bebe (French Edition) (p. 308)
—Cahier de Coloriage Enfant (French Edition) (p. 308)
—Cahier de Coloriage Fille (French Edition) (p. 308)
—Cahier de Coloriage Princesse (French Edition) (p. 308)
—Cahier de Coloriage Zen (French Edition) (p. 308)
—Camión de Bomberos: Libro de niños para Colorear (Spanish Edition) (p. 314)
—Camion de Pompier: Livre À Colorier Pour Enfants (French Edition) (p. 314)
—Camion Dei Pompieri: Libro Da Colorare (Italian Edition) (p. 314)
—Can I Get an A? Alphabet Book for Preschoolers. (p. 317)
—Cassie & Lilly's Secret. (p. 339)
—Catholic Coloring Book. (p. 345)
—Cerebro Libro para Colorear (Spanish Edition) (p. 353)
—Chemistry Coloring Book. (p. 365)
—Childrens Coloring Book. (p. 373)
—Christian Coloring Book. (p. 382)
—Christian Coloring Pages. (p. 382)
—Christmas Coloring Book. (p. 384)
—Circo Libro para Colorear (Spanish Edition) (p. 393)
—Cocina Libro de niños para Colorear (Spanish Edition) (p. 410)
—Color Elephant Mandalas! a Coloring Book. (p. 420)
—Color Me Coloring Book. (p. 420)
—Color Wonder Coloring Book. (p. 421)
—Colorear Del Mar (Spanish Edition) (p. 422)
—Colorear Dinosaurios (Spanish Edition) (p. 422)
—Colorear Mandalas (Spanish Edition) (p. 422)
—Colorear Vehiculos (Spanish Edition) (p. 422)
—Colorific Fun: Colors & Numbers Then Shapes for Kids. (p. 422)
—Coloring for Adults, a Doodling Coloring Book. (p. 425)
—Connect the Dots Adult Activity Book — Form Interesting Pictures! (p. 440)
—Connecting the Dots for Adults. (p. 441)
—Connecting the Dots for Relaxation for Adults. (p. 441)
—Crazy Circus Animals Coloring Book. (p. 468)
—Cute Babies Coloring Book. (p. 491)
—Debajo Del Agua Libro de niños para Colorear (Spanish Edition) (p. 522)
—Decorazioni Floreali: Libro Da Colorare (Italian Edition) (p. 524)
—Deep Blue Sea Underwater Coloring Book. (p. 524)
—Delfines: Libro para Colorear (Spanish Edition) (p. 526)
—Delfini: Libro Da Colorare (Italian Edition) (p. 526)
—Delphine: Malbuch (German Edition) (p. 527)
—Demoiselle D'Honneur: Livre À Colorier Pour Enfants (French Edition) (p. 528)
—día de Los Enamorados Libro de niños para Colorear (Spanish Edition) (p. 537)
—Dinosaur Color Book: Super Fun Edition. (p. 548)
—Dinosaur Coloring Book. (p. 548)
—Dinosaur Coloring Book for Boys. (p. 548)
—Dinosaur Puzzles & Mazes with Word Games. (p. 549)
—Dinosaurier-Malbuch (German Edition) (p. 550)
—Dolphins: Coloring Book. (p. 580)
—Doodle at the Zoo: Awesome Doodling Fun. (p. 584)
—Doodle Book: Doodle Fun Made Easy. (p. 584)
—Doodle Book for Kids: Doodle Me - Doodle You! (p. 584)
—Doodle Crazy Images: Super Fun Edition. (p. 584)
—Doodle Magic! Become a Doodling Expert. (p. 584)
—Doodle Manga Skills Made Easy. (p. 584)
—Doodling Book for Super Fun. (p. 585)
—Dot to Dot 100 Connect the Dot Fun Puzzles. (p. 587)
—Dot to Dot Book Extreme Fun for Kids & Adults. (p. 588)
—Dot to Dot Book for Children: Play & Learn Edition. (p. 588)
—Dot to Dot Book for Older Children: Super Fun Edition. (p. 588)
—Dot to Dot Book Includes Puzzles & Mazes. (p. 588)
—Dot to Dot Counting Book for Kids: Play & Learn. (p. 588)
—Dot to Dot Super Fun: Play & Learn. (p. 588)
—Drachen: Malbuch (German Edition) (p. 592)
—Draghi: Libro Da Colorare (Italian Edition) (p. 593)
—Dragones: Libro para Colorear (Spanish Edition) (p. 594)
—Dragons: Coloring Book. (p. 595)
—Easter Coloring Book. (p. 619)
—Espacio Libro de niños para Colorear (Spanish Edition) (p. 662)
—Fancy Clothes Coloring Book. (p. 705)
—Fancy Dress: Girls Coloring Book Set. (p. 705)
—Fantasia: Libro Da Colorare (Italian Edition) (p. 706)
—Fantasía Libro de niños para Colorear (Spanish Edition) (p. 706)
—Fantastique: Livre À Colorier Pour Enfants (French Edition) (p. 707)
—Fantasy: Coloring Book. (p. 707)
—Farm Animal Coloring Pages. (p. 709)
—Fashion: Coloring Book. (p. 712)
—Fashion Coloring Book. (p. 712)
—Fashion Is Fun: Girls Coloring Books Age 8. (p. 712)
—Fate: Libro Da Colorare (Italian Edition) (p. 714)
—Feen: Malbuch (German Edition) (p. 718)
—Feen: Malbuch 2 (German Edition) (p. 718)
—Feuerwehrauto: Malbuch Für Kinder (German Edition) (p. 721)
—Feuerwehrmann und Feuerwehrleute: Malbuch Für Kinder (German Edition) (p. 721)
—Find & Color Book. (p. 727)
—Find & Seek Book: For Kids (Spot It Edition) (p. 727)
—Fiori: Libro Da Colorare per Ragazzi (Italian Edition) (p. 732)
—Fire Truck Coloring Book. (p. 733)
—Firetruck: Coloring Book. (p. 734)
—First Look & Find Book for Kids: (spot It Fun) (p. 738)
—Flaggen-Malbuch (German Edition) (p. 746)
—Flaggen-Malbuch 2 (German Edition) (p. 746)
—Flags Around the World: Awesome Flags Coloring Fun. (p. 746)
—Flags Book: Color Your Favorite Flag - Activity Books for Kids. (p. 746)
—Flags Coloring Book: Color Around the World. (p. 746)
—Flags Coloring Book. (p. 746)
—Flags of All Nations: Jumbo Coloring Book for Kids. (p. 746)
—Flags of the World: Coloring Fun. (p. 746)
—Fleurs: Livre À Colorier Pour Enfants (French Edition) (p. 748)
—Flower Girl: Coloring Book (Wedding Coloring Book) (p. 752)
—Follow the Dots Book Easy Connect It Fun. (p. 758)
—Follow the Dots for Kids: Dot to Dot Extreme Fun. (p. 758)
—Footwear Super Fun Girls Coloring Books Age 6. (p. 762)
—Fright Night: Halloween Coloring Book. (p. 788)
—Frutas y Verduras Libro de niños para Colorear (Spanish Edition) (p. 796)
—Garniture Florale: Livre À Colorier Pour Enfants (French Edition) (p. 810)
—Gehirn-Malbuch (German Edition) (p. 813)
—Giant Christmas Coloring Book. (p. 830)
—Glasmalerei-Malbuch Für Kinder (German Edition) (p. 841)
—Great de-Stressor — Adult Dot-To-Dot Activity Book. (p. 885)
—Hadas: Libro para Colorear (Spanish Edition) (p. 909)
—Haifisch-Malbuch Für Kinder (German Edition) (p. 909)
—Haifisch-Woche-Malbuch Für Kinder (German Edition) (p. 909)
—Halloween Coloring Book: Super Fun Edition. (p. 912)
—Halloween Coloring Book for Children. (p. 912)
—Halloween Coloring for Kids: We Love Coloring! (p. 912)
—Halloween Libro de niños para Colorear (Spanish Edition) (p. 912)
—Halloween-Malbuch Für Kinder (German Edition) (p. 912)
—Handwriting: Cursive Edition, Grades 2 & Up. (p. 916)
—Hidden Picture Book: Seek & Find Edition. (p. 966)
—Hidden Picture Book for Adults: Spot It Fun for Kids & Adults. (p. 966)
—Hidden Picture Book for Children: Learning Is Fun with Spot It Pictures. (p. 966)
—Hidden Picture Games: I Love Seek & Find Games. (p. 966)
—Hidden Picture Puzzles: Super Fun for Fun Lovers. (p. 966)
—Hidden Pictures Adult Book: Naughty Adult Picture Book. (p. 966)
—Hidden Pictures for Children: Where Ist It? Spot It Fun. (p. 966)
—Hidden Pictures for Kids: Find It If You Can! Seek & Find Fun. (p. 966)
—How to Color Book: With Color Guide Images. (p. 1038)
—How to Color Book for Children: Learning Is Fun for Kids. (p. 1038)
—How to Color for Kids: Learning Is Fun for Kids. (p. 1038)
—How to Color Kids Book: With Color Guide Images. (p. 1038)
—How to Draw: A Simple Step by Step Guide for Kids. (p. 1039)
—How to Draw Anime: We Love Anime! (p. 1039)
—How to Draw Book for Children: Learning Is Fun Edition. (p. 1040)
—How to Draw Book for Kids: Draw This Not That Fun. (p. 1040)
—I Know My Body: Body Parts Baby Book. (p. 1067)
—I Love Babies: Children Coloring Book. (p. 1069)
—I Love Doodling! (p. 1069)
—I Love Sports Coloring Book. (p. 1072)
—Ich Liebe Den Zahnarzt Malbuch (German Edition) (p. 1088)
—Im-Meer-Malbuch Für Kinder (German Edition) (p. 1098)
—Indian Tribes Totem Poles Coloring Book. (p. 1116)
—Insekten-Malbuch Fur Kinder (German Edition) (p. 1122)
—Inside Your Brain Coloring Book. (p. 1124)
—Invierno Libro de niños para Colorear (Spanish Edition) (p. 1132)
—Its Not That Complicated! Mazes & More: Activity Book for Adults. (p. 1146)
—I've Got Senses! Senses Books for Kids. (p. 1149)
—Journal for Girls. (p. 1180)
—Just for Girls Coloring Book. (p. 1193)
—Ka Ching for Kids: Counting Money Book for Kids. (p. 1201)
—Käfer-Malbuch (German Edition) (p. 1201)
—Kinder-Malbuch (German Edition) (p. 1218)
—Knights of the Round Table Coloring Book. (p. 1228)
—Las Mascaras Libro de niños para Colorear (Spanish Edition) (p. 1246)
—Las Muchachas Libro de niños para Colorear (Spanish Edition) (p. 1246)
—Libri per Bambini Animali: Libro Da Colorare (Libri per Bambini e Ragazzi) (Italian Edition) (p. 1285)
—Libri per Bambini Cibo (Libri per Bambini e Ragazzi) (Italian Edition) (p. 1285)
—Libri per Bambini Colorare (Italian Edition) (p. 1285)
—Libro Colorear Animales (Spanish Edition) (p. 1285)
—Libro Colorear Infantil (Spanish Edition) (p. 1285)
—Libro Colorear Princesas (Spanish Edition) (p. 1285)
—Libro Colorear Superheroes (Spanish Edition) (p. 1285)
—Libro Colorear Tren (Spanish Edition) (p. 1285)
—Libro Da Colorare Bambini 3 Anni (Italian Edition) (p. 1285)
—Libro Da Colorare Cars (Italian Edition) (p. 1285)
—Libro Da Colorare con Animali Carini (Italian Edition) (p. 1285)
—Libro Da Colorare con Bimbi (Italian Edition) (p. 1285)
—Libro Da Colorare con le Bandiere (Italian Edition) (p. 1285)
—Libro Da Colorare con Occhi Grandi (Italian Edition) (p. 1285)
—Libro Da Colorare Di Natale (Italian Edition) (p. 1285)
—Libro Da Colorare Mandala (Italian Edition) (p. 1285)
—Libro Da Colorare Matrimonio (Italian Edition) (p. 1285)
—Libro Da Colorare - Mi Piace Andare Dal Dentista (Italian Edition) (p. 1285)
—Libro Da Colorare per Bambini (Italian Edition) (p. 1285)
—Libro Da Colorare per Ragazze (Italian Edition) (p. 1286)
—Libro Da Colorare per Ragazzi con Frutta e Verdura (Italian Edition) (p. 1286)
—Libro Da Colorare per Ragazzi con Mandala (Italian Edition) (p. 1286)
—Libro Da Colorare per Ragazzi con Principesse (Italian Edition) (p. 1286)
—Libro Da Colorare per Ragazzi con Spirografi (Italian Edition) (p. 1286)
—Libro Da Colorare per Ragazzi con Vetrate Policrome (Italian Edition) (p. 1286)
—Libro Da Colorare per Ragazzi Di San Valentino (Italian Edition) (p. 1286)
—Libro Da Colorare per Ragazzi - la Settimana Degli Squali (Italian Edition) (p. 1286)
—Libro Da Colorare per Ragazzi - Nel Mare (Italian Edition) (p. 1286)
—Libro Da Colorare per Ragazzi - Sott'acqua (Italian Edition) (p. 1286)
—Libro Da Colorare per Ragazzi Su Autobus e Camion (Italian Edition) (p. 1286)
—Libro Da Colorare per Ragazzi Su Ricami e Draghi (Italian Edition) (p. 1286)
—Libro Da Colorare per Ragazzi Sugli Insetti (Italian Edition) (p. 1286)
—Libro Da Colorare per Ragazzi Sui Robot (Italian Edition) (p. 1286)
—Libro Da Colorare Planes (Italian Edition) (p. 1286)
—Libro Da Colorare Principesse (Italian Edition) (p. 1286)
—Libro Da Colorare Sugli Animali (Italian Edition) (p. 1286)
—Libro Da Colorare Sugli Scarabei (Italian Edition) (p. 1286)
—Libro Da Colorare Sui Cowboy (Italian Edition) (p. 1286)
—Libro Da Colorare Sui Vestiti (Italian Edition) (p. 1286)
—Libro Da Colorare Sui Vestiti Alla Moda (Italian Edition) (p. 1286)
—Libro Da Colorare Sul Cervello (Italian Edition) (p. 1286)
—Libro Da Colorare Sul Circo (Italian Edition) (p. 1286)
—Libro Da Colorare Super Rilassante (Italian Edition) (p. 1286)
—Libro Di Chimica Da Colorare (Italian Edition) (p. 1287)
—Little Mermaid Coloring Book. (p. 1322)
—Livre À Colorier: Les Fées (French Edition) (p. 1335)
—Livre À Colorier: Les Dragons (French Edition) (p. 1335)
—Livre À Colorier: Les Poupées (French Edition) (p. 1335)
—Livre À Colorier: Les Dauphins (French Edition) (p. 1335)
—Livre À Colorier Pour Enfants (French Edition) (p. 1335)
—Livre À Colorier Pour Enfants Sur Halloween (French Edition) (p. 1335)
—Livre À Colorier Pour Enfants Sur la Cuisine (French Edition) (p. 1335)
—Livre À Colorier Pour Enfants Sur la Princesse (French Edition) (p. 1335)
—Livre À Colorier Pour Enfants Sur la Semaine des Requins (French Edition) (p. 1335)
—Livre À Colorier Pour Enfants Sur les Chevaliers et les Dragons (French Edition) (p. 1335)
—Livre À Colorier Pour Enfants Sur les Fonds Sous-Marins (French Edition) (p. 1335)
—Livre À Colorier Pour Enfants Sur les Masques (French Edition) (p. 1335)
—Livre À Colorier Pour Enfants Sur les Tatouages (French Edition) (p. 1335)
—Livre À Colorier Pour Enfants Sur les Travailleurs (French Edition) (p. 1335)
—Livre À Colorier Pour Enfants Sur l'Espace (French Edition) (p. 1335)
—Livre À Colorier Pour Enfants Sur Mandala (French Edition) (p. 1335)
—Livre À Colorier Sur J'Aime le Dentiste (French Edition) (p. 1335)
—Livre À Colorier Sur la Chimie (French Edition) (p. 1335)
—Livre À Colorier Sur le Cerveau (French Edition) (p. 1335)
—Livre À Colorier Sur les Animaux (French Edition) (p. 1335)
—Livre a Colorier Sur les Cowboys (French Edition) (p. 1335)
—Livre À Colorier Sur les Dinosaures (French Edition) (p. 1335)
—Livre À Colorier Sur les Mignons Animaux (French Edition) (p. 1335)
—Livre À Colorier Sur les Scarabées (French Edition) (p. 1335)
—Livre À Colorier Sur les Vètements de Fantaisie (French Edition) (p. 1335)
—Livre À Colorier Sur Noël (French Edition) (p. 1335)
—Livre À Colorier Sur Pâques (French Edition) (p. 1335)
—Livre de Coloriage de la Nativite / Edition Biblique (French Edition) (p. 1335)
—Livre de Coloriage de Zombies Halloween (French Edition) (p. 1335)
—Livre de Coloriage de Zoologie Animaux (French Edition) (p. 1335)
—Livre de Coloriage des Femmes Merveilleuse Femmes (French Edition) (p. 1335)
—Look & Find Book: Super Fun for Kids. (p. 1344)
—Look & Find Book for Kids: Play & Learn Edition. (p. 1344)
—Look & Find Book for Toddlers: Spot It Fun! (p. 1344)
—Look & Find for Children: Learning Is Fun Edition. (p. 1344)
—Los Animales de la Selva Libro de niños para Colorear (Spanish Edition) (p. 1350)
—Los Animales Libro para Colorear (Spanish Edition) (p. 1350)
—Los Bebés Libros para Colorear (Spanish Edition) (p. 1350)
—Los Deportes Libro de niños para Colorear (Spanish Edition) (p. 1350)
—Los Dinosaurios Libro para Colorear (Spanish Edition) (p. 1350)
—Los Escarabajos Libro para Colorear (Spanish Edition) (p. 1350)
—Los Juguetes Libro de niños para Colorear (Spanish Edition) (p. 1351)
—Los niños Libro para Colorear (Spanish Edition) (p. 1351)
—Los Pasteles Libro para Colorear (Spanish Edition) (p. 1351)
—Los Robots Libro de niños para Colorear (Spanish Edition) (p. 1351)
—Los Tatuajes Libro de niños para Colorear (Spanish Edition) (p. 1351)
—Los Tiburones Libro de niños para Colorear (Spanish Edition) (p. 1351)
—Los Vaqueros Libro para Colorear (Spanish Edition) (p. 1351)
—Los Vitrales Libro de niños para Colorear (Spanish Edition) (p. 1351)
—Malblock Baby (German Edition) (p. 1391)
—Malblock Bauernhof (German Edition) (p. 1391)
—Malblock Buchstaben (German Edition) (p. 1391)
—Malblock Einhörner (German Edition) (p. 1391)
—Malblock Feen (German Edition) (p. 1391)
—Malbuch Bauernhof (German Edition) (p. 1391)
—Malbuch Blumen (German Edition) (p. 1391)
—Malbuch Cars (German Edition) (p. 1391)
—Malbuch der Großen Augen (German Edition) (p. 1391)
—Malbuch Dinosaurier (German Edition) (p. 1391)
—Malbuch Drachen (German Edition) (p. 1391)
—Malbuch Dragons (German Edition) (p. 1391)
—Malbuch Einhorn (German Edition) (p. 1391)
—Malbuch Eule (German Edition) (p. 1391)
—Malbuch Hochzeit Kinder (German Edition) (p. 1391)
—Malbuch Hund (German Edition) (p. 1391)
—Malbuch Im Kindergarten (German Edition) (p. 1391)
—Malbuch Kinder (German Edition) (p. 1391)
—Malbuch Kleinkinder (German Edition) (p. 1391)
—Malbuch Mädchen (German Edition) (p. 1391)
—Malbuch Marchen (German Edition) (p. 1391)
—Malbuch Mit Niedlichen Tieren (German Edition) (p. 1391)
—Malbuch Natur (German Edition) (p. 1391)
—Malbuch Ostern (German Edition) (p. 1391)
—Malbuch Piraten (German Edition) (p. 1391)
—Malbuch Prinzessin (German Edition) (p. 1391)
—Malbuch Superhelden (German Edition) (p. 1391)
—Malbuch Tattoo (German Edition) (p. 1391)
—Malbuch Tiere Zeichnen (German Edition) (p. 1391)
—Malbuch Über Arbeitende Menschen Für Kinder (German Edition) (p. 1391)
—Malbuch Vorschule (German Edition) (p. 1391)
—Malbuch Weltall (German Edition) (p. 1391)
—Mandala Art Made Easy: Designs for Colorists. (p. 1396)
—Mandala Coloring Book Kids Version. (p. 1396)
—Mandala Coloring Fun: Jumbo Mandala Coloring Pages. (p. 1396)
—Mandala Flower Coloring Book. (p. 1396)
—Mandala for Children: Super Coloring Fun. (p. 1396)

S

Spenser, Mary Clare. Benefit of the Doubt (Classic Reprint) (p. 199)
—Brinka: An American Countess (Classic Reprint) (p. 282)
Sper, Emily. Follow the Yarn: A Book of Colors. Sper, Emily, illus. (p. 758)
Speregen, Debra Newberger. How to Train Your Dragon: A Pocket Full of Dreams. Phillipson, Andrew & Shimabukuro, Denise, illus. (p. 1045)
Speregen, Devra Newberger. Barbie: Puppy's Day Out. (p. 166)
—My Little Pony Bracelets for Besties! Nex, Anthony, photos by. (p. 1553)
—My Little Pony Get Ponified Hair! Sparkly Styles Inspired by Equestria. Nex, Anthony, photos by. (p. 1553)
—Nickelodeon Jojo Siwa: Go Big & Bow Big. (p. 1603)
Spergel, Heather. Cloud City: A Child's Journey Through Bereavement. Stylou, Georgia, illus. (p. 407)
—Free to Be Gluten Free! Martino, Anita, illus. (p. 782)
—Gabi Babaroni on Broadway. Vene, Alessandro, illus. (p. 804)
—NiNi Spergelini: Guitar-Ific! Perla, Brian, illus. (p. 1610)
Sperling, Alia, illus. see Kabbani, Shaykh Muhamma & Kabbani, Muhammad Hisham.
Sperling, Karima. Animal Salams. Sperling, Karima, illus. (p. 91)
—Animals of Paradise: Coloring Book. (p. 95)
—Every Day a Thousand Times. (p. 670)
—My Little Lore of Light: Coloring Book. (p. 1553)
Sperling, Karima, illus. see Kabbani, Shaykh Muhamma & Kabbani, Muhammad Hisham.
Sperling, S. David, illus. see Steinbock, Steven E.
Sperling, Thomas, illus. see Asbjornsen, Peter Christen.
Sperling, Thomas, illus. see deRubertis, Barbara.
Sperling, Tom, illus. see Defoe, Daniel.
Sperling, Tom, illus. see Eldridge, Jim.
Sperling, Vatsala. Arjuna: The Gentle Warrior. Weltevrede, Nona & Weltevrede, Pieter, illus. (p. 116)
—Magical Adventures of Krishna: How a Mischief Maker Saved the World. Weltevrede, Pieter, illus. (p. 1379)
Sperling, Vatsala & Johari, Harish. Classic Tales from India: How Ganesh Got His Elephant Head & Other Stories. Weltevrede, Pieter et al, illus. (p. 401)
Spero, J. D. Boy on Hold. (p. 269)
Sperring, Mark. Captain Buckleboots on the Naughty Step. McLaughlin, Tom, illus. (p. 325)
—Dino-Baby. Lloyd, Sam, illus. (p. 547)
—Dino-Daddy. Lloyd, Sam, illus. (p. 547)
—How Many Sleeps 'til Christmas? Braun, Sebastien, illus. (p. 1034)
—How Many Sleeps 'Til My Birthday? Braun, Sebastien, illus. (p. 1034)
—I'll Catch You If You Fall. Marlow, Layn, illus. (p. 1095)
—I'll Love You Always. Brown, Alison, illus. (p. 1095)
—I'll Love You Always (padded Board Book) Brown, Alison, illus. (p. 1095)
—Little Hugs from Little Loves. Frost, Maddie, illus. (p. 1319)
—Littlest Things Give the Loveliest Hugs. Frost, Maddie, illus. (p. 1331)
—Max & the Won't Go to Bed Show. Warburton, Sarah, illus. (p. 1427)
—Most Wonderful Gift in the World. (p. 1509)
—Most Wonderful Gift in the World. Fleming, Lucy, illus. (p. 1509)
—Princess Scallywag & the Brave, Brave Knight. Powell, Claire, illus. (p. 1799)
—Scorch Trials (Maze Runner, Book 2) (p. 1961)
—Shape of My Heart. Paterson, Alys, illus. (p. 2000)
—Sunflower Sword. Latimer, Miriam, illus. (p. 2152)
Sperring, Mark & Teckentrup, Britta. Your Hand in My Hand. (p. 2533)
Sperry, Armstrong. John Paul Jones: The Pirate Patriot. (p. 1174)
Sperry, Brendan. Captain Dino & the Revenge of Roberto. (p. 325)
Sperry, J. E. Kookaburra. (p. 1231)
Speth, Brandilyn, illus. see Garner, Linda.
Spettigue, H. H. Heritage of Eve (Classic Reprint) (p. 959)
Spevack, Donna J. Grandma's Cow. (p. 878)
Speziani, Giulie, jt. auth. see Pryor, Shawn.
Spicer, Brad. Teddy Is Ready: Second Edition. Williams, Sean, illus. (p. 2198)
Spicer, Chris. Jj & the Big Bend. (p. 1169)
Spicer, Henry. Bound to Please, Vol. 1 of 2 (Classic Reprint) (p. 265)
Spicer, Maggee, jt. auth. see Thompson, Richard.
Spicer, Morgan, illus. see Dotsikas, Michael.
Spicer, Morgan, illus. see Greiner, Linda.
Spicer, Morgan, illus. see Medina, Sylvia M.
Spicer, Morgan, illus. see Medina, Sylvia M. & Hill, Krista.
Spicer, Morgan, illus. see Medina, Sylvia M. & Shapiro, Gary.
Spicer, Morgan, illus. see Stevenson, Deborah.
Spicer, Morgen, illus. see Medina, Sylvia M.
Spicer-Dannelly, Doreen. Love Double Dutch. (p. 1359)
Spicer-Wolven, Karen. God's Plan for Nate Nate: An Adoption Story. (p. 853)
—What's Nummy Nadia? (p. 2425)
Spickert, Diane Nelson. Earthsteps: A Rock's Journey Through Time. Wallace, Marianne D., illus. (p. 618)
Spickett, D. M. Adventures of Sarah the Seahorse (p. 27)
Spickett, M. J. Brothers. (p. 286)
Spickler, Henry M. Around the World Without a Cent (Classic Reprint) (p. 119)
Spider, Star. Hey Jude. (p. 964)
Spiegel, Beth, illus. see Bottner, Barbara.
Spiegel, Beth, illus. see Bunting, Eve.
Spiegel, Beth, illus. see Rodman, Mary Ann.
Spiegelman, Art. Jack & the Box Spiegelman, Art, illus. (p. 1151)
Spiegelman, Nadja. Lost in NYC: A Subway Adventure. Garcia Sanchez, Sergio, illus. (p. 1354)
—Lost in NYC: A Subway Adventure. Sánchez, Sergio García, illus. (p. 1354)
—Lost in Nyc: a Subway Adventure. Sanchez, Sergio Garcia, illus. (p. 1354)
—Zig & Wikki in Something Ate My Homework. Loeffler, Trade, illus. (p. 2540)
—Zig & Wikki in the Cow: TOON Level 3. Loeffler, Trade, illus. (p. 2540)
—Zig & Wikki in the Cow. (p. 2540)
—Zig & Wikki in the Cow. Loeffler, Trade, illus. (p. 2540)
Spiegelman, Nadja & Loeffler, Trade. Zig & Wikki in Something Ate My Homework (p. 2540)
—Zig & Wikki in Something Ate My Homework. (p. 2540)
Spiegle, Dan, illus. see Foster, Bob.
Spieker, Diana. Alphabetica: Odes to the Alphabet. Skehan, Krista, illus. (p. 59)
Spielhagen, Frederick. German Pioneers: A Tale of the Mohawk (Classic Reprint) (p. 822)
Spielhagen, Friedrich. Hammer & Anvil: A Novel (Classic Reprint) (p. 913)
—Problematic Characters: A Novel (Classic Reprint) (p. 1803)
Spieller, Lauren. Your Destination Is on the Left. (p. 2533)
Spielman, Gloria. French Toast Sundays. Bousidan, Inbal Gigi, illus. (p. 784)
—Marcel Marceau: Master of Mime. Gauthier, Manon, illus. (p. 1402)
Spielman, Madison. Build It: Skyscrapers (p. 293)
—Craft It: Hand-Blown Glass (p. 466)
—Make It: Chocolate (p. 1386)
—Make It - Chocolate (p. 1386)
Spielmann, M. H. Kate Greenaway (Classic Reprint) (p. 1204)
Spielmann, M h. 1858-1948, jt. auth. see Thackeray, William Makepeace.
Spielmann, Mabel H. My Son & I (Classic Reprint) (p. 1561)
Spielmann, Mabel Henrietta. Rainbow Book: Tales of Fun & Fancy (Classic Reprint) (p. 1836)
Spier, Jo, illus. see Malkus, Alida Sims.
Spier, Peter. Fox Went Out on a Chilly Night: An Old Song. (p. 774)
—We the People: The Constitution of the United States. (p. 2392)
Spier Weaver, Rachel & Haggard, Anna. Brave Big Sister: A Bible Story about Miriam. Skinner, ed. (p. 276)
—Extraordinary Teacher: A Bible Story about Priscilla. Skinner, ed. (p. 685)
—Fearless Leader: A Bible Story about Deborah. Skinner, ed. (p. 717)
Spiero, Simon. Delights of Reading: Written for My Grandchildren. (p. 527)
Spiers, Harry. Souvenir of the Village of Meadowvale-On-the-Credit (Classic Reprint) (p. 2069)
Spiers, Victor. Graduated Course of Translation into French Prose Preceded by Advice to Students (Classic Reprint) (p. 875)
Spies, Adrian. Carolina Magazine, Vol. 70: October, 1940 (Classic Reprint) (p. 333)
Spies, Ben. 2020. (p. 2561)
—Weirdo. Spies, Robert, illus. (p. 2397)
Spies, Karen Bornemann. Buffalo Bill Cody: Legend of the Wild West. (p. 291)
—Heroes in Greek Mythology Rock! Bock, William Sauts, illus. (p. 962)
—Mythology of the Iliad & the Odyssey. (p. 1571)
Spies, Robert, illus. see Spies, Ben.
Spiess, Christian Heinrich. Mountain Cottager, or Wonder upon Wonder: A Tale; Translated from the German (Classic Reprint) (p. 1513)
Spiffy Entertainment. Nature Cat: a Nature Carol. (p. 1580)
Spigarelli, Jane, et al. Oxford Picture Dictionary: Low Beginning. (p. 1689)
Spikes, Leon, Jr., illus. see Spikes, James L.
Spikings, Ashley, illus. see Pelicano, Matt.
Spiliotopoulos, Evan, et al. Beauty & the Beast. (p. 185)
Spillane, Lisa. Six Healing Sounds with Lisa & Ted: Qigong for Children. Spillane, Lisa, illus. (p. 2028)
—Smiling Heart Meditations with Lisa & Ted (And Bingo) (p. 2042)
Spiller, Sara. Bessie Coleman. (p. 205)
—Coretta Scott King. Bane, Jeff, illus. (p. 454)
—Ida B. Wells. Bane, Jeff, illus. (p. 1089)
—Malala Yousafzai. Bane, Jeff, illus. (p. 1391)
—Maya Lin. Bane, Jeff, illus. (p. 1429)
—Nellie Bly. Bane, Jeff, illus. (p. 1586)
—Ruth Bader Ginsburg. Bane, Jeff, illus. (p. 1918)
—Susan B. Anthony. Bane, Jeff, illus. (p. 2166)
Spiller, Trudy. Caillou de Guérison de Trudy. Payette, Marie-Christine, tr. from ENG. (p. 308)
Spilling, Jo-Ann, jt. auth. see Spilling, Michael.
Spilling, Michael. Estonia. (p. 665)
Spilling, Michael, jt. auth. see Sheehan, Sean.
Spilling, Michael & Anderson, Emily. Estonia. (p. 665)
Spilling, Michael & Lark, Liz. Yoga Step-by-Step. (p. 2523)
Spilling, Michael & Spilling, Jo-Ann. Cyprus. (p. 493)
Spilling, Michael & Wong, Winnie. Georgia. (p. 820)
Spilling, Michael, et al. Cyprus (p. 493)
—Georgia. (p. 820)
Spillman, Ken. Absolutely True Adventures of Daydreamer Dev (Omnibus Edition, 3 in 1) (p. 9)
Spilsbury, Louise. Alexander Graham Bell & the Telephone (p. 42)
—Always Broke? Skills to Make More Money. (p. 61)
—Ancient China. (p. 80)
—Animal Bodies: Extreme Anatomies. (p. 88)
—Avoiding Bullies? Skills to Outsmart & Stop Them. (p. 143)
—Baboon (p. 148)
—Backyard Bugs. (p. 156)
—Boa Constrictor. (p. 251)
—Brazil. (p. 277)
—Caterpillar Capers. (p. 344)
—Clean & Healthy. (p. 402)
—Coastal Treasure Hunter. (p. 410)
—Collins Big Cat Phonics for Letters & Sounds - Blackcurrant Jam: Band 05/Green (p. 416)
—Coyote (p. 465)
—Creeping Killers: Extreme Plants. (p. 472)
—Cristales. (p. 475)
—Dams & Hydropower. (p. 499)
—Day in the Life: Grassland Animals Set (p. 513)
—Drinking & Drugs? Skills to Avoid 'Em & Stay Cool. (p. 604)
—Eat or Be Eaten: Extreme Food Chains. (p. 621)
—Family & Friends. (p. 702)
—Family Issues? Skills to Communicate. (p. 702)
—Flight (p. 748)
—Forensic Investigations of the Maya. (p. 765)
—Forensic Investigations of the Romans. (p. 765)
—Fósiles. (p. 770)
—Garbage Can. Hanna, Gary, illus. (p. 808)
—Get Active! (p. 823)
—Global Conflict. Kai, Hanane, illus. (p. 843)
—Harmful Substances. (p. 930)
—Head-to-Toe Body Questions. (p. 942)
—Horrible Jobs in Colonial Times (p. 1003)
—How Bees Make Honey. (p. 1026)
—How Community Gardens Work. (p. 1027)
—How to Survive in the Arctic & Antarctica. (p. 1044)
—How to Survive in the Ocean. (p. 1044)
—How to Survive on a Mountain. (p. 1044)
—Ice Age Animals. (p. 1087)
—Igloos & Inuit Life. (p. 1094)
—Inclined Planes. (p. 1113)
—Indonesia. (p. 1117)
—Industrialization & Empire, 1783 to 1914. (p. 1118)
—Jellyfish (p. 1163)
—Johannes Gutenberg & the Printing Press (p. 1171)
—Kill or Die: Extreme Life Cycles. (p. 1217)
—Kori Bustard (p. 1231)
—Levers. (p. 1282)
—Lion. (p. 1305)
—Mayans. (p. 1429)
—Minerales. (p. 1471)
—Mississippian Culture: The Mound Builders. (p. 1482)
—Mob of Meerkats: And Other Mammal Groups (p. 1485)
—Octopus Set. (p. 1637)
—One Egg. (p. 1659)
—Ostrich (p. 1674)
—Polar Bear: Killer King of the Arctic. (p. 1769)
—Polar Bear. (p. 1769)
—Polar Regions. (p. 1770)
—Pond. Hanna, Gary, illus. (p. 1773)
—Projects with Recycling & Reusing. (p. 1806)
—Projects with Space. (p. 1806)
—Protecting & Caring for Children (p. 1808)
—Pulleys. (p. 1812)
—Racism & Intolerance. Kai, Hanane, illus. (p. 1832)
—Rain Forests. (p. 1835)
—Respiration & Circulation. (p. 1869)
—Robert Goddard & the Rocket (p. 1890)
—Same-Sex Marriage. (p. 1927)
—Save the Cheetah (p. 1937)
—Save the Chimpanzee (p. 1937)
—Save the Humpback Whale (p. 1937)
—Science of Avalanches. (p. 1957)
—Science of Electricity. (p. 1957)
—Science of Magnetism. (p. 1958)
—Science of Sound. (p. 1958)
—Science of the Brain. (p. 1958)
—Screws. (p. 1965)
—Sea Otters (p. 1968)
—Seal (p. 1970)
—Sight (p. 2015)
—Student's Toolbox: Tips for Better Public Speaking. (p. 2144)
—Student's Toolbox: Tips for Better Writing. (p. 2144)
—Suelo. (p. 2147)
—Superstar Birds. (p. 2161)
—Superstar Mammals. (p. 2161)
—Superstar Plants. (p. 2161)
—Superstar Reptiles. (p. 2161)
—Survival of the Fittest: Extreme Adaptations. (p. 2164)
—Surviving the Desert. (p. 2165)
—Surviving the Ice. (p. 2165)
—Surviving the Mountain. (p. 2165)
—Surviving the Rainforest. (p. 2165)
—Surviving the River. (p. 2165)
—Surviving the Sea. (p. 2165)
—Tapestries & Textiles. (p. 2191)
—Threats to Our Water Supply. (p. 2231)
—Tide Pool. Hanna, Gary, illus. (p. 2240)
—Tips for Better Researching (p. 2250)
—Tips for Better Writing (p. 2250)
—Tips for Public Speaking (p. 2250)
—True Cost of Fashion. (p. 2294)
—Vote for Me! How Governments & Elections Work Around the World. Gordon, Mike, illus. (p. 2367)
—Vote for Me! How Governments & Elections Work Around the World. (p. 2367)
—Walruses (p. 2373)
—Waste & Recycling Challenges. (p. 2382)
—Wedges. (p. 2395)
—What Are Food Chains & Food Webs? (p. 2405)
—What Are Habitats & Biomes? (p. 2405)
—What Are Living & Nonliving Things? (p. 2405)
—What Are Natural Disasters? (p. 2405)
—What Are Rivers, Lakes, & Oceans? (p. 2405)
—What Is a Landform? (p. 2414)
—What Is a Life Cycle? (p. 2414)
—What Is the Rock Cycle? (p. 2416)
—What Is the Structure of a Plant? (p. 2417)
—What Is the Structure of an Animal? (p. 2417)
—What Is the Water Cycle? (p. 2417)
—What Is Weather? (p. 2417)
—Wheels & Axles. (p. 2428)
—Wildebeest (p. 2465)
—World Wars & Globalization, 1914 to 2010. (p. 2506)
—Wright Brothers & the Airplane (p. 2511)
—Zits & Hormones? Skills to Handle Puberty. (p. 2541)
—Zoologists in the Field. (p. 2544)
Spilsbury, Louise, jt. auth. see Dickmann, Nancy.
Spilsbury, Louise, jt. auth. see Spilsbury, Richard.
Spilsbury, Louise & Claybourne, Anna. Complete Guide to Extreme Weather. (p. 434)
Spilsbury, Louise and Richard & Spilsbury, Richard. Animal Adaptations. (p. 87)
Spilsbury, Louise & Spilsbury, Richard. Airplane (p. 37)
—Arctic Ocean. (p. 112)
—At the Poles. (p. 131)
—Atlantic Ocean. (p. 133)
—Awesome Forces of Nature (p. 144)
—Cells (p. 350)
—Chimpanzee Troops. (p. 377)
—Crystals (p. 481)
—Desert Biomes. (p. 531)
—Electricity. (p. 631)
—Energy (p. 650)
—Exploring Light. (p. 682)
—Exploring Sound (p. 682)
—Fly to Mars! Forces in Space. (p. 754)
—Fossils (p. 771)
—Freshwater Biomes. (p. 785)
—Grassland Biomes. (p. 881)
—Howling Hurricanes (p. 1047)
—Hurricanes & Tornadoes in Action. (p. 1054)
—In Space. (p. 1107)
—In the Desert. (p. 1108)
—In the Rainforest. (p. 1110)
—Indian Ocean. (p. 1116)
—Killer Plants. (p. 1217)
—Life Processes (p. 1295)
—Light. (p. 1298)
—Light & Dark. (p. 1298)
—Light & Sound (p. 1298)
—Making Noise!: Making Sounds (p. 1389)
—Marine Biomes. (p. 1405)
—Materials (p. 1421)
—Microorganisms (p. 1460)
—Minerals (p. 1471)
—Nature Walk in the City (p. 1581)
—Nature Walk in the Woods (p. 1581)
—Nature Walk on the Beach (p. 1581)
—Nature Walk on the Farm (p. 1581)
—Nature Walks (p. 1581)
—Oceans of the World. (p. 1636)
—Pacific Ocean. (p. 1691)
—Plant Growth. (p. 1756)
—Raging Floods (p. 1834)
—Reflecting Light. (p. 1860)
—Robots in Industry. (p. 1893)
—Robots in Law Enforcement. (p. 1893)
—Robots in Medicine. (p. 1893)
—Robots in Space. (p. 1893)
—Robots in the Military. (p. 1893)
—Robots Underwater. (p. 1893)
—Science of the Digestive System. (p. 1958)
—Science of the Heart & Circulatory System. (p. 1958)
—Science of the Lungs & Respiratory System. (p. 1958)
—Science of the Senses. (p. 1958)
—Science of the Skeleton & Muscles. (p. 1958)
—Shadows. (p. 1997)
—Shattering Earthquakes (p. 2003)
—Shhh! Listen!: Hearing Sounds HL Studios, H. L., illus. (p. 2007)
—Soil (p. 2055)
—Solids, Liquids, & Gases (p. 2057)
—Sources of Light. (p. 2068)
—Southern Ocean. (p. 2069)
—Submarine (p. 2145)
—Sweeping Tsunamis (p. 2168)
—Telephone (p. 2201)
—Terrifying Tornadoes (p. 2207)
—Top 10 Worst Earthquakes. (p. 2263)
—Top 10 Worst Floods. (p. 2263)
—Top 10 Worst Hurricanes. (p. 2263)
—Top 10 Worst Tsunamis. (p. 2263)
—Top 10 Worst Volcanic Eruptions. (p. 2263)
—Top 10 Worst Wildfires. (p. 2263)
—Tsunamis in Action. (p. 2298)
—Tundra Biomes. (p. 2299)
—Turn It up!; Turn It down!: Volume HL Studios Staff, illus. (p. 2300)
—Under the Ground. (p. 2322)
—Violent Volcanoes (p. 2359)
—Why Do Plants Have Flowers? (p. 2456)
Spilsbury, Louise & Spilsbury, Richard, contrib. by. DESERT BIOMES. (p. 531)
—EARTHQUAKE SHATTERS COUNTRY. (p. 617)
—FOREST BIOMES. (p. 765)
—FOREST FIRE CREATES INFERNO. (p. 766)
—FRESHWATER BIOMES. (p. 785)
—GRASSLAND BIOMES. (p. 881)
—HURRICANE HITS THE COAST. (p. 1054)
—MARINE BIOMES. (p. 1405)
—TORNADO: RIPS UP CITY. (p. 2265)
—TSUNAMI: CRUSHES COASTLINE. (p. 2298)
—TUNDRA BIOMES. (p. 2299)
—VOLCANO MELTS VILLAGE. (p. 2366)
Spilsbury, Louise, et al. Essential Physical Science (p. 664)
—Feel the Force. (p. 718)
—Great Scientific Theories. (p. 889)
Spilsbury, Richard. Adaptation & Survival. (p. 14)
—Animal Homes & Hangouts. (p. 90)
—Animal Traps & Lairs. (p. 92)
—Animal Variation & Classification. (p. 92)
—Ask an Expert: Climate Change. (p. 126)
—Autism. (p. 139)
—Bipolar Disorder. (p. 229)
—Bones Speak! Solving Crimes from the Past. (p. 256)
—Born Survivors. (p. 263)
—Burrow. Hanna, Gary, illus. (p. 300)
—Cave. Hanna, Gary, illus. (p. 347)
—Cells, Tissues, & Organs. (p. 351)
—Chemical Reactions: Investigating an Industrial Accident (p. 365)
—Climate Change Catastrophe. (p. 405)
—Cystic Fibrosis. (p. 493)
—Debate about Energy Resources. (p. 522)
—Decorated Pottery. (p. 523)
—Deep Sea Exploration. (p. 524)
—Deforestation. (p. 526)
—Deforestation Crisis. (p. 526)
—Depression. (p. 529)

S

—Emperor's Last Command: Problem-Solving in Action. (p. 645)
—Hidden Valley: Reasoning in Action. (p. 966)
—Lightning Flash: Probability in Action. (p. 1300)
Spoor, Mike, illus. see Bailey, Gerry & Law, Felicia.
Spoor, Mike, illus. see Bailey, Gerry.
Spoor, Mike, illus. see Kennemore, Tim.
Spoor, Mike, illus. see Law, Felicia & Way, Steve.
Spoor, Mike, illus. see Law, Felicia.
Spoor, Mike, illus. see O'Donnell, Liam.
Spoor, Mike, illus. see Taylor, Dereen.
Sporn, Jessica. Old Enough to do Good in the World. (p. 1645)
Sportouche, Thierry. De l'Autre Cote des Nuages. (p. 517)
Sports Illustrated for Kids Editors. 1st & 10: Top 10 Lists of Everything in Football (Revised & Updated) (p. 2546)
—All-Star Activity Book (a Sports Illustrated Kids Book) More Than 100 Games & Activities. (p. 53)
—Baseball: The 101 Stars Every Fan Needs to Know. (p. 168)
—Baseball - Then to Wow! (p. 168)
—Football. (p. 761)
—Hockey: Then to Wow! (p. 985)
—My First Book of Baseball: A Rookie Book. (p. 1542)
—My First Book of Football: A Rookie Book. (p. 1542)
—My First Book of Hockey. (p. 1542)
—My First Book of Lacrosse: A Rookie Book. (p. 1542)
—My First Book of Soccer: Mostly Everything Explained about the Game. (p. 1543)
—Sports Illustrated Kids Big Book of Who Basketball. (p. 2089)
—Sports Illustrated Kids Stats! The Greatest Numbers in Sports. (p. 2089)
—Top 10 of Everything in Sports. (p. 2262)
—Women Athletes Who Rule! The 101 Stars Every Fan Needs to Know. (p. 2486)
Spory, Sheila K., illus. see Heiser, Connie.
Spot 100, Spot 100. Spot 100 1970s Cars: A Spotter's Guide for Kids & Bigger Kids. (p. 2090)
—Spot 100 1980s Cars: A Spotter's Guide for Kids & Bigger Kids. (p. 2090)
—Spot 100 at Christmas: A Spotter's Guide for Kids & Bigger Kids. (p. 2090)
—Spot 100 Classic Vws: A Spotter's Guide for Kids & Bigger Kids. (p. 2090)
—Spot 100 Computers & Video Games: A Spotter's Guide for Kids & Bigger Kids. (p. 2090)
—Spot 100 Minis: A Spotter's Guide for Kids & Bigger Kids. (p. 2090)
Spoth, John Charles. Knight in Homespun (Classic Reprint) (p. 1228)
Spotswood, Jessica. Born Wicked. (p. 263)
—Last Summer of the Garrett Girls. (p. 1249)
—Sisters' Fate. (p. 2027)
—Tyranny of Petticoats. (p. 2311)
Spotswood, Jessica, jt. ed. see Sharpe, Tess.
Spotswood, Jessica, ed. Radical Element: 12 Stories of Daredevils, Debutantes & Other Dauntless Girls. (p. 1833)
—Radical Element: Twelve Stories of Daredevils, Debutantes, & Other Dauntless Girls. (p. 1833)
—Tyranny of Petticoats: 15 Stories of Belles, Bank Robbers & Other Badass Girls. (p. 2311)
Spottiswoode, Amanda. Silver Lining. March, Molly, illus. (p. 2019)
—Up in Arms March, Molly, illus. (p. 2337)
Spottiswoode, Sybil. Her Husband's Country (Classic Reprint) (p. 956)
Spottiswoode, William. Polarisation of Light. (p. 1770)
Spotts, Michele. Zotts & His Unfortunate Spotts. (p. 2544)
Spradlin, Amber L. Cow & the Magic Shoes. Clark, Linda McConeghy, illus. (p. 464)
—Princess, the Cow, & the Corn Maze. (p. 1799)
Spradlin, Leslie, illus. see Gilbert, Drexel.
Spradlin, Leslie, illus. see Thomas, J.D.
Spradlin, Michael. Keeper of the Grail: Book 1 (p. 1208)
—Orphan of Destiny (p. 1672)
—Trail of Fate: Book 2 (p. 2274)
Spradlin, Michael & Smith, Roland. Alamo. (p. 39)
Spradlin, Michael P. Close Calls: How Eleven US Presidents Escaped from the Brink of Death. (p. 407)
—Denali Storm: A 4D Book. Karkavelas, Spiros, illus. (p. 528)
—Enemy Above. (p. 650)
—Feeding Frenzy. (p. 718)
—Into the Killing Seas. (p. 1128)
—Jack & Jill Went up to Kill: A Book of Zombie Nursery Rhymes. Weigel, Jeff, illus. (p. 1151)
—Jack Montgomery: World War II: Gallantry at Anzio. (p. 1152)
—Leo Thorsness: Vietnam: Valor in the Sky. (p. 1267)
—Menace from the Deep. (p. 1447)
—Nile Chaos: A 4D Book. Karkavelas, Spiros, illus. (p. 1609)
—Orphan of Destiny. (p. 1672)
—Out for Blood. (p. 1682)
—Pararescue Corps (p. 1699)
—Pararescue Corps. Karkavelas, Spiros, illus. (p. 1699)
—Ryan Pitts: Afghanistan: a Firefight in the Mountains of Wanat. (p. 1918)
—Sandstorm Blast: A 4D Book. Karkavelas, Spiros, illus. (p. 1931)
—Ultimate Attack. (p. 2314)
—Viper Strike: A 4D Book. Karkavelas, Spiros, illus. (p. 2360)
Spradlin, Michael P., jt. auth. see Smith, Roland.
Spradlin, Michael P. & Smith, Roland. Alcatraz. (p. 41)
Spragg, Iain. Kylian Mbappe: the Ultimate Fan Book. (p. 1234)
Spragg, Patrick. KnightBeard. (p. 1228)
Sprague, Dorothy. Reflector, Vol. 12: November 1933 (Classic Reprint) (p. 1860)
Sprague, Homer B. Six Selections from Irving's Sketch-Book: With Notes, Questions, etc. for Home & School Use (Classic Reprint) (p. 2028)
Sprague, Homer Baxter, jt. auth. see Hillard, George Stillman.
Sprague, Howard Lee. Snowflake's Vacation. Borrajero, Judy, illus. (p. 2049)
Sprague, Isaac, jt. auth. see Gray, Asa.
Sprague, Lila Frost. Shadow People. (p. 1997)
Sprague, Lois, illus. see Pelley, Kathleen T.
Sprague, Miss E. Earnest Trifler (Classic Reprint) (p. 615)
Sprague, Roger. Flamingo's Nest: A Honolulu Story (Classic Reprint) (p. 746)
Sprague, Sarah E. Book One, Vol. 1: A Primer (Classic Reprint) (p. 260)
—Sprague Classic Reader, Vol. 4: Book Four, Part Two (Classic Reprint) (p. 2091)
—Sprague Classic Readers: Book Two. (p. 2091)
—Sprague Classic Readers: Book One, a Primer. (p. 2091)
—Sprague Classic Readers: Book Three (Classic Reprint) (p. 2091)
—Sprague Classic Readers, Vol. 2: Book Two (Classic Reprint) (p. 2091)
—Sprague Classic Readers, Vol. 4: Part One (Classic Reprint) (p. 2091)
—Sprague Classic Readers, Vol. 5 (Classic Reprint) (p. 2091)
Sprague, Shawn. Jackson & Franklin. (p. 1153)
Sprague, Terrell Eastman, illus. see Groover, David L. & Tchaikovsky, Peter Ilich.
Sprague, William C. Felice Constant, or the Master Passion: A Romance (Classic Reprint) (p. 719)
Spranger, Pete. Immigration to North America: Cuban Immigrants Anderson, Stuart, ed. (p. 1101)
Spratlin, J. L. Exciting Adventures of Eli, Cece, & Anderson the Ant - the Great Ant Hill Discovery. (p. 676)
Spratlin, Jennifer. Exciting Adventures of Eli, Cece, & Anderson the Ant: Anderson's Bounce. (p. 676)
Spratt, Dora E. W. Christmas Week at Bigler's Mill: A Sketch in Black & White (Classic Reprint) (p. 387)
Spratt, Niall & Meehan, Patrick. Shamrogues: First Challenge. (p. 1999)
Spratt, R. A. Accidental Blast-Off Nanny Piggins. (p. 10)
—Adventures of Nanny Piggins. Santat, Dan, illus. (p. 26)
—Big Trouble: a Friday Barnes Mystery. Gosier, Phil, illus. (p. 223)
—Danger Ahead. (p. 501)
—Friday Barnes 5: the Plot Thickens. (p. 785)
—Friday Barnes, Girl Detective. (p. 785)
—Friday Barnes, Girl Detective. Gosier, Phil, illus. (p. 785)
—Nanny Piggins: The Daring Rescue. (p. 1574)
—Nanny Piggins: The Rival Ringmaster. (p. 1574)
—Nanny Piggins & the Pursuit of Justice. (p. 1574)
—Nanny Piggins & the Race to Power. (p. 1574)
—Nanny Piggins & the Wicked Plan. (p. 1574)
—No Rules: a Friday Barnes Mystery. Gosier, Phil, illus. (p. 1614)
—Peski Kids: The Mystery of the Squashed Cockroach. (p. 1726)
—Peski Kids 2: Bear in the Woods. (p. 1726)
—Peski Kids 4: near Extinction. (p. 1726)
—Peski Kids 5: the Final Mission. (p. 1726)
—Stuck in the Mud. (p. 2143)
—Under Suspicion. Gosier, Phil, illus. (p. 2321)
Spratt, Sallie Brice. Hickory Log, 1925 (Classic Reprint) (p. 965)
Spray, Jami Lewis. Hiram Ulysses Aloysius Higgenbotham's Special Day. (p. 973)
Spray, John. Next Round: A Young Athlete's Journey to Gold. (p. 1600)
Spray, Sally. Awesome Engineering. (p. 144)
—Awesome Engineering Bridges. (p. 144)
—Awesome Engineering Skyscrapers. (p. 144)
—Awesome Engineering Spacecraft. (p. 144)
—Awesome Engineering Trains, Planes, & Ships. (p. 144)
Spreekmeester, Kevin, jt. auth. see Walters, Eric.
Spreen, Kathe, illus. see Kalar, Bonnie.
Spremulli, Pam. Letter Birds. (p. 1278)
Spremulli, Pam, illus. see Markey, Neil.
Spreng, Robert. Goin' Great in the Lone Star State. (p. 854)
Sprenger, A. Life of Mohammad, from Original Sources. (p. 1294)
Sprigge, S. Squire. Odd Issues (Classic Reprint) (p. 1637)
Spring, Bill, jt. auth. see Castle, Jennifer.
Spring, Gardiner. Essays on the Distinguishing Traits of Christian Character (Classic Reprint) (p. 663)
—Essays on the Distinguishing Traits of Christian Character, Vol. 5 (Classic Reprint) (p. 663)
Spring, Melanie. Practice Makes Perfect. (p. 1784)
—Turn It Up. (p. 2300)
Springate, Georgia. Beyond. (p. 211)
Springdale Elementary 5/6 Class, The Students Of Valerie Dockendorff's. What If ... Springvale (p. 2412)
Springer, Alice G., jt. auth. see Paolicchi, Daniel.
Springer, Audrey. Rusty's Gift. Richards, Kris, illus. (p. 1918)
Springer, Bessie W. Two Dicks: A Comedy in Two Acts (Classic Reprint) (p. 2307)
Springer, Cherish, illus. see Uhrich, Jeremy.
Springer, Helen E. Snap Shots from Sunny Africa (Classic Reprint) (p. 2045)
Springer, Jane, tr. see Machado, Ana Maria.
Springer, Jane, tr. see Starkoff, Vanina.
Springer, Jane, tr. Amazonia: Indigenous Tales from Brazil Popov, Nikolai, illus. (p. 67)
Springer, Kristina. Cotton Candy Wishes: A Swirl Novel. (p. 457)
—Espressologist. (p. 663)
—My Fake Boyfriend Is Better Than Yours. (p. 1538)
Springer, Lisa. Art & Culture of Ancient Egypt. (p. 120)
Springer, Lisa & Morris, Neil. Art & Culture of Ancient Egypt. (p. 120)
Springer, Mark. Beach. (p. 178)
Springer, Mary Elizabeth. Elizabeth Schuyler: A Story of Old New York (Classic Reprint) (p. 636)
—Lady Hancock: A Story of the American Revolution (Classic Reprint) (p. 1237)
Springer, Mary Jane. Story of Baby 'I' (p. 2129)
—Story of Baby 'I' Baby L. Springer, Mary Jane, illus. (p. 2129)
Springer, Nancy. Boy on a Black Horse. (p. 269)
—Case of the Bizarre Bouquets: An Enola Holmes Mystery. (p. 336)
—Case of the Cryptic Crinoline: An Enola Holmes Mystery. (p. 337)
—Case of the Gypsy Goodbye: An Enola Holmes Mystery. (p. 337)
—Case of the Gypsy Good-Bye (p. 337)
—Case of the Peculiar Pink Fan: An Enola Holmes Mystery. (p. 338)
—Enola Holmes: the Case of the Missing Marquess. (p. 655)
—Oddling Prince. (p. 1637)
—Possessing Jessie. (p. 1779)
Springer, Rebecca Ruter. Beechwood (Classic Reprint) (p. 189)
—Intra Muros (Classic Reprint) (p. 1128)
Springer, Sally, illus. see Burrows, Mark.
Springer, Sally, illus. see Slater, Teddy.
Springer, Sally, illus. see Stamper, Judith Bauer & Keyes, Joan Ross.
Springer, Sally, jt. auth. see Slater, Teddy.
Springer, Stephen. Zig Zag Zale. (p. 2540)
Springer, Susan Woodward. Misadventures of Seldovia Sam. Meissner, Amy, illus. (p. 1476)
Springer, T. S. Tyler Builds a Birdhouse. (p. 2310)
Springer, Thomas Grant. Bypath: A City Pastoral (Classic Reprint) (p. 306)
Springett, Isobel, photos by see Springett, Martin.
Springett, Martin. Breakfast on a Dragon's Tail: And Other Book Bites. (p. 278)
—Jousting with Jesters: An ABC for the Younger Dragon (p. 1184)
—Kate & Pippin: An Unlikely Love Story. Springett, Isobel, photos by. (p. 1204)
Springett, Martin, illus. see Thompson, Springett & Thompson, Richard.
Springfield, Pepper. Perfecto Pet Show. Caldwell, Kristy, illus. (p. 1723)
—Scout Camp (Bobs & Tweets #4) Caldwell, Kristy, illus. (p. 1963)
—Trick or Tweet. Caldwell, Kristy, illus. (p. 2287)
Springham, Sarah. Gozo Cat Detectives: Trilogy 2. Galea, Ryan & Taliana, Philip, illus. (p. 873)
Springhouse Publishing Company Staff, ed. see Powell, Robert, et al.
Springman, I. C. More. Lies, Brian, illus. (p. 1504)
Springsguth, Samuel. Fisher-Boy of Weymouth: To Which Are Added, the Pet Donkey, & the Sisters (Classic Reprint) (p. 741)
Springstubb, Tricia. Cody & the Fountain of Happiness. Wheeler, Eliza, illus. (p. 412)
—Cody & the Heart of a Champion. Wheeler, Eliza, illus. (p. 412)
—Cody & the Mysteries of the Universe. Wheeler, Eliza, illus. (p. 412)
—Cody & the Rules of Life. Wheeler, Eliza, illus. (p. 412)
—Every Single Second. Sudyka, Diana, illus. (p. 671)
—Khalil & Mr. Hagerty & the Backyard Treasures. Taherian, Elaheh, illus. (p. 1212)
—Mo Wren, Lost & Found. Ross, Heather, illus. (p. 1485)
—Moonpenny Island. (p. 1503)
—Moonpenny Island. Ford, Gilbert, illus. (p. 1503)
—Phoebe & Digger. Newman, Jeff, illus. (p. 1735)
—What Happened on Fox Street. Ross, Heather, illus. (p. 2411)
Sprinkel, Katy, jt. auth. see Boone, Mary.
Sprinkle, Eric & Evans, Sam. Adventure Devos: Youth Edition: Summer Camp Never Has to End When Your Devotional Takes You Adventuring All Year Long! (p. 18)
Sproles, Clay. Monster Bash: A Halloween Story. Russ, Lamont, illus. (p. 1495)
—Turkey's Thanksgiving Adventure: A Barnyard Tale. Russ, Lamont, illus. (p. 2300)
—Turkey's Thanksgiving Adventure. Russ, Lamont, illus. (p. 2300)
Sprott, Gary. King Cobra. (p. 1220)
—Western Diamondback Rattlesnake. (p. 2402)
Sproul, Avard C. Golden-Rod: May, 1905 (Classic Reprint) (p. 858)
Sproul, R. C. Barber Who Wanted to Pray. Fluharty, T. Lively, illus. (p. 165)
—Priest with Dirty Clothes. Gerard, Justin, illus. (p. 1792)
Sproule, Acquanetta M. Scamp. (p. 1941)
Sproule, Payton a. Immortuos. (p. 1101)
Sproulle, Maria. Max & Milky Make It to Mars. (p. 1427)
—Milky & Max Sail to Saturn. (p. 1467)
Sprouls, Bridget. Gnome at the Laundromat. Sprouls, Bridget, illus. (p. 845)
—Shore Buddies: A Guide to Making Friends at the Beach. Sprouls, Bridget, illus. (p. 2010)
Sprouse, Chris. Infinity Countdown Companion. (p. 1119)
—Star Wars: Age of the Rebellion - Heroes. (p. 2104)
—Star Wars: Age of the Rebellion - Villains. (p. 2104)
Sprouse, Chris, illus. see Coates, Ta-Nehisi.
Sprouse, Chris & Kirk, Leonard. Black Panther Book 5: Avengers of the New World Part 2. (p. 239)
Sprouse, Chris, et al. Amazing Spider-Man: Full Circle. (p. 66)
—Marvel Universe: Time & Again. (p. 1413)
Sprouse, Jackie. Orry & Izzy's Perfect Worm. (p. 1673)
Sproxton, Nick. Girl & the Mutant. (p. 835)
Spruill, Sonya, jt. auth. see Spruill, Edward L.
Sprunger, Reed. Albert Einstein: Brilliant Scientist (p. 40)
—Thomas Edison: Incredible Inventor (p. 2228)
Sprunger, Reed, illus. see Stille, Darlene R.
Sprunt, Hollie, ed. see Sprunt, Matt.
Sprunt, Matt. Ancient Amulet: Lumen Epic Fantasy Series Book 3. Sprunt, Hollie, ed. (p. 79)
Spruza, Janina. Color & Learn Golf! (p. 419)
—Coolest Golf Encyclopedia for Kids... And Even Adult Golf Beginners. (p. 450)
—Più Bella Enciclopedia Di Golf per Bambini... e Anche per Adulti Neofiti. (p. 1752)
Spudich, Giulietta. Amber Giant. (p. 67)
—Ice Giant. (p. 1087)
Spudvilas, Anne. Swan Lake. (p. 2167)
Spudvilas, Anne, illus. see Hartnett, Sonya.
Spunter, Bill. Fish from Head to Tail. (p. 741)
Spurgeon, Aaron, illus. see DiSiena, Laura Lyn & Eliot, Hannah.
Spurgeon, Aaron, illus. see Eliot, Hannah.
Spurgeon, Caroline F. E. Chaucer Devant la Critique en Angleterre et en France: Depuis Son Temps Jusqu'a Nos Jours (Classic Reprint) (p. 362)
Spurgeon, Charles. John Ploughman's Talk (Classic Reprint) (p. 1174)
Spurgeon, Charles H. John Ploughman's Pictures (Classic Reprint) (p. 1174)
—Treasury of David; Volume 5. (p. 2283)
Spurgeon, Hannah. Puppy Angels. (p. 1814)
Spurlin, Barbara & Bernhardt, Michael J. Jellyfish on the Menu. (p. 1163)
Spurll, Barbara, illus. see Metzger, Steve.
Spurll, Barbara, illus. see Moilel, Tololwa M.
Spurll, Barbara, illus. see Ruurs, Margriet.
Spurlock, Katelyn. Baby Bugs' Best Time. (p. 149)
Spurlock, Necole. Rocky & Rudy's Wild Adventure (p. 1896)
Spurr, Elizabeth. At the Beach Oliphant, Manelle, illus. (p. 130)
—Happy Sparkling Halloween. Madden, Colleen, illus. (p. 923)
—Happy Sparkling Hanukkah. Madden, Colleen, illus. (p. 923)
—In the Garden Oliphant, Manelle, illus. (p. 1109)
—In the Rain Oliphant, Manelle, illus. (p. 1110)
—In the Snow Oliphant, Manelle, illus. (p. 1111)
—In the Wind Oliphant, Manelle, illus. (p. 1111)
—In the Woods Oliphant, Manelle, illus. (p. 1112)
—Monsters, Mind Your Manners! Scales, Simon, illus. (p. 1498)
Spurr, George. G. Fight with a Grizzly Bear: A Story of Thrilling Interest (Classic Reprint) (p. 725)
—Land of Gold: A Tale of 49, Illustrative of Early Pioneer Life in California, & Founded upon Fact, Dedicated to California Pioneers (Classic Reprint) (p. 1241)
Spurr, Harry A. Mel; B. Spurr: His Life, Work, Writings, & Recitations (Classic Reprint) (p. 1442)
Spurrell, Chris. Turdsons: Tp's Revenge. Spurrell, Hailey, illus. (p. 2299)
Spurrell, Hailey, illus. see Spurrell, Chris.
Spykman, E. C. Terrible, Horrible Edie. (p. 2207)
Spyri, Johanna. Classic Starts(r): Heidi. Akib, Jamel, illus. (p. 400)
—Cornelli (Classic Reprint) (p. 454)
—Einer Vom Hause Lesa (Klassiker der Kinder- und Jugendliteratur) - Vollständige Ausgabe. (p. 629)
—Gesammelte Werke: Romane + Erzählungen + Briefe + Gedichte (28 Titel - Vollständige Ausgabe) (Band 1/2) (p. 823)
—Geschichten Für Kinder und Auch Für Solche, Welche Die Kinder Lieb Haben: Heimatlos + Moni + Heidi + Rosenresli + Was Die Großmutter Gelehrt Hat und Mehr (Vollständige Ausgabe Mit Illustrationen) Muhlmeister, Karl, illus. (p. 823)
—Gritli's Children a Story for Children & for Those Who Love Children (Classic Reprint) (p. 897)
—Heidi: A Story for Children & Those That Love Children (Classic Reprint) (p. 948)
—Heidi. (p. 948)
—Heidi. Carsey, Alice, illus. (p. 948)
—Heidi. Edwardes, Marian, tr. (p. 948)
—Heidi. Kirk, Maria L., illus. (p. 948)
—Heidi (Classic Reprint) (p. 948)
—Heidi (Weihnachtsedition) (p. 948)
—Heidi: Her Early Lessons & Travels. Bowman, Peter James, tr. (p. 948)
—Heidi, Her Years of Wandering & Learning: A Story for Children & Those Who Love Children (Classic Reprint) (p. 948)
—Heidis Lehr- und Wanderjahre. (p. 948)
—Heimatlos: Two Stories for Children, & for Those Who Love Children (Classic Reprint) (p. 948)
—How Wiseli Was Provided For' (p. 1046)
—In Sicherer Hut: das Abenteuer Auf der Alm (Vollständige Ausgabe) (p. 1107)
—Mazli (Classic Reprint) (p. 1431)
—Moni: The Goat-Boy (Classic Reprint) (p. 1493)
—Moni der Geibub (Classic Reprint) (p. 1493)
—Moni der Geißbub (Classic Reprint) (p. 1493)
—Moni the Goat-Boy (Classic Reprint) (p. 1493)
—Penguin Minis: Heidi. (p. 1716)
—Red-Letter Stories: Swiss Tales (Classic Reprint) (p. 1857)
—Rose Child (Classic Reprint) (p. 1905)
—Schloss Wildenstein (Gruselgeschichte Für Kinder) - Vollständige Ausgabe. (p. 1944)
—Story of Rico (Classic Reprint) (p. 2132)
—Toni: The Little Wood-Carver (Classic Reprint) (p. 2260)
—Uncle Titus & His Visit to the Country. (p. 2320)
—Veronica: And Other Friends Two Stories for Children. (p. 2352)
—Vom This, der Doch Etwas Wird. (p. 2367)
—Was der Grossmutter Lehre Bewirkt (Classic Reprint) (p. 2381)
—Weihnachten Mit Johanna Spyri: Die Beliebtesten Romane & Geschichten Aus Alpengebirge (Band 1/2) (p. 2396)
—Wo Gritlis Kinder Hingekommen Sind. (p. 2483)
Spyri, Johanna & Blaisdell, Robert. Heidi: Adapted for Young Readers. Kliros, Thea, illus. (p. 948)
Spyri, Johanna & Lacey, Mike. Heidi (p. 948)
Spyri, Johanna & Ladybird Books Staff. Heidi. Peluso, Martina, illus. (p. 948)
Spyri, Johanna & Wheelock, Lucy. Red-Letter Stories. (p. 1857)
Squair, John. Exercises in French Prose (Classic Reprint) (p. 676)
Square Pen Books. Color Me... Ninjas! (p. 420)
Squier, Emma-Lindsay. Wild Heart (Classic Reprint) (p. 2463)
Squier, Emma-Lindsay, jt. auth. see Stratton-Porter, Gene.
Squier, Robert. Follow the Drinking Gourd: An Underground Railroad Story (p. 758)
—Story of Cassiopeia: A Roman Constellation Myth (p. 2129)
Squier, Robert, illus. see Anderson, Kirsten & Who HQ.
Squier, Robert, illus. see Berendes, Mary.
Squier, Robert, illus. see Braun, Eric.
Squier, Robert, illus. see Capstone Press Staff.
Squier, Robert, illus. see Demuth, Patricia Brennan & Who HQ.
Squier, Robert, illus. see Frith, Margaret & Who HQ.
Squier, Robert, illus. see Frith, Margaret.
Squier, Robert, illus. see Herman, Gail & Who HQ.
Squier, Robert, illus. see Manzanero, Paula K. & Who HQ.

S

Stafford, Anita. Legend of Sassafras House. King-Morgan, Kristi, ed. (p. 1262)
Stafford, David W. In Defense of the Flag; a True War Story: A Pen Picture of Scenes & Incidents During the Great Rebellion; Thrilling Experiences During Escape from Southern Prisons, etc (Classic Reprint) (p. 1104)
Stafford, Gerry. Young Canaller. Wanecski, Erica Joan, illus. (p. 2530)
Stafford III, Garland E. Odd World of Krisenger Storm. (p. 1637)
Stafford, J. R. When Cattle Kingdom Fell (Classic Reprint) (p. 2429)
Stafford, James & Indovino, Shaina Carmel. Malta. (p. 1392)
Stafford, Jean. Elephi: The Cat with the High IQ. Blegvad, Erik, illus. (p. 635)
Stafford, Jordan, illus. see Gambini, Josephine.
Stafford, Jordan, illus. see Mitchell, Shirley Lipscomb.
Stafford, Justin & Odd Dot. Tiny World: Quilting! Stafford, Justin, illus. (p. 2250)
Stafford, Magdalen. Magdalen Stafford, or a Gleam of Sunshine on a Rainy Day (Classic Reprint) (p. 1376)
Stafford, Ruth. Lasell Leaves, Vol. 58: November 1932 (Classic Reprint) (p. 1246)
Stafford, Sara. Keeper of the Gate, or the Sleeping Giant of Lake Superior (Classic Reprint) (p. 1208)
Stafford, Susan. Pocket Pegasus. (p. 1764)
Stafford, Tiffany, illus. see Stafford, Anita.
Stagg, Benjamin & Stagg, Jacquelyn. Move Like Me - Around the Farm. (p. 1515)
Stagg, Jacquelyn. Kindness Starts with You. (p. 1219)
—Kindness Starts with You - at School. (p. 1219)
—My Hands Were Made for Helping. (p. 1549)
Stagg, John Cecil. King of the School, or Who Will Win? (Classic Reprint) (p. 1221)
Staggenborg, Kim, illus. see Woodfield, Elaine.
Staginnus, Dennis. Emerald Dagger. (p. 641)
—Raiders of Folklore Adventures: An Eye of Odin Prequel. (p. 1835)
Stagliano, Katie. Katie's Cabbage. Heid, Karen, illus. (p. 1206)
Stagnaro, Angelo. Catechist's Magic Kit: 80 Simple Tricks for Teaching Catholicism to Kids. Pryor, Sean, illus. (p. 344)
Stahl, Albert W. Transmission of Power by Wire Ropes (Classic Reprint) (p. 2278)
Stahl, Asa. Big Bang Book. Allen-Fletcher, Carly, illus. (p. 216)
Stahl, Bethany, illus. see Andrus, Kendra.
Stahl, Jon. Dragons Eat Noodles on Tuesdays. Bentley, Tadgh, illus. (p. 595)
Stahl, L. G. Kindergarten: A Boon to Mothers & Teachers on Rainy Days (Classic Reprint) (p. 1218)
Stahl, Miriam Klein, jt. auth. see Schatz, Kate.
Stahl, Nancy. Adventures of Benjamin & Daisy. (p. 21)
Stahl, P. -J. Butterfly Chase (Classic Reprint) (p. 304)
Stahl, Stephanie. Best Snowman Ever. Vasylenko, Veronica, illus. (p. 207)
Stahl, Susan Snyder, jt. auth. see Whitzel, J. a.
Stahl, Todd, illus. see Binder, Bettina.
Stahlberg, Carina, illus. see Lewis, Anne G.
Stahlberg, Carina, illus. see Rydaker, Ewa.
Stahlberg, L. R. Three Musketeers. Cabrera, Eva, illus. (p. 2234)
Stahlberg, L. R. & Peters, Stephanie True. Graphic Revolve: Common Core Editions. Cabrera, Eva & Cano, Fern, illus. (p. 880)
Stahler, David, Jr. Spinning Out. (p. 2082)
Stainero, Giacomo. Perito Arithmetico, e Geometrico (Classic Reprint) (p. 1723)
Staines, Bill. All God's Critters. Nelson, Kadir, illus. (p. 52)
Staines, Sandra. Funny Ha Ha: Rhymes, Riddles & Jokes. (p. 801)
—Wobbly Monsters Coloring Book. (p. 2483)
Staino, Franco. Adventures of Pinocchio (p. 26)
Stainton, Keris. Lily & the Christmas Wish. (p. 1302)
Stainton, Sue. I Love Cats! Staake, Bob, illus. (p. 1069)
—I Love Dogs! Staake, Bob, illus. (p. 1069)
—I Love Dogs. Truesdell, Sue, illus. (p. 1069)
Stair, Grace. Bird of Passage (Classic Reprint) (p. 230)
Stair, Nancy L. Choosing a Career in Mortuary Science & the Funeral Industry. (p. 381)
—Michelle Yeoh. (p. 1458)
Stair, Nancy L., jt. auth. see Wolfe, James.
Staker, Sara. My Baptism Keepsake. (p. 1531)
Stakes, Mary E., jt. auth. see Jackson, Edwin L.
Stalcup, Ann. America's Secret Weapon: Navajo Code Talkers of World War II. (p. 75)
Stalder, Päivi. My Wish Tonight. Wolferman, Iris, illus. (p. 1565)
Staley, Erin. 10 Great Makerspace Projects Using Science. (p. 2549)
—Career Building Through Creating Mobile Apps. (p. 328)
—Careers in Hospitality (p. 330)
—Coping with Sexual Consent (p. 451)
—Defeating Stress & Anxiety (p. 525)
—Grace Murray Hopper (p. 873)
—I'm an Undocumented Immigrant, Now What? (p. 1097)
—Improving Community Health & Safety Through Service Learning (p. 1103)
—Laverne Cox. (p. 1253)
—Maggie Stiefvater. (p. 1376)
—Martin Luther King Jr. & the Speech That Inspired the World. (p. 1411)
—Misty Copeland: Principal Ballerina. (p. 1483)
—Most Influential Female Activists. (p. 1508)
—Nick Swinmurn, Tony Hsieh, & Zappos. (p. 1602)
—Vloggers & Vlogging. (p. 2364)
—What Is Animal Camouflage? (p. 2414)
Staley, G. M., jt. auth. see Kitty, A. T.
Stalfelt, Pernilla. ¿Quién Eres? un Libro Sobre la Tolerancia. (p. 1827)
Stalick, Garyanna. Cocoa's Collar Goodwin, Wendy, illus. (p. 411)
Stalio, Ivan, illus. see Hillert, Margaret.
Stalker, Aileen. One & Only Sam: A Story Explaining Idioms for Children with Asperger Syndrome & Other Communication Difficulties. Spencer, Bob, illus. (p. 1658)
Stallard, Katharine. Focus, Vol. 9: May, 1920 (Classic Reprint) (p. 756)
Stallinga, Jeff. Cross Training. (p. 478)
Stallings, Bree, illus. see Ball, Liz.
Stallings, Gary. Mario's Golden Locket. (p. 1406)
Stallings, Jean. Until the Sky Turns Silver. Forde, Winston, ed. (p. 2336)
Stallings, Laurence. Big Parade (Classic Reprint) (p. 222)
Stallings, Mary. Fuzzy Faith. (p. 803)
Stallings, Ray. Aggies: October, 1927 (Classic Reprint) (p. 35)
—Aggies, Vol. 2: February 1928 (Classic Reprint) (p. 35)
Stallings, Robert. Aggies, Vol. 3: January, 1929 (Classic Reprint) (p. 35)
—Aggies, Vol. 3: October, 1928 (Classic Reprint) (p. 35)
Stallings, Sylvia. Title: Fall, 1946 (Classic Reprint) (p. 2251)
Stallwood, Charles. Senior Booster: January, 1930 (Classic Reprint) (p. 1988)
Stallybrass, James S. Annals of the Poor (Classic Reprint) (p. 98)
Sta.Maria, Ian, illus. see Caputo, Antonella, et al.
Stamatakis, Stella. What's a Yia Yia? A Book about Grandmothers. (p. 2423)
Stamatiadi, Daniela, illus. see Elvgren, Jennifer.
Stamato, Fátima, illus. see Stamm, Linda J.
Stamaty, Mark Alan. Alia's Mission: Saving the Books of Iraq. (p. 44)
Stamaty, Mark Alan, illus. see Asch, Frank.
Stamer, W. Gentleman Emigrant, Vol. 1 Of 2: His Daily Life, Sports, & Pastimes in Canada, Australia & the United States (Classic Reprint) (p. 816)
Stamey, De Keller. Junction of Laughter & Tears. (p. 1189)
Stamford, Tasha. Monet (p. 1492)
Stamm, Linda J. Family Stew for Dads: Building a Family with an Egg Donor & Surrogate. Stamato, Fátima, illus. (p. 703)
—Lilly & Zander: A Children's Story about Equine-Assisted Activities. Whitaker, Suzanne, illus. (p. 1301)
—Phoebe's Family: A Story about Egg Donation. Clipp, Joan, illus. (p. 1735)
—Scarlett's Story: A Tale about Embryo Donation. Clipp, Joan, illus. (p. 1942)
Stamm, Stephanie. Gift of Wings. (p. 832)
Stammen, Jo Ellen McAllister, illus. see Spinelli, Eileen.
Stammen, JoEllen McAllister, illus. see Mason, Cherie.
Stammschroer, Danielle, illus. see Pontefract, Michelle.
Stamp, Anne. Enchanted Bus: Lily & the Lost Soldiers. Collins, Simon, illus. (p. 646)
Stamp, Jorgen. Flying High. (p. 755)
Stamper, C. W. What I Know: Reminiscences of Five Years Personal Attendance upon His Late Majesty King Edward the Seventh (Classic Reprint) (p. 2412)
Stamper, Claire. Color by Numbers: Adding & Subtracting. (p. 419)
—Color by Numbers: Dinosaurs. (p. 419)
—Color by Numbers: Times Tables. (p. 419)
—Color by Numbers: Wild Animals. (p. 419)
—Magical Unicorn Color by Numbers. (p. 1380)
—Search & Find: Animals. (p. 1970)
—Search & Find: Dinosaurs. (p. 1970)
Stamper, Claire, illus. see Allen, Kathy.
Stamper, Claire, jt. auth. see Doyle, Lizzy.
Stamper, Claire, et al. Pocket Fun: Unicorn Activity Book. (p. 1764)
Stamper, Judith. Polar Bear Patrol. Haefele, Steve, illus. (p. 1769)
—Voyage to the Volcano. Speirs, John, illus. (p. 2368)
Stamper, Judith, jt. auth. see Stamper, Judith Bauer.
Stamper, Judith Bauer. Buildings, Buildings, Buildings. (p. 295)
—Caves. (p. 347)
—Earthquakes. (p. 618)
—Eco Dogs. (p. 623)
—Growing Trees. Lowe, Wesley, illus. (p. 899)
—House, Sweet House. (p. 1024)
—Quinceañera. Varma, Ishan, illus. (p. 1828)
—Ragdolls: Alien Cats. (p. 1834)
—Rocks & Minerals. (p. 1896)
—Sam Helps Recycle. (p. 1926)
—Text-Marking Lessons for Active Nonfiction Reading: Reproducible Nonfiction Passages with Lessons That Guide Students to Read Strategically, Identify Text Structures, & Activate Comprehension. (p. 2210)
—Tree Is For- (p. 2284)
—Volcanoes. (p. 2366)
—Who Wears What? (p. 2452)
Stamper, Judith Bauer & Willows, Vicky. Fossils. (p. 771)
Stamper, Phil. Gravity of Us. (p. 882)
Stamper, Terri Dunn. Never Give Up. (p. 1590)
Stamper, Vesper. Cloud of Outrageous Blue. (p. 408)
—What the Night Sings. (p. 2420)
Stampler, Ann Redisch. Afterparty. (p. 34)
—Cats on Ben Yehuda Street Carabelli, Francesca, illus. (p. 346)
—How to Disappear. (p. 1039)
—Where It Began. (p. 2439)
—Wooden Sword. Liddiment, Carol, illus. (p. 2491)
Stampler, Laura. Little Black Dresses, Little White Lies. (p. 1311)
Stamponi, Florencia. Animales a Jugar. (p. 92)
—Practico la Cursiva. (p. 1784)
—Practico la Imprenta Mayúscula. (p. 1784)
Stamponi, Florencia, jt. auth. see Rigiroli, Victoria.
Stamps, Rich, ed. see Stamps, Sarah.
Stamps, Sarah. In the Hills of Arkansas. Stamps, Rich, ed. (p. 1109)
Stampy (Joseph Garrett), Stampy (Joseph. Stick with Stampy! Sticker Book. (p. 2117)
Stan, Adrianna. Letters. (p. 1279)
Stan E Hughes Aka Ha-Gue-A-Dees-Sas. Adventures of Sofia - Warrior Princess. (p. 28)
Stanard, Mary Newton. Dreamer: A Romantic Rendering of the Life-Story of Edgar Allan Poe by Stanard. (p. 602)
—Dreamer: A Romantic Rendering, of the Life-Story of Edgar Allan Poe (Classic Reprint) (p. 602)
Stanborough, Rebecca. 25 Mujeres Que Gobernaron. (p. 2554)
—25 Women Who Dared to Compete. (p. 2554)
—25 Women Who Dared to Create. (p. 2554)
—Exploring the South. (p. 683)
—Golden Gate Bridge. (p. 857)
—Great Pyramid of Giza. (p. 888)
—Great Wall of China. (p. 890)
—Sexual Harassment in the Age Of #MeToo: Crossing the Line. (p. 1995)
—She/He/They/Them: Understanding Gender Identity. (p. 2005)
—Women's Suffrage Time Capsule: Artifacts of the Movement for Voting Rights. (p. 2488)
Stanborough, Rebecca, jt. auth. see Stefoff, Rebecca.
Stanborough, Rebecca J. 25 Women Who Ruled. (p. 2554)
Stanbury, Emily, illus. see Cooper, V. I. X. J.
Stanbury, Emily, illus. see Wall, Jessie.
Stanchfield, Joni. Hazel's Adventures Living with Grandma. Atkinson, Katie, illus. (p. 941)
Stanchfield, Justin. Timewalker. (p. 2247)
Stanciulescu, Diana, illus. see Terbush, Tom.
Stancliff, David. Lee y Juega: Es Tiempo para Amar y Reír Mazali, Gustavo, illus. (p. 1261)
Stancliff, Guy David, jt. auth. see Zondervan.
Stancliffe, Bethany, illus. see Rinker, Jessica.
Standard, Carole K. Arizona. (p. 116)
Standard Publishing Staff. Bible Puzzles for Kids, Ages 6-8. (p. 213)
—Church Programs for Special Days: Plays, Poems, & Ideas for 10 Celebrations! (p. 390)
—God Loves Me Coloring Pages: For Toddlers & 2s. Bausman, Mary, illus. (p. 851)
Standard Publishing Staff & Bookworks Staff. Tell Me about Easter. (p. 2201)
Standiford, Natalie. Boy on the Bridge. (p. 269)
—Confessions of the Sullivan Sisters. (p. 439)
—Countdown (p. 459)
—Only Girl in School: a Wish Novel. (p. 1664)
—Secret Tree. (p. 1979)
—Switched at Birthday. (p. 2171)
—Switched at Birthday: a Wish Novel. (p. 2171)
Standing, Arthur F. One Man's Life: A Memoir. McRae, Dee, ed. (p. 1660)
Standing, Ian, illus. see Mason, P. Harry.
Standing, Jonathan. Through the Wall. (p. 2237)
Standish, Ali. August Isle. (p. 136)
—Bad Bella. (p. 157)
—Ethan I Was Before. (p. 666)
—How to Disappear Completely. (p. 1039)
Standish, Burt L. Frank Merriwell at Yale (Classic Reprint) (p. 777)
—Frank Merriwell down South. (p. 777)
—Frank Merriwell down South (Classic Reprint) (p. 777)
—Frank Merriwell in Camp (Classic Reprint) (p. 777)
—Frank Merriwell's Bravery (Classic Reprint) (p. 777)
—Frank Merriwell's Brother or the Greatest Triumph of All (Classic Reprint) (p. 777)
—Frank Merriwell's Champions (Classic Reprint) (p. 777)
—Frank Merriwell's Chums (Classic Reprint) (p. 777)
—Frank Merriwell's Courage (Classic Reprint) (p. 777)
—Frank Merriwell's Daring (Classic Reprint) (p. 777)
—Frank Merriwell's Faith (Classic Reprint) (p. 777)
—Frank Merriwell's False Friend: A Story for Boys (Classic Reprint) (p. 777)
—Frank Merriwell's Foes (Classic Reprint) (p. 777)
—Frank Merriwell's Hunting Tour (Classic Reprint) (p. 777)
—Frank Merriwell's Lads, or the Boys Who Got Another Chance (Classic Reprint) (p. 777)
—Frank Merriwell's Power: A Story for Boys (Classic Reprint) (p. 777)
—Frank Merriwell's Pursuit: How to Win. (p. 777)
—Frank Merriwell's Races (Classic Reprint) (p. 777)
—Frank Merriwell's Return to Yale (Classic Reprint) (p. 777)
—Frank Merriwell's Reward (Classic Reprint) (p. 777)
—Frank Merriwell's School Days (Classic Reprint) (p. 777)
—Frank Merriwell's Secret (Classic Reprint) (p. 777)
—Frank Merriwell's Setback: A Story for Boys (Classic Reprint) (p. 777)
—Frank Merriwell's Skill (Classic Reprint) (p. 777)
—Frank Merriwell's Sports Afield (Classic Reprint) (p. 777)
—Frank Merriwell's Trip West (Classic Reprint) (p. 777)
—Frank Merriwell's Victories (Classic Reprint) (p. 777)
—Lefty o' the Big League (Classic Reprint) (p. 1261)
—Lefty o' the Bush (Classic Reprint) (p. 1261)
—Making of a Big Leaguer (Classic Reprint) (p. 1389)
Standish, Joyce, ed. Adventures of Ryan Lincoln. Cooper, Nicole, illus. (p. 27)
Standish, Marilyn, jt. auth. see Landes, William-Alan.
Standish, Winn. Jack Lorimer's Champions, or Sports on Land & Lake (Classic Reprint) (p. 1152)
Standke, Linda. Bible Colors & Shapes Fun! (p. 213)
—Bible Dot to Dots ABCs. (p. 213)
—Bible Printing Fun! (p. 213)
Standley, Leigh, illus. see Gates, Mariam.
Stanek, Jack. Space Kitty: The Original. (p. 2071)
Stanek, Linda. Beco's Big Year: A Baby Elephant Turns One. (p. 187)
—Erase un Elefante Bersani, Shennen, illus. (p. 659)
—Once upon an Elephant Bersani, Shennen, illus. (p. 1658)
—Rêves de Guépard. Troff, Sophie, tr. (p. 1873)
Stanek, Linda & Bersani, Shennen. Sueño con Chitas. Bersani, Shennen, illus. (p. 2147)
Stanek, Robert, pseud. Adventures with Letters & Words (Buster Bee's Learning Series #1, the Bugville Critters) (p. 30)
—Break Their Bad Habits: (the Bugville Critters, Lass's Adventures Series #2) (p. 278)
—Break Their Bad Habits. (p. 278)
—Bugville Critters & Catching a Cup of Sunshine. (p. 292)
—Bugville Critters & Every Day Is Different. (p. 292)
—Bugville Critters Explore the Solar System. (p. 292)
—Bugville Critters Go to Camp. (p. 292)
—Bugville Critters Remember Their Manners. (p. 292)
—Bugville Critters Save Their Allowance. (p. 292)
—Bugville Critters So Many Lessons to Learn. (p. 292)
—Bugville Critters Start Summer Vacation. (p. 292)
—Bugville Critters Visit the Library. (p. 292)
—Catching a Cup of Sunshine. (p. 344)
—Every Day Is Different. (p. 670)
—Explore the Solar System. (p. 680)
—Go to Camp. (p. 848)
—Have a Backyard Picnic. (p. 939)
—Have a Bad Day. (p. 939)
—Have a Surprise Party. (p. 939)
—Have Trouble at School. (p. 939)
—Into the Stone Land. (p. 1128)
—Kingdoms & the Elves of the Reaches IV. (p. 1222)
—Reinos y los Elfos de las Quimeras III. (p. 1862)
—Reinos y los Elfos de las Quimeras IV. (p. 1862)
—Remember Their Manners. (p. 1864)
—Rise of the Fallen: Dawn of the Ages. (p. 1885)
—Save Their Allowance. (p. 1938)
—Start Summer Vacation. (p. 2107)
—Stay after School. (p. 2109)
—Visit City Hall. (p. 2362)
—Visit the Library. (p. 2362)
Stanek, Rose. Little Love. (p. 1321)
Stanek, William, see Stanek, Robert, pseud.
Stanek, William, see Stanek, Robert, pseud.
Stanfield, James, ed. see Walker-Hirsch, Leslie & Champagne, Marklyn.
Stanfield, Michael. Bucky & Becky - the Magic of Wigglepoo Mountain. (p. 289)
Stanford, Cody L. Sinews of the Heart. (p. 2023)
Stanford, Dewayne. Everyday Is Not a Rainy Day. (p. 671)
Stanford, Elisa, jt. auth. see Basaluzzo, Constanza.
Stanford, Halle, jt. auth. see Allen, Elise.
Stanford, Michael K. Archive, Vol. 89: Fall 1976 (Classic Reprint) (p. 111)
Stanford, Sara. Minecraft Master Builder: Dragons: A Step-By-step Guide to Creating Your Own Dragons. (p. 1471)
—Minecraft Master Builder-Dinosaurs. (p. 1471)
Stanford, Sarah. Minecraft Master Builder: Monsters. (p. 1471)
Stang, L. Adventures with the Akranoids. (p. 30)
Stange, Albert. Die Zeitalter der Chemie in Wort und Bild (Classic Reprint) (p. 544)
Stangeland, Karin Michaelis. Governor (Classic Reprint) (p. 873)
Stanger, Theophil. Mr. Pickett of Detroit (Classic Reprint) (p. 1520)
Stanghini, Simone, illus. see Amiti, Loreley.
Stangl, Katrin. Strong As a Bear. (p. 2142)
Stangl, Sonja, illus. see Crawford, Leslie.
Stanhope, Charles Lewis Meryon Hester Lu. Memoirs of the Lady Hester Stanhope, Vol. 2 of 3 (Classic Reprint) (p. 1445)
Stanhope, Marianne Spencer. Almack's, Vol. 1 Of 2: A Novel (Classic Reprint) (p. 57)
Stanic Rasin, Irena. When Hen Was on Her Way to Market: A Folktale-Inspired Story of Manners. Rasin, Ivana, illus. (p. 2430)
—When Hen Was on Her Way to Market: A Folktale-Inspired Story of Manners & Nursery Rhyme. Rasin, Ivana, illus. (p. 2430)
Staniford, Linda. Ambulances to the Rescue Around the World. (p. 68)
—Clothes. (p. 407)
—Firefighters to the Rescue Around the World. (p. 734)
—Food & Drink. (p. 759)
—From Farm to Fork: Where Does My Food Come From? (p. 791)
—How Do Animals Give Us Food? (p. 1028)
—Place to Live. (p. 1753)
—Police to the Rescue Around the World. (p. 1770)
—Rescue at Sea Around the World. (p. 1868)
—To the Rescue! (p. 2253)
—Where Do Grains Come From? (p. 2436)
—Where Do Vegetables Come From? (p. 2436)
—Where Does Fruit Come From? (p. 2436)
Staniland, C., illus. see Leslie, Emma.
Staninger Riet-1, Hildegarde. Cricket the K-Town Kitty. (p. 474)
Stanisha, Terésa (Tracey). Especially for Rachel - Butterflies Abound. (p. 662)
Stanislaus. Life of the Viscountess de Bonnault D'Houet: Foundress of the Society of the Faithful Companions of Jesus, 1781-1858 (Classic Reprint) (p. 1295)
Staniszewski, Anna. Dirt Diary. (p. 552)
—Dogosaurus Rex. Hawkes, Kevin, illus. (p. 577)
—Finders Reapers. (p. 729)
—Gossip File. (p. 872)
—I'm with Cupid. (p. 1099)
—Magic Mirror (p. 1378)
—Match Me If You Can. (p. 1420)
—My Epic Fairy Tale Fail. (p. 1538)
—My Sort of Fairy Tale Ending. (p. 1561)
—My Very Unfairy Tale Life. (p. 1564)
—Once upon a Cruise: a Wish Novel. (p. 1657)
—Prank List. (p. 1785)
—Secondhand Wishes. (p. 1974)
—Stolen Slipper (p. 2120)
—Truth Game. (p. 2297)
—Wonder of Wildflowers. (p. 2489)
Stanitsas, Margaux. I Like Art: Rococo. (p. 1067)
—I Like Art: Baroque. (p. 1067)
—I Like Art: Realism. (p. 1067)
—I Like Art: Renaissance. (p. 1067)
—I Like Art: Romanticism. (p. 1067)
—I Like Art: Neoclassical. (p. 1067)
—I Like Art: Expressionism. (p. 1067)
—I Like Art: Impressionism. (p. 1067)
Stankavage, Scott. God Always Has a Plan: The Birth Story of Infants Leo, Ella, Jordan, & Madison. (p. 850)
Stankiewicz, Steven, illus. see Kenney, Karen Latchana.
Stanler, Marina, tr. see Pere, Tuula.
Stanley, Arthur Penrhyn. Suggestions for an Improvement of the Examination Statute. (p. 2147)
Stanley, Brenda. I Am Nuchu. (p. 1059)

Stanley, Caleb & Dennis, Austin. Alternative: Awaken Your Dream, Unite Your Community & Live in Hope (p. 60)
Stanley, Caroline Abbot. Keeper of the Vineyard: A Tale of the Ozarks (Classic Reprint) (p. 1208)
—Modern Madonna (Classic Reprint) (p. 1487)
—Order No. 11: A Tale of the Border (Classic Reprint) (p. 1669)
—Their Christmas Golden Wedding (Classic Reprint) (p. 2215)
Stanley, Charles. Every Day with Jesus: 365 Devotions for Kids (p. 670)
—Spirit-Filled Life: Discover the Joy of Surrendering to the Holy Spirit. (p. 2083)
Stanley, David. Kanga Santa. Stanley, Stephen, illus. (p. 1202)
—Multiple Monkeys. (p. 1525)
Stanley, David J. Lovely Day for Knitting. (p. 1362)
Stanley, Diane. Ada Lovelace, Poet of Science: The First Computer Programmer. Hartland, Jessie, illus. (p. 14)
—Chosen Prince. (p. 382)
—Cup & the Crown. (p. 485)
—Joplin, Wishing. (p. 1177)
—Princess of Cortova. (p. 1798)
—Resist! Peaceful Acts That Changed Our World. (p. 1869)
—Saving Sky. (p. 1939)
—Silver Bowl. (p. 2019)
—Stanley Mid Grade Novel #11. (p. 2101)
Stanley, Diane & Vennema, Peter. Bard of Avon: the Story of William Shakespeare. Stanley, Diane, illus. (p. 166)
Stanley, Edmund. Apple Blossoms & Other Stories: Compiled for Culture & Nature Studies As Outlined in the Course of Study for the Public Schools of Kansas (Classic Reprint) (p. 106)
Stanley, Eleanor. Twenty Years at Court: From the Correspondence of the Hon. Eleanor Stanley, Maid of Honour to Her Late Majesty Queen Victoria, 1842-1862 (Classic Reprint) (p. 2304)
Stanley, Evan, illus. see Flynn, Ian.
Stanley, Gemma, illus. see Kent, R. W.
Stanley, George. Dash. (p. 508)
Stanley, George E. Night Fires. (p. 1605)
—Teddy Kennedy: Lion of the Senate. Faricy, Patrick, illus. (p. 2198)
—Third-Grade Detectives Mystery Masters Collection Murdocca, Salvatore, illus. (p. 2222)
Stanley, Glen F. & Porterfield, Jason. Insider's Guide to Baseball. (p. 1124)
Stanley, Glen F. & Wesley, Ann. Gymnastics: Girls Rocking It (p. 907)
Stanley, Harriet Howard. 550 Children's Books: A Purchase List for Public Libraries (Classic Reprint) (p. 2560)
—Something to Read for Boys & Girls (Classic Reprint) (p. 2061)
Stanley, Heather, illus. see Downing, Johnette.
Stanley, Henry M. My Dark Companions: And Their Strange Stories (Classic Reprint) (p. 1536)
Stanley, Henry Morton. My Kalulu, Prince, King & Slave. (p. 1550)
—My Kalulu, Prince, King, & Slave: A Story of Central Africa (Classic Reprint) (p. 1550)
Stanley, Jane. New Face at the Door, Vol. 1 of 2 (Classic Reprint) (p. 1593)
Stanley, Jo. Play Like a Girl: Dream Team. (p. 1759)
Stanley, John. Idaho: Past & Present. (p. 1089)
—Melvin Monster (p. 1443)
—Melvin Monster: The John Stanley Library (p. 1443)
Stanley, John & Seth. Nancy: Volume 1: The John Stanley Library (p. 1574)
Stanley, Joseph. Big Dipper. (p. 219)
—Delaware (Lenape) (p. 526)
—Grizzly Bear (p. 897)
—Half-Dollars! (p. 910)
—Is It Flat or Is It Solid? Identify & Describe Shapes. (p. 1137)
—John F. Kennedy Assassination: The Shooting That Shook America. (p. 1172)
—Little Dipper. (p. 1315)
—Magnet Magic! (p. 1381)
—Radiant Rubies. (p. 1833)
—Wampanoag (p. 2374)
—What's Freedom of Religion? (p. 2423)
Stanley, Joseph & Jeffries, Joyce. I Learn from My Dad. (p. 1067)
Stanley, Juliet. Minecraft Master Builder: Time Machine. (p. 1471)
—Minecraft Master Builder World Tour: Create Your Own Minecraft Masterpieces from Around the World. (p. 1471)
Stanley, Juliet & Green, Jonathan. Ultimate Minecraft Master Builder: Step-by-Steps & Top Tips to Create 30 Awesome Builds! (p. 2315)
Stanley, Juliet, et al. Minecraft Master Builder Toolkit. (p. 1471)
Stanley, Karen. My Great Granny Moo. (p. 1549)
—Wild Goose Chase. Watson, Mia & Burchell, Scott, illus. (p. 2463)
Stanley, Malaika Rose. Baby Ruby Bawled. Wilson-Max, Ken, illus. (p. 152)
—Miss Bubble's Troubles. Smith, Jan, illus. (p. 1478)
Stanley, Mandy. Arty Friends: Early Learning Through Art. (p. 124)
—Arty Friends. (p. 124)
—Arty Numbers: Early Learning Through Art. (p. 124)
—Arty Numbers Wipe Clean. (p. 124)
—Arty Words. (p. 124)
—Arty Words Wipe Clean. (p. 124)
—Arty World. (p. 124)
—At the Beach. (p. 130)
—At the Zoo. (p. 131)
—Busy Bear's Counting. (p. 302)
—First Words. (p. 740)
—In the Park. (p. 1110)
—Jack & Jill & Other Nursery Favourites. (p. 1151)
—My First English-Spanish Library. (p. 1544)
—My First Mandarin Word Book. (p. 1545)
—My First Spanish Word Book. (p. 1546)
—On the Farm. (p. 1654)
—On the Move. (p. 1655)
—Stencils. (p. 2114)
—Who Tickled Tilly? (p. 2450)
Stanley, Mandy, illus. see Bedford, David.
Stanley, Mandy, illus. see Davidson, Alice Joyce.
Stanley, Mandy, illus. see George, Joshua.
Stanley, Mandy, illus. see Hawksley, Gerald.
Stanley, Mandy, illus. see McKain, Kelly.
Stanley, Maria Josepha. Early Married Life of Maria Josepha, Lady Stanley: With Extracts from Sir John Stanley's Praeeterita (Classic Reprint) (p. 615)
Stanley, Mary. Bruno, Peanut & Me. (p. 288)
Stanley, Monica M. My Diary in Serbia: April 1, 1915-Nov; 1, 1915 (Classic Reprint) (p. 1537)
Stanley, Sanna, illus. see McKissack, Patricia.
Stanley, Shalanda. Drowning Is Inevitable. (p. 606)
—Nick & June Were Here. (p. 1602)
Stanley, Sharon. Haiku, Do You? (p. 909)
—Tootsie Mcpeezalot. Foster, Jack, illus. (p. 2262)
Stanley, Sharon P. Olive Ann. Dragony, Barbara, illus. (p. 1649)
—Why Are the Donkeys Dirty? Dragony, Barbara, illus. (p. 2455)
Stanley, Shelli A. Earthworms Don't Like Pickles, Do They ? (p. 619)
Stanley, Stephanie. Santa's Greatest Gift. (p. 1933)
Stanley, Stephen. City of Lost Mazes. (p. 395)
—Haunted Maze. (p. 938)
—Stephen Stanley's Puzzle Animals. (p. 2115)
—Stephen Stanley's Puzzle Body. (p. 2115)
—Stephen Stanley's Puzzle Kingdoms. (p. 2115)
Stanley, Stephen, illus. see Stanley, David.
Stanley, Susan, illus. see McNamara, Joni Lundin.
Stanley, Susan, illus. see Scaling, Sam T.
Stanley, Wallace P. Our Week Afloat, or How We Explored the Pequonset River (Classic Reprint) (p. 1681)
STANLEY(r) Jr. & Peterson, Chris. Stanley Jr. Woodworking Is Awesome: Projects, Skills, & Ideas for Young Makers - 12 Fun DIY Projects for Ages 8+ (p. 2101)
Stanley-Baker, Penelope, ed. see Beaumont, Oliver.
Stanley-Baker, Penelope, tr. see de Hugo, Pierre & Bour, Laura.
Stanley-Baker, Penelope, tr. see Delafosse, Claude.
Stanley-Baker, Penelope, tr. see Fuhr, Ute, et al.
Stanley-Baker, Penelope, tr. see Peyrols, Sylvaine, et al.
Stanmyer, Jackie F. Jesse Owens: Facing down Hitler. (p. 1165)
Stanmyre, Jackie F. Althea Gibson & Arthur Ashe. (p. 60)
—Coretta Scott King & the Center for Nonviolent Social Change. (p. 454)
—Supporting Groups That Fight for Fairness & Equity. (p. 2162)
—Unification & Reunification of Germany. (p. 2329)
Stanmyre, Jackie F., jt. auth. see King, David C.
Stanmyre, Jackie Friedman. Cam Newton: Trying to Win Them All. (p. 313)
Stannard, M. Memoirs of a Professional Lady Nurse (Classic Reprint) (p. 1444)
Stannard, Russell. www.Here-I-Am. Pugh, Jonathan, illus. (p. 2514)
Stannius, Hermann. Handbuch der Anatomie der Wirbelthiere (Classic Reprint) (p. 915)
Stansberry, Don & Cluster Springs Elementary School Staff. Skipping Through the ABC's of History. Barczak, Marliss & Long, Lisa, eds. (p. 2033)
Stansbie, Stephanie. Dinosaurs: A Busy Sticker Activity Book. Nowowiejska, Kasia, illus. (p. 550)
—Farm Fun: A Busy Sticker Activity Book. Nowowiejska, Kasia, illus. (p. 710)
—I Love You All Year Through. Mason, Suzie, illus. (p. 1078)
—My Friends & Me: A Celebration of Different Kinds of Families. Halford, Katy, illus. (p. 1548)
Stansbie, Stephanie & Smythe, Richard. With All My Heart. (p. 2481)
Stansbury, Lindsey. Adventures of Cody the Mischievous Moose. (p. 22)
Stansfield, Daniel N. Other Men's Flowers. (p. 1674)
Stansfield, Laurie, illus. see Steinberg, D. J.
Stanton. Memories of a Sister of S. Saviour's Priory (Classic Reprint) (p. 1446)
Stanton, A. Ellen. My Life in Paris Fifty Years Ago: From the Journal of an; Ellen Stanton, Paris, 1868-1869 (Classic Reprint) (p. 1552)
Stanton, Andy. Danny Mcgee Drinks the Sea. Layton, Neal, illus. (p. 504)
—Going to the Volcano. Ordonez, Miguel, illus. (p. 855)
—Mr Gum & the Biscuit Billionaire. Tazzyman, David, illus. (p. 1518)
—Mr Gum & the Goblins. Tazzyman, David, illus. (p. 1518)
—Natboff! One Million Years of Stupidity. Tazzyman, David, illus. (p. 1576)
—Sterling & the Canary. (p. 2115)
—You're a Bad Man, Mr. Gum! Tazzyman, David, illus. (p. 2535)
Stanton, Angie. Rock & a Hard Place. (p. 1894)
—Royally Lost. (p. 1910)
—Snapshot. (p. 2045)
—Under the Spotlight. (p. 2323)
—Waking in Time. (p. 2371)
Stanton, Beck & Stanton, Matt. Books That Drive Kids CRAZY!: Did You Take the B from My _ook? (p. 261)
—Books That Drive Kids CRAZY!: This Book Is Red. (p. 261)
—Books That Drive Kids CRAZY!: This Is a Ball. (p. 261)
Stanton, Brandon. Little Humans. Stanton, Brandon, photos by. (p. 1319)
Stanton, Brian, photos by see Van Fleet, Matthew.
Stanton, Coralie. Raven (Classic Reprint) (p. 1843)
Stanton, Debi. Dutchess Scarlett Isabella: A Stanton Pack Adventure. (p. 611)
—Pete the Postman's Neighborhood: The Big Stray Dog. (p. 1728)
Stanton, Elizabeth Rose. Bub. Stanton, Elizabeth Rose, illus. (p. 288)
—Cowie. Stanton, Elizabeth Rose, illus. (p. 464)
—Henny. Stanton, Elizabeth Rose, illus. (p. 954)
—Peddles. Stanton, Elizabeth Rose, illus. (p. 1712)
Stanton, Evan. Ruhainah: A Story of Afghan Life (Classic Reprint) (p. 1913)
Stanton, G. Smith. When the Wildwood Was in Flower: A Narrative Covering the Fifteen Years Experiences of a New Yorker on the Western Plains (Classic Reprint) (p. 2433)
—When the Wildwood Was in Flower: A Narrative, Covering the Fifteen Years' Experiences of a Stockman on the Western Plains, & His Vacation Days in the Open (Classic Reprint) (p. 2433)
Stanton, Henry Thompson. Moneyless Man. (p. 1493)
Stanton, Joe, illus. see Ganeri, Anita.
Stanton, Karen. Monday, Wednesday, & Every Other Weekend. Stanton, Karen, illus. (p. 1492)
Stanton, Laura. Animals Animales: A Bilingual ABC Book for all Readers. Richard, P. M., illus. (p. 94)
Stanton, Lidia. Tricky Punctuation in Cartoons. (p. 2288)
Stanton, Matt. Funny Kid #3: Prank Wars. Stanton, Matt, illus. (p. 801)
—Funny Kid for President. Stanton, Matt, illus. (p. 801)
—Funny Kid Stand Up. (p. 801)
—Funny Kid Stand Up. Stanton, Matt, illus. (p. 801)
Stanton, Matt, illus. see Carthew, Mark.
Stanton, Matt, jt. auth. see Miller, Tim.
Stanton, Melissa. My Pen Pal, Santa. Bell, Jennifer A., illus. (p. 1558)
Stanton, P. L. Love & War in Cuba: Including Many Thrilling Scenes of the Last Years of Spanish Rule (Classic Reprint) (p. 1359)
Stanton, Philip, illus. see Hopkins, Lee Bennett.
Stanton, Sherry. Jack & Judy. Ambadikumar, illus. (p. 1151)
Stanton, Terence M. Bill of Rights: What It Means to You. (p. 226)
—Branches of the U. S. Government. (p. 275)
—Declaration of Independence. (p. 523)
Stanton, Theodore. Reminiscences of Rosa Bonheur (Classic Reprint) (p. 1865)
Stanton, Timothy William. Contributions to the Cretaceous Paleontology of the Pacific Coast: The Fauna of the Knoxville Beds (Classic Reprint) (p. 445)
Stanton-Rich, Diane. Lake Junaluska Assembly, Reflections on the Past: The Laughter, the Struggles & the Love (Classic Reprint) (p. 1240)
Stape, J. H., ed. see Conrad, Joseph.
Stapelkamp, Brent, photos by see Hatkoff, Craig, et al.
Stapleford, Julia M. Baker. Wah-See-Ola: The Light of the Tribes at the Meeting Waters (Classic Reprint) (p. 2370)
Stapler, H. B. B. Detailed Description of the Scenes & Incidents: Connected with a Trip Through the Mountains & Parks of Colorado, As Accomplished by H. B. B. Stapler, & Harry T. Gause, July 21 August 20, 1871 (Classic Reprint) (p. 534)
Stapler, Jodi. Cornelia & the Fancy Lunch. Vitale, Brooke, ed. (p. 454)
—Cornelia Needs a Space of Her Own. Flo, Maria, illus. (p. 454)
—Pepper Miss Pepperoni Finds Someone to Love Her. Nam, InSong, illus. (p. 1720)
—Your Christmas Elf. Akhmetzhanova, Aiym, illus. (p. 2533)
Staples, Arthur G. Just Talks on Common Themes. (p. 1194)
—Just Talks on Common Themes (Classic Reprint) (p. 1194)
Staples, Arthur Gray. Jack in the Pulpit (Classic Reprint) (p. 1152)
Staples, Mary Anne. Birds of a Feather. (p. 232)
—When You Hear Hoofbeats. (p. 2434)
Staples, Rhian. Pod. Staples, Rhian, tr. (p. 1764)
Staples, Suzanne Fisher. Haveli. (p. 939)
—House of Djinn. (p. 1023)
—Shabanu: Daughter of the Wind. (p. 1995)
Stapleton, Jean. Boys Just Like Me: Bible Men Who Trusted God. (p. 272)
—Girls Just Like You: Bible Women Who Trusted God. (p. 838)
—Good Choices, Bad Choices: Bible Characters Decide. (p. 862)
—More Good Choices, Bad Choices: Bible Characters Decide. (p. 1504)
Stapleton, Patience. Babe Murphy (Classic Reprint) (p. 147)
Stapleton, Rhonda. Flirting with Disaster. (p. 749)
—Pucker Up. (p. 1810)
—Stupid Cupid. (p. 2145)
Stapley, Craig, illus. see Nielson, Mark S.
Stapley, Giles. Plinktus, the Little Pink Dinosaur. (p. 1763)
Stapp, Laci. Benson's Pals - Take a Bite Out of Bullying. (p. 201)
Stapylton, K. E. Gathering Gray. (p. 811)
Star, B. History of Madamoiselle de St. Phale: Giving a Full Account of the Miraculous Conversion of a Noble French Lady & Her Daughter to the Reformed Religion (Classic Reprint) (p. 978)
Star Bright Books. Carry Me (Portuguese/English) Icibaci, Neusa, tr. (p. 334)
—Families (Portuguese/English) Icibaci, Neusa, tr. (p. 702)
—Families (Spanish/English) Fiol, Maria A., tr. (p. 702)
—My First Words at Home (p. 1547)
—My First Words at Home (Burmese/English) (p. 1547)
—My First Words at HOME (Spanish/English) (p. 1547)
Star Bright Books, creator. Carry Me (Somali/English) (p. 334)
—Carry Me (Vietnamese/English) (p. 334)
—Eating the Rainbow (Vietnamese/English) (p. 622)
—Families (Vietnamese/English) (p. 702)
Star, Danielle. Ice Enchantment. (p. 1087)
—Night of Courage. (p. 1607)
—Secret Book. (p. 1975)
—Surprise Visit. (p. 2163)
Star, Danielle & Powell, Cortney Faye. Melowy Vol. 4: Frozen in Time. Jampole, Ryan, illus. (p. 1443)
Star, Pat, jt. auth. see Mills, Nathan.
Star Stable Entertainment AB, Star Stable. Soul Riders (Book 1) Jorvik Calling. (p. 2066)
—Soul Riders (Book 2) The Legend Awakens. (p. 2066)
Star, T. R. Tic Tac Takes a Tour: The Neighborhood. (p. 2239)
Star Wars. Star Wars Rebel Rescues: Magnetic Fun on Every Page. (p. 2104)
Star Wars, Star. Millennium Falcon. (p. 1467)
—X-Wing Book & Mini Model. (p. 2515)
Starace, Tom, illus. see Knudsen, Michelle.
Starbright Foundation Staff, jt. auth. see Andersen, Hans.
Starbuck, A. War Stories (Classic Reprint) (p. 2377)
Starbuck, Sara & The Born Free Foundation. Leopard Rescue: A True-Life Story. (p. 1267)
—Lion Rescue: A True-Life Story. (p. 1306)
Starch, Daniel. Measurement of Efficiency in Reading, Writing, Spelling & English (Classic Reprint) (p. 1435)
Stardoll. Sticker Holiday Dress Up. (p. 2118)
Starfall Education. Level I Reading & Writing Journal - Block Print: WK201b. Starfall Education, ed. (p. 1281)
Starfall Education, ed. see Hillert, Margaret.
Starfall Education, illus. see Hillert, Margaret.
Starfall Education, photos by see Hillert, Margaret.
Starfall Education, creator. Level II Reading & Writing Journal: Second Edition. (p. 1281)
Stargeon, Bobbi, illus. see Johnson, Sandi, et al.
Starikova, Natalia, illus. see Conner, Tommy.
Starikova, Natalia, illus. see Holman, Aj.
Starin, Liz. Splashdance. (p. 2084)
Starin, Liz, illus. see Mook-Sang, Jennifer.
Starin, Liz, illus. see Sauer, Tammi.
Starinobets, Anna. In the Wolf's Lair: A Beastly Crimes Book. Bugaeva, Jane, tr. (p. 1111)
—Predator's Rights: A Beastly Crimes Book (#2) Bugaeva, Jane, tr. (p. 1787)
Starinsky, Ron & Mizrahi, Amit. Ron & Rona Fight the Corona. Eilat, Eyal, illus. (p. 1901)
Starishevsky, Jill. My Body Belongs to Me: A Book about Body Safety. Padron, Angela, illus. (p. 1534)
Stark, Andrew. 5th Brother. (p. 2548)
Stark, Clifford D. & Bowers, Elizabeth Shimer. Living with Sports Injuries. (p. 1335)
Stark, Cordelia. Female Wanderer, or the Remarkable Disclosures of Cordelia & Edwin (Classic Reprint) (p. 720)
Stark, Edna Sutton. Monologues & Plays: Designed for the Platform Entertainer, the Reader & the Teacher (Classic Reprint) (p. 1494)
Stark, Evan. Todo lo que necesitas saber sobre Pandillas (Everything You Need to Know about Street Gangs) (p. 2256)
Stark, Freddy. Start Exploring: Gray's Anatomy: A Fact-Filled Coloring Book. (p. 2107)
Stark, Gilbert Little. Letters of Gilbert Little Stark, July 23, 1907-March 12, 1908 (Classic Reprint) (p. 1280)
Stark, Griffin. Immortal Girl5. (p. 1101)
Stark, Hannah. Trucker & Train. Kolar, Bob, illus. (p. 2292)
Stark, Kayla. Friends at the Firehouse: Double Booked: 35 Lift-The-flaps Inside! (Firefighter Board Books; Firetruck Books for Toddlers) (p. 787)
Stark, Kayla, illus. see Arrow, Emily.
Stark, Kayla, illus. see Beme, Emma Carlson.
Stark, Kayla, illus. see Ewert, Marcus.
Stark, Kristy. Amazing Animals: Honeybees: Place Value (Grade 2) (p. 63)
—Animales Asombrosos: Abejas Meliferas. (p. 92)
—Best You: Win or Lose (Level K) (p. 208)
—Conteo: Tu Cuerpo. (p. 444)
—Counting: Your Body. (p. 459)
—Dealing with Wildfires. (p. 519)
—Diversión y Juegos: Campos, Pistas y Canchas - Partición de Figuras. (p. 565)
—Dónde Vive la Gente. (p. 581)
—En el Trabajo: Fotógrafo: Valor Posicional. (p. 646)
—Failure: Business Blunders. (p. 694)
—Fantastic Kids: Care for Animals. (p. 707)
—Fun & Games: Comic Conventions: Division (Grade 5) (p. 798)
—Fun & Games: Fields, Rinks, & Courts: Partitioning Shapes (Grade 2) (p. 798)
—Fun & Games: Building Miniature Models: Multiplying Decimals (Grade 5) (p. 798)
—Greta Thunberg. (p. 895)
—History of Telephones: Fractions (Grade 4) (p. 980)
—Legacy: Business Leaders. (p. 1261)
—Life in Numbers. (p. 1292)
—Lo Mejor de Ti: Ganar o Perder. (p. 1338)
—Make It: Pattern Art. (p. 1386)
—Manualidades: Arte con Patrones. (p. 1399)
—Marsai Martin. (p. 1409)
—Money Matters: Young Entrepreneurs: Addition & Subtraction (Grade 4) (p. 1493)
—Niños Fantásticos: Cuidar a Los Animales. (p. 1611)
—Ntando Mahlangu. (p. 1628)
—On the Job: Photographer: Place Value (Grade 2) (p. 1655)
—Outside the Box: Teams (Level K) (p. 1685)
—Powered by Steam. (p. 1783)
—Predicting Earthquakes (Grade 3) (p. 1787)
—Robert Irwin. (p. 1890)
—Spectacular Sports: Quidditch: Coordinate Planes (Grade 5) (p. 2078)
—STEM in the Stanley Cup. (p. 2114)
—Terrarium Pets: Volume (Grade 6) (p. 2207)
—Travel Adventures: Easter Island. (p. 2279)
—vida en números: Tus favoritos (Life in Numbers: Our Favorites) (Spanish Version) (Level K) (p. 2356)
—Where People Live. (p. 2439)
—¡No te limites! Los equipos (Outside the Box: Teams) (Spanish Version) (Level K) (p. 1615)
Stark, Kristy, ed. see Bradley, Timothy J.
Stark M.A.Ed., Kristy. STEM in the Stanley Cup. (p. 2114)
Stark, Paula Allene. Babe the Bear (p. 147)
Stark, Rebecca. Archaeology. (p. 110)
—Middle Ages: A Study Unit to Promote Critical & Creative Thinking. (p. 1460)
—Native American Cultures. (p. 1578)
—War to Constitution. (p. 2377)
—Weather: A Study Unit to Promote Critical & Creative Thinking. (p. 2394)
Stark, Ryan. Why Do Seasons Change? (p. 2456)
Stark, Ryan, illus. see Dunham, Bandhu Scott.
Stark, Sam. Diderot: French Philosopher & Father of the Encyclopedia. (p. 543)

Stark, Shannon. Peas Help Me Lord: Love the Lord with All Thy Heart. (p. 1711)
Stark, Ulf. Midsummer Tomte & the Little Rabbits: A Day-By-day Summer Story in Twenty-one Short Chapters Beard, Susan, tr. (p. 1462)
—Runaways. Crowther, Kitty, illus. (p. 1915)
—Yule Tomte & the Little Rabbits Beard, Susan, tr. (p. 2537)
Stark, William N. Aerosmith: Living the Rock 'n' Roll Dream. (p. 30)
—Mighty Military Aircraft. (p. 1463)
—Mighty Military Land Vehicles. (p. 1463)
—Mighty Military Robots. (p. 1463)
—Mighty Military Ships. (p. 1463)
—Military Machines on Duty. (p. 1466)
Stark, William N., et al. Legends of Rock. (p. 1264)
Starke, Ruth. Armistice. Kennett, David, illus. (p. 117)
Starke, Ruth & Hannaford, Robert. My Gallipoli. (p. 1548)
Starkey, Fiona, illus. see White, June.
Starkey, Richard, see Starr, Ringo, pseud.
Starkey, Scott. Call of the Bully: A Rodney Rathbone Novel. (p. 311)
—Call of the Bully. (p. 311)
—How to Beat the Bully Without Really Trying. (p. 1038)
Starkings, Richard, illus. see Loeb, Jeph & Sale, Tim.
Starkings, Richard, illus. see Seagle, Steven T.
Starkings, Richard & Kelly, Joe. Wounded Animals (p. 2510)
Stark-Mcginnis, Sandy. Extraordinary Birds. (p. 685)
—Space Between Lost & Found. (p. 2070)
Starkoff, Vanina. Along the River Springer, Jane, tr. (p. 58)
Starkoff, Vanina, illus. see Júnior, Otavio.
Starkoff, Vanina, illus. see Júnior, Otávio & Dias, Beatriz C.
Starkoff, Vanina, illus. see Ross, Stewart & Lonely Planet Kids.
Starks, Kyle. Rock Candy Mountain Volume 2. (p. 1894)
Starks, London. I Sing, Do You Hear? Williams, Iris M., ed. (p. 1082)
Starks, Paris. I Dance, Do You See? Williams, Iris M., ed. (p. 1064)
Starlet. Kiera: The Kurious Kat. (p. 1216)
Starlight, Cyandria. Daydreams of a Little Girl. (p. 515)
Starlin, Jim. Art of Jim Starlin: A Life in Words & Pictures. Pruett, Joe & Marts, Mike, eds. (p. 121)
Starlin, Jim, et al. Cult. Thorsland, Dan & O'Neil, Dennis, eds. (p. 483)
Starlin, Jim, text. Marvel Universe: the End. (p. 1413)
Starling, Annie. Olivia's Prince among the Stars: A Supernatural Adventure. (p. 1650)
Starling Lyons, Kelly. Class Act #2. Brantley-Newton, Vanessa, illus. (p. 399)
—Dancing Queen #4. Myers, Nneka, illus. (p. 500)
—Sleepover Scientist #3. Myers, Nneka & Brantley-Newton, Vanessa, illus. (p. 2037)
Starling, Nicolas. Thomas Troll's Travels. (p. 2229)
Starling, Robert. Fergal & the Bad Temper. (p. 720)
—Super Sloth. Starling, Robert, illus. (p. 2158)
Starling, William. Floods of the Mississippi River: Including an Account of Their Principal Causes & Effects, & a Description of the Levee System & Other Means Proposed & Tried for the Control of the River (Classic Reprint) (p. 750)
Starmer, Aaron. Dweeb: Burgers, Beasts, & Brainwashed Bullies. Rash, Andy, illus. (p. 611)
—Espontánea. (p. 662)
—Magic Eraser #1. La Forest, Courtney, illus. (p. 1377)
—Meme. (p. 1443)
—Rewindable Clock #2. La Forest, Courtney, illus. (p. 1874)
—Riverman. (p. 1887)
—Spontaneous. (p. 2086)
Starmer, Anika, illus. see Thomas, Wendy Russell & Ruchman, Laura.
Starner, Lynn, illus. see Salzler, Laurie.
Starnes, Allison. Bernadette the Brave. (p. 204)
StarNews Media, compiled by. Stars of K-Pop: Boys Edition. (p. 2107)
—Stars of K-Pop: Girls Edition. (p. 2107)
Starobinets, Anna. Catlantis. Bugaeva, Jane, tr. from RUS. (p. 345)
—Claws of Rage: A Beastly Crimes Book (#3) Bugaeva, Jane, tr. (p. 402)
—Plucker: A Beastly Crimes Book (#4) Bugaeva, Jane, tr. (p. 1763)
Staron, Berangere, illus. see Clever Publishing.
Starr, Barbara May. Home for Finn: The Tail of an Alaska Rescue Dog (p. 996)
Starr, Branka, illus. see Bodecker, N. M.
Starr, David. Empty Net. (p. 645)
—Golden Game. (p. 857)
—Golden Goal. (p. 857)
Starr, Ida May Hill. Gardens of the Caribbees, Vol. 1 Of 2: Sketches of a Cruise to the West Indies & the Spanish Main (Classic Reprint) (p. 809)
Starr, Jim, illus. see Kimmel, Eric A.
Starr, Joyce, ed. see Frances, Ethel & Miller, Marcia.
Starr, Kimberley. Book of Whispers. (p. 260)
Starr, L. Lee. Huggily Buggily & the Magical Fart of Wind. (p. 1048)
Starr, Laura B. Doll Book (Classic Reprint) (p. 578)
Starr, Ringo, pseud. Octopus's Garden. Cort, Ben, illus. (p. 1637)
Starr Rose, Caroline. Blue Birds. (p. 248)
Starr Taylor, Bridget, illus. see Parkes, Brenda.
Starrenburg, Hasko. Queen's Orb. (p. 1825)
Starrett, Helen Ekin & Allison, Frances Ekin. Future of Educated Women. (p. 803)
Starrett, Vincent. Bookman's Holiday: The Private Satisfactions of an Incurable Collector (Classic Reprint) (p. 261)
—Et Cetera 1924: A Collector's Scrap-Book (Classic Reprint) (p. 665)
Starzyk, Rhoda & Robinson, Jolie. Adventures of Jolie & Her Best Friends Hamilton & Bacorama: A Lesson for Freddie. (p. 24)
Stashko, David. Halloween Society. (p. 912)
Stashwick, Carson. Fledgling. (p. 747)
Stasio, M. L. Imagine If. (p. 1100)
Stasse, Lisa M. Defiant: The Forsaken Trilogy. (p. 525)
—Defiant. (p. 525)
—Forsaken. (p. 769)
—Uprising: The Forsaken Trilogy. (p. 2339)
Stassen, J. P. Deogratias, a Tale of Rwanda. (p. 529)
Stassi, Laura. Pink Floyd. (p. 1746)
Stasuyk, Max, illus. see Levine, Karen R.
Stasuyk, Max, illus. see Rolle, Elvy P.
Stasyuk, Max, illus. see Edwards, Garth.
Stasyuk, Maz, jt. auth. see Edwards, Garth.
State Department, ed. Foreign Relations of the United States: 1977-1980, Foundations of Foreign Policy. (p. 765)
State of New York, University of the. Proceedings of the Eleventh Anniversary of the University Convocation of the State of New York, Held July 7th, 8th And 9th 1874. (p. 1803)
—Proceedings of the Nineteenth Meeting of the University Convocation of the State of New York, Held July 12-14 1881. (p. 1803)
—Proceedings of the Seventh Anniversary of the University Convocation of the State of New York, August 2-4 1870. (p. 1803)
—Proceedings of the Twenty-Fourth Convocation of the University of the State of New York, Held July 6th - 8th, 1886, Pp. 75-303. (p. 1803)
State, Paul. France. (p. 776)
State, Paul F. Brief History of Ireland. (p. 281)
Statham, Leigh. Daughter 4254. (p. 509)
—Imani Unraveled. (p. 1100)
Statia, Andy. Down the Dark Well. Statia, Andy, illus. (p. 590)
—Run, Monster, Run. Statia, Andy, illus. (p. 1914)
—Snow Day That Went Terribly Wrong. (p. 2047)
Station, New Jersey Agricultural Experim, jt. auth. see Smith, John Bernhard.
Staton, Hilarie. Artist. (p. 123)
—Chicago. (p. 367)
—Civil Rights. (p. 396)
—Denver. (p. 529)
—New York City. (p. 1598)
—State Guide to Capitals. (p. 2108)
Staton, Hilarie N. Civil Rights. (p. 396)
—Cowboys & Wild West. (p. 464)
—Industrial Revolution. (p. 1117)
Staton, Joe, illus. see Fisch, Sholly & Ottolini, Horacio.
Staton, Joe, illus. see Fisch, Sholly.
Statts, Leo. Alligators. (p. 56)
—Anacondas. (p. 78)
—Ants. (p. 103)
—Arctic Foxes. (p. 112)
—Baboons. (p. 148)
—Beavers. (p. 186)
—Bees. (p. 189)
—Beetles. (p. 190)
—Beluga Whales. (p. 198)
—Boxers. (p. 267)
—Bulldogs. (p. 296)
—Burmilla Cats. (p. 299)
—Butterflies. (p. 303)
—Camels. (p. 314)
—Capybaras. (p. 327)
—Cardinals. (p. 328)
—Caribou. (p. 330)
—Catfish. (p. 344)
—Chameleons. (p. 355)
—Cheetahs. (p. 364)
—Chickens. (p. 368)
—Chimpanzees. (p. 377)
—Clown Fish. (p. 408)
—Cobras. (p. 410)
—Cows. (p. 464)
—Crocodiles. (p. 477)
—Deer. (p. 525)
—Desert Animals (p. 531)
—Dogs (p. 577)
—Dolphins. (p. 579)
—Dragonflies. (p. 595)
—Eagles. (p. 613)
—Earthworms. (p. 619)
—Elephants. (p. 634)
—Falcons. (p. 699)
—Fireflies. (p. 734)
—Forest Animals (Set) (p. 765)
—German Shepherds. (p. 822)
—Giraffes. (p. 834)
—Goats. (p. 849)
—Golden Retrievers. (p. 858)
—Grasshoppers. (p. 881)
—Great White Sharks. (p. 891)
—Hammerhead Sharks. (p. 913)
—Hummingbirds. (p. 1050)
—Iguanas. (p. 1094)
—Jaguars. (p. 1155)
—Killer Whales. (p. 1217)
—Komodo Dragons. (p. 1231)
—Labrador Retrievers. (p. 1235)
—Largemouth Bass. (p. 1244)
—Leopards. (p. 1268)
—Lions. (p. 1307)
—Maine Coon Cats. (p. 1384)
—Mako Sharks. (p. 1390)
—Manx Cats. (p. 1400)
—Mosquitoes. (p. 1507)
—Newts. (p. 1600)
—Octopuses. (p. 1637)
—Orangutans. (p. 1668)
—Parrots. (p. 1701)
—Penguins. (p. 1716)
—Persian Cats. (p. 1724)
—Pigs. (p. 1744)
—Piranhas. (p. 1749)
—Polar Animals (p. 1769)
—Polar Bears. (p. 1769)
—Puffins. (p. 1811)
—Pugs. (p. 1812)
—Rain Forest Animals. (p. 1835)
—Rattlesnakes. (p. 1843)
—Salamanders. (p. 1924)
—Sand Sharks. (p. 1930)
—Savanna Animals (p. 1937)
—Scottish Fold Cats. (p. 1962)
—Seahorses. (p. 1969)
—Seals. (p. 1970)
—Sheep. (p. 2004)
—Siamese Cats. (p. 2014)
—Skunks. (p. 2033)
—Sloth Bears. (p. 2039)
—Squirrels. (p. 2095)
—Starfish. (p. 2106)
—Sturgeon. (p. 2145)
—Swamp Animals (p. 2167)
—Tarantulas. (p. 2191)
—Ticks. (p. 2240)
—Tiger Sharks. (p. 2241)
—Tigers. (p. 2242)
—Toucans. (p. 2267)
—Trout. (p. 2292)
—Turkeys. (p. 2300)
—Walleyed Pike. (p. 2373)
—Whale Sharks. (p. 2403)
—Wolves. (p. 2485)
—Woodpeckers. (p. 2492)
—Zebras. (p. 2539)
Statuti, Laura. Butterbean Finds a Home. Statuti, Laura, illus. (p. 303)
Statyuk, Max, jt. auth. see Edwards, Garth.
Staub, Leslie. Bedtime for Beasties. Liu, Jia, illus. (p. 188)
—How Do You Say I Love You, Dewey Dew? Mack, Jeff, illus. (p. 1030)
—Shine, Baby, Shine. Nichols, Lori, illus. (p. 2007)
—Time for (Earth) School, Dewey Dew. Mack, Jeff, illus. (p. 2244)
Staub, Leslie, illus. see Danticat, Edwidge.
Staub, Leslie, illus. see Fox, Mem.
St-Aubin, Bruno, illus. see Ellis, Sarah.
Stauche, Arlett. Bellaterra. (p. 197)
Staufenbiel, Beate. Satansbrut und Brauner Bar. (p. 1936)
Stauffacher, Sue. Animal Rescue Team: Gator on the Loose! Lamont, Priscilla, illus. (p. 91)
—Animal Rescue Team: Hide & Seek. Lamont, Priscilla, illus. (p. 91)
—Animal Rescue Team: Show Time. Lamont, Priscilla, illus. (p. 91)
—Gator on the Loose! Lamont, Priscilla, illus. (p. 812)
—Hide & Seek Lamont, Priscilla, illus. (p. 967)
—Nothing but Trouble: The Story of Althea Gibson. Couch, Greg, illus. (p. 1625)
—Space Between Before & After. (p. 2070)
—Special Delivery! Lamont, Priscilla, illus. (p. 2076)
—Special Delivery! Animal Rescue Team. Lamont, Priscilla, illus. (p. 2076)
Stauffer, Byron H. Your Mother's Apron Strings: And Other Talks to Young Men (Classic Reprint) (p. 2534)
Stauffer, Chrystal & International, Bible Visuals. Filling a Little Space: The Susanna Wesley Story. (p. 726)
Stauffer, Chrystal, et al. Occasions for the Gospel Volume 1: Filling a Little Space, Neither Death nor Life, Our Father's House. (p. 1635)
Stauffer, Ed. There Won't Be a Christmas? (p. 2217)
Stauffer, Lara. Unearthed. (p. 2326)
Stauffer, Lisa Lowe. Two by Two Scudamore, Angelika, illus. (p. 2307)
Stauffer, Mack. Humanity & the Mysterious Knight (Classic Reprint) (p. 1050)
Staunton, Aoife. World Sounds. Rosenstock, Gabriel & Jovet, Michel, trs. (p. 2505)
Staunton, Joseph. Dinosaurs in the Sea. (p. 551)
—Dinosaurs in the Sky. (p. 551)
—Meat-Eating Dinosaurs. (p. 1435)
—Plant-Eating Dinosaurs. (p. 1756)
Staunton, Joseph & Flinthart, Dirk. Dinosaurs in the Sea. Rey, Luis, illus. (p. 551)
—Meat Eating Dinosaurs. Rey, Luis, illus. (p. 1435)
Staunton, Joseph & Hynson, Colin. Dinosaurs in the Sky. (p. 551)
Staunton, Mathew, illus. see Rosenstock, Gabriel.
Staunton, Schuyler. Daughters of Destiny (Classic Reprint) (p. 509)
Staunton, Ted. Accord de Puissance: (Power Chord) (p. 10)
—Ace's Basement (p. 10)
—Acting Up (p. 12)
—Coda (p. 411)
—Daredevil Morgan. Slavin, Bill, illus. (p. 505)
—Morgan & the Dune Racer. Slavin, Bill, illus. (p. 1506)
—Morgan on Ice. Slavin, Bill, illus. (p. 1506)
—Morgan"s Got Game. Slavin, Bill, illus. (p. 1506)
—Morgan's Secret Slavin, Bill & Shannon, Ben, illus. (p. 1506)
—Music by Morgan Slavin, Bill, illus. (p. 1528)
—Pov (p. 1782)
—Power Chord (p. 1782)
—Power Chord. (p. 1782)
Staunton, Ted & Staunton, Will. Morgan the Brave. Slavin, Bill, illus. (p. 1506)
Staunton, Will, jt. auth. see Staunton, Ted.
Stavans, Ilan. Golemito. Villegas, Teresa, illus. (p. 860)
Stavans, Ilan, ed. see Singer, Isaac Bashevis.
Stave, Mel. How Harry Found the Meaning of Friendship. (p. 1031)
Staveley, E. F. British Spiders: An Introduction to the Study of the Araneidae of Great Britain & Ireland (Classic Reprint) (p. 283)
Staves, David. Ida Zeke. (p. 1089)
Staves Jr, David C. Bad Day Activity Book. (p. 157)
—Jeepers Creepers. (p. 1162)
—Roy G. Biv. (p. 1909)
Stavreva, Kirilka, et al. Bulgaria. (p. 295)
Stawell, Rodolph. Fairies I Have Met (Classic Reprint) (p. 695)
—Motor Tours in Yorkshire (Classic Reprint) (p. 1512)
Stawniak, Leonie. Little Flamingo on the Move. (p. 1316)
Stawski, Paul. Both Sides. (p. 264)
Stayte, James, illus. see Graham, Ian.
Stayte, James, illus. see Solway, Andrew.
Stayton, Frank. Threads (Classic Reprint) (p. 2231)
Stead, April-Nicole, illus. see Stevens, Gary J.
Stead, Chris. Christmas Chimney Challenge: Action Adventure Story for Kids. (p. 384)
—Fastest Kid in the World: A Fast-Paced Adventure for Your Energetic Kids. (p. 713)
—Follow the Breadcrumbs: An Imaginative Story for Your Energetic Kids. (p. 758)
—Little Green Boat: Action Adventure Book for Kids. (p. 1318)
Stead, Chris D. Follow the Breadcrumbs: An Imaginative Story for Your Energetic Kids. (p. 758)
Stead, Christina. Modern Women in Love: Sixty Twentieth-Century Masterpieces of Fiction (Classic Reprint) (p. 1488)
Stead, Christopher. Little Green Boat: Action Adventure Story. (p. 1318)
Stead, Emily. Frozen II: an Enchanted Adventure. (p. 795)
—Unicorn Creativity Book. (p. 2328)
Stead, Emily, jt. auth. see Feiwel & Friends.
Stead, Erin, illus. see Stead, Philip C.
Stead, Erin, illus. see Twain, Mark, pseud & Stead, Philip C.
Stead, Erin E., illus. see Cuevas, Michelle.
Stead, Erin E., illus. see Fogliano, Julie.
Stead, Erin E., illus. see Galing, Ed.
Stead, Erin E., illus. see Stead, Philip C.
Stead, Estelle Wilson, jt. auth. see Stead, William Thomas.
Stead, Henry. Review of Reviews for Australasia: April, 1913 (Classic Reprint) (p. 1873)
Stead, Judy. Twelve Days of Christmas in North Carolina. (p. 2303)
—Twelve Days of Christmas in North Carolina. Stead, Judy, illus. (p. 2303)
Stead, Judy, illus. see Bair, Sheila.
Stead, Judy, illus. see Jules, Jacqueline.
Stead, Judy, illus. see Raczka, Bob.
Stead, Natalie, illus. see Brookes, John.
Stead, Philip C. All the Animals Where I Live. (p. 53)
—Bear Has a Story to Tell. (p. 179)
—Bear Has a Story to Tell. Stead, Erin E., illus. (p. 179)
—Hello, My Name Is Ruby: A Picture Book. Stead, Philip C., illus. (p. 951)
—Home for Bird. Stead, Philip C., illus. (p. 996)
—Ideas Are All Around. (p. 1089)
—Lenny & Lucy. Stead, Erin E., illus. (p. 1266)
—Music for Mister Moon. Stead, Erin, illus. (p. 1529)
—Only Fish in the Sea. (p. 1664)
—Samson in the Snow. (p. 1928)
—Sebastian & the Balloon: A Picture Book. Stead, Philip C., illus. (p. 1973)
—Sick Day for Amos McGee. (p. 2014)
—Sick Day for Amos McGee. Stead, Erin E., illus. (p. 2014)
—Sick Day for Amos Mcgee: Book & CD Storytime Set. Stead, Erin E., illus. (p. 2014)
—Special Delivery. Cordell, Matthew, illus. (p. 2076)
—Vernon Is on His Way: Small Stories. (p. 2352)
Stead, Philip C., illus. see Zolotow, Charlotte.
Stead, Philip C., jt. auth. see Twain, Mark, pseud.
Stead, Rebecca. Cuando Me Alcances. (p. 481)
—Goodbye Stranger. (p. 867)
—Liar & Spy. (p. 1283)
—List of Things That Will Not Change. (p. 1308)
—When You Reach Me. (p. 2434)
Stead, Rebecca, jt. auth. see Mass, Wendy.
Stead, Robert. Dennison Grant: A Novel of to-Day (Classic Reprint) (p. 529)
—Neighbours (Classic Reprint) (p. 1586)
Stead, Robert J. C. Bail Jumper (Classic Reprint) (p. 159)
—Cow Puncher (Classic Reprint) (p. 464)
—Homesteaders: A Novel of the Canadian West (Classic Reprint) (p. 998)
Stead, Tony. Should There Be Zoos? A Persuasive Text. (p. 2011)
—What's Your Point? Student Book Package, Grade 1. (p. 2427)
Stead, Tony, jt. auth. see Capstone Classroom Staff.
Stead, W. T. Splendid Paupers: A Tale of the Coming Plutocracy; Being the Christmas Number of the Review of Reviews, 1894 (Classic Reprint) (p. 2085)
Stead, William T. How I Know That the Dead Return. (p. 1032)
—How I Know That the Dead Return (Classic Reprint) (p. 1032)
—Real Ghost Stories (Classic Reprint) (p. 1849)
Stead, William Thomas. Real Ghost Stories: Revised Reprint of the Christmas & New Year's Numbers of the Review of Reviews 1891-2 (Classic Reprint) (p. 1849)
Steadman, Amanda. Pin & the Magic Butterflies. Steadman-Robert, Ava & Steadman-Robert, Esme, illus. (p. 1745)
Steadman, Barbara, jt. auth. see Alcott, Louisa May.
Steadman, Ralph. Little. com. (p. 1314)
Steadman, Ralph, illus. see Carroll, Lewis, pseud.
Steadman, Ralph, illus. see Damjan, Mischa.
Steadman-Robert, Ava, illus. see Steadman, Amanda.
Steadman-Robert, Esme, illus. see Steadman, Amanda.
Stealey, Bryan. Motorcross. (p. 1512)
Steam, Karl. How Santa Changed. (p. 1035)
Steamboat Inspection Service, jt. creator see United States.
Stearman, G. G., ed. see Church, J. R.
Stearman, Kaye. Debate about Cosmetic Surgery. (p. 522)
—Debate about Euthanasia. (p. 522)
—Freedom of Information. (p. 782)
—Taking Action Against Homelessness. (p. 2177)
—Travel & Tourism Careers. (p. 2280)
Stearman, Kaye & Savery, Annabel. Travel & Tourism. (p. 2280)
Stearns. Holt World History: Human Legacy California: Student One-Stop (Set of 25) Grades 9-12 2008. (p. 995)
—World History: Human Legacy Indiana: Student One-Stop CD-ROM 2010. (p. 2502)
Stearns, Carolyn. Quiet Please - Eaglets Growing Aiken, David, illus. (p. 1828)
—Where Did All the Water Go? Aiken, David, illus. (p. 2435)

S

—Escape from Haunted Treasure Island: A 4D Book. Reeves, Pauline, illus. (p. 661)
—Fight This Fire! (p. 725)
—Fight This Fire! Primeau, Chuck, illus. (p. 725)
—Fix That Truck! (p. 745)
—Fix That Truck! Dynamo Limited, illus. (p. 745)
—Flash & the Storm of the Century. Schigiel, Gregg, illus. (p. 746)
—Hunt for the Octo-Shark: A 4D Book. Reeves, Pauline, illus. (p. 1053)
—Justice League & the False Destiny. Castellani, Leonel, illus. (p. 1195)
—LEGO City: Catch That Crook! (p. 1264)
—Metallo Attacks! Brizuela, Dario, illus. (p. 1452)
—Monster Mutt Madness. Jeralds, Scott, illus. (p. 1496)
—Movie Magic Madness. Lozano, Omar, illus. (p. 1516)
—Nearly Fearless Monkey Pirates. Reeves, Pauline, illus. (p. 1584)
—Night at the Museum: Secret of the Tomb. (p. 1604)
—Scooby-Doo! Beginner Mysteries. (p. 1960)
—Skeleton Crew Showdown. Jeralds, Scott, illus. (p. 2030)
—Vampire Zoo Hullabaloo. Jeralds, Scott, illus. (p. 2346)
Steele, Michael Anthony, jt. auth. see Cohen, Ivan.
Steele, Michael Anthony & Scholastic Editors. Look Out Below! Kiernan, Kenny, illus. (p. 1346)
Steele, Philip. Activists. (p. 12)
—Afghanistan: From War to Peace? (p. 31)
—Amazing History of Pirates: See What a Buccaneer's Life Was Really Like, with over 350 Exciting Pictures. (p. 65)
—Ancient Egypt. (p. 80)
—Ancient Rome: Step into the Time of the Roman Empire, with 15 Step-by-Step Projects & over 370 Exciting Pictures. (p. 82)
—Build the Train. Forster, Gregor, illus. (p. 293)
—Children's Encyclopedia of Ancient History: Step Back in Time to Discover the Wonders of the Stone Age, Ancient Egypt, Ancient Greece, Ancient Rome, the Aztecs & Maya, the Incas, Ancient China & Ancient Japan. (p. 373)
—China. (p. 377)
—Chinese Empire. (p. 378)
—Cities in Layers. Lozano, Andrés, illus. (p. 394)
—Did Anything Good Come Out of the Civil War? (p. 542)
—Did Anything Good Come Out of the Vietnam War? (p. 542)
—Did Anything Good Come Out of World War I? (p. 542)
—DKfindout! Castles. (p. 569)
—DKfindout! Vikings. (p. 569)
—Documenting Slavery & Civil Rights. (p. 574)
—Documenting World War I. (p. 574)
—Epic!: Empires. (p. 658)
—Expandable Explorations: Big Builds. Kearney, Brendan, illus. (p. 677)
—Global Financial Crisis. (p. 843)
—Hail! Ancient Romans. (p. 909)
—Hail! Tudors. (p. 909)
—Hands-On History! Viking World: Learn about the Legendary Norse Raiders, with 15 Step-By-step Projects & More Than 350 Exciting Pictures. (p. 915)
—Hostage Takers. (p. 1006)
—I Wonder Why Pyramids Were Built. (p. 1086)
—Incas: Step into the Spectacular World of Ancient South America, with 340 Exciting Pictures & 15 Step-by-Step Projects. (p. 1112)
—Iran & the West. (p. 1133)
—Kingdom of Benin: Band 17/Diamond (Collins Big Cat) (p. 1222)
—Kingfisher Readers L4: the Arctic & Antarctica. (p. 1222)
—Middle East. (p. 1460)
—My Body. (p. 1534)
—Race & Crime. (p. 1830)
—Roman Empire. (p. 1899)
—Russia. (p. 1917)
—Saving Water & Energy. (p. 1939)
—Sudan, Darfur & the Nomadic Conflicts. (p. 2146)
—Turkey. (p. 2300)
—Uprisings in the Middle East & North Africa. (p. 2339)
—Vikings in 30 Seconds. (p. 2358)
Steele, Philip, jt. auth. see Jacobs, Pat.
Steele, Philip, jt. auth. see Morris, Neil.
Steele, Philip & Dorling Kindersley Publishing Staff. City Through Time. Noon, Steve, illus. (p. 395)
Steele, Philip & Goldsmith, Mike. My Body. (p. 1534)
Steele, Philip & Kelly, Miles. World Wonders. Kelly, Richard, ed. (p. 2506)
Steele, Philip & Ljosland, Ragnhild. Vikings. (p. 2357)
Steele, Philip & MacDonald, Fiona. Vikings & the Celts: Ancient Warriors & Raiders. (p. 2358)
Steele, Philip & Powell, Anton. History News: the Greek News. (p. 977)
Steele, Philip & Rosso, Norma. History News: the Aztec News. (p. 977)
Steele, Philip, et al. Extreme Planet. (p. 687)
—Weird & Wacky History Book Box: Find Out What Is Fact or Fantasy in 8 Amazing Books (p. 2396)
Steele, Phillip. Lost Journal. Monesi, Mirella, illus. (p. 1354)
Steele, Richard. Lucubrations of Isaac Bickerstaff, Esq. , Vol. 1 (Classic Reprint) (p. 1365)
—Perverse Widow by Sir Richard Steele (Classic Reprint) (p. 1725)
—Poetical Miscellanies: Consisting of Original Poems & Translations (Classic Reprint) (p. 1766)
—Tatler, or Lucubrations of Isaac Bickerstaff, Esq: In Four Volumes (Classic Reprint) (p. 2192)
—Tatler, or Lucubrations of Isaac Bickerstaff, Esq. 1709, Vol. 1 (Classic Reprint) (p. 2192)
—Toasts Rakes & Cits: Being Portraits of Maids, Men,& Matrons Fashionable & Unfashionable 'about Town' in the Eighteenth Century (Classic Reprint) (p. 2254)
Steele, Robert. One Man: A Novel (Classic Reprint) (p. 1660)
Steele, Robert G., illus. see Lakin, Patricia.
Steele, Robert Gantt, illus. see Wilbur, Helen L.
Steele, Rufus. Aces for Industry (Classic Reprint) (p. 10)
Steele, Silas S. Brazen Drum; or the Yankee in Poland: A National Drama, in Two Acts (Classic Reprint) (p. 277)
Steele, W. H. Memories of by-Gone Days (Classic Reprint) (p. 1446)
Steele, Wilbur Daniel. Land's End: And Other Stories. (p. 1243)
—Land's End: And Other Stories (Classic Reprint) (p. 1243)
—Storm (Classic Reprint) (p. 2126)
—Tower of Sand: And Other Stories (Classic Reprint) (p. 2269)
Steele-Card, Adrianna, illus. see Handy, Femida & Carpenter, Carole H.
Steele-Morgan, Alex, illus. see Nolan, Allia Zobel.
Steele-Morgan, Alex, illus. see Schnur, Susan & Schnur-Fishman, Anna.
Steele-Morgan, Alexandra, illus. see Schnur, Susan.
Steele-Saccio, Eva. Headbands & Hairstyles: Make & Wear Super Stylish Headbands. (p. 942)
—Marvelous Book of Magical Horses: Dress up Paper Horses & Their Fairy Friends. (p. 1413)
—Marvelous Book of Magical Mermaids. (p. 1413)
—Ribbon Bangles: Make 5 Beautiful Wrapped Bracelets. (p. 1876)
Steele-Saccio, Eva & Johnson, Anne Akers. Beaded Bands: Super Stylish Bracelets Made Simple. (p. 178)
Steele-Saccio, Eva & Klutz Editors. Thumb Wars: The Ultimate Guide. (p. 2238)
—Twisted Critters: The Pipe Cleaner Book. (p. 2306)
Steelhammer, Ilona, illus. see Cosgrove, Stephen.
Steell, Willis. In Seville: And Three Toledo Days (Classic Reprint) (p. 1107)
—Prospector: A Comedy in Three Acts. (p. 1807)
—Prospector: A Comedy in Three Acts (Classic Reprint) (p. 1807)
Steen, F. J. ACTA Ridleiana, Vol. 2: June, 1892 (Classic Reprint) (p. 12)
Steen, Rob, illus. see Gervais, Ricky.
Steen, Zara. Song of Sirens. (p. 2062)
Steenblik, Kyle J. Tales of Weirderland: Volume 1. (p. 2186)
Steenholdt, Jeff, illus. see Hoeksema, Gertrude.
Steensland, Mark. Behind the Bookcase. Murphy, Kelly, illus. (p. 192)
Steenwyk, Carrie & Witvliet, John D. At Your Baptism. (p. 131)
Steenwyk, Elizabeth Van. Blacksmith's Song Rich, Anna, illus. (p. 240)
Steenz, illus. see Weir, Ivy Noelle.
Steer, Don, jt. auth. see Farwell, Nick.
Steer, Dugald A. Knightology. (p. 1228)
Steer, Dugald A., ed. see Blake, Spencer.
Steer, Dugald A., ed. see Drake, Ernest.
Steer, Dugald A., ed. see Evans, Hestia.
Steer, Dugald A., ed. see Grey, Allan.
Steer, Dugald A., ed. see Lubber, William.
Steer, Dugald A., ed. see Merlin, Master.
Steer, Dugald A., ed. see Merlin.
Steer, Dugald A., ed. see Sands, Emily.
Steer, Dugald A., jt. auth. see Curtie, Lucinda.
Steer, Joanne. Supporting Kids & Teens with Exam Stress in School: A Workbook. Ross, Suzy, illus. (p. 2162)
Steer, Malcolm. Christian's Evangelistic Pocket Guide to Islam. (p. 383)
Steere, Marcia. Tales from My Coloring Book. (p. 2182)
Steers, Billy. Farmers' Market. (p. 711)
—Lift-The-Flap Tab: Tractor Mac: Friends on the Farm. (p. 1297)
—Tractor Mac: New Friend. (p. 2272)
—Tractor Mac Arrives at the Farm. (p. 2273)
—Tractor Mac: Autumn Is Here. Steers, Billy, illus. (p. 2273)
—Tractor Mac Builds a Barn. (p. 2273)
—Tractor Mac Colors on the Farm. Steers, Billy, illus. (p. 2273)
—Tractor Mac Countdown to Christmas. (p. 2273)
—Tractor Mac Family Reunion. (p. 2273)
—Tractor Mac Farm Days. (p. 2273)
—Tractor Mac Farmers Market: Farmer's Market. Steers, Billy, illus. (p. 2273)
—Tractor Mac Farmers' Market. (p. 2273)
—Tractor Mac Harvest Time. (p. 2273)
—Tractor Mac Learns to Fly. (p. 2273)
—Tractor Mac New Friend. (p. 2273)
—Tractor Mac Parade's Best. (p. 2273)
—Tractor Mac Plane Jane's Journey. (p. 2273)
—Tractor Mac Saves Christmas. (p. 2273)
—Tractor Mac School Day. (p. 2273)
—Tractor Mac Sticker Book. (p. 2273)
—Tractor Mac Teamwork. (p. 2273)
—Tractor Mac Tune-Up. (p. 2273)
—Tractor Mac Worth the Wait. (p. 2273)
—Tractor Mac You're a Winner. (p. 2273)
—Tune-Up. (p. 2299)
—You're a Winner. (p. 2535)
Steevens, Christina. Motley Crew: Reminiscences, Observations & Attempts at Play-Writing (Classic Reprint) (p. 1511)
Steevens, George Warrington. With the Conquering Turk: Confessions of a Bashibazouk (Classic Reprint) (p. 2481)
Steevens, G.W. Glimpses of Three Nations (Classic Reprint) (p. 843)
—Things Seen: Impressions of Men, Cities, & Books (Classic Reprint) (p. 2220)
Steeves, J. E. Adventures of Katie & George: Katie & the Dodos. (p. 24)
Steeves, Lynn. Papa's Beach. Siebold, Erin, illus. (p. 1697)
Stefaniuk-Gaudet, Ilara. Secret Wish of Dragon H. (p. 1979)
Stefano, Tony. Tommy & the Dream MacHine — What a Trip! a Boy, a Soda MacHine & a Voyage to Save the Planet. (p. 2259)
Steffan, Jack. Padre Kino & the Trail to the Pacific. (p. 1692)
Steffanelli, Mary. Galileo (p. 806)
Steffen, Jeremy, illus. see Terry, Alana.
Steffen, Mart R. Itinerant Horse Physician (Classic Reprint) (p. 1142)
Steffen, Tim. Big Book of Birds. (p. 217)
—Mom's Cup of Coffee: The (Incr)Edible Adventures of Allie Quirk. (p. 1491)
Steffens, Bradley. Addicted to Video Games. (p. 15)
—Big Data Analyst. (p. 219)
—Biomedical Engineer. (p. 229)
—Careers in Internet Technology. (p. 330)
—Careers in Medical Technology. (p. 330)
—Cell Phone Addiction. (p. 350)
—Cutting Edge Internet Technology. (p. 492)
—Drake. (p. 596)
—Esports & the New Gaming Culture. (p. 663)
—Gun Violence. (p. 905)
—Gun Violence & Mass Shootings. (p. 905)
—How the Internet Is Changing the World. (p. 1036)
—Human Rights in Focus: Torture. (p. 1050)
—Human Rights in Focus: Genocide. (p. 1050)
—Is Marijuana Harmful? (p. 1137)
—J. Cole. (p. 1150)
—Real-World Stem: Securing Cyberspace. (p. 1850)
—Science & Technology of Basketball. (p. 1953)
—Social Media Deception (p. 2053)
—Suicide Epidemic. (p. 2147)
—Thinking Critically: Cell Phones. (p. 2222)
—Thinking Critically: Fossil Fuels. (p. 2222)
—Thinking Critically: Teen Suicide. (p. 2222)
—Threats to Civil Liberties: Privacy. (p. 2231)
—Threats to Civil Liberties: Policing. (p. 2231)
Steffens, Josephine Bontecou. Letitia Berkeley, A. M: A Novel (Classic Reprint) (p. 1269)
Steffens, Lincoln. Shame of the Cities: The Famous Muckraking Expose of Corruption in America's Cities: St. Louis, Chicago, Pittsburgh, Philadelphia & New York. (p. 1999)
—Shame of the Cities: The Famous Muckraking Expose of Corruption in America's Cities: St. Louis, Chicago, Pittsburgh, Philadelphia & New York (Hardcover) (p. 1999)
Steffens, Steffens. John Reed (Classic Reprint) (p. 1174)
Stefflbauer, Thomas, illus. see Jackson, P. D.
Steffora, Tracey. Adding with Ants (p. 15)
—Animal Math. (p. 90)
—Animal Math: Adding, Taking Away, & Skip Counting (p. 90)
—Animal Math: Comparing & Measuring (p. 90)
—Comparing with Cats (p. 433)
—Counting in the City (p. 460)
—Days of the Week (p. 515)
—Estaciones del Año. (p. 664)
—Horas del Día. (p. 1003)
—Horas, Minutos y Segundos. (p. 1003)
—Hours, Minutes, & Seconds (p. 1022)
—Math Around Us (p. 1421)
—Math at the Hospital (p. 1421)
—Math at the Vet (p. 1421)
—Math on the Farm (p. 1424)
—Measuring in the Garden (p. 1435)
—Measuring Time (p. 1435)
—Measuring with Monkeys (p. 1435)
—Medir el Tiempo. (p. 1437)
—Meses del Año. (p. 1451)
—My Five Senses (p. 1547)
—Patterns at the Museum (p. 1706)
—Relojes y Calendarios. (p. 1863)
—Seasons of the Year (p. 1972)
—Shapes in the Kitchen (p. 2000)
—Shapes with Snakes (p. 2000)
—Skip Counting with Meerkats (p. 2032)
—Sorting at the Market (p. 2066)
—Taking Away with Tigers (p. 2178)
—Times of the Day (p. 2247)
—Using Addition at Home (p. 2341)
—Using Subtraction at the Park (p. 2342)
—What Is Math? (p. 2415)
—What Is Time? (p. 2417)
Stefoff, Rebecca. Al Gore. (p. 38)
—Alchemy & Chemistry. (p. 41)
—Astrology & Astronomy. (p. 128)
—Astrology or Astronomy: Is Your Fate in the Stars? (p. 128)
—Building Bridges. (p. 294)
—Building Dams. (p. 294)
—Building Roads. (p. 294)
—Building Skyscrapers. (p. 295)
—Building the Erie Canal. (p. 295)
—Building the Hoover Dam. (p. 295)
—Building Tunnels. (p. 295)
—Captain Kidd. (p. 325)
—Conifer Division. Romagnoli, Robert, illus. (p. 440)
—Corals: Secrets of Their Reef-Making Colonies. (p. 453)
—Crime Labs. (p. 474)
—Criminal Profiling. (p. 474)
—Cybercrime. (p. 492)
—Earth or Sun: Which One Is in the Center? (p. 617)
—Environmental Movement: Then & Now. (p. 657)
—Family Trees - Group 2 (p. 703)
—Famous Forensic Cases. (p. 703)
—First Humans. (p. 737)
—Flat Earth & Round Earth. (p. 747)
—Forensic Techniques. (p. 765)
—Forensics & Medicine. (p. 765)
—Forensics & Modern Disasters. (p. 765)
—Four Elements & the Periodic Table. (p. 772)
—Giants. (p. 831)
—How Animals Communicate. (p. 1025)
—How Animals Feel. (p. 1025)
—How Animals Play. (p. 1025)
—How Animals Think. (p. 1025)
—How Is a Simile Similar to a Metaphor? (p. 1032)
—Humans: An Evolutionary History (p. 1050)
—Ice Age Neanderthals. (p. 1087)
—Idaho. (p. 1089)
—John Brown & Armed Resistance to Slavery. (p. 1172)
—Magic & Medicine. (p. 1376)
—Managing Land Use. (p. 1396)
—Me, Myself, & I—The More Grammar Changes, the More It Remains Th Same. (p. 1433)
—Modern Humans. (p. 1487)
—Moneran Kingdom. (p. 1492)
—Nevada. (p. 1589)
—Origins. (p. 1672)
—Panama Canal. (p. 1695)
—Patriot Act. (p. 1705)
—Polar Bears. (p. 1769)
—Pros & Cons of Coal. (p. 1807)
—Redbeard. (p. 1859)
—Right to Die. (p. 1882)
—Rodent Order. (p. 1897)
—Sea Mammals. (p. 1967)
—Secrets of the Supernatural (p. 1981)
—Smart Spending. (p. 2040)
—Soil for Agriculture. (p. 2055)
—Soil for Building Materials. (p. 2055)
—Solving History's Mysteries. (p. 2058)
—Space Race: An Interactive Space Exploration Adventure. (p. 2072)
—Stephen King. (p. 2115)
—Sun & the Earth. (p. 2151)
—Surviving the Oregon Trail: Stories in American History. (p. 2165)
—Surviving the Oregon Trail. (p. 2165)
—Termites: Secrets of Their Cozy Colonies. (p. 2207)
—U. S. v. Nixon: The Limits of Presidential Privilege. (p. 2312)
—Whale Sharks. (p. 2403)
Stefoff, Rebecca, jt. auth. see Berne, Emma Carlson.
Stefoff, Rebecca, jt. auth. see Sebree, Chet'la.
Stefoff, Rebecca, jt. auth. see Takaki, Ronald.
Stefoff, Rebecca, adapted by. On the Origin of Species: Young Readers Edition. (p. 1655)
—Third Chimpanzee for Young People: On the Evolution & Future of the Human Animal. (p. 2222)
Stefoff, Rebecca & Mead, Wendy. Utah. (p. 2342)
Stefoff, Rebecca & Stanborough, Rebecca. Engineering Wonders. (p. 652)
Stegall, Joel E., illus. see Johns, Isabel G.
Stegall, Kim. Rodney Robbins & the Rainy-Day Pond. Day, Bruce, illus. (p. 1897)
Stegenga, Wil. Sacred Yantra Coloring Book. (p. 1920)
—Spectacular Star Designs. (p. 2078)
Stegenga, Wil & Coloring Books for Adults. Geometric Whirlwind Coloring Book. (p. 818)
Stegenga, Wil & Coloring Books Staff. Geometric Motifs. (p. 818)
Stegman, Ryan. Absolute Carnage. (p. 9)
—Venom by Donny Cates Vol. 1: Rex. (p. 2350)
Stegman, Ryan, jt. illus. see Coello, Iban.
Stegman, Ryan, et al. Sif: Journey into Mystery - the Complete Collection. (p. 2015)
—Venom Unleashed Vol. 1. (p. 2350)
Stegner, Wallace. Women on the Wall (Classic Reprint) (p. 2487)
Stegos, Daniel, illus. see Halfmann, Janet.
Stegos, Daniel, illus. see Korman, Susan.
Stegos, Daniel, jt. auth. see Halfmann, Janet.
Stegos, Daniel J., illus. see Halfmann, Janet.
Stegos, Daniel J., illus. see Hollenbeck, Kathleen M.
Stegos, Daniel J., illus. see Korman, Susan.
Stehlik, Tania Duprey. I Am Violet. Jovanovic, Vanja Vuleta, illus. (p. 1060)
—Violet Jovanovic, Vanja Vuleta & Second Story Press Staff, illus. (p. 2359)
Stehr, Frederic. Bim Bam Boom. Stehr, Frederic, illus. (p. 228)
Steig, Jeanne. Alpha Beta Chowder. Steig, William, illus. (p. 58)
—Consider the Lemming. Steig, William, illus. (p. 442)
—Divine Comedies: The Old Testament Made Easy & a Gift from Zeus. Steig, William, illus. (p. 566)
—Handful of Beans. Steig, William, illus. (p. 915)
Steig, William. Amazing Bone. (p. 64)
—Amazing Bone. Steig, William, illus. (p. 64)
—Amos & Boris. (p. 76)
—Amos & Boris. Steig, William, illus. (p. 76)
—Brave Irene: A Picture Book. Steig, William, illus. (p. 276)
—Brave Irene Storytime Set. (p. 276)
—Doctor de Soto. (p. 573)
—Doctor de Soto. Steig, William, illus. (p. 573)
—Doctor de Soto Book & CD Storytime Set Steig, William, illus. (p. 573)
—Farmer Palmer's Wagon Ride. Steig, William, illus. (p. 711)
—Pete's a Pizza. (p. 1730)
—Roland the Minstrel Pig. (p. 1897)
—Shrek! Steig, William, illus. (p. 2013)
—Shrek! (Book & CD Set) Steig, William, illus. (p. 2013)
—Spinky Sulks. Steig, William, illus. (p. 2082)
—Sylvester & the Magic Pebble. Steig, William, illus. (p. 2173)
—Wizzil. (p. 2483)
—Wizzil. Blake, Quentin, illus. (p. 2483)
—Zabajaba Jungle: A Picture Book. (p. 2537)
Steig, William, illus. see Steig, Jeanne.
Steig, William, illus. see Yorinks, Arthur.
Steiger, A. J. Mindstormer. (p. 1470)
—When My Heart Joins the Thousand. (p. 2432)
Steigerwalt, Charles. Catalogue of the Collection of the Late Royal W. Hutchins, of Lowell, Massachusetts: For Sale by Chas. Steigerwalt, 130 East King St. , Lancaster, Pa (Classic Reprint) (p. 343)
Steil, Debra. Socks the Laundromat Cat. (p. 2054)
Steimle, James. New Adventures of Stephen Crown. (p. 1591)
Stein, A. Little Anna: A Story for Pleasant Little Children; Translated from the German (Classic Reprint) (p. 1310)
Stein, Abraham. Hurrah for the Holidays: Or the Pleasures & Pains of Freedom (Classic Reprint) (p. 1054)
Stein, Arlene G. Serious Henry Is Serious about Studying. (p. 1991)
Stein, Armin. Katharine Von Bora, Dr. Martin Luther's Wife: A Picture from Life (Classic Reprint) (p. 1205)
Stein, Aurel. Mountain Panoramas from the Pamirs & Kwen Lun - Scholar's Choice Edition. (p. 1514)
Stein, Ben P., jt. auth. see Karam, P. Andrew.
Stein, Bob. Bear, a Moose & a Princess. Kalinina, Viktoria, illus. (p. 179)
Stein, Brynn. Ray of Sunlight. (p. 1844)
Stein, Carol. Going Batty. (p. 854)
—Hello, My Friend / Bonjour, Mon Amie (English-French) (Disney Fancy Nancy) Roche, Camille, tr. (p. 951)
—Tea Party Trouble. (p. 2194)
Stein, David Ezra. Because Amelia Smiled. Stein, David Ezra, illus. (p. 186)
—Dinosaur Kisses. Stein, David Ezra, illus. (p. 549)

S

Stephens, C. A. Busy Year at the Old Squire's (Classic Reprint) (p. 302)
—Great Year of Our Lives: At the Old Squire's (Classic Reprint) (p. 891)
—Knockabout Club in the Tropics: The Adventures of a Party of Young Men in New Mexico, Mexico, & Central America (Classic Reprint) (p. 1229)
—Lynx-Hunting, Vol. 4: From Notes by the Author of Camping Out (Classic Reprint) (p. 1370)
—Off to the Geysers: Or the Young Yachters in Iceland, As Recorded by Wade (Classic Reprint) (p. 1640)
—When Life Was Young, at the Old Farm in Maine (Classic Reprint) (p. 2431)
—Young Moose-Hunters: A Backwood's Story (Classic Reprint) (p. 2531)
Stephens, Cassie. Clay Lab for Kids: 52 Projects to Make, Model, & Mold with Air-Dry, Polymer, & Homemade Clay. (p. 402)
Stephens, Charles Asbury. Fox-Hunting: As Recorded by Raed (Classic Reprint) (p. 774)
Stephens, Cyndi, illus. see Stephens, Heather.
Stephens, Dan V. Phelps & His Teachers. (p. 1733)
Stephens, Dan Voorhees. Phelps & His Teachers (Classic Reprint) (p. 1733)
—Silas Cobb: A Story of Supervision (Classic Reprint) (p. 2017)
Stephens, Darrell & Stephens, Tamara. Ashlynn Rose & the Paper Doll Gang: Mystery at Camp Willow Creek. (p. 125)
—Princess Ashlynn & the Crusaders Return to Skull Island. (p. 1796)
Stephens, Darrell & Tamara. Princess Ashlynn & the Crusaders in the Dark Forest. (p. 1796)
Stephens, David. Coastal Habitats. (p. 410)
—Material World: What Is Matter? (p. 1421)
—Sharks: Predators of the Ocean. (p. 2002)
Stephens, David R. Treasure Hunters. (p. 2282)
Stephens, Dawn. Little Pot. (p. 1325)
Stephens, Elaine C., jt. ed. see Brown, Jean E.
Stephens, Elle. All Around Arendelle (Disney Frozen) Disney Storybook Art Team, Disney Storybook, illus. (p. 51)
—Frozen a Day at Arendelle Castle 6-Copy Counter Display Summer 2020 (p. 795)
—Lady & the Tramp: How Lady Met Tramp. (p. 1236)
—Lady & the Tramp: Puppy Love! (p. 1236)
—One Big Party! (p. 1659)
—One Big Party! (DreamWorks Trolls World Tour) Random House, illus. (p. 1659)
—Princess Adventure (Barbie) Random House, illus. (p. 1795)
—Pup on the Run (Barbie) Random House, illus. (p. 1814)
—You Can Do It! (Top Wing) Fruchter, Jason, illus. (p. 2525)
Stephens, H. Marion. Hagar the Martyr; or Passion & Reality: A Tale of the North & South (Classic Reprint) (p. 909)
Stephens, Heather. ABCs Are Delicious. Stephens, Cyndi, illus. (p. 4)
—Where Shall We Go Today? Proulx, Denis, illus. (p. 2439)
Stephens, Helen. Big Adventure of the Smalls. Stephens, Helen, illus. (p. 215)
—Fleabag. (p. 747)
—Gracie Grabbit & Ho. (p. 874)
—How to Hide a Lion. Stephens, Helen, illus. (p. 1042)
—How to Hide a Lion at Christmas. Stephens, Helen, illus. (p. 1042)
—Lam the Nao de Giau Mot Chu Su Tu. (p. 1240)
—Witchety Sticks & the Magic Buttons. Stephens, Helen, illus. (p. 2480)
Stephens, Helen, illus. see Peacock, Lou.
Stephens, Henry Louis. Comic Natural History of the Human Race (Classic Reprint) (p. 429)
Stephens, Henry P. Virginia; or, Ringing the Changes: A New & Original Comic Opera, in Two Acts (Classic Reprint) (p. 2361)
Stephens, J. L. Short-Hand Primer of the Eclectic System of Short-Hand (Classic Reprint) (p. 2010)
Stephens, Jack. Amazing Adventures of Kathy - Dragon Slayer: A Modern Age Fairy Tale. (p. 62)
Stephens, James. Crock of Gold (Classic Reprint) (p. 476)
—Deirdre (Classic Reprint) (p. 526)
—Demi-Gods (Classic Reprint) (p. 527)
—Here Are Ladies (Classic Reprint) (p. 957)
—Irish Fairy Tales. (p. 1134)
—Irish Fairy Tales. Rackhan, Arthur, illus. (p. 1134)
—Mary, Mary (Classic Reprint) (p. 1415)
—Rocky Road to Dublin (Classic Reprint) (p. 1896)
Stephens, James Brunton. Hundred Pounds: A Novelette, to Which Is Added, Bailed up with a Whitewash Brush (Classic Reprint) (p. 1051)
Stephens, Jane. Katie's Too-Big Coat. (p. 1206)
Stephens, Jay, jt. auth. see Weber, Bob.
Stephens, Joan Wilson, illus. see Catalani, Dorothy Kon & Catalani, Jim.
Stephens, Jocelyn. Blended with Care: Filled with Love. (p. 243)
—Renee the Racing Chicken. (p. 1866)
Stephens, John. Black Reckoning. (p. 239)
—Emerald Atlas. (p. 641)
—Fire Chronicle. (p. 732)
Stephens, Kate. College, Quicker: 24 Practical Ways to Save Money & Get Your Degree Faster. (p. 415)
—Life at Laurel Town in Anglo-Saxon Kansas. (p. 1290)
—Life at Laurel Town in Anglo-Saxon Kansas (Classic Reprint) (p. 1290)
Stephens, Kate, jt. auth. see Mabie, Hamilton Wright.
Stephens, Leigh. Birthday Surprise. Artful Doodlers Ltd. Staff, illus. (p. 234)
Stephens, Lori Ann. Novalee & the Spider Secret. (p. 1626)
Stephens, M. C. Eagle & the Beautiful Game. (p. 613)
Stephens, Matt, illus. see Hawes, Alison.
Stephens, Matte, illus. see Kerley, Barbara & Kalt, Rhoda Knight.
Stephens, Pam. Dropping in on ... Puffer Learns about Ceramics. (p. 605)
Stephens, Pamela Geiger. Dropping in on Impressionists. McNeill, Jim, illus. (p. 605)
Stephens, Pat, illus. see Hickman, Pamela.
Stephens, Pat, illus. see Hodge, Deborah.
Stephens, Pat, illus. see Kaner, Etta.
Stephens, Riccardo. Mr. Peters: A Novel (Classic Reprint) (p. 1520)
—Mr. Peters. (p. 1520)
Stephens, Robert Neilson. Bright Face of Danger: Being an Account of Some Adventures of Henri de Launay, Son of the Sieur de la Tournoire; Freely Translated into Modern English (Classic Reprint) (p. 281)
—Captain Ravenshaw, or the Maid of Cheapside a Romance of Elizabethan London, Vol. 2 (Classic Reprint) (p. 326)
—Clementina's Highwayman: A Romance (Classic Reprint) (p. 403)
—Continental Dragoon: A Love Story of Philipse Manor-House in 1778 (Classic Reprint) (p. 445)
—Continental Dragoon. (p. 445)
—Flight of Georgiana: A Story of Love & Peril in England in 1746 (Classic Reprint) (p. 748)
—Gentleman Player: His Adventures on a Secret Mission for Queen Elizabeth (Classic Reprint) (p. 816)
—Gentleman Player. (p. 816)
—Mystery of Murray Davenport: A Story of New York at the Present Day (Classic Reprint) (p. 1569)
—Philip Winwood (p. 1734)
—Road to Paris: A Story of Adventure (Classic Reprint) (p. 1888)
—Soldier of Valley Forge (Classic Reprint) (p. 2056)
—Tales from Bohemia (Classic Reprint) (p. 2182)
Stephens, Ronald, ed. see Etingoff, Kim.
Stephens, Ronald, ed. see Marlowe, Christie.
Stephens, Ronald, ed. Peer Pressure & Relationships. (p. 1714)
—Road Safety. (p. 1888)
—Sports. (p. 2088)
—Stranger Danger. (p. 2138)
—Terrorism & Perceived Terrorism Threats. (p. 2208)
Stephens, Ronnie K. Kaleidoscope Sisters. (p. 1202)
Stephens, Sarah. Angry Birds Movie: Big Trouble on Bird Island. Karacan, Tugrul, illus. (p. 87)
—Angry Birds Movie: Seeing Red. Karacan, Tugrul, illus. (p. 87)
—Big Trouble in Bird City. (p. 223)
—Midway Monkey Madness Baltazar, Art, illus. (p. 1462)
—Pooches of Power! Baltazar, Art, illus. (p. 1773)
—Seeing Red. (p. 1984)
Stephens, Sarah Hines. Backward Bowwow Baltazar, Art, illus. (p. 156)
—Catwoman's Purrfect Plot. Vecchio, Luciano, illus. (p. 346)
—Creature of Chaos. Schoening, Dan, illus. (p. 471)
—Metropolis Mayhem. Brizuela, Dario, illus. (p. 1453)
—Night of the Scaredy Crows Baltazar, Art, illus. (p. 1607)
—Poison Ivy's Rainforest Revenge. Levins, Tim, illus. (p. 1768)
—Show Off: How to Do Absolutely Everything. One Step at a Time. Mann, Bethany, illus. (p. 2012)
—Sleepy Time Crime Baltazar, Art, illus. (p. 2037)
—Superman Classic: Superman & the Mayhem of Metallo. Mada Design Staff, illus. (p. 2160)
—Super-Pets Showdown Baltazar, Art, illus. (p. 2156)
—Superpowered Pony Baltazar, Art, illus. (p. 2161)
Stephens, Sarah Hines, jt. auth. see Harper, Benjamin.
Stephens, Sarah Hines, jt. auth. see Mason, Jane B.
Stephens, Sarah Hines & Hines-Stephens, Sarah. Rumble in the Rainforest Schoening, Dan, illus. (p. 1914)
Stephens, Sarah Hines & Mann, Bethany. Do It Now! Tricks: Rad Stunts & Sneaky Pranks. (p. 570)
Stephens, Simon, jt. auth. see Haddon, Mark.
Stephens, Surplus, illus. see Carter, Kendra.
Stephenson, Alex, illus. see Wagnon, Brad.
Stephenson, Beverly. Bulldog. (p. 296)
Stephenson, Eliza. Aston-Royal, Vol. 2 of 3 (Classic Reprint) (p. 128)
—Blue Ribbon: A Novel (Classic Reprint) (p. 249)
Stephenson, Eliza tabor. Jeanie's Quiet Life: A Novel (Classic Reprint) (p. 1162)
—Senior Songman, Vol. 2 of 3 (Classic Reprint) (p. 1988)
—St. Olave's, Vol. 1 of 3 (Classic Reprint) (p. 2098)
—St. Olave's, Vol. 2 of 3 (Classic Reprint) (p. 2098)
—St. Olave's, Vol. 3 of 3 (Classic Reprint) (p. 2098)
Stephenson, Frederick Charles Arthur. They're a Multitoode, & Other Stories (Classic Reprint) (p. 2219)
Stephenson, Hazel. Black & Gold, Vol. 9: December, 1919 (Classic Reprint) (p. 236)
Stephenson, Henry Thew. Fickle Wheel: A Tale of Elizabethan London (Classic Reprint) (p. 722)
Stephenson, Jessica, jt. auth. see Holley, Bethany.
Stephenson, Karen F., jt. auth. see Anderson, Margaret J.
Stephenson, Kristina. Dinosaur's Return. (p. 551)
—Sir Charlie Stinky Socks & the Really Dreadful Spell. (p. 2025)
—Sir Charlie Stinky Socks & the Really Frightful Night. (p. 2025)
—Sir Charlie Stinky Socks & the Tale of the Terrible Secret. (p. 2025)
—Sir Charlie Stinky Socks & the Tale of the Two Treasures. (p. 2025)
—Sir Charlie Stinky Socks & the Wizard's Whisper. (p. 2025)
—Sir Charlie Stinkysocks - The Pirate's Curse. (p. 2025)
Stephenson, Kristina, illus. see Bauer, Marion Dane.
Stephenson, Kristina, illus. see Piper, Sophie.
Stephenson, Kristina, illus. see Stromberg, Ronica.
Stephenson, Kristina, illus. see Toulmin, Sarah.
Stephenson, Kristina, jt. auth. see Maisner, Heather.
Stephenson, Kristina, Kristina. Sir Charlie Stinky Socks & the Really Big Adventure. (p. 2025)
Stephenson, Mary. Naven's Dream. (p. 1582)
Stephenson, Midji. Ravenous Raven. Gray, Steve, illus. (p. 1844)
—Whose Tail on the Trail at Grand Canyon. Spengler, Kenneth, illus. (p. 2454)
Stephenson, Nathaniel. They That Took the Sword (Classic Reprint) (p. 2219)
Stephenson, Nathaniel W. Day of the Confederacy: Chronicle of the Embattled South. (p. 514)
Stephenson, Nathaniel Wright. Eleanor Dayton (Classic Reprint) (p. 630)
Stephenson, Omri. Freddie Finds Out. (p. 781)
Stephenson, Susan. Monster Maddie. Snider, K. C., illus. (p. 1496)
Stepniak, S. Career of a Nihilist: A Novel (Classic Reprint) (p. 329)
—Career of a Nihilist. (p. 329)
Stepniak, Sergei. New Convert: A Drama in Four Acts (Classic Reprint) (p. 1592)
Stepniak, Sergius. Blind Musician: From the Russian of Korolenko (Classic Reprint) (p. 244)
Stepp, Shirley. Pongo Penquin's Whale of a Tale. (p. 1773)
—Santa Lost His Cell Phone. (p. 1933)
Steps To Literacy Staff. STL Custom Collection. (p. 2120)
Steps To Literacy Staff, compiled by. Beast Quest Collection Grades 2-5: Class Pack (6 Titles, 6 Each) (p. 181)
—Beast Quest Collection Grades 2-5: Variety Pack (6 Titles, 1 Each) (p. 181)
—Eragon/Eldest Box Set: Variety Pack (2 Titles, 1 Each) (p. 659)
—Families: Variety Pack. (p. 701)
—Mercy Watson Collection: Class Pack (4 Titles, 6 Each) (p. 1448)
—Mercy Watson Collection: Variety Pack (4 Titles, 1 Each) (p. 1448)
—Mysterious Benedict Society Collection: Class Pack (3 titles, 6 Each) (p. 1567)
—Mysterious Benedict Society Collection: Variety Pack (3 titles, 1 Each) (p. 1567)
—Percy Jackson & the Olympians Series: Variety Pack (5 Titles, 1 Each) (p. 1721)
—Rhythm & Rhyme Big Books Set 1: Lib600: Variety Pack. (p. 1876)
Steptoe, Javaka. Radiant Child: The Story of Young Artist Jean-Michel Basquiat. (p. 1833)
Steptoe, Javaka, illus. see English, Karen.
Steptoe, Javaka, illus. see Golio, Gary.
Steptoe, Javaka, illus. see Grimes, Nikki.
Steptoe, Javaka, illus. see Medina, Tony.
Steptoe, Javaka, illus. see Pearsall, Shelley.
Steptoe, Javaka, illus. see Schoeder, Alan.
Steptoe, John. Baby Says. Steptoe, John, illus. (p. 152)
—Baby Says Board Book. Steptoe, John, illus. (p. 152)
—Mufaro's Beautiful Daughters. Steptoe, John, illus. (p. 1524)
—Stevie. Steptoe, John, illus. (p. 2116)
Steptoe, John, illus. see Greenfield, Eloise.
Ster, Caroline Rose. Face 2 Face. Jones, Emily, illus. (p. 692)
Sterer, Gideon. From Ed's to Ned's. Cummins, Lucy Ruth, illus. (p. 791)
—Night Knights. Godbey, Cory, illus. (p. 1606)
—Not Your Nest! Tsurumi, Andrea, illus. (p. 1624)
—Skyfishing: (a Grand Tale with Grandpa) Bernatene, Poly, illus. (p. 2034)
Stergios, Tina, illus. see Wong, Linda L.
Sterguiz, Richard, illus. see Stille, Darlene R.
Sterle, Lisa, illus. see Mannino, Nicole.
Sterling, B. K. Cooper Tails Book: My First Snow. Weber, Judy, illus. (p. 451)
—My New Family: A Cooper Tails Book. Weber, Judy, illus. (p. 1558)
Sterling Casil, Amy. Bomb Scares. (p. 254)
—Pancreatic Cancer: Current & Emerging Trends in Detection & Treatment. (p. 1695)
—Tony Hawk: Skateboard Mogul. (p. 2260)
Sterling Children's. Aquarius. (p. 108)
—Aries. (p. 115)
—Cancer. (p. 321)
—Capricorn. (p. 324)
—Gemini. (p. 813)
—Leo. (p. 1267)
—Libra. (p. 1284)
—Pisces. (p. 1751)
—Sagittarius. (p. 1922)
—Scorpio. (p. 1961)
—Taurus. (p. 2193)
—Virgo. (p. 2361)
Sterling Children's Staff. Look & See: What Sound Do You Make? (p. 1345)
Sterling Children's Staff, jt. auth. see La Coccinella.
Sterling Children's, Sterling. Airport. Finn, Rebecca, illus. (p. 37)
—Blackpink: K-Pop Queens: the Unauthorized Fan Guide. (p. 240)
—Builders. Finn, Rebecca, illus. (p. 294)
—C++ for Kids. (p. 306)
—Clothes/la Ropa. (p. 407)
—CSS for Babies. (p. 481)
—Day at the Beach: A Book Of 123s. (p. 512)
—Food/Los Alimentos. (p. 760)
—HTML for Babies. (p. 1047)
—K-Pop: the Ultimate Fan Book: Your Essential Guide to All the Hottest K-Pop Bands. (p. 1201)
—Listful Thinking. (p. 1309)
—M. A. S. H. What Does Your Future Hold? (p. 1370)
—Make a Yellow Dot the Sun. (p. 1386)
—My First Baseball Book. (p. 1540)
—My First Basketball Book. (p. 1540)
—My First Football Book. (p. 1544)
—My First Soccer Book. (p. 1546)
—My New Friend. (p. 1558)
—My Unicorn & Me: My Thoughts, My Dreams, My Magical Friend. (p. 1563)
—Picture Me: A Journal to Get Life Sorted. (p. 1740)
—Super Scratch Art Pads: Mythical Creatures. (p. 2156)
—Super Scratch Art Pads: Nature. (p. 2156)
—Super Scratch Art Pads: Solar System. (p. 2156)
—Super Scratch Art Pads: under the Sea. (p. 2156)
—Taurus. (p. 2193)
—Virgo. (p. 2361)
Sterling Children's, Sterling & Besley, Adrian. Exo: K-Pop Superstars: the Unofficial Biography. (p. 677)
Sterling Children's, Sterling & Jane. Curious Jane. (p. 488)
Sterling Children's, Sterling & Schader Lee, Susan. Secrets of Our Nation's Capital: Weird & Wonderful Facts about Washington, DC. (p. 1980)
Sterling Children's, Sterling & Woodroffe, David. I Heart Origami. (p. 1066)
Sterling Children's, Sterling, et al. Drew & the Camp Color War (Drew Pendous #1) Dress, Robert & Markowitz, Dan, illus. (p. 604)
—Drew Travels to Ancient Egypt (Drew Pendous #2) Dress, Robert & Markowitz, Dan, illus. (p. 604)
Sterling, Garth. Great Ant Colony. (p. 883)
Sterling, Holly. Karate Kids. Sterling, Holly, illus. (p. 1203)
Sterling, Holly, illus. see Harvey, Moira.
Sterling, Holly, illus. see McAllister, Margaret.
Sterling, Isabel. These Witches Don't Burn. (p. 2219)
—This Coven Won't Break. (p. 2224)
Sterling, J. S. Grail of the Grimoire. (p. 875)
Sterling, James Milton. Willy the Mountain Climber. (p. 2470)
Sterling, John. Arthur Coningsby, Vol. 1 of 3 (Classic Reprint) (p. 122)
—Onyx Ring: With a Biographical Preface (Classic Reprint) (p. 1665)
Sterling, Joyce Bea. Guide to Passing the AMP Real Estate Exam. (p. 903)
Sterling, Judith. Sword Unsheathed. (p. 2171)
Sterling, Kristin. Brown Everywhere. (p. 287)
—Exploring Flowers. (p. 681)
—Exploring Leaves. (p. 682)
—Exploring Roots. (p. 682)
—Exploring Seeds. (p. 682)
—Exploring Stems. (p. 683)
—Gray Everywhere. (p. 882)
—Green Everywhere. (p. 894)
—It's Cloudy Today. (p. 1144)
—It's Windy Today. (p. 1148)
—Orange Everywhere. (p. 1668)
—Pink Everywhere. (p. 1746)
—Purple Everywhere. (p. 1816)
—Red Everywhere. (p. 1857)
—White Everywhere. (p. 2443)
—Yellow Everywhere. (p. 2520)
Sterling, L. E. True North. (p. 2294)
—True Storm. (p. 2295)
Sterling, Louse, illus. see Ezinwoke, Patience.
Sterling Publishing Co., Inc. Bebes Animales(Bebes Animales) (p. 186)
—Colors/Colores. (p. 426)
—First Words/Primeras Palabras. (p. 740)
—My First Dance: Ballet. (p. 1543)
—My First Hockey Book. (p. 1544)
—Numbers/Numeros. (p. 1630)
—Oink, Moo, Meow. (p. 1643)
—Oink, Moo, Meow - Oink, Muu, Miau. (p. 1643)
—Things That Go/Cosas Que Se Mueven. (p. 2221)
Sterling Publishing Co., Inc. Staff. Garage. Finn, Rebecca, illus. (p. 808)
—My First Tennis Book. (p. 1546)
Sterling, Richard. Our Own First Reader: For the Use of Schools & Families (Classic Reprint) (p. 1679)
—Our Own Second Reader: For the Use of Schools & Families (Classic Reprint) (p. 1680)
—Our Own Third Reader: For the Use of Schools & Families (Classic Reprint) (p. 1680)
Sterling, Stewart. Too Hot to Handle: A Marshal Pedley Novel (Classic Reprint) (p. 2260)
Sterling Test Prep. Sterling Test Prep SAT Chemistry Practice Questions: High Yield SAT Chemistry Questions with Detailed Explanations. (p. 2116)
Sterling, Zachary, illus. see Sorese, Jeremy.
Sterling, Zachary, illus. see Williams, Leah.
Sterling, Zack, illus. see Corsetto, Danielle.
Stern, A. J. Check, Please! Marts, Doreen Mulryan, illus. (p. 363)
—Doggy Day Care Marts, Doreen Mulryan, illus. (p. 577)
—Fashion Frenzy. Marts, Doreen Mulryan, illus. (p. 712)
—Frankly, Frannie Marts, Doreen Mulryan, illus. (p. 779)
—Funny Business Marts, Doreen Mulryan, illus. (p. 801)
—Here Comes the... Trouble! Marts, Doreen Mulryan, illus. (p. 958)
—Miss Fortune Marts, Doreen Mulryan, illus. (p. 1478)
—Principal for the Day. Marts, Doreen Mulryan, illus. (p. 1800)
—Rocking Out! Marts, Doreen Mulryan, illus. (p. 1895)
Stern, Ariella. Chanukah Guess Who? A Lift the Flap Book. Argoff, Patti, illus. (p. 357)
—Shavous Guess Who? Argoff, Patti, illus. (p. 2003)
Stern, Ashley. My Lost Hug. (p. 1554)
Stern, Beth. Yoda: The Story of a Cat & His Kittens. Crane, Devin, illus. (p. 2523)
—Yoda Gets a Buddy. Crane, Devin, illus. (p. 2523)
Stern, Chani, illus. see Pfeiffer, Chaviva Krohn.
Stern, Elisabeth G. My Mother & I (Classic Reprint) (p. 1556)
Stern, Elsa Charretier: Sarah, illus. see Charretier, Elsa & Colinet, Pierrick.
Stern, Eva L. Little Immigrant: A True Story (Classic Reprint) (p. 1319)
Stern, G. b. China Shop (Classic Reprint) (p. 378)
—Debatable Ground (Classic Reprint) (p. 522)
—Marrying Man (Classic Reprint) (p. 1409)
—Room (Classic Reprint) (p. 1903)
Stern, Gladys Bronwyn. Twos & Threes (Classic Reprint) (p. 2310)
Stern, H. I. Evelyn Gray: Or the Victims of Our Western Turks; a Tragedy in Five Acts (Classic Reprint) (p. 668)
Stern, Joel. In a Spooky Haunted House: A Pop-Up Adventure. Lee, Christopher, illus. (p. 1103)
Stern, Judith M., jt. auth. see Quinn, Patricia O.
Stern, Judith M. & Ben-Ami, Uzi. Many Ways to Learn: A Kid's Guide to LD. Chesworth, Michael & Pearce, Carl, illus. (p. 1400)
Stern, Leonard, jt. auth. see Price, Roger.
Stern, Leonard, jt. creator see Price, Roger.
Stern, Leonard & Price, Roger. Dance Mania Mad Libs. (p. 500)
—Escape from Detention Mad Libs. (p. 661)
—Hello Kitty Loves Mad Libs. (p. 951)
—Luck of the Mad Libs. (p. 1364)
—More Best of Mad Libs. (p. 1504)
—Peace, Love, & Mad Libs. (p. 1709)
Stern, Margaret, creator. Fraction Set. (p. 775)

S

Stern, Michael. White Ticket: Commercialized Vice in the Machine Age, from the Official Records at the New York District Attorney's Office (Classic Reprint) (p. 2445)
Stern, Moritz Abraham. Lehrbuch der Algebraichen Analysis (Classic Reprint) (p. 1265)
Stern, Philip Van Doren. Man Who Killed Lincoln: The Story of John Wilkes Booth & His Part in the Assassination (Classic Reprint) (p. 1395)
Stern, Robin. We Follow the Rules. (p. 2390)
Stern, Robin, jt. auth. see Mills, Nathan.
Stern, Sam & Stern, Susan. Get Cooking. Campbell, Lorne, photos by. (p. 823)
Stern, Simon Adler, jt. auth. see Auerbach, Berthold.
Stern, Steven L. Building Green-Scrapers. (p. 294)
—Cursed Grounds. (p. 489)
—Witchcraft in Salem. (p. 2480)
—Wretched Ruins. (p. 2511)
Sternberg, Charles H. Life of a Fossil Hunter (Classic Reprint) (p. 1293)
Sternberg, Charles Hazelius. Life of a Fossil Hunter - Scholar's Choice Edition. (p. 1293)
Sternberg, Julie. Bedtime at Bessie & Lil's. Gudeon, Adam, illus. (p. 188)
—Everything's Changed. Wright, Johanna, illus. (p. 674)
—Friendship Over. Wright, Johanna, illus. (p. 788)
—Like Bug Juice on a Burger. Cordell, Matthew, illus. (p. 1300)
—Like Carrot Juice on a Cupcake. Cordell, Matthew, illus. (p. 1300)
—Like Pickle Juice on a Cookie. Cordell, Matthew, illus. (p. 1301)
—Puppy, Puppy, Puppy. Koehler, Fred, illus. (p. 1815)
—Secrets Out! Wright, Johanna, illus. (p. 1981)
Sterndale, Mary. Life of a Boy, Vol. 1 of 2 (Classic Reprint) (p. 1293)
Sterndale, Robert A. Natural History of the Mammalia of India & Ceylon. (p. 1579)
Sterndale, Robert Armitage. Seonee, or Camp Life on the Satpura Range: A Tale of Indian Adventure (Classic Reprint) (p. 1989)
Sterne, Elaine. Over the Seas, for Uncle Sam (Classic Reprint) (p. 1686)
—Road of Ambition (Classic Reprint) (p. 1888)
Sterne, Laurence. Beauties of Sterne: Including All His Pathetic Tales, & Most Distinguished Observations on Life; Selected for the Heart of Sensibility (Classic Reprint) (p. 183)
—Beauties of Sterne: Including All His Pathetic Tales, & Most Distinguished, Observations on Life, Selected for the Heart of Sensibility (Classic Reprint) (p. 183)
—Beauties of Sterne: Including Many of His Letters & Sermons, All His Pathetic Tales, Humorous Descriptions, & Most Distinguished Observations of Life (Classic Reprint) (p. 183)
—Beauties of Sterne, Including All His Pathetic Tales, & Most Distinguished Observations on Life: Selected for the Heart of Sensibility (Classic Reprint) (p. 183)
—Complete Works of Laurence Sterne: With a Life of the Author (Classic Reprint) (p. 435)
—Life & Opinions of Tristram Shandy (Classic Reprint) (p. 1289)
—Life & Opinions of Tristram Shandy, Gent: Vol; 4-6 (Classic Reprint) (p. 1289)
—Life & Opinions of Tristram Shandy, Gent, Vol. 1 (Classic Reprint) (p. 1289)
—Life & Opinions of Tristram Shandy, Gentleman: & a Sentimental Journey, Vol. 1 of 2 (Classic Reprint) (p. 1289)
—Life & Opinions of Tristram Shandy, Gentleman (100 Copy Limited Edition) (p. 1289)
—Life & Opinions of Tristram Shandy, Gentleman (Classic Reprint) (p. 1289)
—Life & Opinions of Tristram Shandy, Gentleman, and, a Sentimental Journey Through France & Italy, Vol. 2 of 2 (Classic Reprint) (p. 1289)
—Life & Opinions of Tristram Shandy, Gentleman, Vol. 2: Gentleman (Classic Reprint) (p. 1289)
—Life & Opinions of Tristram Shandy, Gentleman, Vol. 1 (Classic Reprint) (p. 1289)
—Life & Opinions of Tristram Shandy, Gentleman, Vol. 1 of 3 (Classic Reprint) (p. 1289)
—Life Opinions of Tristram Shandy, Gentleman, Vol. 3 of 3 (Classic Reprint) (p. 1295)
—Sentimental Journey Through France & Italy: To Which Are Added the Letters & a Life of the Author (Classic Reprint) (p. 1989)
—Sentimental Journey Through France & Italy: Also a Tale of a Tub Written for the Universal Improvement of Mankind (Classic Reprint) (p. 1989)
—Sentimental Journey Through France & Italy. (p. 1989)
—Sentimental Journey Through France & Italy (Classic Reprint) (p. 1989)
—Sentimental Journey Through France & Italy, Vol. 1 (Classic Reprint) (p. 1989)
—Works of Laurence Sterne: In One Volume, with a Life of the Author (Classic Reprint) (p. 2498)
—Works of Laurence Sterne: With a Life of the Author Written by Himself (Classic Reprint) (p. 2498)
—Works of Laurence Sterne: In One Volume, with a Life of the Author, Written by Himself (Classic Reprint) (p. 2498)
—Works of Laurence Sterne: In One Volume; with a Life of the Author, Written by Himself (Classic Reprint) (p. 2498)
—Works of Laurence Sterne, A. M, Vol. 1 Of 5: To Which Is Prefixed, Some Account of His Life & Writings (Classic Reprint) (p. 2498)
—Works of Laurence Sterne, A. M, Vol. 4 of 5 (Classic Reprint) (p. 2498)
—Works of Laurence Sterne, in Eight Volumes, Vol. 1 of 8 (Classic Reprint) (p. 2498)
—Works of Laurence Sterne, Vol. 1 of 10 (Classic Reprint) (p. 2498)
—Works of Laurence Sterne, Vol. 1 Of 4: Containing the Life & Opinions of Tristram Shandy, Gent. ; a Sentimental Journey Through France & Italy; Sermons, Letters, &c (Classic Reprint) (p. 2498)
—Works of Laurence Sterne, Vol. 1 Of 4: Containing the Life & Opinions of Tristram Shandy, Gent. ; a Sentimental Journey Through France & Italy; Sermons, Letters, &C. , with a Life of the Author (Classic Reprint) (p. 2498)
—Works of Laurence Sterne, Vol. 1 of 4 (Classic Reprint) (p. 2498)
—Works of Laurence Sterne, Vol. 2 (Classic Reprint) (p. 2498)
—Works of Laurence Sterne, Vol. 2 Of 10: Containing, I. the Life & Opinions of Tristram Shandy, Gent;; II. a Sentimental Journey Through France & Italy; III. Sermons; IV. Letters (Classic Reprint) (p. 2498)
—Works of Laurence Sterne, Vol. 2 Of 4: Containing the Life & Opinions of Tristram Shandy, Gent. ; a Sentimental Journey Through France & Italy; Sermons, Lettres, &C. with a Life of the Author, Written by Himself (Classic Reprint) (p. 2498)
—Works of Laurence Sterne, Vol. 2 Of 4: Containing the Life & Opinions of Tristram Shandy, Gent. ; a Sentimental Journey Through France & Italy; Sermons-Letters, &C. ; with a Life of the Author, Written by Himself (Classic Reprint) (p. 2498)
—Works of Laurence Sterne, Vol. 3: The Life & Opinions of Tristram Shandy, Gentleman (Classic Reprint) (p. 2498)
—Works of Laurence Sterne, Vol. 3 Of 6: Tristram Shandy (Classic Reprint) (p. 2499)
—Works of Laurence Sterne, Vol. 3 Of 6: Containing the Life & Opinions of Tristram Shandy, Gent; a Sentimental Journey Through France & Italy; Sermons, Letters, &C. ; with a Life of the Author, Written by Himself (Classic Reprint) (p. 2499)
—Works of Laurence Sterne, Vol. 4: The Life & Opinions of Tristram Shandy Gentleman (Classic Reprint) (p. 2499)
—Works of Laurence Sterne, Vol. 4 Of 10: Containing I. the Life & Opinions of Tristram Shandy, Gent;; II. a Sentimental Journey Through France & Italy; III. Sermons; IV. Letters (Classic Reprint) (p. 2499)
—Works of Laurence Sterne, Vol. 5 Of 10: Containing, I. the Life & Opinions of Tristram Shandy, Gent. , II. a Sentimental Journey Through France & Italy, III. Sermons, IV. Letters (Classic Reprint) (p. 2499)
—Works of Laurence Sterne, Vol. 6 Of 10: The Sermons of Mr. Yorick (Classic Reprint) (p. 2499)
—Works of Laurence Sterne, Vol. 7 Of 10: Containing, I. the Life & Opinions of Tristam Shandy, Gent. ; II. a Sentimental Journey Through France & Italy; III. Sermons; IV. Letters (Classic Reprint) (p. 2499)
—Works of Laurence Sterne, Vol. 7 of 8 (Classic Reprint) (p. 2499)
Sterne, Laurence, jt. auth. see Barrie, J. M.
Sterne, Laurence & Browne, James P. Works of Laurence Sterne. (p. 2498)
Sterne, René, illus. see Van Hamme, Jean.
Sterner, Albert, jt. auth. see Curtis, George William.
Sterner-Radley, Emma. Silver Beasts. (p. 2019)
Sterngass, Jon. Brian Urlacher. (p. 279)
—Crazy Horse: The Wild West for Kids. (p. 469)
—Frederick Douglass. (p. 781)
—John Brown. (p. 1172)
—Reproductive Technology. (p. 1867)
—Same Sex Marriage. (p. 1927)
—Steroids. (p. 2116)
—Terrorism. (p. 2208)
Sterngass, Jon, jt. auth. see Kachur, Matthew.
Sterngass, Jon & McCoy, Erin L. Reproductive Technology: Indispensable or Problematic? (p. 1867)
—Same-Sex Marriage: Cause for Concern or Celebration? (p. 1927)
Sternhagen, Caroline, jt. auth. see Sorensen, Michael.
Sternhagen, Mimi, illus. see Gortler, Rosemarie & Piscitelli, Donna.
Sternin, Joshua & Ventimilia, Jeffrey. Teenage Mutant Ninja Turtles: Pizza Party! (p. 2199)
Sterns, Megan, illus. see Mooney, Carla.
Sternstein, Martin. AP Statistics: With 6 Practice Tests. (p. 105)
—AP Statistics Premium: With 9 Practice Tests. (p. 105)
Sterrett, Frances R. Mary Rose of Mifflin (Classic Reprint) (p. 1416)
—Nancy Goes to Town (Classic Reprint) (p. 1574)
—Rebecca's Promise (Classic Reprint) (p. 1852)
—These Young Rebels (Classic Reprint) (p. 2219)
—Up the Road with Sallie (Classic Reprint) (p. 2338)
—William & Williamina (Classic Reprint) (p. 2468)
Sterrett, Frances Roberta. Amazing Inheritance (Classic Reprint) (p. 65)
Sterrett, Virginia, illus. see Hawthorne, Nathaniel.
Sterrett, Virginia Frances. Arabian Nights. (p. 108)
Sterrett, Virginia Frances, illus. see Comtesse De Segur, Sophie Rostopchine & Saegur, Sophie.
Sterrett, Virginia Frances, illus. see Hawthorne, Nathaniel.
Sterrett, Virginia Frances, jt. auth. see Hawthorne, Nathaniel.
Sterry, J. Ashby. Naughty Girl: A Story of 1893 (Classic Reprint) (p. 1582)
Sterry, Paul. Baby Animals (p. 148)
—Deer, Elk & Mountain Goats (p. 525)
—Insects - Pb: A Portrait of the Animal World. (p. 1122)
—Monkeys & Apes (p. 1494)
Sterry, Paul & Read, Rob. Collins Life-Size Birds: the Only Guide to Show British Birds at Their Actual Size. (p. 417)
Stetson, Charlotte Perkins. Yellow Wall Paper (Classic Reprint) (p. 2520)
Stetson, Clarence. Why Not Cycle Abroad Yourself? (p. 2458)
—Why Not Cycle Abroad Yourself? What a Bicycle Trip in Europe Costs, How to Take It, How to Enjoy It, with a Narrative of Personal Tours, Illustrations & Maps (Classic Reprint) (p. 2458)
Stetson, James Burgess. San Francisco During the Eventful Days of April 1906: Personal Recollections (Classic Reprint) (p. 1929)
Stetson, P. J. Zombies, Fireballs, Snakes, Death, & Candy. (p. 2542)
Stettler, Nicolas & Shelly, Susan. Living with Obesity. (p. 1335)
Steuart, Claude Scott. Ten Days' Trip into the Interior of Japan (Classic Reprint) (p. 2204)
Steuart, John A. Hebrew: A Story of the Time (Classic Reprint) (p. 947)
—In the Day of Battle: A Romance (Classic Reprint) (p. 1108)
—Minister of State: A Novel (Classic Reprint) (p. 1472)
—Red Reaper (Classic Reprint) (p. 1858)
—Wine on the Lees (Classic Reprint) (p. 2472)
Steuart, John Alexander. Faces in the Mist: A Romance of Reality (Classic Reprint) (p. 693)
—Kilgroom, Vol. 2: A Story of Ireland (Classic Reprint) (p. 1217)
—Quicksands (Classic Reprint) (p. 1827)
—Son of Gad: An Anglo-American Story of to-Day (Classic Reprint) (p. 2061)
Steuart, Mary E. Every Day Life on a Ceylon Cocoa Estate (Classic Reprint) (p. 670)
Steuart, Walter. Collections & Observations Methodized, Concerning the Worship, Discipline, & Government of the Church of Scotland, Vol. 1 of 4 (Classic Reprint) (p. 415)
Steudel, Ernst Gottlieb. Nomenclator Botanicus: Enumerans Ordine Alphabetico Nomina Atque Synonyma Tum Generica Tum Specifica et a Linnaeo et Recentioribus de Re Botanica Scriptoribus Plantis Phanerogamis Imposita (Classic Reprint) (p. 1618)
Steuerwald, Joy. Peculiar Pig. Steuerwald, Joy, illus. (p. 1711)
Steuerwald, Joy, illus. see Arrow, Emily.
Steuerwald, Joy, illus. see Garnett, Jaye.
Steuerwald, Joy, illus. see Jordan, Karen.
Steuerwald, Joy, illus. see Redwing, Jack.
Steuerwald, Joy, illus. see Wren, Rosalee.
Stevanovic, Ivica, illus. see Doan, Lisa.
Stevanovic, Ivica, illus. see Hoena, Blake.
Stevanovic, Ivica, illus. see Kimmel, Eric A.
Stevanovic, Ivica, illus. see Olson, Gillia M.
Stevanovic, Tanja, illus. see Berne, Emma Carlson.
Stevans, Andrew L. Two Youth Gangs, Growing up Pittsburgh. (p. 2310)
Steve Chering. There's Something in Granny's Garden! (p. 2218)
Steve, Hart. Mayan & the Legion of Alice. Andrew, Louis, illus. (p. 1429)
Steve, M. C. Awesome Minecraft Activity Book: Whimsical Art for Kids. (p. 145)
—Diary of a Minecraft Alex: Book 2 - Enderman. (p. 539)
—Diary of a Minecraft Alex: Book 1 - Herobrine's Curse. (p. 539)
—Diary of a Minecraft Dork Steve: Book 2 - the Hero. (p. 539)
—Diary of a Minecraft Dork Steve: Book 1 - Forbidden Cave. (p. 539)
—Diary of a Minecraft Noob Steve: Book 1 - Mysterious Fires. (p. 539)
—Diary of a Minecraft Noob Steve: Book 2 - Mysterious Slimes. (p. 539)
—Diary of a Minecraft Wimpy Zombie: Book 2 - the Rivalry. (p. 539)
—Diary of a Minecraft Wimpy Zombie: Book 1 - Middle School. (p. 539)
—Diary of a Minecraft Wimpy Zombie: Book 3 - Monster Christmas. (p. 539)
—Diary of a Minecraft Zombie Alex: Book 1 - the Witch. (p. 539)
—Diary of a Minecraft Zombie Alex: Book 2 - Zombie Army. (p. 539)
—Diary of a Minecraft Zombie Steve: Book 1 - Beep. (p. 539)
—Diary of a Minecraft Zombie Steve: Book 3 - Shipwrecked. (p. 539)
—Diary of a Minecraft Zombie Steve: Book 2 - Restaurant Wars. (p. 539)
—Diary of a Minecraft Zombie Villager: Book 2 - Stagefright. (p. 539)
—Diary of a Minecraft Zombie Villager: Book 1 - Basement Blast. (p. 539)
—Diary of a Minecraft Zombie Villager: Book 3 - Summer Scavenge. (p. 539)
—Goodnight, Wimpy Little Steve: An Unofficial Minecraft Book. (p. 869)
—Super Minecraft Coloring Book: Hours of Minecraft-Filled Fun. (p. 2156)
—Wimpy Zombie's Minecraft Diary: MC Steve Bedtime Stories (an Unofficial Minecraft Book) (p. 2470)
Steve, M. C. & Coloring, Kids. Awesome Minecraft Activity Book: Whimsical Art for Kids (an Unofficial Minecraft Activity Book) (p. 145)
—Super Minecraft Coloring Book: Hours of Minecraft-Filled Fun (an Unofficial Minecraft Coloring Book) (p. 2156)
—Unofficial Awesome Minecraft Activity Book: Whimsical Art for Kids. (p. 2334)
Steven, Earnest G. Sweet Dreams. (p. 2168)
Steven, Kenneth. Fergus Finds a Friend Crowe, Louise, illus. (p. 720)
—Stories for a Fragile Planet: Traditional Tales about Caring for the Earth. Ray, Jane, illus. (p. 2123)
Steven, Kenneth & Torseter, Oyvind. Why Dogs Have Wet Noses. (p. 2457)
Steven, Kenneth C. Biggest Thing in the World. Mitchell, Melanie, illus. (p. 225)
Steven, Laura. Exact Opposite of Okay. (p. 675)
Steven, Peter. News (p. 1600)
Steven, Ruth Lauren & Lauren, Ruth. Prisoner of Ice & Snow. (p. 1801)
Stevens, illus. see Gardner, L. S.
Stevens, Alex, jt. auth. see Mills, Nathan.
Stevens, Anne. Bewitching Berry Men. (p. 211)
—Grandpa's Treasures. (p. 879)
Stevens, April. Heart & Mind of Frances Pauley. (p. 944)
Stevens, Art, illus. see Meuse, Theresa.
Stevens, Arthur A., illus. see Meuse, Theresa.
Stevens, B. M. Poop Book. (p. 1774)
Stevens, Bernardine S. First Alien Christmas. (p. 735)
Stevens, Bethany. Rattlesnake Cake: The Adventures of Buttercup. (p. 1843)
Stevens, Betsy T. Sea Soup: Discovering the Watery World of Phytoplankton. Giebfried, Rosemary, illus. (p. 1968)
Stevens, Bos. If You Went to the Zoo. (p. 1093)
Stevens, C. M. Of Paradise Valley: His Humorous, Pathetic & Tragic Adventures (Classic Reprint) (p. 1640)
—Uncle Jeremiah: And His Neighbors at the St. Louis Exposition (Classic Reprint) (p. 2318)
Stevens, Cara. Nickelodeon PAW Patrol: Group Hug! Jackson, Mike, illus. (p. 1603)
—Zombies Ate My Homework: Redstone Junior High #1. Heddings, Anthony, illus. (p. 2542)
Stevens, Cara J. Alien Conspiracy: An Unofficial Fortnite Novel. (p. 46)
—Battle for the Dragon's Temple: An Unofficial Graphic Novel for Minecrafters, #4. (p. 174)
—Battle Storm: An Unofficial Novel of Fortnite. (p. 175)
—BLACKPINK: Pretty Isn't Everything (the Ultimate Unofficial Guide) (p. 240)
—BTS. el Ascenso de Bangtan Boys. (p. 288)
—BTS: Rise of Bangtan. (p. 288)
—Chasing Herobrine: An Unofficial Graphic Novel for Minecrafters, #5. (p. 362)
—Creepers Crashed My Party: Redstone Junior High #2. Melby, Walker, illus. (p. 472)
—Creepers Crashed My Party. (p. 472)
—Dragons Never Die: Redstone Junior High #3. Melby, Walker, illus. (p. 596)
—Ender Eye Prophecy: An Unofficial Graphic Novel for Minecrafters, #3. Norgren, David & Norgren, Elias, illus. (p. 649)
—Fidget Spinner Tricks, Hacks & Mods: Amaze Your Friends with Spectacular Spinner Secrets! (p. 722)
—Mammoth Book of Graphic Novels for Minecrafters: Three Unofficial Adventures for Minecrafters. (p. 1393)
—My Family & Me: A Family History Fill-In Book. (p. 1538)
—Quest for the Enchanted Sword: An Unofficial Graphic Novel for Minecrafters. Needham, Sam, illus. (p. 1826)
—Revenge of the Zombie Monks: An Unofficial Graphic Novel for Minecrafters, #2. (p. 1873)
—Saving Xenos: An Unofficial Graphic Novel for Minecrafters, #6. Melby, Walker, illus. (p. 1939)
—Spirit in the Stone: An Unofficial Graphic Novel for Minecrafters. Needham, Sam, illus. (p. 2083)
—Superheroes of the Bible: Action & Adventure Stories about Real-Life Heroes. Brack, Amanda, illus. (p. 2160)
—When Endermen Attack: Redstone Junior High #4. Melby, Walker, illus. (p. 2430)
—When Pigmen Fly: Redstone Junior High #6. Creeden, Mitchell, illus. (p. 2432)
—Zombies Ate My Homework: Redstone Junior High #1. Borcherdt, Fred, illus. (p. 2542)
Stevens, Cara J., jt. auth. see Miller, Megan.
Stevens, Charles Wistar. Revelations of a Boston Physician (Classic Reprint) (p. 1872)
Stevens, Charles Woodbury. Fly-Fishing in Maine Lakes: Or Camp-Life in the Wilderness (Classic Reprint) (p. 754)
Stevens, Chris, jt. auth. see Scholastic, Inc. Staff.
Stevens, Court. June Boys (p. 1189)
Stevens, Courtney. Dress Codes for Small Towns. (p. 604)
—Four Three Two One. (p. 773)
—Lies about Truth. (p. 1287)
Stevens, Courtney C. Faking Normal. (p. 699)
Stevens Crummel, Susan, jt. auth. see Stevens, Janet.
Stevens Crummel, Susan, see Crummel, Susan Stevens.
Stevens Crummel, Susan, see Stevens, Janet & Crummel, Susan Stevens.
Stevens, D. K. Lyrics of Eliza (Classic Reprint) (p. 1370)
Stevens, Dan. Magic of the Brass Ring. (p. 1378)
Stevens, Dana J. Sawdust Queen (Classic Reprint) (p. 1939)
Stevens, Daniel, illus. see Fabian, Cynthia.
Stevens, Danielle. Minibeasts. (p. 1472)
Stevens, Dave. Weirdly Wonderful a to Z: Exotic, Aquatic Creatures from the West Coast of British Columbia, Canada. Stevens, Dave, illus. (p. 2397)
Stevens, David. Maid & the Middy: An Operetta (Classic Reprint) (p. 1382)
Stevens, David Kilburn. Lays of a Lazy Dog (Classic Reprint) (p. 1253)
Stevens, David T., illus. see Stevens, Diane M. R.
Stevens, Deborah Bowman, ed. see Zadunajsky, Donna M.
Stevens, Diane M. R. Eccnetric Earthlings A-Z: Fun Land Creatures from British Columbia, Canada. Stevens, David T., illus. (p. 622)
Stevens, Elizabeth. Abba Father's Lullaby. (p. 3)
—Mister D. Frongia, Daniela, illus. (p. 1482)
—Safety in the Friendzone. (p. 1922)
Stevens, Eric. Finn Reeder, Flu Fighter: How I Survived a Worldwide Pandemic, the School Bully, & the Craziest Game of Dodge Ball Ever. Fraser, Kay, illus. (p. 731)
—Flu Fighter: How I Survived a Worldwide Pandemic, the School Bully, & the Craziest Game of Dodge Ball Ever. Fraser, Kay, illus. (p. 753)
—Revenge of Clayface. (p. 1872)
Stevens, Eric & Fuentes, Benny. Skateboard Sonar Sandoval, Gerardo, illus. (p. 2029)
Stevens, Eric & Maddox, Jake. Playing Forward. Tiffany, Sean, illus. (p. 1760)
Stevens, Eric, et al. Menace of Metallo (p. 1447)
Stevens, Ethel Stefana. Allward: A Story of Gypsy Life (Classic Reprint) (p. 57)
—Veil: A Romance of Tunisia (Classic Reprint) (p. 2349)
Stevens, Frank. Adventures in Hiveland (Classic Reprint) (p. 20)
—Adventures in Pondland (Classic Reprint) (p. 20)
Stevens, Gareth, jt. auth. see Connors, Kathleen.
Stevens, Gareth, contrib. by. ENVIRONMENT MOVEMENT. (p. 657)
—LABOR MOVEMENT. (p. 1235)
—LGBTQ+ MOVEMENT. (p. 1283)
—MODERN NERD'S GUIDE TO: COSPLAY. (p. 1487)
—WOMEN'S RIGHTS MOVEMENTS. (p. 2488)
Stevens, Gary J. If I Called You a Hippopotamus! Stead, April-Nicole, illus. (p. 1091)
Stevens, Geo. Alex. Lecture on Deads: To Which Is Added, an Essay on Satire (Classic Reprint) (p. 1260)
Stevens, George Alexander. Adventures of a Speculist, or a Journey Through London, Vol. 1 of 2 (Classic Reprint) (p. 21)

—Beauties of All the Magazines Selected, for the Year 1762, Vol. 1: Including the Several Original Comic Pieces (Classic Reprint) (p. 183)
—Dramatic History of Master Edward, Miss. Ann, & Others, the Extraordinaries of These Times: Collected from Zaphaniel's Original Papers (Classic Reprint) (p. 597)
—History of Tom Fool, Vol. 2: More Know Tom Fool, Than Tom Fool Knows (Classic Reprint) (p. 981)
—Lecture on Heads (Classic Reprint) (p. 1260)
Stevens, Georgina. Finn the Fortunate Tiger Shark & His Fantastic Friends: Learn How to Protect Our Oceans with Finn. Baker, Tom, illus. (p. 731)
Stevens, Grant Eugene. Wicked City (Classic Reprint) (p. 2460)
Stevens, Hazel. Poppy Is Lost in the Garden. Gambrioli, Bianca Camilla, illus. (p. 1776)
—Poppy Veut Préparer un Gâteau. Minguzzi, Roberto, illus. (p. 1776)
—Poppy Vuole Preparare una Torta. (p. 1776)
—Poppy Wants to Bake a Cake. (p. 1776)
Stevens, Helen, illus. see Beckhorn, Susan Williams.
Stevens, Henry Bailey. Cry Out of the Dark: Three Plays: the Meddler; Bolo & Babette; the Madhouse (Classic Reprint) (p. 480)
Stevens, Isaac N. American Suffragette: A Novel (Classic Reprint) (p. 74)
—American Suffragette. (p. 74)
Stevens, Jake Lee, creator. Finlay Finds the Ravens. (p. 731)
Stevens, Janet. Coyote Steals the Blanket: A Ute Tale. (p. 465)
Stevens, Janet, illus. see Beaumont, Karen.
Stevens, Janet, illus. see Crummel, Susan Stevens.
Stevens, Janet, illus. see Kimmel, Eric A.
Stevens, Janet, illus. see Levitt, Paul M., et al.
Stevens, Janet, illus. see Salley, Coleen.
Stevens, Janet, jt. auth. see Crummel, Susan Stevens.
Stevens, Janet & Crummel, Susan Stevens. Donkey Egg. (p. 581)
—Find a Cow Now! Stevens, Janet, illus. (p. 727)
—Great Fuzz Frenzy. (p. 886)
—Help Me, Mr. Mutt! Expert Answers for Dogs with People Problems. (p. 953)
—Jackalope. (p. 1153)
—Little Red Pen. (p. 1326)
—Little Red Pen. Stevens, Janet, illus. (p. 1326)
—Tumbleweed Stew/Sopa de Matojos. Flor Ada, Alma & Campoy, F. Isabel, trs. (p. 2299)
Stevens, Janet & Stevens Crummel, Susan. My Big Dog. Stevens, Janet, illus. (p. 1532)
Stevens, Jennifer. Love You More. (p. 1361)
Stevens, Jenny. Trafalgar Bear. (p. 2274)
Stevens, Jessica. Within Reach: A Novel. (p. 2482)
Stevens, Jim. Baby Cartoon Animals Coloring Book. (p. 149)
—Cartoon Animals Coloring Book. (p. 335)
Stevens, John. Spanish Jilt (Classic Reprint) (p. 2074)
Stevens, Joseph Earle. Yesterdays in the Philippines (Classic Reprint) (p. 2521)
Stevens, Joshua. Tails of Sanctuary: The Dark Sentinel. (p. 2176)
Stevens, Judith. Maths in Stories (p. 1425)
Stevens, Judy, illus. see Denham, Joyce.
Stevens, K. T. Christmas Stories for Children & the Young at Heart! (p. 387)
—Stories for Children. (p. 2123)
Stevens, Kathryn. Cellos. (p. 350)
—Christmas Trees. (p. 387)
—Fish. (p. 741)
—Gorillas. (p. 870)
—Halloween Jack-O'-Lanterns. (p. 912)
—Hamsters. (p. 914)
—Hermit Crabs. (p. 959)
—Lizards. (p. 1336)
—Parakeets. (p. 1699)
—Turtles. (p. 2301)
Stevens, Laird. Harris Goes to Paris (Color Edition) (p. 933)
—New Blue Fairy Book: Part 1: Fairy Tales 1 To 6. (p. 1591)
—New Blue Fairy Book: Part 2: Fairy Tales 7 To 12. (p. 1591)
—New Blue Fairy Book: Part 3: Fairy Tales 13 To 18. (p. 1591)
—New Blue Fairy Book. (p. 1591)
Stevens, Leon H. Letters from Roy, or the Spirit Voice (Classic Reprint) (p. 1280)
Stevens, Leon Herbert. Second Letters from Roy (Classic Reprint) (p. 1973)
Stevens, Linda M. Unlocking the Hidden Treasures. (p. 2333)
Stevens, Liza. Not Today, Celeste! A Dog's Tale about Her Human's Depression. (p. 1624)
Stevens, Madeline. Discovering Mission San Gabriel Arcángel. (p. 556)
—Discovering Mission San José. (p. 556)
—Discovering Mission San Juan Bautista. (p. 556)
—Orange Around Me. (p. 1668)
—Red Around Me. (p. 1856)
Stevens, Madeline, jt. auth. see McGinty, Alice B.
Stevens, Mark. Six Months at the World's Fair (Classic Reprint) (p. 2028)
Stevens, Mary, illus. see Parkinson, Ethelyn.
Stevens, Matt, illus. see Melilli, Julie.
Stevens, Matt, illus. see Peterson, Megan Cooley & Rustad, Martha E. H.
Stevens, Melissa, illus. see Beynon, M. C.
Stevens, Michael J. Silver Spitfire. (p. 2020)
Stevens, Mitchell. Hey! Follow Your Dreams: 7 Steps to Dream Followin' (p. 964)
—Village of Lights. Pritchett, Emily, illus. (p. 2358)
Stevens, Paul. Fables (Classic Reprint) (p. 690)
Stevens, Rob. Would the Real Stanley Carrot Please Stand Up? (p. 2509)
Stevens, Robin. Guggenheim Mystery. (p. 903)
—Jolly Foul Play. (p. 1176)
—Mistletoe & Murder. (p. 1483)
—Murder Is Bad Manners. (p. 1527)
—Poison Is Not Polite. (p. 1768)
Stevens, Roger, jt. auth. see Moses, Brian.
Stevens, Roger & Moses, Brian. What Are We Fighting For? New Poems about War. (p. 2406)
Stevens, S. S. Red Ryder & the Secret of Wolf Canyon (Classic Reprint) (p. 1858)
Stevens, Sara. I Love You All the Time. (p. 1078)
Stevens, Sarah. Circle Line. (p. 392)
Stevens, Sheppard. I Am the King - Scholar's Choice Edition. (p. 1060)
Stevens, Stefan. Understanding Civilizations. (p. 2324)
Stevens, Stevens. History of Tom Fool, Vol. 1 (Classic Reprint) (p. 981)
Stevens, Stewart, Sr. White House Chandeliers: My Experiences While Working for Seven U. S. Presidents. (p. 2444)
Stevens, Tammie, ed. see Rounds, Erin.
Stevens, Thomas. Scouting for Stanley in East Africa (Classic Reprint) (p. 1963)
Stevens, Thomas Wood. Three Wishes: A Comedy in One Act (Classic Reprint) (p. 2235)
Stevens, Tim, illus. see Cross, Gillian.
Stevens, Tim, illus. see Langrish, Katherine.
Stevens, William Dodge, jt. auth. see Kelly, Myra.
Stevenski, Linda. Merry Heart. (p. 1450)
—Prince, the Princess, & Yes, the Frog. (p. 1795)
Stevens-Marzo, Bridget, illus. see Cocagne, Marie-Pascale.
Stevenson, Archibald E. From New York to Alaska, & Back Again (Classic Reprint) (p. 792)
Stevenson, Augusta. Children's Classics in Dramatic Form: A Reader for the Fourth Grade - Scholar's Choice Edition. (p. 373)
—Children's Classics in Dramatic Form. (p. 373)
—Children's Classics in Dramatic Form, Book Two. (p. 373)
—Children's Classics in Dramatic Form, Vol. 1 (Classic Reprint) (p. 373)
—Puppet Princess: Or, the Heart That Squeaked (Classic Reprint) (p. 1814)
Stevenson, Brandon. Eddie Versus the Shadow Shifters: In the Battle for Christmas. (p. 625)
Stevenson, Bryan. Just Mercy (Adapted for Young Adults) A True Story of the Fight for Justice. (p. 1194)
—Just Mercy (Movie Tie-In Edition, Adapted for Young Adults) A True Story of the Fight for Justice. (p. 1194)
Stevenson, Burton E. Destroyer: A Tale of International Intrigue (Classic Reprint) (p. 534)
—King in Babylon (Classic Reprint) (p. 1220)
Stevenson, Burton Egbert. Charm of Ireland (Classic Reprint) (p. 361)
—Heritage: A Story of Defeat & Victory (Classic Reprint) (p. 959)
—Home Book of Verse, American & English, 1580-1912, Vol. 1: With an Appendix Containing a Few Well-Known Poems in Other Languages; Poems of Youth & Age (Classic Reprint) (p. 996)
—Home Book of Verse, American & English, 1580-1912, Vol. 8: With an Appendix Containing a Few Well-Known Poems in Other Languages; Poems of Sorrow, Death & Immortality (Classic Reprint) (p. 996)
—Home Book of Verse, American & English, 1580-1912, Vol. 5: With an Appendix Containing a Few Well-Known Poems in Other Languages; Familiar Verse, & Poems Humorous & Satiric (Classic Reprint) (p. 996)
—Quest for the Rose of Sharon (Classic Reprint) (p. 1826)
—Soldier of Virginia: A Tale of Colonel Washington & Braddock's Defeat (Classic Reprint) (p. 2056)
—Soldier of Virginia. (p. 2056)
—Spell of Holland: The Story of a Pilgrimage to the Land of Dykes (Classic Reprint) (p. 2078)
Stevenson, C. G. R. Betty Stevenson, Y. M. C. A. , Croix de Guerre Avec Palme: Sept. 3, 1896-May 30, 1918 (Classic Reprint) (p. 210)
Stevenson, Charles. Adventures of the Glo-Worm Family. (p. 28)
Stevenson, D. E. Miss. Buncle, Married: Being the Further Adventures of the Celebrated Authoress (Classic Reprint) (p. 1478)
—Miss Buncle's Book. (p. 1478)
—Two Mrs. Abbotts. (p. 2308)
Stevenson, Dave, illus. see Hunter, Erin.
Stevenson, Dave, illus. see Ruby, Laura.
Stevenson, Dave, illus. see Wolverton, Barry.
Stevenson, David. Principles & Practice of Canal & River Engineering (Classic Reprint) (p. 1800)
Stevenson, Deborah. Last Rhino. Hill, Krista, ed. (p. 1249)
—Oy, Elephants! Hill, Krista, ed. (p. 1690)
Stevenson, Edward Irenaeus. Janus: A Novel (Classic Reprint) (p. 1159)
Stevenson, Emma. Hide-and-Seek Science: Animal Camouflage. (p. 967)
—Hide-and-Seek Science: Animal Camouflage. Stevenson, Emma, illus. (p. 967)
Stevenson, Gail. Anna's Day of Gratitude. (p. 98)
Stevenson, George. Little World Apart (Classic Reprint) (p. 1330)
—Topham's Folly (Classic Reprint) (p. 2264)
Stevenson, Hannah A. Once upon a Paper Doll: Color Your Own Fairy Tale Paper Dolls. (p. 1657)
Stevenson, Ian. Trump for Kids: The President, Freedom, & You. (p. 2295)
Stevenson, Irene, illus. see Boyce, Carla.
Stevenson, James, illus. see Blume, Judy.
Stevenson, James, illus. see Prelutsky, Jack.
Stevenson, John. Boy in the Country (Classic Reprint) (p. 269)
Stevenson, John Allen. Archive, Vol. 87: Fall 1974 (Classic Reprint) (p. 111)
Stevenson, John C. Camosun, Vol. 6: February, 1914 (Classic Reprint) (p. 315)
Stevenson, Juliet, jt. auth. see Duffy, Carol Ann.
Stevenson, Lilian. Child's Bookshelf: Suggestions on Children's Reading, with an Annotated, List of Books on Heroism, Service, Patriotism, Friendliness, Joy & Beauty (Classic Reprint) (p. 375)
Stevenson, Lorie. On Top of the World. Roberts, Jp, illus. (p. 1656)
Stevenson, M. I. Letters from Samoa 1891-1895 (Classic Reprint) (p. 1280)
Stevenson, Mabel B. Brown Mouse: A Rural Play in Four Acts (Classic Reprint) (p. 287)
Stevenson, Noelle. Fire Never Goes Out: A Memoir in Pictures. Stevenson, Noelle, illus. (p. 732)
—Nimona. (p. 1609)
—Nimona. Stevenson, Noelle, illus. (p. 1609)
Stevenson, O. J. Country Life Reader (Classic Reprint) (p. 461)
—High School Prose Book: Part I (Classic Reprint) (p. 969)
Stevenson, Orlando John. High School Prose Book, Vol. 2 (Classic Reprint) (p. 969)
Stevenson, Orlando John, jt. auth. see Longfellow, Henry.
Stevenson, Peggy. Meet the Spencers & the Smart Knots. (p. 1440)
Stevenson, Peter. Baby's First Nativity: A CarryAlong Treasury. (p. 154)
—Baby's First Nativity. (p. 154)
Stevenson, Peter, illus. see Zobel-Nolan, Allia.
Stevenson, R. L. Treasure Island. (p. 2282)
—Treasure Island. Ingpen, Robert, illus. (p. 2282)
Stevenson, Rennie. Through Rhodesia with the Sharpshooters (Classic Reprint) (p. 2237)
Stevenson, Robert. Treasure Island. (p. 2282)
Stevenson, Robert Louis. Across the Plains: With Other Memories & Essays (Classic Reprint) (p. 11)
—Across the Plains. (p. 11)
—Amateur Emigrant, and, the Silverado Squatters (Classic Reprint) (p. 62)
—Bed in Summer. Reisch, Jesse, illus. (p. 187)
—Black Arrow: A Tale of Two Roses. (p. 236)
—Black Arrow: A Tale of the Two Roses. (p. 236)
—Black Arrow: A Tale of the Two Roses (Classic Reprint) (p. 236)
—Black Arrow. (p. 236)
—Catriona. (p. 345)
—Catriona a Sequel to Kidnapped Being Memoirs of the Further Adventures of David Balfour at Home & Abroad (Classic Reprint) (p. 345)
—Child's Garden of Verses: A Collection of Scriptures, Prayers & Poems. Peat, Fern Bisel, illus. (p. 376)
—Child's Garden of Verses. (p. 376)
—Child's Garden of Verses. Foreman, Michael, illus. (p. 376)
—Child's Garden of Verses. Robinson, Charles, illus. (p. 376)
—Child's Garden of Verses. McClintock, Barbara, illus. (p. 376)
—Child's Garden of Verses (Classic Reprint) (p. 376)
—Child's Garden of Verses & Underwoods. (p. 376)
—Child's Garden of Verses & Underwoods (Classic Reprint) (p. 376)
—Classic Starts(r): Treasure Island. Corvino, Lucy, illus. (p. 400)
—Correspondence Addressed to Sidney Colvin, November 1890 to October 1894 (Classic Reprint) (p. 456)
—Cruise of the Janet Nichol among the South Sea Islands: A Diary (Classic Reprint) (p. 479)
—Daisies from a Child's Garden of Verses. (p. 497)
—Daisies from a Child's Garden of Verses (Classic Reprint) (p. 497)
—Dr Jekyll & Mr Hyde. Lubach, Vanessa, illus. (p. 591)
—Dr. Jekyll & Mr. Hyde. (p. 591)
—Dr. Jekyll & Mr. Hyde. Gelev, Penko, illus. (p. 591)
—Dr. Jekyll & Mr. Hyde Graphic Novel. (p. 591)
—Dynamiter. (p. 612)
—Ebb-Tide: A Trio & Quartette (Classic Reprint) (p. 622)
—Ebb-Tide Weir of Hermiston Heathercat: The Young Chevalier (Classic Reprint) (p. 622)
—Edinburgh: Picturesque Notes (Classic Reprint) (p. 626)
—Edinburgh: Picturesque Notes, the Silverado Squatters, Memories & Portraits (Classic Reprint) (p. 626)
—Edinburgh, Vol. 3: Picturesque Notes; the Silverdo Squatters Will o' the Mill (Classic Reprint) (p. 626)
—Essays & Criticisms (Classic Reprint) (p. 663)
—Essays of Travel (Classic Reprint) (p. 663)
—Extrano Caso Del Dr. Jekyll y Mr. Hyde. (p. 685)
—Extraño Caso Del Dr. Jekyll y Mr. Hyde. Jacome, Nelson, illus. (p. 685)
—Fables (Classic Reprint) (p. 690)
—Familiar Studies of Men & Books. (p. 701)
—Father Damien: An Open Letter to the Reverend Doctor Hyde of Honolulu (Classic Reprint) (p. 714)
—Father Damien. (p. 714)
—Flight of the Princess: And Other Pieces (Classic Reprint) (p. 749)
—Fraser's Magazine for Town & Country, Vol. 25: January to June, 1842 (Classic Reprint) (p. 779)
—In the South Seas; Letters from Samoa, etc (Classic Reprint) (p. 1111)
—Inland Voyage (Classic Reprint) (p. 1120)
—Inland Voyage & Travels with a Donkey (Classic Reprint) (p. 1120)
—Inland Voyage; Travels with a Donkey; Dr. Jekyll & Mr. Hyde: And Other Tales (Classic Reprint) (p. 1120)
—Inland Voyage; Travels with a Donkey; Edinburgh: And Other Papers (Classic Reprint) (p. 1120)
—Isla Del Tesoro. (p. 1139)
—Island Nights' Entertainments: Consisting of the Beach of Falesa, the Bottle Imp, the Isle of Voices (Classic Reprint) (p. 1139)
—Island Nights' Entertainments. (p. 1139)
—Island Nights Entertainments (Classic Reprint) (p. 1139)
—Kidnapped Fisher, Eric Scott, illus. (p. 1213)
—Kidnapped: Adapted for Young Readers. Kliros, Thea, illus. (p. 1213)
—Kidnapped. (p. 1213)
—Kidnapped. Kumar, Naresh, illus. (p. 1213)
—Kidnapped (100 Copy Collector's Edition) (p. 1213)
—Kidnapped, and, David Balfour (Classic Reprint) (p. 1213)
—Kidnapped Being Memoirs of the Adventures of David Balfour in the Year 1751 (Classic Reprint) (p. 1213)
—Land of Counterpane. Harrison, Nancy, illus. (p. 1241)
—Lay Morals: And Other Papers (Classic Reprint) (p. 1253)
—Letters & Miscellanies of Robert Louis Stevenson: Weir of Herminston; the Plays; Fables (Classic Reprint) (p. 1279)
—Letters & Miscellanies of Robert Louis Stevenson, Vol. 27: New Letters (Classic Reprint) (p. 1279)
—Letters & Miscellanies of Robert Louis Stevenson (Classic Reprint) (p. 1279)
—Letters of Robert Louis Stevenson to His Family & Friends. (p. 1280)
—Letters of Robert Louis Stevenson, Vol. 2 of 4 (Classic Reprint) (p. 1280)
—Letters of Robert Louis Stevenson, Vol. 4 Of 4: 1891-1894 (Classic Reprint) (p. 1280)
—Little Land. Thornburgh, Rebecca McKillip, illus. (p. 1320)
—Master of Ballantrae: A Winter's Tale (Classic Reprint) (p. 1418)
—Master of Ballantrae: A Winters Tale (the Unabridged Illustrated Edition): Historical Adventure Novel. (p. 1418)
—Master of Ballantrae: A Winter's Tale (Illustrated Edition): the Master of Ballantrae: a Winter's Tale (Illustrated Edition) (p. 1418)
—Master of Ballantrae. (p. 1418)
—Master of Ballantrae, and, Prince Otto, Vol. 3: And Other Stories (Classic Reprint) (p. 1418)
—Master of Ballantrae; Weir of Hermiston; Poems (Classic Reprint) (p. 1418)
—Master of Ballantrea. (p. 1418)
—Memories & Portraits; Random Memories; Records of a Family of Engineers (Classic Reprint) (p. 1445)
—Memories & Portraits, Virginibus Puerisque: And Other Papers (Classic Reprint) (p. 1445)
—Merry Men, & Other Tales & Fables (Classic Reprint) (p. 1450)
—Merry Men, & Other Tales & Fables, and, Strange Case of Dr. Jekyll & Mr. Hyde (Classic Reprint) (p. 1450)
—Merry Men, & Other Tales & Fables; Strange Case of Dr. Jeykll & Mr. Hyde; Prince Otto (Classic Reprint) (p. 1450)
—Moby Dick. (p. 1485)
—Moral Emblems: Other Poems (Classic Reprint) (p. 1503)
—Mountain Town in France: A Fragment (Classic Reprint) (p. 1514)
—Mountain Town in France. (p. 1514)
—My Children's Robert Louis Stevenson Paint Book (Classic Reprint) (p. 1535)
—My Shadow. Idle, Molly, illus. (p. 1560)
—My Shadow. Lang, Glenna, illus. (p. 1560)
—My Shadow. Sanchez, Sara, illus. (p. 1560)
—New Arabian Nights: The Dynamiter (Classic Reprint) (p. 1591)
—New Arabian Nights: The Novels & Tales of Robert Louis Stevenson (Classic Reprint) (p. 1591)
—New Arabian Nights. (p. 1591)
—New Arabian Nights, and, the Dynamiter (Classic Reprint) (p. 1591)
—On the Choice of a Profession (Classic Reprint) (p. 1653)
—Poems & Plays, Vol. 8: With an Essay on Stevenson As a Poet (Classic Reprint) (p. 1765)
—Prince Otto: A Romance (Classic Reprint) (p. 1794)
—Prince Otto. (p. 1794)
—Prince Otto Island Nights Entertainments Father Damien (Classic Reprint) (p. 1794)
—Robert Louis Stevenson: Hitherto Unpublished Prose Writings (Classic Reprint) (p. 1890)
—Selections from Robert Louis Stevenson (Classic Reprint) (p. 1986)
—Silverado Squatters (Classic Reprint) (p. 2020)
—Silverado Squatters; Across the Plains; Dr. Jekyll & Mr. Hyde: And Other Stories (Classic Reprint) (p. 2020)
—Sketches, Criticisms, etc (Classic Reprint) (p. 2031)
—South Sea Yarns, Vol. 1 (Classic Reprint) (p. 2069)
—St. Ives: Being the Adventures of a French Prisoner in England (Classic Reprint) (p. 2096)
—St. Ives. (p. 2096)
—St. Ives, Vol. 2 Of 2: Being the Adventures of a French Prisoner in England (Classic Reprint) (p. 2096)
—Stevenson Reader: Selected Passages from the Works of Robert Louis Stevenson. (p. 2116)
—Stevenson Reader: Selected Passages from the Works of Robert Louis Stevenson (Classic Reprint) (p. 2116)
—Story of a Lie: And Other Tales. (p. 2128)
—Story of a Lie: And Other Tales (Classic Reprint) (p. 2128)
—Strange Case of Dr. Jekyll & Mr. Hyde Fisher, Scott, illus. (p. 2137)
—Strange Case of Dr. Jekyll & Mr. Hyde. McKowen, Scott, illus. (p. 2137)
—Swing. Morstad, Julie, illus. (p. 2170)
—Tale & Fantasies, Vol. 4 (Classic Reprint) (p. 2178)
—Tales & Fantasies (Classic Reprint) (p. 2181)
—Tales & Fantasies, Vol. 1 (Classic Reprint) (p. 2181)
—the Strange Case of Dr Jekyll & Mr Hyde. Williamson, Pete, illus. (p. 2214)
—Travels & Essays of Robert Louis Stevenson: The Amateur Emigrant; Across the Plains; the Silverado Squatters (Classic Reprint) (p. 2281)
—Travels with a Donkey in the Cevennes: An Inland Voyage (Classic Reprint) (p. 2281)
—Travels with a Donkey in the Cevennes. (p. 2281)
—Travels with a Donkey in the Cevennes (Classic Reprint) (p. 2281)
—Treasure Island. (p. 2282)
—Treasure Island. Rhead, Louis, illus. (p. 2282)
—Treasure Island. Lawrence, John, illus. (p. 2282)
—Treasure Island. Rossi, Francesca, illus. (p. 2282)
—Treasure Island (Illustrated Edition) Adventure Tale of Buccaneers & Buried Gold. (p. 2282)
—Treasure Island (Illustrated) With Artwork by N. C. Wyeth & Louis Rhead. Wyeth, N. C. & Rhead, Louis, illus. (p. 2282)
—Treasure Island (Unabridged & Fully Illustrated) Louis, Rhead, illus. (p. 2282)
—Treasure Island, and, Kidnapped (Classic Reprint) (p. 2282)
—Treasure Island & Kidnapped (Unabridged & Fully Illustrated) Louis, Rhead, illus. (p. 2282)
—Treasure Island - Scholar's Choice Edition. (p. 2282)
—Vailima Letters, Vol. 1 Of 2: Being Correspondence Addressed by Robert Louis Stevenson to Sidney Colvin, November, 1890-October 1894 (Classic Reprint) (p. 2343)
—Vailima Letters, Vol. 2 Of 2: Being Correspondence Addressed by Robert Louis Stevenson to Sidney Colvin,

November, 1890-October, 1894 (Classic Reprint) (p. 2343)
—Virginibus Puerisque; the Amateur Emigrant; the Pacific Capitals; Silverado Squatters (Classic Reprint) (p. 2361)
—Waif Woman (Classic Reprint) (p. 2370)
—Weir of Hermiston: An Unfinished Romance. (p. 2396)
—Weir of Hermiston: An Unfinished Romance (Classic Reprint) (p. 2396)
—Weir of Hermiston: The Misadventures of John Nicholson; the Story of a Lie; the Body-Snatcher (Classic Reprint) (p. 2396)
—Weir of Hermiston. (p. 2396)
—Works of Robert Louis Stevenson, Vol. 1: South Sea Yarns (Classic Reprint) (p. 2499)
—Works of Robert Louis Stevenson, Vol. 1: Tales & Fantasies (Classic Reprint) (p. 2499)
—Works of Robert Louis Stevenson, Vol. 16: Records of a Family of Engineers; Additional Memories & Portraits; Later Essays; Lay Morals; Prayers Written for Family Use at Vailima (Classic Reprint) (p. 2499)
—Works of Robert Louis Stevenson, Vol. 16 (Classic Reprint) (p. 2499)
—Works of Robert Louis Stevenson, Vol. 2: Vailima Edition (Classic Reprint) (p. 2499)
—Works of Robert Louis Stevenson, Vol. 2: Treasure Island, and, Kidnapped (Classic Reprint) (p. 2499)
—Works of Robert Louis Stevenson, Vol. 21: The Story of a Lie; the Merry Men; Olalla; Heathercat; the Great North Road; the Young Chevalier; Fables (Classic Reprint) (p. 2499)
—Works of Robert Louis Stevenson, Vol. 4: Tale & Fantasies (Classic Reprint) (p. 2499)
—Works of Robert Louis Stevenson, Vol. 6: Memories & Portraits, Virginibus Puerisque, & Other Papers (Classic Reprint) (p. 2499)
—Works of Robert Louis Stevenson, Vol. 6: The Silverado Squatters; Across the Plains; Dr. Jekyll & Mr. Hyde; & Other Stories (Classic Reprint) (p. 2499)
—Works of Robert Louis Stevenson, Vol. 7: Prince Otto, and, the Wrong Box (Classic Reprint) (p. 2499)
—Works of Robert Louis Stevenson, Vol. 7: In the South Seas; Letters from Samoa, etc (Classic Reprint) (p. 2499)
—Works of Robert Louis Stevenson, Vol. 7 (Classic Reprint) (p. 2499)
—Works of Robert Louis Stevenson, Vol. 8: Poems, Ballads & Plays (Classic Reprint) (p. 2499)
—Works of Robert Louis Stevenson, Vol. 8: An Inland Voyage; Travels with a Donkey; Edinburgh; & Other Papers (Classic Reprint) (p. 2499)
—Wrecker (Classic Reprint) (p. 2511)
—Wrong Box: The Ebb Tide (Classic Reprint) (p. 2514)
—Wrong Box. (p. 2514)
—Wrong Box (Classic Reprint) (p. 2514)
—Wrong Box Island Nights' Entertainments Father Damien (Classic Reprint) (p. 2514)
Stevenson, Robert Louis, jt. auth. see Dafoe, Daniel.
Stevenson, Robert Louis, jt. auth. see Korr, Ann.
Stevenson, Robert Louis, jt. auth. see Stevenson, Robert Louis.
Stevenson, Robert Louis & Colvin, Sidney. Weir of Hermiston. (p. 2396)
Stevenson, Robert Louis & Cortes, Jesus. Isla Del Tesoro. (p. 1139)
Stevenson, Robert Louis & Hole, W. B. Kidnapped. (p. 1213)
Stevenson, Robert Louis & Osbourne, Lloyd. Ebb-Tide: A Trio & Quartette. (p. 622)
Stevenson, Robert Louis & Rhead, Louis. Kidnapped. (p. 1213)
Stevenson, Robert Louis & Schlieve, Ngj. At Seven When I Go to Bed: Bed in Summertime. (p. 130)
Stevenson, Robert Louis & Thomas, Roy. Embassy - And Attack. Gully, Mario & Davidson, Pat, illus. (p. 641)
—Mutiny on the Hispaniola. Gully, Mario & Davidson, Pat, illus. (p. 1530)
—Treasure Island Gully, Mario & Davidson, Pat, illus. (p. 2282)
—Treasure Island. Gully, Mario & Davidson, Pat, illus. (p. 2282)
Stevenson, Robert Luis. Extrano Caso Del Dr. Jekyll y el Sr. Hyde. (p. 685)
Stevenson, Robin. Attitude (p. 135)
—Ben's Robot Parkins, David, illus. (p. 201)
—Desolación (p. 533)
—Escape Velocity (p. 662)
—Hummingbird Heart (p. 1050)
—Kid Activists: True Tales of Childhood from Champions of Change. Steinfeld, Allison, illus. (p. 1212)
—Liars & Fools (p. 1283)
—My Body My Choice: The Fight for Abortion Rights (p. 1534)
—Outback (p. 1683)
—Pride: The Celebration & the Struggle. (p. 1791)
—Pride Colors (p. 1791)
—Record Breaker (p. 1854)
—Under Threat (p. 2323)
—Under Threat. (p. 2323)
—World Without Us. (p. 2506)
Stevenson, Robin, jt. auth. see Harvey, Sarah N.
Stevenson, Sarah Jamila. Latte Rebellion. (p. 1251)
Stevenson, Seline, illus. see Tóth-Jones, Dee S.
Stevenson, Steve. Crime on the Norwegian Sea. (p. 474)
—Crown of Venice Turconi, Stefano, illus. (p. 479)
—Crown of Venice. (p. 479)
—Curse of the Pharaoh. (p. 489)
—Curse of the Pharaoh #1 Turconi, Stefano, illus. (p. 489)
—Eiffel Tower Incident. (p. 629)
—Heist at Niagara Falls. (p. 949)
—Hollywood Intrigue. (p. 989)
—Kenyan Expedition. (p. 1210)
—King of Scotland's Sword. (p. 1221)
—King of Scotland's Sword. Turconi, Stefano, illus. (p. 1221)
—Pearl of Bengal. (p. 1710)
—Treasure of the Bermuda Triangle Turconi, Stefano, illus. (p. 2282)
—Treasure of the Bermuda Triangle. (p. 2282)
Stevenson, Suçie, illus. see Rylant, Cynthia.
Stevenson, W. Grant. Pot Pourri of Gifts Literary & Artistic: Contributed As a Souvenir of the Grand Masonic Bazaar in Aid of the Annuity Fund of Scottish Masonic Benevolence, Edinburgh, 1890 (Classic Reprint) (p. 1780)
Stevenson, William. Ricky's Dream Trip to Ancient Egypt. (p. 1877)
—Ricky's Dream Trip to Ancient Greece. (p. 1877)
—Ricky's Dream Trip under the Sea. (p. 1877)
Stevenson, William Yorke. At the Front in a Flivver (Classic Reprint) (p. 131)
Steventon, John. DJing. (p. 567)
Stever, Karen Malloy. Jabin, the Talking Donkey: In Jerusalem. (p. 1151)
Stevermer, Caroline, jt. auth. see Wrede, Patricia C.
Steverson, Sylvia. I LOVE YOU Means... (p. 1079)
Steveson, Nanci Turner. Georgia Rules. (p. 821)
—Lizzie Flying Solo. (p. 1336)
SteveSongs Staff. Shape Song Singalong. Sim, David, illus. (p. 2000)
—Shape Song Swingalong. Sim, David, illus. (p. 2000)
Stevic-Rust, Lori. Lily's Red Shoes of Courage. (p. 1302)
Stevinson, Emma. Open-Air Nursery School (Classic Reprint) (p. 1665)
Stevos, Joyce L., jt. auth. see Currie, David P.
Steward, Ann. Let the Earth Speak (Classic Reprint) (p. 1269)
Steward, David, II, jt. auth. see Flood, Joe.
Steward, Isabella Travers. Interdict, Vol. 1 Of 3: A Novel (Classic Reprint) (p. 1126)
—Interdict, Vol. 2 Of 3: A Novel (Classic Reprint) (p. 1126)
—Interdict, Vol. 3 Of 3: A Novel (Classic Reprint) (p. 1126)
Steward, Musician. Sparks of Laughter: Suggestions to Toastmasters How to Tell a Funny Story (Classic Reprint) (p. 2075)
Steward, Rebecca. Animals in the Clouds. (p. 95)
Steward, Robyn. Autism-Friendly Guide to Periods. (p. 139)
Stewart. Learning Centers: Saints: Saints. (p. 1258)
Stewart, Alan Duff. Heather & Peat (Classic Reprint) (p. 946)
Stewart, Alex. Gladiators. (p. 840)
—Greek Soldiers. (p. 893)
—Pirates. (p. 1750)
Stewart, Alexander. Nether Lochaber: The Natural History, Legends, & Folk-Lore of the West Highland. (p. 1588)
—Nether Lochaber: The Natural History, Legends, & Folk-Lore of the West Highlands (Classic Reprint) (p. 1588)
—Nether Lochaber. (p. 1588)
—Twixt Ben Nevis & Glencoe: Natural History, Legends, & Folk-Lore of the West Highlands (Classic Reprint) (p. 2306)
—Twixt Ben Nevis & Glencoe. (p. 2306)
Stewart, Alexandra. Everest: the Remarkable Story of Edmund Hillary & Tenzing Norgay. Todd-Stanton, Joe, illus. (p. 669)
Stewart, Amber. Herbert Henry & Santa's Secret Society. Albert, Sonia, illus. (p. 957)
Stewart, Amy. Wicked Bugs (Young Readers Edition) The Meanest, Deadliest, Grossest Bugs on Earth. Morrow-Cribbs, Briony, illus. (p. 2460)
Stewart, Anne K. Arrival of Tavish the Tractor. (p. 119)
Stewart, Arlene. Friendship Bracelet. (p. 787)
—Weaving a Wish. (p. 2394)
Stewart, Artney. Hi, I Love You. Yongco, Rumar, illus. (p. 964)
Stewart, Ashleigh, et al. How's the Weather Today? My Feelings Forecast. (p. 1047)
Stewart, Ashley, illus. see Wahi, Ellen.
Stewart, Aubrey. Felix Fabri, Vol. 1: Circa 1480-1483 A. d (Classic Reprint) (p. 719)
Stewart, Audrey. Our Natural Resources. (p. 1679)
Stewart, Balfour. Conservation of Energy: Being an Elementary Treatise on Energy & Its Laws (Classic Reprint) (p. 442)
—Conservation of Energy: Being an Elementary Treatise on Energy & Its Laws - Scholar's Choice Edition. (p. 442)
—Practical Physics for Schools & the Junior Students of Colleges. Vol. I. (p. 1784)
—Practical Physics for Schools & the Junior Students of Colleges; Vol. I, Electricity & Magnetism. (p. 1784)
Stewart, Balfour & Gee, William Winson Haldane. Practical Physics for Schools & the Junior Students of Colleges. (p. 1784)
Stewart, Barbara. In-Between. (p. 1104)
Stewart, Beth. Unbridled Joy. Foster, Jack, illus. (p. 2317)
Stewart, Beth Roper. Bebeaux & Pierre: The Adventure Begins. (p. 186)
—I'm Not Weird, I'm Wonderful. Reynolds, Candler, illus. (p. 1099)
—One Thing Missing. Stewart, Cameron, illus. (p. 1662)
Stewart, Buffy Ford. Blanket & the Bear: A Whimsical Story of the Endless Possibilities of Love. Ford, Noelle Boucher, illus. (p. 243)
Stewart, C. R. Britfield & the Lost Crown. (p. 283)
Stewart, Cal. Uncle Josh's Punkin Centre Stories: 'the Talking Machine Story Teller (Classic Reprint) (p. 2318)
Stewart, Cameron, illus. see Stewart, Beth Roper.
Stewart, Cathy. Dot's Barnyard Caper. (p. 588)
—Sassy Sparrow & the Hungry Owl. (p. 1936)
Stewart, Cathy L. Camo Joe's Bear Scare. (p. 315)
—French Connection. (p. 783)
—Great Escape. (p. 885)
Stewart, Chantal. Tortoise Soup! (p. 2266)
Stewart, Chantal, illus. see Dinbergs, Holly Smith.
Stewart, Chantal, illus. see Zail, Suzy.
Stewart, Charles D. Fugitive Blacksmith (Classic Reprint) (p. 797)
—Partners of Providence (Classic Reprint) (p. 1701)
—Valley Waters (Classic Reprint) (p. 2345)
—Wrong Woman (Classic Reprint) (p. 2514)
Stewart, Charles David. Finerty of the Sand-House (Classic Reprint) (p. 730)
Stewart, Christen, jt. auth. see Ellis, Julie.
Stewart, Christen, jt. auth. see Reilly, Carmel.
Stewart, Chuck. Angels at Rickwood. (p. 86)
Stewart, Cindy. Lewy Kablooey & Sneezy Cheezy. (p. 1282)
Stewart, Clark Emerson. On Randolph Hills: Personal Memories; Anecdotes; Reminiscences; & Characters (Classic Reprint) (p. 1653)
Stewart, Crystie. Sefer: Spring, 1995 (Classic Reprint) (p. 1985)
Stewart, D. D. Tome 3: Here There Color Mix. (p. 2259)
Stewart, Dave, jt. auth. see Wagner, Matt.
Stewart, David. Amaze Franklin, Carolyn, illus. (p. 62)
—Creepy Egyptian Mummies. (p. 473)
—Dinosaurs. Hewetson, Nick, illus. (p. 550)
—What's the Big Idea? 2,400,000 Years of Inventions. (p. 2426)
—World of Wonder Franklin, Carolyn, illus. (p. 2504)
—You Wouldn't Want to Be an Egyptian Mummy! Disgusting Things You'd Rather Not Know. Antram, David, illus. (p. 2528)
—You Wouldn't Want to... Be an Egyptian Mummy! Antram, David, illus. (p. 2528)
—You Wouldn't Want to Be in a Medieval Dungeon! Antram, David, illus. (p. 2528)
—You Wouldn't Want to Be Tutankhamen! Antram, David, illus. (p. 2529)
—You Wouldn't Want to Sail on the Titanic! (p. 2529)
—You Wouldn't Want to Sail on the Titanic! One Voyage You'D Rather Not Make. Antram, David, illus. (p. 2529)
Stewart, David, illus. see Morley, Jacqueline.
Stewart, David, jt. auth. see Franklin, Carolyn.
Stewart, Dawn Lesley. Harriet's Horrible Hair Day White, Michael P., illus. (p. 933)
—Harriet's Horrible Hair Day. (p. 933)
Stewart, Dianne. Dudu's Basket. Pulles, Elizabeth, illus. (p. 609)
—Gift of the Sun. Daly, Jude, illus. (p. 832)
—Lyle the Crocodile. Rankin, Joan, illus. (p. 1369)
—Who's Afraid of the Dark? Rankin, Joan, illus. (p. 2453)
—Zebra's Stripes: And Other African Animal Tales. Pienaar, Kathy, illus. (p. 2539)
Stewart, Dianne C. Longitude - Zero Degrees. (p. 1344)
—Season of the Cold Moon. (p. 1972)
Stewart, Donald J. Tamarack, Vol. 6: December 1914 (Classic Reprint) (p. 2188)
Stewart, Donald Ogden. Parody Outline of History (Classic Reprint) (p. 1700)
—Perfect Behavior (Classic Reprint) (p. 1722)
Stewart, Dorothy. It's Hard to Hurry When You're a Snail Taylor, Thomas, illus. (p. 1145)
Stewart, E. J. Wayfaring Dolphin. (p. 2387)
Stewart, E. M. Lillias Davenant: A Novel (Classic Reprint) (p. 1301)
Stewart, Elinore Pruitt. Letters of a Woman Homesteader (Classic Reprint) (p. 1280)
—Letters on an Elk Hunt: Illustrated (Classic Reprint) (p. 1281)
Stewart, Elizabeth. Blue Gold: A Novel. (p. 248)
—Lynching of Louie Sam. (p. 1370)
Stewart, Emily D., illus. see Barrett, Judith A.
Stewart, Erin. Scars Like Wings. (p. 1942)
Stewart, Es. 52 Seeds for Fertile Soil. (p. 2556)
—Who Made the Moon, Mummy? (p. 2449)
Stewart, Faith. Teens & Rural Education: Opportunities & Challenges. (p. 2200)
Stewart, Fion, illus. see Chen, Julia.
Stewart, Frances. Our Forest Home: Being Extracts from the Correspondence of the Late Frances Stewart (Classic Reprint) (p. 1678)
Stewart, Fred Mustard. Century, Vol. 47: Illustrated Monthly Magazine; November 1893, to April 1894 (Classic Reprint) (p. 352)
Stewart, Gabrielle. That Star Spangled Banner: The War, the Flag & the National Anthem. (p. 2213)
stewart, gail. Trolls. (p. 2290)
—Urban Legends. (p. 2339)
—Water Monsters. (p. 2385)
Stewart, Gail B. Cesar Milan. (p. 353)
—Cold Cases. Gale Editors, ed. (p. 413)
—Fetal Alcohol Syndrome. (p. 721)
—Hauntings. (p. 939)
—Jennifer Lawrence. (p. 1164)
—Missing Persons. (p. 1481)
—Population. (p. 1777)
—Teens & Bullying. (p. 2200)
—Ukraine: Then & Now. (p. 2314)
—Vampires: Do They Exist? (p. 2346)
Stewart, George A. Look after Brown! A Farce, in One Act (Classic Reprint) (p. 1344)
Stewart, George Rippey. Friendship's Offering: Christmas, New Year & Birthday Present, for 1849 (Classic Reprint) (p. 788)
Stewart, Gill. Gemma's Not Sure. (p. 813)
—Lily's Just Fine. (p. 1302)
Stewart, Gregory. Mr. Conklemeyer's Musical Pets. (p. 1518)
Stewart, Gregory J. Immune System. (p. 1101)
—Skeletal & Muscular Systems. (p. 2030)
Stewart, H. E. Patched Heart: A Gift of Friendship & Caring (p. 1704)
—TreeSong (p. 2285)
Stewart III, Freddie Leonard. Night Night Birmingham. (p. 1606)
Stewart, J. J. Grand Canyon National Park. (p. 876)
—Justin Trudeau: Prime Minister of Canada. (p. 1195)
Stewart, Jack. Once There Was a Dot. (p. 1657)
Stewart, Jacqueline. Commodore: Friend of Crab Island. (p. 430)
Stewart, James. Spies & Traitors. (p. 2081)
—There's a Hole in My Garden. (p. 2217)
—Trials of George Frederick Boutelier & John Boutelier, for the Murder of Frederick Eminaud: Before a Special Court of Oyer & Terminer & General Delivery, Held at Lunenburg, in & for the County of Lunenburg, in the Province of Nova-Scotia, at T. (p. 2286)
Stewart, Jennifer J. Twelve Days of Christmas in Arizona. Avril, Lynne, illus. (p. 2303)
Stewart, Joel, illus. see Andersen, Hans.
Stewart, Joel, illus. see Donaldson, Julia.
Stewart, Joel, illus. see Duffy, Carol Ann.
Stewart, Joel, illus. see Schwarz, Viviane.
Stewart, Joel, illus. see Willis, Jeanne.
Stewart, John. Stable Book: Being a Treatise on the Management of Horses, in Relation to Stabling, Grooming, Feeding, Watering & Working; Construction of Stables, Ventilation, Stable Appendages, Management of the Feet (Classic Reprint) (p. 2099)
Stewart, John Alexander, jt. auth. see Plato.
Stewart, K. L., illus. see Hoyes, Amy & Reimann, A. J.
Stewart, Kara. City Street. (p. 395)
Stewart, Katie. What Colour Is the Sea? (p. 2407)
Stewart, Kellie. Journey to Pluto & Other Dwarf Planets (p. 1182)
Stewart, Kelly, ed. Readers' Theater: Scripts for Young Readers. Palacios, John, illus. (p. 1846)
—Readers' Theater: Scripts for Young Readers: the Peach Boy. Palacios, John, illus. (p. 1846)
—Readers' Theater: Scripts for Young Readers: the Monkey & the Crocodile. Palacios, John, illus. (p. 1846)
Stewart, Kenneth. Drop of the Puck. (p. 605)
—Kickball Kid. (p. 1212)
Stewart, Kiera. Fetching. (p. 721)
—Summer of Bad Ideas. (p. 2149)
Stewart, Kitria. Caz & the Lucky Necklace. Illustrations, Blueberry, illus. (p. 348)
Stewart, Laurie. Alone in the Night. Unsplash Com, photos by. (p. 57)
Stewart, Linda. Great Catsby: A Sam the Cat Mystery. (p. 884)
Stewart, Lindzi J. Flying Visit: Book One of the Salute Islands Treasury. Stewart, Phoebe E. L., illus. (p. 755)
Stewart, Lisa, illus. see Kelly, Deborah.
Stewart, Lizzy. Juniper Jupiter: A Real-Life Superhero. (p. 1191)
—Meet the Artist: JMW Turner. (p. 1439)
—There's a Tiger in the Garden. (p. 2218)
Stewart, Lolla. Savannah Dreams. Russell, Elaine, illus. (p. 1937)
Stewart, M. B. N'Th Foot in War (Classic Reprint) (p. 1628)
Stewart, Margaret Taylor, jt. auth. see Baker, David G.
Stewart, Maria. Omelet Fit for a King. Cost, Steve, illus. (p. 1651)
Stewart, Mark. A. C. Milan. (p. 1)
—Arizona Cardinals. (p. 116)
—Arizona Diamondbacks. (p. 116)
—Arsenal F. C. (p. 120)
—Atlanta Braves. (p. 132)
—Atlanta Falcons. (p. 132)
—Atlanta Hawks. (p. 132)
—Auburn Tigers. (p. 136)
—Baltimore Orioles. (p. 162)
—Baltimore Ravens. (p. 162)
—Baseball. (p. 168)
—Basketball. (p. 170)
—Boston Bruins. Gibbons, Denis, ed. (p. 264)
—Boston Red Sox. (p. 264)
—Brooklyn Nets. (p. 285)
—C. A. River Plate. (p. 306)
—Carolina Panthers. (p. 333)
—Chelsea F. C. (p. 365)
—Chicago Bears. (p. 367)
—Chicago Blackhawks. Gibbons, Denis, ed. (p. 367)
—Chicago Bulls. (p. 367)
—Chicago Cubs. (p. 367)
—Chicago White Sox. (p. 367)
—Cincinnati Bengals. (p. 391)
—Cincinnati Reds. (p. 391)
—Classic Rivalries. (p. 400)
—Cleveland Cavaliers. (p. 404)
—Cleveland Indians. (p. 404)
—Clutch Performers. (p. 409)
—Colorado Avalanche. Gibbons, Denis, ed. (p. 421)
—Colorado Rockies. (p. 422)
—Dallas Cowboys. (p. 498)
—Dallas Mavericks. (p. 498)
—Detroit Lions. (p. 535)
—Detroit Pistons. (p. 535)
—Detroit Red Wings. Gibbons, Denis, ed. (p. 535)
—Detroit Tigers. (p. 535)
—Edmonton Oilers. Gibbons, Denis, ed. (p. 626)
—Eli Manning. (p. 635)
—F. C. Barcelona. (p. 689)
—F. C. Bayern Munich. (p. 689)
—Florida Gators. (p. 751)
—Football. (p. 761)
—Georgetown Hoyas. (p. 820)
—Georgia Bulldogs. (p. 820)
—Golden State Warriors. (p. 859)
—Houston Astros. (p. 1024)
—Houston Dynamo. (p. 1025)
—Houston Texans. (p. 1025)
—Illinois Fighting Illini. (p. 1095)
—Indiana Pacers. (p. 1116)
—Jacksonville Jaguars. (p. 1154)
—Kansas City Chiefs. (p. 1203)
—Kansas City Royals. (p. 1203)
—Los Angeles Angels of Anaheim. (p. 1349)
—Los Angeles Clippers. (p. 1349)
—Los Angeles Dodgers. (p. 1349)
—Los Angeles Galaxy. (p. 1349)
—Los Angeles Kings. Gibbons, Denis, ed. (p. 1349)
—Los Angeles Lakers. (p. 1349)
—Manchester United. (p. 1396)
—Maria Sharapova. (p. 1404)
—Memphis Grizzlies. (p. 1446)
—Miami Heat. (p. 1456)
—Miami Marlins. (p. 1456)
—Michigan Wolverines. (p. 1459)
—Milwaukee Brewers. (p. 1468)
—Minnesota Timberwolves. (p. 1473)
—Minnesota Twins. (p. 1473)
—Minnesota Vikings. (p. 1473)
—Montreal Canadiens. Gibbons, Denis, ed. (p. 1500)
—Movie Blockbusters. (p. 1516)
—Movie Characters. (p. 1516)
—Music Legends. (p. 1529)
—New Jersey Devils. Gibbons, Denis, ed. (p. 1594)
—New Orleans Hornets. (p. 1596)
—New Wave (p. 1597)
—New York Knicks. (p. 1599)
—New York Mets. (p. 1599)

S

—New York Rangers. Gibbons, Denis, ed. (p. 1599)
—New York Red Bulls. (p. 1599)
—New York Yankees. (p. 1599)
—Notre Dame Fighting Irish. (p. 1625)
—Oakland Athletics. (p. 1633)
—Oklahoma City Thunder. (p. 1643)
—Olympics. (p. 1651)
—Orlando Magic. (p. 1672)
—Paris Saint-Germain. (p. 1700)
—Philadelphia 76ers. (p. 1734)
—Philadelphia Eagles. (p. 1734)
—Philadelphia Flyers. Gibbons, Denis, ed. (p. 1734)
—Philadelphia Phillies. (p. 1734)
—Pittsburgh Penguins. Gibbons, Denis, ed. (p. 1751)
—Pittsburgh Pirates. (p. 1751)
—Portland Timbers. (p. 1779)
—Rafael Nadal. (p. 1834)
—Real Madrid C. F. (p. 1849)
—Sacramento Kings. (p. 1920)
—San Antonio Spurs. (p. 1929)
—San Diego Padres. (p. 1929)
—San Francisco 49ers. (p. 1929)
—San Francisco Giants. (p. 1930)
—São Paulo F. C. (p. 1934)
—Seattle Mariners. (p. 1972)
—Seattle Seahawks. (p. 1973)
—Seattle Sounders F. C. (p. 1973)
—St. Louis Cardinals. (p. 2097)
—Tampa Bay Buccaneers. (p. 2189)
—Tampa Bay Rays. (p. 2189)
—Television Moments. (p. 2201)
—Tennessee Titans. (p. 2206)
—Texas Rangers. (p. 2209)
—Toronto Blue Jays. (p. 2265)
—Toronto F. C. (p. 2265)
—Toronto Maple Leafs. Gibbons, Denis, ed. (p. 2265)
—Toronto Raptors. (p. 2265)
—Ultimate 10: Sports - Fall 2009 Release Set (p. 2314)
—United States & Canada. (p. 2330)
—Vancouver Canucks. Gibbons, Denis, ed. (p. 2347)
—Washington Nationals. (p. 2382)
—Washington Redskins. (p. 2382)
—Washington Wizards. (p. 2382)
Stewart, Mark, ed. see Harrison, Geoffrey C. & Scott, Thomas F.
Stewart, Mark, jt. auth. see Doeden, Matt.
Stewart, Mark, jt. auth. see Kennedy, Mike.
Stewart, Mark & Kennedy, Mike. Nascar at the Track. (p. 1576)
—Nascar Behind the Scenes. (p. 1576)
—Nascar Designed to Win. (p. 1576)
—Science of NASCAR (p. 1958)
—Science of Nascar. (p. 1958)
—Touchdown: The Power & Precision of Football's Perfect Play. (p. 2268)
Stewart, Mark & Zeysing, Matt. Syracuse Orange. (p. 2174)
Stewart, Mark R. Malcolm's Cubby House. Swope, Brenda, illus. (p. 1391)
Stewart, Martha. Martha Stewart's Favorite Crafts for Kids. (p. 1410)
Stewart, Martha Morley. Greyhound Fanny (Classic Reprint) (p. 896)
Stewart, Martin. Riverkeep. (p. 1887)
—Sacrifice Box. (p. 1920)
Stewart, Mary. Land of Punch & Judy: A Book of Puppet Plays for Children (Classic Reprint) (p. 1242)
—Tell Me a Story I Never Heard Before: From the Story-Tellers of Long Ago for the Story Tellers of to-Day (Classic Reprint) (p. 2201)
—Tell Me a True Story: Tales of Bible Heroes for the Children of to-Day (Classic Reprint) (p. 2201)
Stewart, Melissa. Alligator or Crocodile? How Do You Know? (p. 56)
—Amazing Eyes up Close. (p. 65)
—Beneath the Sun. Bergum, Constance R., illus. (p. 199)
—Bird-Acious. (p. 230)
—Blasts of Gas: The Secrets of Breathing, Burping, & Farting. Hamlin, Janet, illus. (p. 243)
—Blue Animals. (p. 248)
—Butterfly or Moth? How Do You Know? (p. 304)
—Can an Aardvark Bark? Jenkins, Steve, illus. (p. 317)
—Creepy, Crawly Jokes about Spiders & Other Bugs: Laugh & Learn about Science. Kelley, Gerald, illus. (p. 473)
—Daddy Longlegs Isn't a Spider. Himmelman, John, illus. (p. 495)
—Dino-Mite Jokes about Prehistoric Life: Laugh & Learn about Science. Kelley, Gerald, illus. (p. 547)
—Dolphins (1 Hardcover/1 CD) (p. 580)
—Dolphins (1 Paperback/1 CD) (p. 580)
—Dolphins (4 Paperbacks/1 CD) (p. 580)
—Droughts. Ceolin, Andre, illus. (p. 606)
—Eyes Have It: The Secrets of Eyes & Seeing. Hamlin, Janet, illus. (p. 689)
—Fantastic Feet up Close. (p. 707)
—Feathers: Not Just for Flying. Brannen, Sarah S., illus. (p. 717)
—Feathers. (p. 717)
—Frog or Toad? How Do You Know? (p. 789)
—Germ Wars! The Secrets of the Immune System. Hamlin, Janet L., illus. (p. 822)
—Give Me a Hand: The Secrets of Hands, Feet, Arms, & Legs. Hamlin, Janet, illus. (p. 840)
—Green Animals. (p. 893)
—Gross & Goofy Body Hamlin, Janet, illus. (p. 898)
—Here We Grow: The Secrets of Hair & Nails. Hamlin, Janet, illus. (p. 958)
—How Do Bees Make Honey? (p. 1028)
—How Do Chameleons Change Color? (p. 1028)
—How Do Spiders Make Webs? (p. 1029)
—How Does a Bone Become a Fossil? (p. 1030)
—How Does a Seed Sprout? And Other Questions about Plants. Schwartz, Carol, illus. (p. 1030)
—How Is My Brain Like a Supercomputer? And Other Questions about the Human Body. Bull, Peter, illus. (p. 1032)
—Hurricane Watch. Morley, Taia, illus. (p. 1054)
—Incredible Ears up Close. (p. 1113)
—Insect or Spider? How Do You Know? (p. 1122)
—Inside Volcanoes. (p. 1124)
—It's Spit-Acular! The Secrets of Saliva. Hamlin, Janet, illus. (p. 1147)
—Meteors (1 Hardcover/1 CD) (p. 1453)
—Meteors (1 Paperback/1 CD) (p. 1453)
—Meteors (4 Paperback/1 CD) (p. 1453)
—Mountains of Jokes about Rocks, Minerals, & Soil: Laugh & Learn about Science. Kelley, Gerald, illus. (p. 1514)
—Moving & Grooving: The Secrets of Muscles & Bones. Hamlin, Janet, illus. (p. 1516)
—Nifty Noses up Close. (p. 1604)
—Now Hear This! The Secrets of Ears & Hearing. Hamlin, Janet, illus. (p. 1627)
—Orange Animals. (p. 1668)
—Out of This World Jokes about the Solar System: Laugh & Learn about Science. Kelley, Gerald, illus. (p. 1683)
—Pipsqueaks, Slowpokes, & Stinkers: Celebrating Animal Underdogs. Laberis, Stephanie, illus. (p. 1749)
—Place for Bats Bond, Higgins, illus. (p. 1753)
—Place for Birds Bond, Higgins, illus. (p. 1753)
—Place for Fish Bond, Higgins, illus. (p. 1753)
—Place for Frogs Bond, Higgins, illus. (p. 1753)
—Place for Turtles. Bond, Higgins, illus. (p. 1753)
—Predator Face-Off. (p. 1786)
—Pump It Up! The Secrets of the Heart & Blood. Hamlin, Janet, illus. (p. 1812)
—Purple Animals. (p. 1816)
—Red Animals. (p. 1856)
—Robots (1 Hardcover/1 CD) (p. 1893)
—Robots (1 Paperback/1 CD) (p. 1893)
—Robots (4 Paperback/1 CD) (p. 1893)
—Salamander or Lizard? How Do You Know? (p. 1924)
—Seashells: More Than a Home. Brannen, Sarah S., illus. (p. 1972)
—Shark or Dolphin? How Do You Know? (p. 2002)
—Shockingly Silly Jokes about Electricity & Magnetism: Laugh & Learn about Science. Kelley, Gerald, illus. (p. 2008)
—Skin You're In: The Secrets of Skin. Hamlin, Janet, illus. (p. 2032)
—Talented Tails up Close. (p. 2181)
—Tell Me Why, Tell Me How (p. 2202)
—Tell Me Why, Tell Me How - Group 2 (p. 2202)
—Terrific Tongues up Close. (p. 2207)
—Titanic (1 Hardcover/1 CD) (p. 2251)
—Titanic (1 Paperback/1 CD) (p. 2251)
—Titanic (4 Paperback/1 CD) (p. 2251)
—Under the Snow Bergum, Constance, illus. (p. 2323)
—Under the Snow Bergum, Constance R., illus. (p. 2323)
—Up Your Nose! The Secrets of Schnozes & Snouts. Hamlin, Janet, illus. (p. 2338)
—Wacky Weather & Silly Season Jokes: Laugh & Learn about Science. Kelley, Gerald, illus. (p. 2370)
—When Rain Falls Bergum, Constance R., illus. (p. 2432)
—Why Are Animals Orange? (p. 2455)
—Why Are Animals Purple? (p. 2455)
—Why Are Animals Red? (p. 2455)
—Why Are Animals Yellow? (p. 2455)
—Why Does T. Rex Have Such Short Arms? And Other Questions about... Dinosaurs. Csotonyi, Julius, illus. (p. 2457)
—Yellow Animals. (p. 2520)
—You've Got Nerve! The Secrets of the Brain & Nerves. Hamlin, Janet, illus. (p. 2536)
—Zoom in on Bees. (p. 2544)
—Zoom in on Butterflies. (p. 2544)
—Zoom in on Dragonflies. (p. 2544)
—Zoom in on Fireflies. (p. 2544)
—Zoom in on Grasshoppers. (p. 2544)
—Zoom in on Ladybugs. (p. 2544)
Stewart, Melissa & American Museum of Natural History. Caterpillar to Butterfly. (p. 344)
Stewart, Melissa & Brusatte, Steve. Pinocchio Rex & Other Tyrannosaurs. Csotonyi, Julius, illus. (p. 1747)
Stewart, Melissa & Young, Allen. No Monkeys, No Chocolate. Wong, Nicole, illus. (p. 1613)
Stewart, Melissa & Young, Allen M. No Monkeys, No Chocolate. Wong, Nicole, illus. (p. 1613)
Stewart, Melva Lea. Math'n'maddox: Mathemagicians. (p. 1424)
Stewart, Michael, et al. Kim Possible Adventures. Rousseau, Craig & Bancroft, Tom, illus. (p. 1218)
Stewart, Michael F. Assured Destruction. (p. 127)
—Heart Sister. (p. 945)
—Keep in a Cold, Dark Place. (p. 1207)
Stewart, Michael G., illus. see Polisar, Barry Louis.
Stewart, Miss Mary. Unspotted from the World (Classic Reprint) (p. 2335)
Stewart Molesworth, Mary Louisa. Christmas Posy. (p. 386)
Stewart, Morse. Memorial of Mrs. Morse Stewart: Edited by Her Husband (Classic Reprint) (p. 1445)
Stewart, Muriel, illus. see Chambers, Pamela G.
Stewart, Nancy. Bella Saves the Beach. Bell, Samantha, illus. (p. 197)
—Katrina & Winter: Partners in Courage. (p. 1206)
—One Pelican at a Time: A Story of the Gulf Oil Spill. Bell, Samantha, illus. (p. 1661)
Stewart, Pat, illus. see Burgess, Thornton W.
Stewart, Pat Ronson, illus. see Burgess, Thornton W.
Stewart, Pat Ronson, tr. see Burgess, Thornton W.
Stewart, Patricia. Let's Go to the Moon. (p. 1274)
Stewart, Patricia Brooks. Miss Marble's Backyard Critters. (p. 1479)
Stewart, Patricia M. Seagull Who Came to Stay. (p. 1969)
Stewart, Paul. Brian the Brave. Porter, Jane, illus. (p. 279)
—Far-Flung Adventures: Hugo Pepper. (p. 708)
—Little Bit of Winter. Riddell, Chris, illus. (p. 1311)
—Rabbit & Hedgehog Treasury. Riddell, Chris, illus. (p. 1829)
—Zoid: Scavenger 1. Riddell, Chris, illus. (p. 2541)
Stewart, Paul, jt. auth. see Riddell, Chris.
Stewart, Paul, jt. auth. see Stewart, Paul.
Stewart, Paul & Riddell, Chris. Barnaby Grimes: Curse of the Night Wolf. (p. 167)
—Barnaby Grimes: Legion of the Dead. (p. 167)
—Barnaby Grimes: Phantom of Blood Alley. (p. 167)
—Bloodhoney. (p. 246)
—Bone Trail. (p. 255)
—Bumper Blobheads. (p. 297)
—Dragon's Hoard. Riddell, Chris, illus. (p. 595)
—Edge Chronicles: Clash of the Sky Galleons. (p. 625)
—Edge Chronicles: the Winter Knights. (p. 625)
—Far-Flung Adventures: Corby Flood. (p. 708)
—Far-Flung Adventures: Fergus Crane. (p. 708)
—Joust of Honor. Riddell, Chris, illus. (p. 1184)
—Lake of Skulls. Riddell, Chris, illus. (p. 1240)
—Last of the Sky Pirates. (p. 1249)
—Mind Warp: Scavenger 3. (p. 1469)
—Returner's Wealth. (p. 1871)
Stewart, Peter, jt. auth. see Foster, John.
Stewart, Phoebe E. L., illus. see Stewart, Lindzi J.
Stewart, Piper. Mystical, Magical, Spectacular Tale of Abigail Blake. (p. 1571)
Stewart, Rachel M. Angel Inside Me. (p. 85)
Stewart, Reo. Places. (p. 1753)
Stewart, Rhea A., jt. auth. see Egan, Jill.
Stewart, Rhea A. & Technology Education Design Forum Staff. Math in the Real World Set, 10-Volumes. (p. 1424)
Stewart, Roger, illus. see Abell, Tracy.
Stewart, Roger, illus. see Bell, Samantha S.
Stewart, Roger, illus. see Biskup, Agnieszka.
Stewart, Roger, illus. see Gulati, Annette.
Stewart, Roger, illus. see Hand, Carol.
Stewart, Roger, illus. see McGraw, Sally.
Stewart, Roger, illus. see Miller, Mirella S.
Stewart, Rosanne. Santa's Trip to the Bayou. Rivers, Tess, illus. (p. 1934)
Stewart, S. E. Quest of the Thought Travellers. (p. 1826)
Stewart, Sarah. Friend. (p. 786)
—Quiet Place Small, David, illus. (p. 1828)
—This Book of Mine: A Picture Book. Small, David, illus. (p. 2224)
Stewart, Seth Thayer. First Days in School: A Primer (Classic Reprint) (p. 736)
Stewart, Seth Thayer, jt. auth. see Coe, Ida.
Stewart, Shannon. Badir & the Beaver Gendron, Sabrina, illus. (p. 159)
Stewart, Sheila. Celebrity Families. (p. 350)
—Finding My Voice: Kids with Speech Impairment. (p. 729)
—Growing up in Religious Communities. (p. 900)
—Hidden Child: Kids with Autism. (p. 965)
—House Between Homes: Kids in the Foster Care System. (p. 1022)
—I Can Do It! Kids with Physical Challenges. (p. 1061)
—I Don't Keep Secrets. (p. 1064)
—I Like Me. (p. 1067)
—I Live in Two Homes: Adjusting to Divorce & Remarriage. (p. 1068)
—Kid's Guide to Obesity. (p. 1215)
—Kids Have Troubles Too (p. 1215)
—Listening with Your Eyes: Kids Who Are Deaf & Hard of Hearing. (p. 1309)
—My Feelings Have Names. (p. 1540)
—My Name Is Not Slow: Kids with Intellectual Disabilities. (p. 1557)
—Place Called Dead. (p. 1753)
—Psychology of Our Dark Side: Humans' Love Affair with Vampires & Werewolves. (p. 1809)
—Something's Wrong! Kids with Emotional Disturbance. (p. 2061)
—Sometimes My Mom Drinks Too Much. (p. 2061)
—Speed Racer: Kids with Attention-Deficit/Hyperactivity Disorder. (p. 2078)
—What Is a Family? (p. 2413)
—What's Wrong with My Brain? Kids with Brain Injury. (p. 2427)
—When Daddy Hit Mommy. (p. 2429)
—When Life Makes Me Mad. (p. 2431)
—When My Brother Went to Prison. (p. 2432)
—When My Dad Lost His Job. (p. 2432)
—Why Can't I Learn Like Everyone Else? Kids with Learning Disabilities. (p. 2455)
Stewart, Sheila & Flath, Camden. Finding My Voice: Kids with Speech Impairment. (p. 729)
—Hidden Child: Kids with Autism. (p. 965)
—House Between Homes: Kids in the Foster Care System. (p. 1022)
—I Can Do It! Kids with Physical Challenges. (p. 1061)
—Listening with Your Eyes: Kids Who Are Deaf & Hard of Hearing. (p. 1309)
—My Name Is Not Slow: Kids with Intellectual Disabilities. (p. 1557)
—Seeing with Your Fingers: Kids with Blindness & Visual Impairment. (p. 1984)
—Speed Racer: Kids with Attention-Deficit/Hyperactivity Disorder. (p. 2078)
—What's Going to Happen Next? Kids in the Juvenile Court System. (p. 2423)
—What's Wrong with My Brain? Kids with Brain Injury. (p. 2427)
—Why Can't I Learn Like Everyone Else? Kids with Learning Disabilities. (p. 2455)
Stewart, Sheila & Simons, Rae. I Live in Two Homes: Adjusting to Divorce & Remarriage. (p. 1068)
Stewart, Stephnie. Wow! I Can't Believe You Said That! (p. 2510)
Stewart, Sue, jt. auth. see Bassett, Jennifer.
Stewart, Tavis. Ibbie's Fashion Adventures: Around the World to Catch a Thief. (p. 1087)
Stewart, Tiffany. Holly Jolly Summer. (p. 988)
Stewart, Tobi. Colonial Teachers. (p. 418)
Stewart, Todd, illus. see Barss, Patchen.
Stewart, Trenton Lee. Extraordinary Education of Nicholas Benedict. (p. 685)
—Extraordinary Education of Nicholas Benedict. Sudyka, Diana, illus. (p. 685)
—Mysterious Benedict Society. (p. 1567)
—Mysterious Benedict Society: 10th Anniversary Edition. Ellis, Carson, illus. (p. 1567)
—Mysterious Benedict Society & the Perilous Journey. (p. 1567)
—Mysterious Benedict Society & the Perilous Journey. Sudyka, Diana, illus. (p. 1567)
—Mysterious Benedict Society & the Prisoner's Dilemma. Sudyka, Diana, illus. (p. 1567)
—Mysterious Benedict Society & the Riddle of Ages. (p. 1567)
—Mysterious Benedict Society: Mr. Benedict's Book of Perplexing Puzzles, Elusive Enigmas, & Curious Conundrums. Sudyka, Diana, illus. (p. 1567)
—Secret Keepers. (p. 1976)
—Secret Keepers. Sudyka, Diana, illus. (p. 1976)
Stewart, Vicky. Heide Loves to Cheer. (p. 948)
Stewart, Whitney. Catfish Tale: A Bayou Story of the Fisherman & His Wife. Guerlais, Gérald, illus. (p. 344)
—Loving Kindness. Alejandro, Rocio, illus. (p. 1362)
—Marshall, the Sea Dog. (p. 1409)
—Meditation Is an Open Sky: Mindfulness for Kids. Rippin, Sally, illus. (p. 1437)
—Mindful Kids: 50 Activities for Calm, Focus & Peace. Braun, Mina, illus. (p. 1470)
—Mindful Me: Mindfulness & Meditation for Kids. Peterson, Stacy, illus. (p. 1470)
—Mindful Me Activity Book. Peterson, Stacy, illus. (p. 1470)
—Mindful Tots: Animal Antics. Alejandro, Rocio, illus. (p. 1470)
—Mindful Tots: Rest & Relax. Alejandro, Rocio, illus. (p. 1470)
—Mindfulness & Meditation: Handling Life with a Calm & Focused Mind. (p. 1470)
—Tummy Ride. Alejandro, Rocio, illus. (p. 2299)
—What Do You Celebrate? Holidays & Festivals Around the World. Engel, Christiane, illus. (p. 2408)
—What's on Your Plate? Exploring the World of Food. Engel, Christiane, illus. (p. 2425)
—Who Was Walt Disney? (p. 2452)
Stewart, Whitney & Andersson, Hans Christoph. Genomics: A Revolution in Health & Disease Discovery. (p. 816)
Stewart, Whitney & Who HQ. Who Was Walt Disney? Harrison, Nancy, illus. (p. 2452)
Stewart, Willa. Forever Bed. (p. 767)
Stewart, Yale. Alien Superman! Stewart, Yale, illus. (p. 47)
—Battle of the Super Heroes! Stewart, Yale, illus. (p. 174)
—Creatures from Planet X! Stewart, Yale, illus. (p. 471)
—Escape from Future World! Stewart, Yale, illus. (p. 661)
Stewart-Gissy, Julia. Lonnie the Lonely Mailbox. (p. 1344)
Steynor, Ali & Jolly, Hattie. Get Set! Flute Pieces Book 1 with CD. (p. 824)
—Get Set! Flute Tutor Book 1 with CD. (p. 824)
StGermain, Annetta, jt. auth. see Singhose, Rose.
Stiansen, Jon. Hoot the Owl & the Vegetable Rainbow. (p. 1001)
Stiban Izabella. Mazli Kalandjai 1-2. (p. 1431)
Stich, Bill. Let's Make Art! (p. 1275)
Stich, Tim. Paper Crafts: Shapes & Their Attributes. (p. 1697)
Stichter, Katherine. Phonics (Classic Reprint) (p. 1736)
Stickels, Terry & Immanuvel, Anthony. Go!Games Sudoku. (p. 854)
Stickers, jt. auth. see Dahlen, Noelle.
Stickers, jt. auth. see Rechlin, Ted.
Stickland, Emily. Little Bonsai. (p. 1312)
Stickland, Shadra, illus. see Bandy, Michael S. & Stein, Eric.
Stickland, Shadra, illus. see Watson, Renée.
Stickler, Eidi Helen, illus. see Ness, Nikki.
Stickler, John. Land of Morning Calm: Korean Culture Then & Now. Han, Soma, illus. (p. 1241)
Stickler, John C. & Han, Soma. Maya & the Turtle: A Korean Fairy Tale. Han, Soma, illus. (p. 1429)
Stickley, Frances. Love You Always. Blanco, Migy, illus. (p. 1361)
—Mouse's Apples. Litten, Kristyna, illus. (p. 1515)
Stickley, Gustav. Craftsman, Vol. 31: October, 1916 (Classic Reprint) (p. 466)
Stickley, Lisa. Bake Like Mommy. (p. 160)
—Bernard Makes a Splash. (p. 204)
—Handstand. (p. 916)
—New Baby. (p. 1591)
—New Room. (p. 1597)
Stickney, Charles E. Minisink Double Wedding: A Story of Old Minisink Village Between the Minisink Indian War of 1754-8, & the French & Indian War of 1763-5 (Classic Reprint) (p. 1472)
Stickney, Elizabeth, jt. auth. see Schmidt, Gary D.
Stickney, Eva J. Proceedings at the Dedication of the Theophilus Harrington Monument, July 3 1886: Copied from the Rutland Herald of July 5, 1886 (Classic Reprint) (p. 1803)
Stickney, J. H. Bird World: A Bird Book for Children (Classic Reprint) (p. 231)
—Child's Version of Aesop's Fables: With a Supplement Containing Fables from la Fontaine & Krilof (Classic Reprint) (p. 376)
—Child's Version of Aesop's Fables, with a Supplement Containing Fables from la Fontaine & Krilof. (p. 376)
—Earth & Sky, Vol. 2: A Second & Third Grade Nature Reader & Text-Book (Classic Reprint) (p. 616)
Stickney, Jenny H. Earth & Sky: Number 1, a First Grade Nature Reader & Text-Book (Classic Reprint) (p. 616)
—Fifth Reader: With an Introduction on Elocution (Classic Reprint) (p. 724)
—First Reader (Classic Reprint) (p. 739)
—Fourth Reader (Classic Reprint) (p. 773)
—Pets & Companions: A Second Reader (Classic Reprint) (p. 1731)
—Second Reader (Classic Reprint) (p. 1974)
—Third Reader (Classic Reprint) (p. 2222)
Stickney, Mary E. Ouray Jim, & Other Stories (Classic Reprint) (p. 1681)
Stickney, Mary Etta. Brown of Lost River: A Story of the West (Classic Reprint) (p. 287)
Stidger, William L. Flash-Lights from the Seven Seas (Classic Reprint) (p. 746)
—Soldier Silhouettes on Our Front. (p. 2056)
—Soldier Silhouettes on Our Front (Classic Reprint) (p. 2056)

—Thea Stilton & the Chocolate Sabotage. (p. 2214)
—Thea Stilton & the Dancing Shadows. (p. 2214)
—Thea Stilton & the Frozen Fiasco. (p. 2214)
—Thea Stilton & the Frozen Fiasco: a Geronimo Stilton Adventure (Thea Stilton #25) (p. 2214)
—Thea Stilton & the Ghost of the Shipwreck. (p. 2214)
—Thea Stilton & the Great Tulip Heist. (p. 2214)
—Thea Stilton & the Hollywood Hoax. (p. 2214)
—Thea Stilton & the Journey to the Lion's Den. (p. 2214)
—Thea Stilton & the Legend of the Fire Flowers. (p. 2214)
—Thea Stilton & the Lost Letters. (p. 2214)
—Thea Stilton & the Madagascar Madness: A Geronimo Stilton Adventure. (p. 2214)
—Thea Stilton & the Missing Myth. (p. 2214)
—Thea Stilton & the Mystery in Paris. (p. 2215)
—Thea Stilton & the Mystery on the Orient Express. (p. 2215)
—Thea Stilton & the Niagara Splash. (p. 2215)
—Thea Stilton & the Prince's Emerald. (p. 2215)
—Thea Stilton & the Race for the Gold (Thea Stilton #31) (p. 2215)
—Thea Stilton & the Riddle of the Ruins: A Geronimo Stilton Adventure. Schaffer, Andrea, tr. (p. 2215)
—Thea Stilton & the Secret of the Old Castle. (p. 2215)
—Thea Stilton & the Spanish Dance Mission. (p. 2215)
—Thea Stilton & the Star Castaways. (p. 2215)
—Thea Stilton & the Venice Masquerade. (p. 2215)
—Thea Stilton Graphic Novels #1: The Secret of Whale Island Cooper-McGuinness, Nanette, tr. (p. 2215)
—Thea Stilton Graphic Novels #8: The Thea Sisters & the Secret Treasure Hunt. Cooper-McGuinness, Nanette, tr. (p. 2215)
—Thea Stilton Mouseford Academy #10: A Dream on Ice. (p. 2215)
—Thea Stilton Mouseford Academy #12: Mice on the Runway. (p. 2215)
—Thea Stilton Mouseford Academy #9: The Mysterious Love Letter. (p. 2215)
—Treasure of the Sea. (p. 2282)
—Treasure Seekers (p. 2282)
—Tropical Treasure. (p. 2291)
Stilton, Thea, jt. auth. see Stilton, Geronimo.
Stilton, Thea & Dami, Elisabetta. Secret Invention. (p. 1976)
Stilton, Thea & Pizzelli, Anna. Friendship Recipe. Pellizzari, Barbara & Castelli, Francesco, illus. (p. 788)
Stilton, Thea & Schaffer, Andrea. Royal Ball. Pellizzari, Barbara et al, illus. (p. 1909)
Stilton, Thea & Stilton, Geronimo. Secret of the Snow. (p. 1978)
Stilwell, Alexander. Army Rangers. (p. 118)
—Navy SEALs: What It Takes to Join the Elite. (p. 1583)
Stilwell, Debra. Where Does Our Food Come From? (p. 2436)
Stilwell, Dwayne. Levers. (p. 1282)
Stilwell, Norma Minturn. Making Beautiful Music. LaGrange, Tiffany, illus. (p. 1388)
—Thought for Thanksgiving. Bingham, Pamela E., illus. (p. 2230)
Stimart, Mary. Cora Grows Up. (p. 452)
—Cora's Adventures: The Teenage Years. (p. 453)
Stimola, Aubrey. Brain Injuries. (p. 274)
—Cell Biology. (p. 350)
Stimpson, Aaron & Stimpson, Sarah. Story Builders. (p. 2127)
Stimpson, C., jt. auth. see Howard, M.
Stimpson, Colin, illus. see Howard, Martin.
Stimpson, Herbert Baird. Tory Maid (Classic Reprint) (p. 2266)
Stimpson, Mary Stoyell. Child's Book of American Biography (Classic Reprint) (p. 375)
Stimson, Alexander Lovett. Waifwood: A Novel (Classic Reprint) (p. 2370)
Stimson, F. J. First Harvests: An Episode in the Life of Mrs. Lawson Gower; a Satire Without a Moral (Classic Reprint) (p. 737)
—In the Three Zones (Classic Reprint) (p. 1111)
—Jethro Bacon of Sandwich: The Weaker Sex (Classic Reprint) (p. 1167)
—Pirate Gold (Classic Reprint) (p. 1750)
Stimson, Frederic Jessup. Guerndale: An Old Story (Classic Reprint) (p. 902)
—Guerndale. (p. 902)
Stimson, Frederic Jesup. In Cure of Her Soul (Classic Reprint) (p. 1104)
—King Noanett: A Story of Old Virginia & the Massachusetts Bay (Classic Reprint) (p. 1220)
—Mrs. Knollys: And Other Stories (Classic Reprint) (p. 1522)
—Residuary Legatee, or the Posthumous Jest of the Late John Austin (Classic Reprint) (p. 1869)
Stimson, James. Bully Goat Grim: A Maynard Moose Tale. (p. 297)
Stimson, James, illus. see Claflin, Willy.
Stimson, Janet. Tiny Tree. (p. 2250)
Stimson, Joan. Dinosaur Next Door. (p. 549)
—Dinosaur Next Door. Elkerton, Andy, illus. (p. 549)
Stimson, Julia C. Finding Themselves: The Letters of an American Army Chief Nurse in a British Hospital in France (Classic Reprint) (p. 730)
Stinde, Julius. Buchholz Family: Second Part, Sketches of Berlin Life (Classic Reprint) (p. 289)
—Buchholzes in Italy: Travelling Adventures of Wilhelmine Buchholz (Classic Reprint) (p. 289)
—Frau Wilhelmine the Concluding Part of the Buchholz Family (Classic Reprint) (p. 779)
—Woodland Tales (Classic Reprint) (p. 2491)
Stinde, Julius, ed. see Schmitz, L. Dora.
Stinde, Julius & Schmitz, L. Dora. Buchholz Family. (p. 289)
Stine, Kimberly A. Roxy & the Human Body. (p. 1909)
—Roxy & the Nasty Virus (Teaching Kids about Coronavirus) (p. 1909)
—Roxy & the Paleontologists. (p. 1909)
—Roxy's Christmas Wish. (p. 1909)
Stine, Megan. What Was the Age of the Dinosaurs? (p. 2421)
—What Was the Age of the Dinosaurs? Copeland, Gregory, illus. (p. 2421)
—Where Are the Galapagos Islands? (p. 2435)
—Where Is Niagara Falls? (p. 2438)
—Where Is the Brooklyn Bridge? (p. 2438)
—Where Is the White House? (p. 2438)
—Who Is Michelle Obama? (p. 2448)
—Who Is Sonia Sotomayor? (p. 2448)
—Who Was Marie Curie? (p. 2451)
—Who Was Michael Jackson? (p. 2451)
—Who Was Sally Ride? (p. 2451)
—Who Was Sally Ride? Hammond, Ted, illus. (p. 2451)
—Who Was Ulysses S. Grant? (p. 2452)
Stine, Megan & Who HQ. What Was the Age of the Dinosaurs? Copeland, Gregory, illus. (p. 2421)
—Where Are the Galapagos Islands? Hinderliter, John, illus. (p. 2435)
—Where Is Easter Island? Hinderliter, John, illus. (p. 2437)
—Where Is Machu Picchu? O'Brien, John, illus. (p. 2438)
—Where Is Niagara Falls? Foley, Tim, illus. (p. 2438)
—Where Is the Bermuda Triangle? Foley, Tim, illus. (p. 2438)
—Where Is the Brooklyn Bridge? Hinderliter, John, illus. (p. 2438)
—Where Is the Congo? Putra, Dede, illus. (p. 2438)
—Where Is the Vatican? Conley, Laurie A., illus. (p. 2438)
—Where Is the White House? Groff, David, illus. (p. 2438)
—Who Is Michelle Obama? O'Brien, John, illus. (p. 2448)
—Who Is Sonia Sotomayor? Putra, Dede, illus. (p. 2448)
—Who Was Marie Curie? Hammond, Ted, illus. (p. 2451)
—Who Was Richard Nixon? Gutierrez, Manuel, IV & Gutierrez, Manuel, illus. (p. 2451)
—Who Was Sally Ride? Hammond, Ted, illus. (p. 2451)
—Who Was Ulysses S. Grant? Geyer, Mark Edward, illus. (p. 2452)
Stine, Milton H. Niemans (Classic Reprint) (p. 1604)
Stine, R. L. 12 Screams of Christmas. (p. 2551)
—13th Warning (p. 2552)
—Adventures of Shrinkman (p. 27)
—Attack of the Aqua Apes & Nightmare In 3-D: Twice Terrifying Tales. (p. 134)
—Attack of the Graveyard Ghouls. (p. 134)
—Attack of the Jack. (p. 134)
—Attack of the Jack (Goosebumps SlappyWorld #2) (p. 134)
—Attack of the Jack-O'-Lanterns. (p. 134)
—Battle of the Dum Diddys Park, Trip, illus. (p. 174)
—Be Careful What You Wish For. (p. 177)
—Betrayal: The Betrayal; the Secret; the Burning. (p. 208)
—Big Blueberry Barf-Off! Park, Trip, illus. (p. 217)
—Birthday Party of No Return! (p. 233)
—Bitten: Dangerous Girls & the Taste of Night. (p. 235)
—Blob That Ate Everyone. (p. 245)
—Boy Who Ate Fear Street. (p. 270)
—Bride of the Living Dummy. (p. 280)
—Broken Hearts. (p. 284)
—Can You Keep a Secret? (p. 318)
—Claws! (p. 402)
—Creature Teacher: The Final Exam. (p. 471)
—Creatures from Beyond Beyond (p. 471)
—Curse of the Mummy's Tomb. (p. 489)
—Darkest Dawn. (p. 507)
—Dead Boyfriend. (p. 517)
—Don't Scream! (p. 583)
—Don't Stay up Late: A Fear Street Novel. (p. 583)
—Dr. Maniac Will See You Now. (p. 591)
—Drop Dead Gorgeous. (p. 605)
—Dudes, the School Is Haunted! Park, Trip, illus. (p. 609)
—Dummy Meets the Mummy. (p. 610)
—Escape from HorrorLand. (p. 661)
—Escape from Horrorland. (p. 661)
—Escape from Shudder Mansion. (p. 661)
—Fear Street Super Thriller: Party Games & Don't Stay up Late. (p. 716)
—Fear Street Super Thriller: Nightmares: (2 Books in 1: the Dead Boyfriend; Give Me a K-I-L-L) (p. 716)
—Fear Street Super Thriller: Secrets: The Lost Girl; Can You Keep a Secret? (p. 716)
—First Evil. (p. 736)
—Five Masks of Dr. Scream. (p. 744)
—Frankenstein's Dog. (p. 778)
—Fright Knight & the Ooze: Twice Terrifying Tales. (p. 788)
—Ghost Beach. (p. 827)
—Ghost Next Door. (p. 828)
—Ghost of Slappy. (p. 828)
—Good, the Bad & the Very Slimy. Park, Trip, illus. (p. 866)
—Goosebumps. (p. 869)
—Goosebumps 25th Anniversary Retro Set. (p. 869)
—Goosebumps Slappyworld Boxset 1-5. (p. 869)
—Goosebumps Wanted: the Haunted Mask. (p. 869)
—Great Smelling Bee Park, Trip, illus. (p. 889)
—Haunted Car. (p. 937)
—Haunted Mask. (p. 938)
—Haunted Mask II. (p. 938)
—Haunter. (p. 939)
—Headless Ghost. (p. 942)
—Heads, You Lose. (p. 942)
—Heinie Prize Park, Trip, illus. (p. 948)
—Help! We Have Strange Powers! (p. 953)
—Here Comes the Shaggedy. (p. 958)
—Hide & Shriek & Who's Been Sleeping in My Grave? Twice Terrifying Tales. (p. 967)
—Horror at Chiller House. (p. 1004)
—How I Got My Shrunken Head. (p. 1032)
—How I Met My Monster. (p. 1032)
—How to Be a Vampire. (p. 1037)
—I Am Slappy's Evil Twin. (p. 1060)
—It Came from Ohio! - My Life as a Writer. (p. 1141)
—It's Alive! It's Alive! (p. 1144)
—Just Beyond: the Scare School. Matthews, Kelly & Matthews, Nichole, illus. (p. 1192)
—Little Shop of Hamsters. (p. 1327)
—Little Shop of Monsters. Brown, Marc, illus. (p. 1327)
—Lizard of Oz. (p. 1336)
—Lose, Team, Lose! Park, Trip, illus. (p. 1352)
—Mary Mcscary. Brown, Marc, illus. (p. 1415)
—Midsummer Night's Scream. (p. 1462)
—Movie Novel. Scholastic, Inc. Staff, illus. (p. 1516)
—My Alien Parents (p. 1531)
—My Friends Call Me Monster. (p. 1548)
—Night in Terror Tower. (p. 1606)
—Night of the Giant Everything. (p. 1607)
—Night of the Puppet People. (p. 1607)
—Night of the Puppet People (Goosebumps Most Wanted #8) (p. 1607)
—Night of the Werecat. (p. 1607)
—Nightmare Hour TV Tie-In Edition. (p. 1608)
—Nightmare on Clown Street. (p. 1608)
—Party Poopers. Park, Trip, illus. (p. 1702)
—Phantom of the Auditorium. (p. 1732)
—Planet of the Lawn Gnomes. (p. 1755)
—Please Do Not Feed the Weirdo (p. 1762)
—Please Do Not Feed the Weirdo. (p. 1762)
—Please Do Not Feed the Weirdo (Goosebumps SlappyWorld #4) (p. 1762)
—Please Don't Feed the Vampire! A Give Yourself Goosebumps Book. (p. 1762)
—Please Don't Feed the Vampire a Give Yourself Goosebumps Book. (p. 1762)
—Punk'd & Skunked Park, Trip, illus. (p. 1814)
—Red Rain. (p. 1858)
—Return of the Mummy. (p. 1871)
—Revenge of the Lawn Gnomes. (p. 1872)
—Revenge of the Shadow People & the Bugman Lives! Twice Terrifying Tales. (p. 1873)
—Rotten School Park, Trip, illus. (p. 1907)
—Rotten School - Dudes, the School Is Haunted! Park, Trip, illus. (p. 1907)
—Rottenest Angel Park, Trip, illus. (p. 1907)
—Say Cheese & Die! (p. 1940)
—Say Cheese & Die. (p. 1940)
—Say Cheese & Die Screaming! (p. 1940)
—Say Cheese - And Die Screaming! (p. 1940)
—Scarecrow Walks at Midnight. (p. 1941)
—Shake, Rattle, & Hurl! Park, Trip, illus. (p. 1998)
—Shocker on Shock Street. (p. 2008)
—Slappy Birthday to You. (p. 2035)
—Slappy New Year! (p. 2035)
—Slappy's Tales of Horror. (p. 2035)
—Slappy's Tales of Horror (Goosebumps Graphix) Roman, Dave & Naifeh, Ted, illus. (p. 2035)
—Son of Slappy. (p. 2062)
—Stay Out of the Basement. (p. 2109)
—Streets of Panic Park. (p. 2140)
—Teacher from Heck. Park, Trip, illus. (p. 2195)
—Temptation. (p. 2203)
—Three Faces of Me (p. 2232)
—Trick or Trap. (p. 2287)
—Vampire Breath. (p. 2346)
—Weirdo Halloween. (p. 2397)
—Welcome to Camp Nightmare. (p. 2398)
—Welcome to Camp Slither. (p. 2398)
—Welcome to Dead House. (p. 2398)
—Werewolf of Fever Swamp. (p. 2401)
—When the Ghost Dog Howls. (p. 2433)
—Who's Your Mummy? (p. 2454)
—Why I Quit Zombie School. (p. 2458)
—Wizard of Ooze. (p. 2482)
—Wrong Girl. (p. 2514)
—You Can't Scare Me! (p. 2526)
—You May Now Kill the Bride. (p. 2527)
—Young Scrooge: A Very Scary Christmas Story. (p. 2532)
—Zombie Halloween. (p. 2542)
—Zombie Town (p. 2542)
Stine, R. L., jt. auth. see Heller, Jason.
Stine, R. L., jt. auth. see Lurie, Susan.
Stine, R. L., jt. auth. see Scholastic, Inc. Staff.
Stine, R. L. & Ferguson, Jo Ann. Cabinet of Souls. Scholastic, Inc. Staff, illus. (p. 307)
Stine, R. L. & The Topps Company. Welcome to Smellville (Garbage Pail Kids Book 1) Simko, Joe & Zapata, Jeff, illus. (p. 2398)
Stine, R. L., ed. Fear: 13 Stories of Suspense & Horror. (p. 716)
Stine, R. L., et al. Scream & Scream Again! Spooky Stories from Mystery Writers of America. (p. 1964)
Stine, R.l. Dummy Meets the Mummy! (p. 610)
—Fear Street the Beginning: The New Girl; the Surprise Party; the Overnight; Missing. (p. 716)
—Ghost of Slappy (p. 828)
—Heads, You Lose! (Goosebumps Horrorland) (p. 942)
—It's Alive! It's Alive! (p. 1144)
—Just Beyond (Set) (p. 1192)
—Scare School. (p. 1941)
—Scarecrow Walks at Midnight. (p. 1941)
—Streets of Panic Park (Goosebumps Horrorland) (p. 2140)
—Vampire Breath. (p. 2346)
—Volume 1: the Scare School. Matthews, Kelly & Matthews, Nichole, illus. (p. 2367)
—Volume 2: a Strange Discovery. Matthews, Kelly & Matthews, Nichole, illus. (p. 2367)
—Volume 3: a Monster's Lunch. Matthews, Kelly & Matthews, Nichole, illus. (p. 2367)
—Volume 4: No Escape. Matthews, Kelly & Matthews, Nichole, illus. (p. 2367)
—Welcome to Horrorland: A Survival Guide (Goosebumps Horrorland) (p. 2398)
—Welcome to Smellville (Garbage Pail Kids Book 1) (B&N Signed Edition) Zapata, Jeff & Simko, Joe, illus. (p. 2398)
—Young Scrooge: A Very Scary Christmas Story. (p. 2532)
Stine-Shannon, Melanie L., jt. auth. see Stine, Cyarah Felicity.
Sting. There's a Little Black Spot on the Sun Today. Völker, Sven, illus. (p. 2218)
Stinson, Aimee & Sornson, Kathy. Bearless City (p. 180)
Stinson, Anna. Tatler, Vol. 7: A. D. Higgins Junior High School, Thompsonville, Connecticut; June 1928 (Classic Reprint) (p. 2193)
Stinson, Danielle. Before I Disappear. (p. 190)
Stinson, Jennifer. Even Fairies Fart. Ashdown, Rebecca, illus. (p. 668)
Stinson, June. Basset Named Fred. (p. 171)
—Milton Hears a Train. (p. 1468)
—Yellow Kitty Rags. (p. 2520)
Stinson, Kathy. Big or Little? Goffe, Toni, illus. (p. 222)
—Big or Little? Bell, Jennifer A., illus. (p. 222)
—Dance of the Violin. Petricic, Dusan, illus. (p. 500)
—Dog Who Wanted to Fly. Scott, Brandon James, illus. (p. 577)
—Harry & Walter. Leng, Qin, illus. (p. 934)
—Highway of Heroes. (p. 970)
—Man with the Violin. Petricic, Dusan, illus. (p. 1396)
—What Happened to Ivy (p. 2411)
Stinson, Rick. Kyle Busch: NASCAR Driver. (p. 1234)
Stipo, A. J. Adventures of Tobias the Turtle. (p. 29)
Stipp, George H. California Fairy (Classic Reprint) (p. 310)
Stirling, Emma M. Our Children in Old Scotland & Nova Scotia: Being a History of Her Work (Classic Reprint) (p. 1677)
Stirling, Fanny. Sedgely Court, Vol. 1 Of 3: A Tale (Classic Reprint) (p. 1981)
Stirling, Helen. Soldier of the King: A True Story of a Young Canadian Hero (Classic Reprint) (p. 2056)
Stirling, Janet, jt. auth. see Vale, Jenna.
Stirling, Joss. Angel. (p. 85)
—Deadly Nightshade. (p. 519)
—Flare. (p. 746)
—Girl's Best Friend Is Her Wolf: A High School Comedy. (p. 838)
—Glow. (p. 845)
—Peril. (p. 1723)
—Shaken. (p. 1998)
—Summer. (p. 2148)
Stirling, M. C. Minister's Son, Vol. 1 Of 3: Or Home with Honours (Classic Reprint) (p. 1472)
—Minister's Son, Vol. 3 (Classic Reprint) (p. 1472)
Stirling, Maggie. Sushi the Christmas Puppy. (p. 2166)
Stirling, Mark. Low Places in the Road. (p. 1362)
Stirling, Mary Anne. Sedgely Court, Vol. 2 Of 3: A Tale (Classic Reprint) (p. 1981)
Stirling, Tricia. When My Heart Was Wicked. (p. 2432)
Stites, Bill, jt. auth. see Uhl, Xina M.
Stites, Clara. Lixia of Gold Mountain: A Story of Early California. (p. 1336)
Stites, Theresa, illus. see Goodluck, Marquita.
Stites, Theresa, illus. see Porter, Harry.
Stites, Theresa, illus. see Wood, Debbie.
Stith, John. Climbing Tree. Pieletskaya, Yuliya, illus. (p. 405)
Stith, Tai. Fulbeck Six. (p. 797)
—Legacy of the St. Alodia Hotel. (p. 1261)
Stitz, Kathy. Trouble with Tonsils. (p. 2292)
Stitzer, Daniel Ahrens. Stories of the Occult (Classic Reprint) (p. 2125)
Stiver, Megan. Great Bellybutton Cover-Up. (p. 884)
—Say Please to the Honeybees. (p. 1940)
Stivers, Dane. Daniel's Deeds & the Palace of Everywhere. (p. 503)
Stiverson, Charlotte L. Nellie's Walk. Aitken, Kati, illus. (p. 1586)
Stjean, Shawn. Cranky Bear Wakes Up: An Animal Kingdom Story Sketchbook. Stjean, Todd, illus. (p. 467)
Stjean, Todd, illus. see Stjean, Shawn.
StJohn, Amanda. 5 Steps to Drawing Dogs & Cats. Regan, Dana, illus. (p. 2548)
—5 Steps to Drawing Magical Creatures. Close, Laura Ferraro, illus. (p. 2548)
—5 Steps to Drawing Monsters. Girouard, Patrick, illus. (p. 2548)
—5 Steps to Drawing Sea Creatures. Close, Laura Ferraro, illus. (p. 2548)
—Bouki Cuts Wood: A Haitian Folktale. Revell, Cindy, illus. (p. 265)
—Bridget & Bo Build a Blog. McDee, Katie, illus. (p. 280)
—Evan & Erin Build an Essay. Rooney, Ronnie, illus. (p. 668)
—Frog Went A-Traveling: A Russian Folktale. Wenzel, David, illus. (p. 789)
—How a Library Works. Ostrom, Bob, illus. (p. 1025)
—How an e-Book Works. Ostrom, Bob, illus. (p. 1025)
—How to Check Out a Book. Ostrom, Bob, illus. (p. 1038)
—How to Find a Book. Ostrom, Bob, illus. (p. 1042)
—How to Find Information Online. Ostrom, Bob, illus. (p. 1042)
—How to Treat a Book. Ostrom, Bob, illus. (p. 1045)
—Medio Pollito (Half-Chick) A Mexican Folktale. Todd, Sue, illus. (p. 1437)
—Pied Piper of Hamelin: A German Folktale. Bonder, Dianna, illus. (p. 1742)
—Sophie & Sadie Build a Sonnet. Marten, Luanne, illus. (p. 2064)
St-Laurent, Carole. Funky Town: (Diversity, LGBTQ, Inclusion, Ages 3 To 5) (p. 801)
—Not So Bad Piranha: (Preschool, Ages 6-8, Early Reader, Bullying, Emotions) (p. 1623)
Stobart, Clair. Flaming Sword: In Serbia & Elsewhere (Classic Reprint) (p. 746)
Stobie, Janet. Elizabeth Gets Her Wings. Phillips, Olivia, illus. (p. 636)
Stobo, Robert. Memoirs of Major Robert Stobo, of the Virginia Regiment: Arma Virumque (Classic Reprint) (p. 1444)
Stock, Catherine, illus. see Figley, Marty Rhodes.
Stock, Catherine, illus. see Kent, Allegra.
Stock, Catherine, illus. see Lunde, Darrin.
Stock, Catherine, illus. see Mohammed, Khadra & Williams, Karen Lynn.
Stock, Catherine, illus. see Moreillon, Judi.
Stock, Catherine, illus. see Sanchez, Anita.
Stock, Catherine, illus. see Walter, Mildred Pitts.
Stock, Catherine, illus. see Williams, Karen Lynn.
Stock, Catherine, jt. auth. see Lunde, Darrin P.
Stock, Etta Florence. Redemption of Charley Phillips (Classic Reprint) (p. 1859)
—To Every Man His Work (Classic Reprint) (p. 2252)
Stock, Gregory. Kids' Book of Questions. (p. 1214)
Stock, Lisa. Battle for Naboo. (p. 174)
—DK Readers L1: Star Wars : What Is a Droid? (p. 568)
—DK Readers L2: Star Wars: Rey to the Rescue! (p. 568)
—DK Readers L2: LEGO Friends Perfect Pets. (p. 568)
—Perfect Pets. (p. 1722)
—Rey to the Rescue! (p. 1874)
—What Is a Droid? (p. 2413)
Stock, Lisa, jt. auth. see Dorling Kindersley Publishing Staff.

Stoll, Albert. Clever Business Sketches (Classic Reprint) (p. 404)
Stoll, Heinrich Wilhelm. Die Sagen des Classischen Alterthums, Vol. 2: Erzählungen Aus der Alten Welt (Classic Reprint) (p. 544)
Stoll, Kristen, jt. auth. see Stoll, Scott.
Stoll, Lillian. Trying Them Out: A Comedy in One Act (Classic Reprint) (p. 2297)
Stoll, Scott. Cupcake Boy. Stoll, Scott, ed. (p. 485)
Stoll, Scott & Stoll, Kristen. God's Garden Friends. (p. 853)
Stoll, Scott & Williams, Sara Elizabeth. Dream It! A Playbook to Spark Your Awesomeness. (p. 601)
Stolle, Jeannette. Our Home. (p. 1678)
Stolle, Rachel Jeanette Hall. Why Do Our Loved Ones Die, Aunt Lou? (p. 2456)
Stoller, Bryan Michael. Harry Potter: Imagining Hogwarts: A Beginner's Guide to Moviemaking. (p. 935)
—Smartphone Movie Maker. (p. 2041)
Stollers, Veronica & Keyishian, Elizabeth. Frequently Asked Questions about Smoking. (p. 784)
Stollinger, Heide, illus. see Dahiméne, Adelheid.
Stols, Victor, tr. see Pere, Tuula.
Stoltenberg, Nathan, illus. see Marler, Jerilyn.
Stoltman, Joan. 1,000-Year-Old Sponges! (p. 2560)
—20 Fun Facts about Congress. (p. 2553)
—20 Fun Facts about the 13 Colonies. (p. 2553)
—20 Fun Facts about the Gold Rush. (p. 2553)
—20 Fun Facts about the Supreme Court. (p. 2553)
—20 Fun Facts about Westward Expansion. (p. 2553)
—Barack Obama. (p. 164)
—Beethoven. (p. 190)
—Cooking Great Cuisine with a Chef. (p. 447)
—Did the Abolition Movement Abolish Slavery? (p. 543)
—Digging Deep with an Archaeologist. (p. 546)
—Dwayne Johnson. (p. 611)
—Eleanor Roosevelt. (p. 630)
—Elizabeth Cady Stanton. (p. 636)
—Ellen Ochoa. (p. 637)
—Following Extreme Weather with a Storm Chaser. (p. 758)
—Frederick Douglass. (p. 781)
—Gareth's Guide to Becoming a Brain Surgeon. (p. 809)
—Get to Work! Looking for Clues with a Detective. (p. 825)
—Harriet Tubman: Little Biographies of Big People. (p. 933)
—Harriet Tubman. (p. 933)
—Hillary Clinton. (p. 971)
—Jane Goodall. (p. 1158)
—Jim Henson. (p. 1168)
—Malala Yousafzai. (p. 1391)
—Malcolm X. (p. 1391)
—Melania Trump. (p. 1442)
—Michelle Obama. (p. 1458)
—Mohandas Gandhi. (p. 1488)
—My First Bird. (p. 1542)
—My First Bunny. (p. 1543)
—My First Cat. (p. 1543)
—My First Dog. (p. 1543)
—My First Fish. (p. 1544)
—My First Hamster. (p. 1544)
—Native American Art: From Totems to Textiles. (p. 1578)
—Planning to Build with an Architect. (p. 1756)
—Prohibition: Social Movement & Controversial Amendment. (p. 1805)
—Protests & Riots That Changed America. (p. 1808)
—Rise & Fall of the Aztec Empire. (p. 1885)
—Rosa Parks. (p. 1904)
—Shooting for the Stars with a Rocket Scientist. (p. 2009)
—Thomas Edison. (p. 2228)
—Thurgood Marshall. (p. 2238)
—Weird Beauty Inventions. (p. 2397)
—Weird Medical Inventions. (p. 2397)
—What Are Stars Made Of? (p. 2406)
Stoltzfus, Donna J. Captive (p. 326)
Stoltzfus, Sherman Matthew. Little Bear Builds a Wigwam. Zimmerman, Edith Fay Martin & Kanagy, Audrey Ann Zimmerman, illus. (p. 1311)
Stolz, Donald R. Classroom Times: Charactoons & Rhymes. Thornton, Barbara, illus. (p. 401)
Stolz, Mary. Storm in the Night. Cummings, Pat, illus. (p. 2126)
Stone. William Langshawe, Vol. 1 Of 2: The Cotton Lord (Classic Reprint) (p. 2468)
Stone, A. American Pep: A Tale of America's Efficiency (Classic Reprint) (p. 73)
—Fighting Byng a Novel of Mystery, Intrigue & Adventure (Classic Reprint) (p. 725)
Stone, A. R., illus. see McKinna, Caelaach.
Stone, Adam. Apollo 13 Mission. (p. 106)
—Bermuda Triangle. (p. 203)
—Big Show. (p. 223)
—Challenger Explosion. (p. 354)
—Deepwater Horizon Oil Spill. (p. 525)
—Edge. (p. 625)
—Esp. (p. 662)
—Ghosts. (p. 829)
—Haunted Houses. (p. 938)
—John Cena. (p. 1172)
—Kane. (p. 1202)
—Near-Death Experiences. (p. 1584)
—Randy Orton. (p. 1840)
—Titanic Disaster. (p. 2251)
—Triple H. (p. 2289)
—Undertaker. (p. 2326)
Stone, Adrian, illus. see Mayhew, Jon.
Stone, Amy M., jt. auth. see Dwyer, Helen.
Stone, Ana F., illus. see Kaufman, Kendra L.
Stone Arch Books. Christmas & New Year's Eve Nguyen, Dustin, illus. (p. 383)
—Halloween & Thanksgiving Nguyen, Dustin, illus. (p. 912)
—Valentine's Day & the Lunar New Year Nguyen, Dustin, illus. (p. 2344)
Stone Arch Books Staff. John Henry - Hammerin' Hero. Evergreen, Nelson, illus. (p. 1173)
—Legend of Johnny Appleseed. Lamoreaux, M. A. & Lamoreaux, Michelle, illus. (p. 1262)
—Pecos Bill: Colossal Cowboy. Weber, Lisa K., illus. (p. 1711)
—Robin Hood Tobon, Sara, tr. (p. 1891)
—Tall Tale of Paul Bunyan. Blecha, Aaron, illus. (p. 2188)
Stone Arch Books Staff, jt. auth. see Andersen, Hans.
Stone Arch Books Staff, jt. auth. see Meister, Cari.
Stone, Bev. Hug a Bug? (p. 1047)
—Snowpuppies: Little Bean & MR. Fox. (p. 2049)
—Where Is Maya's Smile? (p. 2438)
Stone, Bob. Missing Beat. (p. 1480)
Stone, Bryan, illus. see Blobaum, Cindy.
Stone, Bryan, illus. see Brown, Cynthia Light & Brown, Grace.
Stone, Bryan, illus. see Brown, Cynthia Light & Brown, Nick.
Stone, Bryan, illus. see Diehn, Andi.
Stone, Bryan, illus. see Fisher, Verna.
Stone, Bryan, illus. see Latham, Donna.
Stone, Bryan, illus. see Mooney, Carla.
Stone, Bryan, illus. see Reilly, Kathleen M.
Stone, Bryan, illus. see Swanson, Jennifer.
Stone, Bryan, illus. see Van Vleet, Carmella.
Stone, Bryan, illus. see Yasuda, Anita.
Stone, Clarence Eastman. Poems & Sketches (Classic Reprint) (p. 1765)
Stone, Danika. All the Feels. (p. 54)
—Internet Famous. (p. 1127)
—Switchback. (p. 2171)
Stone, Danton. Basketball. (p. 170)
Stone, David. Adventures of Tom, Jack & Joe. (p. 29)
Stone, Dori. Beyond the Fence: A Journey to the Roots of the Migration Crisis. (p. 212)
Stone, Elizabeth T. Sketch of the Life of Elizabeth T. Stone, & of Her Persecutions: With an Appendix of Her Treatment & Sufferings While in the Charlestown Mclean Assylum, Where She Was Confined under the Pretence of Insanity (Classic Reprint) (p. 2030)
Stone, Ernest. Battery B Thru the Fires of France: Being a Very Human & Intimate Sketch of a Few Men Who Served Stem a Tiny Eddy in One of the Greatest of Cataclysms the World War (Classic Reprint) (p. 173)
Stone, Evelyn. Hugh Moore, Vol. 1 Of 2: A Novel (Classic Reprint) (p. 1048)
—Hugh Moore, Vol. 2 Of 2: A Novel (Classic Reprint) (p. 1048)
Stone, Forrest. George Washington, Farewell Address: Set Of 6. (p. 820)
—George Washington, Farewell Address. (p. 820)
—Upton Sinclair, the Jungle: Set Of 12. (p. 2339)
—Upton Sinclair, the Jungle. (p. 2339)
Stone, Forrest & Benchmark Education Co., LLC Staff. Ponce de león y la Verdadera Fuente de la Juventud; ¡Navega, Colón! Set of 6 with Common Core Teacher Materials. (p. 1773)
—Tarea Del Futuro y la Aplicación Estimuladora: Set of 6 with Common Core Teacher Materials. (p. 2191)
—Varuna Trabaja en el Censo; un Ataque a la Nave Mayflower en el Año 2647: Set of 6 with Common Core Teacher Materials. (p. 2348)
Stone, George, jt. auth. see Politzer, Adam.
Stone, Gertrude L. Days & Deeds: A Hundred Years Ago (Classic Reprint) (p. 515)
—Every Day Life in the Colonies (Classic Reprint) (p. 670)
Stone, Gertrude Lincoln. Famous Days in the Century of Invention (Classic Reprint) (p. 703)
Stone, Grace Zaring. Letters to a Djinn (Classic Reprint) (p. 1281)
Stone, Heather Duffy. Over the Tracks. (p. 1687)
Stone, Helen, illus. see Bennett, Anna Elizabeth.
Stone, Herbert S. Book of American Prose Humor: Being a Collection of Humorous & Witty Tales, Sketches, etc (Classic Reprint) (p. 258)
Stone, James. Night Night Dance: A Classic Lullaby. (p. 1606)
Stone, James A. Fourteenth Annual Report of the Illinois State Bee-Keepers' Association: Organized February 26, 1891, at Springfield, Illinois (Classic Reprint) (p. 773)
—Fourth Annual Report of the Illinois State Bee-Keepers' Association: Organized February 26, 1891, at Springfield, Ill (Classic Reprint) (p. 773)
Stone, James S. Heart of Merrie England (Classic Reprint) (p. 945)
—Over the Hills to Broadway (Classic Reprint) (p. 1686)
Stone, James Samuel. Woods & Dales of Derbyshire (Classic Reprint) (p. 2492)
Stone, Jamie, ed. Danny Dino Ventures Out. (p. 504)
Stone, Janet, jt. auth. see Miller, Reagan.
Stone, Jeff. Five Ancestors Out of the Ashes (p. 743)
—Lion: Five Ancestors Out Of The Ashes #2. (p. 1305)
—Lion. (p. 1305)
—Phoenix: Out of the Ashes. (p. 1735)
—Phoenix: Five Ancestors Out Of The Ashes #1. (p. 1735)
Stone, Jerry, jt. auth. see Sparrow, Giles.
Stone, Joanie, illus. see Bader, Bonnie.
Stone, Joanie, illus. see Bass, Beverley & Williams, Cynthia.
Stone, Joanie, illus. see Doering, Amanda.
Stone, Joanie, illus. see Kimmel, Allison Crotzer.
Stone, Joanie, illus. see Mabry Bestor, Sheri.
Stone, Joanie, illus. see Mabry, Sheri.
Stone, Joanie, illus. see Puffinton, Brick.
Stone, John, ed. see Stone, Christopher L.
Stone, John A. Put's Golden Songster: Containing the Largest & Most Popular Collection of California Songs Ever Published (Classic Reprint) (p. 1818)
—Put's Original California Songster: Giving in a Few Words What Would Occupy Volumes, Detailing the Hopes, Trials & Joys of a Miner's Life (Classic Reprint) (p. 1818)
Stone, Jon. Another Monster at the End of This Book (Sesame Street) Smollin, Michael, illus. (p. 101)
—Monster at the End of This Book. Smollin, Michael, illus. (p. 1495)
—Monsters at the End of This Book (Sesame Street) Smollin, Michael, illus. (p. 1497)
—Sesame Street: Another Monster at the End of This Book: An Interactive Adventure. (p. 1992)
—Sesame Street: the Monster at the End of This Book: An Interactive Adventure. (p. 1992)
—Sesame Street: the Monster at the End of This Sound Book. Smolin, Michael, illus. (p. 1992)
Stone, Jon & Albee, Sarah. Sesame Street Little Golden Book Library 5-Book Boxed Set: My Name Is Elmo; Elmo Loves You; Elmo's Tricky Tongue Twisters; the Monster on the Bus; the Monster at the End of This Book Smollin, Michael & Swanson, Maggie, illus. (p. 1992)
Stone, Jonny, illus. see Salter, Michelle Lewis.
Stone, Joyce M., illus. see Stone, Kelly P.
Stone, Julia. I Spy Bible: A Picture Puzzle Bible for the Very Young. Meredith, Samantha, illus. (p. 1082)
—I Spy Bible Sticker Book. Meredith, Samantha, illus. (p. 1082)
—Lion Book of Fairy Tales. Jatkowska, Ag, illus. (p. 1305)
—Lion Book of Nursery Rhymes. (p. 1305)
—Little Angels Christmas Story. Kolanovic, Dubravka, illus. (p. 1310)
—Little Bear's Sparkly Christmas. Muss, Angela, illus. (p. 1311)
Stone, Julia, jt. auth. see Dodd, Sarah J.
Stone, Juliana. Some Kind of Normal. (p. 2059)
Stone, Justus R. Bleeding Worlds Book Four: Ragnarok. (p. 243)
—Bleeding Worlds Book One: Harbinger. (p. 243)
—Bleeding Worlds Book Three: Resonance. (p. 243)
—Bleeding Worlds Book Two: Suture. (p. 243)
—Harbinger. (p. 924)
—Ragnarok. (p. 1834)
—Resonance. (p. 1869)
—Suture. (p. 2166)
Stone, Karen, ed. see Shadrick, Crystal Star.
Stone, Kate. ABC Train. (p. 4)
—Happy Birthday, Mouse! (p. 921)
—Heads & Tails. (p. 942)
—Mouse Goes to School. (p. 1514)
Stone, Kate, illus. see Andrews McMeel Publishing, LLC Staff.
Stone, Kate, jt. auth. see Accord Publishing Staff.
Stone, Kate & Accord Publishing Staff. Bunnies for Tea. (p. 298)
Stone, Kazuko, illus. see Gollub, Matthew.
Stone, Kazuko G., illus. see Gollub, Matthew W.
Stone, Kazuko G., illus. see Gollub, Matthew, et al.
Stone, Kazuko G., illus. see Gollub, Matthew.
Stone, Kazuko G., jt. auth. see Gollub, Matthew.
Stone, Kelly P. What Do Pets Do When They Go up to Heaven? Stone, Kelly P. & Stone, Joyce M., illus. (p. 2408)
Stone, Ken. Make Me the Best at Track & Field. (p. 1386)
Stone, Kyle M., illus. see Lewis, J. Patrick.
Stone, Laura. Little Lulu Learns a Lesson. (p. 1321)
—Miss Clarissa & Her Musical Shoes. (p. 1478)
—Tulia Turtle Finds Her Talents. (p. 2299)
Stone, Leia. Fallen Academy: Year One. (p. 700)
—Queen Fae. (p. 1823)
Stone, Leia & Eve, Jaymin. Queen Alpha. (p. 1823)
—Queen Heir. (p. 1823)
—Queen Mecca. (p. 1823)
Stone, Lyn, illus. see Taylor, Dereen.
Stone, Lynn M. Exotic Cats. (p. 677)
Stone Magc Mapc Lpc, Delores A. God's Relocated Kids. (p. 854)
Stone, Mary Louise. Life Hacks: Letting God Sort It. (p. 1291)
Stone, Mason. Bridge to Forever. (p. 280)
—Perry Normal & the Moons of Titan. (p. 1724)
—Pirate Curse. (p. 1750)
—Two Miss Busbys. (p. 2308)
Stone, Matilda Woods. Every Man His Chance (Classic Reprint) (p. 670)
Stone, Mike. Dog Who Would Be Prime Minister (the Dog Prime Minister Series Book 1) (p. 577)
—Terrrence Goes Too Far (the Dog Prime Minister Series Book 3) (p. 2208)
—Terrrence Minister for Dogs (the Dog Prime Minister Series Book 2) (p. 2208)
Stone, Mitzie, illus. see White, Porchanee a.
Stone, Nancy Medaris, jt. auth. see Loendorf, Lawrence L.
Stone, Nic. Clean Getaway. (p. 402)
—Dear Martin. (p. 520)
—Indie Signed Jackpot 6-Copy Pre-Pack (p. 1117)
—Jackpot. (p. 1153)
—Odd One Out. (p. 1637)
Stone, Norman, illus. see Magnusson, Sally.
Stone, Oliver & Kuznick, Peter. Untold History of the United States: Young Readers Edition, 1898-1963. Vol. 1 (p. 2336)
—Untold History of the United States, 1898-1945 (p. 2336)
—Untold History of the United States, Volume 2: Young Readers Edition, 1945-1962. (p. 2336)
Stone, Omar. Bumblebees. (p. 297)
—Chickasaw (p. 368)
—Ecology. (p. 623)
Stone, Pam. Watermelon Party. (p. 2386)
Stone, Pat, ed. see Stone, Christopher L.
Stone, Peter. Perfect Candidate. (p. 1722)
Stone, Phoebe. Boy on Cinnamon Street. (p. 269)
—Deep down Popular. (p. 524)
—Paris for Two. (p. 1700)
—Romeo & Juliet Code. (p. 1901)
—Romeo Blue. (p. 1901)
Stone, Phoebe, illus. see Sasso, Sandy Eisenberg.
Stone, Rex. Grotte Dinosaures N01 Attaque. (p. 898)
Stone, R.H. In Afric's Forest & Jungle: Or Six Years among the Yorubans (Classic Reprint) (p. 1104)
Stone, Robert H. Touchdown for Riley. (p. 2268)
Stone, Sara Elizabeth. Animals. (p. 93)
—Colors. (p. 426)
Stone, Sonja. Dark Divide. (p. 506)
—Desert Dark. (p. 531)
Stone, Steve, illus. see Allcock, Phil.
Stone, Steve, illus. see Montgomery, Heather L.
Stone, Steve, illus. see Pearson, Maggie.
Stone, Stuart Basham. Kingdom of Why: Being the Strange Story of Lucile's Adventures with the Sapient Sage, the Foolish Idea, the Striped Jester, & Other Folk, Creatures, Kings, Beasts, Bogies, Wizards & Witches Who Dwell in That Wonderful Land (Classic Reprint) (p. 1222)
Stone, Tamara. Lo poco que sabemos. (p. 1338)
Stone, Tamara Ireland. Every Last Word. (p. 670)
—Little Do We Know. (p. 1315)
—Swap'd. (p. 2167)
—Time after Time. (p. 2243)
—Time & Time Again. (p. 2243)
—Time Between Us. (p. 2243)
Stone, Tanya Lee. Almost Astronauts: 13 Women Who Dared to Dream. (p. 57)
—Courage Has No Color - The True Story of the Triple Nickles: America's First Black Paratroopers. (p. 462)
—Elizabeth Leads the Way: Elizabeth Cady Stanton & the Right to Vote. Gibbon, Rebecca, illus. (p. 636)
—Girl Rising: Changing the World One Girl at a Time. (p. 836)
—House That Jane Built: A Story about Jane Addams. Brown, Kathryn, illus. (p. 1024)
—Is for America: A Patriotic Alphabet Book. Kelley, Gerald, illus. (p. 1136)
—Pass Go & Collect $200: The Real Story of How Monopoly Was Invented. Salerno, Steven, illus. (p. 1702)
—T Is for Turkey. Kelley, Gerald, illus. (p. 2174)
—Who Says Women Can't Be Doctors? The Story of Elizabeth Blackwell. (p. 2449)
Stone, Tess, illus. see Hirsh, Ananth.
Stone, Tiffany. Knot Cannot. Lowery, Mike, illus. (p. 1229)
—Tallulah Plays the Tuba. Nichols, Sandy, illus. (p. 2188)
—Teatime. van der Linde, Jori, illus. (p. 2196)
—Tree Song. Hatam, Holly, illus. (p. 2284)
Stone, William Leete. Letter to Doctor A. Brigham, on Animal Magnetism: Being an Account of a Remarkable Interview Between the Author & Miss. Loraina Brackett While in a State of Somnambulism (Classic Reprint) (p. 1279)
Stone, William McDonough. Weeds & Flowers: A Collection of Sketches of East Tennessee; Its Scenery, Folk Lore & People (Classic Reprint) (p. 2396)
Stoneback, Paula. North Pole East: Santa's New Town. (p. 1621)
Stone-Barker, Holly, illus. see de Las Casas, Dianne.
Stone-Barker, Holly, illus. see Horning, Sandra.
Stonehouse, Andy. Where Are You Moosehead? (p. 2435)
Stoneman Douglas Students, Stoneman Douglas. Parkland Speaks: Survivors from Marjory Stoneman Douglas Share Their Stories. Lerner, Sarah, ed. (p. 1700)
Stoner, Alexis, illus. see Gerbracht, Edie.
Stoner, Andrew. Mr. Lollypop Makes a Friend. (p. 1519)
Stoner, Burton. Jim Crow Tales (Classic Reprint) (p. 1168)
Stoner, Sherri. Gone Fishing! (Disney Junior: Mickey & the Roadster Racers) Golden Books, illus. (p. 861)
—Mickey's Perfecto Day! (p. 1459)
Stoner, Sherri, adapted by. Mickey's Perfecto Day. (p. 1459)
Stoner, Sherri & Mendoza, Ashley. Mickey Mouse Roadster Racers: Mickey's Perfecto Day! Loter, Inc., illus. (p. 1459)
Stoner, Winifred Sackville. Facts in Jingles (Classic Reprint) (p. 694)
—Jingles Written for Dear Friends (Classic Reprint) (p. 1169)
Stonerook, S. B. Off the Beaten Track: Through the Big Bald, Big Horn, Shoshone, & the Rocky Mountains, to Yellowstone National Park; an Accurate & Concise Description of the Entire Trip from Ottumwa, Iowa, to Yellowstone National Park & Return (Classic Reprint) (p. 1640)
—Off the Beaten Track. (p. 1640)
Stones, Annabel & Savery, Annabel. Flags of the World Activity Book. (p. 746)
—Make a Mobile: Magical Unicorns. Loman, Sam, illus. (p. 1385)
Stones, Brenda, jt. auth. see Feldman, Thea.
Stones, Greg, illus. see Rayner, Abigail.
Stonestreet, John & Kunkle, Brett. Practical Guide to Culture: Helping the Next Generation Navigate Today's World. (p. 1784)
—Student's Guide to Culture. (p. 2143)
Stoney, Annaliese, illus. see Canavan, Roger.
Stoney, Annaliese, illus. see Graham, Ian.
Stoney, Annaliese, illus. see Macdonald, Fiona.
Stoney, Annaliese, illus. see Woolf, Alex.
Stong, Phil. Young Settler (Classic Reprint) (p. 2532)
St-Onge, Donna Na-Tasa Katherine. Eye of Isis (p. 688)
Stooke, Andrew, illus. see Blacklaws, Troy.
Stoop, Naoko. All Creatures Great & Small. (p. 51)
—Love Is Patient, Love Is Kind. (p. 1360)
—Red Knit Cap Girl & the Reading Tree. (p. 1857)
—Red Knit Cap Girl to the Rescue. (p. 1857)
—Sing with Me! (p. 2023)
Stoop, Naoko, illus. see Banks, Kate.
Stoop, Naoko, illus. see Collins Thoms, Susan.
Stoop, Naoko, illus. see Heo, Yumi.
Stoop, Naoko, illus. see Thoms, Susan Collins.
Stoop, Trautie. Casey's North Pole Adventure. (p. 339)
Stopes, Marie C. Conquest or a Piece of Jade: A New Play in Three Acts (Classic Reprint) (p. 442)
—Journal from Japan: A Daily Record of Life As Seen by a Scientist (Classic Reprint) (p. 1180)
Stops, Stops. Punctuation Personified, or Pointing Made Easy (Classic Reprint) (p. 1814)
Stoqnova, Kremena P., illus. see Davis, Siobhan.
Storace, Stephen. Haunted Tower: A Comic Opera in Three Acts (Classic Reprint) (p. 938)
Storad, Conrad. Fang & Stinger, an Arachnid Tale. (p. 706)
Storad, Conrad J. Bat Book. (p. 171)
—Day & Night. (p. 512)
—Earth Is Tilting! (p. 616)
—Earth Is Tilting! Lew, Kristi, ed. (p. 616)
—Earth's Changing Surface. (p. 618)
—Galápagos Tortoises. (p. 805)
—Lizards for Lunch: A Roadrunner's Tale. (p. 1336)
—Mars. (p. 1409)
—Monster in the Rocks. (p. 1496)
—Piranhas. (p. 1749)
—Rattlesnake Rules. Jensen, Nathaniel P., illus. (p. 1843)
—Studying Weather & Climates. (p. 2144)
—Uncovering Earth's Crust. (p. 2320)
—What's the Weather Like Today? (p. 2426)
Storch, Ellen N., illus. see Muench-Williams, Heather.
Storch, Ellen N., illus. see Mullican, Judy & Williams, Heather L.

S

Storch, Ellen N., illus. see Williams, Heather L. & Muench-Williams, Heather.
Storck, Karl. Die Kulturelle Bedeutung der Musik, Vol. 1: Die Musik ALS Kulturmacht des Seelischen und Geistigen Lebens (ALS Vortrag Gehalten Beim 3. Musikpädagogischen Kongress Zu Berlin) (Classic Reprint) (p. 544)
Storck, Kelly Sherman. Gender Identity Workbook for Kids: A Guide to Exploring Who You Are. (p. 814)
Storck, Patrick. Dreamworks Shrek Comics Collection. (p. 603)
—Muppet Sherlock Holmes. Mebberson, Amy, illus. (p. 1527)
Storck, Patrick & Rik Hoskin. Dreamworks Madagascar Comics Collection. (p. 603)
Storden, Thom. Amazing Baseball Records (p. 64)
—Amazing Basketball Records (p. 64)
—Amazing Football Records (p. 65)
—Amazing Hockey Records (p. 65)
—Basketball's Greatest Buzzer-Beaters & Other Crunch-Time Heroics. (p. 171)
—Epic Sports Records (p. 658)
—Hockey's Greatest Game-Winning Goals & Other Crunch-Time Heroics. (p. 986)
Storden, Thom, jt. auth. see Chandler, Matt.
Storer, Florence, illus. see Field, Eugene.
Storer, Jen. Clarrie's Pig Day Out. deGennaro, Sue, illus. (p. 399)
—Fourteenth Summer of Angus Jack. Gifford, Lucinda, illus. (p. 773)
Storer, June. Kip, Brenda & Emong's Adventure. (p. 1223)
Storer, Wendy. Bring Me Sunshine. (p. 282)
Storey, Andrea. Heavens Gate Secrets Revealed. (p. 947)
Storey, G. A. Sketches from Memory (Classic Reprint) (p. 2031)
Storey, Geri, illus. see McFarlane, Brian.
Storey, Jay Allan. Black Heart: Arrival (Black Heart Series, Book 2) (p. 238)
—Black Heart of the Station. (p. 238)
Storey, Jim, illus. see Eggleton, Jill.
Storey, Jim, illus. see Holden, Pam.
Storey, Lela Belle, illus. see Lozzi, Annette.
Storey, Linda, illus. see Carlson, Glenn E.
Storey, Margaret & Storey, Mags. If Only You Knew (p. 1092)
Storey, Rita. Animals. (p. 93)
—Art for Fall. (p. 121)
—Art for Spring. (p. 121)
—Art for Summer. (p. 121)
—Art for Winter. (p. 121)
—Christmas Book. (p. 384)
—Dinosaurs. (p. 550)
—Easter Book. (p. 619)
—Fairies. (p. 695)
—How to Build Aircraft. (p. 1038)
—How to Build Cars. (p. 1038)
—Knights & Castles. (p. 1228)
—Make Your Own Creative Cards. (p. 1387)
—Make Your Own Creative Cards (Do It Yourself Projects!) (p. 1387)
—Make Your Own Toys. (p. 1387)
—Make Your Own Toys (Do It Yourself Projects!) (p. 1387)
—Masks. Rhodes, Harry, illus. (p. 1417)
—Pirates. (p. 1750)
—Recorder & Other Wind Instruments. (p. 1854)
—Tasty Breakfast. (p. 2192)
—Tasty Dinner. (p. 2192)
—Tasty Lunch. (p. 2192)
—Tasty Snacks & Drinks. (p. 2192)
—Tractors & Trucks. (p. 2273)
—Violin & Other Stringed Instruments. (p. 2360)
—Voice & Singing. (p. 2365)
Stories, Brimoral. Car Theme Park. (p. 327)
—Hotel Hero. Stories, Brimoral, illus. (p. 1007)
—Recogn Eyes. (p. 1853)
storiesbypj.com. Willow, Too Soon, Too Late. Manny, illus. (p. 2469)
Storino, Sara, illus. see Corteggiani, François.
Stork, Charles Wharton. Modern Swedish Masterpieces: Short Stories Selected & Translated (Classic Reprint) (p. 1487)
Stork, E. B. Illustrations of Scripture Precept: For the Young (Classic Reprint) (p. 1097)
Stork, Elisabeth P., tr. see Spyri, Johanna.
Stork, Francisco X. Disappeared. (p. 553)
—Irises. (p. 1134)
—Last Summer of the Death Warriors. (p. 1249)
—Marcelo in the Real World. (p. 1402)
—Memory of Light. (p. 1446)
Stork, Theophilus. Home-Scenes of the New Testament: Or, Christ in the Family (Classic Reprint) (p. 997)
Storm, A. D. Jestine Needs to Clean. (p. 1165)
Storm, Ashley. Haunted Battle Sites. (p. 937)
Storm, Falcon. Natalie the Not-So-Nasty: Tales from upon A. Time Series. (p. 1576)
—Persnickety Princess (Tales from upon A. Time - Book 1) (p. 1725)
Storm, Jeff. No Return Land: You Are the Hero of This Book! Chan, Harvey, illus. (p. 1614)
—Petrified World, Determine Your Destiny No. 1: You Are the Hero of This Book! Chan, Harvey, illus. (p. 1731)
—Young Masters of Time, Determine Your Destiny No. 3: You Are the Hero of This Book! Chan, Harvey, illus. (p. 2531)
Storm, Jillian. Burden of Secrets. (p. 299)
Storm, Jo. Snowhook. (p. 2049)
Storm, Marysa. Aliens. (p. 47)
—Beagles. (p. 178)
—Bermuda Triangle. (p. 203)
—Bulldogs. (p. 296)
—Chihuahuas. (p. 369)
—Dirt Bikes. (p. 552)
—Dolphins. (p. 579)
—Eagles. (p. 613)
—Formula 1 Cars. (p. 768)
—Frogs. (p. 790)
—German Shepherds. (p. 822)
—Ghosts. (p. 829)
—Gray Wolves. (p. 883)
—Highlights of the Chicago Bears. (p. 970)
—Highlights of the Dallas Cowboys. (p. 970)
—Highlights of the Denver Broncos. (p. 970)
—Highlights of the Green Bay Packers. (p. 970)
—Highlights of the Indianapolis Colts. (p. 970)
—Highlights of the Kansas City Chiefs. (p. 970)
—Highlights of the Miami Dolphins. (p. 970)
—Highlights of the Minnesota Vikings. (p. 970)
—Highlights of the New England Patriots. (p. 970)
—Highlights of the New York Giants. (p. 970)
—Highlights of the Pittsburgh Steelers. (p. 970)
—Highlights of the San Francisco 49ers. (p. 970)
—Highlights of the Seattle Seahawks. (p. 970)
—Highlights of the Washington Redskins. (p. 970)
—Indy Cars. (p. 1118)
—Labrador Retrievers. (p. 1235)
—Lions. (p. 1307)
—Mapache. (p. 1401)
—Mice. (p. 1457)
—Motorcycles. (p. 1512)
—Orangutans. (p. 1668)
—Owls. (p. 1689)
—Penguins. (p. 1716)
—Pugs. (p. 1812)
—Raccoons. (p. 1830)
—Rana (Frogs) (p. 1839)
—Ratón (Mice) (p. 1843)
—Ring-Tailed Lemurs. (p. 1883)
—Sloths. (p. 2039)
—Stock Cars. (p. 2120)
—Supercars. (p. 2159)
Storm, Rayne. Elemental Tarot for Kids (p. 632)
—In the Night Sky: The Astrological Zodiac for Children (p. 1110)
Storm, Tallia & Courtenay, Lucy. Pop Girl. (p. 1775)
Storm, Theodor. Immensee (Classic Reprint) (p. 1100)
Storm, Zed. Will Solvit & the Cannibal Cavemen. (p. 2467)
—Will Solvit & the Deadly Gladiator. (p. 2467)
—Will Solvit & the Dreaded Droids. (p. 2467)
—Will Solvit & the Mission of Menace. (p. 2467)
—Will Solvit & the Mummy's Curse. (p. 2467)
—Will Solvit & the T-Rex Terror. (p. 2467)
Stormonth, Mary E. B. Manual of Lipreading (Classic Reprint) (p. 1399)
Storms, L. Ryan. Thousand Years to Wait. (p. 2231)
Storms, Patricia. Never Let You Go. (p. 1590)
Storms, Patricia, illus. see Bozik, Chrissy.
Storms, Patricia, illus. see Jenkins, Diana R.
Storms, Patricia, illus. see Montgomery, Monte.
Storms, Patricia, illus. see Todd, Barbara.
Storr, Catherine. Chinese Egg. (p. 378)
—Complete Polly & the Wolf. Watts, Marjorie Anne & Bennett, Jill, illus. (p. 435)
—Marianne Dreams. (p. 1404)
Storr, Francis. Half a Hundred Hero Tales of Ulysses & the Men of Old (Classic Reprint) (p. 910)
Storr, Nicola, illus. see Sims, Janice.
Storrie, Paul D. Beowulf: Monster Slayer. (p. 201)
—Perseus: The Hunt for Medusa's Head. (p. 1724)
Storrs, Landon R. Y. Second Red Scare & the Unmaking of the New Deal Left. (p. 1974)
Storrs, Lewis Austin. Koheleth: A Novel (Classic Reprint) (p. 1230)
Storrs, Richard Salter. Sermon Delivered Before His Excellency Edward Everett, Governor, His Honor George Hull, Lieutenant Governor, the Honorable Council, & the Legislature of Massachusetts, on the Anniversary Election, January 3, 1838 (Classic Reprint) (p. 1991)
Stortz, Diane. Biblia Di y Ora: Primeras Palabras, Historias y Oraciones (p. 214)
—Devociones Di y Ora: Primeras Palabras, Historias y Oraciones (p. 536)
—God's Words to Dream On: Bedtime Bible Stories & Prayers Le Feyer, Diane, illus. (p. 854)
—I Am: 40 Reasons to Trust God (p. 1056)
—I Am: The Names of God for Little Ones Le Feyer, Diane, illus. (p. 1056)
—I Am Devotional: 100 Devotions about the Names of God (p. 1058)
—Say & Pray Devotions (p. 1940)
—Stop-and-Go Devotional: 52 Devotions for Busy Families Marks, Hannah, illus. (p. 2122)
—Yo Soy. (p. 2522)
Stortz, Diane & Holder, Jennifer. I Can Pray! Nobens, C. A., illus. (p. 1063)
Stortz, Diane & Thomas Nelson & Sons Staff. Say & Pray Bible (p. 1940)
Stortz, Diane M. Say & Pray Bible Seek & Find: First Words, Stories, & Prayers WARD, Sarah, illus. (p. 1940)
—Sweetest Story Bible: Sweet Thoughts & Sweet Words for Little Girls Bailey, Sheila, illus. (p. 2169)
—Sweetest Story Bible for Toddlers Bailey, Sheila, illus. (p. 2169)
Story a. We Are the Future Inventors 26. (p. 2389)
Story, Dan. Where Wild Things Live: Wildlife Watching Techniques & Adventures. (p. 2440)
Story, Florence M. Master Travers (Classic Reprint) (p. 1419)
Story, James P. Choisy: A Novel (Classic Reprint) (p. 381)
Story, Jenny. Dysnomia: Outcasts on a Distant Moon. (p. 612)
Story, Joseph. Power of Solitude: A Poem in Two Parts (Classic Reprint) (p. 1782)
Story Pirates Staff, jt. auth. see Rodkey, Geoff.
Story Pirates, Story. Story Pirates Present: Digging up Danger. (p. 2135)
Story Pirates, Story & Rodkey, Geoff. Story Pirates Present: Stuck in the Stone Age. Aly, Hatem, illus. (p. 2135)
Story, William Wetmore. Fiammetta: A Summer Idyl (Classic Reprint) (p. 722)
Storybook Art Team, Disney. Disney Frozen. (p. 559)
—Disney: the Lion King: Friends Forever. (p. 563)
—Disney: the Lion King: Songs with Simba. (p. 563)
Storybook Art Team, Disney, illus. see Broderick, Kathy.
Storybook Art Team, Disney, illus. see Brooke, Susan Rich.
Storybook Art Team, Disney, illus. see Harmening, Derek.
Storybook Art Team, Disney, illus. see Keast, Jennifer H.
Storybook Art Team, Disney, illus. see Skwish, Emily.
Storybots. Amazing Planet Earth (StoryBots) (p. 66)
—Cars Are Cool! (StoryBots) JibJab Bros Studios, illus. (p. 334)
—Moon's Time to Shine. (p. 1503)
—Moon's Time to Shine (StoryBots) (p. 1503)
—Triceratops (StoryBots) (p. 2287)
—Tyrannosaurus Rex (StoryBots) (p. 2311)
Storybots Staff. Triceratops (StoryBots) (p. 2287)
Storybots Staff, jt. auth. see JibJab Bros Studios.
Storybots Staff & JibJab Bros. Studios Staff. ABC Jamboree over 250 Words. (p. 4)
—Trucks Are Terrific! (p. 2293)
Stosch, Dawn. Science Math. (p. 1957)
Stossel, Sage. On the Loose in Boston. (p. 1655)
—On the Loose in New York City. (p. 1655)
—On the Loose in Washington, D. C. (p. 1655)
Stossel, Sage, illus. see Wile, Mary Lee.
Stosuy, Brandon. Music Is ... Martin, Amy, illus. (p. 1529)
—We Are Music. Radford, Nick, illus. (p. 2389)
Stothard, Thomas, jt. auth. see Day, Thomas.
Stothert, Richard. My Life on Request: Pieces of Me. (p. 1552)
Stoto, Tiziana. Millie Micro Nano Pico Book 2 in Which a Scarecrow Gives Millie a Brilliant Idea about Magnets. (p. 1467)
—Millie Micro Nano Pico Book 3 in Which Millie Meets Some Photons at the Playground. (p. 1467)
—Millie Micro Nano Pico Book 4 in Which Millie Has Fun in a Sea of Electrons. (p. 1467)
—Millie Micro Nano Pico Book 5 in Which Millie Wishes She Were More Attractive & Wonders about Quarks. (p. 1467)
—Millie Micro Nano Pico Book 6 in Which Millie Meets Two Neutrinos & Watches Them Race to the Moon & Back. (p. 1467)
—Millie Micro Nano Pico Book 7 in Which the Electrons Invite Millie to a Party & She Is Shocked by Antimatter. (p. 1467)
—Millie Micro Nano Pico Book 8 in Which Millie Wants to Give the Particles a Sleeping Lesson. (p. 1467)
—Millie Micro Nano Pico Book 9 in Which Millie Goes Inside a Red Laser Beam. (p. 1467)
—Millie Micro Nano Pico Libro 1 in Cui Millie Incontra Due Elettroni e Cominciano le Sue Avventure. (p. 1467)
—Millie Micro Nano Pico Libro 2 in Cui Millie Ha un'idea Geniale Grazie Ad uno Spaventapasseri. (p. 1467)
—Millie Micro Nano Pico Libro 3 in Cui Millie Incontra Tre Fotoni Al Parco Giochi. (p. 1467)
—Millie Micro Nano Pico Libro 4 in Cui Millie Si Diverte in un Mare Di Elettroni. (p. 1467)
—Millie Micro Nano Pico Libro 5 in Cui Millie Vorrebbe Incontare I Quark Ed Essere Piu Attraente. (p. 1467)
—Millie Micro Nano Pico Libro 6 in Cui Millie Incontra Due Neutrini Ed Assiste Ad una Gara Di Velocita. (p. 1467)
—Millie Micro Nano Pico Libro 8 in Cui Millie Vuole Dare Lezioni Di Sonno Alle Particelle. (p. 1467)
—Millie Micro Nano Pico Libro 9 in Cui Millie S'Intrufola in un Raggio Laser Rosso. (p. 1467)
—Millie Micro Nano Pico Livre 1 Dans Lequel Millie Rencontre Deux Electrons et Ses Aventures Commencent. (p. 1467)
—Millie Micro Nano Pico Livre 2 Dans Lequel un Epouvantail Donne a Millie une Idee Geniale Sur les Aimants. (p. 1467)
—Millie Micro Nano Pico Livre 3 Dans Lequel Millie Rencontre Trois Photons a l'Aire de Jeux. (p. 1467)
—Millie Micro Nano Pico Livre 5 Dans Lequel Millie Voudrait Rencontrer les Quarks et ?tre Plus Attirante. (p. 1467)
—Millie Micro Nano Pico Livre 6 Dans Lequel Millie Rencontre Deux Neutrinos et Assiste ? une Comp?tition de Vitesse. (p. 1467)
Stott, Ann. I'll Be There. Phelan, Matt, illus. (p. 1095)
—Nana Says I Will Be Famous One Day. Joyner, Andrew, illus. (p. 1573)
—Want to Play Trucks? Graham, Bob, illus. (p. 2375)
—What to Do When You're Sent to Your Room. Gilpin, Stephen, illus. (p. 2420)
Stott, Apryl. Brigid & the Butter: A Legend about Saint Brigid of Ireland. (p. 281)
Stott, Apryl, illus. see Lazurek, Michelle S.
Stott, Apryll, illus. see Monchamp, Genny.
Stott, Carole. Eye Wonder: Space: Open Your Eyes to a World of Discovery. (p. 688)
—I Wonder Why Stars Twinkle. (p. 1086)
—Mission: Space: Explore the Galaxy. (p. 1481)
—Wow! Look What's in Space! Johnson, Ste, illus. (p. 2510)
Stott, Dorothy. Ten in the Bed. (p. 2204)
Stott, Dorothy, illus. see Balsley, Tilda.
Stott, Dorothy, illus. see Capucilli, Alyssa Satin.
Stott, Dorothy, illus. see Simon, Mary Manz.
Stott, Jon C. Book of Tricksters: Tales from Many Lands Dombrowski, Theo, illus. (p. 260)
Stott, M. D. Real Algeria (Classic Reprint) (p. 1848)
Stotter, Mike. World of North American Indians. (p. 2503)
Stotter, Ruth. Loop of String: String Stories & String Stunts: Traditional & Original String Figures & Stories. Coffey, Kevin, illus. (p. 1348)
Stotts, Jeffery. King Everything. (p. 1220)
Stotts, Stuart. Father Groppi: Marching for Civil Rights. (p. 714)
—Lucius Fairchild: Civil War Hero. (p. 1364)
Stotts, Traci Jo. Don't Tell Jessie. (p. 583)
Stotz, Allyn M. Grumpy Kyle. (p. 901)
—Snazzy Razzy. Saint Louis, Ahha Studios, illus. (p. 2045)
Stouck, Mary-Ann. Jeannie Houdini: A Hamster's Tale. Evans, Rebecca, illus. (p. 1162)
Stoudemire, Amar'e. Double Team. Jessell, Tim, illus. (p. 589)
—Home Court. (p. 996)
—Home Court. Jessell, Tim, illus. (p. 996)
—Most Valuable. (p. 1508)
—Schooled. (p. 1947)
—Slam Dunk: Standing Tall & Talented Jessell, Tim, illus. (p. 2034)
—Slam Dunk. (p. 2034)
—Standing Tall & Talented - Most Valuable. Jessell, Tim, illus. (p. 2101)
—STAT #4: Schooled. Jessell, Tim, illus. (p. 2108)
Stouffer, Janice. Little Boys Like Pink Too. (p. 1313)
Stouffer, Mikahla. Laborers of Love. (p. 1235)
Stouffer, Rebecca, illus. see Wilke, Cheryl Weibye.
Stout, Carol. Desert Critters Wacky Wisdom. (p. 531)
Stout, Frankie. Bats: Nature's Night Flyers. (p. 173)
—Bugs: In Flight. (p. 292)
—Bugs in Flight. (p. 292)
—Hummingbirds: Hovering in Nature. (p. 1050)
—Nature's Strongest Animals. (p. 1582)
—Ostriches: Nature's Biggest Birds. (p. 1674)
—Pelicans: Soaring the Seas. (p. 1714)
—Penguins: Nature's Coolest Birds. (p. 1716)
Stout, Glenn. Able to Play: Overcoming Physical Challenges. (p. 6)
—Baseball Heroes. (p. 168)
—Soldier Athletes. (p. 2056)
—Yes, She Can! Women's Sports Pioneers. (p. 2521)
Stout, Glenn, jt. auth. see Christopher, Matt.
Stout, Glenn & Williams, Ike. Against All Odds: Never Give Up. (p. 34)
—From Hardships to Championships. (p. 791)
Stout, Katie M. Hello, I Love You. (p. 951)
Stout, Mary. Blackfoot History & Culture. (p. 240)
—Shoshone History & Culture. (p. 2011)
Stout, Mary, jt. auth. see Dwyer, Helen.
Stout, Mary A. Native American Boarding Schools (p. 1578)
Stout, Mary A., jt. auth. see Dwyer, Helen.
Stout, Mary A., jt. auth. see Stout, Mary.
Stout, Rex. Under the Andes. (p. 2321)
Stout, Se. Doxie Adventure Mysteries the Cheep-Chirp Mystery. (p. 591)
Stout, Shawn K. Ballerina Weather Girl. Martini, Angela, illus. (p. 161)
—Don't Chicken Out. Ying, Victoria, illus. (p. 582)
—Fiona Finkelstein, Big-Time Ballerina!! Martini, Angela, illus. (p. 732)
—Fiona Finkelstein Meets Her Match!! Martini, Angela, illus. (p. 732)
—Miss Matched. Martini, Angela, illus. (p. 1479)
—Penelope Crumb. (p. 1715)
Stout, William, illus. see Smith, Sherwood.
Stoute, June. Anansi & Herald, the Fowl-Cock. Silva-Freimane, Jehanne, illus. (p. 79)
Stoutenburg, Adrien. American Tall Tales. (p. 74)
Stovall, Dennis H. Gold Bug Story Book: Mining Camp Tales (Classic Reprint) (p. 855)
Stovall, Isaiah. Where Is My Dad? (p. 2438)
Stovall, Shami. Dread Pirate Arcanist. (p. 600)
Stovell, Samantha. Clip the Crab. (p. 406)
Stover, Beth, illus. see Bentley, Dawn.
Stover, Jo Ann. If Everybody Did. (p. 1090)
Stover, Kellan, illus. see Doering, Amanda.
Stow, Baron. Little Mary: An Illustration of the Power of Jesus to Save Even the Youngest (Classic Reprint) (p. 1321)
—Little Mary. (p. 1321)
Stow, Edith. Nancy the Joyous (Classic Reprint) (p. 1574)
Stow, J. W. Probate Chaff: Or Beautiful Probate; or Three Years Probating in San Francisco; a Modern Drama Showing the Merry Side of a Dark Picture (Classic Reprint) (p. 1803)
Stowasser, Peter & Burnett, James. Cupcake Capers: A Book about Take-Away Subtraction. (p. 485)
Stowe, Amber. Beautiful And. (p. 183)
—Special Person Battles Cancer. (p. 2077)
Stowe, Beecher. Cabana Del Tio Tom. (p. 307)
Stowe, Debbie. Baby Animals. (p. 148)
Stowe, Harriet Beecher. Betty's Bright Idea: Also, Deacon Pitkin's Farm, & the First Christmas of New England (Classic Reprint) (p. 210)
—Betty's Bright Idea. (p. 210)
—Cabaña Del Tío Tom. (p. 307)
—Case de l'Oncle Tom (Classic Reprint) (p. 336)
—Dialogues & Scenes from the Writings of Harriet Beecher Stowe (Classic Reprint) (p. 537)
—Dog's Mission, or the Story of the Old Avery House: And Other Stories (Classic Reprint) (p. 578)
—Dred: A Tale of the Great Dismal Swamp (Classic Reprint) (p. 603)
—Dred, a Tale of the Great Dismal Swamp: A Drama, in Four Acts, Founded on the Novel of the Same Title (Classic Reprint) (p. 603)
—Dred, a Tale of the Great Dismal Swamp, Vol. 2 Of 2: Together with Anti-Slavery Tales & Papers, & Life in Florida after the War (Classic Reprint) (p. 603)
—Dred, Vol. 1 Of 2: A Tale of the Great Dismal Swamp (Classic Reprint) (p. 603)
—Dred, Vol. 2 Of 2: A Tale of the Great Dismal Swap (Classic Reprint) (p. 603)
—He's Coming to-Morrow (Classic Reprint) (p. 963)
—Library of Famous Fiction: Embracing the Nine Standard Masterpieces of Imaginative Literature (Unabridged); with an Introduction (Classic Reprint) (p. 1285)
—May Flower, & Miscellaneous Writings (Classic Reprint) (p. 1429)
—Mayflower: Or Tales & Pencilings (Classic Reprint) (p. 1430)
—Mayflower: Or, Sketches of Scenes & Characters among the Descendants the Pilgrims (Classic Reprint) (p. 1430)
—Minister's Wooing (Classic Reprint) (p. 1472)
—My Wife & I: Or Harry Henderson's History (Classic Reprint) (p. 1565)
—Oldtown Fireside Stories (Classic Reprint) (p. 1649)
—Oldtown Folks (Classic Reprint) (p. 1649)
—Oldtown Folks, Vol. 1 Of 2: And Sam Lawson's Oldtown Fireside Stories (Classic Reprint) (p. 1649)
—Our Charley: And What to Do with Him (Classic Reprint) (p. 1677)
—Palmetto-Leaves (Classic Reprint) (p. 1694)
—Pearl of Orr's Island: A Story of the Coast of Maine (Classic Reprint) (p. 1710)
—Pictures & Stories from Uncle Tom's Cabin (Classic Reprint) (p. 1741)

—Pink & White Tyranny: A Society Novel (Classic Reprint) (p. 1746)
—Pink & White Tyranny. (p. 1746)
—Poganuc People: Their Loves & Lives (Classic Reprint) (p. 1767)
—Poganuc People, Their Loves & Lives, and, Pink & White Tyranny, a Society Novel (Classic Reprint) (p. 1767)
—Queer Little People (Classic Reprint) (p. 1825)
—Stories & Sketches for the Young (Classic Reprint) (p. 2123)
—Stories, Sketches & Studies (Classic Reprint) (p. 2126)
—Sunny Memories of Foreign Lands (Classic Reprint) (p. 2152)
—Sunny Memories of Foreign Lands, Vol. 2 of 2 (Classic Reprint) (p. 2152)
—Uncle Sam's Emancipation: Earthly Care, a Heavenly Discipline; & Other Sketches (Classic Reprint) (p. 2319)
—Uncle Tom's Cabin: With Original 1852 Illustrations by Hammett Billings. Billings, Hammatt, illus. (p. 2320)
—Uncle Tom's Cabin. (p. 2320)
—Uncle Tom's Cabin (Classic Reprint) (p. 2320)
—Uncle Tom's Cabin, or Life among the Lowly (Classic Reprint) (p. 2320)
—Uncle Tom's Cabin, or Life among the Lowly, Vol. 1 Of 2: With an Introduction Setting Forth the History of the Novel, & a Key to Uncle Tom's Cabin (Classic Reprint) (p. 2320)
—Uncle Tom's Cabin, or Life among the Lowly, Vol. 1 (Classic Reprint) (p. 2320)
—Uncle Tom's Cabin, Vol. 1: Or Life among the Lowly (Classic Reprint) (p. 2320)
—Uncle Tom's Cabin - Young Folks' Edition. (p. 2320)
—We & Our Neighbors: Or the Records of an Unfashionable Street (Sequel to My Wife & I) (Classic Reprint) (p. 2388)
—We & Our Neighbors. (p. 2388)
Stowe, Harriet Beecher & Aiken, George L. Uncle Tom's Cabin: Or, Life among the Lowly: a Domestic Drama in Six Acts - Scholar's Choice Edition. (p. 2320)
—Uncle Tom's Cabin; or, Life among the Lowly. a Domestic Drama in Six Acts, Dramatized by George L. Aiken [of the Novel by Harriet Beecher Stowe] As Performed at the Principal English & American Theatres - Scholar's Choice Edition. (p. 2320)
Stowe, Harriet Beecher & And Others. Six of One by Half a Dozen of the Other. (p. 2028)
Stowe, Harriet Beecher & Weaver, Emily. Dialogues & Scenes from the Writings of Harriet Beecher Stowe. (p. 537)
Stowe, Lisa, ed. see Burke, Joy A.
Stowell, Bellanne. Manxland: A Tale; with an Introductory Sketch of Manx Home Missions (Classic Reprint) (p. 1400)
Stowell, Brian, jt. auth. see Carroll, Lewis, pseud.
Stowell, Cinci, jt. auth. see Miller, Reagan.
Stowell, Elena. Frango & Chicken: (in Portugese) Stowell, Elena, illus. (p. 776)
—Frango & Chicken. Stowell, Elena, illus. (p. 776)
Stowell, Elena, illus. see Davis, Bev.
Stowell, Louie. Astronaut's Handbook IR. (p. 128)
—Brer Rabbit down the Well. Muszynski, Eva, illus. (p. 279)
—Coding for Beginners Using Python IR. (p. 412)
—Look Inside Your Body. (p. 1346)
—Spooky Sticker Dressing. (p. 2087)
—Sticker Dressing Second World War. (p. 2118)
—Story of Astronomy & Space: Internet-Referenced. Allen, Peter, illus. (p. 2129)
—Usborne Big Book of Big Monsters. Fiorin, Fabiano, illus. (p. 2341)
—Wind-Up Pirate Ship. Fox, Christyan, illus. (p. 2471)
—Write & Draw Your Own Comics IR. (p. 2511)
—¡Mira Debajo! Tu Cuerpo(Look Inside Your Body) (p. 1474)
Stowell, Louie, jt. auth. see Davidson, Susanna.
Stowell, Louie, jt. auth. see Davies, Kate.
Stowell, Louie, jt. auth. see Milbourne, Anna.
Stowell, Louie, jt. auth. see Pratt, Leonie.
Stowell, Louie, jt. auth. see Reid, Struan.
Stowell, Louie, jt. auth. see Sims, Lesley.
Stowell, Thomas Blanchard. Syllabus of Lectures in Anatomy & Physiology: For Students of the State Normal & Training School, at Cortland, N. y (Classic Reprint) (p. 2172)
Stower, Adam. Naughty Kitty! Stower, Adam, illus. (p. 1582)
—Troll & the Oliver. Stower, Adam, illus. (p. 2290)
Stower, Adam, illus. see Clements, Andrew.
Stower, Adam, illus. see Crompton, Richmal.
Stower, Adam, illus. see Greenwald, Tom.
Stower, Adam, illus. see Greenwald, Tommy.
Stower, Adam, illus. see Johnson, Jane.
Stower, Adam, illus. see Jones, Marcia & Dadey, Debbie.
Stower, Adam, illus. see Jones, Pip.
Stower, Adam, illus. see Pinkwater, Daniel M.
Stower, Adam, illus. see Sherry, Maureen.
Stowers, Hal, jt. auth. see Stowers, B. J.
Stoyanova, Mariya, illus. see Holiday, Josalyn Ironette.
Stoyanova, Mariya, illus. see Sarkisyan, Mary.
Stoye, Eline. Beyond the Hedge. (p. 212)
Stoyles, Pennie. A-Z of Health. (p. 2)
Stoyles, Pennie & Pentland, Peter. Earth & Space. (p. 616)
—Everyday Technology. (p. 672)
—Human Body. (p. 1049)
—Life on Earth. (p. 1295)
—Medicine & Health. (p. 1436)
—Power & Fuel. (p. 1782)
Stoyva, Mei, illus. see Birdsong, Minnie.
Stoyva, Mei, illus. see Byrd, Ruby.
Stoyva, Mei, illus. see Love-Byrd, Cheri.
Stoyva, Mei, illus. see VonFeder, Rosa.
Stozub, Julia. Am I Perfect Enough. (p. 61)
Stp Books. 11+ Verbal Reasoning Tests for GL Assessment Practice Papers with Detailed Answers & Challenging Words List: Volume I (Ages 10-11) (p. 2550)
—11+ Verbal Reasoning Tests for GL Assessment Practice Papers with Detailed Answers & Challenging Words List: Volume II (Ages 10-11) (p. 2550)
—11+ Verbal Reasoning Tests for GL Assessment Practice Papers with Detailed Answers & Challenging Words Lists Bumper Edition: Volumes I & II (Ages 10-11) (p. 2550)
—Ks2 English Grammar, Punctuation & Spelling 10-Minute Tests for the 2019 Tests. (p. 1232)
—Year 6 SATs Spelling Workbook KS2 English: New Edition Updated for 2020 with Free Additional Content Online. (p. 2518)
St'phane, Bataillon. Mon Comptinier. (p. 1491)
St'phane, Clerget. Comment Obtenir Ce Que Tu Veux (Ou Presque) de Tes Parents. (p. 430)
—Comment Plaire Aux Filles et Surtout l'un d'Entre Elles. (p. 430)
—Comment Plaire Aux Garons et Surtout l'un d'Entre Eux. (p. 430)
St'phanie, Ledu-Frattini. Conte Sur Eux Pour Grandir. (p. 444)
St.Pierre, Joe, illus. see Cousteau, Fabien & Fraioli, James O.
St.Pierre, Joe, illus. see Fraioli, James O. & Cousteau, Fabien.
Straathof, Alette, illus. see Wing, Scarlett.
Stracener, Mark W. Beacon of Ligjt. (p. 178)
Strachan, Andrew. Greatest Save Ever. (p. 892)
Strachan, Linda. Dangerous Lives of the Jacobites: Fact-Tastic Stories from Scotland's History Gate, Darren, illus. (p. 502)
Stracher, Cameron. Water Wars. (p. 2385)
Strachey, John St Loe. Cat & Bird Stories from the Spectator: To Which Are Added Sundry Anecdotes of Horses, Donkeys, Cows, Apes, Bears, & Other Animals, As Well As of Insects & Reptiles (Classic Reprint) (p. 341)
—Cat & Bird Stories from the Spectator. (p. 341)
—Dog Stories from the Spectator: Being Anecdotes of the Intelligence, Reasoning Power (Classic Reprint) (p. 576)
Strachey, Lionel. World's Wit & Humor: An Encyclopedia of the Classic Wit & Humor of All Ages & Nations (Classic Reprint) (p. 2508)
—World's Wit & Humor, Vol. 1: An Encyclopedia of the Classic Wit & Humor of All Ages & Nations (Classic Reprint) (p. 2508)
—World's Wit & Humor, Vol. 10: French; Ruteboeuf to Balzac (Classic Reprint) (p. 2508)
—World's Wit & Humor, Vol. 11: French, International Caricature; Musset to Rostand; Two Centuries of Cartoons (Classic Reprint) (p. 2508)
—World's Wit & Humor, Vol. 14 Of 15: Russian, Scandinavian, Miscellaneous; Khemnitzer to Gorki, Holberg to Strindberg, Erasmus to Sienkiewicz (Classic Reprint) (p. 2508)
—World's Wit & Humor, Vol. 7: British; Fielding to Burney (Classic Reprint) (p. 2508)
—World's Wit & Humor, Vol. 8: British; Austen to Thackeray (Classic Reprint) (p. 2508)
—World's Wit & Humor, Vol. 9: British; Dickens to Kipling (Classic Reprint) (p. 2508)
Strachey, Marjorie. David, the Son of Jesse (Classic Reprint) (p. 511)
—Savitri & Other Women (Classic Reprint) (p. 1939)
Strachey, Strachey. Nursery Lyrics: And Other Verses for Children (Classic Reprint) (p. 1631)
Strack, Beth. Sammy the Snail's Bright Ideas. (p. 1928)
Strack, Hermann L. Jew & Human Sacrifice; [Human Blood & Jewish Ritual]. an Historical & Sociological Inquiry. (p. 1167)
Strader, Irm. What Came First. (p. 2406)
Stradley, Don. Schooled. (p. 1947)
Stradling, Genene. Chance for Solinea. (p. 355)
Stradling, Matthew. Chronicle of the Fermors, Vol. 1 Of 2: Horace Walpole in Love (Classic Reprint) (p. 388)
Strady, Sophie. Memory of an Elephant: An Unforgettable Journey. Martin, Jean-Francois, illus. (p. 1446)
Strahan, Clare. Learning Curves of Vanessa Partridge. (p. 1258)
Strahan, Edward. New Hyperion: From Paris to Marly by Way of the Rhine (Classic Reprint) (p. 1594)
Strahan, Kay Cleaver. Peggy-Mary (Classic Reprint) (p. 1714)
Strahorn, Carrie Adell. Fifteen Thousand Miles by Stage: A Woman's Unique Experience During Thirty Years of Path Finding & Pioneering from the Missouri to the Pacific & from Alaska to Mexico (Classic Reprint) (p. 724)
Strain, Christopher. Bernard the Sneezy Dragon. (p. 204)
Strain, E. H. Man's Foes, Vol. 1 (Classic Reprint) (p. 1398)
—Man's Foes, Vol. 3 (Classic Reprint) (p. 1398)
Strain, Euphans H. Man's Foes (Classic Reprint) (p. 1398)
Strain, Jennifer. Forgotten Lands: Dragon Island. (p. 768)
—Forgotten Lands: Stormy Mountain. (p. 768)
Strain, Shiloh, illus. see Clower, Dawn.
Strain Truett, Trudi & Truett, Trudi Strain. Christmas. (p. 383)
—Valentine's Day. (p. 2344)
Strain-Truett, Trudi, jt. auth. see Truett, Trudi Strain.
Strait, Mark, et al. HearBuilder Auditory Memory Software Program: Home Edition. (p. 944)
—HearBuilder Auditory Memory Software Program: Professional Edition. (p. 944)
Straker, Bethany. Funny Bunny Fly. (p. 801)
Straker, Bethany, illus. see Atherton, Isabel.
Straker, Bethany, illus. see Duffett-Smith, James.
Straker, Bethany, illus. see DuMont, Brianna.
Straker, Bethany, illus. see Louise, Kate.
Straker, Bethany, illus. see Mannering, Rose.
Straker, Bethany, illus. see Sky Pony Editors.
Straker, Bethany, jt. auth. see Atherton, Isabel.
Straley, Linda Broten. Altar of Gold. (p. 60)
Strambini, Karla. Extraordinary Mr. Qwerty. Strambini, Karla, illus. (p. 685)
Stramm, August. Bride of the Moor, Vol. 6 (Classic Reprint) (p. 280)
Stranaghan, Crystal. 13th Floor: Colouring Outside the Lines. Bzymek, Izabela, illus. (p. 2552)
Stranaghan, Crystal J. & Bzymek, Izabela. Safety Superheroes: Preventing Grandparents from Falling. (p. 1922)
Strand, Jeff. Bad Day for Voodoo. (p. 157)
—Greatest Zombie Movie Ever. (p. 892)
—How You Ruined My Life. (p. 1046)
—I Have a Bad Feeling about This. (p. 1065)
—Stranger Things Have Happened. (p. 2138)
Strand, Jennifer. Abigail Adams. (p. 5)
—Abraham Lincoln. (p. 7)
—Alexander Graham Bell. (p. 42)
—Anne Frank. (p. 98)
—Arthur Ashe. (p. 122)
—Babe Didrikson Zaharias. (p. 147)
—Barack Obama. (p. 164)
—Barbara Bush. (p. 165)
—Benjamin Franklin. (p. 200)
—Beyoncé. (p. 211)
—Bill Gates. (p. 226)
—Billie Jean King. (p. 226)
—Bruno Mars. (p. 288)
—Cesar Chavez. (p. 353)
—Charles Schulz. (p. 359)
—Chief Joseph. (p. 369)
—Chien-Shiung Wu. (p. 369)
—Crazy Horse. (p. 469)
—Dr. Seuss. (p. 592)
—Eleanor Roosevelt. (p. 630)
—Ferdinand Magellan. (p. 720)
—George Washington. (p. 819)
—George Washington Carver. (p. 820)
—Great Women (p. 891)
—Henry Ford. (p. 955)
—Hillary Clinton. (p. 971)
—Incredible Inventors (p. 1114)
—Jackie Robinson. (p. 1153)
—Jacqueline Kennedy. (p. 1154)
—Jacques Cousteau. (p. 1154)
—Jane Goodall. (p. 1158)
—Jeff Bezos. (p. 1162)
—Jerry Yang. (p. 1164)
—Justin Timberlake. (p. 1195)
—Katy Perry. (p. 1206)
—Lady Bird Johnson. (p. 1236)
—Laura Bush. (p. 1252)
—Laura Ingalls Wilder. (p. 1252)
—Legendary Leaders (p. 1263)
—Lewis & Clark. (p. 1282)
—Mae Jemison. (p. 1375)
—Mahatma Gandhi. (p. 1382)
—Malala Yousafzai. (p. 1391)
—Marco Polo. (p. 1403)
—Marie Curie. (p. 1405)
—Martha Washington. (p. 1410)
—Mary Todd Lincoln. (p. 1416)
—Maurice Sendak. (p. 1426)
—Melania Trump. (p. 1442)
—Mercer Mayer. (p. 1447)
—Michelle Obama. (p. 1458)
—Mother Teresa. (p. 1510)
—Muhammad Ali. (p. 1524)
—Nancy Reagan. (p. 1574)
—Neil Armstrong. (p. 1586)
—Nelson Mandela. (p. 1587)
—Oprah Winfrey. (p. 1667)
—Pam Munoz Ryan. (p. 1694)
—Pharrell Williams. (p. 1733)
—Pioneering Explorers (p. 1748)
—Pocahontas. (p. 1763)
—Roberto Clemente. (p. 1891)
—Rosa Parks. (p. 1904)
—Sacagawea. (p. 1920)
—Sequoyah. (p. 1990)
—Sitting Bull. (p. 2027)
—Steve Jobs. (p. 2116)
—Taylor Swift. (p. 2193)
—Thomas A. Edison. (p. 2227)
—Trailblazing Athletes (p. 2275)
—Wright Brothers. (p. 2511)
Strand, Jessica. Holiday Crafting & Baking with Kids: Gifts, Sweets, & Treats for the Whole Family. Herring, Aimée & Herring, Aimée, photos by. (p. 987)
Strand, Kai. Save the Lemmings. (p. 1937)
—Wishing Well. (p. 2479)
Strandberg, Lbsw Tracy. Nancy's Neighborhood. (p. 1574)
Strandberg, Mats. End. (p. 648)
Strande, Wilhelm Vom. Chicago in Tears & Smiles (Classic Reprint) (p. 367)
Stranex, Glenn. Paws & Claws. Wynn, Kim, illus. (p. 1708)
—Paws & Claws 2. Wynn, Kim, illus. (p. 1708)
Strang, H. I. Practical Exercises in English Composition: For Public & Private Schools & the Junior Classes in High Schools (Classic Reprint) (p. 1784)
Strang, Herbert. Adventures of Harry Rochester: A Tale of the Days of Marlborough & Eugene (Classic Reprint) (p. 23)
—Brown of Moukden: A Story of the Russo-Japanese War (Classic Reprint) (p. 287)
—With Marlborough to Malplaquet: A Story of the Reign of Queen Anne. (p. 2481)
Strang, Kay, ed. see Lamb, Charles & Lamb, Mary.
Strang, Kay, ed. see Lamb, Charles, et al.
Strange, Calthorpe. Two Worlds of Fashion, Vol. 3: A Novel (Classic Reprint) (p. 2310)
Strange, Cordelia. Environmental Science & Protection: Keeping Our Planet Green. (p. 657)
—How Does Water Pollution Affect Your Health? (p. 1030)
—Medical Technicians: Health-Care Support for the 21st Century. (p. 1436)
—Physicians Assistants & Nurses: New Opportunities in the 21st-Century Health System. (p. 1738)
Strange, J. R. Tree & the Light. Massivebrain.com, illus. (p. 2283)
Strange, Jason. 23 Crow's Perch Evergreen, Nelson & Kendall, Bradford, illus. (p. 2554)
—Basement of the Undead Parks, Phil, illus. (p. 169)
—Demon Card Evergreen, Nelson & Kendall, Bradford, illus. (p. 528)
—Faceless Friend Parks, Phil, illus. (p. 693)
—Full Moon Horror Parks, Phil & Dal Lago, Alberto, illus. (p. 797)
—Graveyard Plot Evergreen, Nelson & Kendall, Bradford, illus. (p. 882)
—Mothman's Shadow Parks, Phil, illus. (p. 1511)
—Mothman's Shadow Soleiman, Serg & Parks, Phil, illus. (p. 1511)
—Realm of Ghosts Parks, Phil, illus. (p. 1851)
—Strays Evergreen, Nelson & Kendall, Bradford, illus. (p. 2139)
—Text 4 Revenge Parks, Phil & Dal Lago, Alberto, illus. (p. 2210)
—To Wake the Dead Parks, Phil, illus. (p. 2254)
—Zombie Winter Parks, Phil, illus. (p. 2542)
—Zombie Winter Soleiman, Serg & Parks, Phil, illus. (p. 2542)
Strange, John Le. Set Them As a Banner (Classic Reprint) (p. 1993)
Strange, Katie, illus. see Hoffmann, Sara E.
Strange, Lucy. Our Castle by the Sea. (p. 1677)
—Secret of Nightingale Wood. (p. 1977)
Strange, Matthew. America at War: Military Conflicts, Home & Abroad in the 1800s. (p. 69)
—Bleeding, Blistering, & Purging: Health & Medicine in The 1800s. (p. 243)
—Guardians of the Home: Women's Lives in The 1800s. (p. 902)
—Jump Ropes, Jacks, & Endless Chores: Children's Lives in The 1800s. (p. 1188)
Strange, Nora K. Kenya Dawn (Classic Reprint) (p. 1210)
Strange, Sheila. Hotdog the Hippo: Hotdog's Messy Room. (p. 1007)
Strange, Vera. Part of Your Nightmare (Disney Chills, Book One) (p. 1701)
Strangeway, Ji. Red As Blue. Fleites, Juan, illus. (p. 1856)
Strangis, Raimo. Kingdom of Grape. (p. 1222)
Strangway, Melissa. Finding Hope. (p. 729)
Straparola, Giovanni Francesco. Facétieuses Nuits du Seigneur J. -F. Straparole (Classic Reprint) (p. 693)
—Facetious Nights of Straparola, Vol. 2 of 4 (Classic Reprint) (p. 693)
—Nights of Straparola, Vol. 1 (Classic Reprint) (p. 1608)
Strasnick, Lauren. 16 Ways to Break a Heart. (p. 2552)
—Her & Me & You. (p. 956)
—Nothing Like You. (p. 1625)
—Then You Were Gone. (p. 2215)
Strassen, Otto L. Zur, jt. auth. see Brehm, Alfred Edmund.
Strasser, Gayle. Harold & Darby. (p. 931)
Strasser, Susanne. So Far Up. Strasser, Susanne, illus. (p. 2050)
—So Light, So Heavy. Strasser, Susanne, illus. (p. 2050)
Strasser, Todd. American Terrorist. (p. 74)
—Beast of Cretacea. (p. 181)
—Boot Camp. (p. 262)
—Can't Get There from Here. (p. 322)
—Fallout. (p. 701)
—Famous. (p. 703)
—Give a Boy a Gun: 20th Anniversary Edition. (p. 839)
—If I Grow Up. (p. 1091)
—Is That an Angry Penguin in Your Gym Bag? (p. 1137)
—Is That an Unlucky Leprechaun in Your Lunch? Swearingen, Greg, illus. (p. 1137)
—No Place. (p. 1614)
—Price of Duty. (p. 1791)
—Summer Of '69. (p. 2149)
—Wave. (p. 2386)
—Wish You Were Dead. (p. 2478)
Strasser, Todd & Thacker, Nola. Shore: Shirt & Shoes Not Required; LB (Laguna Beach) (p. 2010)
Strat, Liana. Guess My Name: With Veggies & Fruits. (p. 902)
Strate, M. G. Abc's for a Child of God. (p. 4)
Stratemeyer, Edward. American Boy's Life of Theodore Roosevelt. (p. 71)
—Between Boer & Briton, or Two Boys' Adventures in South Africa (Classic Reprint) (p. 210)
—Dave Porter & His Classmates: Or for the Honor of Oak Hall (Classic Reprint) (p. 510)
—Dave Porter & His Double: Or the Disappearance of the Basswood Fortune (Classic Reprint) (p. 510)
—Dave Porter & His Rivals, or the Chums & Foes of Oak Hall (Classic Reprint) (p. 510)
—Dave Porter & the Runaways, or Last Days at Oak Hall (Classic Reprint) (p. 510)
—Dave Porter at Bear Camp: Or the Wild Man of Mirror Lake (Classic Reprint) (p. 510)
—Dave Porter at Oak Hall: At Oak Hall, the Schooldays of an American Boy (Classic Reprint) (p. 510)
—Dave Porter at Star Ranch (Classic Reprint) (p. 510)
—Dave Porter in the Far North: Or the Pluck of an American Schoolboy (Classic Reprint) (p. 510)
—Dave Porter in the Gold Fields: Or the Search for the Landslide Mine (Classic Reprint) (p. 510)
—Dave Porter on Cave Island, or a Schoolboy's Mysterious Mission (Classic Reprint) (p. 510)
—Dave Porter's Return to School, or Winning the Medal of Honor (Classic Reprint) (p. 510)
—For the Liberty of Texas. (p. 763)
—Marching on Niagara: The Soldier Boys of the Old Frontier. (p. 1402)
—On the Trail of Pontiac: Or, the Pioneer Boys of the Ohio. (p. 1656)
—Rover Boys at College. (p. 1908)
—Rover Boys in Camp: The Rivals of Pine Island. (p. 1908)
—Rover Boys in the Air from College Campus to the Clouds. (p. 1908)
—Rover Boys on Snowshoe Island. (p. 1908)
—Rover Boys on Snowshoe Island or, the Old Lumberman's Treasure Box. (p. 1908)
—Rover Boys on Treasure Isle: Or, the Strange Cruise of the Steam Yacht. (p. 1908)
—Rover Boys on Treasure Isle the Strange Cruise of the Steam Yacht. (p. 1908)
—True to Himself: Or, Roger Strong's Struggle for Place. (p. 2295)
—True to Himself, or Roger Strong's Struggle for Place (Classic Reprint) (p. 2295)
—With Washington in the West: A Soldier Boy's Battles in the Wilderness. (p. 2482)

—Young Auctioneers (Classic Reprint) (p. 2530)
—Young Volunteer in Cuba, Fighting for the Single Star (Classic Reprint) (p. 2532)
Stratford, Jordan. Case of the Counterfeit Criminals (the Wollstonecraft Detective Agency, Book 3) Murphy, Kelly, illus. (p. 337)
—Case of the Girl in Grey (the Wollstonecraft Detective Agency, Book 2) Murphy, Kelly, illus. (p. 337)
—Case of the Perilous Palace (the Wollstonecraft Detective Agency, Book 4) Murphy, Kelly, illus. (p. 338)
Stratford, S. J., jt. auth. see Matters, Print.
Stratford, Stevan, illus. see Jones, Ayesha.
Stratford, Stevan, illus. see Qamaruddin, Rizwana.
Strathearn, Chris. Ant-Man: The Incredible Shrinking Suit. (p. 101)
—Superman Versus Bizarro. Mada Design, Inc Staff, illus. (p. 2160)
Strathesk, John. Bits from Blinkbonny: Or Bell o the Manse, a Tale of Scottish Village Life Between 1841 & 1851 (Classic Reprint) (p. 235)
Strathgryffe, Alexander. Drizzleys. (p. 605)
Strathie, Chae. Dear Dinosaur: With Real Letters to Read! O'Byrne, Nicola, illus. (p. 520)
—Gorilla Loves Vanilla. O'Byrne, Nicola, illus. (p. 870)
—T. Rex on Tour: With Real Letters to Read! O'Byrne, Nicola, illus. (p. 2174)
Strathmore, Mary Eleanor Bowes. Confessions of the Countess of Strathmore: Carefully Copied from the Original, Lodged in Doctor's Commons (Classic Reprint) (p. 439)
Stratman, Kay, illus. see Martin, Maria G.
Stratton, Allan. Borderline. (p. 262)
—Chanda's Wars. (p. 355)
—Grave Robber's Apprentice. (p. 882)
Stratton, Clarence. Ruby Red: A Play in One Act (Classic Reprint) (p. 1911)
Stratton, Connor. Animal Coverings. (p. 88)
—Animal Ears. (p. 89)
—Animal Eyes. (p. 89)
—Animal Horns. (p. 90)
—Animal Legs. (p. 90)
—Animal Mouths. (p. 90)
—Animal Noses. (p. 90)
—Animal Parts (Set Of 8) (p. 91)
—Animal Tails. (p. 92)
—People at Work (Set Of 6) (p. 1718)
—We Celebrate Holidays. (p. 2390)
—We Exercise. (p. 2390)
—We Help at Home. (p. 2391)
—We Learn at School. (p. 2391)
—We Make a Garden. (p. 2391)
—We Make Music. (p. 2391)
—We Play Outside. (p. 2392)
—Working at a Construction Site. (p. 2495)
—Working at a Fire Station. (p. 2495)
—Working at a Hospital. (p. 2495)
—Working at a School. (p. 2495)
—Working at an Airport. (p. 2495)
—Working on a Farm. (p. 2496)
Stratton, Debra a. Mixed Hope. (p. 1484)
Stratton, Erin. There's Nothing Wrong with Boys. Gregeory, Vicki, illus. (p. 2218)
Stratton, George Frederick. Richard Elliott, Financier (Classic Reprint) (p. 1876)
Stratton, Helen, illus. see MacDonald, George.
Stratton, Mary. Fellowship Books: A Spark Divine (Classic Reprint) (p. 719)
Stratton, Steve. Plainridge. (p. 1754)
Stratton-Porter, Gene. After the Flood (Classic Reprint) (p. 34)
—At the Foot of the Rainbow (Classic Reprint) (p. 131)
—Birds of the Bible (Classic Reprint) (p. 232)
—Daughter of the Land. (p. 509)
—Daughter of the Land (Classic Reprint) (p. 509)
—Freckles. (p. 780)
—Freckles (Classic Reprint) (p. 780)
—Friends in Feathers (p. 787)
—Girl of the Limberlost. (p. 836)
—Girl of the Limberlost (Classic Reprint) (p. 836)
—Harvester (Classic Reprint) (p. 936)
—Homing with the Bird: The History of a Lifetime of Personal Experience with the Birds (Classic Reprint) (p. 998)
—Laddie: A True Blue Story. (p. 1236)
—Laddie: Story Blue Story (Classic Reprint) (p. 1236)
—Michael o'Halloran (Classic Reprint) (p. 1458)
—Song of the Cardinal (Classic Reprint) (p. 2062)
—White Flag (Classic Reprint) (p. 2444)
—Wonder, Hope, Love, & Loss: The Selected Novels of Gene Stratton-Porter. (p. 2488)
Straub, Josh & Straub, Christi. What Am I Feeling? (p. 2404)
Straub-Martin, Susan M. Legends, Loves & Great Lakes. (p. 1263)
Straugh, Phil. Mysterious Traveler: And His Return to the Country of His Boyhood (Classic Reprint) (p. 1568)
Straughn, William R. Home Authors-Pennsylvania (Classic Reprint) (p. 995)
Straus, Ralph. Pengard Awake (Classic Reprint) (p. 1715)
—Scandalous Mr. Waldo (Classic Reprint) (p. 1941)
Straus, Susan Farber. Healing Days: A Guide for Kids Who Have Experienced Trauma. Bogade, Maria, illus. (p. 943)
—Somebody Cares: A Guide for Kids Who Have Experienced Neglect. Keay, Claire, illus. (p. 2060)
Strauss, Alice J. What If Ants Wore Orange Pants. (p. 2413)
Strauss, Bob. Field Guide to Dinosaurs of North America: And Prehistoric Megafauna (p. 723)
Strauss, Ed. Know Your Bible for Kids: Noah's Ark: My First Bible Reference for 5-8 Year Olds. (p. 1229)
Strauss, Elle. Clockwise: (a Young Adult Time Travel Novel) (p. 406)
—Clockwiser: A Young Adult Time Travel Romance. (p. 406)
—Clockwork Crazy: A Young Adult Time Travel Romance. (p. 406)
—Counter Clockwise: A YA Time Travel Romance. (p. 459)
—Love, Tink: The Complete Series. (p. 1361)
—Seaweed. (p. 1973)
Strauss, Elle Lee, jt. auth. see Strauss, Lee.
Strauss, Elle Lee & Strauss, Lee. Clockwise: A Young Adult Time Travel Romance. (p. 406)
—ClockwiseR: A Young Adult Time Travel Romance. (p. 406)
—Clockwork Crazy: A Young Adult Time Travel Romance. (p. 406)
—Counter Clockwise: A Young Adult Time Travel Romance. (p. 459)
—Like Clockwork: A Young Adult Time Travel Romance. (p. 1300)
Strauss, G. L. M. Old Ledger, Vol. 1 of 3 (Classic Reprint) (p. 1646)
Strauss, Gustave Louis Maurice. Old Ledger, Vol. 2 of 3 (Classic Reprint) (p. 1646)
—Old Ledger, Vol. 3 of 3 (Classic Reprint) (p. 1646)
Strauss, Gwen. Hiding Game Leonhard, Herb, illus. (p. 967)
Strauss, Holden. Animal Migration. (p. 90)
—Chef's Tools. (p. 365)
—Jobs in Science: Solve Problems Involving Measurement & Estimation. (p. 1170)
—Wolves. (p. 2485)
Strauss, Joanne. Charlie & His Friends. (p. 359)
Strauss, Kevin. Pecos Bill Invents the Ten-Gallon Hat Harrington, David, illus. (p. 1711)
Strauss, Lee. Gingerbread Man: A Marlow & Sage Mystery. (p. 834)
—Hickory Dickory Dock: A Marlow & Sage Mystery. (p. 965)
—Love, Tink: The Complete Series. (p. 1361)
—Perception. (p. 1721)
—Seaweed: A Young Adult Merfolk Tale. (p. 1973)
—Twinkle Little Star: A Marlow & Sage Mystery. (p. 2305)
—Volition. (p. 2366)
Strauss, Lee & Strauss, Elle Lee. Gingerbread Man: A Marlow & Sage Mystery. (p. 834)
—Like Clockwork: A Young Adult Time Travel Romance. (p. 1300)
—Volition: A Thrilling Dystopian Romance. (p. 2366)
Strauss, Linda Leopold. Different Kind of Passover. Tugeau, Jeremy, illus. (p. 545)
Strauss, Michael J. Investigating the Natural World of Chemistry with Kids: Experiments, Writing, & Drawing Activities for Learning Science. (p. 1131)
Strauss, Michael L. Timothy Cooper's Quest for Balloon Bay: Quest for Balloon Bay. (p. 2247)
—Timothy Cooper's- Boone's Magical Adventure: Boone's Magical Adventure. Strauss, Michael L., illus. (p. 2247)
Strauss, Rochelle. Tree of Life: The Incredible Biodiversity of Life on Earth. Thompson, Margot, illus. (p. 2284)
Strauss, Victoria. Color Song (p. 421)
Strauss, Whitney. Sweet Child Born in Texas. (p. 2168)
Strausser, A., jt. auth. see Wasson, E.
Stravinskas, Janice. Pam the Dog: A Hawaiian Adventure. (p. 1694)
Straw, Wendy. 5 Little Ducks. (p. 2548)
—Action Rhymes Musical Songbook. (p. 12)
—Counting Rhymes Musical Songbook. (p. 460)
—I'm a Little Teapot. (p. 1097)
—Little Engine That Could. (p. 1316)
—My Best Ever Book of Nursery Songs: With CD. (p. 1532)
—My Kitten's Baby Book. (p. 1551)
—My Puppy's Baby Book. (p. 1559)
—Nursery Rhymes Musical Songbook. (p. 1631)
—Peter Peter Pumpkin Eater & Friends. (p. 1729)
—Twinkle Twinkle Little Star Book N' Puzzle Pack. (p. 2305)
—Wendy Straw's Action Rhymes. (p. 2400)
—Wendy Straw's Action Rhymes with CD. (p. 2400)
—Wheels on the Bus. (p. 2428)
—Wheels on the Bus Book N' Puzzle Pack. (p. 2428)
Straw, Wendy, illus. see Adam, Luisa.
Straw, Wendy, illus. see Grace, Christine.
Straw, Wendy, jt. auth. see Lear, Edward.
Strayer, E. Ward. Making Good with Margaret (Classic Reprint) (p. 1389)
Strazzabosco, Jeanne M. Learning about Responsibility from the Life of Colin Powell. (p. 1257)
Strazzabosco, John. Aircraft Carriers Supplies for a City at Sea: Multiplying Multidigit Numbers with Regrouping. (p. 37)
Stream, G. K. Amnesia: Colony 1: Alex & Trish. (p. 76)
Streamer, D. Baby's Baedeker: An International Guide-Book for the Young of All Ages; Peculiarly Adapted to the Wants of 1st 2nd Childhood (Classic Reprint) (p. 153)
—Perverted Proverbs: A Manual of Immorals for the Many (Classic Reprint) (p. 1725)
—Ruthless Rhymes for Heartless Homes. (p. 1918)
Streamer, Volney. World Awheel: With Fac-Similes of Water-Color Paintings (Classic Reprint) (p. 2501)
—World Awheel. (p. 2501)
Streater, Carmel O. Thomas Tyrone Jones Gets Away. (p. 2229)
Streatfeild, Frank Newton. Reminiscences of an Old un (Classic Reprint) (p. 1865)
Streatfeild, Noel. Ballet Shoes. (p. 162)
—Ballet Shoes (Classic Reprint) (p. 162)
—Bell Family. Hughes, Shirley, illus. (p. 196)
—Far to Go. (p. 709)
—Skating Shoes. (p. 2030)
Streatfeild, Richard Alexander. Opera: A Sketch of the Development of Opera. with Full Descriptions of All Works in the Modern Repertory. (p. 1666)
Strebor, Eiggam. Ambition, or the Launch of a Skiff upon the Sea of Life (Classic Reprint) (p. 67)
—Home Scenes During the Rebellion (Classic Reprint) (p. 997)
Strecker, Michael. Jokes for Crescent City Kids Smith, Vernon, illus. (p. 1176)
—Young Comic's Guide to Telling Jokes (p. 2530)
Stredder, Eleanor. Alive in the Jungle: A Story for the Young. (p. 48)
—Alive in the Jungle: A Story for the Young (Classic Reprint) (p. 48)
Streed, Sam. Alfred's Book of Monsters. Streed, Sam, illus. (p. 43)
Street, Alfred B. Woods & Waters, or, the Saranacs & Racket: With Map of the Route & Nine Illustrations on Wood (Classic Reprint) (p. 2492)
Street, G. S. Book of Stories (Classic Reprint) (p. 260)
—Trials of the Bantocks (Classic Reprint) (p. 2286)
—Wise & the Wayward (Classic Reprint) (p. 2478)
Street, James, illus. see Garner, Ellen.
Street, Julian. After Thirty (Classic Reprint) (p. 34)
—My Enemy the Motor: A Tale in Eight Honks & One Crash. (p. 1538)
—My Enemy the Motor: A Tale in Eight Honks & One Crash (Classic Reprint) (p. 1538)
—Need of Change (Classic Reprint) (p. 1585)
—Rita Coventry (Classic Reprint) (p. 1886)
—Ship-Bored (Classic Reprint) (p. 2007)
—Sunbeams, Inc (Classic Reprint) (p. 2151)
—Violets & Vexation (Classic Reprint) (p. 2360)
—Welcome to Our City (Classic Reprint) (p. 2398)
Street, Pat & Brace, Eric. You're Pulling My Leg! 400 Human-Body Sayings from Head to Toe. Brace, Eric, illus. (p. 2535)
Street-Ely, Linda. Cowlick. Reynarde, Niccola, illus. (p. 464)
Streeter, Edward. As You Were, Bill (Classic Reprint) (p. 125)
—Beany, Gangleshanks, & the Tub (Classic Reprint) (p. 179)
—Dere Mable: Love Letters of a Rookie (Classic Reprint) (p. 530)
—Love Letters of Bill to Mable Comprising Dere Mable: Thats Me All over, Mable; Same (Classic Reprint) (p. 1360)
—Same Old Bill, Eh Mable (Classic Reprint) (p. 1927)
—Thats Me All over, Mable (Classic Reprint) (p. 2213)
Streeter, John Williams. Doctor Tom: The Coroner of Brett (Classic Reprint) (p. 573)
—Fat of the Land: The Story of an American Farm. (p. 713)
—Fat of the Land: The Story of an American Farm (Classic Reprint) (p. 713)
Streeter, Nelson R. Gems from an Old Drummer's Grip (Classic Reprint) (p. 813)
Streeter, Talena, illus. see Currie, Colleen & Currie, David.
Streetman, Randy J. What Has God Made? (p. 2412)
Streetman, Susan. It's How We Survive: The Tale of an American Dreamer. (p. 1145)
Stref, illus. see Hutton, Alasdair.
Strehle Hartman, Ashley. Entertainment Robots. (p. 656)
—Teens & STDs. (p. 2200)
Streissguth, Thomas. Albania in Pictures. (p. 40)
—Denmark in Pictures. (p. 529)
—Investigating the D.B. Cooper Hijacking. (p. 1131)
—Korean War. (p. 1231)
—Perspectives on Reconstruction. (p. 1725)
—Perspectives on Westward Expansion. (p. 1725)
—Suriname in Pictures. (p. 2163)
—Truth about Stress Management. (p. 2296)
Streissguth, Thomas, jt. auth. see Simon, Emma.
Streissguth, Thomas & Streissguth, Tom. Senegal in Pictures. (p. 1988)
Streissguth, Tom. Art of Anime & Manga. (p. 121)
—Battle of Antietam (p. 174)
—Battle of Britain (p. 174)
—Battle of Gettysburg (p. 174)
—Belize in Pictures. (p. 196)
—Biotech Careers. (p. 229)
—D. B. Cooper Hijacking. (p. 494)
—District of Columbia V. Heller: The Right to Bear Arms Case. (p. 565)
—Extreme Weather. (p. 687)
—Fashion & Dress Codes: A How-to Guide. (p. 712)
—Fashion & Dress Codes. (p. 712)
—France. (p. 776)
—Great Jobs in Technology. (p. 887)
—Inside the Coal Industry. (p. 1123)
—Inside the Tobacco Industry. (p. 1124)
—It's Great to Be a Fan in Michigan. (p. 1145)
—Korean War. (p. 1231)
—Manson Family Murders. (p. 1398)
—Mayflower Story. (p. 1430)
—Rosalind Franklin: DNA Discoverer. (p. 1904)
—Security Agencies of the United States: How the CIA, FBI, NSA, & Homeland Security Keep Us Safe. (p. 1981)
—Sherman's March to the Sea. (p. 2006)
—Vietnam War. (p. 2357)
—Welcome to America? A Pro/con Debate over Immigration. (p. 2398)
—Welfare & Welfare Reform. (p. 2399)
Streissguth, Tom, jt. auth. see Harris, Duchess.
Streissguth, Tom, jt. auth. see Jd, Duchess Harris.
Streissguth, Tom, jt. auth. see Streissguth, Thomas.
Streissguth, Tom, contrib. by. 2016 Presidential Election. (p. 2561)
Streit, Jakob. Brother Francis: The Life of Francis of Assisi Kuettel, Nina, tr. (p. 286)
—Liputto: Stories of Gnomes & Trolls Kuettel, Nina, tr. (p. 1307)
—Liputto: Stories of Gnomes & Trolls Mitchell, David, ed. (p. 1307)
—Three Knight Tales (p. 2233)
Strelitz Haber, Tiffany. Monster Who Lost His Mean. Edmunds, Kirstie, illus. (p. 1497)
Strelkoff, Tatiana. Changer. (p. 356)
Strelow, Michael. Alyssa Chronicle: The Princess Gardener, Book II. (p. 61)
—Jake's Book: Book III of the Princess Gardener Series. (p. 1156)
—Princess Gardener. (p. 1797)
Stren, Ariella. Bracha Do You Know? Argoff, Patti, illus. (p. 273)
Strength, Ras Jah. My African Me. (p. 1531)
Stresing, Fred C., illus. see Logan, Sam & Trueheart, Eric.
Stresing, Fred C., illus. see Logan, Sam.
Stresing, Fred C., illus. see Trueheart, Eric & Logan, Sam.
Stretar, Elizabeth Duncan. Acorn Gert & Brother Bert. (p. 11)
Strettell, Alma, tr. see Sylva, Carmen.
Stretton, Charles. Sport & Sportsmen: A Book of Recollections (Classic Reprint) (p. 2087)
Stretton, Hesba. Christmas Child (Illustrated) Children's Classic. (p. 384)
—Cobwebs & Cables (Classic Reprint) (p. 410)
—Crew of the Dolphin. (p. 474)
—Doctor's Dilemma (Classic Reprint) (p. 574)
—Highway of Sorrow: At the Close of the Nineteenth Century (Classic Reprint) (p. 970)
—In Prison & Out (Classic Reprint) (p. 1106)
—Jessica's First Prayer: Jessica's Mother (Classic Reprint) (p. 1165)
—Jessica's First Prayer. (p. 1165)
—Jessica's First Prayer (Classic Reprint) (p. 1165)
—Little Meg's Children & Alone in London (Classic Reprint) (p. 1321)
—Night & a Day: Also Apple-Tree Court, & the Worth of a Baby (Classic Reprint) (p. 1604)
—Through a Needle's Eye, Vol. 1 of 2 (Classic Reprint) (p. 2236)
—Through Needle's Eye (Classic Reprint) (p. 2237)
Stretton, Julia Cecilia. Lords & Ladies, Vol. 1 of 3 (Classic Reprint) (p. 1349)
—Margaret & Her Bridesmaids, Vol. 1 of 3 (Classic Reprint) (p. 1403)
—Mr. & Mrs. Asheton, Vol. 1 of 3 (Classic Reprint) (p. 1517)
—Queen of the County (Classic Reprint) (p. 1824)
—Three Wives, Vol. 1 of 3 (Classic Reprint) (p. 2235)
—Valley of a Hundred Fires, Vol. 1 of 3 (Classic Reprint) (p. 2345)
—Woman's Devotion, Vol. 1 Of 3: A Novel (Classic Reprint) (p. 2486)
Stretton, Julia Cecilia Collinson. Margaret & Her Bridesmaids (Classic Reprint) (p. 1403)
Stretton-Stephens, Paul a. Enemies Rising Part 1: A Tacrem Adventure. (p. 650)
Streuvels, Stijn. Path of Life (Classic Reprint) (p. 1704)
Strevens-Marzo, Bridget, illus. see Bedford, David.
Strevens-Marzo, Bridget, illus. see Sturges, Philemon.
Strevens-Marzo, Bridget, illus. see Wild, Margaret.
Strevens-Marzo, Bridget, jt. auth. see Wild, Margaret.
Streza, Katrina. Discover Big Cats. (p. 554)
—Discover Castles. (p. 554)
—Discover Cats: Level 2 Reader. (p. 554)
—Discover China: Level 2 Reader. (p. 554)
—Discover Deadly Animals: Level 3 Reader. (p. 554)
—Discover Deserts: Level 2 Reader. (p. 554)
—Discover Ocean Animals: Level 2 Reader. (p. 554)
—Discover Sewing: Level 2 Reader. (p. 555)
—Dog for Everyone. (p. 576)
—Dog for Everyone / un Perro para Todo el Mundo. (p. 576)
—I Saw a Friend. Katz, Michele, illus. (p. 1080)
—Let's Go to the Hospital: Level 1 Reader. (p. 1274)
—Letters from Santa: a Christmas Alphabet Book: A Christmas Alphabet Book. (p. 1280)
—Mi Gato Esta Triste. Ponnay, Brenda, illus. (p. 1455)
—My Cat Is Sad. Ponnay, Brenda, illus. (p. 1535)
—My Cat Is Sad / Mi Gato Esta Triste. Ponnay, Brenda, illus. (p. 1535)
—My Cat, My Dog. Ponnay, Brenda, illus. (p. 1535)
—My Good Dog. Ponnay, Brenda, illus. (p. 1548)
—Perro para Todo el Mundo (a Dog for Everyone) Sandoval, Lenny, tr. (p. 1724)
—Tiempo de Trenes (Train Time) Sandoval, Lenny, tr. (p. 2240)
—Train Time / Tiempo de Trenes. Sandoval, Lenny, tr. (p. 2275)
—Vámonos a la Playa: (Let's Go to the Beach) (p. 2345)
—We Play: Level 1 Reader. Goegebuer, Jade, illus. (p. 2392)
Streza, Katrnia. Discover Horses: Level 1 Reader. (p. 554)
Streza, Nancy. Cowboy Time: Level 1 Reader. (p. 464)
—Discover Firefighters: Level 2 Reader. (p. 554)
—Let's Clean the House: Level 1 Reader. (p. 1270)
—Let's Eat Dinner: Level 1 Reader. (p. 1271)
—Let's Go Hunting with Our Eyes. (p. 1273)
—Let's Go to the Beach / Vámonos a la Playa. (p. 1274)
—My Favorite Sport: Golf. (p. 1539)
—My Favorite Sport: Hockey. (p. 1539)
—My Favorite Sport: Soccer. (p. 1539)
—My Favorite Sport: Tennis. (p. 1539)
—My Favorite Sport: Cricket. (p. 1539)
—My Favorite Sport: Baseball. (p. 1539)
—My Favorite Sport: Football. (p. 1539)
—My Favorite Sport: Swimming. (p. 1539)
—My Favorite Sport: Basketball. (p. 1539)
—My Favorite Sport: Gymnastics. (p. 1539)
—My Favorite Sport: Volleyball. (p. 1539)
—My Favorite Sport: Cheerleading. (p. 1539)
—My Favorite Sport: Skateboarding. (p. 1539)
—My Favorite Sport: Horseback Riding. (p. 1539)
—Nos Vamos a la Granja. Pryce, Adam, illus. (p. 1622)
—Nos Vamos a la Playa. Sandoval, Lenny, tr. (p. 1622)
—We're Going to the Beach / Nos Vamos a la Playa. Sandoval, Lenny, tr. (p. 2400)
—We're Going to the Farm / Nos Vamos a la Granja. Sandoval, Lenny, tr. (p. 2400)
Striar Rohner, Patricia. Willameana the Witch. (p. 2468)
Stribling, Anne & Benchmark Education Co., LLC Staff. Get up, Meg! (p. 825)
Stribling, T. S. Birthright: A Novel (Classic Reprint) (p. 234)
—Birthright. (p. 234)
Strickland, A. M. Beyond the Black Door. (p. 212)
Strickland, A. W. Adventures of Ralph & Elmer This Potato Is for You. (p. 27)
Strickland, AdriAnne, jt. auth. see Miller, Michael.
Strickland, Agnes. How Will It End?, Vol. 1 of 3 (Classic Reprint) (p. 1046)
—Juvenile Forget Me Not, or Cabinet of Entertainment & Instruction (Classic Reprint) (p. 1195)
—Narratives of Nature, & History Book for Young Naturalists (Classic Reprint) (p. 1575)
—Old Friends & New Acquaintances (Classic Reprint) (p. 1645)
—Stories from History (Classic Reprint) (p. 2124)
—Tales from English History: For Children (Classic Reprint) (p. 2182)
—Tales of the School-Room (Classic Reprint) (p. 2186)
Strickland, Brad. Dragon's Plunder. (p. 596)
Strickland, Brad, jt. auth. see Bellairs, John.
Strickland, Dorothy S., jt. ed. see Alvermann, Donna E.
Strickland, Gail. Oracle of the Song. (p. 1668)
Strickland, Jennifer. Pretty from the Inside Out: Discover All the Ways God Made You Special. Kerr, Kathleen, ed. (p. 1790)
Strickland, Karen L., jt. auth. see Leighton, Davis L.

S

Strickland, Marion. Suggestions for Kindergarten Work (Classic Reprint) (p. 2147)
Strickland, Sarrah. Sefer: Literary Magazine 2014 (Classic Reprint) (p. 1985)
Strickland, Shadra, illus. see Bandy, Michael S. & Stein, Eric.
Strickland, Shadra, illus. see Derby, Sally.
Strickland, Shadra, illus. see Morrison, Toni & Morrison, Slade.
Strickland, Shadra, illus. see Nolen, Jerdine.
Strickland, Shadra, illus. see Powell, Patricia Hruby.
Strickland, Shadra, illus. see Randall, Alice & Randall Williams, Caroline.
Strickland, Shadra, illus. see Watson, Renée.
Strickland, Shadra, jt. auth. see Elliott, Zetta.
Strickland, Stanley. Motorcycle Road Trip! Jefferys, Rhys, illus. (p. 1512)
—Police Car Patrol! Jefferys, Rhys, illus. (p. 1770)
—Rocket Ship Adventure! Sordo, Paco, illus. (p. 1895)
Strickland, Terésa Hammond. Under the Ban: A South Carolina Romance. (p. 2321)
—Under the Ban: A South Carolina Romance (Classic Reprint) (p. 2321)
Strickland, Tessa, jt. auth. see Lallemand, Orianne.
Strickland, Tessa & DePalma, Kate. Barefoot Book of Children. Dean, David, illus. (p. 166)
—Barefoot Books Children of the World. Dean, David, illus. (p. 166)
Strickland, W. W. North West Slav Legends & Fairy Stories: A Sequel to Segnius Irritant (Classic Reprint) (p. 1621)
Strickland-Egans, Joycelyn. Sunday Kind of Joy: 1 Thessalonians 5:16-18. (p. 2152)
Strickling, Jacob. Make Science Fun. (p. 1386)
—Make Science Fun Experiments: Science Experiments to Blow Your Socks Off! (p. 1386)
Strictly Spanish, LLC., tr. see Harbo, Christopher L.
Strictly Spanish, LLC., tr. see Miller, Connie Colwell, et al.
Strictly Spanish, LLC., tr. see Olson, Nathan.
Strictly Spanish LLC. Staff, tr. see Edison, Erin & Saunders-Smith, Gail.
Strictly Spanish LLC. Staff, tr. see Miller, Connie Colwell.
Strictly Spanish LLC. Staff, tr. see Nichols, Cheyenne.
Strictly Spanish LLC. Staff, tr. see Schuh, Mari C.
Strictly Spanish Translation Services Staff, tr. see Biskup, Agnieszka & Martin, Cynthia.
Strictly Spanish Translation Services Staff, tr. see Nichols, Cheyenne.
Strictly Spanish Translation Services Staff, tr. see O'Brien, Kim.
Strictly Spanish Translation Services Staff, tr. see Rustad, Martha E. H.
Stride, Lottie. Girls Miscellany: Fascinating Information Every Girl Should Know. Tambellini, Stefano, illus. (p. 839)
—Time Travel: How to Be the Best Time Traveller Ever. Pavlic, Dusan, illus. (p. 2245)
—Write Every Time. (p. 2512)
Stride, Lottie & Oliver, Martin. Girls Only: How to Survive Anything! Geremia, Daniela & Ecob, Simon, illus. (p. 839)
Strindberg, August. Advent: A Play in Five Acts (Classic Reprint) (p. 18)
—Advent: Ein Weihnachtsspiel (Classic Reprint) (p. 18)
—Easter (a Play in Three Acts) And Stories (Classic Reprint) (p. 619)
—Fair Haven & Foul Strand (Classic Reprint) (p. 695)
—Historical Miniatures (Classic Reprint) (p. 976)
—In Midsummer Days & Other Tales (Classic Reprint) (p. 1106)
—Inferno (Classic Reprint) (p. 1118)
—Married (Classic Reprint) (p. 1408)
—On the Seaboard: A Novel of the Baltic Islands (Classic Reprint) (p. 1655)
—Plays: Comrades; Facing Death; Pariah; Easter. (p. 1761)
—Plays: Swanwhite; Advent; the Storm (Classic Reprint) (p. 1761)
—Plays: Swanwhite; Simoom; Debit & Credit; Advent; the Thunderstorm; after the Fire (Classic Reprint) (p. 1761)
—Plays (Classic Reprint) (p. 1761)
—Red Room (Classic Reprint) (p. 1858)
—Son of a Servant (Classic Reprint) (p. 2061)
—There Are Crimes & Crimes: A Comedy. (p. 2216)
String, Margaret Lancaster. Miss. Wistaria at Home: A Tale of Modern Japan (Classic Reprint) (p. 1480)
Stringam, Jean. How Not to Cry in Public. (p. 1034)
Stringberg, August. Lucky Pehr: A Drama in Five Acts (Classic Reprint) (p. 1365)
Stringer, Arthur. Hand of Peril (Classic Reprint) (p. 914)
—House of Intrigue (Classic Reprint) (p. 1023)
—Lonely O'Malley: A Story of Boy Life (Classic Reprint) (p. 1342)
—Man Who Couldn't Sleep (Classic Reprint) (p. 1395)
—Prairie Child (Classic Reprint) (p. 1784)
—Prairie Mother (Classic Reprint) (p. 1785)
—Prairie Omnibus: Containing Two Complete Novels (Classic Reprint) (p. 1785)
—Prairie Stories: Containing the Prairie Wife; the Prairie Mother; the Prairie Child (Classic Reprint) (p. 1785)
—Prairie Wife (Classic Reprint) (p. 1785)
—Silver Poppy: A Novel (Classic Reprint) (p. 2019)
—Silver Poppy (Classic Reprint) (p. 2019)
—Stranger (Classic Reprint) (p. 2138)
—Supertales of Modern Mystery (Classic Reprint) (p. 2162)
—Twin Tales: Are All Men Alike & the Lost Titian (Classic Reprint) (p. 2305)
—Wire Tappers (Classic Reprint) (p. 2477)
—Woman in the Rain: And Other Poems (Classic Reprint) (p. 2485)
Stringer, Arthur J. Loom of Destiny (Classic Reprint) (p. 1348)
Stringer, David. Charlie Jack. (p. 360)
Stringer, Lauren. Yellow Time. Stringer, Lauren, illus. (p. 2520)
Stringer, Lauren, illus. see Fox, Mem.
Stringer, Lauren, illus. see George, Kristine O'Connell.
Stringer, Lauren, illus. see Going, K. L.
Stringer, Lauren, illus. see Orr, Wendy.
Stringer, Lauren, illus. see Peters, Lisa Westberg.
Stringer, Lauren, illus. see Ray, Mary Lyn.
Stringer, Lauren, illus. see Rylant, Cynthia.
Stringer, Lynne. Crown. (p. 479)
Stringer, Rupert Michael. Curse of Tavicombe. (p. 488)
Stringer Sr, William B. Puppy. (p. 1814)
Stringfield, Joni, illus. see Brokamp, Elizabeth.
Stringham, Jean. Balance. (p. 160)
Stripland, Rubye Weldon. Lucy Bell, Queen of the Pasture Book Four. (p. 1365)
Stritzko, Jos A. V. Anatole France (of the Academie Francaise) The Queen Pedauque (la Rotisserie de la Reine Pedauque) (Classic Reprint) (p. 79)
Strobbart, Darran. Multiplying & Dividing Activity Book. (p. 1525)
Strobbart, Darran, jt. auth. see Reynolds, Eddie.
Strobel, Lee. Case for a Creator for Kids (p. 336)
—Case for Christ Young Reader's Edition: Investigating the Toughest Questions about Jesus (p. 336)
—Case for Faith: A Journalist Investigates the Toughest Objections to Christianity (p. 336)
—Case for Faith for Kids (p. 336)
—Case for Grace for Kids (p. 336)
—Case for Miracles for Kids (p. 336)
—Case for Miracles Student Edition: A Journalist Explores the Evidence for the Supernatural (p. 336)
—Case for the Real Jesus: A Journalist Investigates Current Challenges to Christianity (p. 336)
Strobel, Lee & Suggs, Rob. Case for Christ for Kids (p. 336)
Strobel, Miranda, et al. Quail Tails: The Adventures of Button. (p. 1821)
Strobel, Zachary & Bacos, Camille. Friendship Sanctuary. (p. 788)
Strobel, Zachary & Umrikar, Sakharam. Grand Prize Beagle. (p. 877)
Strobel, Zachary, et al. Debra the Substitute Teacher. (p. 522)
Strobhart, Strobhart. Saved by a Woman: Or, the Hidden Romance; a Story of the Late War (Classic Reprint) (p. 1938)
Strobridge, Idah Meacham. Land of Purple Shadows (Classic Reprint) (p. 1242)
—Loom of the Desert (Classic Reprint) (p. 1348)
Strock, Carren. Grandpa & Me & the Park in the City. Strock, Carren, illus. (p. 879)
—Secret Survivors. (p. 1979)
Stroebe, Clara. Danish Fairy Book (Classic Reprint) (p. 503)
—Norwegian Fairy Book (Classic Reprint) (p. 1622)
—Swedish Fairy Book (Classic Reprint) (p. 2168)
Stroebe, Clara, ed. Swedish Fairy Book: [Illustrated Edition]. Hood, George W., illus. (p. 2168)
—Swedish Fairy Book: [Illustrated Edition]. Hood, George W., illus. (p. 2168)
Stroede, Paul, illus. see Rogala, Judy.
Stroede, Paul, illus. see Stadler, Kristina.
Stroer, Barbara, illus. see Pinner, Vivian.
Stroh, Mary, jt. auth. see Woodward, John.
Strohm, Gertrude. Word Pictures: Thoughts & Descriptions from Popular Authors; Pictures of the Mind, Heart, & Life, Selected from the Works of Great Artists in Literature (Classic Reprint) (p. 2493)
Strohm, Stephanie Kate. Confederates Don't Wear Couture: A Tale of Heartache, Haunting, & Hoop Skirts. (p. 438)
—Date to Save. (p. 509)
—It's Not Me, It's You. (p. 1146)
—No Soy Yo, Eres Tú / It's Not Me, It's You. Dominguez Palomo, Ana Isabel, tr. (p. 1615)
—Pilgrims Don't Wear Pink. (p. 1744)
—Taming of the Drew. (p. 2189)
—That's Not What I Heard. (p. 2214)
Strohmeyer, Sarah. How Zoe Made Her Dreams (Mostly) Come True. (p. 1046)
—Secrets of Lily Graves. (p. 1980)
—Smart Girls Get What They Want. (p. 2040)
—This Is My Brain on Boys. (p. 2225)
Strojny, Shelley. Do You Know Bailey? Zoromski, Ariel & Zoromski, Leia, illus. (p. 571)
Strologo, Doriano, illus. see George, Anya.
Strom, Allison, illus. see Roberts, Rachel.
Strom, Chris. 3D Game Programming for Kids: Create Interactive Worlds with JavaScript. (p. 2547)
Strom, Frank. Scooby-Doo & the Mystery Date Deporter. Vincent, illus. (p. 1960)
Strom, Frank & Barrios, Roberto. Scooby-Doo in Welcome to the Jungle (p. 1961)
Strom, Laura Layton. It's Raining, It's Pouring: Set Of 6. Colombo, Alexandra, illus. (p. 1147)
—It's Raining, It's Pouring Book Set. Colombo, Alexandra, illus. (p. 1147)
—Meaningful Mini-Lessons & Practice: Comprehension Gr 1 Teacher Resource. (p. 1434)
—Opinions about Two Fairy Tales - Baba Yaga & Hansel & Gretel: Set Of 6. Czernichowska, Joanna & Leonidou, Niki, illus. (p. 1667)
—Patito Feo. Palmer, James, illus. (p. 1705)
—Princesa y el Guisante. Leonidou, Niki, illus. (p. 1795)
—Rapunzel. Leonidou, Niki, illus. (p. 1841)
—Rey Midas y el Toque de Oro. Parrish, Kirk, illus. (p. 1874)
—Sight Walk: Set Of 6. (p. 2016)
—Sight Walk Book Set. (p. 2016)
—We Need a Seed: Set Of 6. (p. 2391)
—We Need a Seed Book Set. (p. 2391)
—Who Do You See? a Rain Forest Rap: Set Of 6. (p. 2447)
—Who Do You See? a Rain Forest Rap Book Set. (p. 2447)
Strom, Laura Layton, et al. Opinions about Two Fairy Tales: Baba Yaga & Hansel & Gretel. Czernichowska, Joanna, illus. (p. 1667)
Strombeck, J. F. Freight Classification: A Study of Underlying Principles. (p. 783)
—Hart Schaffner & Marx Prize Essays, XII: Freight Classification, a Study of Underlying Principles. (p. 935)
Stromberg, David, ed. In the Land of Happy Tears: Yiddish Tales for Modern Times: Collected & Edited by David Stromberg. (p. 1109)
Stromberg, Ronica. Living It up to Live It Down. (p. 1333)
—Shadow in the Dark. (p. 1996)
—Time-for-Bed Angel. Stephenson, Kristina, illus. (p. 2244)
Strömgård, Katarina. Secret Cat. (p. 1975)
Stromoski, Rick, illus. see Curry, Don L.
Stromoski, Rick, illus. see Meltzer Kleinhenz, Sydnie.
Stromp, Stephen. In the Graveyard Antemortem. (p. 1109)
Stromsten, Frank Albert, jt. auth. see Davison, Alvin.
Stronach, Ann. Flight to Riches. (p. 749)
Strong, Abigail. Troggins Tales. (p. 2290)
Strong, Amanda. Monsters among Us. (p. 1497)
Strong, Anna Louise. King's Palace (Classic Reprint) (p. 1223)
Strong, Augustus Hopkins. Union with Christ, a Chapter of Systematic Theology. (p. 2329)
Strong, B. L. Troll & His Bridge. (p. 2290)
Strong, B. Norman. Correct Spelling, Vol. 6 (Classic Reprint) (p. 456)
Strong, Belinda. Hold & Touch Bedtime. (p. 987)
Strong, Belinda, illus. see Hane, Tori, et al.
Strong, Belinda, illus. see Hane, Tori.
Strong, Belinda, illus. see Vogel, Cheri.
Strong, Charles Augustus. Wisdom of the Beasts (Classic Reprint) (p. 2477)
Strong, Cynda. Resurrection. (p. 1870)
Strong, Frances L. All the Year Round: A Nature Reader (Classic Reprint) (p. 54)
—All the Year Round, Vol. 1: A Nature Reader (Classic Reprint) (p. 54)
—All the Year Round, Vol. 2: A Nature Reader; Part II: Winter (Classic Reprint) (p. 54)
—Nature Reader, Vol. 1: Autumn (Classic Reprint) (p. 1581)
Strong, Grace. Worst Foe: A Temperance Story (Classic Reprint) (p. 2509)
Strong, Isobel. Girl from Home: A Story of Honolulu (Classic Reprint) (p. 835)
—Memories of Vailima (Classic Reprint) (p. 1446)
—Robert Louis Stevenson (Classic Reprint) (p. 1890)
Strong, J. D. Pacific Monthly, Vol. 10: Devoted to the Arts, Science, Literature & Life of the Pacific Coast; June, 1863 (Classic Reprint) (p. 1691)
Strong, Jeremy. Armadillo & Hare: Tales from the Forest. Bagley, Rebecca, illus. (p. 117)
Strong, Karen. Just South of Home. (p. 1194)
Strong, L. A. G. Patricia Comes Home (Classic Reprint) (p. 1705)
Strong, M. D. Orphan Brothers: A Story of California (Classic Reprint) (p. 1672)
Strong, Nathan. Littlest Shepherd: A Personal Christmas. (p. 1331)
Strong, R. M. Flash. (p. 746)
—Karis. (p. 1203)
Strong, Sydney. Talks to Boys & Girls: Kite Talks; Random Talks; the Life I Ought to Live (Classic Reprint) (p. 2188)
Strong, T. W. Yankee Notions, 1854, Vol. 3 (Classic Reprint) (p. 2517)
Stroppiana, Annamaria. Bruco Peppo e Altre Favole. (p. 287)
Strother, David Hunter. Harper's New Monthly Magazine, 1857, Vol. 14: March 1857 (Classic Reprint) (p. 932)
—Virginia: Containing a Visit to the Virginian Canaan, & the Adventures of Porte Crayon & His Cousins; Illustrated (Classic Reprint) (p. 2360)
—Virginia Illustrated: Containing a Visit to the Virginian Canaan, & the Adventures of Porte Crayon & His Cousins (Classic Reprint) (p. 2361)
Strother, David Hunter & Crayon, Porte. Virginia Illustrated: Containing a Visit to the Virginian Canaan, & the Adventures of Porte Crayon & His Cousins. [New York]. (p. 2361)
Strother, Emily Vielé. Eve Dorre: The Story of Her Precarious Youth (Classic Reprint) (p. 668)
Strother, Michael, ed. see DeLonge, Tom & Young, Suzanne.
Strother, Ruth. B Is for Blue Planet: An Earth Science Alphabet. Marstall, Robert, illus. (p. 146)
—Red Foxes. (p. 1857)
—Tarantula (p. 2191)
—Tarantula Paperback. (p. 2191)
—W Is for Woof: A Dog Alphabet. Frankenhuyzen, Gijsbert van, illus. (p. 2369)
Strother, Ruth & Van Valkenburgh, Blaire. Coyote. (p. 465)
Strothmann, Frederick, jt. auth. see Twain, Mark, pseud.
Strouble, Shery. Bad Baby Chronicles: Book 1 the Fairy Tale Caper. (p. 157)
Stroud, Albert. Verdigris Valley Verse: A Volume of Original Poems (Classic Reprint) (p. 2351)
Stroud, Bettye. World's Wide Open. Cummings, Pat, illus. (p. 2508)
Stroud, Bettye, jt. auth. see Ramsey, Calvin Alexander.
Stroud, Bettye & Ramsey, Calvin Alexander. Belle, the Last Mule at Gee's Bend: A Civil Rights Story. Holyfield, John, illus. (p. 197)
Stroud, Brenda, illus. see Ennis, Ryan R.
Stroud, Brenda D., illus. see Finley, Ucal P.
Stroud, Joanne, illus. see West, Tracey.
Stroud, Jonathan. Heroes of the Valley. (p. 962)
—Heros de la Vallee. (p. 963)
—LOCKWOOD & CO. : the CREEPING SHADOW. (p. 1339)
—LOCKWOOD & CO. : the EMPTY GRAVE. (p. 1339)
—LOCKWOOD & CO. : the HOLLOW BOY. (p. 1339)
—Lockwood & Co. the Screaming Staircase. (p. 1339)
—LOCKWOOD & CO. : the WHISPERING SKULL. (p. 1339)
—Screaming Staircase. (p. 1964)
Stroud, Sean. Dog's Advice. (p. 577)
Strouse, Benjamin. Hey, Boy. Phelan, Jennifer, illus. (p. 964)
Strouse, Stephanie, illus. see Day, Sophia & Johnson, Megan.
Strouse, Stephanie, illus. see Day, Sophia, et al.
Strousse, Flora. Margaret Haughery: Bread Woman of New Orleans. (p. 1403)
Stroyer, Jacob. My Life in the South (Classic Reprint) (p. 1552)
—Sketches of My Life in the South, Vol. 1 (Classic Reprint) (p. 2031)
Strozier, M. Stefan, ed. see Phillips, Louis.
Struck, Karen. Three Paws. (p. 2234)
—Three Paws' New Family. (p. 2234)
Strudwick, Gina. Mummy Sometimes Goes Funny! Strudwick, Gina, illus. (p. 1526)
Strudwick, Leslie. Alaska: The Last Frontier. (p. 39)
—Alaska. (p. 39)
—Inuit with Code. (p. 1129)
—Maori with Code. (p. 1400)
—Oklahoma: The Sooner State. (p. 1643)
—Oklahoma. (p. 1643)
—South Dakota: The Mount Rushmore State. (p. 2068)
—South Dakota. (p. 2068)
—Washington: The Evergreen State. (p. 2381)
—Washington. (p. 2381)
Strugnell, Ann, illus. see Cameron, Ann.
Strumolo, Vinnie. Adventures of George & His Blended Family. (p. 23)
Strunsky, Rose, tr. see Gorky, Maxim.
Strunsky, Simeon. Belshazzar Court: Or Village Life in New York City (Classic Reprint) (p. 198)
—Belshazzar Court; or, Village Life in New York City. (p. 198)
—Belshazzar Court or Village Life in New York City (Classic Reprint) (p. 198)
—Patient Observer: And His Friends. (p. 1705)
—Patient Observer: And His Friends (Classic Reprint) (p. 1705)
—Professor Latimer's Progress: A Novel of Contemporaneous Adventure (Classic Reprint) (p. 1804)
—Sinbad & His Friends (Classic Reprint) (p. 2023)
—Through the Outlooking Glass (Classic Reprint) (p. 2237)
Struntz, D. J., photos by see Doherty, Patrick.
Struthers, Alfred M. Phantom Vale. (p. 1733)
Struthers, C. B. Diary Around the World: 30 Countries, 160 Places, 37, 460 Miles, Expense, $555 (Classic Reprint) (p. 539)
Struthers, Clarence Bruce. How to Be Happy Though Married (Classic Reprint) (p. 1037)
Struthers, John. Memoir on the Anatomy of the Humpback Whale, Megaptera Longimana. (p. 1444)
Strutt, Joseph. Queenhoo-Hall, a Romance, and, Ancient Times, a Drama, Vol. 3 of 4 (Classic Reprint) (p. 1824)
—Queenhoo-Hall a Romance; & Ancient Times, a Drama, Vol. 1 of 4 (Classic Reprint) (p. 1824)
—Queenhoo-Hall, a Romance, Vol. 2 Of 4: And Ancient Times, a Drama (Classic Reprint) (p. 1824)
Strutt, Lesley. On the Edge. (p. 1654)
Strutton, Richard. True Relation of the Cruelties & Barbarities of the French, upon the English Prisoners of War: Being a Journal of Their Travels from Dinan in Britany, to Thoulon in Provence, & Back Again (Classic Reprint) (p. 2294)
Struwin, Mike. Campfire Stu & the Backwoods Jamboree. (p. 316)
Struyk-Bonn, Chris. Nice Girls Endure. (p. 1602)
—Whisper (p. 2442)
Strychalski, Irene. Silk Vol. 3: The Clone Conspiracy. (p. 2018)
Strychalski, Irene, illus. see McGuire, Seanan, et al.
Strydom, Benetta. Land, Sea, Air- Babysitter Coloring Sets. (p. 1242)
Strydom, Sanette, illus. see Du Toit, Lydia.
Stryk, Suzanne, illus. see Person, Naomi, et al.
Stryker, Dale, jt. auth. see Stryker, Stephanie.
Stryker, Elizabeth. E Free Island. (p. 612)
Stryker, H. M. Cale the Corgi Learns Common Sense. (p. 309)
Stryker, Laura Kirby. Incredibly Tall Mrs. Tippet. (p. 1114)
—Mrs. Tippet Adventure Series: Mrs. Tippet Learns to Drive. (p. 1523)
Strykowski, Marcia. Call Me Amy. (p. 311)
Stuart, Arthur T. Chronicles of Service Life in Malta (Classic Reprint) (p. 389)
Stuart, B. S., illus. see Gates, Josephine Scribner.
Stuart, Carrie. Kinds of Coins: Learning the Values of Pennies, Nickels, Dimes & Quarters. (p. 1219)
Stuart, Catterson, illus. see Hil, Gibb.
Stuart, Charles Duff. Casa Grande: A California Pastoral (Classic Reprint) (p. 336)
Stuart, Colin. Astonishing Atoms & Matter Mayhem: Science. (p. 128)
—Astonishing Atoms & Matter Mayhem. (p. 128)
—Fabulous Figures & Cool Calculations: Math. (p. 692)
—Fabulous Figures & Cool Calculations. (p. 692)
—Speed of Starlight: An Exploration of Physics, Sound, Light, & Space. Abadia, Ximo, illus. (p. 2078)
—Why Space Matters to Me. (p. 2459)
Stuart, Eleanor. Stonepastures (Classic Reprint) (p. 2121)
Stuart, Elizabeth Billings. Delightful Stories for Children. (p. 527)
Stuart, Emma, illus. see Grace, Lani.
Stuart, Esme. Harum Scarum: The Story of a Wild Girl (Classic Reprint) (p. 935)
—Mine of Wealth, Vol. 1 of 3 (Classic Reprint) (p. 1470)
—Sent to Coventry (Classic Reprint) (p. 1989)
—Woman of Forty: A Monograph (Classic Reprint) (p. 2485)
—Woman of Forty, Vol. 1 Of 2: A Monograph (Classic Reprint) (p. 2485)
Stuart, Evan. Ellia the Elephant: Outside the Herd. (p. 637)
Stuart, Florence. Punchinello (Classic Reprint) (p. 1813)
Stuart, Florence Partello. Adventures of Piang the Moro Jungle Boy: A Book for Young & Old. (p. 26)
—Adventures of Piang, the Moro Jungle Boy: A Book for Young & Old (Classic Reprint) (p. 26)
Stuart, George R. Sermons (Classic Reprint) (p. 1991)
Stuart, Gordon. Boy Scouts of the Air on Lost Island. (p. 270)
Stuart, Hazel. Where the Cat Led. Beable, Georgie, illus. (p. 2439)
Stuart, Henry Longan. Fenella: A Novel (Classic Reprint) (p. 720)
Stuart, John Sobieski. Tales of the Century: Or Sketches of the Romance of History Between the Years 1746 & 1846 (Classic Reprint) (p. 2185)
Stuart, Jon, illus. see Baker, Catherine.
Stuart, Jon, illus. see DeRidder, Mauritz.
Stuart, Jon, illus. see Pritchard, Gabby.
Stuart, Katharine. True Women, Vol. 1 Of 3: A Love Story (Classic Reprint) (p. 2295)
—True Women, Vol. 2 Of 3: A Love Story (Classic Reprint) (p. 2295)
—True Women, Vol. 3 Of 3: A Love Story (Classic Reprint) (p. 2295)
Stuart, Liam. Parade: Understand Place Value. (p. 1698)

Suben, Eric. Elves & the Shoemaker. Won, Annie, illus. (p. 640)
—Spanish Missions of Florida. (p. 2074)
Suber, Lisa Martin. There's a Bee in My Book Bag! A Tale with Two Sides. (p. 2217)
Suber, Melissa, illus. see Meng, Cece.
Subi, illus. see Obiols, Anna.
Subisak, Tracy, illus. see Davis-Pyles, Barbara.
Subisak, Tracy, illus. see Larson, Kirsten W.
Subisak, Tracy, illus. see Stephens, Ann Marie.
Subramaniam, Manasi. Dancing Bear. Gwangjo & Park, Jung-a, illus. (p. 500)
—Story & the Song. Sankaranarayanan, Ayswarya, illus. (p. 2127)
Subramanian, Mathangi. Bullying: The Ultimate Teen Guide (p. 297)
Subramanian, Samanth. Following Fish: Travels Around the Indi. (p. 758)
Subrina. Jacko the Monkey. (p. 1153)
Subzwari, Noumaan, jt. auth. see Goh, Matthew Kai Jun.
Sucheta, Rawal. Beato Goes to Israel. (p. 183)
Suchy, Julianne. Leaf Me Alone. (p. 1254)
Sudbury, Richard. Two Gentlemen in Touraine (Classic Reprint) (p. 2307)
Sudbury, Wayside Inn. Wayside Inn Diary (Classic Reprint) (p. 2388)
—Wayside Inn Front Door Diaries: April-June, 1931 (Classic Reprint) (p. 2388)
—Wayside Inn Front Door Diaries, 1938 (Classic Reprint) (p. 2388)
Suddeth, Charles. Spearfinger: English/Cherokee Version. (p. 2076)
Sudeith, Alaina. Superman Classic: The Superman Reusable Sticker Book. (p. 2160)
Suderman, Colleen C. Norgee & the Christmas Tree: A Norgee Story. (p. 1619)
Sudermann, Hermann. Dame Care (Classic Reprint) (p. 499)
—Far-Away Princess: A Comedy in One Act (Classic Reprint) (p. 708)
—Indian Lily: And Other Stories (Classic Reprint) (p. 1116)
—Iolanthe's Wedding (Classic Reprint) (p. 1133)
—Regina: Or the Sins of the Fathers (Classic Reprint) (p. 1861)
—Silent Mill (Classic Reprint) (p. 2017)
—Song of Songs (Classic Reprint) (p. 2062)
—St. John's Fire: A Drama in Four Acts (Classic Reprint) (p. 2096)
—Undying Past (Classic Reprint) (p. 2326)
—Wish: A Novel (Classic Reprint) (p. 2478)
Sudermann, Hermann, et al. Wish. (p. 2478)
Sudha, Murthy. How I Taught My Grand Mother to Read. (p. 1032)
Sudha Murti. Bird with Golden Wings: Stories of Wit & Magic. (p. 231)
Sudipta, Dasgupta, illus. see Blom, Tracy.
Sudo, Kumiko. Coco-Chan's Kimono. Sudo, Kumiko, illus. (p. 411)
Sudworth, George Bishop. Check List of the Forest Trees of the United States, Their Names & Ranges (Classic Reprint) (p. 363)
Sudyka, Diana, illus. see Barrett, Hayley.
Sudyka, Diana, illus. see Buzzeo, Toni.
Sudyka, Diana, illus. see Fleming, Meg.
Sudyka, Diana, illus. see Springstubb, Tricia.
Sudyka, Diana, illus. see Stewart, Trenton Lee.
Sudyka, Diana, illus. see Ward, Jennifer.
Sudzuka, Goran, et al. Daredevil: Back in Black Vol. 4: Identity. (p. 505)
Sue, Bright-Moore, jt. auth. see Miller, Reagan.
Sue, Eugene. Abbatial Crosier: Or Bonaik & Septimine, a Tale of a Medieval Abbess (Classic Reprint) (p. 3)
—Brass Bell: Or the Chariot of Death; a Tale of Caesar's Gallic Invasion (Classic Reprint) (p. 275)
—Casque's Lark: Or Victoria, the Mother of the Camps, a Tale (Classic Reprint) (p. 339)
—Gold Sickle: Or Hena, the Virgin of the Isle of Sen; a Tale of Druid Gaul (Classic Reprint) (p. 856)
—Infant's Skull: Or the End of the World, a Tale of the Millennium (Classic Reprint) (p. 1118)
—Iron Pincers: Or Mylio & Karvel; a Tale of the Albigensian Crusades (Classic Reprint) (p. 1135)
—Martin, the Foundling, or Memoirs of a Valet de Chambre (Classic Reprint) (p. 1411)
—Mysteries of Paris: (volume I) (p. 1566)
—Mysteries of Paris: (volume V) (p. 1566)
—Mysteries of Paris: (volume II) (p. 1566)
—Mysteries of Paris: (volume IV) (p. 1566)
—Mysteries of Paris: (volume VI) (p. 1566)
—Mysteries of Paris: (volume III) (p. 1566)
—Mysteries of Paris: A Novel (Classic Reprint) (p. 1566)
—Mysteries of Paris, Vol. 1 (Classic Reprint) (p. 1566)
—Poniard's Hilt, or Karadeucq & Ronan: A Tale of Bagauders & Vagres (Classic Reprint) (p. 1773)
—Seven Cardinal Sins, Vol. 4 Of 5: Avarice, Anger (Classic Reprint) (p. 1993)
—Silver Cross, or the Carpenter of Nazareth: A Tale of Jerusalem (Classic Reprint) (p. 2019)
—Wandering Jew, Vol. 1 of 3 (Classic Reprint) (p. 2375)
—Work of Eugene Sue, Vol. 4 Of 20: Illustrated with Original Etchings (Classic Reprint) (p. 2495)
Sue, Grandma. Zibbins: The Golden Necklace. (p. 2540)
Sue, Wickstead. Christmas Play Rehearsal. (p. 386)
—Daisy Daydream the Nursery Rhyme Bus. (p. 497)
Sue-C, Professor. Auggie the Dragon Who Lives on Gramma Sue's Roof. (p. 136)
Suedkamp, Shirley M. Cat Who Lost His Meow. (p. 342)
Suen, Anastasia. Arctic Foxes. (p. 112)
—Asociación para la prevención de la crueldad de los animales, ASPCA (the Association for the Prevention of Cruelty to Animals) (p. 126)
—Association for the Prevention of Cruelty to Animals. (p. 127)
—Aviones supersónicos (Supersonic Jets) (p. 143)
—Baby Born Chang, Chih-Wei, illus. (p. 149)
—Big Catch: A Robot & Rico Story Laughead, Mike, illus. (p. 219)
—Birthday Gifts. (p. 233)
—Calves. (p. 312)
—Career Building Through Using Search Engine Optimization Techniques. (p. 328)
—Careers with Swat Teams. (p. 330)
—Chicks. (p. 369)
—Circuitry & Electronics. (p. 393)
—Craft & Design 3-D. (p. 466)
—Cruz Roja (the Red Cross) (p. 480)
—Cuerpo de Paz (the Peace Corps) (p. 483)
—Dino Hunt: A Robot & Rico Story. Laughead, Mike, illus. (p. 547)
—Doctors Without Borders. (p. 574)
—Downloading & Online Shopping Safety & Privacy. (p. 591)
—Ducklings. (p. 608)
—Father's Day Gifts. (p. 715)
—Foals. (p. 755)
—From Accident to Hospital. (p. 790)
—Getting a Job in Child Care. (p. 825)
—Great Idea? An Up2U Character Education Adventure Dippold, Jane, illus. (p. 887)
—Gulf Coast Region. (p. 905)
—Habitat for Humanity. (p. 908)
—Hábitat para la Humanidad (Habitat for Humanity) (p. 908)
—historia del baloncesto (the Story of Basketball) (p. 975)
—historia del béisbol (the Story of Baseball) (p. 975)
—historia del fútbol (the Story of Soccer) (p. 975)
—historia del fútbol americano (the Story of Football) (p. 975)
—historia del hockey (the Story of Hockey) (p. 975)
—historia del patinaje artístico (the Story of Figure Skating) (p. 975)
—Holiday Gifts. (p. 987)
—How to Bake a Cake. (p. 1037)
—How to Make a Piñata. (p. 1043)
—How to Make an Ant Farm. (p. 1043)
—How to Start a Lemonade Stand. (p. 1044)
—In the Big City. Myer, Ed, illus. (p. 1108)
—IPod & Electronics Visionary Tony Fadell. (p. 1133)
—Johnny Appleseed. Myer, Ed, illus. (p. 1174)
—Kids. (p. 1213)
—Kittens. (p. 1226)
—Lambs. (p. 1240)
—Main Street School ~Kids with Character Set 2 - 6 Titles (p. 1383)
—Médicos sin Fronteras (Doctors Without Borders) (p. 1436)
—Miniature Robots. (p. 1472)
—Mother's Day Gifts. (p. 1510)
—Mountain Region. (p. 1514)
—Moving Machines. (p. 1516)
—New Girl: An Up2U Character Education Adventure Dippold, Jane, illus. (p. 1594)
—Noche de Terror. Heck, Claudia M., tr. (p. 1617)
—Orcas. (p. 1669)
—Peace Corps. (p. 1709)
—Pirate Map: A Robot & Rico Story. Laughead, Mike, illus. (p. 1750)
—Polar Bears. (p. 1769)
—Premio Adentro. Heck, Claudia M., tr. (p. 1787)
—Prize Inside: A Robot & Rico Story Laughead, Mike, illus. (p. 1802)
—Puppies. (p. 1814)
—Read & Write Sports: Readers Theatre & Writing Activities for Grades 3-8 (p. 1845)
—Recién Nacido Chang, Chih-Wei, illus. (p. 1853)
—Red Cross. (p. 1856)
—Reindeer. (p. 1862)
—Respecting Diversity. (p. 1869)
—Scary Night: A Robot & Rico Story Laughead, Mike, illus. (p. 1943)
—Sea Otters. (p. 1968)
—Skate Trick: A Robot & Rico Story Laughead, Mike, illus. (p. 2029)
—Snow Games: A Robot & Rico Story. Laughead, Mike, illus. (p. 2047)
—Snowy Owls. (p. 2049)
—Story of Baseball. (p. 2129)
—Story of Basketball. (p. 2129)
—Story of Soccer. (p. 2132)
—Test Drive: A Robot & Rico Story. Laughead, Mike, illus. (p. 2208)
—Toco Toucans: Bright Enough to Disappear. (p. 2254)
—Top STEM Careers in Science. (p. 2264)
—Trucos en la Patineta. Heck, Claudia M., tr. (p. 2293)
—Unicef. (p. 2328)
—Unicef (unicef) (p. 2328)
—Up! up! up! Skyscraper. O'Rourke, Ryan, illus. (p. 2338)
—Valentine's Day Gifts. (p. 2344)
—Video Animation & Photography. (p. 2356)
—We're Going on a Dinosaur Dig. Myer, Ed, illus. (p. 2400)
Suen, Anastasia & Heck, Claudia M. Gran Pesca. Laughead, Mike, illus. (p. 876)
Suerken, Kathy & Suerken, John. Story of Yani's Goal: Yani Learns How to Become a Teacher. (p. 2135)
—Story of Yani's Goal: Yani Learns How to Use Clouds to Solve Problems. (p. 2135)
—Story of Yani's Goal: Yani Learns How to Achieve Goals by Creating a Plan to Overcome Obstacles. (p. 2135)
Suerth, Renata. Wig: Cold Feet (Book 4) (p. 2461)
—Wig: When Pigs Fly (Book 5) (p. 2461)
Suess, Eduard, jt. auth. see Sollas, William Johnson.
Suesse et al., Lynne. Pixar Toy Story Look & Find Collection. (p. 1752)
Suffling, E. R. Jethou or Crusoe Life in the Channel Isles. (p. 1167)
—Jethou, or Crusoe Life in the Channel Isles (Classic Reprint) (p. 1167)
Suffling, Ernest R. Innocents on the Broads (Classic Reprint) (p. 1121)
Sugar Snap Studio, jt. auth. see Ford, Jessie.
Sugar Snap Studio & Ford, Jessie. ABC for Me: ABC What Can I Be? YOU Can Be Anything YOU Want to Be, from a to Z. (p. 4)
Sugarek, Trisha. Exciting Exploits of an Effervescent Elf. (p. 676)
Sugarman, Dorothy Alexander, jt. auth. see Herwick Rice, Dona.
Sugarman, Dorothy Alexander, jt. auth. see Rice, Dona Herwick.
Sugeeta, Fribourg. Enfants de Titaniah(les) (p. 651)
Sugg, Zoe. Girl Online: On Tour. (p. 836)
—Girl Online: Going Solo. (p. 836)
—Girl Online: The First Novel by Zoella. (p. 836)
—Girl Online. (p. 836)
Suggs, Eliza. Shadow & Sunshine (Classic Reprint) (p. 1996)
Suggs, Elizabeth, ed. see Pardew, David.
Suggs, Margaret, illus. see Magee, Wes.
Suggs, Margaret Anne, illus. see Hartman, Davida.
Suggs, Margaret Anne, illus. see Jessop, Connie.
Suggs, Margaret Anne, illus. see La Branche, Eric.
Suggs, Margaret Anne, illus. see Watkins, Kathleen.
Suggs, Rob. Comic Book Bible. (p. 429)
Suggs, Rob, jt. auth. see Strobel, Lee.
Suggs, Robb, jt. auth. see Wilkinson, Bruce.
Sugimoto, Nao. 100 Shapes. (p. 2557)
Sugisaki, Yukiru, jt. auth. see Clamp Staff.
Sugita, Yataka, illus. see Beach, Stewart.
Sugiura, Misa. It's Not Like It's a Secret. (p. 1146)
—This Time Will Be Different. (p. 2227)
Sugralinov, Dan. Apostle of the Sleeping Gods (Disgardium Book #2) LitRPG Series. (p. 106)
—Gefahrenklasse a (Disgardium Buch #1) LitRPG-Serie. (p. 813)
Suhrie, Ambrose L. Spell to-Write Spelling Books, Vol. 3 (Classic Reprint) (p. 2079)
—Spell-To-Write Spelling Books. (p. 2079)
—Spell-To-Write, Spelling Books, Book One. (p. 2079)
—Spell-To-Write Spelling Books. Book Two. (p. 2079)
—Spell-To-Write Spelling Books, Vol. 2 (Classic Reprint) (p. 2079)
Suhrie, Ambrose Leo. Spell-To-Write Spelling Books (Classic Reprint) (p. 2079)
—Spell-To-Write Spelling Books, Vol. 1 (Classic Reprint) (p. 2079)
Suits, Barbara Bradford. Hidden Treasure. (p. 966)
Suits, Danial a. Assignment. (p. 127)
—Diner by the Lake. (p. 547)
Suits, Rosella, illus. see Ostrom, Gladys.
Suk, Amanda. Life Lessons with Libra Ryan. (p. 1293)
Sukaczer, Veronica. Nombres Prestados. (p. 1618)
Sukanada, I. Gusti Made, illus. see Bowler, Ann Martin.
Sukarno, Achmad, illus. see Lowry, Jane.
Sukhin, Igor. Gary's Adventures in Chess Country. (p. 810)
Sukhomlinsky, Vasily. Meide Shijie. (p. 1442)
—Mir Krasoty: Pavlyshskie Skazki. (p. 1474)
—Svit Krasy: Kazki Z Pavlysha. (p. 2167)
—World of Beauty: Tales from Pavlysh. (p. 2502)
Sukloff, Marie. Life-Story of a Russian Exile: The Remarkable Experience of a Young Girl, Being an Account of Her Peasant Childhood, Her Girlhood in Prison, Her Exile to Siberia, & Escape from There (Classic Reprint) (p. 1296)
Sukmanindya, Windha, illus. see Reich, Tina.
SukWon, Sa, illus. see SungJa, Cho.
Sulayman, X., jt. auth. see X, Sulayman.
Suleiman, C. A., ed. see Burke, Kealan Patrick, et al.
Suleman, Shilo Shiv, illus. see R. N., Lavanya.
Suleman, Shilo Shiv, illus. see Ranade, Soumitra.
Suleyman, R. H. Tales Within. (p. 2187)
Sulik, Alberta, illus. see Mancuso, Kathleen.
Sulit, William, illus. see Kephart, Beth.
Sulivan, Robert. Raff Hall, Vol. 1 of 3 (Classic Reprint) (p. 1834)
—Raff Hall, Vol. 2 of 3 (Classic Reprint) (p. 1834)
—Raff Hall, Vol. 3 of 3 (Classic Reprint) (p. 1834)
Sulkin, Sidney. Latin School Register, Vol. 54: November 1934 (Classic Reprint) (p. 1251)
Sullen, Jordan. Mally in the Middle. (p. 1392)
Sullen, Jordan C. Flower, Flower, Give Her Power. (p. 752)
Sullens, Anais, illus. see Diabate, Keba & Sumnicht, Patricia.
Sulley, Robert. First Aid in Mathematics. (p. 735)
Sullivan, Erin. Matemáticas en la Luna. Hanner, Albert, illus. (p. 1421)
Sullivan, Alan. Blantyre-Alien (Classic Reprint) (p. 243)
—Cariboo Road (Classic Reprint) (p. 330)
—Inner Door (Classic Reprint) (p. 1121)
—Passing of Oul-I-But & Other Tales (Classic Reprint) (p. 1703)
—Rapids (Classic Reprint) (p. 1841)
Sullivan, Alesha. Funny Tricks & Practical Jokes to Play on Your Friends. (p. 801)
—Wacky Word Games to Play with Your Friends. (p. 2370)
Sullivan, Alesha, jt. auth. see Dahl, Michael.
Sullivan & Buchanan. Programmed Reading 1. (p. 1805)
Sullivan, Ann. Florida: The Sunshine State. (p. 751)
—Florida. (p. 751)
Sullivan, Ann, jt. auth. see Durrie, Karen.
Sullivan, Anne Marie. Albert Einstein: Great Scientist. (p. 40)
—Dalai Lama: Spiritual Leader of Tibet. (p. 498)
—Mother Teresa: Religious Humanitarian. (p. 1510)
—Syria (p. 2174)
—Syria. (p. 2174)
Sullivan, Annie. Curse of Gold (p. 488)
—Tiger Queen (p. 2241)
—Touch of Gold (p. 2268)
Sullivan, Arabella Jane. Recollections of a Chaperon (Classic Reprint) (p. 1853)
—Recollections of a Chaperon, Vol. 1 of 3 (Classic Reprint) (p. 1853)
—Tales of the Peerage & the Peasantry (Classic Reprint) (p. 2186)
Sullivan, Arthur. Cox & Box, or the Long Lost Brothers: A Comic Opera in One Act (Classic Reprint) (p. 465)
—Flashes from the Pan: A Fantasia in Retrospectio & Imaginatio (Classic Reprint) (p. 747)
—H. M. S. Pinafore, or the Lass That Loved a Sailor: An Entirely Original Nautical Comic Opera, in Two Acts (Classic Reprint) (p. 908)
—H. M. S. Pinafore, or the Lass That Loved a Sailor (Classic Reprint) (p. 908)
Sullivan, Arthur, jt. auth. see Gilbert, William Schwenck.
Sullivan, Ayn Cates. Sparkle & the Light. duCray, Belle Crow, illus. (p. 2075)
Sullivan, Candida. Zippy & the Stripes of Courage. (p. 2541)
—Zippy y Las Rayas de Valor. Foster, Jack, illus. (p. 2541)
Sullivan, Colleen Baxter. Charlotte & the Police Officer. (p. 360)
—Doctor Sam & the Ice Cream Stand. (p. 573)
—My Dentist & a Trip to the Stars. (p. 1537)
Sullivan, Collen Baxter. Grace's Missing Ball. (p. 873)
Sullivan, Courtney. Reptiles at the Zoo: Divide Within 100 (p. 1867)
Sullivan, Dana. Deadening: Book 1. Sullivan, Dana, illus. (p. 518)
—Kay Kay's Alphabet Safari. Sullivan, Dana, illus. (p. 1207)
—My Red Velvet Cape. Sullivan, Dana, illus. (p. 1559)
—Ozzie & the Art Contest. Sullivan, Dana, illus. (p. 1690)
—Rocking Dead: Book 2. Sullivan, Dana, illus. (p. 1895)
Sullivan, Dana, illus. see Kertell, Lynn Maslen.
Sullivan, Dana, illus. see Young, Judy.
Sullivan, Dana, jt. auth. see Young, Judy.
Sullivan, Daniel. Spun Yarns from the Full Reel of Daniel Sullivan, Ex-Liar Laureate to His Highness, the Late Baron Munchausen: A Record of Wonderful Things (Classic Reprint) (p. 2093)
Sullivan, Debbie. Lucy & Henrietta the Hummingbird. (p. 1365)
Sullivan, Deena. Finn Beloomey & His Great Big Giant Ears. (p. 731)
Sullivan, Deirdre. Ming & Her Poppy. Löfdahl, Maja, illus. (p. 1471)
—Ming Goes to School. Löfdahl, Maja, illus. (p. 1471)
—Tangleweed & Brine. Vaughan, Karen H., illus. (p. 2190)
Sullivan, Derek, illus. see MacDonald, Margaret Read.
Sullivan, Derek, illus. see Sullivan, Kyle.
Sullivan, Derek E. Biggie. (p. 225)
Sullivan, Don, jt. auth. see Boniface, William.
Sullivan, Edmund Joseph, jt. auth. see Hughes, Thomas.
Sullivan, Erin. Baseball Math. (p. 169)
—Baseball Math & el juego de Béisbol: 6 English, 6 Spanish Adaptations (p. 169)
—Cookie Count! (p. 446)
—Cookie Count! & la venta de Galletas: 6 English, 6 Spanish Adaptations (p. 446)
—Juego de Béisbol: Set Of 6. (p. 1186)
—Los Matemáticos. (p. 1351)
—Matemáticas en los Deportes: Set Of 6. (p. 1421)
—Math on the Moon & Matemáticas en la Luna: 6 English, 6 Spanish Adaptations Hanner, Albert, illus. (p. 1424)
—Mathematical Thinkers & Los Matemáticos: 6 English, 6 Spanish Adaptations (p. 1424)
—Probabilidad: Set Of 6. (p. 1802)
—Probability. (p. 1802)
—Sports Math & Matemáticas en los Deportes: 6 English, 6 Spanish Adaptations (p. 2089)
—Tesoro: Set Of 6. (p. 2208)
—Treasure Hunt & el Tesoro: 6 English, 6 Spanish Adaptations (p. 2281)
—Venta de Galletas: Set Of 6. (p. 2350)
Sullivan, Erin Ash. Ancient Rome: Set Of 6. (p. 82)
—Class Election: Set Of 6. (p. 399)
—Communities Helping Communities: Set Of 6. (p. 431)
—Counting Clues: Set Of 6. (p. 460)
—Counting Clues. (p. 460)
—Holidays Around the World: Set Of 6. (p. 988)
—Human Body Math: Set Of 6. (p. 1049)
—Human Body Math & Matemáticas del cuerpo Humano: 6 English, 6 Spanish Adaptations. (p. 1049)
—Liquids & Gases: Set Of 6. (p. 1308)
—Math Around the Globe: Set Of 6. (p. 1421)
—Math Around the Globe & Matemáticas alrededor del Mundo: 6 English, 6 Spanish Adaptations. (p. 1421)
—Math at the Olympics: Set Of 6. (p. 1421)
—Math at the Olympics & Matemáticas en las Olimpiadas: 6 English, 6 Spanish Adaptations. (p. 1421)
—Math in a Democracy: Set Of 6. (p. 1423)
—Math in a Democracy & Matemáticas en una Democracia: 6 English, 6 Spanish Adaptations. (p. 1423)
—Measuring Matter: Set Of 6. (p. 1435)
—Metric Math: Set Of 6. (p. 1453)
—Metric Math & Matemáticas Métricas: 6 English, 6 Spanish Adaptations. (p. 1453)
—Music Counts: Set Of 6. (p. 1528)
—Music Counts & Cálculos Musicales: 6 English, 6 Spanish Adaptations. (p. 1528)
—Patterns in Nature: Set Of 6. (p. 1706)
—Pyramids: Set Of 6. (p. 1819)
—Pyramids. (p. 1819)
—Seven Wonders of the Ancient World. (p. 1994)
—Seven Wonders of the Ancient World & Las siete maravillas del mundo Antiguo: 6 English, 6 Spanish Adaptations. (p. 1994)
Sullivan, Erin Ash, jt. auth. see Sohn, Emily.
Sullivan, Erin Ash & Benchmark Education Company, LLC Staff. Líquidos y Gases: Set of 6 Common Core Edition. (p. 1308)
—Matemáticas en una Democracia: Set of 6 Common Core Edition. (p. 1421)
—Medir la Materia: Set of 6 Common Core Edition. (p. 1437)
—Puentes líquidos y Gases: Set of 6 with Common Core Teacher Materials. (p. 1811)
—Puentes Medir la Materia: Set of 6 with Common Core Teacher Materials. (p. 1811)
Sullivan et al., Steve. Mission Paw. (p. 1481)
Sullivan, Francis William. Children of Banishment (Classic Reprint) (p. 371)
—Star of the North (Classic Reprint) (p. 2102)
Sullivan, George. Book of U. S. Presidents. (p. 260)
—Click! Click! Click! Photography for Children. (p. 404)
Sullivan, Jaclyn. What's in Your Chicken Nugget? (p. 2424)
—What's in Your Hamburger? (p. 2424)
—What's in Your Hot Dog? (p. 2424)
—What's in Your Pizza? (p. 2424)
—What's in Your Soda? (p. 2424)

Full bibliographic information is available on the Title Index page number referenced in parentheses at the end of each entry

Sullivan, James Frank. British Working Man by One Who Does Not Believe in Him: And Other Sketches (Classic Reprint) (p. 284)
Sullivan, James William. So the World Goes (Classic Reprint) (p. 2050)
Sullivan, Jas F. Queer Side Stories (Classic Reprint) (p. 1825)
Sullivan, Jillian. Rigby Reading Sails: Leveled Reader Emerald Grades 4-5 Book 5: Out of Bounds. (p. 1881)
—Rigby Reading Sails: Leveled Reader Silver Grades 4-5 Book 15: Billy & the Thrush. (p. 1881)
—Rigby Reading Sails: Leveled Reader Silver Grades 4-5 Book 23: Ela & the Dog Choice. (p. 1881)
Sullivan, Jody. Crabs [Scholastic]. (p. 465)
—Sea Stars [Scholastic]. (p. 1969)
Sullivan, Jody, jt. auth. see Lindeen, Carol K.
Sullivan, John. Kitten & the Night Watchman. Yoo, Taeeun, illus. (p. 1225)
Sullivan, Kate. On Linden Square. Sullivan, Kate, illus. (p. 1652)
—What Do You Hear? (p. 2409)
Sullivan, Kathleen, jt. auth. see Craft, Jerry.
Sullivan, Kathryn. Crystal Throne. (p. 481)
—Michael & the Elf. Dunningham, Jo, illus. (p. 1457)
—Talking to Trees. (p. 2187)
Sullivan, Kathy, jt. auth. see Van Vleet, Carmella.
Sullivan, Kayla. Talkin' to Angels. (p. 2187)
Sullivan, Kelsey. This Is Captain Marvel. (p. 2224)
Sullivan, Kevin. New Beginning. (p. 1591)
Sullivan, Kevin & Goldman, Leslie. Anne & the Bully. (p. 98)
—Anne's Babysitting Blues. (p. 99)
—Anne's Red Hair. (p. 99)
Sullivan, Kevin & Morgan, Elizabeth. Anne's New Home. (p. 99)
Sullivan, Kiki. Dolls. (p. 579)
—Midnight Dolls. (p. 1461)
Sullivan, Kimberly L. Slobodan Milosevic's Yugoslavia. (p. 2038)
Sullivan, Kitty. Silence of Nellie. (p. 2017)
Sullivan, Kyle. Don't Eat Me, Chupacabra! / ¡No Me Comas, Chupacabra! A Delicious Story with Digestible Spanish Vocabulary. Sullivan, Derek, illus. (p. 582)
—Get Dressed, Sasquatch! Sullivan, Derek, illus. (p. 823)
—Goodnight Krampus. Sullivan, Derek, illus. (p. 867)
—Hazy Dell Press 5-Book Gift Set: Monster ABC, Goodnight Krampus, Get Dressed, Sasquatch!, Hush Now Banshee! & Don't Eat Me, Chupacabra!/¡No Me Comas, Chupacabra! Sullivan, Derek, illus. (p. 941)
—Hush Now, Banshee! A Not-So-Quiet Counting Book. Sullivan, Derek, illus. (p. 1055)
—Monster ABC. Sullivan, Derek, illus. (p. 1495)
Sullivan, Laura. Colonial Cook. (p. 418)
—Flowering & Nonflowering Plants Explained. (p. 752)
—Insects & Arachnids Explained. (p. 1122)
—Saltwater & Freshwater Creatures Explained. (p. 1925)
Sullivan, Laura L. 24 Hours in an Estuary. (p. 2554)
—24 Hours in the Ocean. (p. 2554)
—Black Bart Roberts. (p. 236)
—Blackbeard. (p. 240)
—Blue-Ringed Octopus. (p. 249)
—Bonnie & Clyde: A Deadly Duo. Abbott, Graham, illus. (p. 256)
—Box Jellyfish. (p. 266)
—Building the Empire State Building. (p. 295)
—Building the Statue of Liberty. (p. 295)
—Charles Darwin: Groundbreaking Naturalist & Evolutionary Theorist (p. 358)
—Colonial Dressmaker. (p. 418)
—Colonial Minuteman. (p. 418)
—Colonial Slave Family. (p. 418)
—Colonial Wigmaker. (p. 418)
—Colonial Woodworker. (p. 418)
—Cuba (p. 482)
—Deathstalker Scorpion. (p. 522)
—Delusion. (p. 527)
—Gail Carson Levine. (p. 805)
—Geronimo (p. 823)
—How Animals Taste. (p. 1025)
—How Do Objects Move? (p. 1029)
—How Does Sound Move? (p. 1030)
—Jacqueline Woodson. (p. 1154)
—Ladies in Waiting. (p. 1236)
—Life As a Cowboy in the American West. (p. 1290)
—Life As a Mississippi Riverboat Captain. (p. 1290)
—Life As a Passenger on the Mayflower. (p. 1290)
—Life As a Spy in the American Revolution. (p. 1290)
—Life As an Ambulance Driver in World War I. (p. 1290)
—Life As an Explorer with Lewis & Clark. (p. 1290)
—Malaysia. (p. 1391)
—Myanmar. (p. 1566)
—Pallas Athena (p. 1694)
—Pocahontas (p. 1763)
—Poison Dart Frog. (p. 1767)
—Pros & Cons of Solar Power. (p. 1807)
—Romania (p. 1900)
—Saudi Arabia. (p. 1937)
—Sir Henry Morgan. (p. 2025)
—Soil for Fossils & History. (p. 2055)
—South Korea. (p. 2069)
—Sri Lanka. (p. 2095)
—Under the Green Hill (p. 2322)
—Under the Green Hill. (p. 2322)
—Venezuela (p. 2350)
—What Is Gravity? (p. 2415)
—What Is Heat? (p. 2415)
—What Is Motion? (p. 2415)
—Yo-Yo Ma: Cellist (p. 2522)
Sullivan, Laura L., jt. auth. see Pateman, Robert.
Sullivan, Laura L., jt. auth. see Sabic-El-Rayess, Amra.
Sullivan, Laura L., jt. auth. see Shankman, Adam.
Sullivan, Laura L., et al. Georgia. (p. 820)
—Tennessee. (p. 2206)
—Virginia. (p. 2360)
Sullivan, Lauren M. & Lewis, Samantha. Chipwrecked. (p. 379)
Sullivan, Lee. Have You Ever Felt Angry? (p. 939)
—Have You Ever Felt Anxious? Supporting Parents to Talk to Their Children about Uncomfortable or Unfamiliar Feelings. (p. 939)
—Have You Ever Felt Down? (p. 939)
—Have You Ever Felt Like Crying? (p. 939)
Sullivan, Licsw. Mindfully Me! (p. 1470)
Sullivan, Lisa, compiled by. Happy Days. (p. 921)
Sullivan, Margaret Davies. Goddess of the Dawn: A Romance (Classic Reprint) (p. 852)
Sullivan, Mark. Collier's, Vol. 50: The National Weekly; September 21, 1912 (Classic Reprint) (p. 416)
—Collier's, Vol. 57: The National Weekly; September 9, 1916 (Classic Reprint) (p. 416)
Sullivan, Martha. Around My City: Describe & Compare Measurable Attributes. (p. 118)
—If You Love Honey. Morrison, Cathy, illus. (p. 1093)
—Pitter & Patter Morrison, Cathy, illus. (p. 1751)
Sullivan, Mary. Ball. (p. 161)
—Frankie. (p. 778)
—Nobody's Duck. (p. 1617)
—Up on Bob. (p. 2338)
Sullivan, Mary, illus. see Connolly, Timothy.
Sullivan, Mary, illus. see Gaydos, Nora.
Sullivan, Mary, illus. see Jones, Christianne C.
Sullivan, Mary, illus. see Mortensen, Lori.
Sullivan, Mary, illus. see Sateren, Shelley Swanson.
Sullivan, Mary, illus. see Stiefel, Chana.
Sullivan, Mary, illus. see Swanson Sateren, Shelley.
Sullivan, Mary, illus. see Wax, Wendy.
Sullivan, Mary Ann. Owen Castle, or Which Is the Heroine?, Vol. 2 Of 4: A Novel (Classic Reprint) (p. 1688)
—Owen Castle, Vol. 1 Of 4: Or Which Is the Heroine? a Novel (Classic Reprint) (p. 1688)
Sullivan, Mary C. Bugs! a Counting Book. Sullivan, Mary C., illus. (p. 292)
Sullivan, Maureen. Cabbages & Queens. Ferrando, Carol, illus. (p. 307)
—Custard & Mustard: Carlos in Coney Island. Josephs, Alison, illus. (p. 490)
Sullivan, May Kellogg. Trail of a Sourdough: Life in Alaska (Classic Reprint) (p. 2274)
—Woman Who Went to Alaska (Classic Reprint) (p. 2486)
Sullivan, Megan. Clarissa's Disappointment: And Resources for Families, Teachers & Counselors of Children of Incarcerated Parents. Jay, Daniel, illus. (p. 399)
Sullivan, Melody. Lillibit's Dream. Grof, Stanislav, illus. (p. 1301)
Sullivan, Michael John & Petrone, Susan. Sockkids Meet Lincoln. (p. 2054)
Sullivan Moore, Carolyn. Chance, the Incredible, Wonderful, Three-Legged Dog & Making Friends. (p. 355)
Sullivan, Myra L., ed. see Sullivan, R. J.
Sullivan, Nancy & Sullivan, Eddie. Magical Town of Freezyville: Secret Adventures of the North Pole. (p. 1380)
—Wish for a Christmas Fish: Secret Adventures of the North Pole. (p. 2478)
Sullivan, Navin. Measure Up! (p. 1434)
Sullivan, Neil. Little House That Didn't Have a Home. Burke, Steven, illus. (p. 1319)
—My Grandad Can Draw Anything: But, He Can't Draw Hands! Burke, Steven, illus. (p. 1548)
Sullivan, Otha Richard. African American Inventors. Haskins, Jim, ed. (p. 32)
Sullivan, Paul. Breaker at Dawn. (p. 278)
Sullivan, R. K. Because of You. (p. 186)
Sullivan, Rebecca. Night Owls & Summer Skies. (p. 1607)
Sullivan, Richard. Fresh & Open Sky: And Other Stories (Classic Reprint) (p. 784)
Sullivan, Richard T. R. Principles of Powerful Prayer: A Practical Plan for Prayer. (p. 1800)
Sullivan, Robert & Vanloon, Hendrik Willem. Story of Mankind. (p. 2131)
Sullivan, Rosana. Mommy Sayang: Pixar Animation Studios Artist Showcase. Sullivan, Rosana, illus. (p. 1491)
Sullivan, Sarah. All That's Missing. (p. 53)
—Day for Skating. Valentine, Madeline, illus. (p. 513)
—Passing the Music Down. Root, Barry, illus. (p. 1703)
Sullivan, Simon, illus. see Lakin, Patricia.
Sullivan, Simon, illus. see Redmond, Shirley Raye & Redmond, Shirley Raye.
Sullivan, Steve & Guerdat, Andy. Mission Paw. Lovett, Nate, illus. (p. 1481)
Sullivan, Syd. Prime Suspect. (p. 1793)
—Unsolved Case. (p. 2335)
Sullivan, T. R. Day & Night Stories (Classic Reprint) (p. 512)
—Hand of Petrarch: And Other Stories (Classic Reprint) (p. 914)
—Heart of Us: A Novel (Classic Reprint) (p. 945)
—Roses of Shadow: A Novel (Classic Reprint) (p. 1906)
Sullivan, Tara. Bitter Side of Sweet. (p. 235)
—Golden Boy. (p. 856)
Sullivan, Thomas. Story of Tom Fogarty: The Autobiography of a Criminal (Classic Reprint) (p. 2135)
Sullivan, Thomas Russell. Tom Sylvester: A Novel (Classic Reprint) (p. 2258)
Sullivan, Tom. Blue vs. Yellow. Sullivan, Tom, illus. (p. 249)
—I Used to Be a Fish. Sullivan, Tom, illus. (p. 1083)
—Out There. Sullivan, Tom, illus. (p. 1683)
Sullivan, Tracey. Tebow Tails: Parker's Pride. (p. 2196)
—Tebow Tails: Caspar's Conquest. (p. 2196)
Sullivan, Troy, illus. see Giuffre, Mary & Clark, Paul L.
Sullivan, Vincent F. With the Yanks in France: A Story of America in France (Classic Reprint) (p. 2482)
Sullivan, W. F. History of More Persons Than One, or Entertaining & Instructive Anecdotes for Youth (Classic Reprint) (p. 979)
Sullivan, William D. St. Joseph's Collegian, Vol. 3: January, 1897 (Classic Reprint) (p. 2096)
—St. Joseph's Collegian, Vol. 3: October, 1896 (Classic Reprint) (p. 2096)
Sullivan, William Francis. History of Master George Freeland: Or, How to Spend Your Time; Intended for the Amusement & Instruction of Youth (Classic Reprint) (p. 978)
Sullivan, William John L. Twelve Years in the Saddle for Law & Order on the Frontiers of Texas (Classic Reprint) (p. 2304)
Sullivan-Fraser, Deannie. Johnny & the Gypsy Moth Rose, Hilda, illus. (p. 1174)
Sullivan-Simon, Stacie. I Am Me & You Are You. (p. 1059)
Sullivant, Holly. Ferrets. (p. 721)
—Hamsters. (p. 914)
Sully, Katherine. Night-Night Alabama. Poole, Helen, illus. (p. 1606)
—Night-Night America. Poole, Helen, illus. (p. 1606)
—Night-Night Arizona. Poole, Helen, illus. (p. 1606)
—Night-Night Arkansas. Poole, Helen, illus. (p. 1606)
—Night-Night Boston. Kolanovic, Dubravka & Poole, Helen, illus. (p. 1606)
—Night-Night Buffalo. Poole, Helen, illus. (p. 1606)
—Night-Night Calgary. Poole, Helen, illus. (p. 1606)
—Night-Night California. Kolanovic, Dubravka & Poole, Helen, illus. (p. 1606)
—Night-Night Canada. Poole, Helen, illus. (p. 1606)
—Night-Night Chicago. Kolanovic, Dubravka & Poole, Helen, illus. (p. 1606)
—Night-Night Colorado. Kolanovic, Dubravka & Poole, Helen, illus. (p. 1606)
—Night-Night Delaware. Poole, Helen, illus. (p. 1606)
—Night-Night Florida. Kolanovic, Dubravka & Poole, Helen, illus. (p. 1606)
—Night-Night Georgia. Kolanovic, Dubravka & Poole, Helen, illus. (p. 1606)
—Night-Night Idaho. Poole, Helen, illus. (p. 1606)
—Night-Night Illinois. Poole, Helen, illus. (p. 1606)
—Night-Night Indiana. Poole, Helen, illus. (p. 1606)
—Night-Night Iowa. Poole, Helen, illus. (p. 1606)
—Night-Night Kansas. Kolanovic, Dubravka & Poole, Helen, illus. (p. 1606)
—Night-Night Kansas City. Poole, Helen, illus. (p. 1606)
—Night-Night Kentucky. Poole, Helen, illus. (p. 1606)
—Night-Night Los Angeles. Poole, Helen, illus. (p. 1606)
—Night-Night Louisiana. Poole, Helen, illus. (p. 1606)
—Night-Night Maryland. Poole, Helen, illus. (p. 1606)
—Night-Night Massachusetts. Poole, Helen, illus. (p. 1606)
—Night-Night Michigan. Kolanovic, Dubravka & Poole, Helen, illus. (p. 1606)
—Night-Night Minnesota. Kolanovic, Dubravka & Poole, Helen, illus. (p. 1606)
—Night-Night Mississippi. Poole, Helen, illus. (p. 1606)
—Night-Night Missouri. Poole, Helen, illus. (p. 1606)
—Night-Night Montana. Poole, Helen, illus. (p. 1606)
—Night-Night Nebraska. Poole, Helen, illus. (p. 1606)
—Night-Night New England. Poole, Helen, illus. (p. 1606)
—Night-Night New Jersey. Kolanovic, Dubravka & Poole, Helen, illus. (p. 1606)
—Night-Night New York. Poole, Helen, illus. (p. 1606)
—Night-Night New York City. Kolanovic, Dubravka & Poole, Helen, illus. (p. 1606)
—Night-Night North Carolina. Poole, Helen, illus. (p. 1606)
—Night-Night North Dakota. Poole, Helen, illus. (p. 1606)
—Night-Night Ohio. Kolanovic, Dubravka & Poole, Helen, illus. (p. 1606)
—Night-Night Oklahoma. Poole, Helen, illus. (p. 1606)
—Night-Night Oregon. Poole, Helen, illus. (p. 1606)
—Night-Night Pennsylvania. Kolanovic, Dubravka & Poole, Helen, illus. (p. 1606)
—Night-Night Philadelphia. Poole, Helen, illus. (p. 1606)
—Night-Night Pittsburgh. Poole, Helen, illus. (p. 1606)
—Night-Night San Francisco. Poole, Helen, illus. (p. 1606)
—Night-Night South Carolina. Poole, Helen, illus. (p. 1606)
—Night-Night South Dakota. Poole, Helen, illus. (p. 1606)
—Night-Night St. Louis. Poole, Helen, illus. (p. 1606)
—Night-Night Tennessee. Poole, Helen, illus. (p. 1606)
—Night-Night Texas. Kolanovic, Dubravka & Poole, Helen, illus. (p. 1606)
—Night-Night Toronto. Poole, Helen, illus. (p. 1606)
—Night-Night Utah. Poole, Helen, illus. (p. 1606)
—Night-Night Vancouver. Poole, Helen, illus. (p. 1606)
—Night-Night Virginia. Poole, Helen, illus. (p. 1606)
—Night-Night Washington. Poole, Helen, illus. (p. 1606)
—Night-Night Washington, D. C. Poole, Helen, illus. (p. 1606)
—Night-Night West Virginia. Poole, Helen, illus. (p. 1606)
—Night-Night Wisconsin. Kolanovic, Dubravka & Poole, Helen, illus. (p. 1606)
—Night-Night Wyoming. Poole, Helen, illus. (p. 1606)
—Santa Is Coming to Wales Colouring Book. (p. 1932)
Sultan, Lana. Amazing Adventures of Eco Boy Vol. 1. (p. 62)
Sultan, Simon. Thanksgiving Tale, & Other Poems (Classic Reprint) (p. 2212)
Sulurayok, Matilda. Kamik's First Sled Leng, Qin, illus. (p. 1202)
Sulzer, James. Card People: Part 1: the Scissors of Fate. (p. 328)
—Crisis: The Card People 3. (p. 475)
—Identity Swap: The Card People 2. (p. 1089)
Suma, Nova Ren. Dani Noir. (p. 502)
—Fade Out. (p. 694)
—Imaginary Girls. (p. 1100)
—Room Away from the Wolves. (p. 1903)
—Walls Around Us. (p. 2373)
Suma, Scott. Twenty Feet Ahead & Thirty Feet High. (p. 2304)
Sumberac, Manuel, illus. see Andersen, Hans.
Sumberac, Manuel, illus. see Dougherty, John.
Sumberac, Manuel, illus. see Moore, Clement C.
Sumerak, Marc. Ororo: Before the Storm. Barberi, Carlo, illus. (p. 1672)
—Playing Hero. Greene, Sanford, illus. (p. 1760)
—Star Wars: Droidography. (p. 2104)
—Survival Handbook: An Essential Companion to the Great Outdoors. (p. 2164)
Sumiko, Kanda. Shoku Bun. (p. 2009)
Sumino, Yoru. I Want to Eat Your Pancreas (Light Novel) loundraw, illus. (p. 1085)
Sumizawa, Katsuyuki. Mobile Suit Gundam WING, 10: Glory of the Losers. Ogasawara, Tomofumi, illus. (p. 1485)
—Mobile Suit Gundam WING, 8: Glory of the Losers. Ogasawara, Tomofumi, illus. (p. 1485)
Summer, L. S. Rosa Parks. (p. 1904)
Summer, Lily. Comment Beau le Chat a Appris le Chinois: Un Livre Bilingue. (p. 430)
—Comment Beau le Chat a Appris l'Espagnol / Como Beau el Gato Ha Aprendido el Espanol: Un Livre Bilingue. (p. 430)
—How Beau the Cat Learned Chinese. (p. 1026)
—How Beau the Cat Learned French / Comment Beau le Chat a Appris le Francais: A Bilingual Book. (p. 1026)
Summer, Mary Elizabeth. Trust Me, I'm Lying. (p. 2296)
Summer, Sunny W. Color Me Panama * Coloreame Panama. Skidmore, Donna, illus. (p. 420)
Summerer, Eric Michael. Frédéric Chopin. (p. 781)
—Ludwig van Beethoven. (p. 1366)
Summerer, Marilyn. First Christmas Present. van der Sterre, Johanna, illus. (p. 735)
Summerhayes, Martha. Vanished Arizona: Recollections of the Army Life by a New England Woman. (p. 2347)
—Vanished Arizona: Recollections of the Army Life of a New England Woman; with Twenty-Eight Illustrations (Classic Reprint) (p. 2347)
Summerhill, Abby & Summerhill, Noni. Ducklings on the Run. Mazon, Alyssa, illus. (p. 608)
Summerhill, Abby & Summerhill, Noni (Gail). Patitos Al Escape. Mazon, Alyssa, illus. (p. 1705)
Summerill, Erin. Ever the Brave. (p. 669)
—Ever the Hunted. (p. 669)
—Once a King. (p. 1657)
Summerly, Felix. Little Red Riding Hood: An Entirely New Edition; with New Pictures by an Eminent Artist (Classic Reprint) (p. 1326)
—Traditional Faery Tales of Little Red Riding Hood, Beauty & the Beast,& Jack & the Bean Stalk (Classic Reprint) (p. 2273)
—Traditional Nursery Songs of England: With Pictures by Eminent Modern Artists (Classic Reprint) (p. 2273)
Summers, Alex. Airplane. (p. 37)
—Boat. (p. 251)
—Haunted Battlefields & Cemeteries. (p. 937)
—Haunted Houses. (p. 938)
—Subway. (p. 2146)
—Taxi Cab. (p. 2193)
—Train. (p. 2275)
Summers, Cathryn. It's Time for a Haircut. (p. 1148)
Summers, Courtney. All the Rage. (p. 54)
—Cracked up to Be: A Novel. (p. 466)
—Fall for Anything. (p. 700)
—Sadie: A Novel. (p. 1921)
—Sadie. (p. 1921)
—Some Girls Are: A Novel. (p. 2059)
—This Is Not a Test. (p. 2225)
—What Goes Around. (p. 2410)
Summers, Dorothy. Renunciation (Classic Reprint) (p. 1866)
Summers, Elizabeth. Tools of War. (p. 2261)
—Weapons & Vehicles of the Iraq War. (p. 2393)
—Weapons & Vehicles of the Vietnam War. (p. 2393)
—Weapons & Vehicles of World War I. (p. 2393)
Summers, Florence Elizabeth. Dere Bill: Mable's Love Letters to Her Rookie (Classic Reprint) (p. 530)
Summers, Helen. Why Can't I Play Football? (p. 2455)
Summers, Jacque. Disgusting Jobs in Modern America: The down & Dirty Details. (p. 558)
—Escaping a POW Camp. (p. 662)
Summers, Janine. Emmy & the Stone of Faith. (p. 644)
Summers, Jean. Kids' Guide to Writing Great Thank-You Notes. (p. 1215)
Summers, Kay & Summers, Amanda. Aven on Earth. (p. 142)
Summers, Kimberly Dillon. Miley Cyrus: A Biography (p. 1466)
—United Kingdom (p. 2330)
Summers, Laura. Petey & the Housekeeper: Scaredy Bird. (p. 1730)
—Summer of Telling Tales. (p. 2149)
Summers, Mark. Riddle Horse. (p. 1878)
Summers, Mark, illus. see Frisch, Aaron.
Summers, Maud. First Reader (Classic Reprint) (p. 739)
—Primer (Classic Reprint) (p. 1793)
—Thought Reader, Vol. 1: Book I (Classic Reprint) (p. 2230)
Summers, Portia. Adding Coins & Bills. (p. 15)
—Community of Our Military Base. (p. 432)
—Counting Coins & Bills. (p. 460)
—Hillary Clinton: Politician & Activist. (p. 971)
—Kate Middleton: Duchess of Cambridge. (p. 1204)
—My Neighborhood. (p. 1557)
—My Rural Community. (p. 1560)
—My School Community. (p. 1560)
—My Suburban Community. (p. 1562)
—My Urban Community. (p. 1563)
—Subtracting Coins & Bills. (p. 2146)
—Was Atlantis Real? (p. 2381)
—Was King Arthur Real? (p. 2381)
—What Is Money? (p. 2415)
—Word Problems with Money. (p. 2493)
Summers, Portia, jt. auth. see Yearling, Tricia.
Summers, Portia & Grady, Colin. Coniferous Forest Biome. (p. 440)
—Deciduous Forest Biome. (p. 523)
—Desert Biome. (p. 531)
—Grassland Biome. (p. 881)
—Ocean Biome. (p. 1635)
—Tundra Biome. (p. 2299)
Summers, Portia & Rau, Dana Meachen. Are Aliens Real? (p. 112)
—Are Dragons Real? (p. 112)
—Are Mermaids Real? (p. 112)
—Are Monsters Real? (p. 112)
—Are Unicorns Real? (p. 113)
Summers, Susan. Greatest Gift: The Story of the Other Wise Man. Morris, Jackie, illus. (p. 891)
Summers, Tamara. Never Bite a Boy on the First Date. (p. 1589)
Summers, Terry. Peter Wanted a Pet. Kai, illus. (p. 1730)
Summersdale. KEEP CALM & COLOUR Mermaids. (p. 1207)
Summersett, Henry. Happy at Last, or Sigh No More Ladies: A Comedy, in Five Acts; As Performed at the

Theatre-Royal, Kendal, March 13th, 1805 (Classic Reprint) (p. 920)
—Martyn of Fenrose, or the Wizard & the Sword (Classic Reprint) (p. 1411)
—Martyn of Fenrose, or the Wizard & the Sword, Vol. 3: A Romance (Classic Reprint) (p. 1411)
Summerton, Winter. Will He Find Her? A Romance of New York & New Orleans (Classic Reprint) (p. 2467)
Summerville, Justin. Forgetful Freddie. (p. 768)
Summitt, April R. Sequoyah & the Invention of the Cherokee Alphabet (p. 1990)
Summy, Barrie. I So Don't Do Famous. (p. 1082)
—I So Don't Do Makeup. (p. 1082)
—I So Don't Do Mysteries. (p. 1082)
—I So Don't Do Spooky. (p. 1082)
Sumner, Charles A. Notes of Travel in Northern Europe (Classic Reprint) (p. 1624)
Sumner, Charles Allen. Depreciation: A Play in Four Acts (Classic Reprint) (p. 529)
Sumner, Charles Allen, jt. auth. see Sumner, Samuel Barstow.
Sumner, Esther. My Nativity ABCs. (p. 1557)
Sumner, Esther Yu. My Nativity 1-2-3s. Davis, Robert, illus. (p. 1557)
Sumner, Francis Bertody. Biological Survey of the Waters of Woods Hole & Vicinity: In Two Parts (Classic Reprint) (p. 229)
Sumner, Jamie. Roll with It. (p. 1898)
Sumner Johnson, Janet. Help Wanted, Must Love Books. Dawson, Courtney, illus. (p. 953)
—Last Great Adventure of the PB & J Society. (p. 1248)
Sumner, M. C. Lost Soul. (p. 1355)
—Unseen Powers. (p. 2335)
Sumner, Ray, ed. World Geography (p. 2501)
Sumner, Samuel Barstow. Poem. (p. 1765)
Sumner, Santana. Blah Blah Blah Blah Blah Blah. (p. 242)
Sumner, Tracy M. & Landreth, Jane. Big Bible Guide: Kids' Guide to Creation & Bible Animals: Fun & Fascinating Bible Reference for Kids Ages 8-12. (p. 216)
Sumner, William, jt. auth. see Halls, Kelly Milner.
Sumonja, Nicholas. Dual Souls: Shadow. (p. 607)
Sumpter, Anthony. Amelia the Fart Detector. Morris, Jordynn, illus. (p. 69)
—Rebel the Superhero. Morris, Jordynn, illus. (p. 1852)
Sumpter, Rachell, illus. see Baum, L. Frank.
Sumrow, Melanie. Inside Battle. (p. 1122)
—Prophet Calls. (p. 1807)
Sumulong, Mike Justin. Final Destiny: The First Key. (p. 727)
Sun, Amanda. Heir to the Sky. (p. 949)
—Ink. (p. 1120)
—Storm. (p. 2126)
Sun, Ann Ruozhu, illus. see Hughes, Mónica.
Sun, Antuanette, illus. see Dellas, Melanie & Woodworth, John.
Sun, Boya & Petty, Kate Reed. Chasma Knights. (p. 362)
Sun, Child Of The. Summer-Land: A Southern Story (Classic Reprint) (p. 2149)
Sun, Irene & Sun, Irene. God Counts: Numbers in His Word & His World. Foster, Alex, illus. (p. 851)
Sun, Jennie. Design It! FASHION. (p. 532)
—Doodle Design & Draw ROCK STAR FASHIONS. (p. 584)
—Fashion. (p. 712)
Sun, Jun, illus. see Chen, Bill.
Sun, Ming-Ju. Creative Haven Japanese Kimono Designs Coloring Book. (p. 470)
—Flower Fashion Fantasies Paper Dolls. (p. 752)
Sun, Ming-Ju & Creative Haven Staff. Creative Haven Art Nouveau Fashions Coloring Book. (p. 470)
—Flower Fashion Fantasies. (p. 752)
Sun, Priya. Chronicles of a Barnyard Life: Smile Mr. Cow! Santos, Ana, illus. (p. 388)
Sun, Wei, tr. see Pere, Tuula.
Sun, Yuhu. Mu Di Jiang Jing Pin Tong Hua: Yu Jian Kong Kong Ru Ye. (p. 1523)
Sundance, Kyra. 101 Dog Tricks, Kids Edition: Fun & Easy Activities, Games, & Crafts. (p. 2558)
Sundara, Kate. United States of Us. (p. 2332)
Sundaram, Renuka. Sammy, the Galapagos Sea Lion. (p. 1928)
Sundaravej, Sittisan, illus. see Montgomery, R. A.
Sundaravej, Sittisan, illus. see Wallace, Jim.
Sunday, William Ashley. Burning Truths from Billy's Bat: A Graphic Description of the Remarkable Conversion of REV. Billy Sunday (the World's Famous Evangelist), Embodying Anecdotes, Terse Sayings, etc., Compiled from Various Sources (Classic Reprint) (p. 300)
Sundberg, Ingrid. All We Left Behind. (p. 55)
Sundberg, Lawrence D. Dinétah, an Early History of the Navajo People. (p. 547)
Sundberg, Mary Rose, tr. see Blondin, John & Blondin, George.
Sundell, Joanne. Arctic Shadow. (p. 112)
—Arctic Will. (p. 112)
Sundem, Garth. Real Kids, Real Stories, Real Challenges: Overcoming Adversity Around the World. (p. 1849)
—Real Kids, Real Stories, Real Change: Courageous Actions Around the World. (p. 1849)
—Real Kids, Real Stories, Real Character: Choices That Matter Around the World. (p. 1849)
—STEAM in a Jar: Experiments, Activities & Trivia for Your Classroom. (p. 2110)
Sunder, Ashwin. Fear of Dreaming. (p. 716)
Sunderland, Alan. Octavius o'Malley & the Mystery of the Criminal Cats. (p. 1636)
—Octavius o'Malley & the Mystery of the Exploding Cheese. (p. 1636)
Sunderland, John, illus. see Combes, Alan.
Sunderland, Margot. Frog Who Longed for the Moon to Smile: A Story for Children Who Yearn for Someone They Love (p. 789)
—Helping Children Locked in Rage or Hate: A Guidebook. (p. 953)
—Helping Children Who Are Anxious or Obsessional: A Guidebook. (p. 953)
—Helping Children with Fear: A Guidebook (p. 953)
—Helping Children with Low Self-Esteem: A Guidebook. (p. 953)
—How Hattie Hated Kindness: A Story for Children Locked in Rage of Hate. (p. 1031)
—Nifflenoo Called Nevermind: A Story for Children Who Bottle up Their Feelings. (p. 1604)
—Pea Called Mildred: A Story to Help Children Pursue Their Hopes & Dreams. (p. 1709)
—Ruby & the Rubbish Bin: A Story for Children with Low Self-Esteem. (p. 1911)
—Wibble Called Bipley: A Story for Children Who Have Hardened Their Hearts or Becomes Bullies (p. 2460)
—Willy & the Wobbly House: A Story for Children Who Are Anxious or Obsessional. (p. 2470)
Sunderland, Margot & Hancock, Nicky. Helping Children Who Bottle up Their Feelings: A Guidebook. (p. 953)
Sunderland, Margot, et al. Using Story Telling As a Therapeutic Tool with Children. (p. 2342)
Sundgaard, Arnold. Lamb & the Butterfly. Carle, Eric, illus. (p. 1240)
Sundquist, Josh. Love & First Sight. (p. 1359)
—We Should Hang Out Sometime: Embarrassingly, a True Story. (p. 2392)
Sundram, Steve, illus. see Kita, Suzanne.
Sundreamz, Hope & Owens, Sky. Amir's First Haircut: The Ongoing Saga of Life's Lessons Through the Eyes of a Young Boy. (p. 75)
Sundy, Jonathan, illus. see Benoist, Cathy & Gilmore, Cathy.
Sundy, Jonathan, illus. see Gilmore, Cathy & Benoist, Carol.
Suneby, Elizabeth. Iqbal & His Ingenious Idea: How a Science Project Helps One Family & the Planet. Green, Rebecca, illus. (p. 1133)
—Razia's Ray of Hope: One Girl's Dream of an Education. Verelst, Suana, illus. (p. 1844)
Suneby, Liz. Razia's Ray of Hope: One Girl's Dream of an Education. Verelst, Suana, illus. (p. 1844)
Suneby, Liz & Heiman, Diane. It's a ... It's a ... It's a Mitzvah. Molk, Laurel, illus. (p. 1143)
—Mitzvah Project Book: Making Mitzvah Part of Your Bar/Bat Mitzvah & Your Life. (p. 1484)
Sunflower Education Staff. Golden Thread. (p. 859)
Sung, Haeun, illus. see Ludwig, Mike.
Sung Ku, Min, illus. see Paley, Rebecca, et al.
SungJa, Cho. Bubbly & Grumpy. SukWon, Sa, illus. (p. 289)
Suni, Hanna, illus. see Tucci, Michele M.
Sunluvr, Amy, illus. see Bates, Melony.
Sunmi, Hwang. niño de la Pegatina Amarilla. Kwon, Sa-Woo, illus. (p. 1610)
Sunseri, Heather. Mindsiege. (p. 1470)
Sunseri, Sophia Natasha. Working As a Teacher in Your Community. (p. 2495)
Sunshine, Mary Lou, illus. see Orth, Jack.
Suo, Raymond & Jetty, Karthik. Origami & Related Mathematics. (p. 1670)
Suorsa, Michael, illus. see Gregory, Caroline.
Super Explorers, jt. auth. see Hartson, Tamara.
Super Explorers, jt. auth. see Pirk, Wendy.
Super Explorers & Carrière, Nicholle. Big Trucks (p. 223)
—Excavators & Diggers (p. 676)
Super Why Staff. Ghost Who Was Afraid of Halloween. (p. 828)
Supercern, Seymour. Truth Will Out: An Emergence from Chaos & Subterfuge into Light & Reality (Classic Reprint) (p. 2297)
Supercivicos, Los. Nomas Tantito: Van Por Las Calles Dando Lecciones de Urbanidad a Los Ciudadanos. (p. 1618)
Superle, Michelle. Black Dog Dream Dog Balance, Millie, illus. (p. 237)
Superstars!. Superstars! One Direction. (p. 2162)
Superstars! Editors. Superstars! One Direction: Inside Their World. Superstars! Editors, ed. (p. 2162)
Suphandagi, Lale. Dream Bird. (p. 601)
Suplee, Etta. Outlines & Suggestions for Primary Teachers (Classic Reprint) (p. 1685)
Supplee, Kathryn. Choose Happy. (p. 381)
Supplee, Suzanne. Artichoke's Heart. (p. 123)
—Somebody Everybody Listens To. (p. 2060)
Sur, Duendes Del. Scooby-Doo! Picture Clue Books (p. 1961)
Sur, Duendes Del, illus. see Abdo Publishing & Gelsey, James.
Sur, Duendes del, illus. see ABDO Publishing Company Staff.
Sur, Duendes Del, illus. see Balaban, Mariah.
Sur, Duendes Del, illus. see Barbo, Maria S.
Sur, Duendes Del, illus. see Class 1-208.
Sur, Duendes Del, illus. see Gelsey, James.
Sur, Duendes del, illus. see Guidone, Ellen.
Sur, Duendes Del, illus. see Ip, Ivy S.
Sur, Duendes Del, illus. see McCann, Jesse Leon.
Sur, Duendes del, illus. see Nagler, Michelle H.
Sur, Duendes Del, illus. see Soderberg, Erin.
Sur, Duendes del, illus. see Wasserman, Robin.
Sur, Paola B. Shorty Tales: Cuentitos Spanish & English. (p. 2011)
Suratos, Don, illus. see Mendolla, Robyn & Rabbit, Frankie B.
Surber, Mary Brigid. Last Stork Summer. (p. 1249)
Surducan, Maria, illus. see Kimmel, Eric A.
Sure, Grace. Robot Coloring Book My Monster Robot Coloring Fun for Kids. (p. 1892)
Surein, Manuel, illus. see Besson, Agnès.
Surell, Alexandre. Étude Sur les Torrents des Hautes-Alpes (Classic Reprint) (p. 666)
—Étude Sur les Torrents des Hautes-Alpes, Vol. 2 (Classic Reprint) (p. 666)
Surendranath, Nayantara, illus. see Venkat, Srividhya.
Suresh, Shreyas. Joy! a Book of Poems. (p. 1184)
—Magic Lighthouse & other Stories. (p. 1378)
Surette, Janet. Scarlett's Spectacles: A Cheerful Choice for a Happy Heart. Crampton, Shane, illus. (p. 1942)
Surev, Surev. Uncle Carl (Classic Reprint) (p. 2318)
Surface, Harvey Adam. First Report on the Economic Features of Turtles of Pennsylvania, Vol. 6: September 1, 1908 (Classic Reprint) (p. 739)
Surgal, Jon. Have You Seen My Dinosaur? Mathieu, Joe, illus. (p. 939)
Surgery, Baltimore College of Dental. College Annual, 1903 (Classic Reprint) (p. 415)
Surgery, Chicago College of Dental. Dentos, 1923 (Classic Reprint) (p. 529)
Surges, James, tr. see Grimm, Jacob & Grimm, Wilhelm K.
Surget, Alain. Escape from Veracruz. (p. 661)
—Ghost Ship. (p. 828)
—Plumed Serpent's Gold. (p. 1763)
—Renard de Morlange. (p. 1865)
—Shark Island. (p. 2002)
Surget, Alain & Yeardley, Glynne. Caesar, Who's He? Parme, Fabrice, illus. (p. 308)
—Cleopatra Must Be Saved! Parme, Fabrice, illus. (p. 403)
—Danger at the Circus! Parme, Fabrice, illus. (p. 501)
—Prisoners in the Pyramid. Parme, Fabrice, illus. (p. 1801)
Suriano, Andy, illus. see Torres, J.
Suriano, Andy, illus. see Wayne, Matt.
Suritsch, Gina. Magical Tales from India: The Secret of the White Elephant & Mukti the Lion Finds Himself. (p. 1380)
Surlin, Janice. Greatest Ten. Krinsky, Rivka Siegel, illus. (p. 892)
Surmelis, Angelo. Dangerous Art of Blending In. (p. 501)
Surnaite, Margarita. Lost Book. (p. 1352)
Surnaite, Margarita, illus. see Gates, Mariam.
Surojegin, Nora. Otto & the Secret Light of Christmas Timbers, Jill, tr. (p. 1676)
Surojegin, Pirkko-Liisa, illus. see Makinen, Kirsti, ed.
Surojegin, Pirkko-Liisa, illus. see Surojegin, Nora.
Surovec, Yasmine. I See Kitty. Surovec, Yasmine, illus. (p. 1081)
—My Pet Human. (p. 1559)
—My Pet Human Takes Center Stage. (p. 1559)
Surplice, Holly. About a Bear. Surplice, Holly, illus. (p. 6)
—I Love You, Little One. Surplice, Holly, illus. (p. 1079)
—Peek-A-Boo Bunny. Surplice, Holly, illus. (p. 1712)
—Snow Still. Surplice, Holly, illus. (p. 2048)
Surplice, Holly, illus. see Nosy Crow.
Surr, T. S. George Barnwell: A Novel (Classic Reprint) (p. 818)
—Mask of Fashion, Vol. 2: A Plain Tale, with Anecdotes Foreign & Domestic (Classic Reprint) (p. 1417)
—Splendid Misery, Vol. 1: A Novel; in Three Volumes (Classic Reprint) (p. 2085)
—Splendid Misery, Vol. 3 Of 3: A Novel (Classic Reprint) (p. 2085)
—Winter in London, or Sketches of Fashion, Vol. 1 Of 2: A Novel (Classic Reprint) (p. 2475)
—Winter in London, or Sketches of Fashion, Vol. 1 Of 3: A Novel, in Three Volumes (Classic Reprint) (p. 2475)
—Winter in London, Vol. 2 Of 3: Or, Sketches of Fashion: a Novel (Classic Reprint) (p. 2475)
Surr, Thomas Skinner. George Barnwell, or the Merchant's Clerk (Classic Reprint) (p. 818)
—Mask of Fashion, Vol. 1 Of 2: A Plain Tale (Classic Reprint) (p. 1417)
—Splendid Misery, Vol. 1 Of 3: A Novel (Classic Reprint) (p. 2085)
—Winter in London, or Sketches of Fashion, Vol. 1 Of 3: A Novel (Classic Reprint) (p. 2475)
Surratt, Christopher. Antic Circle. (p. 102)
Surratt, Tereasa & Charlton-Perrin, Donna. Forever Tree. Roode, Daniel, illus. (p. 767)
Surratt, Tereasa & Lukas, Donna. Forever Tree. Slater, Nicola, illus. (p. 767)
Surrell M D, James A. Laughter Is Good Medicine: Doc's Silly Clean Groaner Jokes. (p. 1252)
Surrey, Ellen. Giving Thanks: More Than 100 Ways to Say Thank You. (p. 840)
Surrey, Michael, illus. see Harner, Ron.
Surridge, David. Penelope Pondhead. Slack, Alex, illus. (p. 1715)
Surridge, Jenny. Woggle's Wishes. (p. 2483)
Surrisi, C. M. Maypop Kidnapping: A Quinnie Boyd Mystery. (p. 1430)
—Side of Sabotage: A Quinnie Boyd Mystery. (p. 2014)
—Vampires on the Run: A Quinnie Boyd Mystery. (p. 2346)
Surrisi, Cynthia. Best Mother. Goode, Diane, illus. (p. 206)
Surtees, R. S. Jorrocks's Jaunts & Jollities: Being the Hunting, Shooting, Racing, Driving, Sailing, Eating, Eccentric & Extravagant Exploits of That Renowned Sporting Citizen, Mr. John Jorrocks (Classic Reprint) (p. 1178)
Surtees, Robert. Hunts with Jorrocks: From Handley Cross (Classic Reprint) (p. 1054)
Surtees, Robert Smith. Ask Mamma, or the Richest Commoner in England (Classic Reprint) (p. 126)
—Handley Cross, or Mr. Jorrocks's Hunt (Classic Reprint) (p. 915)
—Handley Cross, Vol. 1: Or the Spa Hunt; a Sporting Tale (Classic Reprint) (p. 915)
—Handley Cross, Vol. 2 Of 3: Or the Spa Hunt; a Sporting Tale (Classic Reprint) (p. 915)
—Hawbuck Grange: Or the Sporting Adventures of Thomas Scott, Esq. (Classic Reprint) (p. 940)
—Hillingdon Hall: Or the Cockney Squire; a Tale of Country Life (Classic Reprint) (p. 972)
—Hillingdon Hall, or the Cockney Squire, Vol. 3 Of 3: A Tale of Country Life (Classic Reprint) (p. 972)
—Hillingdon Hall, Vol. 1 Of 3: Or the Cockney Squire; a Tale of Country Life (Classic Reprint) (p. 972)
—Horseman's Manual: Being a Treatise on Soundness, the Law of Warranty, & Generally on the Laws Relating to Horses (Classic Reprint) (p. 1005)
—Jorrocks on 'Unting (Classic Reprint) (p. 1178)
—Mr. Jorrocks' Lectors from Handley Cross (Classic Reprint) (p. 1519)
—Plain of Ringlets? (Classic Reprint) (p. 1754)
Surveyor-, New Zealand., jt. auth. see Smith, Stephenson Percy.
Susaeta, Equipo. 365 ADIVINANZAS. (p. 2560)
—BELLA DURMIENTE/SLEEPING BEAUTY. (p. 197)
—BLANCANIEVES/SNOW WHITE. (p. 242)
Susan, Krupp, illus. see Gonzalez de Freire, Aurora Margarita.
Susan, Marlene. Time to Wean. Lowe, Hayley, illus. (p. 2245)
Susan, Morris-Carter. Eco-Leena: Goes to Washington. (p. 623)
Susan, Paradis. Edna. Susan, Paradis, illus. (p. 626)
Susan, Susan. Gold of Chickaree (Classic Reprint) (p. 856)
Susan, Turnbull, illus. see Eastman, Charles A. & Eastman, Elaine Goodale.
Susan Wheelock Freeman, Julia. Boys in White: The Experience of a Hospital Agent in & Around Washington - Scholar's Choice Edition. (p. 272)
Susanna, Davide. Beautiful, the Crummy & the Brave. (p. 184)
Suseata Publishing, Inc. Circulación Vial: Un Juego de Niños. (p. 393)
Susedik, Tina. Hat Peddler. Comstock, Chris, illus. (p. 936)
Susedik, Tina & Heers, Alli. Uncle Bills Farm: True Stories of His Crazy Farm Animals. Sutula, Hollie, illus. (p. 2318)
Susienka, Kristen. America the Beautiful (p. 70)
—Battle Hymn of the Republic (p. 174)
—Frederick Douglass (p. 781)
—Harriet Tubman (p. 933)
—Kamala Harris (p. 1202)
—Rosa Parks (p. 1904)
Susini, Brigitte, illus. see La Fontaine, Jean de.
Suska, Monika, illus. see Lumsden, Zoa.
Susko, Mark D. Sally Sassafras, the Girl with Monster Hair. (p. 1925)
Sussman, Elaine. Boy Who Opened Our Eyes. Matsick, Anni, illus. (p. 271)
Sussman, Elissa. Burn. (p. 299)
—Stray. (p. 2139)
Sussman, Joni Kibort. Grover Goes to Israel Leigh, Tom, illus. (p. 899)
—Grover's Hanukkah Party. Leigh, Tom, illus. (p. 899)
—My First Yiddish Word Book. Marzel, Pépi, illus. (p. 1547)
—My First Yiddish Word Book. Marzel, Pepi, illus. (p. 1547)
—Seder for Grover Leigh, Tom, illus. (p. 1981)
—Shanah Tovah, Grover! Leigh, Tom, illus. (p. 1999)
Sussman, Michael. Duckworth, the Difficult Child. Sardà, Júlia, illus. (p. 608)
Susumu, Shingu. Little Pond. (p. 1325)
Sutcliff, Rosemary. Beowulf, Dragon Slayer. (p. 201)
—Black Ships Before Troy. Lee, Alan, illus. (p. 239)
—Dawn Wind. (p. 512)
—Eagle. (p. 613)
—Eagle of the Ninth. (p. 613)
—Eagle of the Ninth. Hodges, C. Walter, illus. (p. 613)
—Heather, Oak, & Olive. Ambrus, Victor, illus. (p. 946)
—Lantern Bearers. (p. 1244)
—Mark of the Horse Lord. (p. 1407)
—Silver Branch. (p. 2019)
Sutcliffe, Charlie. Zubert. (p. 2545)
Sutcliffe, Halliwell. Bachelor in Arcady (Classic Reprint) (p. 155)
—Benedick in Arcady (Classic Reprint) (p. 199)
—Lone Adventure (Classic Reprint) (p. 1342)
—Priscilla of the Good Intent: A Romance of the Grey Fells (Classic Reprint) (p. 1801)
—Red o' the Feud (Classic Reprint) (p. 1858)
—Ricroft of Withens (Classic Reprint) (p. 1877)
—Through Sorrow's Gates: A Tale of the Lonely Heath (Classic Reprint) (p. 2237)
—Under the White Cockade (Classic Reprint) (p. 2323)
Sutcliffe, Jane. Barack Obama. (p. 164)
—Helen Keller. (p. 949)
—Leonardo's Monster Leonhard, Herb & Leonard, Herb, illus. (p. 1267)
—Sacagawea. (p. 1920)
—Stone Giant: Michelangelo's David & How He Came to Be. Shelley, John, illus. (p. 2121)
—White House Is Burning: August 24 1814. Farquharson, Alexander, illus. (p. 2444)
—Will's Words: How William Shakespeare Changed the Way You Talk. Shelley, John, illus. (p. 2470)
Sutcliffe, Jane & Kodera, Craig. Chester Nimitz & the Sea (p. 366)
Sutcliffe, Jane & Walt Disney Company Staff. Walt Disney. (p. 2373)
Sutcliffe, Kathy. When Romeo Kissed Mercutio. (p. 2432)
Sutcliffe, Kristen. Fabric Paper Thread: 26 Projects to Stitch with Friends. (p. 692)
Sutcliffe, Mandy. Belle & Boo: Friends Make Everything Better. (p. 197)
—Hop along Boo, Time for Bed. (p. 1001)
Sutcliffe, Mandy, jt. auth. see Jarman, Julia.
Sutcliffe, Sangorski And. Great Bastard, Protector of the Little One: Done Out of French (Classic Reprint) (p. 884)
Sutcliffe, Tim, illus. see Harrison, Paul.
Sutcliffe, William. Bad Influence. Anderson, Laura Ellen & Busby, Allie, illus. (p. 158)
—Circus of Thieves & the Comeback Caper. Tazzyman, David, illus. (p. 393)
—Circus of Thieves on the Rampage. Tazzyman, David, illus. (p. 393)
Suteev, V. Skazki. (p. 2030)
Suter, Janine. Day the World Went Wacky. Gunther, Richard, illus. (p. 514)
—Noah's Floating Animal Park. Gunther, Richard, illus. (p. 1616)
Suthar, Himanshu J. Becoming a Big Brother. (p. 187)
Sutherl, Millicent. Winds of the World: Seven Love Stories (Classic Reprint) (p. 2472)
Sutherland, Adam. Amazon: The Business Behind the Everything Store. (p. 67)
—Armed Services. (p. 117)
—Fact or Fiction Behind Pirates. (p. 694)
—Political Leaders. (p. 1771)
—Soccer Stars. (p. 2052)
—Story of Google. (p. 2130)
Sutherland, Alexander. Tales of a Pilgrim (Classic Reprint) (p. 2183)
Sutherland, Celeste, illus. see Ballantyne, Sonya.

S

—Play These Games: 101 Delightful Diversions Using Everyday Items. (p. 1759)
—Selfish Elf Wish. (p. 1987)
Swain, I. C. In the Right Place. (p. 1110)
—In the Right Place, Coloring Book. (p. 1110)
—In the Right Place the Beginning. (p. 1110)
Swain, Robert. Memoir of Robert Swain (Classic Reprint) (p. 1444)
Swain, Wilson, illus. see Covert, Ralph & Mills, G. Riley.
Swain-Bates, Crystal. I'm a Pretty Princess. (p. 1097)
—Naturally Me. (p. 1580)
Swajeski, Donna M. One Magic Kiss: Snow White & the Seven Dwarfs. (p. 1660)
Swales, Susan Matilda. Old Scrap Book (Classic Reprint) (p. 1648)
Swallow, Gerry. Blue in the Face: A Story of Risk, Rhyme, & Rebellion. Fabretti, Valerio, illus. (p. 248)
—Long Live the Queen: A Blue in the Face Novel. Fabretti, Valerio, illus. (p. 1343)
Swallow, Mark. Zero per Cent. (p. 2540)
Swallow, Pamela. It Only Looks Easy. (p. 1141)
Swampy, Lloyd, illus. see McLellan, Joe, et al.
Swampy, Lloyd, illus. see McLellan, Joseph, et al.
Swan, Angela, illus. see Bentley, Sue.
Swan, Annie S. Airlie's Mission (Classic Reprint) (p. 37)
—Aldersyde: A Border Story of Seventy Years Ago (Classic Reprint) (p. 41)
—Aldersyde. (p. 41)
—Bachelor in Search of a Wife: And Roger Marcham's Ward (Classic Reprint) (p. 155)
—Bondage of Riches (Classic Reprint) (p. 255)
—Bonnie Jean (Classic Reprint) (p. 256)
—Bridge Builders (Classic Reprint) (p. 280)
—Carlowrie, or among Lothian Folk (Classic Reprint) (p. 332)
—Elizabeth Glen. M. B: The Experiences of a Lady Doctor (Classic Reprint) (p. 636)
—Gates of Eden: A Story of Endeavour (Classic Reprint) (p. 811)
—Gates of Eden. (p. 811)
—Guinea Stamp: A Tale of Modern Glasgow (Classic Reprint) (p. 904)
—Hazell & Sons, Brewers (Classic Reprint) (p. 941)
—Holidays at Sunnycroft & a Year at Coverley (Classic Reprint) (p. 988)
—Ne'er-Do-Weel (Classic Reprint) (p. 1585)
—Sheila (Classic Reprint) (p. 2005)
—Son of Erin (Classic Reprint) (p. 2061)
—Thankful Rest: A Tale (Classic Reprint) (p. 2211)
—Thomas Dryburgh's Dream: Story of the Sick Children's Hospital (Classic Reprint) (p. 2228)
—Varner's Chase: Or, the Gentle Heart (Classic Reprint) (p. 2348)
—Wyndham's Daughter: A Story of to-Day (Classic Reprint) (p. 2515)
—Year at Coverley. (p. 2518)
Swan, Aurelie Ml. Avènement de L'Ombre. (p. 142)
Swan, Bill. Fourteen & Sentenced to Death: The Story of Steven Truscott. (p. 773)
—Man-to-Man (p. 1395)
—Real Justice: Jailed for Life for Being Black: The Story of Rubin Hurricane Carter (p. 1849)
Swan, Carroll Judson. My Company (Classic Reprint) (p. 1536)
Swan, E. F. O. Tales of the Western Tropics (Classic Reprint) (p. 2186)
Swan, Eliza a. Opal Queen (Classic Reprint) (p. 1665)
Swan, Erin. Bright Star. (p. 281)
Swan, Felicity, illus. see Hirschi, Hans M.
Swan, Finn, illus. see Hirschi, Hans M.
Swan, Geoff. Mystery of the Spaced Out Blue Grouse. (p. 1570)
Swan, Gloria, illus. see Finke, Margot.
Swan, Graham. Kimmy the Koala Helps the Honey Bees in Summertown Wood. (p. 1218)
Swan, H. E. It Might Be: A Story of the Future Progress of the Sciences, the Wonderful Advancement in the Methods, of Government & the Happy, State of the People (Classic Reprint) (p. 1141)
Swan, Henry, jt. auth. see Mills, Nathan.
Swan, Maggie. For the Sake o' the Siller: A Fifeshire Story of Forty Years Ago (Classic Reprint) (p. 763)
Swan, Mark. Her Own Money: A Comedy in Three Acts (Classic Reprint) (p. 956)
Swan, Miranda Eliot. Daisy: The Autobiography of a Cat (Classic Reprint) (p. 497)
Swan, Myra. Ballast: A Novel (Classic Reprint) (p. 161)
Swan, Owen, illus. see Cummings, Phil.
Swan, Owen, illus. see Fenton, Corinne.
Swan, Phoebe. King Leonard's Teddy. Swan, Phoebe, illus. (p. 1220)
Swan, Richard. Melody's Unicorn: A Story of Here & There. (p. 1443)
—Pardoner's Prologue & Tale. (p. 1699)
Swan, Ruth Osborne. Mr. & Mrs. Europe (Classic Reprint) (p. 1517)
Swan, S. How Reindeer Learn How to Fly. Swan, S., illus. (p. 1034)
Swan, Susan, illus. see Chernesky, Felicia Sanzari.
Swan, Susan, illus. see Glaser, Linda.
Swan, Susan, illus. see Pearson, Carrie A.
Swan, Susan, illus. see Profiri, Charline.
Swan, Susan, illus. see Rusch, Elizabeth.
Swan, Susan, illus. see Slade, Suzanne.
Swan, Susan, jt. auth. see Sidman, Joyce.
Swan, William D. Primary School Reader, Vol. 3: Designed for the First Class in Primary Schools, & for the Lowest Class in Grammar Schools (Classic Reprint) (p. 1792)
Swan, William Draper. American Comprehensive Reader: For the Use of Schools (Classic Reprint) (p. 71)
Swanberg, Arvon & Spicer, Carolyn. Big, Blue, Overstuffed Chair. (p. 217)
Swanepoel, Sharon. Adventures of Seek & Save Volume 3: The Village. Locsinto, Lucas, illus. (p. 27)
Swaney, Julianna, illus. see Gaines, Joanna.
Swaney, Julianna, illus. see Gilbert, Frances.
Swaney, Julianna, illus. see Krishnaswami, Uma.
Swaney, Julianna, illus. see Kulling, Monica.
Swaney, Julianna, illus. see Wetzel, JoAnne Stewart.
Swank, Denise Grover. One Paris Summer (p. 1661)
Swank, Samantha. Character Guide. (p. 357)
Swann, Chelsy. Maginty's Quest: A Swashbuckling Adventures Story for All Readers from 10 Years Old To 90! (p. 1381)
Swann, Delyth. Tales from the Trig Points — the Discovery. (p. 2183)
Swann, Michelle. Angels Watching over Me. (p. 86)
Swann, Peter J. My First Barbecue Book. (p. 1540)
Swann, Rick. Our School Garden! Hale, Christy, illus. (p. 1680)
Swann, Stephen. Blooter Boys. (p. 247)
—Magical TV. (p. 1380)
—Where's Our Submarine. (p. 2440)
Swann, Tammy & Benchmark Education Co., LLC Staff. Roy Makes a Choice. (p. 1909)
—Stop! It's a Frog! (p. 2122)
Swansborough, W. Newfoundland Months, a Poem: Newfoundland's National Anthem, Seal Fishery (Classic Reprint) (p. 1600)
Swanson, Angie. Hawaii. (p. 940)
—Idaho. (p. 1089)
—Indiana. (p. 1116)
—Iowa. (p. 1133)
—Kansas. (p. 1203)
—Louisiana. (p. 1358)
—Maine. (p. 1383)
—Maryland. (p. 1416)
Swanson, Bruce. Gray Wolf's Search Peterson, Gary, illus. (p. 883)
Swanson, Cher. Bender Boys: Short Stories. (p. 199)
Swanson, David. Tube World. Burke, Shane, illus. (p. 2298)
Swanson, David C. N. Tube World. Burke, Shane, illus. (p. 2298)
Swanson, Diane. Nibbling on Einstein's Brain: The Good, the Bad & the Bogus in Science. Blake, Francis, illus. (p. 1602)
—Welcome to the World of Animals (p. 2399)
—You Are Weird: Your Body's Peculiar Parts & Funny Functions. Boake, Kathy, illus. (p. 2525)
Swanson, Edward I. Link, Vol. 30: July, 1972 (Classic Reprint) (p. 1304)
—Link, Vol. 30: June, 1972 (Classic Reprint) (p. 1304)
—Link, Vol. 30: December 1972 (Classic Reprint) (p. 1304)
—Link, Vol. 31: December 1973 (Classic Reprint) (p. 1304)
—Link, Vol. 31: A Magazine for Armed Forces Personnel; March 1973 (Classic Reprint) (p. 1304)
—Link, Vol. 31: A Magazine for Armed Forces Personnel; October, 1973 (Classic Reprint) (p. 1304)
—Link, Vol. 31: A Magazine for Armed Forces Personnel; February, 1973 (Classic Reprint) (p. 1304)
—Link, Vol. 31: January, 1973 (Classic Reprint) (p. 1305)
—Link, Vol. 31: November, 1973 (Classic Reprint) (p. 1305)
—Link, Vol. 32: A Magazine for Armed Forces Personnel; June 1974 (Classic Reprint) (p. 1305)
Swanson, James L. Bloody Times: The Funeral of Abraham Lincoln & the Manhunt for Jefferson Davis. (p. 246)
—Chasing King's Killer: The Hunt for Martin Luther King, Jr.'s Assassin. (p. 362)
—Chasing Lincoln's Killer: The Search for John Wikes Booth. (p. 362)
—Manhunt. (p. 1397)
—President Has Been Shot! The Assassination of John F. Kennedy. (p. 1789)
Swanson, Jennifer. Amazing Feats of Electrical Engineering (p. 65)
—Attractive Truth about Magnetism. Lum, Bernice, illus. (p. 135)
—Bartolomeu Dias: First European Sailor to Reach the Indian Ocean. (p. 168)
—Body Bugs: Invisible Creatures Lurking Inside You (p. 253)
—Bridges! With 25 Science Projects for Kids. Stone, Bryan, illus. (p. 280)
—Building with Poop. (p. 295)
—Busting Boredom with Experiments. (p. 301)
—Environmental Activist Wangari Maathai. (p. 657)
—Explore Force & Motion! With 25 Great Projects. Stone, Bryan, illus. (p. 679)
—Lewis & Clark. (p. 1282)
—Metamorphic Rocks (p. 1452)
—Pearl Harbor. McMorris, Kelley, illus. (p. 1710)
—Save the Crash-Test Dummies Grooms, TeMika, illus. (p. 1937)
—Shocking Truth about Electricity. Lum, Bernice, illus. (p. 2008)
—Spies, Lies, & Disguise: The Daring Tricks & Deeds That Won World War II. O'Malley, Kevin, illus. (p. 2081)
—Top Secret Science: Projects You Aren't Supposed to Know About (p. 2264)
—Tsunamis. (p. 2298)
—Uninvited Guests: Invisible Creatures Lurking in Your Home. (p. 2329)
—Zoology: Cool Women Who Work with Animals. Chandhok, Lena, illus. (p. 2544)
Swanson, Jennifer, jt. auth. see Omoth, Tyler.
Swanson, Jennifer, jt. auth. see Workman Publishing.
Swanson, Jennifer A. How Have Animals Evolved & Adapted? (p. 1031)
—Smart Strategies for Turning an Idea into a Product or Service. (p. 2041)
—Top 10 Secrets for Saving Successfully. (p. 2263)
—Wonderful World of Wearable Devices (p. 2490)
Swanson, Jennifer & Larson, Kirby. Pearl Harbor. McMorris, Kelley, illus. (p. 1710)
Swanson, Jennifer & Leet, Karen M. Tiny Creepy Creatures. (p. 2248)
Swanson, Jennifer Ann. Shocking Truth about Electricity Lum, Bernice, illus. (p. 2008)
Swanson, Jennifer, et al. LOL Physical Science. Lum, Bernice, illus. (p. 1340)
Swanson, Jill K., tr. see Shakespeare, William, et al.
Swanson, Katharine, jt. auth. see Delacre, Lulu.
Swanson, Linnea C., jt. auth. see Gritzner, Charles F.
Swanson, Maggie. Awesome Animals Coloring Book. (p. 144)
—Best-Loved Aesop's Fables Coloring Book. (p. 206)
—Easy Christmas Crafts: 12 Holiday Cut & Make Decorations. (p. 620)
—Easy Easter Tabletop Crafts. (p. 620)
—Floral Fantasies Stained Glass Coloring Book. (p. 750)
—Let's Color Together — Sun, Moon & Stars. (p. 1270)
—Lucky Cats Stickers. (p. 1364)
—My Backyard Color by Number. (p. 1531)
—My Storybook Paper Dolls. (p. 1561)
—SPARK Circles of Fun Animals Coloring Book. (p. 2074)
—Spark - Flower Fun Coloring Book. (p. 2074)
—SPARK Sea Life Designs Coloring Book. (p. 2074)
—Spark - Sun, Moon & Stars Coloring Book. (p. 2074)
—Sun, Moon & Stars Designs to Color. (p. 2151)
—Zany Zoo Stained Glass Jr. Coloring Book. (p. 2538)
Swanson, Maggie, illus. see Albee, Sarah, et al.
Swanson, Maggie, illus. see Albee, Sarah.
Swanson, Maggie, illus. see Allen, Constance.
Swanson, Maggie, illus. see Davidson, Alice Joyce.
Swanson, Maggie, illus. see Dreyer, Ellen.
Swanson, Maggie, illus. see Muntean, Michaela.
Swanson, Maggie, illus. see Stone, Jon & Albee, Sarah.
Swanson, Maggie, tr. see Dreyer, Ellen.
Swanson, Maggie & Paper Dolls. Lucky Cats. (p. 1364)
Swanson, Matthew. Babies Ruin Everything. Behr, Robbi, illus. (p. 147)
—Everywhere, Wonder. Behr, Robbi, illus. (p. 674)
—Real Mccoys. Behr, Robbi, illus. (p. 1849)
—Real Mccoys: Two's a Crowd. Behr, Robbi, illus. (p. 1849)
—Real Mccoys: Wonder Undercover. Behr, Robbi, illus. (p. 1849)
Swanson, Michlin. First Flying Car. (p. 737)
Swanson, Peter Joseph, illus. see Bond, Alan.
Swanson Sateren, Shelley. Adventures at Hound Hotel. Melmon, Deborah, illus. (p. 19)
—Adventures at Tabby Towers Melmon, Deborah, illus. (p. 19)
—Adventures of Hound Hotel Collection. Melmon, Deborah, illus. (p. 24)
—Boxing Bootsie. Melmon, Deborah, illus. (p. 267)
—Cool Crosby. Melmon, Deborah, illus. (p. 448)
—Disappearing Darcy. Melmon, Deborah, illus. (p. 553)
—Drooling Dudley. Melmon, Deborah, illus. (p. 605)
—Fishing Frankie. Melmon, Deborah, illus. (p. 742)
—Leaping Lizzie. Melmon, Deborah, illus. (p. 1255)
—Max & Zoe. Sullivan, Mary, illus. (p. 1427)
—Mighty Murphy. Melmon, Deborah, illus. (p. 1463)
—School in Colonial America. (p. 1946)
—Stinky Stanley. Melmon, Deborah, illus. (p. 2120)
Swanson Sateren, Shelley, et al. It's Back to School ... Way Back! (p. 1144)
Swanson, Shari. Honey, the Dog Who Saved Abe Lincoln. Groenink, Chuck, illus. (p. 999)
Swanson, Tom. Twas the Night Before Christmas. (p. 2302)
Swanton, John R. Myths & Tales of the Southeastern Indians (Classic Reprint) (p. 1572)
Swanton, John Reed. Tlingit Myths & Texts, Recorded by John R. Swanton (Classic Reprint) (p. 2252)
Swarbrick, David. Happy Root Beer. White, Greg, illus. (p. 923)
—Trucks: The Legend of Beverly Joe Breece. Moran, Bruce, illus. (p. 2293)
Swarbrick, David E. Boats the Story of Billy Lee Telliot & the Bay Blaster Shootout. Moran, Bruce, illus. (p. 251)
—Peggy's Play House. (p. 1714)
—Twenty Goofy Gumballs: Counting Made Fun. (p. 2304)
Sward, Adam, illus. see Cook, Gary.
Swardstrom, Will, et al. Tales from the Canyons of the Damned 28. (p. 2182)
Swarmer, Kristina. Festival Poems. (p. 721)
Swarner, Kristina. Modeh Ani: A Good Morning Book. (p. 1485)
Swarner, Kristina, illus. see Gillen, Lynea.
Swarner, Kristina, illus. see Joslin, Mary.
Swarner, Kristina, illus. see Jules, Jacqueline.
Swarner, Kristina, illus. see McCaughrean, Geraldine & Hoffmann, E. T. A.
Swarner, Kristina, illus. see Rostoker-Gruber, Karen.
Swarte, Joost, illus. see Lewis, Catherine.
Swartout, Jenny. Little One Behind the Badge. (p. 1323)
Swartout, Norman Lee. Arrival of Kitty: A Farce in Three Acts (Classic Reprint) (p. 119)
Swarts, Katherine, ed. Genetic Disorders. (p. 815)
Swartz, Clay. Who Wins? 100 Historical Figures Go Head-To-Head & You Decide the Winner! Booth, Tom, illus. (p. 2452)
Swartz, Daniel. Bim & Bom, 2nd Edition: A Shabbat Tale Iwai, Melissa, illus. (p. 227)
Swartz, Daniel, illus. see Drury, David.
Swartz, Elly. Finding Perfect. (p. 730)
—Give & Take. (p. 839)
—Smart Cookie. (p. 2040)
Swartz, Karen, illus. see Schulze, Christine E.
Swartz, Nancy Sohn. In Our Image: God's First Creatures. Hall, Melanie, illus. (p. 1106)
Swartz Pepper, Kenda. Well Earth Well Me! (p. 2399)
Swartzberg, Noreen. Do You Believe in Angels? (p. 571)
Swasey, Robert. Kendall's Sister (Classic Reprint) (p. 1209)
Swatling, Todd. What Happens to Space Probes? (p. 2411)
—What Is Space Junk? (p. 2416)
Swatsley, Scott. Crossover Chronicles: Book 3 (of 3): Dream Wars. (p. 478)
Swayne, Martin. Lord Richard in the Pantry (Classic Reprint) (p. 1348)
Swayze, Alan. End of World War I: The Treaty of Versailles & Its Tragic Legacy. (p. 649)
Swayze, J. C. Ossawattomie Brown; or the Insurrection at Harpers Ferry: A Drama in Three Acts (Classic Reprint) (p. 1674)
Swazey, Arthur. Boston Girl: A Story of Boston, Bar Harbor, & Paris (Classic Reprint) (p. 264)
Swazinski, Ed. At the Carnival: Understand & Apply Properties of Operations. (p. 130)
Sweaney, Deborah. Spirit of the Limestone House. (p. 2083)
Swearingen, Greg, illus. see Donaldson, Julia.
Swearingen, Greg, illus. see Easton, Kelly.
Swearingen, Greg, illus. see Niner, Holly L.
Swearingen, Greg, illus. see Strasser, Todd.
Swearingen, Hala Wittwer, illus. see Hays, Anna Jane.
Swearingen, Sara. Lost Space Warrior. (p. 1355)
—Lost Space Warrior (Volume 3) (p. 1355)
Swears, Herbert. Unknown Quantity: A Play in Three Acts (Classic Reprint) (p. 2333)
Sweat, Jeff. Mayfly. (p. 1430)
—Scorpion. (p. 1962)
Sweat, Lynn, illus. see Parish, Herman.
Sweat, Lynn, illus. see Parish, Peggy & Parish, Herman.
Sweat, Lynn, illus. see Parish, Peggy.
Sweazey, Davy. Ball Pythons. (p. 161)
—Bush Vipers. (p. 301)
—Death Adders. (p. 521)
—King Cobras. (p. 1220)
Swedeen, Staci. Abraham Lincoln, the Lincoln-Douglas Debates: Set Of 6. (p. 7)
—Abraham Lincoln, the Lincoln-Douglas Debates. (p. 7)
—Harriet Beecher Stowe, Uncle Tom's Cabin: Set Of 12. (p. 933)
—Harriet Beecher Stowe, Uncle Tom's Cabin. (p. 933)
—Rumor Report, the Big Jump. (p. 1914)
Swedeen, Staci & Benchmark Education Co., LLC Staff. Rumor y el Gran Salto: Set of 6 with Common Core Teacher Materials. (p. 1914)
Sweeney, Alyse. Canyons. (p. 323)
—Frogs (p. 790)
—High-Rise Thriller. (p. 968)
—Mudpuppies. (p. 1524)
—Rivers (p. 1887)
—Toads (p. 2254)
Sweeney, Alyse & Rustad, Martha E. H. Masked Mob Mystery: A Zoo Animal Mystery (p. 1417)
Sweeney, Isaac, ed. see Alva, Kristian.
Sweeney, Jewel. Adventures of Bugaboo & Ladybug: Out of This World. (p. 22)
—Adventures of Bugaboo & Ladybug: The Fire Breathing Dragon. (p. 22)
Sweeney, Joan. Me & My Amazing Body. (p. 1432)
—Me & My Amazing Body. Miller, Ed, illus. (p. 1432)
—Me & My Family Tree. (p. 1433)
—Me & My Family Tree. Trithart, Emma, illus. (p. 1433)
—Me & My Place in Space. (p. 1433)
—Me & My Place in Space. Gore, Christine, illus. (p. 1433)
—Me & the Measure of Things. Kath, Katie, illus. (p. 1433)
—Me Counting Time: From Seconds to Centuries. Willmore, Alex, illus. (p. 1433)
—Me on the Map. (p. 1433)
—Me on the Map. Leng, Qin, illus. (p. 1433)
Sweeney, Jon M. Margaret & the Pope Go to Assisi. DeLeon, Roy, illus. (p. 1403)
—Margaret's First Holy Week. DeLeon, Roy, illus. (p. 1403)
—Margaret's Night in St. Peter's (a Christmas Story) DeLeon, Roy, illus. (p. 1403)
—Pope's Cat. DeLeon, Roy, illus. (p. 1776)
Sweeney, Kevin, jt. auth. see Carroll, Lewis, pseud.
Sweeney, Linda Booth. When the Snow Falls. Christy, Jana, illus. (p. 2433)
Sweeney, Monica. How the Crayons Saved the Rainbow. Parker-Thomas, Feronia, illus. (p. 1035)
Sweeney, Monica & Thomas, Becky. Loom Magic Charms! 25 Cool Designs That Will Rock Your Rainbow. (p. 1348)
—Loom Magic Creatures! 25 Awesome Animals & Mythical Beings for a Rainbow of Critters. (p. 1348)
Sweeney, Monica & Yelvington, Lauren. Can You Yawn Like a Fawn? A Help Your Child to Sleep Book. Watkins, Laura, illus. (p. 319)
Sweeney, Samantha, et al. My First Farm Stories. Harry, Rebecca, illus. (p. 1544)
—My First Night-Night Stories. (p. 1545)
Sweeny, Elizabeth Mifflin, illus. see Sweeny, Vell.
Sweeny, Sheila. Scyther, Heart of a Champion. (p. 1966)
Sweeny, Vell. Second Hand Cat. Sweeny, Elizabeth Mifflin, illus. (p. 1973)
Sweers, Carolyn. Encountering Christmas. (p. 648)
Sweet, Alex. Three Dozen Good Stories: From Texas Siftings (Classic Reprint) (p. 2232)
Sweet, Alex Edwin. On a Mexican Mustang, Through Texas, from the Gulf to the Rio Grande (Classic Reprint) (p. 1652)
Sweet, Alexander Edwin. Sketches from Texas Siftings (Classic Reprint) (p. 2031)
Sweet Briar School, illus. see Wolf, Penny, et al.
Sweet, E. M. Aces the Cat & the Bird Feeder. (p. 10)
Sweet, Frank Herbert. Golden Stories: A Selection of the Best Fiction by the Foremost Writers (Classic Reprint) (p. 859)
Sweet, George H. Lord Byron's Dream Book (Classic Reprint) (p. 1348)
Sweet, Henry. History of English Sounds from the Earliest Period: With Full Word-Lists (Classic Reprint) (p. 977)
—History of English Sounds from the Earliest Period: Including an Investigation of the General Laws of Sound Change, & Full Word Lists (Classic Reprint) (p. 977)
—History of English Sounds from the Earliest Period: Including an Investigation of Th General Laws of Sound Change, & Full Word Lists; Series D. Miscellaneous. (p. 977)
—New English Grammar, Logical & Historical: By Henry Sweet, Volume 2 - Scholar's Choice Edition. (p. 1593)
—Second Middle English Primer: Extracts from Chaucer, with Grammar & Glossary (Classic Reprint) (p. 1973)
—Second Middle English Primer; Extracts from Chaucer, with Grammar & Glossary. (p. 1973)
—Student's Dictionary of Anglo-Saxon (Classic Reprint) (p. 2143)
Sweet, Henry, jt. auth. see Chaucer, Geoffrey.
Sweet, J. H. Bloodstone Miracles (Clock Winders) (p. 246)
—Clock of the Universe (Clock Winders Book Four) (p. 406)
—Foo & Friends Storybook. (p. 759)
—Lost Genie Diaries (Clock Winders) (p. 1353)
—Netherwind & Laurelstone (Clock Winders Book Three) (p. 1589)
—Noontime in the Peacock Garden (Clock Winders) (p. 1619)

—Good Dog! (p. 862)
—Here, Kitty! (p. 958)
Swinney, Nicola Jane. Complete Guide to Cats & Dogs. (p. 434)
—Complete Guide to Horses. (p. 434)
—I Love Dogs & Puppies: Over 50 Breeds. (p. 1069)
—I Love Dogs & Puppies. (p. 1069)
—I Love Horses & Ponies. (p. 1069)
—My Little Book of Dogs & Puppies. (p. 1552)
—My Little Book of Horses & Ponies. (p. 1552)
—My Little Book of Horses & Ponies. Langrish, Bob, illus. (p. 1552)
Swinton, Charles. Jock o' Rippon (Classic Reprint) (p. 1170)
Swinton, Ernest Dunlop. Green Curve: And Other Stories (Classic Reprint) (p. 894)
Swinton, Patty. What's Life Like with a Single Parent? (p. 2425)
—Why Do We Celebrate Presidents' Day? (p. 2457)
Swinton, Robert Blair. Indian Tale or Two: Reprinted from the Blackheath Local Guide; with an Introduction (Classic Reprint) (p. 1116)
Swinton, William. New Word-Analysis, or School Etymology of English Derivative Words: With Practical Exercises in Spelling, Analyzing, Defining, Synonyms & the Use of Words (Classic Reprint) (p. 1598)
—New Word-Analysis, or School Etymology of English Derivative Words: With Practical Exercises in Spelling, Analyzing, Defining, Synonyms, & the Use of Words (Classic Reprint) (p. 1598)
—Readings in Nature's Book (Classic Reprint) (p. 1847)
—School Manual of English Composition: For Advanced Classes in Public Schools, & for High Schools, Academies, etc (Classic Reprint) (p. 1946)
—Standard Supplementary Readers: Book of Tales Being School Readings, Imaginative & Emotional in Prose & Poetry (Classic Reprint) (p. 2100)
—Swinton's: Third Reader (Classic Reprint) (p. 2170)
—Swinton's Advanced First Reader (Classic Reprint) (p. 2170)
—Swinton's Advanced Fourth Reader (Classic Reprint) (p. 2170)
—Swinton's Advanced Third Reader (Classic Reprint) (p. 2170)
—Swinton's First Reader (Classic Reprint) (p. 2170)
—Swinton's Fourth Reader (Classic Reprint) (p. 2170)
—Swinton's Primer & First Reader (Classic Reprint) (p. 2170)
—Word Book of English Spelling. (p. 2493)
—Word Book of English Spelling (Classic Reprint) (p. 2493)
—Word Primer: A Beginner's Book in Oral & Written Spelling (Classic Reprint) (p. 2493)
—Word-Book of English Spelling, Oral & Written: Designed to Attain Practical Results in the Acquisition of the Ordinary English Vocabulary, & to Serve As an Introduction to Word-Analysis (Classic Reprint) (p. 2493)
—Word-Primer: A Beginner's Book in Oral & Written Spelling (Classic Reprint) (p. 2493)
Swinyer, William F. Wilmerding Life, Vol. 10: October, 1912 (Classic Reprint) (p. 2470)
—Wilmerding Life, Vol. 10: December, 1912 (Classic Reprint) (p. 2470)
Swiridoff, Sandi & Dunham, Wendy. Reagandoodle & Little Buddy Find a Forever Family. Sparks, Michal, illus. (p. 1848)
—Reagandoodle & Little Buddy Welcome Baby: The Blessing & Fun of a New Little One. (p. 1848)
Swisher, Bella French. Struggling up to the Light: The Story of a Woman's Life. (p. 2142)
—Struggling up to the Light: The Story of a Woman's Life (Classic Reprint) (p. 2142)
Swisher, Dianne. To Save a Mockingbird. (p. 2253)
Swisher, Elizabeth, illus. see Sanders, Nancy I.
Swisher, Michael-Che, illus. see Troeger, Virginia B.
Swisher, Michael-Che, tr. see Troeger, Virginia B.
Switek, Brian. Prehistoric Predators. Csotonyi, Julius, illus. (p. 1787)
—T Rex Handbook. Csotonyi, Julius, illus. (p. 2174)
Switzer, Bobbi, illus. see Menge, Dawn.
Switzer, Bobbi, illus. see Moore, S. D.
Switzer, Holly. Attitude of Gratitude. (p. 135)
Switzer Hutson, Betty. History of the Christian Methodist Episcopal Church for Children. (p. 980)
Switzer, Jennie Bartlett. Elder Northfield's Home: Or, Sacrificed on the Mormon Altar; a Story of Territorial Days in Utah (Classic Reprint) (p. 630)
Switzer, Maurice. Mrs. Goose, Her Book (Classic Reprint) (p. 1522)
—Satire & Song: Simple Lays & Careless Rhymes of Olden Days & Modern Times (Classic Reprint) (p. 1936)
—Trying It on the Dog (Classic Reprint) (p. 2297)
Switzerland, Knight of Chillon of. Mormon of the Little Manitou Island: An Historical Romance (Classic Reprint) (p. 1506)
Swoboda, Lois. Old Neb & the Ghost Ship Wallace, Leslie, illus. (p. 1647)
—Old Neb & the Lighthouse Treasure. Wallace, Leslie, illus. (p. 1647)
Swofford, Conover. Brave Boys Bible Trivia: 50 Adventurous Quizzes. (p. 276)
Swofford, Morgan, illus. see Rogers, Rachel & Lineberry, Joe.
Swope, Bob. Teach'n Beginning Defensive Basketball Drills, Plays, & Games Free Flow Handbook. (p. 2195)
—Teach'n Beginning Defensive Football Drills, Plays, & Games Free Flow Handbook. (p. 2195)
—Teach'n Beginning Hunting & Hunter Safety Free Flow Handbook. (p. 2195)
—Teach'n Beginning Offensive Basketball Drills, Plays, & Games Free Flow Handbook. (p. 2195)
—Teach'n Beginning Offensive Soccer Drills, Plays, Strategies, & Games Free Flow Handbook. (p. 2195)
Swope, Brenda, illus. see Blace, Maria.
Swope, Brenda, illus. see Calabrese, Diane Marie.
Swope, Brenda, illus. see Cardona, Nancy.
Swope, Brenda, illus. see Doman, Dave.
Swope, Brenda, illus. see Dubrule, Jackie.
Swope, Brenda, illus. see Emanuel, Lora.
Swope, Brenda, illus. see Fass, Amanda L.
Swope, Brenda, illus. see Ferry, Ann.
Swope, Brenda, illus. see Hart-Plaugher, Teresa.
Swope, Brenda, illus. see Joseph, Beverly L.
Swope, Brenda, illus. see Kirkland, Kim M.
Swope, Brenda, illus. see Lawson, Barbara.
Swope, Brenda, illus. see Mattingly, Robin.
Swope, Brenda, illus. see McDade Jr, Bert M.
Swope, Brenda, illus. see Murray, Rosalie.
Swope, Brenda, illus. see Ramirez, Iz.
Swope, Brenda, illus. see Robinson Ed. D., Shannon R.
Swope, Brenda, illus. see Seaman, Lucy.
Swope, Brenda, illus. see Stewart, Mark R.
Swope, Brenda, illus. see Trimoglie, Mario.
Swore, Wendy S. Monster Like Me. (p. 1496)
Swynnerton, Charles. Indian Nights' Entertainment: Or, Folk-Tales from the Upper Indus; with Numerous Illustrations by Native Hands (Classic Reprint) (p. 1116)
—Indian Nights' Entertainment. (p. 1116)
Sy, Cleoward, illus. see Mallorey, Gemma.
Sy, Cleoward, illus. see Shirley, Cindy L.
Sy, Cleoward, illus. see Shirley, Cindy.
Sy, James O. Elixir (p. 636)
Sybesma, Lila Jeanne Elliot. Yours: The Civil War, a Love Triangle, & the Steamboat Sultana. (p. 2535)
Sycamore, Beth. Who Needs a Hug? A Finding Dory Story. Disney Storybook Artists, illus. (p. 2449)
—Who Needs a Hug? A Finding Dory Story. Disney Storybook Artists, Disney Storybook, illus. (p. 2449)
Sycamore-Batty, Sharon, illus. see Gwynn, Michele E.
Sycolin Creek Elementary School (Leesburg, Va.) Staff, contrib. by. Greatest Homework Excuse Book Ever. (p. 891)
Sydenham, Alvin Humphrey, jt. auth. see King, Charles.
Syder, Andrew, illus. see Howard, Mike.
Sydnor, Parker J. When I Feel... ! (p. 2430)
Sydor, Colleen. Fishermen Through & Through Kerrigan, Brooke, illus. (p. 742)
—McGuillicuddy Book of Personal Records (p. 1432)
—Timmerman Was Here. Debon, Nicolas, illus. (p. 2247)
Syed, Anoosha, illus. see Barnaby, Hannah.
Syed, Anoosha, illus. see Brown, Karamo & Brown, Jason
Syed, Anoosha, illus. see Harper, Benjamin & Stephens, Sarah Hines.
Syed, Anoosha, illus. see Harper, Benjamin, et al.
Syed, Anoosha, illus. see Harrington, Claudia.
Syed, Anoosha, illus. see Ragsdale, Linda.
Syed, Anoosha, illus. see Saeed, Aisha.
Syed, Anoosha, illus. see Soderberg, Erin.
Syed, Anoosha, illus. see Stabler, David.
Syed, Hafsa N. Piggy Wanted to Learn. (p. 1743)
Syed, Mansha. Discovery: The Four Syeds. (p. 556)
Syed, Matthew. You Are Awesome. Triumph, Toby, illus. (p. 2524)
—You Are Awesome Journal. (p. 2524)
Syed, Raahem. You Never See Me Coming. Qadri, Rumaysa Adnan and Zaina, illus. (p. 2528)
Syed, Saba. Acquaintance. (p. 11)
Syed, Tayyaba. Islam. (p. 1139)
Sygh, Rian, illus. see Mientus, Andy.
Sygh, Rian, illus. see Ostertag, Molly Knox, et al.
Sygh, Rian, illus. see Tynion Iv, James & Johns, Sam.
Syken, Bill, jt. auth. see The Editors of Sports Illustrated Kids.
Sykes, Arthur Alkin, jt. auth. see Gogol, Nikolai.
Sykes, C. A. Service & Sport on the Tropical Nile: Some Records of the Duties & Diversions of an Officer among Natives & Big Game During the Re-Occupation of the Nilotic Province (Classic Reprint) (p. 1991)
Sykes, Ella C. Home-Help in Canada (Classic Reprint) (p. 996)
Sykes, Frederick Henry. Elementary English Composition (Classic Reprint) (p. 632)
—French Elements in Middle English: Chapters Illustrative of the Origin & Growth of Romance Influence on the Phrasal Power of Standard English in Its Formative Period (Classic Reprint) (p. 783)
Sykes, Julie. Ava & Star (p. 141)
—Bella at the Ball. Morgan, Richard, illus. (p. 196)
—I Don't Want to Go to Bed! Warnes, Tim, illus. (p. 1064)
—Isabel & Cloud (p. 1138)
—Layla & Dancer (p. 1253)
—Olivia & Snowflake (p. 1650)
—Scarlett & Blaze (p. 1942)
—Sophia & Rainbow (p. 2064)
—Sparkle. (p. 2075)
—Unicorn Academy (p. 2328)
—Unicorn Academy #1: Sophia & Rainbow. Truman, Lucy, illus. (p. 2328)
—Unicorn Academy #2: Scarlett & Blaze. Truman, Lucy, illus. (p. 2328)
—Unicorn Academy #3: Ava & Star. Truman, Lucy, illus. (p. 2328)
—Unicorn Academy #4: Isabel & Cloud. Truman, Lucy, illus. (p. 2328)
—Unicorn Academy #5: Layla & Dancer. Truman, Lucy, illus. (p. 2328)
—Unicorn Academy #6: Olivia & Snowflake. Truman, Lucy, illus. (p. 2328)
—Unicorn Academy #7: Rosa & Crystal. Truman, Lucy, illus. (p. 2328)
—Unicorn Academy #8: Ariana & Whisper. Truman, Lucy, illus. (p. 2328)
—Unicorn Academy: Magic of Friendship Boxed Set (Books 5-8) Truman, Lucy, illus. (p. 2328)
—Unicorn Academy: Rainbow of Adventure Boxed Set (Books 1-4) Truman, Lucy, illus. (p. 2328)
Sykes, Julie, jt. auth. see Warnes, Tim.
Sykes, Julie & Reed, Nathan. Pet Sitter: Beware the Werepup & Other Stories. (p. 1726)
Sykes, Julie, et al. Five Minute Christmas Stories. (p. 744)
Sykes, K B. Nicholas. (p. 1602)
Sykes M D, Robin a, illus. see MacGregor, Nancy.
Sykes, Mark. D'Ordel's Pantechnicon: An Universal Directory of the Mechanical Art of Manufacturing Illustrated Magazines, Intended As a Course of Learning for Future Writers; Containing an Account of the Advance of Literature in Modern Times (Classic Reprint) (p. 586)
—Through Five Turkish Provinces (Classic Reprint) (p. 2236)
Sykes, Sam. Brave Chef Brianna. Espiritu, Selina, illus. (p. 276)
Sykes, Shannon, illus. see Love, Pamela.
Sykes, Shelley & Szymanski, Lois. Soldier in the Cellar. (p. 2056)
Sykes, Tina. Elliot Makes a Friend. (p. 638)
Sykes-Bell, Lakeisha, jt. auth. see Lewis, Tameka.
Syler, Rachel, illus. see Ivey, Casi.
Syliboy, Alan. Mi'kmaw Animals (p. 1465)
—Thundermaker (p. 2238)
—Wolverine & Little Thunder: A Story of the First Canoe (p. 2484)
Sylliboy, Helen, tr. see Trottier, Maxine.
Sylte, Darren. Grandpa Wins the Big Game. Margolis, Al, illus. (p. 879)
Sylva, Carmen. Edleen Vaughan, or Paths of Peril (Classic Reprint) (p. 626)
—From Memory's Shrine: The Reminiscences of Carmen Sylva (H. M. Queen Elisabeth of Roumania) (Classic Reprint) (p. 792)
—Heart Regained: A Novel (Classic Reprint) (p. 945)
—How I Spent My Sixtieth Birthday (Classic Reprint) (p. 1032)
—Legends from River Mountain (Classic Reprint) (p. 1263)
Sylva, Rowan. Kleiner Fuchs und Die Regenstäbe. (p. 1227)
—Little Fox & the Rainsticks. Gast, Daniela, illus. (p. 1317)
Sylvada, Peter, illus. see Bunting, Eve.
Sylvada, Peter, illus. see Thomas, Patricia.
Sylvada, Peter, illus. see Whelan, Gloria.
Sylvain, Diez. Couleurs CAM'l'on. (p. 458)
Sylvain, Lignac. Avatars de Gaspard. le Coffre Ensorcel'(les) (p. 141)
—Avatars de Gaspard - le Jardin Myst'rieux(les) (p. 141)
Sylvaine, Jenny, illus. see Malaspina, Ann.
Sylvan Learning. 1st Grade Basic Math Success Workbook: Numbers & Operations, Geometry, Time & Money, Measurement & More; Activities, Exercises & Tips to Help Catch up, Keep up, & Get Ahead. (p. 2546)
—1st Grade Jumbo Language Arts Success Workbook: 3 Books in 1 # Reading Skill Builders, Spellings Games, Vocabulary Puzzles; Activities, Exercises, & Tips to Help Catch up, Keep up & Get Ahead. (p. 2546)
—1st Grade Jumbo Math Success Workbook: 3 Books in 1—Basic Math, Math Games & Puzzles, Shapes & Geometry; Activities, Exercises, & Tips to Help Catch up, Keep up, & Get Ahead. (p. 2546)
—1st Grade Reading Skill Builders Workbook: Letters & Sounds, Short & Long Vowels, Compound Words, Contractions, Syllables, Reading Comprehension, Plurals, & More. (p. 2546)
—2nd Grade Jumbo Language Arts Success Workbook: 3 Books in 1—Reading Skill Builders, Spelling Games & Activities, Vocabulary Puzzles; Activities, Exercises, & Tips to Help Catch up, Keep up & Get Ahead. (p. 2546)
—Kindergarten Basic Math Success Workbook: Counting to 5 & 10, Ordinal Numbers, Classifying & Sorting, Number Patterns, Picture Patterns, Geometry & Shapes, Measurement, & More. (p. 1218)
—Kindergarten Jumbo Math Success Workbook: 3 Books in 1—Basic Math, Math Games & Puzzles, Shapes & Geometry; Activities, Exercises, & Tips to Help You Catch up, Keep up, & Get Ahead. (p. 1218)
—Kindergarten Page per Day: Math Skills: Numbers & Counting, Estimating & Comparing, Picture & Number Patterns, Classification & Sorting, Shapes & Sizes. (p. 1218)
—Kindergarten Page per Day: Reading Skills: Consonant Sounds, Short Vowell Sounds, Beginning & Ending Sounds, Story Characters, Story Setting, Story Sequence. (p. 1218)
—Kindergarten Reading Readiness Workbook: Letters, Consonant Sounds, Beginning & Ending Sounds, Short Vowels, Rhyming Sounds, Sight Words, Color Words, & More. (p. 1218)
—Pre-K Beginning Letters Workbook: Uppercase Letters, Lowercase Letters, Tracing Activities, Alphabet Art, Letter Sounds, More; Activities, Exercises & Tips to Help Catch up, Keep up & Get Ahead. (p. 1786)
—Pre-K Beginning Numbers Workbook: Numbers 1-5, Numbers 6-10, Tracing Exercises, Color by Number, Number Recognition Number Games, & More. (p. 1786)
—Pre-K Letters, Numbers & Shapes Jumbo Workbook: 3 Books in 1 —Beginning Letters, Beginning Numbers, Shapes & Measurement; Ctivities, Exercises, & Tips to Help Catch up, Keep up, & Get Ahead. (p. 1786)
—Pre-K Page per Day: Letters: Alphabet Recognition, Uppercase Letters, Lowercase Letters, Writing Letters. (p. 1786)
—Pre-K Page per Day: Numbers: Number Recognition, Writing Numbers 1-10, Counting to 10, Less & More, Comparing & Matching. (p. 1786)
—Sylvan Kick Start for First Grade. (p. 2172)
—Sylvan Summer Smart Workbook: Between Grades 1 & 2. (p. 2173)
—Sylvan Summer Smart Workbook: Between Grades Pre-K & Kindergarten. (p. 2173)
Sylvan Learning Staff. First Grade Spelling Games & Activities (Sylvan Workbooks) (p. 737)
—Kindergarten Word Games (Sylvan Fun on the Run Series) (p. 1219)
Sylvan, Lu. Vladimir Putin. (p. 2364)
Sylvanus, Sylvanus. Pedestrian & Other Reminiscences at Home & Abroad: With Sketches of Country Life (Classic Reprint) (p. 1712)
—Rambles in Sweden & Gottland: With Etchings by the Way-Side (Classic Reprint) (p. 1839)
Sylvester, Alden W. Five Minutes in America a Voyage in Life. (p. 744)
Sylvester, Charles H. Journeys Through Bookland, Vol. 2: A New & Original Plan for Reading Applied to the World's Best Literature for Children (Classic Reprint) (p. 1183)
—New & Original, Plan for Reading Applied to the Applied Best Literature for Children, Vol. 10 (Classic Reprint) (p. 1591)
Sylvester, Charles Herbert. Journeys Through Bookland, Vol. 1: A New & Original Plan for Reading Applied to the World's Best Literature for Children (Classic Reprint) (p. 1183)
Sylvester, Emma, jt. auth. see Wade, Joseph Henry.
Sylvester, Herbert Milton. Homestead Highways (Classic Reprint) (p. 998)
Sylvester, Kevin. Baseballogy: Tons of Things You Never Knew. (p. 169)
—Basketballogy. (p. 171)
—Gargantua (Jr!) Defender of Earth (p. 810)
—MiNRS. (p. 1473)
—MiNRS 3. (p. 1473)
—Neil Flambé & the Aztec Abduction. (p. 1586)
—Neil Flambé & the Aztec Abduction. Sylvester, Kevin, illus. (p. 1586)
—Neil Flambé & the Bard's Banquet. Sylvester, Kevin, illus. (p. 1586)
—Neil Flambé & the Crusader's Curse. Sylvester, Kevin, illus. (p. 1586)
—Neil Flambé & the Duel in the Desert. Sylvester, Kevin, illus. (p. 1586)
—Neil Flambé & the Marco Polo Murders. (p. 1586)
—Neil Flambé & the Marco Polo Murders. Sylvester, Kevin, illus. (p. 1586)
—Neil Flambé & the Tokyo Treasure. Sylvester, Kevin, illus. (p. 1586)
—Neil Flambé Capers Collection: Neil Flambé & the Marco Polo Murders; Neil Flambé & the Aztec Abduction; Neil Flambé & the Crusader's Curse; Neil Flambé & the Tokyo Treasure. Sylvester, Kevin, illus. (p. 1586)
—Showtime: Meet the People Behind the Scenes. (p. 2013)
—Splinters. (p. 2085)
Sylvester, Kevin, illus. see Holomis, Lauri & Gretzky, Glen.
Sylvester, Kevin, illus. see Hoyte, Carol-Ann.
Sylvester, Kevin, illus. see Rondina, Catherine.
Sylvester, Kevin, jt. auth. see Hlinka, Michael.
Sylvester, Kevin & Hlinka, Michael. Follow Your Stuff: Who Makes It, Where Does It Come from, How Does It Get to You? (p. 758)
Sylvester, Merrill. Ho-Ho Where Did All My Reindeer Go? The Chicken Leg Detective Service. (p. 985)
Sylvester, Natalia. Running. (p. 1915)
Sylvester, Oscar. Life on a Commercial Fishing Boat. (p. 1295)
Sylvester, Sr. Land of the Angels Morrison, Nancy, illus. (p. 1242)
—Talking Memories. Morrison, Nancy, illus. (p. 2187)
Sylvestre, Daniel, illus. see Gingras, Charlotte.
Sylvie, Misslin. Alphabet Prend l'Avion Pour Zanzibar (Ne(l') (p. 59)
—Parle-Moi D'Amour. Adolescence: D'Couvertes et Nouvelles Questions. (p. 1700)
Syme, Daniel B., jt. auth. see Sonsino, Rifat.
Syme, David. Soul: A Study & an Argument (Classic Reprint) (p. 2066)
—Soul: A Study & an Argument - Scholar's Choice Edition. (p. 2066)
Symes, R. F. DK Eyewitness Books: Crystal & Gem: Admire the Beauty & Versatility of Crystals & Gems from Their Use in Elegant. (p. 567)
—DK Eyewitness Books: Rocks & Minerals: Unearth the Vast Wealth of the Rocks & Minerals Beneath Our Feet from Their Formation to Their Everyday Uses. (p. 567)
Symes, Richard. Monkey du - Life Is an Open Book. (p. 1493)
—Monkey du - Siblings. (p. 1493)
Symes, Ruth. Bella Donna: Too Many Spells. Lindsay, Marion, illus. (p. 197)
—Snowball: The Baby Bigfoot. McNaughton, Tina, illus. (p. 2048)
Symes, Ruth Louise. Mondays at Monster School. Reeve, Rosie, illus. (p. 1492)
Symes, Sally. Funny Face, Sunny Face. Beardshaw, Rosalind, illus. (p. 801)
—Little Baby's Busy Day: a Finger Wiggle Book. Sharratt, Nick, illus. (p. 1311)
—Little Baby's Playtime: a Finger Wiggle Book. Sharratt, Nick, illus. (p. 1311)
—Whose Toes Are Those? Sharratt, Nick, illus. (p. 2454)
—Yawn. Sharratt, Nick, illus. (p. 2518)
Symington, Andrew James. Pen & Pencil Sketches of Faröe & Iceland: With an Appendix Containing Translations from the Icelandic & 51 Illustrations Engraved on Wood W. J. Linton (Classic Reprint) (p. 1715)
—Samuel Lover: A Biographical Sketch with Selections from His Writings & Correspondence (Classic Reprint) (p. 1929)
Symington, Andrew James & Palsson, Olafur. Pen & Pencil Sketches of Faröe & Iceland. (p. 1715)
Symington, Lindsay, illus. see Benson, Robert Hugh.
Symington, Martha M. Global Heart Warming: Dream Believe Achieve Series. Sanderson, Jessica B., illus. (p. 843)
Symington, Sabrina, illus. see Karten, Ryan.
Symmons, Sheeres, illus. see Leslie, Emma.
Symon, Andrew. Jack Shian & the Destiny Stone: Book 3 in The Shian Quest Trilogy. (p. 1152)
—Jack Shian & the Mapa Mundi: In the Shian Quest Trilogy. (p. 1152)
Symon Simbotah, Symon, tr. see Pere, Tuula.
Symonds, Brandreth. Manual of Chemistry for the Use of Medical Students (Classic Reprint) (p. 1399)
Symonds, John Addington. Our Life in the Swiss Highlands (Classic Reprint) (p. 1679)
—Some Further Recollections of a Happy Life: Selected from the Journals of Marianne North, Chiefly Between the Years 1859 & 1869 (Classic Reprint) (p. 2059)
—Wine, Women, & Song: Medieval Latin Students' Songs Now First Translated into English Verse with an Essay. (p. 2472)
—Wine, Women, & Song. (p. 2472)
Symonds, Joseph White. Bowdoin Quill, Vol. 20: November, 1916 (Classic Reprint) (p. 266)

Symonds, Margaret. Child of the Alps (Classic Reprint) (p. 370)
—Days Spent on a Doge's Farm (Classic Reprint) (p. 515)
Symonds, Margaret, jt. auth. see Symonds, John Addington.
Symonds, William. Holiday Trips, in Extempore Doggerel (Classic Reprint) (p. 988)
Symons, Arthur. Cities & Sea-Coasts & Islands (Classic Reprint) (p. 394)
—London: A Book of Aspects (Classic Reprint) (p. 1340)
—Savoy: An Illustrated Monthly; July 1896 (Classic Reprint) (p. 1939)
—Savoy (Classic Reprint) (p. 1939)
—Savoy, Vol. 1 Of 5: An Illustrated Quarterly of 1896; Number One, January 1896 (Classic Reprint) (p. 1939)
—Savoy, Vol. 2: July, 1896 (Classic Reprint) (p. 1939)
—Savoy, Vol. 3: An Illustrated Monthly; October December 1896 (Classic Reprint) (p. 1939)
—Savoy, Vol. 4 Of 5: An Illustrated Monthly of 1896 (Classic Reprint) (p. 1939)
—Spiritual Adventures (Classic Reprint) (p. 2084)
Symons, F. A. Cicely in Ceylon (Classic Reprint) (p. 390)
Symons, Mitchell. Why Spacemen Can't Burp. (p. 2459)
Sympher, Leo. Die Neuen Wasserwirtschaftlichen Gesetze in Preußen: In Auftrage des Preußischen Herrn Ministers der Öffentlichen Arbeiten Für Den X. Internationalen Schiffahrt-Kongreß in Mailand (Classic Reprint) (p. 544)
Synarski, Susan, illus. see Gordon, Lynn & Chronicle Books Staff.
Synarski, Susan, illus. see Gordon, Lynn.
Synder, Gail. Teens & Smoking. (p. 2200)
Syndreamz, Hope. Amir's First Haircut: The Ongoing Saga of Life's Lessons Through the Eyes of a Young Boy. Owens, Sky, illus. (p. 75)
Synge, E. M., illus. see Synge, M. B.
Synge, E. M., jt. auth. see Synge, M. B.
Synge, Georgina M. Ride Through Wonderland (Classic Reprint) (p. 1878)
Synge, John M. Aran Islands: Parts I & II (Classic Reprint) (p. 109)
—Aran Islands: Parts III & IV (Classic Reprint) (p. 109)
—Aran Islands (Classic Reprint) (p. 109)
—Five Great Modern Irish Plays: The Playboy of the Western World; Juno & the Paycock Riders to the Sea; Spreading the News; Shadow & Substance; with a Foreword (Classic Reprint) (p. 743)
—In Wicklow & West Kerry (Classic Reprint) (p. 1112)
—In Wicklow, West Kerry & Connemara (Classic Reprint) (p. 1112)
—Playboy of the Western World: A Comedy in Three Acts (Classic Reprint) (p. 1760)
—Plays (Classic Reprint) (p. 1761)
—Tinker's Wedding: A Comedy in Two Acts (Classic Reprint) (p. 2248)
—Tinker's Wedding; Riders to the Sea; & the Shadow of the Glen (Classic Reprint) (p. 2248)
—Well of the Saints: A Comedy in Three Acts (Classic Reprint) (p. 2399)
—Works of John M. Synge, Vol. 1 (Classic Reprint) (p. 2498)
Synge, M. B. Reign of Queen Victoria. Edwards, Amy M. & Mugglin, Christina J., eds. (p. 1862)
—Struggle for Sea Power: A History of the British, French & Spanish Empires & Their Naval Wars Across Europe. Synge, E. M., illus. (p. 2142)
—Struggle for Sea Power. (p. 2142)
Synge, M. B. & Synge, E. M. Discovery of New Worlds: A History of the Roman, English, Spanish & Portuguese Empires; How Each Explored & Colonized New Lands. (p. 557)
Syntipas, Syntipas. Trattati Diversi Di Sendebar Indiano Filosopho Morale: Allo Illustriss. et Eccellentiss. S. Cosimo de Medici Dedicati (Classic Reprint) (p. 2279)
Syratt, Becky. Batsford Book of Music for Children. (p. 173)
Syrett, Netta. Day Journey (Classic Reprint) (p. 513)
—Fairy Doll, & Other Plays for Children (Classic Reprint) (p. 696)
—Magic London (Classic Reprint) (p. 1378)
—Old Miracle Plays of England (Classic Reprint) (p. 1647)
—Robin Goodfellow, & Other Fairy Plays for Children (Classic Reprint) (p. 1891)
—Rose Cottingham: A Novel (Classic Reprint) (p. 1905)
—Six Fairy Plays for Children (Classic Reprint) (p. 2028)
Syrewicz, Connor. Arts: Dance, Music, Theater, & Fine Art. (p. 123)
—Energizing Energy Markets: Clean Coal, Shale, Oil, Wind, & Solar. (p. 650)
—Farming, Ranching, & Agriculture. (p. 711)
—Masseur & Massage Therapist. (p. 1418)
—Personal Assistant. (p. 1725)
—Truck Driver. (p. 2292)
Syrewicz, Connor & Morkes, Andrew. Farmer: Feeding the World. (p. 710)
—Massage Therapist: Providing Relief & Relaxation. (p. 1418)
Syromiatnikof, S. N. Little Russian Masterpieces (Classic Reprint) (p. 1327)
Syson, Lydia. That Burning Summer. (p. 2212)
System, Eminence, illus. see Dione, Donald.
System, Eminence, illus. see Patterson, Keyonna.
Syswerda, Jean E. My Bedtime Story Bible for Little Ones Howarth, Daniel, illus. (p. 1532)
—Super Heroes Holy Bible (p. 2155)
—Super Heroes Storybook Bible O'Brien, Josh, illus. (p. 2155)
Syverson, Carolyn. Community Helpers. (p. 432)
—Places to Go! (p. 1753)
Szabla, Liz, ed. see Cordell, Matthew.
Szabla, Liz, ed. see Tanner, Lian.
Szabo, Balazs. Csipesz Mipesz: Egy Igaz Történet Fiataloknak Es Felnoteknek Egyarant. (p. 481)
—Hawaiian Legend: Of Love & Betrayal. (p. 940)
—HAWAII-I Legenda: Szerelemröl és Hütlenségröl. (p. 940)
—Tweezer Beezer: A True Story. (p. 2302)
Szabo, Erika M. Terry & the Number Fairy. (p. 2208)
Szabo, Levente, illus. see Kaufman, Amie.
Szac, Murielle. Adventures of Hermes, God of Thieves: 100 Journeys Through Greek Mythology. Provata-Carlone, Mika, tr. (p. 24)
Szafranski, Trevor. Never Walk Alone. (p. 1590)
Szalay, Dave, illus. see Bennett, Artie.
Szalay, Dave, jt. auth. see Meyer, Eileen R.
Szanyi, Joshua, illus. see Roemisch, Matt.
Szarka, Balazs. European Folk Tales. (p. 667)
Szcsesniak, Janet. Frog Who Made Friends. (p. 789)
Szczebak, Patricia & Peterson, Mary Joseph. Jesus Our Savior: The Story of God's Son for Children. (p. 1166)
Szczelaszczyk, Jeanette. Someplace in Time. (p. 2060)
Szecsi, Susan, illus. see Carlson, Jon C.
Szecsi, Susan, illus. see Metzger, Steve.
Szecsi, Susan, illus. see Reveno, Katie.
Szegedi, Katalin, illus. see Nobisso, Josephine.
Szegedi, Katalin, illus. see Sorenson, Margo.
Szekeres, Cyndy, illus. see Appelt, Kathi.
Szeps-Fralin, Christiane, jt. auth. see Fralin, Alfred G.
Szereszewski, Haley Rose, illus. see Silver, Avi.
Szewczyk, Elizabeth F. Lottery Dog: As Told by Mac. (p. 1356)
—Lottery Dog 2 the Great Rescue. (p. 1356)
Szewczyk, Manda, illus. see Weber, Roopa.
Szilagyi, Mary, illus. see Krauss, Ruth.
Szilagyi, Mary, illus. see Rylant, Cynthia.
Szitas, Kathie, ed. see Santora, L. Steven.
Szlapa, Rafal, illus. see Yomtov, Nel.
Szmidt, Aleksandra. I Love You, World. (p. 1079)
—Merry Christmas, World. (p. 1450)
Szmidt, Aleksandra, illus. see Hall, Hannah C.
Szold, Edwin. Valenian, 1918 (Classic Reprint) (p. 2344)
Szot, Karolyn. Breakfast Buddies & the Wild Waffle West. (p. 278)
Szpirglas, Jeff. Evil Eye. (p. 674)
—Tales from Beyond the Brain Hughes, Steven P., illus. (p. 2182)
—Tales from the Fringes of Fear. Hughes, Steven P., illus. (p. 2183)
—Wild Cards (p. 2463)
Szpirglas, Jeff & Saint-Onge, Danielle. Heads up! Concussion Awareness. (p. 942)
—Messy Miranda Whamond, Dave, illus. (p. 1452)
—Train Your Brain: How Your Brain Learns Best. (p. 2275)
—Your Brain: Understanding Your Body's Control Center. (p. 2533)
—Your Changing Brain: A Guidebook. (p. 2533)
Szuc, Jeff, illus. see Kaner, Etta.
Szucs, Barbara Szepesi. If You're Happy & You Know It (p. 1093)
Szulyovszky, Sarolta, illus. see Hillert, Margaret, et al.
Szulyovszky, Sarolta, illus. see Hillert, Margaret.
Szumski, Bonnie. Career in Electrical Engineering. (p. 329)
—Careers in Biotechnology. (p. 329)
—Careers in Fashion. (p. 329)
—Cheating. (p. 363)
Szumski, Bonnie & Karson, Jill. Angelina Jolie. Greenhaven Press Staff, ed. (p. 86)
—Careers in Engineering. (p. 329)
Szydlowski, Mary Vigliante. Are We There Yet? (p. 113)
—Ghoul School. (p. 830)
—Little Sowbug & the Big Flood. (p. 1328)
—Millie Muldoon & the Case of the Halloween Haunting. (p. 1467)
—Millie Muldoon & the Case of the Thanksgiving Turkey-Napper. (p. 1467)
—Millie Muldoon & the Christmas Mystery. (p. 1468)
Szymanski, Jennifer. All about Bears. (p. 48)
—Buzz, Bee! (p. 305)
—Climb, Koala! (p. 405)
—Here to There. (p. 958)
Szymanski, Lois. Chincoteague Pony Identification Cards (p. 378)
—Out of the Sea: Today's Chincoteague Pony (p. 1683)
—Surfer Dude: The Legendary Stallion of Chincoteague Kantjas, Linda, illus. (p. 2163)
—True Story of Miracle Man (p. 2295)
—True Story of Quintilius (p. 2295)
—Wild Colt Kantjas, Linda, illus. (p. 2463)
Szymanski, Lois K. Grandfather's Secret (p. 877)
—True Story of Sea Feather (p. 2295)
Szymona, Marlene L. My Sister Beth's Pink Birthday. Battuz, Christine, illus. (p. 1560)

T

T. Adventures of Sugar the Pup. Baker, David, illus. (p. 28)
—It's Prime Time, to Sleep. (p. 1147)
T Adams, William. Spelling-Book for Advanced Classes. (p. 2079)
T, C. J. Folk-Lore & Legends: Germany (Classic Reprint) (p. 757)
—Folk-Lore & Legends. (p. 757)
T Francis, Preston. Fictionals: Secrets in Crimson. (p. 722)
T, H. B. Letters from Abroad: Or, Scraps from New Zealand, Australia, & America (Classic Reprint) (p. 1279)
T, J. C. Sketches of Early Methodism in the Black Country: With the Romantic Story of the Leek-Seed Chapel (Classic Reprint) (p. 2031)
T J Chronos, Professor. Tolling Town @ One O'Clock. (p. 2256)
T, J. I. Young Wanderer's Cave: And Other Tales (Classic Reprint) (p. 2532)
T K R. Have You Seen the Sleep Fairy? (p. 939)
T, M. O., illus. see Wolly, Paul T.
T, N., illus. see Tinti, Natalie.
T, Otis. Paul Bunyan & His Loggers (Classic Reprint) (p. 1707)
T Smith, Alex. Claude All at Sea: A Picture Book. (p. 401)
T. W. Zimmerman, illus. see Dodgson, Y. K.
Ta, Vinh. Carter Meets His New Brother. (p. 335)
Taaffe, Gary. Bowels of Hell: Billy's Gotta Survive the City. (p. 266)
—Budgie Smugglers: Billy's Gotta Survive the City. (p. 290)
—Bullies: Billy's Gotta Survive the City. (p. 296)
—Final Straw: Amber's Story. (p. 727)
—Four Small Stones: Billy's Gotta Find Some Girls. (p. 772)
—Orphanage: Billy's Gotta Survive the City. (p. 1672)
—Tribal Scarring: Billy's Gotta Find Some Girls. (p. 2286)
—Walkabout: Billy's Gotta Find Some Girls. (p. 2372)
—WANTED! New Dad: Billy's Gotta Find a Family. (p. 2375)
Tab Books. Roads from Rome (Classic Reprint) (p. 1889)
Tabachnik, Anna T. Greece. (p. 892)
Taback, Simms. Joseph Had a Little Overcoat. (p. 1178)
Taback, Simms, illus. see Hennessy, B. G.
Taback, Simms, illus. see Ziefert, Harriet.
Tabacon, Marvin, illus. see Copeland, Billy M.
Tabain, Dave & Worland, Nadia. Powman 2: Discover the Strength Within. Ogilvie, Shane, illus. (p. 1783)
Tabak, John. Biofuels. (p. 228)
—Coal & Oil. (p. 410)
—Natural Gas & Hydrogen. (p. 1579)
—Nuclear Energy. (p. 1628)
—Solar & Geothermal Energy. (p. 2055)
—Wind & Water. (p. 2471)
Tabak, Lawrence. In Real Life. (p. 1106)
Tabares, Bridgitt, illus. see Tabares, Veronica.
Tabares, Veronica. Monkeys on an Island. Tabares, Bridgitt, illus. (p. 1494)
Tabarie, Hues De. Ordene de Chevalerie: Avec une Dissertation Sur l'Origine de la Lange Francoise, un Essai Sur les Etimologies, Quelques Contes Anciens, et un Glossaire Pour en Faciliter l'Intelligence (Classic Reprint) (p. 1669)
—Ordene de Chevalerie: Avec une Dissertation Sur l'Origine de la Langue Francoise; un Essai Sur les Etimologies; Quelques Contes Anciens; et un Glossaire Pour en Faciliter l'Intelligence (Classic Reprint) (p. 1669)
Tabart, Benjamin. Popular Fairy Tales, or a Lilliputian Library: Containing Twenty-Six Choice Pieces of Fancy & Fiction, by Those Renowned Personages, King Oberon, Queen Mab, Mother Goose, Mother Bunch, Master Puck, & Other Distinguished Personages at the Court of the F. (p. 1777)
Tabart, Tabart. Tabart's Collection of Popular Stories for the Nursery, Vol. 1: From the French, Italian, & Old English Writers (Classic Reprint) (p. 2174)
Tabary, illus. see Goscinny, René.
Tabary, Armelle, illus. see Goscinny, René.
Tabary, Jean, illus. see Goscinny, René.
Tabary, Jean, jt. auth. see Goscinny, René.
Tabatabaei, Maryam, illus. see Glaser, Linda.
Tabb, John B. Quips & Quiddits: Ques for the Qurious (Classic Reprint) (p. 1828)
Tabbaa, Ahmad. Camp. (p. 315)
—Lamp. (p. 1241)
Tabbutt, Steven, illus. see Gates Galvin, Laura.
Tabby, Abigail. Hokey Pokey Elmo (Sesame Street) Brannon, Tom, illus. (p. 986)
—KnitWits Make a Move! Wildish, Lee, illus. (p. 1229)
—Merry Christmas, Baby. Wong, Alice, illus. (p. 1450)
—Monsters Munch Lunch! (p. 1498)
—Welcome Home, Baby! Williams, Sam, illus. (p. 2397)
—¡Bienvenido a Casa, Bebé! (Welcome Home, Baby!) Romay, Alexis, tr. (p. 215)
Taber, Harry Persons. Rubaiyat of the Commuter: Being Quatrains Concerning the Affairs of Everyday (Classic Reprint) (p. 1911)
Taber, Kristen. Ærenden - the Child Returns. (p. 1865)
Taber, Mary J. Bathsheba's Letters to Her Cousin Deborah, 1831-1861 (Classic Reprint) (p. 172)
Taber, Melissa, illus. see Hamilton, Bailey & Hormel, Margaret.
Taber, Ralph Graham. Chained Lightning: A Story of Adventure in Mexico (Classic Reprint) (p. 353)
Taber, Susan. Jewel of Their Souls (Classic Reprint) (p. 1167)
Taber-Montgomery, Kathy. We Live in a Zoo. (p. 2391)
Tabet, Jonathon, ed. see Kostov, Nayden.
Tabibzadeh, M. R. Angels' Whisper. Sholevar, Bahman, ed. (p. 86)
Tablason, Jamie, illus. see Greenway, Beth.
Tablason, Jamie, illus. see Prokos, Anna.
Tabler, Judith. Rat Terrier (p. 1842)
Tableson, Jamie, illus. see Wagenbach, Debbie.
Tabon, Natasha & Wood, Angela. Misadventures of TOOD & TABOON: The Good, the Bad, & the Mischievous! (p. 1476)
Tabone, Francis. ASD Independence Workbook: Transition Skills for Teens & Young Adults with Autism. (p. 125)
Tabor, Corey R. Fox & the Bike Ride. Tabor, Corey R., illus. (p. 774)
—Fox & the Jumping Contest. Tabor, Corey R., illus. (p. 774)
—Fox Is Late. Tabor, Corey R., illus. (p. 774)
—Fox the Tiger. Tabor, Corey R., illus. (p. 774)
—Snail Crossing. Tabor, Corey R., illus. (p. 2044)
Tabor, Eliza. Alec's Bride, Vol. 3 of 3 (Classic Reprint) (p. 41)
—Aston-Royal, Vol. 1 of 3 (Classic Reprint) (p. 128)
—Double Wedding, Vol. 1 of 3 (Classic Reprint) (p. 589)
—Eglantine: A Novel (Classic Reprint) (p. 628)
—Eglantine, Vol. 2 of 3 (Classic Reprint) (p. 628)
—Hagar, Vol. 1 of 3 (Classic Reprint) (p. 909)
—Hagar, Vol. 3 of 3 (Classic Reprint) (p. 909)
—Hester's Sacrifice, Vol. 1 of 3 (Classic Reprint) (p. 963)
—Hope Meredith, Vol. 1 of 3 (Classic Reprint) (p. 1002)
—Janita's Cross, Vol. 2 of 3 (Classic Reprint) (p. 1159)
—Lady Lowater's Companion, Vol. 2 of 3 (Classic Reprint) (p. 1237)
—Last of Her Line, Vol. 1 of 3 (Classic Reprint) (p. 1248)
—Little Miss. Primrose, Vol. 1 of 3 (Classic Reprint) (p. 1322)
—Man's Mistake (Classic Reprint) (p. 1398)
—Man's Mistake, Vol. 3 of 3 (Classic Reprint) (p. 1398)
—Master of Marton, Vol. 1 of 3 (Classic Reprint) (p. 1418)
—Rachel's Secret, Vol. 1 of 3 (Classic Reprint) (p. 1832)
—Senior Songman, Vol. 1 of 3 (Classic Reprint) (p. 1988)
—St. Olave's: A Novel (Classic Reprint) (p. 2098)
—When I Was a Little Girl: Stories for Children (Classic Reprint) (p. 2431)
Tabor, Louis. Spread Your Wings. (p. 2091)
Tabor, Nathan, illus. see Sims, Nat.
Tabor, Sierra, ed. see Brown, Lori.
Tabor, Sierra, ed. see Jeffries, Jo Ann.
Tabor, Stephen A. When I Wished ... Shamp, Danielle, illus. (p. 2431)
Tabor, Tabor. Hagar, Vol. 2 of 3 (Classic Reprint) (p. 909)
—Jeanie's Quiet Life, Vol. 3 of 3 (Classic Reprint) (p. 1162)
Tabrar, Pauline. Bumble Bee Story Collection. (p. 297)
Tacchella, Benjamin. Derby School Register, 1570-1901 (Classic Reprint) (p. 530)
Taccone, Jorma. Little Fox & the Wild Imagination. Santat, Dan, illus. (p. 1317)
Tacey, Romaine, illus. see del Re, Joey.
Tacey, Romaine, illus. see Frances, Renee.
Tachibana, Mikio. Disney Manga: Pirates of the Caribbean: at World's End. (p. 561)
—Pirates of the Caribbean: Dead Man's Chest. (p. 1751)
Tachibana, Momo, et al. Little Witch Academia (light Novel) The Nonsensical Witch & the Country of the Fairies. (p. 1330)
Tachikawa, Carter. Half-Baked Kate. (p. 910)
Tackaberry, William. Mira the Speedy Sloth. (p. 1474)
Tacoma Historical Society, jt. auth. see Freedman, Deborah K.
Tad, Tad. Daffydils, 1911 (Classic Reprint) (p. 495)
Tada, Hiroshi. Happy Mice. (p. 923)
—Who's There. Perry, Mia, tr. (p. 2454)
Tadaki, Imaizumi. Grow, & I Love You. (p. 899)
—Most Interesting Book That Explores Why Creatures Extincted or Not Extincted. (p. 1508)
Taddeo, John, jt. auth. see Chilman-Blair, Kim.
Taddonio, Lea. Along for the Ride (Set) Aly, Hatem, illus. (p. 58)
—Are You Fur Real? Lamoreaux, Michelle, illus. (p. 113)
—Book 1: First Dance. Price, Mina, illus. (p. 257)
—Book 1: Hair Today, Gone Tomorrow. Lamoreaux, Michelle, illus. (p. 257)
—Book 1: Shake It Off. Aly, Hatem, illus. (p. 257)
—Book 2: Fashion Police. Aly, Hatem, illus. (p. 257)
—Book 2: First Date. Price, Mina, illus. (p. 257)
—Book 2: off on the Wrong Foot. Lamoreaux, Michelle, illus. (p. 257)
—Book 3: Center Stage. Aly, Hatem, illus. (p. 257)
—Book 3: First Fight. Price, Mina, illus. (p. 257)
—Book 3: I'm Squatching You. Lamoreaux, Michelle, illus. (p. 257)
—Book 4: First Kiss. Price, Mina, illus. (p. 257)
—Book 4: Solo ACT. Aly, Hatem, illus. (p. 257)
—Camp Nowhere (Set) Lamoreaux, Michelle, illus. (p. 315)
—Curse of Deadwood Hill: Book 2. Trunfio, Alessia, illus. (p. 488)
—Deadwood Hill Strikes Back: Book 3. Trunfio, Alessia, illus. (p. 519)
—Deadwood Hill Trap: Book 4. Trunfio, Alessia, illus. (p. 519)
—Frankensteve. (p. 778)
—Hairy Problem. (p. 910)
—Hallow-Weenie. (p. 911)
—Head over Heels (Set) Price, Mina, illus. (p. 942)
—Pain in the Neck. (p. 1692)
—Shiverwood Academy (Set) (p. 2008)
—Welcome to Deadwood Hill: Book 1. Trunfio, Alessia, illus. (p. 2398)
Taddonio, Susan A., jt. auth. see Moss, Wendy L.
Tadema, Laurence Alma. Wings of Icarus: Being the Life of One Emilia Fletcher (Classic Reprint) (p. 2473)
Tadgell, Nicole, illus. see Birtha, Becky.
Tadgell, Nicole, illus. see Capozzi, Suzy.
Tadgell, Nicole, illus. see Derby, Sally.
Tadgell, Nicole, illus. see Elster, Jean Alicia.
Tadgell, Nicole, illus. see Filigenzi, Courtney.
Tadgell, Nicole, illus. see Grigsby, Susan.
Tadgell, Nicole, illus. see LaFaye, A.
Tadgell, Nicole, illus. see Lambert, Megan Dowd & Daniels, Peter.
Tadgell, Nicole, illus. see Lyons, Kelly Starling.
Tadgell, Nicole, illus. see Murphy, Frank.
Tadgell, Nicole, illus. see Noble, Trinka Hakes.
Tadgell, Nicole, illus. see Scholastic, Inc. Staff & Grimes, Nikki.
Tadgell, Nicole, illus. see Slade, Suzanne.
Tadiello, Ed, illus. see Wiggin, Kate Douglas.
Tadjo, Veronique. Little Girl Who Didn't Want to Grow Up* (p. 1317)
Tadlock, Clara Moyse. Solomon Grinder's Christmas Eve & Other Poems. (p. 2057)
Taeeun, Yoo. You Are a Lion! & Other Fun Yoga Poses. (p. 2524)
Taekema, Sylvia. Bad Shot. (p. 158)
—Ripple Effect (p. 1885)
Taesoo Kim, John, illus. see Crute, Josh.
Tafolla, Carmen. What Can You Do with a Paleta? Morales, Magaly, illus. (p. 2407)
—What Can You Do with a Rebozo? / ¿Qué Puedes Hacer con un Rebozo? Cordova, Amy, illus. (p. 2407)
—¿Qué Puedes Hacer con una Paleta? (What Can You Do with a Paleta Spanish Edition) Morales, Magaly, illus. (p. 1823)
Tafoya, Jody. Sammy: A Day in the Life of a Snail. (p. 1928)
Tafoya, Nathan. Great Cricket Picket. (p. 885)
Taft, Christopher C. Witch of Green Spring. (p. 2479)
Taft, Israel Plummer. Maid of the Combahee: A Romance of the South from the Manuscript of Sir Thomas Yeld, Bart (Classic Reprint) (p. 1383)
Taft, Jean. Worm Weather. Hunt, Matt, illus. (p. 2508)
Taft, Kevin. Oil's Deep State: How the petroleum industry undermines democracy & stops action on global warming. (p. 1643)
Taft, Linwood. Woodcutter's Christmas: A Play for Children (Classic Reprint) (p. 2491)
Taftaf, Randa. Zaydo Potato: Allah Loves Me. (p. 2538)
Taftaf, Randa & Galini, Maz. Zaydo Potato: Can Allah See Me Now? (p. 2538)

T

Tafuni, Gabriele. Math Mazes: Adding & Subtracting. (p. 1424)
—Under the Sea Dot-To-Dots. Costamagna, Beatrice, illus. (p. 2322)
Tafuni, Gabriele, illus. see Fullman, Joe & Lindley, Sally.
Tafuni, Gabriele & Casey, Catherine. Math Mazes: Times Tables. Scudamore, Angelika, illus. (p. 1424)
Tafuni, Gabriele, et al. Pocket Fun: Mazes Activity Book. (p. 1764)
Tafuri, Nancy. All Kinds of Kisses. (p. 52)
—Big Storm: A Very Soggy Counting Book. Tafuri, Nancy, illus. (p. 223)
—Blue Goose. Tafuri, Nancy, illus. (p. 248)
—Busy Little Squirrel. Tafuri, Nancy, illus. (p. 302)
—Daddy Hugs. (p. 495)
—Five Little Chicks. Tafuri, Nancy, illus. (p. 743)
—Whose Chick Are You? Board Book. Tafuri, Nancy, illus. (p. 2454)
Tag, Ralph W. Conquest of Helen (Classic Reprint) (p. 442)
Tagani, Iliriana Bisha, tr. see Pere, Tuula.
Tagawa, Mi. Fox & the Little Tanuki, Vol. 1. (p. 774)
Tageau, Jerry, illus. see Edgers, Geoff.
Tagel, Peggy, illus. see McGrath, Barbara Barbieri.
Tagel, Peggy, jt. auth. see McGrath, Barbara Barbieri.
Tagert-Paul, Kimberley. God's Ten Promises: Helping Children Understand the Ten Commandments. (p. 854)
Taggak Arnatsiaq, Daniel, tr. see Meijer, Margreet.
Taggart, B., ed. see Cruse, Howard.
Taggart, Mabel G. Story of the Three Goblins (Classic Reprint) (p. 2134)
Taggart, Marion Ames. Annes (Classic Reprint) (p. 99)
—Captain Sylvia (Classic Reprint) (p. 326)
—Nancy Porter's Opportunity (Classic Reprint) (p. 1574)
—Pilgrim Maid: A Story of Plymouth Colony in 1620 (Classic Reprint) (p. 1744)
—Pilgrim Maid. (p. 1744)
—Who Is Sylvia? (Classic Reprint) (p. 2448)
—Winnetou, the Apache Knight: Adapted for Our Boys & Girls from C May (Classic Reprint) (p. 2473)
—Wyndham Girls (Classic Reprint) (p. 2515)
Tagliaferri, Saria & Spada, Alberto. My Baby Teeth (p. 1531)
—Why That Face (p. 2459)
Tagliaferro, Linda. Animals Babies Pack [Scholastic]. (p. 94)
—Bears & Their Cubs [Scholastic]. (p. 180)
—Bears & Their Dens [Scholastic]. (p. 180)
—Bees & Their Hives [Scholastic]. (p. 189)
—Birds & Their Nests [Scholastic]. (p. 231)
—Dogs & Their Puppies: A 4D Book. (p. 577)
—Dogs & Their Puppies [Scholastic]. (p. 577)
—How Does a Volcano Become an Island? (p. 1030)
—Palace of Versailles. (p. 1694)
—Rabbits & Their Burrows [Scholastic]. (p. 1830)
—Who Lands Planes on a Ship? Working on an Aircraft Carrier. (p. 2448)
Tagliaferro, Linda, jt. auth. see Hall, Margaret.
Tagliere, Georgina. Turtle Tales - Book One: The Baby Turtle who Wanted to Fly. (p. 2301)
Taglietti, Emanuele, illus. see Carr, Simonetta.
Tagnetti, Stefano & Watt, Fiona. Busy Car. (p. 302)
Tago, Anita. Traditional Stories from Binandere in Oro Province, Papua New Guinea. (p. 2273)
Tagore, Abanindranath, et al. Fantasy Fictions from the Bengal Renaissance: The Make-Believe Prince; Toddy-Cat the Bold. (p. 708)
Tagore, Rabindranath. Astronomer. (p. 128)
—Champa Flower. (p. 355)
—Crescent Moon: Poems & Stories. (p. 473)
—Crescent Moon. (p. 473)
—Friday Fair. (p. 785)
—Gitanjali: A Collection of Nobel Prize Winning Poems. (p. 839)
—Gitanjali. (p. 839)
—Gitanjali (Song Offerings) A Collection of Prose Translations - Scholar's Choice Edition. (p. 839)
—Glimpses of Bengal: Selected from the Letters of Sir Rabindranath Tagore; 1885 to 1895 (Classic Reprint) (p. 842)
—Home & the World (Classic Reprint) (p. 995)
—Hungry Stones: And Other Stories (Classic Reprint) (p. 1052)
—King of the Dark Chamber (Classic Reprint) (p. 1221)
—Letters: Extracts from Old Letters of Rabindranath Tagore (Classic Reprint) (p. 1279)
—Mashi: And Other Stories (Classic Reprint) (p. 1417)
—Nationalism. (p. 1578)
—Post Office (Classic Reprint) (p. 1780)
—Single Night: Short Stories by Rabindranath Tagore. (p. 2024)
—Stories from Tagore. (p. 2124)
—Wreck (Classic Reprint) (p. 2511)
Tagore, Rabindranath, jt. auth. see Yeats, William Butler.
Tagore, Rabindranath & Ray, Sukhendu. Chirakumar Sabha: The Bachelor's Club: a Comedy in Five Acts. (p. 379)
Tagore, Sir Rabindranath. My Reminiscences (Classic Reprint) (p. 1560)
Tahe, Rose Ann, et al. First Laugh—Welcome, Baby! (p. 738)
Taher, Ronak, illus. see Ayres, Eddie.
Taherian, Elaheh, illus. see Springstubb, Tricia.
Tahir, Rana. Countee Cullen. (p. 459)
Tahir, Sabaa. Ember Backlist 10-Copy MIXED Floor Display W/ Riser (p. 641)
—Ember in the Ashes. (p. 641)
—Reaper at the Gates. (p. 1851)
—Torch Against the Night. (p. 2264)
Tahir, Samar. Ahlam an Akun Katibah. Shayibi, Sundus, illus. (p. 36)
—Ahlam an Akun Tahyan. Nurullah, Sawsan, illus. (p. 36)
Tahirkheli, Sabir Ali Khan. Revenge. (p. 1872)
—Story a Day Keeps You Fresh All the Way. (p. 2127)
Tahiti, Api, ed. see Chastel, Patrick.
Tahmaseb, Charity & Vance, Darcy. Geek Girl's Guide to Cheerleading. (p. 813)
Tai, Elise See. Write & Draw Dinosaurs. (p. 2511)
Tai, Hâtim. Adventures of Hatim Tai: A Romance (Classic Reprint) (p. 23)
Taib, Saadah. Prophet Adam & Wicked Iblis. Rosli, Shazana, illus. (p. 1807)
—Prophet Ibrahim & the Little Bird Activity Book. Rosli, Shazana, illus. (p. 1807)
—Prophet Ismail & the ZamZam Well Activity Book. Rosli, Shazana, illus. (p. 1807)
—Prophet Muhammad & the Crying Camel Activity Book. Rosli, Shazana, illus. (p. 1807)
—Prophet Nuh & the Great Ark. Rosli, Shazana, illus. (p. 1807)
—Prophet Sulaiman & the Talking Ants. Rosli, Shazana, illus. (p. 1807)
Taibah, Nadia Jameel, jt. auth. see MacDonald, Margaret Read.
Taibl, Judy. Ike Is Loved. (p. 1094)
Taibo, Benito. Mundo Sin Dioses 2. la Razón y la Ira. (p. 1526)
Taiki, illus. see Kaidou, Sakon.
Tailfeather, Speck Lee. Architecture According to Pigeons. (p. 111)
Tailfeather, Speck Lee, jt. auth. see Gurney, Stella.
Taill, Madame Saint Taill Rene. Soul of the C. R: B a French View of the Hoover Relief Work (Classic Reprint) (p. 2066)
Tailor, John. Old King Cole: John Martin (Morgan Shepard) (Classic Reprint) (p. 1646)
Taimy Studios, illus. see Turnbull, Betty Turnbull.
Tain, M. R. For the Children. (p. 763)
Taine, H. Life & Opinions of M. Frederic-Thomas Graindorge: Doctor of Philosophy at the University of Jena Special Partner in the House of Graindorce Co;, Oils & Salt Pork; Cincinnati, U. S. a; Collected & Published (Classic Reprint) (p. 1289)
Taine, H. A. Journeys Through France: Being Impressions of the Provinces (Classic Reprint) (p. 1183)
Taine, Hippolyte. Essai Sur les Fables de la Fontaine: Thèse Sur le Doctorat Ès Lettres Présentée À la Faculté de Paris (Classic Reprint) (p. 663)
—Fontaine et Ses Fables (Classic Reprint) (p. 759)
Taine, Hippolyte Adolphe. Journeys Through France: Being Impressions of the Provinces (Classic Reprint) (p. 1183)
—Tour Through the Pyrenees (Classic Reprint) (p. 2269)
Tainsh, Edward Campbell. One Maiden Only, Vol. 1 of 3 (Classic Reprint) (p. 1660)
Tainter, Helen Davies. Reveries of a Spinster (Classic Reprint) (p. 1873)
Tait, A. L., pseud. Breath of the Dragon: Mapmaker Chronicles. (p. 278)
—Breath of the Dragon. (p. 278)
—Prisoner of the Black Hawk: Mapmaker Chronicles. (p. 1801)
—Prisoner of the Black Hawk. (p. 1801)
—Race to the End of the World. (p. 1831)
Tait, Agnes. Crimson & Gray, Vol. 9: 1925-1926 (Classic Reprint) (p. 475)
Tait, Allison, see Tait, A. L., pseud.
Tait, Anne. Li Jun & the Iron Road. (p. 1283)
Tait, Barbara. Timothy Toot.... Finds A Hat. Margolis, Al, illus. (p. 2247)
—Timothy Toot... Goes Fishing. Margolis, Al, illus. (p. 2247)
—Timothy Toot... Goes to the Zoo. (p. 2247)
Tait, Carys, illus. see Landman, Tanya.
Tait, Chris. Diablo & the Leprechaun Figurehead. (p. 537)
—Ridiculous Knock-Knocks. Zahnd, Mark, illus. (p. 1878)
—Ridiculous Tongue Twisters. Jones, Buck, illus. (p. 1878)
Tait, Jackie. Adventures of Abuelito. Johnson, Katherine, illus. (p. 21)
Tait, James Selwin. My Friend Pasquale, & Other Stories (Classic Reprint) (p. 1547)
Tait, Leia. Cinco de Mayo. (p. 391)
—Mice. (p. 1457)
Tait, Leia, jt. auth. see Wiseman, Blaine.
Tait, Mat, illus. see Meredith, Courtney Sina.
Tait, William. Tait's Edinburgh Magazine for 1842, Vol. 9 (Classic Reprint) (p. 2176)
—Tait's Edinburgh Magazine for 1843, Vol. 10 (Classic Reprint) (p. 2176)
Taixi, Su, illus. see Ma, Zheng & Li, Zheng.
Tajima, Nobumoto. Kodomo Ga Nemuru Mae ni Yonde Agetai Sanbyakurokujugo No Mijikai Ohanashi. (p. 1230)
Tak, Bibi Dumon. Mikis & the Donkey. Hopman, Philip, illus. (p. 1465)
—Soldier Bear. Watkinson, Laura, tr. (p. 2056)
Tak, Bibi Dumon & Dumon Tak, Bibi. Soldier Bear. Hopman, Philip, illus. (p. 2056)
Takabatake, Jun, illus. see Iwasa, Megumi.
Takacova, Magdalena, illus. see Bartikova, Petra.
Takacs-Moore, Mary, jt. auth. see Reilly, Kathleen M.
Takahama, Valerie. Get Moving! (p. 824)
Takahashi, Hideko, illus. see Balsley, Tilda.
Takahashi, Kazue. Kuma-Kuma Chan's Home. (p. 1233)
Takai, Hiroaki, jt. auth. see Ono, Mari.
Takaki, Ronald. Different Mirror for Young People: A History of Multicultural America. (p. 545)
Takaki, Ronald & Stefoff, Rebecca. Different Mirror for Young People. (p. 545)
Takanaga, Hinako. Love Round!! (p. 1361)
Takano, Hitomi. My Boy, Volume 3. (p. 1534)
Takano, Noriko. Origami Picturebook. (p. 1671)
Takaoka, Masae. Dotchi Ga Osu Dotchi Ga Mesu: Osu Mesu Zukan (Is It Male of Female?) (p. 588)
Takara, Kathryn Waddell. Timmy Turtle Teaches. Driver, Audrey, illus. (p. 2247)
Takara, Marcio, illus. see Waid, Mark & Walker, Landry.
Takara, Marcio, illus. see Waid, Mark.
Takara, Marcio, illus. see Walker, Landry.
Takarai, Saori. Manga Moods: 40 Faces + 80 Phrases. (p. 1397)
Takashi, Fuuji, illus. see Boston, Jennifer.
Takashi, Fuuji, illus. see Fungchung, Nikko M.
Takata, George. Timeout's Great Baseball Adventure: How Fresno State's Favorite Bulldog Helped the Diamond Dogs Win the College World Series. Thiessen, Marci, illus. (p. 2247)
Takaya, Machiko. Deru Deru Deruzo. (p. 530)
Takaya, Natsuki. Fruits Basket Collector's Edition, Vol. 11. (p. 796)
—Fruits Basket Collector's Edition, Vol. 7. (p. 796)
Takehiko, Uyeki. Gikio Den: A Japanese Romance (Classic Reprint) (p. 833)
Takei, George, et al. They Called Us Enemy: Expanded Edition. (p. 2219)
Takemiya, Yuyuko. Toradora! (Light Novel) Vol. 1. Yasu, illus. (p. 2264)
Takemori, Ginny Tapley, tr. see Inui, Tomiko.
Takemori, Ginny Tapley, tr. see Nosaka, Akiyuki.
Takemori, Lianne K. Four Dog Blues Band, or How Chester Boy, Dog in the Fog, & Diva Took the Big City by Storm. Dietrick, Robin C. & Klein, Bradley S., eds. (p. 772)
Takenashi, Eri. Kannagi Volume 2. (p. 1202)
Takenouche, Keichu, jt. auth. see Hearn, Lafcadio.
Takeshita, Fumiko. Soratobu Kureyon. (p. 2065)
—Umi e Iku Pinpon Basu. (p. 2316)
Takeshita, Gene, illus. see Block, Cheryl.
Taketomo, Torao. Paulownia Seven Stories from Contemporary Japanese Writers (Classic Reprint) (p. 1708)
Takeuchi, Chihiro. Colors. Takeuchi, Chihiro, illus. (p. 426)
—Paper Peek: Animals. Takeuchi, Chihiro, illus. (p. 1697)
Takeuchi, Naoko. Sailor Moon (p. 1923)
—Sailor Moon 1 (p. 1923)
—Sailor Moon 10 (p. 1923)
—Sailor Moon 11 (p. 1923)
—Sailor Moon 12 (p. 1923)
—Sailor Moon 2. (p. 1923)
—Sailor Moon 3 (p. 1923)
—Sailor Moon 4. (p. 1923)
—Sailor Moon 5. (p. 1923)
—Sailor Moon 8. (p. 1923)
—Sailor Moon 9. (p. 1923)
Takidaira, Jiro, jt. auth. see Saito, Ryusuke.
Tako, Rony & Seijas, Hugo. Doodlers Anonymous Epic Coloring Book: An Extraordinary Mashup of Doodles & Drawings Begging to Be Filled in with Color. (p. 584)
Takuna, John Fred. I Am a Big Fish. Skinner, Meg, illus. (p. 1056)
Takuski, Camille. Respect the Flag. Takuski, Camille, ed. (p. 1869)
Takvorian, Nadine. Jason & the Argonauts (p. 1160)
—Odysseus & the Cyclops (p. 1638)
Takvorian, Nadine, illus. see Bullard, Lisa.
Takvorian, Nadine, illus. see Hoena, Blake.
Takvorian, Nadine, illus. see Koontz, Robin Michal.
Takvorian, Nadine, illus. see Koontz, Robin.
Takvorian, Nadine, illus. see Muehlenhardt, Amy Bailey.
Takvorian, Rick, tr. see Ende, Michael.
Tal, Eve. Cursing Columbus. (p. 489)
Talai, Bahar, tr. see Renz, Ulrich.
Talaris Institute. Baby Feelings. (p. 150)
Talbert, Cj. Lila's Harbor. Sodano, Meg, illus. (p. 1301)
Talbert, Jesica D. Little Traveler. (p. 1329)
Talbert, Lilian E. Expression Primer (Classic Reprint) (p. 684)
Talbot, Charles Remington. Parlor Comedies: No Questions Asked & More Than They Bargained for (Classic Reprint) (p. 1700)
Talbot, Fannie Sprague. Poems (Classic Reprint) (p. 1765)
Talbot, Hannah Lincoln. At Miss. Penhallow's: Boarding House Scenes (Classic Reprint) (p. 130)
—Not in the Prospectus (Classic Reprint) (p. 1623)
Talbot, Jim, illus. see Lerangis, Peter.
Talbot, Josh, illus. see Doxey, Heidi.
Talbot, Josh, illus. see Rubin, Elycia.
Talbot, L. A. Jehane of the Forest (Classic Reprint) (p. 1163)
—Lance-In-Rest (Classic Reprint) (p. 1241)
Talbot, L. Raymond. French Composition (Classic Reprint) (p. 783)
Talbot, L. T. Dr Bakewell & the Three Chocolatiers. (p. 591)
Talbot, Mary Elizabeth. Rurality: Original Desultory Tales (Classic Reprint) (p. 1916)
Talbot, Michael, illus. see Kemp-Davis, Valrie.
Talbot, Ralph. Year Book 1915: Weymouth High School (Classic Reprint) (p. 2518)
Talbot, Sophie. Chloe. (p. 379)
—Fabulous Terrible: The Adventures of You. (p. 692)
Talbot, Sophronia Maria. Little Boy Philosophy (Classic Reprint) (p. 1313)
Talbot, Thomas. Granvilles, an Irish Tale, Vol. 3 of 3 (Classic Reprint) (p. 880)
—Granvilles, Vol. 1 Of 3: An Irish Tale (Classic Reprint) (p. 880)
—Granvilles, Vol. 2 Of 3: An Irish Tale (Classic Reprint) (p. 880)
Talbot, Virginia. Do You See the Sea Horse? Book of Homophones. Cuentas, Joel, illus. (p. 572)
Talbott, Hudson. From Wolf to Woof: The Story of Dogs. Talbott, Hudson, illus. (p. 794)
—It's All about Me-Ow. Talbott, Hudson, illus. (p. 1144)
—Picturing America: Thomas Cole & the Birth of American Art. Talbott, Hudson, illus. (p. 1741)
—River of Dreams: The Story of the Hudson River. Talbott, Hudson, illus. (p. 1887)
—United Tweets of America: 50 State Birds Their Stories, Their Glories. Talbott, Hudson, illus. (p. 2332)
Talbott, Hudson, illus. see Fritz, Jean.
Talbott, Hudson, illus. see Woodson, Jacqueline.
Talbott, Sherri, illus. see Rose, Sandra.
Talburt, Tony. History on the Page: Adventures in Black British History. (p. 981)
Talen, Hunter. Xander Nash Kleid, Neil, illus. (p. 2516)
Talens, Valeri. Missa & Her Magnificent Bubbles Learn to Tidy Up. (p. 1480)
Tales & Fables Staff. Star Bilingual Story Cinderella. (p. 2102)
—Star Bilingual Story Jack & the Beanstalk. (p. 2102)
—Star Bilingual Story Little Red Riding Hood. (p. 2102)
—Star Bilingual Story Sleeping Beauty. (p. 2102)
—Star Bilingual Story Snow White & the 7 Dwarfs. (p. 2102)
—Star Bilingual Story Three Little Pigs. (p. 2102)
Taletell, George. Recreations of George Taletell, F. Y. C (Classic Reprint) (p. 1855)
Talhah, Abu & Books, Greenbird. My Sister Saarah. Fowler, Claire, illus. (p. 1561)
Taliaferro, Al, illus. see Karp, Bob.
Taliana, Philip, illus. see Springham, Sarah.
Talib, Binny, illus. see Chandab, Taghred.
Talib, Binny, illus. see Diller, Kevin & Lowe, Justin.
Talib, Binny, illus. see Kenah, Katharine.
Talk, Talk. Talk of the Town; a Novel, Vol. 3 Of 3: In Three Volumes (Classic Reprint) (p. 2187)
Talkington, Amy. Liv, Forever. (p. 1332)
Tallant, Miss Anne. Octavia Elphinstone, Vol. 1 Of 2: A Manx Story, & Lois, a Drama (Classic Reprint) (p. 1636)
Tallant, Wesley. Little Big Toe. (p. 1311)
—Wishing Elf. Conder, Jonathan Paul, illus. (p. 2479)
Tallardy, Laura, illus. see Bergen, Lara.
Tallardy, Laura, illus. see Dunham, Kelli.
Tallardy, Laura, illus. see Speregen, Debra Newberger.
Tallarico, Tony. Hunt for Hector. (p. 1052)
—Sports Spot-The-Differences Activity Book. (p. 2089)
—Things That Go. (p. 2221)
Tallarico, Tony & Drawing Staff. Quick Draw Animals. (p. 1827)
Tallarico, Tony J., Jr. Baseball Activity Book. (p. 168)
—Baseball Facts & Fun Activity Book. (p. 168)
—Bugs! Bugs! Bugs! (p. 292)
—Eco-Logical Brain Games. (p. 623)
—English - Spanish Word Search: Sopa de Letras (p. 652)
—English-Spanish Word Search. (p. 655)
—Famous Firsts Activity Book. (p. 703)
—Frightfully Fun Halloween Activity Book. (p. 788)
—Presidents Activity Book. (p. 1789)
—SPARK Favorite Sports Spot-The-Differences. (p. 2074)
—Spot-the-Differences Around the World. (p. 2090)
—U. S. A. Constitution Activity Book. (p. 2311)
—U. S. A. Secret Code Puzzles for Kids. (p. 2311)
—Worldwide Secret Code Puzzles for Kids. (p. 2508)
Tallarico, Tony J., Jr., jt. auth. see Tallarico, Tony, Sr.
Tallarico, Tony J., Jr. & Tallarico, Tony, Sr. Merry Christmas Activity Book. (p. 1449)
—SPARK Nature Fun Facts Mazes. (p. 2074)
Tallarico, Tony, Sr. Everyday Fun for Kids. (p. 671)
Tallarico, Tony, Sr., jt. auth. see Tallarico, Tony J., Jr.
Tallarico, Tony, Sr. & Activity Books Staff. More Little Hidden Pictures. (p. 1505)
Tallarico, Tony, Sr. & Drawing Staff. Drawing & Cartooning Monsters: A Step-by-Step Guide for the Aspiring Monster-Maker. (p. 598)
Tallarico, Tony, Sr. & Tallarico, Tony J., Jr. Cars & Trucks Mazes. (p. 334)
Tallec, Olivier. It's MY Tree. Tallec, Olivier, illus. (p. 1146)
—Life as a Mini Hero. Bedrick, Claudia Zoe, tr. (p. 1290)
—Louis I, King of the Sheep. (p. 1357)
—Waterloo & Trafalgar. (p. 2386)
—What's Going on Here? A Tell-Your-Own-Tale Book. (p. 2423)
—Who Done It? (p. 2447)
—Who Was That? (p. 2452)
—Who What Where? (p. 2452)
Tallec, Olivier, illus. see Babin, Claire.
Tallec, Olivier, illus. see Brun-Cosme, Nadine.
Tallec, Olivier, illus. see Daywalt, Drew.
Tallec, Olivier, illus. see Dunlap, Cirocco.
Tallec, Olivier, illus. see Ferry, Beth.
Tallec, Olivier, illus. see Lenain, Thierry.
Tallec, Olivier, illus. see Moundlic, Charlotte.
Tallec, Olivier, illus. see Scanlon, Liz Garton & Vernick, Audrey.
Tallec, Olivier, illus. see Sorman, Joy.
Tallent, Alyssa, illus. see Bolger, Z. C.
Tallent, Alyssa, illus. see Christensen, Catherine.
Tallents, Stephen. Dancer, & Other Tales (Classic Reprint) (p. 500)
Tallents, Stephen G. Tales Pool, & Other Tales (Classic Reprint) (p. 2186)
Tallentyre, S. G. Basset: A Village Chronical (Classic Reprint) (p. 171)
—Matthew Hargraves (Classic Reprint) (p. 1426)
Tallentyre, Stephen G. Love Laughs Last (Classic Reprint) (p. 1360)
Talley, Gigi T. Fairest Florabell. (p. 695)
Talley, Pam, illus. see Bevis, Brittany.
Talley, Robin. Lies We Tell Ourselves. (p. 1287)
—Music from Another World. (p. 1529)
Talley, Terrence. Secrets Anonymous: Our Story. (p. 1980)
Talley, Thomas W. Negro Folk Rhymes: Wise & Otherwise, with a Study (Classic Reprint) (p. 1585)
Tallian, Aimee. Sophie the Sea Otter. (p. 2065)
Tallie, Mariahadessa Ekere. Layla's Happiness. Corrin, Ashleigh, illus. (p. 1253)
Tallinda, Theodore. Math at Henry Ford's Factory: Identify & Explain Patterns in Arithmetic (p. 1421)
Tallman, Mariana M. Pleasant Places in Rhode Island, & How to Reach Them. (p. 1762)
—Pleasant Places in Rhode Island, & How to Reach Them (Classic Reprint) (p. 1762)
Tallman, Myrtle Catherine. Traveling Trio (Classic Reprint) (p. 2280)
Tallman, Teresa. Fun with Statistics: What Vary Means. (p. 800)
—Fun with Statistics. (p. 800)
Talmadge Salle, Katherine. Daily Life Around the World: Set Of 6. (p. 496)
Talmage, T. De Witt. 500 Selected Sermons, Vol. 11 of 20 (Classic Reprint) (p. 2560)
—Abominations of Modern Society (Classic Reprint) (p. 6)
—Crumbs Swept up (Classic Reprint) (p. 480)
—Evils of the Cities: A Series of Practical & Popular Discourses Delivered in the Brooklyn Tabernacle (Classic Reprint) (p. 674)
—Frank Leslie's Sunday Magazine, Vol. 22: July to December, 1887 (Classic Reprint) (p. 777)
—Wedding Ring: A Series of Discourses for Husbands & Wives & Those Contemplating Matrimony (Classic Reprint) (p. 2395)
Talmage, Thomas De Witt. Around the Tea-Table (Classic Reprint) (p. 118)
Talmage, Thomas Dewitt. One Thousand Gems: Striking Passages, Incidents & Illustrations (Classic Reprint) (p. 1662)

Talmon, Thrace. Heroine of the Revolution: Or, Captain Molly, the Brave Woman (Classic Reprint) (p. 963)
—Heroine of the Revolution. (p. 963)
—Red Bridge: A Temperance Story (Classic Reprint) (p. 1856)
Talsma, Nynke, illus. see Gordon Ekster, Carol.
Talsma, Nynke Mare, illus. see Koppens, Judith & Engel, Andy.
Talty, Caryn. Cilie Yack Is under Attack: This Is the story of how one boy turned his problems into a Triumph (p. 391)
Talvi, Talvi. Heloise, or the Unrevealed Secret: A Tale (Classic Reprint) (p. 952)
—Life's Discipline: A Tale of the Annals of Hungary (Classic Reprint) (p. 1296)
Talvitie, Virpi, illus. see Parvela, Timo.
Talvj, Talvj. Exiles: A Tale (Classic Reprint) (p. 677)
Talwar, Robert B., jt. auth. see Peto, Judith E.
Tamaki, Jillian. Our Little Kitchen. (p. 1679)
—They Say Blue. (p. 2219)
Tamaki, Jillian, illus. see Beasley, Kate.
Tamaki, Jillian, illus. see Fogliano, Julie.
Tamaki, Jillian, illus. see Tamaki, Mariko.
Tamaki, Lauren, illus. see Paul, Caroline.
Tamaki, Mariko. Adventure Time Vol. 14. McGinty, Ian, illus. (p. 19)
—Disney/PIXAR Onward: Tales of the Manticore. (p. 564)
—Laura Dean Keeps Breaking up with Me. (p. 1252)
—Lumberjanes BEASTiary: The Most Amazing Guide to All the Coolest Creatures You've Ever Heard of & a Few You Haven't. Allen, Brooklyn & BOOM! Studios, illus. (p. 1368)
—Lumberjanes: Ghost Cabin (Lumberjanes #4) Allen, Brooklyn, illus. (p. 1368)
—Lumberjanes: the Good Egg (Lumberjanes #3) Allen, Brooklyn & BOOM! Studios, illus. (p. 1368)
—Lumberjanes: Unicorn Power! (Lumberjanes #1) Allen, Brooklyn & BOOM! Studios, illus. (p. 1368)
—Saving Montgomery Sole. (p. 1938)
—Supergirl: Being Super. Jones, Joelle, illus. (p. 2159)
—This One Summer. Tamaki, Jillian, illus. (p. 2226)
—Unicorn Power! (Lumberjanes) Allen, Brooklyn & BOOM! Studios, illus. (p. 2328)
Tamaki, Mariko & BOOM! Studios. Lumberjanes: Ghost Cabin (Lumberjanes #4) Allen, Brooklyn, illus. (p. 1368)
—Lumberjanes: the Good Egg (Lumberjanes #3) Allen, Brooklyn, illus. (p. 1368)
—Lumberjanes: the Moon Is Up (Lumberjanes #2) Allen, Brooke, illus. (p. 1368)
—Lumberjanes: the Moon Is Up (Lumberjanes #2) Allen, Brooklyn, illus. (p. 1368)
Tamang, Mayan. Captain Remarkable; Girls can be Superheroes Too! (p. 326)
Tamang, Mayan, illus. see O'Neal-Thorpe, Rochelle.
Tamani, Liara. All the Things We Never Knew. (p. 54)
—Calling My Name. (p. 312)
Tamanini, Kara T. I Promised Not to Tell. (p. 1080)
Tamar, Erika, jt. auth. see Kinkade, Thomas.
Tamar Marano, Nina. Clippety Clippety Clop. (p. 406)
Tamara, Visco, illus. see Colon De Mejias, Leticia.
Tamarit, Núria, illus. see Ralphs, Matt.
Tamarkin, Annette. Mon Petit Busy Day. Tamarkin, Annette, illus. (p. 1491)
Tamaro, Susanna. Gran Arbol. (p. 876)
Tamas, Emanuel, illus. see Pere, Tuula.
Tamayo, Alex. Horizons Set 1 Shea, Steve, ed. (p. 1003)
Tamayo, Natalia, illus. see Vasco, Irene.
Tamayo y Baus, Manuel. Drama Nuevo: Drama en Tres Actos. (p. 596)
Tambascio, Jocelyn. King's Drapes. (p. 1223)
Tambellini, Stefano. Frightlopedia: An Encyclopedia of Everything Scary, Creepy, & Spine-Chilling, from Arachnids to Zombies. (p. 788)
Tambellini, Stefano, illus. see Dolan, Penny.
Tambellini, Stefano, illus. see Stride, Lottie.
Tamblyn, Amber. Free Stallion: Poems. (p. 782)
Tamblyn, Catherine M. 40 Fabulous Social Studies Activities: Easy Projects That Work with the Topics You Teach & Help Build Reading, Writing, & Research Skills. (p. 2555)
Tameka. What Matters Most. (p. 2419)
Tamer, Abdul Hakeem. Ideas & Daily Life in the Muslim World Today Pecastaing, Camille, ed. (p. 1089)
Tamez, Eugenia, tr. see Kubiak, Jeff.
Tamez, Juliza. Trixie & Dixie: The Mystery of the Missing Cape. Almanza, Roberto, illus. (p. 2290)
Tamir, Rony. Masada: Judea's Last Stand. (p. 1416)
Tamm, Vali, tr. see De Saint-Exupéry, Antoine.
Tammen, Christina. C h u m P. (p. 306)
—Chump II Every Team Has an Undiscovered Secret Weapon! (p. 390)
Tammi, Elizabeth. Outrun the Wind. (p. 1685)
—Weight of a Soul. (p. 2396)
Tammi Reichel, tr. see Schrocke, Kathrin.
Tamua, Evotia, photos by see Riley, David.
Tamula, Elis, illus. see Lhuissier, Marie.
Tamura, Marikka. Penguins Don't Wear Sweaters! Rieley, Daniel, illus. (p. 1716)
Tan. Stickers Mortelle Adele. (p. 2118)
Tan, Amy Rebecca. Kind of Paradise. (p. 1218)
—Summer at Meadow Wood. (p. 2148)
Tan, Billy. League of Legends: Lux. (p. 1254)
Tan, Billy, et al. Thor by Kieron Gillen: the Complete Collection. (p. 2229)
TAN Books. Our Lady of Fatima: The Graphic Novel. (p. 1678)
Tan, Chung Lee, jt. auth. see Schmermund, Elizabeth.
Tan, Eustacia. Twilight Children: Coming from Darkness #4. (p. 2304)
Tan, Haifang. Scorecard for 38 Chinese Chancellors. (p. 1961)
Tan, Philip, et al. X-Men: Trial of the Juggernaut. (p. 2515)
Tan, Richard. Bridges & Tunnels of New York City. (p. 280)
—Bugs, Bugs, Bugs. (p. 292)
—Dutch New Amsterdam & English New York. (p. 611)
—Famous Explorers of New York City. (p. 703)
—Farm Field Trip. (p. 710)
—Fast & Slow. (p. 713)
—George's Banana. (p. 820)
—Native American Peoples of New York City. (p. 1578)
—New York City's Neighborhoods. (p. 1598)
Tan, Shaun. Bird King: An Artist's Notebook. (p. 230)
—Cicada. Tan, Shaun, illus. (p. 390)
—Lost & Found. Tan, Shaun, illus. (p. 1352)
—Rules of Summer. (p. 1913)
—Rules of Summer. Tan, Shaun, illus. (p. 1913)
—Singing Bones. Tan, Shaun, illus. (p. 2024)
—Tales from Outer Suburbia. (p. 2182)
—Tales from Outer Suburbia. Tan, Shaun, illus. (p. 2182)
—Tales from the Inner City. (p. 2183)
Tan, Shaun, illus. see Crew, Gary.
Tan, Sheri. Handshake in Space: The Apollo-Soyuz Test Project. Bond, Higgins, illus. (p. 916)
—Linus Gets Glasses. (p. 1305)
—Toy Story: Toyography. (p. 2271)
Tan Su Linn. Ten Little Bunnies Go to Town. (p. 2204)
Tan, Susan. Cilla Lee-Jenkins: Future Author Extraordinaire. Wulfekotte, Dana, illus. (p. 391)
—Cilla Lee-Jenkins: the Epic Story. Wulfekotte, Dana, illus. (p. 391)
—Cilla Lee-Jenkins: This Book Is a Classic. Wulfekotte, Dana, illus. (p. 391)
—Piece by Piece. Wong, Justine, illus. (p. 1742)
Tan, Ying Hui, illus. see Garcia, Gabi.
Tana, Hoban. I Read Signs. (p. 1080)
Tanahashi, Kazuaki. Heart of the Brush: The Splendor of East Asian Calligraphy. (p. 945)
Tanaka, Akira. Satoshi Tajiri. (p. 1936)
Tanaka, Hiroshi. Kodomo Zukan Tokei Sansai Nanasai Eigotsuki. (p. 1230)
Tanaka, Ken. Mount Fuji Is Beautiful. (p. 1512)
Tanaka, Masashi. Gon 1. (p. 861)
—Gon 2. (p. 861)
—Gon 3. (p. 861)
Tanaka, Rika. Kilala Princess. (p. 1217)
Tanaka, Shelley. Nobody Knows (p. 1617)
Tanaka, Shelley, tr. see Berner, Rotraut Susanne.
Tanaka, Shelley, tr. see Jang, Iris.
Tanaka, Shelley, tr. see Lapointe, Stéphanie.
Tanaka, Shelley, tr. see Leduc, Émilie.
Tanaka, Shelley, tr. see Pasquet, Jacques.
Tanaka, Shelley, tr. see Simard, Rémy.
Tanaka, Shelley, tr. see Teckentrup, Britta.
Tanaka, Shelley & Doron, Anita. Breadwinner: A Graphic Novel (p. 277)
Tanaka, Yoko. Dandelion's Dream. Tanaka, Yoko, illus. (p. 501)
Tanaka, Yoko, illus. see DiCamillo, Kate.
Tanaka, Yoko, illus. see Godwin, Laura.
Tanaka, Yoko, illus. see LaFevers, R. L.
Tanaka, Yoko, illus. see McGowan, Keith.
Tanaka, Yoko, illus. see Pennypacker, Sara.
Tanaka, Yoshiki. Heroic Legend of Arslan 8. Arakawa, Hiromu, illus. (p. 962)
Tanana, Mary. Christmas to Color: Coloring Book for Adults & Kids to Share. Tanana, Mary, illus. (p. 387)
Tanchez, Plinio, illus. see Garcia, Elizabeth.
Tanco, Miguel. Cuenta Conmigo. (p. 483)
—Mom & Me, Me & Mom. (p. 1490)
—You & Me, Me & You: Brothers. (p. 2524)
—You & Me, Me & You. (p. 2524)
Tanco, Miguel, illus. see Cali, Davide.
Tanco, Miguel, illus. see Kim, YeShil.
Tandy, Russell H., illus. see Keene, Carolyn.
Tandy, William. Foundling of Sebastopol: A Drama (Classic Reprint) (p. 771)
Taneja, Sweta. Krishna - The Defender of Dharma. Nagulakonda, Rajesh, illus. (p. 1232)
Tanen, Sloane. Are You Going to Kiss Me Now? (p. 113)
Tang, Andrea. Rebelwing. (p. 1852)
Tang, Betty, illus. see Patterson, James & Grabenstein, Chris.
Tang, Charles, illus. see Warner, Gertrude Chandler.
T'Ang, Li Chu, illus. see Pitman, Norman Hinsdale.
Tang, Muniu. Al Chi Shui Guo de Niu. (p. 36)
—Xia Yu Le. (p. 2516)
Tang, Sandara, illus. see Duey, Kathleen.
Tang, Sanmu. Celebrating Chinese Festivals: A Collection of Holiday Tales, Poems & Activities. (p. 349)
—Celebrating the Chinese New Year. Ying, Wu, tr. (p. 349)
—Celebrating the Dragon Boat Festival. Tenison, Mina, tr. (p. 349)
—Celebrating the Mid-Autumn Festival. Tenison, Mina, tr. (p. 350)
—Chinese Zodiac Animals. Jingwen, Zhu, tr. (p. 379)
Tang, Sanmu & and Film Studio, Shanghai Animation. Attempt to Scoop up the Moon. Ying, Wu, tr. (p. 135)
—Monkey Makes Havoc in Heaven. Xiaozhen, Wu, tr. (p. 1494)
—Nezha Conquers the Dragon King. Yawtsong, Lee, tr. (p. 1601)
—Tadpoles Looking for Their Mother. Xiaozhen, Wu, tr. (p. 2175)
—Three Monks. Ying, Wu, tr. (p. 2234)
Tang, Wenjia, illus. see Redwing, Jack.
Tang, Wenjia, illus. see Royal Horticultural Society.
Tang, Youshan, illus. see De La Paz, Myrna J.
Tang, Youshan, illus. see de la Paz, Myrna J.
Tang, Youshan, illus. see Mehta, Lila.
Tangen, Nick, illus. see Trombello, William.
Tangerine Designs Ltd. Who Am I? Roar, I Am a Tiger! Peep Through the Eyes. Who Are You Today? (p. 2446)
Tangerine, Tracey. Buddy Zooka: In the French Quarter & Beyond. (p. 290)
Tango-Schurmann, Ann, illus. see Mariotti, Celine Rose.
Tanguay, Dave. Legacy of Mr. Banjo! Vaughns, Byron, illus. (p. 1261)
Tanguy. Can I Keep It? Small Pets Guide: 39 Cool, Easy-To-Care-for Insects, Reptiles, Mammals, Amphibians, & More. (p. 317)
Tangvald, Christine, jt. auth. see Cook, David C. Publishing Staff.
Tangvald, Christine Harder. Best Thing about Christmas. Nobens, C. A., illus. (p. 208)
—Someone I Love Died. (p. 2060)
—Someone I Love Died-10 Pack. (p. 2060)
Tangye, Richard. English Notes for American Circulation: With Apologies to Charles Dickens (Classic Reprint) (p. 654)
—Notes of My Fourth Voyage to the Australian Colonies, Including Australia, Tasmania, & New Zealand (Classic Reprint) (p. 1624)
Tani, Branca. Art for Thanksgiving. (p. 121)
—Baby Farm Animals. (p. 150)
—Beth's Butterfly Garden. (p. 208)
—Dwayne's Safari. (p. 611)
—New York in The 1700s. (p. 1598)
—New York in The 1800s. (p. 1598)
—New York in The 1900s. (p. 1599)
—Sam the Cat. (p. 1926)
Tani, Toshihiko, illus. see Yamanushi, Toshiko.
Tanigawa, Nagaru. Boredom of Haruhi Suzumiya (light Novel) (p. 262)
—[Consternation of Haruhi Suzumiya Vol. 2of 2]. (p. 443)
—Indignation of Haruhi Suzumiya (light Novel) (p. 1117)
—Melancholy of Suzumiya Haruhi-Chan, Vol. 6. (p. 1442)
—Sigh of Haruhi Suzumiya. (p. 2015)
Tanigawa, Nico, creator. No Matter How I Look at It, It's You Guys' Fault I'm Not Popular!, Vol. 11. (p. 1613)
Tanis, Joel E., illus. see Klein, Pamela.
Tanis, Katy, illus. see CARRON BROWN.
Tanis, Katy, illus. see Hurt, Melissa.
Taniwan, Andrias, illus. see Kennard, Jennifer Lynne.
Tankard, Hermione, jt. auth. see Tankard, Jeremy.
Tankard, Jeremy. Boo Hoo Bird. Tankard, Jeremy, illus. (p. 256)
—Grumpy Bird. (p. 900)
—Hungry Bird. Tankard, Jeremy, illus. (p. 1052)
—Sleepy Bird. Tankard, Jeremy, illus. (p. 2037)
Tankard, Jeremy, illus. see LaRochelle, David.
Tankard, Jeremy, illus. see Peters, Diane.
Tankard, Jeremy & Tankard, Hermione. Yorick & Bones. Tankard, Jeremy, illus. (p. 2523)
Tanksley, Ann, illus. see Hurston, Zora Neale & Thomas, Joyce Carol.
Tanksley, David. Michael Waylon & His Dinosaur Crew. (p. 1458)
Tannan, Sonny. Through the Eyes of Om: Exploring Malaysia. (p. 2237)
Tannas, Kathy. Diaries of Polly Aster. Laura, Bachynski, illus. (p. 538)
Tanner, James T. Messenger Boy: A New & Original Musical Play (Classic Reprint) (p. 1451)
—Orchid: A Musical Play in Two Acts (Classic Reprint) (p. 1669)
Tanner, Jane. Lily & the Fairy House. (p. 1302)
Tanner, Jane, illus. see Brennan, Sarah.
Tanner, Jane, illus. see Palmer, Anthony.
Tanner, Jennifer. Robin Hood. (p. 1891)
Tanner, Jennifer, illus. see Stone Arch Books Staff.
Tanner, Karen & Kirby, Karen. Mr Magic Mouse. (p. 1519)
Tanner, Lian. Battlesong. (p. 175)
—Battlesong. Szabla, Liz, ed. (p. 175)
—City of Lies. (p. 395)
—Museum of Thieves. (p. 1528)
—Path of Beasts. (p. 1704)
Tanner, Matthew J. Winds of Aragon. (p. 2472)
Tanner, Minnie H. Cinderella: A Drama (Classic Reprint) (p. 391)
Tanner, S. Clouds: Learning the CL Sound. (p. 408)
—Wild Wolf: Learning the W Sound. (p. 2465)
Tanner, Suzanne. Oluby-Loon Travels in Her Balloon: Oluby Visits Kenya. Bushnell, Holly, illus. (p. 1651)
Tanner, Suzy-Jane. Nursery Rhymes. (p. 1631)
Tanner-Moore, Margie. What Noah Knows. (p. 2419)
Tanquerey, Frederic Joseph. Deux Poemes Moraux Anglo-Francais: Le Roman des Romans, et, le Sermon en Vers (Classic Reprint) (p. 535)
—Deux Poèmes Moraux Anglo-Français: Le Roman des Romans, et, le Sermon en Vers (Classic Reprint) (p. 535)
—Plaintes de la Vierge en Anglo-Francais: Xiile et Xive Siecles (Classic Reprint) (p. 1754)
Tans, Adrian, illus. see Gribnau, Joe.
Tans, Adrian, illus. see Knowlton, Laurie Lazzaro.
Tans, Adrian, illus. see Peck, Jan.
Tans, Adrian, illus. see Pilegard, Virginia.
Tanser, Julie. Nanny Annie & the Magic Word. (p. 1574)
Tansley, Jennifer Sarah. Bedtime Butterfly Kisses. (p. 188)
Tanton, James. Without Words - Walk the Complete Walk Poster. (p. 2482)
Tanuki, Kawo. Dragon Goes House-Hunting Vol. 1. Aya, Choco, illus. (p. 593)
Tanumihardja, Pat. Amazing Islands Around the World. (p. 65)
—Amazing Mountains Around the World. (p. 66)
Tanwar, Rajesh. Goldilocks & the Three Bears. (p. 860)
Tanzosh, Edward, illus. see McKenzie, Precious.
Tao, Wong. Adventurers Bond: Book 5 of the Adventures on Brad. (p. 19)
—Adventurer's Heart: Book 2 of the Adventures on Brad. (p. 19)
—Arena's Call: Book 4 of the Adventures on Brad. (p. 114)
—Dungeon's Soul: Book 3 of the Adventures on Brad. (p. 610)
—Forest's Silence: Book 6 of the Adventures on Brad. (p. 767)
—Healer's Gift: Book 1 of the Adventures on Brad. (p. 943)
Taor, Adam. There's a Worm on My Eyeball: The Alien Zoo of Germs, Worms & Lurgies That Could Be Living Inside You. Holgate, Douglas, illus. (p. 2218)
Tapalansky, Nick. Cast No Shadow. (p. 339)
Tapia, Alfredo, illus. see Wynne-Jones, Tim.
Tapia, Alfredo, jt. auth. see Wynne-Jones, Tim.
Tapia, Karina. Alma Oscura. (p. 57)
Tapia, Rayner. Magnificent Reveal: The Adventures of Tom Mcguire Vol. 5. (p. 1382)
Tapia, Sonia, tr. see Bach, Richard & Gardner, Sally.
Tapia, Sonia, tr. see Cabot, Meg.
Tapia, Sonia, tr. see Gardner, Sally.
Tapia-Bowes, Sally. Saami & the White Wolf. Ward, Danielle, illus. (p. 1919)
Tapia-Bowes, Sally-Anne. MR Crocodile Adventures: Magenta the Witch Works Her Magic on a Bored MR Crocodile. Bushnell, Holly Faith, illus. (p. 1518)
Taplin, Sam. 50 Optical Illusions. Seckel, Al, illus. (p. 2555)
—Animal. (p. 87)
—Are You There Little Bunny? (p. 113)
—Are You There Little Elephant? (p. 113)
—Are You There Little Unicorn? (p. 113)
—Baby Animals. (p. 148)
—Baby's Bedtime Storybook CV. (p. 153)
—Baby's Quiet Time Music Book. (p. 154)
—Cucú, ¿estás Ahí? ¿dónde Estás, Conejito?(Are You There Ltl Bunny?) (p. 482)
—Cucú, ¿estás Ahí? ¿dónde Estás, Elefantita?(Are You There Little Elephant?) (p. 482)
—Cuentos Cortos para Ir a Dormir(Five Minute Bedtime Stories) (p. 483)
—Dinosaurs. Lamb, Stacey, illus. (p. 550)
—Drumming Book IR (was Drum Kit Book) (p. 606)
—Easter Bunny Flap Book. (p. 619)
—Famous Classical Tunes Keyboard Book IR. (p. 703)
—Farm Sounds. (p. 710)
—First Encyclopedia of Dinosaurs II. (p. 736)
—First Sticker Book Santa. (p. 740)
—First Sticker Book Trains. (p. 740)
—Grammar & Punctuation IR. (p. 875)
—Libros para Bebé ¿Quién Está Ya Dormidito?(Who's Fallen Asleep?) (p. 1287)
—Libros para Bebé ¿Quién Lleva Sombrerito?(Who's Wearing a Hat?) (p. 1287)
—Listen & Learn First English Words. (p. 1308)
—Little Stories for Bedtime. Chiara, Francesca De, illus. (p. 1328)
—Little Stories for Christmas. (p. 1328)
—My First Christmas Keyboard Book. (p. 1543)
—My First Drumming Book IR. (p. 1544)
—My First Xylophone Book IR. (p. 1547)
—Night Sounds. (p. 1607)
—Night-Night Stories. (p. 1606)
—Noisy Diggers. (p. 1617)
—Noisy Dinosaurs (NEW) (p. 1617)
—Noisy Orchestra. (p. 1617)
—Noisy Pirates. Chambers, Mark, illus. (p. 1618)
—Noisy Spooky Book. (p. 1618)
—Noisy Zoo. Wildish, Lee, illus. (p. 1618)
—Optical Illusions Tin. (p. 1667)
—Pirates First Coloring Book. (p. 1751)
—Poppy & Sam's Animal Sounds. (p. 1776)
—Poppy & Sam's Animal Sticker Book. (p. 1776)
—Poppy & Sam's Easter Egg Hunt. (p. 1776)
—Poppy & Sam's Fingerprint Activities. (p. 1776)
—Poppy & Sam's First Word Book. (p. 1776)
—Poppy & Sam's Halloween Party (with PEEK THROUGH PAGES) (p. 1776)
—Poppy & Sam's Little Wipe-Clean Activities. (p. 1776)
—Poppy & Sam's LITTLE Wipe-Clean Christmas Activities. (p. 1776)
—Poppy & Sam's Magic Painting Book. (p. 1776)
—Poppy & Sam's Noisy Train Book REVISED/REPLACEMENT. (p. 1776)
—Pop-Up Haunted House. (p. 1775)
—Santa Flap Book. Bonnett, Rosalind, illus. (p. 1932)
—Sleepytime Stories. Chaira, Francesca di, illus. (p. 2038)
—This Is My Dinosaur. (p. 2225)
—Tricky Words to Spell IR. (p. 2288)
—Trucks Sticker Book REVISED BINDING. (p. 2293)
—Twinkly, Twinkly Bedtime Book. (p. 2305)
—Where's the Busy Bee? (p. 2440)
—Where's the Butterfly. (p. 2440)
—Where's the Little Mouse? (p. 2441)
—Who's Fallen Asleep? (p. 2453)
—Who's up in the Air? (p. 2454)
—Who's Wearing a Hat? (p. 2454)
—Winter Wonderland Sound Book. (p. 2476)
—Woodland Sounds. (p. 2491)
—Zoo (First Sticker Book) Johansson, Cecilia, illus. (p. 2543)
—Zoo Sounds. (p. 2543)
—¿dónde Está la Patita? Where's the Butterfly? (p. 581)
—¿dónde Estás, Pequeño Unicornio? Are You There Little Unicorn. (p. 581)
Taplin, Sam, jt. auth. see Brooks, Felicity.
Taplin, Sam, jt. auth. see Greenwell, Jessica.
Taplin, William. Compendium of Practical & Experimental Farriery (Classic Reprint) (p. 433)
—Compendium of Practical & Experimental Farriery, Originally Suggested by Reason & Confirmed by Practice: Equally Adapted for the Convenience of the Gentleman, the Farmer, the Groom, & the Smith (Classic Reprint) (p. 433)
—Compendium of Practical & Experimental Farriery, Originally Suggested by Reason & Confirmed by Practice, Equally Adapted for the Convenience of the Gentleman, the Farmer, the Groom, & the Smith: Interspersed with Such Remarks, & Elucidated With. (p. 433)
—Gentleman's Stable Directory, or Modern System of Farriery: Comprehending All the Most Valuable Prescriptions & Approved Remedies, Accurately Proportioned & Properly Adapted to Every Known Disease to Which the Horse Is Incident (Classic Reprint) (p. 817)
—Gentleman's Stable Directory, or Modern System of Farriery, Vol. 2: Containing Experimental Remarks, upon Breeding, Breaking, Shoeing, Stabling, Exercise & Rowelling; to Which Are Added, Particular Instructions for the General Management of Hunters. (p. 817)
—Taplin Improved, or a Compendium of Farriery: Wherein Is Fully Explained the Nature & Structure of That Useful Creature, a Horse, with the Diseases & Accidents He Is Liable to, & the Methods of Cure, Exemplified by Ten Elegant Cuts, Each the Full Fi. (p. 2191)
Taplinger, Lee, photos by see Florian, Douglas.
Tapora, Lorrie. Frog Named Sandy. Estrada, Jomar, illus. (p. 789)
Tappan, Eva March. Book of Humor (Classic Reprint) (p. 258)
—Children's Hour: Stories from Seven Old Favorites; Volume V. (p. 374)
—Children's Hour, Volume 4. Stories of Legendary Heroes. (p. 374)
—Dixie Kitten (Classic Reprint) (p. 566)

—Egypt, Africa, & Arabia, the World's Story, Vol. 3: A History of the World in Story Song & Art (Classic Reprint) (p. 628)
—Farmer & His Friends. (p. 710)
—Golden Goose: And Other Fairy Tales (Classic Reprint) (p. 857)
—Heroes of the Middle Ages: A Biographic History of the Greatest Kings, Artists & Military Generals of Medieval Times. (p. 962)
—Heroes of the Middle Ages. (p. 962)
—House with the Silver Door (Classic Reprint) (p. 1024)
—In the Days of Alfred the Great (Classic Reprint) (p. 1108)
—In the Days of Queen Elizabeth. (p. 1108)
—In the Days of Queen Elizabeth (Classic Reprint) (p. 1108)
—In the Days of Queen Victori. (p. 1108)
—In the Days of Queen Victoria. (p. 1108)
—In the Days of Queen Victoria (Classic Reprint) (p. 1108)
—Letters from Colonial Children (Classic Reprint) (p. 1279)
—Modern Stories (Classic Reprint) (p. 1487)
—Myths from Many Lands (Classic Reprint) (p. 1572)
—Old Ballads in Prose (Classic Reprint) (p. 1644)
—Old Fashioned Stories & Poems (Classic Reprint) (p. 1645)
—Out-Of-Door Book (Classic Reprint) (p. 1682)
—Robin Hood: His Book (Classic Reprint) (p. 1891)
—Russia, Austria-Hungary, the Balkan States & Turkey, Vol. 6: The World's Story; a History of the World in Story, Song, & Art (Classic Reprint) (p. 1917)
—Sports & Pastimes (Classic Reprint) (p. 2088)
—Stories from Seven Old Favorites: Selected Arranged by Eva March Thappan (Classic Reprint) (p. 2124)
—Stories of Nature (Classic Reprint) (p. 2125)
—World's Story, Vol. 4: A History of the World in Story, Song & Art; Greece & Rome (Classic Reprint) (p. 2508)
—World's Story, Vol. 7: A History of the World in Story, Song, & Art (Classic Reprint) (p. 2508)
Tapper, Alice Paul. Raise Your Hand. Kissi, Marta, illus. (p. 1838)
Tapper, Lucy, illus. see Wilson, Steve.
Tapper, Thomas, jt. auth. see Stevenson, Robert Louis.
Tappin, Christine, illus. see Viswanath, Shobha.
Tappin, Jennifer, et al. Jack & the Wood Pile: A Christmas Story. (p. 1151)
Tapsell, Florence A. Brave & True (Classic Reprint) (p. 276)
Tara, Zann. Wild Child: Forest's First Day of School. (p. 2463)
—Wild Child: Forest's First Home. (p. 2463)
Tarakson, Stella. Apollo's Mystic Message! (p. 106)
—Apollo's Mystic Message! Roberts, Nick, illus. (p. 106)
—Arachne's Golden Gloves! (p. 109)
—Arachne's Golden Gloves! Roberts, Nick, illus. (p. 109)
—Bizarre Animals. (p. 235)
—Circe's Beastly Feast! Roberts, Nick, illus. (p. 392)
—Disgusting Animals. (p. 557)
—Freaky Animals. (p. 780)
—Hera's Terrible Trap! (p. 957)
—Hera's Terrible Trap! Roberts, Nick, illus. (p. 957)
—Here Comes Hercules! (p. 958)
—Here Comes Hercules! Roberts, Nick, illus. (p. 958)
—Jason's Wild Winds! Roberts, Nick, illus. (p. 1161)
—Lethal Animals. (p. 1269)
—Odysseus' Trojan Trick! Roberts, Nick, illus. (p. 1638)
—Problems with Pythagoras! (p. 1803)
—Problems with Pythagoras! Roberts, Nick, illus. (p. 1803)
—Scary Animals. (p. 1942)
—Stinky Animals. (p. 2120)
Taranggana, illus. see Denchukwu, Nkem.
Taranta, Mary. Shimmer & Burn. (p. 2007)
—Splendor & Spark. (p. 2085)
Tarantino, Mardijah Aldrich. Marvellous Stories from the Life of Muhammad. (p. 1413)
Tarantino, Mardiyah A. Prince Harjo & the Enchanted Stream. (p. 1794)
Tarantino, Scott & Ruggiero, David. High Sticking: Xylophone & Marimba Pieces for Grades 4 - 8. (p. 969)
Taraschi-Carr, Gola, jt. auth. see Hickman, Pamela.
Taravella, Emily. Hope & River. (p. 1001)
Tarbeaux, Frank. Autobiography of Frank Tarbeaux As Told to Donald Henderson Clarke (Classic Reprint) (p. 140)
Tarbell, Ida M. Father Abraham (Classic Reprint) (p. 714)
—He Knew Lincoln (Classic Reprint) (p. 941)
—He Knew Lincoln & Other Billy Brown Stories. (p. 941)
—He Knew Lincoln, & Other Billy Brown Stories (Classic Reprint) (p. 941)
—In Lincoln's Chair (Classic Reprint) (p. 1105)
—Rising of the Tide: The Story of Sabinsport (Classic Reprint) (p. 1886)
—Rising of the Tide. (p. 1886)
Tarbell, Ida Minerva. Reporter for Lincoln: Story of Henry E. Wing, Soldier & Newspaperman (Classic Reprint) (p. 1866)
Tarbett, Debbie. 5 Little Ducks. (p. 2548)
—5 Stomping Elephants. (p. 2548)
—Ten Cheepy, Chirpy Chicks. (p. 2203)
—Ten Splishy, Splashy Fish. (p. 2205)
—Ten Wriggly, Wiggly Caterpillars. (p. 2205)
Tarbett, Debbie, illus. see Brooks, Susie.
Tarbett, Debbie, illus. see Tiger Tales.
Tarbot, Jerry. Jerry Tarbot: The Living Unknown Soldier (Classic Reprint) (p. 1164)
Tarbox, A. D. Arctic Tundra Food Chain: Nature's Bounty. (p. 112)
—Desert Food Chain: Nature's Bounty. (p. 531)
—Desert Food Chain. (p. 531)
—Mountain Food Chain: Nature's Bounty. (p. 1513)
—Mountain Food Chain. (p. 1513)
—Nature's Bounty: an Arctic Tundra Food Chain. (p. 1581)
—Nature's Bounty: Ocean. (p. 1581)
—Nature's Bounty: Rainforest. (p. 1581)
—Ocean Food Chain: Nature's Bounty. (p. 1635)
—Prairie Food Chain: Nature's Bounty. (p. 1785)
—Prairie Food Chain. (p. 1785)
—Rainforest Food Chain: Nature's Bounty. (p. 1837)
—Rainforest Food Chain. (p. 1837)
Tarbox, Charlene. Creative Haven Beautiful Flower Arrangements Coloring Book. (p. 470)
—Glow-in-the-Dark Tattoos Flowers. (p. 845)
Tarcov, Susan. Raisins & Almonds: A Yiddish Lullaby. Sánchez, Sonia, illus. (p. 1838)
Tardieu, Émile. Ennui: Etude Psychologique (Classic Reprint) (p. 655)
Tardif, Benoit. Metropolis. Tardif, Benoit, illus. (p. 1453)
Tardif, Elizabeth. Bunny Named Apple. Buehrle, Jacquelyn, illus. (p. 298)
Tardif, Lindi. Daughter of Apartheid (p. 509)
Taree, Aerle. Taree. Marie, :Donna, ed. (p. 2191)
Taree, Aerle Ms. Molly's Mental Health: Love Me Too. (p. 1490)
Tarendash, Albert. Regents Exams & Answers: Chemistry—Physical Setting 2020. (p. 1861)
Tarendash, Albert S. Let's Review Regents: Chemistry—Physical Setting 2020. (p. 1277)
—Regents Chemistry—Physical Setting Power Pack 2020. (p. 1861)
Targ Brill, Marlene, jt. auth. see Keranen, Rachel.
Targett, Zoe. Unbound: A Siren's Quest for Freedom. (p. 2317)
Targioni-Tozzetti, Giovanni. Zanetto: Le Passant, Di F. Coppe (Classic Reprint) (p. 2538)
Tarico, Valerie. Deas & Other Imaginings: Ten Spiritual Folktales for Children. Troy, Tony, illus. (p. 521)
Tario, Francisco. Entre Nosches y Fantasmas. Esquivel, Isidro R., illus. (p. 657)
Tarkela, Johanna, illus. see Garnett, Jaye.
Tarkington, Antonio. Bucky's Day Out. (p. 289)
Tarkington, Booth. Alice Adams: Illustrated by Arthur William Brown (Classic Reprint) (p. 44)
—Alice Adams. (p. 44)
—Beasley's Christmas Party (Classic Reprint) (p. 181)
—Beautiful Lady (Classic Reprint) (p. 184)
—Cherry (Classic Reprint) (p. 366)
—Conquest of Canaan: A Novel (Classic Reprint) (p. 442)
—Conquest of Canaan. (p. 442)
—Country Cousin (Classic Reprint) (p. 461)
—Flirt (Classic Reprint) (p. 749)
—Gentle Julia (Classic Reprint) (p. 816)
—Gentleman from Indiana (Classic Reprint) (p. 816)
—Harlequin & Columbine: Front, by Stetson Crawford (Classic Reprint) (p. 930)
—His Own People (Classic Reprint) (p. 974)
—In the Arena: Stories of Political Life (Classic Reprint) (p. 1107)
—Magnificent Ambersons: (+ Audiobook) (p. 1382)
—Magnificent Ambersons: Illustrated (Classic Reprint) (p. 1382)
—Monsieur Beaucaire: The Beautiful Lady; His Own People (Classic Reprint) (p. 1495)
—Monsieur Beaucaire. (p. 1495)
—Monsieur Beaucaire (Classic Reprint) (p. 1495)
—Penrod. (p. 1718)
—Penrod (Classic Reprint) (p. 1718)
—Penrod & Sam (Classic Reprint) (p. 1718)
—Quest of Quesnay (Classic Reprint) (p. 1826)
—Ramsey Milholland. (p. 1839)
—Ramsey Milholland (Classic Reprint) (p. 1839)
—Seventeen: A Tale of Youth & Summer Time & the Baxter Family Especially William (Classic Reprint) (p. 1994)
—Spring Concert (Classic Reprint) (p. 2092)
—Turmoil: A Novel (Classic Reprint) (p. 2300)
—Turmoil. (p. 2300)
—Two Vanrevels (Classic Reprint) (p. 2309)
—Works of Booth Tarkington, Vol. 8: Harlequin & Columbine, & Other Stories (Classic Reprint) (p. 2496)
—Works of Booth Tarkington, Vol. 9: Monsieur Beaucaire, the Beautiful Lady, His Own People, & Other Stories (Classic Reprint) (p. 2496)
—World Does Move (Classic Reprint) (p. 2501)
Tarkington, Booth, jt. auth. see Wilson, Harry Leon.
Tarkington, Booth & Milholland, Ramsey. Works of Booth Tarkington, Vol. XIV. (p. 2496)
Tarkoff, Sarah. Sinless. (p. 2024)
Tarlow, Ellen. Mole Catches the Sky. Bogacki, Tomek, illus. (p. 1488)
Tarman, Mel. Judah: The Story of Judah P. Benjamin, Confederate Statesman. (p. 1185)
Tarn, W. W. Treasure of the Isle of Mist (Classic Reprint) (p. 2282)
Tarnow, Georgette H. Special Secret Hearts: A Child's Introduction to Dementia & Pink Curls - a Santa Claus Story. (p. 2077)
Tarnowska. Conte des Mille et une Nuits. Henaff, Carole, illus. (p. 444)
Tarnowska, Wafa'. Arabian Nights. Henaff, Carole, illus. (p. 108)
—Arabian Nights Chapter. Hénaff, Carole, illus. (p. 108)
Tarnowski, Mark, illus. see Treanor, H. T.
Taro, Gomi. This Is a Hand. (p. 2224)
—This Is a String. (p. 2224)
Tarou, Miura. Little King. (p. 1320)
Tarpinian, Steve. Mouse in the House: A True Story about the Mice Who Came into Our Home after Hurricane Sandy. Dansereau, Steve, illus. (p. 1515)
Tarpley, Natasha. Harlem Charade. (p. 930)
Tarpley, Natasha Anastasia. Bippity Bop Barbershop. Lewis, E. B., illus. (p. 229)
—Harlem Charade. (p. 930)
—I Love My Hair! Lewis, E. B., illus. (p. 1071)
Tarpley, Todd. Beep! Beep! Go to Sleep! Rocco, John, illus. (p. 189)
—How to Become a Knight (in Ten Easy Lessons) Harney, Jennifer, illus. (p. 1038)
—My Grandma's a Ninja. Chatzikonstantinou, Danny, illus. (p. 1548)
—Naughty Ninja Takes a Bath. Vogel, Vin, illus. (p. 1582)
—Ten Tiny Toes. (p. 2205)
—Three Grumpy Trucks. Parker-Rees, Guy, illus. (p. 2233)
Tarr, Lisa M., illus. see Perry, Phyllis J.
Tarr, P. J. Behold Mary's Little Lamb. (p. 193)
Tarr, William Arthur. Tables for the Determination of the Common Minerals & Rocks (Classic Reprint) (p. 2175)
Tarrac, Carlos F. Veva & the Beaver. (p. 2354)
Tarrant, Daniel, illus. see Lakin, Patricia.
Tarrant, Marcus Adrian. Friendly Ness Goes Fishing: You'll Never Guess What Clever Ness Catches! Nick, Watson, illus. (p. 786)
—Friendly Ness Sings the Friendly Ness Song: Sing along with the Ness Monsters. Watson, Nick, illus. (p. 786)
—Ness Monsters Learn First Aid: Guess Who Ends up Looking Like a Mummy! Nick, Watson, illus. (p. 1588)
Tarrant, Percy. Tom's Boy (Classic Reprint) (p. 2259)
Tarrant, Percy, illus. see Vaizey, George de Horne.
Tarruella, Ramón. Conquista Española de America Contada para Niños. (p. 442)
Tarruella, Ramón, frwd. Llegada de Los Españoles a América Contada para Niños. (p. 1338)
—Revolución Francesa Contada para Niños. (p. 1873)
—Revolución Industrial Contada para Niños. (p. 1873)
Tarshis, Lauren. American Revolution, 1776. (p. 74)
—Attack of the Grizzlies, 1967. (p. 134)
—Attacks of September 11th, 2001. Dawson, Scott, illus. (p. 135)
—Domestic (p. 580)
—El Naufragio del Titanic, 1912. Dawson, Scott, illus. (p. 630)
—Emma-Jean Lazarus Fell in Love. (p. 643)
—I Survived: True Stories, Five Epic Disasters. (p. 1083)
—I Survived Collector's Toolbox (I Survived) (p. 1083)
—I Survived Hurricane Katrina 2005. (p. 1083)
—I Survived Hurricane Katrina 2005. Dawson, Scott, illus. (p. 1083)
—I Survived the Attack of the Grizzlies 1967 (p. 1083)
—I Survived the Attack of the Grizzlies, 1967. (p. 1083)
—I Survived the Battle of D-Day 1944 (p. 1083)
—I Survived the Battle of D-Day 1944. (p. 1083)
—I Survived the Battle of D-Day, 1944. (p. 1083)
—I Survived the Battle of Gettysburg 1863. (p. 1083)
—I Survived the Bombing of Pearl Harbor 1941. (p. 1083)
—I Survived the Bombing of Pearl Harbor 1941. Dawson, Scott, illus. (p. 1083)
—I Survived the Children's Blizzard 1888. (p. 1083)
—I Survived the Destruction of Pompeii, 79 A. D. (p. 1083)
—I Survived the Destruction of Pompeii, AD 79. Dawson, Scott, illus. (p. 1083)
—I Survived the Eruption of Mount St. Helens, 1980. (p. 1083)
—I Survived the Great Chicago Fire 1871. (p. 1083)
—I Survived the Hindenburg Disaster 1937. (p. 1083)
—I Survived the Japanese Tsunami 2011. (p. 1083)
—I Survived the Japanese Tsunami 2011. Dawson, Scott, illus. (p. 1083)
—I Survived the Joplin Tornado 2011. Dawson, Scott, illus. (p. 1083)
—I Survived the Nazi Invasion 1944. (p. 1083)
—I Survived the San Francisco Earthquake 1906. (p. 1083)
—I Survived the San Francisco Earthquake 1906. Dawson, Scott, illus. (p. 1083)
—I Survived the Shark Attacks of 1916. (p. 1083)
—I Survived the Shark Attacks of 1916. Dawson, Scott, illus. (p. 1083)
—I Survived the Sinking of the Titanic 1912. (p. 1083)
—I Survived the Sinking of the Titanic 1912. Dawson, Scott, illus. (p. 1083)
—Nature Attacks! (p. 1580)
—Sobreviví el Terremoto de San Francisco 1906. Dawson, Scott, illus. (p. 2051)
—Tornado Terror: True Tornado Survival Stories & Amazing Facts from History & Today. (p. 2265)
Tarshis, Lauren & Dawson, Scott. Sobreviví - Los Ataques de Tiburones de 1916. Dawson, Scott, illus. (p. 2051)
Tarshis, Lauren, comment. I Survived the Great Molasses Flood 1919 (p. 1083)
Tarshis, Thomas Paul. Living with Peer Pressure & Bullying. (p. 1335)
Tarsky, Sue. Brown Bear Starts School. Aizen, Marina, illus. (p. 286)
—Fall in the Country. Lordon, Claire, illus. (p. 700)
—Spring in the Woods. Lordon, Claire, illus. (p. 2092)
—Summer at the Seashore. Lordon, Claire, illus. (p. 2148)
—Wheels on The... Uh-Oh! Willmore, Alex, illus. (p. 2428)
—Whose Ears? (p. 2454)
—Whose Feet? (p. 2454)
—Whose Nose? Garton, Michael, illus. (p. 2454)
—Whose Tail? Garton, Michael, illus. (p. 2454)
—Winter in the City. Lordon, Claire, illus. (p. 2475)
Taruhi, Furuta. Doggy's Stroll License. (p. 577)
Tarver, John Charles. James, or Virtue Rewarded (Classic Reprint) (p. 1157)
Tarver, Linda. Jesus, Who Is Christmas Is Born. (p. 1167)
Tarver, Monroe S. Tales from the Mapmaker: Imagia & the Magic Pearls. (p. 2183)
Taschek, Karen. Civil War. (p. 396)
—Risen Horse. (p. 1886)
Tash, Sarvenaz. Geek's Guide to Unrequited Love. (p. 813)
—Mapmaker & the Ghost. (p. 1401)
—Three Day Summer. (p. 2232)
—Virtually Yours. (p. 2361)
Tashiro, Chisato. Five Nice Mice & the Great Car Race. Tashiro, Chisato, illus. (p. 744)
Tashjian, Jake, illus. see Tashjian, Janet.
Tashjian, Janet. Einstein the Class Hamster. Tashjian, Jake, illus. (p. 629)
—Einstein the Class Hamster & the Very Real Game Show. Tashjian, Jake, illus. (p. 629)
—Einstein the Class Hamster Saves the Library. Tashjian, Jake, illus. (p. 629)
—For What It's Worth: A Novel. (p. 764)
—Larry & the Meaning of Life. (p. 1244)
—Marty Frye, Private Eye Bk. 2. Keller, Laurie, illus. (p. 1411)
—Marty Frye, Private Eye: The Case of the Missing Action Figure. Keller, Laurie, illus. (p. 1411)
—Marty Frye, Private Eye: the Case of the Busted Video Games. Keller, Laurie, illus. (p. 1411)
—Marty Frye, Private Eye: the Case of the Busted Video Games & Other Mysteries. Keller, Laurie, illus. (p. 1411)
—Marty Frye, Private Eye: the Case of the Stolen Poodle Bk. 2. Keller, Laurie, illus. (p. 1411)
—Marty Frye, Private Eye: the Case of the Stolen Poodle. Keller, Laurie, illus. (p. 1411)
—My Life As a Book. (p. 1551)
—My Life As a Book. Tashjian, Jake, illus. (p. 1551)
—My Life As a Cartoonist. Tashjian, Jake, illus. (p. 1551)
—My Life As a Coder. Tashjian, Jake, illus. (p. 1551)
—My Life As a Gamer. Tashjian, Jake, illus. (p. 1551)
—My Life As a Joke. Tashjian, Jake, illus. (p. 1551)
—My Life As a Meme. Tashjian, Jake, illus. (p. 1551)
—My Life As a Ninja. Tashjian, Jake, illus. (p. 1551)
—My Life As a Stuntboy. (p. 1551)
—My Life As a Stuntboy. Tashjian, Jake, illus. (p. 1551)
—My Life as a Stuntboy. Tashjian, Jake, illus. (p. 1551)
—My Life As a Youtuber. Tashjian, Jake, illus. (p. 1551)
—Sticker Girl. (p. 2118)
—Sticker Girl. Wilmink, Inga, illus. (p. 2118)
—Sticker Girl & the Cupcake Challenge Wilmink, Inga, illus. (p. 2118)
—Sticker Girl Rules the School. Wilmink, Inga, illus. (p. 2118)
Tashlikowich, Natasha. Secret of the Seven Stones. (p. 1978)
Tashlin, Frank. Bear That Wasn't. (p. 180)
—Possum That Didn't. (p. 1780)
Tashlin, Frank, jt. auth. see Minarik, Else Holmelund.
Tasma, Tasma. In Her Earliest Youth: A Novel (Classic Reprint) (p. 1105)
—Not Counting the Cost, Vol. 2 of 3 (Classic Reprint) (p. 1623)
—Penance of Portia James (Classic Reprint) (p. 1715)
—Sydney Sovereign: And Other Tales (Classic Reprint) (p. 2172)
—Uncle Piper of Piper's Hill: An Australian Novel (Classic Reprint) (p. 2318)
Taso, Alex, illus. see Grahame, Kenneth.
Tassell, Charles Van. Truthful Lies (Classic Reprint) (p. 2297)
—Truthful Lies of Yellowstone Park, 1921 (Classic Reprint) (p. 2297)
Tassi, Marguerite, jt. auth. see Shakespeare, William.
Tassin, Algernon. Rainbow String (Classic Reprint) (p. 1837)
Tasso, Torquato. Aminta: Favola Boschereccia (Classic Reprint) (p. 75)
—Aminta: Favola Boscareccia con Gl'intermezzi (Classic Reprint) (p. 75)
—Aminta, Favola Boschereccia; l'Amor Fuggitivo, Idillio; Carme (Classic Reprint) (p. 75)
Taste of Home Editorial Staff. Cake Mix Creations: 216 Easy Desserts That Start with a Mix. (p. 309)
Tata, Cb. Ernie the Eagle Goes to Maine. Hanley, Zachary, illus. (p. 660)
Tatam, Michelle. Chameleon. (p. 355)
—Midnight Running. (p. 1461)
Tatar, Janev. Answer in Your Heart. (p. 101)
Tatar, M., tr. see Andersen, Hans Christian.
Tatar, Maria, ed. see Andersen, Hans Christian.
Tatarnikov, Pavel, illus. see Andersen, Hans.
Tatarsky, Daniel. Cool Philosophy: 50 Fantastic Facts for Kids of All Ages. (p. 449)
Tatchell, J., jt. auth. see Smith, A.
Tatchell, Judy, ed. see Dalby, Elizabeth.
Tate, Allen. Southern Vanguard: The John Pearle Bishop Memorial Volume (Classic Reprint) (p. 2069)
Tate, Beverly A. Being Grace. Antounian, Raffi, illus. (p. 194)
Tate Billingsley, ReShonda. Boy Trouble. (p. 270)
—You Don't Know Me Like That. (p. 2527)
Tate, C. M. Chinook As Spoken by the Indians of Washington Territory, British Columbia & Alaska: For the Use of Traders, Tourists & Others Who Have Business Intercourse with the Indians; Chinook-English; English-Chinook (Classic Reprint) (p. 379)
Tate, Connie. Roll On. Bridge, Sam, illus. (p. 1898)
—Scooter Boy. Bridge, Sam, illus. (p. 1961)
—Sylvester's Cat-Astrophic Tale. Bridge, Sam, illus. (p. 2173)
—Sylvester's CAT-Astropic Tale. Bridge, Sam, illus. (p. 2173)
Tate, Corey. Zwataru: The Otherworld Series: Book 2. (p. 2545)
Tate, Don. Poet: The Remarkable Story of George Moses Horton. (p. 1766)
—Poet: The Remarkable Story of George Moses Horton. Tate, Don, illus. (p. 1766)
—William Still & His Freedom Stories: The Father of the Underground Railroad. Tate, Don, illus. (p. 2468)
Tate, Don, illus. see Barton, Chris & Tate, Don, II.
Tate, Don, illus. see Barton, Chris.
Tate, Don, illus. see Blue, Rose & Naden, Corinne.
Tate, Don, illus. see Bolden, Tonya.
Tate, Don, illus. see Bunting, Eve.
Tate, Don, illus. see Celenza, Anna Harwell.
Tate, Don, illus. see Christie, R. Gregory.
Tate, Don, illus. see Greenfield, Eloise.
Tate, Don, illus. see Hopkinson, Deborah.
Tate, Don, illus. see Hubbell, Patricia.
Tate, Don, illus. see Lyons, Kelly Starling.
Tate, Don, illus. see Mahin, Michael.
Tate, Don, illus. see Mandel, Peter.
Tate, Don, illus. see Vernick, Audrey.
Tate, Don, illus. see Wiggins, Thalia.
Tate, Don, jt. auth. see Hubbell, Patricia.
Tate, Don, II, jt. auth. see Barton, Chris.
Tate, Eleanora E. Celeste's Harlem Renaissance. (p. 350)
—Minstrel's Melody. (p. 1473)
Tate, Elizabeth Dawn. There's a Storm Brewing Outside. (p. 2218)
Tate, Hakim. Twin's Adventures: A Race with an Officer Friendly. Bryant, Jacquelyn, illus. (p. 2306)
Tate, Jean Annette. Daddy & Me. (p. 494)
Tate, Judith. Crawly & Splosh! (p. 467)
Tate, Kelly. Selling Popcorn: Understand Place Value. (p. 1987)
Tate, Kristy. Melange. (p. 1442)
—Menagerie. (p. 1447)
Tate, Meredith. Freedom Trials. (p. 783)
—Red Labyrinth. (p. 1857)
Tate, Mumsy. I Am 1. (p. 1056)
Tate, Nancy. Grandmother Ellie's Attic. (p. 879)
Tate, Nikki. Better Together: Creating Community in an Uncertain World (p. 209)
—Choosing to Live, Choosing to Die: The Complexities of Assisted Dying Wuthrich, Belle, illus. (p. 381)
—Deadpoint (p. 519)

—Deadpoint. (p. 519)
—Deep Roots: How Trees Sustain Our Planet (p. 524)
—Down to Earth: How Kids Help Feed the World (p. 590)
—Fallout (p. 701)
—Home Base: A Mother-Daughter Story. Kath, Katie, illus. (p. 996)
—Razor's Edge (p. 1844)
—Venom (p. 2350)
Tate, Nikki & Tate-Stratton, Dani. Birthdays: Beyond Cake & Ice Cream (p. 234)
—Take Shelter: At Home Around the World (p. 2177)
Tate, Nikki & Tate-Stratton, Danielle. Christmas: From Solstice to Santa (p. 383)
Tate, Richard, illus. see Grantham, Leslie.
Tate, Singleton M. Laugh a Little. Vorella2000, illus. (p. 1251)
Tate, Suzanne. Teena Tortoise: A Tale of a Little Giant. Melvin, James, illus. (p. 2199)
Tate, W. K. Child's World: Fifth Reader (Classic Reprint) (p. 376)
Tate, William J. East Coast Scenery: Rambles Through Towns & Villages; Nutting, Blackberrying, & Mushrooming; Sea Fishing, Wild-Fowl Shooting, Etc. (p. 619)
—East Coast Scenery: Rambles Through Towns & Villages; Nutting, Blackberrying, & Mushrooming; Sea Fishing, Wild-Fowl Shooting, etc (Classic Reprint) (p. 619)
Tate, William Knox. Child's World: Fourth Reader (Classic Reprint) (p. 376)
Tate-Stratton, Dani, jt. auth. see Tate, Nikki.
Tate-Stratton, Danielle, jt. auth. see Tate, Nikki.
Tatic, Mihailo, illus. see Zapple, Elias.
Tatlock, Ann. Backyard Jungle Safari Opossums: Opossums. (p. 157)
—Medieval England. (p. 1436)
—My Friend Is Christian. (p. 1547)
—My Home Is My Castle Hearst Castle: Hearst Castle. (p. 1550)
Tatlow, Richard H. Orpah: A Religious & Historical Novel with the Principal Scenes in Missouri, Immediately Preceeding, During & Following the Great Civil War (Classic Reprint) (p. 1672)
Tatlow-Lord, Robin, illus. see Graham, Brooke.
Tatman, Lianna. Gun Control Debate: From Classrooms to Congress (p. 905)
Tatoian, Julia. God's Creation - Day 3. (p. 853)
—Life of Honey. (p. 1294)
Tatro, MaryAnn. Milton the Square Shell Turtle. Lucas, Diane, illus. (p. 1468)
Tatsi, Andreanna, tr. see Downie, David.
Tatsunoko Production. Samurai Pizza Cats: Official Fan Book. (p. 1929)
Tatsuya, Hamazaki, jt. auth. see Hamazaki, Tatsuya.
Tattam, Mark, jt. auth. see Phillips, Sarah.
Tattoos, jt. auth. see Dover.
Tatuem, Kimberly. Backyard Adventure. (p. 156)
Tatuki, Ru. Poyo Poyo's Observation Diary (Volume 3 Of 6) (p. 1783)
—Poyo Poyo's Observation Diary Vol. 2. (p. 1783)
Tatulli, Mark. Big Break. (p. 218)
—Daydreaming: A Picture Book. (p. 515)
—Desmond Pucket & the Cloverfield Junior High Carnival of Horrors. (p. 533)
—Desmond Pucket & the Mountain Full of Monsters. (p. 533)
—Desmond Pucket Makes Monster Magic. (p. 533)
—Lio: Making Friends. (p. 1305)
—Lio: There's a Monster in My Socks. (p. 1305)
—Short & Skinny. (p. 2010)
—They Came. (p. 2219)
Tatulli, Mark, et al. Lio: Making Friends. (p. 1305)
—Lio: "There's a Monster in My Socks" (p. 1305)
Tatulli, Sandra & Nitsis, Erika. Adventures of Lucy Ladybug: Felicia's Family. (p. 25)
Tatum, Ariana. World of Secrets. (p. 2504)
Tatum, Edith. When the Bugle Called (Classic Reprint) (p. 2433)
Tatum, Frances C. Old Westtown: A Collection (Classic Reprint) (p. 1648)
Taua, Julie Bella. Oh Where Oh Where Can Harawene Be? (p. 1642)
Taub, Melinda. Still Star-Crossed. (p. 2119)
Taub, Udi, illus. see Davis, Linda.
Taub, Udi, illus. see Shaked, S.
Tauber, Sabine. Architecture: Create Your Own City!—Sticker Book. (p. 111)
—Hieronymus Bosch: Sticker Book. (p. 968)
—Hieronymus Bosch: Coloring Book. (p. 968)
—Medieval Creatures Sticker Book. (p. 1436)
Taufick, Roberto. Boa Noite, Bicho Papao. Galvao, Elder, illus. (p. 251)
Taul, Jonas. Serious Thought (p. 1991)
Taunton, Thomas Henry. Portraits of Celebrated Racehorses of the Past & Present Centuries, Vol. 2 Of 4: In Strictly Chronological Order, Commencing in 1702 & Ending in 1870, Together with Their Respective Pedigrees & Performances Recorded in Full (Classic Reprint) (p. 1779)
—Portraits of Celebrated Racehorses of the Past & Present Centuries, in Strictly Chronological Order, Commencing in 1702 & Ending in 1870, Vol. 4 Of 4: Together with Their Respective Pedigrees & Performances Recorded in Full; from 1842 To 1870. (p. 1779)
-Taunton, Winefride Trafford. Threshold (Classic Reprint) (p. 2236)
Taus-Bolstad, Stacy. From Wheat to Bread. (p. 794)
Tauss, Marc, illus. see Ehrmann, Max.
Tauszik, Karleen. When I Grow up, I Want to Be... The Annual Career Possibility Journal for Kids. (p. 2431)
Tautphoeus, Baroness. Initials, Vol. 2: A Story of Modern Life (Classic Reprint) (p. 1120)
—Quits: A Novel, Vol. 2 of 3 (Classic Reprint) (p. 1828)
Tautphoeus, Jemima Montgomery. At Odds: A Novel (Classic Reprint) (p. 130)
Tautphoeus, Jemima Von. At Odds, Vol. 1 Of 2: A Novel (Classic Reprint) (p. 130)
Tautphoeus, Tautphoeus. Initials: A Novel (Classic Reprint) (p. 1120)
—Quits, Vol. 3 Of 3: A Novel (Classic Reprint) (p. 1828)
Tauzin, Louis, contrib. by. Carnet Blanc Route des Pyrenees. (p. 332)
—Carnet Ligne Route des Pyrenees. (p. 332)
Tavares, Matt. Becoming Babe Ruth. Tavares, Matt, illus. (p. 187)
—Crossing Niagara: The Death-Defying Tightrope Adventures of the Great Blondin. Tavares, Matt, illus. (p. 478)
—Dasher: How a Brave Little Doe Changed Christmas Forever. Tavares, Matt, illus. (p. 508)
—Dasher 6-Copy Counter Display (p. 508)
—Growing up Pedro: How the Martinez Brothers Made It from the Dominican Republic All the Way to the Major Leagues. Tavares, Matt, illus. (p. 900)
—Growing up Pedro: Candlewick Biographies: How the Martinez Brothers Made It from the Dominican Republic All the Way to the Major Leagues. Tavares, Matt, illus. (p. 900)
—Henry Aaron's Dream. Tavares, Matt, illus. (p. 954)
—Mudball. Tavares, Matt, illus. (p. 1524)
—Red & Lulu. Tavares, Matt, illus. (p. 1856)
—There Goes Ted Williams: The Greatest Hitter Who Ever Lived. Tavares, Matt, illus. (p. 2216)
—Zachary's Ball. Tavares, Matt, illus. (p. 2538)
Tavares, Matt, illus. see Anonymous.
Tavares, Matt, illus. see Kladstrup, Kristin.
Tavares, Matt, illus. see Nesbit, E.
Tavares, Matt, illus. see Rappaport, Doreen.
Tavares, Matt, illus. see Rosen, Michael J.
Tavares, Matt, illus. see Smith, Matthew Clark.
Tavares, Victor, illus. see Sims, Lesley.
Tavares, Victor, illus. see Williams, Brenda.
Tavares, Victore, illus. see Levene, Rebecca, ed.
Tavcar, Samantha, illus. see Medina, Sylvia M.
Tavengerwei, Rutendo. Hope Is Our Only Wing. (p. 1002)
Tavenner, James W. Fernwood Community Center (Classic Reprint) (p. 721)
Taverna, Pietro. Nuovo Sistema Di Vetture Atto Ad Ogni Genere Di Trasporti Sulle Strade Ordinaire: Un Nuovo Apparecchio Di Sala per Facilitare il Moto Dei Waggons Sulle Curve Delle Strade Ferrate (Classic Reprint) (p. 1631)
Tavernier, Joshua. Senior Year. (p. 1988)
Taves, Julia. Never the Same. (p. 1590)
Tavner, Gill, jt. auth. see Moore, Alan.
Tavner, Gill & Dickens, Charles. David Copperfield. Donnelly, Karen, illus. (p. 511)
—Hard Times. Donnelly, Karen, illus. (p. 929)
Tawa, Renee. Disney Junior Minnie: I'm Ready to Read: Minnie. Disney Storybook Art Team, illus. (p. 560)
—Tink's Magical Day. (p. 2248)
Tawn Bergren, Lisa. Familia Es un Regalo de Dios. (p. 701)
Tawney, C.H. Malavikagnimitra: A Sanskrit Play Kalidasa, Literally Translated into English Prose (Classic Reprint) (p. 1391)
Taxali, Gary. This Is Silly! (p. 2225)
Taxali, Gary, illus. see DePrisco, Dorothea.
Taxali, Gary, illus. see Iodice, Frank.
Tay, Johny. Gwan Anthology, Volume Two. (p. 907)
Tayal, Amit, illus. see Dumas, Alexandre.
Tayal, Amit, illus. see Gunderson, Jessica & Loewen, Nancy.
Tayal, Amit, illus. see Helfand, Lewis.
Tayal, Amit, illus. see Hoena, B. A.
Tayal, Amit, illus. see Loewen, Nancy.
Tayal, Amit, illus. see Poskitt, Kjartan.
Tayal, Amit, illus. see Shaskan, Trisha Speed & Loewen, Nancy.
Tayal, Amit, illus. see Shaskan, Trisha Speed.
Tayal, Amit, illus. see Troupe, Thomas Kingsley.
Tayal, Amit, illus. see Wyss, Johann David.
Tay-Audouard, L. K., illus. see Seow, David.
Tay-Audouard, L. K., jt. auth. see Taylor, Diane.
Taykutgul, Selcuk & Akin, Ferruh. Uthman: Bearer of Two Pure Lights. (p. 2342)
Tayler, Amber. What Do Monsters Look Like? Birth, Ryan, illus. (p. 2408)
Tayler, Charles B. Christmas at Old Court: A Fireside Book (Classic Reprint) (p. 383)
—Legends & Records: Chiefly Historical (Classic Reprint) (p. 1263)
—Mark Wilton, the Merchant's Clerk (Classic Reprint) (p. 1407)
Tayler, Charles Benjamin. Angels' Song: A Christmas Token (Classic Reprint) (p. 86)
—Lady Mary, or Not of the World (Classic Reprint) (p. 1237)
—May You Like It (Classic Reprint) (p. 1429)
—Records of a Good Man's Life (Classic Reprint) (p. 1855)
—Social Evils: And Their Remedy (Classic Reprint) (p. 2053)
—Social Evils, & Their Remedy, Vol. 1: Mechanic, and, the Lady & the Lady's Maid (Classic Reprint) (p. 2053)
—Social Evils, & Their Remedy, Vol. 2 Of 4: The Pastor of Dronfells, and, the Labourer & His Wife (Classic Reprint) (p. 2053)
—Social Evils, & Their Remedy, Vol. 3: The Country Town; Live & Let Live, or the Manchester Weavers (Classic Reprint) (p. 2053)
Tayleur, Karen. Famous (Scholastic) The Awesome Life of David Mortimore Baxter. Garvey, Brann, illus. (p. 704)
Tayleure, Floyd. Professions, Vol. 1 Of 3: A Novel (Classic Reprint) (p. 1804)
—Professions, Vol. 3 Of 3: A Novel (Classic Reprint) (p. 1804)
Tayloe, McConnell Dubay, ed. see Muller, Seth.
Taylor. Correspondence: Between a Mother & Her Daughter at School (Classic Reprint) (p. 456)
Taylor, A. E. Land of the Scarlet Leaf (Classic Reprint) (p. 1242)
Taylor, Adam. George in the UK: The Unknown Kingdom. Taylor, Adam & West, Jeannette, eds. (p. 819)
Taylor, Adam, illus. see Heidari, Mahdi.
Taylor, Adam, illus. see Hickman, Debbie.
Taylor, Adam, illus. see Murphy, T. M.
Taylor, Alex. Breathe. (p. 279)
Taylor, Alex & Patterson, R. J. Breathe. (p. 279)
Taylor, Alfred. Watch & the Clock (Classic Reprint) (p. 2382)
Taylor, Ali. Cotton Wool. (p. 457)
Taylor, Allan & Parish, James Robert. Library & Information Science. (p. 1284)
Taylor, Allison Wagner, jt. auth. see Hurst, Donna L.
Taylor, Amber, illus. see Reyes, S. L.
Taylor, Amber L., illus. see Reyes, Shawntie L.
Taylor, Andrew. Christmas Carol for Evie. (p. 384)
Taylor, Angela. Finch. (p. 727)
—Izzy's Quest for Gold. (p. 1150)
—Poppy Trilogy. (p. 1776)
Taylor, Ann. Select Circulating Library, or Youth's Companion, Vol. 1 (Classic Reprint) (p. 1985)
Taylor, Ann, jt. auth. see Taylor, Jane.
Taylor, Anna. Sophia's Favorite Squirrel Browny. (p. 2064)
Taylor, Aron. Eye of Horus. (p. 688)
—Origin: Rise of Ares Part 2. (p. 1671)
—Rise of Ares Part 1. (p. 1885)
—Rise of Ares Part 2. (p. 1885)
Taylor, Arthur Russell. Mr. Squem & Some Male Triangles (Classic Reprint) (p. 1520)
Taylor, Ashley, illus. see Eckstein, Ashley & Kravetz, Stacy.
Taylor, Barbara. Amazing History of Castles & Knights. (p. 65)
—Encyclopedia of Sharks. Kelly, Richard, ed. (p. 648)
—Exploring Nature: Fantastic Penguins. (p. 682)
—Exploring Nature - Amazing Snakes: An Exciting Insight into the Weird & Wonderful World of Snakes & How They Live, with 190 Pictures. (p. 682)
—Exploring Nature - Sensational Spiders: A Comprehensive Guide to Some of the Most Intriguing Creatures in the Animal Kingdom, with over 220 Pictures. (p. 682)
—I Wonder Why Soap Makes Bubbles: And Other Questions about Science. (p. 1086)
—I Wonder Why Zippers Have Teeth. (p. 1086)
—In Focus: Bugs. (p. 1105)
—In Focus: Reptiles. (p. 1105)
—Incredible Crocodiles: Look at the Fascinating World of Crocodiles, Alligators, Caimans & Gharials, Shown in over 180 Exciting Images. (p. 1113)
—Incredible Elephants: A Fascinating Guide to the Gentle Giants That Dominate Africa & Asia, Shown in More Than 190 Pictures. (p. 1113)
—Inside Plants. (p. 1123)
—Inventions. (p. 1130)
—Sharks. (p. 2002)
—Slimy Spawn & Other Gruesome Life Cycles. (p. 2038)
—Snakes. (p. 2044)
—Stinky Skunks & Other Animal Adaptations. (p. 2120)
—Turtles & Tortoises: An In-Depth Look at Chelonians, the Shelled Reptiles That Have Existed since the Time of the Dinosaurs. (p. 2301)
Taylor, Barbara, jt. auth. see Zommer, Yuval.
Taylor, Barbara & Green, Jen. Explore the Deadly World of Bugs, Snakes, Spiders, Crocodiles: The Dramatic Lives & Conflicts of the World's Strangest Creatures Shown in 1500 Amazing Close-Up Photographs. (p. 680)
Taylor, Barbara & O'Shea, Mark. Ultimate Book of Snakes & Reptiles: Discover the Amazing World of Snakes, Crocodiles, Lizards & Turtles. (p. 2314)
Taylor, Barbara & Parker, Steve. Animals. (p. 93)
Taylor, Barbara Brown. Home by Another Way: A Christmas Story. Cataldo, Melanie, illus. (p. 996)
Taylor, Barbara, et al. Bugs & Minibeasts: Beetle, Bugs, Butterflies, Moths, Insects, Spiders. (p. 292)
—Wild Animals the Best-Ever Box of Books: A Fabulous Collection of Eight Wildlife Books with Fascinating Facts & over 1600 Amazing Photographs (p. 2462)
Taylor, Bayard. At Home & Abroad: A Sketch-Book of Life, Scenery & Men (Classic Reprint) (p. 129)
—At Home & Abroad: A Sketch-Book of Life, Scenery, & Men (Classic Reprint) (p. 129)
—Beauty & the Beast: Tales of Home (Classic Reprint) (p. 185)
—Beauty & the Beast & Tales of Home. (p. 185)
—Boys of Other Countries: Stories for American Boys (Classic Reprint) (p. 273)
—Boys of Other Countries. (p. 273)
—Hannah Thurston: A Story of American Life (Classic Reprint) (p. 918)
—Hannah Thurston. (p. 918)
—Hannah Thurston, a Story of American Life (Classic Reprint) (p. 918)
—Home Ballads (Classic Reprint) (p. 995)
—John Godfrey's Fortunes; Related by Himself: A Story of American Life (Classic Reprint) (p. 1173)
—Joseph & His Friend: A Story of Pennsylvania (Classic Reprint) (p. 1178)
—Joseph & His Friend. (p. 1178)
—Joseph & His Friends. (p. 1178)
—Journey to Central Africa, or Life & Landscapes from Egypt to the Negro Kingdoms of the White Nile (Classic Reprint) (p. 1182)
—Lands of the Saracen, or Pictures of Palestine, Asia Minor Sicily, & Spain (Classic Reprint) (p. 1243)
—Lars: A Pastoral of Norway. (p. 1245)
—Northern Travel: Summer & Winter Pictures of Sweden, Lapland & Norway (Classic Reprint) (p. 1622)
—Northern Travel. (p. 1622)
—Story of Kennett (Classic Reprint) (p. 2131)
—Works of Bayard Taylor, Vol. 1: Views a-Foot; Beauty & the Beast (Classic Reprint) (p. 2496)
—Works of Bayard Taylor, Vol. 2: Eldorado; the Story of Kennett (Classic Reprint) (p. 2496)
—Works of Bayard Taylor, Vol. 3: A Journey to Central Africa; Joseph & His Friend (Classic Reprint) (p. 2496)
—Works of Bayard Taylor, Vol. 4: The Lands of the Saracen, and, John Godfrey's Fortunes (Classic Reprint) (p. 2496)
—Works of Bayard Taylor, Vol. 5: By-Ways of Europe, and, Hannah Thurston (Classic Reprint) (p. 2496)
Taylor, Belle Gray. Sardonyx Seal: A Romance of Normandy (Classic Reprint) (p. 1935)
Taylor, Benj. F. Summer-Savory: Gleaned from Rural Nooks in Pleasant Weather (Classic Reprint) (p. 2150)
Taylor, Benjamin F. Between the Gates (Classic Reprint) (p. 210)
—Pictures of Life in Camp & Field. (p. 1741)
—Pictures of Life in Camp & Field (Classic Reprint) (p. 1741)
Taylor, Benjamin Franklin. Theophilus Trent: Old Times in the Oak Openings (Classic Reprint) (p. 2216)
—World on Wheels & Other Sketches (Classic Reprint) (p. 2504)
Taylor, Bert Leston. Bilioustine 1901: A Periodical of Knock (Classic Reprint) (p. 226)
—Charlatans (Classic Reprint) (p. 358)
—Line-O'-Verse or Two. (p. 1303)
—Line-O-Verse or Two. (p. 1304)
—Log of the Water Wagon, or the Cruise of the Good Ship Lithia (Classic Reprint) (p. 1339)
—So-Called Human Race. (p. 2050)
—So-Called Human Race (Classic Reprint) (p. 2050)
—Well in the Wood (Classic Reprint) (p. 2399)
Taylor, Betty Ann. Mari's Miracle. (p. 1406)
Taylor, Bill. After Our Heart Attacks. (p. 33)
Taylor, Bobbie & Jenny, Krzoska. But I Don't Want a Haircut! (p. 302)
Taylor, Brian, illus. see Kline, Adam.
Taylor, Bridget Starr, illus. see Edwards, Pamela Duncan.
Taylor, Bridget Starr, illus. see Troupe, Thomas Kingsley.
Taylor, C. Bryson. In the Dwellings of the Wilderness (Classic Reprint) (p. 1108)
Taylor, C. J. Spirits, Fairies, & Merpeople: Native Stories of Other Worlds. (p. 2083)
Taylor, C. M. Caramel Mystical. (p. 327)
—Grandkids in a Box! (p. 877)
—Professor Lije - & the Light Show. (p. 1804)
—When God Came down for a Visit. (p. 2430)
Taylor, C. M. & Moore, Jefferson. Cuando Dios Descendio para una Visita. (p. 481)
Taylor, Carolyn, illus. see Johnson, Esther A.
Taylor, Carrie Ann, ed. Ethics of Wikileaks. (p. 666)
Taylor, Carroll S. Chinaberry Summer: On the Other Side. (p. 378)
Taylor, Catherine, illus. see Taylor, Douglas.
Taylor, Centrella P. Little Miss Sunshine (p. 1322)
Taylor, Chad. All about Earthquakes. (p. 49)
—All about Meadows. (p. 49)
—Drums Save the Day. (p. 607)
—Drums Send a Signal. (p. 607)
—Equal under the Law. (p. 659)
—Mountain Man Malik. (p. 1513)
—Our Community Is in the Mountains. (p. 1677)
—United States Has Rules & Laws. (p. 2331)
—We Catch Butterflies. (p. 2390)
—When the Ground Shook. (p. 2433)
Taylor, Charles. Introduction to the Ancient & Modern Geometry of Conics. (p. 1129)
Taylor, Charles & Editors of Kingfisher. Kingfisher Science Encyclopedia. (p. 1222)
Taylor, Charles Jay. In the 400 & Out (Classic Reprint) (p. 1107)
Taylor, Charles Mundy. Winning Buddha's Smile: A Korean Legend (Classic Reprint) (p. 2474)
Taylor, Charlotte. Bridges (p. 280)
—Celebrating U. S. Holidays (p. 350)
—Crispus Attucks: A Hero of the American Revolution. (p. 475)
—Electing U. S. Leaders (p. 631)
—Get to Know Andy Warhol. (p. 825)
—Get to Know Edward Hopper. (p. 825)
—Get to Know Georgia O'Keeffe. (p. 825)
—Get to Know John Singer Sargent. (p. 825)
—Get to Know Mary Cassatt. (p. 825)
—Get to Know Norman Rockwell. (p. 825)
—Get to Know Willem de Kooning. (p. 825)
—Highways & Roads (p. 970)
—Lebron James. (p. 1260)
—Phillis Wheatley: Colonial African-American Poet. (p. 1735)
—Sojourner Truth: Abolitionist & Activist. (p. 2055)
—United States: a Melting Pot (p. 2330)
—Volunteers: Making Our Country Better (p. 2367)
—Ways to Make Money Working Outside (p. 2388)
Taylor, Charlotte & Feinstein, Stephen. Barack Obama: First African-American President. (p. 164)
—Harriet Tubman: Hero of the Underground Railroad. (p. 933)
—LeBron James: Basketball Champion. (p. 1260)
—Lebron James: Basketball Champion. (p. 1260)
—Mae Jemison: First African-American Woman in Space. (p. 1376)
Taylor, Charlotte & Kent, Deborah. Internment of Japanese Americans. (p. 1127)
Taylor, Charlotte & Miller, Mara. Little Rock Nine & School Desegregation. (p. 1327)
Taylor, Charlotte & Stein, R. Conrad. Underground Railroad. (p. 2323)
Taylor, Chloë. Bursting at the Seams. (p. 300)
—Change of Lace. (p. 356)
—Clothes Minded. Zhang, Nancy, illus. (p. 407)
—Cut from the Same Cloth. Zhang, Nancy, illus. (p. 491)
—Cute As a Button. Zhang, Nancy, illus. (p. 491)
—Dressed to Frill. Zhang, Nancy, illus. (p. 604)
Taylor, Chloe. Knot Too Shabby! Zhang, Nancy, illus. (p. 1229)
—Lights, Camera, Fashion! Zhang, Nancy, illus. (p. 1300)
—On Pins & Needles. Zhang, Nancy, illus. (p. 1653)
—On Pins & Needles. Christy, Jana & Zhang, Nancy, illus. (p. 1653)
—Ready to Wear. Zhang, Nancy, illus. (p. 1848)
Taylor, Chloë. Sewing in Circles. Zhang, Nancy, illus. (p. 1995)
Taylor, Chloe. Stitches & Stones. Zhang, Nancy, illus. (p. 2120)
—Swatch Out! Zhang, Nancy, illus. (p. 2167)
Taylor, Chloë. Tangled Thread. Zhang, Nancy, illus. (p. 2190)
Taylor, Chris, illus. see Irwin, Jonathan.
Taylor, Christy Lee, jt. auth. see Bowman, Crystal.
Taylor, Clif. Snowflake. Whitmire, Anna, illus. (p. 2049)
Taylor, Clive, illus. see Eggleton, Jill.
Taylor, Colin, et al. Plains Indians. (p. 1754)
Taylor, Cora. Finding Melissa (p. 729)
Taylor, Corey. House of Gold & Bones. Hahn, Sierra, ed. (p. 1023)
Taylor, Courtney. Teddy Bear's Birthday Bash. Mykalevych, Viktoriia, illus. (p. 2198)
—Vacation Time! A Captain Carlos Adventure. (p. 2343)

T

Taylor, Courtney N. Treasure Box Pops: A Captain Carlos Adventure. (p. 2281)
Taylor, Dale B. Biomedical Foundations of Music as Therapy. (p. 229)
Taylor, Damien T. Enigma: Awakening. (p. 655)
Taylor, Dan. Cinderella. (p. 391)
—First Stories: Nutcracker. (p. 740)
Taylor, Dan, illus. see Fischer, Maggie.
Taylor, Dan, illus. see Sauer, Tammi.
Taylor, Dan, illus. see Sparrow, Leilani.
Taylor, Dan, illus. see Veitch, Catherine.
Taylor, Dan, illus. see Wing, Scarlett.
Taylor, Dan, jt. auth. see Harper, E. T.
Taylor, Darlene. Thank You Notes from Grandma. (p. 2211)
Taylor, David. Sony A77: The Expanded Guide. (p. 2064)
Taylor, David C., illus. see Hughes, Megan Hoert.
Taylor, David W., Jr., illus. see Redmond, Stephanie L.
Taylor, Dawn. Pei Pei Service Dog Reporting for Duty. (p. 1714)
Taylor, Debbie, illus. see Fletcher, E. B.
Taylor, Debbie A. Sweet Music in Harlem. Morrison, Frank, illus. (p. 2169)
Taylor, Debbie MacDonald. Huey the Lost Canadian Goose: Adventures on the Trent River. (p. 1047)
Taylor, Deems. Pictorial History of the Movies (Classic Reprint) (p. 1739)
Taylor, Deems, jt. auth. see Noyes, Alfred.
Taylor, Dereen. Alien Adventure: Peek Inside the Pop-Up Windows! Hutchinson, Tim, illus. (p. 46)
—Celts. (p. 351)
—Dragon's Magic Wish. Hutchinson, Tim, illus. (p. 596)
—Fairy Midnight Surprise Party. Stone, Lyn, illus. (p. 696)
—Journey to the World of the Dinosaurs: Peek Inside the Pop-Up Windows! Kavanagh, Peter, illus. (p. 1183)
—Knight's First Tournament. Kavanagh, Peter, illus. (p. 1228)
—Lost Treasure of the Jungle Temple: Peek Inside the 3D Windows! Hutchinson, Tim, illus. (p. 1356)
—Mystery of the Vampire Boy: Dare You Peek Through the Pop-Up Windows? Spoor, Mike, illus. (p. 1570)
—Paulo & the Football Thieves: Peek Inside the Pop-Up Windows! Hutchinson, Tim, illus. (p. 1708)
—Popcorn: in the Past: Toys. (p. 1776)
—Robo-Pup to the Rescue! Hutchinson, Tim, illus. (p. 1892)
—Rosie Rides to the Rescue: Peek Inside the Pop-Up Windows! Stone, Lyn, illus. (p. 1906)
—Trapped in the Witch's Lair: Peek Inside the Pop-Up Windows! Catchpole, Diana, illus. (p. 2279)
—Vikings. (p. 2357)
Taylor, Derrick & Garnett, Kaila. Jessica & Madison: Being Beautiful. Peters, Rob, illus. (p. 1165)
Taylor, Des. Cartoons & Manga. (p. 335)
Taylor, Devin, illus. see Nefcy, Daron, et al.
Taylor, Devon. Ghost Seekers. (p. 828)
—Soul Keepers. (p. 2066)
Taylor, Di. Lost Kitten. Wright, Craig, ed. (p. 1354)
—Moving House. Wright, Craig, ed. (p. 1516)
Taylor, Diane. Engineers: With Stem Projects for Kids. Li, Hui, illus. (p. 652)
Taylor, Diane C. Renaissance Artists: With History Projects for Kids. (p. 1865)
—Renaissance Thinkers: With History Projects for Kids. (p. 1865)
Taylor, Dorothea. There's a Dragon in My Closet. Palmer, Charly, illus. (p. 2217)
Taylor, Dorothy. Abbot Academy Class Book, 1908 (Classic Reprint) (p. 3)
Taylor, Drew Hayden. Night Wanderer: A Graphic Novel. Wyatt, Michael, illus. (p. 1608)
Taylor, Dwayne L. I Am an Eagle! No More Scratching with Chickens. (p. 1057)
Taylor, E. Dee. Lots of Cats. Taylor, E. Dee, illus. (p. 1356)
Taylor, Ed. Dirty Bombers: Terrorism with a Twist. (p. 552)
Taylor, Edgar, tr. see Grimm, Wilhelm.
Taylor, Edward Harrison. Edward H. Taylor: Recollections of an Herpetologist (Classic Reprint) (p. 627)
Taylor, Edwardian, illus. see Fliess, Sue.
Taylor, Edwardian, illus. see Funk, Josh.
Taylor, Edwardian, illus. see Lynch, Brian.
Taylor, Eleanor, illus. see Almond, David.
Taylor, Eleanor, illus. see Durango, Julia.
Taylor, Eleanor, illus. see Elworthy, Jo.
Taylor, Eleanor, illus. see Potter, Beatrix.
Taylor, Eleanor, illus. see Thompson, Emma.
Taylor, Eleonor, illus. see Thompson, Emma, et al.
Taylor, Elizabeth. Quixstar (Classic Reprint) (p. 1829)
Taylor, Emerson Gifford. Daughter of Dale (Classic Reprint) (p. 509)
—Upper Hand (Classic Reprint) (p. 2339)
Taylor, Emily. Boy & the Birds (Classic Reprint) (p. 268)
—Irish Tourist, or the People & the Provinces of Ireland (Classic Reprint) (p. 1135)
Taylor, Emily, jt. auth. see Pierpont, John.
Taylor, Emma. Color Me: Dinosaurs. McDonald, Jake, illus. (p. 420)
Taylor, Erin, illus. see Birdsong, Minnie.
Taylor, Erin, illus. see Coe, Catherine.
Taylor, Erin, illus. see Evans, Rosemary R.
Taylor, Erin, illus. see Heald, Robin.
Taylor, Erin, illus. see Lee, Bonnie.
Taylor, Erin, illus. see Meadowsweet, Felicity.
Taylor, Ernest M. University Gazette, Vol. 1: January 1st, 1874 (Classic Reprint) (p. 2333)
Taylor, Everett. Mira, the Misfit Sea Dragon. (p. 1474)
Taylor Fonzone, jt. auth. see Reher, Matt.
Taylor, Frances Lilian. Beginnings in English: Oral & Written Language for Primary Schools (Classic Reprint) (p. 192)
—Taylor School Readers: First Reader (Classic Reprint) (p. 2193)
—Taylor School Readers Second Reader (Classic Reprint) (p. 2193)
Taylor, Frank Bursley. Planetary System: A Study of Its Structure & Growth (Classic Reprint) (p. 1755)
Taylor, Gayle & Taylor, Roland. Cody's Rome Dig. (p. 412)
Taylor, Geo B. Oakland Stories: Kenny (Classic Reprint) (p. 1633)
Taylor, Geoff, illus. see Paver, Michelle.
Taylor, George. Antinous: A Romance of Ancient Rome (Classic Reprint) (p. 103)
—Klytia, Vol. 1 Of 2: A Story of Heidelberg Castle (Classic Reprint) (p. 1227)
Taylor, Georgie. Follow That Dinosaur! Meredith, Sam, illus. (p. 757)
—Follow That Tractor! Meredith, Sam, illus. (p. 757)
—Follow That Unicorn! Meredith, Sam, illus. (p. 758)
—la Llamas! (p. 1235)
—Search & Find Animals. Boot, Maaike, illus. (p. 1970)
—Search & Find Dinosaurs. Boot, Maaike, illus. (p. 1970)
—Search & Find under the Sea. Boot, Maaike, illus. (p. 1970)
—Search & Find Unicorns. Boot, Maaike, illus. (p. 1970)
—Snackasaurus! (p. 2044)
—Ten Sleeps to Christmas. (p. 2205)
Taylor, Georgie & Meredith, Sam. Follow That Truck! (p. 758)
Taylor, Gerad, illus. see Maier, Paul L.
Taylor, Greg. Killer Pizza (p. 1217)
—Killer Pizza: the Slice. (p. 1217)
Taylor, Greg R. High Places. (p. 968)
Taylor, Gypsy, illus. see Harmer, Wendy.
Taylor, Gypsy, jt. auth. see Harmer, Wendy.
Taylor Harris Photography, photos by see Harris, Patricia Taylor.
Taylor, Helen. Emu Can't Fly. Gilles-Gray, Carolyn, illus. (p. 645)
—Indigo Bird. (p. 1117)
—Kakapo Dance. (p. 1201)
Taylor, Helen & Harris, Andrew J. R., eds. Learning & Teaching Mathematics 0-8. (p. 1258)
Taylor, Henry C. After the Town Goes Dry. (p. 34)
—After the Town Goes Dry (Classic Reprint) (p. 34)
Taylor, Henry D. 16 Old Maids: And Other Stories (Classic Reprint) (p. 2552)
Taylor, Henry, et al. #justagobbler. (p. 1194)
Taylor, Hobart Chatfield. With Edge Tools (Classic Reprint) (p. 2481)
Taylor, Howard. In the Far East; Letters from Geraldine Guinness in China: Now Mrs. Howard Taylor (Classic Reprint) (p. 1108)
—One of China's Scholars: The Culture & Conversion of a Confucianist. (p. 1661)
Taylor, Howard P. Wiggins of Pop-Over Farm: A Comedy-Drama in Four Acts (Classic Reprint) (p. 2461)
Taylor, Isaac. Family Pen, Vol. 2 Of 2: Memorials Biographical & Literary, of the Taylor Family of Ongar (Classic Reprint) (p. 702)
—Mine: Or Sketches of the Mines of Different Countries, the Modes of Working Them, & Their Various Productions (Classic Reprint) (p. 1470)
—Physical Theory of Another Life. - Scholar's Choice Edition. (p. 1737)
—Physical Theory of Another Life - Scholar's Choice Edition. (p. 1737)
Taylor, J. Glen, et al. Minor Prophets. (p. 1473)
Taylor, J. H. Joe Taylor Barnstormer: His Travels, Troubles & Triumphs During Fifty Years in Footlight Flashes (Classic Reprint) (p. 1171)
Taylor, Jacqui, illus. see Jones, Jack.
Taylor, Jane. Contributions of Q. Q. to a Periodical Work, Vol. 2 Of 2: Miscellaneous Pieces (Classic Reprint) (p. 445)
—Contributions of Q. Q. to a Periodical Work, Vol. 1 Of 2: With Some Pieces Not Before Published; Religious & Didactic Pieces (Classic Reprint) (p. 445)
—Contributions of Q. Q. to a Periodical Work, with Some Pieces Not Before Published. in Two Volumes. Vol. II. (p. 445)
—Display: A Tale (Classic Reprint) (p. 564)
—Little Ann: And Other Poems (Classic Reprint) (p. 1310)
—Original Poems & Others (Classic Reprint) (p. 1671)
—Original Poems, for Infant Minds, Vol. 2 (Classic Reprint) (p. 1671)
—Peep into London, for Good Children (Classic Reprint) (p. 1713)
—Pleasures of Taste, & Other Stories: Selected from the Writings of Miss. Jane Taylor, with a Sketch of Her Life (Classic Reprint) (p. 1762)
—Rhymes for the Nursery (Classic Reprint) (p. 1875)
—Tales: Essays & Poems; with a Memoir (Classic Reprint) (p. 2181)
—Twinkle, Twinkle Little Star. Duffy, Katherine, illus. (p. 2305)
—Writings of Jane Taylor, Vol. 3 Of 3: Containing, Correspondence Between a Mother & Her Daughter at School; Original Poems for Infant Minds; & Display, a Tale (Classic Reprint) (p. 2514)
—Writings of Jane Taylor, Vol. 5 Of 5: In Five Volumes (Classic Reprint) (p. 2514)
—Writings of Jane Taylor, Vol. 5 Of 5: Correspondence & Original Poem (Classic Reprint) (p. 2514)
Taylor, Jane & MacKenzie, Carine. Jesus: The Promised Child. (p. 1165)
—Saul: The Miracle on the Road. Apps, Fred, illus. (p. 1937)
Taylor, Jane & Macleod, Una. God Made Animals. Matthews, Derek, illus. (p. 851)
—God Made Me. Matthews, Derek, illus. (p. 852)
Taylor, Jane, et al. God Made Colours. (p. 851)
—God Made the World. (p. 852)
Taylor, Janet B. Into the Dim. (p. 1128)
—Sparks of Light. (p. 2075)
Taylor, Janice West. Petey, the Purple Pig. (p. 1730)
Taylor, JaRabia, illus. see Brown, Renee.
Taylor, Jasmine. Animal Farts Coloring Book. (p. 89)
—Baby Lovers Coloring Book. (p. 151)
—Dungeons & Dragons Coloring Book. (p. 610)
—Nursery Rhymes Coloring Book. (p. 1631)
Taylor, Jason C. Color & Learn with Lemonade. (p. 419)
—Little Sue's Pink & Blue Shoes. (p. 1328)
Taylor, Jeannie St. John, illus. see Mehl, Ron, et al.
Taylor, Jefferys. Aesop in Rhyme: With Some Originals (Classic Reprint) (p. 30)
—Forest, or Rambles in the Woodland (Classic Reprint) (p. 766)
—Young Islanders: A Tale of the Last Century (Classic Reprint) (p. 2531)
Taylor, Jen, illus. see Berry Byrd, Holly.
Taylor, Jen, illus. see Bovis, Ali.
Taylor, Jen, illus. see Calvert, Pam.
Taylor, Jen, illus. see Crowe, Carmen.
Taylor, Jen, illus. see Fliess, Sue.
Taylor, Jen, illus. see Redwing, Jack.
Taylor, Jen, illus. see VonFeder, Rosa.
Taylor, Jennifer, ed. see Callella, Trisha.
Taylor, Jenny, illus. see McDougall, Jill.
Taylor, Jeremy. Holy Living & Dying: With Prayers: Containing the Complete Duty of a Christian (Classic Reprint) (p. 995)
—Strength of Love. (p. 2140)
Taylor, Jessica. Map for Wrecked Girls. (p. 1400)
—Wandering Wild. (p. 2375)
Taylor, Jessica Sarah. Onion, a North Carolina Dolphin. Bowles, Nan, illus. (p. 1663)
Taylor, Jo. Back to School Sticker Paper Dolls. (p. 155)
—My Happiness Journal. (p. 1549)
—Sneaker Designs Coloring Book. (p. 2045)
—Thank You Working Heroes Coloring Book: We're All in This Together! (p. 2211)
Taylor, Jo, illus. see Higgins, M. G.
Taylor, Jo-Ann. Alchemist's Secret. (p. 41)
Taylor, John. London Magazine, Vol. 5: January to June 1822 (Classic Reprint) (p. 1341)
—Pennyles Pilgrimage or the Money-Lesse Perambulation of John Taylor: Alias the Kings Majesties Water-Poet (Classic Reprint) (p. 1717)
Taylor, John, illus. see Boddy, Catharine.
Taylor, John Ellor. Geological Stories. (p. 817)
—Our Common British Fossils & Where to Find Them: A Handbook for Students (Classic Reprint) (p. 1677)
—Our Common British Fossils & Where to Find Them. (p. 1677)
—Sagacity & Morality of Plants. (p. 1922)
Taylor, Jon. My Dog Monkey. Mosler, Robin, illus. (p. 1537)
Taylor, Jonathan, illus. see Ham, Ken.
Taylor, Jordyn. Paper Girl of Paris. (p. 1697)
Taylor, Joseph. Allison Investigates. (p. 56)
—Apparitions, or the Mystery of Ghosts, Hobgoblins, & Haunted Houses, Developed: Being a Collection of Entertaining Stories, Founded on Fact (Classic Reprint) (p. 106)
—Apparitions, or the Mystery of Ghosts, Hobgoblins, & Haunted Houses, Developed: Being a Collection of Entertaining Stories, Founded on Fact, & Selected for the Purpose of Eradicating Those Fears, Which the Ignorant, the Weak, & the Superstitious, AR. (p. 106)
Taylor, Joseph Henry. Kaleidoscopic Lives: A Companion Book to Frontier & Indian Life (Classic Reprint) (p. 1202)
Taylor, Joseph Russell. Our Dancing Days (Classic Reprint) (p. 1677)
Taylor, Josh, illus. see Blocker, Adam P.
Taylor, Joye. Little Bells: And Other Verses for Children (Classic Reprint) (p. 1311)
Taylor, Julia V. Body Image Workbook for Teens: Activities to Help Girls Develop a Healthy Body Image in an Image-Obsessed World. (p. 253)
Taylor, Julia V., jt. auth. see Lohmann, Raychelle Cassada.
Taylor, Justin. Computer Code Mystery. Hornsby, Lindsay, illus. (p. 437)
Taylor, K. L. Adventures of Jax & Riley: Jax & Riley Meet Their New Brother. (p. 24)
Taylor, Kara. Deadly Little Sins. (p. 518)
—Prep School Confidential. (p. 1787)
—Wicked Little Secrets: A Prep School Confidential Novel. (p. 2460)
Taylor, Katharine Haviland. Cecilia of the Pink Roses (Classic Reprint) (p. 348)
—Modern Trio in an Old Town (Classic Reprint) (p. 1488)
Taylor, Kathleen. Eddie & Bingo: A Friendship Tale. Taylor, Kathleen, illus. (p. 624)
Taylor, Kelda. Look at My Feet Feet Go! (p. 1345)
Taylor, Kelly. Skutterskelfe Farm. (p. 2033)
Taylor Kent, Derek. Perro con Sombrero: A Bilingual Doggy Tale. Henry, Jed, illus. (p. 1724)
Taylor, Keren, jt. ed. see Reber, Deborah.
Taylor, Kristen Michelle, illus. see Mbonu, Ngozi Elizabeth.
Taylor, L. D. Motive Games. (p. 1511)
Taylor, Laini. Blackbringer. (p. 240)
—Daughter of Smoke & Bone. (p. 509)
—Days of Blood & Starlight. (p. 515)
—Dreams of Gods & Monsters. (p. 603)
—Lips Touch: Three Times. Di Bartolo, Jim, illus. (p. 1307)
—Musa de Las Pesadillas / Musa of Nightmares. (p. 1527)
—Muse of Nightmares. (p. 1528)
—Night of Cake & Puppets. Di Bartolo, Jim, illus. (p. 1607)
—Strange the Dreamer. (p. 2138)
Taylor, Laura. Bee-Attitudes: Bee-Atrice the Bumblebee Becomes a Humble Bee. (p. 189)
Taylor, Lauren Nicolle. Breaker & the Sun. (p. 278)
—Hiro Loves Kite. (p. 973)
—Travel Diaries of the Dead & Delusional. (p. 2280)
Taylor, Laurette. Greatest of These (Classic Reprint) (p. 892)
Taylor, Lawrie, illus. see Andrews, Jackie.
Taylor, Lee Mays. Texan: A Tale of Texas (Classic Reprint) (p. 2209)
Taylor, Lenette. Brutus the French Mastiff: The Case of the Missing Sock. (p. 288)
Taylor, Lillian Webb. Santa's Musical Elves. (p. 1933)
Taylor, Linda Colquitt. ABCs of LSU. Casteel, Erin, illus. (p. 5)
Taylor, Lindsay, jt. auth. see Smith, Suzanne.
Taylor, Lynda. Clouds Dance. (p. 408)
—Sea Child. (p. 1967)
Taylor, M. Imlay. Cobbler of Nimes (Classic Reprint) (p. 410)
—House of the Wizard (Classic Reprint) (p. 1023)
Taylor, Malcolm Stewart. Afflicted Family, or a Doctor Without a Diploma: A Farce-Comedy, in Four Acts (Classic Reprint) (p. 31)
—Rags & Bottles, Vol. 8: The Two Waifs, an Original Commedy, in Two Acts (Classic Reprint) (p. 1834)
Taylor, Malcolm Stuart. Auld Robin Gray: Am Emotional Drama, in Five Acts (Classic Reprint) (p. 136)
Taylor, Malcolm Stuart & Barnard, Anne Lindsay. Auld Robin Gray. (p. 136)
Taylor, Maria. Adventures of Kooky the Goat. (p. 25)
—Alpaca Laca Shish Boom Bang! (p. 58)
Taylor, Marian S. Coming down, Looking Up. (p. 430)
Taylor, Marianne. What If... Humans Were Like Animals? Moran, Paul, illus. (p. 2412)
Taylor, Marilyn. 17 Martin Street. (p. 2552)
Taylor, Marjorie, illus. see Bankier, William.
Taylor, Marjorie, illus. see Cruise, Robin.
Taylor, Mark. Henry Explores the Jungle. Booth, Graham, illus. (p. 955)
—Henry Explores the Mountains. (p. 955)
—Henry the Castaway. Booth, Graham, illus. (p. 955)
—Henry the Explorer. Booth, Graham, illus. (p. 955)
Taylor, Mark, illus. see Younge, Cathy.
Taylor, Mart. Local Lyrics, & Miscellaneous Poems (Classic Reprint) (p. 1338)
Taylor, Martin. Lost Treasure of the Sunken City. Catling, Andy, illus. (p. 1356)
Taylor, Mary Ellen. Maniac Magee. (p. 1397)
Taylor, Mary G. Something for Nothing: An Entertainment in One Act (Classic Reprint) (p. 2060)
Taylor, Mary Imlay. Anne of the People of (Classic Reprint) (p. 99)
—Cardinal's Musketeer (Classic Reprint) (p. 328)
—Lotus Lantern (Classic Reprint) (p. 1357)
—My Lady Clancarty Being the True Story of the Earl of Clancarty & Lady Elizabeth Spencer (Classic Reprint) (p. 1551)
—Rebellion of the Princess (Classic Reprint) (p. 1852)
—Yankee Volunteer (Classic Reprint) (p. 2517)
Taylor, Matt, illus. see Gibson, Gerry.
Taylor, Matt, illus. see Lonely Planet Kids & Butterfield, Moira.
Taylor, Matt, illus. see Lonely Planet Kids & Claybourne, Anna.
Taylor, Matt, illus. see Lonely Planet Kids & Greathead, Helen.
Taylor, Meadows. Confessions of a Thug, Vol. 2 of 3 (Classic Reprint) (p. 439)
—Noble Queen: A Romance of Indian History (Classic Reprint) (p. 1616)
—Noble Queen. (p. 1616)
—Noble Queen, Vol. 1 Of 3: A Romance of Indian History (Classic Reprint) (p. 1616)
—Noble Queen, Vol. 2 Of 3: A Romance of Indian History (Classic Reprint) (p. 1616)
—Ralph Darnell (Classic Reprint) (p. 1838)
—Ralph Darnell, Vol. 1 of 3 (Classic Reprint) (p. 1838)
—Tara: A Mahratta Tale (Classic Reprint) (p. 2191)
—Tara. (p. 2191)
—Tara, Vol. 1 Of 3: A Mahratta Tale (Classic Reprint) (p. 2191)
—Tippoo Sultaun: A Tale of the Mysore War (Classic Reprint) (p. 2250)
—Tippoo Sultaun, Vol. 1 Of 3: A Tale of the Mysore War (Classic Reprint) (p. 2250)
Taylor, Michael. Red Light, Green Light. Bassani, Srimalie, illus. (p. 1857)
Taylor, Mike, illus. see West, David.
Taylor, Mildred D. All the Days Past, All the Days to Come. (p. 54)
—Friendship. (p. 787)
—Roll of Thunder, Hear My Cry: 40th Anniversary Special Edition. (p. 1898)
—Roll of Thunder, Hear My Cry (Puffin Modern Classics) (p. 1898)
Taylor, Minnie, ed. see Wright, Chris.
Taylor, Miya. Miss Gorilla Lost Her Keys. Johnson, Steven, illus. (p. 1478)
Taylor, Monica. Monarch Butterfly & the Cecropia Moth: Miraculous Stages & Changes. (p. 1492)
Taylor, Myonna. Show & Tell. Phillips, Hope Ann, illus. (p. 2012)
Taylor, N. Morgan Goes to Kindy. (p. 1506)
Taylor, Nadia, illus. see Baker, Laura.
Taylor, Nandi. Given. (p. 840)
Taylor, Natascha, illus. see Taylor, Natascha Rosina.
Taylor, Natascha Rosina. Angry Potato Man: ... & the Jellybellies! Taylor, Natascha, illus. (p. 87)
—Beetle, Barabus. Taylor, Natascha, illus. (p. 190)
Taylor, Nate, illus. see Rothfuss, Patrick.
Taylor, Ned. Night Before Christmas. (p. 1605)
—Santa's Snow Globe: Join the Snowy Fun & Discover Adventure Friends & Love. (p. 1934)
Taylor, Ned, illus. see Davies, Gill.
Taylor, Nell. Potatoland & the Fable of Thunder & Lightning. Weinstein, Holly, illus. (p. 1781)
Taylor, Nellie Rosilla. Heart Messages from the Trenches (Classic Reprint) (p. 944)
Taylor, Neville. Ibex Shooting on the Himalayas (Classic Reprint) (p. 1087)
Taylor, Nicole. Schooled on Fat: What Teens Tell Us about Gender, Body Image, & Obesity. (p. 1947)
Taylor, Nicole, illus. see Church, Anna.
Taylor, Nicole & Watts, Michael. SpongeBob Squarepants: Wormy. (p. 2086)
Taylor, Nicole M. Extra Girl. (p. 685)
—#freenattypage. (p. 783)
—Hunting Party. (p. 1053)
—Killers (Set) (p. 1217)
—No Faith in Cats. (p. 1612)
—Our Lady of the River's Mouth. (p. 1678)
—Reconstructed. (p. 1854)
Taylor, Nina, illus. see Kee, Kate.
Taylor, Nina, illus. see Narracott, J. E.
Taylor, Olivia a. Attack. (p. 134)
Taylor, Pat, jt. auth. see Shuter, Jane.
Taylor, Pat Eytcheson. Scamper Tangles with Christmas. (p. 1941)
Taylor, Patricia. Bella & Hippo in Mystery of the Black Forest. Oehlert, Mark, illus. (p. 196)
—Catch a Winner Leaves Ranch - Bilingual. (p. 343)
Taylor, Patty. Critical World Issues: Animal Rights (p. 476)
Taylor, Pauline. Maldwyn's Quest. (p. 1391)

T

—Survivor Girl. (p. 2165)
Teagarden, Janine. Dog Named Opposite. Kennedy, Kelly, illus. (p. 576)
Teagle, Caitlyn, illus. see Spalding, Brenda M.
Teague, David. Henry Cicada's Extraordinary Elktonium Escapade. (p. 954)
—How Oscar Indigo Broke the Universe (and Put It Back Together Again) (p. 1034)
Teague, Jim. Molly the Meek & Kizzie the Bully Dog. (p. 1489)
Teague, Mark. Felipe & Claudette. Teague, Mark, illus. (p. 719)
—Firehouse! Teague, Mark, illus. (p. 734)
—Fly! Teague, Mark, illus. (p. 753)
—Jack & the Beanstalk & the French Fries. Teague, Mark, illus. (p. 1151)
—Pirate Jamboree. Teague, Mark, illus. (p. 1750)
—Sky Is Falling! Teague, Mark, illus. (p. 2033)
—Three Little Pigs & the Somewhat Bad Wolf. Teague, Mark, illus. (p. 2234)
—Three Little Pigs & the Somewhat Bad Wolf (a StoryPlay Book) Teague, Mark, illus. (p. 2234)
Teague, Mark, illus. see Rylant, Cynthia.
Teague, Mark, illus. see Verburg, Bonnie.
Teague, Mark, illus. see Yolen, Jane.
Teague, Mark, jt. auth. see Yolen, Jane.
Teague Meyer, Terry. Female Genital Cutting. (p. 719)
—Optimism. (p. 1667)
—Vo-Tech Track to Success in Information Technology. (p. 2364)
Teague, Monica. Diary of a Teenager in Junior High. (p. 540)
Teakle, Hannah, illus. see Teakle, Ruth.
Teakle, Ruth. Joshua Wonders: What Does the Tooth Fairy Do with My Teeth? Teakle, Hannah, illus. (p. 1179)
Teal, Angeline. John Thom's Folks: A Study of Western Life (Classic Reprint) (p. 1174)
—John Thom's Folks. (p. 1174)
Teal, Marion. I Like Me. (p. 1067)
Teal, Val. Little Woman Wanted Noise. Lawson, Robert, illus. (p. 1330)
Teall, Francis Horace. English Compound Words & Phrases (Classic Reprint) (p. 653)
Team, Air, illus. see Albbie.
Team, Air, illus. see REDCODE & Albbie.
Team, Black Ink, illus. see Meng, Author & Slaium, Author.
Team, Disney Storybook Art, illus. see Amerikaner, Susan, et al.
Team, Disney Storybook Art, illus. see Auerbach, Annie & Carleton, Jessica.
Team, Disney Storybook Art, illus. see Baer, Jill & Gerber, Craig.
Team, Disney Storybook Art, illus. see Group, Disney Book.
Team, Disney Storybook Art, illus. see Higginson, Sheila Sweeny & Ansolabehere, Joe.
Team, Disney Storybook Art, illus. see Higginson, Sheila Sweeny & Nee, Chris.
Team, Disney Storybook Art, illus. see LaRose, Melinda & Dubuc, Nicole.
Team, Disney Storybook Art, illus. see Marsoli, Lisa Ann & Cooney, Doug.
Team, Disney Storybook Art, illus. see Marsoli, Lisa Ann & Ruderman, Rachel.
Team, Disney Storybook Art, illus. see Miller, Sara & Riley, Ford.
Team, Disney Storybook Art, illus. see Miller, Sara & Rose, Darrin.
Team, Disney Storybook Art, illus. see Olson, Michael & Carleton, Jessica.
Team, Disney Storybook Art, illus. see Olson, Michael & Williams, Harland.
Team, Disney Storybook Art, illus. see Rogers, Tom.
Team, Disney Storybook Art, illus. see Scollon, Bill & Johnson, Greg.
Team, Disney Storybook Art, illus. see Scollon, Bill & Rabb, Michael.
Team, Disney Storybook Art, illus. see Scollon, Bill & Redeker, Kent.
Team, Disney Storybook Art, illus. see Scollon, Bill & Valentine, Ed.
Team Golfwell. JOKES for VERY FUNNY KIDS (Big & Little) A Treasury of Funny Jokes & Riddles Ages 9 - 12 & Up. (p. 1176)
Team, The Disney Storybook Art, illus. see Beyl, Chelsea & Braun, Travis.
Team, The Disney Storybook Art, illus. see Beyl, Chelsea & Nee, Chris.
Team, The Disney Storybook Art, illus. see Beyl, Chelsea.
Team, The Disney Storybook Art, illus. see Miller, Sara.
Team, The Loud House Creative. Loud House #10: The Many Faces of Lincoln Loud. (p. 1357)
—Loud House 3-In-1: There Will Be Chaos, There Will Be More Chaos, & Live Life Loud! (p. 1357)
—Loud House 3-In-1 #2: After Dark, Loud & Proud, & Family Tree. (p. 1357)
—Loud House 3-In-1 #3: The Struggle Is Real, Livin' la Casa Loud, Ultimate Hangout. (p. 1357)
—Loud House #6: Loud & Proud. (p. 1357)
—Loud House #7: The Struggle Is Real. (p. 1357)
—Loud House #8: Livin' la Casa Loud! (p. 1357)
—Loud House #9: Ultimate Hangout. (p. 1357)
—Loud House Winter Special. (p. 1357)
Teare, Steve, illus. see Ericson, Staci.
Tearle, Christian. Legal Practitioner: Being Certain of My Own Experiences (Classic Reprint) (p. 1261)
—Pilgrim from Chicago Being More Rambles with an American (Classic Reprint) (p. 1744)
—Rambles with an American (Classic Reprint) (p. 1839)
Teasdale, Nancy, ed. see Carlson, Dale.
Teba, Alicia, illus. see Eig, Jonathan.
Tebben, Alexa. Finding Joy. (p. 729)
Tebbetts, Chris, jt. auth. see Patterson, James.
Tebbetts, Chris & Patterson, James. Middle School, the Worst Years of My Life. Park, Laura, illus. (p. 1461)
Tebbetts, Christopher. Me, Myself, & Him. (p. 1433)
Tebbetts, Christopher, jt. auth. see Patterson, James.
Tebbit, Jake, illus. see MacKey, Cindy.
Tebbit, Jake, illus. see Odom, Rebecca.
Tebbs, Victoria. Christmas Story Mitchell, Melanie, illus. (p. 387)
—My Best Ever Bible. (p. 1532)
—Noah's Ark Story Mitchell, Melanie, illus. (p. 1616)
—¡Mi Biblia Favorita! / My Best Ever Bible! (p. 1454)
Tebbutt, C. G., jt. auth. see Heathcote, John Moyer.
Tebow, Tim. Shaken: Young Reader's Edition: Fighting to Stand Strong No Matter What Comes Your Way. (p. 1998)
—Through My Eyes: A Quarterback's Journey (p. 2237)
Tech, Sawsan. Little Red Riding Hood: Augmented Reality. (p. 1326)
—Three Little Pigs: Augmented Reality. (p. 2234)
Tech Tron. How Things Work: The Inside Out of Cellphones, TV, Drones, Race Cars & More! Machinery & Tools. (p. 1036)
—How Things Work: The Inside Out of Cellphones, TV, Drones, Race Cars & More! - Machinery & Tools. (p. 1036)
—Most Famous Inventors Who Ever Lived Inventor's Guide for Kids Children's Inventors Books. (p. 1508)
—Most Important Inventions of All Time Inventions for Kids Children's Inventors Books. (p. 1508)
Techentrup, Britta. Cat & Mouse. (p. 341)
Tech-It-Fwd, *. Super Duper CSS Coloring-In-Book. (p. 2155)
Technology, Carnegie Institute of. Soldier's Progress, from the War Letters of Carnegie Tech Men (Classic Reprint) (p. 2057)
Teckentrup, Britta. Bee: a Peek-Through Picture Book. (p. 189)
—Before I Wake Up (p. 190)
—Birds & Their Feathers. (p. 231)
—Chanson de Petit Loup. (p. 357)
—Don't Wake up the Tiger. Teckentrup, Britta, illus. (p. 584)
—Egg. (p. 628)
—Fast & Slow Spanish. (p. 713)
—Fish Everywhere. Teckentrup, Britta, illus. (p. 741)
—Get Out of My Bath! Teckentrup, Britta, illus. (p. 824)
—Grande y Pequeno. (p. 877)
—Grumpy Cat. (p. 900)
—Kindness Grows. Teckentrup, Britta, illus. (p. 1219)
—Little Owl. (p. 1323)
—Little Squirrel. (p. 1328)
—Look at the Weather. Tanaka, Shelley, tr. from GER. (p. 1345)
—Memory Tree. (p. 1446)
—Mi Gatito. (p. 1455)
—Mi Pequeño Pato. (p. 1455)
—Moon: a Peek-Through Picture Book. (p. 1501)
—My Book of Opposites. (p. 1534)
—My Little Book of Big Questions. (p. 1552)
—Ocean: a Peek-Through Picture Book. (p. 1635)
—Odd One Out. Teckentrup, Britta, illus. (p. 1637)
—One Is Not a Pair. Teckentrup, Britta, illus. (p. 1660)
—Oskar & Mo. (p. 1673)
—Oskar Can... (p. 1673)
—Oskar Loves... (p. 1673)
—Oval Submarine & Other Shapes. (p. 1686)
—Red Train & Other Colors. (p. 1859)
—School: Come in & Take a Closer Look. (p. 1945)
—Seedling That Didn't Want to Grow. (p. 1983)
—Sleep Tight, Little Bear. (p. 2036)
—Tree: a Peek-Through Picture Book. (p. 2283)
—Up & Down. Teckentrup, Britta, illus. (p. 2337)
—We Are Together. Teckentrup, Britta, illus. (p. 2389)
—Where's the Baby? (p. 2440)
—Where's the Baby? Teckentrup, Britta, illus. (p. 2440)
—Where's the Pair? Teckentrup, Britta, illus. (p. 2441)
Teckentrup, Britta, illus. see Books, Barefoot.
Teckentrup, Britta, illus. see Clarke, Jane.
Teckentrup, Britta, illus. see Fletcher, Corina.
Teckentrup, Britta, illus. see Harding, Thomas.
Teckentrup, Britta, illus. see Murray, Lily.
Teckentrup, Britta, illus. see Nosy Crow Staff.
Teckentrup, Britta, jt. auth. see Sperring, Mark.
Teckentrup, Britta, creator. Mr. Lion Dresses Up! (p. 1519)
Tectum, compiled by. Our Amazing World: Discover cultural sites 1, from the Unesco World Heritage (p. 1676)
Tectum Publishers Staff, compiled by. Our Amazing World: Discover cultural sites 2, from the Unesco World Heritage (p. 1676)
Ted, Hood, Jr., photos by see Dealia, Yancey.
Teddy, Meddy. Meddy Teddy: Mindful Poses for Little Yogis. (p. 1436)
Tedesco, Ralph, ed. see Tyler, Joe, et al.
Tedham, Lucy. Growing God's Gifts: The Fruit of the Spirit. (p. 899)
Tedla, Berhanu, tr. see Umar, Mohammed.
Tee, Jacqueline, illus. see Blackwell, Michelle.
Tee, Jacqueline, illus. see France, Dawn Maria.
Tee, Jacqueline, illus. see Halvorsen, Lyn.
Tee, Jacqueline, illus. see Heath, Liz.
Tee, Jacqueline, illus. see Imlay, Mandy.
Tee, Jacqueline, illus. see Newman, P. R.
Tee, Jacqueline, illus. see Piddington, Lorraine.
Tee, Jacqueline, illus. see Smith, Paul.
Tee, Jacqueline, illus. see Webb, Deborah.
Tee, Nicky. Drone: Poems. (p. 605)
Tee, Susanna. Gross Cookbook: Awesome Recipes for (deceptively) Disgusting Treats Kids Can Make. (p. 898)
Teedon, Samuel. Diary of Samuel Teedon: 17 October 1791 to 2 February 1794. (p. 540)
—Diary of Samuel Teedon: 17 October 1791 to 2 February 1794 (Classic Reprint) (p. 540)
Teel, Karen. Robot Rhymes. Teets, Ashley, illus. (p. 1892)
Teele, Elinor. Mechanical Mind of John Coggin. (p. 1435)
—Treasure of Mad Doc Magee. (p. 2282)
Teen Vogue Staff. Teen Vogue Handbook: An Insider's Guide to Careers in Fashion. (p. 2199)
Teeple, Jackie, illus. see Muench-Williams, Heather.
Teer, Robert & Demartino, Damian. Gloom & Dread. (p. 844)
Teer, Samuel. Veda: Assembly Required. Park, Hyeondo, illus. (p. 2348)
Teerdhala, Swati. Archer at Dawn. (p. 110)
—Tiger at Midnight. (p. 2241)
Tees, Levin C. Row in the Kitchen, and, a Politician's Breakfast: Two Irish Monologues (Classic Reprint) (p. 1908)
Teesdale, Marmaduke J. Goethe's Hermann & Dorothea: Translated into English Hexameter Verse (Classic Reprint) (p. 854)
Teeter, Diana. Patchwork Circus. (p. 1704)
Teeter, Linda. Cold Dome. (p. 413)
Teeters, Jim. Beware of Dog: Fun Poems & Pictures for School Kids. Ayers, Lana Hechtman, ed. (p. 211)
Teetgen, A. D. A. B. White Passion (Classic Reprint) (p. 2445)
Teets, Ashley, illus. see Benedetti, Debra.
Teets, Ashley, illus. see Teel, Karen.
Teets, Ashley, illus. see Wilson, Angie.
Teevee, Ningeokuluk. Alego Manning-Toonoo, Nina, tr. (p. 41)
Teffeteller, Juniper, illus. see Heil, Jill.
Tegen, Katherine. Snowman Magic. Dorman, Brandon, illus. (p. 2049)
—Story of the Easter Bunny Board Book. Lambert, Sally Anne, illus. (p. 2133)
—Story of the Jack O'Lantern. Dorman, Brandon, illus. (p. 2133)
—Story of the Leprechaun. Lambert, Sally Anne, illus. (p. 2133)
Tegen, Katherine Brown. Story of the Leprechaun. Lambert, Sally Anne, illus. (p. 2133)
Tegg, Thomas. Rise, Progress, & Termination of the O. P. War, in Poetic Epistles, or Hudibrastic Letters, from AP Simpkins in Town, to His Friend AP Davies in Wales: Including All the Best Songs, Placards, Toasts, &C. , &C. , Which Were Written, Exhibited, & Give. (p. 1886)
Teich, Karsten, illus. see Grosche, Erwin.
Teichman, Diane E., tr. see Van Scoyoc, Pam.
Teichmann, Howard. Solid Gold Cadillac: A Comedy (Classic Reprint) (p. 2057)
Teichreb, Mike, illus. see McGilvery, Alex.
Teis, Kyra, illus. see Baer, Edith.
Teis, Kyra, illus. see Moreillon, Judi.
Teis, Kyra, illus. see Serani, Deborah.
Teis, Sean P. After the Ark: Eli & Ella the Little Elephants - Children of the King! Boutheyette, Valerie, illus. (p. 33)
Teitelbaum, Clancy. Amnesty #4. (p. 76)
—Expansion Pack #2. (p. 677)
—Floating Eye #3. (p. 750)
—Press Start #1. (p. 1790)
—Reunion Tour #5. (p. 1872)
—Suzanne's Dream #6. (p. 2166)
Teitelbaum, Michael. Batman: Meet the Super Heroes. Gordon, Steven E., illus. (p. 172)
—Cave of No Return. (p. 347)
—Curse of the Haunted House. (p. 489)
—Disney Princess Little Golden Book Favorites Williams, Don et al, illus. (p. 563)
—Electrician. (p. 631)
—Ghastly Ghost Town. (p. 827)
—Ghost at the Grand Inn. (p. 827)
—Halloween Howlers: Frightfully Funny Knock-Knock Jokes. Ho, Jannie, illus. (p. 912)
—I Am Superman. (p. 1060)
—I Am Superman. Farley, Rick, illus. (p. 1060)
—Jackie Robinson: Champion for Equality. (p. 1153)
—Mars & Venus Space Exploration: Set Of 6. (p. 1409)
—Meet the Super Heroes. (p. 1440)
—Mutant Origin: Michelangelo/Raphael (Teenage Mutant Ninja Turtles) Random House Staff, illus. (p. 1530)
—Night of the Gravedigger. (p. 1607)
—On the Move! Shannon, David et al, illus. (p. 1655)
—Phantom Pharaoh. (p. 1733)
—Sailing. (p. 1923)
—Scuba Diving. (p. 1966)
—Secret Life of Black Cat. Sazaklis, John, illus. (p. 1976)
—Secret of the Tragic Theater. (p. 1978)
—Steer the Wheel! Shannon, David et al, illus. (p. 2112)
—Superman Versus Mongul. Mada Design Staff, illus. (p. 2160)
—Teenage Mutant Ninja Turtles Wheel Power Book & Skateboard. (p. 2200)
—Trial by Fire. (p. 2285)
—Tricked Out Zalme, Ron, illus. (p. 2287)
—Wild Man of the Woods! Following in the Footsteps of Bigfoot. (p. 2464)
—Wild Man of the Woods! Where's the Creature with the Big Feet? (p. 2464)
Teitelbaum, Michael, jt. auth. see Helfand, Lewis.
Teitelbaum, Michael, jt. auth. see Kiland, Taylor Baldwin.
Teitelbaum, Michael, adapted by. Volcano to the Rescue! (p. 2366)
Teitelbaum, Michael, et al. Disney Princess. Random House Disney Staff, illus. (p. 562)
Teixeira De Mattos, Alexander, jt. auth. see Couperus, Louis.
Teixeira De Mattos, Alexander, jt. auth. see Maeterlinck, Maurice.
Teixeira, Doug, illus. see Teixeira, G. Ann.
Teixeira, G. Ann. Mystery at the O'Reilly Farm. Teixeira, Doug, illus. (p. 1568)
Teixeira, Lucas. Mi Pequeña Biblia Hispana. (p. 1455)
Teixeira, Thiago Jorge. Neymar. (p. 1601)
Tejado, Irene, illus. see Ibarrola, Begonia.
Tejido, Jomike. Jumbo Stickers for Little Hands: Dinosaurs: Includes 75 Stickers. (p. 1188)
—Jumbo Stickers for Little Hands: Fairy Tale Adventures: Includes 75 Stickers. (p. 1188)
—Jumbo Stickers for Little Hands: Farm Animals: Includes 75 Stickers. (p. 1188)
—Jumbo Stickers for Little Hands: Funny Faces: Includes 75 Stickers. (p. 1188)
—Jumbo Stickers for Little Hands: Jungle Animals: Includes 75 Stickers. (p. 1188)
—Jumbo Stickers for Little Hands: under the Sea: Includes 75 Stickers. (p. 1188)
—There Was an Old Woman Who Lived in a Book. (p. 2217)
Tejido, Jomike, illus. see Abrams, Kelsey.
Tejido, Jomike, illus. see Edgar, Amy.
Tejido, Jomike, illus. see Patterson, James & Grabenstein, Chris.
Tejido, Jomike, illus. see Patterson, James & Tebbetts, Chris.
Tejido, Jomike, illus. see Patterson, James.
Tejido, Jomike, illus. see Peabody, Erin.
Tejido, Jomike, illus. see Sanderson, Whitney.
Tejido, Jomike, illus. see Troupe, Thomas Kingsley.
Tejpar, Iman, illus. see Abdullah, Shaila.
Tekavec, Heather. Different? Same! Cumick, Pippa, illus. (p. 545)
—Manners Are Not for Monkeys. Huyck, David, illus. (p. 1397)
—Stop, Thief! Pratt, Pierre, illus. (p. 2122)
—Wanted! Criminals of the Animal Kingdom. Batori, Susan, illus. (p. 2375)
Teke Mwambo, Francis. Four Level Guide Manual. (p. 772)
Tekiela, Stan. C Is for Cardinal (p. 306)
—Can You Count the Critters? (p. 318)
—Critter Litter. (p. 476)
—Critter Litter Southwest (p. 476)
—Do Beavers Need Blankets? Kemp, Kathie, illus. (p. 570)
—Floppers & Loppers (p. 750)
—Hidden Critters: Can You Find Them All? (p. 965)
—Kids' Guide to Birds of Florida: Fun Facts, Activities & 85 Cool Birds. (p. 1215)
—Kids' Guide to Birds of Michigan: Fun Facts, Activities & 86 Cool Birds. (p. 1215)
—Kids' Guide to Birds of Michigan. (p. 1215)
—Kids' Guide to Birds of Minnesota: Fun Facts, Activities & 85 Cool Birds. (p. 1215)
—Kids' Guide to Birds of Minnesota. (p. 1215)
—Kids' Guide to Birds of Ohio: Fun Facts, Activities & 85 Cool Birds. (p. 1215)
—Kids' Guide to Birds of Texas: Fun Facts, Activities & 85 Cool Birds. (p. 1215)
—Our Love of Owls. (p. 1679)
—Paws & Claws (p. 1708)
—Peepers & Peekers (p. 1713)
—Snouts & Sniffers (p. 2046)
—Whose Baby Butt? (p. 2454)
—Whose Butt? (p. 2454)
—Whose Track Is That? (p. 2454)
Tekiela, Stan, photos by see Bauer, Marion Dane.
Tekriwal, Gaurav. Maths Sutra: The Art of Vedic Speed Calculation. (p. 1425)
—Maths Sutras from Around the World. (p. 1425)
Tekulsky, Mathew. Martin Luther King Mitzvah. AlohaHawaii & Lightfield Studios, illus. (p. 1411)
Tela, Donna L., illus. see Tela, Carl M.
Telapary, Michael, illus. see Rushin, Paul R.
Telchin, Eric. Color Factory. Funck, Diego, illus. (p. 420)
Telemachus Thomas Timayenis, jt. creator see Aesop, Aesop.
Telep, Trisha, ed. Kiss Me Deadly: 13 Tales of Paranormal Love. (p. 1224)
Telescope, Tom & Patterson, Robert. Newtonian System of Philosophy: Explained by Familiar Objects, in an Entertaining Manner, for T - Scholar's Choice Edition. (p. 1600)
Telesmanic, Shayna. Food for You. Rafferty, Kavel, illus. (p. 760)
Telfer, Philip. Why Save Alexander (p. 2458)
Telfer, Tori & Telfer, Rhonda. Hunter's Pyjamas. Conger, Holli, illus. (p. 1053)
Telford, Jane, illus. see Welton, Jude.
Telford, Jeremy. Balloonology: 32 Fun Projects to Take You from Beginner to Expert (p. 162)
Telford, Tony. Tramp Life: Part 1 of the Pearly James Chronicles. (p. 2277)
Telgemeier, Raina. Agallas. (p. 34)
—Claudia & Mean Janine (p. 402)
—Club de Las Baby-Sitters: ¡Buena Idea, Kristy! (p. 409)
—Drama. (p. 596)
—Drama. Telgemeier, Raina, illus. (p. 596)
—Ghosts. Telgemeier, Raina, illus. (p. 829)
—Kristy's Great Idea (p. 1232)
—Mary Anne Saves the Day (p. 1414)
—Sisters. (p. 2027)
—Sisters. Telgemeier, Raina, illus. (p. 2027)
—Smile. (p. 2041)
—Smile. Telgemeier, Raina, illus. (p. 2041)
—Truth about Stacey (p. 2296)
Telgemeier, Raina, illus. see Martin Ann, M.
Telgemeier, Raina, illus. see Martin, Ann M.
Telgemeier, Raina, illus. see Martin, Ann M. & Martin Ann, M.
Telgen, Diane. Ghostly Tales of Michigan's West Coast. (p. 829)
—Ghostly Tales of Pittsburgh. (p. 829)
—Gilded Age. (p. 833)
Telias, Ari. Tales of the Chocolate River: How to Make Your Dreams Come True. (p. 2185)
Teliatnik, L., tr. see E-Collen, D.
Telich, Elizabeth. In Other Words. (p. 1106)
Telielska, M. Magdalena, illus. see Doolittle, Eva M.
Telle, Anita. Always Time for Kindness. (p. 61)
—Little Different All Perfect. (p. 1315)
Tellegen, Toon. I Wish. Colmer, David, tr. (p. 1086)
Tellekamp, Lynda, illus. see McKnight, Alex.
Teller, Charlotte. Cage (Classic Reprint) (p. 308)
Teller, Jackson. Free Running. (p. 782)
—Skateboarding. (p. 2029)
Teller, Janne. Nothing. (p. 1624)
—Nothing. Aitken, Martin, tr. (p. 1624)
Teller, Margaret E. Fred Lawrence: Or, the World College (Classic Reprint) (p. 780)
Teller, Thomas. Parent's Offering, or My Mother's Story of Her Own Home & Childhood (Classic Reprint) (p. 1699)
—Pleasant Journey, & Scenes in Town & Country (Classic Reprint) (p. 1762)
Tellez, Martha Cecilia, tr. see Antoinette, Nicole.
Tellier, Derek. Anderson's Heat. (p. 83)
Tellier, Derek, et al. What's Your Dream? (p. 2427)
Tello, Jimena. Mamá Al Galope. (p. 1392)

—Vikings. (p. 2358)
—What Is a Solstice? (p. 2414)
—Wind. (p. 2471)
Terp, Gail, contrib. by. Moose. (p. 1503)
Terpin, Michele. Toby Lost & Found. (p. 2254)
—Toby Takes a Walk. (p. 2254)
Terracher, Adolphe Louis. Chevalerie Vivien, Vol. 1: Chanson de Geste; Textes (Classic Reprint) (p. 366)
Terrana, Diane. World on Either Side (p. 2504)
Terrana-Hollis, Kristen, illus. see Ginns, Russell.
Terrazzini, Daniela Jaglenka, illus. see Dahl, Roald.
Terrazzini, Daniela Jaglenka, illus. see Green, Roger Lancelyn & Green, Richard.
Terrazzini, Daniela Jaglenka, illus. see London, Jack.
Terrell, Brandon. 12 Frightening Tales of Alien Encounters. (p. 2551)
—12 Immigrants Who Made American Entertainment Great. (p. 2551)
—12 Unsolved Mysteries. (p. 2552)
—30,000-Foot Ghost. Pinelli, Amerigo, illus. (p. 2562)
—8-Bit Baseball Ferrara, Eduardo, illus. (p. 2549)
—Above. Cano, Fernando, illus. (p. 6)
—Archie Strikes Gold. (p. 110)
—Break to the Goal. (p. 278)
—Calling His Shot: Babe Ruth's Legendary Home Run. Garcia, Eduardo, illus. (p. 312)
—Cursed Stage. Epelbaum, Mariano, illus. (p. 489)
—Daydream Receiver. (p. 515)
—Dive for the Goal Line. (p. 565)
—Don't Look Down: A Tale of Terror. Epelbaum, Mariano, illus. (p. 583)
—Double Scribble. (p. 589)
—Eyes on the Puck. (p. 689)
—Gear Hero. Garcia, Eduardo, illus. (p. 812)
—Greatest Sports Moments. (p. 892)
—Grit & Gold. Max, Iman & Garcia, Eduardo, illus. (p. 897)
—Guarding Air Force One. (p. 902)
—Guarding Area 51. (p. 902)
—Harmony & Hoops. Max, Iman & Garcia, Eduardo, illus. (p. 931)
—High Drama. (p. 968)
—Incredible Shrinking Horror. Nobati, Eugenia, illus. (p. 1114)
—Limbo's Diner. (p. 1302)
—Mars for Humanity. Foti, Anthony J., illus. (p. 1409)
—No Escape: A Tale of Terror. Epelbaum, Mariano, illus. (p. 1612)
—Pass for the Basket. (p. 1702)
—Phantom of the Library. Epelbaum, Mariano, illus. (p. 1733)
—Pluck & Perfection. Max, Iman, illus. (p. 1763)
—Police Dogs on the Job. (p. 1770)
—Race down the Slopes. (p. 1831)
—Science Fair Sabotage. Epelbaum, Mariano, illus. (p. 1955)
—Second Chance Delivery. (p. 1973)
—Soccer Showdown: U. S. Women's Stunning 1999 World Cup Win. Garcia, Eduardo, illus. (p. 2052)
—Strange Boarders. Muniz, Bere, illus. (p. 2137)
—Strike Out the Side. (p. 2141)
—Summer Freeze! Beavers, Ethen, illus. (p. 2149)
—Time Machine Magazine. (p. 2245)
—Tracking Champ. Epelbaum, Mariano, illus. (p. 2272)
—Undercover Cheerleader. Epelbaum, Mariano, illus. (p. 2323)
—Valor & Victory. Max, Iman, illus. (p. 2345)
—Vanishing Treasure. Epelbaum, Mariano, illus. (p. 2347)
—Win for Women: Billie Jean King Takes down Bobby Riggs. Garcia, Eduardo, illus. (p. 2470)
Terrell, Brandon, jt. auth. see Collins, Ailynn.
Terrell, Brandon, jt. auth. see Darke, J. A.
Terrell, Brandon & Fuentes, Benny. Quarterback Scramble Sandoval, Gerardo, illus. (p. 1822)
Terrell, Brandon, et al. Riptide Pride (p. 1885)
Terrell, Cheryl. Beginning of a Good Friendship. (p. 192)
Terrell, Heather. Boundary. Cortes, Ricardo, illus. (p. 265)
—Eternity: A Fallen Angel Novel. (p. 666)
—Fallen Angel. (p. 700)
—Relic (the Books of Eva I) Cortes, Ricardo, illus. (p. 1863)
—Relic: the Books of Eva 1. (p. 1863)
Terrell, Monica. There's a Big World Past the City Limit Sign. (p. 2217)
Terrell, P. M. Adventures of Blade & Rye. Fitzgerald, Susan, illus. (p. 22)
Terreros, Luis. Memorias de una Senda Inexplorada. (p. 1445)
Terrett, Chali-Ray, jt. auth. see Terrett, Lanyi-May.
Terrica, Joseph. Treasure. (p. 2281)
Terrill, Cristin. Here Lies Daniel Tate. (p. 958)
Terrill, Lucy Stone. Thing Apart (Classic Reprint) (p. 2220)
Terris, Susan, jt. ed. see Follett, C. B.
Terron Tamez, Irma Ilia. Ana y Su Perra Nana. (p. 78)
—Coqui y Sus Amigos. (p. 452)
—Mancha Pegajosa. Ortiz Bello, Frank Joseph, ed. (p. 1396)
—Mi Raton Bufon. Ortiz Bello, Frank Joseph, illus. (p. 1456)
Terron Tamez, Irma Ilia, illus. see Ortiz Bello, Frank Joseph, ed.
Terrones, Tyler, jt. auth. see Durango, Julia.
Terry, Alana. What Hurricane? My Solar-Powered History on a Supply Ship to the Jamestown Colony. Steffen, Jeremy, illus. (p. 2412)
—What, No Sushi? Steffen, Jeremy, illus. (p. 2419)
Terry, Anne. Honest Bob, the Dog, Has a Tea Party. (p. 998)
Terry Anne. Honest Bob, the Dog, Plays Ball. (p. 998)
—Honest Bob, the Dog, Tells the Truth. (p. 998)
Terry, Arthur Guy. Tales from Far & near (Classic Reprint) (p. 2182)
Terry, Barbara. Sr Waldorf Viaja Al Salvaje Estado de Alaska. Kirichenko, Vladimir, illus. (p. 2095)
Terry, Barbara, jt. auth. see Stifflemire, Beth Ann.
Terry, Barbara & Stifflemire, Beth Ann. Spectacular World of Waldorf: Mr. Waldorf Travels to Montana, Big Sky Country. (p. 2078)
—Spectacular World of Waldorf: Mr. Waldorf Travels to the Empire State of New York. (p. 2078)
Terry, Bellamuray a. My Heart Was Made for Loving. (p. 1549)
Terry, Charles L. Sing Mama's Boy Sing. (p. 2023)
Terry, Dianne Dickinson. Dragonfly Dance. (p. 595)
Terry, Eleanore S. New Delilah (Classic Reprint) (p. 1592)
Terry, Ellen. Story of My Life (Classic Reprint) (p. 2131)
Terry, Elliah. Forget Me Not. (p. 767)
Terry, Ellie. Forget Me Not. (p. 767)
Terry, J.E. Harold. General Post: A Comedy in Three Acts (Classic Reprint) (p. 814)
—Man Who Stayed at Home: A Play in Three Acts (Classic Reprint) (p. 1395)
Terry, Laura. Graveyard Shakes. Terry, Laura, illus. (p. 882)
Terry, Laura, illus. see Alberti, Enigma.
Terry, Michael, illus. see Charles, Faustin.
Terry, Michael, illus. see Reader's Digest Editors & Zobel-Nolan, Allia.
Terry, Michael, jt. auth. see Charles, Faustin.
Terry, Michael, jt. auth. see French, Vivian.
Terry, Paul. Top 10 for Kids Deadly Animals. (p. 2262)
—Top 10 for Kids Gaming. (p. 2262)
—Top 10 for Kids Nature. (p. 2262)
—Top 10 for Kids Pets. (p. 2262)
—Top 10 of Everything 2015. (p. 2262)
Terry, Roger, illus. see Miceli, Mary Anne.
Terry, Teri. Book of Lies. (p. 259)
—Contagion. (p. 444)
—Deception. (p. 523)
—Fated. (p. 714)
—Fractur'E. Effac'e, Tome 2. (p. 775)
—Fractured. (p. 775)
—Shattered. (p. 2003)
—Slated. (p. 2035)
Terry, Trueman & Trueman. Stuck in Neutral. (p. 2143)
Terry, Will. Frog with the Big Mouth. (p. 789)
—Little Rooster's Diamond Button. (p. 1327)
Terry, Will, illus. see Corey, Shana.
Terry, Will, illus. see Cuyler, Margery.
Terry, Will, illus. see Holub, Joan.
Terry, Will, illus. see Ketteman, Helen.
Terry, Will, illus. see Kimmelman, Leslie.
Terry, Will, illus. see Pallotta, Jerry.
Terry, Will, illus. see Vaughan, Marcia.
Terry, Will, jt. auth. see Cuyler, Margery.
Terry-Bryant, Wincey. Bullying Is Wrong. (p. 297)
Terry-Todd, Terlene. Sweetie's Healthy Start. (p. 2169)
Tertrais, Gaelle. My Prayer Book. Flusin, Marie, illus. (p. 1559)
—Who Is Jesus? His Life, His Land, His Time. Avril, Adeline, illus. (p. 2448)
Terwilliger, Kelly. Barnyard Purim. Newman, Barbara Johansen, illus. (p. 167)
Terzi, Marinella. Rodando, Rodando... con Plan Lector. (p. 1897)
Terzi, Merve, illus. see Lassa, Julia.
Terzi, Merve, illus. see Mallorey, Gemma.
Terzi, Merve, illus. see Morris, Shanon.
Terzis, Kara. Frayed. (p. 779)
Tesar, Jenny E., jt. auth. see Bunch, Bryan H.
Tesch, Ranah. Biblioteca Secreta. (p. 215)
Tesdorf, Karin-Ann. Case of False Identity. (p. 336)
Tesh, Jane & Klein-Higger, Joni. Land of Lost Socks: A Children's Musical. (p. 1241)
Teshima, Fuminori. Archdemon's Dilemma: How to Love Your Elf Bride: Volume 1. Hikoki, tr. (p. 110)
Tesiero-Miller, E. J. & Miller, Robbin. Stray. (p. 2139)
Teske, Lindsey, ed. see Michelle, Sofia.
Teske, Steven. Natural State Notables: Twenty-One Famous People from Arkansas. (p. 1580)
Teskey, Adeline M. Village Artist (Classic Reprint) (p. 2358)
—Where the Sugar Maple Grows: Idylls of a Canadian Village (Classic Reprint) (p. 2439)
—Where the Sugar Maple Grows; Idylls of a Canadian Village. (p. 2439)
Teskey, Adeline Margaret. Candlelight Days (Classic Reprint) (p. 321)
—Little Child Shall Lead Them (Classic Reprint) (p. 1313)
—Village Artist (Classic Reprint) (p. 2358)
—Yellow Pearl: A Story of the East & the West (Classic Reprint) (p. 2520)
Teskey, Donald, illus. see Conlon-McKenna, Marita.
Teskey, Donald, illus. see MacUistin, Liam.
Tesla, Marco. Progetto Erika. (p. 1805)
Tesla, Nikola. Experiments with Alternate Currents of High Potential & High Frequency: A Lecture Delivered Before the Institution of Electrical Engineers, London... - Scholar's Choice Edition. (p. 678)
—Experiments with Alternate Currents of High Potential & High Frequency - Scholar's Choice Edition. (p. 678)
Tesler, Monica. Bounders. (p. 265)
—Forgotten Shrine. (p. 768)
—Heroes Return. (p. 962)
—Tundra Trials. (p. 2299)
Tesler Stein, Mara, jt. auth. see Davis, Deborah L.
Tess, Jennifer. Dream Runner. Redd, Michael, ed. (p. 602)
Tess, Ruby. Forgetful Teddy Bear. (p. 768)
Tessaro, Gek. Little Duckling Who Wouldn't Get Wet. (p. 1316)
Tessen, Daryl D., jt. auth. see Janssen, Robert B.
Tessier, Beth Marie, photos by see Barry, Debra R.
Tessier, Greg. Chloe #2: The Queen of High School. Amandine, Amandine, illus. (p. 379)
—Chloe #3: Frenemies. (p. 379)
—Chloe #3: Frenemies. (p. 379)
—Chloe #5: Carnival Party. Amandine, Amandine, illus. (p. 379)
Tessier, Greg & Amandine, Amandine. Chloe & Cartoon. (p. 379)
Tessier, Lori-Ann. That Teacher Uses Crutches! Teaching Children about Cerebral Palsy. (p. 2213)
Tessin, Kit Elaine. Never Enough Frogs Whitman, Jennifer, illus. (p. 1589)
Tessler, Daria, illus. see Kaufman, Jeanne.
Testa, Dom. Galahad Archives Book One: Leaving Earth (the Comet's Curse; the Web of Titan) (p. 805)
—Galahad Archives Book Two: Into Deep Space (the Cassini Code; the Dark Zone) (p. 805)
—Web of Titan: A Galahad Book. (p. 2395)
Testa, Fulvio. If You Take a Pencil. (p. 1093)
Testa, Fulvio, illus. see Collodi, Carlo.
Testa, Fulvio, illus. see Waters, Fiona.
Testa, Fulvio, et al. Aesop's Fables. Waters, Fiona, ed. (p. 31)
Testa, Maggie. Baby in Charge. (p. 151)
—Batman Is Fast! (p. 172)
—Bo & Friends. (p. 250)
—Books Are the Best. (p. 261)
—Buddy & Pals. (p. 290)
—Daniel Finds a New Friend. (p. 502)
—Daniel Finds a New Friend. Fruchter, Jason, illus. (p. 502)
—Daniel Gets Scared. (p. 502)
—Daniel Plays Ball. (p. 503)
—Friends Are the Best! Fruchter, Jason, illus. (p. 787)
—Gift of the Night Fury. (p. 832)
—Hello, Teletubbies! Style Guide Staff, illus. (p. 952)
—I'm a True Blue Friend! (p. 1097)
—I'm a True Blue Friend! Rossiter, Clair, illus. (p. 1097)
—I'm Having a Sky Blue Day! A Colorful Book about Life. Rossiter, Clair, illus. (p. 1098)
—Max's Big Show. Shannon, David et al, illus. (p. 1428)
—Meet the Heroes ... & the Villains, Too! Style Guide, illus. (p. 1440)
—Meet the New Dragons. Johnson, Shane L., illus. (p. 1440)
—My First 100 Neighborhood Words. Fruchter, Jason, illus. (p. 1540)
—New Friend. (p. 1593)
—Olivia & Her Alien Brother. (p. 1650)
—Olivia & the Rain Dance. (p. 1650)
—Peppermint Patty Goes to Camp. (p. 1720)
—Power of Po. (p. 1782)
—Ride Through the Neighborhood. Style Guide, illus. (p. 1878)
—Train Ride Fun! (p. 2275)
—We Can Ride down the Slide. Fruchter, Jason, illus. (p. 2390)
—Who Can? Daniel Can! (p. 2446)
—Who Can? Daniel Can! Fruchter, Jason, illus. (p. 2446)
Testa, Maggie, adapted by. Boss Babysitter. (p. 263)
—Catboy Does It Again. (p. 343)
—Dinosaur Egg Day! (p. 549)
—Gekko Saves Christmas. (p. 813)
—Good Night, Heroes. (p. 864)
—Miffy at the Library. (p. 1462)
—New Friend. (p. 1593)
—Owlette Gets a Pet. (p. 1689)
—Vacation Day! (p. 2343)
Testa, Maggie, comment. We Can Ride down the Slide: Daniel Tiger's Neighborhood. (p. 2390)
Testa, Nicole. Lili Macaroni. Boulanger, Annie, illus. (p. 1301)
Testa, Rylan Jay, et al. Gender Quest Workbook for Teens: A Guide for Teens & Young Adults Exploring Gender Identity. (p. 814)
Testa, Susan L. Myra the House Cat & the Garbage Can Monster. (p. 1566)
TETHER, Graham. Hair Book. Joyner, Andrew, illus. (p. 910)
Tetley, Nigel. It's a Funny Old World: Twenty Poems for Teenage Readers. (p. 1143)
Tetley, William C. Blanco y Colorado: Old Days among the Gauchos of Uruguay (Classic Reprint) (p. 243)
Tetlow, John, jt. auth. see Kingsley, Charles.
Tetlow, Karin. Harry Goes Rowing. Guze, Tessa, illus. (p. 934)
—Harry the Carousel Horse. Guze, Tessa, illus. (p. 935)
Tetri, Emily. Tiger vs. Nightmare. Tetri, Emily, illus. (p. 2241)
Tetsuko, Kuroyanagi. Little Dou Dou Who Forgets a Lot. (p. 1315)
Teukolsky, Roselyn. AP Computer Science A: With 6 Practice Tests. (p. 104)
Teulie, Henri. Version Provençale du Traité d'Oculistique de Benvengut de Salem (Classic Reprint) (p. 2352)
Tew, Thomas. Cold Water Magazine, 1843, Vol. 3 (Classic Reprint) (p. 413)
Tewinkel, Naomi, illus. see Winchester, Tonia.
Tewkesbury, Alexa. Benny & Paul's Topz 10 Heroes of the Bible. (p. 200)
—Crinkly Cousins & Other Mishaps. (p. 475)
—Danny's Daring Days (p. 504)
—John's Jam-Packed Jottings (p. 1175)
—Pens Special Edition: Prayer. (p. 1718)
—Pens - Surprise! (p. 1718)
—Purring Wombat & Other Mishaps. (p. 1816)
—Sarah & Josie's Topz 10 Heroes of the Bible. (p. 1935)
—Topz Activity Bible. (p. 2264)
—Topz Gospels: Christmas. (p. 2264)
—Topz Gospels - John. (p. 2264)
—Topz Gospels - Luke. (p. 2264)
—Topz Gospels - Mark. (p. 2264)
—Topz Gospels - Matthew. (p. 2264)
—Topz Tips for Prayer. (p. 2264)
Texidor, Dee, jt. auth. see Millett, Peter.
Texier, Jean, illus. see O'Brien, Joe.
Tey, Priscilla. In-Between Things. Tey, Priscilla, illus. (p. 1104)
Tey, Rachel. Tea in Pajamas. (p. 2194)
Teymorian, Anahita. There's Room for Everyone. Ghanimifard, Delaram, tr. (p. 2218)
Tezuka, Osamu. Atomcat. (p. 134)
—Princess Knight (p. 1797)
Th, H. Nh Ninh, illus. see Varnell, Brandon.
Thach, James Otis. Seal Pup. Cutler, Warren, illus. (p. 1970)
Thacher, Barbara M. Student's Pen, Vol. 13: Graduation Number, June 1934 (Classic Reprint) (p. 2143)
Thacher, Lucy W. S., jt. auth. see Higginson, Thomas Wentworth.
Thacher, Mary P. Seashore & Prairie (Classic Reprint) (p. 1972)
Thacher, Meg. Sky Gazing: A Guide to the Moon, Sun, Planets, Stars, Eclipses, & Constellations. (p. 2033)
Thacker, Marci, illus. see Jacobs, Mary T.
Thacker, Nola, jt. auth. see Strasser, Todd.
Thackeray, Amanda. Lily Bell: Worthy of Love (p. 1302)
Thackeray, Anne Isabella. Story of Elizabeth: With Other Tales & Sketches (Classic Reprint) (p. 2130)
—Writings of Anne Isabella Thackeray (Classic Reprint) (p. 2513)
Thackeray, Anne Isabella Ritchie. Miss. Williamson's Divagations (Classic Reprint) (p. 1480)
Thackeray, Frank W., ed. see ABC-CLIO Inc. Staff, Inc.
Thackeray, M. Half-Hours with Great Authors (Classic Reprint) (p. 911)
Thackeray, Miss. Beauty & the Beast (Classic Reprint) (p. 185)
—Bluebeard's Keys & Other Stories (Classic Reprint) (p. 249)
—Five Old Friends: And a Young Prince (Classic Reprint) (p. 745)
—Old Kensington (Classic Reprint) (p. 1646)
—Story of Elizabeth: Two Hours, & from an Island (Classic Reprint) (p. 2130)
Thackeray, Thackeray. To Esther: And Other Sketches (Classic Reprint) (p. 2252)
Thackeray, William Makepeace. Adventures of Philip on His Way Through the World: Showing Who Robbed Him, Who Helped Him, & Who Passed Him by (Classic Reprint) (p. 26)
—Adventures of Philip on His Way Through the World: Showing Who Robbed Him, Who Helped Him, & Who Passed Him by to Which Is Prefixed a Shabby Genteel Story (Classic Reprint) (p. 26)
—Adventures of Philip on His Way Through the World, Vol. 1 Of 3: Shewing Who Robbed Him, Who Helped Him, & Who Passed Him (Classic Reprint) (p. 26)
—Adventures of Philip on His Way Through the World, Vol. 2 Of 3: Shewing Who Robbed Him, Who Helped Him, & Who Passed Him by (Classic Reprint) (p. 26)
—Adventures of Philip on His Way Through the World, Vol. 1 Of 2: Showing Who Robbed Him, Who Helped Him, & Who Passed Him by (Classic Reprint) (p. 26)
—Adventures of Philip on His Way Through the World, Vol. 3 Of 3: Showing Who Robbed Him, Who Helped Him & Who Passed Him by; Catherine: a Story (Classic Reprint) (p. 26)
—Adventures of Philip on His Way Through the World, Vol. 1 Of 2: Shewing Who Robbed Him, Who Helped Him, & Who Passed Him by; to Which Is Now Prefixed a Shabby Genteel Story (Classic Reprint) (p. 26)
—Adventures of Philip on His Way Through the World Shewing Who Robbed Him, Who Helped Him & Who Passed Him by, Vol. 1 Of 3: To Which Is Prefixed a Shabby Genteel Story (Classic Reprint) (p. 26)
—Adventures of Philip on His Way Through the World, Showing Who Robbed Him, Who Helped Him & Who Passed Him by, Vol. 2 Of 2: To Which Is Now Prefixed a Shabby Genteel Story, Catherine, a Story by Ikey Solomons, Esq. , Junior (Classic Reprint) (p. 26)
—Adventures of Philip, Vol. 2 Of 2: On His Map Through the World Showing Who Robbed Him, Who Helped Him & Who Passed Him by to Which Is Now Prefixed a Shabby Genteel Story (Classic Reprint) (p. 26)
—Adventures of Philip, Vol. 3 Of 3: On His Way Through the World; Shewing Who Robbed Him, Who Helped Him, & Who Passed Him (Classic Reprint) (p. 26)
—Ballads, a Legend of the Rhine, Etc. (p. 161)
—Ballads a Legend of the Rhine, etc (Classic Reprint) (p. 161)
—Ballads & Contributions to 'Punch', 1842-1850 (Classic Reprint) (p. 161)
—Ballads & Tales (Classic Reprint) (p. 161)
—Ballads, and, the Rose & the Ring (Classic Reprint) (p. 161)
—Book of Snobs: Character Sketches; Stories (Classic Reprint) (p. 259)
—Book of Snobs: And Sketches & Travels in London (Classic Reprint) (p. 259)
—Book of Snobs. (p. 259)
—Book of Snobs (Classic Reprint) (p. 259)
—Book of Snobs; Character Sketches; Stories (Classic Reprint) (p. 259)
—Burlesques (p. 299)
—Burlesques: From Cornhill to Grand Cairo, & Juvenilia (Classic Reprint) (p. 299)
—Burlesques: Novels by Eminent Hands; Jeames's Diary; the History of the Next French Revolution; a Legend of the Rhine; Adventures of Major Gahagan (Classic Reprint) (p. 299)
—Burlesques. (p. 299)
—Burlesques, Novels by Eminent Hands, Vol. 1 Of 2: Jeames's Diary; Adventures of Major Gahagan; the Fatal Boots; Little Travels & Roadside Sketches (Classic Reprint) (p. 299)
—Burlesques, Vol. 2 Of 2: Rebecca & Rowena; the History of the Next French Revolution; Cox's Diary; a Legend of the Rhine Stories; Little Travels & Roadside Sketches (Classic Reprint) (p. 299)
—Catherine a Shabby Genteel Story: The Second Funeral of Napoleon; & Miscellanies, 1840 I (Classic Reprint) (p. 345)
—Catherine, a Story; Little Travels; the Fitz-Boodle Papers (Classic Reprint) (p. 345)
—Catherine a Story; Little Travels; the Fitz-Boodle Papers; Reviews; the Wolves (Classic Reprint) (p. 345)
—Catherine, and, Lovel the Widower, etc (Classic Reprint) (p. 345)
—Catherine; Lovel the Widower; Denis Duval; Ballads; etc (Classic Reprint) (p. 345)
—Catherine; Major Gahagan; etc (Classic Reprint) (p. 345)
—Christmas Books of Mr. M. a Titmarsh: Mrs. Perkins's Ball; Our Street; Dr. Birch; the Kickleburys on the Rhine; the Rose & the Ring (Classic Reprint) (p. 384)
—Christmas Books of Mr. M. A. Titmarsh: Mrs. Perkins's Ball; Our Street; Dr. Birch; the Kickleburys on the Rhine; the Rose & the Ring; Ballads (Classic Reprint) (p. 384)
—Christmas Books of Mr. M. A. Titmarsh: Mrs. Perkins's Ball, Our Street, Dr. Birch & His Young Friends, Rebecca & Rowena, the Kickleburys on the Rhine (Classic Reprint) (p. 384)
—Christmas Books of Mr. M. A. Titmarsh: Mrs. Perkins's Ball, Our Street, Dr. Birch & His Young Friends, the Kickleburys on the Rhine, the Rose & the Ring (Classic Reprint) (p. 384)
—Christmas Books of Mr. M. A. Titmarsh, Vol. 2 of 2 (Classic Reprint) (p. 384)
—Christmas Books; Rebecca & Rowena; Later Minor Papers, 1849-1861 (Classic Reprint) (p. 384)
—Christmas Stories; Ballads & Other Poems; Tales (Classic Reprint) (p. 387)

—Lion's Share (Classic Reprint) (p. 1307)
—Man of the Hour (Classic Reprint) (p. 1395)
—Missionary Sheriff: Being Incidents in the Life of a Plain Man Who Tried to Do His Duty (Classic Reprint) (p. 1481)
—Otto the Knight, & Other Trans-Mississippi Stories (Classic Reprint) (p. 1676)
—Slave to Duty & Other Women. (p. 2035)
—Slave to Duty Other Women (Classic Reprint) (p. 2035)
—Step on the Stair (Classic Reprint) (p. 2114)
—Stories by American Authors, Vol. 7: The Bishop's Vagabond; Lost; Kirby's Coals of Fire; Passages from the Journal of a Social Wreck; Stella Grayland; the Image of San Donato (Classic Reprint) (p. 2123)
—Stories by American Authors, Vol. 7 (Classic Reprint) (p. 2123)
—Stories of a Western Town (Classic Reprint) (p. 2124)
—Stories That End Well (Classic Reprint) (p. 2126)
—Tales from Mcclure's: The West (Classic Reprint) (p. 2182)
—We All (Classic Reprint) (p. 2388)
Thanet, Octave & Wilson, E. V. Tales from Mcclure. (p. 2182)
Thanh Le, Xuan, illus. see Elliot, Rachel.
Thanner, Eric. Leaping Lengths! Relate Addition & Subtraction to Length (p. 1255)
Thannhauser, Stephanie, illus. see Best, Elanor.
Thannhauser, Stephanie, illus. see Creese, Sarah.
Thannhauser, Stephanie, illus. see Make Believe Ideas Ltd & Best, Elanor.
Thannhauser, Stephanie, illus. see Make Believe Ideas Ltd.
Thapa, Diptee, illus. see Bramsted, Dino Theodoor.
Thapar, Bindia, illus. see Dharmarajan, Geeta.
Thapp, Manjit, illus. see Bennett, Sophia.
Thapp, Manjit, illus. see Elliott, Elizabeth.
Tharan Sanders, Diwa. Kaya's Heart Song. Canzi, Nerina, illus. (p. 1207)
Tharani, Nadir, illus. see Tharani, Nishant.
Tharani, Nishant. When Trees Walked Miti Ilipokuwa Yatembea: Bilingual English & Swahili. Kitunga, Demere, tr. (p. 2434)
Tharlet, Eve. Happy Birthday, Davy Tuff Book. (p. 920)
—Mommy, Daddy, & Me. (p. 1491)
—Sharing Christmas. Westerlund, Kate, illus. (p. 2001)
Tharlet, Eve, illus. see Balpe, Anne-Gaëlle.
Tharlet, Eve, illus. see Knister.
Tharlet, Eve, illus. see Leblanc, Catherine.
Tharlet, Eve, illus. see Lucado, Max.
Tharlet, Eve, illus. see Luciani, Brigitte.
Tharlet, Eve, illus. see Weninger, Brigitte.
Tharlet, Eve, jt. auth. see Luciani, Brigitte.
Tharlet, Eve, jt. auth. see Weninger, Brigitte.
Tharoor, Shashi. Pax Indica. (p. 1708)
Tharp, Barbara, et al. Tillena Lou's Day in the Sun. Denk, James, ed. (p. 2242)
Tharp, Jason. Bunny Will Not Be Quiet! Tharp, Jason, illus. (p. 298)
—Bunny Will Not Smile! (p. 298)
—Bunny Will Not Smile! Ready-To-Read Level 1. Tharp, Jason, illus. (p. 298)
—It's Okay to Be a Unicorn! Tharp, Jason, illus. (p. 1146)
—Kiwi Cannot Reach! (p. 1226)
—Kiwi Cannot Reach! Tharp, Jason, illus. (p. 1226)
—Monsta Doodle (p. 1495)
Tharp, Jason, jt. auth. see Rose, J. B.
Tharp, Jason & Rose, J. B. Haunted Halls. Tharp, Jason, illus. (p. 938)
Tharp, Lauren R., illus. see Barlow, C. E.
Tharp, Shari. Gertrude & Toby's Friday Adventure Heath, Jim, illus. (p. 823)
Tharp, Theodore A. Sword of Damocles, Vol. 1 of 3 (Classic Reprint) (p. 2171)
Tharp, Tim. Badd. (p. 158)
—Knights of the Hill Country. (p. 1228)
—Mojo. (p. 1488)
—Spectacular Now. (p. 2077)
Tharp, Tricia, illus. see Lee, Calee M.
Thatch, Jaina Marie. My Superhero Mind. Cole, Mernie Gallagher, illus. (p. 1562)
Thatcher, G. W. Key to the Arabic Grammar of the Written Language (Classic Reprint) (p. 1212)
Thatcher, George. Talks (Classic Reprint) (p. 2188)
Thatcher, Henry. Capybaras & Pygmy Mice (p. 327)
—Clydesdales & Miniature Horses (p. 409)
—Komodo Dragons & Geckos (p. 1231)
—Mandrills & Marmosets (p. 1397)
—Pythons & Garter Snakes (p. 1819)
—Wild Boars & Teacup Pigs (p. 2463)
Thatcher Murcia, Rebecca. We Visit Colombia. (p. 2392)
—What Its Like to Be Marta Vieira. de la Vega, Eida, tr. (p. 2417)
—What It's Like to Be Shakira. de la Vega, Eida, tr. from SPA. (p. 2417)
Thatcher, Stephanie. Polly Does NOT Want a Cracker. (p. 1772)
Thaumazo, F. Warrant: A Play in Five Acts (Classic Reprint) (p. 2379)
Thaumazo, Fred. Voices in the Hills (Classic Reprint) (p. 2365)
Thaxter, Celia. Stories & Poems for Children (Classic Reprint) (p. 2122)
Thayer, Albert L. Uncle Zenos (Classic Reprint) (p. 2320)
Thayer, Alexander W. Signor Masoni: And Other Papers of the Late I. Brown (Classic Reprint) (p. 2016)
Thayer, E. H. Mortgage Foreclosed: A Story of the Farm (Classic Reprint) (p. 1507)
Thayer, Ernest L. & Gardner, Martin. Casey at the Bat. Hull, Jim, illus. (p. 339)
Thayer, George B. In Hell Shut in at the Outbreak of the Great War, 1914 (Classic Reprint) (p. 1105)
Thayer, George Burton. Pedal & Path: Across the Continent Awheel & Afoot (Classic Reprint) (p. 1712)
Thayer, James Bradley. Western Journey with Mr. Emerson (Classic Reprint) (p. 2402)
Thayer, Jane. Gus & the Baby Ghost. Fleishman, Seymour, illus. (p. 906)
Thayer, Kristi. Pajama Knights. Willis, Caleb, illus. (p. 1693)
Thayer, Lee. Q. E. d (Classic Reprint) (p. 1821)
Thayer, Mary Dixon. Intellectuals: A Friendly Satire (Classic Reprint) (p. 1125)
Thayer, Nancy. Nantucket Wedding: A Novel. (p. 1574)
Thayer, Pam, illus. see Lindeen, Mary.
Thayer, Pamela D. I Can Draw. Thayer, Pamela D., illus. (p. 1062)
—Yo Sé Dibujar - 6 Pack. (p. 2522)
Thayer, Pamela D., illus. see Corriols, Carmen.
Thayer, Pamela D., illus. see Lindeen, Mary.
Thayer, Pamela D. & Newmark Learning, LLC. I Can Draw: Set Of 6. (p. 1062)
Thayer, Robert Scott. Kobee Manatee: Shipwreck Sea Friends. Korman, Susan, ed. (p. 1230)
—Kobee Manatee: Heading Home to Florida. Korman, Susan, ed. (p. 1230)
Thayer, S. Proctor. Barnes's New National Reader: New National Third Reader (Classic Reprint) (p. 167)
Thayer, William M. Ethics of Success, Vol. 1 Of 3: A Reader for the Lower Grades of Schools; Inspiring Anecdotes from the Lives of Successful Men & Women (Classic Reprint) (p. 666)
—Farmer Boy: And How He Became Commander-In-Chief (Classic Reprint) (p. 710)
Thayer, William Makepeace. Bobbin Boy, or How Nat Got His Learning: An Example for Youth (Classic Reprint) (p. 252)
—Nelson, or How a Country Boy Made His Way in the City (Classic Reprint) (p. 1587)
Thayer, William Roscoe. In the Meshes, or a Drop of Boston Blue Blood (Classic Reprint) (p. 1109)
The 2nd & 7 Foundation. Hog Mollies & the Camp Carmen Campfire. (p. 986)
The Aguilar Sisters, The Aguilar, illus. see Weill, Cynthia.
The Artifact Group, illus. see Banks, Steven.
The Author, By, illus. see Fernanda Heredia, Maria.
The Be Cool Be Nice Movement, The Be. Be Cool Be Nice. (p. 177)
The Bookworm of Edwards, compiled by. Ungoverned Children 2016. (p. 2327)
The Born Free Foundation, jt. auth. see French, Jess.
The Born Free Foundation, jt. auth. see Johnson, Jinny.
The Born Storytellers. Eye of the Tiger: A Born Storyteller Collection of Fantasy & Horror Stories. Price, Kevin, ed. (p. 688)
The Boy Fitz Hammond, The Boy, illus. see Lowe, Dave.
The Broons. Broons Colouring Book. (p. 286)
The Brothers Grimm. Grimm's Fairy Tales. (p. 897)
—Hans in Luck. (p. 918)
The Brothers Grimm, jt. auth. see Racehorse for Young Readers.
The Brothers Grimm & Watts, Bernadette. Grimm. (p. 896)
the Cat, Pete, jt. auth. see Kehret, Peg.
The Child of Achievement(tm) Awards, compiled by. Giggle-A-Day Joke Book. (p. 832)
The Ciletti Publishing Group. Story Time Cafe Maisy's Blue Bath Set. The Ciletti Publishing Group, illus. (p. 2135)
The Coder School. Coding with Basher: Code Your Own Website. Basher, Simon, illus. (p. 412)
—Coding with Basher: Coding with Scratch. Basher, Simon, illus. (p. 412)
The Concerned Group, prod. See Baby Jesus. (p. 1981)
The Daisy Chain Project. Garden Broom. (p. 809)
The Disney Storybook Art Team, illus. see Amerikaner, Susan.
The Disney Storybook Art Team, illus. see Depken, Kristen L.
The Disney Storybook Art Team, illus. see Julius, Jessica.
The Disney Storybook Art Team, illus. see Marsham, Liz & Francis, Suzanne.
The Disney Storybook Art Team, illus. see RH Disney.
The Disney Storybook Art Team, illus. see Webster, Christy.
The Duchess of Northumberland, The Duchess, jt. auth. see Wood, Maryrose.
The Editors at Michael O'Mara. Big Book of Amazing Activities. (p. 217)
The Editors of Popular Science. Popular Science Hacker's Manual. (p. 1777)
The Editors of Sports Illustrated Kids. Greatest Football Teams of All Time (a Sports Illustrated Kids Book) A G. O. A. T. Series Book. (p. 891)
—My First Book of Basketball: A Rookie Book (a Sports Illustrated Kids Book) (p. 1542)
The Editors of Sports Illustrated Kids & Syken, Bill. United States of Sports: An Atlas of Teams, Stats, Stars, & Facts for Every State in America (a Sports Illustrated Kids Book) (p. 2332)
The Experts at Gold's Gym. Find the Balance with Yoga & Pilates. (p. 728)
—Make a Fitness Plan. (p. 1385)
—Take the Cardio Challenge. (p. 2177)
—Train for Strength. (p. 2275)
The Exploratorium, The. Exploralab. (p. 679)
—Exploring - Kitchen Science. (p. 681)
The Fairy, Faye. MY TRIBE; WOODLAND ANIMALS PLAY BOOK [Paperback Teacher Edition]. (p. 1563)
The Fan Brothers, illus. see Hadfield, Chris.
The Fillbach Brothers, jt. auth. see Blackman, Haden.
The Global Fund for Children. American Babies. (p. 70)
—Global Babies/Bebes Del Mundo. (p. 843)
The Grandma. Storm: A Little Dog & Miss Kitty (the Tailless Cat) Adventure. (p. 2126)
The Guide Dog, Thelma. For the Love of My Pet. Hartley, Joshua, illus. (p. 763)
The Indigo Bunting, illus. see Mudpuppy.
The Infamous. Crackheads. (p. 466)
The Intuitive Writing Project, The Young. Declare What You Know to Be True. (p. 523)
The Islamic Foundation, The Islamic. Children's Book of Islam: Part One. (p. 372)
The Jim Henson Company. Dive In, Lend a Fin! (p. 565)
—My Colorful Reef. (p. 1535)
—So Many Sea Creatures! (p. 2050)
—Splash & Bubbles: Double Bubbles. (p. 2084)
—Splash & Bubbles: Double Bubbles with Sticker Play Scene. (p. 2084)
—Splash & Bubbles: I Love to Swim! Tabbed Board Book. (p. 2084)
—Splash & Bubbles: Penguins! (p. 2084)
—Splash & Bubbles: Rhythm of the Reef. (p. 2084)
—Splash & Bubbles: Rhythm of the Reef with Sticker Play Scene. (p. 2084)
—Splash & Bubbles: Shark Surprise. (p. 2084)
—Splash & Bubbles: Shark Surprise with Sticker Play Scene. (p. 2084)
—Splash & Bubbles: Sharks! (p. 2084)
—Splash & Bubbles: Splash's Swim School. (p. 2084)
—Splash & Bubbles: Spook & Seek! Touch & Feel Board Book. (p. 2084)
—Splash & Bubbles: the Greatest Treasure of All. (p. 2084)
—Splash & Bubbles: the Greatest Treasure of All with Sticker Play Scene. (p. 2084)
The Jim Henson Company, illus. see Candlewick Press.
The Jim Henson Company, illus. see Cascardi, Andrea.
The Laugh Factory, The Laugh. Gut Busters! Over 600 Jokes That Pack a Punch.... Line! (p. 906)
—Most Ginormous Joke Book in the Universe! More Laughs for Everyone! More Jokes for Every Occasion! More Jokes for Every Situation! More, More, More! (p. 1508)
—Side Splitters: Over 600 Funtastic Jokes & Riddles. (p. 2015)
The Learning Company, The Learning. Achieve! Grade 1: Think. Play. Achieve! (p. 10)
—Achieve! Grade 2: Think. Play. Achieve! (p. 10)
—Achieve! Grade 3: Think. Play. Achieve! (p. 10)
—Curious George Adventures in Learning, Grade 1: Story-Based Learning. (p. 486)
—Curious George Adventures in Learning, Kindergarten: Story-Based Learning. (p. 486)
—Curious George Adventures in Learning, Pre-K: Story-Based Learning. (p. 486)
The Loud House Creative Team, The Loud, jt. auth. see Nickelodeon.
the Mad, Johanna, illus. see Pacat, C. S.
The Mailbox Books Staff. Totally for Twos: Art Age 2. (p. 2266)
The March for Our Lives Founders. Glimmer of Hope: How Tragedy Sparked a Movement. (p. 842)
The Metropolitan Museum of Art. Christmas Is Coming! Celebrate the Holiday with Art, Stories, Poems, Songs, & Recipes. (p. 386)
—Christmas Story [Deluxe Edition]. (p. 387)
The Metropolitan Museum of Art, illus. see Rubin, Susan Goldman.
The Mouse, Madgewick. Da'vid's Tale. Book One: Nessie's Request. (p. 511)
The Museum of Modern Art, contrib. by. MoMA Topsy-Turvy Stacking Blocks. (p. 1490)
The New York Times, jt. auth. see Shortz, Will.
The New York Times Editorial, ed. Activist Athletes: When Sports & Politics Mix (p. 12)
—Adolf Hitler. (p. 16)
—American Billionaires: Privilege, Politics & Power (p. 70)
—Clean Energy: The Economics of a Growing Market. (p. 402)
—Climate Change. (p. 405)
—Cristiano Ronaldo. (p. 475)
—Disruptive Innovation: Uber, Airbnb, & Other Companies Reshaping the Market. (p. 564)
—Drug Kingpins: the People Behind Drug Trafficking (p. 606)
—Fake News: Read All about It. (p. 699)
—Hacking & Data Privacy: How Exposed Are We? (p. 908)
—Health Tech: The Apps & Gadgets Redefining Wellness. (p. 943)
—Immigration. (p. 1101)
—Net Neutrality: Seeking a Free & Fair Internet. (p. 1588)
—Opioid Epidemic: Narcan & Other Tools to Fight the Opioid Crisis. (p. 1667)
—Royal Couples: Harry & Meghan Markle, William & Kate Middleton, & Charles & Diana. (p. 1909)
—School Shootings: How Can We Stop Them? (p. 1947)
—Seeking Asylum: the Human Cost (p. 1984)
—Space Entrepreneurship: Facing the Next Frontier. (p. 2071)
—Transgender Activists & Celebrities. (p. 2278)
—Transgender Rights: Striving for Equality. (p. 2278)
—Tweet Your Policy: Governance Through Social Media (p. 2302)
—War. (p. 2376)
—Women's Roles. (p. 2488)
The New York Times Editorial Staff, ed. Adapting to Climate Change (p. 14)
—Casualties of War (p. 340)
—Consumer Culture: Feeding Capitalism (p. 444)
—Homeless: An Increasing Population (p. 997)
—Hunting & Gun Ownership (p. 1053)
—Journalism: The Need for a Free Press (p. 1180)
—Plastic: Can the Damage Be Repaired? (p. 1758)
—Political Correctness: Too Far or Not Far Enough? (p. 1771)
—Political Extremism: How Fringe Groups Operate (p. 1771)
—Social Media Influencers: Apps, Algorithms & Celebrities (p. 2053)
—Tech Addiction (p. 2196)
—Vaping: Big Business (p. 2348)
The Official Minecraft Team & Mojang Ab. Minecraft: Guide to Enchantments & Potions. (p. 1471)
—Minecraft: Guide to Farming. (p. 1471)
—Minecraft: Guide to PVP Minigames. (p. 1471)
The Parent-Child Dino Research Team, The Parent-Child. How to Be a Virus Warrior. Loyal Kids, Loyal, illus. (p. 1037)
The Poetic Shivers Editions, ed. see Ginestet, Sylvie.
The Pokemon Company International, The Pokemon. Pokémon Alola Region Sticker Book. (p. 1768)
—Pokémon Origami: Fold Your Own Alola Region Pokémon. (p. 1768)
The Pope Twins, illus. see Kim, YeShil.
The Puppet Company Ltd. Goldilocks & the Three Bears Finger Puppets & Book Set. (p. 860)
The Puppet Company Ltd, creator. Three Billy Goats Gruff. (p. 2232)
The Reduced Shakespeare Co., The Reduced. Pop-Up Shakespeare. Maizels, Jennie, illus. (p. 1775)
The Royal Canadian Geographical Society/Canadian Geographic. Indigenous Peoples Atlas of Canada. (p. 1117)
The School of Life, The School. Big Ideas for Curious Minds: An Introduction to Philosophy. Doherty, Anna, illus. (p. 221)
—What Can I Do When I Grow Up: A Children's Career Guide. Mason, Tyla, illus. (p. 2406)
The Sisters Spurlock. I Give You the Olive Tree. (p. 1065)
—No Mask, No Home! (p. 1613)
The Sparkler Princess. Anything's Possible: Anything Goes! Paramore, Scott, ed. (p. 104)
—Anything's Possible. Anything Goes! Paramore, Scott, ed. (p. 104)
The St. Louis Herb Society. Herbs a to Z. Fathman, Liz, ed. (p. 957)
The Staff of The Undefeated, The Staff. Fierce 44: Black Americans Who Shook up Our World. Ball, Robert, illus. (p. 723)
The Story Pirates & West, Jacqueline. Story Pirates Present. Aly, Hatem, illus. (p. 2135)
The Sun & The Sun Brain Teasers, The Sun. Sun Wordsearch Book 1 (p. 2151)
The Templar Company LTD. Alice in Wonderland: a Puzzle Adventure. Artymoska, Aleksandra, illus. (p. 45)
—I Thought I Saw a Monkey! Nichols, Lydia, illus. (p. 1083)
—I Thought I Saw a Penguin! Nichols, Lydia, illus. (p. 1083)
The, Tienny, illus. see Lee, Karen.
The Times Mind Games. Times MindGames Number & Logic Puzzles Book 1. (p. 2247)
The Topps Company, jt. auth. see Stine, R. L.
The Toy Box, illus. see Wolfe, Jane.
The Trustees of the British Museum, illus. see Goodhart, Pippa.
The Trustees of the British Museum, illus. see Nosy Crow.
The Wanted, The. Wanted: 100% Official: Our Story, Our Way. (p. 2375)
The Wiggles. Wiggles: Colour & Activity Book. (p. 2461)
—Wiggles Emma! Big Sticker for Little Hands. (p. 2461)
—Wiggles Emma! Dance Around the World Dress up Kit. (p. 2461)
—Wiggles Emma! the Ultimate Emma Make & Do. (p. 2461)
—Wiggles: Go Santa Go! A Wiggly Christmas Song Book. (p. 2461)
—Wiggles Jumbo Colouring Book. (p. 2461)
—Wiggles: Old MacDonald Had a Farm. (p. 2461)
—Wiggles: Singalong Slipcase: Includes 4 Wiggly Lift-The-Flap Song Books (p. 2461)
—Wiggles: Words Lift-The-Flap Book. (p. 2462)
The Wiggles, The. Rock-A-Bye Bear. (p. 1894)
—Wiggles: Baa Baa Black Sheep: Nursery Rhyme Sound Book! (p. 2461)
—Wiggles: Big Stickers for Little Hands: With over 200 Big Stickers. (p. 2461)
—Wiggles Emma!: Book & Paint by Numbers Canvas. (p. 2461)
—Wiggles Emma!: CinderEmma Book & Costume. (p. 2461)
—Wiggles Emma!: Colouring & Activity Pack. (p. 2461)
—Wiggles Emma!: Emma's Dress up Day. (p. 2461)
—Wiggles Emma!: Giant Sticker & Activity Pad. (p. 2461)
—Wiggles: Five Little Monkeys: Nursery Rhyme Sound Book! (p. 2461)
—Wiggles: Giant Sticker & Activity Pad. (p. 2461)
—Wiggles: Stories on the Move: a Wiggly Dance: Book & CD. (p. 2461)
—Wiggles Wiggly Songs Sticker Fun Book. (p. 2462)
The Writer, Marques. 56 Life Lessons for Teens. (p. 2556)
Thea Mammen, Eileen. Mean Gene on the Scene. (p. 1434)
Thea Stilton Staff. Cloud Castle. (p. 407)
Theadorer, Theadorer. Finest Baby in the World: Being Letters from a Man to Himself about His Child (Classic Reprint) (p. 730)
Theagene, Jeannisse, illus. see Jackman, Vernon.
Thebaud, A. J. Louisa Kirkbride: A Tale of New York (Classic Reprint) (p. 1357)
Thebaud, Augustus J. Twit-Twats: A Christmas Allegorical Story of Birds; Connected with the Introduction of Sparrows into the New World (Classic Reprint) (p. 2306)
Thebaud, Augustus J. & Bross, R. S. Twit-Twats. (p. 2306)
Thebeau, Anthony W. On the Way to Grandpa's (p. 1656)
Thebo, Mimi. Dreaming the Bear. (p. 603)
—Hospital High: Based on a True Story. (p. 1006)
Thebussem, Thebussem. Fabulas Fabulosas (Classic Reprint) (p. 692)
Theer, Justine M. Backwards Town (p. 156)
Theis, Grover. Numbers: And Other One Act Plays (Classic Reprint) (p. 1630)
Theisen, Manfred. Ohne Fehl und Makel: Ein Junge im Lebensborn-Heim. (p. 1643)
Theisen, Paul. Bigfoot. (p. 224)
Theiss, Lewis E. Journey Through Pennsylvania Farmlands (Classic Reprint) (p. 1182)
—Secret Wireless: Or, the Spy Hunt of the Camp Brady Patrol. (p. 1979)
—Young Wireless Operator, with the U. S. Secret Service: Winning His Way in the Secret Service (Classic Reprint) (p. 2532)
—Young Wireless Operator-As a Fire Patrol: The Story of a Young Wireless Amateur Who Made Good As a Fire Patrol. (p. 2532)
Theiss, Lewis Edwin. Champion of the Foothills (Classic Reprint) (p. 355)
Theiss-Whaley, M. L. By Earthquake & Fire, or the Checkered Romance of Two Generations (Classic Reprint) (p. 305)
Thelen, Mary, illus. see Shahan, Sherry.
Thembeka, Flabia. Esther Becomes Queen. (p. 664)
—Ruth: The Journey, Struggle, & Triumph of a Woman. (p. 1918)
Themerson, Franciszka & Themerson, Franciszka. My First Nursery Book. (p. 1545)
Themerson, Stefan & Wright, Barbara. Mr Rouse Builds His House. (p. 1520)
Themm, Richard. Maddie's Poppa. (p. 1374)
Thenen, Peter Von & Creative Haven Staff. Creative Haven Prismatic Designs Coloring Book. (p. 471)

T

Thomas, Eric, illus. see Wohlrabe, Sarah C.
Thomas, Erin. Boarder Patrol (p. 251)
—Haze (p. 941)
—In My National Park Backyard. (p. 1106)
Thomas, Ethel. Only a Factory Boy: And from Ball Room to Weave Room (Classic Reprint) (p. 1664)
Thomas, Franselica, illus. see Isabel, Michelle.
Thomas, Frederick W. Howard Pinckney: A Novel (Classic Reprint) (p. 1046)
—John Randolph, of Roanoke, & Other Sketches of Character, Including William Wirt: Together with Tales of Real Life (Classic Reprint) (p. 1174)
Thomas, Frederick William. East & West, Vol. 1 Of 2: A Novel (Classic Reprint) (p. 619)
—East & West, Vol. 2 Of 2: A Novel (Classic Reprint) (p. 619)
Thomas, G. D. Keep Your Head Down. (p. 1207)
Thomas, Geraint. Agent Mouse: Snowdon Adventure. (p. 35)
Thomas, Glenn, illus. see Bond, Gwenda & Rowe, Chistopher.
Thomas, Glenn, illus. see Doering, Amanda.
Thomas, Glenn, illus. see Ghigna, Charles.
Thomas, Glenn, illus. see Hoena, Blake.
Thomas, Glenn, illus. see Inches, Alison.
Thomas, Glenn, illus. see Ventura, Bonnie.
Thomas, Greg. Patrick Porcupine's Personal Space. (p. 1705)
Thomas, Gwendolyn. Hiphops: Baby Bunny Comes Home. (p. 973)
Thomas, Helen & Thomas, Hilton. Tom & Tilly's Christmas Play. (p. 2257)
Thomas, Henry Wilton. Last Lady of Mulberry: A Story of Italian New York (Classic Reprint) (p. 1248)
Thomas II, L. Maiin. Boys Can Journal Too. (p. 272)
—You're Never Too Young to Evolve (R. E. A. D. Edition) (p. 2535)
—You're Never Too Young to Evolve (W. R. I. T. E. Edition) (p. 2535)
—You're Never Too Young to Express Yourself Journal. (p. 2535)
—You're Never Too Young to Illustrate. (p. 2535)
Thomas, Isabel. Alphabet Fun: Making Letters with Your Body (p. 59)
—Animal Athletics. (p. 88)
—Animal Gymnastics. (p. 89)
—Animal Strength & Combat Sports. (p. 91)
—Animal Swimming & Diving. (p. 92)
—Animalympics. (p. 96)
—Beaky's Guide to Caring for Your Bird Peterson, Rick, illus. (p. 178)
—Board Sports. (p. 251)
—Brilliant Birds (p. 282)
—City Safari (p. 395)
—Collages (p. 414)
—Collins Big Cat Phonics for Letters & Sounds - Bear Spotting: Band 05/Green (p. 416)
—Collins Big Cat Phonics for Letters & Sounds - Eggs on Toast: Band 04/Blue Byrne, Eva, illus. (p. 416)
—Collins Big Cat Phonics for Letters & Sounds - What's It Made from?: Band 07/Turquoise (p. 417)
—Cool Cat Projects. (p. 448)
—Crazy Creepy Crawlies (p. 468)
—Dealing with Feeling... (p. 519)
—Dealing with Feeling... Angry. Elsom, Clare, illus. (p. 519)
—Dealing with Feeling... Caring. Elsom, Clare, illus. (p. 519)
—Dealing with Feeling Happy Elsom, Clare, illus. (p. 519)
—Dealing with Feeling... Jealous. Elsom, Clare, illus. (p. 519)
—Dealing with Feeling... Sad. Elsom, Clare, illus. (p. 519)
—Designer Dog Projects. (p. 532)
—Drawing (p. 598)
—Elephant vs. Rhinoceros. (p. 634)
—Experiments with Electricity. (p. 678)
—Experiments with Forces. (p. 678)
—Experiments with Heating & Cooling. (p. 678)
—Experiments with Light. (p. 678)
—Experiments with Magnets. (p. 678)
—Experiments with Materials. (p. 678)
—Experiments with Plants. (p. 678)
—Experiments with Sound. (p. 678)
—Fantastic Fish (p. 707)
—Fox: City Safari (p. 773)
—Freestyle BMX. (p. 783)
—Giggle's Guide to Caring for Your Gerbils Peterson, Rick, illus. (p. 833)
—Gordon's Guide to Caring for Your Guinea Pigs Peterson, Rick, illus. (p. 870)
—Handy Horse Projects. (p. 917)
—Hansel, Gretel, & the Pudding Plot. Carretero-Suarez, Mónica, illus. (p. 919)
—Henrietta's Guide to Caring for Your Chickens Peterson, Rick, illus. (p. 954)
—Hip Hamster Projects. (p. 972)
—How to Build a House: Band 16/Sapphire (Collins Big Cat) (p. 1038)
—Latin Dance. (p. 1250)
—Marvelous Mammals (p. 1413)
—Masks & Face Painting (p. 1417)
—Mercury & Venus (p. 1448)
—Moth. Egnéus, Daniel, illus. (p. 1509)
—My Turn. (p. 1563)
—Mysterious World of Microorganisms: Band 18/Pearl (Collins Big Cat) (p. 1568)
—Number Fun: Making Numbers with Your Body (p. 1629)
—Painting (p. 1693)
—Pet Projects. (p. 1726)
—Photographs (p. 1736)
—Pigeon: City Safari (p. 1743)
—Prints (p. 1801)
—Raccoon: City Safari (p. 1830)
—Rat: City Safari (p. 1842)
—Read & Experiment. (p. 1845)
—Remarkable Reptiles (p. 1864)
—Scorpion vs. Tarantula. (p. 1962)
—Sculptures (p. 1966)
—Seagull: City Safari (p. 1969)
—Shark vs. Killer Whale. (p. 2002)
—Should Scientists Pursue Cloning? (p. 2011)
—Slinky's Guide to Caring for Your Snake Peterson, Rick, illus. (p. 2038)
—Squeak's Guide to Caring for Your Pet Rats or Mice Peterson, Rick, illus. (p. 2094)
—Squirrel: City Safari (p. 2095)
—Stars & Galaxies (p. 2107)
—What Is the Controversy over Stem Cell Research? (p. 2416)
—Why Do I Burp? Digestion & Diet (p. 2456)
—Why Do I Have Periods? Menstruation & Puberty (p. 2456)
—World's First Women Doctors: Elizabeth Blackwell & Elizabeth Garrett Anderson: Band 16/Sapphire (Collins Big Cat) (p. 2507)
—You Are Here. (p. 2524)
Thomas, Isabel & Thomas, Marilyn. Stargazing from Nowhere. (p. 2106)
Thomas, Isabel, et al. Cinderella & the Incredible Techno-Slippers. Moor, Becka, illus. (p. 392)
Thomas, Iulian, illus. see Allen, Victoria.
Thomas, J. Meredith. Professor & His Daughters, Vol. 1 Of 3: A Novel (Classic Reprint) (p. 1804)
Thomas, Jacob L. Daniel & the Golden Fleece. (p. 502)
Thomas, Jacquelin. It's a Curl Thing. (p. 1143)
—Split Ends. (p. 2085)
Thomas, Jaliea. Oh Little Garden Girl. (p. 1641)
Thomas, James, illus. see Kesecker, Jennifer.
Thomas, James, jt. auth. see James, Thomas.
Thomas, James Eames, jt. auth. see Tennyson, Alfred Lord.
Thomas, Jan. Can You Make a Scary Face? Thomas, Jan, illus. (p. 318)
—Doghouse. (p. 577)
—Easter Bunny's Assistant. Thomas, Jan, illus. (p. 619)
—Here Comes the Big, Mean Dust Bunny! Thomas, Jan, illus. (p. 958)
—Is Everyone Ready for Fun? Thomas, Jan, illus. (p. 1136)
—Is Everyone Ready for Fun? Classroom Edition. Thomas, Jan, illus. (p. 1136)
—Is That Wise, Pig? Thomas, Jan, illus. (p. 1137)
—Let's Sing a Lullaby with the Brave Cowboy. Thomas, Jan, illus. (p. 1277)
—My Friends Make Me Happy! (p. 1548)
—My Toothbrush Is Missing! (p. 1562)
—Pumpkin Trouble. Thomas, Jan, illus. (p. 1813)
—Rhyming Dust Bunnies. Thomas, Jan, illus. (p. 1875)
—There's a Pest in the Garden! (p. 2218)
—What Is Chasing Duck? (p. 2414)
Thomas, Jan, illus. see Fox, Mem.
Thomas, Janet. Love in a Mist. (p. 1359)
Thomas, Janine, jt. auth. see Thomas, Aiden.
Thomas, Jared. Calypso Summer. (p. 313)
Thomas, J.D. Merry Christmas Sandy. Spradlin, Leslie, illus. (p. 1450)
Thomas, Jeff. Mat with Only One T. Alemanno, Andrea, illus. (p. 1420)
Thomas, Jeffrey, illus. see Marsham, Liz & Francis, Suzanne.
Thomas, Jeffrey, illus. see Sky Koster, Amy & Patrick, Ella.
Thomas, Jenni, jt. auth. see Jay, Caroline.
Thomas, Jennifer, ed. see Whitehouse, Kay.
Thomas, Jerry D. Who Was Ellen White? (p. 2450)
Thomas, Jesse Lee. Ghost House. Daily, Rick, illus. (p. 827)
Thomas, Jewel, jt. auth. see Bouk, T. A.
Thomas, Joan, ed. see McKinnon, Darrell A.
Thomas, John E., jt. auth. see Thomas, Danita.
Thomas, John J. Fifty Years on the Rail (Classic Reprint) (p. 724)
Thomas, John, Jr., illus. see Bullard, Lisa.
Thomas, John Wes, illus. see Bullard, Lisa.
Thomas, Joseph. Randigal Rhymes & a Glossary of Cornish Words. (p. 1840)
—Randigal Rhymes, & a Glossary of Cornish Words. (p. 1840)
—Randigal Rhymes & a Glossary of Cornish Words (Classic Reprint) (p. 1840)
Thomas, Joyce Carol. In the Land of Milk & Honey. Cooper, Floyd, illus. (p. 1109)
Thomas, Jr Darryl W. Today... I Win: When Tests Go Beyond the Classroom. (p. 2254)
Thomas, Judi. Pile of Laundry. (p. 1744)
Thomas, Julia E. K. Super Nit 2: Return to Planet Nit. (p. 2156)
Thomas, Julia E. K. & King, Julia. Super Nit: Rescue Mission. (p. 2156)
Thomas, Julie M. Poncho's Rescue: A Baby Bull & a Big Flood. (p. 1773)
Thomas, K. Clyde the Long Fingered Lemur. (p. 409)
Thomas, Kara. Cheerleaders. (p. 364)
—Darkest Corners. (p. 507)
—Little Monsters. (p. 1323)
Thomas, Katherine Elwes. Not All the King's Horses a Novel of Washington Society (Classic Reprint) (p. 1623)
Thomas, Katherine Fenn. Lewis & Clark, Come Home Before Dark! (p. 1282)
—What Can I Play? (p. 2406)
Thomas, Kelly L. Bumpile: Surviving the Crash, My Mother, & Myself. (p. 300)
Thomas, Keltie. Do Fish Fart? Answers to Kids' Questions about Lakes. Ouseley, Deryk, illus. (p. 570)
—Rising Seas: Flooding, Climate Change & Our New World. (p. 1886)
Thomas, Kerrie Annette. Jinja of the Munjyburr. Jacobs, D. K., illus. (p. 1169)
Thomas, Kiah. Allergic Alpaca. Brecon, Connah, illus. (p. 56)
—Foothand, Elbownose. Brecon, Connah, illus. (p. 762)
Thomas, Kimberly. Kammie's Dream. (p. 1202)
Thomas, Kitty, jt. auth. see Thomas, Jerry D.
Thomas, L. E. Star Runners. (p. 2102)
Thomas, Laura Michelle. Polly Wants to Be a Writer - the Junior Authors Guide to Writing & Getting Published. (p. 1772)
Thomas, Leah. Because You'll Never Meet Me. (p. 186)
—Nowhere near You. (p. 1628)
—When Light Left Us. (p. 2431)
—Wild & Crooked. (p. 2462)
Thomas, Leanne & Schiebold, Olivia. Puppylicious. (p. 1815)
Thomas, LeSean, illus. see David, Peter.
Thomas, Lillie Michelle, illus. see Q., Bev.
Thomas, Lin Rajan. Every Sparrow Was Made to Fly. (p. 671)
Thomas, Lisa. Wake up, Lil Miss New York. (p. 2371)
Thomas, Louis. Hug It Out! (p. 1048)
—Music of Life. (p. 1529)
Thomas, Louis, illus. see Barton, Chris.
Thomas, Louis, illus. see Goodner, David.
Thomas, Louis, illus. see Krulik, Nancy.
Thomas, Louis, illus. see McCurry, Chris & Waddington, Emma.
Thomas, Louis, jt. auth. see Goodner, David.
Thomas, Lyn. 100% Pure Fake: Gross Out Your Friends & Family with 25 Great Special Effects! (p. 2557)
Thomas, M. I Jog Around: Learning the J Sound. (p. 1066)
—Summer at the Beach: Learning the EA Sound. (p. 2148)
Thomas, M. J. Secret of the Hidden Scrolls: Journey to Jericho, Book 4. (p. 1977)
—Secret of the Hidden Scrolls: Miracles by the Sea, Book 8. (p. 1977)
—Secret of the Hidden Scrolls: Race to the Ark, Book 2. (p. 1977)
—Secret of the Hidden Scrolls: the Beginning, Book 1. (p. 1977)
—Secret of the Hidden Scrolls: the Great Escape, Book 3. (p. 1977)
—Secret of the Hidden Scrolls: the King Is Born, Book 7 Reed, Lisa, illus. (p. 1977)
—Secret of the Hidden Scrolls: the Shepherd's Stone, Book 5. (p. 1977)
Thomas, Mack, jt. auth. see Wilkinson, Bruce.
Thomas, Mar Andres. Mi Primer Libro Bilingue: la Comida/My First Bilingual Book: Food. (p. 1455)
Thomas, Maribel. Party in the Sky. (p. 1702)
Thomas, Marilyn, jt. auth. see Thomas, Isabel.
Thomas, Marion & McFarland, John T. Primary Lesson Detail: International Graded Series; Pp. 1-228. (p. 1792)
Thomas, Mark. Akashi-Kaikyo Bridge: World's Longest Bridge. (p. 38)
—Buddhism. (p. 290)
—Discoverer Enterprise: World's Largest Offshore Drilling Rig. (p. 555)
—Discoverer Enterprise: La plataforma de perforación más grande del mundo (the Discoverer Enterprise: World's Largest Offshore Drilling Rig) (p. 555)
—Itaipu Dam: World's Biggest Dam. (p. 1142)
—Maracana: World's Largest Soccer Stadium. (p. 1402)
—Maracaná: El estadio de fútbol más grande del mundo (the Maracaná: World's Largest Soccer Stadium) (p. 1402)
—Petronas Twin Towers: World's Tallest Buildings. (p. 1731)
—puente Akashi Kaikyo: El puente más largo del mundo (the Akashi-Kaikyo Bridge: World's Longest Bridge) (p. 1811)
—represa de Itaipú: La represa más grande del mundo (the Itaipu Dam: World's Biggest Dam) (p. 1867)
—Seikan Railroad Tunnel: World's Longest Tunnel. (p. 1985)
—Torres Gemelas Petronas: Los Edificios Más Altos del Mundo (The Petronas Twin Towers: World'S Tallest Building) (p. 2266)
—túnel ferroviario Seikan: El túnel más largo del mundo (the Seikan Railroad Tunnel: World's Longest Tunnel) (p. 2299)
Thomas, Mark Lawton. My Lemonade Stand Can't Stand Me. Hoke, Jeenhyun, illus. (p. 1551)
Thomas, Martha McCannon. Captain Phil: A Boy's Experience in the Western Army During the War of the Rebellion (Classic Reprint) (p. 326)
—Captain Phil. (p. 326)
—Life's Lesson: A Tale (Classic Reprint) (p. 1297)
Thomas, Martin. Dad Can Do Anything. Jatkowska, Ag, illus. (p. 494)
—My Mom Is There. Jatkowska, Ag, illus. (p. 1556)
Thomas, Mary Ann. Our Train Trip: Learning to Add Times by the Half Hour. (p. 1681)
Thomas, Mary Von. Winning the Battle: Or One Girl in Ten Thousand (Classic Reprint) (p. 2474)
Thomas, Mary Von-Erden. Winning the Battle: Or One Girl in Ten Thousand (Classic Reprint) (p. 2474)
Thomas, Maz. My Big Magic Fish. (p. 1533)
Thomas Media. 365 Writing Prompts for Kids. (p. 2560)
Thomas, Michael Lee, illus. see James-Carde, Genice.
Thomas, Michele. Sodium. (p. 2054)
Thomas, Middy, illus. see Lois, Lowry.
Thomas, Middy, illus. see Lowry, Lois.
Thomas, Mike. Mysterious Treasure of Jerry Lee Thorton. (p. 1568)
Thomas, Mikey. Mouse & the House. (p. 1514)
Thomas, Mindy & Raz, Guy. Wow in the World: Two Whats?! & a Wow! Think & Tinker Playbook: Activities & Games for Curious Kids. (p. 2510)
Thomas, Muller. Ann'e Avec les Hirondelles. (p. 98)
Thomas Nelson. Activity Books Keep It Zipped! (p. 13)
—All Things Bright & Beautiful. (p. 55)
—Annie the Apple Pie Fairy. (p. 100)
—Art Book Neon Art. (p. 120)
—Art Books Best Friends Art. (p. 120)
—Art Books Weave Art. (p. 120)
—Artist Pads Creative Art. (p. 123)
—B is for Breakdancing Bear 123 Wipe Clean. (p. 146)
—Babytown Bible Stories. (p. 155)
—Babytown Noisy Farm. (p. 155)
—Beat the Book. (p. 182)
—Bubble Buddies Things That Go. (p. 288)
—Bugs. (p. 292)
—Butterfly Art. (p. 303)
—Can You Beat the Book? (p. 318)
—Color Me Portrait: Cities. (p. 420)
—Color Me Portrait: London. (p. 420)
—Color Me Portrait: New York. (p. 420)
—Color Me Portrait: Paris. (p. 420)
—Cute & Cuddly: Make Believe Ideas. (p. 491)
—Daring Dinosaur Alphabet. (p. 505)
—Designer Diva. (p. 532)
—Dinosaurs. (p. 550)
—Divine Divas. (p. 566)
—Dress-Up Princess. (p. 604)
—Emily's Room: Butterfly Garden. (p. 642)
—Emily's Room: Monogram Art. (p. 642)
—Emily's Room: Silhouette Art. (p. 642)
—Everyone Is Entitled to My Opinion. (p. 672)
—Extreme Animals. (p. 686)
—Fairy Tales. (p. 697)
—Farm Animals. (p. 709)
—Farmyard Fun. (p. 711)
—Feel-And-Fit Tractors. (p. 718)
—First 100 Farm Words. (p. 734)
—First 100 Things That Go. (p. 735)
—First 100 Words. (p. 735)
—First Words. (p. 740)
—Fit & Feel Moo. (p. 742)
—Fit & Feel Vroom. (p. 742)
—Five Little Speckled Frogs. (p. 744)
—Flip Flap Fun Counting. (p. 749)
—God Loves You Little One (p. 851)
—Guess Where. (p. 903)
—Hey Diddle Diddle. (p. 964)
—Hickory Dickory Dock. (p. 965)
—Hide & Seek ABC. (p. 967)
—Holiday Coloring Fun. (p. 987)
—I Am Using My Inside Voice. (p. 1060)
—I Am Using My Words. (p. 1060)
—Instant Einstein Fast & Fantastic. (p. 1125)
—Izzy the Ice Cream Fairy Sticker Activity Book. (p. 1150)
—Jigsaw Puzzle & Book Hide & Seek ABC Set. (p. 1168)
—Jigsaw Puzzle & Book My First Bible Stories Set. (p. 1168)
—Jolly Christmas. (p. 1176)
—Learn on the Go Pink Sticker Workbook. (p. 1255)
—Learn on the Go Sticker Workbook. (p. 1255)
—Little Mermaid. (p. 1321)
—Look & Tell Bible Stories. (p. 1345)
—Look & Tell Fairytales. (p. 1345)
—Lots of Love Coloring Fun. (p. 1356)
—Maze Activity Books Halloween. (p. 1430)
—Meow! (p. 1447)
—My Awesome Counting. (p. 1531)
—My Awesome Farm. (p. 1531)
—My Cute Kitten. (p. 1536)
—My Fabulous Fox Sewing Kit. (p. 1538)
—My First Dictionary. (p. 1543)
—My First Pink ABC Flashcards. (p. 1545)
—My First Words Bible (p. 1547)
—My First Write & Wipe ABC. (p. 1547)
—My Olivia Owl Sewing Kit. (p. 1558)
—My Pepper Puppy Sewing Kit. (p. 1559)
—My Perfect Pug Doodle Pet. (p. 1559)
—My Pirate Activity Book. (p. 1559)
—My Pretty Pink Bible Purse. (p. 1559)
—My Pretty Pink Prayer Purse. (p. 1559)
—My Princess Activity Book. (p. 1559)
—Noah's Noisy Friends (p. 1616)
—Oola the Owl Who Lost Her Hoot! (p. 1665)
—Owltastic. (p. 1689)
—Petite Boutique Alphabet. (p. 1731)
—Petite Boutique Counting. (p. 1731)
—Pippa the Pumpkin Fairy Coloring Book. (p. 1749)
—Pippa the Pumpkin Fairy Sticker Dolly Dress Up. (p. 1749)
—Pippa the Pumpkin Fairy Story Book. (p. 1749)
—Playdate Pals Bear Learns to Share. (p. 1760)
—Playdate Pals Hamster Learns to Help. (p. 1760)
—Playdate Pals Kitten Learns to Listen. (p. 1760)
—Playdate Pals Puppy Says Please. (p. 1760)
—Posie the Kitten in Pink. (p. 1779)
—Princess Palace. (p. 1798)
—Pug Sticker Activity Book. (p. 1811)
—Rapunzel. (p. 1841)
—Scratch & Sparkle Princess Stencil Art. (p. 1963)
—Sea Life. (p. 1967)
—Sharks. (p. 2002)
—Shut up! I'm Coloring. (p. 2013)
—Sparkle Town Fairies Daphne the Diamond Fairy. (p. 2075)
—Sparkle Town Fairies Daphne the Diamond Fairy Sticker Activity Book. (p. 2075)
—Sparkle Town Fairies Rosie the Ruby Fairy. (p. 2075)
—Star Stylist. (p. 2103)
—Sticker Books My First ABC Activity Book. (p. 2117)
—Story Book Five Little Pumpkins. (p. 2127)
—Story Book Trick or Treat! (p. 2127)
—Supersqueak Comics: the Mystery of the Missing Cheese. (p. 2161)
—Ten Little Teddy Bears Splashing in the Bath. (p. 2204)
—Things That Go Bingo. (p. 2221)
—Three Little Pigs. (p. 2233)
—Totally Glitz. (p. 2266)
—Touch & Feel Never Touch a Monster. (p. 2267)
—Touch & Feel Robbie Reindeer's Snowy Adventure. (p. 2268)
—Touch & Sparkle Baby Animals. (p. 2268)
—Touch & Sparkle Farm Animals. (p. 2268)
—Touch & Sparkle Pets. (p. 2268)
—Touch & Sparkle Wild Animals. (p. 2268)
—Ultimate Sticker File: Dinosaur. (p. 2316)
—Ultimate Sticker File Farm. (p. 2316)
—Ultimate Sticker File Fashion Wardrobe. (p. 2316)
—We Three Kings. (p. 2392)
—Write & Wipe Pink ABC. (p. 2512)
Thomas Nelson & Sons Staff. Christmas Truck Willmore, Alex, illus. (p. 387)
—Super-Funny ROFL Jokes: More Than 444 Jokes for Kids (p. 2155)
Thomas Nelson & Sons Staff, jt. auth. see Peretti, Frank E.
Thomas Nelson & Sons Staff, jt. auth. see Stortz, Diane.
Thomas Nelson Community College Staff. God's Love in My Heart (p. 853)
Thomas Nelson Publishing Staff. Brave Girls - Better Than Perfect: A 90-Day Devotional for Brave Girls Like You! (p. 276)
—Brave Girls Bible Stories (p. 276)
—Daddy Loves You So Much Parry, Jo, illus. (p. 495)
—Faith Journal (p. 698)
—Grandma Kisses (p. 878)

T

—Nieve. Mlawer, Teresa, tr. from ENG. (p. 1604)
—Noo-Noos! (p. 1618)
—Rain. Thompson, Carol, illus. (p. 1835)
—Run! Thompson, Carol, illus. (p. 1914)
—Sing. Thompson, Carol, illus. (p. 2023)
—Snow. Thompson, Carol, illus. (p. 2046)
—Sol. Mlawer, Teresa, tr. from ENG. (p. 2055)
—Sun. Thompson, Carol, illus. (p. 2151)
—Viento. Mlawer, Teresa, tr. from ENG. (p. 2356)
—Wind. Thompson, Carol, illus. (p. 2471)
—¡Bailo!/Dance! ¡Soy Sorprendente!/Amazing Me! Mlawer, Teresa, tr. (p. 159)
—¡Canto!/Sing! ¡Soy Sorprendente!/Amazing Me! Mlawer, Teresa, tr. (p. 323)
—¡Me Disfrazo!/Dressing Up! ¡Soy Sorprendente!/Amazing Me! Mlawer, Teresa, tr. (p. 1433)
—¡Toco Música!/Music! ¡Soy Sorprendente!/Amazing Me! Mlawer, Teresa, tr. (p. 2254)
Thompson, Carol, illus. see Bernstein, Owen.
Thompson, Carol, illus. see Cleary, Beverly.
Thompson, Carol, illus. see Crum, Shutta.
Thompson, Carol, illus. see Newman, Lesléa.
Thompson, Carol, illus. see Ormerod, Jan.
Thompson, Carol, illus. see Zolotow, Charlotte.
Thompson, Carol, jt. auth. see Thompson, Carol.
Thompson, Carolyn. BJ S Bean Patch. (p. 236)
Thompson, Chad. If You're Happy & You Know It. (p. 1093)
—Itsy Bitsy Spider (p. 1148)
—Itsy Bitsy Spider. (p. 1148)
—Old Mother Hubbard (p. 1647)
—Viera Madre Hubbard. (p. 2356)
—Yankee Doodle. (p. 2517)
Thompson, Chad, illus. see Brohart, Karen.
Thompson, Chad, illus. see Bykowski, Christy.
Thompson, Chad, illus. see Crow, Melinda Melton.
Thompson, Chad, illus. see Gibbons, Dawn M.
Thompson, Chad, illus. see Gnap, Jean.
Thompson, Chad, illus. see Houghton, Jill Zierels.
Thompson, Chad, illus. see Umina, Lisa.
Thompson, Chad, jt. auth. see Rice, Dona Herweck.
Thompson, Chad J. Rhymes with Claire. Thompson, Chad J., illus. (p. 1875)
—Rhymes with Doug. Thompson, Chad J., illus. (p. 1875)
Thompson, Chantal, jt. auth. see Hirsch, Bette G.
Thompson, Charles Miner. Army Mule (Classic Reprint) (p. 118)
—Calico Cat (Classic Reprint) (p. 310)
—Nimble Dollar: With Other Stories (Classic Reprint) (p. 1609)
Thompson, Cheryl. Adventures of T. J. & Dodge. Petitt, Tiffany, illus. (p. 28)
Thompson, Chrissy. Christian's Curious Adventure to the Special Room. (p. 383)
—Jesus' Birthday Party: Book Three of the Church House Mouse Series. (p. 1165)
—Our Church House Mouse: Book One. (p. 1677)
Thompson, Clara M. Chapel of St. Mary (Classic Reprint) (p. 357)
—Rectory of Moreland, or My Duty (Classic Reprint) (p. 1855)
Thompson, Clifford. Archaeologists! (p. 110)
—Climatologists! (p. 405)
Thompson, Colin. Amazing Illustrated Floodsopedia. Thompson, Colin, illus. (p. 65)
—Barry. Thompson, Colin, illus. (p. 167)
—Bicycle. (p. 215)
—Fearless. Davis, Sarah, illus. (p. 716)
—Floods Family Files. Thompson, Colin, illus. (p. 750)
—In the Pink. (p. 1110)
—Mordred. (p. 1504)
—Out to Launch. (p. 1683)
—Second Forever. (p. 1973)
—Stanley. (p. 2101)
Thompson, Colin & Lissiat, Amy. Norman & Brenda. (p. 1620)
Thompson, Connie J. What Can You Do with a Mud Pie? Georgetta, illus. (p. 2407)
Thompson, Cornelia. Galesburg's Mighty Horse Market: Leroy Marsh Sales Barn, 1877-1920, and, Memories of a Horseman (Classic Reprint) (p. 806)
Thompson, Craig. ABC's of Black Inventors: A Children's Guide. (p. 4)
—Space Dumplins. (p. 2071)
—Space Dumplins. Thompson, Craig, illus. (p. 2071)
Thompson, Cynthia. Princess Esmeralda of the Land of Ur: The Sharing of Gifts Book Two. (p. 1797)
Thompson, Dan. Li'l Rip Haywire Adventures: Escape from Camp Cooties. (p. 1301)
Thompson, Dana, illus. see Ishida, S. E. M.
Thompson, Daniel P. Locke Amsden: Or the Schoolmaster, a Tale (Classic Reprint) (p. 1339)
—Locke Amsden. (p. 1339)
Thompson, Daniel Pierce. Green Mountain Boys: A Historical Tale of the Early Settlement of Vermont (Classic Reprint) (p. 894)
—Lucy Hosmer, or the Guardian & Ghost: A Tale of Avarice & Crime Defeated (Classic Reprint) (p. 1366)
—May Martin, or the Money Diggers: A Green Mountain Tale (Classic Reprint) (p. 1429)
Thompson, Danna H., ed. see Thompson, James M.
Thompson, D'Arcy Wentworth. Bibliography of Protozoa, Sponges, Coelenterata, & Worms: Including Also the Polyzoa (Classic Reprint) (p. 215)
—Bibliography of Protozoa, Sponges, Coelenterata, & Worms: Including Also the Polyzoa, Brachiopoda, & Tunicata, for the Years 1861-1883 (Classic Reprint) (p. 215)
—Fun & Earnest, or Rhymes with Reason (Classic Reprint) (p. 798)
Thompson, David. Daddy's Big Bike Race. (p. 495)
—Nine Clues of Christmas (p. 1609)
Thompson, Dawn. Double Trouble. (p. 589)
Thompson, Dawn Marie. Sedwick the Seagull. (p. 1981)
Thompson, Debra. Crumb Snatchers. Dennis, Tammy D., illus. (p. 480)
Thompson, Denman. Old Homestead: Novelized from Denman Thompson's Great Play (Classic Reprint) (p. 1646)
Thompson, Dorcas, jt. auth. see Thompson, William.
Thompson, Dorothy B. Ancient Shopping Center: The Athenian Agora. (p. 82)
—Miniature Sculpture from the Athenian Agora. (p. 1472)
Thompson, Dorothy B. & Griswold, Ralph E. Garden Lore of Ancient Athens. (p. 809)
Thompson, Elisabeth C. What If... Watt, Andy, illus. (p. 2412)
Thompson, Elissa. Drawing California's Sights & Symbols. (p. 599)
—Drawing Florida's Sights & Symbols. (p. 599)
—Drawing Illinois's Sights & Symbols. (p. 599)
—Drawing New York's Sights & Symbols. (p. 599)
—Drawing North Carolina's Sights & Symbols. (p. 599)
—Drawing Pennsylvania's Sights & Symbols. (p. 599)
—Drawing South Carolina's Sights & Symbols. (p. 600)
—Drawing Tennessee's Sights & Symbols. (p. 600)
—Drawing Texas's Sights & Symbols. (p. 600)
—James till & Ernest McCulloch: The Team That Discovered Stem Cells. (p. 1157)
Thompson, Elissa & Johanson, Paula. Coping with HIV & AIDS (p. 451)
Thompson, Elissa & Kahaner, Ellen. Become a Great Communicator at Work (p. 187)
Thompson, Elissa & Roza, Greg. Learn How to Network at Work (p. 1255)
Thompson, Elissa & Sommers, Michael A. Develop Your Interpersonal Skills at Work (p. 535)
Thompson, Elizabeth, illus. see Trollinger, Patsi B.
Thompson, Elizabeth Ballard. Times That Were (Classic Reprint) (p. 2247)
Thompson, Ella. Saved from Tuberculosis: Or the Happy Sunshine School (Classic Reprint) (p. 1938)
Thompson, Ella W. Beaten Paths: Or, a Woman's Vacation (Classic Reprint) (p. 182)
Thompson, Ellen. Book of Hours (Classic Reprint) (p. 258)
—Story of Joseph (Classic Reprint) (p. 2131)
Thompson, Emily Skeffington. Moy O'Brien: A Tale of Irish Life (Classic Reprint) (p. 1517)
Thompson, Emily Weisner & Hussey, Mandy. But What If There's No Chimney? Lampe, Kate, illus. (p. 303)
Thompson, Emma. Christmas Tale of Peter Rabbit. Taylor, Eleanor, illus. (p. 387)
—Further Tale of Peter Rabbit. Taylor, Eleanor, illus. (p. 802)
—Spectacular Tale of Peter Rabbit. Taylor, Eleanor, illus. (p. 2078)
Thompson, Emma, et al. Sgeulachd Eile Mu Pheader Rabaid. Taylor, Eleonor, illus. (p. 1995)
Thompson, Ernest Seton. Woodland Tales. (p. 2491)
Thompson, Evelyn S. Yes I Can: Stories That Inspire Our Youth to Realize That All Dreams Are Possible. (p. 2521)
—Yes I Can. (p. 2521)
Thompson, Floyd, illus. see Hambrick, Brandy Yvonne.
Thompson, G. R., jt. auth. see Poe, Edgar Allen.
Thompson, Gabrielle. Candy Art. (p. 322)
—Daphne the Diamond Fairy. (p. 504)
—My First Sticker Art. (p. 1546)
—My Super Sparkly Sticker Purse. (p. 1562)
Thompson, Gare. Main Idea & Details/Determine Importance - Forward, March! (p. 1383)
—Mount St. Helens 1980: Fiery Eruption! Inspiring Tales of Courage & Friendship. (p. 1513)
—Shaping the Constitution: Set Of 6. (p. 2001)
—Underground Railroad 1854: Perilous Journey: Inspiring Tales of Courage & Friendship. (p. 2324)
—Whaling Community: Set of 6: New Bedford, Mass. (p. 2404)
Thompson, Gare, jt. auth. see O'Brien, John A.
Thompson, Gare & Benchmark Education Company, LLC Staff. Elaboración de la Constitución: Set of 6 Common Core Edition. (p. 630)
Thompson, Gare & Peratt, Karen. Seeking the American Revolution - History Comes Alive! (p. 1985)
Thompson, Gare & West, Elizabeth. Main Idea & Details/Determine Importance: Symbols of Freedom. (p. 1383)
Thompson, Garnet. 20/20 Vision Dreams. (p. 2554)
Thompson, George. Venus in Boston: A Romance of City Life (Classic Reprint) (p. 2351)
Thompson, George, illus. see Jungman, Ann.
Thompson, George E. Around the Roman Campagna (Classic Reprint) (p. 118)
Thompson, Graham. Physical Education: Anatomy & Exercise Physiology. (p. 1737)
Thompson, Haley a, illus. see Almendinger, Barbara-Jo.
Thompson, Hamilton. River Road: A Novel of New England Seacoast Folk (Classic Reprint) (p. 1887)
Thompson, Hannah. Living with the Fall. (p. 1335)
Thompson, Harry. Phil May's Illustrated Winter Annual: Season 1901-1902 (Classic Reprint) (p. 1734)
—Phil May's Illustrated Winter Annual: Season 1902-1903 (Classic Reprint) (p. 1734)
Thompson, Heather M. If the World Were Made of Chocolate (p. 1092)
Thompson, Helen. Banking Math. (p. 164)
—Business & the Government: Law & Taxes. Madrian, Brigitte, ed. (p. 301)
—Cookies or Carrots? You Are What You Eat. (p. 446)
—Cost of Living. (p. 457)
—Culinary Math. (p. 483)
—Investing Money. (p. 1132)
—Managing Employees. Madrian, Brigitte, ed. (p. 1396)
—Shopping Math. (p. 2009)
—Travel Math. (p. 2280)
—Understanding Business Math & Budgets. Madrian, Brigitte, ed. (p. 2324)
—Understanding Credit. (p. 2324)
—Understanding the Stock Market. (p. 2326)
—Weighted Down: When Being Overweight makes You Sick. (p. 2396)
Thompson, Helen Stuart. Windy Creek (Classic Reprint) (p. 2472)
Thompson, Herbert. Student of Wake Forest College, Vol. 59: October 1942 (Classic Reprint) (p. 2143)
Thompson, Hilary. Balance Broken. (p. 160)
—Destiny Risen. (p. 534)
—Justice Buried. (p. 1194)
Thompson, Holly. One Wave at a Time: A Story about Grief & Healing. Crowley, Ashley, illus. (p. 1663)
—One Wave at a Time. (p. 1663)
—Orchards. (p. 1669)
—Twilight Chant. Betton, Jen, illus. (p. 2304)
Thompson, Holly Sue. Molly, the Good Furry Friend. Thompson, Kristi June, illus. (p. 1489)
—Molly's Muffins. (p. 1490)
Thompson, Hunter S. Night of the Crown. (p. 1607)
Thompson, I. Owen. Adventures & Day Dreams (Classic Reprint) (p. 19)
Thompson, Ian. Shoal Creek, the Second Twenty Years: A Pictorial History. (p. 2008)
Thompson, Ian, illus. see Farndon, John.
Thompson III, Bill. Young Birder's Guide to Birds of North America. (p. 2530)
Thompson, J. E. Disappearance at Hangman's Bluff. (p. 553)
—Girl from Felony Bay. (p. 835)
Thompson, James C. Sketches from Life: Being Tales on the Ten Commandments & Various Texts of Scripture, Including Remarks on the Service of the Episcopal Church, Intended for the Use of Sunday Schools (Classic Reprint) (p. 2031)
Thompson, James Henry. Real Diary of a Rochester Boy: 1864 (Classic Reprint) (p. 1849)
Thompson, James M. Runaway Train: A Metaphor of the Plight of African American Children. Thompson, Danna H., ed. (p. 1915)
Thompson, Janice. When Jesus Speaks to a Girl's Heart. (p. 2431)
Thompson, Jean May. Over Indian & Animal Trails (Classic Reprint) (p. 1686)
—Three Bears of Porcupine Ridge: Wild Dwellers of Forest, Marsh & Lake (Classic Reprint) (p. 2232)
Thompson, Jeffrey, illus. see Doering Tourville, Amanda.
Thompson, Jeffrey, illus. see Mortensen, Lori.
Thompson, Jeffrey, illus. see Tourville, Amanda Doering.
Thompson, Jeffrey, illus. see Wohlrabe, Sarah C.
Thompson, Jerry D., contrib. by. Symbols of American Freedom Set, 10-Volumes. (p. 2173)
Thompson, Jessica, illus. see Burt, Vickie.
Thompson, Jill. Magic Trixie & the Dragon. Thompson, Jill, illus. (p. 1379)
—Scary Godmother. (p. 1942)
—Scary Godmother Comic Book Stories. (p. 1942)
—Scary Godmother Omnibus. (p. 1942)
Thompson, Jill, illus. see Gaiman, Neil.
Thompson, Jill, illus. see Stine, R. L.
Thompson, Jim. My Cousin Is in the National Guard (p. 1536)
Thompson, Jimmy, illus. see Greene, Sara Beth.
Thompson, Jo. Ted & His Head Full of Worries. (p. 2198)
Thompson, Joe. Life & Adventures of Joe Thompson, Vol. 2: A Narrative Founded on Fact (Classic Reprint) (p. 1288)
Thompson, John. Life of John Thompson, a Fugitive Slave: Containing His History of 25 Years in Bondage, & His Providential Escape (Classic Reprint) (p. 1294)
Thompson, John, illus. see Chall, Marsha Wilson.
Thompson, John, illus. see Clark, Clara Gillow.
Thompson, John, illus. see Lewis, J. Patrick.
Thompson, John, jt. auth. see Lewis, J. Patrick.
Thompson, John G. Fairy Tale & Fable, Second Year: An Introduction to Literature & Art (Classic Reprint) (p. 697)
—New Century Readers; Nature, Myth & Story: Third Year (Classic Reprint) (p. 1592)
—Thompson Readers: Book Two (Classic Reprint) (p. 2229)
—Word from Word Readers, Vol. 1 (Classic Reprint) (p. 2493)
Thompson, John Gilbert. Fables & Rhymes for Beginners: The First Two Hundred Words (Classic Reprint) (p. 690)
—New Century Readers for Childhood Days: First Year (Classic Reprint) (p. 1592)
Thompson, Josephine, illus. see Gilpin, Rebecca & Pratt, Leonie.
Thompson, Josephine, illus. see Watt, Fiona.
Thompson, Josephine Et Al, illus. see Pratt, Leonie.
Thompson, Judy. Dah Dzahge Esigits (p. 495)
Thompson, Julia Carrie. Trye's Year among the Hindoos (Classic Reprint) (p. 2297)
Thompson, Julian & Millett, Allan R. World War II Told Through 100 Artifacts. (p. 2506)
Thompson, Julie. Timeless Love. (p. 2246)
Thompson, Justin K., jt. auth. see Oswald, Pete.
Thompson, Karin, illus. see Lord, Pia.
Thompson, Karla Harney. At Home in the Big Back Yard: The Messy Situation. (p. 129)
—Home in the Big Backyard. Logsdon, Catherine, illus. (p. 996)
Thompson, Karri. Ascendancy. (p. 125)
Thompson, Kate. Highway Robbery. Dress, Robert, illus. (p. 970)
—I'm Just a Little Cow. Green, Barry, illus. (p. 1098)
—I'm Just a Little Horse. Green, Barry, illus. (p. 1098)
—I'm Just a Little Kitten. Green, Barry, illus. (p. 1098)
—I'm Just a Little Pig. Green, Barry, illus. (p. 1098)
—I'm Just a Little Pig. Reasoner, Charles, illus. (p. 1098)
—I'm Just a Little Puppy. Green, Barry, illus. (p. 1098)
—I'm Just a Little Sheep. Green, Barry, illus. (p. 1098)
—Salteador de Caminos/Highway Robbery. Acevedo, Adriana, tr. (p. 1925)
—Sneaky Snappy Mr Croc. Green, Barry, illus. (p. 2045)
—Sneezy Wheezy Mr Shark. Green, Barry, illus. (p. 2045)
—White Horse Trick. (p. 2444)
Thompson, Kathy. Lessons from the Vine Second Grade Spring Quarter. Fahringer, Sarah, illus. (p. 1269)
Thompson, Kay. Eloise & Friends. Knight, Hilary, illus. (p. 639)
—Eloise at the Ball Game. (p. 639)
—Eloise at the Plaza. Knight, Hilary, illus. (p. 639)
—Eloise Has a Lesson. (p. 639)
—On the Go with Eloise! Eloise Throws a Party!; Eloise Skates!; Eloise Visits the Zoo; Eloise & the Dinosaurs; Eloise's Pirate Adventure; Eloise at the Ball Game. Knight, Hilary, illus. (p. 1654)
Thompson, Kay & Knight, Hilary. Eloise Ready-To-Read Value Pack #2: Eloise Breaks Some Eggs; Eloise & the Dinosaurs; Eloise at the Ball Game; Eloise Has a Lesson; Eloise Skates!; Eloise's New Bonnet. (p. 639)
Thompson, Keith, illus. see Oppel, Kenneth.
Thompson, Keith, illus. see Westerfeld, Scott.
Thompson, Kelly. Captain Marvel Vol. 1: Re-Entry. (p. 325)
Thompson, Kerri-Anne. Felicitee the Manatee: Wants to Be a Famous Celebrity. (p. 719)
Thompson, Kim. Caillou, Easter Egg Surprise. Sévigny, Eric, illus. (p. 308)
—Christmas Countdown Gift Set: Storybook & Elf Plush Toy. Duhameau, Élodie, illus. (p. 385)
—Shadow Wrack. (p. 1997)
Thompson, Kim, ed. see Bagge, Peter & Hernandez, Gilbert.
Thompson, Kim, illus. see Regan, Lisa.
Thompson, Kim & Carder, Ken. Phonics. Billman, Dave et al, illus. (p. 1736)
Thompson, Kim Mitzo. Bible Songs. (p. 213)
—Bible Stories. (p. 214)
—Birthday Party. (p. 233)
—Easter Story. (p. 620)
—Five Little Monkeys Jumping on the Bed. Girouard, Patrick, illus. (p. 744)
—Old MacDonald Had a Farm. Girouard, Patrick, illus. (p. 1646)
—Wheels on the Bus. Holm, Sharon Lane, illus. (p. 2428)
Thompson, Kim Mitzo, jt. auth. see Twin Sisters(r) Staff.
Thompson, Kim Mitzo & Hilderbrand, Karen Mitzo. Alphabet. (p. 58)
—Counting. (p. 459)
—Farm Animals. (p. 709)
Thompson, Kim Mitzo & Hilderbrand, Karen Mitzo, adapted by. Multiplication. (p. 1525)
Thompson, Kim Mitzo & Hilderbrand, Karen Mitzo. Wild Animals. (p. 2462)
Thompson, Kim Mitzo & Thompson, Bailey. I Love You More. (p. 1079)
Thompson, Kim Mitzo, et al. My First Bible Cut & Glue Book. (p. 1540)
—Trace & Learn Sticker Fun: Numbers & Counting. (p. 2271)
Thompson, Kimberly. Toulouse Tangled up in Lights. Easey, Chris, illus. (p. 2268)
Thompson, Kristi June, illus. see Thompson, Holly Sue.
Thompson, Landy. Altamaha River. (p. 60)
Thompson, Larry Clinton. William Scott Ament & the Boxer Rebellion: Heroism, Hubris & the Ideal Missionary (p. 2468)
Thompson, Larry G. Dirtball. (p. 552)
Thompson, Larry K., jt. auth. see Kaiter, Manfred E. E.
Thompson, Laura L. In the Butterfly Kingdom There Is Kindness. (p. 1108)
—In the Butterfly Kingdom There Is Love. (p. 1108)
Thompson, Lauren. Chew, Chew, Gulp! Krosoczka, Jarrett J., illus. (p. 367)
—Christmas Magic. Muth, Jon J., illus. (p. 386)
—Cuaquito (Little Quack) Anderson, Derek, illus. (p. 481)
—Good Night, Bunny. Yue, Stephanie, illus. (p. 864)
—Hop, Hop, Jump! Krosoczka, Jarrett J., illus. (p. 1001)
—Leap Back Home to Me. Cordell, Matthew, illus. (p. 1255)
—Little Bunny. Butler, John, illus. (p. 1313)
—Little Chick. Butler, John, illus. (p. 1313)
—Little Chick/Little Bunny Vertical 2-Pack. Butler, John, illus. (p. 1313)
—Little Lamb. Butler, John, illus. (p. 1320)
—Little Quack Counts. Anderson, Derek, illus. (p. 1325)
—Little Quack Loves Colors. Anderson, Derek, illus. (p. 1325)
—Little Quack's ABC's. Anderson, Derek, illus. (p. 1325)
—Little Quack's Bedtime. Anderson, Derek, illus. (p. 1325)
—Little Quack's Opposites. Anderson, Derek, illus. (p. 1325)
—Mouse Loves Fall. Erdogan, Buket, illus. (p. 1515)
—Mouse Loves Love. Erdogan, Buket, illus. (p. 1515)
—Mouse Loves School. Erdogan, Buket, illus. (p. 1515)
—Mouse Loves Snow. (p. 1515)
—Mouse Loves Snow. Erdogan, Buket, illus. (p. 1515)
—Mouse Loves Spring. (p. 1515)
—Mouse Loves Spring. Erdogan, Buket, illus. (p. 1515)
—Mouse Loves Summer. Erdogan, Buket, illus. (p. 1515)
—Mouse's First Day of School. Erdogan, Buket, illus. (p. 1515)
—Mouse's First Fall. Erdogan, Buket, illus. (p. 1515)
—Mouse's First Snow. Erdogan, Buket, illus. (p. 1515)
—Mouse's First Spring. Erdogan, Buket, illus. (p. 1515)
—Mouse's First Summer. Erdogan, Buket, illus. (p. 1515)
—Mouse's First Valentine. Erdogan, Buket, illus. (p. 1515)
—On the Go with Mouse! Mouse Loves Summer; Mouse Loves Fall; Mouse Loves Snow; Mouse Loves Spring; Mouse Loves School, Mouse Loves Love. Erdogan, Buket, illus. (p. 1654)
—Polar Bear Morning. Savage, Stephen, illus. (p. 1769)
—Wee Little Bunny. Butler, John, illus. (p. 2395)
—Wee Little Lamb. Butler, John, illus. (p. 2395)
Thompson, Lauren, comment. Mouse Loves Fall. (p. 1515)
—Mouse Loves Love. (p. 1515)
Thompson, Laurie Ann. Be a Changemaker: How to Start Something That Matters. (p. 176)
—Elizabeth Warren's Big, Bold Plans. Chapman, Susanna, illus. (p. 636)
—Emmanuel's Dream: the True Story of Emmanuel Ofosu Yeboah. Qualls, Sean, illus. (p. 643)
—My Dog Is the Best. Schmid, Paul, illus. (p. 1537)
Thompson, Laurie Ann, jt. auth. see Paquette, Ammi-Joan.
Thompson, Lesley & Oxford Editors. Zombie Attack! (p. 2542)
Thompson, Leslie, illus. see Makhlouf, Jack.
Thompson, Leslie Thompson, illus. see Makhlouf, Jack.
Thompson, Lindsay & Thompson, Chelsea. Abel & the Twelve Keys of Israel. (p. 5)
Thompson, Lisa. Goldfish Boy. (p. 860)
—Light Jar. (p. 1298)
Thompson, Logan. Beyond the Content: Unlocking the Other Half of Test Prep with a Tailored Mindfulness Approach. (p. 212)
Thompson, Louisa. Rex, or Winning the Victoria Cross (Classic Reprint) (p. 1874)
Thompson, Louise. Cold Weather Readers. (p. 413)
Thompson, Loyd Oscar. For Old Eli: A Comedy of Male Life in 4 Acts (Classic Reprint) (p. 763)
Thompson, Luke. Earth. (p. 615)

Full bibliographic information is available on the Title Index page number referenced in parentheses at the end of each entry

—Neptune. (p. 1587)
Thompson, Luther Oliver. Samson's Bee-Hive (Classic Reprint) (p. 1928)
Thompson, M. G. Gaius. Secret Passage. (p. 1978)
Thompson, Maravene. Persuasive Peggy (Classic Reprint) (p. 1725)
—Woman's Law (Classic Reprint) (p. 2486)
Thompson, Maravene Kennedy. Fun in a Theatrical Office: A Vaudeville Entertainment (Classic Reprint) (p. 799)
Thompson, Marcia. Akbar's India. (p. 38)
Thompson, Margaret L. Dragon Daze. (p. 593)
Thompson, Margot, illus. see Lee, Dora.
Thompson, Margot, illus. see Mason, Adrienne.
Thompson, Margot, illus. see Strauss, Rochelle.
Thompson, Marsha. Spoilers: The Rise & Fall. (p. 2085)
Thompson, Martha F. Fables in Verse (Classic Reprint) (p. 691)
Thompson, Martin. Critical World Issues: Genetic Engineering (p. 476)
Thompson, Mary Breckinridge. Breckie, His Four Years: 1914-1918 (Classic Reprint) (p. 279)
Thompson, Mary Langer. Como el Escinco de Lengua Azul Llego a Tener la Lengua Azul. (p. 432)
Thompson, Maurice. Alice of Old Vincennes (Classic Reprint) (p. 45)
—At Love's Extremes (Classic Reprint) (p. 130)
—Banker of Bankersville: A Novel (Classic Reprint) (p. 164)
—Fortnight of Folly (Classic Reprint) (p. 769)
—His Second Campaign (Classic Reprint) (p. 974)
—Hoosier Mosaics (Classic Reprint) (p. 1001)
—How to Train in Archery: Being a Complete Study of the York Round. (p. 1045)
—How to Train in Archery: Being a Complete Study of the York Round, Comprising an Exhaustive Manual of Long-Range Bow Shooting for the Use of Those Archers Who Wish to Become Contestants at the Grand National Association Meetings (Classic Reprint) (p. 1045)
—My First Voyage (Classic Reprint) (p. 1546)
—My Winter Garden: A Nature-Lover under Southern Skies (Classic Reprint) (p. 1565)
—Ocala Boy: A Story of Florida Town & Forest (Classic Reprint) (p. 1635)
—Rosalynde's Lovers (Classic Reprint) (p. 1904)
—Tallahassee Girl (Classic Reprint) (p. 2188)
Thompson, Max. Emperor of San Francisco. (p. 644)
—Ozoo. (p. 1690)
Thompson, Michael. Los Otros Osos Thompson, Michael, illus. (p. 1351)
—Los Otros Osos / the Other Bears. Thompson, Michael, illus. (p. 1351)
—Other Bears Thompson, Michael, illus. (p. 1674)
—World of the Orb. (p. 2504)
Thompson, Michael D., jt. auth. see Meriwether, Louise.
Thompson, Michelle. Day or Forever, I'll Love You the Same: To My 6 Forevers You Are Loved More Than You Will Ever Know (p. 514)
—Taming the Wind. (p. 2189)
Thompson, Mick. Great Tractor Day. (p. 890)
Thompson, Mills, illus. see Wiggin, Kate Douglas.
Thompson, Mya. Ruby's Birds Davila, Claudia, illus. (p. 1911)
—Ruby's Birds Dávila, Claudia, illus. (p. 1911)
Thompson, Nathan David. Royal Gallery of Poetry & Art: An Illustrated Book of the Favorite Poetic Gems of the English Language, the Choicest Productions of Authors, Living & Dead, for the Uncrowned Kings & Queens of American Homes (Classic Reprint) (p. 1909)
Thompson, Nina C. Puzzle King. (p. 1818)
Thompson, Norcliffe G. Hand-In-Hand Figure-Skating (Classic Reprint) (p. 914)
Thompson, Ofa, jt. auth. see Thompson, Richard.
Thompson, Paul B. Battle for the Brightstone: Book III of the Brightstone Saga. (p. 174)
—Brightworking (p. 281)
—Brightworking: Book I of the Brightstone Saga. (p. 281)
—Devil's Door: A Salem Witchcraft Story. (p. 536)
—Fortune-Teller: Book II of the Brightstone Saga. (p. 769)
—Liberty's Son: A Spy Story of the American Revolution. (p. 1284)
—Lost Republic. (p. 1355)
Thompson, Peter. Summer on Earth (p. 2150)
Thompson, Plumly Ruth, jt. auth. see Baum, L. Frank.
Thompson, R. Campbell. Pilgrim's Scrip (Classic Reprint) (p. 1745)
Thompson, Rex. Characters on Wheels (Classic Reprint) (p. 358)
Thompson, Richard. Mighty Alice Goes Round & Round: A Cul de Sac Book. (p. 1462)
Thompson, Richard, illus. see Shields, Carol Diggory.
Thompson, Rick E. Sophie. (p. 2064)
Thompson, Rikkaine. Shift. (p. 2007)
—Twist. (p. 2306)
Thompson, Robbie. Spidey (Set) Bradshaw, Nick et al, illus. (p. 2081)
—Spidey #1. Bradshaw, Nick & Campbell, Jim, illus. (p. 2081)
—Spidey #10: Bad Reputation. (p. 2081)
—Spidey #11: Missing Out. Stockman, Nathan, illus. (p. 2081)
—Spidey #12: Spidey No More! Stockman, Nathan, illus. (p. 2081)
—Spidey #2. Bradshaw, Nick & Campbell, Jim, illus. (p. 2081)
—Spidey #3. Bradshaw, Nick & Campbell, Jim, illus. (p. 2081)
—Spidey #4. Araujo, Andre Lima & Rosenberg, Rachelle, illus. (p. 2081)
—Spidey #5. Araujo, Andre Lima & Campbell, Jim, illus. (p. 2081)
—Spidey #6. Araujo, Andre Lima & Campbell, Jim, illus. (p. 2081)
—Spidey #7: Weekdays. Lima Araujo, Andre, illus. (p. 2081)
—Spidey #8: Blackout! Randolph, Khary, illus. (p. 2081)
—Spidey #9: To Catch a Spider! Stockman, Nathan, illus. (p. 2081)
Thompson, Robert H. Cat with the Question Mark Tail. (p. 342)
Thompson, Robin, illus. see Hayes, Sean & Icenogle, Scott.
Thompson, Rod & McBride, Scott. Mystery of the Baffling Blackout. (p. 1569)
Thompson, Ruth. Type Stories of the World for Little Folk (Classic Reprint) (p. 2310)
Thompson, Ruth Plumly. Kabumpo in Oz (Classic Reprint) (p. 1201)
—Royal Book of Oz (p. 1909)
Thompson, Ruth Plumly, jt. auth. see Baum, L. Frank.
Thompson, Sally Jane, illus. see Moore, Leah & Reppion, John.
Thompson, Sandra Heitmeier. Happy Thanksgiving to Auntie Yammy. (p. 924)
Thompson, Sandy Heitmeier. Case of the Secret Admirer. (p. 338)
—Double Trouble Halloween. (p. 589)
—In the Path of a Hurricane. (p. 1110)
—Stanford to the Rescue. (p. 2101)
—Tricky Leprechaun. (p. 2287)
Thompson, Shannon A. Bad Bloods: July Thunder. (p. 157)
—Bad Bloods: July Lightning. (p. 157)
Thompson, Sharon, illus. see Wolfer, Dianne.
Thompson, Sophie. Zoo Boy. (p. 2543)
—Zoo Boy & the Jewel Thieves. (p. 2543)
Thompson, Stephen P., ed. Teens at Risk. (p. 2200)
Thompson, Sunnie R., illus. see Thompson, Deanna T.
Thompson, Susan, illus. see Allen, Mary.
Thompson, Susan, jt. auth. see Helms, Selah.
Thompson, Susan, jt. auth. see Thompson, John.
Thompson, Susan F. Twins & the Whys: A Fairy Tale Worth While (Classic Reprint) (p. 2306)
Thompson, T. D. Flight of the Wild Geese (p. 749)
Thompson, T. F. Truth Series: Christmas Tree, Not for Me!; Ho, Ho, Ho, Santa Must Go!; the Truth about Christmas. Lovice, Ommi, illus. (p. 2297)
Thompson, Tamara. Before You Were Born. (p. 191)
Thompson, Tamara, ed. see Greenhaven Press Staff.
Thompson, Tamara, jt. ed. see Gale, G.
Thompson, Tamara, jt. ed. see Greenhaven Press Editors.
Thompson, Tamara, jt. ed. see Greenhaven Press Staff.
Thompson, Tamara, ed. Ethics of Medical Testing. (p. 666)
—Rap & Hip-Hop. (p. 1841)
—Solar Storms. (p. 2056)
—Transgender People. (p. 2278)
Thompson, Tara V. Morgan Otter Saves the Sea Turtles: Saves the Sea Turtles. Andersen, Candace, illus. (p. 1506)
Thompson, Tavia. Made by God Wonderfully. (p. 1374)
Thompson, Thelma B. Children's Day. (p. 373)
Thompson, Timothy. Adam & Eve. (p. 14)
Thompson, Travis a. Always Just Be You! Thompson, Travis a, illus. (p. 61)
—Color Wheel Kids. (p. 421)
Thompson, Tyler. Sneaker Freak (p. 2045)
Thompson, Vance. Carnival of Destiny (Classic Reprint) (p. 332)
—Ego Book: A Book of Selfish Ideals (Classic Reprint) (p. 628)
—Strindberg & His Plays (Classic Reprint) (p. 2141)
Thompson, Vanessa J. Song of the Armadillo: Activity Workbook. (p. 2062)
—Song of the Armadillo: Coloring & Activity Book One. (p. 2062)
—Song of the Armadillo: Coloring & Activity Book Three. (p. 2062)
—Song of the Armadillo. (p. 2062)
Thompson, Veronica. Earth-Friendly Animal Crafts. Thompson, Veronica, photos by. (p. 616)
—Earth-Friendly Earth Day Crafts. Thompson, Veronica, photos by. (p. 616)
—Earth-Friendly Engineering Crafts. Thompson, Veronica, photos by. (p. 616)
—Earth-Friendly Math Crafts. Thompson, Veronica, photos by. (p. 616)
—Earth-Friendly Tech Crafts. Thompson, Veronica, photos by. (p. 616)
Thompson, Veronica M. Earth-Friendly Science Crafts. Thompson, Veronica M., photos by. (p. 616)
Thompson, Will H., jt. auth. see Thompson, Maurice.
Thompson, William. Wigwam Wonder Tales (Classic Reprint) (p. 2462)
Thompson, William & Thompson, Dorcas. Iraq. (p. 1133)
Thompson, William Tappan. Chronicles of Pineville: Embracing Sketches of Georgia Scenes, Incidents, & Characters (Classic Reprint) (p. 389)
Thompson-Hernandez, Walter. Compton Cowboys: Young Readers' Edition: And the Fight to Save Their Horse Ranch. (p. 437)
Thompson-Ochoa, Danielle. Elsa & the Motmot. (p. 639)
Thompson-Seton, Ernest. Animal Story Book (Classic Reprint) (p. 91)
Thompson-Swift, Joseph. Adventures of Primrose Perfect. (p. 27)
Thoms, Annie. With Their Eyes: September 11th: the View from a High School at Ground Zero. (p. 2482)
Thoms, Gigi. Noble Pocket. (p. 1616)
Thoms, Nathan. Changing Faces: Happy Halloween! Pintachan, illus. (p. 356)
Thoms, Peter Perring. Affectionate Pair; or the History of Sung-Kin: A Chinese Tale (Classic Reprint) (p. 31)
—Chinese Courtship, in Verse: To Which Is Added, an Appendix, Treating of the Revenue of China, &C (Classic Reprint) (p. 378)
Thoms, Susan Collins. Jonah & the Big Fish. Stoop, Naoko, illus. (p. 1177)
—My First Communion. le Joly Sénoville, Tinou, illus. (p. 1543)
—Twelve Days of Christmas in Michigan. Pilutti, Deb, illus. (p. 2303)
Thoms, William J. Anecdotes & Traditions Illustrative of Early English History & Literature. (p. 84)
Thoms, William John. Early English Prose Romances, Vol. 2: With Bibliographical & Historical Introductions (Classic Reprint) (p. 614)
—Gammer Gurton's Famous Histories of Sir Guy of Warwick, Sir Bevis of Hampton, Tom Hickathrift, Friar Bacon, Robin Hood, & the King & the Cobbler (Classic Reprint) (p. 808)
—Lays & Legends of Various Nations: Illustrative of Their Traditions, Popular Literature, Manners, Customs, & Superstitions (Classic Reprint) (p. 1253)
—Old Story Books of England: Illustrated with Twelve Pictures by Eminent Artists (Classic Reprint) (p. 1648)
Thomsen, Amanda. Backyard Adventure: Get Messy, Get Wet, Build Cool Things, & Have Tons of Wild Fun! 51 Free-Play Activities. (p. 156)
Thomsen, K. a. Hidden Valley. (p. 966)
Thomsen, Keith Stuart. Finding Gods. (p. 729)
Thomsen, Marita, tr. see Oskarsson, Bárdur.
-Thomsett, Richard Gillham. Kohat, Kuram, & Khost: Or, Experiences & Adventures in the Late Afghan War (Classic Reprint) (p. 1230)
—Kohât, Kuram, & Khost: Or, Experiences & Adventures in the Late Afghan War (Classic Reprint) (p. 1230)
Thomson. Pride of Ancestry: Or, Who Is She?, Vol. 2 of 4: a Novel, in Four Volumes (Classic Reprint) (p. 1791)
—Pride of Ancestry, or Who Is She?, Vol. 4 Of 4: A Novel (Classic Reprint) (p. 1791)
Thomson, A. T. Constance, Vol. 1 Of 3: A Novel (Classic Reprint) (p. 443)
—Constance, Vol. 2 Of 3: A Novel (Classic Reprint) (p. 443)
—Constance, Vol. 3 Of 3: A Novel (Classic Reprint) (p. 443)
—Rosabel, Vol. 1 Of 3: A Novel (Classic Reprint) (p. 1904)
—Rosabel, Vol. 2 Of 3: A Novel (Classic Reprint) (p. 1904)
—Rosabel, Vol. 3 Of 3: A Novel (Classic Reprint) (p. 1904)
Thomson, Andrew, illus. see Belviso, Meg, et al.
Thomson, Andrew, illus. see Brown, Dinah & Who HQ.
Thomson, Andrew, illus. see Brown, Dinah.
Thomson, Andrew, illus. see Buckley, James & Who HQ.
Thomson, Andrew, illus. see Buckley, James, Jr., et al.
Thomson, Andrew, illus. see Elling, Brian & Who HQ.
Thomson, Andrew, illus. see Frith, Margaret & Who HQ.
Thomson, Andrew, illus. see Herman, Gail & Who HQ.
Thomson, Andrew, illus. see Medina, Nico & Who HQ.
Thomson, Andrew, illus. see Payne, M. D. & Who HQ.
Thomson, Andrew, illus. see Pollack, Pam & Belviso, Meg.
Thomson, Andrew, illus. see Pollack, Pam, et al.
Thomson, Andrew, illus. see Rau, Dana Meachen.
Thomson, Andrew, illus. see Waterfield, Kathryn, et al.
Thomson, Andy, illus. see Gunning, Mark.
Thomson, Anstruther. Eighty Years' Reminiscences, Vol. 1 of 2 (Classic Reprint) (p. 629)
Thomson, Bill. Chalk (p. 354)
—Fossil Thomson, Bill, illus. (p. 770)
Thomson, Bill, illus. see Nevius, Carol.
Thomson, C. M. Drummeldale Lights & Shadows from the Border Hills: Sketches & Poems (Classic Reprint) (p. 606)
Thomson, Carly. Truth Seekers. (p. 2297)
Thomson, Charles Goff. Terry a Tale of the Hill People (Classic Reprint) (p. 2208)
Thomson, Cindy. Kenny Chesney. (p. 1209)
Thomson, David. Japanese Fairy Tale Series, Vol. 2: The Tongue Cut Sparrow (Classic Reprint) (p. 1160)
—Princes Fire-Flash & Fire-Fade (Classic Reprint) (p. 1795)
Thomson, E. Gertrude, illus. see Carroll, Lewis, pseud.
Thomson, Edward William. Between Earth & Sky: And Other Strange Stories of Deliverance (Classic Reprint) (p. 210)
—Old Man Savarin Stories: Tales of Canada & Canadians (Classic Reprint) (p. 1647)
Thomson, Emma. Princess Pearl: A Royal Ballet. (p. 1798)
—Princess Pearl: A Friend to Treasure. (p. 1798)
Thomson, G. F. Charmed Fawn: A New & Original Fairy Extravaganza in One Act (Classic Reprint) (p. 361)
Thomson, George N. Confessions, Trials, & Biographical Sketches of the Most Cold Blooded Murderers, Who Have Been Executed in This Country from Its First Settlement down to the Present Time: Compiled Entirely from the Most Authentic Sources; Containing Also, Accounts of V. (p. 439)
Thomson, Hugh, jt. auth. see Austen, Jane.
Thomson, Hugh, jt. auth. see Dobson, Austin.
Thomson, J. Public & Private Life of Animals: Adapted from the French of Balzac, Droz, Jules Janin, E. Lemoine, A. de Musset, Georges Sand, &C (Classic Reprint) (p. 1810)
Thomson, James. Recollections of a Speyside Parish (Classic Reprint) (p. 1854)
Thomson, Jamie. Dark Lord: 4: Headmaster of Doom. (p. 506)
Thomson, Jimmy. Koala Bounces Back. Lobbecke, Eric, illus. (p. 1230)
Thomson, John Stuart. Bud & Bamboo (Classic Reprint) (p. 290)
—Fil & Filippa: Story of Child Life in the Philippines (Classic Reprint) (p. 726)
Thomson, Joseph. Ulu, Vol. 1 Of 2: An African Romance (Classic Reprint) (p. 2316)
—Ulu, Vol. 2 Of 2: An African Romance (Classic Reprint) (p. 2316)
Thomson, Joseph John. Treatise on the Motion of Vortex Rings - an Essay to Which the Adams Prize Was Adjudged in 1882, in the University of Cambridge. (p. 2283)
Thomson, Kate. 555 Sticker Fun Aliens. (p. 2560)
—Fuzzy Christmas. Green, Barry, illus. (p. 803)
—Loud Proud Lenny Lion. Green, Barry, illus. (p. 1357)
Thomson, Linda. Harry the Hypno-Potamus: More Metaphorical Tales for Children. (p. 935)
Thomson, Lu. Ruby & the Magic Key. Patrick, J. J., ed. (p. 1911)
—Worry Box. (p. 2509)
Thomson, Maureen, jt. auth. see Smith, Craig.
Thomson, Melissa. Keena Ford & the Field Trip Mix-Up. (p. 1207)
—Keena Ford & the Second-Grade Mix-Up. (p. 1207)
—Keena Ford & the Secret Journal Mix-Up. Morrison, Frank, illus. (p. 1207)
—Tito the Bonecrusher. (p. 2251)
Thomson, Pat. Monkey's Magic Pipe. Cimatoribus, Alessandra, illus. (p. 1494)
Thomson, Permelia Corey. How the Coreys Went West: Fifty Years in Crossing the Continent (Classic Reprint) (p. 1035)
Thomson, Permellin Corey. How the Coreys Went West: Fifty Years in Crossing the Continent (Classic Reprint) (p. 1035)
Thomson, Rachel Starr. Theodore Pharris Saves the Universe. (p. 2216)
Thomson, Regan, illus. see Kootstra, Kara.
Thomson, Richard. Tales of an Antiquary, Vol. 1 Of 3: Chiefly Illustrative of the Manners, Traditions, & Remarkable Localities of Ancient London (Classic Reprint) (p. 2183)
Thomson, Ruth. Bee's Life Cycle. (p. 190)
—Chicken's Life Cycle. (p. 369)
—Coasts. (p. 410)
—Countries (p. 460)
—DK Readers L1: Dinosaur's Day. (p. 568)
—Fairy Tales: Writing Activities with Your Favorite Fairy Tale Characters. (p. 697)
—France. (p. 776)
—Frog's Life Cycle. (p. 790)
—India. (p. 1115)
—Let's Look at Life Cycles (p. 1275)
—Life Cycle of a Crab. (p. 1290)
—Life Cycle of a Ladybug. (p. 1291)
—Life Cycle of a Rose. (p. 1291)
—Life Cycle of an Apple. (p. 1291)
—Life Cycle of an Oak Tree. (p. 1291)
—Life Cycle of an Owl. (p. 1291)
—Mountains. (p. 1514)
—Photos Framed: A Fresh Look at the World's Most Memorable Photographs. (p. 1737)
—Poland. (p. 1769)
—Rain Forests. (p. 1835)
—Rivers. (p. 1887)
—Science & Inventions Creativity Book: Games, Models to Make, High-Tech Craft Paper, Stickers, & Stencils. (p. 1953)
—Spain. (p. 2073)
—Sunflower's Life Cycle. (p. 2152)
—Terezin: Voices from the Holocaust. (p. 2206)
—Vincent Van Gogh (p. 2359)
Thomson, Sarah, jt. auth. see Ford, Gabrielle.
Thomson, Sarah, adapted by. Three Cups of Tea. (p. 2232)
Thomson, Sarah & Relin, David Oliver. Three Cups of Tea. (p. 2232)
Thomson, Sarah L. Ancient Animals: Plesiosaur. Plant, Andrew, illus. (p. 79)
—Around the Neighborhood: A Counting Lullaby Christy, Jana, illus. (p. 118)
—Cinderella Ceccoli, Nicoletta, illus. (p. 391)
—Cub's Big World. Cepeda, Joe, illus. (p. 482)
—Deadly Flowers: A Ninja's Tale. (p. 518)
—Deadly Wish: A Ninja's Journey. (p. 519)
—Eagle's Quill. (p. 613)
—Eureka Key. (p. 667)
—Mercy: The Last New England Vampire (p. 1448)
—Pirates, Ho! Gilpin, Stephen, illus. (p. 1751)
—Quick, Little Monkey! Judge, Lita, illus. (p. 1827)
—Ring of Honor. (p. 1883)
—Saber-Toothed Cat. Plant, Andrew, illus. (p. 1919)
—Terror Birds. Plant, Andrew, illus. (p. 2208)
—What Lincoln Said. Ransome, James E., illus. (p. 2418)
—What's for Lunch? Aye, Nila, illus. (p. 2423)
—Where Do Polar Bears Live? Chin, Jason, illus. (p. 2436)
Thomson, Sarah L., jt. auth. see McGuinness, Denis E.
Thomson, Sarah L., jt. auth. see Mendell, David.
Thomson, Sarah L., jt. auth. see Piven, Hanoch.
Thomson, Sarah L. & Plant, Andrew. Ancient Animals: Terror Bird. (p. 79)
Thomson, Thomas. Sketch of the Progress of Physical Science (Classic Reprint) (p. 2030)
—Works of the Ettrick Shepherd (Classic Reprint) (p. 2499)
Thomson, W. R. In Dickens Street (Classic Reprint) (p. 1104)
Thomson, Wendy Sura. Ted & Ned. (p. 2198)
Thomson-Swift, Joe. Monkeyboy & the Gruffits. (p. 1494)
—Twig People of Mossdown Woods. (p. 2304)
Thomson-Swift, Joseph & Thomson-Swift, Joe. Giant, the Antman & the Mermaid. (p. 831)
Thong, Roseanne. Fly Free. Neilan, Eujin Kim, illus. (p. 754)
—Round Is a Mooncake: A Book of Shapes. Lin, Grace, illus. (p. 1907)
—Round Is a Tortilla: A Book of Shapes. Parra, John, illus. (p. 1907)
Thong, Roseanne Greenfield. Dia de Los Muertos. Ballesteros, Carles, illus. (p. 537)
—Dia de los Muertos. Ballesteros, Carles, illus. (p. 537)
—Green Is a Chile Pepper: A Book of Colors. (p. 894)
—Green Is a Chile Pepper: A Book of Colors. Parra, John, illus. (p. 894)
—Green Is a Chile Pepper. (p. 894)
—Noodle Magic. So, Meilo, illus. (p. 1618)
—One Is a Drummer: A Book of Numbers. (p. 1660)
—One Is a Piñata: a Book of Numbers (Learn to Count Books, Numbers Books for Kids, Preschool Numbers Book) Parra, John, illus. (p. 1660)
—Red Is a Dragon: A Book of Colors. (p. 1857)
—Red Is a Dragon. Lin, Grace, illus. (p. 1857)
—Round Is a Mooncake: A Book of Shapes. (p. 1907)
—Round Is a Tortilla: A Book of Shapes. (p. 1907)
—Round Is a Tortilla: A Book of Shapes. Parra, John, illus. (p. 1907)
Thonger, M. Ellen. Bees: The Story of the B Triplets & Their Aunt (Classic Reprint) (p. 189)
—Jock & I & the Hydra (Classic Reprint) (p. 1170)
Thoolen, Jai D. My Beard. Whitson, Fred, illus. (p. 1532)
—Myself & Things about Me: An Activity Journal. (p. 1566)
—Myself & Things about Me (Hb) An Activity Journal. (p. 1566)
—Selected Collection of Rhymes for Inspection. Greenwood, Sarah G., illus. (p. 1986)
Thor, Annika. Deep Sea. Schenck, Linda, tr. from SWE. (p. 524)
—Faraway Island. Schenck, Linda, tr. (p. 709)
—Lily Pond Schenck, Linda, tr. (p. 1302)
—Lily Pond. Schenck, Linda, tr. (p. 1302)
Thorburn, Mark. President & the Executive Branch: How Our Nation Is Governed. (p. 1789)

T

Thorburn, Thomas James. Critical Examination of the Evidences for the Doctrine of the Virgin Birth (Classic Reprint) (p. 475)
Thordsen, Narona, tr. see Renz, Ulrich.
Thore, Maria Nilsson. Stay-At-Home Sammy & the Runaway Spot. (p. 2109)
Thoreau, Henry. Autumn: From the Journal of Henry David Thoreau (Classic Reprint) (p. 140)
—Canoeing in the Wilderness. (p. 322)
—Early Spring in Massachusetts 1881: From the Journal of Henry D. Thoreau (Classic Reprint) (p. 615)
—Excursions (Classic Reprint) (p. 676)
—In American Fields & Forests (Classic Reprint) (p. 1104)
—Journal of Henry David Thoreau, Vol. 11: July 2, 1858 February 28, 1859 (Classic Reprint) (p. 1180)
—Journal of Henry David Thoreau, Vol. 12: March 2, 1859 November 30, 1859 (Classic Reprint) (p. 1180)
—Journal of Henry David Thoreau, Vol. 13: December 1, 1859 July 31, 1860 (Classic Reprint) (p. 1180)
—Journal of Henry David Thoreau, Vol. 2: 1850 September 15, 1851 (Classic Reprint) (p. 1180)
—Journal of Henry David Thoreau, Vol. 9: August 16, 1856 August 7, 1857 (Classic Reprint) (p. 1180)
—Notes on New England Birds (Classic Reprint) (p. 1624)
—Selections from Thoreau: Edited, with an Introduction (Classic Reprint) (p. 1986)
—Succession of Forest Trees, & Wild Apples (Classic Reprint) (p. 2146)
—Thoreau: A Book of Quotations. Blaisdell, Bob, ed. (p. 2230)
—Walden, Vol. 1 of 2 (Classic Reprint) (p. 2371)
—Walking. Clifton Johnson, illus. (p. 2372)
—Writings of Henry David Thoreau (Classic Reprint) (p. 2513)
—Writings of Henry David Thoreau, Vol. 11 of 20 (Classic Reprint) (p. 2513)
—Writings of Henry David Thoreau, Vol. 14: Journal, Vol; 8; November 1, 1855 August 15, 1856 (Classic Reprint) (p. 2513)
—Writings of Henry Thoreau, Vol. 13: Journal, Vol; 7; September 1, 1854 October 30, 1855 (Classic Reprint) (p. 2513)
Thoreau, Henry David. Year in the Woods. Manna, Giovanni, illus. (p. 2519)
Thorgeirsson, Sigmundur, illus. see Johnston, Thomas Anguti.
Thorgeirsson, Sigmundur, illus. see Lawrence, Margaret.
Thorley, Wilfrid C. Primer of English: For Foreign Students (Classic Reprint) (p. 1793)
Thormanby, Thormanby. Boxers & Their Battles: Anecdotal Sketches & Personal Recollections of Famous Pugilists (Classic Reprint) (p. 267)
—Romances of the Road (Classic Reprint) (p. 1900)
Thorn, Ismay. Only Five: Or Pussie's Frolics in Farm & Field (Classic Reprint) (p. 1664)
Thorn, Nicole. Dollhouse. (p. 578)
Thorn, Shawn. Don't Tease Mr. Beeze. Coia, Vincenzo, ed. (p. 583)
Thorn, Theresa. It Feels Good to Be Yourself: A Book about Gender Identity. Grigni, Noah, illus. (p. 1141)
Thornberry, Laurie. Haunting of a House. (p. 939)
—Mack at Rainbow Bridge. (p. 1372)
Thornborough, Kathy. Animals. Petelinsek, Kathleen, illus. (p. 93)
—Colors & Shapes. Petelinsek, Kathleen, illus. (p. 426)
—Days & Times. Petelinsek, Kathleen, illus. (p. 515)
—Food. Petelinsek, Kathleen, illus. (p. 759)
—School. Petelinsek, Kathleen, illus. (p. 1945)
—Seasons. Petelinsek, Kathleen, illus. (p. 1972)
—Weather. Petelinsek, Kathleen, illus. (p. 2393)
—Work. Petelinsek, Kathleen, illus. (p. 2495)
Thornborough, Tim. Daniel & the Very Hungry Lions. Davison, Jennifer, illus. (p. 502)
—David & the Very Big Giant. Davison, Jennifer, illus. (p. 511)
—Fright of Your Life (p. 788)
—Jonah & the Very Big Fish. Davison, Jennifer, illus. (p. 1177)
—Noah & the Very Big Boat. Davison, Jennifer, illus. (p. 1616)
—Very Noisy Christmas. Davison, Jennifer, illus. (p. 2353)
Thornborrow, Nick, illus. see Walker, Persephone.
Thornborrow, Nick, illus. see Wallace, Carey.
Thornburg, Laura Loehle. Teacher's Practical Guide (Classic Reprint) (p. 2195)
Thornburgh, Blair. Ordinary Girls. (p. 1669)
—Second Banana. Berube, Kate, illus. (p. 1973)
—Skulls! Campbell, Scott, illus. (p. 2033)
—Who's That Girl. (p. 2453)
Thornburgh, Rebecca, illus. see deRubertis, Barbara.
Thornburgh, Rebecca, illus. see Driscoll, Laura.
Thornburgh, Rebecca, illus. see Dussling, Jennifer.
Thornburgh, Rebecca, illus. see Hillert, Margaret.
Thornburgh, Rebecca, illus. see Hopkins, Jackie Mims.
Thornburgh, Rebecca, illus. see Moncure, Jane Belk.
Thornburgh, Rebecca, illus. see Pingry, Patricia A.
Thornburgh, Rebecca, illus. see Redbank, Tennant.
Thornburgh, Rebecca, illus. see Rollins, Jack & Nelson, Steve.
Thornburgh, Rebecca McKillip, illus. see Driscoll, Laura.
Thornburgh, Rebecca McKillip, illus. see Hopkins, Jackie Mims.
Thornburgh, Rebecca McKillip, illus. see Smith, Sherry Weaver.
Thornburgh, Rebecca McKillip, illus. see Stevenson, Robert Louis.
Thornbury, Walter. British Artists from Hogarth to Turner, Vol. 1 Of 2: A Series of Biographical Sketches (Classic Reprint) (p. 283)
—Cross Country (Classic Reprint) (p. 477)
—Greatheart, Vol. 1 of 3 (Classic Reprint) (p. 892)
—Greatheart, Vol. 2 of 3 (Classic Reprint) (p. 892)
—Greatheart, Vol. 3 of 3 (Classic Reprint) (p. 892)
—Ice Bound, Vol. 2 of 3 (Classic Reprint) (p. 1087)
—Ice Bound, Vol. 3 of 3 (Classic Reprint) (p. 1087)
—Life in Spain, Past & Present (Classic Reprint) (p. 1292)
—Life in Spain, Vol. 1 Of 2: Past & Present (Classic Reprint) (p. 1292)
—Turkish Life & Character, Vol. 1 (Classic Reprint) (p. 2300)
—Vicar's Courtship, Vol. 1 of 3 (Classic Reprint) (p. 2355)
—Vicar's Courtship, Vol. 3 (Classic Reprint) (p. 2355)
Thorndike, Ashley Horace, jt. auth. see Baker, Franklin Thomas.
Thorndike, Edward L. English Composition: 150 Specimens Arranged for Use in Psychological & Educational Experiments (Classic Reprint) (p. 653)
—Teacher's Word Book (Classic Reprint) (p. 2195)
Thorndike, Edward Lee. Teacher's Word Book of 30, 000 Words (Classic Reprint) (p. 2195)
Thorndike, John. Student's Pen, Vol. 7: June, 1926 (Classic Reprint) (p. 2143)
Thorne, Adelaide. Anamnesis. Todd, Darren, ed. (p. 79)
—Integer. Todd, Darren, ed. (p. 1125)
—Trace. (p. 2271)
—Trace. Todd, Darren, ed. (p. 2271)
Thorne, Author of Dora. Wedded & Parted (Classic Reprint) (p. 2395)
Thorne, Bella. Autumn's Kiss. (p. 141)
—Autumn's Wish. (p. 141)
Thorne, Bertha. Scaredy-Cat Penguin. (p. 1941)
Thorne, Eglanton. Widowhood of Gabrielle Grant (Classic Reprint) (p. 2461)
Thorne, Frank. Prodigal: Egg of First Light: Egg of First Light. (p. 1803)
Thorne, Guy. Angel (Classic Reprint) (p. 85)
—Chance in Chains: A Story of Monte Carlo. (p. 355)
—Chance in Chains: A Story of Monte Carlo (Classic Reprint) (p. 355)
—Chance in Chains. (p. 355)
—Secret Service Submarine: A Story of the Present War (Classic Reprint) (p. 1979)
—Serf (Classic Reprint) (p. 1990)
—Sharks (Classic Reprint) (p. 2002)
—Socialist (Classic Reprint) (p. 2053)
Thorne, Jack. Recollections of a Sleeping Car Porter (Classic Reprint) (p. 1854)
Thorne, Jenn Marie. Inside of Out. (p. 1123)
—Night Music. (p. 1606)
—Wrong Side of Right. (p. 2514)
Thorne, Jenn Marie & Thorne, Jennifer. Construction Zoo. Hammer, Susie, illus. (p. 444)
Thorne, Jennifer, jt. auth. see Thorne, Jenn Marie.
Thorne, Jenny. Jungle Book. (p. 1189)
Thorne, Jenny, illus. see Adair, Gilbert.
Thorne, Jenny, illus. see Baxter, Nicola, ed.
Thorne, Jenny, illus. see Baxter, Nicola.
Thorne, Jenny, illus. see Dickens, Charles.
Thorne, Jenny, illus. see Jeffs, Stephanie.
Thorne, Jenny, illus. see Kipling, Rudyard.
Thorne, Jenny, illus. see Wilde, Oscar.
Thorne, K. C. Troll of MacKinac. Johnson, Vickie, illus. (p. 2290)
Thorne, Nancy. Victorian Town. (p. 2355)
Thorne, Paul. Secret Toll (Classic Reprint) (p. 1979)
Thorne, Robert. Fugitive Facts (p. 797)
—Fugitive Facts: An Epitome of General Information, Obtained in Large Part from Sources Not Generally Accessible, & Covering More Than One Thousand Topics of General Interest & Frequent Inquiry (Classic Reprint) (p. 797)
Thorne, Troy. Getting Started in Pinewood Derby: Step-by-Step Workbook to Building Your First Car. (p. 826)
Thorne-Thomsen, Gudren. Birch & the Star: And Other Stories (Classic Reprint) (p. 230)
Thorne-Thomsen, Gudrun. East o' the Sun & West o' the Moon: With Other Norwegian Folk Tales. (p. 619)
—East o' the Sun & West o' the Moon: With Other Norwegian Folk Tales (Classic Reprint) (p. 619)
—East O' the Sun & West O' the Moon. Richardson, Frederick, illus. (p. 619)
Thorne-Thomsen, Kathleen. Frank Lloyd Wright for Kids: His Life & Ideas. (p. 777)
Thorney, Kerisha. Different Types of Families. (p. 545)
—Todd the Boastful Fox. (p. 2255)
Thorneycroft, T. Trip to America (Classic Reprint) (p. 2288)
Thornhill, Chris, jt. auth. see King, Michael.
Thornhill, Jan. I Am Josephine (and I Am a Living Thing) Lee, Jacqui, illus. (p. 1059)
—Is This Panama? A Migration Story. Kim, Soyeon, illus. (p. 1138)
—Kyle Goes Alone. Barron, Ashley, illus. (p. 1234)
—Tragic Tale of the Great Auk (p. 2274)
—Triumphant Tale of the House Sparrow (p. 2290)
—Wildlife 123: A Nature Counting Book. (p. 2466)
—Wildlife ABC: A Nature Alphabet Book. Thornhill, Jan, illus. (p. 2466)
—Winter's Coming: A Story of Seasonal Change. Bisaillon, Josée & Bisaillon, Josée, illus. (p. 2476)
Thornhill, Samantha. Card for My Father. Clement, Morgan, illus. (p. 327)
Thornhorn. Kestrel Waters: A Tale of Love & Devil. (p. 1210)
Thornley, Blair, illus. see Tillmanns, Maria Davenza.
Thornley, John, tr. see Zei, Alki.
Thornley, Stew. Kevin Garnett: Champion Basketball Star. (p. 1210)
—Sports Jokes to Tickle Your Funny Bone. (p. 2089)
Thornley, Thomas. Cotton Spinning (Honours, or Third Year). Being a Companion Volume to First Year Cotton Spinning & Intermediate, or Second Year Cotton Spinning. (p. 457)
Thornton, Amy. Meet Sambam. (p. 1439)
Thornton, Barbara, illus. see Stolz, Donald R.
Thornton, Bonnell. Connoisseur, 1755, Vol. 3: By Mr. Town, Critic & Censor-Genera (Classic Reprint) (p. 441)
—Connoisseur, Vol. 3 (Classic Reprint) (p. 441)
Thornton, Caroline L. Blustery Day. Karabach, Alena, illus. (p. 250)
—Scared of the Dark. Boldrin, Elisa, illus. (p. 1941)
Thornton, Catherine & Panckridge, Michael. Be Bully Free. (p. 177)
Thornton, Champ. Radical Book for Kids: Exploring the Roots & Shoots of Faith. (p. 1833)
Thornton, D. S. Scrap City. Bowater, Charlie, illus. (p. 1963)
Thornton, Denise. Living with Cancer: The Ultimate Teen Guide (p. 1334)
Thornton, Edward. Illustrations of the History & Practices of the Thugs: And Notices of Some of the Proceedings of the Government of India, for the Suppression of the Crime of Thuggee (Classic Reprint) (p. 1097)
Thornton, Elizabeth. Truth & Falsehood, Vol. 3 Of 3: A Romance (Classic Reprint) (p. 2296)
Thornton, Harry & Hunter-Higgins, Emily. I Heart Kawaii. (p. 1066)
Thornton, Jeremy. Famous Women of the American Revolution. (p. 704)
—New Industries, New Jobs: British Immigrants Come to America(1830s-1890s) (p. 1594)
Thornton, Jessy Quinn. California Tragedy (Classic Reprint) (p. 311)
Thornton, John. Human Physiology. (p. 1050)
Thornton Jones, Jan. Angel in the Park. (p. 85)
Thornton, Marcellus Eugene. Lady of New Orleans: A Novel of the Present (Classic Reprint) (p. 1237)
Thornton, Marshall. Never Rest. (p. 1590)
Thornton, Mary Taylor. When Pan Pipes: A Fantastic Romance (Classic Reprint) (p. 2432)
Thornton, Peter J., illus. see Dooley, Norah.
Thornton, Randy. Star Wars the Original Trilogy Read-Along Storybook & CD Collection: Read-Along Storybook & CD. Rood, Brian, illus. (p. 2105)
Thornton, Stephen. Alfie & Reid: A Fine Partnership Indeed. Olivier-Argyle, Daniel, illus. (p. 43)
Thornton, Susan, jt. auth. see Steffen, Tim.
Thornton, Susan Ann, jt. auth. see Steffen, Tim.
Thornton W (Thornton Waldo), Burgess. Burgess Bird Book for Children - Scholar's Choice Edition. (p. 299)
Thornton, William Wheeler. Law of Railroad Fences & Private Crossings: Including Injuries to Animals on Right of Way Caused by Negligence (Classic Reprint) (p. 1253)
Thornycroft, Paul. Adventures of Horatio Mowzl: Little Humans. (p. 24)
Thorogood, Keith. Milli Meets the Tooth Fairies. (p. 1467)
Thorold, Arthur. Letters from Brussels, in the Summer Of 1835. (p. 1279)
—Letters from Brussels, in the Summer of 1835 (Classic Reprint) (p. 1279)
Thorold, David, et al. Roman Invaders & Settlers. (p. 1899)
Thoroman, A. M. Classics for the Kansas Schools: Eighth Grade (Classic Reprint) (p. 401)
Thoron, Joe. Kaleidoscope Natural Disasters Group 1 (p. 1202)
Thorp, Michael C. Ben Brown & the Return of the Nephilim. Mazumdar, Sintu, illus. (p. 198)
Thorp, Nathan Howard. Songs of the Cowboys (Classic Reprint) (p. 2063)
Thorpe, Benjamin. Yule-Tide Stories: A Collection of Scandinavian & North German Popular Tales & Traditions, from the Swedish, Danish, & German (Classic Reprint) (p. 2537)
Thorpe, Del, illus. see Kanani, Sheila.
Thorpe, E. G. Pioneering in the Never-Never (Classic Reprint) (p. 1748)
Thorpe, Fred. Ahead of the Show, or the Adventures of Al Allston, Advance Agent (Classic Reprint) (p. 36)
Thorpe, Gary S. AP Environmental Science: With 2 Practice Tests. (p. 104)
—AP Environmental Science Premium: With 5 Practice Tests. (p. 104)
Thorpe, Jack. Little Mix: Test Your Super-Fan Status. (p. 1322)
Thorpe, Jessica. Atheism for Kids. Barnes, Teal, illus. (p. 132)
Thorpe, Judy. Should Gun Control Laws Be Stronger? (p. 2011)
Thorpe, Kiki. Before the Bell. (p. 190)
—Before the Bell. RH Disney Staff & Christy, Jana, illus. (p. 190)
—Beyond Never Land (p. 211)
—Beyond Never Land. (p. 211)
—Dandelion Wish. Christy, Jana, illus. (p. 501)
—Dandelion Wish/from the Mist (Disney: the Never Girls) Christy, Jana, illus. (p. 501)
—Dark Forest. (p. 506)
—Fairy's Gift (Disney: the Never Girls) Christy, Jana, illus. (p. 698)
—Fairy's Gift (Disney: the Never Girls) RH Disney Staff, illus. (p. 698)
—Far from Shore. (p. 708)
—Finding Tinker Bell #1: Beyond Never Land (Disney: the Never Girls) Christy, Jana, illus. (p. 730)
—Finding Tinker Bell #2 (Disney: the Never Girls) Christy, Jana, illus. (p. 730)
—Finding Tinker Bell #2: Through the Dark Forest (Disney: the Never Girls) Christy, Jana, illus. (p. 730)
—Finding Tinker Bell: Books #1-6 (Disney: the Never Girls) Christy, Jana, illus. (p. 730)
—In a Blink. Christy, Jana, illus. (p. 1103)
—In the Game. (p. 1109)
—Into the Waves. (p. 1128)
—Lost & Found Weekend. Bongini, Barbara, illus. (p. 1352)
—Never Girls #1: in a Blink (Disney: the Never Girls) Christy, Jana, illus. (p. 1590)
—Never Girls #10: on the Trail (Disney: the Never Girls) Christy, Jana, illus. (p. 1590)
—Never Girls #11: into the Waves (Disney: the Never Girls) Christy, Jana, illus. (p. 1590)
—Never Girls #12: in the Game (Disney: the Never Girls) Christy, Jana, illus. (p. 1590)
—Never Girls #2: the Space Between (Disney: the Never Girls) Christy, Jana, illus. (p. 1590)
—Never Girls #3: a Dandelion Wish (Disney: the Never Girls) Christy, Jana, illus. (p. 1590)
—Never Girls #4: from the Mist (Disney: the Never Girls) Christy, Jana, illus. (p. 1590)
—Never Girls #5: Wedding Wings (Disney: the Never Girls) Christy, Jana, illus. (p. 1590)
—Never Girls #6: the Woods Beyond (Disney: the Never Girls) Christy, Jana, illus. (p. 1590)
—Never Girls #7: a Pinch of Magic (Disney: the Never Girls) Christy, Jana, illus. (p. 1590)
—Never Girls #8: Far from Shore (Disney: the Never Girls) Christy, Jana, illus. (p. 1590)
—Never Girls #9: Before the Bell (Disney: the Never Girls) Christy, Jana, illus. (p. 1590)
—Never Girls: Books 4-6 (Disney: the Never Girls) Christy, Jana, illus. (p. 1590)
—Never Girls Collection #1 (Disney: the Never Girls) Books 1-4 RH Disney, illus. (p. 1590)
—Never Girls Collection #2 (Disney: the Never Girls) Books 5-8 Christy, Jana, illus. (p. 1590)
—Never Girls Collection #3 (Disney: the Never Girls) Books 9-12 Christy, Jana, illus. (p. 1590)
—Never Girls Volume 1: Books 1-3 (Disney: the Never Girls) Christy, Jana, illus. (p. 1590)
—Never Girls Volume 3: Books 7-9 (Disney: the Never Girls) Christy, Jana, illus. (p. 1590)
—On the Lost Coast (p. 1655)
—Pinch of Magic. (p. 1745)
—Runaway Chicken: Woodworking. Diaz, Maine, illus. (p. 1915)
—Space Between. Christy, Jana, illus. (p. 2070)
—Through the Dark Forest (p. 2237)
—Under the Lagoon. Christy, Jana, illus. (p. 2322)
—Up the Misty Peak. Christy, Jana, illus. (p. 2338)
—Wedding Wings. (p. 2395)
—Woods Beyond. Christy, Jana, illus. (p. 2492)
Thorpe, Kiki, see McCoy, Mimi, pseud.
Thorpe, McKenzie, illus. see Helein, Collin Matthew.
Thorpe, Nicholas, illus. see Powers, Elaine A.
Thorpe, Patricia A. Canada Goslings: Lilly & Scooter a Lesson Learned. (p. 320)
—Chucky the Black Squirrel: A Lesson Learned. (p. 390)
—Harry the Hummingbird: A Lesson Learned. (p. 935)
Thorpe, Patrick, ed. see Himekawa, Akira, et al.
Thorpe, Patrick, ed. see Norton, Mike & Hopeless, Dennis.
Thorpe, Patrick, ed. see Remender, Rick.
Thorpe, Rochelle O'Neal. Gabe & the Park & His Big Toy Box: Learning Your Environment, Numbers, & Shapes. Arias, Cinday, illus. (p. 804)
—Gabe's Nantucket Adventure: Daffodils, Dogs, & Cars. Nakell, Eugenie, ed. (p. 804)
—Surprise Pour Dolly: Dolly's Winter Surprise. Brovender, Jacqueline Grenez, tr. (p. 2163)
Thorpe, Rose (Hartwick). White Lady of la Jolla (Classic Reprint) (p. 2444)
Thorpe, Scott & Field Character Staff. Draw a d*ck on It: A Naughty Drawing Game. (p. 597)
Thorpe, Thomas Bangs. Hive of the Bee-Hunter: A Repository of Sketches, Including Peculiar American Character (Classic Reprint) (p. 982)
—Master's House: A Tale of Southern Life (Classic Reprint) (p. 1419)
Thorpe, Yvonne. Snowboarding. (p. 2048)
—Ultimate Guide to Women's Football. (p. 2315)
Thorpe, Yvonne, jt. auth. see Downing, David.
Thorndyke, Julie. Watching Through the Day. Vines, Nandina, illus. (p. 2384)
Thorsland, Dan, ed. see Starlin, Jim, et al.
Thorson, Robert & Thorson, Kristine. Stone Wall Secrets. Moore, Gustav, illus. (p. 2121)
Thrace, Mischa. My Whole Truth. (p. 1565)
Thrall, Sara & Thrall, Gloria. Mud Stew for Two. (p. 1524)
Thran, Nick. Halifax Hal. Foreman, Gabe, illus. (p. 911)
Thrash, Maggie. Honor Girl: A Graphic Memoir. (p. 999)
—Honor Girl: A Graphic Memoir. Thrash, Maggie, illus. (p. 999)
—Lost Soul, Be at Peace. Thrash, Maggie, illus. (p. 1355)
—Strange Lies. (p. 2138)
—Strange Truth. (p. 2138)
—Watch Your Back (W. T.) (p. 2383)
—We Know It Was You. (p. 2391)
Thrasher, Amanda M. Fairy Match in the Mushroom Patch. (p. 696)
—Ghost of Whispering Willow. (p. 828)
—Mischief in the Mushroom Patch. (p. 1477)
Thrasher, Brian, illus. see Bowlin, Serina.
Thrasher, David. Adventures of Super-Newsboy. (p. 28)
Thrasher, Grady. Tim & Sally's Year in Poems. Rabon, Elaine Hearn, illus. (p. 2243)
Thrasher, Jeanni. Gumbo the Bayou Dog. Browne, Stephanie, illus. (p. 905)
—Surfing, Dancing Seeds of Glory. (p. 2163)
Thrasher, Sarah Murray. As God Made Her: A Story of a Fair Californian (Classic Reprint) (p. 124)
Thrasher, Travis. Tommy Nelson's Brave Girls Confidential: Stories & Secrets about Faith & Friendship Ivanov, Olga and Aleksey, illus. (p. 2259)
Thrasher, Travis, jt. auth. see MattyB.
Three-Thirty, Inc., illus. see Bazaldua, Barbara.
Threlfall, Evelyn. Starlight Songs. (p. 2106)
Thrift, Lynda. Traveller's Tales. (p. 2280)
Thrift, Tim. Tim Talks (Classic Reprint) (p. 2243)
—Tim Thoughts (Classic Reprint) (p. 2243)
Thring, C. H. M. Trials & Pleasures of an Uncompleted Tour (Classic Reprint) (p. 2286)
Thronson, Lloyd. Gomer the Goat & His New Home. (p. 861)
—White Rockets with Four Hooves. (p. 2445)
Throop, George Higby. Bertie, or Life in the Old Field: A Humorous Novel (Classic Reprint) (p. 204)
Throp, Claire. All about Flowers. (p. 49)
—All about Leaves. (p. 49)
—All about Plants. (p. 50)
—All about Roots. (p. 50)
—All about Seeds. (p. 50)
—All about Stems. (p. 50)
—Curling (p. 488)
—Day Inside the Human Body: Fantasy Science Field Trips (p. 513)
—England (p. 652)
—Exploring Other Worlds: What Is Science Fiction? (p. 682)
—Fantasy Science Field Trips (p. 708)
—Figure Skating (p. 726)
—Heroes of World War Two. (p. 962)
—Horrors of the Bubonic Plague. (p. 1004)
—Horrors of the Holocaust. (p. 1004)
—Ice Dancing. (p. 1087)
—Israel (p. 1140)
—Italy (p. 1142)

T

Tiegreen, Alan, illus. see Cole, Joanna & Calmenson, Stephanie.
Tiehel, Amy. Long Ago & Far Away Ancient Egypt: Ancient Egypt. (p. 1342)
Tiel, C. Van. Literary Reading Book, Vol. 2: Containing Specimens of Poetry & Prose from Chaucer to the Present Day; the 19th Century (Classic Reprint) (p. 1309)
Tielesh, Simone. Kindness Is... Cartwrigth, Aidan, illus. (p. 1219)
Tien, Wai, illus. see Robertson, David A.
Tieran, Mary Spear Nicholas. Homoselle (Classic Reprint) (p. 998)
Tieri, Frank & Williams, Leah. Absolute Carnage: Lethal Protectors. Alburquerque, Alberto Jimenez & Larroca, Salvador, illus. (p. 9)
Tiernan, Cate. Darkest Fear. (p. 507)
—Darkness Falls. (p. 508)
—Eternally Yours. (p. 665)
—Immortal Beloved. (p. 1101)
—Sweep: Reckoning, Full Circle, & Night's Child. Vol. 5 (p. 2168)
—Sweep: Book of Shadows, the Coven, & Blood Witch: Volume 1. (p. 2168)
Tiernan, Mary Spear. Jack Horner: A Novel (Classic Reprint) (p. 1152)
Tierney, Adam. Afraid of Everything. Cousin, Matthieu, illus. (p. 31)
Tierney, James. Keeper of the Sword: The Legend of Ziems. (p. 1208)
Tierney, James B. Legend of Ziems: The Coming of Ziems. (p. 1263)
Tierney, Jim, illus. see Albert, Melissa.
Tierney, Jim, illus. see Oppel, Kenneth.
Tierney, John. Jack, Tommy & the Phoenix Street Firefighters. Algar, James, illus. (p. 1153)
Tierney, Josh. Spera: Ascension of the Starless Vol. 2. Rebelka, Jakub, illus. (p. 2079)
—Warm Blood Vol. 1. (p. 2379)
Tierney, Josh & Maybury, Paul. Hunters. (p. 1053)
Tierney, Kathleen & Kiernan, Caitlin R. Cherry Bomb. (p. 366)
Tierney, Kendra. Little Book about Confession for Children. (p. 1312)
Tierney, Leslie. Freddy the Firefly Shines His Light. (p. 781)
Tierney, Mitchell. Heather Cassidy & the Magnificent MR Harlow. (p. 946)
Tierney, Tom. Byzantine Fashions. (p. 306)
—Famous Movie Dance Stars Paper Dolls. (p. 704)
—Fashions from India. (p. 712)
—Fashions of the Roaring Twenties Coloring Book. (p. 712)
—Givenchy Paper Dolls. (p. 840)
—Greek & Roman Fashions. (p. 892)
—Legendary Baseball Stars. (p. 1263)
—Life's a Drag! Paper Dolls. (p. 1296)
—Mexican Folk Dance Paper Dolls. (p. 1454)
—Michelle Obama Paper Dolls. (p. 1458)
—Movie Mobsters Paper Dolls. (p. 1516)
—Nelson Mandela Paper Dolls. (p. 1587)
—Pin-Up Girls of World War II. (p. 1745)
—Woodstock Paper Dolls: 50th Anniversary Edition. (p. 2492)
Tierney, Tom & Paper Dolls for Grownups Staff. Betty Grable Paper Dolls. (p. 209)
Tierney, Tom, et al. Award-Winning Fashions of Edith Head Paper Dolls. (p. 143)
Tierra, Lesley. Kid's Herb Book: For Children of All Ages. Wilson, Susie, illus. (p. 1215)
Tietjen, Amy. Birds I've Met Through the Alphabet. Fitts, Seth, illus. (p. 232)
—Bugs I've Met Through the Alphabet. Fitts, Seth, illus. (p. 292)
Tietjens, Eunice. Jake (Classic Reprint) (p. 1155)
Tietz, Heather. Giving Plate. Foster, Jack, illus. (p. 840)
—Rockabye Baby Jesus. Miller, Nancy, illus. (p. 1894)
—Yes, Jesus Loves You. Miller, Nancy, illus. (p. 2521)
Tietz, Joan Peterson. O Holy Night! (p. 1633)
Tiffany, Charles Comfort. Prayer Book & the Christian Life: Or, the Conception of the Christian Life Implied in the Book of Common Prayer. (p. 1785)
Tiffany, Esther B. Way to His Pocket: A Comedy in One Act (Classic Reprint) (p. 2387)
Tiffany, Esther Brown. Autograph Letter: A Comedy in Three Acts (Classic Reprint) (p. 140)
Tiffany, Flavel Benjamin. Trip to the Land of the Midnight Sun: Summer of 1905 (Classic Reprint) (p. 2289)
Tiffany, Linn. Let's Cheer with Big Al. (p. 1270)
Tiffany, Osmond. Brandon, or a Hundred Years Ago: A Tale of the American Colonies (Classic Reprint) (p. 275)
Tiffany, Sean, illus. see Maddox, Jake.
Tiffany, Sean, illus. see Pryor, Shawn & Maddox, Jake.
Tiffany, Sean, illus. see Stevens, Eric & Maddox, Jake.
Tiffany, Sean, illus. see Suen, Anastasia & Maddox, Jake.
Tiffanyj. Super Beauty Saves the Day. (p. 2154)
TIG, Thomas. Illustrated Treasury of Classic Stories. Kelly, Richard, ed. (p. 1096)
—Illustrated Treasury of Princess Stories. Kelly, Richard, ed. (p. 1096)
Tig, Thomas, jt. auth. see Blake, Carly.
Tigas, Francis. Polluted Asia 2080. (p. 1771)
Tigay, Betty S. Rich People, & Other Stories (Classic Reprint) (p. 1876)
Tiger Tales. 100 First Words. (p. 2557)
—123 Count with Me. Birkett, Georgie, illus. (p. 2559)
—123 Counting Sticker Book. Galloway, Fhiona, illus. (p. 2559)
—ABC Alphabet Sticker Book. Galloway, Fhiona, illus. (p. 3)
—Baby Animals. (p. 148)
—Baby Firsts: Record Cards for Baby's Important Milestones! Ward, Sarah, illus. (p. 150)
—Baby Peekaboo! Delahaye, Genine, illus. (p. 152)
—Baby's First Bear. Ward, Sarah, illus. (p. 154)
—Baby's First Bunny. Ward, Sarah, illus. (p. 154)
—Bedtime Prayer. Rescek, Sanja, illus. (p. 188)
—Chicken Little. East, Nick, illus. (p. 368)
—Christmas: Holiday Fun. (p. 383)
—Christmas Prayer. Rescek, Sanja, illus. (p. 386)
—Christmas Sticker Activities. Ordas, Emi, illus. (p. 387)
—Christmas Surprise. (p. 387)
—Count 123. (p. 458)
—Dinosaur, Dinosaur, Say Good Night. Rescek, Sanja, illus. (p. 548)
—Elves & the Shoemaker. Waters, Erica-Jane, illus. (p. 640)
—Farm. (p. 709)
—First ABC. (p. 735)
—First Colors. (p. 736)
—First Numbers. (p. 738)
—First Words. (p. 740)
—Five Little Pumpkins. Mantle, Ben, illus. (p. 744)
—Fun on the Farm. Lucas, Gareth, illus. (p. 799)
—Funny Faces Sticker Fun! Tiger Tales, illus. (p. 801)
—Gingerbread Man. Latimer, Miriam, illus. (p. 834)
—Good Night Baby! Ward, Sarah, illus. (p. 863)
—Halloween Sticker Activities. Ordas, Emi, illus. (p. 912)
—Halloween Surprise. (p. 912)
—Happy Snappy Crab. Lucas, Gareth, illus. (p. 923)
—Hello Baby! Ward, Sarah, illus. (p. 950)
—He's Got the Whole World in His Hands. Ho, Hanh Dung, illus. (p. 963)
—Hey, Diddle, Diddle: And Other Favorite Nursery Rhymes. Wood, Hannah, illus. (p. 964)
—Hickory, Dickory, Dock. Delahaye, Genine, illus. (p. 965)
—Hug! Mantle, Ben, illus. (p. 1047)
—I Love Mommy! Ward, Sarah, illus. (p. 1070)
—I Love You, Grandma. Tyger, Rory, illus. (p. 1078)
—I Love You, Little One. Mason, Suzie, illus. (p. 1079)
—Is for Apple. Birkett, Georgie, illus. (p. 1136)
—Let's Find the Dinosaur. Willmore, Alex, illus. (p. 1273)
—Let's Find the Kitten. Willmore, Alex, illus. (p. 1273)
—Let's Find the Mermaid. Willmore, Alex, illus. (p. 1273)
—Let's Find the Penguin. Willmore, Alex, illus. (p. 1273)
—Let's Find the Puppy. Willmore, Alex, illus. (p. 1273)
—Let's Find the Tiger. Willmore, Alex, illus. (p. 1273)
—Lift & See Farm. (p. 1297)
—Love You, Baby! Ward, Sarah, illus. (p. 1361)
—My Busy Day. (p. 1535)
—My First Bedtime Prayers. Jones, Anna, illus. (p. 1540)
—My First Listen, Play, & Say! Ward, Sarah, illus. (p. 1544)
—My First Touch, Feel, & Play! Ward, Sarah, illus. (p. 1546)
—My Little Book of Bedtime Prayers. Jones, Anna, illus. (p. 1552)
—Noisy Farm. (p. 1617)
—Noisy Trucks. (p. 1618)
—Nursery Rhymes. Galloway, Fhiona, illus. (p. 1631)
—Old MacDonald Had a Farm: And Other Favorite Children's Songs. Wood, Hannah, illus. (p. 1646)
—Peekaboo Baby! Ward, Sarah, illus. (p. 1713)
—Peekaboo Baby Animals. Frost, Maddie, illus. (p. 1713)
—Pets. (p. 1731)
—Pinocchio. Watson, Richard, illus. (p. 1747)
—Rumpelstiltskin. Schauer, Loretta, illus. (p. 1914)
—Snow White. Demidova, Olga, illus. (p. 2048)
—Teddy Bear, Teddy Bear: And Other Favorite Nursery Rhymes. Lenton, Steven, illus. (p. 2198)
—Ten in the Bed. Guile, Gill, illus. (p. 2204)
—Ten Little Dinosaurs. Barlow, Lisa & Barlow, Damien, illus. (p. 2204)
—Ten Little Lovebugs. Galloway, Ruth, illus. (p. 2204)
—Ten Sparkly Snowflakes. Julian, Sean, illus. (p. 2205)
—Ten Splishy, Splashy Fish. Tarbett, Debbie, illus. (p. 2205)
—Ten Tiny Gingerbread Men. Galloway, Fhiona, illus. (p. 2205)
—Ten Twinkly Stars. Julian, Russell, illus. (p. 2205)
—Things to Learn. (p. 2221)
—Things to See. (p. 2221)
—This Little Light of Mine. Kolvanovic, Dubravka, illus. (p. 2226)
—This Little Piggy: And Other Favorite Action Rhymes. Wood, Hannah, illus. (p. 2226)
—This Little Piggy. Delahaye, Genine, illus. (p. 2226)
—Three Billy Goats Gruff. Pankhurst, Kate, illus. (p. 2232)
—Three Little Pigs. Jatkowska, Ag, illus. (p. 2233)
—Twinkle, Twinkle, Little Baby. Ward, Sarah, illus. (p. 2305)
—Twinkle, Twinkle, Little Star: A Book of Bedtime Rhymes with a Soft Star Lovey. Rescek, Sanja, illus. (p. 2305)
—Twinkle, Twinkle, Little Star. Rescek, Sanja, illus. (p. 2305)
—Ugly Duckling. Eastland, Sue, illus. (p. 2313)
Tiger Tales Staff. 5 Minute Nursery Rhymes. (p. 2548)
—Five Minute Bedtime Stories. (p. 744)
—Lift & See Animals. (p. 1297)
—Peek-A-Boo! Mantle, Ben, illus. (p. 1712)
Tiger Tales Staff, ed. see Kanzler, John.
Tiger Tales Staff, ed. see Vasylenko, Veronica.
Tiger Tales Staff, creator. 100 First Animals. (p. 2557)
—100 First Words. (p. 2557)
—5 Minute Farm Tales. (p. 2548)
—Farm Puzzle + Book. (p. 710)
—Things That Go. (p. 2221)
Tiger Tales Staff, ed. Animals Go. Emily, Bolam, illus. (p. 94)
—Animals Talk. Emily, Bolam, illus. (p. 95)
—Easter Surprise: My First Lift & Learn. (p. 620)
—Jingle Bells: A Collection of Songs & Carols. Kolvanovic, Dubravka, illus. (p. 1169)
—Kittens. (p. 1226)
—Puppies. (p. 1814)
—Stories for Boys. (p. 2123)
—Stories for Girls. (p. 2123)
Tigerstedt, Robert. Text-Book of Human Physiology (Classic Reprint) (p. 2210)
Tigga, Amrit, illus. see Clouser, Lisa M.
Tighe, Francis O. Sullivan. Portion of a Champion (Classic Reprint) (p. 1779)
Til, Books, jt. auth. see Cherry, T. S.
Tiitinen, Esko-Pekka. Drops of Life. Claret Pyrhonen, Emma, tr. (p. 605)
Tiitinen, Nikolai, illus. see Tiitinen, Esko-Pekka.
Tijerina, Arnold G., III, ed. see Schlaht, Kim.
Tijms, Henk. Basic Probability: What Every Math Student Should Know. (p. 169)
Tiki Machine, LLC Staff, creator. Deus Libris: An Illustrated Collection. (p. 535)
Tiki Papier, Tiki, illus. see Ware, Lesley.
Tikulin, Tomislav, illus. see Collins, A. L.
Tilak, Brian, illus. see Elliott, Sherria L.
Tilby, Ginny. You Should, You Should! (p. 2528)
Tilde, photos by see Kim, Sue.
Tilden, Catherine. First Patient: A Story, Written in Aid of the Fair for the Channing Home (Classic Reprint) (p. 738)
Tilden, Freeman. Khaki: How Tredick Got into the War (Classic Reprint) (p. 1212)
—Mr. Podd (Classic Reprint) (p. 1520)
—That Night & Other Satires (Classic Reprint) (p. 2213)
Tilden, Len Ellsworth. Emigrant's Daughter: A Border Drama, in Three Acts (Classic Reprint) (p. 641)
—Stolen Will: A Comedy Drama, in Three Acts (Classic Reprint) (p. 2121)
—Stolen Will. (p. 2121)
Tilden, Mark. Adventures of Princess Mikaila & Prince Pete. (p. 27)
Tilden, Thomasine E. Lewis. Flesh Wound: A Minor Injury Takes a Deadly Turn. (p. 748)
—Mind Games! Can a Psychic Tell What You're Thinking? (p. 1469)
—Worms! Parasites Plague a Village. (p. 2508)
Tildes, Phyllis Limbacher. Baby Animals Day & Night. Tildes, Phyllis Limbacher, illus. (p. 148)
—Baby Animals Spots & Stripes. Tildes, Phyllis Limbacher, illus. (p. 148)
—Baby's First Book of Birds & Colors. Tildes, Phyllis Limbacher, illus. (p. 154)
—Bunny's Big Surprise. Tildes, Phyllis Limbacher, illus. (p. 298)
—Magic Babushka. Tildes, Phyllis Limbacher, illus. (p. 1377)
—Will You Be Mine? A Nursery Rhyme Romance. Tildes, Phyllis Limbacher, illus. (p. 2467)
Tildes, Phyllis Limbacher, illus. see Arnold, Marsha Diane.
Tildes, Phyllis Limbacher, illus. see Farmer, Jacqueline.
Tildes, Phyllis Limbacher, illus. see Goodman, Emily.
Tileston, Amelia Peabody. Amelia Peabody Tileston: And Her Canteens for the Serbs (Classic Reprint) (p. 69)
Tileston, Eleanor Boies. Eleanor Boies Tileston, (1886-1912) (Classic Reprint) (p. 630)
Tileston, Mary W. Sugar & Spice: And All That's Nice (Classic Reprint) (p. 2147)
Tileston, Merrill. Chiquita an American Novel; the Romance of an Ute Chief's Daughter (Classic Reprint) (p. 379)
Tilford, Greg L., jt. auth. see Wulff, Mary L.
Tilford, Tilden. Butternut Jones: A Lambkin of the West (Classic Reprint) (p. 304)
Till, Tom. Photographing the World: A Guide to Photographing 201 of the Most Beautiful Places on Earth. Martres, Laurent, ed. (p. 1736)
Tillen, James. Close Look at Soil. (p. 407)
Tiller, Amy. My Sister Is Like a Baby Bird. Tiller, Amy, illus. (p. 1561)
Tiller, Bill, illus. see Kobren, Myles Scott.
Tiller, Martin. Charlotte Morgan & the Lemonade Stand. (p. 361)
Tiller, Paul, illus. see Tiller, Jerome.
Tiller, Richard. Sid Smart: Eating. (p. 2014)
—Sid Smart: Moving. Tiller, Richard, illus. (p. 2014)
Tillery, Paul, jt. auth. see Tillery, Paul, IV.
Tillery, Paul, IV. Thundercluck! Chicken of Thor. Wittwer, Meg & Tillery, Paul, IV, illus. (p. 2238)
—Thundercluck! Chicken of Thor: Recipe for Revenge. Tillery, Paul, IV & Wittwer, Meg, illus. (p. 2238)
—Thundercluck! Chicken of Thor: Recipe for Revenge. Wittwer, Meg & Tillery, Paul, IV, illus. (p. 2238)
Tillery, Paul, IV & Tillery, Paul. Thundercluck! Tillery, Paul, IV et al, illus. (p. 2238)
Tilley. Damaged. (p. 499)
Tilley, Adrian. Spider's Web. (p. 2081)
Tilley, Cecilia Frances. Chollerton: A Tale of Our Own Times (Classic Reprint) (p. 381)
Tilley, Debbie, illus. see Danzig, Dianne.
Tilley, Debbie, illus. see George, Kristine O'Connell.
Tilley, Debbie, illus. see Gilson, Jamie.
Tilley, Debbie, illus. see Hurwitz, Johanna.
Tilley, Debbie, illus. see Jane, Pamela.
Tilley, Debbie, illus. see Kudlinski, Kathleen V.
Tilley, R. Sudgen, ed. see Salten, Felix.
Tilley, Scott, illus. see Herman, Gail.
Tilley, Scott, illus. see Saxon, Victoria & RH Disney Staff.
Tilley, Scott, illus. see Uyeda, Laura.
Tilley, Shiho, illus. see Francis, Suzanne.
Tilley, Sophie. Sparkly Shoes & Picnic Parties. (p. 2075)
Tillie, C. Dawn. Imani's Bad Day. Tillie, Chiquanda, illus. (p. 1100)
Tillie, Chiquanda. Believe: A Coloring Book of Positive Affirmations: Coloring Book. Tillie, Chiquanda, illus. (p. 196)
—Oh Boy. (p. 1641)
—Search for the Perfect Snack. (p. 1971)
Tillie, Chiquanda, illus. see Alston, Ronalyn T.
Tillie, Chiquanda, illus. see Tillie, C. Dawn.
Tillie, Chiquanda D. Believe- a Book of Positive Affirmations. (p. 196)
Tillie, V. Little Tom (Classic Reprint) (p. 1329)
Tillier, Claude. Belle-Plante & Cornelius (Classic Reprint) (p. 197)
—My Uncle Benjamin: A Humorous, Satirical, & Philosophical Novel (Classic Reprint) (p. 1563)
—My Uncle Benjamin (Classic Reprint) (p. 1563)
Tillinger, Theresa D. & Freeman, Patti Bowman. Homecoming: Shafer's Tale of Lost & Found. Brock, Jason S., illus. (p. 997)
Tillit, L. B. 2 Days. (p. 2546)
—Unchained. (p. 2317)
Tillman, Charles. Middle School Rules of Charles Tillman. (p. 1460)
Tillman, Gloria J. Teeth for Thanksgiving. Tillman, Gloria J., ed. (p. 2201)
Tillman, Katherine Davis. Fifty Years of Freedom, or from Cabin to Congress: A Drama in Five Acts (Classic Reprint) (p. 724)
Tillman, Nancy. Because You're Mine. (p. 186)
—Crown on Your Head. Tillman, Nancy, illus. (p. 479)
—Heaven of Animals. Tillman, Nancy, illus. (p. 947)
—I Knew You Could Do It! Tillman, Nancy, illus. (p. 1067)
—I'd Know You Anywhere, My Love. Tillman, Nancy, illus. (p. 1089)
—Nancy Tillman's the World Is a Wonderland Collection: (the World Is a Wonderland; If You Were an Animal; Let It Snow!; If I Owned the Moon; Sweet Dreams) (p. 1574)
—On the Night You Were Born (p. 1655)
—On the Night You Were Born. (p. 1655)
—Spirit of Christmas. Tillman, Nancy, illus. (p. 2083)
—Tumford the Terrible. (p. 2299)
—Tumford the Terrible. Tillman, Nancy, illus. (p. 2299)
—Tumford's Rude Noises. (p. 2299)
—Wherever You Are: My Love Will Find You. Tillman, Nancy, illus. (p. 2441)
—You & Me & the Wishing Tree. (p. 2524)
—You Are Loved: Welcome Wishes for New Babies. (p. 2524)
—You're All Kinds of Wonderful. Tillman, Nancy, illus. (p. 2535)
—You're Here for a Reason. (p. 2535)
Tillman, Nancy, illus. see Tutu, Desmond.
Tillmanns, Maria Davenza. Why We Are in Need of Tails. Thornley, Blair, illus. (p. 2459)
Tillmar, Kimberly. Kalli & the Cants. (p. 1202)
Tillotson, Katherine, illus. see Jackson, Richard.
Tillotson, Katherine, illus. see Lyon, George Ella.
Tillotson, Katherine, illus. see Mcdonald, Megan.
Tillson, Linda L., illus. see Ryan, Christopher.
Tillworth, Mary. Aladdin. (p. 39)
—All Bottled up! (Shimmer & Shine) Laviosa, Mattia Francesco, illus. (p. 51)
—All-Star Pups! (Paw Patrol) Petrossi, Fabrizio, illus. (p. 53)
—Backyard Ballet (Shimmer & Shine) Hee, Liana, illus. (p. 156)
—Barbie Fall 2014 DVD Little Golden Book. (p. 165)
—Barbie in Princess Power. (p. 165)
—Big Monster, Little Monster. Random House Disney Staff, illus. (p. 221)
—Big Truck Show! (p. 223)
—Blaze Loves to Race! (Blaze & the Monster Machines) Kobasic, Kevin, illus. (p. 243)
—Boots & Dora Forever! (Dora & Friends) Aikins, David, illus. (p. 262)
—Bouncy Tires! (Blaze & the Monster Machines) Burch, Benjamin, illus. (p. 265)
—Bubble Trouble! (Blaze & the Monster Machines) Kobasic, Kevin, illus. (p. 289)
—Busy as a Bee! Moroney, Christopher, illus. (p. 301)
—Color Fiesta! (Dora & Friends) Random House, illus. (p. 420)
—Cupcake Challenge! (p. 485)
—Cupcake Challenge! (Barbie: Life in the Dreamhouse) (p. 485)
—Dino Parade! (Blaze & the Monster Machines) Martinez, Heather, illus. (p. 547)
—Dora in Wonderland. (p. 585)
—Dora in Wonderland (Dora the Explorer) Miller, Victoria, illus. (p. 585)
—Dora's Christmas Star (Dora the Explorer) Miller, Victoria, illus. (p. 586)
—Dump Truck Trouble/Let's Build a Doghouse! (Bubble Guppies) Random House Beginners Books Staff & MJ Illustrations Staff, illus. (p. 610)
—Fairytale Adventure. (p. 698)
—Fairytale Adventure (Dora the Explorer) Jackson, Mike, illus. (p. 698)
—Falcon Quest! (Blaze & the Monster Machines) Aikins, Dave, illus. (p. 699)
—Fall 2017 Cars 3 Deluxe Step into Reading (Disney/Pixar Cars 3) (p. 699)
—Firefighter Gil! (Bubble Guppies) Nunn, Paul E., illus. (p. 733)
—Happy Holidays, Bubble Guppies! (Bubble Guppies) Jackson, Mike, illus. (p. 922)
—Here Come the Bubble Guppies! (Bubble Guppies) Random House Staff, illus. (p. 957)
—I Am Buzz Lightyear (Disney/Pixar Toy Story) RH Disney, illus. (p. 1058)
—It's Time for Ballet! (Bubble Guppies) MJ Illustrations, illus. (p. 1148)
—King for a Day! (PAW Patrol) Jackson, Mike, illus. (p. 1220)
—Leah's Dream Dollhouse (Shimmer & Shine) Yum, Heekyoung, illus. (p. 1255)
—Licensed to Drive. (p. 1287)
—Magical Manners! (Shimmer & Shine) Golden Books & Cartobaleno Staff, illus. (p. 1380)
—Meet Rusty Rivets! (p. 1439)
—Mermaid Treasure Hunt. (p. 1449)
—Mermaid Treasure Hunt (Dora & Friends) Aikins, David, illus. (p. 1449)
—Movie Night Magic! (p. 1516)
—Movie Night Magic! (Shimmer & Shine) Aikins, David, illus. (p. 1516)
—Mulan. (p. 1525)
—Mulan Deluxe Step into Reading (Disney Princess) RH Disney, illus. (p. 1525)
—My Heart Is Bright! (Nella the Princess Knight) Haskett, Dan & Goddard-Laurence, Brenda, illus. (p. 1549)
—Nala & Simba. (p. 1573)
—Nala & Simba (Disney the Lion King) Disney Storybook Artists, illus. (p. 1573)
—Nickelodeon 5-Minute Stories Collection. Random House, illus. (p. 1603)
—Old Racers, New Racers. (p. 1648)
—Old Racers, New Racers (Disney/Pixar Cars 3) RH Disney, illus. (p. 1648)
—Police Officer Blaze! (Blaze & the Monster Machines) Aikins, Dave, illus. (p. 1770)
—Ready, Set, Tow! (Blaze & the Monster Machines) Golden Books, illus. (p. 1848)
—Rock & Rule. Golden Books, illus. (p. 1894)
—Rusty Rocks! (Rusty Rivets) Aikins, Dave, illus. (p. 1917)
—Show Your Love! (Shimmer & Shine) Golden Books Staff & Aikins, Dave, illus. (p. 2012)
—Skate Like a Ninja! (Teenage Mutant Ninja Turtles) Golden Books, illus. (p. 2029)
—Sleepover Surprise (Sunny Day) Watermark Rights Limited, illus. (p. 2037)
—Spark Bug Rescue! (Blaze & the Monster Machines) Aikins, Dave, illus. (p. 2074)

—Stuntmania! (Blaze & the Monster Machines) Hechtenkopf, Omar, illus. (p. 2145)
—Sweet Smells of Zahramay Falls (Shimmer & Shine) Random House & Cartobaleno Staff, illus. (p. 2169)
—Sweetest Cupcake (Shimmer & Shine) Cartobaleno, illus. (p. 2169)
—Treasure Twins! (Shimmer & Shine) Cartobaleno, illus. (p. 2282)
—Triple-Track Train Race! (Bubble Guppies) Unten, Eren, illus. (p. 2289)
—Up in the Air/under the Waves! (PAW Patrol) Random House, illus. (p. 2338)
—Welcome to Fairy World! (Dora & Friends) Aikins, David, illus. (p. 2398)
—Who's Afraid of Monsters? (Sesame Street) Mathieu, Joe, illus. (p. 2453)
—Wish upon a Sleepover (Shimmer & Shine) Hee, Liana, illus. (p. 2478)
—Wonder Woman: an Amazing Hero! (DC Super Friends) Doescher, Erik, illus. (p. 2489)
—Zeg & the Egg. Foley, Niki, illus. (p. 2539)
—Zeg & the Egg (Blaze & the Monster Machines) Foley, Niki, illus. (p. 2539)
Tillworth, Mary, jt. auth. see Depken, Kristen L.
Tillworth, Mary, jt. auth. see Golden Books Staff.
Tillworth, Mary, jt. auth. see Man-Kong, Mary.
Tillworth, Mary, jt. auth. see Random House.
Tillworth, Mary, jt. auth. see Sky Koster, Amy.
Tillworth, Mary, adapted by. Pua & Heihei. (p. 1810)
—Sherlock Gnomes Movie Novelization. (p. 2006)
—Sherlock Gnomes the Deluxe Movie Novelization. (p. 2006)
Tilly, illus. see Claybourne, Anna.
Tilma, Taralee, illus. see Em, Charlie.
Tilma, Taralee, illus. see Reid, Kimm.
Tilmont, Amy. Man vs. Animal: Species at Risk. (p. 1395)
—Trash Talk: What You Throw Away. (p. 2279)
Tilney, F. C. Tales for Children from Many Lands (Classic Reprint) (p. 2181)
Tilney, Fredk. Colin. Original Fables of la Fontaine: Rendered into English Prose (Classic Reprint) (p. 1671)
Tilson, Sonia. Disappearing Boy (p. 553)
Tilthem, Sam. Pete Plan Pup. (p. 1727)
Tilton, Dwight. Golden Greyhound: A Novel (Classic Reprint) (p. 857)
—Miss. Petticoats (Classic Reprint) (p. 1479)
—My Lady Laughter: A Romance of Boston Town in the Days of the Great Siege (Classic Reprint) (p. 1551)
—On Satan's Mount (Classic Reprint) (p. 1653)
Tilton, Eliza. Catching Ivy. (p. 344)
Tilton, Howard W. Lay Sermons (Classic Reprint) (p. 1253)
Tilton, Isabel. Ember's Dragons. (p. 641)
Tilton, J. E. Tailor Boy (Classic Reprint) (p. 2176)
Tilton, Theodore. Fly (Classic Reprint) (p. 754)
—Golden-Haired Gertrude: A Story for Children (Classic Reprint) (p. 857)
—Tempest-Tossed: A Romance (Classic Reprint) (p. 2203)
—Tempest-Tossed, Vol. 2: A Romance (Classic Reprint) (p. 2203)
Tim, Fireball. Fireball Tim's Big Book of Wacky Rides! (p. 733)
Tim, Hamilton, illus. see Stevenson, Robert Louis.
Timbaland & Myers, Christopher. Nighttime Symphony. Myers, Christopher & Kaa Illustration, illus. (p. 1608)
Timberlake, Amy. One Came Home. (p. 1659)
Timbers, Jill, tr. see Kunnas, Mauri.
Timbers, Jill, tr. see Surojegin, Nora.
Timbers, Suzanne. Sepia & the Big Ocean. Timbers, Suzanne, illus. (p. 1989)
Timblin, Stephen. Kitesurfing. (p. 1225)
Timbres, Harry, jt. auth. see Timbres, Rebecca.
Timbres, Rebecca. We Didn't Ask Utopia: A Quaker Family in Soviet Russia (Classic Reprint) (p. 2390)
Timbs, John. Knowledge for the People, or the Plain Why & Because, Vol. 7: Familiarizing Subjects of Useful Curiosity & Amusing Research; Mechanics (Classic Reprint) (p. 1230)
—Knowledge for the Time. (p. 1230)
—Mirror Monthly Magazine, Vol. 3: January to June, 1848 (Classic Reprint) (p. 1475)
—Signs Before Death. (p. 2016)
—Signs Before Death: A Record of Strange Apparitions, Remarkable Dreams, &c (Classic Reprint) (p. 2017)
—Things Not Generally Known: Familiarly Explained, a Book for Old & Young (Classic Reprint) (p. 2220)
—Things Not Generally Known, Familiarly Explained: A Book for Old & Young (Classic Reprint) (p. 2220)
Time for Kids Editors. Abigail Adams: Eyewitness to America's Birth. (p. 5)
—Time for Kids Big Book of How. (p. 2244)
—TIME for Kids Weather Kit. (p. 2244)
Time for Kids Editors, jt. auth. see Iorio, Nicole.
Time for Kids Editors, jt. auth. see Patrick, Denise Lewis.
Time for Kids Magazine Staff. TIME for Kids Big Book of What. (p. 2244)
Time, Nicholas O. Going, Going, Gone. (p. 854)
—Hang Ten for Dear Life! (p. 917)
—Houston, We Have a Klutz! (p. 1025)
—Stay a Spell. (p. 2109)
—Wrong Place, (Really) Wrong Time. (p. 2514)
Timlin, James M. Shadows, Vol. 23: Literary Magazine of the Creighton University; May, 1932 (Classic Reprint) (p. 1998)
—Shadows, Vol. 23: Literary Magazine of the Creighton University; April, 1932 (Classic Reprint) (p. 1998)
Timlow, Elizabeth Westyn. Cricket (Classic Reprint) (p. 474)
—Cricket at the Seashore (Classic Reprint) (p. 474)
—Eunice & Cricket (Classic Reprint) (p. 667)
Timmerman, Charles. Everything Large-Print Travel Word Search Book: Find Your Way Through 150 Easy-To-read Puzzles. (p. 673)
Timmers, Carol, illus. see Morgan, Railin.
Timmers, Leo. Casa para Tom. (p. 336)
—Franky. Timmers, Leo, illus. (p. 779)
—Gus's Garage. Timmers, Leo, illus. (p. 906)
—Magical Life of Mr. Renny. (p. 1380)
—Monkey on the Run. Timmers, Leo, illus. (p. 1494)
—Who Is Driving? Timmers, Leo, illus. (p. 2447)
Timmers, Leo, illus. see Reidy, Jean.
Timmins, Jeffrey Stewart, illus. see Andersen, Hans & Capstone Press Staff.
Timmins, Jeffrey Stewart, illus. see Andersen, Hans & Stone Arch Books Staff.
Timmins, Jeffrey Stewart, illus. see Andersen, Hans.
Timmins, Jeffrey Stewart, illus. see Capstone Press Staff.
Timmins, Jeffrey Stewart, illus. see Lewis, J. Patrick & Yolen, Jane.
Timmins, Jeffrey Stewart, illus. see Soup, Cuthbert.
Timmins, Jeffrey Stewart, illus. see Stone Arch Books Staff.
Timmins, Jeffrey Stewart, illus. see Yolen, Jane & Lewis, J. Patrick.
Timmins, William, illus. see Stone, Ethel B.
Timmons, Angie. American Witches (p. 74)
—Enemy Asteroids. (p. 650)
—Everything You Need to Know about Reporting Sexual Assault (p. 674)
—Exploring Controlled Investigations Through Science Research Projects. (p. 681)
—Identifying & Documenting a Community Problem for a Political Campaign (p. 1089)
—Kate Middleton & Prince William (p. 1204)
—Leakeys: The Family That Traced Human Origins to Africa. (p. 1255)
—Making the Most of Communications & Social Media in a Political Campaign (p. 1390)
—Nanjing Massacre. (p. 1574)
—Real-World Projects to Explore World War II. (p. 1850)
—U2. (p. 2313)
—Ways to Make Money with Art (p. 2388)
—Ways to Make Money Writing (p. 2388)
Timmons, Angie, contrib. by. Nanjing Massacre. (p. 1574)
Timmons, Anne, illus. see Biskup, Agnieszka Józefina.
Timmons, Anne, illus. see Biskup, Agnieszka.
Timmons, Anne, illus. see Jolley, Dan.
Timmons, Anne, illus. see Krohn, Katherine.
Timmons, Anne, illus. see Robbins, Trina & Capstone Press Staff.
Timmons, Bonnie, illus. see Settel, Joanne.
Timmons, Bonnie, illus. see Truss, Lynne.
Timmons, Darlene P. Hands Up. (p. 916)
Timmons, Johnny, illus. see Serling, Rod & Kneece, Mark.
Timmons, Joshua, illus. see Babaian, Edward & Anderson, Kenny.
Timmons, Robin. Hezekiah. (p. 964)
Timmons, Shelli. Ghostly Tales of the Queen Mary. (p. 829)
Timmons-Hanselka, Angela. How to Create Digital Portfolios to Show What You Know. (p. 1039)
—Leakeys: the Family That Traced Human Origins to Africa (p. 1255)
Timms, Barry. I'm Sorry! (p. 1099)
—I'm Sorry! Julian, Sean, illus. (p. 1099)
Timms, Christopher Noel. Adam Jack Goes in to Space: An Adam Jack Adventure. (p. 14)
Timms, E. H. Ring of Nine. (p. 1883)
Timonen Wahlstrom, Mai-Le, tr. see Pere, Tuula.
Timothy, Chanté, illus. see Adero, Malaika.
Timothy, Preacher, jt. auth. see Anthony, Alexandria.
Timpko, D. H. Firma Twins & the Flute of Enchantment. (p. 734)
—Firma Twins & the Purple Staff of Death. (p. 734)
Timreck, Caitlyn, illus. see Harkins, Debra Ann.
Timroth, Stephen. Dreamhawk. (p. 602)
Tims, Laura. Art of Feeling. (p. 121)
—Please Don't Tell. (p. 1762)
Timsol, Robert. Alien from the Commonwealth: The Romance of an Odd Young Man (Classic Reprint) (p. 47)
—Alien from the Commonwealth. (p. 47)
—Pessimist: In Theory & Practice (Classic Reprint) (p. 1726)
Tina, Dunnier, illus. see Kneisley, Amy.
Tinarelli, Beatrice, illus. see Holowaty, Lauren.
Tinarelli, Beatrice, illus. see Murphy, Patricia J.
Tinari, Leah. Limitless: 24 Remarkable American Women of Vision, Grit, & Guts. Tinari, Leah, illus. (p. 1303)
—Presidents: Portraits of History. Tinari, Leah, illus. (p. 1789)
Tinayre, Marcelle. Madeleine at Her Mirror: A Woman's Diary (Classic Reprint) (p. 1375)
—Shadow of Love (Classic Reprint) (p. 1997)
Tincker, Mary Agnes. By the Tiber: By the Author of Signor Monaldini's Niece (Classic Reprint) (p. 306)
—San Salvador (Classic Reprint) (p. 1930)
Tincknell, Cathy. Amazing Things for Boys to Make & Do. Kelly, John, illus. (p. 66)
—Amazing Things for Girls to Make & Do. Kelly, John, illus. (p. 66)
Tindall, Kelly, illus. see Buckley, James, Jr.
Tindall, Kelly, illus. see Shulman, Mark.
Tindall, Samuel. Progressive German Idioms (Classic Reprint) (p. 1805)
Tine, Val Lynn. Jj. (p. 1169)
Ting, Jasmine, illus. see Colwill, Simone.
Ting, Mary. Jaclyn & the Beanstalk. (p. 1154)
—Three Best Friends: Fabulous Day (p. 2232)
Ting, Renee. Chinese History Stories: Stories from the Imperial Era (p. 378)
—Chinese History Stories: Stories from the Zhou Dynasty. (p. 378)
Tingay, Graham, jt. auth. see Marks, Anthony.
Tingle, Tim. Danny Blackgoat, Navajo Prisoner. (p. 504)
—How I Became a Ghost: A Choctaw Trail of Tears Story (p. 1032)
—No More No Name. (p. 1613)
—No Name. (p. 1614)
—Saltypie: A Choctaw Journey from Darkness into Light. Clarkson, Karen, illus. (p. 1925)
—Trust Your Name. (p. 2296)
Tingle, Tim & Moore, Doc. More Spooky Texas Tales. Benas, Jeanne, illus. (p. 1505)
Tingley, Cindy. Lily's Desert Adventure. (p. 1302)
—Lily's Secret. (p. 1302)
Tingley, Janice Ramos. Nolan's Dream. Tingley, Janice Ramos, illus. (p. 1618)
Tingley, John H. Santa Claus' Book of Games & Puzzles: Collection of Riddles, Charades, Enigmas, Rebuses, Anagrams, Labyrinths, Acrostics, etc. ; with a Hieroglyphic Preface (Classic Reprint) (p. 1932)
Tinkelman, Murray, illus. see Stolz, Mary.
Tinkelman, Murray, jt. auth. see Saroyan, William.
Tinker, Rebecca. Who in the World Is Carmen Sandiego? (p. 2447)
—¿Quién Es Carmen Sandiego? (p. 1827)
Tinkle, Brad T. & Darr, Laurren. Bendy Wendy & the (Almost) Invisible Genetic Syndrome: A Story of One Tween's Diagnosis of Ehlers-Danlos Syndrome / Joint Hypermobility. (p. 199)
Tinling, Molly, illus. see Wand, Dana.
Tinne, J. Ernest. Wonderland of the Antipodes: And Other Sketches of Travel in the North Island of New Zealand (Classic Reprint) (p. 2490)
—Wonderland of the Antipodes. (p. 2490)
Tinnes Lord, Pam. Furry Tales. (p. 802)
Tinney, Sherralee. Eli: More Than Just a Kitten with Ambition to Go on a Mission (New Edition) (p. 635)
Tinnon, Gwendolyn. Pancake Bandit. (p. 1695)
Tinsley, Helen. Me & My Grandma: A Story for Children about AIDS. (p. 1433)
Tinsley, Henry C. Observations of a Retired Veteran (Classic Reprint) (p. 1634)
Tinsley, Jillian. Wally the Warthog. Wood, Douglas, illus. (p. 2373)
Tinsley, Larry, illus. see Li, Marci.
Tinsley, Lily. Cinders (Classic Reprint) (p. 392)
—In the Ring, Vol. 1 Of 3: A Novel (Classic Reprint) (p. 1110)
—In the Ring, Vol. 2 Of 3: A Novel (Classic Reprint) (p. 1110)
—In the Ring, Vol. 3 Of 3: A Novel (Classic Reprint) (p. 1110)
Tinsman, Kaya, illus. see Borzilleri, Sophia.
Tintera, Amy. Alianza. (p. 44)
—Allied. (p. 56)
—Avenged. (p. 142)
—Rebel. (p. 1852)
—Rebeldes. (p. 1852)
—Reboot. (p. 1852)
—Reiniciados. (p. 1862)
—Ruina. (p. 1913)
—Ruined. (p. 1913)
—Venganza. (p. 2350)
Tinti, Natalie. Magic in Us. the Healing Circle Tinti, Natalie, illus. (p. 1377)
—Magic in Us. the Healing Circle: The Healing Circle Tinti, Natalie, illus. (p. 1377)
—Magic in Us. the Power of Imagination Tinti, Natalie, illus. (p. 1377)
—Magic in Us. the Power of Imagination: The Power of Imagination T, N., illus. (p. 1377)
—Sewing a Friendship. Tinti, Natalie, illus. (p. 1995)
—Sewing a Friendship 1: I Wish I Have Friends. Tinti, Natalie, illus. (p. 1995)
Tinto, Davide, illus. see Dawson, Delilah S.
Tious. 13 'Trange(s) un Album d'Activit's et Coloriages Monstrueux. (p. 2552)
Tipa, Rob. Ka Aroha Hoki! (p. 1201)
Tipene, Tania. Seed's Journey Home: Book 2: Orange Gate. Luecke, Amber Leigh, illus. (p. 1983)
Tipene, Tim. Maui - Sun Catcher. Ruha, Rob, tr. (p. 1426)
Tiphys. Practical Canoeing; a Treatise on the Management & Handling of Canoes. (p. 1783)
Tiplady, Thomas. Soul of the Soldier: Sketches from the Western Battle-Front (Classic Reprint) (p. 2066)
Tipler, M. J. New National Framework Mathematics 9+ Pupil's Book. (p. 1596)
Tipper, Sarah. Eviscerated Panda: Back in Bamboo. (p. 674)
Tippett, Edwin James. Who Won the War? Letters & Notes of an M. P. in Dixie, England, France & Flanders (Classic Reprint) (p. 2452)
Tippin, Debra P. & Tippin, Ph D. Brigette. Capellio: The New Adventures of Pinocchio's Son. (p. 323)
Tipping, Judith. Squirrel Who Split His Trousers. (p. 2095)
Tipping, Naomi, illus. see Safran, Sheri.
Tipping, Rosie. Giant Pool: The Continuing Adventures of Matty the Hermit Crab & Friends. (p. 831)
—Shell Exchange: A Story about a Hermit Crab Running a Shell Exchange for Other Hermit Crabs. (p. 2005)
Tipton, Annie. Diary of a Real Payne Book 3: Oh Baby! (p. 539)
Tipton, Denton J. X-Files: JFK Disclosure. Menton3, illus. (p. 2515)
Tipton, Denton J. & Smith, Matthew Dow. Goosebumps: Horrors of the Witch House. Fenoglio, Chris, illus. (p. 869)
Tipton, Erica. Monkey Named Haha. Tipton, Erica, illus. (p. 1494)
Tipton, Sarah. Betrayal of the Band. (p. 208)
Tipton, Scott. Teenage Mutant Ninja Turtles: New Animated Adventures Brizuela, Dario, illus. (p. 2199)
Tipton, Scott, et al. Best of Klingons. Messina, David et al, illus. (p. 207)
Tirebuck, William Edwards. Meg of the Scarlet Foot: A Novel (Classic Reprint) (p. 1441)
—Miss. Grace of All Souls (Classic Reprint) (p. 1478)
—'Twixt God & Mammon (Classic Reprint) (p. 2306)
Tireman, Loyd. 3 Toes. Douglass, Ralph, illus. (p. 2547)
—Baby Jack & Jumping Jack Rabbit. Douglass, Ralph, illus. (p. 151)
—Big Fat. Douglass, Ralph, illus. (p. 220)
—Cocky. Douglass, Ralph, illus. (p. 411)
—Dumbee. Douglass, Ralph, illus. (p. 609)
—Hop-a-Long: Stories. Douglass, Ralph, illus. (p. 1001)
—Quills. Douglass, Ralph, illus. (p. 1828)
Tiritilli, Robert A., illus. see Hellman, Charles S.
Tiritilli, Robert A., jt. auth. see Hellman, Charles S.
Tirkey, Evelynn Thea. Little Helpers. (p. 1318)
Tirone, Lisa & TIRONE, Lisa. Chef It Up! (p. 364)
Tischer, Gustav, jt. auth. see Cicero, Marcus Tullius.
Tischler, Molly. Adventures of Kermit the Newf: Kermit Gets a Puppy. (p. 24)
Tischner, August. Fixed Idea of Astronomical Theory. (p. 745)
—Sun: Changes Its Position in Space, Therefore Fore It Cannot Be Regarded As Being in a Condition of Rest (Classic Reprint) (p. 2151)
Tischner, Lukasz. Milosz & the Problem of Evil. Bill, Stanley, tr. (p. 1468)
Tisdale, Alice. Pioneering Where the World Is Old: Leaves from a Manchurian Note-Book (Classic Reprint) (p. 1748)
Tisdale, Rachel. Brown V. Board of Education (p. 287)
—Freedom Riders (p. 783)
—Little Rock Nine (p. 1327)
—March on Washington (p. 1402)
—Montgomery Bus Boycott (p. 1499)
—Woolworth's Sit-In (p. 2493)
Tisdale, Rachel, jt. auth. see Loveless, Antony.
Tisdale, Towanda. Wallace Mack Has a Bug Attack! (p. 2373)
Tisdale, Towanda L. Kelcey Reed Loves to Read. (p. 1208)
Tisdall, Sarah, illus. see Rosen, Michael.
Tisdel, L. L, illus. see Bryson, Karen Mueller.
Tissandier, Gaston, jt. auth. see Frith, Henry.
Tisserand, Felix. Traite de Mecanique Celeste. Theorie de la Figure des Corps Celestes et de Leur Mouvement: De Rotation. (p. 2276)
—Traite de Mecanique Celeste. Theorie des Satellites de Jupiter et de Saturne. Perturbations: Des Petites Planetes. (p. 2276)
Tisserand, François. Traite de Mecanique Celeste, Vol. 1: Perturbations des Planetes d'Apres la Methode de la Variation des Constantes Arbitaires (Classic Reprint) (p. 2276)
—Traite de Mecanique Celeste, Vol. 3: Expose de l'Ensemble des Theories Relatives Au Mouvement de la Lune (Classic Reprint) (p. 2276)
Tissot, Caperton. Pirates on the Saranac. (p. 1751)
Tissot, Joseph. Imagination: Ses Bienfaits et Ses Égarements, Surtout Dans le Domaine du Merveilleux (Classic Reprint) (p. 1100)
Tissot Lcsw, Jennifer. Grateful Gracie: A Story about Gratitude. Washburn, Cecilia, illus. (p. 881)
Tissot, Samuel Auguste David. De la Santé des Gens de Lettres (Classic Reprint) (p. 517)
Tissot, Victor. Unknown Hungary, Vol. 1 of 2 (Classic Reprint) (p. 2333)
—Unknown Switzerland: Reminiscences of Travel (Classic Reprint) (p. 2333)
Tit, Tom. Eagle's Masque (Classic Reprint) (p. 613)
—Scientific Amusements. Knott, Cargill, tr. (p. 1959)
Titan & Lapuss, Stephane. Secret Life of Pets. (p. 1976)
Titan Books Staff & Korman, Susan. Noah - Ila's Story. (p. 1615)
Titan Books Staff, et al. Monsters vs. Aliens: the M Files. Dalton, Alex & Laguna, Fabio, illus. (p. 1498)
Titan Comics Staff. Penguins of Madagascar (p. 1716)
—Underworld (p. 2326)
Titan Comics Staff, jt. auth. see Furman, Simon.
Titan Comics Staff & Furman, Simon. Dangers of the Deep Max, Iman, illus. (p. 502)
—Dragon Down Nazif, Iwan, illus. (p. 593)
Titan Comics, Titan. Ice Castle Lawrence, Jack, illus. (p. 1087)
Titan Comics, Titan & Ah-Koon, Didier. Minions (p. 1472)
Titchen, Annette. Garden Shed Olive & Sylvia. (p. 809)
Titcomb, Gordon. Last Train. Minor, Wendell, illus. (p. 1249)
Tite, Jack. Mega Meltdown: The Weird & Wonderful Animals of the Ice Age. (p. 1441)
Titherington, Jeanne. Pumpkin Pumpkin. (p. 1813)
Titherington, Karen M. Gavin Goes to Kindergarten! Prepare Your Child for the First Day of School. (p. 812)
Tithof, Rose Klopf. My Michigan Summer: With My Cousin, My Best Buddy. (p. 1555)
Titlebaum, Ellen, jt. auth. see Hapka, Cathy, pseud.
Titley, Alan, jt. auth. see Tolkien, J. R. R.
Titmarsh, . Interesting Event (Classic Reprint) (p. 1126)
Titmarsh, M. A. Doctor Birch: And His Young Friends (Classic Reprint) (p. 573)
—Irish Sketch-Book, Vol. 1 of 2 (Classic Reprint) (p. 1135)
—Notes of a Journey from Cornhill to Grand Cairo (Classic Reprint) (p. 1624)
—Our (Classic Reprint) (p. 1677)
Titmarsh, Michael Angelo. Second Funeral of Napoleon, and, Critical Reviews (Classic Reprint) (p. 1973)
Titmarsh, Titmarsh. Paris Sketch Book, Vol. 1 (Classic Reprint) (p. 1700)
Titmus, Dawn. Birds. (p. 231)
—Cats. (p. 345)
—Dogs. (p. 577)
—Fish. (p. 741)
—Horses & Ponies. (p. 1005)
—Insects & Spiders. (p. 1122)
—Rabbits, Mice, & Rats. (p. 1830)
—Reptiles & Amphibians. (p. 1867)
Titra, Stephen, illus. see Thiry, Joan.
Titterton, W. R. London Scenes (Classic Reprint) (p. 1341)
Titterwell, Timo. Yankee Notions: A Medley. (p. 2517)
—Yankee Notions: A Medley (Classic Reprint) (p. 2517)
Tittle, Peg. Exile. (p. 677)
Tittle, Walter. Colonial Holidays (Classic Reprint) (p. 418)
Titus, Debra. Time Out for Daddy. (p. 2245)
Titus, Esther. Milo the Word Eater. (p. 1468)
Titus, Eve. Anatole & the Cat. (p. 79)
—Basil & the Cave of Cats. Galdone, Paul, illus. (p. 170)
—Basil & the Lost Colony. Galdone, Paul, illus. (p. 170)
—Basil in Mexico. Galdone, Paul, illus. (p. 170)
—Basil of Baker Street. Galdone, Paul, illus. (p. 170)
Titus, Eve & Hapka, Cathy. Great Mouse Detective Mastermind Collection Books 1-8: Basil of Baker Street; Basil & the Cave of Cats; Basil in Mexico; Basil in the Wild West; Basil & the Lost Colony; Basil & the Big Cheese Cook-Off; Basil & the Royal Dare; Basil & the Library Ghost. Galdone, Paul & Mottram, David, illus. (p. 888)
Titus, Harold. Bruce of the Circle (Classic Reprint) (p. 287)
—I Conquered (Classic Reprint) (p. 1064)
—Last Straw (Classic Reprint) (p. 1249)
—Timber (Classic Reprint) (p. 2243)
Tiwi College Students, illus. see James, Margaret.
Tize W. Clark. Street Jokes: 1st Edition. (p. 2140)

—Twin Poems. (p. 2305)
Tjernagel, Kelsi Turner. Animals That Live in Groups. (p. 96)
—Gross Recipes (p. 898)
Tjernagel, Nehemias. Paragraphs of a Pedestrian (Classic Reprint) (p. 1699)
—Walking Trips in Norway (Classic Reprint) (p. 2372)
Tjia, Sherwin, illus. see Lawson, JonArno.
Tjong-Khing, Thé. Birthday Cake Mystery. (p. 233)
Tkachenko, Olha, illus. see Mitchell, Liliana.
Tlc. Benjamin's Adventure: Building Self-Esteem in Children. (p. 200)
Tller, Jerome. Sammy's Day at the Fair: The Digestive System,featuring Gut Feelings & Reactions. Tiller, Paul, illus. (p. 1928)
Tnt. Gospel Parables, the Easter Story & Parables on the Second Coming. (p. 871)
—Samson, Ruth, Samuel & Saul Christian Focus Publications (CFP) Staff, ed. (p. 1928)
TNT Ministries Staff, jt. auth. see Blundell, T.
TNT Resource Material Staff. Beginning with the Bible: A Class above - A Child's Further Lessons in Knowing God. (p. 192)
—Beginning with the Bible. (p. 192)
—On the Way, 11-14yr (p. 1656)
—On the Way 3-9's (p. 1656)
—On the Way for 3 - 9's (p. 1656)
TNT Resource Material Staff, jt. auth. see Blundell, T.
To Be Announced. Doozers Make a Rainbow. (p. 585)
—Meechee's Top-Secret Society. (p. 1437)
To Be Announced & Cassel, Alexandra. Daniel Loves You. Fruchter, Jason, illus. (p. 503)
To Be Announced, To Be. My First Origami Book: 35 Fun Papercrafting Projects for Children Aged 7+ (p. 1545)
To, Marcus. Age of X-Man: NextGen. (p. 35)
—All-New Guardians of the Galaxy Vol. 3: Infinity Quest. (p. 53)
—Excalibur by Tini Howard Vol. 1. (p. 676)
To, Vivienne, illus. see Ballarini, Joe.
To, Vivienne, illus. see Enderle, Dotti.
To, Vivienne, illus. see Fiedler, Lisa.
To, Vivienne, illus. see Fields, Jan.
To, Vivienne, illus. see Lazar, Tara.
To, Vivienne, illus. see Naylor, Phyllis Reynolds.
To, Vivienne, illus. see Rhodes, O. K. & Spencer, Octavia.
To, Vivienne, illus. see Wild, Margaret.
Toaldo, Giuseppe. Completa Raccolta Di Opuscoli, Osservazioni, e Notizie Diverse, Vol. 4: Contenute Nei Giornali Astro-Meteorologici Dall'anno 1773. Sino All'anno 1798 (Classic Reprint) (p. 434)
—Completa Raccolta Di Opuscoli, Osservazioni, e Notizie Diverse Contenute Nei Giornali Astro-Meteorologici Dall'anno 1773 Sino All'anno 1798, Vol. 1 (Classic Reprint) (p. 434)
—Completa Raccolta Di Opuscoli, Osservazioni, e Notizie Diverse Contenute Nei Giornali Astro-Meteorologici Dall' Anno 1773 Sino All'anno 1798, Vol. 2 (Classic Reprint) (p. 434)
Toalson, R. L. Colors of the Rain. (p. 426)
—Woods. (p. 2492)
Toaspern, H., jt. auth. see Sewell, Anna.
Toaspern, Otto, jt. auth. see Goodrich, Arthur Frederick.
Toast, Sarah. Panda: Wildlife 3D Puzzle & Book. Pinkney, Debbie, illus. (p. 1695)
Tobar, Jorge, illus. see Tobar, Malena & Oyola, Milta, eds.
Tobar, Malena, illus. see Brannan, Dara, ed.
Tobar, Malena, illus. see Jingling, Kathy, ed.
Tobar, Malena & Oyola, Milta, eds. Cuaderno de la Margarita Tomo 2 (p. 481)
—Cuaderno de la Rosa Tomo 4 Tobar, Jorge, illus. (p. 481)
Tobenkin, Elias. House of Conrad (Classic Reprint) (p. 1022)
—Road (Classic Reprint) (p. 1888)
—Witte Arrives: A Novel (Classic Reprint) (p. 2482)
Tobey, Danny. God Game: A Novel. (p. 851)
Tobey, Marian E. Guide for Grown-Ups to Books of Prose & Poetry for Wee Little Folks & Big Little Folks (Classic Reprint) (p. 903)
Tobia, Lauren, illus. see Atinuke.
Tobia, Lauren, illus. see Hart, Caryl.
Tobia, Lauren, illus. see Hest, Amy.
Tobia, Lauren, illus. see Manushkin, Fran.
Tobia, Lauren, illus. see Schaefer, Carole Lexa.
Tobia, Lauren, illus. see Shields, Carol Diggory.
Tobias, Harris. Moon Saga: How Dancing Turtle Captured the Moon. Mitsopoulos, Dimitris, illus. (p. 1502)
Tobias, Jack. New Home for Mopgolly Mole. (p. 1594)
Tobias, Tamara. Bella Bella Brush. Klein, Isabel, illus. (p. 197)
Tobias, Tom, illus. see Tobias, Anne B.
Tobin, Bertha Irene. Recitations, Drills & Plays for Children (Classic Reprint) (p. 1853)
Tobin, Christine. Brightest Star. Pryor, Frank, illus. (p. 281)
Tobin, Denise. Hydro the Raindrop. (p. 1055)
Tobin, George T. Our National Songs: With Numerous Original Illustrations (Classic Reprint) (p. 1679)
Tobin, Irene. Tidy Bunch. (p. 2240)
Tobin, Jason. Algebra (p. 44)
Tobin, Jim. Sue MacDonald Had a Book. (p. 2147)
—Very Inappropriate Word. Coverly, Dave, illus. (p. 2353)
Tobin, Marc, illus. see Woik, Julie.
Tobin, Nancy. Awesome Bird Hullabaloo. (p. 144)
Tobin, Paul. Avengers (p. 142)
—Bandette Volume 1: Presto! Coover, Colleen, illus. (p. 163)
—Battle Extravagonzo #1. Lattie, Tim, illus. (p. 173)
—Boom Boom Mushroom #1. Chabot, Jacob, illus. (p. 261)
—Doll Winners Squad. Brizuela, Dario, illus. (p. 578)
—Garden Warfare #1. Chabot, Jacob, illus. (p. 809)
—Garden Warfare #2. Chabot, Jacob, illus. (p. 809)
—Garden Warfare #3. Chabot, Jacob, illus. (p. 809)
—Genius Factor: How to Capture an Invisible Cat. Lafontaine, Thierry, illus. (p. 815)
—Genius Factor - How to Capture an Invisible Cat. Lafontaine, Thierry, illus. (p. 815)
—How to Capture an Invisible Cat. (p. 1038)
—How to Outsmart a Billion Robot Bees. Lafontaine, Thierry, illus. (p. 1043)
—How to Outsmart a Billion Robot Bees. Lafontaine, Thierry & Abey, Katie, illus. (p. 1043)
—How to Tame a Human Tornado. (p. 1044)
—Lawn of Doom #1. Chan, Ron, illus. (p. 1253)
—Lawn of Doom #2. Chan, Ron, illus. (p. 1253)
—Lawn of Doom #3. Chan, Ron, illus. (p. 1253)
—Lawnmageddon #1. Chan, Ron & Rainwater, Matthew J., illus. (p. 1253)
—Lawnmageddon #2. Chan, Ron & Rainwater, Matthew J., illus. (p. 1253)
—Lawnmageddon #3. Chan, Ron & Rainwater, Matthew J., illus. (p. 1253)
—Ms. Isaacson's Third Grade Field Trip. Camagni, Jacopo, illus. (p. 1523)
—Petal to the Metal #1. Chan, Ron, illus. (p. 1726)
—Plants vs. Zombies Boxed Set 5. Chan, Ron et al, illus. (p. 1757)
—Plants vs. Zombies: Garden Warfare Volume 2. Lattie, Tim, illus. (p. 1757)
—Plants vs. Zombies Set 3 (Set) (p. 1758)
—Plants vs. Zombies Volume 1: Lawnmageddon (p. 1758)
—Plants vs. Zombies Volume 10: Rumble at Lake Gumbo. Chan, Ron, illus. (p. 1758)
—Plants vs. Zombies Volume 11: War & Peas. Breckel, Heather et al, illus. (p. 1758)
—Plants vs. Zombies Volume 12: Dino-Might. Chan, Ron, illus. (p. 1758)
—Plants vs. Zombies Volume 13: Snow Thanks. Farris, Cat, illus. (p. 1758)
—Plants vs. Zombies Volume 14: a Little Problem. Chan, Ron & Soler, Sara, illus. (p. 1758)
—Plants vs. Zombies Volume 15: Better Homes & Guardens. Gillenardo-Goudreau, Christian, illus. (p. 1758)
—Plants vs. Zombies Volume 16: the Garden Path. Dwyer, Kieron, illus. (p. 1758)
—Plants vs. Zombies Volume 6: Boom Boom Mushroom. Chabot, Jacob, illus. (p. 1758)
—Plants vs. Zombies Volume 7: Battle Extravagonzo. Rainwater, Matt J. & Lattie, Tim, illus. (p. 1758)
—Plants vs. Zombies Volume 8: Lawn of Doom. Chan, Ron, illus. (p. 1758)
—Plants vs. Zombies Volume 9: the Greatest Show Unearthed. Chabot, Jacob & Rainwater, Matt J., illus. (p. 1758)
—Spider-Man & the Secret Wars GN. Scherberger, Patrick, illus. (p. 2080)
—Which Wish? Camagni, Jacopo, illus. (p. 2441)
Tobin, Paul & Dominguez, Horacio. Don't Follow the Leader. (p. 582)
Tobin, Paul & Gray, Scott. Marvel Vault of Heroes: Captain America. Rousseau, Craig & Cliquet, Ronan, illus. (p. 1413)
Tobin, Paul & Korhonen, Kari. Angry Birds Comics: Flight School. Mastantuono, Corrado & Cavazzano, Giorgio, illus. (p. 87)
Tobin, Paul, et al. Angry Birds Comics: Furious Fowl. Dalena, Antonello, illus. (p. 87)
—Angry Birds Comics: Game Play Cavazzano, Giorgio, illus. (p. 87)
Tobin, Richard K. Skating on Thick Ice. LeBlanc, Rebecca, ed. (p. 2030)
Tobin, Sharon. My Name Is Squirt. Hamm, Jolie, illus. (p. 1557)
—My Name Is Squirt Coloring Book Pages. Hamm, Jolie, illus. (p. 1557)
Tobin, Sophia. Vanishing. (p. 2347)
Tobler, Adolf. Mittheilungen Aus Altfranzosischen Handschriften, Vol. 1: Aus der Chanson de Geste Von Auberi Nach Einer Vaticanischen Handschrift (Classic Reprint) (p. 1484)
—Mittheilungen Aus Altfranzösischen Handschriften, Vol. 1: Aus der Chanson de Geste Von Auberi, Nach Einer Vaticanischen Handschrift (Classic Reprint) (p. 1484)
—Mittheilungen Aus Altfranzsischen Handschriften, Vol. 1: Aus der Chanson de Geste Von Auberi Nach Einer Vaticanischen Handschrift (Classic Reprint) (p. 1484)
Tobler, Elise. Chameleons Change Color! (p. 355)
—Geckos Walk on Walls! (p. 813)
—Gila Monsters Have a Deadly Bite! (p. 833)
—Iguanas Have an Extra Eye! (p. 1094)
—Komodo Dragons Are the Largest Lizards! (p. 1231)
—Snapping Turtles Eat Anything! (p. 2045)
—Sulfur. (p. 2148)
—Zinc. (p. 2540)
Tobon, Sara, tr. see Irving, Washington & Gutierrez, Dave.
Tobon, Sara, tr. see Stone Arch Books Staff.
Toboni, Barbara. Bunny Poets. Ferguson Fuller, Sandy, illus. (p. 298)
—Bunny Poets Dyslexic Edition: Dyslexic Font. Ferguson Fuller, Sandy, illus. (p. 298)
—Bunny Poets Dyslexic Font. Ferguson Fuller, Sandy, illus. (p. 298)
Toby Forward Staff. Doubleborn. (p. 589)
—Fireborn. (p. 733)
Tocalli-Beller, Agustina. Boris y el Ajolote Albino. (p. 263)
—Reunión Pendiente. (p. 1872)
Tocchini, Greg, illus. see Ciencin, Scott.
Tocci, Salvatore. Science Fair Projects with Everyday Stuff. (p. 1955)
Tocher, Timothy. Bill Pennant, Babe Ruth, & Me. (p. 226)
Tochor, Jocelyn & Rhydderch, Jena. Faraway Families. (p. 709)
Tocqueville, Alexis de. Democracy in America, Vol. 2 (Classic Reprint) (p. 528)
Tocquigny, Rick. Life Lessons from Family Vacations. (p. 1293)
Todaro, Dianne. How to Talk to Boys. (p. 1044)
Todaro, Joseph. Blockchain. (p. 245)
Today, Holy Ground. Samson's Great Adventures. (p. 1928)
Todd, Alice Adele. Nature in the Old English & Scottish Ballads (Classic Reprint) (p. 1581)
Todd, Allan. Soviet Union & Post-Soviet Russia (1924-2000) (p. 2070)
Todd, Anne. Teddy Powers: The Stone Keepers. (p. 2198)
Todd, Anne, jt. auth. see Manolis, Kay.
Todd, Anne M. Susan B. Anthony: Activist. (p. 2166)
—Tyra Banks. (p. 2311)
—Venus & Serena Williams. (p. 2351)
Todd, Anne M. & Bankston, John. Jacqueline Wilson. (p. 1154)
Todd, Barbara. Edward & the Eureka Lucky Wish Company. Storms, Patricia, illus. (p. 626)
Todd, Brandon, illus. see Petty, Dev.
Todd, Chuck, illus. see Bogue, Gary.
Todd, Darren, ed. see Sheets, Parris.
Todd, Darren, ed. see Thorne, Adelaide.
Todd, David Peck & Lynn, William Thynne. Stars & Telescopes. (p. 2107)
Todd, Emma G. Discoveries of Misconceptions Regarding the Properties of Matter Within the Science of Chemistry. (p. 555)
Todd, Emma J. Normal Course in Reading: First Reader; First Step in Reading (Classic Reprint) (p. 1619)
—Normal Course in Reading: Fourth Reader; the Wonderful Things Around Us (Classic Reprint) (p. 1619)
—Normal Course in Reading: First Reader, Word Pictures & Language Lessons (Classic Reprint) (p. 1619)
—Normal Course in Reading: Alternate Third Reader; How to Read with Open Eyes (Classic Reprint) (p. 1619)
—Normal Course in Reading: Alternate Second Reader; Progressive Readings in Nature (Classic Reprint) (p. 1619)
—Normal Course in Reading: Fifth Reader; Advanced Readings in Literature; Scientific, Geographical, Historical, Patriotic & Miscellaneous, with Analyses of Authors (Classic Reprint) (p. 1619)
—Normal Course in Reading (Classic Reprint) (p. 1619)
—Normal Course in Reading, Primer: First Steps in Reading (Classic Reprint) (p. 1619)
Todd, G. Little Fan; or, the Life & Fortunes of a London Match-Girl. (p. 1316)
Todd, Gretchen. Smith College Monthly, Vol. 20: October, 1912-June, 1913 (Classic Reprint) (p. 2042)
Todd, Hannah, ed. Hello Me, It's You: The Second Edition. (p. 951)
Todd, Ilima. Remake. (p. 1863)
Todd, John. Angel of the Iceberg: And Other Stories, Illustrating Great Moral Truths; Designed Chiefly for the Young (Classic Reprint) (p. 85)
—Lectures to Children: Familiarly Illustrating Important Truth (Classic Reprint) (p. 1260)
—Lost Sister of Wyoming: An Authentic Tale (Classic Reprint) (p. 1355)
—Nuts for Boys to Crack: Earthly Stories with a Heavenly Meaning. (p. 1632)
—Questions on the Lives of the Patriarchs: Embracing the Book of Genesis (Classic Reprint) (p. 1826)
—Raft: Or the Widow's Two Sons (Classic Reprint) (p. 1834)
—Simple Sketches by Rev. John Todd (Classic Reprint) (p. 2022)
—Simple Sketches, Vol. 2 (Classic Reprint) (p. 2022)
—Summer Gleanings: Or Sketches & Incidents of a Pastor's Vacation (Classic Reprint) (p. 2149)
Todd, Justin, illus. see Stevenson, Robert Louis.
Todd, Justin, jt. auth. see Grahame, Kenneth.
Todd Kaplan, Delia Angelescu, tr. see Creanga, Ion.
Todd, Kim D. Jean Jennings Bartik: Computer Pioneer. (p. 1162)
Todd, Lillie. Possibility of You & Me. (p. 1780)
Todd, Mark. Food Trucks! (p. 760)
Todd, Mark, illus. see Harris, John.
Todd, Mary Ives. American Abelard & Heloise: A Love Story (Classic Reprint) (p. 70)
—American Madonna: A Story of Love (Classic Reprint) (p. 73)
Todd, Michelle. Santa's Workshop. (p. 1934)
Todd, Michelle, illus. see Dougherty, Brandi.
Todd, Michelle, illus. see Little Bee Books.
Todd, Michelle, illus. see Taylor, Saranne.
Todd, Mort, illus. see Van Lente, Fred, et al.
Todd, Richard E. Baptism: A Bible Study Wordbook for Kids. (p. 164)
—Church: A Bible Study Wordbook for Kids. (p. 390)
—Communion: A Bible Study Wordbook for Kids. (p. 431)
—Giving: A Bible Study Wordbook for Kids. (p. 840)
—Salvation: A Bible Study Wordbook for Kids. (p. 1926)
Todd, Ruthven. Space Cat. Galdone, Paul, illus. (p. 2071)
—Space Cat & the Kittens. Galdone, Paul, illus. (p. 2071)
—Space Cat Meets Mars. Galdone, Paul, illus. (p. 2071)
—Space Cat Visits Venus. Galdone, Paul, illus. (p. 2071)
Todd, Sereno Edwards. Apple Culturist. (p. 106)
Todd Stanton, Joe. Kai & the Monkey King: Brownstone's Mythical Collection 3. (p. 1201)
Todd, Strasser. Give a Boy a Gun. (p. 839)
Todd, Sue, illus. see Alary, Laura.
Todd, Sue, illus. see Coleman, Wim & Perrin, Pat.
Todd, Sue, illus. see StJohn, Amanda.
Todd, Sue, illus. see Walters, Eric.
Todd, Thomas Olman. Hydesville: The Story of the Rochester Knockings, Which Proclaimed the Advent of Modern Spiritualism (Classic Reprint) (p. 1055)
Todd, Traci N. Wiggle Waggle Bee. Barner, Bob, illus. (p. 2461)
Todd, Walter E. Fireside Musings (Classic Reprint) (p. 734)
—Gathered Treasures (Classic Reprint) (p. 811)
—Little Sunshine (Classic Reprint) (p. 1328)
—Parson Johnson's Lecture (Classic Reprint) (p. 1701)
Todd-Stanton, Joe. Arthur & the Golden Rope: Brownstone's Mythical Collection 1. (p. 122)
—Kai & the Monkey King (Literati Edition) Brownstone's Mythical Collection 3. (p. 1201)
—Marcy & the Riddle of the Sphinx: Brownstone's Mythical Collection 2. (p. 1403)
—Mouse Called Julian. (p. 1514)
—Secret of Black Rock. (p. 1977)
Todd-Stanton, Joe, illus. see Bondor-Stone, Annabeth, et al.
Todd-Stanton, Joe, illus. see Queen, Ben.
Todd-Stanton, Joe, illus. see Stewart, Alexandra.
Toddy, Irving, illus. see Gowan, Barbara.
Toddy, Irving, illus. see Shoulders, Michael & Shoulders, Debbie.
Todhunter, Isaac. Elements of Euclid for the Use of Schools & Colleges: Comprising the First Two Books & Portions of the Eleventh & Twelfth Books; with Notes & Exercises (Classic Reprint) (p. 633)
Todkill, Anas. True Relation of Virginia (Classic Reprint) (p. 2294)
Todorov, Boriana & Todorov, Vladimir. Oliver's Tantrums. (p. 1650)
Todras, Ellen & Bjorklund, Ruth. New Mexico. (p. 1595)
Todras, Ellen H., jt. auth. see Bjorklund, Ruth.
Toenjes, Leonard P., jt. auth. see Proctor, Thomas E.
Toews, Rita. Bully: A Discussion & Activity Story. Ljungberg, Jon, illus. (p. 296)
Tofield, Simon, creator. Simon's Cat off to the Vet ... & Other Adventures. (p. 2021)
Toft, Barbara. Complete Guide to Animals. (p. 434)
—Complete Guides Animals. (p. 434)
Toft, Di. Wolven (p. 2484)
Toft, Lis, illus. see Cameron, Ann.
Toft, Ryen. Bee a Dreamer. Yiwing, Vivian, illus. (p. 189)
Toft, Tony. Dancing for Mr. Dee. (p. 500)
Togden, Ra Chel. Legendary Rabbit of Death - Volume One [Paperback]. (p. 1263)
Togden, Rchel. Legendary Rabbit of Death - Volume Five. (p. 1263)
—Legendary Rabbit of Death - Volume Three. (p. 1263)
Togel, Peggy, jt. auth. see McGrath, Barbara Barbieri.
Together!. Come & See - Leader's Manual. (p. 428)
Tognoni Miller, Christine, illus. see Ozoude, Alexander.
Togo, Narisa. Magnificent Birds. (p. 1382)
Togoe, Andreea & Amazing, Rosie. My Nice Friend Theodore. (p. 1558)
Toht, Dave. Goose That Fell from the Sky. (p. 869)
Toht, Patricia. All Aboard the London Bus. Usher, Sam, illus. (p. 48)
—Dress Like a Girl. Tu-Dean, Lorian, illus. (p. 604)
—Pick a Pine Tree. Jarvis, illus. (p. 1738)
—Pick a Pumpkin. Jarvis, illus. (p. 1738)
Tok, Stephanie, illus. see Eng, Paul.
Tok, Stephanie, jt. auth. see Rielly, Robin L.
Tokarz, Brenda. Curious Jane's: A Balloon Adventure. (p. 488)
Toki, Sela Tuita. Pati Loves to Walk Barefoot to School. (p. 1705)
Tokuda-Hall, Maggie. Also an Octopus. Davies, Benji, illus. (p. 60)
—Mermaid, the Witch, & the Sea. (p. 1449)
Tokuhama, Kelly. Penelope's Christmas in New York. (p. 1715)
Tokutomi, Kenjiro. Heart of Nami-San (Hototogisu) a Story of War, Intrigue & Love (Classic Reprint) (p. 945)
—Nami-Ko: A Realistic Novel (Classic Reprint) (p. 1573)
—Nami-Ko: Novela Popular Japonesa (Classic Reprint) (p. 1573)
Tokyopop and Art Impression Staff & Peymani, Christine. Skelanimals: It's a Wonderful Afterlife. Vol. 1 (p. 2030)
Tol, Alex Van. Sonia Sotomayor: U.S. Supreme Court Justice. (p. 2063)
Tol, Alex Van & National Geographic Learning Staff. Dolores Huerta: Voice for the Working Poor. (p. 579)
Tola, Olsi, illus. see West, Luthie M.
Tolan, R. J., jt. auth. see Tolan, Stephanie S.
Tolan, Stephanie S. Applewhites at Wit's End. (p. 107)
—Surviving the Applewhites. (p. 2165)
—Wishworks, Inc. Bates, Amy June, illus. (p. 2479)
Tolan, Stephanie S. & Tolan, R. J. Applewhites Coast to Coast. (p. 107)
Toland, Darrell, illus. see Holechek, Max.
Toland, Edward D. Aftermath of Battle: With the Red Cross in France (Classic Reprint) (p. 34)
Toland, Mary Bertha McKenzie. Onti Ora: A Metrical Romance (Classic Reprint) (p. 1664)
—Stella (Classic Reprint) (p. 2113)
Tolar, Cam. Crayons. (p. 468)
Tolbert, Tami. Oodles of Poodles. (p. 1665)
Tolcser, Sarah. Canción de la Corriente. (p. 321)
—Song of the Current. (p. 2062)
—Susurro de la Marea. (p. 2166)
—Whisper of the Tide. (p. 2442)
Toledano, Diana, illus. see Kuipers, Alice.
Toledano, Diana, illus. see Meister, Cari.
Toledano, Diane, illus. see Murray, Diana.
Toledo, Eymard. Best Tailor in Pinbauê. (p. 208)
Tolentino, Angela, illus. see Heimbach, William.
Tolentino, Blaine Namahana, tr. see Loebel-Fried, Caren.
Toler, Pamela. War Of 1812 Musteen, Jason R., ed. (p. 2376)
Toler, Pamela D. Causes of the War of 1812. (p. 347)
—Matt Damon. (p. 1425)
—Transatlantic Slave Networks. (p. 2277)
Toler, Sidney. Golden Age: A Play in Four Acts (Classic Reprint) (p. 856)
Tolin, Rosanne. More Than Marmalade: Michael Bond & the Story of Paddington Bear. (p. 1505)
Tolish, Alexander. Gravity Explained. (p. 882)
Toliver, Edward. Our Folks at Home: Or Life at the Old Manor House (Classic Reprint) (p. 1678)
—Sequel to Our Folks at Home, or Life at the Old Manor House (Classic Reprint) (p. 1989)
Toliver, Wendy. Lifted. (p. 1297)
—Miss Match. (p. 1479)
—Once upon a Time: Red's Untold Tale. (p. 1658)
—Once upon a Time Red's Untold Tale. (p. 1658)
—Once upon a Time Regina Rising. (p. 1658)
Tolkien, Baillie, ed. see Tolkien, J. R. R.
Tolkien, J. R. R. Fermier Gilles de Ham. (p. 720)
—Hobbit. (p. 985)
—Hobbit. Tolkien, J. R. R., illus. (p. 985)
Tolkien, J. R. R. & Titley, Alan. Hobad: Nó Anonn Agus Ar Ais Arís. (p. 985)
Tolkien, J. R. R., et al. Hobad: Nó Anonn Agus Ar Ais Arís. (p. 985)
Tolkien, Michael. Woodsy. (p. 2492)
Toll, Damien. Drawing Is Awesome! (p. 599)
Tolland, Margaret, illus. see Hay, Gay.
Tolland, Margaret, illus. see McKinnon, Natalie.
Tolland, Margaret, jt. auth. see Hay, Gay.

Tolle, Glenn, illus. see Hranjec, Stephanie.
Tollefson, Carol. McTavich That Rascal Squirrel. (p. 1432)
Tollefson, Connie Kittleson. Papa Gnome's Magical Mirror Tree Stump Home. (p. 1696)
Tollemache, Beatrix L. Jonquille, or the Swiss Smuggler: Translated from the French of T. Combe (Classic Reprint) (p. 1177)
—Village Priest: And Other Stories from the Russian of Militsina Saltikov (Classic Reprint) (p. 2358)
Tollemache, Beatrix Lucia. Russian Sketches, Chiefly of Peasant Life (Classic Reprint) (p. 1917)
Toller, Ernst. Brokenbrow: A Tragedy (Classic Reprint) (p. 285)
Toller, Frederick. Poetical Version of the Fables of Phaedrus (Classic Reprint) (p. 1766)
Tolley, Diane Stringam. Kris Kringle's Magic. (p. 1232)
Tolley, Diane Stringham & Tolley, Diane Stringam. Carving Angels. (p. 336)
Tolley, S. L. H. Elemental Staff: Book One - the Spreading Darkness-Evolved. (p. 632)
—Elemental Staff Book Two: Courage & Sacrifice-Evolved. (p. 632)
Tolli, Jenna. Changing Coastline Environments (p. 356)
—Earth's Geosphere. (p. 618)
—Federal Courts (p. 717)
—Highest Peak: How Mount Everest Formed (p. 969)
—Plead the Fifth: A Look at the Fifth Amendment. (p. 1761)
—Raising Emus (p. 1838)
Tollison, Hal. Cartooning. (p. 335)
Tolman, Marije, illus. see Heede, Sylvia Vanden.
Tolman, Marije, illus. see Heide, Iris van der.
Tolman, Marije, illus. see Vanden Heede, Sylvia.
Tolman, Marije & Tolman, Ronald. Island. (p. 1139)
—Tree House. (p. 2284)
Tolman, Stacia. Spaces Between Us. (p. 2073)
Tolman, Tom, illus. see Reid, Pamela Carrington.
Tolosa Sisteré, Mariona. Secret Life of Boogers. (p. 1976)
Tolson, Hannah. My Mommy Is a Hero. (p. 1556)
Tolson, Hannah, illus. see Jenkins, Martin.
Tolson, Hannah, illus. see Murphy, Julie.
Tolson, Hannah, illus. see Quarmby, Katharine & O'Neill, Richard.
Tolson, Hannah, illus. see Williams, Susie.
Tolson, Maria, illus. see Khalfani, Natasha M. & Khalfani, Jabari N.
Tolson, Scott, illus. see Owens, L. L.
Tolstikova, Daria, illus. see Esbaum, Jill.
Tolstikova, Dasha. Year Without Mom (p. 2519)
Tolstikova, Dasha, illus. see Esbaum, Jill.
Tolstikova, Dasha, illus. see Grabill, Rebecca.
Tolstikova, Dasha, illus. see Hall, Kirsten.
Tolstikova, Dasha, illus. see Sobol, John.
Tolstoi, Aleksey. Lame Princ: A Story (Classic Reprint) (p. 1240)
Tolstoi, Leon. Resurrección. (p. 1870)
Tolstoi, Loyf N. Invaders & Other Stories (Classic Reprint) (p. 1130)
Tolstoi, Lyof N. Master & Man: A Story (Classic Reprint) (p. 1418)
—Master & Man: The Kreutzer Sonata Dramas (Classic Reprint) (p. 1418)
—Novels & Other Works of Lyof N. Tolstoi. the Death of Ivan Ilyitch & Other Stories. (p. 1626)
—Novels & Other Works of Lyof N. Tolstoi, Vol. 11: The Cossacks, and, Sevastopol (Classic Reprint) (p. 1626)
—Novels & Other Works of Lyof N. Tolstoi, Vol. 2: Resurrection (Classic Reprint) (p. 1626)
—Novels & Other Works of Lyof N. Tolstoi, Vol. 3: War & Peace (Classic Reprint) (p. 1626)
—Sevastopol (Classic Reprint) (p. 1993)
—Where Love Is There God Is Also (Classic Reprint) (p. 2439)
Tolstoi, Tolstoi. Tolstoi for the Young: Select Tales from Tolstoi (Classic Reprint) (p. 2256)
Tolstot, Lyof N. Childhood, Boyhood, Youth (Classic Reprint) (p. 370)
Tolstoy, Aleksei, et al. Gigantic Turnip. (p. 832)
Tolstoy, Ilya. Visions: Tales from the Russian (Classic Reprint) (p. 2362)
Tolstoy, Leo. Boyhood: A Story (Classic Reprint) (p. 271)
—Boyhood. (p. 271)
—Childhood & a Letter to a Hindu. (p. 370)
—Childhood, Boyhood, & Youth (Classic Reprint) (p. 370)
—Childhood, Boyhood, Youth (Classic Reprint) (p. 370)
—Complete Works of Count Tolstoy, Vol. 1: Childhood, Boyhood, Youth; the Incursion (Classic Reprint) (p. 435)
—Complete Works of Count Tolstoy, Vol. 14 (Classic Reprint) (p. 435)
—Complete Works of Count Tolstoy, Vol. 8 (Classic Reprint) (p. 435)
—Complete Works of Lyof N. Tolstoi: War & Peace, III-IV (Classic Reprint) (p. 435)
—Complete Works of Lyof N. Tolstoi, Vol. 6: The Cossacks; Sevastopol; the Invaders; & Other Stories (Classic Reprint) (p. 435)
—Complete Works of Lyof N. Tolstoi, Vol. 7: A Russian Proprietor; the Death of Ivan Ilyitch, & Other Stories (Classic Reprint) (p. 435)
—Complete Works of Lyof N. Tolstoi, Vol. 8: The Long Exile; Master & Man; the Kreutzer Sonata; Dramas (Classic Reprint) (p. 435)
—Complete Works of Lyof N. Tolstoi, Volume IX. (p. 435)
—Cossacks: A Tale Of 1852. (p. 457)
—Cossacks: A Tale of the Caucasus in the Year 1852 (Classic Reprint) (p. 457)
—Fables for Children, Stories for Children, Natural Science Stories, Popular Education, Decembrists, Moral Tales (Classic Reprint) (p. 691)
—Father Sergius: And Other Stories (Classic Reprint) (p. 714)
—Hadji Murad (Classic Reprint) (p. 909)
—Hadji Murd (Classic Reprint) (p. 909)
—In Pursuit of Happiness (Classic Reprint) (p. 1106)
—Ivan the Fool, or the Old Devil & the Three Small Devils: Also a Lost Opportunity & Polikushka (Classic Reprint) (p. 1149)
—Landed Proprietor; the Cossacks; Sevastopol (Classic Reprint) (p. 1242)
—Life Is Worth Living: And Other Stories (Classic Reprint) (p. 1293)
—Master & Man: And Other Parables & Tales (Classic Reprint) (p. 1418)
—Master & Man. (p. 1418)
—Master & Man (Classic Reprint) (p. 1418)
—Master & Man, & Other Parables & Tales. (p. 1418)
—More Tales from Tolstoi (Classic Reprint) (p. 1505)
—My Youth (Classic Reprint) (p. 1565)
—Novels & Other Works of Lyof N. Tolstoï: The Long Exile, & Other Stories (Classic Reprint) (p. 1626)
—Novels & Other Works of Lyof N. Tolstoi. Resurrection, Volume II. (p. 1626)
—Novels & Other Works of Lyof N. Tolstoi, Vol. 3: Anna Karenina (Classic Reprint) (p. 1626)
—Popular Stories & Legends (Classic Reprint) (p. 1777)
—Russian Proprietor: And Other Stories (Classic Reprint) (p. 1917)
—Sebastopol (Classic Reprint) (p. 1973)
—Sevastopol & Other Military Tales (Classic Reprint) (p. 1993)
—Shoemaker Martin. Watts, Bernadette, illus. (p. 2009)
—Three Days in the Village & Other Sketches: Written from September to July (Classic Reprint) (p. 2232)
—Tolstoi for the Young. (p. 2256)
—Twenty-Three Tales (Classic Reprint) (p. 2304)
—Two Generations (Classic Reprint) (p. 2307)
—War & Peace, Vol. 1 Of 2: A Historical Novel (Classic Reprint) (p. 2376)
—War & Peace, Vol. 2 Of 2: A Historical Novel; the Invasion, 1807 1812 (Classic Reprint) (p. 2376)
—War & Peace, Vol. 2 Of 2: A Historical Novel; Before Tilsit, 1805 1807 (Classic Reprint) (p. 2376)
—War & Peace, Vol. 2 of 3 (Classic Reprint) (p. 2376)
—What Men Live (Classic Reprint) (p. 2419)
—What Men Live by, & Other Stories (Classic Reprint) (p. 2419)
Tolstoy, Leo & Riordan, James. Lion & the Puppy: And Other Stories for Children. Riordan, James, tr. (p. 1305)
Tolstoy, Lev N. Childhood; Boyhood; Youth; the Incursion; a Landed Proprietor; the Cossacks; Sevastopol (Classic Reprint) (p. 370)
—Death of Ivan Ilich; Dramatic Works; the Kreutzer Sonata (Classic Reprint) (p. 521)
—Father Sergius: The Forged Coupon, Miscellaneous Stories (Classic Reprint) (p. 714)
—Moscow Acquaintance; Snow-Storm; Domestic Happiness; Polikushka; Pedagogical Articles; Linen-Measurer (Classic Reprint) (p. 1507)
—Moscow Acquaintance; the Snow Storm; Domestic Happiness; Miscellanies (Classic Reprint) (p. 1507)
—War & Peace, Vol. 1 (Classic Reprint) (p. 2376)
Tolstoy, Lev Nikolayevich. Anna Karenin, Vol. 3: Fables & Stories for Children; Miscellaneous Articles (Classic Reprint) (p. 97)
Tolton, Laura, illus. see Aboff, Marcie.
Tolton, Laura, illus. see Eason, Cassandra.
Tolutis, Vytenis, illus. see MacNeill, Lance Joseph.
Tom Adams. Administration of Sacraments in Combat (Classic Reprint) (p. 16)
Tom, Alan. Disgusting Adventures of Bugaboo & Buzz Buzz. (p. 557)
Tom, Darcy, ed. see Phillips, Heather.
Tom, Darcy, illus. see Phillips, Heather.
Tom, Darcy, illus. see Shiotsu, Vicky.
Tom Jellett, illus. see Arena, Felice.
Tom, Leonard, illus. see Riggs, Kate.
Tomalin, Chris Fedorka. If I Had a Tail. (p. 1091)
Tomalin, Emmaline. Rocking Rosetta. (p. 1895)
Tomamichel, Marco, jt. auth. see Ferrie, Chris.
Tomasek, Dean, illus. see Marshall, Jane Garrett.
Tomasello, Sam, illus. see Hanneman, Monika, et al.
Tomasi, Peter J. Bridge: How the Roeblings Connected Brooklyn to New York. DuVall, Sara, illus. (p. 280)
—Bridge: How the Roeblings Connected Brooklyn to New York. DuVall, Sara et al, illus. (p. 280)
Tomasi, Peter J., ed. see Goyer, David S., et al.
Tomasi, Peter J., ed. see Johns, Geoff, et al.
Tomasinelli, Francesco. Bugs of the World: 250 Creepy-Crawly Creatures from Around Planet Earth. Yumenokaori, illus. (p. 292)
Tomasino, Steven. Special & Different: The Autistic Traveler Volume 1: the Beginning of the Autism Adventure. (p. 2076)
Tomaszewski, Grammy Ellen. Grandkids Read about Stupid Stuff. (p. 877)
Tomato Farm, illus. see Carbone, Courtney.
Tomb, R. W. B., illus. see Griffey, A. F. B.
Tombers, Monica, ed. see Mitchell, Shirley Lipscomb.
Tombleson, Alan, ed. Tour Through Dragon Dreamland. Tombleson, Drew, illus. (p. 2269)
Tombleson, Drew, illus. see Tombleson, Alan, ed.
Tomblin, Mark. Itchy-Scratchy Caterpillar. Jones, Doug, illus. (p. 1142)
Tomczyk, Tara & Smith, Terry L. Nutrition & Food Safety. (p. 1632)
Tome. Adventure down Under Saincantin, Jerome, tr. (p. 18)
—Spirou & Fantasio in New York. Janry, illus. (p. 2084)
Tome, Angeles. niño Que Vive Junto Al Mar. Mena, Virginia, illus. (p. 1610)
Tomecek, Stephen M. Animal Communication. (p. 88)
—Plate Tectonics. (p. 1758)
Tomecek, Stephen M. & West, Krista. Animal Courtship. (p. 88)
Tomecek, Steve. Dirt. (p. 552)
Tomes, Margot, illus. see Fritz, Jean.
Tometich, Annabelle. Fruits Group. (p. 796)
—I Know Basketball. (p. 1067)
—I Know Gymnastics. (p. 1067)
—Judo (p. 1185)
—Lacrosse (p. 1235)
—Mixed Martial Arts (p. 1484)
—Superstars of the New York Yankees. (p. 2161)
—Superstars of the Philadelphia Phillies. (p. 2161)
—Superstars of the San Francisco Giants. (p. 2161)
—Superstars of the St. Louis Cardinals. (p. 2161)
—Today's 12 Hottest TV Superstars. (p. 2255)
—Vegetables Group. (p. 2349)
Tomic, Tomislav. Cómo Encontrar un Cuento de Hadas. (p. 432)
—Cómo Encontrar una Criatura Fantástica. (p. 432)
Tomic, Tomislav, illus. see Bell, Alex.
Tomic, Tomislav, illus. see Hamilton, Libby.
Tomkies, Kelly Kagamas. National Counterterrorism Center. (p. 1577)
Tomkinson, E. M. World's Workers: Sarah Robinson, Agnes Weston, Mrs. Meredith (Classic Reprint) (p. 2508)
Tomkinson, Julia Redford. Doris, a Mount Holyoke Girl (Classic Reprint) (p. 586)
Tomkinson, Tim, illus. see Holub, Joan & Who HQ.
Tomkinson, Tim, illus. see Krull, Kathleen & Who HQ.
Tomko, Diana. Ten-Second Race. (p. 2205)
Tomkow, Brittanee. Poppy the Pageant Princess. (p. 1776)
Tomlin, Chris & Barrett, Pat. Buen Buen Padre (p. 290)
—Good Good Father (p. 862)
—Good Good Father for Little Ones (p. 862)
Tomlin, Sarah-Lou. Baked with Love. Alejandro, Shiela, illus. (p. 160)
—Little Dreamers, Big Ideas. Alejandro, Shiela, illus. (p. 1315)
Tomlins, Ann Marie. Leopold the Lion: Escapes from the Zoo. McCarthy, Hailey, illus. (p. 1268)
—Where Foxes Roam. McCarthy, Hailey, illus. (p. 2437)
—Where Foxes Roam 2nd Ed: Prince Edward Island & Panmure Island. McCarthy, Hailey, illus. (p. 2437)
Tomlins, Karen, illus. see Daynes, Katie.
Tomlinson, Carole a. Flying Dog. (p. 754)
Tomlinson, Charles. Magnet: Familiarly Described & Illustrated by a Box of Magnetic Toys. (p. 1381)
Tomlinson, Everett. Elder Boise: A Novel (Classic Reprint) (p. 630)
Tomlinson, Everett T. Boys of Old Monmouth: A Story of Washington's Campaign in New Jersey In 1778. (p. 273)
—Carl Hall of Tait (Classic Reprint) (p. 331)
—Four Boys in the Yosemite (Classic Reprint) (p. 772)
—Rider of the Black Horse: A Story of the American Revolution (Classic Reprint) (p. 1878)
—Scouting with General Funston (Classic Reprint) (p. 1963)
—Stories of the American Revolution, Vol. 1 (Classic Reprint) (p. 2125)
—War for Independence (Classic Reprint) (p. 2376)
—Washington's Young AIDS: A Story of the New Jersey Campaign, 1776-1777 (Classic Reprint) (p. 2382)
Tomlinson, Everett Titsworth. Four Boys in the Land of Cotton: Where They Went, What They Saw, & What They Did (Classic Reprint) (p. 772)
—In the Camp of Cornwallis: Being the Story of Reuben Denton & His Experiences During the New (Classic Reprint) (p. 1108)
—Sergeant Ted Cole, United States Marines (Classic Reprint) (p. 1990)
—Ward Hill at Weston: A Story of American School Life (Classic Reprint) (p. 2378)
Tomlinson, Fiona. Collins Big Cat Phonics for Letters & Sounds - Pack It: Band 01B/Pink B. (p. 416)
—Collins Big Cat Phonics for Letters & Sounds - the Big Nut: Band 01B/Pink B. Aranda, Omar, illus. (p. 417)
Tomlinson, H. M. Old Junk (Classic Reprint) (p. 1646)
—Waiting for Daylight (Classic Reprint) (p. 2370)
Tomlinson, Heather. Aurelie: A Faerie Tale. (p. 137)
Tomlinson, Henry. Tide Marks: Being Some Records of a Journey to the Beaches of the Moluccas & the Forest of Malaya in 1923 (Classic Reprint) (p. 2240)
—Waiting for Daylight (Classic Reprint) (p. 2370)
Tomlinson, Jill. Cat Who Wanted to Go Home. Howard, Paul, illus. (p. 342)
—Gorilla Who Wanted to Grow Up. Howard, Paul, illus. (p. 870)
—Otter Who Wanted to Know. Howard, Paul, illus. (p. 1675)
—Owl Who Was Afraid of the Dark. Howard, Paul, illus. (p. 1689)
—Penguin Who Wanted to Find Out. Howard, Paul, illus. (p. 1716)
Tomlinson, John. Stories & Sketches Relating to Yorkshire (Classic Reprint) (p. 2123)
Tomlinson, Kate. Very Skinny Whippety Dog. (p. 2354)
Tomlinson, Kellom. Art of Dancing Explained by Reading & Figures: Whereby the Manner of Performing the Steps Is Made Easy by a New & Familiar Method (Classic Reprint) (p. 121)
Tomlinson, Laurea a. Elaytay's Adventures in Space & Time: Part Two - We Meet at Last. (p. 630)
—Elaytay's Adventures in Space & Time: Part Two - We Meet at Last. Tomlinson, Lauresa, illus. (p. 630)
Tomlinson, Lauresa. Crazy Deja' Vu. Tomlinson, Lauresa, illus. (p. 469)
—There's an Alien in My Cereal. Tomlinson, Lauresa, illus. (p. 2218)
—Turning Stone. Tomlinson, Lauresa, illus. (p. 2301)
Tomlinson, Lauresa, illus. see Tomlinson, Laurea a.
Tomlinson, Lauresa, illus. see Tomlinson, Lauresa A.
Tomlinson, Lauresa A. Crazy Deja Vu - Not Again. Tomlinson, Lauresa A., illus. (p. 469)
—Elaytay's Adventures in Space & Time: We Came to Visit. (p. 630)
—Elaytay's Adventures in Space & Time: We Came to Visit. Tomlinson, Lauresa, illus. (p. 630)
—My Interview with a Fairy. Tomlinson, Lauresa, illus. (p. 1550)
Tomlinson, M. Sea & the Jungle (Classic Reprint) (p. 1966)
Tomlinson, Paul G. Bob Cook & the German Spy (Classic Reprint) (p. 251)
Tomlinson, Paul Greene. Princeton Boy under the King (Classic Reprint) (p. 1800)
Tomlinson, Rane. Quiet Warrior. (p. 1828)
tomlinson, rick. Adventures of Bob & Mr. Ant the MAZE. (p. 22)
Tomlinson, Shawn M. Pig Abides. (p. 1743)
—Why the Pig Stole Autumn. (p. 2459)
Tomljanovic, Tatiana. All about Wedges. (p. 51)
—Bison. (p. 234)
—Bluenose: Canadian Icons. (p. 250)
—Borrowing. (p. 263)
—Cougars. (p. 457)
—Rallying. (p. 1838)
—Ramadan with Code. (p. 1839)
—Skiing. (p. 2032)
—Wedges. (p. 2395)
Tomllin, Melanie. Lucy Vampoosy: The Little Vampire Dog. (p. 1366)
Tomm, Nora, illus. see Wills, Anna.
Tommalieh, Fakhri & Hujeer, Majeda. 1st Grade Learning Arabic Language Step - by - Step Approach Workbook Part 2,Third Edition: Learn Arabic Language. Al-Ghussinu, Wa'ad Diab, illus. (p. 2546)
Tommaso, Joshua. Milkman. (p. 1467)
Tommer, Sarah, illus. see Penn, M. W.
Tommer, Sarah, illus. see Penn, Mw.
Tommy. Bubba & Cecil. (p. 288)
Tomorrow, Tom. Very Silly Mayor. (p. 2354)
Tomos, Morgan, illus. see Edwards, Meinir Wyn.
Tomova, Veselina, illus. see Dawe, Tom.
Tomova, Veselina, illus. see Parsons, Marnie & Parsons, Marnie.
Tomp, Sarah. Easy Part of Impossible. (p. 621)
Tompert, Ann. Little Fox Goes to the End of the World Bryant, Laura J., illus. (p. 1317)
Tompkins, Abigail, illus. see Olitzky, Kerry.
Tompkins, Edward Staats De Grote. Suffragent, a Social Satire: An Original Play in Three Acts (Classic Reprint) (p. 2147)
Tompkins, Edward Staats DeGrote. Suffragent, a Social Satire: An Original Play in Three Acts (Classic Reprint) (p. 2147)
Tompkins, Elizabeth Knight. Her Majesty: A Romance of to-Day (Classic Reprint) (p. 956)
—Things That Count (Classic Reprint) (p. 2220)
—Unlessoned Girl: A Story of School Life (Classic Reprint) (p. 2333)
Tompkins, Ellen Wilkins. Egotistical I (Classic Reprint) (p. 628)
—Enlightenment of Paulina: A Novel (Classic Reprint) (p. 655)
Tompkins, Erle, illus. see Barrett, Steve.
Tompkins, John Thomas, jt. auth. see Bullard, William Hannum Grubb.
Tompkins, Juliet Wilbor. At the Sign of the Oldest House: A Modern Romance (Classic Reprint) (p. 131)
—At the Sign of the Oldest House; a Modern Romance. (p. 131)
—Diantha (Classic Reprint) (p. 538)
—Dr. Ellen (Classic Reprint) (p. 591)
—Ever after (Classic Reprint) (p. 669)
—Girl Named Mary (Classic Reprint) (p. 836)
—Joanna Builds a Nest (Classic Reprint) (p. 1170)
—Line a Day (Classic Reprint) (p. 1303)
—Mothers & Fathers (Classic Reprint) (p. 1510)
—Open House (Classic Reprint) (p. 1665)
—Seed of the Righteous (Classic Reprint) (p. 1982)
—Starling (Classic Reprint) (p. 2106)
—Top of the Morning (Classic Reprint) (p. 2263)
Tompkins, Michael A. & Barkin, Jonathan R. Relaxation & Stress Reduction Workbook for Teens: CBT Skills to Help You Deal with Worry & Anxiety. (p. 1862)
Tompkins, Michael A. & Martinez, Katherine A. My Anxious Mind: A Teen's Guide to Managing Anxiety & Panic. Sloan, Michael, illus. (p. 1531)
Tompkins, Michael A. & Thompson, Monique A. Insomnia Workbook for Teens: Skills to Help You Stop Stressing & Start Sleeping Better. (p. 1124)
Tompkins, William Henry. Mostly Boy (Classic Reprint) (p. 1509)
Toms, K. 10 Little Penguins. (p. 2549)
—10 Little Penguins Mini Book & Plush. (p. 2549)
Toms, Kate. Duckie Duck. (p. 608)
—I Udderly Love You. (p. 1083)
—Itsy Bitsy Spider Halloween. (p. 1148)
—Twelve Days of Christmas. (p. 2303)
Toms, Kate & Make Believe Ideas Staff. Itsy Bitsy Spider. (p. 1148)
Toms, Kate, et al. God Knows All about Me. (p. 851)
Toms, Suzette. Surfing Surprise. (p. 2163)
Tomsic, Kim. 11:11 Wish. (p. 2550)
—12th Candle. (p. 2552)
—Guitar Genius: How les Paul Engineered the Solid-Body Electric Guitar & Rocked the World (Children's Music Books, Picture Books, Guitar Books, Music Books for Kids) Helquist, Brett, illus. (p. 904)
Tonatiuh, Duncan. Danza! Amalia Hernández & Mexico's Folkloric Ballet. (p. 504)
—Dear Primo: Una Carta para Ti. (p. 520)
—Dear Primo: A Letter to My Cousin. (p. 520)
—Diego Rivera: His World & Ours. (p. 544)
—Feathered Serpent & the Five Suns: A Mesoamerican Creation Myth. (p. 717)
—Funny Bones: Posada & His Day of the Dead Calaveras. (p. 801)
—Pancho Rabbit & the Coyote: A Migrant's Tale. (p. 1695)
—Princesa y el Guerrero. (p. 1795)
—Princess & the Warrior: A Tale of Two Volcanoes. (p. 1796)
—Separate Is Never Equal: Sylvia Mendez & Her Family's Fight for Desegregation. (p. 1989)
—Soldier for Equality: José de la Luz Sáenz & the Great War. (p. 2056)
Tone, Satoe. Very Big Carrot. (p. 2352)
—Where the Heart Is. (p. 2439)
Tonel, illus. see Dole, Mayra L.
Toner, Jacqueline B., jt. auth. see Freeland, Claire A.B.
Toner, Jacqueline B. & Freeland, Claire A.B. What to Do When It's Not Fair: A Kid's Guide to Handling Envy & Jealousy. (p. 2420)
Toney, Cynthia T. Other Side of Freedom. (p. 1675)
Toney, Toni. Ecotarian Kids(tm) & the Big Four. Sekaz, Jennah, illus. (p. 624)
Toney, Wilson & Fanning, Lee. Tom Sawyer & Huckleberry Finn: St. Petersburg Adventures: the Legendary Tom Sawyer (Super Science Showcase) (p. 2257)
Tong, Andie. Justice League Reading Collection. (p. 1195)
Tong, Andie, illus. see Angleberger, Tom.

T

Tong, Andie, illus. see Black, Jake & Kane, Bob.
Tong, Andie, illus. see Black, Jake.
Tong, Andie, illus. see Finnegan, Delphine, et al.
Tong, Andie, illus. see Finnegan, Delphine.
Tong, Andie, illus. see Huelin, Jodi.
Tong, Andie, illus. see Le, Minh.
Tong, Andie, illus. see Lee, Stan & Moore, Stuart.
Tong, Andie, illus. see Lee, Stan.
Tong, Andie, illus. see Lemke, Donald B.
Tong, Andie, illus. see Lemke, Donald.
Tong, Andie, illus. see Rosen, Lucy.
Tong, Andie, illus. see Sazaklis, John & Merkel, Joe F.
Tong, Andie, illus. see Sutter, Marcus.
Tong, Anthony. Over in My City: Boston. Anderson, Penny, illus. (p. 1686)
—Over in My City: San Francisco. Perruzzi, Diane, illus. (p. 1686)
Tong, Jia. Exercise to Eliminate Tension. (p. 676)
Tong, Kimberly. Grower. (p. 899)
Tong, Paul, illus. see Krensky, Stephen.
Tong, Paul, illus. see Ransom, Candice.
Tong Tong, Tong, illus. see Million, So.
Tong, Vivian, illus. see Curley, Grace H.
Tonge, Lucy I. Stories from Mother's Note Book (Classic Reprint) (p. 2124)
Tonge, Neil. Banished, Beheaded, or Boiled in Oil: A Hair-Raising History of Crime & Punishment Throughout the Ages! (p. 164)
Tonges Wilshire, et al. Slurping Soup & Other Confusions. (p. 2039)
Tongue, Catherine. Little Hunchback of Clothespin Alley (Classic Reprint) (p. 1319)
Tongue, Mary V. Tipyn o'Bob, Vol. 10: November, 1912 (Classic Reprint) (p. 2251)
Toni, Alessandra, illus. see Hao, K. T.
Tonkin, Michelle. Simon the Seahorse & the Adventure of the Shipwreck Treasure. (p. 2020)
—Simon the Seahorse & the Legend of the Great White Shark. (p. 2020)
—Simon the Seahorse & the Lost City. (p. 2020)
—Simon the Seahorse & the Mysteries of the Deep. (p. 2020)
—Simon the Seahorse Goes Camping! (p. 2021)
—Simon the Seahorse Takes a Vacation. (p. 2021)
Tonkin, Rachel. Acorn to Oak Tree. Fizer Coleman, Stephanie, illus. (p. 11)
—Egg to Butterfly. Fizer Coleman, Stephanie, illus. (p. 628)
—Egg to Chicken. Fizer Coleman, Stephanie, illus. (p. 628)
—Egg to Frog. Fizer Coleman, Stephanie, illus. (p. 628)
Tonn, Jessica. Bluebell & Snowflake: The Story of an Unlikely Friendship. Prescott, Clara, illus. (p. 249)
Tonn, Mary Jane. Jolly Old Santa Claus. (p. 1176)
Tontiuh, Duncan, illus. see Wood, Susan.
Tony Flowers, illus. see Gwynne, Phillip.
Tony, Ryan, ed. see Caleb, McLean James.
Toohey, Cathy, jt. auth. see Mattern, Joanne.
Toohey, John Peter. Fresh Every Hour: Detailing the Adventures, Comic & Pathetic of One Jimmy Martin, Purveyor of Publicity, a Young Gentleman Possessing Sublime Nerve, Whimsical Imagination, Colossal Impudence, and, Withal, the Heart of a Child (Classic Reprint) (p. 784)
Tooke, Andrew. Pantheon. (p. 1696)
Tooke, Hana. Unadoptables. (p. 2317)
Tooke, Mary E. Just How: Suggestive Points for the Teacher, to Be Used with a Reading Chart for First Year's Work (Classic Reprint) (p. 1193)
Tooke, Susan, illus. see Bastedo, Jamie.
Tooke, Susan, illus. see Clarke, George Elliott.
Tooke, Susan, illus. see Grant, Shauntay.
Tooke, Susan, illus. see Grassby, Donna.
Tooke, Wes. King of the Mound: My Summer with Satchel Paige. (p. 1221)
—Lucky: Maris, Mantle, & My Best Summer Ever. (p. 1364)
Tooker, Gertrude Fulton. Everychild: A Play in Three Acts (Classic Reprint) (p. 671)
Tooker, L. Frank. Under Rocking Skies (Classic Reprint) (p. 2321)
Tool Kits for Kids LLC Staff, creator. Build up Your Resilience - Tool Kit for Kids: Elementary School Edition. (p. 293)
—Build up Your Resilience - Tool Kit for Kids: High School / Middle School Edition. (p. 293)
—Charge up Your Confidence - Tool Kit for Kids: High School / Middle School Edition. (p. 358)
Toole, Anne. Crystal Cadets Vol. 1. O'Neill, Katie, illus. (p. 481)
Toole, Spencer. Finn Follows Rules: Understanding Citizenship. (p. 731)
—Flowers Need Sun: If... Then. (p. 753)
—One Goal of Gabby the Ghost: What's Your Goal? (p. 1660)
—Pete the Pirate's Problem: What's the Problem? (p. 1728)
—Roxy the Rabbit Shows Respect: Giving Respect (p. 1909)
—Selena Saves Money: Checking Your Work. (p. 1987)
—Starting a Petition: Taking Civic Action. (p. 2108)
—You Can Volunteer! Civic Virtues. (p. 2526)
Tooley, Edward. Rounding Third & Headed for Home. (p. 1908)
Tooley, Sarah A. Life of Queen Alexandra (Classic Reprint) (p. 1295)
Toombs, Aisha. Place in the Chase: A Nerdi Bunny Brief. Wijesiri, Tina, illus. (p. 1753)
Toombs, Robert. Dottie the Bus Driver in Bicycle Safety. Barnett, Linda, illus. (p. 588)
Toombs, Tom. Big Camping Adventure: Little Tommy Learns Lessons from the Great Outdoors. Wells-Smith, Abby, illus. (p. 218)
—Mysterious Money Tree: Little Tommy Learns a Lesson in Giving. Smith, Abby, illus. (p. 1568)
—Way to Be a Winner: Little Tommy Learns a Lesson in Working Together. Wells Smith, Abby, illus. (p. 2387)
Toomey, Randy & Smith, Tim D. Still the Same. (p. 2119)
Toon, Paige. Accidental Life of Jessie Jefferson. (p. 10)
—All about the Hype. (p. 50)
—I Knew You Were Trouble: A Jessie Jefferson Novel. (p. 1067)
Toope, Jeremiah. Crock of Gold: Twelve Fairy Tales, Old & New (Classic Reprint) (p. 476)
Toor, Rachel. Misunderstood: A Book about Rats. (p. 1483)
Tooth, Lucy. Star the Tooth Fairy from Treasure Cloud Shares Secrets with You! (p. 2103)
—Star the Tooth Fairy Haunted by Mr. Jack-O-Lantern in Pumpkinland! (p. 2103)
—Star the Tooth Fairy Is Checking on You! (p. 2103)
—Star the Tooth Fairy Takes A Holiday to Visit Santa at the North Pole! (p. 2103)
—Star the Tooth Fairy Wants to Know If You Need Braces? (p. 2103)
—Tooth Fairy Loose & Lost Baby Tooth Coloring Log. (p. 2262)
—Tooth Fairy Loose & Lost Tooth Coloring Log. (p. 2262)
Tooty. Patches in Winter. (p. 1704)
Top That!, creator. Animals with Martha the Monkey. (p. 96)
—Counting with Billy the Bear. (p. 460)
—Journey to the Bottom of the Sea. (p. 1182)
—Old MacDonald's Farm. (p. 1647)
—Shapes with Penny the Penguin. (p. 2000)
Top That Publishing Staff, ed. see Cabral, Jeane.
Top That Publishing Staff, ed. see Lambert, Nat.
Top That Publishing Staff, ed. see Munton, Gill.
Top That Publishing Staff, ed. see Ranson, Erin.
Top That! Staff, ed. see Ranson, Erin.
Topacio, Francine. Creatures in a Dark Cave. (p. 471)
—Creatures in a Hot Desert (p. 471)
—Creatures in a Wet Rain Forest (p. 471)
—Creatures in the Icy Tundra (p. 471)
—Modoc. (p. 1488)
—What Do You Know about Animals with Armor? (p. 2409)
—What Do You Know about Animals with Pouches? (p. 2409)
—What Do You Know about Underground Animals? (p. 2409)
Topaz, Ksenia, illus. see Lehman-Wilzig, Tami.
Topaz, Ksenia, illus. see Levine, Anna.
Topelius, Z. Surgeon's Stories: A Series of Swedish Historical Romances, in Six Cycles (Classic Reprint) (p. 2163)
—Times of Frederick I (Classic Reprint) (p. 2247)
Topelius, Zacharias. Surgeon's Stories: Times of Linnæus (Classic Reprint) (p. 2163)
—Surgeon's Stories: Times of Linnaeus (Classic Reprint) (p. 2163)
—Surgeon's Stories: Times of Battle & of Rest (Classic Reprint) (p. 2163)
—Times of Gustaf Adolf (Classic Reprint) (p. 2247)
Topham, Anne. Daphne in the Fatherland (Classic Reprint) (p. 504)
—Julia & I in Canada (Classic Reprint) (p. 1186)
—Memories of the Kaiser's Court (Classic Reprint) (p. 1446)
Topinka, Joseph Baar. Just Judy: A Citizen & Leader for Illinois. (p. 1193)
Topix Media Lab Editors. Force Awakens: The Official Lucas Collector's Edition. (p. 764)
Topka, U. P. Magic Fifteen. (p. 1377)
Topol, Carolyn LeVine. Run for It All. (p. 1914)
Toponce, Alexander. Reminiscences of Alexander Toponce, Pioneer, 1839-1923 (Classic Reprint) (p. 1865)
Topping, Delores. My Superpower. (p. 1562)
Topsel, Edward. History of Four-Footed Beasts & Serpents: Describing at Large Their True & Lively Figure, Their Several Names, Conditions, Kinds, Virtues (Both Natural & Medicinal) Countries of Their Breed, Their Love & Hatred to Mankind, & the Wonderful Wo. (p. 978)
Topsell, John. How to Raise & Keep a Dragon. Nigg, Jospeh, ed. (p. 1043)
Tor, Seidler, jt. auth. see Seidler, Tor.
Torain, Janie Sheeley. If I Could Quit School for a Day! (p. 1091)
Torba, Edward. Matt Monroe & the Haunted House. (p. 1425)
Torbergson, Paige B., illus. see Vines, Heather Glenn.
Torbert, Wayne E. Twelve for Thebes, a Tale of Ancient Greece. Torbert, Wayne E., illus. (p. 2303)
Torbett, D. Land of Promise: A Novelization of W. Somerset Maugham's Play (Classic Reprint) (p. 1242)
—Life: A Novelization of Thompson Buchanan's Play (Classic Reprint) (p. 1287)
—Sinners: A Novelization of Owen Davis's Play (Classic Reprint) (p. 2024)
Torchinsky, Oleg, et al. Russia. (p. 1917)
Torday, E., jt. auth. see Tormay, Cecile.
Torday, Piers. Box of Delights. (p. 266)
—Last Wild. (p. 1250)
Tordoff, Brian G. Letters & Words Sudoku. (p. 1279)
Toreeva, Natalia G. Battle on the Kalinov-Bridge: A Russian Fairy Tale. (p. 175)
—Greg & the Sea Monster. (p. 895)
Torelli, Giuseppe. Iosephi Torelli Veronensis Geometrica (Classic Reprint) (p. 1133)
Toretto, Jordana. Runaway Children. (p. 1915)
Torgan, Keith & Siesel, Barbara. Green Golly & Her Golden Flute. Langelier-Lebeda, Suzanne, illus. (p. 894)
Torgent, Sherry. King's Oracle. (p. 1223)
Torgrimsen, Reidun. Timmy's Christmas, a Very Special Pig from Sugar Valley & His Best Friend. (p. 2247)
Toriello, James. Stomach: Learning How We Digest. (p. 2121)
Toriello, James, jt. auth. see Bayden, Maya.
Torino, Universita Di. Physicae Experimentalis Lineamenta Ad Subalpinos, Vol. 2 (Classic Reprint) (p. 1737)
—Physicæ Experimentalis Lineamenta Ad Subalpinos, Vol. 1 (Classic Reprint) (p. 1737)
Toriyama, Akira. Dragon Ball Full Color Freeza Arc, Volume 1. (p. 593)
Torke, Kyle, ed. see Phillips, Louis.
Torke, Kyle & Torke, Barbara. Hiking the Grand Mesa: A Clementine the Rescue Dog Story. (p. 971)
—Ice Breaking: The Adventures of Clementine the Rescue Dog. (p. 1087)
Tormay, Cecile. Old House: A Novel (Classic Reprint) (p. 1646)
—Outlaw's Diary: Revolution (Classic Reprint) (p. 1685)
—Outlaw's Diary: The Commune (Classic Reprint) (p. 1685)
Tormo, Bea, illus. see McGee, Joe.
Tornatore, Carol, illus. see Judson, Susan Ryan.
Tornatore, Carol, illus. see Salisbury, Linda G.
Tornatore, Carol, illus. see Salisbury, Linda.
Tornio, Jack & Tornio, Stacy. 101 Outdoor Adventures to Have (p. 2558)
TORNIO, Keffer. Kids Ultimate Animal Adventure Book: 745 Quirky Facts & Hands-On Activities for Year-Round Fun (p. 1216)
Tornio, Stacy. Bird Nests. (p. 230)
—Cathy's Animal Garden: Enter at Your Own Risk. Bell, Samantha, illus. (p. 345)
—Ranger Rick's Amazing Animals: Butterflies. (p. 1840)
Tornio, Stacy, jt. auth. see National Wildlife Federation Staff.
Tornio, Stacy & Keffer, Ken. Kids' Outdoor Adventure Book: 448 Great Things to Do in Nature Before You Grow Up. (p. 1216)
—National Parks! (p. 1577)
—Ranger Rick Goes to the National Parks! (p. 1840)
—Secret Lives of Animals: 1,001 Tidbits, Oddities, & Amazing Facts about North America's Coolest Animals. (p. 1977)
—Truth about Nature: A Family's Guide to 144 Common Myths about the Great Outdoors (p. 2296)
Torno, Shane. Every Cake Has a Baker. Carson, Chuck, illus. (p. 670)
Tornow, Chani, jt. auth. see Burton, Jeffrey.
Tornqvist, Marit. Charlie's Magical Carnival (p. 360)
—Wake up, Let's Play! (p. 2371)
Tornqvist, Marit, illus. see Lindgren, Astrid.
Tornqvist, Marit, illus. see Tornqvist-Verschuur, Rita.
Tornqvist-Verschuur, Rita. Tom's Christmas Fish Tornqvist, Marit, illus. (p. 2259)
Toro, Jorge, tr. see Hoffmann, E. T. A.
Toro, Sandra. Dona Gracia: Beacon of Hope. (p. 581)
Toro, Tom. How to Potty Train Your Porcupine. (p. 1043)
Toro, Valentina, illus. see Lowell, Barbara.
Toron, Eli, illus. see Mindel, Nissan.
Toronto, Grand Opera House. Grand 1915: No. 11 (Classic Reprint) (p. 876)
Toronto, Toronto. Living the Christmas Spirit, Lost on Christmas Eve (Classic Reprint) (p. 1334)
Toronto, University Of. ACTA Victoriana, Vol. 42: January, 1918 (Classic Reprint) (p. 12)
—Epistaxis, 1920 (Classic Reprint) (p. 658)
—Epistaxis, 1921 (Classic Reprint) (p. 658)
—Epistaxis, 1922 (Classic Reprint) (p. 658)
—Epistaxis, 1923, Vol. 25 (Classic Reprint) (p. 658)
—Epistaxis, 1924 (Classic Reprint) (p. 658)
—Epistaxis, 1925 (Classic Reprint) (p. 658)
—Epistaxis, 1926 (Classic Reprint) (p. 658)
—Epistaxis, 1927 (Classic Reprint) (p. 658)
—Epistaxis, 1928 (Classic Reprint) (p. 658)
—Epistaxis, 1933, Vol. 22 (Classic Reprint) (p. 658)
—Epistaxis, 1934, Vol. 23 (Classic Reprint) (p. 658)
—Epistaxis, 1936, Vol. 25 (Classic Reprint) (p. 658)
—Epistaxis, 1937, Vol. 26 (Classic Reprint) (p. 658)
—Epistaxis, 1938, Vol. 27 (Classic Reprint) (p. 658)
—Epistaxis, 1939, Vol. 28 (Classic Reprint) (p. 658)
—Goblin, Vol. 1: March, 1921 (Classic Reprint) (p. 850)
—Goblin, Vol. 1: February, 1921 (Classic Reprint) (p. 850)
—Goblin, Vol. 2: April, 1922 (Classic Reprint) (p. 850)
Torr, Cecil. Small Talk at Wreyland (Classic Reprint) (p. 2040)
Torr, John Berry. Uncle's Legacy, Vol. 1: A Novel in Three Volumes (Classic Reprint) (p. 2320)
—Uncle's Legacy, Vol. 2 Of 3: A Novel in Three Volumes (Classic Reprint) (p. 2320)
Torralba, Enrique, illus. see Pastrana, Miguel.
Torre, Attilio, illus. see Patrick, B.
Torre, Beatriz Gonzalez, illus. see Esposito, Kathleen Christina.
Torre, Beatriz Gonzalez, tr. see Esposito, Kathleen Christina.
Torre, Cristina de la. About Mammals: A Guide for Children = Sobre Los Mamíferos: Una Guía para Niños. Sill, Cathryn P. & Sill, John, illus. (p. 6)
Torrecilla, Pablo, illus. see Zepeda, Gwendolyn.
Torrecilla, Pablo, jt. auth. see Benatar, Raquel.
Torrecilla, Pablo, jt. auth. see Caraballo, Samuel.
Torrence, Jaala. Eli Makes Room. Myers, Garrett, illus. (p. 635)
—Eli Meets Someone New. Myers, Garrett, illus. (p. 635)
Torrence, Jaala & Myers, Garrett. Eli Makes Room. Myers, Garrett, illus. (p. 635)
Torrence, Jack. Light Show: Reflection & Absorption. (p. 1299)
Torrence, Ridgely. Granny Maumee; the Rider of Dreams; Simon the Cyrenian: Plays for a Negro Theater (Classic Reprint) (p. 880)
Torrens, Robert. Victim of Intolerance, Vol. 1: Or, the Hermit of Killarney; a Catholic Tale (Classic Reprint) (p. 2355)
Torrent, Dani, illus. see Leannah, Michael.
Torrent, Dani, illus. see Sayalero, Myriam.
Torres, Ben. Kingpin: Born Against. (p. 1222)
Torres, Carlos, tr. see Poe, Edgar Allan.
Torres, Diana, illus. see Bronstein, Arlene.
Torres, Dottie, illus. see Sobel, Gerrie.
Torres, J. Batman: the Brave & the Bold. Beatty, Terry et al, illus. (p. 172)
—Batman Versus the Yeti! Barberi, Carlo & Beatty, Terry, illus. (p. 172)
—Bring It On. (p. 282)
—BroBots & the Mecha Malarkey! Dove, Sean, illus. (p. 284)
—BroBots And the Shoujo Shenanigans! Dove, Sean, illus. (p. 284)
—Charge of the Army Eternal Davis, Dan & Suriano, Andy, illus. (p. 358)
—Checkers & Dot at the Beach. Lum, J., illus. (p. 363)
—Checkers & Dot at the Zoo. Lum, J., illus. (p. 363)
—Checkers & Dot on the Farm. Lum, J., illus. (p. 363)
—How to Spot a Sasquatch. Grand, Aurélie, illus. (p. 1044)
—Jinx - Little Miss Steps. Burchett, Rick & Austin, Terry, illus. (p. 1169)
—Little Miss Steps. Burchett, Rick & Austin, Terry, illus. (p. 1322)
—Lola: A Ghost Story. Or, Elbert & Beaton, Jill, illus. (p. 1340)
—Power Lunch: First Course Trippe, Dean, illus. (p. 1782)
—Power Lunch Vol. 2: Seconds. Bk. 2 Trippe, Dean, illus. (p. 1782)
—Smells Like Teen Titans Spirit (p. 2041)
—Sound of Thunder. Hicks, Faith Erin, illus. (p. 2067)
—Titans Together! (p. 2251)
Torres, J., jt. auth. see Wayne, Matt.
Torres, J., jt. auth. see Wheeler, Shannon.
Torres, J., et al. Beast Boy Who Cried Wolf (p. 181)
—Demo (p. 528)
—Monster Zit! (p. 1497)
—Thunder & Lightning Strike! (p. 2238)
Torres, Jennifer. Battle. (p. 173)
—Disappearing. (p. 553)
—Finding the Music Alarcão, Renato, illus. (p. 730)
—Flor & Miranda Steal the Show. (p. 750)
—Fresh New Face of Griselda. (p. 785)
—Return. (p. 1870)
—Stef Soto, la Reina Del Taco: Stef Soto, Taco Queen (Spanish Edition) (p. 2112)
—Stef Soto, Taco Queen. (p. 2112)
Torres, Jickie, illus. see Walter Foster Publishing & Berry, Bob.
Torres, John. Carmelo Anthony. (p. 332)
—Cristiano Ronaldo: Champion Soccer Star. (p. 475)
—Critical Perspectives on Minors Playing High-Contact Sports. (p. 476)
—How Barack Obama Fought the War on Terrorism. (p. 1026)
—Neymar: Champion Soccer Star. (p. 1601)
—Sonia Sotomayor: First Latina Supreme Court Justice. (p. 2063)
—Tim Tebow. (p. 2243)
—We Visit Puerto Rico. (p. 2393)
—We Visit the Dominican Republic. (p. 2393)
Torres, John A. Famous Immigrant Athletes. (p. 704)
—Guatemalan Genocide of the Maya People. (p. 902)
—Lil Wayne. (p. 1301)
—Racing Soap Box Derby Stock Cars. (p. 1832)
Torres, John Albert. Dwight Howard: A Basketball Star Who Cares. (p. 611)
—Haruki Murakami: Best-Selling Author. (p. 935)
—Hong Kong. (p. 999)
—Jay-Z: Hip-Hop Mogul. (p. 1161)
—Lionel Messi. (p. 1306)
—Ludacris: Hip-Hop Mogul. (p. 1366)
—Meet Our New Student from Nicaragua. (p. 1439)
—Meet Our New Student from Zambia. (p. 1439)
—People Behind Murderous Crime Sprees. (p. 1718)
—People Behind School Shootings & Public Massacres. (p. 1718)
—Real-Life Zombies (p. 1849)
—Shaun White: A Snowboarder & Skateboarder Who Cares. (p. 2003)
—Soccer Star Cristiano Ronaldo. (p. 2052)
—Soccer Star Lionel Messi. (p. 2052)
—Top 25 Basketball Skills, Tips, & Tricks. (p. 2263)
—Top 25 Football Skills, Tips, & Tricks. (p. 2263)
Torres, John & Healey, Tim. World's Weirdest News Stories. (p. 2508)
Torres, Laura. Rock Your Party. (p. 1894)
—Rock Your Room. (p. 1894)
—Rock Your School Stuff. (p. 1894)
—Rock Your Wardrobe. (p. 1894)
Torres, Mario. My Fun Wonderworld: Children's Stories Book (p. 1548)
Torres, Nora Estela, illus. see Calderon, Eduardo Caballero.
Torres, Rosa, tr. see Clarke, Denise B.
Torres, Stacey M. Let's Take a Trip To: The Beginning. (p. 1277)
Torres Vanga, Tony. Jimmy Wheelz & the Minilights. (p. 1169)
Torres, Veronica Hilda. My Mommy's Sweater. Rottinger, Amy, illus. (p. 1556)
Torres, Victoria. Ducklings Grow up - 6 Pack: Set of 6 Common Core Edition. (p. 608)
—Rainy Day - 6 Pack: Set of 6 Common Core Edition. (p. 1837)
Torres, Walter, illus. see Flor Ada, Alma.
Torres, Walter, illus. see Montero, Mayra.
Torres, Zoe. At the Block Sale: Add & Subtract Within 20. (p. 130)
Torrest, T. Incredibly True Adventures of Clyde the Betta Fish. (p. 1114)
Torretta, Sara, illus. see Dahl, Michael.
Torrey Balsara, Andrea, illus. see Roy, Philip.
Torrey, Bradford. Birds in the Bush (Classic Reprint) (p. 232)
—Clerk of the Woods (Classic Reprint) (p. 403)
—Everyday Birds: Elementary Studies (Classic Reprint) (p. 671)
—Field-Days in California (Classic Reprint) (p. 723)
—Florida Sketch-Book (Classic Reprint) (p. 751)
—Footing It in Franconia (Classic Reprint) (p. 762)
—Foot-Path Way (Classic Reprint) (p. 761)
—Nature's Invitation: Notes of a Bird-Gazer North & South (Classic Reprint) (p. 1582)
—Rambler's Lease (Classic Reprint) (p. 1839)
—Spring Notes from Tennessee. (p. 2092)
—Spring Notes from Tennessee (Classic Reprint) (p. 2092)
—World of Green Hills: Observations of Nature, & Human Nature, in the Blue Ridge (Classic Reprint) (p. 2503)
—World of Green Hills. (p. 2503)
Torrey, Mary Ide. City & Country Life: Or Moderate Better Than Rapid Gains (Classic Reprint) (p. 394)
Torrey, Michele. Case of the Barfy Birthday. Newman, Barbara Johansen, illus. (p. 336)
—Case of the Crooked Carnival. Newman, Barbara Johansen, illus. (p. 337)
—Case of the Gasping Garbage. Torrey, Michele & Newman, Barbara Johansen, illus. (p. 337)
—Case of the Graveyard Ghost. Newman, Barbara Johansen, illus. (p. 337)
—Case of the Mossy Lake Monster. Torrey, Michele & Newman, Barbara Johansen, illus. (p. 338)
—Case of the Terrible T. Rex Newman, Barbara Johansen, illus. (p. 338)
Torrey, Rich, illus. see Pérez-Mercado, Mary Margaret.
Torrey, Rich, illus. see Stiles, Amanda.
Torrey, Rich, illus. see Torrey, Richard.

Torrey, Richard. Ally-Saurus & the First Day of School. (p. 57)
—Almost. Torrey, Richard, illus. (p. 57)
—Almost Terrible Playdate. Torrey, Rich, illus. (p. 57)
—Because. Torrey, Richard, illus. (p. 186)
—Moe is Best. (p. 1488)
—My Dog, Bob. (p. 1537)
—My Dog, Bob. Torrey, Richard, illus. (p. 1537)
—Why? Torrey, Richard, illus. (p. 2454)
Torrey, Richard L., illus. see Pérez-Mercado, Mary Margaret.
Torricelli, Dr Richard & Torricelli, Richard. Tale of a Schnauzer. (p. 2178)
Torris, Sophie. Etait une Fois l'Intimidation (Theatre Pour les Adolescents) Texte a Jouer Pour les 10 a 14 ANS. (p. 665)
—Y'a Pas de lézard (Théâtre Pour Tout-Petits) Texte À Jouer Pour les 4 À 7 ANS. (p. 2516)
Torrisi, Cathy. Eat All Your Colors. (p. 621)
—Get up & Go! (p. 825)
—Healthy Day. (p. 943)
—I Know First Aid. (p. 1067)
—Take a Stand. (p. 2176)
—Tell Someone You Trust. (p. 2202)
Torrisi, Gary, illus. see Urmston, Kathleen.
Torsen, Patricia. Wren Nest. (p. 2511)
Torseter, Oyvind. Heartless Troll. Dickson, Kari, tr. (p. 946)
Torseter, Oyvind, illus. see Lunde, Stein Erik.
Torseter, Oyvind, illus. see Ovreas, Hakon.
Torseter, Oyvind, jt. auth. see Steven, Kenneth.
Torseter, Oyvind, creator. Hole. (p. 987)
Torsiello, David P. Michael Phelps: Swimming for Olympic Gold. (p. 1458)
—Read about Alex Rodriguez. (p. 1845)
—Read about Carmelo Anthony. (p. 1845)
—Read about Derek Jeter. (p. 1845)
—Read about Drew Brees. (p. 1845)
—Read about Eli Manning. (p. 1845)
—Read about Kobe Bryant. (p. 1845)
Torstensson, Elisabeth, tr. see Pere, Tuula.
Tort, Lambert le. Li Romans d'Alixandre (Classic Reprint) (p. 1283)
Tortland, Christy. Heavy-Machine Operators on the Job. (p. 947)
Tortoise Dreaming Staff. Hook-Nosed Einiosaurus. Tortoise Dreaming Staff, illus. (p. 1000)
—Suchomimus Smiles Like a Crocodile. Tortoise Dreaming Staff, illus. (p. 2146)
—Three-Horned Triceratops. Tortoise Dreaming Staff, illus. (p. 2233)
Tortop, Anil, illus. see Hogan, Tamara Anne.
Tortop, Anil, illus. see Sillett, Devon.
Tortorella, Jackie. Our Father: Living the Lord's Prayer (p. 1678)
Tortosa, Wilson, illus. see Bowen, Carl & Fuentes, Benny.
Tortosa, Wilson, illus. see Bowen, Carl.
Tortosa, Wilson, illus. see Yomtov, Nel.
Torvi, Soumya. Princesss Quest for Knowledge. (p. 1800)
Torvund, Helge & Johnsen, Mari Kanstad. Vivaldi. Shaterian, Jeanie & Reinhard, Thilo, trs. (p. 2364)
Torzsas Andrea. Állatmesés Tanoda. (p. 55)
Toscano, Leesa. Eat Your Vegetables. Bodoff, Janet, illus. (p. 622)
Toscano, Rodrigo. Explosion Rocks Springfield. (p. 684)
Tosh, Anita. Zella Chronicles. (p. 2539)
Tosh, Peter. African: A Children's Picture Book. Moss, Rachel, illus. (p. 32)
Toshifumi, Futamase. Astronomy Law Theorem Terminology. (p. 129)
Toshiley. Sponge & the River of Sleepiness. (p. 2086)
Toska, Mary Lou. Ernest's Dream: A Young Boy Wanting to Spend the Summer in the High Alps. (p. 660)
—Shepherd Boy. (p. 2005)
Tosolini, Nicola, illus. see Savini, Alberto & Gilbert, Janet.
Tossell, David H. Charlie & Chippo Meet a Ghost. Pritchard, Louise, illus. (p. 359)
Toten, Teresa. Beware That Girl. (p. 211)
—Beyond Blonde: Book Three of the Series. (p. 211)
—Unlikely Hero of Room 13B. (p. 2333)
Toth, Dorothy, illus. see Weissman, D. S.
Toth, Em. Adventures of Jelly, Bean, & Sophia. (p. 24)
Toth, Henrietta. Career As a Heavy Equipment Operator (p. 328)
—Coping with Life in Homeless Shelters. (p. 451)
—Henry Hudson. (p. 955)
—Ibn Battuta: The Greatest Traveler of the Muslim World. (p. 1087)
—Iron. (p. 1135)
—Lil Nas X: Record-Breaking Musician Who Blurs the Lines. (p. 1301)
—Lilly Singh: Actor & Comedian with More Than 3 Billion Views (p. 1302)
—Lindsey Stirling: Violinist with More Than 2 Billion Views (p. 1303)
—Murder of Emmett Till. (p. 1527)
—Silver. (p. 2019)
—Theocracy (p. 2215)
—Viking Explorers. (p. 2357)
Toth, Henrietta & Pang, Guek Cheng. Mongolia. (p. 1493)
Toth, M., jt. auth. see Rieder, E.
Toth, Shannon, illus. see Wittrock, Jeni.
Toth, Vince. My Sister Is in the Coast Guard (p. 1561)
Toth-Chernin, Jan. E-Textiles. (p. 612)
Totheroh, Dan. Wild Birds, Vol. 1: A Play in Three Acts (Classic Reprint) (p. 2463)
Tóth-Jones, Dee S. Street Cats of Marrakech. Stevenson, Seline, illus. (p. 2140)
Totire, Valerie, illus. see Coulton, Mia.
Totire, Valerie, illus. see Ketch, Ann.
Totten, Cindy. Argus, Vol. 4: Fall 1979 (Classic Reprint) (p. 115)
Totten, Cindy Jo. Argus, Vol. 3: Spring 1979 (Classic Reprint) (p. 115)
Tottenham, G. L. Harry Egerton, or the Younger Son of the Day, Vol. 2 (Classic Reprint) (p. 934)
—Harry Egerton, or the Younger Son of the Day, Vol. 1 of 3 (Classic Reprint) (p. 934)
Tottenham, George L. Charlie Villars at Cambridge, Vol. 2 of 2 (Classic Reprint) (p. 360)
Tottenham, George Loftus. Charlie Villars at Cambridge, Vol. 1 of 2 (Classic Reprint) (p. 360)
—Terence Mcgowan, the Irish Tenant, Vol. 1 of 2 (Classic Reprint) (p. 2206)
Totti, Paolo. Flauto a 7 Diesis: The Flute That Goes to Seven Sharps. (p. 747)
Tottisi, Gary, illus. see Urmston, Kathleen.
Tottman, Julie. Superstar Cats: 25 Easy Tricks to Make Your Cat Shine in the Spotlight. (p. 2161)
—Superstar Cats: 25 Easy Tricks to Make Your Cat Shine in the Spotlight. Santos, Emanuel, illus. (p. 2161)
—Superstar Dogs: 35 Easy Tricks to Make Your Dog Shine in the Spotlight. (p. 2161)
Touche, Maria Price La. Letters of a Noble Woman: Mrs. la Touche of Harristown; Edited by Margaret Ferrier Young (Classic Reprint) (p. 1280)
Touchell, Dianne. Small Madness (p. 2039)
—Sticky Notes. (p. 2118)
Toufexis, George. Alexander Hamilton Activity Book. (p. 42)
—At the Zoo Stickers. (p. 131)
—Big Apple Brain Busters Activity Book. (p. 216)
—Chicago Challenge Activity Book. (p. 367)
—Demonic Dragons Stickers. (p. 528)
—Discovering Washington D. C. Activity Book: Awesome Activities about Our Nation's Capital. (p. 556)
—Glitter Tattoos Day of the Dead. (p. 843)
—Great Explorers Activity Book. (p. 886)
—Halloween Super Sticker Book. (p. 912)
—History's Mysteries! Animals: Activity Book. (p. 982)
—History's Mysteries! Dinosaurs: Activity Book. (p. 982)
—Let's Explore! Sharks Sticker Coloring Book: With 30 Stickers! (p. 1272)
—Monster Mall Activity Book. (p. 1496)
—MONSTER MASH-Up—Aliens Meet Their Match. (p. 1496)
—MONSTER MASH-Up—Dinosaurs Face Destruction. (p. 1496)
—MONSTER MASH-Up—Rise of the Predators. (p. 1496)
—MONSTER MASH-Up—Robots' Revenge. (p. 1496)
—Monster Matrix Activity Book. (p. 1496)
—My Human Body Coloring Book. (p. 1550)
—Nelson Mandela Coloring Book. (p. 1587)
—Outrageous Human Body Activity Book. (p. 1685)
—River Monsters of the World. (p. 1887)
—U. S. A. Facts & Fun Activity Book. (p. 2311)
—Ultimate Horse-Athon Facts & Activity Book. (p. 2315)
—Ultimate Shark-Athon Facts & Activity Book. (p. 2315)
—Unbelievable Cryptozoology Coloring Book. (p. 2317)
—World Atlas Activity & Coloring Book. (p. 2501)
Toufexis, George & Coloring Books Staff. Sharks! Coloring Book. (p. 2002)
Toufexis, George, et al. Sharks. (p. 2002)
Toufidou, Calliopi. In My Grandmother's Footsteps. (p. 1106)
Tougas, Chris. Dojo Daycare. (p. 578)
—Dojo Surprise. (p. 578)
—Mechanimals (p. 1435)
—Tinkle, Tinkle, Little Star. Tougas, Chris, illus. (p. 2248)
Tougas, Janine. Gabriel Entre Chien et Loup. Flower, Alexis, illus. (p. 804)
—Henri et le Cheval Noir. Flower, Alexis, illus. (p. 954)
—Sylvianne Aux Couleurs du Corbeau. Flower, Alexis, illus. (p. 2173)
Tougas, Joe. Beatles: Defining Rock 'n' Roll. (p. 182)
—Heroic Comeback. (p. 962)
—Mind-Blowing Movie Stunts. (p. 1469)
—New York. (p. 1598)
—President Garfield's Killer & the America He Left Behind: The Assassin, the Crime, the Hapless Doctors, & a President's Slow, Grim Death. (p. 1789)
—President Kennedy's Killer & the America He Left Behind: The Assassin, the Crime, & the End of a Hopeful Vision in Chaotic Times. (p. 1789)
—Virginia. (p. 2360)
Tougas, Joe, jt. auth. see Gunderson, Jessica.
Tougas, Joe & Gunderson, Jessica. Assassins' America. (p. 127)
Tougas, Joe, et al. Wild Stunts. (p. 2464)
Tougas, Shelley. Birmingham 1963: How a Photograph Rallied Civil Rights Support (p. 233)
—Finders Keepers. (p. 728)
—Girls Rock! Amazing Tales of Women in Music (p. 839)
—Girls Rule! Amazing Tales of Female Leaders (p. 839)
—Girls Star! Amazing Tales of Hollywood's Leading Ladies (p. 839)
—Laura Ingalls Is Ruining My Life. (p. 1252)
—Little Rock Girl 1957: How a Photograph Changed the Fight for Integration (p. 1327)
—Patron Saint for Junior Bridesmaids. (p. 1706)
—Science of Weapons (p. 1958)
—Weapons, Gear, & Uniforms of the Iraq War (p. 2393)
—Weapons, Gear, & Uniforms of the Vietnam War (p. 2393)
Touger, Malka. Door That's Never Locked. (p. 585)
Tougias, Kristin. Good Night Hong Kong. Keele, Kevin, illus. (p. 864)
Tougias, Michael J. Into the Blizzard: Heroism at Sea During the Great Blizzard of 1978 [the Young Readers Adaptation]. (p. 1128)
Tougias, Michael J. & Sherman, Paul Casey. Finest Hours (Young Readers Edition) The True Story of a Heroic Sea Rescue. (p. 730)
Touhey Storrs, Mary-Chandler. Hurricane Christmas Trees. (p. 1054)
Touliatou, Sophia, illus. see Lewis, Carrie.
Touliatou, Sophia, illus. see McGlen, Tim.
Touliatou, Sophia, illus. see Poitier, Anton.
Touliatou, Sophia, illus. see Welsh, Clare Helen.
Toulmin, Sarah. Baby's Little Bible Stephenson, Kristina, illus. (p. 154)
Toulmin-Rothe, Ann, illus. see Sabin, Francene & Macken, JoAnn Early.
Toulouse, Isadore, tr. see Robertson, Joanne.
Toumazou, Lydia. Legend of the Eltanin Warrior. (p. 1262)
Tour, Anat. Huge, Gigantic, Humongous Lizard in My Living Room. (p. 1048)
—Mama's Bag. Tour, Anat, illus. (p. 1393)
Tour, Anat, illus. see Tseng, C. K. Thomas.
Toure, Khari. Love Yourself. (p. 1361)
Tourgee, Albion W. Black Ice (Classic Reprint) (p. 238)
—Bricks Without Straw: A Novel (Classic Reprint) (p. 280)
—Button's Inn (Classic Reprint) (p. 304)
—John Eax & Mamelon: Or the South Without the Shadow (Classic Reprint) (p. 1172)
—Man Who Outlived Himself. (p. 1395)
—Man Who Outlived Himself (Classic Reprint) (p. 1395)
—Royal Gentleman (Classic Reprint) (p. 1909)
—Son of Old Harry a Novel (Classic Reprint) (p. 2062)
Tourgee, Albion Winegar. Figs & Thistles: A Romance of the Western Reserve (Classic Reprint) (p. 726)
—Hot Plowshares: A Novel (Classic Reprint) (p. 1006)
—Hot Plowshares. (p. 1006)
Tourgenief, Ivan Sergeevich. Virgin Soil (Classic Reprint) (p. 2360)
Tourghenieff, Ivan. Russian Life in the Interior: Or the Experiences of a Sportsman (Classic Reprint) (p. 1917)
Tourgueneff, Ivan. Poems in Prose (Classic Reprint) (p. 1765)
Tourjee, Eben, jt. auth. see Brewer, Ebenezer Cobham.
Tourlonias, Joëlle, illus. see Engler, Michael & Watkinson, Laura.
Tourlonias, Joëlle, illus. see Engler, Michael.
Tournemille, Harry. Attention Deficit Hyperactivity Disorder. (p. 135)
Tourneville, Harry. Attention-Deficit Hyperactivity Disorder. (p. 135)
Tournier, Bertrand, illus. see Ferre, Gil.
Tournier, Michel. Contes du Medianoche. (p. 444)
—Couleuvrine. (p. 458)
—Rois Mages Tournier. (p. 1897)
Tourtel, Mary. Strange Adventures of Billy Rabbit (Classic Reprint) (p. 2137)
Tourville, Amanda Doering. Alimenta Tu Cuerpo. Rooney, Ronnie, illus. (p. 47)
—Animal Invaders. (p. 90)
—Bulldozers Trover, Zachary, illus. (p. 296)
—Comportamiento y Modales en la Cafetería. Lensch, Chris, illus. (p. 436)
—Count the Critters: 6 Titles Holm, Sharon Lane, illus. (p. 458)
—Cranes Trover, Zachary, illus. (p. 467)
—Fire Trucks Trover, Zachary, illus. (p. 733)
—Friends with Disabilities Sorra, Kristin, illus. (p. 787)
—Garbage Trucks Trover, Zachary, illus. (p. 808)
—Helen Keller: Courageous Learner & Leader (p. 949)
—Lávate. Rooney, Ronnie, illus. (p. 1253)
—Manners at a Friend's House Lensch, Chris, illus. (p. 1397)
—Manners with a Library Book Lensch, Chris, illus. (p. 1398)
—My Friend Has ADHD Sorra, Kristin, illus. (p. 1547)
—My Friend Has Autism Sorra, Kristin, illus. (p. 1547)
—My Friend Has down Syndrome Sorra, Kristin, illus. (p. 1547)
—My Friend Has Dyslexia Sorra, Kristin, illus. (p. 1547)
—Out of the Dark: Coping with Emotional Challenges (p. 1682)
—Tractors Trover, Zachary, illus. (p. 2273)
—Transportation in the City Thompson, Jeffrey, illus. (p. 2278)
—Whose Equipment Is This? (p. 2454)
—Whose Tools Are These? (p. 2454)
Tourville, Amanda Doering & Sorra, Kristin. Mi Amiga Tiene Sindrome de Down. Translations.com Staff, tr. (p. 1454)
—Mi Amigo Tiene ADHD. Translations.com Staff, tr. (p. 1454)
Tourville, Jacqueline. Albie's First Word: A Tale Inspired by Albert Einstein's Childhood. Evans, Wynne, illus. (p. 41)
Tourville, Jacqueline & Guglielmo, Amy. Pocket Full of Colors: The Magical World of Mary Blair, Disney Artist Extraordinaire. Barrager, Brigette, illus. (p. 1764)
Tous, Mercè, illus. see Essa, Huda.
Toussaint, Jonathan. How to Talk to Girls. (p. 1044)
Toussaint-Samson, Toussaint-Samson. Parisian in Brazil (Classic Reprint) (p. 1700)
Tout, Frank. Teddy Bear Rescuer. (p. 2198)
Touvay, Monique, jt. auth. see Chic, Suzy.
Touzet, Bzrznice. Lilou. une Vie Sans Voix. (p. 1302)
Tov, Basia, illus. see Bennett, Larry.
Tovahleh, illus. see Rotenberg, Yael.
Tovar, Alicia. Boston Tea Party: No Taxation Without Representation. (p. 264)
Tovar, Juan, tr. see Mendez, Matt.
Tovar, Virgie. Flawless: Radical Body Positivity for Girls of Color. (p. 747)
Tovey, Imogen. Maddy's Dolphin. (p. 1374)
Tovey, Peter. Chester the Crab. Hinkler Books Staff, ed. (p. 366)
Towbin, Meredith. Straightjacket. (p. 2136)
Tōwe, Nina. Jack & the Beanstalk: A Folktale. Tōwe, Nina, illus. (p. 1151)
Towell, Ann. Grease Town. (p. 883)
Towell, Colin. Survival! A Step-By-Step Guide to Camping & Outdoor Skills. (p. 2164)
Towell, Katy. Skary Childrin & the Carousel of Sorrow. (p. 2029)
Towell, Mary Lee Campbell. Finley's Feathers. (p. 731)
Tower, Cory L. Adventures of Courtney, Morgan & the Magic Toy Bears Book 2: In the Beginning. (p. 22)
Tower, David Bates. Gradual Reader: First Step, or Exercises in Articulation; Designed to Develop & Strengthen the Organs of Speech, & to Facilitate the Correct Utterance of the Elementary Sounds & Their Combinations (Classic Reprint) (p. 875)
—Gradual Reader: First Step, or Exercises in Articulation; Designed to Develope & Strengthen the Organs of Speech, & to Facilitate the Correct Utterance of the Elementary Sounds & Their Combinations (Classic Reprint) (p. 875)
—Intermediate Reader: Or, Primary School First Class Book (Classic Reprint) (p. 1126)
—Introduction to the Gradual Reader, or Primary School Enunciator, Vol. 2: The Child's Second Step, Taken at the Right Time (Classic Reprint) (p. 1129)
—North American Second Class Reader: The Fourth Book of Tower's Series for Common Schools; Developing Principles of Elocution, Practically Illustrated by Elementary Exercises, with Reading Lessons (Classic Reprint) (p. 1620)
—Sequel to the Gradual Reader (Classic Reprint) (p. 1989)
Tower, Eric. Unofficial Guide to Building Towns in Minecraft. (p. 2334)
Tower, Eric J. Unofficial Guide to Growing Plants in Minecraft. (p. 2334)
—Unofficial Guide to Mining in Minecraft. (p. 2334)
Towers, Isabella Jane. Wanderings of Tom Starboard, or the Life of a Sailor: His Voyages & Travels, Perils & Adventures, by Sea & Land (Classic Reprint) (p. 2375)
Towers, Maureen. Magic Path: The Making of Magic Wherever You Go! (p. 1378)
Towle, Ben, illus. see Taylor, S. S.
Towler, Grayson. Dragon Waking. (p. 594)
Town, Charles H., jt. auth. see Sue, Eugene.
Town, Salem. Grammar School Reader: Containing the Essential Principles of Elocution & a Series of Exercises in Reading; Designed for Classes in Grammar Schools (Classic Reprint) (p. 876)
—Little Thinker: Comprising Reading Lessons So Arranged As to Exhibit the Obvious Sense of Words (Classic Reprint) (p. 1329)
—Progressive Fifth or Elocutionary Reader; in Which the Principles of Elocution Are Illustrated by Reading Exercises in Connection with the Rules: For the Use of Schools & Academies (Classic Reprint) (p. 1805)
—Second Reader: Consisting of Easy & Progressive Lessons (Classic Reprint) (p. 1974)
—Third Reader: Consisting of Interesting & Progressive Lessons (Classic Reprint) (p. 2222)
—Town's Spelling & Defining Book: Being an Introduction to Town's Analysis (Classic Reprint) (p. 2270)
—Town's Spelling & Defining Book: Containing Rules for Designating the Accented Syllable in Most Words in the Language; Being an Introduction to Town's Analysis (Classic Reprint) (p. 2270)
Town, Town. Connoisseur, 1774, Vol. 3 (Classic Reprint) (p. 441)
Town, Vicky. Mayhem in the Museum. (p. 1430)
—Runaway Pumpkin Pie Man Baird, Roberta, illus. (p. 1915)
Towne, Belle Kellogg. On the Mountain Top (Classic Reprint) (p. 1655)
Towne, Charles Hanson. Autumn Loiterers (Classic Reprint) (p. 140)
—Bad Man: A Novel (Classic Reprint) (p. 158)
—Chain: A Novel (Classic Reprint) (p. 353)
—Loafing down Long Island (Classic Reprint) (p. 1338)
—Shaking Hands with England (Classic Reprint) (p. 1999)
—Shop of Dreams: A Tale of Love, Youth & Books (Classic Reprint) (p. 2009)
Towne, Charles Wayland. Altogether New Foolish Dictionary: Perpetrated for the Second Time, after Ten Years of National Peace & Good Will (Classic Reprint) (p. 60)
Towne, Ellis, et al. Lill's Travels in Santa Claus Land & Other Stories. (p. 1301)
Towne, Florence Hayden. Neighbors: Stories of Neighborhood House Work in a Great City (Classic Reprint) (p. 1586)
Towne, Isobel & MacAdam, Lea. Dealing with Family Rules (p. 519)
Towne, Isobel & Porterfield, Jason. Strategic Searches Using Digital Tools (p. 2139)
Towne, Isobel & Viegas, Jennifer. Mouth & Nose in 3D. (p. 1515)
Towne, Russ. Ducks That Flew Every Which Way. (p. 608)
—Flora Belle & Dreami Dragon. (p. 750)
—Sir Alex Sleighs a Dragon. (p. 2025)
Towneley, John, jt. auth. see Butler, Samuel.
Townes, Tara Lynn. Tiny but Mighty. (p. 2248)
—Tiny but Mighty. Aguayo, Amanda, illus. (p. 2248)
Townley, Alice Ashworth. Opinion of Mary (Classic Reprint) (p. 1666)
Townley, Alvin. Captured: An American Prisoner of War in North Vietnam. (p. 326)
Townley, Houghton. Gay Lord Waring (Classic Reprint) (p. 812)
Townley, James. High Life below Stairs: A Farce of Two Acts; As It Is Performed at the Theatre-Royal in Drury-Lane (Classic Reprint) (p. 968)
—High Life below Stairs: Das Ist, Die Vornehmthuenden Bedienten, Oder Die Groe Welt in der Bedientenstube, eine Farce (Classic Reprint) (p. 968)
Townley, Morris M. Two Plays Nothing Else to Do-Caught (Classic Reprint) (p. 2309)
Townley, Roderick. Bitter Magic. (p. 235)
—Red Thread: A Novel in Three Incarnations. (p. 1859)
—Sky. (p. 2033)
Townley, Susan. Indiscretions' of Lady Susan (Classic Reprint) (p. 1117)
Townsan, Judy. Wishing Flower Rosado, Michael, illus. (p. 2479)
Townsend, A. M. In Memoriam: Walter Ewen Townsend; Born at Yokohama, Japan, 1879; Died There, 1900 (Classic Reprint) (p. 1106)
Townsend, Angela J. River of Bones. (p. 1887)
Townsend, Beth. Publishing (p. 1810)
Townsend, Brenda. Toad S Trilogy. (p. 2254)
Townsend, Charlene. Trap & the Trip. (p. 2279)
Townsend, Charles. Early Vows: A Comedy in Two Acts (Classic Reprint) (p. 615)
—Mahoney Million (Classic Reprint) (p. 1382)
Townsend, Charles Wendell. Beach Grass (Classic Reprint) (p. 178)
—Birds of Essex County, Massachusetts (Classic Reprint) (p. 232)
—Sand Dunes & Salt Marshes (Classic Reprint) (p. 1930)
Townsend, Chris. Global Recruitment by ISIS. (p. 843)
—Inside the NSA (p. 1124)
—ISIS Hostages. (p. 1138)
—Life under the Caliphate. (p. 1296)
—Violent Rise of ISIS. (p. 2359)
—What Does a Member of the Armed Forces Do? (p. 2409)
—What Does a Taxpayer Do? (p. 2409)
—What Does an Office Holder Do? (p. 2409)

T

Townsend, Christopher. ... ... You Happened ... ... (p. 2527)
Townsend, Clint. Xn: X to the Nth (p. 2516)
Townsend, Dominique. Shantideva: How to Wake up a Hero. Norbu, Tenzing, illus. (p. 2000)
Townsend, E. J., tr. see Hilbert, David.
Townsend, E. S. Lost Legacy of St. Benedict's. (p. 1354)
Townsend, Edward W. Chimmie Fadden: Major Max; & Other Stories (Classic Reprint) (p. 377)
—Climbing Courvatels (Classic Reprint) (p. 405)
—Daughter of the Tenements (Classic Reprint) (p. 509)
—Fort Birkett: A Story of Mountain Adventure (Classic Reprint) (p. 769)
—Near a Whole City Full. (p. 1584)
—Near a Whole City Full (Classic Reprint) (p. 1584)
—Reuben Larkmead: A Story of Worldlings (Classic Reprint) (p. 1872)
Townsend, Edward Waterman. Chimmie Fadden Explains: Major Max Expounds (Classic Reprint) (p. 377)
—Days Like These: A Novel (Classic Reprint) (p. 515)
Townsend, Emily Rose. Polar Animals (p. 1769)
Townsend, F. H., illus. see Dickens, Charles.
Townsend, F. H., illus. see Kipling, Rudyard.
Townsend, F. L. In the Nantahalas: A Novel (Classic Reprint) (p. 1110)
Townsend, Geo. Alfred. Bohemian Days: Three American Tales (Classic Reprint) (p. 254)
—Tales of the Chesapeake (Classic Reprint) (p. 2185)
Townsend, George Alfred. Campaigns of a Non-Combatant & His Romaunt Abroad During the War. (p. 316)
—Campaigns of a Non-Combatant, & His Romaunt Abroad During the War (Classic Reprint) (p. 316)
—Columbus in Love (Classic Reprint) (p. 427)
—Entailed Hat, or Patty Cannon's Times: A Romance (Classic Reprint) (p. 656)
—Katy of Catoctin or the Chain-Breakers: A National Romance (Classic Reprint) (p. 1206)
—Life, Crime & Capture of John Wilkes Booth. (p. 1290)
—Life, Crime, & Capture of John Wilkes Booth: And the Pursuit, Trial & Execution of His Accomplices (Classic Reprint) (p. 1290)
Townsend, George Fyler. Arabian Nights Entertainments (Classic Reprint) (p. 109)
Townsend, George Fyler, tr. see Aesop, Aesop.
Townsend, Horace. Handful of Silver: Six Stories of Silversmiths (Classic Reprint) (p. 915)
Townsend, Howard. Sunbeam & the Spectrascope: Read Before the Albany Institute, Feb. 17th, 1863 (Classic Reprint) (p. 2151)
Townsend, Jessica. Nevermoor: the Trials of Morrigan Crow. (p. 1590)
—Wundersmith: The Calling of Morrigan Crow. (p. 2514)
Townsend, John. 101 Things You Didn't Know about Your Body (p. 2558)
—Air Force. (p. 37)
—Amazing Animal Communicators (p. 63)
—Amazing Animal Senses (p. 63)
—Amazing Animal Survivors (p. 63)
—Amazing Predators (p. 66)
—Animal Facts & Jokes. Antram, David, illus. (p. 89)
—Army. (p. 117)
—Body Facts & Jokes. Antram, David, illus. (p. 253)
—Bow! Wow! Meow! Enright, Amanda, illus. (p. 266)
—Cars & Motorcycles (p. 334)
—Famous Forensic Cases. (p. 703)
—Ghost Stories. Lundie, Isobel, illus. (p. 828)
—Gone Missing. (p. 861)
—History Facts & Jokes. Antram, David, illus. (p. 977)
—Hoppity! Cheep! Quack! Enright, Amanda, illus. (p. 1002)
—Is Our Weather Getting Worse? (p. 1137)
—Life-Sized Animal Poop. (p. 1296)
—Life-Sized Animal Tracks. (p. 1296)
—Life-Sized Bugs. (p. 1296)
—Mayflower Facts & Jokes. Antram, David, illus. (p. 1430)
—Navy. (p. 1582)
—Never Odd or Even. (p. 1590)
—Pirate Stories. Lundie, Isobel, illus. (p. 1750)
—Robberies & Heists. (p. 1889)
—Rotters: Decomposition. (p. 1907)
—Science Facts & Jokes. Antram, David, illus. (p. 1954)
—Space Facts & Jokes. Antram, David, illus. (p. 2071)
—Special Operations. (p. 2077)
—Strange Creatures. (p. 2137)
—Unsolved Crimes. (p. 2335)
—Who's That Hiding in the Chimney? Solis, Fermin, illus. (p. 2453)
—Who's That Hiding in the Dark? Solis, Fermin, illus. (p. 2453)
Townsend, Juliana. Seven Sprays & a Golden Poppy: Poems, a Song & a Story (Classic Reprint) (p. 1994)
Townsend, Kristy Ann. Different but the Same As You. (p. 545)
Townsend, Laura, jt. auth. see Sohn, Emily.
Townsend, Michael. Cute & Cuter. (p. 491)
—Kit Feeny: On the Move (p. 1225)
—Ugly Necklace (p. 2314)
Townsend, Mike. Where Do Presidents Come From? And Other Presidential Stuff of Super Great Importance. (p. 2436)
Townsend, Peter, illus. see Whiting, Sue.
Townsend, R. S. Confessions of a Little Man During Great Days: Translated from the Russian of Leonid Andreyev (Classic Reprint) (p. 439)
Townsend, Renice. Chicken Stories: Our Stories with Grandma. (p. 368)
—Dinosaur Stories: Our Stories with Grandma. (p. 549)
—Nature Stories: Our Stories with Grandma. (p. 1581)
Townsend, Tamela Ann. Finding Pumpkin (p. 730)
Townsend, Thomas. Home Afloat, or the Boy Trappers of the Hackensack (Classic Reprint) (p. 995)
Townsend, Una Belle. Great Elephant Escape Hechter, Janice, illus. (p. 885)
—Toby & the Secret Code. Coleman Lester, Gwen, illus. (p. 2254)
Townsend, Virginia F. Battle-Fields of Our Fathers (Classic Reprint) (p. 173)
—Boston Girl's Ambitions (Classic Reprint) (p. 264)
—But a Philistine (Classic Reprint) (p. 302)
—Darryll Gap: Or Whether It Paid (Classic Reprint) (p. 508)
—Hollands (Classic Reprint) (p. 988)
—Janet Strong (Classic Reprint) (p. 1159)
—Margery Keith (Classic Reprint) (p. 1404)
—Only Girls (Classic Reprint) (p. 1664)
—Sirs, Only Seventeen (Classic Reprint) (p. 2026)
Townsend, Virginia Frances. Mills of Tuxbury (Classic Reprint) (p. 1468)
—Woman's Word: And How She Kept It (Classic Reprint) (p. 2486)
Townsend, Wendy. Blue Iguana. (p. 248)
—Lizard Love. (p. 1336)
—Sundown Rule. (p. 2152)
Townsend, Will. Princess & Her King. Bicknelle, Millie, illus. (p. 1795)
Townsend, William Capron. Love & Liberty: A Romance of Anti-Slavery Days (Classic Reprint) (p. 1359)
Townshend, Katie, illus. see Rath, Tom H.
Townshend, Marchioness. Widening Circle: A Chronicle (Classic Reprint) (p. 2461)
Townshend, R.B. Girl from Mexico (Classic Reprint) (p. 835)
—Lone Pine: The Story of a Lost Mine (Classic Reprint) (p. 1342)
Townsley, Diane. 'Twas the Night Before 'Christ'-Mas. (p. 2302)
Townson, H., jt. auth. see Peschke, Marci.
Towslee, Frank. Summerville Bazar: An Entertainment in One Act (Classic Reprint) (p. 2150)
Towson, State Teachers College at. Tower Light, Vol. 10: October, 1936 (Classic Reprint) (p. 2269)
—Tower Light, Vol. 18: October, 1944 (Classic Reprint) (p. 2269)
Toy Box Staff, illus. see Wolfe, Jane.
Toy, Mary Florilla Seymour. When Summer Goes: A Novel (Classic Reprint) (p. 2433)
Toybox Innovations Staff & Toybox Innovations, creators. Disney Read along Little Mermaid Collection (p. 563)
Toye, Derek, illus. see Troupe, Thomas Kingsley.
Toymil, Debra. I Love My Bear. (p. 1070)
Toynbee, Paget. Specimens of Old French (IX-XV Centuries) With Introduction, Notes, & Glossary (Classic Reprint) (p. 2077)
Toynbee, William. Lays of Common Life (Classic Reprint) (p. 1254)
Toyne, Jessica. Dali (p. 498)
—Justin Bieber. (p. 1195)
Toynton, Ian. Hooligan Bear Home. Dietrich, Andrea, illus. (p. 1000)
—Hooligan Bear New Friends. Dietrich, Andrea, illus. (p. 1000)
Toyota, Kazuhiko. Barubonsan No Odekake. (p. 168)
—Coochy-Coochy-Coo, Momon. (p. 446)
—Watermelon Is. (p. 2386)
Toz, Karen Pokras. Millicent Marie Is Not My Name. (p. 1467)
—Nate Rocks the World. (p. 1576)
Tozer, Sarah. MI29: Mouseweb International to the Rescue! Salaman, Rosy, illus. (p. 1456)
Tozier, Christopher. Olivia Brophie & the Pearl of Tagelus. (p. 1650)
—Olivia Brophie & the Sky Island. (p. 1650)
Tozier, Josephine. Among English Inns: The Story of a Pilgrimage to Characteristic Spots of Rural England (Classic Reprint) (p. 76)
—Spring Fortnight in France (Classic Reprint) (p. 2092)
—Susan in Sicily: Her Adventures & Those of Her Friends During Their Travels & Sojourns in the Garden of the Mediterranean (Classic Reprint) (p. 2166)
Tozzi, Federigo. Three Crosses (Classic Reprint) (p. 2232)
Tra, Frank. Masterpiece Robot: And the Ferocious Valerie Knick Knack! Evans, Rebecca, illus. (p. 1419)
—Spy School. O'Reilly, Sean Patrick, ed. (p. 2093)
Trabalka, Pegy, illus. see Rudner, Barry.
Trabbold, Andrew, illus. see Qitsualik-Tinsley, Rachel & Qitsualik-Tinsley, Sean.
Trabbold, Andrew, illus. see Tremblay, Kaitlin.
Trace, Casie, illus. see Le Raff, Jack.
Tracey, Alice. Animal Friends. (p. 89)
Tracey, Andrée. Buddies NOT Bullies Rule! (p. 290)
—Marvelous Me! a Personalized Coloring Book. (p. 1413)
—Storyland: Poppy & Her Magic Hat: A Story Coloring Book. (p. 2136)
Tracey, Jaclyn. Trying to Pull off a Miracle. (p. 2297)
Tracey Sr, Jeffery. Brainwashed by Foster Parents. (p. 275)
Trachok, Cathy, illus. see Otto, Carolyn B.
Trachtenberg, Stanley. Elevator Man. Cox, Paul, illus. (p. 635)
Traci Dibble, jt. auth. see Murphy, Sara.
Tracosas, L. J. Amazing World: Bugs: Get to Know 20 Crazy Bugs. (p. 67)
—Cursed Castle: an Escape Room in a Book: Use Your Wits to Survive & Decipher the Clues to Escape. Tran, Turine, illus. (p. 489)
—Hot Wheels Unleash the Beasts: a Street Race: A Look-Through Storybook. (p. 1007)
—White House Winners: What You Don't Know about the Presidents. Lynch, Josh, illus. (p. 2444)
Tracosas, L. J., jt. auth. see Scholastic.
Tract Society, The Religious. Thoughts among Flowers. (p. 2231)
Tracy, J. L. Grace & Shu Mai: The Dumpling Dog. (p. 873)
Tracy, Kathleen. Ancient Assyria. (p. 79)
—Bessie Smith. (p. 205)
—Cerberus. (p. 352)
—Day by Day with Eli Manning. (p. 512)
—Demi Lovato. (p. 528)
—Edouard Manet. (p. 626)
—Emma Watson. (p. 643)
—Evolution of Government & Politics in Iraq. (p. 675)
—Frog in Our Class. (p. 789)
—Hamster in Our Class. (p. 914)
—Historic Fight for the 2008 Democratic Presidential Nomination: The Clinton View. (p. 975)
—Justin Bieber. (p. 1195)
—Medusa. (p. 1437)
—Megan Fox. (p. 1442)
—Orianthi. (p. 1670)
—Prince William of Wales. (p. 1795)
—Railroad Grows into an Industry (1840-1850) (p. 1835)
—San Diego. (p. 1929)
—Seattle. (p. 1972)
—Troy Polamalu. (p. 2292)
—Turtle in Our Class. (p. 2301)
—We Visit Brazil. (p. 2392)
—We Visit Cuba. (p. 2392)
—We Visit Kuwait. (p. 2392)
—We Visit Saudi Arabia. (p. 2393)
—What It's Like to Be Mark Sanchez. de la Vega, Eida, tr. from ENG. (p. 2417)
Tracy, Keegan Connor. This Is a Job for Mommy! An a-Z Adventure. MacLean, Roz, illus. (p. 2224)
Tracy, Kristen. Bessica Lefter Bites Back. (p. 204)
—Camille McPhee Fell under the Bus. (p. 314)
—Camille Mcphee Fell under the Bus... (p. 314)
—Hung Up. (p. 1052)
—Project (un)Popular Book #1. (p. 1806)
—Project (un)Popular Book #2: Totally Crushed. (p. 1806)
—Reinvention of Bessica Lefter. (p. 1862)
—Too Cool for This School. (p. 2260)
—Totally Crushed. (p. 2266)
Tracy, Louis. American Emperor: The Story of the Fourth Empire of France (Classic Reprint) (p. 71)
—American Emperor. (p. 71)
—At the Court of the Maharaja: A Story of Adventure (Classic Reprint) (p. 130)
—Cynthia's Chauffeur (Classic Reprint) (p. 493)
—Day of Wrath: A Story of 1914 (Classic Reprint) (p. 514)
—Karl Grier: The Strange Story of a Man with a Sixth Sense (Classic Reprint) (p. 1203)
—King of Diamonds: A Tale of Mystery & Adventure (Classic Reprint) (p. 1220)
—Lost Provinces, How Vansittart Came Back to France (Classic Reprint) (p. 1355)
—Message (Classic Reprint) (p. 1451)
—Mind the Paint Girl: Being a Novelization of Sir Arthur Pinero's Comedy (Classic Reprint) (p. 1469)
—Mirabel's Island (Classic Reprint) (p. 1474)
—Pillar of Light (Classic Reprint) (p. 1745)
—Revellers (Classic Reprint) (p. 1872)
—Silent Barrier (Classic Reprint) (p. 2017)
—Sirdar's Sabre: Being for the Most Part the Adventures of Sirdar Bahadur Mohammed Khan (Classic Reprint) (p. 2026)
—Son of the Immortals (Classic Reprint) (p. 2062)
—Strange Case of Mortimer Fenley (Classic Reprint) (p. 2137)
—Terms of Surrender (Classic Reprint) (p. 2207)
—Wheel o' Fortune (Classic Reprint) (p. 2427)
—Wings of the Morning (Classic Reprint) (p. 2473)
Tracy, Roger Sherman. Outlines of Anatomy, Physiology, & Hygiene. (p. 1685)
Tracy, Tammy McCammon. Beau's Beary Scary Adventure. (p. 183)
Tracy, Virginia. Merely Players: Stories of Stage Life (Classic Reprint) (p. 1448)
Tradewind Books Staff, jt. auth. see Keens-Douglas, Richardo.
Traditional. VeggieTales Away in a Manger. Reed, Lisa, illus. (p. 2349)
Traditional & Cloke, Rene. My Book of Favourite Tales & Rhymes. (p. 1534)
Traditional Staff. Dayenu! A Favorite Passover Song. Latimer, Miriam, illus. (p. 515)
Traditional, Traditional. Jesus Loves Me. (p. 1166)
Trafford, Adrienne. Cat & Dog See the World Coloring Book. (p. 341)
—Journey Coloring Book (p. 1181)
—SPARK Cat & Dog Around the World Coloring Book. (p. 2074)
—Tarot Designs Coloring Book. (p. 2192)
Trafford, F. G. George Geith of Fen Court: A Novel (Classic Reprint) (p. 819)
—George Geith of Fen Court, Vol. 1 Of 2: A Novel (Classic Reprint) (p. 819)
—Phemie Keller, Vol. 2 Of 3: A Novel (Classic Reprint) (p. 1733)
—Too Much Alone: A Novel (Classic Reprint) (p. 2261)
—Too Much Alone. (p. 2261)
Trafford-Taunton, Winefride. Romance of a State Secret (Classic Reprint) (p. 1900)
Trafton, Adeline. American Girl Abroad (Classic Reprint) (p. 71)
—His Inheritance (Classic Reprint) (p. 974)
Trafton, Jennifer. Henry & the Chalk Dragon: Curriculum Guide. (p. 954)
—Rise & Fall of Mount Majestic. Helquist, Brett, illus. (p. 1885)
Trafton, Miss Adeline. Katherine Earle (Classic Reprint) (p. 1205)
Trager, Hannah. Festival Stories of Child Life in a Jewish Colony in Palestine. (p. 721)
—Festival Stories of Child Life in a Jewish Colony in Palestine (Classic Reprint) (p. 721)
—Stories of Child Life in a Jewish Colony in Palestine (Classic Reprint) (p. 2124)
Trahan, Virginia A. Where Is Sidney? (p. 2438)
Trail, Florence. My Journal in Foreign Lands (Classic Reprint) (p. 1550)
Trail, George. Moby & Family. (p. 1485)
Trail, Sara. Sew with Sara: Fun Stuff to Keep, Give, Sell! (p. 1995)
Traill, Catharine Parr. Backwoods of Canada: Being Letters from the Wife of an Emigrant Officer (Classic Reprint) (p. 156)
—Canadian Crusoes: A Tale of the Rice Lake Plains (Classic Reprint) (p. 320)
—Fables for the Nursery: Original & Select (Classic Reprint) (p. 691)
—In the Forest (Classic Reprint) (p. 1109)
—Pearls & Pebbles: Or, Notes of an Old Naturalist (Classic Reprint) (p. 1711)
—Step-Brothers: A Tale (Classic Reprint) (p. 2114)
—Young Emigrants, or Pictures of Canada: Calculated to Amuse & Instruct the Minds of Youth (Classic Reprint) (p. 2530)
Train, Arthur. Butler's Story (p. 303)
—Cornell University or in the Wireless House (Classic Reprint) (p. 454)
—Earthquake (Classic Reprint) (p. 617)
—Hermit of Turkey Hollow: The Story of an Alibi, Being an Exploit of Ephraim Tutt Attorney Counselor at Law (Classic Reprint) (p. 959)
—McAllister & His Double (Classic Reprint) (p. 1431)
—Mortmain (Classic Reprint) (p. 1507)
—Needle's Eye (Classic Reprint) (p. 1585)
—Tutt & Mr. Tutt (Classic Reprint) (p. 2302)
—World & Thomas Kelly (Classic Reprint) (p. 2501)
Train, Arthur Cheney. True Stories of Crime from the District Attorney's Office. (p. 2294)
Train, Elizabeth Phipps. Autobiography of a Professional Beauty (Classic Reprint) (p. 140)
—Madam of the Ivies (Classic Reprint) (p. 1374)
—Social Highwayman (Classic Reprint) (p. 2053)
Train, Ethel. Bringing Out Barbara (Classic Reprint) (p. 282)
—Son: And Other Stories of Childhood & Age (Classic Reprint) (p. 2061)
—Son (Classic Reprint) (p. 2061)
Train, M. Ray Burton: A Chicago Tale (Classic Reprint) (p. 1844)
—Ray Burton. (p. 1844)
Trainer, Maria T. Kids Are Gifts from Heaven (p. 1214)
Traini, Agostino. Christmas Find & Color. (p. 385)
—Jesus Is Risen! An Easter Pop-Up Book (p. 1166)
—Lord Is My Shepherd: A Psalm 23 Pop-Up Book. (p. 1348)
—Springtime Find & Color. (p. 2092)
Trainor, Marissa. Amazing Adventure of Ava Appleby. Villanueva, Catherine, illus. (p. 62)
—Good Night, Little Star. (p. 864)
Trammel, Howard K. Galaxies. (p. 805)
—Solar System. (p. 2056)
—Wildfires. (p. 2466)
Trammell, Brandon, illus. see Birt, Michael.
Trammell, Fredi. Journey Through the Bible for Kids. (p. 1182)
Trammell, Jeremiah, illus. see Crews, Marcia.
Trammell, Jeremiah, illus. see Galligan, Michael.
Trammell, Jeremiah, illus. see Stihler, Cherie B.
Trammell, Jeremiah, illus. see Vanasse, Deb.
Trammell, Jeremiah, illus. see Vaughan, Richard & Crews, Marcia.
Trammell, Jeremiah, illus. see Vaughan, Richard Lee & Vaughn, Marcia.
Trammell, Menlia Moss. Rob & Rex Prevent a Poaching. (p. 1889)
Trammell, Norma Jeanne, illus. see DeGarmo, John & DeGarmo, Kelly.
Tramontano, Priscilla, illus. see Flynn, Ian.
Tramontozzi, Lidia Morson, jt. auth. see Stilton, Geronimo.
Tramp, Tim. War Life: Illustrated by Stories of the Camp & Field (Classic Reprint) (p. 2376)
Tran, Andrew K. Don't Eat the Sun... or You Can Die to Death! & Other Survival Tips from a First Grader. (p. 582)
Tran Art, Dahn, illus. see Blom, Tracy & Sheridan, Scott.
Tran Art, Danh, illus. see Culbreth, Kelly Lee.
Tran, Basia, illus. see Nicholas, Susan.
Tran, Basia, illus. see Phi, Bao.
Tran, Danh, illus. see Jimerson, John.
Tran, Melinda M. Pablo & Koji Best Friends Forever. Jensen, Nate P., illus. (p. 1690)
Tran Phan, Aliosa, illus. see Blum, Ingo.
Tran, Phuoc Thi Minh. My First Book of Vietnamese Words: An ABC Rhyming Book of Vietnamese Language & Culture. Nguyen, Dong & Nguyen, Hop Thi, illus. (p. 1543)
Tran, Quincy. Angela. (p. 85)
Tran, Richard, illus. see Gould, Jonathan.
Tran, Turine, illus. see Hay, Sam.
Tran, Turine, illus. see Tracosas, L. J.
Tranco, Miguel, illus. see Benni, Stefano & Curtis, Howard.
Tran-Davies, N. Daddy Is a Conundrum! (p. 495)
Tran-Davies, Nhung. Grain of Rice (p. 875)
Tran-Davies, Nhung N. Ten Cents a Pound Bisaillon, Josée, illus. (p. 2203)
Trane, Amanda. Discover Airplanes: Level 2 Reader. (p. 553)
—Discover Ancient Egypt: Level 2 Reader. (p. 554)
—Discover Bugs: Level 2 Reader. (p. 554)
—Discover Crabs: Level 2 Reader. (p. 554)
—Discover Dogs: Level 2 Reader. (p. 554)
—Discover Heavy Equipment. (p. 554)
—Discover Mammals: Level 2 Reader. (p. 554)
—Discover Military Equipment. (p. 554)
—Discover the Circus: Level 1 Reader. (p. 555)
Tranfa, Regina. My Dad Took Me to Outer Space (the Took Me Series) (p. 1536)
Translation Services Staff, tr. see Clay, Kathryn.
Translation Services Staff, tr. see Lindeen, Carol K.
Translations.com Staff, tr. see Boothroyd, Jennifer.
Translations.com Staff, tr. see Clay, Kathryn.
Translations.com Staff, tr. see Dahl, Michael & Jensen, Brian.
Translations.com Staff, tr. see Jango-Cohen, Judith.
Translations.com Staff, tr. see Johnson, Rebecca L.
Translations.com Staff, tr. see Kalz, Jill.
Translations.com Staff, tr. see Kudela, Katy R.
Translations.com Staff, tr. see Lessem, Don.
Translations.com Staff, tr. see Limke, Jeff.
Translations.com Staff, tr. see Lindeen, Carol K.
Translations.com Staff, tr. see Lowery, Linda.
Translations.com Staff, tr. see Markle, Sandra.
Translations.com Staff, tr. see Marshall, Pam.
Translations.com Staff, tr. see Mayesky & Kalz, Jill.
Translations.com Staff, tr. see Nelson, Kristin L.
Translations.com Staff, tr. see Nelson, Robin.
Translations.com Staff, tr. see Patrick, Jean L. S.
Translations.com Staff, tr. see Posada, Mia.
Translations.com Staff, tr. see Riley, Joelle.
Translations.com Staff, tr. see Schulz, Walter A.
Translations.com Staff, tr. see Sherrow, Victoria.

Trevelyan, L. R. Year in Peshawur, & a Lady's Ride into the Khyber Pass (Classic Reprint) (p. 2519)
Trevelyan, Marie. From Snowdon to the Sea: Stirring Stories of North & South Wales (Classic Reprint) (p. 793)
Trevena, John. Armin of the West (Classic Reprint) (p. 117)
—Bracken (Classic Reprint) (p. 274)
—By Violence (Classic Reprint) (p. 306)
—Drake by George (Classic Reprint) (p. 596)
—Furze the Cruel (Classic Reprint) (p. 802)
—Granite: A Novel (Classic Reprint) (p. 880)
—Heather (Classic Reprint) (p. 946)
—Moyle Church-Town: A Novel (Classic Reprint) (p. 1517)
—Raindrops (Classic Reprint) (p. 1837)
—Sleeping Waters: A Novel (Classic Reprint) (p. 2037)
—Wintering Hay (Classic Reprint) (p. 2476)
Trevenen, Emily. Little Derwent's Breakfast (Classic Reprint) (p. 1315)
Treves, Frederick. Elephant Man & Other Reminiscences. (p. 634)
—Elephant Man & Other Reminiscences (Classic Reprint) (p. 634)
—Made in the Trenches, Composed Entirely from Articles Sketches Contributed by Soldiers: Edited by Sir Frederick Treves & George Goodchild (Classic Reprint) (p. 1374)
—Tale of a Field Hospital (Classic Reprint) (p. 2178)
Treves, Frederick, jt. auth. see Laurence, E. C.
Trevethan, Glenn A. Adventures of Sammi Snake: Sammi's Coat. (p. 27)
Trevia, Rick & Benchmark Education Co., LLC Staff. City Lights. (p. 395)
—Squid Twins. (p. 2094)
Trevinio, Juan, illus. see Johnson, Sandi.
Trevino, David. Colorful Carnival of Kids in the Kingdom of Marbles: Mission #2. (p. 422)
—Colorful Carnival of Kids in the Kingdom of Marbles: Mission #3. (p. 422)
—Colorful Carnival of Kids in the Kingdom of Marbles: Mission #1 the Cemetery Ghost. (p. 422)
Trevino, Esther, jt. auth. see Corman, Clifford L.
Trevino Garcia, Luis R. & Dobarro, Irene. Invasores Invadidos una F?bula Muy Real. (p. 1130)
Trevino, Juan, illus. see Johnson, Sandi.
Trevino, Ruby. Chocolate Feet (p. 380)
Trevisan, Marco, illus. see Belloni, Giulia.
Trevor-Battye, Aubyn. Ice-Bound on Kolguev: A Chapter in the Exploration of Arctic Europe to Which Is Added a Record of the Natural History of the Island (Classic Reprint) (p. 1087)
—Northern Highway of the Tsar (Classic Reprint) (p. 1621)
—Pictures in Prose of Nature, Wild Sport, & Humble Life. (p. 1741)
—Pictures in Prose of Nature, Wild Sport, & Humble Life (Classic Reprint) (p. 1741)
Trevorec, Marie Ryan. Marie: Or Glimpses of Life in France (Classic Reprint) (p. 1404)
Trewartha, James. Poetic Memoirs of the World War, Vol. 1 (Classic Reprint) (p. 1766)
Trewin, Anna, adapted by. Amazing Composers : A2-B1 (Collins Amazing People ELT Readers) (p. 64)
—Amazing Mathematicians : A2-B1 (Collins Amazing People ELT Readers) (p. 65)
Trexler, David. Dinosaur Bone Doctor. (p. 548)
Trexler, Jennifer Suther, illus. see Ritch, Catherine.
Trey, Don. Knight Blazer: Goblet of Truth - Book 3. (p. 1228)
—Knight Blazer: Defender of the Realm - Book 2. (p. 1228)
Triana, Gaby. Summer of Yesterday. (p. 2150)
—Wake the Hollow. (p. 2371)
Triano, Jay. Basketball Basics: How to Play Like the Pros (p. 170)
Trias Trueta, Katy. Sueve: El Valiente Asturcón. Wilkins, Cristina Luz, illus. (p. 2147)
Tribaudeau, Denis. How to Survive on a Desert Island: Operation Robinson! Maincent, Karine, illus. (p. 1044)
Tribbett, Carmen R. Monster Dog: A Small Dog with a Big Heart Learns about Alzheimer's Disease. Hunerdosse, Katie L., illus. (p. 1495)
Tribus, Theresa, illus. see Noel, Carmel.
Tribuzi, Luke. What's the Difference Between Forests & Prairies? (p. 2426)
Tricario, Christine. Advo-Cats. (p. 30)
Tricchinelli, Rob. Arizona Diamondbacks (p. 116)
—Golden State Warriors (p. 859)
Trice III, Andrew Jones. Pirate's Progress. (p. 1751)
Trice, Linda. Kenya's Art. Mitchell, Hazel, illus. (p. 1210)
—Kenya's Song. Johnson, Pamela, illus. (p. 1210)
Triche, Trina. Andre's Great Day. Marino, Natalie, illus. (p. 83)
Trick, Simon. Yesterday Never, Ever Dies. (p. 2521)
Trier, Walter, illus. see Kastner, Erich.
Trifer, Jen. Turtles from Head to Tail. (p. 2301)
Trifle, Trifle. Trifleton Papers (Classic Reprint) (p. 2288)
Trifunov, David. Freerunner. (p. 783)
—Ice Time (p. 1088)
—Snow Soccer. (p. 2048)
Trigant Gautier-J-P. Petit Livre Bon a Consulter, Ou Examen Critique et Impartial Sur les Chemins de Grande Communication. (p. 1730)
Trigg, Elizabeth Ann. Diary of a Teenage Mom. (p. 540)
—Would the Real Mr. Right Please Stand Up! (p. 2509)
Trigg, Michael J. Greanwold & the Mystery Cave: Greanwold & the Minosaurs Story Books. (p. 883)
Triggle, David J., ed. see Olive, M. Foster.
Triggle, David J., ed. see Toufexis, Donna & Hammack, Sayamwong E.
Triggle, David J., jt. auth. see May, Suellen.
Triggle, David J., ed. Drugs: The Straight Facts Set, 32-Volumes. (p. 606)
Trigiani, Adriana. Viola in Reel Life. (p. 2359)
—Viola in the Spotlight. (p. 2359)
Trillia Newbell. God's Very Good Idea. (p. 854)
Trillin, Calvin. No Fair! No Fair! And Other Jolly Poems of Childhood. Chast, Roz, illus. (p. 1612)
Trilling, Richard J. More Stories of Stephanie & Friends: Volume 2 in the Stephanie Stories. (p. 1505)
—Still More Stories of Stephanie & Friends: Volume 3 in the Stephanie Series. (p. 2119)
—Stories of Stephanie & Friends. (p. 2125)
Trim, Tom. Society As It Is in Charlottetown: A Satire on Its Ecclesiastical, Musical, Social & Moral Aspects (Classic Reprint) (p. 2053)
Trimble, Gina. Little Tiny Mouse (p. 1329)
Trimble, Irene. Winter Fun for Everyone! (Disney Princess) RH Disney Staff, illus. (p. 2475)
Trimble, Tonya. Curiosity, with a Capital S. Enik, Ted, illus. (p. 486)
Trimmer. Easy Introduction to the Knowledge of Nature, & Reading the Holy Scriptures: Adapted to the Capacities of Children (Classic Reprint) (p. 620)
—History of the Robins: For the Instruction of Children on Their Treatment of Animals (Classic Reprint) (p. 980)
—Instructive Tales, for Young Persons, Intended to Amuse & Inform the Youthful Mind, Comprising Lascelles, or the Young Soldier: Leland, or the Wanderings of Youthful Romance (Classic Reprint) (p. 1125)
—Servant's Friend; an Exemplary Tale: Designed to Enforce the Religious Instructions Given at Sunday & Other Charity Schools (Classic Reprint) (p. 1991)
Trimmer, Christian. Mimi & Shu in I'll Race You! Van der Paardt, Melissa, illus. (p. 1469)
—Simon's New Bed. van der Paardt, Melissa, illus. (p. 2021)
—Snow Pony & the Seven Miniature Ponies. Sima, Jessie, illus. (p. 2047)
—Teddy's Favorite Toy. Valentine, Madeline, illus. (p. 2198)
Trimmer, Edward Everett, jt. auth. see Hale, Edward Everett.
Trimmer, F. Mortimer. Golden Crocodile (Classic Reprint) (p. 857)
Trimmer, Joshua. Practical Geology & Mineralogy: With Instructions for the Qualitative Analysis of Minerals (Classic Reprint) (p. 1784)
Trimmer, Mary, jt. auth. see Bewick, Thomas.
Trimmer, Sarah. Fabulous Histories: Designed for the Instruction of Children, Respecting Their Treatment of Animals (Classic Reprint) (p. 692)
—History of the Robins (Classic Reprint) (p. 981)
—Leading-Strings to Knowledge: Thirty-Two Easy Stories (Classic Reprint) (p. 1254)
—Mrs. Trimmer's Introduction to Natural History: In an Easy & Familiar Style, Adapted to the Capacities of Children (Classic Reprint) (p. 1523)
Trimmer, Tony, illus. see Kingfisher Editors.
Trimmer, Tony, illus. see Rooke, Thom.
Trimmer, Tony, illus. see Slade, Suzanne.
Trimoglie, Mario. Rivers. Swope, Brenda, illus. (p. 1887)
—Story of Ocos: King of the Sky, Master of the Water. Buehrle, Jacquelyn, illus. (p. 2132)
—Thorn. (p. 2230)
Trimpe, Herb, illus. see Gerani, Gary.
Trimpe, Herb & Buscema, Sal. Incredible Hulk Epic Collection: in the Hands of Hydra. (p. 1114)
Trimpe, Herb, et al. Captain Britain: Legacy of a Legend. (p. 325)
—Wolverine Omnibus Vol. 1. (p. 2484)
Trine, Greg. Brotherhood of the Traveling Underpants. (p. 286)
—Brotherhood of the Traveling Underpants. Montijo, Rhode, illus. (p. 286)
—Dinomighty! (graphic Novel) Blecha, Aaron, illus. (p. 548)
—Dinos Are Forever. Dormer, Frank W., illus. (p. 548)
—George at the Speed of Light. (p. 818)
—Giant. (p. 830)
—Goldilocks Private Eye. (p. 860)
—Invasion from Planet Dork. Montijo, Rhode, illus. (p. 1130)
—Pinkbeard's Revenge. Dormer, Frank W., illus. (p. 1747)
—Shifty Business. Dormer, Frank W., illus. (p. 2007)
—Stinky Cheese Caper. (p. 2120)
—Willy Maykit in Space. Burks, James, illus. (p. 2470)
—Wyatt Burp Rides Again. Dormer, Frank W., illus. (p. 2514)
Trine, Greg, jt. auth. see RH Disney Staff.
Trine, Ralph Waldo. What All the World's A-Seeking: Or, the Vital Law of True Life, True Greatness Power & Happiness. (p. 2404)
Trinidad, Jose, illus. see Swift, Grace M.
Trinidad, Jose, illus. see Swift, Grace Marie.
Trinidad, Leo, illus. see Potter, William.
Trinidad, Leo, illus. see Ventura, Marne.
Trinidad, Leo & Potter, William. Dangerous Mazes. (p. 502)
Trinity, Shaya, illus. see Kirkendol, Karin.
Trinkle, Paul. Man with Pigeons on His Feet. (p. 1396)
Trinko, Regina. Fio Funkelstein. (p. 732)
Trionfetti, Rossella. Weird & Wonderful Animals. (p. 2396)
Trionfo, Nikki. Shatter. (p. 2003)
Trip, Tom. History of Giles Gingerbread, a Little Boy, Who Lived upon Learning (Classic Reprint) (p. 978)
Tripathi, Siddhartha, illus. see Nainy, Mamta.
Triplett, Annette. From the Farm to You Coloring Book. Vale, Joe, ed. (p. 793)
Triplett, Chris Harper, illus. see Kreitz, Tina.
Triplett, Donald & Eiland, Marie. Castle Club Leader Manual: ... Children walking in the way of the Lord Rdm, tr. from SPA. (p. 340)
—Castle Club - Student Guide: Children Walking in the Way of the Lord Rdm, tr. (p. 340)
Triplett, Gina, illus. see Malone, Marianne.
Triplett, Ginger, illus. see James, Anne.
Triplett, Ginger, illus. see Roark, Algernon Michael.
Triplett, Kari. Buttercup the Unicorn. (p. 303)
Triplett-McGee, Jasmine. Secret Door World. (p. 1975)
Tripodi, Pina. Sunny Finds Her Shine. Tripodi, Pina, illus. (p. 2152)
Tripp, Analisa. A Is for Acorn: A California Indian ABC. Risling, Lyn, illus. (p. 1)
Tripp, Christine, illus. see Brimner, Larry Dane.
Tripp, F. J., illus. see Preussler, Otfried.
Tripp, George Henry. Student-Life at Harvard (Classic Reprint) (p. 2143)
Tripp, Howland. In Whaling Days (Classic Reprint) (p. 1112)
Tripp, Karyn. Math Art & Drawing Games for Kids: 40+ Fun Art Projects to Build Amazing Math Skills. (p. 1421)
Tripp, Natalie. We Care! Making Care Packages: Understand the Relationship Between Multiplication & Division. (p. 2390)
Tripp, Valerie. Camille's Mermaid Tale. Thai, Thu, illus. (p. 314)
—Chances & Changes: My Journey with Molly. (p. 355)
—Clippity-Cloppity Carnival. Thai, Thu, illus. (p. 406)
—Emerson & Princess Peep. Thai, Thu, illus. (p. 641)
—Mystery of Mr. E. Thai, Thu, illus. (p. 1569)
—Rainstorm Brainstorm. Thai, Thu, illus. (p. 1837)
—Willa's Wilderness Campout. Thai, Thu, illus. (p. 2468)
Tripp, Valerie, jt. auth. see Jazynka, Kitson.
Tripp, Wallace, illus. see Brock, Betty.
Trippe, Dean, illus. see Torres, J.
Trippel, H. F. Flag: The Book of the Union Jack Club (Classic Reprint) (p. 745)
Triptych, John. Eye of Balor. (p. 688)
—Fomorians. (p. 758)
—Pagan Apocalypse. (p. 1692)
Trissler, Rebecca Johns, ed. see Bonk, John J.
Trissler, Rebecca Johns, ed. see Butler, Dori Hillestad.
Tristante, Manuel. Bajo el Arcoiris. (p. 159)
—Esfera. (p. 662)
Tristen, Sienna, ed. see Silver, Avi.
Tristram, Matilda. Phone Book. (p. 1736)
Tristram, W. Outram. Coaching Days & Coaching Ways (Classic Reprint) (p. 409)
Trites, B. John Cave (Classic Reprint) (p. 1172)
Trites, W. B. Barbara Gwynne (Life) (Classic Reprint) (p. 165)
Trites, William Budd. Brian Banaker's Autobiography up to the Age of Twenty-Four (Classic Reprint) (p. 279)
Trithart, Emma. Crocodile's Burp. (p. 477)
—Leopard's Snore. (p. 1268)
Trithart, Emma, illus. see Burton, Jeffrey.
Trithart, Emma, illus. see Compassion International, Compassion.
Trithart, Emma, illus. see Giroux, Lindsay Nina.
Trithart, Emma, illus. see Lawrence, Sandra.
Trithart, Emma, illus. see Sweeney, Joan.
Triton, Willie. Fisher Boy (Classic Reprint) (p. 741)
Trittin, Paul S., illus. see Baker, Marvin G.
Tritto, Alexandra. Ways to Make Money Working with Kids (p. 2388)
Trittschuh, Erwin. Chief, Vol. 7: May, 1917 (Classic Reprint) (p. 369)
Triumph Books. Legend of Kobe Bryant: Basketball's Modern Superstar. (p. 1262)
—Legend of Michael Jordan. (p. 1262)
Triumph Books Staff. Austin Mahone: Startin' Something Spectacular. (p. 138)
—Baseball All-Stars. (p. 168)
—Believe. (p. 196)
—Jennifer Lawrence: Burning Bright. (p. 1164)
—One Direction: Where We Are. (p. 1659)
—One Direction: What Makes You Beautiful. (p. 1659)
—Super World of Mario: The Ultimate Unofficial Guide to Super Mario(r). (p. 2159)
Triumph Books Staff, ed. see Kidder, Lisa & Kidder, Lisa Damian.
Triumph, Toby, illus. see Syed, Matthew.
Trius, Mireia. Je Mesure Tout ! (p. 1162)
Trivas, Irene, illus. see Davol, Marguerite W.
Trivas, Tracy. Wish Stealers. (p. 2478)
Trivedi, Harish, ed. see Kipling, Rudyard.
Trivedi, Ishan, illus. see Lee, Erin.
Trivelli, Jenifer & Hammond-Brouwer, Brinsley. Jamie's Gift: A Young Teen's Guide to Fears, Worries, & Other Life Challenges (Like Being Irritated by Other People) (p. 1157)
Trivette, Donna K. Friend for Ringo & Girl. (p. 786)
—One Special Christmas. (p. 1662)
—Ringo & Girl. (p. 1883)
Trivizas, Eugene. Three Little Wolves & the Big Bad Pig. Oxenbury, Helen, illus. (p. 2234)
Trock, Kathleen. Hiding Places. (p. 967)
Trockstad, Marcy, illus. see Unger-Pengilly, Elaine.
Trod, Mariano, illus. see Montgomery, R. A.
Trodd, Mark. Hippo in the Stable. Hallam, Steve, illus. (p. 973)
Troeger, John W. Nature-Study Readers: III Harold's Quests (Classic Reprint) (p. 1581)
Trofa, Sara. Taxi Ride with Victor. Klever, Elsa, illus. (p. 2193)
Troff, Sophie, tr. see Cohn, Scotti.
Troff, Sophie, tr. see Curtis, Jennifer Keats.
Troff, Sophie, tr. see Hall, Katharine.
Troff, Sophie, tr. see Holland, Mary.
Troff, Sophie, tr. see Kurtz, Kevin.
Troff, Sophie, tr. see Mayer, Lynne.
Troff, Sophie, tr. see Rock, Brian.
Troff, Sophie, tr. see Stanek, Linda.
Trofin, Charmaine. Luigi's Spaghetti: A Story of Balance. (p. 1366)
Trogdon, Carter & Trogdon, Lauren. My Defender Sets Me Free. (p. 1537)
Trogdon, Kathryn, illus. see DeVogt, Rindia M.
Troiano, Jaden. What Happens When I Burp? (p. 2411)
Troïanowski, Johan. Runaway Princess. (p. 1915)
Troies, Crestien von. Li Romans Dou Chevalier Au Lyon (Classic Reprint) (p. 1283)
Trois-Etoiles, Trois-Etoiles. Member for Paris: A Tale of the Second Empire (Classic Reprint) (p. 1443)
—Member for Paris, Vol. 2 Of 3: A Tale of the Second Empire (Classic Reprint) (p. 1443)
Troisi, Licia. Chroniq Monde Emerge T1 Nihal. (p. 389)
—Chroniq Monde Emerge T2 Missio. (p. 389)
Troisi-Paton, Kimberly, ed. see Tubb, Kristin O'Donnell.
Troll. Butt Detective: Detective vs Strange Thief. (p. 303)
—Butt Detective: SOS from the Ruins. (p. 303)
—Butt Detective: the Giant Gone into the Dark Night. (p. 303)
—Butt Detective: the Strange Thief & Kidnapped Bride. (p. 303)
—Butt Detective: the Weird Detective Agency. (p. 303)
—Butt Detective: Where Is the Lucky Cat? (p. 303)
—Dective Story in a Mysterious House. (p. 524)
Troller, Leah. Cactus Book. (p. 307)
—Great White Shark. (p. 891)
—Look at the Snakes. (p. 1345)
Troller, Leah, jt. auth. see Córdova, Alina Karam.
Troller, Leah, jt. auth. see Karam Córdova, Alina.
Trolle-Steenstrup, H. When I Was a Boy in Denmark: A Chronicle of Happy Days (Classic Reprint) (p. 2431)
Trollinger, Patsi B. Thrill in The 'Ville. Thompson, Elizabeth, illus. (p. 2236)
Trollinger, Valerie L., jt. auth. see Flohr, John W.
Trollope. Barnabys in America, Vol. 2 Of 3: Or, Adventures of the Widow Wedded (Classic Reprint) (p. 167)
—Belgium & Western Germany in 1833, Vol. 1 Of 2: Including Visits to Baden-Baden, Wiesbaden, Cassel, Hanover, the Harz Mountains, &C. &C (Classic Reprint) (p. 195)
—Belgium & Western Germany in 1833, Vol. 2: Including Visits to Baden-Baden, Wiesbaden, Cassel, Hanover, the Harz Mountains, &C, &C (Classic Reprint) (p. 195)
—Can You Forgive Her?, Vol. 1 of 2 (Classic Reprint) (p. 318)
—Father Eustace, Vol. 2 Of 3: A Tale of the Jesuits (Classic Reprint) (p. 714)
—How the Mastiffs Went to Iceland (Classic Reprint) (p. 1036)
—Kellys & the o'Kellys (Classic Reprint) (p. 1209)
—Last Chronicle of Barset, Vol. 1 (Classic Reprint) (p. 1247)
—Marion Fay, Vol. 1 Of 2: A Novel (Classic Reprint) (p. 1406)
—Miss. MacKenzie, Vol. 1 of 2 (Classic Reprint) (p. 1479)
—Orley Farm, Vol. 2 (Classic Reprint) (p. 1672)
—Petticoat Government, Vol. 1 Of 3: A Novel (Classic Reprint) (p. 1731)
—Small House at Allington, Vol. 1 (Classic Reprint) (p. 2039)
—Tales of All Countries (Classic Reprint) (p. 2183)
—Three Clerks: A Novel (Classic Reprint) (p. 2232)
—Three Clerks, Vol. 3 Of 3: A Novel (Classic Reprint) (p. 2232)
—Young Heiress, Vol. 1 Of 3: A Novel (Classic Reprint) (p. 2531)
Trollope, Anthony. American Senator: A Novel (Classic Reprint) (p. 74)
—Autobiographyand Other Writings. Shrimpton, Nicholas, ed. (p. 140)
—Ayala's Angel, Vol. 1 of 3 (Classic Reprint) (p. 145)
—Barchester Towers. (p. 166)
—Barchester Towers (Classic Reprint) (p. 166)
—Barchester Towers, Vol. 1 (Classic Reprint) (p. 166)
—Can You Forgive Her? [complete & Illustrated]. (p. 318)
—Can You Forgive Her? (the Classic Unabridged Edition) (p. 318)
—Can You Forgive Her? (Unabridged) Victorian Classic. (p. 318)
—Can You Forgive Her? - Scholar's Choice Edition. (p. 318)
—Can You Forgive Her, Vol. 1 (Classic Reprint) (p. 318)
—Can You Forgive Her?, Vol. 1 of 2 (Classic Reprint) (p. 318)
—Can You Forgive Her, Volume I - Scholar's Choice Edition. (p. 318)
—Can You Forgive Her, Volume III - Scholar's Choice Edition. (p. 318)
—Christmas at Thompson Hall (Classic Reprint) (p. 383)
—Cousin Henry: A Novel (Classic Reprint) (p. 463)
—Cousin Henry. (p. 463)
—Cousin Henry, Vol. 1 Of 2: A Novel (Classic Reprint) (p. 463)
—Cousin Henry, Vol. 2 Of 2: A Novel (Classic Reprint) (p. 463)
—Doctor Thorne, Vol. 1 (Classic Reprint) (p. 573)
—Dr. Wortle's School. (p. 592)
—Editor's Tales (Classic Reprint) (p. 626)
—Eye for an Eye (Classic Reprint) (p. 688)
—Eye for an Eye, Vol. 1 of 2 (Classic Reprint) (p. 688)
—Framley Parsonage (Classic Reprint) (p. 775)
—Framley Parsonage, Vol. 1 (Classic Reprint) (p. 775)
—Harry Heathcote of Gangoil: A Tale of Australian Bush Life (Classic Reprint) (p. 934)
—How the Mastiffs Went to Iceland. (p. 1036)
—How the Mastiffs Went to Iceland (Classic Reprint) (p. 1036)
—John Caldigate (Classic Reprint) (p. 1172)
—John Caldigate, Vol. 1 (Classic Reprint) (p. 1172)
—Kellys & the o'Kellys (Classic Reprint) (p. 1209)
—Last Chronicle of Barset, Vol. 3 (Classic Reprint) (p. 1247)
—Lotta Schmidt & Other Stories. (p. 1356)
—Lotta Schmidt & Other Stories (Classic Reprint) (p. 1356)
—Macdermots of Ballycloran (Classic Reprint) (p. 1371)
—Marion Fay (Classic Reprint) (p. 1406)
—Marion Fay, Vol. 1 Of 2: A Novel (Classic Reprint) (p. 1406)
—Miss. MacKenzie, Vol. 1 of 2 (Classic Reprint) (p. 1479)
—Miss. Mackenzie, Vol. 1 of 2 (Classic Reprint) (p. 1479)
—Mr. Scarborough's Family, Vol. 1 of 3 (Classic Reprint) (p. 1520)
—Orley Farm: A Novel (Classic Reprint) (p. 1672)
—Orley Farm. (p. 1672)
—Orley Farm (Classic Reprint) (p. 1672)
—Orley Farm, Vol. 1 of 2 (Classic Reprint) (p. 1672)
—Orley Farm, Vol. 10 (Classic Reprint) (p. 1672)
—Orley Farm, Vol. 11 (Classic Reprint) (p. 1672)
—Orley Farm, Vol. 12 (Classic Reprint) (p. 1672)
—Orley Farm, Vol. 13 (Classic Reprint) (p. 1672)
—Orley Farm, Vol. 14 (Classic Reprint) (p. 1672)
—Orley Farm, Vol. 15: May 1862 (Classic Reprint) (p. 1672)
—Orley Farm, Vol. 17: July, 1862 (Classic Reprint) (p. 1672)
—Orley Farm, Vol. 19 (Classic Reprint) (p. 1672)
—Orley Farm, Vol. 2 (Classic Reprint) (p. 1672)
—Orley Farm, Vol. 2 of 2 (Classic Reprint) (p. 1672)
—Orley Farm, Vol. 20 (Classic Reprint) (p. 1672)
—Orley Farm, Vol. 3: May, 1861 (Classic Reprint) (p. 1672)
—Orley Farm, Vol. 3 (Classic Reprint) (p. 1672)
—Orley Farm, Vol. 4: June 1861 (Classic Reprint) (p. 1672)
—Orley Farm, Vol. 5 (Classic Reprint) (p. 1672)
—Orley Farm, Vol. 7: September 1861 (Classic Reprint) (p. 1672)
—Orley Farm, Vol. 8 (Classic Reprint) (p. 1672)
—Phineas Finn, Vol. 1: The Irish Member (Classic Reprint) (p. 1735)
—Ralph the Heir (Classic Reprint) (p. 1838)
—Saint Pauls Magazine, 1871, Vol. 9 (Classic Reprint) (p. 1923)
—Saint Pauls Magazine, Vol. 10: January to June, 1872 (Classic Reprint) (p. 1923)
—Saint Pauls Magazine, Vol. 12 (Classic Reprint) (p. 1923)
—Saint Pauls Magazine, Vol. 13: July to December, 1873 (Classic Reprint) (p. 1923)
—Saint Pauls Magazine, Vol. 8: April 1871, to September, 1871 (Classic Reprint) (p. 1923)
—Sir Harry Hotspur of Humblethwaite. (p. 2025)

—Small House at Allington (Chronicles of Barsetshire) - Unabridged: Romantic Classic. (p. 2039)
—Small House at Allington, Vol. 1 (Classic Reprint) (p. 2039)
—Struggles of Brown, Jones, & Robinson: By One of the Firm (Classic Reprint) (p. 2142)
—Struggles of Brown, Jones, & Robinson. (p. 2142)
—Tales of All Countries (Classic Reprint) (p. 2183)
—Three Clerks: A Novel (Classic Reprint) (p. 2232)
—Three Clerks, Vol. 2 Of 3: A Novel (Classic Reprint) (p. 2232)
—Three Clerks, Vol. 3 Of 3: A Novel (Classic Reprint) (p. 2232)
—Warden (Classic Reprint) (p. 2378)
—Why Frau Frohmann Raised Her Prices: And Other Stories (Classic Reprint) (p. 2458)
—Writings of Anthony Trollope, Vol. 29 (Classic Reprint) (p. 2513)
Trollope, Frances. Blue Belles of England, Vol. 2 of 3 (Classic Reprint) (p. 248)
—Life & Adventures of Jonathan Jefferson Whitlaw, or Scenes on the Mississippi (Classic Reprint) (p. 1288)
—Life & Adventures of Michael Armstrong, the Factory Boy, Vol. 3 of 3 (Classic Reprint) (p. 1288)
—One Fault, Vol. 3 Of 3: A Novel (Classic Reprint) (p. 1659)
—Robertses on Their Travels, Vol. 2 of 3 (Classic Reprint) (p. 1891)
—Tremordyn Cliff, Vol. 2 of 3 (Classic Reprint) (p. 2285)
—Vienna & the Austrians, Vol. 1 Of 2: With Some Account of a Journey Through Swabia, Bavaria, the Tyrol, & the Salzbourg (Classic Reprint) (p. 2356)
—Widow Barnaby (Classic Reprint) (p. 2461)
—Widow Barnaby, Vol. 1 of 3 (Classic Reprint) (p. 2461)
—Widow Married: A Sequel to the Widow Barnaby (Classic Reprint) (p. 2461)
—Widow Married, Vol. 1 Of 3: A Sequel to the Widow Barnaby (Classic Reprint) (p. 2461)
Trollope, Frances Eleanor. American Medium in England (Classic Reprint) (p. 73)
—Among Aliens, Vol. 1 Of 2: A Novel (Classic Reprint) (p. 76)
—Among Aliens, Vol. 2 Of 2: A Novel (Classic Reprint) (p. 76)
—Black Spirits & White, Vol. 3 (Classic Reprint) (p. 239)
—Charming Fellow, Vol. 1 of 3 (Classic Reprint) (p. 361)
—Like Ships upon the Sea: A Novel (Classic Reprint) (p. 1301)
—That Unfortunate Marriage, Vol. 1 (Classic Reprint) (p. 2213)
—That Unfortunate Marriage, Vol. 3 of 3 (Classic Reprint) (p. 2213)
—That Wild Wheel a Novel (Classic Reprint) (p. 2213)
Trollope, Frances Milton. Barnabys in America, or Adventures of the Widow Wedded (Classic Reprint) (p. 167)
—Barnabys in America, Vol. 1 Of 3: Or Adventures of the Widow Wedded (Classic Reprint) (p. 167)
—Belgium & Western Germany In 1833: Including Visits to Baden-Baden, Wiesbaden, Cassel, Hanover, the Harz Mountains, &C. , &C (Classic Reprint) (p. 195)
—Charles Chesterfield, or the Adventures of a Youth of Genius, Vol. 1 of 3 (Classic Reprint) (p. 358)
—Life & Adventures of Michael Armstrong: The Factory Boy (Classic Reprint) (p. 1288)
—Life & Adventures of Michael Armstrong, the Factory Boy, Vol. 1 (Classic Reprint) (p. 1288)
—Life & Adventures of Michael Armstrong, the Factory Boy, Vol. 2 of 3 (Classic Reprint) (p. 1288)
—Mother's Manual: Or, Illustrations of Matrimonial Economy; an Essay in Verse (Classic Reprint) (p. 1510)
—One Fault, Vol. 2 Of 3: A Novel (Classic Reprint) (p. 1659)
—Petticoat Government, Vol. 2 Of 3: A Novel (Classic Reprint) (p. 1731)
—Robertses on Their Travels, Vol. 1 of 3 (Classic Reprint) (p. 1891)
—Widow Barnaby, Vol. 2 of 3 (Classic Reprint) (p. 2461)
—Young Heiress: A Novel (Classic Reprint) (p. 2531)
—Young Heiress, Vol. 2 Of 3: A Novel (Classic Reprint) (p. 2531)
Trollope, Frank. Broken Fetters, Vol. 2 Of 3: A Novel (Classic Reprint) (p. 284)
—Captain Haverty's Wooing, Vol. 2 Of 3: A Novel (Classic Reprint) (p. 325)
—Gladstones, Vol. 1 Of 3: A Novel, in Three Volumes (Classic Reprint) (p. 840)
—Gladstones, Vol. 2 Of 3: A Novel (Classic Reprint) (p. 840)
—Gladstones, Vol. 3 Of 3: A Novel (Classic Reprint) (p. 840)
—Lawyer's Daughter, Vol. 1 Of 3: A Novel (Classic Reprint) (p. 1253)
—Old Times Revived, Vol. 1 Of 2: A Novel Two Volumes (Classic Reprint) (p. 1648)
—Old Times Revived, Vol. 2 Of 2: A Novel (Classic Reprint) (p. 1648)
—Rival Doctors, Vol. 1 Of 2: A Novel (Classic Reprint) (p. 1886)
Trollope, Her. Captain a Wooing, Vol. 1 Of 3: A Novel by Frank Trollope, Qi of the Most Honourable, the Marchioness of Salisbury These Volumes Are, by Kind Permission & Profound Respect (Classic Reprint) (p. 324)
Trollope, T. a. Leonora Casaloni, Vol. 2 Of 2: A Novel (Classic Reprint) (p. 1267)
Trollope, T. Adolphus. Artingale Castle, Vol. 3 (Classic Reprint) (p. 123)
—Beata, Vol. 1 of 2 (Classic Reprint) (p. 182)
—Beata, Vol. 2 of 2 (Classic Reprint) (p. 182)
—Lindi Chase: A Novel (Classic Reprint) (p. 1303)
Trollope, Thomas Adolphus. Artingale Castle, Vol. 1 of 3 (Classic Reprint) (p. 123)
—Diamond Cut Diamond: A Story of Tuscan Life (Classic Reprint) (p. 538)
—Dream Numbers, Vol. 1 Of 3: A Novel (Classic Reprint) (p. 602)
—Garstang Grange: A Novel (Classic Reprint) (p. 810)
—Garstangs of Garstang Grange, Vol. 1 of 2 (Classic Reprint) (p. 810)
—Giulio Malatesta, Vol. 2 Of 3: A Novel (Classic Reprint) (p. 839)
—Leonora Casaloni, Vol. 1 Of 2: A Novel (Classic Reprint) (p. 1267)
—Marietta, Vol. 1 Of 2: A Novel (Classic Reprint) (p. 1405)
—Marietta, Vol. 2 Of 2: A Novel (Classic Reprint) (p. 1405)
Troly-Curtin, Marthe. Phrynette (Classic Reprint) (p. 1737)
—Phrynette & London (Classic Reprint) (p. 1737)
—Phrynette Married (Classic Reprint) (p. 1737)
Trombello, William. Trains & Tow Boats. Tangen, Nick, illus. (p. 2276)
Trombetta, Lynn Alison. I Go to the Ocean & Talk to Myself. (p. 1065)
Trombley, Carl L. Animals, Questions, & One Big Tale. (p. 95)
Trombley, Stacey. Pushing the Boundaries. (p. 1817)
Tromholt, Sophus. Under the Rays of the Aurora Borealis, Vol. 1 Of 2: In the Land of the Lapps & Kvaens (Classic Reprint) (p. 2322)
Tromly, Stephanie. Trouble Makes a Comeback. (p. 2291)
—Trouble Never Sleeps. (p. 2291)
Tronci, Nicoletta. Teach Me to Knit: Super Simple for Kids & Other Beginners! (p. 2194)
Trondheim, Lewis. Mickey's Craziest Adventures. Keramidas, Nicolas, illus. (p. 1459)
Trondheim, Lewis, jt. auth. see Sfar, Joann.
Trone, Jo, illus. see Glass, Graeme.
Trone, Melody, illus. see Beserra, Donna.
Trone, Melody, jt. auth. see Beserra, Donna.
Trone, Melody Karns, illus. see Beserra, Donna.
Trone, Melody Karns, illus. see Davis, Lynda S. & Weisel, Kaitlyn E.
Tronslin, Andrea, ed. see Nelson, Ray & Nelson, Douglas.
Tronson, Louis. Examens Particuliers Sur Divers Sujets, Vol. 1: Propres Aux Ecclesiastiques, et a Toutes les Personnes Qui Veulent S'Avancer Dans la Perfection (Classic Reprint) (p. 675)
Trooboff, Rhoda. Punkinhead's Veggie Adventure: And the Strange Contraption in the Kitchen. Easton, Susan, illus. (p. 1814)
Troon, Kourtney. Adventures of Benjamin Boogie. (p. 21)
Trope, Nicole. Forgotten. (p. 768)
Tropics, Author of in the. Prince of Kashna a West Indian Story (Classic Reprint) (p. 1794)
Trosper, Chad. Apples in a Pail. (p. 107)
Trotandot, John. Rambles, Roamings & Recollections (Classic Reprint) (p. 1839)
Trotman, Felicity. Exploration of Space. (p. 679)
Trotman, Phd Gloria, et al. Fun Time with Jesus. (p. 800)
Trotman, Rita. Tiger Tails. Sandhu, Param, illus. (p. 2241)
Trotman, Tamara. Jared & the Sacred Emerald. (p. 1160)
Trotman, Wayne Gerard. Elephant's Advice. (p. 634)
—Last Honey Bee. (p. 1248)
—Mattie Boombalatty. (p. 1426)
—Tiger's Tale. (p. 2242)
Trotsky, Rebecca. Goodbye Little Dude. (p. 866)
Trotsky, Rebecca & Smyth, Marie. Goodbye Little Dude: A Remarkable Story of Kindness, Hope, & Love. Dansereau, Steve, illus. (p. 866)
Trott, Magda. Pommerle (Gesamtausgabe: Buch 1-6) (p. 1772)
Trotta, Lee. California Cheese. Trotta, Lee & Saemann, Kara, illus. (p. 310)
Trotta Sr, Richard. Nicky's Fire. (p. 1604)
Trotter, Bob. Curious Tale of Marmalade Tuttle - Book Two Marmalade Tuttle & the Battle of Caldor. (p. 488)
—Up the Wooden Hill: Bedtime Stories for Little Ones. Edgar, Barrie, illus. (p. 2338)
Trotter, Isabella Strange. First Impressions of the New World: On Two Travellers from the Old in the Autumn Of 1858. (p. 737)
Trotter, Melvin E. Jimmie Moore of Bucktown (Classic Reprint) (p. 1168)
Trotter, Rick. Black Shadow - Chapter One. (p. 239)
Trotter, Robert de Bruce. Galloway Gossip Sixty Years Ago: Being a Series of Articles Illustrative of the Manners, Customs, & Peculiarities of the Aboriginal Picts of Galloway (Classic Reprint) (p. 806)
Trotter, Stuart. What Am I? Asked Butterfly. (p. 2404)
Trotter, Stuart, illus. see Hawes, Alison.
Trotter, Stuart, illus. see Larkin, Susan.
Trotter, Stuart, illus. see Mayes, Susan.
Trotter, Stuart, illus. see Smith, Lucy.
Trotter, Stuart, illus. see Williams, Sam.
Trottier, Doug. Crow & His Boy. (p. 478)
Trottier, Maxine. Migrant Arsenault, Isabelle, illus. (p. 1464)
—Walking Stick Galouchko, Annouchka, illus. (p. 2372)
Trottot, Tammy. Little Judy Talks to God. (p. 1320)
Troughton, Guy, illus. see Evans, Lynette.
Trounce, Charlotte. San Francisco: A 3D Keepsake Cityscape. Trounce, Charlotte, illus. (p. 1929)
Trounce, Charlotte, illus. see Broom, Jenny.
Trounce, Charlotte, illus. see Candlewick Press Staff.
Troup, Roxanne. Amazing Lakes Around the World. (p. 65)
—Amazing Waterfalls Around the World. (p. 66)
—Deep-Sea Creatures (p. 524)
—Detection Dogs on the Job. (p. 534)
—Military Dogs on the Job. (p. 1466)
—Nasty Parasites (p. 1576)
Troupe, Thomas Kingsley. Animal Robots. (p. 91)
—Apollo's First Moon Landing: A Fly on the Wall History. Tejido, Jomike, illus. (p. 106)
—Are Bowling Balls Bullies? Learning about Forces & Motion with the Garbage Gang. Toye, Derek, illus. (p. 112)
—Battle Zone: The Inspiring Truth Behind Popular Combat Video Games. (p. 175)
—Battling Robots. (p. 175)
—Big Hairy Secret Gilpin, Stephen, illus. (p. 220)
—Birth of the Star-Spangled Banner: A Fly on the Wall History. Tejido, Jomike, illus. (p. 233)
—Blizzard - A Tale of Snow-Blind Survival. Fagan, Kirbi, illus. (p. 245)
—Build Buzz-Worthy Video Blogs: 4D an Augmented Reading Experience. (p. 293)
—Carma Comes Home. Tayal, Amit, illus. (p. 332)
—Centaurs. (p. 351)
—Could You Survive the New Stone Age? An Interactive Prehistoric Adventure. Calle Velez, Juan, illus. (p. 458)
—Create Crazy Stop-Motion Videos: 4D an Augmented Reading Experience. (p. 469)
—Crush It! (p. 480)
—Dark Lens. (p. 506)
—Darling Doll. Faber, Rudy, illus. (p. 508)
—Diggin' Dirt: Science Adventures with Kitanai the Origami Dog Christoph, Jamey, illus. (p. 546)
—Do Ants Get Lost? Learning about Animal Communication with the Garbage Gang Toye, Derek, illus. (p. 570)
—Do Bees Poop? Learning about Living & Nonliving Things with the Garbage Gang Toye, Derek, illus. (p. 570)
—Do Plants Have Heads? Learning about Plant Parts with the Garbage Gang. Toye, Derek, illus. (p. 570)
—Extreme Alien Stories. (p. 686)
—Extreme Ghost Stories. (p. 686)
—Extreme Monster Stories. (p. 687)
—Extreme Near-Death Stories. (p. 687)
—Extreme near-Death Stories. (p. 687)
—Extreme Stories about Disappearances. (p. 687)
—Extreme Stories about ESP. (p. 687)
—Fairies. (p. 695)
—Fantastic Worlds: The Inspiring Truth Behind Popular Role-Playing Video Games. (p. 707)
—Fighting Game Esports: The Competitive Gaming World of Super Smash Bros. , Street Fighter, & More! (p. 725)
—Final Frankenstein. Bonet, Xavier, illus. (p. 727)
—First-Person Action Esports: The Competitive Gaming World of Overwatch, Counter-Strike, & More! (p. 738)
—Flight Down. (p. 748)
—Fly on the Wall History. Tejido, Jomike, illus. (p. 754)
—Garbage Gang's Super Science Questions Toye, Derek, illus. (p. 808)
—Ghostly Goalie. Faber, Rudy, illus. (p. 829)
—Giants. (p. 831)
—Glowing with Electricity: Science Adventures with Glenda the Origami Firefly Christoph, Jamey, illus. (p. 845)
—Gulliver Giant. Bonet, Xavier, illus. (p. 905)
—Harriet Tubman's Escape: a Fly on the Wall History. Tejido, Jomike, illus. (p. 933)
—Hauntiques Faber, Rudy, illus. (p. 939)
—I Want to Be... (p. 1084)
—I Want to Be a Bald Eagle. Rodriguez, Christina Ann, illus. (p. 1084)
—I Want to Be a Brachiosaurus. Tejido, Jomike, illus. (p. 1084)
—I Want to Be a Crocodile. Wald, Christina, illus. (p. 1084)
—I Want to Be a Great White Shark. Boey, Stephanie, illus. (p. 1084)
—I Want to Be a Lion. Beavers, Melinda, illus. (p. 1084)
—I Want to Be a Triceratops. Tejido, Jomike, illus. (p. 1084)
—I Want to Be a Tyrannosaurus Rex. Tejido, Jomike, illus. (p. 1084)
—I Want to Be a Velociraptor. Tejido, Jomike, illus. (p. 1084)
—If I Were a Firefighter Reid, Mick, illus. (p. 1091)
—If I Were the President [Scholastic]. Heyworth, Heather, illus. (p. 1091)
—Jewel of the Galaxy. Tayal, Amit, illus. (p. 1167)
—Keep It Simple, Rapunzel! The Fairy-Tale Physics of Simple Machines. Tejido, Jomike, illus. (p. 1207)
—Kitanai & Cavity Croc Brush Their Teeth. Christoph, Jamey, illus. (p. 1225)
—Kitanai & Filthy Flamingo Wash Up. Christoph, Jamey, illus. (p. 1225)
—Kitanai & Hungry Hare Eat Healthfully. Christoph, Jamey, illus. (p. 1225)
—Kitanai & Lazy Lizard Get Fit. Christoph, Jamey, illus. (p. 1225)
—Kitanai's Healthy Habits. Christoph, Jamey, illus. (p. 1225)
—Kraken. (p. 1231)
—Legend of Atlantis Cressy, Mike, illus. (p. 1261)
—Legend of Bigfoot Dumm, Brian Caleb, illus. (p. 1261)
—Legend of the Loch Ness Monster Ice, D. C., illus. (p. 1262)
—Legend of the Vampire Kemarskaya, Oksana, illus. (p. 1263)
—Legend of the Werewolf Ice, D. C., illus. (p. 1263)
—Legend of UFOs Vignaga, Francesca Dafne, illus. (p. 1263)
—Lost - A Wild Tale of Survival. Fagan, Kirbi, illus. (p. 1352)
—Magnet Power! Science Adventures with MAG-3000 the Origami Robot Christoph, Jamey, illus. (p. 1381)
—Make a Movie! 4D. (p. 1385)
—Make Mind-Blowing Music Videos: 4D an Augmented Reading Experience. (p. 1386)
—Medical Robots. (p. 1436)
—Military Robots. (p. 1466)
—Minotaur Maze. Bonet, Xavier, illus. (p. 1473)
—Misplaced Mummy Gilpin, Stephen, illus. (p. 1477)
—Mount Rushmore Skeens, Matthew, illus. (p. 1513)
—Move on up That Beanstalk, Jack! The Fairy-Tale Physics of Forces & Motion. Tejido, Jomike, illus. (p. 1515)
—My First Day at School. Uno, Kat, illus. (p. 1543)
—Paul Revere's Ride: a Fly on the Wall History. Tejido, Jomike, illus. (p. 1707)
—Phantom's Favorite. Faber, Rudy, illus. (p. 1733)
—Phoenixes. (p. 1736)
—Pilgrims' Voyage to America: a Fly on the Wall History. Tejido, Jomike, illus. (p. 1745)
—Problems with Goblins Gilpin, Stephen, illus. (p. 1803)
—Robot Ruckus. Tayal, Amit, illus. (p. 1892)
—Schools Have Rules. Zhai, Rea, illus. (p. 1947)
—Sea Serpents. (p. 1968)
—Searching for Bermuda Triangle Answers. (p. 1971)
—Searching for Bigfoot. (p. 1971)
—Searching for Ghosts. (p. 1971)
—Shoot Epic Short Documentaries: 4D an Augmented Reading Experience. (p. 2009)
—Skeletons in City Park Gilpin, Stephen, illus. (p. 2030)
—Sneaky Spies: The Inspiring Truth Behind Popular Stealth Video Games. (p. 2045)
—Solemn Golem. Gilpin, Stephen, illus. (p. 2057)
—Space Robots. (p. 2072)
—Spaceship Named Judy. Tayal, Amit, illus. (p. 2073)
—Sphinxes. (p. 2080)
—Squadron. (p. 2094)
—Star Belchers (p. 2101)
—Staying Safe at School. Uno, Kat, illus. (p. 2110)
—Stegosaurus Would Not Make a Good Pirate. Calvert, Steph, illus. (p. 2112)
—Survive! (p. 2164)
—Surviving a Bigfoot Attack. (p. 2164)
—Surviving a Shipwreck at Sea. (p. 2164)
—Surviving a Zombie Attack. (p. 2164)
—Surviving Alone in the Jungle. (p. 2165)
—Surviving an Alien Attack. (p. 2165)
—Surviving on a Desert Island. (p. 2165)
—Time for Action: The Inspiring Truth Behind Popular Adventure Video Games. (p. 2244)
—Titanic's Tragic Journey: A Fly on the Wall History. Tejido, Jomike, illus. (p. 2251)
—Tornado - A Twisting Tale of Survival. Fagan, Kirbi, illus. (p. 2265)
—T-Rex Would Not Make a Good Knight. Calvert, Steph, illus. (p. 2174)
—Trolls. (p. 2290)
—Truth about Elves Squier, Robert, illus. (p. 2296)
—Truth about Trolls Taylor, Bridget Starr, illus. (p. 2296)
—Tuskegee Airmen's Mission to Berlin: A Fly on the Wall History. Tejido, Jomike, illus. (p. 2302)
—Underwater Robots. (p. 2326)
—Video Games vs. Reality. (p. 2356)
—Voiceless Vampire. Gilpin, Stephen, illus. (p. 2365)
—Volcano - A Fiery Tale of Survival. Fagan, Kirbi, illus. (p. 2366)
—Wandering Wagon. Faber, Rudy, illus. (p. 2375)
—Werewolves. (p. 2401)
—What's That Sound, Cinderella? The Fairy-Tale Physics of Sound. Tejido, Jomike, illus. (p. 2426)
—What's the Matter with the Three Little Pigs? The Fairy-Tale Physics of Matter. Tejido, Jomike, illus. (p. 2426)
—What's with the Long Naps, Bears? Learning about Hibernation with the Garbage Gang. Toye, Derek, illus. (p. 2427)
—Why Do Dead Fish Float? Learning about Matter with the Garbage Gang Toye, Derek, illus. (p. 2456)
—Why Does My Body Make Bubbles? Learning about the Digestive System with the Garbage Gang. Toye, Derek, illus. (p. 2457)
—Wild Weather: Science Adventures with Sonny the Origami Bird Christoph, Jamey, illus. (p. 2465)
—Wright Brothers' First Flight: a Fly on the Wall History. Tejido, Jomike, illus. (p. 2511)
—You Call That a Nose? Learning about Human Senses with the Garbage Gang. Toye, Derek, illus. (p. 2525)
—Your Life as a Settler in Colonial America. Canga, C. B., illus. (p. 2534)
—Your Life As an Explorer on a Viking Ship. Ebbeler, Jeffrey, illus. (p. 2534)
Troupe, Thomas Kingsley, jt. auth. see Mauleon, Daniel.
Trout, Ethel Wendell, jt. auth. see Faris, John Thomson.
Trout Fishing in America Staff & Jorisch, Stéphane. Chicken Joe Forgets Something Important. (p. 368)
Trout Fishing in America Staff, et al. My Name Is Chicken Joe. Jorisch, Stéphane, illus. (p. 1557)
Trout, Holly Christian. Firefly Who Lost Her Way. (p. 734)
Trout, Jenny. Such Sweet Sorrow. (p. 2146)
Trout, Laura. POGIL Activities for High School Biology. (p. 1767)
—POGIL Activities for High School Chemistry. (p. 1767)
Trout, Richard. Eclipse of the Jaguar (p. 623)
Troutman, John W. Kika Kila: How the Hawaiian Steel Guitar Changed the Sound of Modern Music. (p. 1216)
Trouvé, Marianne Lorraine. Saint Catherine Labouré: And Our Lady of the Miraculous Medal. (p. 1923)
—Saint Clare of Assisi: A Light for the World. Peterson, Mary Joseph, illus. (p. 1923)
—Saint Thomas Aquinas: Missionary of Truth. Morrison, Cathy, illus. (p. 1924)
Trover, Zachary. Spring Chicken! (p. 2092)
Trover, Zachary, illus. see Aboff, Marcie.
Trover, Zachary, illus. see Dahl, Michael.
Trover, Zachary, illus. see Jones, Christianne C.
Trover, Zachary, illus. see Random House Staff.
Trover, Zachary, illus. see Roop, Peter & Roop, Connie.
Trover, Zachary, illus. see Tourville, Amanda Doering.
Trover, Zachary, illus. see Wagner, Veronica.
Trovillion, Hal W. Sharing My Note Book (Classic Reprint) (p. 2001)
Trowbridge, J. T. Chance for Himself, or Jack Hazard & His Treasure (Classic Reprint) (p. 355)
—Darius Green & His Flying-Machine (Classic Reprint) (p. 505)
—Lucy Arlyn (Classic Reprint) (p. 1365)
—Neighbor Jackwood (Classic Reprint) (p. 1585)
—Neighbors Wives (Classic Reprint) (p. 1586)
—Our Young Folks, 1872, Vol. 8: An Illustrated Magazine for Boys & Girls (Classic Reprint) (p. 1681)
—Three Scouts (Classic Reprint) (p. 2235)
Trowbridge, John. Electrical Boy, or the Career of Greatman & Greatthings (Classic Reprint) (p. 631)
—Great Match, & Other Matches (Classic Reprint) (p. 887)
—Philip's Experiments: Or Physical Science at Home (Classic Reprint) (p. 1734)
—Story of a Wireless Telegraph Boy (Classic Reprint) (p. 2128)
Trowbridge, John Townsend. Adventures of David Vane & David Crane (Classic Reprint) (p. 23)
—Banking House of George P. Bissell Dealers in Safe Eight per Cent: Bonds, Government Securities, & First-Class Investments (Classic Reprint) (p. 164)
—Biding His Time, or Andrew Hapnell's Fortune (Classic Reprint) (p. 215)
—Bound in Honor: Or a Harvest of Wild Oats (Classic Reprint) (p. 265)
—Burrcliff: Its Sunshine & Its Coulds (Classic Reprint) (p. 300)
—Chance for Himself, or Jack Hazard & His Treasure (Classic Reprint) (p. 355)
—Coupon Bonds: And Other Stories (Classic Reprint) (p. 461)
—Coupon Bonds: A Play in Four Acts (Classic Reprint) (p. 461)
—Coupon Bonds, & Other Stories (Classic Reprint) (p. 461)
—Cudjo's Cave, by J. T Trowbridge (Classic Reprint) (p. 483)
—Doing His Best (Classic Reprint) (p. 578)
—Drummer Boy (Classic Reprint) (p. 606)
—Farnell's Folly (Classic Reprint) (p. 711)
—Fast Friends (Classic Reprint) (p. 713)
—Father Bright Hopes: Or an Old Clergyman's Vacation (Classic Reprint) (p. 714)
—Ferry-Boy & the Financier (Classic Reprint) (p. 721)
—His One Fault (Classic Reprint) (p. 974)
—Jack Hazard: His Fortunes (Classic Reprint) (p. 1152)

T

—Kelp-Gatherers: A Story of the Maine Coast (Classic Reprint) (p. 1209)
—Lawrence's Adventures: Among the Ice-Cutters, Glass-Makers, Coal-Miners, Iron-Men, & Ship-Builders (Classic Reprint) (p. 1253)
—Little Master (Classic Reprint) (p. 1321)
—Lottery Ticket (Classic Reprint) (p. 1356)
—Man Who Stole a Meeting-House: And Preaching for Selwyn (Classic Reprint) (p. 1395)
—Man Who Stole a Meeting-House (Classic Reprint) (p. 1395)
—Martin Merrivale: His X Mark (Classic Reprint) (p. 1411)
—Neighbor Jackwood: A Romantic Drama, in Five Acts (Classic Reprint) (p. 1585)
—Our Young Folks, 1865, Vol. 1: An Illustrated Magazine for Boys & Girls (Classic Reprint) (p. 1681)
—Our Young Folks, Vol. 3: An Illustrated Magazine for Boys & Girls (Classic Reprint) (p. 1681)
—Our Young Folks, Vol. 4 (Classic Reprint) (p. 1681)
—Pair of Madcaps (Classic Reprint) (p. 1693)
—Phil & His Friends (Classic Reprint) (p. 1733)
—Pocket-Rifle (Classic Reprint) (p. 1764)
—Prize Cup (Classic Reprint) (p. 1802)
—Question of Damages (Classic Reprint) (p. 1826)
—Scarlet Tanager: And Other Bipeds (Classic Reprint) (p. 1942)
—Silver Medal Stories (Classic Reprint) (p. 2019)
—Start in Life: A Story of the Genesee Country (Classic Reprint) (p. 2107)
—Tinkham Brothers' Tide-Mill (Classic Reprint) (p. 2248)
—Two Biddicut Boys: And Their Adventures with a Wonderful Trick-Dog (Classic Reprint) (p. 2307)
—Two Biddicut Boys. (p. 2307)
—Vagabonds (Classic Reprint) (p. 2343)
—Woodie Thorpe's Pilgrimage & Other Stories. (p. 2491)
—Woodie Thorpe's Pilgrimage & Other Stories (Classic Reprint) (p. 2491)
—Young Joe & Other Boys (Classic Reprint) (p. 2531)
—Young Surveyor: Or, Jack on the Prairies (Classic Reprint) (p. 2532)
—Young Surveyor. (p. 2532)
Trowbridge, W. R. H. Collection of British Authors, Vol. 255 Of 1: Tauchnitz Edition; a Dazzling Reprobate (Classic Reprint) (p. 414)
—Letters of Her Mother to Elizabeth (Classic Reprint) (p. 1280)
—That Little Marquis of Brandenburg (Classic Reprint) (p. 2213)
Trowbridge, William Rutherford Hayes. Dazzling Reprobate (Classic Reprint) (p. 516)
—Gossip of the Caribbees: Sketches of Anglo-West-Indian Life (Classic Reprint) (p. 872)
Troxell, Melanie. David Asks Why: Ellen G. White's Classic Steps to Christ Adapted to Children. (p. 511)
Troy, Andy, illus. see Wyatt, Chris.
Troy, Don. Booker T. Washington. (p. 260)
Troy, Michael. Fame: Adele. Davis, Darren G., ed. (p. 701)
—Fame: Nicki Minaj. Davis, Darren, ed. (p. 701)
—Fame: One Direction #2. Davis, Darren G., ed. (p. 701)
—Fame: One Direction Omnibus. Davis, Darren G., ed. (p. 701)
Troy, Michael, ed. see Davis, Darren G.
Troy, Michael, illus. see Morris, Elizabeth.
Troy, Michael & Davis, Darren G. Fame: Tom Daley. (p. 701)
Troy, Tony, illus. see Tarico, Valerie.
Troyansky, Judie. Parlor Tricks. (p. 1700)
Troyer, Gloria Irene. Beatrice & the Snow People. (p. 183)
Troyer, Joy, illus. see Martignacco, Carole.
Troyes, Chretien de. Li Romans Dou Chevalier Au Lyon (Classic Reprint) (p. 1283)
Troyes, Chrétien De. Li Romans Dou Chevalier Au Lyon Von Crestien Von Troies (Classic Reprint) (p. 1283)
Troyes, Chretien de. Löwenritter: Yvain (Classic Reprint) (p. 1363)
—Roman de la Charrette, d'Après Gauthier Map et Chrestien de Troies (Classic Reprint) (p. 1899)
Troyes, Christian von. löwenritter (Yvain) (Classic Reprint) (p. 1363)
Truax, Lois. Grandmothers Are Magic. (p. 879)
Trudden, Christina. Billy & Gracie: Unplugged Adventures-The Pirate Ship. (p. 227)
Trudgian, Sherri. Psalm 1 for Kidz: I'm So Happy I Want to Shout! Moreland Krass, Melanie, illus. (p. 1809)
True, Charles Kittredge. Word to Lads on Tobacco (Classic Reprint) (p. 2494)
True, E. Th. Spoken English: Everyday Talk with Phonetic Transcription (Classic Reprint) (p. 2086)
True, Emma J. Listen Ladies! A Comedy in Two Acts (Classic Reprint) (p. 1308)
Trueblood, Amy. Across a Broken Shore. (p. 11)
—Nothing but Sky. (p. 1624)
Trueheart, Eric, illus. see Vasquez, Jhonen.
Trueheart, Eric, jt. auth. see Logan, Sam.
Trueheart, Eric & Crosland, Dave. Invader ZIM Vol. 5 Crosland, Dave et al, illus. (p. 1129)
Trueheart, Eric & Logan, Sam. Invader ZIM Vol. 4: Deluxe Edition. Sherron, Kate & Stresing, Fred C., illus. (p. 1129)
Trueheart, Eric & Vasquez, Jhonen. Invader ZIM Vol. 3 Wucinich, Warren, illus. (p. 1129)
Trueheart, Eric, et al. Invader ZIM Vol. 6. Graley, Sarah et al, illus. (p. 1129)
Trueit, Trudi. Explorer Academy - (Vol. 1 of 2) the Nebula Secret. (p. 680)
—Explorer Academy - (Vol. 2 of 2) the Falcon's Feather. (p. 680)
—Mom, There's a Dinosaur in Beeson's Lake Paillot, Jim, illus. (p. 1490)
—Mom, There's a Dinosaur in Beeson's Lake. Paillot, Jim, illus. (p. 1490)
—My Top Secret Dares & Don&'ts. (p. 1562)
—My Top Secret Dares & Don'ts. (p. 1562)
—No Girls Allowed (Dogs Okay) Paillot, Jim, illus. (p. 1613)
—Scab for Treasurer? Paillot, Jim, illus. (p. 1941)
—Sister Solution. (p. 2027)
—Stealing Popular. (p. 2110)
Trueit, Trudi Strain. Animal Physical Therapist. (p. 91)
—Animal Trainer. (p. 92)
—Ants. (p. 103)
—Beetles. (p. 190)
—Birds. (p. 231)
—Birthday Crafts. Gallagher-Cole, Mernie, illus. (p. 233)
—Caterpillars. (p. 344)
—Caterpillars & Butterflies. (p. 344)
—Christmas. (p. 383)
—Cloudy Days. (p. 408)
—Detecting Avalanches. (p. 534)
—Detecting Volcanic Eruptions. (p. 534)
—Dragonflies. (p. 595)
—Frogs & Toads. (p. 790)
—Giant Pandas. (p. 831)
—Grasshoppers. (p. 881)
—Grizzly Bears. (p. 897)
—Halloween. (p. 912)
—Hanukkah. (p. 919)
—Horse Care. (p. 1004)
—Jellyfish. (p. 1163)
—Kwanzaa. (p. 1233)
—Massachusetts. (p. 1417)
—Mother's Day Crafts. Gallagher-Cole, Mernie, illus. (p. 1510)
—Octopuses. (p. 1637)
—Polar Bears. (p. 1769)
—Rainy Days. (p. 1837)
—Sharks. (p. 2002)
—Slugs, Snails, & Worms. (p. 2039)
—Snowy Days. (p. 2049)
—Spiders. (p. 2081)
—Squirrels. (p. 2095)
—Starfish. (p. 2106)
—Stormy Days. (p. 2127)
—Sunny Days. (p. 2152)
—Thanksgiving. (p. 2212)
—Thomas Jefferson. (p. 2228)
—Valentine's Day. (p. 2344)
—Veterinarian. (p. 2354)
—Vikings. (p. 2358)
—What Is Poetry? (p. 2416)
—Wildlife Conservationist. (p. 2466)
—Windy Days. (p. 2472)
—Worms. (p. 2508)
Trueit, Trudi Strain, jt. auth. see Bjorklund, Ruth.
Trueit, Trudi Strain, jt. auth. see Strain Trueit, Trudi.
Truelle, Auguste. Des Poires et des Pommes (Fruits de Table et de Pressoir) Choix, Classement, Commerce, Basés Sur l'Analyse Chimique (Classic Reprint) (p. 530)
Truelove, Dame. Gift Story Book, or Short Tales Written for Children (Classic Reprint) (p. 832)
Trueman, Matthew, illus. see Buhrman-Deever, Susannah.
Trueman, Matthew, illus. see Elliott, David.
Trueman, Matthew, illus. see Kimmel, Eric A.
Trueman, Matthew, illus. see Lasky, Kathryn.
Trueman, Matthew, illus. see London, Jonathan.
Trueman, Matthew, illus. see Rockwell, Anne.
Trueman, Terry. Life Happens Next. (p. 1291)
—No Right Turn. (p. 1614)
—Stuck in Neutral. (p. 2143)
Truemner-Caron, Lili, illus. see Goguen, Martha.
Truesdale, Lisa. Miami. (p. 1456)
—Tourism. (p. 2269)
Truesdell, Ann. Being Respectful Online. Petelinsek, Kathleen, illus. (p. 194)
—Find New Words with Dictionaries. (p. 728)
—Find the Facts with Encyclopedias. (p. 728)
—Fire Away: Asking Great Interview Questions. (p. 732)
—Get to the Right Site. (p. 825)
—How to Handle Cyberbullies. Petelinsek, Kathleen, illus. (p. 1042)
—Make Your Point: Creating Powerful Presentations. (p. 1387)
—Present It! Creating & Sharing a Slide Show. (p. 1788)
—Respecting Others Online. McLean, Rachael, illus. (p. 1869)
—Super Smart Information Strategies: Find the Right Site. (p. 2158)
—Wonderful Wikis. (p. 2490)
Truesdell, Ann, jt. auth. see Fontichiaro, Kristin.
Truesdell, Ann & Fontichiaro, Kristin. Starting Your Own Blog. Petelinsek, Kathleen, illus. (p. 2108)
Truesdell, Sue, illus. see Byars, Betsy.
Truesdell, Sue, illus. see George, Jean Craighead.
Truesdell, Sue, illus. see Grant, Judyann Ackerman.
Truesdell, Sue, illus. see Hamburg, Jennifer.
Truesdell, Sue, illus. see Little, Jean.
Truesdell, Sue, illus. see Stainton, Sue.
Truet, Turin & Gilman, Laura Anne. Searching for Yeti: The Abominable Snowman. (p. 1971)
Truette, Charlotte. Adam's Adventure: Walking in the Footsteps of History in His Hometown. (p. 14)
Truffle, illus. see CHIROLU.
Truitt, Gloria. Jesus bendice a los ninos (Jesus Blesses the Children)- Bilingual. Fernández, Cecilia, ed. (p. 1165)
Trujillo, Angela. Elizabeth Gets Healed. (p. 636)
Trujillo, Francisco. Batallas de Aquiles, Las. (p. 172)
—Medea la Hechicera. (p. 1436)
Trujillo, Janette. Why Do Snowmen Wear Hats? (p. 2456)
Trujillo, Josh. Lost Beast, Found Friend. Kennedy, Nick & Lapovich, Melanie, illus. (p. 1352)
Trujillo, Luis Francisco. Mitologia Maravillosa para Ninos. (p. 1483)
Trujillo, Rafael E. Mira: La Granja. Liu, Kimi, illus. (p. 1474)
—Mira. Liu, Kimi, illus. (p. 1474)
—ultima ola de Marianela. Liu, Kimi, illus. (p. 2314)
Trujillo, Robert, illus. see Bertrand, Diane Gonzales & Ventura, Gabriela Baeza.
Trujillo, Ron. Bird & the Butterfly. (p. 230)
Trukhan, Ekaterina. Apples for Little Fox. (p. 107)
—Five Little Ducks. (p. 744)
—Indestructibles: Baby, Find the Shapes! (p. 1115)
—Indestructibles: Baby, Let's Count! (p. 1115)
—Indestructibles: Baby, See the Colors! (p. 1115)
—Indestructibles: Hanukkah Baby. (p. 1115)
—Indestructibles: Let's Be Kind. (p. 1115)
—Indestructibles: Let's Go Outside! (p. 1115)
—Little Fox & the Missing Moon. (p. 1317)
Trukhan, Ekaterina, illus. see Berger, Samantha.
Trukhan, Ekaterina, illus. see Deutsch, Georgiana.
Trukhan, Ekaterina, illus. see R.A. Strong, R. A.
Trull, George H. Latin American Stories (Classic Reprint) (p. 1250)
Truly, Mary. Adventures of Captain Bentley. (p. 22)
Truly, Mary B. Alien on the Stoop. (p. 47)
—Vortex Magic. (p. 2367)
Truman, Farlo Ben. All the Ways You Can Face the Sky. (p. 54)
Truman, Howard J. Echoes. (p. 623)
Truman, J. K. & Whisenant, Dj. Miracle on the Mountain. (p. 1474)
Truman, Lucy, illus. see Sykes, Julie.
Truman, Lucy, illus. see Teagan, Erin.
Truman, Timothy, illus. see Dixon, Chuck.
Trumbauer, Lisa. Abraham Lincoln & the Civil War. (p. 7)
—First Americans. (p. 735)
—Great Reindeer Rebellion. Ho, Jannie, illus. (p. 889)
—Life Cycle of a Butterfly. (p. 1290)
Trumbauer, Lisa & Gray, Steve. Diente Está Flojo. Gray, Steve, illus. (p. 544)
Trumbauer, Mary. Stoney & Desperate. (p. 2122)
Trumble, Alfred. Mysteries of New York: A Sequel to Glimpses of Gotham, & New York by Day & Night (Classic Reprint) (p. 1566)
Trumble, David, illus. see Collen, Jane F.
Trumbo, Kim & Liem, Fanny. Ally the Accepting Alligator. (p. 57)
Trumbo, Stephen. Dreamers, Fantasies & Thrill Seekers. (p. 602)
Trumbore, Cindy. New Year's Around the World. (p. 1598)
—Three Cheers for Liberty! Elkerton, Andy, illus. (p. 2232)
Trumbore, Cindy, jt. auth. see Roth, Susan L.
Trumbull, Annie Eliot. Christmas Accident & Other Stories. (p. 383)
—Christmas Accident, & Other Stories (Classic Reprint) (p. 383)
—Mistress Content Cradock (Classic Reprint) (p. 1483)
—Rod's Salvation (Classic Reprint) (p. 1897)
Trumbull, Annie Slossen. Local Colorist (Classic Reprint) (p. 1338)
Trumbull, Jamie. Barney Ford: Pioneer Businessman. (p. 167)
Trumbull, John. Poetical Works of John Trumbull, Volume I - Scholar's Choice Edition. (p. 1766)
Trump, D. I'm Dougal Trump... - Where's My Tarantula? (p. 1098)
Trump, Odd. Novel (Classic Reprint) (p. 1626)
Trumper, May. Catalog of Library Books Recommended for School Districts in the State of Montana, 1920 (Classic Reprint) (p. 342)
Trundle, Victoria C. Magic of Manners. (p. 1378)
—Pins & Needles. (p. 1747)
Trunfio, Alessia, illus. see Alikhan, Salima.
Trunfio, Alessia, illus. see Bybee, Veeda, et al.
Trunfio, Alessia, illus. see Bybee, Veeda.
Trunfio, Alessia, illus. see Feldman, Thea.
Trunfio, Alessia, illus. see Gilbert, Julie Kathleen.
Trunfio, Alessia, illus. see Lord, Jill Roman.
Trunfio, Alessia, illus. see Shimose Poe, Mayumi.
Trunfio, Alessia, illus. see Smith, Nikki Shannon.
Trunfio, Alessia, illus. see Taddonio, Lea.
Trunfio, Alessia, illus. see Vawter, Vince.
Trunkhill, Brenda. Christmas Around the World. Camehl, Jeff, illus. (p. 383)
Trunko, Emily. Last Message Received. Ingram, Zoe, illus. (p. 1248)
Truong, Tom, illus. see Hegarty, Patricia.
Trupiano, Katie Belle, jt. auth. see Durango, Julia.
Truran, Stacy. Troy's Tree Fort: Measure Lengths in Standard Units. (p. 2292)
Truscelli, John J. Can P B Find the Jelly? (p. 317)
Truscott, Frederick Wilson. Elementary German Composition, for High Schools & Colleges (Classic Reprint) (p. 632)
Truscott, L. Parry. Mother of Pauline (Classic Reprint) (p. 1510)
Truscott, Wendy B. Haunted Journey. (p. 938)
Trusdell, Brian. 12 Reasons to Love Soccer. (p. 2551)
—Great Moments in Olympic Skiing (p. 888)
—James Harden. (p. 1157)
—Miracle on Ice (p. 1474)
—Neymar: Soccer Superstar. (p. 1601)
—Paul Pogba: Making His Mark on the Soccer World. (p. 1707)
—Pel: Soccer Star & Ambassador (p. 1714)
—Soccer Record Breakers (p. 2052)
—US Women Win the World Cup (p. 2340)
Trusler, John. Works of William Hogarth: In a Series of Engravings: with Descriptions, & a Comment on Their Moral Tendency (Classic Reprint) (p. 2500)
Truss, Lynne. Eats MORE, Shoots & Leaves: Why, ALL Punctuation Marks Matter! Timmons, Bonnie, illus. (p. 622)
Trussell, Jessica. Adventures with Venturous. (p. 30)
Trussell-Cullen, Alan. Edmund Hillary. (p. 626)
—Jackie Robinson. (p. 1153)
—Lonely Penguin's Blog (p. 1342)
—Mahatma Gandhi. (p. 1382)
—Mother Teresa. (p. 1510)
—Nelson Mandela. (p. 1587)
—Princess Diana. (p. 1797)
—Sam the Incredible Inventor (p. 1926)
—Seagull & the Fish. Teo, Ali, illus. (p. 1969)
—Shoo! Shoo! Shoo! Woodford-Robinson, Rieko, illus. (p. 2009)
—Twin Competition. Hurst, Elise, illus. (p. 2305)
—Winston Churchill. (p. 2474)
Trust, The Gunston, ed. see Barrie, J. M.
Trust, The Gunston, ed. see Garis, Howard R.
Trust, The Gunston, ed. see Gruelle, Johnny.
Trust, The Gunston, ed. see Kipling, Rudyard.
Trust, The Gunston, ed. see Nesbit, Edith.
Trust, The Gunston, ed. see Potter, Beatrix.
Trust, The Gunston, ed. see Wais, Louis & Garis, Howard R.
Trust, The Gunston, ed. see Wisa, Louis & Garis, Howard R.
Trust, T'He Gunston Q., ed. see Garis, Howard R.
Trusta, H. Last Leaf from Sunny Side (Classic Reprint) (p. 1248)
—Little Mary: Or Talks & Tales for Children (Classic Reprint) (p. 1321)
—Peep at Number Five, or a Chapter in the Life of a City Pastor (Classic Reprint) (p. 1713)
—Sunny Side: Or, the Country Minister's Wife (Classic Reprint) (p. 2152)
—Tell-Tale: Or Home Secrets Told by Old Travellers (Classic Reprint) (p. 2202)
Trustees, Lick Observatory. Publications of the Lick Observatory of the University of California, 1900, Vol. 4 (Classic Reprint) (p. 1810)
Trusty, Brad & Trusty, Cindy. Kids' Guide to Balloon Twisting (p. 1215)
Trusz, Shane & Frayne, Darryl. Across the Fourwinds. (p. 11)
—Beyond the Hollowtangle. (p. 212)
Truth and Tails. Roxy the Raccoon: A Truth & Tails Story. (p. 1909)
Tryon, Leslie, illus. see Flor Ada, Alma.
Tryon, Lillian Hart. Speaking of Home: Being Essays of a Contented Woman (Classic Reprint) (p. 2076)
Tryst, Cecil's. Woman's Vengeance, Vol. 1 Of 3: A Novel (Classic Reprint) (p. 2486)
Trywhitt, Thomas, jt. auth. see Chaucer, Geoffrey.
Trzpil, Monika Filipina. Bear Who Never Gave Up. (p. 180)
Tsai, Addie. Dear Twin. (p. 521)
Tsaioun, Katya & Kates, Steven A., eds. ADMET for Medicinal Chemists: A Practical Guide. (p. 16)
Tsairis, Jeannie Brett, illus. see Crane, Carol.
Tsakiridis, Dimitra. Art & Culture of Ancient Greece. (p. 120)
Tsakiridis, Dimitra & Bardi, Matilde. Art & Culture of Ancient Greece. (p. 120)
Tsang, Katie & Tsang, Kevin. Sam Wu Is Not Afraid of Sharks. Reed, Nathan, illus. (p. 1927)
—Sam Wu Is Not Afraid of the Dark. Reed, Nathan, illus. (p. 1927)
Tsang, Katie, et al. Sam Wu Is Not Afraid of Ghosts. (p. 1927)
—Sam Wu Is Not Afraid of Spiders. (p. 1927)
Tsang, Nina, jt. auth. see Sohn, Emily.
Tsang, Reginald. Coffee with Uncle Reggie Chatting with Uncle Zeng. (p. 412)
Tsao, Hsüeh-Chin. Dream of the Red Chamber (Classic Reprint) (p. 602)
Tsarfati, Einat. Neighbors. Appel, Annette, tr. (p. 1586)
—Sandcastle. Tsarfati, Einat, illus. (p. 1930)
Tsarfati, Einat, illus. see Smith, Shoham.
-Tsavaris-Lecourezos, Demetra. Letters from Around the World: Learning the Greek Alphabet. (p. 1279)
Tsavaris-Lecourezos, Demetra. Ready, Set, Opa! Saumell, Marina, illus. (p. 1848)
Tschudi, Bob & Tschudi, Marilyn Howard. Club4Girls: #1: the Girls with Boys' Names. (p. 409)
Tseitlin, Michael. Animal Olympics Violin Score. (p. 90)
Tseng, C. K. Thomas. A Is Not Only for Apple. Tour, Anat, illus. (p. 1)
Tseng, Jean, illus. see Park, Linda Sue.
Tseng, Kevin. One Snowy Morning. Wulfekotte, Dana, illus. (p. 1662)
Tseng, Mou-Sien, illus. see Park, Linda Sue.
Tsiang, Sarah. Flock of Shoes. Leng, Qin, illus. (p. 750)
—Sugar & Snails. Wimmer, Sonja, illus. (p. 2147)
Tsiang, Sarah Yi-Mei. Breathing Fire (p. 279)
—Toesy Toes (p. 2256)
Tsilis, Thanos, illus. see Homer.
Tsintziras, Aya. Pretty Bones (p. 1790)
Tsioumanis, Marina. Mum & Dad Are Separating: A Practical Resource for Separating Families & Family Therapy Professionals (p. 1526)
Tso, Anna. Herstory: A Hong Kong Mother. Lo, Joanne, illus. (p. 963)
—Taming Babel. Lo, Joanne, illus. (p. 2189)
—Unforgettable Neighbours. Lo, Joanne, illus. (p. 2327)
Ts'o, Pauline. Whispers of the Wolf (p. 2443)
Tsong, Jing Jing. Counting Birds. (p. 459)
—Sam Surfs. (p. 1926)
Tsong, Jing Jing, illus. see Ahulii, Gabrielle.
Tsong, Jing Jing, illus. see Hutchens, Verlie.
Tsong, Jing Jing, illus. see Hyde, Heidi Smith.
Tsong, Jing Jing, illus. see Melmed, Laura Krauss.
Tsong, Jing Jing, illus. see Sehgal, Kabir & Sehgal, Surishtha.
Tsong, Jing Jing, illus. see Ward, Jennifer.
Tsong, Jing Jing & BeachHouse Publishing. Aloha Zoo. (p. 57)
Tsosie, Dennison, illus. see Alexander, Carmen.
Tsou, Page, illus. see Baker, Kate.
Tsoukanelis, Erika Alexia. Latin Music Scene: The Stars, the Fans, the Music. (p. 1250)
Tsubomi No Yume, illus. see Seigneur, Francoise.
Tsuei, Jon. Sera & the Royal Stars Vol. 1. Wassel, Adrian F., ed. (p. 1990)
Tsukirino, Yumi. Stitch! (p. 2120)
Tsun, Zaawaazit Mkwa, jt. auth. see Chartrand, Jane.
Tsunetomo, Yamamoto & Wilson, William Scott. Hagakure: The Code of the Samurai Kutsuwada, Chie, illus. (p. 909)
Tsurumi, Andrea. Accident! (p. 10)
—Accident! (lap Board Book) (p. 10)
—Crab Cake: Turning the Tide Together. (p. 465)
Tsurumi, Andrea, illus. see Kalan, Elliott.
Tsurumi, Andrea, illus. see Sterer, Gideon.
Tsurusaki, Takahiro, illus. see Murasaki, Yukiya.
Tsutsumi, Robert Kondo and Dice. Dam Keeper. (p. 499)
Tsvetayeva, Elena, illus. see Clever Publishing.
T?s?ygankova, I., illus. see Usache?v, Andrei?.
Ttocs, Asil. Life of Asil: The Life of Asil. (p. 1294)
Ttofa, Juliette. Boat Star: A Story about Loss. (p. 251)
—Boy Who Longed to Look at the Sun: A Story about Self-Care. (p. 271)

—Cool Raw Food Recipes: Delicious & Fun Foods Without Cooking (p. 450)
—Cool Sandwich Food Art: Easy Recipes That Make Food Fun to Eat! (p. 450)
—Cool Snack Food Art: Easy Recipes That Make Food Fun to Eat! (p. 450)
—Cool Sugar-Free Recipes: Delicious & Fun Foods Without Refined Sugar. (p. 450)
—Cool Wheat-Free Recipes: Delicious & Fun Foods Without Gluten. (p. 450)
—Dixie's Big Heart: A Story about Alabama. Doucet, Bob, illus. (p. 566)
—Let's Cook with Apples! Delicious & Fun Apple Dishes Kids Can Make. (p. 1270)
—Let's Cook with Cereal! Delicious & Fun Cereal Dishes Kids Can Make. (p. 1270)
—Let's Cook with Cheese! Delicious & Fun Cheese Dishes Kids Can Make. (p. 1270)
—Let's Cook with Eggs! Delicious & Fun Egg Dishes Kids Can Make. (p. 1270)
—Let's Cook with Noodles! Delicious & Fun Noodle Dishes Kids Can Make. (p. 1270)
—Let's Cook with Popcorn! Delicious & Fun Popcorn Dishes Kids Can Make. (p. 1270)
—Missy the Show-Me Mule: A Story about Missouri. Doucet, Bob, illus. (p. 1482)
—Super Simple Bend & Stretch: Healthy & Fun Activities to Move Your Body. (p. 2157)
—Super Simple Breakfasts: Easy No-Bake Recipes for Kids. (p. 2157)
—Super Simple Cooking (p. 2157)
—Super Simple Desserts: Easy No-Bake Recipes for Kids. (p. 2157)
—Super Simple Dinners: Easy No-Bake Recipes for Kids (p. 2157)
—Super Simple Holiday Treats: Easy No-Bake Recipes for Kids. (p. 2157)
—Super Simple Lunches: Easy No-Bake Recipes for Kids. (p. 2157)
—Super Simple Move & Shake: Healthy & Fun Activities to Move Your Body. (p. 2157)
—Super Simple Punch & Kick: Healthy & Fun Activities to Move Your Body (p. 2157)
—Super Simple Snacks: Easy No-Bake Recipes for Kids. (p. 2157)
—Super Simple Throw & Catch: Healthy & Fun Activities to Move Your Body. (p. 2158)
—Super Simple Walk & Run: Healthy & Fun Activities to Move Your Body. (p. 2158)
Tuminelly, Nancy, jt. auth. see ABDO Publishing Company Staff.
Tuminelly, Nancy, jt. auth. see Doudna, Kelly.
Tuminelly, Nancy, jt. auth. see Salzmann, Mary Elizabeth.
Tummie, Loulou &. Paper Toys: Aliens: 11 Paper Aliens to Build. (p. 1697)
Tumminello, Giovanna, illus. see Isler, Linda Germano.
Tumulak, Ken, illus. see Lim, Adele M.
Tunberg, Jennifer Morrish, tr. see Seuss, Dr.
Tunberg, Terence O., tr. see Seuss, Dr.
Tunbridge, Emma. Feeling Well: Emotional Alchemy for Children. (p. 718)
Tunbridge, J. L. Jellybean Tree. (p. 1163)
Tunbridge, Jill. Fairy of the Night & Still. (p. 697)
Tunby, Benjamin. Arctic Tern's Journey. (p. 112)
—Dragonfly's Journey. (p. 595)
—Hammerhead Sharks in Action. (p. 913)
—Surviving a Space Disaster: Apollo 13. (p. 2164)
—Whale Sharks in Action. (p. 2403)
—Whale's Journey. (p. 2404)
Tune, Riley. Omega: An Icon Story. (p. 1651)
—Paragon: An Icon Story. (p. 1699)
—Warper: Origins. (p. 2379)
—Warper: Echoes of Etangria. (p. 2379)
Tunell, Ken, illus. see Shiotsu, Vicky.
Tung, Kadhima Ren, illus. see Currim, Nazli.
Tungate, Ara. Hugh. (p. 1048)
Tunic, Blue. From the Peasantry to the Peerage, Vol. 2 Of 3: A Novel (Classic Reprint) (p. 794)
Túnica, Martín, illus. see Morhain, Jorge C. & Túnica, Pablo.
Tunis, John R., jt. auth. see Tunis, John Roberts.
Tunks, Karyn. Jubilee! Buckner, Julie, illus. (p. 1185)
Tunmann, Otto. Pflanzenmikrochemie: Ein Hilfsbuch Beim Mikrochemischen Studium Pflanzlicher Objekte (Classic Reprint) (p. 1732)
Tunnell, Amber. Night Sky: Stories of the Stars (Bedtime Shadow Book) Zschock, Martha Day, illus. (p. 1607)
Tunnell, Michael O. Candy Bomber: The Story of the Berlin Airlift's Chocolate Pilot. (p. 322)
—Mailing May. Rand, Ted, illus. (p. 1383)
Tunnicliffe, C. F., illus. see Darling, F. Fraser.
Tunold, E. Ir. Zebra That Has No Stripes: The Adventures of Unique. (p. 2538)
Tunstall, Mark. Cautionary Tales for Kidults. (p. 347)
Tunstall, Nannie Whitmell. No. 40: A Romance of Fortress Monroe & the Hygeia (Classic Reprint) (p. 1612)
Tunstall, Tricia. Note by Note: A Celebration of the Piano Lesson. (p. 1624)
Tunstel Jr., Robert L., illus. see Griffin, Ramona Rorie.
Tuohy, Hannah, illus. see Alt, Jeff.
Tuohy, Hannah, illus. see Dunham, Traci.
Tuozzo, Danielle & Squires, Maryann. Geekdazzle: Gems for Life, Love & Everything in Between. (p. 813)
Tupa, Christopher, illus. see Dorham, Sylvia.
Tupac-Amaru, José Gabriel De. Last Inca, or the Story of Tupac Amaru, Vol. 1 (Classic Reprint) (p. 1248)
Tupera, Tupera. Make Faces. (p. 1386)
—Make More Faces: Doodle & Sticker Book with 52 Faces + 6 Sticker Sheets. (p. 1386)
—Panda Sento. (p. 1695)
—Polar Bear's Underwear. (p. 1769)
—What Does Baby Want? (p. 2409)
—¿Qué Quiere el Bebé? (What Does Baby Want?) (Spanish Edition) (p. 1823)
Tuplin, Luke. Tree & Me. (p. 2283)
Tupper, Edith Sessions. By Whose Hand? (Classic Reprint) (p. 306)
—Stuff of Dreams (Classic Reprint) (p. 2144)
Tupper, Ellin Isabelle. My First Story-Book: The Letterpress (Classic Reprint) (p. 1546)
Tupper Ling, Nancy. My Sister, Alicia May. Bersani, Shennen, illus. (p. 1560)
Tupper, Martin Farquhar. Crock of Gold: A Rural Novel (Classic Reprint) (p. 476)
—Paterfamilias's Diary of Everybody's Tour: Belgium & the Rhine, Munich, Switzerland, Milan, Geneva & Paris (Classic Reprint) (p. 1704)
—Proverbial Philosophy: Being Thoughts & Arguments Originally Treated. (p. 1808)
—Rides & Reveries of the Late Mr. Aesop Smith (Classic Reprint) (p. 1878)
—Stephan Langton (Classic Reprint) (p. 2115)
—Stephan Langton, Vol. 2 (Classic Reprint) (p. 2115)
—Twins: A Domestic Novel (Classic Reprint) (p. 2306)
—Twins: A Tale of Concealment (Classic Reprint) (p. 2306)
Tupper, Susan. Fran & Frederick Hamerstrom: Wildlife Conservation Pioneers. (p. 775)
Tupta, Frank. How to Build a Haunted House. Beckett, Kyle, illus. (p. 1038)
Turan, Kemal. Essence of Wisdom: Parables from Prophet Muhammad. (p. 663)
Turano, Ruth. No They Are My Dinosaurs. (p. 1615)
Turati, Valeria, illus. see Driscoll, Laura & Disney Book Group.
Turati, Valeria, illus. see Driscoll, Laura.
Turati, Valeria, illus. see Vitale, Brooke.
Turcanu, Alexander. Hurricane & the Menace of the Fishchomper. (p. 1054)
Turchan, Monique. Mydoit. Turchan, Monique, illus. (p. 1566)
Turchan, Monique, illus. see Demonia, Lori.
Turchan, Monique, illus. see Nero, Molly.
Turchan, Monique, illus. see Roth, Irene.
Turchan, Monique, illus. see Wamsley, Jody.
Turcios, Guadalupe Vanessa, tr. see Villaseñor, Victor.
Turcios, Omar. David, Fish & Penguins... Brokenbrow, Jon, tr. (p. 511)
—David, Peces, Pinguinos ... Turcios, Omar, illus. (p. 511)
Turco, Laura Lo, illus. see Mann, Elizabeth.
Turconi, Stefano, illus. see Disney & Radice, Teresa.
Turconi, Stefano, illus. see Radice, Teresa.
Turconi, Stefano, illus. see Secchi, Richard & Salati, Giorgio.
Turconi, Stefano, illus. see Stevenson, Steve.
Turcotte, Derek, illus. see Turcotte, Michael.
Turcotte, Michael. Colours Made in Heaven Turcotte, Derek, illus. (p. 427)
Turczynowicz, Laura De Gozdawa. When the Prussians Came to Poland: The Experiences of an American Woman During the German Invasion (Classic Reprint) (p. 2433)
—When the Prussians Came to Poland; the Experiences of an American Woman During the German Invasion. (p. 2433)
Turdera, Cristian, illus. see Vanden-Heuvel, John C., Sr.
Turetsky, Bianca. Time-Traveling Fashionista at the Palace of Marie Antoinette. (p. 2246)
Turetsky, Bianca, jt. auth. see Sheinmel, Courtney.
Turgenef, Ivan Sergheievitch. Annouchka: A Tale (Classic Reprint) (p. 100)
Turgénev, Iván. Diary of a Superfluous Man: And Other Stories (Classic Reprint) (p. 539)
—Dream Tales & Prose Poems. (p. 602)
—Dream Tales & Prose Poems (Classic Reprint) (p. 602)
—Knock, Knock, Knock & Other Stories (Classic Reprint) (p. 1229)
—Lear of the Steppes: And Other Stories (Classic Reprint) (p. 1255)
—Rudin: A Novel (Classic Reprint) (p. 1912)
—Rudin. (p. 1912)
—Sportsman's Sketches (Classic Reprint) (p. 2090)
—Sportsman's Sketches, Vol. 2 (Classic Reprint) (p. 2090)
—Virgin Soil, Vol. 2: Translated from the Russian (Classic Reprint) (p. 2360)
Turgénev, Iván & Garnett, Constance. Dream Tales & Prose Poems. (p. 602)
Turgenev, Ivan S. Fathers & Sons (Classic Reprint) (p. 714)
—First Love & Punin & Baburin (Classic Reprint) (p. 738)
Turgenev, Ivan Sergeevich. Annals of a Sportsman (Classic Reprint) (p. 98)
—Brigadier & Other Stories (Classic Reprint) (p. 281)
—Diary of a Superfluous Man. Garnett, Constance, tr. (p. 539)
—Diary of a Superfluous Man & Other Stories: A Novels & Stories of Ivan Turgenieff (Classic Reprint) (p. 539)
—Diary of a Superfluous Man & Other Stories. (p. 539)
—Dimitri Roudine: A Novel (Classic Reprint) (p. 547)
—Fathers & Children (Classic Reprint) (p. 714)
—First Love & Other Stories (Classic Reprint) (p. 738)
—Memoirs of a Sportsman, Vol. 2: Translated from the Russian (Classic Reprint) (p. 1444)
—Nobleman's Nest (Classic Reprint) (p. 1616)
—Novels & Stories of Ivan Turgenieff: Spring Freshets & Others Stories (Classic Reprint) (p. 1626)
—On the Eve (Classic Reprint) (p. 1654)
—Phantoms & Other Stories (Classic Reprint) (p. 1733)
—Smoke (Classic Reprint) (p. 2043)
—Sportsman's Sketches, Vol. 1 (Classic Reprint) (p. 2090)
—Spring Freshets: And Other Stories; Smoke (Classic Reprint) (p. 2092)
—Stories by Foreign Authors: Russian; Mumu; the Shot; St. John's Eve; an Old Acquaintance (Classic Reprint) (p. 2123)
—Virgin Soil (Classic Reprint) (p. 2360)
—Works of Ivan Turgenieff: Rudin, a Romance; a King Lear of the Steppes; Phantoms, & Other Stories (Classic Reprint) (p. 2498)
Turgenev, Ivan Sergeyevich. Fathers & Sons (Classic Reprint) (p. 714)
—First Love & Punin & Baburin (Classic Reprint) (p. 738)
—Rudin: A Novel (Classic Reprint) (p. 1912)
—Spring Freshets: And Other Stories; Smoke (Classic Reprint) (p. 2092)
—Virgin Soil, Vol. 2: Translated from the Russian (Classic Reprint) (p. 2360)
—Works of Ivan Turgenieff: First Love, & Other Stories; the Jew (Classic Reprint) (p. 2498)
Turgenieff, Ivan. Annals of a Sportsman (Classic Reprint) (p. 98)
—Memoirs of a Sportsman (Classic Reprint) (p. 1444)
—Memoirs of a Sportsman, Vol. 2: Translated from the Russian (Classic Reprint) (p. 1444)
—Reckless Character: And Other Stories (Classic Reprint) (p. 1853)
—Virgin Soil, Vol. 2 (Classic Reprint) (p. 2360)
—Works of Ivan Turgenieff: Spring Freshets, and, Smoke (Classic Reprint) (p. 2498)
—Works of Ivan Turgenieff: Virgin Soil, Reckless Character, & Other Stories (Classic Reprint) (p. 2498)
Turgenieff, Ivan Gergiyevitch. And the Diary of a Superfluous Man (Classic Reprint) (p. 83)
Turgenieff, Ivan S. On the Eve: A Tale (Classic Reprint) (p. 1654)
Turgenieff, Ivan Sergeevich. Rudin, a Romance, and, a King Lear of the Steppes (Classic Reprint) (p. 1912)
Turgenieff, Turgenieff. Virgin Soil (Classic Reprint) (p. 2360)
Turhan, Sedat. New Bilingual Visual Dictionary (English-Arabic) (p. 1591)
—New Bilingual Visual Dictionary (English-Bengali) (p. 1591)
—New Bilingual Visual Dictionary (English-Farsi) (p. 1591)
—New Bilingual Visual Dictionary (English-Urdu) (p. 1591)
—New Bilingual Visual Dictionary (English-Vietnamese) (p. 1591)
Turhan, Sedat, jt. auth. see Hambleton, Laura.
Turiel, Isaac. How Do We Know the Size of the Solar System? (p. 1029)
Turk, Caron, illus. see Elwell, Ellen Banks.
Turk, Caron, illus. see Larsen, Carolyn.
Turk, Caron, jt. illus. see Elwell, Ellen Banks.
Turk, Cheri. Little Beth of the Forest. Turk, Cheri, illus. (p. 1311)
—Pequeña Bety de la Selva. Oceguera, Aracely, tr. (p. 1720)
—Stone Between Kings. Turk, Cheri, illus. (p. 2121)
Turk, Evan. Heartbeat. Turk, Evan, illus. (p. 946)
—Storyteller. Turk, Evan, illus. (p. 2136)
—You Are Home: An Ode to the National Parks. Turk, Evan, illus. (p. 2524)
Turk, Evan, illus. see Gandhi, Arun & Hegedus, Bethany.
Turk, Evan, illus. see Mahin, Michael.
Turk, Hanne, illus. see Landa, Norbert.
Turkienicz, Rachael, jt. auth. see Morgan, Anna.
Turkle, Brinton. Obadiah the Bold. (p. 1634)
—Thy Friend, Obadiah. (p. 2239)
Turkoglu, Nurcay, jt. auth. see Cornell, Kari.
Turkowski, Einar. Houses Floating Home. (p. 1024)
Turland-Estlin, Penelope. Book of Mirrors. (p. 259)
Turley, Beth. If This Were a Story. (p. 1092)
Turley, Charles. Band of Brothers (Classic Reprint) (p. 163)
Turley, Gerry, illus. see Duval, Kathy.
Turley, Gerry, illus. see Nosy Crow.
Turley, Joyce Mihran, illus. see Haukos, Jill.
Turley, Joyce Mihran, illus. see Larsen, Laurel.
Turley, Joyce Mihran, illus. see Love, Donna.
Turley, Joyce Mihran, tr. see Love, Donna.
Turley, LuAnn & Whiteman, Rita. View, a Clue, & You: Poetry & American Art at the Museum of Fine Arts, Houston. (p. 2357)
Turley/Alber. And the Tide Comes In. (p. 83)
Turman, Cheryl. Percy: The Goose That Wanted to Be an Ostrich. (p. 1721)
Turnage, Cyndy. Trip to Washington, D. C. A Capital Idea. Fagan, Martin, illus. (p. 2289)
Turnage, Leceila. Keona Browne. (p. 1210)
Turnage, Sheila. Ghosts of Tupelo Landing. (p. 829)
—Law of Finders Keepers. (p. 1253)
—Odds of Getting Even. (p. 1638)
—Three Times Lucky. (p. 2235)
Turnbaugh, Kay. Mountain Pine Beetle: Tiny but Mighty. Brooks, David, illus. (p. 1514)
Turnbaugh, Rosa. Virgil Learns about God ABCs. (p. 2360)
Turnbloom, Lucas, illus. see Allabach, P. R.
Turnbloom, Lucas, illus. see Grunberg, Greg.
Turnbloom, Lucas, jt. auth. see Grunberg, Greg.
Turnbull, A. R. R. Tales from Natal: Stories about Boers & Blacks (Classic Reprint) (p. 2182)
Turnbull, Alexandra C. Little Orange Cat's Dream. (p. 1323)
—Lost Dog. (p. 1353)
—Lost Dog Part 2. (p. 1353)
Turnbull, Aneika Asharee. Little Girl's Dream. (p. 1317)
Turnbull, Ann. Deep Water. (p. 525)
—Greek Myths. Young, Sarah, illus. (p. 892)
—Josie under Fire. (p. 1179)
—Mary Ann & Miss Mozart. (p. 1414)
Turnbull, Betty. Abigail & the Royal Thread. Adasikov, Igor, illus. (p. 5)
—Isobel's New World. Adasikov, Igor, illus. (p. 1140)
—Man Who Saved the King. Adasikov, Igor, illus. (p. 1395)
—Sergeant in the House. Senning, Susan, illus. (p. 1990)
Turnbull, Betty J. Sergeant in the House. Senning, Susan, illus. (p. 1990)
Turnbull, Betty Turnbull. Isobel's New World. Taimy Studios, illus. (p. 1140)
Turnbull, Brian, illus. see Maclean, Fiona.
Turnbull, Colin M. Forest People (Classic Reprint) (p. 766)
Turnbull, E. G., illus. see Francis, Wendy.
Turnbull, Elizabeth. Bonnwit Kabrit. Vaganos, Erin, illus. (p. 256)
—Janjak & Freda Go to the Iron Market. Turnbull, Wally, tr. (p. 1159)
Turnbull, Elizabeth J. Janjak & Freda Go to the Iron Market. Turnbull, Wally R., tr. (p. 1159)
Turnbull, Frances. Magical Musical Kingdom Song Book. (p. 1380)
—Musical Munchies Song Book. (p. 1529)
—Passport to Transport Song Book. (p. 1703)
—Under the Sea Songbook. (p. 2322)
Turnbull, Kathie. Because Everyone Needs a Friend. (p. 186)
Turnbull, Laurence. Clinical Manual of the Diseases of the Ear (Classic Reprint) (p. 406)
Turnbull, Margaret. Looking after Sandy: A Simple Romance (Classic Reprint) (p. 1347)
Turnbull, Peter. Aftermath. (p. 34)
Turnbull, Samantha. Cruise Control: The Anti-Princess Club 5. Davis, Sarah, illus. (p. 479)
Turnbull, Stacy. Robert Speer: Denver's Building Mayor. (p. 1890)
Turnbull, Stephanie. Accessories: Style Secrets for Girls. (p. 10)
—Acting Skills. (p. 12)
—Actor. (p. 13)
—Alligator. (p. 56)
—Art Skills. (p. 122)
—Artist. (p. 123)
—Baking. (p. 160)
—Beauty Blitz. (p. 185)
—Bedroom Makeovers. (p. 188)
—Camel. (p. 314)
—Canoeing & Kayaking. (p. 322)
—Card Tricks. (p. 328)
—Cards & Gifts: Style Secrets for Girls. (p. 328)
—Castles IR (Rev Cover) (p. 340)
—Caving. (p. 348)
—Chef. (p. 364)
—Circus Skills. (p. 393)
—Circus Star. (p. 393)
—Close-Up Tricks. (p. 407)
—Cold! (p. 413)
—Collecting. (p. 414)
—Cooking Skills. (p. 447)
—Cool Crafts. (p. 448)
—Cool Stuff to Bake. (p. 450)
—Cool Stuff to Collect. (p. 450)
—Cool Stuff to Grow. (p. 450)
—Cool Stuff to Make with Paper. (p. 450)
—Cool Stuff to Photograph. (p. 450)
—Cool Stuff to Sew. (p. 450)
—Craft Skills. (p. 466)
—Craft Star. (p. 466)
—Diaries & Keepsakes: Style Secrets for Girls. (p. 538)
—Do You Really Want to Visit Neptune? (p. 572)
—Do You Really Want to Visit Uranus? (p. 572)
—Dolphin. (p. 579)
—Dolphins. (p. 579)
—Eagle. (p. 613)
—Easy Card Tricks. (p. 620)
—Easy Coin Tricks. (p. 620)
—Easy Dinner Table Tricks. (p. 620)
—Easy Mind & Body Tricks. (p. 621)
—Easy Pen & Paper Tricks. (p. 621)
—Easy Scarf & Rope Tricks. (p. 621)
—Elephant. (p. 633)
—Emergency! (p. 641)
—Essential Atlas of the World. (p. 663)
—Fabulous Food. (p. 692)
—Fall. (p. 699)
—Fun & Games. (p. 798)
—Fun with Friends: Style Secrets for Girls. (p. 800)
—Gardening. (p. 809)
—Giraffe. (p. 834)
—Gorilla. (p. 870)
—Health & Fitness: Style Secrets for Girls. (p. 943)
—Hiking. (p. 971)
—Hippo. (p. 973)
—Hungry! (p. 1052)
—Incredible Illusions. (p. 1114)
—Kangaroo. (p. 1202)
—Komodo Dragon. (p. 1230)
—Leyendo Aprendo el Cuerpo(Your Body IR) (p. 1282)
—Lion. (p. 1305)
—Looking Good: Style Secrets for Girls. (p. 1347)
—Lost! (p. 1352)
—Magic Skills. (p. 1379)
—Magician. (p. 1381)
—Mind-Reading Tricks. (p. 1469)
—Mountain Biking. (p. 1513)
—Panda. (p. 1695)
—Papercraft. (p. 1698)
—Photography. (p. 1737)
—Polar Bear. (p. 1769)
—Ponies. (p. 1773)
—Prop Tricks. (p. 1807)
—Racehorses. (p. 1831)
—Rock Climbing. (p. 1894)
—Sewing. (p. 1995)
—Shark. (p. 2001)
—Show Horses. (p. 2012)
—Snake. (p. 2044)
—Sports Horses. (p. 2089)
—Spring. (p. 2092)
—Stranded! (p. 2137)
—Summer. (p. 2148)
—Thirsty! (p. 2223)
—Tiger. (p. 2241)
—Trains. (p. 2276)
—Transformation & Vanishing Tricks. (p. 2277)
—Vanishing Tricks. (p. 2347)
—Wardrobe Makeovers. (p. 2379)
—Whale. (p. 2403)
—Wild Horses. (p. 2463)
—Winter. (p. 2475)
—Working Horses. (p. 2496)
Turnbull, Stephanie, ed. see Brocklehurst, Ruth.
Turnbull, Stephanie, jt. auth. see Gulliver, Amanda.
Turnbull, Stephanie, jt. auth. see Morgan, Philip.
Turnbull, Stephanie, jt. auth. see Turnbull, Stephaniel.
Turnbull, Stephaniel. Cool Stuff to Photograph. (p. 450)
Turnbull, Stephaniel & Turnbull, Stephanie. Cool Stuff to Bake. (p. 450)
—Cool Stuff to Grow. (p. 450)
—Cool Stuff to Make with Paper. (p. 450)
Turnbull, Stephen. Real Samurai: Over 20 True Stories about the Knights of Old Japan! Field, James, illus. (p. 1850)

T

—True Manliness: Or, the Landscape Gardener; a Book for Boys & Girls (Classic Reprint) (p. 2294)
Tuthill, Louisa C. Get Money (Classic Reprint) (p. 824)
—Hurrah for New England! or the Virginia Boy's Vacation (Classic Reprint) (p. 1054)
Tuthill, Louisa Caroline. Beautiful Bertha (Classic Reprint) (p. 183)
—I Will Be a Lady: A Book for Girls (Classic Reprint) (p. 1085)
Tutino, Stefania, ed. see Bellarmine, Robert.
Tutor, Margaret. Make-Do Christmas (p. 1386)
Tutos, Joanna, ed. see Wright, Joe.
Tutos, Joanna, ed. see Wright, Joseph B.
Tuttle, Ada Alice. Overseas Girl Overseas: Extracts from Letters Written to Her Parents (Classic Reprint) (p. 1688)
Tuttle, Emma Rood. Angell Prize-Contest Recitations: To Advance Humane Education in All Its Phases; Compiled to Be Used in Entertainments Managed by Churches, Societies, Lyceums, Sunday Schools, Bands of Mercy, or Individuals Aiming to Establish Right over Wrong, Kindness O. (p. 86)
Tuttle, Ervilla. Gleaner in Clover Fields (Classic Reprint) (p. 841)
Tuttle, Florence Guertin. Give My Love to Maria: And Other Stories (Classic Reprint) (p. 840)
Tuttle, J. F. Curious Adventures of Fletch Highfield. (p. 486)
Tuttle, Jane. Life with Grandfather Conwell & His Acres of Diamonds (Classic Reprint) (p. 1296)
Tuttle, Lisa, jt. auth. see Martin, George R. R.
Tuttle, Margaretta. His Worldly Goods (Classic Reprint) (p. 974)
Tuttle, Mark. Lexi's Tea Party. Combs, Bradley, illus. (p. 1282)
Tuttle, Mary McArthur T. Follow the Gleam (Classic Reprint) (p. 758)
—Mother of an Emperor: Reprints from Pen & Brush (Classic Reprint) (p. 1510)
Tuttle, Sarah Grace. Spot, Spike, Spiral. Nerlove, Miriam, illus. (p. 2090)
Tuttle, Walter A. Tongo: The Hero of the Luray Caverns (Classic Reprint) (p. 2260)
Tutu, Desmond. Children of God Storybook Bible (p. 371)
—Desmond & the Very Mean Word. Ford, A. G., illus. (p. 533)
—Let There Be Light Tillman, Nancy, illus. (p. 1269)
—My Jesus Story Collection: 18 New Testament Bible Stories (p. 1550)
Tuvey, John. NFL Underdog Stories. (p. 1601)
Tuwim, Julian & Anon. Locomotive. Lewitt and Him Staff & Anon, illus. (p. 1339)
Tuxbury, Larry David, jt. auth. see McElligott, Matthew.
Tuxworth, Nicola. Animals. (p. 93)
—Baby Animals. (p. 148)
—Bodies. (p. 253)
—Clothes. (p. 407)
—Colours. (p. 427)
—Diggers & Dumpers. (p. 546)
—Farm Animals. (p. 709)
—Funny Faces. (p. 801)
—Messy. (p. 1452)
—Mix & Match. (p. 1484)
—Nature. (p. 1580)
—Patterns: Learn-a-Word Book. (p. 1706)
—Peekaboo! (p. 1713)
—Pets. (p. 1731)
—Puppies. (p. 1814)
—Shapes. (p. 2000)
—Sizes. (p. 2029)
—Splish Splash. (p. 2085)
—Things That Go. (p. 2221)
Tuxworth, Nicole. Kittens. (p. 1226)
Tuya, Angela. Dancing with Time. (p. 500)
Tuya, Jez, illus. see Churnin, Nancy.
Tuya, Jez, illus. see Demuth, Patricia Brennan.
Tuya, Jez, illus. see Gibson, Douglas.
Tuya, Jez, illus. see Lowell, Barbara.
Tuya, Jez, illus. see Peet, Mal & Graham, Elspeth.
Tuyl, Christine Van. Media Violence. Merino, Noël, ed. (p. 1436)
Tveite, William P. Adventures of Maximillian P. Dogg - Rescue Dog: Max Finds a New Home. Steele, Gregory D., illus. (p. 25)
Twaddle, Cheryl. Fire. (p. 732)
—Wind. (p. 2471)
Twain. Adventures of Huckleberry Finn. (p. 24)
—Adventures of Tom Sawyer (1000 Copy Limited Edition) (p. 29)
—Adventures of Tom Sawyer & Huckleberry Finn (1000 Copy Limited Edition) (p. 29)
—Celebrated Jumping Frog of Calaveras County: And Other Sketches (Classic Reprint) (p. 349)
—Connecticut Yankee in King Arthur's Court (Classic Reprint) (p. 441)
—Double Barrelled Detective Story (Classic Reprint) (p. 588)
—Europe & Elsewhere, Vol. 29 (Classic Reprint) (p. 667)
—Idle Excursion (Classic Reprint) (p. 1090)
—Mark Twain's Library of Humor: Women & Things (Classic Reprint) (p. 1407)
—Mark Twain's Library of Humor: The Primrose Way (Classic Reprint) (p. 1407)
—Mississippi Pilot; Two Men of Sandy Bar; Poems (Classic Reprint) (p. 1482)
—Pudd'nhead Wilson (Classic Reprint) (p. 1810)
—Sketches New & Old (Classic Reprint) (p. 2031)
—Wit & Humor of the Age: Comprising Wit, Humor, Pathos, Ridicule, Satires, Dialects, Puns, Conundrums, Riddles, Charades, Jokes & Magic (Classic Reprint) (p. 2479)
Twain, Mark, jt. auth. see Beecher, Alvah C.
Twain, Mark, jt. auth. see Harte, Bret.
Twain, Mark, jt. auth. see Lawson, Jessica.
Twain, Mark, jt. auth. see Paine, Albert Bigelow.
Twain, Mark, pseud. $30, 000 Bequest: And Other Stories (Classic Reprint) (p. 2554)
—Adventures of Huckleberry Finn. (p. 24)
—Adventures of Huckleberry Finn. Powell, Eric, illus. (p. 24)
—Adventures of Huckleberry Finn. McWilliam, Howard, illus. (p. 24)
—Adventures of Huckleberry Finn (100 Copy Limited Edition) (p. 24)
—Adventures of Huckleberry Finn (Illustrated) American Classics Series. (p. 24)
—Adventures of Huckleberry Finn (Tom Sawyer's Comrade) [Complete & Unabridged. 174 Original Illustrations.]. Kemble, E. W., illus. (p. 24)
—Adventures of Tom Sawyer: A Novel. (p. 29)
—Adventures of Tom Sawyer. (p. 29)
—Adventures of Tom Sawyer. Ingpen, Robert, illus. (p. 29)
—Adventures of Tom Sawyer (100 Copy Limited Edition) (p. 29)
—Adventures of Tom Sawyer (1000 Copy Limited Edition) (p. 29)
—Adventures of Tom Sawyer (Illustrated) American Classics Series. (p. 29)
—Adventures of Tom Sawyer (Unabridged. Complete with All Original Illustrations) (p. 29)
—Adventures of Tom Sawyer / Las Aventuras de Tom Sawyer. (p. 29)
—Adventures of Tom Sawyer & Huck Finn (Illustrated) American Classics Series. (p. 29)
—Advice to Little Girls. Radunsky, Vladimir, illus. (p. 30)
—American Claimant: And Other Stories & Sketches (Classic Reprint) (p. 71)
—American Claimant (Classic Reprint) (p. 71)
—Celebrated Jumping Frog of Calaveras County: And Other Sketches (Classic Reprint) (p. 349)
—Classic Starts(r): the Adventures of Huckleberry Finn. Andreasen, Dan, illus. (p. 400)
—Classic Starts(r): the Adventures of Tom Sawyer. Corvino, Lucy, illus. (p. 400)
—Complete Works of Mark Twain: Tom Sawyer, Abroad (Classic Reprint) (p. 435)
—Complete Works of Mark Twain: Mark Twain's Speeches (Classic Reprint) (p. 435)
—Connecticut Yankee in King Arthur's Court. (p. 441)
—Connecticut Yankee in King Arthur's Court (Classic Reprint) (p. 441)
—Dog's Tale (Classic Reprint) (p. 578)
—Double Barrelled Detective Story (Classic Reprint) (p. 588)
—Editorial Wild Oats (Classic Reprint) (p. 626)
—Europe & Elsewhere, Vol. 29 (Classic Reprint) (p. 667)
—Eve's Diary: Translated from the Original Ms. (Classic Reprint) (p. 674)
—Extract from Captain Stormfield's Visit to Heaven (Classic Reprint) (p. 685)
—Extracts from Adam's Diary: Translated from the Original Ms. (Classic Reprint) (p. 685)
—Eye Openers: Good Things, Immensely Funny Sayings Stories That Will Bring a Smile upon the Gruffest Countenance (Classic Reprint) (p. 688)
—Following the Equator, Vol. 1 Of 2: A Journey Around the World (Classic Reprint) (p. 758)
—Gilded Age: A Tale of to-Day (Classic Reprint) (p. 833)
—Gilded Age, Vol. 1 Of 2: A Tale of to-Day (Classic Reprint) (p. 833)
—Gilded Age, Vol. 2 Of 2: A Tale of to-Day (Classic Reprint) (p. 833)
—Horse's Tale (Classic Reprint) (p. 1005)
—Huckleberry Finn. (p. 1047)
—Idle Excursion (Classic Reprint) (p. 1090)
—Innocents Abroad (Classic Reprint) (p. 1121)
—Innocents Abroad or the New Pilgrims Progress, Being Some Account of the Steamship Quaker City's, Pleasure Excursion to Europe & the Holy Land, Vol. 1 of 2 (Classic Reprint) (p. 1121)
—Innocents Abroad, or the New Pilgrims' Progress, Vol. 2 Of 2: Being Some Account of the Steamship Quaker City's Pleasure Excursion to Europe & the Holy Land (Classic Reprint) (p. 1121)
—Jumping Frog: In English, Then in French, Then Clawed Back into a Civilized Language Once More by Patient, Unremunerated Toil (Classic Reprint) (p. 1188)
—King Leopold's Soliloquy; a Defense of His Congo Rule. (p. 1220)
—King Leopold's Soliloquy a Defense of His Congo Rule (Classic Reprint) (p. 1220)
—Las Aventuras de Tom Sawyer. (p. 1245)
—Man That Corrupted Hadleyburg: And Other Essays & Stories (Classic Reprint) (p. 1395)
—Man That Corrupted Hadleyburg: And Other Stories & Essays (Classic Reprint) (p. 1395)
—Mark Twain's a Connecticut Yankee in King Arthur's Court: You Can't Depend on Your Eyes When Your Imagination Is Out of Focus. (p. 1407)
—Mark Twain's Library of Humor: Women & Things (Classic Reprint) (p. 1407)
—Mark Twain's Library of Humor: The Primrose Way (Classic Reprint) (p. 1407)
—Mark Twain's Library of Humor (Classic Reprint) (p. 1407)
—Men & Things: America's Best Funny Stories (Classic Reprint) (p. 1446)
—Merry Tales (Classic Reprint) (p. 1450)
—Mississippi Pilot; Two Men of Sandy Bar; Poems (Classic Reprint) (p. 1482)
—Moments with Mark Twain (Classic Reprint) (p. 1490)
—More Tramps Abroad (Classic Reprint) (p. 1505)
—Mysterious Stranger: And Other Stories (Classic Reprint) (p. 1568)
—Mysterious Stranger a Romance (Classic Reprint) (p. 1568)
—Personal Recollections of Joan of Arc; Volume 2. (p. 1725)
—Prince & the Pauper. (p. 1793)
—Prince & the Pauper: A Tale for Young People of All Ages (Classic Reprint) (p. 1794)
—Prince & the Pauper. (p. 1794)
—Principe y el Mendigo. (p. 1800)
—Pudd'nhead Wilson (Classic Reprint) (p. 1810)
—Roughing It (Classic Reprint) (p. 1907)
—Roughing It, Vol. 1 of 2 (Classic Reprint) (p. 1907)
—Roughing It, Vol. 2 of 2 (Classic Reprint) (p. 1907)
—Simon Wheeler, Detective (Classic Reprint) (p. 2021)
—Sketches (Classic Reprint) (p. 2031)
—Sketches New & Old (Classic Reprint) (p. 2031)
—Some Funny Things: Very Funny, Not Too Funny, Just Funny Enough; a Careful Selection of the Freshest & Best Sketches (Classic Reprint) (p. 2059)
—Stolen White Elephant. (p. 2121)
—Stolen White Elephant etc (Classic Reprint) (p. 2121)
—Tom Sawyer Le Fevebvre, Severine, illus. (p. 2257)
—Tom Sawyer Mullarkey, Lisa & McWilliam, Howard, illus. (p. 2257)
—Tom Sawyer. (p. 2257)
—Tramp Abroad (Classic Reprint) (p. 2277)
—Tramp Abroad, Vol. 1 (Classic Reprint) (p. 2277)
—Tramp Abroad, Vol. 1 of 2 (Classic Reprint) (p. 2277)
—Tramp Abroad, Vol. 2 of 2 (Classic Reprint) (p. 2277)
—Unexpected Acquaintance (Classic Reprint) (p. 2327)
—Wilson of Mark Twain (Classic Reprint) (p. 2470)
—Wit & Humor of the Age: Comprising Wit, Humor, Pathos, Ridicule, Satires, Dialects, Puns, Conundrums, Riddles, Charades, Jokes & Magic (Classic Reprint) (p. 2479)
—Writings of Mark Twain the Round, Vol. 2 of 2 (Classic Reprint) (p. 2514)
—£1, 000, 000 Bank-Note: And Other New Stories (Classic Reprint) (p. 2545)
Twain, Mark, pseud & Bott, William. Adventures of Jane Sawyer. (p. 24)
Twain, Mark, pseud & Kemble, E. W. Adventures of Huckleberry Finn (Tom Sawyer's Comrade) [Complete & Unabridged. 174 Original Illustrations.]. (p. 24)
Twain, Mark, pseud & Racehorse Publishing. Classics to Color: the Adventures of Huckleberry Finn. (p. 401)
Twain, Mark, pseud & Stead, Philip C. Purloining of Prince Oleomargarine. Stead, Erin, illus. (p. 1816)
Twain, Mark, pseud, et al. Prince & the Pauper. Kliros, Thea, illus. (p. 1794)
Twain, Mark, pseud, tr. Slovenly Peter. Kredel, Fritz, illus. (p. 2039)
Twead, Victoria. Morgan & the Martians. (p. 1506)
Tweddle, Beth. Becoming an Olympic Gymnast: Band 18/Pearl (Collins Big Cat) (p. 187)
Twede, Shane K. Adventures of Derby & Charlie: Derby & Charlie Go to the Beach-The Power of Influence. Sangngg, illus. (p. 23)
—Adventures of Derby & Charlie - Derby & Charlie Go Fishing: The Magic of Attitude. Nguyen, Sang, illus. (p. 23)
Tweed, Anna. Fairy Tales Everyone Should Know (Classic Reprint) (p. 697)
Tweed, Benjamin Franklin. First Lessons in Natural History & Language: Entertaining & Instructive Lessons in Natural History & Language for Primary & Grammar Schools (Classic Reprint) (p. 738)
Tweed, Susan Larned. Sailor's Adventure: Sailing Stormy Seas. (p. 1923)
Tweedale, Elizabeth. How to Code 2. 0: Pushing Your Skills Further with Python: Learn How to Code with Python in 10 Easy Lessons. (p. 1038)
Tweedale, Elizabeth, jt. auth. see Lyons, Heather.
Tweedale, Violet. Beautiful Mrs. Davenant: A Novel of Love & Mystery (Classic Reprint) (p. 184)
Tweedie, Alec. Behind the Footlights (Classic Reprint) (p. 192)
—Girl's Ride in Iceland (Classic Reprint) (p. 839)
—Through Finland in Carts (Classic Reprint) (p. 2236)
—Wilton, Q. C: Or, Life in a Highland Shooting Box (Classic Reprint) (p. 2470)
Tweedy, John R. Clancy the Lonesome Little Donkey. (p. 398)
Tweet, Jonathan. Grandmother Fish: A Child's First Book of Evolution. Lewis, Karen, illus. (p. 879)
Twells, J. H. Souci: A Novel (Classic Reprint) (p. 2066)
Twelsiek, Monika, ed. Animals: 30 Easy Piano Pieces for Children. (p. 93)
Twelve, One of the. June Days on Alaska Waters (Classic Reprint) (p. 1189)
Twemlow, Nick. Josh Gibson. (p. 1179)
Twentieth Century Fox Home Entertainment Staff & Anderson, Wes. Making of Fantastic Mr. Fox. (p. 1389)
Twenty-Third Publications, creator. Celebrating Eucharist: A Mass Book for Children. (p. 349)
Twersky, Atara. Curlee Girlee. Wolcott, Karen, illus. (p. 488)
Twichell, Joseph Hopkins. John Winthrop, First Governor of the Massachusetts Colony. (p. 1174)
—Makers of America. John Winthrop, First Governor of the Massachusetts Colony. (p. 1388)
Twiddy, Robin. France. (p. 776)
—UK. (p. 2314)
Twigum, Xtopher. Cambridge in the Long Vacation: Poetically Described. (p. 313)
—Cambridge in the Long Vacation: Poetically Described (Classic Reprint) (p. 313)
Twin, Kalysta. Jane et John. (p. 1158)
Twin Sister Prodution & Galvin, Laura Gates. Sesame Street Abby Cadabby's Nursery Rhymes. (p. 1992)
—Sesame Street What Did Elmo Say? (p. 1992)
Twin Sister Prodution & Shepherd, Jodie. Sesame Street Big Red Riding Hood. (p. 1992)
—Sesame Street Rosita & the Beanstalk. (p. 1992)
Twin Sister Prodution Staff & Galvin, Laura Gates. Sesame Street What Did Elmo Say? (p. 1993)
Twin Sister Prodution Staff & Shepherd, Jodie. Sesame Street Big Red Riding Hood. (p. 1992)
—Sesame Street Rosita & the Beanstalk. (p. 1992)
Twin Sisters(r) Staff. 12 Days of Christmas. (p. 2551)
—Abc Nursery Rhymes. (p. 4)
—B-I-N-G-O. (p. 146)
—B-i-n-g-o. (p. 146)
—Christmas Songs 4 Kids 3. (p. 387)
—Christmas Story. (p. 387)
—Down by the Bay. (p. 590)
—Down Through the Chimney. (p. 590)
—Farmer in the Dell. (p. 710)
—Five Little Monkeys Jumping on the Bed. (p. 744)
—Five Little Skunks. (p. 744)
—Five Trick or Treaters. (p. 745)
—Gruesome Grub. (p. 900)
—Humpty Dumpty & More. (p. 1051)
—Jesus Loves the Little Children. (p. 1166)
—Jolly Old St.Nicholas. (p. 1176)
—Kids' Favorite Songs & Stories- 4books. (p. 1215)
—Kids' Halloween Party. (p. 1215)
—Kids Learn Spanish Handlebox- 4 books. (p. 1215)
—Learning with Elmo: Animals. (p. 1259)
—Lord Is My Shepherd. (p. 1348)
—Multiplication Workbook & Music CD. (p. 1525)
—Old MacDonald Had a Farm. (p. 1646)
—Old Testament Handlebox-4 books. (p. 1648)
—Rise & Shine. (p. 1885)
—Santa Songs & More Boxed Set- 2 books. (p. 1933)
—Six Little Ducks. (p. 2028)
—Spanish Workbook. (p. 2074)
—Story of Jesus Handlebox-4books. (p. 2130)
—Ten in the Bed. (p. 2204)
—Twelve Days of Christmas. (p. 2303)
—Up on the Housetop. (p. 2338)
—Wheels on the Bus. (p. 2428)
—When I Go Trick or Treating. (p. 2430)
Twin Sisters(r) Staff & Hilderbrand, Karen Mitzo, adapted by. Subtraction. (p. 2146)
—Ten in the Bed. (p. 2204)
Twin Sisters(r) Staff & Thompson, Kim Mitzo. My First Old Testament Bible Stories. (p. 1545)
—Night-Night Song. (p. 1606)
—Subtraction. (p. 2146)
Twin Sisters(r) Staff, et al. Best Thing about Christmas Sing-Along Storybook. (p. 208)
—Bible Fun: Color & Trace. (p. 213)
—Bible Fun: Cut & Glue. (p. 213)
—Bible Songs for Little Hearts. (p. 213)
—Bible Story Word Searches for Kids. (p. 214)
—Celebrate Easter! Prayer & Activity Book. (p. 348)
—Celebrating Christmas Coloring & Activity Book. (p. 349)
—Christmas Carols for Kids: a Sing-Along Book. (p. 384)
—Christmas Joy Black & White Board Book. (p. 386)
—Create Your Own Christmas Cards Activity Box. (p. 469)
—David & Goliath Padded Board Book & CD (p. 510)
—Easy-To-Make Christmas Crafts for Kids. (p. 621)
—Everyday Blessings: a Creative Journal for Girls. (p. 671)
—Five Little Bunnies. (p. 743)
—Fun Bible Story Rhymes for Kids. (p. 798)
—Glitter Christmas Scripture Art: 16 Fun Designs. (p. 843)
—Happy Birthday, Jesus: A Sing-Along Storybook. (p. 920)
—He Is Risen! Activity Book & Free Album Download. (p. 941)
—I Can Read Bible Stories. (p. 1063)
—I Can Read the Christmas Story. (p. 1063)
—I Thank God for You. (p. 1083)
—It's Christmas Day Sing-A-Story Book. (p. 1144)
—It's Silly Time. (p. 1147)
—J Is for JESUS Black & White Board Book. (p. 1150)
—Jesus Is Born Sticker & Activity Book. (p. 1166)
—Jesus Is in My Heart Sing-A-Story Book (p. 1166)
—Jesus Loves Me More Than... (p. 1166)
—Jonah & the Whale Padded Board Book & CD (p. 1177)
—Jumbo Christmas Activity Book. (p. 1188)
—Marvelous Plan in Bethlehem. (p. 1413)
—Mommy & Me Coloring Christmas: Creativity Inspired by Faith. (p. 1490)
—My First Bedtime Prayers for Boys. (p. 1540)
—My First Bedtime Prayers for Girls. (p. 1540)
—My First Bible Promises for Boys. (p. 1540)
—My First Bible Promises for Girls. (p. 1540)
—My First Christmas Coloring & Activity Book. (p. 1543)
—My First Christmas Storybook. (p. 1543)
—My First New Testament Bible Stories. (p. 1545)
—My First Old Testament Bible Stories. (p. 1545)
—My First Read-Along Christmas Story. (p. 1545)
—My First Read-Along Easter Story: Includes Music CD with Read-Along Story. (p. 1545)
—Story of Easter: Read-Along Book with CD. (p. 2130)
—Trace & Learn Sticker Fun: ABCs. (p. 2271)
—Where Is Baby Jesus? a Lift-The-Flap Book. (p. 2437)
—Year-Round Crafts for Kids. (p. 2519)
Twin Sisters(r) Staff, et al, adapted by. B-i-n-g-o. (p. 146)
—Six Little Ducks. (p. 2028)
Twin Sisters(r) Staff, prod. Alphabet & Counting: Songs That Teach. (p. 58)
—Preschool: Songs That Teach. (p. 1788)
Twine, Alice. Alligators/Caimanes. (p. 56)
—Bears. (p. 180)
—Bears/Osos. (p. 181)
—Cats of the Wild/Gatos Salvajes. (p. 346)
—Ducks/Patos. (p. 608)
—Elephants/Elefantes Bebé. (p. 635)
—Horses/Caballos. (p. 1005)
—Kangaroos/Canguros. (p. 1202)
—Kittens/Gatitos. (p. 1226)
—Monkeys/Monos. (p. 1494)
—Penguins/Pinguinos. (p. 1716)
—Puppies/Cachorros. (p. 1814)
—Seals/Focas. (p. 1970)
Twinem, Neecy, illus. see Bentley, Dawn.
Twinem, Neecy, illus. see James, Helen Foster.
Twinney, Dick, illus. see Davies, Gill.
Twins, Pope. Poke-A-Dot!: Who's in the Ocean? (30 Poke-able Poppin' Dots) (p. 1768)
Twins, Swedish. Little Swedish Baron (Classic Reprint) (p. 1328)
Twiss, Jill. Everyone Gets a Say. Keller, E. G., illus. (p. 672)
—Someone New. Keller, E. G., illus. (p. 2060)
Twiss, Johan. 4 Years Trapped in My Mind Palace. (p. 2547)
—I Am Sleepless: Sim 299 (Book 1) (p. 1060)
—I Am Sleepless: Traitors (Book 3) (p. 1060)
—I Am Sleepless: The Huntress (Book 2) (p. 1060)
Twist, Clint. Cleopatra: Queen of Egypt. Andrew, Ian, illus. (p. 403)
—Electricity. (p. 631)
—Extreme Earth. (p. 686)
—Life Cycle of Army Ants. (p. 1291)
—Light & Sound: The Best Start in Science. (p. 1298)
—Light & Sound. (p. 1298)
—Little Book of Slime: Everything That Oozes, from Killer Slime to Living Mold. (p. 1312)
—Marco Polo: History's Great Adventurer. (p. 1403)
Twist, Clint, ed. see Aronnax, Pierre.
Twist, Clint, ed. see Calhoun, Marmaduke Randolph.

Twist, Clint, jt. auth. see Parker, Steve.
Twist, Clint & Wells-Cole, Catherine. Charles Dickens: England's Most Captivating Storyteller. (p. 358)
Twist, Clint, et al. Extreme Earth. (p. 686)
Twist, Sean, jt. auth. see Southwell, David.
Twitchell, Alice Bentley. Triumphs of an Or: Maid or (Classic Reprint) (p. 2290)
Two Bulls, Marty Grant, illus. see Meierhenry, Mark V. & Volk, David.
Two Little Hands Productions, creator. Good Night, Alex & Leah. (p. 863)
—What Do You See Outside? (p. 2409)
Two Little Hands Productions, prod. Board Book 4: Family, Feelings & Fun. (p. 251)
—Board Book 5: ABC Signs. (p. 251)
—Board Book 6: My Favorite Things. (p. 251)
Two Sisters Circle. Lady of the Lane. (p. 1238)
Twohig, Chloe. Donald the Magic Farty Bum. (p. 581)
Twohy, Mike. Mouse & Hippo. Twohy, Mike, illus. (p. 1514)
—Oops, Pounce, Quick, Run! An Alphabet Caper. Twohy, Mike, illus. (p. 1665)
—Outfoxed. Twohy, Mike, illus. (p. 1684)
—Poindexter Makes a Friend. Twohy, Mike, illus. (p. 1767)
—Stop, Go, Yes, No! A Story of Opposites. Twohy, Mike, illus. (p. 2122)
—Wake up, Rupert! Twohy, Mike, illus. (p. 2371)
Twombly, Frances Doane. Romance of Labor, Scenes from Good Novels Depicting, Joy in Work (Classic Reprint) (p. 1900)
Twomey, Emily Golden. Buster's Brilliant Dot to Dot. Twomey, Emily Golden, illus. (p. 301)
—Kids' Book of Dot to Dot. (p. 1214)
Twomey, Kevin, photos by see Smith, Amber.
Twomey, Patty. Grace, Little & Their Pot Bellied Pigs. Pugh, Carson & Goss, Rebecca, illus. (p. 873)
Tyack, Lena. Girl Who Lost Things (Classic Reprint) (p. 837)
Tyacke, R. H. How I Shot My Bears, or Two Years Tent Life in Kullu & Lahoul (Classic Reprint) (p. 1032)
Tybout, Ella Middleton. Poketown People or Parables in Black (Classic Reprint) (p. 1768)
—Smuggler (Classic Reprint) (p. 2043)
—Wife of the Secretary of State (Classic Reprint) (p. 2461)
Tye, Peter. Crocodile Tours. Howe, Norma, illus. (p. 477)
Tyer, Francesca. Firestone. (p. 734)
Tyger, Rory, illus. see Freedman, Claire.
Tyger, Rory, illus. see Tiger Tales.
Tyhurst, Robert. Robert Tyhurst's Olio Folio (Classic Reprint) (p. 1890)
Tyldesley, Joyce & Heath, Julian. Stories from Ancient Greece & Rome. (p. 2123)
Tyler, Anna Cogswell. Twenty-Four Unusual Stories: For Boys & Girls (Classic Reprint) (p. 2304)
—Twenty-Four Unusual Stories for Boys & Girls. (p. 2304)
Tyler, Barbara A. Picture Yourself Writing Drama: Using Photos to Inspire Writing. (p. 1741)
Tyler, Brenda. Tomtes of Hilltop Stream (p. 2259)
—Tomtes of Hilltop Wood (p. 2259)
Tyler, Bridget. Pioneer. (p. 1748)
—Survivor: a Pioneer Novel. (p. 2165)
Tyler, C. W. K. K. K (Classic Reprint) (p. 1201)
—Scout: A Tale of the Civil War (Classic Reprint) (p. 1962)
Tyler, Darlene Misconish. Tu Mundo: Chicle Bomba: Suma y Resta. (p. 2298)
Tyler, Gemma. Crocodile. (p. 477)
Tyler, Georgie Vere. Daughter of a Rebel a Novel (Classic Reprint) (p. 509)
Tyler, Gillian, illus. see Chaconas, Dori.
Tyler, Gillian, illus. see Rosen, Michael.
Tyler, Jay. Mr. Tyler Rocks!!! (p. 1521)
Tyler, Jenny. Animal Stories for Little Children. (p. 91)
—Baby's Very First Getting Dressed. (p. 154)
—Baby's Very First Mealtime Book. (p. 154)
—Poppy & Sam's Animal Hide-And-Seek (REVISED) (p. 1776)
Tyler, Jenny, ed. see Amery, Heather.
Tyler, Jenny, ed. see Bryant-Mole, Karen.
Tyler, Jenny, ed. see Dowswell, Paul.
Tyler, Jenny, ed. see Marks, Anthony.
Tyler, Jenny, ed. see Roxbee Cox, Phil.
Tyler, Jenny, jt. auth. see Brooks, Felicity.
Tyler, Jenny, jt. auth. see Bryant-Mole, Karen.
Tyler, Joe, et al. Grimm Fairy Tales Volume 4 Tedesco, Ralph & Gregory, Raven, eds. (p. 896)
Tyler, Josephine. Waymarks, or Sola in Europe (Classic Reprint) (p. 2388)
Tyler, Katharine E. Story of a Scandinavian Summer (Classic Reprint) (p. 2128)
Tyler Kazmier, Kit. Piece It Together Family Puzzle: Purrmaid Paradise. (p. 1742)
Tyler, Kip, jt. auth. see Tyler, Marya Washington.
Tyler, Madeline. Mapping Money & Trade (p. 1401)
—Mapping People (p. 1401)
—Marsupials (p. 1409)
—Mollusks (p. 1489)
—Monster Counting. Li, Amy, illus. (p. 1495)
—Monster Measuring. Li, Amy, illus. (p. 1496)
—Monster Patterns. Li, Amy, illus. (p. 1496)
—Monster Shapes. Li, Amy, illus. (p. 1497)
—Surviving a Megatsunami. (p. 2164)
—Surviving a Vampire Invasion. (p. 2164)
—Surviving an Ice Age. (p. 2165)
—Surviving in a World Without Water. (p. 2165)
—Surviving the Rise of the Mummies. (p. 2165)
—Why Do I Grow? (p. 2456)
—Why Do I Itch? (p. 2456)
—Why Do I Sneeze? (p. 2456)
Tyler, Madeline, jt. auth. see Duhig, Holly.
Tyler, Misconish Darlene. Amazing Animals: Alligators: Multiplication (Grade 4) (p. 63)
—Your World: Bubblegum: Addition & Subtraction (Grade 2) (p. 2534)
Tyler, Odette. Boss (Classic Reprint) (p. 263)
Tyler, Robert. Baptism on the Bayou: Story of Bo Bob & Skipper. (p. 164)
Tyler, Robert D. Baptism on the Bayou: Story of Bo Bob & Skipper. (p. 164)
Tyler, Roland Winthrop. Pictorial Elements in Spenser's Faerie Queene: Thesis Submitted in Partial Fulfillment of the Requirements for the Degree of Master of Arts, 1931 (Classic Reprint) (p. 1739)
Tyler, Royall. Contrast: A Comedy in Five Acts (Classic Reprint) (p. 445)
Tyler, Simon. Adventures on Earth. (p. 29)
—Bugs. (p. 292)
—Exploring Space. (p. 682)
Tyler, Tara. Cradle Rock. (p. 466)
Tyler, Therese. Dusty Road (Classic Reprint) (p. 611)
Tyler, Thomas, jt. auth. see Shakespeare, William.
Tyler, Tim, illus. see Mazur, Cathy May.
Tyler, Toni Kaye. Annie Em's Red Shoes. (p. 100)
Tyler, Wm. N. Dispatch Carrier (p. 564)
Tyler-Laws, Sadiya. Princess Escape. Laws, Jerl L., illus. (p. 1797)
Tyler-Laws, Sadiya Robin. Princess Escape. (p. 1797)
Tylers, Michael. Predators of North America. (p. 1787)
—Predators of South America & Antarctica. (p. 1787)
—Surviving a Nuclear War. (p. 2164)
Tylicki, Gene & Tylicki, Jo a. I Lost My Boss: As Told by Tuxie. (p. 1068)
Tylicki, Gene J. & Tylicki, Jo. Lonesome George: The First Three Weeks (p. 1342)
—More Cat Tails As Told by George to Guy: A Lonesome George Work. (p. 1504)
—Saga Continues As Told by George to Guy: A Lonesome George Work. (p. 1922)
Tyminski, Lori, illus. see Driscoll, Laura & Disney Book Group.
Tyminski, Lori, illus. see Driscoll, Laura & Disney Books.
Tyminski, Lori, illus. see Driscoll, Laura.
Tyminski, Lori, illus. see Redbank, Tennant, et al.
Tyminski, Lori, illus. see Vitale, Brooke.
Tynan, Katharine. Cluster of Nuts: Being Sketches among My Own People (Classic Reprint) (p. 409)
—Cluster of Nuts. (p. 409)
—Countrymen All (Classic Reprint) (p. 461)
—Daughter of the Fields (Classic Reprint) (p. 509)
—Dear Irish Girl (Classic Reprint) (p. 520)
—Denys the Dreamer (Classic Reprint) (p. 529)
—Dick Pentreath (Classic Reprint) (p. 541)
—Freda (Classic Reprint) (p. 780)
—Girl of Galway (Classic Reprint) (p. 836)
—Handsome Brandons (Classic Reprint) (p. 916)
—Handsome Quaker: And Other Stories (Classic Reprint) (p. 916)
—House (Classic Reprint) (p. 1022)
—House of the Secret (Classic Reprint) (p. 1023)
—Isle in the Water (Classic Reprint) (p. 1140)
—Lord Edward: A Study in Romance (Classic Reprint) (p. 1348)
—Lost Angel (Classic Reprint) (p. 1352)
—Love of Brothers (Classic Reprint) (p. 1360)
—Love of Sisters (Classic Reprint) (p. 1360)
—Luck of the Fairfaxes (Classic Reprint) (p. 1364)
—Mary Gray (Classic Reprint) (p. 1415)
—Middle Years (Classic Reprint) (p. 1461)
—Midsummer Rose (Classic Reprint) (p. 1462)
—Oh, What a Plague Is Love (Classic Reprint) (p. 1642)
—Paradise Farm (Classic Reprint) (p. 1698)
—Princess Katharine (Classic Reprint) (p. 1797)
—Red, Red Rose (Classic Reprint) (p. 1858)
—Story of Bawn. (p. 2129)
—Story of Bawn (Classic Reprint) (p. 2129)
—That Sweet Enemy (Classic Reprint) (p. 2213)
—Three Fair Maids, or the Burkes of Derrymore (Classic Reprint) (p. 2232)
—Twenty-Five Years Reminiscences (Classic Reprint) (p. 2304)
—Wandering Years (Classic Reprint) (p. 2375)
—Way of a Maid (Classic Reprint) (p. 2387)
—Years of the Shadow (Classic Reprint) (p. 2520)
Tynan, Tim. Adventures of Snibbles Mcgibbons: First Day of School. (p. 28)
Tyndale & Livingstone, creators. NLT Girls Life Application Study Bible (LeatherLike, Teal/Pink Flowers) (p. 1612)
Tyndale, creator. Biblia para niños NTV (Tapa Dura) (p. 214)
—Biblia para niños NTV (Tapa Rústica) (p. 214)
Tyndale House Publisher Staff, creator. Arca. (p. 109)
Tyndale House Publishers Staff & Livingstone Publishing Staff, creators. Girls Life Application. (p. 838)
Tyndale House Publishers Staff, creator. Gigantic Coloring Book of Bible Stories. (p. 832)
—Gigantic Coloring Book of God's World. (p. 832)
—I Can Follow Jesus. (p. 1062)
Tyndale, Walter. Artist in Egypt (Classic Reprint) (p. 123)
—Japan the Japanese (Classic Reprint) (p. 1159)
Tyndale-Biscoe, C. E. Character Building in Kashmir (Classic Reprint) (p. 357)
Tyndale-Biscoe, Cecil Earle. Character Building in Kashmir (Classic Reprint) (p. 357)
Tyndall, C. H. Object-Lessons for Children: Or, Hooks & Eyes, Truth Linked to Sight, Pp. 8-242. (p. 1634)
Tyndall, Charles Herbert. Object-Lessons for Children: Or Hooks & Eyes, Truth Linked to Sight (Classic Reprint) (p. 1634)
Tyndall, John. Forms of Water in Clouds & Rivers, Ice & Glaciers. (p. 768)
—Lectures on Light: Delivered in the United States in 1872-'73 (Classic Reprint) (p. 1260)
—Lectures on Light. (p. 1260)
—Notes of a Course of Nine Lectures on Light: Delivered at the Royal Institution of Great Britain, April 8 June 3, 1869 (Classic Reprint) (p. 1624)
—Notes of a Course of Nine Lectures on Light. (p. 1624)
—On Radiation: The Rede Lecture Delivered in the Senate-House Before the University of Cambridge on Tuesday, May 16, 1865 (Classic Reprint) (p. 1653)
—Schall: Acht Vorlesungen Gehalten in der Royal Institution Von Grossbritannien (Classic Reprint) (p. 1944)
Tyndall, John, et al. Licht: Sechs Vorlesungen. (p. 1287)
Tyndall, Nita. Who I Was with Her. (p. 2447)
Tyndall, W. J. De Lucky Garcon: And Other French Canadian Poems (Classic Reprint) (p. 517)
Tyner, Artika R. So You Want to Be a Supreme Court Justice. (p. 2051)
Tyner, P. T. Mysteries of URAGH. (p. 1567)
Tyner, Stuart. Meanest Man in the Army: And Other Stories of Grace. (p. 1434)
Tynion Iv, James & Johns, Sam. Backstagers Vol. 3. Sygh, Rian et al, illus. (p. 156)
Typaldos, Melanie. Celeste & the Adorable Kitten. Tayts, Alexandra, illus. (p. 350)
Tyre, Lisa Lewis. Hope in the Holler. (p. 1002)
Tyrell, Wes, illus. see Kelly, Dave.
Tyro, Theresa. Feast of the Fishes, or the Whale's Invitation to His Brethren of the Deep (Classic Reprint) (p. 717)
Tyron, Leslie. Thumbtack Dancer. Spivey Gilchrist, Jan, illus. (p. 2238)
Tyrpak, Joseph & International, Bible Visuals. Life & Death of David Brainerd. (p. 1289)
Tyrrell, Andrea. Chewy's Day. (p. 367)
Tyrrell, Christina. Lizzie of the Mill, Vol. 1 Of 2: From the German of W. Heimnurg (Classic Reprint) (p. 1337)
Tyrrell, Colm. Snow Day. (p. 2047)
Tyrrell, Colm, jt. auth. see Scollon, Bill.
Tyrrell, Eleanor. More about the Squirrels (Classic Reprint) (p. 1504)
Tyrrell, Frances, illus. see Jules, Jacqueline.
Tyrrell, Karen. Bailey Beats the Blah. Pocock, Aaron, illus. (p. 159)
—Battle of Bug World. (p. 174)
—Great Barrier Reef Rescue. (p. 884)
—Rainforest Rescue. (p. 1837)
—Ready. Set. Discover Logan. Pocock, Aaron, illus. (p. 1848)
Tyrrell, Karen & Pocock, Aaron. Ready. Set. Discover Logan. (p. 1848)
Tyrrell, Ross. Pathway of Adventure (Classic Reprint) (p. 1704)
Tyrwhitt, Richard St John. Our Sketching Club: Letters & Studies on Landscape Art (Classic Reprint) (p. 1680)
Tyrwhitt, T. Canterbury Tales of Chaucer, Vol. 3: With an Essay upon His Language & Versification, an Introductory Discourse, Notes, & a Glossary (Classic Reprint) (p. 323)
Tyrwhitt, Thomas, jt. auth. see Chaucer, Geoffrey.
Tysoe, Laurence. Henge. (p. 954)
Tyson, Anne Arrington. Price of Honor (Classic Reprint) (p. 1791)
Tyson, E. C. Key to Bonnycastle's Introduction to Mensuration (Classic Reprint) (p. 1211)
Tyson, Edward. Orang-Outang, Sive Homo Sylvestris: Or the Anatomy of a Pygmie Compared with That of a Monkey, an Ape, & a Man (Classic Reprint) (p. 1668)
—Orang-Outang, Sive Homo Sylvestris. (p. 1668)
—Philological Essay Concerning the Pygmies of the Ancients. (p. 1735)
Tyson, Frank H. American Legion Monthly, Vol. 18: June, 1935 (Classic Reprint) (p. 72)
Tyson, Ian. Primera: The Story of Wild Mustangs. Halvorson, Adeline, illus. (p. 1793)
Tyson, Leigh Ann. Good Night, Little Dragons. (p. 864)
Tyson, Neil deGrasse, jt. auth. see Graubart, Norman D.
Tyson, Neil deGrasse & Mone, Gregory. Astrophysics for Young People in a Hurry. (p. 129)
Tyson, Peter K. Winning Touch: A story about football for teenage boys (and maybe a few Girls) (p. 2474)
Tytler, Ann Fraser. Leila: Or the Island (Classic Reprint) (p. 1265)
Tytler, Sarah. Beauty & the Beast, Vol. 1 Of 3: A Novel (Classic Reprint) (p. 185)
—Blackhall Ghosts (Classic Reprint) (p. 240)
—Bubble Fortune (Classic Reprint) (p. 288)
—Buried Diamonds, Vol. 1 of 3 (Classic Reprint) (p. 299)
—By the Elbe, Vol. 1 of 3 (Classic Reprint) (p. 306)
—By the Elbe, Vol. 2 of 3 (Classic Reprint) (p. 306)
—By the Elbe, Vol. 3 of 3 (Classic Reprint) (p. 306)
—Citoyenne Jacqueline: A Woman's Lot in the Great French Revolution (Classic Reprint) (p. 394)
—Citoyenne Jacqueline, Vol. 1: A Woman's Lot in the Great French Revolution (Classic Reprint) (p. 394)
—Citoyenne Jacqueline, Vol. 2 Of 3: A Woman's Lot in the Great French Revolution (Classic Reprint) (p. 394)
—Days of Yore, Vol. 1 (Classic Reprint) (p. 515)
—French Janet: A Novel (Classic Reprint) (p. 784)
—Girl Neighbors: Or, the Old Fashion & the New (Classic Reprint) (p. 836)
—Honor Ormthwaite: A Novel (Classic Reprint) (p. 999)
—Huguenot Family (Classic Reprint) (p. 1048)
—Huguenot Family, Vol. 1 of 3 (Classic Reprint) (p. 1048)
—Lady Bell: A Story of the Last Century (Classic Reprint) (p. 1236)
—Lady Bell, Vol. 1 Of 3: A Story of Last Century (Classic Reprint) (p. 1236)
—Lady Bell, Vol. 2: A Story of Last Century (Classic Reprint) (p. 1236)
—Lady Bell, Vol. 3 Of 3: A Story of Last Century (Classic Reprint) (p. 1236)
—Machinations of Janet (Classic Reprint) (p. 1372)
—Noblesse Oblige: An English Story of to-Day (Classic Reprint) (p. 1616)
—Papers for Thoughtful Girls: With Illustrative Sketches of Some Girls' Lives (Classic Reprint) (p. 1698)
—Saint Mungo's City, Vol. 1 Of 3: A Novel (Classic Reprint) (p. 1923)
—Saint Mung's City, Vol. 3 Of 3: A Novel (Classic Reprint) (p. 1923)
—Sapphira, Vol. 1 Of 2: A Novel (Classic Reprint) (p. 1934)
—Scotch Marriages, Vol. 1 of 3 (Classic Reprint) (p. 1962)
—Wearing the Willow; or Bride Fielding: A Tale of Ireland & of Scotland Sixty Years Ago (Classic Reprint) (p. 2393)
Tzannes, Robin, jt. auth. see Paul, Korky.
Tzekov, Jack, illus. see Soares, Valérie.
Tzingoker, Lilach. Sonny's Adventure in Mystery Park. (p. 2064)
Tzouganatos, Dimitris. Competition Law in Greece. (p. 433)
Tzu, Sun. Arte de la Guerra. (p. 122)
Tzvieli, Neta. Private Eyes & the Mysterious Submarine. (p. 1801)

U

U, Deoghwan. Why? Korean History: Friendship & Competition. (p. 2454)
U, Gertrude M. Van Vranken Cleveland. Frederick Cleveland: The Story of His Life, Suffering & Patient Service (Classic Reprint) (p. 781)
U. S. National Geographic Society Staff. National Geographic Kids Almanac 2011. (p. 1577)
—You Are the World! (p. 2525)
U X L, ed. UXL Encyclopedia of Science (p. 2343)
—UXL Man-Made Disasters (p. 2343)
—UXL Money, Banking & Trading (p. 2343)
Uchard, Mario. My Uncle Barbassou (Classic Reprint) (p. 1563)
Uchida, Rintaro. Kindergarten Transformed! (p. 1219)
Uchida, Yoshiko. Journey to Topaz. Carrick, Donald, illus. (p. 1183)
Uchiyama, Akira & Kodaira, Hiromi. Yubisashi Yubinazori Aiueo. (p. 2536)
Udasi, Harshikaa. Friends Behind Walls. (p. 787)
Udayabaskar, Nachimuthu, ed. see Ananya, Swaminathan.
Udayabaskar, Nachimuthu, ed. see Shah, Radhika.
Udelhoven, Hermann-Josef, jt. auth. see Hattstein, Markus.
Uderzo, Albert. ADIVINO. (p. 16)
—Astérix en América: El álbum de la Película. (p. 127)
—ASTÉRIX EN BÉLGICA. (p. 127)
—ASTÉRIX EN BRETAÑA. (p. 127)
—ASTÉRIX EN HELVECIA. (p. 127)
—ASTÉRIX EN HISPANIA. (p. 127)
—ASTÉRIX EN LA INDIA. (p. 127)
—ASTÉRIX GLADIADOR. (p. 127)
—ASTÉRIX LEGIONARIO. (p. 127)
—ASTÉRIX Y CLEOPATRA. (p. 127)
—ASTÉRIX Y EL CALDERO. (p. 127)
—Astérix y Latraviata. (p. 127)
—ASTÉRIX Y LOS GODOS. (p. 127)
—CIZAÑA. (p. 397)
—COMBATE DE LOS JEFES. (p. 428)
—ESCUDO ARVERNO. (p. 662)
—Golpe de Menhir: El álbum de la Película. (p. 861)
—Gran Zanja. (p. 876)
—HIJO DE ASTÉRIX. (p. 970)
—HOZ DE ORO. (p. 1047)
—LOS LAURELES DEL CÉSAR. (p. 1351)
—Mal Trago de Obélix. (p. 1391)
—OBÉLIX Y COMPAÑÍA. (p. 1634)
—Odisea de Astérix. (p. 1638)
—REGALO DEL CÉSAR. (p. 1861)
—VUELTA A LA GALIA DE ASTÉRIX. (p. 2368)
Uderzo, Albert, illus. see Goscinny, René.
Uderzo, Albert, jt. auth. see Goscinny, René.
Uderzo, M., illus. see Lefèvre-Garros, J. P.
Uderzo, M., illus. see Rideau, J. & Asso, B.
Uderzo, M., jt. auth. see Goscinny, René.
Udon Studios Staff. VENT Volume 1. (p. 2350)
Udovic, David, illus. see Cleary, Brian P.
Udraoni, Rose, tr. see Pere, Tuula.
Udry, Janice May. Moon Jumpers. Sendak, Maurice, illus. (p. 1501)
Udumalagala, Daphni. Space Master. Yahathugoda, Chethanika & Yahathugoda, Thissarika, illus. (p. 2071)
Udvari, Joseph G. Courage. (p. 462)
Udzenija, Mario, jt. auth. see Gran, Meredith.
Uegaki, Chieri. Hana Hashimoto, Sixth Violin. Leng, Qin, illus. (p. 914)
—Ojiichan's Gift. Simms, Genevieve, illus. (p. 1643)
Uehara, Sho, illus. see Karpik, Joanasie.
Uehashi, Nahoko. Beast Player. Hirano, Cathy, tr. (p. 181)
Uehashi, Nahoko & Hirano, Cathy. Guardian of the Darkness. Shimizu, Yuko, illus. (p. 901)
Ueno, Haruki. Big Hero 6 (p. 220)
Ufer, David A. Giraffe Who Was Afraid of Heights in Chinese. Ping, He, tr. (p. 834)
Uff, Caroline, illus. see Nimmo, Jenny.
UFlipp. You & Your Military Hero: Building Positive Thinking Skills During Your Hero's Deployment. (p. 2524)
UG, Philippe. Funny Birds. (p. 801)
Ug, Philippe. In the Butterfly Garden. (p. 1108)
UG, Philippe. Robots: Watch Out, Water About! (p. 1893)
Ugalde Alcantara, Felipe, illus. see Villaseñor, Victor.
Ugalde, Felipe, illus. see Argueta, Jorge, et al.
Ugalde, Felipe, illus. see Argueta, Jorge.
Ugalde, Raquel, tr. see Harter, Debbie.
Ugliano, Natascia, illus. see Gellman, Ellie B.
Ugliano, Natascia, illus. see Jules, Jacqueline.
Ugo, Kachi. Mewranters: Attack of the Sea Monster: A Novel. (p. 1453)
Uhelski, Casey, illus. see Jones, Shannon.
Uhl, Xina M. Cleopatra: Queen of Egypt. (p. 403)
—Economics of Global Trade (p. 624)
—Extreme Aerial Silks (p. 686)
—Francisco de Vasquez Coronado. (p. 776)
—Harry S. Truman. (p. 935)
—How STEM Built the Egyptian Empire (p. 1035)
—How STEM Built the Roman Empire (p. 1035)
—Juan Rodriguez Cabrillo: Explorer of the American West Coast (p. 1184)
—Kobe Bryant. (p. 1230)
—Loch Ness Monster. (p. 1338)
—Most Influential Female Inventors. (p. 1508)
—Pharrell Williams: Music Industry Star. (p. 1733)
—Preventing & Treating Addiction. (p. 1791)
—Railroad, the Telegraph, & Other Technologies. (p. 1835)
—Settlers, Traders, & Trails. (p. 1993)
—Strengthening Collaborative Project Skills. (p. 2140)
—Texas Revolution. (p. 2209)

U

—Theodore Roosevelt. (p. 2216)
—Thomas Jefferson. (p. 2228)
—Tom Brady. (p. 2257)
—Using Computer Science in Film & Television Careers. (p. 2341)
—Vampires. (p. 2346)
—Werewolves. (p. 2401)
—What Is Oral History? (p. 2415)
—Who Is Using Opioids & Opiates? (p. 2448)
—Women in Television. (p. 2487)
Uhl, Xina M., ed. see Byers, Ann.
Uhl, Xina M. & Alagna, Magdalena. Mae Jemison (p. 1375)
Uhl, Xina M. & Apel, Melanie Ann. Virginia Apgar (p. 2361)
Uhl, Xina M. & Brezina, Corona. Dictatorship (p. 541)
—Primary Source Investigation of the Industrial Revolution. (p. 1792)
Uhl, Xina M. & Buell, Tonya. Primary Source Investigation of Slavery. (p. 1792)
Uhl, Xina M. & Burnett, Betty. Primary Source Investigation of the Continental Congress. (p. 1792)
Uhl, Xina M. & Canino, Kate. Insider Tips for Hunting Turkey. (p. 1124)
Uhl, Xina M. & Flanagan, Timothy. Primary Source Investigation of Reconstruction. (p. 1792)
Uhl, Xina M. & Freedman, Jeri. Managing Bank Accounts & Investments (p. 1396)
Uhl, Xina M. & Harmon, Daniel E. Getting Your First Job (p. 826)
Uhl, Xina M. & Jarnow, Jesse. Socialism (p. 2053)
Uhl, Xina M. & Link, Theodore. Communism (p. 431)
Uhl, Xina M. & Marx, Christy. Grace Hopper: Computer Pioneer (p. 873)
Uhl, Xina M. & Moriarty, J. T. Primary Source Investigation of Manifest Destiny. (p. 1792)
Uhl, Xina M. & Orr, Tamra. Primary Source Investigation of the Lewis & Clark Expedition. (p. 1792)
Uhl, Xina M. & Peterson, Judy Monroe. Insider Tips for Hunting Big Game. (p. 1124)
—Insider Tips for Hunting Small Game. (p. 1124)
—Insider Tips for Hunting Varmint. (p. 1124)
—Making a Budget (p. 1388)
—Managing Finances & Shopping Online (p. 1396)
Uhl, Xina M. & Poolos, Jamie. Primary Source Investigation of the Mayflower. (p. 1792)
Uhl, Xina M. & Schiel, Katy. Monarchy (p. 1492)
Uhl, Xina M. & Stites, Bill. Democracy (p. 528)
Uhl, Xina M. & White, Katherine. Sylvia Earle: Oceanographer & Conservationist (p. 2173)
Uhl, Xina M. & Wolny, Philip. Colonialism (p. 418)
—Insider Tips for Hunting Waterfowl. (p. 1124)
Uhlberg, Myron. Bar Mitzvah Boys. Arcabascio, Carolyn, illus. (p. 164)
—Me & Mcgee. Sosa, Daniela, illus. (p. 1432)
—My Name Is Helen Keller. Kocsmiersky, Jenn, illus. (p. 1557)
—Sound of All Things Papoulas, Ted, illus. (p. 2067)
—Sound of Silence: Growing up Hearing with Deaf Parents. (p. 2067)
—Sound of Silence. (p. 2067)
—Storm Called Katrina Bootman, Colin, illus. (p. 2126)
—Storm Called Katrina. (p. 2126)
Uhlenbeck, C. C. New Series of Blackfoot Texts: From the Southern Peigans Blackfoot Reservation, Teton County, Montana, with the Help of Joseph Tatsey, Collected & Pubwith an English Translation (Classic Reprint) (p. 1597)
Uhler, Matt, ed. Right to a Living Wage. (p. 1882)
Uhles, Mary, illus. see Enderle, Dotti.
Uhles, Mary, illus. see Lewis, J. Patrick.
Uhles, Mary, illus. see Lindeen, Mary.
Uhles, Mary, illus. see Riehle, Mary Ann McCabe.
Uhles, Mary Reaves, illus. see Duncan, Alice Faye.
Uhles, Mary Reaves, illus. see Lindeen, Mary.
Uhles, Mary Reaves, illus. see McGillian, Jamie.
Uhles, Mary Reaves, illus. see Wilbur, Helen L.
Uhles, Talmadge G. Tale of a Toad. (p. 2178)
Uhlig, Elizabeth. I See America! Uhlig, Elizabeth, illus. (p. 1081)
Uhlig, Elizabeth, illus. see Anderson, Lillian.
Uhlig, Elizabeth, illus. see Laub, Frima.
Uhlig, Elizabeth, illus. see Rothstein, Evelyn.
Uhlig, William Cullen. Nitrogen Contents of Commercial Distilled Water (Classic Reprint) (p. 1611)
Uhlman, Tom, illus. see Rusch, Elizabeth.
Uhlman, Tom, photos by see Carson, Mary Kay.
Uhre, Mark, illus. see Nuttall, Susan.
Uhren, Anja, illus. see Mathias, Irene.
Uhrich, Jeremy. Appropriate Behavior Counts: A Guide for Young Athletes. Springer, Cherish, illus. (p. 107)
Uhrig, Betsy. Double the Danger & Zero Zucchini. (p. 589)
Uihlein, Mary. Hello Little Owl. Uihlein, Mary, illus. (p. 951)
—Hello Little Owl, I Am Hermit Crab! Uihlein, Mary, illus. (p. 951)
Uistin, Liam Mac, see MacUistin, Liam.
Ujdur, Sr Richard R. & Ann Ujdur-Vendl, Sherri. Too Damn Young to Know. (p. 2260)
Ukazu, Ngozi. Check, Please! Book 1: # Hockey (p. 363)
—Check, Please! Book 2: Sticks & Scones. Ukazu, Ngozi, illus. (p. 363)
—Check, Please!: # Hockey (p. 363)
Ukpong, Caitlin. Thoughts in My Head. (p. 2231)
Ukray, Murat, ed. see De Saint-Exupéry, Antoine.
Ukropina, Jovan, illus. see Johnson, Terry Lynn.
Ulasevich, Olga, ed. see AZ Books Staff.
Ulasl, Zekeriya, et al. Umar Ibn Al-Khattab. (p. 2316)
Ulbrich, Jasper. Little Owl. (p. 1323)
Ulbricht, Jaryd. Higgs Mechanism Explained. (p. 968)
Ulbricht, Juliet, illus. see Rucker, Diana Lynn.
Ulene, Nancy, illus. see Peterson, Scott.
Ulerio, Michelle. Lily Finds Her Way Home. (p. 1302)
Ulery, Dodie. Freedom Song. (p. 783)
Ulfers, S. Idylls of a Dutch Village (Eastloom) (Classic Reprint) (p. 1090)
Ulh, Xina M. Using Computer Science in Military Service. (p. 2341)
Ulinski, Michael. Why Do Animals Hibernate? (p. 2455)
Ulkutay & Co Ltd, illus. see Gerlings, Rebecca, ed.
Ulkutay Design Group, illus. see Landolf, Diane Wright.
Ulkutay Design Group Staff, illus. see Gerlings, Rebecca, ed.
Ulkutay Design Group Staff & Random House Children's Books Staff, contrib. by. My Book of Kittens. (p. 1534)
Ullah, Akmal. Accidental Rich Boy. (p. 10)
Ullas, Sharmi. What Happened with Chikunkun? (p. 2411)
Ullman, Albert Edward. Line's Busy (Classic Reprint) (p. 1304)
Ullman, Alice Woods. Gingham Rose (Classic Reprint) (p. 834)
Ullman, B. B. Bad Order. (p. 158)
Ullman, Barb Bentler. Whistle Bright Magic: A Nutfolk Tale. (p. 2443)
Ullmann, Carol & Zott, Lynn M., eds. Religious Liberty. (p. 1863)
Ullmann, Margaret. Pocahontas: A Pageant (Classic Reprint) (p. 1764)
Ullyett, Henry. Rambles of a Naturalist Round Folkestone: With Occasional Papers on the to & Are Added, Lists of Plants, Which Are & Land & Freshwater Shells (Classic Reprint) (p. 1839)
—Rambles of a Naturalist Round Folkestone. (p. 1839)
Ulmer, George T. Adventures & Reminiscences of a Volunteer (Classic Reprint) (p. 19)
Ulmer, Michael. C Is for Canada. Daigneault, Sylvie, illus. (p. 306)
—H Is for Horse: An Equestrian Alphabet. Frankenhuyzen, Gijsbert van, illus. (p. 908)
—J Is for Jump Shot: A Basketball Alphabet. Braught, Mark, illus. (p. 1150)
—M Is for Maple Leafs. Rose, Melanie, illus. (p. 1370)
—S Is for the Stanley Cup: A Hockey Championship Alphabet. Benoit, Renné & Lyons, Chris, illus. (p. 1919)
Ulmer, Mikaila. Bee Fearless: Dream Like a Kid. (p. 189)
Ulmer, Wendy K. Zero, Zilch, Nada: Counting to None. Knorr, Laura, illus. (p. 2540)
Ulrich, Charles. In Plum Valley: A Rural Comedy Drama in Four Acts (Classic Reprint) (p. 1106)
—Political Editor: A Comedy of Newspaper & Political Life (Classic Reprint) (p. 1771)
Ulrich, George, illus. see Christopher, Matt.
Ulrich, George, illus. see Kramer, Sydelle & Who HQ.
Ulrich, George, illus. see McKay, Sindy.
Ulrich, Hub. Arche Part 8 Heures(l') (p. 110)
Ulrich, Joyce. Halloween Explained for Children. (p. 912)
Ulrich, Kelly, illus. see Fedorowich, Mike.
Ulrich, Kelly, illus. see Griffiths, Allen & Godinez, Mary.
Ulrich, Kelly, illus. see Yrjana, Colleen.
Ulrich, Maureen. Face Off (p. 693)
Ulshafer, Katherine S. I Love You. Emms, Sarah Frushour, illus. (p. 1078)
Ulsifer, Shannon. Suns of Magic: Return of the Phoenix. (p. 2153)
Ultman, Suzy. Masha & Her Sisters. (p. 1417)
—Masha's World: Coloring & Activity Book. (p. 1417)
—Tiny Town. (p. 2250)
—to Z Menagerie. (p. 2254)
Ultman, Suzy, illus. see Chronicle Books Staff.
Uluadluak, Donald. Inuit Puppy Story Leng, Qin, illus. (p. 1129)
Ulz, Ivan. Fire Truck! Kaida, Garrett, illus. (p. 733)
Umansky, Kaye. Belinda & the Bears & the New Chair (Early Reader) (p. 196)
—Cinderella. Crossland, Caroline, illus. (p. 391)
—Clover Twig & the Perilous Path. Wright, Johanna, illus. (p. 408)
—Emperor's New Clothes. Crossland, Caroline, illus. (p. 645)
—Noah's Ark. Richardson-Jones, Tessa, illus. (p. 1616)
—Sleeping Beauty. Crossland, Caroline, illus. (p. 2036)
Umar, Mohammed. Enemies Inside. (p. 650)
—Enemies Inside (Macedonian Edition) (p. 650)
—Samad in the Desert: English-Afrikaans Bilingual Edition. Simes, Wyno, tr. (p. 1927)
—Samad in the Desert: English-Sesotho Bilingual Edition. Khumalo, Virginia, tr. (p. 1927)
—Samad in the Desert: English-Kinyarwanda Bilingual Edition. Mudacumura, Fiston, tr. (p. 1927)
—Samad in the Desert: English-Chichewa Bilingual Edition. Masamba, Maureen Lynda, tr. (p. 1927)
—Samad in the Desert: English-Zulu Bilingual Edition. Zungu Oshin, Glenrose Nonhlala, tr. (p. 1927)
—Samad in the Desert: English-Xhosa Bilingual Edition. Saliwa-Mogale, Ncebakazi Faith, tr. (p. 1927)
—Samad in the Desert. (p. 1927)
—Samad in the Desert (Bilingual English-Acholi Edition) (p. 1927)
—Samad in the Desert (Bilingual English-Fulfulde Edition) (p. 1927)
—Samad in the Desert (Bilingual English-Hausa Edition) (p. 1927)
—Samad in the Desert (Bilingual English-Kirundi Edition) (p. 1927)
—Samad in the Desert (English - Amharic Bilingual Edition) Beyene, Brook, tr. (p. 1927)
—Samad in the Desert (English - Oromo Bilingual Edition) Tedla, Berhanu, tr. (p. 1927)
—Samad in the Desert (English - Swahili Bilingual Edition) Rajab, Ahmed, tr. (p. 1927)
—Samad in the Desert (English - Tigrinya Bilingual Edition) Markos, Tewodros, tr. (p. 1927)
—Samad in the Desert. English-Somali Bilingual Edition. Hassan, Mohammed Sh, tr. (p. 1927)
—Samad in the Forest: English-Luo Bilingual Edition. Atoh, Fred Ochieng, tr. (p. 1927)
—Samad in the Forest: English-Sesotho Bilingual Edition. Khumalo, Virginia, tr. (p. 1927)
—Samad in the Forest: English-Somali Bilingual Edition. Hassan, Mohammed Ali, tr. (p. 1927)
—Samad in the Forest: English-Bemba Bilingual Edition. Siulapwa, Christopher Kaule, tr. (p. 1927)
—Samad in the Forest: English-Zulu Bilingual Edition. Glenrose Nonhlala, Zungu Oshin, tr. (p. 1927)
—Samad in the Forest: English-Xhosa Bilingual Edition. Saliwa-Mogale, Ncebakazi Faith, tr. (p. 1927)
—Samad in the Forest (Bilingual English-Acholi Edition) (p. 1927)
—Samad in the Forest (Bilingual English-Fulfulde Edition) (p. 1927)
—Samad in the Forest (Bilingual English-Hausa Edition) (p. 1927)
—Samad in the Forest (Bilingual English-Igbo Edition) (p. 1927)
—Samad in the Forest (Bilingual English-Kirundi Edition) (p. 1927)
—Samad in the Forest (English - Amharic Bilingual Edition) Beyene, Brook, tr. (p. 1927)
—Samad in the Forest (English - Oromo Bilingual Edition) Tedla, Berhanu, tr. (p. 1927)
—Samad in the Forest (English - Swahili Bilingual Edition) Rajab, Ahmed, tr. (p. 1927)
—Samad in the Forest (English - Tigrinya Bilingual Edition) Markos, Tewodros, tr. (p. 1927)
Umar, Mohammed & Greene, Soukaina Lalla. Samad in the Forest: English-Afrikaans Bilingual Edition. Simes, Wyno, tr. (p. 1927)
—Samad in the Forest: English-Kinyarwanda Bilingual Edition. Mudacumura, Fiston, tr. (p. 1927)
Umar, Mohammed & Siulapwa, Christopher Kaule. Samad in the Desert: Bilingual English-Bemba Edition. Greene, Soukaina Lalla, illus. (p. 1927)
Umayra, Hadi. Piece of Night. (p. 1742)
Umbach, Andrea. Conquer Your Fears & Phobias for Teens: How to Overcome Scary Situations & Increase Your Freedom. (p. 441)
Umbstaetter, Herman Daniel. Red-Hot Dollar & Other Stories from the Black Cat (Classic Reprint) (p. 1857)
Umeed, Rubayata. Zero: Dream. Football. Alfresco. (p. 2539)
Umezawa, Rui. Strange Light Afar: Tales of the Supernatural from Old Japan Fujita, Mikiko, illus. (p. 2138)
Umicini, Roberta, tr. see Hambleton, Laura.
Umicini, Roberta, tr. see McKee, David.
Umina, Lisa. Milo Finds His Best Friend. Thompson, Chad, illus. (p. 1468)
Umpherville, Tina. Spring Celebration Rice, Christie, illus. (p. 2092)
Umrigar, Thrity. Binny's Diwali. Chanani, Nidhi, illus. (p. 228)
Umrigar, Thrity & Chen, Ziyue. When I Carried You in My Belly. (p. 2430)
Umrikar, Sakharam, illus. see Ludka, Richard.
Umsted, Lillie Devereux Blake. Southwold: A Novel (Classic Reprint) (p. 2069)
Unabridged, Illustrated -, jt. auth. see Austen, Jane.
Unamuno, Miguel de. San Manuel Bueno, Mártir. (p. 1930)
Unchained, Fly Ty. Fly Ty Unchained Presents: Destiny's First Day... a Look at Black Hair Issues in Our Community. (p. 754)
Uncle Chuck. Monkey Puzzle Tree. (p. 1494)
Undercuffler, Gary, illus. see Allen, Nancy Kelly.
Undercuffler, Gary, illus. see Hillert, Margaret, et al.
Undercuffler, Gary, illus. see Hillert, Margaret.
Undercuffler, Gary, illus. see Klepeis, Alicia & Ventura, Gabriela Baeza.
Underdown, Emily. Stories from Chaucer (Classic Reprint) (p. 2123)
Underhill, Alecia, illus. see Wilsdon, Christina.
Underhill, Alice Mertie. Dookie, Sookie, & Big Mo. (p. 585)
Underhill, Edwin H. How It Happened & Other Poems (Classic Reprint) (p. 1032)
Underhill, Evelyn. Column of Dust (Classic Reprint) (p. 427)
—Practical Mysticism: A Little Book for Normal People. (p. 1784)
—Practical Mysticism - Scholar's Choice Edition. (p. 1784)
Underhill, Evelyn T. Credible Chronicles of the Patchwork Village: 'Sconset by the Sea (Classic Reprint) (p. 472)
Underhill, George F. Gone to Ground: A Hunting Novel. (p. 861)
—Gone to Ground: A Hunting Novel (Classic Reprint) (p. 861)
—Helterskelter Hounds: Or Mr. Flopkin's Sporting Memoirs (Classic Reprint) (p. 954)
—In & Out of the Pig-Skin (Classic Reprint) (p. 1104)
Underwood, Deborah. 101 Ways to Save the Planet (p. 2559)
—Bad Bye, Good Bye. Bean, Jonathan, illus. (p. 157)
—Bearnard's Book. Saburi, Misa, illus. (p. 180)
—Christmas Quiet Book. Liwska, Renata, illus. (p. 386)
—Creature Camouflage (p. 471)
—Ducks! McBeth, T. L., illus. (p. 608)
—Every Little Letter. Ruiz, Joy Hwang, illus. (p. 670)
—Finding Kindness. Chan, Irene, illus. (p. 729)
—Good Night, Baddies. Kangas, Juli, illus. (p. 863)
—Here Comes Santa Cat. (p. 958)
—Here Comes Teacher Cat. Rueda, Claudia, illus. (p. 958)
—Here Comes the Easter Cat. Rueda, Claudia, illus. (p. 958)
—Here Comes the Tooth Fairy Cat. Rueda, Claudia, illus. (p. 958)
—Here Comes Valentine Cat. Rueda, Claudia, illus. (p. 958)
—Hiding in Deserts (p. 967)
—Hiding in Forests (p. 967)
—Hiding in Grasslands (p. 967)
—Hiding in Mountains (p. 967)
—Hiding in Oceans (p. 967)
—Hiding in Rain Forests (p. 967)
—Hiding in the Polar Regions (p. 967)
—Hiding in Wetlands (p. 967)
—Loud Book! (p. 1357)
—Loud Book! Liwska, Renata, illus. (p. 1357)
—Loud Book! Padded Board Book. Liwska, Renata, illus. (p. 1357)
—Monster & Mouse Go Camping. Chapman, Jared, illus. (p. 1495)
—Ogilvy. McBeth, T. L., illus. (p. 1641)
—Outside In. Derby, Cindy, illus. (p. 1685)
—Panda Problem. Marks, Hannah, illus. (p. 1695)
—Part-Time Princess. Evans, Cambria, illus. (p. 1701)
—Quiet Book. (p. 1827)
—Quiet Book. Liwska, Renata, illus. (p. 1827)
—Reading Beauty: (Empowering Books, Early Elementary Story Books, Stories for Kids, Bedtime Stories for Girls) (p. 1846)
—Super Saurus & the Egg. Young, Ned, illus. (p. 2156)
—Super Saurus Saves Kindergarten. Young, Ned, illus. (p. 2156)
—Walrus in the Bathtub. Hunt, Matt, illus. (p. 2373)
Underwood, Deborah, jt. auth. see Goldberg, Whoopi.
Underwood, Deborah & Whoopi, Goldberg. Sugar Plum Ballerinas in Two Acts: Plum Fantastic & Toeshoe Trouble. Roos, Maryn, illus. (p. 2147)
Underwood, Deborah K. Balloon for Isabel. Rankin, Laura, illus. (p. 162)
Underwood, Earl. Representing John Marshall Co: Being Confessions of Edward R. Ward, a Drummer (Classic Reprint) (p. 1867)
Underwood, Edna. Famous Stories from Foreign Countries (Classic Reprint) (p. 704)
Underwood, Edna Worthley. Penitent (Classic Reprint) (p. 1716)
—Short Stories from the Balkans: Translated into English (Classic Reprint) (p. 2010)
—Short Stories from the Balkans. (p. 2010)
Underwood, Edna Worthyley. Whirlwind (Classic Reprint) (p. 2442)
Underwood, Edward, illus. see Hart, Caryl.
Underwood, Edward, illus. see Nosy Crow.
Underwood, Francis Henry. Man Proposes: A Novel (Classic Reprint) (p. 1395)
—Man Proposes. (p. 1395)
Underwood, Gary. Frogs. (p. 790)
—Reptiles. (p. 1867)
Underwood, John Curtis. Americans. (p. 74)
Underwood, Kim. Wonderful World of Sparkle Girl & Doobins. Goldman, Garnet, illus. (p. 2490)
Underwood, L. . H. With Tommy Tompkins in Korea (Classic Reprint) (p. 2482)
Underwood, Mary Lanman. American Mother: And Other Stories (Classic Reprint) (p. 73)
Underwood, Mia. My First Needle-Felting Book: 30 Adorable Animal Projects for Children Aged 7+ (p. 1545)
Underwood, Michelle, ed. see Dora, Liza.
Underwood, Ruth. Living Legacy (Classic Reprint) (p. 1333)
Underwood, Sandi. Secret at One Belmont Lane. (p. 1974)
Underwood, Sandy, illus. see Alice the Pony.
Underwood, Shelley. Insects. (p. 1122)
—Minibeasts. (p. 1472)
Underwood, Steve. Borrowed Princess: The Daughters of the Lost King Series. Ashby, Amy, ed. (p. 263)
Underwood, William Lyman. Wild Brother: Strangest of True Stories from the North Woods (Classic Reprint) (p. 2463)
Undset, Sigrid. Happy Times in Norway. (p. 924)
—Sigurd & His Brave Companions: A Tale of Medieval Norway. Bull Tellman, Gunvor, illus. (p. 2017)
Undset, Sigrid, ed. True & Untrue & Other Norse Tales. Chapman, Frederick T., illus. (p. 2293)
Ung, Elisa. Coping with ADD, ADHD, & ODD. (p. 451)
Ungaro, Ellen. Diamonds: Set Of 6. (p. 538)
—Inquiry & Investigation - 6 Pack: Set of 6 with Common Core Teacher Materials. (p. 1121)
—Inquiry & Investigation - 6 Pack: Set of 6 Bridges Edition with Common Core Teacher Materials. (p. 1121)
—Tools of Scientists - 6 Pack: Set of 6 with Common Core Teacher Materials. (p. 2261)
—Tools of Scientists - 6 Pack: Set of 6 Bridges Edition with Common Core Teacher Materials. (p. 2261)
Ungaro, Marley. Darling Dozen of the Deep. (p. 508)
Unger, David, tr. see Montejo, Victor.
Unger, Erin, illus. see Gragg, Karla.
Ungerer, Tomi. Adelaide: The Flying Kangaroo. (p. 15)
—Beast of Monsieur Racine. (p. 181)
—Blue Cloud. (p. 248)
—Christmas Eve at the Mellops' (p. 385)
—Christmas Eve at the Mellops', the Mellops Go Diving for Treasure, the Mellops Go Spelunking, the Mellops Strike Oil, the Mellops Go Flying - 5 Volumes. (p. 385)
—Die Blaue Wolke. (p. 543)
—Emile: The Helpful Octopus. (p. 642)
—Fog Island IBook. (p. 756)
—Mellops Go Spelunking. (p. 1443)
—Mellops Strike Oil. (p. 1443)
—Moon Man. (p. 1502)
—No Kiss for Mother. (p. 1613)
—Nonstop. (p. 1618)
—One, Two, Where's My Shoe? (p. 1663)
—Otto-Autobiography of a Teddy Bear. (p. 1676)
—Rufus: The Bat Who Loved Colors. (p. 1912)
—Rufus: The Bat Who Loved Colours. (p. 1912)
—Snail, Where Are You? (p. 2044)
Unger-Pengilly, Elaine. Rat. Trockstad, Marcy, illus. (p. 1842)
—There's a Rat in This City. Pengilly, Gordon, ed. (p. 2218)
Ungs, Tim. Paul Mccartney & Stella Mccartney. (p. 1707)
Ungureanu, Dan. Nara & the Island. Ungureanu, Dan, illus. (p. 1575)
Ungureanu, Dan Paul, illus. see DeLong, Lucianne.
Uni, North Georgia College and State. Cadet Bugler, Vol. 1: Nov. 15, 1934 (Classic Reprint) (p. 308)
Unicorn, Pretty. Unicorn Coloring Books: For Kids Ages 4-8 (Special Edition) (p. 2328)
Union, American Civil Liberties. What Shocked the Censors! A Complete Record of Cuts in Motion Picture Films Ordered by the New York State Censors from January, 1932 to March, 1933 (Classic Reprint) (p. 2419)
Union, American Study School. Fanny Graham, or a Peep at the Heart: A Story for Children (Classic Reprint) (p. 706)
Union, American Sunday. Amaranth: A Gift for All Seasons (Classic Reprint) (p. 62)
—Cottage Scenes (Classic Reprint) (p. 457)
—Grandfather Merrie, or the Command & the Promise (Classic Reprint) (p. 877)
—Little Missionary, or a Biographical Sketch of Gratia Olive Leonard (Classic Reprint) (p. 1322)
—Maria Cheeseman, or the Candy-Girl: With a Preface (Classic Reprint) (p. 1404)
—Natural History, for Infant Schools (Classic Reprint) (p. 1579)
—Pink Slippers, or Cure of Vanity (Classic Reprint) (p. 1746)
—School Days Reviewed: Or Stories of Schoolboys (Classic Reprint) (p. 1945)

College of Duke University, at Durham, North Carolina (Classic Reprint) (p. 111)
—Archive, Vol. 48: October 1934 (Classic Reprint) (p. 111)
—Archive, Vol. 49: October 1935 (Classic Reprint) (p. 111)
—Archive, Vol. 52: October, 1938 (Classic Reprint) (p. 111)
—Archive, Vol. 53: October, 1939 (Classic Reprint) (p. 111)
—Archive, Vol. 54: October, 1940 (Classic Reprint) (p. 111)
—Archive, Vol. 55: October, 1941 (Classic Reprint) (p. 111)
—Archive, Vol. 56: September, 1942 (Classic Reprint) (p. 111)
—Archive, Vol. 64: October 1950 (Classic Reprint) (p. 111)
—Archive, Vol. 68: October, 1955 (Classic Reprint) (p. 111)
—Archive, Vol. 69: October, 1956 (Classic Reprint) (p. 111)
—Archive, Vol. 75: November 1963 (Classic Reprint) (p. 111)
—Archive, Vol. 81: Winter 68-69 (Classic Reprint) (p. 111)
—Little German Drummer Boy (Classic Reprint) (p. 1317)
University, Fordham. Fordham Monthly, Vol. 37: February, 1919 (Classic Reprint) (p. 764)
University, Harvard. Harvard Advocate, Vol. 46 (Classic Reprint) (p. 935)
—Harvard Advocate, Vol. 74: September 25, 1902 (Classic Reprint) (p. 935)
University, Illinois State Normal. Index, 1926 (Classic Reprint) (p. 1115)
University, Indiana. Blanche Dearwood: A Tale of Modern Life (Classic Reprint) (p. 242)
—Winnie & I (Classic Reprint) (p. 2474)
University, James Madison. Schoolma'am, 1912, Vol. 3 (Classic Reprint) (p. 1947)
—Schoolma'am, 1917, Vol. 8 (Classic Reprint) (p. 1947)
—Schoolma'am, 1918, Vol. 9 (Classic Reprint) (p. 1947)
University, Johns Hopkins. Johns Hopkins University Circular, No. 10, December 1908; in Memoriam Daniel Colt Gilman 1831-1908. (p. 1175)
University, Kent State. Chestnut Burr, 1914 (Classic Reprint) (p. 366)
—Chestnut Burr, 1919 (Classic Reprint) (p. 366)
University, Lake Forest. Forester, 1967 (Classic Reprint) (p. 766)
—Forester, 1985 (Classic Reprint) (p. 766)
University, Lehigh. Lehigh Burr, Vol. 15: February, 1896 (Classic Reprint) (p. 1265)
University, Michigan. Quarter-Centennial Reunion, Class of Eighteen-Ninety-Two, University of Michigan, June Twenty-Fifth to Twenty-Seventh, Nineteen Hundred & Seventeen: And Addresses of All Classmates (Classic Reprint) (p. 1822)
University, Millikin. Millidek, 1906 (Classic Reprint) (p. 1467)
University, National-Louis. N. K. E. C. Year Book, 1919, Vol. 4 (Classic Reprint) (p. 1572)
—N. K. E. C. Year Book, 1923 (Classic Reprint) (p. 1572)
—N. K. E. C. Year Book, 1925, Vol. 10 (Classic Reprint) (p. 1572)
University, North Carolina. Coraddi, Vol. 38: Member of the North Carolina Collegiate Press Association; March, 1934 (Classic Reprint) (p. 453)
University, North Carolina Baptist Femal. Oak Leaves, 1904, Vol. 1 (Classic Reprint) (p. 1633)
University, Northern Illinois. Norther: A Story of the Castle on the Hill (Classic Reprint) (p. 1621)
University, Northwestern. Northwestern Purple Parrot, Vol. 2: March, 1922 (Classic Reprint) (p. 1622)
—Purple Parrot, Vol. 11: April, 1931 (Classic Reprint) (p. 1816)
—Purple Parrot, Vol. 2: May, 1922 (Classic Reprint) (p. 1816)
—Purple Parrot, Vol. 2: April, 1922 (Classic Reprint) (p. 1816)
—Purple Parrot, Vol. 2: January, 1922 (Classic Reprint) (p. 1816)
—Purple Parrot, Vol. 2: December, 1921 (Classic Reprint) (p. 1816)
—Purple Parrot, Vol. 2: November, 1921 (Classic Reprint) (p. 1816)
—Purple Parrot, Vol. 2 (Classic Reprint) (p. 1816)
—Purple Parrot, Vol. 3: October, 1922 (Classic Reprint) (p. 1816)
—Purple Parrot, Vol. 3: December, 1922 (Classic Reprint) (p. 1816)
—Syllabus, 1903 (Classic Reprint) (p. 2172)
University, Northwestern State. Argus, 1984 (Classic Reprint) (p. 115)
—Argus, 1985, Vol. 9 (Classic Reprint) (p. 115)
—Argus, 1988 (Classic Reprint) (p. 115)
—Argus, 1991 (Classic Reprint) (p. 115)
—Argus, 1993 (Classic Reprint) (p. 115)
—Argus, 1994 (Classic Reprint) (p. 115)
—Argus, 1995 (Classic Reprint) (p. 115)
—Argus, 1996 (Classic Reprint) (p. 115)
—Argus, 1999 (Classic Reprint) (p. 115)
—Argus, 2002-2003 (Classic Reprint) (p. 115)
—Argus 2004: Art & Literary Magazine (Classic Reprint) (p. 115)
—Argus 2006: Student Literary Magazine; the Refrigerator Issue (Classic Reprint) (p. 115)
—Argus 2007: Art & Literary Magazine (Classic Reprint) (p. 115)
—Argus, 2008 (Classic Reprint) (p. 115)
—Argus, 2009 (Classic Reprint) (p. 115)
—Argus 2011: Northwestern State University's Annual Art & Literary Magazine (Classic Reprint) (p. 115)
—Argus, 2012 (Classic Reprint) (p. 115)
—Argus 98 (Classic Reprint) (p. 115)
—Argus, Vol. 11: Spring 1978 (Classic Reprint) (p. 115)
—Argus, Vol. 3: Fall, 1978 (Classic Reprint) (p. 115)
—Potpourri 1915: The Annual of the Louisiana State Normal School, Being a Record of the Life, Activities, & Interests of Its Students (Classic Reprint) (p. 1781)
—Potpourri, 1916 (Classic Reprint) (p. 1781)
—Voices Argus, 2010 (Classic Reprint) (p. 2365)
University of Ghana. Fate's Promise: Sequel to the Lost Princess. (p. 714)
University of Minnesota Libraries Publishing, University of. Sociology: Understanding & Changing the Social World. (p. 2054)
University of Phoenix Staff. Dragon Who Learned to Fly. (p. 594)
University of Texas System Academy of Distinguished Teachers, The. Little Orange Book II: Student Voices on Excellent Teaching. (p. 1323)
University, Otterbein. Sibyl, 1902, Vol. 2 (Classic Reprint) (p. 2014)
University, Southern Illinois Normal. Obelisk, 1920, Vol. 6: Annual of the Southern Illinois Normal University (Classic Reprint) (p. 1634)
University, Southwestern. Sou'wester, 1912, Vol. 9 (Classic Reprint) (p. 2069)
—Sou'wester, 1913, Vol. 10 (Classic Reprint) (p. 2069)
University, Student of Yale. Yale Literary Magazine, Vol. 84: Conducted by the Students of Yale University; December 1918 (Classic Reprint) (p. 2517)
University, Troy State Normal. Palladium, 1926 (Classic Reprint) (p. 1694)
University, Victoria. ACTA Victoriana, Vol. 38: December, 1913 (Classic Reprint) (p. 12)
—ACTA Victoriana, Vol. 38: February, 1914 (Classic Reprint) (p. 12)
University, West Virginia. Monticola, 1909 (Classic Reprint) (p. 1500)
University, Westfield State. Tekoa, 1924 (Classic Reprint) (p. 2201)
—Westfield Normal School, 1909 (Classic Reprint) (p. 2402)
University, Winthrop. Lang Syne, 1904 (Classic Reprint) (p. 1243)
—Tatler, 1917 (Classic Reprint) (p. 2192)
University, Woman's College of the N. C. Coraddi, Vol. 39: March, 1935 (Classic Reprint) (p. 453)
—Coraddi, Vol. 45: November, 1940 (Classic Reprint) (p. 453)
University, Yale. Yale Courant, 1898, Vol. 35 (Classic Reprint) (p. 2517)
—Yale Literary Magazine, Vol. 73: October, 1907 June, 1908 (Classic Reprint) (p. 2517)
—Yale Literary Magazine, Vol. 82: April, 1917 (Classic Reprint) (p. 2517)
—Yale Literary Magazine, Vol. 83: April, 1918 (Classic Reprint) (p. 2517)
Unka, Vasanti. Boring Book. (p. 262)
—Who Stole the Rainbow? One Hundred Book Covers in One Box. (p. 2450)
Unka, Vasanti, illus. see Mewburn, Kyle.
Unknown. Comical People. (p. 430)
—Golden Moments: Bright Stories for Young Folks. (p. 858)
—Goody Two-Shoes. (p. 869)
—Meg in the Jungle. (p. 1441)
—Nursery Rhyme Book. (p. 1631)
—Story of the White Mouse. (p. 2135)
—Villains on the Loose. (p. 2358)
—Where in Tinga Tinga Is Tickbird? (p. 2437)
Unknown, jt. auth. see Steck-Vaughn Company.
Unknown & BBC Children's Books Staff. Official Annual 2018. (p. 1641)
Ünlükoç, Müge. Real Race. (p. 1850)
Uno, Kat, illus. see Broderick, Kathy.
Uno, Kat, illus. see Rose, Robin.
Uno, Kat, illus. see Troupe, Thomas Kingsley.
Unruh, Charlotte Love, illus. see Sanchez, Gary.
Unruh, Cindy. Sierra, the Black Lab Who Loved to Eat: (a True Story) Krehbiel, Angie, illus. (p. 2015)
—What to Expect When Your Family Becomes a Foster Family. (p. 2421)
Unruh, Terri. Moving Hat. (p. 1516)
Unsplash Com, photos by see Stewart, Laurie.
Unstead, Sue. DK Readers L2: Amazing Bees: Buzzing with Bee Facts! (p. 568)
Unstead, Sue, jt. auth. see Dorling Kindersley Publishing Staff.
Unswood, Cassie. Exploring Plane Figures: Understand Concepts of Area (p. 682)
Unsworth, Tania. Brightwood. (p. 281)
—One Safe Place. (p. 1662)
Unten, Eren, illus. see Capozzi, Suzy.
Unten, Eren, illus. see Gilbert, Frances.
Unten, Eren, illus. see Golden Books.
Unten, Eren, illus. see Tillworth, Mary.
Unten, Eren Blanquet, illus. see Golden Books Staff.
Unten, Eren Blanquet, illus. see Nicholas, Christopher.
Untermeyer, Louis. Modern American Poetry: An Anthology (Classic Reprint) (p. 1486)
—Modern American Poetry: An Introduction (Classic Reprint) (p. 1486)
—Modern American Poetry: An Introduction - Scholar's Choice Edition. (p. 1486)
—New Era in American Poetry (Classic Reprint) (p. 1593)
—One & One & One. Jones, Robert, illus. (p. 1658)
Unwin, Cobden. Hungry Forties: Life under the Bread Tax (Classic Reprint) (p. 1052)
Unwin, Cynthia. Birds of Paradise: Winged Wonders. (p. 232)
—Cheetahs. (p. 364)
Unwin, Dave, illus. see Holland, Bradley R.
Unwin, M. Science Activities. (p. 1948)
Unwin, Mike. Migration: Incredible Animal Journeys. Desmond, Jenni, illus. (p. 1464)
Unwin, Mike, illus. see Davidson, Susanna.
Unwin, Mike, jt. auth. see Davidson, Susanna.
Unwin, Shelly. You're Five! Battersby, Katherine, illus. (p. 2535)
—You're Four! Battersby, Katherine, illus. (p. 2535)
—You're One! Battersby, Katherine, illus. (p. 2535)
—You're Three! Battersby, Katherine, illus. (p. 2535)
—You're Two! Battersby, Katherine, illus. (p. 2535)
Unwin, T. Fisher. Century Illustrated Monthly Magazine, Vol. 44: May 1892 to October 1892 (Classic Reprint) (p. 352)
—Century Illustrated Monthly Magazine, Vol. 55: November, 1897, to April, 1898 (Classic Reprint) (p. 352)
Unwin, Thomas Fisher. Century Illustrated Monthly Magazine, Vol. 60: May, 1900, to October, 1900 (Classic Reprint) (p. 352)
Unzner, Christa, illus. see Paquette, Ammi-Joan.
Unzner, Christa, illus. see Wilson, Karma.
Upadhyay, Karla. I'm Hungry, but No Bugs Please! (p. 1098)
Upadhyay, Vikas, illus. see Knight, Bridget.
Upadhyay, Vikas, illus. see Neckles, Nadine.
Upchurch, J. T. Bravest of the Brave or a Mother's Influence (Classic Reprint) (p. 277)
Updale, Eleanor. Johnny Swanson. (p. 1175)
—Vengeance de Montmorency. (p. 2350)
Updegraff, Allan. Second Youth: Being, in the Main, Some Account of the Middle Comedy in the Life of a New York Bachelor; a Novel (Classic Reprint) (p. 1974)
—Strayed Revellers a Novel of Modernistic Truth & Intruding War (Classic Reprint) (p. 2139)
Updegraff, Nicole, illus. see Anyabwele, Talitha.
Updike, John. Child's Calendar (20th Anniversary Edition) Hyman, Trina Schart, illus. (p. 375)
Uphall, Margaret. U. S. Postal Service: The History of America's Mail System. (p. 2312)
Upham, Francis William. Debate Between the Church & Science, or the Ancient Hebraic Idea of the Six Days of Creation: With an Essay on the Literary Character of Tayler Lewis (Classic Reprint) (p. 522)
Upham, Janice, illus. see Jones, Donna.
Upholz, Matt. Adventures of the Baby Shark. (p. 28)
Upitis, Alvis, photos by see Patrick, Jean L. S.
Upitis, Alvis, photos by see Peterson, Cris.
Upjohn, Rebecca. Last Loon (p. 1248)
—Secret of the Village Fool Benoit, Renne, illus. (p. 1978)
Upjohn, Rebecca & Benoit, Renne. Secreto Del Tonto Del Pueblo. (p. 1979)
Upjohn, Rebecca, et al. Patrick's Wish (p. 1705)
Upperman, Katy. How the Light Gets In. (p. 1036)
—Impossibility of Us. (p. 1102)
—Kissing Max Holden. (p. 1225)
Upright, Blanche. Losing Gain (Classic Reprint) (p. 1352)
Upton, Bridget. Archibald Trotter. (p. 110)
Upton, Camp. Army Lessons in English: Book I-VI (Classic Reprint) (p. 118)
—Army Lessons in English: Military Stories (Classic Reprint) (p. 118)
Upton, Charles Elmer. Down Wild Goose Canyon. (p. 590)
—Down Wild Goose Canyon (Classic Reprint) (p. 591)
Upton, Elizabeth. Maxi the Little Taxi. Cole, Henry, illus. (p. 1428)
Upton, George. Johann Sebastian Bach. (p. 1171)
—Mozart's Youth. (p. 1517)
Upton, George P. Letters of Peregrine Pickle (Classic Reprint) (p. 1280)
—Youth of the Great Elector: Translated from the German of Ferdinand Schmidt (Classic Reprint) (p. 2536)
Upton, J. Katie, the Curious Kitty. Victoria, A., illus. (p. 1205)
Upton, Lawrence, et al, eds. Salt Companion to Maggie O'Sullivan. (p. 1925)
Upton, Matthew & Upton, Luisa. Secret Life of Grandpas. (p. 1976)
Upton, Rachael. Disney Villains: the Evilest of Them All. Artists, Disney Storybook, illus. (p. 564)
—My Little Pony Cutie Mark Crew Collector's Guide. (p. 1553)
Upton, Rachael, adapted by. My Little Pony the Movie: Book & Magnetic Playset. (p. 1554)
Upton, Robert Jesten. Milo & the Dragon Cross: A Novel. (p. 1468)
Upton, S. T. Dreamnesia: Retrospect. (p. 603)
Upton, Shawn T. Death Dot. (p. 521)
Upton, William C. Uncle Pat's Cabin: A Story of Irish Life (Classic Reprint) (p. 2318)
Upward, Asia. Lovable Lottie & the Lost Toy. (p. 1358)
—Lovable Lottie & the Shy Sheep. (p. 1358)
Upward, Bernard. Sons of Han: Stories of Chinese Life & Mission Work (Classic Reprint) (p. 2064)
Upward Books. Secret Notes. (p. 1977)
Uranas, Chuck, photos by see Doeden, Matt.
Urbain, Christophe, photos by. Emma in Paris. (p. 643)
Urban, A. Teachers Handbook to Bible History: A Practical Commentary upon the Principal Events of the Old & New Testament with Directions for Their Application in the Religious & Moral Training of Children (Classic Reprint) (p. 2195)
Urban, Chieu Anh. Color Wonder Winter Is Here! Urban, Chieu Anh, illus. (p. 421)
—Hooray for Spring! Urban, Chieu Anh, illus. (p. 1001)
Urban, Chiêu Anh. Quiet As a Mouse: And Other Animal Idioms. (p. 1827)
Urban, Diana. All Your Twisted Secrets. (p. 55)
Urban, Friedrich Maria. Application of Statistical Methods to the Problems of Psychophysics (Classic Reprint) (p. 107)
Urban, Helle, illus. see Brennan-Nelson, Denise.
Urban, Helle, illus. see Crane, Carol.
Urban, Helle, illus. see Gagliano, Eugene M.
Urban, Helle, illus. see James, Helen Foster & Wilbur, Helen L.
Urban, Helle, illus. see Wargin, Kathy-jo.
Urban, Helle, illus. see Young, Judy & Wargin, Kathy-jo.
Urban, Keith, illus. see Urban, Joyce.
Urban, Kerri. Day in the Life of Dexter: Dexter Goes to the Zoo. (p. 513)
—Day in the Life of Dexter: Dexter Goes to the Zoo. Jul Saavedra, Jescae, illus. (p. 513)
Urban, Linda. Center of Everything. (p. 351)
—Crooked Kind of Perfect. (p. 477)
—Little Red Henry. Valentine, Madeline, illus. (p. 1326)
—Mabel & Sam at Home. Hooper, Hadley, illus. (p. 1371)
—Milo Speck, Accidental Agent. (p. 1468)
—Mouse Was Mad. Cole, Henry, illus. (p. 1515)
—Road Trip with Max & His Mom. Kath, Katie, illus. (p. 1888)
—Weekends with Max & His Dad. (p. 2396)
—Weekends with Max & His Dad. Kath, Katie, illus. (p. 2396)
Urban, Lynne Martin. Annie Lynne & Jackie Lee: I Help You & You Help Me. (p. 100)
Urban, Sergei. Thedadiab. (p. 2215)
Urban, Sylvanus. Gentleman's Magazine: July, 1832 (Classic Reprint) (p. 816)
—Gentleman's Magazine: January June, 1873 (Classic Reprint) (p. 816)
—Gentleman's Magazine: July December, 1873 (Classic Reprint) (p. 816)
—Gentleman's Magazine, 1871 (Classic Reprint) (p. 816)
—Gentleman's Magazine, 1876, Vol. 16 (Classic Reprint) (p. 816)
—Gentleman's Magazine, Vol. 10: January June, 1873 (Classic Reprint) (p. 816)
—Gentleman's Magazine, Vol. 13: July-December, 1874 (Classic Reprint) (p. 816)
—Gentleman's Magazine, Vol. 13: January to June, Inclusive, 1840 (Classic Reprint) (p. 816)
—Gentleman's Magazine, Vol. 14: July to December Inclusive, 1840 (Classic Reprint) (p. 816)
—Gentleman's Magazine, Vol. 14: July to December, Inclusive, 1840 (Classic Reprint) (p. 816)
—Gentleman's Magazine, Vol. 17: July to December, 1876 (Classic Reprint) (p. 816)
—Gentleman's Magazine, Vol. 240: January to June, 1877 (Classic Reprint) (p. 816)
—Gentleman's Magazine, Vol. 249: July to December 1880 (Classic Reprint) (p. 816)
—Gentleman's Magazine, Vol. 249: July to December, 1880 (Classic Reprint) (p. 816)
—Gentleman's Magazine, Vol. 255: January to June 1885 (Classic Reprint) (p. 816)
—Gentleman's Magazine, Vol. 274: January to June, 1893 (Classic Reprint) (p. 817)
—Gentleman's Magazine, Vol. 275: July to December, 1893 (Classic Reprint) (p. 817)
—Gentleman's Magazine, Vol. 284: January to June 1898 (Classic Reprint) (p. 817)
Urban, William. Wyatt Earp: The O. K. Corral & the Law of the American West. (p. 2514)
Urbana-Champaign, University Of Illinois At. Siren, 1924-1925 (Classic Reprint) (p. 2026)
Urbano, Aide, jt. auth. see Pingry, Patricia A.
Urbano, Emilio, illus. see Behling, Steve, et al.
Urbano, Emilio, illus. see Caramagna, Joe & Behling, Steve.
Urbano, Emilio, illus. see Mulazzi, Paola, et al.
Urbanovic, Jackie. Duck & Cover. Urbanovic, Jackie, illus. (p. 607)
—Ducks in a Row. Urbanovic, Jackie & Mathieu, Joe, illus. (p. 608)
—Happy Go Ducky. Urbanovic, Jackie & Mathieu, Joe, illus. (p. 922)
—Prince of a Frog. (p. 1794)
—Sitting Duck. Urbanovic, Jackie, illus. (p. 2028)
Urbanovic, Jackie, illus. see Bateman, Teresa.
Urbanovic, Jackie, illus. see Fretz, Denette.
Urbanovic, Jackie, illus. see Hester, Denia Lewis.
Urbanovic, Jackie, illus. see Isaacs, Ronald H. & Rostoker-Gruber, Karen.
Urbanovic, Jackie, illus. see McConnaughhay, JoDee H.
Urbanovic, Jackie, illus. see Prelutsky, Jack.
Urbanovic, Jackie, illus. see Ransom, Jeanie Franz.
Urbanovic, Jackie, illus. see Sayre, April Pulley.
Urbanowich, Evelyn, illus. see Feravolo, Rocco V.
Urbanowicz, Kana, illus. see Wang, Andrea.
Urbantschitsch, Victor. Lehrbuch der Ohrenheilkunde. (p. 1265)
Urberuaga, Emilio. Gilda, la Oveja Gigante. Urberuaga, Emilio, illus. (p. 833)
—Gilda the Giant Sheep. Dawlatly, Ben, tr. (p. 833)
Urberuaga, Emilio, illus. see Ganges, Montse.
Urberuaga, Emilio, illus. see Lindo, Elvira.
Urberuaga, Emilio, illus. see Sobrino, Javier.
Urberuaga, Emilio, jt. auth. see Ganges, Montse.
Urbigkit, Cat. Guardian Team: On the Job with Rena & Roo. (p. 901)
Urbino, L. B. Home Angel (Classic Reprint) (p. 995)
Urbino, Levina Buoncuore. Miss. Kate: Or, the Village Teacher; a True Character (Classic Reprint) (p. 1479)
Urbino, S. R. American Woman in Europe: The Journal of Two Years & a Half Sojourn in Germany, Switzerland, France, & Italy (Classic Reprint) (p. 74)
Urda, Gary. Love You More. Bell, Jennifer A., illus. (p. 1361)
Urdahl, Catherine. Polka-Dot Fixes Kindergarten. Kemble, Mai S., illus. (p. 1771)
—Virginia Was a Spy. Kelley, Gary, illus. (p. 2361)
Ure, Jean. Born to Dance (Dance Trilogy, Book 1) (p. 263)
—Boys Beware. (p. 272)
—Buster (Chums) (p. 301)
—Daisy May. Donnelly, Karen, illus. (p. 497)
—Dazzling Danny. Donnelly, Karen, illus. (p. 516)
—Family Fan Club. Donnelly, Karen, illus. (p. 702)
—Flower Power Collection. (p. 752)
—Fortune Cookie. (p. 769)
—Hunky Dory. (p. 1052)
—Ice Lolly. (p. 1088)
—Jelly Baby. (p. 1163)
—Kissing Game. (p. 1225)
—Love & Kisses. (p. 1359)
—Showtime (Dance Trilogy, Book 3) (p. 2013)
—Shrinking Violet. (p. 2013)
—Star Quality (Dance Trilogy, Book 2) (p. 2102)
—Strawberry Crush. (p. 2139)
Ure, Regan. Descendant. (p. 530)
—Destined. (p. 533)
—Mason. (p. 1417)
Ureel, Jessica & Jacobs, Jessica. Peanut Pickle: A Story about Peanut Allergy. Roslyn, Jacquelyn, illus. (p. 1710)
Urell, Catherine. Carontawan 1919: Alias the Little Town on the Hill (Classic Reprint) (p. 333)
Uren, Alfred E. Bob & Bill See Canada: A Travel Story in Rhyme for Boys & Girls (Classic Reprint) (p. 251)
U'Ren, Andrea, illus. see DeFelice, Cynthia.
U'Ren, Andrea, illus. see Moss, Marissa.
U'Ren, Victoria, illus. see Green, Tom.
Urena, Pedro Henriquez, tr. see Barrie, J. M.
Urey, Gary. Escaped. (p. 662)
—Pursued. (p. 1816)
—Super Schnoz & the Gates of Smell. Long, Ethan, illus. (p. 2156)
—Super Schnoz & the Invasion of the Snore Snatchers. Frawley, Keith, illus. (p. 2156)
—Super Schnoz Boxed Set #1-3. Long, Ethan & Frawley, Keith, illus. (p. 2156)
Urfe, Honore D. Conclusion et Dernière Partie d'Astree, Ou Par Plusieurs Histoires et Sous Personnes de Bergers et

d'Autres, Sont déduits les Divers Effects de l'Honneste Amitié (Classic Reprint) (p. 438)
Urias, Abraham, illus. see Amado, Elisa.
Uribe, Luisa, illus. see Burnett, Frances Hodgson.
Uribe, Luisa, illus. see Churnin, Nancy.
Uribe, Luisa, illus. see Gianferrari, Maria.
Uribe, Luisa, illus. see Haydu, Corey Ann.
Uribe, Luisa, illus. see Houghton Mifflin Harcourt, Houghton Mifflin.
Uribe, Luisa, illus. see Mangal, Mélina.
Uribe, Luisa, illus. see Montgomery, L. M.
Uribe, Luisa, illus. see Perez de la Iglesia, Janina.
Uribe, Luisa, jt. auth. see Haydu, Corey Ann.
Uribe Urbieta, Kirmen & Lete, Nere. Garmendia & the Black Rider. (p. 810)
Uribe, Verónica. Aquí Veo. (p. 108)
Uribe, Verónica, tr. see Young, Ed, ed.
Urío, Bàrbara Castro. Goodnight, Rainbow Cats: (Baby Shower Gift, Bedtime Board Book, Children's Cat Themed Board Book) (p. 868)
Urish, J. D. Adventures of Rex Bolton Volume 1. (p. 27)
Urmston, Kathleen. When Sammy Was a Puppy. Torrisi, Gary, illus. (p. 2432)
—When Sammy Was a Puppy (6 Pack) Tottisi, Gary, illus. (p. 2432)
Urmy, William Smith. Lost & Found (Classic Reprint) (p. 1352)
Urner, Mabel Herbert. Journal of a Neglected Wife, 1909 (Classic Reprint) (p. 1180)
—Woman Alone (Classic Reprint) (p. 2485)
Urner, Nathan D. Never: A Hand-Book for the Uninitiated & Inexperienced Aspirants to Refined Society's Giddy Heights & Glittering (Classic Reprint) (p. 1589)
—Never. (p. 1589)
Urosevic, Irena, illus. see Manning, James & Ridgeway, Nicola.
Urquhart, Debra. Storm Riders. (p. 2126)
Urquhart, Elizabeth. Suited at Last or Sauce Bordelaise: A Comedy in One Act (Classic Reprint) (p. 2148)
Urquhart, Jessie. Wayside (Classic Reprint) (p. 2388)
Urquhart, Kristina Mercedes. Making Music with Magnets. (p. 1389)
Urquhart, M. Wheel: A Book of Beginnings (Classic Reprint) (p. 2427)
Urquhart, Mercedes Kristina. Botanical Illustration (Grade 3) (p. 264)
Urquhart, Thomas. Works of Francis Rabelais, Vol. 2 Of 2: Translated from the French (Classic Reprint) (p. 2497)
Urquhart, Thomas, jt. auth. see Rabelais, Francois.
Urquhart, Tiffany. Many Hats of Hank. (p. 1400)
Urru, Franco, illus. see Lynch, Brian.
Urruela, Maria Cristina, tr. see McCalla Njee, Lena.
Ursache, Daniela, tr. see Popescu, Sinziana.
Ursell, Martin. You Can Draw Cartoons: A Step-By-Step Guide to Drawing Great Cartoons. (p. 2525)
—You Can Draw Horses. (p. 2525)
—You Can Draw Wild Animals. (p. 2526)
Ursell, Martin, illus. see Benton, Lynne.
Ursell, Martin, illus. see Goodhart, Pippa.
Ursell, Martin, illus. see Julia, Donaldson.
Ursell, Martin, illus. see Laird, Elizabeth.
Ursell, Martin, illus. see Martineau, Susan.
Ursell, Martin, illus. see Rabley, Stephen.
Ursida, Francis. Kiddy Tales. (p. 1213)
Ursu, Anne. Breadcrumbs. (p. 277)
—Breadcrumbs. McGuire, Erin, illus. (p. 277)
—Immortal Fire. Swaab, Neil, illus. (p. 1101)
—Lost Girl. (p. 1353)
—Real Boy. McGuire, Erin, illus. (p. 1849)
Ursula, Ursula. Mrs. Greville, Vol. 1 Of 3: The Story of a Woman's Life (Classic Reprint) (p. 1522)
Uruno, Munetsugu, jt. auth. see Rost, Michael.
Urwin, Kirsten. Betsy Ross & the Creation of the American Flag. (p. 209)
Ury, Laura, illus. see Redmond, Mark L.
Urzi, Giuseppe. Fatti Sentire! Come Migliorare la Tua Voce per Migliorare le Tue Relazioni. (p. 715)
U.S. Defense Dept. & Defense Department Staff, eds. Julie & the Atom. (p. 1187)
Us Now, illus. see Whitfield, Jakob.
USA Today Staff, contrib. by. USA Today Weather Wonders: Discover What's up & What's Coming Down. (p. 2341)
Usache?v, Andrei?. Veselye Stikhi. T?s?ygankova, I., illus. (p. 2354)
Usai, Luca, illus. see Cavalieri, Joey & Caramagna, Joe.
Usai, Luca, illus. see Ferrari, Alessandro.
Usai, Luca, illus. see Macchetto, Augusto.
Usai, Luca, illus. see Stilton, Geronimo & Heim, Julia.
Usai, Luca, illus. see Stilton, Geronimo & Schaffer, Andrea.
Usai, Luca, illus. see Stilton, Geronimo, et al.
Usatsuka, Eiji, illus. see Fuyuhara, Patora.
Usborne Books, creator. Usborne Big Book of Christmas Things to Make & Do. (p. 2341)
Usborne Books Staff, creator. Usborne Doodle Pad for Boys. (p. 2341)
—Usborne Doodle Pad for Girls. (p. 2341)
USCCB Department of Justice, Peace, and Human Development. Drop by Drop. (p. 605)
—Everyone Belongs. (p. 672)
—Green Street Park. (p. 895)
Uschan, Michael, jt. auth. see Pina, Andrew.
Uschan, Michael V. Alex Rodriguez. (p. 42)
—Apolo Anton Ohno. (p. 106)
—Blues. (p. 250)
—Careers If You Like Government & Politics. (p. 329)
—Careers in Law Enforcement. (p. 330)
—Chinese Mythology. (p. 378)
—Civil Rights Movement. (p. 396)
—Comic Art. (p. 429)
—Golf. Greenhaven Press Editors, ed. (p. 860)
—Graffiti. (p. 875)
—Halle Berry. (p. 911)
—Human Rights in Focus: Refugees. (p. 1050)
—James Foreman & SNCC. Greenaven Press Staff, ed. (p. 1156)
—Jet Li. (p. 1167)
—Joe Biden. (p. 1171)
—Michelle Obama. (p. 1458)
—Serena Williams. (p. 1990)
—Transcontinental Railroad. (p. 2277)
—Watergate. (p. 2386)
Uschan, Michael V., jt. auth. see Crewe, Sabrina.
Uschan, Michael V., jt. auth. see Goff, Elizabeth Hudson.
Uschan, Michael V., jt. auth. see Hudson Goff, Elizabeth.
Uschan, Michael V., jt. auth. see Lucent Books Staff.
Uschan, Michael V. & Juettner, Bonnie. Will Smith. (p. 2467)
Usdin, Carly. Avant-Guards Vol. 1. Hayes, Noah, illus. (p. 141)
—Avant-Guards Vol. 2. Hayes, Noah, illus. (p. 141)
—Heavy Vinyl: Y2K-O! Vakueva, Nina, illus. (p. 947)
used), Sherry Anne (not. Quiet Wyatt Is a Riot! (p. 1828)
Usher, M. D. Golden Ass of Lucius Apuleius. Motley, T., illus. (p. 856)
Usher, Roland G. Story of the Pilgrims for Children, Vol. 1 (Classic Reprint) (p. 2134)
Usher, Sam. Snow. Usher, Sam, illus. (p. 2046)
—Storm. Usher, Sam, illus. (p. 2126)
—Sun. Usher, Sam, illus. (p. 2151)
Usher, Sam, illus. see Booth, Anne.
Usher, Sam, illus. see Goodhart, Pippa.
Usher, Sam, illus. see McAllister, Cameron.
Usher, Sam, illus. see Toht, Patricia.
Ushinski?, K. D. Skazki Za Piat' Minut. (p. 2030)
Ushler, John, illus. see Reilly, Frank.
Usikova, Nasia. Boris Wants a Dog. (p. 263)
Uslan, Michael. Dinosaucers Vol. 1. (p. 548)
Usova, Victoria, illus. see Ross, Warren.
Usry, Tralyne. Sweet Jambalaya. (p. 2169)
Uss, Christina. Adventures of a Girl Called Bicycle. (p. 21)
—Colossus of Roads. (p. 427)
Uss, John & Benchmark Education Co., LLC Staff. Dan & Ed. (p. 499)
Usual Gang of Idiots Staff. Totally Useless Mad. (p. 2267)
Utchenko, Olga, illus. see Clever Publishing.
Uthoff, Jessie K. Courage to Be You: Empowering Notes for Girls & Women. (p. 462)
Utkin, Alexander. Gamayun Tales I: An Anthology of Modern Russian Folk Tales (Volume I) (p. 806)
—Tyna of the Lake: Gamayun Tales Vol. 3. (p. 2310)
—Water Spirit: Gamayun Tales Vol. 2. (p. 2385)
Utkina, Olga, jt. auth. see Clever Publishing.
Utkina, Olga & Clever Publishing. Clever Colors Photo Book: 700 Things to Learn. (p. 404)
—Fun Things to Do: Puzzles, Mazes & More. (p. 800)
—Things That Vroom! (p. 2221)
Utley, J. Stacy, illus. see Harvey Mph, Janera P.
Utomo, Gabhor, illus. see DeGezelle, Terri.
Utomo, Gabhor, illus. see Ditto, Denise.
Utomo, Gabhor, illus. see Gilligan, Alison.
Utomo, Gabhor, illus. see Hillert, Margaret, et al.
Utomo, Gabhor, illus. see Hillert, Margaret.
Utomo, Gabhor, illus. see Lake, Joan.
Utomo, Gabhor, illus. see Laviera, Tato.
Utomo, Gabhor, illus. see Leibold, Jay.
Utomo, Gabhor, illus. see Montgomery, R. A.
Utomo, Gabhor, illus. see Ruiz-Flores, Lupe.
Utomo, Gabhor, illus. see Simpson, C. E.
Utomo, Gabhor, illus. see Windover, Liz.
Utopia, illus. see Shears, William.
Utsey, Jan. Sefer, Vol. 3: A Literary Magazine Presented by the Baptist College at Charleston; Spring, 1973 (Classic Reprint) (p. 1985)
—Sefer, Vol. 4: Fall, 1973 (Classic Reprint) (p. 1985)
Utt, Mary Ann, jt. illus. see Rader, Laura.
Utterly Global Youth Empowerment. Anti-Bullying Club/Project Manual. (p. 102)
Uttley, Alison & Bray, Phyllis. Traveller in Time. (p. 2280)
Uttley, Colin. Experiments with Force & Motion. (p. 678)
Utton, Peter, illus. see Grindley, Sally.
Uttridge, Sarah. Dinosaurs Around the World. (p. 551)
—Horses Around the World. (p. 1005)
—Jungle Animals Around the World. (p. 1189)
—Mammals Around the World. (p. 1393)
—Ocean Animals Around the World. (p. 1635)
—Sharks & Sea Creatures Around the World. (p. 2002)
—Snakes & Reptiles Around the World. (p. 2044)
—Spiders & Bugs Around the World. (p. 2081)
Utz, Brigitte. Mathilde. (p. 1424)
Uwabami. Bam Bam & a Bun Go to an Adventure. (p. 163)
Uwiringiyimana, Sandra & Abigail Pesta. How Dare the Sun Rise: Memoirs of a War Child. (p. 1027)
Uwiringiyimana, Sandra & Pesta, Abigail. How Dare the Sun Rise: Memoirs of a War Child. (p. 1027)
Uxó, Carlos, tr. see O'Reilly, Bill.
Uya, Nivola, illus. see Ayats, Marc.
Uya, Nivola, illus. see Eulate, Ana.
Uya, Nivola, illus. see Pavon, Mar.
Uyeda, Laura. Bing Bong Book. Tilley, Scott, illus. (p. 228)
Uyeh, Orezime A. Girls for Medicine. (p. 838)
Uyetake, Neil, illus. see Anderson, Ted.
Uyetake, Neil, illus. see Cook, Katie & Nuhfer, Heather.
Uyetake, Neil, illus. see Rice, Christina.
Uyetake, Neil, illus. see Zahler, Thom.
Uzelac, Rosemary J., jt. auth. see Downing, James B.
Uzon, Jorge. Go, Baby, Go! (p. 845)
—Look Around, Baby! (p. 1345)
—Not a Baby Anymore! (p. 1622)
Uzorova, Olga & Clever Publishing. Palm Painting. Level 1: Stickers Inside! Strengthens Fine Motor Skills, Develops Patience, Sparks Conversation, Inspires Creativity. (p. 1694)
Uzorova, Olga & Nefedova, Elena. Finger Painting. Level 1: Stickers Inside! Strengthens Fine Motor Skills, Develops Patience, Sparks Conversation, Inspires Creativity. Sergeeva, Masha, illus. (p. 731)
—Finger Painting Level 2: Stickers Inside! Strengthens Fine Motor Skills, Develops Patience, Sparks Conversation, Inspires Creativity. Sergeeva, Masha, illus. (p. 731)
—Palm Painting Level 2: Stickers Inside! Strengthens Fine Motor Skills, Develops Patience, Sparks Conversation, Inspires Creativity. Sergeeva, Masha, illus. (p. 1694)
Uzzell, Ashley. Tales of Mentara: Book One: the Portal. (p. 2184)
—Tales of Mentara: Book Two: the Ritual. (p. 2184)
—Where's My Kitty? (p. 2440)

V

V Alexandrov, John. Axdorian Fairy Tales. (p. 145)
V Chellappan Iyer. Interview an Innerview: Job & Joy... . for You. (p. 1127)
V, Ram. Essential Singularity. (p. 664)
V Ramos, Caio H. Mar. (p. 1402)
V, Sarah. Old Man. DuBois, Claude, illus. (p. 1647)
V, V. Special Day Programme Bulletin: For Use in Virginia Public Schools & Community Leagues (Classic Reprint) (p. 2076)
V, Vasanthi. Toy-Gobbling Monster. Lee, Anais, illus. (p. 2270)
Va, State Normal School Farmville. Focus, Vol. 4: Alumnae Number; June, 1914 (Classic Reprint) (p. 756)
—Focus, Vol. 6: March, 1916 (Classic Reprint) (p. 756)
—Focus, Vol. 8: May, 1918 (Classic Reprint) (p. 756)
Vaca, Sally, illus. see Darden, Hunter.
Vacaresco, Helene. Kings & Queens I Have Known (Classic Reprint) (p. 1222)
Vacaro, Matt. Sleepy Monkey. (p. 2037)
Vacca, John, et al. Identity Theft. (p. 1089)
Vacca, Richard T., jt. auth. see Marrow, Lesley Mandel.
Vaccarini, Franco. Fuiste Vos, Robot. Bustos, Ignacio, illus. (p. 797)
—Sombrero Del Muerto y Otros Cuentos Extraños. (p. 2058)
Vaccarino, Lucia. Escalofríos en Halloween. (p. 661)
Vaccaro Seeger, Laura. Bear in the Chair. (p. 179)
—Blue. (p. 247)
—Bully. Vaccaro Seeger, Laura, illus. (p. 296)
Vaccaro Seeger, Laura, illus. see Jackson, Richard.
Vachell, Horace Annesley. Brothers: The True History of a Fight Against Odds (Classic Reprint) (p. 286)
—Brothers, Vol. 1 Of 2: The True History of a Fight Against Odds (Classic Reprint) (p. 286)
—Bunch Grass: A Chronicle of Life on a Cattle Ranch. (p. 297)
—Bunch Grass: A Chronicle of Life on a Cattle Ranch (Classic Reprint) (p. 297)
—Drama in Sunshine: A Novel (Classic Reprint) (p. 596)
—Face of Clay: An Interpretation (Classic Reprint) (p. 693)
—Fishpingle: A Romance of the Countryside (Classic Reprint) (p. 742)
—Fourth Dimension (Classic Reprint) (p. 773)
—Her Son: A Chronicle of Love (Classic Reprint) (p. 956)
—Hill: A Romance of Friendship. (p. 971)
—Hill: A Romance of Friendship (Classic Reprint) (p. 971)
—John Charity: A Romance of Yesterday, Containing Certin Adventures & Love-Passages in Alta California of John Charity, Yeoman of Cranberry-Orcas in the County of Hampshire, England, As Set down by Himself (Classic Reprint) (p. 1172)
—John Verney (Classic Reprint) (p. 1174)
—Other Side: The Record of Certain Passages in the Life of a Genius (Classic Reprint) (p. 1675)
—Pinch of Prosperity (Classic Reprint) (p. 1745)
—Quinneys' (Classic Reprint) (p. 1828)
—Some Happenings (Classic Reprint) (p. 2059)
—Soul of Susan Yellam (Classic Reprint) (p. 2066)
—Sport & Life on the Pacific Slope (Classic Reprint) (p. 2087)
—Spragge's Canyon: A Character Study (Classic Reprint) (p. 2091)
—Triumph of Tim (Classic Reprint) (p. 2290)
—Waters of Jordan (Classic Reprint) (p. 2386)
—Whitewash (Classic Reprint) (p. 2445)
Vachss, Andrew. Heart Transplant. Caruso, Frank, illus. (p. 946)
Vachula, Monica, illus. see Longfellow, Henry & Boyds Mills Press Staff.
Vachula, Monica, illus. see Longfellow, Henry.
Vachula, Monica, illus. see Shea, Pegi Deitz.
Vachutinsky, Yuri, illus. see Boger, Yuval S.
Vacura, Merri, illus. see McAlpine, Janice.
Vadalia, Hemali, illus. see Graham, Rita Z.
Vadivelu, Avanti Pradhan. Not So Lucky Brother: The Not So Lucky Brother. (p. 1623)
Vadney, Jackie. Pokey's Promise: A Charming Tale of Telling Time. Balogh, Jared, illus. (p. 1768)
Vaganos, Erin, illus. see Turnbull, Elizabeth.
Vagin, Vladimir, illus. see Asch, Frank.
Vagin, Vladimir, illus. see Paterson, Katherine.
Vagin, Vladimir, illus. see Yolen, Jane.
Vagner, Bohdanka. Bullying, Change, Friendship & Trust. Montgomerie, Genevieve, illus. (p. 297)
Vagnozzi, Barbara, illus. see Atkins, Jill.
Vagnozzi, Barbara, illus. see Rock, Lois.
Vagnozzi, Barbara, illus. see Scribens, Sunny.
Vagnozzi, Barbara, illus. see Shand, Jennifer.
Vago, Mike. Rocket: A Journey Through the Pages Book. Rockefeller, Matt, illus. (p. 1895)
—Train: A Journey Through the Pages Book. Rockefeller, Matt, illus. (p. 2275)
Vagues, Terrains. DIY Afternoon: Paper. (p. 566)
Vahdani, Kataneh. Kat & Juju. (p. 1204)
Vahidi, Mohd, tr. see King, Dedie.
Vahle, Joseph. Jerico Papers: A Quaint & Amusing Side of Early New England Life (Classic Reprint) (p. 1164)
Vahrenkamp, William. House the Blind-Man Built, Illustrated: A Synopsis of a Blind-Man's Methods of Building a House, Showing Courage & Patience Seldom Found in Human Beings (Classic Reprint) (p. 1024)
Vaicikonis, Kris. Puzzle Me-Brain Twisters. (p. 1818)
Vaid, Michelle. MR Peter's Adventures in Siracusa, Sicily: Le Avventure Di Peter a Siracusa, Sicilia. Tusa, Paola, illus. (p. 1520)
Vaid, Stephen. Moo's Walk. (p. 1503)
Vaid-Menon, Alok. Beyond the Gender Binary. Lukashevsky, Ashley, illus. (p. 212)
Vaidyanathan, Sheena. Creative Coding in Python: 30+ Programming Projects in Art, Games, & More. (p. 470)
Vail, Barry. Little Book of Too Familiar Family Verse: To Which Are Added a Few Philuppics (Classic Reprint) (p. 1312)
Vail, Grace. Bird Watcher's Guide to Sparrows. (p. 231)
—Death Valley. (p. 522)
—Dolphin Doubles. (p. 579)
—Earthquakes: Energy in Motion. (p. 618)
—Hunting with Hawks (p. 1054)
—Jaguars. (p. 1155)
—More Freaky Weather Stories (p. 1504)
—Motors & Generators. (p. 1512)
Vail, Noah. Stover in Bones (Classic Reprint) (p. 2136)
Vail, Rachel. Bad Best Friend. (p. 157)
—Big Mouth Elizabeth. Keiser, Paige, illus. (p. 221)
—Brilliant. (p. 282)
—Cat Ears on Elizabeth. Keiser, Paige, illus. (p. 341)
—Doodlebug Elizabeth. Keiser, Paige, illus. (p. 584)
—Gorgeous. (p. 870)
—Is for Elizabeth. Keiser, Paige, illus. (p. 1136)
—Justin Case: School, Drool, & Other Daily Disasters. Cordell, Matthew, illus. (p. 1195)
—Justin Case: Shells, Smells, & the Horrible Flip-Flops of Doom Cordell, Matthew, illus. (p. 1195)
—Kiss Me Again. (p. 1224)
—Lucky. (p. 1364)
—Rules, Tools, & Maybe a Bully. (p. 1913)
—Shells, Smells, & the Horrible Flip-Flops of Doom. Cordell, Matthew, illus. (p. 2005)
—Unfriended. (p. 2327)
—Well, That Was Awkward. (p. 2399)
Vail, Rachel, jt. auth. see Avi.
Vail, Sue, tr. see Powers, David M. F.
Vaile, Charlotte M. M. M. C: A Story of the Great Rockies (Classic Reprint) (p. 1370)
—Sue Orcutt a Sequel to the Orcutt Girls (Classic Reprint) (p. 2147)
—Wheat & Huckleberries or Dr. Northmore's Daughters (Classic Reprint) (p. 2427)
Vaile, Cyril. Liza of Bourke's & Other Stories. (p. 1336)
—Liza of Bourke's, & Other Stories (Classic Reprint) (p. 1336)
Vaillancourt, François, jt. auth. see Tibo, Gilles.
Vaillant, Tom, illus. see Daugey, Fleur.
Vainreb, M., illus. see Irenshtain, Hadas.
Vairous. Diamond Fairy Book: From the Many Countries. Pape, Frank & Millar, H. R., illus. (p. 538)
—More Celtic Fairy Tales: [Illustrated Edition]. Jacobs, Joseph, ed. (p. 1504)
—More Celtic Fairy Tales: [illustrated Edition]. Jacobs, Joseph, ed. (p. 1504)
Vaisberg, Diego, illus. see Graham, Ian.
Vaisberg, Diego, illus. see Hubbard, Ben C.
Vaisberg, Diego, illus. see Hubbard, Ben.
Vaisberg, Diego, illus. see Walter Foster Jr. Creative Team.
Vaisberg, Diego & DGPH Stufio Staff. Dino. Vaisberg, Diego & DGPH Stufio Staff, illus. (p. 547)
Vaitonis, Steven. Edison the Christmas Elf & the Imperfect Perfect Toy. Blue, Melissa, illus. (p. 626)
Vaizey, G. de Horne. Daughters of a Genius: A Story of Brave Endeavour (Classic Reprint) (p. 509)
Vaizey, George de Horne. Lady Cassandra (Classic Reprint) (p. 1236)
—Question of Marriage (Classic Reprint) (p. 1826)
Vajda, Joseph. Great Orange. Kis, Gabor Norbert, illus. (p. 888)
—Michael Jones -. the First Encounter. (p. 1457)
Vaka, Demetra. Child of the Orient (Classic Reprint) (p. 370)
—Grasp of the Sultan (Classic Reprint) (p. 881)
—Haremlik: Some Pages from the Life of Turkish Women (Classic Reprint) (p. 930)
—Heart of the Balkans (Classic Reprint) (p. 945)
—In the Shadow of Islam (Classic Reprint) (p. 1111)
—Modern Greek Stories (Classic Reprint) (p. 1486)
Vakueva, Nina. League of Legends: Ashe - Warmother. (p. 1254)
Vakueva, Nina, illus. see Usdin, Carly.
Vala, Courtney. Tippi Tie Toe: The Adventures of Bits N Boots. (p. 2250)
Valadi, Nashmin, illus. see Webster, William, ed.
Valan, photos by see Fowler, Allan.
Valat, Pierre-Marie. My First Discoveries - Fruits. (p. 1543)
—Pirates. (p. 1750)
—Water. Valat, Pierre-Marie, illus. (p. 2384)
Valat, Pierre-Marie, et al. Inside the Body. Best, Clare, tr. (p. 1123)
Valay, Ana Patricia. Giovani Dos Santos. (p. 834)
Valay, Ana Patricia & Sandoval, Ana Valay. Arnoldo Iguaran. (p. 118)
Valckx, Catharina. Bruno: Some of the More Interesting Days in My Life So Far. Hubesch, Nicolas, illus. (p. 287)
—Zanzibar. Valckx, Catharina, illus. (p. 2538)
Valde S, A. Palacio. Fourth Estate (Classic Reprint) (p. 773)
Valder, Hayim. Di Vunderlikhe Ertseylung Fun Moti. Heler, Moti, illus. (p. 536)
Valder, Justin, illus. see Valder, Margret.
Valder, Margret. Henry the Honey Bee. Valder, Justin, illus. (p. 955)
Valderrama, Linda N. Brush Barry Brush. Memarzadeh, Sudabeh, illus. (p. 288)
Valdes, Alisa. Perdition: A Kindred Novel. (p. 1721)
—Temptation: A Kindred Novel. (p. 2203)
Valdes, Armando Palacio. Fourth Estate, Vol. 2: Translated from the Spanish (Classic Reprint) (p. 773)
—Froth: A Novel (Classic Reprint) (p. 795)
—Grandee: A Novel (Classic Reprint) (p. 877)
—Jose (Classic Reprint) (p. 1178)
—José (Classic Reprint) (p. 1178)
Valdes, Don Armando Palacio. Maximina (Classic Reprint) (p. 1428)
Valdes, Ernesto R., illus. see Ruano, Tony.
Valdes, Palacio. Fourth Estate, Vol. 1 (Classic Reprint) (p. 773)

—Marquis of Penalta (Marta y Maria) A Realistic Social Novel (Classic Reprint) (p. 1408)
Valdez, Joseph G. Lean on Me, Lee. Martinez, Gayle Denise, illus. (p. 1255)
Valdez, Max. SINNER & the SERVANT. (p. 2024)
Valdez, Patricia. Joan Procter, Dragon Doctor: The Woman Who Loved Reptiles. Sala, Felicita, illus. (p. 1170)
Valdez Y Alanis, Erik, illus. see Capstone Press Staff.
Valdivia, Paloma. Up above & down Below. (p. 2337)
Valdivia, Paloma, illus. see Giménez de Ory, Beatriz.
Valdivia, Paloma, illus. see Ortiz, Estrella.
Valdrighi, Alessandro, illus. see Apps, Roy.
Valdrighi, Alessandro, illus. see Braun, Eric Mark, et al.
Valdrighi, Alessandro, illus. see Braun, Eric Mark.
Valdrighi, Alessandro, illus. see Ganeri, Anita.
Valdrighi, Alessandro, illus. see Grennan, Conor.
Valdrighi, Alessandro, illus. see Hoena, Blake.
Valdrighi, Alessandro, illus. see Yomtov, Nel.
Vale, Ferna. Natalie: Or, a Gem among the Sea-Weeds (Classic Reprint) (p. 1576)
Vale, Jenna. Tracking Ghosts & Hauntings. (p. 2272)
—Tracking the Loch Ness Monster. (p. 2272)
Vale, Jenna & Gilman, Laura Anne. Tracking the Yeti. (p. 2272)
Vale, Jenna & Rosenberg, Aaron. Tracking the Bermuda Triangle. (p. 2272)
Vale, Jenna & Stirling, Janet. Tracking UFOs. (p. 2272)
Vale, Joe, ed. see Triplett, Annette.
Vale, Lillie. Small Town Hearts. (p. 2040)
Valencia, Esau Andrade, illus. see Sáenz, Benjamin Alire.
Valencia, Vanessa. Mamma's Planet Earth. (p. 1393)
Valens, Victor Manuel, jt. auth. see Behnke, Alison.
Valente, Catherynne M. Boy Who Lost Fairyland. Juan, Ana, illus. (p. 271)
—Girl Who Circumnavigated Fairyland in a Ship of Her Own Making. (p. 837)
—Girl Who Circumnavigated Fairyland in a Ship of Her Own Making. Juan, Ana, illus. (p. 837)
—Girl Who Fell Beneath Fairyland & Led the Revels There. Juan, Ana, illus. (p. 837)
—Girl Who Soared over Fairyland & Cut the Moon in Two. Juan, Ana, illus. (p. 837)
—Glass Town Game. (p. 841)
—Glass Town Game. Green, Rebecca, illus. (p. 841)
—Smoky & the Feast of Mabon: A Magical Child Story. (p. 2043)
Valente, Dominique. Starfell #1: Willow Moss & the Lost Day. (p. 2106)
Valente, Gianna Josephina, illus. see Overstreet, Karen LaFaye.
Valente, Peter Isaiah, illus. see Overstreet, Karen LaFaye.
Valente, Sarah Hawkes & Hawkes Jr, George W. Jobear. Mykhalevych, Viktoriia, illus. (p. 1170)
Valenti, Joseph. NERO Rule Book: 8th Edition. (p. 1588)
Valenti, Karla. Marie Curie & the Power of Persistence. Beghelli, Annalisa, illus. (p. 1405)
Valentin, Gabriel. Grundriss der Physiologie des Menschen: Fur das Erste Studium und Zur Selbstbelehrung (Classic Reprint) (p. 901)
—Lehrbuch der Physiologie des Menschen, Vol. 1 Of 2: Für Ärzte und Studirende (Classic Reprint) (p. 1265)
—Lehrbuch der Physiologie des Menschen, Vol. 2 Of 2: Für Aerzte und Studirende (Classic Reprint) (p. 1265)
Valentin, Jean. Bravery of Amelia Earhart. (p. 277)
Valentin, Karen. Allie's World: Abuela & Abuelo Move: Abuela & Abuelo Move. (p. 56)
—Block Party. (p. 245)
—What Did Abuela Say? (p. 2407)
—When Are We Going to the Beach? (p. 2429)
Valentina, Serena, jt. auth. see Gray, Amy.
Valentine. Eastern Tales (Classic Reprint) (p. 620)
—Old Fairy Tales (Classic Reprint) (p. 1645)
Valentine, Allison, illus. see Cook, Julia & Jana, Laura.
Valentine, Allison, illus. see Cook, Julia.
Valentine, Amanda, ed. see Harris, Carrie.
Valentine, Bridget. Building with Shapes: Analyze, Compare, Create, & Compose Shapes. (p. 295)
Valentine Davies Estate, et al. Dear Santa & Miracle on 34th Street Picture Book Gift Set: Christmas Books for Kids. Newman Gray, James & Joseph, John, illus. (p. 520)
Valentine Davis Estate Staff & Hill, Susanna Leonard. Miracle on 34th Street. (p. 1474)
Valentine, E. Seton. Travels in Space: A History of Aerial Navigation (Classic Reprint) (p. 2281)
Valentine, Ed, jt. auth. see Scollon, Bill.
Valentine, Edward Uffington. Hecla Sandwith (Classic Reprint) (p. 947)
Valentine, James. Stuff Happens: Luke. (p. 2144)
Valentine, Jenny. Broken Soup. (p. 285)
—Fire Color One. (p. 732)
—Hello Now. (p. 951)
—Me, the Missing, & the Dead. (p. 1433)
Valentine, L. We Three Boys: Or a Year of Adventure (Classic Reprint) (p. 2392)
Valentine, L. D. Rising. (p. 1886)
Valentine, Luke, illus. see Sparer, E. G.
Valentine, Luna, illus. see Lute, Renee Beauregard.
Valentine, M. K., illus. see Fantastik, B.
Valentine, Madeline. George in the Dark. (p. 819)
—I Want That Nut! (p. 1084)
Valentine, Madeline, illus. see Detlefsen, Lisl H.
Valentine, Madeline, illus. see Sullivan, Sarah.
Valentine, Madeline, illus. see Trimmer, Christian.
Valentine, Madeline, illus. see Urban, Linda.
Valentine, Madeline, illus. see Ziarnik, Natalie.
Valentine, Mann Satterwhite. Mock Auction: Ossawatomie Sold, a Mock Heroic Poem (Classic Reprint) (p. 1485)
Valentine, Nancy. I Heart My Dentist. (p. 1066)
Valentine, Nicole. Time Traveler's Theory of Relativity. (p. 2246)
Valentine, Salisia. God Loves Me So Much. (p. 851)
Valentine, Sophie. Zoo Hullabaloo (p. 2543)
Valentine, Stephen J. Lazarus Game. (p. 1254)
Valentine, Susan. Molly & Ollie: The Great Adventure to France. (p. 1489)
Valentine, Tanya. Little Taco Truck. Martin, Jorge, illus. (p. 1328)
Valentine, Teresa, ed. see Marsh, Carole.
Valentine, Valerie, ed. see Fitzgerald, J.D.
Valentine, William. Budget of Wit & Humour (Classic Reprint) (p. 290)
—Dr. Valentine & Yankee Hill's Metamorphoses: Being the Second Series of Dr. Valentine's Comic Lectures, with Characters As Given by the Late Yankee Hill (Classic Reprint) (p. 592)
Valentini, Cristiana. Stay, Little Seed. Giordano, Philip, illus. (p. 2109)
Valentini, Enzo. Letters & Drawings of Enzo Valentini: Conte Di Laviano, Italian Volunteer & Soldier (Classic Reprint) (p. 1279)
Valentini, Julian A. Defiant. (p. 525)
Valentin-Natale, Zoraida. Blossom & Friends. (p. 247)
Valentino, Russell Scott, tr. see Tamaro, Susanna.
Valentino, Serena. Beast Within: A Tale of Beauty's Prince. Disney Storybook Art Team, illus. (p. 182)
—Evil Thing. (p. 674)
—Fairest of All: A Tale of the Wicked Queen. (p. 695)
—How to Be a Werewolf: The Claws-On Guide for the Modern Lycanthrope. (p. 1037)
—Mistress of All Evil: A Tale of the Dark Fairy. (p. 1483)
—Mother Knows Best: A Tale of the Old Witch. (p. 1510)
—Odd Sisters: A Villains Novel. (p. 1637)
—Poor Unfortunate Soul: A Tale of the Sea Witch. Disney Storybook Art Team, illus. (p. 1775)
—Serena Valentino's Villains Box Set: Books 1-3 Disney Storybook Art Team, illus. (p. 1990)
Valentino, Serena, jt. auth. see Calle, Juan.
Valentino, Serena & Disney Book Group. Fairest of All: A Tale of the Wicked Queen. Disney Storybook Art Team, illus. (p. 695)
Valenza, Bryan, illus. see Higgins, Kyle.
Valenzuela, Anabelle. Day an Angel Ran into My Room. Latham, Sarah, illus. (p. 512)
Valenzuela, Jose Ignacio. Hashtag / Hashtag. (p. 936)
—Mi Tío Pachunga / My Uncle Pachunga. (p. 1456)
Valenzuela, José Ignacio. ¿De Qué Color Es Tu Sombra? (p. 517)
Valenzuela, Kristine. Secret Sydney. Green, Matthew, illus. (p. 1979)
Valenzuela, Liliana, tr. see Alvarez, Julia.
Valenzuela, Luisa. ABC de Las Microfabulas. (p. 3)
Valerga, Susan L. Esperanza (Classic Reprint) (p. 662)
Valeri, Jennifer. God from A-Z: A Child's Guide to Learning about God. (p. 851)
Valeria, Leonova, illus. see Nicoloro-Tanner, Nancy.
Valério, Geraldo. At the Pond (p. 131)
—Blue Rider (p. 249)
—Blue Rider. (p. 249)
—Egg. (p. 628)
—Go to Sleep, Gecko! A Balinese Folktale. (p. 848)
—Moose, Goose, Animals on the Loose! A Canadian Wildlife ABC. (p. 1503)
—My Book of Birds (p. 1534)
—Turn on the Night (p. 2300)
Valerio, Geraldo, illus. see Harby, Melanie.
Valério, Geraldo, illus. see Heneghan, James & McBay, Bruce.
Valério, Geraldo, illus. see Hickman, Pamela.
Valério, Geraldo, illus. see MacDonald, Margaret Read.
Valério, Geraldo, illus. see Spinelli, Eileen.
Valério, Geraldo, jt. auth. see Valério, Geraldo.
Valério, Geraldo & Valério, Geraldo. Canadian Animals 123. (p. 320)
—Canadian Animals ABC. (p. 320)
—Canadian Animals in Colour. (p. 320)
—Jump, Leap, Count Sheep! A Canadian Wildlife 123. (p. 1188)
—Splish, Splash, Foxes Dash! Canadian Wildlife in Colour. (p. 2085)
Valero, Andrew Stephan, creator. Hero's Helmet Saga (full Version) (p. 963)
Vales, Chrissie, illus. see Paticoff, Melanie.
Valett, Ann. Clique Bait. (p. 406)
Vali, Ali. Blue Skies. (p. 249)
Valiant, Kristi, illus. see Accord Publishing Staff.
Valiant, Kristi, illus. see Galante, Cecilia.
Valiant, Kristi, illus. see Lazo Gilmore, Dorina K.
Valiant, Kristi, illus. see Matthies, Jana.
Valiant, Kristi, illus. see Matthies, Janna.
Valiant, Kristi, illus. see Ohrt, Kate.
Valiant, Kristi, illus. see Pataki, Allison & Myers, Marya.
Valiant, Kristi, illus. see Steel, Danielle.
Valice, Kimberly Lynn Perez. Orca Scientists. Comins, Andy, photos by. (p. 1669)
Valk, Laurens. Lego Mindstorms NXT 2. 0 Discovery Book: A Beginner's Guide to Building & Programming Robots. (p. 1265)
Valko, Danna. Dee & Maya Are Best Friends. (p. 524)
Valko, Diane, illus. see Kupperstein, Joel.
Valko, Diane, illus. see McFarren, Kathleen & Graf, Mike.
Valla, Susanne, illus. see Ehnes, Tiffany.
Valladares, Ellen Wolfson. Crossing the Line. (p. 478)
Valladares, Ellen Wolfson & Wolfson, Steve. Filbert the Lonely Flamingo. (p. 726)
Vallade, Jean François. Discours Philosophique Sur la Creation et l'Arrangement du Monde: Où l'on Fait Voir les Rapports Qu'il y a Entre les Creatures, et Leur Dependance Sous les Loix de la Providence (Classic Reprint) (p. 553)
Vallageas, Coralie, illus. see Fowler, Cherry.
Vallance, Ashley. Sandy the Sea Turtle. (p. 1931)
Vallarino, Elisa, illus. see Macri, Giancarlo, et al.
Vallarino, Sacco, illus. see Lavagno, Enrico.
Vallat, Christelle. Celia. Augusseau, Stphanie, illus. (p. 350)
Valle, Anita. Best Princess Coloring Book. (p. 207)
Valle, Elizabeth, illus. see Lihn, Henry.
Valle, Isabel. Epitaphs of Some Dear Dumb Beasts (Classic Reprint) (p. 659)
Vall'e, Jean-Louis. Chouette(la) (p. 382)
Valle, Mercedes, jt. auth. see Miller, Sara.
Valle, Nick Della. Inn Keeper of Bethlehem (p. 1120)
Valle, Suzette. 101 Movies to See Before You Grow Up: Be Your Own Movie Critic—The Must-see Movie List for Kids. (p. 2558)
—101 Movies to See Before You Grow Up. (p. 2558)
Valleau, Gailon, illus. see Daulby, Joan.
Valleau, Gailon, illus. see Hearn, Emily.
Vallecchi, Alessandro, photos by see Williams, Megan K.
Vallejo, Esperanza, illus. see Quiroga, Horacio.
Vallejo, Francis, illus. see Orgill, Roxane.
Vallejo, Monse, illus. see Smit, Fb.
Vallejo, Monserratt, illus. see Smit, Fb.
Vallencourt, Margaret. History of Photography. (p. 979)
—Technology of the Industrial Revolution (p. 2197)
Vallepur, Shalini. Australia. (p. 138)
—People Did What in Ancient Egypt? (p. 1718)
—People Did What in Ancient Greece? (p. 1718)
—People Did What in the Viking Age? (p. 1718)
—USA. (p. 2340)
Valliant, Kristi, illus. see Cunningham, Elaine.
Vallières, Nathalie & Guion, Marine. Ocean Fun Box: Includes a Storybook & a 2-in-1 Puzzle. Miller, Jonathan & Dupuis, Karina, illus. (p. 1635)
Vallings, Harold. Transgression of Terence Clancy, Vol. 2 of 3 (Classic Reprint) (p. 2278)
—Transgression of Terencec Clancy, Vol. 1 of 3 (Classic Reprint) (p. 2278)
Vallone, Theresa. Lost Little Goslings. (p. 1355)
Vallorani, Giorgio, illus. see Driscoll, Laura & Disney Books.
Vallotton, Benjamin. Heart of Alsace (Classic Reprint) (p. 945)
—In the Land of Death (Classic Reprint) (p. 1109)
—Potterat & the War (Classic Reprint) (p. 1781)
Valls, Maribel Garcia. I Love You Because: Dad & Me Gratitude Book. (p. 1078)
—I Love You Because: Grandma & Me Gratitude Book. (p. 1078)
—I Love You Because: Grandpa & Me Gratitude Book. (p. 1078)
—I Love Your Because: Mom & Me Gratitude Book. (p. 1079)
—Te Amo Porque: Mama y Yo Libro de Gratitud. (p. 2194)
—Te Amo Porque: Papa y Yo Libro de Gratitud. (p. 2194)
—Te Amo Porque: Abuela y Yo Libro de Gratitud. (p. 2194)
—Te Amo Porque: Abuelo y Yo Libro de Gratitud. (p. 2194)
Valmond, T. S. Courier's Collection: The Bolaji Kingdoms Books 1-3. (p. 462)
Valney, Mona. Pluie. (p. 1763)
Valney, Mona & Dore, Bruno. Léon Ou Celui Qui Ne Savait Pas Changer de Couleur. (p. 1267)
Valney, Mona & Dutertre, Cedric. Étoiles de Loup. (p. 666)
—Loup et le Mystère de la Mort. (p. 1358)
Valois, Jane de St Remy de. Life of Jane de St. Remy de Valois, Heretofore Countess de la Motte, Vol. 1 Of 2: Containing a Circumstantial & Exact Detail of the Many Extraordinary Events Which Have Attended This Unfortunate Lady from Her Birth, & Contributed to Raise Her to T. (p. 1294)
Valois, Jean. Cours D'Hippiatrique: Comprenant des Notions Sur la Charpente Osseuse du Cheval, la Description de Toutes Ses Parties Extérieures, les Beautés et le Defectuosités Naturelles Ou Accidentelles Dont Elles Sont Susceptibles (Classic Reprint) (p. 462)
Valois, Jeanne De Saint. Life of Jane de St. Remy de Valois, Heretofore Countess de la Motte, Vol. 2 Of 2: Containing a Circumstantial & Exact Detail of the Many Extraordinary Events Which Have Attended This Unfortunate Lady from Her Birth, & Contributed to Raise Her to T. (p. 1294)
Valois, Jeanne De Saint-Re My De. Life of Jane de St. Remy de Valois, Heretofore Countess de la Motte, Vol. 2 Of 2: Containing a Circumstantial & Exact Detail of the Many Extraordinary Events Which Have Attended This Unfortunate Lady from Her Birth, & Contributed to Raise Her to T. (p. 1294)
Valois, Rob. Sonic the Hedgehog Mad Libs. (p. 2063)
Valois, Rob & Caravan Studios Staff. Spyro & the Giants. (p. 2094)
Valor, Caroline. Zesty's Starstruck Challenge. (p. 2540)
Valt, Cindy. Adventures of Couki & Broni: The Great Departure. (p. 22)
—Aventures de Couki et Broni: Le Grand Départ. Gagne, Alexandra, illus. (p. 142)
Valverde, Mariana. Force of Law (p. 764)
Valverde, Mikel, illus. see Atxaga, Bernardo & Costa, Margaret Jull.
Vamba, Vamba. Prince & His Ants (Ciondolino) (Classic Reprint) (p. 1793)
Vamos, Lesley, illus. see Brown, Ruby.
Vamos, Lesley, illus. see Diamond, Jill.
Vamos, Lesley, illus. see Helliar, Peter.
Vamos, Lesley, illus. see Sellner, Joelle.
Vamos, Lesley, jt. auth. see Helliar, Peter.
Vamos, Samantha R. Alphabet Boats. O'Rourke, Ryan, illus. (p. 58)
—Alphabet Trains. (p. 59)
—Alphabet Trains. O'Rourke, Ryan, illus. (p. 59)
—Cazuela That the Farm Maiden Stirred. López, Rafael, illus. (p. 348)
—Cazuela That the Farm Maiden Stirred. López, Rafael & López, Rafael, illus. (p. 348)
—Piñata That the Farm Maiden Hung. Serra, Sebastià, illus. (p. 1745)
Vamos, Samantha R., et al. Struttin' with Some Barbecue: Lil Harden Armstrong Becomes the First Lady of Jazz. O'Rourke, Ryan, illus. (p. 2142)
Vample, J. B. College Life 401: Senior Experience. (p. 415)
—College Life 402: Undergrad Completion. (p. 415)
Vample, Jessyca. College Life 202: Core Principles. (p. 415)
Van Allen, Lily. Lost & Found: Five People. Three Stories. New Beginnings. (p. 1352)
Van Allsburg, Chris. Jardin de Abdul Gazasi. (p. 1160)
—Jumanji. (p. 1188)
—Just a Dream. (p. 1192)
—Just a Dream. Van Allsburg, Chris, illus. (p. 1192)
—Just a Dream 25th Anniversary Edition. (p. 1192)
—Misadventures of Sweetie Pie. (p. 1476)
—Polar Express. (p. 1769)
—Polar Express Big Book. (p. 1770)
—Queen of the Falls. (p. 1824)
—Sweetest Fig. (p. 2169)
—Two Bad Ants. (p. 2307)
—Widow's Broom (25th Anniversary Edition) (p. 2461)
—Wreck of the Zephyr. (p. 2511)
Van Allsburg, Chris, et al. Chronicles of Harris Burdick: Fourteen Amazing Authors Tell the Tales. (p. 389)
Van Alst, Danielle. Delilah's Birthday Surprise. (p. 527)
Van Alstyne, B. W. Sweet Adventures of Henry P. Twist. (p. 2168)
Van Alstyne, Bruce W. Sweet Adventures of Henry P. Twist: The Island of Milk & Honey. (p. 2168)
Van, Andi. Magic Fell. (p. 1377)
Van, Annelies, illus. see Rabou, John.
van Arsdale, Peternelle. Beast Is an Animal. (p. 181)
—Cold Is in Her Bones. (p. 413)
Van Baarland, Adriaan, jt. auth. see Aesop, Aesop.
Van Bakel, Danielle. Alpha-Mania Adventures: The Fantastic Floating Feast: an Alliteration Book. Henry, Jalisa, illus. (p. 58)
Van Bakkum, Ramona, illus. see Harvey, Sarah.
Van Bergen, Beppie, jt. auth. see Leunissen, Ron.
Van Biesen, Koen & Watkinson, Laura. Roger Is Reading a Book. (p. 1897)
Van Bolswert, Boëce, jt. auth. see Williams, Isaac.
Van Booy, Simon. Gertie Milk & the Keeper of Lost Things. (p. 823)
Van Brunt, K. D. Red Sun Rises. (p. 1859)
Van Buren, David. I Love You As Big As the World. Warnes, Tim, illus. (p. 1078)
Van Buren, Nancy, illus. see Doran, Christine L. & Doran, Thomas P.
Van Buskirk, Venyce. Santa's Bag of Magic. (p. 1933)
Van Camp, Katie. CookieBot! Agnew, Lincoln, illus. (p. 446)
—Harry & Horsie. Agnew, Lincoln, illus. (p. 934)
Van Camp, Richard. Kiss by Kiss: A Counting Book for Families (p. 1224)
—Little You Flett, Julie, illus. (p. 1330)
—Little You / Nîya-K'apisîsisîyân Collins, Mary, tr. (p. 1330)
—May We Have Enough to Share (p. 1429)
—We Sang You Home Flett, Julie, illus. (p. 2392)
—We Sang You Home / Ka Kîweh Nikâmôstamâtinân Collins, Mary, tr. (p. 2392)
—Welcome Song for Baby / ni Nikamon 'Tawâw Nipepîmis' Collins, Mary, tr. (p. 2397)
—What's the Most Beautiful Thing You Know about Horses? Littlechild, George, illus. (p. 2426)
Van Campen, Elizabeth, illus. see Jajou, Rafee.
Van Cleve, Kathleen. Drizzle. (p. 605)
Van Clief, Sylvia Worth, jt. auth. see Heide, Florence Parry.
van Dam, Katrin. Come November. (p. 428)
van de Beek, Mariella, illus. see Priess, Brett.
Van De Car, Nikki. Junior Witch's Handbook: A Kid's Guide to White Magic, Spells, & Rituals. Krogmann, Uta, illus. (p. 1191)
Van de Graaff, Arie. Scripture Power. (p. 1966)
van de Liejgraaf, Deborah, illus. see Vermeulen, Mariska.
van de Liejgraaf, Deborah, illus. see Wehrmeijer, Annelien.
van de Liejgraaf, Deborah, illus. see Wejrmeijer, Annelien.
Van de Peelt, Vrani. Degaz! (p. 526)
van de Ruit, John. Spud-The Madness Continues. (p. 2093)
Van De Stevenson, Fanny Grift, jt. auth. see Stevenson, Robert Louis.
Van de Vendel, Edward. Dog That Nino Didn't Have. Van Hertbruggen, Anton, illus. (p. 576)
Van de Vendel, Edward & van der Linden, Martijn. For You & No One Else. (p. 764)
van Deelen, Fred, illus. see Gregory, Philippa.
Van Den Berg, Jonathan, tr. see Renz, Ulrich.
Van Den Berg, Jonathan, tr. Schlaf Gut, Kleiner Wolf - Slaap Lekker, Kleine Wolf (Deutsch - Holländisch) Zweisprachiges Kinderbuch Mit Mp3 Hörbuch Zum Herunterladen, Ab 2-4 Jahren. Brinkmann, Barbara, illus. (p. 1944)
Van Den Bosch, Alexander P. M. Schaapje Is Een Aapje. (p. 1944)
Van Den Hoonaard, Will. Did You Ever Wonder: The Story of the Bab As a Child. (p. 543)
van der Does, Ellis, illus. see Tea, Michelle.
van der Hammen, Gijs. Little Wise Wolf. Watkinson, Laura, tr. (p. 1330)
Van Der Helm, Wil. Elf Dancer. (p. 635)
Van Der Hoeven, Jan, jt. auth. see Clark, William.
Van Der Ley, Leny. Sandy from Sterrenduin. (p. 1931)
van der Linde, Jori, illus. see Lewis, J. Patrick.
van der Linde, Jori, illus. see Riggs, Kate.
van der Linde, Jori, illus. see Stone, Tiffany.
van der Linde, Jori, illus. see Yolen, Jane.
van der Linde, Laurel. So, You Want to Be a Dancer? The Ultimate Guide to Exploring the Dance Industry. (p. 2051)
van der Linden, Elly. Larry & Lola. What Do We Buy? Diederen, Suzanne, illus. (p. 1244)
Van Der Linden, Gerdien, illus. see Stein, Mathilde.
Van Der Linden, Martijn, illus. see Rinck, Maranke.
van der Linden, Martijn, jt. auth. see Rinck, Maranke.
van der Linden, Martijn, jt. auth. see Van de Vendel, Edward.
van der Meer, Ron. Interactive Art Book. (p. 1125)
van der Meer, Sjors & Suijker, Job. Forest Woodworker: A Step-By-Step Guide to Working with Green Wood. (p. 766)
Van Der Meide, Shelley, illus. see Watson, Art.
Van der Merwe, Avril. How Cheetah Got His Tears. Greeff, Heidi-Kate, illus. (p. 1027)
—Once upon a Rhinoceros. Greeff, Heidi-Kate, illus. (p. 1657)
Van Der Merwe, Mia-Lize. Untouchable Love. (p. 2336)
Van Der Merwe, Stefan. ABC of All the Questions We Never Dare to Ask. (p. 4)
Van der Paardt, Melissa, illus. see Trimmer, Christian.
van der Peijl, Liza Rebecca. Mog. Filippi, Mirko, illus. (p. 1488)
Van Der Put, Klaatje, illus. see Chronicle Books & ImageBooks.

V

Van Steenwyk, Mark. Wolf at the Gate. Hedstrom, Joel, illus. (p. 2483)
Van Stockum, Hilda. Borrowed House. (p. 263)
Van Straaten, Harmen. My Car Book. (p. 1535)
Van Tassel, Mary. Beach Ball's Journey (p. 178)
Van Tassel, Mary A. Beach Ball's Discovery. (p. 178)
—Beach Ball's Return. DeBroech, Sarah, illus. (p. 178)
Van Tine, Laura, illus. see Sharp, Michael.
Van Tol, Alex. Aliens among Us: Invasive Animals & Plants in British Columbia Deas, Mike, illus. (p. 47)
—Dolores Huerta: Voice for the Working Poor. (p. 579)
—Food Freak (p. 760)
—Food Freak. (p. 760)
—Gravity Check (p. 882)
—Knifepoint (p. 1227)
—Oracle (p. 1668)
—Punta de Cuchillo (p. 1814)
—Redline (p. 1859)
—Redline. (p. 1859)
—Shallow Grave (p. 1999)
—Sonia Sotomayor: U. S. Supreme Court Justice. (p. 2063)
—Viral (p. 2360)
Van Tol, Alex, jt. auth. see McAllister, Ian.
Van Valkenburgh, Blaire, jt. auth. see Strother, Ruth.
Van Veen, Marleen. Acorn Man's Search for the Golden Heart. (p. 11)
Van Velzer, Charles Ambrose, jt. auth. see Shutts, George Clinton.
Van Vierzen, Ruth. Edgar: The Mouse Who Left His Field & Discovered the Ocean. Ansheen, Anda, illus. (p. 625)
Van Vleet, Carmella. Ancient Civilizations: Egyptians! With 25 Social Studies Projects for Kids. Casteel, Tom, illus. (p. 80)
—Ancient Civilizations: Greeks! With 25 Social Studies Projects for Kids. Casteel, Tom, illus. (p. 80)
—Aviation: Cool Women Who Fly. Chandhok, Lena, illus. (p. 143)
—Eliza Bing Is (Not) a Big, Fat Quitter. (p. 636)
—Eliza Bing Is (Not) a Star. (p. 636)
—Explore Electricity! With 25 Great Projects. Stone, Bryan, illus. (p. 679)
—Robotics! With 25 Science Projects for Kids. Casteel, Tom, illus. (p. 1893)
—Seven Wonders of the World: Discover Amazing Monuments to Civilization with 20 Projects. Rizvi, Farah, illus. (p. 1994)
—To the Stars! (p. 2253)
Van Vleet, Carmella & Sullivan, Kathy. To the Stars! The First American Woman to Walk in Space. Wong, Nicole, illus. (p. 2253)
Van Vliet, Amanda. By Dragon's Light. (p. 305)
Van Vloten, Kristin, ed. see Flynn, Julie.
Van Voorn, Rineke. Stories of Children Who Dream on How the World Began. (p. 2124)
van Voorst, Jenny Fretland. Igneous Rocks. (p. 1094)
—Metamorphic Rocks. (p. 1452)
—Sedimentary Rocks. (p. 1981)
Van Vorst, Dwight D. Compassion for Lou. (p. 433)
Van Waes, Mike. Peeves. (p. 1714)
Van Wagenen, Kate. Dictation Day by Day: A Modern Speller; Sixth Year. (p. 541)
Van Wagenen, Maya. Popular: A Memoir. (p. 1777)
—Popular: How a Geek in Pearls Discovered the Secret to Confidence. (p. 1777)
Van Wagoner, Traci, illus. see Knutson, Julie.
Van Wagoner, Traci, illus. see McAdam, Claudia Cangilla.
Van Wagoner, Traci, illus. see Metivier, Gary.
Van Wagoner, Traci, illus. see Schoettler, Joan.
Van Wagoner, Traci, illus. see Van Scott, Miriam.
Van Wakeren, Kari. Bubble Wrap Girl. (p. 289)
Van Wemmer, Deby. Wishes & Walnuts. (p. 2479)
Van Wijk, Bert, illus. see Gibert, Jimena & Cornum, Lindsey, eds.
Van Winkle, Diana. Ur Bible Study Devotion Companion: 6-Week Devotional on Self-Image. (p. 2339)
Van Wright, Cornelius, illus. see Bridges, Ruby & Maccarone, Grace.
Van Wright, Cornelius, illus. see Day, Nancy Raines.
Van Wright, Cornelius, illus. see Glass, Susan.
Van Wright, Cornelius, illus. see Grubman, Bonnie.
Van Wright, Cornelius, illus. see Hoffman, Mary.
Van Wright, Cornelius, illus. see Levinson, Lara.
Van Wright, Cornelius, illus. see Medearis, Angela Shelf.
Van Wright, Cornelius, illus. see Rappaport, Doreen.
Van Wright, Cornelius, illus. see Scholastic, Inc. Staff & Black, Sonia.
Van Wright, Cornelius, illus. see Scholastic, Inc. Staff & Medearis, Angela Shelf.
Van Wright, Cornelius, illus. see Schroeder, Alan.
Van Wright, Cornelius, illus. see Shahan, Sherry.
Van Wright, Cornelius, illus. see Starr, Meg.
Van Wright, Cornelius, illus. see Williamson, Dorena.
Van Wright, Cornelius, tr. see Shahan, Sherry.
Van Wyk, Chris, illus. see Bouma, Paddy.
Van Wyk, Hanri, illus. see Brooks, Felicity & Litchfield, Jo.
Van Wyk, Hanri, illus. see Brooks, Felicity.
Van Wyk, Hanri, illus. see Helbrough, Emma & Brooks, Felicity.
Van Wyk, Hanri, illus. see Taplin, Sam.
Van Wyk, Rupert, illus. see al-Qadi, Charlotte.
Van Wyk, Rupert, illus. see Cuillain, Adam, et al.
Van Wyk, Rupert, illus. see Guillain, Adam, et al.
Van Wyk, Rupert, illus. see Mackey, Cindy.
Van Wyk, Rupert, illus. see Nelson, Jo.
van Wyk, Rupert, illus. see Platt, Richard.
Van Zee, Amy. How to Analyze the Works of C. S. Lewis (p. 1037)
Van Zeyl, Marjan, illus. see Grimm, Wilhelm K. & Grimm, Jacob.
van Zeyl, Marjan, illus. see van Dort, Evelien.
Van Zuyen, Gregory. Levi's Book of Barnyard Animals. (p. 1282)
Van Zyle, Daniel, illus. see Miller, Debbie S.
Van Zyle, Jon, illus. see Carlstrom, Nancy White.
Van Zyle, Jon, illus. see Flowers, Pam.
Van Zyle, Jon, illus. see Heinz, Brian J.
Van Zyle, Jon, illus. see London, Jonathan.
Van Zyle, Jon, illus. see McDaniel, Jequita Potts.
Van Zyle, Jon, illus. see Miller, Debbie S.
Van Zyle, Jon, illus. see Miller, Debbie S. & Eiler, John H.
Van Zyle, Jon, jt. auth. see Miller, Debbie S.
Vana, Dan. Joey & the Magic Dream Pillow. Ware, Quinton, illus. (p. 1171)
Vanamee, Lida Ostrom. Adirondack Idyl (Classic Reprint) (p. 16)
—Two Women, or over the Hills & Far Away (Classic Reprint) (p. 2310)
Van-Anderson, Helen. Story of Teddy (Classic Reprint) (p. 2132)
Vanardy, Varick. Up Against It (Classic Reprint) (p. 2337)
Vanardy, Varrick. Night Wind's Promise (Classic Reprint) (p. 1608)
VanArsdale, Anthony. Boxcar Children Great Adventure 5-Book Set. (p. 266)
—Clue in the Papyrus Scroll. (p. 409)
—Journey on a Runaway Train. (p. 1181)
—Khipu & the Final Key. (p. 1212)
—Mystery at Camp Survival. (p. 1568)
—Mystery at the Calgary Stampede. (p. 1568)
—Mystery of the Forgotten Family. (p. 1570)
—Science Fair Sabotage. (p. 1955)
—Shackleton Sabotage. (p. 1996)
—Skeleton Key Mystery. (p. 2030)
—Sleepy Hollow Mystery. (p. 2037)
VanArsdale, Anthony, illus. see Cooper, James Fenimore.
VanArsdale, Anthony, illus. see London, Jack.
Vanarsdale, Anthony, illus. see Norwich, Grace.
VanArsdale, Anthony, illus. see Warner, Gertrude Chandler.
Vanartsdalen, Renee. Kobe Saves the Day. (p. 1230)
Vanasse, Deb. Cold Spell. (p. 413)
—Lucy's Dance. (p. 1366)
Vanasse, Patricia. Resilient. Shalaby, Asharaf, illus. (p. 1869)
Vanbeek, Lauren. Jack: The Ice Dog. (p. 1151)
Vancata, Brad, jt. auth. see Sazaklis, John.
Vance, Alexander. Book of the Knight of the Tower, Landry: Which He Made for the Instruction of His Daughters (by Way of Selection); Now Done into English (Classic Reprint) (p. 260)
—Heartbreak Messenger. (p. 946)
—Romantic Episodes of Chivalric & Mediaeval France. (p. 1901)
—Romantic Episodes of Chivalric & Medieval France (Classic Reprint) (p. 1901)
Vance, Arthur T. Real David Harum: The Wise Ways & Droll Sayings of One Dave Hannum, of Homer, the Original of the Hero of Mr. Westcott's Popular Book; How He Made & Lost a Fortune, His Many Deeds of Charity, Amusing Anecdotes about Him (Classic Reprint) (p. 1849)
Vance, Ashlee. Elon Musk & the Quest for a Fantastic Future Young Readers' Edition. (p. 639)
Vance, Colleen. Flip Flop Family. Kinra, Richa, illus. (p. 749)
Vance, Hiram Albert, jt. auth. see Stevenson, Robert Louis.
Vance, Keione. Hammy the Hamster Counts to Ten. (p. 913)
VanCe, Lilo. Once upon a Time & Other Stories. (p. 1658)
Vance, Louis Joseph. Bandbox (Classic Reprint) (p. 163)
—Black Bag (Classic Reprint) (p. 236)
—Brass Bowl (Classic Reprint) (p. 276)
—Bronze Bell (Classic Reprint) (p. 285)
—Fortune Hunter (Classic Reprint) (p. 769)
—Linda Lee Incorporated. (p. 1303)
—Linda Lee, Incorporated: A Novel (Classic Reprint) (p. 1303)
—Nobody (Classic Reprint) (p. 1616)
—Woman in the Shadow (Classic Reprint) (p. 2485)
Vance, Lucian. Fake News & Media Bias. (p. 699)
Vance, Michael. Klockwerks. (p. 1227)
Vance, Susa S. Leap-Year: A Comedy in Four Acts, for Nine Characters (Classic Reprint) (p. 1255)
—Nature Wins: A Comedy in Four Acts (Classic Reprint) (p. 1581)
Vance, Wilson. God's War (Classic Reprint) (p. 854)
VanCleave, Janice. Even More of Janice VanCleave's Wild, Wacky, & Weird Earth Science Experiments. (p. 669)
—Janice VanCleave's Wild, Wacky, & Weird Science Experiments: Set 4. (p. 1159)
—More of Janice VanCleave's Wild, Wacky, & Weird Astronomy Experiments. (p. 1505)
—More of Janice VanCleave's Wild, Wacky, & Weird Biology Experiments. (p. 1505)
—More of Janice VanCleave's Wild, Wacky, & Weird Earth Science Experiments. (p. 1505)
—Step-by-Step Science Experiments in Astronomy. (p. 2114)
—Step-by-Step Science Experiments in Biology. (p. 2114)
—Step-by-Step Science Experiments in Earth Science. (p. 2114)
—Step-by-Step Science Experiments in Energy. (p. 2114)
VanCleave, Janice Pratt. Even More of Janice Vancleave's Wild, Wacky, & Weird Biology Experiments. (p. 668)
—Even More of Janice VanCleave's Wild, Wacky, & Weird Astronomy Experiments. (p. 668)
—Even More of Janice Vancleave's Wild, Wacky, & Weird Physics Experiments. (p. 669)
—Janice VanCleave's Crazy, Kooky, & Quirky Astronomy Experiments. (p. 1159)
—Janice VanCleave's Crazy, Kooky, & Quirky Biology Experiments. (p. 1159)
—Janice VanCleave's Crazy, Kooky, & Quirky Earth Science Experiments. (p. 1159)
—Janice Vancleave's Crazy, Kooky, & Quirky Physics Experiments. (p. 1159)
—Janice VanCleave's Wild, Wacky, & Weird Astronomy Experiments. (p. 1159)
—Janice Vancleave's Wild, Wacky, & Weird Biology Experiments. (p. 1159)
—Janice VanCleave's Wild, Wacky, & Weird Earth Science Experiments. (p. 1159)
—Janice VanCleave's Wild, Wacky, & Weird Physics Experiments. (p. 1159)
—Many More of Janice Vancleave's Wild, Wacky, & Weird: Earth Science Experiments. (p. 1400)
—Many More of Janice VanCleave's Wild, Wacky, & Weird Biology Experiments. (p. 1400)
—Many More of Janice VanCleave's Wild, Wacky, & Weird Astronomy Experiments. (p. 1400)
VanCleve, Rhonda. Concrete & Cranes: 100 Devotions Building on the Love of Jesus. (p. 438)
Vancouver, Charles. General View of the Agriculture in the County of Essex: With Observations on the Means of Its Improvement (Classic Reprint) (p. 814)
—General View of the Agriculture of the County of Devon: With Observations on the Means of Its Improvement; Drawn up for the Consideration of the Board of Agriculture; & Internal Improvement (Classic Reprint) (p. 814)
Vand, Rochel, jt. auth. see Yerushalmi, Miriam.
Vande Griek, Susan. Hawks Kettle, Puffins Wheel: And Other Poems of Birds in Flight. Hoffmann, Mark, illus. (p. 940)
Vande Velde, Vivian. 8 Class Pets + 1 Squirrel ÷ 1 Dog = Chaos. Björkman, Steve & Björkman, Steve, illus. (p. 2549)
—Deadly Pink. (p. 519)
—Frogged. (p. 789)
—Magic Can Be Murder. (p. 1377)
—Prince Problem. (p. 1795)
—Princess Imposter. (p. 1797)
—Rumpelstiltskin Problem. (p. 1914)
—Squirrel in the House. Björkman, Steve, illus. (p. 2095)
—Squirrel in the House. Björkman, Steve & Björkman, Steve, illus. (p. 2095)
—Squirrel in the Museum. Björkman, Steve, illus. (p. 2095)
—User Unfriendly. (p. 2341)
Vandegrift, April, illus. see McKetta, Elisabeth Sharp & Stead, James.
Vandegrift, Margaret. Doris & Theodora (Classic Reprint) (p. 586)
—Holidays at Home: For Boys & Girls (Classic Reprint) (p. 988)
—Holidays at Home. (p. 988)
—Little Helpers (Classic Reprint) (p. 1318)
—Queen's Body-Guard: A Story of American Life for Girls (Classic Reprint) (p. 1824)
—Ways & Means (Classic Reprint) (p. 2388)
Vandeloo, Helene. Gracie's Wheels. Murphy, Frank, ed. (p. 874)
Vanden Berg, Myra, illus. see Kreder Sr., Edward G. & Kreder, Mary Ellen DeLuca.
Vanden Broeck, Fabricio, illus. see Rincón García, Luis Antonio.
Vanden Heede, Sylvia. Wolf & Dog. Tolman, Marije, illus. (p. 2483)
Vandenberg, Kimberly, illus. see Lingelbach, Anne.
Vandenberg, Kimberly, illus. see Mackey, Madame.
Vandenberg, Kimberly, illus. see Schram, Stephen T.
Vandenbos, Scarlet, illus. see Eernisse, Rachel.
VandenBroeck, Fabricio, illus. see Durango, Julia.
VandenBroeck, Fabricio, illus. see Markle, Sandra.
VandenBroeck, Fabricio, jt. auth. see Durango, Julia.
Vandenheede, Ruben, illus. see Hockensmith, Laura.
Vanden-Heuvel, John C., Sr. Web Design for Kids. Turdera, Cristian, illus. (p. 2395)
Vanden-Heuvel, John C., Sr. & Ostrovsky, Andrey. ABCs of the Web. Holmes, Tom, illus. (p. 5)
VanDenhoven, Godelieve. Louis in Kindergarten. (p. 1357)
Vander Hook, Sue. Adolf Hitler: German Dictator (p. 16)
—Building the Panama Canal (p. 295)
—Colin Powell: General & Statesman (p. 414)
—Communism (p. 431)
—Democracy (p. 528)
—Dust Bowl (p. 610)
—Frederick Douglass: Fugitive Slave & Abolitionist (p. 781)
—How to Analyze the Roles of Paul Newman (p. 1036)
—Johannes Gutenberg: Printing Press Innovator (p. 1171)
—Louis Pasteur: Groundbreaking Chemist & Biologist (p. 1357)
—Mahatma Gandhi: Proponent of Peace (p. 1382)
—Rupert Murdoch: News Corporation Magnate (p. 1916)
—Steven Spielberg: Groundbreaking Director (p. 2116)
—Trail of Tears (p. 2274)
—United States Enters World War I. (p. 2331)
—Winston Churchill: British Prime Minister & Statesman (p. 2474)
Vander Mey, Paula. View from the Upper Deck. (p. 2357)
Vander Pluym, Andrea. Mission: Sisterhood. Waters, Susy Pilgrim, illus. (p. 1481)
Vander Pol, Matt, illus. see Crouch, Cheryl.
Vander Pol, Matt, jt. auth. see Crouch, Cheryl.
Vander Stoep, Jenaya. Six Tribes. (p. 2029)
Vander Zee, Ruth. Next Year. Kelley, Gary, illus. (p. 1601)
Vanderberg, Hope, ed. see Youth Communication.
Vanderbilt, David. Up & down on the Elevator: Add & Subtract Within 20. (p. 2337)
Vanderbilt, Gertrude Lefferts. Jack's Story (Classic Reprint) (p. 1153)
Vandercook, Maragaret. Red Cross Girls with Pershing to Victory (Classic Reprint) (p. 1856)
Vandercook, Margaret. Camp Fire Girls at Sunrise Hall. (p. 315)
—Camp Fire Girls at Sunrise Hill: First of a Series. (p. 315)
—Camp Fire Girls in after Years. (p. 315)
—Camp Fire Girls in the Outside World. (p. 315)
—Girl Scouts in Beechwood Forest. (p. 837)
—Girl Scouts in Beechwood Forest (Classic Reprint) (p. 837)
—Loves of Ambrose (Classic Reprint) (p. 1362)
—Ranch Girls & Their Great Adventure. (p. 1840)
—Ranch Girls at Home Again. (p. 1840)
—Ranch Girls at Rainbow Lodge. (p. 1840)
—Ranch Girls at Rainbow Lodge (Classic Reprint) (p. 1840)
—Ranch Girls in Europe. (p. 1840)
—Ranch Girls' Pot of Gold (Classic Reprint) (p. 1840)
—Red Cross Girls with Pershing to Victory. (p. 1856)
—Red Cross Girls with the Russian Army. (p. 1856)
Vanderem, Fernand. Two Banks of the Seine: Les Deux Rives (Classic Reprint) (p. 2307)
Vandergrift, Adam. Slime Sorcery: 97 Magical Concoctions Made from Almost Anything - Including Fluffy, Galaxy, Crunchy, Magnetic, Color-Changing, & Glow-in-the-Dark Slime. (p. 2038)
Vanderhoof, Gabrielle. Air Force. (p. 37)
—Basketball. (p. 170)
—Cheerleading. (p. 364)
—Hockey. (p. 985)
—Lacrosse. (p. 1235)
—Track & Field. (p. 2272)
—Volleyball. (p. 2367)
Vanderhoof, Gabrielle, jt. auth. see Earl, C. F.
Vanderhoof, Herbert. Canada Monthly, Vol. 20: May, 1916 (Classic Reprint) (p. 320)
—Canada Monthly, Vol. 21: November, 1916 (Classic Reprint) (p. 320)
—Canada Monthly, Vol. 4: November, 1910-October, 1910 (Classic Reprint) (p. 320)
—Canada West, Vol. 2: May, 1907 (Classic Reprint) (p. 320)
—Canada West, Vol. 5: November, 1908 (Classic Reprint) (p. 320)
—Canada West, Vol. 7: November, 1909 (Classic Reprint) (p. 320)
—Canada-West Magazine, Vol. 3: November, 1907 (Classic Reprint) (p. 320)
Vanderklugt, Kyla. Science Comics: Crows: Genius Birds. (p. 1954)
Vanderlinden, Kathy, jt. auth. see Suzuki, David.
VanderMeer, Jeff. Peculiar Peril. (p. 1711)
VanderMey, Paula. Kaibab: The Quest. (p. 1201)
VanderMey, P.E. Kaibab: Family Ties (p. 1201)
Vandermolen, Cynthia. My Super Scar. (p. 1562)
VanderPloeg, Libby, illus. see Gates, Mariam.
VanderPloeg, Libby, illus. see Sohn, Amy & Le Pape, Orna.
Vanderpool, Clare. Moon over Manifest. (p. 1502)
—Navigating Early. (p. 1582)
VanDerpool, Jessie. Little Rose Becomes a Hunter. (p. 1327)
Vanderpoole, Lew. Red Mountain Mines (Classic Reprint) (p. 1857)
Vanderstelt, Adrianna, illus. see Porter, Marisa Grace.
Vanderveen, Cary, illus. see Devisser, Dave.
Vanderveer, Lettie C. Any-Day Entertainments: A Collection of Monologues, Dialogues, One-Act Sketches, & Novelty Recitations (Classic Reprint) (p. 104)
VanDervleuten, Robin M. Keepers of the Fairy Moon. (p. 1208)
Vanderwal, Andrew H. Battle for Duncragglin. (p. 173)
—Death of a King. (p. 521)
Vanderwater, Amy Ludwig. Dreaming of You. DeWitt, Aaron, illus. (p. 603)
VanDerwater, Amy Ludwig. Every Day Birds. Metrano, Dylan, illus. (p. 670)
Vanderwater, Amy Ludwig. Read! Read! Read! O'Rourke, Ryan, illus. (p. 1845)
VanDerwater, Amy Ludwig. With My Hands: Poems about Making Things. Fancher, Lou & Johnson, Steve, illus. (p. 2481)
Vanderwater, Amy Ludwig. Write! Write! Write! O'Rourke, Ryan, illus. (p. 2512)
Vandevelde, Lucie, illus. see Elschner, Géraldine.
Vandever, Daniel W. Fall in Line, Holden. Frank, LaFrenda, ed. (p. 700)
Vandewiele, Agnès. Chevaux. (p. 367)
Vandewièle, Agnès. Monster Machines! on the Farm. Lepretre, Jean-Marc, illus. (p. 1496)
Vandezande, Cody. Chuck Book: An Interactive ABC Storybook for Everyone. (p. 389)
Vandiver, Melissa, illus. see Asher, Sally.
Vandome, Nick. Photoshop Elements 2018 Tips, Tricks & Shortcuts in Easy Steps. (p. 1737)
Vandoni, Antonio. Favolette Morali Ad USO Della Gioventu Italiana (Classic Reprint) (p. 715)
VanDycke, Lilian Claudine. Mystery Fire. (p. 1569)
Van-Dyke-Hempenstall, Clare, illus. see Yeo, Julia.
Vane, Capel. Desire of the Moth, Vol. 1 of 2 (Classic Reprint) (p. 533)
Vane, Derek. Ferrybridge Mystery (Classic Reprint) (p. 721)
—Paradise of Fools (Classic Reprint) (p. 1698)
Vane, Mitch, illus. see Arena, Felice & Kettle, Phil.
Vane, Mitch, illus. see Clarke, Lorin.
Vane, Mitch, illus. see Dubosarsky, Ursula.
Vane, Mitch, illus. see French, Jackie.
Vane, Mitch, illus. see Green, Jessica.
Vane, Mitch, illus. see Katz, Danny.
Vane, Mitch, illus. see Lasky, Kathryn.
Vane, Mitch, illus. see Plourde, Lynn.
Vane, Mitch, illus. see Williamson, John.
Vaneck Holub, Helen. Beloved Companion. (p. 198)
Vanellis, Latoya. Thank You, God, for the Sun. (p. 2211)
Vanessa, Balleza, illus. see Kianny, Antigua N.
Vaney, Barry de. Walk with the Rainbow Family. (p. 2372)
vanFrankenhuyze, Gijsbert, illus. see Ulmer, Michael.
Vang Nyman, Ingrid, illus. see Lindgren, Astrid.
Vang Nyman, Ingrid, jt. auth. see Lindgren, Astrid.
Vangrifter, Zachary Philemon. Sayings & Doings at the Tremont House, in the Year 1832 (Classic Reprint) (p. 1940)
Vangrifter, Zachary Philmon, jt. auth. see Sly, Costard.
VanHecke, Susan. Apple Pie for Dinner Baicker-McKee, Carol, illus. (p. 106)
—Raggin' Jazzin' Rockin' A History of American Musical Instrument Makers. (p. 1834)
—Under the Freedom Tree. (p. 2321)
—Under the Freedom Tree. Ladd, London, illus. (p. 2321)
Vanhee, Jason. Engines of the Broken World. (p. 652)
Vanholme, Virginie. Malevolence & Mandrake. (p. 1392)
Vanier, Jean. I Meet Jesus: He Tells Me "I Love You" (p. 1079)
—I Walk with Jesus. (p. 1083)
Vaniere, Jacques. Jacobi Vanierii Prædium Rusticum (Classic Reprint) (p. 1154)
—Oeconomie Rurale, Vol. 1: Traduction du Poeme (Classic Reprint) (p. 1638)
Vankirk Schue, Lori, illus. see Giddan, Norman & Giddan, Jane.
Vankirk Schue, Lori, illus. see Schue, Lori.
Vanmeter, Michelle Lynn. Old Rag Doll. (p. 1648)
Vann, Russell. Ghetto Bastard III: Life after Death. (p. 827)
Vanner, Chelsey, illus. see Mitchell, Mae.

V

Vaughn, Richard. Rowena & the Magic Hawk, the First Adventure. (p. 1909)
Vaughn, Sarah. Sleepless Volume 1. (p. 2037)
Vaughn, Sarah & Luna, Jonathan. Eternal Empire Volume 1. (p. 665)
Vaughn, Sharon & Wolfe, Hillary. Phonics Connections Teacher's Resource Guide. (p. 1736)
Vaughn, Stanton. 700 Limerick Lyrics: A Collection of Choice Humorous Versifications (Classic Reprint) (p. 2560)
Vaughn, Sydney. At the Track Meet: Understand Place Value. (p. 131)
Vaughn-Jackson, N. Vanessa. I Say! Smith, Samayyah, illus. (p. 1081)
Vaughns, Byron, illus. see Tanguay, Dave.
Vaught, Mike. Crossroads. (p. 478)
Vaught, Susan. Footer Davis Probably Is Crazy. (p. 762)
—Footer Davis Probably Is Crazy. Reinhardt, Jennifer Black, illus. (p. 762)
—Freaks Like Us. (p. 780)
—Insanity. (p. 1121)
—Me & Sam-Sam Handle the Apocalypse. (p. 1433)
—Super Max & the Mystery of Thornwood's Revenge. (p. 2155)
—Things Too Huge to Fix by Saying Sorry. (p. 2221)
Vaun, Missouri. Birthright. (p. 234)
Vaux, Georgia, jt. auth. see Scott-Smith, Louise.
Vaux, James Hardy. Memoirs of James Hardy Vaux, Vol. 1 of 2 (Classic Reprint) (p. 1444)
Vaux, Patricia, illus. see Andrews McMeel Publishing Staff & Wang, Dorthea Deprisco.
Vaux, Patricia, illus. see Wang, Dorthea Deprisco.
Vavasour, Anne. My Last Tour & First Work: Or, a Visit to the Baths of Wildbad & Rippoldsau (Classic Reprint) (p. 1551)
Vavouri, Elisa, illus. see Hyde, Heidi Smith.
Vawter, Clara. Rabbit's Ransom: Being a New Edition of of Such Is the Kingdom (Classic Reprint) (p. 1830)
Vawter, Vince. Copyboy. Trunfio, Alessia, illus. (p. 452)
—Paperboy. (p. 1698)
Vawter, Will, jt. auth. see Riley, James Whitcomb.
Vaysset, Ghyslaine, illus. see Craddock, Petra.
Vaysset, Ghyslaine, illus. see Lindeen, Mary.
Vaysset, Ghyslaine, illus. see Mortensen, Lori.
Vayssiere, Frederique, illus. see Hooper, Mary.
Vaz De Carvalho, Joao, illus. see Pavón, Mar.
Vaz, Mark Cotta. Twilight Saga Breaking Dawn Part 1: the Official Illustrated Movie Companion Pt. 1. (p. 2305)
Vaz, Mark Cotta, ed. see Macauley, Michael.
Vazan, Sandy, illus. see Braun, Anne.
Vazeer, Author. Vords: Vinci on a Roadside. (p. 2367)
Vazoff, Ivan. Under the Yoke: A Romance of Bulgarian Liberty. (p. 2323)
—Under the Yoke: A Romance of Bulgarian Liberty (Classic Reprint) (p. 2323)
Vazquez, Esteban. Halloween Warriors: Parts 1, 2 And 3. (p. 912)
—Halloween Warriors Part 4 And 5. (p. 912)
Vazquez, Gustavo & Vargas, Fredrico. Chicharito Hernndez. (p. 367)
Vazquez, Hector. Billy Zoomer's Interview Search for the Biggest Fear. (p. 227)
Vazquez, Joey. Ms. Marvel by Saladin Ahmed Vol. 2: Stormranger. (p. 1523)
—Ms. Marvel Team-Up. (p. 1523)
Vázquez-Figueroa, Alberto. Anaconda. (p. 78)
Vazquez-Lozano, Gustavo. Ivan Cordoba. (p. 1149)
Vazquez-Lozano, Gustavo & Benard, Federico Vargas. Luis Suarez. (p. 1366)
Veach, Janie. Chloe. (p. 379)
Veal, Pat J. Veal House: A Family Refuge for Furry Friends. (p. 2348)
Veasey, Michele, illus. see Bohlken, Robert L.
Veasey, Nick. X-Treme X-Ray: See the World Inside Out! (p. 2515)
Vebæk, Mâlâraq. Journey to the Mother of the Sea. Høegh, Aka, illus. (p. 1182)
Vecchia, Fabio Marco Dalla, jt. auth. see Cunningham, Mark.
Vecchini, Silvia. 10 Commandments Explained. Vincenti, Antonio, illus. (p. 2549)
—Beatitudes Explained. Vincenti, Antonio, illus. (p. 182)
Vecchini, Silvia & Daughters of St. Paul Staff. Creed Explained. Vincenti, Antonio, illus. (p. 472)
Vecchini, Silvia & Sualzo. Red Zone: An Earthquake Story. (p. 1859)
Vecchio, Luciano, illus. see Beatty, Scott, et al.
Vecchio, Luciano, illus. see Beatty, Scott.
Vecchio, Luciano, illus. see Biskup, Agnieszka & Enz, Tammy.
Vecchio, Luciano, illus. see Biskup, Agnieszka.
Vecchio, Luciano, illus. see Black, Jake.
Vecchio, Luciano, illus. see Bright, J. E.
Vecchio, Luciano, illus. see Bright, J. E. & Sutton, Laurie S.
Vecchio, Luciano, illus. see Cohen, Ivan & Eltaeb, Gabe.
Vecchio, Luciano, illus. see Cohen, Ivan, et al.
Vecchio, Luciano, illus. see Dahl, Michael.
Vecchio, Luciano, illus. see Enz, Tammy & Biskup, Agnieszka.
Vecchio, Luciano, illus. see Enz, Tammy.
Vecchio, Luciano, illus. see Hult, Gene & Bright, J. E.
Vecchio, Luciano, illus. see Manning, Matthew K.
Vecchio, Luciano, illus. see Manning, Matthew K. & Sazaklis, John.
Vecchio, Luciano, illus. see Sazaklis, John.
Vecchio, Luciano, illus. see Simonson, Louise.
Vecchio, Luciano, illus. see Snider, Brandon T.
Vecchio, Luciano, illus. see Sonneborn, Scott.
Vecchio, Luciano, illus. see Stephens, Sarah Hines.
Vecchio, Luciano, illus. see Sutton, Laurie S.
Vecchio, Luciano, illus. see Tulien, Sean.
Vecchio, Luciano & Geoffrey, Beaulieu. Ironheart Vol. 2: Ten Rings. (p. 1136)
Vecchione, Patrice & Raymond, Alyssa, eds. Ink Knows No Borders: Poems of the Immigrant & Refugee Experience. (p. 1120)
Vecellio, Stephanie. Twinkle Twinkle Little Star: A Spinning Star Book. (p. 2305)
Vechten, Carl Van. Lords of the Housetops: Thirteen Cat Tales (Classic Reprint) (p. 1349)
—Peter Whiffle: His Life & Works (Classic Reprint) (p. 1730)
—Tiger in the House (Classic Reprint) (p. 2241)
Vedder, David. Story of Reynard the Fox (Classic Reprint) (p. 2132)
Vedder, Elihu. Digressions of V: Written for His Own Fun & That of His Friends (Classic Reprint) (p. 546)
Vedder, Erik, illus. see Beechen, Adam & Age, Heroic.
Vedder, Mark. What Gifts We Give. (p. 2410)
Vedere, D. Autour de la Ferme Mes Pts Alb. (p. 140)
Veech, Alyssa. Small but Mighty. Weber, Penny, illus. (p. 2039)
Veenendall, Jennifer. Why Does Izzy Cover Her Ears? Dealing with Sensory Overload. (p. 2457)
Veenstra, Rosa. Tale of Norman the Nutcracker & the Sour Pickle: A Story from the Christmas Tree. (p. 2179)
Veer, Willem de. Battle Royal: A Western Drama in an Eastern Land (Classic Reprint) (p. 175)
Veera Das. Rhyme Time: Read Aloud Poems. (p. 1875)
Veerkamp, Misty J. Oh What I Could Do with a Neck Like a Giraffe. (p. 1642)
Veerman, David R. & Schmitt, Betsy. 365 Trivia Twist Devotions: Fun Facts & Spiritual Truths for Every Day of the Year. (p. 2560)
Vega, Ali. Brains, Brains, & Other Horrifying Breakfasts. (p. 275)
—Cat Litter Cake & Other Horrifying Desserts. (p. 341)
—Hideously Delicious Recipes to Disgust & Delight Your Friends. (p. 967)
—Little Kitchen of Horrors: Hideously Delicious Recipes That Disgust & Delight. (p. 1320)
—Mummy Dogs & Other Horrifying Snacks. (p. 1526)
—Tombstone Sandwiches & Other Horrifying Lunches. (p. 2259)
—Witches' Brew & Other Horrifying Party Foods. (p. 2480)
—Zombie-Gut Chili & Other Horrifying Dinners. (p. 2542)
Vega, Alison, illus. see Foster, Marilyn.
Vega, Anne, illus. see Kanellos, Nicolás.
Vega, Danielle. Crueles. (p. 479)
—Exorcism of Sofia Flores. (p. 677)
—Haunted. (p. 937)
—Merciless. (p. 1448)
—Merciless II: The Exorcism of Sofia Flores. (p. 1448)
—Merciless III: Origins of Evil. (p. 1448)
—Merciless IV: Last Rites. (p. 1448)
—Unleashed. (p. 2333)
Vega, Denise. If Your Monster Won't Go to Bed. OHora, Zachariah, illus. (p. 1093)
—Rock On: A Story of Guitars, Gigs, Girls, & a Brother (not Necessarily in That Order) (p. 1894)
Vega, Eida de la, jt. auth. see Curtis, Christopher Paul.
Vega, Eida de la, see de la Vega, Eida, tr.
Vega, Eida de la, tr. see Kondrchek, Jamie & Rasemas, Joe.
Vega, Eida de la, tr. see Kondrchek, Jamie.
Vega, Eida de la, tr. see Leavitt, Amie Jane.
Vega, Eida de la, tr. see Sherman, Patrice.
Vega, G. K. Little Boy Who Was Different. (p. 1313)
Vega, Lope de. Desprecio Agradecido. (p. 533)
—Hamete de Toledo. (p. 913)
—Principe Perfeto: Parte Primero. (p. 1800)
—Principe Perfeto: Parte Segunda. (p. 1800)
Vegara, Isabel Sanchez. Vivienne Westwood. Callaghan, Laura, illus. (p. 2364)
Vegara, Isabel Sanchez & Albero, Ana. Coco Chanel. (p. 411)
Vegara, Isabel Sanchez & Fan, Eng Gee. Frida Kahlo. (p. 785)
Vegara, Isabel Sanchez & Martín, Raquel. Maria Montessori. (p. 1404)
Vegas, Peter. Bones of the Sun God. (p. 256)
—Iron Tomb. (p. 1136)
Vegetta777 & Willyrex. Wigetta en Las Dinolimpiadas. (p. 2461)
Vegetta777, Vegetta777 & Willyrex, Willyrex. Wigetta y la Momia de Ra-Mon. (p. 2461)
VeggieTales. Bob & Larry's Book of Colors. Reed, Lisa, illus. (p. 251)
—Bob & Larry's Book of Numbers. Reed, Lisa, illus. (p. 251)
—My Time with God: 365 Daily Devos for Boys. (p. 1562)
—My Time with God: 365 Daily Devos for Girls. (p. 1562)
Vehanen, Kosti. Marian Anderson: A Portrait (Classic Reprint) (p. 1404)
Veiby, John. Direct Action: An One Act Play (Classic Reprint) (p. 552)
Veiga, Dirceu, illus. see Cross, Shiloh.
Veigas, Jennifer, ed. Critical Perspectives on Natural Disasters. (p. 476)
Veil, Karney. Sun & Moon Play Hide & Seek: A Children's Story. (p. 2151)
Veillé, Eric. Bureau of Misplaced Dads. Martin, Pauline, illus. (p. 299)
—Encyclopedia of Grannies. Veillé, Eric, illus. (p. 648)
—My Pictures after the Storm. Veillé, Eric, illus. (p. 1559)
Veillette, Roseanne M. Buck & Ben Junior: Colors. Veillette, Roseanne M., illus. (p. 289)
Veilleux, Tam, illus. see Fontanella, Lisa.
Veill'res, Claire. Malek, Youssef et Boussana Vivent en Gypte. (p. 1392)
Veirs, Laura. Libba: The Magnificent Musical Life of Elizabeth Cotten. Fazlalizadeh, Tatyana, illus. (p. 1283)
Veissid, Jacqueline. Caspian Finds a Friend. Brown, Merrilees, illus. (p. 339)
—Ruby's Sword. Zakimi, Paola, illus. (p. 1912)
Veit, Benjamin. Safety First for Children: A Reader for City Schools That Will Help to Prevent Fires & Accidents (Classic Reprint) (p. 1922)
Veit, Henry C. Redwood, Vol. 18: November 1918 (Classic Reprint) (p. 1860)
Veitch, Catherine. Allosaurus: The Troublesome Tooth Brown, Steve, illus. (p. 57)
—Amphibian Babies (p. 77)
—Animal Babies. (p. 88)
—Big Machines (p. 221)
—Big Machines Build! (p. 221)
—Big Machines Float! (p. 221)
—Big Machines Fly! (p. 221)
—Big Machines Rescue! (p. 221)
—Big Machines Ride Rails! (p. 221)
—Bird Babies (p. 230)
—Brachiosaurus: The Nosy Dinosaur Forshaw, Louise, illus. (p. 274)
—Bug Babies (p. 291)
—Changing Designs: Band 10/White (Collins Big Cat) (p. 356)
—Collins Big Cat Phonics for Letters & Sounds - Stunt Jets: Band 03/Yellow (p. 417)
—Farms Around the World (p. 711)
—Fish Babies (p. 741)
—Gymnastics (p. 907)
—Iguanodon: The Noisy Night Taylor, Dan, illus. (p. 1094)
—Learning about Animals (p. 1257)
—Learning about Insects (p. 1257)
—Learning about Plants (p. 1257)
—Learning about Trees (p. 1258)
—Mammal Babies (p. 1393)
—Natural World. (p. 1580)
—Remember 10 with Explorer Ben. Beedie, Duncan, illus. (p. 1864)
—Reptile Babies. (p. 1867)
—Sports & My Body (p. 2088)
—Stegosaurus: The Thoughtful Surprise Bakos, Barbara, illus. (p. 2112)
Veitch, Sophie F. F. James Hepburn: Free Church Minister (Classic Reprint) (p. 1157)
Veitelle, I. de. Lessons for Children in English & French, after Mrs. Barbauld's Method (Classic Reprint) (p. 1268)
Vejjajiva, Jane. Histoire de Kati. (p. 975)
Vekaria, Alka, jt. auth. see Dicker, Katie.
Vela, David, illus. see Marzo, José.
Vela, Eugenio H. Twinkle, Twinkle Little Harold. (p. 2305)
Velarde, Chase, illus. see Etherly, L. D.
Velasco, Catherine Ann. Behind the Scenes of Pro Baseball. (p. 193)
—Behind the Scenes of Pro Basketball. (p. 193)
Velasco, Cecilia. Tony. (p. 2260)
Velasco, Francisco Ruiz, illus. see Kennedy, Mike.
Velasco, M. G. Cardslinger. (p. 328)
Velasco, Ruth, illus. see Verne, Julio.
Velasquez, Crystal. Circle of Lies. (p. 393)
—Hunters of Chaos. (p. 1053)
—Jasmine's Big Idea. (p. 1160)
—Just Princesses. (p. 1194)
—Keiko's Pony Rescue. (p. 1208)
—Madison's New Buddy. (p. 1375)
—Sofia's Puppy Love. (p. 2054)
—Your Life, but Cooler. (p. 2534)
—Your Life, but Sweeter (p. 2534)
Velasquez, Eric. Grandma's Gift. Velasquez, Eric, illus. (p. 878)
—Grandma's Records. (p. 878)
—Looking for Bongo. (p. 1347)
—Looking for Bongo. Velasquez, Eric, illus. (p. 1347)
—Octopus Stew. (p. 1637)
Velasquez, Eric, illus. see Bolden, Tonya & Roberts, Cokie.
Velasquez, Eric, illus. see Boswell, Addie.
Velasquez, Eric, illus. see Brigham, Marilyn.
Velasquez, Eric, illus. see Grimes, Nikki.
Velasquez, Eric, illus. see Haskins, Jim.
Velasquez, Eric, illus. see Ieronimo, Christine.
Velasquez, Eric, illus. see Krull, Kathleen.
Velasquez, Eric, illus. see Malaspina, Ann.
Velasquez, Eric, illus. see McKissack, Patricia C.
Velasquez, Eric, illus. see Meyer, Susan Lynn.
Velasquez, Eric, illus. see Naidoo, Beverley.
Velasquez, Eric, illus. see Rappaport, Doreen.
Velasquez, Eric, illus. see Tuck, Pamela M.
Velasquez, Eric, illus. see Watkins, Angela Farris.
Velasquez, Eric, illus. see Weatherford, Carole Boston.
Velásquez, Gloria. Forgiving Moses. (p. 768)
—Rudy's Memory Walk. (p. 1912)
Velasquez, Isabella. Catholic Puppies: Therese & the Golden Bible. (p. 345)
—Catholic Puppies: Bernadette Gets Lost in the Holy Land. (p. 345)
—Catholic Puppies * Lucy's Big Adventure. (p. 345)
Velasquez, Liliana. Dreams & Nightmares: I Fled Alone to the United States When I Was Fourteen. (p. 603)
Velasquez, Lizzie. Se Bella, Se Tu Misma. (p. 1966)
Velasquez, Rebecca R., et al. Sunshine & His Sack of Snakes. (p. 2153)
Velástegui, Cecilia. Olinguito Speaks Up. (p. 1649)
Velazquez, Catherine. Dirty Birdie. (p. 552)
Velázquez de León, Mauricio. 20 Soccer Legends. (p. 2553)
—Top Soccer Tournaments Around the World. (p. 2264)
Velazquez De Leon, Mauricio, tr. see Houghton, Gillian.
Velazquez De Leon, Mauricio, tr. see Johnston, Marianne.
Velazquez, Eric, illus. see Johnson, Angela.
Velazquez, Jaqueline, illus. see Guczka Pacheco, Christel Rosemarie.
Velázquez Press, creator. Diario de Escritura Académica para Matemáticas. (p. 538)
—Velázquez Biliteracy Program PreK Hora de la Comida Set. (p. 2349)
Velázquez Press Staff & Velázquez Press, creators. Velázquez Biliteracy Program PreK Meal Time Set. (p. 2349)
Velázquez Press Staff, creator. Mi Cuaderno de Vocabulario Académico. (p. 1454)
Velde, David. David & Braveheart. (p. 510)
—No Nonsense Mr. Booboo & Boo Meets Sam. (p. 1614)
Velde, Marie, tr. see Brun, Cecile & Pichard, Olivier.
Velde, Vivian Vande. 23 Minutes. (p. 2554)
Veldhoven, Marijke, illus. see Eason, Sarah.
Veldhuijzen, Lorena. Plastic Fantastic: Real Heroes in a World That Wants to Be Saved. Charbonneau, Saskia, tr. (p. 1758)
—Plastic Fantastic: Echte Helden in Een Wereld Die Schreeuwt Om Hulp. Moerman, Cilla, illus. (p. 1758)
Veldhuis-Kemperman, Rietta. Reiki Adventure for Children. (p. 1862)
Veldkamp, Tjibbe. Tom the Tamer. Hopman, Philip, illus. (p. 2258)
Velemir, Gundula. Swetja und Die Späte Liebe. (p. 2169)
Veley, Margaret. Garden of Memories; Mrs. Austin; Lizzie's Bargain, Vol. 1 (Classic Reprint) (p. 809)
—Mitchelhurst Place, Vol. 1 Of 2: A Novel (Classic Reprint) (p. 1483)
Velez, Walter, illus. see Albee, Sarah.
Velhuijs, Max. Kind-Hearted Monster. (p. 1218)
Velica, Teodora, illus. see Myers, Janice Limb.
Velikan, Phil, illus. see Doyle, Mary K.
Velikan, Phil, illus. see Francine, Gabriella & Vayanian, Solara.
Velikanje, Kathryn. A Is for Alligator. Wilson, Lynda Farrington, illus. (p. 1)
—B Is for Boys & Bees. Wilson, Lynda Farrington, illus. (p. 146)
—Bike of Bees. Hovhannisyan, Nune, illus. (p. 225)
—C Is for Crazy Cats. Wilson, Lynda Farrington, illus. (p. 306)
—D Is for Dragon. Wilson, Lynda Farrington, illus. (p. 494)
—E Is for Elephant. Wilson, Lynda Farrington, illus. (p. 612)
—F Is for Face. Wilson, Lynda Farrington, illus. (p. 689)
—G Is for Girly Girls. Wilson, Lynda Farrington, illus. (p. 804)
—H Is for Horse. Wilson, Lynda Farrington, illus. (p. 908)
—I Is for Ice Cream. Wilson, Lynda Farrington, illus. (p. 1066)
—Zebras Paint Themselves Rainbow. Hovhannisyan, Nune, illus. (p. 2539)
Veloy Planas, Mariano. Mozart (esp.) (p. 1517)
Velthuijs, Max. Frog & the Stranger. (p. 789)
—Where Is Frog? (p. 2437)
Velthuijs, Max, illus. see Bell, Anthea.
Velthuis, Max. Little Boy & the Big Fish. (p. 1312)
Veltkamp, Jane, jt. auth. see Rose, Deborah Lee.
Velvin, Ellen. Rataplan, a Rogue Elephant: And Other Stories (Classic Reprint) (p. 1842)
—Wild Creatures Afield (Classic Reprint) (p. 2463)
—Wild-Animal Celebrities (Classic Reprint) (p. 2462)
Venable, Alan, jt. auth. see Stevenson, Robert Louis.
Venable, Charles S. Venable's Arithmetics-New Two-Book Series. Elementary Arithmetic. (p. 2350)
Venable, Charles Scott, jt. auth. see Legendre, Adrien Marie.
Venable, Colleen A. F. Going, Going, Dragon! Yue, Stephanie, illus. (p. 854)
—Raining Cats & Detectives. Yue, Stephanie, illus. (p. 1837)
Venable, Colleen Af. Amy the Red Panda Is Writing the Best Story in the World. Chan, Ruth, illus. (p. 77)
—Kiss Number 8. Crenshaw, Ellen T., illus. (p. 1224)
—Mervin the Sloth Is about to Do the Best Thing in the World. Chan, Ruth, illus. (p. 1451)
Venable, Colleen Af & Odd Dot. One More Wheel! A Things-That-Go Counting Book. Russo, Blythe, illus. (p. 1661)
Venable, Edward C. Pierre Vinton: The Adventures of a Superfluous Husband (Classic Reprint) (p. 1742)
Venable, James, illus. see Chandler, Ann.
Venable Jr, Al B. Captain Tom, the Sea Adventurer. (p. 326)
Venable, Ronny, jt. auth. see Grabenstein, Chris.
Venable, William Henry. Dream of Empire, or the House of Blennerhassett. (p. 602)
—Dream of Empire, or the House of Blennerhassett (Classic Reprint) (p. 602)
—Tom Tad (Classic Reprint) (p. 2258)
Vendera, Jaime & McGee, Anne Loader. Sing Out Loud Book I: Discovering Your Voice. Bastien, Valerie & Bingham, Jerry, illus. (p. 2023)
—Sing Out Loud Book II: Developing Your Voice. Bastien, Valerie, illus. (p. 2023)
—Sing Out Loud Book III: Owning Your Voice. Bastien, Valerie, illus. (p. 2023)
—Sing Out Loud Book IV: Owning the Stage. Bingham, Jerry, illus. (p. 2023)
Vendittelli, Marie. Chiens Racont's(les) (p. 369)
—Colors. (p. 426)
Venditti, Maria Cristina, illus. see Kameneva, Aleksandra S.
Venditti, Robert. Attack of the Alien Horde. Higgins, Dusty, illus. (p. 134)
—Battle of the Labyrinth. (p. 174)
—Last Olympian. (p. 1249)
—Lightning Thief. (p. 1300)
—Rise of the Robot Army. Higgins, Dusty, illus. (p. 1885)
—Sea of Monsters. (p. 1968)
—Titan's Curse. (p. 2251)
Venditti, Robert, jt. auth. see Riordan, Rick.
Venditti, Robert & de la Cruz, Melissa. Isle of the Lost: the Graphic Novel (a Descendants Novel) Fajardo, Kat, illus. (p. 1140)
—Isle of the Lost: the Graphic Novel (the Descendants Series) Fajardo, Kat, illus. (p. 1140)
—Return to the Isle of the Lost: the Graphic Novel. (p. 1871)
Venditti, Robert & Riordan, Rick. Percy Jackson & the Olympians the Titan's Curse: the Graphic Novel. Futaki, Attila & Guilhaumond, Gregory, illus. (p. 1721)
—Sea of Monsters. (p. 1968)
Vendlinger, Joan. Littlest Chair. (p. 1331)
Vene, Alessandro, illus. see Cervone, Shannon.
Vene, Alessandro, illus. see Schleuning, Todd & Schleuning, Cheryl.
Vene, Alessandro, illus. see Spergel, Heather.
Venegas, Leah. Wobbles. Rauch, Micah, illus. (p. 2483)
Venema, Lisa J., illus. see Coppage, Merry Ann.
Venerable, Trae Q. L. Grandpa I Just Wanna Be a Cowboy: Rodeo Cowboys. (p. 879)
—Grandpa I Just Wanna Be a Cowboy: Women in the West. (p. 879)
—Grandpa I Just Wanna Be a Cowboy: Notables from the West. (p. 879)
Veness, Kimberley. Let's Eat: Sustainable Food for a Hungry Planet (p. 1271)
Venetta, D. S. Wild Tales & Garden Thrills Garden Activity Book. (p. 2465)

—Regal Academy #2: Happily Ever After. Barone, Bendetta, illus. (p. 1861)
Verger, Victor. Epigrammes de M. Val. Martial, Vol. 4 (Classic Reprint) (p. 658)
Vergne, George H. De La. At the Foot of the Rockies: Stories of Mountain & Plain or Boy Life on the Old Ranche (Classic Reprint) (p. 131)
Vergne, H. De La. Hawaiian Sketches (Classic Reprint) (p. 940)
Verg'r, Victor. Epigrammes de M. Val. Martial, Vol. 4 (Classic Reprint) (p. 658)
Verhaeren, Emile. Dawn - Scholar's Choice Edition. (p. 511)
Verheijen, Jan, illus. see Sehlin, Gunhild.
Verhille, Alexandre & Tavernier, Sarah. Illustrated Atlas of Architecture & Marvelous Monuments. (p. 1096)
—Legendary Routes of the World. (p. 1263)
—Recordmania: Atlas of the Incredible. (p. 1855)
Verhoef, Sharon, illus. see Roland-James, Patricia & James, Robert L.
Verhoeff, Nelleke, illus. see DePalma, Kate.
Verhoosky, Michele. Molly Marie & the Amazing Jimmy. Verhoosky, Michele, illus. (p. 1489)
Verhoosky, Michele, illus. see Fonte, Mary Roessler & Hoppe, Jessica.
Verhoye, Annabelle, illus. see Asai, Carrie.
Verien, Nicolas. Emblemes et Devises Latines, Espagnoles et Italiennes, Vol. 1: Avec Leurs Explications Francoises (Classic Reprint) (p. 641)
Verity, Art. Tucson Charlie: Lost in the Zoo. Wilkinson, Nancy, illus. (p. 2298)
—Tucson Charlie: Lost in the Desert. Wilkinson, Nancy, illus. (p. 2298)
Verjan, Isaac M. Regeneration. (p. 1861)
Verkaik, Marcia, illus. see Bowden, Kristina.
Verkruysse, Toni, illus. see Gould, Susan Lynn.
Verlag, Arena, jt. auth. see Sterling Publishing Co., Inc.
Verlag, Don Bosco Medien. Relaxation & Concentration. Portmann, Rosemarie & Schneid, Elisabeth, eds. (p. 1862)
Verlag, Kelebek, ed. see Butzler, Annika.
Verlag, Kelebek, ed. see Gol, Ines.
Verlag, Kelebek, ed. see Schenk, Margareta.
Verlag, Kelebek, ed. Anthologie Halloween. (p. 102)
—Fabelhaft und Drachenstark. (p. 690)
Verlomme, Hugo. Homme des Vagues. (p. 998)
Verlot, Bernard. Guide du Botaniste Herborisant: Conseils Sur la Recolte des Plantes, la Preparation des Herbiers, l'Exploration des Stations de Plantes Phanerogames et Cryptogames et les Herborisations (Classic Reprint) (p. 903)
Verma, Dheeraj, illus. see Abnett, Dan.
Verma, Dheeraj, illus. see Jeffrey, Gary.
Verma, Dinesh, et al. Hindi Alphabet Activity Book International Edition. (p. 972)
Verma, Jatinder. Prince of Fire PB. (p. 1794)
Verma, Prachand, illus. see Luongo, Charlotte.
Verma, Sushant Sunita. I Failed to Read Her Heart. (p. 1064)
Verme, Julio. De la Tierra a la Luna. (p. 517)
—Viaje Al Centro de la Tierra. (p. 2354)
Vermette, Katherena. Northwest Resistance. Henderson, Scott B. & Yaciuk, Donovan, illus. (p. 1622)
—Pemmican Wars Henderson, Scott B. & Yaciuk, Donovan, illus. (p. 1715)
—Red River Resistance Henderson, Scott B. & Yaciuk, Donovan, illus. (p. 1858)
Vermeule, C. C. Report on Forestry in Northern New Jersey. Report on Forest Fires for Season 1895; Pp. 99-187. (p. 1866)
Vermeulen, Mariska. James & Cooper Finger Puppet Book. van de Liejgraaf, Deborah, illus. (p. 1156)
Vermeulen, Rob. Over Kabouters, Trollen en Draken. (p. 1686)
Vermeulen, Thomas. Gabangani Guinea Fowl & Huzu the Bird Eating Spider. (p. 804)
Vermillion, Danny, illus. see McGhee, Patti Gray.
Vermillion, Gail. Playground Personalities. Stukey, James, illus. (p. 1760)
Vermillion, Patricia. Hound Dawg. Pilgrim, Cheryl, illus. (p. 1021)
—Texas Chili? Oh My! Smith, Kuleigh, illus. (p. 2209)
—¿Chili Texano? ¡Ay Dios! Guadalupe, Jezabel, tr. (p. 376)
Vermillion, Veerle, illus. see Wijnberg, John Paul.
Vermillion, Veerle, illus. see Wijnberg, John.
Vermond, Kira. Growing Up, Inside & Out. (p. 900)
—Why Don't Cars Run on Apple Juice? Real Science Questions from Real Kids. Ogawa, Suharu, illus. (p. 2457)
Vermond, Kira & Hanmer, Clayton. Half-Truths & Brazen Lies: An Honest Look at Lying. (p. 911)
—Trending: How & Why Stuff Gets Popular. (p. 2285)
Vern, Lynn. Chocolate Is Better: Part 2. (p. 380)
Verne, Geo La. Photo-Play Journal, Vol. 1: May, 1916 (Classic Reprint) (p. 1736)
Verne, Ilian. Phil, the Scout, or a Fight for Beauregard's Dispatches, Vol. 7: A Story of Pittsburg Landing (Classic Reprint) (p. 1734)
Verne, Jules. 20,000 Leagues under the Sea Fisher, Eric Scott, illus. (p. 2561)
—20,000 Leagues under the Sea. (p. 2561)
—20,000 Leagues under the Sea (100 Copy Limited Edition) (p. 2561)
—20000 Lieues Sous. (p. 2562)
—Adventures of a Chinaman in China (Classic Reprint) (p. 21)
—Adventures of a Special Correspondent. (p. 21)
—All Around the Moon. (p. 51)
—Around the World in 80 Days. (p. 119)
—Around the World in 80 Days (100 Copy Limited Edition) (p. 119)
—Around the World in Eighty Days. (p. 119)
—Around the World in Eighty Days. Ingpen, Robert, illus. (p. 119)
—Cinq Semaines en Ballon. (p. 392)
—Eight Hundred Leagues on the Amazon: (world Classics, Unabridged) (p. 629)
—Eight Hundred Leagues on the Amazon. (p. 629)
—Eight Hundred Leagues on the Amazon Jules Verne. (p. 629)
—English at the North Pole. (p. 653)
—Facing the Flag: Pirate Adventure. (p. 693)
—Fantaisie du Docteur Ox. (p. 706)
—Five Hundred Millions of the Begum; the Tribulations of a Chinaman in China; the Giant Raft, Eight Hundred Leagues on the Amazon, Vol. 11 (Classic Reprint) (p. 743)
—Five Weeks in a Balloon: Journeys & Discoveries in Africa by Three Englishmen. (p. 745)
—Ile Mysterieuse. (p. 1095)
—Journey to the Center of the Earth Fisher, Eric Scott, illus. (p. 1182)
—Journey to the Center of the Earth. (p. 1182)
—Journey to the Center of the Earth. Kumar, Vinod, illus. (p. 1182)
—Journey to the Center of the Earth. Freeberg, Eric, illus. (p. 1182)
—Journey to the Center of the Earth. Rossi, Francesca, illus. (p. 1182)
—Journey to the Center of the Earth (100 Copy Limited Edition) (p. 1182)
—Journey to the Centre of the Earth: A Sci-Fi Adventure. (p. 1182)
—Journey to the Centre of the Earth. (p. 1182)
—Journey to the Centre of the Earth. Malleson, Frederick Amadeus, tr. (p. 1182)
—Master of the World. (p. 1419)
—Mysterious Island. (p. 1567)
—Mysterious Island. Kingston, W. H. G., tr. (p. 1567)
—Revoltes de la Bounty. (p. 1873)
—Special Correspondent: Or the Adventures of Claudius Bombarnac (Classic Reprint) (p. 2076)
—Topsy-Turvy. Ogilvie, J. G., tr. (p. 2264)
—Tour du Monde en Quatre-Vingts Jours (Classic Reprint) (p. 2268)
—Twenty Thousand Leagues under the Sea. (p. 2304)
—Twenty Thousand Leagues under the Sea. Rossi, Francesca, illus. (p. 2304)
—Twenty Thousand Leagues under the Sea (Classic Reprint) (p. 2304)
—Twenty Thousand Leagues under the Sea (World Classics, Unabridged) (p. 2304)
—Twenty Thousand Leagues under the Seas. (p. 2304)
—Voyage Au Centre de la Terre. 13e Édition. (p. 2368)
—Vuelta Al Mundo en 80 Dias. (p. 2369)
—Works of Jules Verne, Vol. 10: Dick Sands, a Captain at Fifteen; the Dark Continent; Measuring a Meridian (Classic Reprint) (p. 2498)
—Works of Jules Verne, Vol. 11: The Five Hundred Millions of the Begum; the Tribulations of a Chinaman in China; the Giant Raft, Eight Hundred Leagues on the Amazon (Classic Reprint) (p. 2498)
Verne, Jules, jt. auth. see Verne, Julio.
Verne, Jules & Cortes, Jesus. Vuelta Al Mundo en 80 Dias. (p. 2369)
Verne, Jules & D'Ennery, Adolphe. Around the World in 80 Days - the 1874 Play (hardback) (p. 119)
Verne, Jules & Lokus, Rex. Around the World in 80 Days. Smith, Tod G., illus. (p. 119)
Verne, Jules, et al. 20,000 LEAGUES under the SEA (Illustrated) A Thrilling Saga of Wondrous Adventure, Mystery & Suspense in the Wild Depths of the Pacific Ocean. (p. 2562)
Verne, Julio. 20 000 Leguas de Viaje Submarino. (p. 2553)
—20,000 Leguas de Viaje Submarino (Bilinge) La Gran Aventura Marítima. (p. 2562)
—De la Tierra a la Luna. (p. 517)
—De la Tierra a la Luna. Duran, Jesus, illus. (p. 517)
—Isla Misteriosa. (p. 1139)
—Julio Verne. (p. 1187)
—Veinte Mil Leguas de Viaje Submarino. (p. 2349)
—Viaje Al Centro de la Tierra. (p. 2354)
—Vuelta Al Mundo en 80 Días. Velasco, Ruth, illus. (p. 2369)
Verne, Julio, jt. auth. see Verne, Jules.
Verne, Julio, jt. auth. see Wells, H. G.
Verne, Julio & Verne, Jules. Veinte Mil Leguas de Viaje Submarino. (p. 2349)
Vernede, R. E. Fair Dominion: A Record of Canadian Impressions (Classic Reprint) (p. 695)
—Judgement of Illingborough (Classic Reprint) (p. 1185)
—Letters to His Wife (Classic Reprint) (p. 1281)
—Port Allington Stories (Classic Reprint) (p. 1778)
—Quietness of Dick (Classic Reprint) (p. 1828)
Vernede, Robert Ernest. Flight of Faviel (Classic Reprint) (p. 748)
Vernell, Jerome, illus. see Guerrero, Elsie.
Vernell Jr, Jerome, illus. see Guerrero, Elsie.
Vernera, Justīne, tr. see Pere, Tuula.
Verness, Lucile Driftmier. Story of an American Family (Classic Reprint) (p. 2129)
Verney, Frances. Sketches from Nature: With Pen & Pencil (Classic Reprint) (p. 2031)
Verney, John. February's Road. (p. 717)
—Friday's Tunnel. (p. 785)
Vernick, Audrey. After the Worst Thing Happens. (p. 34)
—Brothers at Bat: The True Story of an Amazing All-Brother Baseball Team. Salerno, Steven, illus. (p. 286)
—Edgar's Second Word. Burris, Priscilla, illus. (p. 625)
—First Grade Dropout. (p. 737)
—First Grade Dropout. Cordell, Matthew, illus. (p. 737)
—Funniest Man in Baseball: The True Story of Max Patkin. Bower, Jennifer, illus. (p. 801)
—I Won a What? Neubecker, Robert, illus. (p. 1086)
—Is Your Buffalo Ready for Kindergarten? Jennewein, Daniel, illus. (p. 1138)
—Second Grade Holdout. Cordell, Matthew, illus. (p. 1973)
—She Loved Baseball: The Effa Manley Story. Tate, Don, illus. (p. 2004)
—Take Your Octopus to School Day. Schoenbrun, Diana, illus. (p. 2177)
—Teach Your Buffalo to Play Drums. Jennewein, Daniel, illus. (p. 2194)
Vernick, Audrey, jt. auth. see Rhuday-Perkovich, Olugbemisola.
Vernick, Audrey, jt. auth. see Scanlon, Liz Garton.
Vernick, Shirley. I Love You, Michigan Baby. Bergin, Molly, illus. (p. 1079)
Vernick, Shirley & La Forest, Courtney. Boston Baby: A Local Baby Book. (p. 264)
Vernick, Shirley Reva. Black Butterfly. (p. 237)
—Blood Lie. (p. 246)
—Remember Dippy. (p. 1864)
Verniero, Joan C., jt. auth. see Rappaport, Doreen.
Vernieux, C. Hermit of Motee Jhurna, or Pearl Spring: Also Indian Tales & Anecdotes, Moral & Instructive (Classic Reprint) (p. 959)
—Hermit of Motee Jhurna, or Pearl Spring. (p. 959)
—Hermit of Motee Jhurna, or Pearl Spring; Also Indian Tales & Anecdotes, Moral & Instructive. (p. 959)
Vernon, Caitlyn. Nowhere Else on Earth: Standing Tall for the Great Bear Rainforest (p. 1628)
Vernon, Carolyn. Where Are My Playmates? (p. 2435)
Vernon, Charlie. Mary Barker: A Thrilling Narrative of Early Life in North Carolina (Classic Reprint) (p. 1414)
Vernon, Elisient Maeve. Ava's Bad Day. (p. 141)
—More Ava Stories. (p. 1504)
Vernon, Geneva. Jubilee Gems (Classic Reprint) (p. 1185)
Vernon, Henry. Life & Remains of Wilmot Warwick: Edited by His Friend (Classic Reprint) (p. 1289)
Vernon, Horace. Horace Vernon, or Life in the West, Vol. 1 of 3 (Classic Reprint) (p. 1003)
Vernon, Jeff, illus. see Boritzer, Etan.
Vernon, Rion, illus. see Langteau, Scott.
Vernon, Ruth. Bride of Love: Or the True Greatness of Female Heroism (Classic Reprint) (p. 280)
Vernon, Steve. Maritime Monsters Solway, Jeff, illus. (p. 1406)
Vernon, Ursula. Attack of the Ninja Frogs. (p. 134)
—Castle Hangnail. (p. 340)
—Curse of the Were-Wiener. (p. 489)
—Dani Bocafuego. la Cueva Del Murcielago Gigante. (p. 502)
—Dani Bocafuego. la Salchicha Maldita. (p. 502)
—Dragonbreath. (p. 594)
—Dragonbreath #1. (p. 594)
—Dragonbreath #11: The Frozen Menace. (p. 594)
—Dragonbreath #2: Attack of the Ninja Frogs. (p. 594)
—Dragonbreath #3: Curse of the Were-Wiener. (p. 594)
—Dragonbreath #4: Lair of the Bat Monster. (p. 594)
—Dragonbreath #5: No Such Thing As Ghosts. (p. 594)
—Dragonbreath #9: The Case of the Toxic Mutants. (p. 594)
—Hamster Princess: Harriet the Invincible. (p. 914)
—Hamster Princess: Giant Trouble. (p. 914)
—Hamster Princess: Ratpunzel. (p. 914)
—Harriet the Invincible. (p. 933)
—Knight-Napped! (p. 1228)
—Lair of the Bat Monster. (p. 1240)
—Little Red Rodent Hood. (p. 1326)
—Nightmare of the Iguana. (p. 1608)
—Of Mice & Magic. (p. 1640)
—Revenge of the Horned Bunnies (p. 1872)
—When Fairies Go Bad (p. 2430)
—Whiskerella. (p. 2442)
Vernon-Melzer, Gabby. Amazing Ancients!: Egypt. DGPH Stufio, illus. (p. 63)
Veronica, M. Bearers of Freedom. (p. 180)
Veronica, M., ed. see Theresine, Mary.
Veronica, Nick. Icebreakers. (p. 1088)
Veronica, Roth. Divergente. (p. 565)
—Las marcas de la muerte. (p. 1246)
Verplancke, Klaas. Magritte's Apple. (p. 1382)
Verploegh, Harry, ed. see MacDonald, George.
Verr, Harry Coe. Let's Fly a Kite, Charlie Brown! (Peanuts) Ellis, Kim & Schulz, Charles, illus. (p. 1273)
Verrall, Lisa, illus. see Litton, Jonathan.
Verrett, Michael. Beyond the Wall. (p. 212)
—Cozmo the Elf. (p. 465)
—Dinosaur Tree. (p. 549)
—Galid's Christmas Wish. (p. 806)
—Goat on Cow. (p. 849)
—Good Too Too & Bad Too Too. (p. 866)
—How High How Far. (p. 1031)
—It Followed Me Home Can I Keep It? (p. 1141)
—It Followed Me Home Can I Keep It? (full Color) (p. 1141)
—Luca Got What for Christmas. (p. 1363)
—Monday Morning March with Rainey Estelle. (p. 1492)
—No Hug for a Kaylea Bug. (p. 1613)
—Pontolong & Duckie. (p. 1773)
—Pontolong & Duckie. Verrett, Michael, illus. (p. 1773)
—Prettiest Girl on Planet X. (p. 1790)
—Rhymes of the Gray Beard Tree. (p. 1875)
—Speckle the Annoying Freckle. (p. 2077)
—White Alligator (paper Back) (p. 2443)
—White Alligator (paperback full Color) (p. 2443)
—White Alligator Crown Quatro. (p. 2443)
—Zac Zap the Great Big Canoe Race. (p. 2537)
Verrett, Michael, illus. see Bankston, Pamela Cali.
Verrett, Michael, illus. see Wilson, Janet.
Verrico, Susan. Privateer's Apprentice. (p. 1802)
Verrill, A. Hyatt. Boy Adventurers in the Forbidden Land (Classic Reprint) (p. 267)
—Radio Detectives (Classic Reprint) (p. 1833)
Verrill, Alpheus Hyatt. Harper's Aircraft Book: Why Aeroplanes Fly, How to Make Models, & All about Aircraft, Little & Big (Classic Reprint) (p. 931)
—Uncle Abner's Legacy (Classic Reprint) (p. 2318)
Verrill, William, illus. see Puppel, Douglas.
Verrone, Patric C. W. Sharktooth. (p. 2003)
Verseghy, Lauren a, illus. see Miller, Michael A.
Versteeg, Lizelot. Squirrel in Autumn. (p. 2095)
—Squirrel in Winter. (p. 2095)
Verstraete, Elaine, illus. see Alphin, Elaine Marie.
Verstraete, Elaine, illus. see Pfeffer, Wendy.
Verstraete, Elaine, illus. see Sutcliffe, Jane.
Verstraete, Elaine, illus. see Walker, Sally M.
Verstraete, Larry. Coop the Great. (p. 451)
—G Is for Golden Boy: A Manitoba Alphabet. Lund, Brian, illus. (p. 804)
—Innovations in Everyday Technologies. (p. 1121)
—Innovations in Transportation. (p. 1121)
—S Is for Scientists: A Discovery Alphabet. Geister, David, illus. (p. 1919)
—Surviving the Hindenburg. (p. 2165)
Verstraete, Majanka. Doll Maker: Weirdville. (p. 578)
—Fright Train: Weirdville. (p. 788)
—House of Horrors: Weirdville. (p. 1023)
—Valentina & the Haunted Mansion (Valentina's Spooky Adventures - 1) Giffin, Noelle, illus. (p. 2344)
—Valentina & the Whackadoodle Witch: Valentina's Spooky Adventures. Giffin, Noelle, illus. (p. 2344)
Vert, Octavia Walton Le. Souvenirs of Travel, Vol. 2 (Classic Reprint) (p. 2069)
Vertical Inc. Staff, ed. see Tezuka, Osamu.
Vertilus, Nathan, tr. My First Haitian Creole Dictionary. (p. 1544)
Verveen, Wim. Karel en de Elementen. (p. 1203)
Verville, Béroalde de. Moyen de Parvenir, Oevvre Contenant la Raison de Tout Ce Qui a Esté, Est, et Sera: Auec Demonstrations Certaines et Necessaires, Selon la Rencontre des Effets de Vertu (Classic Reprint) (p. 1517)
Verville, Kathleen. Testicular Cancer. (p. 2209)
Verwey, Albert, jt. auth. see Sidney, Philip.
Verwey, Amanda, illus. see Tea, Michelle.
Very, Lydia Louisa Anna. Old-Fashioned Garden, & Walks & Musings Therein (Classic Reprint) (p. 1645)
Very, Pierre. Assassinat du Pere Noel. (p. 127)
Verzini, Daniele, illus. see Stilton, Geronimo & Heim, Julia.
Verzini, Daniele, illus. see Stilton, Geronimo & Pizzelli, Anna.
Verzini, Daniele, illus. see Stilton, Geronimo & Schaffer, Andrea.
Verzini, Daniele, illus. see Stilton, Geronimo & Tramontozzi, Lidia Morson.
Verzini, Daniele, illus. see Stilton, Geronimo, et al.
Verzov, Ella & Oirechman, Chana. Moshe of Japan. (p. 1507)
—Tamar of Venice. (p. 2188)
Vescelius-Sheldon, Louise. I. D. B. in South Africa (Classic Reprint) (p. 1064)
—Yankee Girls in Zulu Land (Classic Reprint) (p. 2517)
Vescia, Monique. Battle Reenactments (p. 175)
—Culture & Science of Implants. (p. 484)
—Culture of Scarification. (p. 484)
—David Karp & Tumblr. (p. 511)
—Emancipation Proclamation. (p. 640)
—Engineers at Work. (p. 652)
—Extreme Parkour (p. 687)
—Extreme Trampoline (p. 687)
—Fashion. (p. 712)
—Kim Kardashian West & Kanye West (p. 1218)
—Markus Zusak (p. 1407)
—What Is Animal Behavior? (p. 2414)
—Zachary Quinto (p. 2537)
Vescia, Monique, jt. auth. see Rauf, Don.
Vescia, Monique & Judson, Karen. Do You Get into Arguments? (p. 571)
Vescia, Monique & Nicholson, Michael. Mahatma Gandhi: Champion of the Indian Independence Movement. (p. 1382)
Vescia, Monique, et al. What You Can Do about ADHD. (p. 2422)
—What You Can Do about Sickle Cell Disease. (p. 2422)
Vescia, Peter. Pikes Peak Gold Rush (p. 1744)
Vescio, Robert. Box Cars. King, Cara, illus. (p. 266)
—Finn & Puss. Mackie, Melissa, illus. (p. 731)
—Ganz Gleich Mit Wem Wir Zusammen Sind. Beer, Michele, tr. from ENG. (p. 808)
—No Matter Who We're With. Scholten, Cheri, illus. (p. 1613)
Vescio, Robert & Creamer, Kathy. Bigger Than Yesterday, Smaller Than Tomorrow. (p. 224)
Vesey, Arthur Henry. Clock & the Key (Classic Reprint) (p. 406)
Vesey, Ernest Blakeman. Beowulf: Guide Dog to the Blind (Classic Reprint) (p. 201)
Vess, Charles, illus. see De Lint, Charles.
Vess, Charles, illus. see Gaiman, Neil.
Vess, Charles, illus. see Lachenmeyer, Nathaniel.
Vess, Charles, illus. see Smith, Jeff.
Vessel, Celestine. Boy Who Became a Cheetah: Reflections of Donelo. (p. 270)
Vest, Dale G., jt. auth. see Overstreet, Tommy.
Vest, Sam, illus. see Bunt, Stephanie Marie.
Vestergaard, Hope. Digger, Dozer, Dumper. (p. 545)
—Digger, Dozer, Dumper. Slonim, David, illus. (p. 545)
—Potty Animals: What to Know When You've Gotta Go! Petrone, Valeria, illus. (p. 1781)
Vestita, Marisa. Bronto's Search for Dad. (p. 285)
—Terri's First Flight. (p. 2207)
—Toothbrush for Rex. (p. 2262)
—Trixie Faces Her Fear. (p. 2290)
Vetenskapsakademien, Kungl. Svenska, jt. auth. see Berzelius, Jöns Jakob.
Vetere, Lori. Jungle Bugs & Vegetation (p. 1190)
—Jungle Facts & Figures (p. 1190)
—Jungle Tribes. (p. 1190)
—Jungle Wildlife (p. 1190)
—Pharrell (p. 1733)
Vetleseter, Tonje, tr. see Bringsvaerd, Tor Age.
Vetromile, Eugene. Abnakis & Their History; or, Historical Notices on the Aborigines of Acadia. (p. 6)
Vetsch, Rita Kaye. Many Colors of Friendship. (p. 1400)
Vetter, Sandra. Lunartiks(r) (p. 1368)
Vetto, Mandana. President Wears Pink. Foresti, Sara, illus. (p. 1789)
Vevers, Rachel. Quest for the Unicorn. (p. 1826)
Veyret, Yvette. NUESTRO PLANETA, LA TIERRA. (p. 1629)
Veysey, Arthur Henry. Pedigree in Pawn (Classic Reprint) (p. 1712)
—Two White Elephants (Classic Reprint) (p. 2310)
Vezeau, Sheila. Sky, the Blue Bunny. Ostrowski, Justin, illus. (p. 2034)
ViacomCBS, Arthur Desin, illus. see Nickel, Scott, et al.
Vial-Andru, Mauricette. Let's Pray the Rosary. Beaudesson, Emmanuel, illus. (p. 1277)
Viana, Tatio, illus. see Farndon, John.

Viana, Tatio, illus. see Hall, Mark & West, Matthew.
Viana, Tatio, illus. see Oxlade, Chris.
Vianch. Salto Cu. (p. 1925)
Viancha, Yesid. Salto Cuántico. (p. 1925)
Vianney, M. John, illus. see Dominic, Sister M.
Viano, Hannah. Arrow to Alaska: A Pacific Northwest Adventure. (p. 119)
—B Is for Bear: A Natural Alphabet. Viano, Hannah, illus. (p. 146)
—S Is for Salmon: A Pacific Northwest Alphabet. Viano, Hannah, illus. (p. 1919)
Viau, Nancy. Beauty & Bernice Young, Timothy, illus. (p. 184)
—City Street Beat. (p. 395)
—First Snow. Shipman, Talitha, illus. (p. 739)
—Just One Thing! Young, Timothy, illus. (p. 1194)
—Samantha Hansen Has Rocks in Her Head (p. 1927)
—Something Is Bugging Samantha Hansen (p. 2060)
—Storm Song Gynux, illus. (p. 2127)
—Today Is a Beach Day! Alder, Charlie, illus. (p. 2255)
Viau, Théophile de. Nouvelles Oeuvres de Feu Mr. Theophile: Composées d'Excellentes Lettres Françoises et Latines (Classic Reprint) (p. 1626)
—Oeuvres de Théophile, Divisées en Trois Parties: La Premiere, Contenant l'Immortalité de l'Ame, Avec Plusieurs Autres Pieces; la Seconde, les Tragedies; et la Troisiesme, les Pieces Qu'il a Faites Pendant Sa Prison, Iusques À Present. (p. 1639)
Vicar, Henry. Company Owns the Tools (Classic Reprint) (p. 433)
Vicario, Evelyn. Mathematics for Life - Moses Meets the Triangles. Vicario, Evelyn, illus. (p. 1424)
—Mathematics for Life - Moses Teaches Properties of Addition. (p. 1424)
—Mathematics for Life Practice Workbook - Kindergarten. (p. 1424)
Vicario, Miguel Medina & Miguel, Medina Vicario. Quico: El Nino Que Quiso Ser Comico. (p. 1827)
Vicary, John Fulford. Danish Parsonage (Classic Reprint) (p. 503)
Vicary, Tim. Hitchhiker (p. 982)
Vicens, Paula, tr. see Solotareff, Gregoire.
Vicent, Al. Amazing Stories. (p. 66)
Vicente, Alidis. Case of the Three Kings / el Caso de Los Reyes Magos: The Flaca Files / Los Expedientes de Flaca. (p. 338)
—Missing Chancleta & Other Top-Secret Cases / la Chancleta Perdida y Otros Casos Secretos. (p. 1480)
—Shameless Shenanigans of Mister Malo / Las Terribles Travesuras de Mister Malo: The Mister Malo Series / Serie Mister Malo. (p. 1999)
Vicente, Fernando, illus. see Barrie, J. M.
Vichitraa. Bali Farm Adventures. (p. 161)
Vichuras, Michael J. St. Joseph's Collegian, Vol. 21: March 15, 1933 (Classic Reprint) (p. 2096)
Vick, E. M. Top Hat Society. (p. 2263)
Vick, Jacqueline. Logical Larry. (p. 1339)
Vick, Kari, illus. see Arrowsmith Decoux, Rose.
Vick, Kari, illus. see Lunge-Larsen, Lise.
Vick, Wm T. Identical Opposites: The Apocalypse Trilogy Book One. (p. 1089)
Vickers, Brant. Dewey: The Silent Boy. (p. 536)
Vickers, Elaine. Like Magic. Not, Sara, illus. (p. 1300)
—Paper Chains. Not, Sara, illus. (p. 1697)
Vickers Givens, Belinda. I Am Blessed to Have You. (p. 1058)
Vickers, Rebecca. 101 Ways to Be Smart about Money. (p. 2559)
—Every Person Has a History (p. 670)
—Every Possession Has a History (p. 670)
—Industrial Age Medicine (p. 1117)
—Medicine (p. 1436)
—Punctuation & Spelling: Rules That Make Things Clear (p. 1814)
—Types of Words: Unleashing Powerful Parts of Speech (p. 2310)
Vickers, Rebecca & Langley, Andrew. Everything Has a History (p. 673)
Vickers, Roy, illus. see Weisman, Kay.
Vickers, Roy Henry, illus. see Bouchard, David.
Vickers, Roy Henry & Budd, Robert. Cloudwalker. (p. 408)
—Hello Humpback! Vickers, Roy Henry, illus. (p. 951)
—One Eagle Soaring. (p. 1659)
—Orca Chief. (p. 1669)
—Peace Dancer. (p. 1709)
—Raven Brings the Light: A Northwest Coast Legend. (p. 1843)
—Raven Squawk, Orca Squeak. Vickers, Roy Henry, illus. (p. 1843)
—Sockeye Silver, Saltchuck Blue. Vickers, Roy Henry, illus. (p. 2054)
Vickers, Sheree. Drama Scripts for People with Special Needs: Inclusive Drama for PMLD, Autistic Spectrum & Special Needs Groups. (p. 596)
Vickers-Hulse, Karan. Surf School. (p. 2162)
Vicki, Jones, ed. see Jones, Carl L.
Vickie Washington and Carla Watts, ed. see Young, T. M.
Victor, Frances Fuller. New Penelope, & Other Stories & Poems (Classic Reprint) (p. 1596)
Victor, Irving a. Gleaner: June, 1923 (Classic Reprint) (p. 841)
Victor, M. V. Unionist's Daughter: A Tale of the Rebellion in Tennessee (Classic Reprint) (p. 2329)
Victor, Metta V. Alice Wilde, the Raftsman's Daughter: A Forest Romance (Classic Reprint) (p. 46)
—Passing the Portal, or a Girl's Struggle: An Autobiography (Classic Reprint) (p. 1703)
Victor, Metta Victoria. Two Hunters, or the Canon Camp: A Romance of the Santa Fe Trail (Classic Reprint) (p. 2308)
Victor, Metta Victoria (Fuller). Blunders of a Bashful Man (Classic Reprint) (p. 250)
—Dead Letter: An American Romance (Classic Reprint) (p. 517)
—Mrs. Rasher's Curtain Lectures (Classic Reprint) (p. 1523)
Victor, Ralph. Boy Scouts Patrol. (p. 270)
Victor, Verity. Behind the Scenes: A Story of the Stage (Classic Reprint) (p. 193)
Victoria, A., illus. see Upton, J.
Victoria, Amber & Brian, Reinker. Magic Chocolate Shop. Christina, Linsin, ed. (p. 1377)
Victoria Assanelli, illus. see Miller, Connie Colwell.
Victoria, Danna, illus. see Williams, Kay.
Victoria, Dionne, illus. see Joy, Elissa.
Victoria, Empress. Empress Frederick Writes to Sophie Her Daughter, Crown Princess & Later Queen of the Hellenes: Letters 1889-1901 (Classic Reprint) (p. 645)
Victoria, Kirton, illus. see Redmond, Valerie.
Victoria Lerae, Moreno. Arbez the Friendly Zebra. (p. 109)
Victoria, Lisa, illus. see Davis, L. J.
Victoria, Marie Alexandra. Christmas Tale. (p. 387)
Victoria, Queen. More Leaves from the Journal of a Life in the Highlands: From 1802 to 1888 (Classic Reprint) (p. 1505)
Victoria, Roberts. Best Pet Ever. Deborah, Allwright, illus. (p. 207)
Victoria, Sarah. Little Boy & His Red Glasses. (p. 1312)
Victoria Washington and Carla Watts, ed. see Young, T. M.
Victorin, B. M. Roiser de la Vierge: The Madonna's Rosebush (Classic Reprint) (p. 1897)
Victorio, Ricci Mann. Emily's Book of Words. (p. 642)
Victor-Larsen, Jennifer & Korby, Katy. Baby Thunder. (p. 153)
Victory Productions, Inc. Staff, tr. see Gordon, Sharon & Ricciuti, Edward R.
Victory Productions, Inc. Staff, tr. see Rau, Dana Meachen.
Vicuna, Claudio Orrego. Surprising Adventures of Balthazar. (p. 2163)
Vida, Marco Girolamo. Vida's Art of Poetry: Translated into English Verse (Classic Reprint) (p. 2356)
Vidal, Aleta, illus. see Carreras, Hernan.
Vidal, Alexander, illus. see Parhad, Elisa.
Vidal, Beatriz, illus. see Jamba, Dashdondog & Pellowski, Anne.
Vidal, Beatriz, illus. see Killion, Bette.
Vidal, Gayle. Magic Diamond. (p. 1377)
—Magic Garden. (p. 1377)
—Magic Smile. (p. 1379)
Vidal, Jordi, tr. see Hulme, John & Wexler, Michael.
Vidal, Oriol. Build a Picture Monsters Sticker Book. (p. 293)
Vidal, Oriol, illus. see Bailey, Catherine.
Vidal, Oriol, illus. see Dahl, Michael.
Vidal, Oriol, illus. see Fields, Jan.
Vidal, Oriol, illus. see George, K.
Vidal, Oriol, illus. see George, Kallie.
Vidal, Oriol, illus. see Mass, Wendy.
Vidal, Oriol, illus. see Mullen, Diane C.
Vidal, Séverine. Mega Bunny. Barroux, Stephane, illus. (p. 1441)
—Mega Mouse. Barroux, Stephane, illus. (p. 1441)
—Mega Pig. Barroux, Stephane, illus. (p. 1441)
—Mega Wolf. Barroux, Stephane, illus. (p. 1441)
—Pipe Por Fin Dice No. (p. 1748)
Vidali, Valerio, illus. see Bozzi, Riccardo.
Vidali, Valerio, illus. see Rodari, Gianni.
Vidali, Valerio & Uman, Jennifer. Jemmy Button. Vidali, Valerio & Uman, Jennifer, illus. (p. 1163)
Vidaurri, S. M. All My Friends Are Ghosts. Krieger, Hannah, illus. (p. 53)
—Steven Universe: Harmony. Rose, Mollie, illus. (p. 2116)
Videau, Valerie. Gde Fete Pinkie Pie Litt Pony. (p. 812)
Videbeck, Sheila, jt. auth. see Wilder, Laura Ingalls.
Vides Campbell, Maria & Gugliara, Therese. Gia Maria's World True Accounts of Autism. (p. 830)
Vidi, Vidi. Mr. Frank: The Underground Mail-Agent (Classic Reprint) (p. 1518)
VIDIC, Bostjan, tr. see Pere, Tuula.
VIDILI, Laura, illus. see Zedda, Claudia.
Vidinhas, Catia, illus. see Magalhaes, Alvaro.
Vidocq, Eugene Francois. Memoirs of Vidocq, Principal Agent of the French Police until 1827, Vol. 2 of 2 (Classic Reprint) (p. 1445)
Vidrine, Gabriel D. On a Summer Night. (p. 1652)
Viebig, Clara. Absolution (Classic Reprint) (p. 9)
—Our Daily Bread (Classic Reprint) (p. 1677)
—Son of His Mother (Classic Reprint) (p. 2061)
Vieceli, Emma, illus. see Horowitz, Anthony & Johnston, Antony.
Vieceli, Emma, illus. see Mead, Richelle.
Vieceli, Emma, illus. see Shakespeare, William.
Viegas, Jennifer. Eye: Learning How We See. (p. 688)
—Pierre Omidyar: The Founder of EBay. (p. 1742)
—William James: American Philosopher, Psychologist, & Theologian. (p. 2468)
Viegas, Jennifer, jt. auth. see Huddle, Rusty.
Viegas, Jennifer, jt. auth. see Kingston, Anna.
Viegas, Jennifer, jt. auth. see Wolfe, James.
Viegas, Jennifer & Baum, Margaux. Fungi & Molds. (p. 801)
—Parasites. (p. 1699)
Viegas, Marneta. Magic Box. (p. 1377)
—Relax Kids: The Wishing Star. (p. 1862)
—Relax Kids: Little Book of Stars. (p. 1862)
—Relax Kids - Aladdin's Magic Carpet: Let Snow White, the Wizard of Oz & Other Fairytale Characters Show You & Your Child How to Meditate & Relax. (p. 1862)
Viegas-Barros, Rocio, tr. see Bertrand, Diane Gonzales.
Vieira, Derek, jt. auth. see Loach, Claire.
Vieira, Eduardo, illus. see Skye, Obert.
Vieira, Eileen. Let's Celebrate Our Differences. (p. 1270)
Vieira, Gloria, illus. see Medina, Jennette.
Vieira, Margie. When Shadows Fade. (p. 2433)
Vieira, Nuno Alexandre, illus. see Highley, Rainey Marie.
Vieira, Rayanne, illus. see Shepherd, Kat.
Vieira, Rayanne, illus. see Virr, Paul & Potter, William.
Vieira, Rayanne, illus. see Woolf, Alex.
Viele, Herman Knickerbocker. Heartbreak Hill: A Comedy Romance (Classic Reprint) (p. 946)
—Inn of the Silver Moon (Classic Reprint) (p. 1121)
—Last of the Knickerbockers: A Comedy Romance (Classic Reprint) (p. 1248)
—Myra of the Pines (Classic Reprint) (p. 1566)
—On the Lightship (Classic Reprint) (p. 1655)
Viele, Steven. My Dog Is the Tooth Fairy. McKeown, Ashley, illus. (p. 1537)
Viel-Taschereau, Geneviève, illus. see Weber, Vicky.
Vien, Ashley. Justin Fights Sleep. Stenton, Murray, illus. (p. 1195)
Viennet, Jean-Pons-Guillaume. Fables Completes (Classic Reprint) (p. 690)
Vierow, Wendy. Battle of Bull Run: Confederate Forces Overwhelm Union Troops. (p. 174)
—Battle of Trenton. (p. 174)
—Battle of Yorktown. (p. 175)
—Capture of New Orleans: Union Fleet Takes Control of the Lower Mississippi. (p. 326)
—Shots Fired at Fort Sumter: Civil War Breaks Out! (p. 2011)
Viers, Ric. Make Some Noise: Sound Effects Recording for Teens. (p. 1386)
Vieth, Gerhard Ulrich Anthony. Pleasing Preceptor, or Familiar Instructions in Natural History & Physics, Vol. 2: Adapted to the Capacities of Youth, & Calculated Equally to Inform & Amuse Their Minds During the Intervals of More Dry & Severe Study (Classic Reprint) (p. 1762)
—Pleasing Preceptor, or Familiar Instructions in Natural History & Physics, Vol. 1: Adapted to the Capacities of Youth, & Calculated Equally to Inform & Amuse Their Minds During the Intervals of More Dry & Severe Study; Taken Chiefly from the G. (p. 1762)
Vietor, Wilhelm. Englisches Lesebuch (Classic Reprint) (p. 652)
Vietze, Andrew. Life & Death of Malcolm X. (p. 1289)
—Life & Death of Martin Luther King Jr. (p. 1289)
—Samuel de Champlain. (p. 1929)
—Zheng He: China's Greatest Navigator. (p. 2540)
Vieweg, Olivia. Bibi & Miyu, Vol. 1. (p. 212)
Vig, P. S. Den Danske Udvandring Til Amerika: Dans Aarsager Og Veje. (p. 528)
Vigg, Vigg, illus. see Sadler, Judy Ann.
Viggers, Katie. 1 to 20, Animals Aplenty. (p. 2546)
—Almost an Animal Alphabet. (p. 57)
Vigil, Angel. Papi, How Many Stars Are in the Sky? Ahmad, Aadil & James, Martin, illus. (p. 1698)
Vigil, Luis Gerardo Sanchez, illus. see Romeu, Emma.
Vigla, Vincent, illus. see Broski, Julie.
Viglione, Julia Douthwaite. Frankenstein de la Caja de Manzanas: Una Historia Posiblemente Verdadera de Los orígenes Del Monstruo. Dela Cruz, Jeremy Llanes, tr. (p. 778)
—Frankenstein du Cageot à Pommes: Ou Comment le Monstre Est Né, de Source (presque) Sûre. Jauneau, Vincent, tr. (p. 778)
—Frankenstein of the Apple Crate: A Possibly True Story of the Monster's Origins. Neis, Karen, illus. (p. 778)
Vignaga, Francesca Dafne, illus. see Magni, Aurora.
Vignaga, Francesca Dafne, illus. see Troupe, Thomas Kingsley.
Vigneault, Gilles. Cadeau Pour Sophie: Conte et Chansons. Jorisch, Stéphane, illus. (p. 308)
—Gift for Sophie. Jorisch, Stéphane, illus. (p. 832)
Vigneras, Marcel. Chansons de France: Transcrites Avec Accompagnement de Piano, Notes Historiques et Explicatives, et Guide de Prononciation (Classic Reprint) (p. 357)
Vignocchi, Chiara, et al. Shake the Tree! A Minibombo Book. (p. 1998)
Vignoli, Daniella, illus. see Visconti, Guido.
Vignolli, David Jesus. Girl in the Himalayas. (p. 836)
Vignolo, Enrique, illus. see Durant, Sybrina & Johnson, Sandi.
Vignolo, Enrique, illus. see Johnson, Sandi.
Vignolo, Enrique, illus. see McMillan, Dawn.
Vignolo, Enrique, illus. see Sommer, Carl.
Vigny, Alfred de. Imperial Grandeur, or the Family from Souvenirs of Count Alfred de Vigny (Classic Reprint) (p. 1102)
—Military Servitude & Grandeur (Classic Reprint) (p. 1466)
Vigourt, Renaud, illus. see Etherington, Robin.
Vigovszky, Rita, illus. see Zabel, Alanna.
Viguié, Debbie. Scarlet Moon. (p. 1942)
—Spring of Candy Apples (p. 2092)
Viguie, Debbie, jt. auth. see Holder, Nancy.
Viguié, Debbie, jt. auth. see Viguié, Debbie.
Viguie, Debbie & Holder, Nancy. Unleashed. (p. 2333)
Viguié, Debbie & Viguié, Debbie. Violet Eyes. (p. 2360)
ViiiZ. Photo Doodles: 200 Photos for You to Complete. (p. 1736)
Vijay, Sakthika. Outcast. (p. 1684)
Vik, Lyn, illus. see Pentelechuk, Mariane.
Vik, Peter. Hope. (p. 1001)
Vikara, John A. My Lonely Room. (p. 1554)
Vikas. Lekhak Sahab: Khud Se Khud Tak Ka Safar. (p. 1266)
Vikre, Caron. What's the Matter with Milford? (p. 2426)
Vil, Steve. Arvid & Hornschwatz Go Skunk Scoffing. Witt, Eddie, illus. (p. 124)
Vila, Alvaro F., illus. see Capstone Press Staff.
Vilanova, Guiu, et al. Ruins of Ravencroft. (p. 1913)
Vilardi, Debbie. 3-D Printers. (p. 2547)
—Amazing Human Feats of Speed. (p. 65)
—Amazing Human Feats of Strength. (p. 65)
—Electric Cars. (p. 631)
—How Do Airplanes Stay Up? (p. 1028)
—Science Questions (Set Of 8) (p. 1959)
—What Are Clouds Made Of? (p. 2405)
—What Makes a Rainbow? (p. 2418)
—Why Do Birds Fly South for Winter? (p. 2456)
—Why Do Camels Have Humps? (p. 2456)
—Why Do Spiders Make Webs? (p. 2457)
—Why Is the Ocean Salty? (p. 2458)
—Why Is the Sky Blue? (p. 2458)
Vilardi, Debbie & Gagne, Tammy. 21st Century Inventions (Set Of 6) (p. 2554)
Vilas, Charles Harrison. Spectacles, & How to Choose Them: An Elementary Monograph (Classic Reprint) (p. 2077)
Vilas, Faith Van Valkenburgh. Fiat (Let There Be Light) A Modern Mystery Play, in One Act (Classic Reprint) (p. 722)
Vilela, Caio, photos by see Taylor, Sean.
Vilela, Fernando. Along the Tapajós. Hahn, Daniel, tr. (p. 58)
Vilela, Fernando, illus. see Argueta, Jorge.
Vilela, Luiz, illus. see Osborne, Mary Pope & Boyce, Natalie Pope.
Viles, Edward. Black Bess; or the Knight of the Road: A Tale of the Good Old Times (Classic Reprint) (p. 237)
—Black Bess, or the Knight of the Road, Vol. 2 (Classic Reprint) (p. 237)
—Black Bess, or the Knight of the Road, Vol. 3: A Tale of the Good Old Times (Classic Reprint) (p. 237)
—Blueskin, Vol. 2: A Romance (Classic Reprint) (p. 250)
Villa, Alvaro F. Flood (p. 750)
Villa, Carlos. Shatterstar: Reality Star. (p. 2003)
Villa, Carlos & Gomez, Carlos. Secret Warps. (p. 1979)
Villa, Francisco, illus. see Nostlinger, Christine.
Villa, Ruben. Granola Farm. (p. 880)
Villabona, Nancy Sue. Little Car in Spring: Anti-Bullying. Hooker, Terry, ed. (p. 1313)
Villacis, Felix. la Cuenta de Tres. (p. 1234)
Village Earth. Nutrition: a Global View (5-Volume Series) (p. 1632)
Villagrán, Jazmin. ¿Qué Esta Pasando Allá Arriba? (p. 1822)
Villalba, Ana, illus. see Harper, Kathryn.
Villalobos, Cinta, illus. see Bonilla, Lindsay.
Villalobos, Ethel M., illus. see Pierce, Terry.
Villalobos, Juan Pablo. Other Side: Stories of Central American Teen Refugees Who Dream of Crossing the Border. (p. 1675)
Villalobos, Miguel, illus. see Yellen, David.
Villalobos, Yana Alfaro, tr. see Yoder, Eric & Yoder, Natalie.
Villamaria, Villamaria. Fairy Circles: Tales & Legends of Giants, Dwarfs, Fairies, Water-Sprites, & Hobgoblins (Classic Reprint) (p. 696)
Villamuza, Noemi, illus. see Keselman, Gabriela.
Villamuza, Noemí, illus. see Sobrino, Javier.
Villamuza, Noemí, tr. see Sobrino, Javier.
Villanea, Alpha. Prince Juan. (p. 1794)
Villanelli, Paolo. Star Wars: Lando - Double or Nothing. (p. 2104)
—Star Wars: Vader - Dark Visions. (p. 2105)
Villanelli, Paolo, illus. see Houser, Jody.
Villanelli, Paolo, illus. see Random House.
Villanelli, Paolo, jt. illus. see Schiti, Valerio.
Villanes Cairo, Carlos. Oro de Indias. (p. 1672)
Villano, Christina. Victoria Velvet. (p. 2355)
Villanueva, Catherine, illus. see Trainor, Marissa.
Villanueva, Clara. Enigma. (p. 655)
Villanueva Jr, David. Baby Bee, Where Are You? (Paperback) (p. 149)
—Butterfly Princesses. (p. 304)
—Caleb's Birthday Wish. (p. 310)
—Extraordinary Capers of Lochlin de Carlo. Kantar, Fran Keleher, illus. (p. 685)
—Legend of Ms. Tutu Larue. (p. 1262)
—Little Bea, Where Are You? (p. 1311)
—Little Writer. (p. 1330)
—Sebastian's Moon. (p. 1973)
Villanueva, Muriel. Amarillo y Redondo. (p. 62)
Villanueva, Pedro. Chronicle of a New Kid. (p. 388)
Villard, Erik B. Combat Operations: Staying the Course, October 1967-September 1968: Staying the Course, October 1967-September 1968. (p. 427)
—Combat Operations: Staying the Course October 1967-September 1968: Staying the Course October 1967-September 1968. (p. 427)
Villard, Marc. Doigts Rouges. (p. 578)
Villard, Ray. Supertelescopios: Por dentro y por fuera (Large Telescopes: Inside & Out) (p. 2162)
Villard, Raymond. Large Telescopes: Inside & Out. (p. 1244)
Villareal, Mark. Adventures of Park Ranger Brock Cliffhanger & His Jr. Park Rangers: The Missing Hikers of Allegany State Park. (p. 26)
—Adventures of Park Ranger Brock Cliffhanger & His Jr. Park Rangers: Mountain Rescue: Preserving Our Great Smoky Mountains National Park. (p. 26)
Villareal, Ray. Body Slammed! (p. 253)
—Don't Call Me Hero. (p. 582)
—On the Other Side of the Bridge. (p. 1655)
—Who's Buried in the Garden? (p. 2453)
Villari, Dominic Robert. Don't Poke the Bear. (p. 583)
—Tan's Tile: A Tale of Creative Thought Featuring Tangram. (p. 2190)
—Way Forward. (p. 2387)
—You Have to Wear Pants. (p. 2527)
Villari, Laura, illus. see Pilgrim, Will Corona & Di Vito, Andrea.
Villari, Linda. On Tuscan Hills Venetian Waters (Classic Reprint) (p. 1656)
Villarreal, Alberto. Ocho Lugares Que Me Recuerdan a Ti. (p. 1636)
—Todo lo Que Fuimos. (p. 2255)
Villarreal, Tanya E. Izzie's First Christmas Villarreal, Tanya E., illus. (p. 1150)
Villarroel, Carolina, jt. auth. see Garza, Xavier.
Villarroel, Carolina, jt. auth. see Luna, James.
Villarroel, Carolina, tr. see Baca, Ana.
Villarroel, Carolina, tr. see Saldana, Rene.
Villarroel, Carolina, tr. see Saldaña, René.
Villarrubia, Jose, illus. see Riordan, Rick & Venditti, Robert.
Villars, Mary H. Stories of Home & Home Folks, or Leaves from a Parsonage Portfolio, Vol. 1 (Classic Reprint) (p. 2125)
Villasante, Alexandra. Grief Keeper. (p. 896)
Villaseñor, Victor. Stranger & the Red Rooster / el Forastero y el Gallo Rojo. Jara, José, illus. (p. 2138)
Villavert, Armand, Jr., illus. see Beedle, Tim.
Villegas, Francisco De Quevedo. Visions of Dom Francisco de Quevedo Villegas: Knight of the Order of St. James (Classic Reprint) (p. 2362)
Villegas, Mercedes, tr. see Ahlberg, Allan.
Villegas, Teresa, illus. see Stavans, Ilan.
Villella, Jessica, illus. see Branda, Barnabus.
Villeneuve, Anne. Loula & Mister the Monster. Villeneuve, Anne, illus. (p. 1358)
—Loula Is Leaving for Africa. Villeneuve, Anne, illus. (p. 1358)
—Red Scarf. (p. 1858)

V

Villeneuve, Mylène, illus. see Audet, Dre Nicole.
Villeneuve, Mylène, illus. see Audet, Nicole.
Villeneuve, Mylène & Audet, Nicole. Félix Au Musée du Corps Humain: Corps Humain. (p. 719)
Villet, Olivia, illus. see French, Vivian.
Villeuve, Mylene, illus. see Audet, Dre Nicole.
Villeuve, Mylene, illus. see Audet, Nicole.
Villiers, Frederic. Peaceful Personalities & Warriors Bold (Classic Reprint) (p. 1709)
—Villiers His Five Decades of Adventure, Vol. 2 (Classic Reprint) (p. 2359)
—Villiers, Vol. 1: His Five Decades of Adventure (Classic Reprint) (p. 2359)
Villiers, Katharine. Memoirs of a Maid of Honour (Classic Reprint) (p. 1444)
Villiers-Stuart, Gerald. Soul of Croesus (Classic Reprint) (p. 2066)
Villing, Alexandra. Ancient Greeks: Their Lives & Their World. (p. 81)
Villiot, Bernard. Mariage de Mme Edouard. (p. 1404)
—Mephisto. Guilloppe, Antoine, illus. (p. 1447)
Villnave, Erica. Sophie's Lovely Locks Villnave, Erica, illus. (p. 2065)
Villnave, Erica Pelton, illus. see Burns, Ellen Flanagan.
Villnave, Erica Pelton, illus. see Galvin, Laura Gates.
Villnave, Erica Pelton, illus. see Galvin, Laura.
Villnave, Erica Pelton, illus. see Wallingford, Stephanie & Rynders, Dawn.
Villorente, David, ed. ABCs of Style: A Graffiti Alphabet. (p. 5)
Villoro, Juan. Autopista Sanguijuela. (p. 140)
—Te de Tomillo Del Profesor Ziper. (p. 2194)
—Wild Book. Schimel, Lawrence, tr. (p. 2463)
Villoro, Juan & Gmez Morin, Mauricio. Las Golosinas Secretas. (p. 1246)
Vilsack, Gladys Brace. Unpardonable Sin (Classic Reprint) (p. 2334)
Vimar, A. Clown the Circus Dog (Classic Reprint) (p. 408)
—Curly Haired Hen: Text & Illustrations (Classic Reprint) (p. 488)
Vimislik, Matthew, illus. see Bean, Raymond.
Viña, Rose. Ice Breaker: How Mabel Fairbanks Changed Figure Skating. Almon, Claire, illus. (p. 1087)
Vinberger, Naftali Yehiel ben Shelomoh Avraham, et al. Story of Rebbetzin Kanievsky: A Biography for Young Readers. (p. 2132)
Vince, Charles. Street of Faces: Glimpses of Town (Classic Reprint) (p. 2140)
—Wayfarers in Arcady (Classic Reprint) (p. 2387)
Vince, Charli. Heroes of Space: Who Changed the World. (p. 962)
Vince Crandall, Vince. Village Baker. (p. 2358)
Vince, Dawn, illus. see McAllister, Margaret.
Vince, Henry Scott. Two Pardons, Vol. 1 Of 3: A Novel (Classic Reprint) (p. 2309)
—Two Pardons, Vol. 2 Of 3: A Novel (Classic Reprint) (p. 2309)
Vince, Paula. Picking up the Pieces. (p. 1739)
Vince, Sarah, illus. see Make Believe Ideas Ltd.
Vincent, Abhishek. Book of My Life: A True Love Journey. (p. 259)
Vincent, Andrew M., illus. see Fox, Frances Margaret.
Vincent, Annick. My Brain Needs Glasses: ADHD Explained to Kids. (p. 1534)
Vincent, Benjamin, illus. see Abercrombie, Josephine.
Vincent, Benjamin, illus. see Casad, Mary Brooke.
Vincent, Beverly & Greenberger, Robert. Frequently Asked Questions about Birth Control. (p. 784)
Vincent, Bruno. School for Villains. (p. 1946)
—So You Want to Be a Ninja? Akiyama, Takayo, illus. (p. 2051)
Vincent, Clarence Augustus. Night & the Stars: A Tale of the Western Reserve (Classic Reprint) (p. 1604)
Vincent, Denis & Francis, Peter. Non-Verbal Reasoning, Age 8-10. (p. 1618)
Vincent, Eleanor. Hugh Meredith: The Story of a Boy Who Conquered Circumstances by Knowing the Truth about Them (Classic Reprint) (p. 1048)
Vincent, Francis. Arundel, Vol. 1 Of 3: A Tale of the French Revolution (Classic Reprint) (p. 124)
Vincent, Geraldine. Story of the Sea Unicorn. (p. 2134)
Vincent, Jacques. Return of the Princess (Classic Reprint) (p. 1871)
Vincent, Jessica. Gnome in My Home. (p. 845)
Vincent, Joan. Legend of the Lost Lilies. (p. 1262)
Vincent, John H. My Mother's Bible Stories: Told in the Language of a Gentle, Loving Mother Conversing with Her Children; Designed for Family Use During the Children's Hour Around the Evening Lamp (Classic Reprint) (p. 1556)
Vincent, Joyce. Sellbridge Co: An Australian Story (Classic Reprint) (p. 1987)
Vincent, Kay. Bedtime Baby Cloth Book. (p. 188)
—Playtime Baby Cloth Book. (p. 1761)
Vincent, Kelly. Finding Frances. (p. 729)
Vincent, Mathy. Boucle d'or et les Trois Ours. (p. 265)
Vincent, Monica-Marie. Roses are Red...Violet Is Dead. (p. 1906)
Vincent, Rachel. 100 Hours. (p. 2557)
—99 Lies. (p. 2556)
—Brave New Girl. (p. 276)
—My Soul to Take. (p. 1561)
—Strange New World. (p. 2138)
—With All My Soul (p. 2481)
Vincent, Rd. Donbridge: The Ring of Lazarus. (p. 581)
Vincent, Victor H. American Girl: Operetta for Young Ladies (in Two Acts) (Classic Reprint) (p. 71)
Vincent, Vincent. Braver, Stronger, Smarter: A Fun & Easy Guide to Being More Mindful, More Confident, & More YOU! (p. 277)
Vincent, W. T. Recollections of Fred Leslie, Vol. 1 (Classic Reprint) (p. 1854)
Vincent, Zu. Catherine the Great: Empress of Russia. (p. 345)
Vincenti, Antonio, illus. see Vecchini, Silvia & Daughters of St. Paul Staff.
Vincenti, Antonio, illus. see Vecchini, Silvia.
Vincentini, Federico, illus. see Ahmed, Saladin.
Vincer, Carole, illus. see Watson, Mary Gordon.
Vinci, Rosaria, illus. see Jones, Sherry a.
Vincolisi, Marnie. House Who Found Its Home. Clarke, Benjamin S., illus. (p. 1024)
Vine, Deryth. Fiskers Meets Santa Claus. (p. 742)
Vine, Lucy, illus. see Simon Dietz, Suzanne.
Vine, Mary. Biju Silver Lining. Dowling, Kaylynne, illus. (p. 225)
—Dragon Gilby. Dowling, Kaylynne, illus. (p. 593)
Vine, Rachel, jt. auth. see Renzetti, Rob.
Vine, Rachel Shana, illus. see Sherman, Paulette Kouffman.
Vine, Vernon. Farm Credit Club Grapevine, Vol. 2: December 29, 1943 (Classic Reprint) (p. 710)
—Farm Credit Club Grapevine, Vol. 3: April 5, 1944 (Classic Reprint) (p. 710)
Viner, Callie. Pebbles Wants a Friend. Mosley, Bonita K., illus. (p. 1711)
Viner, Callie Lee. Pebbles Loves Counting. Viner, Callie Lee, photos by. (p. 1711)
—Pebbles Wants a Friend. Mosley, Bonita K., illus. (p. 1711)
Viner, Constance. Golden Rod: December, 1936 (Classic Reprint) (p. 858)
Vines, Heather Glenn. Love, Sun. (p. 1361)
—That's One Odd Duck! Torbergson, Paige B., illus. (p. 2214)
Vines, Nandina, illus. see Thorndyke, Julie.
Vines, Sydney Howard, jt. auth. see Bower, Frederick Orpen.
Vinesse, Cecilia. Seven Days of You. (p. 1993)
—Summer of Us. (p. 2150)
Viney, Peter. Case of the Dead Batsman (p. 337)
—Casualty! (p. 341)
—Collector (p. 415)
—Space Romance (p. 2072)
—Strawberry & the Sensations (p. 2139)
—Sunnyvista City (p. 2153)
—Tidy Ghost (p. 2240)
—Underground (p. 2323)
Vingut, Francisco Javier. Clave de Los Ejercicios Del Maestro de Ingles, Metodo Practico para Aprender a Leer, Escribir y Hablar la Lengua Inglesa: Segun el Sistema de Ollendorff (Classic Reprint) (p. 402)
—Lecturas Inglesas Escogidas, o Sea Trozos de Los Mejores Escritores Ingleses y Americanos, en Prosa y Verso: Arreglados en Lecciones con Notas Gramaticales y Fraseologicas, Traduccion Interlinear y un Vocabulario con la Pronunciacion y Definiciones. (p. 1260)
Vingut, Gertrude F. De. Naomi Torrente: The History of a Woman (Classic Reprint) (p. 1574)
Vink, Amanda. And We Call It Love. (p. 83)
—Dangers of Digital Addiction (p. 502)
—Dragonflies up Close (p. 595)
—Fake News at Newton High (p. 699)
—Is a Dog a Good Pet for Me? (p. 1136)
—Jaguars (p. 1155)
—Jellyfish Are Brainless! (p. 1163)
—Missing Persons: What Happens When Someone Disappears? (p. 1481)
—Modern Nerd's Guide to Miniatures (p. 1487)
—Online Activism: Social Change Through Social Media. (p. 1663)
—Peculiar Sequence of Events. Gennari, Joel, illus. (p. 1711)
—Postmodern Artists: Creators of a Cultural Movement. (p. 1780)
—Sea Urchins Are Brainless! (p. 1969)
—Simulated Friend. Gennari, Joel, illus. (p. 2023)
—Suffragists & Those Who Opposed Them (p. 2147)
—Team Time Machine Crosses the Delaware (p. 2196)
Vinloft, Al & M, Aniq. Mae Day: SOS for Love. (p. 1375)
Vinod, et al. Aakash # 1: Clash with the Legion of Darkness. (p. 2)
—Rudra: The Origin. (p. 1912)
Vinsh, Aara J. Ben, the Miracle Horse (p. 199)
—Playtime Adventures. Leijs, Tommie, illus. (p. 1761)
Vinson, Haley. Horizons Set 2 Shea, Steve, ed. (p. 1003)
Vinson, Susan. Silence. (p. 2017)
Vinson, Wentworth Webster Julien. Basque Legends, Vol. 4: Collected, Chiefly in the Labourd (Classic Reprint) (p. 171)
Vinten, C. R. Aggie Squib, 1921 (Classic Reprint) (p. 35)
Vinton, Arthur Dudley. Pomfret Mystery: A Novel of Incident (Classic Reprint) (p. 1772)
Vints, Kostya, illus. see Dewar, Andrew.
Viola, Herman J. Houghton Mifflin Social Studies Florida: Student Edition Level 4studies Florida Studies 2006. (p. 1021)
Viola, Jason. Science Comics: Polar Bears: Survival on the Ice. Giallongo, Zack, illus. (p. 1954)
Viola, Karen, illus. see Froeb, Lori C.
Viola, Karen, illus. see Pulles, Christina.
Violet, Anna, illus. see Cooke, Trish.
Violet, Thao Nguyen, illus. see Jean, Rose S. & Zaidan, Asim.
Violette, Henry. Nouvelles Manipulations Chimiques Simplifiees, Ou Laboratoire Economique de L'Etudiant: Ouvrage Contenant la Description d'Appareils Simples et Nouveaux, Suivi d'un Cours de Chimie Pratique a l'Aide des Instruments (Classic Reprint) (p. 1626)
Violi, Daniela, illus. see Horvath, Polly.
Violi, Daniela, illus. see Lavin, Monica.
Violi, Daniela, illus. see MacHado, Ana Maria.
Violi, Daniela, illus. see Scholes, Katherine.
Viollet, Paul. Établissements de Saint Louis, Vol. 1: Accompagnés des Textes Primitifs et de Textes dérivés Avec une Introduction et des Notes (Classic Reprint) (p. 665)
—Etablissements de Saint Louis, Vol. 2: Accompagnes des Textes Primitifs et de Textes Derives, Avec une Introduction et des Notes; Texte des Etablissements (Classic Reprint) (p. 665)
—Établissements de Saint Louis, Vol. 2: Accompagnés des Textes Primitifs et de Textes dérivés, Avec une Introduction et des Notes; Texte des Établissements (Classic Reprint) (p. 665)
—Établissements de Saint Louis, Vol. 3: Accompagnés des Textes Primitifs et de Textes dérivés Avec une Introduction et des Notes; Textes Primitifs, Textes dérivés, Notes (Classic Reprint) (p. 665)
—Etablissements de Saint Louis, Vol. 3: Accompagnes des Textes Primitifs et de Textes Derives, Avec une Introduction et des Notes; Publies, Pour la Societe de l'Histoire de France; Textes Primitifs, Textes Derivees, Notes (Classic Reprint) (p. 665)
—Établissements de Saint Louis, Vol. 4: Accompagnés des Textes Primitifs et de Textes dérivés Avec une Introduction et des Notes; Notes (Suite et Fin), Table-Glossaire (Classic Reprint) (p. 665)
Viollet-Le-Duc, Emmanuel Louis Nicolas. Ancien Théâtre François, Ou Collection des Ouvrages Dramatiques les Plus Remarquables Depuis les Mystères Jusqu'à Corneille, Vol. 10: Publié Avec des Notes et Éclaircissements; Glossaire (Classic Reprint) (p. 79)
Viollet-P. Établissements de Saint Louis, Accompagnés des Textes Primitifs et des Textes dérivéS. Tome 2. (p. 665)
Viorst, Judith. Alexander & the Terrible, Horrible, No Good, Very Bad Day: Lap Edition. Cruz, Ray, illus. (p. 42)
—Alexander & the Terrible, Horrible, No Good, Very Bad Day. (p. 42)
—Alexander & the Terrible, Horrible, No Good, Very Bad Day. Cruz, Ray, illus. (p. 42)
—Alexander, Who's Not (Do You Hear Me? I Mean It!) Going to Move. Glasser, Robin Preiss, illus. (p. 43)
—Alexander, Who's Trying His Best to Be the Best Boy Ever. (p. 43)
—Earrings! (p. 615)
—Earrings! Malone, Nola Langner, illus. (p. 615)
—I'll Fix Anthony. Lobel, Arnold, illus. (p. 1095)
—Just in Case. Bluthenthal, Diana Cain, illus. (p. 1193)
—Lulu & the Brontosaurus. (p. 1367)
—Lulu & the Brontosaurus. Smith, Lane, illus. (p. 1367)
—Lulu Collection (If You Don't Read Them, She Will NOT Be Pleased) Lulu & the Brontosaurus; Lulu Walks the Dogs; Lulu's Mysterious Mission; Lulu Is Getting a Sister. Smith, Lane & Cornell, Kevin, illus. (p. 1367)
—Lulu Is Getting a Sister: (Who WANTS Her? Who NEEDS Her?) Cornell, Kevin, illus. (p. 1367)
—Lulu Walks the Dogs. (p. 1367)
—Lulu Walks the Dogs. Smith, Lane, illus. (p. 1367)
—Lulu's Mysterious Mission. (p. 1367)
—What Are You Glad about? What Are You Mad About? Poems for When a Person Needs a Poem. White, Lee, illus. (p. 2406)
Vipah Interactive, illus. see Rey, Margret.
Vipah Interactive Staff, illus. see Rey, H. A.
Vipah Interactive Staff, illus. see Rey, H. A. & Rey, Margret.
Vipah Interactive Staff, illus. see Rey, Margret & Rey, H. A.
Virag, Nicolas. Fruits-Conteurs. (p. 796)
Viraraghavan, Chitra. Delhi Thaatha: A Great Grand Story. Banerjee, Sunandini, illus. (p. 526)
Virata Books. Ravi, the Victorious. (p. 1844)
Virden, William & Borg, Mary. My Colorado Teacher Guide. (p. 1535)
Virella, Nik & Unzueta, Angel. Star Wars: Poe Dameron Vol. 4: Legend Found. (p. 2104)
Viresalingamu, Kandukuri. Fortune's Wheel: A Tale of Hindu Domestic Life (Classic Reprint) (p. 770)
Virgil. Aeneid. (p. 30)
—Aeneid. Dryden, John, tr. (p. 30)
Virgil, jt. auth. see Church, Alfred J.
Virgili, Marta Costa, illus. see Potter, Joe.
Virginia, State Female Normal School. Virginian, 1905 (Classic Reprint) (p. 2361)
Virginia, State Normal School. Focus, Vol. 7: March, 1917 (Classic Reprint) (p. 756)
—Focus, Vol. 9: May, 1919 (Classic Reprint) (p. 756)
Virginia, State Normal School in Frederi. Battlefield in Seven Chapters: With the Biographical Memoirs of the Illustrious Graduates of 1917 (Classic Reprint) (p. 175)
Virginian, Virginian. American Wanderer, Through Various Parts of Europe, in a Series of Letters to a Lady: Interspersed with a Variety of Interesting Anecdotes (Classic Reprint) (p. 74)
—Kentuckian in New York, Vol. 2 Of 2: Or the Adventures of Three Southerns (Classic Reprint) (p. 1209)
Virginie, Desmoulins. Mes Petits Animaux de Laine. (p. 1451)
Virginie, Pfeiffer. Et l'Homme Rit ! (p. 665)
Virgo, Seán. Shadow Mother Pérez, Javier Serrano, illus. (p. 1996)
Virjan, Emma J. What This Story Needs Is a Bang & a Clang. Virjan, Emma J., illus. (p. 2420)
—What This Story Needs Is a Munch & a Crunch. Virjan, Emma J., illus. (p. 2420)
—What This Story Needs Is a Pig in a Wig. Virjan, Emma J., illus. (p. 2420)
Virmani, Anjna. Click Start 3 Primary: Computer Science for Schools. (p. 404)
—Click Start 4 Primary: Computer Science for Schools. (p. 404)
—Click Start 5 Primary: Computer Science for Schools. (p. 404)
Virnig, Christine. Dung for Dinner: A Stomach-Churning Look at the Animal Poop, Pee, Vomit, & Secretions That People Have Eaten (and Often Still Do!) Briggs, Korwin, illus. (p. 610)
Virr, Paul. Animal Antics Enright, Amanda, illus. (p. 87)
—Car Record Breakers. (p. 327)
—Kitchen Capers Enright, Amanda, illus. (p. 1225)
—Monster Laughs Enright, Amanda, illus. (p. 1496)
—Silly Stories Enright, Amanda, illus. (p. 2018)
—Trailblazers: Albert Einstein: The Greatest Mind in Physics. (p. 2275)
Virr, Paul & Potter, William. Math Adventures: Solve the Puzzles, Save the World! Vieira, Rayanne, illus. (p. 1421)
Virta, Juha. Piano Maijala, Marika, illus. (p. 1738)
Virtue, Doreen. Cambiaria Mi Vida Su Tubiera Mas Tiempo! (p. 313)
—Los Milagros Del Arcangel Gabriel. (p. 1351)
Visaggio, Magdalene. Quantum Teens Are Go Volume 1. (p. 1822)
Visaggio, Magdelene & Cates, Donny, texts. Marvel Legacy Companion. (p. 1412)
Visaya, Artemio, illus. see Schliewen, Richard.
Visca, illus. see Gomes, Alexandre de Castro.
Visca, Curt. How to Draw Cartoon Careers. (p. 1040)
—How to Draw Cartoon Holiday Symbols. (p. 1040)
—How to Draw Cartoon Spacecraft & Astronauts in Action. (p. 1040)
—How to Draw Cartoon Symbols of the United States. (p. 1040)
—How to Draw Cartoon Symbols of the Wild West. (p. 1040)
Visca, Kelley, jt. auth. see Visca, Curt.
Visca, Kelly. How to Draw Cartoon Birds. (p. 1040)
—How to Draw Cartoon Crustaceans. (p. 1040)
—How to Draw Cartoon Fish. (p. 1040)
—How to Draw Cartoon Rodents. (p. 1040)
Vischer, Frans. Fuddles. Vischer, Frans, illus. (p. 797)
—Fuddles & Puddles. Vischer, Frans, illus. (p. 797)
—Very Fuddles Christmas. Vischer, Frans, illus. (p. 2353)
Vischer, Frans, afterword by. Fuddles. (p. 797)
Vischer, Phil. Buck Denver's Bad, Bad Day: A Lesson in Thankfulness. (p. 289)
—Buck Denver's Big, Big Bubble: A Lesson in Courage. (p. 289)
—Buck Denver's Giant Robot Suit: A Lesson in Friendship. (p. 289)
—Buck Denver's Hammer of Strength: A Lesson in Loving Others. (p. 289)
—I Thank God for This Day! (p. 1083)
—Laugh & Grow Bible for Little Ones: The Gospel in 15 One-Minute Bible Stories. (p. 1251)
Visconti, Guido. Genius of Leonardo. Landmann, Bimba, illus. (p. 815)
Visher, Frans, notes. Very Fuddles Christmas. (p. 2353)
Vishpriya. Tales from Indi: Character Counts! RESPECT. Ruble, Eugene, illus. (p. 2182)
Vishwanath, Vindhya. Bonnie & a Ball of Yarn. (p. 256)
Visiani, Roberto de. Trattato Di Virtu Morali (Classic Reprint) (p. 2279)
—Trattato Di Virtù Morali (Classic Reprint) (p. 2279)
Vision, David. Who's That Crying! Alcantara, Ignacio, illus. (p. 2453)
Vision, David & Vision, Mutiya. What Makes Me Beautiful? ¿Qué Es lo Que Me Hace Hermoso? (p. 2418)
Vision, David & Vision, Mutiya Sahar. Daddy Loves His Baby Girl. Vision, Mutiya Sahar, illus. (p. 495)
—If Only I Could! Alcantara, Ignacio, illus. (p. 1092)
—Missing You. Alcantara, Ignacio, illus. (p. 1481)
—What Makes Me Beautiful? Alcantara, Ignacio, illus. (p. 2418)
Vision, David, et al. My Very Breast Friend. Alcantara, Ignacio, illus. (p. 1563)
Vision, Mutiya, jt. auth. see Vision, David.
Vision, Mutiya & Vision, David. Land of Expression. Alcantara, Ignacio, illus. (p. 1241)
—My Choices Make Me Who I Am. Alcantara, Ignacio, illus. (p. 1535)
Vision, Mutiya Sahar. Disabilities. Alcantara, Ignacio, illus. (p. 552)
Vision, Mutiya Sahar, jt. auth. see Vision, David.
Vision, Willi. Love Makes a Family: Friends, Family, & Significant Others. (p. 1360)
Visions, Chris, jt. illus. see Rodriguez, Robbi.
Visitacion, Ayin, illus. see Herrera, James/H.
Vismes, Marie Josephe Henriette De. Petite Poule Blanche: Falbe en Deux Tableaux (Classic Reprint) (p. 1731)
Visram, Zahra M. Missing Crown. (p. 1480)
—Not My Universe. (p. 1623)
—One, Two, Squiggle: Count Your Way from 1-20 Through the Royal Kingdom. (p. 1663)
—Princess & the Polar Bear. (p. 1796)
—Royal Mess. (p. 1910)
Visscher, William Lightfoot. Poems of the South, & Other Verse (Classic Reprint) (p. 1765)
—Vissch: A Book of Sketches, Rhymes, & Other Matters Credited to Matthew Mattox, N. P. R (Classic Reprint) (p. 2363)
—Way Out Yonder, the Romance of a New City (Classic Reprint) (p. 2387)
Visser, Annie, illus. see Visser, Shaina Elizabeth.
Visser, Nisse & Going, Cair Emma. On Brighton Streets. (p. 1652)
Visser, Shaina Elizabeth. Tale of an Apple Tree. Visser, Annie, illus. (p. 2178)
Vissicchio, Joseph R. Grandpa & Dad's Counsel. (p. 879)
Visto, Joy. How Much Is Infinity? (p. 1034)
—What Are the Chances? (p. 2406)
—When Does a Line Become a Shape? (p. 2430)
—Where Does a Graph Go? (p. 2436)
—Whose Foot Is a Foot? (p. 2454)
—Why Do Math with Letters? (p. 2456)
Visuals International, Bible, jt. auth. see Lyster, R. Iona.
Visuals, Roi. Drawmaster Robocar Poli: Super Stencil Kit: 4 Easy Steps to Draw Your Heroes. (p. 600)
Viswanath, Shobha. Blue Jackal. Joshi, Dileep, illus. (p. 248)
—Elephant in My Backyard. Jawa, Sadhvi, illus. (p. 634)
—One Rainy Day: A Counting Book. P.S., Ashwathy, illus. (p. 1661)
—Tangle of Brungles. Fox, Culpeo, illus. (p. 2190)
—Whose Lovely Child Can You Be? Tappin, Christine, illus. (p. 2454)
Vitale, Ann. Manager. Riggs, Ernestine G. & Gholar, Cheryl, eds. (p. 1396)
—Sexual Disorders. McDonnell, Mary Ann & Esherick, Donald, eds. (p. 1995)
Vitale, Brooke. Boris & the Missing Monkey. (p. 262)
—Bubble Trouble (Corn & Peg) Petrossi, Fabrizio, illus. (p. 289)
—Disney Bunnies: Thumper & the Egg. Tyminski, Lori & Turati, Valeria, illus. (p. 559)
—Fingerlings: Let the Games Begin! a Sticker & Activity Book. Johnson, Shane L., illus. (p. 731)
—Happy Birthday, Mickey! Read-Along Storybook & CD. Disney Storybook Art Team, illus. (p. 921)
—I Am Cleopatra. (p. 1058)
—I Am Harry Houdini. (p. 1058)
—I Am Theodore Roosevelt. (p. 1060)
—Lucky Pups! (p. 1365)
—Mickey & Friends Best Friends Day. Disney Storybook Art Team, illus. (p. 1459)

—Sorcerer's Apprentice: A Classic Mickey Mouse Tale. Disney Storybook Art Team, illus. (p. 2065)
—Thumper & the Egg. (p. 2238)
—Vote for Minnie. (p. 2367)
—We Are the Brontë Sisters. (p. 2389)
—World of Reading: Minnie Vote for Minnie (Level 2 Reader Plus Fun Facts) (p. 2503)
—World of Reading: Puppy Dog Pals Lucky Pups (Level 1 Word Swap Reader) Disney Storybook Art Team, illus. (p. 2503)
Vitale, Brooke, ed. see Stapler, Jodi.
Vitale, Brooke, jt. auth. see Hosten, Colin.
Vitale, Brooke & Disney Storybook Artists Staff, adapted by. Disney Classics. (p. 559)
Vitale, Brooke & Petrower, Scott. Disney Who's Who: An a to Z of Disney Characters. (p. 564)
Vitale, Debbie. Adventures of Amanda. (p. 21)
Vitale, Guido. Chinese Folklore: Pekinese Rhymes (Classic Reprint) (p. 378)
—Chinese Folklore. (p. 378)
Vitale, Mary Ann. Formiche Sui Miei Jeans. (p. 768)
Vitale, Raoul, illus. see Coatsworth, Elizabeth.
Vitale, Raoul, illus. see Rodda, Emily.
Vitale, Stefano, illus. see Franco, Betsy.
Vitali, Keith & Oates, Sam. Victor Stops the School Bully. (p. 2355)
Vitaliev, Vitali. Granny Yaga. (p. 880)
Vitantoni, Valerio. Gelsomina & il Filato Lunare. (p. 813)
—Gelsomina & the Moon Yarn. (p. 813)
Vitelli, Alessandra, illus. see Lavatelli, Anna.
Vitello, Suzy. Moment Before. (p. 1490)
Vitman, Fulgenzio. Summa Plantarum Quae Hactenus Innotuerunt Methodo Linnaeana per Genera et Species, Vol. 4 (Classic Reprint) (p. 2148)
Vito, Andrea Di, illus. see Wong, Clarissa.
Vitsky, Sally, illus. see Schwacber, Barbie Heit.
Vitsky, Sally, illus. see Schwaeber, Barbie.
Vitt, Karren, illus. see Kerr, Mike.
Vittachi, Nury. Young Scientists Series, the (in 12 Volumes) (p. 2532)
Vittachi, Nury & Cheung, Step. First of Everything. (p. 738)
Vitterito, Joseph A., 2nd. My Sister Is a Preemie: A Children's Guide to the NICU Experience. Chuzzlewit, Abraham R., illus. (p. 1561)
Vium-Olesen, Jacob. Mi Primera Biblia para Memorizar L'amour, Sandrine, illus. (p. 1456)
Viva, Frank. Outstanding in the Rain. (p. 1686)
—Sea Change. Viva, Frank, illus. (p. 1967)
—Trip to the Bottom of the World with Mouse: TOON Level 1. (p. 2289)
—Trip to the Bottom of the World with Mouse. (p. 2289)
—Trip to the Top of the World with Mouse. (p. 2289)
—Young Frank, Architect. (p. 2531)
Viva, Frank, illus. see Hrab, Naseem.
Viva, Giuseppe. Come le Zanzare in una Notte D'Estate. (p. 428)
Vivanco, Kelly, illus. see Andersen, Hans Christian.
Vivanco, Kelly, illus. see Grimm, Brothers.
Vivanco, Sylvia, illus. see Lindeen, Mary.
Vivanti, Anna. Journey to Crete, Constantinople, Naples, & Florence: Three Months Abroad (Classic Reprint) (p. 1182)
—Journey to Crete, Constantinople, Naples, & Florence. (p. 1182)
Vivanti, Annie. Outrage (Classic Reprint) (p. 1685)
Vivaria, Kassandra. Via Lucis: A Novel (Classic Reprint) (p. 2354)
Vivas, Chad, illus. see Denton, Mitchell James.
Vivas, Julie, illus. see Fox, Mem.
Vivas, Julie, illus. see Saxby, Claire.
Vivas, Julie, illus. see Wild, Margaret.
Vivas, Julie, illus. see Williams, Sue.
Vivat, Booki. Frazzled: Everyday Disasters & Impending Doom. Vivat, Booki, illus. (p. 779)
—Frazzled #2: Ordinary Mishaps & Inevitable Catastrophes. Vivat, Booki, illus. (p. 779)
—Frazzled #3: Minor Incidents & Absolute Uncertainties. Vivat, Booki, illus. (p. 779)
Vivekânanda, Swami. Notes of Some Wanderings with the Swami Vivekananda (Classic Reprint) (p. 1624)
Vivès, Bastien, et al. Chase. (p. 361)
—Royal Cup. (p. 1909)
Vives, Juan Luis. Tudor School-Boy Life: The Dialogues of Juan Luis Vives (Classic Reprint) (p. 2298)
Vivian, Bart. Imagine. Vivian, Bart, illus. (p. 1100)
Vivian, Evelyn Charles. Following Feet (Classic Reprint) (p. 758)
Vivian, H. W. Kylie's Stories. (p. 1234)
Vivian, Harold Acton. Theatrical Primer (Classic Reprint) (p. 2215)
Vivian, Herbert. Francis Joseph & His Court: From the Memoirs of Count Roger de Rességuier: (Son of Francis Joseph's Court Chamberlain) (p. 776)
—Francis Joseph & His Court: From the Memoirs of Count Roger de Rességuier (Son of Francis Joseph's Court Chamberlain) (Classic Reprint) (p. 776)
—Italy at War (Classic Reprint) (p. 1142)
Vivian, Martha Campbell. Down the Avenue of Ninety Years (Classic Reprint) (p. 590)
Vivian, Siobhan. Last Boy & Girl in the World. (p. 1247)
—List. (p. 1308)
—Little Friendly Advice. (p. 1317)
—Not That Kind of Girl. (p. 1623)
—Same Difference. (p. 1927)
—Siempre Dulce. (p. 2015)
—Stay Sweet. (p. 2109)
—We Are the Wildcats. (p. 2389)
Vivian, Siobhan, jt. auth. see Han, Jenny.
Vivian, Thomas Jondrie. Seven Smiles & a Few Fibs (Classic Reprint) (p. 1994)
Viviane, Faudi-Khourdifi. Patrouille des Oies(la) (p. 1706)
Viviani, Luisa. There Is Something Special Inside of Me. (p. 2216)
—There Is Something Special Inside of Me Too. (p. 2216)
—Where Is the Love? (p. 2438)
Viz Media. Fairy Dreams. (p. 696)
—Time for Magic. (p. 2244)
Vizcarra, Daniel, illus. see Peters, Tracy.
Vize, Bonnie. Mystery of the Park Pavilion. (p. 1570)
Vizetelly, Ernest Alfred, tr. see Zola, Emile.
Vizetelly, Henry. Christmas with the Poets: A Collection of Songs, Carols, & Descriptive Verses Relating to the Festival of Christmas. (p. 388)
—Christmas with the Poets: A Collection of Songs, Carols, & Descriptive Verses, Relating to the Festival of Christmas, from the Anglo-Normand Period to the Present Time (Classic Reprint) (p. 388)
Vizzini, Med. Be More Chill. (p. 177)
Vizzini, Ned. It's Kind of a Funny Story. (p. 1145)
—Other Normals. (p. 1674)
—Teen Angst? Naaah... A Quasi-Autobiography. (p. 2198)
Vlahos, Len. Hard Wired. (p. 930)
—Life in a Fishbowl. (p. 1291)
Vlasek, Mary C. Advent of Modern Spiritualism, or Great Oaks from Acorns Grow: A Playlet (Classic Reprint) (p. 18)
Vliestra, David. Timmy's Tornado. Denef, Barbara, illus. (p. 2247)
Vlock, Rob. Sven Carter & the Android Army. (p. 2167)
—Sven Carter & the Trashmouth Effect. (p. 2167)
Vlymen, William T. Second Reading Book (Classic Reprint) (p. 1974)
Vo, Dzung X. Mindful Teen: Powerful Skills to Help You Handle Stress One Moment at a Time. (p. 1470)
Vo, Nancy. Outlaw (p. 1685)
—Ranger (p. 1840)
Voake, Charlotte. Melissa's Octopus & Other Unsuitable Pets. Voake, Charlotte, illus. (p. 1443)
—Some Dinosaurs Are Small. Voake, Charlotte, illus. (p. 2058)
Voake, Charlotte, ed. see Beaumont, Oliver.
Voake, Charlotte, illus. see Babin, Pierre.
Voake, Charlotte, illus. see Butterworth, Chris.
Voake, Charlotte, illus. see Donaldson, Julia.
Voake, Charlotte, illus. see Du Bouchet, Paule.
Voake, Charlotte, illus. see Farjeon, Eleanor.
Voake, Charlotte, illus. see French, Vivian.
Voake, Charlotte, illus. see Hopkinson, Deborah.
Voake, Charlotte, illus. see Khoury, Marielle D. & du Bouchet, Paule.
Voake, Charlotte, illus. see Scholastic, Inc. Staff & La Bretesche, Genevieve de.
Voake, Charlotte, illus. see Voake, Steve.
Voake, Charlotte, illus. see Walcker, Yann.
Voake, Charlotte, illus. see Zolotow, Charlotte.
Voake, Charlotte, jt. auth. see Butterworth, Chris.
Voake, Charlotte, et al. Little Guide to Trees. (p. 1318)
Voake, Steve. Daisy Dawson & the Big Freeze. Meserve, Jessica, illus. (p. 497)
—Daisy Dawson & the Secret Pond. Meserve, Jessica, illus. (p. 497)
—Daisy Dawson at the Beach. Meserve, Jessica, illus. (p. 497)
—Daisy Dawson is on Her Way! Meserve, Jessica, illus. (p. 497)
—Daisy Dawson on the Farm. Meserve, Jessica, illus. (p. 497)
—Hooey Higgins & the Shark. Dodson, Emma, illus. (p. 1000)
—Hooey Higgins & the Tremendous Trousers. Dodson, Emma, illus. (p. 1000)
—Insect Detective. (p. 1121)
—Insect Detective. Voake, Charlotte, illus. (p. 1121)
Voboril, Evan T. Poems about the Natural World (p. 1765)
Voce, Karma. Forever Inspired Coloring Book: Paris Fashions. (p. 767)
Vodicka-Parades, Lenka & Currie, Asia. Magical Forest Fairy Crafts Through the Seasons: Make 25 Enchanting Forest Fairies, Gnomes & More from Simple Supplies. (p. 1380)
Vodicka-Paredes, Lenka & Curte, Asia. Forest Fairy Crafts: Enchanting Fairies & Felt Friends from Simple Supplies. (p. 766)
Vo-Dinh, Mai, illus. see Tran, Kim-Lan & Millar, Louise.
Voege, Debra, jt. auth. see Herman, Gail.
Voege, Debra, jt. auth. see Prokos, Anna.
Voege, Debra, jt. auth. see Ruscoe, Michael.
Voege, Debra & Science Applications, inc Staff. Science in the Real World Set, 10-Volumes. (p. 1955)
Voegelin, Anna M. My Trip to Europe (Classic Reprint) (p. 1563)
Voelkel, J&p. Lost City. (p. 1353)
Voelkel, Jon & Voelkel, Pamela. End of the World Club (p. 649)
Voerg, Kathy. Animal Alphabet Fun Coloring Book. (p. 87)
—Hooray for Unicorns! Coloring Book. (p. 1001)
Voerg, Kathy, illus. see Tuchman, Gail.
Vogel, Carole Garbuny & Leshem, Yossi. Man Who Flies with Birds (p. 1395)
Vogel, Cheri. Everybody Potties: Shaped Board Book down SPEC. Cottage Door Press, ed. (p. 671)
Vogel, Dawn. Trouble with the Tick-Tock Tabby. (p. 2292)
Vogel, Elizabeth. Big Cats (p. 219)
—Cheetahs. (p. 364)
—Conflict Resolution Library: Set 4: Facing Changes (p. 440)
—Eating Right. (p. 622)
—Jaguars. (p. 1155)
—Leopards. (p. 1268)
—Let's Exercise / ¡A hacer Ejercicio! (p. 1271)
—Lions. (p. 1307)
—Meet My Teacher. (p. 1439)
—Meet the Cafeteria Workers. (p. 1439)
—Meet the Librarian. (p. 1440)
—Meet the Principal. (p. 1440)
—Meet the School Nurse. (p. 1440)
—My School (p. 1560)
—Pumas. (p. 1812)
—Taking Care of My Hair. (p. 2178)
—Taking Care of My Hair / ¡el cuidado de tu Cabello! (p. 2178)
—Taking My Bath. (p. 2178)
—Taking My Bath / ¡Al agua Patos! (p. 2178)
—Tigers. (p. 2242)
—¡A comer sanamente! (Eating Right) (p. 1)
—¡A hacer ejercicio! (Let's Exercise) (p. 1)
—¡A lavarse las manos! (Washing My Hands) (p. 1)
—¡A lavarse los dientes! (Brushing My Teeth) (p. 1)
—¡Al agua patos! (Taking My Bath) (p. 38)
—¡el cuidado de tu cabello! (Taking Care of My Hair) (p. 630)
Vogel, Henry. I'm in Charge! & Other Stories. (p. 1098)
Vogel, Jarom, illus. see Volant, Iris.
Vogel, Julia. City Food Chains Adams, Hazel, illus. (p. 394)
—Deciduous Forest Food Chains Adams, Hazel, illus. (p. 523)
—Desert Food Chains Adams, Hazel, illus. (p. 531)
—Discover Air. Yamada, Jane, illus. (p. 553)
—Discover Electricity. Yamada, Jane, illus. (p. 554)
—Discover Energy. Yamada, Jane, illus. (p. 554)
—Length. (p. 1266)
—Measuring Length. Marten, Luanne, illus. (p. 1435)
—Measuring Temperature. Marten, Luanne, illus. (p. 1435)
—Measuring Time: The Clock. Marten, Luanne, illus. (p. 1435)
—Measuring Time: The Calendar. Marten, Luanne, illus. (p. 1435)
—Measuring Volume. Marten, Luanne, illus. (p. 1435)
—Measuring Weight. Marten, Luanne, illus. (p. 1435)
—Save the Planet: Local Farms & Sustainable Foods. (p. 1937)
—Solar Power. (p. 2056)
—Tigers: Built for the Hunt. (p. 2242)
—Weight. (p. 2396)
—What Are Food Chains & Food Webs? Adams, Hazel, illus. (p. 2405)
Vogel, Julius. Mikroskop, ein Mittel der Belehrung und Unterhaltung Für Jedermann Sowie des Gewinns Für Biese. (p. 1465)
Vogel, Kimberly. Sticks & Stones. (p. 2118)
Vogel, Malvina G., ed. see Doyle, A. Conan.
Vogel, Mark A. This Fun Family Has Fun with Numbers. (p. 2224)
Vogel, Michael. My Little Pony: Good Night, Baby Flurry Heart. (p. 1553)
Vogel, Naomi. Do You Know Big Tiny Bunny? (p. 571)
—Happy Animal Alphabet! Vogel, Naomi, illus. (p. 920)
Vogel, Sean. Celtic Run. (p. 351)
Vogel, Vin. Bedtime for Yeti. (p. 188)
—Thing about Yetis. (p. 2220)
Vogel, Vin, illus. see Brandt, Lois.
Vogel, Vin, illus. see McCleery, Peter.
Vogel, Vin, illus. see Tarpley, Todd.
Vogel, Vin, illus. see Weinstone, David.
Vogeler, Edward Jerome. War Is a Bore (Classic Reprint) (p. 2376)
Vogel-Placides, Joan Katherine. Safe Place. Placides, Del S., illus. (p. 1922)
Voght, Victor A. Fun with Huff & Puff (p. 800)
Vogl, Virginia Douglass Hyde. Echoes & Prophecies: Dramatic Sparks Struck from the Anvil of the Times by the Hammer of the Spirit (Classic Reprint) (p. 623)
Vogler, Sara & Burchett, Jan. Oh, Jack! Murfin, Teresa, illus. (p. 1641)
Vogler, Sarah A. Poseidon's Academy. (p. 1779)
—Poseidon's Academy & the Deadly Disease. (p. 1779)
—Poseidon's Academy & the Vanishing Students. (p. 1779)
Vogt, Benjamin N. Revolt. (p. 1873)
Vogt, Gregory. Building Reusable Rockets. (p. 294)
—Dwarf Planet Pluto. (p. 611)
—Is There Life on Other Planets? And Other Questions about Space. (p. 1138)
—Mercury. (p. 1448)
—Meteorology in the Real World. (p. 1453)
—Meteors & Comets. (p. 1453)
—Milky Way. (p. 1467)
—Missions to Mars. (p. 1481)
—Pluto: A Dwarf Planet. (p. 1763)
—Solar System. (p. 2056)
—Stars. (p. 2106)
—Uranus. (p. 2339)
Vogt, Gregory & Shearer, Deborah. 5-Minute Science: Grades 1-3. (p. 2548)
Vogt, Gregory & Waxman, Laura. Sun. (p. 2151)
Vogt, Gregory L. Building Reusable Rockets. (p. 294)
—Missions to Mars. (p. 1481)
Vogt, Johannes, illus. see Horstschafer, Felicitas.
Vogt, Richard C. Rain Forests. (p. 1835)
Vohra, Chetan, et al. Sochu - Think Outside the Box. (p. 2052)
—Sochu - When I Grow Up. (p. 2052)
Vohra Manasvi. Children's Encyclopedia - Life Sciences. (p. 373)
Vohra, Manasvi. Children's Encyclopedia - Physics. (p. 373)
—Children's Encyclopedia - Space Science. (p. 373)
—Children's Encyclopedia - the Earth. (p. 373)
—Children's Encyclopedia - Transportation. (p. 373)
Vohra, Sibi, illus. see Asbjornsen, Peter Christen.
Vohra, Subhash. Little Red Hen. (p. 1326)
Voight, Lisa, illus. see Drez, Jennifer & Bumstead, Robin.
Voigt, Cynthia. Book of Secrets. (p. 259)
—Come a Stranger. (p. 428)
—Dicey's Song. (p. 540)
—Little Bird. (p. 1311)
—Mister Max: the Book of Kings: Mister Max 3. Bruno, Iacopo, illus. (p. 1482)
—Mister Max: the Book of Lost Things: Mister Max 1. Bruno, Iacopo, illus. (p. 1482)
—Mister Max: the Book of Secrets: Mister Max 2. Bruno, Iacopo, illus. (p. 1482)
—Orfe. (p. 1670)
—Runner. (p. 1915)
—Solitary Blue. (p. 2057)
—Sons from Afar. (p. 2064)
—Tale of Birle. (p. 2179)
—Tale of Elske. (p. 2179)
—Tale of Oriel. (p. 2179)
—Teddy & Co. Zakimi, Paola, illus. (p. 2198)
—The Book of Kings. Bruno, Iacopo, illus. (p. 2214)
—Toaff's Way. (p. 2254)
—Young Fredle. Yates, Louise, illus. (p. 2531)
Voigt, David & Voigt, Grady. Socky, the Soft-Hearted Soccer Ball. Wagner, Steve, illus. (p. 2054)
Voigt, F. A. Combed Out (Classic Reprint) (p. 428)
Voigt, Frederick Augustus. Combed Out. (p. 428)
Voiklis, Charlotte Jones & Roy, Léna, contrib. by. Becoming Madeleine: A Biography of the Author of a Wrinkle in Time by Her Granddaughters. (p. 187)
Voiland, Adam. ABCs from Space: A Discovered Alphabet. Voiland, Adam, photos by. (p. 4)
Voisin, Mandy Madson. Star of Deliverance. (p. 2102)
Voitsehovskiy, Boris, et al. Captain Billy Finds a Friend. Barenbaum, Elena, illus. (p. 325)
Voje, Patty, illus. see Cox, Barbara G.
Vojnovic, Ivo. Trilogy of Dubrovnik (Classic Reprint) (p. 2288)
Vojtech, Anna, illus. see St. James, Rebecca.
Vojtech, Anna, illus. see Wadsworth, Olive A.
Vol, Vera, ed. see AZ Books Staff.
Volant, Iris. Ancient Warriors. Lillington, Joe, illus. (p. 82)
—Ancient Wonders. Nuovo, Avalon, illus. (p. 82)
—Ancient Wonders (Literati Edition) Nuovo, Avalon, illus. (p. 82)
—Boats: Fast & Slow. Vogel, Jarom, illus. (p. 251)
—Horses: Wild & Tame. Vogel, Jarom, illus. (p. 1005)
—Under the Canopy: Tales of Trees. Alonso, Cynthia, illus. (p. 2321)
Volbeda, Ludwig, illus. see Lindelauf, Benny.
Volinski, Jess. Notebook Doodles Amazing Me: Coloring & Activity Book. (p. 1624)
—Notebook Doodles Fabulous Fashion Guided Journal. (p. 1624)
—Notebook Doodles Peace Love & Music Guided Journal. (p. 1624)
Volk, Gretchen. Amazing Adventures of Tristy Ruth, Raisin Girl. (p. 62)
Völker, Sven, illus. see Sting.
Volkov, Alexander. Tales of Magic Land 1. (p. 2184)
Vollard, Ambroise. Degas: An Intimate Portrait (Classic Reprint) (p. 526)
—Recollections of a Picture Dealer (Classic Reprint) (p. 1853)
Vollbracht, James. Mishan's Garden. Brooke, Janet, illus. (p. 1477)
Volley, Will, illus. see Shakespeare, William.
Vollmer, Cheryl. Hungry Lion in My Tummy. Dimitriadis, Nick, illus. (p. 1052)
Vollstadt, Elizabeth Weiss. Pairs at Nationals. (p. 1693)
—Pairs on Ice. (p. 1693)
Volmer, Glenn. Legend of Angelgreen. (p. 1261)
Voloschuk, Myroslava, illus. see Smith, Vicki.
Volpari, Daniela, illus. see Wallace, Rich.
Volpari, Daniela, illus. see Weakland, Mark.
Volpe, Julia. Fox & the Castle. Girgenti, Antonio, illus. (p. 774)
Volpe, Karen. Get to Know Levers. (p. 825)
—Get to Know Pulleys. (p. 825)
Volpe, Mamie O. Senior Annual 1919: Class Book of the East Bethlehem Township High School (Classic Reprint) (p. 1988)
Volpi, Giovanni. Great Poplar Mystery. (p. 888)
Volpin, Lucy. Crocodali. (p. 476)
—We Love Dinosaurs. Volpin, Lucy, illus. (p. 2391)
Volponi, Paul. Final Four. (p. 727)
—Hand You're Dealt. (p. 914)
—Homestretch. (p. 998)
—Hurricane Song: A Novel of New Orleans. (p. 1054)
—Hurricane Song. (p. 1054)
—Response. (p. 1870)
—Rikers High. (p. 1883)
—Top Prospect. (p. 2263)
Voltaire. Candide: And Other Romances (Classic Reprint) (p. 321)
—Candide. (p. 321)
—Romances, Novels, & Tales, Vol. 1 (Classic Reprint) (p. 1900)
—Romances, Tales, & Smaller Pieces of M. de Voltaire, Vol. 1 Of 2: Zadig; the World As It Goes; Micromegas; the White Bull; Travels of Scaramentado; How Far We Ought to Impose upon the People (Classic Reprint) (p. 1900)
—Voltaire, Vol. 1: Part I. ; Introductory & Biographical; Victor Hugo's Oration; Candide; Poetical Dissertations (Classic Reprint) (p. 2367)
—Works of M. de Voltaire, Translated from the French, Vol. 11: With Notes, Historical & Critical (Classic Reprint) (p. 2499)
—Works of M. de Voltaire, Vol. 1: Translated from the French; with Notes Historical & Critical (Classic Reprint) (p. 2499)
—Works of M. de Voltaire, Vol. 13: Translated from the French, with Notes, Historical & Critical; Prose Works (Classic Reprint) (p. 2499)
—Works of M. de Voltaire, Vol. 14: Translated from the French; with Notes, Historical & Critical (Classic Reprint) (p. 2499)
—Works of M. de Voltaire, Vol. 25 (Classic Reprint) (p. 2499)
—Works of Voltaire, Vol. 1: Introductory & Biographical; Victor Hugo's Oration; Candide; Poetical Dissertations, Part I (Classic Reprint) (p. 2500)
—Works of Voltaire, Vol. 2 Of 22: A Contemporary Version; Romances (Classic Reprint) (p. 2500)
—Works of Voltaire, Vol. 2 Of 3: Romances (Classic Reprint) (p. 2500)
—Zadig, & Other Tales (Classic Reprint) (p. 2538)
Voltaire, jt. auth. see Voltaire.
Voltaire & Dodsley, P. Romances, Tales & Smaller Pieces of Voltaire. (p. 1900)
Voltaire, Aurelio. Call of the Jersey Devil. (p. 311)
Voltaire, M. De. Romances, Novels, & Tal, Vol. 2 (Classic Reprint) (p. 1900)
Voltz, Christian. Mon Cahier d'Activit's Nature Automne Hiver. (p. 1491)
Voltz, Ralph, illus. see Dorrier, Nancy.
Voltz, Ralph, illus. see Holmes, Andy.
Voltz, Ralph, illus. see Ikids Staff.
Volz, Carole A. Tiggy Finds a Home. (p. 2242)
—Tiggy Finds a Home. Volz, Katie, illus. (p. 2242)
Volz, Heiko, tr. see Kuehn, Birgit.
Volz, Katie, illus. see Volz, Carole A.
Von Bidder, Alex, jt. auth. see McGuirk, Leslie.
Von Braun, Jessica, illus. see Brooks, Charlie.
von Buhler, Cynthia, illus. see Fradin, Dennis Brindell.
von Buhler, Cynthia, illus. see Rockwell, Anne.
von Buhler, Cynthia, tr. see Fradin, Dennis Brindell.
Von Chamisso, Adelbert. Peter Schlemihl. Bowring, John, tr. (p. 1729)

V

Von Collins, Christopher. Mary's Misfortune. (p. 1416)
Von Dahn, Therese Droste-Hülshoff, jt. auth. see Dahn, Felix.
Von Däniken, Erich. Alien Contact in Ancient Greece (p. 46)
—Aliens of the Ancient World (p. 47)
—Mysterious Master Builders of the Stone Age (p. 1567)
Von Denffer, Ahmad. Islam for Children. (p. 1139)
von der Gathen, Katharina. Tell Me: What Children Really Want to Know about Bodies, Sex, & Emotions. Kuhl, Anke, illus. (p. 2201)
von der Sterre, Johanna, illus. see Bader, Joanne.
Von Finn, Denny. Concept Cars. (p. 437)
—Funny Cars. (p. 801)
—Jet Fighters. (p. 1167)
—Powerboats. (p. 1783)
—Snowmobiles. (p. 2049)
—Sprint Cars. (p. 2093)
—Super Cars. (p. 2154)
—Torque: 4X4 Trucks. (p. 2265)
—Torque - Cool Rides (p. 2266)
Von Finn, Denny, jt. auth. see McClellan, Ray.
Von Frantzius, Alexander, jt. auth. see Aristotle.
Von Goethe, Johann Wolfgang. Eleanora, Vol. 1: From the Sorrows of Werter; a Tale (Classic Reprint) (p. 630)
—Elective Affinities: A Novel (Classic Reprint) (p. 631)
—Goethe's Works, Vol. 5: Wilhelm Meister's Travels, a Romance; Elective Affinities (Classic Reprint) (p. 854)
—Hermann & Dorothea: From the German (Classic Reprint) (p. 959)
—Letters from Switzerland: Letters from Italy; Iphigenia in Tauris; Torquato Tasso; Goetz Von Berlichingen (Classic Reprint) (p. 1280)
—Letters of Charlotte, Vol. 1: During Her Connexion with Werter (Classic Reprint) (p. 1280)
—Novels & Tales (Classic Reprint) (p. 1626)
—Prose Translation of Goethe's Hermann & Dorothea (Classic Reprint) (p. 1807)
—Reynard the Fox: After the German Version of Goethe (Classic Reprint) (p. 1874)
—Sorrows of Werter (Classic Reprint) (p. 2066)
—Wilhelm Meister's Apprenticeship & Travels (Classic Reprint) (p. 2467)
—Wilhelm Meister's Apprenticeship & Travels, Vol. 1 Of 2: From the German (Classic Reprint) (p. 2467)
—Wilhelm Meister's Apprenticeship & Travels, Vol. 3 Of 3: From the German; Travels (Classic Reprint) (p. 2467)
—Wilhelm Meister's Apprenticeship, Vol. 1 of 2 (Classic Reprint) (p. 2467)
—Wilhelm Meister's Travels (Classic Reprint) (p. 2467)
—Wilhelm Meister's Travels; the Recreations of the German Emigrants; the Sorrows of Young Werther; Elective Affinities (Classic Reprint) (p. 2467)
—Works of J. W. Von Goethe, Vol. 1 Of 14: With His Life (Classic Reprint) (p. 2498)
—Works of J. W. Von Goethe, Vol. 19: With His Life by George Henry Lewes (Classic Reprint) (p. 2498)
von Holleben, Jan & Helms, Antje. Does This Happen to Everyone? A Budding Adult's Guide to Puberty. (p. 575)
Von Humboldt-A. Voyage Aux Regions Equinoxiales du Nouveau Continent. Tome 11. (p. 2368)
von Innerebner, Jessika. Kevin the Unicorn: It's Not All Rainbows. von Innerebner, Jessika, illus. (p. 1210)
—Kevin the Unicorn: Why Can't We Be Bestie-Corns? von Innerebner, Jessika, illus. (p. 1210)
von Innerebner, Jessika, illus. see Anderson, Teddy.
von Innerebner, Jessika, illus. see Archambault, Nathan & Lecocq, Mara.
von Innerebner, Jessika, illus. see Bellisario, Gina.
von Innerebner, Jessika, illus. see Hitchcock, Laura.
von Innerebner, Jessika, illus. see Jaadee, Kung.
von Innerebner, Jessika, illus. see Kelley, Jane.
von Innerebner, Jessika, illus. see Larsen-Jonasson, Theresa.
von Innerebner, Jessika, illus. see Locke, Kevin.
von Innerebner, Jessika, illus. see Snider, Brandon T.
von Innerebner, Jessika, illus. see Spiller, Trudy.
von Innerebner, Jessika, illus. see Wunsch, Emma.
Von Kanel, Liz. Search for Cuddles & Jonathan's Dream. (p. 1971)
Von Kitzing, Constanze. Pearls of Wisdom. (p. 1711)
Von Kitzing, Constanze, illus. see Munton, Gill.
Von Klan, Stella and Laurene. Beauty & the Boy. (p. 185)
von Klitzing, Maren. Lecturas Acogedoras para Leer Juntos: Suenos, Estrellas y Dias de Lluvia. (p. 1260)
—Lecturas Magicas para Compartir: Princesas, Hadas y Sirenas. (p. 1260)
von Königslöw, Andrea Wayne, illus. see Parkinson, Curtis.
von Königslöw, Andrea Wayne, jt. auth. see Waisberg, Brigitte.
Von Linne, Carl, jt. auth. see Stillingfleet, Benjamin.
Von Martens, Eduard, jt. auth. see Albers, Johann Christian.
Von Meck. My Name Is Vaselinetjie. (p. 1557)
Von Minckwitz, Richard Alexander, jt. auth. see Homer.
von Olfers, Sibylle. Mother Earth & Her Children Coloring Book: Color the Wonderful World of Nature As You See It! 24 Magical, Mythical Coloring Scenes. Zipes, Jack, tr. (p. 1509)
—My First Snow Children (p. 1546)
—Story of the Snow Children (p. 2134)
—Story of the Wind Children: Mini Edition (p. 2135)
Von Schlichten, David. H-E-Double Hockey Stick. (p. 907)
Von Schrenk, Hermann. U. S. Department of Agriculture. Bureau of Forestry-Bulletin No. 51; Report on the Condition of Treated Timbers Laid in Texas, February 1902. (p. 2312)
Von Sperber, Annabelle. Great Big Art History Colouring Book. (p. 884)
—Where's the Artist? From Cave Paintings to Modern Art - A Look & Find Book. (p. 2440)
Von Sperber, Annabelle, illus. see Rebscher, Susanne.
Von Tessin, Marion. Haarige Elefantenkind. (p. 908)
Von Wielligh, G. R. Animal Tales Bankenaar, Dale, illus. (p. 92)
von Ziegesar, Cecily. Adored. (p. 17)
—Dark Horses. (p. 506)
—Gossip Girl: A Novel by Cecily Von Ziegesar. (p. 872)
—I Will Always Love You: A Gossip Girl Novel. (p. 1085)
—It Had to Be You: The Gossip Girl Prequel. (p. 1141)
—You Know You Love Me: A Gossip Girl Novel. (p. 2527)
von Ziegesar, Cecily, creator. Love the One You're With (p. 1361)
Von Zumbusch, Amelie. Ancient Roman Culture. (p. 82)
—Ancient Roman Daily Life. (p. 82)
von Zumbusch, Amelie. Cheetahs: World's Fastest Cats. (p. 364)
—Cheetahs. (p. 364)
—Cheetahs/Guepardos. (p. 364)
Von Zumbusch, Amelie. Dangerous Cats (p. 501)
von Zumbusch, Amelie. Elephants. (p. 634)
—Elephants/Elefantes. (p. 634)
—Giraffes. (p. 834)
—Giraffes/Jirafas. (p. 835)
—Hippos. (p. 973)
—Hippos/Hipopótamos. (p. 973)
—Jaguars: World's Strongest Cats. (p. 1155)
—Leopards: Silent Stalkers. (p. 1268)
—Lions: King of the Beasts. (p. 1307)
—Lions. (p. 1307)
—Lions/Leones. (p. 1307)
—Pumas: Lone Hunters. (p. 1812)
Von Zumbusch, Amelie. Safari Animals (p. 1921)
von Zumbusch, Amelie. Tigers: World's Largest Cats. (p. 2242)
—True Story of the American Flag. (p. 2295)
—True Story of the Battle of Lexington & Concord. (p. 2295)
—True Story of the Salem Witch Hunts. (p. 2295)
—Zebras. (p. 2539)
—Zebras/Cebras. (p. 2539)
Vondebur, M. Colleen. Sammy & the Terrible Storm. (p. 1928)
Vonder Brink, Tracy. Aztec Civilization. (p. 146)
—Microwaves. (p. 1460)
—Protecting the Amazon Rainforest. (p. 1808)
VonFeder, Rosa. Babies Love Halloween: Chunky Lift a Flap Board Book. Cottage Door Press, ed. (p. 147)
—Baby's First Halloween. Cottage Door Press, ed. (p. 154)
—Boo: Chunky Peek a Flap Board Book. Cottage Door Press, ed. (p. 256)
—Brave Little Camper Saves Halloween: Square Padded Board Book. Cottage Door Press, ed. (p. 276)
—Funny Little Ghost. Cottage Door Press, ed. (p. 801)
—Happy Halloween: Chunky Peek a Flap Board Book. Cottage Door Press, ed. (p. 922)
—Happy Halloween, Little Baby! Cottage Door Press, ed. (p. 922)
—Little Vampire's Big Smile: Small Padded Board Book. Dale-Scott, Lindsay, illus. (p. 1329)
—Peek-A-Bright Halloween: Tall Tiered Board Book. Cottage Door Press, ed. (p. 1713)
—Spooky Little Kitten. Cottage Door Press, ed. (p. 2087)
—Spooky, Spooky Little Bat. Cottage Door Press, ed. (p. 2087)
—Trick or Treat: 3 Button Handle Book. Cottage Door Press, ed. (p. 2287)
—Trick or Treat Little Pumpkin. Cottage Door Press, ed. (p. 2287)
—Trick or Treat Songs. Cottage Door Press, ed. (p. 2287)
Vonne, Gertrude Hauck. Paris: The Magic City by the Seine (Classic Reprint) (p. 1699)
Vonne, Mira. Gross Facts about Pirates. (p. 898)
—Gross Facts about the American Civil War. (p. 898)
—Gross Facts about the American Colonies. (p. 898)
—Gross Facts about the Middle Ages. (p. 898)
—Gross Facts about the Roman Empire. (p. 898)
—Gross Facts about Vikings. (p. 898)
—Gross History. (p. 898)
Vonne, Mira, jt. auth. see Clay, Kathryn.
Vonnegut, Kurt. Sun Moon Star. Chermayeff, Ivan, illus. (p. 2151)
VonRecht, illus. see Kay, Susan.
Vonthron-Laver, Sarah, illus. see Mueller, Kirk Jay.
Voorhees, Coert. Benny the Adverb: Grammaropolis. (p. 201)
—Brothers Torres. (p. 286)
—Connie the Conjunction: Grammaropolis. (p. 441)
—Grammaropolis: the Parts of Speech Workbook, Grade 1. (p. 876)
—Grammaropolis: the Punctuation Workbook. (p. 876)
—Izzy the Interjection: Grammaropolis. (p. 1150)
—Jake the Adjective: Grammaropolis. (p. 1156)
—Li'l Pete the Preposition: Grammaropolis. (p. 1301)
—Nelson the Noun: Grammaropolis. (p. 1587)
—Roger the Pronoun: Grammaropolis. (p. 1897)
—Vinny the Action Verb & Lucy the Linking Verb: Grammaropolis. (p. 2359)
Voorhees, James Paxton. Caverns of Dawn (Classic Reprint) (p. 347)
Voorhies, Frank C. Love Letters of an Irishwoman (Classic Reprint) (p. 1360)
Vorderman, Carol. 10 Minutes a Day Math, 1st Grade. (p. 2550)
—10 Minutes a Day Math Kindergarten: Helps Develop Strong Math Habits. (p. 2550)
—10 Minutes a Day Multiplication, 3rd Grade. (p. 2550)
—10 Minutes a Day Phonics Kindergarten. (p. 2550)
—10 Minutes a Day Spelling, 2nd Grade. (p. 2550)
—10 Minutes a Day Spelling, 4th Grade: Helps Develop Strong English Skills. (p. 2550)
—How to Be an Engineer. (p. 1037)
—Math Dictionary. (p. 1422)
Vorella2000, illus. see Tate, Singleton M.
Voremberg, Linda. Robbie: A Journey of Hope (p. 1889)
Vorhand, Rachel, illus. see Yerushalmi, Miriam.
Vornicu, Roxana. Dincolo de Ocean. (p. 547)
Voros, Kevin. Bo N' Joe: Digger Buddies, the Bridge. (p. 250)
Vorse, Mary Heaton. Autobiography of an Elderly Woman (Classic Reprint) (p. 140)
—Breaking in of a Yachtsman's Wife, Vol. 5 (Classic Reprint) (p. 278)
—Growing up (Classic Reprint) (p. 900)
—Heart's Country (Classic Reprint) (p. 946)
—Men & Steel (Classic Reprint) (p. 1446)
—Ninth Man: A Story. (p. 1611)
—Ninth Man: A Story (Classic Reprint) (p. 1611)
—Prestons (Classic Reprint) (p. 1790)
—Second Cabin (Classic Reprint) (p. 1973)
Vorsheck, John, III. Ghost House. (p. 827)
Vorst, John Van. Cry of the Children: A Study of Child-Labor (Classic Reprint) (p. 480)
—Issues of Life: A Novel of the American Woman of to-Day (Classic Reprint) (p. 1141)
—Woman Who Toils: Being the Experiences of Two Ladies As Factory Girls (Classic Reprint) (p. 2486)
—Woman Who Toils: Being the Experiences of Two Gentlewomen As Factory Girls (Classic Reprint) (p. 2486)
Vorst, Marie Van. Amanda of the Mill (Classic Reprint) (p. 61)
—Bagsby's Daughter (Classic Reprint) (p. 159)
—Big Tremaine: A Novel (Classic Reprint) (p. 223)
—Broken Bell (Classic Reprint) (p. 284)
—Fairfax & His Pride: A Novel (Classic Reprint) (p. 695)
—First Love (Classic Reprint) (p. 738)
—Girl from His Town (Classic Reprint) (p. 835)
—His Love Story (Classic Reprint) (p. 974)
—Man from Rome: And Other Stories (Classic Reprint) (p. 1394)
—Mary Moreland: A Novel (Classic Reprint) (p. 1415)
—Philip Longstreth: A Novel (Classic Reprint) (p. 1734)
—Queen of Karmania (Classic Reprint) (p. 1824)
—Tradition (Classic Reprint) (p. 2273)
—War Letters of an American Woman (Classic Reprint) (p. 2376)
Vorster, Claire. Ellie Sparrow & the Great Fire of London: Sizzling Adventure Story for Girls Ages 9-12. (p. 638)
Vort, Carl. Ask Mummy or Daddy. Waterkeyn, Lana, illus. (p. 126)
Vorys, George W. Billikin & Others: Being a Collection of Express Stories (Classic Reprint) (p. 226)
Vosburg, L., illus. see Latham, Frank Brown.
Vosburg, M., illus. see Schauer, M.
Vosburg, Mike, et al. What If? Classic: the Complete Collection Vol. 4. (p. 2412)
Vosburgh, Leonard, illus. see De Leeuw, Cateau.
Vosburgh, Leonard, illus. see Malkus, Alida Sims.
Vosburgh, Leonard, illus. see Webb, Robert N.
Vosburgh, Maude B. Home-Makers: A Play of the Pilgrims in Three Acts (Classic Reprint) (p. 996)
Voshell, Denise Laura. Charlie's Muddy, Yucky, Smelly Day. (p. 360)
—Just Looking for a Friend. (p. 1193)
Voskuil, Hannah. Horus & the Curse of Everlasting Regret. (p. 1006)
Vosloo, Ninette. Pretty on the Outside. (p. 1790)
Vosmaer, Carl. Amazon (Classic Reprint) (p. 67)
Voss, Fred. My House Was Not a Home. (p. 1550)
Voss, Jay Grotius. Just a Rimey Few (Classic Reprint) (p. 1192)
Voss, Johann Heinrich. Luise: Ein ländliches Gedicht in Drei Idyllen (Classic Reprint) (p. 1366)
Voss, Jonathan, illus. see Gianferrari, Maria.
Voss, Jonathan D. Brave Enough for Two. (p. 276)
—Imagine That: A Hoot & Olive Story. Voss, Jonathan D., illus. (p. 1100)
Voss, Jonathan D., illus. see Walker, Sally M.
Votaw, Clarence Ely. Jasper Hunnicutt of Jimpsonhurst (Classic Reprint) (p. 1161)
Voto, Bernard De. Hour (Classic Reprint) (p. 1022)
Votruba, Erik C. Cowboy Mile. (p. 464)
Votsis, Joan. Hollywood, 1941, Vol. 30 (Classic Reprint) (p. 988)
—Hollywood, 1942, Vol. 31 (Classic Reprint) (p. 988)
—Hollywood, Vol. 32: January 1943 (Classic Reprint) (p. 989)
Voudrie, Krista. Sisters of Destiny. (p. 2027)
Vourvoulias, Sabrina. Nuestra América: 30 Inspiring Latinas/Latinos Who Have Shaped the United States. Félix, Gloria, illus. (p. 1629)
—Nuestra América: 30 Latinas/latinos Inspiradores Que Han Forjado la Historia de Los Estados Unidos. F¿lix, Gloria, illus. (p. 1629)
Vous, Nous. Show & Tell: Transport Activities. (p. 2012)
Voute, Emile. Passport (Classic Reprint) (p. 1703)
Voute, Kathleen, illus. see Biemiller, Carl L.
Voutila, Ritva, illus. see Lamond, Margrete.
Voutila, Ritva, illus. see Wild, Margaret.
Vowel, Chelsea, et al. This Place: 150 Years Retold Chomichuk, G. M. B. et al, illus. (p. 2226)
Vox, Everett. U. S. Mint: The History of U. S. Money. (p. 2312)
Voye, Marin De La. Eugenie, the Young Laundress of the Bastille, Vol. 1 of 3 (Classic Reprint) (p. 667)
Voyer, Dorothy May. Henry Hedgehog's Holiday. (p. 955)
Voynich, E. L. E Gadfly (Classic Reprint) (p. 612)
—Humour of Russia (Classic Reprint) (p. 1051)
—Jack Raymond (Classic Reprint) (p. 1152)
—Olive Latham (Classic Reprint) (p. 1649)
Voynich, Ethel Lillian. Interrupted Friendship (Classic Reprint) (p. 1127)
Voyt, Sherri. Party Beneath the Oak Tree: The Ant & The... (p. 1702)
Voz, Samuel. Exploring the Great Basin. (p. 683)
Vrabel, Beth. Blind Guide to Normal. (p. 244)
—Blind Guide to Stinkville. (p. 244)
—Bringing Me Back. (p. 282)
—Caleb & Kit. (p. 309)
—Camp Dork. (p. 315)
—Humiliations of Pipi Mcgee. (p. 1050)
—Newspaper Club. Franco, Paula, illus. (p. 1600)
—Newspaper Club: the Cubs Get the Scoop. (p. 1600)
—Pack of Dorks. (p. 1691)
—Reckless Club. (p. 1853)
—Super Dorks. (p. 2154)
Vranich, Belisa & Eagleson, Holly. Boys Lie: How Not to Get Played. (p. 272)
Vrba, Christina. Good Night Connecticut. Rosen, Anne, illus. (p. 864)
—Stable Cat's Christmas. Yerrill, Gail, illus. (p. 2099)
Vreeland, Suzy. Nose-Blowing 101 for Super Kids: When Little Noses Need Help Learning How. (p. 1622)
Vrettos, Adrienne Maria. Best Friends for Never. (p. 206)
—Burnout. (p. 300)
—Exile of Gigi Lane. (p. 677)
Vries, Anne De, see De Vries, Anne.
Vries, Lizzette de & Vries, Cecile de. How the Tooth Mouse Met the Tooth Fairy. Suwannakit, Tul, illus. (p. 1036)
Vries, Maggie De, see De Vries, Maggie.
Vriesen, Giselle, illus. see King, Alexandria.
Vroman, Lynn. Into the Hollow. (p. 1128)
Vroman, Martin Andrew. Sabbath Readings for the Home Circle (Classic Reprint) (p. 1919)
Vry, Silke. 13 Art Illusions Children Should Know. (p. 2552)
—Trick of the Eye: Art & Illusion. (p. 2287)
—Trick of the Eye: How Artists Fool Your Brain. (p. 2287)
Vry, Silke & Klee, Paul. Paul Klee for Children. (p. 1707)
Vs Editorial Board. Alien Encounters. (p. 46)
—UFO Encounters. (p. 2313)
Vsetula, Maren. Going Fishing (English) Sandland, Amanda, illus. (p. 854)
—Land Skills (English) (p. 1242)
—Ukaliq & Kalla Go Camping (English) Sandland, Amanda, illus. (p. 2314)
Vu, Thi, illus. see Johnson, Sandi.
Vu, Tuan Anh. Manners Handbook for Kids. (p. 1398)
Vue, Jeng Tong & Vue, See. Baby Chick & the Fox. (p. 149)
Vue, Tou, illus. see Brezenoff, Steve.
Vue, Tou, illus. see Dahl, Michael.
Vuillamy, Clara. Bear with Sticky Paws Won't Go to Bed. Vuillamy, Clara, illus. (p. 180)
Vuillemin, Paul. Subordination des Caracteres de la Feuille Dans le Phylum des Anthyllis, et, Propositions Donnees Par la Faculte: Theses (Classic Reprint) (p. 2145)
Vukelic, Deneen. Soaring - a Teen's Guide to Spirit & Spirituality. (p. 2051)
Vukov, Ana. Noory Tree: We Are Friends. (p. 1619)
Vukovic, Elizabet, illus. see Arnold, Elana K.
Vukovic, Elizabet, illus. see Calkhoven, Laurie.
Vukovic, Elizabet, illus. see Diterlizzi, Angela.
Vukovic, Elizabet, illus. see Florence, Debbi Michiko.
Vukovic, Elizabet, illus. see Michiko Florence, Debbi.
Vulliamy, Clara. Bear with Sticky Paws Goes to School. Vuillamy, Clara, illus. (p. 180)
—Birthday Surprise (Dotty Detective, Book 5) (p. 234)
—Dotty Detective (Dotty Detective, Book 1) (p. 588)
—Lost Puppy (Dotty Detective, Book 4) (p. 1355)
—Midnight Mystery (Dotty Detective, Book 3) (p. 1461)
—Paw Print Puzzle (Dotty Detective, Book 2) (p. 1708)
—Vacation Mystery (Dotty Detective, Book 6) (p. 2343)
Vulliamy, Clara, illus. see Andreae, Giles.
Vulliamy, Clara, illus. see Faber, Polly.
Vulliamy, Clara, illus. see Hughes, Shirley.
Vulliamy, Clara, illus. see Mayhew, James.
Vulliamy, Clara, illus. see Rae, Gwynned.
Vulpius, Christian August. History of Rinaldo Rinaldini, Captain of Banditti, Vol. 1 of 2 (Classic Reprint) (p. 979)
Vuoriaro, Paivi, tr. see Pere, Tuula.
Vvoodrovv, Woodrow. Bird of Time: Being Conversations with Egeria (Classic Reprint) (p. 230)
Vyas, Bhavana, illus. see Padma, T. V.
Vyas-Myall, Nisha. Anamchara: Connections. (p. 79)
Vynne, Harold Richard. Woman That's Good: A Story of the Undoing of a Dreamer (Classic Reprint) (p. 2485)
Vynne, Nora. Blind Artist's Pictures: And Other Stories (Classic Reprint) (p. 244)
Vyver, Marita van der. Swemlesse Vir 'n Meermin. (p. 2169)
Vyvyan, Taylor. Beyond the Waterfall. (p. 212)
—Dragon's Odyssey. (p. 596)

W

W, A. M. Patty William's Voyage: A Story Almost Wholly True (Classic Reprint) (p. 1706)
—Patty William's Voyage. (p. 1706)
W, Anais. Au-Dela des Tours. (p. 135)
W B, R., illus. see Griffey, A. F. B.
W, Bernardina. Who Am I? (p. 2446)
W Burgess, Thornton. Bed Time Stories - the Adventures of Buster Bear. (p. 187)
—Bed Time Stories - the Adventures of Danny Meadow Mouse. (p. 187)
—Bed Time Stories - the Adventures of Grandfather Frog. (p. 187)
—Bed Time Stories - the Adventures of Jerry Muskrat. (p. 187)
—Bed Time Stories - the Adventures of Johnny Chuck. (p. 187)
—Bed Time Stories - the Adventures of Poor Mrs. Quack. (p. 187)
—Bed Time Stories - the Adventures of Reddy Fox. (p. 187)
—Burgess Animal Book for Children. (p. 299)
W, C. H. Five Hundred Dollars: And Other Stories of New England Life (Classic Reprint) (p. 743)
W, C. O. John Gutenberg: First Master Printer, His Acts, & Most Remarkable Discourses & His Death (Classic Reprint) (p. 1173)
W, Chris, illus. see Shivers, Ellen C.
W., E., illus. see Leslie, Emma.
W, F. Big Bruce & Little Moss (Classic Reprint) (p. 218)
W, F. E. Sketches of Native Life & Character in Southern India (Classic Reprint) (p. 2031)
W, J. L. Buck & a Puck. (p. 289)
W, L. C. Haydocks' Testimony (Classic Reprint) (p. 941)
W, Maurice. See Me. (p. 1982)
W, N. History of George A. Green, Pindar of the Town of Wakefield: His Birth, Calling, Valour, & Reputation in the Country (Classic Reprint) (p. 978)
W Paul, Herbert. English Men of Letters; Matthew Arnold. (p. 654)
W Robison, Marcus. Butterfly Kite. (p. 304)
W, S. Visit to a Farm House; or, an Introduction to Various Subjects: Connected with Rural Economy, Embellished with Beautiful Plates (Classic Reprint) (p. 2362)

W

Wagner, Lucyann & Blackstone, Delia. Lucy Patoocy & Her Pink Piggy Racer. (p. 1366)
Wagner, Madge Morris. Autobiography of a Tame Coyote (Classic Reprint) (p. 140)
Wagner, Mary. Kelsey Hates the Needle. Almora, Krystal, illus. (p. 1209)
Wagner, Mary M., jt. auth. see Mitten, Luana K.
Wagner, Matt. Mage: The Hero Discovered. (p. 1376)
—Mage: The Hero Defined. Bk. 2, Vol. 3 (p. 1376)
—Mage: The Hero Defined. Bk. 2, Vol. 4 (p. 1376)
Wagner, Mckenzie. Amulet Chase. (p. 77)
—Benotripia Trilogy. (p. 201)
—Casters of Doovik. (p. 340)
—Keys to the Dream World. (p. 1212)
—Rescue. (p. 1868)
Wagner, Michael. Little Ned. Carruthers, Adam, illus. (p. 1323)
—Why I Love Footy. Jellett, Tom, illus. (p. 2458)
—Why I Love Summer. Jellett, Tom, illus. (p. 2458)
Wagner, Michael, jt. auth. see Godwin, Jane.
Wagner, Obe, jt. auth. see Wagner, Kathi.
Wagner, Rachel A. Bogie the Boxer: Gardens. (p. 254)
Wagner, Rob. Film Folk: Close-Ups of the Men, Women, & Children Who Make the Movies (Classic Reprint) (p. 726)
Wagner, Robert Leicester. Rob Wagner's California Almanack (Classic Reprint) (p. 1889)
Wagner, Ron, illus. see Hama, Larry.
Wagner, Samuel. American Bee Journal, 1872, Vol. 7 (Classic Reprint) (p. 70)
—American Bee Journal, Vol. 7: 1871-72 (Classic Reprint) (p. 70)
Wagner, Sandra Glahn. Ants Have Dyed. Wagner, Sandra Glahn, illus. (p. 103)
—Trickle, the Water Cycler. Wagner, Sandra Glahn, illus. (p. 2287)
Wagner, Steve, illus. see Voigt, David & Voigt, Grady.
Wagner, Tina L. Puddles the Skunk in What Stinks? (p. 1810)
Wagner, Tricia & Wagner, Tricia Martineau. North Carolina, the First Golden State Camling, Candace, illus. (p. 1621)
Wagner, Tricia Martineau. Wacky Things about Animals—Volume 1: Weird & Amazing Animal Facts! Ballesteros, Carles, illus. (p. 2369)
Wagner, Veronica. Animal Stories: 8 Animal Stories, over 35 Sounds. Carle, Eric, illus. (p. 91)
—Baby Einstein: Look & See with Me! Shutterstock.com, photos by. (p. 150)
—Disney: Mickey & the Roadster Racers: Go, Go, Go! (p. 561)
—Disney Mickey Mouse Clubhouse: 3 Book Play-A-Sound Set (p. 561)
—Disney Princess Beauty & the Beast Look & Find. (p. 562)
—DreamWorks: Trolls: Meet the Trolls! (p. 603)
—DreamWorks: Trolls. (p. 603)
—Dreamworks Trolls Look & Find. (p. 603)
—Go, Go, Go! (p. 846)
—Hasbro My Little Pony the Movie Look & Find. (p. 936)
—Lion Guard Look & Find. (p. 1306)
—Nickelodeon: Bubble Guppies. Moore, Harry & Trover, Zachary, illus. (p. 1603)
—Nickelodeon: Meet PAW Patrol: Meet PAW Patrol. (p. 1603)
—Nickelodeon PAW Patrol. Moore, Harry & Petrossi, Fabrizio, illus. (p. 1603)
—Star Look & Find. (p. 2102)
—Trolls Little Music Note. (p. 2290)
Wagner, Veronica, jt. auth. see Skwish, Emily.
Wagner, Veronica, jt. ed. see Wage, Erin Rose.
Wagner, Veronica, adapted by. Disney. (p. 558)
—Nickelodeon PAW Patrol: Ruff Ruff Rhythms. (p. 1603)
Wagner, Veronica & P. I. Kids Staff. Bedtime Sound Storybook. (p. 188)
—Dreamworks, Trolls. (p. 603)
—Nickelodeon, Paw Patrol: ABCs My Write-and-Erase Book. Moore, Harry & Petrossi, Fabrizio, illus. (p. 1603)
—Nickelodeon, Paw Patrol. (p. 1603)
Wagner, Veronica, ed. Nickelodeon PAW Patrol: My Little Bucket of Books. (p. 1603)
Wagner, Viqi & Wyborny, Sheila. Muammar Qaddafi. Greenhaven Press Staff, ed. (p. 1523)
Wagner, Wilhelm. Epics & Romances of the Middle Ages (Classic Reprint) (p. 658)
Wagner, William. Ryan Flying Reporter, Vol. 4: July 17, 1942 (Classic Reprint) (p. 1918)
Wagner, Zoey Abbott, illus. see Ehrlich, Nikki.
Wagner-Robertson, Garry. Evil Mailbox & the Super Burrito Wagner, Connie, illus. (p. 674)
Wagnon, Brad. Land of the Great Turtles. Stephenson, Alex, illus. (p. 1242)
Wagstaff, Janiel. Stella & Class: Information Experts. (p. 2112)
—Stella & Class: Information Experts. (p. 2112)
—Stella Tells Her Story. (p. 2113)
—Stella Writes an Opinion. (p. 2113)
Wagstaff, Janiel M. 85 Differentiated Word Sorts: One-Page Leveled Word Sorts for Building Decoding & Spelling Skills. (p. 2556)
—Stella: Poet Extraordinaire. (p. 2113)
—Stella Tells Her Story. (p. 2113)
—Stella Writes an Opinion. (p. 2113)
—Stella Writes Set. (p. 2113)
Wagstaff, Tiffany. Fairies of Kawakawa. (p. 696)
Wagstaffe, Johanna. Fault Lines: Understanding the Power of Earthquakes (p. 715)
—Little Cloud: The Science of a Hurricane. McLaughlin, Julie, illus. (p. 1314)
Wagstaffe, William Warwick. Student's Guide to Human Osteology (Classic Reprint) (p. 2143)
Waguespack, Michael. Deer Hunting Book. (p. 525)
Wahab, Shaista & Youngerman, Barry. Afghanistan. (p. 31)
Wahi, Ellen. Full Moon Lore. Stewart, Ashley, illus. (p. 797)
Wahid, Kelli. As Children Grow: Poetry for Children. (p. 124)
Wahl, Charis. Rosario's Fig Tree Melanson, Luc, illus. (p. 1904)
Wahl, Charis, jt. auth. see Falcone, L. M.
Wahl, Charis, jt. auth. see MacDonald, Anne Louise.
Wahl, Elizabeth. Do You Have a Friend Who Is Suicidal? (p. 571)
Wahl, J. New Familiar & Progressive Dialogues in English & Italian (Classic Reprint) (p. 1593)
Wahl, Jan. Art Collector. Bonnet, Rosalinde, illus. (p. 120)
—Cobweb Castle. (p. 410)
—Hedy & Her Amazing Invention. Wallace, Morgana, illus. (p. 948)
—Hunter. Jessell, Tim, illus. (p. 1053)
—I Met a Dinosaur. Sheban, Chris, illus. (p. 1079)
—Long Tall Journey. Gapaillard, Laurent, illus. (p. 1343)
Wahl, Leslea. Perfect Blindside. (p. 1722)
Wahl, Phoebe. Backyard Fairies. (p. 157)
—Blue House. (p. 248)
—Sonya's Chickens. (p. 2064)
Wahl, Phoebe, illus. see Lloyd, Megan Wagner.
Wahl, Valerie. Ayat Jamilah: Beautiful Signs: A Treasury of Islamic Wisdom for Children & Parents. (p. 145)
Wahl, Valerie, illus. see Conover, Sarah.
Wahlenberg, Anna. Swedish Fairy Tales (Classic Reprint) (p. 2168)
Wahler, Pat. Midnight the Cat. (p. 1461)
Wahlert, Jennie. Child Development Readers: Meeting Our Neighbors (Classic Reprint) (p. 369)
Wahlstrom, Mai-Le, tr. see Pere, Tuula.
Wahman, Wendy. Don't Lick the Dog: Making Friends with Dogs. Wahman, Wendy, illus. (p. 583)
—Rabbit Stew. (p. 1829)
Waibel, Mary. Charmed Memories: A Princess of Valendria Novel. (p. 361)
—Different Kind of Knight: A Princess of Valendria Novel. (p. 545)
—Quest of the Hart: A Princess of Valendria Novel. (p. 1826)
Waibel, Stacy Raye. Rudy's Incredible Kidney Machine. Gruebele, Michelle, illus. (p. 1912)
Waid, Mark. Captain America Molina, Jorge, illus. (p. 324)
—Champions, Volume 1: Change the World (p. 355)
—City of Incredibles Takara, Marcio, illus. (p. 395)
—Family Matters. Takara, Marcio, illus. (p. 702)
—Incorruptible. Takara, Marcio, illus. (p. 1113)
—Incredibles: City of Incredibles Takara, Marcio, illus. (p. 1114)
—Man Out of Time. Molina, Jorge, illus. (p. 1395)
Waid, Mark & Haspiel, Dean. Fox - Freak Magnet. Haspiel, Dean, illus. (p. 773)
Waid, Mark & Peyer, Tom. Captain Kid Volume 1. Mike, Marts, ed. (p. 325)
Waid, Mark & Walker, Landry. Revenge from Below. Takara, Marcio, illus. (p. 1872)
Waid, Mark, text. Avengers & Champions: Worlds Collide (p. 142)
Waight, Peter Robin. When Shakespeare Lost the Plot. (p. 2433)
Wailly, Gustave De. Oreiller Qui Pleure: Monologue (Classic Reprint) (p. 1670)
Wain, Doug. War Against Violence Everywhere. (p. 2376)
Wain, John. Living in the Present: A Novel (Classic Reprint) (p. 1333)
Waines, Frances Drummond. Humpi, the Orphan Camel (p. 1051)
Wainewright, Max. 20 Games to Create with Scratch. (p. 2553)
—25 Scratch 3 Games for Kids: A Playful Guide to Coding. (p. 2554)
—Code Your Own Jungle Adventure. Smith, Henry, illus. (p. 411)
—Code Your Own Knight Adventure. Smith, Henry, illus. (p. 412)
—Design, Animate, & Create with Computer Graphics. (p. 532)
—How to Code: A Step-By-Step Guide to Computer Coding. (p. 1038)
—I'm a JavaScript Games Maker: Advanced Coding. (p. 1097)
—I'm a Javascript Games Maker. (p. 1097)
—I'm a Python Programmer. (p. 1097)
—I'm a Scratch Coder. (p. 1097)
—I'm an App Developer. (p. 1097)
—I'm an HTML Web Page Builder. (p. 1097)
—Level 2: A Step-By-Step Guide to Computer Coding. Henson, Mike, illus. (p. 1281)
—Level 3. Henson, Mike, illus. (p. 1281)
—Saving Adventure. Smith, Henry, illus. (p. 1938)
—Scratch Code Robots. (p. 1963)
—Scratch Code Smart Homes. (p. 1963)
—Scratch Code Space Tech. (p. 1963)
—Scratch Code Transportation. (p. 1963)
Wainter, Erica Zappy. Curious George Lemonade Stand. (p. 487)
Wainwright, Debra. That Kind of Dog. (p. 2213)
Wainwright, Jen, ed. Winter Wonderland Doodles: Festive Full-Color Pictures to Complete & Create. (p. 2476)
Waipara, Zak, illus. see Tipene, Tim.
Wairy, Louis Constant. Memoirs of Constant, the Emperor Napoleon's Head Valet, Vol. 3 Of 4: Containing Details of the Private Life of Napoleon, His Family & His Court (Classic Reprint) (p. 1444)
Waisanen, Emily. Book Monster. Konecny, John, illus. (p. 257)
Waisberg, Brigitte. Bed Tales (Big Kid Books) Koultourides, Ariana, illus. (p. 187)
—Shirt Tales (Big Kid Books) Koultourides, Ariana, illus. (p. 2008)
Waisberg, Brigitte & von Königslöw, Andrea Wayne. Toilet Tales (Big Kid Books) Koultourides, Ariana, illus. (p. 2256)
Waisbrooker, Lois. Alice Vale: A Story for the Times (Classic Reprint) (p. 45)
—Alice Vale. (p. 45)
Waisman, Shirley, illus. see MacLeod, Jennifer Tzivia.
Wait, Frona Eunice. Stories of el Dorado (Classic Reprint) (p. 2125)
Wait, Lea. Contrary Winds: A Novel of the American Revolution. (p. 445)
—For Freedom Alone: A Novel of the Highland Clearances. (p. 762)
Waite, Alice Vinton. Modern Masterpieces of Short Prose Fiction (Classic Reprint) (p. 1487)
Waite, Campbell Waldo. Among the Moonshiners (Classic Reprint) (p. 76)
Waite, Cpt John Carnahan. Splinter Island: The Splinter Island Mystery. (p. 2085)
Waite, D. Byron. O-Neh-Da Te-Car-Ne-O-Di; or up & down the Hemlock: Including History, Commerce, Accidents, Incidents, Guide, etc (Classic Reprint) (p. 1633)
Waite, Donald E., jt. auth. see Calderwood, Damon.
Waite, Donald E., jt. photos by see Calderwood, Damon.
Waite, E. S. Corn-Husking: A Farce (Classic Reprint) (p. 454)
Waite, Jim. Better Than Best: Be a Friend. (p. 209)
—Better Than Best. (p. 209)
Waite, Tyler, illus. see Bishop, Sabrena.
Waites, Joan. Artist's Night Before Christmas (p. 123)
—Colorful Tail: Finding Monet at Giverny (p. 422)
Waites, Joan, illus. see Butler, Dori Hillestad.
Waites, Joan, illus. see Slade, Suzanne.
Waites, Joan, illus. see St. Romain, Rose Anne.
Waites, Joan, illus. see Wallace, Susan Helen.
Waites, Joan, jt. auth. see Slade, Suzanne.
Waites, Joan C., illus. see Allen, Nancy Kelly.
Waites, Joan C., illus. see Butler, Dori Hillestad.
Waites, Joan C., illus. see Nicholas, J. B.
Waites, Joan C., illus. see St. Romain, Rose Anne.
Waitt Cu-Banc, Mw & Co Bkp, jt. auth. see Tate, C. M.
Waitt, Isabel Woodman. What-Shall-I-Do Girl (Classic Reprint) (p. 2419)
Waitt, Paul. Further Adventures of Mollie, Waddy & Tony (Classic Reprint) (p. 802)
Wajsbort, Rochel. Advanced Kriah Level 2: Level 2. (p. 18)
Wakatoon. Coloriages Animes Wakatoon - Tome 1: Trois Dessins Animes a Colorier. (p. 422)
Wake, Charlotte. Beavers & the Elephant: Stories in Natural History, for Children (Classic Reprint) (p. 186)
Wake, Clara. Modern Myth. (p. 1487)
Wake, Katherine, illus. see Steven, Kenneth.
Wake, Rich, illus. see Lazar, Tara.
Wake, Rich, illus. see Murphy, Angela.
Wakefield, Alice, ed. see Chute, Phillip B.
Wakefield, Beth. Cleaner. (p. 402)
Wakefield, Chris. Dad Did It! (p. 494)
Wakefield, Priscilla. Instinct Displayed in a Collection of Well-Authenticated Facts: Exemplifying the Extraordinary Sagacity of Various Species of the Animal Creation (Classic Reprint) (p. 1125)
—Introduction to Botany: In a Series of Familiar Letters, with Illustrative Engravings. (p. 1129)
Wakefield, S. A. Selected Adventures of Bottersnikes & Gumbles. Digby, Desmond, illus. (p. 1986)
Wakefield, Scott, illus. see Namm, Diane.
Wakefield, Scott, illus. see Olmstead, Kathleen.
Wakefield, Scott J., illus. see Graham, Billy.
Wakefield, Scott J., illus. see McFadden, Deanna.
Wakefield, Scott J., illus. see Namm, Diane.
Wakefield, Vikki. Ballad for a Mad Girl. (p. 161)
—Friday Never Leaving. (p. 785)
—In-Between Days. (p. 1104)
—This Is How We Change the Ending. (p. 2224)
Wakeham, Kate. Moby-Dick Tempest, Annabel, illus. (p. 1485)
—Pride & Prejudice Tempest, Annabel, illus. (p. 1791)
—Secret Garden Newland, Jane, illus. (p. 1975)
Wakelin, Kirsti Anne, illus. see Bar-el, Dan.
Wakelin, Kirsti Anne, illus. see Gilmore, Rachna.
Wakelin, Kirsti Anne, illus. see Lloyd, Jennifer.
Wakelin, Kirsti Anne, illus. see McFarlane, Sheryl.
Wakelin, Kirsti Anne, jt. auth. see Lloyd, Jennifer.
Wakeman, Bill, illus. see Ferguson, Don.
Wakeman, Joel. Mysterious Parchment, or the Satanic License: Dedicated to Maine Law Progress (Classic Reprint) (p. 1568)
Wakeman, Marion Freeman, illus. see Hatch, Richard W.
Wakil, Landen. Some Place Better Than Here. (p. 2059)
Wakiyama, Hanako, illus. see Archer, Peggy.
Wakiyama, Hanako, illus. see Dealey, Erin.
Wakiyama, Hanako, illus. see Novesky, Amy.
Wal, K. B. Cerebral Labyrinth. (p. 353)
Walberg, Herbert J., ed. see Greenhaven Press Editors.
Walbridge, Helen Isabel. Smith College Monthly, Vol. 9: October, 1901-June, 1902 (Classic Reprint) (p. 2042)
Walburg, Lori. Legend of the Candy Cane: The Inspirational Story of Our Favorite Christmas Candy Bernardin, James & Cowdrey, Richard, illus. (p. 1262)
Walburg, Lori, jt. auth. see Mackall, Dandi Daley.
Walburg, Lori, jt. auth. see Zondervan Staff.
Walch, Garnet. Little Tin Plate & Other Verses (Classic Reprint) (p. 1329)
Walckenaer, C. A. Fables et Oeuvres Diverses de J. la Fontaine: Avec des Notes et une Nouvelle Notice Sur Sa Vie (Classic Reprint) (p. 691)
Walckenaer, Charles Athanase. Histoire Naturelle des Insectes, Vol. 1: Apteres (Classic Reprint) (p. 975)
Walcker, Yann. Ludwig Van Beethoven Voake, Charlotte, illus. (p. 1366)
Walcot, Charles M. Good Fellow: Petite Comedy in One Act (Classic Reprint) (p. 862)
—Nothing to Nurse: An Original Farce, in One Act (Classic Reprint) (p. 1625)
Walcot, Charles Melton. One Coat for Two Suits, an Entirely Original Comic Drama, in Two Acts (Classic Reprint) (p. 1659)
Walcott, Charles Doolittle. Second Contribution to the Studies on the Cambrian Faunas of North America (Classic Reprint) (p. 1973)
Walcott, Earle Ashley. Apple of Discord (Classic Reprint) (p. 106)
—Blindfolded (Classic Reprint) (p. 244)
Walcott, Frederica A. Letters from the Far East: Notes of a Visit to China, Korea & Japan, 1915-1916 (Classic Reprint) (p. 1280)
Walcott, Stuart. Above the French Lines: Letters of Stuart Walcott, American Aviator: July 4, 1917, to December 8 1917. (p. 7)
—Above the French Lines: Letters of Stuart Walcott, American Aviator, July 4, 1917 to December 8, 1917 (Classic Reprint) (p. 7)
—Life Story of an American Airman in France: Extracts from the Letters of Stuart Walcott, Who, Between July & December, 1917, Learned to Fly in French Schools of Aviation, Won Fame at the Front, & Fell near Saint Souplet (Classic Reprint) (p. 1296)
Walczak, Krystyna. Shadownose & the Kingdom of Shadows. (p. 1997)
Wald, Christina, illus. see Bowman, Donna H.
Wald, Christina, illus. see Buchanan, Buck.
Wald, Christina, illus. see Cooper, Sharon Katz.
Wald, Christina, illus. see Downing, Johnette.
Wald, Christina, illus. see Driscoll, Laura.
Wald, Christina, illus. see East, Cathy.
Wald, Christina, illus. see Gerber, Carole.
Wald, Christina, illus. see Keener, Anna.
Wald, Christina, illus. see Kieber-King, Cynthia.
Wald, Christina, illus. see Lay, Kathryn.
Wald, Christina, illus. see Love, Donna.
Wald, Christina, illus. see Patent, Dorothy Hinshaw.
Wald, Christina, illus. see Pearson, Carrie A.
Wald, Christina, illus. see Robinson, Tom.
Wald, Christina, illus. see Singleton, Linda Joy.
Wald, Christina, illus. see Spangler, Lois.
Wald, Christina, illus. see Troupe, Thomas Kingsley.
Wald, Christina, jt. auth. see Pearson, Carrie A.
Wald, Heywood. Spanish Is Fun: Book 1 Student Edition. (p. 2074)
Walda, Angela & Yalda, Angelina. Space Race: How We Set Our Sights on Thge Stars & Conquered Space. (p. 2072)
Waldeck, Aaron. Space Rocks: A Look at Asteroids & Comets. (p. 2072)
Waldek, Kelly, illus. see Richemont, Enid.
Walden, Katherine. Baboons. (p. 148)
—Leopards of the African Plains. (p. 1268)
—Meerkats. (p. 1437)
—Rhinoceroses. (p. 1875)
—Warthogs. (p. 2381)
—Wildebeests. (p. 2466)
Walden, Katherine & Watson, Stephanie. Conquering Anorexia (p. 441)
Walden, Kelly. Rory Story: Rory Loves Robots. (p. 1904)
—V Is for Virus. (p. 2343)
Walden, Libby. Across the Savannah. Robin, Clover, illus. (p. 11)
—Bear Hugs. Riley, Vicky, illus. (p. 179)
—Construction. Artful Doodlers, Artful, illus. (p. 443)
—Emergency Services. Artful Doodlers, Artful, illus. (p. 641)
—Finding First Animals & More! Galloway, Fhiona, illus. (p. 729)
—Finding First Words & More! Galloway, Fhiona, illus. (p. 729)
—Hidden World: Forest. Coleman, Stephanie Fizer, illus. (p. 966)
—Hidden World: Ocean. Coleman, Stephanie Fizer, illus. (p. 966)
—In Focus. Tucker, Tracey et al, illus. (p. 1105)
—In Focus: Cities. Easton, Grace et al, illus. (p. 1105)
—Lots to Spot: Farm. Meredith, Samantha, illus. (p. 1356)
—Noisy Animals. (p. 1617)
—Noisy First Words. (p. 1617)
—Noisy Things That Go. (p. 1618)
—Noisy Touch & Feel: Cow Says Moo. Enright, Amanda, illus. (p. 1618)
—Noisy Touch & Feel: Owl Says Hoot. Enright, Amanda, illus. (p. 1618)
—Search & Find: Dinosaurs. Solís, Fermín, illus. (p. 1970)
—Ten Tiny Dinosaurs. Fennell, Clare, illus. (p. 2205)
—Things That Grow. Stadtlander, Becca, illus. (p. 2221)
—Touch-And-Feel First Words. Galloway, Fhiona, illus. (p. 2267)
Walden, Mark. Aftershock. (p. 34)
—Deadlock. (p. 518)
—Dreadnought. (p. 600)
—Earthfall. (p. 617)
—Escape Velocity. (p. 662)
—Redemption. (p. 1859)
—Retribution. (p. 1870)
—Rogue. (p. 1897)
—Zero Hour. (p. 2540)
Walden, Pamela Charlene. Puff Bear Goes to the Hospital. (p. 1811)
Walden, Tillie. Are You Listening? Walden, Tillie, illus. (p. 113)
—On a Sunbeam. (p. 1652)
Waldendorf, Kurt. Hooray for Chefs! (p. 1000)
—Hooray for Construction Workers! (p. 1000)
—Hooray for Farmers! (p. 1000)
—Hooray for Veterinarians! (p. 1001)
—How Big Is a Blue Whale? (p. 1026)
—How Deep Is the Ocean? (p. 1027)
—How Far Is the Sun? (p. 1031)
—How Fast Is a Cheetah? (p. 1031)
—How Slow Is a Sloth? (p. 1035)
—How Small Is a Hummingbird? (p. 1035)
—How Strong Is an Ant? (p. 1035)
—How Tall Is a Giraffe? (p. 1035)
—Que Vivan los Obreros de Construccion! (Hooray for Construction Workers!) (p. 1823)
—Que Vivan los Veterinarios! (p. 1823)
—¡Que Vivan los Chefs! (p. 1823)
—¡Que Vivan los Granjeros! (p. 1823)
Walder, Johan, illus. see Richle, Urs.
Waldherr, Kris. Bad Princess: True Tales from Behind the Tiara. (p. 158)
Waldie, John. Adventures of a Valet, Vol. 1 of 2 (Classic Reprint) (p. 21)
Waldman, Alan/A. Erica from America & the Start of the Gang of Four. Scobie, Andrea, illus. (p. 659)
Waldman, Bruce, illus. see Peter Pauper Press Staff, et al.
Waldman, Cantor. Song Divine: An Autobiography (Classic Reprint) (p. 2062)
Waldman, David K. How Teddy Bears Find Their Homes. Danner, Maggie, illus. (p. 1035)
Waldman, Debby. Addy's Race (p. 15)
—Clever Rachel Revell, Cindy, illus. (p. 404)
—Miriam's Secret (p. 1475)
Waldman, Debby & Feutl, Rita. Room Enough for Daisy Revell, Cindy, illus. (p. 1903)
Waldman, Loretta. 3D Materials & Construction Possibilities. (p. 2547)

Waldman, Neil. Al & Teddy. (p. 38)
—Land of Big Dreamers: Voices of Courage in America. Waldman, Neil, illus. (p. 1241)
—Voyages: Reminiscences of Young Abe Lincoln. (p. 2368)
Waldman, Nomi J. Deadwood, South Dakota A Frontier Community: Set Of 6. (p. 519)
Waldman, Scott. Gunfight at the O. K. Corral: Wyatt Earp Upholds the Law. (p. 905)
—Victory at Sea: John Paul Jones & the Continental Navy. (p. 2356)
Waldman, Stacey. Primary Paintsville. (p. 1792)
Waldman, Stuart. Last River: John Wesley Powell & the Colorado River Exploring Expedition. Manchess, Gregory, illus. (p. 1249)
Waldmann, Alfred. Die Begriffliche Entwicklung des Lateinischen Super (Supra) und Sursum Im Französischen; Mit Berücksichtigung der Übrigen Romanischen Sprachen: Inaugural-Dissertation (Classic Reprint) (p. 543)
Waldo Cutler, U. Stories of King Arthur & His Knights. (p. 2125)
Waldo, Dorothy. Idowanna: A Play for Children in One Act (Classic Reprint) (p. 1090)
Waldo, Edith H. Aunt Hester's Dilemma: A Farce in Two Acts (Classic Reprint) (p. 137)
Waldo, Frank. Modern Meteorology: An Outline of the Growth & Present Condition of Some of Its Phases (Classic Reprint) (p. 1487)
Waldo, Fullerton L. Seashell a Comedy in One Act (Classic Reprint) (p. 1972)
—With Grenfell on the Labrador (Classic Reprint) (p. 2481)
Waldo, Fullerton Leonard. America at the Front (Classic Reprint) (p. 69)
Waldo, Harold. Stash of the Marsh Country (Classic Reprint) (p. 2108)
Waldo, Lillian M. Safety First for Little Folks: First Steps in Civics (Classic Reprint) (p. 1922)
Waldo, Nigel. Wallflowers (Classic Reprint) (p. 2373)
Waldon, Ruth. Wife of 'Ostler Joe: A Travesty (Classic Reprint) (p. 2461)
Waldorf, Heather. Leftovers (p. 1261)
Waldorf, Marjorie Bleau. Three Mothers for Margie. (p. 2234)
Waldrep, Evelyn L., ed. see Lundy, Charlotte.
Waldrep Poole, Lynnette. Dragon Dreams. (p. 593)
Waldrep, Richard, illus. see Crowe, Ellie.
Waldrod, Amy, illus. see Howe, James.
Waldron, Ann. Who Was Claude Monet? (p. 2450)
Waldron, Ann & Who HQ. Who Was Claude Monet? Marchesi, Stephen, illus. (p. 2450)
Waldron, Douglas Edward. Pathway to Montan: The Settlers Rest (p. 1705)
Waldron, Kevin. Harold Tiene Hambre (Harold's Hungry Eyes) (Spanish Edition) (p. 931)
—Mr. Peek & the Misunderstanding at the Zoo. Waldron, Kevin, illus. (p. 1519)
—Panda-Monium at Peek Zoo. Waldron, Kevin, illus. (p. 1695)
Waldron, Kevin, illus. see Rosen, Michael.
Waldron, Malcolm. Snow Man: John Hornby in the Barren Lands (Classic Reprint) (p. 2047)
Waldron, Melanie. Adaptation (p. 14)
—Deserts (p. 532)
—Flowers (p. 753)
—Geography Matters in Ancient Egypt. (p. 817)
—Geography Matters in Ancient Greece. (p. 817)
—Geography Matters in Ancient Rome. (p. 817)
—Human Body. (p. 1049)
—Iceland (p. 1088)
—Ireland (p. 1134)
—Let's Get Mapping! (p. 1273)
—Lithuania (p. 1309)
—Mapping Communities (p. 1401)
—Mapping Information (p. 1401)
—Mapping the Land & Weather (p. 1401)
—Mapping the World (p. 1401)
—Mountains (p. 1514)
—Plant Parts (p. 1756)
—Plants (p. 1757)
—Polar Regions (p. 1770)
—Rivers (p. 1887)
—Roots (p. 1903)
—Scotland (p. 1962)
—Seeds & Fruits (p. 1983)
—Types of Maps (p. 2310)
—Variation & Classification (p. 2348)
—Your Body by Numbers (p. 2533)
—Your Brain: Understand It with Numbers (p. 2533)
—Your Digestive System: Understand It with Numbers (p. 2533)
—Your Respiration & Circulation: Understand Them with Numbers (p. 2534)
—Your Skin & Bones: Understand Them with Numbers (p. 2534)
Waldron, Melanie, et al. Essential Life Science (p. 664)
Waldron, Webb. Road to the World (Classic Reprint) (p. 1888)
Waldron, William Watson. Pocahontas, Princess of Virginia: And Other Poems (Classic Reprint) (p. 1764)
Waldrop, Thomas A. & Goodrick, Scott L. Introduction to Prescribed Fire in Southern Ecosystems. Forest Service (U.S.) & Southern Research Station (U.S.), eds. (p. 1129)
Waldrup, Carole Chandler. Wives of the American Presidents, 2d Ed (p. 2482)
Waldvogel, K. M. Spies, Soldiers, Couriers, & Saboteurs: Women of the American Revolution. (p. 2082)
Waldy, Frances Helen. Frolic a Scarborough Romance (Classic Reprint) (p. 790)
Wales, Dirk. Further Adventures of a Lucky Dog: Owney, U. S. Rail Mail Mascot. DeJong Artman, Catherine & Artman, Townsend, illus. (p. 802)
Wales, Hubert. Cynthia in the Wilderness (Classic Reprint) (p. 493)
—Mr. & Mrs. Villiers (Classic Reprint) (p. 1517)
—Yoke (Classic Reprint) (p. 2523)
Wales, Johnny, illus. see King, Thomas.
Wales, Johnny, illus. see King, Tom.
Wales, Sid. Freddie & Mee. Bryant, Kerry, illus. (p. 781)
Waley, Arthur. More Translations from the Chinese (Classic Reprint) (p. 1505)
Waley, Arthur, tr. Hundred & Seventy Chinese Poems. (p. 1051)
Walford, Austin. Confession of the Hills (Classic Reprint) (p. 439)
Walford, L. B. Baby's Grandmother (Classic Reprint) (p. 154)
—Baby's Grandmother, Vol. 2 of 3 (Classic Reprint) (p. 154)
—Cousins, Vol. 1 of 3 (Classic Reprint) (p. 463)
—Cousins, Vol. 2 of 3 (Classic Reprint) (p. 463)
—Cousins, Vol. 3 of 3 (Classic Reprint) (p. 463)
—Iva Kildare: A Matrimonial Problem (Classic Reprint) (p. 1149)
—Little Legacy: And Other Stories (Classic Reprint) (p. 1320)
—Matchmaker: A Novel (Classic Reprint) (p. 1420)
—Memories of Victorian London (Classic Reprint) (p. 1446)
—Mr. Smith, Vol. 1 Of 2: A Part of His Life (Classic Reprint) (p. 1520)
—Mr. Smith, Vol. 2 Of 2: A Part of His Life (Classic Reprint) (p. 1520)
—Pauline (Classic Reprint) (p. 1708)
—Pinch of Experience (Classic Reprint) (p. 1745)
—Recollections of a Scottish Novelist (Classic Reprint) (p. 1854)
—Troublesome Daughters, Vol. 1 of 3 (Classic Reprint) (p. 2292)
Walford, Lucy Bethia. Archdeacon (Classic Reprint) (p. 110)
—Baby's Grandmother, Vol. 1 of 3 (Classic Reprint) (p. 154)
—Charlotte (Classic Reprint) (p. 361)
—Cousins (Classic Reprint) (p. 463)
—Dick Netherby (Classic Reprint) (p. 541)
—Fair Rebel: And Other Stories (Classic Reprint) (p. 695)
—Frederick (Classic Reprint) (p. 781)
—Her Great Idea, & Other Stories (Classic Reprint) (p. 956)
—Leddy Marget (Classic Reprint) (p. 1260)
—Mischief of Monica (Classic Reprint) (p. 1477)
—Mr. Smith: A Part of His Life (Classic Reprint) (p. 1520)
—One Good Guest (Classic Reprint) (p. 1660)
—Ploughed & Other Stories (Classic Reprint) (p. 1763)
—Sage of Sixteen (Classic Reprint) (p. 1922)
—Sir Patrick: The Puddock (Classic Reprint) (p. 2026)
—Stay at Homes (Classic Reprint) (p. 2109)
—Stiff-Necked Generation, Vol. 3 of 3 (Classic Reprint) (p. 2119)
—Successors to the Title (Classic Reprint) (p. 2146)
—Troublesome Daughters (Classic Reprint) (p. 2292)
—Troublesome Daughters, Vol. 2 of 3 (Classic Reprint) (p. 2292)
Walford, N. E. Island Hunters: The Legend of Brown Eyed James (p. 1139)
—Island Hunters - Book I: The Backyard Pirate Adventure. (p. 1139)
—Island Hunters - Book II: Trail of the Tomb Robbers. (p. 1139)
—Island Hunters - Book III: The Legend of Brown Eyed James. N Gallerie Studios, illus. (p. 1139)
Walfrid Johnson, Lois. Adventures of the Northwoods Set 1: First 5 Books. (p. 28)
—Adventures of the Northwoods Set 2. (p. 28)
Wali, Anbara. Overview: Who Are the Muslims? Pecastaing, Camille, ed. (p. 1688)
Waling-Palmer, Mary E. Papa Tom's Toast. (p. 1697)
Walji, Zehaan. Adventure of Kakenya. (p. 18)
Walk, Charles Edmonds. Crimson Cross (Classic Reprint) (p. 475)
—Silver Blade: The True Chronicle of a Double Mystery (Classic Reprint) (p. 2019)
—Time Lock (Classic Reprint) (p. 2244)
Walker. Cousin George, & Other Tales, Vol. 3 of 3 (Classic Reprint) (p. 463)
—Cousin George, Vol. 2 Of 3: And Other Tales (Classic Reprint) (p. 463)
Walker, Abbie Phillips. Sandman Tales: Stories for Bedtime (Classic Reprint) (p. 1931)
—Sandman Twilight Stories (Classic Reprint) (p. 1931)
Walker, A.J. Bond of a Dragon: Fall of the Kings. (p. 255)
—Bond of a Dragon: Rise of the Dragonriders. (p. 255)
—Bond of a Dragon: Secrets of the Sapphire Soul. (p. 255)
Walker, Alcee Howard. Substitute #8. (p. 2146)
Walker, Alexandra Boyden, et al. Unplugged: Hundreds of Activities for Teens to Do Without a Screen. (p. 2334)
Walker, Alice Johnstone. Little Plays from American History for Young Folks (Classic Reprint) (p. 1324)
Walker, Amy. Anchor Moon. (p. 79)
Walker, Anita R. Beyond Male & Female: The Gender Identity Spectrum. (p. 211)
Walker, Anna. Florette. (p. 751)
—Hurry up, Alfie! (p. 1055)
—I Love Birthdays. Walker, Anna, illus. (p. 1069)
—I Love Christmas. Walker, Anna, illus. (p. 1069)
—I Love My Dad. Walker, Anna, illus. (p. 1070)
—I Love My Mom. Walker, Anna, illus. (p. 1071)
—I Love to Dance. Walker, Anna, illus. (p. 1073)
—I Love to Sing. Walker, Anna, illus. (p. 1077)
—I Love Vacations. Walker, Anna, illus. (p. 1078)
—Lottie & Walter. (p. 1356)
—Peggy: A Brave Chicken on a Big Adventure. (p. 1714)
Walker, Anna, illus. see Godwin, Jane.
Walker, Annie Louisa, jt. auth. see Oliphant, Margaret.
Walker, Archibald Stodart. Beggar's Wallet: Containing Contributions in Prose, Verse & Pictorial Illustration, Gathered from Certain Workers in Art & Letters (Classic Reprint) (p. 191)
Walker, Barbara M. Little House Cookbook. Williams, Garth, illus. (p. 1319)
—Little House Cookbook: New Full-Color Edition: Frontier Foods from Laura Ingalls Wilder's Classic Stories. Williams, Garth, illus. (p. 1319)
Walker, Brad. Thanos Imperative. (p. 2212)
Walker, Brad, et al. Heroes for Hire by Abnett & Lanning: the Complete Collection. (p. 962)
Walker, Bradley, illus. see Schuette, Leslie Elaine.
Walker, Brandy, illus. see Collar, C. L.
Walker, Brett. Trm. Larose, Trina, ed. (p. 2290)
Walker, Brian F. Black Boy White School. (p. 237)
Walker, Carol J. Mustang Babies! (p. 1530)
Walker, Carolina. You Can Work in Music. (p. 2526)
Walker, Charles Rumford. Steel: The Diary of a Furnace Worker (Classic Reprint) (p. 2112)
Walker, Charmaine. Jon & Alex: Goes to School. (p. 1176)
—Our Voices Through Writing. (p. 1681)
Walker, Chase, illus. see Pailey, Robtel Neajai.
Walker, Christian. Artak & the Forgotten Mark. (p. 122)
Walker, Christopher. Man in the Mango Tree. (p. 1394)
Walker, Claire. Power of Me! a Dragon Book Series - Barbian & the Wishing Star. (p. 1782)
Walker, Colin. Plants Grow Almost Anywhere. Simons, Sally, illus. (p. 1757)
Walker, Cornelius, jt. auth. see Tower, David Bates.
Walker, Cory, illus. see Kirkman, Robert.
Walker, Courtney King. Chasing Midnight. (p. 362)
Walker, Curtis. My Own Little Story: Volume 1: about Me. (p. 1558)
Walker, Dan L. Secondhand Summer. (p. 1974)
Walker, David, illus. see Boelts, Maribeth.
Walker, David, illus. see Engle, Margarita.
Walker, David, illus. see Gershator, Phillis & Green, Mim.
Walker, David, illus. see Gershator, Phillis.
Walker, David, illus. see Gibby, Bayne.
Walker, David, illus. see Greene, Rhonda Gowler.
Walker, David, illus. see Knapman, Timothy.
Walker, David, illus. see Martin, David.
Walker, David, illus. see Morgan, Michaela.
Walker, David, illus. see Parenteau Shirley, Shirley.
Walker, David, illus. see Parenteau, Shirley.
Walker, David, illus. see Paul, Ann Whitford.
Walker, David, illus. see Wharton, Eileen.
Walker, David, jt. auth. see Gershator, Phillis.
Walker, David F. Superb Vol. 3: The Youth Are Getting Restless. Martinez, Alitha, illus. (p. 2159)
Walker, David L., illus. see Cuyler, Margery.
Walker, David M., illus. see Boelts, Maribeth.
Walker, David M., illus. see Martin, David.
Walker, David M., illus. see Muldrow, Diane.
Walker, David M., illus. see Root, Phyllis.
Walker, Demosthenes. Stanley, or Playing for Amusement, & Betting to Count the Game: Scenes in the South (Classic Reprint) (p. 2101)
Walker, Denise M. Hannah's Heart: The Broken Pieces. (p. 918)
Walker, Dolores. Peter, the Pouting Puzzle Piece. (p. 1730)
Walker, Dugald Stewart. Dream Boats, & Other Stories: Portraits & Histories of Fauns, Fairies, Fishes & Other Pleasant Creatures (Classic Reprint) (p. 601)
Walker, Dugald Stewart, illus. see Andersen, Hans.
Walker, E. O. Romance of Ceylon (Classic Reprint) (p. 1900)
Walker, Edith Jean. Sarah Banksia. (p. 1935)
Walker, Edward Ashley. Little Leaven, & What It Wrought at Mrs. Blake's School (Classic Reprint) (p. 1320)
—Watson's Woods, or Margaret Huntington's Experiment (Classic Reprint) (p. 2386)
Walker, Eldred G. F. Canadian Trails: Hither & Thither in the Great Dominion (Classic Reprint) (p. 321)
Walker, Elizabeth J. M. This Night Sucks. (p. 2226)
Walker, Elliot. Cat Tales in Verse (Classic Reprint) (p. 342)
Walker, Erica R. Through the Lens: A Book of Short Stories. (p. 2237)
Walker, Francis. Prince's Pigeon: A Japanese Play in One Act (Classic Reprint) (p. 1795)
Walker Franklin, P. J. Amira, Princess of the Flowers. (p. 75)
Walker, Frederick. Aerial Navigation: A Practical Handbook on the Construction of Dirigible Balloons, Aerostats, Aeroplanes, & Aeromotors (Classic Reprint) (p. 30)
Walker, George. Don Raphael, Vol. 1 Of 3: A Romance (Classic Reprint) (p. 581)
—Don Raphael, Vol. 2 Of 3: A Romance (Classic Reprint) (p. 581)
—Don Raphael, Vol. 3 Of 3: A Romance (Classic Reprint) (p. 581)
—Theodore Cyphon, or the Benevolent Jew, Vol. 1 Of 3: A Novel (Classic Reprint) (p. 2215)
—Three Spaniards, Vol. 1 Of 2: A Romance (Classic Reprint) (p. 2235)
—Vagabond, Vol. 2 Of 2: A Novel (Classic Reprint) (p. 2343)
—Voyages & Cruises of Commodore Walker, During the Late Spanish & French Wars, Vol. 2 (Classic Reprint) (p. 2368)
Walker, George F. Moss Park & Tough! The Bobby & Tina Plays. (p. 1507)
Walker, Guy Morrison. Skeletons: A Claim Agent's Stories (Classic Reprint) (p. 2030)
Walker, H. Wilfrid. Wanderings among South Sea Savages: And in Borneo & the Philippines (Classic Reprint) (p. 2375)
Walker, Harvey Jeanne. Honey Girl: The Hawaiian Monk Seal. Bersani, Shennen, illus. (p. 999)
Walker, Herbert W. Review, Vol. 1: November, 1919 (Classic Reprint) (p. 1873)
Walker, Hugh. Selected English Short Stories, XIX Century (First Series) (Classic Reprint) (p. 1986)
Walker, Ida. Addiction in America: Society, Psychology & Heredity. (p. 15)
—Addiction in America: Society, Psychology, & Heredity. (p. 15)
—Addiction in America: Society, Psychology & Heredity. Henningfield, Jack E., ed. (p. 15)
—Addiction Treatment: Escaping the Trap. (p. 15)
—Around the World. (p. 118)
—France (p. 776)
—Homelessness. Merino, Noël, ed. (p. 997)
—Natural & Everyday Drugs: A False Sense of Security. (p. 1579)
—Natural & Everyday Drugs: A False Sense of Security. Henningfield, Jack E., ed. (p. 1579)
—Nigeria. (p. 1604)
—Nigeria. Rotberg, Robert I., ed. (p. 1604)
—Nutrition & You. (p. 1632)
—Painkillers: Prescription Dependency. (p. 1692)
—Painkillers: Prescription Dependency. Henningfield, Jack E., ed. (p. 1692)
—Sedatives & Hypnotics: Deadly Downers. (p. 1981)
—Sedatives & Hypnotics: Deadly Downers. Henningfield, Jack E., ed. (p. 1981)
—un Security Council & the Center of Power Russett, Bruce, ed. (p. 2317)
—William Blackstone & Commentaries upon the Laws of England. (p. 2468)
Walker, Ida, jt. auth. see McIntosh, Kenneth.
Walker, Ida, jt. auth. see Nelson, Sheila.
Walker, Ida & Indovino, Shaina C. Belgium. Bruton, John, ed. (p. 195)
—Germany. Bruton, John, ed. (p. 822)
Walker, Ida & Indovino, Shaina Carmel. Belgium. (p. 195)
—Germany. (p. 822)
—Ireland. (p. 1134)
—Ireland. Bruton, John, ed. (p. 1134)
Walker, Ida J. Alcohol Addiction: Not Worth the Buzz. (p. 41)
—Sedatives & Hypnotics: Deadly Downers. (p. 1981)
Walker, J. A. Canadian Magazine, Vol. 55: Toronto, May, 1920; the Legal Minimum Wage (Classic Reprint) (p. 321)
Walker, J. P. Fighting the Stars. (p. 726)
Walker, Jack, illus. see Kelly, Diana.
Walker, Jane. Ancient Egypt. (p. 80)
—Knights & Castles. (p. 1228)
Walker, Janice. Awesome Gratitude Journal: Write in 5 Good Things a Day for Happiness 365 Days a Year. Gratitude Journal for Kids. (Cute Llama & Cactus Custom Diary) (p. 144)
—Drama Need No Llama: 5 Good Things a Day for Happiness 365 Days a Year. Daily Gratitude Journal for Kids to Write in. (Llama Custom Diary) (p. 596)
—Gratitude Journal: 5 Good Things a Day, Simple Gratitude Journal for Greater Happiness 365 Days a Year. (p. 881)
—Gratitude Journal: Awesome Llama Journal for Kids to Write & Draw in. for Confidence, Goal Setting & Inspiration. (p. 881)
—Gratitude Journal: Girl Power. Daily Gratitude Journal to Write & Draw in. for Confidence, Inspiration & Fun (Happy Kids, Rainbow Diary) (p. 881)
—Gratitude Journal: Dream Big. Llama Gratitude Journal for Kids. Write in 5 Good Things a Day for Greater Happiness 365 Days a Year (Custom Diary) (p. 881)
—Gratitude Journal: Cute Flamingo Daily Gratitude Journal for Kids to Write & Draw in. for Confidence, Inspiration & Happiness (Fun Diary, Dream Big) (p. 881)
—Gratitude Journal: Cute Sloth Daily Gratitude Journal for Kids to Write & Draw in. for Confidence, Inspiration & Happiness (Fun Diary, Happy Dreams) (p. 881)
—Gratitude Journal: Cute Unicorn & Mermaid Gratitude Journal for Kids. Write in 5 Good Things a Day for Greater Happiness 365 Days a Year (Rainbow Stars) (p. 881)
—Gratitude Journal: Follow Your Dreams. Gratitude Journal for Kids. Write in 5 Good Things a Day for Greater Happiness 365 Days a Year (Unicorn, Rainbow) (p. 881)
—Gratitude Journal: Don't Forget to Be Awesome. Daily Gratitude Journal for Kids to Write & Draw in. for Confidence, Self-Esteem & Happiness (Fun Notebook) (p. 881)
—Gratitude Journal: Believe in Yourself. Mermaid Gratitude Journal for Kids. Write in 5 Good Things a Day for Greater Happiness 365 Days a Year (Custom Keepsake) (p. 881)
—Gratitude Journal: Awesome Llama, Daily Gratitude Journal for Kids to Write & Draw in. for Confidence, Inspiration & Happiness Everyday (Fun Notebook, Cactus Diary) (p. 881)
—Gratitude Journal: Dream Big. Cute Unicorn Gratitude Journal for Kids to Write & Draw in. for Confidence, Fun, Inspiration, Self-Esteem & Goal Setting (Daily Kids Diary) (p. 881)
—Gratitude Journal: Cute Giant Panda, Daily Gratitude Journal for Kids to Write & Draw in. for Confidence, Fun, Inspiration & Happiness (Children's Notebook, Feathers Diary) (p. 881)
—Gratitude Journal: Dream. Believe. Achieve. Magical Unicorn Gratitude Journal for Kids. Write in 5 Good Things a Day for Greater Happiness 365 Days a Year (Custom Keepsake) (p. 881)
—Gratitude Journal: Good Vibes, Happiness & Fun Through Positivity. (p. 882)
—Gratitude Journal: Gratitude Journal for Kids. Write in 5 Good Things a Day for Greater Happiness 365 Days a Year (Love Llama) (p. 882)
—Gratitude Journal: You Are Awesome. Daily Gratitude Journal to Write & Draw in. for Confidence, Happiness & Fun (Pug Diary, Dog Lover) (p. 882)
—Gratitude Journal: Love Llamas. Gratitude Journal for Kids. Write in 5 Good Things a Day for Greater Happiness 365 Days a Year (Custom Diary) (p. 882)
—Gratitude Journal: I Love Unicorn. Rainbow Gratitude Journal for Kids. Write in 5 Good Things a Day for Greater Happiness 365 Days a Year (My Best Friend) (p. 882)
—Gratitude Journal: I Love You Lots. Gratitude Journal for Kids. Write in 5 Good Things a Day for Greater Happiness 365 Days a Year (Llama, Custom Keepsake) (p. 882)
—Gratitude Journal: Mermaids Are Real. Daily Gratitude Journal for Kids to Write & Draw in. for Confidence, Inspiration & Happiness (Lovely Diary, Cute Little Mermaid) (p. 882)
—Gratitude Journal: I Love You to the Moon & Back, Gratitude Journal for Kids to Write & Draw in. for Confidence, Inspiration & Happiness (Fun Notebook, Cute Kids Diary) (p. 882)
—You Are Awesome: Cute Sloth Gratitude Journal for Kids. Write in 5 Good Things a Day for Happiness 365 Days a Year (Jungle Sloth Custom Diary) (p. 2524)
Walker, Janis P. Kids to the Rescue. (p. 1216)
Walker, Jason M. Crosby vs. Ovechkin vs. McDavid vs. Gretzky (p. 477)
Walker, Jerome. How We Raised Our Baby (Classic Reprint) (p. 1046)
Walker, Jess. Black Gold Deception. (p. 238)
Walker, Jessica, illus. see Babbott-Klein, Libby.
Walker, Joe. Belief & Science. (p. 196)
Walker, John. Critical Pronouncing Dictionary & Expositor of the English Language: In Which Not Only the Meaning of Every Word Is Clearly Explained, & the Sound of Every

W

Syllable Distinctly Shown, but Where Words Are Subject to Different Pronunciations, the Reaso. (p. 476)
—Critical Pronouncing Dictionary, & Expositor of the English Language: In Which the Meaning of Every Word Is Explained, & the Sound of Every Syllable Distinctly Shown; & Where Words Are Subject to Different Pronunciations, the Preferable One Is Poi. (p. 476)
—Critical Pronouncing Dictionary, & Expositor of the English Language: In Which Not Only the Meaning of Every Word Is Clearly Explained, & the Sound of Every Syllable Distinctly Shown, but, Where Words Are Subject to Different Pronunciations, the Aut. (p. 476)
—Critical Pronouncing Dictionary, & Expositor of the English Language (Classic Reprint) (p. 476)
—Dictionary of the English Language: Answering at Once the Purposes of Rhyming, Spelling, & Pronouncing, on a Plan Not Hitherto Attempted (Classic Reprint) (p. 542)
—Walker's Critical Pronouncing Dictionary & Expositor of the English Language: Abridged for the Use of Schools; to Which Is Annexed, an Abridgment of Walker's Key to the Pronunciation of Greek, Latin, & Scripture Proper Names (Classic Reprint) (p. 2372)
—Walker's Critical Pronouncing Dictionary & Expositor of the English Language (Classic Reprint) (p. 2372)
—Walker's Pronouncing Dictionary: In Which the Accentuation, Orthography, & Pronunciation of the English Language Is Distinctly Shown According to the Present Practice of the Most Eminent Lexicographers (Classic Reprint) (p. 2372)
—Walker's Pronouncing Dictionary of the English Language: Abridged for the Use of Schools Containing a Compendium of the Principles of English Pronunciation, with the Proper Names That Occur in the Sacred Scriptures to Which Is Likewise Added, a Selection. (p. 2372)
Walker, John, illus. see Mackall, Dandi Daley.
Walker, John, illus. see Rainey, Barbara.
Walker, John, jt. auth. see Johnson, Samuel.
Walker, John, tr. see Hichs, Donald E. & Demers, Aimee.
Walker, John Anthony. Frel. (p. 783)
Walker, Jonathan. Bat Cave. Zahn, Lisa, ed. (p. 171)
—Bill & the Little Red Plane. Zahn, Lisa, ed. (p. 226)
Walker, Juanita. Maggie, a Christmas Story of Simple Gifts of Love. (p. 1376)
Walker, Kaisa. Importance of Jury Service. (p. 1102)
Walker, Karen, illus. see London, Jack.
Walker, Kate. Air. (p. 37)
—Clothing. Vanzet, Gaston, illus. (p. 407)
—Food & Garden Waste. Vanzet, Gaston, illus. (p. 759)
—Glass. Vanzet, Gaston, illus. (p. 841)
—Metal Cans. Vanzet, Gaston, illus. (p. 1452)
—Paper. Vanzet, Gaston, illus. (p. 1697)
—Plants. (p. 1757)
—Plastic Bottles & Bags. Vanzet, Gaston, illus. (p. 1758)
—Rocks. (p. 1896)
—Soil. (p. 2055)
—Water. Hopgood, Andrew, illus. (p. 2384)
—Weather. (p. 2393)
Walker, Katherine, illus. see Cottringer, Anne.
Walker, Kathryn. My Family Remembers: The 1950s. (p. 1538)
—Mysteries of the Ancients. (p. 1567)
—Mysteries of the Cosmic Joker. (p. 1567)
—Mysteries of the Mind. (p. 1567)
—Mysterious Healing. (p. 1567)
—Mysterious Predictions. (p. 1568)
—Mystery of Atlantis. (p. 1569)
—See How Cats Grow. (p. 1981)
—See How Dogs Grow. (p. 1981)
—See How Horses & Ponies Grow. (p. 1981)
—See How Rabbits Grow. (p. 1981)
Walker, Kathryn, jt. auth. see Hunter, Rebecca.
Walker, Kev. Black Panther Book 7: The Intergalactic Empire of Wakanda Part 2. (p. 239)
—Star Wars: Doctor Aphra Vol. 1: Aphra. (p. 2104)
Walker, Kev & Laming, Marc. Star Wars: Doctor Aphra Vol. 2: Doctor Aphra & the Enormous Profit. (p. 2104)
Walker, Kev, et al. Avengers Arena: the Complete Collection. (p. 142)
—Nova by Abnett & Lanning: the Complete Collection Vol. 1 (p. 1626)
Walker, Kevin. Bmw M4. (p. 250)
—Bmw X6m. (p. 250)
—Field Trips, Yes or No. (p. 723)
—Learning a Second Language, Yes or No. (p. 1257)
—Mercedes AMG G-65. (p. 1447)
—Social Media. (p. 2053)
—STEAM Guides in Inventions. (p. 2110)
Walker, Kristin. 7 Clues to Winning You. (p. 2549)
Walker, Landry. Moviemaking Magic of Star Wars: Ships & Battles. (p. 1516)
—Secrets & Lies. Takara, Marcio, illus. (p. 1979)
—Supergirl: Cosmic Adventures of the 8th Grade. (p. 2159)
—Teenage Mutant Ninja Turtles Amazing Adventures, Vol. 1. (p. 2199)
Walker, Landry, jt. auth. see Waid, Mark.
Walker, Landry G. Heroes of the Galaxy. (p. 962)
Walker, Landry Q. Election Day Mad Libs. (p. 631)
—Fast & Furious: Spy Racers: Training Academy: A Sticker & Activity Book. (p. 712)
—Secret Entity! #4 Jones, Eric, illus. (p. 1975)
—Star Wars Adventures Vol. 2: Unexpected Detour Charm, Derek, illus. (p. 2104)
—Star Wars Encyclopedia of Starfighters & Other Vehicles. (p. 2104)
—Stolen Vault. Spaziante, Patrick, illus. (p. 2121)
—Super Hero School: #3 Jones, Eric, illus. (p. 2155)
—Supergirl: Cosmic Adventures in the 8th Grade. Jones, Eric, illus. (p. 2159)
Walker, Landry Q., jt. auth. see Scott, Cavan.
Walker, Landry Q. & Dawson, Delilah S. Star Wars Adventures #5: the Trouble at Tibrin, Part 2. Jones, Eric et al, illus. (p. 2103)
Walker, Landry Q. & Mason, Joey. Evil in a Skirt! #5 Jones, Eric, illus. (p. 674)
—Her First Extra-Ordinary Adventure! #1 Jones, Eric, illus. (p. 956)
—My Own Best Frenemy: #2 Jones, Eric, illus. (p. 1558)
—Off to Save the Day... Jones, Eric, illus. (p. 1640)
Walker, Landry Q. & Scott, Cavan. Star Wars Adventures Omnibus, Vol. 1. Charm, Derek et al, illus. (p. 2104)
Walker, Landry Q., et al. Star Wars Adventures #3: Pest Control. Jones, Eric et al, illus. (p. 2103)
—Star Wars Adventures #4: the Trouble at Tibrin, Part 1. Jones, Eric et al, illus. (p. 2103)
Walker, Landry Quinn. Star Wars the Force Awakens: Tales from a Galaxy Far, Far Away. Scarlet, Tyler, illus. (p. 2105)
—Supergirl Cosmic Adventures of the 8th Grade. (p. 2159)
Walker, Lane. Boss on Redemption Road. (p. 263)
—Day It Rained Ducks. (p. 513)
—Hunt for Scarface. (p. 1052)
—Legend of the Ghost Buck. (p. 1262)
—Terror at Deadwood Lake. (p. 2207)
Walker, Lee Jay. Mavis & the Magic Curtain. (p. 1427)
—Mavis the Magic Dog: Sakura the Squirrel & the Terrible Storm. (p. 1427)
Walker, Lillie M. Her Sacrifice: An Entertainment for Churches, Sunday Schools & Societies Connected with the Church (Classic Reprint) (p. 956)
Walker, Lillie Nolting. That Girl (Classic Reprint) (p. 2212)
Walker, Lisa & Coyne, Adrian. Boy Who Brought Thunder. (p. 270)
Walker, Margaret Coulson. Bird Legend & Life (Classic Reprint) (p. 230)
—Lady Hollyhock & Her Friends: A Book of Nature Dolls & Others. (p. 1237)
—Lady Hollyhock & Her Friends: A Book of Nature Dolls & Others (Classic Reprint) (p. 1237)
Walker, Mario. Little Red Cup. (p. 1326)
Walker, Marion. Technala, Vol. 9: March, 1916 (Classic Reprint) (p. 2197)
Walker, Mark. Lost in a Book: A Library of Mazes. (p. 1354)
Walker, Mark, jt. auth. see Riley, Peter D.
Walker, Mark Evan, illus. see Lorenzo, Amanda.
Walker, Mary Spring. Family Doctor: Or Mrs. Barry & Her Bourbon (Classic Reprint) (p. 702)
—Rev. Dr. Willoughby & His Wine. (p. 1872)
—REV. Dr. Willoughby & His Wine (Classic Reprint) (p. 1872)
Walker, Maryalice. Entomology & Palynology. Noziglia, Carla Miller & Siegel, Jay A., eds. (p. 656)
—Pathology. Noziglia, Carla Miller & Siegel, Jay A., eds. (p. 1704)
Walker, Megan, illus. see Leet, Rhonda.
Walker, Melissa. Ashes to Ashes. (p. 125)
—Dust to Dust. (p. 611)
—Let's Pretend We Never Met. (p. 1277)
—Lovestruck Summer. (p. 1362)
—Small Town Sinners. (p. 2040)
—Unbreak My Heart. (p. 2317)
—Why Can't I Be You. (p. 2455)
Walker, Melissa & Walker, Richard. Place for Delta. (p. 1753)
Walker, Mj. Cloud Seekers. (p. 408)
Walker, Nan. Day Camp. (p. 513)
—Follow That Clue! Palmisciano, Diane, illus. (p. 757)
—Otto & the New Girl: Symmetry. Wummer, Amy, illus. (p. 1676)
—Rainy Day, Sunny Day - 6 Pack: Set of 6 with Teacher Materials Common Core Edition. Cammell, Sandra, illus. (p. 1837)
—Spork Out of Orbit. Warrick, Jessica, illus. (p. 2087)
—Spork Out of Orbit (Book 1) Respect. Warrick, Jessica, illus. (p. 2087)
—Thanksgiving Then & Now. (p. 2212)
—Weather. (p. 2393)
—Yum-Yum House. Pilz, M. H., illus. (p. 2537)
Walker, Nan, jt. auth. see Kulling, Monica.
Walker, Nan & Kulling, Monica. Messiest Room on the Planet. (p. 1452)
Walker, Nancy. Koobla the Camel. (p. 1231)
Walker, Niki. Why Do We Fight? Conflict, War, & Peace. (p. 2457)
Walker, Niki, jt. auth. see Kalman, Bobbie.
Walker, Niki & Kalman, Bobbie. Kittens. (p. 1226)
Walker, Niki, et al. Chatons. (p. 362)
Walker, Pam & Wood, Elaine. Ecology Experiments. (p. 623)
—Ecosystem Science Fair Projects, Revised & Expanded Using the Scientific Method. (p. 624)
—Human Body Experiments. (p. 1049)
—Marine Science Experiments. (p. 1406)
Walker, Pamela, jt. auth. see Coster, Patience.
Walker, Pamela & Wood, Elaine. Chemistry Experiments. (p. 365)
—Genetics Experiments. (p. 815)
Walker, Patricia M., illus. see Goguen, Martha M.
Walker, Patricius. Rambles (Classic Reprint) (p. 1839)
Walker, Paul. Chameleon, 1927, Vol. 6 (Classic Reprint) (p. 355)
Walker, Paul Robert. American Indians. (p. 72)
—Theodore Roosevelt & the Progressive Era: Set Of 6. (p. 2216)
—Theodore Roosevelt & the Progressive Era: Bridges Edition. Ginerva, Dante, illus. (p. 2216)
—Theodore Roosevelt & the Progressive Era: Bridges Edition Set of 6 with Common Core Indicators. Ginerva, Dante, illus. (p. 2216)
Walker, Persephone. Brain Quest Workbook: Grade 6. Thornborrow, Nick, illus. (p. 275)
Walker, Persephone, et al. Summer Brain Quest: Between Grades 2 And 3. Cummings, Matt & Yan, Edison, illus. (p. 2148)
—Summer Brain Quest: Between Grades 3 And 4. Yan, Edison, illus. (p. 2148)
Walker, Peter. Biblical Repertory & Princeton Review for the Year 1850, Vol. 22 (Classic Reprint) (p. 214)
Walker Productions LTD. We're Going on a Bear Hunt: My First 123. (p. 2400)
Walker, Rachel. Be Kind to Bees. (p. 177)
—Book Art. (p. 257)
—Farming. (p. 711)
—Help Our Oceans. (p. 953)
—Polar Bear Survival. (p. 1769)
Walker, Richard. Body: [an Amazing Tour of Human Anatomy]. (p. 253)
—Build the Human Body. Bernstein, Galia & Ruffle, Mark, illus. (p. 293)
—DK Eyewitness Books: Human Body: Explore How the Human Body Works from the Smallest Cells to the Systems That Keep Us Alive. (p. 567)
—Jack & the Beanstalk. (p. 1151)
—Jack & the Beanstalk. Sharkey, Niamh, illus. (p. 1151)
Walker, Richard, jt. auth. see Walker, Melissa.
Walker, Rob. Mapping Towns & Cities. (p. 1401)
Walker, Robert. Bar & Bat Mitzvahs. (p. 164)
—Eid Al-Adha. (p. 629)
—Flag Day. (p. 745)
—Happy Birthday! (p. 920)
—Labor Day. (p. 1235)
—Live It: Optimism. (p. 1332)
—Live It: Integrity. (p. 1332)
—Live It: Initiative. (p. 1332)
—Maserati. (p. 1417)
—Porsche. Crabtree, ed. (p. 1778)
—Pushes & Pulls: Why Do People Migrate? (p. 1817)
—Sheamus. (p. 2004)
—Transportation Inventions: Moving Our World Forward. (p. 2278)
—Transportation Inventions. (p. 2278)
—Veterans Day. (p. 2354)
—What Is the Theory of Evolution? (p. 2417)
—World War I: 1917-1918 - The Turning of the Tide. (p. 2505)
Walker, Robert, jt. auth. see Miller, Reagan.
Walker, Robin & Harding, Keith. Tourism, Level 2. (p. 2269)
Walker, Rory, illus. see Graham, Ian.
Walker, Rory, illus. see Pipe, Jim.
Walker, Roxanne M. Hairables. (p. 910)
Walker, Rysa. Delphi Effect. (p. 527)
—Timebound (p. 2246)
—Time's Divide (p. 2247)
—Time's Edge (p. 2247)
Walker, S. E. Fitting In. (p. 743)
Walker, S. L., jt. auth. see Walker, Suzettra L.
Walker, Sally M. Blizzard of Glass: The Halifax Explosion Of 1917. (p. 245)
—Boundaries: How the Mason-Dixon Line Settled a Family Feud & Divided a Nation. (p. 265)
—Champion: The Comeback Tale of the American Chestnut Tree. (p. 355)
—Deadly Aim: The Civil War Story of Michigan's Anishinaabe Sharpshooters. (p. 518)
—Earth Verse: Haiku from the Ground Up. Grill, William, illus. (p. 617)
—Fiery Night: A Boy, His Goat, & the Great Chicago Fire. Harren, Kayla, illus. (p. 723)
—Figuring Out Fossils. (p. 726)
—Freedom Song: The Story of Henry Box Brown. Qualls, Sean, illus. (p. 783)
—Ghost Walls: The Story of a 17th-Century Colonial Homestead. (p. 828)
—Investigating Electricity. (p. 1131)
—Investigating Heat. (p. 1131)
—Investigating Light. (p. 1131)
—Investigating Magnetism. (p. 1131)
—Investigating Matter. (p. 1131)
—Investigating Sound. (p. 1131)
—Libros de Energía para Madrugadores (Early Bird Energy) King, Andy, photos by. (p. 1287)
—Marveling at Minerals. (p. 1413)
—Opossum at Sycamore Road. Snyder, Joel, illus. (p. 1667)
—Researching Rocks. (p. 1869)
—Sinking the Sultana: A Civil War Story of Imprisonment, Greed, & a Doomed Journey Home. (p. 2024)
—Studying Soil. (p. 2144)
—Winnie: The True Story of the Bear Who Inspired Winnie-the-Pooh. Voss, Jonathan D., illus. (p. 2474)
—Written in Bone: Buried Lives of Jamestown & Colonial Maryland. (p. 2514)
Walker, Sally M., jt. auth. see Feldman, Roseann.
Walker, Sally M. & Feldmann, Roseann. Palancas. King, Andy, photos by. (p. 1694)
—Planos Inclinados. King, Andy, photos by. (p. 1756)
—Tornillos. King, Andy, photos by. (p. 2265)
Walker, Sam, jt. ed. see Goswell, Emma.
Walker, Sarah, jt. auth. see Dorling Kindersley Publishing Staff.
Walker, Scott, illus. see Lloyd, Victoria.
Walker, Sherry. My Amazing Mom. Walker, Sherry & Gibbons, Myla, illus. (p. 1531)
Walker, Sholto, illus. see Durant, Alan.
Walker, Sholto, illus. see Fuerst, Jeffrey B.
Walker, Sholto, illus. see Lane, Alex.
Walker, Steven, illus. see Kittinger, Jo S.
Walker, Stuart. Portmanteau Adaptations (Classic Reprint) (p. 1779)
—Portmanteau Plays (Classic Reprint) (p. 1779)
—Six Who Pass While the Lentils Boil (Classic Reprint) (p. 2029)
Walker, Susan Eileen. Not Enough Time (p. 1623)
Walker, Susan Sandvig. Gingerbread Man: A Favorite Story in Rhythm & Rhyme. Karabatzia, Villie, illus. (p. 834)
Walker, Suzanne. Mooncakes. Xu, Wendy, illus. (p. 1502)
Walker, Sylvia. At the Wedding. (p. 131)
—Halloween ABC Coloring Book. (p. 912)
—Happy New Year Around the World. (p. 923)
—Let's Color Together — My Sleepover. (p. 1270)
—My Sleepover Coloring Book. (p. 1561)
—Our New Baby Coloring Book. (p. 1679)
—Storyland: We're Moving! A Story Coloring Book. (p. 2136)
Walker, Sylvia, illus. see Hooks, Gwendolyn.
Walker, Sylvia, illus. see Scholastic, Inc. Staff & Hooks, Gwendolyn.
Walker, Sylvia & Coloring Books Staff. Easter Egg Hunt Coloring Book. (p. 619)
Walker, Tanisha. Rainbow Tots- 10-28. (p. 1837)
Walker, Teresa M. P. K. Subban: Making His Mark on the Hockey World. (p. 1690)
Walker, Theo. Feeding Time: the Feeding Habits of Animals High Beginning Book with Online Access. (p. 718)
—Swing, Slither, Swim Low Intermediate Book with Online Access. (p. 2170)
Walker, Tigh, illus. see Hopeless, Dennis.
Walker, Tigh & Bagley, Mark. Venom Vol. 4: The Nativity. (p. 2350)
Walker, Timothy. Elements of Geometry: With Practical Applications, for the Use of Schools (Classic Reprint) (p. 633)
Walker, Trenton, illus. see Hughes, Annette.
Walker, Vicki, illus. see Thurston, Dorothy Dawn.
Walker, W. F. Arithmetic: As Taught in the Troy Episcopal Institute. (p. 116)
Walker, W. S. Between the Tides: Comprising Sketches, Tales & Poems, Including Hungry Land (Classic Reprint) (p. 210)
—Between the Tides. (p. 210)
Walker, Whimsical. From Sawdust to Windsor Castle (Classic Reprint) (p. 793)
Walker, William Hall. Sir Charlton Richards' Last Kiss (Classic Reprint) (p. 2025)
Walker, William Henry. Five Minutes with the Boys' & Girls' Congregation (Classic Reprint) (p. 744)
Walker, William Sylvester. From the Land of the Wombat (Classic Reprint) (p. 794)
—What Lay Beneath: A Story of the Queensland Bush (Classic Reprint) (p. 2418)
Walker, Wm Sylvester. Silver Queen: A Tale of the Northern Territory (Classic Reprint) (p. 2019)
Walker-Cox, Krysten. Amber's Metal Singlet. (p. 67)
Walker-Hirsch, Leslie & Champagne, Marklyn. Circles I, Level 1: Intimacy & Relationships. Stanfield, James, ed. (p. 393)
Walker-Jones, Alexandra & Herrera, Hanna. Adventures of Hobnob & Raisin - Paris Airport. (p. 24)
Walker-Smith, G. J. Sand Jewels. (p. 1930)
WalkerTheo. CITY EXPERIMENT: REBUILDING GREENSBURG, KANSAS LOW INTERMEDIATE BOOK WITH ONLINE ACCESS. (p. 394)
—EAT UP! BEGINNING BOOK WITH ONLINE ACCESS. (p. 622)
—SUGAR: OUR GUILTY PLEASURE LOW INTERMEDIATE BOOK WITH ONLINE ACCESS. (p. 2147)
Walkes, Irvin, illus. see Ardanaz, Nicolas.
Walkington, Jen. I Wonder If George Washington Owned a Pooper Scooper? Hinton, David W., illus. (p. 1086)
Walkins, Anne S. Basketful of All Sorts of Eggs (Classic Reprint) (p. 171)
Walkley, Lizzie, illus. see Ferreri, Della Ross.
Walkley, Lizzie, illus. see Graham, Oakley.
Walkley, Lizzie, illus. see Nelson, Steve & Rollins, Jack.
Walko. Amigos: Friends Forever. (p. 75)
Walkup, ed. see Evans, Tony.
Walkup, ed. see Merritt, James.
Walkup, ed. see Rothschild, Jennifer.
Walkup, ed. see Walsh, Sheila.
Walkup, Jennifer. Second Verse. (p. 1974)
Wall, Billy James. Mystery of Marcy & the Stony Squirrel. (p. 1569)
Wall, Charles H., tr. see Molière.
Wall, Deborah. Base Camp Las Vegas: 101 Hikes in the Southwest. (p. 168)
Wall, Dorothy. Complete Adventures of Blinky Bill. (p. 434)
Wall, George A. Jacob Valmont, Manager: A Novel (Classic Reprint) (p. 1154)
Wall, James Charles. Devils (Classic Reprint) (p. 536)
Wall, Jessie. Philomena, the Cat Who Thinks She's a Dog. Stanbury, Emily, illus. (p. 1735)
Wall, Joanne. Anna of Allegheny. Wall, Joanne, ed. (p. 97)
Wall, Karen, illus. see Helmore, Jim.
Wall, Karen, jt. auth. see Helmore, Jim.
Wall, Kathy. Oscar the Oak. Cash-Walsh, Tina, illus. (p. 1673)
Wall, Laura. Goose. Wall, Laura, illus. (p. 869)
—Goose Goes to School. Wall, Laura, illus. (p. 869)
—Goose Goes to the Zoo. Wall, Laura, illus. (p. 869)
—Goose on the Farm. Wall, Laura, illus. (p. 869)
—Goose on the Farm Board Book. Wall, Laura, illus. (p. 869)
Wall, M. S. Blue Crown. (p. 248)
Wall, Mary Virginia. Daughter of Virginia Dare (Classic Reprint) (p. 509)
Wall, Matthew. So You Want to Learn: Juggling. Wall, Matthew, illus. (p. 2051)
—So You Want to Learn: Juggling. (p. 2051)
Wall, Mike, illus. see Katschke, Judy.
Wall, Mike, illus. see Posner-Sanchez, Andrea.
Wall, Mike, illus. see Rubiano, Brittany.
Wall, Molly & Mandryk, Jason. Window on the World: An Operation World Prayer Resource. (p. 2472)
Wall, Peter & Wall, Christyane. Potatoes & Tomatoes. (p. 1781)
Wall, Sheelagh, illus. see Asheya.
Wallace, Adam. Better Out Than In: Number Twos. McKenzie, Heath, illus. (p. 209)
—Cómo atrapar a una sirena. (p. 432)
—Dawn of the Zombie Knights. (p. 512)
—How to Catch a Dinosaur. (p. 1038)
—How to Catch a Dinosaur. Elkerton, Andy, illus. (p. 1038)
—How to Catch a Dragon. Elkerton, Andy, illus. (p. 1038)
—How to Catch a Leprechaun. Elkerton, Andy, illus. (p. 1038)
—How to Catch a Snowman. Elkerton, Andy, illus. (p. 1038)
—How to Catch a Unicorn. Elkerton, Andy, illus. (p. 1038)
—How to Catch a Yeti. Elkerton, Andy, illus. (p. 1038)
—How to Catch an Elf. Elkerton, Andy, illus. (p. 1038)
—How to Catch the Easter Bunny. Elkerton, Andy, illus. (p. 1038)
—Incredible Journey of Pete McGee. (p. 1114)
—Invisible Jerry. Poli, Giuseppe, illus. (p. 1132)
—Mac O'Beasty McKenzie, Heath, illus. (p. 1371)
—Only YOU Can Save Christmas! A Help-The-Elf Adventure. Bruner, Garth, illus. (p. 1664)
—Rhymes with Art: Learn Cartooning the Fun Way! Wallace, Adam, illus. (p. 1875)
Wallace, Adam, jt. auth. see Wallace, Adam.

W

Waller, Sally. Imperial Russia, Revolution & the Establishment of the Soviet Union (1855-1924) (p. 1102)
Waller, Steven H. My Child: Girl. Fincher, Kathy, illus. (p. 1535)
Walles, Dwight, illus. see Coleman, William L.
Walley, Keith. Angel to Guide Me. (p. 85)
Walleystack, Phillip & Caisley, Raewyn. Rocky & Louie. Dub Leffler, illus. (p. 1896)
Walliams, David. Bad Dad. Ross, Tony, illus. (p. 157)
—Billionaire Baim: Billionaire Boy in Scots. Fitt, Matthew, tr. (p. 226)
—Demon Dentist. (p. 528)
—Demon Dentist. Ross, Tony, illus. (p. 528)
—Grandpa's Great Escape. Ross, Tony, illus. (p. 879)
—Grandpa's Great Escape . (p. 879)
—Increíble Historia de... la Cosa Más Rara Del Mundo / Fing. Ross, Tony, illus. (p. 1114)
—Increíble Historia... Del Monstruo de Hielo / the Ice Monster. (p. 1114)
—Midnight Gang. Ross, Tony, illus. (p. 1461)
—World's Worst Children. Ross, Tony, illus. (p. 2508)
Walliams, Patrick. Hollow Tree Children. (p. 988)
Walliman, Dominic. Astro Kittens: Cosmic Machines. Newman, Ben, illus. (p. 128)
—Astro Kittens: into the Unknown. Newman, Ben, illus. (p. 128)
—Professor Astro Cat's Atomic Adventure. Newman, Ben, illus. (p. 1804)
—Professor Astro Cat's Deep Sea Voyage. Newman, Ben, illus. (p. 1804)
—Professor Astro Cat's Frontiers of Space. Newman, Ben, illus. (p. 1804)
—Professor Astro Cat's Solar System. Newman, Ben, illus. (p. 1804)
—Professor Astro Cat's Space Rockets. Newman, Ben, illus. (p. 1804)
—Professor Astro Cat's Stargazing. Newman, Ben, illus. (p. 1804)
Wallin, Clarence Monroe. Gena of the Appalachians (Classic Reprint) (p. 813)
Wallin, Marisa. Find & Point Birthday. Michael, Joan, illus. (p. 727)
Walling, Burns Tracy. Electrical Installations of the United States Navy: A Manual of the Latest Approved Material, Including Its Use, Operation, Inspection, Care & Management & Method of Installation on Board Ship (Classic Reprint) (p. 631)
Wallingford, Stephanie & Rynders, Dawn. Day at the Lake. Villnave, Erica Pelton, illus. (p. 512)
Wallis, Angie, illus. see Gallardo-Walker, Gloria.
Wallis, Arthur F. Idonia: A Romance of Old London (Classic Reprint) (p. 1090)
Wallis, Becky, illus. see Bentley, Dawn.
Wallis, Diz, illus. see Calhoun, Marmaduke Randolph.
Wallis, Emily. Journey Through the Jungle. (p. 1182)
—Sea Voyage: Anti-Stress Dot-To-Dot. (p. 1969)
Wallis, Emily, illus. see Greaves, David.
Wallis, Emily, illus. see Green, D. L.
Wallis, Ginger. Finch Discoveries: An Inspiring Tale of Adaptation to a Changing Environment. Dodson, Bert, illus. (p. 727)
Wallis, Jenny. Sandman: His Songs & Rhymes (Classic Reprint) (p. 1931)
Wallis, Pete & Wilkins, Joseph. What Are You Staring At? A Comic about Restorative Justice in Schools. (p. 2406)
Wallis, Quvenzhané. Night Out with Mama. Brantley Newton, Vanessa, illus. (p. 1607)
—Shai & Emmie Star in Dancy Pants! Miller, Sharee, illus. (p. 1998)
—Shai & Emmie Star in to the Rescue! Miller, Sharee, illus. (p. 1998)
Wallis, Quvenzhané, jt. auth. see Wallis, Quvenzhané.
Wallis, Quvenzhané & Wallis, Quvenzhané. Shai & Emmie Star in Break an Egg! Miller, Sharee, illus. (p. 1998)
Wallis, Rachel, illus. see Bartlett, Debbie.
Wallis, Thomas. Farrier's & Horseman's Complete Dictionary: Containing the Art of Farriery in All Its Branches; with Whatever Relates to the Manage, & to the Knowledge, Breeding, Feeding, & Dieting of Horses (Classic Reprint) (p. 711)
—Farrier's & Horseman's Complete Dictionary: Containing the Art of Farriery in All Its Branches; with Whatever Relates to the Manage, & to the Knowledge, Breeding, Feeding & Dieting of Horses; As Delivered by the Best Writers upon These Subjects. (p. 711)
Wallis, Velma. Two Old Women. (p. 2309)
Wallis-Tayler, Alexander James. Modern Cycles: A Practical Handbook on Their Construction & Repair (Classic Reprint) (p. 1486)
Wallmann, Joanna Barbara, tr. see Renz, Ulrich.
Wallmark, Laurie. Ada Byron Lovelace & the Thinking Machine. Chu, April, illus. (p. 13)
—Grace Hopper: Queen of Computer Code. Wu, Katy, illus. (p. 873)
—Hedy Lamarr's Double Life: Hollywood Legend & Brilliant Inventor. Wu, Katy, illus. (p. 948)
—Numbers in Motion: Sophie Kowalevski, Queen of Mathematics. Nayberg, Yevgenia, illus. (p. 1630)
Wallner, Alexandra. Susan B. Anthony. Wallner, Alexandra, illus. (p. 2166)
Wallner, Alexandra, illus. see Adler, David A.
Wallner, Alexandra, illus. see Woelfle, Gretchen.
Wallner, John, illus. see Adler, David A.
Walloth, Wilhelm. Empress Octavia: A Romance of the Reign of Nero (Classic Reprint) (p. 645)
—King's Treasure House: A Romance of Ancient Egypt (Classic Reprint) (p. 1223)
Walls, Anthony. Toddler Bay Presents Todd's First Day. (p. 2255)
Walls, Suzanne L. Insects & Spiders. Maiden, D. W. & Govoni, Dennis, photos by. (p. 1122)
Walls, Vicki. Maybe God Just Needed a Puppy. (p. 1429)
Wallsten, Karen. Adventures of Shiko & Walter. (p. 27)
Walluk, Wilbur. Alaskan Ten-Footed Bear & Other Legends. (p. 40)
Wallus Sammons, Sandra. Ponce de Leon & the Discovery of Florida. (p. 1773)
—Three Marjories: Marjory Stoneman Douglas, Marjorie Kinnan Rawlings, Marjorie Harris Carr & Their Contributions to Florida (p. 2234)
—Zora Neale Hurston (p. 2544)
Wallwork, Heather Louise. Enchanted Sonata. (p. 647)
Wallys, Philip. About New York: An Account of What a Boy Saw in His Visit to the City (Classic Reprint) (p. 6)
Walmesley, Charles. Analyse des Mesures, des Rapports et des Angles, Ou Reduction des Integrales Aux Logarithmes, et Aux Arcs de Cercle (Classic Reprint) (p. 79)
Walmsley, Jane, illus. see Dahl, Roald.
Walmsley, Lucy Ela. Faery Tales. (p. 694)
Waln, Nora. House of Exile (Classic Reprint) (p. 1023)
Waln, Sara. But I'm Afraid of Spiders! (p. 302)
Walpole, Brenda. I Wonder Why the Sun Rises: And Other Questions about Time & Seasons. (p. 1086)
Walpole, Hugh. Captives, Vol. 1 Of 4: A Novel in Four Parts (Classic Reprint) (p. 326)
—Cathedral: A Novel (Classic Reprint) (p. 344)
—Cathedral. (p. 344)
—Dark Forest (Classic Reprint) (p. 506)
—Fortitude: Being a True & Faithful Account of the Education of an Adventurer (Classic Reprint) (p. 769)
—Gods & Mr. Perrin: A Tragi-Comedy (Classic Reprint) (p. 853)
—Golden Scarecrow (Classic Reprint) (p. 859)
—Green Mirror: A Quiet Story (Classic Reprint) (p. 894)
—Jeremy (Classic Reprint) (p. 1164)
—Maradick at Forty: A Transition (Classic Reprint) (p. 1402)
—Old Ladies (Classic Reprint) (p. 1646)
—Prelude to Adventure (Classic Reprint) (p. 1787)
—Secret City: A Novel in Three Parts. (p. 1975)
—Secret City: A Novel in Three Parts (Classic Reprint) (p. 1975)
—Thirteen Travellers (Classic Reprint) (p. 2223)
—Wooden Horse (Classic Reprint) (p. 2491)
—Young Enchanted: A Romantic Story (Classic Reprint) (p. 2530)
Walpole, Hugh & Kendall, Bridget. Secret City. (p. 1975)
Walpole-Bond, J. A. Bird Life in Wild Wales (Classic Reprint) (p. 230)
Walrath, Dana. I Am a Bird. Kim, Jaime, illus. (p. 1057)
Walrod, Amy, illus. see Howe, James.
Walrod, Amy, jt. auth. see Howe, James.
Walrond, Beth, illus. see Little Gestalten, Little, ed.
Walsch, Daniel. Hilltop in Jymbob. (p. 972)
Walser, David. Meg & the Romans. Pienkowski, Jan, illus. (p. 1441)
—Thousand Nights & One Night. Pienkowski, Jan, illus. (p. 2231)
Walser, David, jt. auth. see Pienkowski, Jan.
Walser, Jo. Chasing the Rising Moon. (p. 362)
Walser, Lee. Kitty Island. (p. 1226)
Walser, Richard. North Carolina Parade: Stories of History & People. (p. 1621)
Walsh, Alice. Buried Truth (p. 299)
—Change of Heart Banks, Erin Bennett, illus. (p. 356)
—Gift of Music: Emile Benoit & His Fiddle Butler, Geoff, illus. (p. 832)
—Long Way from Home (p. 1343)
—Uncle Farley's False Teeth Martchenko, Michael, illus. (p. 2318)
Walsh, Alison. Hugh O'Flaherty: His Wartime Adventures. (p. 1048)
Walsh, Aly. My Mum Says Blah Blah Blah. Walsh, Marilyn, illus. (p. 1557)
Walsh, Angeline. Memento Mortale. (p. 1443)
Walsh, Ann. Moses, Me, & Murder: A Barkerville Mystery. (p. 1507)
—Whatever. (p. 2423)
Walsh, Aoife. Lost for Words. (p. 1353)
Walsh, Barbara. Sammy in the Sky. Wyeth, Jamie, illus. (p. 1928)
Walsh, Barbara E. Poppy Lady: Moina Belle Michael & Her Tribute to Veterans. Johnson, Layne, illus. (p. 1776)
Walsh, Becki. Deep in the Woods: A Benjamin Owl Book. Walsh, Madeleine Riley, illus. (p. 524)
Walsh, Bee. Manning Up (p. 1398)
Walsh, Bill. Dog Show. (p. 576)
Walsh, Brendan. Greek & Roman Gods & Goddesses: Set Of 6. (p. 892)
—Hats off to the President - a White House Mystery: Set Of 6. McEvenue, Tim, illus. (p. 937)
Walsh, Brendan & Benchmark Education Co., LLC. Greek & Roman Gods & Goddesses. (p. 892)
—Hats off to the President: A White House Mystery. McEvenue, Tim, illus. (p. 937)
Walsh, Brendan & Clark, Donna Schmeltekopf. Opinions about Three Victorian-Era Poets - Christina Rossetti, Robert Louis Stevenson, & Emily Dickinson: Set Of 6. (p. 1667)
Walsh, Brendan, et al. Opinions about Three Victorian Era Poets: Christina Rossetti, Robert Louis Stevenson, Emily Dickinson. (p. 1667)
Walsh, Brian Everard. Thinking, Reading, Remembering: Brain-Friendly Tips & Techniques for a Student's Enriched Learning. (p. 2222)
Walsh, C. C. Early Days on the Western Range: A Pastoral Narrative (Classic Reprint) (p. 614)
Walsh, Christopher. Tucker's Tale. Lavar, Vanda, illus. (p. 2298)
Walsh, Christopher J. Cowboys Triviology: Fascinating Facts from the Sidelines. (p. 464)
—Packers Trivology: Fascinating Facts from the Sidelines. (p. 1691)
Walsh, D. T., illus. see Smith, Sherri Graves.
Walsh, D. T., illus. see Smith, Sherri.
Walsh, Dale M. Wesley's Adventures: Mystery Stories. (p. 2401)
—Wesley's Adventures: The Watchdog Stories. (p. 2401)
—Wesley's Adventures: Who Runs Faster? Stories. (p. 2401)
Walsh, David. British Redcoats. (p. 283)
Walsh, Ellen Stoll. Balancing Act. Walsh, Ellen Stoll, illus. (p. 160)
—Dot & Jabber & the Big Bug Mystery. (p. 587)
—Dot & Jabber & the Mystery of the Missing Stream. (p. 587)
—Mouse Paint - Pintura de Ratón. (p. 1515)
—Mouse Shapes. (p. 1515)
—Where Is Jumper? Walsh, Ellen Stoll, illus. (p. 2438)
Walsh, Enda. Chatroom: A Play. (p. 362)
Walsh, Francis. Daring Women of the American Revolution. (p. 505)
Walsh, George Ethelbert. Allin Winfield: A Romance (Classic Reprint) (p. 56)
Walsh, Illustrated by T. B. R., illus. see Pinder, Eric.
Walsh, J. M. Lost Valley (Classic Reprint) (p. 1356)
Walsh, Jenni L. Bethany Hamilton. (p. 208)
—Malala Yousafzai. (p. 1391)
Walsh, Jennifer, illus. see Yager, Karen & Williams, Kiersten.
Walsh, Jill Paton & Paton Walsh, Jill. Green Book. Bloom, Lloyd, illus. (p. 893)
Walsh, Joanna. Biggest Kiss. Abbot, Judi, illus. (p. 225)
—Did You Ever See? (p. 543)
—I Love Dad. Abbot, Judi, illus. (p. 1069)
—I Love Mom. Abbot, Judi, illus. (p. 1070)
—Perfect Hug. Abbot, Judi, illus. (p. 1722)
Walsh, Joanna & Abbot, Judi. I Love Dad. (p. 1069)
Walsh, John. Ballads of an Old Soldier (Classic Reprint) (p. 161)
—Our Lady of Lourdes: Lourdes, Its Grotto, Apparitions & Cures (Classic Reprint) (p. 1678)
Walsh, John H. CAM Clarke (Classic Reprint) (p. 313)
—Glenwood of Shipbay (Classic Reprint) (p. 842)
—New Primary Arithmetic. (p. 1596)
—Walsh-Suzzallo Arithmetic: By Grades, Fifth Year. (p. 2373)
—Walsh-Suzzallo Arithmetic: By Grades, Third Year. (p. 2373)
—Walsh-Suzzallo Arithmetic: By Grades, Fourth Year. (p. 2373)
—Walsh-Suzzallo Arithmetic. (p. 2373)
—Walsh-Suzzallo Arithmetics; by Grades, Eighth Year. (p. 2373)
Walsh, John Henry. Dogs of Great Britain, America, & Other Countries. (p. 578)
—Dogs of the British Islands: Being a Series of Articles & Letters by Various Contributors, Reprinted from the Field Newspaper (Classic Reprint) (p. 578)
—Dogs of the British Islands. (p. 578)
—New Grammar School Arithmetic, Vol. 1 (Classic Reprint) (p. 1594)
Walsh, Judith E. India. (p. 1115)
Walsh, Kay. Amy Carmichael - Rescuer by Night. (p. 77)
Walsh, Kenneth. Our Earth (p. 1677)
—Outer Space (p. 1684)
—Solar System (p. 2056)
Walsh, Kenneth C. H. You Are There! San Francisco 1906. (p. 2525)
Walsh, Kent D. Legend of Beards Hollow. (p. 1261)
Walsh, Liam Francis. Fish. (p. 741)
—Make a Wish, Henry Bear. (p. 1386)
Walsh, Liza Gardner. Do Fairies Bring the Spring Mitchell, Hazel, illus. (p. 570)
—Fairies 1, 2, 3. Mitchell, Hazel, illus. (p. 695)
—Fall Fairy Gathering. Mitchell, Hazel, illus. (p. 700)
—Ghost Hunter's Handbook (p. 827)
—How Do Fairies Have Fun in the Sun? Mitchell, Hazel, illus. (p. 1028)
—Muddy Boots: Outdoor Activities for Children. (p. 1524)
—Treasure Hunters Handbook (p. 2282)
Walsh, Louis J. On My Keeping, & in Theirs: A Record of Experiences on the Run, in Derry Gaol, & in Ballykinlar Internment Camp (Classic Reprint) (p. 1653)
Walsh, Madeleine Riley, illus. see Walsh, Becki.
Walsh, Marie A. My Queen: A Romance of the Great Salt Lake (Classic Reprint) (p. 1559)
Walsh, Marilyn, illus. see Walsh, Aly.
Walsh, Mary Elizabeth. Reminiscences of a Sunny Clime (Classic Reprint) (p. 1865)
Walsh, Mary Lou Oakley. Samuel K. Cat. (p. 1929)
Walsh, Melanie. 10 Things I Can Do to Help My World. Walsh, Melanie, illus. (p. 2550)
—Isaac & His Amazing Asperger Superpowers! Walsh, Melanie, illus. (p. 1138)
—Living with Mom & Living with Dad. Walsh, Melanie, illus. (p. 1335)
—My Green Day. (p. 1549)
—My Green Day: 10 Green Things I Can Do Today. Walsh, Melanie, illus. (p. 1549)
—Trick or Treat? Walsh, Melanie, illus. (p. 2287)
Walsh, Michael. Mercantile Arithmetic, Adapted to the Commerce of the United States, in Its Domestic & Foreign Relations: With an Appendix, Containing Practical Systems of Mensuration, Gauging, & Book-Keeping (Classic Reprint) (p. 1447)
Walsh, Michael, jt. illus. see Romero, Leonardo.
Walsh, Miss. Officer's Daughter, or a Visit to Ireland in 1790, Vol. 1 Of 4: By the Daughter of a Captain in the Navy, Deceased (Classic Reprint) (p. 1640)
WALSH, Mitchell. How Do Fairies Have Fun in The (p. 1028)
Walsh, Molly, illus. see Sooy, Julia.
Walsh, Pat. Crowfield Curse. (p. 479)
—Crowfield Demon. (p. 479)
Walsh, Patricia. Wizecatz & Dogz. (p. 2483)
Walsh, Patrick M., Jr. Derby: A Timmy Wallings Story. McGriff, Aaron C., ed. (p. 530)
—Who Says Timmy Can't Play: The Derby: A Timmy Wallings Story. McGriff, Aaron, ed. (p. 2449)
Walsh, Rebecca, illus. see Ehrlich, Amy.
Walsh, Richard H., illus. see Brennan, Lynda.
Walsh, Richard J. Kidd: A Moral Opuscule (Classic Reprint) (p. 1213)
Walsh, Robert. Museum of Foreign Literature & Science, Vol. 25: July to December, 1834 (Classic Reprint) (p. 1528)
—Museum of Foreign Literature, Science & Art, Vol. 34: September to December, 1838 (Classic Reprint) (p. 1528)
—Museum of Foreign Literature, Science, & Art, Vol. 31: For the Year 1837 (Classic Reprint) (p. 1528)
—Museum of Foreign Literature, Science, & Art, Vol. 39: May to August, 1840 (Classic Reprint) (p. 1528)
Walsh, Russ. Eternity: Where Will You Spend It? (p. 666)
Walsh, Sandy E. Gift of the Monkey Pajamas. Schubbe, Matt, illus. (p. 832)
Walsh, Sara. Dark Light. (p. 506)
Walsh, Sarah, illus. see Burningham, Sarah O'Leary.
Walsh, Sarah, illus. see Chronicle.
Walsh, Sarah, illus. see Cohan, Medeia.
Walsh, Sarah, illus. see Halligan, Katherine.
Walsh, Sarah, illus. see Lerwill, Ben.
Walsh, Sarah, illus. see Nosy Crow Staff.
Walsh, Sarah, illus. see Parker, Amy.
Walsh, Sarah, illus. see Steinberg, Billy & Kelly, Tom.
Walsh, Sarah, jt. auth. see Parker, Amy.
Walsh, Sheila. Bible Is My Best Friend Bible Storybook. (p. 213)
—Bible Is My Best Friend—Flip Book. (p. 213)
—God's Little Princess Treasury Johnson, Meredith, illus. (p. 853)
—Where Do I Find Jesus? Home, Sarah, illus. (p. 2436)
—You're Worth It for Girls: God Thinks You Rock! Walkup, ed. (p. 2535)
Walsh Shepherd, Donna. New Zealand. (p. 1599)
Walsh, Sidonie. No Country for Young Fools: Book One - NCFYF Series. (p. 1612)
Walsh, Stephen & O'Donovan, Marita. Brendan & the Blarney Stone. Le Feyer, Diane, illus. (p. 279)
—Vinnie Goes to Vegas. Le Feyer, Diane, illus. (p. 2359)
Walsh, Steve. Chief Ouray: Ute Chief & Man of Peace. (p. 369)
—Enos Mills: Rocky Mountain Conservationist. (p. 655)
—Zebulon Montgomery Pike: Explorer & Military Officer. (p. 2539)
Walsh, Stuart P. Thirteen Years of Scout Adventure (Classic Reprint) (p. 2223)
Walsh, Tania. Stories of Wonder. (p. 2126)
Walsh, Tina, illus. see Guettier, Nancy.
Walsh, Walsh. Officer's Daughter, or a Visit to Ireland in 1790, Vol. 2 of 4 (Classic Reprint) (p. 1640)
Walsh, William Shepard. Extravaganza: Grey Dolphin; Moses, the Sassy; Mr. Columbus Coriander's Gorilla; the Fate of Young Chubb; Boots at the Holly-Tree Inn; the Enthusiast in Anatomy; the Light Princess; the Legend of the Little Weaver (Classic Reprint) (p. 686)
Walsh, William Thomas. Mirage of the Many (Classic Reprint) (p. 1475)
Walshaw, Rodney, jt. auth. see Challoner, Jack.
Walshaw, Rodney, jt. auth. see Farndon, John.
Walshaw, Sam. Lulu Ladybug. (p. 1367)
Walshaw, Sam, illus. see Ackland, Nick.
Walshe, Blayney. Sporting & Military Adventures in Nepaul & the Himalayas: A Narrative of Personal Encounters & Narrow Escapes (Classic Reprint) (p. 2088)
Walshe, Dermot, illus. see Helmer, Marilyn.
Walshe, E. H. Foster-Brothers of Doon: A Tale of the Irish Rebellion of 1798 (Classic Reprint) (p. 771)
Walshe, Elizabeth Hely. Cedar Creek: From the Shanty to the Settlement; a Tale of Canadian Life (Classic Reprint) (p. 348)
—Under the Inquisition: A Story of the Reformation in Italy. (p. 2322)
Walshon, Jay. Eye See You Africa. (p. 688)
Walsleben, Edda Brigitte. Little Bee Who Would Be Queen. (p. 1311)
—Scotty the Little Westie Dog & His Diary. (p. 1962)
Walstead, Curt, illus. see Brill, Patricia Ann.
Walstead, Curt, illus. see Ormond, Jennifer.
Walt Disney Animation Research Library. Walt Disney Animation Studios the Archive Series Layout & Background. (p. 2374)
Walt Disney Company Staff, illus. see Bedford, Annie North & Golden Books Staff.
Walt Disney Company Staff, illus. see Golden Books Staff & Random House Disney Staff.
Walt Disney Company Staff, illus. see Random House Disney Staff.
Walt Disney Company Staff, jt. auth. see Sutcliffe, Jane.
Walt Disney Imagineering & Jungle Cruise Skippers. Disney Parks Presents: Jungle Cruise: Purchase Includes a CD with Narration! Madrid, Erwin, illus. (p. 561)
Walt Disney Pictures. Mary Poppins Returns: Everything Is Possible - Leveled Reader. (p. 1416)
Walt Disney Studio, illus. see Dempster, Al.
Walt Disney Studio, illus. see Hazen, Barbara Shook.
Walt Disney Studio, illus. see North Bedford, Annie.
Walt Disney Studio, illus. see Watson, Jane Werner.
Walt Disney Studio, illus. see Werner, Jane.
Walt Disney Studios Staff, illus. see Golden Books Staff.
Walt Disney Studios Staff, illus. see Random House Disney Staff.
Walta, Gabriel Hernandez. Doctor Strange by Donny Cates Vol. 1: God of Magic (p. 573)
—Vision. (p. 2362)
—Vision: the Complete Collection. (p. 2362)
Walta, Gabriel Hernandez, et al. Doctor Strange by Donny Cates. (p. 573)
Waltch, illus. see Shuky.
Walter, Alan, illus. see Pike, Diane.
Walter, Carmel M. Caterpillar & the Black Cherry Tree. (p. 344)
Walter, Carrie Stevens. Idyl of Santa Barbara: A Fragmentary Tale Half Told & Half Inferred; As Full of Sighs & Heartache Tones As Song of Prisoned Bird (Classic Reprint) (p. 1090)
—Idyl of Santa Barbara. (p. 1090)
Walter, Deborah, illus. see Rigg, Diana.
Walter, Ekaterina & Walter, Taya. Amber & Sapphire: The Magic Spell. Wisniewski, Jim "Wiz", illus. (p. 67)
Walter, Eugene. Easiest Way: A Play in Four Acts (Classic Reprint) (p. 619)
—Easiest Way: Representative Plays by American Dramatists: 1856-1911. (p. 619)
—Great Issue, or the Undertow (Classic Reprint) (p. 887)
—Paid in Full (Classic Reprint) (p. 1692)
—Wolf (Classic Reprint) (p. 2483)
Walter Foster (Firm) Staff, contrib. by. Learn to Draw Walt Disney's Mickey Mouse. (p. 1257)

W

—Let's Ride a Bike. (p. 1277)
Walton, Sally. I Can Do Crafts: Creative Things for Young Children to Make, Shown Step by Step. (p. 1061)
Walton, Sally, jt. auth. see Walton, Stewart.
Walton, Sally & Donaldson, Stephanie. Show Me How: I Can Grow Things. (p. 2012)
Walton, Sally, et al. Fun Projects & Amazing Things to Make, Do, Play & Give: Two Fantastic Books in a Box - the Ultimate Rainy-Day Collection with 220 Exciting Step-By-Step Projects Shown in over 3000 Photographs (p. 800)
Walton, Stephen, illus. see Cotton, Katie.
Walton, Thomas. Know Your Own Ship (p. 1229)
—Know Your Own Ship: A Simple Explanation of the Stability, Construction, Tonnage & Freeboard - Scholar's Choice Edition. (p. 1229)
—Sins of the Fathers: Or the Wye Valley Mystery (Classic Reprint) (p. 2025)
Walton, Tj. Elijah the Prophet: Volume 1. Walton, Haley, illus. (p. 635)
Walton, Tony, illus. see Andrews, Julie & Hamilton, Emma Walton.
Walton, Tony, illus. see Andrews, Julie.
Walton, Vikki. Will God Still Find Me? Walton, Jori, illus. (p. 2467)
Walton, Will. Anything Could Happen. (p. 104)
—I Felt a Funeral in My Brain. (p. 1065)
Walton, William J. Polly. Walton, William J., illus. (p. 1771)
Waltower, A. C. Hydro. (p. 1055)
Waltrip, Mildred, illus. see Morris, Richard B.
Waltz, Elizabeth Cherry. Ancient Landmark: A Kentucky Romance (Classic Reprint) (p. 81)
Waltz, Michael. Hen & I. (p. 954)
Waltz, Tom. Little Jackie Lantern. Hickman, Jessica, illus. (p. 1319)
Waltz, Tom, jt. auth. see Burnham, Erik.
Waltz, Tom, jt. auth. see Lynch, Brian.
Waltz, Tom & Eastman, Kevin. Teenage Mutant Ninja Turtles Volume 1: Change Is Constant. Duncan, Dan, illus. (p. 2200)
—Teenage Mutant Ninja Turtles Volume 1: Change Is Constant Deluxe Edition. Duncan, Dan, illus. (p. 2200)
—Teenage Mutant Ninja Turtles Volume 2: Enemies Old, Enemies New. Duncan, Dan & Santolouco, Mateus, illus. (p. 2200)
—Teenage Mutant Ninja Turtles Volume 4: Sins of the Fathers Kuhn, Andy, illus. (p. 2200)
Waltz, Tom & Eastman, Kevin B. Teenage Mutant Ninja Turtles Enemies Old, Enemies New. Santolouco, Mateus & Duncan, Dan, illus. (p. 2200)
—Teenage Mutant Ninja Turtles Volume 5: Krang War Bates, Ben, illus. (p. 2200)
Walworth, Ellen H. Old World: As Seen Through Young Eyes, or, Travels Around the World (Classic Reprint) (p. 1649)
Walworth, J. H. Baldy's Point (Classic Reprint) (p. 161)
—New Man at Rossmere (Classic Reprint) (p. 1595)
—Strange Pilgrimage: A Novel (Classic Reprint) (p. 2138)
Walworth, Janet H. Heavy Yokes (Classic Reprint) (p. 947)
Walworth, Jeannette H. Bar-Sinister: A Social Study (Classic Reprint) (p. 164)
—Fortune's Tangled Skein: A Novel (Classic Reprint) (p. 770)
—Fortune's Tangled Skein. (p. 770)
—Southern Silhouettes (Classic Reprint) (p. 2069)
—Uncle Scipio: A Story of Uncertain Days in the South (Classic Reprint) (p. 2319)
Walworth, Jeannette Hadermann. Martlet Seal (Classic Reprint) (p. 1411)
Walworth, Mansfield T. Hotspur: A Tale of the Old Dutch Manor (Classic Reprint) (p. 1007)
Walworth, Mansfield Tracy. Beverly: Or, the White Mask, a Novel (Classic Reprint) (p. 211)
—Lulu: A Tale of the National Hotel Poisoning (Classic Reprint) (p. 1367)
—Stormcliff a Tale of the Highlands (Classic Reprint) (p. 2127)
Walworth, Nathan, et al. Correspondence of Nathan Walworth & Peter Seddon of Outwood. (p. 456)
Walz, Annerose. Your Travel Stories: A Colorful Journal for Travelling Teens & Those Who Are Young at Heart. (p. 2534)
Walz, Jason. Last Pick. (p. 1249)
—Last Pick: Born to Run. (p. 1249)
—Last Pick: Rise Up. (p. 1249)
Walz, Richard, illus. see Kulling, Monica.
Walz, Richard, illus. see Murphy, Frank.
Wambach, Abby. Forward: My Story Young Readers' Edition. (p. 770)
—Wolfpack (Young Readers Edition) (p. 2484)
Wampol, Pam & Woodard, Heather. Oscar's Dreamzz: The Story of Santa's First Elf. (p. 1673)
Wamsley, Jody. What Am I Gonna Do? Turchan, Monique, illus. (p. 2404)
Wan, Joyce. Are You My Mommy? Wan, Joyce, illus. (p. 113)
—Bear in My Bed. (p. 179)
—Dream Big. (p. 601)
—Good Night, Sweetie. Wan, Joyce, illus. (p. 865)
—Hug You, Kiss You, Love You. Wan, Joyce, illus. (p. 1048)
—My Lucky Little Dragon. Wan, Joyce, illus. (p. 1555)
—Peek-A-Boo Farm. (p. 1712)
—Peek-A-Boo Zoo. (p. 1712)
—Sleepy Farm: a Lift-The-Flap Book. (p. 2037)
—We Belong Together. Wan, Joyce, illus. (p. 2389)
—Whale in My Swimming Pool. (p. 2403)
—You Are My Cupcake. Wan, Joyce, illus. (p. 2524)
—You Are My Cupcake: a Cloth Book. Wan, Joyce, illus. (p. 2524)
—You Are My Magical Unicorn. Wan, Joyce, illus. (p. 2524)
—You Are My Merry Little Christmas. Wan, Joyce, illus. (p. 2524)
—You Are My Pumpkin. Wan, Joyce, illus. (p. 2524)
—You Are My Sweetheart. Wan, Joyce, illus. (p. 2524)
Wan, Joyce, illus. see Gallion, Sue Lowell.
Wan, Joyce, illus. see Gehl, Laura.
Wan, Joyce, illus. see Howatt, Sandra J.
Wan, Stephanie, illus. see Wisma, Mare.
Wanardi, Jennifer, illus. see Iyengar, Malathi Michelle.
Wanasundera, Nanda P. & Spilling, Jo-Ann. Sri Lanka. (p. 2095)
Wand, Dana. Shanie June Jumped over the Moon. Tinling, Molly, illus. (p. 1999)
—Those Bad, Bad Bedtime Boys. (p. 2230)
Wand, Dana D. Those Bad, Bad Bedtime Boys. (p. 2230)
Wandelmaier, Michael, illus. see Hughes, Susan.
Wander, Diane C. Anything Is Possible! (p. 104)
—Maddie Hoffman Gymnastics Superstar: Triple Trouble Plus One Book 2. (p. 1374)
—Sleepaway Camp-The Hoffman's Best Summer Ever! Triple Trouble Plus One: Book 3. (p. 2036)
Wander, Sharon Lee. Child of the Wind. Even, William C., ed. (p. 370)
Wanderer, Wanderer. Across Country (Classic Reprint) (p. 11)
—Glamour, Vol. 1 Of 3: A Novel (Classic Reprint) (p. 841)
—Glamour, Vol. 2 Of 3: A Novel (Classic Reprint) (p. 841)
—Loose Rein (Classic Reprint) (p. 1348)
Wandersman, Aldo. Ronaldinho. (p. 1902)
—Ronaldo. (p. 1902)
Wandless, David. Natural Magic. (p. 1580)
—Natural Magic Book 3 - the Milk Stone & the Tauren. (p. 1580)
Wandulu, Timothy, jt. auth. see Warugaba, Christine.
Wanecski, Erica Joan, illus. see Stafford, Gerry.
Wanert, Amandine, illus. see Bonnewijn, Olivier.
Wanert, Amandine, illus. see Davidson, Susanna.
Wanert, Amandine, illus. see Johnson, Elizabeth Crispina.
Wang, Amann, illus. see Wang, Wenhua.
Wang, Andrea. How Can We Reduce Fossil Fuel Pollution? (p. 1026)
—Learning about Asia. (p. 1257)
—Magic Ramen: The Story of Momofuku Ando. Urbanowicz, Kana, illus. (p. 1378)
—Malala Yousafzai: Nobel Peace Prize Winner & Education Activist (p. 1391)
—Nian Monster. Chau, Alina, illus. (p. 1602)
—What's Great about Georgia? (p. 2424)
—What's Great about Maine? (p. 2424)
Wang, Annie, illus. see Bozzo, Alessandro.
Wang, Corrie. City of Beasts. (p. 395)
—Takedown. (p. 2177)
Wang, Dorthea Deprisco. Five Minutes until Bed. Vaux, Patricia, illus. (p. 744)
Wang, Dorthea Deprisco, jt. auth. see Andrews McMeel Publishing Staff.
Wang, Emily, jt. auth. see Smith, Michael.
Wang, Gabrielle. Pearlie Stories. (p. 1711)
Wang, Helen, tr. see Lin, Man-Chiu.
Wang, Helen, tr. see Wenxuan, Cao.
Wang, Hilary & Wang, Julian. Enchanted Cello Case. (p. 646)
Wang, Holman. Great Job, Dad! (p. 887)
—Great Job, Mom! (p. 887)
Wang, Holman & Wang, Jack. Cozy Classics: Great Expectations. (p. 465)
—Star Wars Epic Yarns: Return of the Jedi. (p. 2104)
Wang, Jack, jt. auth. see Wang, Holman.
Wang, Jack & Wang, Holman. War & Peace. (p. 2376)
Wang, Jack, et al. Adventures of Huckleberry Finn. (p. 24)
—Cozy Classics: Emma. (p. 465)
—Cozy Classics: The Adventures of Tom Sawyer. (p. 465)
Wang, Jen. Fionna & Cake Card Wars. (p. 732)
—Prince & the Dressmaker. (p. 1793)
—Stargazing. Wang, Jen, illus. (p. 2106)
Wang, Jen, illus. see Doctorow, Cory.
Wang, Jianwei, ed. see Bo, Zhiyue.
Wang, Jianwei, ed. see Hollihan-Elliot, Sheila.
Wang, Jianwei, ed. see Liao, Yan.
Wang, Jianwei, ed. see Lin, Zhimin.
Wang, Jianwei, ed. see Lu, Jia.
Wang, Jianwei, ed. see Luh, Shu Shin.
Wang, Jianwei, ed. see Yu, Bin.
Wang, Jiazhen. Hu Gu Po. (p. 1047)
—Tong Hua Jing Ling. (p. 2260)
Wang, Lei, illus. see Haag, Tiffany.
Wang, Lin, illus. see Branscombe, Allison.
Wang, Lin, illus. see Konrad, Maria Stewart.
Wang, Lin, illus. see Manley, Curtis.
Wang, Lin, illus. see Qu, Zhi.
Wang, Lin, illus. see Yoo, Paula.
Wang, Lin, jt. auth. see Yoo, Paula.
Wang, Lucy. Art of Chinese Brush Painting. (p. 121)
Wang, M. S. Rosie. Seeing the Underwater World with Abby & Josh. Grijalva, M. S. Laurah, illus. (p. 1984)
Wang, Mengji. Legend of Ji Gong. (p. 1262)
Wang, Mengting. Latchkey Kid. (p. 1250)
Wang, Michael. Liam the Brave. (p. 1283)
—Stray. (p. 2139)
Wang, Qi, ed. see Lo, Yuet-Wan.
Wang, Qi, illus. see Schwaeber, Barbie.
Wang, Qi Z., illus. see Brill, Marlene Targ.
Wang, Qijun, illus. see Sadlier, Rosemary.
Wang, Rosie C. Seeing the Underwater World with Abby & Josh. (p. 1984)
Wang, Sean. Carnival Capers! (p. 332)
—Space Justice. (p. 2071)
Wang, Sean, illus. see Esquivel, Eric.
Wang, Sean, illus. see King, Trey.
Wang, Sean, illus. see Steele, Michael Anthony.
Wang, Shaoli. Chinese Fairy Tale Feasts: A Literary Cookbook. (p. 378)
Wang, Shaoli, illus. see Yee, Paul.
Wang, Shifu. [Record of the Western Chamber]. (p. 1854)
Wang, Suling, illus. see Bauer, Marion Dane.
Wang, Suling, illus. see Yep, Laurence.
Wang, Tom, tr. Disney Mulan: Movie Storybook / Diàn Yǐng Tóng Huà Gù Shi (English-Mandarin) Disney Storybook Art Team, illus. (p. 561)
Wang, wen hua. Learn, Read, & Write with Wang Wenhua: A Superman Who Only Listen Half Way. (p. 1255)
—Learn, Read, & Write with Wang Wenhua: The Talking Class of Teacher Wu Po Po. (p. 1255)
Wang, Wenhua. Chief Cellist. Chen, Yu Yan, tr. (p. 369)
—Jiuge's Best Chinese Children's Literature Of 2013. (p. 1169)
—MR Horton's Violin. Chen, Yu Yan, tr. (p. 1518)
—Shepherd's Pipe Award Series: I Am No Little Monster. (p. 2006)
Wang, X. I. Chinese Zodiac. (p. 379)
Wang, Xinyu. Shoot down the Suns, Fly to the Noon. (p. 2009)
Wang, Yanxing, tr. see Renz, Ulrich.
Wang, Yinan. 50 State Fossils: A Guidebook for Aspiring Paleontologists Levy, Jane, illus. (p. 2555)
Wang, Yiqun Sophia. Adventures of Mumu. (p. 26)
Wang, Yujia, illus. see Hosten, Colin & Dey, Sia.
Wang, Zong-Zhou, illus. see Crane, Carol.
Wangerin, Albert. Ueber Die Anziehung Homogener Ellipsoide Abhandlungen Von Laplace 1782. (p. 2313)
Wangler, Val. When the Climate Changed. (p. 2433)
Wanjie, Anne, ed. Basics of Animal Systems. (p. 170)
—Basics of Biochemistry. (p. 170)
—Basics of Biology. (p. 170)
—Basics of Ecology. (p. 170)
—Basics of Evolution. (p. 170)
—Basics of Genetics. (p. 170)
—Basics of Microbes. (p. 170)
—Basics of Plant Structures. (p. 170)
—Basics of Reproduction. (p. 170)
—Basics of the Human Body. (p. 170)
Wanker, William Paul. Ziby & the Island of Izbuk. (p. 2540)
Wanless, Andrew. Sketches & Anecdotes (Classic Reprint) (p. 2031)
Wanley, Nathaniel. Wonders of the Little World, or a General History of Man, Vol. 1 Of 2: Displaying the Various Faculties, Capacities, Powers & Defects of the Human Body & Mind (Classic Reprint) (p. 2491)
Wannamaker, L. S. Earning the Blue Stripe (Classic Reprint) (p. 615)
Wanner, Carole, illus. see Green, Tom.
Wanner, Zukiswa. Africa. (p. 32)
—Refilwe: Best Loved Tales for Africa. Hinrichsen, Tamsin, illus. (p. 1860)
Wapahi, Robert, illus. see Hay, John & Harwich, Mary Belle.
Waples, Evelyn. Lantern, Vol. 11: December, 1930 (Classic Reprint) (p. 1244)
War Department, Bureau of Insular Affairs. Report of the Commissioner of Education of Porto Rico, 1910, from the Report of the Governor of Porto Rico, 1910, Pages 153 - 203, Inclusive. (p. 1866)
Warbrick, Caroline. Taking Action Against Eating Disorders. (p. 2177)
Warbrick, Margaret. Charlie Takes the Lead. (p. 360)
Warburg, Geraldine. Counterpoint: Fall, 1948 (Classic Reprint) (p. 459)
Warburg, Sandol Stoddard. Thinking Book. (p. 2222)
Warburton, Cecil. Spiders - Scholar's Choice Edition. (p. 2081)
Warburton, Eliot. Reginald Hastings: Or a Tale of the Troubles in 164 (Classic Reprint) (p. 1861)
—Reginald Hastings, or a Tale of the Troubles in 164-, Vol. 2 of 3 (Classic Reprint) (p. 1861)
—Reginald Hastings, Vol. 1 Of 3: Or a Tale of the Troubles (Classic Reprint) (p. 1861)
Warburton, Emma. Mabel, Vol. 1 Of 3: A Novel (Classic Reprint) (p. 1371)
Warburton, R. E. Egerton. Hunting Songs (Classic Reprint) (p. 1053)
Warburton, Ruth. Witchfinder: Witch Finder. (p. 2480)
Warburton, Sarah, illus. see Bradman, Tony.
Warburton, Sarah, illus. see Hart, Caryl.
Warburton, Sarah, illus. see Holabird, Katharine.
Warburton, Sarah, illus. see Holabird, Katherine.
Warburton, Sarah, illus. see Magee, Wes.
Warburton, Sarah, illus. see Sperring, Mark.
Warburton, Thomas, tr. see Jansson, Tove.
Ward (Katydid in the Morning), Sharon K. All the Animals Gave Their Gifts: A Native Christmas. (p. 53)
Ward (Willard), Bernice. God Says, Momma Says, & Children Says. (p. 852)
Ward, A. B. Sage Brush Parson (Classic Reprint) (p. 1922)
Ward, A. W. Works of Mrs. Gaskell, Vol. 6 Of 8: With Introductions; Sylvia's Lovers, etc (Classic Reprint) (p. 2499)
—Works of Mrs. Gaskell, Vol. 8 Of 8: Wives & Daughters (Classic Reprint) (p. 2499)
Ward, Aaron. Report of the International Meteorological Congress: At Paris, France, September 19-26, 1889 (Classic Reprint) (p. 1866)
Ward, Ada L. My Greatest Adventure, Vol. 25 (Classic Reprint) (p. 1549)
Ward, Adam. Critical World Issues: Capital Punishment (p. 476)
Ward, Albert. Critical World Issues: Genocide (p. 476)
Ward, Amy M. & Cayenne, Olivia. Secrets Above: Book 1 of the Secrets Series. (p. 1979)
—Secrets Below: Book 2 of the Secrets Series. (p. 1980)
Ward, Annie. My Mother, or Home Scenes in Yorkshire (Classic Reprint) (p. 1556)
Ward, April, illus. see Brown, Monica.
Ward, April, illus. see Feldman, Thea.
Ward, April, illus. see Garza, Xavier.
Ward, April, illus. see Zepeda, Gwendolyn & Ventura, Gabriela Baeza.
Ward, Artemus, pseud. Artemus Ward: His Book, with Many Comic Illustrations (Classic Reprint) (p. 122)
—Artemus Ward (His Travels) among the Mormons, Vol. 1 (Classic Reprint) (p. 122)
—Artemus Ward, His Book. (p. 122)
—Artemus Ward, His Book (Classic Reprint) (p. 122)
—Artemus Ward, His Travels: Part I., Miscellaneous; Part II., among the Mormons (Classic Reprint) (p. 122)
—Artemus Ward, His Travels, Part I. - Miscellaneons, Part II. - among the Mormons. (p. 122)
—Artemus Ward, Vol. 1: His Travels (Classic Reprint) (p. 122)
—Complete Works of Artemus Ward: With a Biographical Sketch (Classic Reprint) (p. 435)
—Sandwiches (Classic Reprint) (p. 1931)
Ward, Arthur Henry Sarsfield, see Rohmer, Sax, pseud.
Ward, Austin N. Male Life among the Mormons: Or the Husband in Utah; Detailing Sights & Scenes among the Mormons; with Remarks on Their Moral & Social Economy (Classic Reprint) (p. 1392)
Ward, B. J. Farty Marty. Kellogg, Steven, illus. (p. 712)
Ward, Babs. Connectrix. (p. 441)
Ward, Brian. History of Medicine: Healthcare Around the World & Through the Ages. (p. 978)
Ward, Brian R. Story of Medicine. (p. 2131)
—Tunas. (p. 2299)
Ward, Brittney. Grace the Gorilla. (p. 873)
—Sam the Snake. (p. 1926)
Ward, Candace, ed. Children's Christmas Stories & Poems. (p. 373)
Ward, Catherine G. Cottage on the Cliff: A Sea-Side Story (Classic Reprint) (p. 457)
—Family Portrait, or Descendants of Trelawney (Classic Reprint) (p. 703)
—Fishers Daughter, or the Wanderings of Wolf, & the Fortunes of Alfred: Being the Sequel to That So Greatly Admired & Popular Work, Entitled, the Cottage on the Cliff, or a Sea-Side Story (Classic Reprint) (p. 742)
—Fisher's Daughter, or the Wanderings of Wolf, & the Fortunes of Alfred: Being the Sequel to That So Greatly Admired & Popular Work, Entitled, the Cottage on the Cliff, a Seaside Story (Classic Reprint) (p. 742)
—Fisher's Daughter, Vol. 2: Or the Wanderings of Wolf & the Fortunes of Alfred (Classic Reprint) (p. 742)
—Son & the Nephew, or More Secrets Than One, Vol. 2 Of 3: A Novel (Classic Reprint) (p. 2061)
—Son & the Nephew, Vol. 3 Of 3: Or More Secrets Than One; a Novel (Classic Reprint) (p. 2061)
Ward, Catherine George. Family Portraits, or Descendants of Trelawney (Classic Reprint) (p. 703)
—Fisher's Daughter, or the Wanderings of Wolf, & the Fortunes of Alfred: Being the Sequel to That So Greatly Admired & Popular Work, Entitled, the Cottage on the Cliff, or a Sea-Side Story (Classic Reprint) (p. 742)
—Mysterious Marriage, or the Will of My Father (Classic Reprint) (p. 1567)
Ward, Charles Frederick. Epistles on the Romance of the Rose & Other Documents in the Debate: A Dissertation, Submitted to the Faculty of the Graduate School of Arts & Literature in Candidacy for the Degree of Doctor of Philosophy, Department of Romance Languages & Lite. (p. 658)
Ward, Cherise, illus. see Hillhouse, Joanne C.
Ward, Cherise, illus. see Mitchell, Carol.
Ward, Cherise, illus. see Picayo, Mario, et al.
Ward, Chris. Adventures of Seaborne Morse. (p. 27)
—Discover Australia. (p. 554)
—Discover Kenya. (p. 554)
—Discover South Africa. (p. 555)
Ward, Chris, jt. auth. see Wilson, Rosie.
Ward, Christian, et al. Black Bolt. (p. 237)
Ward, Christopher. Mac on the Road to Marseille. (p. 1371)
Ward, Cindy. Cookie's Week. dePaola, Tomie, illus. (p. 446)
Ward, D. J. How a City Works. Lemay, Violet, illus. (p. 1025)
—Simple Machines. Lowery, Mike, illus. (p. 2022)
—What Happens to Our Trash? Meisel, Paul, illus. (p. 2411)
Ward, Damian. Everyone Has Feelings (p. 672)
Ward, Damian, illus. see Aboff, Marcie.
Ward, Damian, illus. see Coleman, Wim & Perrin, Pat.
Ward, Damian, illus. see Higgins, Nadia.
Ward, Damian, illus. see Meister, Cari.
Ward, Damian, illus. see Schwaeber, Barbie Heit.
Ward, Danielle, illus. see Tapia-Bowes, Sally.
Ward, David J. I Heard a Sound. Comstock, Eric, illus. (p. 1066)
Ward, E. Fresh from the Fens: A Story of Three Lincolnshire Lasses (Classic Reprint) (p. 784)
—Pair of Originals: A Story (Classic Reprint) (p. 1693)
Ward, E. F., illus. see Webb, Robert N.
Ward, Edward. History of the London Clubs, or, the Citizens' Pastime (Part I) (p. 980)
—History of the London Clubs, or the Citizens Pastime, Vol. 1 (Classic Reprint) (p. 980)
—Mars Stript of His Armour, or the Army Displayed in All Its True Colours (Classic Reprint) (p. 1409)
—Second Volume of the Writings of the Author of the London-Spy (Classic Reprint) (p. 1974)
—Vade Mecum for Malt-Worms, or a Guide to Good Fellows: Being a Description of the Manners & Customs of the Most Eminent Publick Houses, in & about the Cities of London & Westminster; with a Hint on the Props (or Principal Customers) of Each House. (p. 2343)
—Wooden World Dissected, in the Character of a Ship of War: As Also the Characters of All the Officers, from the Captain to the Common Sailor (Classic Reprint) (p. 2491)
Ward, Edward G. Rational Method in Readin: An Original Presentation of Sight & Sound Work That Leads Rapidly to Independent & Intelligent Reading; Second Reader (Third Half-Year's Work) (Classic Reprint) (p. 1842)
—Rational Method in Reading: Additional Second Reader (Classic Reprint) (p. 1842)
—Rational Method in Reading: An Original Presentation of Sight & Sound Work That Leads Rapidly to Independent & Intelligent Reading (Classic Reprint) (p. 1842)
—Rational Method in Reading. (p. 1842)
—Rational Method in Reading (Classic Reprint) (p. 1842)
—Rational Method in Reading, Vol. 2: An Original Presentation of Sight & Sound Work That Leads Rapidly to Independent & Intelligent Reading (Classic Reprint) (p. 1843)
Ward, Edward Gendar. Rational Method in Reading: Primer (Classic Reprint) (p. 1842)
—Rational Method in Reading: Introductory Second Reader (Classic Reprint) (p. 1842)
—Rational Method in Reading: An Original Presentation of Sight & Sound Work That Leads Rapidly to Independent & Intelligent Reading (Classic Reprint) (p. 1842)
—Rational Method in Reading: An Original Presentation of Sight & Sound Work That Leads Rapidly to Independent & Intelligent Reading; First Reader (Second Half-Year's Work) (Classic Reprint) (p. 1842)
—Rational Method in Reading: An Original Presentation of Sight & Sound Work That Leads Rapidly to Independent

Waring, George. Squirrels & Other Animals: Or, Illustrations of the Habits & Instincts of Many of the Smaller British Quadrupeds (Classic Reprint) (p. 2095)
Waring, George E. Whip & Spur (Classic Reprint) (p. 2442)
Waring, Kerry Jones. Soil for Minerals & Medicine. (p. 2055)
Waring, Kerry Jones, jt. auth. see Gaines, Ann Graham.
Waring, Kerry Jones, et al. Arizona. (p. 116)
—New Hampshire. (p. 1594)
—Pennsylvania. (p. 1717)
Waring, William. Call to the Fountain: To Turn from Shadow & Imitation, & to Press after Substance; the Power That Quickens the Life That Is Eternal (Classic Reprint) (p. 312)
—Call to the Fountain: To Turn from Shadow & Imitation & to Press after Substance; the Power That Quickens — the Life That Is Eternal. Addressed to All, Especially to Those of Every Class Professing to Be Friends. (p. 312)
Waring, Zoe. No Hugs for Porcupine. (p. 1613)
Waring, Zoe, illus. see Burton, Jeffrey.
Waring, Zoe, illus. see Conway, Sara.
Waring, Zoe, illus. see Houghton Mifflin Harcourt, Houghton Mifflin.
Waring, Zoe, illus. see Houghton Mifflin Harcourt, Houghton Mifflin & Gryta, Thomas.
Waring, Zoe, illus. see Jardine, Hannah & Clever Publishing.
Waring, Zoe, illus. see Maier, Brenda.
Waring, Zoe, illus. see Oswald, Helen.
Waring, Zoe, illus. see Sauer, Tammi.
Waring, Zoe, illus. see Swift, Ginger.
Warlick, Sonya. King's Love for His Daughter. (p. 1223)
Warloch, Daniel M. Stories Paint Perfect Pictures. (p. 2126)
Warm Day, Jonathan, illus. see Orona-Ramirez, Kristy.
Warman, Cy. Express Messenger, & Other Tales of the Rail (Classic Reprint) (p. 684)
—Last Spike: And Other Railroad Stories (Classic Reprint) (p. 1249)
—Prospector: Story of the Life of Nicholas C. Creede (Classic Reprint) (p. 1807)
—Prospector. (p. 1807)
—Silver Queen: A Romance of the Early Days of Creede Camp (Classic Reprint) (p. 2019)
—Snow on the Headlight: A Story of the Great Burlington Strike (Classic Reprint) (p. 2047)
—Tales of an Engineer: With Rhymes of the Rail (Classic Reprint) (p. 2183)
—Tales of an Engineer with Rhymes of the Rail. (p. 2183)
—Weiga of Temagami: And Other Indian Tales (Classic Reprint) (p. 2396)
—White Mail (Classic Reprint) (p. 2444)
Warman, Jessica. Breathless. (p. 279)
—Last Good Day of the Year. (p. 1248)
Warmbrodt, Sue. Remington: The Gentle Giant. (p. 1864)
Warmington, Amy, illus. see Smith, Fiona Veitch.
Warms, Breanna, illus. see Lavergne, Angele.
Warms, Ed. Immigration to North America: Middle Eastern Immigrants Anderson, Stuart, ed. (p. 1101)
Warnaar, Dawn. DIY Lettering. (p. 566)
Warnaar, Dawn Nicole. Adventures in Lettering: 40 Exercises to Improve Your Lettering Skills. (p. 20)
Warnasuriya, Chandrani. Spooky Tales from the Orient: Tales of Ogres, Demons, Ghosts, Spells, Charms & the Enchanted (p. 2087)
Warne. My Father's Flying Machine. (p. 1538)
Warne, jt. auth. see Barker, Cicely Mary.
Warne, Francis Wesley. Darjeeling Disaster, Its Bright Side: The Triumph of the Six Lee Children (Classic Reprint) (p. 505)
Warne, Frederick. Bunny Trouble. (p. 298)
—Garden Party Sticker Book. (p. 809)
—Little Rabbit, Big City! (p. 1325)
—Little Rabbit, Big City! Peter Rabbit 2: the Runaway. (p. 1325)
—Peter Rabbit 2, Based on the Major New Movie: Peter Rabbit 2: the Runaway. (p. 1729)
—Peter Rabbit 2 Coloring Activity Book: Peter Rabbit 2: the Runaway. (p. 1729)
—Peter Rabbit 2 Sticker Activity Book: Peter Rabbit 2: the Runaway. (p. 1729)
Warne, Frederick, jt. auth. see Potter, Beatrix.
Warne, Jude. Big Reveal. (p. 222)
—Girls Who Go to Parties. (p. 839)
—Henley High Poetry Club. (p. 954)
—It Factor. (p. 1141)
—Landlocked. (p. 1242)
—Rules of the Range. (p. 1913)
Warneford, Warneford. Phantom Cruiser (Classic Reprint) (p. 1732)
Warner, A. Bartlett. My Brother's Keeper (Classic Reprint) (p. 1535)
Warner, Agnes. My Beloved Poilus (Classic Reprint) (p. 1532)
Warner, Allison H., jt. auth. see Johnson, Alice W.
Warner, Anna. Three Little Spades (Classic Reprint) (p. 2234)
—Tired Church Members (Classic Reprint) (p. 2251)
Warner, Anna B. Cross Corners (Classic Reprint) (p. 477)
—Susan Warner: Elizabeth Wetherell (Classic Reprint) (p. 2166)
—West Point Colors (Classic Reprint) (p. 2402)
Warner, Anna Bartlett. Hard Maple (Classic Reprint) (p. 929)
—Stories of Vinegar Hill (Classic Reprint) (p. 2126)
Warner, Anne. Gay & Festive Claverhouse an Extravaganza (Classic Reprint) (p. 812)
—How Leslie Loved (Classic Reprint) (p. 1033)
—In a Mysterious Way (Classic Reprint) (p. 1103)
—Just Between Themselves (Classic Reprint) (p. 1192)
—Original Gentleman (Classic Reprint) (p. 1671)
—Rejuvenation of Aunt Mary: A Three-ACT Comedy (Classic Reprint) (p. 1862)
—Rejuvenation of Aunt Mary (Classic Reprint) (p. 1862)
—Seeing England with Uncle John (Classic Reprint) (p. 1984)
—Seeing France with Uncle John (Classic Reprint) (p. 1984)
—Sunshine Jane (Classic Reprint) (p. 2153)
—Susan Clegg: And Her Love Affairs (Classic Reprint) (p. 2166)
—Susan Clegg: Her Friend & Her Neighbors (Classic Reprint) (p. 2166)
—Susan Clegg & a Man in the House (Classic Reprint) (p. 2166)
—Susan Clegg & Her Neighbors' Affairs (Classic Reprint) (p. 2166)
—Susan Clegg: And Her Friend Mrs. Lathrop (Classic Reprint) (p. 2166)
—Tigress (Classic Reprint) (p. 2242)
—When Woman Proposes (Classic Reprint) (p. 2434)
—Your Child & Mine (Classic Reprint) (p. 2533)
Warner, Beverley Ellison. Troubled Waters: A Problem of to-Day (Classic Reprint) (p. 2292)
Warner Bros. Consumer Products Inc., . Harry Potter Poster Collection: The Quintessential Images. (p. 935)
—Harry Potter Poster Collection: The Definitive Movie Posters. (p. 935)
Warner Bros Staff. Hidden Creatures. (p. 965)
Warner Brothers. Flash: Ultimate Guidebook. (p. 747)
—Supergirl: the Secret Files of Kara Danvers: The Ultimate Guide to the Hit TV Show. (p. 2159)
Warner, Chalene, illus. see Wrzosek, Jennifer.
Warner, Charles D. Saunterings (Classic Reprint) (p. 1937)
Warner, Charles Dudley. A-Hunting of the Deer & Other Essays. (p. 1)
—A-Hunting of the Deer & Other Essays (Classic Reprint) (p. 1)
—Ancient & Modern, Vol. 1 of 46 (Classic Reprint) (p. 79)
—Backlog Studies (Classic Reprint) (p. 156)
—Baddeck, & That Sort of Thing. (p. 158)
—Baddeck, & That Sort of Thing (Classic Reprint) (p. 158)
—Being a Boy (Classic Reprint) (p. 193)
—Complete Writings of Charles Dudley Warner, Vol. 1 of 15 (Classic Reprint) (p. 436)
—Golden House; a Novel: Illustrated by W. T. Smedley (Classic Reprint) (p. 858)
—In the Wilderness (Classic Reprint) (p. 1111)
—Library of the World's Best Literature, Ancient & Modern, Vol. 9 (Classic Reprint) (p. 1285)
—Library of the World's Best Literature, Ancient & Modern, Vol. 41 (Classic Reprint) (p. 1285)
—Library of the World's Best Literature, Ancient & Modern, Vol. 3 of 31 (Classic Reprint) (p. 1285)
—Library of the World's Best Literature, Ancient & Modern, Vol. 11 of 31 (Classic Reprint) (p. 1285)
—Library of the World's Best Literature, Vol. 10 Of 45: Ancient & Modern (Classic Reprint) (p. 1285)
—Library of the World's Best Literature, Vol. 4 Of 30: Ancient & Modern (Classic Reprint) (p. 1285)
—Little Journey in the World: A Novel (Classic Reprint) (p. 1319)
—My Summer in a Garden (Classic Reprint) (p. 1562)
—On Horseback: A Tour in Virginia, North Carolina & Tennessee, with Notes of Travel in Mexico & California (Classic Reprint) (p. 1652)
—Their Pilgrimage (Classic Reprint) (p. 2215)
Warner, Charles Forbes. Picturesque Hampden, Vol. 2: West (Classic Reprint) (p. 1741)
Warner, Chris. Infinities: A\New Hope Johnson, Drew, illus. (p. 1119)
—New Hope. Johnson, Drew, illus. (p. 1594)
Warner, Christopher S., ed. see Richardson, Mike.
Warner, Claire. Amber Sky. (p. 67)
Warner, Danielle, illus. see Warner, Jeremy.
Warner, Darrell, illus. see Brontë, Emily.
Warner, Frances. Life's Minor Collisions (Classic Reprint) (p. 1297)
—Noot's in Charge! (p. 1619)
Warner, Frances Lester. Endicott & I (Classic Reprint) (p. 649)
—Pilgrim Trails: A Plymouth-To-Provincetown Sketchbook (Classic Reprint) (p. 1744)
Warner, Frank A. Bobby Blake at Rockledge School or Winning the Medal of Honor (Classic Reprint) (p. 252)
Warner, Gaylee. Snuggly House. Macomber, C. R., illus. (p. 2050)
Warner, Gertrude Chandler. Amusement Park Mystery. Tang, Charles, illus. (p. 77)
—Bicycle Mystery Dunn, Joeming W. & Dunn, Ben, illus. (p. 215)
—Blue Bay Mystery Dubisch, Michael, illus. (p. 248)
—Blue Bay Mystery. Gringhuis, Dirk, illus. (p. 248)
—Box Car Children: Facsimile of 1924 First Edition with Illustrations in Color. (p. 266)
—Boxcar Children. Deal, L. Kate, illus. (p. 266)
—Box-Car Children: The Original 1924 Edition. (p. 266)
—Boxcar Children. Gilbert, Anne Yvonne & Powers, Gretchen Ellen, illus. (p. 266)
—Box-Car Children. Gregory, Dorothy Lake, illus. (p. 266)
—Boxcar Children (Set) (p. 266)
—Boxcar Children (the Boxcar Children: Time to Read, Level 2) Clester, Shane, illus. (p. 266)
—Boxcar Children DVD & Book Set. (p. 266)
—Boxcar Children Early Reader Set #1 (the Boxcar Children: Time to Read, Level 2) Clester, Shane, illus. (p. 266)
—Boxcar Children Graphic Novels Dunn, Ben, illus. (p. 266)
—Boxcar Children Graphic Novels Dubisch, Mike, illus. (p. 266)
—Boxcar Children Graphic Novels - 6 Titles Dubisch, Michael, illus. (p. 266)
—Boxcar Children Guide to Adventure: A How-To for Mystery Solving, Make-It-Yourself Projects, & More. (p. 266)
—Boxcar Children Mysteries Boxed Set #13-16. (p. 266)
—Boxcar Children Mysteries Boxed Set #9-12. (p. 266)
—Castle Mystery. Tang, Charles, illus. (p. 340)
—Clue in the Papyrus Scroll. (p. 409)
—Creepy Clues Special. (p. 472)
—Day of the Dead Mystery. (p. 514)
—Detour of the Elephants. VanArsdale, Anthony, illus. (p. 535)
—Dog-Gone Mystery. (p. 576)
—Doughnut Whodunit. (p. 589)
—Great Spy Showdown. (p. 890)
—Haunted Cabin Mystery Bloodworth, Mark, illus. (p. 937)
—Haunted Cabin Mystery. Tang, Charles, illus. (p. 937)
—Houseboat Mystery Dunn, Joeming W. & Dunn, Ben, illus. (p. 1024)
—Hundred-Year Mystery. (p. 1051)
—Isla de Las Sorpresas (Surprice Island) (p. 1139)
—Journey on a Runaway Train. (p. 1181)
—Legend of the Howling Werewolf. (p. 1262)
—Los Chicos Del Vagon de Carga (the Boxcar Children) (p. 1350)
—Midnight at the Haunted Hotel: A Boxcar Children Interactive Mystery. (p. 1461)
—Mike's Mystery Dubisch, Michael, illus. (p. 1464)
—Mike's Mystery. Gringhuis, Dirk, illus. (p. 1464)
—Mike's Mystery (the Boxcar Children: Time to Read, Level 2) Clester, Shane, illus. (p. 1464)
—Misterio de la Casa Amarilla (the Yellow House Mystery) (p. 1482)
—Mystery of the Grinning Gargoyle. VanArsdale, Anthony, illus. (p. 1570)
—Mystery of the Soccer Snitch. VanArsdale, Anthony, illus. (p. 1570)
—Mystery Ranch. Gringhuis, Dirk, illus. (p. 1570)
—Mystery Ranch Dubisch, Michael, illus. (p. 1571)
—Mystery Ranch (the Boxcar Children: Time to Read, Level 2) Clester, Shane, illus. (p. 1571)
—Pizza Mystery. Tang, Charles, illus. (p. 1752)
—Power down Mystery. VanArsdale, Anthony, illus. (p. 1782)
—Rancho Del Misterio (Mystery Ranch) (p. 1840)
—Robot Ransom. (p. 1892)
—Sea Turtle Mystery. (p. 1969)
—Secret on the Thirteenth Floor. VanArsdale, Anthony, illus. (p. 1978)
—Snowbound Mystery. Cunningham, David, illus. (p. 2048)
—Snowbound Mystery Dubisch, Mike, illus. (p. 2049)
—Snowbound Mystery. Dubisch, Mike, illus. (p. 2049)
—Star Stories for Little Folks (Classic Reprint) (p. 2103)
—Surprise Island. Gehr, Mary, illus. (p. 2163)
—Surprise Island (the Boxcar Children: Time to Read, Level 2) Clester, Shane, illus. (p. 2163)
—Tree House Mystery. Cunningham, David, illus. (p. 2284)
—Yellow House Mystery Dubisch, Mike, illus. (p. 2520)
—Yellow House Mystery Dubisch, Michael, illus. (p. 2520)
—Yellow House Mystery. Gehr, Mary, illus. (p. 2520)
—Yellow House Mystery (the Boxcar Children: Time to Read, Level 2) Clester, Shane, illus. (p. 2520)
Warner, Gertrude Chandler, jt. auth. see Denton, Shannon Eric.
Warner, Gertrude Chandler, jt. auth. see Dunn, Joeming.
Warner, Gertrude Chandler, jt. auth. see Long, Christopher E.
Warner, Gertrude Chandler, jt. auth. see Worley, Rob M.
Warner, Gertrude Chandler, creator. Boxcar Children (p. 266)
—Celebrity Cat Caper. (p. 350)
—Election Day Dilemma. (p. 631)
—Garden Thief. (p. 809)
—Ghost-Hunting Special. (p. 827)
—Haunted Legends Special. (p. 938)
—Hidden in the Haunted School. (p. 965)
—Legend of the Irish Castle. (p. 1262)
—Mystery at the Calgary Stampede. (p. 1568)
—Mystery of the Missing Pop Idol. (p. 1570)
—Mystery of the Stolen Dinosaur Bones. (p. 1570)
—Sleepy Hollow Mystery. (p. 2037)
Warner, H. H. Songs of the Spindle & Legends of the Loom: Selected & Arranged (Classic Reprint) (p. 2063)
Warner, Henry Edward. That House I Bought: A Little Leaf from Life (Classic Reprint) (p. 2212)
Warner, J. C., jt. auth. see Brandt, Daniel A.
Warner, J. F. Massachusetts. (p. 1417)
—Rhode Island. (p. 1875)
Warner, J. Franklin. Arctic: Or, the North Pole Expedition, in Three Acts (Classic Reprint) (p. 111)
Warner, Jeremy. Hidden Mickeys: A Mouse in the Land. Warner, Danielle, illus. (p. 966)
Warner, Jessica, illus. see Chiang, George.
Warner, Jody Nyasha. Viola Desmond Won't Be Budged! Rudnicki Rudnicki, Richard, illus. (p. 2359)
Warner, Katie. Father Ben Gets Ready for Mass. Whalen, Meg, illus. (p. 714)
—I Went to Mass: What Did I See? Whalen, Meg, illus. (p. 1085)
—Let Us Pray: A Child's First Book of Prayers. Whalen, Meg, illus. (p. 1269)
—Lily Lolek: Future Saint. (p. 1302)
Warner, Kelli. Moment We Fell. (p. 1490)
Warner, Kenneth Fisher. Farm & Home Visits: A Training Leaflet in Eight Parts (Classic Reprint) (p. 709)
Warner, Laverne, jt. auth. see Lynch, Sharon Ann.
Warner, Linda, illus. see Love, Pamela.
Warner, Matthew, tr. see CHIROLU.
Warner, Michael N. Tales to Make You Scream for Your Momma. Warner, Robert, illus. (p. 2186)
—Titanic Game. Ordaz, Frank, illus. (p. 2251)
Warner, Michelle L. Adventures of Tommy & Goldnugget. (p. 29)
Warner, Paula. Harry Grainger New Boy in High School. (p. 934)
Warner, Penny. Haunted Lighthouse (p. 938)
—Hunt for the Missing Spy. (p. 1053)
—Mummy's Curse. (p. 1526)
—Mystery of the Missing Mustangs. (p. 1570)
—Mystery of the Pirate's Treasure. (p. 1570)
—Secret of the Puzzle Box. (p. 1978)
—Secret of the Skeleton Key (p. 1978)
—Secret of the Skeleton Key. (p. 1978)
Warner Press. Agents of God Word Search Ittybitty Activity Book. (p. 35)
—a-Maze-Ing Christmas (8-10) (p. 2)
—Baby Moses (2-4) (p. 151)
—Bible Fun Dot-To-Dot (5-7) (p. 213)
—Bible Heroes Coloring Book. (p. 213)
—Bible Trips & Travelers. (p. 214)
—Bible Verses in Secret Code (8-10) (p. 214)
—C&a Bks Adv of David 6pk (p. 321)
—C&a Bks Armor God Lwr ELM 6pk (p. 321)
—C&a Bks Hidden Pict 6cy (p. 321)
—C&a Bks Jesus Is Born PS 6pk (p. 321)
—C&a Bks Jesus Is Friend PS 6pk (p. 321)
—C&a Bks Jesus Lvs Chldrn 6pk (p. 321)
—C&a Bks Sunny Xmas Lwr ELM 6pk (p. 321)
—C&a Bks the Bible Sys Wht 6cy. (p. 321)
—C&a Bks Xmas 1st Xmas 6pk (p. 321)
—C&a Bks Xmas CC Lower Elem 6pk (p. 321)
—Christmas Story (5-7) (p. 387)
—Coloring & Activity Book - a-Maze-Ing Bible Stories (8-10) 6-Pack Coloring & Activity Books. (p. 422)
—Coloring & Activity Book - Bible Story Dot-To-Dots (2-4) 6-Pack Coloring & Activity Books. (p. 422)
—Coloring & Activity Book - Maxine's Markers (2-4) 6-Pack Coloring & Activity Books. (p. 422)
—Coloring & Activity Book - My Favorite Bible Verses (5-7) 6-Pack Coloring & Activity Books. (p. 422)
—Coloring & Activity Book - Parables of Jesus (8-10) 6-Pack Coloring & Activity Books. (p. 422)
—Coloring & Activity Book - the Lord's Prayer (5-7) 6-Pack Coloring & Activity Books. (p. 422)
—Countdown to Xmas. (p. 459)
—Easter Coloring & Activity Book - Easter Fun (5-7) 6-Pack Coloring & Activity Books. (p. 619)
—Easter Coloring/Activity Book - Easter Hidden Pictures (8-10) 6-Pack Coloring & Activity Books. (p. 619)
—Easter Coloring/Activity Book - My Easter Pictures- (2-4) 6-Pack Coloring & Activity Books. (p. 619)
—Faith in Action 6pk: Word Search Puzzles from the Book of Acts. (p. 698)
—First Christmas (2-4) (p. 735)
—Get Ready for Christmas! Advent Activity Book-48 Pg. (p. 824)
—God Made Me Special (2-4) (p. 852)
—God Made the World Coloring & Activity Book. (p. 852)
—Happy Birthday, Jesus Coloring Book: Coloring Activity Books] Christmas—2-4. (p. 920)
—Iba Bk Xmas Wrd Srch Vol 2 6pk (p. 1087)
—If I Were a Butterfly: Coloring/Activity Book Ages 2-5. (p. 1091)
—It's Time for Christmas: Coloring Activity Books] Christmas—8-10. (p. 1148)
—Itty Bitty ACT Bk Aog 6pk (p. 1148)
—Itty Bitty Christmas. (p. 1149)
—Ittybitty Activity Book - Jelly Bean Prayer: 6-Pack Ittybitty Activity Books. (p. 1149)
—Ittybitty Activity Book - Psalms of David Word Search: 6-Pack Ittybitty Activity Books. (p. 1149)
—Itty-Bitty Christmas & Advent Activity Book. (p. 1149)
—Jesus & His Friends 6pk. (p. 1165)
—Jonah & the Big Fish (5-7) (p. 1177)
—Kids' All-Time Favorite Bible Stories: Itty-Bitty Bible Activity Book. (p. 1213)
—Let's Learn the Bible from Genesis to Revelation Puzzle Book 48pg. (p. 1274)
—Lord Is My Shepherd. (p. 1348)
—My Jumbo Bible Story Activity Book. (p. 1550)
—Nativity Color & Cut Out: Coloring Activity Books] Christmas—5-7. (p. 1579)
—New Testament Crossword Puzzles: Ittybitty Bible Activity Book (6pk) (p. 1597)
—New Testament Ittybitty Bible Activity Book 6pk (p. 1597)
—Noah & His Animal Friends: Itty-Bitty Bible Activity Book. (p. 1615)
—Old Testament Ittybitty Bible Activity Book 6pk. (p. 1648)
—Paul's Journeys Word Search Puzzles: Itty-Bitty Bible Activity Book. (p. 1708)
—Prodigal Son - Coloring & Activity Book. (p. 1804)
—Stories Jesus Told 6pk: Hidden Pictures. Ball, Liz, illus. (p. 2124)
—Too Little (Jesus Blesses Children) Coloring Book for Ages 2-5. (p. 2260)
—What Does Jesus Do? (8-10) (p. 2410)
—What Is Salvation? Activity Book. (p. 2416)
Warner Press, creator. Best Loved Bible Stories (p. 206)
—Coloring & Activity Book - Easter 2-4: He Loves You Jelly Bean Prayer Match U9215 Bk Mk the Jelly Bean Prayer Coloring Book. (p. 422)
—Coloring & Activity Book - Easter 5-7: Easter Color & Cut Out Activity Book. (p. 422)
—Coloring & Activity Book - Easter 8-10: A Joyful Easter Coloring & Activity Book. (p. 422)
—Coloring & Activity Book - Easter 8-10: Jesus Has Risen! Hidden Pictures Activity Book. (p. 422)
—Coloring Book - Easter 2-4: Jesus Lives! Easter Coloring Bk. (p. 422)
—Coloring Book - Easter 5-7: Jesus Is Our Savior Easter Coloring Bk. (p. 422)
—Fun Wth Hidden Pictures Activity Book. (p. 800)
—God Is So Good! Coloring Book 6pk: E4726. (p. 851)
—It Was So Yucky 6pk Coloring Bk: Coloring Book about Paul & Silas. (p. 1142)
—Itty Bit - Gen: Salvation Activity Book. (p. 1148)
—Itty Bitty - Easter: Easter Week Word Puzzle Book. (p. 1148)
—My Favorite Bible Stories Coloring Book. (p. 1539)
—New Testament Word Search Puzzles (p. 1597)
—Ten Commandments Activity Book. (p. 2203)
—Ten Commandments Coloring Book. (p. 2203)
—Zacchaeus Climbs a Tree Coloring Book. (p. 2537)
Warner Press Kids, creator. Jelly Bean Prayer Coloring & Activity Book. (p. 1163)
—Jelly Bean Witness. (p. 1163)
Warner, Richmond. Bel & the Kittens. (p. 195)
—Green Children. (p. 893)
Warner, Robert, illus. see Warner, Michael N.
Warner, Roxie & Warner, Christian. Land of the Free, A to Z. Schartup, Adam, illus. (p. 1242)
Warner, Sally. Absolutely Alfie & the First Week Friends. Malone, Shearry, illus. (p. 9)
—Absolutely Alfie & the Furry, Purry Secret. Malone, Shearry, illus. (p. 9)
—Absolutely Alfie & the Princess Wars Malone, Shearry, illus. (p. 9)
—Absolutely Alfie & the Princess Wars. Malone, Shearry, illus. (p. 9)
—Absolutely Alfie & the Worst Best Sleepover. (p. 9)
—Absolutely Alfie & the Worst Best Sleepover. Malone, Shearry, illus. (p. 9)
—EllRay Jakes & the Beanstalk. (p. 638)
—EllRay Jakes & the Beanstalk. Biggs, Brian, illus. (p. 638)
—EllRay Jakes Is a Rock Star Harper, Jamie, illus. (p. 638)

W

Washburne, Sophie. African American Inventors: Overcoming Challenges to Change America. (p. 32)
—Alternative Energy Sources: The End of Fossil Fuels? (p. 60)
—American Revolution (p. 73)
—Clues in Corpses: A Closer Look at Body Farms. (p. 409)
—Should Kids Get an Allowance? (p. 2011)
Washburne, Sophie & Sheen, Barbara. Steve Jobs: Computer Visionary. (p. 2116)
Washington. Jack the Boogey Is My Real Name: The Truth about the Boogeyman. (p. 1153)
Washington, Andre & Washington, Angela. Donovan & Winslow in Obey Your Parents. (p. 582)
Washington, Angel D. Always Remember You Are Loved: When a Child Seeks Guidance on Cyber & Peer Bullying. Perry, Curtis, illus. (p. 61)
Washington, Beatrice. Story of Juliette: A Child's Romance (Classic Reprint) (p. 2131)
—Story of Juliette. (p. 2131)
Washington, Booker T. Up from Slavery: Collector's Edition. (p. 2337)
Washington, C. E., illus. see Washington, Ida H.
Washington, Danny. Funny & Wild Adventures of Mr. Stubstitute the Substitute. (p. 801)
Washington, Donna, jt. auth. see Washington, Donna L.
Washington, Donna L. Li'l Rabbit's Kwanzaa. Evans, Shane W., illus. (p. 1301)
Washington, George. Diary of George Washington: September-December, 1785 (Classic Reprint) (p. 540)
Washington, James Madison. How Beauty Was Saved: And Other Memories of the Sixties (Classic Reprint) (p. 1026)
Washington, Janae. Bye Bye Black Skin. (p. 306)
—Dad Assignment. (p. 494)
Washington, Janice Blue. Princess Alyssa's Big Birthday Party. (p. 1795)
Washington, Janice Hutto. Half a Rabbit. (p. 910)
—Half a Rabbit. Linen, Mark, illus. (p. 910)
Washington, Joi. Ant. (p. 101)
—Ants. (p. 103)
—Dragonflies. (p. 595)
—Dragonfly. (p. 595)
—Jumping Spiders. (p. 1189)
—Mantises. (p. 1399)
—Pink Book. (p. 1746)
—Pink Book. Washington, Joi, illus. (p. 1746)
—Robber Flies. (p. 1889)
—Wasp. (p. 2382)
—Wasps. (p. 2382)
—Wolf Spider. (p. 2484)
Washington, Joi, illus. see Fleischer, Jayson.
Washington, Joi, illus. see Lynch, Michelle.
Washington, Joi, illus. see Taylor, Trace, et al.
Washington, Joi, jt. auth. see Dibble, Traci.
Washington, Joi, jt. auth. see Sánchez, Lucía M.
Washington, Joi & Byerly, Robbie. Ants. Byerly, Robbie, illus. (p. 103)
Washington, Joi & Dibble, Traci. Robber Flies. Dibble, Traci, illus. (p. 1889)
Washington, Joi & Fleischer, Jayson. These Are Wolves. (p. 2219)
Washington, Joi & Sanchez, Lucia M. AraÑAs Saltadoras: Jumping Spiders. (p. 109)
—Avispas: Wasps. (p. 143)
Washington, Joi & Sánchez, Lucía M. Las Mantis: Mantises. (p. 1246)
Washington, Joi & Sanchez, Lucia M. Las Mantis (Mantises) (p. 1246)
Washington, Joi, et al. Hormigas: Ants. (p. 1003)
—Moscas Predadoras. (p. 1507)
Washington, Jordan Caleb, illus. see Ag, Tarsha M. Washington Illustrations B.
Washington, Kathy. Three Colors of Katie. Farina, Kathy, illus. (p. 2232)
Washington, LaVonne & Washington, LaShawn. Parables of Humpty Dumpty: Volume 1. (p. 1698)
Washington, Linda. Children of the World Storybook Bible. (p. 372)
Washington, Linda D. Mommy I Don't Want to Die! (p. 1491)
Washington, Maryam. Careers for Tech Girls in Web Development. (p. 329)
Washington Sr., Terence B. Terry, Bear & Duck (p. 2208)
Washington, Tanya. Battle Is the Lord's- David & Goliath. (p. 174)
—Fear Not - Daniel & the Lions' Den. (p. 716)
—In All Things Give Thanks. (p. 1104)
Washington, University of Mary. Battlefield, 1914 (Classic Reprint) (p. 175)
—Battlefield, 1915 (Classic Reprint) (p. 175)
—Battlefield, 1915-1916 (Classic Reprint) (p. 175)
—Battlefield 1921: State Normal School for Women (Classic Reprint) (p. 175)
—Battlefield, 1922 (Classic Reprint) (p. 175)
—Battlefield, 1927 (Classic Reprint) (p. 175)
—Thw Battlefield (Classic Reprint) (p. 2239)
Washington, Victoria, ed. see Du Lac, Leo J.
Washington, Victoria, ed. see Young, T. M.
Wasiak, Maria. Mango, the Scaredy Bat. Wasiak, Maria, illus. (p. 1397)
Wasielewski, Margaret, illus. see Markarian, Marianne.
Wasielewski, Margaret M., illus. see Markarian, Marianne.
Wasikhongo, Odalo Magruder. My First Book of Numbers. Wasikhongo, Odalo Magruder, illus. (p. 1542)
Wasko, Denise. Roxy Remembers. (p. 1909)
Wasley, S. D. Deluge. (p. 527)
—Strange Truths. (p. 2138)
Wasmann, Erich. Vergleichende Studien Ber das Seelenleben der Ameisen und der Hhern Thiere (Classic Reprint) (p. 2351)
—Vergleichende Studien Uber das Seelenleben der Ameisen und der Hohern Thiere (Classic Reprint) (p. 2351)
Wason, Rigby. Some Volunteer Verse (Classic Reprint) (p. 2059)
Wason, Robert Alex. Knight-Errant a Novel of to-Day (Classic Reprint) (p. 1228)
—Steering Wheel (Classic Reprint) (p. 2112)
Wason, Robert Alexander. And Then Came Jean: A Novel (Classic Reprint) (p. 83)
—Dog & the Child & the Ancient Sailor Man. (p. 575)
—Dog & the Child & the Ancient Sailor Man (Classic Reprint) (p. 575)
—Friar Tuck: Being the Chronicles of the Reverend John Carmichael, of Wyoming, U. S. an;, As Set Forth & Embellished by His Friend & Admirer; Happy Hawkins (Classic Reprint) (p. 785)
—Happy Hawkins (Classic Reprint) (p. 922)
—Knight-Errant: A Novel of to-Day (Classic Reprint) (p. 1228)
Wasowicz, Pawel, illus. see Koons, Linda.
Wass, Chip, illus. see Capote, Lori.
Wass, Chip, illus. see Doherty, Kathleen.
Wass, Eliza. Cresswell Plot. (p. 473)
—Life & Death Parade. (p. 1289)
Wassel, Adrian F., ed. see Rebmann, Chad & Nicholas, Matt.
Wassel, Adrian F., ed. see Tsuei, Jon.
Wasserman, Eleanor B. Linda (Classic Reprint) (p. 1303)
Wasserman, Michelle. Dancing Tree. (p. 500)
Wasserman, Robin. Book of Blood & Shadow. (p. 258)
—Crashed. (p. 467)
—Frozen. (p. 795)
—Game of Flames: Voyagers. (p. 807)
—Life, Starring Me! (p. 1296)
—Lumen. un Secret Enfoui Depuis Cinq Si'cles Ressurgit. (p. 1368)
—Scooby-Doo & the Missing Scooby-Snacks Sur, Duendes del, illus. (p. 1960)
—Scooby-Doo & the Snow Monster Scare Sur, Duendes del, illus. (p. 1960)
—Search for Scooby Snacks Sur, Duendes Del, illus. (p. 1971)
—Seven Deadly Sins Vol. 1: Lust; Envy. (p. 1993)
—Seven Deadly Sins Vol. 2: Pride; Wrath. Vol. 2 (p. 1993)
—Seven Deadly Sins Vol. 3: Sloth; Gluttony; Greed. Vol. 3 (p. 1993)
—Shattered. (p. 2003)
—Torn. (p. 2265)
—Waking Dark. (p. 2371)
—Wired. (p. 2477)
Wasserman, Robin, jt. auth. see Soderberg, Erin.
Wasserman, Robin & Carman, Patrick. Voyagers Mission Launch (p. 2368)
Wasserman, S. Paragon Expedition. (p. 1699)
Wasserman, Sand. Sun's Special Blessing: Happens Only Once in 28 Years - HC. Koffsky, Ann, illus. (p. 2153)
—Sun's Special Blessing: Happens Only Once in 28 Years - French Flap. Koffsky, Ann, illus. (p. 2153)
Wassermann, Jacob. World's Illusion, Vol. 1: Eva (Classic Reprint) (p. 2507)
Wassermann, Jakob. Goose Man (Classic Reprint) (p. 869)
—World's Illusion (Classic Reprint) (p. 2507)
Wasserstrom, Randy. Finding God in North Carolina (Classic Reprint) (p. 729)
Wassmann, Marilyn B. What the Wind Blew In: 6 Stories to Read with Children (New Edition) (p. 2420)
Wassmer, J. Smudge. (p. 2043)
Wasson, Dave. Big Ideas of Buster Bickles. Wasson, Dave, illus. (p. 221)
Wasson, Dianne. Learning to Dance on My Daddy's Shoes. (p. 1258)
Wasson, George S. Home from Sea (Classic Reprint) (p. 996)
Wastasecoot, Brenda Isabel. Granny's Giant Bannock McKay-Fleming, Kimberly, illus. (p. 880)
Wasvary, Marcia, illus. see George, Francis.
Watami. Female Force: Mother Teresa- a Graphic Novel. Davis, Darren, ed. (p. 719)
Watanabe, Bryce, illus. see Kapaona, Alyssa.
Watanabe, Chinatsu. Magic Cooking. (p. 1377)
—Magic Rainbow. (p. 1378)
Watanabe, Kaori, illus. see Grace, Will.
Watanabe, Kaori, illus. see Michalak, Jamie.
Watanabe, Lynne M. Squirrels. (p. 2095)
Watanabe, Rui, illus. see Mashima, Hiro.
Watanabe, Wataru. Yowamushi Pedal, Vol. 7. (p. 2536)
Watanabe-Rocco, Sarah, illus. see Berger, Melvin & Berger, Gilda.
Watanna, Onoto. Daughters of Nijo: A Romance of Japan (Classic Reprint) (p. 509)
—Heart of Hyacinth (Classic Reprint) (p. 945)
—Honorable Miss. Moonlight (Classic Reprint) (p. 1000)
—Japanese Blossom (Classic Reprint) (p. 1159)
—Japanese Nightingale (Classic Reprint) (p. 1160)
—Miss Numè of Japan. (p. 1479)
—Miss Numè of Japan; A Japanese-American Romance. (p. 1479)
—Miss. Nume of Japan: A Japanese-American Romance (Classic Reprint) (p. 1479)
—Sunny-San (Classic Reprint) (p. 2152)
—Tama (Classic Reprint) (p. 2188)
Watari, Wataru. My Youth Romantic Comedy Is Wrong, As I Expected, Vol. 1 (light Novel) (p. 1565)
Watchorn, Sara. Sara Fay & the Elementals: Book 5: Quazzie & the Rock Kingdom. Watchorn, Sara, illus. (p. 1935)
—Sara Fay & the Elementals: Book 5: Quest & Meditation Journal. Watchorn, Sara, illus. (p. 1935)
Water, Virginia Terhune Van De. In the Web of Life (Classic Reprint) (p. 1111)
—Two Sisters (Classic Reprint) (p. 2309)
—Why I Left My Husband: And Other Human Documents of Married Life (Classic Reprint) (p. 2458)
Waterbury, M. Seven Years among the Freedmen (Classic Reprint) (p. 1994)
Waterbury, Mary F. Light for Little Ones (Classic Reprint) (p. 1298)
Waterbury, Matthew. Little Pig. Muro, Jenny, illus. (p. 1324)
Waterbury, Norma Rose. Around the World with Jack & Janet: A Study of Missions (Classic Reprint) (p. 119)
Waterbury, Ruth. Photoplay, 1937, Vol. 51 (Classic Reprint) (p. 1737)
—Photoplay, Vol. 49: January June, 1936 (Classic Reprint) (p. 1737)
—Photoplay, Vol. 50: July, 1936 (Classic Reprint) (p. 1737)
—Silver Screen, Vol. 1: November, Nineteen Thirty (Classic Reprint) (p. 2019)
Waterby, Ralph. Muscogee (Creek) (p. 1528)
Waterfield, Kathryn, et al. Who Was Alexander the Great? Thomson, Andrew, illus. (p. 2450)
Waterfield, Sarah, illus. see Brown, Beatrice.
Waterfield, Sarah, illus. see Gothard, Nicola.
Waterfield, Susan. Spunkie's Magical Garden. (p. 2093)
Waterford, Cliff. Hurricane Harvey. (p. 1054)
Waterford Press Staff, jt. auth. see Kavanagh, James.
Waterhouse, J. H. L. New Britain Phrase Book (Classic Reprint) (p. 1591)
Waterhouse, Stephen, illus. see Ganeri, Anita.
Watering-Places, English. Love Stories of the English Watering-Places, Vol. 1 of 3 (Classic Reprint) (p. 1361)
Waterkeyn, Lana, illus. see Vort, Carl.
Waterloo, Stanley. Cassowary: What Chanced in the Cleft Mountains (Classic Reprint) (p. 339)
—How It Looks (Classic Reprint) (p. 1032)
—Launching of a Man (Classic Reprint) (p. 1252)
—Odd Situation (Classic Reprint) (p. 1637)
—Son of the Ages: The Reincarnations & Adventures of Scar, the Link (Classic Reprint) (p. 2062)
—Story of AB: A Tale of the Time of the Cave Man. (p. 2128)
—Story of AB: A Tale of the Stone Age (Classic Reprint) (p. 2128)
—Story of AB: A Tale of the Time, of the Cave Man (Classic Reprint) (p. 2128)
—Story of Ab. (p. 2128)
—Wolf's Long Howl (Classic Reprint) (p. 2484)
Waterman, A. N. Century of Caste (Classic Reprint) (p. 352)
Waterman, Jill & Walker, Elizabeth. Helping At-Risk Students: A Group Counselling Approach for Grades 6-9. (p. 953)
Waterman, Nixon. Boy Wanted: A Book of Cheerful Counsel (Classic Reprint) (p. 270)
Watermark Rights Limited, illus. see Huntley, Tex.
Watermark Rights Limited, illus. see Tillworth, Mary.
Waters. Through Grace & Mercy, I Made It Out Against All Odds. (p. 2236)
Waters, Alice. Fanny in France: With French Adventures & French Recipes. Arnold, Ann, illus. (p. 706)
Waters, Alice, illus. see Coren, Giles.
Waters, Alyson, tr. see Hong, Chen Jiang.
Waters, Alyson, tr. see Ponti, Claude.
Waters, Bella. Zambia in Pictures. (p. 2538)
Waters, Bernard. Modern Training & Handling. (p. 1488)
Waters, Beth. Child of St Kilda. Waters, Beth, illus. (p. 370)
Waters, Cassie. Cool Down. (p. 448)
—Dive In! (p. 565)
—Heat Wave. (p. 946)
Waters, Charles, jt. auth. see Latham, Irene.
Waters, Charles & Latham, Irene. Can I Touch Your Hair? Poems of Race, Mistakes, & Friendship. Alko, Selina & Qualls, Sean, illus. (p. 317)
Waters, Daniel. Break My Heart 1,000 Times. (p. 277)
—Kiss of Life. (p. 1224)
Waters, De. Glad Tidings (Classic Reprint) (p. 840)
Waters, Elizur W. Journal of Incidents Connected with the Travels of the Twenty-Second Regiment Conn; Volunteers: For Nine Months, in Verse by an Orderly Sergeant (Classic Reprint) (p. 1180)
Waters, Erica. Ghost Wood Song. (p. 828)
Waters, Erica-Jane. If the Hat Fits. Waters, Erica-Jane, illus. (p. 1092)
—Light As a Feather. Waters, Erica-Jane, illus. (p. 1298)
—Penny for Your Thoughts. Waters, Erica-Jane, illus. (p. 1717)
—Petticoat Pirates: The Mermaids of Starfish Reef. (p. 1731)
Waters, Erica-Jane, illus. see Guillian, Adam, et al.
Waters, Erica-Jane, illus. see Jakubowski, Michele.
Waters, Erica-Jane, illus. see Lewis, Jill & Blue Bananas.
Waters, Erica-Jane, illus. see Meister, Cari.
Waters, Erica-Jane, illus. see Milbourne, Anna.
Waters, Erica-Jane, illus. see Perelman, Helen.
Waters, Erica-Jane, illus. see Press, Judy.
Waters, Erica-Jane, illus. see Tiger Tales.
Waters, Erica-Jane, jt. auth. see Waters, Erica-Jane.
Waters, Erica-Jane & Waters, Erica-Jane. Light As a Feather. Waters, Erica-Jane, illus. (p. 1298)
Waters, Fiona. Aesop's Forgotten Fables. Testa, Fulvio, illus. (p. 31)
Waters, Fiona, ed. see Crow, Nosy.
Waters, Fiona, ed. see Testa, Fulvio, et al.
Waters, Fiona, illus. see Hall, Amanda.
Waters, Galadriel, ed. Plot Thickens... Harry Potter Investigated by Fans for Fans. Rogers, Melissa & Heran, Michelle, illus. (p. 1763)
Waters, Ginny B. Miracle House. (p. 1474)
Waters, Grace, jt. auth. see Mills, Nathan.
Waters, Jacob. Adventures of Spot the Pig. (p. 28)
Waters, Jennifer. Todo Tipo de Movimiento. (p. 2256)
Waters, John F. Sharks Have Six Senses. Barner, Bob, illus. (p. 2002)
Waters, Kate. Curious about Fossils. (p. 486)
—Curious about the White House. (p. 486)
—Curious about Worms. (p. 486)
—Monarch Butterflies. (p. 1492)
—Ocean Giants. (p. 1635)
—Penguins. (p. 1716)
Waters, Kathleen. My Favorite Place to Be. (p. 1539)
Waters, Lilly. Hurry Harry! Hurry! Quinn, Valerie, illus. (p. 1055)
Waters, Michael. Tommy & his Flying Saucer of Milk. (p. 2259)
Waters, Rod. Eric's Big Day: A Bicycle Race Unlike Any Other. (p. 659)
Waters, Rosa. Anger. Croft, Cindy, ed. (p. 86)
—Emotional Self-Awareness. (p. 644)
—Empathy & Compassion. Croft, Cindy, ed. (p. 644)
—Instagram: How Kevin Systrom & Mike Krieger Changed the Way We Take & Share Photos. (p. 1125)
—Legal & Developmental Consequences. Borus, Joshua, ed. (p. 1261)
—Marijuana: Legal & Developmental Consequences. Borus, Joshua, ed. (p. 1405)
—Methamphetamine & Other Amphetamines. Borus, Joshua, ed. (p. 1453)
—My Daily Diet: Dairy. (p. 1536)
—My Daily Diet: Fruits. Prock, Lisa Albers, ed. (p. 1536)
—My Daily Diet: Grains. Prock, Lisa Albers, ed. (p. 1536)
—Over-The-Counter Medications. Borus, Joshua, ed. (p. 1686)
—Oxycontin(r), Percocet(r), Vicodin(r), & Other Addictive Analgesics. Borus, Joshua, ed. (p. 1690)
—Pinterest(r): How Ben Silbermann & Evan Sharp Changed the Way We Share What We Love. (p. 1747)
—Ritalin(r), Adderall(r), & Other Addictive Stimulants. Borus, Joshua, ed. (p. 1886)
—Stress & Tension. Croft, Cindy, ed. (p. 2140)
—Surprise & Flexibility. Croft, Cindy, ed. (p. 2163)
—Yung Joc. (p. 2537)
Waters, Russell Judson. Estranjero: The Stranger; a Story of Southern California (Classic Reprint) (p. 665)
Waters, Ruth, illus. see Masson, Sophie.
Waters, Summer. High Tide (Silver Dolphins, Book 9) (p. 969)
—Rising Star. (p. 1886)
—River Rescue (Silver Dolphins, Book 10) (p. 1887)
—Stormy Skies (Silver Dolphins, Book 8) (p. 2127)
Waters, Susy Pilgrim, illus. see Vander Pluym, Andrea.
Waters, Tawni. Beauty of the Broken. (p. 185)
—Long Ride Home. (p. 1343)
Waters, Thomas. Recollections of a Policeman (Classic Reprint) (p. 1854)
Waters, Todd. Cuenta la Historia de la Quiropractica. (p. 483)
Waters, Treea Forest. Earth School: Making the World a Better Place. (p. 617)
Waters, W. G. Italian Novelists, Vol. 1 (Classic Reprint) (p. 1142)
Waterston, Elizabeth, ed. see Montgomery, L. M.
Waterton, Betty. Salmon for Simon Blades, Ann, illus. (p. 1925)
Waterton, Charles. Essays on Natural History: Chiefly Ornithology (Classic Reprint) (p. 663)
—Essays on Natural History (Classic Reprint) (p. 663)
—Essays on Natural History, Chiefly Ornithology - Scholar's Choice Edition. (p. 663)
—Wanderings in South America: The North-West of the United States & the Antilles in the Years 1812, 1816, 1820 & 1824 (Classic Reprint) (p. 2375)
—Wanderings in South America: The North-West of the United States & the Antilles in the Years 1812, 1816, 1820, & 1824; with Original Instructions for the Perfect Preservation of Birds, etc. for Cabinets of Natural History (Classic Reprint) (p. 2375)
—Wanderings in South America: The North-West of the United States, & the Antilles, in the Years 1812, 1816, 1820, & 1824; with Original Instructions for the Perfect Preservation of Birds, etc; for Cabinets of Natural History (Classic Reprint) (p. 2375)
Watkin, Vikki. Yala & Sunnie Meet Sam: A Gender Neutral Story in a New Age World. DuBois, Marc, illus. (p. 2517)
Watkins, Abbey, illus. see Hurley, Tonya.
Watkins, Adam, illus. see Loewen, Nancy.
Watkins, Adam F. R Is for Robot: A Noisy Alphabet. Watkins, Adam F., illus. (p. 1829)
—Raybot. Watkins, Adam F., illus. (p. 1844)
Watkins, Amanda Lee, illus. see Hunter, Larisa C. & Haseleu, N. L.
Watkins, Angela Farris. Love Will See You Through: Martin Luther King Jr. 's Six Guiding Beliefs (as Told by His Niece) Comport, Sally Wern, illus. (p. 1361)
—My Uncle Martin's Big Heart. Velasquez, Eric, illus. (p. 1563)
—My Uncle Martin's Words for America: Martin Luther King Jr. 's Niece Tells How He Made a Difference. Velasquez, Eric, illus. (p. 1563)
Watkins, Ben. Complete Choctaw Definer: English with Choctaw Definition (Classic Reprint) (p. 434)
—Complete Choctaw Definer. (p. 434)
Watkins, Caroline. Giraccula Tuchman, Mark, illus. (p. 834)
Watkins, Caroline, ed. see Rose, Deborah Lee.
Watkins, Carolyn. Knock: A Collection of Childhood Memories. Erickson, Lindsey, illus. (p. 1229)
Watkins, Christine. Biological Warfare. (p. 229)
Watkins, Christine, ed. see Haugen, David M.
Watkins, Christine, ed. see Haugen, David.
Watkins, Christine, jt. ed. see Greenhaven Press Editors.
Watkins, Christine, ed. Alcohol Abuse. (p. 41)
—Are Adoption Policies Fair? (p. 112)
—Ethics of Capital Punishment. (p. 666)
—Is Selling Body Parts Ethical? (p. 1137)
—Sports & Athletes (p. 2088)
Watkins, Courtney. Dream It! Draw It! Think It! Do It! Activities to Spark Creative Adventures. (p. 601)
Watkins, Dwight Everett. Freddie Goes to College (Classic Reprint) (p. 781)
Watkins, Elaine. Billy Bobbin at Mystery Farm. (p. 227)
—Tornado Nine. (p. 2265)
Watkins, Eleanor. Wind of Change. (p. 2471)
Watkins, Essence, jt. auth. see Watkins, Schertevear Q.
Watkins, Francis. Popular Sketch of Electro-Magnetism, or Electro-Dynamics: With Plates of the Most Approved Apparatus for Illustrating the Principal Phenomena of the Science, & Outlines of the Parent Sciences Electricity & Magnetism (Classic Reprint) (p. 1777)
—Popular Sketch of Electro-Magnetism, or Electro-Dynamics. (p. 1777)
Watkins, Fred L. Sue, Mary & Charles (p. 2147)
Watkins, Gwen. Trip. (p. 2288)
Watkins, Harry. Ups & Downs: Of an Ill-Spent Life (Classic Reprint) (p. 2339)
Watkins, Heidi, ed. Dropping Out of School. (p. 605)
—Homeschooling. (p. 998)
Watkins, [James Andrew]. Watkins Brothers' Repertoire: The Power of Expression, or Life in Action (Classic Reprint) (p. 2386)
Watkins, Joe E. Story of the Choctaw Indians: From the Past to the Present (p. 2133)
Watkins, John. Magic Frisbee. (p. 1377)
Watkins, Kathleen. Pigín of Howth. Suggs, Margaret Anne, illus. (p. 1743)
Watkins, Katy. Baptism Is a Promise (a Choose-The-Light Book) (p. 164)
Watkins, Laura, illus. see David, Donna.

W

Watson, Stephanie Elaine. Elvis & Olive: Super Detectives. (p. 640)
Watson, Sydney. In the Twinkling of an Eye (Classic Reprint) (p. 1111)
—Life's Look Out: An Autobiography (Classic Reprint) (p. 1297)
—Life's Look Out. (p. 1297)
Watson, T. E. Going West / the Pioneer Journey: Going to California. (p. 855)
—Mom Can I Have a Dragon? Ferchaud, Steve, illus. (p. 1490)
—Mountain. Ferchaud, Steve, illus. (p. 1513)
Watson, Tammy. Growing up Down's. (p. 900)
Watson, Terry H. Clock That Lost Its Tick & Other Tales. Freeman, Lynda, illus. (p. 406)
Watson, Thomas E. Bethany: A Story of the Old South (Classic Reprint) (p. 208)
—Tom Watson's Magazine for April (Classic Reprint) (p. 2258)
—Watson's Jeffersonian Magazine, Vol. 2: April, 1908 (Classic Reprint) (p. 2386)
Watson, Thomas Edward. Tom Watson's Magazine, Vol. 1: April, 1905 (Classic Reprint) (p. 2258)
Watson, Thos. E. Prose Miscellanie (Classic Reprint) (p. 1807)
—Watson's Jeffersonian Magazine, Vol. 1: December, 1907 (Classic Reprint) (p. 2386)
—Watson's Jeffersonian Magazine, Vol. 5: December, 1910 (Classic Reprint) (p. 2386)
Watson, Tom. Stick Cat: A Tail of Two Kitties. (p. 2117)
—Stick Cat: Cats in the City. (p. 2117)
—Stick Cat: Two Catch a Thief. (p. 2117)
—Stick Cat: Two Cats & a Baby. (p. 2117)
—Stick Cat: Two Cats to the Rescue. (p. 2117)
—Stick Dog. (p. 2117)
—Stick Dog Box Set: Two Servings of Stick Dog: Stick Dog & Stick Dog Wants a Hot Dog. (p. 2117)
—Stick Dog Chases a Pizza. (p. 2117)
—Stick Dog Crashes a Party. (p. 2117)
—Stick Dog Craves Candy. (p. 2117)
—Stick Dog Dreams of Ice Cream. (p. 2117)
—Stick Dog Gets the Tacos. (p. 2117)
—Stick Dog Meets His Match. (p. 2117)
—Stick Dog Slurps Spaghetti. (p. 2117)
—Stick Dog Tries to Take the Donuts. (p. 2117)
—Stick Dog Wants a Hot Dog. (p. 2117)
—Stick Dog Wants a Hot Dog. Long, Ethan, illus. (p. 2117)
—Trouble at Table 5 #1: the Candy Caper. Kissi, Marta, illus. (p. 2291)
—Trouble at Table 5 #2: Busted by Breakfast. Kissi, Marta, illus. (p. 2291)
—Trouble at Table 5 #3: the Firefly Fix. (p. 2291)
Watson, Tom & Long, Ethan. Stick Dog Dreams of Ice Cream. (p. 2117)
—Stick Dog Slurps Spaghetti. (p. 2117)
Watson, Vicki. Bob & the Alien Escapade. (p. 251)
—History on Horseback the Early Years: 1493 To 1866. (p. 981)
Watson, Virginia. Princess Pocahontas. (p. 1798)
—Princess Pocahontas (Classic Reprint) (p. 1798)
Watson, W. H. L. Adventures of a Despatch Rider (Classic Reprint) (p. 21)
Watson, Walker, jt. auth. see Youatt, William.
Watson, Wayne. I'm a Leader Now. Gourdeau, Brigitte, illus. (p. 1097)
—Je Suis un Leader, Mamie. Gourdeau, Brigitte, illus. (p. 1162)
Watson, Wendy. Bedtime Bunnies (padded Board Book) (p. 188)
Watson, William. Wordsworth's Grave & Other Poems. (p. 2495)
—Wordsworth's Grave, & Other Poems. (p. 2495)
Watson, William Davy. Trevethlan, Vol. 1 Of 3: A Cornish Story (Classic Reprint) (p. 2285)
—Trevethlan, Vol. 2 Of 3: A Cornish Story (Classic Reprint) (p. 2285)
—Trevethlan, Vol. 3 Of 3: A Cornish Story (Classic Reprint) (p. 2285)
Watson-Doost, Valeria. Issa. (p. 1141)
Watt, Agnes Craig Paterson. Agnes C. P. Watt: Twenty-Five Years' Mission Life on Tanna, New Hebrides (Classic Reprint) (p. 35)
Watt, Andy, illus. see Thompson, Elisabeth C.
Watt, Charles. Chemist, or Reporter of Chemical Discoveries & Improvements, & Protector of the Rights of the Chemist & Chemical Manufacturer, Vol. 6 (Classic Reprint) (p. 365)
Watt, Coulter, illus. see Ward, L. B. B.
Watt, D. Healing the Temple of the Soul. (p. 943)
Watt, E. Melanie. Giraffes. (p. 834)
—Leatherback Turtles, with Code. (p. 1259)
—Tigers. (p. 2242)
Watt, Erin. Broken Prince: A Novel. (p. 285)
—Cracked Kingdom. (p. 466)
—One Small Thing. (p. 1662)
—Paper Princess: A Novel. (p. 1697)
—Twisted Palace: A Novel. (p. 2306)
Watt, F., jt. auth. see Gibson, R.
Watt, F., jt. auth. see Watt, Fiona.
Watt, Fiona. 365 Things to Draw & Paint. (p. 2560)
—ABC. Elkerton, Andy, illus. (p. 3)
—Animals Magic Painting Book. (p. 95)
—Baby's First Christmas. (p. 154)
—Baby's Very First Book of Little Babies. (p. 154)
—Baby's Very First Little Touchy-Feely Play Book. (p. 154)
—Baby's Very First Noisy Book Jungle. (p. 154)
—Baby's Very First Slide & See Animals. (p. 154)
—Baby's Very First Slide & See under the Sea. (p. 154)
—Baby's Very First Word Book. (p. 154)
—Bats: Internet- Referenced. (p. 173)
—Bébé Toca y Habla Animales(Baby's Very First Play Book Animals Words) (p. 186)
—Beep Beep. (p. 189)
—Big Dinosaur Sticker Book. (p. 219)
—Big Doodling Book. (p. 219)
—Big Drawing Book. Thompson, Josephine & Day, Caroline, illus. (p. 219)
—Busy Bug Book. Mantle, Ben, illus. (p. 302)
—Busy Helicopter Book. (p. 302)
—Busy Santa Book. (p. 302)
—Cars. (p. 334)
—Choo Choo. (p. 381)
—Christmas Decorations to Cut, Fold & Stick. (p. 385)
—Christmas Doodles. (p. 385)
—Christmas Magic Painting Book. (p. 386)
—Christmas Things to Draw. (p. 387)
—Complete Book of First Experiences. (p. 434)
—Cut-Out Paper Dolls. (p. 491)
—Dinosaur Fun. Lovell, Katie, illus. (p. 549)
—Drawing, Doodling & Coloring Fashion. Miller, Antonia, illus. (p. 599)
—Easter Fun. (p. 620)
—Esta No Es Mi Sirenita(That's Not My Mermaid) (p. 664)
—Éste No Es Mi Dinosaurio(That's Not My Dinosaur) (p. 664)
—Éste No Es Mi Perrito... (That's Not My Puppy) (p. 664)
—Este No Es Mi Tren(That's Not My Train) (p. 664)
—Farm Stroller Book. Baggott, Stella, illus. (p. 710)
—Fashion Designer Summer Collection. Baggott, Stella & Miller, Antonia, illus. (p. 712)
—Fingerprint Activities. (p. 731)
—Fingerprint Activities Backyard. (p. 731)
—Fingerprint Activities Christmas. (p. 731)
—Fingerprint Activities under the Sea. (p. 731)
—Go to Sleep Little Baby. Watt, Fiona, illus. (p. 848)
—Halloween Magic Painting. (p. 912)
—Jungle. Elkerton, Andy, illus. (p. 1189)
—Little Children's Christmas Music Book. (p. 1313)
—Little Children's Music Book. (p. 1313)
—Little Sticker Dolly Dressing Christmas. (p. 1328)
—Little Sticker Dolly Dressing Kittens. (p. 1328)
—Little Sticker Dolly Dressing Pixies. (p. 1328)
—Little Sticker Dolly Dressing Snow White. (p. 1328)
—Lots of Things to Draw. (p. 1356)
—Lots of Things to Find & Color. (p. 1356)
—Mermaids Magic Painting Book. (p. 1449)
—Mi Primer Toca, Toca Animales(Baby's Very 1St Touchy-Feely Animals) (p. 1456)
—Monster Doodles. (p. 1495)
—Nursery Rhymes Touchy-Feely Board Book. Meyer, Kerry, illus. (p. 1631)
—Nutcracker Sound Book. (p. 1632)
—Penguins Luxury Touchy-Feely Board Book. (p. 1716)
—Pequeñines Curiosos Veo, Veo en la Calle(Very 1St Bk Things to Spot Out & About) (p. 1720)
—Pequeñines Curiosos Veo, Veo Por Casa(Very 1St Bk Things to Spot at Home) (p. 1720)
—Pequeñines Curiosos Veo, Veo(Very 1St Bk Things to Spot) (p. 1720)
—Pirate Sticker Book. Nichols, Paul, illus. (p. 1750)
—Planes: Internet-Referenced. (p. 1754)
—Polar Bears. Chiara, Francesca De, illus. (p. 1769)
—Pop-Up Christmas. (p. 1775)
—Pull-Back Busy Train. Field, Jim, illus. (p. 1812)
—Rainy Day Stroller Book. Baggott, Stella, illus. (p. 1837)
—Rubber Stamp Activities. (p. 1911)
—Rubber Stamp Activities Animals. (p. 1911)
—Rubber Stamp Activities Backyard (was Garden) (p. 1911)
—Seaside Stroller Book. Baggott, Stella, illus. (p. 1972)
—Sing-Along Christmas Carols. Bonnet, Rosalinde, illus. (p. 2023)
—Sing-along Nursery Rhymes. Bordoni, Chiara, illus. (p. 2023)
—Space Sticker Book. (p. 2072)
—Spooky Things to Make & Do. (p. 2087)
—Sports Sticker Book. (p. 2089)
—Sticker Dolly Dressing Back to School. (p. 2117)
—Sticker Dolly Dressing Costumes Around the World. (p. 2117)
—Sticker Dolly Dressing Dancers. Baggott, Stella, illus. (p. 2117)
—Sticker Dolly Dressing Fashion Activity Book. (p. 2117)
—Sticker Dolly Dressing Fashion Designer Home Designer. (p. 2117)
—Sticker Dolly Dressing Parties. Moore, Jo, illus. (p. 2117)
—Sticker Dolly Dressing Sportsgirls. (p. 2117)
—Sticker Dolly Dressing Travel. (p. 2117)
—Sticker Dolly Dressing Weddings. Baggott, Stella, illus. (p. 2117)
—Sticker Dressing Explorers. (p. 2118)
—Taller & Shorter. (p. 2188)
—That's Not My Angel. (p. 2213)
—That's Not My Angel REVISED. (p. 2214)
—That's Not My Baby (Boy) (p. 2214)
—That's Not My Baby (Girl) (p. 2214)
—That's Not My Bat. (p. 2214)
—That's Not My Chick. (p. 2214)
—That's Not My Cow. (p. 2214)
—That's Not My Dolly. (p. 2214)
—That's Not My Donkey. Wells, Rachel, illus. (p. 2214)
—That's Not My Dragon. (p. 2214)
—That's Not My Duck... Wells, Rachel, illus. (p. 2214)
—That's Not My Elephant. Wells, Rachel, illus. (p. 2214)
—That's Not My Flamingo. (p. 2214)
—That's Not My Frog. Wells, Rachel, illus. (p. 2214)
—That's Not My Giraffe. (p. 2214)
—That's Not My Hamster. (p. 2214)
—That's Not My Llama. (p. 2214)
—That's Not My Meerkat. (p. 2214)
—That's Not My Mermaid. (p. 2214)
—That's Not My Mermaid REVISED (Sparkly) (p. 2214)
—That's Not My Otter. (p. 2214)
—That's Not My Panda. (p. 2214)
—That's Not My Pig... Its Nose Is Too Fuzzy. Wells, Rachel, illus. (p. 2214)
—That's Not My Plane. (p. 2214)
—That's Not My Polar Bear. (p. 2214)
—That's Not My Polar Bear (REVISED) (p. 2214)
—That's Not My Prince. Wells, Rachel, illus. (p. 2214)
—That's Not My Reindeer... Wells, Rachel, illus. (p. 2214)
—That's Not My Snowman. (p. 2214)
—That's Not My Tiger. Wells, Rachel, illus. (p. 2214)
—That's Not My Truck. (p. 2214)
—That's Not My Unicorn. (p. 2214)
—That's Not My Zebra. (p. 2214)
—Tractors. King, Sue, illus. (p. 2273)
—Tweet Tweet. (p. 2302)
—Under the Sea Baby Jigsaw Book. (p. 2322)
—Unicorns Sticker Book. (p. 2329)
—Usborne Book of Drawing, Doodling & Coloring Book. Harrison, Erica & Lovell, Katie, illus. (p. 2341)
—Usborne Book of Drawing, Doodling & Coloring for Christmas. Harrison, Erica, illus. (p. 2341)
—Usborne Color by Numbers Book. Harrison, Erica, illus. (p. 2341)
—Visto a Mis Amigas - Bailarinas(Little Sdd Ballerinas) (p. 2363)
—Visto a Mis Amigas Princesas(Little Sdd Princesses) (p. 2363)
—Visto a Mis Amigas Sirenas(Little Sdd Mermaids) (p. 2363)
—Visto a Mis Amigas Unicornios(Little Sdd Unicorns) (p. 2363)
—Vivaldi's Four Seasons. (p. 2364)
—Water Baby. (p. 2384)
—Winter Wonderland Sticker Book. (p. 2476)
—Winter Wonderland Sticker Book (holographic with 1 Spread Foil Stickers) (p. 2476)
Watt, Fiona, ed. see Bowman, Lucy & MacLaine, James.
Watt, Fiona, ed. see Civardi, Anne.
Watt, Fiona, ed. see MacLaine, James & Bowman, Lucy.
Watt, Fiona, ed. see MacLaine, James.
Watt, Fiona, jt. auth. see Bone, Emily.
Watt, Fiona, jt. auth. see Wilkes, Angela.
Watt, Fiona, jt. ed. see Daynes, Katie.
Watt, Fiona, des. Sticker Dolly Dressing Princess Kit. (p. 2117)
Watt, Gertrude Balmer. Town & Trail (Classic Reprint) (p. 2270)
—Woman in the West (Classic Reprint) (p. 2485)
Watt, Hansard. Myths about Monarchs (Classic Reprint) (p. 1571)
Watt, Jewell Kimball. Survey of Haskell Institute: A Thesis (Classic Reprint) (p. 2164)
Watt, Lauchlan MacLean. Heart of a Soldier (Classic Reprint) (p. 945)
—In France & Flanders, with the Fighting Men (Classic Reprint) (p. 1105)
Watt, Marg. Tales from Hallowed Hollow: Karma. Finn, Jenny, illus. (p. 2182)
Watt, Mary. Broadcaster, Vol. 4: June 6, 1928 (Classic Reprint) (p. 284)
—Broadcaster, Vol. 4: March 21, 1928 (Classic Reprint) (p. 284)
Watt, Mélanie. Bug in a Vacuum. (p. 291)
—Chester's Masterpiece. Watt, Mélanie, illus. (p. 366)
—Leatherback Turtles. (p. 1259)
—Scaredy Squirrel. (p. 1942)
—Scaredy Squirrel. (p. 1942)
—Scaredy Squirrel at the Beach. Watt, Mélanie, illus. (p. 1942)
—Scaredy Squirrel Has a Birthday Party. (p. 1942)
Watt, Mélanie, jt. auth. see Watt, Mélanie.
Watt, Mélanie & Watt, Mélanie. Chester. Watt, Mélanie & Watt, Mélanie, illus. (p. 366)
—Chester's Back! Watt, Mélanie & Watt, Mélanie, illus. (p. 366)
—Chester's Masterpiece. Watt, Mélanie & Watt, Mélanie, illus. (p. 366)
—Have I Got a Book for You! Watt, Mélanie & Watt, Mélanie, illus. (p. 939)
—Scaredy Squirrel at Night. Watt, Mélanie & Watt, Mélanie, illus. (p. 1942)
—Scaredy Squirrel Has a Birthday Party Watt, Mélanie & Watt, Mélanie, illus. (p. 1942)
Watt, R. a. As Silver Is to the Moon. (p. 124)
Wattenberg, Jane, illus. see Lear, Edward.
Watters, Bertha Alice. Smith College Monthly, Vol. 1: October, 1893 (Classic Reprint) (p. 2042)
Watters, Kristyn Mikayla, illus. see Little, Paul D.
Watters, Shannon & Kat Leyh. Stone Cold. (p. 2121)
Watters, Shannon, creator. Lumberjanes: Campfire Songs. (p. 1368)
—Lumberjanes: to the Max Vol. 6. (p. 1368)
Watters, Shannon, ed. Adventure Time: Eye Candy Vol. 1 (p. 19)
Watters, Shannon, et al. Band Together. (p. 163)
Watters, Shannon, et al, creators. Lumberjanes Vol. 12. (p. 1368)
Watters, Thomas. Stories of Everyday Life in Modern China (Classic Reprint) (p. 2125)
Watters, Timothy Teruo. When Piglets Fly. Watters, Timothy Teruo, illus. (p. 2432)
Watterston, George. Lawyer, or Man As He Ought Not to Be: A Tale (Classic Reprint) (p. 1253)
Wattles, W. D. Hell-Fire Harrison (Classic Reprint) (p. 950)
Wattles, Willard Austin. Funston Double Track (Classic Reprint) (p. 801)
Watton, Ross, illus. see Petty, Kate.
Watton, Ross, illus. see West, David.
Watts, Alan. Fish Who Found the Sea. Le, Khoa, illus. (p. 741)
Watts, Alaric Alexander. Poetical Sketches: The Profession; the Broken Heart, etc;; with Stanzas for Music; & Other Poems (Classic Reprint) (p. 1766)
Watts, Anna. You're Not Alone. (p. 2535)
Watts, Bernadette. Bernadette Watts Collection: Stories & Fairy Tales. (p. 204)
—Golden Plate. (p. 858)
—Little Drummer Boy. (p. 1315)
—Peter's Tree (p. 1730)
—Star Child. (p. 2102)
—Tortoise & the Hare. (p. 2266)
Watts, Bernadette, illus. see Andersen, Hans Christian.
Watts, Bernadette, illus. see Grimm, Brothers.
Watts, Bernadette, illus. see Scheidl, Gerda Marie.
Watts, Bernadette, illus. see Tolstoy, Leo.
Watts, Bernadette, jt. auth. see The Brothers Grimm.
Watts, Bernadette & Grimm, Jacob and Wilhelm. Enchanted Nightingale: The Classic Grimm's Tale of Jorinda & Joringel (p. 647)
Watts, C. Galaxia & Her Quest to Save the Universe Chapter 1: #thebeginning (8+) (p. 805)
Watts, Catherine & Phillips, Hilary. Bringing French to Life: Creative Activities For 5-11. (p. 282)
—Bringing German to Life: Creative Activities For 5-11. (p. 282)
—Bringing Spanish to Life: Creative Activities For 5-11. (p. 282)
Watts, Claire & Day, Trevor. DK Eyewitness Books: Natural Disasters: Confront the Awesome Power of Nature from Earthquakes & Tsunamis to Hurricanes. (p. 567)
Watts, Clark. Galaxia & Her Quest to Save the Universe Chapter 1: #thebeginning (Picture Book) (p. 805)
Watts, Clark & Chavez Campero, Laura. Gio the Worldly Dog in Hong Kong: Muchokids. (p. 834)
—Gio the Worldly Dog in New York City: Muchokids. (p. 834)
—Gio the Worldly Dog in Paris: Muchokids. (p. 834)
—Muchokids: Galaxia & Her Quest to Save the Universe Chapter 1: #TheBeginning (Picture Book) (p. 1524)
—Muchokids: Galaxia & Her Quest to Save the Universe Chapter 3: #TheIntruder: Galaxia's Quest (Picture Book) (p. 1524)
—Muchokids: Galaxia & Her Quest to Save the Universe Chapter 2: #TrainingCamp: Galaxia's Quest (Picture Book) (p. 1524)
—Muchokids in England: #TheFreezing: Earth Adventures (Picture Book) (p. 1524)
—Muchokids in Kenya: #TheVanishing: Earth Adventures (Picture Book) (p. 1524)
Watts, David, et al. Disney Pixar Read-Along Storybook & CD Box Set. (p. 562)
Watts, Erika. Road Signs Coloring & Activity Book. (p. 1888)
Watts, Fraces. Middle Sheep. Watson, Judy, illus. (p. 1461)
Watts, Frances. Extraordinary Ernie & Marvelous Maud. Watson, Judy, illus. (p. 685)
—Goodnight, Mice! Watson, Judy, illus. (p. 867)
—Greatest Sheep in History. Watson, Judy, illus. (p. 892)
—Heroes of the Year. Watson, Judy, illus. (p. 962)
—Kisses for Daddy. Legge, David, illus. (p. 1224)
—Pigeon Problems. Rogers, Gregory, illus. (p. 1743)
—Poison Plot. Rogers, Gregory, illus. (p. 1768)
—Rat in a Stripy Sock. Francis, David, illus. (p. 1842)
—Secret of the Swords. Rogers, Gregory, illus. (p. 1978)
—Song of the Winns: the Spies of Gerander. (p. 2063)
—Terrible Trickster. Rogers, Gregory, illus. (p. 2207)
Watts, Franklin. Beating Odds. (p. 182)
—Fifth Harmony - the Dream Begins... (p. 724)
Watts, Gail Eileen. Kevin Thinks: ...About Outer Space, Confusing Expressions & the Perfectly Logical World of Asperger Syndrome. (p. 1210)
Watts, Gillian. Creatures Close Up. Martin, Philippe, photos by. (p. 471)
Watts, Henry. Index to Gmelin's Handbook of Chemistry (Classic Reprint) (p. 1115)
Watts Hicks, Eartha, des. Everyday Excellence Student Planner: Featuring Celai West. (p. 671)
Watts, Irene. Seeking Refuge Shoemaker, Kathryn, illus. (p. 1985)
Watts, Irene N. Escape from Berlin. (p. 661)
—Munsch at Play: Eight Stage Adaptations for Young Performers. (p. 1527)
—No Moon. (p. 1613)
—Touched by Fire. (p. 2268)
Watts, Isaac. Divine & Moral Songs for Children. (p. 566)
—Divine & Moral Songs for Children (Classic Reprint) (p. 566)
—Knowledge of the Heavens & the Earth Made Easy, or the First Principles of Astronomy & Geography, Explained by the Use of Globes & Maps: With a Solution of the Common Problems by a Plain Scale & Compasses, As Well As by the Globe; Written Seve. (p. 1230)
Watts, J. Museum of Remarkable & Interesting Events, Vol. 1: Containing Historical & Other Accounts of Adventures, Incidents of Travels & Voyages, Scenes of Peril, & Escapes, Military Achievements, Eccentric Personages, Noble Examples of Fortitude & P. (p. 1528)
Watts, James. Quest Begins: Magic Bag Trilogy Book One. Leonhard, Herb, illus. (p. 1825)
Watts, James, illus. see Curry, Jane Louise.
Watts, James, illus. see Mozelle, Shirley.
Watts, Jan. CAKE! A comedy script for young People. (p. 309)
—Zipline. (p. 2541)
Watts, Jeri. Kizzy Ann Stamps. (p. 1226)
—On Snowden Mountain. (p. 1653)
—Piece of Home. Yum, Hyewon, illus. (p. 1742)
Watts, Jeri Hanel. Keepers. Marshall, Felicia, illus. (p. 1208)
Watts, Julia. Free Spirits. (p. 782)
—Revived Spirits. (p. 1873)
—Secret City. (p. 1975)
Watts, Juliette, illus. see Burzynski, Roberta.
Watts, Leander. Meet Me in the Strange. (p. 1438)
Watts, Leslie. Just Leah. (p. 1193)
Watts, Leslie, illus. see Fitch, Sheree.
Watts, Leslie Elizabeth, illus. see Gilmore, Rachna.
Watts, Leslie Elizabeth, illus. see Spalding, Andrea.
Watts, Lou Ellen. Round-Em-Up & the Marshmallow Treat. (p. 1907)
—Round-Em-Up & the Marshmallow Treat Coloring Book. (p. 1907)
Watts, Louisa. Pretty Little Poems, for Pretty Little People: Explanatory of the Operations of Nature, in a Style Suited to Their Capacities, from the Age of Two to Twelve Years (Classic Reprint) (p. 1790)
Watts, Marjorie Anne, illus. see Storr, Catherine.
Watts, Martha E. Letters of David (Classic Reprint) (p. 1280)
Watts, Mary S. Boardman Family (Classic Reprint) (p. 251)
—Fabric of the Loom (Classic Reprint) (p. 692)
—From Father to Son (Classic Reprint) (p. 791)
—Legacy: A Story of a Woman (Classic Reprint) (p. 1261)
—Nathan Burke (Classic Reprint) (p. 1577)
—Noon-Mark (Classic Reprint) (p. 1619)
—Rise of Jennie Cushing (Classic Reprint) (p. 1885)
—Rudder: A Novel with Several Heroes (Classic Reprint) (p. 1912)
—Tenants: An Episode of the '80s (Classic Reprint) (p. 2205)
—Three Short Plays (Classic Reprint) (p. 2235)
—Van Cleve (Classic Reprint) (p. 2347)
Watts, Mary Stanbery. House of Rimmon (Classic Reprint) (p. 1023)
Watts, Michael, jt. auth. see Taylor, Nicole.
Watts, Pam. Gasoline Engines. (p. 811)
—Grassland Ecosystems (p. 881)
—Rock Cycle. (p. 1894)
—Soil. (p. 2055)

W

—Seahorses: World of Wonder: Underwater Life. (p. 1970)
—Seahorses. (p. 1970)
—Smell. (p. 2041)
—Taste. (p. 2192)
—Winter: WOW Study of Day & Seasons. (p. 2475)
—World of Wonder: Underwater Life (p. 2504)
Wearing, Judy, jt. auth. see Riddolls, Tom.
Wearing, Judy & Diemer, Lauren. Winter. (p. 2475)
Wearing, Judy & Riddolls, Tom. Golden Gate Bridge. (p. 857)
Wearing, Judy & Yasuda, Anita. Lebron James. (p. 1260)
Wearing, Judy, et al. Golden Gate Bridge. (p. 857)
Weatherbee, Ruth Cole. Lessons for the Sunday Kindergarten (Classic Reprint) (p. 1268)
Weatherbee, Tabatha. Dream Sharers: Love/Hate. (p. 602)
Weatherby, Georgie Ann. Little Big Bedtime Tales. (p. 1311)
—Sea Tales Tiny & Tall. (p. 1969)
Weatherford, Carole Boston. Be a King: Dr. Martin Luther King Jr. 's Dream & You. Ransome, James E., illus. (p. 176)
—Beatitudes: From Slavery to Civil Rights. Ladwig, Tim, illus. (p. 182)
—Beauty Mark: A Verse Novel of Marilyn Monroe. (p. 185)
—BOX: Henry Brown Mails Himself to Freedom. Wood, Michele, illus. (p. 266)
—By & By: Charles Albert Tindley, the Father of Gospel Music. Collier, Bryan, illus. (p. 305)
—Dorothea Lange. (p. 586)
—Dorothea Lange. Green, Sarah, illus. (p. 586)
—Gordon Parks: How the Photographer Captured Black & White America. Christoph, Jamey, illus. (p. 869)
—How Sweet the Sound: The Story of Amazing Grace. Morrison, Frank, illus. (p. 1035)
—In Your Hands. Pinkney, Brian, illus. (p. 1112)
—Legendary Miss Lena Horne. Zunon, Elizabeth, illus. (p. 1263)
—Leontyne Price: Voice of a Century. ón, Raul, illus. (p. 1267)
—Respect: Aretha Franklin, the Queen of Soul. Morrison, Frank, illus. (p. 1869)
—Schomburg: The Man Who Built a Library. (p. 1945)
—Schomburg: el Hombre Que Creó una Biblioteca. Velasquez, Eric, illus. (p. 1945)
—Schomburg: the Man Who Built a Library. Velasquez, Eric, illus. (p. 1945)
—Sound That Jazz Makes (p. 2067)
—Sugar Hill: Harlem's Historic Neighborhood. (p. 2147)
—Sugar Hill: Harlem's Historic Neighborhood. Christie, R. Gregory, illus. (p. 2147)
—Voice of Freedom: Fannie Lou Hamer: The Spirit of the Civil Rights Movement. Holmes, Ekua, illus. (p. 2365)
—You Can Fly: The Tuskegee Airmen. Weatherford, Jeffery Boston, illus. (p. 2526)
Weatherford, Jeffery Boston, illus. see Weatherford, Carole Boston.
Weatherford, Robert, illus. see Johnston, Tony.
Weatherly, Frederic Edward. Out of Town (Classic Reprint) (p. 1683)
—Told in the Twilight (Classic Reprint) (p. 2256)
Weatherly, George. Little Folks Painting Book: A Series of Outline Engravings for Water-Colour Painting (Classic Reprint) (p. 1316)
Weatherly, L. A. Angel Burn. (p. 85)
—Angel Fever. (p. 85)
—Angel Fire. (p. 85)
—Them. (p. 2215)
—Watcher. (p. 2383)
Weatherly, Myra. Nebraska. (p. 1584)
Weaver, A. J. Big Cats, Little Cats. Budgen, Tim, illus. (p. 219)
Weaver, Alison. Three Moms & the Magical Manny. (p. 2234)
Weaver, Alyssa. Sefer 2012: Literary Magazine (Classic Reprint) (p. 1985)
Weaver, Anna E. Stories From Grandma's Day. (p. 2124)
Weaver, Anne H. Children of Time: Evolution & the Human Story. Celeskey, Matt, illus. (p. 372)
Weaver, Brian M., illus. see Reynolds, Aaron.
Weaver, Charles Edwin. Tertiary Faunal Horizons of Western Washington (Classic Reprint) (p. 2208)
Weaver, Clare, jt. auth. see MacDonald, Fiona.
Weaver, Dustin. S. H. I. E. L. D. by Hickman & Weaver: the Human Machine. (p. 1919)
Weaver, Emily. Rainproof Invention: Or Some Tangled Threads (Classic Reprint) (p. 1837)
Weaver, Emily, jt. auth. see Stowe, Harriet Beecher.
Weaver, Emily P. Search for Molly Marling (Classic Reprint) (p. 1971)
Weaver, Emily Poynton. Search for Molly Marling (Classic Reprint) (p. 1971)
—Trouble Man, or the Wards of St. James (Classic Reprint) (p. 2291)
Weaver, Greg & Weaver, Allie. Mickey the Monkey Makes a Friend. (p. 1459)
Weaver, J. Denny, jt. auth. see Weaver, Lisa.
Weaver, Jack, jt. auth. see Gaspar, Joe.
Weaver, Jack W. Cat & Dog Breath Meet the Last Pirates: How to Fly a Basset Hound. (p. 341)
Weaver, Janice. Hudson. Craig, David, illus. (p. 1047)
Weaver, Jo. Little Tigers. Weaver, Jo, illus. (p. 1329)
—Little Whale Weaver, Jo, illus. (p. 1329)
—Paul Bunyan: A Very Tall Tale (p. 1707)
Weaver, Jo, illus. see Lewis, Gill.
Weaver, John Van Alstyne. In American-Poems (Classic Reprint) (p. 1104)
—Margey Wins the Game (Classic Reprint) (p. 1404)
Weaver, Joyce A. Mckissick. Adventures of Mopey Bear & His Two Brothers (p. 25)
Weaver, Karen. Alphabet Job Buddies. Fox, Kat, illus. (p. 59)
—Australian Animal Walkabout. (p. 138)
—Australian Animal Walkabout. Lees, Jeanette, illus. (p. 138)
—Bumble Bee Rock Around the Clock. Lees, Jeanette, illus. (p. 297)
—Irish Dancing Girl. (p. 1134)
—Minky Monkey Meets Alex the Astronaut. Fox, Kat, illus. (p. 1472)
—Minky Monkey Meets Barney the Brickie. Fox, Kat, illus. (p. 1472)
—Roly Poly Rainbow Princess: Soft Cover. (p. 1899)
—Roly Poly Rainbow Princess. (p. 1899)
Weaver, Lila Quintero. My Year in the Middle. Weaver, Lila Quintero, illus. (p. 1565)
Weaver, Lisa, illus. see Martin, Rebecca.
Weaver, Lisa & Weaver, J. Denny. Living the Anabaptist Story: A Guide to Early Beginnings with Questions for Today. (p. 1334)
Weaver, Louise Bennett. Thousand Ways to Please a Husband with Bettina's Best Recipes (Classic Reprint) (p. 2231)
Weaver, Louise Bennett & Lecron, Helen Cowles. Thousand Ways to Please a Husband: With Bettina's Best Recipes. (p. 2231)
Weaver, Madeline. Near & Far at the Park: Describe & Compare Measurable Attributes. (p. 1584)
Weaver, Nicole. Colton & Chloe: A Trilingual Story- English Spanish French. Smith, Clara Batton, illus. (p. 427)
Weaver, Rachel Spier & Haggard, Anna. Unexpected Hero: A Bible Story about Rahab. (p. 2327)
Weaver, Steve, illus. see Cussen, Sarah.
Weaver, Steve, illus. see Magellan, Marta.
Weaver, Steve, illus. see Nickel, Bonnie.
Weaver, Steve, illus. see Wicker, Jan L.
Weaver, Steve, illus. see Wicker, Jan Lee.
Weaver, Sue. Llamas & Alpacas: Small-Scale Herding for Pleasure & Profit. (p. 1337)
Weaver, Susan B. Forever Friend: Activities for Kids Who Have Lost a Pet. (p. 767)
—Heroes! Activities for Kids Dealing with Deployment. (p. 961)
—Love & Memories: Activities for Kids Who Have Lost a Loved One. (p. 1359)
Weaver, Verity. Fitness Fiasco. Huddleston, Courtney, illus. (p. 742)
—Lab Mice Heist. Huddleston, Courtney, illus. (p. 1235)
—Math Test Mischief. Huddleston, Courtney, illus. (p. 1424)
—Sandwich Shenanigans. Huddleston, Courtney, illus. (p. 1931)
—Showtime Sabotage. Huddleston, Courtney, illus. (p. 2013)
—Stage Two Hullabaloo. Huddleston, Courtney, illus. (p. 2099)
—Switchback Switcheroo. Huddleston, Courtney, illus. (p. 2171)
—Trojan Horse Trouble. Huddleston, Courtney, illus. (p. 2290)
—What Happened? (Set Of 4) Huddleston, Courtney, illus. (p. 2411)
—What Happened? Set 2 (Set Of 4) Huddleston, Courtney, illus. (p. 2411)
Weaver, Will. Checkered Flag Cheater: A Motor Novel. (p. 363)
—Saturday Night Dirt: A MOTOR Novel. (p. 1936)
Webb, Amanda & Webb, Rory. Legends of Aukera: The Ascendants - Volume One. Webb, Amanda, illus. (p. 1263)
—Legends of Aukera: The Ascendants - Volume Three. Webb, Amanda, illus. (p. 1263)
Webb, Amy. When Charley Met Emma Liddiard, Merrilee, illus. (p. 2429)
Webb, Anne Aldridge. Appalachian State, A to Z. Bostian, Laurie, illus. (p. 106)
Webb, Aquilla. Christian Athlete: A Sermon Story (Classic Reprint) (p. 382)
Webb, Arch, illus. see Brereton, F. S.
Webb, Barbara L. Hot or Cold? (p. 1006)
Webb, Blair, illus. see Perry, Brien.
Webb, Brandon & Feldman, Thea. Navy SEALs: Mission at the Caves. (p. 1583)
Webb, C. H. Liffith Lank, or Lunacy (Classic Reprint) (p. 1297)
—Wickedest Woman in New York (Classic Reprint) (p. 2460)
Webb, Celia, illus. see Webb, Mack H., Jr.
Webb, Charles Henry. Californian, Vol. 1: May 28, 1864 (Classic Reprint) (p. 311)
—Californian, Vol. 3: May 27, 1865 (Classic Reprint) (p. 311)
—Sea-Weed & What We Seed: My Vacation at Long Branch & Saratoga (Classic Reprint) (p. 1969)
Webb, Charles Henry, jt. auth. see Twain, Mark, pseud.
Webb, Christina & Lonely Planet Kids. Doodle Spots Flintham, Thomas, illus. (p. 584)
—Let's Explore... Mountain Shephard, David & Zamazing, Cherie, illus. (p. 1272)
—Let's Explore... Safari Curnick, Pippa, illus. (p. 1272)
Webb, Christina, et al. Let's Explore... City Love, Mike et al, illus. (p. 1271)
—Let's Explore... Desert Love, Mike et al, illus. (p. 1271)
Webb, Deborah. Remember Remember the Fifth of November. Tee, Jacqueline, illus. (p. 1864)
Webb, Derek & Webb, Arthur. Is. (p. 1136)
Webb, Dirk. Warm Summer's Day. (p. 2379)
Webb, Donald. Grim Reaper's Calling Card. (p. 896)
Webb, Dorothy Newman. Historical Pageant of Winthrop, Maine: Thesis (Classic Reprint) (p. 976)
Webb, Edith. Coraddi, Vol. 33: April, 1929 (Classic Reprint) (p. 452)
—Coraddi, Vol. 33: March, 1929 (Classic Reprint) (p. 452)
—Coraddi, Vol. 33: December, 1928 (Classic Reprint) (p. 452)
Webb, Edward. Hindoo Life: With Pictures of the Men, Women, & Children of India (Classic Reprint) (p. 972)
Webb, Edward Meryon. Runaway Jo (Classic Reprint) (p. 1915)
Webb, Genie. Princess Lydi & the Baby Brother. Nelson, Joe, illus. (p. 1798)
Webb, George James. Little Songster: Consisting of Original Songs for Children; Together with Directions to Teachers for Cultivating the Ear & the Voice, & Exercises for Teaching Children the First Rudiments of Singing; for the Use of Primary Schools & Families. (p. 1328)
Webb, Glenn. Critical World Issues: Terrorism (p. 476)
Webb, Harrison Emmett, jt. auth. see Betz, William.
Webb, Holly. Abandoned Puppy. Williams, Sophy, illus. (p. 3)
—Alone in the Night. Williams, Sophy, illus. (p. 57)
—Brave Kitten. Williams, Sophy, illus. (p. 276)
—Case of the Feathered Mask: The Mysteries of Maisie Hitchins, Book 4. Lindsay, Marion, illus. (p. 337)
—Case of the Feathered Mask. Lindsay, Marion, illus. (p. 337)
—Case of the Phantom Cat. Lindsay, Marion, illus. (p. 338)
—Case of the Secret Tunnel. Lindsay, Marion, illus. (p. 338)
—Case of the Vanishing Emerald. Lindsay, Marion, illus. (p. 338)
—Curious Kitten. Williams, Sophy, illus. (p. 488)
—Dog Magic. (p. 576)
—Harry the Homeless Puppy. Williams, Sophy, illus. (p. 935)
—Home for Sandy. Williams, Sophy, illus. (p. 996)
—Homeless Kitten. Williams, Sophy, illus. (p. 997)
—Jessie the Lonely Puppy. Williams, Sophy, illus. (p. 1165)
—Kitten Nobody Wanted. Williams, Sophy, illus. (p. 1225)
—Kitten Nobody Wanted & Other Tales. Williams, Sophy, illus. (p. 1225)
—Leo All Alone. Williams, Sophy, illus. (p. 1267)
—Little Princess Finds Her Voice. (p. 1325)
—Loneliest Kitten. Williams, Sophy, illus. (p. 1342)
—Lost in the Snow. Williams, Sophy, illus. (p. 1354)
—Lost Puppy. Williams, Sophy, illus. (p. 1355)
—Magical Venice Story: the Girl of Glass: Book 4 (p. 1380)
—Magical Venice Story: the Maskmaker's Daughter: Book 3. (p. 1380)
—Magical Venice Story: the Mermaid's Sister: Book 2. (p. 1380)
—Missing Kitten. Williams, Sophy, illus. (p. 1480)
—Missing Kitten & Other Tales. Williams, Sophy, illus. (p. 1480)
—Missing Puppy & Other Tales. Williams, Sophy, illus. (p. 1481)
—Misty the Abandoned Kitten. Williams, Sophy, illus. (p. 1483)
—Mystery Kitten. Williams, Sophy, illus. (p. 1569)
—Oscar's Lonely Christmas. Williams, Sophy, illus. (p. 1673)
—Perfect Kitten. Williams, Sophy, illus. (p. 1722)
—Puppy Who Couldn't Sleep. Williams, Sophy, illus. (p. 1815)
—Reindeer Girl. Mendez, Simon & Artful Doodlers, Artful, illus. (p. 1862)
—Rescued Puppy. Williams, Sophy, illus. (p. 1868)
—Return to the Secret Garden. (p. 1871)
—Rose. (p. 1904)
—Rose & the Lost Princess. (p. 1905)
—Rose & the Magician's Mask. (p. 1905)
—Rose & the Silver Ghost. (p. 1905)
—Sad Puppy. Williams, Sophy, illus. (p. 1920)
—Sam the Stolen Puppy. Williams, Sophy, illus. (p. 1926)
—Sammy the Shy Kitten. Williams, Sophy, illus. (p. 1928)
—Scruffy Puppy. Williams, Sophy, illus. (p. 1966)
—Secret Kitten. Williams, Sophy, illus. (p. 1976)
—Secret Puppy. Williams, Sophy, illus. (p. 1978)
—Secret Puppy & Other Tales. Williams, Sophy, illus. (p. 1978)
—Sky the Unwanted Kitten. Williams, Sophy, illus. (p. 2034)
—Snow Bear. Mendez, Simon, illus. (p. 2047)
—Teddy in Trouble. Williams, Sophy, illus. (p. 2198)
—Tiniest Puppy. Williams, Sophy, illus. (p. 2248)
—Unwanted Puppy. Williams, Sophy, illus. (p. 2337)
Webb, Holly & Lindsay, Marion. Case of the Stolen Sixpence. Lindsay, Marion, illus. (p. 338)
Webb, Jane K. My Super Stupendous Day at the Beach. Cupolo, Eileen, illus. (p. 1562)
Webb, John Russell. Model Fourth Reader: In Two Parts, for Intermediate & Higher Grades (Classic Reprint) (p. 1485)
—Model Second Reader: Sentence Method (Classic Reprint) (p. 1486)
—Model Third Reader (Classic Reprint) (p. 1486)
Webb, Karen C. Rising Star. (p. 1886)
Webb, Kate Cope. Arthur in Shadow & Sunshine (Classic Reprint) (p. 122)
Webb, Leann. BB & Betty. (p. 176)
Webb, Lexy, jt. auth. see Webb, Melissa.
Webb, Lisa. Kids Who Travel the World: Rome. (p. 1216)
—Kids Who Travel the World: Paris. (p. 1216)
—Kids Who Travel the World: London. (p. 1216)
—Kids Who Travel the World: Indonesia. (p. 1216)
—Kids Who Travel the World: African Safari. (p. 1216)
Webb, Lois Sinaiko, jt. auth. see Roten, Lindsay Grace.
Webb, Lois Sinaiko & Roten, Lindsay Grace. Holidays of the World Cookbook for Students (p. 988)
Webb, M. L. GayBCs. (p. 812)
Webb, Mack H. Webb's Wondrous Tales Book 3. (p. 2395)
Webb, Mack H., Jr. Webb's Wondrous Tales Book 4. Webb, Celia, illus. (p. 2395)
Webb, Margaret. Pump It up Cheerleading. (p. 1812)
Webb, Margaret, jt. auth. see Crabtree Staff.
Webb, Mary. Gone to Earth (Classic Reprint) (p. 861)
—House in Dormer Forest (Classic Reprint) (p. 1022)
Webb, Mary & Ni Laoghaire, Ide. My Ireland Counting Book. Ryan, Eoin, illus. (p. 1550)
Webb, Melanie. Merveilleux Voyage de Claude le Raton Laveur. (p. 1451)
—Wonderful Journey of Claude the Raccoon. (p. 2489)
Webb, Melissa. How the Ladybug Got Her Spots: A Pourquoi Story. (p. 1036)
Webb, Melissa, illus. see Haydon, Julie.
Webb, Melissa, illus. see Pryor, Kimberley Jane.
Webb, Melissa, jt. auth. see Brasch, Nicolas.
Webb, Mick. Book of Languages: Talk Your Way Around the World. (p. 259)
Webb, Naomi. Ben's Rubbish Day. Graham, Hannah, illus. (p. 201)
Webb, Pam. Someday We Will: A Book for Grandparents & Grandchildren. Leach, Wendy, illus. (p. 2060)
Webb, Philip, illus. see Burslem, Diana & Freeman, Diana.
Webb, Philip, illus. see Cowley, Joy.
Webb, Philip, illus. see Dale, Jay.
Webb, Philip, illus. see Eggleton, Jill.
Webb, Philip, illus. see Holden, Pam.
Webb, Philip, illus. see Punter, Russell.
Webb, Phillip, illus. see Cowley, Joy.
Webb Quest, Sara. Angel's Shore. (p. 86)
Webb, Richard. Me & Lawson: Humpty Hotfoots Little Run in with Frenzied Copper, Amalgamated Gas & Scrambled Oil (Classic Reprint) (p. 1432)
Webb, Rita. Tears. (p. 2196)
Webb, Robert N. We Were There at the Boston Tea Party. Ward, E. F., illus. (p. 2393)
Webb, Ros, illus. see Briseno, Kellie Ann.
Webb, Ros, illus. see Grand, Robert Alan.
Webb, Ros, illus. see Hunter, T. E.
Webb, Ros, illus. see Kinsey, Michael C.
Webb, Ros, illus. see Levi, Sheli.
Webb, Ros, illus. see McGinnis, Deborah Ann.
Webb, Ros, illus. see McGinnis, Deborah.
Webb, Ros & Hunter, T. E. Davey, Daisy & Pete: Bubble Bath Ocean: Imagine with Davey, Daisy & Pete. (p. 510)
Webb, Ross, illus. see Grand, Robert.
Webb, Ross, illus. see Litscher Debruin, Kari.
Webb, Ryan. Buddy: Dog of the Smoky Mountains. (p. 290)
Webb, Samantha. Glub. Webb, Samantha, illus. (p. 845)
Webb, Sarah. Ask Amy Green: Boy Trouble. (p. 126)
—Ask Amy Green: Love & Other Drama-Ramas! (p. 126)
—Ask Amy Green: Dancing Daze. (p. 126)
—Ask Amy Green: Wedding Belles. (p. 126)
—Blazing a Trail: Irish Women Who Changed the World. O'Neill, Lauren, illus. (p. 243)
—Boy Trouble. (p. 270)
—Bridesmaid Blitz. (p. 280)
—Dare to Dream: Irish People Who Took on the World (and Won)! Corcoran, Graham, illus. (p. 505)
—Sailor Went to Sea, Sea, Sea: Favourite Rhymes from an Irish Childhood. McCarthy, Steve, illus. (p. 1923)
Webb, Sarah, illus. see Claus, Fred J.
Webb, Sarah & Ranson, Claire. Sally Go Round the Stars: Favourite Rhymes for an Irish Childhood. McCarthy, Steven, illus. (p. 1924)
Webb, Sarah Powers. American Revolution. (p. 73)
—Marie Antoinette: Fashionable Queen or Greedy Royal? (p. 1405)
—When They Came: A Chronology of North American Exploration. (p. 2434)
Webb, Shirley G., jt. auth. see Moreland, Janet.
Webb, Sophie. Far from Shore: Chronicles of an Open Ocean Voyage. (p. 708)
Webb, Stephanie, illus. see Coolidge, Kevin.
Webb, Steve. City Kitty Cat. Le Huche, Magali, illus. (p. 395)
—Happy Zappa Cat. Le Huche, Magali, illus. (p. 924)
—Spangles Mcnasty & the Diamond Skull. Mould, Chris, illus. (p. 2073)
Webb, Stuart. UFOs. (p. 2313)
Webb, Susan Hankey, jt. auth. see Webb, Jack B.
Webb, Trudi, illus. see Graham, Cece.
Webb, Trudi, jt. auth. see Regan, Lisa.
Webb, Virginia. One American Girl (Classic Reprint) (p. 1658)
Webb, Walter F. Auction Catalogue of Choice Foreign & American Gold, All Series of American Silver & Copper, Rare Medals, Foreign Crowns, Ancient Greek, Roman Gold, Patterns & Bargain Lots, Many Fascinating Items If You Take the Time to Dig Them Out: To Be Sold Feb. (p. 136)
—Auction Catalogue of Choice Foreign & United States Gold, Extensive Series of Dollars to Cents in Uncirculated & Brilliant Proof, Rare Crowns & Other Choice Material Mostly Contributed by My Friends: To Be Sold Saturday, June 10 1944. (p. 136)
—Auction Catalogue of Choice Foreign & United States Gold, Foreign Crowns & Hundreds of Proof Coins from Cents to Dollars, Ancient Greek Silver, Commemorative Half Dollars, Medals & Many Other Fascinating Items: To Be Sold December 4 1943. (p. 136)
—Auction Catalogue of Foreign & United States Gold, Hundreds of Minor Coins in Uncirculated & Proof, Foreign Crowns, Choice Medals & Many Other Fine Lots for Your Collection: To Be Sold Saturday, October 7th, 1944 (Classic Reprint) (p. 136)
Webb, Yarns By the Kentucky Girl. Johnny & Dad & the Red Canoe. (p. 1174)
Webbe, Cornelius. Glances at Life in City & Suburb (Classic Reprint) (p. 841)
—Man about Town, Vol. 1 of 2 (Classic Reprint) (p. 1394)
Webber, B. Seriously, Kitty! Webber, B., illus. (p. 1991)
Webber, Byron. Pigskin & Willow, Vol. 1 Of 3: With Other Sporting Stories (Classic Reprint) (p. 1744)
Webber, C. W. Hunter-Naturalist: Romance of Sporting; or, Wild Scenes & Wild Hunters (Classic Reprint) (p. 1053)
Webber, Charles W. Tales of the Southern Border (Classic Reprint) (p. 2186)
Webber, Charles Wilkins. Wild Scenes in the Forest & Prairie, or the Romance of Natural History (Classic Reprint) (p. 2464)
Webber, Diane. Celebrity's Son Snatched: Can Handwriting Help Nab the Perp? (p. 350)
Webber, Donna and Reagan. Allergy Adventures with Cari the Cupcake. (p. 56)
Webber, Jake. Lafitte's Black Box: Boit Noir. (p. 1239)
Webber, James Plaisted. Bowdoin Quill, Vol. 3: May, 1899 (Classic Reprint) (p. 266)
—Bowdoin Quill, Vol. 3: January, 1899 (Classic Reprint) (p. 266)
Webber, Jennie, illus. see Knowles, Laura.
Webber, Katherine. Heartbeats of Wing Jones. (p. 946)
—Only Love Can Break Your Heart. (p. 1664)
Webber, Lissa. Pipsqueak the Puppy. Boyce, Tami, illus. (p. 1749)
Webber, Mike, illus. see Wozniak, Paul.
Webber, Penny, illus. see Njenga, Wamoro P.
Webber, Sharon, et al. Party Pups: The Game of Prepositional Fun! Ink, Bruce, illus. (p. 1702)
Webber-Bey, Deimosa & Fitzgerald, Stephanie. Martin Luther King, Jr. Memorial. (p. 1411)
Webb-Jones, Darlene Y. a, illus. see Munir, Jamilah.
Webb-Peploe, Alex. Light in the Darkness: The Christmas Story from Luke 1-2 (Hcsb) (p. 1298)
Webb-Peploe, Annie. Marco Griffi, the Italian Patriot (Classic Reprint) (p. 1403)
Weber, Adele. Fortunes of the Van der Bergs (Classic Reprint) (p. 770)
Weber, Alice. Angela: A Sketch (Classic Reprint) (p. 85)
Weber, Amy, ed. see Rosa-Mendoza, Gladys.
Weber, Amy & Creative Haven Staff. Creative Haven Curious Creatures Coloring Book. (p. 470)
Weber, Andra, illus. see Sirotzky, Sara.
Weber, Belinda. Discover Science: Animal Disguises. (p. 555)
—Discover Science: Reptiles. (p. 555)
—I Wonder Why Caterpillars Eat So Much: And Other Questions about Life Cycles. (p. 1086)
—Kingfisher Young Knowledge - Reptiles. (p. 1222)

W

Wedekind, Frank. Awakening of Spring: A Tragedy of Childhood (Classic Reprint) (p. 143)
—Awakening of Spring. (p. 143)
—Grisley Suitor: A Story (Classic Reprint) (p. 897)
—Princess Russalka (Classic Reprint) (p. 1799)
—Rabbi Ezra; the Victim, Vol. 2: Two Stories (Classic Reprint) (p. 1829)
Wedel, Mathew J. Totally Amazing Facts about Dinosaurs. (p. 2266)
Wedel, Mathew J. & Potts, Nikki. Mind Benders. (p. 1469)
Wedel, Steven E., jt. auth. see Jones, Carrie.
Wedelich, Sam. Chicken Little: the Real & Totally True Tale. Wedelich, Sam, illus. (p. 368)
Wedemeyer, K. Mark. But Grandpa, I'm Only Twelve! Why Do We Have to Talk about Retirement? Grandpa's Little Book of Financial Wisdom. (p. 302)
Wedeven, Carol. arca de Noé (Noah's 2-by-2 Adventure) - Bilingual. (p. 109)
Wedge, Hayden. Examining Shipwrecks. (p. 675)
Wedgeworth, Anthony G. Nums of Shoreview: Baka's Curse. (p. 1630)
Wedgeworth, Anthony Glenn. Nums of Shoreview: AC Epic Fantasy Adventures. Wedgeworth, Frederick & Ott, Steve, illus. (p. 1630)
Wedgeworth, Frederick, illus. see Wedgeworth, Anthony Glenn.
Wedgwood, A. F. Shadow of a Titan (Classic Reprint) (p. 1996)
Wedgwood, Julia. Framleigh Hall, Vol. 1 Of 3: A Novel (Classic Reprint) (p. 775)
Wedl, Carl. Pathologie der Zahne: Mit Besonderer Rucksicht Auf Anatomie und Physiologie (Classic Reprint) (p. 1704)
Wedman, Belgin K., jt. auth. see Novesky, Amy.
Wedmore, Frederick. Dream of Provence (Orgeas & Miradou) (p. 602)
—Dream of Provence (Orgeas & Miradou) (Classic Reprint) (p. 602)
—Orgeas & Miradou: With Other Pieces (Classic Reprint) (p. 1670)
—Pastorals of France (Classic Reprint) (p. 1704)
—Renunciations: A Chemist in the Suburbs a Confidence at the Savile the North Coast & Eleanor (Classic Reprint) (p. 1866)
—Renunciations. (p. 1866)
—Snapt Gold Ring, Vol. 1 of 2 (Classic Reprint) (p. 2045)
Wedzin, James, illus. see Football, Virginia & Mantla, Rosa.
Wedzin, James, illus. see Football, Virginia.
Wee, Charlyn. Sometimes with Ghosts. (p. 2061)
Wee Society. Wee Hee Hee: A Collection of Pretty Funny Jokes & Pictures. (p. 2395)
Weeber, Jochen. What in the World Is Wrong with Gisbert? Gholizadeh, Fariba, illus. (p. 2413)
Weeber, Stephanie B., jt. auth. see Beach, Kathleen H.
Weed, Walter Harvey. Formation of Travertine & Siliceous Sinter by the Vegetation of Hot Springs. (p. 768)
Weeden, Edward St. Clair. Year with the Gaekwar of Baroda (Classic Reprint) (p. 2519)
Weedn, Flavia, illus. see York Lumbard, Alexis.
Weedon, Christopher. Adventures of Humphrey the Guinea Pig: Humphrey's Night Out. Weedon, Sandra, illus. (p. 24)
—Adventures of Humphrey the Guinea Pig: Humphrey Meets Father Christmas! Weedon, Sandra, illus. (p. 24)
Weedon, Sandra, illus. see Weedon, Christopher.
Weedon, William. See My Savior's Hands. (p. 1982)
Week, Jason, illus. see Meyerhoff, Jenny.
Weekes, Agnes Russell. Clair de Lune (Classic Reprint) (p. 397)
—Marqueray's Duel (Classic Reprint) (p. 1408)
Weekes, Cora Anna. Athenaeum & California Critic, Vol. 1: For the Cultivation of the Memorable & the Beautiful; March 20, 1858 (Classic Reprint) (p. 132)
Weekes, Patrick. Feeder. (p. 718)
Weekes, Rose Kirkpatrick. Convict B 14: A Novel (Classic Reprint) (p. 446)
Weekes, T. J. Dragon Rider. (p. 594)
Weekly, Debbie, illus. see Schiller, Pamela Byrne.
Weeks, Allen Ticknor Tuttle and. Child's Annual, 1834 (Classic Reprint) (p. 375)
Weeks, Arland D. Squaw Point (Classic Reprint) (p. 2094)
Weeks, Clara Winslow. Story of a China Plate (Classic Reprint) (p. 2128)
Weeks, George F. Seen in a Mexican Plaza: A Summer's Idyll of an Idle Summer (Classic Reprint) (p. 1985)
Weeks, Helen C. White & Red: A Narrative of Life among the Northwest Indians (Classic Reprint) (p. 2443)
Weeks, Helen Campbell. Ainslee Stories (Classic Reprint) (p. 36)
Weeks, J. Hatton. Tin Kitchen (Classic Reprint) (p. 2247)
Weeks, Jan. Once upon a Time in Fairyland. (p. 1658)
Weeks, Jan, jt. auth. see Rigby.
Weeks, Jeanne G., illus. see Weeks, Timothy A.
Weeks, Kermit. Spirit of Lindy. Premise Entertainment, illus. (p. 2083)
Weeks Millard, Mary. Bilingual Parrot. (p. 225)
Weeks, Sarah. Angel Face. Diaz, David, illus. (p. 85)
—As Simple As It Seems. (p. 124)
—Catfish Kate & the Sweet Swamp Band. Smith, Elwood H., illus. (p. 344)
—Cheese: A Combo of Oggie Cooder & Oggie Cooder, Party Animal. (p. 364)
—Glamourpuss. Small, David, illus. (p. 841)
—Lizzy Mctizzy & the Busy Dizzy Day. Wildish, Lee, illus. (p. 1337)
—Mac & Cheese. Manning, Jane, illus. (p. 1371)
—Mac & Cheese & the Perfect Plan. Manning, Jane, illus. (p. 1371)
—Oggie Cooder - Party Animal! (p. 1641)
—Pie. (p. 1742)
—So B. It. (p. 2050)
—Soof. (p. 2064)
—Sophie Peterman Tells the Truth! Neubecker, Robert, illus. (p. 2065)
—Woof: a Love Story. Berry, Holly, illus. (p. 2492)
Weeks, Sarah & Varadarajan, Gita. Save Me a Seat. (p. 1937)
Weeks, Sophie. Soured Earth. (p. 2068)
Weeks, Timothy A. Goldie's Search for Silver: The Wise Mullet Finale! Weeks, Timothy A. & Weeks, Jeanne G., illus. (p. 860)
Weel, Rosalinda. Dream Clouds: Float Away with Seven Enchanting Children's Stories for Relaxation & Bedtime. (p. 601)
Weems, Mason L. God's Revenge Against Adultery: Awfully Exemplified in the Following Cases of American Crim; con (Classic Reprint) (p. 854)
Weems, Mason Locke. God's Revenge Against Murder, or the Drown'd Wife: A Tragedy, Lately Performed, with Unbounded Applause, (of the Devil & His Court) by Ned Findley, Esquire, One of the Grand Company of Tragedians in the Service of the Black Prince (Classic Reprint) (p. 854)
—Life of Benjamin Franklin: With Many Choice Anecdotes & Admirable Sayings of This Great Man, Never Before Published by Any of His Biographers (Classic Reprint) (p. 1294)
—Life of Gen. Francis Marion: A Celebrated Partizan Officer, in the Revolutionary War, Against the British & Tories, in South Carolina & Georgia (Classic Reprint) (p. 1294)
Weenie, Gayle, tr. see Florence, Melanie.
Weerasekera, Becky. 10 Magical Mermaids. Schofield, Jayne & Dupuis, Karina, illus. (p. 2549)
—10 Pesky Pirates: a Lift-The-Flap Book. Schofield, Jayne & Dupuis, Karina, illus. (p. 2550)
Weerts, Christine. Hero of Faith - Rosa Young. (p. 961)
Wees, Alyssa. Waking Forest. (p. 2371)
Wees, Janet. When We Were Shadows (p. 2434)
Weesner, Stephen. Heroes of the Old Testament: Joseph, Daniel, & Captain Naaman. (p. 962)
Weetman, Nova. Hot Cold Summer: Choose Your Own Ever After. (p. 1006)
—Marvelous Moleon Kennett, Chris, illus. (p. 1413)
—Speedy Spidersaurus Kennett, Chris, illus. (p. 2078)
—Tumbling Tigerdillo Kennett, Chris, illus. (p. 2299)
Weetwood, E. m. Lure of the Land (Classic Reprint) (p. 1369)
Weever, Edwin. Uncle Zeberiah, or Just Plain Folks: A Rural Comedy-Drama in Four Acts (Classic Reprint) (p. 2320)
Weevers, Peter, illus. see Wahl, Jan.
Wefer, Harold. Under the Onion Dome. (p. 2322)
Wegelius, Jakob. Murderer's Ape. (p. 1527)
Wegelius, Jakob & Graves, Peter. Murderer's Ape. (p. 1527)
Wegener, Scott, illus. see Alberti, Enigma.
Wegeng, Pamela Kay. Keepsakes Forever. (p. 1208)
Weger, Pauline & Williamson, Alicia. Useful Gifts: Colorful Quotes & True Stories to Inspire Everyday Living. (p. 2341)
Weglein, David Emrich. Correlation of Abilities of High School Pupils: A Dissertation. (p. 456)
Weglinski, Michaela. NGR in the Desert (Pre-Reader) (p. 1601)
Wegman, Marcia. Lula Belle. Wegman, Marcia, illus. (p. 1367)
Wegman, William. 3... 2... 1... Circus! (p. 2546)
Wegner, Fritz, illus. see Ahlberg, Allan.
Wegner, Fritz, illus. see Winterfeld, Henry.
Wegwerth, A. L. Little Bo Peep & Her Bad, Bad Sheep: A Mother Goose Hullabaloo. Flowers, Luke, illus. (p. 1312)
—Stegosaurus (p. 2112)
—Tyrannosaurus Rex (p. 2311)
Wehde, Albert. Since Leaving Home (Classic Reprint) (p. 2023)
Wehlen Morrison, Joan. Home Front Girl: A Diary of Love, Literature, & Growing up in Wartime America. Signe Morrison, Susan, ed. (p. 996)
Wehm, Darusha. Floating Point. (p. 750)
Wehman, A. Mother Shipton's Gipsy Fortune Teller & Dream Book: With Napoleon's Oraculum (Classic Reprint) (p. 1510)
Wehman, Henry J. Wehman's Black Jokes, for Blue Devils: Chuck Full of Darkey Fun! Colored Philosophy & Nigger Witticisms; Consisting of Plantation & High Life Stories, Highfalutin Sermons, Die-Away Songs, Ivory Opening Jokes, Complicated Conunderfums & an Endl. (p. 2396)
—Wehman's Brudder Bones' 4 11-44 Joker: Containing a Jolly Lot of Sable Conundrums, Ethiopian Jokes, Burnt Cork Comicalities & Darkey Dialogues (Classic Reprint) (p. 2396)
Wehner, Lauren, et al. Honduras. (p. 998)
Wehrheim, Carol A. Baptism Promises. Fulcher, Roz, illus. (p. 164)
—Dedication Promises. Fulcher, Roz, illus. (p. 524)
—Feasting on the Word Childrens's Sermons for Year A. (p. 717)
—Word & Picture Books: For Year C/A Set 2 (p. 2493)
—Word & Picture Books: For Year A/B Set 3 (p. 2493)
Wehrheim, Carol A., jt. auth. see Caldwell, Elizabeth F.
Wehrman, Richard, illus. see Martin, Rafe.
Wehrman, Tom. Grandpa's a Martian. Dunnier, Tina, illus. (p. 879)
Wehrman, Vicki, illus. see Ehrmantraut, Brenda.
Wehrman, Vicki, illus. see Lehman-Wilzig, Tami.
Wehrmeijer, Annelien. Anik & Yukon. van de Liejgraaf, Deborah, illus. (p. 87)
Wei, Chen. Secrets of the Terracotta Army. Yang, Peng, illus. (p. 1981)
Wei, Miao, illus. see Ma, Zheng & Li, Zheng.
Wei, Rouyi. My Parisian Uncle's Dinner Table. (p. 1558)
Wei, Valerie, illus. see Krishnan, Laura.
Wei, Yuheng. Bischofia Javanica School in the Storm. (p. 234)
Weibel, Suzy, jt. auth. see Gresh, Dannah K.
Weibel, Suzy, jt. contrib. by see Gresh, Dannah.
Weicker, Gretchen. Kanye West: Hip-Hop Star. (p. 1203)
Weidemann, Christiane. Year in Art: The Activity Book. (p. 2519)
Weidenbach, Kristin. Meet Banjo Paterson. Hancock, James Gulliver, illus. (p. 1438)
Weider, Nicole. Project Inspired: Tips & Tricks for Staying True to Who You Are (p. 1806)
Weider, Shoshana, jt. auth. see Dorling Kindersley Publishing Staff.
Weider, Shoshana Z. Moon Landings. (p. 1501)
Weidman, Bella. Hedgie's Nantucket Dawn. (p. 948)
Weidner, Brittany L., illus. see Halloran, T.
Weidner, Teri. Always Twins. Weidner, Teri, illus. (p. 61)
—Sleep, Baby, Sleep. (p. 2036)
—Three Little Kittens. Weidner, Teri, illus. (p. 2233)
Weidner, Teri, illus. see Brown, Margaret Wise.
Weidner, Teri, illus. see Plourde, Lynn.
Weidner, Teri, illus. see Shoulders, Michael.
Weidner, Teri, illus. see Stutson, Caroline.
Weigall, Arthur. Burning Sands (Classic Reprint) (p. 300)
—Madeline of the Desert (Classic Reprint) (p. 1375)
Weigall, Arthur Edward Pearse Brome. Bedouin Love (Classic Reprint) (p. 188)
Weigand, John, photos by see Dyan, Penelope.
Weigand, John, photos by see Hillan, Pamela & Dyan, Penelope.
Weigand, John D. Wonderful, Wonderful Copenhagen! a Kid's Guide to Copenhagen, Denmark. Dyan, Penelope, photos by. (p. 2490)
Weigand, John D., illus. see Dyan, Penelope.
Weigand, John D., photos by see Dyan, Penelope.
Weigand, John D., photos by see Hillan, Pamela & Dyan, Penelope.
Weigandt, Elizabeth. Queen Bee. (p. 1823)
Weigel, Hans, ed. see Schnitzler, Arthur.
Weigel, Jeff. Dragon Girl: The Secret Valley. (p. 593)
—Quantum Mechanics. (p. 1822)
Weigel, Jeff, illus. see Latta, Sara L.
Weigel, Jeff, illus. see Latta, Sara.
Weigel, Jeff, illus. see Spradlin, Michael P.
Weigel, Marlene. U-X-L Encyclopedia of Biomes. (p. 2313)
Weigelt, Udo. Wild Wombat. Weigelt, Udo, illus. (p. 2465)
Weighill, Damien, illus. see Cox, Lizzie.
Weighill, Damien, illus. see Hutton, Sarah.
Weightman, Magnus. All along the River. (p. 51)
—Welcome Home, Beaver. (p. 2397)
Weightman, Paul. Adventure of Syvannah & Haelyn. (p. 18)
—Chase & His Dinosaur Friend Called Cute. (p. 361)
—Diary of the Sentinel. (p. 540)
—Dream-Catcher's Curse. (p. 601)
—Little Stories for Little Children. (p. 1328)
—Old Man of Dolby Forest. (p. 1647)
—Summer Duke. (p. 2149)
—Summer Duke & the Old Man of Epping Forest. (p. 2149)
—?the Wizard Family Schmitt? (Syvannah & Haelyn Mystical Adventure in Ireland) (p. 2214)
Weigl Publishers, creator. Crab & Its Mother: What Is the Best Way to Teach Others? (p. 465)
—Crow & the Raven: Why Should You Be Yourself? (p. 478)
—Farmer & His Sons: Why Should You Work Hard? (p. 710)
—Goose & the Golden Egg: What Happens When You Are Greedy? (p. 869)
—Lion & the Mouse: Can Little Friends Be Great Friends? (p. 1305)
—Milk Woman & Her Pail: What Happens If You Count on Getting Something Before You Have It? (p. 1467)
—Shoemaker & His Medicine: Why Should You Tell the Truth? (p. 2009)
—Snake & His Tail: How Can You Support Your Team? (p. 2044)
—Wild Donkey & the Tame Donkey: Why Should You Not Judge Others by Their Appearance? (p. 2463)
Weihenmayer, Erik & Levy, Buddy. No Barriers (the Young Adult Adaptation) A Blind Man's Journey to Kayak the Grand Canyon. (p. 1612)
Weihs, Erika, illus. see Chaikin, Miriam.
Weihs, Erika, illus. see Kimmel, Eric A.
Weil, Ann. Australia (p. 138)
—Bomb-Sniffing Dogs. (p. 254)
—Geronimo (p. 823)
—Italy in Our World. (p. 1142)
—Medgar Evers (p. 1436)
—Meet Our New Student from Quebec. (p. 1439)
—Pro Wrestling Greats. (p. 1802)
—Sitting Bull (p. 2027)
—Story Behind Silk (p. 2127)
—World's Most Amazing Castles (p. 2507)
—World's Most Amazing Dams (p. 2507)
—World's Most Amazing Lost Cities (p. 2507)
—World's Most Amazing Monuments (p. 2507)
—World's Most Amazing National Parks (p. 2507)
—World's Most Amazing Pyramids (p. 2507)
Weil, Ann & Guillain, Charlotte. American Indian Cultures (p. 72)
Weil, Cynthia. I'm Glad I Did. (p. 1098)
Weil, Eliot. Golden Rod, Vol. 36: April 1924 (Classic Reprint) (p. 859)
Weil, Jamie. Asking Questions about What's on Television. (p. 126)
—First Break. (p. 735)
—Jeff Bezos: Founder of Amazon. com (p. 1162)
—Mark Zuckerberg: Creator of Facebook (p. 1407)
Weil, Joseph R. Yellow Kid Weil: The Autobiography of America's Master Swindler (Classic Reprint) (p. 2520)
Weil, Susan. Trees. (p. 2284)
Weil, Sylvie. Elvina's Mirror. (p. 640)
—My Guardian Angel. Rosner, Gillian, tr. (p. 1549)
Weiland, Jeanette. Red Beans & Rice. Loflin, Van Zandt Roberta, illus. (p. 1856)
Weiland, Peter. So Big yet So Small. Coffey, Kevin, illus. (p. 2050)
Weiland, Samantha. Learning with Tasha & Benji: This Is Tasha & This Is Benji. Kumar, Ambadi, illus. (p. 1259)
Weilerstein, Sadie Rose. K'tonton's Sukkot Adventure. (p. 1233)
Weill, Alexander. Village Tales from Alsatia (Classic Reprint) (p. 2358)
Weill, Blanche C. Through Children's Eyes: True Stories Out of the Practice of a Consultant Psychologist (Classic Reprint) (p. 2236)
Weill, Catherine. Frédéric Chopin. (p. 781)
Weill, Cynthia. ABeCedarios - Mexican Folk Art ABCs in English & Spanish. (p. 5)
—Animal Talk: Mexican Folk Art Animal Sounds in English & Spanish. (p. 92)
—Animal Talk. (p. 92)
—Colores de la Vida: Mexican Folk Art Colors in English & Spanish. (p. 422)
—Colores de la Vida. (p. 422)
—Count Me In: A Parade of Mexican Folk Art Numbers in English & Spanish. The Aguilar Sisters, The Aguilar, illus. (p. 458)
—Count Me In! (p. 458)
—Let's Work. (p. 1278)
—Mi Familia Calaca / My Skeleton Family. Zarate, Jesus, illus. (p. 1455)
—My Skeleton Family. Zarate, Jesus, illus. (p. 1561)
—Opuestos: Mexican Folk Art Opposites in English & Spanish. (p. 1667)
—Opuestos. (p. 1667)
Weills, Isaac Mosheim. Bright Spots in Camp Life (Classic Reprint) (p. 281)
Weiman, Jon, illus. see Hollenbeck, Kathleen M.
Weiman, Jon, illus. see Lingemann, Linda.
Weiman, Tracy. Larp. McWryat, Aine, illus. (p. 1244)
Weimer, Anissa C. When Ray Loses His Moo! (p. 2432)
Weimer, Brandon. Mom Serves Monsters. Salmond, Jared, illus. (p. 1490)
Weimer, Heidi. You're My Little Love Bug! (p. 2535)
Weimer, Heidi R. You're My Little Love Bug. Smart Kidz, ed. (p. 2535)
Weimer, Liza. Hello? (p. 950)
Wein, Elizabeth. Black Dove White Raven. (p. 238)
—Code Name Verity. (p. 411)
—Pearl Thief. (p. 1710)
—Rose under Fire. (p. 1905)
—Star Wars: the Last Jedi Cobalt Squadron. Noto, Phil, illus. (p. 2105)
—Thousand Sisters: The Heroic Airwomen of the Soviet Union in World War II. (p. 2231)
Wein, Len, et al. House of Mystery (p. 1023)
Weinbach, Shaindel, tr. see Matov, G.
Weinberg, Bruce P. Fabulous Feats of Mr. B: Opposite Day. Palomo, Gabriela M., illus. (p. 692)
—Fabulous Feats of Mr. B: Mr. B's First Day. Palomo, Gabriela M., illus. (p. 692)
Weinberg, Devorah, illus. see Yerushalmi, Miriam.
Weinberg, Devorah, jt. auth. see Yerushalmi, Miriam.
Weinberg, Elisabeth & Stine, Matt. Little Chef. Keiser, Paige, illus. (p. 1313)
Weinberg, James. Contrary Creatures: Unique Animal Opposites. (p. 445)
Weinberg, James, illus. see Nayeri, Daniel.
Weinberg, Jennifer, et al. Race for the Stars. Melaranci, Elisabetta et al, illus. (p. 1831)
Weinberg, Jennifer Liberts. Doc Mcstuffins: Blame It on the Rain. (p. 572)
—Happy Birthday, Mike! (p. 921)
—Happy Birthday, Mike! (Disney/Pixar Monsters, Inc.) RH Disney Staff, illus. (p. 921)
—Happy Birthday, Princess! (p. 921)
—Princess Hearts. (p. 1797)
—Princess Hearts (Disney Princess) Legramandi, Francesco, illus. (p. 1797)
—Princesses & Puppies. (p. 1800)
—This Little Piggy (Disney Junior: Minnie's Bow-Toons) RH Disney, illus. (p. 2226)
Weinberg, Jennifer Liberts, jt. auth. see Posner-Sanchez, Andrea.
Weinberg, Steven. Fred & the Lumberjack. Weinberg, Steven, illus. (p. 780)
—Rex Finds an Egg! Egg! Egg! Weinberg, Steven, illus. (p. 1874)
—You Must Be This Tall. Weinberg, Steven, illus. (p. 2527)
Weinberg, Steven, illus. see Scieszka, Jon.
Weinberger, Caspar W. Account of the Pilgrimage to the Tomb of General Grant (Classic Reprint) (p. 10)
Weinberger, David J. Answers to a Christmas Question. (p. 101)
—Answers to a Christmas Question Coloring Book. (p. 101)
Weinberger, Justin. Reformed. (p. 1860)
Weinbrecht, William. Stories for Amand. (p. 2123)
Weinbrenner, Darlene. My Silly Willy Loose Tooth. Weinbrenner, Jacquelyn, illus. (p. 1560)
Weinbrenner, Jacquelyn, illus. see Weinbrenner, Darlene.
Weineger, Brigitte. Aunt Fanny's Star. Oral, Feridun, illus. (p. 137)
Weiner, Andrew. Down by the River: A Family Fly Fishing Story. Chu, April, illus. (p. 590)
Weiner, Ellis. Templeton Twins Have an Idea: Book. Holmes, Jeremy, illus. (p. 2203)
—Templeton Twins Have an Idea: Book 1. Holmes, Jeremy, illus. (p. 2203)
—Templeton Twins Have an Idea: Book One. Holmes, Jeremy, illus. (p. 2203)
Weiner, Eric, jt. auth. see Inches, Alison.
Weiner, Jennifer. Little Bigfoot, Big City. (p. 1311)
—Littlest Bigfoot. (p. 1330)
Weiner, Jonathan, illus. see English, Karen.
Weiner, Jordan. Junior & Tipper Learn to Deal with the Bully. (p. 1190)
Weiner, Marcella Bakur, jt. auth. see Neimark, Jill.
Weiner, Marcella Bakur & Neimark, Jill. I Want Your Moo: A Story for Children about Self-Esteem. Adinolfi, JoAnn, illus. (p. 1085)
Weiner, Miriam. Shakespeare's Seasons. Whitt, Shannon, illus. (p. 1999)
Weinert, Matthias. No Bath, No Cake! Polly's Pirate Party. (p. 1612)
Weinert, Stella, compiled by. Come on Clouds, Fly Away! (p. 428)
Weing, Drew. Creepy Case Files of Margo Maloo. (p. 472)
—Creepy Case Files of Margo Maloo: the Monster Mall. (p. 472)
Weingarten, A. J. Rock Climbing. (p. 1894)
Weingarten, E. T. Fishing. (p. 742)
—Hunting with Killer Whales (p. 1054)
—I See a Deer. (p. 1081)

W

Wells, Karen, jt. auth. see McCloud, Carol.
Wells, Kate Gannett. In the Clearings (Classic Reprint) (p. 1108)
—Miss. Curtis: A Sketch (Classic Reprint) (p. 1478)
—Two Modern Women: A Novel (Classic Reprint) (p. 2308)
Wells, L. R. Trusting Pup. (p. 2296)
Wells, Leah. Furry Foot Notes. Rosenblatt, Naomi, illus. (p. 802)
Wells, Lee. Tom's Christmas Wishes. (p. 2259)
Wells, Lorraine, illus. see Pingry, Patricia A.
Wells, Lucy Colton. Children of the Old Stone House (Classic Reprint) (p. 372)
Wells, Maggie. Aleecia #2. (p. 41)
—Candace #1. (p. 321)
—Isabella #4. (p. 1138)
—Jasmine #3. (p. 1160)
—Luciana #6. (p. 1363)
—Shawna #5. (p. 2004)
Wells, Marcia. Doom at Grant's Tomb. Calo, Marcos, illus. (p. 585)
—Mystery in Mayan Mexico. (p. 1569)
—Mystery in Mayan Mexico. Calo, Marcos, illus. (p. 1569)
—Mystery on Museum Mile. Calo, Marcos, illus. (p. 1570)
Wells, Mark & Wells, Meagan. Tommy's Lost Tooth. Wells, Mark, illus. (p. 2259)
Wells, Mary G. Marie Derville: A Story of a French Boarding-School (Classic Reprint) (p. 1405)
Wells, Morris B. Five Gallons of Gasoline (Classic Reprint) (p. 743)
Wells, Naomi. Astronauts Believe in Themselves! Believing in Yourself (p. 128)
—Gia the Giraffe Gets Started! Getting It Done! (p. 830)
—I Find Signs: Looking at Data. (p. 1065)
—My Class Decides Together: Civic Virtues. (p. 1535)
—Prince Makes a Plan: What Could Happen? (p. 1794)
—Sophie Helps at School: Taking Civic Action. (p. 2065)
—Stars at the Science Museum: What Will Happen? (p. 2107)
—What Does Citizenship Mean? Digital Citizenship. (p. 2410)
—What Happens at City Hall? Understanding Government. (p. 2411)
Wells, Patricia Taylor. Eyes of the Doe. (p. 689)
Wells, Percival W. Great Corrector: More or Less a Vital Satire (Classic Reprint) (p. 885)
Wells, Philip. Alien Guide from Inner Space: And Other Poems. (p. 47)
—Daddy Island. Daly, Niki, illus. (p. 495)
Wells, Polly. Freaking Out: Real-Life Stories about Anxiety. Mitchell, Peter, illus. (p. 779)
Wells, Quierra LaQuelle, illus. see Wells-Sanders, Glenora.
Wells, R., jt. auth. see Watt, Fiona.
Wells, Rachel. Alfie Cat in Trouble. (p. 43)
—Alfie Far from Home. (p. 43)
—Farm. (p. 709)
—That's Not My Christmas Coloring Book. (p. 2214)
—That's Not My Sticker Book Christmas. (p. 2214)
—That's Not My Sticker Book Farm. (p. 2214)
Wells, Rachel, illus. see Durber, Matt & Brooks, Felicity.
Wells, Rachel, illus. see Watt, Fiona.
Wells, Rachel, jt. auth. see Watt, Fiona.
Wells, Rachel, jt. ed. see Watt, Fiona.
Wells, Rebecca Kim. Shatter the Sky. (p. 2003)
Wells, Rebekah, illus. see Pearse, Kaye Saoirse.
Wells, Robert, jt. auth. see Wells, Robert E.
Wells, Robert E. Can We Share the World with Tigers? Wells, Robert E., illus. (p. 318)
—Can You Count to a Googol? (p. 318)
—Did a Dinosaur Drink This Water? (p. 542)
—How Do You Know What Time It Is? Wells, Robert E., illus. (p. 1030)
—How Do You Lift a Lion? (p. 1030)
—Is a Blue Whale the Biggest Thing There Is? (p. 1136)
—Polar Bear, Why Is Your World Melting? Wells, Robert E., illus. (p. 1769)
—What's Faster Than a Speeding Cheetah? (p. 2423)
—What's Older Than a Giant Tortoise? Wells, Robert E., illus. (p. 2425)
—What's Smaller Than a Pygmy Shrew? (p. 2425)
—What's So Special about Planet Earth? (p. 2425)
—What's So Special about Planet Earth? Wells, Robert E., illus. (p. 2425)
—Why Do Elephants Need the Sun? (p. 2456)
—Why Do Elephants Need the Sun? Wells, Robert E., illus. (p. 2456)
Wells, Robert G., illus. see Jeffrey, Maggie.
Wells, Robin. Sarah's Day at Kindergarten. Grott, Isabella, illus. (p. 1935)
—Sarah's Day in Kindergarten. Grott, Isabella, illus. (p. 1935)
—So Many Classes. Piworski, Marcin, illus. (p. 2050)
—So Many Classes. Piwowarski, Marcin, illus. (p. 2050)
—Trick or Treat. Grott, Isabella, illus. (p. 2287)
—Where Is Santa? Bassani, Srimalie, illus. (p. 2438)
Wells, Robison. Blackout. (p. 240)
—Dark Energy. (p. 506)
—Dead Zone. (p. 518)
—Feedback. (p. 718)
—Variant. (p. 2348)
Wells, Robyn, jt. auth. see Button, Joshua.
Wells, Ronnie. Legend of Catfish & Little Bream. (p. 1261)
Wells, Rosemary. Bunny Cakes (Edición en Español) Wells, Rosemary, illus. (p. 298)
—Felix Eats Up. Wells, Rosemary, illus. (p. 719)
—Felix Stands Tall. Wells, Rosemary, illus. (p. 719)
—Fiona's Little Accident. Wells, Rosemary, illus. (p. 732)
—Fiona's Little Lie. Wells, Rosemary, illus. (p. 732)
—Following Grandfather. Denise, Christopher, illus. (p. 758)
—Hand in Hand. (p. 914)
—Hand in Hand. Wells, Rosemary, illus. (p. 914)
—Hungry Bunny Tales. (p. 1052)
—Ivy Takes Care. LaMarche, Jim, illus. (p. 1150)
—Kindergators: Hands off, Harry! Wells, Rosemary, illus. (p. 1219)
—Kindergators: Miracle Melts Down. Wells, Rosemary, illus. (p. 1219)
—Kit & Kaboodle. (p. 1225)
—Love Waves: Midi Edition. Wells, Rosemary, illus. (p. 1361)
—Love Waves. Wells, Rosemary, illus. (p. 1361)
—Max & Ruby & Twin Trouble. Wells, Rosemary, illus. (p. 1427)
—Max & Ruby at the Warthogs' Wedding. Wells, Rosemary, illus. (p. 1427)
—Max & Ruby's Bedtime Book. (p. 1427)
—Max & Ruby's Preschool Pranks. (p. 1427)
—Max & the Fall Parade. (p. 1427)
—Max at School. (p. 1427)
—Max at School. Grey, Andrew, illus. (p. 1427)
—Max's Bug. (p. 1428)
—Max's Bug. Grey, Andrew, illus. (p. 1428)
—Max's Christmas. (p. 1428)
—Max's Half Birthday. Grey, Andrew, illus. (p. 1428)
—Max's Lunch. (p. 1428)
—Max's Lunch. Grey, Andrew, illus. (p. 1428)
—McDuff Moves In. Jeffers, Susan, illus. (p. 1432)
—On the Blue Comet. Ibatoulline, Bagram, illus. (p. 1653)
—Otto Runs for President. Wells, Rosemary, illus. (p. 1676)
—Ruby's Rainbow. (p. 1912)
—Say Hello, Sophie! (p. 1940)
—Sleep, My Bunny. Wells, Rosemary, illus. (p. 2036)
—Sophie's Christmas Surprise. (p. 2065)
—Sophie's Halloween Disguise. (p. 2065)
—Sporty Bunny Tales. (p. 2090)
—Stella's Starliner. Wells, Rosemary, illus. (p. 2113)
—Time-Out for Sophie. Wells, Rosemary, illus. (p. 2245)
—Use Your Words, Sophie. (p. 2341)
—Visit to Dr. Duck. Wells, Rosemary, illus. (p. 2362)
—Voyage to the Bunny Planet. (p. 2368)
—Yoko. Wells, Rosemary, illus. (p. 2523)
—Yoko Finds Her Way. (p. 2523)
—You Can Do It, Noisy Nora! (p. 2525)
Wells, Rosemary, illus. see Opie, Iona, ed.
Wells, Rosemary, illus. see Opie, Iona.
Wells, Rosemary, illus. see White, E. B.
Wells, Rosemary, jt. auth. see Carbone, Elisa.
Wells, Rosemary, jt. auth. see London, Jonathan.
Wells, Rosemary, jt. auth. see Marino, Gianna.
Wells, Rosemary, jt. auth. see Pinkney, Andrea Davis.
Wells, Rosemary, jt. auth. see Winchester, Simon.
Wells, Rosemary & Jeffers, Susan. McDuff Moves In. (p. 1432)
Wells, Rosemary & Rosemary, Wells. Yoko. (p. 2523)
Wells, Rosemary, et al. My Havana: Memories of a Cuban Boyhood. Ferguson, Peter, illus. (p. 1549)
Wells, S. J. Windy Blabs & His Bad Mouth. (p. 2472)
Wells, Samuel E. Valmond the Crank: The Forbidden Book (Classic Reprint) (p. 2345)
Wells, Shannon Nicole. Gold! A Tall Tale. (p. 855)
Wells Smith, Abby, illus. see Toombs, Tom.
Wells, Tina. Mackenzie Blue. (p. 1372)
—Mackenzie Blue #2: the Secret Crush. (p. 1372)
—Mackenzie Blue #3: Friends Forever? (p. 1372)
—Mackenzie Blue #4: Mixed Messages. (p. 1372)
—Mackenzie Blue #5: Double Trouble Vol. 5. Segawa, Michael, illus. (p. 1372)
Wells, Webster. Essentials of Geometry. (p. 664)
—New Plane & Solid Geometry (Classic Reprint) (p. 1596)
Wells, William Bittle. Pacific Monthly, Vol. 1: July, 1905 (Classic Reprint) (p. 1691)
—Pacific Monthly, Vol. 12: July, 1904 December, 1904 (Classic Reprint) (p. 1691)
—Pacific Monthly, Vol. 15: January, 1906-June, 1906 (Classic Reprint) (p. 1691)
—Pacific Monthly, Vol. 25: January to June, 1911 (Classic Reprint) (p. 1691)
Wells, Zeb. Carnage, U. S. A. Crain, Clayton, illus. (p. 332)
—Inauguration Day. Nauck, Todd, illus. (p. 1112)
Wells-Cole, Catherine. Slavery & the Forging of Early America. (p. 2035)
Wells-Cole, Catherine, jt. auth. see Twist, Clint.
Wells-Sanders, Glenora. Trinny Bear & Dallas. Wells, Quierra LaQuelle, illus. (p. 2288)
Wells-Strozier, Marsay Latrice. Keira & Me: Homonyms & Homophones. Brittany, Jackson, illus. (p. 1208)
Welsh, Anne Marie. It's Your Planet-Love It! Breathe. (p. 1148)
Welsh, Anne Marie & Fenly, Leigh. Wow! Wonders of Water. Garcia, Helena, illus. (p. 2510)
Welsh, Anne Marie & Tuchman, Laura. World of Girls. Garcia, Helena, illus. (p. 2503)
Welsh, C. E. L. Space Race. Jones, K. L., illus. (p. 2072)
Welsh, Charles. Book of Nursery Rhymes: Being Mother Goose's Melodies, Arranged in the Order of Attractiveness & Interest (Classic Reprint) (p. 259)
—Bookseller of the Last Century - Scholar's Choice Edition. (p. 261)
—Chauffeur Chaff or Automobilia (Classic Reprint) (p. 363)
—Famous Tales & Laughter Stories (Classic Reprint) (p. 704)
—Story of a Donkey: Abridged from the French of Madame la Comtesse de Segur (Classic Reprint) (p. 2128)
Welsh, Charles, tr. see Perrault, Charles.
Welsh, Clare Helen. Cookie Blast Off! Touliatou, Sophia, illus. (p. 446)
—Tide. (p. 2240)
Welsh, Hayley, illus. see Bennett, Sandra.
Welsh, Herbert. New Gentleman of the Road (Classic Reprint) (p. 1594)
Welsh, James. White Baby (Classic Reprint) (p. 2443)
Welsh, James C. Underworld: The Story of Robert Sinclair, Miner. (p. 2326)
—Underworld: The Story of Robert Sinclair, Miner (Classic Reprint) (p. 2326)
Welsh, Lora Jagla. Chicken Who Ate Cheese off of China. (p. 368)
Welsh, Lucie D. Some of Our Friends (Classic Reprint) (p. 2059)
Welsh, Mary Reddick. Sammy, the Little Green Snake Who Wanted to Fly. Welsh, Mary Reddick, illus. (p. 1928)
Welsh, Moe. Time for Bed. (p. 2244)
Welshman, Kate. Anais Butt & the Hairy-Handed Gent. (p. 78)
—Make up or Break Up: Choose Your Own Ever After. (p. 1387)
—Make up or Break Up. (p. 1387)
—Posse. (p. 1779)
Welsh-Mason, C. Rape of the Gamp, Vol. 3 Of 3: Or, Won at Last; a Novel (Classic Reprint) (p. 1841)
—Rape of the Gamp; or, Won at Last, Vol. 2 Of 3: A Novel (Classic Reprint) (p. 1841)
Welters, M. Andrine. My Confession Book: A Child's Preparation for the Sacrament of Penance. (p. 1536)
Weltevrede, Nona, illus. see Sperling, Vatsala.
Weltevrede, Pieter, illus. see Johari, Harish & Sperling, Vatsala.
Weltevrede, Pieter, illus. see Sperling, Vatsala & Johari, Harish.
Weltevrede, Pieter, illus. see Sperling, Vatsala.
Weltman, Relly, illus. see Martwick, Alica.
Welton, Darlene. Dinohumes. Gibson, Maria, illus. (p. 548)
—Rufus, the Rac. Gibson, Maria, illus. (p. 1912)
Welton, Jude. Tomas Loves... A Rhyming Book about Fun, Friendship - & Autism. Telford, Jane, illus. (p. 2258)
Welty, Carolyn. Look at Little Lucy Pratt. Susan, illus. (p. 1345)
Welty, E. A. Self-Made: Or, Living for Those We Love (Classic Reprint) (p. 1987)
Welty, Tara. Jane Goodall. (p. 1158)
Welty, Tara & Banas, Sharon L. Handling Teamwork & Respect for Others. (p. 915)
Welvaert, Scott R. 13th Floor. (p. 2552)
—Alabaster Ring. (p. 39)
—Grotesque. (p. 898)
Welwood, Margaret. Scissortown (Faith-Based Application) (p. 1960)
—Scissortown (Life Application) (p. 1960)
Welzen, Jon. I Know Numbers. (p. 1067)
—I Know Shapes. (p. 1067)
—I Know the Seasons. (p. 1067)
Wemyss, George. Grannie for Granted (Classic Reprint) (p. 880)
—Jaunty in Charge (Classic Reprint) (p. 1161)
—Secret Book (Classic Reprint) (p. 1975)
—Things We Thought Of: Told from a Child's Point of View (Classic Reprint) (p. 2221)
Wemyss, Mary C. E. Impossible People (Classic Reprint) (p. 1102)
—Lost Interest (Classic Reprint) (p. 1354)
—People of Popham (Classic Reprint) (p. 1719)
—Professional Aunt (Classic Reprint) (p. 1804)
—Prudent Priscilla (Classic Reprint) (p. 1809)
Wen, Abigail Hing. Loveboat, Taipei. (p. 1361)
Wen, Kang. Legend of the Unknowns. (p. 1263)
Wenberg, Michael. Seattle Blues. (p. 1972)
—Stringz. (p. 2141)
Wencel, Dave. UFOs. (p. 2313)
Wenckebach, L. W. R., illus. see Hoffmann, E. T. A.
Wency, Mélanie. Resurrection (l'Envers du Paradis - Tome 1) (p. 1870)
Wendel, Carie, illus. see Everett, Melissa.
Wendel, Carrie, illus. see Everett, Melissa.
Wendel, Gretchen Schomer & Schomer, Adam Anthony. All Around Town. Renthrope, Damon, illus. (p. 51)
—Becka Goes to India. Renthrope, Damon, illus. (p. 186)
—Becka Goes to the North Pole. Renthrope, Damon, illus. (p. 186)
Wendel, S. E. Across the Pond (p. 11)
—Across the Pond. (p. 11)
—Demons in the North #2. (p. 528)
—Expedition #1. (p. 677)
—Others #4. (p. 1675)
—Rebirth #6. (p. 1852)
—Time of Trying Souls #3. (p. 2245)
—World at War #5. (p. 2501)
Wendel, S. E. & Siemens, Jared. WNBA Finals. (p. 2483)
Wendell, Barrett. Rankell's Remains: An American Novel (Classic Reprint) (p. 1841)
Wendell Holton, William. Imaginative Adventures of Penelope Ellerbee. (p. 1100)
Wendig, Chuck. Force Awakens: Volume 1. Ross, Luke & Martin, Frank, illus. (p. 764)
—Force Awakens: Volume 3. Laming, Marc & Martin, Frank, illus. (p. 764)
—Hunt (p. 1052)
Wendinger, Jennifer. Unusual & Awesome Jobs Using Science: Hollywood Animal Trainer, Cave Diver, & More. (p. 2336)
Wendland, Paula, illus. see Hillert, Margaret.
Wendland, Paula, illus. see Malaspina, Ann.
Wendland, Paula Zinngrabe, illus. see Hillert, Margaret & Andersen, Hans.
Wendland, Paula Zinngrabe, illus. see Hillert, Margaret, et al.
Wendling, Émile. Alsatiana, or the Faithful Daughter: A Fairy Tale of the Present Day (Classic Reprint) (p. 60)
—Alsatiana, or, the Faithful Daughter: A Fairy Tale of the Present Day. (p. 60)
Wendling, Nathalie & Glatzmayer, Thomas. Melanie & Tommy Have Two Pet Rats & One Syndrome. (p. 1442)
Wendling, Peter. Magic of the Dark Ravine. Durie, Sally, illus. (p. 1378)
Wendorff, Anne. Bear Cubs. (p. 179)
—Blastoff! Readers - Watch Animals Grow (p. 243)
—Eaglets. (p. 613)
—Fawns. (p. 716)
—Gymnastics. (p. 907)
—Lambs. (p. 1240)
—Pugs. (p. 1812)
—Saint Bernards. (p. 1923)
—Shetland Sheepdogs. (p. 2006)
—Siberian Huskies. (p. 2014)
—Soccer. (p. 2051)
—Swimming. (p. 2170)
—Tennis. (p. 2206)
Wendt, Caitlin. Mr. Dill Pickles. (p. 1518)
Wendt, Frederick W. Transatlantics (Classic Reprint) (p. 2277)
Wendt, Jennifer. Showing Chickens at the Fair. (p. 2012)
—Showing Cows at the Fair. (p. 2012)
—Showing Horses at the Fair. (p. 2012)
—Showing Pigs at the Fair. (p. 2013)
—Showing Rabbits at the Fair. (p. 2013)
—Showing Sheep at the Fair. (p. 2013)
Wendt, K. Where Did My Stars Go? Parkerson, Hannah, illus. (p. 2435)
Wendt, Matt, illus. see Jolley, Dan.
Wendt, Yohanna, illus. see Saint, Mimi.
Wendte, Charles W. At Christmas Time (Classic Reprint) (p. 129)
Wendy Lee Jungling; Illustrated By My Fa. Who Do You Want to Be? (p. 2447)
Wendy, Watson, illus. see Keen, Marian.
Weng, Yi Shan. Busy New Year Eve. (p. 302)
Wenger, Amanda, illus. see Edwards, Aylan.
Wenger, Amanda, jt. auth. see Edwards, Aylan.
Wenger, Brahm. Dewey's Helping Heart: To Beneift the Larry King Cardiac Foundation. (p. 536)
Weninger, Brigitte. 24 Stories for Advent. Tharlet, Eve, illus. (p. 2554)
—Davy Loves the Baby. Tharlet, Eve, illus. (p. 511)
—Davy's Summer Vacation. Tharlet, Eve, illus. (p. 511)
—Happy Birthday, Davy! Tharlet, Eve, illus. (p. 920)
—Happy Easter, Davy! Tharlet, Eve, illus. (p. 921)
—Merry Christmas Davy. Tharlet, Eve, illus. (p. 1450)
—Silent Night: The Story of the Famous Carol. Wintz-Litty, Julie, illus. (p. 2017)
Weninger, Brigitte & Tharlet, Eve. Davy Loves His Mommy. (p. 511)
Wenisch, Tanja. Friends Always. (p. 786)
Wenley, R. M. University Extension Movement in Scotland. (p. 2333)
Wenner, George U. Lutherans of New York: Their Story & Their Problems. (p. 1369)
Wennick, Elizabeth. Whatever Doesn't Kill You (p. 2423)
Wenning, Jeremy. Coco & Pebbles: Bath Night. Barrett, Casey, illus. (p. 411)
—Coco & Pebbles: That's My Duck! Barrett, Casey, illus. (p. 411)
—Roscoe the Volunteer Emt. Burns, Sandra, illus. (p. 1904)
Wensell, Ulises, illus. see Campoy, F. Isabel & Ada, Alma Flor.
Wensell, Ulises, illus. see Reviejo Hernandez, Carlos.
Wensink, Patrick. Go Go Gorillas: A Romping Bedtime Tale. Wragg, Nate, illus. (p. 846)
—Gorillas Go Bananas. Wragg, Nate, illus. (p. 870)
Wensley, Arin. Counting Frogs. (p. 460)
Wentk, Richard. Getting Started with Raspberry Pi. (p. 826)
—Raspberry Pi for Kids for Dummies. (p. 1842)
Wentworth, E. Arithmetical Problems, Arranged for Drill & Review in Primary, Grammar, & High Schools. (p. 116)
Wentworth, G. A. First Steps in Number, Part II. - Second Year: Numbers Ten to Twenty Inclusive, Pp. 212-327. (p. 739)
—First Steps in Number. Teacher's Edition. Part I. - First Year: Number One to Nine Inclusive. (p. 739)
—First Steps in Number, Teacher's Edition, Part I. - First Year: Numbers One to Nine Inclusive. (p. 739)
Wentworth, George. Machine-Shop Mathematics. (p. 1372)
Wentworth, George, jt. auth. see Smith, David Eugene.
Wentworth, George Albert. New Plane & Spherical Trigonometry, Surveying & Navigation (Classic Reprint) (p. 1596)
—New Plane & Spherical Trigonometry, Surveying, & Navigation (Classic Reprint) (p. 1596)
Wentworth, Hiram. Sold by His Wife in Mexico! The Bard of Mount Madonna (Classic Reprint) (p. 2056)
Wentworth, Marjory. Shackles. Pratt-Thomas, Leslie, illus. (p. 1996)
Wentworth, Mary. Golden Dawn: And Other Stories (Classic Reprint) (p. 857)
Wentworth, May. Fairy Tales from Gold Lands: Second Series (Classic Reprint) (p. 698)
—Fairy Tales from Gold Lands. (p. 698)
—Fairy Tales from Gold Lands (Classic Reprint) (p. 698)
Wentworth, Patricia. Devil's Wind (Classic Reprint) (p. 536)
—Fire Within (Classic Reprint) (p. 733)
Wentworth-James, Gertie De S. House of Chance (Classic Reprint) (p. 1022)
Wentz, Holly. Stars Forbade Us (p. 2107)
Wentz, Lorraine. Who Has Barney. (p. 2447)
Wentz, Sara A. Smiles & Frowns (Classic Reprint) (p. 2042)
Wentz, Tim. Dark Secret at Twenty-Five Feet. (p. 507)
Wentzloff, Linden, illus. see Nunn, Lori.
Wenxuan, Cao. Bronze & Sunflower. So, Meilo, illus. (p. 285)
—Bronze & Sunflower. Wang, Helen, tr. from CHI. (p. 285)
—Summer: Animals Share in a Poetic Tale of Kindness. Rong, Yu, illus. (p. 2148)
Wenxuan, Cao & Meilo, Roger. Feather. Garcia-roberts, Chloe, tr. (p. 717)
Wenzel, Angela. 13 Art Mysteries Children Should Know. (p. 2552)
—13 Art Techniques Children Should Know. (p. 2552)
—13 Artists Children Should Know. (p. 2552)
—13 Paintings Children Should Know. (p. 2552)
—13 Sculptures Children Should Know. (p. 2552)
Wenzel, Anna. Male Privilege (p. 1392)
Wenzel, Brendan. Hello Hello. (p. 951)
—Hello Hello (Books for Preschool & Kindergarten, Poetry Books for Kids) (p. 951)
—Stone Sat Still. (p. 2121)
—They All Saw a Cat. (p. 2219)
—They All Saw a Cat. Wenzel, Brendan, illus. (p. 2219)
—They All Saw a Cat (Cat Books for Kids, Beginning Reading Books, Preschool Prep Books) (p. 2219)
Wenzel, Brendan, illus. see Bernstrom, Daniel.
Wenzel, Brendan, illus. see DiTerlizzi, Angela.
Wenzel, Brendan, illus. see Jackson, Ellen.
Wenzel, Brendan, illus. see Rylant, Cynthia.
Wenzel, Connie S. Fiona's Story - Featuring Fiona the Sea Turtle. (p. 732)
Wenzel, David, illus. see Deutsch, Stacia & Cohon, Rhody.
Wenzel, David, illus. see Lucado, Max, et al.
Wenzel, David, illus. see Lucado, Max.
Wenzel, David, illus. see Ross, Dev.
Wenzel, David, illus. see Spinelli, Eileen.
Wenzel, David, illus. see StJohn, Amanda.
Wenzel, David, jt. auth. see Lepp, Bil.

W

—Titanium Ninja. (p. 2251)
—Treasure of the Gold Dragon (p. 2282)
—Treasure of the Gold Dragon. Foresti, Sara, illus. (p. 2282)
—Waking the Rainbow Dragon (p. 2371)
—Waking the Rainbow Dragon. Jones, Damien, illus. (p. 2371)
—What Should Riley Do? Random House Disney Staff, illus. (p. 2420)
—World of Ninjago Official Guide. (p. 2503)
—You Are Magic: a Guided Journal to Unlock the Power of Your Inner Unicorn, Llamacorn, & Narwhal. Potter, Alice, illus. (p. 2524)
—Zeus & the Dreadful Dragon (p. 2540)
—Zeus & the Dreadful Dragon. Phillips, Craig, illus. (p. 2540)
West, Tracey, jt. auth. see Barbo, Maria S.
West, Tracey, jt. auth. see Scholastic, Inc. Staff.
West, Tracey, jt. auth. see Scholastic.
West, Tracey, jt. auth. see Simon, Coco.
West, Tracey, adapted by. Abominable Movie Novelization. (p. 6)
—Independence Day Resurgence Movie Novelization: Young Readers Edition. (p. 1115)
—More Monsters, More Problems (p. 1505)
—Smallfoot Movie Novelization. (p. 2040)
—Star Deluxe Junior Novelization. (p. 2102)
—Star Junior Novelization. (p. 2102)
West, Tracey & Dewin, Howie. Four-Star Challenge. (p. 773)
West, Tracey & Howard, Kate. Team Divided. (p. 2196)
West, Tracey, et al. Hermes & the Horse with Wings. (p. 959)
West, Venesa V. What Can I Be? (p. 2406)
West, W. L. Common Sense Speller: For Second & Third Grades (Classic Reprint) (p. 431)
—Common Sense Speller: For Sixth & Seventh Grades (Classic Reprint) (p. 431)
West, Woman's College of Due. Arrow, 1924, Vol. 4 (Classic Reprint) (p. 119)
Westall, Robert. Blitzcat. (p. 245)
—Machine Gunners. (p. 1372)
Westall, W. Tales & Legends of Saxony & Lusatia (Classic Reprint) (p. 2181)
Westall, William. Birch Dene: A Novel (Classic Reprint) (p. 230)
—Birch Dene. (p. 230)
—Birch Dene a Novel, Vol. 3 of 3 (Classic Reprint) (p. 230)
—Birch Dene, Vol. 1 Of 3: A Novel (Classic Reprint) (p. 230)
—Birch Dene, Vol. 2 Of 3: A Novel (Classic Reprint) (p. 230)
—For Honor & Life: A Novel (Classic Reprint) (p. 762)
—For Honor & Life. (p. 762)
—Her Two Millions, Vol. 1 of 3 (Classic Reprint) (p. 956)
—Her Two Millions, Vol. 2 of 3 (Classic Reprint) (p. 957)
—Old Factory: A Lancashire Story (Classic Reprint) (p. 1645)
—Old Factory, Vol. 3 Of 3: A Lancashire Story (Classic Reprint) (p. 1645)
—Princes of Peele (Classic Reprint) (p. 1795)
—Red Ryvington, Vol. 1 of 3 (Classic Reprint) (p. 1858)
—Sons of Belial (Classic Reprint) (p. 2064)
—Tales & Traditions of Switzerland (Classic Reprint) (p. 2181)
—Trust-Money, Vol. 1 Of 3: A Novel (Classic Reprint) (p. 2296)
—Trust-Money, Vol. 2 Of 3: A Novel (Classic Reprint) (p. 2296)
—Trust-Money, Vol. 3 Of 3: A Novel (Classic Reprint) (p. 2296)
—Two Pinches of Snuff, Vol. 1 of 3 (Classic Reprint) (p. 2309)
Westaway, Kylie. Whale in the Bathtub. Jellett, Tom, illus. (p. 2403)
—Why Can't I Be a Dinosaur? Jellett, Tom, illus. (p. 2455)
Westberg, Hannah. Hannah: My True Story of Drugs, Cutting, & Mental Illness. (p. 918)
Westberg, Jan, illus. see Freese, Susan M.
Westberg, Jan, illus. see Freese, Susan M., ed.
Westberg, Marijke De Roo. More about Vermont Gnomes. Westberg, Marijke De Roo, illus. (p. 1504)
Westbrook, Charles. Kabalyon Key. (p. 1201)
Westbrook, Dick, illus. see Sommer, Carl.
Westbrook, Emily. Vale of Glendor: Or, Memoirs of Emily Westbrook (Classic Reprint) (p. 2344)
—Vale of Glendor, or Memoirs of Emily Westbrook, Vol. 1 of 2 (Classic Reprint) (p. 2344)
Westbrook, Henrietta Payne. West-Brook Drives (Classic Reprint) (p. 2401)
Westbrook, Joe, jt. auth. see Chaffey, Tim.
Westbrook, Leah. Ballad of Cowboy Justin. (p. 161)
Westbury, Atha. Australian Fairy Tales (Classic Reprint) (p. 138)
—Shadow of Hilton Fernbrook: A Romance of Maoriland (Classic Reprint) (p. 1997)
Westbury, Hugh. Frederick Hazzleden, Vol. 1 Of 3: A Novel (Classic Reprint) (p. 782)
—Frederick Hazzleden, Vol. 2: A Novel (Classic Reprint) (p. 782)
Westcott, Anne & Hu, C. C. Alicia. Bomji & Spotty's Frightening Adventure: A Story about How to Recover from a Scary Experience. Kuo, Ching-Pang, illus. (p. 255)
—How Little Coyote Found His Secret Strength: A Story about How to Get Through Hard Times. Kuo, Ching-Pang, illus. (p. 1033)
—How Sprinkle the Pig Escaped the River of Tears: A Story about Finding Comfort after a Loss. Kuo, Ching-Pang, illus. (p. 1035)
Westcott, Edward Noyes. Christmas Story from David Harum (Classic Reprint) (p. 387)
—David Harum: A Story of American Life (Classic Reprint) (p. 511)
—David Harum. (p. 511)
—Teller a Story (Classic Reprint) (p. 2202)
Westcott, Frank N. Dabney Todd (Classic Reprint) (p. 494)
—Hepsey Burke (Classic Reprint) (p. 956)
Westcott, Jim. Gift. (p. 831)
—Greece. (p. 892)
—Natural Disasters. (p. 1579)
—Olympic Greats. (p. 1651)
—Performance Cars. (p. 1723)
—Tea Party, Libertarian, & Other Political Parties. (p. 2194)
—Upper Plains: Montana, North Dakota, South Dakota (p. 2339)
Westcott, Margaret. Bessie Wilmerton; or, Money, & What Came of It: A Novel (Classic Reprint) (p. 205)
Westcott, Nadine B., illus. see Harris, Robie H.
Westcott, Nadine Bernard, illus. see Ayres, Katherine.
Westcott, Nadine Bernard, illus. see Bateman, Teresa.
Westcott, Nadine Bernard, illus. see Buzzeo, Toni.
Westcott, Nadine Bernard, illus. see Harris, Robie H.
Westcott, Nadine Bernard, illus. see Hoberman, Mary Ann.
Westcott, Nadine Bernard, illus. see Lewison, Wendy Cheyette.
Westcott, Nadine Bernard, illus. see London, Jonathan.
Westcott, Nadine Bernard, illus. see Pirner, Connie White.
Westcott, Neva. Jack My Mechanic & What He Does to Your Car. (p. 1152)
Westell, W. Percival. Country Rambles: Being a Field Naturalist's & Country Lover's Note Book for a Year (Classic Reprint) (p. 461)
—My Life As a Naturalist (Classic Reprint) (p. 1551)
—Year with Nature (Classic Reprint) (p. 2519)
Westen, Leah. Jack the Tooth Rat. (p. 1153)
Westen, Robin. Oprah Winfrey: A Biography of a Billionaire Talk Show Host. (p. 1667)
Westendorf, Sandra. World According to August: One Good Friend. Rand, Tracy, illus. (p. 2501)
Wester, Jennifer. Spring Break Activity Book Presented by Arborcreek Montessori Academy. (p. 2092)
—Tear & Crumple 1 Dual Language: Russian / English. (p. 2196)
—Tear & Crumple Book 1. (p. 2196)
—Tracing, Cutting & Taping Activity Book [Wrapping Craft Edition]. (p. 2272)
Westerfeld, Scott. Afterworlds. (p. 34)
—Behemoth. (p. 192)
—Behemoth. Thompson, Keith, illus. (p. 192)
—Extras. (p. 686)
—Goliath. (p. 861)
—Goliath. Thompson, Keith, illus. (p. 861)
—Horizon. (p. 1003)
—Impostors. (p. 1102)
—Leviathan: Leviathan; Behemoth; Goliath. Thompson, Keith, illus. (p. 1282)
—Leviathan. (p. 1282)
—Leviathan. Thompson, Keith, illus. (p. 1282)
—Leviathan T1. (p. 1282)
—Manual of Aeronautics: An Illustrated Guide to the Leviathan Series. Thompson, Keith, illus. (p. 1399)
—Mind-Rain: Your Favorite Authors on Scott Westerfeld's Uglies Series. (p. 1469)
—Pretties. (p. 1790)
—Specials. (p. 2077)
—Spill Zone. (p. 2082)
—Spill Zone. Puvilland, Alex, illus. (p. 2082)
—Spill Zone Book 1. Puvilland, Alex, illus. (p. 2082)
—Spill Zone Book 2: The Broken Vow. Puvilland, Alex, illus. (p. 2082)
—Uglies: Uglies; Pretties; Specials; Extras. (p. 2313)
—Uglies. (p. 2313)
—Uglies & Pretties: Uglies; Pretties. (p. 2313)
—Uglies Collection: Uglies; Pretties; Specials; Extras. (p. 2313)
Westerfeld, Scott & Grayson, Devin. Cutters. (p. 491)
—Shay's Story. (p. 2004)
—Uglies: Cutters (Graphic Novel) Cummings, Steven, illus. (p. 2313)
Westerfeld, Scott & Lanagan, Margo. Swarm. (p. 2167)
Westerfeld, Scott, et al. Nexus. (p. 1601)
—Swarm. (p. 2167)
—Zeroes. (p. 2540)
—Zeroes Trilogy: Zeroes; Swarm; Nexus. (p. 2540)
Westergard, Tim. Jesus Box (p. 1165)
Westerink, Gerda, jt. auth. see West, Judy.
Westerlund, Kate. Message of the Birds. Oral, Feridun, illus. (p. 1451)
—Mr. Hollyberry's Christmas Gift. Pacovska, Kveta, illus. (p. 1518)
—Whisper in the Snow. Oral, Feridun, illus. (p. 2442)
Westerlund, Kate, illus. see Tharlet, Eve.
Westerman, Johanna, illus. see Carson, Jana.
Westerman, Johanna, illus. see Cuyler, Margery.
Westerson, Jeri. Serpent in the Thorns. (p. 1991)
—Veil of Lies. (p. 2349)
Westervelt, Josephine Hope. Lure of the Leopard Skin: A Story of the African Wilds (Classic Reprint) (p. 1369)
Westervelt, Leonidas. Puppet-Show: A Sketch (Classic Reprint) (p. 1814)
Westervelt, Mildred. Allerlei, 1913 (Classic Reprint) (p. 56)
Westfall, Rachel & Westfall, Ursula. One Faceted Eye: A Sasquatch Tale. (p. 1659)
Westgard, Erik, jt. auth. see Johnson, Mark Stephen.
Westgate, Adam. Biscuit Learns about Bullying. (p. 234)
—Cody's West Virginia University Basketball Game. (p. 412)
Westgate, Alex, illus. see Heos, Bridget.
Westgate, Alex, illus. see Lyons, Heather & Tweedale, Elizabeth.
Westgate, Alex, illus. see Lyons, Heather.
Westgate, Vanessa. To Catch an Elephant. (p. 2252)
Westheimer, Ruth K. Leopold. (p. 1268)
Westheimer, Ruth K. & Lehu, Pierre A. Rollercoaster Grandma! The True Story of Dr. Ruth. Simmons, Marc, illus. (p. 1898)
Westheimer, Ruth K., et al. Dr. Ruth Talks with the Animals. Decker, C. B., illus. (p. 592)
Westing, Jemma. Out of the Box: 25 Cardboard Engineering Projects for Makers. (p. 1682)
Westlake, Donald E. Risk Profession. (p. 1886)
Westley, Elaine. Legacy Lost. (p. 1261)
Westley, G. Hembert. Strange Adventure of Richard Cartel (Classic Reprint) (p. 2137)
Westlund, Emmaline. Fatim. (p. 715)
Westlund, Laura, illus. see Kenney, Karen Latchana.
Westmacott, C. M. Punster's Pocket-Book: Or the Art of Punning Enlarged by Bernard Blackmantle, Illustrated with Numerous Original Designs by Robert Cruikshank (Classic Reprint) (p. 1814)
Westmacott, Charles Molloy. English Spy, Vol. 1: An Original Work, Characteristic, Satirical, & Humorous (Classic Reprint) (p. 655)
—Spirit of the Public Journals for 1799, Vol. 3: Being an Impartial Selection of the Most Exquisite Essays & Jeux d'Esprits, Principally Prose, That Appear in the Newspapers & Other Publications, with Explanatory Notes (Classic Reprint) (p. 2083)
—Spirit of the Public Journals for 1802, Vol. 6: Being an Impartial Selection of the Most Exquisite Essays & Jeux d'Esprits, Principally Prose, That Appear in the Newspapers & Other Publications (Classic Reprint) (p. 2083)
—Spirit of the Public Journals for 1804, Vol. 8: Being an Impartial Selection of the Most Ingenious Essays & Jeux d'Esprits, That Appear in the Newspapers & Other Publications; with Explanatory Notes, & Anecdotes of Many of the Persons Alluded To. (p. 2083)
—Spirit of the Public Journals for 1812, Vol. 16: Being an Impartial Selection of the Most Ingenious Essays & Jeux d'Esprits That Appear in the Newspapers & Other Publications (Classic Reprint) (p. 2083)
Westmacott, Marion, illus. see Cronin, Leonard.
Westmark, Jon. Iraq War: 12 Things to Know. (p. 1133)
—Smoke Jumpers in Action. (p. 2043)
Westminster, School. Looking after Our Fascinating Earth. Westminster, School, illus. (p. 1347)
Westmoreland, Susan, jt. auth. see Good Housekeeping Editors.
Westmorland, Priscilla Anne Fane. Letters of Lady Burghersh (Afterwards Countess of Westmorland) From Germany & France During the Campaign of 1813-14 (Classic Reprint) (p. 1280)
Weston, Albert Edmund. Boy Scouts' Good Turn: A Three-ACT Play Depicting Typical Scout Activities & Camp Life (Classic Reprint) (p. 269)
Weston, Avalon. All the Sky. (p. 54)
—Rubic's Return. (p. 1911)
—Running. (p. 1915)
—Sian & the Winterwife: A Fairy Tale. Booth, Kevin, ed. (p. 2014)
—Sian y la Matrona Del Invierno: Un Cuento de Hadas. (p. 2014)
Weston, Carol. Ava & Pip. (p. 141)
—Speed of Life. (p. 2078)
Weston, Carrie. What Noise Does a Rabbit Make? Byrne, Richard, illus. (p. 2419)
Weston, Danny. Scarecrow. (p. 1941)
Weston, Dpa. Girl Who Couldn't Read: Until She Discovered Her Super Powers. Ak, Leena, illus. (p. 837)
Weston, George. Apple-Tree Girl: The Story of Little Miss. Moses, Who Led Herself into the Promised Land (Classic Reprint) (p. 107)
—Mary Minds Her Business. (p. 1415)
—Mary Minds Her Business (Classic Reprint) (p. 1415)
—Oh, Mary, Be Careful! (Classic Reprint) (p. 1641)
Weston, Greg. Charlie Cornwall & the Historymakers. (p. 360)
—Inventors. (p. 1130)
Weston, Jessie. Sir Gawain & the Green Knight. (p. 2025)
Weston, Jessie L. Sir Gawain & the Lady of Lys. (p. 2025)
Weston, Joanna M. Frame & the McGuire (p. 775)
Weston, Laura. Butterfly Garden. Weston, Laura, illus. (p. 304)
Weston, Linda, illus. see Birks, Alison a.
Weston, M. R. Dawn of the Shadowcasters. (p. 512)
Weston, Margeaux. Clothing Inspired by Nature (p. 407)
Weston, Mark. Finding the Speed of Light Evans, Rebecca, illus. (p. 730)
Weston, Martha, illus. see Greene, Stephanie.
Weston, Martha, illus. see Rey, H. A. & Rey, Margret.
Weston, Martha, illus. see Rey, Margret & Rey, H. A.
Weston, Martha, illus. see Sharmat, Marjorie Weinman & Sharmat, Mitchell.
Weston, Martha, illus. see Winters, Kay.
Weston, Paul, illus. see Bone, Emily.
Weston, Paula. Shadows. (p. 1997)
—Undercurrent. (p. 2323)
Weston, Rhonda. Playing to Distraction. (p. 1760)
Weston, Richard. Visit to the United States & Canada In 1833: With the View of Settling in America, Including a Voyage to & from New York (Classic Reprint) (p. 2362)
Weston, Robert Paul. Creature Department. Framestore, illus. (p. 471)
—Dust City. (p. 611)
—Natsumi's Song of Summer. Saburi, Misa, illus. (p. 1579)
—Prince Puggly of Spud & the Kingdom of Spiff. (p. 1795)
—Sakura's Cherry Blossoms. Saburi, Misa, illus. (p. 1924)
—Zorgamazoo. (p. 2544)
Weston, Steve & Field, James. Mahakala & Other Insect-Eating Dinosaurs (p. 1382)
—Saurophaganax & Other Meat-Eating Dinosaurs (p. 1937)
Weston, Tony. Catching the Arrow. (p. 344)
Weston, Wendy J., illus. see Keen, Marian E.
Weston Woods Staff, creator. Anansi the Spider. (p. 79)
—And Then What Happened, Paul Revere? (p. 83)
—Biggest Bear. (p. 224)
—Brave Irene. (p. 276)
—Caps for Sale. (p. 324)
—Casi. (p. 339)
—Caterpillar & the Polliwog. (p. 344)
—Children Make Terrible Pets. (p. 371)
—Clown of God. (p. 408)
—Corduroy. (p. 453)
—Crazy Hair Day. (p. 469)
—Crictor. (p. 474)
—Crow Boy. (p. 478)
—Crow Call. (p. 478)
—Day of the Dead / el Día de Los Muertos. (p. 514)
—Doctor de Soto. (p. 573)
—Duck on a Bike. (p. 608)
—Duke Ellington. (p. 609)
—Each Peach Pear Plum. (p. 613)
—Elizabeti's Doll. (p. 636)
—Ella Fitzgerald. (p. 637)
—Emily's First 100 Days of School. (p. 642)
—Five Creatures. (p. 743)
—Fletcher & the Falling Leaves. (p. 748)
—Fletcher & the Snowflake Christmas. (p. 748)
—Frog Went A-Courtin' (p. 789)
—George Washington's Mother. (p. 820)
—Giving Thanks. (p. 840)
—Goldilocks & the Three Bears. (p. 860)
—Goodnight Moon. (p. 867)
—Grandfather's Journey. (p. 877)
—Gym Teacher from the Black Lagoon. (p. 907)
—Hansel & Gretel. (p. 919)
—Harold & the Purple Crayon. (p. 931)
—Harold's Fairy Tale. (p. 931)
—Henry Hikes to Fitchburg. (p. 955)
—Henry's Freedom Box. (p. 956)
—Hiawatha. (p. 964)
—Hiawatha Weston Woods. (p. 964)
—Hondo & Fabian. (p. 998)
—How Do Dinosaurs Eat Their Food? (p. 1028)
—How Do Dinosaurs Get Well Soon? (p. 1028)
—How Do Dinosaurs Go to School? (p. 1028)
—I Like Me! (p. 1067)
—I Stink! (p. 1083)
—In the Night Kitchen. (p. 1110)
—In the Small, Small Pond. (p. 1111)
—Inch by Inch. (p. 1112)
—Island of the Skog. (p. 1140)
—James Marshall's Cinderella. (p. 1157)
—Johnny Appleseed. (p. 1174)
—Kiss for Little Bear. (p. 1224)
—Kitten's First Full Moon. (p. 1226)
—Little Bear's Visit. (p. 1311)
—Little Drummer Boy. (p. 1315)
—Little House. (p. 1319)
—Little Old Lady Who Was Not Afraid of Anything. (p. 1323)
—Little Red Lighthouse & the Great Gray Bridge. (p. 1326)
—Lon Po Po. (p. 1340)
—Madeline's Rescue. (p. 1375)
—Make Way for Ducklings. (p. 1387)
—Man Who Walked Between the Towers. (p. 1395)
—March on! the Day My Brother Martin Changed the World. (p. 1402)
—May I Bring a Friend? (p. 1429)
—Mike Mulligan & His Steam Shovel. (p. 1464)
—Millions of Cats Weston Woods. (p. 1468)
—Miss Nelson Is Missing. (p. 1479)
—Morris's Disappearing. (p. 1506)
—Morris's Disappearing Bag. (p. 1506)
—Mr Rabbit & the Lovely Present. (p. 1520)
—Mr. Rabbit & the Lovely Present. (p. 1520)
—Mufaro's Beautiful Daughters. (p. 1524)
—Napping House. (p. 1575)
—Norman the Doorman. (p. 1620)
—North Star. (p. 1621)
—One Fine Day. (p. 1659)
—Open Wide- Tooth School Inside. (p. 1666)
—Otto Runs for President. (p. 1676)
—Owen. (p. 1688)
—Pet Show! (p. 1726)
—Peter's Chair. (p. 1730)
—Pete's a Pizza. (p. 1730)
—Petunia. (p. 1732)
—Picture for Harold's Room. (p. 1740)
—Pigeon Finds a Hot Dog. (p. 1743)
—Pinkerton, Behave! (p. 1747)
—Planting a Rainbow. (p. 1757)
—Possum Magic. (p. 1780)
—Ready, Freddy! #1: Tooth Trouble. (p. 1848)
—Ready, Freddy! #3: Homework Hassles. (p. 1848)
—Ready, Freddy! #4: Don't Sit on My Lunch! (p. 1848)
—Red Riding Hood. (p. 1858)
—Rikki-Tikki-Tavi. (p. 1883)
—Rosa. (p. 1904)
—Scrambled States of America Talent Show. (p. 1963)
—Seven Blind Mice. (p. 1993)
—Stone Soup. (p. 2121)
—Story about Ping. (p. 2127)
—Story-A Story. (p. 2127)
—Story-Astory. (p. 2127)
—Sylvester & the Magic Pebble. (p. 2173)
—T Is for Terrible. (p. 2174)
—There Was an Old Lady Who Swallowed a Fly. (p. 2217)
—This Is the House That Jack Built. (p. 2225)
—Three Cheers for Catherine the Great. (p. 2232)
—Three Little Pigs. (p. 2233)
—Time of Wonder. (p. 2245)
—Too Many Toys! (p. 2261)
—True Story of the 3 Little Pigs. (p. 2295)
—Ugly Duckling. (p. 2313)
—What to Do about Alice? (p. 2420)
—Whistle for Willie. (p. 2443)
—Wild about Books. (p. 2462)
—Wilfrid Gordon Mcdonald Partridge. (p. 2467)
—Will I Have a Friend? (p. 2467)
—Will You Sign Here, John Hancock? (p. 2468)
—Wings: A Tale of Two Chickens. (p. 2473)
Westover, Clyde C. Dragon's Daughter (Classic Reprint) (p. 595)
Westover, Gail. Mrs Mouse's Garden Party in Giggleswick Village. Daly, Karen Anne, illus. (p. 1522)
Westover, Steve. Crater Lake: Battle for Wizard Island. (p. 467)
—Nothing Named Silas. (p. 1625)
—Return of the Mystic Gray. (p. 1871)
Westphal, A. J. In Green Bay Waters: : a Bildungsroman. (p. 1105)
Westphal, Jeremy. Mummy's Curse. (p. 1526)
Westphal, Laurie E. Science Dictionary for Kids: The Essential Guide to Science Terms, Concepts, & Strategies. (p. 1954)
—Stress-Free Science: A Visual Guide to Acing Science in Grades 4-8. (p. 2140)
West-Pratt, Judy Lea. Just Like Me! (p. 1193)
Westrick, A. B. Brotherhood. (p. 286)
Westropp, J. E. Summer Experiences of Rome, Perugia, & Siena, in 1854, & Sketches of the Islands in the Bay of Naples: With Illustrations (Classic Reprint) (p. 2149)
Westrup, Hugh. Electricity. (p. 631)
—Mixtures & Solutions. (p. 1484)
Westrup, Hugh & Barchers, Suzanne I. Let's Explore Physical Science Grades 4-5 (p. 1272)

Westrup, Margaret. Elizabeth in Retreat (Classic Reprint) (p. 636)
—Greater Mischief a Novel, Vol. 1 (Classic Reprint) (p. 891)
—Tide Marks (Classic Reprint) (p. 2240)
Westwell, Ian. World War I. (p. 2505)
Westwood, Chris. Graveyard Shift. (p. 882)
Westwood, John Obadiah, jt. auth. see Rennie, James.
Westwood, Jon, illus. see Cella, Clara.
Westwood, Thomas. Literary Friendship: Letters to Lady Alwyne Compton 1869-1881 (Classic Reprint) (p. 1309)
Wetherald, Ethelwyn. Tree-Top Mornings (Classic Reprint) (p. 2284)
Wethered, Charles. Richer Than Wealth, Vol. 1 Of 3: A Novel (Classic Reprint) (p. 1877)
—Richer Than Wealth, Vol. 2: A Novel (Classic Reprint) (p. 1877)
Wethered, Frank Joseph. Medical Microscopy. (p. 1436)
Wetherell, Elizabeth. Queechy (Classic Reprint) (p. 1823)
—Queechy, Vol. 1 of 2 (Classic Reprint) (p. 1823)
—Queechy, Vol. 2 of 2 (Classic Reprint) (p. 1823)
—Wide, Wide World (Classic Reprint) (p. 2460)
—Wide, Wide World, Vol. 1 (Classic Reprint) (p. 2460)
—Wide, Wide World, Vol. 2 of 2 (Classic Reprint) (p. 2460)
Wetherell, Elizabeth, jt. auth. see Warner, Susan.
Wetherell, Ellen F. In Free America: Or Tales from North & South (Classic Reprint) (p. 1105)
Wethington, Constance. Adventures of One-Eyed Jack. (p. 26)
Wethington. Constance. Butterfly's Ball. (p. 304)
Wethington, Julie & Wethington, Lang. Yes I Can! Have My Cake & Food Allergies Too. Wethington, Julie & Wethington, Lang, illus. (p. 2521)
Wetmore, Barry, illus. see Frankel, Fred.
Wetmore, Helen Cody. Last of the Great Scouts: Buffalo Bill (Classic Reprint) (p. 1248)
Wetmore, Mary B. Sounds from Home & Echoes of a Kingdom. (p. 2067)
—Sounds from Home & Echoes of a Kingdom (Classic Reprint) (p. 2067)
Wetta, J. Augustine. Humility Rules: Saint Benedict's Twelve-Step Guide to Genuine Self-Esteem. (p. 1050)
Wette, Adelheid. Ha Nsel & Gretel: A Fairy Opera in Three Acts (Classic Reprint) (p. 908)
—Hansel & Gretel: A Fairy Opera in Three Acts (Classic Reprint) (p. 919)
—Hänsel & Gretel: A Fairy Opera in Three Acts (Classic Reprint) (p. 919)
Wetterer, Charles M., jt. auth. see Wetterer, Margaret K.
Wetterer, Margaret K. Midnight Adventure of Kate Shelley, Train Rescuer. (p. 1461)
Wetterer, Margaret K., jt. auth. see Wetterer, Charles M.
Wetterer, Margaret K. & Wetterer, Charles M. Snowshoeing Adventure of Milton Daub, Blizzard Trekker. (p. 2049)
Wettersten, Laura. My Faire Lady. (p. 1538)
Wetterwald, Florence. Night-Night, Wooly (a Blabla Book) Wetterwald, Florence, illus. (p. 1606)
—Peekaboo, Pierre (a Blabla Book) Wetterwald, Florence, illus. (p. 1713)
Wettstein, Frances. Language Plan for the Wisconsin Day Schools for the Deaf (Classic Reprint) (p. 1243)
Wetzel, Dan. Epic Athletes: Alex Morgan. Thomas, Cory, illus. (p. 657)
—Epic Athletes: Kevin Durant. Baez, Marcelo, illus. (p. 657)
—Epic Athletes: Lebron James. Fiadzigbey, Setor, illus. (p. 657)
—Epic Athletes: Lionel Messi. Reed, Jay, illus. (p. 657)
—Epic Athletes: Patrick Mahomes. Baez, Marcelo, illus. (p. 657)
—Epic Athletes: Serena Williams. Leong, Sloane, illus. (p. 657)
—Epic Athletes: Simone Biles. Baez, Marcelo, illus. (p. 657)
—Epic Athletes: Stephen Curry. Peña, Zeke, illus. (p. 657)
—Epic Athletes: Tom Brady. Iskander, Kazimir Lee, illus. (p. 657)
—Epic Athletes: Tom Brady. Iskander, Kazimir Lee, illus. (p. 658)
Wetzel, Eduard. Allgemeine Himmelskunde: Eine Populare Darstellung Dieser Wissenschaft Nach Den Neuesten Forschungen (Classic Reprint) (p. 56)
Wetzel, Franz Xaver. Dutiful Child: From the German (Classic Reprint) (p. 611)
Wetzel, JoAnne Stewart. Mermaid School. Swaney, Julianna, illus. (p. 1449)
—Playing Juliet. (p. 1760)
Weulersse, Odile & Merz, Kathleen. Nasreddine. Dautremer, Rebecca, illus. (p. 1576)
Wevers, Lydia. Reading on the Farm: Victorian Fiction & the Colonial World. (p. 1847)
Wewer, Iris. My Wild Sister & Me. (p. 1565)
Wexler, Django. City of Stone & Silence. (p. 395)
—Fall of the Readers: The Forbidden Library. (p. 700)
—Forbidden Library. (p. 764)
—Palace of Glass: The Forbidden Library: Volume 3. (p. 1694)
—Ship of Smoke & Steel: The Wells of Sorcery, Book One. (p. 2008)
Weyant, Christopher, illus. see Gehl, Laura.
Weyant, Christopher, illus. see Kang, Anna.
Weyl, Maurice. Choice (Classic Reprint) (p. 380)
—Happy Woman (Classic Reprint) (p. 924)
Weyland, Jack. Brianna, My Brother, & the Blog. (p. 280)
Weyler, Carrie & Weyler, Katie. Charlie Tractor & Pickles. (p. 360)
—Charlie Tractor & the Garden. (p. 360)
Weyler, Katie & Weyler, Carrie. Charlie Tractor & the Big Fish. (p. 360)
Weyman, Stanley J. Castle Inn: Illustrated by Walter Appleton Clark (Classic Reprint) (p. 340)
—Castle Inn. (p. 340)
—Chippinge (Classic Reprint) (p. 379)
—Chippinge Borough (Classic Reprint) (p. 379)
—For the Cause (Classic Reprint) (p. 763)
—From the Memoirs of a Minister of France (Classic Reprint) (p. 794)
—Gentleman of France, Vol. 1 Of 3: Being the Memoirs of Gaston de Bonne, Sieur de Marsac (Classic Reprint) (p. 816)
—Great House (Classic Reprint) (p. 887)
—In Kings' Byways: Short Stories - Scholar's Choice Edition. (p. 1105)
—In Kings' Byways (Classic Reprint) (p. 1105)
—Little Wizard (Classic Reprint) (p. 1330)
—Man in Black (Classic Reprint) (p. 1394)
—Ovington's Bank (Classic Reprint) (p. 1688)
—Shrewsbury; a Romance: With Illus, by Claude a Shepperson (Classic Reprint) (p. 2013)
—Sophia (Classic Reprint) (p. 2064)
—Starvecrow Farm (Classic Reprint) (p. 2108)
—Story of Francis Cludde (Classic Reprint) (p. 2130)
—When Love Calls (Classic Reprint) (p. 2432)
—Wild Geese (Classic Reprint) (p. 2463)
Weymouth, Laura E. Light Between Worlds. (p. 1298)
—Treason of Thorns. (p. 2281)
Weyn, Suzanne. Bar Code Tattoo. (p. 164)
—Beaten. (p. 182)
—Bionic. (p. 229)
—Cursed Scarab. (p. 489)
—Daring to Dream. (p. 505)
—Empty. (p. 645)
—Faces of the Dead. (p. 693)
—Full Impact. (p. 797)
—Haunted Museum - The Cursed Scarab. (p. 938)
—Learning to Fly. (p. 1258)
—Pearl Earring. (p. 1710)
—Phantom Music Box. (p. 1732)
—Recruited. (p. 1855)
—Snapstreak: A New School, a Head Injury, & How My Best Friends Saved My (Social) Life. (p. 2045)
—Titanic Locket. (p. 2251)
—Water Song: A Retelling of the Frog Prince (p. 2385)
Weyn, Suzanne, jt. auth. see Windham, Ryder.
Weyr, Garret. Language of Spells. Harnett, Katie, illus. (p. 1243)
Wezeman, Phyllis Vos. Petra's Pier Picnic. Joyo, Oscar, illus. (p. 1731)
WFM Services, illus. see Walsh, Patrick M., Jr.
WGBH, illus. see Candlewick Press Staff.
WGBH Educational Foundation Staff, illus. see Candlewick Press Staff.
WGBH Kids. Crane Song. (p. 466)
—Little Dog Lost. (p. 1315)
—Party Moose. (p. 1702)
WGBH Kids, Wgbh. Molly of Denali: a-Maze-ing Snow. WGBH Kids, Wgbh, illus. (p. 1489)
—Molly of Denali: an Alaskan Adventures Reading Collection. (p. 1489)
—Molly of Denali: Berry Itchy Day. WGBH Kids, Wgbh, illus. (p. 1489)
—Molly of Denali: Crane Song. WGBH Kids, Wgbh, illus. (p. 1489)
—Molly of Denali: Little Dog Lost. WGBH Kids, Wgbh, illus. (p. 1489)
—Molly of Denali: Molly's Awesome Alaska Guide. WGBH Kids, Wgbh, illus. (p. 1489)
—Molly of Denali: Party Moose. WGBH Kids, Wgbh, illus. (p. 1489)
—Molly of Denali: Tubing Rocks! WGBH Kids, Wgbh, illus. (p. 1489)
Whaite, Michael. Diggersaurs. (p. 546)
—Diggersaurs Explore. (p. 546)
Whalen, E. C. Uncle Dick's Mistake (Classic Reprint) (p. 2318)
Whalen, Linda. Little Red Rolls Away. Morris, Jennifer E., illus. (p. 1326)
Whalen, Meg, illus. see Warner, Katie.
Whalen, Molly. I've Lost My Special Power! (p. 1149)
Whalen, Raymond J., illus. see Guiles, Glenn S.
Whaler, Norman. Am I Black or Am I White? Mills, Jasmine, illus. (p. 61)
—Jack. Mkhoiani, Nina, illus. (p. 1151)
—Oink & Gobble & the Men in Black. Firestone, Ellie, ed. (p. 1643)
—Oink & Gobble & the Missing Cupcakes. Randell, Esther, ed. (p. 1643)
—Oink & Gobble & the 'no One Can Ever Know Secret' Firestone, Ellie, ed. (p. 1643)
—Oink y Gobble y el 'secreto Que Nadie Debe Saber' Shayan, Mohammad, illus. (p. 1643)
—Oink y Gobble y Los Cupcakes Desaparecidos. Randell, Esther, ed. (p. 1643)
—Tiny Tree. (p. 2250)
Whaley, Jason. Joseph & His Dragon Samuel & the World Around Sarena Had a Dream. (p. 1178)
Whaley, John Corey. Highly Illogical Behavior. (p. 970)
—Noggin. (p. 1617)
—Where Things Come Back. (p. 2440)
Whaley, Thomas. Luke's Rainforest Adventure. (p. 1367)
Whalley, Jim. Baby's First Bank Heist. Collins, Stephen, illus. (p. 154)
Whalley, Mary Frances. Of European Descent (Classic Reprint) (p. 1639)
Whamhower, Shogun. Nerdy Ninjas vs the Really Really Bad Guys. McKenzie, Heath, illus. (p. 1588)
Whamond, Dave. Alien Nate. Whamond, Dave, illus. (p. 47)
—Nick the Sidekick. Whamond, Dave, illus. (p. 1602)
—Oddrey. (p. 1638)
—Oddrey & the New Kid. (p. 1638)
—Oddrey Joins the Team. (p. 1638)
—Rosie's Glasses. Whamond, Dave, illus. (p. 1906)
Whamond, Dave, illus. see Birmingham, Maria.
Whamond, Dave, illus. see Brouwer, Sigmund.
Whamond, Dave, illus. see Munsch, Robert.
Whamond, Dave, illus. see Rovetch, L. Bob.
Whamond, Dave, illus. see Stuchner, Joan Betty.
Whamond, Dave, illus. see Szpirglas, Jeff & Saint-Onge, Danielle.
Whamond, Dave, illus. see Wyatt, Valerie.
Whamsby, Dawud. Picnic of Poems: In Allah's Green Garden. (p. 1739)
Wharry, Remy, illus. see Lashe, Tyia.
Wharton, Anne Hollingsworth. Colonial Days & Dames - Scholar's Choice Edition. (p. 418)
—English Honeymoon (Classic Reprint) (p. 653)
—Italian Days & Ways (Classic Reprint) (p. 1142)
—Last Century Maid: And Other Stories for Children (Classic Reprint) (p. 1247)
Wharton, Anthony. Joan of Overbarrow (Classic Reprint) (p. 1170)
Wharton, Anthony P. At the Barn: An Idyll in Three Acts (Classic Reprint) (p. 130)
Wharton, Charles. Hand-Book on the Treatment of the Horse in the Stable & on the Road: Or, Hints to Horse Owners (Classic Reprint) (p. 914)
—Hand-Book on the Treatment of the Horse in the Stable & on the Road, or Hints to Horse Owners (Classic Reprint) (p. 914)
Wharton, Edith. Book of the Homeless: Le Livre des Sans-Foyer (Classic Reprint) (p. 260)
—Crucial Instances (Classic Reprint) (p. 479)
—Crucial Instances Sanctuary (Classic Reprint) (p. 479)
—Custom of the Country (Classic Reprint) (p. 491)
—Descent of Man: And Other Stories (Classic Reprint) (p. 531)
—Descent of Man: And Other Stories, Madame de Treymes (Classic Reprint) (p. 531)
—Fruit of the Tree (Classic Reprint) (p. 796)
—Fruit of the Tree, Vol. 1 of 2 (Classic Reprint) (p. 796)
—Greater Inclination: The Touchstone (Classic Reprint) (p. 891)
—Greater Inclination. (p. 891)
—Greater Inclination (Classic Reprint) (p. 891)
—Hermit & the Wild Woman: And Other Stories (Classic Reprint) (p. 959)
—House of Mirth (Classic Reprint) (p. 1023)
—Marne: A Tale of the War (Classic Reprint) (p. 1408)
—Summer: A Novel (Classic Reprint) (p. 2148)
—Tales of Men & Ghosts (Classic Reprint) (p. 2184)
—Touchstone (Classic Reprint) (p. 2268)
—Valley of Decision: A Novel (Classic Reprint) (p. 2345)
—Valley of Decision, Vol. 1: A Novel (Classic Reprint) (p. 2345)
—War on All Fronts: Fighting France; from Dunkerque to Belfort (Classic Reprint) (p. 2377)
—Xingu: And Other Stories (Classic Reprint) (p. 2516)
Wharton, Edith & Gardner, Anthony. World Over. (p. 2504)
Wharton, Eileen. Shmoogly Boo. Walker, David, illus. (p. 2008)
Wharton, Ellie. Michael Recycle's Environmental Adventures. Colombo, Alexandra & Zahler, Thom, illus. (p. 1458)
Wharton, George M. New Orleans Sketch Book (Classic Reprint) (p. 1596)
Wharton, H. M. Pulpit, Pew & Platform (Classic Reprint) (p. 1812)
Wharton, Jennifer Heyd, illus. see Blackistone, Mick.
Wharton, Jennifer Heyd, illus. see Henderson, Richard.
Wharton, Laura Spanton, et al. Mystery at the Phoenix Festival. (p. 1568)
Wharton, Ruth. Phoenix, 1999-1910, Vol. 1: A Record of the Year 1910 (Classic Reprint) (p. 1735)
Wharton, Thomas Isaac. Bobbo & Other Fancies (Classic Reprint) (p. 252)
—Latter Day Saint: Being the Story of the Conversion of Ethel Jones Related by Herself (Classic Reprint) (p. 1251)
Whately, E. J. Life & Work of Mary Louisa Whately (Classic Reprint) (p. 1290)
Whately, M. L. Child-Life in Egypt (Classic Reprint) (p. 370)
Whately, Mary. Letters from Egypt: To Plain Folks at Home. (p. 1279)
Whately, Mary Louisa. Ragged Life in Egypt (Classic Reprint) (p. 1834)
—Scenes from Life in Cairo: A Glimpse Behind the Curtain (Classic Reprint) (p. 1943)
Whately, Richard. Lectures on Some of the Scripture Parables - Scholar's Choice Edition. (p. 1260)
Whatley, April. Tucker's Adventures in America. (p. 2298)
Whatley, Bruce. I Wanna Be Famous. (p. 1083)
—Little Drummer Boy. Whatley, Bruce, illus. (p. 1315)
—Little White Dogs Can't Jump. (p. 1329)
—That Magnetic Dog. (p. 2213)
—Ugliest Dog in the World. (p. 2313)
Whatley, Bruce, illus. see Crew, Gary.
Whatley, Bruce, illus. see French, Jackie.
Whatley, Bruce, illus. see Gwynne, Phillip.
Whatley, Bruce, illus. see Kimmel, Eric A. & Korelitz, Jean Hanff.
Whatley, Bruce, illus. see Moore, Clement C.
Whatley, Bruce, illus. see Palatini, Margie.
Whatley, Bruce, illus. see Rox, John.
Whatley, Bruce, illus. see Smith, Rosie.
Whatley, Bruce, jt. auth. see French, Jackie.
Whatley, Bruce, jt. auth. see Smith, Rosie.
Whatley, Charlotte. Peter Pan Paper Dolls. (p. 1729)
Whatmore, Candace. Monsters Coloring Book. (p. 1497)
Whatmore, Candice. 25 Postcards to Color. (p. 2554)
Whatmore, Candice, illus. see Dalby, Elizabeth.
Whatmore, Candice, illus. see Khan, Sarah.
Whatmore, Candice, illus. see Marks, Anthony.
Wheat, Lu. Helen: A Story of Things to Be (Classic Reprint) (p. 949)
—Third Daughter: A Story of Chinese Home Life (Classic Reprint) (p. 2222)
Wheat, Tiffany. There's a Gopher in My Garden! (p. 2217)
Wheat, Valerie A. Kid Who Loved Mac & Cheese. (p. 1213)
Wheatcroft, Ryan, illus. see Hegarty, Patricia.
Wheatle, Alex. Crongton Knights. (p. 477)
—Home Girl. (p. 996)
Wheatley, Abigail. Book of Growing Food IR. (p. 258)
—Children's Cupcake Kit. (p. 373)
—History of Science in 100 Pictures IR. (p. 979)
—Little Transfer Book Fairies. (p. 1329)
—Magical Creatures Magic Painting Book. (p. 1380)
Wheatley, Abigail, jt. auth. see Lacey, Minna.
Wheatley, Daniel. Zanna Function. (p. 2538)
Wheatley, Doug, illus. see DeBlois, Dean & Hamilton, Richard.
Wheatley, Doug, illus. see DeBlois, Dean, et al.
Wheatley, Doug, illus. see Lane, Miles.
Wheatley, Doug, jt. auth. see Lane, Miles.
Wheatley, H. B., jt. auth. see Gomme, G. I.
Wheatley, Henry B. Diary of Samuel Pepys Clerk: Clerk of the Acts & Secretary to the Admiralty (Classic Reprint) (p. 540)
—Diary of Samuel Pepys, M. A. , F. R. S, Vol. 2: Clerk of the Acts & Secretary to the Admiralty, Completely Transcribed by the Late REV. Mynors Bright, M. A. , from the Shorthand Mauscript in the Pepysian Library, Magdalene College, Cambridge, with Lord. (p. 540)
Wheatley, Louise Knight. Ashes of Roses (Classic Reprint) (p. 125)
Wheatley, Sarah. Christmas Fire-Side: Or the Juvenile Critics (Classic Reprint) (p. 385)
Wheatman, Sarina. Twisted Wires. (p. 2306)
Wheaton, Emily. Russells in Chicago (Classic Reprint) (p. 1917)
Wheaton, Sheila. Fab Vocab: Greek & Latin Roots: Reproducible Games & Activities That Teach 25 Key Roots. (p. 690)
—Fab Vocab: Prefixes & Suffixes: Reproducible Games & Activities That Teach 50 Key Prefixes & Suffixes. (p. 690)
Wheatonnovember. Little Hermit Ant. (p. 1318)
Wheble, J. Sporting Magazine, or Monthly Calendar, of the Transactions of the Turf, the Chase, & Every Other Diversion Interesting to the Man of Pleasure, Enterprize, & Spirit, Vol. 19: 1801-1802 (Classic Reprint) (p. 2088)
—Sporting Magazine, or Monthly Calendar of the Transactions of the Turf, the Chace, & Every Other Diversion Interesting to the Man of Pleasure, Enterprize & Spirit, for April 1797, Vol. 10 (Classic Reprint) (p. 2088)
Whedon, Joss, et al. Buffy the Vampire Slayer Allie, Scott & Hahn, Sierra, eds. (p. 291)
Whedon, Zack & Horse, Dark. Dr. Horrible. Rugg, Jim, illus. (p. 591)
Wheeler, A. C. Iron Trail: A Sketch. (p. 1136)
—Iron Trail: A Sketch (Classic Reprint) (p. 1136)
Wheeler, A. O. Eye-Witness; or, Life Scenes in the Old North State. (p. 688)
—Eye-Witness, or Life Scenes in the Old North State: Depicting the Trials & Sufferings of the Unionists During the Rebellion (Classic Reprint) (p. 688)
Wheeler, Alex. Firefight (p. 733)
Wheeler, Alex, jt. auth. see Scholastic, Inc. Staff.
Wheeler, Andrew. Valentin & the Widow: the Mandrake Machine. (p. 2344)
Wheeler, Ann. Westmoreland Dialect in Four Familiar Dialogues: In Which an Attempt Is Made to Illustrate the Provincial Idiom (Classic Reprint) (p. 2402)
Wheeler, Billy E., jt. auth. see Jones, Loyal.
Wheeler, Catherine. Bright Little Poems for Bright Little People (Classic Reprint) (p. 281)
Wheeler, Charles Gardner, jt. auth. see Wheeler, William Adolphus.
Wheeler, Charlotte. New Speller for Foreigners: A Sounding & Pronouncing System (Classic Reprint) (p. 1597)
Wheeler, Christine. Tapping Solution for Teenage Girls: How to Stop Freaking Out & Keep Being Awesome. (p. 2191)
Wheeler, Cindy. Ralph's Hospital Adventures. (p. 1838)
Wheeler, Curtis. Letters from an American Soldier to His Father (Classic Reprint) (p. 1279)
Wheeler, David & Twigg, Natalie. My Pirate Grandad. (p. 1559)
Wheeler, David Cole, illus. see Nemmers, Lee.
Wheeler, Dora. Prize Painting Book: Good Times (Classic Reprint) (p. 1802)
Wheeler, Duchess Harris: Jill C. LGBTQ Service in the Armed Forces. (p. 1283)
Wheeler, E. B. Haunting of Springett Hall. (p. 939)
Wheeler, Eliza. Home in the Woods. Wheeler, Eliza, illus. (p. 996)
—Miss Maple's Seeds. (p. 1479)
—Miss Maple's Seeds. Wheeler, Eliza, illus. (p. 1479)
Wheeler, Eliza, illus. see Bajaj, Varsha.
Wheeler, Eliza, illus. see Black, Holly.
Wheeler, Eliza, illus. see DiOrio, Rana.
Wheeler, Eliza, illus. see Doyen, Denise.
Wheeler, Eliza, illus. see Mcghee, Alison.
Wheeler, Eliza, illus. see Miller, Pat Zietlow.
Wheeler, Eliza, illus. see Nobleman, Marc Tyler.
Wheeler, Eliza, illus. see Rockliff, Mara.
Wheeler, Eliza, illus. see Springstubb, Tricia.
Wheeler, Eliza, illus. see Wood, Maryrose.
Wheeler, Eliza, jt. auth. see Bajaj, Varsha.
Wheeler, Elizabeth. Asher's Fault. (p. 125)
—Asher's Out. (p. 125)
—Asher's Shot. (p. 125)
Wheeler, Elizabeth, illus. see Davis, Rebecca Harding.
Wheeler, Esther Gracie. Stray Leaves from Newport (Classic Reprint) (p. 2139)
Wheeler, Francis Rolt. Boy with the U. S. Census. (p. 271)
—Boy with the U. S. Fisheries. (p. 271)
-Wheeler, Francis William Rolt. Aztec-Hunters (Classic Reprint) (p. 146)
Wheeler, Francis William Rolt-. Boy with the U. S. Weather Men. (p. 271)
Wheeler, George W. Captain Wheeler's Narrative of His Wanderings in Brazil, South America (Classic Reprint) (p. 326)
Wheeler, Griswold. Return, & Other Stories (Classic Reprint) (p. 1870)
Wheeler, Henry M. Recollections of Two New England Houses: Built by REV. Joseph Wheeler, of Worcester, a Paper Read Before the Worcester Society of Antiquity on November 3, 1903 (Classic Reprint) (p. 1854)
Wheeler, Herman Henry. Up-To-Date Minstrel Jokes, & Female Minstrel Jokes (Classic Reprint) (p. 2338)
Wheeler, James Cooper. Captain Pete of Cortesana (Classic Reprint) (p. 326)
Wheeler, Janet D. Billie Bradley & Her Inheritance: The Queer Homestead at Cherry Corners. (p. 226)
—Billie Bradley at Three Towers Hall: Leading a Needed Rebellion. (p. 226)
Wheeler, Jeff. Hollow Crown. (p. 988)
—Veneno para la Reina. (p. 2350)
Wheeler, Jenny Lee. Weird Is Normal When Teenagers Grieve. (p. 2397)

W

Wheeler, Jill C. Abigail Adams (p. 5)
—Alvin Schwartz (p. 60)
—American Wirehair Cats (p. 74)
—Antonia Novello: Fantastic Physician. (p. 103)
—Bengal Cats (p. 199)
—Bernese Mountain Dogs (p. 204)
—Boston Terriers (p. 264)
—British Shorthair Cats (p. 283)
—Cats: Designer Cats (p. 345)
—Chausie Cats (p. 363)
—Chien-Shiung Wu: Phenomenal Physicist. (p. 369)
—Children's Authors (p. 372)
—Christopher Paul Curtis (p. 388)
—Cynthia Kadohata (p. 493)
—Dav Pilkey (p. 510)
—Donald Trump. (p. 581)
—E. B. White (p. 612)
—Edith Wilson (p. 626)
—Egyptian Mau Cats (p. 628)
—Ellen DeGeneres: Groundbreaking Entertainer. (p. 637)
—Eye on Energy (p. 688)
—Fidel Castro: Cuban Revolutionary Leader. (p. 722)
—First Ladies (p. 737)
—Flickr (p. 748)
—Fun & Food with Guy Fieri (p. 798)
—Gary Paulsen (p. 810)
—Grace Hopper: Computer Scientist. (p. 873)
—Grace Lin (p. 873)
—Harriet Lane (p. 933)
—Havana Brown Cats (p. 939)
—Hayat Sindi: Brilliant Biochemist. (p. 941)
—Iowa (p. 1133)
—Japanese Bobtail Cats (p. 1159)
—Joanne Simpson: Magnificent Meteorologist. (p. 1170)
—Julia Alvarez (p. 1186)
—Kansas (p. 1203)
—L. Frank Baum (p. 1234)
—Mae Jemison: Awesome Astronaut. (p. 1375)
—Mamie Eisenhower (p. 1393)
—New Jersey (p. 1594)
—New Mexico (p. 1595)
—Newfoundlands (p. 1600)
—Nikki Grimes (p. 1609)
—Patricia Nixon (p. 1705)
—Pennsylvania (p. 1717)
—Pinterest (p. 1747)
—Pioneer Practices with Ree Drummond (p. 1748)
—Pixiebob Cats (p. 1752)
—Portuguese Water Dogs (p. 1779)
—Rachel Carson: Extraordinary Environmentalist. (p. 1832)
—Ragdoll Cats (p. 1834)
—Reality TV Titans (p. 1851)
—Rick Riordan (p. 1877)
—Safari Cats (p. 1921)
—Savannah Cats (p. 1937)
—Scott O'Dell (p. 1962)
—Sharon Creech (p. 2003)
—Simple Solutions with Rachael Ray (p. 2022)
—Suzanne Collins (p. 2166)
—Tasteful Fashion with Tim Gunn (p. 2192)
—Toyger Cats (p. 2271)
—Travis Scott: lo-Fi Hip-Hop Creator. (p. 2281)
—Vine (p. 2359)
—Walter Dean Myers (p. 2374)
—Weimaraners (p. 2396)
—Welsh Corgis (p. 2400)
—Yuyi Morales (p. 2537)
Wheeler, Jill C., jt. auth. see ABDO Publishing Company Staff.
Wheeler, Jill C., jt. auth. see Harris, Duchess.
Wheeler, Jody, illus. see Alcott, Louisa May.
Wheeler, Jody, illus. see Davis, Viola.
Wheeler, Jody, illus. see Hennessy, B. G.
Wheeler, Jody, illus. see Lindemann, Lindy.
Wheeler, Jody, illus. see Sharmat, Andrew & Sharmat, Marjorie Weinman.
Wheeler, Jody, illus. see Sharmat, Marjorie Weinman & Sharmat, Andrew.
Wheeler, Jody, illus. see Sharmat, Marjorie Weinman & Sharmat, Mitchell.
Wheeler, Jody, illus. see Wilder, Laura Ingalls.
Wheeler, Jordan. Brothers in Arms (p. 286)
—Chuck in the City Auchter, Christopher, illus. (p. 389)
—Just a Walk (p. 1192)
Wheeler, Jordan, ed. see Smith, M. Jane.
Wheeler, Keith. Mimi's Adventure. Aveira, Harry, illus. (p. 1469)
—One Bad Call. (p. 1658)
Wheeler, Kim. Adventures of Jonny Plumb. (p. 24)
—Even More Adventures of Jonny Plumb. (p. 668)
—Jonny Plumb's New Adventures... (p. 1177)
Wheeler, Kimberly. Emma's Extravagant Expedition. (p. 644)
Wheeler, L. Christine, jt. auth. see Dean, Carolyn.
Wheeler, Lawrence Eric. Tales from Nettlefold Cottage. (p. 2182)
Wheeler, Lindy. It's All about Bodd Parent Guide. (p. 1144)
Wheeler, Lindy & Lawley, Tom. It's All about Bodd. (p. 1144)
Wheeler, Lisa. Babies Can Sleep Anywhere. Buzio, Carolina, illus. (p. 147)
—Babies Can Sleep Anywhere. Búzio, Carolina, illus. (p. 147)
—Bubble Gum, Bubble Gum. Huliska-Beith, Laura, illus. (p. 288)
—Christmas Boot. Pinkney, Jerry, illus. (p. 384)
—Dino-Baseball. Gott, Barry, illus. (p. 547)
—Dino-Basketball. Gott, Barry, illus. (p. 547)
—Dino-Boarding. Gott, Barry, illus. (p. 547)
—Dino-Christmas. Gott, Barry, illus. (p. 547)
—Dino-Dancing. Gott, Barry, illus. (p. 547)
—Dino-Football. Gott, Barry, illus. (p. 547)
—Dino-Halloween. Gott, Barry, illus. (p. 547)
—Dino-Racing. Gott, Barry, illus. (p. 547)
—Dino-Soccer. Gott, Barry, illus. (p. 547)
—Dino-Swimming. Gott, Barry, illus. (p. 548)
—Dino-Thanksgiving. Gott, Barry, illus. (p. 548)
—Dino-Wrestling. Gott, Barry, illus. (p. 548)
—Even Monsters Go to School. Van Dusen, Chris, illus. (p. 668)
—Even Monsters Need to Sleep. Van Dusen, Chris, illus. (p. 668)
—Farmer Dale's Red Pickup Truck. Bates, Ivan, illus. (p. 710)
—Hug Is for Holding Me. Feng, Lisk, illus. (p. 1048)
—People Don't Bite People. Idle, Molly, illus. (p. 1718)
—People Share with People. Idle, Molly, illus. (p. 1719)
—Pet Project: Cute & Cuddly Vicious Verses. OHora, Zachariah, illus. (p. 1726)
—Spinster Goose: Twisted Rhymes for Naughty Children. Blackall, Sophie, illus. (p. 2082)
—Ugly Pie. Solomon, Heather, illus. (p. 2314)
—Uncles & Antlers. Floca, Brian, illus. (p. 2320)
Wheeler, Lisa, jt. auth. see RH Disney Staff.
Wheeler, Martha Thorne. Catalogue of the Emmanuel Baptist Church Sunday School Library, Albany, N. y (Classic Reprint) (p. 343)
Wheeler, Mary. Twirling & Dancing with Annie & Friends. Wheeler, Mary, illus. (p. 2306)
Wheeler, Patti & Hemstreet, Keith. Travels with Gannon & Wyatt: Botswana. (p. 2281)
Wheeler, Ron. Stinky Stevens: The Missing Soggy Soccer Shoe (Book 3) (p. 2120)
—Stinky Stevens: Escape from Aunt Smoochie-Kiss (Book 4) (p. 2120)
Wheeler, Ron, illus. see Gould, Judith S. & Gould, Evan Jay.
Wheeler, Ron, illus. see Hein, Marilyn B.
Wheeler, Ron, illus. see Kumpe, Pam.
Wheeler, Ron, illus. see Woodman, Ros.
Wheeler, S. A. Daughters of Armenia (Classic Reprint) (p. 509)
Wheeler, Samuel, illus. see Ecrivain, M. S. Belle.
Wheeler, Shannon & Torres, J. Wall E: Recharge. Vol. 1 Luthi, Morgan, illus. (p. 2373)
Wheeler, Shannon, et al. Wall-E: Recharge. Vol. 1 Luthi, Morgan & Barks, Carl, illus. (p. 2373)
Wheeler, Sherrie Leigh. Defending Americ: A Children's Guide to Understanding the Circumstances & Sacrifices of War. (p. 525)
Wheeler, Thomas. Cursed. Miller, Frank, illus. (p. 489)
Wheeler, Tonika Yvonne. Damaged Goods. Attaway, Anelda, ed. (p. 499)
Wheeler, Ty. If You Were a Bandicoot. Myers, Courtney, illus. (p. 1093)
Wheeler, Van Zandt. Creed of Her Father: A Novel (Classic Reprint) (p. 472)
Wheeler, Wesley, illus. see Gardner, Holly.
Wheeler, William Adolphus. Mother Goose's Melodies: Or Songs for the Nursery (Classic Reprint) (p. 1509)
Wheeler, William H., jt. auth. see Calmerton, Gail.
Wheeler, William Henry. Tidal Rivers: Their (1) Hydraulics, (2) Improvement, (3) Navigation (Classic Reprint) (p. 2240)
—Wheeler's Graded Literary Readers with Interpretations: A Sixth Reader (Classic Reprint) (p. 2427)
—Wheeler's Graded Literary Readers with Interpretations: A Fourth Reader (Classic Reprint) (p. 2427)
Wheeler, William Lamont. Washington Symphony (Classic Reprint) (p. 2382)
Wheeler, Zachry. Mortal Vestige: Book Three of the Immortal Wake. (p. 1507)
—Thursday Midnight: Book Two of the Immortal Wake. (p. 2238)
Wheeler-Cribb, Peggy. Madeline Becomes a Star. Bensch, April, illus. (p. 1375)
Wheeler-Nicholson, Malcolm & Wheeler-Nicholson, Nicky. DC Comics Before Superman: Major Malcolm Wheeler-Nicholson's Pulp Comics. Herman, Daniel, ed. (p. 516)
Wheeler-Toppen, Jodi. Amazing Cardboard Tube Science. (p. 64)
—Cat Science Unleashed. (p. 342)
—Cool Chemistry Activities for Girls (p. 448)
—Dog Science Unleashed. (p. 576)
—Ghosts & Atoms Haus, Estudio, illus. (p. 829)
—Orchid Mantises & Other Extreme Insect Adaptations (p. 1669)
—Science Experiments That Explode & Implode: Fun Projects for Curious Kids. (p. 1954)
—Science Experiments That Fizz & Bubble: Fun Projects for Curious Kids. (p. 1954)
—This Is a Book to Read with a Worm. MCCARTNEY, Margaret, illus. (p. 2224)
Wheeler-Toppen, Jodi, jt. auth. see Enz, Tammy.
Wheeler-Toppen, Jodi, et al. Extreme Adaptations (p. 686)
—Girls Science Club. (p. 839)
Wheeler-Toppen, Jodi Lyn. Gross Science Projects (p. 898)
—Our Amazing Senses. (p. 1676)
—Our Ears Can Hear. (p. 1677)
—Our Eyes Can See. (p. 1677)
—Our Mouths Can Taste. (p. 1679)
—Our Noses Can Smell. (p. 1679)
—Our Skin Can Touch. (p. 1680)
Wheeler-Toppen, Jodi Lyn, jt. auth. see Enz, Tammy.
Wheelhouse, M. V., illus. see Ewing, Juliana Horatia.
Wheelhouse, M. V., jt. auth. see Ewing, Juliana Horatia Gatty.
Wheelock, Irene Grosvenor. Nestlings of Forest & Marsh (Classic Reprint) (p. 1588)
Wheelock, John Hall. Harvard Monthly, Vol. 46: March, 1908, to July, 1908 (Classic Reprint) (p. 936)
—Love & Liberation: The Songs of Adsched of Meru & Other Poems. (p. 1359)
—Love & Liberation: The Songs of Adsched of Meru & Other Poems (Classic Reprint) (p. 1359)
Wheelock, Lucy. Talks to Mothers (Classic Reprint) (p. 2188)
Wheelock, Lucy, jt. auth. see Spyri, Johanna.
Wheelon, Joshua. Departure. (p. 529)
Wheelwright, John Tyler. Rollo's Journey to Cambridge (Classic Reprint) (p. 1899)
Wheiler, Robert. Herphus & the importance of Aroooo. (p. 963)
—Snowflake a Christmas Gift. (p. 2049)
—Wink's , Boo, & Who! (p. 2473)
Whelan, Charles Elbert. BASCOM Clarke the Story of a Southern Refugee (Classic Reprint) (p. 168)
Whelan, Daniel. Box of Demons. (p. 266)
Whelan, Gloria. After the Train. (p. 34)
—All My Noble Dreams & Then What Happens. (p. 53)
—Boy Who Wanted to Cook. Adams, Steve, illus. (p. 271)
—Hedge School. (p. 947)
—Listeners. Benny, Mike, illus. (p. 1308)
—Megan's Year: An Irish Traveler's Story. Peck, Beth, illus. (p. 1442)
—Small Acts of Amazing Courage. (p. 2039)
—Waiting for the Owl's Call. Milelli, Pascal, illus. (p. 2370)
Whelan, Gloria & Nolan, Jenny. K Is for Kabuki: A Japan Alphabet. Han, Oki S., illus. (p. 1201)
Whelan, Gloria & Swain, Gwenyth. Voices for Freedom. Geister, David et al, illus. (p. 2365)
Whelan, Joan Marie. Intuition Girl: You Have Girl Power. (p. 1129)
Whelan, Kat, illus. see Moore, Clement C.
Whelan, Kat, illus. see Salzano, Tammi.
Whelan, Kevin, illus. see Cook, Peter.
Whelan, Kevin, jt. auth. see Cook, Peter.
Whelan, Lucy. Oh Why, Oh Why Can I Not Fly? (p. 1642)
Whelan, Olwyn, illus. see Maidment, Stella & Wilde, Oscar.
Whelan, Olwyn, illus. see Walker, Richard.
Whelan, Olwyn, tr. see Maidment, Stella & Wilde, Oscar.
Whelan, Piper. Clown Fish. (p. 408)
—Gravity. (p. 882)
—Trees. (p. 2284)
—Water Buffalo. (p. 2384)
Whelan, Piper & Willis, John. Wind. (p. 2471)
Whelen, Christine Crosby. Jolts & Jars of Amanda Hunter, and, a Family Jar (Classic Reprint) (p. 1176)
Whelon, Chuck. 3-D Mazes—Treasure Hunters. (p. 2547)
—Alien Invasion! Mazes. (p. 47)
—Alien Invasion! Stickers. (p. 47)
—Comical Festivals. (p. 430)
—Create Your Own Dinosaurs Sticker Activity Book. (p. 469)
—Create Your Own Monsters Sticker Activity Book. (p. 469)
—Dinoscenes. (p. 551)
—FLIP OUTS — Dinosaurs: Color Your Own Cartoon! (p. 749)
—Funny Families. (p. 801)
—Hysterical History. (p. 1056)
—Jokes, Riddles & Tongue Twisters. (p. 1176)
—Merry Magic. (p. 1450)
—Nutty Nature. (p. 1632)
—Sea Animals Finger Tattoos. (p. 1967)
—Smiley Things That Go Sticker Activity Book. (p. 2042)
—Treasure Hunter Activity Book. (p. 2282)
—What to Doodle? Adventure Stories! Pirates, Robots & More. (p. 2420)
—What to Doodle? Adventure Stories! Princesses, Fairies & More. (p. 2420)
—What to Doodle? All Sorts of Sports! (p. 2420)
—What to Doodle? Amazing Animals! (p. 2420)
—What to Doodle? Best Friends Forever! (p. 2421)
—What to Doodle Big Book #1 (for Costco) (p. 2421)
—What to Doodle? Christmas Creations! (p. 2421)
—What to Doodle? Dinosaurs! (p. 2421)
—What to Doodle? Fantastic Fantasy! (p. 2421)
—What to Doodle? Happy Halloween! (p. 2421)
—What to Doodle? in the Garden! (p. 2421)
—What to Doodle? Things That Go! (p. 2421)
—Where's the Elf? (p. 2440)
—Where's the Mermaid: A Mermazing Search-And-Find Adventure. (p. 2441)
—Where's the Princess? And Other Fairy Tale Searches. Whelon, Chuck, illus. (p. 2441)
—Where's the Witch? A Spooky Search-And-Find Book. (p. 2441)
—Witty Wandering. (p. 2482)
—Word Play: Write Your Own Crazy Comics (p. 2493)
—Word Play - Write Your Own Crazy Comics (p. 2493)
—Word Play! - Write Your Own Crazy Comics (p. 2493)
—Zoo Animals Finger Tattoos. (p. 2543)
Whelon, Chuck, illus. see Jones, Bryony.
Whelon, Chuck, jt. auth. see Altmann, Scott.
Whelon, Chuck, jt. auth. see Donahue, Peter.
Whelon, Chuck, jt. auth. see Woodworth, Viki.
Whelon, Chuck, jt. auth. see Wynne, Patricia J.
Whelon, Chuck & Brown, Helen. Where's the Bunny? A Search-And-Find Book. (p. 2440)
Whelon, Chuck & Dinosaurs. Dinosaur Rampage Activity Book. (p. 549)
Whelpley, Henry Milton. Chemical Lecture Notes: Taken from Prof. C. o Curtman's Lectures at the St. Louis College of Pharmacy (Classic Reprint) (p. 365)
Whelpton, Edwin. Meadow Sweet, or the Wooing of Iphis, Vol. 2 Of 3: A Pastoral (Classic Reprint) (p. 1434)
—Meadow Sweet, Vol. 1 Of 3: Or the Wooing of Iphis; a Pastoral (Classic Reprint) (p. 1434)
Whenman, Allison. Omega Project. (p. 1651)
Wherry, Edith. Red Lantern: Being the Story of the Goddess of the Red Lantern Light (Classic Reprint) (p. 1857)
—Wanderer on a Thousand Hills (Classic Reprint) (p. 2374)
Whetstone, Davidson. Brave for My Family. (p. 276)
Whetung, James. Vision Seeker Morin, Paul, illus. (p. 2362)
Whewell, William. Lectures on Systematic Morality Delivered in Lent Term 1846. (p. 1260)
Whibley, Charles. Book of Scoundrels (Classic Reprint) (p. 259)
Whidden, Dawn Kopman & Faye, O. M. Harold Peabody & the Magic Glasses. (p. 931)
Whigham, Rod, illus. see Fandel, Jennifer.
Whigham, Rod, illus. see Sautter, Aaron.
Whigham, Rod, illus. see Seidman, David.
Whigham, Rod, illus. see Wade, Mary Dodson.
Whilldin, Sunny. Alex P. Maxwell's Rainy Day Adventure. (p. 42)
Whimp, Pauline, illus. see Holden, Pam.
Whipp, Jo. Otis & Baby Jean. Whipp, Katie, illus. (p. 1675)
Whipp, Katie, illus. see Whipp, Jo.
Whipple, Annette. Africa. (p. 32)
—Flowers. (p. 753)
—Insects As Producers. (p. 1122)
—Laura Ingalls Wilder Companion: A Chapter-By-Chapter Guide. (p. 1252)
—Soil. (p. 2055)
Whipple, Chris. That's Not My Name. (p. 2214)
Whipple, Frances Harriet. Mechanic (Classic Reprint) (p. 1435)
Whipple, Guy Montrose. Classes for Gifted Children: An Experimental Study of Methods of Selection & Instruction (Classic Reprint) (p. 400)
—Classes for Gifted Children: An Experimental Study of Methods of Selection & Instruction - Scholar's Choice Edition. (p. 400)
Whipple, Kevin, illus. see Jones, Marcia Thornton.
Whipple, Natalie. House of Ivy & Sorrow. (p. 1023)
—Sidekick. (p. 2015)
—Transparent. (p. 2278)
Whipple, Rick, illus. see Drummond, Ree.
Whipple, Rick, illus. see Grogan, John.
Whipple, Rick, illus. see O'Connor, Jane & Glasser, Robin Preiss.
Whipple, S. A. D. Arthur St. Clair of Old Fort Recovery (Classic Reprint) (p. 123)
Whipple, Vicky. Little Weed Flower. Barcita, Pamela, illus. (p. 1329)
—Little Weed Flower/La Florecita de la Maleza. Barcita, Pamela, illus. (p. 1329)
Whipple, Wayne. Tad Lincoln: A True Story (Classic Reprint) (p. 2175)
Whipple, Wayne & Aaron, S. F. Radio Boys Cronies. (p. 1833)
—Radio Boys Loyalty Bill Brown Listens In. (p. 1833)
Whishaw, Bernhard. My Spanish Year (Classic Reprint) (p. 1561)
Whishaw, Fred. Countess Ida (Classic Reprint) (p. 459)
—Tsars Gratitude (Classic Reprint) (p. 2298)
Whishaw, Frederick. Boyar of the Terrible: A Romance of the Court of Ivan the Cruel, First Tsar of Russia (Classic Reprint) (p. 271)
—Romance of the Woods (Classic Reprint) (p. 1900)
Whishaw, Frederick J. Out of Doors in Tsarland: A Record of the Seeings & Doings of a Wanderer in Russia (Classic Reprint) (p. 1682)
Whisker, Dan, illus. see Meister, Cari.
Whiskerin, Yuri. Yuri Whiskerin's True Tale of the Invasion of the Shrews. Lukowiak, Michael, illus. (p. 2537)
Whisp, Kennilworthy, pseud. Quidditch Through the Ages. (p. 1827)
Whispering Pine Press International, ed. see Hood, James G.
Whispering Pine Press International, ed. see Hood, Kared Jean Matsko.
Whispering Pine Press International, ed. see Hood, Karen Jean Matsko.
Whispering Pine Press International, ed. Petting Farm Fun, Translated Amharic Artistic Design Service Staff, illus. (p. 1732)
Whispering Pine Press International, Inc. Staff, ed. see Hilderbrandt, Sandra June.
Whispering Pine Press International, Inc. Staff, ed. see Hood, Karen Jean Matsko.
Whispering Pine Press International Staff, ed. see Hood, Karen Jean Matsko.
Whistlecraft, William. Prospectus & Specimen of an Intended National Work: Intended to Comprise the Most Interesting Particulars, Relating to King Arthur & His Round Table (Classic Reprint) (p. 1807)
Whistler, Charles W. King Alfred's Vikings, a Story of the First English Fleet. (p. 1219)
—Prince of Cornwall: A Story of Glastonbury & the West in the Days of Ina of Wessex (Classic Reprint) (p. 1794)
—Sea Queen's Sailing. (p. 1968)
—Sea-Queen's Sailing. Groome, W. H. C., illus. (p. 1968)
Whistler, Charles Watts. King's Comrade: A Story of Old Hereford. (p. 1222)
Whitaker, Alecia. Queen of Kentucky. (p. 1824)
—Way Back Home. (p. 2387)
Whitaker, David. Doctor Who & the Crusaders. (p. 574)
—Doctor Who & the Daleks. (p. 574)
Whitaker, Edward. Lucy Fitzadam, Vol. 1 Of 2: An Autobiography (Classic Reprint) (p. 1366)
Whitaker, Evelyn. Belle (Classic Reprint) (p. 197)
—Dear (Classic Reprint) (p. 520)
—For the Fourth Time of Asking. (p. 763)
—For the Fourth Time of Asking (Classic Reprint) (p. 763)
—Laddie (Classic Reprint) (p. 1236)
—Miss. Toosey's Mission (Classic Reprint) (p. 1480)
—Miss. Toosey's Mission & Laddie (Classic Reprint) (p. 1480)
—Our Little Ann (Classic Reprint) (p. 1679)
—Rob & Kit (Classic Reprint) (p. 1889)
—Zoe (Classic Reprint) (p. 2541)
Whitaker, Fess. History of Corporal Fess Whitaker (Classic Reprint) (p. 977)
Whitaker, Herman. Cross Trails: The Story of One Woman in the North Woods (Classic Reprint) (p. 478)
—Mystery of the Barranca (Classic Reprint) (p. 1569)
—Planter a Novel (Classic Reprint) (p. 1757)
—Probationer: And Other Stories (Classic Reprint) (p. 1803)
—Settler (Classic Reprint) (p. 1993)
—West Winds: California's Book of Fiction Written by California Authors & Illustrated by California Artists (Classic Reprint) (p. 2402)
Whitaker, J. British Duck Decoys of to-Day, 1918 (Classic Reprint) (p. 283)
Whitaker, Jimmy. Lilly & Twinkle Eyes (p. 1301)
Whitaker, Joan. Cartwheeling. Cusack, Elizabeth, illus. (p. 335)
Whitaker, Kenneth. Hood-Hearted Child, Life as a Nobody: Based on a True Story (p. 1000)
Whitaker, Nathan. Snap Decision (p. 2045)
Whitaker, Olivar B. Evenings with Uncle 'Bijah, or Christian Fellowship (Classic Reprint) (p. 669)
Whitaker Playhouse. Away in a Manger: Wipe-Clean Color Play & Learn. (p. 144)
—Bible 123's: Wipe-Clean Activity Book. (p. 213)
—Bible ABC's: Wipe-Clean Activity Book. (p. 213)

W

—Hija de Las Tinieblas. (p. 970)
—Illusions of Fate. (p. 1096)
—Mind Games. (p. 1469)
—Now I Rise. (p. 1627)
—Oscuro Descenso de Elizabeth Frankenstein. (p. 1673)
—Paranormalcy. (p. 1699)
—Perfect Lies. (p. 1722)
—Slayer. (p. 2035)
—Supernaturally. (p. 2161)
White, Kiersten, jt. auth. see Lasky, Kathryn.
White, Kiersten & Di Bartolo, Jim. In the Shadows. Di Bartolo, Jim, illus. (p. 1111)
White, Kiersten & Kotaki, Kekai. Chosen. (p. 381)
White, Kinga. Animalphabetical Adventures. (p. 93)
White, Kris. Third Gate: Book One in the Gates Trilogy. (p. 2222)
White, Lee, illus. see Agosin, Marjorie & Agosain, Marjorie.
White, Lee, illus. see Agosin, Marjorie.
White, Lee, illus. see Britt, Paige.
White, Lee, illus. see Brockenbrough, Martha.
White, Lee, illus. see Case, Julie.
White, Lee, illus. see Davies, Jacqueline.
White, Lee, illus. see Odanaka, Barbara.
White, Lee, illus. see Ribke, Simone T.
White, Lee, illus. see Rosen, Michael J.
White, Lee, illus. see Scanlon, Liz Garton.
White, Lee, illus. see Scillian, Devin.
White, Lee, illus. see Smith, Danna.
White, Lee, illus. see Viorst, Judith.
White, Lee, illus. see Weatherford, Carole Boston.
White, Leslie, illus. see Hitchcock, S. C. & Flynn, Tom.
White, Lia. Alkis. (p. 48)
White, Linda. Too Many Pumpkins. (p. 2261)
White, Linda & White, Katherine. Pocket Guide to Camping (p. 1764)
White, Loricia. Little Tail's Rhyming Roots. (p. 1328)
White, Lowell. Chief, 1915 (Classic Reprint) (p. 369)
White, Lydia E. Success in Society: A Manual of Good Manners. (p. 2146)
—Success in Society: A Manual of Good Manners, Social Etiquette, Rules (Classic Reprint) (p. 2146)
White, Lyn, ed. see Beale, Fleur.
White, Lyn, ed. see Chim, Wai.
White, Lyn, ed. see Daniel, Zoe.
White, Lyn, ed. see Heffernan, John.
White, M. Agnes. Gordon Lodge, or Retribution: An Autobiography (Classic Reprint) (p. 869)
White, M. L. History of the Life of Amos Owens, the Noted Blockader, of Cherry Mountain, N. C (Classic Reprint) (p. 980)
White, Mack, illus. see Kearby, Mike.
White, Mandy. Imagine with Me. (p. 1100)
White, Mark. Ant & the Grasshopper: A Retelling of Aesop's Fable Pérez, Sara Rojo, illus. (p. 101)
—Lion & the Mouse: A Retelling of Aesop's Fable Pérez, Sara Rojo, illus. (p. 1305)
—Wolf in Sheep's Clothing: A Retelling of Aesop's Fable Pérez, Sara Rojo, illus. (p. 2484)
White, Mark & Aesop Enterprise Inc. Staff. Ant & the Grasshopper: A Retelling of Aesop's Fable Pérez, Sara Rojo, illus. (p. 101)
—Fox & the Grapes: A Retelling of Aesop's Fable Pérez, Sara Rojo, illus. (p. 774)
—Lion & the Mouse: A Retelling of Aesop's Fable Pérez, Sara Rojo, illus. (p. 1305)
—Wolf in Sheep's Clothing: A Retelling of Aesop's Fable Pérez, Sara Rojo, illus. (p. 2484)
White, Martin. Blood Price. (p. 246)
White, Matthew. Born Aristocrat: A Story of the Stage (Classic Reprint) (p. 263)
—Harry Ascott Abroad (Classic Reprint) (p. 934)
White, Matthew, Jr. Two Boys & a Fortune or the Tyler Will (Classic Reprint) (p. 2307)
White, Maude Valerie. Friends & Memories (Classic Reprint) (p. 787)
White, Maude Valerie, jt. auth. see Munthe, Axel.
White, Maureen. Butterfly Shell: Tbc. (p. 304)
White, May Langdon. Story Readers (Classic Reprint) (p. 2135)
White, Melissa. Purple Frogs, Imagine High. (p. 1816)
White, Mia. Femme FATALE - FAITH STORIES When Good Girls Are Caught in BAD Situations They Become Femme Fatales: Vamp. White, Mia, illus. (p. 720)
—VAMP -Chronicles - Pin up Heros don't become BaD: Vamp Series 2 the Golden Vessel. White, Mia, illus. (p. 2345)
—VAMP Courtesan - Beauties in Tough Spots an Historic Graphic Novel: Vamp's Adventures Time Travel Chronicles. White, Mia, illus. (p. 2345)
White, Michael. Garden of Indra (Classic Reprint) (p. 809)
White, Michael P., illus. see Deedy, Carmen Agra.
White, Michael P., illus. see Stewart, Dawn Lesley.
White, Mike, illus. see Hynes, Margaret.
White, Mus, jt. auth. see Andersen, Hans.
White, Mus, tr. see Andersen, Hans.
White, Nancy. Aviation Firefighters. (p. 143)
—Black Mambas: Sudden Death! (p. 238)
—Coral Snakes: Beware the Colors! (p. 453)
—Creeping Land Snails. (p. 472)
—Death Adders: Super Deadly! (p. 521)
—Diamondback Rattlers: America's Most Venomous Snakes! (p. 538)
—Fer-De-Lance: Master Killer! (p. 720)
—King Cobras: The Biggest Venomous Snakes of All! (p. 1220)
—Maine Coons: Super Big. (p. 1384)
—Paramedics to the Rescue. (p. 1699)
—Police Officers to the Rescue. (p. 1770)
—Por qué hay osos polares en la nieve ... y no hay Flamencos. (p. 1778)
—Siamese: Talk to Me! (p. 2014)
—Using Earth's Underground Heat. (p. 2341)
—Why Polar Bears Like Snow... & Flamingos Don't & Por qué hay osos polares en la nieve ... y no hay Flamencos: 6 English, 6 Spanish Adaptations (p. 2458)
White, Nancy, jt. auth. see Lunis, Natalie.
White, Nancy & Benchmark Education Company, LLC Staff. Por Qué Hay Osos Polares en la Nieve ... y No Hay Flamencos: Set of 6 Common Core Edition. (p. 1778)
White, Nick. Meet the Artist: Alberto Giacometti. (p. 1439)
White, Nina. Town Called Crayonville: Underneath We Are All the Same. (p. 2270)
White, N.m. Unlock Level 1 Listening & Speaking Skills Student's Book & Online Workbook (p. 2333)
White, Oli. Generation Next: the Takeover. (p. 814)
White, Paul. Jungle Doctor & the Whirlwind. (p. 1190)
—Jungle Doctor in Slippery Places. (p. 1190)
—Jungle Doctor Looks for Trouble. (p. 1190)
—Jungle Doctor Meets a Lion. (p. 1190)
—Jungle Doctor on Safari. (p. 1190)
—Jungle Doctor on the Hop. (p. 1190)
—Jungle Doctor Operates. (p. 1190)
—Jungle Doctor to the Rescue. (p. 1190)
—Jungle Doctor's Africa. (p. 1190)
—Jungle Doctor's Crooked Dealings. (p. 1190)
—Jungle Doctor's Enemies. (p. 1190)
White, Pauline. Jewel Baxter & Friends (p. 1167)
White, Pearl. Just Me (Classic Reprint) (p. 1194)
White, Percy. Andria (Classic Reprint) (p. 84)
—Grip of the Bookmaker (Classic Reprint) (p. 897)
—Heart of the Dancer (Classic Reprint) (p. 945)
—Mr. John Strood (Classic Reprint) (p. 1519)
—New Christians (Classic Reprint) (p. 1592)
—Passionate Pilgrim (Classic Reprint) (p. 1703)
White, Porchanee a. #bookpusher. Stone, Mitzie, illus. (p. 261)
White, Queonna. Giant Snake & the Brave Little Mouse. (p. 831)
White, Rachel. Helping Children to Improve Their Gross Motor Skills: The Stepping Stones Curriculum. (p. 953)
White, Randy Wayne. Fins: A Sharks Incorporated Novel. (p. 731)
White, Rebecca. Holly's Not So Plain & Ordinary Day. (p. 988)
White, Rebecca B. Sweet Briar Magazine, Vol. 3: Published Quarterly by the Students of Sweet Briar College; November, 1911 (Classic Reprint) (p. 2168)
White, Rex, illus. see White, Kevin.
White, Rhoda E. Memoir & Letters of Jenny C. White Del Bal (Classic Reprint) (p. 1443)
White, Richard Grant. Adventures of Sir Lyon Bouse. (p. 28)
—Adventures of Sir Lyon Bouse, Bart. , in America, During the Civil War: Being Extracts from His Diary (Classic Reprint) (p. 28)
White, Robb. Deathwatch. (p. 522)
White, Robin L. Santa's Christmas Memoirs: Volume 1. (p. 1933)
White, Rod. Longnose & Rainbow Tail. (p. 1344)
White, Ruth. Belle Prater's Boy. (p. 197)
—Month of Sundays. (p. 1499)
—Way down Deep (p. 2387)
—You'll Like It Here (Everybody Does) (p. 2529)
White, S. A. Stampeder (Classic Reprint) (p. 2100)
White, Sam, illus. see Fleishman, Brett.
White, Sam Jordan. Gourds & Brains (Classic Reprint) (p. 872)
White, Sam O., illus. see Decesare, Jason F.
White, Samuel Alexander. Foaming Fore Shore (Classic Reprint) (p. 755)
—Wildcatters (Classic Reprint) (p. 2465)
White, Samuel O., illus. see Decesare, Jason F.
White, Sarah. Let Me List the Ways. (p. 1269)
—Our Broken Pieces. (p. 1676)
White, Selden F. Book of Cranford Village (Classic Reprint) (p. 258)
White, Shannon. Tough Stuff. (p. 2268)
White, Sierra. Ballad of a Whip Cream Bird. (p. 161)
—Goodnight Library. (p. 867)
—Have You Seen My Mom? (p. 939)
White, Siobhán, illus. see Rankin, H. L.
White, Stanley I. & White, Rachael. Absence Abbey (p. 9)
White, Stephanie. Ludwig Van Beethoven: Famous Composer. (p. 1366)
White, Stephen. Thoughts & Obsessions. (p. 2231)
White, Stephen & Barrie, J. M. J. M. Barrie's Peter Pan. (p. 1150)
White, Steve. Cleo the Curious Cat. (p. 403)
White, Steve & McKenzie-Ray, Mark. Hunting Vampires. (p. 1054)
White, Stewart Edward. Adventures of Bobby Orde (Classic Reprint) (p. 22)
—African Camp Fires (Classic Reprint) (p. 32)
—Arizona Nights (Classic Reprint) (p. 116)
—Cabin (Classic Reprint) (p. 307)
—Claim Jumpers: A Romance (Classic Reprint) (p. 397)
—Conjuror's House: A Romance of the Free Forest. (p. 440)
—Conjuror's House: A Romance of the Free Forest (Classic Reprint) (p. 440)
—Gold (Classic Reprint) (p. 855)
—Gray Dawn (Classic Reprint) (p. 882)
—Killer (Classic Reprint) (p. 1217)
—Leopard Woman (Classic Reprint) (p. 1268)
—Mountains (Classic Reprint) (p. 1514)
—Mystery (Classic Reprint) (p. 1568)
—No Title (Classic Reprint) (p. 1615)
—On Tiptoe: A Romance of the Redwoods (Classic Reprint) (p. 1656)
—Pass (Classic Reprint) (p. 1702)
—Riverman (Classic Reprint) (p. 1887)
—Rose Dawn (Classic Reprint) (p. 1905)
—Rules of the Game (Classic Reprint) (p. 1913)
—Sign at Six. (p. 2016)
—Simba (Classic Reprint) (p. 2020)
—Westerners (Classic Reprint) (p. 2402)
—Works of Stewart Edward White. (p. 2499)
—Works of Stewart Edward White (Classic Reprint) (p. 2499)
—Works of Stewart Edward White. Camp & Trail. (p. 2499)
White, Susan. Headliner (p. 942)
White, Susan K. Jesus Does Good Things. McQuitty, LaVonia Corbin, illus. (p. 1166)
White, Sylvia. And They Laughed Ha Ha, Ha Ha, Ha Ha. (p. 83)
White, Tara. I Like Who I Am (p. 1068)
—Where I Belong (p. 2437)
White, Tara B., illus. see Hughes, John P.
White, Teagan. Adventures with Barefoot Critters. (p. 30)
—Counting with Barefoot Critters. (p. 460)
White, Teagan, illus. see Chronicle Books Staff.
White, Teagan, illus. see Darwin, Charles.
White, Teagan, illus. see DeStefano, Lauren.
White, Teagan, illus. see Kelly, Jacqueline.
White, Teagan, illus. see Kokias, Kerri.
White, Teagan, illus. see Marr, Melissa.
White, Teagan, illus. see Rosenthal, Amy Krouse.
White, Teagan, illus. see Silvestro, Annie.
White, Teagan, jt. auth. see Rogge, Robie.
White, Ten Eyck. Lakeside Musings (Classic Reprint) (p. 1240)
White, Terry, jt. auth. see Maynard, Christopher.
White, T.h. Master: An Adventure Story (Classic Reprint) (p. 1418)
White, Timothy, ed. see White, Franicia.
White, Tina Jorgenson, illus. see Briceno, Carole.
White, Tom and Erica. Aggie over the Fence. (p. 35)
White, Tryphena Ely. Tryphena Ely White's Journal, 1805-1905: Being a Record, Written One Hundred Years Ago, of the Daily Life of a Young Lady of Puritan Heritage (Classic Reprint) (p. 2297)
White, Valarie. Dinosaurs Still Rule the Earth. (p. 551)
White, Vernon. Birdhouse. (p. 231)
White, Vicky, illus. see Jenkins, Martin.
White, Virginia K. Little Honker Saves the Day. (p. 1318)
—Little Honker's Backyard Adventures. (p. 1318)
—Little Honker's Patriotic Paws. (p. 1318)
—Little Honker's Winter Concert. (p. 1318)
White, Vivian Elliott. Memories of Grandmother (Classic Reprint) (p. 1446)
White, W. H. Some Women of to-Day (Classic Reprint) (p. 2059)
White, W. L., III. Flux: Celestial Genesis. Malakar, Nilanjan, illus. (p. 753)
—Flux: Sequence of Astrometry. Malakar, Nilanjan, illus. (p. 753)
White, Wade Albert. Adventurer's Guide to Dragons (and Why They Keep Biting Me) (p. 19)
—Adventurer's Guide to Successful Escapes. (p. 19)
—Adventurer's Guide to Treasure (and How to Steal It) (p. 19)
White, Walter. All Round the Wrekin (Classic Reprint) (p. 53)
—Eastern England, Vol. 2 Of 2: From the Thames to the Humber (Classic Reprint) (p. 620)
—July Holiday in Saxony, Bohemia, & Silesia (Classic Reprint) (p. 1188)
—Month in Yorkshire (Classic Reprint) (p. 1499)
—Northumberland, & the Border (Classic Reprint) (p. 1622)
—On Foot Through Tyrol, in the Summer of 1855 (Classic Reprint) (p. 1652)
—To Mont Blanc: And Back Again (Classic Reprint) (p. 2253)
White, William Allen. Certain Rich Man (Classic Reprint) (p. 353)
—Court of Boyville (Classic Reprint) (p. 463)
—God's Puppets (Classic Reprint) (p. 854)
—Heart of a Fool (Classic Reprint) (p. 945)
—In Our Town (Classic Reprint) (p. 1106)
—In the Heart of a Fool (Classic Reprint) (p. 1109)
—Martial Adventures, of Henry & Me (Classic Reprint) (p. 1410)
—Real Issue: A Book of Kansas Stories (Classic Reprint) (p. 1849)
—Stratagems & Spoils: Stories of Love & Politics (Classic Reprint) (p. 2139)
White, William Ellis, jt. auth. see Wilson, Gustavus James Nash.
White, William Patterson. Heart of the Range (Classic Reprint) (p. 945)
—Hidden Trails (Classic Reprint) (p. 966)
—Lynch Lawyers (Classic Reprint) (p. 1370)
—Owner of the Lazy d (Classic Reprint) (p. 1689)
—Paradise Bend (Classic Reprint) (p. 1698)
—RIDER of GOLDEN BAR (a Western Adventure) (p. 1878)
—Rider of Golden Bar (Classic Reprint) (p. 1878)
Whiteaves, Joseph Frederick. Descriptions of Eight New Species of Fossils from the Cambro-Silurian Rocks of Manitoba (Classic Reprint) (p. 531)
—Notes on the Cretaceous Fossils Collected by Mr. James Richardson, at Vancouver & the Adjacent Islands (Classic Reprint) (p. 1624)
Whitebeach, Terry & Enadio, Sarafino Wani. Trouble Tomorrow. (p. 2292)
Whitechurch, Victor L. Downland Echoes (Classic Reprint) (p. 591)
Whitechurch, Victor Lorenzo. Canon in Residence (Classic Reprint) (p. 322)
Whited, Melissa F. Bear Brothers' Big Adventure (p. 179)
Whited, Susanne. Little Baby Poot-Poot. Whited, Susanne, illus. (p. 1310)
Whited, Susanne, ed. see Clark, Rhonda.
Whited, Wayne & Burns, Robert David. Adventures of Orie Alexander - the Story Thief (Paperback Edition) (p. 26)
Whitefield, Charles T. Plain American in England (Classic Reprint) (p. 1754)
Whitefield, George. Sermons of George Whitefield: The 57 Preaching Lectures on Christian Theology, History, Bible Doctrine & Prophecy, Complete. (p. 1991)
—Sermons of George Whitefield: The 57 Preaching Lectures on Christian Theology, History, Bible Doctrine & Prophecy, Complete (Hardcover) (p. 1991)
—Sermons of George Whitefield. (p. 1991)
Whiteford, Gary T., jt. auth. see Salter, Christopher L.
Whiteford, Rhona, jt. auth. see Fitzsimmons, Jim.
Whitefriars, Author of. Whitehall, or the Days of Charles the First, Vol. 1: An Historical Romance (Classic Reprint) (p. 2445)
Whitehair, Charles W. Out There (Classic Reprint) (p. 1683)
—Pictures Burned into My Memory (Classic Reprint) (p. 1741)
Whitehall, Jean-Paul. Raven Prince & Other Stories. (p. 1843)
White-Hartman, K. L. Drake the Dragon. (p. 596)
Whitehead, A. C. Standard Bearer: A Story of Army Life in the Time of Caesar. (p. 2100)
—Standard Bearer: A Story of Army Life in the Time of Caesar (Classic Reprint) (p. 2100)
Whitehead, Albert Carlton. Makers of Georgia's Name & Fame (Classic Reprint) (p. 1388)
Whitehead, Alfred North. Concept of Nature: The Tarner Lectures Delivered in Trinity College. (p. 437)
—Concept of Nature: The Tarner Lectures Delivered in Trinity College, November 1919 (Classic Reprint) (p. 437)
Whitehead, Brynne E., illus. see Whitehead, Brynne.
Whitehead, C. Lives & Exploits of English Highwaymen, Pirates, & Robbers, Vol. 1 Of 2: Drawn from the Earliest & Most Authentic Sources, & Brought down to the Present Time (Classic Reprint) (p. 1332)
Whitehead, Charles. Autobiography of Jack Ketch (Classic Reprint) (p. 140)
—Lives & Exploits of the Most Noted Highwaymen, Robbers & Murderers, of All Nations: Drawn from the Most Authentic Sources & Brought down to the Present Time (Classic Reprint) (p. 1332)
Whitehead, Charles Edward, jt. auth. see Gerard, Jules.
Whitehead, D. P. Captain Shellfish & the Meanest Pirate on the Sea. (p. 326)
—Princess Deodara & the Golden Leaf. (p. 1797)
Whitehead, Harold. Business Career of Peter Flint (Classic Reprint) (p. 301)
Whitehead, Jenny. You're a Crab! A Moody Day Book. Whitehead, Jenny, illus. (p. 2535)
Whitehead, Jenny, illus. see Bruno, Elsa Knight.
Whitehead, Joan. Four Seasons of Sammy Snail. (p. 772)
Whitehead, Kim. Afghanistan (p. 31)
Whitehead, Paul, illus. see Auerbach, Annie.
Whitehead, Pete, illus. see Highlights for Children Editorial Staff.
Whitehead, Pete, illus. see Inches, Alison.
Whitehead, Rachael, illus. see Angman, Pauline Hagen.
Whitehead, Ralph Radcliffe. Folk-Songs of Eastern Europe (Classic Reprint) (p. 757)
Whitehead, Russell. Jelly Fish Bit My Bum. Gillespie, Martin, illus. (p. 1163)
Whitehead, S. B., illus. see Leno, Jay.
Whitehead, S. R. Nelly Armstrong, Vol. 2 Of 2: A Story of the Day (Classic Reprint) (p. 1586)
Whitehead, T. C. Village Sketches: Descriptive of Club & School Festivals & Other Village Gatherings & Institutions (Classic Reprint) (p. 2358)
Whitehead, Vickie. Just Like Me. Whitehead, Vickie, illus. (p. 1193)
Whitehead, Victoria E., illus. see Gerber, Mary Lichty.
Whitehead, William. Country Money. Beech, Mark, illus. (p. 461)
—Family Money. Beech, Mark, illus. (p. 702)
Whitehead, William, et al. Country Money. Beech, Mark, illus. (p. 461)
Whitehead, Zollicofer Wiley. Trial of D. A. Mcdougald for the Murder of Simeon Conoley, at Fayetteville, N. C (Classic Reprint) (p. 2286)
Whitehill, Dorothy. Books for Young Girls: The Polly Pendleton Series (Classic Reprint) (p. 261)
—Phyllis: A Twin (Classic Reprint) (p. 1737)
—Polly Sees the World at War (Classic Reprint) (p. 1772)
Whitehill, Simcha. All about Pikachu. (p. 50)
—Alola Region Adventure Guide. (p. 57)
—Battle with the Ultra Beast. (p. 175)
—Battle with the Ultra Beast (Pokémon: Graphic Collection #1) (p. 175)
—First Partner. (p. 738)
—Grand Trial Showdown. (p. 877)
—Grand Trial Showdown (Pokémon: Graphic Collection #2) (p. 877)
—Kalos Beginner's Handbook. (p. 1202)
—Legendary & Mythical Pokémon Guide. (p. 1263)
—Now You See It! Watch Pokémon Evolve— Right Before Your Eyes! (p. 1628)
—Official Guide to Legendary & Mythical Pokemon. (p. 1641)
—Official Guide to Mythical & Legendary Pokémon. (p. 1641)
—Prima Games Reader Level 2 Pokemon: Legends of Alola. (p. 1792)
—Prima Games Reader Level 3 Pokemon: Ash's Epic Island Challenge. (p. 1792)
—Training Manual. (p. 2275)
—World of Sinnoh. (p. 2504)
Whitehill, Simcha & Rusu, Meredith. Pokemon - Detective Pikachu's Case Files. (p. 1768)
Whitehorn, Harriet. Violet & the Hidden Treasure. Moor, Becka, illus. (p. 2359)
—Violet & the Mummy Mystery. Moor, Becka, illus. (p. 2359)
—Violet & the Pearl of the Orient. Moor, Becka, illus. (p. 2359)
—Violet & the Smugglers. Moor, Becka, illus. (p. 2359)
Whitehouse, Anna. Last Sant. (p. 1249)
Whitehouse, Ben. Dinner for Dinos: Gulp, Guzzle, Chomp, Chew (p. 547)
Whitehouse, Ben, illus. see Berne, Emma Carlson.
Whitehouse, Ben, illus. see Davies, Becky.
Whitehouse, Ben, illus. see Donald, Alison.
Whitehouse, Ben, illus. see Durst, Sarah Beth.
Whitehouse, Ben, illus. see Kahler, Alex R.
Whitehouse, Ben, illus. see Karanja, Caroline.
Whitehouse, Ben, illus. see Meister, Cari.
Whitehouse, Ben, illus. see Styles, Walker.
Whitehouse, Ben, illus. see Yasiejko, Roman.
Whitehouse, Ben & Clever Publishing. Porcupine Pete's Sports Corner: Ice Hockey. (p. 1778)
—Porcupine Pete's Sports Corner: Ice Skating. (p. 1778)
Whitehouse, Howard. Zombie Elementary: The Real Story. (p. 2542)
Whitehouse, Kay. Dolly, a Dog, & a Camper. Thomas, Jennifer, ed. (p. 579)
Whitehurst, Susan. Mayflower. (p. 1430)
—Pilgrims Before the Mayflower. (p. 1744)
—Plymouth Partnership: Pilgrims & Native Americans. (p. 1763)
—William Bradford & Plymouth: A Colony Grows. (p. 2468)
Whiteing, Richard. All Moonshine (Classic Reprint) (p. 52)

W

Whitman, Sylvia. Milk of Birds. (p. 1467)
—Under the Ramadan Moon Williams, Sue, illus. (p. 2322)
—Under the Ramadan Moon. Williams, Sue, illus. (p. 2322)
Whitman, Walt. Autobiographia: Or the Story of a Life (Classic Reprint) (p. 139)
—Complete Prose Works of Walt Whitman, Vol. 2 (Classic Reprint) (p. 435)
—Gesang Von Mir Selbst. (p. 823)
—Leaves of Grass: Including Sands at Seventy, Good Bye My Fancy, Old Age Echoes, & a Backward Glance o'Er Travel'd Roads - Scholar's Choice Edition. (p. 1260)
—Specimen Days in America (Classic Reprint) (p. 2077)
Whitmarsh, H. Phelps. Golden Talisman (Classic Reprint) (p. 859)
Whitmarsh, John & Hunloke, Max. Call Me Max: A Life in Radio. (p. 311)
Whitmer, T. W. Down on Devil's Creek (Classic Reprint) (p. 590)
Whitmire, Anna, illus. see Taylor, Clif.
Whitmire, Denise. Tree. (p. 2283)
Whitmore, Frederic. Florida Farm (Classic Reprint) (p. 751)
Whitmore, Hugh. Three Madelines. Wilson, Raylene Jenee & Gibbons, Deanna, illus. (p. 2234)
Whitmore, Patrick Charles. Cookie & the Golden Quill. (p. 446)
Whitney, A. D. T. Ascutney Street: A Neighborhood Story (Classic Reprint) (p. 125)
—Biddy's Episodes (Classic Reprint) (p. 215)
—Bonnyborough (Classic Reprint) (p. 256)
—Boys at Chequasset: Or, a Little Leaven (Classic Reprint) (p. 272)
—Faith Gartney's Girlhood (Classic Reprint) (p. 698)
—Gayworthys: A Story of Threads & Thrums (Classic Reprint) (p. 812)
—Golden Gossip: Neighborhood Story Number Two (Classic Reprint) (p. 857)
—Hitherto: A Story of Yesterdays (Classic Reprint) (p. 982)
—Homespun Yarns (Classic Reprint) (p. 998)
—Mother Goose: For Grown Folks (Classic Reprint) (p. 1509)
—Odd, or Even? (Classic Reprint) (p. 1637)
—Other Girls (Classic Reprint) (p. 1674)
—Patience Strong's Outings (Classic Reprint) (p. 1705)
—Real Folks (Classic Reprint) (p. 1849)
—Sights & Insights, Vol. 1: Patience Strong's Story of over the Way (Classic Reprint) (p. 2016)
—Square Pegs (Classic Reprint) (p. 2094)
—Summer in Leslie Goldthwaite's Life. (p. 2149)
—Summer in Leslie Goldthwaite's Life (Classic Reprint) (p. 2149)
—We Girls: A Home Story. (p. 2390)
—We Girls: A Home Story (Classic Reprint) (p. 2390)
—Zerub Throop's Experiment (Classic Reprint) (p. 2540)
Whitney, Adeline Dutton Train. Faith Gartney S Girlhood. (p. 698)
—We Girls. (p. 2390)
Whitney, Atwell. Almond-Eyed: A Story of the Day (Classic Reprint) (p. 57)
Whitney, Cara. Unbridled Faith Devotions for Young Readers (p. 2317)
Whitney, Chris. Composition Year 5 Pupil Book (Treasure House) (p. 436)
—Composition Year 6 Pupil Book (Treasure House) (p. 436)
Whitney, Daisy. Mockingbirds. (p. 1485)
—Rivals. (p. 1887)
—Starry Nights. (p. 2106)
—When You Were Here. (p. 2434)
Whitney, David. Get Coding 2! Build Five Computer Games Using HTML & JavaScript. Beedie, Duncan, illus. (p. 823)
Whitney, E. Transition Primer (Classic Reprint) (p. 2278)
Whitney, E. C. Easy Entertainments for Young People: Containing, the Court of the Year; a Carnival of Sports; the Sniggles Family; Doctor Cure-All; the Courting of Mother Goose; Vice Versa; My Country (Classic Reprint) (p. 620)
Whitney, Elliott. Blind Lion of the Congo. (p. 244)
—Blind Lion of the Congo (Classic Reprint) (p. 244)
—King Condor of the Andes (Classic Reprint) (p. 1220)
—Rogue Elephant: The Boys' Big Game Series. (p. 1897)
Whitney, Gertrude Capen. Above the Shame of Circumstance (Classic Reprint) (p. 7)
—House of Landell, or Follow & Find (Classic Reprint) (p. 1023)
—I Choose (Classic Reprint) (p. 1063)
—Where the Sun Shines (Classic Reprint) (p. 2439)
—Yet Speaketh He (Classic Reprint) (p. 2521)
Whitney, Jason. Seed. (p. 1982)
Whitney, Jennifer, photos by see Burtwell, Ross & Celeste Rosenfeld, Julia.
Whitney, Kim Ablon. Other Half of Life. (p. 1674)
Whitney, Louisa M. Goldie's Inheritance, Vol. 47: A Story of the Siege of Atlanta (Classic Reprint) (p. 860)
Whitney, Thomas Richard. Republic, Vol. 3: A Monthly Magazine of American Literature, Politics & Art; January, 1852 (Classic Reprint) (p. 1868)
Whitson, Andrew, illus. see Doyle, Malachy.
Whitson, Andrew, jt. auth. see Doyle, Malachy.
Whitson, Chris. Salty Strong: The Whole Cajun Story. (p. 1925)
Whitson, Fred, illus. see Thoolen, Jai D.
Whitson, John H. Castle of Doubt (Classic Reprint) (p. 340)
—Justin Wingate Ranchman (Classic Reprint) (p. 1195)
—Rainbow Chasers: A Story of the Plains (Classic Reprint) (p. 1836)
Whitson, John Harvey. Barbara, a Woman of the West (Classic Reprint) (p. 165)
—Young Ditch Rider: A Story of the Plains (Classic Reprint) (p. 2530)
Whitson, L. D. Gilbert St. Maurice (Classic Reprint) (p. 833)
Whitson, Savannah. I Wish I Were a Superhero! (p. 1086)
Whitt, Carlynn, illus. see Mackall, Dandi Daley.
Whitt, Carlynn, illus. see Snyder, Laurel.
Whitt, Kelly Kizer. Pronóstico Del Sistema Solar Klein, Laurie Allen, illus. (p. 1807)
—Solar System Forecast Klein, Laurie Allen, illus. (p. 2056)
Whitt, Pennie. Fun Lessons Learned: All 9 Stories for Boys & Girls. (p. 799)
Whitt, Shannon, illus. see Weiner, Miriam.
Whittaker, Frederick. Cadet Button: A Novel of American Army Life (Classic Reprint) (p. 308)
Whittaker, Heather. Different Little Doggy. Alberts, Scott, illus. (p. 545)
Whittaker, Helen. Food. Porcellato, Nives, illus. (p. 759)
—How Toys Roll. (p. 1046)
—How Toys Slide. (p. 1046)
—How Toys Spin. (p. 1046)
—Waste. Porcellato, Nives, illus. (p. 2382)
Whittaker, Helen & Lewis, Helen. Clothing. (p. 407)
—Energy. (p. 650)
—Leisure. (p. 1266)
—Water. (p. 2384)
Whittaker, Joseph. Tumblefold (Classic Reprint) (p. 2299)
Whittemore, Emma Mott. Delia, Formerly the Blue-Bird of Mulberry Bend (Classic Reprint) (p. 526)
Whittemore, Jo. Brooke's Bad Luck (p. 285)
—Colonial Madness. (p. 418)
—Confidentially Yours #1: Brooke's Not-So-Perfect Plan. (p. 439)
—Confidentially Yours #2: Vanessa's Fashion Face-Off. (p. 439)
—Confidentially Yours #3: Heather's Crush Catastrophe. (p. 439)
—Confidentially Yours #4: the Secret Talent. (p. 439)
—Confidentially Yours #6: Vanessa's Design Dilemma. (p. 439)
—D Is for Drama. (p. 494)
—Front Page Face-Off. (p. 795)
—Lights, Music, Code! #3. (p. 1300)
—Odd Girl In. (p. 1637)
—Supergirl: Age of Atlantis. (p. 2159)
—Supergirl: Age of Atlantis: (Supergirl Book 1) (p. 2159)
—Supergirl: Curse of the Ancients: (Supergirl Book 2) (p. 2159)
—Supergirl: Curse of the Ancients. (p. 2159)
—Supergirl: Master of Illusion: (Supergirl Book 3) (p. 2159)
—Supergirl: Master of Illusion. (p. 2159)
Whittemore, Susan. Circulatory System. (p. 393)
—Respiratory System. (p. 1869)
Whittemore, W. B. Reminiscences of the Civil War (Classic Reprint) (p. 1865)
Whitten, A. J. Cellar. (p. 350)
—Well. (p. 2399)
Whitten, Elizabeth, et al. RTI Success: Proven Tools & Strategies for Schools & Classrooms. (p. 1910)
Whitten, Robin. Rae. (p. 1833)
Whitten, Samantha & Lee, Jeannie. How to Draw Manga Chibis & Cute Critters. (p. 1041)
—You Can Draw Manga Chibi Characters, Critters & Scenes: A Step-By-step Guide for Learning to Draw Cute & Colorful Manga Chibis & Critters. (p. 2525)
—You Can Draw Manga Chibis: A Step-By-step Guide for Learning to Draw Basic Manga Chibis. (p. 2525)
Whittier, James. Believe... If You Want To. (p. 196)
Whittier, John Greenleaf. Child Life in Prose (Classic Reprint) (p. 370)
—Leaves from Margaret Smith's Journal in the Province of Massachusetts Bay, 1678-9, Vol. 1 of 2 (Classic Reprint) (p. 1259)
—Literary Recreations & Miscellanies (Classic Reprint) (p. 1309)
—Margaret Smith's Journal: Tales Sketches (Classic Reprint) (p. 1403)
Whittingham, Charles. Miscellanies of the Philobiblon Society, Vol. 7 (Classic Reprint) (p. 1477)
Whittingham, Jane. Good Day for Ducks. Tuazon, Noel, illus. (p. 862)
—Queenie Quail Can't Keep Up. Pedersen, Emma, illus. (p. 1824)
—Wild One. Tuazon, Noel, illus. (p. 2464)
Whittingham, Kim, illus. see Brynie, Faith Hickman.
Whittingham, Stephen. Best Summer Holiday. (p. 208)
Whittingham, Wendy, illus. see Sherrard, Valerie.
Whittingham, Zane, illus. see Shackleton, Kath, ed.
Whittington, Mark R. Gender Equality. (p. 814)
—Health Care. (p. 943)
—Jobs & Economy. (p. 1170)
Whittington, Nancy. Wilma the Wonderdog. (p. 2470)
Whittington, Thea. Dragon's Back. (p. 595)
Whittle, Chelsey J. Ordinary Girl. (p. 1669)
Whittle, D. W. Gospel Pictures & Story Sermons, Vol. 1 (Classic Reprint) (p. 871)
Whittlesea, P. J. Complicated Blue: The Extraordinary Adventures of the Good Witch Anais Blue. (p. 436)
Whittlesey, Sarah Johnson Cogswell. Bertha the Beauty: A Story of the Southern Revolution (Classic Reprint) (p. 204)
Whitton, Joseph. Wags of the Stage (Classic Reprint) (p. 2370)
Whitton, Marie. Camping with Mr. Mcdoogle. (p. 316)
—Day at Mr. Mcdoogle's Zoo. (p. 512)
—How Does Your Garden Grow Mr. Mcdoogle? (p. 1030)
—In Mr. Mcdoogle's Silver Spaceship. (p. 1106)
—Into the Cave with Mr. Mcdoogle. (p. 1128)
—Mr. Mcdoogle Visits the Dinosaurs. (p. 1519)
—Mr. Mcdoogle's Dune Buggy Trip. (p. 1519)
—Mr. Mcdoogle's Farm. (p. 1519)
—Mr. Mcdoogle's Yellow Submarine. (p. 1519)
—To the Swamp with Mr. Mcdoogle. (p. 2253)
Whitty, E. M. Friends of Bohemia, Vol. 1 Of 2: Or, Phases of London Life (Classic Reprint) (p. 787)
—Friends of Bohemia, Vol. 2 Of 2: Or Phases of London Life (Classic Reprint) (p. 787)
Whitty, Edward Michael. Knaves & Fools, or Friends of Bohemia: A Satirical Novel of London Life (Classic Reprint) (p. 1227)
Whitty, Hannah, illus. see Platt, Cynthia.
Whitwell, Stephen. Battles of Lexington & Concord: First Shots of the American Revolution. (p. 175)
Whitworth, Amber Harmon, illus. see Harmon, Coy Michie.
Whitworth, Christy. Come Back, o Tiger! A Jataka Tale. (p. 428)
Whitworth, Geoffrey Arundel, jt. auth. see Coster, Charles de.
Whitworth, John, illus. see Whitworth, Melissa.
Whitworth, Melissa. Lizzy & Buster's Time for Fall. Whitworth, John, illus. (p. 1337)
Whitworth, Robert Percy. Shimmer of Silk: A Volume of Melbourne Cup Stories (Classic Reprint) (p. 2007)
Whitzel, J. a. Kingdom X: The Secret of the Tower - Book Two of the Kingdom X Series. (p. 1222)
Whitzel, J. a & Stahl, Susan Snyder. Kingdom X. (p. 1222)
Whizpops, The. Forest Communities: Living in Harmony with Fire. Lawson, Glory, illus. (p. 766)
Who, Carrie Lou, illus. see Klitzner, Irene.
Who HQ. Who HQ 3-Book Collection: Inventors (p. 2447)
—Who HQ 3-Book Collection: Presidents (p. 2447)
Who HQ, jt. auth. see Abramson, Ann.
Who HQ, jt. auth. see Alexander, Heather.
Who HQ, jt. auth. see Anastasio, Dina.
Who HQ, jt. auth. see Anderson, Kirsten.
Who HQ, jt. auth. see Bader, Bonnie.
Who HQ, jt. auth. see Bailey, Diane.
Who HQ, jt. auth. see Brown, Dinah.
Who HQ, jt. auth. see Buckley, James.
Who HQ, jt. auth. see Burgan, Michael.
Who HQ, jt. auth. see Cooper, Gabriel P.
Who HQ, jt. auth. see Demuth, Patricia Brennan.
Who HQ, jt. auth. see Edgers, Geoff.
Who HQ, jt. auth. see Edwards, Roberta.
Who HQ, jt. auth. see Elling, Brian.
Who HQ, jt. auth. see Ellison, Katie.
Who HQ, jt. auth. see Fabiny, Sarah.
Who HQ, jt. auth. see Fradin, Dennis Brindell.
Who HQ, jt. auth. see Frith, Margaret.
Who HQ, jt. auth. see Gigliotti, Jim.
Who HQ, jt. auth. see Harris, Michael C.
Who HQ, jt. auth. see Herman, Gail.
Who HQ, jt. auth. see Holub, Joan.
Who HQ, jt. auth. see Hopkinson, Deborah.
Who HQ, jt. auth. see Johnson, Varian.
Who HQ, jt. auth. see Keenan, Sheila.
Who HQ, jt. auth. see Kelley, True.
Who HQ, jt. auth. see Kinney, Patrick.
Who HQ, jt. auth. see Koontz, Robin.
Who HQ, jt. auth. see Kramer, Barbara.
Who HQ, jt. auth. see Krull, Kathleen.
Who HQ, jt. auth. see Labrecque, Ellen.
Who HQ, jt. auth. see Manzanero, Paula K.
Who HQ, jt. auth. see McDonough, Yona Zeldis.
Who HQ, jt. auth. see Medina, Nico.
Who HQ, jt. auth. see Milton, Joyce.
Who HQ, jt. auth. see Morgan, Ellen.
Who Hq, jt. auth. see O'Connor, Jim.
Who HQ, jt. auth. see Pascal, Janet B.
Who HQ, jt. auth. see Payne, M. D.
Who HQ, jt. auth. see Prince, April Jones.
Who HQ, jt. auth. see Rau, Dana Meachen.
Who HQ, jt. auth. see Reed, Avery.
Who HQ, jt. auth. see Sabol, Stephanie.
Who HQ, jt. auth. see Smith, Sherri L.
Who HQ, jt. auth. see Spinner, Stephanie.
Who HQ, jt. auth. see St. George, Judith.
Who HQ, jt. auth. see Stewart, Whitney.
Who HQ, jt. auth. see Stine, Megan.
Who HQ, jt. auth. see Thompson, Gare.
Who HQ, jt. auth. see Waldron, Ann.
Who HQ, jt. auth. see Yacka, Douglas.
Who HQ & Brallier, Jess. What Was the Bombing of Hiroshima? Foley, Tim, illus. (p. 2421)
Who HQ & Gigliotti, Jim. Who Was Stephen Hawking? Copeland, Gregory, illus. (p. 2452)
Who HQ & Korte, Steve. What Is the Story of Looney Tunes? Hinderliter, John, illus. (p. 2417)
—What Is the Story of Wonder Woman? Murray, Jake, illus. (p. 2417)
Who HQ & Leonard, Jill. Who Is Greta Thunberg? Gutierrez, Manuel, illus. (p. 2448)
Who HQ & O'Connor, Jane. Who Is Ralph Lauren? Marchesi, Stephen, illus. (p. 2448)
Who HQ & O'Connor, Jim. What Is LEGO? Hammond, Ted, illus. (p. 2415)
—What Is Rock & Roll? Copeland, Gregory, illus. (p. 2416)
—What Was Pompeii? Hinderliter, John, illus. (p. 2421)
—What Was the Battle of Gettysburg? Mantha, John, illus. (p. 2421)
—What Was the Vietnam War? Foley, Tim, illus. (p. 2421)
—What Were the Twin Towers? Hammond, Ted, illus. (p. 2422)
—Where Is the Colosseum? O'Brien, John, illus. (p. 2438)
—Where Is the Grand Canyon? Colon, Daniel, illus. (p. 2438)
—Who Is Bob Dylan? O'Brien, John, illus. (p. 2447)
WHO Regional Office for the Western Pacific. Responding to Questions about the 100% Condom Use Programme: A Job Aid for Programme Staff. (p. 1870)
Whooley, Karen. Crochet Projects That Will Hook You. (p. 476)
Whooley, Karen, et al. Crafty Creations. (p. 466)
Whoopi, Goldberg, jt. auth. see Underwood, Deborah.
whurley, jt. auth. see Ferrie, Chris.
Why Don't We, Why Don't. Why Don't We: in the Limelight. (p. 2457)
Whybrow, Ian. Bedtime Bear. Scheffler, Axel, illus. (p. 188)
—Bedtime Bear Sticker Book. Scheffler, Axel, illus. (p. 188)
—Best Little Bullfrog in the Forest Orange Band. Smillie, Natalie, illus. (p. 206)
—Boy Racer. (p. 269)
—Christmas Bear. Scheffler, Axel, illus. (p. 383)
—Christmas Bear Sticker Book. Scheffler, Axel, illus. (p. 383)
—Flying Diggers. Melling, David, illus. (p. 754)
—Harry & the Bucketful of Dinosaurs. Reynolds, Adrian, illus. (p. 934)
—Harry & the Dinosaurs Go to School. Reynolds, Adrian, illus. (p. 934)
—Harry & the Dinosaurs - The Flying Save! (p. 934)
—It's Much Too Early! Watson, Laura, illus. (p. 1146)
—Little Fennec Fox & Jerboa Turquoise Band. Batori, Susan, illus. (p. 1316)
—Say Boo to the Animals! Warnes, Tim, illus. (p. 1940)
—Say Goodnight to the Sleepy Animals! Eaves, Edward, illus. (p. 1940)
—Say Hello to the Animals! Warnes, Tim, illus. (p. 1940)
—Say Hello to the Baby Animals! Eaves, Edward, illus. (p. 1940)
—Say Hello to the Jungle Animals! Eaves, Edward, illus. (p. 1940)
—Say Hello to the Snowy Animals! Eaves, Edward, illus. (p. 1940)
—Sinbad & the Roc Purple Band. Schon, Nick, illus. (p. 2023)
—Sinbad Goes to Sea Turquoise Band. Schon, Nick, illus. (p. 2023)
—Tale of Two Sinbads 3 Explorers. Shamshirsaz, Shabab, illus. (p. 2180)
—That Naughty Meerkat! Parsons, Garry, illus. (p. 2213)
—Tickle Book. Scheffler, Axel, illus. (p. 2239)
—Tim, Ted & the Pirates. Ayto, Russell, illus. (p. 2243)
—Where's Tim's Ted? It's Time for Bed! Ayto, Russell, illus. (p. 2441)
Whyman, Matt. Bad Apple. (p. 157)
—Boy Kills Man. (p. 269)
—Goldstrike: A Thriller. (p. 860)
—Icecore: A Thriller. (p. 1088)
—Our Planet: the One Place We All Call Home. Jones, Richard, illus. (p. 1680)
Whymper, Edward. Halcyon Days (Classic Reprint) (p. 910)
—Home at the Haven: A Tale (Classic Reprint) (p. 995)
—King & the Bondmen (Classic Reprint) (p. 1219)
—Louis Duval: A Tale of the French Revolution (Classic Reprint) (p. 1357)
—Poacher & His Family (Classic Reprint) (p. 1763)
Whymper, Josiah W., jt. auth. see Jennings, Louis J.
Whymper, Josiah Wood. Puss in Boots (Classic Reprint) (p. 1817)
Whyte, Alexander. Bunyan Characters, Third Series: Lectures Delivered in St. George's Free Church Edinburgh. (p. 299)
Whyte, Cara. Ocean, Sea & Me. Nguyen, Ann, illus. (p. 1636)
Whyte, Christen A., illus. see Lopez, Daniela J.
Whyte, Elizabeth. Making Tally Charts. (p. 1390)
—Tigers. (p. 2242)
Whyte, Harlinah. England. (p. 652)
Whyte, Harlinah & Frank, Nicole. Japan. (p. 1159)
Whyte, Janet M. Rescue Rider (p. 1868)
Whyte, Mariam & Yong, Jui Lin. Bangladesh. (p. 163)
Whyte, Mariam, et al. Bangladesh. (p. 163)
Whyte, Mary, illus. see Joosse, Barbara M.
Whyte, S. L. Finding Tir Na Nog: Finding Tir Na Nog: Finding Tir Na Nog. Ronsley, Jill, ed. (p. 730)
Whyte, Tracey. Zak's Tales. (p. 2538)
Whyte-Melville, G. Digby Grand, an Autobiography (Classic Reprint) (p. 545)
—M. or N. Similia Similibus Curantur (Classic Reprint) (p. 1370)
—Roy's Wife (Classic Reprint) (p. 1910)
Whyte-Melville, G. J. Black but Comely (Classic Reprint) (p. 237)
—Black but Comely, or the Adventures of Jane Lee, Vol. 3 of 3 (Classic Reprint) (p. 237)
—Black but Comely, Vol. 2 Of 3: Or the Adventures of Jane Lee (Classic Reprint) (p. 237)
—Bones & I: Or the Skeleton at Home (Classic Reprint) (p. 255)
—Brookes of Bridlemere (Classic Reprint) (p. 285)
—Brookes of Bridlemere, Vol. 3 of 3 (Classic Reprint) (p. 285)
—Cerise: A Tale of the Eighteenth Century (Classic Reprint) (p. 353)
—Cerise, Vol. 1 Of 3: A Tale of the Last Century (Classic Reprint) (p. 353)
—Contraband: Or a Losing Hazard (Classic Reprint) (p. 445)
—Contraband, Vol. 1 Of 2: Or a Losing Hazard (Classic Reprint) (p. 445)
—Contraband, Vol. 2 Of 2: Or a Losing Hazard (Classic Reprint) (p. 445)
—Digby Grand, Vol. 1 Of 2: An Autobiography (Classic Reprint) (p. 545)
—Digby Grand, Vol. 2 Of 2: An Autobiography (Classic Reprint) (p. 545)
—General Bounce: Or the Lady & the Locusts (Classic Reprint) (p. 814)
—General Bounce. (p. 814)
—Gladiators: A Tale of Rome & Judaea (Classic Reprint) (p. 840)
—Gladiators, Vol. 1 Of 3: A Tale of Rome & Judaea (Classic Reprint) (p. 840)
—Interpreter: A Tale of the War (Classic Reprint) (p. 1127)
—Interpreter. (p. 1127)
—Kate Coventry: An Autobiography (Classic Reprint) (p. 1204)
—Katerfelto: A Story of Exmoor (Classic Reprint) (p. 1204)
—M. or Similia Similibus Curantur, Vol. 1 of 2 (Classic Reprint) (p. 1370)
—Market Harborough & Inside the Bar (Classic Reprint) (p. 1407)
—Roy's Wife, Vol. 1 Of 2: A Novel (Classic Reprint) (p. 1910)
—Satanella: A Story of Punchestown (Classic Reprint) (p. 1936)
—Satanella a Story of Punchestown, Vol. 2 of 2 (Classic Reprint) (p. 1936)
—Satanella, Vol. 1 Of 2: A Story of Punchestown (Classic Reprint) (p. 1936)
—Sister Louise or the Story of a Woman's Repentance: Rosine (Classic Reprint) (p. 2027)
—Tilbury Nogo (Classic Reprint) (p. 2242)
—Uncle John: A Novel (Classic Reprint) (p. 2318)
—Uncle John, Vol. 1 Of 3: A Novel (Classic Reprint) (p. 2318)
—Uncle John, Vol. 2 Of 3: A Novel (Classic Reprint) (p. 2318)
—Uncle John, Vol. 3 Of 3: A Novel (Classic Reprint) (p. 2318)
—White Rose (Classic Reprint) (p. 2445)
—White Rose, Vol. 1 (Classic Reprint) (p. 2445)
—White Rose, Vol. 3 (Classic Reprint) (p. 2445)
Whyte-Melville, George J. Good for Nothing: Or All down Hill (Classic Reprint) (p. 862)
Whyte-Melville, George John. Black but Comely, or the Adventures of Jane Lee, Vol. 1 of 3 (Classic Reprint) (p. 237)

Wiggin, Kate Douglas Smith, jt. auth. see Smith, Nora Archibald.
Wiggin, Kate Douglas Smith & Smith, Nora Archibald. Arabian Nights: Their Best-Known Tales. (p. 108)
Wiggin, Samuel B. Streak of Luck: An American Comedy, in Five Tableaux (Classic Reprint) (p. 2139)
Wiggins, Amari Tyler. Moving from Place to Place. (p. 1516)
Wiggins, Bethany. Cured: A Stung Novel. (p. 485)
—Dragon's Curse (a Transference Novel) (p. 595)
—Dragon's Price (a Transference Novel) (p. 596)
—Stung. (p. 2145)
Wiggins, D. L. Where Dreams Are Born. Carter, Kelly, illus. (p. 2437)
Wiggins, L. J., ed. see Evans, Laneta Fullenwiley.
Wiggins, Mick, illus. see Lyon, George Ella & Lyon, Benn.
Wiggins, Mick, illus. see Lyon, George Ella.
Wiggins, Myra Albert. Letters from a Pilgrim (Classic Reprint) (p. 1279)
Wiggins, Robert Lemuel. Life of Joel Chandler Harris: From Obscurity in Boyhood to Fame in Early Manhood, with Short Stories & Other Early Literary Work Not Heretofore Published in Book Form (Classic Reprint) (p. 1294)
Wiggins Sr, Raymond E. Paw Paw & the Po-Po: Respecting & Protecting. (p. 1708)
Wiggins, Thalia. Greg & the Cheat Sheets Tate, Don, illus. (p. 895)
—Greg & the Mural Tate, Don, illus. (p. 895)
—Greg's Game Dilemma Tate, Don, illus. (p. 895)
—James Cheats! Tate, Don, illus. (p. 1156)
—James Makes a Choice Tate, Don, illus. (p. 1157)
—James the Rock's Boys Tate, Don, illus. (p. 1157)
Wiggins-James, Nesta. AS/A-Level Physical Education: Historical Factors & Contemporary Issues. (p. 125)
Wiggles Press Staff, jt. auth. see Five Mile.
Wiggles Staff, jt. auth. see Five Mile.
Wiggles, The. Little Wiggles: the Toilet Song: Sing-Along Sound Book. (p. 1329)
—Wiggles Book & Tambourine. (p. 2461)
—Wiggles: Emma's Ballet Alphabet. (p. 2461)
—Wiggles: Welcome to Wiggle Town: Press-Out & Build. (p. 2461)
Wigglesworth, Laura. Bekalu: From Ethiopia with Love. Somina, Yulia, illus. (p. 195)
Wigglesworth, Michael. Day of Doom: Or, a Poetical Description of the Great & Last Judgement; with Other Poems; Also a Memoir of the Author, Autobiography, & Sketch of His Funeral Sermon by REV. Cotton Mather (Classic Reprint) (p. 513)
Wiggs. Lovey Mary (Classic Reprint) (p. 1362)
Wiggs, A. R. Hal's Travels in Europe, Egypt, & the Holy Land: A Twelve Months Tour During Which He Saw Many Wonderful Things & a Vast Deal of Fun (Classic Reprint) (p. 913)
—Hal's Travels in Europe, Egypt, & the Holy Land. (p. 913)
Wight, Carol. Scallop Shanty: A Chatham Play (Classic Reprint) (p. 1941)
Wight, Emma Howard. Little Maid of Israel. (p. 1321)
Wight, Eric. Frankie Pickle & the Closet of Doom. Wight, Eric, illus. (p. 778)
—Frankie Pickle & the Mathematical Menace. Wight, Eric, illus. (p. 778)
—Frankie Pickle & the Pine Run 3000. Wight, Eric, illus. (p. 778)
Wight, Eric, illus. see Bardhan-Quallen, Sudipta.
Wight, Eric, illus. see DiPucchio, Kelly.
Wight, Eric, illus. see Egan, Kate & Lane, Mike.
Wight, Eric, illus. see Scaletta, Kurtis.
Wight, Estella. Vineyard Story (Classic Reprint) (p. 2359)
Wight, J. B. Tobacco: Its Use & Abuse. (p. 2254)
Wight, Joe, jt. auth. see Bozanich, Tony L.
Wight, John. Mornings at Bow Street 1875: A Selection of the Most Humorous & Entertaining Reports Which Have Appeared in the Morning Herald (Classic Reprint) (p. 1506)
Wight, Karol. Paperweight Pals. (p. 1698)
Wight, Orlando Williams. Quinland, Vol. 1: Or, Varieties in American Life (Classic Reprint) (p. 1828)
Wight, Pamela S. Birds of Paradise. Steinle, Shelley a, illus. (p. 232)
—Molly Finds Her Purr. Steinle, Shelley a, illus. (p. 1489)
Wight, Robert. Prodromus Florae Peninsulae Indiae Orientalis, Vol. 1: Containing Abridged Descriptions of the Plants Found in the Peninsula of British India, Arranged According to the Natural System (Classic Reprint) (p. 1804)
Wight, Tamra. Mystery of the Bear Cub (p. 1569)
—Mystery of the Bear Cub DiRocco, Carl, illus. (p. 1569)
—Mystery of the Eagle's Nest (p. 1569)
—Mystery of the Missing Fox (p. 1570)
—Mystery on Pine Lake: A Cooper & Packrat Mystery DiRocco, Carl, illus. (p. 1570)
Wightman, Francis P. Last Egyptian: A Romance of the Nile (Classic Reprint) (p. 1247)
Wightman, Gregory J. Origins of Religion in the Paleolithic. (p. 1672)
Wightwick, George. Life & Remains of Wilmot Warwick (Classic Reprint) (p. 1289)
Wigley, Audrey Watson, illus. see Igneri, David S.
Wigmore, Kitty, illus. see Januarius & Botteley, Gerald.
Wignall, K. J. Death. (p. 521)
Wignall, Kevin. When We Were Lost. (p. 2434)
Wignell, Edel. Bilby: Secrets of an Australian Marsupial. Jackson, Mark, illus. (p. 225)
Wigram, W. Knox. Five Hundred Pounds Reward. (p. 743)
—Five Hundred Pounds Reward, Vol. 3: A Novel (Classic Reprint) (p. 743)
Wigram, William Knox. Twelve Wonderful Tales: Told in Rhyme (Classic Reprint) (p. 2304)
Wigsby, Nick, illus. see Peacock, L. A.
Wigston, Rebecca. Tommy Wallis, the Knight of the Hollows. (p. 2259)
Wigu Publishing. When I Grow up I Want to Be... a Teacher! Carlee Learns a Surprising Lesson! (p. 2431)
Wijesiri, Tina, illus. see Toombs, Aisha.
Wijnberg, John. Old Man & the Fat Ginger Cat. Balsdon, Lizette, ed. (p. 1647)
Wijnberg, John Paul. Old Man & the Fat Ginger Cat. Balsdon, Lizette, ed. (p. 1647)
Wijngaard, Caspar. Star Wars: Doctor Aphra Vol. 7: A Rogue's End. (p. 2104)
Wijngaard, Caspar, illus. see Edginton, Ian.
Wijngaard, Juan, illus. see Peet, Mal & Graham, Elspeth.
Wik, Jenny, illus. see Reuterstrand, Siri.
Wik, John. Visual Chaos Stained Glass Coloring Book. (p. 2363)
Wik, John & Coloring Books for Adults. Deco Tech: Geometric Coloring Book. (p. 523)
Wik, John & Creative Haven Staff. Creative Haven Tessellation Patterns Coloring Book. (p. 471)
Wikland, Ilon, illus. see Lagerlöf, Selma.
Wikland, Ilon, illus. see Lindgren, Astrid.
Wiklund, Melody. Eleven Dancing Sisters. (p. 635)
Wilbanks, April. How Gracie See's Christmas. (p. 1031)
Wilberforce, Bert. Black Holes (p. 238)
—Can I Have a Pet Giraffe? (p. 317)
—Can I Have a Pet Gorilla? (p. 317)
—Can I Have a Pet Polar Bear? (p. 317)
—Comets, Asteroids, & Meteoroids (p. 429)
—Galaxies (p. 805)
—Moon (p. 1501)
Wilberforce, Bertram. Why We Need Laws. (p. 2459)
Wilberforce, Samuel. Agathos, & Other Sunday Stories (Classic Reprint) (p. 35)
—Agathos; the Rocky Island: And Other Sunday Stories (Classic Reprint) (p. 35)
—Agathos the Rocky Island & Other Sunday Stories & Parables. (p. 35)
—Note Book of a Country Clergyman, Vol. 1 of 2 (Classic Reprint) (p. 1624)
—Rocky Island: And Other Parables (Classic Reprint) (p. 1896)
Wilberforce, T. Twentieth Century Vacation: Travels after My Own Notion at the Seashore & Mountains of New England (Classic Reprint) (p. 2304)
Wilbor, Elsie M. Delsarte Recitation Book (Classic Reprint) (p. 527)
Wilborn, Beth G. Little Brown Turkey. Goncalves, Edison, illus. (p. 1313)
Wilbraham, Frances M. For & Against, or Queen Margaret's Badge, Vol. 1 Of 2: A Domestic Chronicle of the Fifteenth Century (Classic Reprint) (p. 762)
—Phil Thorndyke's Adventures (Classic Reprint) (p. 1734)
Wilbrandt, Adolf. Fridolin's Mystical Marriage (Classic Reprint) (p. 785)
—New Humanity or the Easter Island (Classic Reprint) (p. 1594)
Wilbur, Harriette. Calendar Days: An Entertainment in One Act (Classic Reprint) (p. 310)
Wilbur, Helen. Little New York. Brett, Jeannie, illus. (p. 1323)
Wilbur, Helen & L Wilbur, Helen. E Is for Eiffel Tower: A France Alphabet. (p. 612)
Wilbur, Helen L. B Is for Beacon: A Great Lakes Lighthouse Alphabet. Graef, Renee, illus. (p. 146)
—D Is for Derby: A Kentucky Derby Alphabet. Corum, Jaime, illus. (p. 494)
—E Is for Eiffel Tower: A France Alphabet. Nascimbene, Yan, illus. (p. 612)
—F Is for Friendship: A Quilt Alphabet. van Frankenhuyzen, Gijsbert, illus. (p. 690)
—Finnegan & Fox: The Ten-Foot Cop. Manders, John, illus. (p. 731)
—Lily's Victory Garden. Steele, Robert Gantt, illus. (p. 1302)
—Tuba Christmas. Uhles, Mary Reaves, illus. (p. 2298)
Wilbur, Helen L., jt. auth. see James, Helen Foster.
Wilbur, Henry W. Friends with Lincoln in the White House: Adapted from Nellie Blessing-Eyster's Story. (p. 787)
Wilbur, Richard. Loudmouse. (p. 1357)
Wilburn, Belinda. Louie, Louie! The Story of a Very Scared Kitty. (p. 1357)
Wilburn, George T. Auto-Biography of Sam Simple: Giving an Account of the Administration of the Affairs of the Simple Family from the Year 1829 to 1837, by His Aunt Deborah Crabstick, Together with a History of Some New & Important Experiments in Government Never Before T. (p. 139)
Wilburn, John C. Larry, the Leaf. (p. 1245)
Wilburn, Kathy. Scrooge. (p. 1966)
Wilburn, Kathy, illus. see Hall, Kirsten.
Wilby, Thomas W. Motor Tour Through Canada (Classic Reprint) (p. 1512)
—On the Trail to Sunset (Classic Reprint) (p. 1656)
Wilce, Ysabeau S. Flora's Fury: How a Girl of Spirit & a Red Dog Confound Their Friends, Astound Their Enemies, & Learn the Importance of Packing Light. (p. 750)
Wilcox, Brad. Hip, Hip, Hooray! for Annie Mcrae Olson, Julie, illus. (p. 972)
Wilcox, Brad & Olson, Julie. Hip, Hip, Hooray for Annie McRae! (p. 972)
Wilcox, Brindy. Through Time to London. (p. 2237)
Wilcox, Cathy, illus. see Gervay, Susanne.
Wilcox, Cathy, jt. auth. see Gervay, Susanne.
Wilcox, Charlotte. Greyhounds. (p. 896)
Wilcox, Chelsea, illus. see MC Dermott, Karen.
Wilcox, Chelsea, illus. see McDermott, Karen.
Wilcox, Christine. Careers in Emergency Response. (p. 329)
—Careers in Environmental Conservation. (p. 329)
—Careers in Information Technology. (p. 330)
—Cell Phones & Teens. (p. 350)
—Engineering Careers. (p. 651)
—Gambling Addiction. (p. 806)
—Health Care Careers. (p. 943)
—How Is Online Pornography Affecting Society? (p. 1032)
—Justin Bieber. Greenaven Press Staff, ed. (p. 1195)
—Oscar Pistorius. (p. 1673)
—Real-World Stem: Reverse-Engineer the Brain. (p. 1850)
—Shaun White. Greenhaven Press Editors, ed. (p. 2003)
—Teens & Body Image. (p. 2200)
—Teens, Nutrition, & Dieting. (p. 2200)
—Thinking Critically: Abortion. (p. 2222)
—Thinking Critically: Opioid Abuse. (p. 2222)
—Thinking Critically: Online Privacy. (p. 2222)
—Understanding Family & Personal Relationships. (p. 2324)
—Understanding Violent Behavior. (p. 2326)
—Young Adult Authors. (p. 2529)
Wilcox, Constance. Pan Pipes: A Woodland Play in One Act (Classic Reprint) (p. 1695)
—Princess in the Fairy Tale: A Garden Fairy Story for Children in One Act (Classic Reprint) (p. 1797)
—Told in a Chinese Garden & Four Other Fantastic Plays, for Out-Doors or in-Doors (Classic Reprint) (p. 2256)
Wilcox, Constance Grenelle. Told in a Chinese Garden: A Play Pageant for a Garden, in One Act (Classic Reprint) (p. 2256)
Wilcox, Dominic & Mengardon, Katherine. Little Inventors Go Green!: Inventing for a Better Planet. (p. 1319)
—Little Inventors Handbook. (p. 1319)
Wilcox, Ella Wheeler. Beautiful Land of Nod. (p. 184)
—Beautiful Land of Nod (Classic Reprint) (p. 184)
—Men, Women & Emotions - Scholar's Choice Edition. (p. 1447)
—New Hawaiian Girl: A Play (Classic Reprint) (p. 1594)
—Perdita, & Other Stories (Classic Reprint) (p. 1721)
—Sailing Sunny Seas: A Story of Travel in Jamaica, Haiti, Porto Rico, Dominica, Honolulu, Santo Domingo St. Thomas, Martinique, Trinidad & the West Indies (Classic Reprint) (p. 1923)
—Sweet Danger (Classic Reprint) (p. 2168)
Wilcox, Frank N. Blind Goddess: A Drama (Classic Reprint) (p. 244)
Wilcox, Gail. Friend of Many Colors. (p. 786)
Wilcox, Henry S. Strange Flaw (Classic Reprint) (p. 2137)
Wilcox, Jean A. Winston's New Camelot. (p. 2475)
Wilcox, Leah. Waking Beauty. Monks, Lydia, illus. (p. 2371)
Wilcox, Marrion. Vengeance of the Female (Classic Reprint) (p. 2350)
Wilcox, Mary, ed. see Rey, H. A.
Wilcox, Mary Emily Donelson. Christmas under Three Flags: Being Memories of Holiday Festivities in the White House with Old Hickory, in the Palace of Prince of Prussia, Afterwards Emperor William I, & at the Alamo with the Alcalde's Daughter (Classic Reprint) (p. 387)
Wilcox, Merrie-Ellen. After Life: Ways We Think about Death (p. 33)
—What's the Buzz? Keeping Bees in Flight (p. 2426)
Wilcox, Ray. Extra Ordinary: The Adventures of Shawna Ray & Christa Lynn. (p. 685)
Wilcox, Sara. Serious History. (p. 1991)
Wild, Ailsa. Squishy Taylor. (p. 2095)
—Squishy Taylor Wood, Ben, illus. (p. 2095)
—Squishy Taylor & a Question of Trust. (p. 2095)
—Squishy Taylor & the Bonus Sisters. (p. 2095)
—Squishy Taylor & the Mess Makers. (p. 2095)
—Squishy Taylor & the Tunnel of Doom. (p. 2095)
—Squishy Taylor & the Vase That Wasn't. (p. 2095)
—Squishy Taylor in Zero Gravity. (p. 2095)
Wild, Ailsa, et al. Zobi & the Zoox: A Story of Coral Bleaching. (p. 2541)
Wild, Alisa. Squishy Taylor Wood, Ben, illus. (p. 2095)
—Squishy Taylor & a Question of Trust. Wood, Ben, illus. (p. 2095)
—Squishy Taylor & the Bonus Sisters. Wood, Ben, illus. (p. 2095)
—Squishy Taylor & the Mess-Makers. Wood, Ben, illus. (p. 2095)
—Squishy Taylor & the Vase That Wasn't. Wood, Ben, illus. (p. 2095)
Wild, Charlotte Sullivan. Amazing Idea of You. Lundquist, Mary, illus. (p. 65)
Wild, Ida. Drum's House (Classic Reprint) (p. 606)
—House-Room (Classic Reprint) (p. 1024)
Wild, Jonnie. Monstruo de Barro. (p. 1498)
—Yum Yum Tree. Granstrom, Brita, illus. (p. 2537)
Wild, Margaret. Boo! Freya Blackwood & Joyner, Andrew, illus. (p. 256)
—Chalk Boy. Ord, Mandy, illus. (p. 354)
—Dream of the Thylacine. Brooks, Ron, illus. (p. 602)
—Feather. Blackwood, Freya, illus. (p. 717)
—Let the Celebrations Begin. Vivas, Julie, illus. (p. 1269)
—Nighty Night! Argent, Kerry, illus. (p. 1608)
—No More Kisses! Rycroft, Nina, illus. (p. 1613)
—No More Kisses. Rycroft, Nina, illus. (p. 1613)
—Old Pig. Brooks, Ron, illus. (p. 1647)
—Piglet & Papa. King, Stephen Michael, illus. (p. 1743)
—Ruby Roars. Argent, Kerry, illus. (p. 1911)
—Sloth Who Slowed Us Down. To, Vivienne, illus. (p. 2039)
—Stone Lion. Voutila, Ritva, illus. (p. 2121)
—This Little Piggy Went Dancing. Niland, Deborah, illus. (p. 2226)
—Treasure Box. Blackwood, Freya, illus. (p. 2281)
—Vanishing Moment. (p. 2347)
Wild, Margaret & Gamble, Kim. First Day. (p. 736)
Wild, Maureen. Story of Lexi: And a Dream That Follows Her. (p. 2131)
Wildavsky, Rachel. Secret of Rover. Caparo, Antonio, illus. (p. 1977)
Wilde, Cindy, et al. Color with Mom. (p. 421)
Wilde, Elizabeth. Oracle, the Alicorn, & the Long-Lost Princess. (p. 1668)
Wilde, Fran. Riverland. (p. 1887)
Wilde, Irma & dePaola, Tomie. Christmas Puppy. Wilde, Irma, illus. (p. 386)
Wilde, Jen. Brightsiders. (p. 281)
—Going off Script. (p. 854)
—Queens of Geek. (p. 1825)
Wilde, Kristie. It's a Jungle in Here. Wilde, Kristie, illus. (p. 1143)
—Made for a Purpose. Wilde, Kristie, illus. (p. 1374)
—So Great a Love. (p. 2050)
Wilde, M. Vaughan. Juleps & Clover (Classic Reprint) (p. 1186)
Wilde, Michael John. Billy Chen & the Holy Wars. (p. 227)
Wilde, Oscar. Ben Kutcher's: Illustrated Edition of a House of Pomegranates (Classic Reprint) (p. 199)
—Canterville Ghost. (p. 323)
—Complete Works of Oscar Wilde: Reviews (Classic Reprint) (p. 435)
—Complete Works of Oscar Wilde: Salome; a Florentine Tragedy; Vera (Classic Reprint) (p. 435)
—Complete Works of Oscar Wilde: Duchess of Padua, and, de Profundis (Classic Reprint) (p. 435)
—Complete Works of Oscar Wilde: The Picture of Dorian Gray, and, a House of Pomegranates (Classic Reprint) (p. 435)
—Complete Works of Oscar Wilde: Lady Windermere's Fan & the Importance of Being Earnest. Robert Ross, Editor, ed. (p. 435)
—Complete Works of Oscar Wilde: The Happy Prince, & Other Tales; Lord Arthur Saville's Crime, & Other Prose Pieces (Classic Reprint) (p. 435)
—Complete Works of Oscar Wilde, Vol. 12: Criticisms & Reviews (Classic Reprint) (p. 435)
—Complete Works of Oscar Wilde. Volume 8. (p. 435)
—Fairy Tales of Oscar Wilde. Shimizu, Yuko, illus. (p. 698)
—Fairy Tales of Oscar Wilde: the Complete Hardcover Set 1-5. Russell, P. Craig, illus. (p. 698)
—Fairy Tales of Oscar Wilde: the Happy Prince Signed & Numbered. Russell, P. Craig, illus. (p. 698)
—Fantasma de Canterville. Bilingüe. (p. 706)
—Happy Prince: And Other Tales (Classic Reprint) (p. 923)
—Happy Prince: And Other Fairy Tales (Classic Reprint) (p. 923)
—Happy Prince. Russell, P. Craig, illus. (p. 923)
—Happy Prince, & Other Fairy Stories (Classic Reprint) (p. 923)
—Happy Prince & Other Stories. (p. 923)
—Happy Prince & Other Stories. Robinson, Charles, illus. (p. 923)
—Happy Prince & Other Tales. (p. 923)
—Happy Prince & Other Tales. Charles Robinson, illus. (p. 923)
—Happy Prince & Other Tales - Scholar's Choice Edition. (p. 923)
—Happy Prince Signed & Numbered. Russell, P. Craig, illus. (p. 923)
—House of Pomegranates. King, Jessie Marion, illus. (p. 1023)
—Importance of Being Earnest: A Trivia Comedy for Serious People. (p. 1102)
—Importance of Being Earnest: A Trivial Comedy for Serious People - Scholar's Choice Edition. (p. 1102)
—Importance of Being Earnest. (p. 1102)
—Importance of Being Earnest. Stokes, John, illus. (p. 1102)
—Importance of Being Earnest the Graphic Novel Quick Text: (American English) Stokes, John, illus. (p. 1102)
—Lord Arthur Savile's Crime: And Other Stories (Classic Reprint) (p. 1348)
—Lord Arthur Savile's Crime: The Portrait of Mr. W. H & Other Stories (Classic Reprint) (p. 1348)
—Lord Arthur Savile's Crime & Other Prose Pieces. (p. 1348)
—Novels & Fairy Tales of Oscar Wilde (Classic Reprint) (p. 1626)
—Oscar Wilde: The Importance of Being Earnest. (p. 1673)
—Oscar Wilde: Die Erzählungen (Vollständige Deutsche Ausgaben) Meyerfeld, Max, tr. (p. 1673)
—Oscar Wilde Fairy Tales. (p. 1673)
—Picture Dorian Gray (Classic Reprint) (p. 1740)
—Picture of Dorian Gray Fisher, Eric Scott, illus. (p. 1740)
—Portrait de Dorian Gray. (p. 1779)
—Prince Heureux Gean. (p. 1794)
—Príncipe Feliz y Otros Cuentos. Cicero, Julián, illus. (p. 1800)
—Retrato de Dorian Gray. (p. 1870)
—Retrato de Dorian Gray y el Principe Feliz. (p. 1870)
—Selfish Giant. Bowman, Jeanne, illus. (p. 1987)
—Selfish Giant. Zwerger, Lisbeth, illus. (p. 1987)
—Selfish Giant & Other Classic Tales. Thorne, Jenny, illus. (p. 1987)
—Woman's World (Classic Reprint) (p. 2486)
—Young King: The Star-Child (Classic Reprint) (p. 2531)
—Young King. (p. 2531)
Wilde, Oscar, jt. auth. see Maidment, Stella.
Wilde, Oscar & Hollingsworth, Mary. Oscar Wilde's the Selfish Giant. Bell, Bill, illus. (p. 1673)
Wilde, Oscar, et al. Happy Prince. (p. 923)
—Oscar Wilde Pomplun, Tom, ed. (p. 1673)
Wilde, Percival. Dawn: With the Noble Lord, the Traitor, a House of Cards, Playing with Fire, the Finger of God; One-Act Plays of Life to-Day (Classic Reprint) (p. 511)
—Dyspeptic Ogre: A Modernized Fairy Play; Opus 57 (Classic Reprint) (p. 612)
—Eight Comedies for Little Theatres (Classic Reprint) (p. 629)
—Question of Morality & Other Plays (Classic Reprint) (p. 1826)
—Unseen Host, & Other War Plays: The Unseen Host, Mothers of Men Pawns, in the Ravine Valkyrie (Classic Reprint) (p. 2335)
Wildenbruch, Ernst von. Francesca Da Rimini (Classic Reprint) (p. 776)
—Noble Blood: A Prussian Cadet Story (Classic Reprint) (p. 1616)
Wildenstein, Olivia. Not Another Love Song. (p. 1623)
Wilder, Ben. Big & Small, God Made Them All. Carin, Siegfried, ed. (p. 216)
Wilder, Beth. Bugs in Shoes (p. 292)
Wilder, Chase. Pyramid Peril. (p. 1819)
Wilder, Laura Ingalls. Animal Adventures: Reillustrated Edition. (p. 87)
—Christmas in the Big Woods. (p. 386)
—Christmas Stories: Reillustrated Edition. Kim, Ji-Hyuk, illus. (p. 387)
—Laura & Nellie: Reillustrated Edition. Kim, Ji-Hyuk, illus. (p. 1252)
—Little House Complete 9-Book Box Set: Books 1 To 9 Williams, Garth, illus. (p. 1319)
—Little House on the Prairie. (p. 1319)
—Little House Picture Book Treasury: Six Stories of Life on the Prairie. Graef, Renee, illus. (p. 1319)
—Little House Traveler: Writings from Laura Ingalls Wilder's Journeys Across America. (p. 1319)
—Pioneer Sisters: Reillustrated Edition. Kim, Ji-Hyuk, illus. (p. 1748)

—School Days: Reillustrated Edition. Kim, Ji-Hyuk, illus. (p. 1945)
Wilder, Laura Ingalls, jt. auth. see Henson, Heather.
Wilder, Laura Ingalls & Videbeck, Sheila. Little House on the Prairie. Williams, Garth, illus. (p. 1319)
Wilder, Marshall P. People I've Smiled: Recollections of a Merry Little Life (Classic Reprint) (p. 1718)
—Sunny Side of the Street (Classic Reprint) (p. 2153)
—Ten Books of the Merrymakers, Vol. 1 (Classic Reprint) (p. 2203)
—Ten Books of the Merrymakers, Vol. 10 (Classic Reprint) (p. 2203)
—Wit & Humor of America, Vol. 5 (Classic Reprint) (p. 2479)
—Wit & Humor of America, Vol. III, Pp. 403-584. (p. 2479)
Wilder, Marshall Pinckney. Smiling Round the World (Classic Reprint) (p. 2042)
—Ten Books of the Merrymakers, Vol. 2 (Classic Reprint) (p. 2203)
—Wit & Humor of America (Classic Reprint) (p. 2479)
—Wit & Humor of America, Vol. 2 (Classic Reprint) (p. 2479)
—Wit & Humor of America, Vol. 8 of 10 (Classic Reprint) (p. 2479)
Wilder, Nellie. Changing Weather (p. 356)
—On Land (p. 1652)
—On Water (p. 1656)
—Staying Afloat. (p. 2110)
—Taking Food to Go. (p. 2178)
—What Is the Weather? (p. 2417)
Wilder, Nellie, jt. auth. see Rice, Dona.
Wilder, S. Fannie Gerry. Boston Girls at Home & Abroad. (p. 264)
—Boston Girls at Home & Abroad (Classic Reprint) (p. 264)
Wilder, Susan. Broadcaster, Vol. 2: June 11, 1926 (Classic Reprint) (p. 284)
Wilder, Van. Outrepasseurs - la Reine des Neiges T2(les) (p. 1685)
Wilder, Vickie. Umbrella. (p. 2316)
Wilder, Walter. Seaside Scenes & Thoughts, Some Extracts from a Diary: Originally Selected & Edited for the Springfield Republican, Mass, Republican, & Now Done into a Book (Classic Reprint) (p. 1972)
Wildermuth, Ottalie. Ottalie's Stories for the Little Folks: Translated from the German (Classic Reprint) (p. 1675)
Wildermuth, Ottilie. Aus Schloss und Hutte: Erzahlungen Fur Kinder Von 8 Bis 12 Jahren (Classic Reprint) (p. 138)
Wilderness, Dale. Drift in Your Pillow's Eyes. (p. 604)
Wilderspin, Samuel. On the Importance of Educating the Infant Poor, from the Age of Eighteen Months to Seven Years: Containing an Account of the Spitalfields Infant School, & the New System of Instruction There Adopted; to Which Is Added, a Reply to the Strictures of Dr. P. (p. 1654)
Wildes, Cynthia. Trees Please. Illustrations, Blueberry, illus. (p. 2284)
Wildes, Emma. Mr. Poot's Christmas [a Scary Baby Adventure]. (p. 1520)
Wildfong, Tonya. Bee in the Barn. Cichos, Tomek, illus. (p. 189)
Wildfowler, Lewis Clements. Shooting & Fishing Trips (Classic Reprint) (p. 2009)
Wildfowler, Wildfowler. Shooting & Fishing Trips, Vol. 2 Of 2: In England, France, Alsace, Belgium, Holland, & Bavaria (Classic Reprint) (p. 2009)
Wildgoose, Chris, illus. see Lu, Marie.
Wildgrube, Erich Otto. Empress & the Archer. (p. 645)
Wildgrube, Paula C. To Catch a Thief. (p. 2252)
Wilding, Valerie. Grumpy Queen. Sanfilippo, Simona, illus. (p. 901)
Wildish, Lee, illus. see Adam, Guillain & Guillain, Charlotte.
Wildish, Lee, illus. see Clarke, Jane.
Wildish, Lee, illus. see Crum, Shutta.
Wildish, Lee, illus. see Delmege, Sarah.
Wildish, Lee, illus. see Gray, Kes.
Wildish, Lee, illus. see Greenwell, Jessica.
Wildish, Lee, illus. see Guillain, Adam & Guillain, Charlotte.
Wildish, Lee, illus. see Guillain, Adam.
Wildish, Lee, illus. see Guillain, Charlotte & Guillain, Adam.
Wildish, Lee, illus. see Reagan, Jean.
Wildish, Lee, illus. see Richtel, Matt.
Wildish, Lee, illus. see Tabby, Abigail.
Wildish, Lee, illus. see Taplin, Sam.
Wildish, Lee, illus. see Waddell, Martin.
Wildish, Lee, illus. see Weeks, Sarah.
Wildish, Lee, jt. auth. see Reagan, Jean.
Wildish, Lee & Mayhew, James. Katie & the Starry Night. (p. 1205)
Wildlife Conservation Society, photos by see Thomson, Sarah L.
Wildman, Andrew, et al. Spider-Man 2099 vs. Venom 2099. (p. 2080)
Wildman, Rounsevelle. Overland Monthly, Vol. 24: July-December, 1894 (Classic Reprint) (p. 1687)
Wilds, Kazumi, illus. see Moore, Sandra.
Wilds, Kazumi, illus. see Moore, Willamarie.
Wilds, Kazumi, illus. see Thompson, Holly.
Wildsmith, Brian. Animal Colors (p. 88)
—Animal Colors wintranslation.com, tr. (p. 88)
—Bear's Adventure Wildsmith, Brian, illus. (p. 180)
—Brian Wildsmith's Amazing Animal Alphabet Book (p. 279)
—Brian Wildsmith's Animal Gallery. Wildsmith, Brian, illus. (p. 279)
—Brian Wildsmith's Animals to Count Wildsmith, Brian, illus. (p. 279)
—Brian Wildsmith's Opposites (p. 279)
—Daisy Wildsmith, Brian, illus. (p. 497)
Wildsmith, Brian, illus. see Ikeda, Daisaku.
Wildsmith, Brian, illus. see Stevenson, Robert Louis.
Wildsmith, Sarah. Princess Charming. Paramonova, Lea, illus. (p. 1796)
Wildwood, Gretchen. Ancient Mesopotamian Civilization. Cantucci, Alessandro & Morandi, Andrea, illus. (p. 81)
Wildwood, W. R. Violent World. (p. 2359)
Wile, Jay L., ed. see Fulbright, Jeannie.
Wile, Jay L., ed. see Seligson, Sherri.
Wile, Mary Lee. Season of Angels. Stossel, Sage, illus. (p. 1972)
Wiles, Deborah. Aurora County All-Stars. (p. 137)
—Countdown (p. 459)
—Countdown. (p. 459)
—Freedom Summer: Celebrating the 50th Anniversary of the Freedom Summer. Lagarrigue, Jerome, illus. (p. 783)
—Kent State. (p. 1209)
—Long Line of Cakes. (p. 1343)
—Revolution. (p. 1873)
Wiles, Frank, illus. see Smith, Evelyn.
Wiles, Jon. Landon's Local Government. (p. 1242)
Wiles, Patricia. My Mom's a Mortician. (p. 1556)
Wiley, Bee, illus. see Aiken, Joan.
Wiley, Belle. Children of the Cliff (Classic Reprint) (p. 372)
—Mother Goose Primer (Classic Reprint) (p. 1509)
—Rago & Goni: The Tree-Dweller Children (Classic Reprint) (p. 1834)
Wiley, Brandie. Why Won't He Look at Me? A Book for Children Struggling to Understand Autism. (p. 2460)
Wiley, C. H. Alamance, or the Great & Final Experiment (Classic Reprint) (p. 39)
Wiley, C. R. Purloined Boy. (p. 1816)
Wiley, Calvin Henderson. Adventures of Old Dan Tucker, & His Son Walter: A Tale of North Carolina (Classic Reprint) (p. 26)
Wiley, Chris. Purloined Boy. (p. 1816)
Wiley, Hugh. Jade: And Other Stories. (p. 1154)
—Lady Luck (Classic Reprint) (p. 1237)
—Lily (Classic Reprint) (p. 1302)
—Wildcat (Classic Reprint) (p. 2465)
Wiley, I. W. Ladies' Repository, Vol. 30: A Monthly Periodical, Devoted to Literature & Religion; January-June, 1870 (Classic Reprint) (p. 1236)
Wiley, Jean. Sweet Dreams for Sydney: A Book to Help Dissipate Nightmares Green, Burt, illus. (p. 2168)
Wiley, Jennie. Everybody Just Be Quiet. Russo, Maria Octavia, illus. (p. 671)
—Make a Wish on a Fish. Anguelova, Mina, illus. (p. 1386)
Wiley, Jesse. Alone in the Wild. (p. 57)
—Calamity in the Cold. (p. 309)
—Gold Rush! (p. 856)
—Hit the Trail! (Two Books in One) The Race to Chimney Rock & Danger at the Haunted Gate. (p. 982)
—Oregon City or Bust! (Two Books in One) The Search for Snake River & the Road to Oregon City. (p. 1670)
—Pick Your Own Path on the Oregon Trail: A Tabbed Expedition with More Than 50 Story Possibilities. (p. 1739)
—Wagon Train Trek. (p. 2370)
Wiley, Jesse, jt. auth. see Houghton Mifflin Harcourt Staff.
Wiley, Jessica a. Mother's Assurance. (p. 1510)
Wiley, Kate. Pet Marjorie & Sir Walter Scott: The Story of Marjorie Fleming (Classic Reprint) (p. 1726)
Wiley, Lisa Manuzak, illus. see Gallion, Sue Lowell.
Wiley, Melissa. Fox & Crow Are Not Friends. Braun, Sebastien, illus. (p. 773)
—Fox & Crow Are Not Friends. (p. 774)
—Inch & Roly & the Sunny Day Scare. Jatkowska, Ag, illus. (p. 1112)
—Inch & Roly & the Very Small Hiding Place. Jatkowska, Ag, illus. (p. 1112)
—Inch & Roly Make a Wish. Jatkowska, Ag, illus. (p. 1112)
—Nerviest Girl in the World. (p. 1588)
—Prairie Thief. Madrid, Erwin, illus. (p. 1785)
Wiley, Nancy, illus. see Carroll, Lewis, pseud.
Wiley, Thom. Big Earth, Little Me. Endle, Kate, illus. (p. 219)
Wilfley, Denise E., et al. Childhood Obesity (p. 370)
Wilford, Florence. Dominie Freylinghausen (Classic Reprint) (p. 580)
—Holiday Tales. (p. 988)
Wilgus, Alison. Mars Challenge: The Past, Present, & Future of Human Spaceflight. Yates, Wyeth, illus. (p. 1409)
—Science Comics: Flying Machines: How the Wright Brothers Soared. Brooks, Molly, illus. (p. 1954)
Wilgus, Nick. Raise It Up. (p. 1838)
Wilham, Lou. Tales of a Sea Witch. (p. 2183)
Wilharm, Sabine, illus. see Ludwig, Sabine.
Wilhelm, Doris L., illus. see Rogers, Leslie E.
Wilhelm, Doug. Alexander the Great: Master of the Ancient World. (p. 43)
—Alexander the Great. (p. 43)
—Curse of the Pirate Mist. (p. 489)
—Revealers. (p. 1872)
—Snake Invasion. Semionov, Vlad, illus. (p. 2044)
Wilhelm, Eric. Marcus Aurelius & Musa the Frog Go to Boston. (p. 1403)
—Marcus Aurelius & Musa the Frog Go to the Dentist. (p. 1403)
Wilhelm, Hans. Buddy for President. Wilhelm, Hans, illus. (p. 290)
—Bunny Trouble Treasury. (p. 298)
—Guess Which Hand: A Turn-And-Seek Book. Guarducci, Ilaria, illus. (p. 903)
—Hole in the Wall. (p. 987)
—I Love Rainy Days! Wilhelm, Hans, illus. (p. 1072)
—I Love School! Wilhelm, Hans, illus. (p. 1072)
—I Love Valentine's Day! (p. 1078)
—I Won't Share! Wilhelm, Hans, illus. (p. 1086)
—Little Whale in Deep Trouble: A Story Inspired by a True Event. (p. 1329)
—Noodles & the Bully. (p. 1619)
—Pigs in a Blanket. Salcedo, Erica, illus. (p. 1744)
Wilhelm, Hans, illus. see Harrison, David L.
Wilhelm, James J., ed. see Schachner, Judy.
Wilhelm, Jeffrey. Ulysses S. Grant: From Failure to Hero. (p. 2316)
Wilhelm, Lauren, illus. see Merker, Patricia D.
Wilhelm, Richard. 100 Chinesische Märchen Mit Illustrationen (das Zauberfaß, der Panther, das Grosse Wasser, der Fuchs und der Tiger, der Feuergott, Morgenhimmel und Mehr) - Vollständige Deutsche Ausgabe. (p. 2556)
Wilhelmine H Bauregger. Fliege Agathe. (p. 748)
Wilhite, Becca. Bright Blue Miracle. (p. 281)
Wilhite, Cindy. Santa He Sees You When. (p. 1932)
Wilhite, Kenneth. Little Black Bear's Lunch. (p. 1311)
Wilhite, Susan L., jt. auth. see Lewis, Calvin, Jr.
Wilhoite, Joellen. Safety Safari. Paraschiv, Doina, illus. (p. 1922)
Wiliams, Cornelius, jt. auth. see Melvin E., Meggan.
Wilinski, Bethany. When Pre-K Comes to School: Policy, Partnerships, & the Early Childhood Education Workforce. (p. 2432)
Wilk, David. There's a Duck in My Bathtub! Ahlbum, Joey, illus. (p. 2217)
Wilke, Cheryl Weibye. At the Cabin: In the Woods by the Lake up North. Stouffer, Rebecca, illus. (p. 130)
Wilke, Daria & Schwartz, Marian. Playing a Part. (p. 1760)
Wilken, Scott. Spooky Historical Sites. (p. 2087)
Wilkens, Karen & Benchmark Education Co., LLC Staff. ABC. (p. 3)
—I Like. (p. 1067)
Wilkens, Karen & Johnson, Tiffany. ABC - I - I Like: StartUp Unit 1 Lap Book. Litwin, Mike, illus. (p. 3)
Wilkenstanley, Ellen. Berryville Bully. (p. 204)
Wilker, Ian, jt. auth. see Kelly, Evelyn B.
Wilkerson, Bessie T. Grasshopper. Schafrath, Richard "ty", illus. (p. 881)
—It's Been a Good Day Ha Sido un Buen Dia: English & in Spanish. (p. 1144)
—My Friend the Wind. (p. 1548)
Wilkerson, Dana. Mustang Macy. (p. 1530)
Wilkerson, David, et al. Cross & the Switchblade: The True Story of One Man's Fearless Faith. Foley, Tim, illus. (p. 477)
Wilkerson, Dawn. Katie & Katoa Travel down the River. (p. 1205)
Wilkerson, Lori. Light & I. (p. 1298)
Wilkerson, Ramona, et al. Twinning. (p. 2305)
Wilkerson, Teresa, illus. see Major, Wayne A. & Major, Ralphine.
Wilkes, Angela. Discover Science: Animal Homes. (p. 555)
—Science Encyclopedia. Bhachu, Verindr, illus. (p. 1954)
—Wild Places: Combined Volume. (p. 2464)
Wilkes, Angela, jt. auth. see Watt, Fiona.
Wilkes, C. Gene. Jesus on Leadership: Discovering the Secrets of Servant Leadership from the Life of Christ. (p. 1166)
Wilkes, Clement. Sidney Forrester (Classic Reprint) (p. 2015)
Wilkes, Larry. Folktales of Eastern Europe: The Flying Ship & Other Traditional Stories. (p. 757)
Wilkes, Paula. Annie & the Butterfly Fairies. (p. 99)
—Tilly & Ted. (p. 2243)
Wilkes, Ruth. Dancing Fruit Put on a Show! Cross, James, illus. (p. 500)
Wilkes, Sally R. Harry's First Holiday. (p. 935)
Wilkes, Thomas G. E. Hell's Cauldron (Classic Reprint) (p. 952)
Wilkie, Cleve. Just Lookin' Around (Classic Reprint) (p. 1193)
Wilkie, Eunice. Bible Activity Book Volume 1. (p. 213)
—Faithful Scar. (p. 699)
—Garden of Eden Adventure. (p. 809)
—Noah's Ark Adventure. (p. 1616)
—Princess Precious & the Great King of Everything. (p. 1799)
Wilkie, Franc B. Gambler: A Story of Chicago Life (Classic Reprint) (p. 806)
—Walks about Chicago, 1871-1881: And Army & Miscellaneous Sketches (Classic Reprint) (p. 2372)
Wilkie, G. Lamar. Christopher's Tornado. Smith, Wd, illus. (p. 388)
—Puppy for Athena. Smith, W. D., illus. (p. 1815)
Wilkie, James. St. Michael & Inveresk (Classic Reprint) (p. 2097)
Wilkie, Judith & Wilkie, Colin. Lost Shoe. (p. 1355)
Wilkie, Katharine Elliott. Mary Todd Lincoln: Girl of the Bluegrass (Classic Reprint) (p. 1416)
Wilkie, Kylie. Memories Are Forever. (p. 1446)
Wilkie, Sara. Super Smart Information Strategies: Social Studies Projects That Shine. (p. 2158)
Wilkie, Sue, illus. see Unger-Pengilly, Elaine.
Wilkie, William P. Dina, or Familiar Faces, Vol. 3 of 3 (Classic Reprint) (p. 547)
Wilkie, William Patrick. Dina, or Familiar Faces, Vol. 1 of 3 (Classic Reprint) (p. 547)
Wilkin, Eloise, illus. see Cushman, Jean, et al.
Wilkin, Eloise, illus. see Golden Books Staff, et al.
Wilkin, Eloise, illus. see Golden Books.
Wilkin, Eloise, illus. see Johnson, Florence.
Wilkin, Eloise, illus. see Watson, Jane Werner.
Wilkin, Eloise, illus. see Wilkin, Esther.
Wilkin, Eloise, illus. see Williams, Garth & Wise Brown, Margaret.
Wilkin, Esther. Baby Listens. Wilkin, Eloise, illus. (p. 151)
—Baby's Christmas. Wilkin, Eloise, illus. (p. 153)
Wilkin, Wendy. Bible Stories for Children. Cloke, Rene, illus. (p. 214)
Wilkins, Benjamin. Grateful Jill & the Giant. Else, Somebody, illus. (p. 881)
Wilkins, Charles. Red Dragon, Vol. 1: The National Magazine of Wales; February to July, 1882 (Classic Reprint) (p. 1856)
—Tales & Sketches of Wales (Classic Reprint) (p. 2181)
Wilkins, Cristina Luz, illus. see Trias Trueta, Katy.
Wilkins, Ebony Joy. Claudette Colvin Refuses to Move: Courageous Kid of the Civil Rights Movement. Simmons, Mark, illus. (p. 401)
—DK Life Stories: Katherine Johnson. Ager, Charlotte, illus. (p. 568)
—Malcolm X: Get to Know the Civil Rights Activist. (p. 1391)
—Perron Family Haunting: The Ghost Story That Inspired Horror Movies. (p. 1724)
—Trailblazers: Beyoncé: Queen of the Spotlight. (p. 2275)
Wilkins, Ed G. P. Young New York: Comedy, in Three Acts (Classic Reprint) (p. 2531)
Wilkins, Eva. Brogues of Kilavain Glen: A Play (Classic Reprint) (p. 284)
—Weaver's Children: A True Story of Pioneering Times (Classic Reprint) (p. 2394)
Wilkins, James Francis. Queen & Mr Brown: A Day for Dinosaurs. (p. 1823)
—Queen & Mr Brown - A Day for Dinosaurs. (p. 1823)
—Queen & Mr Brown: a Night in the Natural History Museum. (p. 1823)
—Queen & Mr Brown: Meet the Rats. (p. 1823)
—Queen & Mr Brown: the Ugliest Fish in the Sea. (p. 1823)
Wilkins, Jessica. Date Rape. (p. 509)
—Street Pharma. (p. 2140)
Wilkins, John. Autobiography of an English Gamekeeper (John Wilkins of Stanstead, Essex) (Classic Reprint) (p. 140)
Wilkins, John, et al. Autobiography of an English Gamekeeper. (p. 140)
Wilkins, John-Paul. What Can Live in the River? (p. 2407)
—What Can Live in the Snow? (p. 2407)
Wilkins, Joseph, jt. auth. see Bigwood, John.
Wilkins, Marcella Fanny. Slave Son (Classic Reprint) (p. 2035)
Wilkins, Mary E. Comfort Pease & Her Gold Ring (Classic Reprint) (p. 429)
—Decorative Plaques (Classic Reprint) (p. 523)
—Heart's Highway: A Romance of Virginia in the Seventeenth Century (Classic Reprint) (p. 946)
—Humble Romance, & Other Stories (Classic Reprint) (p. 1050)
—In Colonial Times: The Adventures of Ann, the Bound Girl of Samuel Wales, of Braintree, in the Province of Massachusetts Bay (Classic Reprint) (p. 1104)
—Jamesons (Classic Reprint) (p. 1157)
—Jerome a Poor Man: A Novel (Classic Reprint) (p. 1164)
—Madelon: A Novel (Classic Reprint) (p. 1375)
—Pembroke: A Novel (Classic Reprint) (p. 1714)
—Portion of Labor (Classic Reprint) (p. 1779)
—Pot of Gold: And Other Stories (Classic Reprint) (p. 1780)
—Understudies: Short Stories (Classic Reprint) (p. 2326)
—Young Lucretia: And Other Stories (Classic Reprint) (p. 2531)
Wilkins, Mary-Jane. Asteroids, Comets, & Meteors. (p. 127)
—Deep Sea. (p. 524)
—Deserts. (p. 532)
—Earth. (p. 615)
—Frozen Lands. (p. 795)
—Grasslands. (p. 881)
—Inner Planets. (p. 1121)
—Moon. (p. 1501)
—Mountains. (p. 1514)
—Outer Planets. (p. 1684)
—Rain Forests. (p. 1835)
—Sun. (p. 2151)
Wilkins, Nalini. Doby's First Christmas. Robb, Jonathan, illus. (p. 572)
Wilkins, Peter, jt. auth. see Paltock, Robert.
Wilkins, Remy. Strays. (p. 2139)
Wilkins, Tiana. Adulation. (p. 17)
Wilkins, W. A. Cleverdale Mystery: Or, the Machine & Its Wheels; a Story of American Life (Classic Reprint) (p. 404)
Wilkins, W. H. Green Bay Tree, Vol. 11: A Tale of to-Day (Classic Reprint) (p. 893)
—Green Bay Tree, Vol. 2: A Tale of to-Day (Classic Reprint) (p. 893)
—Holy Estate: A Study in Morals (Classic Reprint) (p. 995)
Wilkins, W. Henri. Rock Allen the Orphan, Vol. 2: Or Lost & Found; with Cast of Characters, Stage Business, Costumes, Relative Positions of the Performers, etc (Classic Reprint) (p. 1894)
—Turn of the Tide, or Wrecked in Port: A Nautical & Temperance Drama, in Three Acts (Classic Reprint) (p. 2300)
Wilkins, Wendy H., illus. see Frederick, H. J.
Wilkins, William Henry. Forbidden Sacrifice, Vol. 1 of 3 (Classic Reprint) (p. 764)
—Green Bay Tree: A Tale of to-Day (Classic Reprint) (p. 893)
—Green Bay Tree, Vol. 3: A Tale of to-Day (Classic Reprint) (p. 893)
Wilkins, William Henry, jt. auth. see Burton, Isabel.
Wilkins-Freeman, Mary E. Doc Gordon (Classic Reprint) (p. 572)
Wilkinson, jt. auth. see Price.
Wilkinson, A. a. Archive, Vol. 39: October, 1926 (Classic Reprint) (p. 111)
Wilkinson, Andrews. Plantation Stories of Old Louisiana (Classic Reprint) (p. 1757)
Wilkinson, Annie, illus. see Barrie, J. M. & Ladybird Books Staff.
Wilkinson, Annie, illus. see Cooke, Brandy.
Wilkinson, Annie, illus. see Marks, Allison & Marks, Wayne.
Wilkinson, Annie Margaret. Lady's Life & Travels in Zululand & the Transvaal During Cetewayo's Reign: Being the African Letters & Journals of the Late Mrs. Wilkinson (Classic Reprint) (p. 1239)
Wilkinson, Brenda. Ludell. (p. 1366)
Wilkinson Brown, Valerie. Me & My Faith. (p. 1433)
Wilkinson, C. Allix. Reminiscences of Eton (Keate's Time) (Classic Reprint) (p. 1865)
Wilkinson, Carl. Albert Einstein's Theory of Relativity. (p. 40)
Wilkinson, Charles Henry. Effects of Electricity in Paralytic & Rheumatic Affections, Gutta Serena, Deafness, Indurations of the Liver, Dropsy, Chlorosis, & Many Other Female Complaints, &C: Illustrated with a Variety of Cases Which Have Occurred at the Medico-Electrical R. (p. 627)
Wilkinson, Colin. Everything You Need to Know about Digital Privacy. (p. 673)
—Gaming: Playing Safe & Playing Smart. (p. 808)
—Mobile Platforms: Getting Information on the Go. (p. 1485)
—Twitter & Microblogging: Instant Communication with 140 Characters or Less. (p. 2306)
Wilkinson, Colin, contrib. by. Using Math in Construction. (p. 2341)
Wilkinson, Dean. Sheerluck Versus the Paranormal Volume 1. Keen, Joseph, illus. (p. 2005)
Wilkinson, Elizabeth Hays. Lane to Sleepy Town, & Other Verses (Classic Reprint) (p. 1243)
Wilkinson, Ella Crane. Freddy's Great Aunt: A Play for Female Characters (Classic Reprint) (p. 781)

W

Wilkinson, Florence. Lady of the Flag-Flowers (Classic Reprint) (p. 1238)
—Silent Door (Classic Reprint) (p. 2017)
—Strength of the Hills: A Novel (Classic Reprint) (p. 2140)
Wilkinson, George. Chronicles of Southport In 1845: With a Variety of Other Miscellaneous Pieces, Written Expressly for the Southport Visiter (Classic Reprint) (p. 389)
Wilkinson, James H. Yang the Dragon Tells His Story, Halloween Train. Blake, Carol, illus. (p. 2517)
Wilkinson, Janet. Around the World on a Bicycle. (p. 119)
Wilkinson, Joshua Lucock. Wanderer, or a Collection of Anecdotes & Incidents, Vol. 1: With Reflections, Political & Religious, During Two Excursions, in 1791 & 1793, in France, Germany, & Italy (Classic Reprint) (p. 2374)
Wilkinson, Kate, illus. see Pulford, Elizabeth.
Wilkinson, Lili. Boundless Sublime. (p. 265)
—Green Valentine. (p. 895)
—Pink. (p. 1746)
—That Christmas Feeling. Francey, Amanda, illus. (p. 2212)
Wilkinson, Lisa Diane Crislip. Dog's Bill of Rights. (p. 577)
Wilkinson, Louis. Brute Gods (Classic Reprint) (p. 288)
—Buffoon (Classic Reprint) (p. 291)
—Chaste Man (Classic Reprint) (p. 362)
Wilkinson, Marguerite. Dingbat of Arcady (Classic Reprint) (p. 547)
Wilkinson, Nancy, illus. see Verity, Art.
Wilkinson, Naomi. One Hundred Things to Spot. (p. 1660)
—Spot the Difference: at the Beach. (p. 2090)
Wilkinson, Nevile. Yvette in Italy & Titania's Palace (Classic Reprint) (p. 2537)
Wilkinson, Phil. Child Through Time: The Book of Children's History. Noon, Steve, illus. (p. 370)
Wilkinson, Philip. DK Readers L3: Spacebusters: the Race to the Moon. (p. 568)
—Myths & Legends: An Illustrated Guide to Their Origins & Meanings. (p. 1571)
—Myths, Legends, & Sacred Stories: A Visual Encyclopedia. (p. 1572)
—Spacebusters: The Race to the Moon. (p. 2072)
—Spacebusters. (p. 2072)
Wilkinson, Phyllis. College Greetings, Vol. 1: February, 1917 (Classic Reprint) (p. 415)
Wilkinson, Richard, illus. see Nelson, Jo.
Wilkinson, Richard James. Vocabulary of Central Sakai: Dialect of the Aboriginal Communities in the Gopeng Valley (Classic Reprint) (p. 2364)
Wilkinson, Rita. Girl Who Never Stops Asking. (p. 837)
Wilkinson, Robbie. Garbage Dog. Little Gestalten, Little, ed. (p. 808)
Wilkinson, Ron, illus. see White, Ken.
Wilkinson, Sheena. Taking Flight (p. 2178)
Wilkinson, Sheena Maria. Street Song. (p. 2140)
Wilkinson, Steve, jt. auth. see Knudson, Mike.
Wilkinson, Tate. Memoirs of His Own Life, Vol. 1 of 4 (Classic Reprint) (p. 1444)
Wilkinson, Thomas M. Forest Through the Trees. (p. 766)
—Willie-off-the-Pickleboat. (p. 2469)
Wilkinson, William L. Glorious Praise. Blackmon, Kim, illus. (p. 844)
Wilkinson-Latham, Christopher. Boer War. Roffe, Michael, illus. (p. 253)
Wilkon, Józef, illus. see Herrmann, Svenja.
Wilks, John. Tory Baronet, or Tories, Whigs, & Radicals, Vol. 1 of 3 (Classic Reprint) (p. 2266)
—Tory Baronet, or Tories, Whigs, & Radicals, Vol. 3 (Classic Reprint) (p. 2266)
Wilks, Mike. Weather Works. Wilks, Mike, illus. (p. 2394)
Wilks, Seth. Hatmaker. Wilks, Seth, illus. (p. 937)
Wilks, Vernell. Leaving the Nest. (p. 1260)
—Messy Mia. (p. 1452)
Will, Charles James. Pit Town Coronet, Vol. 2 Of 3: A Family Mystery (Classic Reprint) (p. 1751)
Will, Clark Moor, illus. see Kopp, J. J.
Will, Herbert. Weak Man & Weak Woman (Classic Reprint) (p. 2393)
Will, John McArthur. Out of Darkness into Light: A Story of the Pioneer West (Classic Reprint) (p. 1682)
Will, Julianne, jt. auth. see Ball, Ann.
Will, Julianne M., jt. auth. see Ball, Ann.
Will, Kip. Bombo's Big Question (Mandarin) (p. 254)
Will, R. Maisy, the Motorcycle Mutt. (p. 1384)
Will, R. K. Harry's Flowers. (p. 935)
Willams, Brian, tr. see Perelman, Yakov.
Willan, Alex. Jasper & Ollie. (p. 1161)
Willan, Alex, illus. see Rinker, Sherri Duskey.
Willard, Baron And Mary. Hugs Are for Every One... Willard, Mary, illus. (p. 1048)
Willard, Carolyn, jt. auth. see Erickson, John.
Willard, Christopher. Mindfulness for Teen Anxiety: A Workbook for Overcoming Anxiety at Home, at School, & Everywhere Else. (p. 1470)
Willard, Christopher, jt. auth. see Abblett, Mitch R.
Willard, Christopher & O'Leary, Wendy. Breathing Makes It Better: A Book for Sad Days, Mad Days, Glad Days, & All the Feelings In-Between. (p. 279)
Willard, Christopher & Rechtschaffen, Daniel. Alphabreaths: The ABCs of Mindful Breathing. Clifton-Brown, Holly, illus. (p. 59)
Willard, Christopher & Weisser, Olivia. Breathing Book. (p. 279)
Willard Crompton, Samuel. Discovering Ancient Rome (p. 555)
Willard, Edgar Lincoln. Ideal Speller (Classic Reprint) (p. 1089)
Willard, Eleanor Withey. Children's Garden (Classic Reprint) (p. 374)
Willard, Ellen M. Yuletide Entertainments: Christmas Recitations, Monologues, Drills, Tableaux, Motion Songs, Exercises, Dialogues, & Plays; Suitable for All Ages (Classic Reprint) (p. 2537)
Willard, Eugene S. Kin-Da-Shon's Wife: An Alaskan Story (Classic Reprint) (p. 1218)
Willard, Frances E. Nineteen Beautiful Years: Or Sketches of a Girl's Life (Classic Reprint) (p. 1610)
Willard, Gerald. Amy Firefly. (p. 77)
Willard, Hugh. Goodwill Vultures Club: No Time for Play. Holjes, Kerry, ed. (p. 869)
—Goodwill Vultures Club: The Gift of the Vulture. Dozier, Dolly, ed. (p. 869)
—Goodwill Vultures Club. Holjes, Kerry, ed. (p. 869)
Willard, J. H., jt. auth. see De Segur, Comtesse.
Willard, Madeline Deaderick. King's Highway: A Romance of the Franciscan Order in Alta California. (p. 1223)
—King's Highway: A Romance of the Franciscan Order in Alta California (Classic Reprint) (p. 1223)
Willard, Mary, illus. see Willard, Baron And Mary.
Willard, Nancy. Adventures of Anatole. McPhail, David, illus. (p. 21)
—Be Positively Powerful: A Guide for Teens on Achieving Resilience & Empowerment. (p. 177)
—Starlit Snowfall. Pinkney, Jerry, illus. (p. 2106)
—Three Mouths of Little Tom Drum. Hawkes, Kevin, illus. (p. 2234)
—Way of the Donkey. (p. 2387)
Willard, Renee. Mama Who Didn't Work. (p. 1392)
—Memommy's Miracles. (p. 1445)
Willard, Samuel. Secondary Lessons, or the Improved Reader: Intended As a Sequel to the Franklin Primer (Classic Reprint) (p. 1974)
Willcock, Jennifer. Exit Stage Right. (p. 677)
Willcocks, M. P. Eyes of the Blind: A Novel (Classic Reprint) (p. 689)
—Man of Genius: A Story of the Judgment of Paris (Classic Reprint) (p. 1394)
—Will to Live (Classic Reprint) (p. 2467)
—Wingless Victory (Classic Reprint) (p. 2473)
—Wings of Desire (Classic Reprint) (p. 2473)
Willcocks, Mary Patricia. Way up (Classic Reprint) (p. 2387)
—Widdicombe (Classic Reprint) (p. 2460)
Willcox, Helen L. Sunlight or Candlelight (Classic Reprint) (p. 2152)
Willcox, Helen Lida. Kanjundu, or from Fear of the Enemy (Classic Reprint) (p. 1202)
Willebrandt, Avery. Spitting Cobra / Cobra Escupidora. (p. 2084)
—Spitting Cobras. (p. 2084)
Willebrandt, Isabella. Why Do My Teeth Fall Out? (p. 2456)
Willebrant, Avery. Meat-Eating Plants. (p. 1435)
Willeford, Tammy Jean. Alphabear. Hopkins, Emily, illus. (p. 58)
Willem Van Loon, Hendrik. Story of Mankind. (p. 2131)
Willems, J. F. Roman du Renard: Traduit Pour la Première Fois d'Après un Texte Flamand du Xiie Siècle (Classic Reprint) (p. 1899)
Willems, Kristen. Adventures of Roobear & Aj. (p. 27)
Willems, Mo. Are You Ready to Play Outside? (p. 113)
—Because. Ren, Amber, illus. (p. 186)
—Big Guy Took My Ball! (an Elephant & Piggie Book) Willems, Mo, illus. (p. 220)
—Busy Creature's Day Eating! (p. 302)
—Can I Play Too? (p. 317)
—Can I Play Too? (an Elephant & Piggie Book) Willems, Mo, illus. (p. 317)
—Cat the Cat, Who Is That? Willems, Mo, illus. (p. 342)
—Cautionary Tale. Willems, Mo, illus. (p. 347)
—City Dog, Country Frog. Muth, Jon J., illus. (p. 394)
—Conejito Knuffle. Campoy, F. Isabel, tr. (p. 438)
—Don't le the Pigeon Drive the Bus. Campoy, F. Isabel, tr. (p. 583)
—Dont Let the Pigeon Drive. (p. 583)
—Don't Let the Pigeon Drive the Bus! (p. 583)
—Don't Let the Pigeon Drive the Bus! (Big Book Edition) (a Pigeon Series Book) Willems, Mo, illus. (p. 583)
—Don't Let the Pigeon Finish This Activity Book! (Pigeon Series) Willems, Mo, illus. (p. 583)
—Don't Let the Pigeon Stay up Late! (p. 583)
—Duckling Gets a Cookie!? (Pigeon Series) Willems, Mo, illus. (p. 608)
—Elephant & Piggie: Happy Pig Day. (p. 633)
—Elephant & Piggie: I Broke My Trunk. (p. 633)
—Elephant & Piggie: I Love My New Toy. (p. 633)
—Elephant & Piggie: Pigs Make Me Sneeze. (p. 633)
—Elephant & Piggie: Are You Ready to Play Outside. (p. 633)
—Elephant & Piggie Biggie! Willems, Mo, illus. (p. 633)
—Elephant & Piggie Biggie Volume 2! (p. 633)
—Elephant & Piggie Biggie! Volume 3. Willems, Mo, illus. (p. 633)
—Elephant & Piggie: the Complete Collection (an Elephant & Piggie Book) Willems, Mo, illus. (p. 633)
—Elephants Cannot Dance! (p. 634)
—Elephants Cannot Dance! (an Elephant & Piggie Book) Willems, Mo, illus. (p. 634)
—Goldilocks & the Three Dinosaurs: As Retold by Mo Willems. Willems, Mo, illus. (p. 860)
—Happy Pig Day! (an Elephant & Piggie Book) Willems, Mo, illus. (p. 923)
—Hooray for Amanda & Her Alligator! Willems, Mo, illus. (p. 1000)
—I Am Going! (an Elephant & Piggie Book) Willems, Mo, illus. (p. 1058)
—I Am Invited to a Party! (p. 1058)
—I Broke My Trunk! (an Elephant & Piggie Book) Willems, Mo, illus. (p. 1061)
—I Lost My Tooth! (an Unlimited Squirrels Book) Willems, Mo, illus. (p. 1068)
—I Really Like Slop! (an Elephant & Piggie Book) Willems, Mo, illus. (p. 1080)
—I Will Take a Nap! (an Elephant & Piggie Book) Willems, Mo, illus. (p. 1085)
—I'm a Frog! (an Elephant & Piggie Book) Willems, Mo, illus. (p. 1097)
—Knuffle Bunny. (p. 1230)
—Knuffle Bunny Free: An Unexpected Diversion. (p. 1230)
—Knuffle Bunny Free: An Unexpected Diversion. Willems, Mo, illus. (p. 1230)
—Knuffle Bunny Free: Un Unexpected Diversion. Willems, Mo, illus. (p. 1230)
—Knuffle Bunny Free. (p. 1230)
—Knuffle Bunny Too. (p. 1230)
—Let's Go for a Drive! (an Elephant & Piggie Book) Willems, Mo, illus. (p. 1273)
—Let's Say Hi to Friends Who Fly! Willems, Mo, illus. (p. 1277)
—Listen to My Trumpet! (an Elephant & Piggie Book) Willems, Mo, illus. (p. 1308)
—Mi Amigo Está Triste (Spanish Edition) (p. 1454)
—My New Friend Is So Fun! (an Elephant & Piggie Book) Willems, Mo, illus. (p. 1558)
—Naked Mole Rat Gets Dressed. Willems, Mo, illus. (p. 1573)
—Nanette's Baguette. Willems, Mo, illus. (p. 1574)
—Pigeon HAS to Go to School! (p. 1743)
—Pigeon Needs a Bath! Willems, Mo, illus. (p. 1743)
—Pigeon Needs a Bath Book! (p. 1743)
—Pigeon Needs a Bath Book with Pigeon Bath Toy! (p. 1743)
—Pigeon Wants a Puppy! (p. 1743)
—Pigs Make Me Sneeze! (an Elephant & Piggie Book) Willems, Mo, illus. (p. 1744)
—Sam, the Most Scaredy-Cat Kid in the Whole World: A Leonardo, the Terrible Monster Companion. Willems, Mo, illus. (p. 1926)
—Should I Share My Ice Cream? (an Elephant & Piggie Book) Willems, Mo, illus. (p. 2011)
—Story of Diva & Flea. DiTerlizzi, Tony, illus. (p. 2130)
—Thank You Book (an Elephant & Piggie Book) Willems, Mo, illus. (p. 2211)
—That Is Not a Good Idea! (p. 2213)
—That Is Not a Good Idea! Willems, Mo, illus. (p. 2213)
—Time to Pee! Board Book. (p. 2245)
—Time to Sleep, Sheep the Sheep! Willems, Mo, illus. (p. 2245)
—Waiting Is Not Easy! (an Elephant & Piggie Book) Willems, Mo, illus. (p. 2371)
—Watch Me Throw the Ball! (an Elephant & Piggie Book) Willems, Mo, illus. (p. 2383)
—We Are in a Book! (an Elephant & Piggie Book) Willems, Mo, illus. (p. 2389)
—We Are in an ART-ivity Book! Willems, Mo, illus. (p. 2389)
—Welcome: a Mo Willems Guide for New Arrivals. Willems, Mo, illus. (p. 2397)
—What's Your Sound, Hound the Hound? Willems, Mo, illus. (p. 2427)
—Who Flies, Cat the Cat? Willems, Mo, illus. (p. 2447)
—Who Is That, Cat the Cat? Willems, Mo, illus. (p. 2448)
—Who Is the Mystery Reader? (p. 2448)
—Who Says That, Cat the Cat? Willems, Mo, illus. (p. 2449)
—Who Sleeps, Cat the Cat? Willems, Mo, illus. (p. 2449)
—¡Escucha Mi Trompeta! (an Elephant & Piggie Book, Spanish Edition) Willems, Mo, illus. (p. 662)
—¡Esperar No Es Fácil! (Spanish Edition) Willems, Mo, illus. (p. 662)
—¡Estamos en un Libro! (Spanish Edition) Willems, Mo, illus. (p. 664)
—¡He Perdido un Diente! (Spanish Edition) Willems, Mo, illus. (p. 942)
—¡Hoy Volaré! (Spanish Edition) Willems, Mo, illus. (p. 1047)
—¡la Paloma Encuentra un Perro Caliente! Willems, Mo, illus. (p. 1235)
—¡Me Rompí la Trompa! (Spanish Edition) (p. 1433)
—¡No Dejes Que la Paloma Conduzca el Autobus! Willems, Mo, illus. (p. 1612)
—¡Tienes un Pájaro en la Cabeza! (an Elephant & Piggie Book, Spanish Edition) Willems, Mo, illus. (p. 2240)
—¡un Tipo Grande Se Llevó Mi Pelota! (Spanish Edition) Willems, Mo, illus. (p. 2317)
—¡Vamos a Dar una Vuelta! (an Elephant & Piggie Book, Spanish Edition) Willems, Mo, illus. (p. 2345)
—¿Debo Compartir Mi Helado? (Spanish Edition) Willems, Mo, illus. (p. 522)
—¿Estás Lista para Jugar Afuera? (an Elephant & Piggie Book, Spanish Edition) Willems, Mo, illus. (p. 664)
—¿Puedo Jugar Yo También? (an Elephant & Piggie Book, Spanish Edition) Willems, Mo, illus. (p. 1811)
Willems, Mo, jt. auth. see Santat, Dan.
Willems, Mo & Collier, Bryan. It's Shoe Time! Willems, Mo & Collier, Bryan, illus. (p. 1147)
Willems, Mo & Harper, Charise Mericle. Good for Nothing Button! Willems, Mo & Harper, Charise Mericle, illus. (p. 862)
Willems, Mo & Keller, Laurie. We Are Growing! Willems, Mo & Keller, Laurie, illus. (p. 2389)
Willems, Mo & Pham, Leuyen. Itchy Book! (Elephant & Piggie Like Reading!) Willems, Mo & Pham, Leuyen, illus. (p. 1142)
Willems, Mo & Scieszka, Jon, narrated by. Don't Let the Pigeon Drive the Bus! (p. 583)
Willems, Mo & Willems, Trixie, narrated by. Knuffle Bunny Too: A Case of Mistaken Identity. (p. 1230)
—Pigeon Finds a Hot Dog! (p. 1743)
Willems, Mo, et al, narrated by. Naked Mole Rat Gets Dressed. (p. 1573)
Willems, Mo, narrated by. Leonardo, the Terrible Monster. (p. 1267)
Willems, Trixie, jt. narrated by see Willems, Mo.
Willemse, Y. K. Rafen. (p. 1834)
Willemsen, Tricia. Willis: Something Was about to Happen. (p. 2469)
Willen, Janet & Gann, Marjorie. Speak a Word for Freedom: Women Against Slavery. (p. 2076)
Willet, Edward. Rock Sport Climbing: Techniques & Tricks. (p. 1894)
—Skateboarding: Techniques & Tricks. (p. 2029)
Willet, W. N. Charles Vincent, or the Two Clerks, Vol. 1 Of 2: A Tale of Commercial Life (Classic Reprint) (p. 359)
Willett, Edward. Andy Warhol: Fighting to Revolutionize Art. (p. 84)
—Andy Warhol. (p. 84)
—Angela Merkel: Chancellor of Germany. (p. 85)
—Around the House: Rhymes. (p. 118)
—Around the House: Rhymes (Classic Reprint) (p. 118)
—Bounty Mutiny: From the Court Case to the Movie. (p. 265)
—Career As a Mason (p. 328)
—Career Building Through Using Digital Design Tools. (p. 328)
—Disease-Hunting Scientist: Careers Hunting Deadly Diseases. (p. 557)
—Hurricane Irma. (p. 1054)
—Infectious Disease Specialists: Hunting down Disease. (p. 1118)
—Jimi Hendrix: Kiss the Sky. (p. 1168)
—Johnny Cash: "The Man in Black" (p. 1174)
—Johnny Cash: Fighting for the Underdog. (p. 1174)
—Johnny Cash. (p. 1174)
—Kiera Cass (p. 1216)
—Loyal Spectre, or the True Hearts of Atlanta (Classic Reprint) (p. 1363)
—Magnesium. (p. 1381)
—Powering a City. (p. 1783)
—Search for the Star: A Tale of Life in the Wild Woods (Classic Reprint) (p. 1971)
—Space. (p. 2070)
—Space Q&a. (p. 2072)
—Speed. (p. 2078)
—Spirit Singer. (p. 2083)
—Tale of the War in the West: Bob Brant, Patriot & Spy (Classic Reprint) (p. 2180)
—What Is the Milky Way? (p. 2416)
—What You Can Do about Ebola. (p. 2422)
—Worldshaper. (p. 2508)
Willett, Edward & Warhol, Andy. Andy Warhol: "Everyone Will Be Famous for 15 Minutes" (p. 84)
Willett, Mindy. Viens Avec Moi, Nous Apprendrons Ensemble! Ewo, Séh Keddh MacIntosh, Tessa & Macintosh, Tessa, photos by. (p. 2356)
Willett, Mindy, jt. auth. see André, Julie-Ann.
Willett, Mindy, jt. auth. see Beaver, Henry.
Willett, Mindy & Enyagotailak, Darla. No Borders Macintosh, Tessa, photos by. (p. 1612)
Willett, Mindy & Enzoe, Peter. Caribou Feed My Soul Macintosh, Tessa, photos by. (p. 330)
Willett, Mindy & Pokiak, James. Proud to Be Inuvialuit: Quviahuktunga Inuvialuugama Macintosh, Tessa, photos by. (p. 1808)
Willett, Walter, jt. auth. see Katzen, Mollie.
Willetts, Lucy & Waite, Polly. Can I Tell You about Anxiety? A Guide for Friends, Family & Professionals. (p. 317)
Willey, jt. auth. see Wallace, Karen.
Willey, Bee, illus. see Alrawi, Karim.
Willey, Bee, illus. see Hooper, Meredith.
Willey, Bee, illus. see Husain, Shahrukh.
Willey, Bee, illus. see Matthews, Andrew.
Willey, Bee, illus. see McCaughrean, Geraldine.
Willey, Bee, illus. see Page, Nick & Page, Claire.
Willey, Bee, jt. auth. see McCaughrean, Geraldine.
Willey, George Franklyn. Soltaire a Romance of the Willey Slide & the White Mountains (Classic Reprint) (p. 2058)
Willey, Kira. Breathe Like a Bear: 30 Mindful Moments for Kids to Feel Calm & Focused Anytime, Anywhere. Betts, Anni, illus. (p. 279)
—Mindfulness Moments for Kids: Breathe Like a Bear. Betts, Anni, illus. (p. 1470)
—Mindfulness Moments for Kids: Bunny Breaths. Betts, Anni, illus. (p. 1470)
—Mindfulness Moments for Kids: Listen Like an Elephant. Betts, Anni, illus. (p. 1470)
Willey, Toni. Princess Petunia & Me: Based on the Life of Petunia the Possum. (p. 1798)
Willia, Sarah, illus. see Lafaye, Gwarmekia.
William. Recollections of Rambles at the South (Classic Reprint) (p. 1854)
will.i.am & Johnson, Brian David. WaR: Wizards & Robots. (p. 2377)
William Hill, Christopher. Bleakley Brothers Mystery: What Manor of Murder? (p. 243)
William Jones, George. Logarithmic Tables. (p. 1339)
William, Lorna, illus. see Klepeis, Alicia Z.
William, Lorna, illus. see McMeans, Julia.
William Miles, jt. auth. see Myers, Walter Dean.
William Milton. Tome. (p. 2259)
—Valentine. (p. 2344)
William Prevost, Edward, jt. auth. see Dickinson, William.
William, William. Alexis, the Tyrant of the East: A Persian Tale (Classic Reprint) (p. 43)
—Rich Boy & the Poor Boy: Or, a Contented Mind Is the Best Feast (Classic Reprint) (p. 1876)
—Stories of English & Foreign Life (Classic Reprint) (p. 2125)
Williams, A. Bryan. Rod & Creel in British Columbia. (p. 1897)
—Rod Creel in British Columbia (Classic Reprint) (p. 1897)
Williams, Adene. Girl Warriors: A Book for Girls (Classic Reprint) (p. 837)
Williams, Adrian & Sassoon, Rosemary. Penpals for Handwriting Font CD-ROM. (p. 1718)
Williams, Albert Rhys. In the Claws of the German Eagle. (p. 1108)
—In the Claws of the German Eagle (Classic Reprint) (p. 1108)
Williams, Alfred. Round about the Upper Thames (Classic Reprint) (p. 1907)
Williams, Alfred Henry. Afoot & Afloat in Burma (Classic Reprint) (p. 31)
Williams, Alicia D. Genesis Begins Again. (p. 814)
Williams, Allen, illus. see del Toro, Guillermo & Funke, Cornelia.
Williams, Amanda Schaefer. Sadie in Heaven. (p. 1921)
Williams, Amber, jt. auth. see Sandelin, Karen.
Williams, Amy. Gertrude the Silly Puppy. (p. 823)
Williams, Andrea. Goodbye Kindergarten. (p. 866)
Williams, Andy. Moon River. Hopgood, Tim, illus. (p. 1502)
Williams, Angela L. PTSD & Coping with Trauma Information for Teens, First Edition. (p. 1810)
—Traveler's Health Information for Teens. (p. 2280)
Williams, Angela L., ed. Abuse & Violence Information for Teens. (p. 9)
Williams, Angie, photos by see Martin, Paige.
Williams, Anthony. Creating Superhero Comics (p. 470)
—Dracula: A Classic Pop-Up Tale. (p. 592)
Williams, Anthony, illus. see Abnett, Dan.
Williams, Anthony, illus. see Busch, Robbie.
Williams, Anthony, illus. see Doyle, Arthur Conan, ed.
Williams, Anthony, illus. see Shelley, Mary.
Williams, Anthony, illus. see Stoker, Bram.
Williams, Archibald. Romance of Modern Mechanism: With Interesting Descriptions in Non-Technical Language of

W

—Shasta of California. (p. 2003)
Williams, Jack S. Craftsmen & Craftswomen of the California Mission Frontier. (p. 466)
—Indians of the California Mission Frontier. (p. 1117)
—Luiseno of California. (p. 1366)
—Padres of the California Mission Frontier. (p. 1692)
—Sailors, Merchants, & Muleteers of the California Mission Frontier. (p. 1923)
—Soldiers & Their Families of the California Mission Frontier. (p. 2057)
—Townspeople & Ranchers of the California Mission Frontier. (p. 2270)
Williams, Jaimeann Melissa. Meekah's Nana Went to Heaven. (p. 1437)
Williams, Jake. Darwin's Voyage of Discovery. (p. 508)
—Remarkable Reptiles. (p. 1864)
Williams, James. Life & Adventures of James Williams, a Fugitive Slave: With a Full Description of the Underground Railroad (Classic Reprint) (p. 1288)
—Narrative of Events, since the First of August, 1834 (Classic Reprint) (p. 1575)
—Narrative of James Williams, an American Slave, Who Was for Several Years a Driver on a Cotton Plantation in Alabama (Classic Reprint) (p. 1575)
Williams, James Douglas. Reading Conversation Composition (Classic Reprint) (p. 1846)
Williams, James E. Pray It Kiddo. (p. 1785)
Williams, Jan. Amazing Storytelling Cat. Peecock, Simon & McKissock, Charmaine, illus. (p. 66)
—Essex Folk Tales for Children. (p. 664)
Williams, Jane. Days Like These: New & Selected Poems 1998-2013. (p. 515)
Williams, Jane Stouffer. Super Duck of the Chesapeake: A True Story. (p. 2154)
Williams, Janet Yvette. Flower That Finally Bloomed. (p. 752)
Williams, Jared T. Rabbit Ninja. Williams, Jared T., illus. (p. 1829)
Williams, Jared T., illus. see Kovacs, Deborah.
Williams, Jarrett. Super Pro K. O. Vol. 3: Gold for Glory. (p. 2156)
Williams, Jay & Blickenstaff, Wayne. Puppy Pie. (p. 1815)
Williams, Jayne, illus. see Cutrer, Elisabeth.
Williams, Jean Ann. Just Claire. (p. 1192)
Williams, Jean K. Perils of the Santa Fe Trail. (p. 1723)
Williams, Jean Kinney. Empire of Ancient Greece, Revised Edition. (p. 645)
Williams, Jemima, illus. see Scheuer, Benjamin.
Williams, Jennifer. Oobleck, Slime & Dancing Spaghetti: Twenty Terrific at Home Science Experiments Inspired by Favorite Children's Books. (p. 1665)
Williams, Jenny. Little Red Riding Hood. (p. 1326)
Williams, Jenny, illus. see Mahy, Margaret.
Williams, Jenny, illus. see Riley, Kana.
Williams, Jenny, illus. see Young, Lesley.
Williams, Jerome, jt. auth. see Walters, Eric.
Williams, Jerry Richard. Fairy Tale: A Gay Adventure. (p. 697)
Williams, Jesse Lynch. Adventures of a Freshmen (Classic Reprint) (p. 21)
—Day-Dreamer: Being the Full Narrative of the Stolen Story (Classic Reprint) (p. 513)
—Girl & the Game: And Other College Stories (Classic Reprint) (p. 835)
—Married Life of the Frederic Carrolls (Classic Reprint) (p. 1408)
—Mr. Cleveland: A Personal Impression (Classic Reprint) (p. 1518)
—Mr. Cleveland, a Personal Impression (Classic Reprint) (p. 1518)
—My Lost Duchess: An Idyl of the Town (Classic Reprint) (p. 1554)
—Princeton Stories (Classic Reprint) (p. 1800)
—Stolen Story: And Other Newspaper Stories (Classic Reprint) (p. 2120)
Williams, Jessica. Mama's Cloud. Ark, Mateya, illus. (p. 1393)
—Mealtime Monster. Lavrova, Daria, illus. (p. 1434)
—My Koala Doesn't Take Baths. Williams, Jessica, illus. (p. 1551)
—Nuage de Maman. Marion, Renee-Alexandra, tr. (p. 1628)
—Scaredy Cali. Moncao, Nathan, illus. (p. 1941)
—Sleeping Brilliant. Williams, Jessica, illus. (p. 2037)
—You Can't Invite a Fish to a Dance Party. de la Vega, Jimena, illus. (p. 2526)
Williams, Jo. Golden Dolphin. (p. 857)
Williams, Joel Strother. Missourian in the Far West: Or the World As Seen by a Stranger (Classic Reprint) (p. 1482)
Williams, John. Eccentricities of John Edwin, Comedian, Vol. 2: Collected from His Manuscripts, & Enriched with Several Hundred Original Anecdotes (Classic Reprint) (p. 622)
Williams, John, illus. see Layburn, Joe.
Williams, John Alfred. Sissie (Classic Reprint) (p. 2026)
Williams, John Joseph. Frightened Garden. (p. 788)
—Vak's War. (p. 2343)
Williams, Josh, jt. auth. see O'Neill, Terence.
Williams, Joyce. Daddy's Love Through a Girl's Eye. Petroff, Kathryn, illus. (p. 495)
Williams Jr., Anthony, illus. see Williams-Ashe, Marcella Norton.
Williams Jr., Floyd. Lenney the Lightning Bug. Roberts, Joel, illus. (p. 1266)
Williams, Judith. Does the Sun Make Weather? (p. 575)
—Forensic Scientist: Careers Solving Crimes & Scientific Mysteries. (p. 765)
—How Come It's Raining? (p. 1027)
—How Come It's Snowing? (p. 1027)
—How Come It's Windy? (p. 1027)
—Matt's Forever Home. (p. 1426)
Williams, Judith, jt. auth. see Rauf, Don.
Williams, Judith M. Montana. (p. 1499)
Williams, Judy. 50 Recipes for Kids to Cook: Tasty Food to Make Yourself Shown in Step-By-Step Pictures. (p. 2555)
Williams, Julie. Adventures of Susie Duck: Susie Visits Memphis, Tennessee. (p. 28)
—Adventures of Susie Duck: Susie Visits St. Louis, Missouri. (p. 28)
—Drama Queens in the House. (p. 596)
—Smiling Tree. (p. 2042)
Williams, Julie-Anne. Bully Me Not. (p. 297)
Williams, Justine. Nobody Likes Me: What Am I Doing Wrong? Martinez, Michael, illus. (p. 1617)
Williams, K. L. Tag You're It. (p. 2176)
Williams, Kara. Frequently Asked Questions about My Pyramid: Eating Right. (p. 784)
Williams, Kara, jt. auth. see Faulkner, Nicholas.
Williams, Karen Lynn. Beach Tail. Cooper, Floyd, illus. (p. 178)
—Circles of Hope. (p. 393)
—Facing Fear. Palacios, Sara, illus. (p. 693)
—Galimoto. Stock, Catherine, illus. (p. 806)
—Lubuto Means Light. Grifalconi, Ann, illus. (p. 1363)
Williams, Karen Lynn & Mohammad, Khadra. Four Feet, Two Sandals. Chayka, Doug, illus. (p. 772)
Williams, Kate M. Babysitters Coven. (p. 155)
Williams, Kathryn. Pizza, Love, & Other Stuff That Made Me Famous. (p. 1752)
—Plants. (p. 1757)
Williams, Katie. Space Between Trees. (p. 2070)
Williams, Katina T. Jeremiah Pie. (p. 1164)
Williams, Kay. Adventures in the Pond: The Big Move. Victoria, Danna, illus. (p. 20)
—Adventures in the Pond: Gizmo Escapes. Victoria, Danna, illus. (p. 20)
—Adventures in the Pond: Bob & the Duck. Victoria, Danna, illus. (p. 20)
—Adventures in the Pond: Jaws Gets Toothache. Victoria, Danna, illus. (p. 20)
—Adventures in the Pond: Snapper & the Hiccups. Victoria, Danna, illus. (p. 20)
—Adventures in the Pond: Tiddles Caught in a Trap. Victoria, Danna, illus. (p. 20)
—Adventures in the Pond: The Day the Fish Got a Shock. Victoria, Danna, illus. (p. 20)
—Adventures in the Pond: Fido the Fish at the Bottom of the Pond. Victoria, Danna, illus. (p. 20)
—Big Move. Victoria, Danna, illus. (p. 221)
—Bob & the Duck. Victoria, Danna, illus. (p. 251)
—Day the Fish Got a Shock. (p. 514)
—Dragon Who Lost His Fire. Victoria, Danna, illus. (p. 594)
—House at the Bottom of the Garden. Victoria, Danna, illus. (p. 1022)
—Snapper & the Hiccups. Victoria, Danna, illus. (p. 2045)
—Talking Carrier Bag. Victoria, Danna, illus. (p. 2187)
Williams, Kelly Ann. Pye. (p. 1818)
Williams, Kj Johnny. Devil Fell in Love with Her. (p. 535)
Williams, Kristen. Sheepy Sue & the Bedtime Blues. (p. 2005)
Williams, Kristjana S., illus. see Rundell, Katherine.
Williams, Kristy. Buttercup: Poodles on Parade. Gates, Leslie, illus. (p. 303)
Williams, L.A. Cave of Mystery. (p. 347)
Williams, Lambert. Heart of the Furnace (Classic Reprint) (p. 945)
Williams, Laura E. Father Damien. Kofsky, Kristen, illus. (p. 714)
Williams, Laura E. & Orback, Craig. Can Man (p. 317)
Williams, Laura M. Why Was Jesus Born. (p. 2459)
Williams, Lawrence. Little Book, Jody Bill. (p. 1312)
—Search Is On. (p. 1971)
Williams, Leah. Adventure Time Original Graphic Novel: Marceline the Pirate Queen: Marceline the Pirate Queen. Sterling, Zachary, illus. (p. 19)
—Alchemy of Being Fourteen. (p. 41)
Williams, Lee. Seaweed, the Purrfect Cat. Johnson, Tamaris, illus. (p. 1973)
—Twin Dragons. Johnson, Tamaris, illus. (p. 2305)
Williams, Leonard. Granada: Memories, Adventures, Studies & Impressions (Classic Reprint) (p. 876)
Williams, Letitia y. Fruit in the Garden Clubhouse. (p. 796)
Williams, Lily. If Elephants Disappeared. Williams, Lily, illus. (p. 1090)
—If Polar Bears Disappeared. Williams, Lily, illus. (p. 1092)
—If Sharks Disappeared. (p. 1092)
Williams, Lily, illus. see Schwartz, Ella.
Williams, Linda. Little Old Lady Who Was Not Afraid of Anything. Lloyd, Megan, illus. (p. 1323)
Williams, Linda D. Careers in Forensics. (p. 329)
Williams, Linda J. Keys of Wisdom. (p. 1212)
Williams, Lisa, illus. see French, Vivian.
Williams, Lisa, illus. see Graves, Sue.
Williams, Lisa, illus. see Griffiths, Sarah.
Williams, Lisa, illus. see Hughes, Mónica.
Williams, Lisa, illus. see Lennon, Jude.
Williams, Lorraine, illus. see Reid, Rob.
Williams, Lucy Langdon. Too Short Vacation (Classic Reprint) (p. 2261)
Williams, M. Williams Intelligence Test for Children with Defective Vision: A Test for Blind & Partially Sighted Children (Classic Reprint) (p. 2469)
Williams, M. B. Mike: Or the Cutting of a Slum Diamond (Classic Reprint) (p. 1464)
Williams, M. Ed. Friends in the Meadow - Squirrels the Frolics of Scamp & Scooter. (p. 787)
Williams, Mabel, jt. as told by see Williams, Robert F.
Williams, Maggy. Celia & the Glue Man: A Girl's Journey to Becoming Gluten-Free & Happy. Agresta, Elizabeth, illus. (p. 350)
—"I'm Mixed!" Agresta, Elizabeth, illus. (p. 1098)
Williams, Maiya. Fizzy Whiz Kid. (p. 745)
Williams, Marcia. Elephant's Friend & Other Tales from Ancient India. Williams, Marcia, illus. (p. 634)
—Greek Myths. Williams, Marcia, illus. (p. 892)
—Hooray for Inventors! Williams, Marcia, illus. (p. 1001)
—Hooray for Women! Williams, Marcia, illus. (p. 1001)
—Lizzy Bennet's Diary: Inspired by Jane Austen's Pride & Prejudice. Williams, Marcia, illus. (p. 1337)
—Romans: Gods, Emperors, & Dormice. (p. 1901)
—Romans: Gods, Emperors, & Dormice. Williams, Marcia, illus. (p. 1901)
—Tudors: Kings, Queens, Scribes, & Ferrets! Williams, Marcia, illus. (p. 2298)
Williams, Marcia, jt. auth. see Yang, Belle.
Williams, Marcy. Teen Entrepreneurship Workbook. (p. 2199)
Williams, Margery. New Five-And-a-Half Club (Classic Reprint) (p. 1593)
—Peeps at Great Cities: Paris (Classic Reprint) (p. 1713)
—Price of Youth (Classic Reprint) (p. 1791)
—Velveteen Rabbit Spirin, Gennady, illus. (p. 2350)
—Velveteen Rabbit: Or How Toys Become Real (Classic Reprint) (p. 2350)
—Velveteen Rabbit: The Original 1922 Edition in Full Color. Nicholson, William, illus. (p. 2350)
—Velveteen Rabbit. (p. 2350)
—Velveteen Rabbit. Berg, Maria, illus. (p. 2350)
—Velveteen Rabbit. Nicholson, William, illus. (p. 2350)
—Velveteen Rabbit. Nicholson, William S., illus. (p. 2350)
—Velveteen Rabbit Board Book: The Classic Edition. Santore, Charles, illus. (p. 2350)
—Velveteen Rabbit Coloring Book. Kliros, Thea, illus. (p. 2350)
—Velveteen Rabbit Hardcover: The Classic Edition. Santore, Charles, illus. (p. 2350)
—Velveteen Rabbit Oversized Padded Board Book: The Classic Edition. Santore, Charles, illus. (p. 2350)
—Velveteen Rabbit Plush Gift Set: The Classic Edition Board Book + Plush Stuffed Animal Toy Rabbit Gift Set. Santore, Charles, illus. (p. 2350)
Williams, Marilyn & Caspersen, Barbara. Peggy & Barbie on the Farm. (p. 1714)
Williams, Mark. Hooty & Pig: The Missing Christmas Pudding. Garrett, Keith, illus. (p. 1001)
—Little Welsh Football Fan. (p. 1329)
Williams, Mark R. Adventures of the Jungle Buddies. (p. 28)
Williams, Martha McCullough. Two of a Trade (Classic Reprint) (p. 2308)
Williams, Mary. Brothers in Hope: The Story of the Lost Boys of Sudan Christie, R. Gregory, illus. (p. 286)
Williams, Mary E. Mark Zuckerberg. Greenhaven Press Staff, ed. (p. 1407)
Williams, Mary E., ed. see Greenhaven Press Editors.
Williams, Mary E., jt. ed. see Gale, G.
Williams, Mary E., jt. ed. see Greenhaven Press Editors.
Williams, Mary E., ed. Gangs. (p. 808)
—Growth Disorders. (p. 900)
—Lyme Disease. (p. 1370)
—Self-Injury. (p. 1987)
—Tourette Syndrome. (p. 2269)
Williams, Mary Raymond. July & August of 1914 (Classic Reprint) (p. 1188)
Williams, Mary Wilhelmine. Cousin-Hunting in Scandinavia (Classic Reprint) (p. 463)
Williams, Matt, illus. see Milan, Stefani.
Williams, Matt, jt. auth. see Milan, Stefani.
Williams, Maude Newell. Least of These in Colombia (Classic Reprint) (p. 1259)
Williams, Megan K. Maddy's Amazing African Birthday Vallecchi, Alessandro et al, photos by. (p. 1374)
Williams, Mel. Robert Pattinson: Fated for Fame. (p. 1890)
—Stars in the Arena: Meet the Hotties of the Hunger Games. (p. 2107)
—Taylor Lautner: Overnight Sizzlin' Sensation. (p. 2193)
Williams, Melissa. Crazy, Curly Chae. (p. 469)
Williams, Melissa, compiled by. I Write Short Stories by Kids for Kids Vol. 8. (p. 1086)
Williams, Melissa M., compiled by. I Write Short Stories by Kids for Kids Vol. 8. (p. 1086)
Williams, Melyssa. Shadows Lost. (p. 1998)
Williams, Mercedes. Little Tree. (p. 1329)
Williams, Merriwether, jt. auth. see Jakobs, D.
Williams, Michael. Diamond Boy. (p. 538)
—Now Is the Time for Running. (p. 1628)
Williams, Michael, jt. auth. see Van Ee, Yvonne E.
Williams, Michael E. Bowtown Curvy. Gierhart, Steve & Duke, Doyle, eds. (p. 266)
Williams, Mignon. Somebody Save Scotty. Knight, Rhonda, illus. (p. 2060)
Williams, Minnie Olcott. Indiana Authors: A Representative Collection for Young People (Classic Reprint) (p. 1116)
Williams, Morgan. Careers for People Who Love Kids (p. 329)
—Careers for People Who Love Traveling (p. 329)
Williams, Nana & Wiltz, Kaley. Yes You Can. Illustrations, rks, illus. (p. 2521)
Williams, Nancy E., ed. see Barnes, Brenda J.
Williams, Nancy E., ed. see Carty, Amy.
Williams, Nancy E., ed. see Davis, Mary Perrone.
Williams, Nancy E., ed. see Dixon, Dallas L.
Williams, Nancy E., ed. see Ghani, Samna.
Williams, Nancy E., ed. see Ratliff, Barbara Tiffany.
Williams, Nancy Noel. Don't Lose It, Reuse It. (p. 583)
—Have a Ball. (p. 939)
—Rice Is Nice. (p. 1876)
Williams, Naomi Jean. Annabell Unlocks the Case in London. (p. 98)
—Dave Saves the City That Never Sleeps. (p. 510)
—Jamie Wraps It up in Rio. (p. 1157)
Williams, Nat. Little Chick. (p. 1313)
—Little Chick Gets Bullied! (p. 1313)
Williams, Natalee S. Nat's Inspirational Treats: Words of Encouragement for Kids in Business. (p. 1579)
Williams, Natalie J. & Williams, Deanna. Adventures of a Pretty Awesome Kid: Melvins Gift. (p. 21)
Williams, Nate, illus. see Bodden, Valerie.
Williams, Nate, illus. see Riggs, Kate.
Williams, Nate & Snow, Virginia Brimhall. Spring Walk (p. 2092)
Williams, Neil. Little Bear Sam from Greeley Square. (p. 1311)
Williams, Neil Wynn. Electric Theft (Classic Reprint) (p. 631)
Williams, Nicholas, jt. auth. see Carroll, Lewis, pseud.
Williams, Nicholas, jt. auth. see Grahame, Kenneth.
Williams, Nicholas, tr. see Nesbit, E.
Williams, Nicole. Almost Impossible. (p. 57)
—Clash (p. 399)
—Crash (p. 467)
—Crush (p. 480)
—Girl Upside Down. (p. 837)
—Trusting You & Other Lies. (p. 2296)
Williams, Noele. Little Red Frog. Kern, Debb, illus. (p. 1326)
Williams, Olin Dale. Precious Love. (p. 1786)
Williams, Oneeka. Dr. Dee Dee Dynamo: Ice Worm Intervention. (p. 591)
—Dr Dee Dee Dynamo Bee More Breakthru Coloring Book. (p. 591)
—Dr. Dee Dee Dynamo's Beemore Breakthru. Bouthyette, Valerie, illus. (p. 591)
—Dr. Dee Dee Dynamo's Meteorite Mission. (p. 591)
Williams, Owen, illus. see Goddard, Sam.
Williams, Pam. Remixing Toys. (p. 1865)
—Starting a Makerspace. (p. 2108)
Williams, Pamela. Sasquatch Summer. (p. 1936)
Williams, Patrick A. Erin's Gift. Shauf, Rob, illus. (p. 659)
Williams, Paula. Tom's Wish. Graham, Carl, illus. (p. 2259)
Williams, Peggy Ann. Peaks: Land of the Sky Number; December, 1926 (Classic Reprint) (p. 1709)
Williams, Pharrell. Happy! (p. 920)
Williams, R. L. Three Small Bears & Christmas. (p. 2235)
Williams, R. M. Freckles & His East Coast Adventure: R. M. Williams, Illustrated by Mary Cotter. (p. 780)
Williams, Rachel. Atlas of Adventures: A Collection of Natural Wonders, Exciting Experiences & Fun Festivities from the Four Corners of the Globe. Letherland, Lucy, illus. (p. 133)
—Illuminature: Discover 180 Animals with Your Magic Three Color Lens. Carnovsky, illus. (p. 1096)
—Little Pear Tree. Bowers, Jenny, illus. (p. 1324)
—Slow Down: 50 Mindful Moments in Nature. Hartas, Freya, illus. (p. 2039)
Williams, Rachel, illus. see Rogers, Debbie.
Williams, Rachel & Hawkins, Emily. Atlas of Animal Adventures: A Collection of Nature's Most Unmissable Events, Epic Migrations & Extraordinary Behaviours. Letherland, Lucy, illus. (p. 133)
Williams, Rachel, ed. Read to Your Baby Every Day: 30 Classic Nursery Rhymes to Read Aloud. (p. 1845)
Williams, Rain & Pirnat, Joyce. Houdini's Big Adventures: Finding a Forever Home. (p. 1007)
Williams, Rasheda Kamaria. Be Empowered: How to Live above & Beyond Life's Drama. (p. 177)
Williams, Raymond. House of Useful Things. (p. 1023)
—Tales from the Willow Tree. (p. 2183)
Williams, Raymond, illus. see Williams, Brenda May.
Williams, R.H. With the Border Ruffians: Memories of the Far West, 1852-1868 (Classic Reprint) (p. 2481)
Williams, Ricardo. Angel de Mi Guarda (Libro + CD) Chamorro, Marco, illus. (p. 85)
—Monstruos (Libro + CD) Sozapato, illus. (p. 1498)
—Verde Manzana. Cornejo, Eulalia, illus. (p. 2351)
—Verde Manzana (Libro + CD) Cornejo, Eulalia, illus. (p. 2351)
Williams, Richard Brady, ed. Stonewall's Prussian Mapmaker: The Journals of Captain Oscar Hinrichs. (p. 2122)
Williams, Rob, illus. see Eldridge, Sherrie.
Williams, Robert & Wood, Robert. Stacked Deck: A Program to Prevent Problem Gambling: Facilitator's Guide. (p. 2099)
Williams, Robert F. Mephistophiles in England, or the Confessions of a Prime Minister, Vol. 2 of 2 (Classic Reprint) (p. 1447)
Williams, Robert Fellow. Shakespeare the Admirers & of the Other Illustrious Spirits of the Golden Age of England, These Volumes: With True Humbleness, & Entire Devotedness Their the & Are Respectfully Inscribed (Classic Reprint) (p. 1999)
Williams, Robert Folkestone. Lady Eureka, or the Mystery, Vol. 3 Of 3: A Prophecy of the Future (Classic Reprint) (p. 1237)
—Lady Eureka, Vol. 2 Of 3: Or the Mystery; a Prophecy of the Future (Classic Reprint) (p. 1237)
—Maids of Honour, Vol. 1 Of 3: A Tale of the Court of George I (Classic Reprint) (p. 1383)
—Mephistophiles in England, Vol. 1 Of 2: Or the Confessions of a Prime Minister (Classic Reprint) (p. 1447)
—Secret Passion (Classic Reprint) (p. 1978)
—Shakspeare & His Friends, or the Golden Age of Merry England (Classic Reprint) (p. 1999)
—Shakspeare & His Friends, Vol. 1 Of 3: Or the Golden Age of Merry England (Classic Reprint) (p. 1999)
—Strawberry Hill: An Historical Novel (Classic Reprint) (p. 2139)
—Strawberry Hill, Vol. 2 Of 3: An Historical Novel (Classic Reprint) (p. 2139)
—Youth of Shakspeare (Classic Reprint) (p. 2536)
—Youth of Shakspeare, Vol. 2 of 3 (Classic Reprint) (p. 2536)
Williams, Robert L., jt. auth. see Long, James D.
Williams, Robin. Adventures of Great George. (p. 23)
Williams, Rozanne. A-Counting We Will Go. (p. 1)
—All Through the Week with Cat & Dog. (p. 55)
—Barney Bear Gets Dressed. (p. 167)
—Bear Went over the Mountain. (p. 180)
—Birthday. (p. 233)
—Bugs Go Marching. (p. 292)
—Buttons, Buttons. (p. 304)
—By Myself or with My Friends. (p. 305)
—Can You Read a Map? (p. 318)
—Caring for Our Lizard. (p. 331)
—Cat & Dog at School. (p. 341)
—Cat & Dog Have Fun with Science. (p. 341)
—Cat & Dog Make the Biggest, Best Sandwich. (p. 341)
—Cat & Dog on Playground Patrol. (p. 341)
—Cat, Dog & the Tooth Fairy. (p. 341)
—City Mouse & Country Mouse. (p. 395)
—Collecting Things Is Fun! (p. 414)
—Colors of My Day. (p. 426)
—Come See My Bugs. (p. 428)
—Costume Parade. (p. 457)
—Count & Add with Me! (p. 458)
—Crayola Counting Book. (p. 468)
—Dog. (p. 575)
—Families Share. (p. 702)
—Five Little Monsters. (p. 744)
—Five Little Monsters Went to School. (p. 744)
—Four Seasons. (p. 772)

W

Williamson, Judithe Anne. Princess Kara in Her Village (p. 1797)
—Tiny with a Twist: Book 3 of the Tiny Village Series (p. 2250)
Williamson, Julia. Lion Sleeps Tonight. (p. 1306)
—Night of the Living. (p. 1607)
Williamson, Karen. Adam & Eve Conner, Sarah, illus. (p. 14)
—Christmas Story Barnard, Lucy, illus. (p. 387)
—First Easter Conner, Sarah, illus. (p. 736)
—Joseph Conner, Sarah, illus. (p. 1178)
—Lift the Flap Bible Anglicas, Louise, illus. (p. 1297)
—Mary & Martha Conner, Sarah, illus. (p. 1414)
—More Bible Sliders Selbert, Kathryn, illus. (p. 1504)
—My First Bible Stories Allen, Marie, illus. (p. 1540)
—My Little Life of Jesus Enright, Amanda, illus. (p. 1553)
—Noah & Other Stories Barnard, Lucy, illus. (p. 1615)
—Noah & the Animals Hanton, Sophie, illus. (p. 1615)
—Paul Conner, Sarah, illus. (p. 1706)
—Play-Time Noah Anglicas, Louise, illus. (p. 1759)
—Prodigal Son Conner, Sarah, illus. (p. 1804)
—Samuel Conner, Sarah, illus. (p. 1929)
—Wise Men's Story Barnard, Lucy, illus. (p. 2478)
—Zacchaeus Conner, Sarah, illus. (p. 2537)
Williamson, Karen, jt. auth. see David, Juliet.
Williamson, Karen & Rock, Lois. Good Samaritan Conner, Sarah & Allsopp, Sophie, illus. (p. 866)
Williamson, Katie, photos by see Ling, Mary & Dorling Kindersley Publishing Staff.
Williamson, Leah. Froggo Family Adventure. (p. 789)
Williamson, Linda. Groundhog Breakfast, Soft Petals, & a Roof That Don't Leak Too Much Mollett, Irene, illus. (p. 898)
Williamson, Linda, ed. see Williamson, Duncan.
Williamson, Linda K., illus. see Birkholz, Gay Lyn.
Williamson, Lisa. All about Mia. (p. 49)
—Art of Being Normal: A Novel. (p. 121)
—Malala Yousafzai (the First Names Series) Smith, Mike, illus. (p. 1391)
Williamson, Lisa Reid, illus. see Henderson, Rema Frazier.
Williamson, Liza. Emily to the Rescue. Keddy, Brian, illus. (p. 642)
Williamson, M. R. Can You See Me? (p. 319)
Williamson, Margaret. First Book of Bugs (Classic Reprint) (p. 735)
—John & Betty's History Visit (Classic Reprint) (p. 1172)
—John & Betty's Scotch History Visit (Classic Reprint) (p. 1172)
Williamson, Mary. My Beach Adventure. (p. 1531)
Williamson, Mary L. Life of Gen. Robert E. Lee: For Children, in Easy Words; Illustrated with Colored Plates (Classic Reprint) (p. 1294)
—Life of Robert E. Lee (Classic Reprint) (p. 1295)
Williamson, Melanie. Las Ruedas Del Autobús. (p. 1246)
Williamson, Melanie, illus. see Amador Family Staff & Barefoot Books Staff.
Williamson, Melanie, illus. see Barefoot Books Staff & Amador Family Staff.
Williamson, Melanie, illus. see Bedford, David.
Williamson, Melanie, illus. see Conway, David.
Williamson, Melanie, illus. see Don, Lari.
Williamson, Melanie, illus. see Sykes, Julie.
Williamson, Natalie. Rules We're Meant to Break: A Novel. (p. 1913)
Williamson, Pete, illus. see Bass, Guy.
Williamson, Pete, illus. see Davis, Mandie.
Williamson, Pete, illus. see Stevenson, Robert Louis.
Williamson, Roland. Love Shall Not Pass (Classic Reprint) (p. 1361)
—Star Well: And Other Stories (Classic Reprint) (p. 2105)
Williamson, Rose. Look at Me! Look at Me! Marts, Doreen, illus. (p. 1345)
Williamson, Ryan. Auston Matthews: Hockey Superstar. (p. 138)
—College Basketball Hot Streaks. (p. 415)
—David Pastrnak: Hockey Superstar. (p. 511)
—John Tavares: Hockey Superstar. (p. 1174)
—NFL Hot Streaks. (p. 1601)
—NHL Hot Streaks. (p. 1601)
—Nikita Kucherov: Hockey Superstar. (p. 1608)
—Olympic Hot Streaks. (p. 1651)
—Zion Williamson: Basketball Superstar. (p. 2541)
Williamson, Sarah. Cactus & Flower: A Book about Life Cycles. Williamson, Sarah, illus. (p. 307)
—Let's Go! (p. 1273)
—Where Are You? (p. 2435)
Williamson, Sharon. Grandma Says, Don't Climb the Peach Tree. (p. 878)
Williamson, Susan. Riding Lesson. McGannon, Cj, illus. (p. 1879)
Williamson, Thames. Flint Chipper (Classic Reprint) (p. 749)
Williamson, Victoria. Boy with the Butterfly Mind (p. 271)
—Fox Girl & the White Gazelle (p. 774)
Williamson, W. H. Prince's Marriage (Classic Reprint) (p. 1795)
Williamson, William Florence. Only to Be Married, a Novel, Vol. 1 of 3 (Classic Reprint) (p. 1664)
Williamson, William Henry. Average Woman (Classic Reprint) (p. 143)
Williams-Rogers, Steppi G. Through the Eyes of a Child. (p. 2237)
Williams-Sanchez, Valerie. Eddie & the Hot Cocoa Hot Rod. Russell, Brooklyn, illus. (p. 624)
—Isaiah & the Chocolate Mountain. (p. 1138)
—Lorena & the Magic Mocha Mirror. (p. 1349)
Williams-Sonoma & American Girl, American. American Girl Cooking: Recipes for Delicious Snacks, Meals & More. (p. 71)
Williams-Sonoma Staff. Junior Chef Cookbook. (p. 1190)
Williams-Walker, Carol. Our Dolls' Enchanted Wedding. Cenizal, I., illus. (p. 1677)
Willians, Rozanne Lanczak. Sing & Read with Greg & Steve All-in-One Pack. (p. 2023)
Williaon, Karen. Baby Jesus Conner, Sarah, illus. (p. 151)
—Daniel & the Lions Conner, Sarah, illus. (p. 502)
—David & Goliath Conner, Sarah, illus. (p. 510)
—My Little Bible Memory Game Enright, Amanda, illus. (p. 1552)
Williby, D. J. Larry & His Cat Named Blue. (p. 1244)
Willier, Russell, et al. Cree Healer & His Medicine Bundle: Revelations of Indigenous Wisdom—Healing Plants, Practices, & Stories. (p. 472)
Willier, Shelley, jt. auth. see Bouchard, David.
Willing, Jennie Fowler. Dozen Be's for Boys (Classic Reprint) (p. 591)
Willingham, Bob, jt. auth. see Chesterman, Barnaby.
Willink, Jocko. Marc's Mission: Way of the Warrior Kid (a Novel) Bozak, Jon, illus. (p. 1403)
—Way of the Warrior Kid: From Wimpy to Warrior the Navy SEAL Way: a Novel. Bozak, Jon, illus. (p. 2387)
Willis, A. F. Tales from the Middle Kingdom: Stories of China (Classic Reprint) (p. 2183)
Willis, Alexander A. Story of Laulii: A Daughter of Samoa (Classic Reprint) (p. 2131)
Willis, Brian L. Airlis. (p. 37)
—Kirus. (p. 1224)
Willis, Caleb, illus. see Thayer, Kristi.
Willis, Carolyn Sahaja Jean. Keisha's Wondrous Christmas. (p. 1208)
Willis, Chris. Dutch Clark: The Life of an NFL Legend & the Birth of the Detroit Lions (p. 611)
Willis, Cynthia Chapman. Dog Gone. (p. 576)
Willis, Danny. Why Pigeons? a Young Boy Discovers Gods Masterpieces. (p. 2458)
Willis, Drew, illus. see Bell, Hilari.
Willis, Drew, illus. see Freeman, Philip.
Willis, Drew, illus. see Packard, Edward.
Willis, Drew, illus. see Paulsen, Gary.
Willis, Drew, illus. see Weissman, Elissa Brent.
Willis, E. B. Make a Face Exercise Book: E. B. Willis Children's Exercise Book. Hunt, Sally K., photos by. (p. 1385)
Willis, Grant. Camosun, Vol. 30: June 1938 (Classic Reprint) (p. 315)
Willis, Helena, illus. see Widmark, Martin.
Willis Hudson, Cheryl, jt. ed. see Hudson, Wade.
Willis, Jaymie Janaye. Deal. (p. 519)
Willis, Jeanne. Blue Monster Wants It All! Desmond, Jenni, illus. (p. 249)
—Boa's Bad Birthday. Ross, Tony, illus. (p. 251)
—Caterpillar Dreams. Ross, Tony, illus. (p. 344)
—Chicken Clicking. Ross, Tony, illus. (p. 368)
—Como Era Yo Cuando Era un Bebe? (p. 432)
—Cow Tripped over the Moon: a Nursery Rhyme Emergency. Stewart, Joel, illus. (p. 464)
—Don't Go There! Bragadottir, Hrefna, illus. (p. 583)
—Dr Xargle's Book of Earth Tiggers. Ross, Tony, illus. (p. 592)
—Dr Xargle's Book of Earthlets. Ross, Tony, illus. (p. 592)
—Elephants Can't Jump! Reynolds, Adrian, illus. (p. 634)
—Empanada de Mamut. (p. 644)
—Flabby Cat & Slobby Dog. Ross, Tony, illus. (p. 745)
—Fly, Chick, Fly! Ross, Tony, illus. (p. 754)
—Frockodile. Laberis, Stephanie, illus. (p. 789)
—Goldilocks. Ross, Tony, illus. (p. 860)
—Goldilocks (a Hashtag Cautionary Tale) Ross, Tony, illus. (p. 860)
—Hippospotamus. Ross, Tony, illus. (p. 973)
—I'm in Charge! Jarvis, illus. (p. 1098)
—I'M Sure I Saw a Dinosaur. Reynolds, Adrian, illus. (p. 1099)
—Lucinda Belinda Melinda Mccool. Ross, Tony, illus. (p. 1364)
—Mammoth Pie. Ross, Tony, illus. (p. 1393)
—Never Too Little to Love. Fearnley, Jan, illus. (p. 1590)
—Not Just a Book. Ross, Tony, illus. (p. 1623)
—Penguin Pandemonium. (p. 1716)
—Pet Person. Ross, Tony, illus. (p. 1726)
—Poles Apart. Jarvis, illus. (p. 1770)
—Prince Charmless. Ross, Tony, illus. (p. 1794)
—Really Rude Rhino. (p. 1851)
—Shamanka. (p. 1999)
—Slug Needs a Hug! Ross, Tony, illus. (p. 2039)
—Stardust. Smith, Briony May, illus. (p. 2106)
—Supercat vs the Party Pooper (Supercat, Book 2) (p. 2159)
—Supercat vs the Pesky Pirate (Supercat, Book 3) (p. 2159)
—Tadpole's Promise. Ross, Tony, illus. (p. 2175)
—Tale of Georgie Grub. Chamberlain, Margaret, illus. (p. 2179)
—Tell Me a Story, Rory. Clifton Brown, Holly, illus. (p. 2201)
—T-Rex Who Lost His Specs! Ross, Tony, illus. (p. 2174)
—Troll Stinks. Ross, Tony, illus. (p. 2290)
—Upside down Babies. Reynolds, Adrian, illus. (p. 2339)
—We're Going to a Party! Ross, Tony, illus. (p. 2400)
—Who's in the Loo? Reynolds, Adrian, illus. (p. 2453)
Willis, Jeanne, et al. Best Bear in All the World. Burgess, Mark, illus. (p. 205)
Willis, Jerrne. Dinosaur Olympics. Robins, Arthur, illus. (p. 549)
—Dinosaur Scramble. Robins, Arthur, illus. (p. 549)
Willis, John. Airport. (p. 37)
—Baboon. (p. 148)
—Biological Adaptations. (p. 229)
—Carnivorous Plants. (p. 332)
—Herbivores. (p. 957)
—Moto X. (p. 1511)
—Natural Resources. (p. 1580)
—Orca. (p. 1669)
—Piranha. (p. 1749)
Willis, John, jt. auth. see Austic, Greg.
Willis, John, jt. auth. see Daly, Ruth.
Willis, John, jt. auth. see Furstinger, Nancy.
Willis, John, jt. auth. see Gagne, Tammy.
Willis, John, jt. auth. see Gleisner, Jenna Lee.
Willis, John, jt. auth. see Lomberg, Michelle.
Willis, John, jt. auth. see Siemens, Jared.
Willis, John, jt. auth. see Spalding, Maddie.
Willis, John, jt. auth. see Whelan, Piper.
Willis, John, jt. auth. see Woods, Bob.
Willis, John, jt. auth. see York, M. J.
Willis, John & Gillespie, Katie. Seasons. (p. 1972)
—Stars. (p. 2106)
—Taste. (p. 2192)
Willis Jr., Joseph H. Silly the Scarecrow. (p. 2019)
Willis, Kathryn. Coraddi, Vol. 24: April May, 1920 (Classic Reprint) (p. 452)
—Coraddi, Vol. 24: Magazine of the North Carolina College; November, 1919 (Classic Reprint) (p. 452)
—Coraddi, Vol. 24: Magazine of the North Carolina College; February-March, 1920 (Classic Reprint) (p. 452)
Willis, Kathy. Botanicum: Welcome to the Museum. Scott, Katie, illus. (p. 264)
Willis, Kip N. Kid That Needed a Pet. (p. 1213)
Willis, Laurie, ed. see Greenhaven Press Editors.
Willis, Laurie, ed. Culture of Beauty. (p. 484)
—Electronic Devices in Schools. (p. 632)
—Exercise & Fitness. (p. 676)
—Extremism. (p. 688)
—Holocaust. (p. 989)
—Teen Parenting. (p. 2199)
Willis, Meredith Sue. Blazing Pencils. (p. 243)
—Meli's Way. (p. 1443)
Willis, N. P. Loiterings of Travel, Vol. 1 of 3 (Classic Reprint) (p. 1340)
—Out-Doors at Idlewild, or the Shaping of a Home on the Banks of the Hudson (Classic Reprint) (p. 1682)
—Pencillings by the Way: Written During Some Years of Residence & Travel in France, Italy, Greece, Asia Minor, Turkey, & England (Classic Reprint) (p. 1715)
Willis, N. Parker. Fun-Jottings: Or, Laughs I Have Taken a Pen to (Classic Reprint) (p. 799)
Willis, Nathaniel. Youth's Companion, Vol. 3: May 28, 1829 May 19, 1830 (Classic Reprint) (p. 2536)
—Youth's Companion, Vol. 4: May 26, 1830 May 18, 1381 (Classic Reprint) (p. 2536)
Willis, Nathaniel Parker. Convalescent (Classic Reprint) (p. 446)
—Dashes at Life with a Free Pencil (Classic Reprint) (p. 508)
—Famous Persons & Places (Classic Reprint) (p. 704)
—Fun-Jottings, or Laughs I Have Taken a Pen to (Classic Reprint) (p. 799)
—Health Trip to the Tropics (Classic Reprint) (p. 943)
—Inklings of Adventure, Vol. 1 of 2 (Classic Reprint) (p. 1120)
—Legendary, Consisting of Original Pieces, Vol. 2: Principally Illustrative of American History, Scenery, & Manners (Classic Reprint) (p. 1263)
—Letters from under a Bridge (Classic Reprint) (p. 1280)
—Life, Here & There: Or Sketches of Society & Adventure at Far-Apart Times & Places (Classic Reprint) (p. 1291)
—Miscellaneous Works of N. P. Willis (Classic Reprint) (p. 1476)
—Pencillings by the Way: Written During Some Years of Residence & Travel in Europe (Classic Reprint) (p. 1715)
—Pencillings by the Way (Classic Reprint) (p. 1715)
—Pencillings by the Way, Vol. 2 of 2 (Classic Reprint) (p. 1715)
—People I Have Met: Or Pictures of Society & People of Mark, Drawn under a Thin Veil of Fiction (Classic Reprint) (p. 1718)
—Poems of Early & after Years - Scholar's Choice Edition. (p. 1765)
—Prose Writings of Nathaniel Parker Willis (Classic Reprint) (p. 1807)
—Romance of Travel: Comprising Tales of Five Lands (Classic Reprint) (p. 1900)
—Rural Letters & Other Records of Thought at Leisure: Written in the Intervals of More Hurried Literary Labor (Classic Reprint) (p. 1916)
—Winter Wreath (Classic Reprint) (p. 2476)
Willis, Oliver Rivington, jt. auth. see Wood, Alphonso.
Willis, Peter, illus. see Pattison, Darcy.
Willis, Sabien T., illus. see Dumas, Dionne Blackmon.
Willis, Stephen J. Spirits of the Dead: A Supernatural Adventure. (p. 2084)
Willis, Tania, illus. see Debram, Mio.
Willis, Terry. Book of Poems about Minecraft. (p. 259)
—Tale of Rusty the Squirrel. (p. 2179)
Willis, Uncle. Mrs. Partington's Mother Goose's Melodies: Containing All the Original Rhymes of Mother Goose, Besides Many Others of a Similar Character, & Full Directions for Costumes & Acting Some of the Principal Pieces; with a Choice Selection of Music, Especial. (p. 1522)
Willis, W. N. White Slaves of London (Classic Reprint) (p. 2445)
Willis-Crowley, Kate, illus. see O'Connor, Jenny.
Willison, John. Balm of Gilead for Healing a Diseased Land: With the Glory of the Ministration of the Spirit; & a Scripture Prophecy of the Increase of Christ's Kingdom & the Destruction of Antichrist (Classic Reprint) (p. 162)
Willis-Sell, Melissa. Escapades of Nae. (p. 661)
Williston, Samuel Wendell. Synopsis of the North American Syrphidae (Classic Reprint) (p. 2173)
Williston, Seth. Lectures on the Moral Imperfection of Christians: Designed to Show, That While Sinless Perfection Is Obligatory on All, It Is Attained by None (Classic Reprint) (p. 1260)
Williston, Teresa Peirce. Japanese Fairy Tales (Classic Reprint) (p. 1160)
Willman, Lisa. Art & Culture: Patterns of the Past: Partitioning Shapes (Grade 2) (p. 120)
—Travel Adventures: Kruger National Park: Repeated Addition (Grade 2) (p. 2279)
Willman, Lisa A. Diseños Del Pasado: Partición de Figuras. (p. 557)
Willmore, Alex. It's MY Sausage. Willmore, Alex, illus. (p. 1146)
Willmore, Alex, illus. see Conway, Sara.
Willmore, Alex, illus. see Donald, Alison.
Willmore, Alex, illus. see Grahame, Kenneth.
Willmore, Alex, illus. see Houran, Lori Haskins.
Willmore, Alex, illus. see Linn, Susie.
Willmore, Alex, illus. see Skwish, Emily.
Willmore, Alex, illus. see Sweeney, Joan.
Willmore, Alex, illus. see Tarsky, Sue.
Willmore, Alex, illus. see Thomas Nelson & Sons Staff.
Willmore, Alex, illus. see Tiger Tales.
Willmore, J. Selden. Key to the Exercises in the Spoken Arabic of Egypt (Classic Reprint) (p. 1212)
Willmott, Erica. Sockz at Christmas. (p. 2054)
—Sockz in New York City. (p. 2054)
—Sockz in Paris. (p. 2054)
Willmott, H. P., et al. World War II. (p. 2505)
Willmott, Poppy. Importance of Being Ivy. (p. 1102)
Willner-Pardo, Gina. Hard Kind of Promise. (p. 929)
Willocks, Tim. Doglands. (p. 577)
Willoughby, Barrett. Where the Sun Swings North (Classic Reprint) (p. 2439)
Willoughby, Bryan, et al. Walking God's Trail: End of the Spear. (p. 2372)
Willoughby, F. Fairy Guardians (Classic Reprint) (p. 696)
Willoughby, Frank. For Zion's Sake: A Tale of Real Life. (p. 764)
—For Zion's Sake: A Tale of Real Life (Classic Reprint) (p. 764)
Willoughby, Jennie Evelyn. Written Exercises on Direct & Indirect Quotations (Classic Reprint) (p. 2514)
Willoughby, Katrina. So You Want to Learn about Reptiles & Amphibians. (p. 2051)
Willoughby, Nick. Digital Filmmaking for Kids for Dummies. (p. 546)
—Making YouTube Videos: Star in Your Won Video! (p. 1390)
Willoughby, Yuko, illus. see Carvin, Rose-Mae.
Willoughby, Yuko, illus. see Hershey, Katherine.
Willoughby, Yuko, illus. see Lyster, R. Iona.
Willoughby, Yuko, illus. see Piepgrass, Arlene & Hershey, Katherine.
Willoughby, Yuko, illus. see Weitzel, Karen E.
Willow, Anwyn. Lola: The Lonely Vampire. (p. 1340)
Willow, Bim. I-Can't & I-Can! Morales, Jose, illus. (p. 1063)
Willowmeana. Memoirs of the In-Between. (p. 1445)
Willowraven, Aidana, illus. see Cioffi, Karen.
WillowRaven, Aidana, illus. see Laughter, Jim.
WillowRaven, Aidana, illus. see Sansone, V. K.
Willows, Vicky. Clever Critters. (p. 404)
—Colossal Creatures. (p. 426)
Willows, Vicky, jt. auth. see Stamper, Judith Bauer.
Willowtree, Sabbath Oshel. Banshee & Nightshade. Oshel, Susie L., ed. (p. 164)
Wills, Anna. Who Believes What? Exploring the World's Major Religions. Tomm, Nora, illus. (p. 2446)
Wills, Anthony E. Football Romance: A College Play in Four Acts (Classic Reprint) (p. 762)
—Just Plain Folks: A Comedy Drama of Rural Life in Three Acts (Classic Reprint) (p. 1194)
Wills, Aurelia. Someone I Wanted to Be. (p. 2060)
Wills, Barbro K. E., tr. see Wills, Michael E.
Wills, C. I. Behind an Eastern Veil: A Plain Tale, of Events Occurring in the Experience of a Lady, Who Had an Unique Opportunity of Observing, the Inner Life of Ladies of the Upper Class in Persia (Classic Reprint) (p. 192)
Wills, C. J. Laura Ruthven's Widowhood, Vol. 1 (Classic Reprint) (p. 1252)
Wills, Charles J. Pit Town Coronet, Vol. 3 Of 3: A Family Mystery (Classic Reprint) (p. 1751)
Wills, Charles James. In the Land of the Lion & Sun, or Modern Persia: Being Experiences of Life in Persia During a Residence of Fifteen Years in Various Parts of That Country from 1866 to 1881 (Classic Reprint) (p. 1109)
—Laura Ruthven's Widowhood, Vol. 2 (Classic Reprint) (p. 1252)
—Pit Town Coronet, Vol. 1 Of 3: A Family Mystery (Classic Reprint) (p. 1751)
—Was He Justified? A Novel (Classic Reprint) (p. 2381)
Wills, Cheryl. Emancipation of Grandpa Sandy Wills. Pearson, Randell, illus. (p. 640)
Wills, Fred. Just Stand by Me: Working Together in Groups. Wills, Fred, illus. (p. 1194)
Wills, Henrietta. Wind Twins & the Oracle of Secrets. (p. 2471)
Wills, Joseph. World. (p. 2501)
Wills, Julia. Fleeced! an Aries Adventure. (p. 747)
Wills, Mary H. Summer in Europe (Classic Reprint) (p. 2149)
—Winter in California (Classic Reprint) (p. 2475)
Wills, Sarah-Leigh, illus. see Bennett, Clayre.
Wills, Sarah-Leigh, illus. see Henwood, Jenny.
Wills, Sarah-Leigh, jt. auth. see Henwood, Jenny.
Wills, W. G. Notice to Quit, Vol. 2 of 3 (Classic Reprint) (p. 1625)
Wills, William Gorman. Notice to Quit, Vol. 1 of 3 (Classic Reprint) (p. 1625)
—Wife's Evidence: A Novel (Classic Reprint) (p. 2461)
Wills, William Henry. Old Leaves, Gathered from Household Words (Classic Reprint) (p. 1646)
—Poets' Wit & Humour (Classic Reprint) (p. 1767)
Wills, Z. J., jt. auth. see Wills, R. E.
Willsea, Hedley. Heath of the Graves. (p. 946)
Willshire, W. H. Land of the Dawning: Being Facts Gleaned from Cannibals in the Australian Stone Age (Classic Reprint) (p. 1242)
Willsie, Honore. Benefits Forgot: A Story of Lincoln & Mother Love (Classic Reprint) (p. 199)
—Forbidden Trail (Classic Reprint) (p. 764)
—Heart of the Desert: Kut-Le of the Desert (Classic Reprint) (p. 945)
—Judith of the Godless Valley (Classic Reprint) (p. 1185)
—Still Jim (Classic Reprint) (p. 2119)
Willson, Beckles. Harold: An Experiment (Classic Reprint) (p. 931)
Willson, Dixie. Honey Bear. (p. 999)
—Pinky Pup & the Empty Elephant (Classic Reprint) (p. 1747)
Willson, Marcius. Fifth Reader of the Popular Series (Classic Reprint) (p. 724)
—Fifth Reader of the School & Family Series (Classic Reprint) (p. 724)
—First Reader of the School & Family Series (Classic Reprint) (p. 739)
—Fourth Reader of the Popular Series (Classic Reprint) (p. 773)
—Fourth Reader of the School & Family Series (Classic Reprint) (p. 773)
—School & Family Primer: Introductory to the Series of School & Family Readers (Classic Reprint) (p. 1945)
—Second Reader of the School & Family Series (Classic Reprint) (p. 1974)
—Third Reader, of a Grade Between the Second & Third Readers of the School & Family Series (Classic Reprint) (p. 2222)

W

Wilson, Herbert Michael. Topographic Surveying: Including Geographic, Exploratory, & Military Mapping, with Hints on Camping, Emergency Surgery, & Photography (Classic Reprint) (p. 2264)
Wilson, Herbert Wrigley. Hush: Or the Hydrophone Service (Classic Reprint) (p. 1055)
Wilson, Howard E. Our Ways of Living: Where Our Ways of Living Come from (Classic Reprint) (p. 1681)
Wilson, J. M., jt. auth. see Simpson, Selwyn G.
Wilson, Jacqueli. Mon Amie Pour la Vie. (p. 1491)
Wilson, Jacqueline. Beauty & the Beast. Kavanagh, Peter, illus. (p. 185)
—Best Friends. Sharratt, Nick, illus. (p. 206)
—Cookie. Sharratt, Nick, illus. (p. 446)
—Double Vie de Charlotte. (p. 589)
—Kiss. (p. 1224)
—Lola Rose. (p. 1340)
—Maman Ma Soeur et Moi. (p. 1392)
—Mi Hermana Es lo Peor / the Worst Thing about My Sister. (p. 1455)
—Mi Mamá Es la Bomba / My Mom Is the Bomb: the Illustrated Mom. (p. 1455)
—Monster Eyeballs. Lewis, Stephen, illus. (p. 1495)
—Nous Deux. (p. 1625)
—Nouv Defi Pour Jenny B. (p. 1625)
—Poisson d Avril. (p. 1768)
—Role en or Pour Jenny B. (p. 1898)
Wilson, James. Fire-Eater (Classic Reprint) (p. 732)
Wilson, James Mikel. Mr. Froggy's Dilemma. (p. 1518)
Wilson, Jamia. ABCs of AOC: Alexandria Ocasio-Cortez from a to Z. (p. 4)
—Big Ideas for Young Thinkers: 20 Questions about Life & the Universe. Pippins, Andrea, illus. (p. 221)
—Step into Your Power: 23 Lessons on How to Live Your Best Life. Pippins, Andrea, illus. (p. 2114)
—Young Gifted & Black: Meet 52 Black Heroes from Past & Present. Pippins, Andrea, illus. (p. 2531)
Wilson, Janet. LSU Night Before Christmas. Verrett, Michael, illus. (p. 1363)
—Our Earth: How Kids Are Saving the Planet (p. 1677)
—Our Future: How Kids Are Taking Action (p. 1678)
—Our Heroes: How Kids Are Making a Difference (p. 1678)
—Our Rights: How Kids Are Changing the World (p. 1680)
—Severn & the Day She Silenced the World (p. 1995)
—Shannen & the Dream for a School (p. 1999)
Wilson, Janet, illus. see Spalding, Andrea.
Wilson, Janice Marie. Eliana, Where Do Thoughts Come From? Windle, Shayda, illus. (p. 635)
Wilson, Jd. Volcano Girl. Roffler, Crystal H., ed. (p. 2366)
Wilson, Jeanette. Miniature Schnauzer. (p. 1472)
Wilson, Jennifer. New World Ashes. (p. 1598)
—New World Inferno. (p. 1598)
Wilson, Joe, jt. auth. see Rooney, Anne.
Wilson, John. Alchemist's Dream. (p. 41)
—And in the Morning. (p. 82)
—Battle Scars: Fields of Conflict: The American Civil War, Part Two. (p. 175)
—Bones (p. 255)
—Broken Arrow (p. 284)
—Crusade (p. 480)
—Crusade: The Heretic's Secret. Pt. 1 (p. 480)
—Death on the River (p. 521)
—Fiery Sky. (p. 723)
—Flags of War: Fields of Conflict-The American Civil War, Part One. (p. 746)
—Flames of the Tiger: Fields of Conflict—Germany 1945. (p. 746)
—Foresters: A Tale of Domestic Life (Classic Reprint) (p. 766)
—Ghost Moon (p. 827)
—Gold (p. 855)
—Grail. (p. 875)
—Little Hannah Lee: A Winter Story; from Lights & Shadows of Scottish Life; Adapted to Children (Classic Reprint) (p. 1318)
—Lost (p. 1352)
—Lost. (p. 1352)
—Lost Cause (p. 1353)
—Lost in Spain. (p. 1354)
—Stolen (p. 2120)
—Synopsis of British Plants, in Mr. Ray's Method: With Their Characters, Descriptions, Places of Growth, Time of Flowering, & Physical Virtues, According to the Most Accurate Observations, & the Best Modern Authors (Classic Reprint) (p. 2173)
—Third Act (p. 2222)
—Trials of Margaret Lyndsay (Classic Reprint) (p. 2286)
—Victorio's War (p. 2356)
—Wilson's Historical, Traditionary, & Imaginative Tales of the Borders, & of Scotland, Vol. 1: With a Glossary of Scotch Words (Classic Reprint) (p. 2470)
—Written in Blood (p. 2514)
Wilson, John, illus. see DiMare, Joseph S.
Wilson, John, illus. see Wilson, Angela.
Wilson, John Dover. Life in Shakespeare's England: A Book of Elizabethan Prose (Classic Reprint) (p. 1292)
Wilson, John Fleming. Land Claimers (Classic Reprint) (p. 1241)
—Princess of Sorry Valley (Classic Reprint) (p. 1798)
—Scouts of the Desert (Classic Reprint) (p. 1963)
Wilson, John Mackay. Historical, Traditionary, & Imaginative Tales of the Borders & of Scotland, Vol. 6: With an Illustrative Glossary of the Scottish Dialect (Classic Reprint) (p. 976)
—Selections from Tales of the Border's: And of Scotland (Classic Reprint) (p. 1986)
—Wilson's Historical, Traditionary, & Imaginative Tales of the Borders & of Scotland, Vol. 1: With an Illustrative Glossary of the Scottish Dialect (Classic Reprint) (p. 2470)
—Wilson's Historical, Traditionary, & Imaginative Tales of the Borders, & of Scotland, Vol. 2: With an Illustratius Glossary of the Scottish Dialect (Classic Reprint) (p. 2470)
—Wilson's Historical, Traditionary, & Imaginative, Tales of the Borders, & of Scotland, Vol. 2: With a Glossary of Scotch Words (Classic Reprint) (p. 2470)
—Wilson's Tales of the Borders & of Scotland, Vol. 2: Historical, Traditionary, & Imaginative (Classic Reprint) (p. 2470)
—Wilson's Tales of the Borders & of Scotland, Vol. 7: Historical, Traditionary, & Imaginative; with a Glossary (Classic Reprint) (p. 2470)
—Wilson's Tales of the Borders, & of Scotland, Vol. 3: Historical, Traditionary, & Imaginative (Classic Reprint) (p. 2470)
—Wilson's Tales of the Borders, & of Scotland, Vol. 1: Historical, Traditionary, & Imaginative; with a Glossary (Classic Reprint) (p. 2470)
Wilson, Jon. Statue of Liberty. (p. 2109)
—White House. (p. 2444)
Wilson, Joseph Kennard. Longcove Doings (Classic Reprint) (p. 1343)
Wilson, Judith Vt. Growing Smarter. Saghy, Christopher, illus. (p. 899)
Wilson, Jules. Child of This Earth. (p. 370)
Wilson, Julia. Voice, Vol. 1: June, 1929 (Classic Reprint) (p. 2365)
—Voice, Vol. 1: February, 1929 (Classic Reprint) (p. 2365)
Wilson, Julia Phelps. Leaves from My Diary: Containing Incidents Connected with a Sea Voyage Taken May 20, 1899, from New York to Naples (Classic Reprint) (p. 1259)
Wilson, Julia Rae. Most Miserable, Awful Day of the Year: A Mostly True Story on Forgiveness. Written for Children of All Ages. (p. 1508)
Wilson, Julius & Benchmark Education Co. Staff. I Was a 21st Century Civil War Reporter. (p. 1085)
Wilson, K. Anthony. Back to You. (p. 156)
Wilson, Karl M. Study of the Status of Composition in Kansas High Schools (Classic Reprint) (p. 2144)
Wilson, Karma. Baby, I Love You. Williams, Sam, illus. (p. 151)
—Bear Can't Sleep. Chapman, Jane, illus. (p. 179)
—Bear Counts. Chapman, Jane, illus. (p. 179)
—Bear Feels Scared. Chapman, Jane, illus. (p. 179)
—Bear Feels Sick. Chapman, Jane, illus. (p. 179)
—Bear Says Thanks. Chapman, Jane, illus. (p. 180)
—Bear Sees Colors. Chapman, Jane, illus. (p. 180)
—Bear Stays up for Christmas. Chapman, Jane, illus. (p. 180)
—Bear's Loose Tooth. Chapman, Jane, illus. (p. 180)
—Bear's New Friend. Chapman, Jane, illus. (p. 181)
—Beautiful Babies: A Touch-And-Feel Book. (p. 183)
—Big Bear, Small Mouse. Chapman, Jane, illus. (p. 216)
—Cow Loves Cookies. Hall, Marcellus, illus. (p. 464)
—Dog Named Doug. Myers, Matt, illus. (p. 576)
—Don't Be Afraid, Little Pip. Chapman, Jane, illus. (p. 582)
—Duddle Puck: The Puddle Duck. Hall, Marcellus, illus. (p. 609)
—Frog in the Bog. Rankin, Joan, illus. (p. 789)
—Hogwash! McMullan, Jim, illus. (p. 986)
—Mama, Why? Mendez, Simon, illus. (p. 1392)
—Mortimer's First Garden. Andreasen, Dan, illus. (p. 1507)
—Sleepyhead. Segal, John, illus. (p. 2037)
—Trick or Treat, Calico! Erdogan, Buket, illus. (p. 2287)
—What's in the Egg, Little Pip? Chapman, Jane, illus. (p. 2424)
—What's the Weather Inside? Blitt, Barry, illus. (p. 2426)
—Who Goes There? Currey, Anna, illus. (p. 2447)
Wilson, Karma & Chapman, Jane. Bear Snores On. (p. 180)
Wilson, Kate, illus. see Bentley, Paula.
Wilson, Kathleen Curtis. Adventurous Max Flax. (p. 30)
Wilson, Katie. 123s. (p. 2559)
—ABC's. (p. 4)
—Animals. (p. 93)
—Colors. (p. 426)
—Joy: A Celebration of Mindfulness. (p. 1184)
—Landmarks. (p. 1242)
—Numbers. (p. 1630)
—Peace: A Celebration of Mindfulness. (p. 1709)
—Sounds. (p. 2067)
Wilson, Katie, illus. see Flowerpot Press.
Wilson, Kay, illus. see Mika, Sharon Ann.
Wilson, Keith, ed. Aircraft. (p. 37)
Wilson, Kelly. Cameo, the Street Pony. (p. 314)
—Casper, the Spirited Arabian. (p. 339)
—Chessy, the Welsh Pony. (p. 366)
—Koolio: The Problem Pony. (p. 1231)
Wilson, Kelly B. Dandy, the Mountain Pony. (p. 501)
Wilson, Kendell, illus. see Wilson, Patsy Hobbs.
Wilson, Kip. White Rose. (p. 2445)
Wilson, Kris E. & Maurer, Toby. How Putter Learned His ABC's: An alphabet Book for Your Littlest Golfer. (p. 1034)
Wilson, Kyla. Stretch It Yoga. (p. 2141)
Wilson, L. L. W. United States History in Elementary Schools (Classic Reprint) (p. 2331)
Wilson, Lady Campbell. Letters from India (Classic Reprint) (p. 1279)
Wilson, Lakita. Lizzo: Breakout Artist. (p. 1337)
—Michelle Obama: Get to Know the Influential First Lady & Education Advocate. (p. 1458)
—Rosa Parks. (p. 1904)
—Thurgood Marshall. (p. 2238)
Wilson, Land. Sofia's Dream. O'Malley, Judy, ed. (p. 2054)
—Sofia's Dream. Cornelison, Sue, illus. (p. 2054)
Wilson, Laurie Harman. Treasures of Destiny. (p. 2283)
Wilson, Lesley. Oric & the Alchemist's Key. (p. 1670)
—Oric & the Lockton Castle Mystery (p. 1670)
Wilson, Liesl-Yvette. Balloon & a Bear. (p. 162)
Wilson, Lillian P. Fruit of Toil: And Other One-Act Plays (Classic Reprint) (p. 796)
Wilson, Lorna, illus. see Leighton, Noreen.
Wilson, Louis N. Bibliography of Child Study. (p. 214)
Wilson, Louise Latham. Case of Suspension: A Comedietta in One Act (Classic Reprint) (p. 336)
—Priscilla's Room (Classic Reprint) (p. 1801)
—Where Is Helen? (Classic Reprint) (p. 2437)
Wilson, Lucia. Adventures of Cedric the Bear. Bowes, Anne, illus. (p. 22)
Wilson, Lucy Langdon Williams. History Reader for Elementary Schools, 1898, Vol. 3: Arranged with Special Reference to Holidays; March, April (Classic Reprint) (p. 981)
—History Reader for Elementary Schools, Vol. 4: Arranged with Special Reference to Holidays; May, June (Classic Reprint) (p. 981)
—History Reader for Elementary Schools, Vol. 5: Arranged with Special Reference to Holidays (Classic Reprint) (p. 981)
—Nature Study in Elementary Schools: First Reader (Classic Reprint) (p. 1581)
—Nature Study in Elementary Schools: Second Reader; Myths, Stories, Poems (Classic Reprint) (p. 1581)
—Nature Study in Elementary Schools. (p. 1581)
—Nature Study in Elementary Schools Second: Reader, Myths, Stories, Poems (Classic Reprint) (p. 1581)
Wilson, Lucy Sarah Atkins. Fruits of Enterprize Exhibited in the Adventures of Belzoni in Egypt & Nubia: With an Account of His Discoveries in the Pyramids, among the Ruins of Cities, & in the Ancient Tombs (Classic Reprint) (p. 796)
—Scripture Histories for Little Children (Classic Reprint) (p. 1966)
—Visit to Grove Cottage: For the Entertainment & Instruction of Children (Classic Reprint) (p. 2362)
Wilson, Lynda Farrington, illus. see Shan Shan, Kathryn Velikanje.
Wilson, Lynda Farrington, illus. see Shan Shan, Kathryn.
Wilson, Lynda Farrington, illus. see Velikanje, Kathryn.
Wilson, Lynda Farrington, illus. see Yacio, Jennifer Gilpin.
Wilson, M. Fairy's Gift. (p. 698)
Wilson, M. A. Adventure on Whalebone Island. (p. 19)
—Mystery of the Missing Mask. (p. 1570)
—SOS at Night. (p. 2066)
Wilson, Mabel Fitzroy. When the World Went Wry (Classic Reprint) (p. 2434)
Wilson, Marcius. School & Family Primer: Introductory to the Series of School & Family Readers (Classic Reprint) (p. 1945)
Wilson, Mark. Owling: Enter the World of the Mysterious Birds of the Night. (p. 1689)
Wilson, Mark, illus. see McLaughlin, Richard.
Wilson, Marlys, jt. auth. see Henne, R. J.
Wilson, Marshall, jt. auth. see Wilson, Robert.
Wilson, Martin. What They Always Tell Us. (p. 2420)
Wilson, Matthew. Scrooge & Santa GN. (p. 1966)
Wilson, Megan, illus. see Whitley, Jeremy.
Wilson, Melvin Douglas. Jimmy's Got a Gun: The Crash Brothers Forever. (p. 1169)
—Parable of the Spirit That Whispers: Study for a Bright Future. (p. 1698)
Wilson, Meredith, illus. see Adcox, Norman.
Wilson, Mg. History Mashups for Teens: From Lou Gehrig to Derek Jeter. (p. 977)
—History Mashups for Teens: From Sleeping Beauty to Beyonce. (p. 977)
Wilson, Michael R. Endocrine System: Hormones, Growth, & Development. (p. 650)
—Frequently Asked Questions about How the Teen Brain Works. (p. 784)
—Hunger: Food Insecurity in America. (p. 1052)
—Hunger: Food Insecurity in the United States. (p. 1052)
—Living a Heart-Healthy Life. (p. 1332)
Wilson, Michelle Longega. Dangerously Deep / Acque Pericolose (a Bilingual Book in English & Italian) (p. 502)
Wilson, Minden. History of Behar Indigo Factories: Reminiscences of Behar; Tirhoot & Its Inhabitants of the Past; History of Behar Light Horse Volunteers (Classic Reprint) (p. 977)
—History of Behar Indigo Factories; Reminiscences of Behar; Tirhoot & Its Inhabitants of the Past; History of Behar Light Horse Volunteers. (p. 977)
Wilson, Miriam. Spirit of Christmas: An Original Fantasy in Two Short Acts (Classic Reprint) (p. 2083)
Wilson, Mitchell. My Brother, My Enemy (Classic Reprint) (p. 1534)
Wilson, Mollie. Duck Tape 2. (p. 608)
Wilson, N. D. Chestnut King (100 Cupboards Book 3) (p. 366)
—Dandelion Fire. (p. 500)
—Door Before (100 Cupboards Prequel) (p. 585)
—Dragon's Tooth. (p. 596)
—Dragon's Tooth (Ashtown Burials #1) (p. 596)
—Drowned Vault (Ashtown Burials #2) (p. 606)
—Empire of Bones (Ashtown Burials #3) (p. 645)
—Hello, Ninja. Dickison, Forrest, illus. (p. 951)
—Hello, Ninja. Hello, Georgie. Dickison, Forrest, illus. (p. 951)
—Outlaws of Time #2: the Song of Glory & Ghost. (p. 1685)
—Outlaws of Time #3: the Last of the Lost Boys. (p. 1685)
—Outlaws of Time: the Legend of Sam Miracle. (p. 1685)
Wilson, Nancy. Our Mother Tongue: An Introductory Guide to English Grammar. (p. 1679)
Wilson, Natashya. Bats. (p. 173)
—Bears. (p. 180)
—Bears / Osos. (p. 180)
—How to Draw the Life & Times of William Howard Taft. (p. 1041)
Wilson, Nathaniel. Jessie's Big Move. Shoopik, Marina, illus. (p. 1165)
Wilson, Nicole. Callie Gang: Who Said Cats Don't Talk? (p. 312)
Wilson, Norah & Doherty, Heather. Embrace the Night. (p. 641)
Wilson, Obed Gray. My Adventures in the Sierras (Classic Reprint) (p. 1531)
Wilson, Olivia, illus. see Gilbert, Jon.
Wilson, P. A. Elven Stones: Family: an Elven Legend Quest. (p. 640)
—Elven Stones: Abundance: an Elven Legend Quest. (p. 640)
—Elven Stones; Orphan. (p. 640)
Wilson, Patricia. Rocking Horse & the Fighting Fish. (p. 1895)
Wilson, Patricia P. Rocking Horse & the Fighting Fish. (p. 1895)
Wilson, Patrick. Ropes & Knots for Survival. Carney, John, ed. (p. 1903)
—Survival Equipment. Carney, John, ed. (p. 2164)
—Survival First Aid. Carney, John, ed. (p. 2164)
—Surviving by Trapping, Fishing, & Eating Plants. Carney, John, ed. (p. 2165)
—Surviving Natural Disasters. Carney, John, ed. (p. 2165)
—Surviving with Navigation & Signaling. Carney, John, ed. (p. 2165)
Wilson, Patsy Hobbs. Holding the Father's Hand. Wilson, Kendell, illus. (p. 987)
Wilson, Patten. Nature Round the House (Classic Reprint) (p. 1581)
Wilson, Patten, jt. auth. see Bryant, Sara Cone.
Wilson, Paul. Screech Owl: Dec. , 1932 (Classic Reprint) (p. 1964)
Wilson, Paula M. Cavachon: Cavalier King Charles Spaniels Meet Bichon Frises! (p. 347)
—Cockapoo: Cocker Spaniels Meet Poodles! (p. 410)
—Cute & Unusual Pets. (p. 491)
—Hedgehogs. (p. 947)
—Mini Pigs. (p. 1472)
—Miniature Horses. (p. 1472)
—Sugar Gliders. (p. 2147)
Wilson, Peter L., jt. ed. see Mandl, Dave.
Wilson, Phil, illus. see Brown, Charlotte Lewis & Brown, Charlotte L.
Wilson, Phil, illus. see DeLand, M. Maitland.
Wilson, Phil, illus. see Livshits, Larisa.
Wilson, Philip, retold by. Celtic Fairy Tales: Sixteen Mystical Myths & Legends from the Celtic Lands. (p. 351)
—Irish Fairy Tales: Sixteen Enchanting Myths & Legends from Ireland. (p. 1134)
—Scottish Fairytales: Sixteen Magical Myths & Legends from the Highlands & Islands. (p. 1962)
—Welsh Fairytales: Sixteen Mysterious Myths & Legends from the Hills & Valleys of Wales. (p. 2400)
Wilson, Rachel M. Don't Touch. (p. 584)
Wilson, Ray. Kelsey's Lessons on Africa Vol 2. (p. 1209)
Wilson, Raylene Jenee, illus. see Whitmore, Hugh.
Wilson, Rene. Kenny Chesney. (p. 1209)
Wilson, Richard. Russian Story Book: Containing Tales from the Song-Cycles of Kiev & Novgorod & Other Early Sources (Classic Reprint) (p. 1917)
—Russian Story Book. Pape, Frank C., illus. (p. 1917)
Wilson, Richard Henry. Preposition a, the Relation of Its Meanings Studied in Old French, Vol. 1: Dissertation Presented to the Board of the University Studies of the John Hopkins University for the Degree of Doctor of Philosophy, June 1898; Situation (Classic Reprint) (p. 1787)
—Preposition À, the Relation of Its Meanings Studied in Old French, Vol. 1: Dissertation Presented to the Board of the University Studies of the John Hopkins University for the Degree of Doctor of Philosophy, June 1898; Situation (Classic Reprint) (p. 1787)
—Venus of Cadiz: An Extravaganza (Classic Reprint) (p. 2351)
Wilson, Rob, illus. see Blanco, Alberto.
Wilson, Robert. In the Land of the Tui 1894: My Journal in New Zealand (Classic Reprint) (p. 1109)
Wilson, Robert Burns. Until the Day Break: A Novel (Classic Reprint) (p. 2336)
Wilson, Robert C. Archive, Vol. 51: October, 1937 (Classic Reprint) (p. 111)
Wilson, Robert H. Wilmerding Life, Vol. 7: March, 1910 (Classic Reprint) (p. 2470)
Wilson, Roberta, illus. see Jacobson, John.
Wilson, Robin M., ed. see Dell, Jacob J. & Dell, Rachel E.
Wilson, Rock. If I Had My Way—/By Rock S. Wilson ; Illustrated by Carol Dixon. Dixon, Carol, illus. (p. 1091)
Wilson, Roman. How Does a Battery Work? (p. 1030)
Wilson, Romer. Grand Tour (Classic Reprint) (p. 877)
—Martin Schuler (Classic Reprint) (p. 1411)
Wilson, Ron. Wolfpack: the Complete Collection. (p. 2484)
Wilson, Ron, jt. illus. see Kirby, Jack.
Wilson, Ron, et al. Master of Kung Fu Epic Collection: Weapon of the Soul. (p. 1418)
Wilson, Ros. Bonkers Boris Meets the Mayor. (p. 256)
Wilson, Rosalee. Mushy Mouse Tale. (p. 1528)
Wilson, Rosie. Discover Iran. (p. 554)
—Discover Poland. (p. 554)
—Fashion Industry. (p. 712)
—Media & Communications Industry. (p. 1436)
Wilson, Rosie & Ward, Chris. Discover Poland. (p. 554)
—Discover South Africa. (p. 555)
Wilson, Sam, illus. see Wilson, Todd.
Wilson, Samuel. George Paull of Benita, West Africa. (p. 819)
—George Paull, of Benita, West Africa: A Memoir (Classic Reprint) (p. 819)
Wilson, Samuel Graham. Mariam: A Romance of Persia. (p. 1404)
—Mariam: A Romance of Persia (Classic Reprint) (p. 1404)
Wilson, Samuel Sheridan. Anglo-Greek Primer, or First Step to a Practical Knowledge of the English & Greek Languages (Classic Reprint) (p. 87)
Wilson, Samuel Troy. America ABC Board Book. Chan, Irene, illus. (p. 69)
Wilson, Sandra. Anxious Alligator. (p. 104)
—Bravo Bear. (p. 277)
—Courageous Caterpillar. (p. 462)
—Determined Dog. (p. 535)
—Dino Stars. (p. 548)
—Empathy Elephant. (p. 644)
—EXcited Xerus. (p. 676)
—Fabulous Flamingo. (p. 692)
—Grateful Giraffe. (p. 881)
—Hopeful Hippo. (p. 1002)
—Impatient Iguana. (p. 1102)
—Jealous Jaguar. (p. 1162)
—Lovable Lion. (p. 1358)
—Messy Monkey. (p. 1452)
—Nervous Newt. (p. 1588)
—Optimistic Octopus. (p. 1667)
—Pleasant Penguin. (p. 1762)
—Purrfect Place. (p. 1816)
—Question Quetzal. (p. 1826)
—Reckless Raccoon. (p. 1853)
—Sensitive Sea Lion. (p. 1989)
—Super Kids vs the Energy Monster. (p. 2155)
—Super Kids vs the Garbage Monster. (p. 2155)
—Timid Turtle. (p. 2247)

W

—Rover Boys at Colby Hall: The Struggles of the Young Cadets. (p. 1908)
—Rover Boys at Colby Hall: Or the Struggles of the Young Cadets (Classic Reprint) (p. 1908)
—Rover Boys at College: Or the Right Road & the Wrong (Classic Reprint) (p. 1908)
—Rover Boys at School: Or the Cadets of Putnam Hall (Classic Reprint) (p. 1908)
—Rover Boys at School. (p. 1908)
—Rover Boys down East: Or the Struggle for the Stanhope Fortune (Classic Reprint) (p. 1908)
—Rover Boys in Business: The Search for the Missing Bonds. (p. 1908)
—Rover Boys in Business: Or the Search for the Missing Bonds (Classic Reprint) (p. 1908)
—Rover Boys in Camp, or the Rivals of Pine Island (Classic Reprint) (p. 1908)
—Rover Boys in New York: Saving Their Father's Honor. (p. 1908)
—Rover Boys in New York: Or Saving Their Father's Honor (Classic Reprint) (p. 1908)
—Rover Boys in the Air: Or from College Campus to the Clouds (Classic Reprint) (p. 1908)
—Rover Boys in the Land of Luck, or Stirring Adventures in the Oil Fields (Classic Reprint) (p. 1908)
—Rover Boys in the Mountains. (p. 1908)
—Rover Boys in the Mountains, or a Hunt for Fun & Fortune (Classic Reprint) (p. 1908)
—Rover Boys on a Hunt: The Mysterious House in the Woods. (p. 1908)
—Rover Boys on a Hunt: Or the Mysterious House in the Woods (Classic Reprint) (p. 1908)
—Rover Boys on a Hunt, or the Mysterious House in the Woods (Classic Reprint) (p. 1908)
—Rover Boys on a Tour: Or Last Days at Brill College (Classic Reprint) (p. 1908)
—Rover Boys on Land & Sea the Crusoes of Seven Islands. (p. 1908)
—Rover Boys on Snowshoe Island: Or the Old Lumberman's Treasure Box (Classic Reprint) (p. 1908)
—Rover Boys on the Farm: Last Days at Putnam Hall. (p. 1908)
—Rover Boys on the Great Lakes: The Secret of the Island Cave. (p. 1908)
—Rover Boys on the Ocean: A Chase for a Fortune. (p. 1908)
—Rover Boys on the Ocean: Or, a Chase for a Fortune. (p. 1908)
—Rover Boys on the Ocean: Or a Chase for a Fortune (Classic Reprint) (p. 1908)
—Rover Boys on the Ocean. (p. 1908)
—Rover Boys on the Ocean, or a Chase for a Fortune (Classic Reprint) (p. 1908)
—Rover Boys on the Plains: Or the Mystery of Red Rock Ranch (Classic Reprint) (p. 1908)
—Rover Boys on the River: Or the Search for the Missing Houseboat (Classic Reprint) (p. 1908)
—Rover Boys on the River the Search for the Missing Houseboat. (p. 1908)
—Rover Boys Out West: The Search for a Lost Mine. (p. 1908)
—Rover Boys under Canvas: The Mystery of the Wrecked Submarine. (p. 1908)
—Rover Boys under Canvas, or the Mystery of the Wrecked Submarine (Classic Reprint) (p. 1908)
Winfrey, Kerry. Love & Other Alien Experiences. (p. 1359)
—Things Jolie Needs to Do Before She Bites It. (p. 2220)
Wing, Carol. Lio the Carousel Horse. Moen, Ruth, illus. (p. 1305)
Wing, Francis Marion. Fambly Album: Another Fotygraft Album, Shown to the New Preacher by Rebecca Sparks Peters, Aged Eleven; the Bigger Album from Upstairs (Classic Reprint) (p. 701)
Wing, Frank. Fotygraft Album: Shown to the New Neighbor by Rebecca Sparks Peters. (p. 771)
—Fotygraft Album: Shown to the New Neighbor by Rebecca Sparks Peters Aged Eleven (Classic Reprint) (p. 771)
Wing, Henry E. My Horse Jesse: A Sequel to When Lincoln Kissed Me (Classic Reprint) (p. 1550)
Wing, J. C., ed. see Pace, Guy L.
Wing, Joseph E. In Foreign Fields: Sketches of Travel in South America & Western Europe (Classic Reprint) (p. 1105)
Wing, Natasha. Bagel in Love. Dardik, Helen, illus. (p. 159)
—Buzz Off! 600 Jokes about Things with Wings. (p. 305)
—Lettuce Laugh: 600 Corny Jokes about Food. (p. 1281)
—Night Before Class Picture Day. (p. 1605)
—Night Before Class Picture Day. Wummer, Amy, illus. (p. 1605)
—Night Before Easter: Special Edition. Couri, Kathy, illus. (p. 1605)
—Night Before Election Day. Wummer, Amy, illus. (p. 1605)
—Night Before Father's Day. (p. 1605)
—Night Before Father's Day. Wummer, Amy, illus. (p. 1605)
—Night Before Groundhog Day. (p. 1605)
—Night Before Groundhog Day. Wummer, Amy, illus. (p. 1605)
—Night Before Halloween Activity Book. Fisher, Cynthia, illus. (p. 1605)
—Night Before Hanukkah Wummer, Amy, illus. (p. 1605)
—Night Before Hanukkah. (p. 1605)
—Night Before Kindergarten. Durrell, Julie, illus. (p. 1605)
—Night Before Kindergarten Graduation. (p. 1605)
—Night Before Kindergarten Graduation. Wummer, Amy, illus. (p. 1605)
—Night Before Mother's Day. Wummer, Amy, illus. (p. 1605)
—Night Before My Birthday. (p. 1605)
—Night Before My Birthday. Wummer, Amy, illus. (p. 1605)
—Night Before My Dance Recital. (p. 1605)
—Night Before My Dance Recital. Wummer, Amy, illus. (p. 1605)
—Night Before My First Communion. Wummer, Amy, illus. (p. 1605)
—Night Before New Year's. Wummer, Amy, illus. (p. 1605)
—Night Before Preschool. Wummer, Amy, illus. (p. 1605)
—Night Before St. Patrick's Day. Wummer, Amy, illus. (p. 1605)
—Night Before the Fourth of July. Wummer, Amy, illus. (p. 1605)
—Night Before the New Pet. (p. 1605)
—Night Before the New Pet. Wummer, Amy, illus. (p. 1605)
—Night Before the Snow Day. Wummer, Amy, illus. (p. 1605)
—When Jackie Saved Grand Central. Bolger, Alexandra, illus. (p. 2431)
Wing, Scarlett. 100 Curious Things to Count: Case Bound Big Book. Cottage Door Press, ed. (p. 2556)
—100 Dinosaur & Prehistoric Words to Know. Cottage Door Press, ed. (p. 2556)
—ABC & 123 Learning Songs: Deluxe Sound Book Wood Module. Cottage Door Press, ed. (p. 3)
—At the Beach: Look up, Look Around, Look Down: 3-In-1 Board Book. Cottage Door Press, ed. (p. 130)
—Baa Baa, Llama Llama, Ding Dong! Cottage Door Press, ed. (p. 147)
—Babies Love Animales. Cottage Door Press, ed. (p. 147)
—Babies Love Animals, First Words, Things That Go, & Opposites 4 Pack: Chunky Lift a Flap Board Book 4 Pack. Cottage Door Press, ed. (p. 147)
—Babies Love Kittens. Cottage Door Press, ed. (p. 147)
—Babies Love Numbers: Life-A-Flap Book. Cottage Door Press, ed. (p. 147)
—Babies Love Opposites: Chunky Lift a Flap Board Book. Cottage Door Press, ed. (p. 147)
—Babies Love Opuestos. Cottage Door Press, ed. (p. 147)
—Babies Love Primeras Palabras. Cottage Door Press, ed. (p. 147)
—Babies Love Puppies. Cottage Door Press, ed. (p. 147)
—Babies Love Vehículos. Cottage Door Press, ed. (p. 147)
—Backyard All Year: Touch & Feel Multi Board Book. Cottage Door Press, ed. (p. 156)
—Bedtime Songs: Deluxe Sound Book Wood Module. Rescek, Sanja, illus. (p. 188)
—Big & Little: Chunky Lift a Flap Board Book. Crisp, Dan, illus. (p. 216)
—Big Bed for Little Bear: Shaped Board Book. Rizzo, Letizia, illus. (p. 216)
—Brush, Flush, Wash: 5 Color Lift a Flap. Cottage Door Press, ed. (p. 288)
—Butterflies & Moths: First Discovery Books. Cottage Door Press, ed. (p. 303)
—Campfire Songs. Cottage Door Press, ed. (p. 316)
—Circles & Squares: Chunky Lift a Flap Board Book. Cottage Door Press, ed. (p. 393)
—Colors Everywhere: Shake & Play. Cottage Door Press, ed. (p. 426)
—Daniel Takes Care of Snowball: 3 Button Handle Book. Cottage Door Press, ed. (p. 503)
—Daniel's Marching Band. Cottage Door Press, ed. (p. 503)
—Discover 100 First Words: Case Bound Big Book. Crisp, Dan, illus. (p. 553)
—Early Bird Library: Early Learning: Early Bird Library Book Set. (p. 614)
—Early Bird Library: Good Morning Good Night: Early Bird Library Book Set. (p. 614)
—Farm Animals. Cottage Door Press, ed. (p. 709)
—Favorite First Words: Lift-A-Tab Book. Cottage Door Press, ed. (p. 715)
—First Words & Animals 2 Pack: Chunky Lift a Flap Board Book 2 Pack. Cottage Door Press, ed. (p. 740)
—Friendly Songs. Cottage Door Press, ed. (p. 786)
—Friends Help Each Other! Cottage Door Press, ed. (p. 787)
—Going to Grandma's House: Shaped Board Book. Chen, Yuyi, illus. (p. 855)
—Hat, Socks, Shoes: 5 Color Lift a Flap. Cottage Door Press, ed. (p. 936)
—Hug, Kiss, Love: 5 Color Lift a Flap. Cottage Door Press, ed. (p. 1048)
—I Love You More. Cottage Door Press, ed. (p. 1079)
—It's You I Like! Cottage Door Press, ed. (p. 1148)
—Laugh & Sing: Silly Animal Songs. Cottage Door Press, ed. (p. 1251)
—Let's Imagine. Cottage Door Press, ed. (p. 1274)
—Let's Learn in My Neighborhood. Cottage Door Press, ed. (p. 1274)
—Lights & Music Bedtime Songs: Lights & Music Board Book. Cottage Door Press, ed. (p. 1300)
—Numeros: Lif-A-Flap Book. Cottage Door Press, ed. (p. 1630)
—Old MacDonald Had a Band: Board Book with Handle. Cottage Door Press, ed. (p. 1646)
—Play & Learn Activity Cards: Activity Card Set. Crisp, Dan, illus. (p. 1758)
—Play & Learn Together: Flip a Flap Board Book. Crisp, Dan, illus. (p. 1759)
—Potty Time! Cottage Door Press, ed. (p. 1781)
—Sing & Smile: Wheels on the Bus & Itsy Bitsy Spider: Board Book with Handle 2 Pack. Cottage Door Press, ed. (p. 2023)
—Sip, Chew, Yum: 5 Color Lift a Flap. Cottage Door Press, ed. (p. 2025)
—Snowflake Songs. Cottage Door Press, ed. (p. 2049)
—There's a Doctor for You: Shaped Board Book. Aparicio, Núria, illus. (p. 2217)
—Trains Then & Now: First Discovery Books. Cottage Door Press, ed. (p. 2276)
—Under the Stars: Turn & Learn Wood Disc Board Book. Cottage Door Press, ed. (p. 2323)
—Wheels on the Bus: Board Book with Handle. Cottage Door Press, ed. (p. 2428)
—Who Am I? Mirror & Me. Cottage Door Press, ed. (p. 2446)
Wing, Scarlett, jt. auth. see Rhodes-Conway, Michelle.
Wing, Scarlett & Cottage Door Press. 100 Curious Words to Know: Case Bound Big Book. Smithsonian Kids, photos by. (p. 2556)
Wing, Scarlett & Finch, Rusty. Spring in the Forest. Longhi, Katya, illus. (p. 2092)
Wingard, Lucinda. Turn-Around Bird. (p. 2300)
Wingard-Nelson, Rebecca. Addition & Subtraction: Ace Your Math Test. (p. 15)
—Addition & Subtraction. (p. 15)
—Algebra & Pre-Algebra: It's Easy. (p. 44)
—Algebra I & Algebra II Smarts! (p. 44)
—Algebra Word Problems: No Problem! (p. 44)
—Big Truck & Car Word Problems Starring Multiplication & Division. (p. 223)
—Data, Graphing, & Statistics Smarts! (p. 509)
—Decimals & Fractions: It's Easy. (p. 523)
—Division & Multiplication: It's Easy. (p. 566)
—Fractions & Decimals: Ace Your Math Test. (p. 775)
—Fractions & Decimals. (p. 775)
—Fun Food Word Problems Starring Fractions: Math Word Problems Solved. (p. 799)
—Geometry: It's Easy. (p. 818)
—Geometry: Ace Your Math Test. (p. 818)
—Geometry. (p. 818)
—Geometry, It's Easy. (p. 818)
—How Many Pennies Make a Dollar? (p. 1033)
—I Can Add Bills & Coins. (p. 1061)
—I Can Count Money. (p. 1061)
—I Can Do Money Word Problems. (p. 1062)
—I Can Name Bills & Coins. (p. 1063)
—I Can Subtract Bills & Coins. (p. 1063)
—Multiplication & Division: Ace Your Math Test. (p. 1525)
—Multiplication & Division. (p. 1525)
—Multiplication & Division Word Problems: No Problem! (p. 1525)
—Percents & Ratios: Ace Your Math Test. (p. 1721)
—Percents & Ratios. (p. 1721)
—Pre-Algebra & Algebra: Ace Your Math Test. (p. 1786)
—Pre-Algebra & Algebra. (p. 1786)
—Problem Solving & Word Problem Smarts! (p. 1803)
—Ratios & Percents: It's Easy. (p. 1843)
—Ready for Addition. (p. 1847)
—Ready for Addition. LaBaff, Tom, illus. (p. 1847)
—Ready for Division. LaBaff, Tom, illus. (p. 1847)
—Ready for Fractions & Decimals. LaBaff, Tom, illus. (p. 1847)
—Ready for Multiplication. LaBaff, Tom, illus. (p. 1847)
—Ready for Subtraction. LaBaff, Tom, illus. (p. 1847)
—Ready for Word Problems & Problem Solving. LaBaff, Tom, illus. (p. 1848)
—Space Word Problems Starring Ratios & Proportions: Math Word Problems Solved. (p. 2072)
—Subtraction & Addition: It's Easy. (p. 2146)
Wingard-Nelson, Rebecca, jt. auth. see Williams, Zella.
Wingard-Nelson, Rebecca & Library. Geometry Word Problems: No Problem! (p. 818)
—Graphing & Probability Word Problems: No Problem! (p. 881)
—Math Measurement Word Problems: No Problem! (p. 1424)
Wingard-Nelson, Rebecca & Williams, Zella. Word Problems Using Decimals & Percentages. (p. 2493)
—Word Problems Using Fractions. (p. 2493)
—Word Problems Using Ratios & Proportions. (p. 2493)
Wingate, Barbara. Petey the One Lopped Eared Dog Mignano, Daniel, illus. (p. 1730)
Wingate, Brian. BMX Bicycle Racing: Techniques & Tricks. (p. 250)
—Saddam Hussein. (p. 1921)
—Violence at Sports Events. (p. 2359)
Wingate, Edmund. Britton (Classic Reprint) (p. 284)
Wingate, Kate. Political Reforms: American Citizens Gain More Control over Their Government. (p. 1771)
Wingate, Philippa, ed. see Foster, Juliana.
Wingate, Philippa, ed. see Heywood, Rosie.
Wingerter, Linda. Home on the Range. (p. 997)
Wingerter, Linda, illus. see Sherman, Josepha.
Winget, D. H. Anecdotes of Buffalo Bill: Which Have Never Before Appeared in Print (Classic Reprint) (p. 84)
Winget, Dan. Anecdotes of Buffalo Bill That Have Never Appeared in Print (Classic Reprint) (p. 84)
Winget, Dianna Dorisi. Million Ways Home. (p. 1468)
—Smidgen of Sky. (p. 2041)
Winget, Rosie. ABC on the Farm. Cottage Door Press, ed. (p. 4)
—Other Colors. Cottage Door Press, ed. (p. 1674)
—Ready to Learn. Bianda, Junissa, illus. (p. 1848)
—Silly Animal Stories. Cottage Door Press, ed. (p. 2018)
—Sunny Day Point N Match: Hardcover Board Book. Lane, Lily, illus. (p. 2152)
—Zoom Zoom Point N Match: Hardcover Board Book. Ho, Jannie, illus. (p. 2544)
Winget, Susan, illus. see Moore, Clement C., ed.
Winget, Susan, illus. see Moulton, Mark Kimball.
Winget, Susan, tr. see Moulton, Mark Kimball.
Wingfield, Anthony. True Coppie of a Discourse Written by a Gentleman, Employed in the Late Voyage of Spaine & Portingale: Sent to His Particular Friend, & by Him Published, for the Better Satisfaction of All Such, As Having Been Seduced by Particular Report, Have Entr. (p. 2294)
Wingfield, George & Gritzner, Charles F. Belgium. (p. 195)
Wingfield, Hayley. Little Johnny's Book of Wild & Crazy Friends. (p. 1319)
Wingfield, Hon Lewis. Maid of Honour, Vol. 2 of 3 (Classic Reprint) (p. 1383)
Wingfield, Lewis. Abigel Rowe, Vol. 1 Of 3: A Chronicle of the Regency (Classic Reprint) (p. 6)
—Abigel Rowe, Vol. 2 Of 3: A Chronicle of the Regency (Classic Reprint) (p. 6)
—Abigel Rowe, Vol. 3 Of 3: A Chronicle of the Regency (Classic Reprint) (p. 6)
—Barbara Philpot, Vol. 1 Of 3: A Study of Manners & Morals; 1727 to 1737 (Classic Reprint) (p. 165)
—Barbara Philpot, Vol. 3 Of 3: A Study of Manners & Morals; (1727 to 1737) (Classic Reprint) (p. 165)
—Gehenna or Havens of Unrest, Vol. 3 of 3 (Classic Reprint) (p. 813)
—Gehenna or, Vol. 2 Of 3: Havens of Unrest (Classic Reprint) (p. 813)
—Gehenna, Vol. 1 Of 3: Or Havens of Unrest (Classic Reprint) (p. 813)
—In Her Majesty's Keeping, Vol. 2 Of 3: The Story of a Hidden Life (Classic Reprint) (p. 1105)
—Lady Grizel, Vol. 3 Of 3: An Impression of a Momentous Epoch (Classic Reprint) (p. 1237)
—Maid of Honour, Vol. 1 Of 3: A Tale of the Dark Days of France (Classic Reprint) (p. 1383)
—My Lords of Strogue, Vol. 1 Of 3: A Chronicle of Ireland, from the Convention to the Union (Classic Reprint) (p. 1554)
—Storm of a Hidden Life, Vol. 1 of 3 (Classic Reprint) (p. 2126)
—Wanderings of a Globe-Trotter in the Far East, Vol. 1 of 2 (Classic Reprint) (p. 2375)
Wingfield, Lewis Strange. Lady Grizel, Vol. 1 Of 3: An Impression of a Momentous Epoch (Classic Reprint) (p. 1237)
—Lady Grizel, Vol. 2 Of 3: An Impression of a Momentous Epoch (Classic Reprint) (p. 1237)
Wingfield, Robert. Mystery of the Lake. (p. 1570)
—Mystery of the Midnight Sun. (p. 1570)
Wingham, Peter, illus. see Somper, Justin.
Wings, Tanina. Little Seagull. (p. 1327)
Winick, Judd. Hilo (p. 972)
—Hilo Book 1: the Boy Who Crashed to Earth. (p. 972)
—Hilo Book 2: Saving the Whole Wide World. (p. 972)
—Hilo Book 3: the Great Big Boom. (p. 972)
—Hilo Book 4: Waking the Monsters. (p. 972)
—Hilo Book 5: Then Everything Went Wrong. (p. 972)
—Hilo Book 6: All the Pieces Fit. (p. 972)
—Hilo: Out-Of-This-World Boxed Set (p. 972)
—Pedro & Me: Friendship, Loss, & What I Learned. (p. 1712)
Winick, Judd, illus. see Nickel, Scott & Evanier, Mark.
Winicki, Danielle, illus. see Allsopp, Nigel.
Winik, Edward. Horse's Tale. (p. 1005)
Winkel, Andrew. Raceboy & Super Qwok Adventures. Brault, Christopher, illus. (p. 1831)
Winkelman, Barbara Gaines, jt. auth. see RH Disney Staff.
Winkelmann, Mirja. Odd Couples: One Word, Two Meanings. (p. 1637)
Winkel-Schmelz, Annegret. Märchen-Bärchen Geht Auf Wanderschaft. (p. 1402)
Winkelstein, Steven Paul. Brisko: A True Tale of Holocaust Survival. Juliano, Dana, illus. (p. 282)
Winkk. Misleading. (p. 1477)
Winkler, Dorianne Allister. Pukey Poetry: Tale Ticklers by Mz Millipede. (p. 1812)
Winkler, Henry, jt. auth. see Oliver, Lin.
Winkler, Henry & Oliver, Lin. Alien Superstar (Book #1) (p. 47)
—Always Dance with a Hairy Buffalo. (p. 61)
—Always Watch Out for the Flying Potato Salad! (p. 61)
—Always Watch Out for the Flying Potato Salad! #9. Garrett, Scott, illus. (p. 61)
—Bookmarks Are People Too! (p. 261)
—Bookmarks Are People Too! #1. Garrett, Scott, illus. (p. 261)
—Brand-New Me! #17. (p. 275)
—Dump Trucks & Dogsleds #16: I'm on My Way, Mom! (p. 610)
—Everybody Is Somebody #12. Garrett, Scott, illus. (p. 671)
—Fake Snakes & Weird Wizards #4. Garrett, Scott, illus. (p. 699)
—Hooray! My Butt Left the Bench! #10. Garrett, Scott, illus. (p. 1001)
—How to Hug an Elephant #6. Garrett, Scott, illus. (p. 1042)
—How to Scare the Pants off Your Pets (p. 1044)
—Robot on the Loose. (p. 1892)
—Robot on the Loose #11. (p. 1892)
—Short Tale about a Long Dog. (p. 2011)
—Short Tale about a Long Dog #2. Garrett, Scott, illus. (p. 2011)
—Soggy, Foggy Campout #8 Garrett, Scott, illus. (p. 2055)
—Stop That Frog! (p. 2122)
—Stop That Frog! #3. Garrett, Scott, illus. (p. 2122)
—You Can't Drink a Meatball Through a Straw #7. Garrett, Scott, illus. (p. 2526)
Winkler, Kathleen. Are You Being Bullied? How to Deal with Taunting, Teasing, & Tormenting. (p. 113)
Winkler, Susan Elliott. Haylee & the Mud Puddle. (p. 941)
Winkley, J. W. John Brown the Hero: Personal Reminiscences (Classic Reprint) (p. 1172)
Winlock, Joseph. Tables to Facilitate the Reduction of Places of the Fixed Stars: Prepared for the Use of the American Ephemeris & Nautical Almanac (Classic Reprint) (p. 2175)
Winlow, Alice Maud. Mornin'-Glory Girl (Classic Reprint) (p. 1506)
Winmilawe. Shango's Son. Melchishua, Tewodross, illus. (p. 1999)
Winn, Anthony, et al. Star Wars Legends Epic Collection: Rise of the Sith Vol. 2. (p. 2104)
Winn, Christopher, illus. see Winn, Sheridan.
Winn, Don M. Chipper the Clown. (p. 379)
—Tortoise & the Hairpiece. Hefflin, Toby, illus. (p. 2266)
Winn, Sheridan. Sprite Sisters: Magic at Drysdale's School (Vol 7) Winn, Christopher, illus. (p. 2093)
Winn, T. Allen. Come Here Getouttahere: Tyler's Tail Wagging Tale. (p. 428)
—Mister Twix Mystery: A Cat Scene Investigation. (p. 1482)
Winn, Whee. Lots of Christmas Jokes for Kids (p. 1356)
—Lots of Jokes & Riddles Box Set: Over 750 Jokes for Kids (p. 1356)
—Lots of Knock-Knock Jokes for Kids (p. 1356)
—Lots of Tongue Twisters for Kids (p. 1356)
Winner, Cherie. Everything Reptile. (p. 673)
—Ranger Rick Kids' Guide to Camping: All You Need to Know about Having Fun in the Outdoors. (p. 1840)
Winnick, Judd. Pedro & Me. (p. 1712)
Winnick, Karen B. Sybil's Night Ride. (p. 2172)
Winnick, Neil. Hearing. (p. 944)
Winnick, Nick. Build Green. (p. 293)
—Butterflies. (p. 303)
—Green Buildings. (p. 893)
—Green Energy. (p. 894)
—Green Power. (p. 894)
—Moose. (p. 1503)
—Owls. (p. 1689)
—Reduce Waste. (p. 1860)
—Reducing Waste. (p. 1860)
—Salamanders. (p. 1924)
—Summer: Wow Study of Day & Seasons. (p. 2148)
—Summer. (p. 2148)
Winnie, Aunt. Two Sixpences (Classic Reprint) (p. 2309)
Winnie, Joanne. Long Tradition. (p. 1343)
Winnie, Joanne M. Long Tradition. (p. 1343)
Winnie the Pooh. Close-up Day. (p. 407)

—Goodbye, Honeypot! (p. 866)
—Spring Cleaning. (p. 2092)
—Winnie the Pooh Nature's True Colors. (p. 2474)
Winningham, Barbara. Turtle Pit. (p. 2301)
Winnipeg, Havergal College. Havergal Magazine, Vol. 7: May, 1914 (Classic Reprint) (p. 940)
Winquist, Gloria & McCarthy, Matt. Coding IPhone Apps for Kids: A Playful Introduction to Swift. (p. 412)
Winscom, Jane Anne. Onward: Or, the Mountain Clamberers; a Tale of Progress (Classic Reprint) (p. 1664)
—Rest & Resurrection, or the Sabbath & the Sunday (Classic Reprint) (p. 1870)
Winser, Lilian. Lays & Legends of the Weald of Kent. (p. 1253)
—Lays & Legends of the Weald of Kent (Classic Reprint) (p. 1253)
Winship, A. E. American Primary Teacher, Vol. 14: Devoted to the Methods & Principles of Teaching; from September, 1896, to June, 1897, Inclusive (Classic Reprint) (p. 73)
—Danger Signals for Teachers. (p. 501)
Winship, Albert Edward. Fastidious Prisoner (Classic Reprint) (p. 713)
Winship, Daniel. Tortoise & the Hare: The Tortoise & the Hare. (p. 2266)
Winship, Daniel, illus. see Parker, Theron.
Winslade, Jayn. Curse of Aggara. (p. 488)
Winslade, Jayn E. Emily & Jen Dance for Deeron. (p. 642)
Winslow, Barbara. Dance on a Sealskin. Sloat, Teri, illus. (p. 500)
Winslow, Claire. Book in Four Languages: My Numbers. de Alba, Arlette et al, trs. (p. 257)
—Disney Baby: Let's Learn Together. Disney Storybook Art Team, illus. (p. 558)
—Disney Junior Fancy Nancy. Disney Storybook Art Team, illus. (p. 560)
—Disney Junior Fancy Nancy. Disney Storybook Art Team & Imaginism Studio, illus. (p. 560)
—Disney Puppy Dog Pals: Fun on the Farm. Disney Storybook Art Team, illus. (p. 563)
—Nickelodeon Jojo Siwa: Out of This World! (p. 1603)
—Peppa Pig: First Look & Find Book & Blocks. (p. 1719)
—Peppa Pig: My Family & Me. (p. 1720)
—Sesame Street: ABCs with Elmo! Brannon, Tom, illus. (p. 1992)
—Sesame Street: Big Bird's Road Trip. Goldberg, Barry, illus. (p. 1992)
—Thomas & Friends: All Aboard! Chilvers, Nigel, illus. (p. 2227)
Winslow, Claire, jt. auth. see Wage, Erin Rose.
Winslow, Claire, adapted by. Encyclopedia Britannica Kids: Around the World: Sights & Sounds for Adventure Seekers. (p. 648)
Winslow, Elizabeth Bruce R. Rosamond of Monterre: A Canadian Pastoral (Classic Reprint) (p. 1904)
Winslow, Erving, jt. auth. see Maeterlinck, Maurice.
Winslow, Helen M. Pleasuring of Susan Smith (Classic Reprint) (p. 1762)
—Salome Shepard, Reformer (Classic Reprint) (p. 1925)
Winslow Johnson, Franklin. University of Chicago Publications in Religious Education; the Problems of Boyhood: A Course in Ethics for Boys of High-School Age. (p. 2333)
Winslow, Justin. Perro y el Gato. (p. 1724)
Winslow, Justin, illus. see Hines, Chrissie & Ferreras, Alberto.
Winslow, Margaret E. Katie Robertson, or in All Thy Ways Acknowledge Him: A Tale of Factory Life (Classic Reprint) (p. 1205)
—Three Years at Glenwood: A Sequel to Katie Robertson (Classic Reprint) (p. 2236)
Winslow, Marjorie. Mud Pies & Other Recipes: A Cookbook for Dolls. Blegvad, Erik, illus. (p. 1524)
Winslow, Theresa. Katie the Bear & Her Adventure for Honey (p. 1205)
Winslow, William Henry. Sea Letter: A Mystery of Martha's Vineyard (Classic Reprint) (p. 1967)
—Southern Buds & Sons of War (Classic Reprint) (p. 2069)
Winsor, Dorothy. Wind Reader. (p. 2471)
Winsor, Dorothy A. Deep As a Tomb. (p. 524)
—Wysman. (p. 2515)
Winsor, Henry. Pebblebrook, & the Harding Family (Classic Reprint) (p. 1711)
Winstanley, Eliza. Shifting Scenes in Theatrical Life (Classic Reprint) (p. 2007)
Winstanley, L. Scholar Vagabond (Classic Reprint) (p. 1944)
Winstanley, Liz. Adventures of Abra & His Magic Carpet. (p. 21)
Winstanley, Nicola. How to Give Your Cat a Bath: In Five Easy Steps. Martz, John, illus. (p. 1042)
—Mel & Mo's Marvelous Balancing Act. Ferrer, Marianne, illus. (p. 1442)
—Pirate's Bed. (p. 1750)
Winstead, Leo, illus. see Jackson, Mary Helene.
Winstead, Rosie, illus. see Spinelli, Eileen.
Winstedt, R. O. Malayan Memories (Classic Reprint) (p. 1391)
—Shaman Saiva & Sufi: A Study of the Evolution of Malay Magic. (p. 1999)
Winstock, April. Eating & Drinking Difficulties in Children: A Guide for Practitioners. (p. 622)
Winston, Alfonso, tr. see Jones, Kizzie Elizabeth.
Winston, Alfonso, tr. see Jones, Kizzie.
Winston, Annie. Admiral Wright's Heroical Storicals: Daniel Boone & the Battle of Boonesborough. (p. 16)
Winston, Annie Steger. Memoirs of a Child (Classic Reprint) (p. 1444)
Winston, David Lorenz, illus. see Wolfman, Judy.
Winston, David Lorenz, photos by see Wolfman, Judy.
Winston, Dulcie. Birthday Surprise. (p. 234)
—Just Being You. (p. 1192)
Winston, Jeannie, illus. see Winters, Kay.
Winston, Mary A. Rural Ruse (Classic Reprint) (p. 1916)
Winston, Nannie B. Waters That Pass Away (Classic Reprint) (p. 2386)
Winston, Robert. Ask a Scientist: Professor Robert Winston Answers 100 Big Questions from Kids Around the World! (p. 126)
—Inventors: Incredible Stories of the World's Most Ingenious Inventions. Hawke, Jessamy, illus. (p. 1130)
—It's Elementary! Big Questions about Chemistry. (p. 1145)
—My Amazing Body Machine: A Colorful Visual Guide to How Your Body Works. Gildersleeve, Owen, illus. (p. 1531)
—Science Rocks! Unleash the Mad Scientist in You! (p. 1959)
—Steam Team Explains: More Than 100 Amazing Science Facts. (p. 2110)
Winston, Robert, jt. auth. see Dorling Kindersley Publishing Staff.
Winston, Robert M. L. Evolution Revolution. (p. 675)
Winston, Sam. Nina Hecha de Libros. Jeffers, Oliver, illus. (p. 1609)
Winston, Sam, jt. auth. see Jeffers, Oliver.
Winston, Sherri. Great Escapes #2: Journey to Freedom 1838. Bernardin, James, illus. (p. 885)
—Jada Sly, Artist & Spy. (p. 1154)
—President of the Whole Fifth Grade. (p. 1789)
—President of the Whole Sixth Grade: Girl Code. (p. 1789)
—Sweetest Sound. (p. 2169)
Wint, Florence, illus. see Grossman, Bill.
Wint, P. Grade Six Achievement Tests Language Arts. (p. 874)
Winter, A. P. Boy Who Went Magic. (p. 271)
Winter, Ali. Peace & Me: Inspired by the Lives of Nobel Peace Prize Laureates. El Fathi, Mickael, illus. (p. 1709)
Winter, Alice Ames. Jewel Weed (Classic Reprint) (p. 1167)
—Prize to the Hardy (Classic Reprint) (p. 1802)
Winter, Ariel S. One of a Kind. Hitch, David, illus. (p. 1661)
Winter, Charles Edwin. Ben Warman (Classic Reprint) (p. 199)
Winter, Christopher. Henrietta the Farmer & the Long, Long, Long, Long Vacation! O'Shea, Bonnie, illus. (p. 954)
Winter, Elizabeth C. Spanish Treasure a Story (Classic Reprint) (p. 2074)
Winter, Isobelle. Weather. Odgers, Sally, ed. (p. 2393)
Winter, J. B. From Switzerland to the Mediterranean on Foot (Classic Reprint) (p. 793)
Winter, J. S. Cavalry Life, or Sketches & Stories in Barracks & Out (Classic Reprint) (p. 347)
Winter, Jane Kohen & Baguley, Kitt. Venezuela. (p. 2350)
Winter, Jane Kohen & Roraff, Susan. Chile. (p. 376)
Winter, Jane Kohen & Spilling, Jo-Ann. Italy. (p. 1142)
Winter, Jeanette. Biblioburro: A True Story from Colombia. Winter, Jeanette, illus. (p. 214)
—Henri's Scissors. Winter, Jeanette, illus. (p. 954)
—Librarian of Basra: A True Story from Iraq. (p. 1284)
—Mr. Cornell's Dream Boxes. Winter, Jeanette, illus. (p. 1518)
—Nanuk the Ice Bear. Winter, Jeanette, illus. (p. 1574)
—Nasreen's Secret School: A True Story from Afghanistan. Winter, Jeanette, illus. (p. 1576)
—Our House Is on Fire: Greta Thunberg's Call to Save the Planet. Winter, Jeanette, illus. (p. 1678)
—Sisters: Venus & Serena Williams. Winter, Jeanette, illus. (p. 2027)
—Wangari's Trees of Peace: A True Story from Africa. (p. 2375)
—Wangari's Trees of Peace. (p. 2375)
—Watcher: Jane Goodall's Life with the Chimps. Winter, Jeanette, illus. (p. 2383)
—World Is Not a Rectangle: A Portrait of Architect Zaha Hadid. Winter, Jeanette, illus. (p. 2502)
Winter, Jeanette, illus. see Winter, Jonah.
Winter, John Strange. Army Society: Life in a Garrison Town; a Discursive Story (Classic Reprint) (p. 118)
—Army Society. (p. 118)
—Beautiful Jim, of the Blankshire Regiment. (p. 184)
—Beautiful Jim, of the Blankshire Regiment (Classic Reprint) (p. 184)
—Binks Family: The Story of a Social Revolution (Classic Reprint) (p. 228)
—Blaze of Glory (Classic Reprint) (p. 243)
—Bootles' Baby: A Story of the Scarlet Lancers (Classic Reprint) (p. 262)
—Born Soldier (Classic Reprint) (p. 263)
—Cavalry Life, Vol. 1 Of 2: Or Sketches & Stories in Barracks & Out (Classic Reprint) (p. 347)
—Cavalry Life, Vol. 2 Of 2: Or Sketches & Stories in Barracks & Out (Classic Reprint) (p. 347)
—Cherry's Child: A Novel (Classic Reprint) (p. 366)
—Christmas Fairy (Classic Reprint) (p. 385)
—Everybody's Favourite: A Novel (Classic Reprint) (p. 671)
—Experiences of a Lady Help (Classic Reprint) (p. 678)
—Good-Bye (Classic Reprint) (p. 861)
—Grip (Classic Reprint) (p. 897)
—He Went for a Soldier (Classic Reprint) (p. 942)
—In Luck's Way (Classic Reprint) (p. 1106)
—In Quarters with the 25th (the Black Horse) Dragoons (Classic Reprint) (p. 1106)
—Into an Unknown World: A Novel (Classic Reprint) (p. 1128)
—Into an Unknown World. (p. 1128)
—Little Gervaise: And Other Stories (Classic Reprint) (p. 1317)
—Little Vanities of Mrs. Whittaker: A Novel (Classic Reprint) (p. 1329)
—Love & Twenty (Classic Reprint) (p. 1359)
—Lumley, the Painter (Classic Reprint) (p. 1368)
—Magic Wheel: A Novel (Classic Reprint) (p. 1379)
—Magnificent Young Man, Vol. 1: A Novel (Classic Reprint) (p. 1382)
—Major's Favourite a Novel (Classic Reprint) (p. 1385)
—Marty: A Novel (Classic Reprint) (p. 1411)
—Matter of Sentiment (Classic Reprint) (p. 1426)
—Money Sense: A Novel (Classic Reprint) (p. 1493)
—Name to Conjure with (Classic Reprint) (p. 1573)
—Only Human: A Novel (Classic Reprint) (p. 1664)
—Peacemakers (Classic Reprint) (p. 1709)
—Price of a Wife (Classic Reprint) (p. 1791)
—Private Tinker: And Other Stories (Classic Reprint) (p. 1802)
—Self-Made Countess: The Justification of a Husband (Classic Reprint) (p. 1987)
—Seventh Child: A Novel (Classic Reprint) (p. 1994)
—Strange Story of My Life: A Novel (Classic Reprint) (p. 2138)
—Strange Story of My Life. (p. 2138)
—Stranger Woman (Classic Reprint) (p. 2138)
—Summer Jaunt: Being a Rambling Autobiography. (p. 2149)
—Summer Jaunt: Being a Rambling Autobiography of John Strange Winter (Classic Reprint) (p. 2149)
—Those Girls (Classic Reprint) (p. 2230)
—Truth-Tellers: A Novel (Classic Reprint) (p. 2297)
—Truth-Tellers. (p. 2297)
—Wedlock (Classic Reprint) (p. 2395)
Winter, John Strange, et al. Christmas Fairy & Other Stories. (p. 385)
Winter, John T. Gumwood Tales Story Two: The Trouble with Swill. (p. 905)
Winter, John W. Rhymes for Ramblers, Amblers & Scramblers. (p. 1875)
Winter, Jonah. Barack (p. 164)
—Beisbol! Pioneros y Leyendas del Beisbol Latino Del Risco, Enrique, tr. (p. 195)
—Born & Bred in the Great Depression. Root, Kimberly Bulcken, illus. (p. 263)
—Elvis Is King! Red Nose Studio, illus. (p. 640)
—Fabulous Feud of Gilbert & Sullivan. Egielski, Richard, illus. (p. 692)
—Founding Fathers! Those Horse-Ridin', Fiddle-Playin', Book-Readin', Gun-Totin' Gentlemen Who Started America. Blitt, Barry, illus. (p. 771)
—Gertrude Is Gertrude Is Gertrude Is Gertrude. Brown, Calef, illus. (p. 823)
—Hillary. ón, Raul, illus. (p. 971)
—How Jelly Roll Morton Invented Jazz. Mallett, Keith, illus. (p. 1033)
—Jazz Age Josephine: Dancer, Singer—Who's That, Who? Why, That's MISS Josephine Baker, to You! Priceman, Marjorie, illus. (p. 1162)
—JFK. Ford, A. G., illus. (p. 1167)
—Lillian's Right to Vote: A Celebration of the Voting Rights Act Of 1965. Evans, Shane W., illus. (p. 1301)
—Mickey Mantle: the Commerce Comet. Payne, C. F., illus. (p. 1459)
—Mother Jones & Her Army of Mill Children. Carpenter, Nancy, illus. (p. 1510)
—My Name Is James Madison Hemings. Widener, Terry, illus. (p. 1557)
—Oil. Winter, Jeanette, illus. (p. 1643)
—Peaceful Heroes. Addy, Sean, illus. (p. 1709)
—Ruth Bader Ginsburg: The Case of R. B. G. vs. Inequality. Innerst, Stacy, illus. (p. 1918)
—Sad Little Fact. Oswald, Pete, illus. (p. 1920)
—Secret Project. Winter, Jeanette, illus. (p. 1978)
—Sonia Sotomayor: A Judge Grows in the Bronx/la Juez Que Creció en el Bronx. Rodriguez, Edel, illus. (p. 2063)
—Sonia Sotomayor. Rodriguez, Edel, illus. (p. 2063)
—Thurgood. Collier, Bryan, illus. (p. 2238)
—You Never Heard of Casey Stengel?! Blitt, Barry, illus. (p. 2527)
—You Never Heard of Sandy Koufax?! Carrilho, Andre, illus. (p. 2527)
—You Never Heard of Willie Mays?! Widener, Terry, illus. (p. 2527)
—¡Beisbol! Latino Baseball Pioneers & Legends (p. 195)
Winter, Jonah & Addy, Sean. Peaceful Heroes. (p. 1709)
Winter, Judy A. Joke Books (p. 1176)
—Jokes about Animals (p. 1176)
—Jokes about Bugs (p. 1176)
—Jokes about Monsters (p. 1176)
—Jokes about School (p. 1176)
—Jokes about Sports (p. 1176)
—Knock-Knock Jokes (p. 1229)
Winter, Judy A. & Shores, Erika L. Joke Books. (p. 1176)
Winter, Juliane. Wishweaver. (p. 2479)
Winter, Julianne. Fairy Flights & Neverland Nights: Corgi Adventures. (p. 696)
Winter, Laurel. Growing Wings. (p. 900)
Winter, Max. Afghanistan War. (p. 31)
—Civil Rights Movement (p. 396)
—Japan. (p. 1159)
—Powering up a Career in Artificial Intelligence. (p. 1783)
Winter, Milo. Aesops Fables for Children. (p. 31)
—Aesop's Favorite Fables: More Than 130 Classic Fables for Children! (p. 31)
—Arabian Nights Entertainments (Classic Reprint) (p. 109)
—Tales from the Arabian Nights. (p. 2182)
Winter, Milo, illus. see Aesop, Aesop.
Winter, Milo, illus. see Faulkner, Georgene.
Winter, Milo, illus. see Loveland, Seymour.
Winter, Milo, illus. see Mother Goose, Mother.
Winter, Milo, jt. auth. see Aesop.
Winter, Milo 1888-1956, jt. auth. see Olcott, Frances Jenkins.
Winter, Milo & Aesop. Aesop's Fables for Children: With MP3 Downloads. (p. 31)
Winter, Rosalind. Mice of St Goran. (p. 1457)
Winter, Susan, illus. see Ashman, Linda.
Winter, William. Life, Stories, & Poems of John Brougham: Comprising; I. His Autobiography a Fragment; II. a Supplementary Memoir; III. Sketch of His Miscellaneous Writings (Classic Reprint) (p. 1296)
—Winner (Classic Reprint) (p. 2473)
Winter, William West. Louisiana Lou: A Western Story (Classic Reprint) (p. 1358)
Winterberg, Jenna. Balanced & Unbalanced Forces (p. 160)
—Chemical Reactions. (p. 365)
—Conservation of Mass. (p. 442)
—Electromagnetism (p. 632)
—Light & Its Effects. (p. 1298)
—Parks for All: U. S. National Parks (Level 4) (p. 1700)
—Parques para Todos: Parques Nacionales de EE.UU. (p. 1701)
—Sound Waves & Communication. (p. 2067)
—Tech World: 20th Century Inventions (Level 3) (p. 2197)
—Watch Me Draw a Boy's Adventure. Fisher, Diana, illus. (p. 2383)
—Watch Me Draw Dinosaurs. Fisher, Diana, illus. (p. 2383)
Winterbotham, Russell Robert. Joyce of the Secret Squadron: A Captain Midnight Adventure (Classic Reprint) (p. 1184)
Winterbottom, Julie. Frightlopedia: An Encyclopedia of Everything Scary, Creepy, & Spine-Chilling, from Arachnids to Zombies. (p. 788)
—Frightlopedia: An Encyclopeidia of Everything Scary, Creepy, & Spine-Chilling, from Arachnids to Zombies. (p. 788)
—Pranklopedia: The Funniest, Grossest, Craziest, Not-Mean Pranks on the Planet! (p. 1785)
Winterbourne, Dale E. Star Shell, Vol. 1: Of, for & by the Men of the U. S. A. General Hospital, Markleton, Pa.; December 24, 1918 (Classic Reprint) (p. 2102)
Winterbourne, Septimus. Impossible Winterbourne Presents... the Alphabots. (p. 1102)
Winterburn, Florence Hull. Liberty Hall: A Story for Girls (Classic Reprint) (p. 1284)
—Southern Hearts (Classic Reprint) (p. 2069)
Winterfeld, Henry. Star Girl. Schabert, Kyrill, tr. (p. 2102)
Winterhalt, Tara, illus. see Dias, Denise.
Winterhaven School, Winterhaven, creator. O Is for Oregon: Written by Kids for Kids. (p. 1633)
Winterholler, Elisabeth, tr. Schlaf Gut, Kleiner Wolf - Schlof Guad, Gloana Wolf (Deutsch - Bairisch) Zweisprachiges Kinderbuch Mit Mp3 Hörbuch Zum Herunterladen, Ab 2-4 Jahren Zum Herunterladen, Ab 2-4 Jahren. Brinkmann, Barbara, illus. (p. 1944)
Winterich, John T. American Legion Monthly, Vol. 1: October, 1926 (Classic Reprint) (p. 72)
—American Legion Monthly, Vol. 21: December, 1936 (Classic Reprint) (p. 72)
—American Legion Monthly, Vol. 3: August, 1927 (Classic Reprint) (p. 72)
—American Legion Monthly, Vol. 7: September, 1929 (Classic Reprint) (p. 72)
Winteringham, Claire. Claire Winteringham's Alphabet Parade. (p. 397)
Winterroth, Martha Ann. Big Adventure. (p. 215)
—Explorer Extraordinaire. (p. 680)
—One Crazy Squirrel: Humphrey. (p. 1659)
Winters, Alexandria, illus. see Ashford, Marcia.
Winters, Ben H. Mystery of the Missing Everything. (p. 1570)
—Secret Life of Ms. Finkleman. (p. 1976)
Winters, Cat. Cure for Dreaming. (p. 485)
—In the Shadow of Blackbirds. (p. 1111)
—Odd & True. (p. 1637)
—Raven's Tale. (p. 1844)
—Steep & Thorny Way. (p. 2112)
Winters, Eleanor. 1-2-3 Calligraphy! Letters & Projects for Beginners & Beyond. (p. 2545)
Winters, Erastus. In the 50th Ohio Serving Uncle Sam: Memoirs of One Who Wore the Blue, Battle of Perryville, Camp Scenes in Old Kentucky & Tennessee, the Atlanta Campaign, Back in Tennessee, Battle of Franklin, Captured by the Enemy, a Hot Place Between the Firing Lines. (p. 1107)
Winters, Jaime. Breakaway! The History of Hockey. (p. 278)
—Carve It Snowboarding. (p. 335)
—Center Court: The History of Basketball. (p. 351)
—Center Field: The History of Baseball. (p. 351)
—Center Ice: The Stanley Cup. (p. 351)
—For the Win: The World Series. (p. 764)
—Get into Smoothies. (p. 824)
—Get into Yoga. (p. 824)
—Haunted at Sea. (p. 937)
—Ruling the Court: Basketball's Biggest Wins. (p. 1913)
—Shred It Skateboarding. (p. 2013)
Winters, Julian. Summer of Everything. (p. 2149)
Winters, Kari-Lynn. Buzz about Bees (p. 305)
—French Toast. Thisdale, François, illus. (p. 784)
—Gift Days Taylor, Stephen, illus. (p. 832)
—Good Pirate. Griffiths, Dean, illus. (p. 865)
—No-Matter-What Friend Pratt, Pierre, illus. (p. 1613)
—On My Bike Leist, Christina, illus. (p. 1653)
—On My Skis Leist, Christina, illus. (p. 1653)
—On My Swim Leist, Christina, illus. (p. 1653)
—On My Walk Leist, Christina, illus. (p. 1653)
—Runaway Alphabet. Frey, Ben, illus. (p. 1915)
—Stinky Skunk Mel. Opal, Paola, illus. (p. 2120)
Winters, Kari-Lynn & Mercurio, Ishta. Bite into Bloodsuckers (p. 235)
Winters, Kari-Lynn & Sherritt-Fleming, Lori. Hungry for Math: Poems to Munch On Collins, Peggy, illus. (p. 1052)
—Hungry for Science Collins, Peggy, illus. (p. 1052)
Winters, Karissa. Your Guide to All Things Caticorn. (p. 2533)
Winters, Kay. Bears Go to School (a Pete & Gabby Book) (p. 180)
—Colonial Voices: Hear Them Speak: The Outbreak of the Boston Tea Party Told from Multiple Points-Of-View! Day, Larry, illus. (p. 418)
—Did You Hear What I Heard? Poems about School. Barton, Patrice, illus. (p. 543)
—Did You See What I Saw? Weston, Martha, illus. (p. 543)
—This School Year Will Be the BEST! Andriani, Renee, illus. (p. 2227)
—Voices from the Underground Railroad. Day, Larry, illus. (p. 2365)
—Whooo's That? Winston, Jeannie, illus. (p. 2453)
Winters, Nellie, illus. see Oberndorfer, Erica, ed.
Winters, Nicole. TT: Full Throttle (p. 2298)
Winters, P. A. Alexander & Avery's Great Adventure (p. 42)
Winters, Pierre. My Body. Van Lindenhuizen, Eline, illus. (p. 1534)
—Traveling by Airplane. Meirink, Tineke, illus. (p. 2280)
Winters, Robert, ed. see Tubb, Kristin O'Donnell.
Winters, Ryan, illus. see Rose, Emmaline.
Winters, Talena. Undine's Tear. (p. 2326)
Winters, Terra, jt. auth. see Scholastic.
Winterson, Jeanette. Watcher. (p. 2383)
Winthrop, Elizabeth. Battle for the Castle. (p. 174)
—Castle in the Attic (35th Anniversary Edition) (p. 340)
Winthrop, John. Reading for Children: History (Classic Reprint) (p. 1846)
Winthrop, Sophy. Miss. Roberts' Fortune: A Story for Girls (Classic Reprint) (p. 1480)
Winthrop, Theodore. Edwin Brothertoft (Classic Reprint) (p. 627)
—John Brent (Classic Reprint) (p. 1172)

W

—Life in the Open Air, & Other Papers (Classic Reprint) (p. 1293)
—Mr. Waddy's Return (Classic Reprint) (p. 1521)
Winton, Alais. Fun Games & Activities for Children with Dyslexia. Salerno, Joe, illus. (p. 799)
Winton, Julia de. Yr Ynys Unyg: The Lonely Island. (p. 2536)
Winton, W. H. De. Forbidden Sacrifice, Vol. 3 of 3 (Classic Reprint) (p. 764)
Wintor, Quinton, illus. see Brooks, Ben.
wintranslation.com, tr. see Wildsmith, Brian.
wintranslation.com, tr. Carry Me (French/English) (p. 334)
—Eating the Rainbow (French/English) (p. 622)
Wintringham, Clifton. Experimental Inquiry on Some Parts of the Animal Structure (Classic Reprint) (p. 678)
Wintrob, Kitty. I'm Not Going Back: Wartime Memoir of a Child Evacuee. (p. 1098)
Wintz-Litty, Julie, illus. see Weninger, Brigitte.
Winward, Makenzie, illus. see Meyer, Lisa O.
Winzenried, Chandra. Epic Adventures of Chandrini Yogini: Chandrini Yogini Goes to India. Sil, Avijit, illus. (p. 657)
Wipf, Arden. Legacy for the Living. (p. 1261)
Wipo. Learn from the Past, Create the Future - the Arts & Copyright. (p. 1255)
Wirbeleit, Patrick. Box (Book One) Heidschötter, Uwe, illus. (p. 266)
Wireman, Katharine R., illus. see Wiggin, Kate Douglas.
Wirkala, Rita, tr. see Shah, Idries.
Wirkner, Linda. Learning about America's Industrial Growth & Expansion with Graphic Organizers. (p. 1257)
Wirrenga, Shannon, illus. see Ficocelli, Elizabeth.
Wirsén, Stina, illus. see Nilsson, Frida.
Wirt, Mildred A. Guilt of the Brass Thieves. (p. 904)
—Saboteurs on the River. (p. 1920)
—Signal in the Dark. (p. 2016)
—Swamp Island. (p. 2167)
—Voice from the Cave. (p. 2365)
—Whispering Walls. (p. 2443)
Wirth, Margie & Sherfinski, Julie. BF: the Carrot Monster. (p. 212)
Wirths, Claudine G., jt. auth. see Bowman-Kruhm, Mary.
Wisa, Louis, illus. see Garis, Howard R.
Wisa, Louis, jt. auth. see Garis, Howard Roger.
Wisdom, Sahara. ABCs Our Way. (p. 5)
—Cultural Counting. (p. 484)
—Free to Be Modest. (p. 782)
Wise, Anna. Vala of Trinity: Book One Norse Series (p. 2343)
Wise Bauer, Susan, ed. see Bauer, Susan Wise.
Wise, Bill. If You Played Hide-And-Seek with a Chameleon Evans, Rebecca, illus. (p. 1093)
Wise Brown, Margaret. PÁJARO MUERTO. (p. 1693)
Wise Brown, Margaret, jt. auth. see Sebring Lowrey, Janette.
Wise Brown, Margaret, jt. auth. see Williams, Garth.
Wise, Caroline. Sulky Sue (Classic Reprint) (p. 2148)
Wise, Daniel. Boy Travelers in Arabia; or, from Boston to Bagdad: Including Pictures, Sketches, & Anecdotes of the Wandering Arabs, & of the City of Good Haroun Alraschid; (Classic Reprint) (p. 270)
—Jessie Carlton: The Story of a Girl Who Fought with the Little Impulse, the Wizard, & Conquered Him (Classic Reprint) (p. 1165)
—Jessie Carlton. (p. 1165)
—Kate Carlton: The Story of a Proud, Vain Girl (Classic Reprint) (p. 1204)
—Summer Days on the Hudson. (p. 2149)
Wise, J. K. Natural Disasters. (p. 1579)
Wise, John Sergeant. Diomed: The Life, Travels, & Observations of a Dog (Classic Reprint) (p. 551)
Wise, Keith. Isabella's Playmate. (p. 1138)
Wise, Loveis, illus. see Elliott, Zetta.
Wise, Rachel. Black & White & Gray All Over (p. 236)
—Black & White & Gray All Over. (p. 236)
—Breaking News. (p. 278)
—Cast Your Ballot! (p. 339)
—Digital Disaster! (p. 546)
—Everyone's a Critic (p. 672)
—Everyone's a Critic. (p. 672)
—Late Edition. (p. 1250)
—Level Playing Field (p. 1281)
—Level Playing Field. (p. 1281)
—Old Story, New Twist (p. 1648)
—Old Story, New Twist. (p. 1648)
—Read All about It! (p. 1845)
—Set the Record Straight! (p. 1993)
—Stop the Presses! (p. 2122)
—Texting 1, 2, 3 (p. 2210)
—Texting 1, 2, 3. (p. 2210)
Wise, Steve. Critical World Issues: Euthanasia (p. 476)
Wise, Tama. Street Dreams. (p. 2140)
Wise, Terry, illus. see Rodgers, Lenora.
Wise-Douglas, Terri. Wonderful World of Cupcakes. Duckworth, Jeffrey, illus. (p. 2490)
Wisehart, Randall. Luke's Summer Secret. (p. 1367)
Wisely, Linda, contrib. by. Theopolda's Quest. (p. 2216)
Wiseman, A. H. Toby Gets Lost. (p. 2254)
Wiseman, Blaine. Airbnb. (p. 37)
—Argentina. (p. 114)
—Baseball. (p. 168)
—Basketball. (p. 170)
—Beavers. (p. 186)
—Blizzards. (p. 245)
—Boeing. (p. 253)
—Budgeting. (p. 290)
—Bulldozers. (p. 296)
—Chinese. (p. 378)
—Colombia. (p. 417)
—Dump Trucks: WOW: Big Machines. (p. 610)
—Dump Trucks. (p. 610)
—Ecologist. (p. 623)
—Excavators. (p. 676)
—Extreme Excavators. (p. 686)
—Father's Day: Canadian Celebrations. (p. 715)
—Fête des Pères: Les Célébrations Canadiennes. Karvonen, Tanjah, tr. from ENG. (p. 721)
—Football. (p. 761)
—Haiti. (p. 910)
—Indonesia. (p. 1117)
—Iran. (p. 1133)
—Johnson & Johnson. (p. 1175)
—Jumbo Jets: WOW: Big Machines. (p. 1188)
—Jumbo Jets. (p. 1188)
—Lynxes. (p. 1370)
—Martial Arts. (p. 1410)
—Midwest. (p. 1462)
—Mighty Bulldozers. (p. 1462)
—Monster Trucks: WOW: Big Machines. (p. 1497)
—Monster Trucks. (p. 1497)
—MotoX. (p. 1512)
—Nigeria. (p. 1604)
—Nineteen Eighty-Four. (p. 1610)
—Northeast. (p. 1621)
—Persians. (p. 1725)
—Record Breakers (p. 1854)
—Shaun White. (p. 2003)
—Skateboarding. (p. 2029)
—Snowboarding. (p. 2048)
—Snowmobiling. (p. 2049)
—Soccer. (p. 2051)
—South Korea. (p. 2069)
—Southeast. (p. 2069)
—Southwest. (p. 2069)
—Stanley Cup. (p. 2101)
—Surfing. (p. 2163)
—Tough Tractors. (p. 2268)
—Tractors: WOW: Big Machines. (p. 2273)
—UFC Championship: Sporting Championships. (p. 2313)
—UFC Championship. (p. 2313)
—United Kingdom. (p. 2330)
—Volcanoes. (p. 2366)
—West. (p. 2401)
—World of Wonder: Big Machines (p. 2504)
Wiseman, Blaine & Gillespie, Katie. Alchemist. (p. 41)
Wiseman, Blaine & Kissock, Heather. Aztecs. (p. 146)
Wiseman, Blaine & Tait, Leia. Hockey Records. (p. 986)
Wiseman, Daniel, illus. see Bell, Kristen & Hart, Benjamin.
Wiseman, Daniel, illus. see Gehl, Laura.
Wiseman, Daniel, illus. see Hill, Susanna Leonard.
Wiseman, Daniel, illus. see Young, Jessica.
Wiseman, Daniel, jt. auth. see Bustard, Anne.
Wiseman, Daniel, jt. auth. see White, Dianne.
Wiseman, Eva. Last Song. (p. 1249)
—Puppet. (p. 1814)
—World Outside. (p. 2504)
Wiseman, H. E. Cardinal. Dramas: The Witch of Rosenburg; the Hidden Gem (Classic Reprint) (p. 596)
Wiseman, Nicholas Patrick. Dramas: The Witch of Rosenburg; the Hidden Gem (Classic Reprint) (p. 596)
—Dramas. (p. 596)
—Fabiola (Classic Reprint) (p. 690)
—Fabiola, or the Church of the Catacombs (Classic Reprint) (p. 690)
Wiseman, Rosalind. Boys, Girls & Other Hazardous Materials. (p. 272)
Wiseman, T. P. Julius Caesar: Roman General. (p. 1187)
Wisenfeld, Alison, illus. see Joslin, Mary.
Wisenrich, Athena. Sitar: Legend of the Morning Star. (p. 2027)
Wish, Katia, illus. see Dixon, Amy.
Wish, Katia, illus. see Smith, Bryan.
Wishar, John Herman. Transformation (Classic Reprint) (p. 2277)
Wisher, Mark. Don't kiss the Prince. (p. 583)
Wishinsky, Frieda. Avis Dolphin Dawson, Willow, illus. (p. 143)
—Blob (p. 245)
—Camp Disaster (p. 315)
—Camp Disaster. (p. 315)
—How Emily Saved the Bridge Nelson, Natalie, illus. (p. 1031)
—Maggie Can't Wait Griffiths, Dean, illus. (p. 1376)
—Man Who Made Parks: The Story of Parkbuilder Frederick Law Olmsted. Zhang, Song Nan, illus. (p. 1395)
—No Frogs for Dinner Hendry, Linda, illus. (p. 1613)
—Profiles #4: Freedom Heroines. (p. 1805)
—Remembering the Titanic. (p. 1864)
—What's up, Bear? A Book about Opposites. Moore, Sean L., illus. (p. 2426)
—Where Are You, Bear? A Canadian Alphabet Adventure. Moore, Sean L., illus. (p. 2435)
Wishinsky, Frieda, jt. auth. see MacLeod, Elizabeth.
Wishinsky, Frieda, jt. auth. see Weaver, Janice.
Wishinsky, Frieda & MacLeod, Elizabeth. How to Become an Accidental Genius Playford, Jenn, illus. (p. 1038)
Wisinski, Ed, illus. see Harper, Benjamin.
Wisken, Steven, illus. see Beale, Alan.
Wisler, Joelle. Ariana Gold. (p. 115)
Wisma, Mare. Adventures of Hazar the Golden Canary. Wan, Stephanie, illus. (p. 23)
—Cat with the Hemingway Paw. Cruz, Bruno, illus. (p. 342)
—Trials & Tribulations of Mischief the Extraordinary Cat. Cruz, Bruno, illus. (p. 2286)
—Trials & Tribulations of Mischief the Extraordinary Cat. Cruz, Bruno D., illus. (p. 2286)
Wismer, C. L. Missing Chocolate Chip Oatmeal Peanut Butter Raisin Cookie. (p. 1480)
Wisnewski, Andrea. Little Old Farm Folk. (p. 1323)
—Little Red Riding Hood. (p. 1326)
—Trio: The Tale of a Three-Legged Cat. (p. 2288)
Wisnewski, Andrea, illus. see Millen, C. M.
Wisnia, Chris. Doris Danger: Giant Monster Adventures. Vol. 1 (p. 586)
Wisnia, Saul. Miracle at Fenway: The Inside Story of the Boston Red Sox 2004 Championship Season. (p. 1474)
Wisniewski, David, illus. see Bunting, Eve.
Wisniewski, Gaya. My Bison. (p. 1533)
Wisniewski, Lori. Importance of Being Uu. (p. 1102)
Wison, Sarah K. L. Dragon School: Episodes 16 - 20. (p. 594)
Wissing, Caroline. Voiceless. (p. 2365)
Wissinger, Tamera Will. Gone Camping: A Novel in Verse. Cordell, Matthew, illus. (p. 861)
—Gone Fishing. Cordell, Matthew, illus. (p. 861)
—There Was an Old Lady Who Gobbled a Skink. Bermejo, Ana, illus. (p. 2217)
—This Old Band. Loveridge, Matt, illus. (p. 2226)
Wissinger, Tamera Will & Long, Earlene R. Gone Fishing: A Novel. Cordell, Matthew & Brown, Richard, illus. (p. 861)
Wissink-Tressler, Lynne. Crazy Bones! the Tale of a Waggy Tail. (p. 468)
Wist, S. J. Whispering Stone. (p. 2442)
Wister, A. L. Bailiff's Maid: A Romance from the German of E. Marlitt (Classic Reprint) (p. 159)
—Enchanting & Enchanted: From the German of Hacklander (Classic Reprint) (p. 647)
—Erlach Court: Translated from the German of Ossip Schubin (Classic Reprint) (p. 660)
—Gold Elsie: From the German of E. Marlitt (Classic Reprint) (p. 855)
—Leaves from the Life of a Good-For-Nothing (Classic Reprint) (p. 1259)
—Old Mam'selle's Secret (Classic Reprint) (p. 1647)
—Too Rich: A Romance after the German of Adolph Streckfuss (Classic Reprint) (p. 2261)
—Violetta: A Romance after the German of Ursula Zoge Von Manteuffel (Classic Reprint) (p. 2360)
Wister, Jones. Jones Wister's Reminiscences (Classic Reprint) (p. 1177)
Wister, Owen. Dragon of Wantley: His Tale (Classic Reprint) (p. 594)
—Dragon of Wantley. (p. 594)
—How Doth the Simple Spelling Bee (Classic Reprint) (p. 1030)
—Jimmyjohn Boss, & Other Stories (Classic Reprint) (p. 1169)
—Journey in Search of Christmas (Classic Reprint) (p. 1181)
—Lady Baltimore (Classic Reprint) (p. 1236)
—Lin Mclean (Classic Reprint) (p. 1303)
—Members of the Family (Classic Reprint) (p. 1443)
—Mother (Classic Reprint) (p. 1509)
—Neighbors Henceforth (Classic Reprint) (p. 1586)
—New Swiss Family Robinson: A Tale for Children of All Ages (Classic Reprint) (p. 1597)
—Philosophy a Story of Harvard University (Classic Reprint) (p. 1735)
—Red Men & White (Classic Reprint) (p. 1857)
—Virginian: A Horseman of the Plains (Classic Reprint) (p. 2361)
Wister, Sally. Diary of Sally Wister: A Colonial Quaker Girl (p. 540)
Wister, T. F., illus. see Jefferson, W. C.
Wisuri, Marlene, jt. auth. see Peacock, Thomas Love.
Wiszowaty, Robin. My Maasai Life: From Suburbia to Savannah (p. 1555)
Witanto, Shiella, illus. see Gottesfeld, Jeff.
Witchell, Charles A. Evolution of Bird-Song: With Observations on the Influence of Heredity & Imitation (Classic Reprint) (p. 675)
—Evolution of Bird-Song. (p. 675)
—Nature's Story of the Year (Classic Reprint) (p. 1582)
Witek, Jo. All My Treasures: A Book of Joy. Roussey, Christine, illus. (p. 53)
—Brave As Can Be: A Book of Courage. Roussey, Christine, illus. (p. 276)
—Dico de la Jeune Fille. (p. 541)
—Hello in There! A Big Sister's Book of Waiting. Roussey, Christine, illus. (p. 951)
—In My Heart: A Book of Feelings. Roussey, Christine, illus. (p. 1106)
—In My Room: A Book of Creativity & Imagination. Roussey, Christine, illus. (p. 1106)
—My Little Gifts: A Book of Sharing. Roussey, Christine, illus. (p. 1552)
—My Tree & Me: A Book of Seasons. Roussey, Christine, illus. (p. 1563)
—Ventre de Ma Maman. Toi Dedans, Moi Devant(le) (p. 2350)
—With My Daddy: A Book of Love & Family. Roussey, Christine, illus. (p. 2481)
Witesman, Owen, jt. auth. see Simukka, Salla.
Witesman, Owen, tr. see Hakkola, Kalle.
Witesman, Owen Frederick, tr. see Simukka, Salla.
Witherall, Sharon. Granddad & Nanny Sharon Meet the Mermaids. (p. 877)
Witherell, Nancy L., jt. auth. see McMackin, Mary C.
Withering, William. Systematic Arrangement of British Plants (Classic Reprint) (p. 2174)
Withers, John William. Euclid's Parallel Postulate: Its Nature, Validity, & Place in Geometrical Systems: Thesis Presented to the Philosophical Faculty of Yale University for the Degree of Doctor of Philosophy (Classic Reprint) (p. 667)
Withers, Kyrja. Rupert's Tales: The Price of Carrots: Friendship Is Magick, Too. Pringle-Burke, Lesli, illus. (p. 1916)
—Seeing Through the Storm: Friendship Is Magick, Too. Pringle-Burke, Lesli, illus. (p. 1984)
—What's in a Name? Magick Is Friendship, Too. Pringle-Burke, Lesli, illus. (p. 2424)
Withers, Margaret. Welcome to the Lord's Table: A Practical Course for Preparing Children to Receive Holy Communion. (p. 2398)
Withers, Pam. Andreo's Race. (p. 83)
—Casse-Cous: (Daredevil Club) (p. 339)
—First Descent. (p. 736)
—Respira (p. 1869)
—Stowaway. (p. 2136)
—Tracker's Canyon. (p. 2272)
Withers, Sarah. Child's World: Primer (Classic Reprint) (p. 376)
—Child's World: First Reader (Classic Reprint) (p. 376)
—Child's World: Third Reader (Classic Reprint) (p. 376)
—Child's World: Primer-... - Scholar's Choice Edition. (p. 376)
Witherspoon, Pattie French. Through Two Administrations: Character Sketches of Kentucky (Classic Reprint) (p. 2237)
Witherup, Anne Warrington. Peeps at People: Being Certain Papers from the Writings of Anne Warrington Witherup (Classic Reprint) (p. 1714)
Withey, John Franklin. Uncle Frank's Fish Stories: With Poems of a Fish Flavor (Classic Reprint) (p. 2318)
Withrow, Brandon & Withrow, Mindy. Peril & Peace: Chronicles of the Ancient Church (p. 1723)
Withrow, Lesley Breen, illus. see Dopirak, Kate.
Withrow, Mindy & Withrow, Brandon. Courage & Conviction: Chronicles of the Reformation Church (p. 462)
—Rescue & Redeem: Chronicles of the Modern Church. Vol. 5 (p. 1868)
Withrow, W. H. King's Messenger, or Lawrence Temple's Probation: A Story of Canadian Life (Classic Reprint) (p. 1223)
Witkin, Kim. Butterfly Blessings. (p. 304)
Witkowski, Teri. Bitty Bear, Flower Girl. Ackley, Peggy Jo, illus. (p. 235)
—Bitty Bunny's Slipper Search. Ackley, Peggy Jo, illus. (p. 235)
Witman, David. First Seed. (p. 739)
Witman, Melissa Buyer. Mishkan HaNefesh for Youth: A Machzor for Youth & Families. Podwal, Mark H., illus. (p. 1477)
Witmer, Edith. Helping Grandfather. Reinford, Luanne & Horst, Melissa, illus. (p. 953)
Witmer, Nicole. Active Minds My First Book of Planets. Allen, Marie, illus. (p. 12)
Witmer, Ruth, illus. see Martin, Mabel.
Witmer, Scott. Political Systems (p. 1771)
—Sports & Society (p. 2088)
Witnes, Vitus, illus. see Baia, Edward.
Witschger, Anne-Laure. 7 Artistes et Moi. (p. 2548)
Witschonke, Alan, illus. see Mann, Elizabeth.
Witschonke, Alan, illus. see Robb, Don.
Witschonke, Alan, jt. auth. see Mann, Elizabeth.
Witsil, Grace. Ida from Idaho & the Boise River Afternoon. (p. 1089)
Witt, David, illus. see Fontes, Ron & Fontes, Justine.
Witt, David, illus. see Jolley, Dan.
Witt, David, illus. see Limke, Jeff.
Witt, David, illus. see Schweizer, Chris.
Witt, David, illus. see Storrie, Paul D.
Witt, De. Original Dialogues, or Conversations: Designed for the Use of Schools & the Family Circle (Classic Reprint) (p. 1671)
Witt, Eddie, illus. see Vil, Steve.
Witt, Edwin D. de. Nassau Herald of the Class of 1900 of Princeton University, Vol. 36: Class-Day, June 11th, 1900 (Classic Reprint) (p. 1576)
Witt, Janice. Harold Discovers Santa's Secret: A Very Long Dog with a Very Big Heart. Reznicek, Curtis, illus. (p. 931)
Witt, Jennie De. Kate Weston, or to Will & to Do (Classic Reprint) (p. 1204)
Witt, John De. Versatile Verse (Classic Reprint) (p. 2352)
Witt, Louis. Pictures Out of the Past: A Hanukkah Play (Classic Reprint) (p. 1741)
Witt, Madame Guizot De. Parisian Family (Classic Reprint) (p. 1700)
Witt, Rici, illus. see Rose, Alea.
Witt, Robert M. De. Free & Easy Comic Songster: Being a Choice Collection of Amusing, Broadly Burlesque, Dry, Droll, Humorous, & Truly Original Songs; All Adapted to Very Popular Airs (Classic Reprint) (p. 782)
—Webster's Little Folks' Speaker: Comprising Many Standard Pieces, As Well As a Great Many Entirely Original, Both Sentimental & Humorous (Classic Reprint) (p. 2395)
Witt, Sandy. We Are All Different... but That's Okay. (p. 2388)
Witte, Anna. Fandango de Lola. Archer, Micha, illus. (p. 706)
—Lola's Fandango. Archer, Micha, illus. (p. 1340)
—Lola's Fandango. Masse, Josée & Archer, Micha, illus. (p. 1340)
—Loro Tico Tango. Witte, Anna, illus. (p. 1349)
—Parrot Tico Tango. Witte, Anna, illus. (p. 1701)
Witte, Anna & Amador, Brian. Parrot Tico Tango. Witte, Anna, illus. (p. 1701)
Witte, Brianna. Witches & Vampires. (p. 2480)
Witte, Iris. Portal der Magie: Glimmerwelt der Phantasie. (p. 1779)
—Samedo und der Glutblutstein. Witte, Iris, illus. (p. 1927)
—Samedo und der Zauberwald. (p. 1927)
Witte, J. S. Rescue of Charles de Simpson: Book One in the Dorchester Chronicles (p. 1868)
Witte, Jessica Pierce. Dexter the Duck Gets His Quack. York, Shane, illus. (p. 536)
Witte, Sam. Gamal Abdel Nasser. (p. 806)
Wittebrood, Menno, illus. see Coxall, Darcy.
Wittekind, Erika. Afghanistan (p. 31)
—Amazon. com: The Company & Its Founder (p. 67)
—Argentina (p. 114)
—Benjamin Banneker: Brilliant Surveyor, Mathematician, & Astronomer (p. 200)
—Big Push: How Popular Culture Is Always Selling (p. 222)
—Gloria Steinem: Women's Liberation Leader (p. 844)
—James Madison's Presidency. (p. 1157)
—Violence as Entertainment: Why Aggression Sells. (p. 2359)
—What's Great about Wisconsin? (p. 2424)
Wittekind, Erika & Gerhardt, Michael J. United States v. Nixon: The Watergate Scandal & Limits to Us Presidential Power (p. 2332)
Witteman, Mina. Nido de Mia. (p. 1604)
Wittemund, Fatima. Magic Net. (p. 1378)
Witten, George. Outlaw Trails: A Yankee Hobo Soldier of the Queen (Classic Reprint) (p. 1685)
Witten, Jonathan. Football Freddie & Fomble the Dog: Gameday in Chicago. (p. 761)
Witten, Suzy. 10/10ths: A Young Adult Novel of la Carrera Panamericana. (p. 2550)
Wittenbach, Jennie Gannon. Nito & the Witch. (p. 1611)
Wittenberg, Stella, illus. see Ende, Michael.
Wittenstein, Barry. Boo-Boos That Changed the World: A True Story about an Accidental Invention (Really!) Hsu, Chris, illus. (p. 256)
—Place to Land: Martin Luther King Jr. & the Speech That Inspired a Nation. Pinkney, Jerry, illus. (p. 1753)
Wittenstein, Barry & Ladd, London. Waiting for Pumpsie. (p. 2370)
Wittenstein, Barry & Mallett, Keith. Sonny's Bridge: Jazz Legend Sonny Rollins Finds His Groove. (p. 2064)

Wittenstein, Vicki Oransky. Reproductive Rights: Who Decides? (p. 1867)
Witthaus, A. S. Frankie the Frog Saves Christmas. (p. 778)
—Princess Sach. (p. 1799)
Wittigschlager, Wilhelmina. Minna, Wife of the Young Rabbi: A Novel (Classic Reprint) (p. 1473)
Wittkamp, Frantz, illus. see Nöstlinger, Christine.
Wittkamp, Frantz, tr. see Nöstlinger, Christine.
Wittlinger, Ellen. Saturdays with Hitchcock. (p. 1936)
—Someone Else's Shoes. (p. 2060)
—This Means War! (p. 2226)
Wittlin-Leger, Heddie. Sofa Dog. Berner Coble, Lynn, ed. (p. 2054)
Wittman, Kathy A. Raina's Vision Quest (p. 1836)
Wittman, Kelly. Botswana. Rotberg, Robert I., ed. (p. 264)
Wittman, Patricia. Scrabble Creek. (p. 1963)
Wittman, Susan S. Heroes of the Civil War (p. 962)
—Reconstruction: Outcomes of the Civil War (p. 1854)
Wittmann, Kelly. Bone Wars: The Race to Dig up Dinosaurs. (p. 255)
—Botswana. (p. 264)
—Botswana. Rotberg, Robert I., ed. (p. 264)
—Building the Transcontinental Railroad: Race of the Railroad Companies. (p. 295)
—Freedom of Assembly. (p. 782)
—Race to Sail Around the World. (p. 1831)
—Right to Bear Arms. (p. 1882)
Wittmann, Patricia, illus. see Murray, Marjorie Dennis.
Wittner, David G. Commodore Matthew Perry & the Perry Expedition to Japan. (p. 430)
Witton, Hannah. Doing It. (p. 578)
Wittrock, Jeni. ABCs. Banks, Timothy, illus. (p. 4)
—Ancient Armadillos. (p. 79)
—Baby Rabbit Story. (p. 152)
—How Honest Are You? (p. 1032)
—Laika the Space Dog: First Hero in Outer Space Toth, Shannon, illus. (p. 1239)
—Pet Hermit Crabs up Close. (p. 1726)
—Pet Rabbits up Close. (p. 1726)
—Tarantulas (p. 2191)
—W. E. B. du Bois. (p. 2369)
Wittrock, Jeni, jt. auth. see Jones, Jen.
Wittrock, Jeni & Rustad, Martha E. H. Baby Animals. (p. 148)
Wittrock, Jeni, et al. Animal Heroes (p. 90)
—Great African-Americans (p. 883)
Wittwer, Hala, illus. see Loehr, Mallory.
Wittwer, Hala Swearingen, illus. see Hays, Anna Jane.
Wittwer, Meg, illus. see Tillery, Paul, IV & Tillery, Paul.
Witwer, Meg, illus. see Tillery, Paul, IV.
Witwer, Beverly. Triplet Ballerinas. Sonke, Sandie, illus. (p. 2289)
Witwer, H. C. Alex the Great (Classic Reprint) (p. 42)
—Kid Scanlan (Classic Reprint) (p. 1213)
—Leather Pushers (Classic Reprint) (p. 1259)
—Rubyiat of a Freshman (Classic Reprint) (p. 1911)
—There's No Base Like Home (Classic Reprint) (p. 2218)
Witwer, Harry Charles. From Baseball to Boches (Classic Reprint) (p. 791)
Wiviott, Meg. Benno & the Night of Broken Glass Bisaillon, Josée & Bisaillon, Josée, illus. (p. 200)
—Benno & the Night of Broken Glass. Bisaillon, Josée, illus. (p. 200)
—Paper Hearts. (p. 1697)
Wizard, Prodigy. Colors Workbook Prek-Grade 1 - Ages 4 To 7. (p. 426)
—First Words Matching Game: Children's Reading & Writing Education Books. (p. 740)
Wlodarski, Loran. Felina's New Home: A Florida Panther Story Clayton, Lew, illus. (p. 719)
—If a Dolphin Were a Fish in Chinese. Shuqi, Yang, tr. (p. 1090)
Wloszczyna, Susan, jt. auth. see Johnson, Jordan.
Wodehouse, P. G. Aunt's Aren't Gentlemen. (p. 137)
—Gold Bat. (p. 855)
—Head of Kay's. (p. 942)
—Love among the Chickens. (p. 1358)
—Mike. (p. 1464)
—Mike & Psmith. (p. 1464)
—Tales of St. Austin's. (p. 2185)
—White Feather. (p. 2444)
Wodehouse, Pelham Grenville. Gold Bat. (p. 855)
—Head of Kay's (Classic Reprint) (p. 942)
—Heart of a Goof (Classic Reprint) (p. 945)
—Indiscretions of Archie (Classic Reprint) (p. 1117)
—Intrusion of Jimmy, Vol. 5 (Classic Reprint) (p. 1129)
—Little Nugget (Classic Reprint) (p. 1323)
—Love among the Chickens: A Story of the Haps & Mishaps on an English Chicken Farm - Scholar's Choice Edition. (p. 1358)
—Love among the Chickens: A Story of the Haps & Mishaps on an English Chicken Farm (Classic Reprint) (p. 1359)
—Meet Mr. Mulliner (Classic Reprint) (p. 1438)
—Mike: A Public School Story (Classic Reprint) (p. 1464)
—Mike at Wrykyn. (p. 1464)
—Piccadilly Jim (Classic Reprint) (p. 1738)
—Pothunters. (p. 1781)
—Pothunters - Scholar's Choice Edition. (p. 1781)
—Prince & Betty (Classic Reprint) (p. 1793)
—Tales of St. Austin's (Classic Reprint) (p. 2185)
—Their Mutual Child (Classic Reprint) (p. 2215)
—Three Men & a Maid (Classic Reprint) (p. 2234)
—Uneasy Money (Classic Reprint) (p. 2327)
—White Feather. (p. 2444)
—White Feather (Classic Reprint) (p. 2444)
—William Tell Told Again - Illustrated in Color. Philip Dadd, illus. (p. 2468)
Woden, George. Little Houses a Tale of Past Years (Classic Reprint) (p. 1319)
Wodson, Harry M. Private Warwick: Musings of a Canuck in Khaki (Classic Reprint) (p. 1802)
Wodson, Harry Milner. Whirlpool: Scenes from Toronto Police Court (Classic Reprint) (p. 2442)
Wodzak, Mango. Arnold Trevor Cirrus. (p. 118)
Woelfle, Gretchen. Answering the Cry for Freedom: Stories of African Americans & the American Revolution. Christie, R. Gregory, illus. (p. 101)
—Mumbet's Declaration of Independence. Delinois, Alix, illus. (p. 1526)
—Wind at Work: An Activity Guide to Windmills. (p. 2471)
—Write on, Mercy! The Secret Life of Mercy Otis Warren. Wallner, Alexandra, illus. (p. 2512)
Woellner, Elyse. It's Bedtime: New Edition. (p. 1144)
Woerle, Hans. Erschütterungsbezirk des Grossen Erdbebens Zu Lissabon: Ein Beitrag Zur Geschichte der Erdbeben (Classic Reprint) (p. 660)
Woerner, J. G. Rebel's Daughter: A Story of Love, Politics & War (Classic Reprint) (p. 1852)
Woerth, George. Book of Hard Facts. (p. 258)
Woffington, Sandra. Evil Speaks. (p. 674)
Wofford, Delaney. For Courage. (p. 762)
Wofford, Sherry Lynn. Introducing the Adventures of Jerry Giraffe & Feather Bird. (p. 1129)
—Jerry Giraffe & Feather Bird on Safari: The Adventures Continue! (p. 1164)
Wohl, David. Fathom Volume 5: Cold Destiny. Hernandez, Vince & Mastromauro, Frank, eds. (p. 715)
Wohl, Julie Schwartz. Make, Create, Celebrate! Jewish Holidays Through Art. (p. 1386)
Wohl, Lauren L. Blueberry Bonanza Tuchman, Mark, illus. (p. 249)
—Eighth Menorah. Hughes, Laura, illus. (p. 629)
—Extravaganza at the Plaza Tuchman, Mark, illus. (p. 686)
—Teeny Tiny Halloween Cole, Henry, illus. (p. 2200)
—Zooapalooza in the Park Tuchman, Mark, illus. (p. 2543)
Wohlenhaus, Kim, ed. Suicide Information for Teens. (p. 2147)
Wohlfarth, Julia Helen. New-World Speller: Grades One & Two (Classic Reprint) (p. 1598)
—New-World Speller: Grades Six, Seven, & Eight (Classic Reprint) (p. 1598)
—New-World Speller: Second Book for Grades Four, Five, & Six, Pp. 137-280. (p. 1598)
—Self-Help English Lessons (Classic Reprint) (p. 1987)
Wohlleben, Peter. Can You Hear the Trees Talking? Discovering the Hidden Life of the Forest (p. 318)
—Peter & the Tree Children. Atkinson, Cale, illus. (p. 1728)
Wohlleber, Dan. Harry: The Very Hairy Hare. (p. 934)
Wohlman, Ronald. Kingdom of Nothing. Hewitt, Dylan, illus. (p. 1222)
Wohlrabe, Sarah C. Visit to the Library. Thompson, Jeffrey, illus. (p. 2362)
Wohnoutka, Mike. Croc & Turtle. (p. 476)
—Croc & Turtle: Snow Fun! (p. 476)
—Dad's First Day. (p. 495)
—Head, Shoulders, Knees, & Toes. (p. 942)
—So Big! (p. 2050)
Wohnoutka, Mike, illus. see Beil, Karen Magnuson.
Wohnoutka, Mike, illus. see Buzzeo, Toni.
Wohnoutka, Mike, illus. see Hill, Susanna Leonard.
Wohnoutka, Mike, illus. see Kehoe, Tim.
Wohnoutka, Mike, illus. see Kimmel, Eric A.
Wohnoutka, Mike, illus. see LaRochelle, David.
Wohnoutka, Mike, illus. see Pace, Anne Marie.
Wohnoutka, Mike, illus. see Random House.
Wohnoutka, Mike, illus. see Roemer, Heidi Bee.
Wohnoutka, Mike, illus. see Schotter, Roni.
Wohnoutka, Mike, illus. see Van Hoven, Constance.
Woik, Julie. Life & Times of Lilly the Lash: The Garden Gathering. Tobin, Marc, illus. (p. 1290)
Wojahn, Rebecca Hogue & Donald. Australian Outback Food Chain: A Who-Eats-What Adventure. (p. 138)
—Desert Food Chain: A Who-Eats-What Adventures in North America. (p. 531)
—Rain Forest Food Chain: A Who-Eats-What Adventures in South America. (p. 1835)
—Savanna Food Chain: A Who-Eats-What Adventure in Africa. (p. 1937)
—Tundra Food Chain: A Who-Eats-What in the Arctic. (p. 2299)
Wojahn, Rebecca Hogue & Wojahn, Donald. Cloud Forest Food Chain: A Who-Eats-What Adventure in Africa. (p. 407)
—Coral Reef Food Chain: A Who-Eats-What Adventure in the Caribbean Sea. (p. 453)
—Desert Food Chain: A Who-Eats-What Adventure in North America. (p. 531)
—Estuary Food Chain: A Who-Eats-What Adventure in North America. (p. 665)
—Temperate Forest Food Chain: A Who-Eats-What Adventure in North America. (p. 2202)
—Tundra Food Chain: A Who-Eats-What Adventure in the Arctic. (p. 2299)
Wojahn, Rebecca Hogue & Wojahn, Rebecca. Dr. Kate: Angel on Snowshoes. (p. 591)
Wojciechowska, Maia. Kingdom in a Horse. (p. 1221)
—Shadow of a Bull. (p. 1996)
Wojciechowska, Marisha. Bangkok: City of Angels (My Globetrotter Book): Global Adventures... in the Palm of Your Hands! (p. 163)
—New York (My Globetrotter Book) Travel Activity Book for Children 6-12 Years Old. (p. 1599)
—Paris (My Globetrotter Book) Global Adventures... in the Palm of Your Hands! (p. 1700)
—Québec et Montréal. (p. 1823)
Wojciechowska, Marisha & Gyaurov, Angel. Tokyo (My Globetrotter Book) Global Adventures... in the Palm of Your Hands! (p. 2256)
Wojciechowski, Susan. Best Halloween of All. Meddaugh, Susan, illus. (p. 206)
—Christmas Miracle of Jonathan Toomey. Lynch, P. J., illus. (p. 386)
Wojcik, Chelsea A. Bible Journaling with Kids. (p. 213)
Wojcik, Joe. Call Me Yubbie. (p. 311)
Wojick, Luke. I Can Draw Shapes: Shapes & Their Attributes. (p. 1062)
—I Can Draw Shapes. (p. 1062)
Wojnar, Stella. Tatler, Vol. 9: June, 1930 (Classic Reprint) (p. 2193)
Wojtkiewicz, Maciej. Julia vs Olympics: A Novellette. (p. 1187)
Wojton, Nick. Oops! They're X-Rays! (p. 1665)
Wojton, Roxane. My Mommy & Me & Baby Makes Three. (p. 1556)
Wojtowicz, Jen. Boy Who Grew Flowers. Adams, Steve, illus. (p. 271)
—Des Fleurs Pour Angélina. Adams, Steve, illus. (p. 530)
Wojtowycz, David. Elephant Joe, Brave Firefighter! (p. 634)
Wojtowycz, David, illus. see Andreae, Giles.
Wojzowitz, Jen, jt. auth. see Wojtowicz, Jen.
Wokes, Paul & Cummings, Delphine. Percy the Pebble. Dynes, Katy, illus. (p. 1721)
—Poddle's First Flight. Dynes, Katy, illus. (p. 1764)
Wokkel, Ulla. Domi und Die Hohle der Schwarzen Drachen. (p. 580)
Wolanksi Ma Lpc, Kristy. Giraffe That Lost His Footprint. (p. 834)
Wolber, Lee. Porcupine Polly Needs a Hug. (p. 1778)
Wolcott, Grace. Coraddi, Vol. 32: May, 1928 (Classic Reprint) (p. 452)
—Coraddi, Vol. 32: Member of North Carolina Collegiate Press Association; June, 1928 (Classic Reprint) (p. 452)
Wolcott, K. Hannah, ed. see Wolcott, P. A.
Wolcott, Karen, illus. see Gordh, Bill & Pugliano-Martin, Carol.
Wolcott, Karen, illus. see Jordan, Apple & RH Disney Staff.
Wolcott, Karen, illus. see Parker, Jessie.
Wolcott, Karen, illus. see Roberts, Angela.
Wolcott, Karen, illus. see Twersky, Atara.
Wolcott, Laura. Gray Dream, Vol. 1 Of 2: And Other Stories of New England Life (Classic Reprint) (p. 882)
—Maddalena's Day: And Other Sketches (Classic Reprint) (p. 1374)
Wolcott, P. A. Bumble in the Barrel. (p. 297)
—Fox the Badger & the Bunny. (p. 774)
—Fox, the Badger, & the Bunny: A Dales Tale. Wolcott, K. Hannah, ed. (p. 774)
—Pear Tree. (p. 1710)
Wolcott-Whitten, Sue. Stalker. (p. 2099)
Wold, Bruce. Lil' Red Pepper. McGinty, Lupi, illus. (p. 1301)
Wolds, Clara. Greedy Gran. (p. 892)
Wolek, Guy, illus. see Dungy, Tony & Dungy, Lauren.
Wolek, Guy, illus. see Horender, Philip M.
Wolek, Guy, illus. see Huneke, Amanda.
Wolek, Guy, illus. see Kipling, Rudyard.
Wolek, Guy, illus. see Niner, Holly L.
Wolek, Guy, illus. see Oberschneider, Michael.
Wolek, Guy, jt. auth. see Baum, L. Frank.
Wolek, Katia. Vengeance D'Ulysse(la) (p. 2350)
Woleslagle, Amie. Snowball & the Missing Apple. (p. 2048)
Wolf, Alice S. House of Cards (Classic Reprint) (p. 1022)
Wolf, Aline D. Our Peaceful Classroom. (p. 1680)
Wolf, Allan. Day the Universe Exploded My Head: Poems to Take You into Space & Back Again. Raff, Anna, illus. (p. 514)
—Snow Fell Three Graves Deep: Voices from the Donner Party. (p. 2047)
—Watch That Ends the Night: Voices from the Titanic. (p. 2383)
—Who Killed Christopher Goodman? (p. 2448)
—Who Killed Christopher Goodman? Based on a True Crime. (p. 2448)
Wolf, Alyssa, jt. auth. see Ring, Susan.
Wolf, Annie S. Pictures & Portraits of Foreign Travel. (p. 1741)
—Pictures & Portraits of Foreign Travel (Classic Reprint) (p. 1741)
Wolf, Beverly. Mimi & K. Bug. (p. 1468)
Wolf, Bree. Butterflies: A Tale of Love & Friendship. (p. 303)
—Dragonflies: A Tale of Courage & Respect. (p. 595)
—Fireflies: A Tale of Life & Death. (p. 734)
—Heroes Next Door Box Set: The Complete Series. (p. 962)
Wolf, Bruce, illus. see Abrams, Pam.
Wolf, Bruce, photos by see Rudy, Maggie & Abrams, Pam.
Wolf, Cassandra. Hannah's Magical Horse Farm. (p. 918)
Wolf, Cathrine, ed. see Sweeny, Sheila.
Wolf, Clarissa. Cat, Cat, Feral Cat. Messer, Corey, illus. (p. 341)
—Orange Fizz. Wolf, Myron, photos by. (p. 1668)
Wolf, Claudia, illus. see Mackall, Dandi Daley.
Wolf Dreisbach, Kristina. Tale from a Fox Hound Beagle Named Bailey: Are We Going to the Lake Yet? (p. 2178)
Wolf, Elaine. Camp: A Novel. (p. 315)
—Camp. (p. 315)
Wolf, Elizabeth, illus. see Bader, Bonnie & Who HQ.
Wolf, Elizabeth, illus. see Bader, Bonnie.
Wolf, Elizabeth, illus. see Lehman-Wilzig, Tami.
Wolf, Elizabeth, illus. see Milton, Joyce & Who HQ.
Wolf, Elizabeth, illus. see Thompson, Gare & Who HQ.
Wolf, Elizabeth, illus. see Thompson, Gare.
Wolf, Ema. ¡Silencio, Niños! y Otros Cuentos. Pez, illus. (p. 2017)
Wolf, Emma. Heirs of Yesterday (Classic Reprint) (p. 949)
—Other Things Being Equal (Classic Reprint) (p. 1675)
—Prodigal in Love: A Novel (Classic Reprint) (p. 1803)
—Prodigal in Love. (p. 1803)
Wolf, Jamieson. Sophie's Choice. (p. 2065)
Wolf, Jennifer Shaw. Breaking Beautiful. (p. 278)
—Dead Girls Don't Lie. (p. 517)
Wolf, Joan M. Runs with Courage. (p. 1916)
—Someone Named Eva. (p. 2060)
Wolf, Karina. I Am Not a Fox. Groenink, Chuck, illus. (p. 1059)
Wolf, Laurie Goldrich. Crafty Princess: Green & Groovy. (p. 466)
—Lonely Sock Club: One Sock, Tons of Cool Projects! (p. 1342)
Wolf, LeeHee, illus. see Honey, Steve.
Wolf, Linda. Cozy Kitty (p. 465)
Wolf, Mari. Empty Bottle. (p. 645)
Wolf, Marie E. GHB & Analogs: High-Risk Club Drugs. (p. 827)
Wolf, Matt, illus. see Stilton, Geronimo.
Wolf, Matt, jt. auth. see Stilton, Geronimo.
Wolf, Myron, photos by see Wolf, Clarissa.
Wolf, Ned. Nandia's Apparition: Book II of the Nandia Trilogy. (p. 1574)
—Nandia's Copper. (p. 1574)
Wolf, Penny, et al. Bea's Almost Bad Day. Sweet Briar School, illus. (p. 181)
Wolf, Rachel Jepson. Unplugged Family Activity Book: 60+ Simple Crafts & Recipes for Year-Round Fun. (p. 2334)
Wolf, Rudolf. Handbuch der Mathematik, Physik, Geodäsie und Astronomie, Vol. 1 of 2 (Classic Reprint) (p. 915)
Wolf, Ryan. Control Room (p. 445)
—Watches & Warnings (p. 2383)
Wolf, Sallie. Peter's Trucks. (p. 1730)
—Truck Stuck. Davies, Andy Robert, illus. (p. 2292)
Wolf, Sallie & Bornstein, Micah. Robin Makes a Laughing Sound: A Birder's Journal. (p. 1891)
Wolf, Sara. Bring Me Their Hearts. (p. 282)
—Find Me Their Bones. (p. 728)
—Forget Me Always. (p. 767)
—Love Me Never. (p. 1360)
Wolf, Szanne & Grace, Guy. Room 23 & the Lock down Drill. Nethercot, Michelle, illus. (p. 1903)
Wolfe, Alyce, illus. see Chesnutt, Van.
Wolfe, Art, photos by see Helman, Andrea.
Wolfe, Austin. Legend. (p. 1261)
—Lumiere. (p. 1368)
Wolfe, Benjamin. Buzz -N- Zipp. (p. 305)
Wolfe, Bradley W. Upside Downside Up. (p. 2339)
Wolfe, Brian & Wolfe, Nick. Fun Face Painting Ideas for Kids: 40 Step-By-Step Demos. (p. 798)
Wolfe, Carolyn. Am I Your Pet? Patil, Amruta, illus. (p. 61)
—Bedtime of the Sky & Other Sleepy-Bye Stories. Mathis, Leslie, illus. (p. 188)
—Unhappy Little Dragon: Lessons Begin. Mathis, Leslie, illus. (p. 2327)
Wolfe, Daniel. Trees Are Not Umbrellas. (p. 2284)
Wolfe, Diane, illus. see Cornell, Kari A., ed.
Wolfe, Diane, photos by see Cornell, Kari A., ed.
Wolfe, Elisabeth, jt. auth. see Monaghan, Annabel.
Wolfe, Gillian. Look! Drawing the Line in Art. (p. 1345)
Wolfe, Greg. Shmelf the Hanukkah Elf. McWilliam, Howard, illus. (p. 2008)
Wolfe, Helen. Terrific Women Teachers (p. 2207)
Wolfe, Hillary, jt. auth. see Rice, William B.
Wolfe, Hillary & Rice, William B. Blast off to Space Camp (p. 243)
Wolfe, Humbert. Circular Saws (Classic Reprint) (p. 393)
Wolfe, James. Colonial Period (p. 418)
—Genetic Testing & Gene Therapy. (p. 815)
—Industrial Revolution: Steam & Steel. (p. 1117)
Wolfe, James & Callahan, Kerry P. Understanding the Articles of Confederation. (p. 2325)
Wolfe, James & Moe, Barbara A. Understanding the Charter of the Massachusetts Bay Colony. (p. 2325)
Wolfe, James & Stair, Nancy L. Understanding the Bill of Rights. (p. 2325)
Wolfe, James & Viegas, Jennifer. Understanding the Declaration of Independence. (p. 2325)
Wolfe, James, ed. Industrial Revolution. (p. 1117)
Wolfe, James, et al. Understanding the Iroquois Constitution. (p. 2325)
Wolfe, Jane. Cheeky Frog. Benham, Tors, illus. (p. 363)
—Crazy Cow. Benham, Tors, illus. (p. 468)
—Dizzy Duck. Benham, Tors, illus. (p. 567)
—Happy Cat. Benham, Tors, illus. (p. 921)
—Hungry Horse. Benham, Tors, illus. (p. 1052)
—Messy Pig. Benham, Tors, illus. (p. 1452)
—Noisy Dog. Benham, Tors, illus. (p. 1617)
—Pull the Lever: Who Are You? The Toy Box, illus. (p. 1812)
—Pull the Lever: Who Does What? Benham, Tors, illus. (p. 1812)
—Pull the Lever: Who's in Here? Benham, Tors, illus. (p. 1812)
—Sleepy Sheep. Benham, Tors, illus. (p. 2037)
—Who Lives Here? Toy Box Staff, illus. (p. 2448)
—Who Says Moo? Toy Box Staff, illus. (p. 2449)
—Who's Hiding? Toy Box Staff, illus. (p. 2453)
Wolfe, Jane & Baxter, Nicola. Who's on the Farm? Lawson, Peter, illus. (p. 2453)
Wolfe, Jaymie Stuart. Adoring Jesus with the Holy Father. (p. 17)
—Family Matters: Thirteen Short Stories. (p. 702)
Wolfe, Jaymie Stuart, jt. auth. see Monge, Marlyn.
Wolfe, Julie Leavitt. Dear Jack: A Letter from a Special Needs Child to Her Sibling. (p. 520)
Wolfe, K. M. & Moose, L. G. Deekin Duck & His Sleepytime Nursery Rhymes. (p. 524)
Wolfe, Kathryn. Deekin Duck & the Road to Find Purpose. (p. 524)
—Deekin Duck & the Road to Find Purpose. Comahig, Aljon, illus. (p. 524)
Wolfe, Laura E. Sasha & the Dragon. Malara, Nicholas, illus. (p. 1936)
Wolfe, Lynn, illus. see Majumdar, Debu.
Wolfe, Madeline. Historia de la Sra. Inez. Franco, George, illus. (p. 975)
Wolfe, Margaret. Beauty's Daughters (Classic Reprint) (p. 185)
Wolfe, Mary Eleanor. Candlelight Stories: Volume One. (p. 322)
—Candlelight Stories: Volume Two. (p. 322)
Wolfe, Mike & Sprengelmeyer, Lily. Kid Pickers: How to Turn Junk into Treasure. Right, Mike, illus. (p. 1213)
Wolfe, Myra & Monescillo, Maria. Charlotte Jane Battles Bedtime. Monescillo, Maria, illus. (p. 361)
Wolfe, Percival. Red Ralph, or the Daughter of the Night: A Romance of the Road in the Days of Dick Turpin (Classic Reprint) (p. 1858)
Wolfe, Robert Hewitt. Fallen Star: Billy Smith & the Goblins, Book 2. (p. 701)
—Final Drop: Billy Smith & the Goblins, Book 3. (p. 727)
—Goblin Crown: Billy Smith & the Goblins, Book 1. (p. 849)
Wolfe, Robert L., illus. see Cornell, Kari A., ed.
Wolfe, Robert L., photos by see Cornell, Kari A., ed.
Wolfe, Sean Fay. Elementia Chronicles #1: Quest for Justice: An Unofficial Minecraft-Fan Adventure. (p. 633)
—Elementia Chronicles #2: the New Order: An Unofficial Minecraft-Fan Adventure. (p. 633)
Wolfe, Sharon. Conrad the Collector. (p. 442)
Wolfe, Steven F. Hi. I'm Oliver. (p. 964)

W

Wolfe, Sue. Lily Bouquet & a Special May Day. (p. 1302)
Wolfe, Susan Markle. Deer from Ponchatoula Welch, Gracie, illus. (p. 525)
Wolfe, Suzanne. There Was a Young Rabbi: A Hanukkah Tale. Ebbeler, Jeffrey, illus. (p. 2217)
Wolfe, Theodore Frelinghuysen. Literary Shrines: The Haunts of Some Famous American Authors (Classic Reprint) (p. 1309)
—Literary Shrines. (p. 1309)
Wolfelt, Alan D. & Maloney, Raelynn. Healing after Divorce: 100 Practical Ideas for Kids. (p. 943)
Wolfelt, Jaimie A. Living with Diabetes: A Journal for Teens. (p. 1335)
Wolfe-Murray, Caroline, illus. see Hayman, Judy.
Wolfenden, Heidi. If a Python Puts on Your Pj's What Should You Do? Wolfenden, Heidi, illus. (p. 1090)
Wolfenstein, Martha. Idyls of the Gass (Classic Reprint) (p. 1090)
—Renegade: And Other Tales (Classic Reprint) (p. 1866)
Wolfer, Dianne. Choices. (p. 380)
—In the Lamplight. Simmonds, Brian, illus. (p. 1109)
—Light Horse Boy. Simmonds, Brian, illus. (p. 1298)
—Nanna's Button Tin. Potter, Heather, illus. (p. 1574)
Wolferman, Fred. Nelson. (p. 1587)
Wolferman, Iris, illus. see Hachler, Bruno.
Wolferman, Iris, illus. see Stalder, Päivi.
Wolff, Ariana. Khan Academy & Salman Khan (p. 1212)
Wolff, Ariana, ed. see Barrington, Richard.
Wolff, Ashley. Baby Bear Counts One. Wolff, Ashley, illus. (p. 149)
—Baby Bear Sees Blue. Wolff, Ashley, illus. (p. 149)
—Baby Chicks Are Singing/Los Pollitos Dicen: Sing along in English & Spanish!/Vamos a Cantar Junto en Ingles y Espanol! Wolff, Ashley, illus. (p. 149)
—Where, Oh Where, Is Baby Bear? Wolff, Ashley, illus. (p. 2439)
Wolff, Ashley, illus. see Elsohn Ross, Michael.
Wolff, Ashley, illus. see Scanlon, Liz Garton.
Wolff, Ashley, illus. see Siddals, Mary McKenna.
Wolff, Ashley, illus. see Slate, Joseph.
Wolff, Christian. Entdeckung der Wahren Ursache Von der Wunderbahren Vermehrung des Getreydes: Dadurch Zugleich der Wachsthum der Baeume und Pflantzen Überhaupt Erläutert Wird, ALS Die Erste Probe der Untersuchungen Von Dem Wachsthume der Pflanzen (Classic Reprint) (p. 656)
Wolff, Danielle. Spider-Verse #1. Caramagna, Joe, illus. (p. 2081)
Wolff, Danielle, jt. auth. see Caramagna, Joe.
Wolff, Ferida. Rachel's Roses. Lucas, Margeaux, illus. (p. 1832)
Wolff, Ferida & Savitz, Harriet May. Story Blanket. Odriozola, Elena, illus. (p. 2127)
Wolff, H. Drummond. Madrilenia; or, Pictures of Spanish Life. (p. 1375)
—Madrilenia, or Pictures of Spanish Life (Classic Reprint) (p. 1375)
Wolff, Jason, illus. see Lay, Kathryn.
Wolff, Jason, illus. see Lenhard, Elizabeth.
Wolff, Jason, illus. see Rauchwerger, Diane Levin.
Wolff, Jason, illus. see Rosa-Mendoza, Gladys.
Wolff, Julius. Salt Master of lüneburg, Vol. 1 (Classic Reprint) (p. 1925)
Wolff, Kathy & Byrne, Richard. What George Forgot. (p. 2410)
Wolff, Susan. Quackers Wants to Fly. Currie, Justin, illus. (p. 1821)
Wolff, Tracy. Book 1: Crisis. Kinsella, Pat, illus. (p. 257)
—Book 2: Sabotage. Kinsella, Pat, illus. (p. 257)
—Book 3: Restoration. Kinsella, Pat, illus. (p. 257)
—Book 4: Arrival. Kinsella, Pat, illus. (p. 257)
—Crave. (p. 467)
—Crush. (p. 480)
—Mars Bound (Set) Kinsella, Pat, illus. (p. 1409)
Wolff, Ulla Hirschfeld. Simon Eichelkatz: The Patriarch; Two Stories of Jewish Life (Classic Reprint) (p. 2020)
Wolff, Virginia Euwer. This Full House. (p. 2224)
Wolff, William Almon. Hero, Robert Lansing; the Girl, Mary Brewster; the Villain, Jim Hazzard: With an Exceptionally Strong Company (Classic Reprint) (p. 961)
Wolf-Ferrari, Ermanno. Jewels of the Madonna: Opera in Three Acts on Neapolitan Life (Classic Reprint) (p. 1167)
Wolfgang, Jane. Art Today. (p. 122)
Wolfhard, Steve, illus. see Kloepfer, John.
Wolfhard, Steve, illus. see Pla, Sally J.
Wolf-Heffner, Lori. Between Worlds: Books 1-3. Fish, Susan, ed. (p. 210)
—Between Worlds 1: The Move. Fish, Susan, ed. (p. 210)
—Between Worlds 1: The Move (Large Print) Fish, Susan, ed. (p. 210)
—Between Worlds 2: The Distance. Fish, Susan, ed. (p. 210)
—Between Worlds 2: The Distance (Large Print) Fish, Susan, ed. (p. 210)
—Between Worlds 3: The First Step. Fish, Susan, ed. (p. 210)
—Between Worlds 3: The First Step (Large Print) Fish, Susan, ed. (p. 210)
—Between Worlds 4: What Friends Do. Fish, Susan, ed. (p. 210)
—Between Worlds 4: What Friends Do (large Print) Fish, Susan, ed. (p. 210)
—Between Worlds 5: Hide & Seek. Fish, Susan, ed. (p. 210)
—Between Worlds 5: Hide & Seek (large Print) Fish, Susan, ed. (p. 210)
—Between Worlds 6: Missing Home. Fish, Susan, ed. (p. 210)
—Between Worlds 6: Missing Home (large Print) Fish, Susan, ed. (p. 210)
Wolfle, Brittany. Sidd & the Four Noble Truths. (p. 2014)
—Sidd the Buddhist Cat. (p. 2014)
Wolfman, Judy. Gatita y Yo. Greiman, Brett, illus. (p. 811)
—Kitty & Me. Greiman, Brett, illus. (p. 1226)
—Kitty & Me / Gatita y Yo. Greiman, Brett, illus. (p. 1226)
Wolfman, Marv. 10th Muse Omnibus. (p. 2550)
—Defex (p. 525)
Wolford, Merle & Harvey, Karen. Pau Pua & the Watering Hole. (p. 1706)
Wolfram, Amy. DC Super Hero Girls: Midterms. Labat, Yancey, illus. (p. 516)
—DC Super Hero Girls: Powerless. Garbowska, Agnes, illus. (p. 516)
Wolfram, Amy, jt. auth. see Fisch, Sholly.
Wolfram, Amy & Fisch, Sholly. Robin the First & Teen Titans Go ... Fish! Corona, Jorge & Gugliotti, Chris, illus. (p. 1891)
Wolfram, Amy & Labat, Yancey. DC Super Hero Girls: At Metropolis High. (p. 516)
Wolfram, Amy & Sanchez, Ricardo. Party, Party & Silicon Valley Cyborg. Corona, Jorge & Bates, Ben, illus. (p. 1702)
Wolfrom, Anna. Human Wisps: Six One-Act Plays (Classic Reprint) (p. 1050)
Wolfsgruber, Linda. Daisy Is a Daisy Is a Daisy (Except When It's Girl's Name) (p. 497)
Wolfsgruber, Linda, illus. see Lecis, Alessandro & Shirtliffe, Leanne.
Wolfsgruber, Linda, illus. see Ondaatje, Griffin.
Wolfson, Elissa & Barker, Margaret. Audubon Birding Adventures for Kids: Activities & Ideas for Watching, Feeding, & Housing Our Feathered Friends. (p. 136)
Wolfson, Evelyn. Mythology of King Arthur & His Knights. (p. 1571)
—Mythology of the American Indians. (p. 1571)
—Mythology of the Romans. (p. 1571)
—Native Americans. (p. 1578)
Wolfson, Ron. Be Like God: God's To-Do List for Kids. (p. 177)
Wolfson, Steve. Elephants at the Airport. Brulot, Heleen, illus. (p. 634)
—Monster Cheese. Johnson, Bill, illus. (p. 1495)
Wolfson, Steve, jt auth. see Valladares, Ellen Wolfson.
Wolfzorn, Gene, photos by see Wolfzorn, Mary Ann.
Wolfzorn, Mary Ann. Ducks of Park Place. Wolfzorn, Gene, photos by. (p. 608)
Wolin, Steven. ELSB STUDENT ASSESSMENT Level 2&3. (p. 639)
Wolitzer, Meg. Belzhar. (p. 198)
—Fingertips of Duncan Dorfman. (p. 731)
Wolitzer, Meg, jt. auth. see Sloan, Holly Goldberg.
Wolk, Lauren. Beyond the Bright Sea. (p. 212)
—Echo Mountain. (p. 623)
—Wolf Hollow. (p. 2484)
Wolkenstein, M. Evan. Turtle Boy. (p. 2301)
Wolkin, Joseph Steven. Superfast Indy Car Racing. (p. 2159)
Wolk-Stanley, Jessica, illus. see Geiger, Beth & Fuerst, Jeffrey B.
Woll, Kris. Nelson Mandela: South African President & Civil Rights Activist (p. 1587)
—Pope Francis: Catholic Spiritual Leader (p. 1776)
—Wind Energy. (p. 2471)
Wollard, Kathy. How Come? Every Kid's Science Questions Explained. Solomon, Debra, illus. (p. 1027)
Wollering, Loretta. Tai Chi (p. 2176)
Wolley, John. Ootheca Wolleyana, Vol. 1: An Illustrated Catalogue of the Collection of Birds' Eggs; Accipitres (Classic Reprint) (p. 1665)
—Ootheca Wolleyana, Vol. 1: An Illustrated Catalogue of the Collection of Birds' Eggs, Begun by the Late John Wolley, Jun;, M. A. , F. Z. S. , & Continued with Additions by the Editor Alfred Newton (Classic Reprint) (p. 1665)
Wollman, Neil & Fuller, Abigail. What Animal Needs a Wig? Fuller Baldwin, Fran, illus. (p. 2404)
Wollocombe, John B. Tetcott Hunt Week: Antecedents & Consequences (Classic Reprint) (p. 2209)
Wollstonecraft, Mary. Letters Written During a Short Residence in Sweden, Norway, & Denmark (Classic Reprint) (p. 1281)
—Mary Wollstonecraft - Original Stories: All the Sacred Rights of Humanity Are Violated by Insisting on Blind Obedience. (p. 1416)
—Mary Wollstonecraft's Original Stories: With Five Illustrations (Classic Reprint) (p. 1416)
—Original Stories from Real Life: With Conversations, Calculated to Regulate the Affections, & Form the Mind to Truth & Goodness (Classic Reprint) (p. 1671)
Wollstonecraft Shelley, Mary, see Shelley, Mary & Shelley, Mary.
Wollstonecraft Shelley, Mary, see Shelley, Mary.
Wolly, Paul T. My Secret Super-Powers 2: A Hilarious Adventure for Kids of All Ages 2. Adventure Books, ed. (p. 1560)
Wolny, Philip. 21st Century Ships. (p. 2554)
—21st Century Skyscrapers. (p. 2554)
—Aaron Rodgers. (p. 2)
—African American Entrepreneurs: Stories of Success. (p. 32)
—Avoiding Danger on the Hunt. (p. 143)
—Chris Rock: Comedian & Actor. (p. 382)
—Constructing, Using, & Interpreting Spreadsheets. (p. 443)
—Creating Electronic Graphic Organizers. (p. 470)
—Defeating Gangs in Your Neighborhood & Online (p. 525)
—Delaware: Past & Present. (p. 526)
—Discovering Dark Matter (p. 555)
—Discovering the Empire of Mali. (p. 556)
—Everything You Need about Protests & Public Assembly. (p. 673)
—Extreme Skateboarding (p. 687)
—Fight for the Environment (p. 725)
—Food Supply Collapse. (p. 760)
—Foursquare & Other Location-Based Services: Checking in, Staying Safe, & Being Savvy. (p. 773)
—Geologists at Work. (p. 817)
—Getting a Job in Building Maintenance. (p. 825)
—Getting a Job in the Construction Industry. (p. 825)
—Google & You: Maximizing Your Google Experience. (p. 869)
—Gun Rights: Interpreting the Constitution. (p. 905)
—High-Risk Construction Work: Life Building Skyscrapers, Bridges, & Tunnels. (p. 968)
—Holodomor: The Ukrainian Famine-Genocide. (p. 989)
—How Do You Read Maps? (p. 1030)
—I Have an STD. Now What? (p. 1066)
—Investigating Atlantis & Other Lost Cities (p. 1131)
—Iran & Iraq: Religion, War, & Geopolitics. (p. 1133)
—Isaac Asimov. (p. 1138)
—James Dashner. (p. 1156)
—Joan of Arc: French Soldier & Saint. (p. 1170)
—Liza Koshy (p. 1336)
—Ludacris. (p. 1366)
—Mark Markiplier Fischbach: Star YouTube Gamer with 10 Billion+ Views (p. 1407)
—Markiplier (p. 1407)
—Money-Making Opportunities for Teens Who Are Handy. (p. 1492)
—Muslims Around the World Today. (p. 1529)
—Native American Treatment & Resistance. (p. 1578)
—Ryan Higa: Actor & Comedian with More Than 4 Billion Views (p. 1918)
—Stephen Chbosky (p. 2115)
—Strengthening Research Paper Skills. (p. 2140)
—Sylvia Mendez: Civil Rights Activist (p. 2173)
—Truth about Heroin. (p. 2296)
—Understanding Financial Frauds & Scams. (p. 2324)
—Water Fowl. (p. 2384)
—What Are Deserts? (p. 2405)
—Write Like a Scientist. (p. 2512)
Wolny, Philip, ed. see Baum, Margaux & Hopkins, Andrea.
Wolny, Philip, jt. auth. see Uhl, Xina M.
Wolny, Philip, jt. ed. see Killcoyne, Hope Lourie.
Wolny, Philip & Green, Meg. Louis Sachar (p. 1357)
Wolny, Philip & Solomon, Dane. Fishing (p. 742)
Wolny, Philip, contrib. by. Holodomor: The Ukrainian Famine-Genocide. (p. 989)
Wolny, Philip, ed. 100 Most Influential Religious Leaders of All Time. (p. 2557)
—Earth Science (p. 617)
—New Nation (p. 1596)
Woloszynek, Olivia, illus. see Young, Barbara E.
Wolpe, Nina. Forest of Trees Does Not Grow There in Rows. Cable, Annette, illus. (p. 766)
Wolpert, Carys. How to Take Care of an Alien the Hard Way. (p. 1044)
Wolsak, Wendy, illus. see Evyindson, Peter.
Wolsak-Frith, Wendy, illus. see Eyvindson, Peter.
Wolsey, Chris. Trees Call Charlie. (p. 2284)
Wolski, Igor, illus. see Poskitt, Kjartan & Casey, Catherine.
Wolski, Igor, illus. see Poskitt, Kjartan & Litton, Jonathan.
Wolstenholm, Jessica & Rupe, Heather. Pregnancy Companion: A Faith-Filled Guide for Your Journey to Motherhood. (p. 1787)
Wolstenholme, Susan, ed. see Baum, L. Frank.
Wolter II, Russel Tracy. Adventure Story. (p. 19)
Woltmann, C. Von. White Lady: A Romance (Classic Reprint) (p. 2444)
Woltz, Anna. Hundred Hours of Night. Watkinson, Laura, tr. (p. 1051)
Wolverton, Barry. Dragon's Gate. Stevenson, Dave, illus. (p. 595)
—Neversink. Nielson, Sam, illus. (p. 1590)
—Sea of the Dead. (p. 1968)
—Vanishing Island. Stevenson, Dave, illus. (p. 2347)
Wolverton, Margery. Window to Christmas. (p. 2472)
Wolzogen, Ernst Von. Florian Mayr (der Kraft-Mayr) A Humorous Tale of Musical Life (Classic Reprint) (p. 751)
—Third Sex (Classic Reprint) (p. 2223)
Womac Cook, Meredith. Polar Bear Songbook. (p. 1769)
Womack, Rowena. L'Élan du Yellowstone. Archer, Angela, illus. (p. 1266)
—Popcorn. Archer, Angela, illus. (p. 1775)
—Tommy Two Shoes. (p. 2259)
—Yellowstone Moose: The Translated Japanese Version of the English Original. Slotsve, Kaoru, tr. (p. 2521)
—Yellowstone Moose. (p. 2521)
Womack-Whye, Cheryl. Michael Makes Maps. (p. 1457)
Woman, Magpie Sleeping. Big Eyes: The Keeper of the Night. (p. 220)
Woman, Plain. My Trivial Life & Misfortune, Vol. 1 Of 3: A Gossip with No Plot in Particular (Classic Reprint) (p. 1563)
Woman, Woman. Woman's Vengeance, Vol. 3 Of 3: A Novel (Classic Reprint) (p. 2486)
Wombacker, Sharon. Grandma, the Moon, & Me. (p. 878)
Womble, Louis, illus. see Kleinberg, Naomi.
Womble, Susan Larned. Opal's Brigade. (p. 1665)
Women, Athens College for Young. Maid of Athens, 1928 (Classic Reprint) (p. 1383)
Women, Baptist University for. Oak Leaves, 1908, Vol. 5 (Classic Reprint) (p. 1633)
Women, Chicora College for. Nods & Becks, 1917 (Classic Reprint) (p. 1617)
—Résumé, 1914 (Classic Reprint) (p. 1870)
Women, Columbia College for. College Follies Wisdom, 1914 (Classic Reprint) (p. 415)
Women, Florida State College for. Flastacowo, 1913, Vol. 4 (Classic Reprint) (p. 747)
—Flastacowo, 1914, Vol. 5 (Classic Reprint) (p. 747)
—Flastacowo, Vol. 2 (Classic Reprint) (p. 747)
—Flastacowo, Vol. 3 (Classic Reprint) (p. 747)
Women, Greensboro College for. Echo 17 (Classic Reprint) (p. 623)
—Echo, 1918 (Classic Reprint) (p. 623)
Women, Gulf Park College for. Sea Gull, 1944 (Classic Reprint) (p. 1967)
—Tammy Howl, Vol. 13: Dec. 15, 1938 (Classic Reprint) (p. 2189)
—Tammy Howl, Vol. 13: Feb. 14, 1939 (Classic Reprint) (p. 2189)
—Tammy Howl, Vol. 15: March 24, 1942 (Classic Reprint) (p. 2189)
—Tammy Howl, Vol. 16: May 29, 1943 (Classic Reprint) (p. 2189)
—Tammy Howl, Vol. 16: February, 1943 (Classic Reprint) (p. 2189)
—Tammy Howl, Vol. 17: May 27, 1944 (Classic Reprint) (p. 2189)
—Tammy Howl, Vol. 17: February 14, 1944 (Classic Reprint) (p. 2189)
—Tammy Howl, Vol. 18: December 14, 1944 (Classic Reprint) (p. 2189)
Women, Lasell Seminary for Young. Allerlei, 1893, Vol. 2 (Classic Reprint) (p. 56)
—Allerlei, 1894, Vol. 3 (Classic Reprint) (p. 56)
—Allerlei, 1896, Vol. 5 (Classic Reprint) (p. 56)
—Allerlei, 1898, Vol. 7 (Classic Reprint) (p. 56)
—Allerlei, 1899, Vol. 8 (Classic Reprint) (p. 56)
—Allerlei, 1905 (Classic Reprint) (p. 56)
—Allerlei, 1910 (Classic Reprint) (p. 56)
—Allerlei, 1911 (Classic Reprint) (p. 56)
Women, North Carolina College For. Carolinian, 1909, Vol. 1 (Classic Reprint) (p. 333)
—Carolinian, 1910, Vol. 2 (Classic Reprint) (p. 333)
—Carolinian, 1911, Vol. 3 (Classic Reprint) (p. 333)
—Coraddi, 1923, Vol. 28 (Classic Reprint) (p. 452)
—Coraddi, 1924-1925, Vol. 29 (Classic Reprint) (p. 452)
—Coraddi, Vol. 25: Member of the North Carolina Collegiate Press Association; June, 1921 (Classic Reprint) (p. 452)
—Coraddi, Vol. 29: December, 1924 (Classic Reprint) (p. 452)
—Coraddi, Vol. 30: March, 1926 (Classic Reprint) (p. 452)
—Coraddi, Vol. 31: March, 1927 (Classic Reprint) (p. 452)
—Coraddi, Vol. 32: December, 1927 (Classic Reprint) (p. 452)
—Coraddi, Vol. 32: Member of North Carolina Collegiate Press Association; October, 1927 (Classic Reprint) (p. 452)
—Coraddi, Vol. 33: May, 1929 (Classic Reprint) (p. 452)
—Coraddi, Vol. 35: May, 1931 (Classic Reprint) (p. 452)
—Coraddi, Vol. 35: October, 1930 (Classic Reprint) (p. 452)
—Coraddi, Vol. 35: November, 1930 (Classic Reprint) (p. 452)
—Coraddi, Vol. 35: Member of the North Carolina Collegiate Press Association; February, 1931 (Classic Reprint) (p. 452)
—Coraddi, Vol. 36: April, 1932 (Classic Reprint) (p. 452)
—Coraddi, Vol. 36: October, 1931 (Classic Reprint) (p. 452)
—Coraddy, Vol. 26: October, 1921 (Classic Reprint) (p. 453)
—Corradi, Vol. 30: October, 1925 (Classic Reprint) (p. 456)
Women, Pennsylvania College for. Arrow, 1945, Vol. 25 (Classic Reprint) (p. 119)
—Be Sorosis March, 1910 (Classic Reprint) (p. 177)
—Pennsylvanian, 1947 (Classic Reprint) (p. 1717)
—Sorosis: Vols; 20-21; January, 1914 June, 1915 (Classic Reprint) (p. 2065)
—Sorosis, Vol. 12: October, 1905 (Classic Reprint) (p. 2065)
—Sorosis, Vol. 15: October, 1908 June, 1909 (Classic Reprint) (p. 2065)
—Sorosis, Vol. 17: October, 1910 June, 1911 (Classic Reprint) (p. 2065)
—Sorosis, Vol. 18: October, 1911 (Classic Reprint) (p. 2065)
—Sorosis, Vol. 22: September, 1915 (Classic Reprint) (p. 2065)
—Sorosis, Vol. 23: October, 1916 (Classic Reprint) (p. 2065)
—Sorosis, Vol. 24: October, 1917-June, 1918 (Classic Reprint) (p. 2065)
Women, St Joseph. Loria: Fall, 1943 (Classic Reprint) (p. 1349)
—Loria: Fall, 1944 (Classic Reprint) (p. 1349)
Women, St Joseph's College for. Footprints, 1926, Vol. 7 (Classic Reprint) (p. 762)
—Loria: Fall 1942 (Classic Reprint) (p. 1349)
—Loria: Fall, 1943 (Classic Reprint) (p. 1349)
—Loria: Fall, 1944 (Classic Reprint) (p. 1349)
—Loria, Vol. 10: November, 1932 (Classic Reprint) (p. 1349)
—Loria, Vol. 11: Fall 1934 (Classic Reprint) (p. 1349)
—Loria, Vol. 13: Fall, 1936 (Classic Reprint) (p. 1349)
—Loria, Vol. 15: Fall, 1938 (Classic Reprint) (p. 1349)
—Loria, Vol. 7: November, 1929 (Classic Reprint) (p. 1349)
—Loria, Vol. 9: November, 1931 (Classic Reprint) (p. 1349)
Women, State Normal School For. Class Book 1919: State Normal School for Women (Classic Reprint) (p. 399)
—Class Book, 1920 (Classic Reprint) (p. 399)
Womick, Chip. Phantom Fishing with Gramps. Saumell, Marina, illus. (p. 1732)
Wommack, Linda. Ann Bassett: Colorado's Cattle Queen. (p. 97)
Won, Annie, illus. see Brown, Margaret Wise.
Won, Annie, illus. see Crow, Kristyn.
Won, Annie, illus. see Rosen, Michael J.
Won, Annie, illus. see Suben, Eric.
Won, Brian. Hooray for Books! (p. 1000)
—Hooray for Hat! (p. 1001)
—Hooray for Hat! (Board Book) (p. 1001)
—Hooray for Today! (p. 1001)
Won, Brian, illus. see Brockenbrough, Martha.
Won, Brian, illus. see Dunklee, Annika.
Won, Brian, illus. see LaReau, Kara.
Won, Brian, illus. see Martin, Bill & Sampson, Michael R.
Won, Brian, illus. see Nayeri, Daniel.
Won, Brian, illus. see Wynne-Jones, Tim.
Wonder, Yvonne. Mrs. Claus Saves Christmas. Sarganis, Brad, illus. (p. 1521)
Wonderland, Morgan's. Wonderland Welcome: A Fun 'n Learn Activity Guide to Morgan's Wonderland. (p. 2490)
Wonderly, William Carey. World to Live in (Classic Reprint) (p. 2505)
Wonders, Junia. Tobia e la Grande Catastrofe Delle Patate. Lombardo, Giulia, illus. (p. 2254)
—Zachary & the Great Potato Catastrophe. Lombardo, Giulia, illus. (p. 2537)
Wondriska, William. Puff. (p. 1811)
Wong, Alice, illus. see Tabby, Abigail.
Wong, Alice & Tabori, Lena, eds. Big Book for Toddlers. (p. 217)
—Goodnight Book for Moms & Little Ones. (p. 867)
Wong, Angi Ma. Barack Obama: Historymaker. (p. 164)
—Meet President Obama: America's 44th President. (p. 1439)
Wong, Clarissa. Guardians of the Galaxy: These Are the Guardians Lim, Ron & Pinto, Marcelo, illus. (p. 902)
—Hawkeye: This Is Hawkeye. Vito, Andrea Di & Rosenberg, Rachelle, illus. (p. 940)
—This Is Black Widow. Di Vito, Andrea & Pantazis, Pete, illus. (p. 2224)
—This Is Black Widow. Di Vito, Andrea & Pantazis, Peter, illus. (p. 2224)
—This Is Hawkeye. (p. 2224)
Wong, Clarissa S. Story of the Guardians of the Galaxy. (p. 2133)
Wong, Edward. Merlion: A Fairy Tale of Singapore. (p. 1448)
Wong, Eva & Ho, June. Mina's Magic Malong. (p. 1469)

W

—Argosy, Vol. 15: January to June, 1873 (Classic Reprint) (p. 114)
—Argosy, Vol. 17: January to June, 1874 (Classic Reprint) (p. 114)
—Argosy, Vol. 18: July to December, 1874 (Classic Reprint) (p. 114)
—Argosy, Vol. 19: January to June, 1875 (Classic Reprint) (p. 114)
—Argosy, Vol. 20: July to December, 1875 (Classic Reprint) (p. 114)
—Argosy, Vol. 21: January to June, 1876 (Classic Reprint) (p. 114)
—Argosy, Vol. 22: July to December, 1876 (Classic Reprint) (p. 114)
—Argosy, Vol. 23: January to June, 1877 (Classic Reprint) (p. 114)
—Argosy, Vol. 24: July to December, 1877 (Classic Reprint) (p. 114)
—Argosy, Vol. 25: January to June, 1878 (Classic Reprint) (p. 114)
—Argosy, Vol. 26: July to December, 1878 (Classic Reprint) (p. 114)
—Argosy, Vol. 27: January to June, 1879 (Classic Reprint) (p. 114)
—Argosy, Vol. 28: July to December, 1879 (Classic Reprint) (p. 114)
—Argosy, Vol. 29: January to June, 1880 (Classic Reprint) (p. 114)
—Argosy, Vol. 30: July to December, 1880 (Classic Reprint) (p. 114)
—Argosy, Vol. 31: January to June, 1881 (Classic Reprint) (p. 114)
—Argosy, Vol. 32: July to December, 1881 (Classic Reprint) (p. 114)
—Argosy, Vol. 33 (Classic Reprint) (p. 114)
—Argosy, Vol. 34: July to December, 1882 (Classic Reprint) (p. 114)
—Argosy, Vol. 35: January to June, 1883 (Classic Reprint) (p. 114)
—Argosy, Vol. 36: July to December, 1883 (Classic Reprint) (p. 114)
—Argosy, Vol. 37: January to June, 1884 (Classic Reprint) (p. 114)
—Argosy, Vol. 38: July to December, 1884 (Classic Reprint) (p. 114)
—Argosy, Vol. 39 (Classic Reprint) (p. 114)
—Argosy, Vol. 40: July to December, 1885 (Classic Reprint) (p. 114)
—Argosy, Vol. 41: January to June, 1886 (Classic Reprint) (p. 114)
—Argosy, Vol. 42 (Classic Reprint) (p. 114)
—Argosy, Vol. 49 (Classic Reprint) (p. 114)
—Argosy, Vol. 5: December, 1867, to May, 1868 (Classic Reprint) (p. 114)
—Ashley, & Other Stories (Classic Reprint) (p. 125)
—Bessy Ra, Vol. 1 Of 3: A Novel (Classic Reprint) (p. 205)
—Bessy Rane: A Novel (Classic Reprint) (p. 205)
—Bessy Rane. (p. 205)
—Bessy Rane, Vol. 2 Of 3: A Novel (Classic Reprint) (p. 205)
—Bessy Rane, Vol. 3 Of 3: A Novel (Classic Reprint) (p. 205)
—Bessy Wells (Classic Reprint) (p. 205)
—Court Netherleigh, Vol. 2 Of 3: A Novel (Classic Reprint) (p. 462)
—Danesbury House (Classic Reprint) (p. 501)
—Dene Hollow: A Novel (Classic Reprint) (p. 528)
—Dene Hollow. (p. 528)
—East Lynne (Classic Reprint) (p. 619)
—East Lynne, Vol. 2 of 3 (Classic Reprint) (p. 619)
—East Lynne, Vol. 3 of 3 (Classic Reprint) (p. 619)
—Edina: A Novel (Classic Reprint) (p. 626)
—Edina: A Novel, Vol. 1 of 3 (Classic Reprint) (p. 626)
—Edina: A Novel, Vol. 3 of 3 (Classic Reprint) (p. 626)
—Edina, Vol. 2 Of 3: A Novel (Classic Reprint) (p. 626)
—George Canterbury's Will (Classic Reprint) (p. 818)
—George Canterbury's Will, Vol. 1 Of 3: A Novel (Classic Reprint) (p. 818)
—George Canterbury's Will, Vol. 2: A Novel (Classic Reprint) (p. 818)
—House of Halliwell: A Novel (Classic Reprint) (p. 1023)
—House of Halliwell, Vol. 1 Of 3: A Novel (Classic Reprint) (p. 1023)
—It May Be True. (p. 1141)
—It May Be True, Vol. 1 Of 3: A Novel (Classic Reprint) (p. 1141)
—Johnny Ludlow: Third Series (Classic Reprint) (p. 1175)
—Johnny Ludlow (Classic Reprint) (p. 1175)
—Johnny Ludlow, Vol. 1 of 3 (Classic Reprint) (p. 1175)
—Johnny Ludlow, Vol. 5 (Classic Reprint) (p. 1175)
—Lady Grace: A Novel (Classic Reprint) (p. 1237)
—Lady Grace. (p. 1237)
—Lady Grace & Other Stories, Vol. 2 of 3 (Classic Reprint) (p. 1237)
—Lady Grace, Vol. 1 Of 3: And Other Stories (Classic Reprint) (p. 1237)
—Life's Secret: A Story (Classic Reprint) (p. 1297)
—Life's Secret, Vol. 1 of 2 (Classic Reprint) (p. 1297)
—Lord Oakburn's Daughters (Classic Reprint) (p. 1348)
—Lord Oakburn's Daughters, Vol. 1 of 3 (Classic Reprint) (p. 1348)
—Master of Greylands: A Novel (Classic Reprint) (p. 1418)
—Master of Greylands. (p. 1418)
—Master of Greylands, Vol. 1 Of 3: A Novel (Classic Reprint) (p. 1418)
—Mrs. Halliburton's Troubles, Vol. 1 of 3 (Classic Reprint) (p. 1522)
—Mrs. Halliburton's Troubles, Vol. 2: A Novel (Classic Reprint) (p. 1522)
—Orville College: A Story (Classic Reprint) (p. 1673)
—Orville College. (p. 1673)
—Orville College, Vol. 1: A Story (Classic Reprint) (p. 1673)
—Oswald Cray, Vol. 1 of 3 (Classic Reprint) (p. 1674)
—Oswald Cray, Vol. 2 of 3 (Classic Reprint) (p. 1674)
—Oswald Cray, Vol. 3 of 3 (Classic Reprint) (p. 1674)
—Parkwater (Classic Reprint) (p. 1700)
—Red Court Farm: A Novel (Classic Reprint) (p. 1856)
—Red Court Farm. (p. 1856)
—Red Court Farm a Novel, Vol. 1 of 3 (Classic Reprint) (p. 1856)
—Red Court Farm, Vol. 2 Of 3: A Novel (Classic Reprint) (p. 1856)
—Shadow of Ashlydyat (Classic Reprint) (p. 1996)
—Shadow of Ashlydyat, Vol. 1 of 3 (Classic Reprint) (p. 1996)
—Shadow of Ashlydyat, Vol. 3 of 3 (Classic Reprint) (p. 1997)
—Story of Charles Strange: A Novel (Classic Reprint) (p. 2129)
—Story of Charles Strange, Vol. 1 Of 3: A Novel (Classic Reprint) (p. 2129)
—Trevlyn Hold: A Novel (Classic Reprint) (p. 2285)
—Trevlyn Hold. (p. 2285)
—Trevlyn Hold, Vol. 1 Of 3: Or, Squire Trevlyn's Heir (Classic Reprint) (p. 2285)
—Trevlyn Hold, Vol. 2 Of 3: Or Squire Trevlyn's Heir (Classic Reprint) (p. 2285)
—Trevlyn Hold, Vol. 3 Of 3: Or Squire Trevlyn's Heir (Classic Reprint) (p. 2285)
—Under the Rose (Classic Reprint) (p. 2322)
—Unholy Wish: And Other Stories (Classic Reprint) (p. 2327)
—Verner's Pride (Classic Reprint) (p. 2352)
—Verner's Pride, Vol. 1 of 3 (Classic Reprint) (p. 2352)
—William Allair: Or, Running Away to Sea (Classic Reprint) (p. 2468)
—William Allair. (p. 2468)
—Within the Maze a Novel (Classic Reprint) (p. 2482)
Wood, Henry Firth. Good-Humor for Reading & Recitation (Classic Reprint) (p. 863)
Wood, Holly J. Invaluable. (p. 1130)
Wood, I. Sharks: Learning the SH Sound. (p. 2002)
Wood, Ira. How to Stay Safe at Home & On-line. (p. 1044)
—Mexican Feast: The Foods & Recipes of Mexico. (p. 1454)
Wood, Isaac L. Dansville Poisoning Case (Classic Reprint) (p. 504)
Wood, J. G. Man & Beast: Here & Hereafter (Classic Reprint) (p. 1394)
—My Feathered Friends (Classic Reprint) (p. 1540)
Wood, Jacqui. Cliff Dreamers. (p. 404)
Wood, Jamie Robyn. Bearskin. (p. 181)
Wood, Jay Hickory. Dan Leno (Classic Reprint) (p. 499)
Wood, Jennifer, illus. see Chin, Oliver, ed.
Wood, Jennifer, illus. see Chin, Oliver.
Wood, Jerome James. Child of Genius: A Sketch Book for Winter Evenings, & Summer Afternoons (Classic Reprint) (p. 370)
—Wilderness & the Rose: A Story of Michigan. (p. 2466)
—Wilderness & the Rose: A Story of Michigan (Classic Reprint) (p. 2466)
Wood, Joanna E. Daughter of Witches: A Romance (Classic Reprint) (p. 509)
—Untempered Wind (Classic Reprint) (p. 2336)
Wood, John. Alarming Animal Collection (p. 39)
—Animals in the Arctic. (p. 94)
—Animals in the Desert. (p. 95)
—Animals in the Forest. (p. 95)
—Animals in the Mountains. (p. 95)
—Animals in the Ocean. (p. 95)
—Animals in the Rain Forest. (p. 95)
—Card Magic. (p. 327)
—Classic Magic. (p. 400)
—Coin Magic. (p. 413)
—Gaming Technology: Streaming, VR, & More. (p. 808)
—Harrowing Human Gallery (p. 934)
—Hideous House Exhibit (p. 967)
—Illusions. (p. 1096)
—Magic Stunts. (p. 1379)
—Mapping the Weather (p. 1401)
—Medical Technology: Genomics, Growing Organs, & More. (p. 1436)
—Mind Magic. (p. 1469)
—Moviemaking Technology: 4D, Motion Capture, & More. (p. 1516)
—Nightmare Nature Tour (p. 1608)
—Relationships & Consent. (p. 1862)
—Space Technology: Landers, Space Tourism, & More. (p. 2072)
—Sports Technology: Cryotherapy, LED Courts, & More. (p. 2089)
—Travel Technology: Maglev Trains, Hovercrafts, & More. (p. 2280)
—Where Animals Live. (p. 2435)
Wood, John & Brundle, Harriet. Skeleton. (p. 2030)
Wood, John George. Half Hours with a Naturalist. (p. 911)
—Petland Revisited (Classic Reprint) (p. 1731)
—Romance of Animal Life: Short Chapters in Natural History (Classic Reprint) (p. 1900)
Wood, John Seymour. College Days: Or Harry's Career at Yale (Classic Reprint) (p. 415)
—Daughter of Venice (Classic Reprint) (p. 509)
—Gramercy Park: A Story of New York (Classic Reprint) (p. 875)
—Gramercy Park. (p. 875)
—Yale Yarns: Sketches of Life at Yale University (Classic Reprint) (p. 2517)
—Yale Yarns. (p. 2517)
Wood, Judith V., illus. see Driscoll, Laura.
Wood, Julie K. Pooks & Boots Meet Jesus. Goodway, Simon, illus. (p. 1774)
—Pooks & Boots Put on the Armor of God. Goodway, Simon, illus. (p. 1774)
Wood, Julie M. Learn to Read with Tug the Pup & Friends! Box Set 1: Levels Included: A-C Braun, Sebastien, illus. (p. 1257)
Wood, Karen. Diamond Spirit. (p. 538)
—Golden Stranger. (p. 859)
—Moonstone Promise. (p. 1503)
Wood, KariAnne. 52 Room Makeover Ideas for Girls: Pretty Projects to Decorate Your Bedroom. (p. 2556)
Wood, Kate. Sir Cyrus of Stonycleft, Vol. 1 Of 3: A Novel (Classic Reprint) (p. 2025)
—Twinkle. (p. 2305)
Wood, Kathleen Kennedy. Finding Broly. (p. 729)
Wood, Katie. Friendly Scarecrow Draft2. (p. 786)
Wood, Katie, illus. see Canasi, Brittany.
Wood, Katie, illus. see Gurtler, Janet.
Wood, Katie, illus. see Maddox, Jake & Berne, Emma Carlson.
Wood, Katie, illus. see Maddox, Jake & Brandes, Wendy L.
Wood, Katie, illus. see Maddox, Jake.
Wood, Katie, illus. see Mudpuppy.
Wood, Katie, illus. see Robertson, K. A.
Wood, Katie, illus. see Steinkraus, Kyla.
Wood, Kelly & Fletcher, Douglas. Stand up to OCD! A CBT Self-Help Guide & Workbook for Teens. (p. 2100)
Wood, Kerry & Muskat, Carrie. All You Can Be: Learning & Growing Through Sports. (p. 55)
Wood, Kevin. Create an Animation with Scratch. McBeth, Glen, illus. (p. 469)
—Create Computer Games with Scratch. McBeth, Glen, illus. (p. 469)
—Create Music with Scratch. McBeth, Glen, illus. (p. 469)
—Create Your Own Story with Scratch. McBeth, Glen, illus. (p. 469)
Wood, Kristen. Find Albert Alberta Too. (p. 727)
—Find Big Al. (p. 727)
—Find Reveille. (p. 728)
—Find Uga Hairy Dawg Too. (p. 728)
Wood, Lady. Seadrift, Vol. 1 Of 3: A Novel (Classic Reprint) (p. 1969)
—Seadrift, Vol. 3 Of 3: A Novel (Classic Reprint) (p. 1969)
Wood, Lansing P. Book of the Pageant of Ridgewood, N. J (Classic Reprint) (p. 260)
Wood, Laura, illus. see Dillemuth, Julie.
Wood, Laura, illus. see Fischer, Ellen.
Wood, Laura, illus. see Preston, Ian.
Wood, Laura, illus. see Steinberg, D. J.
Wood, Lily. Skeletons. (p. 2030)
Wood, Lydia Cope. For a Free Conscience (Classic Reprint) (p. 762)
Wood, M. K. Piper's Pond: The Unwritten Fairytale. (p. 1749)
Wood, M. S. Henry. Mrs. Halliburton's Troubles (Classic Reprint) (p. 1522)
Wood, Madeline, illus. see Schmidt, Mollie.
Wood, Mandy. My First Kitty. (p. 1544)
—My First Puppy. (p. 1545)
Wood, Marilyn, jt. auth. see Streissguth, Tom.
Wood, Martha Buckingham. Trip to the Land of the Midnight Sun: A Narrative of Personal Experiences (Classic Reprint) (p. 2289)
Wood, Martha C. Tales of Old Times in Rhode Island: An Ancient Book Now Republished with Some New Illustrations & Additional Notes (Classic Reprint) (p. 2185)
Wood, Mary. Pebbles Gathered by the Wayside: A Monthly Visitor, Devoted to Temperance, Truth & Virtue (Classic Reprint) (p. 1711)
Wood, Mary, jt. auth. see Low, Emma.
Wood, Mary Ann. Pricklebottoms: A Collection of Short Stories. (p. 1791)
Wood, Mary Rosalie Alling. Turn of the Current: A Study of the New Consciousness (Classic Reprint) (p. 2300)
Wood, Maryrose. Alice's Farm: A Rabbit's Tale. (p. 46)
—Hidden Gallery. Klassen, Jon, illus. (p. 965)
—Incorrigible Children of Ashton Place: Book I: The Mysterious Howling. Klassen, Jon, illus. (p. 1113)
—Incorrigible Children of Ashton Place: Book II: The Hidden Gallery. Klassen, Jon, illus. (p. 1113)
—Incorrigible Children of Ashton Place: Book III: The Unseen Guest. Klassen, Jon, illus. (p. 1113)
—Incorrigible Children of Ashton Place: Book IV: The Interrupted Tale. Bk. 4 Wheeler, Eliza, illus. (p. 1113)
—Incorrigible Children of Ashton Place: Book IV: The Interrupted Tale. Bk. IV Wheeler, Eliza, illus. (p. 1113)
—Incorrigible Children of Ashton Place: Book V: The Unmapped Sea. Wheeler, Eliza, illus. (p. 1113)
—Incorrigible Children of Ashton Place: Book V: The Unmapped Sea. Bk. 5 Wheeler, Eliza, illus. (p. 1113)
—Incorrigible Children of Ashton Place: Book VI: The Long-Lost Home. Wheeler, Eliza, illus. (p. 1113)
—Mysterious Howling. Klassen, Jon, illus. (p. 1567)
—What I Wore to Save the World. (p. 2412)
Wood, Maryrose & The Duchess of Northumberland, The Duchess. Poison Diaries. (p. 1767)
Wood, Mathew Brenden. Science of Science Fiction. Casteel, Tom, illus. (p. 1958)
Wood, Matthew Brenden. Planetary Science: Explore New Frontiers. Carbaugh, Samuel, illus. (p. 1755)
—Projectile Science: The Physics Behind Kicking a Field Goal & Launching a Rocket with Science Activities for Kids. (p. 1806)
Wood, Michael. White Island (Classic Reprint) (p. 2444)
—Willow Weaver & Seven Other Tales (Classic Reprint) (p. 2469)
Wood, Michele, illus. see Grady, Cynthia.
Wood, Michele, illus. see Grimes, Nikki.
Wood, Michele, illus. see Igus, Toyomi.
Wood, Michele, illus. see Rockliff, Mara.
Wood, Michele, illus. see Weatherford, Carole Boston.
Wood, Muriel, illus. see Lowery, Lawrence F.
Wood, Muriel, illus. see Skrypuch, Marsha Forchuk.
Wood, Natasha Tabon and Angela. Misadventures of Tood & Taboon. Marino, Natalie, illus. (p. 1476)
Wood, Oliver Ellsworth. West Point Scrap Book: A Collection of Stories, Songs, & Legends of the United States Military Academy (Classic Reprint) (p. 2402)
—West Point Scrap Book. (p. 2402)
Wood, Paul. Cousin Albert's Day at the Zoo. (p. 463)
Wood, Pearl Beaudry. Dramatic Reader for Seventh & Eighth Years (Classic Reprint) (p. 597)
Wood, Ramona. Kids' Book of Bible Feast Days: And Their Secrets to the Future. (p. 1214)
Wood, Rev James. Nuttall Encyclopaedia: Being a Concise & Comprehensive Dictionary of General Knowledge; Volume 1. (p. 1632)
Wood, Robert. Day Robby the Rat Became a Hero Maker. Wood, Will, illus. (p. 514)
—Indelible Images. (p. 1114)
Wood, Robert E. My New Friend, Squatchette: A True Story As Told to Robert E. Wood. Matic, Jaclyn, illus. (p. 1558)
Wood, Robert Muir. Discovering Prehistory. (p. 556)
Wood, Robert Williams. Animal Analogues: Verses & Illustrations (Classic Reprint) (p. 87)
—How to Tell the Birds from the Flowers: A Manual of Flornithology for Beginners (Classic Reprint) (p. 1045)
—How to Tell the Birds from the Flowers. (p. 1045)
—How to Tell the Birds from the Flowers. a Manual of Flornithology for Beginners. (p. 1045)
—How to Tell the Birds from the Flowers & Other Wood-Cuts: A Revised Manual of Flornithology for Beginners (Classic Reprint) (p. 1045)
—How to Tell the Birds from the Flowers, & Other Wood-Cuts: A Revised Manual of Flornithology for Beginners (Classic Reprint) (p. 1045)
Wood, Ruth Kedzie. Honeymooning in Russia (Classic Reprint) (p. 999)
Wood, Ryan, illus. see Bardhan-Quallen, Sudipta.
Wood, Samantha. Lumps on a Log. (p. 1368)
Wood, Selina. Snakes. (p. 2044)
—Spiders. (p. 2081)
Wood, Selina & March, Julia. LEGO Halloween Ideas. (p. 1264)
Wood, Selina, et al. LEGO Halloween Ideas: With Exclusive Spooky Scene Model. (p. 1264)
Wood, Steve, illus. see Hillyer, Rhonda.
Wood, Steven, illus. see Dale, Elizabeth.
Wood, Steven, illus. see Gippetti, Rachel.
Wood, Steven, illus. see Kenney, Karen Latchana.
Wood, Steven, illus. see Regan, Lisa.
Wood, Steven, illus. see Winget, Rosie.
Wood, Susan. American Gothic: The Life of Grant Wood. MacDonald, Ross, illus. (p. 71)
—Elizabeth Warren: Nevertheless, She Persisted. Green, Sarah, illus. (p. 636)
—Esquivel! Space-Age Sound Artist. Tontiuh, Duncan, illus. (p. 663)
—Holy Squawkamole! Little Red Hen Makes Guacamole. Gonzalez, Laura, illus. (p. 995)
—Skydiving Beavers of Idaho: A True Tale. Frankenhuyzen, Gijsbert van, illus. (p. 2034)
—Vaccine Innovators Pearl Kendrick & Grace Eldering. (p. 2343)
—¡Esquivel! un Artista Del Sonido de la Era Espacial. Calvo, Carlos E., tr. (p. 663)
Wood, T. L. Eldohr Adventures: Quest for Windsoar (Book 2) (p. 630)
Wood, T. L. B. Great Locomotive Chase, 1862 (the Symbiont Time Travel Adventures Series, Book 4) (p. 887)
—Titanic, 1912 (the Symbiont Time Travel Adventures Series, Book 5) Young Adult Time Travel Adventure. (p. 2251)
Wood, Thomas. Poetical Works of Thomas Wood, Vol. 5: With Some Account of the Author (Classic Reprint) (p. 1766)
Wood, Tony. Mermaid's Kiss. (p. 1449)
Wood, Tracey, illus. see Heiman, Diane & Suneby, Liz.
Wood, Virginia. Coraddi, Vol. 27: Spring, 1923 (Classic Reprint) (p. 452)
Wood, W. Supplement to the Index Testaceologicus; or Acatalogue of Shells - Scholar's Choice Edition. (p. 2162)
Wood, Will, illus. see Wood, Robert.
Wood, William. Index Testaceologicus, or a Catalogue of Shells, British & Foreign, Arranged According to the Linnean System: With the Latin & English Names, References to Authors, & Places Where Found (Classic Reprint) (p. 1115)
—New Englands Prospect: A True, Lively, & Experimental Description of That Part of America, Commonly Called New England (Classic Reprint) (p. 1593)
—New Englands Prospect: A True, Lively, & Experimentall Description of That Part of America, Commonly Called New England; Discovering the State of That Countrie, Both As It Stands to Our New-Come English Planters, & to the Old Native Inhabitants. (p. 1593)
—New-England's Prospect: Being a True, Lively, & Experimental Description of That Part of America, Commonly Called New-England; Discovering the State of That Country, Both As It Stands to Our New-Come English Planters, & to the Old Native Inhabitants. (p. 1593)
Wood, Wood. Seadrift, Vol. 2 Of 3: A Novel (Classic Reprint) (p. 1969)
Wood-Allen, Mary. Making the Best of Our Children: Eight to Sixteen Years of Age (Classic Reprint) (p. 1390)
—Making the Best of Our Children: First Series, One to Eight Years of Age (Classic Reprint) (p. 1390)
Woodard, April & White-Petaway, Davida. Adventures of Frankie & Lucy. (p. 23)
Woodard, Brad, illus. see Roeser, Matt.
Woodard, Chris. Ugo's Fantastic African Voyage. (p. 2314)
Woodard, Kate. Mary & Me. (p. 1414)
—No One to Hug. (p. 1614)
Woodard, Patricia L. Ava & Salome: Welcome to Cali! (p. 141)
Woodard, Sorah Junkin, illus. see Murdock, Bob E.
Wood-Bradford, Sarah. Spike's Adventures: Don't Cross the Road. (p. 2082)
Woodbridge, Elisabeth. Jonathan Papers (Classic Reprint) (p. 1177)
—More Jonathan Papers (Classic Reprint) (p. 1505)
Woodbridge, H. Horatio. Dig, Two Heads Wanted: A Novel (Classic Reprint) (p. 545)
Woodbridge, William W. That Something (Classic Reprint) (p. 2213)
Woodbury, Charles J. Potato Child & Others (Classic Reprint) (p. 1780)
Woodbury et al, Charles H., illus. see Burroughs, John.
Woodbury, Sarah E. Dramatization in the Grammar Grades (Classic Reprint) (p. 597)
Woodcock, Fiona. Hello. Woodcock, Fiona, illus. (p. 950)
—Hiding Heidi. (p. 967)
—Look. Woodcock, Fiona, illus. (p. 1344)
—Poppy, Buttercup, Bluebell, & Dandy. (p. 1776)
Woodcock, Fiona, illus. see Burgess, Matthew.
Woodcock, Jane. Boy Who Dug. Roberts, Alice Jane, illus. (p. 270)
Woodcock, John. Color & Doodle Your Way Across the USA. (p. 419)

Woodward, Arthur Smith. Fossil Fishes of the Hawkesbury Series at Gosford (Classic Reprint) (p. 770)
Woodward, Barbara. Curious Place. (p. 488)
Woodward, Brinton W. Old Wine in New Bottles: For Old & New Friends (Classic Reprint) (p. 1648)
Woodward, Caroline. Singing Away the Dark. Morstad, Julie, illus. (p. 2024)
—West Coast Summer. Evans, Carol, illus. (p. 2401)
Woodward, David R. World War I Almanac. (p. 2505)
Woodward, Fred E. Line Lost Limericks: A Guest Book (Classic Reprint) (p. 1303)
Woodward, Henry. Guide to the Exhibition Galleries of the Department of Geology & Paleontology, Vol. 1: In the British Museum (Natural History), Cromwell Road, London, S. W. ; Fossil Mammals & Birds (Classic Reprint) (p. 903)
—Guide to the Exhibition Galleries of the Department of Geology & Palaeontology in the British Museum (Natural History), Part I. -Fossil Mammals & Birds. (p. 903)
Woodward, Houston. Year for France: War Letters (Classic Reprint) (p. 2519)
Woodward II, Ed, illus. see Francis, JennaKay.
Woodward, Joe, jt. auth. see Ross, Stewart.
Woodward, John. Along the Shore. (p. 58)
—Ant. (p. 101)
—Bee. (p. 189)
—Beetle. (p. 190)
—Butterfly. (p. 303)
—Cricket. (p. 474)
—Deep, Deep Ocean. (p. 524)
—Dragonfly. (p. 595)
—Garden Minibeasts up Close (p. 809)
—Life Through Time: The 700-Million-Year Story of Life on Earth. (p. 1296)
—On the Seabed. (p. 1655)
—Snail. (p. 2044)
—Spider. (p. 2080)
—Temperate Forests (p. 2202)
—Under the Waves. (p. 2323)
Woodward, John & Dorling Kindersley Publishing Staff. Horses: The Ultimate Treasury. (p. 1005)
Woodward, Jonathan. Dino Pops. (p. 547)
Woodward, Jonathan, illus. see Brooks, Susie.
Woodward, Jonathan, illus. see Butterfield, Moira.
Woodward, Jonathan, illus. see French, Jess.
Woodward, Jonothan, photos by see Warren, Mike.
Woodward, Junko Kaga, tr. see Kurtz, Kevin.
Woodward, Kate, jt. auth. see Unwin, Mike.
Woodward, Kay. Dancing Danger. (p. 500)
—Frozen Wish. (p. 796)
—Giggling Tree. (p. 833)
—Sleeping Handsome & the Princess Engineer. de Ruiter, Jo, illus. (p. 2037)
—What Would She Do? 25 True Stories of Trailblazing Rebel Women. (p. 2422)
Woodward, M. E. Vocabulary of English-Chinyanja & Chinyanja-English As Spoken at Likoma, Lake Nyasa (Classic Reprint) (p. 2364)
Woodward, Mac. Sam Houston: For Texas & the Union. (p. 1926)
Woodward, Marcus. Arcadian Calendar (Classic Reprint) (p. 109)
—How to Enjoy the Countryside (Classic Reprint) (p. 1042)
—In Nature's Ways: A Book for All Young Lovers of Nature Being an Introduction to Gilbert White's, Natural History of Selborne (Classic Reprint) (p. 1106)
Woodward, Marcus, jt. auth. see White, Gilbert.
Woodward, Molly. It's Nice to Be a Kit Fox. Quintana, Donald, photos by. (p. 1146)
—It's Nice to Be a Mountain Lion. Leeson, Pat and Tom, photos by. (p. 1146)
—It's Nice to Be an Otter. Leeson, Tom and Pat, photos by. (p. 1146)
Woodward, Molly, jt. auth. see Schindel, John.
Woodward, Morgan S. His Last Log (Classic Reprint) (p. 974)
Woodward, R. Pitcher. On a Donkey's Hurricane Deck: A Tempestuous Voyage of Four Thousand & Ninety-Six Miles Across the American Continent on a Burro, in 340 Days & 2 Hours, Starting Without a Dollar & Earning My Way (Classic Reprint) (p. 1652)
Woodward, Rachel. Out, Out Away from Here. Miao, Sang, illus. (p. 1683)
Woodward, Robert Pitcher. Trains That Met in the Blizzard: A Composite Romance; Being a Chronicle of the Extraordinary (Classic Reprint) (p. 2276)
Woodward, Scott. Life Pictures: In Prose & Verse (Classic Reprint) (p. 1295)
Woodward, Stephanie Lynn. Wildwoods. (p. 2467)
Woodwell, Dennis. Happy Jack at the Farm. (p. 923)
Woodworth, Francis C. Boy's & Girl's Country Book: With Illustrations (Classic Reprint) (p. 272)
—Diving Bell, or Pearls to Be Sought For: With Tinted Illustrations (Classic Reprint) (p. 566)
—Jack Mason, the Old Sailor. (p. 1152)
—Peddler's Boy; or, I'll Be Somebody. (p. 1712)
—Woodworth's Youth's Cabinet, Vol. 4 (Classic Reprint) (p. 2492)
Woodworth, Francis Channing. Jack Mason: The Old Sailor; with Illustrations (Classic Reprint) (p. 1152)
—Peep at Our Neighbors: The Sequel to the Willow Lane Budget; with Illustrations (Classic Reprint) (p. 1713)
—Stories about Birds: With Pictures to Match (Classic Reprint) (p. 2122)
—Stories about the Country (Classic Reprint) (p. 2122)
Woodworth, Herbert G. In the Shadow of Lantern Street (Classic Reprint) (p. 1111)
Woodworth, Laurence Conger. Morris Book Shop: Impressions of Some Old Friends in Celebration of the Xxvth Anniversary. (p. 1506)
—Morris Book Shop: Impressions of Some Old Friends in Celebration of the Xxvth Anniversary (Classic Reprint) (p. 1506)
Woodworth, Samuel. Beasts at Law, or Zoologian Jurisprudence: A Poem, Satirical, Allegorical, & Moral; in Three Cantos (Classic Reprint) (p. 182)
Woodworth, Viki. 50 States: Facts & Fun. (p. 2555)
—Princess Mazes. (p. 1798)
—United States Maze Craze. (p. 2332)
Woodworth, Viki, illus. see Hillert, Margaret.
Woodworth, Viki & Whelon, Chuck. 3-D Mazes—Maze Mania. (p. 2547)
Woodworth, William McMichael. Harbard College Library: Bequest of William Mcmichael Woodworth (Class of 1888) (Classic Reprint) (p. 924)
Woody, illus. see Howell, Gill.
Woody, John. Alberto Otter Singing Star. (p. 40)
—Ernie Tales. Byars, Bob M., illus. (p. 660)
Woody, Thomas. Furstenschulen in Germany after the Reformation. (p. 802)
Woodyard, Benjamin, illus. see Green, Stella.
Woodyard, Janelle Valido. Girl's Guide to Softball (p. 838)
Woodyard, Sandy Lilly, illus. see Young, Norene.
Woog, Adam. Billy the Kid. (p. 227)
—Bionic Hand. (p. 229)
—Blake Shelton. (p. 242)
—Careers in Forensic Science. (p. 329)
—Careers in Homeland Security. (p. 330)
—Careers in State, County, & City Police Forces. (p. 330)
—Careers in the ATF. (p. 330)
—Careers in the FBI. (p. 330)
—Careers in the Secret Service. (p. 330)
—Derrick Rose. (p. 530)
—Early Middle Ages. (p. 615)
—Emancipation Proclamation: Ending Slavery in America. (p. 640)
—Giants. (p. 831)
—History of Gospel Music. Greenhaven Press Editors, ed. (p. 978)
—Jacques Cartier. (p. 1154)
—Jesse James: The Wild West for Kids. (p. 1165)
—LaDainian Tomlinson. (p. 1236)
—Life During the Spanish Inquisition. (p. 1291)
—Military Might & Global Intervention. (p. 1466)
—Oprah Winfrey. (p. 1667)
—Pearl Harbor. (p. 1710)
—Reggie Bush. (p. 1861)
—Robert Kirkman. (p. 1890)
—SCRATCHbot. (p. 1963)
—Trey Parker, Matt Stone, & South Park: South Park. (p. 2285)
—Vampires in the Movies. (p. 2346)
Woog, Adam, jt. auth. see Malaspina, Ann.
Wookey, Alfred John. Secwana & English Phrases: With Short Introduction to Grammar & a Vocabulary (Classic Reprint) (p. 1981)
Wool, Henry. East Lynne, Vol. 1 of 3 (Classic Reprint) (p. 619)
Woolet, A. Wellington. Woolet Papers (Classic Reprint) (p. 2493)
Woolf, Alex. Arab-Israeli War Since 1948 (p. 108)
—Asteroid Strike. (p. 127)
—Buildings (p. 295)
—Ciencia de la Caca y Los Pedos. (p. 391)
—Encounters with the Past. (p. 648)
—Expedition to the Arctic. (p. 677)
—Impact of Technology in Art. (p. 1101)
—Impact of Technology in History & Archaeology. (p. 1101)
—Isaac Newton & Gravity. Stoney, Annaliese, illus. (p. 1138)
—Journey along the Amazon. (p. 1181)
—Let's Think about the Internet & Social Media (p. 1278)
—Meet the Ancient Romans. (p. 1439)
—Meet the Tudors. (p. 1440)
—Meet the Vikings. (p. 1440)
—My Life in India. (p. 1551)
—My Life in Indonesia. (p. 1551)
—My Life in Kenya. (p. 1551)
—Powder Treason. (p. 1782)
—Sailing the Great Barrier Reef. (p. 1923)
—Science Adventures: Solve the Puzzles, Save the World! Vieira, Rayanne & Rodríguez, Geraldine, illus. (p. 1948)
—Science of Acne & Warts: The Itchy Truth about Skin. (p. 1957)
—Science of Acne & Warts. (p. 1957)
—Science of Buildings: The Sky-Scraping Story of Structures. Lundie, Isobel & Beach, Bryan, illus. (p. 1957)
—Science of Flying Reptiles: The Terrifying Truth about the Pterosaurs. Beach, Bryan, illus. (p. 1957)
—Science of Flying Reptiles. Beach, Bryan, illus. (p. 1957)
—Science of Natural Disasters: The Devastating Truth about Volcanoes, Earthquakes, & Tsunamis. Rowlands, Andy, illus. (p. 1958)
—Science of Poop & Farts: The Smelly Truth about Digestion. (p. 1958)
—Science of Poop & Farts. (p. 1958)
—Science of Rocks & Minerals: The Hard Truth about the Stuff Beneath Our Feet. Sordo, Paco, illus. (p. 1958)
—Science of Sea Monsters: Prehistoric Reptiles of the Sea. Rowland, Andy, illus. (p. 1958)
—Science of Spacecraft: The Cosmic Truth about Rockets, Satellites, & Probes. Myer, Ed & Beach, Bryan, illus. (p. 1958)
—Stories from the Bible. (p. 2124)
—Story of Food: Chocolate. (p. 2130)
—Terrorism. (p. 2208)
—Trailblazers: Neil Armstrong: First Man on the Moon. (p. 2275)
—Trailblazers: Stephen Hawking: A Life Beyond Limits. (p. 2275)
—Trekking in the Congo Rainforest. (p. 2285)
—Women in Science - Jane Goodall. Lundie, Isobel, illus. (p. 2487)
—You Wouldn't Want to Live Without Bees! (p. 2529)
—You Wouldn't Want to Live Without Bees! Antram, David, illus. (p. 2529)
—You Wouldn't Want to Live Without Boogers! Antram, David, illus. (p. 2529)
—You Wouldn't Want to Live Without Books! Antram, David, illus. (p. 2529)
—You Wouldn't Want to Live Without Soap! Bergin, Mark, illus. (p. 2529)
—You Wouldn't Want to Live Without Vegetables! Antram, David, illus. (p. 2529)
—¡No Te Gustaría Vivir Sin Fuego! (p. 1615)
Woolf, Alex, ed. see Elgin, Kathy.
Woolf, Alex, ed. see Hibbert, Clare & Hibbert, Adam.
Woolf, Alex, ed. see Rooney, Anne.
Woolf, Alex, ed. see Steele, Philip.
Woolf, Alex, jt. auth. see Farndon, John.
Woolf, Alex, jt. auth. see Graham, Ian.
Woolf, Alex, jt. auth. see Loughrey, Anita.
Woolf, Alex & Anniss, Matthew. Impact of Technology. (p. 1101)
Woolf, Alex & Graham, Ian. Science of Prehistoric Giants. (p. 1958)
Woolf, Alex, et al. World After. (p. 2501)
Woolf, Benjamin E. Pounce & Co;, or Capital vs; Labor: An Original Comic Opera; in Two Acts (Classic Reprint) (p. 1781)
Woolf, Dwight Homer. Tramping & Camping (Classic Reprint) (p. 2277)
Woolf, Jennifer. Adventures in Writing: A Fun Guide to Figurative Language. (p. 20)
Woolf, Julia. Duck & Penguin Are NOT Friends. Woolf, Julia, illus. (p. 607)
—Jack's Room. (p. 1153)
Woolf, Julia, illus. see Albee, Sarah.
Woolf, Julia, illus. see Ghigna, Charles.
Woolf, Julia, illus. see Hegarty, Patricia.
Woolf, Julia, illus. see Kuenzler, Lou.
Woolf, Julia, illus. see Moore, Katrina.
Woolf, Julia, illus. see Stockland, Patricia M.
Woolf, L. S. Village in the Jungle (Classic Reprint) (p. 2358)
Woolf, Michael Angelo. Sketches of Lowly Life in a Great City (Classic Reprint) (p. 2031)
Woolf, Pemberley. Tale of Paddlewick. (p. 2179)
Woolf, Virginia. Jacob's Room (Classic Reprint) (p. 1154)
—Mark on the Wall. (p. 1407)
—Mark on the Wall (Classic Reprint) (p. 1407)
—Monday or Tuesday (Classic Reprint) (p. 1492)
—Mrs Dalloway: a-Level Set Text Student Edition (Collins Classroom Classics) (p. 1522)
—Night & Day (Classic Reprint) (p. 1604)
—Voyage Out (Classic Reprint) (p. 2368)
Woolfolk Sr, Oscar. Bird & the Mirror. (p. 230)
Woolford, Mary. I Don't Feel Like It. (p. 1064)
Woollacott, Angela, et al. History NSW Syllabus for the Australian Curriculum Year 7 Stage 4. (p. 977)
—History NSW Syllabus for the Australian Curriculum Year 7 Stage 4 Workbook. (p. 977)
Woollam, Wilfred. All for Naught, Vol. 1 of 3 (Classic Reprint) (p. 52)
Woollam, Wilfrid. With the Help of the Angels: A Novel (Classic Reprint) (p. 2482)
Woollard, Elli. Adventures of Swashbuckle Lil. Anderson, Laura Ellen, illus. (p. 28)
—Dilly the Donkey. Lenton, Steven, illus. (p. 547)
—Dinosaurs Don't Draw. Lenton, Steven, illus. (p. 551)
—Dragon & the Nibblesome Knight. Davies, Benji, illus. (p. 593)
—Great Gran Plan. Lenton, Steven, illus. (p. 886)
—Swashbuckle Lil: the Secret Pirate. Anderson, Laura Ellen, illus. (p. 2167)
Woollatt, Margaret. Twelve Days of Christmas in New Jersey. Rossi, Rich, illus. (p. 2303)
Woollatt, Sue, illus. see Farrington, Karen.
Woollcombe, Walter George. Practical Work in Physics for Use in Schools & Colleges, Vol. 4 (Classic Reprint) (p. 1784)
Woollcott, Alexander. Mr. Dickens Goes to the Play (Classic Reprint) (p. 1518)
—Shouts & Murmurs: Echoes of a Thousand & One First Nights (Classic Reprint) (p. 2012)
Woollcott, Tory. Science Comics: the Brain: The Ultimate Thinking Machine. Graudins, Alex, illus. (p. 1954)
Woollett, Laura A. Big Top Burning: The True Story of an Arsonist, a Missing Girl, & the Greatest Show on Earth. (p. 223)
Woolley, C. Leonard. Dead Towns & Living Men: Being Pages from an Antiquary's Notebook (Classic Reprint) (p. 518)
Woolley, Celia Parker. Love & Theology (Classic Reprint) (p. 1359)
Woolley, Edward Mott. Cub Reporter (Classic Reprint) (p. 482)
Woolley, John. I Am with You: For Young People & for Those Young at Heart. (p. 1060)
Woolley, Justin. City Called Smoke: the Territory 2. (p. 394)
—Town Called Dust: the Territory 1. (p. 2270)
—We Are Omega. (p. 2389)
—World of Ash: the Territory 3. (p. 2502)
Woolley, Katie. Meat-Eating Dinosaurs. (p. 1435)
—Plant-Eating Dinosaurs. (p. 1756)
—School Success: Telling the Time: Wipe-Clean Book with Pen. Heard, Tom, illus. (p. 1947)
—Story of the Dinosaurs. (p. 2133)
—Tyrannosaurus Rex. (p. 2311)
Woolley, Kim, illus. see Sansone, Emma.
Woolley, Sara, illus. see Sosin, Deborah.
Woolley, Steph. Where's Sonic? A Search-and-Find Adventure. (p. 2440)
Woolley, Tom, illus. see Burton, Jesse.
Woolley, Tom, illus. see Perkins, Chloe & Silva, Reg.
Woolley, Tom, illus. see Perkins, Chloe.
Woolliscroft, Kittie M. Little Drummer Boy Grows Up. (p. 1315)
Woollvin, Bethan. Bo the Brave. Woollvin, Bethan, illus. (p. 251)
—Hansel & Gretel. Woollvin, Bethan, illus. (p. 919)
—Little Red. Woollvin, Bethan, illus. (p. 1325)
—Rapunzel Woollvin, Bethan, illus. (p. 1841)
Woollvin, Bethan, illus. see Nicholls, Sally.
Woolrych, Humphry William. Our Island, Vol. 1 Of 2: Comprising Forgery, a Tale; & the Lunatic, a Tale (Classic Reprint) (p. 1678)
Wools, Katie, illus. see DeBarbieri, Lili.
Woolsey, Isaac. Baby Mercy. (p. 151)
Woolsey, Sarah Chauncey. Diary & Letters of Frances Burney, Vol. 1 Of 2: Madame d'Arblay (Classic Reprint) (p. 539)
Woolson, Abba Goold. Browsing among Books, & Other Essays (Classic Reprint) (p. 287)
Woolson, Constance Fenimore. Anne: A Novel (Classic Reprint) (p. 98)
—Castle Nowhere: Lake-Country Sketches (Classic Reprint) (p. 340)
—Castle Nowhere. (p. 340)
—East Angels (Classic Reprint) (p. 619)
—For the Major: A Novelette (Classic Reprint) (p. 763)
—For the Major. (p. 763)
—Front Yard: And Other Italian Stories (Classic Reprint) (p. 795)
—Horace Chase: A Novel (Classic Reprint) (p. 1003)
—Horace Chase. (p. 1003)
—Jupiter Lights (Classic Reprint) (p. 1192)
—Mentone, Cairo, & Corfu (Classic Reprint) (p. 1447)
—Rodman the Keeper: Southern Sketches (Classic Reprint) (p. 1897)
—Rodman the Keeper. (p. 1897)
—Solomon (Classic Reprint) (p. 2057)
—Stories by American Authors: Miss. Grief; Love in Old Cloathes; Two Buckets in a Well; Friend Barton's Concern; an Inspired Lobbyist; Lost in the Fog (Classic Reprint) (p. 2123)
Woolston, Blythe. MARTians. (p. 1410)
Woolworth, Solomon. Experiences in the Civil War (Classic Reprint) (p. 678)
Woomer, Jean Nelson. Flower Fairies of the World. (p. 752)
Woommavovah, Mark E. L. Little Indian Runner. Koenig, James, illus. (p. 1319)
Woop Studios. Zeal of Zebras: An Alphabet of Collective Nouns. (p. 2538)
Wooster, Devin Ann. Barbie & Her Sisters in the Great Puppy Adventure. (p. 165)
—Big Dinosaur, Little Dinosaur. (p. 219)
—Horses to the Rescue. (p. 1005)
—Horses to the Rescue (Barbie & Her Sisters in a Puppy Chase) (p. 1005)
—Sing It Out. (p. 2023)
Wooster, Devin Ann, jt. auth. see Lagonegro, Melissa.
Wooster, Lizzie E. Wooster Fourth Reader: Wheat Field Kay County, Oklahoma (Classic Reprint) (p. 2493)
—Wooster Primer (Classic Reprint) (p. 2493)
Wooster, Lorraine Elizabeth. Wooster First Reader (Classic Reprint) (p. 2493)
Wooster, Patricia. Fashion Designer. (p. 712)
—Flickr Cofounder & Web Community Creator Caterina Fake. (p. 748)
—Ignite Your Spark: Discovering Who You Are from the Inside Out. (p. 1094)
—Illustrated Timeline of U. S. States Morgan, Rick, illus. (p. 1096)
—Music Producer. (p. 1529)
—Show Me Rocks & Minerals: My First Picture Encyclopedia (p. 2012)
—Show Me Rocks & Minerals. (p. 2012)
—Show Me the United States: My First Picture Encyclopedia (p. 2012)
—So, You Want to Be a Leader? An Awesome Guide to Becoming a Head Honcho. (p. 2051)
—Youtube Founders Steve Chen, Chad Hurley, & Jawed Karim. (p. 2536)
Wooster, Patricia & Dell, Pamela. My First Picture Encyclopedias. (p. 1545)
Wooster, Robert, jt. ed. see Kessel, William B.
Wooten, Arthur. Wise Bear William: A New Beginning. Santora, Bud, illus. (p. 2478)
Wooten, Chandra & Crowder, Liz, eds. My Day at School: A Bullying Awareness Book. Murkey, Lee, illus. (p. 1536)
Wooten, Deborah. Another Jar of Tiny Stars: Poems by More NCTE Award-Winning Poets. Cullinan, Bernice E., ed. (p. 101)
Wooten, Jason, illus. see Carver, Dale.
Wooten, Neal. Cedric the Bulge. (p. 348)
—Insomniant: A Human Holiday Story. Duarte, Javier, illus. (p. 1124)
Wooten, Neal, illus. see Austin, Antoinette & Austin, John.
Wooten, Rosalie. Tippy Tales: The Story of Tippy the Neighborhood Dog. (p. 2250)
Wooten, Sara McIntosh. Donald Trump: Real Estate Mogul & President. (p. 581)
—Donald Trump: From Real Estate to Reality TV. (p. 581)
—Tim McGraw. (p. 2243)
Wooten, Vernon Lee, illus. see Briggs-Anderson, Naomi.
Wopat, Christy. Always Ours. Wells, Julie, illus. (p. 61)
Wopschall, Kayla, illus. see Petitt, Karlene.
Woram, Catherine. Christmas Crafting with Kids. Wreford, Polly, photos by. (p. 385)
—What Shall We Do Today? 60 Creative Crafting Projects for Kids. (p. 2419)
Woram, Catherine & Youngs, Clare. Rainy Day Book of Things to Make & Do. (p. 1837)
Worboise, Emma Jane. Grey & Gold (Classic Reprint) (p. 896)
—Joan Carisbroke (Classic Reprint) (p. 1169)
—Lady Clarissa (Classic Reprint) (p. 1236)
—Lillingstones of Lillingstone (Classic Reprint) (p. 1301)
Worcester, Daryl D. Traves Travislot: The North American Adventure (p. 2281)
—Traves Travislot's Going South for the Winter. (p. 2281)
Worcester, Retta, illus. see Collyer, Barbara & Foley, John R.
Worcester, Samuel. Second Book for Reading & Spelling (Classic Reprint) (p. 1973)
—Third Book for Reading & Spelling: With Simple Rules & Instructions for Avoiding Common Errors, & a Vocabulary of Words Used in the Lessons, That Are to Be Defined (Classic Reprint) (p. 2222)
Worcester, Samuel Thomas. American Primary Spelling-Book (Classic Reprint) (p. 73)

W

—Sea & Its Marvels. (p. 1966)
—Searching for Atlantis. (p. 1971)
—Searching for the Real Dracula. (p. 1971)
—Seasonal Forests. (p. 1972)
—Secrets of Ancient Tombs. (p. 1980)
—Secrets of the Pharachs. (p. 1981)
—Shih Tzu & Other Toy Dogs. (p. 2007)
World Book, Inc. Staff, contrib. by. Smoke Signals to Smartphones: A Timeline of Long-Distance Communication. (p. 2043)
World Book, Inc Staff, contrib. by. Solar System. (p. 2056)
—Sound. (p. 2067)
—South Africa's Anti-Apartheid Movement. (p. 2068)
—Space Exploration. (p. 2071)
World Book, Inc. Staff, contrib. by. Sports. (p. 2088)
World Book, Inc Staff, contrib. by. Spring Celebrations. (p. 2092)
World Book, Inc. Staff, contrib. by. Stargazing to Space Travel: A Timeline of Space Exploration. (p. 2106)
World Book, Inc Staff, contrib. by. Stars— Birth & Death. (p. 2106)
—Stars— the Inside Story. (p. 2106)
—Subtraction. (p. 2146)
World Book, Inc. Staff, contrib. by. Sugar. (p. 2147)
World Book, Inc Staff, contrib. by. Swim with a Manta Ray? (p. 2170)
—Tales Through Time: A Supplement to Childcraft-The How & Why Library. (p. 2186)
—Technology. (p. 2197)
World Book, Inc. Staff, contrib. by. Terrific Trees. (p. 2207)
World Book, Inc Staff, contrib. by. Things I Like. (p. 2220)
—Tornadoes. (p. 2265)
—Traits & Heredity. (p. 2276)
—Transportation. (p. 2278)
—Treasures of the Ocean. (p. 2283)
—Treasures of the Oceans. (p. 2283)
—Tropical Regions & Rain Forests. (p. 2291)
World Book, Inc. Staff, contrib. by. Ugh! Yuck! & Whoa! What a Jerk! (p. 2313)
—Ugh! Yuck! & Whoa! Don't Bite Me! (p. 2313)
—Ugh! Yuck! & Whoa! Back off, Buddy! (p. 2313)
—Ugh! Yuck! & Whoa! Where Did It Go? (p. 2313)
—Ugh! Yuck! & Whoa! Ugh, That's Ugly! (p. 2313)
—Ugh! Yuck! & Whoa! Yuck, That's Gross! (p. 2313)
—Ugh! Yuck! & Whoa! Whoa, That's Strange! (p. 2313)
—Ugh! Yuck! & Whoa! What on Earth Is That? (p. 2313)
World Book, Inc Staff, contrib. by. Understanding Climate Change. (p. 2324)
—Universe—A Cosmic Tour. (p. 2332)
—Universe— Mysteries & Marvels. (p. 2332)
World Book, Inc. Staff, contrib. by. Video Games. (p. 2356)
World Book, Inc Staff, contrib. by. Volcanoes. (p. 2366)
—Voyages of Exploration. (p. 2368)
—Warfare. (p. 2379)
World Book, Inc. Staff, contrib. by. Weather. (p. 2393)
World Book, Inc. Staff, contrib. by. Weather & Climate Change. (p. 2394)
World Book, Inc. Staff, contrib. by. Weird Robots. (p. 2397)
—Where in the World Can I... A Supplement to Childcraft, the How & Why Library. (p. 2437)
—Why Are Monkeys So Flexible? World Book Answers Your Questions about Wild Animals. (p. 2455)
—Wildfires. (p. 2466)
World Book, Inc Staff, contrib. by. Wildlife & Climate Change. (p. 2466)
—Winter Celebrations. (p. 2475)
—Wonders of the World. (p. 2491)
World Book, Inc. Staff, contrib. by. Wooden Spears to Military Drones: A Timeline of Warfare. (p. 2491)
World Book, Inc Staff, contrib. by. World Book Encyclopedia 2013. (p. 2501)
World Book, Inc. Staff, contrib. by. World of Birds. (p. 2502)
World Book, Inc. Staff, contrib. by. World of Pets. (p. 2503)
World Book, Inc. Staff, contrib. by. World War II: Asian & Pacific Fronts. (p. 2505)
World Book, Inc Staff, contrib. by. World War II in Europe. (p. 2506)
—World War II in the Pacific. (p. 2506)
—Worlds Beneath Our Feet. (p. 2506)
—Zac Newton Investigates Beasts & Bugs. (p. 2537)
World Book, Inc. Staff, contrib. by. Zac Newton Investigates Bodies & Brains. (p. 2537)
—Zac Newton Investigates Extraordinary Electricity. (p. 2537)
—Zac Newton Investigates Spectacular Space. (p. 2537)
—Zac Newton Investigates Wild Weather. (p. 2537)
World Book Staff. Cells to Organ Systems. (p. 351)
—Circulatory System. (p. 393)
World Book-Childcraft International Staff, contrib. by. Brain Games: A Supplement to Childcraft—The How & Why Library. (p. 274)
World Health Organization. Quality Assessment Guidebook: A Guide to Assessing Health Services for Adolescent Clients. (p. 1822)
World of Happy Staff, jt. auth. see Andreae, Giles.
World Peace, Metta & McBride, Heddrick. Metta's Bedtime Stories. Pax, H. H., illus. (p. 1453)
World, Toronto. Toronto World, Book of English Proverbs: Including All the Proverbs to Be Used in the Toronto World's Proverb Contest (Classic Reprint) (p. 2265)
World-Famous San Diego Zoo Staff, photos by see Ryder, Joanne.
Worlds Beyond Art, illus. see Jeffries, Jo Ann.
Worley, Ashley. Mystery of Pineville Woods. Sharp, Cheryl, illus. (p. 1569)
Worley, Brandi. Crumb Snatchers, Part I. (p. 480)
Worley, C. L. Luckiest Sheep in the World. (p. 1364)
—Tales from Mousey Row - a Test of Faith. (p. 2182)
Worley, Carla. Freedom Choice: A Book that Allows You to Consider Your Options. (p. 782)
Worley, John W. Inside Insight: Worley's Identity Discovery Profile (WIDP) (p. 1123)
Worley, Karen E., jt. auth. see Pearce, Claudia.
Worley, Kayla M. Aspirations: An Alphabet Coloring Book of Women in the Workforce. (p. 126)
Worley, Rob M. Heimdall. Moll, Shawn, illus. (p. 948)
—Loki. McKinney, Brandon, illus. (p. 1340)
—Scratch9: Cat of Nine Worlds: Cat of Nine Worlds. (p. 1963)
Worley, Rob M. & Aesop, Aesop. Ants & the Grasshopper. Bloodworth, Mark, illus. (p. 103)
Worley, Rob M. & Warner, Gertrude Chandler. Pizza Mystery Dubisch, Mike, illus. (p. 1752)
—Surprise Island Dubisch, Michael, illus. (p. 2163)
Worley, Roger A. 14 Wishes (p. 2552)
Wormeley, Elizabeth. Amabel: A Family History (Classic Reprint) (p. 61)
Wormeley, Katharine Prescott. Saint: Translated from Cu Paul Bourget's Pastels of Men (Classic Reprint) (p. 1923)
Wormeley, Mary Elizabeth. Our Cousin Veronica: Or Scenes & Adventures over the Blue Ridge (Classic Reprint) (p. 1677)
Wormell, Chris. Eric!... The Hero? (p. 659)
—Molly & the Night Monster. Wormell, Chris, illus. (p. 1489)
Wormell, Chris, illus. see Lewis, J. Patrick.
Wormell, Chris, illus. see Mangus, Lily.
Wormell, Chris, illus. see Prinja, Raman.
Wormell, Christopher. Scruffy Bear & the Lost Ball. (p. 1966)
Wormell, Christopher, illus. see Green, Kate.
Wormell, Christopher, illus. see Lewis, J. Patrick.
Wormley, Theodore George, jt. auth. see Marshall, John.
Worms, Ina, illus. see Hoppenstedt, Gila & Richardson, Karen.
Worms, Penny. Brain Boosters: Adding & Subtracting Activities. Rich, Graham, illus. (p. 274)
—Brain Boosters: Times Tables Activities. Rich, Graham, illus. (p. 274)
—Dinosaur Creativity Book. (p. 548)
—Motorcycles. (p. 1512)
—Off-Road Vehicles. (p. 1640)
—Race Cars. (p. 1831)
—Super Stars! Phonics Activity Book. Rimmington, Natasha, illus. (p. 2158)
—Super Stars! Spelling Activity Book. Rimmington, Natasha, illus. (p. 2158)
—Trucks. (p. 2293)
Wormser, G. Ranger. Scarecrow & Other Stories (Classic Reprint) (p. 1941)
Wormser, Richard. All's Fair (Classic Reprint) (p. 57)
Wormwood, Edyth M. Doll That Saved an Army, an Historical Play in Four Scenes (Classic Reprint) (p. 578)
—New Woman in Mother Goose Land: A Play for Children (Classic Reprint) (p. 1598)
Woronowicz, Travis & Pannell, Titus. Return to Eden. (p. 1871)
Worrall, Lechmere. White Feather (Classic Reprint) (p. 2444)
Worrell, Edna Randolph. Two Merry Wagers: A Farce (Classic Reprint) (p. 2308)
Worron, Harriet B. Trustum & His Grandchildren (Classic Reprint) (p. 2296)
Worsdale, David H. Pedro & the Magic Marbles. (p. 1712)
Worsley, Arlene. Gymnastics. (p. 907)
—Veterans Day. (p. 2354)
Worsley, Belinda, illus. see Adamson, Jean.
Worsley, Belinda, illus. see Gurney, Stella.
Worsley, Belinda, illus. see Harrison, Paul.
Worsley, Belinda, illus. see Powell, Jillian.
Worsley, George. Advice to the Young! Honesty Is the Trade Mark & Perseverance Is a Pearl of Great Price (Classic Reprint) (p. 30)
Worsley, Lucy. Maid of the King's Court. (p. 1383)
—My Name Is Victoria. (p. 1557)
Worsley, R. M. Sour Puss Grumpy Face. (p. 2067)
—Tiger Shark the Terrible. (p. 2241)
Worster, W. W. Egholm & His God (Classic Reprint) (p. 628)
—Growth of the Soil, Vol. 2 (Classic Reprint) (p. 900)
—Wanderers (Classic Reprint) (p. 2375)
Wortabet, John. English-Arabic Dictionary: For the Use of Schools (Classic Reprint) (p. 653)
Wortche, Allison. I Love Engineering: Explore with Sliders, Lift-The-flaps, a Wheel, & More! Mack, Steve, illus. (p. 1069)
—I Love Genetics: Explore with Sliders, Lift-The-flaps, a Wheel, & More! Mack, Steve, illus. (p. 1069)
—I Love Science. Mack, Steve, illus. (p. 1072)
—I Love Space. Mack, Steve, illus. (p. 1072)
—Rosie Sprout's Time to Shine. Barton, Patrice, illus. (p. 1906)
Worth, Barbara E., ed. see Jenkins, Derek.
Worth, Bonnie. Cows Can Moo! Can You? All about Farms. (p. 465)
—Happy Pi Day to You! Ruiz, Aristides & Mathieu, Joe, illus. (p. 923)
—Hark! a Shark! All about Sharks. Ruiz, Aristides & Mathieu, Joe, illus. (p. 930)
—Ice Is Nice! All about the North & South Poles. Ruiz, Aristides & Mathieu, Joe, illus. (p. 1088)
—If I Ran the Horse Show: All about Horses. Ruiz, Aristides & Mathieu, Joe, illus. (p. 1091)
—Looking for Bigfoot. Nelson, Jim, illus. (p. 1347)
—Oh, the Things They Invented! All about Great Inventors. (p. 1642)
—Once upon a Mastodon: All about Prehistoric Mammals. (p. 1657)
—One Vote, Two Votes, I Vote, You Vote. Ruiz, Aristides & Mathieu, Joe, illus. (p. 1663)
—Safari, So Good! All about African Wildlife. Ruiz, Aristides & Mathieu, Joe, illus. (p. 1921)
—Would You Rather Be a Pollywog? All about Pond Life. Ruiz, Aristides & Mathieu, Joseph, illus. (p. 2510)
Worth, Bonnie & Klimo, Kate. Ginger. Jessell, Tim, illus. (p. 833)
Worth, Bonnie & Rabe, Tish. Oh, the Places on Earth! A Cat in the Hat's Learning Library Collection (p. 1642)
Worth, Boys and Girls Club of Greater Fort. T Is for Texas: Written by Kids for Kids. (p. 2174)
Worth, K. D. Grim Life. (p. 896)
—Lost Souls. (p. 1355)
—Wounded Heart. (p. 2510)
Worth, Patience. Hope Trueblood (Classic Reprint) (p. 1002)
Worth, Pauline Wilson. Death-Valley Slim: And Other Stories (Classic Reprint) (p. 522)
Worth, Richard. 1950s to 1960s. (p. 2561)
—1970s to the 1980s. (p. 2561)
—Adaptación y Biodiversidad. (p. 14)
—Adaptación y Biodiversidad - 6 Pack: Set of 6 Common Core Edition. (p. 14)
—Adaptation & Biodiversity: Prime Bridges Edition. Greenhead, Bill, illus. (p. 14)
—Adaptations & Biodiversity: Set Of 10. Greenhead, Bill, illus. (p. 14)
—Adaptations & Biodiversity: Bridges Edition, Set Of 10. Greenhead, Bill, illus. (p. 14)
—Amistad Revolt & the Transatlantic Slave Trade. (p. 76)
—Black Culture in Bloom: The Harlem Renaissance. (p. 237)
—Christina Aguilera: Pop Singer. (p. 383)
—Earth's Hydrosphere: Set Of 10. Freeman, Gary, illus. (p. 618)
—Earth's Hydrosphere: Prime Bridges Edition. Freeman, Gary, illus. (p. 618)
—Earth's Hydrosphere: Bridges Edition, Set Of 10. Freeman, Gary, illus. (p. 618)
—Eva Longoria: Actress, Activist, & Entrepreneur. (p. 668)
—Gambling: Winner or Loser? (p. 806)
—George Catlin: Painter of Indian Life: Painter of Indian Life. (p. 818)
—Helping a Friend Who Is Depressed. (p. 953)
—Hidrosfera de la Tierra. (p. 967)
—Hidrosfera de la Tierra - 6 Pack: Set of 6 Common Core Edition. (p. 967)
—Huella Humana. (p. 1047)
—Huella Humana - 6 Pack: Set of 6 Common Core Edition. (p. 1047)
—Human Footprint: Set Of 10. Chiu, Andrew, illus. (p. 1049)
—Human Footprint: Prime Bridges Edition. Chiu, Andrew, illus. (p. 1049)
—Human Footprint: Bridges Edition, Set Of 10. Chiu, Andrew, illus. (p. 1049)
—Illegal Drugs: Condone or Incarcerate? (p. 1095)
—Immigration 1850-1925: Set Of 6. (p. 1101)
—Immigration 1850-1925: Bridges Edition. Canas, Alex, illus. (p. 1101)
—Immigration 1850-1925: Bridges Edition Set of 6 with Common Core Indicators. Canas, Alex, illus. (p. 1101)
—Lewis Hine: Photographer of Americans at Work: Photographer of Americans at Work. (p. 1282)
—Life at School & in the Community. (p. 1290)
—Light: Set Of 10. Carloni, Marco, illus. (p. 1298)
—Light: Prime Bridges Edition. Carloni, Marco, illus. (p. 1298)
—Light: Bridges Edition, Set Of 10. Carloni, Marco, illus. (p. 1298)
—Los Angeles Police Department. (p. 1349)
—Pope Francis: The People's Pope. (p. 1776)
—Prohibition: The Rise & Fall of the Temperance Movement. (p. 1805)
—Puerto Rico: From Colony to Commonwealth. (p. 1811)
—Sherman Antitrust Act. (p. 2006)
—Social Security Act. (p. 2053)
—Toussaint L'Ouverture: Fighting for Haitian Independence. (p. 2269)
—United States Becomes a World Power: 1890-1918: Set Of 6. (p. 2330)
—United States Becomes a World Power: 1890-1918: Bridges Edition. Ginerva, Dante, illus. (p. 2330)
—United States Becomes a World Power: 1890-1918: Bridges Edition Set of 6 with Common Core Indicators. Ginerva, Dante, illus. (p. 2330)
—Vasco da Gama. (p. 2348)
—Vera Wang: Fashion Designer. (p. 2351)
—Weight Control Drugs. (p. 2396)
Worth, Richard, jt. auth. see Hasday, Judy L.
Worth, Richard & Benchmark Education Co., LLC. Adaptation & Biodiversity. (p. 14)
Worth, Richard & McCoy, Erin L. Illicit Drug Use: Treatment or Punishment? (p. 1095)
Worth, Sharon. Jacob's Garden (p. 1154)
Worth, Valerie. Pug: And Other Animal Poems. Jenkins, Steve, illus. (p. 1811)
Wortham, B. Hale. Enchanted Parrot: Being a Selection from the Suka Saptati, or the Seventy Tales of a Parrot (Classic Reprint) (p. 647)
Worthen, Alex, illus. see Hall, Annalisa.
Worthen, Johnny. Celeste. (p. 350)
Worthen, Olivia. Cute As a Bug's Ear. (p. 491)
—Sight for Sore Eyes. (p. 2016)
Worthen, Rashawn. Three Wishes from a Leprechaun. Proulx, Denis, illus. (p. 2235)
Worthington, D. Broken Sword or a Pictorial Page in Reconstruction. (p. 285)
—Broken Sword, or a Pictorial Page in Reconstruction (Classic Reprint) (p. 285)
Worthington, Edward D. Reminiscences of Student Life & Practice (Classic Reprint) (p. 1865)
Worthington, Elizabeth Strong. Gentle Art of Cooking Wives (Classic Reprint) (p. 816)
—How to Cook Husbands (Classic Reprint) (p. 1038)
Worthington, Frank. Witch Doctor & Other Rhodesian Studies (Classic Reprint) (p. 2479)
Worthington, Heather Hill. Miles of Smiles: The Story of Roxey, the Long Island Rail Road Dog. Farnsworth, Bill, illus. (p. 1465)
Worthington, Holli. Jubilee & the Legend of the Donkey's Cross: An Easter Story. (p. 1185)
Worthington, Katharine, ed. see Ludwig, Mike.
Worthington, Leonie, illus. see Bedford, David.
Worthington, Leonie, jt. auth. see Bedford, David.
Worthington, Michelle. Noah Chases the Wind. Cowman, Joseph, illus. (p. 1616)
—Start of the Ocean. Finn, Ann-Marie, illus. (p. 2107)
Worthington, Michelle & Ferre, Adyna. Wind & the Mouse. (p. 2471)
Worthington, Niles. Bee's Nest. (p. 190)
—Bird's Nest. (p. 232)
—Chef's Job. (p. 364)
—Plumber's Job. (p. 1763)
—Rabbit's Burrow. (p. 1830)
—Vet's Job. (p. 2354)
Worthington, Sandi. Adventure with Rainy Twostep. (p. 19)
Worthy, Shanya. LeBron James: Basketball Legend. (p. 1260)
—Taipan. (p. 2176)
—Taipan / Taipán. (p. 2176)
Worthy, Shanya, jt. auth. see Mills, Nathan.
Worthy, Vera. Chocolate. (p. 380)
WorthyKids/Ideals. God Knows Me: 365 Daily Devos for Boys. (p. 851)
—God Knows Me: 365 Daily Devos for Girls. (p. 851)
—My First Book of Prayers. Flint, Gillian, illus. (p. 1543)
Wortley, Emmeline Stuart. Visit to Portugal & Madeira (Classic Reprint) (p. 2362)
Wortley, Isabel. Elf & Her Friends: A Horse Story Founded on Fact (Classic Reprint) (p. 635)
Wos, Joe. A-Maze-Ing America: 50 Mazes of the 50 States. (p. 2)
—Maze-O-zoic: 50 Dinosaur Mazes. (p. 1430)
—Myths & Monsters: 50 Mazes for Kids. (p. 1571)
Wotherspoon, John, jt. auth. see Park, Barbara.
Wotton, Jon, illus. see Williams, Vivienne.
Wotton, Joy. My First Word Book: Pictures & Words to Start Toddlers Reading & to Help Pre-Schoolers Develop Vocabulary Skills. Tulip, Jenny, illus. (p. 1546)
Wouk, Henry. Hearing Disorders. (p. 944)
—Organ Transplants. (p. 1670)
—Tuberculosis. (p. 2298)
Woupio, Amy, illus. see Woupio, Isaac Jay.
Woyt, Barbara A. Geology. (p. 817)
Wozniak, Erin, illus. see Miletsky, Jay.
Wozniak, Lana, illus. see Miletsky, Jay.
Wozniak, Paul. Stranded in a Snowstorm! Webber, Mike, illus. (p. 2137)
Wozny, Sharon. Jamie's Journey: Cancer from the Voice of a Sibling. Bailey, Melissa, illus. (p. 1157)
Wrag, Elizabeth. Secret History of the Most Renowned Q. Elizabeth & the E. of Essex (Classic Reprint) (p. 1976)
Wrage, Hermann D. Lehrbuch der Englischen Sprache. (p. 1265)
—Lehrbuch der Englischen Sprache (Classic Reprint) (p. 1265)
Wragg, Cynthia a. What Color Is God? (p. 2407)
Wragg, Nate, illus. see Denise, Anika.
Wragg, Nate, illus. see Esbaum, Jill.
Wragg, Nate, illus. see Kerstein, Lauren H.
Wragg, Nate, illus. see Masessa, Ed.
Wragg, Nate, illus. see Paul, Miranda.
Wragg, Nate, illus. see Schwartz, Corey Rosen & Coulton, Beth.
Wragg, Nate, illus. see Wensink, Patrick.
Wragge, Clement L. Romance of the South Seas (Classic Reprint) (p. 1900)
Wraith, Steve. Ghost Who Couldn't Scare. Joey, Alfie, illus. (p. 828)
Wrate, Richard. Din-o-mite in Aarons Closet. (p. 547)
Wratislaw, A. H. Sixty Folk-Tales: From Exclusively Slavonic Sources (Classic Reprint) (p. 2029)
Wraxall, Lascelles. Backwoodsman, or Life on the Indian Frontier (Classic Reprint) (p. 156)
Wray, Angelina W. Glimpses of Child Nature: For Teachers & Parents (Classic Reprint) (p. 842)
—Jean Mitchell's School (Classic Reprint) (p. 1162)
Wray, Brian. Max's Box: Letting Go of Negative Feelings Penfield, Shiloh, illus. (p. 1428)
—Unraveling Rose Penfield, Shiloh, illus. (p. 2335)
Wray, Brian & Penfield, Shiloh. Maia & the Very Tall Wall. (p. 1382)
Wray, Fitzwater. We Others: Stories of Fate, Love & Pity (Classic Reprint) (p. 2392)
Wray, J. Mess. (p. 1451)
Wray, J. Jackson. Nestleton Magna: A Story of Yorkshire Methodism (Classic Reprint) (p. 1588)
Wray, Jordan. My Christmas ABCs (an Alphabet Book) (p. 1535)
Wray, Jordan, illus. see Atkins, Jill.
Wray, Jordan, illus. see Cottrell, Jane.
Wray, Melissa. Destiny Road. (p. 534)
Wray, Zoe, illus. see Daynes, Katie.
Wray, Zoe, illus. see Milbourne, Anna.
Wray, Zoe, illus. see Patchett, Fiona.
Wray, Zoe, illus. see Turnbull, Stephanie.
Wray, Zoe, jt. auth. see Daynes, Katie.
Wrecks, Billy. Ant-Man. Spaziante, Patrick, illus. (p. 101)
—Batman: Adventures of the Dark Knight. (p. 172)
—Batman! (DC Super Friends) Beavers, Ethen, illus. (p. 172)
—Batman's Hero Files. (p. 173)
—Batman's Hero Files (DC Super Friends) Doescher, Erik & Spaziante, Patrick, illus. (p. 173)
—Big Freeze (Marvel) Borkowski, Michael & Atiyen, Michael, illus. (p. 220)
—Big Heroes! (DC Super Friends) Golden Books, illus. (p. 220)
—Bizarro Day! (p. 235)
—Bizarro Day! (DC Super Friends) Legramandi, Francesco, illus. (p. 235)
—Catch Catwoman! (p. 343)
—Courageous Captain America. Golden Books Staff, illus. (p. 462)
—Crime Wave! (p. 474)
—Dino Hybrid. Random House, illus. (p. 547)
—Eye of the Dragon (Marvel: Iron Man) Spaziante, Patrick, illus. (p. 688)
—Green Lantern vs. the Meteor Monster! (DC Super Friends) Random House, illus. (p. 894)
—Here Come the Heroes! (DC Super Friends) DeCarlo, Mike et al, illus. (p. 957)
—Heroes vs. Villains/Space Chase! (DC Super Friends) Doescher, Erik et al, illus. (p. 962)
—Incredible Hulk (Marvel: Incredible Hulk) Spaziante, Patrick, illus. (p. 1114)
—Invincible Iron Man (Marvel: Iron Man) Spaziante, Patrick, illus. (p. 1132)
—Marvel Black Panther Rules! Discover What It Takes to Be a Super Hero. (p. 1412)
—Marvel Black Panther Rules! (Library Edition) Discover What It Takes to Be a Super Hero. (p. 1412)
—Mighty Avengers (Marvel: the Avengers) Spaziante, Patrick, illus. (p. 1462)
—Mighty Thor (Marvel: Thor) Golden Books, illus. (p. 1463)

W

—Third Reader Stories of Birds & Beasts (Classic Reprint) (p. 2222)
—Tommy-Anne & the Three Hearts. (p. 2259)
—Tommy-Anne & the Three Hearts (Classic Reprint) (p. 2259)
—Wabeno the Magician: The Sequel to Tommy-Anne & the Three Hearts (Classic Reprint) (p. 2369)
—Wabeno the Magician. (p. 2369)
—Woman Errant: Being Some Chapters from the Wonder Book of Barbara, the Commuter's Wife (Classic Reprint) (p. 2485)
Wright, Mabel Osgood, jt. auth. see Coues, Elliott.
Wright, Mabel Osgood & Fuertes, Louis Agassiz. Birdcraft. (p. 231)
Wright, Mabel Osgood & Wright, Mabel O. Birdcraft. (p. 231)
Wright Mabie, Hamilton. Myths That Every Child Should Know: A Selection of the Classic Myths of All Times for Young People. (p. 1572)
Wright, Mance Ian. City of Abundance. (p. 395)
Wright, Marcy. Juan Pablo Montoya. (p. 1184)
Wright, Margaret B. Hired Furnished: Being Certain Economical Housekeeping Adventures in England (Classic Reprint) (p. 973)
—Hired Furnished. (p. 973)
Wright, Mary. Co-Man & Poppa Meet Kanka. Dewitt, Levi, illus. (p. 409)
Wright, Mary F. Co-Man the Dolphin. (p. 409)
Wright, Mary H. & Frontiera, Deborah K. Simon & Company: Flea Market Mice. Scott, Korey, illus. (p. 2020)
Wright, Mary Tappan. Aliens (Classic Reprint) (p. 47)
—Tower: A Novel (Classic Reprint) (p. 2269)
—Truce & Other Stories (Classic Reprint) (p. 2292)
Wright, Maureen. Barnyard Fun de Tagyos, Paul Rátz, illus. (p. 167)
—Earth Day, Birthday! Kim, Violet, illus. (p. 616)
—Sleep, Big Bear, Sleep! Hillenbrand, Will, illus. (p. 2036)
—Sneeze, Big Bear, Sneeze! Hillenbrand, Will, illus. (p. 2045)
Wright, Melissa, jt. auth. see Wallace, Susan Helen.
Wright, Michael. Jake Starts School. Wright, Michael, illus. (p. 1156)
Wright, Mike, illus. see Blank, Eva, et al.
Wright, Natalie. Slime 101: How to Make Stretchy, Fluffy, Glittery & Colorful Slime! (p. 2038)
Wright, Nathan T., illus. see Wright, Karla.
Wright, Nicky. Mustang: The American Muscle Car. (p. 1530)
Wright, Olivia. Malarie Jane Learns to Help. (p. 1391)
Wright, Pam, jt. auth. see Sohn, Emily.
Wright, Pamela. Rant Room. (p. 1841)
Wright, Pamela, jt. auth. see Bair, Diane.
Wright, Peter. Teddy the Psychic. (p. 2198)
—Three-Foot Stool (Classic Reprint) (p. 2233)
Wright, Peter M. Stone Prince (p. 2121)
Wright, Pj. When Your Dino Gets the Downers. (p. 2434)
—When Your Dragon Gets the Drowsies. (p. 2434)
—When Your Hippo Gets the Huggies. (p. 2434)
—When Your Monkey Gets the Junkies. (p. 2435)
—When Your Monster Gets the Munchies. (p. 2435)
—When Your Weasel Gets the Sneezles. (p. 2435)
Wright, Priscilla Hovey. Car Belongs to Mother (Classic Reprint) (p. 327)
Wright, R. H. Greatness in My Community. (p. 892)
Wright, Randall, jt. auth. see Deedy, Carmen Agra.
Wright, Rebecca. Simon & the Magic Drums. (p. 2020)
—Ups & Downs: Elementary Monologues That Explore Emotions. (p. 2339)
Wright, Rebecca Hu-Van & Asbjornsen, Peter Christen. Three Billy Goats Gruff Hu, Ying-Hwa, illus. (p. 2232)
Wright, Richard. Rite of Passage. (p. 1886)
Wright, Richard & Crews, Nina. Seeing into Tomorrow: Haiku by Richard Wright. Crews, Nina, illus. (p. 1984)
Wright, Richardson. Open Door (Classic Reprint) (p. 1665)
Wright, Richardson Little. Letters to the Mother, of a Soldier (Classic Reprint) (p. 1281)
—Truly Rural: Adventures in Getting Back to Earth (Classic Reprint) (p. 2295)
Wright, Robert, illus. see McDonnell, Thomas.
Wright, Robert A., illus. see McDonnell, Tom.
Wright, Robert M. Dodge City, the Cowboy Capital & the Great Southwest: In the Days of the Wild Indian, the Buffalo, the Cowboys, Dance Halls, Gambling Halls & Bad Men (Classic Reprint) (p. 574)
Wright, Rowe. Everygirl's Magazine (Formerly Wohelo), Vol. 10: Magazine of the Camp Fire Girls; September 1922 (Classic Reprint) (p. 672)
Wright, S. 1683-1746, jt. auth. see Dafoe, Daniel.
Wright, S. B. Lissa Discovers the Secrets of the Castle (p. 1308)
Wright, S. K. It Ends with You. (p. 1141)
Wright, Sally Ann. Bible Adventures & Activities. Maclean, Moira, illus. (p. 213)
—Child's Book of Prayers. Ayres, Honor, illus. (p. 375)
—Christmas Activity Book. Grudina, Paola Bertolini, illus. (p. 383)
—Mix & Match Bible. (p. 1484)
Wright, Sally Ann & Wright, Lesley. My Keepsake Bible. Ayres, Honor, illus. (p. 1550)
Wright, Samantha, illus. see Belkin, Dick.
Wright, Sara Ann, illus. see Morimoto, Diana.
Wright, Sarah A. Crimson Star: Or the Midnight Vision (Classic Reprint) (p. 475)
Wright, Sarah Jane, illus. see Beha, Eileen.
Wright, Sarah Jane, illus. see Buck, Nola.
Wright, Sarah Jane, illus. see Fleming, Meg.
Wright, Sarah Jane, illus. see Wright, Kenneth.
Wright, Sasha. Malik Chooses Generosity. (p. 1392)
Wright, Saul. Surf: A Summer Pilgrimage (Classic Reprint) (p. 2162)
Wright, Shamekia. Mr. Fatty Mcfatterton. (p. 1518)
Wright, Shannon. Children's Secret Diary: Kid's Diary. (p. 375)
—Dinosaurs & Monsters Coloring Book. (p. 550)
—Wild Wild Animals Coloring Book. (p. 2465)
Wright, Shannon, illus. see Danticat, Edwidge.
Wright, Shannon, illus. see Wright, Jasmyn.
Wright, Simeon & Boyd, Herb. Simeon's Story: An Eyewitness Account of the Kidnapping of Emmett Till. (p. 2020)
Wright, Sky'asia. Big, Blue Raspberry. (p. 217)
Wright, Susan. Civil Rights Act Of 1964: Landmark Anti-Discrimination Legislation. (p. 396)
—Georgia O'Keefe: An Eternal Spirit (p. 821)
Wright, Sylvia. Get Away from Me with Those Christmas Gifts: And Other Reactions (Classic Reprint) (p. 823)
—Lantern, Vol. 17: November, 1937 (Classic Reprint) (p. 1244)
Wright, Theodore Lyman. Beloit Pageant from the Turtle Pageant: To the Flaming Wheel (Classic Reprint) (p. 198)
Wright, Thomas. Anecdota Literaria; a Collection of Short Poems in English, Latin, & French: Illustrative of the Literature & History of England in the Thirteenth Century, & More Especially of the Conditions & Manners of the Different Classes of Society. (p. 84)
—Autobiography of Thomas Wright: Of Birkenshaw, in the County of York, 1736-1797 (Classic Reprint) (p. 140)
—Pinch of Poverty: Sufferings & Heroism of the London Poor (Classic Reprint) (p. 1745)
—Romance of the Shoe: Being the History of Shoemaking in All Ages, & Especially in England & Scotland (Classic Reprint) (p. 1900)
—Seven Sages in English Verse: Edited from a Manuscript in the Public Library, of the University of Cambridge (Classic Reprint) (p. 1994)
—Seven Sages, in English Verse: Edited from a Manuscript in the Public Library of the University of Cambridge (Classic Reprint) (p. 1994)
—Songs & Carols: From a Manuscript in the British Museum of the Fifteenth Century (Classic Reprint) (p. 2063)
—Specimens of Lyric Poetry, Composed in England in the Reign of Edward the First: Edited from Ms. Harl. 2253, in the British Museum (Classic Reprint) (p. 2077)
—Tale of the Basyn & the Frere & the Boy: Two Early Tales of Magic Printed from Manuscripts Preserved in the Public Library of the University of Cambridge (Classic Reprint) (p. 2180)
—Vision & Creed of Piers Ploughman, Vol. 1 Of 2: Edited, from a Contemporary Manuscript, with a Historical Introduction, Notes, & a Glossary (Classic Reprint) (p. 2362)
Wright, Thomas, jt. auth. see Chaucer, Geoffrey.
Wright, Thomas & Langland, William. Vision & Creed of Piers Ploughman. (p. 2362)
Wright, Timothy. Real Christmas Story. (p. 1849)
Wright, W. Aldis. Generydes: A Romance in Seven-Line Stanzas; Edited from the Unique Paper Ms. in Trinity College, Cambridge (about 1440 A. D.) (Classic Reprint) (p. 814)
Wright, Waugh. Aspects, Bright & Fair: Book One of the Cordelian Chronicles. (p. 126)
Wright, Wendy L., illus. see Terrill Holdman, Shirley.
Wright, Willard Huntington. Great Modern French Stories: A Chronological Anthology (Classic Reprint) (p. 887)
Wright, William Aldis. Generydes: A Romance in Seven-Line Stanzas (Classic Reprint) (p. 814)
—Generydes, a Romance in Seven-Line Stanzas: Edited from the Unique Paper Ms. in Trinity College, Cambridge (about 1440 A. D.) (Classic Reprint) (p. 814)
Wright, William Greenwood. Butterflies of the West Coast of the United States: Illustrated with 940 Figures in Color-Photography of Butterflies from the West Coast, Nearly All of Which Were Captured by the Author, with Accurate Data for Each Specimen (Classic Reprint) (p. 303)
Wright, William H. Black Bear (Classic Reprint) (p. 236)
Wright, William Henry. Grizzly Bear: The Narrative of a Hunter-Naturalist - Scholar's Choice Edition. (p. 897)
—Grizzly Bear: The Narrative of a Hunter-Naturalist, Historical, Scientific & Adventurous - Scholar's Choice Edition. (p. 897)
Wright, William Henry Kearley, jt. auth. see Gay, John.
Wright, William Lord. Photoplay Writing (Classic Reprint) (p. 1737)
Wright, Willie Etta. Grandma Mable, Are You Able? Illustrations, Blueberry, illus. (p. 878)
Wright, Winifred. Colonnade, Vol. 4: May, 1942 (Classic Reprint) (p. 419)
—Colonnade, Vol. 5: March, 1943 (Classic Reprint) (p. 419)
WrightGroup/McGraw-Hill. Dlm Early Childhood Express: Sing a Song of Opposites Little Book English. (p. 569)
WrightGroup/McGraw-Hill Staff, jt. auth. see Wagner, B. J.
WrightGroup/McGraw-Hill Staff, jt. auth. see Wagner, B.J.
WrightGroup/McGraw-Hill Staff, jt. auth. see WrightGroup/McGraw-Hill.
Wright-Mcadoo, Joyce, jt. auth. see Wright-McAdoo, Joyce.
Wright-Phillips, Leanne. Magic Word. (p. 1379)
Wrightson, Bernie. Bernie Wrightson: Art & Designs for the Gang of Seven Animation Studio. Herman, Daniel, ed. (p. 204)
Wrightson, Bernie & Lee, Pat. Marvel Knights Punisher by Golden, Sniegoski, & Wrightson: Purgatory. (p. 1412)
Wrightson, John. Sheep. (p. 2004)
Wrigley, Annabel. We Love to Sew: 28 Pretty Things to Make. (p. 2391)
—We Love to Sew—Bedrooms: 23 Projects, Cool Stuff for Your Space. (p. 2391)
Wrigley, John. Notes on the Bird Life of Formby (Classic Reprint) (p. 1624)
Wrike, Jessica, illus. see Blake, Nyron.
Wrinkler et al., Henry. Always Watch Out for the Flying Potato Salad! (p. 61)
—Everybody Is Somebody (p. 671)
—Hooray! My Butt Left the Bench (p. 1001)
—Robot on the Loose (p. 1892)
—Soggy, Foggy Campout (p. 2055)
Wriothesley, William. Ambassadress (Classic Reprint) (p. 67)
Write Planners and Notebooks. Sports Enthusiast's Record Keeping Sporting Journal. (p. 2088)
Writer, The Dark. Grim. (p. 896)
Writers, Cairns Collection Of American W. Women's Husbands (Classic Reprint) (p. 2488)
Writers, Contemporary French. Tales of Wartime France (Classic Reprint) (p. 2186)
Writers, Famous American. Pansy's Sunday Book (Classic Reprint) (p. 1696)
Writers, Great. Original Stories, Poems, & Essays (Classic Reprint) (p. 1671)
Writers, Hgps. Scribblers in the Grove. (p. 1965)
Writers, Many Eminent. International Library of Famous Literature, Vol. 15 Of 20: Selections from the World's Great Writers (Classic Reprint) (p. 1126)
—International Library of Famous Literature, Vol. 17 Of 20: Selections from the World's Great Writers Ancient, Mediaeval, & Modern, with Biographical & Explanatory Notes & Critical Essays (Classic Reprint) (p. 1126)
—International Library of Famous Literature, Vol. 8 Of 20: Selection from the World's Great Writers, Ancient, Mediaeval, & Modern, with Biographical & Explanatory Notes, & Critical Essays (Classic Reprint) (p. 1126)
—International Library of Famous Literature, Vol. 9 Of 20: Selections from the Worlds Great Writers Ancient, Mediaeval, & Modern, with Biographical & Explanatory Notes & Critical Essays (Classic Reprint) (p. 1126)
Writers, Townsville. Scribblerz Anthology 2. (p. 1965)
Writers, Young. Adventures of Dreamtopia. (p. 23)
Writing and Editorial Services, Jmd, ed. see McNally, Emma R.
Writing Clubs, Oak Tree Arts. Oak Tree Chronicles. (p. 1633)
Written By Dana Wright; Illustrated By S. Crazy Pants. (p. 469)
Written By Doretta Elaine Wilson; Illust. Ultimate Heart. Baker, Jonathan, illus. (p. 2315)
Written by Elli Matthews; Illustrated by, illus. see Matthews, Elli.
Written By Kimberly M Sosnowski; Illustr. Ace's Wish for a Forever Home. Sosnowski, Tiffany, illus. (p. 10)
Written By Pamela McFarland; Illustrated. Guide Me Home, Sunny. Bates, Bill, illus. (p. 903)
Written by Shelia West; Illustrated by D, illus. see West, Shelia.
Written By Susan J. Perry; Illustrated B. Snuckle-Bee & Snuckle-Bun: The Bee-Attitudes. Dedering, Victoria, illus. (p. 2050)
Written By Tori Velle; Illustrated By Al. Tia Tot Rules! Aguila, Alicia del, illus. (p. 2239)
Written, L. & By Hope Martin, Illustrated. What Does the Tooth Fairy Do with All Those Teeth? (p. 2410)
Wroath, Tami. ABC: Art by the Letter. (p. 3)
Wrobel, C. J., ed. see Beddor, Frank & Cavalier, Liz.
Wroble, Lisa A. Dealing with Stress. (p. 519)
—Right to Counsel: From Gideon V. Wainwright to Gideon's Trumpet. (p. 1882)
—Starving: Can We Feed Everyone? (p. 2108)
Wroble, Lisa A. & Library. Food for a Greener Planet: What You Can Do. (p. 759)
Wroblewski, Nick, illus. see Casanova, Mary.
Wroe, Dameon K., ed. see Banks, Kimberly E.
Wronski, Gareth. Holly Farb & the Princess of the Galaxy. (p. 988)
Wroth, Dean, illus. see Castro, Anita.
Wroth, Dean, illus. see Chamberlin, Kate.
Wroth, Dean, illus. see Feuerbach, Jennifer.
Wroth, Warwick. London Pleasure Gardens of the Eighteenth Century (Classic Reprint) (p. 1341)
Wrucke, Mary. Timmy the Tadpole Cooke, Bev., illus. (p. 2247)
Wrzosek, Jennifer. Jumping Fish. Malekoff, Stephanie & Warner, Chalene, illus. (p. 1188)
Wshington, Ned. When You Wish upon a Star. Puybaret, Eric, illus. (p. 2434)
Wspk, ed. Great Source Write Source: Interactive CD Site License Grade K 2006. (p. 889)
Wu, Amelia. Alphabet Book for Children of the Heavenly Way: A Parent Read- along Book. Gao, Gloria, illus. (p. 58)
Wu, Annie, illus. see Acker, Ben & Blacker, Ben.
Wu, Annie, illus. see Ireland, Justina.
Wu, Bill. Survive! (Set) (p. 2164)
Wu, Cheng'En. [Journey to the West]. (p. 1183)
Wu, Donald, illus. see Boelts, Maribeth.
Wu, Donald, illus. see Brennan-Nelson, Denise.
Wu, Donald, illus. see Hubbell, Patricia.
Wu, Donald, illus. see Loewen, Nancy.
Wu, Donald, illus. see Sherman, Caroline.
Wu, Faye-Lynn. Chinese & English Nursery Rhymes: Little Mouse & Other Charming Chinese Rhymes (Audio Disc in Chinese & English Included) Dutcher, Kieren, illus. (p. 378)
—Mulan: The Legend of the Woman Warrior. Ang, Joy, illus. (p. 1525)
—My First Book of Chinese Words: An ABC Rhyming Book. Padron, Aya, illus. (p. 1542)
—My First Book of Chinese Words: An ABC Rhyming Book of Chinese Language & Culture. Padron, Aya, illus. (p. 1542)
Wu, Helen, illus. see Rock, Nic.
Wu, Helen H., illus. see Patrick, Jill O.
Wu, Julie, illus. see Crowe, Ellie.
Wu, Junyi, illus. see Heidicker, Christian McKay.
Wu, Junyi, illus. see Metcalf, Lindsay H.
Wu, Junyi, illus. see Robeson, Teresa.
Wu, Katy, illus. see Burleigh, Robert.
Wu, Katy, illus. see Clickard, Carrie.
Wu, Katy, illus. see Freeman, Martha.
Wu, Katy, illus. see Furst, Joshua.
Wu, Katy, illus. see Wallmark, Laurie.
Wu, Leslie, illus. see Bauer, Marion Dane.
Wu, Leslie, illus. see Markle, Sandra.
Wu, Mike. Ellie. Wu, Mike, illus. (p. 637)
—Ellie in Color. (p. 638)
—Ellie in Concert. Wu, Mike, illus. (p. 638)
—Ellie Makes a Friend. Wu, Mike, illus. (p. 638)
—Henri's Hats: Pixar Animation Studios Artist Showcase. Wu, Mike, illus. (p. 954)
Wu, Mike, illus. see Griffin, Adele.
Wu, Nicholas. Bears' Story by Baldwin B. Bear (p. 181)
—Princess & the Pea (p. 1796)
—Princess & the Pea: A Retelling of Hans Christian Andersen's Story (p. 1796)
—Tiddalick, the Greedy Frog: An Aboriginal Dreamtime Story (p. 2240)
Wu, Vivien, illus. see Bardhan-Quallen, Sudipta.
Wu, Vivien, illus. see Giuliani, Alfred.
Wu, Vivien, illus. see RH Disney Staff.
Wu, Vivien, illus. see Saxon, Victoria.
Wu, Vivien, illus. see Sutherland, Kari & L'Engle, Madeleine.
Wu, Yi-Hsaun. Sing & Slide: Old MacDonald Had a Farm. (p. 2023)
—Sing & Slide: the Itsy Bitsy Spider. (p. 2023)
—Sing & Slide: the Wheels on the Bus. (p. 2023)
Wu, Yi-Hsuan. Who Said Boo? (p. 2449)
—Who Said Moo? (p. 2449)
Wu, Yi-Hsuan, illus. see Amiot, Karine-Marie.
Wu, Yi-Hsuan, illus. see Crowe, Carmen.
Wu, Yi-Hsuan, illus. see Downy, Rufus.
Wu, Yi-Hsuan, illus. see Editors of Silver Dolphin Books.
Wu, Yi-Hsuan, illus. see Marx, Jonny.
Wu, Yi-Hsuan, illus. see Redd, R. I.
Wu, Yi-Hsuan, illus. see Wing, Scarlett.
Wucinich, Carrie. Where the Sugar Bugs Live. (p. 2439)
Wucinich, Warren, illus. see Logan, Sam.
Wucinich, Warren, illus. see Naifeh, Ted.
Wucinich, Warren, illus. see Trueheart, Eric & Crosland, Dave.
Wucinich, Warren, illus. see Trueheart, Eric & Vasquez, Jhonen.
Wucinich, Warren, illus. see Wagner, Justin.
Wuest, Marcia. Twelve Things to Do at Age 12. (p. 2304)
Wukovits, John F. Bombing of Pearl Harbor. (p. 254)
—George Clooney. (p. 818)
—Manhattan Project. Greenhaven Press Editors, ed. (p. 1397)
—Victorian Era. Greenhaven Press Editors, ed. (p. 2355)
Wukovits, John F. & Hay, Jeff. Internment of Japanese Americans. (p. 1127)
Wulf, Jessica, jt. auth. see Lebsock, K. B.
Wulfekotte, Dana. Rabbit & Possum. Wulfekotte, Dana, illus. (p. 1829)
Wulfekotte, Dana, illus. see Oliveros, Jessie.
Wulfekotte, Dana, illus. see Tan, Susan.
Wulfekotte, Dana, illus. see Tseng, Kevin.
Wulff, Mary L. & Tilford, Greg L. Herbs for Pets: The Natural Way to Enhance Your Pet's Life. (p. 957)
Wulffson, Don. Toys. Keller, Laurie, illus. (p. 2271)
—Toys! Amazing Stories Behind Some Great Inventions. (p. 2271)
Wulfing, Amy J., illus. see Baretz, Susie.
Wulfing, Amy J., illus. see Shortle, Stacy & Mooney, Dean J. M.
Wulfing, Ernst Anton, jt. auth. see Rosenbusch, Harry.
Wulfing, J. Ernst. Sand Iron Book, Vol. 1: A Romance of about 1400 A. D. Now First Edited from the Unique Ms. (Laud, Misc, 595) in the Bodleian Library, Oxford, with Introduction, Notes, I Glossary (Classic Reprint) (p. 1930)
Wulfing, Johann Ernst. Laud Troy Book: A Romance of about 1400 A. d (Classic Reprint) (p. 1251)
Wullie, Oor. Oor Wullie Colouring Book. (p. 1665)
—Oor Wullie's Big Bucket of Laughs Joke Book. (p. 1665)
Wume, Cindy. Best Sound in the World. (p. 207)
Wummel, Jeanette. Zendoodle Color-By-Number: Sea Life: Underwater Worlds to Color & Display. (p. 2539)
Wummer, Amy, illus. see Adams, Michelle Medlock.
Wummer, Amy, illus. see Bishop, Jennie.
Wummer, Amy, illus. see Buzzeo, Toni.
Wummer, Amy, illus. see Clarke, Ginjer L.
Wummer, Amy, illus. see Driscoll, Laura.
Wummer, Amy, illus. see Dussling, Jennifer.
Wummer, Amy, illus. see Harkrader, Lisa.
Wummer, Amy, illus. see Hepker, Sue.
Wummer, Amy, illus. see Jordan, Taylor.
Wummer, Amy, illus. see Kennedy, Pamela & Kennedy, Douglas.
Wummer, Amy, illus. see Kennedy, Pamela.
Wummer, Amy, illus. see Kline, Suzy.
Wummer, Amy, illus. see Knudsen, Michelle.
Wummer, Amy, illus. see Lansky, Bruce.
Wummer, Amy, illus. see Lord, Jill Roman.
Wummer, Amy, illus. see May, Eleanor.
Wummer, Amy, illus. see Montgomery, Lewis B.
Wummer, Amy, illus. see Walker, Nan.
Wummer, Amy, illus. see Wing, Natasha.
Wunder, Wendy. Probability of Miracles. (p. 1802)
Wunderli, Stephen. Little Boo. Zeltner, Tim, illus. (p. 1312)
Wunderlich, Jordan. Colorado Barn Cats - Skunk & Chauncey. (p. 421)
Wunderlich, Richard. Math on the Job. (p. 1424)
Wunderlich, Rick. Math on the Job: Working in Sports. (p. 1424)
—Math on the Job: Building a Business. (p. 1424)
—Math on the Job: Keeping People Healthy. (p. 1424)
—Math on the Job: Working in Construction. (p. 1424)
—Math on the Job: Caring for Marine Animals. (p. 1424)
Wundt, Wilhelm. Lehrbuch der Physiologie des Menschen (Classic Reprint) (p. 1265)
Wung-Sung, Jesper. Last Execution. van Rooyen, Lindy Falk, tr. (p. 1247)
Wunsch, Emma. Banana Pants! (Miranda & Maude #2) von Innerebner, Jessika, illus. (p. 163)
—Movie Version. (p. 1516)
—Princess & the Absolutely Not a Princess (Miranda & Maude #1) von Innerebner, Jessika, illus. (p. 1795)
—Princess & the Absolutely Not a Princess (Miranda & Maude #1) von Innerebner, Jessika, illus. (p. 1795)
—Recess Rebels (Miranda & Maude #3) von Innerebner, Jessika, illus. (p. 1853)
Wurdz, Gideon. Eedotic Etiquette: An up-To-Date Manual of the Manners of Men & Women for Men & Women of Manners, & a Complete Catalogue of the Social Dues & Most of the Don'ts for All Disciples of Deportment (Classic Reprint) (p. 627)
—Foolish Dictionary: An Exhausting Work of Reference to un-Certain English Words, Their Origin, Meaning, Legitimate & Illegitimate Use, Confused by a Few Pictures (Classic Reprint) (p. 761)
Wurge, B. B. Last Notebook of Leonardo. (p. 1248)
—Squiggle. (p. 2094)
Wuthrich, Belle, illus. see Ayer, Paula & Banyard, Antonia.

X

—Black Sheep, Vol. 2 Of 3: A Novel (Classic Reprint) (p. 239)
—Black Sheep, Vol. 3 Of 3: A Novel (Classic Reprint) (p. 239)
—Broken to Harness, Vol. 1 Of 3: A Story of English Domestic Life (Classic Reprint) (p. 285)
—Business of Pleasure, Vol. 1 of 2 (Classic Reprint) (p. 301)
—Castaway, Vol. 2 Of 3: A Novel (Classic Reprint) (p. 339)
—Castaway, Vol. 3 Of 3: A Novel (Classic Reprint) (p. 339)
—Dr. Wainwright's Patient, Vol. 1 Of 3: A Novel (Classic Reprint) (p. 592)
—Forlorn Hope: A Novel (Classic Reprint) (p. 768)
—Forlorn Hope: A Novel in Threee Volumes, Vol. III. (p. 768)
—Going to the Bad: A Novel (Classic Reprint) (p. 855)
—Impending Sword, Vol. 2 Of 3: A Novel (Classic Reprint) (p. 1102)
—Kissing the Rod: A Novel (Classic Reprint) (p. 1225)
—Land at Last, Vol. 1 Of 3: A Novel; Making for Shore (Classic Reprint) (p. 1241)
—Righted Wrong, Vol. 1: A Novel (Classic Reprint) (p. 1882)
—Rock Ahead, Vol. 1 Of 2: A Novel (Classic Reprint) (p. 1894)
—Running the Gauntlet, Vol. 1 Of 3: A Novel (Classic Reprint) (p. 1916)
—Silent Witness: A Novel (Classic Reprint) (p. 2018)
—Time, 1880, Vol. 2: A Monthly Miscellany of Interesting & Amusing Literature (Classic Reprint) (p. 2243)
—Time, 1883, Vol. 9: A Monthly Miscellany of Interesting & Amusing Literature (Classic Reprint) (p. 2243)
—Two, by Tricks: A Novel (Classic Reprint) (p. 2307)
—Waiting Race: A Novel (Classic Reprint) (p. 2371)
—Wrecked in Port, Vol. 1 Of 3: A Novel (Classic Reprint) (p. 2511)
—Yellow Flag (Classic Reprint) (p. 2520)
—Yellow Flag, Vol. 1 Of 3: A Novel (Classic Reprint) (p. 2520)
—Yellow Flag, Vol. 2 Of 3: A Novel (Classic Reprint) (p. 2520)
—Yellow Flag, Vol. 3 Of 3: A Novel (Classic Reprint) (p. 2520)
Yates, Edmund H. My Haunts & Their Frequenters. (p. 1549)
—My Haunts & Their Frequenters (Classic Reprint) (p. 1549)
Yates, Edmund Hodgson. Broken to Harness: A Story of English Domestic Life (Classic Reprint) (p. 285)
—Broken to Harness. (p. 285)
—Broken to Harness, Vol. 2 Of 3: A Story of English Domestic Life (Classic Reprint) (p. 285)
—Castaway, Vol. 1: A Novel (Classic Reprint) (p. 339)
—Forlorn Hope, Vol. 1 Of 3: A Novel (Classic Reprint) (p. 768)
—Impending Sword, Vol. 1 Of 3: A Novel (Classic Reprint) (p. 1102)
—Our Miscellany, Which Ought to Have Come Out, but Didn't (Classic Reprint) (p. 1679)
—Righted Wrong, Vol. 2 Of 3: A Novel (Classic Reprint) (p. 1882)
—Time, 1889, Vol. 2: A Monthly Magazine (Classic Reprint) (p. 2243)
—Time, Vol. 6 (Classic Reprint) (p. 2246)
Yates, Irene & Ladybird Books Staff. Enormous Turnip. (p. 655)
Yates, Jane. 3-D Art Skills Lab. (p. 2546)
—Awesome Hamster Crafts. (p. 144)
—Creative Cat Crafts. (p. 470)
—Dollar Bill Origami. (p. 578)
—Duct Tape Creations. (p. 609)
—Fantastic Horse Crafts. (p. 707)
—Fun with Felt. (p. 800)
—I Can Draw! Mythical Creatures (Set) (p. 1062)
—I Can Draw Mermaids. (p. 1062)
—I Can Draw Unicorns. (p. 1062)
—Paper-Mache Masks. (p. 1697)
—Pipe Cleaner Projects. (p. 1748)
—Sensational Bird Crafts. (p. 1988)
—Superfun Dog Crafts. (p. 2159)
—Terrific Bunny Crafts. (p. 2207)
—Tissue Paper Creations. (p. 2251)
Yates, Jane, contrib. by. I Can Draw Mermaids. (p. 1062)
—I Can Draw Unicorns. (p. 1062)
—I Can Draw Vampires. (p. 1062)
—I Can Draw Witches. (p. 1062)
Yates, Katherine M. Along the Trail: In Which Marjorie Finds That Everyone Does Not Hurry Past the Rough Places on the Rail, & Why (Classic Reprint) (p. 58)
—Chet (Classic Reprint) (p. 366)
—Grey Story Book (Classic Reprint) (p. 896)
Yates, Katherine Merritte. On the Way There: A Wonder Tale for Boys & Girls Both Little & Grown Tall (Classic Reprint) (p. 1656)
—On the Way There: A Wonder Tale for Boys & Girls, Both Little & Grown Tall (Classic Reprint) (p. 1656)
Yates, Kelly, illus. see Krovatin, Christopher.
Yates, L. B. Picking Winners with Major Miles (Classic Reprint) (p. 1739)
Yates, Louise. Dog Loves Books. (p. 576)
—Dog Loves Counting. (p. 576)
—Dog Loves Fairy Tales. (p. 576)
—Toad & I. (p. 2254)
Yates, Louise, illus. see Voigt, Cynthia.
Yates, Marie. Frankie & Me: The Third Book in the Dani Moore Trilogy. (p. 778)
—Reggie & Me: The First Book in the Dani Moore Trilogy. (p. 1861)
—Sammy & Me: The Second Book in the Dani Moore Trilogy. (p. 1928)
Yates, Martha, jt. auth. see Blake, Kevin.
Yates, Philip. Pirate's Twelve Days of Christmas. Serra, Sebastià, illus. (p. 1751)
Yates, Sarah-Jane. Marmalade & Fatso. (p. 1408)
Yates, Vicki. Life at Home. (p. 1290)
Yates, W. Dictionary, Hindustani & English (Classic Reprint) (p. 541)
Yates, Wyeth, illus. see Reed, M. K. & Smith, Brian
Yates, Wyeth, illus. see Wilgus, Alison.
Yatoo, Altaf Hussain. Legacy of Kashmir- a Study of the Ancient Faiths of Kashmir. (p. 1261)
Yatscoff, E. R. Ransom. (p. 1841)
—Rumrunner's Boy: Crime Writers of Canada Award Finalist. (p. 1914)
Yatscoff, Edward R. Archie's Gold. (p. 110)
Yaun, Katherine. Drones in the Classroom. (p. 605)
—Etiquette at School. (p. 666)
—Getting a Job in the Transportation Industry. (p. 825)
Yaw, Valerie. Color-Changing Animals. (p. 420)
Yaweera, Sasiprapa, illus. see Montgomery, R. A.
Yawtsong, Lee, tr. see Tang, Sanmu & and Film Studio, Shanghai Animation.
Yaya. Adventures of Milo & Pookie Part III. (p. 25)
Yaya, Silly, et al. Pete Comes to America. (p. 1727)
Yayo. Pikiq (p. 1744)
Yayo, illus. see Fitch, Sheree.
Yayo, illus. see McMaster, Juliet & Cote, Patricia.
Yayo, illus. see New, William.
Yazawa, Nao. Moon & Blood (p. 1501)
Yazdani, Ashley Benham. Green Place to Be: the Creation of Central Park. Yazdani, Ashley Benham, illus. (p. 894)
Yazzie, Peterson, illus. see Flood, Nancy Bo.
Yazzie, Seraphine G. Beauty Beside Me: Stories of My Grandmother's Skirts. Ruffenach, Jessie Eve, ed. (p. 185)
Yazzie, Serphine G. Beauty Beside Me: Stories of My Grandmother's Skirts. (p. 185)
Ybarra, Andres. Arizona Cardinals (p. 116)
—Chicago Bears (p. 367)
—Great Basketball Debates. (p. 884)
—Phoenix Suns (p. 1736)
Ybarra, Janice a. Pass the Magic Key. (p. 1702)
—Tooth Fairy & Canary. (p. 2262)
Ybarra, Katherine. Just a Little More Christmas. (p. 1192)
Ybarra, Thomas. Davy Jones's Yarns: And Other Salted Songs (Classic Reprint) (p. 511)
Yber, A. Death. (p. 521)
—Resurrection. (p. 1870)
Ycaza, Roger. Emocionante Historia de un Valiente Gato Que Subió a la Rama Más Alta de un Arbol... y Luego no Pudo Bajar. (p. 644)
Ycaza, Roger, illus. see Fernanda Heredia, Maria.
Ye, Ting-Xing. Chinese Thought of It: Amazing Inventions & Innovations. (p. 379)
Ye, Yong Lie. Xiao Liuliu Slips Away. (p. 2516)
Yeager, Anne H. American Tall Tales. (p. 74)
Yeager, Jackie. Flip the Silver Switch. (p. 749)
—Spin the Golden Light Bulb. (p. 2082)
Yeagle, Dean, illus. see Frost, Robert.
Yeahquo, Timothy. Magpie & the Turtle: A Native American-Inspired Folk Tale. Gledhill, Sarah, illus. (p. 1382)
Yeardley, Glynne, jt. auth. see Surget, Alain.
Yearling, A. K. My Little Pony: the Daring Do Adventure Collection: A Three-Book Boxed Set with Exclusive Figure. Set (p. 1554)
Yearling, Tricia. Computers: What They Are & How to Use Them. (p. 437)
—E-Mail: What It Is & How to Use It. (p. 612)
—How Do I Find Information Online? (p. 1028)
—How Do I Keep My Privacy Online? (p. 1028)
—How Do I Play Games Online? (p. 1028)
—How Do I Stay Safe from Cyberbullies? (p. 1028)
—How Do I Stay Safe from Online Predators? (p. 1028)
—How Do I Use Social Networking? (p. 1028)
—Internet: What It Is & How to Use It. (p. 1127)
—World Wide Web: What It Is & How to Use It. (p. 2506)
Yearling, Tricia & Summers, Portia. One Dollar: How Many Pennies? (p. 1659)
Years, A. Gentleman. London Guide, & Stranger's Safeguard Against the Cheats, Swindlers, & Pickpockets That Around Within the Bills of Mortality: Forming a Picture of London; As Regrads Active Life, Collected from the Verbal Communication of William Perry, & Others, (p. 1341)
Yeates, Thomas, illus. see Fontes, Justine & Fontes, Ron.
Yeates, Thomas, illus. see Jolley, Dan.
Yeates, Thomas, illus. see Limke, Jeff.
Yeates, Thomas, illus. see Storrie, Paul D.
Yeaton, Clyde Elizabeth. Boy of the Backwoods (Classic Reprint) (p. 269)
Yeats, Jack Butler, jt. auth. see Yeats, William Butler.
Yeats, Sidney Levett. Orrain: A Romance (Classic Reprint) (p. 1673)
Yeats, W. B. Celtic Twilight (Classic Reprint) (p. 351)
—Collected Works in Verse & Prose of William Butler Yeats, Vol. 8: Discoveries; Edmund Spenser; Poetry & Tradition; & Other Essays (Classic Reprint) (p. 414)
—Collected Works in Verse & Prose of William Butler Yeats, Vol. 3: The Countess Cathleen; the Land of Heart's Desire; the Unicorn from the Stars (Classic Reprint) (p. 414)
—Countess Cathleen (Classic Reprint) (p. 459)
—Fairy Tales of Ireland. Lynch, P. J., illus. (p. 698)
—Hour Glass (Classic Reprint) (p. 1022)
—Hour-Glass, Vol. 2: And Other Plays, Being of Plays for an Irish Theatre (Classic Reprint) (p. 1022)
—In the Seven Woods: Being Poems Chiefly of the Irish Heroic Age (Classic Reprint) (p. 1111)
—Irish Fairy & Folk Tales (Classic Reprint) (p. 1134)
—Irish Fairy Tales: Edited with an Introduction (Classic Reprint) (p. 1134)
—John Sherman & Dhoya (Classic Reprint) (p. 1174)
—King's Threshold, Vol. 3: And on Baile's Strand (Classic Reprint) (p. 1223)
—Moon Spun Round: W. B. Yeats for Children. Doody, Noreen, ed. (p. 1502)
—On Baile's Strand (Classic Reprint) (p. 1652)
—Plays in Prose & Verse: Written for an Irish Theatre, & Generally with the Help of a Friend (Classic Reprint) (p. 1761)
—Secret Rose; Rosa Alchemica; the Tables of the Law; the Adoration of the Magi; John Sherman & Dhoya: Being the Collected Works in Verse & Prose of William Butler Yeats (Classic Reprint) (p. 1978)
—Stories from Carleton: With an Introduction (Classic Reprint) (p. 2123)
—Stories of Red Hanrahan: The Secret Rose Rosa Alchemica (Classic Reprint) (p. 2125)
—Visions & Beliefs in the West of Ireland (Classic Reprint) (p. 2362)
—Where There Is Nothing, Vol. 1 (Classic Reprint) (p. 2440)
Yeats, W. B. & Schlieve, Ngj. Lake Isle of Innisfree: The Song of Wandering Aengus. (p. 1240)
Yeats, W. B. & Wade, Allan. Collected Works in Verse & Prose of William Butler Yeats. the Secret Rose. Rosa Alchemica. the Tables of the Law. the Adoration of the Magi. 7th Volume. (p. 414)
Yeats, William B. Unicorn from the Stars: And Other Plays (Classic Reprint) (p. 2328)
Yeats, William Butler. Collected Works in Verse & Prose of William Butler Yeats, Vol. 3: The Countess Cathleen; the Land of Heart's Desire; the Unicorn from the Stars (Classic Reprint) (p. 414)
Yeats, William Butler & Yeats, Jack Butler. Irish Fairy Tales. (p. 1134)
Yeatts, Tabatha. Weisel, Wiesenthal, Klarsfeld: The Holocaust Survivors. (p. 2397)
—Wiesel, Wiesenthal, Klarsfeld: The Holocaust Survivors. (p. 2461)
Yeatts, Tabatha, ed. Imperfect: Poems about Mistakes: an Anthology for Middle Schoolers. (p. 1102)
Yechton, Barbara. Christine's Inspiration (Classic Reprint) (p. 383)
—Dorothy's Temptation (Classic Reprint) (p. 587)
—Fortune's Boats (Classic Reprint) (p. 770)
—Little Saint Hilary: And Other Stories (Classic Reprint) (p. 1327)
—Lovable Crank, or More Leaves from the Roses (Classic Reprint) (p. 1358)
—Matter of Honor, & Other Stories (Classic Reprint) (p. 1426)
—Molly (Classic Reprint) (p. 1489)
—Roland Gentleheart (Classic Reprint) (p. 1897)
—Some Adventures of Jack Jill (Classic Reprint) (p. 2058)
—'Toinette: And Other Stories (Classic Reprint) (p. 2256)
—Two Young Americans Philip & Molly (Classic Reprint) (p. 2310)
—Young Savage (Classic Reprint) (p. 2532)
Yee, Christian. Épica Conquista de Genie Lo. (p. 658)
Yee, F. C. Avatar, the Last Airbender: the Rise of Kyoshi. (p. 141)
—Avatar, the Last Airbender: the Shadow of Kyoshi. (p. 141)
—Epic Crush of Genie Lo. (p. 658)
—Iron Will of Genie Lo. (p. 1136)
Yee, Jeanne, illus. see Oshiro, Kimberley.
Yee, Josie, illus. see Hecht, Tracey.
Yee, Josie, illus. see Higginson, Sheila Sweeny.
Yee, Karen. My First Everyday Words in Cantonese & English: With Jyutping Pronunciation. (p. 1544)
Yee, Lisa. Absolutely Maybe. (p. 9)
—Batgirl at Super Hero High (DC Super Hero Girls) (p. 172)
—Bobby the Brave (Sometimes) Santat, Dan, illus. (p. 252)
—Bobby vs. Girls (Accidentally) Santat, Dan, illus. (p. 252)
—Bumblebee at Super Hero High (DC Super Hero Girls) Random House, illus. (p. 297)
—DC Super Hero Girls Adventure Collection #1 (DC Super Hero Girls) Wonder Woman at Super Hero High; Supergirl at Super Hero High Random House, illus. (p. 516)
—Harley Quinn at Super Hero High (DC Super Hero Girls) Random House, illus. (p. 930)
—Kidney Hypothetical: or How to Ruin Your Life in Seven Days:Or How to Ruin Your Life in Seven Days. (p. 1213)
—Kidney Hypothetical, or, How to Ruin Your Life in Seven Days. (p. 1213)
—Las Aventuras de Supergirl en Super Hero High / Supergirl at Super Hero High. (p. 1245)
—Supergirl at Super Hero High (DC Super Hero Girls) Random House, illus. (p. 2159)
—Warp Speed. (p. 2379)
—Wonder Woman at Super Hero High (DC Super Hero Girls) Random House, illus. (p. 2489)
Yee, Nong, illus. see Low, Lk.
Yee, Patrick, illus. see Conger, David & Romulo, Liana.
Yee, Patrick, illus. see Fu, Shelley.
Yee, Paul. Bone Collector's Son (p. 255)
—Ghost Train Chan, Harvey, illus. (p. 828)
—Shu-Li & Diego Wang, Shaoli, illus. (p. 2013)
—ShuLi & the Magic Pear Tree Wang, Shaoli, illus. (p. 2013)
—Tales from Gold Mountain Ng, Simon, illus. (p. 2182)
Yee, Rebecca. My Family Tree. (p. 1538)
Yee, Reimena, illus. see Laskow, Sarah.
Yee, Sennah. My Day with Gong Gong. Chen, Elaine, illus. (p. 1537)
Yee, Tammy. Easy Butterfly Origami. (p. 620)
Yee, Tammy, illus. see Fredericks, Anthony D.
Yee, Tammy, illus. see Greenway, Beth.
Yee, Tammy, illus. see Hirschi, Ron.
Yee, Tammy, jt. auth. see Curtis, Jennifer Keats.
Yee, Wong Herbert. Abracadabra! Magic with Mouse & Mole. (p. 7)
—Brand-New Day with Mouse & Mole. (p. 275)
—Fine Feathered Friends. Yee, Wong Herbert, illus. (p. 730)
—Mouse & Mole, a Winter Wonderland. Yee, Wong Herbert, illus. (p. 1514)
—Mummies at the Museum. (p. 1526)
—My Autumn Book. Yee, Wong Herbert, illus. (p. 1531)
—Perfect Halloween. (p. 1722)
—Secret Valentine. (p. 1979)
—Secret Valentine. Yee, Wong Herbert, illus. (p. 1979)
—Summer Days & Nights. Yee, Wong Herbert, illus. (p. 2149)
Yee, Wong Herbert, illus. see Brandon, Anthony G.
Yee, Wong Herbert, illus. see Friend, Catherine.
Yeesman, Vinit, illus. see Russell, Elaine.
Yeh, Chun-Liang. Autre Bout du Monde (l') (p. 140)
—Calligraphe(le) (p. 312)
—CICI H'Risson. (p. 390)
—Deux Paysages de L'Empereur. (p. 535)
—Duc Aime le Dragon(le) (p. 607)
—Face Au Tigre. (p. 692)
—Got de la Pche(le) (p. 872)
—Mais o Est Donc le Lapin ? (p. 1384)
—Yexian et le Soulier D'or. (p. 2521)
Yeh, Jessica. Something Tragic. (p. 2061)
Yeh, Kat. Friend Ship. Groenink, Chuck, illus. (p. 786)
—Truth about Twinkie Pie. (p. 2296)
—Way to Bea. (p. 2387)
Yehoash, Yehoash. Feet of the Messenger (Classic Reprint) (p. 719)
Yehoshua, A. B. & Dostoevsky, Fyodor. Story of Crime & Punishment. Schoffman, Stuart, tr. (p. 2129)
Yeigh, Kate Westlake. Specimen Spinster (Classic Reprint) (p. 2077)
Yelchin, Eugene. Arcady's Goal. Yelchin, Eugene, illus. (p. 110)
—Breaking Stalin's Nose. (p. 278)
—Breaking Stalin's Nose. Yelchin, Eugene, illus. (p. 278)
—Haunting of Falcon House. (p. 939)
—Pip & Pup. (p. 1748)
—Spring Hare. Yelchin, Eugene, illus. (p. 2092)
—Spy Runner. Yelchin, Eugene, illus. (p. 2093)
Yelchin, Eugene, illus. see Anderson, M. T.
Yelchin, Eugene, illus. see Beaumont, Karen.
Yelchin, Eugene, illus. see Deedy, Carmen Agra.
Yelchin, Eugene, illus. see Fleming, Candace.
Yelchin, Eugene, illus. see Gerber, Carole.
Yelchin, Eugene, illus. see Javaherbin, Mina & Jalal al-Din Rumi.
Yelchin, Eugene, illus. see Wardlaw, Lee.
Yelchin, Eugene, jt. auth. see Anderson, M. T.
Yelchin, Eugene & Kuryla, Mary. Next Door Bear. Yelchin, Eugene & Kuryla, Mary, illus. (p. 1600)
Yellen, David. Hair Wars Coloring Book. Villalobos, Miguel, illus. (p. 910)
Yellich, Patricia. Penelope the People Pleaser. (p. 1715)
Yellowhale s.r.l. Rudolph the Red-Nosed Reindeer Read-Along Book & CD. (p. 1912)
Yellowhawk, James Mark, illus. see Marshall, Joseph, III & Marshall, Joseph.
Yellowhead & Giggles. Areoke Cub Blueberry Syrup: Areoke & the Pals. (p. 114)
Yellowhorn, Eldon & Lowinger, Kathy. Turtle Island: The Story of North America's First People. (p. 2301)
—What the Eagle Sees: Indigenous Stories of Rebellion & Renewal. (p. 2420)
Yelsew, Jean. Mountaineers: Or, Bottled Sunshine for Blue Mondays (Classic Reprint) (p. 1514)
Yelverton, Therese. Zanita a Tale of the Yo-Semite (Classic Reprint) (p. 2538)
Yelvington, Lauren, jt. auth. see Sweeney, Monica.
Yen, Brandon, tr. see Li, Tong.
Yen Mah, Adeline. Chinese Cinderella: True Story of an Unwanted Daughter. (p. 378)
Yen, W. W. Manual of Translation: One Hundred & Twenty Lessons (Classic Reprint) (p. 1399)
Yenne, Bill, jt. auth. see Johnson, Michael.
Yeo, Julia. Ryan the Gnome Adventures: The Garden Man & the Big Bang! Van-Dyke-Hempenstall, Clare, illus. (p. 1918)
Yeo, Margaret. Don John of Austria. (p. 581)
Yeo, Miranda, illus. see Acampora, Courtney.
Yeo, Miranda, illus. see Berrios, Frank.
Yeo, Miranda, illus. see Matheis, Mickie.
Yeo, Yeo. Soldier Men (Classic Reprint) (p. 2056)
Yeoman, John. All the Year Round. Blake, Quentin, illus. (p. 54)
—Bear's Water Picnic. Blake, Quentin, illus. (p. 181)
—Bear's Winter House. Blake, Quentin, illus. (p. 181)
—Heron & the Crane. Blake, Quentin, illus. (p. 963)
—Mouse Trouble. Blake, Quentin, illus. (p. 1515)
—Mr. Nodd's Ark. Blake, Quentin, illus. (p. 1519)
—Quentin Blake's Amazing Animal Stories. (p. 1825)
—Quentin Blake's the Seven Voyages of Sinbad the Sailor. Blake, Quentin, illus. (p. 1825)
—Sixes & Sevens. Blake, Quentin, illus. (p. 2029)
—Wild Washerwomen. Blake, Quentin, illus. (p. 2465)
—Young Performing Horse. Blake, Quentin, illus. (p. 2532)
Yeoman, John & Blake, Quentin. Boy Who Sprouted Antlers. (p. 271)
—Drink of Water. (p. 604)
—Fabulous Foskett Family Circus. (p. 692)
Yeoman, John & Quentin, Blake. Up with Birds! (p. 2338)
Yeomans, Ellen. Other Ducks. (p. 1674)
—Some Snow Is... Offermann, Andrea, illus. (p. 2059)
Yep, Kathleen S., jt. auth. see Yep, Laurence.
Yep, Laurence. Dragon Prince: A Chinese Beauty & the Beast Tale. (p. 594)
—Skunk Scout. (p. 2033)
—Staking a Claim. (p. 2099)
Yep, Laurence & Ryder, Joanne. Dragon's Guide to Making Perfect Wishes. (p. 595)
—Dragon's Guide to Making Your Human Smarter. GrandPre, Mary, illus. (p. 595)
—Dragon's Guide to the Care & Feeding of Humans. GrandPré, Mary, illus. (p. 595)
Yep, Laurence & Yep, Kathleen S. Dragon's Child: A Story of Angel Island. (p. 595)
Yerdon, Joe. America's Oddest Foods. (p. 75)
Yeretskaya, Yevgeniya. Snow Queen: A Pop-Up Adaption of a Classic Fairytale. (p. 2048)
Yeretskaya, Yevgeniya, illus. see Preston Chushcoff, Jennifer.
Yerger, Susan M. Mighty Little Samuel Seagull. (p. 1463)
Yerkes, Helen K. Our City: A City Reader (Classic Reprint) (p. 1677)
Yerkes, Lane, illus. see Casterline, L. C.
Yerkes, Lane, illus. see Slater, Teddy.
Yerko, Vladyslav, illus. see Andersen, Hans.
Yerrill, Gail. Gingerbread Man. (p. 834)
—Starry Night, Sleep Tight. (p. 2106)
Yerrill, Gail, illus. see Amen, Daniel.
Yerrill, Gail, illus. see Freedman, Claire.
Yerrill, Gail, illus. see Howard, Debbie.
Yerrill, Gail, illus. see Moss, Stephanie.
Yerrill, Gail, illus. see Nellist, Glenys.
Yerrill, Gail, illus. see Vrba, Christina.
Yerrinton, James Manning Winchell. Official Report of the Trial of Sarah Jane Robinson: For the Murder of Prince Arthur Freeman, in the Supreme Judicial Court of Massachusetts (Classic Reprint) (p. 1641)
Yerta, Gabrielle Marguerite. Six Women & the Invasion (Classic Reprint) (p. 2029)

Y

—Georgia. (p. 820)
—Grimy, Gross Unusual History of the Toilet (p. 897)
—Haiti. (p. 910)
—How to Write a Comic Book. Petelinsek, Kathleen, illus. (p. 1045)
—Indonesia. (p. 1117)
—Internet Inventors. (p. 1127)
—Internet Security: From Concept to Consumer. (p. 1127)
—Iraq: Enchantment of the World. (p. 1133)
—Israel. (p. 1140)
—Medical Illustrator. (p. 1436)
—Modern Pirates. (p. 1487)
—Nepal. (p. 1587)
—New Hampshire. (p. 1594)
—New Jersey. (p. 1594)
—Poachers. (p. 1763)
—Polar Ice Caps in Danger: Expedition to Antarctica. (p. 1770)
—Puerto Rico. (p. 1811)
—Rhode Island. (p. 1875)
—Sarah Palin: Political Rebel D'Ottavi, Francesca, illus. (p. 1935)
—Scotland. (p. 1962)
—Terrors from the Deep: True Tales of Surviving Shark Attacks. (p. 2208)
—Titanic Disaster! Nickolas Flux & the Sinking of the Great Ship. Simmons, Mark, illus. (p. 2251)
—Tracking an Assassin! Nickolas Flux & the Assassination of Abraham Lincoln Pinelli, Amerigo, illus. (p. 2272)
—Trapped in Antarctica! Nickolas Flux & the Shackleton Expedition. Simmons, Mark, illus. (p. 2279)
—True Stories of the Civil War Molinari, Carlo, illus. (p. 2294)
—True Stories of World War I Proctor, Jon, illus. (p. 2295)
—United States & Mexico. (p. 2330)
—When Volcanoes Erupt! O'Neill, Sean, illus. (p. 2434)
Yomtov, Nelson & Rogers, Stillman. Russia. (p. 1917)
Yonay, Shahar & Yonay, Rina. Ha-Mikraah Shel: Osef Kite Keriah Le-Talmidim Ba-Tefutsot: Kolel Targile Lashon U-Fituah Ha-Habah Ve-Havanat Ha-Nikra. (p. 908)
Yonce, G. V. First Steps in Language: A Primer. Designed for Use in the Philippine Islands. (p. 739)
—First Steps in Language: A Primer Designed for Use in the Philippine Islands (Classic Reprint) (p. 739)
Yonetani, Takane. Make More Love & Peace (p. 1386)
Yoneyama, Natsuko, illus. see Medina, Melissa & Colting, Fredrik.
Yonezu, Yusuke. Seek & Count. Yonezu, Yusuke, illus. (p. 1984)
—We Love Each Other. Yonezu, Yusuke, illus. (p. 2391)
Yong, Billy, illus. see Scott, Jenny.
Yong, Jui Lin, jt. auth. see Heale, Jay.
Yong, Jui Lin, jt. auth. see Sheehan, Sean.
Yongco, Rumar, illus. see Smith, Amelia.
Yongco, Rumar, illus. see Stewart, Artney.
Yonge, Charlotte. Lances of Lynwood. Deangeli, Marguerite, illus. (p. 1241)
Yonge, Charlotte M. Armourer's Prentices (Classic Reprint) (p. 117)
—Armourer's Prentices, Vol. 1 of 2 (Classic Reprint) (p. 117)
—Beechcroft at Rockstone (Classic Reprint) (p. 189)
—Beechcroft at Rockstone, Vol. 2 of 2 (Classic Reprint) (p. 189)
—Beechcroft, Vol. 1 Of 2: At Rockstone (Classic Reprint) (p. 189)
—Chantry House, Vol. 2 of 2 (Classic Reprint) (p. 357)
—Chaplet of Pearls (Classic Reprint) (p. 357)
—Disturbing Element, or, Chronicles of the Blue-Bell Society. (p. 565)
—Disturbing Element or Chronicles of the Blue-Bell Society (Classic Reprint) (p. 565)
—Dove in the Eagle's Nest (Classic Reprint) (p. 590)
—Founded on Paper: Or Uphill & Downhill Between the Two Jubilees (Classic Reprint) (p. 771)
—Grisly Grisell, Vol. 2 Of 2: Or the Laidly Lady of Whitburn a Tale of the Wars of the Roses (Classic Reprint) (p. 897)
—Heartsease: Or the Brother's Wife (Classic Reprint) (p. 946)
—Heir of Redclyffe (Classic Reprint) (p. 948)
—Hopes & Fears: Or Scenes from the Life of a Spinster (Classic Reprint) (p. 1002)
—Little Lucy's Wonderful Globe. (p. 1321)
—Long Vacation (Classic Reprint) (p. 1343)
—Love & Life: An Old Story in Eighteenth Century Costume (Classic Reprint) (p. 1359)
—Love & Life; An Old Story in Eighteenth Century Costume - Vol. 2. (p. 1359)
—Love & Life, Vol. 1 Of 2: An Old Story in Eighteenth Century Costume (Classic Reprint) (p. 1359)
—Magnum Bonum: Or Mother Carey's Brood (Classic Reprint) (p. 1382)
—Magnum Bonum or Mother Carey's Brood, Vol. 1 of 3 (Classic Reprint) (p. 1382)
—Magnum Bonum, or Mother Carey's Brood, Vol. 2 of 3 (Classic Reprint) (p. 1382)
—Magnum Bonum, Vol. 3 Of 3: Or Mother Carey's Brood (Classic Reprint) (p. 1382)
—Monthly Packet of Evening Readings for Members of the English Church, Vol. 10: July December, 1885 (Classic Reprint) (p. 1499)
—Monthly Packet of Evening Readings for Members of the English Church, Vol. 15: Parts LXXXV to XC; January-June, 1888 (Classic Reprint) (p. 1499)
—Monthly Packet of Evening Readings, Vol. 26: For Members of the English Church, July December, 1878 (Classic Reprint) (p. 1499)
—Monthly Packet of Evening Readings, Vol. 4: For Members of the English Church (Classic Reprint) (p. 1499)
—Monthly Packet of Evening Readings, Vol. 8: For Members of the English Church; Parts XLIII. to XLVIII. July December, 1884 (Classic Reprint) (p. 1499)
—Monthly Packet of Evening Readings, Vol. 9: For Members of the English Church; January June, 1885 (Classic Reprint) (p. 1499)
—More Bywords (Classic Reprint) (p. 1504)
—Novels & Tales, Vol. 24: Scenes & Characters (Classic Reprint) (p. 1626)
—Nuttie's Father (Classic Reprint) (p. 1632)
—Nuttie's Father, Vol. 1 (Classic Reprint) (p. 1632)
—Old Woman's Outlook in a Hampshire Village. (p. 1649)
—Old Woman's Outlook in a Hampshire Village (Classic Reprint) (p. 1649)
—Our New Mistress, or Changes at Brookfield Earl (Classic Reprint) (p. 1679)
—Pigeon Pie (Classic Reprint) (p. 1743)
—Pillars of the House, Vol. 1 Of 2: Or, under Wode, under Rode (Classic Reprint) (p. 1745)
—Prince & the Page: A Story of the Last Crusade. (p. 1793)
—Prince & the Page: A Story of the Last Crusade (Classic Reprint) (p. 1793)
—P's & Q's: Or, the Question of Putting Upon. (p. 1809)
—P's & Q's: Or the Question of Putting upon & Little Lucy's Wonderful Globe (Classic Reprint) (p. 1809)
—Release or Caroline's French Kindred (Classic Reprint) (p. 1863)
—Reputed Changeling, Vol. 1 Of 2: Or Three Seventh Years Two Centuries Ago (Classic Reprint) (p. 1868)
—Sides of the Shield, Vol. 2 of 2 (Classic Reprint) (p. 2015)
—Stray Pearls, Vol. 1: Memoirs of Margaret de Ribaumont, Viscountess of Bellaise (Classic Reprint) (p. 2139)
—Stray Pearls, Vol. 1 Of 2: Memoirs of Margaret de Ribaumont, Viscountess of Bellaise (Classic Reprint) (p. 2139)
—That Stick, Vol. 2 of 2 (Classic Reprint) (p. 2213)
—Three Brides, Vol. 1 of 2 (Classic Reprint) (p. 2232)
—Three Brides, Vol. 2 of 2 (Classic Reprint) (p. 2232)
—Two Penniless Princesses, Vol. 2 of 2 (Classic Reprint) (p. 2309)
—Two Sides of the Shield, Vol. 1 of 2 (Classic Reprint) (p. 2309)
—Unknown to History, Vol. 1: A Story of the Captivity of Mary of Scotland (Classic Reprint) (p. 2333)
Yonge, Charlotte Mary. Aunt Charlotte's Roman History. (p. 136)
—Aunt Charlotte's Stories of Bible History (Classic Reprint) (p. 136)
—Aunt Charlotte's Stories of Greek History for the Little Ones. (p. 137)
—Book of Golden Deeds of All Times & All Lands (Classic Reprint) (p. 258)
—Book of Golden Deeds of All Times & All Lands, Vol. 1 (Classic Reprint) (p. 258)
—Bye-Words a Collection of Tales, New & Old (Classic Reprint) (p. 306)
—Caged Lion (Classic Reprint) (p. 308)
—Castle Builders (Classic Reprint) (p. 340)
—Chantry House (Classic Reprint) (p. 357)
—Chantry House, Vol. 1 of 2 (Classic Reprint) (p. 357)
—Chaplet of Pearls, Vol. 1 Of 2: Or, the White & Black Ribaumont (Classic Reprint) (p. 357)
—Constable's Tower: Or the Times of Magna Charta (Classic Reprint) (p. 443)
—Countess Kate: And the Stokesley Secret (Classic Reprint) (p. 459)
—Countess Kate, and, the Stokesley Secret (Classic Reprint) (p. 459)
—Danvers Papers: An Invention (Classic Reprint) (p. 504)
—Dove in the Eagle's Nest, Vol. 1 of 2 (Classic Reprint) (p. 590)
—Dynevor Terrace: Or the Clue of Life (Classic Reprint) (p. 612)
—Dynevor Terrace, Vol. 1 Of 2: Or, the Clue of Life (Classic Reprint) (p. 612)
—Grisly Grisell or the Laidly Lady of Whitburn: A Tale of the Wars of the Roses (Classic Reprint) (p. 897)
—Grisly Grisell or the Laidly Lady of Whitburn, Vol. 1 Of 2: A Tale of the Wars of the Roses (Classic Reprint) (p. 897)
—Heartsease, or the Brother's Wife, Vol. 2 of 2 (Classic Reprint) (p. 946)
—Heir of Redclyffe, Vol. 1 (Classic Reprint) (p. 948)
—Henrietta's Wish; or Domineering: A Tale (Classic Reprint) (p. 954)
—Henrietta's Wish; or, Domineering. (p. 954)
—History of Sir Thomas Thumb (Classic Reprint) (p. 980)
—Hopes & Fears, Vol. 1 Of 2: Or, Scenes from the Life of a Spinster (Classic Reprint) (p. 1002)
—Kenneth, or the Rear-Guard of the Grand Army (Classic Reprint) (p. 1209)
—Lances of Lynwood: Chivalry in England (Classic Reprint) (p. 1241)
—Little Duke: Richard the Fearless (Classic Reprint) (p. 1316)
—Little Lucys Wonderful Globe. (p. 1321)
—Little Lucy's Wonderful Globe (Classic Reprint) (p. 1321)
—Love & Life an Old Story in Eighteenth Century Costume, Vol. 2 of 2 (Classic Reprint) (p. 1359)
—Modern Broods: Or Developments Unlooked for (Classic Reprint) (p. 1486)
—Modern Telemachus (Classic Reprint) (p. 1488)
—Modern Telemachus, Vol. 1 of 2 (Classic Reprint) (p. 1488)
—Monthly Packet of Evening Readings for Members of the English Church, Vol. 1: Parts I. to VI. , Jan. -June, 1891 (Classic Reprint) (p. 1499)
—Monthly Packet of Evening Readings for Members of the English Church, Vol. 2: Parts VII to XII; July-Dec. , 1891 (Classic Reprint) (p. 1499)
—Monthly Packet of Evening Readings for Members of the English Church, Vol. 9: Parts XLIX to LIV, January-June, 1870 (Classic Reprint) (p. 1499)
—Monthly Packet of Evening Readings for Members of the English Church, Vol. 4: Parts XIX to XXIV; July-December, 1867 (Classic Reprint) (p. 1499)
—Monthly Packet of Evening Readings for Members of the English Church, Vol. 5: Parts XXV. to XXX. , January-June, 1883 (Classic Reprint) (p. 1499)
—Monthly Packet of Evening Readings for Members of the English Church, Vol. 3: Parts XIII. to XVIII. ; Jan. -June, 1892 (Classic Reprint) (p. 1499)
—Monthly Packet of Evening Readings for Members of the English Church, Vol. 5: Parts XXVI. to XXX. , January-June, 1868 (Classic Reprint) (p. 1499)
—Monthly Packet of Evening Readings for Members of the English Church, Vol. 3: Parts XIII. to XVIII. , January-June, 1882 (Classic Reprint) (p. 1499)
—Monthly Packet of Evening Readings for Members of the English Church, Vol. 12: Parts 67-72; July-December 1886 (Classic Reprint) (p. 1499)
—Monthly Packet of Evening Readings for Members of the English Church, Vol. 10: Parts LV to LX; July-December, 1870 (Classic Reprint) (p. 1499)
—Monthly Packet of Evening Readings for Members of the English Church, Vol. 19: Parts 109 to 114; January-June, 1890 (Classic Reprint) (p. 1499)
—Monthly Packet of Evening Readings for Members of the English Church, Vol. 11: Parts LXI to LXVI; January-June 1871 (Classic Reprint) (p. 1499)
—Monthly Packet of Evening Readings for Members of the English Church, Vol. 20: Parts 115 to 120, July-December, 1890 (Classic Reprint) (p. 1499)
—Monthly Packet of Evening Readings for Members of the English Church, Vol. 17: Parts XCVII to CII; January-June, 1874 (Classic Reprint) (p. 1499)
—Monthly Packet of Evening Readings for Members of the English Church, Vol. 19: Parts CIX. to CXIV. , January-June, 1875 (Classic Reprint) (p. 1499)
—Monthly Packet of Evening Readings for Members of the English Church, Vol. 20: Parts CXV. to CXX. ; July-December, 1875 (Classic Reprint) (p. 1499)
—Monthly Packet of Evening Readings for Members of the English Church, Vol. 11: Parts LXI. to LXVI. , January-June, 1886 (Classic Reprint) (p. 1499)
—Monthly Packet of Evening Readings for Members of the English Church, Vol. 13: Parts LXXIII to LXXVII; January-June 1872 (Classic Reprint) (p. 1499)
—Monthly Packet of Evening Readings for Members of the English Church, Vol. 84: Parts CCCCXCVII. to DII. , July-Dec. , 1892 (Classic Reprint) (p. 1499)
—Monthly Packet of Evening Readings for Members of the English Church, Vol. 18: Parts CIII. to CVIII. ; July December, 1874 (Classic Reprint) (p. 1499)
—Monthly Packet of Evening Readings for Members of the English Church, Vol. 12: Parts LXVII. to LXXII. , July-December, 1871 (Classic Reprint) (p. 1499)
—Monthly Packet of Evening Readings for Members of the English Church, Vol. 14: Parts LXXIX. to LXXXIV. , July-December, 1887 (Classic Reprint) (p. 1499)
—Monthly Packet of Evening Readings for Members of the English Church, Vol. 13: Parts LXXIII. to LXXVIII. , January June, 1887 (Classic Reprint) (p. 1499)
—Monthly Packet of Evening Readings for Members of the English Church, Vol. 17: Third Series; Parts XCVII to CII; January-June, 1889 (Classic Reprint) (p. 1499)
—Monthly Packet of Evening Readings for Members of the English Church, Vol. 28 (Classic Reprint) (p. 1499)
—Monthly Packet of Evening Readings for Younger Members of the English Church, Vol. 16: Parts XCI. to XCVI. , July-December, 1888 (Classic Reprint) (p. 1499)
—Monthly Packet of Evening Readings, Vol. 6: For Members of the English Church; July December, 1868 (Classic Reprint) (p. 1499)
—Monthly Packet of Evening Readings, Vol. 7 (Classic Reprint) (p. 1499)
—Monthly Packet or Evening Readings for Members of the English Church, Vol. 29: Parts 169 to 174, January-June, 1880 (Classic Reprint) (p. 1499)
—Monthly Packet, Vol. 21 (Classic Reprint) (p. 1500)
—Monthly Packet, Vol. 96: Half-Yearly Volume (Classic Reprint) (p. 1500)
—My Young Alcides: A Faded Photograph (Classic Reprint) (p. 1565)
—My Young Alcides, Vol. 1: A Faded Photograph (Classic Reprint) (p. 1565)
—Nuttie's Father, Vol. 2 (Classic Reprint) (p. 1632)
—Reputed Changeling - or Three Seventh Years Two Centuries Ago. (p. 1868)
—Reputed Changeling, or Three Seventh Years Two Centuries Ago (Classic Reprint) (p. 1868)
—Sowing & Sewing: A Sexagesima Story. (p. 2070)
—Stokesley Secret (Classic Reprint) (p. 2120)
—Storehouse of Stories: Storehouse the First (Classic Reprint) (p. 2122)
—Stray Pearls, Vol. 2: Memoirs of Margaret de Ribaumont, Viscountess of Bellaise (Classic Reprint) (p. 2139)
—That Stick (Classic Reprint) (p. 2213)
—That Stick, Vol. 1 of 2 (Classic Reprint) (p. 2213)
—Treasures in the Marshes (Classic Reprint) (p. 2283)
—Trial: Or, More Links of the Daisy Chain. (p. 2285)
—Trial: More Links of the Daisy Chain; Two Volumes in One (Classic Reprint) (p. 2285)
—Trial. (p. 2285)
—Trial, Vol. 1: More Links of the Daisy Chain (Classic Reprint) (p. 2286)
—Trial, Vol. 2: More Links of the Daisy Chain (Classic Reprint) (p. 2286)
—Two Guardians, or Home in This World (Classic Reprint) (p. 2308)
—Two Penniless Princesses. (p. 2309)
—Two Penniless Princesses (Classic Reprint) (p. 2309)
—Two Penniless Princesses, Vol. 1 of 2 (Classic Reprint) (p. 2309)
—Two Sides of the Shield (Classic Reprint) (p. 2309)
—Under the Storm, or Steadfast's Charge (Classic Reprint) (p. 2323)
—Unknown to History: A Story of the Captivity of Mary of Scotland (Classic Reprint) (p. 2333)
—Unknown to History, Vol. 2: A Story of the Captivity of Mary of Scotland (Classic Reprint) (p. 2333)
—Young Step-Mother (Classic Reprint) (p. 2532)
—Young Step-Mother, Vol. 2 Of 2: Or a Chronicle of Mistakes (Classic Reprint) (p. 2532)
Yonge, J. D., illus. see Bell, Madeline.
Yonts, Barbara, photos by see Hawkins, Linda J.
Yoo, David. Detention Club. (p. 535)
Yoo, Hajin. Totally Captivated (p. 2266)
Yoo, Paula. Good Enough. (p. 862)
—Lily's New Home. Ng-Benitez, Shirley, illus. (p. 1302)
—Perfect Gift Ng-Benitez, Shirley, illus. (p. 1722)
—Sixteen Years in Sixteen Seconds: The Sammy Lee Story Lee, Dom, illus. (p. 2029)
—Story of Movie Star Anna May Wong Wang, Lin, illus. (p. 2131)
—Story of Olympic Diver Sammy Lee Lee, Dom, illus. (p. 2132)
—Twenty-Two Cents: Muhammad Yunus & the Village Bank. Akib, Jamel, illus. (p. 2304)
—Want to Play? Ng-Benitez, Shirley, illus. (p. 2375)
Yoo, Paula & Wang, Lin. Shining Star: The Anna May Wong Story. (p. 2007)
Yoo, Seong Min. Bear's Dancing Shoes. (p. 180)
—Beaver's Crazy Sleepover. (p. 186)
—Memories of Korea. (p. 1446)
Yoo, Taeeun. You Are a Lion! And Other Fun Yoga Poses. Yoo, Taeeun, illus. (p. 2524)
Yoo, Taeeun, illus. see Ashman, Linda.
Yoo, Taeeun, illus. see Mantchev, Lisa.
Yoo, Taeeun, illus. see McGhee, Alison.
Yoo, Taeeun, illus. see Sidman, Joyce.
Yoo, Taeeun, illus. see Sullivan, John.
Yooju, Cheon. In Blossom. (p. 1104)
Yoon, Audrey Kai. Joy. (p. 1184)
Yoon, David. Frankly in Love. (p. 779)
—Tenía Que Pasar / Frankly in Love. (p. 2205)
Yoon, Helen, illus. see Sanders, Rob.
Yoon, Jenny. Gnome, Sweet Gnome. (p. 845)
Yoon, JooHee. Beastly Verse. (p. 182)
—Up down Inside Out. (p. 2337)
Yoon, JooHee, illus. see Thurber, James.
Yoon, Nicola. Everything, Everything. (p. 673)
—Everything, Everything Movie Tie-In Edition. (p. 673)
—Nicola Yoon Boxed Set (p. 1604)
—Sun Is Also a Star. (p. 2151)
—Sun Is Also a Star Movie Tie-In Edition. (p. 2151)
—Todo, Todo. (p. 2256)
Yoon, Salina. At the Beach. (p. 130)
—Be a Friend. (p. 176)
—Bear's Big Day. (p. 180)
—Bug Hunt. (p. 291)
—Busy Little Bee. Yoon, Salina, illus. (p. 302)
—Busy Little Fishy. Yoon, Salina, illus. (p. 302)
—Christmas Puppy: A Wag My Tail Book. Yoon, Salina, illus. (p. 386)
—Deep Sea Dive. (p. 524)
—Dinosaur Discovery. (p. 548)
—Do Cows Meow? (p. 570)
—Do Crocs Kiss? (p. 570)
—Duck, Duck, Porcupine! (p. 608)
—Easter Bunny: A Wag My Tail Book. Yoon, Salina, illus. (p. 619)
—Five Trick-or-Treaters. (p. 745)
—Found. Yoon, Salina, illus. (p. 771)
—Halloween Kitty. Yoon, Salina, illus. (p. 912)
—Humpty Dumpty. Yoon, Salina, illus. (p. 1051)
—Jack & Jill: A Halloween Nursery Rhyme. Yoon, Salina, illus. (p. 1151)
—My Chanukah Playbook. Yoon, Salina, illus. (p. 1535)
—My Kite Is Stuck! & Other Stories. (p. 1550)
—Opposnakes: A Lift-the-Flap Book about Opposites. Yoon, Salina, illus. (p. 1667)
—Peek-A-Love. Yoon, Salina, illus. (p. 1713)
—Penguin & Pinecone. (p. 1715)
—Penguin & Pinecone. Yoon, Salina, illus. (p. 1715)
—Penguin & Pumpkin. (p. 1715)
—Penguin Gets Dressed! Yoon, Salina, illus. (p. 1716)
—Penguin Gets Ready for Bed! Yoon, Salina, illus. (p. 1716)
—Penguin Goes to the Farm! Yoon, Salina, illus. (p. 1716)
—Penguin in Love. Yoon, Salina, illus. (p. 1716)
—Penguin on Vacation. (p. 1716)
—Penguin on Vacation. Yoon, Salina, illus. (p. 1716)
—Penguin's Big Adventure. (p. 1716)
—Penguin's Christmas Wish. (p. 1716)
—Pingüino Enamorado. (p. 1745)
—Pinwheel. (p. 1747)
—Space Walk. (p. 2072)
—Stormy Night. (p. 2127)
—Tap to Play! (p. 2191)
—That's My Book! & Other Stories. (p. 2213)
—Where's Boo? (p. 2440)
—Where's Ellie? A Hide-And-Seek Book. (p. 2440)
—Where's Santa Boo? (p. 2440)
—Who Loves Boo? (p. 2449)
—Wings: A Book to Touch & Feel. Yoon, Salina, illus. (p. 2473)
Yoon, Salina, jt. auth. see Kondo, Marie.
Yoon, Selina, ed. see Chan, Hingman.
Yopp, William Isaac. Dual Role: A Romance (Classic Reprint) (p. 607)
Yoran, Elad, jt. auth. see DiOrio, Rana.
Yorick, Yorick. Sentimental Journey Through France & Italy, Vol. 1 (Classic Reprint) (p. 1989)
Yorinks, Arthur. Flappy & Scrappy. Ivanov, Aleksey & Ivanov, Olga, illus. (p. 746)
—Flappy & Scrappy. Ivanov, Olga & Ivanov, Aleksey, illus. (p. 746)
—Flying Latke. Steig, William, illus. (p. 755)
—Invisible Man. Cushman, Doug, illus. (p. 1132)
—Making Scents. Lamb, Braden & Paroline, Shelli, illus. (p. 1390)
—One Mean Ant. Ruzzier, Sergio, illus. (p. 1661)
Yorinks, Arthur & Sendak, Maurice. Presto & Zesto in Limboland. Sendak, Maurice, illus. (p. 1790)
York, A. Citizen of New. Cabinet, or a Collection of Choice Things: Comprising the Beauties of American Miscellanies for the Last Thirty Years (Classic Reprint) (p. 307)
York, Andy. Ultimate College Football Road Trip. (p. 2314)
York, Arcadie Camp New. Etchings: Camp Arcadie; Summer, 1920 (Classic Reprint) (p. 665)
York, Children's Aid Society New. Second Annual Report of the Children's Aid Society: February, 1855 (Classic Reprint) (p. 1973)
York, Court of Appeals of New. Court of Appeals, State of New York, Vol. 5: The People of the State of New York, Plaintiff-Respondent; Against Ruth Snyder & Henry Judd Gray, Defendants-Appellants; Case on Appeal; Pages 2001-2500 (Classic Reprint) (p. 462)
York, Debbie. Ephraim & Jasper. (p. 657)

—Noah, the Ark & Celia. (p. 1616)
York, Eva Rose. White Letter: A Tale of Retribution & Reward (Classic Reprint) (p. 2444)
York, Frances. Book for Kids about Pandas: The Giant Panda Bear. (p. 257)
York, George W. American Bee Journal, 1895, Vol. 35: Devoted Exclusively to the Interests of Honey Producers (Classic Reprint) (p. 70)
—American Bee Journal, 1897, Vol. 37: The Oldest Bee-Paper in America, Devoted Exclusively to the Interests of Honey Producers (Classic Reprint) (p. 70)
—American Bee Journal, 1899, Vol. 39 (Classic Reprint) (p. 70)
—American Bee Journal, Vol. 31: Devoted Exclusively to Bee-Culture; January 5, 1893 (Classic Reprint) (p. 70)
—American Bee Journal, Vol. 32: July 6, 1893 (Classic Reprint) (p. 70)
—American Bee Journal, Vol. 38: January 6, 1898 (Classic Reprint) (p. 70)
—American Bee Journal, Vol. 41: January 3, 1901 (Classic Reprint) (p. 70)
—American Bee Journal, Vol. 44: Jan. 7, 1904 (Classic Reprint) (p. 70)
—American Bee Journal, Vol. 48: January, 1908 (Classic Reprint) (p. 70)
—American Bee Journal, Vol. 50: Golden Jubilee Year, January 1910 (Classic Reprint) (p. 70)
—American Bee Journal, Vol. 52: January, 1912 (Classic Reprint) (p. 70)
York, Gerorge W. American Bee Journal, Vol. 49: January, 1909 (Classic Reprint) (p. 70)
York, J. Igneous Rocks. (p. 1094)
York, John Randall. King Bronty in the Days of the Dinosaurs. (p. 1220)
York, Kelley. Modern Monsters. (p. 1487)
York, Lesley. Henry the Naughty Raven Stories. (p. 955)
York Lumbard, Alexis. Angels Weedn, Flavia, illus. (p. 86)
—Everyone Prays: Celebrating Faith Around the World Sadeghian, Alireza, illus. (p. 672)
York, M. J. 12 Ancient Mysteries. (p. 2550)
—12 Entertainers Who Changed the World. (p. 2551)
—Animals in Spring. (p. 94)
—Butterflies & Moths. (p. 303)
—Camping. (p. 316)
—Canoeing. (p. 322)
—Celebrating Earth Day. (p. 349)
—Celebrating St. Patrick's Day. (p. 349)
—Constellation Hercules: The Story of the Hero. Morrow, J. T., illus. (p. 443)
—Henry Ford: Manufacturing Mogul (p. 955)
—Hiking. (p. 971)
—It's Mother's Day! (p. 1146)
—Learn Arabic Words. Petelinsek, Kathleen, illus. (p. 1255)
—Learn German Words. Petelinsek, Kathleen, illus. (p. 1255)
—Learn Hindi Words. Petelinsek, Kathleen, illus. (p. 1255)
—Learn Japanese Words. Petelinsek, Kathleen, illus. (p. 1255)
—Learn Korean Words. Petelinsek, Kathleen, illus. (p. 1255)
—Learn Portuguese Words. Petelinsek, Kathleen, illus. (p. 1255)
—Learn Russian Words. Petelinsek, Kathleen, illus. (p. 1255)
—Learn Tagalog Words. Petelinsek, Kathleen, illus. (p. 1255)
—Learn Vietnamese Words. Petelinsek, Kathleen, illus. (p. 1257)
—Plants in Spring. (p. 1757)
—Pond in Spring. (p. 1773)
—Rock Climbing. (p. 1894)
—Spring on the Farm. (p. 2092)
—Toads & Frogs. (p. 2254)
—Weather in Spring. (p. 2394)
—Woodrow Wilson. (p. 2492)
York, M. J. & Willis, John. Animals. (p. 93)
—Plants. (p. 1757)
—Weather. (p. 2393)
York, Marion. Happy to Be Me. (p. 924)
York, N. Historical Publishing Company N. Modern Gilpin: A Ballad of Bull Run (Classic Reprint) (p. 1486)
York Notes Staff, jt. auth. see Duffy, Carol Ann.
York Notes Staff, jt. auth. see Shakespeare, William.
York, Penelope, et al. Natural World. (p. 1580)
York, Rayna. Everything I Knew to Be True. (p. 673)
York, Saint Joseph. 1934 Footprints (Classic Reprint) (p. 2561)
York, Saint Joseph's College New. 1934 Footprints (Classic Reprint) (p. 2561)
York, Shane, illus. see Witte, Jessica Pierce.
York, St Joseph. Loria, Vol. 17: Nov. 1940 (Classic Reprint) (p. 1349)
York, St Joseph's College for Women Ne. Loria, Vol. 5: November, 1927 (Classic Reprint) (p. 1349)
York, St Joseph's College New. Loria, Vol. 17: Nov. 1940 (Classic Reprint) (p. 1349)
—Loria, Vol. 8: November, 1930 (Classic Reprint) (p. 1349)
York, University Society New. Book of Nature & Outdoor Life, Vol. 2 (Classic Reprint) (p. 259)
Yorke, Anthony. Margaret's Travels: Letters from Margaret Lee of New York to Florence Jackson of Chicago (Classic Reprint) (p. 1403)
Yorke, Curtis. Brown Portmanteau: And Other Stories (Classic Reprint) (p. 287)
—Medlicotts: An Uneventful Family Chronicle (Classic Reprint) (p. 1437)
—Other Sara (Classic Reprint) (p. 1675)
—Romance of Modern London: A Novel (Classic Reprint) (p. 1900)
—Romance of Modern London. (p. 1900)
—Romance of Modern London, Vol. 1 Of 3: A Novel (Classic Reprint) (p. 1900)
Yorkey, Mike & Florea, Jesse. Linspired: The Jeremy Lin Story (p. 1305)
Yoshi, illus. see Clements, Andrew.
Yoshi, illus. see Wood, Douglas.
Yoshida, Akira, jt. auth. see ABDO Publishing Company Staff.
Yoshida, Amanda. Greatest Wish. (p. 892)
Yoshifumi, Hasegawa. Yamada's Weather Report. (p. 2517)
Yoshikawa, Sachiko. Boy from the Dragon Palace: A Folktale from Japan. (p. 268)
—Boy from the Dragon Palace. (p. 268)
Yoshikawa, Sachiko, illus. see Buzzeo, Toni.
Yoshikawa, Sachiko, illus. see Cuyler, Margery.
Yoshikawa, Sachiko, illus. see Hopkins, Lee Bennett.
Yoshikawa, Sachiko, illus. see Loewen, Nancy.
Yoshikawa, Sachiko, illus. see MacDonald, Margaret Read.
Yoshimura, Takumi. Neon Genesis Evangelion: the Shinji Ikari Detective Diary Volume 1: The Shinji Ikari Detective Diary Volume 1. Horn, Carl Gustav, ed. (p. 1587)
Yoshinari, Yoh & TRIGGER. Little Witch Academia, Vol. 1 (manga) (p. 1330)
Yoshitake, Shinsuke. Boring Book: (Childrens Book about Boredom, Funny Kids Picture Book, Early Elementary School Story Book) (p. 262)
—I Cannot See It. (p. 1063)
—"I Wonder . . ." Bookstore. (p. 1086)
—Still Stuck. (p. 2119)
Yoshitani, Yoshi, illus. see Cody, Matthew.
Yoshiyasu. Zen Scratch Art: Magical Woodlands. (p. 2539)
Yoshizaki, Mine. Sgt. Frog (p. 1995)
Yoshizumi, Carol, illus. see Hawes, Alison.
Yost, Casper Salathiel. Making of a Successful Wife: Letters of a Father to His Daughter (Classic Reprint) (p. 1389)
Yotter, Tate, illus. see Bowman, Chris.
Yotter, Tate, illus. see Hoena, Blake.
Yotter, Tate, illus. see Leaf, Christina.
You Are Here Books, creator. All Around Ashland: Doodle, Color, & Learn All about Your Hometown! (p. 51)
—All Around Aspen: Doodle, Color, & Learn All about Your Hometown! (p. 51)
—All Around Bellingham: Doodle, Color, & Learn All about Your Hometown! (p. 51)
—All Around Bend: Doodle, Color, & Learn All about Your Hometown! (p. 51)
—All Around Boise: Doodle, Color, & Learn All about Your Hometown! (p. 51)
—All Around Coeur D'Alene: Doodle, Color, & Learn All about Your Hometown! (p. 51)
—All Around Colorado Springs: Doodle, Color, & Learn All about Your Hometown! (p. 51)
—All Around Denver: Doodle, Color, & Learn All about Your Hometown! (p. 51)
—All Around Fresno: Doodle, Color, & Learn All about Your Hometown! (p. 51)
—All Around Lincoln: Doodle, Color, & Learn All about Your Hometown! (p. 51)
—All Around Los Angeles: Doodle, Color, & Learn All about Your Hometown! (p. 51)
—All Around Monterey: Doodle, Color, & Learn All about Your Hometown! (p. 51)
—All Around Oakland: Doodle, Color, & Learn All about Your Hometown! (p. 51)
—All Around Olympia: Doodle, Color, & Learn All about Your Hometown! (p. 51)
—All Around Omaha: Doodle, Color, & Learn All about Your Hometown! (p. 51)
—All Around Portland: Doodle, Color, & Learn All about Your Hometown! (p. 51)
—All Around Provo: Doodle, Color, & Learn All about Your Hometown! (p. 51)
—All Around Salt Lake City: Doodle, Color, & Learn All about Your Hometown! (p. 51)
—All Around San Diego: Doodle, Color, & Learn All about Your Hometown! (p. 51)
—All Around San Francisco: Doodle, Color, & Learn All about Your Hometown! (p. 51)
—All Around San Luis Obispo: Doodle, Color, & Learn All about Your Hometown! (p. 51)
—All Around Seattle: Doodle, Color, & Learn All about Your Hometown! (p. 51)
—All Around Spokane: Doodle, Color, & Learn All about Your Hometown! (p. 51)
—All Around St. George: Doodle, Color, & Learn All about Your Hometown! (p. 51)
—All Around Tacoma: Doodle, Color, & Learn All about Your Hometown! (p. 51)
You, Catherina. Winter Stays with Me. (p. 2476)
You Fu Bian Ji Bu. Children's Atlas of Marine Life in 3 Dar Interactive Games. (p. 372)
—Children's Edition of Chinese Idioms (Book+cd) (p. 373)
—Engnali Bai & Confucius. (p. 655)
—Engnaludwig Van Beethoven & Wolfgang Amadeus Mozart. (p. 655)
You Fu Bian Ji Bu, compiled by. Cheng Yu Gu Shi Yi Ben Tong (Ping Zhuang Ban) (p. 365)
—Ming Ren Wei Ren Yi Ben Tong (Ping Zhuang Ban) (p. 1471)
Youcat Foundation. Youcat for Kids. (p. 2529)
Youd, Pauline. I Wonder . . . Books: Pack 1 Garvin, Elaine, illus. (p. 1086)
—I Wonder . . . Books: Pack 2 Garvin, Elaine, illus. (p. 1086)
YouDae, Kim, illus. see InSeon, Chae.
Youmans, Edward Livingston. Alcohol & the Constitution of Man: Being a Popular Scientific Account of the Chemical History & Properties of Alcohol, & Its Leading Effects upon the Healthy Human Constitution (Classic Reprint) (p. 41)
Youmans, Edward Livingston, jt. auth. see Grove, William Robert.
Youmans, Eliza Ann. Descriptive Botany. (p. 531)
Younce, W. H. Adventures of a Conscript (Classic Reprint) (p. 21)
Yound, Florence Ethel Mills. Wine Farm (Classic Reprint) (p. 2472)
YouNeek Studios, illus. see Buckley, James, Jr.
Young, A. From Chicago to the Canyon (p. 791)
Young, Adam, illus. see O'Hearn, Darcee.
Young, Adrienne. Fable: A Novel. (p. 690)
—Girl the Sea Gave Back: A Novel. (p. 837)
—Sky in the Deep. (p. 2033)
Young, Alicia, illus. see Benishek, Becky.
Young, Alicia, illus. see Dembowski, Becky.
Young, Allen, jt. auth. see Stewart, Melissa.
Young, Allen M., jt. auth. see Stewart, Melissa.
Young, Amy. Belinda in Paris. (p. 196)
—Belinda the Ballerina. (p. 196)
—New Friend for Sparkle. (p. 1593)
—Unicorn Named Sparkle. Young, Amy, illus. (p. 2328)
—Unicorn Named Sparkle & the Pumpkin Monster. Young, Amy, illus. (p. 2328)
—Unicorn Named Sparkle's First Christmas. Young, Amy, illus. (p. 2328)
Young, Andrea. Finny & the Boy from Horse Mountain. (p. 731)
Young, Ann Eastman. Once Blue. (p. 1657)
Young, Annemarie, jt. auth. see Rosen, Michael.
Young, Art. Hell up to Date: The Reckless Journey of R. Palasco Drant, Newspaper Correspondent, Through the Infernal Regions, As Reported by Himself; with Illustrations (Classic Reprint) (p. 950)
Young, Art, jt. auth. see Riley, James Whitcomb.
Young Authors Guild, Pebbles & the. Sam, Eli, & the Bully Sharks. Jicha, Brenda & Stuebs, Debby, eds. (p. 1926)
Young, Barbara D. Larry's Adventure. (p. 1245)
Young, Beryl. Follow the Elephant. (p. 758)
—Miles to Go (p. 1465)
Young, Beverley, illus. see Dorion, Christian.
Young, Beverley, illus. see Dorion, Christiane.
Young, Beverley, jt. auth. see Dorion, Christiane.
Young, Bill, illus. see Austin, Laurie.
Young, Bill, illus. see Paul, John.
Young, Bill, illus. see Rodhe, Paul & Wallas Reidy, Sarah.
Young, Blamire. Children's Bread; an One Act Play, Being a Tragedy or a Farce: According, to How You Look at It (Classic Reprint) (p. 373)
Young, Brandon. Daughter of Etheron. (p. 509)
Young, Brigit. Prettiest. (p. 1790)
—Worth a Thousand Words. (p. 2509)
Young, C. Howard. Sunny Life of an Invalid (Classic Reprint) (p. 2152)
Young, Candice June. My Name Is Wes & My Mema Has Ms. (p. 1557)
Young, Caroline. Big Bug Search. (p. 218)
—First Sticker Book Bugs. (p. 739)
—Guide to Potty Training Internet-Referenced. (p. 903)
—Wipe-Clean Starting Cursive. (p. 2477)
Young, Cathleen. Pumpkin War. (p. 1813)
Young, Charles Augustus. Lessons in Astronomy Including Uranography. (p. 1269)
—Sun. (p. 2151)
—Text-Book of General Astronomy for Colleges & Scientific Schools (Classic Reprint) (p. 2210)
—Uranography. (p. 2339)
Young, Cheryl a. Spellbreaker. (p. 2079)
Young, Cheyanne. Last Wish of Sasha Cade. (p. 1250)
Young, Chuck. Day We Lost Pet. Sobieski, Aniela, illus. (p. 514)
Young, Clare, jt. auth. see Youngs, Clare.
Young, Clarence. Jack Ranger's Schooldays: Or the Rivals of Washington Hall (Classic Reprint) (p. 1152)
—Motor Boys on the Border: Or Sixty Nuggets of Gold (Classic Reprint) (p. 1512)
—Racer Boys to the Rescue (Classic Reprint) (p. 1831)
Young, Craig. Arrr Marks the Spot. (p. 119)
Young, Cybele. Few Bites (p. 722)
—Few Blocks (p. 722)
Young, Cybèle. Nancy Knows. (p. 1574)
Young, Cybele. Out the Window (p. 1683)
Young, Cybèle, illus. see Fagan, Cary.
Young, Cybèle, jt. auth. see Young, Cybèle.
Young, Cybèle & Young, Cybèle. Queen's Shadow: A Story about How Animals See. Young, Cybèle & Young, Cybèle, illus. (p. 1825)
Young, Cynthia Anne. Muddy Little Piggy's. (p. 1524)
Young, Dalandra. Noonimals: First Day of School. Young, Dalandra, illus. (p. 1619)
Young, Dan. Life among the Inuit. (p. 1287)
Young, David W. Adventures of Sam. (p. 27)
Young, Dawn. Abcs of Making Good Choices. Keaggy, Sarah, illus. (p. 5)
—Counting Elephants. Solis, Fermin, illus. (p. 460)
—Melvin Fastidious the Sailor. (p. 1443)
—Night Baafore Christmas. Pino, Pablo, illus. (p. 1604)
Young, Debra. Gingersnap! (p. 834)
Young, Dianne. Grampa, Will You Tell Me a Story: A 'Pickles' Children's Book. (p. 876)
Young, Dot, illus. see Rives, J. G.
Young, Drew. Meaning of Your Mission. (p. 1434)
Young, E. Ryerson. Camp Doctor: And Other Stories (Classic Reprint) (p. 315)
—Duck Lake: Stories of the Canadian Backwoods (Classic Reprint) (p. 608)
Young, Ed. Cat from Hunger Mountain. Young, Ed, illus. (p. 341)
—Catastrophe by the Sea. (p. 343)
—House Baba Built: An Artist's Childhood in China. (p. 1022)
—Mighty Moby. (p. 1463)
—Seven Blind Mice. Young, Ed, illus. (p. 1993)
—Should You Be a River: A Poem about Love. (p. 2011)
—Voices of the Heart. Young, Ed, illus. (p. 2365)
—Weather's Bet. Young, Ed, illus. (p. 2394)
Young, Ed, illus. see Burleigh, Robert.
Young, Ed, illus. see Cheng, Andrea.
Young, Ed, illus. see Golio, Gary.
Young, Ed, illus. see Grimes, Nikki.
Young, Ed, illus. see Guiberson, Brenda Z.
Young, Ed, illus. see Kajikawa, Kimiko.
Young, Ed, illus. see Oppenheim, Shulamith.
Young, Ed, illus. see Reibstein, Mark.
Young, Ed, illus. see Singer, Marilyn.
Young, Ed, illus. see Yolen, Jane.
Young, Ed, jt. auth. see Cheng, Andrea.
Young, Ed, ed. Siete Ratones Ciegos. Uribe, Verónica, tr. (p. 2015)
Young, Egerton R. Algonquin Indian Tales (Classic Reprint) (p. 44)
—Indian Life in the Great North-West (Classic Reprint) (p. 1116)
—On the Indian Trail: And Other Stories of Missionary Work among the Cree & Salteaux Indians (Classic Reprint) (p. 1655)
—Winter Adventures of Three Boys in the Great Lone Land (Classic Reprint) (p. 2475)
Young, Egerton Ryerson. Battle of the Bears: Life in the North Land (Classic Reprint) (p. 174)
—By Canoe & Dog-Train: Among the Cree & Salteaux Indians (Classic Reprint) (p. 305)
—By Canoe & Dog-Train. (p. 305)
—By Canoe & Dog-Train among the Cree & Salteaux Indians. (p. 305)
—Children of the Forest: A Story of Indian Love (Classic Reprint) (p. 372)
—My Dogs in the Northland (Classic Reprint) (p. 1537)
—Oowikapun, or How the Gospel Reached the Nelson River Indians (Classic Reprint) (p. 1665)
—Stories from Indian Wigwams & Northern Camp-Fires (Classic Reprint) (p. 2124)
Young, Eileen Parrigin. Cousins & the Cave of Fire (p. 463)
Young, Elizabeth. ed up Platypus. Seabrooks, Lydia, illus. (p. 624)
—Plight of the Enchanted Forest. (p. 1763)
Young, Elizabeth G. Homestead Ranch (Classic Reprint) (p. 998)
Young, Elizabeth L. Dozens & Dozens of Cousins & Cousins. Perkins, Ruth, illus. (p. 591)
—Oodles & Oodles of Poodles. (p. 1665)
Young, Ella. Celtic Wonder-Tales. Gonne, Maud, illus. (p. 351)
Young, Ella Flagg. Young & Field Literary Readers. Book One, a Primer & First Reader. (p. 2530)
—Young & Field Literary Readers, Vol. 1: A Primer & First Reader (Classic Reprint) (p. 2530)
—Young & Field Literary Readers, Vol. 2 (Classic Reprint) (p. 2530)
Young, Ellsworth, illus. see Babbitt, Ellen C.
Young, Ellsworth, jt. auth. see Babbitt, Ellen C.
Young, Emma. She, Myself, & I. (p. 2004)
Young, Eric, illus. see Temple, Teri & Temple, Emily.
Young, Erin. Brendan the Drummer Boy. (p. 279)
Young, Ernest. Kingsway Geography Readers, Vol. 2: At Work in Many Lands (Classic Reprint) (p. 1223)
—Kingsway Geography Readers, Vol. 3: Travellers' Tales (Classic Reprint) (p. 1223)
—Kingsway Geography Readers, Vol. 4: At Home in Distant Lands (Classic Reprint) (p. 1223)
Young, Ernest A. Only a Woman's Heart, or Barbara's Rival (Classic Reprint) (p. 1664)
—Wife's Honor: A Novel (Classic Reprint) (p. 2461)
Young, Ethan. Battles of Bridget Lee Volume 2: the Miracle Child. (p. 175)
Young, F. E. Mills. Almonds of Life (Classic Reprint) (p. 57)
—Grit Lawless (Classic Reprint) (p. 897)
—Imprudence (Classic Reprint) (p. 1103)
—Shadow of the Past (Classic Reprint) (p. 1997)
—Stronger Influence (Classic Reprint) (p. 2142)
Young, Filson. Letters from Solitude: And Other Essays (Classic Reprint) (p. 1280)
—Memory Harbour: Essays Chiefly in Description (Classic Reprint) (p. 1446)
—Sands of Pleasure (Classic Reprint) (p. 1931)
—Wagner Stories: Retold from the Music-Dramas (Classic Reprint) (p. 2370)
—When the Tide Turns (Classic Reprint) (p. 2433)
Young, Florence. Take His Hand. (p. 2177)
Young, Florence Ethel Mills. Coelebs, the Love Story of a Bachelor (Classic Reprint) (p. 412)
—Triumph of Jill (Classic Reprint) (p. 2290)
Young, Francis Brett. Black Diamond (Classic Reprint) (p. 237)
—Crescent Moon, Vol. 5 (Classic Reprint) (p. 473)
—Red Knight: A Romance (Classic Reprint) (p. 1857)
—Young Physician (Classic Reprint) (p. 2532)
Young, Franklin. S P o T S. (p. 1919)
Young, G. Bayard. Strangers at the Door: A Christmas Story (Classic Reprint) (p. 2139)
Young, Gary. More Than Two: Under the Sea. (p. 1505)
Young, Georgie. Magdalen's Life (Classic Reprint) (p. 1376)
Young, Gladys I. Taming of Horrors: A Girl Scout Play in Four Acts (Classic Reprint) (p. 2189)
Young, Harry. Hard Knocks: A Life Story of the Vanishing West (Classic Reprint) (p. 929)
Young, Heather, illus. see Lasterday, J.
Young, Helen Ann. Hellie & the Sensational Magic Carpet. Young, Tim, illus. (p. 950)
—Hello to Hellie's World. Young, Tim Blair, illus. (p. 952)
—Your World Discovery Scrapbook. Young, Tim Blair, illus. (p. 2535)
Young, Ife Gail. Bina & the Beanpole Vol. 2: Working for Unity in the Community. (p. 228)
Young, Ife Gail F. Mama Rue: A Celebratory & Empowerment Experience. (p. 1392)
Young III, Estrell. I Prayed & Everything. (p. 1080)
Young III, Estrell S. Painting of a Gentleman. (p. 1693)
Young, Iza, jt. auth. see Sienkiewicz, Henryk.
Young, J. Blue Diamond Box. (p. 248)
Young, Jacob. Examining Earthquakes. (p. 675)
Young, James, illus. see Salsi, Lynn.
Young, James H., jt. auth. see Gummere, John.
Young, Jan. Starting the Colt. (p. 2108)
Young, Janet Ruth. Babysitter Murders. (p. 155)
—My Beautiful Failure. (p. 1532)
—Things I Shouldn't Think. (p. 2220)
Young, Janice L. Sunshine & Butterflies. (p. 2153)
Young, Jeanna. Princess Prayers Aranda, Omar, illus. (p. 1799)
—Royal Christmas to Remember Aranda, Omar, illus. (p. 1909)
Young, Jeanna Stolle & Johnson, Jacqueline. Princess Hope & the Hidden Treasure Aranda, Omar, illus. (p. 1797)
Young, Jeanna Stolle & Johnson, Jacqueline Kinney. Princess Grace & the Little Lost Kitten Aranda, Omar, illus. (p. 1797)
—Princess Joy's Birthday Blessing Aranda, Omar, illus. (p. 1797)

Y

Young, Jeff C. Adrenaline Adventure (p. 17)
—Albert Pujols: A Baseball Star Who Cares. (p. 40)
—Amazing African-American Actors. (p. 62)
—Belaying the Line: Mountain, Rock, & Ice Climbing. (p. 195)
—Brilliant African-American Scientists: Nine Exceptional Lives. (p. 282)
—Dropping the Flag: Auto Racing. (p. 605)
—Dwyane Wade. (p. 611)
—Henry Hudson: Discoverer of the Hudson River. (p. 955)
—Hernando de Soto: Spanish Conquistador in the Americas. (p. 959)
—Inspiring African-American Inventors: Nine Extraordinary Lives. (p. 1124)
—Joe Biden. (p. 1171)
—Leading the Pack: Dogsled Racing. (p. 1254)
—Michelle Wie. (p. 1458)
—Motorcycles: The Ins & Outs of Superbikes, Choppers, & Other Motorcycles. (p. 1512)
—Pheasant Hunting for Kids (p. 1733)
—Pulling the Rip Cord: Skydiving. (p. 1812)
—Running the Rapids: White-Water Rafting, Canoeing, & Kayaking. (p. 1916)
—Shooting the Curl: Surfing. (p. 2009)
—Trucks: The Ins & Outs of Monster Trucks, Semis, Pickups, & Other Trucks. (p. 2293)
—True Underground Rescue Stories. (p. 2295)
Young, Jeff C., et al. Into the Great Outdoors. (p. 1128)
Young, Jeffrey, jt. auth. see Patent, Dorothy Hinshaw.
Young, Jennifer Law, jt. auth. see Young, Bruce.
Young, Jessica. All Paws on Deck (p. 53)
—All Paws on Deck. Burks, James, illus. (p. 53)
—Art-Rageous. Sécheret, Jessica, illus. (p. 121)
—Boy & Toy. (p. 268)
—Digging for Dinos (p. 546)
—Digging for Dinos. Burks, James, illus. (p. 546)
—Finley Flowers Collection. Sécheret, Jessica, illus. (p. 731)
—Fin-Tastic Fashion. Sécheret, Jessica, illus. (p. 727)
—Howl at the Moon. (p. 1047)
—Howl at the Moon: a Branches Book (Haggis & Tank Unleashed #3) Burks, James, illus. (p. 1047)
—My Blue Is Happy. Chien, Catia, illus. (p. 1534)
—Nature Calls. Sécheret, Jessica, illus. (p. 1580)
—New & Improved. Sécheret, Jessica, illus. (p. 1591)
—Original Recipe. Sécheret, Jessica, illus. (p. 1671)
—Pet This Book. Wiseman, Daniel, illus. (p. 1726)
—Pet-Rified. Sécheret, Jessica, illus. (p. 1726)
—Play This Book. Wiseman, Daniel, illus. (p. 1759)
—Room to Bloom. Sécheret, Jessica, illus. (p. 1903)
—Spy Guy: The Not-So-Secret Agent. Santoso, Charles, illus. (p. 2093)
—Super Spooktacular. Sécheret, Jessica, illus. (p. 2158)
—Wish Is a Seed. Pritelli, Maria Cristina, illus. (p. 2478)
Young, John. Descriptive Catalogue of the Works of Hogarth: Placed in the Gallery of the British Institution for Exhibition (Classic Reprint) (p. 531)
—Farewell Tour of a Terminal Optimist (p. 709)
Young, Josephine. Journals of Josephine Young (Classic Reprint) (p. 1180)
Young, Judy. Book for Black-Eyed Susan. Ettlinger, Doris, illus. (p. 257)
—Danger at the Dinosaur Stomping Grounds. (p. 501)
—Digger & Daisy Go Camping. Sullivan, Dana, illus. (p. 545)
—Digger & Daisy Go on a Picnic. Sullivan, Dana, illus. (p. 545)
—Digger & Daisy Go to the Doctor. Sullivan, Dana, illus. (p. 545)
—Digger & Daisy Go to the Zoo. (p. 545)
—Digger & Daisy Plant a Garden. Sullivan, Dana, illus. (p. 545)
—Digger et Daisy Vont Au Docteur (Digger & Daisy Go to the Doctor) Sullivan, Dana, illus. (p. 545)
—Digger y Daisy Van a la Ciudad (Digger & Daisy Go to the City) Sullivan, Dana, illus. (p. 545)
—Digger y Daisy Van Al Médico (Digger & Daisy Go to the Doctor) Sullivan, Dana, illus. (p. 545)
—Digger y Daisy Van de Picnic (Digger & Daisy Go on a Picnic) Sullivan, Dana, illus. (p. 545)
—H Is for Hook: A Fishing Alphabet. Palmer, Gary, illus. (p. 908)
—Hidden Bestiary of Marvelous, Mysterious, & (Maybe Even) Magical Creatures. Filippucci, Laura Francesca, illus. (p. 965)
—Hu-Wan & the Sleeping Dragon. Solano, Jordi, illus. (p. 1047)
—Marty's Mission: An Apollo 11 Story. Miles, David, illus. (p. 1411)
—Minnow & Rose: An Oregon Trail Story. Farnsworth, Bill, illus. (p. 1473)
—Missing Grizzly Cubs. (p. 1480)
—Pet for Miss Wright. Wesson, Andrea, illus. (p. 1726)
—Promise. (p. 1806)
—Sleepy Snoozy Cozy Coozy: A Book of Animal Beds. Monroe, Michael Glenn, illus. (p. 2037)
—Star in a Play. Sullivan, Dana, illus. (p. 2102)
—Tuki & Moka: A Tale of Two Tamarins. Madsen, Jim, illus. (p. 2299)
Young, Judy, jt. auth. see Scillian, Devin.
Young, Judy & A12. R Is for Rhyme: A Poetry Alphabet. Juhasz, Victor, illus. (p. 1829)
Young, Judy & Sullivan, Dana. Digger & Daisy Go to the City. (p. 545)
Young, Judy & Wargin, Kathy-jo. Little Missouri. Urban, Helle, illus. (p. 1322)
Young, Judy Dockrey. Missouri Reader. Darnell, Kate, illus. (p. 1482)
Young, Julia Ditto. Adrift: A Story of Niagara (Classic Reprint) (p. 17)
Young, Julian. Daniel Model: Understanding the Pathway to Promotion & Power in the Kingdom of God. (p. 503)
—Peter Model: Understanding the Key That Unlock Maximum Kingdom Impact. (p. 1728)
Young, Julian Charles. Memoir of Charles Mayne Young, Tragedian 1871: With Extracts from His Son's Journal (Classic Reprint) (p. 1443)
—Memoir of Charles Mayne Young, Tragedian, 1871, Vol. 2: With Extracts from His Son's Journal (Classic Reprint) (p. 1443)
—Memoir of Charles Mayne Young, Vol. 1: Tragedian, with Extracts from His Son's Journal (Classic Reprint) (p. 1443)
Young, K. L. Cardboard Castles. (p. 328)
Young, Karen, jt. auth. see Reilly, Carmel.
Young, Karen L., illus. see Bronstein, Christine.
Young, Karen Romano. Doodlebug: A Novel in Doodles. (p. 584)
—Girl, a Raccoon, & the Midnight Moon: (Juvenile Fiction, Mystery, Young Reader Detective Story, Light Fantasy for Kids) Bagley, Jessixa, illus. (p. 835)
—Hundred Percent. (p. 1051)
—Shark Quest: Protecting the Ocean's Top Predators. (p. 2002)
—Space Junk: The Dangers of Polluting Earth's Orbit. (p. 2071)
—Stuck in the Middle (of Middle School) A Novel in Doodles. (p. 2143)
—Whale Quest: Working Together to Save Endangered Species. (p. 2403)
Young, Karen Romano & dePaola, Tomie. Oceans Doodle Book. (p. 1636)
Young, Katherine A. Stories of the Maple Land: Tales of the Early Days of Canada for Children (Classic Reprint) (p. 2125)
—Stories of the Maple Land. (p. 2125)
Young, L. F. Ryan's Legend: The Early Adventures. (p. 1919)
Young, Latesha. Hair in My Brush. (p. 910)
Young, Lawrence Ditto. Iceman: A Farce in One Act (Classic Reprint) (p. 1088)
Young, Lesley. Storyteller Book - Red Riding Hood. Williams, Jenny, illus. (p. 2136)
—Storyteller Book Sleeping Beauty. Press, Jenny, illus. (p. 2136)
Young, Lesley, retold by. Children's Treasury of Tales. (p. 375)
Young, Lili. Incredible Dreams: Your Light Guides the Way. (p. 1113)
Young, Linda. Backyard Adventures of Anna & Andy Hummingbird: Book 1 Of 10. (p. 156)
Young Lowery, Tamara. Little Pirate Goes to Kindergarten. (p. 1324)
Young, Lynn. Adventures with Looka (p. 30)
Young, Lynne. Bee's Lullaby. Kennedy, Karen J., illus. (p. 190)
Young, M. Alan. Little Betty's Big Idea. (p. 1311)
—Little Bobby's Big Idea. (p. 1312)
Young, Margaret. Self-Supporting: A Duologue (Classic Reprint) (p. 1987)
Young, Mariabelle & Buchwald, Ann. White Gloves & Party Manners. Christiane, illus. (p. 2444)
Young, Mark. Beware of the Giant Brain! Epelbaum, Mariano, illus. (p. 211)
—Creature in Room #YTH-125. Epelbaum, Mariano, illus. (p. 471)
—Robot Who Knew Too Much. Epelbaum, Mariano, illus. (p. 1892)
Young, Martha. Minute Dramas: The Kodak at the Quarter (Classic Reprint) (p. 1474)
—Two Little Southern Sisters & Their Garden Plays (Classic Reprint) (p. 2308)
—When We Were Wee: Tales of the Ten Grandchildren (Classic Reprint) (p. 2434)
Young, Mary. Nos Gusta Vivir Verde: We Like to Live Green. Parker, Zachary, illus. (p. 1622)
—We Like to Nurse Too. Parker, Zac, illus. (p. 2391)
Young, Mary, illus. see Wetterer, Margaret K. & Wetterer, Charles M.
Young, Mary & Parker, Zac. También a Nosotros Nos Gusta Amamantar We Like to Nurse Too. (p. 2189)
Young, Mary Julia. Right & Wrong, or the Kinsmen of Naples, Vol. 2 Of 4: A Romantic Story (Classic Reprint) (p. 1882)
—Right & Wrong; or the Kinsmen of Naples, Vol. 3 Of 4: A Romantic Story (Classic Reprint) (p. 1882)
—Right & Wrong, Vol. 1 Of 4: Or, the Kinsmen of Naples; a Romantic Story (Classic Reprint) (p. 1882)
—Summer at Brighton, Vol. 1 Of 3: A Modern Novel (Classic Reprint) (p. 2148)
—Summer at Weymouth, or the Star of Fashion, Vol. 1 Of 3: A Novel (Classic Reprint) (p. 2148)
—Summer at Weymouth, or the Star of Fashion, Vol. 2 (Classic Reprint) (p. 2148)
Young, Mary O'Keefe, illus. see Rey, H. A. & Hapka, Catherine.
Young, Mary O'Keefe, illus. see Anderson, R. P., et al.
Young, Mary O'Keefe, illus. see Capucilli, Alyssa Satin.
Young, Mary O'Keefe, illus. see Fishman, Cathy Goldberg.
Young, Mary O'Keefe, illus. see Rey, H. A.
Young, Mary O'Keefe, illus. see Rey, H. A., et al.
Young, Mary O'Keefe, illus. see Wetterer, Margaret K. & Wetterer, Charles M.
Young, Mary OKeefe, jt. auth. see Rey, H. A.
Young, Mary Stuart. Griffins: A Colonial Tale (Classic Reprint) (p. 896)
Young, Melanie. Fearless Fabulous You! (p. 717)
Young, Michael. Living with a Cheetah... or More. (p. 1334)
—Portrait of a Mother. (p. 1779)
Young, Miriam. Miss Suzy. (p. 1480)
Young, Mitchell, ed. see Greenhaven Press Editors.
Young, Mitchell, ed. For-Profit Education. (p. 763)
—Political Corruption. (p. 1771)
Young, Moira. Blood Red Road (p. 246)
—Blood Red Road. (p. 246)
—Raging Star. (p. 1834)
—Rebel Heart. (p. 1852)
Young, N. G. Illegal: A Hip-Hop Tale. (p. 1095)
Young, Ned. Zoomer. Young, Ned, illus. (p. 2544)
—Zoomer's Out-Of-This-World Christmas. Young, Ned, illus. (p. 2544)
Young, Ned, illus. see Swenson, Jamie A.
Young, Ned, illus. see Underwood, Deborah.
Young, Norene. Cathy, the Castaway Cat. Woodyard, Sandy Lilly, illus. (p. 345)
Young, Norman, illus. see Amery, Heather.
Young, Norman, illus. see Castor, Harriet.
Young, Norman, illus. see Dickins, Rosie & Pratt, Leonie.
Young Nz Writers. Something Strange Happened in Rotorua: Write off Line - NZ Secondary School Writing Competition 2019. Gavel & Bridges, Grace, eds. (p. 2061)
Young, O. E. Betsey's Boarders: A Farce in One Act (Classic Reprint) (p. 208)
—Little Red Mare (Classic Reprint) (p. 1326)
—Pickled Polliwog: A Farce in One Act (Classic Reprint) (p. 1739)
Young, Owen. Our Camping Trip: Subtract Within 20. (p. 1677)
Young, Paige. Homework Dilemm. (p. 998)
Young, Paul, illus. see McQuinn, Anna.
Young, Pauline, illus. see Joe, Rita.
Young, Pauline, illus. see Thomas, Rebecca.
Young, Pearl. I'm a Little Different. (p. 1097)
Young, Phil. Best Book on Northern Brown Snakes. (p. 205)
Young, R. E. Sally of Missouri (Classic Reprint) (p. 1925)
Young, Rachel & Young, Jackie. Tale of Squabbit. Lynch, Stephanie, illus. (p. 2179)
Young, Rae. Drawing Appaloosas & Other Handsome Horses Q2AMedia Services Private Ltd, Q2AMedia Services, illus. (p. 598)
—Drawing Arabians & Other Amazing Horses Q2AMedia Services Private Ltd, Q2AMedia Services, illus. (p. 599)
—Drawing Barrel Racers & Other Speedy Horses Q2AMedia Services Private Ltd, Q2AMedia Services, illus. (p. 599)
—Drawing Friesians & Other Beautiful Horses Q2AMedia Services Private Ltd, Q2AMedia Services, illus. (p. 599)
—Drawing Horses Q2AMedia Services Private Ltd, Q2AMedia Services, illus. (p. 599)
—Drawing Mustangs & Other Wild Horses Q2AMedia Services Private Ltd, Q2AMedia Services, illus. (p. 599)
—Drawing Thoroughbreds & Other Elegant Horses Q2AMedia Services Private Ltd, Q2AMedia Services, illus. (p. 600)
—Ultimate Guide to Drawing Horses Q2AMedia Services Private Ltd Staff, illus. (p. 2315)
Young, Rebecca. 102 Great Monologues: A versatile collection of monologues & duologues for student Actors (p. 2559)
—Teacup. Ottley, Matt, illus. (p. 2195)
Young, Rebecca & Accord Publishing Staff. Hop, Pop, & Play: A Mini Animotion Book. (p. 1001)
Young Rewired State. Get Coding!: Learn HTML, CSS & JavaScript & Build a Website, App & Game. (p. 823)
—Get Coding! Learn HTML, CSS, & JavaScript & Build a Website, App, & Game. (p. 823)
Young, Reyna. Bride of Hamsterstein. (p. 280)
—Christmas Creature. (p. 385)
—Halloween Zombie Party. (p. 912)
—Hamsterstein: Monsters: Book Eight. (p. 914)
—Horror Lullubies. (p. 1004)
—Mr. Torture. (p. 1521)
—Nevermore Books: Two Tales of Terror. (p. 1590)
—Once upon a Horror. (p. 1657)
Young, Rida Johnson. Brown of Harvard: A Play in Four Acts (Classic Reprint) (p. 287)
—Brown of Harvard (Classic Reprint) (p. 287)
—Captain Kidd: Jr. a Farcical Adventure in Three Acts New York Johnson Young November by Messrs. Cohan Present Harris, Kidd, by Samuel French All Rights Reserved Captain Kidd, Jr. a Farcical Adventure in Three Acts (Classic Reprint) (p. 325)
—Girl & the Pennant: A Base-Ball Comedy, in Three Acts (Classic Reprint) (p. 835)
Young, Robert. Gujarati Exercises, or a New Mode of Learning to Read, Write, & Speak the Gujarati Language in Six Months, on the Ollendorffian System: With Appendix (Classic Reprint) (p. 904)
—Hebrew & Chaldee Vocabulary: Consisting of Every Word in the Old Testament Scriptures, Whether Verb, Noun, PR Particle, the Verbs with Their Conjugations, & the Nouns with Their Genders, to Which Is Added, the Number of Times in Which Each Word Occurs. (p. 947)
Young, Rose E. Henderson (Classic Reprint) (p. 954)
Young, Ross, illus. see Young, Judy.
Young, Ruth. Aunty Marmalade. (p. 137)
Young, S. Hall. Klondike Clan: A Tale of the Great Stampede (Classic Reprint) (p. 1227)
Young, Samantha. Fragile Ordinary. (p. 775)
—Impossible Vastness of Us. (p. 1102)
Young, Samuel. History of My Life: Being a Biographical Outline of the Events of a Long & Busy Life (Classic Reprint) (p. 979)
Young, Samuel Hall. Adventures in Alaska (Classic Reprint) (p. 20)
Young, Samuel Oliver. True Stories of Old Houston & Houstonians: Historical & Personal Sketches (Classic Reprint) (p. 2294)
—True Stories of Old Houston & Houstonians, with a Thumbnail History of Houston. (p. 2294)
Young, Sandra Goodwin. Grandpa's Orchard: And the Christmas Pie. (p. 879)
Young, Sandy de. Look Up! Lee, Kathy, illus. (p. 1346)
Young, Sarah. 365 Devotions for Kids (p. 2560)
—Gasparilla's Key & the Revenge of the Purple Mermaid. (p. 811)
—Jesus Always: 365 Devotions for Kids (p. 1165)
—Jesus Calling: Family Devotional: 100 Devotions for Families to Enjoy Peace in His Presence. (p. 1165)
—Jesus Calling: 365 Devotions for Kids (p. 1165)
—Jesus Calling - 365 Devotions for Kids (p. 1165)
—Jesus Calling: 50 Devotions for a Thankful Heart (p. 1165)
—Jesus Calling: 50 Devotions for Busy Days (p. 1166)
—Jesus Calling: 50 Devotions to Grow in Your Faith (p. 1166)
—Jesus Calling for Little Ones Woodward, Antonia, illus. (p. 1166)
—Jesus Calling Little Book of Prayers (p. 1166)
—Jesus Calling My First Bible Storybook (p. 1166)
—Jesus Calling: the Story of Christmas (board Book) Longhi, Katya, illus. (p. 1166)
—Jesus Calling: the Story of Christmas (picture Book) Longhi, Katya, illus. (p. 1166)
—Jesus Calling: the Story of Easter (board Book) Longhi, Katya, illus. (p. 1166)
—Jesus Calling: the Story of Easter (picture Book) Longhi, Katya, illus. (p. 1166)
—Jesus Today Devotions for Kids (p. 1167)
—Jesus Today Teen Cover: Experience Hope in His Presence (p. 1167)
Young, Sarah, illus. see Turnbull, Ann.
Young, Sarah & Candlewick Press Staff. Endangered Animals: a 3D Pocket Guide. Young, Sarah, illus. (p. 649)
Young, Sarah & Fortner, Tama. Jesus Calling: 365 Devotions for Kids (Boys Edition) (p. 1165)
Young, Scott Alexander. Wild Cats of Piran. Christe, Moreno, illus. (p. 2463)
Young, Selina, illus. see French, Vivian.
Young, Shane, photos by see Gardner, Carol.
Young, Shaun. Castor. (p. 340)
Young, Sierra. Opa Wizard. (p. 1665)
Young, Skott, illus. see Andrews, Kaare.
Young, Skottie. Bully Wars. (p. 297)
—Middlewest (p. 1461)
—Oz: the Complete Collection - Ozma/Dorothy & the Wizard. (p. 1690)
—Oz: the Complete Collection - Wonderful Wizard/Marvelous Land. (p. 1690)
—Rocket Raccoon #1: a Chasing Tale Part One. Young, Skottie & Beaulieu, Jean-François, illus. (p. 1895)
—Rocket Raccoon #2: a Chasing Tale Part Two. Young, Skottie & Beaulieu, Jean-François, illus. (p. 1895)
—Rocket Raccoon #3: a Chasing Tale Part Three. Young, Skottie & Beaulieu, Jean-François, illus. (p. 1895)
—Rocket Raccoon #4: a Chasing Tale Part Four. Young, Skottie & Beaulieu, Jean-François, illus. (p. 1895)
—Rocket Raccoon #5: Storytailer. Young, Skottie et al, illus. (p. 1895)
—Rocket Raccoon #6: Misfit Mechs. Young, Skottie et al, illus. (p. 1895)
—Rocket Raccoon & Groot, Volume 1. (p. 1895)
Young, Skottie, illus. see Connolly, MarcyKate.
Young, Skottie, illus. see Gaiman, Neil.
Young, Skottie, illus. see Shanower, Eric & Baum, L. Frank.
Young, Skottie, illus. see Shanower, Eric.
Young, Stephanie, illus. see Fischer, Luke.
Young, Steve, jt. auth. see Gentner, Norma L.
Young, Stuart. Merely a Negress: A West African Story (Classic Reprint) (p. 1448)
Young, Susan. Becoming a Star Detective: Your Detective's Notebook for Finding Clues to How You Feel. (p. 187)
Young, Susan, illus. see Barton, Brittney B.
Young, Susan, illus. see Mackey, Cindy.
Young, Susan G., illus. see Newman, Adam T.
Young, Suzanne. Adjustment. (p. 16)
—All in Pieces. (p. 52)
—Complication. (p. 436)
—Epidemic. (p. 658)
—Girls with Razor Hearts. (p. 839)
—Girls with Sharp Sticks. (p. 839)
—Hotel for the Lost. (p. 1007)
—Hotel Ruby. (p. 1007)
—Program. (p. 1805)
—Program Complete Collection: The Program; the Treatment; the Remedy; the Epidemic; the Adjustment; the Complication. (p. 1805)
—Remedy. (p. 1864)
—Treatment. (p. 2283)
Young, Suzanne, jt. auth. see Patrick, Cat.
Young, Suzanne Marie. Dedication to Free Spirit. (p. 524)
Young, T. M. My Ten Cents. Victoria Washington and Carla Watts, ed. (p. 1562)
—Playing Church. Washington, Victoria, ed. (p. 1760)
—What's Love Got to Do with It. Vickie Washington and Carla Watts, ed. (p. 2425)
Young, Thomas. How Do Hair & Nails Grow? (p. 1028)
Young, Tiffany. Amaiya & Friends See a Counselor: Coloring Book. Taylor, Tamara & Overman, Britani, eds. (p. 61)
—Amaiya & Friends See a Counselor. Taylor, Tamara & Overman, Britani, eds. (p. 61)
Young, Tim, illus. see Young, Helen Ann.
Young, Tim Blair, illus. see Young, Helen Ann.
Young, Timothy. Angry Little Puffin (p. 87)
—Creatures & Characters: Drawing Amazing Monsters, Aliens, & Other Weird Things! (p. 471)
—Do Not Open the Box (p. 570)
—I Hate Picture Books! (p. 1065)
—If You Give the Puffin a Muffin (p. 1092)
—I'm Going to Outer Space! (p. 1098)
—More Creatures & Characters: Drawing Awesomely Wild, Wacky, & Funny Animals (p. 1504)
—Shadows on My Wall (p. 1998)
—They're Coming! (p. 2219)
—Untitled (p. 2336)
Young, Timothy, illus. see Pinckney, Julia.
Young, Timothy, illus. see Viau, Nancy.
Young, Tracie & Hewett, Katie. Cool Math: 50 Fantastic Facts for Kids of All Ages. (p. 449)
Young, Virginia D. Beholding As in a Glass: A Novel (Classic Reprint) (p. 193)
Young, W. Arthur. Dictionary of the Characters & Scenes in the Stories & Poems, of Rudyard Kipling, 1886-1911 (Classic Reprint) (p. 542)
Young, Walter H. Merry Banker in the Far East (and South America) (Classic Reprint) (p. 1449)
Young, William. Mathieu Ropars: Et Cetera. (p. 1424)
—Mathieu Ropars: Et Cetera (Classic Reprint) (p. 1424)
—Tales of a School Bus. (p. 2183)
Young, Yvonne. Children's Coloring Book of the Saints & Leavened & Unleavened Bread. (p. 373)
Youngberg, Norma R. Jungle Thorn. (p. 1190)
—Singer on the Sand: The True Story of an Occurance on the Island of Great Sangir, North of the Celebes, More Than a Hundred Years Ago. (p. 2024)
Youngblood, David W., illus. see Nicol, Scott Thomas.
Youngblood, J. E. Chronicle, Vol. 25: December, 1926 (Classic Reprint) (p. 388)
Youngblood Rabalais, Rita. Seventy Times Seven. (p. 1995)
Young-Brown, Fiona. Chelsea FC (p. 365)
—Declaring War. (p. 523)

—Edward Snowden: NSA Contractor & Whistle-Blower. (p. 627)
—Fake News & Propaganda (p. 699)
—Nuclear Fusion & Fission. (p. 1628)
—Plate Tectonics. (p. 1758)
—Seeing Through Internet Hoaxes. (p. 1984)
—Universe to Scale: Similarities & Differences in Objects in Our Solar System. (p. 2333)
Youngdahl, Nancy. Remembering Joseph Chickadee. (p. 1864)
Youngdahl, Shana. As Many Nows As I Can Get. (p. 124)
Younge, Annemina De. Joy, or New Dramatical Charades for Home Performance (Classic Reprint) (p. 1184)
Younge, Cathy. Tale of Sidney Elderberry - an Ordinary Boy with Extraordinary Bowels. Taylor, Mark, illus. (p. 2179)
Younge, Leigh. Golden Grain (Classic Reprint) (p. 857)
Younger, David. Mysterious Moat Maiden: A Wandering Firefly Fairy Adventure (p. 1568)
Younger, Hudibras The. Sultan Sham, & His Seven Wives: An Historical, Romantic, Heroic Poem, in Three Cantos (Classic Reprint) (p. 2148)
Younger, Marshal, jt. auth. see Hering, Marianne.
Younger, Nathan C., illus. see Blythe, Kenton.
Younge-Ullman, Danielle. Everything Beautiful Is Not Ruined. (p. 672)
—He Must Like You. (p. 942)
—Lola Carlyle's 12-Step Romance. (p. 1340)
Younghusband, Ethel. Glimpses of East Africa & Zanzibar (Classic Reprint) (p. 842)
Younghusband, George. Soldier's Memories: In Peace & War (Classic Reprint) (p. 2057)
Younging, Greg, ed. Gatherings XV: Youth Water Anthology (p. 811)
Youngman, William Ernest. Gleanings: Western Prairies (Classic Reprint) (p. 842)
Youngmark, Matt. Robot the Robot Is Here to Help! (p. 1892)
Youngquist, Jeff, ed. see Bendis, Brian Michael.
Youngquist, Jeff, ed. see Busiek, Kurt.
Youngquist, Jeff, ed. see David, Peter.
Youngquist, Jeff, ed. see Jones, Bruce.
Youngquist, Jeff, ed. see Starlin, Jim.
Youngquist, Jeff, ed. see Straczynski, J. Michael.
Youngs, Bettie, jt. auth. see Jennifer, Youngs L.
Youngs, Clare. My First Painting & Collage Book: 35 Fun & Easy Art Projects for Children Aged 7 Plus. (p. 1545)
Youngs, Clare, jt. auth. see Woram, Catherine.
Youngs, Clare & Young, Clare. Explorar y Crear. (p. 679)
Youngs, Jennifer & Bettie, Youngs. Managing Stress, Pressure & the Ups & Downs of Life. (p. 1396)
Youngs, Kendahl Brooke. Kendahl Gets a Puppy. (p. 1209)
Youngs, Mary Fanny. When We Were Little, Children's Rhymes of Oyster Bay (Classic Reprint) (p. 2434)
Youngsuk, Ratchanee, illus. see Wing, Scarlett.
Younker, J. Marin. Bleed, Blister, Puke, & Purge: The Dirty Secrets Behind Early American Medicine. (p. 243)
Yount, Lisa. Antoine Lavoisier: Genius of Modern Chemistry. (p. 103)
—Antoine Lavoisier: Founder of Modern Chemistry. (p. 103)
—Antoni Van Leeuwenhoek: Genius Discoverer of Microscopic Life. (p. 103)
—Craig Venter. (p. 466)
—Edward Pickering & His Women Computers. (p. 627)
—Father of Anatomy: Galen & His Dissections. (p. 714)
—Luc Montagnier. (p. 1363)
—Nikola Tesla. (p. 1609)
—Rosalind Franklin. (p. 1904)
—William Harvey: Genius Discoverer of Blood Circulation. (p. 2468)
Yourell, Pam, illus. see Jones, Sandy.
Yourell, Pamela, illus. see Weber, Suzon Babitt & Yingling, Phyllis S.
Yourish, Meryl. Darkness Rising: Book One of the Catmage Chronicles. (p. 508)
Yousaf, Aisha. Adventures of Little Lam: Animals of the World. (p. 25)
Yousaf, Maryam. Fatima Al-Fihri the Founder of the World's First University: Little Muslims Inspiration Series. (p. 715)
—Huda's Hijab. (p. 1047)
—MR Blue in Rainbow Planet: A Story of Staying True to Who You Are. (p. 1518)
Yousafzai, Malala. I Am Malala: The Girl Who Stood up for Education & Was Shot by the Taliban. (p. 1059)
—I Am Malala: How One Girl Stood up for Education & Changed the World (Young Readers Edition) (p. 1059)
—I Am Malala 9c Solid Floor Display: How One Girl Stood up for Education & Changed the World (Young Readers Edition) (p. 1059)
—I Am Malala PB 9c Solid Floor Display: How One Girl Stood up for Education & Changed the World (Young Readers Edition) (p. 1059)
—Malala: My Story of Standing up for Girls' Rights. (p. 1391)
—Malala's Magic Pencil. Kerascoët, illus. (p. 1391)
—Moi, Malala. (p. 1488)
—We Are Displaced: My Journey & Stories from Refugee Girls Around the World. (p. 2389)
Yousafzai, Malala & McCormick, Patricia. I Am Malala: The Girl Who Stood up for Education & Was Shot by the Taliban. (p. 1059)
Youso, Justin, illus. see McNutt, Nan & Miller, Bruce
Youssef, Donia. Monster in Wonderland. (p. 1496)
Youssef, Jagger. Fast Fact Addition. (p. 713)
—Fast Fact Division. (p. 713)
—Fast Fact Fractions. (p. 713)
—Making Bar Graphs. (p. 1388)
—Ponds. (p. 1773)
Youssef, Marcus. Jabber. (p. 1151)
Youssef, Nyamka & Youssef, Maheeyah. Adventures of Nana & Maheeyah Pt. 1. (p. 26)
Youth, A. Friend to. Holiday Tales (Classic Reprint) (p. 988)
Youth and United Nations Global Alliance Staff, jt. auth. see Food and Agriculture Organization of the United Nations Staff.
Youth Communication. My Secret Addiction: Teens Write about Cutting. Desetta, Al, ed. (p. 1560)
—Sticks & Stones: Teens Write about Bullying. Vanderberg, Hope, ed. (p. 2118)
Youzhi, He, illus. see Ma, Zheng & Li, Zheng.
Yovanoff, Brenna. Places No One Knows. (p. 1753)
—Replacement. (p. 1866)
—Stranger Things: Runaway Max. (p. 2138)
Yoxall, J. H. Rommany Stone (Classic Reprint) (p. 1901)
Yoxall, James Henry. Alain Tanger's Wife (Classic Reprint) (p. 39)
—Beyond the Wall (Classic Reprint) (p. 212)
—Chateau Royal (Classic Reprint) (p. 362)
—Château Royal (Classic Reprint) (p. 362)
YoYo. Vermonia 7: Battle for the Turtle Realm (p. 2351)
—Warriors' Trial YoYo, illus. (p. 2381)
Yoyo Books, creator. Baby Animals. (p. 148)
—Farm Animals. (p. 709)
—Numbers. (p. 1630)
—Pets. (p. 1731)
—Vroom. (p. 2368)
—Wild Animals. (p. 2462)
Yraceburu, Maria. Connect to the Earth. (p. 441)
Yriarte, Tomas De. Literary Fables: From the Spanish of Yriarte (Classic Reprint) (p. 1309)
Yrjana, Colleen. Carry Me to Kinshasa Our Adoption Journey. Ulrich, Kelly, illus. (p. 334)
Ystridde, G. Three Dukes (Classic Reprint) (p. 2232)
Ytreeide, Arnold. Amon's Adventure: A Family Story for Easter (p. 76)
—Ishtar's Odyssey: A Storybook for Advent (p. 1138)
—Tabitha's Travels: A Family Story for Advent (p. 2175)
Yu, Bill. Desert Determination. (p. 531)
—Forest Fortitude. (p. 766)
—Island Endurance. (p. 1139)
—Set & Spike. Siragusa, Renato, illus. (p. 1993)
—Star Striker. Siragusa, Renato, illus. (p. 2103)
—Vaulting to Victory. Amormino, Paola, illus. (p. 2348)
—Winter Willpower. (p. 2476)
Yu, Bin. Government of China. (p. 873)
—Government of China. Wang, Jianwei, ed. (p. 873)
Yu, Brenna Burns. Hazel & Twig: the Birthday Fortune. Yu, Brenna Burns, illus. (p. 941)
—Hazel & Twig: the Lost Egg. Burns Yu, Brenna, illus. (p. 941)
Yu, Chao, illus. see Galat, Joan.
Yu, Erica. Disney Learning My First 1,000 Words. (p. 561)
Yu, Eun Sil. In That Autumn. (p. 1107)
Yu, Jennifer. Four Weeks, Five People. (p. 773)
—Talking Flower Garden: A Series of Ricky's Secret Friends Yu, Jennifer, illus. (p. 2187)
—Texas Animal Ranch: Ricky's Secret Friends Series Yu, Jennifer, illus. (p. 2209)
Yu, Leinil Francis. Captain America by Ta-Nehisi Coates Vol. 1: Winter in America. (p. 324)
—Phoenix Resurrection: the Return of Jean Grey. (p. 1736)
—X-Men by Jonathan Hickman Vol. 1. (p. 2515)
Yu, Leinil Francis, illus. see Aaron, Jason.
Yu, Leinil Francis, illus. see Gillen, Kieron.
Yu, Leinil Francis & Kubert, Adam. Captain America by Ta-Nehisi Coates Vol. 1. (p. 324)
Yu, Leinil Francis & Rocafort, Kenneth. Inhumans vs. X-Men. (p. 1120)
Yu, Leinil Francis, et al. Indestructible Hulk by Mark Waid: the Complete Collection. (p. 1115)
—Star Wars Vol. 2. (p. 2105)
—War of the Realms: Strikeforce. (p. 2377)
Yu, Li Qiong. New Year's Reunion: A Chinese Story. Liang, Zhu Chen, illus. (p. 1598)
—New Year's Reunion. Cheng-Liang, Zhu, illus. (p. 1598)
Yu, Mimi. Girl King. (p. 836)
Yu, Myeong-Hwa. Patterns from Nature: The Art of Klimt. Yu, Seung-Beom, illus. (p. 1706)
—Putting Faces to Names: The Art of Raphael. Kim, Yeon Joo, illus. (p. 1818)
Yu, Seung-Beom, illus. see Yu, Myeong-Hwa.
Yu, Sina. Horoscope & Bloddtype. (p. 1003)
Yu, Tae-Won, illus. see Butler, Megan Hewes & Odd Dot.
Yu, Tae-Won, jt. see Conigliaro, Phil.
Yu Wei, Wang. Mr. Cat & the Little Girl. (p. 1518)
Yu, Yi Nuo. Dream Traveler. (p. 602)
Yu, Yun. 9,999-Year-Old Mother. (p. 2561)
Yuan, A. Ikern Shards. (p. 1095)
Yuan, Yidan, illus. see Flores, Angie.
Yucula, jt. auth. see Mackall, Dandi Daley.
Yue, Emily, illus. see McDonald, Trevy A.
Yue, Gui & Farrow, Clare. Little Leap Forward: A Boy in Beijing. Cann, Helen, illus. (p. 1320)
Yue, Stephanie, illus. see Schertle, Alice.
Yue, Stephanie, illus. see Thompson, Lauren.
Yue, Stephanie, illus. see Venable, Colleen A. F.
Yue, Stephanie, illus. see Venable, Colleen Af.
Yueh-Hwa, Lin. Golden Wing: A Sociological Study of Chinese Familism (Classic Reprint) (p. 859)
Yuen, Dan. Charlie the Chopper & the Greatest Toymaker. Davis, Tim, illus. (p. 360)
Yuen, Sammy, illus. see Fisher, Catherine.
Yuen, Sammy, Jr., illus. see Decter, Ed.
Yuichi, Kimura. Hot Hot Pancakes! (p. 1006)
Yuio, illus. see Cetrix.
Yuji, Iwahara, illus. see Watson, Andi.
Yuka. Hello My Name Is Mochi Mochi Panda. (p. 951)
—Mochi Mochi Panda Sticker Activity Book. (p. 1485)
Yuki, Kaori. Alice in Murderland, Vol. 5. (p. 45)
—Demon from Afar, Vol. 5. (p. 528)
Yukihisa, Tokuda. Teacher Banana. (p. 2195)
Yukiko. Futaribeya: A Room for Two. (p. 802)
—Futaribeya Manga Volume 2 (English) (p. 802)
Yukishiro, Kira. Scarlet Soul, Vol. 1. (p. 1942)
—Scarlet Soul, Vol. 2. (p. 1942)
Yuko, Fukui. Ferris Wheel. (p. 721)
Yulia, Lushnikova, illus. see Baghdasaryan, Rouzanna.
Yuliana, Yuffie, illus. see Kenney, Alexis.
Yuliana, Yuffie, illus. see Morris, Hannah.
Yuliana, Yuffie, illus. see Rothman, Suzanne.
Yuly, Toni. Cat Nap. (p. 342)
—Early Bird. (p. 614)
—Early Bird. Yuly, Toni, illus. (p. 614)
—Jelly Bean Tree. (p. 1163)
—Night Owl. (p. 1607)
—Play Day School Day. Yuly, Toni, illus. (p. 1759)
—Thank You, Bees. Yuly, Toni, illus. (p. 2211)
Yum, Heekyoung, illus. see Tillworth, Mary.
Yum, Hyewon. Mom, It's My First Day of Kindergarten! Yum, Hyewon, illus. (p. 1490)
—Puddle. (p. 1810)
—Saturday Is Swimming Day. Yum, Hyewon, illus. (p. 1936)
—Twins' Blanket. Yum, Hyewon, illus. (p. 2306)
—Twins' Little Sister. Yum, Hyewon, illus. (p. 2306)
Yum, Hyewon, illus. see Corman, Avery.
Yum, Hyewon, illus. see Mantchev, Lisa.
Yum, Hyewon, illus. see Van, Muon Thi.
Yum, Hyewon, illus. see Watts, Jeri.
Yum, Hyewon, jt. illus. see Yum, Hyewon.
Yum, Hyewon & Yum, Hyewon. Lion Needs a Haircut. (p. 1306)
Yumeka, Sumomo. Tengu-Jin. (p. 2205)
Yumenokaori, illus. see Tomasinelli, Francesco.
Yun, Gong-Joo, illus. see Yun, Hui-Jeong.
Yun, Heshin. Bed Time Story for My Dear Friend, Atheist Paul. (p. 188)
Yun, Hui-Jeong. Welcome to the Seashore: Seashore Creatures. Yun, Gong-Joo, illus. (p. 2398)
Yun, JiUn, creator. Time & Again, Vol. 2 (p. 2243)
Yun, Ji-yeon. So Thirsty: A Water Story. Kim, Hyeon-ju, illus. (p. 2050)
Yun, Monokuro. Sign: A Novel. (p. 2016)
Yun, Yeji, illus. see Medina, Melissa & Colting, Fredrik.
Yun, Yeo-rim. Liang's Treasure: China. Cowley, Joy, ed. (p. 1283)
—Liang's Treasure: China. Choi, Yang-sook, illus. (p. 1283)
Yundt, Katherine. Thankful Tonight. (p. 2211)
Yung Dong, Venerable & Jacobs, Marjorie. Short March to Wisdom. Martin, Peter, illus. (p. 2010)
Yung Yoo, Sun, illus. see Andersen, Hans & Fowler, Gloria.
Yung-Abu, Samson. Student Exam Passport. (p. 2143)
Yunger, Joshua. Hippo & Monkey. (p. 973)
Yunger, Joshua, illus. see Homeyer, Henry.
Yunker, Kathy. Fox's Birthday Surprise. (p. 774)
Yurksaitis, Anne. Genevieve the Singing Ladybug. Yurksaitis, Stephanie, illus. (p. 815)
—Ingle Bingle. Yurksaitis, Stephanie, illus. (p. 1119)
Yurksaitis, Stephanie, illus. see Yurksaitis, Anne.
Yusagi, Aneko. Reprise of the Spear Hero Volume 01. (p. 1867)
—Rising of the Shield Hero (p. 1886)
Yuste, Patricia, illus. see Canetti, Yanitzia.
Yustiadi, A., illus. see Nelson, Richard.
Yusuf, Katharine. Grandmas Precious Memories. Martin, Marilyn & Bates, Jean, illus. (p. 878)
—Grandma's Precious Memories. Martin, Marilyn & Bates, Jean, illus. (p. 878)
Yusuke, Murata. One Punch Man (Volume 1 Of 21) (p. 1661)
Yutaka, Hara. Kaiketsu Zorori. 17 [Incredible Zorori]. (p. 1201)
—Kaiketsu Zorori. 18 [Incredible Zorori]. (p. 1201)
—Kaiketsu Zorori [Incredible Zorori]: 6. (p. 1201)
—Kaiketsu Zorori [Incredible Zorori]: 7. (p. 1201)
—Kaiketsu Zorori [Incredible Zorori]: 9. (p. 1201)
—Kaiketsu Zorori [Incredible Zorori]: 11. (p. 1201)
—Kaiketsu Zorori [Incredible Zorori]: 13. (p. 1201)
—Kaiketsu Zorori [Incredible Zorori]: 14. (p. 1201)
—Kaiketsu Zorori [Incredible Zorori]: 20. (p. 1201)
—Kaiketsu Zorori [Incredible Zorori]: 22. (p. 1201)
—Kaiketsu Zorori [Incredible Zorori]: 23. (p. 1201)
—Kaiketsu Zorori [Incredible Zorori]: 24. (p. 1201)
—Kaiketsu Zorori [Incredible Zorori]: 25. (p. 1201)
—Kaiketsu Zorori [Incredible Zorori]: 26. (p. 1201)
—Kaiketsu Zorori No Jigoku Ryoko. (p. 1201)
—Kaiketsu Zorori No Mama Daisuki. (p. 1201)
—Kaiketsu Zorori No Tengoku to Jigoku. (p. 1201)
Yuu, Kristen, jt. auth. see Random House Disney Staff.
Yuu, Shiina, illus. see Burnett, Frances Hodgson.
Yuwiler, Janice. Diabetes. (p. 537)
Yuzuru, illus. see Horowitz, Anthony & Johnston, Antony.
Yuzuru, illus. see Horowitz, Anthony.

Z

Z. Guiberson, Brenda. Greatest Dinosaur Ever. Spirin, Gennady, illus. (p. 891)
Z, Z. Business Venture in Los Angeles: Or a Christian Optimist (Classic Reprint) (p. 301)
—Business Venture in Los Angeles; or, a Christian Optimist. (p. 301)
—Drama in Dutch (Classic Reprint) (p. 596)
Zabarsky, Jessi. Witchlight. (p. 2480)
Zabarylo-Duma, Ewa, illus. see deVet, L. J.
Zabbal, Danny. Life Death & Sorcery Volume 01. (p. 1291)
Zabel, Alanna. Being Rosie. Vigovszky, Rita, illus. (p. 194)
—Only Way Out Is In. Vigovszky, Rita, illus. (p. 1664)
Zabel, Anna, illus. see James, Petra.
Zabel, Vivian. Baby Doll from Santy Claus. Brown, Diane, illus. (p. 150)
—I Like Pink. Nielson, Ginger, illus. (p. 1068)
—Louie Finds a Friend: A Louie the Duck Story. Conway, Jeanne, illus. (p. 1357)
—Wave Excitement: A Louie the Duck Story. Conway, Jeanne, illus. (p. 2386)
—Where Did Panther Go? A Panther Adventure. (p. 2435)
—Where Did Panther Go? A Panther Adventure. Salazar, Carrie, illus. (p. 2435)
Zabib, Fadwa, illus. see Al-Bandawi, Jalil Khazal.
Zabini, Eleni & Livanios, Eleni. Best Grandma in the World! Lütje, Susanne, illus. (p. 206)
—Best Grandpa in the World! Lütje, Susanne, illus. (p. 206)
Zabinski, Tanya. Peace, Love, Action! Everyday Acts of Goodness from A-Z. (p. 1709)
Zable, Stacey. City by the Lake. (p. 394)
—Our Families. (p. 1677)
Zable, Stacy. City by the Lake: Set Of 6. (p. 394)
—Four Faces in Rock: Set Of 6. (p. 772)
—Our Families: Set Of 6. (p. 1677)
Zabludoff, Marc. Basilosaurus. Bollinger, Peter, illus. (p. 170)
—Dire Wolf. Bollinger, Peter, illus. (p. 552)
—Doedicurus. Bollinger, Peter, illus. (p. 575)
—Ebox. (p. 622)
—Gastornis. Bollinger, Peter, illus. (p. 811)
—Giant Ground Sloth. Bollinger, Peter, illus. (p. 830)
—Hyracotherium. Bollinger, Peter, illus. (p. 1056)
—Kronosaurus. Bollinger, Peter, illus. (p. 1232)
—Mastodon. Bollinger, Peter, illus. (p. 1420)
—Saber-Toothed Cat. Bollinger, Peter, illus. (p. 1919)
—Woolly Mammoth. Bollinger, Peter, illus. (p. 2493)
Zaboly, Gary. Barack Obama Coloring Book. (p. 165)
—Frederick Douglass Coloring Book. (p. 782)
—Story of World War I. (p. 2135)
Zaborowski, Barbara, jt. auth. see Kohl, MaryAnn F.
Zaboski, Dave, illus. see Edelman, Ric & Edelman, Jean.
Zabower, Melissa. In the Shadow of Mr. Lincoln. (p. 1111)
Zacarias, Betania, illus. see Cortright, Celeste, et al.
Zacarias, Betania, illus. see Cortright, Celeste.
Zacarias, Betania, illus. see Isern, Susanna.
Zacarías, Karen. Chasing George Washington: A White House Adventure. (p. 362)
Zacarias, Karen. Einstein Is a Dummy. (p. 629)
Zacarías, Karen. Einstein Is a Dummy (small-Cast Musical) (p. 629)
Zacarías, Karen. Looking for Roberto Clemente. (p. 1347)
Zaccari, John. Student Body Mafia. (p. 2143)
Zacchilli, Mickey. Space Academy 123. (p. 2070)
Zach. Bedtime Nature Tails: Baby Spider. Zach, William, illus. (p. 188)
—Bedtime Nature Tails: Dumpy the Caterpillar. Zach, William, illus. (p. 188)
Zach, Jacob. Pleasant Nightmares! Schons, Margaret, illus. (p. 1762)
Zach, Nicholas. Bedtime Nature Tails: Squirmy Squid. (p. 188)
—Bedtime Nature Tails: Slithery the Snake. Zach, William, illus. (p. 188)
—Bedtime Nature Tails: Mr. Sowbug & Friends. Zach, William, illus. (p. 188)
Zach, William, illus. see Zach, Nicholas.
Zach, William, illus. see Zach.
Zachariah, Abdul-Razak. Night Is Yours. Bobo, Keturah A., illus. (p. 1606)
Zacharias, Carolyn. Katie, Kristie, & Kevin Go to Camp Meeting. (p. 1205)
Zacharias, Ingrid, ed. see Cheatam, Gail Fluker.
Zacharias, Naomi McNeil. Little Prince, Little Prince: What Will You Be? (p. 1325)
Zacharias, Ravi. Merchant & the Thief: A Folktale from India Fournier, Laure, illus. (p. 1447)
Zacharies, Mae. Farmer's Market: Use Place Value & Properties of Operations to Add. (p. 711)
Zachary, Alyson A. Earth Helpers: Count the Ways to Save Our Planet. (p. 616)
Zacher, Nichola. Marley's Dream Love. (p. 1408)
Zack, Gwendoline. Roman Road (Classic Reprint) (p. 1899)
Zack, Zack. Life Is Life: And Other Tales & Episodes (Classic Reprint) (p. 1293)
—On Trial (Classic Reprint) (p. 1656)
—Tales of Dunstable Weir (Classic Reprint) (p. 2184)
—White Cottage (Classic Reprint) (p. 2443)
Zackeo, Sonny. Secret Side to Sammy the Stowaway Sock. (p. 1979)
Zackrison, Harry. Current State of the Art Electrical & Security Engineering Design. (p. 488)
ZackZeal, tr. see Murasaki, Yukiya.
Zaczek, Alyssa. Martin Mclean, Middle School Queen. Rodil, Risa, illus. (p. 1411)
Zaczek, Iain. Édouard Manet. (p. 626)
—Georges Seurat. (p. 820)
—Leonardo Da Vinci. (p. 1267)
—Mary Cassatt. (p. 1414)
—Paul Cézanne. (p. 1707)
—Vincent Van Gogh. (p. 2359)
Zaczynski, Celine Clemens. Where's Owen Going? (p. 2440)
Zadoff, Allen. I Am the Mission. (p. 1060)
—I Am the Traitor. (p. 1060)
—I Am the Weapon. (p. 1060)
—Wild & Chance. (p. 2462)
Zados, Emilia Kate. Plush Friends: Reflections in the Time of COVID-19. (p. 1763)
Zadunajsky, Donna M. Dead Girl under the Bleachers: A Craven Fall Mystery. (p. 517)
—Help Me! Bowman Stevens, Deborah, ed. (p. 952)
—Talk to Me. Stevens, Deborah Bowman, ed. (p. 2187)
—Tayla Takes a Trip. Bicking, Judith, illus. (p. 2193)
—Tayla's Day at the Beach. Bicking, Judith, illus. (p. 2193)
—Tayla's First Day of School. Bicking, Judith, illus. (p. 2193)
Zadvorkina, Alisa. Elius & the Glimmering Ruby. (p. 636)
Zafon, Carlos. Marina. (p. 1405)
Zafon, Carlos Ruiz. Marina. (p. 1405)
—Midnight Palace. (p. 1461)
—Prince of Mist. (p. 1794)
—Watcher in the Shadows. (p. 2383)
Zafra, José. Palacio de Papel. (p. 1694)
Zafrilla, Marta. Grandpa Monty's Muddles. Brokenbrow, Jon, tr. (p. 879)
—Las camisetas no somos servilletas. Peluso, Martina, illus. (p. 1245)
—Little Chick & Mommy Cat. Brokenbrow, Jon, tr. (p. 1313)
ZAG. Miraculous: Peril in Paris. (p. 1474)
Zag Entertainment, et al. Miraculous: Tales of Ladybug & Cat Noir: Season Two - the Chosen One. (p. 1475)
—Miraculous: Tales of Ladybug & Cat Noir: Season Two - No More Evil-Doing. (p. 1475)
—Miraculous: Tales of Ladybug & Cat Noir: Season Two - Bye Bye, Little Butterfly! (p. 1475)
Zag, Jeremy. Akumatized. (p. 38)
—Claws Out. (p. 402)
—Miraculous: Tales of Ladybug & Cat Noir: Season Two - Gotcha! (p. 1475)

Z

—Miraculous: Tales of Ladybug & Cat Noir: Season Two - a New Hero Emerges. (p. 1475)
Zag, Jeremy & Rudder, Leonie de. Miraculous: Tales of Ladybug & Cat Noir: Bug Out. (p. 1475)
Zag, Jeremy, et al. Miraculous: Tales of Ladybug & Cat Noir: Santa Claws Christmas Special. (p. 1475)
—Miraculous: Tales of Ladybug & Cat Noir: Season Two - Bugheads. (p. 1475)
—Miraculous: Tales of Ladybug & Cat Noir: Season Two - Heroes' Day. (p. 1475)
—Miraculous: Tales of Ladybug & Cat Noir: Season Two - Love Compass. D'Andria, Nicole & Seaton, Bryan, eds. (p. 1475)
—Miraculous: Tales of Ladybug & Cat Noir: Season Two - Double Trouble. (p. 1475)
—Miraculous: Tales of Ladybug & Cat Noir: Season Two - Skating on Thin Ice. (p. 1475)
Zagarenski, Pamela. Henry & Leo. (p. 954)
—Whisper. (p. 2442)
Zagarenski, Pamela, illus. see American Heritage Dictionary Editors, ed.
Zagarenski, Pamela, illus. see American Heritage Dictionary Editors.
Zagarenski, Pamela, illus. see de Sève, Randall.
Zagarenski, Pamela, illus. see Lendler, Ian.
Zagarenski, Pamela, illus. see Logue, Mary.
Zagarenski, Pamela, illus. see Sidman, Joyce.
Zager, Ellen Kahan & Helfand, Harriet Cohen. And There Was Evening, & There Was Morning. Zager, Ellen Kahan, illus. (p. 83)
Zagnoli, Olimpia, illus. see Revah, Noemie.
Zagorski, Steve. River of Wisdom. (p. 1887)
Zagoskin, Michael. Tales of Three Centuries (Classic Reprint) (p. 2186)
Zagoskin, Mikhail Nikolaevich. Young Muscovite, or the Poles in Russia, Vol. 1 (Classic Reprint) (p. 2531)
Zahares, Wade. Frosty the Snowman. (p. 795)
Zahares, Wade, illus. see Shea, Pegi Deitz.
Zaharias, Terrilynn, illus. see Hoercher, Donald F.
Zaharko, Mary. Mystical Computer. (p. 1571)
Zaharopoulos, Spyros, illus. see Andersen, Sofie.
Zahed, Ramin. J. K. Rowling's Wizarding World: Movie Magic Volume Two: Curious Creatures. (p. 1150)
Zahedi, Morteza, illus. see Akbarpour, Ahmad.
Zahensky, Barbara. Diet Fads. (p. 544)
Zahensky, Kenneth. George W. Bush. (p. 819)
Zahensky, Kenneth & Egan, Tracie. Insider's Guide to Water Polo (p. 1124)
Zahensky, Kenneth & Sommers, Michael A. Snowmobiling (p. 2049)
Zahensky, Kenneth, ed. George W. Bush. (p. 819)
Zahler, Diane. Baker's Magic. Price, Mina, illus. (p. 160)
—Black Death. (p. 237)
—Marvelwood Magicians. (p. 1414)
—Princess of the Wild Swans. Gilbert, Yvonne, illus. (p. 1798)
—Sleeping Beauty's Daughters. (p. 2037)
—Thirteenth Princess. (p. 2223)
—True Princess. (p. 2294)
Zahler, Kathy A. Assads' Syria. (p. 126)
Zahler, Thom. Fluttershy & Zecora Fleecs, Tony et al, illus. (p. 753)
—Rainbow Dash & Trixie Garbowska, Agnes & Uyetake, Neil, illus. (p. 1836)
Zahler, Thom, illus. see Wharton, Ellie.
Zahler, Thom, jt. auth. see Maggs, Sam.
Zahler, Thom, jt. auth. see Rice, Christina.
Zahler, Thom & Anderson, Ted. My Little Pony: Friendship Is Magic Volume 11 Fleecs, Tony & Garbowska, Agnes, illus. (p. 1553)
Zahler, Thom, et al. My Little Pony: Friendship Is Magic Volume 15 Vol. 15. Price, Andy & Fleecs, Tony, illus. (p. 1553)
Zahler, Thomas. Twilight Sparkle Zahler, Thomas, illus. (p. 2305)
Zahler, Thomas F., et al. Pony Tales Curnow, Bobby, illus. (p. 1773)
Zahm, John Augustine. Sound & Music. (p. 2067)
Zahn, Ellsworth E. Dudley. Zahn, Ellsworth E., illus. (p. 609)
Zahn, Lisa, ed. see Walker, Jonathan.
Zahn, Mara. Adios (Classic Reprint) (p. 16)
Zahn, Peter. Let's Recycle: Represent & Solve Addition Problems. (p. 1277)
—Let's Recycle. (p. 1277)
Zahn, Timothy. Thrawn (Star Wars) (p. 2231)
Zahnd, Mark, illus. see Tait, Chris.
Zahnow, Vicki. My Little Kitten, Patch. (p. 1553)
Zahova, Borislava, illus. see Coulter, Chrys.
Zaidan, Jurji. Girl of Ghassan. Solounias, Basil, tr. (p. 836)
Zaidi, Anbara. Muslims in America Pecastaing, Camille, ed. (p. 1529)
Zaidi, Ishan. Keep Counting. (p. 1207)
Zaidi, Nadeem, illus. see Singer, Marilyn.
Zaidman, Harriet. City on Strike (p. 395)
Zaiken, Beth, illus. see Persons, W. Scott.
Zaikina, Maria, illus. see Kasbarian, Lucine.
Zail, Suzy. Playing for the Commandant. (p. 1760)
Zain, Damian, illus. see Canavan, Roger.
Zain, Damian, illus. see Catchpole, Barbara.
Zain, Damian, illus. see ED., Stephen Arterburn M. & Brotherton, M. N.
Zain, Damian, illus. see Macdonald, Fiona.
Zainab, Merchant. Stylo de Princesse Siyana. (p. 2145)
Zaitley, Abby. I Like Me & I Love Me: A Self-Love & Like Book of Affirmations for Children. Manav, Begum, illus. (p. 1067)
Zajac, Kristen. Chasing the Spirit of Service. Tucker, Julie, illus. (p. 362)
—Isabella's Aviary. Delaurent, Trisha, photos by. (p. 1138)
Zajac, Kristen J. Ebeneezer's Cousin. Houdeshell, Jennifer T., illus. (p. 622)
Zajac, Kristen K. Ebeneezer's Cousin. Houdeshell, Jennifer Thomas, illus. (p. 622)
—Primo de Ebeneezer. Houdeshell, Jennifer Thomas, illus. (p. 1793)
Zajac, Linda. Unofficial Guide to Minecraft Creative Mode. (p. 2334)
—Unofficial Guide to Minecraft Enchantments. (p. 2334)
—Unofficial Guide to Minecraft Maps. (p. 2334)
—Unofficial Guide to Minecraft Redstone. (p. 2334)
Zajceva, Ira, ed. see AZ Books Staff.
Zajonc, Taylor. Adventures of Samuel Oliver (Set) Rodriguez, Geraldine, illus. (p. 27)
—Ancient Cave. Rodriguez, Geraldine, illus. (p. 80)
—Battleship Rescue. Rodriguez, Geraldine, illus. (p. 175)
—Iron Island. Rodriguez, Geraldine, illus. (p. 1135)
—Monster of the Deep. Rodriguez, Geraldine, illus. (p. 1496)
Zajur, Michel & Zajur, Lisa. Pinata Story. (p. 1745)
Zak, Faith. Naptime Adventures: Train. (p. 1575)
—Naptime Adventures: Christmas Tree. (p. 1575)
Zak, Monica. Alex Dogboy. (p. 42)
—Niña y la Anguila. Orea, Lucia, tr. (p. 1609)
Zak, Murray, jt. auth. see Ames, Lee J.
Zakanitch, Robert Rahway, illus. see Gottfried, Maya.
Zakarin, Debra Mostow. First Fairytales. Fiore, Rob, illus. (p. 736)
—Who's Your Superstar BFF? (p. 2454)
—Who's Your Superstar Soul Mate? (p. 2454)
Zakas, Mary Jane. To the City: A Stretch2smart Book. (p. 2253)
Zaken, Debbie. Colliding Skies. (p. 416)
Zakimi, Paola, illus. see Fleming, Meg.
Zakimi, Paola, illus. see George, Kallie.
Zakimi, Paola, illus. see Silvestro, Annie.
Zakimi, Paola, illus. see Veissid, Jacqueline.
Zakimi, Paola, illus. see Voigt, Cynthia.
Zakiyev, Ilgizar, tr. see Pere, Tuula.
Zakon, Miriam Stark, jt. auth. see Blitz, Shmuel.
Zalben, Jane Breskin. Light. (p. 1298)
—Moon for Moe & Mo. Amini, Mehrdokht, illus. (p. 1501)
—Pearl's Eight Days of Chanukah: With a Story & Activity for Each Night. Zalben, Jane Breskin, illus. (p. 1711)
Zaleski, Laurie Anne. Young Person's Field Guide to Finding Lost Shipwrecks. (p. 2532)
Zalevskaya, Anastacia, illus. see Brereton, Erin.
Zalewski, Aubrey. Area 51. (p. 114)
—Bulldozers. (p. 296)
—Chadwick Boseman. (p. 353)
—Cranes. (p. 467)
—Dirt Bikes. (p. 552)
—Excavators. (p. 676)
—Front-End Loaders. (p. 795)
—Poison Dart Frogs. (p. 1767)
Zalewski, Todd, illus. see Wadsworth, Ginger.
Zalme, Ron. How to Draw Sinnoh Superstars. (p. 1041)
—Pokémon: How to Draw Unova Heroes. (p. 1768)
—Rainy Day Tales. (p. 1837)
—Sunny Day Tales. (p. 2152)
Zalme, Ron, illus. see Barbo, Maria S. & West, Tracey.
Zalme, Ron, illus. see Inches, Alison.
Zalme, Ron, illus. see Larsen, Kirsten.
Zalme, Ron, illus. see Nickel, Scott.
Zalme, Ron, illus. see Teitelbaum, Michael.
Zaloga, Steven J. Most Daring Raid of World War II: D-Day—Pointe-Du-Hoc. (p. 1508)
Zamacois, Eduardo. Their Son, the Necklace (Classic Reprint) (p. 2215)
Zaman, Farida. I Want to Be... A Gutsy Girls' ABC. (p. 1084)
Zaman, Farida, illus. see Beliveau, Kathy.
Zaman, Farida, illus. see Cho, Tina.
Zaman, Farida, illus. see Elissa, Barbara.
Zaman, Farida, illus. see Hillert, Margaret.
Zaman, Farida, illus. see Singh, Rina.
Zaman, Salma. Greedy Gertie. (p. 892)
Zamazing, Cherie. ComicQuest Adventure Island. (p. 430)
Zamazing, Cherie, illus. see Dale, Jay.
Zamazing, Cherie, illus. see Sanders, Jayneen.
Zamazing, Cherie, illus. see Webb, Christina & Lonely Planet Kids.
Zambak Çucok Publishing Staff, ed. Lost: Niloya 3. (p. 1352)
—Onion: Niloya 2. (p. 1663)
—Rainbow: Niloya 1. (p. 1836)
Zamboni, David, illus. see Alpert, Barbara.
Zamboni, David, illus. see Howell, Julie Ann.
Zamboni, David, illus. see James, Julie Ann.
Zamboni, David, illus. see Marie, Jill Jana.
Zambruk, Brett M. Every Boat. (p. 670)
Zame, Andrea. Cloud Fine! (p. 407)
Zamenhof, Robert. Adventures of Armadillo Baby & Annabelli. Baker, Sara, illus. (p. 21)
Zamir, Shamoon. Gift of the Face: Portraiture & Time in Edward S. Curtis's the North American Indian. (p. 832)
Zammit, Edward. Luna Moonies. (p. 1368)
Zammit, Jeanelle, illus. see Pace, David.
Zamor, Nehemie Djose. Adventures of Naoomi. (p. 26)
Zamora, Dulce. How to Draw the Life & Times of John Fitzgerald Kennedy. (p. 1041)
Zamora, J, illus. see Sides, Matthew.
Zamora, Marcelo, illus. see Agrimbau, Diego, et al.
Zamosky, Lisa. Agricultores de Antes y de Hoy. (p. 36)
—Lideres de Gobierno de Antes y de Hoy. (p. 1287)
—Pescadores de Antes y de Hoy. (p. 1726)
—Primera Guerra Mundial (World War I) (p. 1793)
Zamoyski, Adam. Napoleon: A Life. (p. 1574)
Zamudio, David, illus. see Howard, Brooke Leigh.
Zand, Judi. Fuzzy Bears. (p. 803)
Zander, Alex. School Track Meet: Understand Place Value. (p. 1947)
—School Track Meet. (p. 1947)
Zander, Christian, ed. see Kores, M. T.
Zane, Dory. How to Track a Leopard (p. 1045)
—How to Track a Lion (p. 1045)
—How to Track a Rhinoceros (p. 1045)
Zanella, Susy. My Magic Wand: A Magical Sound Book! (p. 1555)
—My Wild Orchestra: A Magical Sound Book! (p. 1565)
Zanelli, Michael. When God Created. (p. 2430)
Zanello, Elisabetta. Genitori: Maestri per I Vostri Bambini. (p. 815)
Zanes, Dan. Dan Zanes' House Party! A Family Roots Music Treasury. Saaf, Donald, illus. (p. 499)
Zang, Hengjing, jt. auth. see Gadient, Augustine.
Zangara, Orion, illus. see Yolen, Jane & Stemple, Adam.
Zangas, Sherri. A Is for Alabama: Roll Tide Roll. Williams, Tim, illus. (p. 1)
Zangenberg, Yasar. Eddie the Fox Goes to London: Children's Travel Book Series. (p. 624)
Zangwill, I. Bachelors Club (Classic Reprint) (p. 155)
—Children of the Ghetto, Vol. 1 of 3 (Classic Reprint) (p. 372)
—Grey Wig, Stories & Novelettes (Classic Reprint) (p. 896)
—Master: A Novel (Classic Reprint) (p. 1418)
—Old Maid's Club (Classic Reprint) (p. 1647)
—Serio-Comic Governess (Classic Reprint) (p. 1991)
—They That Walk in Darkness: Ghetto Tragedies (Classic Reprint) (p. 2219)
Zangwill, Israel. Celibates Club (Classic Reprint) (p. 350)
—Chambers's New Reciter (Classic Reprint) (p. 354)
—Children of the Ghetto: A Study of a Peculiar People (Classic Reprint) (p. 372)
—Children of the Ghetto. (p. 372)
—Children of the Ghetto, Vol. 1: Being Pictures of a Peculiar People (Classic Reprint) (p. 372)
—Ghetto Comedies (Classic Reprint) (p. 827)
—Ghetto Tragedies, Vol. 2 of 2 (Classic Reprint) (p. 827)
—Jinny the Carrier: A Folk-Comedy of Rural England (Classic Reprint) (p. 1169)
—Jinny the Carrier (Classic Reprint) (p. 1169)
—Mantle of Elijah: A Novel (Classic Reprint) (p. 1399)
—Merely Mary Ann (Classic Reprint) (p. 1448)
—Plaster Saints: A High Comedy in Three Movements (Classic Reprint) (p. 1758)
—Premier & the Painter: A Fantastic Romance (Classic Reprint) (p. 1787)
—Works of Israel Zangwill: The King of Schnorrers (Classic Reprint) (p. 2498)
Zangwill, Louis. Cleo the Magnificent, or the Muse of the Real: A Novel (Classic Reprint) (p. 403)
—Engagement of Convenience: A Novel (Classic Reprint) (p. 651)
—One's Womenkind: A Novel (Classic Reprint) (p. 1663)
Zaniewski, Lisa. Stinkin Lincoln. (p. 2119)
Zann, Tara. Wild Child: Forest's First Birthday Party. (p. 2463)
—Wild Child: Forest's First Bully. (p. 2463)
Zanni, Roger, illus. see Son, John.
Zanoni, Anne, ed. see Fiction, Digital.
Zanotti, Carolina. Mario & the Aliens. Phuong, Thai My, illus. (p. 1406)
Zanotti, Francesco Maria. Dell'arte Poetica Ragionamenti Cinque (Classic Reprint) (p. 527)
Zanotto, Lucas. Everimal. (p. 669)
—Miximal. (p. 1484)
Zaozao, Wang. Graine du Petit Moine(la) (p. 875)
Zapata, Jeff, illus. see Stine, R. L. & The Topps Company.
Zapata, Jeff, illus. see Stine, R.I.
Zaper, Monika, illus. see Pennington, Kate.
Zapico, Alfonso. James Joyce: Portrait of a Dubliner—A Graphic Biography. (p. 1157)
Zappa, Ahmet. Because I'm Your Dad. Santat, Dan, illus. (p. 186)
Zappa, Marcia. Black Holes (p. 238)
—Caves (p. 347)
—Chicago Bears (p. 367)
—Coconut Crabs (p. 411)
—Constellations (p. 443)
—Dallas Cowboys (p. 498)
—Denver Broncos (p. 529)
—Echidnas (p. 622)
—Elephant Shrews (p. 634)
—Erosion (p. 660)
—Flying Squirrels (p. 755)
—Fossil Fuels (p. 770)
—Galaxies (p. 805)
—Glaciers (p. 840)
—Green Bay Packers (p. 893)
—Indianapolis Colts (p. 1117)
—Kakapos (p. 1202)
—Minnesota Vikings (p. 1473)
—NASA (p. 1576)
—New England Patriots (p. 1593)
—New Orleans Saints (p. 1596)
—New York Jets (p. 1599)
—NFL's Greatest Teams Set 2 (p. 1601)
—Oakland Raiders (p. 1633)
—Pittsburgh Steelers (p. 1752)
—Proboscis Monkeys (p. 1803)
—Rockets & Satellites (p. 1895)
—Rocks (p. 1896)
—San Francisco 49ers (p. 1929)
—Seattle Seahawks (p. 1973)
—Space Exploration (p. 2071)
—Space Stations (p. 2072)
—Star-Nosed Moles (p. 2102)
—Thorny Devils (p. 2230)
—Universe (p. 2332)
—Washington Redskins (p. 2382)
—Water Cycle (p. 2384)
Zappa, Shana Muldoon & Zappa, Ahmet. Star Darlings Astra's Mixed-Up Mission. Disney Storybook Art Team, illus. (p. 2102)
—Star Darlings Piper's Perfect Dream. Disney Storybook Art Team, illus. (p. 2102)
Zappa, Shana Muldoon, et al. Adora Finds a Friend (p. 17)
—Astra's Mixed-Up Mission (p. 128)
—Cassie Comes Through. (p. 339)
—Leona's Unlucky Mission (p. 1267)
—Libby & the Class Election. (p. 1283)
—Piper's Perfect Dream. (p. 1749)
—Scarlet Discovers True Strength (p. 1942)
—Tessa's Lost & Found (p. 2208)
—Vega & the Fashion Disaster (p. 2348)
Zappia, Francesca. Eliza & Her Monsters. (p. 636)
—Made You Up. (p. 1375)
—Now Entering Addamsville. Zappia, Francesca, illus. (p. 1627)
Zappitella, Katie & International, Bible Visuals. When I Am Weak: The Story of One of America's Founding Fathers. (p. 2430)
Zappitello, Beth, jt. auth. see Lewis, J. Patrick.
Zapple, Elias. Amo a Mi Papá. Terán, Camila Ayala, tr. (p. 76)
—Amo a MIS Mamás. Terán, Camila Ayala, tr. (p. 76)
—Banhado Em Sangue! Marques Vollkopf, Karla, tr. (p. 163)
—Big Fangs. Cabalu, Reimarie, illus. (p. 220)
—Blood, Blood Everywhere. Cabalu, Reimarie, illus. (p. 245)
—Christmas Carol... Slimed: American-English Edition. Cabalu, Reimarie, illus. (p. 384)
—Christmas Carol... Slimed. Cabalu, Reimarie, illus. (p. 384)
—Cyril the Dragon. Cabalu, Reimarie, illus. (p. 493)
—Dead Again. Cabalu, Reimarie, illus. (p. 517)
—Elias Zapple's Book of Slugs: American-English Edition. Salem, Maru & Cabalu, Reimarie, illus. (p. 635)
—Elias Zapple's Book of Slugs. Salem, Maru & Cabalu, Reimarie, illus. (p. 635)
—Elias Zapple's Book of Slugs Coloring Book. Cabalu, Reimarie, illus. (p. 635)
—Elias Zapple's Book of Slugs Colouring Book. Cabalu, Reimarie, illus. (p. 635)
—Elias Zapple's Rhymes from the Cabbage Patch: American-English Edition. Misirlou, Ilaeira, illus. (p. 635)
—Elias Zapple's Rhymes from the Cabbage Patch. Misirlou, Ilaeira, illus. (p. 635)
—Fangless. Cabalu, Reimarie, illus. (p. 706)
—Fillmore the Dragon. Cheshenko, Valentina, illus. (p. 726)
—I Love God. Etorma, Crisanto, illus. (p. 1069)
—I Love My Big Brother. Etorma, Crisanto, illus. (p. 1070)
—I Love My Daddy. Basova, Xenia, illus. (p. 1071)
—I Love My Mama. Ero, Aguilar, illus. (p. 1071)
—I Love My Mamas. Etorma, Crisanto, illus. (p. 1071)
—J'aime Dieu. Kalbfeis, Blanche, tr. (p. 1155)
—J'aime Ma Maman. Blanchet, Jean-François, tr. (p. 1155)
—J'aime Mon Papa. Blanchet, Jean-François, tr. (p. 1155)
—Jellybean the Dragon. Misirlou, Ilaeira, illus. (p. 1163)
—King Tingaling Painting. (p. 1221)
—Mysterious Corridor. (p. 1567)
—Mysterious Corridor. Beavan, Elliott, illus. (p. 1567)
—NICU - the Littlest Vampire: American-English Edition. Cabalu, Reimarie, illus. (p. 1604)
—NICU - the Littlest Vampire. Cabalu, Reimarie, illus. (p. 1604)
—Return of the Nibbles. Cabalu, Reimarie, illus. (p. 1871)
—Sin Colmillos. Manzano, Maria J., tr. (p. 2023)
—Trixy & the Troublesome Egg: Trixy & Friends. Tatic, Mihailo, illus. (p. 2290)
Zapple, Elias, illus. see Terán, Camila Ayala, tr.
Zapple, Elias & Teran. Amo a Dios. Etorma, Crisanto, illus. (p. 76)
Zappy, Erica, ed. see Rey, H. A.
Zarate, Jesus, illus. see Weill, Cynthia.
Zarb, Mike, illus. see Gold, Robin.
Zarb, Mike, illus. see Harmer, Wendy.
Zarbo, Ban. Kamo: Pact with the Spirit World Manga Volume 2 (English) (p. 1202)
—Pact with the Spirit World. (p. 1691)
Zarcinas, Scott. Golden Chalice: A Pilgrim's Chronicle. (p. 857)
Zarco Villarosa, Jorge, illus. see Abad Ros, Irena.
Zarcone, Marley, illus. see Castellucci, Cecil.
Zardes, Cassandra. Cherokee. (p. 365)
Zareba, Lukasz, illus. see Lee, Stephi.
Zarema, Hanieva, tr. see Pere, Tuula.
Zarifian, J. A. Once upon a Mouse. (p. 1657)
Zarin, Cynthia. Saints among the Animals. Gore, Leonid, illus. (p. 1924)
Zaring, Laurie. Who Could You Be at the Zoo? Barlup, Jessica, illus. (p. 2447)
Zarins, Kim. Sometimes We Tell the Truth. (p. 2061)
Zark. Beyond the Evergreens: A Story of a Boy, His Dog, & Their Final Adventure. Gafni, Gabriella, ed. (p. 212)
Zark, Jenna. Fool's Errand. (p. 761)
Zaro, Zoraida. Breve Gatopedia Ilustrada. (p. 279)
Zarr, Sara. Gem & Dixie. (p. 813)
—Goodbye from Nowhere. (p. 866)
—How to Save a Life. (p. 1044)
—Lucy Variations. (p. 1366)
—Sweethearts. (p. 2169)
Zarr, Sara & Altebrando, Tara. Roomies. (p. 1903)
Zarriello, Nancy. Free to Be Me. Illustrations, Blueberry, illus. (p. 782)
Zarrin, Laura. Wheels on the Bus. (p. 2428)
Zarrin, Laura, illus. see Alexander, Heather.
Zarrin, Laura, illus. see Craddock, Petra.
Zarrin, Laura, illus. see Manushkin, Fran.
Zarrin, Laura, illus. see Pope, Elodie.
Zarrin, Laura, jt. auth. see Manushkin, Fran.
Zaslavsky, Claudia. Number Sense & Nonsense: Games, Puzzles, & Problems for Building Creative Math Confidence. (p. 1629)
Zastrow, Gavin. Marshland of His Own. (p. 1409)
Zater, Valeria, illus. see Arlan, Joni.
Zau, illus. see Bourdier, Emmanuel.
Zaü, illus. see Elschner, Géraldine.
Zaugg, Sandra L. Secret of the Desert Lights: A Story about Following God's Laws. (p. 1977)
Zaun, Paris, illus. see Zaun, Sarah.
Zaun, Sarah. My Name Is Destiny. Zaun, Sarah & Zaun, Paris, illus. (p. 1557)
Zavala Fernandez, Citlali. Choco. (p. 380)
Zavala, Paola, illus. see Bair, Christopher.
Zavyalov, Diana. Winter Riddles. (p. 2476)
Zayarny, Jack. Amphibians. (p. 77)
—Camouflage. (p. 315)
—Change & Reform: 1814-1860. (p. 355)
—Civil War: 1856-1865. (p. 396)
—Garbage Collector. (p. 808)
—Humpback Whales. (p. 1051)
—Metamorphosis. (p. 1452)
—Reptiles. (p. 1867)
—Symbiosis. (p. 2173)
Zaya-Ruzo, Anatoly. Fourth Dimension. (p. 773)
Zayas, Alejandro. Worm's Dream. (p. 2508)
Zayas, Eddie. Charli Comet Book I. (p. 359)

Z

—Show-How Guides: Paper Airplanes: The 11 Essential Planes Everyone Should Know! Zoo, Keith, illus. (p. 2012)
—Tiny World: Pins! Zoo, Keith, illus. (p. 2250)
Zoo, La. Activity: Face. (p. 13)
—Activity: Foot. (p. 13)
—Activity: Hand. (p. 13)
ZOO, La. Colors! (p. 426)
—Hidden Animals! (p. 965)
—Holes! A Coloring Book. Oku, Makiko, tr. (p. 987)
—Imagine That! A Coloring Book for Growing Young Minds. (p. 1100)
—Incredible Stickers! An Activity Book with Stickers. Miyakoshi, Junko, tr. (p. 1114)
—Squiggles! A Drawing Book. Oku, Makiko, tr. (p. 2094)
—Stickers! An Activity Book with Stickers. Miyakoshi, Junko, tr. (p. 2118)
ZOO, La, jt. auth. see Lazoo Publishing Staff.
Zook Jr, Aaron M. Isle of Intrigue. (p. 1140)
Zook, Melinda. L-E-t-t-e-r-s. (p. 1234)
Zoological Record Association (London, E., jt. creator see Zoological Society of London.
Zora, Subhi. House of Wisdom: Level 11. (p. 1023)
Zorat, Maurizio, illus. see Kadohata, Cynthia.
Zorka, Shawna. Carter Goes to a Funeral Reyes, Arlene, illus. (p. 335)
Zorn, Claire. Protected. (p. 1807)
—Sky So Heavy. (p. 2034)
Zorn, Frederick J. Stop That Wagon, Please! The Amazing Dessert Chase. Pathak, Varun, illus. (p. 2122)
Zoromski, Ariel, illus. see Strojny, Shelley.
Zoromski, Leia, illus. see Strojny, Shelley.
Zorrilla, Jeff, tr. see Gibert, Jimena & Cornum, Lindsey, eds.
Zorrilla, Jose. Don Juan Tenorio. (p. 581)
—Don Juan Tenorio. para Jovenes. (p. 581)
Zorro, Sephone. Growing Up: Home & School. Baxter, Rhea, illus. (p. 900)
—Welcome. (p. 2397)
Zortman, Bruce. Eight Little Candles Plus: A Hanukkah Tale. (p. 629)
Zorvoc, Karen, illus. see 4 Paws Games and Publishing, ed.
Zorzi, Gina, jt. auth. see Johnson, Gee.
Zorzi, Gina, jt. auth. see Taylor, Trace.
Zorzi, Gina & Cline, Gina. Lion Pride. Dibble, Traci, illus. (p. 1306)
Zorzi, Gina & Dibble, Traci. Lion Pride. (p. 1306)
Zorzi, Gina & Sánchez, Lucía M. Bosques: This Is a Forest. (p. 263)
Zorzi, Gina & Sanchez, Lucia M. Bosques (This Is a Forest) (p. 263)
Zorzi, Gina & Sánchez, Lucía M. Desiertos: This Is a Desert. (p. 532)
Zorzi, Gina & Sanchez, Lucia M. Desiertos (This Is a Desert) (p. 532)
—OcéAnos: This Is an Ocean. (p. 1636)
—Praderas: This Is a Prairie. (p. 1784)
Zosienka. Moon Keeper. Zosienka, illus. (p. 1501)
Zoss, Lori. Bed for Fred. (p. 187)
Zoto, Gabriel Q., illus. see Zoto, Sandra D. C.
Zoto, Maximus B., illus. see Zoto, Sandra D. C.
Zoto, Sandra D. C. Gauntlet. Zoto, Maximus B. & Zoto, Gabriel Q., illus. (p. 812)
Zott, Lynn M., ed. see Greenhaven Press Editors.
Zott, Lynn M. & Haerens, Margaret, eds. US Airport Security. (p. 2340)
Zottoli, Catherine. Manet, Vol. 8: February, 1935 (Classic Reprint) (p. 1397)
Zotz, Mary Kay. Grandma's Wishes of Love from Heaven. (p. 879)
Zou, Bridgette. Norman & the Nom Nom Factory. Zou, Bridgette, illus. (p. 1620)
Zouaghi, Alexandre. Auberge des Nes(l') (p. 135)
Zouev, Alexander & Zouev, Roman. Good University Guide for IB Students UK Edition 2019. (p. 866)
Zouev, Roman, jt. auth. see Zouev, Alexander.
Zourelias, Diana. All Around Chicago Mini Coloring Book. (p. 51)
—Barrel of Monkeys & Other Animal Groups. (p. 167)
—Build a Giant Poster Coloring Book—United States Map. (p. 293)
—Celebrity Parents, Celebrity Kids Paper Dolls. (p. 350)
—Find & Color the Impostor Activity Book. (p. 727)
—First Ladies Fascinating Facts. (p. 737)
—Fun Facts about Everyday Inventions. (p. 798)
—Laugh Out Loud Letters for Boys: The Easy Way to Create Fast & Funny Notes! (p. 1252)
—Laugh Out Loud Letters for Girls! The Easy Way to Create Fast & Funny Notes! (p. 1252)
—Monster Bugs. (p. 1495)
—Monster Reptiles: A Close-Up Coloring Book. (p. 1497)
—My Awesome Superhero Journal: A Fun Fill-In Book for Kids. (p. 1531)
—My Cool Car Trip Journal: A Fun Fill-In Book for Kids. (p. 1536)
—My Fantastic Vacation Journal: A Fun Fill-In Book for Kids. (p. 1538)
—My Merry Christmas Journal: A Fun Fill-In Book for Kids. (p. 1555)
—My Royal Princess Journal: A Fun Fill-In Book for Kids. (p. 1560)
—Presidential Pets Coloring Book. (p. 1789)
—SPARK Adorable Animals Find It! Color It! (p. 2074)
—SPARK Garden Daze Find It! Color It! (p. 2074)
—SPARK Silly Sea Life Find It! Color It! (p. 2075)
—SPARK Things That Go Find It! Color It! (p. 2075)
—SPARK U. S. A. Fun Find It! Color It! (p. 2075)
—SPARK Very Silly Animals Coloring Book. (p. 2075)
—Spot It! Clever & Crazy Picture Puzzles. (p. 2090)
—Weird & Wacky Jobs. (p. 2396)
Zourelias, Diana & Coloring Books Staff. Monster Sea Creatures. (p. 1497)
Zourelias, Diana, et al. Mix & Match PRINCESSES. (p. 1484)
Zowada, Timmy, illus. see Day, Sophia & Pearson, Kayla.
Zowada, Timothy, illus. see Day, Sophia & Pearson, Kayla.
Zowada, Timothy, illus. see Day, Sophia, et al.
Zraick, Robert, illus. see Moor-Doucette, Saba.
Zschock, Martha. Aloha, Hawaii! (p. 57)
—Hello, Adirondacks! (p. 950)
—Hello, Airplane! (p. 950)
—Hello, America! (p. 950)
—Hello, Brooklyn! (p. 950)
—Hello, California! (p. 950)
—Hello, Cape Cod! (p. 950)
—Hello, Chicago! (p. 950)
—Hello, Dinosaurs! (p. 950)
—Hello, Florida! (p. 950)
—Hello, National Parks! (p. 951)
—Hello, New Orleans! (p. 951)
—Hello, New York City! (p. 951)
—Hello, Paris! (p. 951)
—Hello, Philadelphia! (p. 951)
—Hello, Puerto Rico! (p. 951)
—Hello, Reading! (p. 951)
—Hello, Rhode Island! (p. 951)
—Hello, Rockies! (p. 951)
—Hello, San Francisco! (p. 951)
—Hello, Seashore! (p. 951)
—Hello, Smokies! (p. 951)
—Hello, Snow! (p. 951)
—Hello, St. Louis! (p. 952)
—Hello, Yellowstone! (p. 952)
Zschock, Martha Day. Hello Congress! (p. 950)
—Hello, Grandma! (p. 951)
—Scratch & Sketch Sparkle. (p. 1963)
Zschock, Martha Day, illus. see Conlon, Mara.
Zschock, Martha Day, illus. see Gandolfi, Claudine.
Zschock, Martha Day, illus. see Levy, Talia.
Zschock, Martha Day, illus. see Nemmers, Lee.
Zschock, Martha Day, illus. see Paulding, Barbara.
Zschock, Martha Day, illus. see Tunnell, Amber.
Zschock, Martha Day, creator. Hello, Alaska! (p. 950)
—Hello, Aquarium! (p. 950)
—Hello, Arizona! (p. 950)
—Hello, Baby Brother! (p. 950)
—Hello, Baby Sister! (p. 950)
—Hello, Farm! (p. 950)
—Hello, Fourth of July! (p. 950)
—Hello, Grandpa! (p. 951)
—Hello, Lake! (p. 951)
—Hello, Las Vegas! (p. 951)
—Hello, Los Angeles! (p. 951)
—Hello, Mountain! (p. 951)
—Hello, Nashville! (p. 951)
—Hello, New Hampshire! (p. 951)
—Hello, New Jersey! (p. 951)
—Hello, New Mexico! (p. 951)
—Hello, Night Sky! (p. 951)
—Hello, Orlando! (p. 951)
—Hello, Portland! (p. 951)
—Hello, South Carolina! (p. 951)
—Hello, Utah! (p. 952)
—Hello, Virginia! (p. 952)
—Hello, Wisconsin! (p. 952)
—Hello, Wyoming! (p. 952)
—Hello, Zion! (p. 952)
—Hello, Zoo! (p. 952)
Zschokke, Heinrich. Bravo of Venice: A Romance (Classic Reprint) (p. 277)
—Incidents of Social Life amid the European Alps: Translated from the German (Classic Reprint) (p. 1113)
—Labour Stands on Golden Feet: Or, the Life of a Foreign Workman; a Holiday Story for Sensible Apprentices, Journeymen, & Masters (Classic Reprint) (p. 1235)
—Princess of Brunswick-Wolfenbuttel & Other Tales (Classic Reprint) (p. 1798)
—Tales (Classic Reprint) (p. 2181)
Zsembery, Alice M. Real Kids, Real Play: 150+ Activities to Do Around the Home Using Household Items. (p. 1849)
Zsikai-Spiker, Lisa Marie. Buster & Snoopy. Schimmelman, Alex, illus. (p. 301)
Zub, Jim. Advent of Ultron #1. Choi, Woo Bin et al, illus. (p. 18)
—Advent of Ultron #2. Choi, Woo Bin et al, illus. (p. 18)
—Advent of Ultron #3. Choi, Woo Bin et al, illus. (p. 18)
—Advent of Ultron #4. Choi, Woo Bin et al, illus. (p. 18)
—Advent of Ultron #5. Choi, Woo Bin et al, illus. (p. 18)
—Advent of Ultron #6. Choi, Woo Bin et al, illus. (p. 18)
—Assembling the Avengers #1. (p. 127)
—Avengers K Choi, Woo Bin et al, illus. (p. 142)
—Avengers vs. Ultron #1. Choi, Woo Bin et al, illus. (p. 142)
—Disney Kingdoms: Figment Set 2 (Set) Bachs, Ramon & Beaulieu, Jean-François, illus. (p. 561)
—Figment: Journey into Imagination. Andrade, Filipe, illus. (p. 726)
—Figment: Journey into Imagination Andrade, Filipe et al, illus. (p. 726)
—Figment: Journey into Imagination. Andrade, Filipe & Christopher, John Tyler, illus. (p. 726)
—Figment. Andrade, Filipe et al, illus. (p. 726)
—Figment 2: the Legacy of Imagination: Volume 1. Bachs, Ramon & Beaulieu, Jean-François, illus. (p. 726)
—Wayward Deluxe Book 3. (p. 2388)
Zubal, Lynn. Sonoran Desert Frog. Zubal, Lynn, illus. (p. 2064)
Zubarev, Misha. Magnificent Nine. Cohen, Dov Ber, illus. (p. 1382)
Zubek, Adeline. Counting Lions. (p. 460)
—Fast or Slow? (p. 713)
—Foxes in the Dark. (p. 774)
—Front or Back? (p. 795)
—Heavy or Light? (p. 947)
Zubiat, Gabriel, illus. see González Reyes, Amaury.
Zubizarreta, Gabriel M., jt. auth. see Flor Ada, Alma.
Zubizarreta, Gabriel M. & Ada, Alma Flor. Con Cariño, Amalia (Love, Amalia) (p. 437)
—Dancing Home. (p. 500)
—Love, Amalia. (p. 1358)
Zubizarreta, Patxi. Maravilloso Viaje de Xan Tezin. (p. 1402)
Zubizarreta, Rosalma, jt. tr. see Flor Ada, Alma.
Zubizarreta, Rosalma, tr. see Rohmer, Harriet.
Zubizarreta, Rosalma, et al. Woman Who Outshone the Sun (la mujer que brillaba aun mas que el Sol) Olivera, Fernando, illus. (p. 2486)
Zuboff, Sara. Dear Boy, (p. 520)
—Everyday Super Hero. (p. 672)
—Everyday Super Hero Activity & Coloring Book. (p. 672)
Zubro, Mark. Gentle. (p. 816)
Zuccante, Luigi. Lucia Mène L'Enquête. Andre, Frederic, illus. (p. 1363)
Zucchelli-Romer, Claire. TouchThinkLearn: Wiggles: (Childrens Books Ages 1-3, Interactive Books for Toddlers, Board Books for Toddlers) (p. 2268)
Zuccoli, Luciano. Light-Fingered Gentry (Classic Reprint) (p. 1298)
Zuchold, Ernst Amandus. Bibliotheca Chemica: Verzeichniss der Auf Dem Gebiete der Reinen, Pharmaceutischen, Physiologischen und Technischen Chemie in Den Jahren 1840 Bis Mitte 1858 in Deutschland und Im Auslande Erschienenen Schriften (Classic Reprint) (p. 215)
Zuchora-Walske, Christine. Amazing Human Body. (p. 65)
—Andrew Jackson's Presidency. (p. 84)
—Antibiotics (p. 102)
—Bermuda Triangle (p. 203)
—Bionic Eyes. (p. 229)
—Chad in Pictures. (p. 353)
—Dust Bowl: A History Perspectives Book. (p. 610)
—Energy in the Real World. (p. 651)
—Engineering the Pyramids of Giza. (p. 652)
—Honduras in Pictures. (p. 998)
—How Can I Be a Good Digital Citizen? (p. 1026)
—Key Discoveries in Earth & Space Science. (p. 1210)
—Key Discoveries in Engineering & Design. (p. 1210)
—Killer Whales: Built for the Hunt. (p. 1217)
—Let's Look at Prairie Dogs. (p. 1275)
—Mountain Lions (p. 1513)
—Poland (p. 1769)
—Pythons (p. 1819)
—Robots at Home. (p. 1893)
—Science Lab: The Transfer of Energy. (p. 1955)
—Self-Driving Cars. (p. 1987)
—Setters: Loyal Hunting Companions (p. 1993)
—Solar Energy (p. 2055)
—That Bull Is Seeing Red! Science's Biggest Mistakes about Animals & Plants. (p. 2212)
—Transcontinental Railroad (p. 2277)
—Tuskegee Airmen (p. 2301)
—Weather Robots. (p. 2394)
—We're the Center of the Universe! Science's Biggest Mistakes about Astronomy & Physics. (p. 2400)
—Working in Math. (p. 2496)
—Your Mission to Mercury (p. 2534)
—Your Mission to Uranus (p. 2534)
—Your Mission to Venus (p. 2534)
Zuchora-Walske, Christine, jt. auth. see Harris, Duchess.
Zuchora-Walske, Christine & Burroughs, Scott. Your Mission on Earth (p. 2534)
Zucker, Bonnie. Something Very Sad Happened: A Toddler's Guide to Understanding Death. Fleming, Kim, illus. (p. 2061)
—Take Control of OCD: A Kid's Guide to Conquering Anxiety & Managing OCD. (p. 2177)
Zucker, Jonny. Lanterns & Firecrackers: A Chinese New Year Story. Barger Cohen, Jan, illus. (p. 1244)
—Mission 3: In Deep. Woodman, Ned, illus. (p. 1481)
—Mission 3: in Deep. Woodman, Ned, illus. (p. 1481)
—Mission 5: Subzero. Woodman, Ned, illus. (p. 1481)
—Mission 6: Short Circuit. Woodman, Ned, illus. (p. 1481)
—Stunt Girl. (p. 2145)
Zuckerberg, J. R., illus. see G., Mady.
Zuckerberg, Randi. Dot. Berger, Joe, illus. (p. 587)
Zuckerkandl, Emil, jt. auth. see Heitzmann, Carl.
Zuckerman, Andrew. Creature ABC. (p. 471)
Zuckerman, Andrew, photos by. Creature Baby Animals. (p. 471)
—Creature Colors. (p. 471)
—Creature Sounds. (p. 471)
Zuckerman, Gregory & Zuckerman, Elijah. Rising Above: How 11 Athletes Overcame Challenges in Their Youth to Become Stars. (p. 1886)
Zuckerman, Gregory & Zuckerman, Gabriel. Rising above: Inspiring Women in Sports. (p. 1886)
Zuckerman, Gregory, et al. Rising Above: Inspiring Women in Sports. (p. 1886)
—Rising Above: How 11 Athletes Overcame Challenges in Their Youth to Become Stars. (p. 1886)
Zuckerman, Linda. Day Is Waiting Freeman, Don, illus. (p. 513)
Zuehlke, Jeffrey. Alex Rodriguez (Revised Edition) (p. 42)
—Dirk Nowitzki (Revised Edition) (p. 552)
—Earth. (p. 615)
—Grand Canyon. (p. 876)
—Helicopters on the Move. (p. 950)
—Joe Mauer (Revised Edition) (p. 1171)
—Joe Mauer, 2nd Edition. (p. 1171)
—Kevin Garnett (Revised Edition) (p. 1210)
—Michael Phelps (Revised Edition) (p. 1458)
—Motorcycle Road Racing. (p. 1512)
—Pickup Trucks on the Move. (p. 1739)
—Rally Cars. (p. 1838)
Zufelt, Justin, jt. auth. see Gifford, Stephanie.
Zug, Mark, illus. see Haven, Paul.
Zug, Mark, illus. see Sage, Angie.
Zuggo, Violeta & Zuggo, Jutka. Story Time for Kids with Nip by the English Sisters: The Little Grasshopper & the Big Ball of Dung. Kecskés, Anna, illus. (p. 2135)
Zuill, Andrea. Business Pig. (p. 301)
—Dance Is for Everyone. (p. 499)
—Sweety. (p. 2169)
—Wolf Camp. Zuill, Andrea, illus. (p. 2483)
Zuill, Andrea, illus. see Buchet, Nelly.
Zuk, Valentina, ed. see AZ Books Staff.
Zukowski, A. Courting Light. (p. 463)
Zulauf, J. W. Kingdom in Chains. (p. 1221)
Zulewski, Timothy, illus. see Doyle, V. L. & Rohm, Robert.
Zuljevic, Vida. I Was Almost Five. (p. 1085)
Zulkifli, Azhari, illus. see Cara, Anwar.
Zulkifli, Azhari, illus. see D'Oyen, Fatima.
Zulli, Michael, et al. Spider-Man: Webspinners - the Complete Collection. (p. 2080)
Zullo, Allan. 10 True Tales: Young Civil Rights Heroes. (p. 2550)
—Bad Pets: On the Loose! (p. 158)
—Bad Pets Save Christmas! (p. 158)
—Christmas Miracle Pets: Animals Who Saved the Day. (p. 386)
—Fact or Fake? Test Your Smarts! (p. 694)
—Heroes of 9/11. (p. 962)
—Heroes of Hurricane Katrina. (p. 962)
—Miracle Pets: True Tales of Courage & Survival. (p. 1474)
—Surviving Sharks. (p. 2165)
—Titanic: Young Survivors. (p. 2251)
—Titanic Young Survivors. (p. 2251)
—Vietnam War Heroes. (p. 2357)
—War Heroes: Voices from Iraq. (p. 2376)
—World War I Heroes. (p. 2505)
—Worlds Dumbest Crooks 2: True Tales of Goofs, Giggles & Gaffes. (p. 2507)
—Young Survivors of the Holocaust. (p. 2532)
Zullo, Germano. Little Bird. Albertine, illus. (p. 1311)
Zumbusch, Amelie von. Ancient Roman Culture. (p. 82)
—Ancient Roman Daily Life. (p. 82)
—Ancient Roman Economy. (p. 82)
—Ancient Roman Geography. (p. 82)
—Ancient Roman Government. (p. 82)
—Ancient Roman Technology. (p. 82)
—Barack Obama: Man of Destiny. (p. 165)
—Barack Obama's Family Tree: Roots of Achievement. (p. 165)
—First Family: The Obamas in the White House. (p. 736)
—Making History: The Obamas (p. 1389)
—Michelle Obama: Our First Lady. (p. 1458)
—True Story of the American Flag. (p. 2295)
—What Really Happened? (p. 2419)
Zumbusch, Amelie Von & Von Zumbusch, Amelie. Ancient Roman Geography. (p. 82)
—Ancient Roman Technology. (p. 82)
Zummo, Judy. Henry & Hinky: Meet the Little Pirates. (p. 954)
Zungu Oshin, Glenrose Nonhlala, tr. see Umar, Mohammed.
Zuniga, Elisabeth. Egg for Bunny. (p. 628)
Zunon, Elizabeth. Grandpa Cacao: A Tale of Chocolate, from Farm to Family. (p. 879)
Zunon, Elizabeth, illus. see Alonso, Harriet Hyman.
Zunon, Elizabeth, illus. see Carolan, Joanna & Carolan, Terry.
Zunon, Elizabeth, illus. see Grimes, Nikki.
Zunon, Elizabeth, illus. see Harvey, Jeanne Walker.
Zunon, Elizabeth, illus. see Kamkwamba, William & Mealer, Bryan.
Zunon, Elizabeth, illus. see Maclachlan, Patricia.
Zunon, Elizabeth, illus. see Nelson, Vaunda Micheaux.
Zunon, Elizabeth, illus. see Paul, Miranda & Paul, Baptiste.
Zunon, Elizabeth, illus. see Paul, Miranda.
Zunon, Elizabeth, illus. see Rose, Carolyn.
Zunon, Elizabeth, illus. see Weatherford, Carole Boston.
Zupan, Katherine A. a. Young Fashionista. (p. 2530)
Zuppardi, Sam. Jack's Worry. Zuppardi, Sam, illus. (p. 1153)
—Nowhere Box. Zuppardi, Sam, illus. (p. 1628)
—Things to Do with Dad. (p. 2221)
—Things to Do with Dad. Zuppardi, Sam, illus. (p. 2221)
Zuppardi, Sam, illus. see Elliott, David.
Zuppardi, Sam, illus. see McAlpine, Gordon.
Zupsic, Kelly. Mrs. Sneeze & the Three Legged Goat. (p. 1523)
Zur Muehlen, Nersel. Monkey in the Mirror. Sanchez, Sara, illus. (p. 1493)
Zuravicky, Orli. Amazing Animals: Multiplying Multidigit Numbers by a One-Digit Number with Regrouping. (p. 63)
—C Is for City: An Alphabet Book. Castellano, Giuseppe, illus. (p. 306)
—Color for Sketch: A Book about Colors. Castellano, Giuseppe, illus. (p. 420)
—Drama. (p. 596)
—Exploring Pyramids Around the World: Making Models of Geometric Solids. (p. 682)
—Galloping Book / Trotar. (p. 806)
—Happily Ever Afterlife #2: Crushed. (p. 919)
—Map Math: Learning about Latitude & Longitude Using Coordinate Systems. (p. 1400)
—School Spirit. (p. 1947)
—Skipping Book / Avanzar a Saltitos. (p. 2032)
Zurawski, Jackie. Dream a Dream. (p. 601)
Zuric, Vule. Orlovi Ponovo Lete: Nove Price o Magarecim Godinama. (p. 1672)
Zurlo, Tony. United States Congress & the Legislative Branch: How the Senate & House of Representatives Create Our Laws. (p. 2331)
Zuroweste, Rick. Christmas Comes to Prairie Dog Village: A Christmas Adventure Story. (p. 385)
Zusak, Markus. Book Thief. (p. 260)
—Book Thief (Anniversary Edition) (p. 260)
—Cartas Cruzadas. (p. 335)
—I Am the Messenger. (p. 1060)
—Ladrona de Libros. (p. 1236)
—Puente de Clay / Bridge of Clay. (p. 1811)
Zuschlag, Chris. Star Fairy. (p. 2102)
Zusman, Evelyn. Passover Parrot, 2nd Edition. Brooker, Kyrsten, illus. (p. 1703)
Zuss, X. Q. Pinkled Frinft: Don't Wrinkle Your Nose When You Pronounce It a Strange Story of Mystery & Wrath (Classic Reprint) (p. 1747)
Zutautas, Susan. Mr. Beaver Plans a Party: Illustrated Children's Book. Larson, Sannel, illus. (p. 1517)
Zvorc, Karen, illus. see Hathiramani, Susan.
Zvorykin, Boris, illus. see Ransome, Arthur.
Zwaardemaker, Hendrik. Die Physiologie des Geruchs (Classic Reprint) (p. 544)
Zwald, John & DesRochers, Diane O. Mahmoud Meets Moses. Zwald, John, illus. (p. 1382)
Zweber, Rhonda. Mommy's Hats. (p. 1491)

Numeric

ILLUSTRATOR INDEX

Volume 3

A

A

A and J Studios Staff. Dora's Valentine Adventure. Ricci, Christine. 2006. (Dora the Explorer Ser.). (ENG.). 14p. (J). (gr. -1-k). bds. 6.99 *(978-1-4169-1754-0(3)*, Simon Spotlight/Nickelodeon) Simon Spotlight/Nickelodeon.

—Navidad Estelar de Dora. Ricci, Christine. Ziegler, Argentina Palacios, tr. 2005. (Dora the Explorer Ser.). (SPA.). 24p. (J). pap. 3.99 *(978-1-4169-1183-8(9)*, Libros Para Ninos) Libros Para Ninos.

A, Eugenia. Alice's Adventures in Wonderland (Illustrated) Carroll, Lewis. 2018. (ENG.). 66p. (J). pap. 7.00 *(978-1-7293-6813-8(1))* Independently Published.

A Lee, Michael & Lee, Jessica. Not Gonna Write Poems: A Poetry Book for All the Non-Poets. A Lee, Michael. 2019. (ENG.). 168p. (J). (gr. k-6). pap. ***(978-1-927538-44-9(0)***, Agora Cosmopolitan, The) Agora Publishing Consortium.

A Michael, Shumate. The Genie & the Woodcutter. A Michael, Shumate. 2019. (ENG.). 36p. (J). (gr. k-4). pap. *(978-0-9950584-7-7(4))* Elfstone Press.

A, Veeran. Cleopatra (Illustrated) Cleopatra Traveled to Rome. Haggard, H. Rider. 2019. (ENG.). 408p. (J). pap. 14.99 *(978-1-0794-8724-4(7))* Independently Published.

A, Yasmeen. Dare to Be Different: Sketch Book for Kids with Creepy Cute 3in1 Monster: Unicorn-Dinosaur-Mermaid! Sandwitch, St. 2018. (Kids Sketchbooks Ser.: Vol. 1). (ENG.). 100p. (J). pap. 7.99 *(978-1-7902-2626-9(0))* Independently Published.

Aamir, Aisha. I Am Full Truth, I Am Half Truth, I Am All Lie. Marfani, Ayesha. 2018. (ENG.). 64p. (J). (gr. 1-5). pap. 12.99 *(978-1-68160-629-3(1))* Crimson Cloak Publishing.

—Miss Never Pleased. Marfani, Ayesha. 2018. (ENG.). 84p. (J). (gr. 1-6). pap. 7.99 *(978-1-68160-573-9(2))* Crimson Cloak Publishing.

A'Amu. Hiro et Hina: Balades Au Coeur des L. Chastel, Patrick. Tahiti, Api, ed. 2018. (FRE.). 104p. (J). pap. 28.00 *(978-1-7209-2463-0(5))* CreateSpace Independent Publishing Platform.

Aardema, John. The Blizzard Wizard. Plourde, Lynn. ed. 2010. (ENG.). 32p. (J). (gr. -1-3). 16.95 *(978-0-89272-789-6(6))* Down East Bks.

—Slippery Fish in Hawaii. Diamond, Charlotte. 2013. (ENG.). 16p. (J). (gr. -1-1). bds. 7.95 *(978-1-933067-57-5(8))* Beachhouse Publishing, LLC.

Aardvark, D. The Congraduation Fish. Aardvark, D. l.t. ed. 2005. 48p. (J). per. 12.95 *(978-0-9755567-1-9(1))* Aardvark's Weedpatch Pr.

—Merry Kissmoose. Aardvark, D. l.t. ed. 2005. 48p. (J). per. 12.95 *(978-0-9755567-2-6(X))* Aardvark's Weedpatch Pr.

Aardvark, Nathan. Blackbeard & the Monster of the Deep: Band 11 Lime/Band 12 Copper (Collins Big Cat Progress) Murtagh, Ciaran. 2014. (Collins Big Cat Progress Ser.). (ENG.). 32p. (J). (gr. 2-3). pap. 10.99 *(978-0-00-751931-6(1))* HarperCollins Pubs. Ltd. GBR. Dist: Independent Pubs. Group.

Aaron, Glenroy. Musical Youth. Hillhouse, Joanne C. 2014. (ENG.). 275p. (J). pap. 9.99 *(978-0-9899305-1-2(3))* CaribbeanReads.

Aaron, Huw. Find the Dragon! Aaron, Huw. 2019. (ENG.). 32p. (J). pap. 7.99 *(978-1-78461-717-2(2))* Y Lolfa GBR. Dist: Casemate Pubs. & Bk. Distributors, LLC.

Aaron, Rich. Mice Don't Taste Like Chicken. Heydt, Scott. 2011. 188p. pap. 13.00 *(978-0-9830109-2-0(7))* Helm Publishing.

Aarts, Esther. Look, There's a Helicopter! Nosy Crow. 2019. (Look There's Ser.). (ENG.). 10p. (J). (— 1). bds. 7.99 *(978-1-5362-0557-2(5)*, Nosy Crow) Candlewick Pr.

—Look, There's a Rocket! Nosy Crow. 2018. (Look There's Ser.). (ENG.). 10p. (J). (— 1). bds. 7.99 *(978-1-5362-0252-6(5)*, Nosy Crow) Candlewick Pr.

—Look, There's a Submarine! Nosy Crow. 2018. (Look There's Ser.). (ENG.). 10p. (J). (— 1). bds. 7.99 *(978-1-5362-0253-3(3)*, Nosy Crow) Candlewick Pr.

—Look, There's a Tractor! Nosy Crow. 2019. (Look There's Ser.). (ENG.). 10p. (J). (— 1). bds. 7.99 *(978-1-5362-0558-9(3)*, Nosy Crow) Candlewick Pr.

Aarvig, Cindy. Turkeys in Disguise. Honeycutt, Scarlet. 2007. 48p. per. 24.95 *(978-1-4137-4035-6(9))* America Star Bks.

Abad, Miguel. Dragal IV: The Dragon's Lineage. Gallego Abad, Elena. Dunne, Jonathan, tr. 2019. (Galician Wave Ser.: Vol. 19). (ENG.). 272p. (YA). (gr. 7-12). pap. ***(978-954-384-100-4(4))*** Small Stations Pr. = Smol Stejsans Pres.

Abad, Sam. Chronicles of Chloe: Frozen Eden: a Book about Increasing Self-Confidence, Coping with Bullying & Building Friendships. Berg, Melissa. 2020. (Chronicles of Chloe Ser.: Vol. 2). (ENG.). 54p. (J). pap. ***(978-1-7770306-0-5(9))*** Berg, Melissa.

—Chronicles of Chloe: Mean Girls Exodus. Berg, Melissa. 2019. (Chronicles of Chloe Ser.: Vol. 1). (ENG.). 78p. (J). pap. ***(978-1-9995167-7-2(X))*** Berg, Melissa.

Abadia, Ximo. Goliath: The Boy Who Was Different. Little Gestalten, Little, ed. 2019. (ENG.). 48p. 19.95 *(978-3-89955-826-5(X))* Die Gestalten Verlag DEU. Dist: Ingram Publisher Services.

—The Speed of Starlight: An Exploration of Physics, Sound, Light, & Space. Stuart, Colin. 2019. (ENG.). 80p. (J). (gr. 3-7). 24.99 *(978-1-5362-0855-9(8)*, Big Picture Press) Candlewick Pr.

Abadzis, Nick. Laika. Abadzis, Nick. 2007. (ENG.). 208p. (YA). (gr. 5-12). pap. 19.99 *(978-1-59643-101-0(6)*, 900031538, First Second Bks.) Roaring Brook Pr.

Abagiu, Alexandra. Fram: Am un Nume! Barbu, Adrian. 2017. (RUM.). 32p. (J). pap. *(978-606-94329-2-1(4))* Deveo Media.

—Fram: Calatorie Cu Peripetii. Barbu, Adrian. 2017. (RUM.). 32p. (J). pap. *(978-606-94329-1-4(6))* Deveo Media.

—Fram: Cum Am Devenit Celebru. Barbu, Adrian. 2017. (RUM.). 32p. (J). pap. *(978-606-94329-3-8(2))* Deveo Media.

—Fram: Inainte, Spre Nord! Barbu, Adrian. 2017. (RUM.). 32p. (J). pap. *(978-606-94329-5-2(9))* Deveo Media.

—Fram: Nanuk. Barbu, Adrian. 2017. (RUM.). 32p. (J). pap. *(978-606-94329-8-3(3))* Deveo Media.

Abasta, Mary. Simply & the Shiny Quarter. Mendoza, Madeleine. 2011. 24p. pap. 24.95 *(978-1-4560-3792-5(7))* America Star Bks.

Abay, Ismail. Darryl & the Mountain. Ozgur, Lynne Emily. 2009. 32p. (J). (gr. 2-4). 9.95 *(978-1-59784-138-2(2)*, Tughra Bks.) Blue Dome, Inc.

Abboreno, Joseph F. & Fu, Sherwin. Hoyi the Archer & other Classic Chinese Tales. Fu, Shelley. 2005. 144p. (J). (gr. 4-8). reprint ed. 22.00 *(978-0-7567-9713-3(6))* DIANE Publishing Co.

Abbot, Judi. Best Friends Forever. Hart, Owen. 2018. (ENG.). 24p. (J). (gr. -1-2). 16.99 *(978-1-68010-085-3(8))* Tiger Tales.

—The Big Five. Makatini, Bella. 2019. (ENG.). 32p. (J). 17.95 *(978-1-60537-457-4(1))*; 9.95 *(978-1-60537-476-5(8))* Clavis Publishing.

—The Biggest Kiss. Walsh, Joanna. 2011. (ENG.). 32p. (J). (gr. -1-3). 14.99 *(978-1-4424-2769-3(8)*, Simon & Schuster/Paula Wiseman Bks.) Simon & Schuster/Paula Wiseman Bks.

—Glitter. Jones, Stella J. 2017. (ENG.). 32p. (J). (gr. -1-2). 16.99 *(978-1-68010-039-6(4))* Tiger Tales.

—I Am Strong, 1 vol. Zondervan Staff. 2019. (ENG.). 20p. (J). bds. 8.99 *(978-0-310-76828-9(4))* Zonderkidz.

—I Love Dad. Walsh, Joanna. 2019. (Classic Board Bks.). (ENG.). 28p. (J). (gr. -1 — 1). bds. 7.99 *(978-1-5344-3901-6(3)*, Little Simon) Little Simon.

—I Love Mom. Walsh, Joanna. 2019. (Classic Board Bks.). (ENG.). 28p. (J). (gr. -1 — 1). bds. 7.99 *(978-1-5344-3900-9(5)*, Little Simon) Little Simon.

—I Love Mom. Walsh, Joanna. 2014. (ENG.). 32p. (J). (gr. -1-3). 16.99 *(978-1-4814-2808-8(X)*, Simon & Schuster/Paula Wiseman Bks.) Simon & Schuster/Paula Wiseman Bks.

—I Love You, Baby! Freedman, Claire. 2017. (ENG.). 32p. (J). (gr. -1-3). 17.99 *(978-1-4814-9904-0(1)*, Simon & Schuster/Paula Wiseman Bks.) Simon & Schuster/Paula Wiseman Bks.

—My Grandparents Love Me. Freedman, Claire. 2016. (ENG.). 32p. (J). (gr. -1-3). 17.99 *(978-1-4814-7937-0(7)*, Simon & Schuster/Paula Wiseman Bks.) Simon & Schuster/Paula Wiseman Bks.

—The Perfect Hug. Walsh, Joanna. 2012. (ENG.). 32p. (J). (gr. -1-3). 14.99 *(978-1-4424-6606-7(5)*, Simon & Schuster/Paula Wiseman Bks.) Simon & Schuster/Paula Wiseman Bks.

—Snug as a Bug. Murray, Tamsyn. 2013. (ENG.). 32p. (J). *(978-0-85707-108-8(4))* Barnes & Noble, Inc.

—Snug as a Bug. Murray, Tamsyn. 2014. (ENG.). 32p. (J). (gr. -1). pap. 8.99 *(978-0-85707-109-5(2))* Simon & Schuster, Ltd. GBR. Dist: Simon & Schuster, Inc.

—You Can't Scare Me. Grubman, Bonnie. 2020. (Willy & Walter Ser.). (ENG.). 32p. (J). (gr. -1). 17.95 *(978-1-60537-514-4(4))*; 9.95 *(978-1-60537-538-0(1))* Clavis Publishing.

Abbot, Judi. Hugs & Kisses. Abbot, Judi. 2016. (ENG.). 20p. (J). (gr. -1 — 1). bds. 7.99 *(978-1-4814-9168-6(7)*, Little Simon) Little Simon.

—Snow Kisses. Abbot, Judi. 2018. (ENG.). 20p. (J). (gr. -1 — 1). bds. 7.99 *(978-1-5344-3075-4(X)*, Little Simon) Little Simon.

Abbot, Judi & Gaviraghi, Giuditta. Snug As a Bug. Murray, Tamsyn. 2013. (ENG.). 30p. (J). *(978-1-4351-4731-7(6))* Barnes & Noble, Inc.

Abbott, Amory. I Like Being Me. Hartley, Alicia Byrd. 2012. (ENG.). 24p. pap. 15.50 *(978-1-4772-9088-0(5))* AuthorHouse.

Abbott, Graham. Bonnie & Clyde: A Deadly Duo. Sullivan, Laura L. 2018. (American Legends & Folktales Ser.). 32p. (gr. 3-3). pap. 10.58 *(978-1-5026-3684-3(0))*; lib. bdg. 28.50 *(978-1-5026-3682-9(4))* Cavendish Square Publishing LLC.

Abbott, Greg. Everybody's Welcome. Hegarty, Patricia. 2018. (ENG.). 32p. (J). (gr. -1-2). 16.99 *(978-1-5247-7165-2(1)*, Doubleday Bks. for Young Readers) Random Hse. Children's Bks.

—There's a Dragon in Your Book. Fletcher, Tom. (Who's in Your Book? Ser.). (ENG.). (J). 2019. 34p. (— 1). bds. 8.99 *(978-1-9848-5008-9(3))*; 2018. 32p. (gr. -1-2). 17.99 *(978-1-5247-6638-2(0))* Random Hse. Children's Bks. (Random Hse. Bks. for Young Readers).

—There's a Monster in Your Book. Fletcher, Tom. (Who's in Your Book? Ser.). (ENG.). (J). 2018. 34p. (— 1). bds. 8.99 *(978-0-525-64578-8(0))*; 2017. 32p. (gr. -1-2). 17.99 *(978-1-5247-6456-2(6))* Random Hse. Children's Bks. (Random Hse. Bks. for Young Readers).

—There's an Elf in Your Book. Fletcher, Tom. (Who's in Your Book? Ser.). (ENG.). (J). 2020. 34p. (— 1). bds. 8.99 ***(978-0-593-12511-3(8))***; 2019. 32p. (gr. -1-2). 17.99 *(978-1-9848-9344-4(0))* Random Hse. Children's Bks. (Random Hse. Bks. for Young Readers).

Abbott, Jane. Over the Moon. Robinson, Hilary. 2009. (Tadpoles Ser.). (ENG.). 24p. (J). (gr. k-2). pap. *(978-0-7787-3899-2(X))*; lib. bdg. *(978-0-7787-3868-8(X))* Crabtree Publishing Co.

—Over the Moon! Robinson, Hilary. 2009. (Tadpoles Ser.). (ENG.). (J). (gr. k-k). lib. bdg. 17.55 *(978-1-61383-945-4(6))* Perfection Learning Corp.

Abbott, Jason. Bethany Bubbles Makes a Mistake. Edwards, Wysteria. 2011. 34p. pap. 14.50 *(978-1-60911-353-7(5)*, Strategic Bk. Publishing) Strategic Book Publishing & Rights Agency (SBPRA).

—Hot Cross Buns for Everyone. Fuerst, Jeffrey B. 2009. (Reader's Theater Nursery Rhymes & Songs Set B Ser.). 48p. (J). pap. *(978-1-60859-153-4(0))* Benchmark Education Co.

—Little Bo Peep. Smith, Carrie. 2010. (Rising Readers Ser.). (J). 3.49 *(978-1-60719-700-3(6))* Newmark Learning LLC.

—Where Are Bo Peep's Sheep? Smith, Carrie. 2009. (Reader's Theater Nursery Rhymes & Songs Set B Ser.). 48p. (J). pap. *(978-1-60859-171-8(9))* Benchmark Education Co.

Abbott, Kristin. The Baseball Princess: Samantha's Summer & the Unicorn Flu. Hegerhorst, Bethany. 2012. 32p. (J). *(978-0-9871281-5-7(9))* Murray Bks.

—The Six Sisters & Their Flying Carpets. Ford, Adam B. 2012. 34p. (-18). 20.95 *(978-0-9794104-6-8(0))* H Bar Pr.

—The Soccer Princess: Josephina & the Gown Fashion Runway Show, 13 bks., bk. 1. Hegerhorst, Bethany. 2011. 32p. (J). 17.99 *(978-0-615-35488-0(2))* Leo Publishing Works, Inc.

—The Soccer Princess: Josephina & the Gown Fashion Runway Show, 12. Hegerhorst, Bethany. 2011. 32p. (J). *(978-0-9803829-6-9(3))* Murray Bks.

Abbott, Sally. Tidley Squeak. Marshall, Nick. 2018. (ENG.). 72p. (J). pap. *(978-1-78693-631-8(3))* Austin Macauley Pubs. Ltd.

Abbott, Simon. Alphabet. Rainstorm Publishing, ed. 2019. (Let's Get Talking Ser.). (ENG.). 20p. (J). bds. 7.99 ***(978-1-77402-002-9(5))*** Rainstorm Pr.

—Animals. Rainstorm Publishing, ed. 2019. (Let's Get Talking Ser.). (ENG.). 20p. (J). bds. 7.99 ***(978-1-989219-99-7(3))*** Rainstorm Pr.

Abbott, Simon. Bible Journey Storybook, 1 vol. David, Juliet. ed. 2016. (ENG.). 24p. (J). bds. 19.99 *(978-1-78128-148-2(3)*, Candle Bks.) Lion Hudson PLC GBR. Dist: Kregel Pubns.

—Bible Stories Painting Book, 1 vol., Bk. 3. David, Juliet. ed. 2014. (ENG.). 24p. (J). 7.99 *(978-1-85985-995-7(X)*, Candle Bks.) Lion Hudson PLC GBR. Dist: Kregel Pubns.

—Dinosaurs. 2011. (Learn to Draw Ser.). (ENG.). 24p. (J). (gr. k-2). pap. 6.95 *(978-1-84898-202-4(X)*, TickTock Books) Octopus Publishing Group GBR. Dist: Independent Pubs. Group.

—Dinosaurs. Goldsmith, Mike. 2011. (Flip Flap Science Ser.). (ENG.). 10p. (J). (gr. -1-k). 9.95 *(978-1-84898-365-6(4)*, TickTock Books) Octopus Publishing Group GBR. Dist: Independent Pubs. Group.

—Happy Street - School. 2016. (Happy Street Ser.). (ENG.). 10p. (J). (gr. -1-k). bds. 9.99 *(978-1-4052-7522-4(7))* Egmont Bks., Ltd. GBR. Dist: Independent Pubs. Group.

—Happy Street: Bookshop. 2016. (Happy Street Ser.). (ENG.). 10p. (J). (gr. -1-k). bds. 9.99 *(978-1-4052-7517-0(0))* Egmont Bks., Ltd. GBR. Dist: Independent Pubs. Group.

—Happy Street: Pet Shop. 2014. (Happy Street Ser.). (ENG.). 10p. (J). (gr. -1-k). 9.99 *(978-1-4052-6864-6(6))* Egmont Bks., Ltd. GBR. Dist: Independent Pubs. Group.

—Happy Street: Vet. 2016. (Happy Street Ser.). (ENG.). 10p. (J). (gr. -1-k). 9.99 *(978-1-4052-7518-7(9))* Egmont Bks., Ltd. GBR. Dist: Independent Pubs. Group.

—Henry Goes Skating. Biggs, Brian. ed. 2012. (My First I Can Read Ser.). (J). lib. bdg. 13.55 *(978-0-606-26852-3(9))* Turtleback.

—Henry in a Jam. Biggs, Brian. 2013. 32p. (J). *(978-1-4351-5057-7(0))* Barnes & Noble, Inc.

—Learn to Draw: Dragons. 2011. (Learn to Draw Ser.). (ENG.). 24p. (J). (gr. k-2). pap. 6.95 *(978-1-84898-201-7(1)*, TickTock Books) Octopus Publishing Group GBR. Dist: Independent Pubs. Group.

—Learn to Draw: Fairies. 2011. (Learn to Draw Ser.). (ENG.). 24p. (J). (gr. k-2). pap. 6.95 *(978-1-84898-203-1(8)*, TickTock Books) Octopus Publishing Group GBR. Dist: Independent Pubs. Group.

—Learn to Draw: Monsters. 2011. (Learn to Draw Ser.). (ENG.). 24p. (J). (gr. k-2). pap. 6.95 *(978-1-84898-200-0(3)*, TickTock Books) Octopus Publishing Group GBR. Dist: Independent Pubs. Group.

Abbott, Simon. Numbers. Rainstorm Publishing, ed. 2019. (Let's Get Talking Ser.). (ENG.). 20p. (J). bds. 7.99 ***(978-1-77402-000-5(9))*** Rainstorm Pr.

Abbott, Simon. Read It Build It Space. Hayes, Susan. 2015. (Read It Build It Ser.). (ENG.). 16p. (J). (gr. -1-1). 15.99 *(978-1-4052-7165-3(5))* Egmont Bks., Ltd. GBR. Dist: Independent Pubs. Group.

—Space Adventure. Goldsmith, Mike. 2011. (Flip Flap Science Ser.). (ENG.). 10p. (J). (gr. -1-k). 9.95 *(978-1-84898-364-9(6)*, TickTock Books) Octopus Publishing Group GBR. Dist: Independent Pubs. Group.

—Sticker Playbook Spaceship: A Fold-Out Story Activity Book for Toddlers. 2015. (Sticker Playbook Ser.). (ENG.). (J). *(978-1-78209-576-7(4))* Miles Kelly Publishing, Ltd.

—Train: A Fold-Out Story Activity Book for Toddlers. 2015. (Playbooks Ser.). (ENG.). (J). *(978-1-78209-071-7(1))* Miles Kelly Publishing, Ltd.

Abbott, Simon. Words. Rainstorm Publishing, ed. 2019. (Let's Get Talking Ser.). (ENG.). 20p. (J). bds. 7.99 ***(978-1-77402-001-2(7))*** Rainstorm Pr.

Abbott, Simon. 100 Questions about Bugs: And All the Answers, Too! 2018. (J). pap. *(978-1-4413-2618-8(9))* Peter Pauper Pr. Inc.
—100 Questions about Colonial America: And All the Answers Too! 2018. (J). *(978-1-4413-2616-4(2))* Peter Pauper Pr. Inc.
—100 Questions about Outer Space: And All the Answers, Too! 2018. (J). pap. *(978-1-4413-2617-1(0))* Peter Pauper Pr. Inc.
—100 Questions about the Human Body: And All the Answers Too! 2019. (J). *(978-1-4413-3101-4(8))* Peter Pauper Pr. Inc.
Abbott, Simon, jt. illus. see Biggs, Brian.
Abbott, Zoey. Finn's Feather. Noble, Rachel. 2018. (J). (ENG.). 17.95 *(978-1-59270-239-8(2))*; 56p. 9.95 *(978-1-59270-274-9(0))* Enchanted Lion Bks., LLC.
Abby, Mitchell. The Bear & the Price. Bradford, Wilson D. 2012. 48p. (-18). pap. 12.00 *(978-0-9848651-2-3(8))* True Path Pubs.
(abby Zechman), Zechmana. Dragonfly Farms: The Great Adventure. Ortiz, Jennifer Anne. 2019. (Dragonfly Farms Ser.: Vol. 1). (ENG.). 40p. (J). pap. 9.99 *(978-0-578-40926-9(7))* Dragonfly Farms: The Great Adventure.
Abdollahi, Ehsan. Thinker: My Puppy Poet & Me. Greenfield, Eloise. 2019. (ENG.). 32p. (J). (-4). 15.99 *(978-1-4926-7724-6(8)*, Sourcebooks Jabberwocky) Sourcebooks, Inc.
—When I Colored in the World. Ahmadi, Ahmadreza. Rassi, Azita, tr. 2019. (ENG.). 32p. (J). 16.99 *(978-1-910328-49-1(9))* Tiny Owl Publishing Ltd. GBR. Dist: Consortium Bk. Sales & Distribution.
Abdou, Mahmoud. Le Cerf-Volant de R�ves. Abdou, Mahmoud. 2020. (FRE.). 28p. (J). pap. 9.98 ***(978-1-6575-4626-4(8))*** Independently Published.
Abdrasilov, Daniel. George the Dragon: And the Snake Attack. Abdrasilov, Daniel. Abdrasilova, Anna. 2018. (ENG.). 44p. (J). pap. 9.99 *(978-1-7289-9732-2(1))* Independently Published.
Abdullah, Tariq. Goodnight Joy! Brown, Mia. 2010. 20p. 12.49 *(978-1-4520-1492-0(2))* AuthorHouse.
Abe, Hiroshi. One Stormy Night. Kimura & North, Lucy. 2005. 48p. (J). (gr. 1-3). 16.00 *(978-4-7700-2970-6(5))* Kodansha International JPN. Dist: Cheng & Tsui Co.
—One Sunny Day, 2 vols., Vol. 2. Kimura & North, Lucy. 2005. 48p. (J). 16.00 *(978-4-7700-2971-3(3))* Kodansha International JPN. Dist: Cheng & Tsui Co.
Abel, Cami. Kiko the Hawaiian Wave. Navarro, Beth. 2016. (ENG.). 38p. (J). (gr. k-4). 16.95 *(978-0-692-74330-0(8))* Be There Bedtime Stories LLC.
Abel, Jack, et al. The Death of Captain Marvel. 2019. (Death of Captain Marvel Ser.: 1). (ENG.). 168p. (YA). (gr. 8-17). pap. 19.99 *(978-1-302-91593-3(2))* Marvel Worldwide, Inc.
Abel, Simone. Cuddly Critters: Animal Nursery Rhymes, 1 vol. 2007. (Mother Goose Rhymes Ser.). (ENG.). 32p. (J). (gr. -1-2). lib. bdg. 25.99 *(978-1-4048-2344-0(1)*, 1265749, Picture Window Bks.) Capstone.
—Easy Guitar Tunes Internet Referenced. Marks, Anthony. 2004. 32p. (J). pap. 8.95 *(978-0-7945-0775-6(1)*, Usborne) EDC Publishing.
—Rainbow Duck. Lodge, Yvette. 2006. 8p. (J). (gr. -1-k). bds. 9.99 *(978-1-57791-263-7(2))* Brighter Minds Children's Publishing.
—Science with Plants. Edom, Helen. rev. ed. 2007. (Science Activities Ser.). 24p. (J). (gr. 3-7). pap. 5.99 *(978-0-7945-1485-3(5)*, Usborne) EDC Publishing.
—Where Is Caterpillar Look & Play. (Lamaze Ser.). bds. 8.99 *(978-1-58663-731-6(2))* Friedman, Michael Publishing Group, Inc.
Abel, Terry Scalzo. Big Desire. Andries, Kathryn. 2015. (ENG.). 48p. 13.50 *(978-1-940265-16-2(9))* Ozark Mountain Publishing, Inc.
Abelardo, Fernan Allan. Nickelodeon Nella the Princess Knight: Nella & the Dragon Knight: a Peek-Through Story. 2018. (Peek Through Story Ser.). (ENG.). 16p. (J). (gr. -1-k). bds. 10.99 *(978-0-7944-4168-5(8)*, Reader's Digest Children's Bks.) Studio Fun International.
Abello, Analyn. Chucky's Unbelievable Discovery. Adams, Lejoyce. 2017. (ENG.). (J). pap. 12.95 *(978-1-68197-982-3(9))* Christian Faith Publishing.
Abercrombie, Bethaney. Garrett the Firefighter. Garces Iii, Joseph Louis. 2008. 24p. pap. 12.99 *(978-1-59858-716-6(1))* Dog Ear Publishing, LLC.
Aberle, Xylena Apotheloz. Kenzie's Key. Doerr, Bonnie J. 2003. 211p. (J). 16.95 *(978-0-9619155-6-8(0))* Laurel & Herbert, Inc.
Abey, Katie, et al. Life in Colour. 2016. (ENG.). 96p. (J). pap. *(978-1-78202-494-1(8)*, Curious Fox) Raintree Pubs.
Abey, Katie, jt. illus. see Lafontaine, Thierry.
Abey, Katie, jt. illus. see Treleaven, Lou.
Abigail, de Montfort. The Hedgehog's Full Moon Party. Mayers, Richard a. 2018. (ENG.). 36p. (J). (gr. k-3). pap. *(978-0-9573387-6-0(7))* Burton Mayers Bks.
Abirached, Zeina. I Remember Beirut. Abirached, Zeina. 2014. (ENG.). 96p. (YA). (gr. 8-12). pap. 9.99 *(978-1-4677-4458-4(1)*, 9781467744584, Graphic Universe™) Lerner Publishing Group.
Ablett, Barry. Great Expectations. 2008. (Usborne Young Reading: Series Three Ser.). 61p. (J). 8.99 *(978-0-7945-1944-5(X)*, Usborne) EDC Publishing.
—Illustrated Stories from Dickens. Dickens, Charles. 2010. (Illustrated Stories Ser.). 352p. (YA). (gr. 3-18). 19.99 *(978-0-7945-2628-3(4)*, Usborne) EDC Publishing.
—Oliver Twist. Dickens, Charles. 2007. (Young Reading Series 3 Gift Bks.). 63p. (J). (gr. 3). 8.99 *(978-0-7945-1459-4(6)*, Usborne) EDC Publishing.
—See Inside Famous Buildings. Jones, Rob Lloyd. 2009. (See Inside Board Bks). 16p. (J). (gr. 2). bds. 13.99 *(978-0-7945-2350-3(1)*, Usborne) EDC Publishing.
—Tale of Two Cities: Internet-Referenced. Sebag-Montefiore, Mary, ed. 2009. (Young Reading 3 Ser.). 64p. (J). 6.99 *(978-0-7945-2319-0(6)*, Usborne) EDC Publishing.
Ablett, Barry, jt. illus. see Young, Norman.
Abnett, Dan & Eaton, Scot. God Complex, 3 vols. Lanning, Andy. 2011. (Iron Man & Thor Ser.). (ENG.). 24p. (J). (gr. 4-8). 27.07 *(978-1-59961-944-6(X)*, 10022);Pt. 1. 27.07 *(978-1-59961-942-2(3)*, 10020);Pt. 4. 27.07 *(978-1-59961-945-3(8)*, 10023);Set. 27.07 *(978-1-59961-943-9(1)*, 10021) Spotlight. (Marvel Age).
Abolaffio, Ariella. You Are a Star. Abolaffio, Ariella. 2019. (J). 8.99 *(978-1-61067-813-1(3))* Kane Miller.
Abolafia, Yossi. The Golden Bell. Sachs, Tamar. 2019. (ENG.). 24p. (J). (gr. -1-3). 17.99 *(978-1-5415-2612-9(0)*, Kar-Ben Publishing) Lerner Publishing Group.
—Harry's Birthday. Porte, Barbara Ann. 2003. (I Can Read Bks.). 48p. (J). 15.99 *(978-0-06-050355-0(6))*; 16.89 *(978-0-06-050356-7(4))* HarperCollins Pubs.
—Harry's Pony. Porte, Barbara Ann. 2003. (I Can Read Bks.). 64p. (J). 16.89 *(978-0-06-050658-2(X))* HarperCollins Pubs.
—It's Snowing! It's Snowing! Prelutsky, Jack. 2007. (I Can Read Bks.). 48p. (gr. -1-3). 14.00 *(978-0-7569-8057-3(7))* Perfection Learning Corp.
—It's Snowing! It's Snowing! Winter Poems. Prelutsky, Jack. 2006. (I Can Read Bks.). 48p. (J). (gr. -1-3). lib. bdg. 16.89 *(978-0-06-053716-6(7))* HarperCollins Pubs.
—My Parents Think I'm Sleeping. Prelutsky, Jack. (I Can Read Level 3 Ser.). 48p. (J). (gr. k-3). 2008. (ENG.). pap. 4.99 *(978-0-06-053722-7(1))*; 2007. lib. bdg. 16.89 *(978-0-06-053721-0(3))* HarperCollins Pubs.
Abraham, Joe, et al. Planetary Brigade. Giffen, Keith & DeMatteis, J. M. 2007. (ENG.). 128p. per. 14.99 *(978-1-934506-10-3(9))* Boom! Studios.
Abram, Elise. Harry Has a Lot of Energy. Abram, Elise. 2020. (ENG.). 42p. (J). (gr. k-6). ***(978-1-988843-42-1(1))*** EMSA Publishing.
—Heddy Is Sad. Abram, Elise. 2020. (ENG.). 38p. (J). (gr. k-6). ***(978-1-988843-40-7(5))*** EMSA Publishing.
Abram, Keona Venice. The Girl Who Discovered What Was Already There. Albright, Ashley L. 2019. (ENG.). 30p. (J). pap. 12.00 *(978-1-7953-8174-1(4))* Independently Published.
Abrams, Annette. Absolutely No Dogs Allowed. Kranowitz, Asher. 2016. (ENG.). 32p. (J). pap. 14.95 *(978-1-935567-58-5(6))* Sensory Resources.
Abramskaya, Anna. While You Sleep, Little Love (padded) Burke, Michelle Prater. 2018. (ENG.). 20p. (J). (— 1). bds. 9.99 *(978-1-5359-2375-0(X)*, 005806932, B&H Kids) B&H Publishing Group.
Abramson, Cathy. Wild Washington: Animal Sculptures A to Z. Arbuthnoy, Nancy. 2005. pap. 18.00 *(978-1-884878-09-1(1))* Annapolis Publishing Co.
Abramson, Stephen, photos by. Coco. Abramson, Laurin. 2010. 28p. pap. 8.75 *(978-1-935125-95-2(8))* Robertson Publishing.
Abraxas, Matt. Athanasius. Carr, Simonetta. 2011. 64p. (J). 18.00 *(978-1-60178-151-2(2))* Reformation Heritage Bks.
—John Knox. Carr, Simonetta. 2014. (ENG.). 64p. (J). 18.00 *(978-1-60178-289-2(6))* Reformation Heritage Bks.
—John Owen. Carr, Simonetta. 2010. (ENG.). 62p. (J). 18.00 *(978-1-60178-088-1(5))* Reformation Heritage Bks.
—Jonathan Edwards. Carr, Simonetta. 2014. (ENG.). 60p. (J). 18.00 *(978-1-60178-354-7(X))* Reformation Heritage Bks.
—Marie Durand: Christian Biographies for Young Readers. Carr, Simonetta. 2015. (ENG.). 60p. (J). 18.00 *(978-1-60178-390-5(6))* Reformation Heritage Bks.
Abrego, Rii. Steven Universe: Field Researching (Vol. 3), 3. Kraft, Grace. 2018. (Steven Universe Ser.). (ENG.). 112p. (J). (gr. 4-7). pap. 14.99 *(978-1-68415-244-5(5))* Boom! Studios.
—Steven Universe: Find a Way (Vol. 5) Find a Way. Kraft, Grace. 2019. (Steven Universe Ser.: 5). (ENG.). 112p. (J). pap. 14.99 *(978-1-68415-387-9(5))* Boom! Studios.
—Steven Universe: Just Right (Vol. 4) Kraft, Grace. 2019. (Steven Universe Ser.). (ENG.). 112p. (J). (gr. 4-7). pap. 14.99 *(978-1-68415-314-5(X))* Boom! Studios.
—Steven Universe: Playing by Ear (Vol. 6) Playing by Ear. Kraft, Grace. 2020. (Steven Universe Ser.: 6). (ENG.). 112p. (J). pap. 14.99 *(978-1-68415-489-0(8))* Boom! Studios.
Abremski, Kathy. An a-Bee-Sea Book. Burr, Holly. 2012. 28p. pap. 14.95 *(978-1-61493-040-2(6))* Peppertree Pr., The.
—If I Get to Be in Charge of Spelling. Burr, Holly. 2012. 16p. pap. 10.95 *(978-1-61493-039-6(2))* Peppertree Pr., The.
Abreu, Julie de. Operation Imagination with Buddy the Bear: Gone Fishing. Horton, Joshua. 2017. (ENG.). (J). pap. 9.99 *(978-0-9966539-8-5(8))* Lighted Hill.
Abreu, Raquel. Little Ruth Reddingford (and the Wolf) An Old Tale retold by Hank Wesselman, PH. D. 2004. 32p. (J). per. 15.95 *(978-0-9740190-0-0(3))* Illumination Arts Publishing Co., Inc.
—Your Father Forever. Griffith, Travis. 2005. 32p. (J). (gr. -1-3). 15.95 *(978-0-9740190-3-1(8))* Illumination Arts Publishing Co., Inc.
Abril, Mauricio. Meet Everest! 2019. (Abominable Ser.). (ENG.). 24p. (J). (gr. -1-2). pap. 4.99 *(978-1-5344-4874-2(8)*, Simon Spotlight) Simon Spotlight.
—Yi's Journey Home. 2019. (Abominable Ser.). (ENG.). 16p. (J). (gr. -1-2). pap. 6.99 *(978-1-5344-5084-4(X)*, Simon Spotlight) Simon Spotlight.
Abs, Renata. Erase Una Vez Galileo Galilei. Foelker, Rita. 2004. 24p. pap. 2.95 *(978-85-7416-192-1(6))* Callis Editora Ltda BRA. Dist: Independent Pubs. Group.
Abt-Tomkow, Desiree. To Willow's House for Tea. Palin, Cindy. 2019. (ENG.). 32p. (J). (gr. k-1). pap. *(978-1-4866-1833-0(2))* Word Alive Pr.
Abt-Tomkow, Desiree. Willow's Lullaby. Palin, Cindy. 2019. (ENG.). 28p. (J). (gr. k-1). pap. ***(978-1-4866-1835-4(9))*** Word Alive Pr.
Abts, Stacey. I'm Trying to Be Like Jesus. Perry, Janice Kapp. 2003. (J). *(978-1-57008-843-8(8)*, Bookcraft, Inc.) Deseret Bk. Co.
Abul-Maati, Rania. Falfoul's Trunk. Nasser, Amal. 2016. (Stories & Fables from Around the World Ser.). (ENG.). 24p. (J). (gr. 2-1). lib. bdg. 24.60 *(978-1-4777-5693-5(0)*, Windmill Bks.) Rosen Publishing Group, Inc., The.
Abulafia, Yossi. A Kiss for Lily. Nirgad, Lia. 2006. (ENG.). 24p. (J). (gr. -1-1). *(978-1-59692-163-4(3))* MacAdam/Cage Publishing, Inc.
Aburto, Jesus. Battle for Home Plate, 1 vol. Kreie, Chris et al. 2010. (Sports Illustrated Kids Graphic Novels Ser.). (ENG.). 56p. (J). (gr. 3-8). 26.65 *(978-1-4342-1913-8(5)*, Stone Arch Bks.) Capstone.
—Hoop Hustle. Maddox, Jake. 2015. (Jake Maddox Sports Stories Ser.). (ENG.). 72p. (J). (gr. 3-6). lib. bdg. 25.32 *(978-1-4965-0494-4(1)*, Stone Arch Bks.) Capstone.
—Point-Blank Paintball, 1 vol. Ciencin, Scott et al. 2010. (Sports Illustrated Kids Graphic Novels Ser.). (ENG.). 56p. (J). (gr. 3-8). pap. 7.19 *(978-1-4342-2293-0(4)*, Stone Arch Bks.) Capstone.
—Point-Blank Paintball, 1 vol. Ciencin, Scott et al. 2010. (Sports Illustrated Kids Graphic Novels Ser.). (ENG.). 56p. (J). (gr. 3-8). 26.65 *(978-1-4342-1914-5(3)*, Stone Arch Bks.) Capstone.
—Secret Weapons: A Tale of the Revolutionary War, 1 vol. Gunderson, Jessica. 2008. (Historical Fiction Ser.). (ENG.). 56p. (J). (gr. 3-6). pap. 6.25 *(978-1-4342-0848-4(6)*, Stone Arch Bks.) Capstone.
Aburto, Jesus, et al. Snowboard Standoff, 1 vol. Ciencin, Scott et al. 2011. (Sports Illustrated Kids Graphic Novels Ser.). (ENG.). 56p. (J). (gr. 3-8). lib. bdg. 26.65 *(978-1-4342-2242-8(X)*, Stone Arch Bks.) Capstone.
Aburto, Jesus. Soccer Shake-Up. Maddox, Jake. 2015. (Jake Maddox Sports Stories Ser.). (ENG.). 72p. (J). (gr. 3-6). lib. bdg. 25.32 *(978-1-4965-0495-1(X)*, Stone Arch Bks.) Capstone.
—Touchdown Triumph. Maddox, Jake. 2015. (Jake Maddox Sports Stories Ser.). (ENG.). 72p. (J). (gr. 3-6). lib. bdg. 25.32 *(978-1-4965-0492-0(5)*, Stone Arch Bks.) Capstone.
Aburto, Jesus, et al. Track Team Titans, 1 vol. Peters, Stephanie True & Cano, Fernando M. 2011. (Sports Illustrated Kids Graphic Novels Ser.). (ENG.). 56p. (J). (gr. 3-8). pap. 7.19 *(978-1-4342-3072-0(4))*; lib. bdg. 26.65 *(978-1-4342-2224-4(1))* Capstone. (Stone Arch Bks.).
Aburto, Jesus & Cano, Fernando M. Hoop Rat, 1 vol. Ciencin, Scott et al. 2011. (Sports Illustrated Kids Graphic Novels Ser.). (ENG.). 56p. (J). (gr. 3-8). pap. 7.19 *(978-1-4342-3069-0(4))*; lib. bdg. 26.65 *(978-1-4342-2223-7(3))* Capstone. (Stone Arch Bks.).
Aburto, Jesus & Esparza, Andres. Avalanche Freestyle, 1 vol. Ciencin, Scott & Maese, Fares. 2010. (Sports Illustrated Kids Graphic Novels Ser.). (ENG.). 56p. (J). (gr. 3-8). 26.65 *(978-1-4342-2009-7(5))*; pap. 7.19 *(978-1-4342-2783-6(9))* Capstone. (Stone Arch Bks.).
—BMX Blitz, 1 vol. Ciencin, Scott & Maese, Fares. 2011. (Sports Illustrated Kids Graphic Novels Ser.). (ENG.). 56p. (J). (gr. 3-8). pap. 7.19 *(978-1-4342-3071-3(6)*, Stone Arch Bks.) Capstone.
—Paintball Punk, 1 vol. Tulien, Sean & Maese, Fares. 2010. (Sports Illustrated Kids Graphic Novels Ser.). (ENG.). 56p. (J). (gr. 3-8). 26.65 *(978-1-4342-2219-0(5))*; pap. 7.19 *(978-1-4342-2788-1(X))* Capstone. (Stone Arch Bks.).
—Shot Clock Slam. Kreie, Chris & Maese, Fares. 2010. (Sports Illustrated Kids Graphic Novels Ser.). (ENG.). 56p. (J). (gr. 3-8). pap. 7.19 *(978-1-4342-2786-7(3)*, Stone Arch Bks.) Capstone.
Aburto, Jesus, jt. illus. see Esparza, Andres.
Aburto, Jesus, jt. illus. see Maese, Fares.
Aburto Martinez, Jesus Salvador. Fútbol Extremo. Maddox, Jake. 2019. (Jake Maddox Novelas Gráficas Ser.). (SPA.). 72p. (J). (gr. 3-8). pap. 6.95 *(978-1-4965-8590-5(9)*, 141331); lib. bdg. 26.65 *(978-1-4965-8580-6(1)*, 141313) Capstone. (Stone Arch Bks.).
—Jake Maddox Novelas Gráficas. Maddox, Jake. (Jake Maddox Novelas Gráficas Ser.).Tr. of Jake Maddox Graphic Novels. (SPA.). (J). (gr. 3-8). 2020. 213.20 *(978-1-4965-9186-9(0)*, 29930); 2020. pap., pap., pap. 55.60 *(978-1-4965-9335-1(9)*, 30083); 2019. 106.60 *(978-1-4965-8582-0(8)*, 29730); 2019. pap., pap., pap. 27.80 *(978-1-4965-8601-8(8)*, 29741) Capstone. (Stone Arch Bks.).
—Jugada Doble. Maddox, Jake. 2019. (Jake Maddox Novelas Gráficas Ser.). (SPA.). 72p. (J). (gr. 3-8). pap. 6.95 *(978-1-4965-8589-9(5)*, 141330); lib. bdg. 26.65 *(978-1-4965-8578-3(X)*, 141312) Capstone. (Stone Arch Bks.).
Aburtov. Beach Bully, 1 vol. Maddox, Jake. 2013. (Jake Maddox Sports Stories Ser.). (ENG.). 72p. (J). (gr. 3-6). pap. 5.95 *(978-1-4342-6206-6(5)*, Stone Arch Bks.) Capstone.
—Pete Bogg: King of the Frogs. Sonneborn, Scott. 2013. (Pete Bogg Ser.). (ENG.). 48p. (J). (gr. 3-5). pap. 5.95 *(978-1-4342-3872-6(5))*; lib. bdg. 23.99 *(978-1-4342-3284-7(0))* Capstone. (Stone Arch Bks.).
—Point-Blank Paintball, 1 vol. Ciencin, Scott. 2010. (Sports Illustrated Kids Graphic Novels Ser.). (ENG.). 32p. pap. 1.00 *(978-1-4342-2137-7(7)*, Stone Arch Bks.) Capstone.
Aburtov, Jesus. Beach Bully, 1 vol. Maddox, Jake. 2013. (Jake Maddox Sports Stories Ser.). (ENG.). 72p. (J). (gr. 3-6). lib. bdg. 25.32 *(978-1-4342-5973-8(0)*, Stone Arch Bks.) Capstone.
—Kart Competition, 1 vol. Maddox, Jake. 2013. (Jake Maddox Sports Stories Ser.). (ENG.). 72p. (J). (gr. 3-6). lib. bdg. 25.32 *(978-1-4342-5976-9(5)*, Stone Arch Bks.) Capstone.
Aburtov, Jesus Aburto. Battle for Home Plate, 1 vol. Kreie, Chris et al. 2010. (Sports Illustrated Kids Graphic Novels Ser.). (ENG.). 56p. (J). (gr. 3-8). pap. 7.19 *(978-1-4342-2290-9(X)*, Stone Arch Bks.) Capstone.
—Board Battle, 1 vol. Maddox, Jake. 2013. (Jake Maddox Sports Stories Ser.). (ENG.). 72p. (J). (gr. 3-6). pap. 5.95 *(978-1-4342-6208-0(1))*; lib. bdg. 25.32 *(978-1-4342-5975-2(7))* Capstone. (Stone Arch Bks.).
—Caught Stealing. Maddox, Jake. 2015. (Jake Maddox Sports Stories Ser.). (ENG.). 72p. (J). (gr. 3-6). lib. bdg. 25.32 *(978-1-4965-0493-7(3)*, Stone Arch Bks.) Capstone.
—Kart Competition, 1 vol. Maddox, Jake. 2013. (Jake Maddox Sports Stories Ser.). (ENG.). 72p. (J). (gr. 3-6). pap. 5.95 *(978-1-4342-6209-7(X)*, Stone Arch Bks.) Capstone.
—Lacrosse Laser. Maddox, Jake. 2016. (Jake Maddox Sports Stories Ser.). (ENG.). 72p. (J). (gr. 3-6). lib. bdg. 25.32 *(978-1-4965-3051-6(9)*, Stone Arch Bks.) Capstone.
—Paintball Problems, 1 vol. Maddox, Jake. 2013. (Jake Maddox Sports Stories Ser.). (ENG.). 72p. (J). (gr. 3-6). pap. 5.95 *(978-1-4342-6207-3(3))*; lib. bdg. 25.32 *(978-1-4342-5974-5(9))* Capstone. (Stone Arch Bks.).
—Rodeo Challenge. Maddox, Jake. 2018. (Jake Maddox Sports Stories Ser.). (ENG.). 72p. (J). (gr. 3-6). lib. bdg. 25.32 *(978-1-4965-5865-7(0)*, 136944, Stone Arch Bks.) Capstone.
—Second Shot. Maddox, Jake & Anderson, Josh. 2016. (Jake Maddox Sports Stories Ser.). (ENG.). 72p. (J). (gr. 3-6). lib. bdg. 25.32 *(978-1-4965-3052-3(7)*, Stone Arch Bks.) Capstone.
—Secondhand Slice. Maddox, Jake. 2018. (Jake Maddox Sports Stories Ser.). (ENG.). 72p. (J). (gr. 3-6). lib. bdg. 25.32 *(978-1-4965-5864-0(2)*, 136940, Stone Arch Bks.) Capstone.
—Soccer Switch. Maddox, Jake. 2017. (Jake Maddox Graphic Novels Ser.). (ENG.). 72p. (J). (gr. 3-8). lib. bdg. 26.65 *(978-1-4965-3699-0(1)*, Stone Arch Bks.) Capstone.
Abvabi, Chris. The Velveteen Rabbit. Suben, Eric. 2019. (ENG.). 26p. (J). pap. 12.99 *(978-1-7984-8361-9(0))* Independently Published.
Acar, Sinan. Pancakes on Sunday. Cox, Miss Karin & Cox, Karin. 2012. 26p. pap. *(978-0-9873602-2-9(1))* Indelible Ink Pr.
Accardo, Anthony. Benito's Sopaipillas/Las Sopaipillas de Benito. Baca, Ana. Villarroel, Carolina, tr. 2007. (ENG & SPA.). 32p. (J). (gr. -1-2). 16.95 *(978-1-55885-370-6(7)*, Piñata Books) Arte Publico Pr.
—Cesar Chavez: The Struggle for Justice (La Lucha por la Justicia) Griswold del Castillo, Richard. Colin, Jose Juan, tr. 2010. (ENG & SPA.). (J). (gr. 1-3). pap. 18.95 incl. audio compact disk *(978-1-4301-0834-4(7))* Live Oak Media.
—Cesar Chavez: The Struggle for Justice/la Lucha Por la Justicia. Griswold del Castillo, Richard. Colin, Jose Juan, tr. 2008. (Hispanic Civil Rights Ser.). (SPA & ENG.). 32p. (J). (gr. -1-3). pap. 7.95 *(978-1-55885-424-6(X)*, Piñata Books) Arte Publico Pr.
—Chiles for Benito (Chiles para Benito) Baca, Ana. Colin, Jose Juan, tr. (ENG & SPA.). (J). 16.95 *(978-1-55885-389-8(8)*, Piñata Books) Arte Publico Pr.
—Ricardo's Race/la Carrera de Ricardo. Bertrand, Diane Gonzales. Viegas-Barros, Rocio, tr. from ENG. 2007. (SPA.). 32p. (J). (gr. -1-2). 16.95 *(978-1-55885-481-9(9))* Arte Publico Pr.
—Waiting for Papá/Esperando a Papá. Laínez, René Colato.Tr. of Esperando a Papa. (ENG & SPA.). 32p. (gr. 1-3). 16.95 *(978-1-55885-403-1(7)*, Piñata Books) Arte Publico Pr.
Accrocco, Anthony. Stewie Meets New Friends. Seitz, Melissa. 2012. 26p. pap. 12.95 *(978-1-61244-079-8(7))* Halo Publishing International.
Ace, Dani, jt. illus. see Ace Jr, Wesley.
Ace Jr, Wesley & Ace, Dani. Still I Fly: Designed to Help Children Build Confidence, Resilience, Grit, Positive Thinking, & Perseverance. Ace, Nikki. 2019. (Still I ... Ser.: Vol. 1). (ENG.). 42p. (J). (gr. k-3). pap. 9.99 ***(978-0-578-47563-9(4))*** Ace Publishing.
—Still I Shine: Designed to Empower Children to PERSEVERE, Encourage a GROWTH MINDSET, & Embrace the Power of ENDURANCE. Ace, Nikki. 2019. (Still I ... Ser.: Vol. 2). (ENG.). 40p. (J). (gr. k-5). pap. 9.99 ***(978-0-578-58961-9(3))*** Ace Publishing.
Acedera, Kei. How to Talk to Dads. Greven, Alec. 2009. (ENG.). 48p. (J). (gr. 1-5). 9.99 *(978-0-06-172930-0(2)*, Collins) HarperCollins Pubs.
—How to Talk to Girls. Greven, Alec. 2008. (ENG.). 48p. (J). (gr. 1-5). 9.99 *(978-0-06-170999-9(9)*, Collins) HarperCollins Pubs.
—How to Talk to Moms. Greven, Alec. 2009. (ENG.). 48p. (J). (gr. 1-5). 9.99 *(978-0-06-171001-8(6)*, Collins) HarperCollins Pubs.
—How to Talk to Santa. Greven, Alec. 2009. (ENG.). 48p. (J). (gr. 1-5). 9.99 *(978-0-06-180207-2(7))* HarperCollins Pubs.
—Liesl & Po. Oliver, Lauren. 2011. (ENG.). 320p. (J). (gr. 3-7). 16.99 *(978-0-06-201451-1(X))* HarperCollins Pubs.
—Liesl & Po. Oliver, Lauren. 2012. (ENG.). 336p. (J). (gr. 3-7). pap. 7.99 *(978-0-06-201452-8(8)*, HarperCollins) HarperCollins Pubs. Ltd. GBR. Dist: HarperCollins Pubs.
—Rules for School. Greven, Alec. 2010. (ENG.). 48p. (J). (gr. 1-5). 9.99 *(978-0-06-195170-1(6)*, Collins) HarperCollins Pubs.
Acerno, Gerry. Eli Whitney & the Cotton Gin, 1 vol. Gunderson, Jessica Sarah & Barnett, Charles, III. 2007. (Inventions & Discovery Ser.). (ENG.). 32p. (J). (gr. 3-9). per. 8.10 *(978-0-7368-7895-1(5)*, Capstone Pr.) Capstone.
Acevedo, Rey. The Adventures of Wukong & Bajie: The Quest. Penneman, Jon & Ren, Lanbin. 2019. (Adventures of Wukong & Bajie Ser.: Vol. 1). (ENG.). 26p. (J). pap. 9.99 ***(978-1-0993-8992-4(5))*** Independently Published.
Achdé. The Beautiful Province, Vol. 52. Gerra, Laurent. 2015. (Lucky Luke Ser.: 52). (ENG.). 48p. pap. 11.95 *(978-1-84918-249-2(3))* CineBook GBR. Dist: National Bk. Network.
—Lucky Luke Versus the Pinkertons. Pennac, Daniel & Benacquista, Tonino. 2012. (Lucky Luke Ser.: 31). (ENG.). 48p. pap. 11.95 *(978-1-84918-096-6(9))* CineBook GBR. Dist: National Bk. Network.
Acheson, Steve. The Twelve Days of Catmas: A Christmas Tale with Percy the Cat. Collyer, Jeff. 2016. (ENG.). (J). pap. *(978-0-9956325-2-3(9))* Aelurus Publishing.
Achilles, Pat. The Adventures of the Poodle Posse: [happy Tales 1 & 2]. Smith, Chrysa. 2007. 26p. (J). *(978-1-4243-3335-6(0))* Independent Publisher Services.
—Mommy's High Heel Shoes. Finnan, Kristie. 2008. 32p. (J). 16.99 *(978-0-9817565-2-3(2))* Mommy Workshop Bks.

Ackerley, Sarah. Your Fantastic, Elastic Brain: Stretch It, Shape It. Deak, JoAnn. O'Malley, Judy, ed. 2010. 32p. (J). (gr. -1-3). 18.95 *(978-0-9829938-0-4(3),* Little Pickle Pr.) Sourcebooks, Inc.

Ackerley, Sarah. Patrick the Somnambulist. Ackerley, Sarah. 2008. (ENG.). 32p. (J). (gr. -1 — 1). 14.95 *(978-1-933831-07-7(3))* Blooming Tree Pr.

Ackerman, Dena. Me, My Dog, & the Key Mystery. Adler, David A. 2018. 30p. (J). *(978-1-61465-601-2(0))* Menucha Pubs. Inc.

—Red Is My Rimon: A Jewish Child's Book of Colors. Glick, Dvorah. 2012. 32p. (J). 12.95 *(978-1-929628-71-1(4))* Hachai Publishing.

Ackerman, Lauren. Pirates! Mischief on the High Seas. Cooper, Amby. 2019. (ENG.). 48p. (J). pap. 10.99 *(978-1-0778-4686-9(X))* Independently Published.

Ackerman, Michele, et al. Brain Games Kids: Toddler Time. Art Explosion et al, photos by. PI Kids. 2018. (ENG.). 208p. (J). spiral bd. ***(978-1-5037-3758-7(6),*** 735db536-0adb-4ae8-8dba-e578273204a9, p i kids) Phoenix International Publications, Inc.

Ackerman, Michele L. Jack & the Beanstalk Story in a Box. James, Annabelle. 2003. (Story in a Box Ser.). 12p. (J). bds. 8.99 *(978-1-883043-42-1(5))* Straight Edge Pr., The.

Ackison, Wendy Wassink. Catfish Annie to the Rescue. Crowe, Duane E. 2004. (Back River Adventures of Catfish Annie Ser.). 48p. (J). (gr. k-5). *(978-0-9672882-0-8(7))* Back River Company, The, LLC.

Ackley, Peggy Jo. Bitty Bear & the Bugs. Witkowski, Teri. 2008. (J). *(978-1-59369-383-1(4),* American Girl) American Girl Publishing, Inc.

—Bitty Bear, Flower Girl. Witkowski, Teri. 2009. (J). *(978-1-59369-564-4(0),* American Girl) American Girl Publishing, Inc.

—Bitty Bear's Birthday Treats. Witkowski, Teri. 2008. (J). *(978-1-59369-384-8(2),* American Girl) American Girl Publishing, Inc.

—Bitty Bear's New Friend. Witkowski, Teri. 2005. (J). *(978-1-59369-021-2(5))* American Girl Publishing, Inc.

—Bitty Bear's Sleigh Ride. Child, Lydia Maria. 2006. (J). *(978-1-59369-157-8(2))* American Girl Publishing, Inc.

—Bitty Bear's Snowflake Dreams. Witkowski, Teri. 2006. (J). *(978-1-59369-166-0(1))* American Girl Publishing, Inc.

—Bitty Bear's Valentines. Witkowski, Teri. 2004. (J). *(978-1-58485-837-9(0))* American Girl Publishing, Inc.

—Bitty Bear's Walk in the Woods. Witkowski, Teri. 2006. (J). *(978-1-59369-156-1(4))* American Girl Publishing, Inc.

—The Bitty Bunch Bath Book. Witkowski, Teri. 2006. (J). *(978-1-59369-080-9(0))* American Girl Publishing, Inc.

—Bitty Bunny's Bedtime. Witkowski, Teri. 2004. (J). *(978-1-58485-921-5(0))* American Girl Publishing, Inc.

—Bitty Bunny's Slipper Search. Witkowski, Teri. 2009. (J). *(978-1-59369-586-6(1),* American Girl) American Girl Publishing, Inc.

—Bunny & Piggy at the Beach. Witkowski, Teri. 2005. (J). *(978-1-58485-961-1(X))* American Girl Publishing, Inc.

—Happy Birthday, Bitty Bear! Witkowski, Teri. 2005. (J). *(978-1-58485-959-8(8))* American Girl Publishing, Inc.

Ackley, Peggy Jo. If Christmas Were a Poem. Sellers, Ronnie. 2020. (ENG.). 32p. (J). 14.95 ***(978-1-5319-1217-8(6))*** Sellers Publishing, Inc.

Ackley, Peggy Jo. It's Spring, Bitty Bear! Witkowski, Teri. 2007. (J). *(978-1-59369-242-1(0))* American Girl Publishing, Inc.

—Time for Bed, Bitty Bunch. Witkowski, Teri. 2008. (J). *(978-1-59369-380-0(X))* American Girl Publishing, Inc.

—Wait Your Turn, Bitty Froggy! Witkowski, Teri. 2008. (J). *(978-1-59369-285-8(4))* American Girl Publishing, Inc.

ACO. Nick Fury: Deep-Cover Capers, Vol. 1. 2017. (ENG.). 136p. (YA). (gr. 8-17). pap. 17.99 *(978-1-302-90486-9(8))* Marvel Worldwide, Inc.

Acosta, Laura. Christian Grace. Houston, Terence. Reid, Tierra Destiny, ed. 2018. (Chronicles of Christian Grace Ser.: Vol. 1). (ENG.). 26p. (J). pap. 14.95 ***(978-1-947574-29-8(9))*** TDR Brands Publishing.

—Christian the Princess. Houston, Terence. Reid, Tierra Destiny, ed. 2018. (Chronicles of Christian Grace Ser.: Vol. 1). (ENG.). 26p. (J). pap. 14.95 ***(978-1-947574-27-4(2))*** TDR Brands Publishing.

—Following the Rules. Houston, Terence. Reid, Tierra Destiny, ed. 2018. (Chronicles of Christian Grace Ser.: Vol. 1). (ENG.). 26p. (J). pap. 14.95 ***(978-1-947574-24-3(8))*** TDR Brands Publishing.

—Honoring My Boundaries. Houston, Terence. Reid, Tierra Destiny, ed. 2018. (Chronicles of Christian Grace Ser.: Vol. 1). (ENG.). 26p. (J). pap. 14.95 ***(978-1-947574-28-1(0))*** TDR Brands Publishing.

—I Can Do It, Too! Houston, Terence. Reid, Tierra Destiny, ed. 2018. (Chronicles of Christian Grace Ser.: Vol. 1). (ENG.). 26p. (J). pap. 14.95 ***(978-1-947574-26-7(4))*** TDR Brands Publishing.

—KK Cooks Guacamole. Reid, Kylie Renee. Reid, Tierra Destiny, ed. 2017. (ENG.). 24p. (J). pap. 10.00 ***(978-1-947574-00-7(0))*** TDR Brands Publishing.

—KK Loves Gymnastics. Reid, Kylie Renee. Reid, Tierra Destiny, ed. 2017. (ENG.). 24p. (J). pap. 10.00 ***(978-0-9988804-2-6(6))*** TDR Brands Publishing.

—La Princesa Christian. Houston, Terence. Reid, Tierra Destiny, ed. 2019. (Las Cr&#65533;nicas de Christian Grace Ser.: Vol. 1). (SPA.). 26p. (J). pap. 14.95 ***(978-1-947574-38-0(8))*** TDR Brands Publishing.

—Quiero Ser Grande. Houston, Terence. Reid, Tierra Destiny, ed. 2019. (Las Cr&#65533;nicas de Christian Grace Ser.: Vol. 1). (SPA.). 26p. (J). pap. 14.95 ***(978-1-947574-37-3(X))*** TDR Brands Publishing.

—&#65533;Yo Tambi&#65533;n Puedo Hacerlo! Houston, Terence. Reid, Tierra Destiny, ed. 2019. (Las Cr&#65533;nicas de Christian Grace Ser.: Vol. 1). (SPA.). 26p. (J). pap. 14.95 ***(978-1-947574-39-7(6))*** TDR Brands Publishing.

Acosta, Patricia. Adivinario de Diccionanzas. Zambrano, Alicia. 2008. (SPA.). 32p. (J). (gr. 2). 10.95 *(978-958-28-1298-0(2))* Intermedio Editores S.A. COL. Dist: Random Hse., Inc.

—La Alegría de Querer: Poemas de Amor para Ninos. Nino, Jairo Anibal. 2010. (Literatura Juvenil (Panamericana Editorial) Ser.). (SPA.). 70p. (gr. 4-6). pap. 9.99 *(978-958-30-0293-9(3),* PV30142) Panamericana Editorial COL. Dist: Lectorum Pubns., Inc.

—Andres, Perro y Oso en el Pais de los Medios. Ibanez, Francisco Montana. 2003. (SPA.). 84p. (J). (gr. -1-7). pap. *(978-958-30-0997-6(0))* Editorial Medica Panamerican.

—Cuentos, Pombo Rafael. Pombo, Rafael. (SPA.). 68p. (J). (gr. 2). pap. *(978-958-30-0355-4(7),* PV0862) Panamericana Editorial COL. Dist: Lectorum Pubns., Inc.

—Fiodor Mijailovich Dostoievsky. Dostoevsky, Fyodor. 2003. (Cajon de Cuentos Ser.). (SPA.). 223p. (J). (gr. 4-7). *(978-958-30-1027-9(8))* Panamericana Editorial.

—Relatos para Muchachos. Ramirez, Gonzalo Canal. 2003. (Literatura Juvenil (Panamericana Editorial) Ser.). (SPA.). 110p. (YA). (gr. 4-7). pap. *(978-958-30-0351-6(4))* Panamericana Editorial.

Acraman, Helen. Japanese & English Nursery Rhymes: Carp Streamers, Falling Rain & Other Favorite Songs & Rhymes (Audio Disc of Rhymes in Japanese Included) Wright, Danielle. 2019. 32p. (J). (gr. -1-3). 12.99 *(978-4-8053-1459-3(1))* Tuttle Publishing.

—Japanese Nursery Rhymes: Carp Streamers, Falling Rain & Other Traditional Favorites. Wright, Danielle. ed. 2012. (ENG.). 32p. (J). (gr. -1-3). 16.95 *(978-4-8053-1188-2(6))* Tuttle Publishing.

—Korean & English Nursery Rhymes: Wild Geese, Land of Goblins & Other Favorite Songs & Rhymes (Audio Disc in Korean & English Included) Wright, Danielle. ed. 2018. 32p. (J). (gr. -1-3). 12.99 *(978-0-8048-4998-2(6))* Tuttle Publishing.

Acreman, Hayley. Tai & the Tremorfa Troll. Davies, Lewis. 2007. (ENG.). 30p. (J). (gr. -1-k). pap. 7.95 *(978-1-905762-48-4(8))* Parthian Bks. GBR. Dist: Independent Pubs. Group.

Acreman, Hayley. Found You Rabbit! Acreman, Hayley. 2011. (ENG.). 34p. (J). (gr. k-2). pap. 9.95 *(978-1-905762-87-3(9))* Parthian Bks. GBR. Dist: Independent Pubs. Group.

Acton, Sara. Daddy Cuddle. Mayes, Kate. 2017. (ENG.). 32p. (J). (gr. -1-3). 17.99 *(978-1-68152-193-0(8))* Amicus.

—Esther's Rainbow. Kane, Kim. 2015. (ENG.). 32p. (J). (gr. -1-k). 16.99 *(978-1-925266-28-3(1))* Allen & Unwin AUS. Dist: Independent Pubs. Group.

Acton, Sara. Mr Walker Gets the Inside Scoop. 2020. (Mr Walker Ser.). (ENG.). 96p. (J). (gr. k-2). 12.99 ***(978-0-14-379309-0(8),*** Puffin) Penguin Random Hse. AUS. Dist: Independent Pubs. Group.

Acton, Sara. Quick As a Wink, Fairy Pink. Gibbes, Lesley. 2019. 32p. pap. 6.99 *(978-1-921504-87-7(0),* Working Title Pr.) HarperCollins Pubs. Australia AUS. Dist: HarperCollins Pubs.

Acuna, Antonia. Where Are My Teeth? ¿dónde Están MIS Dientes? Letelier, Ada N. 2018. (ENG.). 40p. (J). 25.50 *(978-1-946540-67-6(6))* Strategic Book Publishing & Rights Agency (SBPRA).

Acuna, Daniel. Black Panther Book 6: The Intergalactic Empire of Wakanda Part 1. 2019. (Black Panther by Ta-Nehisi Coates (2018) Ser.: 1). 136p. (J). (gr. 4-17). pap. 17.99 *(978-1-302-91293-2(3))* Marvel Worldwide, Inc.

Acuna, Daniel, et al. Black Widow: Widowmaker. 2020. (ENG.). 464p. (YA). (gr. 8-17). pap. 39.99 *(978-1-302-92144-6(4))* Marvel Worldwide, Inc.

Acuna, Daniel. Captain America: Sam Wilson Vol. 5: End of the Line. 2017. 112p. (YA). (gr. 8-17). pap. 15.99 *(978-1-302-90614-6(3))* Marvel Worldwide, Inc.

Ada, Carol. Bisi's Wonderful World: Childhood Tales from Nigeria. Bolujoko, Morenike. 2019. (ENG.). 20p. (J). (gr. 1-4). pap. 12.99 *(978-1-64438-486-2(8))* Booklocker.com, Inc.

—Jade's Journey. Randall, Julieann T. 2018. (Newness Ser.: Vol. 1). (ENG.). 84p. (J). (gr. 4-6). pap. 9.99 *(978-1-7323622-0-8(3))* Finding the JEMS.

Adair, Kiara. Mommy, Will You Play with Me? Adair, Tierashia. 2018. (ENG.). 32p. (J). pap. 12.99 ***(978-1-948248-13-6(1))*** Authors Pen, LLC, The.

Adalian, Sona. Aladdin's Magic Chest. Reznik, Vladimir. Fairweather-Vega, Shelley, tr. 2018. (ENG.). 120p. (J). pap. 5.84 *(978-1-7226-7497-7(0))* CreateSpace Independent Publishing Platform.

Adam, Mccauley, jt. illus. see McCauley, Adam.

Adam, Morris. Lucky Luke Vol. 70: O. K. Corral. 2018. (Lucky Luke Ser.: 70). (ENG.). 48p. pap. 11.95 *(978-1-84918-417-5(8))* CineBook GBR. Dist: National Bk. Network.

Adam, Sarah E. Abby in Vermont Coloring & Activity Book. 2008. 32p. (J). 4.95 *(978-0-9793790-1-7(6))* Howard Printing, Inc.

Adams, Adrienne. Mouse House. Godden, Rumer. 2016. (ENG.). 72p. (J). (gr. -1-2). 15.95 *(978-1-59017-998-7(6),* NYR Children's Collection) New York Review of Bks., Inc., The.

Adams, Adrienne. A Woggle of Witches. Adams, Adrienne. 2017. (ENG.). 32p. (J). (gr. -1-3). 13.99 *(978-1-5344-1246-0(8),* Aladdin) Simon & Schuster Children's Publishing.

Adams, Allysa. Pine Needle Pedro. Megerdichian, Janet. 2010. 36p. pap. 16.99 *(978-1-4520-4422-4(8))* AuthorHouse.

Adams, Anatol. Alfie Dalfie. Adams, Jon. 2017. (ENG.). (J). pap. 12.45 *(978-0-9797613-6-2(0))* Slack Water Pr.

Adams, Arlene. Locket Out. Bennett, Leonie. 2004. (ENG.). 24p. (J). lib. bdg. 23.65 *(978-1-59646-688-3(X))* Dingles & Co.

Adams, Arthur, et al. Marvel Masterworks: the Uncanny X-Men Vol. 12. 2020. (ENG.). 448p. (YA). (gr. 4-17). 100.00 *(978-1-302-92238-2(6))* Marvel Worldwide, Inc.

Adams, Arthur. Marvel Monograph: the Art of Arthur Adams - X-Men. 2020. (ENG.). 112p. (YA). (gr. 8-17). pap. 19.99 *(978-1-302-92294-8(7))* Marvel Worldwide, Inc.

Adams, Ben. Animals: Lift the Flaps to Find Out about Animals! O'Toole, Janet & Anness Publishing Staff. 2013. 16p. bds. 6.99 *(978-1-84322-793-9(2),* Armadillo) Anness Publishing GBR. Dist: National Bk. Network.

—First Words: Lift the Flaps to Find Out about Words! O'Toole, Janet & Anness Publishing Staff. 2013. 16p. bds. 6.99 *(978-1-84322-795-3(9),* Armadillo) Anness Publishing GBR. Dist: National Bk. Network.

—On the Farm: Lift the Flaps to Find Out about Farms! O'Toole, Janet. 2013. 16p. bds. 6.99 *(978-1-84322-794-6(0),* Armadillo) Anness Publishing GBR. Dist: National Bk. Network.

—Vehicles: Lift the Flaps to Find Out about Vehicles! O'Toole, Janet & Anness Publishing Staff. 2013. 16p. bds. 6.99 *(978-1-84322-728-1(2),* Armadillo) Anness Publishing GBR. Dist: National Bk. Network.

Adams, Beth. Confessions of a Former Bully. Ludwig, Trudy. 48p. (J). 2012. (gr. 3-7). pap. 7.99 *(978-0-307-93113-9(7),* Dragonfly Bks.); 2010. (ENG.). (gr. 1-4). 15.99 *(978-1-58246-309-4(3),* Tricycle Pr.) Random Hse. Children's Bks.

Adams Burque, Hannah. Environmental Health Narratives: A Reader for Youth. Mendenhall, Emily & Koon, Adam, eds. 2012. (ENG.). 400p. pap. 34.95 *(978-0-8263-5166-1(2))* Univ. of New Mexico Pr.

Adams, Craig. Edward of Canterbury & the King of Red. Cash, M. A. 2003. (J). *(978-0-9772711-0-8(2))* Jama Kids.

Adams, Denise H. Annabelle's Angels. Adams, Denise H. 2007. 24p. (J). (gr. -1-3). 11.99 *(978-1-59879-386-4(1))* Lifevest Publishing, Inc.

—Itchy the Witch. Adams, Denise H. 2007. 32p. (J). (gr. -1-3). 13.99 *(978-1-59879-385-7(3))* Lifevest Publishing, Inc.

Adams, Frank & Lawrence, C. H. Puss in Boots. Perrault, Charles. 2009. (ENG.). 16p. (J). (gr. -1-3). pap. 9.95 *(978-1-59583-361-7(7),* 9781595833617) Laughing Elephant.

Adams, Gil & Jessell, Tim. In the Ice Caves of Krog. Abbott, Tony. 2003. (Secrets of Droon Ser.: No. 20). 114p. (J). (gr. 2-5). 12.65 *(978-0-7569-3940-3(2))* Perfection Learning Corp.

Adams, Hazel. City Food Chains, 1 vol. Vogel, Julia. 2010. (Fascinating Food Chains Ser.). (ENG.). 32p. (J). (gr. k-4). 28.50 *(978-1-60270-791-7(X),* 7274, Looking Glass Library) Magic Wagon.

—Deciduous Forest Food Chains, 1 vol. Vogel, Julia. 2010. (Fascinating Food Chains Ser.). (ENG.). 32p. (J). (gr. k-4). 28.50 *(978-1-60270-792-4(8),* 7276, Looking Glass Library) Magic Wagon.

—Deep Ocean Food Chains, 1 vol. Mataya, Marybeth. 2010. (Fascinating Food Chains Ser.). (ENG.). 32p. (J). (gr. k-4). 28.50 *(978-1-60270-793-1(6),* 7278, Looking Glass Library) Magic Wagon.

—Desert Food Chains, 1 vol. Vogel, Julia. 2010. (Fascinating Food Chains Ser.). (ENG.). 32p. (J). (gr. k-4). 28.50 *(978-1-60270-794-8(4),* 7280, Looking Glass Library) Magic Wagon.

—Grassland Food Chains, 1 vol. Mataya, Marybeth. 2010. (Fascinating Food Chains Ser.). (ENG.). 32p. (J). (gr. k-4). 28.50 *(978-1-60270-795-5(2),* 7282, Looking Glass Library) Magic Wagon.

—What Are Food Chains & Food Webs?, 1 vol. Vogel, Julia. 2010. (Fascinating Food Chains Ser.). (ENG.). 32p. (J). (gr. k-4). 28.50 *(978-1-60270-796-2(0),* 7284, Looking Glass Library) Magic Wagon.

Adams, Jean Ekman. Clarence & the Purple Horse Bounce into Town, Vol. Adams, Jean Ekman. 2003. (ENG.). 32p. (J). (gr. -1-3). 15.95 *(978-0-87358-826-3(6),* Rising Moon Bks. for Young Readers) Northland Publishing.

Adams, Kevin & Price, Michael. A Stegosaurus Named Sam. Adams, Kevin. 2004. (J). per. 12.50 *(978-0-9740683-4-3(9))* Authors & Artists Publishers of New York, Inc.

Adams, Lisa. Oliver Brightside: You Don't Want That Penny. Manzo, Christopher. 2016. (ENG.). 36p. (J). 16.95 *(978-0-9963756-4-1(3))* All About Kids Publishing.

Adams, Lisa. The Twelve Days of Christmas in New York City. Adams, Lisa. 2009. (Twelve Days of Christmas in America Ser.). 40p. (J). (gr. k-3). 12.95 *(978-1-4027-6440-0(5))* Sterling Publishing Co., Inc.

Adams, Liz. Brooke's Big Decision, No. 8. Jones, Jen. 2012. (Team Cheer Ser.). (ENG.). 112p. (J). (gr. 4-8). 25.32 *(978-1-4342-4036-1(3),* Stone Arch Bks.) Capstone.

—Faith & the Dance Drama, No. 5. Jones, Jen. 2012. (Team Cheer Ser.: No. 5). (ENG.). 112p. (J). (gr. 4-8). lib. bdg. 25.32 *(978-1-4342-4033-0(9),* Stone Arch Bks.) Capstone.

—Lissa on the Sidelines, No. 6. Jones, Jen. 2012. (Team Cheer Ser.). (ENG.). 112p. (J). (gr. 4-8). lib. bdg. 25.32 *(978-1-4342-4034-7(7),* Stone Arch Bks.) Capstone.

—Save Our Squad, Gaby, No. 7. Jones, Jen. 2012. (Team Cheer Ser.). (ENG.). 112p. (J). (gr. 4-8). lib. bdg. 25.32 *(978-1-4342-4035-4(5),* Stone Arch Bks.) Capstone.

Adams, Lucas. Can a Toucan Hoot Too? A Phonemic Awareness Tale, 10 vols. Carlson, Lavelle. 2003. 32p. (J). (gr. -1-1). per. 16.95 *(978-0-9725803-0-4(1))* Children's Publishing.

—Rocks in My Socks & Rainbows Too, 10 vols. Carlson, Lavelle. 2003. 32p. (J). per. 16.95 *(978-0-9725803-2-8(8))* Children's Publishing.

Adams, Lynn. Bears on the Brain: Animal Tracks. Penner, Lucille Recht. 2006. (Science Solves It! ® Ser.). (ENG.). 32p. (J). (gr. k-2). pap. 5.95 *(978-1-57565-121-7(1))* Astra Publishing Hse.

—Chickens on the Move: Measurement: Perimeter. Pollack, Pam & Belviso, Meg. 2006. (Math Matters ® Ser.). (ENG.). 32p. (J). (gr. k-2). pap. 5.95 *(978-1-57565-113-2(0))* Astra Publishing Hse.

—¿dónde Está Ese Hueso? (Where's That Bone?) Position Words/Mapping. Penner, Lucille Recht. 2006. (Math Matters en Español Ser.). (SPA.). 32p. (J). (gr. k-2). pap. 5.95 *(978-1-57565-156-9(4))* Astra Publishing Hse.

—Gallinas de Aqui para Alla. Pollack, Pam & Belviso, Meg. 2008. (Math Matters en Espanol Ser.). (SPA.). 32p. (J). (gr. -1-3). pap. 5.95 *(978-1-57565-268-9(4))* Astra Publishing Hse.

—Kitten Castle: 3-D Shapes. Friedman, Mel et al. 2006. (Math Matters ® Ser.). (ENG.). 32p. (J). (gr. k-2). pap. 5.95 *(978-1-57565-103-3(3))* Astra Publishing Hse.

—Picky Peggy: Nutrition. Dussling, Jennifer. 2006. (Science Solves It! ® Ser.). (ENG.). 32p. (J). (gr. k-2). pap. 5.95 *(978-1-57565-138-5(6))* Astra Publishing Hse.

—¿Qué es Ese Sonido? (What's That Sound?) Lawrence, Mary. 2009. (Science Solves It! ® en Espanol Ser.). (SPA.). (gr. k-2). pap. 33.92 *(978-0-7613-4801-6(8))* Lerner Publishing Group.

—What's That Sound? Sound. Lawrence, Mary. 2006. (Science Solves It! ® Ser.). (ENG.). 32p. (J). (gr. k-2). pap. 5.95 *(978-1-57565-118-7(1))* Astra Publishing Hse.

—Where's That Bone? Position Words/Mapping. Penner, Lucille Recht. 2006. (Math Matters ® Ser.). (ENG.). 32p. (J). (gr. k-2). pap. 5.95 *(978-1-57565-097-5(5))* Astra Publishing Hse.

Adams, Lynn. Un Castillo para Gatitos. Adams, Lynn. Friedman, Mel et al. 2008. (SPA.). (J). *(978-1-57565-275-7(7))* Astra Publishing Hse.

Adams, Marcella Ryan. Around the World with Rosalie. Redman-Waldeyer, Christine. 2003. pap. 9.00 *(978-0-8059-6185-0(2))* Dorrance Publishing Co., Inc.

Adams, Mark W. My Friendly Giant. Rubenstein, Lauri. 2012. (ENG.). 36p. (J). 16.95 *(978-0-9770391-6-6(1))* Growing Field Bks.

Adams, Mark Wayne. The Belly Button Fairy. Hinman, Bobbie. 2009. (ENG.). 32p. (J). (gr. -1-1). 16.95 *(978-0-9786791-3-2(X))* Best Fairy Bks.

—Dolly, a Dog, & a Camper. Whitehouse, Kay. Thomas, Jennifer, ed. 2018. (Hand Truck Named Dolly Ser.: Vol. 3). (ENG.). 96p. (J). (gr. k-4). pap. 8.95 *(978-1-5323-6549-2(7))* Vance Hardy Publishing.

—The Fart Fairy. Hinman, Bobbie. 2010. (ENG.). 32p. (J). (gr. -1-1). 16.95 *(978-0-9786791-4-9(8))* Best Fairy Bks.

—The Freckle Fairy: Book & Audio CD. Hinman, Bobbie. 2016. (ENG.). 32p. (J). (gr. -1-1). 16.95 *(978-0-9786791-2-5(1))* Best Fairy Bks.

—Jadyn & the Magic Bubble: I Met Gandhi. Benchimol, Brigitte. 2008. (J). 24.95 *(978-0-9799339-7-4(8))* East West Discovery Pr.

Adams Marks, Elizabeth. Comprehension Crosswords Grade 5, 6 vols. Koumpouras, Sally. 2003. 32p. (J). 4.99 *(978-1-56472-189-1(2))* Edupress, Inc.

—Comprehension Crosswords Grade 6, 6 vols. Hemminger, Marcia. 2003. 32p. (J). 4.99 *(978-1-56472-190-7(6))* Edupress, Inc.

—Lewis & Clark Famous Faces. Meinke, Amanda & Stegmann, Lisa. 2003. 2p. (J). pap. 2.99 *(978-1-56472-289-8(9))* Edupress, Inc.

Adams, Matt. Meet Ned Kelly. Brian, Janeen. 2014. (Meet... Ser.). 36p. (J). (gr. k). 13.99 *(978-1-74275-719-3(7))* Random Hse. Australia AUS. Dist: Independent Pubs. Group.

Adams, Michael. Turning the Page: Frederick Douglass Learns to Read. Roos, Am & Hamilton, A. 2011. (Social Studies). (ENG.). 28p. (J). pap. 8.00 *(978-1-61406-683-5(3))* American Reading Co.

Adams, Milancie Hill. Beasties, Ghosties, Goblins, Witches & Things That Go Bump in the Night! Adams, Milancie Hill. 2019. (ENG.). 34p. (J). pap. 9.99 ***(978-1-6996-5520-7(0))*** Independently Published.

Adams, Milancie Hill. The Big Catch. Adams, Milancie Hill. 2019. (ENG.). 34p. (J). pap. 9.99 *(978-1-0764-3666-5(8))* Independently Published.

—Echo of Horse's Soul's Footprint. Adams, Milancie Hill. 2018. (Time's Looking Glass - Echos of Life's Footprints Ser.: Vol. 2). (ENG.). 80p. (J). pap. 17.00 *(978-1-7272-4658-2(6))* CreateSpace Independent Publishing Platform.

—Echo of the Penguin's Soul's Footprint. Adams, Milancie Hill. 2018. (Time's Looking Glass - Echos of Life's Footprints Ser.: Vol. 4). (ENG.). 70p. (J). pap. 15.99 *(978-1-7311-5292-3(2))* Independently Published.

—Echoes of a Deer's Silent Soul's Footprints. Adams, Milancie Hill. 2018. (Time's Looking Glass - Echos of Life's Footprints Ser.: Vol. 7). (ENG.). 58p. (J). pap. 12.00 *(978-1-7927-2810-5(7))* Independently Published.

—Echoes of Lions. Adams, Milancie Hill. 2018. (Time's Looking Glass - Echos of Life's Footprints Ser.: Vol. 5). (ENG.). 64p. (J). pap. 15.00 *(978-1-7903-7640-7(8))* Independently Published.

Adams, Milancie Hill. The Flight of the Dragon Damsel Flies' Daughter. Adams, Milancie Hill. 2019. (ENG.). 34p. (J). pap. 9.99 ***(978-1-6967-7821-3(2))*** Independently Published.

—Mt. Possum & Mr. Turtle - Around the World. Adams, Milancie Hill. 2019. (Mr. Pssum & Mr. Turtle Ser.: Vol. 3). (ENG.). 54p. (J). pap. 11.99 ***(978-1-6768-4331-3(0))*** Independently Published.

—A New Friend. Adams, Milancie Hill. 2019. (ENG.). 38p. (J). pap. 9.99 ***(978-1-7122-1611-8(2))*** Independently Published.

Adams, Milancie Hill. Santa Did Come! Adams, Milancie Hill. 2018. (ENG.). 44p. (J). pap. 11.99 *(978-1-7909-1998-7(3))* Independently Published.

Adams, Milancie Hill. Swans, Witches, & Mermaids: Aphrodite Keeper of the Sea's Foam. Adams, Milancie Hill. 2019. (ENG.). 38p. (J). pap. 12.99 ***(978-1-6877-0867-0(3))*** Independently Published.

—Tristan - the Mouse Who Could Fly. Adams, Milancie Hill. 2019. (ENG.). 42p. (J). pap. 9.99 ***(978-1-7067-3203-7(1))*** Independently Published.

Adams, Neal, et al. Avengers: Kree/Skrull War. 2019. (Avengers: Kree/Skrull War Ser.: 1). (ENG.). 208p. (J). (gr. 4-17). pap. 24.99 *(978-1-302-91548-3(7))* Marvel Worldwide, Inc.

—Mephisto: Speak of the Devil. 2020. 456p. (YA). (gr. 8-17). pap. 39.99 *(978-1-302-92361-7(7))* Marvel Worldwide, Inc.

Adams, Neal. X-Men by Roy Thomas & Neal Adams Gallery Edition. 2019. (ENG.). 208p. (YA). (gr. 4-17). 39.99 *(978-1-302-91936-8(9))* Marvel Worldwide, Inc.

Adams, Pam. The Farmer in the Dell. 2013. (Classic Books with Holes 8x8 with CD Ser.). (ENG.). 16p. (J). (gr. -1). pap. incl. audio compact disk *(978-1-84643-624-6(9))* Child's Play International Ltd.

A

—The First Day. 2009. 10p. (J). bds. *(978-0-85953-149-8(X))* Child's Play International Ltd.

—Había una Vez una Viejecita Que una Mosca Se Tragó. 2019. (Classic Books with Holes 8x8 with CD Ser.). (SPA.). 16p. (J). *(978-1-78628-401-3(4))* Child's Play International Ltd.

—Había una Vez una Viejecita Que una Mosca Se Tragó. 2018. (Classic Books with Holes Big Book Ser.). (SPA.). 16p. (J). *(978-1-78628-165-4(1))* Child's Play International Ltd.

—Old Macdonald Had a Farm. (Classic Books with Holes 8x8 with CD Ser.). (ENG.). 16p. (J). 2007. (gr. -1-1). *(978-1-904550-64-8(9))*; 2004. bds. *(978-0-85953-317-1(4))*; 2003. pap. *(978-0-85953-135-1(X))* Child's Play International Ltd.

—There Was an Old Lady Who Swallowed a Fly. (Classic Books with Holes 8x8 with CD Ser.). (ENG.). (J). 2007. 16p. (gr. -1-1). *(978-1-904550-62-4(2))*; 2005. 20p. (gr. -1-1). bds. *(978-0-85953-314-0(X))*; 2003. 16p. pap. *(978-0-85953-134-4(1))* Child's Play International Ltd.

—This Is the House That Jack Built. 2007. (Classic Books with Holes 8x8 with CD Ser.). (ENG.). 16p. (J). (gr. -1-1). *(978-1-904550-65-5(7))* Child's Play International Ltd.

—This Old Man. 2007. (Classic Books with Holes 8x8 with CD Ser.). (ENG.). 16p. (J). (gr. -1-1). *(978-1-904550-63-1(0))* Child's Play International Ltd.

—El Viejo Macdonald. Child's Play. Mlawer, Teresa, tr. from ENG. (Classic Books with Holes 8x8 with CD Ser.). (SPA.). 16p. (J). 2019. pap. incl. audio compact disk *(978-1-78628-400-6(6))*; 2017. pap. *(978-1-84643-964-3(7))*; 2017. bds. *(978-1-84643-967-4(1))* Child's Play International Ltd.

Adams, Renee. Can Thunder Hurt Me? Adams, Renee. 2012. 24p. pap. 17.99 *(978-1-4685-5852-4(8))* AuthorHouse.

Adams, Rich. Rupert & the Bag. Staman, A. Louise. 2006. (J). 11.99 *(978-0-9787263-0-0(8))* Tiger Iron Pr.

Adams, Ronald. The Adventures of Junior & Mousey in the Land of Puttin Pow: Don't Talk to Strangers. Adams, Jt. 2013. 32p. pap. 24.95 *(978-1-63004-457-2(1))* America Star Bks.

Adams, Shireen. Colours of Islam. 2013. (ENG.). 40p. (J). (gr. k-2). 22.95 *(978-0-86037-591-3(9))* Kube Publishing Ltd. GBR. Dist: Consortium Bk. Sales & Distribution.

—Snow White: An Islamic Tale. Gilani, Fawzia. 2013. (Islamic Fairy Tales Ser.). (ENG.). 40p. (J). (gr. k-3). 14.00 *(978-0-86037-526-5(9))* Kube Publishing Ltd. GBR. Dist: Consortium Bk. Sales & Distribution.

Adams, Stephen. Gracie Lou Tries Something New. Juliano, Larissa. 2019. (ENG.). 24p. (J). 25.99 ***(978-1-4808-8133-4(3))***; pap. 12.45 ***(978-1-4808-8134-1(1))*** Archway Publishing.

Adams, Stephen. Mystery Within. Child, Jodie. 2017. (ENG.). 28p. pap. 20.99 *(978-1-5043-0574-7(4)*, Balboa Pr.) Author Solutions, Inc.

Adams, Steve. A Believe Devotional for Kids: Think, Act, Be Like Jesus: 90 Devotions, 1 vol. Frazee, Randy. 2015. (ENG.). 192p. (J). 12.99 *(978-0-310-75202-8(7))* Zonderkidz.

—Believe Storybook: Think, Act, Be Like Jesus, 1 vol. Frazee, Randy. 2015. (ENG.). 256p. (J). 19.99 *(978-0-310-74590-7(X))* Zonderkidz.

—The Boy Who Grew Flowers. Wojtowicz, Jen & Wojzowitz, Jen. 2005. 32p. (J). (gr. -1-3). 16.99 *(978-1-84148-686-4(8))* Barefoot Bks., Inc.

—The Boy Who Grew Flowers. Wojtowicz, Jen. 2012. 32p. (J). (gr. k-5). pap. 8.99 *(978-1-84686-749-1(5))* Barefoot Bks., Inc.

—The Boy Who Wanted to Cook. Whelan, Gloria. 2011. (Tales of the World Ser.). (ENG.). 40p. (gr. k-5). lib. bdg. 16.95 *(978-1-58536-534-0(3))* Sleeping Bear Pr.

—Des Fleurs Pour Angélina. Wojtowicz, Jen. 2017. (FRE.). 32p. (J). (gr. k-5). pap. 8.99 *(978-1-78285-142-4(9))* Barefoot Bks., Inc.

—If: A Mind-Bending New Way of Looking at Big Ideas & Numbers. Smith, David J. 2014. (ENG.). 40p. (J). (gr. 3-7). 18.95 *(978-1-894786-34-8(3))* Kids Can Pr., Ltd. CAN. Dist: Hachette Bk. Group.

Adamson, Bonnie. Bedtime Monster. Brunell, Heather. 2010. (ENG.). 32p. (J). (gr. -1-12). lib. bdg. 16.95 *(978-1-934960-03-5(9)*, Raven Tree Pr.,Csi) Continental Sales, Inc.

—Feeling Better: A Kid's Book about Therapy. Rashkin, Rachel. 2005. 48p. (J). (gr. -1-7). pap. 9.95 *(978-1-59147-238-4(5)*, Magination Pr.) American Psychological Assn.

—Feeling Better: A Kid's Books about Therapy. Rashkin, Rachel. 2005. 48p. (J). 14.95 *(978-1-59147-237-7(7)*, Magination Pr.) American Psychological Assn.

—I Wish I Had Freckles Like Abby. Heling, Kathryn & Hembrook, Deborah. (I Wish Ser.). (ENG.). 32p. (J). 2010. (gr. 4-7). pap. 7.95 *(978-1-934960-47-9(0))*; 2009. (gr. -1-3). 16.95 *(978-1-934960-46-2(2))* Continental Sales, Inc. (Raven Tree Pr.,Csi).

—I Wish I Had Freckles Like Abby/Quisiera Tener Pecas Como Abby. Heling, Kathryn & Hembrook, Deborah. 2007. (SPA & ENG.). 32p. (J). (gr. -1-3). pap. 7.95 *(978-0-9770906-6-2(3)*, Raven Tree Pr.,Csi) Continental Sales, Inc.

—I Wish I Was Strong Like Manuel. Heling, Kathryn & Hembrook, Deborah. (I Wish Ser.). (ENG.). 32p. (J). 2010. (gr. 4-7). pap. 7.95 *(978-1-934960-53-0(5))*; 2009. (gr. -1-3). 16.95 *(978-1-934960-52-3(7))* Continental Sales, Inc. (Raven Tree Pr.,Csi).

—I Wish I Was Tall Like Willie. Heling, Kathryn & Hembrook, Deborah. (I Wish Ser.). (ENG.). 32p. (J). (gr. 4-7). 2010. pap. 7.95 *(978-1-934960-51-6(9))*; 2009. 16.95 *(978-1-934960-50-9(0))* Continental Sales, Inc. (Raven Tree Pr.,Csi).

—I Wish I Was Tall Like Willie/Quisiera Ser Tan Alto Como Willie. Heling, Kathryn & Hembrook, Deborah. 2008. (I Wish Ser.). (ENG & SPA.). 32p. (J). (gr. 4-7). 16.95 *(978-0-9794462-0-7(1)*, Raven Tree Pr.,Csi) Continental Sales, Inc.

—Postcards from Chicago/Postales Desde Chicago. Crawford, Laura. de La Vega, Eida, tr. 2008. (Traveling with Anna Ser.). (ENG.). 32p. (J). (gr. 4-7). 16.95 *(978-0-9795477-4-4(1)*, Raven Tree Pr.,Csi) Continental Sales, Inc.

—Postcards from New York City/Postales Desde New York City. Crawford, Laura. de La Vega, Eida, tr. 2008. (Traveling with Anna Ser.). (ENG.). 32p. (J). (gr. 4-7). 16.95 *(978-0-9795477-2-0(5))*; per. 7.95 *(978-0-9795477-3-7(3))* Continental Sales, Inc. (Raven Tree Pr.,Csi).

—Postcards from Washington D. C./Postales Desde Washington D. C. Crawford, Laura. de La Vega, Eida, tr. 2008. (Traveling with Anna Ser.). (ENG.). 32p. (J). (gr. 4-7). 16.95 *(978-0-9795477-0-6(9))*; per. 7.95 *(978-0-9795477-1-3(7))* Continental Sales, Inc. (Raven Tree Pr.,Csi).

—Rutabaga Boo! Bardhan-Quallen, Sudipta. 2017. (ENG.). 40p. (J). (gr. -1-3). 15.99 *(978-1-4814-2461-5(0))* Simon & Schuster Children's Publishing.

Adamson, Gareth, jt. illus. see Worsley, Belinda.

Adamson, Ged. Meet the Mckaws. 2015. 32p. (J). (gr. -1-k). 16.95 *(978-1-62914-618-8(8)*, Sky Pony Pr.) Skyhorse Publishing Co., Inc.

Adamson, Ged. Ava & the Rainbow (Who Stayed) Adamson, Ged. 2018. (ENG.). 40p. (J). (gr. -1-3). 17.99 *(978-0-06-267080-9(8))* HarperCollins Pubs.

—Douglas, You Need Glasses! Adamson, Ged. 2016. 40p. (J). (gr. -1-2). 17.99 *(978-0-553-52243-3(4)*, Schwartz & Wade Bks.) Random Hse. Children's Bks.

—Shark Dog! Adamson, Ged. 2017. (ENG.). 40p. (J). (gr. -1-3). 17.99 *(978-0-06-245713-4(6))* HarperCollins Pubs.

—Shark Dog & the School Trip Rescue! Adamson, Ged. 2018. (ENG.). 40p. (J). (gr. -1-3). 17.99 *(978-0-06-245718-9(7))* HarperCollins Pubs.

Adamson, Lynne. First Star I See. Caffrey, Jaye Andras. 2nd ed. 2010. (ENG.). 164p. (J). (gr. 2-7). pap. 12.95 *(978-1-936290-01-7(4))* Central Recovery Pr.

Adancie, Milancie Hill. Beavers, Muskrats, Badgers, Moose & the Sleeping Child. Adams, Milancie Hill. 2019. (ENG.). 48p. (J). pap. 10.99 ***(978-1-6929-7301-8(0))*** Independently Published.

Adasa, Alyssa. 10 Classic Poems for Bedtime. Adasa, Alyssa. 2019. (ENG.). 32p. (J). pap. 10.99 *(978-1-0959-5669-4(8))* Independently Published.

Adasikov, Igor. Abigail & the Royal Thread. Turnbull, Betty. 2014. 44p. (J). pap. 8.95 *(978-1-61153-008-7(3))* Light Messages Publishing.

—Isobel's New World. Turnbull, Betty. 2014. 48p. (J). pap. 8.95 *(978-1-61153-006-3(7))* Light Messages Publishing.

—The Man Who Saved the King. Turnbull, Betty. 2014. 44p. (J). pap. 8.95 *(978-1-61153-004-9(0))* Light Messages Publishing.

—The Megalith Union. LaMar, Brad A. 2013. (Celtic Mythos Ser.). (ENG.). 342p. pap. 16.99 *(978-1-61153-070-4(9))* Light Messages Publishing.

Adb+ge, Emma. Outdoor Math: Fun Activities for Every Season. Adb+ge, Emma. 2016. (ENG.). 26p. (J). (gr. k-3). 15.95 *(978-1-77138-612-8(6))* Kids Can Pr., Ltd. CAN. Dist: Hachette Bk. Group.

Adbage, Lisen. Soda Pop. Lindgren, Barbro. 2017. (ENG.). 112p. (J). (gr. 3-5). 16.99 *(978-1-77657-010-2(3))* Gecko Pr. NZL. Dist: Lerner Publishing Group.

Adcock, Kerry. Bible Animal Tales: 50 Devotionals for Teen Agers. Pearson, Mary Rose. 2004. (J). pap. 13.95 *(978-0-9664803-7-5(6))* Fair Havens Pubns.

Adderley, Peter. God's Wonderful World. Godfrey, Jan. 2008. Orig. Title: Wonderful World. (J). (gr. k-3). 12.95 *(978-0-8198-8317-9(4))* Pauline Bks. & Media.

Addison, Kenneth. We, 1 vol. Schertle, Alice. (ENG.). 32p. (J). (gr. 1-12). 2017. pap. 10.95 *(978-1-62014-573-9(1)*, 8130af1c-bea4-42ab-aee6-c3a2f3692cf7); 2013. 16.95 *(978-1-58430-060-1(4))* Lee & Low Bks., Inc.

Addy, Sean. Peaceful Heroes. Winter, Jonah. 2009. (J). pap. *(978-0-439-62308-7(1)*, Levine, Arthur A. Bks.) Scholastic, Inc.

Addy, Sean & Halsey, Megan. Akira to Zoltan: Twenty-Six Men Who Changed the World. Chin-Lee, Cynthia. 2008. 32p. (J). (gr. 3-7). pap. 7.95 *(978-1-57091-580-2(6))* Charlesbridge Publishing, Inc.

Addy, Sean, jt. illus. see Halsey, Megan.

Adeel, M. Mandy the Sad Unicorn: Short Bedtime Stories about Unicorns, Unicorn Storybook for Children, into the Land of the Unicorns. Cooper, Amby. 2019. (ENG.). 30p. (J). pap. 9.99 *(978-1-0968-3197-6(X))* Independently Published.

Adeff, Jay & Mittan, J. Barry, photos by. Joannie Rochette: Canadian Ice Princess. Dzidrums, Christine & Rendon, Leah. Allison, Elizabeth, ed. 2nd exp. rev. ed. 2010. (Skate Stars Ser.: Vol. 1). 100p. (YA). pap. 12.99 *(978-0-9826435-0-1(0))* Creative Media Publishing.

Adele, Amy. And Then Another Sheep Turned Up. Gehl, Laura. ed. 2015. (ENG.). 32p. (J). (gr. -1-3). E-Book 23.99 *(978-1-4677-1190-6(X)*, Kar-Ben Publishing) Lerner Publishing Group.

Adeola, Dapo. The Last Last-Day-of-Summer. Giles, Lamar. 2019. (Legendary Alston Boys Adventure Ser.). (ENG.). 304p. (J). (gr. 3-7). 16.99 *(978-1-328-46083-7(5)*, 1712835, Versify) Houghton Mifflin Harcourt Publishing Co.

Adeola, Dapo. The Last Last-Day-Of-Summer: A Legendary Alston Boys Adventure. Giles, Lamar. 2020. (Legendary Alston Boys Adventure Ser.). (ENG.). 320p. (J). (gr. 3-7). pap. 7.99 ***(978-0-358-24441-7(2)***, 1767946, Versify) Houghton Mifflin Harcourt Publishing Co.

Adeola, Dapo. Rocket Says Look Up! Bryon, Nathan. 2019. (ENG.). 40p. (J). (gr. -1-2). 17.99 *(978-1-9848-9442-7(0)*, Random Hse. Bks. for Young Readers) Random Hse. Children's Bks.

Adilman, Katarzyna. Everyday Signs for the Newborn Baby. Campbell, Diana & Mosher, Nancy, eds. 2007. 20p. (J). bds. *(978-0-9791059-0-6(0))* Dakitab, Inc.

Adinolfi, JoAnn. A Circle in the Sky. Wilson, Zachary. (Rookie Ready to Learn Ser.). (ENG.). (J). 2011. 40p. pap. 5.95 *(978-0-531-26746-2(6))*; 2006. 32p. lib. bdg. 19.50 *(978-0-531-12570-0(X))* Scholastic Library Publishing. (Children's Pr.).

—Un Circulo en el Cielo. Wilson, Zachary. 2011. (Rookie Ready to Learn Español Ser.). (SPA.). 40p. (J). pap. 5.95 *(978-0-531-26791-2(1)*, Children's Pr.) Scholastic Library Publishing.

—Here Comes Silent E! Hays, Anna Jane. 2004. (Step into Reading Ser.). (ENG.). 32p. (J). (gr. -1-1). pap. 4.99 *(978-0-375-81233-0(4)*, Random Hse. Bks. for Young Readers) Random Hse. Children's Bks.

—I Want Your Moo: A Story for Children about Self-Esteem. Weiner, Marcella Bakur & Neimark, Jill. 2nd ed. 2009. 32p. (J). (gr. -1-3). 14.95 *(978-1-4338-0542-4(1))*; pap. 9.95 *(978-1-4338-0552-3(9))* American Psychological Assn. (Magination Pr.).

—Leaping Lizards. Murphy, Stuart J. 2005. (MathStart 1 Ser.). (ENG.). 40p. (J). (gr. -1). pap. 5.99 *(978-0-06-000132-2(1))* HarperCollins Pubs.

—Leaping Lizards. Murphy, Stuart J. ed. 2005. (Mathstart Level 1 Ser.). 33p. (J). (gr. -1-3). lib. bdg. 16.00 *(978-1-4176-7758-0(9))* Turtleback.

—The Little Tree. Van, Muon. 2015. (ENG.). 32p. (J). (gr. k-3). 16.95 *(978-1-939547-19-4(9))* Creston Bks.

—The Perfect Thanksgiving. Spinelli, Eileen. 2007. (ENG.). 32p. (J). (gr. -1-2). 8.99 *(978-0-312-37505-8(0)*, 900045781) Square Fish.

—This Book Is Haunted. Rocklin, Joanne. 2003. (I Can Read Level 1 Ser.). (ENG.). 48p. (J). (gr. k-3). pap. 4.99 *(978-0-06-444261-9(6))* HarperCollins Pubs.

—This Book Is Haunted. Rocklin, Joanne. 2004. (I Can Read Bks.). 48p. (gr. k-3). 14.00 *(978-0-7569-3081-3(2))* Perfection Learning Corp.

—Toodles & Teeny: A Story about Friendship. Neimark, Jill & Weiner, Marcella Bakur. 2012. 32p. (J). 14.95 *(978-1-4338-1198-2(7))*; pap. 9.95 *(978-1-4338-1199-9(5))* American Psychological Assn. (Magination Pr.).

—Valentine Hearts: Holiday Poetry. Hopkins, Lee Bennett. 2004. (I Can Read Bks.). 32p. (J). (gr. k-3). 15.99 *(978-0-06-008057-0(4))* HarperCollins Pubs.

Adinolfi, JoAnn. The Chilly Adventures of Mr. Small. Adinolfi, JoAnn. 2017. (ENG.). 32p. (J). (gr. k-3). pap. 9.99 *(978-1-939547-35-4(0))* Creston Bks.

—Un Circulo en el Cielo. Adinolfi, JoAnn. Wilson, Zachary. 2011. (Rookie Ready to Learn Español Ser.). (SPA.). 40p. (J). lib. bdg. 23.00 *(978-0-531-26123-1(9)*, Children's Pr.) Scholastic Library Publishing.

—Tina's Diner. Adinolfi, JoAnn. 2014. (ENG.). 32p. (J). (gr. -1-3). 13.99 *(978-1-4814-4459-0(X)*, Simon & Schuster Bks. For Young Readers) Simon & Schuster Bks. For Young Readers.

Adinolfi, Joanne. A Circle in the Sky. Wilson, Zachary. 2011. (ENG.). 40p. (J). (gr. -1-1). lib. bdg. 23.00 *(978-0-531-26446-1(7)*, Children's Pr.) Scholastic Library Publishing.

Adiputri, Maima W. A Night in the Wood. Holt, Gloria Rosella. 2019. (ENG.). 28p. (J). pap. 9.13 *(978-1-0938-7979-7(3))* Independently Published.

—A World Without Failures: Growth Mindset. Cordova, Esther Pia. 2019. (Growth Mindset Ser.: Vol. 2). (ENG.). 32p. (J). pap. *(978-3-948298-03-6(3))* Cordova, Esther Pia Power Of Yet.

Adkins, Jan. Bertha Takes a Drive. Adkins, Jan. 2017. 32p. (J). (gr. k-3). lib. bdg. 17.99 *(978-1-58089-696-2(0))* Charlesbridge Publishing, Inc.

—Moving Heavy Things. Adkins, Jan. 2004. (ENG.). 48p. (J). (gr. -1-3). 13.95 *(978-0-937822-82-1(5))* WoodenBoat Pubns.

Adkins, Loretta B. The Lottie & Annie Upside-down Book. Vogel, Cara Lynn. 2003. 16p. (J). 8.99 *(978-1-56309-627-3(7))* Woman's Missionary Union.

Adkins, Minnie. Mommy Goose: Rhymes from the Mountains. Norris, Mike. 2016. (ENG.). 48p. 19.95 *(978-0-8131-6614-8(4))* Univ. Pr. of Kentucky.

Adkins, Miriam. Creature. Robertson, Miriam & Robertson, Hayley K. 2018. (ENG.). 38p. (J). 23.95 *(978-1-64003-827-1(2))*; pap. 13.95 *(978-1-64003-826-4(4))* Covenant Bks.

Adl, Shirin. Mabrook! a World of Muslim Weddings. Robert, Na'ima B. 2016. (ENG.). 32p. (J). (gr. -1-2). 17.99 *(978-1-84780-588-1(4)*, Frances Lincoln Children's Bks.) Quarto Publishing Group UK GBR. Dist: Hachette Bk. Group.

—Ramadan Moon. Robert, Na'ima B. 2015. (ENG.). 32p. (J). (gr. -1-2). pap. 8.95 *(978-1-84780-206-4(0)*, Frances Lincoln Children's Bks.) Quarto Publishing Group UK GBR. Dist: Hachette UK Distribution.

—Riding a Donkey Backwards: Wise & Foolish Tales of Mulla Nasruddin. Taylor, Sean & Khayaal Theatre Company. 2019. (ENG.). 48p. (J). (gr. -1-3). 18.99 *(978-1-5362-0507-7(9))* Candlewick Pr.

Adlard, Charlie. The X Files, Vol.1. Petrucha, Stefan et al. 2005. (X-Files Ser.: Vol. 1). (ENG.). 200p. (YA). pap. 19.95 *(978-1-933160-02-3(0))* Devil's Due Digital, Inc. - A Checker Digital Co.

Adler, Charlie. Zak's King Arthur Adventure. Cuillain, Adam & Guillain, Charlotte. 2014. (Race Ahead with Reading Ser.). (ENG.). 32p. (J). (gr. 2-2). *(978-0-7787-1315-9(6))* Crabtree Publishing Co.

Adlerman, Kimberly M. Rock-a-Bye Baby. Adlerman, Daniel. 2004. 32p. (J). 15.95 *(978-1-58089-082-3(2))* Charlesbridge Publishing, Inc.

Adnet, Bernard. The Ants & the Grasshopper, Vol. 4262. Williams, Rozanne Lanczak. 2005. (Reading for Fluency Ser.). 16p. (J). pap. 3.49 *(978-1-59198-162-6(X))* Creative Teaching Pr., Inc.

—Bugs in Your Backyard. Williams, Rozanne Lanczak. Hamaguchi, Carla, ed. 2003. (Sight Word Readers Ser.). 16p. (J). (gr. k-2). pap. 3.49 *(978-1-57471-968-0(8)*, 3590) Creative Teaching Pr., Inc.

—Busy Bugs: A Book about Patterns. Harvey, Jayne. 2003. (Penguin Young Readers, Level 2 Ser.: Level 1). 32p. (J). (gr. 1-2). pap. 4.99 *(978-0-448-43159-8(9)*, Penguin Young Readers) Penguin Young Readers Group.

—Writing Dino-Mite Poems. Williams, Rozanne Lanczak. (Learn to Write Ser.). 8p. (J). 2008. (gr. -1-3). pap. 6.99 *(978-1-59198-336-1(3))*; 2006. (gr. k-2). pap. 3.49 *(978-1-59198-285-2(5)*, 6179) Creative Teaching Pr., Inc.

Adobe, Stock. Autumntime in the Forest. Kurtz, Edward Alan. 2016. (ENG.). 60p. (J). (gr. k-2). pap. *(978-1-910370-86-5(X))* Stergiou Ltd.

Adobe Stock. Christmas in the Forest. Kurtz, Edward Alan. 2nd ed. 2016. (ENG.). 62p. (J). (gr. k-2). pap. *(978-1-910370-90-2(8))* Stergiou Ltd.

Adolphe, Joseph. The Night Before Christmas. Moore, Clement C. 2013. (J). 19.95 *(978-1-59530-953-2(5))* Hallmark Card, Inc.

Adona, Nomer. God Made. Miller, Sharon J. 2016. (ENG.). 32p. (J). pap. 9.97 *(978-0-9774756-5-0(4))* Miller, Sharon.

—Jonah. Miller, Sharon J. 2016. (ENG.). 26p. (J). pap. 9.97 *(978-0-9774756-3-6(8))* Miller, Sharon.

—Noah. Miller, Sharon J. 2016. (ENG.). 26p. (J). pap. 9.97 *(978-0-9774756-4-3(6))* Miller, Sharon.

Adore, Jess. The Brave Zombie. Reyland, E. a. 2019. (ENG.). 54p. (J). pap. 12.99 *(978-1-0746-3720-0(8))* Independently Published.

Adreani, Manuela. Alice in Wonderland. Carroll, Lewis. 2018. (ENG.). 80p. (J). (gr. 3). 16.95 *(978-88-544-1255-2(4))* White Star ITA. Dist: Sterling Publishing Co., Inc.

—Bible Stories: Illustrated Stories from the Old Testament. 2019. (ENG.). 80p. (J). (gr. 3). 16.95 *(978-88-544-1353-5(4))* White Star ITA. Dist: Sterling Publishing Co., Inc.

—Boundless Sky. Addison, Amanda. 2020. 40p. (J). (gr. k-2). 17.99 *(978-1-911373-67-4(6))* Lantana Publishing GBR. Dist: Lerner Publishing Group.

—Brothers Grimm: The Most Beloved Fairy Tales. 2019. (ENG.). 80p. (J). (gr. 3). 16.95 *(978-88-544-1530-0(8))* White Star ITA. Dist: Sterling Publishing Co., Inc.

—The Little Prince. Saint-Exupery, Antoine De. 2018. (ENG.). 80p. (J). (gr. 3). 16.95 *(978-88-544-1254-5(6))* White Star ITA. Dist: Sterling Publishing Co., Inc.

—The Owl & the Raven - 6 Pack: Set of 6 with Common Core Teacher Materials. 2015. (Classic Tales Ser.). (J). (gr. k-1). 39.00 *(978-1-5125-8355-7(3))* Benchmark Education Co.

Adriance, Patrick. There Are a Lot of Things I Could Tell You about Myself, but I'll Keep It Short: Student Expectations, Self-Perceptions, Aspirations, & Concerns on the Eve of 7th Grade. Adriance, Patrick. Adriance, John. 2019. (ENG.). 52p. (J). pap. 7.00 ***(978-1-7129-5438-6(5))*** Independently Published.

Adzhigirey, Galina. Pretty Girl: Teaching Girls What Petty Really Is. McCarty, Katara. 2017. 24p. (J). 14.95 *(978-0-9980154-0-8(7))* Fierce Publishing.

Aesop, Aesop. Aesop's Fables. ed. 2006. 32p. (J). (gr. -1-3). 16.95 *(978-0-7358-2068-5(6))* North-South Bks., Inc.

Aesop, Aesop, jt. illus. see Zwerger, Lisbeth.

Affaya, Colette. Arkam, Numero & Numbers, 1 vol. Affaya, Colett & Affaya, Otman. 2009. 16p. pap. 24.95 *(978-1-60749-929-9(0))* America Star Bks.

Affleck, Donna. Mykey Moments. Tiffany, Thomas Charles. 2019. (Volume Ser.: Vol. 1). (ENG.). 110p. (J). pap. 10.00 *(978-1-7956-6601-5(3))* Independently Published.

Affonso, Alexandre & Beach, Bryan. The Science of Medical Technology: From Humble Syringes to Lifesaving Robots. Senker, Cath. 2019. (Science of Engineering Ser.). (ENG.). 32p. (J). (gr. 3-3). lib. bdg. 29.00 *(978-0-531-13193-0(9)*, Watts, Franklin) Scholastic Library Publishing.

—The Science of Seafaring: The Float-Tastic Facts about Ships. Rooney, Anne. 2019. (Science of Engineering Ser.). (ENG.). 32p. (J). (gr. 3-3). lib. bdg. 29.00 *(978-0-531-13196-1(3)*, Watts, Franklin) Scholastic Library Publishing.

Afzal, Zara. Family Shark Tornado: (as Seen on YouTube) Suarez, Mike. 2019. (ENG.). 40p. (J). pap. 11.92 ***(978-1-7059-3624-5(5))*** Independently Published.

AG Jatkowska. Little Seeds [Scholastic]. Ghigna, Charles. 2012. (My Little Planet Ser.). (ENG.). 24p. (gr. -1 — 1). pap. 0.50 *(978-1-4795-1671-1(6)*, Picture Window Bks.) Capstone.

Agaoglu, Basak. These Words I Shaped for You. Merchant, Megan. 2017. 30p. (J). (— 1). bds. 7.99 *(978-0-399-17253-3(X)*, Philomel Bks.) Penguin Young Readers Group.

Agarao, Rowin. The Adventures of Hilary Hickenbottham. Haining, Karen. Carson, Alison, ed. 2017. (Hilary Hickenbottham Ser.: Vol. 1). (ENG.). 256p. (J). (gr. 3-6). pap. *(978-1-9998736-0-8(2))* Haining.

Agata, Boba. Bear Gets a Beating. Magda, Olchawska. 2016. (About Little Boy Ser.: Vol. 3). (ENG.). (J). (gr. k-2). pap. *(978-83-946520-4-3(2))* Olchawska, Magdalena.

Age 6, Eren. The Lost Hat Before Christmas. Mom, Eren's. 2014. (ENG.). (J). pap. *(978-1-928126-05-8(7))* Eren's Mom.

Agee, Cynthia. Gabby Grape Meets Junk Food Junkie. Hodge-McLoud, Linda. McLoud, Harry H., ed. 2018. (ENG.). 34p. (J). (gr. 1-5). pap. *(978-1-988925-10-3(X))* Doyle-Ingram, Suzanne.

Agee, Jon. Potch & Polly. Steig, William. Date not set. (J). 14.99 *(978-0-06-205144-8(X))* HarperCollins Pubs.

Agee, Jon. Nothing. Agee, Jon. 2007. (ENG.). 32p. (gr. -1-3). 16.99 *(978-0-7868-3694-9(6))* Hyperion Pr.

—Palindromania! Agee, Jon. 2009. (ENG.). 112p. (J). (gr. 3-8). pap. 11.11 *(978-0-374-40025-5(3)*, 900058755) Square Fish.

—The Wall in the Middle of the Book. Agee, Jon. 2018. (ENG.). 48p. (J). (gr. -1-3). 17.99 *(978-0-525-55545-2(5)*, Dial Bks) Penguin Young Readers Group.

Agency, Muje Creations. The Holiday Boys Make a New Friend. Daniel, Onicka J. 2018. (ENG.). 62p. (J). pap. 13.99 *(978-0-692-08712-1(5))* Daniel, Onicka J.

Ager, Charlotte. Child of Galaxies. Nuto, Blake. 2020. (ENG.). 40p. (J). (-k). 16.95 *(978-1-912497-42-3(5))* Flying Eye Bks. GBR. Dist: Penguin Random Hse. LLC.

—DK Life Stories: Alexander Hamilton. Buckley, Jim. 2019. (DK Life Stories Ser.). (ENG.). 128p. (J). (gr. 3-7). 16.99 *(978-1-4654-7960-0(0))*; pap. 5.99

(978-1-4654-7961-7(9)) Dorling Kindersley Publishing, Inc. (DK Children).
—DK Life Stories: Anne Frank. Krensky, Stephen. 2019. (DK Life Stories Ser.). (ENG.). 128p. (J). (gr. 3-7). 16.99 (978-1-4654-7029-4(8)); pap. 5.99 (978-1-4654-7543-5(5)) Dorling Kindersley Publishing, Inc. (DK Children).
—DK Life Stories: Florence Nightingale. Jazynka, Kitson. 2019. (DK Life Stories Ser.). (ENG.). 128p. (J). (gr. 3-7). 16.99 (978-1-4654-7844-3(2)); pap. 5.99 (978-1-4654-7843-6(4)) Dorling Kindersley Publishing, Inc. (DK Children).
—DK Life Stories: Gandhi. Bailey, Diane. 2019. (DK Life Stories Ser.). (ENG.). 128p. (J). (gr. 3-7). 16.99 (978-1-4654-7463-6(3)); pap. 5.99 (978-1-4654-7842-9(6)) Dorling Kindersley Publishing, Inc. (DK Children).
—DK Life Stories: Helen Keller. Romero, Libby. 2019. (DK Life Stories Ser.). (ENG.). 128p. (J). (gr. 3-7). 16.99 (978-1-4654-7544-2(3)); pap. 5.99 (978-1-4654-7474-2(9)) Dorling Kindersley Publishing, Inc. (DK Children).
—DK Life Stories: Jane Goodall. Romero, Libby. 2019. (DK Life Stories Ser.). (ENG.). 128p. (J). (gr. 2). pap. 5.99 (978-1-4654-8397-3(7)); (gr. 3-7). 16.99 (978-1-4654-8398-0(5)) Dorling Kindersley Publishing, Inc. (DK Children).
—DK Life Stories: Katherine Johnson. Wilkins, Ebony Joy. 2019. (DK Life Stories Ser.). (ENG.). 128p. (J). (gr. 3-7). 16.99 (978-1-4654-7962-4(7)); pap. 5.99 (978-1-4654-7912-9(0)) Dorling Kindersley Publishing, Inc. (DK Children).
—DK Life Stories: Nelson Mandela. Krensky, Stephen. 2019. (DK Life Stories Ser.). (ENG.). 128p. (J). (gr. 2). pap. 5.99 (978-1-4654-8400-0(0)); (gr. 3-7). 16.99 (978-1-4654-8399-7(3)) Dorling Kindersley Publishing, Inc. (DK Children).
Aggs, John. Cherub: The Recruit (Graphic Novel) Muchamore, Robert & Edginton, Ian. 2012. 176p. (YA). (gr. 7-17). pap. 11.99 (978-1-4449-0318-8(7)) Hodder & Stoughton GBR. Dist: Hachette Bk. Group.
Aggs, Patrice. Un Deux Trois (Dual Language French/English) Dunn, Opal. 2006. (ENG.). 24p. (J). (gr. k-3). pap. 9.99 (978-1-84507-623-8(0), Frances Lincoln Children's Bks.) Quarto Publishing Group UK GBR. Dist: Hachette Bk. Group.
Aggs, Patrice. Bertie Rooster. Aggs, Patrice, tr. Stewart, Maddie. 2007. (Panda Cubs Ser.: 02). (ENG.). 48p. (J). pap. 9.95 (978-0-86278-798-1(X)) O'Brien Pr., Ltd., The IRL. Dist: Dufour Editions, Inc.
Aghhavani Shajari, Benyamin. The Dream Life of Little Paul. Guyon Spennato, Elizabeth. 2019. (ENG.). 56p. (J). (978-99957-96-01-3(5)) Faraxa Publishing.
Agin, Sue. Max - a Griggstown Mystery. Shaw, Mary. Cormilliat, Francois, tr. 2004.Tr. of Max - Un Mystire de Griggstown. (ENG & FRE.). (J). (gr. k-6). pap. 18.50 (978-0-9705404-2-3(6), 0-9705404-2-6) Criqueville Pr.
Agnew, Alicia. Baby Brother Goes to the Hospital. Slanina, Anne M. 2007. (Adventures of Annie Mouse Ser.: Bk. 2). 28p. (J). 18.99 (978-0-9793379-1-8(7)); per. 9.99 (978-0-9793379-0-1(9)) Annie Mouse Bks.
Agnew, Lincoln. CookieBot! Van Camp, Katie. 2011. (Harry & Horsie Adventures Ser.: 2). (ENG.). 32p. (J). (gr. -1-1). 16.99 (978-0-06-197445-8(5), Balzer & Bray) HarperCollins Pubs.
—Harry & Horsie. Van Camp, Katie. 2009. (Harry & Horsie Adventures Ser.: 1). (ENG.). 32p. (J). (gr. -1-1). 16.99 (978-0-06-175598-9(2), Balzer & Bray) HarperCollins Pubs.
Agoussoye, Simone. Ona Judge Outwits the Washingtons: An Enslaved Woman Fights for Freedom. Hooks, Gwendolyn. 2019. (ENG.). 40p. (J). (gr. 3-6). 18.95 (978-1-5435-1280-9(1), 137745, Capstone Editions) Capstone.
Agraso, Alberto. I Am Happy. Agraso, Alberto. Dojeiji, Mony. 2013. 36p. pap. (978-0-9878762-3-2(6)) Walking for Peace Publishing.
—I Am Happy - Je Suis Heureuse - Soy Feliz: (Special Edition) Agraso, Alberto. Dojeiji, Mony. 2018. (ENG.). 70p. (J). pap. (978-1-927803-20-2(9)) Walking for Peace Publishing.
—Je Suis Heureuse. Agraso, Alberto. Dojeiji, Mony. 2013. 36p. pap. (978-1-927803-01-1(2)) Walking for Peace Publishing.
—My Family & I: Ma Famille et Moi - Mi Familia y Yo. Agraso, Alberto. 2017. (ENG.). 60p. (J). pap. (978-1-927803-15-8(2)) Walking for Peace Publishing.
—Soy Feliz. Agraso, Alberto. Dojeiji, Mony. 2013. 36p. pap. (978-0-9878762-4-9(4)) Walking for Peace Publishing.
Agrell, Lewis. We Like to Eat Well. April, Elyse. 2010th rev. ed. 2013. (We Like To Ser.). (ENG.). 32p. (J). pap. 9.95 (978-1-935826-04-0(2)) Kalindi Pr.
—We Like to Eat Well/Nos Gusta Comer Bien. April, Elyse. 2011th alt. ed. 2011. (We Like To Ser.). (ENG.). 32p. (J). pap. 10.95 (978-1-935826-01-9(8)) Kalindi Pr.
Agresta, Elizabeth. Celia & the Glue Man: A Girl's Journey to Becoming Gluten-Free & Happy. Williams, Maggy. 2018. (J). pap. (978-1-61599-390-1(8)) Loving Healing Pr., Inc.
—"I'm Mixed!" Williams, Maggy. 2018. 38p. (J). pap. (978-1-61599-359-8(2)) Loving Healing Pr., Inc.
Agroff, Patti. All about Us. Rosenfeld, Dina. 2008. 28p. (J). 10.95 (978-1-929628-45-2(5)) Hachai Publishing.
—I Am a Torah: A Playful Action Rhyme. Paluch, Beily. 2014. 12p. (J). bds. 6.95 (978-1-929628-84-1(6)) Hachai Publishing.
Aguado, Pili. Harriet Tubman: My First Harriet Tubman. Sanchez Vegara, Maria Isabel. 2019. (Little People, Big Dreams Ser.: Vol. 14). (ENG.). 24p. (J). (gr. -1). bds. (978-0-7112-4311-8(5)) Frances Lincoln Childrens Bks.
Aguayo, Amanda. Tiny but Mighty. Townes, Tara Lynn. 2017. (ENG.). (J). 34.99 (978-1-4984-9504-2(4)); pap. 24.99 (978-1-4984-9503-5(6)) Salem Author Services.
Aguerrebehere, Laura. Diary of a Fairy. Dávila, Valeria et al. Warriner, David, tr. 2018. (Dear Diary Ser.). 32p. (J). (gr. -1-1). 7.99 (978-2-924786-65-9(7), CrackBoom! Bks.) Chouette Publishing CAN. Dist: Publishers Group West (PGW).
—Diary of a Monster. Dávila, Valeria & López, Mónica. Warriner, David, tr. 2018. (Dear Diary Ser.). 32p. (J). (gr. -1-1). 7.99 (978-2-924786-71-0(1), CrackBoom! Bks.) Chouette Publishing CAN. Dist: Publishers Group West (PGW).
—Diary of a Witch. Dávila, Valeria & López, Mónica. Warriner, David, tr. 2018. (Dear Diary Ser.). 32p. (J). (gr. -1-1). 7.99 (978-2-924786-67-3(3), CrackBoom! Bks.) Chouette Publishing CAN. Dist: Publishers Group West (PGW).
—Diary of an Ogre. Dávila, Valeria & López, Mónica. Warriner, David, tr. 2018. (Dear Diary Ser.). 32p. (J). (gr. -1-1). 7.99 (978-2-924786-69-7(X), CrackBoom! Bks.) Chouette Publishing CAN. Dist: Publishers Group West (PGW).
Aguila, Alicia del. Tia Tot Rules! Written By Tori Velle; Illustrated By Al. 2011. 44p. pap. 24.95 (978-1-4241-7833-9(9)) America Star Bks.
Aguilar, Arelys. The Trouble with Cats. Ballard, George Anne & Bolton, Georgia Helen. 2012. 24p. pap. 12.00 (978-0-9855312-1-8(5)) Bolton Publishing LLC.
Aguilar, David A. Space Encyclopedia: A Tour of Our Solar System & Beyond. Pulliam, Christine & Daniels, Patricia. 2013. 191p. (J). (978-1-4263-1629-6(1)) National Geographic Society.
Aguilar, Ero. Amo a Mi Mam� Zapple, Elias. Ter�n, Camila Ayala, tr. 2020. (SPA.). 32p. (J). pap. (978-1-912704-36-1(6)) Heads or Tales Pr.
—J'aime Ma Maman. Zapple, Elias. Blanchet, Jean-Francois, tr. 2020. (J'Aime... Ser.). (FRE.). 32p. (J). pap. (978-1-912704-38-5(2)) Heads or Tales Pr.
—わたしはおかあさんがすき Zapple, Elias. Kondo, Katsunori, tr. 2020. (わたしは ものがたりがす Ser.: Vol. 1). (JPN.). 32p. (J). pap. (978-1-912704-35-4(8)) Heads or Tales Pr.
—我爱我的妈妈 Zapple, Elias. 刘全国, tr. 2020. (我喜欢睡前故事 Ser.: Vol. 1). (CHI.). 32p. (J). pap. (978-1-912704-42-2(0)) Heads or Tales Pr.
Aguilar, Jose. 4 Poemas de Gloria Fuertes y Una Calabaza Vestida de Luna. Fuertes, Gloria. 2007. (SPA.). 36p. (J). (978-84-934160-9-6(6)) Atalante.
Aguilar, Laia. Bonjour Camille. Cano, Felipe. 2014. (ENG.). 32p. (J). (gr. 1-4). 12.99 (978-1-4521-2407-0(8)) Chronicle Bks. LLC.
Aguilar, Sandra. Big Cat. Goodhart, Pippa. 2011. (Tadpoles Ser.). (ENG.). (J). (gr. -1-3). lib. bdg. 17.55 (978-1-61383-943-0(X)) Perfection Learning Corp.
—Queen Ella's Feet. Grindley, Sally. 2011. (My Phonics Readers: Level 3 Ser.). 24p. (J). (gr. -1-1). 24.25 (978-1-84898-513-1(4)) Sea-To-Sea Pubns.
Aguiler, Manny. A Smile: B una Sonrisa. Aguiler, Manny. Smith, Michael. 2015. (SPA & ENG.). 36p. (J). (978-0-9913454-5-8(2)) East West Discovery Pr.
Aguilera, Aurora. I Help at Grandpa's House. Mortmain, Beatrice. 2017. (Ways I Help Ser.). 24p. (J). (gr. 4-6). pap. 8.25 (978-1-5081-5677-2(8), PowerKids Pr.) Rosen Publishing Group, Inc., The.
—I Help at the Store. Woods, Sadie. 2017. (Ways I Help Ser.). 24p. (J). (gr. 4-6). pap. 8.25 (978-1-5081-5678-9(6), PowerKids Pr.) Rosen Publishing Group, Inc., The.
—I Help in the Kitchen. Richards, Cassandra. 2017. (Ways I Help Ser.). 24p. (J). (gr. 4-6). 23.60 (978-1-5081-5739-7(1), PowerKids Pr.) Rosen Publishing Group, Inc., The.
Aguillo, Don Ellis. Boomer, the Missing Pomeranian. 2005. 34p. (J). pap. (978-1-932864-45-8(8)) Masthof Pr.
Aguirre, Alfredo. La Almohada. Mansour, Vivian. 2nd rev. ed. 2003. (Castillo de la Lectura Verde Ser.). (SPA & ENG.). 88p. (J). pap. 7.95 (978-970-20-0140-9(4)) Castillo, Ediciones, S. A. de C. V. MEX. Dist: Macmillan.
Aguirre, Claudia. Hotel Dare. Blas, Terry. 2019. (ENG.). 144p. (J). pap. 9.99 (978-1-68415-205-6(4)) Boom! Studios.
—The Twisted Ones. Cawthon, Scott & Breed-Wrisley, Kira. 2017. (Five Nights at Freddy's Ser.: 2). (ENG.). 304p. (J). (gr. 7-7). pap. 9.99 (978-1-338-13930-3(4)) Scholastic, Inc.
Aguirre, Diego, jt. illus. see Beckman, Jeff.
Aguirre, Freddy. Kids Who Love Lines. Jones, Loman. 2004. (ENG.). 38p. (YA). pap. 20.00 (978-1-4120-2730-4(6)) Trafford Publishing.
Aguirre, Zurine. Alegraa. Gil, Carmen. 2018. (SPA.). 40p. (J). 15.95 (978-84-946926-0-4(7)) NubeOcho Ediciones ESP. Dist: Consortium Bk. Sales & Distribution.
—Joy the Elf. Gil, Carmen. 2018. (ENG.). 40p. (J). 15.95 (978-84-946926-1-1(5)) NubeOcho Ediciones ESP. Dist: Consortium Bk. Sales & Distribution.
Aguirre, Zuriñe & Aguirre, Zuriñe. Sardines of Love. Aguirre, Zuriñe & Aguirre, Zuriñe. 2016. (Child's Play Library). 36p. (J). (978-1-84643-726-7(1)) Child's Play International Ltd.
Aguirre, Zuriñe, jt. illus. see Aguirre, Zuriñe.
Ahanonu, Monica. Serena: the Littlest Sister. Gray, Karlin. 2019. (ENG.). 40p. (J). 17.99 (978-1-62414-694-7(5), 900197962) Page Street Publishing Co.
Ahern, Frank. The Good Night Book. Beckman, Amy. 2006. 28p. per. 16.95 (978-1-59858-255-0(0)) Dog Ear Publishing, LLC.
Aherne, Sue. The Julie Malloy Gang & the Smugglers. Davies, Michael. 2019. (ENG.). 160p. (J). (gr. 4-6). pap. (978-0-6484702-9-8(6)) Dalton, Mickie Foundation, The.
Ahlberg, Allan, jt. illus. see Ahlberg, Janet.
Ahlberg, Janet. Adiós Pequeño! Ahlberg, Janet. Ahlberg, Allan. 2003. (Picture Books Collection).Tr. of Bye Bye Baby. (SPA.). 32p. (J). (gr. k-3). 12.95 (978-84-372-2315-5(6)) Altea, Ediciones, S.A. - Grupo Santillana ESP. Dist: Santillana USA Publishing Co., Inc.
Ahlberg, Janet & Ahlberg, Allan. Adiós Pequeño! Ahlberg, Janet & Ahlberg, Allan. (Historias Para Dormir Ser.).Tr. of Bye Bye Baby. (SPA.). 28p. (J). (gr. k-3). 9.95 (978-968-19-1039-6(7)) Aguilar Editorial MEX. Dist: Santillana USA Publishing Co., Inc.
Ahlberg, Jessica. The Goldilocks Variations: A Pop-Up Book. Ahlberg, Allan. 2012. (ENG.). 40p. (J). (gr. k-4). 17.99 (978-0-7636-6268-4(2)) Candlewick Pr.
—Yucky Worms: Read & Wonder. French, Vivian. 2012. (Read & Wonder Ser.). (ENG.). 32p. (J). (gr. -1-3). pap. 7.99 (978-0-7636-5817-5(0)) Candlewick Pr.
Ahlbum, Joey. There's a Duck in My Bathtub! Wilk, David. 2018. (ENG.). 24p. (J). (gr. -1-k). pap. 4.99 (978-1-947951-08-2(4)) City Point Bks.
Ahmad, Aadil & James, Martin. Papi, How Many Stars Are in the Sky? Vigil, Angel. 2010. (J). (978-1-60617-151-6(8)) Teaching Strategies, LLC.
Ahmad, Abdul-Aziz. Dinosaur in Disguise. Clarke, Leon. 2018. (ENG.). 26p. (J). pap. (978-0-9575103-5-7(7)) Botty Publishing Ltd.
Ahmad, Maryam & Ramotar, Alexandra. One Day. Persaud, Sandhya S. 2009. 12p. pap. 12.99 (978-1-4389-4437-1(3)) AuthorHouse.
Ahmed, Ishrat H. Acts of Kindness Through a City: The Adventures of Maya & Her Modern Day Family. Alvarez, Sheila R. & Alvarez, Ernesto F. 2016. (ENG.). (J). pap. 9.95 (978-0-9972566-1-1(3)) Maya & Me Pubns.
Ahmed, Raziah, jt. illus. see Khan, Ruqayyah.
Ahn, Eun-Jin. Bubble, Bubble! Soap Bubble. Lee, Ji-Hyeon. 2017. (Science Storybooks Ser.). (ENG.). 32p. (J). (gr. k-4). lib. bdg. 27.99 (978-1-925235-42-5(4), Big and SMALL) ChoiceMaker Pty. Ltd., The AUS. Dist: Lerner Publishing Group.
Ahn, Flora. Two's a Crowd. 2018. 119p. (J). (978-1-338-27713-5(8), Scholastic Pr.) Scholastic, Inc.
Ahn, Jae-seon. The People in the Paintings: The Art of Bruegel. Ddang, Haneul. 2017. (Stories of Art Ser.). (ENG.). 36p. (J). (gr. 3-5). lib. bdg. 10.00 (978-1-925235-26-5(2), Big and SMALL) ChoiceMaker Pty. Ltd., The AUS. Dist: Lerner Publishing Group.
Ahokoivu, Mari. Livi & Nate. Hakkola, Kalle. Witesman, Owen, tr. from FIN. 2019. (ENG.). 72p. (J). (gr. 1-5). 16.95 (978-1-77147-372-9(X)) Owlkids Bks. Inc. CAN. Dist: Publishers Group West (PGW).
Ahonen, Elina Johanna. Saga Flyttar: Swedish Edition of Stella & the Berry Bay. Pere, Tuula. Nikolowski-Bogomoloff, Angelika, tr. 2018. (Saga Ser.: Vol. 2). (SWE.). 48p. (J). (gr. k-4). (978-952-357-002-3(1)); pap. (978-952-7107-99-7(7)) Wickwick oy.
—Sanni Ja Laatikkopäivät: Finnish Edition of Stella & the Berry Bay. Pere, Tuula. 2018. (Sanni Ser.: Vol. 2). (FIN.). 48p. (J). (gr. k-4). (978-952-357-001-6(3)); pap. (978-952-7107-98-0(9)) Wickwick oy.
—Stella & the Berry Bay. Pere, Tuula. Korman, Susan, ed. 2018. (Stella Ser.: Vol. 2). (ENG.). 48p. (J). (gr. k-4). (978-952-357-000-9(5)); pap. (978-952-7107-97-3(0)) Wickwick oy.
Ahpornsiri, Helen. Beneath the Waves. Murray, Lily. 2020. (ENG.). 64p. (J). (gr. 1-4). 22.00 (978-1-5362-1040-8(4), Big Picture Press) Candlewick Pr.
Ahpornsiri, Helen. Drawn from Nature. Ahpornsiri, Helen. 2018. (ENG.). 64p. (J). (gr. 1-4). 22.00 (978-0-7636-9898-0(9), Big Picture Press) Candlewick Pr.
Ahrends, Susan. How Willy Got His Wings: The Continuing Adventures of Wheely Willy. Turner, Deborah & Mohler, Diana. 2003. (ENG.). 32p. 15.95 (978-0-944875-88-9(2)) i-5 Publishing LLC.
Ahrens, Niki, photos by. Aladdin Idea Lab. Ahrens, Niki. 2019. (Disney STEAM Projects Ser.). (ENG., 32p. (J). (gr. 2-5). pap. 8.99 (978-1-5415-7400-7(1), 9781541574007, Lerner Pubns.) Lerner Publishing Group.
—Big Hero 6 Idea Lab. Ahrens, Niki. 2019. (Disney STEAM Projects Ser.). (ENG., 32p. (J). (gr. 2-5). 29.32 (978-1-5415-5482-5(5), 9781541554825); pap. 8.99 (978-1-5415-7401-4(X), 9781541574014) Lerner Publishing Group. (Lerner Pubns.).
—Celebrate with Ariel: Plan a Little Mermaid Party. Ahrens, Niki. 2020. (Disney Princess Celebrations Ser.). (ENG., 32p. (J). (gr. 1-4). pap. 6.99 (978-1-5415-8718-2(9)); lib. bdg. 27.99 (978-1-5415-7271-3(8)) Lerner Publishing Group. (Lerner Pubns.).
—Celebrate with Belle: Plan a Beauty & the Beast Party. Ahrens, Niki. 2020. (Disney Princess Celebrations Ser.). (ENG., 32p. (J). (gr. 1-4). pap. 6.99 (978-1-5415-8719-9(7)); lib. bdg. 27.99 (978-1-5415-7276-8(9)) Lerner Publishing Group. (Lerner Pubns.).
—Celebrate with Cinderella: Plan a Royal Party. Ahrens, Niki. 2020. (Disney Princess Celebrations Ser.). (ENG., 32p. (J). (gr. 1-4). pap. 6.99 (978-1-5415-8720-5(0)); lib. bdg. 27.99 (978-1-5415-7274-4(2)) Lerner Publishing Group. (Lerner Pubns.).
—Celebrate with Jasmine: Plan an Aladdin Party. Ahrens, Niki. 2020. (Disney Princess Celebrations Ser.). (ENG., 32p. (J). (gr. 1-4). 27.99 (978-1-5415-7275-1(0)); pap. 6.99 (978-1-5415-8721-2(9)) Lerner Publishing Group. (Lerner Pubns.).
—Celebrate with Moana: Plan a Wayfinding Party. Ahrens, Niki. 2020. (Disney Princess Celebrations Ser.). (ENG., 32p. (J). (gr. 1-4). pap. 6.99 (978-1-5415-8722-9(7)); lib. bdg. 27.99 (978-1-5415-7273-7(4)) Lerner Publishing Group. (Lerner Pubns.).
—Celebrate with Tiana: Plan a Princess & the Frog Party. Ahrens, Niki. 2020. (Disney Princess Celebrations Ser.). (ENG., 32p. (J). (gr. 1-4). pap. 6.99 (978-1-5415-8723-6(5)); lib. bdg. 27.99 (978-1-5415-7272-0(6)) Lerner Publishing Group. (Lerner Pubns.).
—Hack Your Backyard: Discover a World of Outside Fun with Science Buddies? Ahrens, Niki. 2019. (ENG., 32p. (J). (gr. 2-5). 27.99 (978-1-5415-3915-0(X), Lerner Pubns.) Lerner Publishing Group.
—Hack Your Backyard: Discover a World of Outside Fun with Science Buddies®. Ahrens, Niki. 2019. (ENG., 32p. (J). (gr. 2-5). pap. 8.99 (978-1-5415-5717-8(4), Lerner Pubns.) Lerner Publishing Group.
—Moana Idea Lab. Ahrens, Niki. 2019. (Disney STEAM Projects Ser.). (ENG., 32p. (J). (gr. 2-5). 29.32 (978-1-5415-5480-1(9), 9781541554801); pap. 8.99 (978-1-5415-7405-2(2), 9781541574052) Lerner Publishing Group. (Lerner Pubns.).
Ahrin, Jacob. Stop the Bully. Pearl, David R. & Pearl, Tamara R. 2013. 26p. pap. (978-0-646-90104-6(4)) Be Positive Solutions.
Ahumada, Dalia. Rid. Noriega, Eugenia. 2018. (SPA.). 88p. (J). pap. 11.00 (978-1-7198-5347-7(9)) Independently Published.
Aiello, Sara. Bean & Bug - Protect & Respect. Fernan, Kathleen. 2018. (Bean & Bug Ser.: 1). (ENG.). 24p. (J). pap. 14.95 (978-1-5439-2103-8(5)) BookBaby.
Aiers, Daniel. John's Path to Success. Job, Jj. 2019. (ENG.). 30p. (J). pap. 9.99 (978-1-6766-3976-3(4)) Independently Published.
Aihara, Miki. Hot Gimmick, 12 vols. Aihara, Miki. (Hot Gimmick Ser.: 7). (ENG.). 2004. 192p. pap. 9.99 (978-1-59116-502-6(4)); 2004. 192p. pap. 9.95 (978-1-59116-389-3(7)); 2003. 184p. pap. 9.95 (978-1-59116-227-8(0)) Viz Media.
—Hot Gimmick, Vol. 9, 12 vols. Aihara, Miki. 2005. (ENG.). 192p. pap. 9.99 (978-1-59116-845-4(7)) Viz Media.
Aikawa, Yu. Dark Edge. Aikawa, Yu. 2006. (Dark Edge Ser.). (ENG.). 200p. (YA). Vol. 5. pap. 9.95 (978-1-59796-025-0(X)); Vol. 6. pap. 9.95 (978-1-59796-026-7(8)) DrMaster Pubns. Inc.
Aiken, David. Chesapeake 1-2-3, 1 vol. Cummings, Priscilla. 2009. (ENG.). 32p. (J). (gr. -1-2). 11.95 (978-0-87033-542-6(1), 3760, Cornell Maritime Pr./Tidewater Pubs.) Schiffer Publishing, Ltd.
—Chesapeake Rainbow, 1 vol. Cummings, Priscilla. 2009. (ENG.). 30p. (J). 11.95 (978-0-87033-556-3(1), 9780870335563, Cornell Maritime Pr./Tidewater Pubs.) Schiffer Publishing, Ltd.
—Double-Talk: Word Sense & Nonsense, 1 vol. Aiken, Zora & David. 2012. (ENG.). 32p. (J). 14.99 (978-0-7643-3962-2(1), 4438) Schiffer Publishing, Ltd.
—Finding Birds in the Chesapeake Marsh: A Child's First Look, 1 vol. Aiken, Zora. 2009. (ENG.). 30p. (J). 11.95 (978-0-87033-533-4(2), 9780870335334, Cornell Maritime Pr./Tidewater Pubs.) Schiffer Publishing, Ltd.
—Majesty from Assateague, 1 vol. Hagman, Harvey Dixon. 2009. (ENG.). 80p. (J). pap. 8.95 (978-0-87033-552-5(9), 9780870335525, Cornell Maritime Pr./Tidewater Pubs.) Schiffer Publishing, Ltd.
—Quiet Please - Eaglets Growing, 1 vol. Stearns, Carolyn. 2009. (ENG.). 30p. (J). 11.95 (978-0-87033-541-9(3), 9780870335419, Cornell Maritime Pr./Tidewater Pubs.) Schiffer Publishing, Ltd.
—Where Did All the Water Go?, 1 vol. Stearns, Carolyn. 2009. (ENG.). 30p. (J). (gr. 4-7). 12.95 (978-0-87033-506-8(5), 9780870335068, Cornell Maritime Pr./Tidewater Pubs.) Schiffer Publishing, Ltd.
Aiken, David. A to Z: Pick What You'll Be. Aiken, David. Aiken, Zora. 2011. (ENG.). 32p. (J). 14.99 (978-0-7643-3701-7(7), 9780764337017, Schiffer Publishing Ltd) Schiffer Publishing, Ltd.
—Camp ABC: A Place for Outdoor Fun, 1 vol. Aiken, David. Aiken, Zora. 2013. (ENG.). 32p. (J). 16.99 (978-0-7643-4423-7(4), 4809) Schiffer Publishing, Ltd.
Aiken, David & Aiken, David. All about Boats: A to Z, 1 vol. Aiken, Zora. 2012. (ENG.). 32p. (J). 14.99 (978-0-7643-4184-7(7), 4611) Schiffer Publishing, Ltd.
Aiken, David, jt. illus. see Aiken, David.
Aiken, Lara & Schultz, Paul. Kismet Tales from Happy Trails. McDonald, Lisa. 2017. (ENG.). (J). (978-1-5255-0785-4(0)); pap. (978-1-5255-0786-1(9)) FriesenPress.
Aikins, Dave, et al. Animal Adventure. Ricci, Christine. 2007. (Little Life Lessons Ser.). (J). pap. (978-1-4127-8922-6(2)) Publications International, Ltd.
Aikins, Dave. Bailando Al Rescate. 2005. (Dora la Exploradora Ser.). (SPA.). 24p. (J). pap. 3.99 (978-1-4169-1504-1(4), Libros Para Ninos) Libros Para Ninos.
—Big Egg Rescue! (Top Wing) Random House. 2019. (ENG.). 22p. (J). (— 1). bds. 6.99 (978-0-525-64794-2(5), Random Hse. Bks. for Young Readers) Random Hse. Children's Bks.
—Big Sister Dora! Inches, Alison. ed. 2005. (Dora the Explorer Ser.: 13). 32p. (J). lib. bdg. 15.00 (978-1-59054-790-8(X)) Fitzgerald Bks.
—Big Sister Dora! 2005. (Dora the Explorer Ser.: Vol. 13). (ENG.). 24p. (J). pap. 3.99 (978-0-689-87846-6(X), Simon Spotlight/Nickelodeon) Simon Spotlight/Nickelodeon.
—The Big Win. Chipponeri, Kelli. 2008. (SpongeBob SquarePants Ser.: 13). (ENG.). 32p. (J). (gr. k-2). pap. 3.99 (978-1-4169-4938-1(0), Simon Spotlight/Nickelodeon) Simon Spotlight/Nickelodeon.
—The Birthday Dance Party: Daisy's Fiesta de Quinceañera. 2006. (Dora the Explorer Ser.: 19). (ENG.). 24p. (J). (gr. -1-3). pap. 3.99 (978-1-4169-1303-0(3), Simon Spotlight/Nickelodeon) Simon Spotlight/Nickelodeon.
Aikins, Dave. Blue's Winter Day! (Blue's Clue & You) Random House. 2020. (ENG.). 22p. (J). (— 1). bds. 6.99 (978-0-593-17736-5(3), Random Hse. Bks. for Young Readers) Random Hse. Children's Bks.
Aikins, Dave. Botarilla to the Rescue! (Rusty Rivets) Neumann, Casey. 2019. (Pictureback(R) Ser.). (ENG.). 24p. (J). (gr. -1-2). 5.99 (978-0-525-64795-9(3), Random Hse. Bks. for Young Readers) Random Hse. Children's Bks.
—Bunny Business. Golden Books Staff. 2011. (ENG.). 64p. (J). (gr. -1-2). pap. 4.99 (978-0-375-86818-4(6), Golden Bks.) Random Hse. Children's Bks.
—The Chocolate Voyage. Rabe, Tish. 2013. (Little Golden Book Ser.). (ENG.). 24p. (J). (-k). 3.99 (978-0-307-98023-6(5), Golden Bks.) Random Hse. Children's Bks.

Aikins, Dave. Count with Blue! (Blue's Clues & You) Random House. 2020. (ENG.). 26p. (J). (— 1). bds. 7.99 ***(978-0-593-12430-7(8)***, Random Hse. Bks. for Young Readers) Random Hse. Children's Bks.

Aikins, Dave. Dance to the Rescue. Driscoll, Laura. 2005. 24p. (J). lib. bdg. 9.00 *(978-1-4242-0981-1(1))* Fitzgerald Bks.

—Demolition Derby/Class Confusion (SpongeBob SquarePants) Random House Staff. 2013. (Pictureback(R) Ser.). (ENG.). 32p. (J). (gr. -1-2). 4.99 *(978-0-449-81756-8(3)*, Random Hse. Bks. for Young Readers) Random Hse. Children's Bks.

—Dora salva el Reino de Cristal (Dora Saves Crystal Kingdom) Rodriguez, Daynali Flores, tr. from ENG. 2009. (Dora la Exploradora Ser.). (SPA.). 24p. (J). (gr. -1-2). pap. 3.99 *(978-1-4169-9020-8(8)*, Libros Para Ninos) Libros Para Ninos.

—Dora Saves the Snow Princess. 2008. (Dora the Explorer Ser.: 27). (ENG.). 24p. (J). (gr. -1-2). pap. 3.99 *(978-1-4169-5866-6(5)*, Simon Spotlight/Nickelodeon) Simon Spotlight/Nickelodeon.

—Dora y la Princesa de la Nieve (Dora Saves the Snow Princess) Ziegler, Argentina Palacios, tr. 2008. (Dora la Exploradora Ser.). (SPA.). 24p. (J). (gr. -1-2). pap. 3.99 *(978-1-4169-5870-3(3)*, Libros Para Ninos) Libros Para Ninos.

—Dora's Princess Party. Reisner, Molly. 2009. (Dora the Explorer Ser.). (ENG.). 12p. (J). (gr. -1-1). 6.99 *(978-1-4169-9045-1(3)*, Simon Spotlight/Nickelodeon) Simon Spotlight/Nickelodeon.

—Dress up Dora! McMahon, Kara. 2009. (Dora the Explorer Ser.). (ENG.). 12p. (J). 8.99 *(978-1-4169-6067-6(8)*, Simon Spotlight/Nickelodeon) Simon Spotlight/Nickelodeon.

Aikins, Dave. Elbow Grease Magnetic Play Book. Cena, John. 2020. (Elbow Grease Ser.). 8p. (J). (gr. -1-2). bds. 12.99 ***(978-0-525-57763-8(7)***, Random Hse. Bks. for Young Readers) Random Hse. Children's Bks.

Aikins, Dave. Falcon Quest! (Blaze & the Monster Machines) Tillworth, Mary. 2017. (Pictureback(R) Ser.). (ENG.). 24p. (J). (gr. -1-2). pap. 5.99 *(978-1-5247-6529-3(5)*, Random Hse. Bks. for Young Readers) Random Hse. Children's Bks.

—Far-Out Friends! (Rusty Rivets) Finnegan, Delphine. 2017. (Step into Reading Ser.). (ENG.). 24p. (J). (gr. -1-1). pap. 4.99 *(978-1-5247-6801-0(4)*, Random Hse. Bks. for Young Readers) Random Hse. Children's Bks.

—Get Out & Play (Elbow Grease) Cena, John. 2020. (Step into Reading Ser.). 32p. (J). (gr. -1-1). pap. 4.99 *(978-0-525-57758-4(0))*; lib. bdg. 12.99 *(978-0-525-57759-1(9))* Random Hse. Children's Bks. (Random Hse. Bks. for Young Readers).

—The Great Big Parade. Ricci, Christine. 2007. (J). pap. *(978-1-4127-8923-3(0))* Publications International, Ltd.

—The Great Ice Race. Melendez, Renee. 2017. 24p. (J). *(978-1-5182-5217-4(6))* Random Hse., Inc.

—The Great Ice Race (Blaze & the Monster Machines) Melendez, Renee. 2017. (Step into Reading Ser.). (ENG.). 24p. (J). (gr. -1-1). pap. 4.99 *(978-1-5247-6384-8(5))*; lib. bdg. 12.99 *(978-1-5247-6385-5(3))* Random Hse. Children's Bks. (Random Hse. Bks. for Young Readers).

—Happy Birthday to You! Depken, Kristen L. 2018. 24p. (J). *(978-1-5444-0156-0(6))* Random Hse., Inc.

—Happy Birthday to You! (Shimmer & Shine) Depken, Kristen L. 2018. (Step into Reading Ser.). (ENG.). 24p. (J). (gr. -1-1). pap. 4.99 *(978-1-5247-6799-0(9)*, Random Hse. Bks. for Young Readers) Random Hse. Children's Bks.

—The Haunted Cave (Top Wing) Webster, Christy. 2019. (Step into Reading Ser.). (ENG.). 24p. (J). (gr. -1-1). 5.99 *(978-1-9848-4784-3(8)*, Random Hse. Bks. for Young Readers) Random Hse. Children's Bks.

—Hooray for Friends! (Top Wing) Finnegan, Delphine. 2019. (Step into Reading Ser.). (ENG.). 24p. (J). (gr. -1-1). 12.99 *(978-0-593-12209-9(7))*; 5.99 *(978-0-593-12208-2(9))* Random Hse. Children's Bks. (Random Hse. Bks. for Young Readers).

—I Love My Mami! Katschke, Judy. 2006. (Dora the Explorer Ser.: 9). (ENG.). 24p. (J). (gr. -1-k). pap. 3.99 *(978-1-4169-0650-6(9)*, Simon Spotlight/Nickelodeon) Simon Spotlight/Nickelodeon.

—I Love My Mami! (Dora the Explorer) Random House. 2013. (Step into Reading Ser.). (ENG.). 24p. (J). (gr. -1-1). pap. 3.99 *(978-0-449-81439-0(4)*, Random Hse. Bks. for Young Readers) Random Hse. Children's Bks.

—Just Like Dora! Inches, Alison. 2005. (Dora the Explorer Ser.: Vol. 8). (ENG.). 24p. (J). pap. 3.99 *(978-0-689-87675-2(0)*, Simon Spotlight/Nickelodeon) Simon Spotlight/Nickelodeon.

—Lemon Pirates! (Top Wing) Man-Kong, Mary. 2019. (Step into Reading Ser.). (ENG.). 24p. (J). (gr. -1-1). 5.99 *(978-0-525-64772-0(4))*; 12.99 *(978-0-525-64773-7(2))* Random Hse. Children's Bks. (Random Hse. Bks. for Young Readers).

—Magical Mermaids! Swenlin, Brian & Bardekoff, Jennifer. 2017. 24p. (J). *(978-1-5182-3609-9(X))* Random Hse., Inc.

—Magical Mermaids! (Shimmer & Shine) Random House. 2017. (Step into Reading Ser.). (ENG.). 24p. (J). (gr. -1-1). pap. 4.99 *(978-0-399-55886-3(1)*, Random Hse. Bks. for Young Readers) Random Hse. Children's Bks.

—Meet the Animals! Ricci, Christine. 2006. (Dora the Explorer Ser.). (ENG.). 16p. (J). (gr. -1-k). 10.95 *(978-1-4169-1819-6(1)*, Simon Spotlight/Nickelodeon) Simon Spotlight/Nickelodeon.

—My Monster Truck Family (Elbow Grease) Cena, John. 2020. (Step into Reading Ser.). 32p. (J). (gr. -1-1). pap. 4.99 *(978-0-525-57755-3(6))*; lib. bdg. 12.99 *(978-0-525-57756-0(4))* Random Hse. Children's Bks. (Random Hse. Bks. for Young Readers).

—Nazboo's Kazoo! (Shimmer & Shine) Finnegan, Delphine. 2019. (Step into Reading Ser.). (ENG.). 24p. (J). (gr. -1-1). 12.99 *(978-0-525-64828-4(3))*; pap. 5.99 *(978-0-525-64827-7(5))* Random Hse. Children's Bks. (Random Hse. Bks. for Young Readers).

—Ninja Blaze! (Blaze & the Monster Machines) Mangual, Cynthia Ines. 2019. (Step into Reading Ser.). (ENG.). 24p. (J). (gr. -1-1). 12.99 *(978-0-525-64866-6(6))*; pap. 4.99 *(978-0-525-64865-9(8))* Random Hse. Children's Bks. (Random Hse. Bks. for Young Readers).

—Penny to the Rescue! (Top Wing) Neumann, Casey. 2019. (Pictureback(R) Ser.). (ENG.). 24p. (J). (gr. -1-2). 5.99 *(978-1-9848-4782-9(1)*, Random Hse. Bks. for Young Readers) Random Hse. Children's Bks.

—Police Officer Blaze! (Blaze & the Monster Machines) Tillworth, Mary. 2019. (Pictureback(R) Ser.). (ENG.). 24p. (J). (gr. -1-2). 5.99 *(978-1-9848-4940-3(9)*, Random Hse. Bks. for Young Readers) Random Hse. Children's Bks.

—La Quinceañera. Inches, Alison. 2006. (Dora la Exploradora Ser.). (SPA.). 24p. (J). (gr. -1-3). pap. 3.99 *(978-1-4169-2462-3(0)*, Libros Para Ninos) Libros Para Ninos.

—Race to the Tower of Power. 2005. (Backyardigans Ser.: Vol. 1). (ENG.). 24p. (J). pap. 3.99 *(978-1-4169-0799-2(8)*, Simon Spotlight/Nickelodeon) Simon Spotlight/Nickelodeon.

—Rainbow Friends! (Shimmer & Shine) Golden Books. 2018. (ENG.). 128p. (J). (gr. -1-2). pap. 7.99 *(978-1-5247-7276-5(3)*, Golden Bks.) Random Hse. Children's Bks.

—Reach for the Stars! (Shimmer & Shine) Carbone, Courtney. 2019. (Pictureback(R) Ser.). (ENG.). 24p. (J). (gr. -1-2). 5.99 *(978-1-9848-4777-5(5)*, Random Hse. Bks. for Young Readers) Random Hse. Children's Bks.

—Robot Power! (Blaze & the Monster Machines) Sisler, Celeste. 2018. (Step into Reading Ser.). (ENG.). 24p. (J). (gr. -1-1). pap. 4.99 *(978-0-525-57820-8(X))*; lib. bdg. 12.99 *(978-0-525-57821-5(8))* Random Hse. Children's Bks. (Random Hse. Bks. for Young Readers).

—Rusty Rocks! (Rusty Rivets) Tillworth, Mary. 2017. (Pictureback(R) Ser.). (ENG.). 24p. (J). (gr. -1-2). pap. 5.99 *(978-1-5247-1721-6(5)*, Random Hse. Bks. for Young Readers) Random Hse. Children's Bks.

—Save the Rainbow! (Shimmer & Shine) Depken, Kristen L. 2018. (Step into Reading Ser.). (ENG.). 24p. (J). (gr. -1-1). pap. 4.99 *(978-0-525-57751-5(3))*; lib. bdg. 12.99 *(978-0-525-57752-2(1))* Random Hse. Children's Bks. (Random Hse. Bks. for Young Readers).

—Spark Bug Rescue! (Blaze & the Monster Machines) Tillworth, Mary. 2017. (Pictureback(R) Ser.). (ENG.). 16p. (J). (gr. -1-2). pap. 5.99 *(978-1-5247-1717-9(7)*, Random Hse. Bks. for Young Readers) Random Hse. Children's Bks.

—The SpongeBob Movie: Sponge on the Run: Happy Campers! (SpongeBob SquarePants) Lewman, David. 2020. (Step into Reading Ser.). (ENG.). 24p. (J). (gr. -1-1). 12.99 *(978-0-593-12755-1(2))*; 5.99 *(978-0-593-12754-4(4))* Random Hse. Children's Bks. (Random Hse. Bks. for Young Readers).

—The SpongeBob Movie: Sponge on the Run: Official Activity Book (SpongeBob SquarePants) Golden Books. 2020. (ENG.). 48p. (J). (gr. -1-2). pap. 8.99 *(978-0-593-12750-6(1)*, Golden Bks.) Random Hse. Children's Bks.

—The SpongeBob Movie: Sponge on the Run: the Great Gary Rescue! (SpongeBob SquarePants) Lewman, David. 2020. (Pictureback(R) Ser.). (ENG.). 24p. (J). (gr. -1-2). 5.99 *(978-0-593-12753-7(6)*, Random Hse. Bks. for Young Readers) Random Hse. Children's Bks.

—A Very Krabby Christmas (SpongeBob SquarePants) Golden Books Staff. 2011. (ENG.). 64p. (J). (gr. -1-2). pap. 4.99 *(978-0-375-87392-8(9)*, Golden Bks.) Random Hse. Children's Bks.

—Watch Me Draw Dora's Favorite Adventures: Let's Draw! 2012. (J). *(978-1-936309-76-4(9))* Quarto Publishing Group USA.

—Winter Wishes! Depken, Kristen L. 2017. 23p. (J). *(978-1-5182-5212-9(5))* Random Hse., Inc.

—Winter Wishes! (Shimmer & Shine) Depken, Kristen L. 2017. (Step into Reading Ser.). (ENG.). 24p. (J). (gr. -1-1). pap. 4.99 *(978-1-5247-2057-5(7)*, Random Hse. Bks. for Young Readers) Random Hse. Children's Bks.

Aikins, Dave. World of Colors! (Blue's Clues & You) Random House. 2020. (ENG.). 26p. (J). (— 1). bds. 7.99 ***(978-0-593-12419-2(7)***, Random Hse. Bks. for Young Readers) Random Hse. Children's Bks.

Aikins, Dave & Miller, Victoria. Be Nice, Swiper! Ricci, Christine. 2007. (J). pap. *(978-1-4127-8925-7(7))* Publications International, Ltd.

Aikins, Dave, jt. illus. see Golden Books Staff.

Aikins, Dave, jt. illus. see Random House Dictionary Staff.

Aikins, Dave, jt. illus. see Random House Disney Staff.

Aikins, Dave, jt. illus. see Random House Editors.

Aikins, Dave, jt. illus. see Random House Staff.

Aikins, Dave, jt. illus. see Random House.

Aikins, David. Boots & Dora Forever! (Dora & Friends) Tillworth, Mary. 2016. (Pictureback(R) Ser.). (ENG.). 16p. (J). (gr. -1-2). 4.99 *(978-0-553-53836-6(5)*, Random Hse. Bks. for Young Readers) Random Hse. Children's Bks.

—Dora & the Unicorn King (Dora the Explorer) Reisner, Molly. 2011. (Little Golden Book Ser.). (ENG.). 24p. (J). (gr. -1-2). 4.99 *(978-0-375-87226-6(4)*, Golden Bks.) Random Hse. Children's Bks.

—Dora's Birthday Surprise! Reisner, Molly. 2010. (Little Golden Book Ser.). (ENG.). 24p. (J). (gr. -1-2). 4.99 *(978-0-375-86163-5(7)*, Golden Bks.) Random Hse. Children's Bks.

—Find the Dinosaurs! (Team Umizoomi) Golden Books. 2012. (Little Golden Book Ser.). (ENG.). 24p. (J). (gr. -1-k). 4.99 *(978-0-307-92995-2(7)*, Golden Bks.) Random Hse. Children's Bks.

—Follow That Egg! (Team Umizoomi) Random House. 2014. (ENG.). 12p. (J). (-k). bds. 6.99 *(978-0-385-37518-4(2)*, Random Hse. Bks. for Young Readers) Random Hse. Children's Bks.

—Halloween Hoedown! (Dora the Explorer) Reisner, Molly. 2013. (Pictureback Ser.). (ENG.). 24p. (J). (gr. -1-2). 3.99 *(978-0-449-81762-9(8)*, Random Hse. Bks. for Young Readers) Random Hse. Children's Bks.

—I Love My Papi! (Dora the Explorer) Inches, Alison. 2014. (Step into Reading Ser.). (ENG.). 24p. (J). (gr. -1-1). 3.99 *(978-0-385-37459-0(3)*, Random Hse. Bks. for Young Readers) Random Hse. Children's Bks.

—Island of the Lost Horses (Dora & Friends) Depken, Kristen L. 2015. (Step into Reading Ser.). (ENG.). 24p. (J). (gr. -1-1). 4.99 *(978-0-553-52093-4(8)*, Random Hse. Bks. for Young Readers) Random Hse. Children's Bks.

—Mermaid Treasure Hunt (Dora & Friends) Tillworth, Mary. 2015. (Pictureback(R) Ser.). (ENG.). 24p. (J). (gr. -1-2). 3.99 *(978-0-553-51076-8(2)*, Random Hse. Bks. for Young Readers) Random Hse. Children's Bks.

—Monster Magic! (Shimmer & Shine) Depken, Kristen L. 2017. (Big Golden Book Ser.). (ENG.). 48p. (J). (gr. -1-2). 9.99 *(978-1-5247-1671-4(5)*, Golden Bks.) Random Hse. Children's Bks.

—Movie Night Magic! (Shimmer & Shine) Tillworth, Mary. 2016. (Step into Reading Ser.). (ENG.). 24p. (J). (gr. -1-1). 4.99 *(978-1-101-93704-4(1)*, Random Hse. Bks. for Young Readers) Random Hse. Children's Bks.

—Nickelodeon Rusty Rivets: Build a Pet. 2018. (Magnetic Hardcover Ser.). (ENG.). 10p. (J). (gr. -1-k). 12.99 *(978-0-7944-4171-5(8)*, Studio Fun International) Printers Row Publishing Group.

—One Spooky Night (Dora & Friends) Golden Books. 2015. (ENG.). 64p. (J). (gr. -1-2). pap. 4.99 *(978-0-553-52118-4(7)*, Golden Bks.) Random Hse. Children's Bks.

—A Tale of Two Genies (Shimmer & Shine) Lewman, David. 2016. (Big Golden Book Ser.). (ENG.). 32p. (J). (gr. -1-2). 9.99 *(978-0-553-52200-6(0)*, Golden Bks.) Random Hse. Children's Bks.

—We Love to Dance! (Dora & Friends) Depken, Kristen L. 2015. (Step into Reading Ser.). (ENG.). 24p. (J). (gr. -1-1). 4.99 *(978-0-553-50857-4(1)*, Random Hse. Bks. for Young Readers) Random Hse. Children's Bks.

—Welcome to Fairy World! (Dora & Friends) Tillworth, Mary. 2015. (ENG.). 16p. (J). (gr. -1-2). 5.99 *(978-0-553-52119-1(5)*, Random Hse. Bks. for Young Readers) Random Hse. Children's Bks.

Aikins, David, jt. illus. see Golden Books.

Aikins, David, jt. illus. see Random House Staff.

Aileen Co & Dayton, Melissa. In the Beginning: Catholic Bible Study for Children. Watson Manhardt, Laurie. 2008. (Come & See Kids Ser.). 108p. (J). (gr. -1-2). per. 9.95 *(978-1-931018-42-5(1))* Emmaus Road Publishing.

Aime, Luigi. The Dragon with the Girl Tattoo, 1 vol. Dahl, Michael. 2012. (Dragonborn Ser.). (ENG.). 72p. (J). (gr. 4-8). pap. 7.10 *(978-1-4342-4257-0(9))*; lib. bdg. 23.99 *(978-1-4342-4041-5(X))* Capstone. (Stone Arch Bks.).

—Fangs in the Mirror, 1 vol. Dahl, Michael. 2012. (Dragonborn Ser.). (ENG.). 72p. (J). (gr. 4-8). pap. 7.10 *(978-1-4342-4255-6(2))*; lib. bdg. 23.99 *(978-1-4342-4042-2(8))* Capstone. (Stone Arch Bks.).

—Monster Hunter, 1 vol. Dahl, Michael. 2012. (Dragonborn Ser.). (ENG.). 72p. (J). (gr. 4-8). pap. 7.10 *(978-1-4342-4256-3(0))*; lib. bdg. 23.99 *(978-1-4342-4040-8(1))* Capstone. (Stone Arch Bks.).

Aime, Luigi, jt. illus. see Saito, Diogo.

Aines, Diane. Matilda Private Eye: The Case of the Missing Socks. McClafferty, Lisa. 2012. 34p. 29.95 *(978-1-4489-5049-2(X))*; 2007. (ENG.). 31p. 24.95 *(978-1-4241-8637-2(4))* America Star Bks.

Ainslie, Tamsin. A Baby for Loving. Hathorn, Libby. 2015. (ENG.). 32p. (J). (gr. -1-k). 19.99 *(978-1-921894-67-1(9))* Little Hare Bks. AUS. Dist: Independent Pubs. Group.

Ainslie, Tamsin. Collecting Sunshine. Flynn, Rachel. 2018. (ENG.). 32p. (J). (gr. k-k). 23.99 ***(978-0-14-378518-7(4)***, Viking Adult) Penguin Publishing Group.

Ainslie, Tamsin. The Easter Bunny's Helpers. Mangan, Anne. 2017. 32p. 9.99 *(978-0-7322-9576-9(9))* HarperCollins Pubs. Australia AUS. Dist: HarperCollins Pubs.

—The Greatest Father's Day of All. Mangan, Anne. 2017. 32p. 9.99 *(978-0-7322-9577-6(7))* HarperCollins Pubs. Australia AUS. Dist: HarperCollins Pubs.

—Henny Penny. 2016. (Once upon a Timeless Tale Ser.). (ENG.). 24p. (J). (gr. k-2). 9.99 *(978-1-921894-95-4(4))* Little Hare Bks. AUS. Dist: Independent Pubs. Group.

—Our Baby: Little Hare Books. Hathorn, Libby. 2020. (ENG.). 30p. (J). (gr. -1-k). bds. 10.99 *(978-1-76050-339-0(8))* Little Hare Bks. AUS. Dist: Independent Pubs. Group.

Aires, Celeste. Wacky Inventions Throughout History: Weird Inventions That Seem Too Crazy to Be Real! Rhatigan, Joe. 2019. (Wacky Things Ser.). (ENG.). 32p. (J). (gr. 3-5). 27.99 *(978-1-60058-800-6(X)*, Walter Foster Jr) Quarto Publishing Group USA.

—50 Ways to Feel Happy: Fun Activities & Ideas to Build Your Happiness Skills. King, Vanessa et al. 2018. (ENG.). 64p. (J). (gr. 3-6). 14.95 *(978-1-68297-311-0(5))* QEB Publishing Inc.

Aisato, Lisa. The Night of His Birth. Paterson, Katherine. 2019. (ENG.). 32p. (J). (gr. k-4). 18.00 *(978-1-947888-12-8(9)*, Flyaway Bks.) Westminster John Knox Pr.

Aison, Everett. Arthur. Levine, Rhoda. 2015. 48p. (J). (gr. -1-2). 15.95 *(978-1-59017-935-2(8)*, NYR Children's Collection) New York Review of Bks., Inc., The.

Aitch. Easy Peasy: Gardening for Kids. Bradley, Kirsten. Little Gestalten, Little, ed. 2019. (ENG.). 56p. 19.95 *(978-3-89955-824-1(3))* Die Gestalten Verlag DEU. Dist: Ingram Publisher Services.

Aitch, et al. The Magical Unicorn Society: a Brief History of Unicorns. Phipps, Selwyn E. 2019. (Magical Unicorn Society Ser.: 2). (ENG.). 128p. (J). 12.99 *(978-1-250-25187-9(7)*, 900215260) Feiwel & Friends.

Aitch. A World Full of Animal Stories: 50 Folk Tales & Legends. McAllister, Angela. 2017. (ENG.). 128p. (J). (gr. 1-4). 22.99 *(978-1-78603-045-0(4)*, Frances Lincoln Children's Bks.) Quarto Publishing Group UK GBR. Dist: Hachette Bk. Group.

Aitken, Kati. Nellie's Walk. Stiverson, Charlotte L. 2016. (J). *(978-1-935864-62-2(9))* Oncology Nursing Society.

Aitken, Stephen. How to Cure Earth's Fever. 2011. (J). *(978-1-61641-674-4(2))* Magic Wagon.

—People in Trouble. 2011. (J). *(978-1-61641-675-1(0))* Magic Wagon.

Aizen, Marina. Brown Bear Starts School. Tarsky, Sue. 2019. (ENG.). 32p. (J). (gr. -1-3). 16.99 *(978-0-8075-0773-5(3)*, 807507733) Whitman, Albert & Co.

—Mary Had a Little Lamb. (Classic Books with Holes Big Book Ser.). (ENG.). (J). 2014. 16p. *(978-1-84643-669-7(9))*; 2012. 14p. bds. *(978-1-84643-512-6(9))*; 2012. 16p. pap. *(978-1-84643-501-0(3))* Child's Play International Ltd.

Ajhar, Brian. Book of American Heroes. Beck, Glenn. 2011. (ENG.). 276p. (J). 19.99 *(978-1-4424-2332-9(3)*, Simon & Schuster/Paula Wiseman Bks.) Simon & Schuster/Paula Wiseman Bks.

—No Pirates Allowed! Said Library Lou. Greene, Rhonda Gowler. 2013. (ENG.). 40p. (J). (gr. 1-3). 15.95 *(978-1-58536-796-2(6)*, 202364) Sleeping Bear Pr.

—Pinocchio. 2005. (Rabbit Ears Ser.). 36p. (J). (gr. k-5). 25.65 *(978-1-59679-228-9(0))* Spotlight.

—Shipwreckers: The Curse of the Cursed Temple of Curses or We Nearly Died. a Lot a Lot. Peterson, Scott & Pruett, Joshua. 2020. (ENG.). 336p. (J). (gr. 3-7). pap. 7.99 *(978-1-368-02395-5(9))* Hyperion Bks. for Children.

Ak, Leena. The Girl Who Couldn't Read: Until She Discovered Her Super Powers. Weston, Dpa. 2018. (ENG.). 40p. (J). *(978-1-5255-2706-7(1))* FriesenPress.

Akaba, Suekichi. El Gorrion de la Lengua Cortada. Ishii, Momoko.Tr. of Tongue-Cut Sparrow. (SPA.). 40p. (J). (gr. 3-18). 14.95 *(978-980-257-073-7(7))* Ekare, Ediciones VEN. Dist: Kane Miller.

Akamatsu, Ken. A. I. Love You, 8 vols., Vol. 8. Akamatsu, Ken. Ury, David, tr. from JPN. rev. ed. 2005. 224p. (YA). pap. 14.99 *(978-1-59182-944-7(5)*, Tokyopop Adult) TOKYOPOP, Inc.

—Ai Love You, 8 vols., Vol. 7. Akamatsu, Ken. rev. ed. 2005. 216p. pap. 14.99 *(978-1-59182-943-0(7)*, Tokyopop Adult) TOKYOPOP, Inc.

—Love Hina, 14 vols., Vol. 8. Akamatsu, Ken. Rymer, Nan, tr. from JPN. rev. ed. 2003. (JPN & ENG.). 184p. (gr. 9-18). pap. 14.99 *(978-1-59182-019-2(7)*, Tokyopop Adult) TOKYOPOP, Inc.

Akana, Lizzi. Playground. 50 Cent, 50. 2012. (ENG.). 320p. (YA). (gr. 7). pap. 9.99 *(978-1-59514-478-2(1)*, Razorbill) Penguin Young Readers Group.

Akbar, Zoheb. The Ramayana. Harini Gopalswami Srinivasan & Valmiki. 2017. (J). ***(978-93-5085-298-9(5))*** Agarwal, Anuraag.

Akerlund, Sara. If Only My Belt Could Speak (Holocaust Survivor's Story) Harris, Samuel & Harris, Dede. 2020. (ENG.). 48p. (J). (gr. 4-6). 15.98 ***(978-1-64558-231-1(0)***, 4395600) Publications International, Ltd.

Akerman, Emma. Junk Collector School. Dahlin, Adam A. Sandin, Joan, tr. from SWE. 2007. 32p. (J). (gr. -1-3). 16.00 *(978-91-29-66736-3(4))* R & S Bks. SWE. Dist: Macmillan.

Akers-Bell, Mary. Benjamin's Dog Joseph: A Three Legged Hero. Greene, Daryl C. 2003. 48p. (J). (gr. 2-4). pap. 9.95 *(978-0-9700827-4-9(6))*; lib. bdg. 17.95 *(978-0-9700827-5-6(4))* Densmore-Reid Pubns.

Akgul, Semih. Little Squirrel Squish Gets His Christmas Wish. Hammond, Ross. 2019. (Little Christmas Ser.: Vol. 2). (ENG.). 44p. (J). pap. ***(978-1-9993187-2-7(2))*** Blonc Bks.

Akhmetzhanova, Aiym. Your Christmas Elf. Stapler, Jodi. 2019. (ENG.). 34p. (J). 17.99 *(978-1-948256-21-6(5))* Willow Moon Publishing.

Akhmetzhanova, Aiym. Your Christmas Elf. Stapler, Jodi. 2019. (ENG.). 34p. (J). pap. 13.99 ***(978-1-948256-22-3(3))*** Willow Moon Publishing.

Akhtar, Waheed. Mouth Almighty a Play. Agbaje, Salihah. 2012. 144p. pap. *(978-0-9565861-0-0(4))* Spoken World Productions.

Akhter, Sadiqa. The Angels at My School. Bonner, Brandy D. 2019. (ENG.). 28p. (J). pap. 14.99 ***(978-1-6728-4228-0(X))*** Independently Published.

Aki. Baby's First Eames: From Art Deco to Zaha Hadid. Merberg, Julie. 2018. (ENG.). 24p. (J). (gr. -1 — 1). bds. 11.99 *(978-1-941367-39-1(9))* Downtown Bookworks.

Aki. The City Girls. Aki. 2020. (ENG.). 32p. (J). 17.99 *(978-1-250-31395-9(3)*, 900199457, Holt, Henry & Co. Bks. For Young Readers) Holt, Henry & Co.

—The Nature Girls. Aki. 2019. (ENG.). 32p. (J). 16.99 *(978-1-62779-621-7(5)*, 900156982, Holt, Henry & Co. Bks. For Young Readers) Holt, Henry & Co.

Aki, jt. illus. see Mach, Delphine.

Aki, Aki. Toshi's Little Treasures. Robert, Nadine. 2016. (ENG.). 32p. (J). (gr. -1-2). 17.95 *(978-1-77138-573-2(1))* Kids Can Pr., Ltd. CAN. Dist: Hachette Bk. Group.

Aki, Katsu. Psychic Academy. Aki, Katsu. Vol. 6. rev. ed. 2005. 192p. pap. 14.99 *(978-1-59532-425-2(9))*; Vol. 8. rev. ed. 2005. 192p. pap. 14.99 *(978-1-59532-427-6(5))*; Vol. 9. 9th rev. ed. 2005. 192p. per. 14.99 *(978-1-59532-428-3(3))*; Vol. 10. 10th rev. ed. 2005. 200p. per. 14.99 *(978-1-59532-429-0(1))*; Vol. 11. 11th rev. ed. 2006. 204p. (YA). per. 14.99 *(978-1-59532-430-6(5))* TOKYOPOP, Inc. (Tokyopop Adult).

Aki, Katsu. Psychic Academy, Vol. 7. Aki, Katsu, creator. rev. ed. 2005. 192p. pap. 14.99 *(978-1-59532-426-9(7)*, Tokyopop Adult) TOKYOPOP, Inc.

Akia, Kylie, jt. illus. see Bye, Alexandra.

Akib, Jamel. Annie Shapiro & the Clothing Workers' Strike. Brill, Marlene Targ. 2010. (History Speaks: Picture Books Plus Reader's Theater Ser.). (ENG.). 48p. (gr. 2-4). pap. 9.95 *(978-0-7613-6132-9(4))* Lerner Publishing Group.

—Around the World in 80 Days: Retold from the Jules Verne Original. Verne, Jules. 2007. (Classic Starts® Ser.). 160p. (J). (gr. 2-4). 6.95 *(978-1-4027-3689-6(4))* Sterling Publishing Co., Inc.

—Bringing Asha Home, 1 vol. Krishnaswami, Uma. 2006. (ENG.). 32p. (J). (gr. -1-4). pap. 10.95 *(978-1-62014-225-7(2)*, ba4c6c66-6719-47d3-b4bf-35e73626f9b1) Lee & Low Bks., Inc.

Akib, Jamel. Classic Starts®: Heidi. Spyri, Johanna. 2020. (Classic Starts® Ser.). (ENG.). 160p. (J). (gr. 2-4). pap. 6.95 ***(978-1-4549-3796-8(3))*** Sterling Publishing Co., Inc.

—Classic Starts®: the Swiss Family Robinson. Wyss, Johann David. 2020. (Classic Starts® Ser.). (ENG.). 160p. (J). (gr.

2-4). pap. 6.95 ***(978-1-4549-3806-4(4))*** Sterling Publishing Co., Inc.
—Classic Starts®: the Three Musketeers. Dumas, Alexandre. 2020. (Classic Starts® Ser.). (ENG.). 160p. (J). (gr. 2-4). pap. 6.95 ***(978-1-4549-3807-1(2))*** Sterling Publishing Co., Inc.
Akib, Jamel. Dracula: Retold from the Bram Stoker Original. Stoker, Bram. 2007. (Classic Starts® Ser.). 160p. (J). (gr. 2-4). 6.95 *(978-1-4027-3690-2(8))* Sterling Publishing Co., Inc.
—Emanuel & the Whale Oil Lamp. Hyde, Heidi Smith. 2012. (Hanukkah Ser.). (ENG.). 32p. (J). (gr. -1-1). lib. bdg. 17.95 *(978-0-7613-6625-6(3)*, Kar-Ben Publishing) Lerner Publishing Group.
—Frankenstein: Retold from the Mary Shelley Original. Shelley, Mary. 2006. (Classic Starts® Ser.). 160p. (J). (gr. 2-4). 6.95 *(978-1-4027-2666-8(X))* Sterling Publishing Co., Inc.
—Gulliver's Travels. Swift, Jonathan. 2006. (Classic Starts® Ser.). 160p. (J). (gr. 2-4). 6.95 *(978-1-4027-2662-0(7))* Sterling Publishing Co., Inc.
—Heidi: Retold from the Johanna Spyri Original. Spyri, Johanna. 2007. (Classic Starts® Ser.). 160p. (J). (gr. 2-4). 6.95 *(978-1-4027-3691-9(6))* Sterling Publishing Co., Inc.
—Pollyanna. Olmstead, Kathleen & Porter, Eleanor H. 2007. (Classic Starts Ser.). 154p. (J). *(978-1-4287-4209-3(3))* Sterling Publishing Co., Inc.
—Pollyanna. Porter, Eleanor H. 2007. (Classic Starts® Ser.). 160p. (J). (gr. 2-4). 6.95 *(978-1-4027-3692-6(4))* Sterling Publishing Co., Inc.
—The Prince & the Pauper. Twain, Mark. 2007. (Classic Starts® Ser.). 160p. (J). (gr. 2-4). 6.95 *(978-1-4027-3687-2(8))* Sterling Publishing Co., Inc.
—Rebecca of Sunnybrook Farm. Wiggin, Kate Douglas. 2007. (Classic Starts® Ser.). 160p. (J). (gr. 2-4). 6.95 *(978-1-4027-3693-3(2))* Sterling Publishing Co., Inc.
—The Red Badge of Courage. Crane, Stephen. 2006. (Classic Starts® Ser.). 160p. (J). (gr. 2-4). 6.95 *(978-1-4027-2663-7(5))* Sterling Publishing Co., Inc.
—Robinson Crusoe: Retold from the Daniel Defoe Original. Dafoe, Daniel. 2006. (Classic Starts® Ser.). 160p. (J). (gr. 2-4). 6.95 *(978-1-4027-2664-4(3))* Sterling Publishing Co., Inc.
—The Strange Case of Dr. Jekyll & Mr. Hyde: Retold from the Robert Louis Stevenson Original. Stevenson, Robert Louis. 2006. (Classic Starts® Ser.). 160p. (J). (gr. 2-4). 6.95 *(978-1-4027-2667-5(8)*, 1252057) Sterling Publishing Co., Inc.
—The Swiss Family Robinson. Tait, Chris & Wyss, Johann David. 2007. 151p. (J). *(978-1-4287-4213-0(1))* Sterling Publishing Co., Inc.
—The Swiss Family Robinson: Retold from the Johann David Wyss Original. Wyss, Johann David. 2007. (Classic Starts® Ser.). (ENG.). 160p. (J). (gr. 2-4). 6.95 *(978-1-4027-3694-0(0))* Sterling Publishing Co., Inc.
—Tan to Tamarind: Poems about the Color Brown. Iyengar, Malathi Michelle. 2013. (ENG.). 32p. (J). (gr. k). 16.95 *(978-0-89239-227-8(4))* Lee & Low Bks., Inc.
—Tan to Tamarind: Poems about the Color Brown. Iyengar, Malathai. 2017. (ENG.). 32p. (J). pap. 9.95 *(978-0-89239-412-8(9)*, Children's Book Press) Lee & Low Bks., Inc.
—The Three Musketeers: Retold from the Alexandre Dumas Original. Dumas, Alexandre. 2007. (Classic Starts® Ser.). 160p. (J). (gr. 2-4). 6.95 *(978-1-4027-3695-7(9))* Sterling Publishing Co., Inc.
—Twenty-Two Cents: Muhammad Yunus & the Village Bank. Yoo, Paula. 2014. (ENG.). 40p. (J). 18.95 *(978-1-60060-658-8(X))* Lee & Low Bks., Inc.
—The War of the Worlds. Sasaki, Chris & Wells, H. G. 2007. (Classic Starts Ser.). 151p. (J). *(978-1-4287-4208-6(5))* Sterling Publishing Co., Inc.
—The War of the Worlds. Wells, H. G. 2007. (Classic Starts® Ser.). 160p. (J). (gr. 2-4). 6.95 *(978-1-4027-3688-9(6))* Sterling Publishing Co., Inc.
—The Wind in the Willows. Woodside, Martin & Grahame, Kenneth. 2007. (Classic Starts Ser.). 152p. (J). *(978-1-4287-4210-9(7))* Sterling Publishing Co., Inc.
—The Wind in the Willows. Grahame, Kenneth. 2007. (Classic Starts® Ser.). 160p. (J). (gr. 2-4). 6.95 *(978-1-4027-3696-4(7))* Sterling Publishing Co., Inc.
Akib, Jamel, jt. illus. see Jeyaveeran, Ruth.
Akimine, Kamijyo. Samurai Deeper Kyo, 18 vols. Akimine, Kamijyo. 192p. Vol. 3. rev. ed. 2003. (YA). pap. 14.99 *(978-1-59182-227-1(0))*; Vol. 12. 12th rev. ed. 2005. pap. 14.99 *(978-1-59532-452-8(6))* TOKYOPOP, Inc. (Tokyopop Adult).
—Samurai Deeper Kyo: Volume 15, Vol. 15. Akimine, Kamijyo. rev. ed. 2005. (Samurai Deeper Kyo Ser.). 192p. (YA). per. 14.99 *(978-1-59532-455-9(0)*, Tokyopop Adult) TOKYOPOP, Inc.
—Samurai Deeper Kyo: Volume 17, 31 vols., Vol. 17. Akimine, Kamijyo. 17th rev. ed. 2006. (Samurai Deeper Kyo Ser.). 192p. (YA). per. 14.99 *(978-1-59532-457-3(7)*, Tokyopop Adult) TOKYOPOP, Inc.
Akimoto, Nami. Miracle Girls, 9 vols., Vol. 7. Akimoto, Nami. 7th rev. ed. 2003. 192p. (gr. 2-18). pap. 9.99 *(978-1-59182-073-4(1))* TOKYOPOP, Inc.
Akin, Sean. Henny Penny. 2010. (J). *(978-1-60617-133-2(X))* Teaching Strategies, LLC.
Akino, Matsuri. Genju No Seiza, Vol. 1. Akino, Matsuri. 2006. (Genju No Seiza Ser.). 216p. per. 9.99 *(978-1-59816-607-1(7))* TOKYOPOP, Inc.
—Pet Shop of Horrors - Tokyo, 10 vols., Vol. 3. Akino, Matsuri. rev. ed. 2003. (Teen Ser.). 200p. (YA). (gr. 10-18). pap. 14.99 *(978-1-59182-365-0(X)*, Tokyopop Adult) TOKYOPOP, Inc.
—Pet Shop of Horrors - Tokyo, 10 vols., Vol. 4. Akino, Matsuri. Iwo, Tomoharu & Masumoto, Bryan, trs. from JPN. rev. ed. 2004. (Teen Ser.). 210p. (YA). pap. 14.99 *(978-1-59182-501-2(6)*, Tokyopop Adult) TOKYOPOP, Inc.
Akins, Shakera Le-Ann. The Little Brown Girl Experience. Akins, Shakera Le-Ann. 2018. (ENG.). 62p. (J). pap. 19.95 *(978-0-692-98411-6(9))* Akins, ShaKera.
Akins, Tamlyn. In Grandpa's Woods. Addy, Sharon. 2004. (J). *(978-1-931599-42-9(4)*, Trails Bks.) Bower Hse.
Akio, Irene. T Is for Tokyo. Akio, Irene. 2010. (ENG.). 36p. (J). (gr. k-5). 12.95 *(978-1-934159-23-1(9))* ThingsAsian Pr.
Akira, Shouko. Times Two. Akira, Shouko. 2005. (Times Two Ser.). (ENG.). 200p. (YA). pap. 9.99 *(978-1-59116-736-5(1))* Viz Media.
Akiyama, Takayo. So You Want to Be a Ninja? Vincent, Bruno. 2020. (ENG.). 96p. (J). (gr. 3-6). 14.95 ***(978-0-500-65210-7(4)***, 565210) Thames & Hudson.
Akiyama, Tamayo. Mouryou Kiden, Vol. 3. Akiyama, Tamayo, creator. rev. ed. 2005. 192p. pap. 9.99 *(978-1-59532-247-0(7)*, Tokyopop Adult) TOKYOPOP, Inc.
Akridge, Bill. Intrigue at Pine Haven: Civil War in Florida. Bonner, Anne. 2006. 220p. (YA). 12.95 net. *(978-1-878398-76-5(8)*, Blue Note Bks.) Blue Note Pubns.
Akyuz, Sav. Bear Moves. Smith, Ben Bailey. 2018. (ENG.). 40p. (J). (-k). 15.99 *(978-0-7636-9831-7(8)*, Candlewick Entertainment) Candlewick Pr.
Akyüz, Sav. I Am Bear. Smith, Ben Bailey. 2016. (ENG.). (J). (-k). 15.99 *(978-0-7636-7743-5(4)*, Candlewick Entertainment) Candlewick Pr.
Al-Fakhri, Patricia. Fizza the Flamingo. Sheffield, Marilyn. 2003. 3p. pap. 7.95 *(978-1-900988-63-6(1))* Interlink Publishing Group, Inc.
—The Pearl Diver. Johnson, Julia. Stacey International Staff, ed. 2003. (ARA & ENG.). 240p. (J). (gr. 3-6). *(978-1-900988-62-9(3)*, Stacey International) Stacey Publishing.
Al-Ghani, Haitham. Baby Blue Has the Blues, 1 vol. Al-Ghani, K. I. 2011. (ENG.). 32p. (J). (gr. -1-3). 16.99 *(978-0-7643-3732-1(7)*, 9780764337321, Schiffer Publishing Ltd) Schiffer Publishing, Ltd.
—Bertie Bumble Bee: Troubled by the Letter "B" Al-Ghani, K. I. 2012. (ENG.). 44p. (J). (gr. -1-3). 16.99 *(978-0-7643-3993-6(1)*, 9780764339936) Schiffer Publishing, Ltd.
—The Red Beast: Controlling Anger in Children with Asperger's Syndrome. Al-Ghani, Kay. 2008. (K. I. Al-Ghani Children's Colour Story Bks.). (ENG.). 48p. (gr. 3-7). 21.95 *(978-1-84310-943-3(3)*, 691651) Kingsley, Jessica Pubs. GBR. Dist: Hachette UK Distribution.
—Ronnie Raven Recycles, 1 vol. Al-Ghani, K.I. 2011. (ENG.). 44p. (J). (gr. -1-3). 16.99 *(978-0-7643-3840-3(4)*, 9780764338403, Schiffer Publishing Ltd) Schiffer Publishing, Ltd.
Al-Ghani, Haitham. Super Shamia!: Living & Learning with Pathological Demand Avoidance. Al-Ghani, Kay. ed. 2019. (K. I. Al-Ghani Children's Colour Story Bks.). (ENG.). 72p. 19.95 ***(978-1-78775-056-2(6)***, 710028) Kingsley, Jessica Pubs. GBR. Dist: Hachette UK Distribution.
Al-Ghussinu, Wa'ad Diab. 1st Grade Learning Arabic Language Step - by - Step Approach Workbook Part 2,Third Edition: Learn Arabic Language. Tommalieh, Fakhri & Hujeer, Majeda. 2012. (ARA.). 104p. pap. 21.99 *(978-0-9853772-0-5(8))* Dar Asadeeq Publishing & Distribution, Inc.
Al-Greene, Bob. Ghost in the Water. at Science, Editors. 2014. (League of Scientists Ser.). (ENG.). 192p. (J). (gr. 5-9). pap. 12.95 *(978-0-9700106-2-9(1))* Platypus Media, L.L.C.
Al, Parker. Jane's Blanket. Miller, Arthur. 2015. (ENG.). 64p. pap. 9.99 *(978-0-486-79682-6(5))* Dover Pubns., Inc.
Al-Zubaidy, Zaidoon a. Bertie & the Troublesome Mice. Al-Zubaidy, Zaidoon a. 2018. (ENG.). 22p. (J). (gr. k-2). *(978-1-63576-492-5(0))* Malaysian Press Institute.
Alabaster, Rosie. Recipe for Making a Snowman. Lynas, Peter. 2016. (ENG.). (J). *(978-0-9933403-2-1(6))*; pap. *(978-0-9933403-1-4(8))* Lynas, P J.
Alakija, Polly. Catch That Goat! A Market Day in Nigeria. Alakija, Polly. 2007. 40p. (J). (gr. -1-3). pap. 8.99 *(978-1-84686-057-7(1))* Barefoot Bks., Inc.
Alan, Jones. Annabelle & the Strawberry Faerie, & the Magic Comb: And the Magic Comb. Roscoe, P. J. 2016. (Adventures of Faerie Folk Ser.: 1). (ENG.). (J). (gr. k-6). pap. 9.99 *(978-1-68160-189-2(3))* Crimson Cloak Publishing.
Alanguilan, Gerry, et al. Secret Empire. 2017. (ENG.). 432p. (YA). (gr. 8-17). 60.00 *(978-0-7851-9452-1(5))* Marvel Worldwide, Inc.
Alanis, Erik Valdez Y. Rumpelstiltskin: La Novela Grafica, 1 vol. Andersen, Hans & Stone Arch Books Staff. 2010. (Graphic Spin en Español Ser.). (SPA.). 40p. (J). (gr. 3-6). pap. 5.95 *(978-1-4342-2273-2(X)*, Stone Arch Bks.) Capstone.
—Rumpelstiltskin: The Graphic Novel, 1 vol. Stone Arch Books Staff. 2008. (Graphic Spin Ser.). (ENG.). 40p. (J). (gr. 3-6). pap. 5.95 *(978-1-4342-0864-4(8)*, Stone Arch Bks.) Capstone.
Alaniz, Adam. Germ Stories, Vol. Kolter, Roberto, photos by. Kornberg, Arthur. 2007. (ENG.). 84p. (J). (gr. 3-7). 34.00 *(978-1-891389-51-1(3))* Univ. Science Bks.
Alarcão, Renato. The Book of the Heart. Asai, Carrie. 2004. (Samurai Girl Ser.: 6). (ENG.). 240p. (YA). (gr. 11). pap. 11.99 *(978-0-689-86712-5(3)*, Simon Pulse) Simon Pulse.
—The Book of the Pearl. Asai, Carrie. 2003. (Samurai Girl Ser.: 3). (ENG.). 240p. (YA). (gr. 11). pap. 6.99 *(978-0-689-86432-2(9)*, Simon Pulse) Simon Pulse.
—The Book of the Shadow. Asai, Carrie. 2013. (Samurai Girl Ser.: 2). (ENG.). 224p. (YA). (gr. 11). pap. 13.99 *(978-1-4814-1540-8(9)*, Simon Pulse) Simon Pulse.
—Finding the Music, 1 vol. Torres, Jennifer. 2015.Tr. of En Pos de la Música. (ENG & SPA.). 40p. (J). 18.95 *(978-0-89239-291-9(6))* Lee & Low Bks., Inc.
Alarcao, Renato. Roberto's Trip to the Top. Paterson Jr., John B. & Paterson Sr, John B. 2010. 40p. (J). (gr. -1-3). pap. 6.99 *(978-0-7636-4755-1(1))* Candlewick Pr.
—Roberto's Trip to the Top. Paterson, John B., Jr. & Paterson, John B., Sr. 2009. (ENG.). 40p. (J). (gr. -1-3). 16.99 *(978-0-7636-2708-9(9))* Candlewick Pr.
—Soccer Star. Javaherbin, Mina. 40p. (J). (gr. k-3). 2019. 7.99 *(978-1-5362-0713-2(6))*; 2014. (ENG.). 16.99 *(978-0-7636-6056-7(6))* Candlewick Pr.
Alarcão, Renato & Alarcão, Renato. The Book of the Flame. Asai, Carrie. 2004. (Samurai Girl Ser.: 5). (ENG.). 224p. (YA). (gr. 11). pap. 7.99 *(978-0-689-86713-2(1)*, Simon Pulse) Simon Pulse.
—The Book of the Wind. Asai, Carrie. 2003. (Samurai Girl Ser.: 4). (ENG.). 224p. (YA). (gr. 11). pap. 6.99 *(978-0-689-86433-9(7)*, Simon Pulse) Simon Pulse.
Alarcão, Renato, jt. illus. see Alarcão, Renato.
Alarid, Carilyn & Markel, Marilyn. Old Grandfather Teaches a Lesson: Mimbres Children Learn Respect. Alarid, Carilyn & Markel, Marilyn. 2004. 116p. (J). pap. 16.95 *(978-0-86534-418-1(3))* Sunstone Pr.
—Runs Like the Wind Stops in Her Tracks: Mimbres Children Learn about Trustworthiness. 2016. 95p. (J). pap. *(978-1-63293-099-6(4))* Sunstone Pr.
—Talks All Day Has the Courage to Speak: Mimbres Children Learn Citizenship. Alarid, Carilyn & Markel, Marilyn. 2006. 125p. (J). pap. 16.95 *(978-0-86534-470-9(1))* Sunstone Pr.
Alaverdy, Melissa. Introduction to Music. O'Brien, Eileen. 2004. (ENG.). 96p. (J). 7.95 *(978-0-7945-0276-8(8)*, Usborne) EDC Publishing.
Alayon, Gaby. A Dozen Differences. Elaine, Kirsten. 2017. (Dozen Differences Ser.: Vol. 1). (ENG.). (J). (gr. k-2). pap. 12.99 *(978-1-64136-329-7(0))* North Bound Bks.
Alba, Elisabeth. Martin Luther King, Jr. Norwich, Grace. 2012. (I Am Ser.: 4). (ENG.). 128p. (J). (gr. 2-5). pap. 5.99 *(978-0-545-44780-5(1)*, Scholastic Paperbacks) Scholastic, Inc.
—Morgan & the Forty Thieves: A Magic Math Adventure. Abacus, Addie. 2018. (Magic Math Adventures Ser.: Vol. 1). (ENG.). 130p. (J). pap. 8.99 *(978-1-7328813-1-0(6))* Phantom Hill Pr.
Alba, Elisabeth. Morgan & the Monster of the Deep: A Magic Math Adventure. Abacus, Addie. 2019. (Magic Math Adventures Ser.: Vol. 2). (ENG.). 140p. (J). pap. 8.99 ***(978-1-7328813-7-2(5))*** Phantom Hill Pr.
Albanez, Dixie. Isecas the Dream Cat & the Tides of Change. Squire, Preston. 2015. (Dream Cats Ser.: Vol. 2). (ENG.). 46p. (J). pap. *(978-0-9938888-6-1(0))* Squire, Preston Publishing.
Albano, Jennifer. Wanda & Willie. Schultz, Brenda. 2008. 25p. pap. 24.95 *(978-1-60703-446-9(8))* America Star Bks.
Alberg, Nathan. What Happened to Marion's Book? Berg, Brook. 2003. 48p. (J). (gr. -1-2). per. 16.95 *(978-1-932146-05-9(9)*, Upstart Bks.) Highsmith Inc.
—What Marion Taught Willis. Berg, Brook. 2005. (J). 16.95 *(978-1-932146-31-8(8)*, 1242215) Highsmith Inc.
Albergottie, Aziza. Oh, the Green Things! Day, Shantel. 2018. (ENG.). 26p. (J). pap. 9.95 *(978-1-7905-5000-5(9))* Independently Published.
Albergottie, Aziza Latique. JONBOYONDABEAT Presents Tiny Stories: Alie Rose. Saunders, Alvin Jonathan. 2019. (Jonboyondabeat Presents Tiny Stories Ser.: Vol. 1). (ENG.). 26p. (J). pap. 16.00 ***(978-1-0894-7073-1(8))*** Independently Published.
Alberini, Teresa. Do You Really Want to Burn Your Toast? A Book about Heat. Maurer, Daniel D. 2016. (Adventures in Science Ser.). (ENG.). 24p. (J). (gr. k-3). 20.95 *(978-1-60753-961-2(6))* Amicus Publishing.
—Do You Really Want to Create a Mudslide? A Book about Erosion. Maurer, Daniel D. 2016. (Adventures in Science Ser.). (ENG.). 24p. (J). (gr. k-3). 20.95 *(978-1-60753-957-5(8))* Amicus Publishing.
—Do You Really Want to Drive in a Blizzard? A Book about Predicting Weather. Maurer, Daniel D. 2016. (Adventures in Science Ser.). (ENG.). 24p. (J). (gr. k-3). 20.95 *(978-1-60753-959-9(4))* Amicus Publishing.
—Do You Really Want to Skate on Thin Ice? A Book about States of Matter. Maurer, Daniel D. 2016. (Adventures in Science Ser.). (ENG.). 24p. (J). (gr. k-3). 20.95 *(978-1-60753-958-2(6))* Amicus Publishing.
—Do You Really Want to Walk in the Dark? A Book about Light. Maurer, Daniel D. 2016. (Adventures in Science Ser.). (ENG.). 24p. (J). (gr. k-3). 20.95 *(978-1-60753-960-5(8))* Amicus Publishing.
—Do You Really Want to Yell in a Cave? A Book about Sound. Maurer, Daniel D. 2016. (Adventures in Science Ser.). (ENG.). 24p. (J). (gr. k-3). 20.95 *(978-1-60753-956-8(X))* Amicus Publishing.
—My Bones. Dawson, Emily C. 2015. (Inside My Body Ser.). (ENG.). 24p. (J). (gr. 1-3). 19.95 *(978-1-60753-753-3(2))* Amicus Publishing.
—My Brain. Pimentel, Annette Bay. 2015. (Inside My Body Ser.). (ENG.). 24p. (J). (gr. 1-3). 19.95 *(978-1-60753-754-0(0))* Amicus Publishing.
—My Heart. Shaffer, Jody Jensen. 2015. (Inside My Body Ser.). (ENG.). 24p. (J). (gr. 1-3). 19.95 *(978-1-60753-755-7(9))* Amicus Publishing.
—My Lungs. Shaffer, Jody Jensen. 2015. (Inside My Body Ser.). (ENG.). 24p. (J). (gr. 1-3). 19.95 *(978-1-60753-756-4(7))* Amicus Publishing.
—My Muscles. Shaffer, Jody Jensen. 2015. (Inside My Body Ser.). (ENG.). 24p. (J). (gr. 1-3). 19.95 *(978-1-60753-757-1(5))* Amicus Publishing.
—My Stomach. Pimentel, Annette Bay. 2015. (Inside My Body Ser.). (ENG.). 24p. (J). (gr. 1-3). 19.95 *(978-1-60753-758-8(3))* Amicus Publishing.
Albero, Ana. Coco Chanel. Sanchez Vegara, Maria Isabel. 2016. (Little People, BIG DREAMS Ser.: 1). (ENG.). 32p. (J). (gr. -1-2). 14.99 *(978-1-84780-784-7(4)*, Frances Lincoln Children's Bks.) Quarto Publishing Group UK GBR. Dist: Hachette Bk. Group.
Albert, Dar, jt. illus. see Cardillo, Linda.
Albert, Jason. Seaper Powers: The Mystery of the Blue Pearls. Cameron, Kim. 3rd ed. 2016. (Seaper Powers Ser.: Vol. 2). (ENG.). (J). (gr. 1-4). 25.00 *(978-0-692-82883-0(4))* Side FX Partners, LLC.
Albert, Robert & Anthis, Brian. The Lost Kachina. Irbinskas, Heather. 2004. 32p. (J). 15.95 *(978-1-885772-33-6(5))* Kiva Publishing, Inc.
Albert, Sonia. Herbert Henry & Santa's Secret Society. Stewart, Amber. 2018. 220p. (J). (gr. 3-7). 16.99 *(978-1-948206-17-4(X)*, Curiosity Bks.) Curiosity Ink Media, LLC.
Albert, Virginia. La Historia de Peter Rabbit. Potter, Beatrix. 2020. (SPA.). 42p. (J). ***(978-88-3346-496-1(2))***; pap. ***(978-88-3346-494-7(6))*** Ali Ribelli Edizioni.
Albert, Yael. Francesco Tirelli's Ice Cream Shop. Meir, Tamar. 2019. (ENG.). 32p. (J). (gr. 3-6). 17.99 *(978-1-5415-3465-0(4)*, 9781541534650, Kar-Ben Publishing) Lerner Publishing Group.
Albertine. Little Bird. Zullo, Germano. 2012. (ENG.). 72p. (J). (gr. k). 16.95 *(978-1-59270-118-6(3))* Enchanted Lion Bks., LLC.
Alberts, Scott. A Different Little Doggy. Whittaker, Heather. 2013. 28p. (J). 9.99 *(978-0-9820962-1-5(6))* Pen-Tech Professional.
Albon, Lucie. Little Ballerina: A Children's Book Inspired by Edgar Degas. 2011. (ENG.). 32p. (J). (gr. -1-3). 14.95 *(978-3-7913-7081-1(2))* Prestel Verlag GmbH & Co KG. DEU. Dist: Penguin Random Hse. LLC.
Alborough, Jez. Billy the Goat's Big Breakfast. Alborough, Jez. 2014. (ENG.). 32p. (J). 12.99 *(978-1-61067-190-3(2))* Kane Miller.
—The Gobble Gobble Moooooo Tractor Book. Alborough, Jez. 2010. 32p. (J). (gr. -1-1). 15.99 *(978-1-935279-66-2(1))* Kane Miller.
—Hug. Alborough, Jez. (ENG.). 32p. (J). 2009. (gr. -1-k). pap. 4.99 *(978-0-7636-4510-6(9))*; 2005. (— 1). bds. 12.99 *(978-0-7636-2893-2(X))* Candlewick Pr.
—Play. Alborough, Jez. 2018. (ENG.). 32p. (J). (— 1). 15.99 *(978-0-7636-9599-6(8))* Candlewick Pr.
—Where's My Teddy? Alborough, Jez. 2017. (ENG.). 32p. (J). (gr. -1-2). 7.99 *(978-0-7636-9871-3(7))*; 25th ed. 16.99 *(978-0-7636-9816-4(4))* Candlewick Pr.
—Where's My Teddy? 25th Anniversary Edition. Alborough, Jez. 25th ed. 2018. (ENG.). 24p. (J). (-k). bds. 7.99 *(978-0-7636-9980-2(2))* Candlewick Pr.
Alborozo, et al. Sharing, Caring & Friendship Book Set Of 4. Alborozo et al. 2020. (Social & Emotional Learning Sets Ser.). (ENG.). 128p. (J). pap., pap., pap. ***(978-1-78628-535-5(5))*** Child's Play International Ltd.
Alborozo. This Old Dog. Brockenbrough, Martha. 2020. (J). *(978-1-338-28395-2(2)*, Levine, Arthur A. Bks.) Scholastic, Inc.
Alborozo. And Then... Alborozo. 2016. (Child's Play Library). 32p. (J). (ENG.). *(978-1-84643-696-3(6))*; pap. *(978-1-84643-695-6(8))* Child's Play International Ltd.
Alborozo, Gabriel. All the Families. Brown, Margaret Wise. 2019. (Margaret Wise Brown Classics Ser.). (ENG.). 32p. (J). (gr. -1-k). 12.99 *(978-1-68412-751-1(3)*, Silver Dolphin Bks.) Printers Row Publishing Group.
—The Boy on the Bench. Averiss, Corrinne. 2018. (ENG.). 32p. (J). (gr. -1-k). pap. 9.99 *(978-1-4052-7820-1(X))* Egmont Bks., Ltd. GBR. Dist: Independent Pubs. Group.
—This is the Kiss: A StoryPlay Book. Harcup, Claire. 2017. (StoryPlay Ser.). (ENG.). 32p. (J). (gr. -1-k). 5.99 *(978-1-338-18733-5(3)*, Cartwheel Bks.) Scholastic, Inc.
—The Two Tims. Elliott, David. 2016. 32p. (J). (gr. -1-1). 15.99 *(978-0-7636-7264-5(5))* Candlewick Pr.
Alborozo, Gabriel. Flora's Tree House. Alborozo, Gabriel. 2019. (ENG.). 32p. (J). 17.99 *(978-1-62779-226-4(0)*, 900141612, Holt, Henry & Co. Bks. For Young Readers) Holt, Henry & Co.
Albrecht, Jeff. Remarkable Rescue: Saved on Noah's Ark. Dudley, Becki. 2016. (ENG.). 12p. (J). bds. 7.99 *(978-0-89051-976-9(5)*, Master Books) New Leaf Publishing Group.
Albright, Ann. Samuel Sparrow & the Tree of Light. Albright, Ann. 2nd ed. 2003. (ENG.). 28p. (J). pap. *(978-0-9715472-5-4(4))* Ascension Lutheran Church.
Albright, Audrey. Rachel the Homely Rabbit: A Story about Kindness. Kaye, Christian Thomas. 2011. 30p. pap. 9.95 *(978-1-60844-763-3(4))* Dog Ear Publishing, LLC.
Albright, Tawnya, et al. Puppetry Clip Art Book & CD. rev. ed. 2003. 44p. (YA). 25.00 *(978-1-58302-229-0(5))* Creative Ministry Solutions.
Albright, Tawnya. Travel God's Way. VonSeggen, Liz. rev. ed. 2003. 116p. (J). ring bd. 35.00 *(978-1-58302-248-1(1))* Creative Ministry Solutions.
Albuquerque, Rafael. The Savage Brothers. Cosby, Andrew & Stokes, Johanna. 2007. (ENG.). 128p. pap. 14.99 *(978-1-934506-16-5(8))* Boom! Studios.
Alburquerque, Alberto Jimenez & Larroca, Salvador. Absolute Carnage: Lethal Protectors. Tieri, Frank & Williams, Leah. 2020. (ENG.). 112p. (YA). (gr. 8-17). pap. 15.99 *(978-1-302-92013-5(8))* Marvel Worldwide, Inc.
Alca, Bàrbara. Ella Fitzgerald. Sanchez Vegara, Maria Isabel. 2018. (Little People, Big Dreams Ser.: Vol. 11). (ENG.). 32p. (J). (gr. -1-2). ***(978-1-78603-087-0(X))*** Frances Lincoln Childrens Bks.
Alcadia, S. N. C. Giddy-Up, Scooby-Doo, 1 vol. Howard, Lee. 2015. (Scooby-Doo Leveled Readers Ser.). (ENG.). 32p. (J). (gr. k-4). lib. bdg. 27.07 *(978-1-61479-414-1(6)*, 19437) Spotlight.
—A Merry Scary Holiday. Howard, Lee & Khan, Nahnatchka. 2014. (Scooby-Doo Comic Storybook Ser.). (ENG.). 32p. (J). (gr. -1-3). 27.07 *(978-1-61479-282-6(8)*, 1636, Graphic Novels) Spotlight.
—Scooby-Doo & the Battle of the Snowboarders, 1 vol. Sander, Sonia. 2015. (Scooby-Doo Leveled Readers Ser.). (ENG.). 32p. (J). (gr. k-4). lib. bdg. 27.07 *(978-1-61479-415-8(4)*, 19438) Spotlight.
—Scooby-Doo & the Big Catch, 1 vol. Sander, Sonia. 2015. (Scooby-Doo Leveled Readers Ser.). (ENG.). 32p. (J). (gr. k-4). lib. bdg. 27.07 *(978-1-61479-416-5(2)*, 19439) Spotlight.
—Scooby-Doo & the Snow Monster Mystery, 1 vol. Howard, Lee. 2015. (Scooby-Doo Leveled Readers Ser.). (ENG.). 32p. (J). (gr. k-4). lib. bdg. 27.07 *(978-1-61479-417-2(0)*, 19440) Spotlight.
—Scooby-Doo in Bake-Off Mayhem, 1 vol. Howard, Lee. 2015. (Scooby-Doo Leveled Readers Ser.). (ENG.). 32p. (J). (gr. k-4). lib. bdg. 27.07 *(978-1-61479-418-9(9)*, 19441) Spotlight.

—Scooby-Doo in Monkey See, Monkey Doo, 1 vol. Howard, Lee. 2015. (Scooby-Doo Leveled Readers Ser.). (ENG.). 32p. (J). (gr. k-4). lib. bdg. 27.07 *(978-1-61479-419-6(7)*, 19442) Spotlight.

—Scooby-Doo in Raging River Adventure, 1 vol. Sander, Sonia. 2015. (Scooby-Doo Leveled Readers Ser.). (ENG.). 32p. (J). (gr. k-4). lib. bdg. 27.07 *(978-1-61479-420-2(0)*, 19443) Spotlight.

—Scooby-Doo Steals the Dog Show, 1 vol. Sander, Sonia. 2015. (Scooby-Doo Leveled Readers Ser.). (ENG.). 32p. (J). (gr. k-4). lib. bdg. 27.07 *(978-1-61479-421-9(9)*, 19444) Spotlight.

Alcadia SNC Staff. Scooby-Doo Comic Storybook, 4 vols. ABDO Publishing Company Staff & Howard, Lee. 2014. (Scooby-Doo Comic Storybook Ser.: 4). (ENG.). 32p. (J). (gr. -1-3). lib. bdg. 108.28 *(978-1-61479-280-2(1)*, 1634, Graphic Novels) Spotlight.

Alcala, Alfredo, jt. illus. see Leonard, Richard.

Alcantara, Felipe Ugalde. Little Crow to the Rescue/el Cuervito al Rescate. Villasenor, Victor. Munoz, Elizabeth Cummins, tr. 2005. (SPA & ENG.). 32p. (J). (gr. -1-3). pap. 16.95 *(978-1-55885-430-7(4)*, Piñata Books) Arte Publico Pr.

Alcantara, Ignacio. Disabilities. Vision, Mutiya Sahar. 2009. 32p. 17.00 *(978-0-9659538-9-4(0))* Von Curtis Publishing.

—If Only I Could! Vision, David & Vision, Mutiya Sahar. 2009. 32p. 17.00 *(978-0-9659538-8-7(2))* Von Curtis Publishing.

—The Land of Expression. Vision, Mutiya & Vision, David. 2009. (ENG.). 48p. 15.00 *(978-0-9816254-0-9(1))* Von Curtis Publishing.

—Missing You. Vision, David & Vision, Mutiya Sahar. 2009. 32p. 17.00 *(978-0-9659538-6-3(6))* Von Curtis Publishing.

—My Choices Make Me Who I Am. Vision, Mutiya & Vision, David. 2009. 40p. (gr. 2-5). 17.00 *(978-0-9659538-2-5(3))* Von Curtis Publishing.

—My Very Breast Friend. Vision, David et al. 2009. (ENG.). 40p. 17.00 *(978-0-9659538-5-6(8))* Vitally Important.

—What Makes Me Beautiful? Vision, David & Vision, Mutiya Sahar. 2009. 24p. 16.00 *(978-0-9659538-4-9(X))* Von Curtis Publishing.

—Who's That Crying! Vision, David. 2009. 64p. 17.00 *(978-0-9659538-1-8(5))* Von Curtis Publishing.

Alcántara, Jacqueline. The Field. Paul, Baptiste. 2018. (ENG.). 32p. (J). (gr. -1-3). 17.95 *(978-0-7358-4312-7(0))* North-South Bks., Inc.

—Freedom Soup. Charles, Tami. 2019. (ENG.). 32p. (J). (gr. k-4). 16.99 *(978-0-7636-8977-3(7))* Candlewick Pr.

Alcomendas, Jp & Yoga, Afrianas Dwi. My Bee's Keeper. Baier, Antoinette. 2019. (ENG.). 72p. (J). pap. 14.99 ***(978-1-7025-1486-6(2))*** Independently Published.

Alcorn, Jeremiah. The Year of the Pig: Tales from the Chinese Zodiac. Chin, Oliver. 2018. (Tales from the Chinese Zodiac Ser.). (ENG.). 40p. (J). (gr. -1-3). 15.95 *(978-1-59702-143-2(1))* Immedium.

—The Year of the Rat: Tales of the Chinese Zodiac. Chin, Oliver Clyde. 2019. (Tales from the Chinese Zodiac Ser.). 36p. (J). 15.95 *(978-1-59702-147-0(4))* Immedium.

Alcorn, John. Books! McCain, Murray. 2013. (ENG.). 42p. (J). (gr. -1). 17.95 *(978-1-62326-020-0(5))* AMMO Bks., LLC.

—Writing! McCain, Murray. 2016. (ENG.). 48p. 17.95 *(978-1-62326-075-0(2))* AMMO Bks., LLC.

Alcorn, Miah. The Year of the Ox: Tales from the Chinese Zodiac. Chin, Oliver. 2009. (Tales from the Chinese Zodiac Ser.). (ENG.). 36p. (J). (gr. -1-3). 15.95 *(978-1-59702-015-2(X))* Immedium.

Alcorn, Stephen. America at War. Hopkins, Lee Bennett, ed. 2008. (ENG.). 96p. (J). (gr. 3-7). 24.99 *(978-1-4169-1832-5(9)*, McElderry, Margaret K. Bks.) McElderry, Margaret K. Bks.

—Children of the Slaughter: Young People of the Holocaust. Gottfried, Ted. (Holocaust History Ser.). 112p. (YA). (gr. 7-12). 22.95 *(978-1-58013-202-2(2)*, Kar-Ben Publishing) Lerner Publishing Group.

—Days to Celebrate: A Full Year of Poetry, People, Holidays, History, Fascinating Facts, & More. Hopkins, Lee Bennett. 2004. (ENG.). 112p. (J). (gr. 2-7). 18.99 *(978-0-06-000765-2(6)*, Greenwillow Bks.) HarperCollins Pubs.

—Deniers of the Holocaust: Who They Are, What They Do, Why They Do It. Gottfried, Ted. (Holocaust History Ser.). 112p. (YA). (gr. 7-12). 22.95 *(978-1-58013-200-8(6)*, Kar-Ben Publishing) Lerner Publishing Group.

—Displaced Persons: The Liberation & Abuse of Holocaust Survivors. Gottfried, Ted. (Holocaust History Ser.). 112p. (YA). (gr. 7-12). 22.95 *(978-1-58013-201-5(4)*, Kar-Ben Publishing) Lerner Publishing Group.

—Heroes of the Holocaust. Gottfried, Ted. (Holocaust History Ser.). 112p. (YA). (gr. 7-12). 22.95 *(978-1-58013-222-0(7)*, Kar-Ben Publishing) Lerner Publishing Group.

—Holocaust History Series. Gottfried, Ted. (J). 103.28 *(978-1-58013-197-1(2)*, Kar-Ben Publishing) Lerner Publishing Group.

—I, Too, Sing America: Three Centuries of African American Poetry. Clinton, Catherine. 2017. (ENG.). 128p. (J). (gr. 5-7). 9.99 *(978-0-544-58256-9(X)*, 1613659, HMH Books For Young Readers) Houghton Mifflin Harcourt Publishing Co.

—Keep On! The Story of Matthew Henson, Co-Discoverer of the North Pole, 1 vol. Hopkinson, Deborah. (ENG.). 36p. (J). (gr. 1-5). 2015. pap. 7.95 *(978-1-56145-886-8(4))*; 2009. 17.95 *(978-1-56145-473-0(7))* Peachtree Publishing Co. Inc.

—Lincoln in His Own Words. Meltzer, Milton. 2018. (ENG.). 240p. (J). (gr. 7). pap. 12.99 *(978-1-328-89574-5(2)*, 1699521, HMH Books For Young Readers) Houghton Mifflin Harcourt Publishing Co.

—Mary's Song. Hopkins, Lee Bennett. 2012. (ENG.). 32p. (J). 17.00 *(978-0-8028-5397-4(8)*, Eerdmans Bks For Young Readers) Eerdmans, William B. Publishing Co.

—Nazi Germany: The Face of Tyranny. Gottfried, Ted. (Holocaust History Ser.). 112p. (YA). (gr. 7-12). 22.95 *(978-1-58013-203-9(0)*, Kar-Ben Publishing) Lerner Publishing Group.

—Yours for Justice, Ida B. Wells: The Daring Life of a Crusading Journalist, 1 vol. Dray, Philip. 2008. (ENG.). 48p. (J). (gr. 5-9). 18.95 *(978-1-56145-417-4(6))* Peachtree Publishing Co. Inc.

Alcorn, Stephen. A Gift of Days: The Greatest Words to Live By. Alcorn, Stephen. 2009. (ENG.). 128p. (J). (gr. 3-7). 21.99 *(978-1-4169-6776-7(1)*, Atheneum Bks. for Young Readers) Simon & Schuster Children's Publishing.

Alden, Bea. A Bad Night's Sleep. Craig, Joni. 2013. 46p. (J). 16.95 *(978-1-940224-11-4(X))* Taylor and Seale Publishing.

Alden, Carol. Paddy the Pelican Survives the Storm. Fane, Judy B. 2010. 48p. pap. 16.50 *(978-1-60911-448-0(5)*, Eloquent Bks.) Strategic Book Publishing & Rights Agency (SBPRA).

Aldepolla, Arnild. Daggers & Dresses Coloring Book. Van Risseghem, Kristin D. 2018. (ENG.). 52p. (J). pap. 6.99 *(978-1-943207-50-3(X))* Kasian Publishing.

—Swords & Stilettos Coloring Book. Van Risseghem, Kristin D. 2018. (ENG.). 52p. (J). pap. 6.99 *(978-1-943207-42-8(9))* Kasian Publishing.

—Wars & Wings Coloring Book. Van Risseghem, Kristin D. 2018. (ENG.). 52p. (J). pap. 6.99 *(978-1-943207-54-1(2))* Kasian Publishing.

Aldepolla, Arnild, jt. illus. see Aldepolla, Arnild C.

Aldepolla, Arnild C. Landis & the Pink Unicorn. Maldonado, L. A. 2020. (ENG.). 32p. (J). pap. 9.99 ***(978-1-7068-1822-9(X))*** Independently Published.

—Ms. Maggie Undercover K-9: And the Missing Agent. Scholl, Geneieve & Bloom, Faith, eds. 2020. (Ms. Esme Undercover K-9 Ser.: Vol. 5). (ENG.). 134p. (J). pap. 6.50 ***(978-1-9760-9263-3(9))*** CreateSpace Independent Publishing Platform.

Aldepolla, Arnild C. & Aldepolla, Arnild. Ms. Esme Undercover K-9: The Activity & Coloring Book Adventures. Maldonado, L. A. 2019. (Ms. Esme Undercover K-9: Coloring Book Ser.: Vol. 1). (ENG.). 28p. (J). pap. 5.99 *(978-1-9759-5409-3(2))* CreateSpace Independent Publishing Platform.

Alder, Charlie. Collins Big Cat Phonics for Letters & Sounds - Disaster Duck: Band 06/Orange, Bd. 6. Baker, Catherine. 2018. (Collins Big Cat Phonics Ser.). (ENG.). 24p. (J). pap. 6.99 *(978-0-00-825173-4(8))* HarperCollins Pubs. Ltd. GBR. Dist: Independent Pubs. Group.

—Katie Woo's Super Stylish Activity Book, 1 vol. Manushkin, Fran. 2013. (Katie Woo Ser.). (ENG.). 64p. (J). (gr. k-2). pap. 4.95 *(978-1-4795-2047-3(0)*, Picture Window Bks.) Capstone.

—Owen & Eleanor Make Things Up, Vol. Bouwman, H. M. 2018. (Owen & Eleanor Ser.: 2). (ENG.). 136p. (J). (gr. k-3). pap. 7.99 *(978-1-5064-4845-9(3)*, Sparkhouse Family) Augsburg Fortress, Pubs.

—Owen & Eleanor Meet the New Kid, Vol. Bouwman, H. M. 2019. (Owen & Eleanor Ser.: 3). (ENG.). 139p. (J). (gr. k-3). pap. 7.99 *(978-1-5064-5202-9(7)*, Sparkhouse Family) Augsburg Fortress, Pubs.

—Owen & Eleanor Move In, Vol. Bouwman, H. M. 2018. (Owen & Eleanor Ser.: 1). (ENG.). 133p. (J). (gr. 2-5). pap. 7.99 *(978-1-5064-3972-3(1)*, Sparkhouse Family) Augsburg Fortress, Pubs.

Alder, Charlie. Today Is a Beach Day! Viau, Nancy. 2020. (ENG.). 32p. (J). (gr. -1-3). 16.99 ***(978-0-8075-9396-7(6)***, 807593966) Whitman, Albert & Co.

Alder, Charlie. Where Is Carl the Corn Snake?, 1 vol. Dale, Jay. 2012. (Engage Literacy Green Ser.). (ENG.). 32p. (gr. k-2). pap. 5.99 *(978-1-4296-8994-6(3)*, Capstone Pr.) Capstone.

—100th Day of School. Berne, Emma Carlson. 2018. (Holidays in Rhythm & Rhyme Ser.). (ENG.). 24p. (C). (gr. k-2). lib. bdg. 33.99 *(978-1-68410-396-6(7)*, 140356) Cantata Learning.

Alder, Charlotte. Chicken Break! A Counting Book. Berry, Cate. 2019. (ENG.). 32p. (J). 17.99 *(978-1-250-30679-1(5)*, 900197873) Feiwel & Friends.

—Green Princess Saves the Day. Crowne, Alyssa. 2010. (J). (Perfectly Princess Ser.: 3). (ENG.). 80p. (gr. 1-4). 4.99 *(978-0-545-20848-2(3)*, Scholastic Paperbacks); 71p. *(978-0-545-23414-6(X))* Scholastic, Inc.

—Pink Princess Rules the School. Crowne, Alyssa. 2009. 80p. (J). pap. *(978-0-545-16077-3(4))* Scholastic, Inc.

Alder, Kelynn. Moments of Wonder: Life with Moritz. 2008. (ENG.). 68p. (J). 22.00 *(978-0-9721457-4-9(5))* Silent Moon Bks.

Alder, Kelynn Z. Journey to the Bottomless Pit: The Story of Stephen Bishop & Mammoth Cave. Mitchell, Elizabeth. 2019. (ENG.). 112p. (J). (gr. 4-8). pap. 12.99 *(978-1-5040-5770-7(8))* Open Road Integrated Media, Inc.

Alderman, Derrick & Shea, Denise. Una Bandera a Cuadros: Un Libro para Contar Sobre Carreras de Autos. Dahl, Michael. 2010. (Apréndete Tus Números/Know Your Numbers Ser.).Tr. of One Checkered Flag - A Counting Book about Racing. (ENG.). 24p. (J). (gr. -1-2). lib. bdg. 27.32 *(978-1-4048-6295-1(1)*, Picture Window Bks.) Capstone.

—I Drive a Snowplow, 1 vol. Bridges, Sarah. 2004. (Working Wheels Ser.). (ENG.). 24p. (J). (gr. -1-2). 27.32 *(978-1-4048-0617-7(2)*, Picture Window Bks.) Capstone.

—On the Launch Pad: A Counting Book about Rockets, 1 vol. Dahl, Michael. 2004. (Know Your Numbers Ser.). (ENG.). 24p. (J). (gr. -1-2). per. 8.95 *(978-1-4048-1119-5(2)*, Picture Window Bks.) Capstone.

—Yo Manejo un Camión de Volteo. Bridges, Sarah. 2010. (Vehículos de Trabajo/Working Wheels Ser.).Tr. of I Drive a Dump Truck. (ENG.). 24p. (J). (gr. -1-2). lib. bdg. 27.32 *(978-1-4048-6301-9(X)*, Picture Window Bks.) Capstone.

—Yo Manejo Una Niveladora. Bridges, Sarah. 2010. (Vehículos de Trabajo/Working Wheels Ser.).Tr. of I Drive a Bulldozer. (ENG.). 24p. (J). (gr. -1-2). lib. bdg. 27.32 *(978-1-4048-6300-2(1)*, Picture Window Bks.) Capstone.

Aldern, Jackson. Brad Bateman; Brat Ratman. Aldern, Sam. 2018. (ENG.). 152p. (J). pap. 7.99 *(978-1-7250-9503-8(3))* CreateSpace Independent Publishing Platform.

Alderson, Lisa. The Moon Sees You & Me: Padded Board Book. Burroughs, Caleb. 2015. (Love You Always Ser.). (ENG.). 18p. (J). (gr. -1-k). bds. 9.99 *(978-1-68052-006-4(7)*, 1000070) Cottage Door Pr.

—The Night Before Christmas: Peek Inside the 3D Windows. Moore, Clement C. 2013. (ENG.). 12p. (J). (gr. -1-3). 16.99 *(978-1-84322-923-0(4)*, Armadillo) Anness Publishing GBR. Dist: National Bk. Network.

—The Snow Family: A Winter's Tale. 2005. (ENG.). 12p. (J). 12.95 *(978-1-58117-233-1(8)*, Intervisual/Piggy Toes) Bendon, Inc.

—The Snow Family: A Winter's Tale. Feldman, Thea & Auerbach, Annie. 2005. 12p. (J). 13.00 *(978-0-7567-9460-6(9))* DIANE Publishing Co.

Alderton, John. Nerfnerd. Michael, Melanie. 2011. (J). *(978-0-938467-07-6(7))* Headline Bks., Inc.

Aldin, Cecil. Black Beauty. Sewell, Anna. 2018. (ENG.). 240p. 12.99 *(978-1-5098-6598-7(5)*, 900195882, Collector's Library, The) Pan Macmillan GBR. Dist: Macmillan.

Aldous, Kate. Black Beauty. Sewell, Anna. 2003. 288p. (J). 9.98 *(978-1-4054-1675-7(0))* Parragon, Inc.

—A Little Princess. Burnett, Frances Hodgson. 2005. 62p. (J). (gr. 4-7). 8.95 *(978-0-7945-1123-4(6)*, Usborne) EDC Publishing.

Aldous, Kate & McGairy, James. Little Women. 320p. (J). *(978-1-4054-3772-1(3))* Parragon, Inc.

Aldredge, Terry Beckham. The Story of Jesus: Part 1. Laubach, Frank. Woodworth, Ralph, ed. 2005. per. *(978-0-9749168-6-6(2))* FEA Ministries.

—The Story of Jesus: Part 2. Laubach, Frank. Woodworth, Ralph, ed. 2005. per. *(978-0-9749168-8-0(9))* FEA Ministries.

Aldridge, Alan. The Butterfly Ball & the Grasshopper's Feast. Plomer, William. 2009. (ENG.). 96p. (J). (gr. k-12). 22.99 *(978-0-7636-4422-2(6)*, Templar) Candlewick Pr.

Aldridge Deacon, Jack Aldridge. Can I Tell You about Being a Young Carer? A Guide for Friends, Family & Professionals. Aldridge, Jo. 2018. (Can I Tell You About...? Ser.). (ENG.). 56p. (J). pap. 14.95 *(978-1-78592-526-9(1)*, 696866) Kingsley, Jessica Pubs. GBR. Dist: Hachette UK Distribution.

Aldridge, Ethan M. Estranged. Aldridge, Ethan M. 2018. (ENG.). 224p. (J). (gr. 3-7). 21.99 *(978-0-06-265387-1(3))*; pap. 12.99 *(978-0-06-265386-4(5))* HarperCollins Pubs.

—Estranged #2: the Changeling King. Aldridge, Ethan M. 2019. (ENG.). 256p. (YA). (gr. 3-7). 21.99 *(978-0-06-265390-1(3))*; pap. 12.99 *(978-0-06-265389-5(X))* HarperCollins Pubs.

Aldy, Aguirre. A Grain of Hope: A Picture Book about Refugees. Philp, Nicola. 2019. (ENG.). 34p. (J). (gr. 3-6). pap. ***(978-0-6483486-4-1(4))*** Publishink Pr.

Alejandro, Rocio. Loving Kindness. Stewart, Whitney. 2019. (Mindful Tots Ser.). (ENG.). 16p. (J). (gr. -1 — 1). bds. *(978-1-78285-749-5(4))* Barefoot Bks., Ltd.

Alejandro, Rocio. Mindful Tots: Animal Antics. Stewart, Whitney. 2020. (ENG.). (J). bds. ***(978-1-78285-936-9(5))*** Barefoot Bks., Inc.

—Mindful Tots: Rest & Relax. Stewart, Whitney. 2020. (ENG.). (J). bds. ***(978-1-78285-935-2(7))*** Barefoot Bks., Inc.

Alejandro, Rocio. Tummy Ride. Stewart, Whitney. 2019. (Mindful Tots Ser.). (ENG.). 16p. (J). (gr. -1 — 1). bds. *(978-1-78285-748-8(6))* Barefoot Bks., Ltd.

Alejandro, Shiela. Baked with Love. Tomlin, Sarah-Lou. 2017. (ENG.). 22p. (J). *(978-1-912009-57-2(9)*, Compass Publishing) Book Refinery Ltd, The.

—Little Dreamers, Big Ideas. Tomlin, Sarah-Lou. 2017. (ENG.). 20p. (J). *(978-1-912009-91-6(9)*, Compass Publishing) Book Refinery Ltd, The.

Alekos. Un Conejo Es un Ciempies / a Rabbit Is a Centipede (Torre de Papel Naranja) Spanish Edition. 2017. (Torre de Papel Naranja Ser.). (SPA.). (J). (gr. -1-2). pap. *(978-958-8860-28-2(8))* Norma Ediciones, S.A.

—El Leon y el Perrito: Y Otros Cuentos. Tolstoy, Leo. Montaña, Francisco, tr. 2nd ed. 2003. (Cajon de Cuentos Ser.). (SPA.). 177p. (J). (gr. -1-7). *(978-958-30-0333-2(6))* Panamericana Editorial.

Aleksic, Vladimir. Design a Skyscraper. Koll, Hilary & Mills, Steve. 2015. (You Do the Math Ser.). (ENG.). 32p. (J). (gr. 1-3). 17.95 *(978-1-60992-730-1(3))* QEB Publishing Inc.

—Legendary 12: John Rabbit (Vol. 4): Darkness at Camelot. Ngo, Son Bac. 2018. (Legendary 12 Ser.: Vol. 4). (ENG.). 98p. (J). (gr. 2-6). pap. *(978-0-9944947-9-5(3))* Jaguar Ngo Investment Pty Ltd.

Aleksic, Vladimir & Ware, Kate. A Christmas Carol: a Coloring Classic. Random House Disney Staff. 2016. (ENG.). 80p. (gr. k-12). pap. 15.99 *(978-1-5247-1319-5(8)*, Doubleday Bks. for Young Readers) Random Hse. Children's Bks.

Alem�n, Manuel. Sarah Was Waiting for the Shark. Alem�n, Manuel. 2020. (ENG.). 52p. (J). pap. 14.25 ***(978-1-5172-1104-2(2))*** CreateSpace Independent Publishing Platform.

Alemagna, Beatrice. One & Seven. Rodari, Gianni. Anglin, David, tr. from ITA. 2005. (SPA.). 26p. (J). (gr. k-3). 17.95 *(978-0-9628720-6-8(7))* Iaconi, Mariuccia Bk. Imports.

—Songs from the Garden of Eden: Jewish Lullabies & Nursery Rhymes. Soussana, Nathalie et al. 2009. (ENG & MUL.). 52p. (J). (gr. -1-2). 16.95 *(978-2-923163-46-8(X))* La Montagne Secrete CAN. Dist: Independent Pubs. Group.

Alemagna, Beatrice. Harold Snipperpot's Best Disaster Ever. Alemagna, Beatrice. 2019. (ENG.). 48p. (J). (gr. -1-3). 18.99 *(978-0-06-249882-3(7))* HarperCollins Pubs.

—On a Magical Do-Nothing Day. Alemagna, Beatrice. 2017. (ENG.). 48p. (J). (gr. -1-3). 17.99 *(978-0-06-265760-2(7))* HarperCollins Pubs.

Alemán, Manuel, et al. Soñé con Elefantes. 2020. (SPA.). 72p. (J). pap. 18.00 ***(978-1-6581-8086-3(0))*** Independently Published.

Alemanno, Andrea. Between the Walls. Pere, Tuula. Korman, Susan, ed. 2018. (ENG.). 40p. (J). (gr. k-4). *(978-952-7107-09-6(1))*; pap. *(978-952-5878-85-1(6))* Wickwick oy.

—The Fox's City. Pere, Tuula. Korman, Susan, ed. 2018. (ENG.). 44p. (J). (gr. k-4). *(978-952-7107-15-7(6))*; pap. *(978-952-5878-91-2(0))* Wickwick oy.

Alemanno, Andrea. The Fox's Palace. Pere, Tuula. Vuoriaro, Paivi, tr. 2019. (Francis the Fox Ser.: Vol. 2). (ENG.). 44p. (J). (gr. k-4). ***(978-952-357-286-7(5))***; pap. ***(978-952-357-287-4(3))*** Wickwick oy.

Alemanno, Andrea. Ketun Kaupunki: Finnish Edition of the Fox's City. Pere, Tuula. 2018. (FIN.). 44p. (J). (gr. k-4). *(978-952-7107-16-4(4))*; pap. *(978-952-5878-93-6(7))* Wickwick oy.

Alemanno, Andrea. Ketun Palatsi: Finnish Edition of the Fox's Palace. Pere, Tuula. 2019. (Francis the Fox Ser.: Vol. 2). (FIN.). 44p. (J). (gr. k-4). ***(978-952-357-289-8(X))***; pap. ***(978-952-357-290-4(3))*** Wickwick oy.

Alemanno, Andrea. Laakson Kehtolaulu: Finnish Edition of Lullaby of the Valley. Pere, Tuula. 2018. (FIN.). 36p. (J). (gr. k-4). *(978-952-7107-13-3(X))*; pap. *(978-952-5878-89-9(9))* Wickwick oy.

—Lullaby of the Valley: Pacifistic Book about War & Peace. Pere, Tuula. Korman, Susan, ed. 2018. (ENG.). 36p. (J). (gr. k-4). *(978-952-7107-12-6(1))*; pap. *(978-952-5878-88-2(0))* Wickwick oy.

—Mat with Only One T. Thomas, Jeff. 2016. (ENG.). (J). (gr. -1-3). 14.95 *(978-1-63177-596-3(0))* Mascot Bks., Inc.

—Mellan Murarna: Swedish Edition of Between the Walls. Pere, Tuula. Torstensson, Elisabeth, tr. 2018. (SWE.). 40p. (J). (gr. k-4). *(978-952-7107-11-9(3))*; pap. *(978-952-5878-86-8(4))* Wickwick oy.

—Muurien Välissä: Finnish Edition of Between the Walls. Pere, Tuula. 2018. (FIN.). 40p. (J). (gr. k-4). *(978-952-7107-10-2(5))*; pap. *(978-952-5878-87-5(2))* Wickwick oy.

—Rävens Stad: Swedish Edition of the Fox's City. Pere, Tuula. Nikolowski-Bogomoloff, Angelika, tr. 2018. (SWE.). 44p. (J). (gr. k-4). pap. *(978-952-5878-92-9(9))* Wickwick oy.

—Vaggvisan I Dalen: Swedish Edition of Lullaby of the Valley. Pere, Tuula. Torstensson, Elisabeth, tr. 2018. (SWE.). 36p. (J). (gr. k-4). *(978-952-7107-14-0(8))*; pap. *(978-952-5878-90-5(2))* Wickwick oy.

Alemian, Kimberlee. Adventures of Dingle Dee & Lingle Dee. Masella, Rosalie Tagg. 2009. 26p. (J). 19.95 *(978-0-9663730-3-5(0))* Vesper Enterprises, Inc.

Alencar, Rayner. Meena Meets Her Match. Mantemach, Karla. 2019. (Meena Zee Bks.). (ENG.). 192p. (J). (gr. 3-7). 17.99 *(978-1-5344-2817-1(8)*, Simon & Schuster Bks. For Young Readers) Simon & Schuster Bks. For Young Readers.

Alenick, Chaya. Goodnight. Alenick, Chaya. 2018. (ENG.). 26p. (J). 14.99 *(978-0-692-05225-9(9))* Alenick, Chaya.

Aleshina, Nonna. Isabel Saves the Prince: Based on a True Story of Isabel I of Spain. Holub, Joan. 2007. (Young Princesses Around the World Ser.). (ENG.). 48p. (J). (gr. 1-3). pap. 13.99 *(978-0-689-87197-9(X)*, Simon Spotlight) Simon Spotlight.

Alesi, Hugo. Carnet Blanc Chemin de Fer Paris-Lyon. 2016. (Bnf Monuments Ser.). (FRE.). (J). pap. *(978-2-01-116952-5(6))* Hachette Groupe Livre.

—Carnet Blanc Chemins de Fer du MIDI. 2016. (Bnf Monuments Ser.). (FRE.). (J). pap. *(978-2-01-116965-5(8))* Hachette Groupe Livre.

—Carnet Blanc Chemins de Fer P. L. M. 2016. (Bnf Monuments Ser.). (FRE.). (J). pap. *(978-2-01-116963-1(1))* Hachette Groupe Livre.

—Carnet Blanc Paris-Lyon, Dauphine. 2016. (Bnf Monuments Ser.). (FRE.). (J). pap. *(978-2-01-116953-2(4))* Hachette Groupe Livre.

—Carnet Ligne Chemin de Fer Paris-Lyon. 2016. (Bnf Monuments Ser.). (FRE.). (J). pap. *(978-2-01-116977-8(1))* Hachette Groupe Livre.

—Carnet Ligne Chemins de Fer du MIDI. 2016. (Bnf Monuments Ser.). (FRE.). (J). pap. *(978-2-01-116942-6(9))* Hachette Groupe Livre.

—Carnet Ligne Chemins de Fer P. L. M. 2016. (Bnf Monuments Ser.). (FRE.). (J). pap. *(978-2-01-116940-2(2))* Hachette Groupe Livre.

—Carnet Ligne Paris-Lyon, Dauphine. 2016. (Bnf Monuments Ser.). (FRE.). (J). pap. *(978-2-01-116978-5(X))* Hachette Groupe Livre.

Alessandra, Amandine. The Big Letter Hunt: London: an Architectural a-Z Around the City. Ferreira, Rute Nieto. 2016. 64p. pap. 14.95 *(978-1-84994-366-6(4)*, Batsford) Pavilion Bks. GBR. Dist: Sterling Publishing Co., Inc.

Alex, Green. Fun Tongue Twisting ABCs: Creative & Easy Way to Learn Alphabet. Graham, Inna. 2018. (ENG.). 28p. (J). pap. 9.99 *(978-1-5136-4148-5(4))* Graham, Inna.

Alex, Ioan. My First Words, 1 vol. 2004. (ENG.). 64p. (J). 9.95 *(978-1-59496-000-0(3))* Teora USA LLC.

Alex, Smith. Home. Alex, Smith. 2010. (ENG.). 32p. (J). (gr. -1-2). 15.95 *(978-1-58925-088-8(5))* Tiger Tales.

Alexa, Melton. Buddemut Adventures: Gamma Loves Strawberries Just Like Aurielle. Outlaw, Rebecca a. 2020. (ENG.). 48p. (J). 15.00 ***(978-1-0878-7149-3(2))*** Independently Published.

Alexander, Claire. Back to Front & Upside Down. 2012. (ENG.). 26p. (J). 16.00 *(978-0-8028-5414-8(1)*, Eerdmans Bks For Young Readers) Eerdmans, William B. Publishing Co.

—The Snowbear. Taylor, Sean. 2017. (ENG.). 32p. (J). (gr. -1-k). 17.95 *(978-1-910277-43-0(6)*, Words & Pictures) Quarto Publishing Group UK GBR. Dist: Hachette Bk. Group.

Alexander, Claire. Lucy & the Bully. Alexander, Claire. 2013. (AV2 Fiction Readalong Ser.). (ENG.). (J). (gr. -1-2). 34.28 *(978-1-62127-882-5(4)*, AV2 by Weigl) Weigl Pubs., Inc.

—Small Florence, Piggy Pop Star. Alexander, Claire. 2013. (AV2 Fiction Readalong Ser.). (ENG.). (J). (gr. -1-2). 32.71 *(978-1-62127-892-4(1)*, AV2 by Weigl) Weigl Pubs., Inc.

Alexander, Cleopatra B. Shiny the Sea Star Surfs the Seas & Meets a Ganges River Tiger. Alexander, Cleopatra B. 2018. (J). (gr. -1-3). 15.95 *(978-0-9968666-9-9(8))* WaveRider Pr.

Alexander, Florence, et al. Come with Me & See... A Total Eclipse in Africa. Alexander, Florence et al. 2003. (ENG & SPA.). 40p. (J). 3.99 *(978-0-915960-50-7(8))* Ebon Research Systems Publishing, LLC.

Alexander, Gregory. The Jungle Book. Rowe, John, ed. 2003. (Chrysalis Childrens Classics Ser.). 159p. (YA). pap. *(978-1-84365-038-6(X)*, Pavilion Children's Books) Pavilion Bks.

Alexander, Jason. Alice's Adventures in Wonderland. 2009. (ENG.). 12p. (J). 8.95 *(978-1-58117-855-5(7)*, Intervisual/Piggy Toes) Bendon, Inc.

Alexander, John. The Adventures of Thunder & Avalanche: Laws of Nature. Alexander, John. 2013. 46p. 18.99 *(978-0-9887625-0-3(1))* Mountain Thunder Publishing.

—The Adventures of Thunder & Avalanche: Up & Away. Alexander, John. 2013. 48p. 15.99 *(978-0-9887625-1-0(X))* Mountain Thunder Publishing.

Alexander, Johnna A. An Angel's Day on Earth. Flora, B. David. 2011. 24p. pap. 24.95 *(978-1-4560-9851-3(9))* PublishAmerica, Inc.

Alexander, Katie Norwood. This Little Light of Mine. Bateman, Claire Boudreaux. ed. 2005. 32p. (J). per. 18.50 *(978-0-9706732-2-0(1))* Shell Beach Publishing, LLC.

Alexander, Kay. The Calico Truck: A Novel for Young Readers — & the Young at Heart. Morrison, Michael F. S. W. 2019. (ENG.). 38p. (J). pap. 6.99 *(978-1-0703-5546-7(1))* Independently Published.

Alexander, Larry, et al. Captain America Epic Collection: Blood & Glory. 2020. (ENG.). 496p. (YA). (gr. 8-17). pap. 39.99 *(978-1-302-92279-5(3))* Marvel Worldwide, Inc.

Alexander, Martha. A You're Adorable. Alexander, Martha. 2011. 20p. (J). (gr. -1 — 1). bds. 6.99 *(978-0-7636-5332-3(2))* Candlewick Pr.

Alexander, Martha. Poems & Prayers for the Very Young. Alexander, Martha, selected by. 32p. (J). Random Hse. Children's Bks.

Alexander, Rebecca. Brad Was Sad: Emotional Intelligence Storybook. Choose Your Outlook & Own Your Feelings. Goldrick, M. C. 2019. (ENG.). 32p. (J). ***(978-1-989579-04-6(3))***; pap. ***(978-1-989579-02-2(7))*** MotherButterfly Bks.

Alexander, Rilla. A Bear Sat on My Porch Today. Yolen, Jane. 2018. (ENG.). 32p. (J). (gr. -1-k). 17.99 *(978-1-4521-0249-8(X))* Chronicle Bks. LLC.

—Clothes. 2019. (ENG.). 16p. (J). (gr. -1 — 1). bds. 16.99 *(978-1-4521-7561-4(6))* Chronicle Bks. LLC.

—Flight: Invent Your Own Mix-and-Match Vehicles! Snape, Emily. 2017. (ENG.). 16p. (J). (gr. -1 — 1). bds. 9.99 *(978-1-4521-4839-7(2))* Chronicle Bks. LLC.

—Motor Mix: Emergency. Snape, Emily. 2017. (ENG.). 16p. (J). (gr. -1 — 1). bds. 9.99 *(978-1-4521-4838-0(4))* Chronicle Bks. LLC.

—Swarm of Bees. Snicket, Lemony. 2019. (ENG.). 48p. (J). (gr. -1-3). 17.99 *(978-0-316-39282-2(0))* Little Brown & Co.

—TouchWords: Animals. 2019. (ENG.). 16p. (J). (gr. -1 — 1). bds. 16.99 *(978-1-4521-7392-4(3))* Chronicle Bks. LLC.

—TouchWords: Food. 2019. (ENG.). 16p. (J). (gr. -1 — 1). bds. 16.99 *(978-1-4521-7391-7(5))* Chronicle Bks. LLC.

—TouchWords: My Day. 2019. (ENG.). 16p. (J). (gr. -1 — 1). bds. 16.99 *(978-1-4521-7562-1(4))* Chronicle Bks. LLC.

Alexander, Yvonne Rabdau. The Adventures of Super Keith! MacPherson, Lorry. 2010. 56p. pap. 19.50 *(978-1-60976-268-1(1)*, Eloquent Bks.) Strategic Book Publishing & Rights Agency (SBPRA).

—Lynne Woke Up! MacPherson, Lorry. 2007. 20p. per. 24.95 *(978-1-4137-2536-0(8))* America Star Bks.

Alexandra Dzhiganskaya. Angels, Angels Way up High. Hood, Karen Jean Matsko. Whispering Pine Press International, ed. 2017. (Hood Picture Book Ser.). (J). bk. 2. pap. 15.95 *(978-1-930948-09-9(3))*; Vol. 2. 24.95 *(978-1-930948-81-5(6))* Whispering Pine Pr. International, Inc.

Alexandria, Miziker. Forever Home. Goulandris, Karen. 2017. 24p. (J). pap. *(978-0-9824899-4-9(3))* Monolith Graphics.

Alexopolous, George. Go with Grace, Vol. 1. Alexopolous, George. Blackman, Ryu. 2017. (ENG.). 192p. (YA). (gr. 8-18). pap. 9.99 *(978-1-59816-709-2(X)*, 14ffd02d-bd5d-4957-ae0d-a7e789cb2eae) TOKYOPOP, Inc.

Alexovich, Aaron. Stitched #2: Love in the Time of Assumption. Huehner, Mariah. 2018. (Stitched Ser.: 2). (ENG.). 96p. (J). 14.99 *(978-1-62991-861-7(X)*, 900185397) Papercutz.

Alexovich, Aaron, jt. illus. see Trueheart, Eric.

Alfandolo, Koffi. I Am the Blues. Gorg, Gwyn. 2012. 26p. pap. 19.95 *(978-0-9840204-2-3(X))* Pacific Raven Pr.

Alfano, Wayne. Saint Bakhita of Sudan: Forever Free. Wallace, Susan Helen. 2006. (Encounter the Saints Ser.: 21). 102p. (J). pap. 7.95 *(978-0-8198-7094-0(3))* Pauline Bks. & Media.

—Saint John Bosco: Champion for the Young. Marsh, Emily Beata. 2015. 128p. (J). pap. 8.95 *(978-0-8198-9045-0(6))* Pauline Bks. & Media.

—Saint Martin de Porres: Humble Healer. Dedomenico, Elizabeth Marie. 2005. (Encounter the Saints Ser.: No. 19). 108p. (J). (gr. 3-7). per. 7.95 *(978-0-8198-7091-9(9))* Pauline Bks. & Media.

Alfaro, Antonio. Garfield: Snack Pack Vol. 1. Nickel, Scott & Evanier, Mark. 2018. (Garfield Ser.). (ENG.). 112p. (J). pap. 14.99 *(978-1-68415-248-3(8))* Boom! Studios.

—Garfield: Snack Pack Vol. 2. Evanier, Mark & Nickel, Scott. 2019. (Garfield Ser.). (ENG.). 112p. (J). pap. 14.99 *(978-1-68415-370-1(0))* Boom! Studios.

—Garfield: Snack Pack Vol. 3. Nickel, Scott. 2019. (Garfield Ser.). (ENG.). 112p. (J). pap. 14.99 *(978-1-68415-436-4(7))* Boom! Studios.

—Garfield: the Monday That Wouldn't End Original Graphic Novel. Evanier, Mark & Nickel, Scott. 2019. (Garfield Ser.). (ENG.). 96p. (J). (gr. 1-3). pap. 14.99 *(978-1-68415-342-8(5))* Boom! Studios.

—The Thing in the Fridge. Nickel, Scott & Evanier, Mark. 2017. (Garfield Ser.: 3). (ENG.). 96p. (J). (gr. 1-3). pap. 9.99 *(978-1-68415-019-9(1))* Boom! Studios.

Alfaro, Antonio & Smart, Kyle. Garfield Original Graphic Novel: Trouble in Paradise: Trouble in Paradise. Nickel, Scott & Evanier, Mark. 2018. (Garfield Ser.). (ENG.). 96p. (J). (gr. 1-1). pap. 9.99 *(978-1-68415-237-7(2))* Boom! Studios.

Alfaro, Luis. Muu muuu dice una Vaca. Salinas, Sonia. 2007.Tr. of Moo Moo Says a Cow. (SPA.). 32p. (J). 15.99 *(978-0-9794710-0-1(1))* S&S Publishing LLC.

Alff, Mary M. The Lazarus Collection: Kimmi Jambo. Alff, Mary M. Alff, Lena N., tr. 2018. (ENG.). 396p. (J). pap. 17.99 *(978-1-7904-1574-8(8))* Independently Published.

Alfonso, Anabel. Giraffe Hears the Drum. Picayo, Mario. 2018. (J). pap. *(978-1-934370-75-9(4))* Editorial Campana.

—When I Grow Up. Grant, Rick S. 2017. (J). pap. *(978-1-934370-67-4(3))* Editorial Campana.

Alfreda. Be Somebody Be Yourself Lesson Plan Reproducibles. Alfreda. 2004. 60p. (gr. 4-7). 29.95 *(978-1-56820-031-6(5))* Story Time Stories That Rhyme.

Algar, James. Jack, Tommy & the Phoenix Street Firefighters. Tierney, John. 2012. (ENG.). 70p. pap. 11.99 *(978-1-78035-416-3(9)*, Fastprint Publishing) Upfront Publishing Ltd. GBR. Dist: Printondemand-worldwide.com.

Ali, Intelaq. The Amazing Discoveries of Ibn Sina, 1 vol. Sharafeddine, Fatima. 2015. (ENG.). 32p. (J). (gr. 1-6). 17.95 *(978-1-55498-710-8(5))* Groundwood Bks. CAN. Dist: Publishers Group West (PGW).

Ali, Nabi. The Fighting Infantryman: The Story of Albert D. J. Cashier, Transgender Civil War Soldier. Sanders, Rob. 2020. (ENG.). 48p. (J). (gr. k-4). 18.99 ***(978-1-4998-0936-7(0))*** Little Bee Books Inc.

Aliaga, Natali Sejuro, et al. Highlights: Farm Fun! First Look & Find. Beck, Riley. 2018. (Look & Find Ser.). (ENG.). 18p. (J). bds. ***(978-1-5037-3618-4(0)***, 9aacb53f-78bf-434a-96dc-de7d0f11c6a1, p i kids) Phoenix International Publications, Inc.

Alibert, Eric, jt. illus. see Hyman, Miles.

Alice, Alex. Castle in the Stars: the Space Race Of 1869. Alice, Alex. 2017. (Castle in the Stars Ser.: 1). (ENG.). 64p. (J). 19.99 *(978-1-62672-493-8(8)*, 900158826, First Second Bks.) Roaring Brook Pr.

—The Valykrie, Vol. 2. Alice, Alex. 2014. (Siegfried Ser.: 2). (ENG.). 144p. 24.95 *(978-1-936393-79-4(4))* Boom Entertainment, Inc.

Alicia, Young. Mason the Bull: A Story Inspired by True Events. Crystal, Day. 2018. (Mason the Bull Ser.: Vol. 1). (ENG.). 40p. (J). (gr. k-2). pap. 12.00 *(978-0-692-87176-8(4))* ODE.

Alikhan, Salima. Lawyer's Week Before Christmas, 1 vol. Justice, Joseph. 2010. (Night Before Christmas Ser.). (ENG.). 32p. (J). (gr. 4-8). 16.99 *(978-1-58980-739-6(1)*, Pelican Publishing) Arcadia Publishing.

—Pieces of Another World, 1 vol. Rockliff, Mara. 2005. (ENG.). 32p. (J). (gr. k-4). 15.95 *(978-0-9764943-2-4(9))* Arbordale Publishing.

—Rocky Mountain Night Before Christmas, 1 vol. Gribnau, Joe. 2007. (Night Before Christmas Ser.). (ENG.). 32p. (J). (gr. k-3). 16.99 *(978-1-58980-317-6(5)*, Pelican Publishing) Arcadia Publishing.

Alikhan, Salima. The Pied Piper of Austin, 1 vol. Alikhan, Salima. 2009. (ENG.). 32p. (J). (gr. k-3). 16.99 *(978-1-58980-629-0(8)*, Pelican Publishing) Arcadia Publishing.

Aliki. Are You Thinking Again, Dear? 2018. (ENG.). 40p. (gr. k-4). 16.95 *(978-0-486-81954-9(X))* Dover Pubns., Inc.

—I Wish I Was Sick, Too! Brandenberg, Franz. 2018. 40p. (J). (gr. -1-2). 16.95 *(978-1-68137-228-0(2)*, NYR Children's Collection) New York Review of Books, Inc., The.

—That's Good, That's Bad. Lexau, Joan M. 2020. (ENG.). 40p. (J). (gr. -1-2). 17.95 *(978-3-7913-7419-2(2))* Prestel Verlag GmbH & Co KG. DEU. Dist: Penguin Random Hse. LLC.

Aliki. Ah, Music! Aliki. 2005. (ENG.). 48p. (J). (gr. k-5). pap. 7.99 *(978-0-06-446236-5(6))* HarperCollins Pubs.

—All by Myself! Aliki. 2003. (ENG.). 32p. (J). (gr. -1-1). pap. 7.99 *(978-0-06-446253-2(6))* HarperCollins Pubs.

—Feelings. Aliki. 2019. (ENG.). 32p. (J). (gr. -1-3). pap. 7.99 *(978-0-688-06518-8(X)*, Greenwillow Bks.) HarperCollins Pubs.

—Fossils Tell of Long Ago. Aliki. 2016. (Let's-Read-And-Find-Out Science 2 Ser.). (ENG.). 32p. (J). (gr. -1-3). pap. 6.99 *(978-0-06-238207-8(1))* HarperCollins Pubs.

—Marianthe's Story: Painted Words & Spoken Memories. Aliki. 2019. (ENG.). 64p. (J). (gr. k-5). pap. 8.99 *(978-0-06-185774-4(2)*, Greenwillow Bks.) HarperCollins Pubs.

—My Five Senses. Aliki. 2015. (Let's-Read-And-Find-Out Science 1 Ser.). (ENG.). 32p. (J). (gr. -1-3). 17.99 *(978-0-06-238191-0(1))* HarperCollins Pubs.

—Play's the Thing. Aliki. 2005. (ENG.). 32p. (J). 16.99 *(978-0-06-074355-0(7))* HarperCollins Pubs.

—Quiet in the Garden. Aliki. 2009. (ENG.). 32p. (J). (gr. -1-2). 17.99 *(978-0-06-155207-6(0)*, Greenwillow Bks.) HarperCollins Pubs.

Alisdan, Bill Q. Ofrio, the Sea Otter (Environmental Series) Baldonado, Estrella C. & Baldonado, Orlino C. 2020. (Ofrio, the Sea Otter Ser.: Vol. 3). (ENG.). 30p. (J). pap. 9.99 ***(978-1-948623-56-8(0))*** ecEmedia, a Div. of The EC Corp.

Alison, Jay & Jay, Alison. Out of the Blue. Books, Barefoot. 2014. 32p. (J). (gr. -1-k). 14.99 *(978-1-78285-042-7(2))* Barefoot Bks., Inc.

Aliste Sunkel, Fernando. A Cavallo Di un Protone. Baroni, Simone. 2019. (ITA.). 168p. (J). pap. 9.90 ***(978-1-6872-5243-2(2))*** Independently Published.

Alizadeh, Kate. All Through the Night. Hughes, John Ceiriog. Boulton, Harold, tr. 2013. (ENG.). 24p. (J). (gr. -1-2). bds. 12.95 *(978-1-927018-09-5(9))* Simply Read Bks. CAN. Dist: Ingram Publisher Services.

—Plenty of Hugs. Manushkin, Fran. 2020. 32p. (J). (-k). 17.99 *(978-0-525-55401-1(7)*, Dial Bks) Penguin Young Readers Group.

—That's MY Blanket, Baby! Morgan, Angie. 2017. (ENG.). 32p. (J). (gr. -1-2). 16.99 *(978-1-68010-074-7(2))* Tiger Tales.

—World So Wide. McGhee, Alison. 2020. (ENG.). 32p. (J). (gr. -1-2). 17.99 *(978-1-5420-0633-0(3)*, 9781542006330, Two Lions) Amazon Publishing.

Alizadeh, Kate. Quiet! Alizadeh, Kate. 2017. (Child's Play Library). 32p. (J). (ENG.). *(978-1-84643-887-5(X))*; pap. *(978-1-84643-888-2(8))* Child's Play International Ltd.

Alko, Selina. The God Around Us: A Child's Garden of Prayer. Pollack-Brichto, Mira. rev. ed. 2004. (ENG & HEB.). 32p. (J). (gr. -1-1). 13.95 *(978-0-8074-0701-1(1)*, 101072) URJ Pr.

—The God Around Us Vol. 2: The Valley of Blessings. Brichto, Mira Pollak. 2004. 32p. (gr. -1-3). 13.95 *(978-0-8074-0738-7(0)*, 101074) URJ Pr.

—Good Morning, Boker Tov. Abraham, Michelle Shapiro. 2004. pap. 6.95 *(978-0-8074-0783-7(6)*, 101974) URJ Pr.

—Good Night, Lilah Tov. Abraham, Michelle Shapiro. 2004. pap. 6.95 *(978-0-8074-0784-4(4)*, 101975) URJ Pr.

—My Fathers World. 2006. 36p. (J). 14.99 *(978-0-7847-1440-9(1)*, 04075) Standard Publishing.

—My Subway Ride, 1 vol. Jacobs, Paul DuBois & Swender, Jennifer. ed. 2004. (ENG.). 32p. (J). (gr. 2-3). 15.99 *(978-1-58685-357-0(0))* Gibbs Smith, Publisher.

Alko, Selina, et al. Shaking Things up: 14 Young Women Who Changed the World. Hood, Susan. 2018. (ENG.). 40p. (J). (gr. -1-3). 18.99 *(978-0-06-269945-9(8))* HarperCollins Pubs.

Alko, Selina. B Is for Brooklyn. Alko, Selina. 2012. (ENG.). 40p. (J). (gr. -1-1). 17.99 *(978-0-8050-9213-4(7)*, 900066076, Holt, Henry & Co. Bks. For Young Readers) Holt, Henry & Co.

—Joni: the Lyrical Life of Joni Mitchell. Alko, Selina. 2020. (ENG.). 48p. (J). (gr. -1-3). 18.99 *(978-0-06-267129-5(4)*, HarperCollins) HarperCollins Pubs. Ltd. GBR. Dist: HarperCollins Pubs.

—One Golden Rule at School: A Counting Book. Alko, Selina. 2020. (ENG.). 40p. (J). 17.99 *(978-1-250-16381-3(1)*, 900186611, Holt, Henry & Co. Bks. For Young Readers) Holt, Henry & Co.

Alko, Selina & Qualls, Sean. Can I Touch Your Hair? Poems of Race, Mistakes, & Friendship. Waters, Charles & Latham, Irene. 2018. (ENG.). 40p. (J). (gr. 3-6). 17.99 *(978-1-5124-0442-5(X)*, 9781512404425, Carolrhoda Bks.) Lerner Publishing Group.

—The Case for Loving: The Fight for Interracial Marriage. Alko, Selina. 2015. (ENG.). 40p. (J). (gr. -1-3). 18.99 *(978-0-545-47853-3(7))* Scholastic, Inc.

—¿Por Qué Yo Soy Yo? Britt, Paige. 2017. (SPA.). 40p. (J). (gr. -1-3). pap. 7.99 *(978-1-338-23344-5(0))* Scholastic, Inc.

Alko, Selina, jt. illus. see Qualls, Sean.

Allain, Moose. Fill-Me-In. Allain, Moose. 2016. (ENG.). 96p. (J). (gr. 1-4). 16.99 *(978-0-7636-8532-4(1)*, Big Picture Press) Candlewick Pr.

Allaire, Gauthier. I Really Don't Like Reading! Curtiss, Dominique. Hill, Rowland, tr. 2012. (ENG.). 44p. (J). pap. *(978-2-89687-303-6(1))* chouetteditions.com.

Allan, Chris & Kazaleh, Mike. Teenage Mutant Ninja Turtles Adventures Volume 9. Clarrain, Dean. 2015. (TMNT Adventures Ser.: 9). (ENG.). 140p. (J). (gr. 4-7). pap. 19.99 *(978-1-63140-208-1(0)*, 9781631402081) Idea & Design Works, LLC.

Allan, Gill. When I Wear My Leopard Hat: Poems for Young Children. Rose, Dilys. 40p. pap. 6.95 *(978-1-899827-70-1(6))* Scottish Children's Pr. GBR. Dist: Gatewood Pr.

Allan, Jo. Hide-and-Seek Hettie, 30 vols. 2018. (ENG.). 24p. (J). 11.95 *(978-1-78250-508-2(3)*, Kelpies) Floris Bks. GBR. Dist: Consortium Bk. Sales & Distribution.

—Hungry Hettie, 50 vols. 2010. (ENG.). 24p. (J). (gr. -1-1). 11.95 *(978-0-86315-779-0(3))* Floris Bks. GBR. Dist: Consortium Bk. Sales & Distribution.

Allan, Nicholas. The Bump. Kelly, Mij. 2012. (ENG.). 32p. (J). *(978-1-58925-107-6(5))* Tiger Tales.

Allanson, Patricia. Parallella's Problem. Allanson, Patricia. 2007. (J). (gr. -1-3). per. 13.99 *(978-1-59879-278-2(4))* Lifevest Publishing, Inc.

Allard, et al. I Can Play Piano. 2017. 24p. (J). (gr. -1-1). 12.99 *(978-2-924786-01-7(0)*, CrackBoom! Bks.) Chouette Publishing CAN. Dist: Publishers Group West (PGW).

Allard, Mario. Caillou: Chinese New Year: Dragon Mask & Mosaic Stickers Included. 2018. (Playtime Ser.). (ENG.). 24p. (J). (gr. -1-1). 4.99 *(978-2-89718-498-8(1))* Caillouet, Gerry.

—Caillou Fall Family Tradition: Picture Dominoes Included. Delporte, Corinne. 2018. (Playtime Ser.). (ENG.). 24p. (J). (gr. -1-1). 4.99 *(978-2-89718-496-4(5))* Caillouet, Gerry.

—Caillou Meets Sophie: a Story about Autism. 2019. (Playtime (Special Edition) Ser.). (ENG.). 24p. (J). (gr. -1-1). 7.95 *(978-2-89718-505-3(8))* Caillouet, Gerry.

Allard, Mario & Dupuis, Karina. Caillou & the Puppies. 2017. (Clubhouse Ser.). (ENG.). 24p. (J). (gr. -1-1). 3.99 *(978-2-89718-445-2(0))* Caillouet, Gerry.

—Caillou at the Sugar Shack. 2018. (Clubhouse Ser.). (ENG.). 24p. (J). (gr. -1-1). 3.99 *(978-2-89718-467-4(1))* Caillouet, Gerry.

—Caillou Plays Hockey. 2017. (Clubhouse Ser.). (ENG.). 24p. (J). (gr. -1-1). 3.99 *(978-2-89718-407-0(8))* Caillouet, Gerry.

—Caillou Takes the Train. 2018. (Clubhouse Ser.). (ENG.). 24p. (J). (gr. -1-1). 3.99 *(978-2-89718-463-6(9))* Caillouet, Gerry.

—Caillou: the Dinosaur Museum. 2019. (Clubhouse Ser.). (ENG.). 24p. (J). (gr. -1-1). 3.99 *(978-2-89718-518-3(X))* Caillouet, Gerry.

Allard, Melanie. Bernadette & the Lunch Bunch, 1 vol. Glickman, Susan. 2009. (Lunch Bunch Ser.: 1). (ENG.). 123p. (J). (gr. 1-3). pap. 6.95 *(978-1-897187-51-7(3))* Second Story Pr. CAN. Dist: Orca Bk. Pubs. USA.

Allegri, Natasha. Adventure Time - Fionna & Cake. Allegri, Natasha, . 2013. (ENG.). 176p. (J). (gr. 4-7). pap. 19.99 *(978-1-60886-338-9(7))* Boom! Studios.

Allegri, Natasha. Fionna & Cake Mathematical. Allegri, Natasha. 2014. (Adventure Time Ser.: 1). (ENG.). 192p. (J). (gr. 4). 39.99 *(978-1-60886-391-4(3))* Boom! Studios.

Allen, Amy Meyer. I Have a Name: The Story of a Pug Named Cass. Montoya, Carlos. 2018. (ENG.). 26p. (J). pap. 11.99 *(978-1-7905-2783-0(X))* Independently Published.

Allen, Brooke. Lumberjanes: the Moon Is Up (Lumberjanes #2) Tamaki, Mariko & BOOM! Studios. 2018. (ENG.). 208p. (J). (gr. 3-7). 14.99 *(978-1-4197-2868-6(7)*, Amulet Bks.) Abrams, Inc.

—Welcome To Wonderland #1: Home Sweet Motel. Grabenstein, Chris. 2016. (Welcome to Wonderland Ser.: 1). 304p. (J). (gr. 3-7). 13.99 *(978-0-553-53602-7(8)*, Random Hse. Bks. for Young Readers) Random Hse. Children's Bks.

Allen, Brooke A. Sandapalooza Shake-Up. Grabenstein, Chris. 2018. (Welcome to Wonderland Ser.: 3). 304p. (J). (gr. 3-7). 13.99 *(978-1-5247-1758-2(4)*, Random Hse. Bks. for Young Readers) Random Hse. Children's Bks.

—Welcome To Wonderland #2: Beach Party Surf Monkey. Grabenstein, Chris. 2017. (Welcome to Wonderland Ser.: 2). 320p. (J). (gr. 3-7). 13.99 *(978-0-553-53610-2(9)*, Random Hse. Bks. for Young Readers) Random Hse. Children's Bks.

Allen, Brooklyn. Lumberjanes: Ghost Cabin (Lumberjanes #4) Tamaki, Mariko. 2020. (Lumberjanes Ser.). (ENG.). 256p. (J). (gr. 3-7). pap. 8.99 ***(978-1-4197-4698-7(7)***, 1193603, Amulet Bks.) Abrams, Inc.

Allen, Brooklyn. Lumberjanes: Ghost Cabin (Lumberjanes #4) Tamaki, Mariko & BOOM! Studios. 2019. (Lumberjanes Ser.). (ENG.). 256p. (J). (gr. 3-7). 14.99 *(978-1-4197-3361-1(3)*, 1193601, Amulet Bks.) Abrams, Inc.

—Lumberjanes: the Good Egg (Lumberjanes #3), Bk. 3. Tamaki, Mariko & BOOM! Studios. 2018. (ENG.). 208p. (J). (gr. 3-7). 14.99 *(978-1-4197-3131-0(9)*, Amulet Bks.) Abrams, Inc.

—Lumberjanes: the Moon Is Up (Lumberjanes #2) Tamaki, Mariko & BOOM! Studios. 2019. (ENG.). 224p. (J). (gr. 3-7). pap. 8.99 *(978-1-4197-3951-4(4)*, Amulet Bks.) Abrams, Inc.

Allen, Brooklyn & BOOM! Studios. The Lumberjanes BEASTiary: The Most Amazing Guide to All the Coolest Creatures You've Ever Heard of & a Few You Haven't. Tamaki, Mariko. 2020. (Lumberjanes Ser.). (ENG.). 144p. (J). (gr. 3-17). 16.99 *(978-1-4197-3644-5(2)*, 1274101, Amulet Bks.) Abrams, Inc.

—Lumberjanes: the Good Egg (Lumberjanes #3) Tamaki, Mariko. 2020. (ENG.). 240p. (J). (gr. 3-7). pap. 8.99 *(978-1-4197-4092-3(X)*, Amulet Bks.) Abrams, Inc.

—Lumberjanes: Unicorn Power! (Lumberjanes #1) Tamaki, Mariko. 2019. (ENG.). 272p. (J). (gr. 5-9). pap. 8.99 *(978-1-4197-2726-9(5)*, Amulet Bks.) Abrams, Inc.

—Unicorn Power! (Lumberjanes) Tamaki, Mariko. 2017. (ENG.). 256p. (J). (gr. 5-9). 14.99 *(978-1-4197-2725-2(7)*, Amulet Bks.) Abrams, Inc.

Allen, Cassandra. Inside My Garden. Carriger, Candace. 2011. 46p. (J). pap. 11.95 *(978-0-9816047-5-6(7))* Sadie Bks.

Allen, Chris. Booker T. Washington, 1 vol. Dunn, Joeming W. 2008. (Bio-Graphics Ser.). (ENG.). 32p. (J). (gr. 3-8). 29.93 *(978-1-60270-177-9(6)*, 3593, Graphic Planet - Fiction) Magic Wagon.

—George Washington Carver, 1 vol. Dunn, Joeming W. 2008. (Bio-Graphics Ser.). (ENG.). 32p. (J). (gr. 3-8). 29.93 *(978-1-60270-171-7(7)*, 3581, Graphic Planet - Fiction) Magic Wagon.

—Henry VIII: Graphic Novel, 1 vol. Shakespeare, William. 2010. (Graphic Shakespeare Ser.). (ENG.). 48p. (J). (gr. 5-10). 31.35 *(978-1-60270-764-1(2)*, 9162, Graphic Planet - Fiction) Magic Wagon.

—King Lear, 1 vol. Farrens, Brian & Shakespeare, William. 2008. (Graphic Shakespeare Ser.). (ENG.). 48p. (J). (gr. 5-10). 31.35 *(978-1-60270-189-2(X)*, 9140, Graphic Planet - Fiction) Magic Wagon.

—Martin Luther King, Jr, 1 vol. Dunn, Joeming W. 2008. (Bio-Graphics Ser.). (ENG.). 32p. (J). (gr. 3-8). 29.93 *(978-1-60270-175-5(X)*, 3589, Graphic Planet - Fiction) Magic Wagon.

—Marvel's Ant-Man & the Wasp Prelude. 2018. (ENG.). 136p. (J). (gr. 4-17). pap. 14.99 *(978-1-302-90944-4(4))* Marvel Worldwide, Inc.

—Othello, 1 vol. Goodwin, Vincent. 2008. (Graphic Shakespeare Ser.). (ENG.). 48p. (J). (gr. 5-10). 31.35 *(978-1-60270-192-2(X)*, 9146, Graphic Planet - Fiction) Magic Wagon.

Allen, Christina. A Farmer's Alphabet. Long, Charles. 2016. (ENG.). 64p. (J). (gr. k-4). 18.00 *(978-0-9907688-2-1(1))* Corn Crib Publishing.

Allen, Dana K. Tales from Poplar Hollow. Deskins, Charlotte H. 2004. 104p. pap. *(978-0-9753671-1-7(0))* Shamus B. Publishing.

Allen, Douglas, jt. illus. see Sweet, Darrell.

Allen, Elanna. Eva & Sadie & the Best Classroom EVER! Cohen, Jeff. 2015. (ENG.). 32p. (J). (gr. -1-3). 17.99 *(978-0-06-224938-8(X))* HarperCollins Pubs.

—Eva & Sadie & the Worst Haircut EVER! Cohen, Jeff. 2014. (ENG.). 32p. (J). (gr. -1-3). 17.99 *(978-0-06-224906-7(1))* HarperCollins Pubs.

—Violet Mackerel's Brilliant Plot. Branford, Anna. 2012. (Violet Mackerel Ser.). (ENG.). 112p. (J). (gr. 1-5). 15.99 *(978-1-4424-3585-8(2))*; pap. 5.99 *(978-1-4424-3586-5(0))* Simon & Schuster Children's Publishing. (Atheneum Bks. for Young Readers).

—Violet Mackerel's Natural Habitat. Branford, Anna. 2013. (Violet Mackerel Ser.). (ENG.). 112p. (J). (gr. 1-5). 15.99 *(978-1-4424-3594-0(1))*; pap. 5.99 *(978-1-4424-3595-7(X))* Simon & Schuster Children's Publishing.

—Violet Mackerel's Outside-The-Box Set Set: Violet Mackerel's Brilliant Plot, Violet Mackerel's Remarkable Recovery, Violet Mackerel's Natural Habitat, Violet Mackerel's Personal Space. Branford, Anna. ed. 2013. (Violet Mackerel Ser.). (ENG.). 464p. (J). (gr. 1-5). pap. 23.99 *(978-1-4424-8859-5(X)*, Atheneum Bks. for Young Readers) Simon & Schuster Children's Publishing.

—Violet Mackerel's Personal Space. Branford, Anna. 2013. (Violet Mackerel Ser.). (ENG.). 128p. (J). (gr. 1-5). 15.99 *(978-1-4424-3591-9(7))*; pap. 5.99 *(978-1-4424-3592-6(5))* Simon & Schuster Children's Publishing. (Atheneum Bks. for Young Readers).

A

—Violet Mackerel's Possible Friend. Branford, Anna. 2014. (Violet Mackerel Ser.). (ENG.). 128p. (J). (gr. 1-5). 17.99 *(978-1-4424-9455-8(7)*, Atheneum Bks. for Young Readers) Simon & Schuster Children's Publishing.

—Violet Mackerel's Remarkable Recovery. Branford, Anna. 2013. (Violet Mackerel Ser.). (ENG.). 128p. (J). (gr. 1-5). pap. 5.99 *(978-1-4424-3589-6(5)*, Atheneum Bks. for Young Readers) Simon & Schuster Children's Publishing.

—Violet Mackerel's Remarkable Recovery. Branford, Anna. 2013. (Violet Mackerel Ser.). (ENG.). 114p. (J). (gr. 1-3). 18.69 *(978-1-4424-3588-9(7))* Simon & Schuster, Inc.

Allen, Elanna. Itsy Mitsy Runs Away. Allen, Elanna. 2011. (ENG.). 40p. (J). (gr. -1-2). 16.99 *(978-1-4424-0671-1(2)*, Atheneum Bks. for Young Readers) Simon & Schuster Children's Publishing.

Allen, Elizabeth. Be Positive! Meiners, Cheri J. 2013. (Being the Best Me Ser.). (ENG.). 40p. (J). (gr. -1-3). pap. 11.99 *(978-1-57542-441-5(X))* Free Spirit Publishing, Inc.

—Feel Confident! Meiners, Cheri J. 2013. (Being the Best Me Ser.). (ENG.). 40p. (J). (gr. -1-3). pap. 11.99 *(978-1-57542-442-2(8))* Free Spirit Publishing, Inc.

—Forgive & Let Go! A Book about Forgiveness. Meiners, Cheri J. 2015. (Being the Best Me® Ser.). (ENG.). 40p. (J). (gr. -1-3). pap. 11.99 *(978-1-57542-487-3(8))* Free Spirit Publishing, Inc.

Allen, Emma. H�ctor Ayuda a Limpiar el Parque. Culliford, Claire. Translations, Tick, tr. 2019. (SPA.). 26p. (J). pap. 9.49 ***(978-1-6930-3465-7(4))*** Independently Published.

—Penny Helps Protect the Polar Ice Caps. Culliford, Claire. 2015. (ENG.). 26p. (J). pap. 9.49 ***(978-1-0858-0972-6(2))*** Independently Published.

Allen-Fletcher, Carly. The Big Bang Book. Stahl, Asa. 2020. (ENG.). 32p. (J). (gr. -1-3). 18.99 *(978-1-939547-64-4(4))* Creston Bks.

Allen-Fletcher, Carly. Beastly Biomes. Allen-Fletcher, Carly. 2019. (ENG.). 32p. (J). (gr. 2-5). 17.99 *(978-1-939547-54-5(7))* Creston Bks.

Allen, Francesca. Creepy-Crawlies. 2005. 10p. (J). 4.99 *(978-0-7945-0856-2(1)*, Usborne) EDC Publishing.

—First Picture Fairytales. 2008. (Usborne First Book Ser.). 14p. (J). (gr. -1). bds. 18.99 incl. audio compact disk *(978-0-7945-1832-5(X)*, Usborne) EDC Publishing.

—Under the Sea. 2005. 10p. (J). 4.99 *(978-0-7945-0857-9(X)*, Usborne) EDC Publishing.

—Vacation. 2006. (Usborne Look & Say Ser.). 10p. (J). (gr. -1-k). bds. 7.99 *(978-0-7945-1315-3(8)*, Usborne) EDC Publishing.

Allen, Francesca, jt. illus. see Litchfield, Jo.

Allen, Jason. The Almighty Organ All: And the Vivacious Vibrakids. Hickox, Norma. 2019. (ENG.). 124p. (J). pap. 6.99 *(978-1-0901-2823-2(1))* Independently Published.

Allen, Joe. The Mission: An Angel's Most Important Assignment. Horner, Susan. 2006. pap. 10.99 *(978-1-59317-148-3(X))* Warner Pr., Inc.

Allen, Jonathan. Hair Scare. Doyle, Malachy. 2005. (ENG.). 24p. (J). lib. bdg. 23.65 *(978-1-59646-724-8(X))* Dingles & Co.

Allen, Jonathan. Banana! Allen, Jonathan. 2006. 32p. (J). pap. *(978-1-905417-02-5(0))* Boxer Bks., Ltd.

Allen, Joshua. Marissa Plans a Princess Tea Party. Hordos, Sandra. 2010. 28p. pap. 12.49 *(978-1-4520-2557-5(6))* AuthorHouse.

—Ouse the Mouse. Beverly-Barrier, Essie. 2009. 20p. pap. 12.99 *(978-1-4389-4518-7(3))* AuthorHouse.

—Twenty Six Fence Posts to the Pond. Herrick, Jeff. 2018. (ENG.). 38p. (J). pap. 13.95 *(978-1-64191-855-8(1))* Christian Faith Publishing.

Allen, Joy. Cam Jansen & the Joke House Mystery. Adler, David A. 2014. (Cam Jansen Ser.: 34). (ENG.). 64p. (J). (gr. 2-5). 14.99 *(978-0-670-01262-6(9)*, Viking Books for Young Readers) Penguin Young Readers Group.

—Cam Jansen & the Millionaire Mystery. Adler, David A. 2013. (Cam Jansen Ser.: 32). (ENG.). 64p. (J). (gr. 2-5). pap. 4.99 *(978-0-14-242747-7(0)*, Puffin Books) Penguin Young Readers Group.

—Cam Jansen & the Spaghetti Max Mystery. Adler, David A. 2014. (Cam Jansen Ser.: 33). (ENG.). 64p. (J). (gr. 2-5). pap. 4.99 *(978-0-14-751232-1(8)*, Puffin Books) Penguin Young Readers Group.

—Cam Jansen & the Sports Day Mysteries. Adler, David A. 2009. (Cam Jansen: A Super Special Ser.). 118p. 16.00 *(978-1-60686-431-9(9))* Perfection Learning Corp.

—Cam Jansen: Cam Jansen & the Mystery Writer Mystery #27. Adler, David A. 27th ed. 2008. (Cam Jansen Ser.: 27). (ENG.). 64p. (J). (gr. 2-5). 4.99 *(978-0-14-241194-0(9)*, Puffin Books) Penguin Young Readers Group.

—Cam Jansen: Cam Jansen & the Sports Day Mysteries: A Super Special. Adler, David A. 2009. (Cam Jansen Ser.). (ENG.). 128p. (J). (gr. 2-5). 5.99 *(978-0-14-241225-1(2)*, Puffin Books) Penguin Young Readers Group.

—Cam Jansen: Cam Jansen & the Wedding Cake Mystery #30, 30 vols. Adler, David A. 2011. (Cam Jansen Ser.: 30). (ENG.). 64p. (J). (gr. 2-5). 4.99 *(978-0-14-241958-8(3)*, Puffin Books) Penguin Young Readers Group.

—Cam Jansen: the Basketball Mystery #29, 29 vols., No. 29. Adler, David A. 2010. (Cam Jansen Ser.: 29). (ENG.). 64p. (J). (gr. 2-5). 4.99 *(978-0-14-241671-6(1)*, Puffin Books) Penguin Young Readers Group.

—Cam Jansen: the Green School Mystery #28, No. 28. Adler, David A. 2009. (Cam Jansen Ser.: 28). (ENG.). 64p. (J). (gr. 2-5). 4.99 *(978-0-14-241456-9(5)*, Puffin Books) Penguin Young Readers Group.

—Carrie Está a la Altura (Carrie Measures Up) Measurement: Length. Williams Aber, Linda. 2006. (Math Matters en Español Ser.). (SPA.). 32p. (J). (gr. 1-3). pap. 5.95 *(978-1-57565-161-3(0))* Astra Publishing Hse.

—Carrie Measures Up: Measurement: Length. Williams Aber, Linda. 2006. (Math Matters ® Ser.). (ENG.). 32p. (J). (gr. k-3). pap. 5.95 *(978-1-57565-100-2(9))* Astra Publishing Hse.

—Fairy Tale Mail. Williams, Rozanne Lanczak. (Learn to Write Ser.). 16p. (J). 2007. pap. 8.99 *(978-1-59198-359-0(2))*; 2006. pap. 3.49 *(978-1-59198-301-9(0)*, 6195) Creative Teaching Pr., Inc.

—I Am the Turkey. Spirn, Michele Sobel. 2006. (I Can Read Level 2 Ser.). (ENG.). 48p. (J). (gr. k-3). pap. 4.99 *(978-0-06-053232-1(7))* HarperCollins Pubs.

—I Am the Turkey. Spirn, Michele Sobel & Spirn, Michele S. 2004. (I Can Read Bks.). 48p. (J). (gr. k-3). 15.99 *(978-0-06-053230-7(0))* HarperCollins Pubs.

—I Am the Turkey. Spirn, Michele Sobel. 2007. (I Can Read Bks.). 48p. (gr. -1-3). 14.00 *(978-0-7569-8055-9(0))* Perfection Learning Corp.

—I Can Listen. Parker, David. 2005. (J). *(978-0-439-79208-0(8))* Scholastic, Inc.

—Mud Pie Annie, 1 vol. Buchanan, Sue & Shafer, Dana. 2008. (I Can Read! Ser.). (ENG.). 32p. (J). (gr. -1-1). pap. 4.99 *(978-0-310-71572-6(5))* Zonderkidz.

—Muffin Man. Scelsa, Greg. Faulkner, Stacey, ed. 2006. (J). pap. 2.99 *(978-1-59198-321-7(5))* Creative Teaching Pr., Inc.

—Prayers for a Child's Day. Derico, Laura. 2003. 32p. (J). 7.99 *(978-0-7847-1273-3(5)*, 04033) Standard Publishing.

—The Summer Camp Mysteries. Adler, David A. 2007. (Cam Jansen Ser.). (ENG.). 128p. (J). (gr. 2-5). 5.99 *(978-0-14-240742-4(9)*, Puffin Books) Penguin Young Readers Group.

—Tressa the Musical Princess. Simon, Charnan. 2005. 25p. (J). *(978-1-58987-112-0(X))* Kindermusik International.

—Two Stories, Two Friends. Williams, Rozanne Lanczak. 2006. (Learn to Write Ser.). 16p. (J). (gr. k-2). pap. 3.49 *(978-1-59198-295-1(2)*, 6186) Creative Teaching Pr., Inc.

—Two Stories, Two Friends. Williams, Rozanne Lanczak. Maio, Barbara, ed. 2006. (J). per. 8.99 *(978-1-59198-343-9(6))* Creative Teaching Pr., Inc.

—Where Is Jake? Packard, Mary. 2003. (My First Reader Ser.). (ENG.). 32p. (J). 18.50 *(978-0-516-22957-7(5)*, Children's Pr.) Scholastic Library Publishing.

Allen, Katherine E. Festival of Light: Deepavali Legends from Around India. 2005. 61p. (J). *(978-81-87111-70-2(4))* Vakils, Feffer & Simons, Ltd.

Allen, Kathy. Grandma & her Amazing Colt, Dripper! Blake, Edna L. & Boatwright, Edith. 2005. 50p. (J). 12.00 *(978-0-9668906-3-1(9))* Blake, Edna.

Allen, Kd & Giraud, Teresa. The Sleepytime Ponies Trick a Trickster. Jordan, Lana. 2004. 32p. (J). 12.95 *(978-0-9710696-1-9(1))* Jorlan Publishing, Inc.

Allen, Keith. What a Mess! A Pop-Up Misadventure. Allen, Keith. 2017. 7p. (J). (gr. 1-3). 35.00 *(978-0-692-81057-6(9))* 5am Pr., LLC.

Allen Klein, Laurie. If a Dolphin Were a Fish in Chinese. Wlodarski, Loran. Shuqi, Yang, tr. 2019. (CHI.). 32p. (J). (gr. -1-2). pap. 11.95 *(978-0-9777423-9-4(3))* Arbordale Publishing.

Allen, Leighyah. The Moon in You: A Period Book for Young Women. King, Alexandria. 2016. (ENG.). (J). (gr. 3-6). pap. *(978-0-9936624-0-9(4))* Vriesen, Andrea.

Allen, Marie. Active Minds My First Book of Planets. Witmer, Nicole. 2021. (ENG.). 10p. (J). bds. ***(978-1-64269-250-1(6)***, a1fe02cb-4fb6-43d7-9e17-838d7f16b9df, Sequoia Publishing & Media LLC) Phoenix International Publications, Inc.

Allen, Marie. All Aboard with Noah, 1 vol. David, Juliet. ed. 2010. (ENG.). 12p. (J). (gr. -1-k). bds. 11.99 *(978-1-85985-864-6(3)*, Candle Bks.) Lion Hudson PLC GBR. Dist: Kregel Pubns.

—Let's Go Aquarium: A Magnetic Storybook. Pennington, Stacey & Pennington, J. C. D. 2008. 6p. (J). (gr. -1-1). bds. 10.99 *(978-2-7641-2184-9(9))* Gardner Pubns.

—My First Bedtime Stories. Baxter, Nicola. 2016. (ENG.). 16p. (J). (gr. -1-12). bds. 10.99 *(978-0-85723-809-2(4)*, Armadillo) Anness Publishing GBR. Dist: National Bk. Network.

—My First Bible Stories, 1 vol. Williamson, Karen. ed. 2014. (ENG.). 108p. (J). (gr. -1-k). spiral bd. 7.99 *(978-1-85985-994-0(1)*, Candle Bks.) Lion Hudson PLC GBR. Dist: Kregel Pubns.

Allen, Matt. Mop Rides the Waves of Life: A Story of Mindfulness & Surfing. Yogis, Jaimal. 2020. (ENG.). 40p. (J). (gr. k-3). 16.95 ***(978-1-946764-60-7(4)***, Plum Blossom Bks.) Parallax Pr.

Allen, Paddy. Tucklebinnie Goes Travelling. Lindsay, Tom. 2017. (ENG.). (J). pap. *(978-1-912192-71-7(3))* Mirador Publishing.

Allen, Pamela. Mr. Archimedes' Bath. Allen, Pamela. 2004. 81p. (J). (gr. -1-1). pap. 11.00 *(978-0-207-17285-4(4))* HarperCollins Pubs.

Allen, Patsy. Buzzbee in a Can. Allen, Patsy. Allen, Tom. 2018. (ENG.). 32p. (J). (gr. 2-6). pap. 10.99 *(978-1-68160-625-5(9))* Crimson Cloak Publishing.

Allen, Peter. Ancient Egypt Jigsaw Book. 2006. (Jigsaw Bks.). 14p. (J). (gr. k-3). bds. 14.99 *(978-0-7945-1236-1(4)*, Usborne) EDC Publishing.

—My First Pirate Book. Reid, Struan & Stowell, Louie. ed. 2012. (My First Book Ser.). 16p. (J). ring bd. 6.99 *(978-0-7945-3228-4(4)*, Usborne) EDC Publishing.

—Pirate Jigsaw Book. Reid, Struan. 2007. (Luxury Jigsaw Bks.). 14p. (J). bds. 14.99 *(978-0-7945-1432-7(4)*, Usborne) EDC Publishing.

—See Inside Space. Daynes, Katie. 2009. (See Inside Board Bks). 16p. (J). (gr. 2). bds. 12.99 *(978-0-7945-2088-5(X)*, Usborne) EDC Publishing.

—Story of Astronomy & Space: Internet-Referenced. Stowell, Louie. 2009. (Science Stories Ser.). 104p. (YA). (gr. 3-18). pap. 10.99 *(978-0-7945-2139-4(8)*, Usborne) EDC Publishing.

Allen, Raul. Frank #3. Alonge, L. J. 2017. (Blacktop Ser.: 3). (ENG.). 128p. (YA). (gr. 7). mass mkt. 6.99 *(978-1-101-99566-2(1)*, Grosset & Dunlap) Penguin Young Readers Group.

—Janae. Alonge, L. J. 2016. (Blacktop Ser.: 2). 144p. (YA). (gr. 7). mass mkt. 6.99 *(978-1-101-99564-8(5)*, Grosset & Dunlap) Penguin Young Readers Group.

—Justin #1. Alonge, L. J. 2016. (Blacktop Ser.: 1). (ENG.). 144p. (YA). (gr. 7). lib. bdg. 15.99 *(978-0-399-54275-6(2)*, Grosset & Dunlap) Penguin Young Readers Group.

Allen, Rick. Battle Cry. Schultz, Jan Neubert. 2006. (ENG.). 240p. (YA). (gr. 6-12). 15.95 *(978-1-57505-928-0(2)*, Carolrhoda Bks.) Lerner Publishing Group.

—Dark Emperor & Other Poems of the Night. Sidman, Joyce. 2010. (ENG.). 32p. (J). (gr. 1-4). 17.99 *(978-0-547-15228-8(0)*, 1051947) Houghton Mifflin Harcourt Publishing Co.

Allen, Russ. Now I Know the 10 Commandments. Allen, Jan. 2005. 32p. (J). (gr. k-5). *(978-0-9765514-0-9(3))* Light Bugs Publishing.

Allen, S. Joan & Graham, Jerry L. The Little Country Girl & Frisky the Squirrel. Graham, Janice C. 2008. 32p. pap. 24.95 *(978-1-60610-312-8(1))* America Star Bks.

Allen, Sandra Hutchins. Rainbows Are the Best. Pimot, Karen Hutchins. 2009. 24p. pap. 12.95 *(978-1-936051-01-4(X))* Peppertree Pr., The.

Allen, Shira. We Can Do Mitzvos from Aleph to Tav. Zoldan, Yael. 2009. 46p. (J). (gr. -1-2). 14.99 *(978-1-59826-395-4(1))* Feldheim Pubs.

Allen, Thomas B. Good-Bye for Today: The Diary of a Young Girl at Sea. Roop, Connie & Roop, Peter. 2008. (ENG.). 48p. (J). (gr. 4-6). 11.99 *(978-1-4169-7573-1(X)*, Simon & Schuster/Paula Wiseman Bks.) Simon & Schuster/Paula Wiseman Bks.

—Sewing Quilts. Turner, Ann Warren. 2012. (ENG.). 32p. (J). (gr. k-3). pap. 16.99 *(978-1-4424-6042-3(3)*, Simon & Schuster Bks. For Young Readers) Simon & Schuster Bks. For Young Readers.

Allen, Timothy. The Land of Phonicia: An Enchanted Tale to Learn Phonics. McKee, Ruby. l.t. ed. 2003. 52p. (J). per. 39.95 *(978-0-9744944-0-1(2))* Jewel Publishing.

Allenstein, Marilynne. The Lonely Feral Cat. Smith, Amy Elizabeth. 2019. (Amy's Animal Stories Ser.: Vol. 1). (ENG.). 32p. (J). pap. 9.99 *(978-1-7268-1191-0(3))* Independently Published.

Allepuz, Anuska. A Bear Is a Bear (except When He's Not) Newson, Karl. 2020. (ENG.). 32p. (J). (-k). 16.99 ***(978-1-5362-1202-0(4)***, Nosy Crow) Candlewick Pr.

Allepuz, Anuska. The Boy, the Bird & the Coffin Maker. Woods, Matilda. (ENG.). 208p. (J). (gr. 3-7). 2019. 7.99 *(978-0-525-51523-4(2)*, Puffin Books); 2018. 16.99 *(978-0-525-51521-0(6)*, Philomel Bks.) Penguin Young Readers Group.

—The Girl Who Sailed the Stars. Woods, Matilda. 2019. (ENG.). 272p. (J). (gr. 3-7). 16.99 *(978-0-525-51524-1(0)*, Philomel Bks.) Penguin Young Readers Group.

—Thank You. Pita, Charo. 2019. (ENG.). 32p. (J). *(978-0-8028-5524-4(5)*, Eerdmans Bks For Young Readers) Eerdmans, William B. Publishing Co.

Allepuz, Anuska. Little Green Donkey. Allepuz, Anuska. 2020. (ENG.). 32p. (J). (gr. -1-2). 16.99 ***(978-1-5362-0937-2(6))*** Candlewick Pr.

Allepuz, Anuska. That Fruit Is Mine! Allepuz, Anuska. 2018. (ENG.). 32p. (J). (gr. -1-k). 16.99 *(978-0-8075-7894-0(0)*, 807578940) Whitman, Albert & Co.

Alley, Amy. The Resisters. Premo Steele, Cassie. 2018. (ENG.). 220p. (J). pap. 14.99 *(978-1-7327237-1-9(0))* All Things That Matter Pr.

Alley, Ashleigh & Norona, Bill. My Elephant Likes to Read. Gerstler, J. C. 2013. 30p. pap. 12.00 *(978-1-4349-3548-9(5)*, RoseDog Bks.) Dorrance Publishing Co., Inc.

Alley, R. W. El Acto de Alejo El Acróbata. deRubertis, Barbara. 2017. (Travesuras de Animales (Animal Antics a to Z ®) Ser.: 1). (SPA.). 32p. (J). (gr. -1-3). pap. 7.99 *(978-1-57565-902-2(6)*, 9781575659022) Astra Publishing Hse.

—Alexander Anteater's Amazing Act. deRubertis, Barbara & DeRubertis, Barbara. 2012. (Animal Antics A to Z Ser.). 32p. (J). (gr. 2 — 1). cd-rom 7.95 *(978-1-57565-394-5(X))* Astra Publishing Hse.

—Alexander Anteater's Amazing Act. deRubertis, Barbara. 2010. (Animal Antics a to Z ® Ser.). (ENG.). 32p. (J). (gr. -1-3). pap. 7.95 *(978-1-57565-300-6(1))* Astra Publishing Hse.

Alley, R. W. Animales a Bordo: Animals on Board (Spanish Edition) Murphy, Stuart J. 2020. (MathStart 2 Ser.). (ENG.). 40p. (J). (gr. -1-3). pap. 5.99 ***(978-0-06-298326-8(1)***, HarperCollins) HarperCollins Pubs. Ltd. GBR. Dist: HarperCollins Pubs.

Alley, R. W. El Baile de la Banana de Beto (Bobby Baboon's Banana Be-Bop) La Letra B (Letter B) deRubertis, Barbara. 2017. (Travesuras de Animales (Animal Antics a to Z ®) Ser.: 2). (SPA.). 32p. (J). (gr. -1-3). pap. 7.99 *(978-1-57565-904-6(2)*, 9781575659046) Astra Publishing Hse.

—El Baile Desastroso de Delia. deRubertis, Barbara. 2017. (Travesuras de Animales (Animal Antics a to Z ®) Ser.: 4). (SPA.). 32p. (J). (gr. -1-3). pap. 7.99 *(978-1-57565-908-4(5)*, 9781575659084) Astra Publishing Hse.

—Be the Star That You Are: A Book for Kids Who Feel Different. O'Keefe, Susan Heyboer. 2005. (Elf-Help Books for Kids). (J). per. 7.95 *(978-0-87029-391-7(5))* Abbey Pr.

—Because Your Daddy Loves You. Clements, Andrew. 2009. (ENG.). 32p. (J). (gr. -1-3). pap. 7.99 *(978-0-547-23764-0(2)*, 1083875) Houghton Mifflin Harcourt Publishing Co.

—Because Your Grandparents Love You. Clements, Andrew. 2015. (ENG.). 32p. (J). (gr. -1-3). 16.99 *(978-0-544-14854-3(1)*, 1548513) Houghton Mifflin Harcourt Publishing Co.

—Being Teddy Roosevelt. Mills, Claudia. 2012. (ENG.). 112p. (J). (gr. 2-5). pap. 18.69 *(978-0-312-64018-7(8)*, 900077669) Square Fish.

—Bobby Baboon's Banana Be-Bop. deRubertis, Barbara & DeRubertis, Barbara. 2012. (Animal Antics A to Z Ser.). 32p. (J). (gr. 2 — 1). cd-rom 7.95 *(978-1-57565-395-2(8))* Astra Publishing Hse.

—Bobby Baboon's Banana Be-Bop. deRubertis, Barbara. 2010. (Animal Antics a to Z ® Ser.). (ENG.). 32p. (J). (gr. -1-3). pap. 7.95 *(978-1-57565-301-3(X))* Astra Publishing Hse.

—A Book of Prayers for All Your Cares. Mundy, Michaelene. 2004. (J). per. 7.95 *(978-0-87029-382-5(6))* Abbey Pr.

—Bratty Brothers & Selfish Sisters: All about Sibling Rivalry. 2007. (Elf-Help Books for Kids Ser.). 28p. (J). (gr. -1-3). per. 7.95 *(978-0-87029-404-4(0))* Abbey Pr.

—Corky Cub's Crazy Caps. deRubertis, Barbara & DeRubertis, Barbara. 2012. (Animal Antics A to Z Ser.). 32p. (J). (gr. 2 — 1). cd-rom 7.95 *(978-1-57565-396-9(6))* Astra Publishing Hse.

—Corky Cub's Crazy Caps. deRubertis, Barbara. 2010. (Animal Antics a to Z ® Ser.). (ENG.). 32p. (J). (gr. -1-3). pap. 7.95 *(978-1-57565-302-0(8))* Astra Publishing Hse.

—Dear Santa: The Letters of James B. Dobbins. Harley, Bill. 2005. 32p. (J). (ENG.). 15.99 *(978-0-06-623778-7(5))*; lib. bdg. 16.89 *(978-0-06-623779-4(3))* HarperCollins Pubs.

—Detective Dinosaur Undercover. Skofield, James. 2010. (I Can Read Level 2 Ser.). (ENG.). 48p. (J). (gr. -1-3). 16.99 *(978-0-06-623878-4(1))*; pap. 4.99 *(978-0-06-444319-7(1))* HarperCollins Pubs.

—Dilly Dog's Dizzy Dancing. deRubertis, Barbara & DeRubertis, Barbara. 2012. (Animal Antics A to Z Ser.). 32p. (J). (gr. 2 — 1). cd-rom 7.95 *(978-1-57565-397-6(4))* Astra Publishing Hse.

—Dilly Dog's Dizzy Dancing. deRubertis, Barbara. 2010. (Animal Antics a to Z ® Ser.). (ENG.). 32p. (J). (gr. -1-3). pap. 7.95 *(978-1-57565-303-7(6))* Astra Publishing Hse.

—Eddie Elephant's Exciting Egg-Sitting. deRubertis, Barbara & DeRubertis, Barbara. 2012. (Animal Antics A to Z Ser.). 32p. (J). (gr. 2 — 1). cd-rom 7.95 *(978-1-57565-398-3(2))* Astra Publishing Hse.

—Eddie Elephant's Exciting Egg-Sitting. deRubertis, Barbara. 2010. (Animal Antics a to Z ® Ser.). (ENG.). 32p. (J). (gr. -1-3). pap. 7.95 *(978-1-57565-309-9(5))* Astra Publishing Hse.

—Ello Se Echa en el Nido (Eddie Elephant's Exciting Egg-Sitting) La Letra e (Letter E) deRubertis, Barbara. 2017. (Travesuras de Animales (Animal Antics a to Z ®) Ser.: 5). (SPA.). 32p. (J). (gr. -1-3). pap. 7.99 *(978-1-57565-910-7(7)*, 9781575659107) Astra Publishing Hse.

—Enzo & the Christmas Tree Hunt! Stein, Garth. 2015. (ENG.). 40p. (J). (gr. -1-3). 17.99 *(978-0-06-229532-3(2))* HarperCollins Pubs.

—Enzo & the Fourth of July Races. Stein, Garth. 2017. (ENG.). 40p. (J). (gr. -1-3). 17.99 *(978-0-06-238059-3(1))* HarperCollins Pubs.

—Enzo Races in the Rain! Stein, Garth. 2014. (ENG.). 40p. (J). (gr. -1-3). 17.99 *(978-0-06-229533-0(0))* HarperCollins Pubs.

—Enzo's Very Scary Halloween. Stein, Garth. 2016. (ENG.). 40p. (J). (gr. -1-3). 17.99 *(978-0-06-238061-6(3))* HarperCollins Pubs.

—Flor y Flora Son Amigas para Siempre (Frances Frog's Forever Friend) La Letra F (Letter F) deRubertis, Barbara. 2017. (Travesuras de Animales (Animal Antics a to Z ®) Ser.: 6). (SPA.). 32p. (J). (gr. -1-3). pap. 7.99 *(978-1-57565-912-1(3)*, 9781575659121) Astra Publishing Hse.

—Forgiveness Is Smart for the Heart. Morrow, Carol. 2003. (Elf-Help Books for Kids). 32p. (J). per. 6.95 *(978-0-87029-370-2(2))* Abbey Pr.

—Four Eyes. McMullan, Kate. 2013. (Pearl & Wagner Ser.: 4). 48p. (J). (gr. 1-3). pap. 4.99 *(978-0-448-47781-7(5)*, Penguin Young Readers) Penguin Young Readers Group.

—Frances Frog's Forever Friend. deRubertis, Barbara & DeRubertis, Barbara. 2012. (Animal Antics A to Z Ser.). 32p. (J). (gr. 2 — 1). cd-rom 7.95 *(978-1-57565-399-0(0))* Astra Publishing Hse.

—Frances Frog's Forever Friend. deRubertis, Barbara. 2010. (Animal Antics a to Z ® Ser.). (ENG.). 32p. (J). (gr. -1-3). pap. 7.95 *(978-1-57565-310-5(9))*; lib. bdg. 22.65 *(978-1-57565-317-4(6))* Astra Publishing Hse.

—The Genie in the Book. Trumbore, Cindy. 2004. (ENG.). 120p. (J). (gr. -1-7). 15.95 *(978-1-59354-042-5(6)*, Handprint Bks.) Chronicle Bks. LLC.

—Gertie Gorilla's Glorious Gift. deRubertis, Barbara & DeRubertis, Barbara. 2012. (Animal Antics A to Z Ser.). 32p. (J). (gr. 2 — 1). cd-rom 7.95 *(978-1-57565-400-3(8))* Astra Publishing Hse.

—Gertie Gorilla's Glorious Gift. deRubertis, Barbara. 2010. (Animal Antics a to Z ® Ser.). (ENG.). 32p. (J). (gr. -1-3). pap. 7.95 *(978-1-57565-311-2(7))*; lib. bdg. 22.65 *(978-1-57565-318-1(4))* Astra Publishing Hse.

—Gladis y Su Glorioso Regalo. deRubertis, Barbara. 2017. (Travesuras de Animales (Animal Antics a to Z ®) Ser.: 7). (SPA.). 32p. (J). (gr. -1-3). pap. 7.99 *(978-1-57565-914-5(X)*, 9781575659145) Astra Publishing Hse.

—God Made Us One by One: How to See Prejudice & Celebrate Differences. Adams, Christine. ed. 2008. (J). mass mkt. 7.95 *(978-0-87029-418-1(0))* Abbey Pr.

—Growing into a Family: A Kids Guide to Living in a Blended Family. Geisen, Cynthia. 2015. 32p. (J). pap. 7.95 *(978-0-87029-684-0(1))* Abbey Pr.

—Hanna Hippo's Horrible Hiccups. deRubertis, Barbara & DeRubertis, Barbara. 2012. (Animal Antics A to Z Ser.). 32p. (J). (gr. 2 — 1). cd-rom 7.95 *(978-1-57565-401-0(6))* Astra Publishing Hse.

—Hanna Hippo's Horrible Hiccups. deRubertis, Barbara. 2010. (Animal Antics a to Z ® Ser.). (ENG.). 32p. (J). (gr. -1-3). pap. 7.95 *(978-1-57565-312-9(5))* Astra Publishing Hse.

—Hilda Tiene un Hipo Horrible (Hanna Hippo's Horrible Hiccups) La Letra H (Letter H) deRubertis, Barbara. 2017. (Travesuras de Animales (Animal Antics a to Z ®) Ser.: 8). (SPA.). 32p. (J). (gr. -1-3). pap. 7.99 *(978-1-57565-916-9(6)*, 9781575659169) Astra Publishing Hse.

—I Don't Want to Go to Church: Turning the Struggle into a Celebration. Falkenhain, John Mark. 2009. (J). pap. 7.95 *(978-0-87029-423-5(7))* Abbey Pr.

—It's Great to Be Grateful! A Kid's Guide to Being Thankful. Mundy, Michaelene. 2012. 32p. (J). pap. 7.95 *(978-0-87029-512-6(8))* Abbey Pr.

—Izzy Impala's Imaginary Illnesses. deRubertis, Barbara & DeRubertis, Barbara. 2012. (Animal Antics A to Z Ser.).

32p. (J). (gr. 2 — 1). cd-rom 7.95 *(978-1-57565-402-7(4))* Astra Publishing Hse.
—Izzy Impala's Imaginary Illnesses. deRubertis, Barbara. 2010. (Animal Antics a to Z ® Ser.). (ENG.). 32p. (J). (gr. -1-3). pap. 7.95 *(978-1-57565-313-6(3))*; lib. bdg. 22.65 *(978-1-57565-320-4(6))* Astra Publishing Hse.
—Jeremy Jackrabbit's Jumping Journey. deRubertis, Barbara & DeRubertis, Barbara. 2012. (Animal Antics A to Z Ser.). 32p. (J). (gr. 2 — 1). cd-rom 7.95 *(978-1-57565-403-4(2))* Astra Publishing Hse.
—Jeremy Jackrabbit's Jumping Journey. deRubertis, Barbara. 2010. (Animal Antics a to Z ® Ser.). (ENG.). 32p. (J). (gr. -1-3). pap. 7.95 *(978-1-57565-314-3(1))*; lib. bdg. 22.65 *(978-1-57565-321-1(4))* Astra Publishing Hse.
—Jigsaw Jones: the Case of the Hat Burglar. Preller, James. 2019. (Jigsaw Jones Mysteries Ser.). (ENG.). 96p. (J). 15.99 *(978-1-250-20752-4(5)*, 900201638); pap. 4.99 *(978-1-250-20768-5(1)*, 900201639) Feiwel & Friends.
—Keeping Family First: A Kid's Guide. Jackson, J. S. 2004. (J). per. 7.95 *(978-0-87029-390-0(7))* Abbey Pr.
—Kylie Kangaroo's Karate Kickers. deRubertis, Barbara & DeRubertis, Barbara. 2012. (Animal Antics A to Z Ser.). 32p. (J). (gr. 2 — 1). cd-rom 7.95 *(978-1-57565-404-1(0))* Astra Publishing Hse.
—Kylie Kangaroo's Karate Kickers. deRubertis, Barbara. 2011. (Animal Antics A to Z Ser.). 32p. (J). pap. 45.32 *(978-0-7613-7657-6(7))*; (ENG.). lib. bdg. 22.60 *(978-1-57565-332-7(X))*; (ENG.). (gr. -1-3). pap. 7.95 *(978-1-57565-323-5(0))* Astra Publishing Hse.
—Lana Llama's Little Lamb. deRubertis, Barbara & DeRubertis, Barbara. 2012. (Animal Antics A to Z Ser.). 32p. (J). (gr. 2 — 1). cd-rom 7.95 *(978-1-57565-405-8(9))* Astra Publishing Hse.
—Lana Llama's Little Lamb. deRubertis, Barbara. 2011. (Animal Antics A to Z Ser.). 32p. (J). pap. 45.32 *(978-0-7613-7658-3(5))*; (ENG.). lib. bdg. 22.60 *(978-1-57565-333-4(8))*; (ENG.). (gr. -1-3). pap. 7.95 *(978-1-57565-324-2(9))* Astra Publishing Hse.
—Las Gorras Chifladas de Carlos (Corky Cub's Crazy Caps) deRubertis, Barbara. 2017. (Travesuras de Animales (Animal Antics a to Z (SPA.) Ser.: 3). (SPA.). 32p. (J). (gr. -1-3). pap. 7.99 *(978-1-57565-906-0(9)*, 9781575659060) Astra Publishing Hse.
—Learning to Be a Good Friend: A Guidebook for Kids. Adams, Christine. 2004. 32p. (J). per. 7.95 *(978-0-87029-388-7(5))* Abbey Pr.
—Making Christmas Count! A Kid's Guide to Keeping the Season Sacred. 2006. (Elf-Help Books for Kids Ser.). (AFA.). 32p. (J). (gr. -1-3). per. 7.95 *(978-0-87029-401-3(6))* Abbey Pr.
—Maxwell Moose's Mountain Monster. deRubertis, Barbara & DeRubertis, Barbara. 2012. (Animal Antics A to Z Ser.). 32p. (J). (gr. 2 — 1). cd-rom 7.95 *(978-1-57565-406-5(7))* Astra Publishing Hse.
—Maxwell Moose's Mountain Monster. deRubertis, Barbara. 2011. (Animal Antics A to Z Ser.). 32p. (J). pap. 45.32 *(978-0-7613-7659-0(3))*; (ENG.). lib. bdg. 22.60 *(978-1-57565-334-1(6))*; (ENG.). (gr. -1-3). pap. 7.95 *(978-1-57565-325-9(7)*, 9781575653259) Astra Publishing Hse.
—Nina Nandu's Nervous Noggin. deRubertis, Barbara & DeRubertis, Barbara. 2012. (Animal Antics A to Z Ser.). 32p. (J). (gr. 2 — 1). cd-rom 7.95 *(978-1-57565-407-2(5))* Astra Publishing Hse.
—Nina Nandu's Nervous Noggin. deRubertis, Barbara. 2011. (Animal Antics A to Z Ser.). 32p. (J). pap. 45.32 *(978-0-7613-7660-6(7))*; (ENG.). lib. bdg. 22.60 *(978-1-57565-335-8(4))*; (ENG.). (gr. -1-3). pap. 7.95 *(978-1-57565-326-6(5)*, 9781575653266) Astra Publishing Hse.
—Oliver Otter's Own Office. deRubertis, Barbara & DeRubertis, Barbara. 2012. (Animal Antics A to Z Ser.). 32p. (J). (gr. 2 — 1). cd-rom 7.95 *(978-1-57565-408-9(3))* Astra Publishing Hse.
—Oliver Otter's Own Office. deRubertis, Barbara. 2011. (Animal Antics A to Z Ser.). 32p. (J). pap. 45.32 *(978-0-7613-7661-3(5))*; (ENG.). (gr. -1-3). pap. 7.95 *(978-1-57565-327-3(3))* Astra Publishing Hse.
—The on-Again, off-Again Friend: Standing up for Friends. Blevins, Wiley. 2015. (Funny Bone Readers (tm) — Dealing with Bullies Ser.). (ENG.). 24p. (J). (gr. k-2). lib. bdg. 19.99 *(978-1-63440-015-2(1))* Red Chair Pr.
—One Funny Day. McMullan, Kate. 2012. (Pearl & Wagner Ser.: 1). 48p. (J). (gr. 1-3). pap. 4.99 *(978-0-448-45866-3(7)*, Penguin Young Readers) Penguin Young Readers Group.
—Paddington. Bond, Michael. (Paddington Ser.). (ENG.). 32p. (J). (gr. -1-3). 2014. 17.99 *(978-0-06-231719-3(9))*; 2007. 17.99 *(978-0-06-117074-4(7))* HarperCollins Pubs.
—Paddington & the Christmas Surprise. Bond, Michael. (Paddington Ser.). (ENG.). 32p. (J). (gr. -1-3). 2015. 17.99 *(978-0-06-231842-8(X))*; 2008. 16.99 *(978-0-06-168740-2(5))* HarperCollins Pubs.
—Paddington & the Magic Trick. Bond, Michael. 2016. (I Can Read Level 1 Ser.). (ENG.). 32p. (J). (gr. -1-3). pap. 4.99 *(978-0-06-243067-0(X))* HarperCollins Pubs.
—Paddington at St. Paul's. Bond, Michael. 2019. (Paddington Ser.). (ENG.). 32p. (J). (gr. -1-3). 17.99 *(978-0-06-288785-6(8))* HarperCollins Pubs.
—Paddington at the Barber Shop. Bond, Michael. 2017. (I Can Read Level 1 Ser.). (ENG.). 32p. (J). (gr. -1-3). 16.99 *(978-0-06-243080-9(7))*; pap. 4.99 *(978-0-06-243079-3(3))* HarperCollins Pubs.
—Paddington at the Beach. Bond, Michael. (Paddington Ser.). (ENG.). 32p. (J). (gr. -1-3). 2015. 17.99 *(978-0-06-231720-9(2))*; 2009. 17.99 *(978-0-06-168767-9(7))* HarperCollins Pubs.
—Paddington at the Circus. Bond, Michael. 2016. (Paddington Ser.). (ENG.). 32p. (J). (gr. -1-3). 17.99 *(978-0-06-231843-5(8))* HarperCollins Pubs.
—Paddington Bear All Day. Bond, Michael. 2004. 12p. (J). *(978-1-85269-442-5(4))*; *(978-1-85269-443-2(2))*; *(978-1-85269-444-9(0))*; *(978-1-85269-445-6(9))*; *(978-1-85269-456-2(4))* Mantra Lingua.
—Paddington Bear All Day Board Book. Bond, Michael. 2014. (Paddington Ser.). (ENG.). 14p. (J). (gr. -1-3). bds. 6.99 *(978-0-06-231721-6(0)*, HarperFestival) HarperCollins Pubs.
—Paddington Bear Goes to Market. Bond, Michael. 2004. 12p. (J). *(978-1-85269-451-7(3))*; *(978-1-85269-455-5(6))* Mantra Lingua.
—Paddington Bear Goes to Market Board Book. Bond, Michael. 2014. (Paddington Ser.). (ENG.). 14p. (J). (gr. -1-3). bds. 7.99 *(978-0-06-231722-3(9)*, HarperFestival) HarperCollins Pubs.
—Paddington Collector's Quintet: 5 Fun-Filled Stories in 1 Box! Bond, Michael. 2018. (I Can Read Level 1 Ser.). (ENG.). 160p. (J). (gr. -1-3). pap. 19.99 *(978-0-06-267138-7(3))* HarperCollins Pubs.
—Paddington Here & Now. Bond, Michael. 176p. (J). 2009. pap. 5.99 *(978-0-06-147366-1(9))*; 2008. (ENG.). (gr. 3-7). 15.99 *(978-0-06-147364-7(2))* HarperCollins Pubs.
—Paddington Here & Now. Bond, Michael. 2018. (Paddington Ser.). (ENG.). 192p. (J). (gr. 3-7). 9.99 *(978-0-06-231723-0(7))* HarperCollins Pubs.
—Paddington Here & Now. Bond, Michael. 2020. (Paddington Ser.). (ENG.). 192p. (J). (gr. 3-7). pap. 7.99 *(978-0-06-243317-6(2)*, HarperCollins) HarperCollins Pubs. Ltd. GBR. Dist: HarperCollins Pubs.
—Paddington in the Garden. Bond, Michael. 2015. (Paddington Ser.). (ENG.). 32p. (J). (gr. -1-3). 17.99 *(978-0-06-231844-2(6))* HarperCollins Pubs.
—Paddington Plays On. Bond, Michael. 2016. (I Can Read Level 1 Ser.). (ENG.). 32p. (J). (gr. -1-3). pap. 4.99 *(978-0-06-243070-0(X))* HarperCollins Pubs.
—Paddington Plays On. Bond, Michael & Webster, Christy. 2016. 32p. (J). *(978-1-5182-3398-2(8))* Harper & Row Ltd.
—Paddington Sets Sail. Bond, Michael. 2016. (I Can Read Level 1 Ser.). (ENG.). 32p. (J). (gr. -1-3). pap. 4.99 *(978-0-06-243064-9(5))* HarperCollins Pubs.
—Paddington Storybook Collection: 6 Classic Stories. Bond, Michael. 2017. (Paddington Ser.). (ENG.). 192p. (J). (gr. -1-3). 11.99 *(978-0-06-266850-9(1))* HarperCollins Pubs.
—Paddington Storybook Favorites: Includes 6 Stories Plus Stickers! Bond, Michael. 2019. (Paddington Ser.). (ENG.). 192p. (J). (gr. -1-3). 13.99 *(978-0-06-297274-3(X))* HarperCollins Pubs.
—The Paddington Treasury: Six Classic Bedtime Stories. Bond, Michael. 2014. (Paddington Ser.). (ENG.). 160p. (J). (gr. -1-3). 21.99 *(978-0-06-231242-6(1))* HarperCollins Pubs.
—Paddington's Day Off. Bond, Michael. 2017. (I Can Read Level 1 Ser.). (ENG.). 32p. (J). (gr. -1-3). pap. 4.99 *(978-0-06-243073-1(4))* HarperCollins Pubs.
—Paddington's Finest Hour. Bond, Michael. 2017. (ENG.). 128p. (J). *(978-0-00-822619-0(9))* HarperCollins Pubs.
—Paddington's Post. Bond, Michael. 2019. (Paddington Ser.). (ENG.). 48p. (J). (gr. -1-3). 16.99 *(978-0-06-296212-6(4)*, HarperFestival) HarperCollins Pubs.
—Paddington's Prize Picture. Bond, Michael. 2017. (I Can Read Level 1 Ser.). (ENG.). 32p. (J). (gr. -1-3). pap. 4.99 *(978-0-06-243076-2(9))* HarperCollins Pubs.
—Paddington's Prize Picture. Bond, Michael. 2017. 29p. (J). *(978-1-5182-4206-9(5))* Harper & Row Ltd.
—Peanut & Pearl's Picnic Adventure. Dotlich, Rebecca. 2008. (My First I Can Read Ser.). (ENG.). 32p. (J). (gr. -1 — 1). pap. 4.99 *(978-0-06-054922-0(X))* HarperCollins Pubs.
—Pearl & Wagner: Five Days till Summer. McMullan, Kate. 2014. (Pearl & Wagner Ser.: 5). (ENG.). 48p. (J). (gr. 1-3). pap. 4.99 *(978-0-448-48137-1(5)*, Penguin Young Readers) Penguin Young Readers Group.
—Pearl & Wagner: Two Good Friends. McMullan, Kate. 2011. (Pearl & Wagner Ser.: 2). 48p. (J). (gr. 1-3). pap. 4.99 *(978-0-448-45690-4(7)*, Penguin Young Readers) Penguin Young Readers Group.
—Playing Fair, Having Fun: A Kid's Guide to Sports & Games. Grippo, Daniel. 2004. 32p. (J). per. 7.95 *(978-0-87029-384-9(2))* Abbey Pr.
—Police Officers on Patrol. Hamilton, Kersten. 2009. 32p. (J). (gr. -1-k). 16.99 *(978-0-670-06315-4(0)*, Viking Books for Young Readers) Penguin Young Readers Group.
—Polly Porcupine's Painting Prize. deRubertis, Barbara. 2011. (Animal Antics A to Z Ser.). 32p. (J). pap. 45.32 *(978-0-7613-7662-0(3))*; lib. bdg. 22.60 *(978-1-57565-337-2(0))* Astra Publishing Hse.
—Polly Porcupine's Painting Prizes. deRubertis, Barbara & DeRubertis, Barbara. 2012. (Animal Antics A to Z Ser.). 32p. (J). (gr. 2 — 1). cd-rom 7.95 *(978-1-57565-409-6(1))* Astra Publishing Hse.
—Polly Porcupine's Painting Prizes. deRubertis, Barbara. 2011. (Animal Antics a to Z ® Ser.). (ENG.). 32p. (J). (gr. -1-3). pap. 7.95 *(978-1-57565-328-0(1))* Astra Publishing Hse.
—The Prince's Tooth Is Loose! 2005. (I'm Going to Read® Ser.). (ENG.). 28p. (J). (gr. -1-k). pap. 3.95 *(978-1-4027-2721-4(6))* Sterling Publishing Co., Inc.
—Quentin Quokka's Quick Questions. deRubertis, Barbara & DeRubertis, Barbara. 2012. (Animal Antics A to Z Ser.). 32p. (J). (gr. 2 — 1). cd-rom 7.95 *(978-1-57565-410-2(5))* Astra Publishing Hse.
—Quentin Quokka's Quick Questions. deRubertis, Barbara. 2011. (Animal Antics A to Z Ser.). 32p. (J). pap. 45.32 *(978-0-7613-7663-7(1))*; (ENG.). (gr. -1-3). pap. 7.95 *(978-1-57565-329-7(X))* Astra Publishing Hse.
—Rosie Raccoon's Rock & Roll Raft. deRubertis, Barbara & DeRubertis, Barbara. 2012. (Animal Antics A to Z Ser.). 32p. (J). (gr. 2 — 1). cd-rom 7.95 *(978-1-57565-411-9(3))* Astra Publishing Hse.
—Rosie Raccoon's Rock & Roll Raft. deRubertis, Barbara. 2011. (Animal Antics A to Z Ser.). 32p. (J). pap. 45.32 *(978-0-7613-7664-4(X))*; (ENG.). (gr. -1-3). pap. 7.95 *(978-1-57565-330-3(3))* Astra Publishing Hse.
—Sammy Skunk's Super Sniffer. Derubertis, Barbara. 2011. (Animal Antics A to Z Set III Ser.). pap. 45.32 *(978-0-7613-8428-1(6))* Astra Publishing Hse.
—Sammy Skunk's Super Sniffer. deRubertis, Barbara & DeRubertis, Barbara. 2012. (Animal Antics A to Z Ser.). 32p. (J). (gr. 2 — 1). cd-rom 7.95 *(978-1-57565-412-6(1))* Astra Publishing Hse.
—Sammy Skunk's Super Sniffer. deRubertis, Barbara. 2011. (Animal Antics a to Z ® Ser.). (ENG.). 32p. (J). (gr. -1-3). pap. 7.95 *(978-1-57565-344-0(3))* Astra Publishing Hse.
—Saying Good-Bye, Saying Hello... When Your Family Is Moving. Mundy, Michaelene. 2005. (Elf-Help Books for Kids). 32p. (J). (gr. -1-3). per. 7.95 *(978-0-87029-393-1(1))* Abbey Pr.
—Standing up to Peer Pressure: A Guide to Being True to You. Auer, Jim. 2003. 32p. (J). per. 7.95 *(978-0-87029-375-7(3))* Abbey Pr.
—Tessa Tiger's Temper Tantrums. Derubertis, Barbara. 2011. (Animal Antics A to Z Set III Ser.). pap. 45.32 *(978-0-7613-8429-8(4))* Astra Publishing Hse.
—Tessa Tiger's Temper Tantrums. deRubertis, Barbara & DeRubertis, Barbara. 2012. (Animal Antics A to Z Ser.). 32p. (J). (gr. 2 — 1). cd-rom 7.95 *(978-1-57565-413-3(X))* Astra Publishing Hse.
—Tessa Tiger's Temper Tantrums. deRubertis, Barbara. 2011. (Animal Antics a to Z ® Ser.). (ENG.). 32p. (J). (gr. -1-3). pap. 7.95 *(978-1-57565-345-7(1))* Astra Publishing Hse.
—Three Secrets. McMullan, Kate. 2013. (Pearl & Wagner Ser.: 3). 48p. (J). (gr. 1-3). pap. 4.99 *(978-0-448-46472-5(1)*, Penguin Young Readers) Penguin Young Readers Group.
—The Treasure of Dead Man's Lane & Other Case Files: Saxby Smart, Private Detective: Book 2. Cheshire, Simon. 2011. (Saxby Smart, Private Detective Ser.: 2). (ENG.). 224p. (J). (gr. 3-7). pap. 14.99 *(978-0-312-67434-2(1)*, 900072849) Square Fish.
—Umma Ungka's Unusual Umbrella. Derubertis, Barbara. 2011. (Animal Antics A to Z Set III Ser.). pap. 45.32 *(978-0-7613-8430-4(8))* Astra Publishing Hse.
—Umma Ungka's Unusual Umbrella. deRubertis, Barbara & DeRubertis, Barbara. 2012. (Animal Antics A to Z Ser.). 32p. (J). (gr. 2 — 1). cd-rom 7.95 *(978-1-57565-414-0(8))* Astra Publishing Hse.
—Umma Ungka's Unusual Umbrella. deRubertis, Barbara. 2011. (Animal Antics a to Z ® Ser.). (ENG.). 32p. (J). (gr. -1-3). pap. 7.95 *(978-1-57565-346-4(X))* Astra Publishing Hse.
—Victor Vicuna's Volcano Vacation. Derubertis, Barbara. 2011. (Animal Antics A to Z Set III Ser.). pap. 45.32 *(978-0-7613-8431-1(6))* Astra Publishing Hse.
—Victor Vicuna's Volcano Vacation. deRubertis, Barbara & DeRubertis, Barbara. 2012. (Animal Antics A to Z Ser.). 32p. (J). (gr. 2 — 1). cd-rom 7.95 *(978-1-57565-415-7(6))* Astra Publishing Hse.
—Victor Vicuna's Volcano Vacation. deRubertis, Barbara. 2011. (Animal Antics a to Z ® Ser.). (ENG.). 32p. (J). (gr. -1-3). pap. 7.95 *(978-1-57565-347-1(8))* Astra Publishing Hse.
—Walter Warthog's Wonderful Wagon. Derubertis, Barbara. 2011. (Animal Antics A to Z Set III Ser.). pap. 45.32 *(978-0-7613-8432-8(4))* Astra Publishing Hse.
—Walter Warthog's Wonderful Wagon. deRubertis, Barbara & DeRubertis, Barbara. 2012. (Animal Antics A to Z Ser.). 32p. (J). (gr. 2 — 1). cd-rom 7.95 *(978-1-57565-416-4(4))* Astra Publishing Hse.
—Walter Warthog's Wonderful Wagon. deRubertis, Barbara. 2011. (Animal Antics a to Z ® Ser.). (ENG.). 32p. (J). (gr. -1-3). pap. 7.95 *(978-1-57565-348-8(6))* Astra Publishing Hse.
—We're off to Find the Witch's House. Krieb & Kreib. 2007. 32p. (J). (gr. -1-2). 7.99 *(978-0-14-240854-4(9)*, Puffin Books) Penguin Young Readers Group.
—What Does Sam Sell? Rothman, Cynthia Anne. l.t. ed. 2005. (Sadlier Phonics Reading Program). 8p. (gr. -1-1). 23.00 net. *(978-0-8215-7342-6(X))* Sadlier, William H. Inc.
—When Bad Things Happen: A Guide to Help Kids Cope. O'Neal, Ted. 2003. (Elf-Help Books for Kids). 32p. (J). per. 7.95 *(978-0-87029-371-9(0)*, 20071) Abbey Pr.
—When Dads Don't Grow Up. Blain Parker, Marjorie. 2012. 32p. (J). (gr. -1-k). 17.99 *(978-0-8037-3717-4(3)*, Dial Bks) Penguin Young Readers Group.
—When Mom or Dad Dies: A Book of Comfort for Kids. Grippo, Daniel. 2008. (J). pap. 7.95 *(978-0-87029-415-0(6))* Abbey Pr.
—When Someone You Love Has Cancer: A Guide to Help Kids Cope. Lewis, Alaric. 2005. (Elf-Help Books for Kids Ser.). 32p. per. 7.95 *(978-0-87029-395-5(8))* Abbey Pr.
—Worry, Worry Go Away. Adams, Christine A. 2012. 32p. (J). pap. 7.95 *(978-0-87029-471-6(7))* Abbey Pr.
—Xavier Ox's Xylophone Experiment. Derubertis, Barbara. 2011. (Animal Antics A to Z Set III Ser.). pap. 45.32 *(978-0-7613-8433-5(2))* Astra Publishing Hse.
—Xavier Ox's Xylophone Experiment. deRubertis, Barbara & DeRubertis, Barbara. 2012. (Animal Antics A to Z Ser.). 32p. (J). (gr. 2 — 1). cd-rom 7.95 *(978-1-57565-417-1(2))* Astra Publishing Hse.
—Xavier Ox's Xylophone Experiment. deRubertis, Barbara. 2011. (Animal Antics a to Z ® Ser.). (ENG.). 32p. (J). (gr. -1-3). pap. 7.95 *(978-1-57565-349-5(4))* Astra Publishing Hse.
—Yoko Yak's Yakety Yakking. deRubertis, Barbara & DeRubertis, Barbara. 2012. (Animal Antics A to Z Ser.). 32p. (J). (gr. 2 — 1). cd-rom 7.95 *(978-1-57565-418-8(0))* Astra Publishing Hse.
—Yoko Yak's Yakety Yakking. deRubertis, Barbara. 2011. (Animal Antics a to Z ® Ser.). (ENG.). 32p. (J). (gr. -1-3). pap. 7.95 *(978-1-57565-350-1(8))*; lib. bdg. 22.65 *(978-1-57565-358-7(3))* Astra Publishing Hse.
—You Are You, I Am Me: Understanding Diversity. Geisen, Cynthia. 2016. 32p. (J). pap. 7.95 *(978-0-87029-699-4(X))* Abbey Pr.
—Zachary Zebra's Zippity Zooming. Derubertis, Barbara. 2011. (Animal Antics A to Z Set III Ser.). pap. 45.32 *(978-0-7613-8435-9(9))* Astra Publishing Hse.
—Zachary Zebra's Zippity Zooming. deRubertis, Barbara & DeRubertis, Barbara. 2012. (Animal Antics A to Z Ser.). 32p. (J). (gr. 2 — 1). cd-rom 7.95 *(978-1-57565-419-5(9))* Astra Publishing Hse.
—Zachary Zebra's Zippity Zooming. deRubertis, Barbara. 2011. (Animal Antics a to Z ® Ser.). (ENG.). 32p. (J). (gr. -1-3). pap. 7.95 *(978-1-57565-351-8(6))*; lib. bdg. 22.65 *(978-1-57565-359-4(1))* Astra Publishing Hse.

Alley, R. W. Because Your Daddy Loves You. Alley, R. W., tr. Clements, Andrew. 2005. (ENG.). 32p. (J). (gr. -1-3). 16.99 *(978-0-618-00361-7(4)*, 112735) Houghton Mifflin Harcourt Publishing Co.
—Bye-Bye, Bully: A Kid's Guide for Dealing with Bullies. Alley, R. W., tr. Jackson, J. S. 2003. (J). per. 6.95 *(978-0-87029-369-6(9))* Abbey Pr.
Alley, R. W., jt. illus. see Fortnum, Peggy.
Alley, R. W., jt. illus. see Ryan, Victoria.
Alley, R. W., jt. illus. see Smith, Jamie.
Alleyne, Paris. Freedom of Expression: Deal with It Before You're Censored. McLaughlin, Danielle S. 2019. (Lorimer Deal with It Ser.). (ENG.). 32p. (J). (gr. 4-9). 22.65 *(978-1-4594-1393-1(8)*, 5702dcb9-cbe0-4464-a190-3e3a933edcf4) James Lorimer & Co. Ltd., Pubs. CAN. Dist: Lerner Publishing Group.
Allibone, Judith & Benson, Patrick. It's a Dog's Life. Morpurgo, Michael. 2010. 32p. (J). *(978-1-4052-1336-3(1))* Egmont Bks., Ltd.
Allie, Beverly. The American Schoolhouse Reader: A Colorized Children's Reading Collection from Post-Victorian America 1890-1925. Allie, Beverly, ed. 2005. (American Schoolhouse Reader Ser.). 151p. 12.95 *(978-0-9747615-3-4(2))* Level 603 LLC.
—The American Schoolhouse Reader, Book II: A Colorized Children's Reading Collection from Post-Victorian America 1890-1925. Allie, Beverly, ed. 2005. (American Schoolhouse Reader Ser.). 151p. 12.95 *(978-0-9747615-2-7(4))* Level 603 LLC.
Allie, Beverly & Allie, Beverly. The American Schoolhouse Reader: A Colorized Children's Reading Collection from Post-Victorian America 1890-1925. Allie, Beverly, ed. 2005. (American Schoolhouse Reader Ser.). 76p. 10.95 *(978-0-9747615-1-0(6))* Level 603 LLC.
Allie, Beverly, jt. illus. see Allie, Beverly.
Alliger, Richard. Classic Literature for Teens: Every Teachers Friend Classroom Plays. Jordan, Pat. 2007. 118p. pap. 25.00 *(978-0-88734-692-7(8))* Players Pr., Inc.
—Mini-Myths for Pre-Teens & Teens Vol. 2: Every Teacher's Friend Classroom Plays. Jordan, Pat. 2008. (Every Teacher's Friend Classroom Plays Ser.: Vol. 2). 122p. pap. 25.00 *(978-0-88734-964-5(1))* Players Pr., Inc.
—Plays from Around the World: Every Teacher's Friend Classroom Plays. Jordan, Pat. 2010. (ENG.). 128p. (J). spiral bd. 25.00 *(978-0-88734-975-1(7))* Players Pr., Inc.
Allin, Nicole. Anansi's Narrow Waist: A Tale from Ghana, 1 vol. Arrington, H. 2017. (ENG.). 32p. (J). (gr. k-3). 16.99 *(978-1-4556-2216-0(8)*, Pelican Publishing) Arcadia Publishing.
Allingham, Andrew. Offbeat. Ainsworth, Marlane. 2006. 128p. (Orig.). (J). pap. 13.50 *(978-1-920731-65-6(2))* Fremantle Pr. AUS. Dist: Independent Pubs. Group.
Allinson, Kate. Maddie's Great Adventure. Allinson, Amy & Allinson, Matt. 2008. (ENG.). 26p. (YA). pap. 12.00 *(978-1-4120-6805-5(3))* Trafford Publishing.
Allison, Charles T. Bobble Stories: The Bobbleup Pup. Allison, Teresa J. 2013. 42p. pap. 12.99 *(978-0-9887612-2-3(X))* Tawnsy Publishing.
—Bobble Stories: The Humbobble's Lost Hum. Allison, Teresa J. 2013. 48p. pap. 12.99 *(978-0-9887612-1-6(1))* Tawnsy Publishing.
—Bobble Stories: The Oddbobble's Visit. Allison, Teresa J. 2013. 48p. pap. 12.99 *(978-0-9887612-0-9(3))* Tawnsy Publishing.
Allison, Diane Worfolk. Julian, Secret Agent. Cameron, Ann. 2018. (Julian's World Ser.). (ENG.). 80p. (J). (gr. 1-4). lib. bdg. 12.99 *(978-0-525-57985-4(0)*, Random Hse. Bks. for Young Readers) Random Hse. Children's Bks.
Allison, John. Bad Machinery Vol. 4 Vol. 4: The Case of the Lonely One, Pocket Edition. Allison, John. 2018. (Bad Machinery Ser.: 4). (ENG.). 136p. (J). pap. 12.99 *(978-1-62010-457-6(1)*, 9781620104576, Lion Forge) Oni Pr., Inc.
—Bad Machinery Vol. 9: The Case of the Missing Piece. Allison, John. 2020. (Bad Machinery Ser.: 9). (ENG.). 128p. (YA). (gr. 8). pap. 12.99 *(978-1-62010-668-6(X)*, Lion Forge) Oni Pr., Inc.
Allison, Ralph. Where Did They Go? Allison, Ray. 2013. 36p. pap. 14.95 *(978-1-61493-191-1(7))* Peppertree Pr., The.
Allen, Katherine. Gloves down Under. Allen, Katherine. 2005. 32p. (J). 15.95 *(978-0-9747278-9-9(X))* Diakonia Publishing.
Allman, Cynthia. Olden Days of Medina: A Children's Guide to Medina History. Lucht, Susan & Wilson, Mollie. 2013. iii, 30p. (J). pap. *(978-0-578-10958-9(1))* History Gal's Publishing.
Allman, Howard, photos by. Children's Book of Baking. Patchett, Fiona et al. 2007. (Children's Cooking Ser.). (ENG., 96p. (J). 17.99 *(978-0-7945-1438-9(3)*, Usborne) EDC Publishing.
—First Numbers. Brooks, Felicity & Litchfield, Jo. 2006. (Usborne First Numbers Ser.). 48p. (J). (gr. -1). pap. 8.99 *(978-0-7945-0746-6(8)*, Usborne) EDC Publishing.
—The Usborne Advent Nativity Book. Doherty, Gillian, ed. 2006. 12p. (J). (gr. -1-3). bds. 14.99 *(978-0-7945-1174-6(0)*, Usborne) EDC Publishing.
—The Usborne Book of Everyday Words. Litchfield, Jo. Treays, Rebecca et al, eds. 2006. (Everyday Words Ser.). 48p. (J). (gr. -1). lib. bdg. 15.99 *(978-1-58086-964-5(5))* EDC Publishing.
—Usborne Lift-The-Flap Nitivity. Litchfield, Jo. 2004. (J). *(978-0-439-68683-9(0))* Scholastic, Inc.
Allman, Howard, jt. photos by see MMStudios.
Allon, Jeffrey. The Chanukah Blessing. Schram, Peninnah. 2004. (J). (gr. -1-3). 13.95 *(978-0-8074-0733-2(X)*, 101973) URJ Pr.
—The 40 Greatest Jewish Stories Ever Told, 4 vols., Set. Goldin, Barbara Diamond et al. 2005. 192p. (J). (gr. 1-4). 49.95 *(978-0-943706-89-4(0)*, Devora Publishing) Simcha Media Group.
Allred, Mike. Good Omens, Vol. 1. Milligan, Peter. 2003. (X-Statix Ser.). 128p. (YA). pap. 11.99 *(978-0-7851-1059-0(3))* Marvel Worldwide, Inc.

—X-Force: Famous, Mutant & Mortal. Milligan, Peter. 2003. (X-Statix Ser.). 352p. (YA). 29.99 (978-0-7851-1023-1(2)) Marvel Worldwide, Inc.

—X-Statix: the Complete Collection Vol. 1. 2020. (ENG.). 504p. (gr. 10-17). pap. 39.99 (978-1-302-92403-4(6)) Marvel Worldwide, Inc.

Allsop, Sophie, et al. Princess: A Glittering Guide for Young Ladies. Sparklington, Madame & Gurney, Stella. 2006. (Genuine & Moste Authentic Guide Ser.: 2). (ENG.). 26p. (J). (gr. 1-4). 15.99 (978-0-7636-3430-8(1)) Candlewick Pr.

Allsop, Sophie. The Ballerina's Handbook. Castle, Kate. 2009. (ENG.). 22p. (J). (gr. 1-4). 14.99 (978-0-7636-4552-6(4), Templar) Candlewick Pr.

—Easter Love Letters from God: Bible Stories, 1 vol. Nellist, Glenys. 2018. (Love Letters from God Ser.). (ENG.). 32p. (J). 16.99 (978-0-310-76065-8(8)) Zonderkidz.

—The Good Samaritan & Other Parables of Jesus. Rock, Lois. ed. 2018. (ENG.). 48p. (J). (gr. k-2). 14.99 (978-0-7459-6557-4(1)) Lion Hudson PLC GBR. Dist: Independent Pubs. Group.

—Goodnight, Angels, 1 vol. Carlson, Melody. 2011. (ENG.). 32p. (J). 15.99 (978-0-310-71687-7(X)) Zonderkidz.

Allsopp, Sophie, et al. Horse: The Essential Guide for Young Equestrians. Stoddard, Rosie & Marshall, Phillip. Hamilton, Libby, ed. 2008. (Genuine & Moste Authentic Guide Ser.: 4). (ENG.). 32p. (J). (gr. 1-4). 16.99 (978-0-7636-3547-3(2)) Candlewick Pr.

Allsopp, Sophie. The Lion Bible to Keep for Ever. Rock, Lois. ed. (ENG.). 320p. (J). (gr. 2-4). 2016. 12.99 (978-0-7459-7635-8(2)); 2014. 19.99 (978-0-7459-6487-4(7)) Lion Hudson PLC GBR. Dist: Independent Pubs. Group.

—The Lion Book of Prayers to Keep for Ever. Rock, Lois. ed. 2016. (ENG.). 64p. (J). (gr. 2-4). 7.99 (978-0-7459-7641-9(7)) Lion Hudson PLC GBR. Dist: Independent Pubs. Group.

—Love Letters from God: Bible Stories, 1 vol. Nellist, Glenys. 2014. (Love Letters from God Ser.). (ENG.). 40p. (J). 16.99 (978-0-310-73384-3(7)) Zonderkidz.

—My Little Golden Book about Balto. Lovitt, Charles. 2019. (Little Golden Book Ser.). 24p. (J). (-k). 4.99 (978-1-9848-9352-9(1), Golden Bks.) Random Hse. Children's Bks.

—Noah's Ark. Rock, Lois. ed. 2012. (ENG.). 32p. (J). (gr. k-2). 6.99 (978-0-7459-6321-1(8)) Lion Hudson PLC GBR. Dist: Independent Pubs. Group.

—Thank You, God! A Year of Blessings & Prayers for Little Ones. 2009. (ENG.). 16p. (J). (gr. -1-3). 12.99 (978-1-4169-4754-7(X), Little Simon Inspirations) Little Simon Inspirations.

Allsopp, Sophie, jt. illus. see Conner, Sarah.

Allwright, Deborah. Best Pet Ever. Roberts, Victoria. 2011. (ENG.). 32p. pap. 7.95 (978-1-58925-432-9(5)) Tiger Tales.

—Dinosaur Sleepover. Edwards, Pamela Duncan. 2013. (J). (978-1-4351-4923-6(8)) Barnes & Noble, Inc.

—Don't Read This Book! Lewis, Jill. 2010. (ENG.). 32p. (J). (gr. -1-2). 15.95 (978-1-58925-094-9(X)) Tiger Tales.

—The Fox in the Dark. Green, Alison. (ENG.). 32p. (J). (gr. -1-1). 2012. pap. 7.95 (978-1-58925-437-4(6)); 2010. 15.95 (978-1-58925-091-8(5)) Tiger Tales.

—Hello! Is This Grandma? Whybrow, Ian. 2008. (Tiger Tales Ser.). 32p. (J). (gr. -1-2). 15.95 (978-1-58925-072-7(9)) Tiger Tales.

—Sinclair the Wonder Bear. Blackman, Malorie. 2nd ed. 2016. (Reading Ladder Ser.). (ENG.). 48p. (J). (gr. k-2). pap. 7.99 (978-1-4052-8203-1(7)) Egmont Bks., Ltd. GBR. Dist: Independent Pubs. Group.

—Sinclair, Wonder Bear. Blackman, Malorie. 2005. (Blue Go Bananas Ser.). (ENG.). 48p. (J). (gr. 1-2). (978-0-7787-2653-1(3)); lib. bdg. (978-0-7787-2631-9(2)) Crabtree Publishing Co.

—There's a Monster in My Fridge: With Fun Split Pages. Hart, Caryl. 2016. (ENG.). 24p. (J). (gr. -1-2). pap. 7.99 (978-1-4380-0824-0(4), B.E.S. Publishing) Peterson's.

—Where Are My Shoes? Wallace, Karen. 2005. (Reading Corner Ser.). 24p. (J). (gr. k-3). lib. bdg. 22.80 (978-1-59771-002-2(4)) Sea-To-Sea Pubns.

Allyn, Virginia. Hush-a-Bye Counting: A Bedtime Book. McLeod, Kris Aro. 2008. (ENG.). 20p. (J). (gr. -1). 14.95 (978-1-58117-785-5(2), Intervisual/Piggy Toes) Bendon, Inc.

—Night Night Bible Stories: 30 Stories for Bedtime, 1 vol. Parker, Amy. 2019. (Night Night Ser.). (ENG.). 208p. (J). 16.99 (978-1-4002-0891-3(2)) Nelson, Thomas Inc.

—Night Night, Bunny, 1 vol. Parker, Amy. 2020. (Night Night Ser.). (ENG.). 20p. (J). bds. 9.99 (978-1-4002-1273-6(1)) Nelson, Thomas Inc.

—Night Night Devotions: 90 Devotions for Bedtime, 1 vol. Parker, Amy. 2019. (Night Night Ser.). (ENG.). 208p. (J). 16.99 (978-1-4002-0890-6(4)) Nelson, Thomas Inc.

—Night Night, Farm, 1 vol. Parker, Amy. 2016. (Night Night Ser.). (ENG.). 20p. (J). bds. 8.99 (978-0-7180-8831-6(X)) Nelson, Thomas Inc.

—Night Night, Farm Touch & Feel, 1 vol. Parker, Amy. 2018. (Night Night Ser.). (ENG.). 18p. (J). bds. 12.99 (978-1-4003-1059-3(8)) Nelson, Thomas Inc.

—Night Night, Jungle, 1 vol. Parker, Amy. 2018. (Night Night Ser.). (ENG.). 20p. (J). bds. 9.99 (978-0-7180-9086-9(1)) Nelson, Thomas Inc.

Allyn, Virginia. Night Night, Pumpkin, 1 vol. Parker, Amy. 2020. (Night Night Ser.). (ENG.). 20p. (J). bds. 9.99 **(978-1-4002-1281-1(2))** Nelson, Thomas Inc.

Allyn, Virginia. Night Night, Sleepytown, 1 vol. Parker, Amy. 2018. (Night Night Ser.). (ENG.). 20p. (J). bds. 9.99 (978-1-4003-1003-6(2)) Nelson, Thomas Inc.

—Night Night, Train, 1 vol. Parker, Amy. 2017. (Night Night Ser.). (ENG.). 20p. (J). bds. 9.99 (978-0-7180-8932-0(4)) Nelson, Thomas Inc.

—Night Night, Zoo, 1 vol. Parker, Amy. 2019. (Night Night Ser.). (ENG.). 20p. (J). bds. 9.99 (978-1-4003-1014-2(8)) Nelson, Thomas Inc.

Almada, Baraciel. Murphie & the Meerkat. Holley, Kim. 2016. (ENG.). (J). (gr. k-3). pap. 14.00 (978-1-939054-75-3(3)) Rowe Publishing.

Almada, Marcos. Marina la Furiosa. Martinez Sandoval, Jaime Alfonso. 2016. (Cuentamelo Otra Vez Ser.). (ENG & SPA.). (J). 16.95 (978-1-68165-259-7(5)) Trialtea USA, LLC.

Almanstotter, Susanne. Pompety-Pooh: Purplest Penguin in Zonkety Zoo. Beggs, Melissa. Laible, Steve William, ed. 2013. 52p. pap. 12.95 (978-0-9844784-9-1(3), Empire Holdings) Kodel Group, LLC, The.

Almanza, Roberto. Trixie & Dixie: The Mystery of the Missing Cape. Tamez, Juliza. 2013. (ENG.). (J). 12.95 (978-1-62086-426-5(6)) Mascot Bks., Inc.

Almara, Dono Sanchez, jt. illus. see Sanchez Almara, Dono.

Almasty. Greek Gods & Heroes: 40 Inspiring Icons. Baussier, Sylvie. 2018. (40 Inspiring Icons Ser.). (ENG.). 88p. (J). (gr. 2-5). 14.99 **(978-1-78603-143-3(4)**, Wide Eyed Editions) Quarto Publishing Group UK GBR. Dist: Hachette Bk. Group.

Almeda, Christine. Sarai & the Meaning of Awesome. Gonzalez, Sarai & Brown, Monica. 2018. (Sarai Ser.: 1). 112p. (J). (gr. 2-5). (ENG.). pap. 5.99 (978-1-338-23668-2(7)); (SPA.). pap. 5.99 (978-1-338-33055-7(1), Scholastic en Espanol) Scholastic, Inc.

—Saraí en Primer Plano. Gonzalez, Sarai & Brown, Monica. 2018. (Saraí Ser.: 2). (SPA.). 112p. (J). (gr. 2-5). pap. 5.99 (978-1-338-33056-4(X), Scholastic en Espanol) Scholastic, Inc.

—Sarai in the Spotlight! Gonzalez, Sarai & Brown, Monica. 2018. (Sarai Ser.: 2). (ENG.). 112p. (J). (gr. 2-5). pap. 5.99 (978-1-338-23669-9(5)) Scholastic, Inc.

Almeyda, Tonito Avalon. Billy's Mountain Adventure, 1 vol. Arnold, Ginger Fudge. 2010. 32p. pap. 24.95 (978-1-4489-5582-4(3)) PublishAmerica, Inc.

Almon, Claire. Ballet Breakdown. Gurevich, Margaret. 2018. (Academy of Dance Ser.). (ENG.). 72p. (J). (gr. 3-6). lib. bdg. 25.32 (978-1-4965-6206-7(2), 137815, Stone Arch Bks.) Capstone.

—BFF Breakup. Gurevich, Margaret. 2018. (Academy of Dance Ser.). (ENG.). 72p. (J). (gr. 3-6). lib. bdg. 25.32 (978-1-4965-6205-0(4), 137814, Stone Arch Bks.) Capstone.

Almon, Claire. The Clue is in the Poop: And Other Things Too. Seed, Andy. 2018. (ENG.). 64p. (J). (gr. k-6). 17.95 **(978-1-68297-371-4(9))** QEB Publishing Inc.

Almon, Claire. Dance Team Bully. Gurevich, Margaret. 2018. (Academy of Dance Ser.). (ENG.). 72p. (J). (gr. 3-6). lib. bdg. 25.32 (978-1-4965-6203-6(8), 137812, Stone Arch Bks.) Capstone.

—Everybody's Favorite Book. Allegra, Mike. 2018. (ENG.). 40p. (J). 17.99 (978-1-250-13276-5(2), 900177152) Imprint IND. Dist: Macmillan.

—Fearless Mary: The True Adventures of Mary Fields, American Stagecoach Driver. Charles, Tami. 2019. (ENG.). 32p. (J). (gr. -1-3). 16.99 (978-0-8075-2305-6(4), 807523054) Whitman, Albert & Co.

—Hip-Hop Road Trip. Gurevich, Margaret. 2018. (Academy of Dance Ser.). (ENG.). 72p. (J). (gr. 3-6). lib. bdg. 25.32 (978-1-4965-6204-3(6), 137813, Stone Arch Bks.) Capstone.

—Ice Breaker: How Mabel Fairbanks Changed Figure Skating. Viña, Rose. 2019. (She Made History Ser.). (ENG.). 32p. (J). (gr. -1-3). 16.99 (978-0-8075-3496-0(X), 080753496X) Whitman, Albert & Co.

—Penny & Penelope. Richards, Dan. 2019. (ENG.). 40p. (J). 17.99 (978-1-250-15607-5(6), 900184824) Imprint IND. Dist: Macmillan.

Almora, Krystal. Kelsey Hates the Needle. Wagner, Mary. 2019. (ENG.). 30p. (J). (gr. -1-3). pap. 14.95 (978-1-64096-776-2(1)) Newman Springs Publishing, Inc.

AlohaHawaii & Lightfield Studios. The Martin Luther King Mitzvah. Tekulsky, Mathew. 2018. (ENG.). 152p. (J). (gr. 4-7). pap. 12.95 (978-1-947548-08-4(5), Fitzroy Bks.) Regal Hse. Publishing, LLC.

Aloise, Frank. Experiments with MacHines & Matter. Sootin, Harry. 2012. 96p. 38.95 (978-1-258-23744-8(X)); pap. 23.95 (978-1-258-24341-8(5)) Literary Licensing, LLC.

Aloisi, Giuliano. Danger on the Reef. Maddox, Jake. 2020. (Jake Maddox Adventure Ser.). (ENG.). 72p. (J). (gr. 3-6). pap. 5.95 (978-1-4965-9206-4(9), 142234); lib. bdg. 25.32 (978-1-4965-8700-8(6), 141436) Capstone. (Stone Arch Bks.).

—The Digestive System: Bridges Edition, Set Of 10. Loughran, Donna. 2013. (Prime Plus Ser.). (J). (gr. 6-8). 99.00 net. (978-1-4509-9945-8(X)) Benchmark Education Co.

—The Digestive System: Prime Bridges Edition. Loughran, Donna. 2013. (Prime Ser.). (YA). (gr. 6-8). pap. (978-1-4509-9696-9(5)) Benchmark Education Co.

—The Digestive System: Set Of 10. Loughran, Donna. 2013. (Prime Plus Ser.). (J). (gr. 6-8). 99.00 net. (978-1-4509-9921-2(2)) Benchmark Education Co.

—Extreme Ice Adventure. Maddox, Jake. 2020. (Jake Maddox Adventure Ser.). (ENG.). 72p. (J). (gr. 3-6). pap. 5.95 (978-1-4965-9205-7(0), 142233); lib. bdg. 25.32 (978-1-4965-8698-8(0), 141435) Capstone. (Stone Arch Bks.).

—Geography of Africa: Bridges Edition. Simpson, Kathleen. 2015. (Prime Plus Ser.). (YA). (gr. 6-8). pap. (978-1-4900-1956-7(1)) Benchmark Education Co.

—Geography of Africa: Bridges Edition Set of 6 with Common Core Indicators. Simpson, Kathleen. 2015. (Prime Plus Ser.). (YA). (gr. 6-8). 69.00 net. (978-1-4900-2052-5(7)) Benchmark Education Co.

—Geography of Asia & Australia: Bridges Edition. Simpson, Kathleen. 2015. (Prime Plus Ser.). (YA). (gr. 6-8). pap. (978-1-4900-1957-4(X)) Benchmark Education Co.

—Geography of Asia & Australia: Bridges Edition Set of 6 with Common Core Indicators. Simpson, Kathleen. 2015. (Prime Plus Ser.). (YA). (gr. 6-8). 69.00 net. (978-1-4900-2053-2(5)) Benchmark Education Co.

—Geography of Europe: Bridges Edition. Simpson, Kathleen. 2015. (Prime Plus Ser.). (YA). (gr. 6-8). pap. (978-1-4900-1959-8(6)) Benchmark Education Co.

—Geography of Europe: Bridges Edition Set of 6 with Common Core Indicators. Simpson, Kathleen. 2015. (Prime Plus Ser.). (YA). (gr. 6-8). 69.00 net. (978-1-4900-2055-6(1)) Benchmark Education Co.

—Geography of the Americas: Bridges Edition. Simpson, Kathleen. 2015. (Prime Plus Ser.). (YA). (gr. 6-8). pap. (978-1-4900-1958-1(8)) Benchmark Education Co.

—Geography of the Americas: Bridges Edition Set of 6 with Common Core Indicators. Simpson, Kathleen. 2015. (Prime Plus Ser.). (YA). (gr. 6-8). 69.00 net. (978-1-4900-2054-9(3)) Benchmark Education Co.

—How to Live Like an Aztec Priest. Farndon, John. 2016. (How to Live Like ... Ser.). (ENG.). 32p. (J). (gr. 3-6). 27.99 (978-1-5124-0628-3(7), 9781512406283, Hungry Tomato ®) Lerner Publishing Group.

—The Human Body Structure & Function: Bridges Edition, Set Of 10. Stiefel, Chana. 2013. (Prime Plus Ser.). (J). (gr. 6-8). 99.00 net. (978-1-4509-9941-0(7)) Benchmark Education Co.

—The Human Body Structure & Function: Prime Bridges Edition. Stiefel, Chana. 2013. (Prime Ser.). (YA). (gr. 6-8). pap. (978-1-4509-9692-1(2)) Benchmark Education Co.

—The Human Body Structure & Function: Set Of 10. Stiefel, Chana. 2013. (Prime Plus Ser.). (J). (gr. 6-8). 99.00 net. (978-1-4509-9917-5(4)) Benchmark Education Co.

—Jake Maddox Adventure. Maddox, Jake. 2020. (Jake Maddox Adventure Ser.). (ENG.). (J). (gr. 3-6). 101.28 (978-1-4965-8702-2(2), 29778); pap., pap., pap. 23.80 (978-1-4965-9251-4(4), 29960) Capstone. (Stone Arch Bks.).

—The Muscular & Skeletal Systems: Prime Bridges Edition. Loughran, Donna. 2013. (Prime Ser.). (YA). (gr. 6-8). pap. (978-1-4509-9695-2(7)) Benchmark Education Co.

—The Muscular & Skeletal Systems Systems: Bridges Edition, Set Of 10. Loughran, Donna. 2013. (Prime Plus Ser.). (J). (gr. 6-8). 99.00 net. (978-1-4509-9944-1(1)) Benchmark Education Co.

—The Muscular & Skeletal Systems Systems: Set Of 10. Loughran, Donna. 2013. (Prime Plus Ser.). (J). (gr. 6-8). 99.00 net. (978-1-4509-9920-5(4)) Benchmark Education Co.

—The Nervous & Endocrine Systems: Bridges Edition, Set Of 10. Montgomery, Heather. 2013. (Prime Plus Ser.). (J). (gr. 6-8). 99.00 net. (978-1-4509-9943-4(3)) Benchmark Education Co.

—The Nervous & Endocrine Systems: Prime Bridges Edition. Montgomery, Heather. 2013. (Prime Ser.). (YA). (gr. 6-8). pap. (978-1-4509-9694-5(9)) Benchmark Education Co.

—The Nervous & Endocrine Systems: Set Of 10. Montgomery, Heather. 2013. (Prime Plus Ser.). (J). (gr. 6-8). 99.00 net. (978-1-4509-9919-9(0)) Benchmark Education Co.

—Obstacle Challenge. Maddox, Jake. 2020. (Jake Maddox Adventure Ser.). (ENG.). 72p. (J). (gr. 3-6). pap. 5.95 (978-1-4965-9204-0(2), 142232); lib. bdg. 25.32 (978-1-4965-8696-4(4), 141434) Capstone. (Stone Arch Bks.).

—Physical & Human Geography: Bridges Edition. Simpson, Kathleen. 2015. (Prime Plus Ser.). (YA). (gr. 6-8). pap. (978-1-4900-1955-0(3)) Benchmark Education Co.

—Physical & Human Geography: Bridges Edition Set of 6 with Common Core Indicators. Simpson, Kathleen. 2015. (Prime Plus Ser.). (YA). (gr. 6-8). 69.00 net. (978-1-4900-2051-8(9)) Benchmark Education Co.

—The Respiratory & Circulatory Systems: Bridges Edition, Set Of 10. Montgomery, Heather. 2013. (Prime Plus Ser.). (J). (gr. 6-8). 99.00 net. (978-1-4509-9942-7(5)) Benchmark Education Co.

—The Respiratory & Circulatory Systems: Prime Bridges Edition. Montgomery, Heather. 2013. (Prime Ser.). (YA). (gr. 6-8). pap. (978-1-4509-9693-8(0)) Benchmark Education Co.

—The Respiratory & Circulatory Systems: Set Of 10. Montgomery, Heather. 2013. (Prime Plus Ser.). (J). (gr. 6-8). 99.00 net. (978-1-4509-9918-2(2)) Benchmark Education Co.

—Trail Trouble. Maddox, Jake. 2020. (Jake Maddox Adventure Ser.). (ENG.). 72p. (J). (gr. 3-6). pap. 5.95 (978-1-4965-9203-3(4), 142231); lib. bdg. 25.32 (978-1-4965-8694-0(8), 141433) Capstone. (Stone Arch Bks.).

Alon Curiel, Gil-Ly. Passing By. Tepper, Yona. Guthman, Deborah, tr. from HEB. 2010. (ENG.). 40p. (J). (gr. -1-3). 9.99 (978-1-935279-36-5(X)) Kane Miller.

Alonso, Cynthia. Aquarium. 2018. (ENG.). 40p. (J). (gr. -1-k). 17.99 (978-1-4521-6875-3(X)) Chronicle Bks. LLC.

—Under the Canopy: Tales of Trees. Volant, Iris. 2018. 56p. (J). (gr. 2). 19.95 (978-1-911171-42-3(9)) Flying Eye Bks. GBR. Dist: Penguin Random Hse. LLC.

Alonso, Denis. Daniel & the Lions' Den. 2017. 32p. (J). (978-1-5182-5384-3(9)) Zonderkidz.

—Frankly, I Never Wanted to Kiss Anybody! The Story of the Frog Prince As Told by the Frog. Loewen, Nancy. 2013. (Other Side of the Story Ser.). (ENG.). 24p. (J). (gr. -1-3). 27.99 (978-1-4048-8304-8(5), Picture Window Bks.) Capstone.

—Frankly, I Never Wanted to Kiss Anybody! The Story of the Frog Prince, As Told by the Frog. Loewen, Nancy. 2013. (Other Side of the Story Ser.). (ENG.). 24p. (J). (gr. -1-3). 9.95 (978-1-4795-1948-4(0), Picture Window Bks.) Capstone.

—Really, Rapunzel Needed a Haircut! The Story of Rapunzel, as Told by Dame Gothel. Gunderson, Jessica. 2013. (Other Side of the Story Ser.). (ENG.). 24p. (J). (gr. -1-3). 27.99 (978-1-4048-7941-6(2), Picture Window Bks.) Capstone.

—Really, Rapunzel Needed a Haircut! The Story of Rapunzel As Told by Dame Gothel. Gunderson, Jessica. 2013. (Other Side of the Story Ser.). (ENG.). 24p. (J). (gr. -1-3). 9.95 (978-1-4795-1946-0(4), Picture Window Bks.) Capstone.

Alonso, Denis & Tayal, Amit. Frankly, I Never Wanted to Kiss Anybody! The Story of the Frog Prince, As Told by the Frog. Loewen, Nancy. 2013. (Other Side of the Story Ser.). (ENG.). 24p. (J). (gr. -1-3). pap. 6.95 (978-1-4795-1952-1(9), Picture Window Bks.) Capstone.

—Really, Rapunzel Needed a Haircut! The Story of Rapunzel As Told by Dame Gothel. Gunderson, Jessica & Loewen, Nancy. 2013. (Other Side of the Story Ser.). (ENG.). 24p. (J). (gr. -1-3). pap. 6.95 (978-1-4795-1950-7(2), Picture Window Bks.) Capstone.

Alonso Díaz-Toledo, Juan Ramón. Anastasia Tiene las Respuestas. Lois, Lowry. Bustelo, Ana, tr. 2003. (Anastasia Krupnik Ser.).Tr. of Anastasia Has the Answers. (SPA.). 160p. (J). 9.95 (978-84-239-6334-8(9)) Espasa Calpe, S.A. ESP. Dist: Planeta Publishing Corp., Lectorum Pubns., Inc.

Alonso, Jesus, jt. illus. see Alvarez, Jose M.

Alonso, Juan. The Early Cretaceous Volume 1: Notes, Drawings, & Observations from Prehistory. Paul, Gregory. 2017. (Ancient Earth Journal Ser.). (ENG.). 48p. (J). (gr. 3-8). lib. bdg. 31.99 (978-1-942875-30-7(4), Walter Foster Jr) Quarto Publishing Group USA.

Alonso, Juan Carlos. The Early Cretaceous Volume 2: Notes, Drawings, & Observations from Prehistory. Alonso, Juan Carlos. Paul, Gregory. 2017. (Ancient Earth Journal Ser.). (ENG.). 48p. (J). (gr. 3-8). lib. bdg. 31.99 (978-1-942875-31-4(2), Walter Foster Jr) Quarto Publishing Group USA.

—The Late Jurassic: Notes, Drawings, & Observations from Prehistory. Alonso, Juan Carlos. Paul, Gregory. 2017. (Ancient Earth Journal Ser.). (ENG.). 48p. (J). (gr. 3-8). lib. bdg. 31.99 (978-1-942875-33-8(9), Walter Foster Jr) Quarto Publishing Group USA.

—The Late Jurassic Vol. 1: Notes, Drawings, & Observations from Prehistory. Alonso, Juan Carlos. Paul, Gregory. 2017. (Ancient Earth Journal Ser.). (ENG.). 48p. (J). (gr. 3-8). lib. bdg. 31.99 (978-1-942875-32-1(0), Walter Foster Jr) Quarto Publishing Group USA.

Alonso, Juan Ramon. Anastasia Vive Aqui. Lois, Lowry. 2003. (Anastasia Krupnik Ser.). (SPA.). 160p. (J). 9.95 (978-84-670-0073-3(2)) Espasa Calpe, S.A. ESP. Dist: Planeta Publishing Corp.

—El Lugar Mas Bonito del Mundo. Cameron, Ann. 2003. (SPA.). 70p. (gr. 3-5). pap. 8.95 (978-968-19-0402-9(8)) Santillana USA Publishing Co., Inc.

—Por Tierras de Pan Llevar. Farias, Juan & Juan, Farias. (SPA.). 96p. (J). (978-84-392-8726-1(7)) Gaviota Ediciones ESP. Dist: Lectorum Pubns., Inc.

Alonso, Marvin. The Fairy Godmother Helps the Monarchs. Stark Ph D, Amy L. 2019. (Fairy Godmother Next Door Ser.: Vol. 3). (ENG.). 38p. (J). pap. 9.99 (978-1-7292-2188-4(2)) Independently Published.

—Great Catch, Sarafina! Bacon, Carol a. 2017. (ENG.). (J). (gr. k-3). pap. 10.99 (978-0-9981543-3-6(4)) Himari Publishing.

Alonso, Marvin. Loolee & Sparty: Welcome Home! Robles, Gina Melissa. 2018. (ENG.). 34p. (J). 19.99 **(978-0-578-50265-6(8))** New Age Beauty Corp.

—Loolee & the Boyz: The Way Loolee Loves. Hartkemeyer, Kirk & Robles, Gina Melissa. 2020. (ENG.). 34p. (J). pap. 9.99 **(978-1-7346298-0-4(0))** New Age Beauty Corp.

Alonso, Marvin. Pepper's Forever Home. Finkbeiner, Betty Ladley. 2013. (ENG.). 24p. pap. 10.99 (978-1-4797-6982-7(7)) Xlibris Corp.

—Sylvander: Finds a Gift of True Happiness. McCray-Garrison, Rispba N. Brenda, Olson, ed. 2018. (Sylvander Ser.: Vol. 1). (ENG.). 38p. (J). (gr. k-6). 19.95 (978-0-692-16987-2(3)) McCray-Garrison, Rispba.

—A Time to Shine: How to Help a Friend Who Is Being Bullied. Phillips, Jacqui. 2018. (Adventures of Stushy & Bello! Ser.: Vol. 1). (ENG.). 46p. (J). (gr. k-3). pap. 9.99 (978-0-9994550-4-3(4)) PHILLIPS, JACQUELINE J. LLC.

—A Time to Shine: How to Help a Friend Who Is Being Bullied - Coloring Book: the Adventures of Stushy & Bello! Phillips, Jacqui. 2018. (Adventures of Stushy & Bello! Ser.: Vol. 1). (ENG.). 28p. (J). (gr. k-3). pap. 8.99 (978-0-9994550-6-7(0)) PHILLIPS, JACQUELINE J. LLC.

Alpaugh, Priscilla. Hold This, 1 vol. Scoppettone, Carolyn Cory. 2015. (ENG.). 32p. (J). 17.95 (978-1-939017-68-0(8), 807eace7-5b53-4e13-842e-5d7e60666fdd) Islandport Pr., Inc.

Alpaugh, Priscilla. Noodle Helps Gabriel Say Goodbye. Rivadeneira, Caryn. 2020. (Helper Hounds Ser.). (ENG.). 72p. (J). (gr. 1-3). pap. 6.99 **(978-1-63440-918-6(3))**; lib. bdg. 12.99 **(978-1-63440-915-5(9))** Red Chair Pr.

Alpaugh, Priscilla. Penny Helps Portia Face Her Fears. Rivadeneira, Caryn. 2020. (Helper Hounds Ser.). (ENG.). 72p. (J). (gr. 1-3). pap. 6.99 (978-1-63440-778-6(4)); lib. bdg. 12.99 (978-1-63440-775-5(X)) Red Chair Pr.

Alpaugh, Priscilla. Robot Helps Max & Lily Deal with Bullies. Rivadeneira, Caryn. 2020. (Helper Hounds Ser.). (ENG.). 72p. (J). (gr. 1-3). pap. 6.99 **(978-1-63440-779-3(2))**; lib. bdg. 12.99 **(978-1-63440-776-2(8))** Red Chair Pr.

—Space Mice. Houran, Lori Haskins. 2020. (ENG.). 32p. (J). (gr. -1-3). 16.99 **(978-0-8075-7553-6(4)**, 807575534) Whitman, Albert & Co.

Alpaugh, Priscilla. Sparky Helps Mary Make Friends. Rivadeneira, Caryn. 2020. (Helper Hounds Ser.). (ENG.). 72p. (J). (gr. 1-3). pap. 6.99 (978-1-63440-777-9(6)); lib. bdg. 12.99 (978-1-63440-774-8(1)) Red Chair Pr.

Alpern, Andrew, photos by. How It's Made: Torah Scroll, Vol. Ofanansky, Allison. 2016. (ENG.). (J). (978-1-68115-516-6(8)) Behrman Hse., Inc.

—How It's Made Matzah. Ofanansky, Allison. 2017. 32p. (J). (978-1-68115-524-1(9)) Behrman Hse., Inc.

Alpern, Eliyahu. Sukkot Treasure Hunt, Vol. Alpern, Eliyahu, photos by. Ofanansky, Allison. 2009. (Sukkot & Simchat Torah Ser.). (ENG.). 32p. (J). (gr. -1-5). 15.95 (978-0-8225-8763-7(7), Kar-Ben Publishing) Lerner Publishing Group.

—What's the Buzz? Honey for a Sweet New Year. Alpern, Eliyahu, photos by. Ofanansky, Allison. 2011. (High Holidays Ser.). (J). (gr. -1-k). lib. bdg. 15.95 (978-0-7613-5640-0(1)) Lerner Publishing Group.

Alpern, Eliyahu, photos by. How It's Made: Hanukkah Menorah. Ofanansky, Allison. 2018. 32p. (J). *(978-1-68115-534-0(6)*, Apples & Honey Pr.) Behrman Hse., Inc.

—New Month, New Moon. Ofanansky, Allison Maile. 2014. (ENG., 32p. (J). (gr. -1-2). 16.95 *(978-1-4677-1945-2(5)*, 9781467719452, Kar-Ben Publishing) Lerner Publishing Group.

—Tisha B'Av: A Jerusalem Journey. Ofanansky, Allison Maile. ed. 2017. (ENG., 32p. (J). (gr. -1-3). E-Book 27.99 *(978-1-5124-2719-6(5)*, 9781512427196); Vol. 16.99 *(978-1-4677-8930-1(5)*, 9781467789301) Lerner Publishing Group. (Kar-Ben Publishing).

Alphenaar, Pamela L. Crackerjack the Christmas Cat. Dorner, Nancy L. 2008. 40p. pap. 16.95 *(978-0-9818488-0-8(X))* Ajoyin Publishing, Inc.

Alphona, Adrian. Ms. Marvel: Kamala Khan. 2019. 120p. (YA). (gr. 4-7). pap. 12.99 *(978-1-302-91640-4(8))* Marvel Worldwide, Inc.

Alphona, Adrian, et al. Ms. Marvel Vol. 3. 2017. 272p. (YA). (gr. 8-17). 34.99 *(978-1-302-90361-9(6))* Marvel Worldwide, Inc.

Alphona, Adrian. Runaways: Pride & Joy. Vaughn, Brian K. 2004. (X-Men Ser.). 144p. (YA). pap. 14.99 *(978-0-7851-1244-0(8))* Marvel Worldwide, Inc.

—Runaways: Pride & Joy Marvel Select Edition. 2020. 152p. (YA). (gr. 8-17). 24.99 *(978-1-302-92124-8(X))* Marvel Worldwide, Inc.

—Runaways Vol. 4: True Believers. 2017. (ENG.). 160p. (YA). (gr. 8-17). pap. 14.99 *(978-1-302-90869-0(3))* Marvel Worldwide, Inc.

—Runaways Vol. 6: Parental Guidance. 2017. (ENG.). 152p. (YA). (gr. 8-17). pap. 14.99 *(978-1-302-90871-3(5))* Marvel Worldwide, Inc.

Alphona, Adrian, jt. illus. see Norton, Mike.

Alrubaye, Salim, jt. illus. see Fiume, Cosimo.

Alsonso, Denis, jt. illus. see Tayal, Amit.

Alston, Brad. The Adventures of Abigale Green in Spain. Green, Elaine. 2012. 38p. (J). 14.95 *(978-1-937406-10-3(5))* Mascot Bks., Inc.

Alston, Sheila Y., photos by. Faith, Love & Life. Alston, Stanley E. Sharps, Angelique, ed. 48p. (YA). (gr. 4-18). pap. 12.95 *(978-0-9719897-0-2(2))* Magnatic Music.

Alter, Amanda. I'm Just a Little Someone. Peters, Sharen S. 2017. (Friends for Life Ser.: Vol. 1). (ENG.). (J). 14.95 *(978-0-9971221-0-7(2))* Lifelong Friends Pub.

Alter, Anna. Priscilla & the Hollyhocks. Broyles, Anne. 32p. (J). (gr. 1-4). 2019. pap. 7.99 *(978-1-57091-676-2(4))*; 2008. 15.95 *(978-1-57091-675-5(6))* Charlesbridge Publishing, Inc.

Alter, Anna. Francine's Day. Alter, Anna. 2003. 32p. (J). lib. bdg. 16.89 *(978-0-06-623937-8(0))* HarperCollins Pubs.

Altés, Marta. Confessions of a Dork Lord. Johnston, Mike. 2020. 352p. (J). (gr. 3-7). 13.99 *(978-1-5247-4081-8(0)*, G.P. Putnam's Sons Books for Young Readers) Penguin Young Readers Group.

—Just So Stories. Kipling, Rudyard. 2020. (ENG.). 96p. (J). (gr. 3-7). 17.99 *(978-1-68412-674-3(6)*, Silver Dolphin Bks.) Printers Row Publishing Group.

Altes, Marta. The King Cat. Altes, Marta. ed. 2016. (ENG.). 32p. (J). (gr. -1-k). pap. 11.99 ***(978-1-4472-5899-5(1)***, Macmillan Children's Bks.) Pan Macmillan GBR. Dist: Independent Pubs. Group.

Althea, Erin & Bertino, Mike. Recipe. Petrella, Angela et al. 2013. 48p. (J). (gr. -1-3). 17.95 *(978-1-936365-84-5(7)*, 9bfc91d0-bde8-495d-be28-6ad121e23930) McSweeney's Publishing.

Altman, Scott. Attack of the Shark-Headed Zombie. Doyle, Bill. 2011. (Stepping Stone Book(TM) Ser.). (ENG.). 112p. (J). (gr. 1-4). 5.99 *(978-0-375-86675-3(2)*, Random Hse. Bks. for Young Readers) Random Hse. Children's Bks.

Altmann, S. Drawing Aliens, Spacecraft, & Other Stuff Beyond the Galaxy: 4D an Augmented Reading Drawing Experience. Cella, Clara. 2018. (Drawing With 4D Ser.). (ENG.). 32p. (J). (gr. 3-9). lib. bdg. 31.99 *(978-1-5435-3187-9(3)*, 138813, Capstone Pr.) Capstone.

Altmann, Scott. Big City Blues: Back to Wonderland, 1 vol. Fields, Jan. 2013. (Adventures in Extreme Reading Ser.). (ENG.). 112p. (J). (gr. 2-5). 29.93 *(978-1-61641-923-3(7)*, 66, Calico Chapter Bks.) ABDO Publishing Co.

—The Calm Before the Storm: A Night in Sleepy Hollow, 1 vol. Fields, Jan. 2013. (Adventures in Extreme Reading Ser.). (ENG.). 112p. (J). (gr. 2-5). 29.93 *(978-1-61641-920-2(2)*, 60, Calico Chapter Bks.) ABDO Publishing Co.

—Crazy Horse: Brave Warrior, 5. Hood, Ann. 2013. (Treasure Chest: the Time-Traveling Adventures of the Robbins Twins Ser.: 5). (ENG.). 192p. (J). (gr. 4-6). 18.69 *(978-0-448-45738-3(5))* Penguin Young Readers Group.

—Fairy Fashion. 2008. (Dover Coloring Bks.). (ENG.). 32p. (gr. k-5). pap. 3.99 *(978-0-486-46684-2(1))* Dover Pubns., Inc.

—Der Geheimnisvolle Mr. Spines - Wings, 1. Lethcoe, Jason. 2010. (Mysterious Mr. Spines Ser.: 1). 256p. (J). (gr. 6-8). 21.19 *(978-0-448-44653-0(7))* Penguin Young Readers Group.

—Hack Attack: A Trip to Wonderland, 1 vol. Fields, Jan. 2013. (Adventures in Extreme Reading Ser.). (ENG.). 112p. (J). (gr. 2-5). 29.93 *(978-1-61641-919-6(9)*, 58, Calico Chapter Bks.) ABDO Publishing Co.

—Lightning Strikes Twice: Escaping Great Expectations, 1 vol. Fields, Jan. 2013. (Adventures in Extreme Reading Ser.). (ENG.). 112p. (J). (gr. 2-5). 29.93 *(978-1-61641-922-6(9)*, 64, Calico Chapter Bks.) ABDO Publishing Co.

—A Novel Nightmare: The Purloined Story, 1 vol. Fields, Jan. 2013. (Adventures in Extreme Reading Ser.). (ENG.). 112p. (J). (gr. 2-5). 29.93 *(978-1-61641-924-0(5)*, 68, Calico Chapter Bks.) ABDO Publishing Co.

—Sea Monsters vs. Dragons: Showdown of the Legends, 1 vol. O'Hearn, Michael. 2011. (Monster Wars Ser.). (ENG.). 32p. (gr. 3-4). pap. 7.95 *(978-1-4296-7263-4(3))*; pap. 47.70 *(978-1-4296-7264-1(1))*; (J). lib. bdg. 28.65 *(978-1-4296-6523-0(8))* Capstone. (Capstone Pr.).

—Trapped in Stormy Seas: Sailing to Treasure Island, 1 vol. Fields, Jan. 2013. (Adventures in Extreme Reading Ser.). (ENG.). 112p. (J). (gr. 2-5). 29.93 *(978-1-61641-921-9(0)*, 62, Calico Chapter Bks.) ABDO Publishing Co.

—Wonder Woman & the Heroes of Myth. Korte, Steve. 2017. (Wonder Woman Mythology Ser.). (ENG.). 32p. (J). (gr. 5-9). lib. bdg. 27.32 *(978-1-5157-4585-3(6)*, Stone Arch Bks.) Capstone.

—Wonder Woman & the Monsters of Myth. Korte, Steve. 2017. (Wonder Woman Mythology Ser.). (ENG.). 32p. (J). (gr. 5-9). lib. bdg. 27.32 *(978-1-5157-4583-9(X)*, Stone Arch Bks.) Capstone.

—Wonder Woman & the Villains of Myth. Korte, Steve. 2017. (Wonder Woman Mythology Ser.). (ENG.). 32p. (J). (gr. 5-9). lib. bdg. 27.32 *(978-1-5157-4584-6(8)*, Stone Arch Bks.) Capstone.

—Wonder Woman & the World of Myth. Korte, Steve. 2017. (Wonder Woman Mythology Ser.). (ENG.). 32p. (J). (gr. 5-9). lib. bdg. 27.32 *(978-1-5157-4582-2(1)*, Stone Arch Bks.) Capstone.

Altmann, Scott & Zilber, Denis. Prince of Air, 4. Hood, Ann. 2012. (Treasure Chest: the Time-Traveling Adventures of the Robbins Twins Ser.: 4). 208p. (J). (gr. 4-6). 21.19 *(978-0-448-45474-0(2))* Penguin Young Readers Group.

Alvarado, Carol. Harry's Last Wish: A Story about Forever. Benz, Suzanne. 2007. (ENG.). 32p. (J). 24.95 *(978-0-944963-23-4(4))* Glastonbury Pr.

Alvarado, Dalia & Pacheco, Luis Gabriel. Maraca. Romero, Alfonso Suárez. rev. ed. 2006. (Castillo de la Lectura Verde Ser.). (SPA & ENG.). 120p. (J). (gr. 2-4). pap. 7.95 *(978-970-20-0128-7(5))* Castillo, Ediciones, S. A. de C. V. MEX. Dist: Macmillan.

Alvarado, Eladia. The Adventures of Simsim: Based on a True Story. Gigi. 2010. 60p. pap. 12.99 *(978-1-4490-6524-9(4))* AuthorHouse.

Alvarado, Juan. The Adventures of Sammy the Saver In: Will Sammy Ride the World's First Space Coaster?, Vol. 2. Renick, Sam X. 2003. 32p. (J). pap. 8.95 *(978-0-9713664-1-1(1))* It's A Habit! Co., The.

Alvarado, Paulo. My Day... at the Zoo. Wagner, Jeff. 2004. 20p. (J). bds. *(978-0-9754515-0-2(2))* Wagner Entertainment.

Alvarenga, Angela, jt. illus. see Goley, Jonathon.

Alvarez, Amber. Wild about Dads. Murray, Diana. 2020. (ENG.). 40p. (J). 17.99 *(978-1-250-31574-8(3)*, 900199711) Imprint IND. Dist: Macmillan.

Álvarez, Cecilia. Antonio's Card: La Tarjeta de Antonio. González, Rigoberto. 2016. (ENG & SPA.). (J). pap. 9.95 *(978-0-89239-387-9(4)*, Children's Book Press) Lee & Low Bks., Inc.

Alvarez, Dave, jt. illus. see Bartolini, Egle.

Alvarez, David. El Mejor Es Mi Papa. Leon, Georgina Lazaro. 2003. (Yellow Ser.). (SPA.). 31p. (gr. k-3). pap. 9.95 *(978-1-57581-442-1(0))* Santillana USA Publishing Co., Inc.

Alvarez, Diego. Dentro del Cubo. Villegas, Aline Guevara. rev. ed. 2006. (Otra Escalera Ser.). (SPA & ENG.). 24p. (J). (gr. 4). pap. 9.95 *(978-968-5920-73-5(7))* Castillo, Ediciones, S. A. de C. V. MEX. Dist: Macmillan.

—El Galeon de Manila: Los Objetos Que Llegaron de Oriente. Durán, Rosa Dopazo. rev. ed. 2006. (Otra Escalera Ser.). (SPA & ENG.). 48p. (J). (gr. 4-7). pap. 10.95 *(978-968-5920-76-6(1))* Castillo, Ediciones, S. A. de C. V. MEX. Dist: Macmillan.

Alvarez, Francesc. An Eagle's Feather, 1 vol. Ho, Minfong. 2018. (ENG.). 36p. (J). (gr. -1-1). 15.95 *(978-1-943645-23-7(X)*, c9689f2b-d893-4edc-82d5-ee35772a077e, Cornell Lab Publishing Group, The) WunderMill, Inc.

Alvarez, Jose M. & Alonso, Jesus. David Crockett. Santillana U. S. A. Publishing Co, Inc. Staff. 2003. (Historias de Siempre Ser.). (SPA.). 95p. (J). (gr. 5-8). pap. 12.95 *(978-84-204-5703-1(5))* Santillana USA Publishing Co., Inc.

Alvarez, Lamberto. Muffler Man el Hombre Mofle. Campos, Tito. 2009. 32p. (J). pap. 7.95 *(978-1-55885-557-1(2)*, Piñata Books) Arte Publico Pr.

Alvarez, Laura, jt. illus. see Luna, Tom.

Alvarez, Leticia Herrera. Dia de Reyes. Alvarez, Leticia Herrera. 2003. (SPA.). 52p. (J). (gr. 3-5). 14.95 *(978-968-19-1043-3(5))* Santillana USA Publishing Co., Inc.

Alvarez, Lorena. A Little Princess. Posner-Sanchez, Andrea. 2017. (Little Golden Book Ser.). 24p. (J). (-k). 4.99 *(978-1-101-93834-8(X)*, Golden Bks.) Random Hse. Children's Bks.

—Nightlights. Gomez, Lorena. 2017. (Nightlights Ser.). 56p. (J). (gr. 3-7). 18.95 *(978-1-910620-13-7(0))* Nobrow Ltd. GBR. Dist: Penguin Random Hse. LLC.

—The Noon Balloon. Brown, Margaret Wise. 2020. (Margaret Wise Brown Classics Ser.). (ENG.). 32p. (J). (gr. -1-k). 12.99 *(978-1-68412-752-8(1)*, Silver Dolphin Bks.) Printers Row Publishing Group.

—Sleep Tight, Snow White. Arena, Jen. 2017. (ENG.). 32p. (J). (-k). 17.99 *(978-1-101-93713-6(0)*, Knopf Bks. for Young Readers) Random Hse. Children's Bks.

Alvarez, Maria de Jesus. I'm Proud of My Past. White, Amy. 2008. (Fácil de Leer / Easy to Read Ser.). (ENG.). 16p. (J). pap. 5.99 ***(978-1-59820-573-2(0)***, Santillana Texto) Santillana USA Publishing Co., Inc.

Alvarez, Maria Jesus. Celebrate a Powwow with Sandy Starbright. Flor Ada, Alma. 2007. (Cuentos para Celebrar / Stories to Celebrate Ser.). 30p. (gr. k-6). per. 11.95 *(978-1-59820-127-7(1))* Santillana USA Publishing Co., Inc.

—La Fiesta de Las Tortillas: The Fiesta of the Tortillas. Argueta, Jorge. Hayes, Joe & Franco, Sharon, trs. from SPA. 2006. (Bilingual Bks). (ENG & SPA.). 32p. (gr. 3-5). 15.95 *(978-1-59820-094-2(1)*, Alfaguara) Santillana USA Publishing Co., Inc.

—Leyendas de Misterio. Fuster, Ana Maria. 2007. (Serie Naranja / Leyendas de Puerto Rico Ser.). (SPA.). 40p. (J). pap. 7.95 *(978-1-63113-917-8(7))* Santillana USA Publishing Co., Inc.

Alvarez Miguens, Marta. Dinosaur Lady. Skeers, Linda. 2020. 40p. (J). (-4). 17.99 *(978-1-7282-0951-7(X))* Sourcebooks, Inc.

—Little Bible Playbook: the First Christmas. 2018. (Little Bible Playbook Ser.). (ENG.). 20p. (J). (— 1). bds. 7.99 *(978-0-7944-4180-7(7)*, Reader's Digest Children's Bks.) Studio Fun International.

Álvarez Miguéns, Marta. My Great Big God: 20 Bible Stories to Build a Great Big Faith, 1 vol. Holmes, Andy. 2017. (ENG.). 40p. (J). bds. 9.99 *(978-0-7180-9737-0(8))* Nelson, Thomas Inc.

—Shark Lady: The Daring Tale of How Eugenie Clark Dove into History. Keating, Jess. 2017. 40p. (J). (-4). 17.99 *(978-1-4926-4204-6(5)*, Sourcebooks Jabberwocky) Sourcebooks, Inc.

Álvarez, Mrinalí. Grano a Grano. Barceló, Josefina. 2006. (SPA.). (J). pap. 8.95 *(978-0-8477-1561-9(2))* Univ. of Puerto Rico Pr.

Alvarez, Mrinali. Mi Silla de Ruedas. Rivera, Lassen. 2006. (SPA.). 28p. 8.95 *(978-0-8477-1568-8(X))* Univ. of Puerto Rico Pr.

—Pon, Pon: ¡A Jugar con el Bebé! 2005. (SPA.). 28p. (J). 8.95 *(978-0-8477-1550-3(7))* Univ. of Puerto Rico Pr.

Álvarez, Mrinalí. Pon pon, a jugar con el Bebé. Barceló, Josefina. 2006. (SPA.). (J). pap. 8.95 *(978-0-8477-1557-2(4))* Univ. of Puerto Rico Pr.

Alvarez, Mrinali. Soy Gordito. Rivera, Lassen. 2006. (SPA.). 28p. 8.95 *(978-0-8477-1565-7(5))* Univ. of Puerto Rico Pr.

Álvarez, Mrinalí. Los tres reyes a Caballo. Rivera, Carmen & Maldonado, Victor. 2006. (SPA.). (J). pap. 8.95 *(978-0-8477-1559-6(0))* Univ. of Puerto Rico Pr.

Alvarez, Mrinali. Los tres reyes a Caballo. Rivera Lassén, Carmen & Maldonado, Víctor. 2005. (SPA.). 28p. (J). 8.95 *(978-0-8477-1552-7(3))* Univ. of Puerto Rico Pr.

Álvarez, Mrinalí. Vamos a Jugar. Barceló, Josefina. 2006. (SPA.). (J). 8.95 *(978-0-8477-1560-2(4))* Univ. of Puerto Rico Pr.

Alvarez O'Neill, Juan. Grano a grano... Refranes Populares. 2005. (SPA.). (J). 8.95 *(978-0-8477-1554-1(X))* Univ. of Puerto Rico Pr.

—¡Vamos a Jugar! 2005. (SPA.). 28p. (J). 8.95 *(978-0-8477-1553-4(1))* Univ. of Puerto Rico Pr.

Alvarez, Silvia. The Last Tree. Quintana Silva, Maria. 2019. (ENG.). 32p. (J). 16.95 *(978-84-16733-46-0(5))* Cuento de Luz SL ESP. Dist: Publishers Group West (PGW).

Alvarez, Silvia. Oso Quiere Volar (Bear Wants to Fly) Isern, Susanna. 2020. (SPA.). 32p. (J). (gr. -1). 9.95 ***(978-84-16733-95-8(3))*** Cuento de Luz SL ESP. Dist: Publishers Group West (PGW).

Alvarez, Silvia. El último árbol. Quintana Silva, Maria. 2019. (SPA.). 32p. (J). 16.95 *(978-84-16733-45-3(7))* Cuento de Luz SL ESP. Dist: Publishers Group West (PGW).

Alvendia, Vince. Dark Agents: Violet & the Trial of Trauma. Scarlet, Janina. 2020. (ENG.). 152p. (YA). (gr. 6-12). pap. 19.95 *(978-1-68403-174-0(5)*, 41740, Instant Help Books) New Harbinger Pubns.

Alves, Fernanda. Carlinhos, o Gnomo e o Natal. Vasconcelos, Sandra. 2019. (POR.). 60p. (J). pap. 15.93 ***(978-1-6994-8830-0(4))*** Independently Published.

Alves, Josh. Ball Hog. Masterson, Hoss. 2017. (Animal All-Stars Ser.). (ENG.). 56p. (J). (gr. 1-3). lib. bdg. 25.32 *(978-1-4965-4308-0(4)*, Stone Arch Bks.) Capstone.

—Owl Ball. Masterson, Hoss. 2017. (Animal All-Stars Ser.). (ENG.). 56p. (J). (gr. 1-3). lib. bdg. 25.32 *(978-1-4965-4309-7(2)*, Stone Arch Bks.) Capstone.

—Soccer Sloth. Masterson, Hoss. 2017. (Animal All-Stars Ser.). (ENG.). 56p. (J). (gr. 1-3). lib. bdg. 25.32 *(978-1-4965-4306-6(8)*, Stone Arch Bks.) Capstone.

—Wild Receiver. Masterson, Hoss. 2017. (Animal All-Stars Ser.). (ENG.). 56p. (J). (gr. 1-3). lib. bdg. 25.32 *(978-1-4965-4307-3(6)*, Stone Arch Bks.) Capstone.

—Zeke Meeks vs His Big Phony Cousin, 1 vol. Green, D. L. 2014. (Zeke Meeks Ser.). (ENG.). 128p. (J). (gr. 2-4). pap. 5.95 *(978-1-4795-3810-2(8))*; 22.65 *(978-1-4795-2167-8(1))* Capstone. (Picture Window Bks.).

—Zeke Meeks vs the Annoying Princess Sing-Along, 1 vol. Green, D. L. 2014. (Zeke Meeks Ser.). (ENG.). 128p. (J). (gr. 2-4). 22.65 *(978-1-4795-4828-6(6)*, Picture Window Bks.) Capstone.

—Zeke Meeks vs the Big Blah-Rific Birthday, 1 vol. Green, D. L. 2013. (Zeke Meeks Ser.). (ENG.). 128p. (J). (gr. 2-4). 8.95 *(978-1-4048-8105-1(0))*; lib. bdg. 22.65 *(978-1-4048-7637-8(5))* Capstone. (Picture Window Bks.).

—Zeke Meeks vs the Crummy Class Play, 1 vol. Green, D. L. 2014. (Zeke Meeks Ser.). (ENG.). 128p. (J). (gr. 2-4). 22.65 *(978-1-4795-4827-9(8)*, Picture Window Bks.) Capstone.

—Zeke Meeks vs the Gruesome Girls, 1 vol. Green, D. L. 2012. (Zeke Meeks Ser.). (ENG.). 128p. (J). (gr. 2-4). pap. 5.95 *(978-1-4048-7221-9(3))*; lib. bdg. 22.65 *(978-1-4048-6805-2(4))* Capstone. (Picture Window Bks.).

—Zeke Meeks vs the Horrendous Halloween, 1 vol. Green, D. L. 2013. (Zeke Meeks Ser.). (ENG.). 128p. (J). (gr. 2-4). lib. bdg. 22.65 *(978-1-4048-7638-5(3)*, Picture Window Bks.) Capstone.

—Zeke Meeks vs the Horrifying TV-Turnoff Week, 1 vol. Green, D. L. 2012. (Zeke Meeks Ser.). (ENG.). 128p. (J). (gr. 2-4). pap. 5.95 *(978-1-4048-7220-2(5))*; lib. bdg. 22.65 *(978-1-4048-6804-5(6))* Capstone. (Picture Window Bks.).

—Zeke Meeks vs the Mother's Day Meltdown. Green, D. L. 2015. (Zeke Meeks Ser.). (ENG.). 128p. (J). (gr. 2-4). 22.65 *(978-1-4795-2168-5(X)*, Picture Window Bks.) Capstone.

—Zeke Meeks vs the No-Fun Fund-Raiser, 1 vol. Green, D. L. 2013. (Zeke Meeks Ser.). (ENG.). 128p. (J). (gr. 2-4). lib. bdg. 22.65 *(978-1-4048-7640-8(5)*, Picture Window Bks.) Capstone.

—Zeke Meeks vs the Pain-In-the-Neck Pets, 1 vol. Green, D. L. 2014. (Zeke Meeks Ser.). (ENG.). 128p. (J). (gr. 2-4). 22.65 *(978-1-4795-2166-1(3)*, Picture Window Bks.) Capstone.

—Zeke Meeks vs the Putrid Puppet Pals, 1 vol. Green, D. L. 2012. (Zeke Meeks Ser.). (ENG.). 128p. (J). (gr. 2-4). pap. 5.95 *(978-1-4048-7223-3(X))*; lib. bdg. 22.65 *(978-1-4048-6803-8(8))* Capstone. (Picture Window Bks.).

—Zeke Meeks vs the Stinkin' Science Fair, 1 vol. Green, D. L. 2012. (Zeke Meeks Ser.). (ENG.). 128p. (J). (gr. 2-4). pap. 5.95 *(978-1-4048-7222-6(1))*; lib. bdg. 22.65 *(978-1-4048-6802-1(X))* Capstone. (Picture Window Bks.).

—Zeke Meeks vs the Stinky Soccer Team. Green, D. L. 2015. (Zeke Meeks Ser.). (ENG.). 128p. (J). (gr. 2-4). 22.65 *(978-1-4795-5768-4(4)*, Picture Window Bks.) Capstone.

—Zeke Meeks vs the Super Stressful Talent Show, 1 vol. Green, D. L. 2013. (Zeke Meeks Ser.). (ENG.). 128p. (J). (gr. 2-4). 8.95 *(978-1-4048-8106-8(9))*; lib. bdg. 22.65 *(978-1-4048-7639-2(1))* Capstone. (Picture Window Bks.).

Alves, Wellinton, et al. Daredevil: Fearless Origins. 2019. (ENG.). 136p. (YA). (gr. -1-17). pap. 15.99 *(978-0-7851-5644-4(5))* Marvel Worldwide, Inc.

Alves, Wellinton. Superhero Therapy: Mindfulness Skills to Help Teens & Young Adults Deal with Anxiety, Depression, & Trauma. Scarlet, Janina. 2017. (ENG.). 112p. (YA). (gr. 6-12). pap. 17.95 *(978-1-68403-033-0(1)*, 40330) New Harbinger Pubns.

Alvim Correa, Henrique. The Time Machine / the Wonderful Visit / the Island of Doctor Moreau / the Invisible Man / the War of the Worlds (Annotated) Wells, H. G. Barry, ed. 2019. (H. G. Wells: Notable Works: Vol. 1). (ENG.). 736p. (J). pap. 39.96 ***(978-1-6982-2375-9(7))*** Independently Published.

Alvitre, Weshoyot. At the Mountain's Base. Sorell, Traci. 2019. 32p. (J). (gr. -1-3). 17.99 *(978-0-7352-3060-6(9)*, Kokila) Penguin Young Readers Group.

Alward, Jeff. Gold Rush. Piotrowski, Robert. 2007. 48p. (J). lib. bdg. 23.08 *(978-1-4242-1628-4(1))* Fitzgerald Bks.

—Hidden Message. Boyd, David. 2007. 48p. (J). lib. bdg. 23.08 *(978-1-4242-1637-6(0))* Fitzgerald Bks.

—In a Class of Her Own. Lundy, Kathleen Gould. 2007. 48p. (J). lib. bdg. 23.08 *(978-1-4242-1629-1(X))* Fitzgerald Bks.

Aly, Hatem. Along for the Ride (Set), 4 vols. Taddonio, Lea. 2017. (Along for the Ride Ser.). 48p. (J). (gr. 3-7). lib. bdg. 114.00 *(978-1-5321-3000-7(7)*, 25546, Spellbound) Magic Wagon.

—The Basque Dragon. Gidwitz, Adam & Casey, Jesse. 2019. (Unicorn Rescue Society Ser.: 2). (ENG.). 208p. (J). (gr. 2-5). 7.99 *(978-0-7352-3175-7(3)*, Puffin Books) Penguin Young Readers Group.

—The Basque Dragon. Gidwitz, Adam et al. 2018. (Unicorn Rescue Society Ser.: 2). 176p. (J). (gr. 2-5). 14.99 *(978-0-7352-3173-3(7)*, Dutton Books for Young Readers) Penguin Young Readers Group.

—Book 1: Shake It Off. Taddonio, Lea. 2017. (Along for the Ride Ser.). (ENG.). 48p. (J). (gr. 3-7). lib. bdg. 29.93 *(978-1-5321-3001-4(5)*, 25548, Spellbound) Magic Wagon.

—Book 2: Fashion Police. Taddonio, Lea. 2017. (Along for the Ride Ser.). (ENG.). 48p. (J). (gr. 3-7). lib. bdg. 29.93 *(978-1-5321-3002-1(3)*, 25550, Spellbound) Magic Wagon.

—Book 3: Center Stage. Taddonio, Lea. 2017. (Along for the Ride Ser.). (ENG.). 48p. (J). (gr. 3-7). lib. bdg. 29.93 *(978-1-5321-3003-8(1)*, 25552, Spellbound) Magic Wagon.

—Book 4: Solo ACT. Taddonio, Lea. 2017. (Along for the Ride Ser.). (ENG.). 48p. (J). (gr. 3-7). lib. bdg. 29.93 *(978-1-5321-3004-5(X)*, 25554, Spellbound) Magic Wagon.

—The Chupacabras of the Río Grande. Gidwitz, Adam & Bowles, David. (Unicorn Rescue Society Ser.: 4). (J). (gr. 2-5). 2020. 224p. 7.99 *(978-0-7352-3181-8(8)*, Puffin Books); 2019. 192p. 14.99 *(978-0-7352-3179-5(6)*, Dutton Books for Young Readers) Penguin Young Readers Group.

—The Creature of the Pines. Gidwitz, Adam. 2019. (Unicorn Rescue Society Ser.: 1). 192p. (J). (gr. 2-5). 7.99 *(978-0-7352-3172-6(9)*, Puffin Books) Penguin Young Readers Group.

—The Creature of the Pines. Gidwitz, Adam et al. 2018. (Unicorn Rescue Society Ser.: 1). 176p. (J). (gr. 2-5). 14.99 *(978-0-7352-3170-2(2)*, Dutton Books for Young Readers) Penguin Young Readers Group.

—How to Feed Your Parents. Miller, Ryan. 2018. (ENG.). 40p. (J). (gr. -1). 16.95 *(978-1-4549-2562-0(0))* Sterling Publishing Co., Inc.

—The Inquisitor's Tale: Or, the Three Magical Children & Their Holy Dog. Gidwitz, Adam. (ENG.). (J). (gr. 5). 2018. 400p. 9.99 *(978-0-14-242737-8(3)*, Puffin Books); 2016. 384p. 17.99 *(978-0-525-42616-5(7)*, Dutton Books for Young Readers) Penguin Young Readers Group.

—The Madre de Aguas of Cuba. Gidwitz, Adam & Otheguy, Emma. 2020. (Unicorn Rescue Society Ser.: 5). 224p. (J). (gr. 2-5). 14.99 *(978-0-7352-3142-9(7)*, Dutton Books for Young Readers) Penguin Young Readers Group.

—Meet Yasmin! Faruqi, Saadia. ed. 2018. (Yasmin Ser.). (ENG.). 96p. (J). (gr. k-2). pap. 5.95 *(978-1-68436-022-2(6)*, 137937, Picture Window Bks.) Capstone.

—Not So Normal Norbert. Patterson, James. 2018. (ENG.). 368p. (J). (gr. 3-9). 13.99 *(978-0-316-46541-0(0))* Little Brown & Co.

—The Proudest Blue: A Story of Hijab & Family. Muhammad, Ibtihaj. 2019. (ENG.). 40p. (J). (gr. -1-3). 17.99 *(978-0-316-51900-7(6))* Little Brown & Co.

Aly, Hatem. Raj's Rule (for the Bathroom at School) Button, Lana. 2020. (ENG.). 32p. (J). (gr. -1-3). 17.95 ***(978-1-77147-340-8(1))*** Owlkids Bks. Inc. CAN. Dist: Publishers Group West (PGW).

Aly, Hatem. Sasquatch & the Muckleshoot. Gidwitz, Adam & Bruchac, Joseph. (Unicorn Rescue Society Ser.: 3). (J). (gr. 2-5). 2020. 156p. 7.99 *(978-0-7352-3178-8(8)*, Puffin Books); 2018. 176p. 14.99 *(978-0-7352-3176-4(1)*, Dutton Books for Young Readers) Penguin Young Readers Group.

—The Story Pirates Present. The Story Pirates & West, Jacqueline. 2019. (Story Pirates Ser.: 2). 288p. (J). (gr. 3-7). 13.99 *(978-1-63565-091-4(7)*, 9781635650914,

Random Hse. Bks. for Young Readers) Random Hse. Children's Bks.
—The Story Pirates Present: Stuck in the Stone Age. Story Pirates, Story & Rodkey, Geoff. 2020. (Story Pirates Ser.: 1). 272p. (J). (gr. 3-7). 7.99 *(978-0-593-12378-2(6)*, Yearling) Random Hse. Children's Bks.
—Stuck in the Stone Age. Rodkey, Geoff & Story Pirates Staff. 2018. (Story Pirates Ser.: 1). 272p. (J). (gr. 3-7). 13.99 *(978-1-63565-089-1(5)*, 9781635650891, Random Hse. Bks. for Young Readers) Random Hse. Children's Bks.
—Stuck in the Stone Age (Signed Edition) Rodkey, Geoff. 2018. (Story Pirates Ser.: 1). (ENG.). 256p. (J). (gr. 3-7). 13.99 *(978-1-63565-383-0(5)*, Rodale Kids) Random Hse. Children's Bks.
—Yasmin. Faruqi, Saadia. (Yasmin Ser.). (ENG.). (J). (gr. k-2). 2020. 247.80 *(978-1-5158-4645-1(8)*, 29717); 2020. pap., pap., pap. 71.40 *(978-1-5158-6034-1(5)*, 29982); 2018. 32p. 82.60 *(978-1-5158-2737-5(2)*, 28046); 2018. 32p. pap., pap., pap. 23.80 *(978-1-5158-2738-2(0)*, 28045) Capstone. (Picture Window Bks.).
Aly, Hatem. Yasmin en Español. Faruqi, Saadia. (Yasmin en Español Ser.).Tr. of Yasmin. (SPA.). (J). (gr. k-2). 2020. 247.80 ***(978-1-5158-7206-1(8)***, 200727); 2020. pap., pap., pap. 71.40 ***(978-1-5158-7345-7(5)***, 201802); 2020. 165.20 *(978-1-5158-5744-0(1)*, 29920); 2020. pap., pap., pap. 47.60 *(978-1-5158-5745-7(X)*, 29921); 2019. 82.60 *(978-1-5158-4687-1(3)*, 29723); 2019. pap., pap., pap. 23.80 *(978-1-5158-4711-3(X)*, 29753) Capstone. (Picture Window Bks.).
—Yasmin la Amiga. Faruqi, Saadia. 2020. (Yasmin en Español Ser.).Tr. of Yasmin the Friend. (SPA.). 32p. (J). (gr. k-2). pap. 5.95 ***(978-1-5158-7317-4(X)***, 201600); lib. bdg. 20.65 ***(978-1-5158-7197-2(5)***, 200644) Capstone. (Picture Window Bks.).
Aly, Hatem. Yasmin la Chef. Faruqi, Saadia. 2020. (Yasmin en Español Ser.).Tr. of Yasmin the Chef. (SPA.). 32p. (J). (gr. k-2). pap. 5.95 *(978-1-5158-5734-1(4)*, 142098); lib. bdg. 20.65 *(978-1-5158-5730-3(1)*, 142095) Capstone. (Picture Window Bks.).
—Yasmin la Constructora. Faruqi, Saadia. 2019. (Yasmin en Español Ser.). (SPA.). 32p. (J). (gr. k-2). pap. 5.95 *(978-1-5158-4697-0(0)*, 141324); lib. bdg. 20.65 *(978-1-5158-4661-1(X)*, 141260) Capstone. (Picture Window Bks.).
Aly, Hatem. Yasmin la Escritora. Faruqi, Saadia. 2020. (Yasmin en Español Ser.).Tr. of Yasmin the Writer. (SPA.). 32p. (J). (gr. k-2). pap. 5.95 ***(978-1-5158-7320-4(X)***, 201603); lib. bdg. 20.65 ***(978-1-5158-7203-0(3)***, 200650) Capstone. (Picture Window Bks.).
—Yasmin la Estrella de Fútbol. Faruqi, Saadia. 2020. (Yasmin en Español Ser.).Tr. of Yasmin the Soccer Star. (SPA.). 32p. (J). (gr. k-2). pap. 5.95 ***(978-1-5158-7319-8(6)***, 201602); lib. bdg. 20.65 ***(978-1-5158-7201-6(7)***, 200648) Capstone. (Picture Window Bks.).
Aly, Hatem. Yasmin la Exploradora. Faruqi, Saadia. 2019. (Yasmin en Español Ser.). (SPA.). 32p. (J). (gr. k-2). pap. 5.95 *(978-1-5158-4698-7(9)*, 141325); lib. bdg. 20.65 *(978-1-5158-4663-5(6)*, 141262) Capstone. (Picture Window Bks.).
—Yasmin la Fashionista. Faruqi, Saadia. 2019. (Yasmin en Español Ser.). (SPA.). 32p. (J). (gr. k-2). pap. 5.95 *(978-1-5158-4699-4(7)*, 141326); lib. bdg. 20.65 *(978-1-5158-4664-2(4)*, 141263) Capstone. (Picture Window Bks.).
—Yasmin, la Guardiana Del Zoo. Faruqi, Saadia. 2020. (Yasmin en Español Ser.).Tr. of Yasmin the Zookeeper. (SPA.). 32p. (J). (gr. k-2). pap. 5.95 *(978-1-5158-5735-8(2)*, 142100); lib. bdg. 20.65 *(978-1-5158-5731-0(X)*, 142096) Capstone. (Picture Window Bks.).
Aly, Hatem. Yasmin la Jardinera. Faruqi, Saadia. 2020. (Yasmin en Español Ser.).Tr. of Yasmin the Gardener. (SPA.). 32p. (J). (gr. k-2). pap. 5.95 ***(978-1-5158-7318-1(8)***, 201601); lib. bdg. 20.65 ***(978-1-5158-7199-6(1)***, 200646) Capstone. (Picture Window Bks.).
Aly, Hatem. Yasmin la Maestra. Faruqi, Saadia. 2020. (Yasmin en Español Ser.).Tr. of Yasmin the Teacher. (SPA.). 32p. (J). (gr. k-2). pap. 5.95 *(978-1-5158-5732-7(8)*, 142097); lib. bdg. 20.65 *(978-1-5158-5728-0(X)*, 142092) Capstone. (Picture Window Bks.).
—Yasmin la Pintora. Faruqi, Saadia. 2019. (Yasmin en Español Ser.). (SPA.). 32p. (J). (gr. k-2). pap. 5.95 *(978-1-5158-4700-7(4)*, 141327); lib. bdg. 20.65 *(978-1-5158-4662-8(8)*, 141261) Capstone. (Picture Window Bks.).
—Yasmin la Superheroína. Faruqi, Saadia. 2020. (Yasmin en Español Ser.).Tr. of Yasmin the Superhero. (SPA.). 32p. (J). (gr. k-2). pap. 5.95 *(978-1-5158-5733-4(6)*, 142099); lib. bdg. 20.65 *(978-1-5158-5729-7(8)*, 142094) Capstone. (Picture Window Bks.).
—Yasmin the Builder. Faruqi, Saadia. 2018. (Yasmin Ser.). (ENG.). 32p. (J). (gr. k-2). 20.65 *(978-1-5158-2727-6(5)*, 137931, Picture Window Bks.) Capstone.
—Yasmin the Chef. Faruqi, Saadia. 2019. (Yasmin Ser.). (ENG.). 32p. (J). (gr. k-2). pap. 5.95 *(978-1-5158-4578-2(8)*, 141178); lib. bdg. 20.65 *(978-1-5158-3784-8(X)*, 139366) Capstone. (Picture Window Bks.).
—Yasmin the Explorer. Faruqi, Saadia. 2018. (Yasmin Ser.). (ENG.). 32p. (J). (gr. k-2). 20.65 *(978-1-5158-2729-0(1)*, 137933, Picture Window Bks.) Capstone.
—Yasmin the Fashionista. Faruqi, Saadia. 2018. (Yasmin Ser.). (ENG.). 32p. (J). (gr. k-2). 20.65 *(978-1-5158-3103-7(5)*, 138807, Picture Window Bks.) Capstone.
—Yasmin the Friend. Faruqi, Saadia. 2020. (Yasmin Ser.). (ENG.). 32p. (J). (gr. k-2). pap. 5.95 *(978-1-5158-5888-1(X)*, 142144); lib. bdg. 20.65 *(978-1-5158-4644-4(X)*, 141250) Capstone. (Picture Window Bks.).
—Yasmin the Gardener. Faruqi, Saadia. 2020. (Yasmin Ser.). (ENG.). 32p. (J). (gr. k-2). pap. 5.95 *(978-1-5158-5885-0(5)*, 142141); lib. bdg. 20.65 *(978-1-5158-4641-3(5)*, 141247) Capstone. (Picture Window Bks.).
—Yasmin the Painter. Faruqi, Saadia. 2018. (Yasmin Ser.). (ENG.). 32p. (J). (gr. k-2). 20.65 *(978-1-5158-2728-3(3)*, 137932, Picture Window Bks.) Capstone.
—Yasmin the Soccer Star. Faruqi, Saadia. 2020. (Yasmin Ser.). (ENG.). 32p. (J). (gr. k-2). pap. 5.95 *(978-1-5158-5886-7(3)*, 142142); lib. bdg. 20.65 *(978-1-5158-4642-0(3)*, 141248) Capstone. (Picture Window Bks.).
—Yasmin the Superhero. Faruqi, Saadia. 2019. (Yasmin Ser.). (ENG.). 32p. (J). (gr. k-2). pap. 5.95 *(978-1-5158-4579-9(6)*, 141179); lib. bdg. 20.65 *(978-1-5158-3783-1(1)*, 139365) Capstone. (Picture Window Bks.).
—Yasmin the Teacher. Faruqi, Saadia. 2019. (Yasmin Ser.). (ENG.). 32p. (J). (gr. k-2). pap. 5.95 *(978-1-5158-4580-5(X)*, 141180); lib. bdg. 20.65 *(978-1-5158-3782-4(3)*, 139364) Capstone. (Picture Window Bks.).
—Yasmin the Writer. Faruqi, Saadia. 2020. (Yasmin Ser.). (ENG.). 32p. (J). (gr. k-2). pap. 5.95 *(978-1-5158-5887-4(1)*, 142143); lib. bdg. 20.65 *(978-1-5158-4643-7(1)*, 141249) Capstone. (Picture Window Bks.).
—Yasmin the Zookeeper. Faruqi, Saadia. 2019. (Yasmin Ser.). (ENG.). 32p. (J). (gr. k-2). pap. 5.95 *(978-1-5158-4581-2(8)*, 141181); lib. bdg. 20.65 *(978-1-5158-3785-5(8)*, 139367) Capstone. (Picture Window Bks.).
—You Can Do It, Yasmin! Faruqi, Saadia. ed. 2020. (Yasmin Ser.). (ENG.). 96p. (J). (gr. k-2). pap. 5.95 *(978-1-5158-6091-4(4)*, 142367, Picture Window Bks.) Capstone.
Alzaga, Gerald. 7 Little Miracles. Junior, Huey. 2019. (ENG.). 26p. (J). pap. 9.29 *(978-1-0714-5543-2(5))* Independently Published.
Amado, Defne. Macaroni on the Moon. Dordick, Barry. 2003. 110p. pap. 11.95 *(978-0-595-26886-3(2))* iUniverse, Inc.
Amalia, Rendon. The Grand High Monster: Dyslexia Friendly Edition. Matt, Beighton. 3rd ed. 2019. (Monstacademy Ser.: Vol. 3). (ENG.). 158p. (J). pap. ***(978-1-9161360-3-8(6))*** Green Monkey Pr.
Amalia, Rendon. The Magic Knight: You're the Monster! Matt, Beighton. 2018. (Monstacademy Ser.: Vol. 2). (ENG.). 126p. (J). (gr. 1-5). pap. *(978-1-9997244-5-0(3))* Green Monkey Pr.
Amanda Dilworth. Artist Notebook: Amanda Dilworth Illustrated Cover Notebook Beautiful Artwork Painters' Book for an Artist, Designer or Illustrator to Jot down Their Notes. Artwork Notebook Publishing. 2019. (ENG.). 108p. (J). pap. 6.99 ***(978-1-6751-4190-8(8))*** Independently Published.
Amanda, Henke. Pocketful of Dreams- Spanish Edition. Long, George. 2016. (SPA.). (J). pap. 8.99 *(978-0-9844946-9-9(3))* Long, George Children's Books.
Amandine, Amandine. Chloe #2: The Queen of High School. Tessier, Greg. 2017. (Chloe Ser.: 2). (ENG.). 112p. (J). 14.99 *(978-1-62991-834-1(2)*, 900181007) Papercutz.
—Chloe #5: Carnival Party. Tessier, Greg. 2020. (Chloe Ser.: 5). (ENG.). 112p. (J). 14.99 *(978-1-5458-0142-0(8)*, 900194331) Papercutz.
Amann, Remy & Stoffel, Dominique, photos by. Face-to-Face with the Ant: Energetic Worker. Gomel, Luc. 2004. (Face to Face Ser.). 28p. (J). (gr. -1-2). 9.95 *(978-1-57091-451-5(6))* Charlesbridge Publishing, Inc.
Amano, Shiro. Kingdom Hearts, 4 vols., Vol. 4. Amano, Shiro. 4th rev. ed. 2006. (Disney Squaresoft Ser.). 131p. pap. 5.99 *(978-1-59816-220-2(9)*, Tokyopop Kids) TOKYOPOP, Inc.
Amante, Mike & Pantoja, Tintin. Unplugged & Unpopular. Heagerty, Mat. 2019. (ENG.). 144p. (J). (gr. 5-8). 19.99 *(978-1-62010-680-8(9)*, Lion Forge) Oni Pr., Inc.
Amante, Mike, jt. illus. see Pantoja, Tintin.
Amati, Susanna. Show Your Style (Barbie) Golden Books. 2017. (ENG.). 24p. (J). (gr. -1-2). pap. 9.99 *(978-1-5247-1644-8(8)*, Golden Bks.) Random Hse. Children's Bks.
Amatisto, Brandi. Oscar: A Cat's Tale. Coleman, William L. 2012. 38p. pap. 16.97 *(978-1-61204-750-8(5)*, Strategic Bk. Publishing) Strategic Book Publishing & Rights Agency (SBPRA).
Amato, Angela. The Picnic at Squirrel Park. Donaghy, Rolla. 2018. (ENG.). 24p. (J). 21.95 *(978-1-64438-259-2(8))* Booklocker.com, Inc.
Amatori, Stephanie. Drat That Cat! Ross, Susan R. 2017. (ENG.). (J). (gr. k-3). pap. *(978-0-9879404-4-5(9))* Susan Ross (self publishing).
Amatrula, Michele. Haven House. Olds, Barbara Anne. 2007. (ENG.). 148p. (J). (gr. 4-6). pap. 10.95 *(978-0-9744446-0-4(X))* All About Kids Publishing.
Ambadikumar. Jack & Judy. Stanton, Sherry. 2019. (ENG.). 34p. (J). (gr. k-2). pap. *(978-1-9995566-0-0(7))* Stanton, Sherry.
Amber, Holly & Davidsson, Ashton. The Little Garden. Johnson, Rhonda & Paladin, Frank. l.t. ed. 2004. 48p. (J). per. 16.95 *(978-0-9763635-7-6(7)*, TLG01) Beyond the Stars Pubns.
Amber, Holly & Lin, Melanie. Hole in My Stocking. Paladin, Frank. 2005. 24p. (J). per. 16.95 *(978-0-9763635-4-5(2))* Beyond the Stars Pubns.
Amber, Malone. Betsy Did It. Patricia, Prevosti. 2017. (ENG.). 42p. (J). (gr. k-5). pap. 12.95 *(978-0-9995258-0-7(8))* Gateway Hse. Publishing.
Ambler, Laura & Brown, Amanda. The Rat Tank, 1 vol. Henry, Kristina. 2011. (ENG.). 40p. (J). (gr. -1-3). 16.99 *(978-0-7643-3842-7(0)*, 9780764338427, Schiffer Publishing Ltd) Schiffer Publishing, Ltd.
—The Turtle Tank, 1 vol. Henry, Kristina. 2011. (ENG.). 32p. (J). (gr. -1-3). 16.99 *(978-0-7643-3843-4(9)*, 9780764338434, Schiffer Publishing Ltd) Schiffer Publishing, Ltd.
Ambrose, Sophie. The Lonely Giant. Ambrose, Sophie. 2016. (ENG.). 32p. (J). (gr. -1-3). 16.99 *(978-0-7636-8225-5(X))* Candlewick Pr.
Ambroz, Mark. Ben, His Helmet & Hats Off. Frances, Nelle. 2012. 16p. (Orig.). pap. *(978-0-646-43174-1(9))* Nelle Frances.
—Ben, His Helmet & the Crashing Cymbals. Frances, Nelle. 2012. 16p. (Orig.). pap. *(978-0-9751168-4-5(3))* Nelle Frances.
—Ben, His Helmet & the Too Tight Hair. Frances, Nelle. 2012. 16p. (Orig.). pap. *(978-0-9751168-1-4(9))* Nelle Frances.
Ambrus, Victor. Heather, Oak, & Olive. Sutcliff, Rosemary. 2015. (ENG.). 120p. (J). (gr. 3-6). pap. 11.95 *(978-1-58988-106-8(0))* Dry, Paul Bks., Inc.
—Olaudah Equiano: from Slavery to Freedom: Band 15/Emerald (Collins Big Cat) Thomas, Paul. 2007. (Collins Big Cat Ser.). (ENG.). 48p. (J). (gr. 3-4). pap. 9.99 *(978-0-00-723096-9(6))* HarperCollins Pubs. Ltd. GBR. Dist: Independent Pubs. Group.
Ambrus, Victor G. The Iliad. 2004. (Kingfisher Epics Ser.). (ENG.). 165p. (YA). (gr. 3-7). pap. 8.99 *(978-0-7534-5722-1(9)*, 900052604, Kingfisher) Roaring Brook Pr.
—Robin Hood: His Life & Legend. Miles, Bernard. 128p. (J). (gr. 4-18). 12.95 *(978-1-56288-412-3(3))* Checkerboard Pr., Inc.
Ambush, Peter. One Million Men & Me. Lyons, Kelly Starling. 2007. 32p. (J). (gr. -1-3). 16.95 *(978-1-933491-07-3(8))* Just Us Bks., Inc.
Amechazurra, G. Anastasia Tiene Problemas. Lois, Lowry. 2003. (Anastasia Krupnik Ser.). (SPA.). 160p. (J). (gr. 5-7). 9.95 *(978-84-239-9026-9(5))* Espasa Calpe, S.A. ESP. Dist: Planeta Publishing Corp., Lectorum Pubns., Inc.
AMEET Studio. Vader's Secret Missions. Landers, Ace. 2015. (LEGO Star Wars Ser.: 2). (ENG.). 64p. (J). (gr. 2-5). pap. 4.99 *(978-0-545-83557-2(7))* Scholastic, Inc.
AMEET Studio. Activity Book with Minifigure (LEGO Ninjago) AMEET Studio. 2020. (LEGO Ninjago Ser.). (ENG.). 32p. (J). (gr. 1-3). 9.99 *(978-1-338-58195-9(3))* Scholastic, Inc.
—Lego Jurassic World - Sticker Activity Book. AMEET Studio. 2020. (LEGO Jurassic World Ser.). (ENG.). 96p. (J). (gr. 1-3). 12.99 *(978-1-338-58194-2(5))* Scholastic, Inc.
—Sticker Activity Book (LEGO Disney Princess) AMEET Studio. 2020. (ENG.). 96p. (J). (gr. 1-3). 12.99 *(978-1-338-58191-1(0))* Scholastic, Inc.
—Under the Sea, 2. AMEET Studio. 2020. (Lego Ser.: 2). (ENG.). 32p. (J). (gr. 1-3). act. bk. ed. 9.99 *(978-1-338-58190-4(2))* Scholastic, Inc.
Ameet Studio Staff. Tales of the Rebellion. Landers, Ace. 2016. (LEGO Star Wars Ser.: 3). 64p. (J). (gr. 2-5). pap. 4.99 *(978-0-545-87326-0(6))* Scholastic, Inc.
—The Tournament of Elements. 2015. (LEGO Ninjago Ser.). (ENG.). 32p. (J). (gr. 1-3). pap., act. bk. ed. 8.99 *(978-0-545-80540-7(6))* Scholastic, Inc.
Ameet Studio Staff. Epic Space Adventures. Ameet Studio Staff. 2016. (LEGO Star Wars Ser.). 32p. (J). (gr. 1-3). pap. 8.99 *(978-0-545-91727-8(1))* Scholastic, Inc.
—Search & Find Adventure. Ameet Studio Staff. 2019. (Lego Ser.). (ENG.). 32p. (J). (gr. k-2). 9.99 *(978-1-338-58189-8(9))* Scholastic, Inc.
Ameling, Charlotte. Musical Instruments. 2018. (My First Music Book Ser.). (ENG.). 16p. (J). bds. 11.95 *(978-2-7338-6148-6(4))* Auzou, Philippe Editions FRA. Dist: Consortium Bk. Sales & Distribution.
Amendola, Dominique. Krishna & the Mystery of the Stolen Calves. Greene, Joshua M. 2013. (ENG.). 24p. (gr. -1). 14.99 *(978-1-60887-173-5(8))* Mandala Publishing.
Amenta, Rob. My Aunt's Ant's Aunt. Loach, Claire. 2018. (ENG.). 20p. (J). *(978-1-5255-3035-7(6))*; pap. *(978-1-5255-3036-4(4))* FriesenPress.
America. Waikiki Lullaby. Greenway, Bethany. 2009. (ENG.). 20p. (J). (gr. -1-1). bds. 7.95 *(978-1-933067-30-8(6))* Beachhouse Publishing, LLC.
Americo, Tiago. A Baby's Guide to Surviving Dad. Bird, Benjamin. 2016. (Baby Survival Guides). (ENG.). 24p. (J). (gr. -1-1). 6.95 *(978-1-62370-610-4(6)*, Capstone Young Readers) Capstone.
—A Baby's Guide to Surviving Mom. Bird, Benjamin. 2016. (Baby Survival Guides). (ENG.). 24p. (J). (gr. -1-1). 6.95 *(978-1-62370-611-1(4)*, Capstone Young Readers) Capstone.
—My First Quiz Picture Book. Clever Publishing. 2019. (Clever Quiz Bks.). (ENG.). 16p. (J). (gr. -1 — 1). bds. 9.99 *(978-1-948418-57-7(6))* Clever Media Group.
—My First Quiz Picture Book of Animals. Clever Publishing. 2019. (Clever Quiz Bks.). (ENG.). 16p. (J). (gr. -1 — 1). bds. 9.99 *(978-1-948418-58-4(4))* Clever Media Group.
—Pinocchio. 2018. (ENG.). 10p. (J). bds. 10.99 *(978-2-7338-5626-0(X))* Auzou, Philippe Editions FRA. Dist: Consortium Bk. Sales & Distribution.
—Space. Krasinski, Géraldine. 2018. (AllAbout Ser.). (ENG.). 20p. (J). (gr. -1-k). 14.99 *(978-2-7459-9550-6(2))* Editions Tourbillon FRA. Dist: Hachette Bk. Group.
Amery, Heather. Christmas Treasury. gif. ed. 2004. (Christmas Treasury Ser.). 128p. (J). act. bk. ed. 7.95 incl. audio compact disk *(978-0-7945-0224-9(5)*, Usborne) EDC Publishing.
Ames, Alexandra. Who Saw the First Snow? Blue, Shari. 2019. (ENG.). 26p. (J). (gr. k-2). 16.99 ***(978-0-578-53714-6(1))*** Blue, Shari.
Ames, Philippe & Hop, Nguyen Thi. A Pebble for Your Pocket. Hanh, Thich Nhat. rev. ed. 2006. 144p. (J). (gr. 3-7). pap. 12.95 *(978-1-935209-45-4(0)*, Plum Blossom Bks.) Parallax Pr.
Amin, Heba. Extraordinary Women from the Muslim World. Maydell, Natalie & Riahi, Sep. 2008. (ENG.). (J). 17.95 *(978-0-9799901-0-6(6))* Global Content Ventures.
Amin, Shadia. The Amazing World of Gumball Original Graphic Novel: the Storm. Sjursen-Lien, Kiernan. 2019. (Amazing World of Gumball Ser.). (ENG.). 144p. (J). pap. 14.99 *(978-1-68415-401-2(4)*, 9781292288529) Boom! Studios.
Amini-Holmes, Liz. Chester Nez & the Unbreakable Code: A Navajo Code Talker's Story. Bruchac, Joseph. 2018. (ENG.). 32p. (J). (gr. 1-5). 16.99 *(978-0-8075-0007-1(0)*, 807500070) Whitman, Albert & Co.
—Fatty Legs (10th Anniversary Edition) Jordan-Fenton, Christy & Pokiak-Fenton, Margaret-Olemaun. ed. 2020. (ENG.). 156p. (J). (gr. 4-7). pap. 12.95 *(978-1-77321-350-7(4))*; 21.95 ***(978-1-77321-351-4(2))*** Annick Pr., Ltd. CAN. Dist: Publishers Group West (PGW).
Amini, Mehrdokht. Behowl the Moon: An Ageless Story from Shakespeare's a Midsummer Night's Dream. Parekh, Erin Nelson. 2017. 22p. (J). (gr. k-3). bds. 9.99 *(978-0-9984397-1-6(1)*, Drivel & Drool) Dramatic Ellipsis.
—Crescent Moons & Pointed Minarets: A Muslim Book of Shapes. Khan, Hena. 2018. (ENG.). 32p. (J). (gr. -1-k). 17.99 *(978-1-4521-5541-8(0))* Chronicle Bks. LLC.
—Dictionary for a Better World: Poems, Quotes, & Anecdotes from a to Z. Latham, Irene & Waters, Charles. 2020. (ENG.). 120p. (J). (gr. 3-6). 19.99 *(978-1-5415-5775-8(1)*, Carolrhoda Bks.) Lerner Publishing Group.
—Golden Domes & Silver Lanterns: A Muslim Book of Colors. Khan, Hena. 2012. (ENG.). 32p. (J). (gr. -1-2). 17.99 *(978-0-8118-7905-7(4))* Chronicle Bks. LLC.
—Golden Domes & Silver Lanterns: A Muslim Book of Colors. Khan, Hena. 2015. (ENG.). 32p. (J). (gr. -1-k). pap. 7.99 *(978-1-4521-4121-3(5))* Chronicle Bks. LLC.
—A Moon for Moe & Mo. Zalben, Jane Breskin. 2018. 32p. (J). (gr. -1-2). lib. bdg. 17.99 *(978-1-58089-727-3(4))* Charlesbridge Publishing, Inc.
—Nimesh the Adventurer. Singh, Ranjit. 2018. 32p. (J). (gr. -1-2). 17.99 *(978-1-911373-24-7(2))* Lantana Publishing GBR. Dist: Lerner Publishing Group.
—Yo Soy Muslim: A Father's Letter to His Daughter. Gonzales, Mark. 2017. (ENG.). 32p. (J). (gr. -1-3). 17.99 *(978-1-4814-8936-2(4)*, Simon & Schuster Bks. For Young Readers) Simon & Schuster Bks. For Young Readers.
Aminov, Iskander R. Mandorla. Braymen, Nathan T. 2018. (ENG.). 40p. (J). (gr. k-6). 24.95 *(978-0-692-11432-2(7))* Aminov, Iskander.
Amir, Amin Abd al-Fattah Mahmud. The Travels of Igal Shidad/Safarada Cigaal Shidaad: A Somali Folktale. Ahmed, Said Salah, tr. 2008. (J). (gr. -1-3). 28p. pap. 7.95 *(978-1-931016-15-5(1))*; 32p. 15.95 *(978-1-931016-14-8(3))* Minnesota Humanities Ctr.
—Wil Waal: A Somali Folktale. Moriarty, Kathleen M. Adam, Jamal, tr. 2007. (SOM & ENG.). 32p. (J). (gr. -1-3). 15.95 *(978-1-931016-16-2(X))*; pap. 7.95 *(978-1-931016-17-9(8))* Minnesota Humanities Ctr.
Amit, Ofra. Angel Girl. Friedman, Laurie. 2008. 32p. (J). (gr. 3-7). 16.95 *(978-0-8225-8739-2(4)*, Carolrhoda Bks.) Lerner Publishing Group.
Ammassari, Rita. Amy Carmichael - Can Brown Eyes Be Made Blue? MacKenzie, Catherine. 2011. (Little Lights Ser.). (ENG.). 24p. (J). (gr. -1-2). 7.99 *(978-1-84550-108-2(X)*, 081a9cf3-c9ef-4715-ab43-3338f1a49d28) Christian Focus Pubns. GBR. Dist: Baker & Taylor Publisher Services (BTPS).
—Corrie Ten Boo - Are All of the Watches Safe? MacKenzie, Catherine. 2011. (Little Lights Ser.). (ENG.). 24p. (J). (gr. -1-2). 7.99 *(978-1-84550-109-9(8)*, 85908963-343f-444a-a14b-4cba4233e990) Christian Focus Pubns. GBR. Dist: Baker & Taylor Publisher Services (BTPS).
—Could Somebody Pass the Salt? MacKenzie, Catherine. 2012. (Little Lights Ser.). (ENG.). 24p. (J). (gr. 4-7). 7.99 *(978-1-84550-111-2(X)*, b226d812-64ea-4019-8c72-5704e6f80735) Christian Focus Pubns. GBR. Dist: Baker & Taylor Publisher Services (BTPS).
Ammirati, Christelle & Second Story Press Staff. Princess to the Rescue, 1 vol. Souza, Cláudia. 2011. (ENG.). 24p. (J). (gr. 1-3). lib. bdg. 15.95 *(978-1-897187-93-7(9))* Second Story Pr. CAN. Dist: Orca Bk. Pubs. USA.
Amna, J. Forever Friends: The Day Troll Lost Rat: Children's Early Learner/Beginner Reader/Bedtime Rhyming Picture Book (ages 2-8) (a Fairytale World of Humour, Fun & Friendship for Kids/Toddlers) Book 4. Melia, Paul R. 2019. (Forever Friends Ser.: Vol. 4). (ENG.). 36p. (J). pap. 9.15 ***(978-1-0815-5197-1(6))*** Independently Published.
Amodeo, Christina. Matisse's Garden. Friedman, Samantha & Matisse, Henri. 2014. (ENG.). 48p. (J). (gr. -1-3). 19.95 *(978-0-87070-910-4(0))* Museum of Modern Art.
Amormino, Paola. Buzzer Beater. Lawrence, David. 2018. (Get in the Game Ser.). 32p. (J). (gr. 3-8). lib. bdg. 29.93 *(978-1-5321-3294-0(8)*, 28493, Graphic Planet - Fiction) Magic Wagon.
—Face-Off. Lawrence, David. 2018. (Get in the Game Ser.). 32p. (J). (gr. 3-8). lib. bdg. 29.93 *(978-1-5321-3295-7(6)*, 28495, Graphic Planet - Fiction) Magic Wagon.
—Vaulting to Victory. Yu, Bill. 2018. (Get in the Game Ser.). 32p. (J). (gr. 3-8). lib. bdg. 29.93 *(978-1-5321-3298-8(0)*, 28501, Graphic Planet - Fiction) Magic Wagon.
Amory, Deanna & O'Hara, Cynthia. Courageous Warrior. Neuhofer, Sheri L. 2010. 28p. pap. 10.95 *(978-0-9787472-7-5(5))* Ajoyin Publishing, Inc.
Amos, Muriel & Olrun, Prudy. Animals of Nunivak Island. Amos, Muriel & Olrun, Prudy. 2006. (Animal Story Collection Ser.). 16p. (J). (gr. 2-6). pap. 9.00 *(978-1-58084-238-9(0))* Lower Kuskokwim Schl. District.
Amoss, Berthe. The Loup Garou, 1 vol. Amoss, Berthe. 2011. (ENG.). 48p. (J). (gr. 1-3). pap. 11.99 *(978-1-58980-893-5(2)*, Pelican Publishing) Arcadia Publishing.
Ampel, Kenneth Robert. Alexander & the Stallion. Westra, Elizabeth. 2003. (Books for Young Learners). 16p. (J). per. 5.75 net. *(978-1-57274-534-6(7)*, 2721, Bks. for Young Learners) Owen, Richard C. Pubs., Inc.
Amrein, Paul. Chasing the Pot of Gold. Soundar, Chitra. 2006. 32p. (J). E-Book 5.00 incl. cd-rom *(978-1-933090-36-8(7))* Guardian Angel Publishing, Inc.
Amstutz, Andre. Chicken, Chips & Peas, Vol. 1. Ahlberg, Allan. 32p. (J). pap. 9.95 *(978-0-14-056397-9(0))* Penguin Publishing Group.
—Master Track's Train. Ahlberg, Allan. (ENG.). 24p. (J). pap. 6.95 *(978-0-14-037881-8(2))* Penguin Bks., Ltd. GBR. Dist: Trafalgar Square Publishing.
Amy Belle Elementary School. The Cupcake Boy. Stoll, Scott, photos by. Stoll, Scott. l.t. ed. 2012. 108p. (J). (gr. k-6). pap. 8.95 *(978-0-9827842-4-2(4))* Argonauts, The.

Amy, Holloway. Hermione: Shipwrecked! in Ocean City, Maryland. Trimper, Marty. 2004. (J). *(978-1-886068-28-5(3))* Fruitbearer Publishing, LLC.

Amy Huntington. Adding with Sebastian Pig & Friends at the Circus. Anderson, Jill. 2009. (Math Fun with Sebastian Pig & Friends! Ser.). 32p. (gr. k-2). pap. 9.35 *(978-0-7660-5973-3(1),* Enslow Elementary) Enslow Publishing, LLC.

—Counting with Sebastian Pig & Friends on the Farm. Anderson, Jill. 2009. (Math Fun with Sebastian Pig & Friends! Ser.). 32p. (gr. k-2). pap. 9.35 *(978-0-7660-5980-1(4),* Enslow Elementary) Enslow Publishing, LLC.

—Finding Shapes with Sebastian Pig & Friends at the Museum. Anderson, Jill. 2009. (Math Fun with Sebastian Pig & Friends! Ser.). 32p. (gr. k-2). pap. 9.35 *(978-0-7660-5981-8(2),* Enslow Elementary) Enslow Publishing, LLC.

—Measuring with Sebastian Pig & Friends on a Road Trip. Anderson, Jill. 2009. (Math Fun with Sebastian Pig & Friends! Ser.). 32p. (gr. k-2). pap. 9.35 *(978-0-7660-5982-5(0),* Enslow Elementary) Enslow Publishing, LLC.

—Money Math with Sebastian Pig & Friends at the Farmer's Market. Anderson, Jill. 2009. (Math Fun with Sebastian Pig & Friends! Ser.). 32p. (gr. k-2). pap. 9.35 *(978-0-7660-5983-2(9),* Enslow Elementary) Enslow Publishing, LLC.

Amy, Preveza. The Sweetest Christmas Eve (Hard Cover) Hallinan, Annie. 2016. (ENG.). 44p. (J). (gr. 2-4). 19.95 *(978-0-9971477-0-4(9))* Turnberry Pr.

Amy, Rodriguez. Marissa the Mermaid: Counting by the Sea. Sims, Brianna. 2019. (ENG.). 26p. (J). (gr. k-2). 18.99 *(978-0-9980949-2-2(7))* Growsies.

An, Carlos. Frankenstein's Monster & Scientific Methods. Harbo, Christopher L. 2013. (Monster Science Ser.). (ENG.). 32p. (gr. 3-4). pap. 47.70 *(978-1-62065-817-8(8),* Capstone Pr.) Capstone.

—Monster Science. Harbo, Christopher L. 2013. (Monster Science Ser.). (ENG.). 32p. (J). (gr. 3-9). pap., pap., pap. 81.00 *(978-1-4765-3674-3(0),* Capstone Pr.) Capstone.

An, Jiyoung. Barbie Loves Pets. Frazer, Rebecca. 2007. (Pictureback(R) Ser.). (ENG.). 16p. (J). (gr. -1-2). pap. 3.99 *(978-0-375-84797-4(9),* Golden Bks.) Random Hse. Children's Bks.

—I Can Be a Pet Vet (Barbie) Man-Kong, Mary. 2010. (Step into Reading Ser.). (ENG.). 32p. (J). (gr. -1-1). pap. 4.99 *(978-0-375-86581-7(0),* Random Hse. Bks. for Young Readers) Random Hse. Children's Bks.

An, Jiyoung, jt. illus. see Golden Books Staff.

An, Jiyoung, jt. illus. see RH Disney Staff.

An, Sang, photos by. A Gracious Welcome: Etiquette & Ideas for Entertaining Houseguests. Nebens, Amy. 2004. (ENG., 120p. (gr. 8-17). 19.95 *(978-0-8118-4083-5(2))* Chronicle Bks. LLC.

Anacleto, Jay. Marvels: Eye of the Camera. 2019. (ENG.). 160p. (YA). (gr. 4-17). pap. 19.99 *(978-1-302-91734-0(X))* Marvel Worldwide, Inc.

Anagost, Karen. The Night Before Cat-Mas. Unser, Virginia. 2007. (Petite Plush Kit Ser.). 64p. (J). (gr. -1-3). 9.95 *(978-1-59359-882-2(3))* Peter Pauper Pr. Inc.

—The Night Before Dog-Mas. Gandolfi, Claudine. 2007. (Petite Plush Kit Ser.). 64p. (J). (gr. -1-3). 9.95 *(978-1-59359-883-9(1))* Peter Pauper Pr. Inc.

Anand, Tara. Blood Tied: (last Moon Rising #4) Ibitz, Dale. Pollock, Chrissie, ed. 2014. (Last Moon Rising Ser.: Vol. 4). (ENG.). 290p. (J). pap. 11.00 *(978-1-7200-5895-3(4))* Independently Published.

Ananth, Mithila. The Manic Panic. Jha, Richa. 2018. (ENG.). 32p. (J). (gr. k-3). 16.99 *(978-1-939547-43-9(1))* Creston Bks.

Anas, Afra. I'm Fasting This Ramadan: A Ramadan Story. Zaneer, Zeneefa. 2019. (ENG.). 38p. (J). pap. 10.00 *(978-1-5470-5648-4(7))* CreateSpace Independent Publishing Platform.

Anaya, Fátima. The Big Splash. McDonald, Kirsten. 2019. (Carlos & Carmen Ser.). (ENG.). 32p. (J). (gr. -1-3). lib. bdg. 28.50 *(978-1-5321-3491-3(6),* 31901, Calico Chapter Bks) Magic Wagon.

—Campout. McDonald, Kirsten. 2019. (Carlos & Carmen Ser.). (ENG.). 32p. (J). (gr. -1-3). lib. bdg. 28.50 *(978-1-5321-3492-0(4),* 31903, Calico Chapter Bks) Magic Wagon.

Anaya, Fatima. Carlos & Carmen Set 4 (Set), 4 vols. McDonald, Kirsten. 2019. (Carlos & Carmen (Spanish Version) Ser.). 32p. (J). (gr. -1-3). lib. bdg. 108.28 *(978-1-5321-3605-4(6),* 31949, Calico Chapter Bks) Magic Wagon.

—Carlos & Carmen Set 5 (Set), 4 vols. McDonald, Kirsten. 2019. (Carlos & Carmen Ser.). 32p. (J). (gr. -1-3). lib. bdg. 108.28 *(978-1-5321-3490-6(8),* 31899, Calico Chapter Bks) Magic Wagon.

Anaya, Fátima. Demasiadas Tarjetas de San Valentín (Too Many Valentines) McDonald, Kirsten. 2019. (Carlos & Carmen (Spanish Version) Ser.). (SPA.). 32p. (J). (gr. -1-3). lib. bdg. 28.50 *(978-1-5321-3608-5(0),* 31955, Calico Chapter Bks) Magic Wagon.

—The Family Time Bible, Vol. Simon, Mary Manz. 2019. (ENG.). 318p. (J). (gr. -1-3). 22.99 *(978-1-5064-4855-8(0),* Beaming Books) Augsburg Fortress, Pubs.

—Far from Home: A Story of Loss, Refuge, & Hope. Rubio, Sarah Parker. 2019. (ENG.). 32p. (J). 14.99 *(978-1-4964-3673-3(3),* 20_31031) Tyndale Hse. Pubs.

—Fenced In. McDonald, Kirsten. 2019. (Carlos & Carmen Ser.). (ENG.). 32p. (J). (gr. -1-3). lib. bdg. 28.50 *(978-1-5321-3493-7(2),* 31905, Calico Chapter Bks) Magic Wagon.

—La Fortaleza Divertida (the Fun Fort) McDonald, Kirsten. 2019. (Carlos & Carmen (Spanish Version) Ser.). (SPA.). 32p. (J). (gr. -1-3). lib. bdg. 28.50 *(978-1-5321-3606-1(4),* 31951, Calico Chapter Bks) Magic Wagon.

—The Fun Fort. McDonald, Kirsten. 2017. (Carlos & Carmen Ser.). (ENG.). 32p. (J). (gr. -1-3). lib. bdg. 28.50 *(978-1-5321-3033-5(3),* 27035, Calico Chapter Bks) Magic Wagon.

—Our Spaces! Over, under, Around, & Between. Dahl, Michael. 2018. (Creative Movement Ser.). (ENG.). 24p. (J). (gr. -1-2). lib. bdg. 33.99 *(978-1-68410-244-0(8),* 138434) Cantata Learning.

—Over the Fence. McDonald, Kirsten. 2017. (Carlos & Carmen Ser.). (ENG.). 32p. (J). (gr. -1-3). lib. bdg. 28.50 *(978-1-5321-3034-2(1),* 27036, Calico Chapter Bks) Magic Wagon.

—Por Encima de la Valla (over the Fence) McDonald, Kirsten. 2019. (Carlos & Carmen (Spanish Version) Ser.). (SPA.). 32p. (J). (gr. -1-3). lib. bdg. 28.50 *(978-1-5321-3607-8(2),* 31953, Calico Chapter Bks) Magic Wagon.

—Problemas de Diente (Tooth Trouble) McDonald, Kirsten. 2019. (Carlos & Carmen (Spanish Version) Ser.). (SPA.). 32p. (J). (gr. -1-3). lib. bdg. 28.50 *(978-1-5321-3609-2(9),* 31957, Calico Chapter Bks) Magic Wagon.

—The Sweet Treasure. McDonald, Kirsten. 2019. (Carlos & Carmen Ser.). (ENG.). 32p. (J). (gr. -1-3). lib. bdg. 28.50 *(978-1-5321-3494-4(0),* 31907, Calico Chapter Bks) Magic Wagon.

—Too Many Valentines. McDonald, Kirsten. 2017. (Carlos & Carmen Ser.). (ENG.). 32p. (J). (gr. -1-3). lib. bdg. 28.50 *(978-1-5321-3035-9(X),* 27037, Calico Chapter Bks) Magic Wagon.

—Tooth Trouble. McDonald, Kirsten. 2017. (Carlos & Carmen Ser.). (ENG.). 32p. (J). (gr. -1-3). lib. bdg. 28.50 *(978-1-5321-3036-6(8),* 27038, Calico Chapter Bks) Magic Wagon.

Anchin, Lisa. I Will Love You. Capucilli, Alyssa Satin. 2017. (ENG.). 40p. (J). (gr. -1-k). 17.99 *(978-0-545-80310-6(1),* Cartwheel Bks.) Scholastic, Inc.

—A Penguin Named Patience: A Hurricane Katrina Rescue Story. Lewis, Suzanne. 2015. (ENG.). 24p. (J). (gr. 1-4). 15.95 *(978-1-58536-840-2(7),* 203732) Sleeping Bear Pr.

Anchin, Lisa. The Polio Pioneer. Marshall, Linda Elovitz. 2020. 40p. (J). (gr. -1-3). 17.99 ***(978-0-525-64651-8(5));*** (ENG.). lib. bdg. 20.99 ***(978-0-525-64652-5(3))*** Random Hse. Children's Bks. (Knopf Bks. for Young Readers).

Anchin, Lisa. The Little Green Girl. Anchin, Lisa. 2019. 40p. (J). (-k). 17.99 *(978-0-7352-3073-6(0),* Dial Bks) Penguin Young Readers Group.

Ancona, George. Boys Dancing: From School Gym to Theater Stage. Ancona, George. 2017. 48p. (J). (gr. k-3). 16.99 *(978-0-7636-8202-6(0))* Candlewick Pr.

—Can We Help? Kids Volunteering to Help Their Communities. Ancona, George. 48p. (J). (gr. k-3). 2019. 7.99 *(978-1-5362-0297-7(5));* 2015. 17.99 *(978-0-7636-7367-3(6))* Candlewick Pr.

—It's Our Garden: From Seeds to Harvest in a School Garden. Ancona, George. 2015. 48p. (J). (gr. k-3). pap. 6.99 *(978-0-7636-7691-9(8))* Candlewick Pr.

—Kids Cooking: Students Prepare & Eat Foods from Around the World. Ancona, George. 2018. 32p. (J). (gr. -1-1). 16.99 *(978-0-7636-9876-8(8))* Candlewick Pr.

—Nuestro Huerto: De la Semilla a la Cosecha en el Huerto Del Colegio. Ancona, George. 2016. 48p. (J). (gr. k-3). 6.99 *(978-0-7636-8771-7(5))* Candlewick Pr.

—¿Podemos Ayudar? Niños Que Ayudan a Sus Comunidades. Ancona, George. 2019. 48p. (J). (gr. k-3). 6.99 *(978-1-5362-0298-4(3))* Candlewick Pr.

Ancona, George, photos by. Arizona. Becker, Michelle Aki. Risco, Eida del, tr. from ENG. 2004. (Rookie Readers Spanish Ser.). (SPA., 32p. (J). 19.50 *(978-0-516-25106-6(6),* Watts, Franklin) Scholastic Library Publishing.

—California. De Capua, Sarah. Risco, Eida del, tr. from ENG. 2004. (Rookie Readers Spanish Ser.). (SPA., 32p. (J). 19.50 *(978-0-516-25107-3(4),* Watts, Franklin) Scholastic Library Publishing.

—Florida. Bredeson, Carmen. Risco, Eida del, tr. from ENG. 2004. (Rookie Readers Spanish Ser.). (SPA., 32p. (J). 19.50 *(978-0-516-25108-0(2),* Watts, Franklin) Scholastic Library Publishing.

—Join Hands! The Ways We Celebrate Life. Mora, Pat. 2008. 32p. (J). (gr. -1-3). 15.95 *(978-1-58089-202-5(7))* Charlesbridge Publishing, Inc.

Ancona, George, photos by. Come & Eat! Ancona, George. 2011. 48p. (J). (gr. k-3). 16.95 *(978-1-58089-366-4(X));* pap. 7.95 *(978-1-58089-367-1(8))* Charlesbridge Publishing, Inc.

—Olé Flamenco! Ancona, George. 2010. (ENG., 48p. (J). (gr. 2-6). 19.95 *(978-1-60060-361-7(0))* Lee & Low Bks., Inc.

—Self Portrait. Ancona, George. 2006. (Meet the Author Ser.). 32p. (J). 14.95 *(978-1-57274-860-6(5),* 733, Meet the Author) Owen, Richard C. Pubs., Inc.

Ancutici, Manuela, photos by. I Spy 123: Totally Crazy Numbers. Sauerhofer, Ulrike. 2017. (ENG., 32p. (J). (gr. -1-2). 14.95 *(978-1-77085-999-9(3),* 14234ad6-3d60-4bab-9508-256d108fa8b8) Firefly Bks., Ltd.

—I Spy ABC: Totally Crazy Letters. Prenting, Ruth. 2017. (ENG., 32p. (J). (gr. -1-2). 14.95 *(978-1-77085-991-6(6),* 175120b6-87af-4a2d-a502-d4fb1a025f6e) Firefly Bks., Ltd.

Ancutici, Manuela, photos by. I Spy ABC: Totally Crazy Letters! Prenting, Ruth. 2020. (ENG., 32p. (J). (gr. -1-2). pap. 6.95 ***(978-0-2281-0262-5(6),*** 599f1e45-1e92-4f2c-be22-fe90e86566d1) Firefly Bks., Ltd.

Anders, Kenzie. The Baby Who Overcame a Dragon: A Surprisingly Accurate Christmas Story. Thompson, Chase a. 2019. (ENG.). 28p. (J). pap. 9.99 ***(978-1-7123-5489-6(2))*** Independently Published.

Andersen, Amy Elliott. The Shroud of the Thwacker. Elliott, Chris. 2006. 368p. pap. 13.95 *(978-1-4013-6011-5(4))* Miramax Bks.

Andersen, Bethane. But God Remembered: Stories of Women from Creation to the Promised Land. Sasso, Sandy Eisenberg. 2008. (ENG.). 32p. pap. 8.99 *(978-1-58023-372-9(4),* 14658449-7565-40e4-9c7f-b0da8c2f75de, Jewish Lights Publishing) LongHill Partners, Inc.

Andersen, Bethanne. The Bear & the Star. Schaefer, Lola M. 2019. (ENG.). 40p. (J). (gr. -1-3). 17.99 *(978-0-06-266037-4(3),* Greenwillow Bks.) HarperCollins Pubs.

—Georgia's Bones. Bryant, Jen. 2005. (ENG.). 32p. (J). 17.00 *(978-0-8028-5217-5(3))* Eerdmans, William B. Publishing Co.

—Seven Brave Women. Hearne, Betsy. 2006. (gr. -1-3). 17.00 *(978-0-7569-6669-0(8))* Perfection Learning Corp.

Andersen, Brooklyn, jt. illus. see Andersen, Richard.

Andersen, Candace. Morgan Otter Saves the Sea Turtles: Saves the Sea Turtles. Thompson, Tara V. 2016. (ENG.). 130p. (J). (gr. k-4). pap. 6.99 *(978-1-944995-01-0(3))* Amberjack Publishing Co.

Andersen, Dana Lynne. Born with a Bang: The Universe Tells Our Cosmic Story. Morgan, Jennifer. 2004. (Sharing Nature with Children Book Ser.). 48p. (YA). (gr. 2-18). 19.95 *(978-1-58469-033-7(X))* Dawn Pubns.

—Born with a Bang: The Universe Tells Our Cosmic Story. Morgan, Jennifer. 2011. (ENG.). 48p. (J). (gr. 2-5). pap. 12.95 *(978-1-58469-032-0(1),* Dawn Pubns.) Sourcebooks, Inc.

—From Lava to Life: The Universe Tells Our Earth Story. Morgan, Jennifer. (ENG.). 48p. (J). 2012. (gr. 2-5). 16.95 *(978-1-58469-043-6(7));* 2003. pap. 8.95 *(978-1-58469-042-9(9))* Sourcebooks, Inc. (Dawn Pubns.).

—Mammals Who Morph: The Universe Tells Our Evolution Story: Book 3. Morgan, Jennifer. 2006. (ENG.). 45p. (J). (gr. 2-5). 19.95 *(978-1-58469-084-9(4));* pap. 9.95 *(978-1-58469-085-6(2))* Sourcebooks, Inc. (Dawn Pubns.).

Andersen, Flemming & Gonzalez, Jose Antonio. Donald Duck Adventures, Vol. 17. Laban, Terry. Clark, John, ed. 2006. (ENG.). 128p. (YA). (gr. 3-7). pap. 7.95 *(978-1-888472-12-7(X),* 9781888472127) Gemstone Publishing, Inc.

Andersen, Gregg, photos by. Adding & Subtracting in Math Club. Ayers, Amy. 2007. (Math in Our World Ser.). 24p. (gr. 1-2). lib. bdg. 23.00 *(978-0-8368-8470-8(1),* Weekly Reader Leveled Readers) Stevens, Gareth Publishing LLLP.

—Bus Drivers. Gorman, Jacqueline Laks & Laks Gorman, Jacqueline. 2010. (People in My Community Ser.). 24p. (gr. k-3). 23.60 *(978-1-4339-3335-6(7))* Stevens, Gareth Publishing LLLP.

—Bus Drivers. Gorman, Jacqueline Laks. 2010. (People in My Community Ser.). 24p. (gr. k-3). pap. 8.15 *(978-1-4339-3336-3(5))* Stevens, Gareth Publishing LLLP.

—Bus Drivers / Conductores de Autobuses. Laks Gorman, Jacqueline. 2010. (People in My Community / Mi comunidad Ser.). (SPA., 24p. (gr. k-3). pap. 8.15 *(978-1-4339-3754-5(9))* Stevens, Gareth Publishing LLLP.

—Counting at the Zoo. Rauen, Amy & Ayers, Amy. 2007. (Math in Our World Ser.). 24p. (gr. 1-2). pap. 8.15 *(978-0-8368-8478-4(7),* Weekly Reader Leveled Readers) Stevens, Gareth Publishing LLLP.

—Firefighters. Gorman, Jacqueline Laks & Laks Gorman, Jacqueline. 2010. (People in My Community Ser.). 24p. (gr. k-3). 23.60 *(978-1-4339-3338-7(1))* Stevens, Gareth Publishing LLLP.

—Firefighters. Gorman, Jacqueline Laks. 2010. (People in My Community Ser.). 24p. (gr. k-3). pap. 8.15 *(978-1-4339-3339-4(X))* Stevens, Gareth Publishing LLLP.

—Firefighters / Bomberos. Laks Gorman, Jacqueline. 2010. (People in My Community / Mi comunidad Ser.). (SPA., 24p. (gr. k-3). pap. 8.15 *(978-1-4339-3757-6(3))* Stevens, Gareth Publishing LLLP.

—I Can Read a Map. Ashley, Susan. 2004. (I Can Do It! Ser.). (ENG., (J). (gr. k-3). lib. bdg. 19.25 *(978-1-61383-787-0(9))* Perfection Learning Corp.

—Librarians. Laks Gorman, Jacqueline. 2010. (People in My Community Ser.). 24p. (gr. k-3). pap. 8.15 *(978-1-4339-3342-4(X))* Stevens, Gareth Publishing LLLP.

—Librarians. Gorman, Jacqueline Laks & Laks Gorman, Jacqueline. 2010. (People in My Community Ser.). 24p. (gr. k-3). 23.60 *(978-1-4339-3341-7(1))* Stevens, Gareth Publishing LLLP.

—Librarians / Bibliotecarios. Laks Gorman, Jacqueline. 2010. (People in My Community / Mi comunidad Ser.). (SPA., 24p. (gr. k-3). pap. 8.15 *(978-1-4339-3760-6(3))* Stevens, Gareth Publishing LLLP.

—Mail Carriers. Early Macken, JoAnn. 2010. (People in My Community Ser.). 24p. (gr. k-3). pap. 8.15 *(978-1-4339-3345-5(4))* Stevens, Gareth Publishing LLLP.

—Mail Carriers / Carteros. Early Macken, JoAnn. 2010. (People in My Community / Mi comunidad Ser.). (SPA., 24p. (gr. k-3). pap. 8.15 *(978-1-4339-3763-7(8))* Stevens, Gareth Publishing LLLP.

—Police Officers. Gorman, Jacqueline Laks & Laks Gorman, Jacqueline. 2010. (People in My Community Ser.). 24p. (gr. k-3). 23.60 *(978-1-4339-3350-9(0))* Stevens, Gareth Publishing LLLP.

—Police Officers. Gorman, Jacqueline Laks. 2010. (People in My Community Ser.). 24p. (gr. k-3). pap. 8.15 *(978-1-4339-3351-6(9))* Stevens, Gareth Publishing LLLP.

—Police Officers / Policías. Laks Gorman, Jacqueline. 2010. (People in My Community / Mi comunidad Ser.). (SPA., 24p. (gr. k-3). pap. 8.15 *(978-1-4339-3769-9(7))* Stevens, Gareth Publishing LLLP.

—Safety at Home. Knowlton, MaryLee. 2008. (Staying Safe Ser.). (ENG., 32p. (J). (gr. -1-3). lib. bdg. *(978-0-7787-4316-3(0))* Crabtree Publishing Co.

—Safety at School. Knowlton, MaryLee & Dowdy, Penny. 2008. (Staying Safe Ser.). (ENG., 32p. (J). (gr. -1-3). pap. *(978-0-7787-4322-4(5))* Crabtree Publishing Co.

—Safety at School. Knowlton, MaryLee. 2008. (Staying Safe Ser.). (ENG., 32p. (J). (gr. -1-3). lib. bdg. *(978-0-7787-4317-0(9))* Crabtree Publishing Co.

—Safety at the Playground. Knowlton, MaryLee & Dowdy, Penny. 2008. (Staying Safe Ser.). (ENG., 32p. (J). (gr. -1-3). pap. *(978-0-7787-4323-1(3))* Crabtree Publishing Co.

—Safety at the Playground. Knowlton, MaryLee. 2008. (Staying Safe Ser.). (ENG., 32p. (J). (gr. -1-3). lib. bdg. *(978-0-7787-4318-7(7))* Crabtree Publishing Co.

—Sumando y Restando en el Club de Matematicas. Rauen, Amy & Ayers, Amy. 2007. (Matemáticas en Nuestro Mundo (Math in Our World) Ser.). (SPA., 24p. (gr. 1-2). lib. bdg. 23.00 *(978-0-8368-8488-3(4),* Weekly Reader Leveled Readers) Stevens, Gareth Publishing LLLP.

—Teachers. Early Macken, JoAnn. 2010. (People in My Community Ser.). 24p. (gr. k-3). pap. 8.15 *(978-1-4339-3348-6(9))* Stevens, Gareth Publishing LLLP.

—Teachers / Maestros. Early Macken, JoAnn. 2010. (People in My Community / Mi comunidad Ser.). (SPA., 24p. (gr. k-3). pap. 8.15 *(978-1-4339-3766-8(2))* Stevens, Gareth Publishing LLLP.

—Using Math to Make Party Plans. Freese, Joan. 2008. (Math in Our World: Level 2 Ser.). 24p. (gr. 1-4). lib. bdg. 23.00 *(978-0-8368-9003-7(5),* Weekly Reader Leveled Readers) Stevens, Gareth Publishing LLLP.

—Vamos A Planear una Fiesta Con Matematicas. Freese, Joan. 2008. (Matemáticas en Nuestro Mundo - Nivel 2 (Math in Our World - Level 2) Ser.). (SPA., 24p. (gr. 1-4). lib. bdg. 23.00 *(978-0-8368-9021-1(3),* Weekly Reader Leveled Readers) Stevens, Gareth Publishing LLLP.

Andersen, Hans. Thumbelina. 2004.Tr. of Tommelise. 32p. 3.99 *(978-1-894998-17-8(0))* Lake, Jack Productions, Inc. CAN. Dist: Hushion Hse. Publishing, Ltd.

Andersen, Lynette. Izzybug. Andersen, Lynette. Andersen, Jake, ed. 2018. (ENG.). 58p. (J). pap. 12.99 *(978-1-7200-6654-5(X))* Independently Published.

—Izzybug Coloring Book. Andersen, Lynette. Andersen, Jake, ed. 2018. (ENG.). 58p. (J). pap. 9.99 *(978-1-7200-8721-2(0))* Independently Published.

Andersen, Richard & Andersen, Brooklyn. The New Fairy. Andersen, Richard. 2019. (Adventures of Little Miss, the Lone Fairy Ser.: Vol. 2). (ENG.). 32p. (J). pap. 9.99 ***(978-1-7040-3466-9(3))*** Independently Published.

Andersen, Sarah. Érase una Vez y Otras Mentiras / Cheshire Crossing. Weir, Andy. 2020. (SPA.). 128p. (YA). (gr. 8-12). pap. 18.95 ***(978-607-31-8911-8(7),*** Montena) Penguin Random House Grupo Editorial ESP. Dist: Penguin Random Hse. LLC.

Anderson, Aaron. Veterans: Heroes in Our Neighborhood. Pfundstein, Valerie. Chernesky, Felicia, ed. 2012. (ENG.). 32p. (J). 18.95 *(978-0-9837186-1-1(X))* Novanglus Publishing, LLC.

Anderson, Adrienne. Marti: The Quarry Lake Monster. Gregory, Jennifer N. 2019. (ENG.). 76p. (J). pap. 19.99 *(978-1-0750-3528-9(7))* Independently Published.

—Mercy. Dalton, Mary. 2019. (ENG.). 48p. (J). pap. 13.50 *(978-1-7954-1592-7(4))* Independently Published.

Anderson, Airlie. Cows in the Kitchen. (Classic Books with Holes 8x8 with CD Ser.). (J). 2013. (ENG.). 16p. (gr. -1). pap. incl. audio compact disk *(978-1-84643-625-3(7));* 2009. (ENG.). 16p. pap. incl. audio compact disk *(978-1-84643-257-6(X));* 2007. 14p. (gr. -1-1). spiral bd. *(978-1-84643-110-4(7));* 2007. 16p. (gr. 1-1). pap. *(978-1-84643-106-7(9))* Child's Play International Ltd.

—Cows in the Kitchen. 2009. (Classic Books with Holes Big Book Ser.). 16p. (J). (gr. -1-1). spiral bd. *(978-1-84643-208-8(1))* Child's Play International Ltd.

—Mini Manners: Hello & Goodbye! Saying Sorry! Please & Thank You!: 3 Books Teach 3 New Skills. Napier, Tanya. 2005. (J). *(978-0-316-74064-7(0))* Little Brown & Co.

—My Name Starts with J. Hayes, Larry E. 2004. (My Name Starts With Ser.). 31p. (J). 14.95 *(978-0-9725292-2-8(5))* Inspire Pubns.

—My Name Starts with K. Hayes, Larry. 2005. (My Name Starts With Ser.). 31p. (J). 14.95 *(978-0-9725292-6-6(8))* Inspire Pubns.

—My Name Starts with M. Hayes, Larry E., photos by. Hayes, Larry E. 2004. (My Name Starts With Ser.). 31p. (J). 14.95 *(978-0-9725292-3-5(3,* 1) Inspire Pubns.

—My Name Starts with S. Hayes, Larry E., photos by. Hayes, Larry E. 2003. (My Name Starts With Ser.). 31p. 14.95 *(978-0-9725292-1-1(7))* Inspire Pubns.

—My Name Starts with S (Library Version) Hayes, Larry E. 2004. (My Name Starts With Ser.). 32p. (J). lib. bdg. 12.95 *(978-0-9725292-8-0(4))* Inspire Pubns.

—A Very Patchy Flap Book. 2004. 10p. (J). bds. 5.95 *(978-1-58925-702-3(2))* Tiger Tales.

—A Very Spotty Flap Book. 2004. 10p. (J). bds. 5.95 *(978-1-58925-703-0(0))* Tiger Tales.

—A Very Stripy Flap Book. 2004. 10p. (J). bds. 5.95 *(978-1-58925-704-7(9))* Tiger Tales.

Anderson, Airlie. Cat's Colors. Anderson, Airlie. 2016. (Child's Play Library). 32p. (J). (gr. k-2). *(978-1-84643-761-8(X))* Child's Play International Ltd.

—Cat's Colours. Anderson, Airlie. 2016. (Child's Play Library). 32p. (J). pap. *(978-1-84643-760-1(1))* Child's Play International Ltd.

Anderson, Alasdair. 2011: Living in the Future. Hoyle, Geoffrey. 2010. (ENG.). 64p. 15.95 *(978-1-59583-430-0(3),* 9781595834300, Darling & Co.) Laughing Elephant.

Anderson, Bethan. Georgia's Bones. Bryant, Jen. 2010. (ENG.). 32p. (J). (gr. -1-5). 9.00 *(978-0-8028-5367-7(6))* Eerdmans, William B. Publishing Co.

Anderson, Betheny, jt. illus. see Jackson, Helston.

Anderson, Bill. How Congress Works. Uni Photo Picture Agency Staff, photos by. Campodonica, Carol A. Miller, Bondell, ed. Date not set. (J). (gr. 4-5). pap. *(978-0-9648489-9-4(9))* Buzzard Pr. International.

—How to Build a California Mission: Santa Cruz, 20 vols. Anderson, Jay, photos by. Campodonica, Carol A. Weber, Francis J. et al, eds. Date not set. (How to Build a California Mission Ser.). (J). (gr. 4-5). pap. *(978-0-9648488-5-6(6))* Buzzard Pr. International.

—The Mesa Verde Cliff Dwellers: An Isabel Soto Archaeology Adventure, 1 vol. Collins, Terry. 2010. (Graphic Expeditions Ser.). (ENG.). 32p. (J). (gr. 3-9). lib. bdg. 31.32 *(978-1-4296-3971-2(7),* Capstone Pr.) Capstone.

Anderson, Bill, jt. illus. see Hoover, Dave.

Anderson, Bill, jt. illus. see Wyman, M. C.

A

Anderson, Billie Ann. My First Bus Ride. Faircloth, Harry W. Date not set. 26p. (J). (gr. -1-4). pap. 9.95 (978-0-9668650-1-1(4)) Maximilian Pr. Pubs.

Anderson, Brent, et al. Power Pack Classic Omnibus Vol. 1. 2020. 1160p. (YA). (gr. 4-17). 125.00 (978-1-302-92367-9(6)) Marvel Worldwide, Inc.

Anderson, C. W. Remus Goes to Town. Paltenghi, Madalena. 2011. 32p. 35.95 (978-1-258-10024-7(X)) Literary Licensing, LLC.

Anderson, C. W. Billy & Blaze Collection: Billy & Blaze; Blaze & the Forest Fire; Blaze Finds the Trail; Blaze & Thunderbolt; Blaze & the Mountain Lion; Blaze & the Lost Quarry; Blaze & the Gray Spotted Pony; Blaze Shows the Way; Blaze Finds Forgotten Roads. Anderson, C. W. ed. 2018. (Billy & Blaze Ser.). (ENG.). 448p. (J). (gr. k-3). pap. 79.99 (978-1-5344-1371-9(5), Aladdin) Simon & Schuster Children's Publishing.

—Blaze Finds Forgotten Roads. Anderson, C. W. 2018. (Billy & Blaze Ser.). (ENG.). 48p. (J). (gr. k-3). pap. 8.99 (978-1-5344-1367-2(7), Aladdin) Simon & Schuster Children's Publishing.

Anderson, Cassie. Lifeformed Volume 2: Hearts & Minds. Lowery, Matt Mair. 2019. (ENG.). 200p. (YA). (gr. 7). pap. 12.99 (978-1-5067-0937-6(0), Dark Horse Books) Dark Horse Comics.

Anderson, Cassie. Lifeformed: Cleo Makes Contact. Anderson, Cassie. Lowery, Matt Mair. 2017. (ENG.). 192p. (YA). (gr. 7). pap. 12.99 (978-1-5067-0177-6(9)) Dark Horse Comics.

Anderson, Constance. Smelling Sunshine, 1 vol. Anderson, Constance. 2013. (ENG.). 32p. (J). 16.99 (978-1-59572-635-3(7)); pap. 6.99 (978-1-59572-636-0(5)) Star Bright Bks., Inc.

Anderson, David. And the Winner Is ... Amazing Animal Athletes. Kaner, Etta. 2013. (ENG.). 32p. (J). (gr. -1-3). 16.95 (978-1-55453-904-8(8)) Kids Can Pr., Ltd. CAN. Dist: Hachette Bk. Group.

—Friend or Foe: The Whole Truth about Animals That People Love to Hate. Kaner, Etta. 2015. (ENG.). 48p. (J). (gr. 3-7). 17.95 (978-1-77147-064-3(X), Owlkids) Owlkids Bks. Inc. CAN. Dist: Publishers Group West (PGW).

—Pretty Ballerina. McRae, G. c. 2013. 44p. pap. (978-0-9876845-3-0(1)) Warne, MacDonald Media.

—The Tooth. McRae, G. c. 2012. 36p. pap. (978-0-9876845-2-3(3)) Warne, MacDonald Media.

Anderson, David. Charlie Sparrow & the Secret of Flight. Anderson, David. 2013. 98p. pap. (978-0-9918003-2-2(X)) Underdog Bks.

Anderson, Debby. Most of All, Jesus Loves You! Piper, Noël. 2004. (ENG.). 24p. (J). 11.99 (978-1-58134-630-5(1)) Crossway.

Anderson, Debby. God Knows My Name. Anderson, Debby. 2003. (ENG.). 32p. (J). 12.99 (978-1-58134-415-8(5)) Crossway.

—Kindness Counts! Anderson, Debby. 2007. (ENG.). 32p. (J). (gr. -1-3). 9.99 (978-1-58134-861-3(4)) Crossway.

Anderson, Dennis E., photos by. Hidden Treasures of San Francisco Bay. 2003. 176p. pap. 29.95 (978-1-890771-75-1(9)) Heyday.

Anderson, Derek. Ballyhoo Bay. Sierra, Judy. 2009. (ENG.). 40p. (J). (gr. -1-3). 19.99 (978-1-4169-5888-8(6), Simon & Schuster/Paula Wiseman Bks.) Simon & Schuster/Paula Wiseman Bks.

—Cuaquito (Little Quack) Thompson, Lauren. 2010. (SPA.). 34p. (J). (gr. -1-1). bds. 7.99 (978-1-4169-9894-5(2), Libros Para Ninos) Libros Para Ninos.

—Hot Rod Hamster. Lord, Cynthia. 2010. (Hot Rod Hamster Ser.). (ENG.). 40p. (J). (gr. -1-1). 18.99 (978-0-545-03530-9(9), Scholastic Pr.) Scholastic, Inc.

—Hot Rod Hamster & the Haunted Halloween Party! Lord, Cynthia. 2015. (ENG.). 32p. (J). (gr. -1-3). 16.99 (978-0-545-81529-1(0), Scholastic Pr.) Scholastic, Inc.

—Hot Rod Hamster & the Wacky Whatever Race! Lord, Cynthia. 2014. (Hot Rod Hamster Ser.). (ENG.). 32p. (J). (gr. -1-2). pap. 3.99 (978-0-545-62678-1(1), Scholastic Pr.) Scholastic, Inc.

—Hot Rod Hamster Meets His Match! Lord, Cynthia. 2016. (Scholastic Reader, Level 2 Ser.). (ENG.). 32p. (J). (gr. -1-2). pap. 3.99 (978-0-545-82591-7(1), Scholastic Pr.) Scholastic, Inc.

—Little Quack Counts. Thompson, Lauren. 2009. (Super Chubbies Ser.). (ENG.). 26p. (J). (gr. -1 — 1). bds. 5.99 (978-1-4169-6093-5(7), Little Simon) Little Simon.

—Little Quack Loves Colors. Thompson, Lauren. 2009. (Super Chubbies Ser.). (ENG.). 26p. (J). (gr. -1 — 1). bds. 5.99 (978-1-4169-6094-2(5), Little Simon) Little Simon.

—Little Quack's ABC's. Thompson, Lauren. 2010. (Super Chubbies Ser.). (ENG.). 26p. (J). (gr. -1 — 1). bds. 5.99 (978-1-4169-6091-1(0), Little Simon) Little Simon.

—Little Quack's Bath Book. Thompson, Lauren. 2006. (ENG.). 8p. (J). (gr. -1 — 1). 9.99 (978-1-4169-0803-6(X), Little Simon) Little Simon.

—Little Quack's Bedtime. Thompson, Lauren. 2009. (Classic Board Bks.). (ENG.). 34p. (J). (gr. -1-k). bds. 8.99 (978-1-4169-6873-3(3), Little Simon) Little Simon.

—Little Quack's Bedtime. Thompson, Lauren. 2005. (ENG.). 32p. (J). (gr. -1-3). 18.99 (978-0-689-86894-8(4), Simon & Schuster Bks. For Young Readers) Simon & Schuster Bks. For Young Readers.

—Little Quack's Hide & Seek. Thompson, Lauren. 2007. (Classic Board Bks.). (ENG.). 34p. (J). (gr. -1-k). bds. 7.99 (978-1-4169-0325-3(9), Little Simon) Little Simon.

—Little Quack's New Friend. Thompson, Lauren. 2008. (Classic Board Bks.). (ENG.). 34p. (J). (gr. -1-1). bds. 7.99 (978-1-4169-4923-7(2), Little Simon) Little Simon.

—Little Quack's New Friend. Thompson, Lauren. 2006. (ENG.). 32p. (J). (gr. -1-3). 19.99 (978-0-689-86893-1(6), Simon & Schuster Bks. For Young Readers) Simon & Schuster Bks. For Young Readers.

—Little Quack's Opposites. Thompson, Lauren. 2010. (Super Chubbies Ser.). (ENG.). 26p. (J). (gr. -1 — 1). bds. 5.99 (978-1-4169-6092-8(9), Little Simon) Little Simon.

—Monster Truck Mania! Lord, Cynthia. 2014. (ENG.). 40p. (J). (gr. -1-k). 18.99 (978-0-545-46261-7(4), Scholastic Pr.) Scholastic, Inc.

—The Potty Train. Hochman, David & Kennison, Ruth. 2008. (ENG.). 32p. (J). (gr. -1-k). 9.99 (978-1-4169-2833-1(2), Simon & Schuster Bks. For Young Readers) Simon & Schuster Bks. For Young Readers.

—Waking Dragons. Yolen, Jane. 2012. (ENG.). 32p. (J). (gr. -1-3). 16.99 (978-1-4169-9032-1(1), Simon & Schuster Bks. For Young Readers) Simon & Schuster Bks. For Young Readers.

Anderson, Derek. Blue Burt & Wiggles. Anderson, Derek. 2014.Tr. of Signed in American Sign Language. (ENG.). 32p. (J). (gr. -1-3). 16.99 (978-1-4814-1933-8(1), Simon & Schuster Bks. For Young Readers) Simon & Schuster Bks. For Young Readers.

—Friends Forever. Anderson, Derek. (Croc & Ally Ser.). 32p. (J). (gr. 1-2). 2019. pap. 4.99 (978-1-5247-8708-0(6)); 2018. 9.99 (978-1-5247-8707-3(8)) Penguin Young Readers Group. (Penguin Workshop).

—Gladys Goes Out to Lunch. Anderson, Derek. 2005.Tr. of Signed in American Sign Language. (ENG.). 40p. (J). (gr. -1-3). 17.99 (978-0-689-85688-4(1), Simon & Schuster Bks. For Young Readers) Simon & Schuster Bks. For Young Readers.

—How the Easter Bunny Saved Christmas. Anderson, Derek. 2006. (ENG.). 40p. (J). (gr. -1-3). 19.99 (978-0-689-87634-9(3), Simon & Schuster Bks. For Young Readers) Simon & Schuster Bks. For Young Readers.

—Romeo & Lou Blast Off. Anderson, Derek. 2014. (ENG.). 32p. (J). (gr. -1-3). 16.99 (978-1-4814-1932-1(3), Simon & Schuster Bks. For Young Readers) Simon & Schuster Bks. For Young Readers.

—The Shark Report #1. Anderson, Derek. 2020. (Benny Mcgee & the Shark Ser.: 1). (ENG.). 64p. (J). (gr. 1-3). 6.99 (978-0-593-09339-9(9)); 15.99 (978-0-593-09338-2(0)) Penguin Young Readers Group. (Penguin Workshop).

—Ten Hungry Pigs: An Epic Lunch Adventure. Anderson, Derek. 2016. 32p. (J). (gr. -1-k). 17.99 (978-0-545-16848-9(1)) Scholastic, Inc.

—Ten Pigs: An Epic Bath Adventure. Anderson, Derek. 2015. (ENG.). 40p. (J). (gr. -1-k). 17.99 (978-0-545-16846-5(5)) Scholastic, Inc.

Anderson, Derek. We Are Famous! #2. Anderson, Derek. 2020. (Benny Mcgee & the Shark Ser.: 2). (ENG.). 64p. (J). (gr. 1-3). 6.99 **(978-0-593-09342-9(9))**; 15.99 **(978-0-593-09341-2(0))** Penguin Young Readers Group. (Penguin Workshop).

Anderson, Derek. What about Harry? Anderson, Derek. 2019. (ENG.). 32p. (J). (gr. -1-3). 17.99 (978-0-06-240259-2(5)) HarperCollins Pubs.

Anderson, Derek & Paprocki, Greg. Hot Rod Hamster Meets His Match! Lord, Cynthia. 2016. (J). (978-1-5182-0993-2(9), Scholastic Pr.) Scholastic, Inc.

Anderson, Doug. 101 Best Magic Tricks. Frederick, Guy. 2012. 130p. 40.95 (978-1-258-23095-1(X)); pap. 25.95 (978-1-258-23889-6(6)) Literary Licensing, LLC.

Anderson, Harold. Get 'Em Mayfield. Sherman, Harold M. 2011. 272p. 47.95 (978-1-258-06451-8(0)) Literary Licensing, LLC.

Anderson, Hayley. Rebecca Finds Happiness. Harris, Gina. 2017. (ENG.). 34p. (J). (gr. k-2). pap. 12.95 (978-1-5069-0465-8(3)) First Edition Design eBook Publishing.

Anderson, Howard. One Sweet Princess. Kornfield, Katie. 2005. (ENG.). 36p. pap. 15.99 (978-1-4134-8581-3(2)) Xlibris Corp.

Anderson, J. Cecil. Getting the Brain Ready for Early Learning. Anderson, J. Cecil. Anderson, Lorraine. 2019. (Habari Bks.: 1). (ENG.). 32p. (J). (gr. k-1). pap. 10.95 **(978-0-578-55615-4(4))** Holy Child Pubns.

—Habari's Book of Letters: A Practical Guide for Learning the Alphabet. Anderson, J. Cecil. Anderson, Lorraine. 2019. (Habari Bks.: 2). (ENG.). 36p. (J). (gr. k-1). pap. 10.95 **(978-0-578-55616-1(2))** Holy Child Pubns.

Anderson, Jan. A Wolf's Tale. Clish, Marian L. unabr. I.t. ed. (J). (gr. k-5). pap. 14.95 incl. audio compact disk (978-1-928632-01-6(7)) Writers Marketplace:Consulting, Critiquing & Publishing.

Anderson, Jan, jt. illus. see Larkins, Mona.

Anderson, Jane A. How Do Hedgehogs Hug? Alford, Douglas J. & Alford, Pakaket. 2013. 58p. pap. 11.99 (978-1-62495-071-1(X)) Manufacturing Application Konsulting Engineering (MAKE)in.

Anderson, Jeff. The Duke's Daughter: A Story of Faith & Love. MacKenzie, Lachlan. 2008. (Story Time Ser.). (ENG.). 24p. (J). (gr. -1-3). 7.99 (978-1-84550-326-0(0), a99aa817-1875-482f-a90f-23d0b21703c8) Christian Focus Pubns. GBR. Dist: Baker & Taylor Publisher Services (BTPS).

—How God Sent a Dog to Save a Family. Beeke, Joel R. & Kleyn, Diana. 2008. (Building on the Rock Ser.). (ENG.). 176p. (J). pap. 8.99 (978-1-85792-819-8(9), ac45ed85-91e2-4253-b12b-270eebf0f0ed, CF4Kids) Christian Focus Pubns. GBR. Dist: Baker & Taylor Publisher Services (BTPS).

—How God Stopped the Pirates. Beeke, Joel R. & Kleyn, Diana. 2008. (Building on the Rock Ser.). (ENG.). 176p. (J). pap. 8.99 (978-1-85792-816-7(4), 917ca6ad-a5cb-4e5a-806f-ec8f683e4ee5, CF4Kids) Christian Focus Pubns. GBR. Dist: Baker & Taylor Publisher Services (BTPS).

—How God Used a Drought & an Umbrella. Beeke, Joel R. & Kleyn, Diana. 2006. (Building on the Rock Ser.). (ENG.). 176p. (J). pap. 8.99 (978-1-85792-818-1(0), 2263551a-78ca-4c87-9939-edffac40b8dc, CF4Kids) Christian Focus Pubns. GBR. Dist: Baker & Taylor Publisher Services (BTPS).

—How God Used a Snowdrift. Beeke, Joel R. & Kleyn, Diana. 2013. (Building on the Rock Ser.). (ENG.). 176p. (J). pap. 8.99 (978-1-85792-817-4(2), 71756dc1-4033-470c-9092-e1ff89eb05bc, CF4Kids) Christian Focus Pubns. GBR. Dist: Baker & Taylor Publisher Services (BTPS).

—How God Used a Thunderstorm. Beeke, Joel R. & Kleyn, Diana. 2007. (Building on the Rock Ser.). (ENG.). 176p. (J). pap. 8.99 (978-1-85792-815-0(6), 710c5983-c426-4257-8b31-2de72923e32d, CF4Kids) Christian Focus Pubns. GBR. Dist: Baker & Taylor Publisher Services (BTPS).

—Jesus: The Real Story. Mackenzie, Carine & MacKenzie, Carine. 2014. (ENG.). 148p. (J). 10.99 (978-1-85792-930-0(6), 1489577f-d71b-44a9-841c-ec4bdb7eb75e, Christian Focus) Christian Focus Pubns. GBR. Dist: Baker & Taylor Publisher Services (BTPS).

—Jesus el Milagroso. Foce, Natalia, tr. from ENG. I.t. ed. 2009. Orig. Title: Jesus the Miracle Worker. (SPA & ENG.). 24p. (J). 3.49 (978-1-932789-28-7(6)) Editorial Sendas Antiguas, LLC.

—Jesus Maestro. Foce, Natalia, tr. from ENG. I.t. ed. 2009. Orig. Title: Jesus the Teacher. (SPA & ENG.). 24p. (J). 3.49 (978-1-932789-26-3(X)) Editorial Sendas Antiguas, LLC.

—Jesus Narrador. Foce, Natalia, tr. from ENG. I.t. ed. 2009. Orig. Title: Jesus the Storyteller. (SPA & ENG.). 24p. (J). 3.49 (978-1-932789-25-6(1)) Editorial Sendas Antiguas, LLC.

—Jesus Niño. Foce, Natalia, tr. from ENG. I.t. ed. 2009. Orig. Title: Jesus the Child. (SPA & ENG.). 24p. (J). 3.49 (978-1-932789-24-9(3)) Editorial Sendas Antiguas, LLC.

—Jesus Salvador. Foce, Natalia, tr. from ENG. I.t. ed. 2009. Orig. Title: Jesus the Saviour. (SPA & ENG.). 24p. (J). 3.49 (978-1-932789-29-4(4)) Editorial Sendas Antiguas, LLC.

—Jesus Sanador. Foce, Natalia, tr. from ENG. I.t. ed. 2009. Orig. Title: Jesus the Healer. (SPA & ENG.). 24p. (J). 3.49 (978-1-932789-27-0(8)) Editorial Sendas Antiguas, LLC.

—Queen Victoria's Request: A Story of Grace & Mercy. Spurgeon, Charles. 2008. (Story Time Ser.). (ENG.). 24p. (J). (gr. -1-3). 7.99 (978-1-84550-325-3(2), 859a0672-cb8d-4103-89cd-95e8a0bb02a6) Christian Focus Pubns. GBR. Dist: Baker & Taylor Publisher Services (BTPS).

Anderson, Jesse. The Graham Cracker Kid & the Calico Girl. Overstreet, Tommy & Vest, Dale G. 2012. 46p. 12.95 (978-1-62016-014-5(5)) AWOC.COM.

Anderson, Josephine. Flight of Maldar. Myers, Veronica. 2019. (Flight of Maldar Ser.: Vol. 1). (ENG.). 202p. (J). pap. 8.13 (978-1-0714-5989-8(9)) Independently Published.

Anderson, Kari A. When I Grow Up. Wilson, Jodi L. 32p. (Orig.). (J). (gr. 1-3). pap. 4.95 (978-0-9628335-0-2(9)) Wilander Publishing Co.

Anderson, Karin, photos by. Impact! Asteroids & the Science of Saving the World. Rusch, Elizabeth. 2017. (Scientists in the Field Ser.). (ENG., 80p. (J). (gr. 5-7). 18.99 (978-0-544-67159-1(7), 1625794, HMH Books For Young Readers) Houghton Mifflin Harcourt Publishing Co.

Anderson, Kelsey. Only God Knows. Anderson, Cori. 2017. (ENG.). (J). 23.95 (978-1-64028-513-2(X)); pap. 13.95 (978-1-64028-511-8(3)) Christian Faith Publishing.

Anderson, Laura. Aladdin. Nadin, Joanna. 2014. (Traditional Tales Ser.). (ENG.). 32p. (J). (gr. 1-2). pap. 7.95 (978-1-62521-532-1(0), Capstone Classroom) Capstone.

Anderson, Laura Ellen. The Adventures of Swashbuckle Lil. Woollard, Elli. 2018. (Swashbuckle Lil: the Secret Pirate Ser.). (ENG.). 192p. (J). (gr. k-3). pap. 10.99 (978-1-5098-8152-9(2)) Pan Macmillan GBR. Dist: Independent Pubs. Group.

—Big Bob, Little Bob. Howe, James. 2016. (ENG.). 32p. (J). (gr. -1-1). 15.99 (978-0-7636-4436-9(6)) Candlewick Pr.

Anderson, Laura Ellen. Harper & the Circus of Dreams. Burnell, Cerrie. (Harper Ser.: 2). (ENG.). 152p. (J). (gr. 1-3). 2020. pap. 7.99 **(978-1-5107-5771-4(6))**; 2017. 14.99 (978-1-5107-1567-7(3)) Skyhorse Publishing Co., Inc. (Sky Pony Pr.).

Anderson, Laura Ellen. Harper & the Fire Star. Burnell, Cerrie. 2018. (Harper Ser.: 4). (ENG.). 168p. (J). (gr. 1-3). 14.99 (978-1-5107-3613-9(1), Sky Pony Pr.) Skyhorse Publishing Co., Inc.

—Harper & the Night Forest. Burnell, Cerrie. 2018. (ENG.). 188p. (J). (gr. 1-3). 14.99 (978-1-5107-3483-8(X), Sky Pony Pr.) Skyhorse Publishing Co., Inc.

—Harper & the Scarlet Umbrella. Burnell, Cerrie. 2017. (ENG.). 128p. (J). (gr. 1-4). 14.99 (978-1-5107-1566-0(5), Sky Pony Pr.) Skyhorse Publishing Co., Inc.

—Izzy the Invisible. Gray, Louise. 2016. (ENG.). 144p. (J). (gr. 2-4). pap. 8.99 (978-1-84812-509-4(7)) Bonnier Publishing GBR. Dist: Independent Pubs. Group.

—Prince George Goes to School. Hart, Caryl. 2018. (Prince George Ser.). 32p. (J). (gr. -1-k). pap. 9.99 (978-1-4083-4610-5(9), Orchard Bks.) Hachette Children's Group GBR. Dist: Hachette Bk. Group.

—Rapunzel & the Prince of Pop. Gorman, Karyn. 2015. (Tadpoles: Fairytale Twists Ser.). (ENG.). 32p. (J). (gr. 1-2). (978-0-7787-1929-8(4)) Crabtree Publishing Co.

—Swashbuckle Lil: the Secret Pirate. Woollard, Elli. 2016. (Swashbuckle Lil: the Secret Pirate Ser.: 1). (ENG.). 128p. (J). (gr. k-2). pap. 10.99 (978-1-5098-0882-3(5)) Pan Macmillan GBR. Dist: Independent Pubs. Group.

—Witch Switch. Pounder, Sibéal. 2017. (Witch Wars Ser.). (ENG.). 272p. (J). 16.99 (978-1-61963-984-3(X), 900154237, Bloomsbury USA Childrens) Bloomsbury Publishing USA.

—Witch Wars. Pounder, Sibéal. 2015. (Witch Wars Ser.). 272p. (J). (gr. 2-4). pap. (978-1-4088-5265-1(9), 251780, Bloomsbury Children's Bks.) Bloomsbury Publishing Plc.

—Witch Wars. Pounder, Sibéal. 2016. (Witch Wars Ser.). (ENG.). 272p. (J). 16.99 (978-1-61963-925-6(4), 9781619639256, Bloomsbury USA Childrens) Bloomsbury Publishing USA.

—Witch Wars. Pounder, Sibéal. 2017. (Witch Wars Ser.). (ENG.). 288p. (J). pap. 7.99 (978-1-68119-296-3(9), 900165545, Bloomsbury USA Childrens) Bloomsbury Publishing USA.

Anderson, Laura Ellen & Busby, Ailie. Bad Influence. Sutcliffe, William. 2015. 224p. (YA). (gr. 9). pap. 15.99 (978-1-4088-3653-8(X), 900139944, Bloomsbury Paperbacks) Bloomsbury Publishing USA.

Anderson, Lena. Linnea in Monet's Garden. Björk, Christina. Sandin, Joan, tr. 2012. (ENG.). 48p. (J). (-3). 16.99 (978-1-4022-7729-0(6), Sourcebooks Jabberwocky) Sourcebooks, Inc.

Anderson, Leo. Leo the Duck. Godfrey, Roy & Godfrey, Craig. 2017. (ENG.). (J). 21.95 (978-1-64003-277-4(0)); pap. 12.95 (978-1-64003-276-7(2)) Covenant Bks.

Anderson, Lesley. Gwendolyn Goes Hollywood. Rottenberg, David Ira & Rottenberg, David Ira. 2011. 40p. (J). 16.99 (978-0-910291-11-8(X)) Cedar Crest Bks.

Anderson, Lexie. All about Me Children's Coloring Journal. Beck, Lauren. 2015. (J). pap. 4.99 (978-1-4621-1707-9(4), Horizon Pubs.) Cedar Fort, Inc./CFI Distribution.

Anderson, Lochlin. The Adventures of Charley Mcchoochoo: Danny & the Whistling Engine. Davis, Trevor. Davis, Natalie, ed. 2012. 34p. pap. 9.99 (978-0-9853650-5-9(6)) Mindstir Media.

—The Adventures of Charley Mcchoochoo: Tank's Glasses. Davis, Trevor. 2018. (ENG.). 46p. (J). pap. 9.99 (978-0-9998275-7-4(X)) Mindstir Media.

Anderson, Mark. For the Love of Cats: An A-to-Z Primer for Cat Lovers of All Ages. Robins, Sandy. 2011. (For the Love Of... Ser.). (ENG.). 48p. 16.95 (978-1-60078-581-8(6)) Triumph Bks.

—For the Love of Dogs: An A-to-Z Primer for Dog Lovers of All Ages. Entrekin, Allison Weiss. 2011. (For the Love Of... Ser.). (ENG.). 48p. 16.95 (978-1-60078-371-5(6)) Triumph Bks.

—For the Love of the Red Sox: An A-to-Z Primer for Red Sox Fans of All Ages. Klein, Fredrick C. 2004. 48p. (J). 16.95 (978-1-57243-667-1(0)) Triumph Bks.

—For the Love of the Yankees: An A-to-Z Primer for Yankees Fans of All Ages. Klein, Fredrick C. 2003. 48p. (J). 19.95 (978-1-57243-579-7(8)) Triumph Bks.

Anderson, Marlene. The Gift. Blythe, Jennifer. 2018. (ENG.). 26p. (J). pap. 12.95 (978-1-64258-486-8(X)) Christian Faith Publishing.

Anderson, Neal. Nephi, Nephi, the Scriptures Are True. Wells, Anita. 2004. 32p. (J). (gr. -1-2). 17.95 (978-1-59038-307-0(9)) Deseret Bk. Co.

Anderson, Nicola. The Boy Who Said Nonsense. Chernesky, Felicia Sanzari. 2016. (ENG.). 32p. (J). (gr. -1-3). 16.99 (978-0-8075-5742-6(0), 807557420) Whitman, Albert & Co.

—Collins Big Cat Phonics for Letters & Sounds - Pog Pops in: Band 01B/Pink B. Baker, Catherine. 2020. (Collins Big Cat Phonics for Letters & Sounds Ser.). (ENG.). 16p. (J). (gr. -1-k). pap. 6.99 (978-0-00-835759-7(5)) HarperCollins Pubs. Ltd. GBR. Dist: Independent Pubs. Group.

Anderson, Nicola. Cuán Grande Es Nuestro Dios: 100 Devocionales Indescriptibles Acerca de Dios y la Ciencia, 1 vol. Giglio, Louie. 2020. (SPA.). 208p. (J). pap. 16.99 **(978-0-8297-4232-9(8))** Grupo Nelson.

Anderson, Nicola. How Great Is Our God: 100 Indescribable Devotions about God & Science, 1 vol. Giglio, Louie. 2019. (ENG.). 208p. (J). 17.99 (978-1-4002-1552-2(8)) Nelson, Thomas Inc.

—In Our Town - Ray Makes a Choice - a Room for Moose: BuildUp Unit 9 Lap Book. Anin, Ravi et al. 2015. (Build up Core Phonics Ser.). (J). (gr. 1). (978-1-4900-2608-4(8)) Benchmark Education Co.

—Mouse in the Haunted House. Litton, Jonathan. 2015. (Planet Pop-Up Ser.). (ENG.). 12p. (J). (gr. -1). 12.95 (978-1-62686-485-6(3), Silver Dolphin Bks.) Readerlink Distribution Services, LLC.

—My First Quran with Pictures: Juz' Amma Part 1. Sharief, Shereen. Aljudai, Abdullah Ibn Yusuf, ed. 2018. (ENG & ARA.). 48p. (J). (gr. 1-6). pap. (978-1-9999183-0-9(4)) Sharief, Shereen.

—Planet Pop-Up: Bear's Merry Christmas. Litton, Jonathan. 2015. (Planet Pop-Up Ser.). (ENG.). 12p. (J). (gr. -1). 12.95 (978-1-62686-486-3(1), Silver Dolphin Bks.) Readerlink Distribution Services, LLC.

—Planet Pop-Up: Monkey on the Moon. Litton, Jonathan. 2015. (Planet Pop-Up Ser.). (ENG.). 12p. (J). (gr. -1). 12.95 (978-1-62686-372-9(5), Silver Dolphin Bks.) Readerlink Distribution Services, LLC.

—Planet Pop-Up: Shark Makes a Splash! Litton, Jonathan. 2015. (Planet Pop-Up Ser.). (ENG.). 12p. (J). (gr. -1). 12.95 (978-1-62686-353-8(9), Silver Dolphin Bks.) Readerlink Distribution Services, LLC.

—Planet Pop-Up: Sheep Rules the Roost! Litton, Jonathan. 2015. (Planet Pop-Up Ser.). (ENG.). 12p. (J). (gr. -1). 12.95 (978-1-62686-354-5(7), Silver Dolphin Bks.) Readerlink Distribution Services, LLC.

—Planet Pop-Up: Tiger Takes Off. Litton, Jonathan. 2015. (Planet Pop-Up Ser.). (ENG.). 12p. (J). (gr. -1). 12.95 (978-1-62686-373-6(3), Silver Dolphin Bks.) Readerlink Distribution Services, LLC.

Anderson, Nicola & Greenhead, Bill. Get Well, Red Hen! - Big Bus - a Sled Club: BuildUp Unit 2 Lap Book. Rogers, Jane et al. 2015. (Build up Core Phonics Ser.). (J). (gr. 1). (978-1-4900-2601-5(0)) Benchmark Education Co.

Anderson, Peggy Perry. To the Tub. Anderson, Peggy Perry. 2004. 52p. (gr. -1-3). 17.00 (978-0-7569-4258-8(6)) Perfection Learning Corp.

Anderson, Penny. Over in My City: Boston. Tong, Anthony. 2019. (Over Bks.: Vol. 2). (ENG.). 36p. (J). pap. 9.99 (978-0-9981412-3-7(2)) Otto PD.

Anderson, Peter & Brightling, Geoff. Gorilas. Redmond, Ian. 2003. (SPA.). 64p. 14.95 (978-84-372-2323-0(7)) Altea, Ediciones, S.A. - Grupo Santillana ESP. Dist: Santillana USA Publishing Co., Inc.

Anderson, Rick. Ancient Mounds of Watson Brake: Oldest Earthworks in North America, 1 vol. Moore, Elizabeth & Couvillon, Alice. 2010. (ENG.). 32p. (J). (gr. k-3). 16.99 (978-1-58980-656-6(5), Pelican Publishing) Arcadia Publishing.

—M Is for Magnolia: A Mississippi Alphabet. Shoulders, Michael. 2003. (Discover America State by State Ser.). (ENG.). 40p. (J). 17.95 (978-1-58536-129-8(1)) Sleeping Bear Pr.

—N Is for Natural State: An Arkansas Alphabet. Shoulders, Michael. 2003. (Discover America State by State Ser.).

(ENG.). 40p. (J). (gr. k-6). 17.95 *(978-1-58536-067-3(8))* Sleeping Bear Pr.

—Natural Numbers: An Arkansas Number Book. Shoulders, Michael. 2008. (Count Your Way Across the U. S. A. Ser.). (ENG.). 40p. (J). 17.95 *(978-1-58536-172-4(0))* Sleeping Bear Pr.

—Racecar Driver's Night Before Christmas, 1 vol. Townsend, Una Belle. 2008. (Night Before Christmas Ser.). (ENG.). 32p. (J). (gr. 1-3). 16.99 *(978-1-58980-565-1(8)*, Pelican Publishing) Arcadia Publishing.

—1 Mississippi 2 Mississippi: A Mississippi Number Book. Shoulders, Michael. 2004. (America by the Numbers Ser.). (ENG.). 40p. (J). (gr. 1-3). 19.99 *(978-1-58536-188-5(7)*, 202034) Sleeping Bear Pr.

Anderson, Sara. Too Big to Dance (Paperback) Anderson, Doug. 2015. (ENG.). 32p. (J). (gr. -1-2). pap. 10.95 *(978-0-9702784-9-4(7))* Sara Anderson Children's Bks.

Anderson, Sara. Noisy City Day (2015 Board Book) Anderson, Sara. 2015. (ENG.). 12p. (J). (gr. -1-1). bds. 10.95 *(978-1-943459-00-1(2))* Sara Anderson Children's Bks.

—Noisy City Night (2015 Board Book) Anderson, Sara. 2015. (ENG.). 12p. (J). (gr. -1-1). bds. 10.95 *(978-1-943459-01-8(0))* Sara Anderson Children's Bks.

Anderson, Sarah. Makoona. Morano, John. 2017. (John Morano Eco-Adventure Ser.: Vol. 2). (ENG.). (YA). (gr. 8-12). pap. 9.99 *(978-1-945760-04-4(4))* Grey Gecko Pr.

—A Wing & a Prayer. Morano, John. 2016. (John Morano Eco-Adventure Ser.: Vol. 1). (ENG.). (J). pap. 9.99 *(978-1-938821-96-7(3))* Grey Gecko Pr.

Anderson, Scoular. The Celts & All That. Burnett, Alan. 2016. (and All That Ser.). 112p. (gr. 4-8). pap. 7.95 *(978-1-78027-392-1(4)*, BC Bks.) Birlinn, Ltd. GBR. Dist: Casemate Pubs. & Bk. Distributors, LLC.

—Columba & All That. Burnett, Allan. 2007. 104p. (J). (gr. 4-8). pap. 5.95 *(978-1-84158-571-0(8))* Birlinn, Ltd. GBR. Dist: Casemate Pubs. & Bk. Distributors, LLC.

—Mary Queen of Scots & All That. Burnett, Allan. 2016. (and All That Ser.). 112p. (gr. 4-8). pap. 7.95 *(978-1-78027-388-4(6))* Birlinn, Ltd. GBR. Dist: Casemate Pubs. & Bk. Distributors, LLC.

—Mei & the Pirate Queen White Band. Bradman, Tony. 2016. (Cambridge Reading Adventures Ser.). (ENG.). 32p. pap. 8.78 *(978-1-316-50090-3(X))* Cambridge Univ. Pr.

—The Pied Piper & the Wrong Song. North, Laura. 2015. (Tadpoles: Fairytale Twists Ser.). (ENG.). 32p. (J). (gr. 1-2). *(978-0-7787-1934-2(0))* Crabtree Publishing Co.

—Robert Burns & All That. Burnett, Allan. 2016. (and All That Ser.). 112p. (gr. 4-8). pap. 7.95 *(978-1-78027-391-4(6))* Birlinn, Ltd. GBR. Dist: Casemate Pubs. & Bk. Distributors, LLC.

—Robert the Bruce. Burnett, Allan. 2006. (ENG.). 105p. pap. *(978-1-84158-497-3(5))* Birlinn, Ltd.

—Robert the Bruce & All That. Burnett, Alan. 2016. (and All That Ser.). 112p. (gr. 4-8). pap. 7.95 *(978-1-78027-390-7(8))* Birlinn, Ltd. GBR. Dist: Casemate Pubs. & Bk. Distributors, LLC.

—The Vikings & All That. Burnett, Alan. 2016. (and All That Ser.). (ENG.). 112p. (gr. 4-8). pap. 7.95 *(978-1-78027-393-8(2)*, Birlinn) Birlinn, Ltd. GBR. Dist: Casemate Pubs. & Bk. Distributors, LLC.

—William Wallace & All That. Burnett, Allan. 2006. (ENG.). 128p. pap. *(978-1-84158-498-0(3))* Birlinn, Ltd.

—William Wallace & All That. Burnett, Allan. 2016. (and All That Ser.). 112p. (gr. 4-8). pap. 7.95 *(978-1-78027-389-1(4))* Birlinn, Ltd. GBR. Dist: Casemate Pubs. & Bk. Distributors, LLC.

Anderson, Scoular. Bubble Trouble (Wizzbang Wizard, Book 2) Anderson, Scoular. 2010. (Wizzbang Wizard Ser.: 2). (ENG.). 96p. (J). (gr. 2-4). pap. 5.99 *(978-0-00-719006-5(9)*, HarperCollins Children's Bks.) HarperCollins Pubs. Ltd. GBR. Dist: HarperCollins Pubs.

—Dragon Danger / Grasshopper Glue (Wizzbang Wizard) Anderson, Scoular. 2011. (Wizzbang Wizard Ser.). (ENG.). 192p. (J). (gr. 2-4). pap. 7.99 *(978-0-00-719007-2(7)*, HarperCollins Children's Bks.) HarperCollins Pubs. Ltd. GBR. Dist: HarperCollins Pubs.

—Fabulous Creatures - Are They Real?: Band 11/Lime (Collins Big Cat) Anderson, Scoular. 2005. (Collins Big Cat Ser.). (ENG.). 32p. (J). (gr. 1-3). pap. 9.99 *(978-0-00-718639-6(8))* HarperCollins Pubs. Ltd. GBR. Dist: Independent Pubs. Group.

—How to Be a Knight: Band 09/Gold (Collins Big Cat) Anderson, Scoular. 2007. (Collins Big Cat Ser.). (ENG.). 24p. (J). (gr. 1-2). pap. 8.99 *(978-0-00-718675-4(4))* HarperCollins Pubs. Ltd. GBR. Dist: Independent Pubs. Group.

—How to Be a Tudor: Band 14/Ruby (Collins Big Cat) Anderson, Scoular. 2007. (Collins Big Cat Ser.). (ENG.). 48p. (J). (gr. 3-4). pap. 10.99 *(978-0-00-723090-7(7))* HarperCollins Pubs. Ltd. GBR. Dist: Independent Pubs. Group.

—How to Be a Viking: Band 12/Copper (Collins Big Cat) Anderson, Scoular. 2007. (Collins Big Cat Ser.). (ENG.). 32p. (J). (gr. 2-4). pap. 10.99 *(978-0-00-723079-2(6))* HarperCollins Pubs. Ltd. GBR. Dist: Independent Pubs. Group.

—Pirate Treasure. Anderson, Scoular. 2009. (Get Set Readers Ser.). 32p. (J). (gr. -1-2). lib. bdg. 25.60 *(978-1-60754-266-7(8))* Windmill Bks.

—Super Splosh (Wizzbang Wizard, Book 1) Anderson, Scoular. 2011. (Wizzbang Wizard Ser.: 1). (ENG.). 96p. (J). (gr. 2-4). pap. 5.99 *(978-0-00-719005-8(0)*, HarperCollins Children's Bks.) HarperCollins Pubs. Ltd. GBR. Dist: HarperCollins Pubs.

—Where on Earth?: Band 11/Lime (Collins Big Cat) Anderson, Scoular. 2005. (Collins Big Cat Ser.). (ENG.). 32p. (J). (gr. 1-3). pap., pap. 9.95 *(978-0-00-718633-4(9))* HarperCollins Pubs. Ltd. GBR. Dist: Independent Pubs. Group.

Anderson, Shauna. Spoofaloof's Adventures: Rainy Day Fun. Anderson, Shel. 2008. 52p. pap. 22.50 *(978-1-4389-1689-7(2))* AuthorHouse.

Anderson-Shorter, Susan. Whitey on the Ranch. Weldon, Stayton. 2010. 52p. pap. 12.95 *(978-1-4490-5474-8(9))* AuthorHouse.

Anderson, Stephanie. Saving Lily. Cladouhos, Tova R. 2019. (ENG.). 32p. (J). pap. 9.99 ***(978-1-63522-003-2(3))*** Rivershore Bks.

Anderson, Stephanie. Sleepy Boy. Kanevsky, Polly. 2006. (ENG.). 32p. (J). (gr. -1-k). 16.99 *(978-0-689-86735-4(2)*, Atheneum/Richard Jackson Bks.) Simon & Schuster Children's Publishing.

—Witch-Hunt: Mysteries of the Salem Witch Trials. Aronson, Marc. (ENG.). 288p. 2003. (J). (gr. 9-18). 19.99 *(978-0-689-84864-3(1))*; 2005. (YA). (gr. 7). reprint ed. pap. 12.99 *(978-1-4169-0315-4(1))* Simon & Schuster Children's Publishing. (Atheneum Bks. for Young Readers).

—You & Me & Home Sweet Home. Lyon, George Ella. 2009. (ENG.). 48p. (J). (gr. -1-3). 19.99 *(978-0-689-87589-2(4)*, Atheneum/Richard Jackson Bks.) Simon & Schuster Children's Publishing.

Anderson, Stephanie. Weaving the Rainbow. Anderson, Stephanie. Lyon, George Ella. 2004. (ENG.). 40p. (J). (gr. -1-2). 19.99 *(978-0-689-85169-8(3)*, Atheneum/Richard Jackson Bks.) Simon & Schuster Children's Publishing.

Anderson, Stephanie, jt. illus. see Ladd, Dave.

Anderson, Stephanie, jt. illus. see Ladd, David.

Anderson, Susan. Amani's World: Amani Goes to Washington D. C. Rutledge, Eddie. 2009. 16p. pap. 8.75 *(978-1-4490-2095-8(X))* AuthorHouse.

—The Queen's 3 Jewels. Gillespie, Tonnika. 2009. 20p. pap. 13.99 *(978-1-4389-3925-4(6))* AuthorHouse.

—Star the Mermaid. Filakosky, Sandra. 2010. 20p. pap. 10.49 *(978-1-4389-8626-5(2))* AuthorHouse.

Anderson, Tara. Pumpkin Orange, Pumpkin Round. Battigelli, Rosanna. 2020. (ENG.). 26p. (J). (gr. -1 — 1). bds. 12.95 ***(978-1-77278-125-0(8))*** Pajama Pr. CAN. Dist: Ingram Publisher Services.

Anderson, Tara. Sapphire the Great & the Meaning of Life. Brenna, Beverley. 2019. (ENG.). 160p. (J). (gr. 2-6). 16.95 *(978-1-77278-069-7(3))* Pajama Pr. CAN. Dist: Ingram Publisher Services.

Anderson, Tara, et al. A World of Kindness. Featherstone, Ann, ed. 2018. (ENG.). 32p. (J). (gr. -1-1). 17.95 *(978-1-77278-050-5(2))* Pajama Pr. CAN. Dist: Ingram Publisher Services.

Anderson, Wayne. The Tin Forest. Ward, Helen. 2003. (ENG.). 32p. (J). (gr. -1-2). 7.99 *(978-0-14-250156-6(5)*, Puffin Books) Penguin Young Readers Group.

—Twenty-five December Lane. Ward, Helen. 2007. 17p. (J). *(978-1-74178-722-1(X))* Five Mile Australia.

Andert, John. Good Night Cape Cod. Gamble, Adam. 2007. (Good Night Our World Ser.). (ENG.). 20p. (J). (gr. k — 1). bds. 9.95 *(978-1-60219-004-7(6))* Good Night Bks.

—Good Night Cape Cod. Gamble, Adam. 2005. (J). bds. 9.95 *(978-0-9758502-5-1(3))* On Cape Pubns.

Ando, Mariko. The Princess Dolls, 1 vol. Schwartz, Ellen. 2018. (ENG.). 144p. (J). (gr. 4-7). pap. 17.95 *(978-1-926890-08-1(6))* Tradewind Bks. CAN. Dist: Orca Bk. Pubs. USA.

—The Princess Dolls, 1 vol. Schwartz, Ellen. 2018. (ENG.). 148p. (J). (gr. 4-7). pap. 10.95 *(978-1-926890-29-6(9))* Tradewind Bks. CAN. Dist: Orca Bk. Pubs. USA.

Andolfo, Mirka, et al. Out of the Bottle. Fontana, Shea. 2020. (DC Super Hero Girls Ser.). (ENG.). 128p. (J). (gr. 2-6). lib. bdg. 31.99 ***(978-1-5158-7436-2(2)***, 202141, Stone Arch Bks.) Capstone.

AndoTwin. The ABCs of Love. Rossner, Rose. 2020. 28p. (J). 8.99 ***(978-1-7282-2095-6(5))*** Sourcebooks, Inc.

AndoTwin. Always More Love. Guendelsberger, Erin. 2020. 40p. (J). (gr. 4-3). 10.99 *(978-1-7282-1376-7(2))* Sourcebooks, Inc.

AndoTwin. Always So Grumpy. Guendelsberger, Erin. 2020. 40p. (J). (-3). 10.99 ***(978-1-7282-1620-1(6))*** Sourcebooks, Inc.

AndoTwin. Around the World with Baxter. Acampora, Courtney. 2018. (ENG.). 32p. (J). (gr. k-k). pap. 12.99 *(978-1-62686-935-6(9)*, Silver Dolphin Bks.) Printers Row Publishing Group.

Andrada, Javier. Pulgarcita. Bailer, Darice et al. 2007. (SPA & ENG.). 28p. (J). *(978-0-545-02099-2(9))* Scholastic, Inc.

Andrade, Filipe, et al. Absolute Carnage: Immortal Hulk & Other Tales. 2020. (ENG.). 112p. (YA). (gr. 8-17). pap. 15.99 *(978-1-302-92448-5(6))* Marvel Worldwide, Inc.

—Figment. Zub, Jim. 2015. (Disney Kingdoms: Figment Ser.). (ENG.). 24p. (J). (gr. 1-5). lib. bdg. 27.07 *(978-1-61479-446-2(4)*, 19186, Graphic Novels) Spotlight.

Andrade, Filipe. Figment: Journey into Imagination. Zub, Jim. 2015. (Disney Kingdoms: Figment Ser.). (ENG.). 24p. (J). (gr. 1-5). lib. bdg. 27.07 *(978-1-61479-448-6(0)*, 19188); lib. bdg. 27.07 *(978-1-61479-447-9(2)*, 19187) Spotlight. (Graphic Novels).

Andrade, Filipe, et al. Figment: Journey into Imagination, Vol. 5. Zub, Jim. 2015. (Disney Kingdoms: Figment Ser.). (ENG.). 24p. (J). (gr. 1-5). lib. bdg. 27.07 *(978-1-61479-449-3(9)*, 19189, Graphic Novels) Spotlight.

Andrade, Filipe. Rocket Raccoon & Groot: Tall Tails. 2020. 232p. (J). (gr. 4-7). pap. 12.99 *(978-1-302-92115-6(0))* Marvel Worldwide, Inc.

Andrade, Filipe, et al. What If? with Great Power. 2019. (ENG.). 136p. (YA). (gr. 8-17). pap. 17.99 *(978-1-302-91615-2(7))* Marvel Worldwide, Inc.

Andrade, Filipe & Christopher, John Tyler. Figment: Journey into Imagination. Zub, Jim. 2015. (Disney Kingdoms: Figment Ser.). (ENG.). 24p. (J). (gr. 1-5). lib. bdg. 27.07 *(978-1-61479-445-5(6)*, 19185, Graphic Novels) Spotlight.

Andrade, Mary J., photos by. Day of the Dead A Passion for Life: Día de los Muertos Pasión por la Vida. Andrade, Mary J., . 2nd ed. 2007. (SPA & ENG., 200p. lib. bdg., stu. ed., tchr.'s training gde. ed. 29.95 *(978-0-9791624-0-4(8))* La Oferta Publishing Co.

Andrade Valencia, Esau. A Perfect Season for Dreaming (Un Tiempo Perfecto para Soñar) Saenz, Benjamin Alire. 2010. (ENG.). 40p. (J). (gr. 1-4). pap. 8.95 *(978-1-933693-62-0(2))* Cinco Puntos Pr.

Andrae, Tom. Sherlock: A Police Dog Story. Goldish, Meish. 2016. (Hound Town Chronicles Ser.). (ENG.). 32p. (J). (gr. 2-6). 28.50 *(978-1-62724-870-9(6))* Bearport Publishing Co., Inc.

Andre, Frederic. Lucia Mène L'Enquête. Zuccante, Luigi. 2015. (FRE.). 78p. (J). pap. *(978-2-9542789-5-7(1))* Le point du jour.

Andreasen, Dan. Across the Puddingstone Dam. Wiley, Melissa. 2004. (Little House Ser.: No. 4). 224p. (J). 16.99 *(978-0-06-027021-6(7))* HarperCollins Pubs.

—The Adventures of Huckleberry Finn: Retold from the Mark Twain Original. Twain, Mark. 2006. (Classic Starts® Ser.). 160p. (J). (gr. 2-4). 6.95 *(978-1-4027-2499-2(3))* Sterling Publishing Co., Inc.

—Alice in Wonderland & Through the Looking-Glass: Retold from the Lewis Carroll Originals. Carroll, Lewis. 2009. (Classic Starts® Ser.). 160p. (J). (gr. 2-4). 6.95 *(978-1-4027-5422-7(1))* Sterling Publishing Co., Inc.

—Anne of Avonlea. Montgomery, L. M. 2009. (Classic Starts® Ser.). 160p. (J). (gr. 2-4). 6.95 *(978-1-4027-5424-1(8))* Sterling Publishing Co., Inc.

Andreasen, Dan. Classic Starts®: Alice in Wonderland & Through the Looking-Glass. Carroll, Lewis. 2020. (Classic Starts® Ser.). (ENG.). 160p. (J). (gr. 2-4). pap. 6.95 ***(978-1-4549-3793-7(9))*** Sterling Publishing Co., Inc.

—Classic Starts®: Peter Pan. Barrie, J. M. 2020. (Classic Starts® Ser.). (ENG.). 160p. (J). (gr. 2-4). pap. 6.95 ***(978-1-4549-3798-2(X))*** Sterling Publishing Co., Inc.

—Classic Starts®: the Adventures of Huckleberry Finn. Twain, Mark. 2020. (Classic Starts® Ser.). (ENG.). 160p. (J). (gr. 2-4). pap. 6.95 ***(978-1-4549-3799-9(8))*** Sterling Publishing Co., Inc.

—Classic Starts®: the Story of King Arthur & His Knights. Pyle, Howard. 2020. (Classic Starts® Ser.). (ENG.). 160p. (J). (gr. 2-4). pap. 6.95 ***(978-1-4549-3805-7(6))*** Sterling Publishing Co., Inc.

Andreasen, Dan. Felicity Story Collection. Tripp, Valerie. 2008. (ENG.). 404p. (J). 29.95 *(978-1-59369-452-4(0))* American Girl Publishing, Inc.

—Firebears, the Rescue Team. Greene, Rhonda Gowler. 2015. (ENG.). 30p. (J). (gr. -1 — 1). bds. 8.99 *(978-1-62779-240-0(6)*, 900142335, Holt, Henry & Co. Bks. For Young Readers) Holt, Henry & Co.

—The Forever Dog. Cochran, Bill. 2007. (ENG.). 32p. (J). (gr. -1-3). 16.99 *(978-0-06-053939-9(9))* HarperCollins Pubs.

—The Hand-Me-Down Doll, 0 vols. Kroll, Steven. 2012. (ENG.). 32p. (J). (gr. k-3). 17.99 *(978-0-7614-6124-1(8)*, 9780761461241, Two Lions) Amazon Publishing.

—The Happy Elf Book & CD. Connick, Harry, Jr. 2011. (ENG.). 32p. (J). (gr. -1-3). 17.99 *(978-0-06-128879-1(9)*, Balzer & Bray) HarperCollins Pubs.

—Hug a Bug. Spinelli, Eileen. 2009. 32p. (J). (gr. -1-3). lib. bdg. 17.89 *(978-0-06-051833-2(2))* HarperCollins Pubs.

—Jeannette Rankin: First Lady of Congress. Marx, Trish. (ENG.). 48p. (J). 2013. (gr. 2-5). 19.99 *(978-1-4424-9618-7(5))*; 2006. (gr. 3-7). 18.95 *(978-0-689-86290-8(3))* McElderry, Margaret K. Bks. (McElderry, Margaret K. Bks.).

—Love Song for a Baby. Bauer, Marion Dane. 2011. (Classic Board Bks.). (ENG.). 40p. (J). (gr. -1 — 1). bds. 7.99 *(978-1-4169-6395-0(2)*, Little Simon) Little Simon.

—The Map Trap. Clements, Andrew. (ENG.). (J). (gr. 3-7). 2016. 160p. pap. 7.99 *(978-1-4169-9728-3(8))*; 2014. 144p. 18.99 *(978-1-4169-9727-6(X)*, Atheneum Bks. for Young Readers) Simon & Schuster Children's Publishing.

—Mortimer's First Garden. Wilson, Karma. 2009. (ENG.). 32p. (J). (gr. -1-3). 19.99 *(978-1-4169-4203-0(3)*, McElderry, Margaret K. Bks.) McElderry, Margaret K. Bks.

—Needle & Thread. Martin, Ann M. 2007. 205p. (J). pap. *(978-0-545-03660-3(7))* Scholastic, Inc.

—Nellie's Promise. Tripp, Valerie. England, Tamara, ed. 2004. (American Girls Collection: Samantha Stories Ser.). (ENG.). 96p. (gr. 2-4). pap. 18.69 *(978-1-58485-890-4(7))* American Girl Publishing, Inc.

—Oliver Twist: Retold from the Charles Dickens Original. Dickens, Charles. 2006. (Classic Starts® Ser.). 160p. (J). (gr. 2-4). 6.95 *(978-1-4027-2665-1(1))* Sterling Publishing Co., Inc.

—Peter Pan. Barrie, J. M. 2009. (Classic Starts® Ser.). 160p. (J). (gr. 2-4). 6.95 *(978-1-4027-5421-0(3))* Sterling Publishing Co., Inc.

—Pilot Pups. Meadows, Michelle. 2008. (ENG.). 32p. (J). (gr. -1-3). 17.99 *(978-1-4169-2484-5(1)*, Simon & Schuster Bks. For Young Readers) Simon & Schuster Bks. For Young Readers.

—A Quiet Place. Wood, Douglas. 2005. (ENG.). 32p. (J). (gr. -1-3). reprint ed. 8.99 *(978-0-689-87609-7(2)*, Simon & Schuster Bks. For Young Readers) Simon & Schuster Bks. For Young Readers.

—River Boy: The Story of Mark Twain. Anderson, William. 2003. (ENG.). 40p. (J). (gr. 2-5). 17.99 *(978-0-06-028400-8(5))* HarperCollins Pubs.

—Sam & the Bag. Jeffries, Alison. 2004. (Green Light Readers Level 1 Ser.). (ENG.). 24p. (J). (gr. -1-3). pap. 4.99 *(978-0-15-205151-8(1)*, 1195546) Houghton Mifflin Harcourt Publishing Co.

—Sam & the Bag. Jeffries, Alison. 2004. (Green Light Readers Level 1 Ser.). (gr. -1-1). 13.95 *(978-0-7569-4331-8(0))* Perfection Learning Corp.

—Samantha's World: A Girl's-Eye View of the Turn of the 20th Century. Goldberg, Judy. 2009. 30p. (YA). (gr. 3-18). 24.95 *(978-1-59369-554-5(3))* American Girl Publishing, Inc.

—Someone's Sleepy. Rose, Deborah Lee. 2013. (ENG.). 32p. (J). (gr. -1-1). 16.95 *(978-1-4197-0539-7(3)*, Abrams Bks. for Young Readers) Abrams, Inc.

—The Sound of Music: A Classic Collectible Pop-Up. Rodgers & Hammerstein & Lindsay & Crouse. 2009. (ENG.). 14p. (J). (gr. -1-3). 34.99 *(978-1-4169-3655-8(6)*, Little Simon) Little Simon.

—Too Many Leprechauns: Or How That Pot O' Gold Got to the End of the Rainbow. Krensky, Stephen. 2007. (ENG.). 32p. (J). (gr. -1-1). 12.99 *(978-0-689-85112-4(X)*, Simon & Schuster Bks. For Young Readers) Simon & Schuster Bks. For Young Readers.

—Traffic Pups. Meadows, Michelle. 2011. (ENG.). 32p. (J). (gr. -1-3). 15.99 *(978-1-4169-2485-2(X)*, Simon & Schuster Bks. For Young Readers) Simon & Schuster Bks. For Young Readers.

—The Twelve Days of Christmas. 2012. (ENG.). 32p. (J). (gr. k-2). 14.99 *(978-1-58536-834-1(2)*, 202344) Sleeping Bear Pr.

—A ValueTales Treasury: Stories for Growing Good People. Johnson, Spencer. 2010. (ENG.). 96p. (J). (gr. k-5). 19.99 *(978-1-4169-9838-9(1)*, Simon & Schuster/Paula Wiseman Bks.) Simon & Schuster/Paula Wiseman Bks.

—White Fang. London, Jack. 2006. (Classic Starts® Ser.). 160p. (J). (gr. 2-4). 6.95 *(978-1-4027-2500-5(0))* Sterling Publishing Co., Inc.

—20,000 Leagues under the Sea: Retold from the Jules Verne Original. Verne, Jules. 2006. (Classic Starts® Ser.). 160p. (J). (gr. 2-4). 6.95 *(978-1-4027-2533-3(7))* Sterling Publishing Co., Inc.

Andreasen, Dan. Saturday with Daddy. Andreasen, Dan. 2017. (ENG.). 26p. (J). bds. 7.99 *(978-1-250-11265-1(6)*, 9781250112651, Holt, Henry & Co. Bks. For Young Readers) Holt, Henry & Co.

Andrejev, Vladislav. Saint Nicholas & the Nine Gold Coins. Forest, Jim. 2015. (J). *(978-0-88141-511-7(1))* St. Vladimir's Seminary Pr.

Andres, Kristina. Good Night Sleep Tight: Eleven-And-a-Half Good Night Stories with Fox & Rabbit. Andres, Kristina. 2018. (ENG.). 60p. (J). (gr. k-3). 17.99 *(978-1-77657-143-7(6))* Gecko Pr. NZL. Dist: Lerner Publishing Group.

Andreu, Meritxell, jt. illus. see Laguna, Fabio.

Andrew, Ian. Cleopatra: Queen of Egypt. Twist, Clint. 2012. (Historical Notebooks Ser.). (ENG.). 30p. (J). (gr. 3-7). 19.99 *(978-0-7636-6095-6(7)*, Templar) Candlewick Pr.

—Colly's Barn. Morpurgo, Michael. 2nd ed. 2016. (Reading Ladder Ser.). (ENG.). 48p. (J). (gr. k-2). 7.99 *(978-1-4052-8253-6(3))* Egmont Bks., Ltd. GBR. Dist: Independent Pubs. Group.

Andrew, Ian, et al. Egyptology: Search for the Tomb of Osiris. Sands, Emily. Steer, Dugald A., ed. 2004. (Ologies Ser.). (ENG.). 32p. (J). (gr. 3-7). 24.99 *(978-0-7636-2638-9(4))* Candlewick Pr.

Andrew, Ian. The Ropemaker. Dickinson, Peter. 2004. 375p. (gr. 7). 17.95 *(978-0-7569-1935-1(5))* Perfection Learning Corp.

—Sixteen String Jack & the Garden of Adventure. Pow, Tom. 2015. 32p. (J). (gr. -1-k). 15.95 *(978-1-78027-226-9(X))* Birlinn, Ltd. GBR. Dist: Casemate Pubs. & Bk. Distributors, LLC.

Andrew, Ian, jt. illus. see Gilbert, Anne Yvonne.

Andrew, Ian P., et al. Egyptology: Search for the Tomb of Osiris. Sands, Emily & Anderson, Wayne. 2004. (ENG.). 30p. *(978-1-84011-852-0(0))* Templar Publishing.

Andrew, Joe. The Three Lady Fish: A Friend in Need. Andrew, Joe. 2007. (J). (gr. -1-3). pap. 9.95 *(978-0-9787995-6-4(9))* High-Pitched Hum Inc.

Andrew, Kate. Chompy the Velociraptor. Morley, J. S. 2019. (ENG.). 26p. (J). pap. ***(978-1-78645-384-6(3))*** Beaten Track Publishing.

Andrew, Louis. Mayan & the Legion of Alice. Steve, Hart. 2019. (ENG.). 44p. (YA). pap. ***(978-0-473-48557-3(5))*** Hart, Steve.

Andrews, Benny. Delivering Justice: W. W. Law & the Fight for Civil Rights. Haskins, Jim. 2005. (ENG.). 30p. (J). (gr. k-3). 22.44 *(978-0-7636-2592-4(2))* Candlewick Pr.

—Delivering Justice: W. W. Law & the Fight for Civil Rights. Haskins, Jim. 2008. (ENG.). 32p. (J). (gr. k-3). pap. 7.99 *(978-0-7636-3880-1(3))* Candlewick Pr.

—John Lewis in the Lead: A Story of the Civil Rights Movement, 1 vol. Benson, Kathleen & Haskins, Jim. 2006. (ENG.). 40p. (gr. 2-7). 17.95 *(978-1-58430-250-6(X))* Lee & Low Bks., Inc.

—Poetry for Young People: Langston Hughes. Roessel, David & Rampersad, Arnold, eds. 2013. (Poetry for Young People Ser.). (ENG.). 56p. (J). (gr. 3). 16.95 *(978-1-4549-0328-4(7))* Sterling Publishing Co., Inc.

Andrews, Gary. Captain Wobbly. Carter, Laura. 2019. (Captain Wobbly Ser.: Vol. 1). (ENG.). 34p. (J). pap. ***(978-0-9955109-0-6(3))*** Wobbly Pr.

—Captain Wobbly & the Invasion from Erm. Carter, Laura. 2020. (Captain Wobbly Ser.: Vol. 2). (ENG.). 34p. (J). pap. ***(978-0-9955109-1-3(1))*** Wobbly Pr.

Andrews, Gary. A Christmas Carol. Dickens, Charles. 2008. (Fast Track Classics Ser.). 46p. (Orig.). (J). (gr. 4-7). pap. 10.00 *(978-1-4190-5087-9(7))* Steck-Vaughn.

—The Strange Case of Dr. Jekyll & Mr. Hyde. Stevenson, Robert Louis. 2008. (Fast Track Classics Ser.). (ENG.). 48p. pap. 10.00 *(978-1-4190-5082-4(6))* Steck-Vaughn.

—Tales from Shakespeare: "A Midsummer Night's Dream" Lamb, Charles & Lamb, Mary. Strang, Kay, ed. rev. ed. 2005. 39p. pap. 4.95 *(978-0-9542905-3-5(4))* Capercaillie Bks., Ltd GBR. Dist: Gatewood Pr.

—Tales from Shakespeare: "King Lear" Lamb, Charles & Lamb, Mary. Strang, Kay, ed. rev. ed. 2005. 35p. pap. 4.95 *(978-0-9542905-6-6(9))* Capercaillie Bks., Ltd GBR. Dist: Gatewood Pr.

—Tales from Shakespeare: "Othello" Lamb, Charles & Lamb, Mary. Strang, Kay, ed. rev. ed. 2005. 36p. pap. 4.95 *(978-0-9542905-4-2(2))* Capercaillie Bks., Ltd GBR. Dist: Gatewood Pr.

Andrews, Jazmine, jt. illus. see Vanner, Chelsey.

Andrews, Kaare. Spider-Man/Doctor Octopus: Year One. 2019. (ENG.). 120p. (YA). (gr. 8-17). pap. 15.99 *(978-1-302-91545-2(2))* Marvel Worldwide, Inc.

Andrews, Kimberly. Song of the River. Cowley, Joy. 2019. (ENG.). 32p. (J). (gr. k-2). 17.99 *(978-1-77657-253-3(X))* Gecko Pr. NZL. Dist: Lerner Publishing Group.

Andrews, LaMont, Jr. Encyclopedia of Activists & Activism in America, Vol. 2 A-Z, Vol. 2. l.t. ed. 2005. 30p. (YA). pap. 10.00 *(978-0-9728975-1-8(8))* JA-M Pubs., LLC.

—Encyclopedia of Activists & Activism in America, Vol. 3 A-Z, Vol. 3. Andrews-McKinney, Joyce. l.t. ed. 2006. 30p. (YA). pap. 10.00 *(978-0-9728975-2-5(6))* JA-M Pubs., LLC.

Andrews, Luke. Sassafras in What Is Metamorphosis? Dontell, Susan L. 2008. 36p. pap. 24.95 *(978-1-60441-776-0(5))* America Star Bks.

A

Andrews-McKinney, Joyce. Jentle & Jewel Fix Things, Andrews-McKinney, Joyce. l.t. ed. 2006. 17p. (J). pap. 8.00 *(978-0-9728975-4-9(2))* JA-M Pubs., LLC.

Andrews, Ryan. The Dollar Kids. Jacobson, Jennifer Richard. 416p. (J). (gr. 5-9). 2020. pap. 8.99 *(978-1-5362-1311-9(X))*; 2018. 17.99 *(978-0-7636-9474-6(6))* Candlewick Pr.

—Mightier Than the Sword #1. Callander, Drew & Harrison, Alana. (Mightier Than the Sword Ser.: 1). (J). (gr. 3-7). 2019. 320p. pap. 9.99 *(978-0-593-09364-1(X))*; 2018. 304p. 13.99 *(978-1-5247-8509-3(1))* Penguin Young Readers Group. (Penguin Workshop).

—Mightier Than the Sword: the Edge of the Word #2. Callander, Drew & Harrison, Alana. 2019. (Mightier Than the Sword Ser.: 2). 336p. (J). (gr. 3-7). 13.99 *(978-1-5247-8510-9(5)*, Penguin Workshop) Penguin Young Readers Group.

Andrews, Ryan. Rise of ZomBert. LaReau, Kara. 2020. (Zombert Chronicles Ser.). (ENG.). 144p. (J). (gr. 3-7). 15.99 ***(978-1-5362-0106-2(5))*** Candlewick Pr.

Andrewson, Natalie. A Fall for Friendship. Atwood, Megan. 2018. (Orchard Novel Ser.: 3). (ENG.). 240p. (J). (gr. 2-6). 12.99 *(978-1-4814-9051-1(6)*, Aladdin) Simon & Schuster Children's Publishing.

—Ice Cream Summer. Atwood, Megan. 2017. (Orchard Novel Ser.: 1). (ENG.). 272p. (J). (gr. 2-6). 12.99 *(978-1-4814-9047-4(8)*, Aladdin) Simon & Schuster Children's Publishing.

—Nooks & Crannies. Lawson, Jessica. 2015. (ENG.). 336p. (J). (gr. 3-7). 19.99 *(978-1-4814-1921-5(8)*, Simon & Schuster Bks. For Young Readers) Simon & Schuster Bks. For Young Readers.

Andrewson, Natalie. The Nutcracker & the Mouse King: the Graphic Novel. Hoffmann, E. T. A. 2020. (ENG.). 144p. (J). 18.99 ***(978-1-59643-681-7(6)***, 900071149, First Second Bks.) Roaring Brook Pr.

Andrewson, Natalie. Once upon a Winter. Atwood, Megan. 2017. (Orchard Novel Ser.: 2). (ENG.). 240p. (J). (gr. 2-6). 12.99 *(978-1-4814-9049-8(4)*, Aladdin) Simon & Schuster Children's Publishing.

—Pixie Piper & the Matter of the Batter. Fisher, Annabelle. (Pixie Piper Ser.: 2). (ENG.). 336p. (J). (gr. 3-7). 2018. pap. 6.99 *(978-0-06-239381-4(2))*; 2017. 16.99 *(978-0-06-239380-7(4))* HarperCollins Pubs. (Greenwillow Bks.).

—The Secret Destiny of Pixie Piper. Fisher, Annabelle. 2016. (Pixie Piper Ser.: 1). (ENG.). 320p. (J). (gr. 3-7). 16.99 *(978-0-06-239377-7(4)*, Greenwillow Bks.) HarperCollins Pubs.

—A Spring to Remember. Atwood, Megan. 2019. (Orchard Novel Ser.: 4). (ENG.). 240p. (J). (gr. 2-6). 12.99 *(978-1-4814-9053-5(2)*, Aladdin) Simon & Schuster Children's Publishing.

Andrezzinho. Los Pájaros No Tienen Fronteras: Leyendas y Mitos de América Latina. Iturralde, Edna. 2015. (Serie Azul Ser.). (SPA.). 280p. (J). (gr. 5-8). pap. 13.95 *(978-958-9002-76-6(5)*, Loqueleo) Santillana USA Publishing Co., Inc.

Andriamanga, Faratiana. Amazing Animals. 2016. (Coloring Studio Ser.: 2). (ENG.). 48p. (J). (gr. 1-17). pap. 8.99 *(978-0-316-39288-4(X))* Little, Brown Bks. for Young Readers.

Andriani, Renée. Don't Know Much about the 50 States. Davis, Kenneth C. 2004. (Don't Know Much About Ser.). (ENG.). 64p. (J). (gr. 1-4). pap. 7.99 *(978-0-06-446227-3(7))* HarperCollins Pubs.

Andriani, Renee. Dudley's Day at Home. Kaufman Orloff, Karen. 2020. (ENG.). 32p. (J). (gr. -1-k). 17.95 *(978-1-947277-26-7(X))* Flashlight Pr.

Andriani, Renée. Earth Day — Hooray! Murphy, Stuart J. 2004. (MathStart 3 Ser.). (ENG.). 40p. (J). (gr. 2-18). 17.99 *(978-0-06-000127-8(5))*; Vol. 50. pap. 5.99 *(978-0-06-000129-2(1))* HarperCollins Pubs.

—Girl Versus Squirrel. Barrett, Hayley. 2020. (ENG.). 32p. (J). (gr. -1-3). 18.99 *(978-0-8234-4251-5(9)*, Margaret Ferguson Books) Holiday Hse., Inc.

—Mall Mania. Murphy, Stuart J. 2006. (MathStart 2 Ser.). (ENG.). 40p. (J). (gr. 1-4). pap. 5.99 *(978-0-06-055777-5(X))* HarperCollins Pubs.

—Teddy Spaghetti. Frank, Dorothea Benton & Frank, Victoria Benton. 2020. (ENG.). 32p. (J). (gr. -1-3). 18.99 *(978-0-06-291542-9(8)*, HarperCollins) HarperCollins Pubs. Ltd. GBR. Dist: HarperCollins Pubs.

Andriani, Renee. This School Year Will Be the BEST! Winters, Kay. 2013. 32p. (J). (gr. 1-3). mass mkt. 6.99 *(978-0-14-242696-8(2)*, Puffin Books) Penguin Young Readers Group.

—This School Year Will Be the BEST! Winters, Kay. 2010. 32p. (J). (gr. 1-3). 17.99 *(978-0-525-42275-4(7)*, Dutton Books for Young Readers) Penguin Young Readers Group.

Andriani, Renee W. Annabel the Actress Starring in Camping It Up. Conford, Ellen. 2005. (Annabel the Actress Ser.). 60p. (J). (gr. 2-5). 11.65 *(978-0-7569-5555-7(6))* Perfection Learning Corp.

—Annabel the Actress Starring in Camping It Up. Conford, Ellen. 2013. (ENG.). 64p. (J). (gr. 2-5). pap. 13.99 *(978-1-4814-0147-0(5)*, Simon & Schuster Bks. For Young Readers) Simon & Schuster Bks. For Young Readers.

—Annabel the Actress Starring in Hound of the Barkervilles. Conford, Ellen. 2003. (ENG.). 96p. (J). (gr. 2-5). pap. 6.99 *(978-0-689-84791-2(2)*, Simon & Schuster/Paula Wiseman Bks.) Simon & Schuster/Paula Wiseman Bks.

—Annabel the Actress Starring in Just a Little Extra. Conford, Ellen. 2013. (ENG.). 64p. (J). (gr. 4-6). pap. 13.99 *(978-1-4814-0148-7(3)*, Simon & Schuster Bks. For Young Readers) Simon & Schuster Bks. For Young Readers.

—Annabel the Actress Starring in the Hound of the Barkervilles. Conford, Ellen. 2004. (Annabel the Actress Ser.). 83p. (gr. 2-5). 14.00 *(978-0-7569-2180-4(5))* Perfection Learning Corp.

—Mall Mania. Murphy, Stuart J. 2006. (MathStart Ser.). (ENG.). 40p. (J). (gr. 1-4). 15.99 *(978-0-06-055776-8(1))* HarperCollins Pubs.

Andriyevskaya, Yevgeniya. Stacy Takes the Train to School. Lupa, Mary R. 2009. 20p. (J). pap. 10.95 *(978-1-4327-1609-7(3))* Outskirts Pr., Inc.

Andronic, Madalina. Jane Eyre. Medina, Melissa & Colting, Fredrik. 2017. (KinderGuides Early Learning Guide to Culture Classics Ser.). 48p. (J). 16.95 *(978-0-9988205-0-7(4))* Moppet Bks.

Andronic, Madalina. A World Full of Spooky Stories: 50 Tales to Make Your Spine Tingle. McAllister, Angela. ed. 2019. (ENG.). 128p. (J). (gr. k-3). 22.99 ***(978-0-7112-4148-0(1)***, Frances Lincoln Children's Bks.) Quarto Publishing Group UK GBR. Dist: Hachette Bk. Group.

Andrules, Jamie L. Why are You my Mother? A Mother's Response to her Adopted Daughter. Hamilton, Deborah E. 2006. (J). 9.99 net. *(978-0-9789202-0-3(1))* Dreams Due Media Group, Inc.

Anegón, Tamara. The Last Lemon Pink B Band. Hawes, Alison. 2016. (Cambridge Reading Adventures Ser.). (ENG.). 16p. pap. 7.37 *(978-1-107-54909-8(4))* Cambridge Univ. Pr.

Anegon, Tamara. Waggers. Nyikos, Stacy. 2014. 32p. (J). (gr. -1-k). 16.95 *(978-1-62914-629-4(3)*, Sky Pony Pr.) Skyhorse Publishing Co., Inc.

Anelli, Liz. Dad's Camera. Watkins, Ross. 2018. (ENG.). 40p. (J). (gr. k-4). 16.99 *(978-1-5362-0138-3(3))* Candlewick Pr.

—Grace & Katie. Merritt, Susanne. 2017. (ENG.). 32p. (J). (gr. -1-3). 17.99 *(978-1-925335-54-5(2)*, EK Bks.) Exisle Publishing Pty Ltd. AUS. Dist: Hachette Bk. Group.

Anfuso, Dennis. The Butterfly & the Bunny's Tail. De Sena, Joseph. 2007. 60p. per. 19.95 *(978-1-4327-0404-9(4))* Outskirts Pr., Inc.

Ang, Joy. Arr, Mustache Baby! Heos, Bridget. 2019. (Mustache Baby Ser.). (ENG.). 40p. (J). (gr. -1-3). 17.99 *(978-1-328-50652-8(5)*, 1718797, Clarion Bks.) Houghton Mifflin Harcourt Trade & Reference Pubs.

—The Atlas Obscura Explorer's Guide for the World's Most Adventurous Kid. Thuras, Dylan & Mosco, Rosemary. 2018. (Atlas Obscura Ser.). (ENG.). 112p. (J). (gr. 3-7). 19.95 *(978-1-5235-0354-4(8)*, 100354) Workman Publishing Co., Inc.

—Behold! a Baby. Watson, Stephanie. 2015. 32p. (J). (gr. -1-1). 16.99 *(978-1-61963-452-7(X)*, 900136955, Bloomsbury USA Childrens) Bloomsbury Publishing USA.

—I Will Not Read This Book. Meng, Cece. 2011. (ENG.). 32p. (J). (gr. -1-3). 17.99 *(978-0-547-04971-7(4)*, 1035388) Houghton Mifflin Harcourt Publishing Co.

—Mulan: The Legend of the Woman Warrior. Wu, Faye-Lynn. 2019. (ENG.). 32p. (J). (gr. -1-3). 17.99 *(978-0-06-280341-2(7)*, HarperCollins) HarperCollins Pubs. Ltd. GBR. Dist: HarperCollins Pubs.

—Mustache Baby. Heos, Bridget. 2016. (Mustache Baby Ser.). (ENG.). 36p. (J). (— 1). bds. 7.99 *(978-0-544-78984-5(9)*, 1639283, HMH Books For Young Readers) Houghton Mifflin Harcourt Publishing Co.

—Mustache Baby. Heos, Bridget. (Mustache Baby Ser.). (ENG.). 40p. (J). (gr. -1-3). 2015. 17.99 *(978-0-544-36375-5(2)*, 1587965); 2013. 17.99 *(978-0-547-77357-5(9)*, 1490719) Houghton Mifflin Harcourt Trade & Reference Pubs. (Clarion Bks.).

Ang, Joy. A Mustache Baby Christmas. Heos, Bridget. 2020. (Mustache Baby Ser.). (ENG.). 36p. (J). (— 1). bds. 8.99 ***(978-0-358-36267-8(9)***, 1784604, HMH Books For Young Readers) Houghton Mifflin Harcourt Publishing Co.

Ang, Joy. A Mustache Baby Christmas. Heos, Bridget. 2019. (Mustache Baby Ser.). (ENG.). 40p. (J). (gr. -1-3). 17.99 *(978-1-328-50653-5(3)*, 1718799, Clarion Bks.) Houghton Mifflin Harcourt Trade & Reference Pubs.

—Mustache Baby (lap Board Book) Heos, Bridget. 2018. (Mustache Baby Ser.). (ENG.). 36p. (J). (— 1). bds. 12.99 *(978-1-328-91048-6(2)*, 1701056, HMH Books For Young Readers) Houghton Mifflin Harcourt Publishing Co.

—Mustache Baby Meets His Match (board Book) Heos, Bridget. 2018. (Mustache Baby Ser.). (ENG.). 36p. (J). (gr. -1-3). bds. 7.99 *(978-1-328-86653-0(X)*, 1695874, HMH Books For Young Readers) Houghton Mifflin Harcourt Publishing Co.

—Petey & Pru & the Hullabaloo. Paquette, Ammi-Joan. 2013. (ENG.). 40p. (J). (gr. -1-3). 16.99 *(978-0-544-03888-2(6)*, 1528603) Houghton Mifflin Harcourt Publishing Co.

Ang, Joy. Princesses Versus Dinosaurs. Bailey, Linda. 2020. (ENG.). 40p. (J). (gr. -1-2). 17.99 ***(978-0-7352-6429-8(5)***, Tundra Bks.) Tundra Bks. CAN. Dist: Penguin Random Hse. LLC.

Ang, Joy. The Qalupalik, 1 vol. Kilabuk, Elisha. 2011. (ENG.). 36p. (J). (gr. 1-3). 12.95 *(978-1-926569-31-4(8))* Inhabit Media Inc. CAN. Dist: Consortium Bk. Sales & Distribution.

Ang, Selvi. Jesus Loves Me: A Bedtime Prayer. Ranga, Katherine. 2011. 26p. pap. 11.95 *(978-1-60976-989-5(9)*, Eloquent Bks.) Strategic Book Publishing & Rights Agency (SBPRA).

Angaramo, Roberta. The Bicklebys' Birdbath. Perry, Andrea. 2010. (ENG.). 40p. (J). (gr. -1-1). 19.99 *(978-1-4169-0624-7(X)*, Atheneum Bks. for Young Readers) Simon & Schuster Children's Publishing.

—Smile, Breathe, & Go Slowly: Slumby the Sloth Goes to School. Carminati, Chiara. 2020. (ENG.). 40p. (J). (gr. -1-2). 18.99 *(978-0-8234-4246-1(2))* Holiday Hse., Inc.

Angel, Carl. The Girl Who Saved Yesterday. Lester, Julius. 2016. (ENG.). 32p. (J). (gr. 2-5). 16.99 *(978-1-939547-24-8(5))* Creston Bks.

—Lakas & the Makibaka Hotel. Robles, Anthony. 2016. (ENG & TGL.). 32p. (J). 9.95 *(978-0-89239-411-1(0)*, Children's Book Press) Lee & Low Bks., Inc.

—Lakas & the Manilatown Fish. Robles, Anthony. 2015. (ENG & TGL.). 32p. (J). pap. 9.95 *(978-0-89239-211-7(8)*, Children's Book Press) Lee & Low Bks., Inc.

—Lakas & the Manilatown Fish (Si Lakas at Ang Isdang Manilatown) Robles, Anthony D. & Children's Book Press Staff. de Jesus, Eloisa D. & de Guzman, Magdalena, trs. 2003.Tr. of Si Lakas at Ang Isdang Manilatown. (ENG & TAG.). 32p. (J). 16.95 *(978-0-89239-182-0(0))* Lee & Low Bks., Inc.

—Willie Wins, 1 vol. Gilles, Almira Astudillo. 2013. (ENG.). 32p. (J). (gr. -1-3). 16.95 *(978-1-58430-023-6(X))* Lee & Low Bks., Inc.

—Xochitl & the Flowers. Argueta, Jorge. 2013. (ENG.). 32p. (J). (gr. k). pap. 10.95 *(978-0-89239-224-7(X))* Lee & Low Bks., Inc.

—Xochitl & the Flowers (Xochitl, la Nina de Las Flores) Argueta, Jorge. 2003.Tr. of Xochitl, la Nina de Las Flores. (ENG & SPA.). 32p. (J). 16.95 *(978-0-89239-181-3(2))* Lee & Low Bks., Inc.

Angel-Rose. The Little Mouse. Lovatt, C. W. 2018. (ENG.). 146p. (J). pap. *(978-1-907954-67-2(8))* Wild Wolf Publishing.

Angela-Lago. Lucas y el Ruisenor. Ventura, Antonio. 2005. (SPA.). 24p. (J). (gr. 1-3). pap., pap. 6.99 *(978-980-257-285-4(3))* Ekare, Ediciones VEN. Dist: Lectorum Pubns., Inc.

Angeletti, Roberta. The Wim Wom from the Mustard Mill. Peters, Polly. 2008. (Child's Play Library). (ENG.). 32p. (J). (gr. -1-3). pap. *(978-1-84643-253-8(7))* Child's Play International Ltd.

Angelini, George. The Oak Inside the Acorn, 1 vol. Lucado, Max. 2006. (ENG.). 48p. 16.99 *(978-1-4003-0601-5(9))* Nelson, Thomas Inc.

Anggareni, Rinandita. You Are So Precious, Rosemarie: A Bilingual Good Night Story to Promote Secure Attachement & Bonding with Your Child. Amador, Ruth-Narumi. 2019. (ENG.). 32p. (J). pap. 10.50 *(978-1-7314-2455-6(8))* Independently Published.

Angle, Scott. Baseball: An Introduction to Being a Good Sport. Derr, Aaron. 2017. (Start Smart (tm) — Sports Ser.). (ENG.). 32p. (J). (gr. k-3). lib. bdg. 26.65 *(978-1-63440-129-6(8))*; E-Book 39.99 *(978-1-63440-141-8(7))* Red Chair Pr.

—Basketball: An Introduction to Being a Good Sport. Derr, Aaron. ed. 2017. (Start Smart (tm) — Sports Ser.). (ENG.). 32p. (J). (gr. k-3). E-Book 39.99 *(978-1-63440-142-5(5))* Red Chair Pr.

—Grammar All-Stars: Parts of Speech, 6 vols. Fisher, Doris & Gibbs, D. L. 2008. (Grammar All-Stars Ser.). 32p. (gr. 2-5). pap. 10.50 *(978-0-8368-8910-9(X))*; pap. 10.50 *(978-0-8368-8912-3(6))*; pap. 10.50 *(978-0-8368-8913-0(4))* Stevens, Gareth Publishing LLLP. (Gareth Stevens Learning Library).

—Half-Pipe Homonyms. Prokos, Anna & Voege, Debra. 2009. (Grammar All-Stars Ser.). 32p. (gr. 2-5). (J). lib. bdg. 27.00 *(978-1-4339-0010-5(6))*; pap. 10.50 *(978-1-4339-0150-8(1))* Stevens, Gareth Publishing LLLP. (Gareth Stevens Learning Library).

—Hole-in-One Adverbs. Fisher, Doris & Gibbs, D. L. 2008. (Grammar All-Stars Ser.). 32p. (gr. 2-5). pap. 10.50 *(978-0-8368-8909-3(6)*, Gareth Stevens Learning Library) Stevens, Gareth Publishing LLLP.

—Slam dunk Pronouns, 6 vols. Fisher, Doris & Gibbs, D. L. 2008. (Grammar All-Stars Ser.). 32p. (gr. 2-5). pap. 10.50 *(978-0-8368-8911-6(8)*, Gareth Stevens Learning Library) Stevens, Gareth Publishing LLLP.

—Soccer: An Introduction to Being a Good Sport. Derr, Aaron. 2017. (Start Smart (tm) — Sports Ser.). (ENG.). 32p. (J). (gr. k-3). lib. bdg. 26.65 *(978-1-63440-132-6(8))*; E-Book 39.99 *(978-1-63440-144-9(1))* Red Chair Pr.

—Tennis: An Introduction to Being a Good Sport. Derr, Aaron. ed. 2017. (Start Smart (tm) — Sports Ser.). (ENG.). 32p. (J). (gr. k-3). E-Book 39.99 *(978-1-63440-145-6(X))* Red Chair Pr.

—Touchdown Nouns. Fisher, Doris & Gibbs, D. L. 2008. (Grammar All-Stars Ser.). 32p. (J). (gr. 2-5). lib. bdg. 27.00 *(978-0-8368-8906-2(1)*, Gareth Stevens Learning Library) Stevens, Gareth Publishing LLLP.

—Volleyball: An Introduction to Being a Good Sport. Derr, Aaron. 2017. (Start Smart (tm) — Sports Ser.). (ENG.). 32p. (J). (gr. k-3). lib. bdg. 26.65 *(978-1-63440-134-0(4))*; E-Book 39.99 *(978-1-63440-146-3(8))* Red Chair Pr.

Angle, Scott & Chandler, Jeff. Bowling Alley Adjectives. Fisher, Doris & Gibbs, D. L. 2008. (Grammar All-Stars Ser.). 32p. (J). (gr. 2-5). lib. bdg. 27.00 *(978-0-8368-8901-7(0)*, Gareth Stevens Learning Library) Stevens, Gareth Publishing LLLP.

Angle, Scott & Roper, Robert. Home Run Verbs. Fisher, Doris & Gibbs, D. L. 2008. (Grammar All-Stars Ser.). 32p. (J). (gr. 2-5). lib. bdg. 27.00 *(978-0-8368-8903-1(7)*, Gareth Stevens Learning Library) Stevens, Gareth Publishing LLLP.

Angleberger, Tom. Rocket & Groot: Keep on Truckin'! Angleberger, Tom. 2017. (Marvel Middle Grade Novel Ser.). (ENG.). 272p. (J). (gr. 3-7). 13.99 *(978-1-4847-8141-8(4)*, Marvel Pr.) Disney Publishing Worldwide.

—Rocket & Groot: Stranded on Planet Strip Mall! Angleberger, Tom. (Marvel Middle Grade Novel Ser.). (ENG.). 224p. (J). (gr. 3-7). 2017. pap. 7.99 *(978-1-368-01392-5(9))*; 2016. 13.99 *(978-1-4847-1452-2(0))* Disney Publishing Worldwide. (Marvel Pr.).

Anglemyer, Jordan. Grandpa's Favorites: A collection of quotes, things to ponder, stories, bits of verse, & Humor. 2007. 77p. (YA). per. 10.95 *(978-0-9796251-2-1(2))* Robertson Publishing.

Anglicas, Loise. Now I Know My ABC's: Musical Sing-Along Book. 2018. (ENG.). 14p. (J). (gr. -1 — 1). bds. 10.99 *(978-1-4380-5055-3(0)*, B.E.S. Publishing) Peterson's.

Anglicas, Louise. Lift the Flap Bible, 1 vol. Williamson, Karen. ed. 2014. (ENG.). 16p. (J). bds. 12.99 *(978-1-78128-130-7(0)*, Candle Bks.) Lion Hudson PLC GBR. Dist: Kregel Pubns.

—Play-Time Noah, 1 vol. Williamson, Karen. ed. 2014. (ENG.). 8p. (J). bds. 9.99 *(978-1-78128-111-6(4)*, Candle Bks.) Lion Hudson PLC GBR. Dist: Kregel Pubns.

Anglund, Joan Walsh. The Cowboy's Christmas. Anglund, Joan Walsh. 2004. (ENG.). 40p. (J). 8.95 *(978-0-7407-4675-8(8))* Andrews McMeel Publishing.

—Little Angels' Book of Christmas. Anglund, Joan Walsh. 2005. (ENG.). 32p. (J). (gr. -1-18). bds. 8.99 *(978-1-4169-1003-9(4))* Simon & Schuster Children's Publishing.

Angold, Mary. Aaliyah P. Rides to Great Grandpa Alvy's Farm! Weeks, Lucinda. 2018. (Little Adventures of Aaliyah P. Ser.: Vol. 9). (ENG.). 40p. (J). pap. 9.15 *(978-1-7273-7020-1(1))* CreateSpace Independent Publishing Platform.

Angorn, Matthew. The Invasion of Planet Wampetter. Pillsbury, Samuel H. 2003. (Planet Wampetter Adventure Ser.). 133p. (J). (gr. 3-8). 15.00 *(978-0-9622036-6-4(1))*; pap. 8.95 *(978-1-930085-05-3(2))* Perspective Publishing, Inc.

Anguelova, Mina. Make a Wish on a Fish. Wiley, Jennie. 2018. (ENG.). 46p. (J). 14.99 *(978-1-948256-11-7(8))*; pap. 10.99 *(978-1-948256-10-0(X))* Willow Moon Publishing.

Angulo, Ruth. La Danta en Pasarela. Rubio, Carlos. 2019. (Torre Roja Ser.). (SPA.). 48p. (J). pap. ***(978-958-776-959-3(7))*** Norma Ediciones, S.A.

Angus, Laurie Ellen. Octopus Escapes Again!, 1 vol. Angus, Laurie Ellen. 2016. (ENG.). 32p. (J). (gr. k-4). 16.95 *(978-1-58469-577-6(3)*, Dawn Pubns.) Sourcebooks, Inc.

—Paddle Perch Climb: Bird Feet Are Neat, 1 vol. Angus, Laurie Ellen. 2018. (ENG.). 32p. (J). (gr. -1-3). 16.95 *(978-1-58469-613-1(3)*, Dawn Pubns.) Sourcebooks, Inc.

Anholt, Catherine & Anholt, Laurence. Catherine & Laurence Anholt's Big Book of Little Children. Anholt, Catherine & Anholt, Laurence. 2003. (ENG.). 80p. (J). (gr. -1-k). 15.99 *(978-0-7636-2210-7(9))* Candlewick Pr.

Anholt, Laurence, jt. illus. see Anholt, Catherine.

Aniel, Isabel. So Big: Keepsake Greeting Card Board Book. Birdsong, Minnie. ed. 2017. (Little Bird Greetings Ser.). (ENG.). 8p. (J). (gr. -1-k). bds. 6.99 *(978-1-68052-208-2(6)*, 1000741) Cottage Door Pr.

Anikeeva, Inna. Amazing Mazes: Level 2. Danilova, Lida & Clever Publishing. 2019. (Clever Mazes Ser.). (ENG.). 48p. (J). (gr. k-17). pap. 4.99 *(978-1-949998-22-1(3))* Clever Media Group.

—Marvelous Mazes: Level 1. Clever Publishing. 2019. (Clever Mazes Ser.). (ENG.). 32p. (J). (gr. -1-17). pap. 4.99 *(978-1-949998-21-4(5))* Clever Media Group.

—Merry Mazes for the Holidays: Level 2. Clever Publishing. 2019. (Clever Mazes Ser.). (ENG.). 48p. (J). (gr. k-17). pap. 4.99 *(978-1-949998-23-8(1))* Clever Media Group.

—Warm & Busy Wintertime. Clever Publishing. 2018. (Clever Activity Pad Ser.). (ENG.). 80p. (J). (gr. -1-1). pap. 4.99 *(978-1-948418-26-3(6))* Clever Media Group.

Animation, Marvel. Take the Milanoand Run, Vol. 4. Robinson, Andrew R. & Caramagna, Joe. 2017. (Guardians of the Galaxy Set 2 Ser.). (ENG.). 24p. (J). (gr. 2-6). lib. bdg. 27.07 *(978-1-5321-4073-0(8)*, 25478, Marvel Age) Spotlight.

—Volume 1: Road to Knowhere. Isenberg, Marty & Caramagna, Joe. 2017. (Guardians of the Galaxy Set 2 Ser.). (ENG.). 24p. (J). (gr. 2-6). lib. bdg. 27.07 *(978-1-5321-4070-9(3)*, 25475, Marvel Age) Spotlight.

—Volume 2: Knowhere to Run. Isenberg, Marty & Caramagna, Joe. 2017. (Guardians of the Galaxy Set 2 Ser.). (ENG.). 24p. (J). (gr. 2-6). lib. bdg. 27.07 *(978-1-5321-4071-6(1)*, 25476, Marvel Age) Spotlight.

—Volume 3: One in a Million You. Melching, Steven & Caramagna, Joe. 2017. (Guardians of the Galaxy Set 2 Ser.). (ENG.). 24p. (J). (gr. 2-6). lib. bdg. 27.07 *(978-1-5321-4072-3(X)*, 25477, Marvel Age) Spotlight.

—Volume 5: Can't Fight This Seedling. McDermott, David & Caramagna, Joe. 2017. (Guardians of the Galaxy Set 2 Ser.). (ENG.). 24p. (J). (gr. 2-6). lib. bdg. 27.07 *(978-1-5321-4074-7(6)*, 25479, Marvel Age) Spotlight.

—Volume 6: Undercover Angle. Griffin, Marsha F. & Caramagna, Joe. 2017. (Guardians of the Galaxy Set 2 Ser.). (ENG.). 24p. (J). (gr. 2-6). lib. bdg. 27.07 *(978-1-5321-4075-4(4)*, 25480, Marvel Age) Spotlight.

Anindito, Ario. Hulkverines. 2019. (ENG.). 112p. (YA). (gr. -1-17). pap. 15.99 *(978-1-302-91835-4(4))* Marvel Worldwide, Inc.

—Weapon H Vol. 2: War for Weirdworld. 2019. (ENG.). 136p. (YA). (gr. 8-17). pap. 17.99 *(978-1-302-91229-1(1))* Marvel Worldwide, Inc.

Anindito, Ario, jt. illus. see Mhan, Pop.

Anka, Kris, et al. Captain Marvel: Earth's Mightiest Hero Vol. 5. 2019. (Captain Marvel: Earth's Mightiest Hero Ser.: 5). (ENG.). 232p. (YA). (gr. 8-17). pap. 24.99 *(978-1-302-91541-4(X))* Marvel Worldwide, Inc.

Anka, Kris. Runaways by Rainbow Rowell & Kris Anka Vol. 3: That Was Yesterday. 2019. (ENG.). 136p. (YA). (gr. 8-17). pap. 17.99 *(978-1-302-91413-4(8))* Marvel Worldwide, Inc.

—Runaways by Rainbow Rowell Vol. 1: Find Your Way Home, Vol. 1. 2018. (ENG.). 136p. (YA). (gr. 8-17). pap. 17.99 *(978-1-302-90852-2(9))* Marvel Worldwide, Inc.

Ann Hollis Rife. The Little Prairie Hen. Leland, Debbie. 2003. 32p. (J). lib. bdg. 14.95 *(978-0-9667086-3-9(6))* Wildflower Run.

Ann Marie Martin, Laurie. Mi'kmaq Campfire Stories of Prince Edward Island, 1 vol. Pellissier-Lush, Julie. 2020. (ENG & MIC.). 32p. (J). pap. 10.95 ***(978-1-77366-054-7(3)***, ee77a7aa-e493-409e-b375-85222905c662) Acorn Pr., The CAN. Dist: Baker & Taylor Publisher Services (BTPS).

Anna, Burstein. Animal Dreams. Burstein, Fred. 2020. (ENG.). 50p. (J). (gr. 1-4). pap. 15.95 ***(978-1-5154-1728-6(X))*** Wilder Pubns., Corp.

Annan, Layal. The Case of the Locker Room Thief. Pietrantonio, Elizabeth. Love, Janice E., ed. 2019. (Stella Hudson High Ser.: Vol. 2). (ENG.). 202p. (J). pap. 11.30 ***(978-1-7121-1172-7(8))*** Independently Published.

Anne, Charlene. Dori's Stories Dori Hiding. Evans, Marjorie. 2018. (ENG.). 20p. (J). pap. 9.99 *(978-1-5456-4983-1(9)*, Mill City Press, Inc) Salem Author Services.

Anne, Zimanski. Grizzly Bears Aren't So Scary! Ewing, Jimmy. 2018. (ENG.). 42p. (J). (gr. k-3). pap. 14.99 *(978-0-578-42526-9(2))* Hound Dog Pr., The.

Annelli, Nikki. Morning. Marshall, Judy. l.t. ed. 2005. 21p. (J). per. 9.99 *(978-1-59879-050-4(1))* Lifevest Publishing, Inc.

Annemarie. The Amazing Adventures of Annemarie & Emily. Corriere, Michael F. 2017. (ENG.). (J). pap. (978-1-4602-9633-2(8)) FriesenPress.
Anno, Moyoco. Happy Mania, 5 vols. Anno, Moyoco. 2003. Vol. 4. 4th rev. ed. 200p. pap. 9.99 (978-1-59182-172-4(X)); Vol. 5. 5th rev. ed. 184p. pap. 9.99 (978-1-59182-173-1(8)) TOKYOPOP, Inc.
Anon. The King & the Magician. Bucay, Jorge. 2014. (ENG.). 52p. (J). (gr. -1). 14.95 (978-0-7892-1204-7(8), 791204, Abbeville Kids) Abbeville Pr., Inc.
—Why Don't Fish Drown? And Other Vital Questions about the Animal Kingdom. Claybourne, Anna & Goble, Claire. 2017. (ENG.). 96p. (J). (gr. 2-7). 19.95 (978-0-500-65126-1(4), 565126) Thames & Hudson.
Anon, jt. illus. see Lewitt and Him Staff.
Anonimo, Silentpilot. Estrellas en el Nochero. Yi, Nur. 2018. (SPA.). 34p. (J). pap. 6.00 (978-1-0886-7917-3(X)) Independently Published.
Anotonini, Gabriele. The Ant & the Grasshopper. 2012. (Tadpoles Tales Ser.). (ENG.). (J). (gr. -1-3). lib. bdg. 17.55 (978-1-61383-953-9(7)) Perfection Learning Corp.
Ansheen, Anda. Edgar: The Mouse Who Left His Field & Discovered the Ocean. Van Vierzen, Ruth. 2018. (ENG.). 38p. (J). (gr. k-3). (978-1-7752047-1-8(5)); pap. (978-1-7752047-2-5(3)) Vierzen, Ruth van.
Ansley, Frank. Invasion of the Pig Sisters. Wheeler, Lisa. 2006. (Fitch & Chip Ser.: 4). (ENG.). 48p. (J). (gr. 1-3). 16.99 (978-0-689-84953-4(2)); pap. 3.99 (978-0-689-84958-9(3)) Simon Spotlight. (Simon Spotlight).
—New Pig in Town. Wheeler, Lisa. ed. 2005. 48p. (J). lib. bdg. 15.00 (978-1-59054-997-1(X)) Fitzgerald Bks.
—New Pig in Town. Wheeler, Lisa. 2003. (Fitch & Chip Ser.: 1). (ENG.). 48p. (J). (gr. 1-3). 16.99 (978-0-689-84950-3(8), Atheneum/Richard Jackson Bks.) Simon & Schuster Children's Publishing.
—New Pig in Town. Wheeler, Lisa. 2005. (Fitch & Chip Ser.: 1). (ENG.). 48p. (J). (gr. 1-3). pap. 3.99 (978-0-689-84955-8(9), Simon Spotlight) Simon Spotlight.
—Turk & Runt: A Thanksgiving Comedy. Wheeler, Lisa. 2005. (ENG.). 32p. (J). (gr. -1-2). 7.99 (978-1-4169-0714-5(9), Atheneum Bks. for Young Readers) Simon & Schuster Children's Publishing.
—When Pigs Fly. Wheeler, Lisa. ed. 2005. 48p. (J). lib. bdg. 15.00 (978-1-59054-996-4(1)) Fitzgerald Bks.
—When Pigs Fly. Wheeler, Lisa. 2005. (Fitch & Chip Ser.). 48p. (gr. 1-3). 14.00 (978-0-7569-5472-7(X)) Perfection Learning Corp.
—When Pigs Fly. Wheeler, Lisa. 2003. (Fitch & Chip Ser.: 2). (ENG.). 48p. (J). (gr. 1-3). 16.99 (978-0-689-84951-0(6), Atheneum/Richard Jackson Bks.) Simon & Schuster Children's Publishing.
—When Pigs Fly. Wheeler, Lisa. 2005. (Fitch & Chip Ser.: 2). (ENG.). 48p. (J). (gr. 1-3). pap. 4.99 (978-0-689-84956-5(7), Simon Spotlight) Simon Spotlight.
—Who's Afraid of Granny Wolf? Wheeler, Lisa. 2006. (Fitch & Chip Ser.: 3). (ENG.). 48p. (J). (gr. 1-3). pap. 4.99 (978-0-689-84957-2(5), Simon Spotlight) Simon Spotlight.
—Willie & Buster Take the Train. DePrisco, Dorothea. 2003. (Stories to Share Ser.). 10p. (J). 10.95 (978-1-58117-183-9(8), Intervisual/Piggy Toes) Bendon, Inc.
Ansley, Frank. Who's Afraid of Granny Wolf? Ansley, Frank. Wheeler, Lisa. 2004. (Fitch & Chip Ser.: 3). (ENG.). 48p. (J). (gr. 1-3). 16.99 (978-0-689-84952-7(4), Simon Spotlight) Simon Spotlight.
Ansley-Gutierrez, Kaisha. My Mommies & I... Father's Day. Ansley-Gutierrez, Susana. 2019. (ENG.). 28p. (J). pap. 9.99 (978-1-0737-7423-4(6)) Independently Published.
Anstee, Ashlyn. The Grumpy Pirate. Demas, Corinne & Roehrig, Artemis. 2020. (ENG.). 40p. (J). (gr. -1-k). 17.99 (978-1-338-22297-5(X), Orchard Bks.) Scholastic, Inc.
Anstee, Ashlyn. Are We There, Yeti? Anstee, Ashlyn. 2015. (ENG.). 40p. (J). (gr. -1-3). 18.99 (978-1-4814-3089-0(0), Simon & Schuster Bks. For Young Readers) Simon & Schuster Bks. For Young Readers.
—No, No, Gnome! Anstee, Ashlyn. 2016. (ENG.). 40p. (J). (gr. -1-3). 17.99 (978-1-4814-3091-3(2), Simon & Schuster Bks. For Young Readers) Simon & Schuster Bks. For Young Readers.
Anstey, David. Ali Baba. Clynes, Kate. 2005. (SWA & ENG.). 32p. (J). pap. (978-1-84444-429-8(5)) Mantra Lingua.
—Jill & the Beanstalk. Gregory, Manju. 2004. (ENG & TUR.). (J). (978-1-84444-495-3(3)) Mantra Lingua.
Antal, Lara. The Legend of Sleepy Hollow: The Headless Horseman. Small, Cathleen. 2016. (American Legends & Folktales Ser.). 32p. (J). (gr. 3-3). pap. 10.58 (978-1-5026-2206-8(8)) Cavendish Square Publishing LLC.
Antal, Lara & Gennari, Joel. Lady Liberty. Shoup, Kate. 2018. (American Legends & Folktales Ser.). 32p. (gr. 3-3). 28.50 (978-1-5026-3686-7(7)) Cavendish Square Publishing LLC.
Antelo, Marta. Rosa Parks. Kaiser, Lisbeth. 2017. (Little People, BIG DREAMS Ser.: 9). (ENG.). 32p. (J). (gr. k-3). 15.99 (978-1-78603-018-4(7), Frances Lincoln Children's Bks.) Quarto Publishing Group UK GBR. Dist: Hachette Bk. Group.
Antelo, Marta. Rosa Parks: My First Rosa Parks. Kaiser, Lisbeth. ed. 2019. (Little People, Big Dreams Ser.: Vol. 9). (ENG.). 24p. (J). (gr. -1). bds. (978-1-78603-263-8(5)) Frances Lincoln Childrens Bks.
Anthis, Brian. Pauly the Adventurous Pallid Bat. Tuttle, Merlin D., photos by. Irbinskas, Heather. 2003. 32p. (J). pap. 7.95 (978-1-58369-032-1(8)) Western National Parks Assn.
Anthis, Brian, jt. illus. see Albert, Robert.
Anthoine, Leila, et al. Trust & Obey: A Visualized Gospel Song. Cunningham, Edie. 2005. 20p. (J). pap. (978-1-932381-20-7(1), 6480) Bible Visuals International, Inc.
Anthony, Alan. 190 Ready-To-Use Activities That Make Math Fun! Watson, George. 2003. (J-B Ed: Ready-To-Use Activities Ser.: 65). (ENG.). 304p. pap. 29.95 (978-0-7879-6585-3(5), Jossey-Bass) Wiley, John & Sons, Inc.
Anthony, Mark. Cracking the Wall: The Struggles of the Little Rock Nine. Lucas, Eileen. 2007. pap. 37.95 incl. audio (978-1-59519-939-3(X)); pap. 39.95 incl. audio compact disk (978-1-59519-943-0(8)) Live Oak Media.
Anthony, Ross. Please Don't Step on the Ants. Anthony, Ross. 2006. (ENG, CHI, SPA & JPN.). (J). per. (978-0-9727894-4-8(8)) Arizona Blueberry Studios.
Antiporda, Enrico. The Adventures of Jimbo, the Homeless Cat. Antiporda, Enrico. 2013. 66p. pap. 14.95 (978-0-9672793-5-0(6)) Blue Owl Editions.
Antkowiak, Meghan. Dragons & Dragonslayers. Chester, Tim. 2020. (ENG.). 98p. (J). pap. 10.99 (978-1-947644-23-6(8), Canonball Bks.) Canon Pr.
Antkowski, Marygrace. What Color Is Spring? Zipf, Sean. 2008. 36p. pap. 24.95 (978-1-60703-005-8(5)) America Star Bks.
Antle, Bhagavan. The Tiger Cubs & the Chimp: The True Story of How Anjana the Chimp Helped Raise Two Baby Tigers. Antle, Bhagavan. Bland, Barry, photos by. 2013. (ENG.). 32p. (J). (gr. -1-3). 16.99 (978-0-8050-9319-3(2), 900069905, Holt, Henry & Co. Bks. For Young Readers) Holt, Henry & Co.
Antle, Bhagavan & Bland, Barry. Suryia & Roscoe: The True Story of an Unlikely Friendship. Antle, Bhagavan. 2011. (ENG.). 32p. (J). (gr. -1-3). 18.99 (978-0-8050-9316-2(8), 900069900, Holt, Henry & Co. Bks. For Young Readers) Holt, Henry & Co.
Anton, Rafa. Meskwaki & the President: A Tale of a Fox & His Urgent Mission to the White House. Santos, Vivaldo Andrade dos. 2019. (ENG.). 64p. (J). pap. 13.15 (978-1-0964-6051-0(3)) Independently Published.
Antonelli, Gina. Who Is Ollie? Antonelli, Gina. 2006. 31p. (J). (gr. -1-3). per. 10.99 (978-1-883573-07-2(6)) Blue Forge Pr.
Antonello, Marisa & Laidley, Victoria. Lessons from a Street Kid, 1 vol. Kielburger, Craig. 2012. (ENG.). 40p. (J). (gr. k-5). 19.95 (978-1-55365-865-8(5), Greystone Bks.) Greystone Books Ltd. CAN. Dist: Publishers Group West (PGW).
Antonia, Miller. Baby's Very First Little Book of Bunnies. ed. 2011. (Baby's Very First Board Bks). 10p. (J). ring bd. 6.99 (978-0-7945-2955-0(0), Usborne) EDC Publishing.
—Baby's Very First Little Book of Kittens. ed. 2011. (Baby's Very First Board Bks). 10p. (J). ring bd. 6.99 (978-0-7945-2956-7(9), Usborne) EDC Publishing.
Antonini, Gabriel. Farm. Rainstorm Publishing, ed. 2018. (First Animal Facts Ser.). (ENG.). 20p. (J). bds. 7.99 (978-1-989219-79-9(9)) Rainstorm Pr.
—Jungle. Rainstorm Publishing, ed. 2018. (First Animal Facts Ser.). (ENG.). 20p. (J). bds. 7.99 (978-1-989219-81-2(0)) Rainstorm Pr.
—Ocean. Rainstorm Publishing, ed. 2018. (First Animal Facts Ser.). (ENG.). 20p. (J). bds. 7.99 (978-1-989219-78-2(0)) Rainstorm Pr.
—Old MacDonald. Rainstorm Publishing, ed. 2019. (Nursery Rhyme Time Ser.). (ENG.). 20p. (J). bds. 7.99 (978-1-989219-69-0(1)) Rainstorm Pr.
—Ten Little Monkey's. Rainstorm Publishing, ed. 2018. (Nursery Rhyme Time Ser.). (ENG.). 20p. (J). bds. 7.99 (978-1-989219-66-9(7)) Rainstorm Pr.
—There Was an Old Lady Who Swallowed a Fly. Rainstorm Publishing, ed. 2018. (Nursery Rhyme Time Ser.). (ENG.). 20p. (J). bds. 7.99 (978-1-989219-67-6(5)) Rainstorm Pr.
—Wheels on the Bus. Rainstorm Publishing, ed. 2018. (Nursery Rhyme Time Ser.). (ENG.). 20p. (J). bds. 7.99 (978-1-989219-68-3(3)) Rainstorm Pr.
Antonini, Gabriele. Brave Little Red: Sound Book Wood Module with Handle. Rose, Robin. Cottage Door Press, ed. 2017. (Early Bird Sound Bks.). (ENG.). 10p. (J). (gr. -1-k). bds. 9.99 (978-1-68052-157-3(8), 1001550) Cottage Door Pr.
Antonini, Gabriele. Garden. Rainstorm Publishing, ed. 2018. (First Animal Facts Ser.). (ENG.). 20p. (J). bds. 7.99 (978-1-989219-80-5(2)) Rainstorm Pr.
Antonini, Gabriele. The Hungry Little Monkey. Blackford, Andy. 2011. (Tadpoles Ser.). (ENG.). (J). (gr. -1-3). lib. bdg. 17.55 (978-1-61383-949-2(9)) Perfection Learning Corp.
—Wheels on the Bus. 2012. 22p. (J). (978-1-4508-3332-5(2)) Publications International, Ltd.
Antonini, Gabriele, jt. illus. see Metzger, Steve.
Antonio & Covi. Manolo Multon y el Mago Guason. Cerda, Alfredo Gomez. 2004.Tr. of Manolo Citation & Boring the Magician. (SPA.). (J). pap. 7.99 (978-84-236-6322-4(1)) Edebé ESP. Dist: Lectorum Pubns., Inc.
Antonio, Mitch. Duck Duck: Thankful for Luck. Aicher, Jennifer. Aicher, Jennifer, ed. 2019. (Bill the Duck Ser.: Vol. 4). (ENG.). 36p. (J). pap. 11.99 (978-1-7117-2116-3(6)) Independently Published.
Antonishak, Tom. The Pony Express. Bailer, Darice. 3rd ed. 2003. (Soundprints' Read-and-Discover Ser.). (ENG.). 48p. (J). (gr. -1-3). pap. 3.95 (978-1-59249-019-6(0), S2008) Soundprints.
Antonucci, Danilo, et al. Disney the Lion King: Wild Schemes & Catastrophes (Graphic Novel) Miller, John Jackson. 2019. (ENG.). 72p. (J). (gr. 3-7). pap. 10.99 (978-1-5067-1273-4(8)) Dark Horse Comics.
Antonsson, Petur. A Daring Rescue (Dolphin Island #1) Hapka, Catherine. 2020. (Dolphin Island Ser.: 1). (ENG.). 112p. (J). (gr. 2-3). pap. 5.99 (978-1-338-29018-9(5), Scholastic Pr.) Scholastic, Inc.
—Lost in the Storm (Dolphin Island #2) Hapka, Catherine. 2020. (Dolphin Island Ser.: 2). (ENG.). 112p. (J). (gr. 2-3). pap. 5.99 (978-1-338-29019-6(3), Scholastic Pr.) Scholastic, Inc.
—The Luck Uglies. Durham, Paul. 2014. (Luck Uglies Ser.: 1). (ENG.). 400p. (J). (gr. 3-7). 16.99 (978-0-06-227150-1(4)) HarperCollins Pubs.
—The Luck Uglies #2: Fork-Tongue Charmers. Durham, Paul. 2016. (Luck Uglies Ser.: 2). (ENG.). 432p. (J). (gr. 3-7). pap. 7.99 (978-0-06-227154-9(7)) HarperCollins Pubs.
—The Luck Uglies #3: Rise of the Ragged Clover. Durham, Paul. 2016. (Luck Uglies Ser.: 3). (ENG.). 400p. (J). (gr. 3-7). 16.99 (978-0-06-227156-3(3)) HarperCollins Pubs.
Antonsson, Petur Atli. The Ancient Amulet: Lumen Epic Fantasy Series Book 3. Sprunt, Matt. Sprunt, Hollie, ed. 2018. (ENG.). 336p. (J). pap. 13.95 (978-0-692-99751-2(2)) Living Room Adventures.
Antonucci, Jason. Captain Jay & the Perfect Pet. Antonucci, Jason. 2020. (ENG.). 24p. (J). (gr. k-3). pap. 15.00 (978-0-578-66897-0(1)) Antonucci, Jason.
Antony, Steve. When I Grow Up. Minchin, Tim. 2018. (ENG.). 32p. (J). (gr. -1-k). 17.99 (978-1-338-23384-1(X)); pap. incl. audio compact disk (978-1-4071-8043-4(6)) Scholastic, Inc.
Antony, Steve. Good Night, Mr. Panda. Antony, Steve. 2018. (ENG.). 32p. (J). (gr. -1-k). 16.99 (978-1-338-27595-7(X), Scholastic Pr.) Scholastic, Inc.
—Good Night, Mr. Panda / Buenas Noches, Sr. Panda. Antony, Steve. 2018. (ENG & SPA.). 32p. (J). (gr. -1-k). pap. 6.99 (978-1-338-29952-6(2), Scholastic en Espanol) Scholastic, Inc.
—Green Lizards vs. Red Rectangles. Antony, Steve. 2015. (ENG.). 32p. (J). (gr. -1-k). 16.99 (978-0-545-84902-9(0), Scholastic Pr.) Scholastic, Inc.
—I'll Wait, Mr. Panda. Antony, Steve. 2016. (ENG.). 32p. (J). (gr. -1-k). 16.99 (978-1-338-02836-2(7), Scholastic Pr.) Scholastic, Inc.
—Please, Mr. Panda. Antony, Steve. 2014. (ENG.). 32p. (J). (gr. -1-k). 16.99 (978-0-545-78892-2(7), Scholastic Pr.) Scholastic, Inc.
—The Queen's Handbag. Antony, Steve. 2017. (ENG.). 32p. (J). (gr. -1-k). 17.99 (978-1-338-03293-2(3), Scholastic Pr.) Scholastic, Inc.
—Thank You, Mr. Panda. Antony, Steve. 2019. (ENG.). 26p. (J). (gr. -1-k). bds. 6.99 (978-1-338-31276-8(6), Scholastic Pr.) Scholastic, Inc.
Antounian, Raffi. Being Grace. Tate, Beverly A. 2020. (ENG.). 62p. (J). pap. 18.95 (978-1-59594-649-2(7), Wingspan Pr.) WingSpan Publishing.
Antram, David. Animal Facts & Jokes. Townsend, John. 2018. (Totally Gross & Awesome Ser.). (ENG.). 128p. (J). (gr. 2). pap. 6.95 (978-1-912233-62-5(2), Scribo) Book Hse. GBR. Dist: Sterling Publishing Co., Inc.
—Assyrian Soldier! An Ancient Army You'd Rather Not Join. Matthews, Rupert. 2007. (You Wouldn't Want to... Ser.). (ENG.). 32p. (J). (gr. 2-5). 29.00 (978-0-531-18727-2(6)) Scholastic Library Publishing.
—Be a Mayan Soothsayer! Fortunes You'd Rather Not Tell. Matthews, Rupert. 2007. (You Wouldn't Want to...: Ancient Civilization Ser.). (ENG.). 32p. (J). (gr. 2-5). 29.00 (978-0-531-18746-3(2), Watts, Franklin) Scholastic Library Publishing.
—Be a Skyscraper Builder! A Hazardous Job You'd Rather Not Take. Malam, John. 2009. (ENG.). 32p. (J). (gr. 3-18). 29.00 (978-0-531-20824-3(9), Watts, Franklin) Scholastic Library Publishing.
—Be a Suffragist! A Protest Movement That's Rougher Than You Expected. MacDonald, Fiona. 2008. (You Wouldn't Want To... Ser.). (ENG.). 32p. (J). (gr. 4-6). 26.19 (978-0-531-20701-7(3)) Scholastic Library Publishing.
—Be a Sumerian Slave! A Life of Hard Labor You'd Rather Avoid. Morley, Jacqueline. 2007. (ENG.). 32p. (J). (gr. 3-7). pap. 9.95 (978-0-531-18921-4(X)); (gr. 4-7). 29.00 (978-0-531-18728-9(4)) Scholastic Library Publishing. (Watts, Franklin).
—Be a Victorian Mill Worker! A Grueling Job You'd Rather Not Have. Malam, John. (You Wouldn't Want To... Ser.). (ENG.). 32p. (J). 2008. (gr. 4-6). 26.19 (978-0-531-18747-0(0)); 2007. (gr. 2-5). pap. 9.95 (978-0-531-13928-8(X)) Scholastic Library Publishing. (Watts, Franklin).
—Be a Worker on the Statue of Liberty! A Monument You'd Rather Not Build. Malam, John. 2008. (You Wouldn't Want to...: American History Ser.). (ENG.). 32p. (J). 29.00 (978-0-531-20700-0(5), Watts, Franklin) Scholastic Library Publishing.
—Be an Aristocrat in the French Revolution! A Horrible Time in Paris You'd Rather Avoid. Pipe, Jim. 2007. (You Wouldn't Want to...: History of the World Ser.). (ENG.). 32p. (J). (gr. 2-5). 29.00 (978-0-531-18745-6(4), Watts, Franklin) Scholastic Library Publishing.
—Be an Inca Mummy! A One-Way Journey You'D Rather Not Make. Hynson, Colin. 2008. (You Wouldn't Want To... Ser.). (ENG.). 32p. (J). (gr. 4-6). 26.19 (978-0-531-18744-9(6)) Scholastic Library Publishing.
—Be in the First Submarine! An Undersea Expedition You'D Rather Avoid. Graham, Ian. 2008. (You Wouldn't Want to...: American History Ser.). (ENG.). 32p. (J). 29.00 (978-0-531-20702-4(1), Watts, Franklin) Scholastic Library Publishing.
—Be in the Forbidden City! A Sheltered Life You'd Rather Avoid. Morley, Jacqueline. 2008. (You Wouldn't Want to Ser.). (ENG.). 32p. (J). (gr. 4-7). 29.00 (978-0-531-18749-4(7), Children's Pr.) Scholastic Library Publishing.
—The Big Scream! The Creepiest, Most Disgusting, Horrifying Things You Should Know. 2018. (ENG.). 208p. (J). (gr. 3). pap. 12.95 (978-1-912233-67-0(3), Scribo) Book Hse. GBR. Dist: Sterling Publishing Co., Inc.
—Body Facts & Jokes. Townsend, John. 2018. (Totally Gross & Awesome Ser.). (ENG.). 128p. (J). (gr. 2). pap. 6.95 (978-1-912233-63-2(0), Scribo) Book Hse. GBR. Dist: Sterling Publishing Co., Inc.
—Book of Ancient Egyptian Mummies - Groan! Salariya, ed. ed. 2019. 128p. (J). (gr. 2). pap. 6.95 (978-1-912537-52-5(4)) Book Hse. GBR. Dist: Sterling Publishing Co., Inc.
—Book of Pirates - Arrr! Salariya, ed. ed. 2019. 128p. (J). (gr. 2). pap. 6.95 (978-1-912537-53-2(2)) Book Hse. GBR. Dist: Sterling Publishing Co., Inc.
—Dinosaurs. Salariya, ed. ed. 2019. 128p. (J). (gr. 2). pap. 6.95 (978-1-912537-51-8(6)) Book Hse. GBR. Dist: Sterling Publishing Co., Inc.
—Egyptian Town. Steedman, Scott. 2017. (Time Traveler's Guide Ser.). 48p. (gr. 3-7). 37.10 (978-1-910706-99-2(X)) Book Hse. GBR. Dist: Black Rabbit Bks.
—Greek Town. Malam, John. 2017. (Time Traveler's Guide Ser.). 48p. (gr. 3-7). 37.10 (978-1-911242-00-0(8)) Book Hse. GBR. Dist: Black Rabbit Bks.
—History Facts & Jokes. Townsend, John. 2018. (Totally Gross & Awesome Ser.). (ENG.). 128p. (J). (gr. 2). pap. 6.95 (978-1-912233-64-9(9), Scribo) Book Hse. GBR. Dist: Sterling Publishing Co., Inc.
—Live in a Medieval Castle! A Home You'D Rather Not Inhabit. Morley, Jacqueline. 2008. (You Wouldn't Want to...: History of the World Ser.). (ENG.). 32p. (J). 29.00 (978-0-531-20703-1(X), Watts, Franklin) Scholastic Library Publishing.
—Live in Pompeii! A Volcanic Eruption You'd Rather Avoid. Malam, John. 2008. (You Wouldn't Want to Ser.). (ENG.). 32p. (J). (gr. 2-5). 29.00 (978-0-531-18748-7(9)); pap. 9.95 (978-0-531-16900-1(6), Watts, Franklin) Scholastic Library Publishing.
Antram, David, et al. Machines & Inventions. Graham, Ian. 2008. (World of Wonder Ser.). (ENG.). 32p. (J). (gr. 1-4). 29.00 (978-0-531-24027-4(4)); pap. 9.95 (978-0-531-23823-3(7)) Scholastic Library Publishing. (Children's Pr.).
Antram, David. Manga Monsters & Pets. Marlborough, Max. ed. 2019. (Art of Drawing Ser.). 64p. (J). (gr. 4). pap. 9.95 (978-1-912537-59-4(1)) Book Hse. GBR. Dist: Sterling Publishing Co., Inc.
—Mayan Soothsayer! Fortunes You'D Rather Not Tell. Matthews, Rupert. 2007. (ENG.). 32p. (J). (gr. 3-5). pap. 9.95 (978-0-531-13925-7(5), Watts, Franklin) Scholastic Library Publishing.
—The Mayflower Facts & Jokes. Townsend, John. 2019. (Totally Gross & Awesome Ser.). (ENG.). 128p. (J). (gr. 2). pap. 6.95 (978-1-912904-58-7(6), Scribo) Book Hse. GBR. Dist: Sterling Publishing Co., Inc.
—The Medieval Chronicles: Vikings, Knights, & Castles. Macdonald, Fiona. 2013. 92p. (J). (978-1-4351-5067-6(8)) Barnes & Noble, Inc.
Antram, David, et al. People & Places. Chesire, Gerald. 2008. (World of Wonder Ser.). (ENG.). 32p. (J). (gr. 1-4). pap. 9.95 (978-0-531-23824-0(5), Children's Pr.) Scholastic Library Publishing.
Antram, David. People & Places. Chesire, Gerald. 2008. (World of Wonder Ser.). (ENG.). 32p. (J). (gr. 1-4). 29.00 (978-0-531-24028-1(2), Children's Pr.) Scholastic Library Publishing.
—Sail on a 19th-Century Whaling Ship! Grisly Tasks You'd Rather Not Do. Cook, Peter & Salariya, David. 2004. (You Wouldn't Want to Ser.). (ENG.). (J). 29.00 (978-0-531-12356-0(1)) Scholastic Library Publishing.
—Sail on an Irish Famine Ship! A Trip Across Teh Atlantic You'd Rather Not Make. Pipe, Jim. 2008. (You Wouldn't Want To... Ser.). (ENG.). 32p. (J). (gr. 4-6). 26.19 (978-0-531-13913-4(1), Watts, Franklin) Scholastic Library Publishing.
Antram, David, et al. Scary Creatures of the Soil. Cheshire, Gerard. 2009. (Scary Creatures Ser.). (ENG.). 32p. (J). (gr. 2-4). 27.00 (978-0-531-21821-1(X), Watts, Franklin); pap. 8.95 (978-0-531-22226-3(8), Children's Pr.) Scholastic Library Publishing.
Antram, David. Science Facts & Jokes. Townsend, John. 2018. (Totally Gross & Awesome Ser.). (ENG.). 128p. (J). (gr. 2). pap. 6.95 (978-1-912233-65-6(7), Scribo) Book Hse. GBR. Dist: Sterling Publishing Co., Inc.
—Space Facts & Jokes. Townsend, John. 2019. (Totally Gross & Awesome Ser.). (ENG.). 128p. (J). (gr. 2). pap. 6.95 (978-1-912904-59-4(4), Scribo) Book Hse. GBR. Dist: Sterling Publishing Co., Inc.
Antram, David, et al. The Story of the Exploration of Space. Clarke, Penny. 2013. 64p. (J). (978-1-4351-5030-0(9)) Barnes & Noble, Inc.
Antram, David. Top 10 Worst Nasty Pirates: You Wouldn't Want to Meet! Macdonald, Fiona & Salariya, Daivid. 2013. 32p. (J). (978-1-4351-5037-9(6)) Barnes & Noble, Inc.
—Top 10 Worst Ruthless Warriors. Macdonald, Fiona. 2012. (Top 10 Worst Ser.). (ENG.). 32p. (J). (gr. 3-6). pap. 10.50 (978-1-4339-6686-6(7)); lib. bdg. 27.60 (978-1-4339-6685-9(9)) Stevens, Gareth Publishing LLLP. (Gareth Stevens Learning Library).
—Top 10 Worst Things about Ancient Egypt. England, Victoria. 2012. (Top 10 Worst Ser.). (ENG.). 32p. (J). (gr. 3-6). pap. 10.50 (978-1-4339-6689-7(1)); lib. bdg. 27.60 (978-1-4339-6688-0(3)) Stevens, Gareth Publishing LLLP. (Gareth Stevens Learning Library).
—Top 10 Worst Things about Ancient Greece. England, Victoria. 2012. (Top 10 Worst Ser.). (ENG.). 32p. (J). (gr. 3-6). pap. 10.50 (978-1-4339-6692-7(1)); lib. bdg. 27.60 (978-1-4339-6691-0(3)) Stevens, Gareth Publishing LLLP. (Gareth Stevens Learning Library).
—Top 10 Worst Things about Ancient Rome. England, Victoria. 2012. (Top 10 Worst Ser.). (ENG.). 32p. (J). (gr. 3-6). pap. 10.50 (978-1-4339-6695-8(6)); lib. bdg. 27.60 (978-1-4339-6694-1(8)) Stevens, Gareth Publishing LLLP. (Gareth Stevens Learning Library).
—Top 10 Worst Vicious Villains. Pipe, Jim. 2012. (Top 10 Worst Ser.). (ENG.). 32p. (J). (gr. 3-6). pap. 10.50 (978-1-4339-6698-9(0)); lib. bdg. 27.60 (978-1-4339-6697-2(2)) Stevens, Gareth Publishing LLLP. (Gareth Stevens Learning Library).
—Top 10 Worst Vicious Villains: You Wouldn't Want to Know! Pipe, Jim & Salariya, David. 2013. 32p. (J). (978-1-4351-5043-0(0)) Barnes & Noble, Inc.
—Top 10 Worst Wicked Rulers. Macdonald, Fiona. 2012. (Top 10 Worst Ser.). (ENG.). 32p. (J). (gr. 3-6). pap. 10.50 (978-1-4339-6701-6(4)); lib. bdg. 27.60 (978-1-4339-6700-9(6)) Stevens, Gareth Publishing LLLP. (Gareth Stevens Learning Library).
—Tutankhamen! A Mummy Who Really Got Meddled With. Stewart, David. 2007. (You Wouldn't Want to... Ser.). (ENG.). 32p. (J). (gr. 2-5). 29.00 (978-0-531-18725-8(X)) Scholastic Library Publishing.
—Unsinkable Titanic - Look Out! Salariya, ed. ed. 2019. 128p. (J). (gr. 2). pap. 6.95 (978-1-912537-54-9(0)) Book Hse. GBR. Dist: Sterling Publishing Co., Inc.
—You Wouldn't Want to Be a 19th-Century Coal Miner in England! A Dangerous Job You'd Rather Not Have.

A

Malam, John. 2006. (You Wouldn't Want to Ser.). (ENG.). 32p. (J). (gr. 2-5). 29.00 *(978-0-531-14971-3(4))* Scholastic Library Publishing.

—You Wouldn't Want to Be a Civil War Soldier! A War You'd Rather Not Fight. Ratliff, Thomas. 2013. (You Wouldn't Want to... Ser.). (ENG.). (J). 32p. 29.00 *(978-0-531-25947-4(1))*; 40p. (gr. 3). pap. 9.95 *(978-0-531-24503-3(9))* Scholastic Library Publishing. (Watts, Franklin).

—You Wouldn't Want to Be a Greek Athlete! Races You'd Rather Not Run. Ford, Michael & Salariya, David. 2004. (You Wouldn't Want to Ser.). (ENG.). 32p. (J). 29.00 *(978-0-531-12352-2(9))* Scholastic Library Publishing.

—You Wouldn't Want to Be a Mammoth Hunter! Dangerous Beasts You'd Rather Not Encounter. Malam, John & Smith, Karen Barker. 2004. (ENG.). 32p. (J). (gr. 3-5). pap. 9.95 *(978-0-531-16397-9(0)*, Watts, Franklin) Scholastic Library Publishing.

—You Wouldn't Want to Be a Medieval Knight! Armor You'd Rather Not Wear. Macdonald, Fiona. 2013. (ENG.). 32p. (J). (gr. 3). pap. 9.95 *(978-0-531-23851-6(2))*; 29.00 *(978-0-531-27100-1(5))* Scholastic Library Publishing. (Watts, Franklin).

—You Wouldn't Want to Be a Ninja Warrior! Malam, John. 2012. (ENG.). 32p. (J). (gr. 3). pap. 9.95 *(978-0-531-20948-6(2)*, Watts, Franklin) Scholastic Library Publishing.

—You Wouldn't Want to Be a Ninja Warrior! A Secret Job That's Your Destiny. Malam, John. 2012. (ENG.). 32p. (J). (gr. 3-12). lib. bdg. 29.00 *(978-0-531-20873-1(7))* Scholastic Library Publishing.

—You Wouldn't Want to... Be a Pirate's Prisoner! Malam, John. rev. ed. 2012. (ENG.). 32p. (J). lib. bdg. 29.00 *(978-0-531-27502-3(7))* Scholastic Library Publishing.

—You Wouldn't Want to Be a Pirate's Prisoner! Horrible Things You'd Rather Not Know. Malam, John. rev. ed. 2012. (ENG.). 40p. (J). (gr. 3). pap. 9.95 *(978-0-531-28027-0(6)*, Watts, Franklin) Scholastic Library Publishing.

—You Wouldn't Want to Be a Polar Explorer! Green, Jen. 2017. (ENG.). 40p. (J). (gr. 3). pap. 9.95 *(978-0-531-23154-8(2)*, Watts, Franklin) Scholastic Library Publishing.

—You Wouldn't Want to Be a Pyramid Builder! A Hazardous Job You'd Rather Not Have. Morley, Jacqueline. rev. ed. 2013. (ENG.). 32p. (J). (gr. 3). 29.00 *(978-0-531-27101-8(3))*; pap. 9.95 *(978-0-531-23852-3(0))* Scholastic Library Publishing. (Watts, Franklin).

—You Wouldn't Want to... Be a Roman Galdiator! Malam, John. rev. ed. 2012. (ENG.). 32p. (J). lib. bdg. 29.00 *(978-0-531-27503-0(5))* Scholastic Library Publishing.

—You Wouldn't Want to Be a Roman Galdiator! Malam, John. rev. ed. 2012. (ENG.). 40p. (J). (gr. 3). pap. 9.95 *(978-0-531-28028-7(4)*, Watts, Franklin) Scholastic Library Publishing.

—You Wouldn't Want to Be a Samurai! A Deadly Career You'd Rather Not Pursue. Macdonald, Fiona. 2009. (You Wouldn't Want to Ser.). (ENG.). 32p. (J). 29.00 *(978-0-531-21325-4(0))* Scholastic Library Publishing.

—You Wouldn't Want to Be a Shakespearean Actor! Some Roles You Might Not Want to Play. Morley, Jacqueline & Salariya, David. 2010. (You Wouldn't Want to Ser.). (ENG.). 32p. (J). 29.00 *(978-0-531-20471-9(5))* Scholastic Library Publishing.

—You Wouldn't Want to Be a Shakespearean Actor! Some Roles You Might Not Want to Play. Morley, Jacqueline. 2010. (You Wouldn't Want to Ser.). (ENG.). 32p. (J). (gr. 3-18). pap. 9.95 *(978-0-531-22826-5(6))* Scholastic Library Publishing.

—You Wouldn't Want to Be a Slave in Ancient Greece! A Life You'd Rather Not Have. Macdonald, Fiona. rev. ed. 2013. (ENG.). 32p. (J). (gr. 3). 29.00 *(978-0-531-27102-5(1))*; pap. 9.95 *(978-0-531-23853-0(9))* Scholastic Library Publishing. (Watts, Franklin).

—You Wouldn't Want to Be a Suffragist! A Protest Movement That's Rougher Than You Expected. MacDonald, Fiona. 2008. (You Wouldn't Want to...: History of the World Ser.). (ENG.). 32p. (J). (gr. 3-18). pap. 9.95 *(978-0-531-21911-9(9)*, Watts, Franklin) Scholastic Library Publishing.

—You Wouldn't Want to Be a Victorian Servant! A Thankless Job You'd Rather Not Have. MacDonald, Fiona & Macdonald, Fiona. 2006. (You Wouldn't Want to Ser.). (ENG.). 32p. (J). (gr. 2-5). 29.00 *(978-0-531-14972-0(2))* Scholastic Library Publishing.

—You Wouldn't Want to Be a Viking Explorer! Voyages You'd Rather Not Make. Langley, Andrew. rev. ed. 2013. (ENG.). 32p. (J). (gr. 3). 29.00 *(978-0-531-27103-2(X))*; pap. 9.95 *(978-0-531-23854-7(7))* Scholastic Library Publishing. (Watts, Franklin).

—You Wouldn't Want to Be a Worker on the Statue of Liberty! A Monument You'd Rather Not Build. Malam, John. 2008. (You Wouldn't Want to...: American History Ser.). (ENG.). 32p. (J). (gr. 3-18). pap. 9.95 *(978-0-531-21910-2(0)*, Watts, Franklin) Scholastic Library Publishing.

—You Wouldn't Want to Be a World War II Pilot! Air Battles You Might Not Survive. Graham, Ian. 2009. (You Wouldn't Want to Ser.). (ENG.). 32p. (J). 29.00 *(978-0-531-21326-1(9))*; (gr. 3-18). pap. 9.95 *(978-0-531-20517-4(7)*, Watts, Franklin) Scholastic Library Publishing.

—You Wouldn't Want to Be an 18th-Century British Convict! A Trip to Australia You'd Rather Not Take. Costain, Meredith. 2006. (You Wouldn't Want to Ser.). (ENG.). 32p. (J). (gr. 2-5). 29.00 *(978-0-531-14973-7(0))*; pap. 9.95 *(978-0-531-16998-8(7)*, Watts, Franklin) Scholastic Library Publishing.

—You Wouldn't Want to Be an American Colonist! A Settlement You'd Rather Not Start. Morley, Jacqueline. 2013. (ENG.). (J). 40p. (gr. 3). pap. 9.95 *(978-0-531-24502-6(0))*; 32p. 29.00 *(978-0-531-25946-7(3))* Scholastic Library Publishing. (Watts, Franklin).

—You Wouldn't Want to... Be an American Pioneer! Morley, Jacqueline. rev. ed. 2012. (ENG.). (J). 32p. lib. bdg. 29.00 *(978-0-531-27500-9(0))*; 40p. (gr. 3). pap. 9.95 *(978-0-531-28025-6(X)*, Watts, Franklin) Scholastic Library Publishing.

—You Wouldn't Want to Be an Aztec Sacrifice: Gruesome Things You'd Rather Not Know. Macdonald, Fiona. rev. ed. 2013. (ENG.). (J). 32p. 29.00 *(978-0-531-27104-9(8))*; 40p. (gr. 3). pap. 9.95 *(978-0-531-23855-4(5))* Scholastic Library Publishing. (Watts, Franklin).

—You Wouldn't Want to... Be an Egyptian Mummy! Stewart, David. rev. ed. 2013. (You Wouldn't Want To... Ser.). (ENG.). 32p. (J). (gr. 4-6). lib. bdg. 26.19 *(978-0-531-27501-6(9)*, Watts, Franklin) Scholastic Library Publishing.

—You Wouldn't Want to Be an Egyptian Mummy! Disgusting Things You'd Rather Not Know. Stewart, David. rev. ed. 2012. (ENG.). 40p. (J). (gr. 3). pap. 9.95 *(978-0-531-28026-3(8)*, Watts, Franklin) Scholastic Library Publishing.

—You Wouldn't Want to Be an Inca Mummy! A One-Way Journey You'd Rather Not Make. Hynson, Colin. 2007. (ENG.). 32p. (J). (gr. 3-3). pap. 9.95 *(978-0-531-13926-4(3)*, Watts, Franklin) Scholastic Library Publishing.

—You Wouldn't Want to Be at the Boston Tea Party! Wharf Water You'd Rather Not Drink. Cook, Peter. 2013. (ENG.). (J). (gr. 3). 32p. 29.00 *(978-0-531-27105-6(6))*; 40p. pap. 9.95 *(978-0-531-23856-1(3))* Scholastic Library Publishing. (Watts, Franklin).

—You Wouldn't Want to Be Cleopatra! An Egyptian Ruler You'd Rather Not Be. Pipe, Jim. 2007. (You Wouldn't Want to... Ser.). (ENG.). 32p. (J). (gr. 2-5). pap. 9.95 *(978-0-531-18923-8(6)*, Watts, Franklin) Scholastic Library Publishing.

—You Wouldn't Want to Be Cleopatra! An Egyptian Ruler You'D Rather Not Be. Pipe, Jim. 2007. (You Wouldn't Want to... Ser.). (ENG.). 32p. (J). (gr. 2-5). 29.00 *(978-0-531-18726-5(8)*, Watts, Franklin) Scholastic Library Publishing.

—You Wouldn't Want to Be Cursed by King Tut! Morley, Jacqueline. 2012. (You Wouldn't Want to... Ser.). (ENG.). 32p. (J). pap. 9.95 *(978-0-531-20949-3(0)*, Watts, Franklin) Scholastic Library Publishing.

—You Wouldn't Want to Be Cursed by King Tut! A Mysterious Death You'd Rather Avoid. Morley, Jacqueline. 2012. (ENG.). 32p. (J). (gr. 3-12). lib. bdg. 29.00 *(978-0-531-20874-8(5))* Scholastic Library Publishing.

—You Wouldn't Want to Be in a Medieval Dungeon! Stewart, David. rev. ed. 2013. (You Wouldn't Want to... Ser.). (ENG.). 32p. (J). 29.00 *(978-0-531-25949-8(8)*, Watts, Franklin) Scholastic Library Publishing.

—You Wouldn't Want to Be in a Medieval Dungeon! Prisoners You'd Rather Not Meet. MacDonald, Fiona & Macdonald, Fiona. 2003. (You Wouldn't Want to Ser.). (ENG.). 32p. (J). 29.00 *(978-0-531-12312-6(X)*, Watts, Franklin) Scholastic Library Publishing.

—You Wouldn't Want to Be in a Medieval Dungeon! Prisoners You'd Rather Not Meet. Macdonald, Fiona. 2013. (ENG.). (J). 40p. (gr. 3). pap. 9.95 *(978-0-531-24504-0(7))*; 32p. 29.00 *(978-0-531-25948-1(X))* Scholastic Library Publishing. (Watts, Franklin).

—You Wouldn't Want to Be in Alexander the Great's Army! Miles You'd Rather Not March. Morley, Jacqueline. 2005. (You Wouldn't Want to... Ser.). (ENG.). 32p. (J). (gr. 2-5). 29.00 *(978-0-531-12410-9(X))*; (gr. 4-7). pap. 9.95 *(978-0-531-12390-4(1))* Scholastic Library Publishing. (Watts, Franklin).

—You Wouldn't Want to Be in the First Submarine! An Undersea Expedition You'd Rather Avoid. Graham, Ian. 2008. (You Wouldn't Want to...: American History Ser.). (ENG.). 32p. (J). (gr. 3-18). pap. 9.95 *(978-0-531-21912-6(7)*, Watts, Franklin) Scholastic Library Publishing.

—You Wouldn't Want to Be Joan of Arc! A Mission You Might Want to Miss. Macdonald, Fiona. 2010. (You Wouldn't Want to Ser.). (ENG.). 32p. (J). 29.00 *(978-0-531-20473-3(1))*; (gr. 3-18). pap. 9.95 *(978-0-531-22828-9(2)*, Watts, Franklin) Scholastic Library Publishing.

—You Wouldn't Want to Be Mary Queen of Scots. MacDonald, Fiona. 2008. (You Wouldn't Want to...: History of the World Ser.). (ENG.). 32p. (J). (gr. 2-5). pap. 9.95 *(978-0-531-14853-2(X)*, Watts, Franklin) Scholastic Library Publishing.

—You Wouldn't Want to Be Mary Queen of Scots: A Ruler Who Really Lost Her Head. MacDonald, Fiona. 2008. (You Wouldn't Want to Ser.). (ENG.). 32p. (J). (gr. 4-7). 29.00 *(978-0-531-13912-7(3))* Scholastic Library Publishing.

—You Wouldn't Want to Be on Apollo 13! Graham, Ian. 2017. (ENG.). 32p. (J). (gr. 3). lib. bdg. 29.00 *(978-0-531-23835-6(0)*, Watts, Franklin) Scholastic Library Publishing.

—You Wouldn't Want to Be on Apollo 13! A Mission You'd Rather Not Go On. Graham, Ian. 2003. (You Wouldn't Want to Ser.). (ENG.). 32p. (J). (gr. 2-5). pap. 9.95 *(978-0-531-16650-5(3)*, Watts, Franklin) Scholastic Library Publishing.

—You Wouldn't Want to Be on the First Flying Machine! A High-Soaring Ride You'd Rather Not Take. Graham, Ian. 2013. (ENG.). 32p. (J). (gr. 3). 29.00 *(978-0-531-25945-0(5))*; pap. 9.95 *(978-0-531-23042-8(2))* Scholastic Library Publishing. (Watts, Franklin).

—You Wouldn't Want to Be Sir Isaac Newton! A Lonely Life You'd Rather Not Lead. Graham, Ian. 2013. (ENG.). 32p. (J). (gr. 3). 29.00 *(978-0-531-25943-6(9))*; pap. 9.95 *(978-0-531-23040-4(6))* Scholastic Library Publishing. (Watts, Franklin).

—You Wouldn't Want to Be Tutankhamen! Stewart, David. 2017. (ENG.). 32p. (J). (gr. 3). lib. bdg. 29.00 *(978-0-531-23837-0(7)*, Watts, Franklin) Scholastic Library Publishing.

—You Wouldn't Want to Climb Mount Everest! A Deadly Journey to the Top of the World. Graham, Ian. 2010. (ENG.). 32p. (J). (gr. 3-18). pap. 9.95 *(978-0-531-13785-7(6)*, Watts, Franklin) Scholastic Library Publishing.

—You Wouldn't Want to Explore with Marco Polo! A Really Long Trip You'd Rather Not Take. Morley, Jacqueline. 2009. (You Wouldn't Want to Ser.). (ENG.). 32p. (J). (gr. 3-12). 29.00 *(978-0-531-21327-8(7))*; pap. 9.95 *(978-0-531-20518-1(5)*, Watts, Franklin) Scholastic Library Publishing.

—You Wouldn't Want to Explore with Sir Francis Drake! A Pirate You'd Rather Not Know. Stewart, David. 2005. (You Wouldn't Want to... Ser.). (ENG.). 32p. (J). (gr. 2-5). 29.00 *(978-0-531-12413-0(4))*; pap. 9.95 *(978-0-531-12393-5(6))* Scholastic Library Publishing. (Watts, Franklin).

—You Wouldn't Want to Live in a Wild West Town! Dust You'd Rather Not Settle. Hicks, Peter. 2013. (ENG.). (J). (gr. 3). 32p. 29.00 *(978-0-531-27106-3(4))*; 40p. pap. 9.95 *(978-0-531-23857-8(1))* Scholastic Library Publishing. (Watts, Franklin).

—You Wouldn't Want to Live in Pompeii! Malam, John. 2017. (ENG.). 32p. (J). (gr. 3). lib. bdg. 29.00 *(978-0-531-23836-3(9)*, Watts, Franklin) Scholastic Library Publishing.

—You Wouldn't Want to Live Without Antibiotics. Rooney, Anne. 2014. (You Wouldn't Want to Live Without... Ser.). (ENG.). 32p. (J). lib. bdg. 29.00 *(978-0-531-21218-9(1)*, Watts, Franklin) Scholastic Library Publishing.

—You Wouldn't Want to Live Without Bees! Woolf, Alex. 2016. (You Wouldn't Want to Live Without... Ser.). (ENG.). 32p. (J). (gr. 3-6). lib. bdg. 29.00 *(978-0-531-22458-8(9)*, Watts, Franklin) Scholastic Library Publishing.

—You Wouldn't Want to Live Without Boogers! Woolf, Alex. 2016. (You Wouldn't Want to Live Without... Ser.). (ENG.). 32p. (J). (gr. 3-6). lib. bdg. 29.00 *(978-0-531-22459-5(7)*, Watts, Franklin) Scholastic Library Publishing.

—You Wouldn't Want to Live Without Books! Woolf, Alex. 2014. (You Wouldn't Want to Live Without... Ser.). (ENG.). 32p. (J). lib. bdg. 29.00 *(978-0-531-21220-2(3)*, Watts, Franklin) Scholastic Library Publishing.

—You Wouldn't Want to Live Without Clean Water! Canavan, Roger. 2014. (You Wouldn't Want to Live Without... Ser.). (ENG.). 32p. (J). lib. bdg. 29.00 *(978-0-531-21219-6(X)*, Watts, Franklin) Scholastic Library Publishing.

—You Wouldn't Want to Live Without Clocks & Calendars! Macdonald, Fiona. 2015. (You Wouldn't Want to Live Without... Ser.). (ENG.). 32p. (J). (gr. 3). lib. bdg. 29.00 *(978-0-531-21928-7(3)*, Watts, Franklin) Scholastic Library Publishing.

—You Wouldn't Want to Live Without Dentists! Macdonald, Fiona. 2015. (You Wouldn't Want to Live Without... Ser.). (ENG.). 32p. (J). (gr. 3). pap. 9.95 *(978-0-531-21410-7(9)*, Watts, Franklin) Scholastic Library Publishing.

—You Wouldn't Want to Live Without Gaming! Pipe, Jim. 2018. (You Wouldn't Want to Live Without... Ser.). (ENG.). 32p. (J). (gr. 3). lib. bdg. 29.00 *(978-0-531-12814-5(8)*, Watts, Franklin) Scholastic Library Publishing.

—You Wouldn't Want to Live Without Money! Woolf, Alex. 2015. (You Wouldn't Want to Live Without Ser.). (ENG.). 12p. (J). (gr. 3-6). 20.75 *(978-1-5311-8766-8(8))* Perfection Learning Corp.

—You Wouldn't Want to Live Without Money! Woolf, Alex. 2015. (You Wouldn't Want to Live Without... Ser.). (ENG.). 32p. (J). (gr. 3). lib. bdg. 29.00 *(978-0-531-21926-3(7)*, Watts, Franklin) Scholastic Library Publishing.

—You Wouldn't Want to Live Without Nurses! MacDonald, Fiona. 2016. (You Wouldn't Want to Live Without... Ser.). (ENG.). 32p. (J). (gr. 3-6). lib. bdg. 29.00 *(978-0-531-22462-5(7)*, Watts, Franklin) Scholastic Library Publishing.

—You Wouldn't Want to Live Without Pain! Macdonald, Fiona. 2016. (You Wouldn't Want to Live Without... Ser.). (ENG.). 32p. (J). (gr. 3). lib. bdg. 29.00 *(978-0-531-21491-6(5)*, Watts, Franklin) Scholastic Library Publishing.

—You Wouldn't Want to Live Without Plastic! Graham, Ian. 2015. (You Wouldn't Want to Live Without... Ser.). (ENG.). 32p. (J). (gr. 3). lib. bdg. 29.00 *(978-0-531-21929-4(1)*, Watts, Franklin) Scholastic Library Publishing.

—You Wouldn't Want to Live Without Poop! Woolf, Alex. 2016. (You Wouldn't Want to Live Without... Ser.). (ENG.). 32p. (J). (gr. 3). lib. bdg. 29.00 *(978-0-531-21489-3(3)*, Watts, Franklin) Scholastic Library Publishing.

—You Wouldn't Want to Live Without Robots! Graham, Ian. 2018. (You Wouldn't Want to Live Without... Ser.). (ENG.). 32p. (J). (gr. 3). lib. bdg. 29.00 *(978-0-531-12813-8(X)*, Watts, Franklin) Scholastic Library Publishing.

—You Wouldn't Want to Live Without Toilets! Macdonald, Fiona. 2014. (You Wouldn't Want to Live Without... Ser.). (ENG.). 32p. (J). lib. bdg. 29.00 *(978-0-531-21215-8(7)*, Watts, Franklin) Scholastic Library Publishing.

—You Wouldn't Want to Live Without Vaccinations! Rooney, Anne. 2015. (You Wouldn't Want to Live Without... Ser.). (ENG.). 32p. (J). (gr. 3). pap. 9.95 *(978-0-531-21409-1(5)*, Watts, Franklin) Scholastic Library Publishing.

—You Wouldn't Want to Live Without Vegetables! Woolf, Alex. 2016. (You Wouldn't Want to Live Without... Ser.). (ENG.). 32p. (J). (gr. 3). lib. bdg. 29.00 *(978-0-531-21490-9(7)*, Watts, Franklin) Scholastic Library Publishing.

—You Wouldn't Want to Meet Typhoid Mary! A Deadly Cook You'd Rather Not Know. Morley, Jacqueline. 2013. (You Wouldn't Want To... Ser.). (ENG.). 32p. (J). (gr. 4-6). 26.19 *(978-0-531-25944-3(7)*, Watts, Franklin) Scholastic Library Publishing.

—You Wouldn't Want to Sail in the Spanish Armada! An Invasion You'd Rather Not Launch. Malam, John. 2006. (You Wouldn't Want to Ser.). (ENG.). 32p. (J). (gr. 2-5). 29.00 *(978-0-531-14974-4(9))*; (gr. 3-5). pap. 9.95 *(978-0-531-16999-5(5)*, Watts, Franklin) Scholastic Library Publishing.

—You Wouldn't Want to Sail on an Irish Famine Ship! A Trip Across the Atlantic You'd Rather Not Make. Pipe, Jim. 2008. (You Wouldn't Want to...: History of the World Ser.). (ENG.). 32p. (J). (gr. 4-7). pap. 9.95 *(978-0-531-14854-9(8)*, Watts, Franklin) Scholastic Library Publishing.

—You Wouldn't Want to Sail on the Titanic! One Voyage You'D Rather Not Make. Stewart, David. rev. ed. 2013. (ENG.). 32p. (J). (gr. 3). pap. 9.95 *(978-0-531-24505-7(5)*, Watts, Franklin) Scholastic Library Publishing.

—You Wouldn't Want to Work on a Medieval Cathedral! A Difficult Job That Never Ends. MacDonald, Fiona. 2010. (ENG.). 32p. (J). (gr. 3-18). pap. 9.95 *(978-0-531-13784-0(8)*, Watts, Franklin) Scholastic Library Publishing.

—You Wouldn't Want to Work on the Great Wall of China! Morley, Jacqueline. 2017. (ENG.). 32p. (J). (gr. 3). lib. bdg. 29.00 *(978-0-531-23838-7(5)*, Watts, Franklin) Scholastic Library Publishing.

—You Wouldn't Want to Work on the Great Wall of China! Defenses You'd Rather Not Build. Morley, Jacqueline. 2006. (You Wouldn't Want to Ser.). (ENG.). 32p. (J). (gr. 2-5). pap. 9.95 *(978-0-531-12449-9(5))*; (gr. 4-6). 26.19 *(978-0-531-12424-6(X))* Scholastic Library Publishing. (Watts, Franklin).

—You Wouldn't Want to Work on the Hoover Dam! An Explosive Job You'd Rather Not Do. Graham, Ian. 2012. (ENG.). 32p. (J). lib. bdg. 29.00 *(978-0-531-20871-7(0))* Scholastic Library Publishing.

Anyabwile, Dawud. The Crossover (Graphic Novel) Alexander, Kwame. 2019. (Crossover Ser.). (ENG.). 224p. (J). (gr. 5-7). 22.99 *(978-1-328-96001-6(3)*, 1706917); pap. 12.99 *(978-1-328-57549-4(7)*, 1727477) Houghton Mifflin Harcourt Publishing Co. (HMH Books For Young Readers).

—Monster. Myers, Walter Dean & Sims, Guy A. ed. 2015. (J). lib. bdg. 20.85 *(978-0-606-37629-7(1))* Turtleback.

—Monster: a Graphic Novel. Sims, Guy A. & Myers, Walter Dean. 2015. (Monster Ser.). (ENG.). 160p. (J). (gr. 8). pap. 10.99 *(978-0-06-227499-1(6)*, Amistad) HarperCollins Pubs.

Anzalone, Frank, photos by. Images & Art of Santana Row. 2nd ed. 2005. 64p. per. 19.95 *(978-0-9770788-0-6(9))* Anzalone, Frank.

Anzalone, Lori. Alligator at Saw Grass Road. Halfmann, Janet. (Smithsonian's Backyard Ser.). (ENG.). 32p. (J). 2011. (gr. -1-3). 19.95 *(978-1-60727-630-2(5))*; 2011. (gr. -1-3). 8.95 *(978-1-60727-631-9(3))*; 2006. pap. 6.95 *(978-1-59249-633-4(4))* Soundprints.

Anziano, Eva. El Correcaminos: Spanish Version. Civin, Todd. 2019. (SPA.). 38p. (J). pap. 15.00 ***(978-1-6918-8548-0(7))*** Independently Published.

—If Every Day Was a Daisy Day. Civin, Todd. 2019. (ENG.). 42p. (J). pap. 14.95 ***(978-1-6704-7271-7(X))*** Independently Published.

Anzur, Thad. The Mismatched Twins. Fanning, Neli. 2018. (Mismatched Twins Ser.: Vol. 1). (ENG.). 30p. (J). 19.00 *(978-0-692-19555-0(6))* Fanning, Neli.

Aoki, Deb. The Best Hawaiian Style Mother Goose Ever! Sullivan, Kevin. 2006. 40p. 16.95 incl. cd-rom *(978-0-9644149-6-9(1))* Hawaya, Inc.

Aoki, Takao. Beyblade. Aoki, Takao. (ENG.). 2004. 200p. (YA). pap. 7.99 *(978-1-59116-621-4(7))*; Vol. 9. 2006. 208p. pap. 7.99 *(978-1-4215-0249-6(6))*; Vol. 10. 2006. 208p. pap. 7.99 *(978-1-4215-0380-6(8))* Viz Media.

—Beyblade: Beyblade Extreme Rotation Shoot, Vol. 2. Aoki, Takao. 2004. (Beyblade Ser.). (ENG.). 192p. (YA). pap. 7.99 *(978-1-59116-697-9(7))* Viz Media.

—Beyblade, Vol. 5. Aoki, Takao. 2005. (ENG.). 192p. (YA). pap. 7.99 *(978-1-59116-793-8(0))* Viz Media.

Aoki, Yuya. Fruits Basket, Volume 3. Takaya, Natsuki. 2004. (Fruits Basket Ser.). 189p. 17.65 *(978-0-7569-6009-4(6))* Perfection Learning Corp.

Aón, Carlos. Aliens & Energy, 1 vol. Biskup, Agnieszka. 2011. (Monster Science Ser.). (ENG.). 32p. (gr. 3-9). (J). pap. 8.10 *(978-1-4296-7325-9(7))*; pap. 47.70 *(978-1-4296-7326-6(5)*, Capstone Pr.); (J). lib. bdg. 31.32 *(978-1-4296-6580-3(7))* Capstone.

—Astro the Alien Learns about Friendship, 28 vols. Sohn, Emily. 2019. (BeginningtoRead Ser.). (ENG.). 32p. (J). (gr. 1-2). pap. 11.94 *(978-1-68404-446-7(4))* Norwood Hse. Pr.

—Astro the Alien Learns about Honesty, 28 vols. Sohn, Emily. 2019. (BeginningtoRead Ser.). (ENG.). 32p. (J). (gr. 1-2). pap. 11.94 *(978-1-68404-444-3(8))* Norwood Hse. Pr.

—Astro the Alien Learns about Patience, 28 vols. Sohn, Emily. 2019. (BeginningtoRead Ser.). (ENG.). 32p. (J). (gr. 1-2). pap. 11.94 *(978-1-68404-447-4(2))* Norwood Hse. Pr.

—Astro the Alien Learns about Sharing, 28 vols. Sohn, Emily. 2019. (BeginningtoRead Ser.). (ENG.). 32p. (J). (gr. 1-2). pap. 11.94 *(978-1-68404-442-9(1))* Norwood Hse. Pr.

Aón, Carlos. Astro the Alien Learns about T-Rex. Sohn, Emily. 2020. (Beginning-To-Read: Astro the Alien Learns about Extinct Animals Ser.). (ENG.). 32p. (J). (gr. 1-2). 22.60 ***(978-1-68450-844-0(4))***; pap. 11.94 ***(978-1-68404-612-6(2))*** Norwood Hse. Pr.

Aón, Carlos. Astro the Alien Learns about Teamwork, 28 vols. Sohn, Emily. 2019. (BeginningtoRead Ser.). (ENG.). 32p. (J). (gr. 1-2). 22.60 *(978-1-68450-930-0(0))* Norwood Hse. Pr.

Aón, Carlos. Astro the Alien Learns about the Dodo. Sohn, Emily. 2020. (Beginning-To-Read: Astro the Alien Learns about Extinct Animals Ser.). (ENG.). 32p. (J). (gr. 1-2). 22.60 ***(978-1-68450-848-8(7))***; pap. 11.94 ***(978-1-68404-608-9(4))*** Norwood Hse. Pr.

—Astro the Alien Learns about the Golden Toad. Sohn, Emily. 2020. (Beginning-To-Read: Astro the Alien Learns about Extinct Animals Ser.). (ENG.). 32p. (J). (gr. 1-2). 22.60 ***(978-1-68450-847-1(9))***; pap. 11.94 ***(978-1-68404-609-6(2))*** Norwood Hse. Pr.

—Astro the Alien Learns about the Passenger Pigeon. Sohn, Emily. 2020. (Beginning-To-Read: Astro the Alien Learns about Extinct Animals Ser.). (ENG.). 32p. (J). (gr. 1-2). 22.60 ***(978-1-68450-849-5(5))***; pap. 11.94 ***(978-1-68404-607-2(6))*** Norwood Hse. Pr.

—Astro the Alien Learns about the Tasmanian Tiger. Sohn, Emily. 2020. (Beginning-To-Read: Astro the Alien Learns about Extinct Animals Ser.). (ENG.). 32p. (J). (gr. 1-2).

22.60 *(978-1-68450-846-4(0))*; pap. 11.94 *(978-1-68404-610-2(6))* Norwood Hse. Pr.

—Astro the Alien Learns about the Woolly Mammoth. Sohn, Emily. 2020. (Beginning-To-Read: Astro the Alien Learns about Extinct Animals Ser.). (ENG.). 32p. (J). (gr. 1-2). 22.60 *(978-1-68450-845-7(2))*; pap. 11.94 *(978-1-68404-611-9(4))* Norwood Hse. Pr.

Aón, Carlos. Astro the Alien Learns How to Calm Down, 28 vols. Sohn, Emily. 2019. (BeginningtoRead Ser.). (ENG.). 32p. (J). (gr. 1-2). pap. 11.94 *(978-1-68404-445-0(6))* Norwood Hse. Pr.

—Frankenstein's Monster & Scientific Methods, 1 vol. Harbo, Christopher L. 2013. (Monster Science Ser.). (ENG.). 32p. (J). (gr. 3-9). pap. 8.10 *(978-1-62065-816-1(X))*; lib. bdg. 31.32 *(978-1-4296-9931-0(0))* Capstone.

Aon, Carlos. Jesse & Jasmine Build a Journal. Lynette, Rachel. 2014. (Writing Builders Ser.). (ENG.). 32p. (J). (gr. 2-4). pap. 11.94 *(978-1-60357-559-1(6))*; lib. bdg. 25.27 *(978-1-59953-585-2(8))* Norwood Hse. Pr.

Aón, Carlos & Lazzati, Laura. The Lonely Existence of Asteroids & Comets. Weakland, Mark. 2012. (Adventures in Science Ser.). (ENG.). 32p. (gr. 3-4). pap. 47.70 *(978-1-4296-8465-1(8))*, Capstone Pr.; (J). lib. bdg. 31.32 *(978-1-4296-7546-8(2))* Capstone.

Aón, Carlos, jt. illus. see Gervasio.

Aón, Carlos Javier. Extraterrestres y Energía. Biskup, Agnieszka Józefina. 2019. (Ciencias Monstruosas Ser.). (SPA.). 32p. (J). (gr. 3-9). lib. bdg. 31.32 *(978-1-5435-8265-9(6))*, 141275) Capstone.

Aoyagi, Nora. Spur: A Wolf's Story, 1 vol. Robertson, Eliza. 2019. 32p. (J). (gr. k-3). 17.95 *(978-1-77164-341-2(2))*, Greystone Bks.) Greystone Books Ltd. CAN. Dist: Publishers Group West (PGW).

Aoyama, Gôshô. Case Closed. Aoyama, Gôshô. 2006. (Case Closed Ser.: 10). (ENG.). 194p. pap. 9.95 *(978-1-4215-0316-5(6))* Viz Media.

—Case Closed, Vol. 1. Aoyama, Gôshô. 2004. (Case Closed Ser.: 1). (ENG.). 200p. pap. 9.99 *(978-1-59116-327-5(7))* Viz Media.

—Case Closed, Vol. 2. Aoyama, Gôshô. 2004. 184p. pap. 9.95 *(978-1-59116-587-3(3))* Viz Media.

—Case Closed, Vol. 3. Aoyama, Gôshô. 2005. (Case Closed Ser.: 3). (ENG.). 200p. pap. 9.95 *(978-1-59116-589-7(X))* Viz Media.

—Case Closed, Vol. 5. Aoyama, Gôshô. 2005. (ENG.). 200p. pap. 9.95 *(978-1-59116-633-7(0))* Viz Media.

—Case Closed, Vol. 6. Aoyama, Gôshô. Yamazaki, Joe, tr. from JPN. 2005. (ENG.). 184p. pap. 9.95 *(978-1-59116-838-6(4))* Viz Media.

—Case Closed, Vol. 7. Aoyama, Gôshô. 2005. (ENG.). 184p. pap. 9.95 *(978-1-59116-978-9(X))* Viz Media.

—Case Closed, Vol. 8. Aoyama, Gôshô. 2005. (Case Closed Ser.: 8). (ENG.). 192p. pap. 9.95 *(978-1-4215-0111-6(2))* Viz Media.

Aoyama, Gosho. Case Closed, Vol. 9, Vol. 9. Aoyama, Gosho. 2006. (Case Closed Ser.: 9). (ENG.). 184p. pap. 9.95 *(978-1-4215-0166-6(X))* Viz Media.

Apa, Ivy Marie. The Adventures of Sir Ambrose Elephant: A Visit to the City. Smith, E. 2012. 19p. pap. 9.95 *(978-1-4691-8378-7(1))* Xlibris Corp.

—Harlow the Helpful Ghost. Brearley, Leeanne. 2012. 60p. pap. 31.99 *(978-1-4797-3178-7(1))* Xlibris Corp.

Aparicio, Ercy Francisco. Melanie: Los Ojos Del Amor. Garcia, Rodrigo Nahuel, ed. 2020. (Reina de Los Espejos Ser.: Vol. 1). (SPA.). 158p. (J). pap. 7.00 ***(978-1-6773-3134-5(8))*** Independently Published.

Aparicio, Núria. Be a Good Citizen. Harimann, Sierra. 2016. 32p. (J). *(978-1-338-03336-6(0))* Scholastic, Inc.

—Caring Classmates. Harimann, Sierra. 2016. 32p. (J). *(978-1-338-03340-3(9))* Scholastic, Inc.

—There's a Doctor for You: Shaped Board Book. Wing, Scarlett. 2017. (I Can Do It Ser.). (ENG.). 11p. (J). (gr. -1-k). bds. 6.99 *(978-1-68052-201-3(9))*, 1001990) Cottage Door Pr.

Aparicio, Raquel. One White Dolphin. Lewis, Gill. 2013. (ENG.). 368p. (J). (gr. 3-7). pap. 8.99 *(978-1-4424-1448-8(0))*, Atheneum Bks. for Young Readers) Simon & Schuster Children's Publishing.

Apel, Peter. Fred Pinsocket Loves Bananas. Apel, Peter. 2015. (ENG.). (J). (gr. -1). bds. 9.99 *(978-0-9907941-0-3(5))* Fred Pinsocket Productions.

Aponte, Carlos. Across the Bay. Aponte, Carlos. 2019. (ENG.). 32p. (J). (gr. -1-2). 17.99 *(978-1-5247-8662-5(4))*, Penguin Workshop) Penguin Young Readers Group.

App, Comipo. El Cambio de Vir. Disuenos, Lapequita. 2018. (SPA.). 106p. (J). pap. 5.99 *(978-1-7201-7190-4(4))* Independently Published.

Appel, Morgan. The Teacher's Classroom Companion: A Handbook for Primary Teachers. Coons, Mary H. 2003. 320p. (J). pap. 24.95 *(978-0-9634938-0-4(9))* Teachers' Handbooks.

Appelhans, Chris. A Greyhound, a Groundhog. Jenkins, Emily. 2017. 40p. (J). (gr. -1-2). 17.99 *(978-0-553-49805-9(3))*, Schwartz & Wade Bks.) Random Hse. Children's Bks.

—Sparky! Offill, Jenny. 2014. (ENG.). 40p. (J). (gr. -1-3). 16.99 *(978-0-375-87023-1(7))*, Schwartz & Wade Bks.) Random Hse. Children's Bks.

Appelt, Kenneth, photos by. Just People & Paper - Pen - Poem: A Young Writer's Way to Begin. Appelt, Kathi. 2004. (Writers & Young Writers Ser.: Vol. 1). 91p. (YA). pap. 11.95 *(978-1-888842-07-4(5))*, 1020) Absey & Co.

Apperley, Dawn. The Tooth Fairy. Hall, Kirsten. (My First Reader Ser.). (ENG.). 32p. (J). (gr. k-1). 2004. pap. 3.95 *(978-0-516-24640-6(2))*; 2003. 18.50 *(978-0-516-22938-6(9))* Scholastic Library Publishing. (Children's Pr.).

Apple, Emma. Hind's Hands: A Story about Autism. Juwayriyah, Umm & Ayed, Juwayriyah. 2013. 16p. (J). pap. 6.00 *(978-1-935437-76-5(3))*, As Sabr Pubns.) Imago Pr.

Apple, Linda. A Dog by Any Other Name Is Not the Same. Piper, J. G. 2017. (ENG.). (J). (gr. k-4). 19.99 *(978-0-9916561-2-7(1))* Piper, J.G.

Apple, Margo. The Chocolate Touch. Catling, Patrick Skene. 2006. (ENG.). 128p. (J). (gr. 3-7). pap. 7.99 *(978-0-688-16133-0(2))* HarperCollins Pubs.

Apple, Margot. Birthday Pony. Haas, Jessie. 2004. 80p. (J). (gr. 2-18). 15.99 *(978-0-06-057359-1(7))* HarperCollins Pubs.

—The Chocolate Touch. Catling, Patrick Skene & Catling, P. ed. 2006. 126p. (J). (gr. 3-7). 17.20 *(978-1-4177-3437-5(X))* Turtleback.

—Me First. Shaw, Nancy. 2015. 32p. pap. 7.00 *(978-1-61003-505-7(4))* Center for the Collaborative Classroom.

—Sheep Blast Off! Shaw, Nancy E. 2011. (Sheep in a Jeep Ser.). (ENG.). 32p. (J). (gr. -1-3). pap. 6.99 *(978-0-547-52025-4(5))*, 1445464) Houghton Mifflin Harcourt Publishing Co.

—Sheep Go to Sleep. Shaw, Nancy. 2015. (Sheep in a Jeep Ser.). (ENG.). 32p. (J). (gr. -1-3). 16.99 *(978-0-544-30989-0(8))*, 1581244, HMH Books For Young Readers) Houghton Mifflin Harcourt Publishing Co.

—Sheep Go to Sleep. Shaw, Nancy E. 2019. (Sheep in a Jeep Ser.). (ENG.). 32p. (J). (gr. -1-3). pap. 7.99 *(978-1-328-60368-5(7))*, 1732077, HMH Books For Young Readers) Houghton Mifflin Harcourt Publishing Co.

—Sheep Go to Sleep (board Book) Shaw, Nancy E. 2016. (Sheep in a Jeep Ser.). (ENG.). 30p. (J). (gr. -1-3). bds. 7.99 *(978-0-544-64053-5(5))*, 1620828, HMH Books For Young Readers) Houghton Mifflin Harcourt Publishing Co.

—Sheep Go to Sleep (lap Board Book) Shaw, Nancy E. 2018. (Sheep in a Jeep Ser.). (ENG.). 30p. (J). (— 1). bds. 12.99 *(978-1-328-91049-3(0))*, 1701058, HMH Books For Young Readers) Houghton Mifflin Harcourt Publishing Co.

—Sheep in a Jeep. Shaw, Nancy E. (Sheep in a Jeep Ser.). (ENG.). (J). (gr. -1-3). 2013. 32p. 26.99 *(978-0-547-99383-6(8))*, 1525236); 2009. 26p. bds. 12.99 *(978-0-547-23775-6(8))*, 1083730); 2006. 32p. 10.99 *(978-0-618-69522-5(2))*, 441919) Houghton Mifflin Harcourt Publishing Co.

—Sheep in a Jeep 5-Minute Stories. Shaw, Nancy E. 2019. (5-Minute Stories Ser.). (ENG.). 224p. (J). (gr. -1-3). 12.99 *(978-1-328-56674-4(9))*, 1726583, HMH Books For Young Readers) Houghton Mifflin Harcourt Publishing Co.

—Sheep in a Shop, 1 vol. Shaw, Nancy E. 2009. (Sheep in a Jeep Ser.). (ENG.). 32p. (J). (gr. -1-3). 10.99 *(978-0-547-23767-1(7))*, 1083884) Houghton Mifflin Harcourt Publishing Co.

—Sheep in a Shop (board Book) Shaw, Nancy E. 2017. (Sheep in a Jeep Ser.). (ENG.). 28p. (J). (— 1). bds. 7.99 *(978-1-328-70286-9(3))*, 1672394, HMH Books For Young Readers) Houghton Mifflin Harcourt Publishing Co.

—Sheep Out to Eat. Shaw, Nancy E. 2005. (Sheep in a Jeep Ser.). (ENG.). 28p. (J). (gr. k — 1). bds. 6.99 *(978-0-618-58339-3(4))*, 587642) Houghton Mifflin Harcourt Publishing Co.

Applefield, Annie. The Beetle & the Berry. Applefield, Annie. 2007. 28p. (J). per. 15.95 *(978-0-9748933-9-6(0))* E & E Publishing.

Appleoff, Sandy. C Is for Cornhusker: A Nebraska Alphabet. Luebs Shepherd, Rajean. 2004. (State Ser.). (ENG.). 40p. (J). 17.95 *(978-1-58536-147-2(X))* Sleeping Bear Pr.

Appolcella, Francesca. Valerie: A Story of a Vase Who Finds Her True Worth: This Book Will Be Helpful to Therapists, Counsellors, Carers, Teachers & Social Workers Who Are Working with Children Struggling with Low Self-Worth and/or Children Who Are Moving Away from Abusive Env. Manning, James & Ridgeway, Nicola. 2018. (ENG.). 74p. (J). pap. *(978-1-78917-380-2(9))* Sketchbook, Sketch Pad, Art Bk., Drawing Paper, and Writing Paper Publishing Co., The.

Apps, Fred. The Back Leg of a Goat: A Tania Abbey Adventure. Reeve, Penny. 2008. (Tania Abbey Adventure Ser.). (ENG.). 96p. (J). pap. 6.99 *(978-1-84550-340-6(6))*, 180a333d-6474-4fcd-bcb0-f479165d62d7) Christian Focus Pubns. GBR. Dist: Baker & Taylor Publisher Services (BTPS).

—Barnabas: The Encourager. MacKenzie, Carine. 2007. (Bible Wise Ser.). (ENG.). 32p. (J). (gr. -1-3). pap. 4.50 *(978-1-84550-290-4(6))*, 484bc7c4-c6de-4dc4-8ef7-b7c6f43a0c94) Christian Focus Pubns. GBR. Dist: Baker & Taylor Publisher Services (BTPS).

—Big Book of Bible Truths, Vol. 1. Ferguson, Sinclair B. 2012. (ENG.). 64p. (J). pap. 14.99 *(978-1-84550-371-0(6))*, 6b29aaac-68e8-4e59-86d1-7ef54646fadb) Christian Focus Pubns. GBR. Dist: Baker & Taylor Publisher Services (BTPS).

—Big Book of Bible Truths 2. Ferguson, Sinclair B. 2008. (ENG.). 64p. (J). pap. 14.99 *(978-1-84550-372-7(4))*, b4b16e6f-086e-4ce4-a6d5-26969e103ca2) Christian Focus Pubns. GBR. Dist: Baker & Taylor Publisher Services (BTPS).

—Daniel: The Praying Prince. MacKenzie, Carine. 2012. (Bible Wise Ser.). (ENG.). 32p. (J). (gr. -1-3). pap. 4.50 *(978-1-85792-155-7(0))*, ecb50659-1d75-4e81-8333-d414504953da) Christian Focus Pubns. GBR. Dist: Baker & Taylor Publisher Services (BTPS).

—Daniel, el Príncipe que Oraba, Mackenzie, Carine. Foce, Natalia, tr. from ENG. l.t. ed. 2004. (Biblewise Ser.). (SPA.). 32p. (J). 4.50 *(978-1-932789-19-5(7))*, 9781932789195, CF4Kids) Christian Focus Pubns. GBR. Dist: Baker & Taylor Publisher Services (BTPS).

—David el Luchador Valiente, Mackenzie, Carin. Foce, Natalia, tr. from ENG. l.t. ed. 2004. (Biblewise Ser.). (SPA.). 32p. (J). 4.50 *(978-1-932789-18-8(9))*, 9781932789188, CF4Kids) Christian Focus Pubns. GBR. Dist: Baker & Taylor Publisher Services (BTPS).

—God's Names. Michael, Sally. 2011. (J). pap. *(978-1-59638-219-0(8))* P & R Publishing.

—La Historia de Pablo — Viajes de Aventura, 1. Mackenzie, Carine. Foce, Natalia, tr. from ENG. l.t. ed. 2004. (Biblewise Ser.). Orig. Title: Journeys of Adventure — the Story of Paul. (SPA.). 32p. (J). 4.50 *(978-1-932789-23-2(5))*, 9781932789232, CF4Kids) Christian Focus Pubns. GBR. Dist: Baker & Taylor Publisher Services (BTPS).

—Jesus Finds His People. MacKenzie, Catherine. 2008. (Sent to Save Ser.). (ENG.). 16p. (J). (gr. -1-3). bds. 3.99 *(978-1-84550-324-6(4))*, 18b8970e-01b9-477d-8a8f-4ebfa51bfe5c) Christian Focus Pubns. GBR. Dist: Baker & Taylor Publisher Services (BTPS).

—Jesus Helps His People. MacKenzie, Catherine. 2008. (Sent to Save Ser.). (ENG.). 16p. (J). (gr. -1-3). bds. 3.99 *(978-1-84550-322-2(8))*, db19d01e-b248-4c0a-833f-a20b8a5f4e81) Christian Focus Pubns. GBR. Dist: Baker & Taylor Publisher Services (BTPS).

—Jesus Is Most Special. Michael, Sally. 2014. (ENG.). 24p. (J). (gr. 4-7). 9.99 *(978-1-62995-029-7(7))* P & R Publishing.

—Jesus Rescues His People. MacKenzie, Catherine. 2008. (Sent to Save Ser.). (ENG.). 16p. (J). (gr. 4-7). bds. 3.99 *(978-1-84550-321-5(X))*, f7cf95d9-69ff-40e8-b8fd-bab56c91c81f) Christian Focus Pubns. GBR. Dist: Baker & Taylor Publisher Services (BTPS).

—Jesus Saves His People. MacKenzie, Catherine. 2008. (Sent to Save Ser.). (ENG.). 16p. (J). (gr. -1-3). bds. 3.99 *(978-1-84550-323-9(6))*, 5cf5792c-9122-4f5f-bb53-5a45a2c8bb48) Christian Focus Pubns. GBR. Dist: Baker & Taylor Publisher Services (BTPS).

—Jonah & the Big Fish. MacKenzie, Carine. 2015. (Board Books Famous Bible Stories Ser.). (ENG.). 12p. (J). (gr. -1-k). bds. 3.99 *(978-1-84550-087-0(3))*, 70535a5e-3c49-4054-9f8f-5f28cbbc7e46, Christian Focus) Christian Focus Pubns. GBR. Dist: Baker & Taylor Publisher Services (BTPS).

—Jonathan: The Faithful Friend. Mackenzie, Carine. 2007. (Bible Wise Ser.). (ENG.). 32p. (J). (gr. -1-2). 4.50 *(978-1-84550-289-8(2))*, a2931b1b-b498-489e-82a1-6cf8128a81fa) Christian Focus Pubns. GBR. Dist: Baker & Taylor Publisher Services (BTPS).

—Jose el Sonador de Dios, Mackenzie, Carine. Foce, Natalia, tr. from ENG. l.t. ed. 2004. (Biblewise Ser.). (SPA.). 32p. (J). 4.50 *(978-1-932789-16-4(2))*, 9781932789164, CF4Kids) Christian Focus Pubns. GBR. Dist: Baker & Taylor Publisher Services (BTPS).

—Joseph: God's Dreamer. Christian Focus Publications (CFP) Staff & MacKenzie, Carine. 2012. (Bible Wise Ser.). (ENG.). 32p. (J). (gr. k-3). pap. 4.50 *(978-1-85792-343-8(X))*, 37b6ff46-b408-42e5-92dd-287bfb1b6b5e) Christian Focus Pubns. GBR. Dist: Baker & Taylor Publisher Services (BTPS).

—Mary & Joseph Love Jesus. MacKenzie, Catherine. 2006. (Board Books Born to Be King Ser.). (ENG.). 16p. (J). (gr. -1-k). bds. 3.99 *(978-1-84550-184-6(5))*, 8992f235-f404-4b75-b316-fc68c8c87c75, Christian Focus) Christian Focus Pubns. GBR. Dist: Baker & Taylor Publisher Services (BTPS).

—My Bible Story Book. Mackenzie, Carine. 2013. (Colour Bks.). (ENG.). 160p. (J). (gr. -1-3). 10.99 *(978-1-84550-129-7(2))*, 0a8d3154-6d72-4c8f-b113-d658d3baf48a) Christian Focus Pubns. GBR. Dist: Baker & Taylor Publisher Services (BTPS).

—Naaman: The Soldier. MacKenzie, Carine. 2015. (Board Books Famous Bible Stories Ser.). (ENG.). 12p. (J). (gr. -1-k). bds. 3.99 *(978-1-84550-085-6(7))*, ecd4a6e7-3b7f-4e89-be2d-9bfc5244aba2, Christian Focus) Christian Focus Pubns. GBR. Dist: Baker & Taylor Publisher Services (BTPS).

—El Nacimiento de Jesús: El Niño Prometido, 1. Mackenzie, Carine. Foce, Natalia, tr. from ENG. l.t. ed. 2004. (Biblewise Ser.). Orig. Title: The Birth of Jesus — the Promised Child. (SPA.). 32p. (J). 4.50 *(978-1-932789-20-1(0))*, 9781932789201, CF4Kids) Christian Focus Pubns. GBR. Dist: Baker & Taylor Publisher Services (BTPS).

—The New Children's Bible. De Vries, Anne. 2014. (Colour Bks.). (ENG.). 288p. (J). 15.99 *(978-1-85792-838-9(5))*, a0114739-0815-49a7-a6f4-d1931c2965f4) Christian Focus Pubns. GBR. Dist: Baker & Taylor Publisher Services (BTPS).

—Noah: Rescue Plan. MacKenzie, Carine. 2013. (Bible Wise Ser.). (ENG.). 32p. (J). (gr. 1-5). pap. 4.50 *(978-1-85792-466-4(5))*, f0e0f83a-ff9c-475f-9c74-0d0645e10ad1) Christian Focus Pubns. GBR. Dist: Baker & Taylor Publisher Services (BTPS).

—El Plan de Rescate: La Historia de Noe, 1. Mackenzie, Carine. Foce, Natalia, tr. from ENG. l.t. ed. 2004. (Biblewise Ser.). Orig. Title: The Rescue Plan. (SPA.). 32p. (J). 4.50 *(978-1-932789-15-7(4))*, 9781932789157, CF4Kids) Christian Focus Pubns. GBR. Dist: Baker & Taylor Publisher Services (BTPS).

—La Resurrección: Jesús Está Vivo, 1. Mackenzie, Carine. Foce, Natalia, tr. from ENG. l.t. ed. 2004. (Biblewise Ser.). Orig. Title: The Resurrection — Jesus Is Alive. (SPA.). 32p. (J). 4.50 *(978-1-932789-21-8(9))*, 9781932789218, CF4Kids) Christian Focus Pubns. GBR. Dist: Baker & Taylor Publisher Services (BTPS).

—Ruth's Journey. Mackenzie, Carine. 2015. (Board Books Famous Bible Stories Ser.). (ENG.). 12p. (J). (gr. -1-k). bds. 3.99 *(978-1-84550-086-3(5))*, 98b900b9-22e7-46a3-bdf3-7629f02555dd, Christian Focus) Christian Focus Pubns. GBR. Dist: Baker & Taylor Publisher Services (BTPS).

—Samuel: The Boy Who Listened. MacKenzie, Carine. 2012. (Bible Wise Ser.). (ENG.). 32p. (J). pap. 4.50 *(978-1-85792-199-1(2))*, 1f7d1620-29fb-4ae7-8a90-db685a37bc06) Christian Focus Pubns. GBR. Dist: Baker & Taylor Publisher Services (BTPS).

—Samuel, el Niño que Escuchaba. Mackenzie, Carine. Foce, Natalia, tr. from ENG. l.t. ed. 2004. (Biblewise Ser.). (SPA.). 32p. (J). 4.50 *(978-1-932789-17-1(0))*, 9781932789171, CF4Kids) Christian Focus Pubns. GBR. Dist: Baker & Taylor Publisher Services (BTPS).

—Samuel's Surprise. MacKenzie, Carine. 2015. (Board Books Famous Bible Stories Ser.). (ENG.). 12p. (J). (gr. -1-k). bds. 3.99 *(978-1-84550-088-7(1))*, 768d65ec-ee40-46c4-91a6-6f7310842996, Christian Focus) Christian Focus Pubns. GBR. Dist: Baker & Taylor Publisher Services (BTPS).

—Sara y Abraham: La maravillosa Promesa. Mackenzie, Carine. Foce, Natalia C., tr. from ENG. 2004. (Biblewise Ser.). Orig. Title: Sarah & Abraham - the Wonderful Promise. (SPA.). 32p. (J). 4.50 *(978-1-932789-14-0(6))*, 9781932789140, CF4Kids) Christian Focus Pubns. GBR. Dist: Baker & Taylor Publisher Services (BTPS).

—Sarah & Abraham: The Wonderful Promise. MacKenzie, Carine. 2013. (Bible Wise Ser.). (ENG.). 32p. (J). (gr. 4-7). pap. 4.50 *(978-1-85792-156-4(9))*, 6064b7ae-31c2-49c8-96cf-41fb1e30ef8f) Christian Focus Pubns. GBR. Dist: Baker & Taylor Publisher Services (BTPS).

—Saul: The Miracle on the Road. Taylor, Jane & MacKenzie, Carine. 2015. (Bible Wise Ser.). (ENG.). 32p. (J). (gr. -1-k). pap. 4.50 *(978-1-85792-296-7(4))*, 985634a2-cd42-4884-8c79-5634029eb054) Christian Focus Pubns. GBR. Dist: Baker & Taylor Publisher Services (BTPS).

—Saúl — el Milagro en el Camino, 1. Mackenzie, Carine. Foce, Natalia, tr. from ENG. l.t. ed. 2004. (Biblewise Ser.). Orig. Title: Saul — the Miracle on the Road. (SPA.). 32p. (J). 4.50 *(978-1-932789-22-5(7))*, 9781932789225, CF4Kids) Christian Focus Pubns. GBR. Dist: Baker & Taylor Publisher Services (BTPS).

—The Shepherds Find Jesus. MacKenzie, Catherine. 2006. (Board Books Born to Be King Ser.). (ENG.). 16p. (J). (gr. -1-k). bds. 3.99 *(978-1-84550-185-3(3))*, ea77db95-04a0-4128-819d-f63c4051984c, Christian Focus) Christian Focus Pubns. GBR. Dist: Baker & Taylor Publisher Services (BTPS).

—Simeon & Anna See Jesus. MacKenzie, Catherine. 2006. (Board Books Born to Be King Ser.). (ENG.). 16p. (J). (gr. -1-k). bds. 3.99 *(978-1-84550-186-0(1))*, 46645ffa-f6fd-4241-a4bd-0097d61af7d7) Christian Focus Pubns. GBR. Dist: Baker & Taylor Publisher Services (BTPS).

—The Singing Soldiers: And Other Bible Stories You've Gotta Hear. Haley, Barbara. 2007. (ENG.). 112p. (J). mass mkt. 7.99 *(978-1-84550-249-2(3))*, 1262c4be-0940-4eca-8516-c7472e7a7e77) Christian Focus Pubns. GBR. Dist: Baker & Taylor Publisher Services (BTPS).

—Water or Goo? Reeve, Penny. 2008. (Tania Abbey Adventure Ser.). (ENG.). 96p. (J). pap. 6.99 *(978-1-84550-341-3(4))*, 349dd7a5-a2da-4674-8869-04e1c81a2b5b) Christian Focus Pubns. GBR. Dist: Baker & Taylor Publisher Services (BTPS).

—The Wise Mean Help Jesus. MacKenzie, Catherine. 2006. (Board Books Born to Be King Ser.). (ENG.). 16p. (J). (gr. -1-k). bds. 3.99 *(978-1-84550-187-7(X))*, 4202d515-cd9b-41f7-b0f7-cc584362358a) Christian Focus Pubns. GBR. Dist: Baker & Taylor Publisher Services (BTPS).

Aprillia, Vinsensiana. Crunch Viaja Al Polo Norte. Valada, Christopher. Utset, George, tr. 2019. (SPA.). 34p. (J). pap. 9.99 ***(978-1-7065-2018-4(2))*** Independently Published.

Apsley. Can I Tell You about Tourette Syndrome? A Guide for Friends, Family & Professionals. Leicester, Mal. 2013. (Can I Tell You About... ? Ser.). (ENG.). 56p. (C). pap. 13.95 *(978-1-84905-407-2(X))*, 694427) Kingsley, Jessica Pubs. GBR. Dist: Hachette UK Distribution.

Aragon Art Studio. The Chocolate Man A Children's Horror Tale. Riddle, Waide Aaron. ed. 2010. (ENG.). 44p. pap. 15.00 *(978-0-615-38560-0(5))* Waide Aaron Riddle.

Aragon, Dolores. Grandma Lale's Magic Adobe Oven: El Horno Magico de Abuelita Lale. García, Nasario. 2018. (SPA & ENG.). (J). pap. *(978-1-943681-64-8(3))*, Rio Grande Bks.) LPD Pr.

—Grandma Lale's Tamales: A Christmas Story. García, Nasario. 2014. (SPA & ENG.). 58p. (J). *(978-1-936744-26-8(0))*, Rio Grande Bks.) LPD Pr.

—Grandma Lale's Tamales: A Christmas Story = Los Tamales de Abuelita Lale: un Cuento Navideano. Garcia, Nasario. 2018. (ENG.). 64p. (J). (gr. 1-3). pap. 17.95 *(978-1-943681-23-5(6))* Nuevo Bks.

—Grandpa Lolo's Matanza: A New Mexico Tradition. Garcia, Nasario. 2018. (ENG.). 74p. (J). (gr. 1-3). pap. 17.95 *(978-1-943681-27-3(9))* LPD Pr.

Aragon, Dolores, jt. illus. see García, Nasario.

Aragon, Rosi. Un Misterio para DOS. Baranda, Maria. 2019. (Torre Azul Ser.). (SPA.). 72p. (J). pap. ***(978-607-9107-92-5(9))*** Norma Ediciones, S.A.

Arai, Ryoji. What What What. Tendo, Arata. Boyd, David, tr. 2017. 48p. (J). (gr. -1-3). 17.95 *(978-1-59270-237-4(6))* Enchanted Lion Bks., LLC.

Arai, Setsuo. Boy's Day in Hawaii. Ching, Tokie. 2008. 32p. (J). 12.95 *(978-1-56647-852-6(9))* Mutual Publishing LLC.

Araizumi, Rui. The Silver Beast, Vol. 5. Kanzaka, Hajime. 2005. (Slayers (Tokyopop) Ser.). 248p. pap. 7.99 *(978-1-59532-581-5(6))* TOKYOPOP, Inc.

—Slayers, Vol. 3. Kanzaka, Hajime. 2005. 232p. pap. 7.99 *(978-1-59532-579-2(4))* TOKYOPOP, Inc.

—Slayers: The Battle of Saillune, Vol. 4. Kanzaka, Hajime. 2005. 232p. pap. 7.99 *(978-1-59532-580-8(8))* TOKYOPOP, Inc.

—Slayers: The Sorcerer of Atlas, 2 vols., Vol. 2. Kanzaka, Hajime. 2004. 192p. pap. 7.99 *(978-1-59532-095-7(4))* TOKYOPOP, Inc.

—Slayers - Vezendi's Shadow, Vol. 6. Kanzaka, Hajime. 2005. (Slayers (Tokyopop) Ser.). 248p. pap. 7.99 *(978-1-59532-582-2(4))* TOKYOPOP, Inc.

Arakawa, Hiromu. The Heroic Legend of Arslan 8. Tanaka, Yoshiki. 2018. (Heroic Legend of Arslan Ser.: 8). (ENG.). 192p. (gr. 8-12). pap. 10.99 *(978-1-63236-484-5(0))* Kodansha America, Inc.

Arakawa, Hiromu. The Art of Fullmetal Alchemist 2. Arakawa, Hiromu. Searleman, Eric, ed. 2007. (Fullmetal Alchemist Ser.: 1). (ENG.). 112p. (gr. 8-18). 19.99 *(978-1-4215-1408-6(7))* Viz Media.

—Fullmetal Alchemist (3-In-1 Edition), Vol. 1: Includes Vols. 1, 2 And 3. Arakawa, Hiromu. 2011. (Fullmetal Alchemist (3-In-1 Edition) Ser.: 1). (ENG.). 576p. pap. 14.99 *(978-1-4215-4018-4(5))* Viz Media.

—Fullmetal Alchemist (3-In-1 Edition), Vol. 2: Includes Vols. 4, 5 And 6. Arakawa, Hiromu. 2011. (Fullmetal Alchemist (3-In-1 Edition) Ser.: 2). (ENG.). 576p. pap. 14.99 *(978-1-4215-4019-1(3))* Viz Media.

—Fullmetal Alchemist, Vol. 1. Arakawa, Hiromu. 2005. (Fullmetal Alchemist Ser.: 1). (ENG.). 192p. (gr. 8-18). pap. 9.99 *(978-1-59116-920-8(8))* Viz Media.

—Fullmetal Alchemist, Vol. 10. Arakawa, Hiromu. 2006. (Fullmetal Alchemist Ser.: 10). (ENG.). 208p. pap. 9.99 *(978-1-4215-0461-2(8))* Viz Media.

—Fullmetal Alchemist, Vol. 11. Arakawa, Hiromu. 2007. (Fullmetal Alchemist Ser.: 11). (ENG.). 208p. pap. 9.99 *(978-1-4215-0838-2(9))* Viz Media.

—Fullmetal Alchemist, Vol. 14. Arakawa, Hiromu. 2007. (Fullmetal Alchemist Ser.: 14). (ENG.). 192p. pap. 9.99 *(978-1-4215-1379-9(X))* Viz Media.

—Fullmetal Alchemist, Vol. 2. Arakawa, Hiromu. 2005. (Fullmetal Alchemist Ser.: 2). (ENG.). 192p. pap. 9.99 *(978-1-59116-923-9(2))* Viz Media.

—Fullmetal Alchemist, Vol. 24. Arakawa, Hiromu. 2011. (Fullmetal Alchemist Ser.: 24). (ENG.). 192p. pap. 9.99 *(978-1-4215-3812-9(1))* Viz Media.

—Fullmetal Alchemist, Vol. 25. Arakawa, Hiromu. 2011. (Fullmetal Alchemist Ser.: 25). (ENG.). 192p. pap. 9.99 *(978-1-4215-3924-9(1))* Viz Media.

—Fullmetal Alchemist, Vol. 26. Arakawa, Hiromu. 2011. (Fullmetal Alchemist Ser.: 26). (ENG.). 193p. pap. 9.99 *(978-1-4215-3962-1(4))* Viz Media.

—Fullmetal Alchemist, Vol. 3. Arakawa, Hiromu. 2005. (Fullmetal Alchemist Ser.: 3). (ENG.). 192p. pap. 9.99 *(978-1-59116-925-3(9))* Viz Media.

—Fullmetal Alchemist, Vol. 4. Arakawa, Hiromu. 2005. (Fullmetal Alchemist Ser.: 4). (ENG.). 200p. pap. 9.99 *(978-1-59116-929-1(1))* Viz Media.

—Fullmetal Alchemist, Vol. 5: Hana Yori Dango. Arakawa, Hiromu. 2006. (Fullmetal Alchemist Ser.: 5). (ENG.). 192p. pap. 9.99 *(978-1-4215-0175-8(9))* Viz Media.

—Fullmetal Alchemist, Vol. 8. Arakawa, Hiromu. 2006. (Fullmetal Alchemist Ser.: 8). (ENG.). 208p. pap. 9.99 *(978-1-4215-0459-9(6))* Viz Media.

—Fullmetal Alchemist, Vol. 9. Arakawa, Hiromu. 2006. (Fullmetal Alchemist Ser.: 9). (ENG.). 208p. pap. 9.99 *(978-1-4215-0460-5(X))* Viz Media.

Arakawa, Shizue. Bunny's Happy Day. 2019. (Buttercup Babies Ser.). (ENG.). 14p. (J). bds. 8.99 *(978-4-05-621079-8(9))* Gakken Plus Co., Ltd. JPN. Dist: Simon & Schuster, Inc.

—Mimi's Picnic. 2019. (Buttercup Babies Ser.). (ENG.). 14p. (J). bds. 8.99 *(978-4-05-621080-4(2))* Gakken Plus Co., Ltd. JPN. Dist: Simon & Schuster, Inc.

Aranda, Amira. Los Mil Anos de Pepe Corcuena. Malpica, Tono. 2010. (SPA.). 104p. (YA). (gr. 6-18). pap. *(978-607-7661-18-4(X))* Ediciones El Naranjo Sa De Cv.

Aranda, Ana. The Chupacabra Ate the Candelabra. Nobleman, Marc Tyler. 2017. 32p. (J). (gr. k-3). 17.99 *(978-0-399-17443-8(5),* Nancy Paulsen Books) Penguin Young Readers Group.

Aranda, Omar. Big Dreams & Powerful Prayers Illustrated Bible: 30 Inspiring Stories from the Old & New Testament, 1 vol. Batterson, Mark. 2020. 224p. (J). 18.99 *(978-0-310-74682-9(5))* Zonderkidz.

—Collins Big Cat Phonics for Letters & Sounds - the Big Nut: Band 01B/Pink B. Tomlinson, Fiona. 2020. (Collins Big Cat Phonics for Letters & Sounds Ser.). (ENG.). 16p. (J). (gr. -1-k). pap. 6.99 *(978-0-00-835760-3(9))* HarperCollins Pubs. Ltd. GBR. Dist: Independent Pubs. Group.

—In the Playhouse, 1 vol. Giulieri, Anne. 2012. (Engage Literacy Magenta Ser.). (ENG.). 32p. (gr. k-2). pap. 5.99 *(978-1-4296-8852-9(1),* Capstone Pr.) Capstone.

—Little Sea Horse & the Big Crab, 1 vol. Giulieri, Anne. 2012. (Engage Literacy Yellow Ser.). (ENG.). 32p. (gr. k-2). pap. 5.99 *(978-1-4296-8968-7(4),* Capstone Pr.) Capstone.

—Little Sea Horse & the Big Storm, 1 vol. Giulieri, Anne. 2012. (Engage Literacy Blue Ser.). (ENG.). 32p. (gr. k-2). pap. 5.99 *(978-1-4296-8992-2(7),* Capstone Pr.) Capstone.

—Once upon a Time Bible for Little Ones, 1 vol. 2017. (ENG.). 32p. (J). bds. 9.99 *(978-0-310-76170-9(0))* Zonderkidz.

—Once upon a Time Storybook Bible, 1 vol. 2017. (ENG.). 144p. (J). 16.99 *(978-0-310-75792-4(4))* Zonderkidz.

—Princess Charity's Courageous Heart, 1 vol. Johnson, Jacqueline & Young, Jeanna Stolle. 2012. (Princess Parables Ser.). (ENG.). 32p. (J). 14.99 *(978-0-310-72701-9(4))* Zonderkidz.

—Princess Grace & the Little Lost Kitten, 1 vol. Young, Jeanna Stolle & Johnson, Jacqueline Kinney. 2011. (Princess Parables Ser.). (ENG.). 32p. (J). (gr. -1-2). 14.99 *(978-0-310-71640-2(3))* Zonderkidz.

—Princess Hope & the Hidden Treasure, 1 vol. Young, Jeanna Stolle & Johnson, Jacqueline. 2012. (Princess Parables Ser.). (ENG.). 32p. (J). 14.99 *(978-0-310-72699-9(9))* Zonderkidz.

—Princess Hope & the Hidden Treasure, 1 vol. Johnson, Young et al. 2012. (I Can Read! / Princess Parables Ser.). (ENG.). 32p. (J). pap. 4.99 *(978-0-310-73250-1(6))* Zonderkidz.

—Princess Joy's Birthday Blessing, 1 vol. Young, Jeanna Stolle & Johnson, Jacqueline Kinney. 2011. (Princess Parables Ser.). (ENG.). 32p. (J). (gr. -1-2). 14.99 *(978-0-310-71639-6(X))* Zonderkidz.

—The Princess Parables Daughters of the King: 90 Devotions, 1 vol. 2017. (Princess Parables Ser.). (ENG.). 192p. (J). 14.99 *(978-0-310-75621-7(9))* Zonderkidz.

—Princess Prayers, 1 vol. Young, Jeanna. 2017. (Princess Parables Ser.). (ENG.). 30p. (J). bds. 9.99 *(978-0-310-75869-3(6))* Zonderkidz.

—A Royal Christmas to Remember, 1 vol. Young, Jeanna. 2016. (Princess Parables Ser.). (ENG.). 32p. (J). 14.99 *(978-0-310-74802-1(X))* Zonderkidz.

Aranda, Tom & Campidelli, Maurizio. The Science of Baseball with Max Axiom, Super Scientist. Dreier, David L. 2015. (Science of Sports with Max Axiom Ser.). (ENG.). 32p. (J). (gr. 3-9). lib. bdg. 31.32 *(978-1-4914-6083-2(0),* Capstone Pr.) Capstone.

Aranda, Tomás & Campidelli, Maurizio. The Science of Basketball with Max Axiom, Super Scientist. Bethea, Nikole Brooks. 2015. (Science of Sports with Max Axiom Ser.). (ENG.). 32p. (J). (gr. 3-9). pap. 7.95 *(978-1-4914-6088-7(1),* Capstone Pr.) Capstone.

Aranega, Merce. Una Medicina para No Llorar. Paloma, David. 3rd ed. (SPA.). 32p. (J). *(978-84-236-4226-7(7))* Edebé ESP. Dist: Lectorum Pubns., Inc.

Aranyi, Jen. Percy the Pigeon. Budge, Katie. 2017. (ENG.). 24p. (J). pap. *(978-1-910565-94-0(6))* Britain's Next Bestseller.

Araujo, Andre. Black Panther: Long Live the King (Marvel Premiere Graphic Novel) 2018. 136p. (J). (gr. 4-17). pap. 14.99 *(978-1-302-90538-5(4))* Marvel Worldwide, Inc.

Araujo, Andre Lima. War of the Realms: Journey into Mystery. 2019. (ENG.). 112p. (YA). (gr. 8-17). pap. 15.99 *(978-1-302-91834-7(6))* Marvel Worldwide, Inc.

Araujo, Andre Lima & Campbell, Jim. Spidey #5. Thompson, Robbie. 2016. (Spidey Ser.). (ENG.). 24p. (J). (gr. 2-8). lib. bdg. 27.07 *(978-1-61479-597-1(5),* 24378, Marvel Age) Spotlight.

—Spidey #6. Thompson, Robbie. 2016. (Spidey Ser.). (ENG.). 24p. (J). (gr. 2-8). lib. bdg. 27.07 *(978-1-61479-598-8(3),* 24379, Marvel Age) Spotlight.

Araujo, Andre Lima & Rosenberg, Rachelle. Spidey #4. Thompson, Robbie. 2016. (Spidey Ser.). (ENG.). 24p. (J). (gr. 2-8). lib. bdg. 27.07 *(978-1-61479-596-4(7),* 24377, Marvel Age) Spotlight.

Araujo, Gabriela. Kizzi the Fire Pug: Book 2 Believe. Shaw, Leroy. 2019. (Kizzi the Fire Pug Ser.: Vol. 2). (ENG.). 44p. (J). pap. *(978-0-9954754-1-0(5))* Tiger Flame Publishing.

Araujo, Katie. Sage Learns to Share, 1 vol. Irwin, Gayle. 2009. 45p. pap. 24.95 *(978-1-60836-409-1(7))* America Star Bks.

Arbat, Carles. The Ants & the Grasshopper, Narrated by the Fanciful but Truthful Grasshopper. Loewen, Nancy. 2018. (Other Side of the Fable Ser.). (ENG.). 24p. (J). (gr. -1-3). lib. bdg. 27.99 *(978-1-5158-2868-6(9),* 138406, Picture Window Bks.) Capstone.

—Barbazul. 2006. (Coleccion Libros para Sonar Ser.). (SPA.). 38p. (J). *(978-84-8464-194-0(5))* Kalandraka Editora, S.L.

—The Emperor's New Clothes (Tales to Grow By) A Story about Honesty. 2020. (Tales to Grow By Ser.). (ENG.). 32p. (J). (gr. k-1). pap. 6.95 *(978-0-531-24624-5(8));* lib. bdg. 26.00 *(978-0-531-23190-6(9))* Scholastic Library Publishing. (Children's Pr.).

—Mr. Tempkin Climbs a Tree. Fagan, Cary. 2019. (ENG.). 32p. (J). (gr. -1-2). 17.99 *(978-1-5415-2173-5(0),* Kar-Ben Publishing) Lerner Publishing Group.

Arbo, Cris. All Around Me, I See. Steinberg, Laya. 2005. (Sharing Nature with Children Book Ser.). 32p. (J). 16.95 *(978-1-58469-068-9(2));* pap. 8.95 *(978-1-58469-069-6(0))* Dawn Pubns.

—All Around Me I See. Steinberg, Laya. 2008. 26p. (J). (gr. -1). bds. 7.95 *(978-1-58469-107-5(7))* Dawn Pubns.

—Champions of the Ocean, 1 vol. Hodgkins, Fran. 2011. (ENG.). 144p. (J). (gr. 5-8). pap. 12.95 *(978-1-58469-119-8(0),* Dawn Pubns.) Sourcebooks, Inc.

—The Dandelion Seed's Big Dream. Anthony, Joseph. 2014. (ENG.). 32p. (J). (gr. k-4). 16.99 *(978-1-58469-496-0(3));* pap. 8.99 *(978-1-58469-497-7(1))* Sourcebooks, Inc. (Dawn Pubns.).

Arbo, Cris. Explore Life Cycles Book Set: Nature Picture Books for Kids. Anthony, Joseph & Rice, David L. 2020. (ENG.). (J). (-4). pap. 35.84 ***(978-1-7282-4203-3(7),*** Dawn Pubns.) Sourcebooks, Inc.

Arbo, Cris. In a Nutshell, 1 vol. Anthony, Joseph. 2011. (ENG.). 32p. (J). (gr. -1-4). pap. 8.95 *(978-1-883220-98-3(X),* Dawn Pubns.) Sourcebooks, Inc.

—In the Trees, Honey Bees. Mortensen, Lori. 2009. 32p. (J). (gr. -1-5). 16.95 *(978-1-58469-114-3(X))* Dawn Pubns.

—In the Trees, Honey Bees, 1 vol. Mortensen, Lori. 2009. (ENG.). 32p. (J). (gr. -1-4). pap. 8.95 *(978-1-58469-115-0(8),* Dawn Pubns.) Sourcebooks, Inc.

—What's in the Garden?, 1 vol. Berkes, Marianne. 2013. (ENG.). 32p. (J). (gr. -1-4). 16.95 *(978-1-58469-189-1(1));* pap. 8.95 *(978-1-58469-190-7(5))* Sourcebooks, Inc. (Dawn Pubns.).

Arbo, Hal. Tom: The Fighting Cowboy. Morgan, Leon. 2011. 426p. 56.95 *(978-1-258-10103-9(3))* Literary Licensing, LLC.

Arbona, Marion. The Good Little Book. MacLear, Kyo. 2015. (ENG.). 40p. (J). (gr. k-4). 16.99 *(978-1-77049-451-0(0),* Tundra Bks.) Tundra Bks. CAN. Dist: Penguin Random Hse. LLC.

—The Magic Clothesline. Poulin, Andree. 2012. 32p. (J). 14.95 *(978-1-4338-1194-4(4));* pap. 9.95 *(978-1-4338-1195-1(2))* American Psychological Assn. (Magination Pr.).

—My Wounded Island, 1 vol. Pasquet, Jacques. Watson, Sophie, tr. from FRE. 2017. (ENG.). 32p. (J). (gr. 1-3). 19.95 *(978-1-4598-1565-0(3))* Orca Bk. Pubs. USA.

—Simon Steps into the Ring. Monette, Marylène. Watson, Sophie B., tr. from FRE. 2020. (ENG.). 32p. (J). (gr. 1-3). 19.95 *(978-1-4598-2181-1(5))* Orca Bk. Pubs. USA.

—Trampoline Boy. Forler, Nan. 2018. (ENG.). 48p. (J). (gr. -1-2). 17.99 *(978-1-77049-830-3(3),* Tundra Bks.) Tundra Bks. CAN. Dist: Penguin Random Hse. LLC.

Arbona, Marion. Window. Arbona, Marion. 2020. (ENG.). 32p. (J). (gr. -1-3). 17.99 *(978-1-5253-0136-0(5))* Kids Can Pr., Ltd. CAN. Dist: Hachette Bk. Group.

Arbour, Danielle. Ready, Set, Kindergarten! Ayer, Paula. 2015. (ENG.). 24p. (J). (gr. -1-k). pap. 8.95 *(978-1-55451-703-9(6),* 9781554517039) Annick Pr., Ltd. CAN. Dist: Publishers Group West (PGW).

Arbuckle, Scott. Mr. Green's Magnificent Machine. Woolley, Bryan. 2003. 32p. 15.95 *(978-1-57168-606-0(1))* Eakin Pr.

Arcabascio, Carolyn. Bar Mitzvah Boys. Uhlberg, Myron. 2019. (ENG.). 32p. (J). (gr. -1-3). 16.99 *(978-0-8075-0570-0(6),* 807505706) Whitman, Albert & Co.

—Olympians vs. Titans: An Interactive Mythological Adventure. Gunderson, Jessica. 2017. (You Choose: Ancient Greek Myths Ser.). (ENG.). 112p. (J). (gr. 3-7). pap. 6.95 *(978-1-5157-4825-0(1));* lib. bdg. 32.65 *(978-1-5157-4820-5(0))* Capstone. (Capstone Pr.).

—Olympians vs. Titans: An Interactive Mytholoical Adventure. Gunderson, Jessica. 2017. (ENG.). 112p. (J). pap. *(978-1-4747-3767-8(6))* Capstone.

—The Quest of Theseus: An Interactive Mythological Adventure. Hoena, Blake. 2017. (You Choose: Ancient Greek Myths Ser.). (ENG.). 112p. (J). (gr. 3-7). pap. 6.95 *(978-1-5157-4826-7(X),* Capstone Pr.) Capstone.

—The Quest of Theseus: An Interactive Mytholoical Adventure. Hoena, Blake. 2017. (You Choose: Ancient Greek Myths Ser.). (ENG.). 112p. (J). (gr. 3-7). lib. bdg. 32.65 *(978-1-5157-4821-2(9),* Capstone Pr.) Capstone.

Arcana Studio Staff. Demolition Day, 1 vol. Everheart, Chris. 2010. (Recon Academy Ser.). (ENG.). 64p. (J). (gr. 4-8). 26.65 *(978-1-4342-1917-6(8),* Stone Arch Bks.) Capstone.

—Mixed Signals, 1 vol. Everheart, Chris. 2010. (Recon Academy Ser.). (ENG.). 64p. (J). (gr. 4-8). 26.65 *(978-1-4342-1915-2(1),* Stone Arch Bks.) Capstone.

—Monster Beach, 1 vol. O'Reilly, Sean. 2012. (Mighty Mighty Monsters Ser.). (ENG.). 48p. (J). (gr. 2-4). pap. 6.10 *(978-1-4342-4608-0(6),* Stone Arch Bks.) Capstone.

—The Monster Crooks, 1 vol. O'Reilly, Sean. 2012. (Mighty Mighty Monsters Ser.). (ENG.). 48p. (J). (gr. 2-4). pap. 6.10 *(978-1-4342-4610-3(8),* Stone Arch Bks.) Capstone.

—The Scare Fair, 1 vol. O'Reilly, Sean. 2012. (Mighty Mighty Monsters Ser.). (ENG.). 48p. (J). (gr. 2-4). pap. 6.10 *(978-1-4342-4611-0(6),* Stone Arch Bks.) Capstone.

—Storm Surge, 1 vol. Everheart, Chris. 2010. (Recon Academy Ser.). (ENG.). 64p. (J). (gr. 4-8). 26.65 *(978-1-4342-1918-3(6),* Stone Arch Bks.) Capstone.

—Teen Agent, 1 vol. Everheart, Chris. 2010. (Recon Academy Ser.). (ENG.). 64p. (J). (gr. 4-8). 26.65 *(978-1-4342-1916-9(X),* Stone Arch Bks.) Capstone.

—The Wolfboy's Wish, 1 vol. O'Reilly, Sean. 2012. (Mighty Mighty Monsters Ser.). (ENG.). 48p. (J). (gr. 2-4). pap. 6.10 *(978-1-4342-4613-4(2),* Stone Arch Bks.) Capstone.

Arcella, Steven. Carl Sandburg. Bolin, Frances Schoonmaker, ed. 2008. (Poetry for Young People Ser.: 4). 48p. (J). (gr. 3-7). pap. 6.95 *(978-1-4027-5471-5(X))* Sterling Publishing Co., Inc.

Archambault, Matthew. Janusz Korczak's Children, Vol. Spielman, Gloria. 2007. (Kar-Ben for Older Readers Ser.). (ENG.). 40p. (J). (gr. 3-7). lib. bdg. 17.95 *(978-1-58013-255-8(3));* (gr. 2-4). pap. 8.95 *(978-0-8225-7050-9(5))* Lerner Publishing Group. (Kar-Ben Publishing).

—Pat & Pea Soup. Stegall, Billy Mark. 2003. (Books for Young Learners). (ENG.). 12p. (J). 5.75 net. *(978-1-57274-278-9(X),* 2757, Bks. for Young Learners) Owen, Richard C. Pubs., Inc.

—Saint Paul: The Thirteenth Apostle. Hill, Mary Lea. 2008. (Encounter the Saints Ser.: 22). 117p. (J). (gr. 3-7). per. 7.95 *(978-0-8198-7102-2(8))* Pauline Bks. & Media.

—Sam Collier & the Founding of Jamestown. Ransom, Candice. (On My Own History Ser.). 48p. (J). 2007. (ENG.). (gr. 2-4). pap. 7.99 *(978-0-8225-6451-5(3),* First Avenue Editions); 2006. (gr. 1-2). 25.26 *(978-1-57505-874-0(X),* Millbrook Pr.) Lerner Publishing Group.

—Sojourner Truth. Swain, Gwenyth. 2005. (On My Own Biography Ser.). 48p. (J). (gr. 1-3). pap. 6.95 *(978-1-57505-827-6(8))* Lerner Publishing Group.

Archbold, Tim. Big Liam, Little Liam. Morgan, Ruth. 2005. (ENG.). 24p. (J). lib. bdg. 23.65 *(978-1-59646-728-6(2))* Dingles & Co.

Archbold, Tim. Lost, Set. Munton, Gill. 2016. (ENG.). 16p. (J). pap. ***(978-0-19-837207-3(8))*** Oxford Univ. Pr., Inc.

Archbold, Tim. Pig in Love. French, Vivian. 2005. 32p. (J). lib. bdg. 9.00 *(978-1-4242-0889-0(0))* Fitzgerald Bks.

—Sam & the Griswalds. Barnes, Emma. 2016. (ENG.). 318p. (J). (gr. 2-4). pap. *(978-0-9935158-1-1(9))* Greyfire Publishing.

—The Secret Dog. Friedman, Joe. 2015. 192p. (J). (gr. 2-4). pap. 12.99 *(978-1-78027-287-0(1))* Birlinn, Ltd. GBR. Dist: Casemate Pubs. & Bk. Distributors, LLC.

—Something's Drastic: Band 12/Copper (Collins Big Cat) Rosen, Michael. 2007. (Collins Big Cat Ser.). (ENG.). 32p. (J). (gr. 2-4). pap. 10.99 *(978-0-00-723077-8(X))* HarperCollins Pubs. Ltd. GBR. Dist: Independent Pubs. Group.

—La Sorprendente Mascota del Señor Pérez. Robinson, Hilary. 2005. (Lectores Relampago / Lightning Readers: Level 3 Ser.). (SPA.). 32p. (J). (gr. 1-2). 16.19 *(978-0-7696-4061-7(3))* School Specialty, Incorporated.

Archembault, Matthew. Logan West, Printer's Devil. Breault, Christie Merriman. 2006. 142p. (J). pap. *(978-1-59336-762-6(7))* Mondo Publishing.

Archer, Angela. L'Élan du Yellowstone. Womack, Rowena. 2018. (FRE.). 28p. (J). (gr. k-1). pap. 14.99 *(978-1-942922-33-9(7))* Wee Creek Pr. LLC.

—Popcorn. Womack, Rowena. 2017. (ENG.). (J). (gr. k-2). pap. 10.99 *(978-1-942922-36-0(1))* Wee Creek Pr. LLC.

—Popcorn. Womack, Rowena. 2013. 26p. (J). 16.99 *(978-1-61160-595-2(4))* Whiskey Creek Restorations.

Archer, Charlotte. Animals. Ackland, Nick & Clever Publishing. 2019. (Clever Colorful Concepts Ser.). (ENG.). 10p. (J). (gr. -1 — 1). bds. 5.99 *(978-1-948418-92-8(4),* 331917) Clever Media Group.

—Colors. Ackland, Nick & Clever Publishing. 2019. (Clever Colorful Concepts Ser.). (ENG.). 10p. (J). (gr. -1 — 1). bds. 5.99 *(978-1-948418-93-5(2),* 331916) Clever Media Group.

—The Great Pond Race: With Four Easy-Stick Characters! 2018. (Pocket Pals Bks.). (ENG.). 8p. (J). (gr. -1 — 1). 6.99 *(978-1-4380-7886-1(2),* B.E.S. Publishing) Peterson's.

—My Growing Garden: Flip-A-Flap. Colombe, Rose. Cottage Door Press, ed. 2019. (Lamaze Activity Bks.). (ENG.). 10p. (J). (gr. -1-k). bds. 9.99 *(978-1-68052-739-1(8),* 1004600) Cottage Door Pr.

—Playtime for Fox. 2017. (J). *(978-1-62885-270-7(4))* Kidsbooks, LLC.

—Vehicles. Clever Publishing & Ackland, Nick. 2019. (Clever Colorful Concepts Ser.). (ENG.). 10p. (J). (gr. -1 — 1). bds. 5.99 *(978-1-948418-96-6(7),* 331935) Clever Media Group.

Archer, Christine. Origami Fortune Tellers. Heiman, Diane & Suneby, Elizabeth. 2011. (Dover Origami Papercraft Ser.). (ENG.). 32p. (J). (gr. 2-7). pap. 7.99 *(978-0-486-47826-5(2))* Dover Pubns., Inc.

Archer, Dosh. Baaad Sheep. Archer, Dosh. 2016. (Urgency Emergency! Ser.). (ENG.). 48p. (J). (gr. -1-3). 12.99 *(978-0-8075-8349-4(9),* 807583499) Whitman, Albert & Co.

—Big Bad Wolf. Archer, Dosh. (Urgency Emergency! Ser.). (ENG.). 48p. (J). (gr. -1-3). 2015. pap. 9.99 *(978-0-8075-8351-7(0),* 807583510); 2013. 12.99 *(978-0-8075-8352-4(9),* 807583529) Whitman, Albert & Co.

—The Case of Piggy's Bank. Archer, Dosh. 2018. (Time to Read Ser.: 1). (ENG.). 48p. (J). (gr. k-2). 12.99 *(978-0-8075-1557-0(4),* 807515574) Whitman, Albert & Co.

Archer, Dosh. The Case of the Icky Ice Cream (Detective Paw of the Law: Time to Read, Level 3) Archer, Dosh. 2020. (Time to Read Ser.). (ENG.). 48p. (J). (gr. k-2). pap. 3.99 ***(978-0-8075-1584-6(1),*** 0807515841); 12.99 ***(978-0-8075-1571-6(X),*** 080751571X) Whitman, Albert & Co.

Archer, Dosh. The Case of the Missing Painting (Detective Paw of the Law: Time to Read, Level 3) Archer, Dosh. 2020. (Time to Read Ser.). (ENG.). 48p. (J). (gr. k-2). pap. 3.99 *(978-0-8075-1570-9(1),* 807515701) Whitman, Albert & Co.

—The Case of the Stolen Drumsticks. Archer, Dosh. 2018. (Time to Read Ser.: 2). (ENG.). 48p. (J). (gr. k-2). 12.99 *(978-0-8075-1556-3(6),* 807515566) Whitman, Albert & Co.

—Humpty's Fall. Archer, Dosh. (Urgency Emergency! Ser.). (ENG.). 48p. (J). (gr. -1-3). 2016. pap. 9.99 *(978-0-8075-8362-3(6),* 807583626); 2015. 12.99 *(978-0-8075-8356-2(1),* 807583561) Whitman, Albert & Co.

—Itsy Bitsy Spider. Archer, Dosh. (Urgency Emergency! Ser.). (ENG.). 48p. (J). (gr. -1-3). 2015. pap. 9.99 *(978-0-8075-8360-9(X),* 080758360X); 2013. 12.99 *(978-0-8075-8358-6(8),* 807583588) Whitman, Albert & Co.

—Little Elephant's Blocked Trunk. Archer, Dosh. (Urgency Emergency! Ser.). (ENG.). 48p. (J). (gr. -1-3). 2015. pap. 9.99 *(978-0-8075-8361-6(8),* 807583618); 2014. 12.99 *(978-0-8075-8354-8(5),* 807583545) Whitman, Albert & Co.

—Urgency Emergency!, 4, Set. Archer, Dosh. 2016. (Urgency Emergency! Ser.). (ENG.). 192p. (J). (gr. -1-3). pap. 19.99 *(978-0-8075-9991-4(3),* 807599913) Whitman, Albert & Co.

Archer, Mary Jane. I Am Her Ears: A Story with Pictures of a Three Year Old Rescued Dog Who Leads a New Life As a Certified Hearing Dog. Archer, Mary Jane, photos by. Peters, Jean Norman. 2004. 26p. (J). *(978-0-9749911-0-8(4),* 1237614) Gizmo Pr.

Archer, Micha. Around the World in a Bathtub. Bradford, Wade. 2017. 32p. (J). (gr. -1-2). lib. bdg. 16.99 *(978-1-58089-544-6(1))* Charlesbridge Publishing, Inc.

—El Fandango de Lola. Witte, Anna. 32p. 2013. pap. 8.99 *(978-1-78285-066-3(X));* 2011. (J). 9.99 *(978-1-84686-359-2(7))* Barefoot Bks., Inc.

—Girl Running. Pimentel, Annette Bay. 2018. 32p. (J). (gr. k-3). 17.99 *(978-1-101-99668-3(4),* Nancy Paulsen Books) Penguin Young Readers Group.

—Lola's Fandango. Witte, Anna. 2018. (ENG.). 32p. (J). (gr. k-4). pap. 9.99 *(978-1-78285-398-5(7))* Barefoot Bks., Inc.

—Prairie Days. MacLachlan, Patricia. 2020. (ENG.). 40p. (J). (gr. -1-3). 17.99 *(978-1-4424-4191-0(7),* McElderry, Margaret K. Bks.) McElderry, Margaret K. Bks.

—Snowman - Cold = Puddle: Spring Equations. Salas, Laura Purdie. 2019. 32p. (J). (gr. -1-3). lib. bdg. 16.99 *(978-1-58089-798-3(3))* Charlesbridge Publishing, Inc.

—We Are Problem Solvers. Giroux, Lindsay Nina. 2016. (J). *(978-0-87659-715-6(0))* Gryphon Hse., Inc.

—The Wise Fool. Husain, Shahrukh. 2012. (ENG.). 64p. (J). (gr. 2-6). pap. 12.99 *(978-1-84686-938-9(2))* Barefoot Bks., Inc.

—Wise Fool: Fables from the Islamic World. Husain, Shahrukh & Barefoot Books. 2015. (ENG.). 64p. (J). (gr. 1-5). pap. 14.99 *(978-1-78285-255-1(7))* Barefoot Bks., Inc.

Archer, Micha. Daniel Finds a Poem. Archer, Micha. 2016. 32p. (J). (gr. k-3). 16.99 *(978-0-399-16913-7(X),* Nancy Paulsen Books) Penguin Young Readers Group.

—Daniel's Good Day. Archer, Micha. 2019. 32p. (J). (-k). 16.99 *(978-0-399-54672-3(3),* Nancy Paulsen Books) Penguin Young Readers Group.

Archer, Micha, jt. illus. see Masse, Josée.

Archeval, Jose. Flying Courage. Brown, Amanda C. 2012. (ENG.). 26p. (J). pap. 9.99 *(978-1-62006-121-3(X))* Sunbury Press, Inc.

Archibald, A. L. The secret of the live Dolls. Gates, Josephine Scribner. 2007. (J). lib. bdg. 59.00 *(978-1-60304-024-2(2))* Dollworks.

Archibald, Odell. P Is for Puffin: A Newfoundland & Labrador Alphabet. Skirving, Janet. rev. ed. 2006. (Discover Canada Province by Province Ser.). (ENG.). 40p. (J). (gr. 1-3). 17.95 *(978-1-58536-287-5(5),* 202098) Sleeping Bear Pr.

Archibold, Tim. Knock Knock! The Best Knock Knock Jokes Ever! 2004. (Sidesplitters Ser.). (ENG.). 64p. (YA). (gr. 1-5). pap. 6.99 *(978-0-7534-5707-8(5),* 9780753457078, Kingfisher) Roaring Brook Pr.

Archimede, Daniele. Spuds & the Spider. Ó Conaill, Séamus. 2018. (ENG.). 32p. (J). pap. 16.00 *(978-0-7171-7995-4(8))* Gill Bks. IRL. Dist: Casemate Pubs. & Bk. Distributors, LLC.

Archipova, Anastasiya. A Favourite Collection of Grimm's Fairy Tales: Cinderella, Little Red Riding Hood, Snow White & the Seven Dwarfs & Many More Classic Stories, 16 vols. Grimm, Jacob & Wilhelm. 2015. Orig. Title: Die Schönsten Märchen der Brüder Grimm. (ENG.). 176p. (J). 16.95 *(978-1-78250-201-2(7))* Floris Bks. GBR. Dist: Consortium Bk. Sales & Distribution.

—Hansel & Gretel, 20 vols. Grimm, Jacob & Grimm, Wilhelm. 2008. (ENG.). 32p. (J). (gr. -1-3). *(978-0-86315-623-6(1))* Floris Bks.

Archipowa, A. Cuentos de los Hermanos Grimm. Archipowa, A. Grimm, Jacob et al. Martínez B. de Quirós, Eladio, tr. (SPA.). 102p. 19.95 *(978-84-241-5770-8(2))* Everest Editora ESP. Dist: Lectorum Pubns., Inc.

Arciero, Susan. Christmas in America. Gingrich, Callista. 2015. (Ellis the Elephant Ser.: 5). (ENG.). 40p. (J). (gr. -1-3). 16.99 *(978-1-62157-345-6(1),* Regnery Kids) Regnery Publishing, Inc., An Eagle Publishing Co.

—From Sea to Shining Sea. Gingrich, Callista. 2014. (Ellis the Elephant Ser.: 4). (ENG.). 40p. (J). (gr. -1-3). 14.99 *(978-1-62157-253-4(6),* Regnery Kids) Regnery Publishing, Inc., An Eagle Publishing Co.

—Hail to the Chief. Gingrich, Callista. 2016. (Ellis the Elephant Ser.: 6). (ENG.). 40p. (J). (gr. -1-4). 16.99 *(978-1-62157-479-8(2),* Regnery Kids) Regnery Publishing, Inc., An Eagle Publishing Co.

—Land of the Pilgrims Pride. Gingrich, Callista. 2012. (Ellis the Elephant Ser.: 2). (ENG.). 28p. (J). (gr. k-3). 14.95 *(978-1-59698-829-3(0),* Little Patriot Pr.) Regnery Publishing, Inc., An Eagle Publishing Co.

—Remember the Ladies. Gingrich, Callista. 2017. (Ellis the Elephant Ser.: 7). (ENG.). 40p. (J). (gr. -1-4). 16.99 *(978-1-62157-480-4(6))* Regnery Publishing, Inc., An Eagle Publishing Co.

—Sweet Land of Liberty. Gingrich, Callista. 2011. (Ellis the Elephant Ser.: 1). (ENG.). 28p. (J). (gr. -1-3). 14.95 *(978-1-59698-292-5(6))* Regnery Publishing, Inc., An Eagle Publishing Co.

—Yankee Doodle Dandy. Gingrich, Callista. 2013. (Ellis the Elephant Ser.: 3). (ENG.). 40p. (J). (gr. -1-3). 14.95 *(978-1-62157-087-5(8),* Regnery Kids) Regnery Publishing, Inc., An Eagle Publishing Co.

Ardizzone, Edward. The Alley. Estes, Eleanor. 2003. (ENG.). 288p. (J). (gr. 3-7). pap. 18.95 *(978-0-15-204918-8(5),* 1194852) Houghton Mifflin Harcourt Publishing Co.

—The Alley. Estes, Eleanor. 2004. (Odyssey/Harcourt Young Classic Ser.). 283p. 15.95 *(978-0-7569-3475-0(3))* Perfection Learning Corp.

—Ann at Highwood Hall. Graves, Robert. 2017. 56p. (J). (gr. k-4). 16.95 *(978-1-60980-743-6(X),* Triangle Square) Seven Stories Pr.

—Desbarolida, the Waltzing Mouse. Langley, Noel. 2008. 80p. pap. *(978-1-905946-01-3(5))* Durrant Publishing.

—Jim at the Corner. Farjeon, Eleanor. 2017. (ENG.). 96p. (J). (gr. 2-4). 15.95 *(978-1-68137-164-1(2),* NYR Children's Collection) New York Review of Bks., Inc., The.

—The Little Bookroom. Farjeon, Eleanor. 2003. (ENG.). 336p. (J). (gr. 4-7). 19.95 *(978-1-59017-048-9(2),* NYR Children's Collection) New York Review of Bks., Inc., The.

—The Little Steamroller. Greene, Graham. 2018. (Little Train Ser.: 2). (ENG.). 48p. (J). (gr. -1-k). pap. 9.99 *(978-1-78295-284-8(5),* Red Fox) Random House Children's Books GBR. Dist: Independent Pubs. Group.

—The Little Train. Greene, Graham. 2018. (Little Train Ser.: 1). (ENG.). 48p. (J). (gr. -1-k). pap. 9.99 *(978-1-78295-281-7(0),* Red Fox) Random House Children's Books GBR. Dist: Independent Pubs. Group.

—Miranda the Great. Estes, Eleanor. 2005. (ENG.). 96p. (J). (gr. 3-7). pap. 7.95 *(978-0-15-205411-3(1),* 1196287) Houghton Mifflin Harcourt Publishing Co.

—Nurse Matilda Goes to Hospital. Brand, Christianna. 128p. *(978-0-7475-7678-5(5))* Bloomsbury Publishing Plc GBR. Dist: Macmillan.

—The Tunnel of Hugsy Goode. Estes, Eleanor. 2003. (ENG.). 256p. (J). (gr. 3-7). pap. 14.95 *(978-0-15-204916-4(9),* 1194845) Houghton Mifflin Harcourt Publishing Co.

Ardizzone, Edward. Sarah & Simon & No Red Paint. Ardizzone, Edward. 2011. (ENG.). 48p. (J). 17.95 *(978-1-56792-410-7(7))* Godine, David R. Pub.

Arégui, Matthias, et al. Before After. Arégui, Matthias et al. 2014. (ENG.). 176p. (J). (gr. -1-3). 19.99 *(978-0-7636-7621-6(7))* Candlewick Pr.

Arégui, Matthias, jt. illus. see Ramstein, Anne-Margot.

Arelys, Aguilar, jt. illus. see James, Melody A.

Arena, Jillayne. Playing Lotería Mexicana: El Juego de la Lotería Mexicana. Laínez, René Colato. 2005. (ENG, MUL & SPA.). 32p. (J). (gr. -1-3). 15.95 *(978-0-87358-881-2(9))* Cooper Square Publishing Llc.

Arenson, Roberta. Kids' Garden: 40 Fun Outdoor Activities & Games. Cohen, Whitney & Life Lab Science Program Staff. 2009. 40p. (J). (gr. k-3). pap. 19.99 *(978-1-84686-367-7(8))* Barefoot Bks., Inc.

—Kids' Kitchen: 40 Fun & Healthy Recipes to Make & Share. Bird, Fiona. 2009. 40p. (J). (gr. 3-18). pap. 19.99 *(978-1-84686-176-5(4))* Barefoot Bks., Inc.

—Three Billy Goats Gruff. Finch, Mary. 2018. (ENG.). 32p. (J). (gr. k-3). pap. 8.99 *(978-1-78285-401-2(0))* Barefoot Bks., Inc.

—Los Tres Chivitos Gruff. Finch, Mary. 2003.Tr. of Three Billy Goats Gruff. 32p. (J). pap. 7.99 *(978-1-84148-145-6(9))* Barefoot Bks., Inc.

Arenson, Roberta. One, Two, Skip a Few! First Number Rhymes. Arenson, Roberta. 2005. 32p. (J). pap. 6.99 *(978-1-84148-130-2(0))* Barefoot Bks., Inc.

Arenson, Roberta & Asbjørnsen, Peter Christen. The Three Billy Goats Gruff. Arenson, Roberta & Finch, Mary. 2003. (ENG.). 32p. (J). 7.99 *(978-1-84148-351-1(6))* Barefoot Bks., Inc.

Arevalo, Jose Daniel. I See Many Colors Around My House: Los Colores que Veo Por Mi Casa. Layne, Carmela C. Layne, Carmela C., ed. l.t. ed. 2005. (SPA.). 24p. (J). (gr. -1-3). pap. 6.95 *(978-0-9769538-0-7(3))* Pannycake Pubn.

Argent, Kerry. Nighty Night!, 1 vol. Wild, Margaret. 2014. (ENG.). 32p. (J). (gr. -1-1). 7.95 *(978-1-56145-812-7(0))* Peachtree Publishing Co. Inc.

—Ruby Roars. Wild, Margaret. 2009. (ENG.). 32p. (J). (gr. -1-2). pap. 12.99 *(978-1-74175-752-1(5))* Allen & Unwin AUS. Dist: Independent Pubs. Group.

Argha, Mondal. Tommy Two-Toes: Teaches the Jungle about Being Vegetarian. Dayton, Mason & Darci, Mason. 2017. (ENG.). (J). pap. *(978-0-9959983-3-9(7))* Green Bamboo Publishing.

Argilli, Genny Wolf. Please Don't Disturb I'm Writing: Quaderno; Notebook; Libro Di Scrittura; Diario, Notepad; Quaderno per Appunti; Sketchbook. Travini, Genny. 2019. (ITA.). 114p. (J). pap. 5.52 ***(978-1-7097-9962-4(5))*** Independently Published.

Argoff, Beily. Braid the Challah: A Playful Action Rhyme. Paluch, Beily. 2004. 12p. (J). bds. 6.95 *(978-1-929628-17-9(X))* Hachai Publishing.

Argoff, Patti. Bracha Do You Know? Stren, Ariella. 2015. 28p. (J). 9.95 *(978-1-929628-76-6(5))* Hachai Publishing.

—Braid the Challah: A Playful Action Rhyme. Paluch, Beily. 2014. 12p. (J). bds. 6.95 *(978-1-929628-83-4(8))* Hachai Publishing.

—Chanukah Guess Who? A Lift the Flap Book. Stern, Ariella. 2012. (ENG.). 32p. (J). 9.95 *(978-1-929628-68-1(4))* Hachai Publishing.

—Happy Birthday to Me! - Boys' Edition. Lieberman, Channah. 2006. 32p. (J). 12.95 *(978-1-929628-27-8(7))* Hachai Publishing.

—Happy Birthday to Me! Girls' Edition. Lieberman, Channah. 2006. 32p. (J). 12.95 *(978-1-929628-31-5(5))* Hachai Publishing.

—I am a Torah: A Playful Action Rhyme. Paluch, Beily. 2004. 12p. (J). bds. 5.95 *(978-1-929628-18-6(8))* Hachai Publishing.

—Miller the Green Caterpillar. House, Darrell. l.t. ed. 2005. 32p. 16.95 *(978-0-9663276-9-4(1))* Red Engine Pr.

—Shavous Guess Who? Stern, Ariella. 2017. (ENG.). 28p. (J). 9.95 *(978-1-945560-00-2(2))* Hachai Publishing.

—What Else Do I Say? A Lift the Flap Book. Goldberg, Malky. 2007. (J). (gr. -1-k). bds. 9.95 *(978-1-929628-34-6(X))* Hachai Publishing.

—When the World Was Quiet. Nutkis, Phyllis. 2003. (J). pap. 10.95 *(978-1-929628-14-8(5))* Hachai Publishing.

Argue, Karon. Barn Cat Buttons: Meets Princess Kylie. Edall-Robson, Ann. Cartwright, Tracy, ed. 2019. (Barn Cat Buttons Ser.: Vol. 1). (ENG.). 40p. (J). (gr. 3-6). pap. ***(978-1-989248-05-8(5))*** 1449511 Alberta Ltd.

Argue, Karon. Sydney's Vacation: Miracles & Mud Puddles. Cowling, Loree & Cowling, Sydney. 2019. (ENG.). 44p. (J). *(978-1-5255-1692-4(2));* pap. *(978-1-5255-1693-1(0))* FriesenPress.

Arguello, Stacie M. Merry Berry Rocker Hound Meets Santa. Arguello, Stacie M. 2018. (ENG.). 122p. (J). pap. 24.99 *(978-1-7310-1081-0(8))* Independently Published.

Arhøj, Anders. Catch Me: A Seek-and-Find Book. 2019. (ENG.). 40p. (J). (gr. k-3). 17.99 *(978-1-4521-6649-0(8))* Chronicle Bks. LLC.

Arias, Cinday. Gabe & the Park & His Big Toy Box: Learning Your Environment, Numbers, & Shapes. Thorpe, Rochelle O'Neal. 2011. (ENG.). 38p. (J). pap. 10.00 ***(978-1-935706-62-5(4))*** Wiggles Pr.

Arias, Fernando. Witchy Travel Tales 2: Sleepless in Stonehenge. Beadle, Sibel. 2017. (Witchy Travel Tales Ser.: Vol. 2). (ENG.). 42p. (J). pap. *(978-1-78623-092-8(5))* Grosvenor Hse. Publishing Ltd.

—Witchy Travel Tales 3: The Golden Bunny of the Lake District. Beadle, Sibel. 2018. (Witchy Travel Tales Ser.: Vol. 3). (ENG.). 62p. (J). pap. *(978-1-78623-158-1(1))* Grosvenor Hse. Publishing Ltd.

—Witchy Travel Tales 4: Nessie's Husband. Beadle, Sibel. 2018. (ENG.). 76p. (J). pap. *(978-1-78623-339-4(8))* Grosvenor Hse. Publishing Ltd.

Aric, Nicholson. I Hope You Dance. gif. ed. 2005. 24p. (J). bds. 9.99 incl. audio compact disk *(978-1-57791-151-7(2),* Little Melody Pr.) Brighter Minds Children's Publishing.

Arihara, Shino. A Song for Cambodia, 1 vol. Lord, Michelle. 2008. (ENG.). 32p. (J). (gr. 1-6). 16.95 *(978-1-60060-139-2(1))* Lee & Low Bks., Inc.

Arijanto, Astrid. Putuguq & Kublu, 1 vol. Christopher, Danny. 2017. (ENG.). 40p. (J). (gr. k-2). pap. 5.95 *(978-1-77227-143-0(8))* Inhabit Media Inc. CAN. Dist: Consortium Bk. Sales & Distribution.

—Putuguq & Kublu & the Qalupalik. Akulukjuk, Roselynn & Christopher, Danny. 2019. (ENG.). 32p. (J). mass mkt. 6.95 *(978-1-77227-228-4(0))* Inhabit Media Inc. CAN. Dist: Consortium Bk. Sales & Distribution.

Arima, Keitaro. Tsukuyomi - Moon Phase, Vol. 1. Arima, Keitaro. 2005. (Tsukuyomi Ser.: Vol. 1). 192p. pap. 9.99 *(978-1-59532-948-6(X))* TOKYOPOP, Inc.

Arinsberg, Norman. The Tush People. Favorite, Deborah. (J). 11.95 *(978-0-9722514-0-2(5))* Tush People, The.

Aristophane. The Zabime Sisters. Aristophane. Madden, Matt, tr. 2010. (ENG.). 96p. (YA). (gr. 7-18). pap. 17.99 *(978-1-59643-638-1(7),* 900068446, First Second Bks.) Roaring Brook Pr.

Arjas, Pirkko & Butcher, Sally K. Friend Owl: A Children's Book. 1000th ed. 2005. 48p. (J). 18.00 *(978-0-9762132-0-8(6))* Old Bess Publishing Co.

Ark, Mateya. Mama's Cloud. Williams, Jessica. 2018. (ENG.). 26p. (J). (gr. k-2). pap. *(978-1-7753456-1-9(0))* All Write Here Publishing.

—Le Nuage de Maman. Williams, Jessica. Marion, Renee-Alexandra, tr. 2019. (FRE.). 26p. (J). (gr. k-2). *(978-1-7753456-6-4(1));* pap. *(978-1-7753456-8-8(8))* All Write Here Publishing.

Arkanov, Elvira. Princess Panny - Not Princess Nobody. Alexander, Janice Marie. 2013. 46p. pap. 21.95 *(978-0-9890410-1-0(8))* Artistic Angels Corp.

Arling, Jackie L. Grace Alone Is Enough, 1 vol. Berning, Terri J. 2010. 34p. 24.95 *(978-1-4512-9045-5(4))* PublishAmerica, Inc.

Arlon, Penelope & Lee, Paul. Super Sharks: A LEGO Adventure in the Real World. Arlon, Penelope & Lee, Paul. 2018. 32p. (J). *(978-1-5490-3671-2(8))* Scholastic, Inc.

Armada, Jorge Parada. Juan, Su Ventana y Rosaflor Enamorada. Armada, Jorge Parada. 2013. (SPA.). (J). pap. *(978-84-941792-7-3(6))* inlibris.

Armand, Anjale Renee. Engraved in Stone. Coleman, Alice Scovell. 2003. 152p. (J). 14.95 *(978-0-9729846-0-7(7))* Tiara Bks. LLC.

Armas, Lourdes. Diana en la Tierra Wayuu. Antillano, Laura. 2003. (SPA.). 121p. (YA). (gr. 5-8). pap. 9.95 *(978-958-24-0180-1(X))* Santillana COL. Dist: Santillana USA Publishing Co., Inc.

Armbrust, Janet. Volcanoes: A Comprehensive Hands-on Science Unit. Storey, Melinda. Mitchell, Judy & Lindeen, Mary, eds. 2007. (Nature's Fury Ser.). 32p. (J). pap. 6.95 *(978-1-57310-530-9(9))* Teaching & Learning Co.

Armbrust, Janet & Skiles, Janet. Under the Sea: A Cross-Curricular Unit for Grades 1-3. Cecchini, Marie E. Mitchell, Judy & Lindeen, Mary, eds. 2007. 32p. (J). pap. 6.95 *(978-1-57310-529-3(5))* Teaching & Learning Co.

Armer, Sidney. Waterless Mountain. Armer, Laura Adams. 2014. (ENG.). 256p. (J). (gr. 5-9). pap. 5.99 *(978-0-486-49288-9(5))* Dover Pubns., Inc.

Armiño, Mónica. At the Boardwalk. Fineman, Kelly Ramsdell. 2012. (ENG.). 32p. (J). *(978-1-58925-104-5(0));* pap. *(978-1-58925-431-2(7))* Tiger Tales.

Armino, Monica. Collins Big Cat Phonics for Letters & Sounds - Pip Pip Pip: Band 01A/Pink A, Bd. 1A. Clarke, Zoë. 2018. (Collins Big Cat Phonics Ser.). (ENG.). 16p. (J). (gr. -1-k). pap. 6.99 *(978-0-00-825133-8(9))* HarperCollins Pubs. Ltd. GBR. Dist: Independent Pubs. Group.

Armiño, Monica. Cómo Cuidar a Tu Dragón. 2020. (SPA.). 22p. (J). (gr. -1-k). 26.00 *(978-607-21-1970-3(0))* Larousse, Editions FRA. Dist: Independent Pubs. Group.

Armiño, Mónica. A Wolf Called Wander. Parry, Rosanne. 2019. (ENG.). 256p. (J). (gr. 3-7). 16.99 *(978-0-06-289593-6(1),* Greenwillow Bks.) HarperCollins Pubs.

Armitage, David. My Brother Sammy Is Special. Armitage, David. Edwards, Becky. 2012. (ENG.). 32p. (J). (gr. -1-k). 16.95 *(978-1-61608-480-6(4),* 608480, Sky Pony Pr.) Skyhorse Publishing Co., Inc.

Armo, Nancy. A Friend for Mole, 1 vol. Armo, Nancy. (ENG.). 32p. (J). (gr. -1-3). 2020. pap. 7.95 *(978-1-68263-153-9(2));* 2016. 16.95 *(978-1-56145-865-3(1))* Peachtree Publishing Co. Inc.

Armour, Steven & Kennard, Thomas. Dr. Tootsie: A Young Girl's Dream. Knoebel, Suzanne B. 2003. 100p. (J). per. 12.97 *(978-0-9679416-1-5(X))* Alexie Bks.

Armstrong, Andrea. Arm Tale. Campbell, Sean. 2019. (Social Emotional Ser.: Vol. 2). (ENG.). 30p. (J). (gr. k-3). pap. *(978-1-7752572-3-3(1))* Education Backpack.

Armstrong, Bev. From Caravels to the Constitution: Puzzles Trageting Historical Themes That Reinforce Logic & Problem-Solving Skills. Duby, Marjorie. 2006. (Learning Works). 112p. (J). (gr. 5-8). per. 13.99 *(978-0-88160-385-9(6),* LW405, Learning Works, The) Creative Teaching Pr., Inc.

Armstrong, Bev & Baker, Don. Centers on the Go: Fun, Creative Activity Folders to Take to Your Seat. Klawitter, Pamela Amick. VanBlaricum, Pam, ed. 2005. 192p. pap. 19.99 *(978-0-88160-378-1(3),* LW435, Learning Works, The) Creative Teaching Pr., Inc.

Armstrong, Bev & Grayson, Rick. Language Critical Thinking, Grades 2-4: Creative Puzzles to Challenge the Brain. Schwartz, Linda. 2005. 64p. (J). pap. 11.99 *(978-0-88160-384-2(8),* LW423, Learning Works, The) Creative Teaching Pr., Inc.

—Math Critical Thinking, Grades 2-4: Creative Puzzles to Challenge the Brain. Schwartz, Linda. VanBlaricum, Pam, ed. 2005. 64p. (J). pap. 11.99 *(978-0-88160-383-5(X),* LW-422) Creative Teaching Pr., Inc.

Armstrong, Beverly. Current Events: Looking at Current Issues from Different Perspectives. Sylvester, Diane. Larson, Eric, ed. 2003. 112p. (YA). (gr. 5-8). pap. 12.99 *(978-0-88160-325-5(2),* LW-1021) Creative Teaching Pr., Inc.

—Language Arts Quiz Whiz. Schwartz, Linda. Larson, Eric, ed. 2003. 128p. (YA). (gr. 5-8). pap. 13.99 *(978-0-88160-344-6(9),* LW-418) Creative Teaching Pr., Inc.

—Language Arts Quiz Whiz 3-5, Vol. 430. Schwartz, Linda. VanBlaricum, Pam, ed. 2004. 128p. (J). (gr. 3-5). pap. 14.99 *(978-0-88160-373-6(2),* LW-430) Creative Teaching Pr., Inc.

—Language Critical Thinking, Grades 5-8 Vol. 412: Creative Puzzles to Challenge the Brain. Klawitter, Pamela Amick. Schwartz, Linda, ed. 2004. 64p. (J). (gr. 5-8). pap. 11.99 *(978-0-88160-338-5(4),* LW412, Learning Works, The) Creative Teaching Pr., Inc.

—Math Critical Thinking, Grades 5-8 Vol. 413: Creative Puzzles to Challenge the Brain. Klawitter, Pamela Amick. Schwartz, Linda, ed. 2004. 64p. (J). (gr. 5-8). pap. 10.99 *(978-0-88160-339-2(2))* Creative Teaching Pr., Inc.

—Math Quiz Whiz 3-5, Vol. 431. Schwartz, Linda. VanBlaricum, Pam, ed. 2004. 128p. (J). (gr. 3-5). pap. 10.99 *(978-0-88160-374-3(0),* LW-431) Creative Teaching Pr., Inc.

—Pick a Project. Klawitter, Pamela Amick. Clark, Kimberly, ed. 2003. 96p. (J). (gr. 4-6). pap. 11.99 *(978-0-88160-337-8(6),* LW-411) Creative Teaching Pr., Inc.

—Social Studies & Science Quiz Whiz 3-5, Vol. 432. Schwartz, Linda. VanBlaricum, Pam, ed. 2004. 128p. (J). (gr. 3-5). pap. 10.99 *(978-0-88160-375-0(9),* LW-432) Creative Teaching Pr., Inc.

Armstrong, Beverly & Grayson, Rick. Conquer Spelling: Word Lists, Roles, & Activities to Help Kids Become Spelling Heros. Schwartz, Linda. Scott, Kelly, ed. 2003. 112p. (J). pap. 13.99 *(978-0-88160-362-0(7),* LW-420, Learning Works, The) Creative Teaching Pr., Inc.

—Critical Thinking Social Studies Vol. 414: Creative Puzzles to Challenge the Brain. Klawitter, Pamela Amick. Schwartz, Linda, ed. 2004. 64p. (J). (gr. 5-8). pap. 10.99 *(978-0-88160-340-8(6))* Creative Teaching Pr., Inc.

—Figuratively Speaking: Using Classic Literature to teach 40 Literary Terms, Vol. 1020. Heidrich, Delana. Clark, Kim, ed. 2004. 136p. (J). (gr. 5-8). pap. 14.99 *(978-0-88160-317-0(1),* LW-1020) Creative Teaching Pr., Inc.

Armstrong-Ellis, Carey. Miss Tutu's Star. Newman, Lesléa & Newman, Lesléa. 2010. (ENG.). 32p. (J). (gr. -1-3). 17.95 *(978-0-8109-8396-0(6),* Abrams Bks. for Young Readers) Abrams, Inc.

—The Spelling Bee Before Recess. Rose, Deborah Lee. 2013. (ENG.). 32p. (J). (gr. k-4). 16.95 *(978-1-4197-0847-3(3),* Abrams Bks. for Young Readers) Abrams, Inc.

—The Twelve Days of Kindergarten: A Counting Book. Rose, Deborah Lee. 2003. (ENG.). 30p. (J). (gr. -1-1). 16.95 *(978-0-8109-4512-8(6))* Abrams, Inc.

Armstrong-Ellis, Carey F. Twelve Days of Winter: A School Counting Book. Rose, Deborah Lee. 2019. (ENG.). 32p. (J). (gr. -1-3). pap. 4.99 *(978-1-4197-3845-6(3),* Abrams Bks. for Young Readers) Abrams, Inc.

—12 Days of Kindergarten: A Counting Book. Rose, Deborah Lee. 2017. (ENG.). 32p. (J). (gr. -1-1). pap. 4.95 *(978-1-4197-2742-9(7),* Abrams Bks. for Young Readers) Abrams, Inc.

Armstrong, Katharine. Mask Parade: Forest Animals. Trelogan, Stephanie. 2008. (ENG.). 14p. (J). (gr. -1). 12.95 *(978-1-58117-790-9(9),* Intervisual/Piggy Toes) Bendon, Inc.

Armstrong, Mark, et al. Peter Porker: the Spectacular Spider-Ham - the Complete Collection Vol. 1. 2019. (ENG.). 424p. (YA). (gr. -1-17). pap. 39.99 *(978-1-302-91843-9(5))* Marvel Worldwide, Inc.

Armstrong, Mark, et al. Spider-Man: Spider-Verse - Spider-Ham. 2020. 120p. (J). (gr. 5-9). pap. 9.99 ***(978-1-302-92521-5(0))*** Marvel Worldwide, Inc.

Armstrong, Matthew S. The Blacksmith's Gift: A Christmas Story. Davis, Dan T. Davis, Jan, ed. 2004. 64p. (J). 14.95 *(978-0-9725977-4-6(3))* Second Star Creations.

—Flight Explorer, Vol. 1. Matte, Johane et al. Kibuishi, Kazu, ed. 2008. (Flight Explorer Ser.). (ENG.). 112p. (YA). pap. 16.00 *(978-0-345-50313-8(9),* Villard Bks.) Random House Publishing Group.

—Rhino, Rhino, Sweet Potato. Prose, Francine. 2009. 32p. (J). (gr. -1-1). lib. bdg. 18.89 *(978-0-06-008079-2(5))* HarperCollins Pubs.

Armstrong, Michelle Hartz. Little Jake Learns to Stop: A Heartwarming Tale about Determination & Succeeding with Attention Difficulties. Beyer, Pamela J. & Bilbrey, Hilary. 2006. (J). per. 9.99 *(978-0-9787074-0-8(0))* Inspired By Family.

Armstrong, Neal. Owen's Choice: The Night of the Halloween Vandals. Butler, Leah & Peters, Trudy. 2005. 64p. (J). (gr. 1-5). 18.95 *(978-0-9771666-0-2(0))* Spencer's Mill Pr.

Armstrong, Samuel. Gene Autry & the Lost Dogie. 2011. 30p. 35.95 *(978-1-258-02476-5(4))* Literary Licensing, LLC.

Armstrong, Shelagh. If America Were a Village: A Book about the People of the United States. Smith, David J. 2009. (CitizenKid Ser.). (ENG.). 32p. (J). (gr. 3-7). 18.99 *(978-1-55453-344-2(9))* Kids Can Pr., Ltd. CAN. Dist: Hachette Bk. Group.

—If the World Were a Village - Second Edition: A Book about the World's People. Smith, David J. (CitizenKid Ser.). (ENG.). 32p. (J). (gr. 3-7). 2020. pap. 10.99 *(978-1-55337-732-0(X));* 2nd ed. 2011. 18.99 *(978-1-55453-595-8(6))* Kids Can Pr., Ltd. CAN. Dist: Hachette Bk. Group.

—This Child, Every Child: A Book about the World's Children. Smith, David J. 2011. (CitizenKid Ser.). (ENG.). 36p. (J). (gr. 3-7). 18.95 *(978-1-55453-466-1(6))* Kids Can Pr., Ltd. CAN. Dist: Hachette Bk. Group.

Armstrong, Tymn. Hidden Dangers: Seek & Find 13 of the World's Deadliest Animals. Schaefer, Lola M. 2017. (ENG.). 40p. (J). (gr. k-3). 16.99 *(978-1-4521-3429-1(4))* Chronicle Bks. LLC.

Arnaktauyok, Germaine. Inukpak & His Son (English) Christopher, Neil. 2020. (Nunavummi Ser.). (ENG.). 36p. 16.95 ***(978-1-77266-554-3(1))*** Inhabit Education CAN. Dist: Consortium Bk. Sales & Distribution.

Arnaktauyok, Germaine. A Sled Dog for Moshi, 1 vol. Bushey, Jeanne. 2005. (ENG.). 32p. (J). (gr. 3-4). pap. 8.95 *(978-1-55041-956-6(0),* b6fcc42d-2922-4ede-a520-8aa5253bbabf) Fitzhenry & Whiteside, Ltd. CAN. Dist: Firefly Bks., Ltd.

—Takannaaluk, 1 vol. Paniaq, Herve. ed. 2018. (ENG & IKU.). 32p. (J). (gr. k-2). 16.95 *(978-1-77227-181-2(0))* Inhabit Media Inc. CAN. Dist: Consortium Bk. Sales & Distribution.

—Those That Cause Fear, 1 vol. Christopher, Neil. 2016. (ENG.). 48p. (J). (gr. 2-4). 16.95 *(978-1-77227-085-3(7))* Inhabit Media Inc. CAN. Dist: Consortium Bk. Sales & Distribution.

Arnaktauyok, Germaine. Tuniit, 1 vol. Hainnu, Rebecca. 2017. (Nunavummi Ser.). (ENG.). 32p. (J). (gr. 2-2). 7.95 ***(978-1-77266-551-2(7))*** Inhabit Education CAN. Dist: Consortium Bk. Sales & Distribution.

Arnaktauyok, Germaine. Way Back Then, 1 vol. Christopher, Neil. ed. 2015. (ENG.). 40p. (J). (gr. -1-k). 16.95 *(978-1-77227-021-1(0))* Inhabit Media Inc. CAN. Dist: Consortium Bk. Sales & Distribution.

Arnaldo, Monica. Lucy & the Rocket Dog. Buckingham, Will. 2017. 160p. (J). (gr. 3-7). 16.99 *(978-0-399-55432-2(7));* (ENG.). lib. bdg. 19.99 *(978-0-399-55433-9(5))* Random Hse. Children's Bks. (Knopf Bks. for Young Readers).

A

Arnaldo, Monica. Time for Bed's Story. Arnaldo, Monica. 2020. (ENG.). 32p. (J). (gr. -1-2). 17.99 ***(978-1-5253-0239-8(6))*** Kids Can Pr., Ltd. CAN. Dist: Hachette Bk. Group.

Arnaquq-Baril, Alethea & Giese, Daniel. The Blind Boy & the Loon, 1 vol. Arnaquq-Baril, Alethea. 2014. (ENG.). 48p. (J). (gr. k-2). 16.95 *(978-1-927095-57-7(3))* Inhabit Media Inc. CAN. Dist: Consortium Bk. Sales & Distribution.

Arnau, Marta. El cartero de los Suenos. 2004. (Cuentos con miga Ser.). 69p. pap. 12.95 *(978-84-931888-2-5(4))* Editorial Brief ESP. Dist: Independent Pubs. Group.

Arnault, Delphine. Tir Na Nog: A New Adventure. Henry, William. 2009. (ENG.). 128p. (J). pap. 25.95 *(978-1-85635-597-1(7))* Mercier Pr., Ltd., The IRL. Dist: Dufour Editions, Inc.

Arndt, Charles T. A Calf Named Polly. Richardson, Lans. 2003. 38p. per. 11.95 *(978-1-59405-022-0(8))* New Age World Publishing.

Arné, Isabelle. Soda Pop Drop. Howell, Mallory. Bulbeck, Leonora, ed. 2018. (ENG.). 30p. (J). pap. 10.99 ***(978-1-7324216-0-8(9))*** Howell, Mallory.

Arnett, Patty, photos by. Look to the Sky. Armacost, Betty. 2004. (J). 5.99 *(978-0-9760409-0-3(5))* Artist Designs.

Arnhold, Heidi. Cottons: the Secret of the Wind. Pascoe, Jim. (Cottons Ser.: 1). (ENG.). 272p. (J). 2020. pap. 14.99 *(978-1-250-30943-3(3)*, 900198488); 2018. 19.99 *(978-1-250-15744-7(7)*, 900185194) Roaring Brook Pr. (First Second Bks.).

—Cottons: the White Carrot. Pascoe, Jim. 2020. (Cottons Ser.: 2). (ENG.). 272p. (J). 19.99 *(978-1-62672-061-9(4)*, 900133963, First Second Bks.) Roaring Brook Pr.

Arnim, Dana. Bartholomew Quill: A Crow Learns to Tell Who's Who in the Animal World. Hanson, Thor. 2016. 32p. (J). (gr. -1-3). 17.99 *(978-1-63217-046-0(9)*, Little Bigfoot) Sasquatch Bks.

Arno. Psalms for Young Children. Delval, Marie-Hélène. 2008. (ENG.). 88p. (J). (gr. -1-3). 16.50 *(978-0-8028-5322-6(6)*, Eerdmans Bks For Young Readers) Eerdmans, William B. Publishing Co.

Arnold Aka Horseinwinter, J. a. Pete Pete the Parakeet. Arnold Aka Horseinwinter, J. a. 2018. (ENG.). 42p. (J). pap. 12.95 *(978-1-64114-935-8(3))* Christian Faith Publishing.

Arnold, Alli. Girl to Girl: Honest Talk about Growing up & Your Changing Body. Burningham, Sarah O'Leary. 2013. (ENG.). 136p. (J). (gr. 3-7). 12.99 *(978-1-4521-0242-9(2))* Chronicle Bks. LLC.

—Goodnight Mr. Darcy Board Book, 1 vol. Coombs, Kate. 2015. 22p. (J). bds. 9.99 *(978-1-4236-4177-3(9))* Gibbs Smith, Publisher.

—I Love You, Little Monster. Weiss, Ellen. 2012. (ENG.). 16p. (J). (gr. -1 — 1). bds. 7.99 *(978-1-4424-2850-8(3)*, Little Simon) Little Simon.

—Mimi & Maty to the Rescue! Book 1: Roger the Rat Is on the Loose! Smith, Brooke. 2014. 88p. (J). (gr. k-4). pap. 9.95 *(978-1-62914-619-5(6)*, Sky Pony Pr.) Skyhorse Publishing Co., Inc.

—Mimi & Maty to the Rescue! Book 2: Sadie the Sheep Disappears Without a Peep! Smith, Brooke. 2014. 96p. (J). (gr. 1-5). 14.95 *(978-1-62636-344-1(7)*, Sky Pony Pr.) Skyhorse Publishing Co., Inc.

—Mimi & Maty to the Rescue! Book 3: C. C. the Parakeet Flies the Coop! Smith, Brooke. 2014. 96p. (J). (gr. k-4). 14.95 *(978-1-62914-620-1(X)*, Sky Pony Pr.) Skyhorse Publishing Co., Inc.

—Mimi & Maty to the Rescue! Bk. 1: Roger the Rat Is on the Loose! Smith, Brooke. 2012. 88p. (J). (gr. 1-4). 14.95 *(978-1-62087-252-9(8)*, 620252, Sky Pony Pr.) Skyhorse Publishing Co., Inc.

Arnold, Ann. Fanny in France: With French Adventures & French Recipes. Waters, Alice. 2016. 184p. (J). (gr. 5). 19.99 *(978-0-670-01666-2(7)*, Viking Books for Young Readers) Penguin Young Readers Group.

Arnold, Beth. Elijah Makes New Friends. Arnold, Beth. 2012. 30p. pap. 9.99 *(978-0-9860272-3-9(5))* Get Happy Tips, LLC.

Arnold, Caroline. Caroline Arnold's Habitats. Arnold, Caroline. 2015. (Caroline Arnold's Habitats Ser.). (ENG.). 24p. (J). (gr. k-3). lib. bdg., lib. bdg., lib. bdg. 114.60 *(978-1-4795-6235-0(1)*, Picture Window Bks.) Capstone.

—A Day & Night in the Desert. Arnold, Caroline. 2015. (Caroline Arnold's Habitats Ser.). (ENG.). 24p. (J). (gr. k-3). lib. bdg. 28.65 *(978-1-4795-6072-1(3)*, Picture Window Bks.) Capstone.

—A Day & Night in the Forest. Arnold, Caroline. 2015. (Caroline Arnold's Habitats Ser.). (ENG.). 24p. (J). (gr. k-3). lib. bdg. 28.65 *(978-1-4795-6075-2(8)*, Picture Window Bks.) Capstone.

—A Day & Night in the Rain Forest. Arnold, Caroline. 2015. (Caroline Arnold's Habitats Ser.). (ENG.). 24p. (J). (gr. k-3). lib. bdg. 28.65 *(978-1-4795-6074-5(X)*, Picture Window Bks.) Capstone.

—A Day & Night on the Prairie. Arnold, Caroline. 2015. (Caroline Arnold's Habitats Ser.). (ENG.). 24p. (J). (gr. k-3). lib. bdg. 28.65 *(978-1-4795-6073-8(1)*, Picture Window Bks.) Capstone.

—A Moose's World, 1 vol. Arnold, Caroline. 2010. (Caroline Arnold's Animals Ser.). (ENG.). 24p. (J). (gr. k-2). lib. bdg. 28.65 *(978-1-4048-5742-1(7)*, Picture Window Bks.) Capstone.

—A Penguin's World, 1 vol. Arnold, Caroline. 2006. (Caroline Arnold's Animals Ser.). (ENG.). 24p. (J). (gr. k-2). 28.65 *(978-1-4048-1323-6(3)*, 1253185, Picture Window Bks.) Capstone.

—A Polar Bear's World, 1 vol. Arnold, Caroline. 2010. (Caroline Arnold's Animals Ser.). (ENG.). 24p. (J). (gr. k-2). lib. bdg. 28.65 *(978-1-4048-5743-8(5)*, Picture Window Bks.) Capstone.

—A Walrus' World, 1 vol. Arnold, Caroline. 2010. (Caroline Arnold's Animals Ser.). (ENG.). 24p. (J). (gr. k-2). lib. bdg. 28.65 *(978-1-4048-5744-5(3)*, Picture Window Bks.) Capstone.

—A Wombat's World, 1 vol. Arnold, Caroline. 2008. (Caroline Arnold's Animals Ser.). (ENG.). 24p. (J). (gr. k-2). lib. bdg. 28.65 *(978-1-4048-3986-1(0)*, Picture Window Bks.) Capstone.

Arnold, Elizabeth. The Greatest Race. Lawati, A. 2018. (ENG.). 74p. (J). (gr. 1-6). 18.99 *(978-1-68160-626-2(7))* Crimson Cloak Publishing.

Arnold, George "Speedy". What's an Elephant Doing in the Ausable River?!! Arnold, George "Speedy". 2012. (ENG.). 64p. (J). 20.00 *(978-0-9836925-5-3(6))* Bloated Toe Publishing.

Arnold, Jeanne. Carlos Digs to China. Stevens, Jan Romero. 2004. (Carlos Digs to China / Carlos Excava Hasta la China Ser.). (ENG, SPA & MUL.). 32p. (J). (gr. k-3). 15.95 *(978-0-87358-764-8(2))* Cooper Square Publishing Llc.

Arnold, Katya. Onions & Garlic: An Old Tale. Kimmel, Eric A. 2005. 29p. (J). (gr. k-4). reprint ed. 16.00 *(978-0-7567-9638-9(5))* DIANE Publishing Co.

Arnold, Katya R., photos by. Elephants Can Paint Too! Arnold, Katya R. Arnold, Katya. 2005. (ENG., 40p. (J). (gr. -1-3). 19.99 *(978-0-689-86985-3(1)*, Atheneum Bks. for Young Readers) Simon & Schuster Children's Publishing.

Arnold, Michael. Hocus Pocus Al I Mi Choo. Ross, Brad. 2012. 62p. pap. 19.95 *(978-0-9834201-0-1(6))* Illusionary Magic LLC.

Arnold, Patricia. Patchwork Trail. Kaderli, Janet. 2005. 59p. (J). 9.95 *(978-0-9754796-2-9(8))* GASLight Publishing.

Arnold, Stephen. Tobi the Little Puppy Dog. Uncle Bob. 2006. (Uncle Bob Ser.). 12p. (J). pap. 3.95 *(978-1-930596-61-0(8))* Amherst Pr.

Arnold, Tedd. Fly Guy Presents: Snakes. 2016. (J). *(978-1-5182-0352-7(3))* Scholastic, Inc.

—Giant Children. Bagert, Brod. 2005. (ENG.). 32p. (J). (gr. -1-3). pap. 7.99 *(978-0-14-240192-7(7)*, Puffin Books) Penguin Young Readers Group.

—Giant Children: Poems. Bagert, Brod. 2005. (ENG.). (J). (gr. -1-3). lib. bdg. 17.60 *(978-0-7569-5055-2(4))* Perfection Learning Corp.

—Police Officers. 2018. (J). *(978-1-5444-0550-6(2))* Scholastic, Inc.

—Reading Placement Tests: Easy Assessments to Determine Students' Levels in Phonics, Vocabulary, & Reading Comprehension. 2003. (ENG.). 32p. pap. 8.95 *(978-0-439-40411-2(8))* Scholastic, Inc.

—Reading Placement Tests: Easy Assessments to Determine Students' Levels of Literacy Development. 2003. (ENG.). 32p. pap. 8.95 *(978-0-439-40413-6(4))* Scholastic, Inc.

—The Yuckiest, Stinkiest, Best Valentine Ever. Ferber, Brenda. 2015. (ENG.). 32p. (J). (gr. -1-2). 8.99 *(978-0-14-751709-8(5)*, Puffin Books) Penguin Young Readers Group.

Arnold, Tedd. Bats. Arnold, Tedd. 2015. (Scholastic Reader, Level 2 Ser.). (ENG.). 32p. (J). (gr. k-2). pap. 3.99 *(978-0-545-77813-8(1)*, Scholastic Reference) Scholastic, Inc.

—Big Family. Arnold, Tedd. 2017. (Fly Guy Ser.: 17). 32p. (J). (gr. -1-3). 6.99 *(978-0-545-66316-8(4))* Scholastic, Inc.

—Buzz Boy & Fly Guy. Arnold, Tedd. 2010. (Fly Guy Ser.: 9). (ENG.). 32p. (J). (gr. -1-3). 6.99 *(978-0-545-22274-7(5)*, Cartwheel Bks.) Scholastic, Inc.

—Dinosaurs. Arnold, Tedd. 2014. (Fly Guy Presents Ser.). (ENG.). 32p. (J). (gr. k-2). pap. 3.99 *(978-0-545-63159-4(9)*, Scholastic Reference) Scholastic, Inc.

—El El Príncipe Hombre Mosca. Arnold, Tedd. 2017. (Hombre Mosca Ser.: 15). (SPA.). 32p. (J). (gr. -1-1). pap. 3.99 *(978-1-338-20866-5(7))* Scholastic, Inc.

—Even More Parts. Arnold, Tedd. 2007. (ENG.). 40p. (J). (gr. -1-3). pap. 7.99 *(978-0-14-240714-1(3)*, Puffin Books) Penguin Young Readers Group.

—Firefighters. Arnold, Tedd. 2014. (Fly Guy Presents Ser.). (ENG.). 32p. (J). (gr. k-2). pap. 3.99 *(978-0-545-63160-0(2)*, Scholastic Reference) Scholastic, Inc.

—Fix This Mess! Arnold, Tedd. 2014. (I Like to Read Ser.). (ENG.). 24p. (J). (gr. -1-3). 14.95 *(978-0-8234-2942-4(3))* Holiday Hse., Inc.

—Fly Guy Meets Fly Girl! Arnold, Tedd. 2010. (Fly Guy Ser.: 8). (ENG.). 32p. (J). (gr. -1-3). 6.99 *(978-0-545-11029-7(7)*, Cartwheel Bks.) Scholastic, Inc.

—Fly Guy Phonics Boxed Set. Arnold, Tedd. 2017. (Fly Guy Ser.). (ENG.). 16p. (J). (gr. k-1). 12.99 *(978-0-545-91801-5(4)*, Cartwheel Bks.) Scholastic, Inc.

—Fly Guy Presents: Garbage & Recycling. Arnold, Tedd. 2019. (Scholastic Reader, Level 2 Ser.: 12). (ENG.). 32p. (J). (gr. k-2). pap. 3.99 *(978-1-338-21719-3(4))* Scholastic, Inc.

—Fly Guy Presents: Police Officers. Arnold, Tedd. 2018. (Scholastic Reader, Level 2 Ser.: 11). (ENG.). 32p. (J). (gr. k-2). pap. 3.99 *(978-1-338-21717-9(8))* Scholastic, Inc.

—Fly Guy Presents: Weather. Arnold, Tedd. 2016. (Scholastic Reader, Level 2 Ser.). 32p. (J). (gr. k-2). 3.99 *(978-0-545-85187-9(4))* Scholastic, Inc.

—Fly Guy Presents - The White House. Arnold, Tedd. 2016. (Scholastic Reader, Level 2 Ser.). (ENG.). 32p. (J). (gr. k-2). pap. 3.99 *(978-0-545-91737-7(9))* Scholastic, Inc.

—Fly Guy Presents: Castles (Scholastic Reader, Level 2) Arnold, Tedd. 2017. (Scholastic Reader, Level 2 Ser.). (ENG.). 32p. (J). (gr. k-2). pap. 3.99 *(978-0-545-91738-4(7))* Scholastic, Inc.

—Fly Guy Presents: Space. Arnold, Tedd. 2013. (Scholastic Reader Ser.). 32p. (J). (gr. -1-3). pap. 3.99 *(978-0-545-56492-2(1)*, Scholastic Reference) Scholastic, Inc.

—Fly Guy vs. the Flyswatter! Arnold, Tedd. 2011. (Fly Guy Ser.: 10). 32p. (J). (gr. -1-3). 6.99 *(978-0-545-31286-8(8)*, Cartwheel Bks.) Scholastic, Inc.

—Fly Guy's Ninja Christmas. Arnold, Tedd. 2016. (Fly Guy Ser.: 16). 32p. (J). (gr. -1-3). pap. 6.99 *(978-0-545-66277-2(X))* Scholastic, Inc.

—Fly High, Fly Guy! Arnold, Tedd. 2008. (Fly Guy Ser.: 5). (ENG.). 32p. (J). (gr. -1-3). 6.99 *(978-0-545-00722-1(4))* Scholastic, Inc.

—Hi! Fly Guy. Arnold, Tedd. (ENG.). 32p. (J). (gr. -1-3). 2006. (Scholastic Reader Level 2 Ser.). pap. 3.99 *(978-0-439-85311-8(7))*; 2005. (Fly Guy Ser.: 1). 6.99 *(978-0-439-63903-3(4))* Scholastic, Inc. (Cartwheel Bks.).

—¡Hombre Mosca Contra el Matamoscas! Arnold, Tedd. 2017. (Hombre Mosca Ser.: 10). (SPA.). 32p. (J). (gr. -1-3). pap. 3.99 *(978-0-545-64613-0(8)*, Scholastic en Espanol) Scholastic, Inc.

—Hooray for Fly Guy! Arnold, Tedd. 2008. (Fly Guy Ser.: 6). (ENG.). 32p. (J). (gr. -1-3). 6.99 *(978-0-545-00724-5(0))* Scholastic, Inc.

—I Spy Fly Guy! Arnold, Tedd. 2009. (Fly Guy Ser.: 7). (ENG.). 32p. (J). (gr. -1-3). 6.99 *(978-0-545-11028-0(9))* Scholastic, Inc.

—I Spy Fly Guy! Arnold, Tedd. ed. 2009. (Fly Guy Ser.: 7). lib. bdg. 17.20 *(978-0-606-07098-0(2))* Turtleback.

—Insects. Arnold, Tedd. 2015. (Fly Guy Presents Ser.). (ENG.). 32p. (J). (gr. -1-3). pap. 3.99 *(978-0-545-75714-0(2)*, Scholastic Reference) Scholastic, Inc.

—Noodlehead Nightmares. Arnold, Tedd. Hamilton, Martha & Weiss, Mitch. 2016. (Noodleheads Ser.: 1). (ENG.). 48p. (J). (gr. 1-4). 15.95 *(978-0-8234-3566-1(0))* Holiday Hse., Inc.

—Noodleheads Find Something Fishy. Arnold, Tedd. Hamilton, Martha & Weiss, Mitch. 2018. (Noodleheads Ser.: 3). 48p. (J). (gr. 1-4). 15.99 *(978-0-8234-3937-9(2))* Holiday Hse., Inc.

—Noodleheads Find Something Fishy. Arnold, Tedd. Hamilton, Martha & Weiss, Mitch. 2020. (Noodleheads Ser.: 3). (ENG.). 48p. (J). (gr. 1-4). pap. 6.99 *(978-0-8234-4437-3(6))* Holiday Hse., Inc.

—Noodleheads See the Future. Arnold, Tedd. Hamilton, Martha & Weiss, Mitch. (Noodleheads Ser.: 2). (ENG.). 48p. (J). (gr. 1-4). 2018. pap. 6.99 *(978-0-8234-4014-6(1))*; 2017. 15.95 *(978-0-8234-3673-6(X))* Holiday Hse., Inc.

—A Pet for Fly Guy. Arnold, Tedd. 2014. (Fly Guy Ser.). (ENG.). 32p. (J). (gr. -1-3). 16.99 *(978-0-545-31615-6(4)*, Orchard Bks.) Scholastic, Inc.

—Ride, Fly Guy, Ride! Arnold, Tedd. 2012. (Fly Guy Ser.: 11). (ENG.). 32p. (J). (gr. -1-3). 6.99 *(978-0-545-22276-1(1)*, Cartwheel Bks.) Scholastic, Inc.

—Sharks. Arnold, Tedd. 2013. (Fly Guy Ser.). (ENG.). 32p. (J). (gr. -1-3). pap. 3.99 *(978-0-545-50771-4(5)*, Scholastic Reference) Scholastic, Inc.

—Shoo, Fly Guy! Arnold, Tedd. 2006. (Fly Guy Ser.: 3). (ENG.). 32p. (J). (gr. -1-3). 6.99 *(978-0-439-63905-7(0)*, Cartwheel Bks.) Scholastic, Inc.

—Snakes. Arnold, Tedd. 2016. (Fly Guy Presents Ser.). (ENG.). 32p. (J). (gr. k-2). pap. 3.99 *(978-0-545-85188-6(2))* Scholastic, Inc.

—Super Fly Guy. Arnold, Tedd. 2006. (Fly Guy Ser.: 2). (ENG.). 32p. (J). (gr. -1-3). 6.99 *(978-0-439-63904-0(2)*, Cartwheel Bks.) Scholastic, Inc.

—There Was an Old Lady Who Swallowed Fly Guy. Arnold, Tedd. 2007. (Fly Guy Ser.: 4). (ENG.). 32p. (J). (gr. -1-3). 6.99 *(978-0-439-63906-4(9))* Scholastic, Inc.

—There's a Fly Guy in My Soup. Arnold, Tedd. 2012. (Fly Guy Ser.: 12). (ENG.). 32p. (J). (gr. -1-3). 6.99 *(978-0-545-31284-4(1)*, Cartwheel Bks.) Scholastic, Inc.

—Why, Fly Guy? Arnold, Tedd. 2017. (Fly Guy Presents Ser.). 128p. (J). (gr. k-2). 14.99 *(978-1-338-05318-0(3))* Scholastic, Inc.

Arnoldson, Teresa. No Music for Skylark City. Foley Mabry, Donna. 2019. (ENG.). 66p. (J). pap. 14.99 ***(978-1-0804-1971-5(3))*** Independently Published.

Arnosky, Deanna, photos by. Whole Days Outdoors: An Autobiographical Album. Arnosky, James. 2006. (Meet the Author Ser.). (ENG., 32p. (J). 14.95 *(978-1-57274-859-0(1)*, 734, Meet the Author) Owen, Richard C. Pubs., Inc.

Arnosky, Jim. Man Gave Names to All the Animals. Dylan, Bob. 2015. 32p. (J). (gr. -1). pap. 6.95 *(978-1-4549-1576-8(5))* Sterling Publishing Co., Inc.

Arnosky, Jim. All about Manatees. Arnosky, Jim. 2008. (All About Ser.). (ENG.). 32p. (J). (gr. -1-3). pap. 6.99 *(978-0-439-90361-5(0)*, Scholastic Nonfiction) Scholastic, Inc.

—All about Turtles. Arnosky, Jim. 2008. (All About Ser.). (ENG.). 32p. (J). (gr. -1-3). pap. 6.99 *(978-0-590-69781-1(1))* Scholastic, Inc.

—Babies in the Bayou. Arnosky, Jim. 2010. (ENG.). 32p. (J). (gr. -1-k). pap. 7.99 *(978-0-14-241463-7(8)*, Puffin Books) Penguin Young Readers Group.

—Crinkleroot's Guide to Knowing Animal Habitats. Arnosky, Jim. 2014. (ENG.). 32p. (J). (gr. -1-3). pap. 14.99 *(978-1-4814-2599-5(4)*, Simon & Schuster Bks. For Young Readers) Simon & Schuster Bks. For Young Readers.

—Following the Coast. Arnosky, Jim. 2004. (ENG.). 32p. (J). (gr. 3-18). 15.99 *(978-0-688-17117-9(6))* HarperCollins Pubs.

—Raccoon on His Own. Arnosky, Jim. 2003. (ENG.). 32p. (J). (gr. -1-k). 7.99 *(978-0-14-250071-2(2)*, Puffin Books) Penguin Young Readers Group.

Arnoux, Lucie. In Their Shoes: Fairy Tales & Folktales. 2016. (ENG.). 128p. (J). (gr. 4-7). pap. 9.99 *(978-1-78269-101-3(4)*, Pushkin Children's Bks.) Steerforth Pr.

—The Snow Queen. Andersen, Hans & Hoekstra, Misha. 2016.Tr. of ??????? ????????. (ENG.). 128p. (J). (gr. 3-7). pap. 9.99 *(978-1-78269-103-7(0)*, Pushkin Children's Bks.) Steerforth Pr.

Aron, Bill, photos by. What You Will See Inside a Synagogue. Hoffman, Lawrence A. & Wolfson, Ron. 2008. (What You Will See Inside ... Ser.). (ENG., 32p. (J). pap. 8.99 *(978-1-59473-256-0(6)*, 0206b87d-4ecf-4a43-af2c-3d2eaf77e346, Skylight Paths Publishing) LongHill Partners, Inc.

Aronson, Jeff & Zephyr, Jay. Little Mike & Maddie's Black Hill's Adventure. Aronson, Jeff & Aronson, Miriam. 2007. 33p. (J). 16.00 *(978-0-9795302-1-0(0)*, CrumbGobbler Pr.) Downtown Wetmore Pr.

—Little Mike & Maddie's Christmas Book. Aronson, Jeff & Aronson, Miriam. 2007. 32p. (J). 16.00 *(978-0-9795302-2-7(9)*, CrumbGobbler Pr.) Downtown Wetmore Pr.

—Little Mike & Maddie's First Motorcycle Ride. Aronson, Jeff & Aronson, Miriam. 2007. 32p. (J). 16.00 *(978-0-9795302-0-3(2)*, CrumbGobbler Pr.) Downtown Wetmore Pr.

Arrasmith, Patrick. Clash of the Demons. Delaney, Joseph. 2009. (Last Apprentice Ser.: 6). 416p. (YA). (gr. 8). lib. bdg. 18.89 *(978-0-06-134463-3(X)*, Greenwillow Bks.) HarperCollins Pubs.

—Dark Eden. Carman, Patrick. 2012. (Dark Eden Ser.: 1). (ENG.). 336p. (YA). (gr. 8). pap. 8.99 *(978-0-06-200971-5(0)*, Tegen, Katherine Bks) HarperCollins Pubs.

—The House of Dead Maids. Dunkle, Clare B. 2011. (ENG.). 176p. (YA). (gr. 7-12). pap. 16.99 *(978-0-312-55155-1(X)*, 9780312551551) Square Fish.

—The Last Apprentice: a Coven of Witches. Delaney, Joseph. (Last Apprentice Short Fiction Ser.: 2). (ENG.). 240p. (YA). (gr. 8). 2011. pap. 10.99 *(978-0-06-196040-6(3))*; 2010. 16.99 *(978-0-06-196038-3(1))* HarperCollins Pubs. (Greenwillow Bks.).

—The Last Apprentice: Attack of the Fiend (Book 4) Delaney, Joseph. 2009. (Last Apprentice Ser.: 4). (ENG.). 576p. (YA). (gr. 8-18). pap. 9.99 *(978-0-06-089129-9(7)*, Greenwillow Bks.) HarperCollins Pubs.

—The Last Apprentice: Clash of the Demons (Book 6) Delaney, Joseph. (Last Apprentice Ser.: 6). (ENG.). (YA). (gr. 8-18). 2009. 416p. 17.99 *(978-0-06-134462-6(1))*; Bk. 6. 2010. 432p. pap. 9.99 *(978-0-06-134464-0(8))* HarperCollins Pubs. (Greenwillow Bks.).

—The Last Apprentice: Fury of the Seventh Son (Book 13), Bk. 13. Delaney, Joseph. (Last Apprentice Ser.: 13). (ENG.). 480p. (YA). (gr. 8). 2015. pap. 10.99 *(978-0-06-219232-5(9))*; 2014. 17.99 *(978-0-06-219231-8(0))* HarperCollins Pubs. (Greenwillow Bks.).

—The Last Apprentice: Grimalkin the Witch Assassin (Book 9), Bk. 9. Delaney, Joseph. 2013. (Last Apprentice Ser.: 9). (ENG.). 416p. (YA). (gr. 8). pap. 9.99 *(978-0-06-208208-4(6)*, Greenwillow Bks.) HarperCollins Pubs.

—The Last Apprentice: Grimalkin the Witch Assassin (Book 9) Bk. 9, Bk. 9. Delaney, Joseph. 2012. (Last Apprentice Ser.: 9). (ENG.). 400p. (YA). (gr. 8). 17.99 *(978-0-06-208207-7(8)*, Greenwillow Bks.) HarperCollins Pubs.

—The Last Apprentice: I Am Alice (Book 12), Bk. 12. Delaney, Joseph. (Last Apprentice Ser.: 12). (ENG.). (YA). (gr. 8). 2014. 464p. pap. 10.99 *(978-0-06-171515-0(8))*; 2013. 448p. 17.99 *(978-0-06-171513-6(1))* HarperCollins Pubs. (Greenwillow Bks.).

—The Last Apprentice: Lure of the Dead (Book 10) Delaney, Joseph. (Last Apprentice Ser.: 10). (ENG.). (YA). (gr. 8). 2013. 448p. pap. 10.99 *(978-0-06-202762-7(X))*; Bk. 10. 2012. 432p. 17.99 *(978-0-06-202760-3(3))* HarperCollins Pubs. (Greenwillow Bks.).

—The Last Apprentice: Rage of the Fallen (Book 8) Bk. 8. Delaney, Joseph. 2012. (Last Apprentice Ser.: 8). (ENG.). 416p. (YA). (gr. 8). pap. 10.99 *(978-0-06-202758-0(1)*, Greenwillow Bks.) HarperCollins Pubs.

—The Last Apprentice: Revenge of the Witch (Book 1), Bk. 1. Delaney, Joseph. (Last Apprentice Ser.: 1). (ENG.). (YA). (gr. 8). 2005. 368p. 17.99 *(978-0-06-076618-4(2))*; 2006. 384p. reprint ed. pap. 9.99 *(978-0-06-076620-7(4))* HarperCollins Pubs. (Greenwillow Bks.).

—The Last Apprentice: Rise of the Huntress (Book 7) Bk. 7, Bk. 7. Delaney, Joseph. 2011. (Last Apprentice Ser.: 7). (ENG.). 464p. (YA). (gr. 8). pap. 10.99 *(978-0-06-171512-9(3)*, Greenwillow Bks.) HarperCollins Pubs.

Arrayás, Albert. ¿de dónde Vienen Las Ideas? Amenós, Jordi. 2019. (SPA.). 48p. (J). (gr. 2-4). pap. 17.95 *(978-84-17440-18-3(6))* Akiara Bks. ESP. Dist: Independent Pubs. Group.

Arrazola, Amaia. Audrey Hepburn. Sanchez Vegara, Maria Isabel. 2017. (Little People, BIG DREAMS Ser.: 7). (ENG.). 32p. (J). (gr. -1-2). 15.99 *(978-1-78603-053-5(5)*, Frances Lincoln Children's Bks.) Quarto Publishing Group UK GBR. Dist: Hachette Bk. Group.

Arreola Alemón, Roberto. De dos mundos = of Two Worlds: Las ranas, sapos y salamandras de la Península de Yucatán, México = the Frogs, Toads & Salamanders of the Yucatan Peninsula, Mexico. Galindo-Leal, Carlos. 2003. (SPA & ENG.). 152p. pap. 19.95 *(978-1-929165-52-0(8))* PANGAEA.

Arreola, Gil. Cesar Chavez: Changing Lives. Gotsch, Patrice. 2006. 19p. pap. 6.30 *(978-1-55501-780-4(0))* Ballard & Tighe Pubs.

—Martin Luther King, Jr: Changing Lives. Gotsch, Patrice. 2006. 19p. pap. 6.30 *(978-1-55501-779-8(7))* Ballard & Tighe Pubs.

Arreola, Manuel. Weenz the Cat: What about Me? Arreola, Perla. 2013. 30p. 14.99 *(978-0-9859298-7-9(1))* Dream&Achieve Bks.

Arrhenius, Ingela P. Alphabet Street. Emmett, Jonathan. 2019. (ENG.). 26p. (J). (-k). bds. 17.99 *(978-1-5362-0827-6(2)*, Nosy Crow) Candlewick Pr.

—Bookscape Board Books: a Forest's Seasons: (Colorful Children's Shaped Board Book, Forest Landscape Toddler Book) 2019. (ENG.). 10p. (J). (gr. -1 — 1). bds. 8.99 *(978-1-4521-7494-5(6))* Chronicle Bks. LLC.

—Bookscape Board Books: Fun at the Fair: (Lift the Flap Book, Block Books for Preschool) 2020. (ENG.). 10p. (J). (gr. -1 — 1). bds. 8.99 *(978-1-4521-7493-8(8))* Chronicle Bks. LLC.

—A Marvelous Museum. 2019. (ENG.). 10p. (J). (gr. -1 — 1). bds. 8.99 *(978-1-4521-7492-1(X))* Chronicle Bks. LLC.

Arrhenius, Ingela P. Peekaboo: Apple. Reid, Camilla. 2020. (ENG.). 8p. (J). (— 1). bds. 9.99 ***(978-1-5362-1445-1(0)***, Nosy Crow) Candlewick Pr.

—Peekaboo: Farm. Reid, Camilla. 2020. (ENG.). 8p. (J). (— 1). bds. 9.99 ***(978-1-5362-1444-4(2)***, Nosy Crow) Candlewick Pr.

Arrhenius, Ingela P. Where's Santa Claus? Nosy Crow. 2018. (Where's The Ser.). (ENG.). 10p. (J). (— 1). bds. 8.99 *(978-1-5362-0697-5(0)*, Nosy Crow) Candlewick Pr.

—Where's the Astronaut? Nosy Crow. 2019. (Where's The Ser.). (ENG.). 10p. (J). (— 1). bds. 8.99 (978-1-5362-0752-1(7), Nosy Crow) Candlewick Pr.
—Where's the Bear? Nosy Crow. 2018. (Where's The Ser.). (ENG.). 10p. (J). (— 1). bds. 8.99 (978-1-5362-0251-9(7), Nosy Crow) Candlewick Pr.
—Where's the Chick? Nosy Crow. 2019. (Where's The Ser.). (ENG.). 10p. (J). (— 1). bds. 8.99 (978-1-5362-0751-4(9), Nosy Crow) Candlewick Pr.
—Where's the Dog? Nosy Crow. 2018. (Where's The Ser.). (ENG.). 10p. (J). (— 1). bds. 8.99 (978-0-7636-9913-0(6), Nosy Crow) Candlewick Pr.
—Where's the Duck? Nosy Crow. 2019. (Where's The Ser.). (ENG.). 10p. (J). (— 1). bds. 8.99 (978-1-5362-0577-0(X), Nosy Crow) Candlewick Pr.
—Where's the Giraffe? Nosy Crow. 2017. (Where's The Ser.). (ENG.). 10p. (J). (— 1). bds. 8.99 (978-0-7636-9334-3(0), Nosy Crow) Candlewick Pr.
—Where's the Hen? Nosy Crow Staff. 2017. (Where's The Ser.). (ENG.). 10p. (J). (— 1). bds. 8.99 (978-0-7636-9640-5(4), Nosy Crow) Candlewick Pr.
—Where's the Kangaroo? Nosy Crow. 2020. (Where's The Ser.). (ENG.). 10p. (J). (— 1). bds. 8.99 (978-1-5362-0590-9(7), Nosy Crow) Candlewick Pr.
—Where's the Ladybug? Nosy Crow. 2017. (Where's The Ser.). (ENG.). 10p. (J). (— 1). bds. 8.99 (978-0-7636-9335-0(9), Nosy Crow) Candlewick Pr.
—Where's the Narwhal? Nosy Crow. 2019. (Where's The Ser.). (ENG.). 10p. (J). (— 1). bds. 8.99 (978-1-5362-0950-1(3), Nosy Crow) Candlewick Pr.
—Where's the Owl? Nosy Crow Staff. 2017. (Where's The Ser.). (ENG.). 10p. (J). (— 1). bds. 8.99 (978-0-7636-9639-9(0), Nosy Crow) Candlewick Pr.
—Where's the Penguin? Nosy Crow. 2018. (Where's The Ser.). (ENG.). 10p. (J). (— 1). bds. 8.99 (978-1-5362-0250-2(9), Nosy Crow) Candlewick Pr.
—Where's the Pirate? Nosy Crow. 2020. (Where's The Ser.). (ENG.). 10p. (J). (— 1). bds. 8.99 (978-1-5362-1222-8(9), Nosy Crow) Candlewick Pr.
Arrhenius, Ingela P. Where's the T. Rex? Nosy Crow. 2020. (Where's The Ser.). (ENG.). 10p. (J). (— 1). bds. 8.99 **(978-1-5362-1438-3(8)**, Nosy Crow) Candlewick Pr.
—Where's the Tiger? Nosy Crow. 2020. (Where's The Ser.). (ENG.). 10p. (J). (— 1). bds. 8.99 **(978-1-5362-1439-0(6)**, Nosy Crow) Candlewick Pr.
Arrhenius, Ingela P. Where's the Unicorn? Nosy Crow. 2018. (Where's The Ser.). (ENG.). 10p. (J). (— 1). bds. 8.99 (978-1-5362-0696-8(2), Nosy Crow) Candlewick Pr.
—Where's the Witch? Nosy Crow. 2019. (Where's The Ser.). (ENG.). 10p. (J). (— 1). bds. 8.99 (978-1-5362-0753-8(5), Nosy Crow) Candlewick Pr.
—Where's the Zebra? Nosy Crow. 2018. (Where's The Ser.). (ENG.). 10p. (J). (— 1). bds. 8.99 (978-0-7636-9914-7(4), Nosy Crow) Candlewick Pr.
Arrhenius, Ingela P. Animals. Arrhenius, Ingela P. 2016. (ENG.). 40p. (J). (gr. -1-2). 22.00 (978-0-7636-9268-1(9)) Candlewick Pr.
—City. Arrhenius, Ingela P. 2018. (ENG.). 40p. (J). (gr. -1-2). 22.00 (978-1-5362-0257-1(6)) Candlewick Pr.
Arrhenius, Ingela P. My First Book of London. Arrhenius, Ingela P. 2020. (ENG.). 32p. (J). (gr. -1-2). 18.99 **(978-1-5362-0991-4(0))** Candlewick Pr.
Arrhenius, Ingela P. My First Book of New York. Arrhenius, Ingela P. 2019. (ENG.). 32p. (J). (gr. -1-2). 18.99 (978-1-5362-0990-7(2)) Candlewick Pr.
—Pop-Up Jungle. Arrhenius, Ingela P. 2019. (ENG.). 30p. (J). (— 1). 12.00 (978-1-5362-0551-0(6)) Candlewick Pr.
—Pop-Up Ocean. Arrhenius, Ingela P. 2018. (ENG.). 30p. (J). (— 1). 12.00 (978-1-5362-0119-2(7)) Candlewick Pr.
—Pop-Up Things That Go! Arrhenius, Ingela P. 2018. (ENG.). 30p. (J). (— 1). 12.00 (978-1-5362-0120-8(0)) Candlewick Pr.
Arrhenius, Ingela Peterson. Little Concepts: ABC Color: Apricot, Burgundy & Chartreuse, 26 Cool New Colors Are Out on the Loose! 2017. (Little Concepts Ser.). (ENG.). 36p. (J). (gr. -1-1). bds. 12.95 (978-1-63322-336-3(1), 225372, Walter Foster Jr) Quarto Publishing Group USA.
Arribas, Cinta. I Hate Everyone. Danis, Naomi. 2018. (ENG.). 32p. (J). (gr. -1-1). 17.99 (978-1-57687-874-3(0), powerHouse Bks.) powerHse. Bks.
—My Best Friend, Sometimes. Danis, Naomi. 2020. (ENG.). 32p. (J). (gr. -1-3). 17.99 (978-1-57687-946-7(1), powerHouse Bks.) powerHse. Bks.
Arrigan, Mary. Milo & One Dead Angry Druid. Arrigan, Mary. 2013. (Milo Adventures Ser.: 1). (ENG.). 112p. (J). pap. 12.95 (978-1-84717-351-5(9)) O'Brien Pr., Ltd., The IRL. Dist: Casemate Pubs. & Bk. Distributors, LLC.
Arrington, Chiquila. Dallas: On Book One: Jo/Jo KIDS. Arrington, Gladys. 2006. 49p. pap. 16.95 (978-1-4241-1162-6(5)) PublishAmerica, Inc.
Arrington, Linda, photos by. Ugly Trees. Arrington, Linda. 2012. 24p. pap. 24.95 (978-1-4626-8925-5(6)) America Star Bks.
Arriola, Ricardo Ramirez. Vivir en el Circo. Arriola, Ricardo Ramirez. rev. ed. 2006. (Otra Escalera Ser.). (SPA & ENG.). 48p. (J). (gr. 2-4). pap. 10.95 (978-968-5920-63-6(X)) Castillo, Ediciones, S. A. de C. V. MEX. Dist: Macmillan.
Arrott, Nancy. Children's Stories from Around the World. Avalon-Pai, Phyllis. 2008. 70p. pap. 9.95 (978-0-9788283-8-7(0)) Acacia Publishing, Inc.
Arrowsmith, Sarah. Over the Creek. Thomas, Jacob. 2020. (ENG.). 26p. (J). pap. 14.95 **(978-1-6588-8389-4(6))** Independently Published.
Arroyo. La Loncheria. Stalcup. 2008. (SPA & ENG.). 28p. (J). pap. 8.95 (978-1-60448-006-1(8)) Lectura Bks.
—La Loncheria. Stalcup. 2008. (SPA & ENG.). 28p. (J). 15.95 (978-1-60448-005-4(X)) Lectura Bks.
Arroyo, Andrea. The Legend of the Lady Slipper. 2004. (ENG.). 32p. (J). (gr. -1-3). reprint ed. pap. 7.99 (978-0-618-43231-8(0), 490423) Houghton Mifflin Harcourt Publishing Co.
Arroyo, Daniel, jt. illus. see Curiel, A. M.
Arroyo, David, jt. illus. see Rio, Adam del.
Arroyo, Felipe, photos by. Healthy Taste of Corona Cookbook. Reddy, Prerana & Strauss, David, eds. Mesalles, Monica, tr. 2008.Tr. of Sabor Saludable de Corona. (ENG & SPA., 130p. (J). pap. (978-1-929641-10-9(9)) Queens Museum of Art.
Arroyo, Fian. Bee Double Bopp: Respecting Others. Cosgrove, Stephen. 2004. (J). (978-1-58804-350-4(9)) P C I Education.
—Big Bubba Bigg, Jr: Dealing with Bullies. Cosgrove, Stephen. 2004. (J). (978-1-58804-352-8(5)) P C I Education.
—The Bigg Family: Getting along with Others. Cosgrove, Stephen. 2004. (J). (978-1-58804-354-2(1)) P C I Education.
—The Bugglar Brothers: Consequences of Stealing. Cosgrove, Stephen. 2007. (J). (978-1-58804-381-8(9)) P C I Education.
—Cricket Clickett: Finding Your Talents. Cosgrove, Stephen. 2004. (J). (978-1-58804-382-5(7)) P C I Education.
—Flynn "Flea" Flicker: Sticking to the Truth. Cosgrove, Stephen. 2004. (J). (978-1-58804-353-5(3)) P C I Education.
—Hickory B. Hopp: Paying Attention. Cosgrove, Stephen. 2004. (J). (978-1-58804-379-5(7)) P C I Education.
—Katy Didd Bigg: Standing up for Yourself. Cosgrove, Stephen. 2004. (J). (978-1-58804-378-8(9)) P C I Education.
—Melody Moth: Practice Makes Perfect. Cosgrove, Stephen. 2004. (J). (978-1-58804-351-1(7)) P C I Education.
—Mizz Buggly: Doing Your Best. Cosgrove, Stephen. 2004. (J). (978-1-58804-380-1(0)) P C I Education.
—Princess Island. Gilligan, Shannon. 2015. (ENG.). 96p. (J). (gr. 2). pap. 7.99 (978-1-937133-50-4(8)) Chooseco LLC.
—Second Dad Summer. Klas, Benjamin. 2020. (ENG.). 224p. (J). (gr. 2-5). 16.99 (978-1-947159-24-2(0), One Elm Books) Red Chair Pr.
—Snugg N. Flitter: Facing Your Fears. Cosgrove, Stephen. 2004. (J). (978-1-58804-377-1(0)) P C I Education.
Arscott, Dean. Spend the Day with Me. Baruch, M. P. 2009. 20p. pap. 10.95 (978-1-936051-27-4(3)) Peppertree Pr., The.
Arscott, Ellie. Night Walk, 1 vol. O'Leary, Sara. 2020. (ENG.). 32p. (J). (gr. -1-2). 18.95 **(978-1-55498-796-2(2))** Groundwood Bks. CAN. Dist: Publishers Group West (PGW).
ARSedition. Winter Magic: Beautiful Holiday Patterns to Color. 2015. (Color Magic Ser.). (ENG.). 80p. pap. 12.99 (978-1-4380-0733-5(7), B.E.S. Publishing) Peterson's.
Arsenault, Isabelle. Captain Rosalie. de Fombelle, Timothee. 2019. (ENG.). 64p. (J). (gr. 3-7). 15.99 (978-1-5362-0520-6(6)) Candlewick Pr.
—The Children of Lir. Buonocore, Maire. 2014. (Traditional Tales Ser.). (ENG.). 32p. (J). (gr. 2-3). pap. 7.95 (978-1-62521-544-4(4), Capstone Classroom) Capstone.
—Cloth Lullaby: The Woven Life of Louise Bourgeois. Novesky, Amy. 2016. (ENG.). 40p. (J). (gr. k-2). 18.95 (978-1-4197-1881-6(9), Abrams Bks. for Young Readers) Abrams, Inc.
—The Honeybee. Hall, Kirsten. 2018. (ENG.). 48p. (J). (gr. -1-3). 18.99 (978-1-4814-6997-5(5)) Simon & Schuster Children's Publishing.
—Jane, the Fox & Me, 1 vol. Britt, Fanny. Ourious, Susan & Morelli, Christelle, trs. 2013. (ENG.). 104p. (J). (gr. 5). 19.95 (978-1-55498-360-5(6)) Groundwood Bks. CAN. Dist: Publishers Group West (PGW).
—Just Because. Barnett, Mac. 2019. (ENG.). 40p. (J). (gr. -1-3). 17.99 (978-0-7636-9680-1(3)) Candlewick Pr.
—Louis Undercover, 1 vol. Britt, Fanny. 2017. (ENG.). 160p. (J). (gr. 5-9). 19.95 (978-1-55498-859-4(4)) Groundwood Bks. CAN. Dist: Publishers Group West (PGW).
—Migrant, 1 vol. Trottier, Maxine. 2011. (ENG.). 40p. (J). (gr. -1-2). 18.95 (978-0-88899-975-7(5)) Groundwood Bks. CAN. Dist: Publishers Group West (PGW).
—Once upon a Northern Night, 1 vol. Pendziwol, Jean E. 2013. (ENG.). 32p. (J). (gr. -1-2). 17.95 (978-1-55498-138-0(7)) Groundwood Bks. CAN. Dist: Publishers Group West (PGW).
—Spork. Maclear, Kyo. 2017. (ENG.). 21p. (J). (gr. -1-2). pap. 8.95 (978-1-77138-805-4(6)) Kids Can Pr., Ltd. CAN. Dist: Hachette Bk. Group.
—That Night's Train, 1 vol. Akbarpour, Ahmad. Saghafi, Majid, tr. 2012. (ENG.). 96p. (J). (gr. 3). 14.95 (978-1-55498-169-4(7)) Groundwood Bks. CAN. Dist: Publishers Group West (PGW).
—Virginia Wolf. Maclear, Kyo. 2012. (ENG.). 32p. (J). (gr. -1-3). 16.95 (978-1-55453-649-8(9)) Kids Can Pr., Ltd. CAN. Dist: Hachette Bk. Group.
Arseneau, Philippe & Drouin, Julie Saint-Onge. Coureurs des Bois a Clark City. Lefrancois, Viateur. 2003. (Collection des 9 Ans: Vol. 32). (FRE.). 136p. 8.95 (978-2-922565-69-0(6)) Editions de la Paix CAN. Dist: World of Reading, Ltd.
Art, Dahn Tran. I Make. DiResta, Jimmy & Blom, Tracy. 2019. (ENG.). 32p. (J). pap. 11.99 (978-1-7336349-0-8(8)) Hom, Jonathan.
Art, Kan Ev. The Earth Plane. DuBay, Eric. 2018. (ENG.). 54p. (J). pap. 20.00 (978-1-7274-3046-2(8)) CreateSpace Independent Publishing Platform.
Art, Tessa Creative. Drawing Chibi: Learn How to Draw Kawaii People, Animals, & Other Utterly Cute Stuff. Sondereker, Kierra, ed. 2020. (How to Draw Bks.). (ENG.). 144p. (J). pap. 10.00 **(978-1-64604-093-3(7))** Ulysses Pr.
Art, Zephyr, jt. illus. see Najm, Fauzia.
Art&Script. Outside Fun, 1. Earley, Catherine. Earley, Catherine, ed. 2005. 12p. (J). 6.95 (978-0-9769589-1-8(0)) Naynay Bks.
Artayudianto, M. S. Caroline. Tardy Goes to Animal School. Keegan, Dan. 2016. (ENG.). (J). pap. (978-1-5272-0355-6(7)) Nielsen Bk. Services.
Arte y Cultura, A.C Staff. La Domadora de Miedos. Lascurain, Guadalupe Aleman. rev. ed. 2006. (Castillo de la Lectura Roja Ser.). (SPA & ENG.). 232p. (YA). (gr. 7). pap. 8.95 (978-970-20-0182-9(X)) Castillo, Ediciones, S. A. de C. V. MEX. Dist: Macmillan.
Arte Y Diseno, Tane, jt. illus. see Sanchez, Andres.
Artell, Mike. 25 Reproducible Literature Circle Role Sheets for Fiction & Nonfiction Books, Grades 4-6 Revised & Updated. Moen, Christine Boardman. Mitchell, Judy, ed. 2004. 64p. (J). (gr. 4-6). pap., tchr. ed. 9.95 (978-1-57310-141-7(9)) Teaching & Learning Co.
Artell, Mike. Jokes Jokes & More Jokes for Kids. Artell, Mike. 2020. (ENG.). 34p. (J). (gr. k-6). pap. 4.99 **(978-1-7324180-2-8(0))** MJA Creative, LLC.
Artell, Mike. You Can Draw Military Aircraft. Artell, Mike. 2016. (ENG.). (J). (gr. 2-6). 19.95 (978-0-9910894-6-8(4)) MJA Creative, LLC.
Artful Doodlers. The Devil Fish. Campbell, Tom, photos by. Williams, Geoffrey T. 2008. (Save Our Seas Adventure Bks.). (ENG.). 64p. (J). (gr. 4-7). 8.95 (978-0-9800444-1-6(3)) Save Our Seas, Ltd.
—The Great White Red Alert. Campbell, Tom, photos by. Williams, Geoffrey T. 2008. (Save Our Seas Adventure Bks.). (ENG.). 64p. (J). (gr. 4-7). 8.95 (978-0-9800444-0-9(5)) Save Our Seas, Ltd.
—Picnic Day! Wax, Wendy. 2006. 24p. (J). lib. bdg. 15.00 (978-1-4242-0952-1(8)) Fitzgerald Bks.
—Thanksgiving Parade. Barbo, Maria S. & Bridwell, Norman. 2010. (J). (978-0-545-25332-1(2)) Scholastic, Inc.
Artful Doodlers, Artful. Construction. Walden, Libby. 2015. (ENG.). 96p. (J). (gr. -1-2). 9.99 (978-1-58925-315-5(9)) Tiger Tales.
—Dinosaurs. Litton, Jonathan. 2015. (ENG.). 96p. (J). (gr. -1-2). 9.99 (978-1-58925-316-2(7)) Tiger Tales.
—Emergency Services. Walden, Libby. 2015. (ENG.). 96p. (J). (gr. -1-2). 9.99 (978-1-58925-314-8(0)) Tiger Tales.
Artful Doodlers, Artful, jt. illus. see Cuniffe, Ian.
Artful Doodlers, Artful, jt. illus. see Isherwood, Matthew.
Artful Doodlers, Artful, jt. illus. see Mendez, Simon.
Artful Doodlers Limited Staff. Alvin & the Chipmunks: Alvin & the Substitute Teacher. Huelin, Jodi. 2013. (I Can Read Level 2 Ser.). 32p. (J). (gr. -1-3). pap. 3.99 (978-0-06-225223-4(2), HarperFestival) HarperCollins Pubs.
—Beastly Feast!, 1 vol. Corderoy, Tracey. 2012. (Grunt & the Grouch Ser.). (ENG.). 112p. (J). (gr. 1-3). pap. 5.19 (978-1-4342-4269-3(2)); 25.32 (978-1-4342-4603-5(5)) Capstone. (Stone Arch Bks.).
—Big Splash!, 1 vol. Corderoy, Tracey. 2012. (Grunt & the Grouch Ser.). (ENG.). 112p. (J). (gr. 1-3). pap. 5.19 (978-1-4342-4268-6(4)); 25.32 (978-1-4342-4602-8(7)) Capstone. (Stone Arch Bks.).
—It's Absolutely True. 2006. (Famous Fables Ser.). (J). 6.99 (978-1-59939-029-1(9)) Cornerstone Pr.
Artful Doodlers Limited Staff & Carzon, Walter. Alvin & the Chipmunks: Alvin's Easter Break. Huelin, Jodi. 2014. 24p. (J). (gr. -1-3). pap. 3.99 (978-0-06-225222-7(4), HarperFestival) HarperCollins Pubs.
Artful Doodlers Ltd. Carlos Gets the Sneezes: Exploring Allergies: a Branches Book (the Magic School Bus Rides Again) Katschke, Judy. 2018. (Magic School Bus Rides Again Ser.: 3). (ENG.). 96p. (J). (gr. 1-3). pap. 4.99 (978-1-338-19446-3(1)) Scholastic, Inc.
Artful Doodlers Ltd. Curious George in Super George! Rey, H. A. & Rey, Margret. 2018. (Curious George's Funny Readers Ser.). (ENG.). 40p. (J). (gr. -1-3). 9.99 (978-1-328-73623-9(7), 1676620, HMH Books For Young Readers) Houghton Mifflin Harcourt Publishing Co.
Artful Doodlers Ltd. The Meet the Class. Brooke, Samantha. 2017. (Magic School Bus Rides Again Ser.). (ENG.). 24p. (J). (gr. -1-k). pap. 4.99 (978-1-338-20236-6(7)) Scholastic, Inc.
—Monster Power. Katschke, Judy. 2017. (Magic School Bus Rides Again Ser.: 2). (ENG.). 96p. (J). (gr. 1-3). pap. 4.99 (978-1-338-19444-9(5)) Scholastic, Inc.
—Satellite Space Mission. Anderson, AnnMarie. 2018. (Magic School Bus Rides Again Ser.: 4). (ENG.). 96p. (J). (gr. 1-3). pap. 4.99 (978-1-338-26251-3(3)) Scholastic, Inc.
—Sink or Swim. Katschke, Judy. 2017. (Magic School Bus Rides Again Ser.: 1). (ENG.). 96p. (J). (gr. 1-3). pap. 4.99 (978-1-338-19445-6(3)) Scholastic, Inc.
Artful Doodlers Ltd., Artful. Carlos Gets the Sneezes: Exploring Allergies: a Branches Book (the Magic School Bus Rides Again) Katschke, Judy. 2018. (Magic School Bus Rides Again Ser.: 3). (ENG.). 96p. (J). (gr. 2-5). lib. bdg. 15.99 (978-1-338-23212-7(6)) Scholastic, Inc.
—Deep-Sea Dive. Brooke, Samantha. 2019. (Scholastic Reader, Level 2 Ser.). (ENG.). 32p. (J). (gr. k-2). pap. 4.99 (978-1-338-25382-5(4)) Scholastic, Inc.
—Ghost Farming. Brooke, Samantha & Polt, Gabe. 2018. (Magic School Bus Rides Again Ser.). (ENG.). 24p. (J). (gr. -1-k). pap. 4.99 (978-1-338-29081-3(9)) Scholastic, Inc.
Artful Doodlers Ltd. Staff. The Birthday Surprise. Stephens, Leigh. 2017. (Shopkins: Shoppies Ser.). (ENG.). 32p. (J). (gr. -1-3). pap. 3.99 (978-1-338-15901-1(1)) Scholastic, Inc.
—Blowing in the Wind. Brooke, Samantha. 2018. (Scholastic Reader, Level 2 Ser.). (ENG.). 32p. (J). (gr. k-2). pap. 4.99 (978-1-338-25377-1(8)) Scholastic, Inc.
Artful Doodlers Ltd Staff. Magic School Bus Rides Again: Hide & Seek. Brooke, Samantha. 2018. (Scholastic Reader, Level 2 Ser.). (ENG.). 32p. (J). (gr. k-2). pap. 4.99 (978-1-338-25379-5(4)) Scholastic, Inc.
Artful Doodlers Ltd. Staff. Monster Power. Katschke, Judy. 2017. (Magic School Bus Rides Again Ser.: 2). (ENG.). 96p. (J). (gr. 2-5). lib. bdg. 15.99 (978-1-338-23213-4(4)) Scholastic, Inc.
Artful Doodlers Ltd., Staff. Presentamos a la Clase. Brooke, Samantha. 2018. (Autobús Mágico Vuelve a Despegar Ser.). (SPA.). 24p. (J). (gr. -1-k). pap. 3.99 (978-1-338-29955-7(7)) Scholastic, Inc.
Artful Doodlers Ltd Staff. The Reason for the Season. Huelin, Jodi. 2013. (Alvin & the Chipmunks Ser.). (ENG.). 24p. (J). (gr. -1-3). pap. 4.99 (978-0-06-225221-0(6), HarperFestival) HarperCollins Pubs.
Artful Doodlers Ltd. Staff. Rock Man vs. Weather Man. Brooke, Samantha. 2018. (Scholastic Reader, Level 2 Ser.). (ENG.). 32p. (J). (gr. k-2). pap. 4.99 (978-1-338-25378-8(6)) Scholastic, Inc.
—Sink or Swim: Exploring Schools of Fish. Katschke, Judy. 2017. (Magic School Bus Rides Again Ser.: 1). (ENG.). 96p. (J). (gr. 2-5). lib. bdg. 24.99 (978-1-338-23214-1(2)) Scholastic, Inc.
—Sundae Fun-Day! Katschke, Judy. 2017. (Shopkins: Shoppies Ser.). 64p. (J). (gr. 1-3). pap. 4.99 (978-1-338-15899-1(6)) Scholastic, Inc.
—Tales Glaciers Tell. Brooke, Samantha. 2018. (Scholastic Reader, Level 2 Ser.). (ENG.). 32p. (J). (gr. k-2). pap. 4.99 (978-1-338-25381-8(6)) Scholastic, Inc.
Artful Doodlers Ltd Staff. Unidos o Nada. Katschke, Judy. 2018. (Autobús Mágico Vuelve a Despegar Ser.: 1). (SPA.). 96p. (J). (gr. 1-3). pap. 4.99 (978-1-338-29956-4(5)) Scholastic, Inc.
Artful Doodlers Ltd. Staff. A Very Special Mama's Day. McCarthy, Rebecca. 2013. (Zoobles! Ser.). (ENG.). 24p. (J). (gr. -1-1). 17.44 (978-0-448-46316-2(4)) Penguin Young Readers Group.
—Vuela con el Viento (el Autobus Mágico Vuelve a Despegar: Lector de Scholastic, Nivel 2) Brooke, Samantha. 2018. (Lector de Scholastic, Nivel 2 Ser.). (SPA.). 32p. (J). (gr. k-2). pap. 3.99 (978-1-338-32971-1(5), Scholastic en Espanol) Scholastic, Inc.
Arthur, Jenny. Monster Mayhem. Murphy, Rose. 2011. (Pat & Sound Stories Ser.). (ENG.). 12p. (gr. -1). 14.95 (978-1-61524-497-3(2), Intervisual/Piggy Toes) Bendon, Inc.
Arthur, Rackham. Gulliver's Travels into Several Remote Nations of the World: Children's Literature, /ILLUSTRATED / Swift, Jonathan. 2019. (ENG.). 338p. (J). pap. 14.60 **(978-1-7042-1030-8(5))** Independently Published.
Arthus-Bertrand, Yann, photos by. Kids Who Are Changing the World. Jankeliowitch, Anne. 2014. (ENG., 144p. (J). (gr. 3-6). pap. 19.99 (978-1-4022-9532-4(4), 9781402295324, Sourcebooks Jabberwocky) Sourcebooks, Inc.
—Our Living Earth: A Story of People, Ecology, & Preservation. 2008. (ENG., 160p. (J). (gr. 3-9). 24.95 (978-0-8109-7132-5(1), Abrams Bks. for Young Readers) Abrams, Inc.
Artifact Group. Welcome to Lalaloopsy Land. Brooke, Samantha. 2011. (Lalaloopsy Ser.). (ENG.). 16p. (J). (gr. -1-3). pap. 6.99 (978-0-545-37999-1(7)) Scholastic, Inc.
Artifact Group Staff. Champions of the Sea! (SpongeBob SquarePants) Golden Books Staff. 2011. (Hologramatic Sticker Book Ser.). (ENG.). 48p. (J). (gr. -1-2). pap. 3.99 (978-0-375-87322-5(8), Golden Bks.) Random Hse. Children's Bks.
Artigas, Alexandra. The Fuzzy Escape Artists. Isaacs, Michael. 2006. 32p. (J). (gr. -1-7). 15.95 (978-0-9742845-8-3(0)) Mystic Ridge Bks.
—Rebecca & the Great Goat Getaway. Furfur, Christopher. 2005. 40p. (J). (gr. -1). per. 15.95 (978-0-9742845-7-6(2)) Mystic Ridge Bks.
Artistic Book and Web Design. Adventures of My Dentist & the Tooth Fairy: Activity & Coloring Book, bk. 2. Hood, Karen Jean Matsko. Whispering Pine Press International, Inc. Staff, ed. 2013. (ENG & JPN.). 174p. (J). pap. 19.95 (978-1-59649-535-7(9)) Whispering Pine Pr. International, Inc.
—Gaited Horse Activity & Coloring Book-English/German/Spanish Edition. Hood, Karen Jean Matsko. Whispering Pine Press International, Inc. Staff, ed. 2010. (ENG, GER & SPA.). 160p. (J). per. 19.95 (978-1-59649-522-7(7)) Whispering Pine Pr. International, Inc.
—Girls Can Do Activity & Coloring Book. Hood, Karen Jean Matsko. Whispering Pine Press International, Inc. Staff, ed. 2010. (ENG & JPN.). 160p. (J). per. 13.95 (978-1-59210-593-9(9)) Whispering Pine Pr. International, Inc.
—My Birth Celebration Journal: A Daily Journal, Vol. 3. Hood, Karen Jean Matsko. Whispering Pine Press International, Inc. Staff, ed. 2014. (Children's Journal Series). 164p. (J). pap. 13.95 (978-1-59210-647-9(1)) Whispering Pine Pr. International, Inc.
Artistic Design Service. Lost Medal, Bk.1. Hood, Karen Jean Matsko. Whispering Pine Press International, Inc. Staff, ed. 2014. (Hood Horse Story Ser.). 160p. (J). (gr. 4-8). 25.95 (978-1-930948-94-5(8)) Whispering Pine Pr. International, Inc.
—Lost Medal, Vol. 1. Hood, Karen Jean Matsko. Whispering Pine Press International, ed. 2014. (Hood Horse Story Ser.). (ENG.). 160p. (J). (gr. 4-8). per. 9.95 (978-1-930948-95-2(6)) Whispering Pine Pr. International, Inc.
—Petting Farm Fun, Bilingual English & Spanish, Bk. 3. Hood, Karen Jean Matsko. Whispering Pine Press International, ed. ed. 2015. (Hood Picture Book Ser.). (ENG & SPA.). 36p. (J). pap. 29.95 (978-1-59808-824-3(6)) Whispering Pine Pr. International, Inc.
—Spokane Falls. Hood, Karen Jean Matsko. Whispering Pine Press International, ed. l.t. ed. 2015. (Banacek & Flannigan Mystery Ser.). 224p. pap. 22.95 (978-1-59434-223-3(7)); Vol. 1. 29.95 (978-1-59434-228-8(8)); Vol. 1. per. 19.95 (978-1-59434-226-4(1)) Whispering Pine Pr. International, Inc.
Artistic Design Service Staff. Apple Delights Cookbook, Translated Italian: A Collection of Apple Recipes, Vol. 1. Hood, Karen Jean Matsko. Whispering Pine Press International, ed. 2014. (Cookbook Delights Translated Ser.). (ITA.). 324p. 27.95 (978-1-59649-100-7(0)) Whispering Pine Pr. International, Inc.
—Apples: Apple Board Book, Vol. 1. Hood, Karen Jean Matsko. Whispering Pine Press International, ed. 2016. (ENG.). 14p. (J). 12.99 (978-1-59649-006-2(3)) Whispering Pine Pr. International, Inc.
—Arizona Saguaro: A Collection of Poetry, Vol. 2. Hood, Karen Jean Matsko. Whispering Pine Press International, ed. 2015. (Hood Regional Poetry Ser.). 224p. pap., tchr. ed. 19.95 (978-1-59649-443-5(3)) Whispering Pine Pr. International, Inc.

A

—Arizona Saguaro: A Collection of Poetry, Vol. 2. Hood, Karen Jean Matsko. Whispering Pine Press International Staff, ed. l.t. ed. 2015. (Hood Regional Poetry Ser.). 224p. pap. 22.95 *(978-1-59649-414-5(X))* Whispering Pine Pr. International, Inc.

—Dewberry Farm. Hood, Karen Jean Matsko. Whispering Pine Press International, ed. 2017. (Magic Farmhouse Ser.). 160p. (J). 25.95 *(978-1-59649-415-2(8))*; per. 14.95 *(978-1-59649-562-3(6))* Whispering Pine Pr. International, Inc.

—Dr. James G. Hood, Author: Book, Freelance Service & Gift Catalog. Hood, James G. Whispering Pine Press International, ed. 2014. 100p. pap. 4.99 *(978-1-59210-603-5(X))* Whispering Pine Pr. International, Inc.

—Gaited Horse Activity & Coloring Book. Hood, Karen Jean Matsko. Whispering Pine Press International, ed. 2014. (Hood Activity & Coloring Book Ser.). 160p. (J). bk. 4. spiral bd. 21.95 *(978-1-59649-628-6(2))*; Vol. 4. (ENG.). per. 19.95 *(978-1-59210-591-5(2))* Whispering Pine Pr. International, Inc.

—Icelandic Horse Activity & Coloring Book, Vol. 6. Hood, Karen Jean Matsko. Whispering Pine Press International, ed. 2nd ed. 2014. (Educational Activity & Coloring Book Ser.). (ENG, ICE & GER.). 160p. (J). spiral bd. 21.95 *(978-1-59649-364-3(X))* Whispering Pine Pr. International, Inc.

—Icelandic Horse Activity & Coloring Book: Activity & Coloring Book, Vol. 6. Hood, Karen Jean Matsko. Whispering Pine Press International, ed. 2014. (Hood Activity & Coloring Book Ser.). (ENG, GER & ICE.). 160p. (J). per. 19.95 *(978-1-59210-595-3(5))* Whispering Pine Pr. International, Inc.

—Jesus Loves the Little Children: Activity & Coloring Book, Vol. 8. Hood, Karen Jean Matsko. Whispering Pine Press International, ed. ed. 2016. (Educational Activity & Coloring Book Ser.). (ENG & SPA.). (J). spiral bd. 21.95 *(978-1-59434-087-1(0))* Whispering Pine Pr. International, Inc.

—Karen Jean Matsko Hood, Inc. Parenting Book & Gift Catalog. Hood, Karen Jean Matsko. Whispering Pine Press International, ed. 2014. 50p. pap. 4.99 *(978-1-59210-715-5(X))* Whispering Pine Pr. International, Inc.

—Kids' Kindness Activity & Coloring Book, Vol. 9. Hood, Karen Jean Matsko. Whispering Pine Press International, ed. 2015. (Hood Activity & Coloring Book Ser.). 170p. (J). spiral bd. 21.95 *(978-1-59808-753-6(3))*; per. 19.95 *(978-1-59808-752-9(5))* Whispering Pine Pr. International, Inc.

—Kids' Kindness Journal: A Daily Journal, bk. 9. Hood, Karen Jean Matsko. Whispering Pine Press International, ed. 2015. (Children's Journal Series). 160p. (J). spiral bd. 15.95 *(978-1-59649-416-9(6))* Whispering Pine Pr. International, Inc.

—My Holiday Memories Scrapbook for Foster Kids: A Holiday Memories Scrapbook for Kids, Bk.1. Hood, Karen Jean Matsko. Whispering Pine Press International, ed. 2014. (Childrens Scrapbook Ser.). 124p. (J). per. 19.95 *(978-1-59649-925-6(7))* Whispering Pine Pr. International, Inc.

—My Special Care Journal for Adopted Children: A Daily Journal, Vol. 7. Hood, Karen Jean Matsko. Whispering Pine Press International, ed. 2014. (Children's Journal Series). 164p. (J). 19.95 *(978-1-59210-279-2(4))* Whispering Pine Pr. International, Inc.

—My Special Care Journal for Foster Children: A Daily Journal, bk. 8. Hood, Karen Jean Matsko. Whispering Pine Press International, ed. 2014. (Children Scrapbook Journal Ser.). 160p. (J). spiral bd. 15.95 *(978-1-59210-274-7(3))* Whispering Pine Pr. International, Inc.

—My Special Care Scrapbook for Adopted Children: A Special Care Scrapbook for Adopted Children, bk. 7. Hood, Karen Jean Matsko. Whispering Pine Press International, ed. 2014. (Childrens Scrapbook Ser.). 124p. (J). spiral bd. 21.95 *(978-1-59649-927-0(3))*; per. 19.95 *(978-1-59649-629-3(0))* Whispering Pine Pr. International, Inc.

—My Special Care Scrapbook for Adopted Children: A Special Scrapbook for Adopted Children, bk. 7. Hood, Karen Jean Matsko. Whispering Pine Press International, ed. 2014. (Childrens Scrapbook Ser.). 124p. (J). 29.95 *(978-1-59210-493-2(2))* Whispering Pine Pr. International, Inc.

—Opening Day. Hood, Karen Jean Matsko. Whispering Pine Press International, ed. l.t. ed. 2014. (Bernadette's Bakery Ser.). 224p. pap. 22.95 *(978-1-930948-27-3(1))* Whispering Pine Pr. International, Inc.

—Petting Farm Fun, Translated Amharic, Vol. 3. Whispering Pine Press International, ed. 2014. (Hood Picture Book Ser.). (AMH.). 42p. (J). per. 19.95 *(978-1-59649-554-8(5))* Whispering Pine Pr. International, Inc.

—Tanka Thoughts: A Collection of Poetry, bk. 11. Hood, Karen Jean Matsko. Whispering Pine Press International, ed. 2014. (Hood Poetry Ser.). 224p. pap. 19.95 *(978-1-930948-52-5(2)*, 1-930948-52-2); pap. 22.95 *(978-1-59808-648-5(0))* Whispering Pine Pr. International, Inc.

—There's a Toad in the Hole: A Big Fat Toad in the Hole, Bk.2. Hood, Karen Jean Matsko. Whispering Pine Press International, ed. 2014. (Hood Poetry Ser.). (J). 29.95 *(978-1-930948-24-2(7))*; per. 19.95 *(978-1-59649-298-1(8))* Whispering Pine Pr. International, Inc.

—Under the Lilacs: A Collection of Children's Poetry, Vol. 1. Hood, Karen Jean Matsko. Whispering Pine Press International, ed. 2014. (Hood Children's Poetry Book Ser.). 160p. (J). 29.95 *(978-1-930948-51-8(4)*, 1-930948-51-4) Whispering Pine Pr. International, Inc.

Artistic Design Services. Girls Can Do Journal: A Daily Journal, bk. 5. Hood, Karen Jean Matsko. Whispering Pine Press International, ed. 2014. (Educational Activity & Coloring Book Ser.). 164p. (J). spiral bd. 15.95 *(978-1-59649-361-2(5))* Whispering Pine Pr. International, Inc.

—Grandma Bert's Favorite Christmas Sweets Recipes: A Collection of Recipes from Grandma Bert, Vol. 8. Hood, Karen Jean Matsko. Whispering Pine Press International, ed. 2014. 324p. 34.95 *(978-1-59210-538-0(6))* Whispering Pine Pr. International, Inc.

Artistic Design Services Staff. Adventure Travel: A Daily Journal, Vol. 1. Hood, Karen Jean Matsko. Whispering Pine Press International, Inc. Staff, ed. 2014. (Hood Journal Ser.). (ENG.). 130p. (J). 19.95 *(978-1-59210-428-4(2))*; per. 13.95 *(978-1-59210-134-4(8)*, 1-59210-134-8) Whispering Pine Pr. International, Inc.

—Gaited Horse Journal: A Daily Journal, Bk.4. Hood, Karen Jean Matsko. Whispering Pine Press International, Inc. Staff, ed. 2014. (Children's Journal Series). 160p. (J). 19.95 *(978-1-59434-790-0(5))*; per. 13.95 *(978-1-59434-791-7(3))*; spiral bd. 15.95 *(978-1-59434-795-5(6))* Whispering Pine Pr. International, Inc.

—Getaway Country Kitchen Catalog: Gourmet & Country Grocery, Take-Out Food & Catering Service Products, no. 3. Hood, Karen Jean Matsko. Whispering Pine Press International, ed. 2014. 160p. pap. 4.99 *(978-1-59210-605-9(6))* Whispering Pine Pr. International, Inc.

—Icelandic Horse: A Daily Journal, bk. 6. Hood, Karen Jean Matsko. Whispering Pine Press International, ed. 2014. (Hood Activity & Coloring Book Ser.). 128p. (J). spiral bd. 15.95 *(978-1-59649-422-0(0))* Whispering Pine Pr. International, Inc.

—Kids' Kindness: Adventures in Learning, Vol. 9. Hood, Karen Jean Matsko. Whispering Pine Press International, ed. 2015. 160p. (J). 29.95 *(978-1-59808-759-8(2))*; per. 19.95 *(978-1-59808-757-4(6))* Whispering Pine Pr. International, Inc.

—Kids' Kindness Journal: A Daily Journal, bk. 9. Hood, Karen Jean Matsko. Whispering Pine Press International, ed. 2015. (Children's Journal Series). 160p. (J). 19.95 *(978-1-59649-431-2(X))* Whispering Pine Pr. International, Inc.

—Lost Medal, Christian Edition: With Bible Verses & Christian Themes. Hood, Karen Jean Matsko. Whispering Pine Press International, ed. 2014. (Hood Christian Horse Story Ser.). 160p. (J). Bk.1. pap. 19.95 *(978-1-59808-618-8(9))*; Vol. 1. 29.95 *(978-1-59808-617-1(0))* Whispering Pine Pr. International, Inc.

—My Adoption Celebration Scrapbook: A Special Celebration of My Adoption, bk. 2. Hood, Karen Jean Matsko. Whispering Pine Press International, ed. 2014. (Childrens Scrapbook Ser.). 124p. (J). 29.95 *(978-1-59210-265-5(4))*; per. 19.95 *(978-1-59649-523-4(5))* Whispering Pine Pr. International, Inc.

—My Birth Celebration Scrapbook: A Celebration of My Birth Scrapbook for Children, Vol. 3. Hood, Karen Jean Matsko. Whispering Pine Press International, Inc. Staff, ed. 2014. (Childrens Scrapbook Ser.). 128p. (J). per. 19.95 *(978-1-59649-520-3(0))* Whispering Pine Pr. International, Inc.

—My Holiday Memories Journal: A Daily Journal, bk. 5. Hood, Karen Jean Matsko. Whispering Pine Press International, ed. 2014. (Children Scrapbook Journal Ser.). 128p. (J). 19.95 *(978-1-59210-645-5(5))* Whispering Pine Pr. International, Inc.

—My Holiday Memories Scrapbook for Adopted Kids: A Holiday Memories Scrapbook for Kids, bk. 4. Hood, Karen Jean Matsko. Whispering Pine Press International, ed. 2014. (Childrens Scrapbook Ser.). 124p. (J). 29.95 *(978-1-59210-476-5(2))*; spiral bd. 21.95 *(978-1-59649-924-9(9))*; per. 19.95 *(978-1-59649-326-1(7))* Whispering Pine Pr. International, Inc.

—My Holiday Memories Scrapbook for Foster Kids: A Holiday Memories Scrapbook for Kids. Hood, Karen Jean Matsko. Whispering Pine Press International, ed. 2014. (Childrens Scrapbook Ser.). 124p. (J). Bk.1. spiral bd. 21.95 *(978-1-59649-633-0(9))*; Vol. 1. 29.95 *(978-1-59210-481-9(9))* Whispering Pine Pr. International, Inc.

—My Holiday Memories Scrapbook for Kids, bk. 5. Hood, Karen Jean Matsko. Whispering Pine Press International, ed. 2014. (Childrens Scrapbook Ser.). (ENG.). 190p. (J). 29.95 *(978-1-59210-620-2(X))* Whispering Pine Pr. International, Inc.

—My Holiday Memories Scrapbook for Kids, Bk.5. Hood, Karen Jean Matsko. Whispering Pine Press International, Inc. Staff, ed. 2014. (Childrens Scrapbook Ser.). (ENG.). 190p. (J). spiral bd. 21.95 *(978-1-59649-926-3(5))* Whispering Pine Pr. International, Inc.

—My Special Care Scrapbook for Children: A Special Scrapbook for Children, bk. 6. Hood, Karen Jean Matsko. Whispering Pine Press International, Inc. Staff, ed. 2014. (Childrens Scrapbook Ser.). 128p. (J). 29.95 *(978-1-59649-631-6(2))*; spiral bd. 21.95 *(978-1-59210-623-3(4))* Whispering Pine Pr. International, Inc.

—My Special Care Scrapbook for Foster Children: A Special Scrapbook for Foster Children, bk. 8. Hood, Kared Jean Matsko. Whispering Pine Press International, ed. 2014. (Childrens Scrapbook Ser.). (ENG.). 122p. (J). pap. 19.95 *(978-1-59649-928-7(1))* Whispering Pine Pr. International, Inc.

—Petting Farm Fun, Bilingual English & Hindi. Hood, Karen Jean Matsko. Whispering Pine Press International, ed. ed. 2015. (Hood Picture Book Ser.). (ENG & HIN.). 36p. (J). Bk. 3. pap. 29.95 *(978-1-59808-646-1(4))*; Vol. 3. 34.95 *(978-1-59808-641-6(3))*; Vol. 3. 94.99 *(978-1-59808-642-3(1))*; Vol. 3. pap. 25.95 *(978-1-59808-657-7(X))* Whispering Pine Pr. International, Inc.

—Petting Farm Fun, Bilingual English & Portuguese. Hood, Karen Jean Matsko. Whispering Pine Press International, ed. ed. 2015. (Hood Picture Book Ser.). (ENG & POR.). 36p. (J). Bk. 3. pap. 29.95 *(978-1-59808-813-7(0))*; Vol. 3. 34.95 *(978-1-59808-811-3(4))*; Vol. 3. 94.95 *(978-1-59808-812-0(2))*; Vol. 3. pap. 25.95 *(978-1-59808-814-4(9))* Whispering Pine Pr. International, Inc.

—Petting Farm Fun, Bilingual English & Spanish, Vol. 3. Hood, Karen Jean Matsko. Whispering Pine Press International, ed. ed. 2015. (Hood Picture Book Ser.). (ENG & SPA.). 36p. (J). 34.95 *(978-1-59808-822-9(X))*; 94.99 *(978-1-59808-823-6(8))*; pap. 25.95 *(978-1-59808-825-0(4))* Whispering Pine Pr. International, Inc.

—Petting Farm Fun, Translated Hindi, bk. 3. Hood, Karen Jean Matsko. Whispering Pine Press International, ed. 2014. (Hood Picture Book Ser.). (HIN.). 46p. (J). 24.95 *(978-1-59808-843-4(2))*; 84.99 *(978-1-59808-844-1(0))*; pap. 15.95 *(978-1-59808-845-8(9))*; pap. 19.95 *(978-1-59808-846-5(7))* Whispering Pine Pr. International, Inc.

—Petting Farm Fun, Translated Portuguese, bk. 3. Hood, Karen Jean Matsko. Whispering Pine Press International, ed. 2014. (Hood Picture Book Ser.). (POR.). 46p. (J). 24.95 *(978-1-59808-864-9(5))*; 84.99 *(978-1-59808-865-6(3))*; pap. 15.95 *(978-1-59808-866-3(1))*; pap. 19.95 *(978-1-59808-867-0(X))* Whispering Pine Pr. International, Inc.

Artists, Disney Storybook. Disney Princess: Princess Dreams. 2017. (ENG.). 12p. (J). (gr. -1-k). 12.99 *(978-0-7944-4073-2(8)*, Reader's Digest Children's Bks.) Studio Fun International.

—Disney Villains: the Evilest of Them All. Upton, Rachael. 2017. (Replica Journal Ser.). (ENG.). 112p. (J). (gr. 1-3). 11.99 *(978-0-7944-4160-9(2)*, Reader's Digest Children's Bks.) Studio Fun International.

artists, Multiple, et al. W is for Welcome: A Celebration of America's Diversity. Herzog, Brad. 2018. (ENG.). 32p. (J). (gr. 1-4). 17.99 *(978-1-58536-402-2(9)*, 204404) Sleeping Bear Pr.

Artists of Troublemaker Studios Staff. The Adventures of Shark Boy & Lava Girl in 3-D: The Illustrated Screenplay. Rodriguez, Robert. 2005. (Shark Boy & Lava Girl Adventures Ser.). 128p. (J). *(978-1-933104-01-0(5))* Troublemaker Publishing, LP.

Artists, Various. A New Take on ABCs - S Is for Smiling Sunrise: An Alphabet Book of Goodness, Beauty, & Wonder [Free Audio-Book Download Included]. Wadhwa, Vick. l.t. ed. 2014. 32p. (J). 16.95 *(978-1-940229-12-6(X))* WordsBright.

Artley, Bob. Grady's in the Silo, 1 vol. Townsend, Una Belle. 2003. (ENG.). 32p. (J). (gr. k-3). 16.99 *(978-1-58980-098-4(2)*, Pelican Publishing) Arcadia Publishing.

—Step Up!, 1 vol. Hahn, Cathe. 2005. (ENG.). 32p. (J). (gr. k-3). 16.99 *(978-1-58980-214-8(4)*, Pelican Publishing) Arcadia Publishing.

Artley, Bob. Christmas on the Farm, 1 vol. Artley, Bob. 2003. (ENG.). 96p. 22.95 *(978-1-58980-108-0(3)*, Pelican Publishing) Arcadia Publishing.

Artist Collection Staff. The Dog from Arf! Arf! to Zzzzzz. Artist Collection Staff. 2007. (Artist Collection: the Dog Ser.). 40p. (J). (gr. -1-3). 6.99 *(978-0-06-059859-4(X))* HarperCollins Pubs.

Artman, Townsend, jt. illus. see DeJong Artman, Catherine.

Arts, Richa Kinra. Teddy Bear Princess: A Story about Sharing & Caring. Kats, Jewel. 2012. 24p. (-18). pap. 13.95 *(978-1-61599-163-1(8)*, Marvelous Spirit Pr.) Loving Healing Pr., Inc.

Artwork, Pandamonium. The Lonely Spider. May, Duckie. 2019. (ENG.). 24p. (J). pap. 12.99 ***(978-1-7124-8123-3(1))*** Independently Published.

Artworks, D. R. I., et al. Thomas & Friends. P. I. Kids Staff. Publications International Ltd. Staff, ed. 2015. (ENG.). 120p. (J). *(978-1-4508-9373-2(2)*, 40a8f10c-e127-4d9b-b1e3-4774c5c901d0, p i kids) Phoenix International Publications, Inc.

Artymoska, Aleksandra. Alice in Wonderland: a Puzzle Adventure. The Templar Company LTD. 2020. (ENG.). 96p. (J). (gr. 2-4). 19.99 *(978-1-5362-1039-2(0)*, Big Picture Press) Candlewick Pr.

Artymoska, Aleksandra. Around the World in 80 Puzzles. Artymoska, Aleksandra. 2018. (ENG.). 96p. (J). (gr. 2-4). 19.99 *(978-1-5362-0308-0(4)*, Big Picture Press) Candlewick Pr.

—20,000 Leagues under the Sea: a Puzzle Adventure. Artymoska, Aleksandra. 2019. (ENG.). 96p. (J). (gr. 2-4). 19.99 *(978-1-5362-0624-1(5)*, Big Picture Press) Candlewick Pr.

Aruego, Jose & Dewey, Ariane. Antarctic Antics: A Book of Penguin Poems. Sierra, Judy. 2003. (ENG.). 32p. (J). (gr. -1-3). pap. 6.99 *(978-0-15-204602-6(X)*, 1193858) Houghton Mifflin Harcourt Publishing Co.

—The Big, Big Wall. Howard, Reginald. ed. 2003. (Green Light Readers Level 1 Ser.). (ENG.). 24p. (J). (gr. -1-3). pap. 3.95 *(978-0-15-204853-2(7)*, 1194654) Houghton Mifflin Harcourt Publishing Co.

—Duck, Duck, Goose! (A Coyote's on the Loose!) Beaumont, Karen. 2004. 32p. (J). (gr. -1-2). lib. bdg. 18.89 *(978-0-06-050804-3(3))* HarperCollins Pubs.

—Duck, Duck, Goose! (a Coyote's on the Loose!) Beaumont, Karen. 2004. (ENG.). 32p. (J). (gr. -1-2). 17.99 *(978-0-06-050802-9(7))* HarperCollins Pubs.

—How Chipmunk Got His Stripes. Bruchac, Joseph & Bruchac, James. 2003. (ENG.). 32p. (J). (gr. k-3). 7.99 *(978-0-14-250021-7(6)*, Puffin Books) Penguin Young Readers Group.

—Lizard's Guest. Shannon, George. 2003. 32p. (J). 16.89 *(978-0-06-009084-5(7))* HarperCollins Pubs.

—Turtle's Race with Beaver. Bruchac, Joseph. 2005. (ENG.). 32p. (J). (gr. k-3). pap. 6.99 *(978-0-14-240466-9(7)*, Puffin Books) Penguin Young Readers Group.

Aruego, Jose, jt. illus. see Dewey, Ariane.

Arvidson, Tracey. The Little Flower: A Parable of St. Therese of Liseux. Arganbright, Becky. 2019. (ENG.). 32p. (J). pap. 10.95 *(978-1-68192-498-4(6))* Our Sunday Visitor, Publishing Div.

Arya, Viki. The Boy Who Became King. Dutta, Arup Kumar. 2004. 122p. (J). *(978-81-291-0405-2(9))* Rupa & Co.

Aryai, Sia, photos by. 1 2 3s. (Baby Bright Board Bks.). 10p. (J). (gr. -1). 5.95 *(978-1-56565-824-0(8)*, 08248W, Roxbury Park Juvenile) Lowell Hse. Juvenile.

Aryan, Kiana. The Real Beauty. Mohr, Kathryn. 2010. 106p. (J). pap. 14.95 *(978-1-61660-000-6(4))* GFC Pr.

Arzoumanian, Alik. So Many Houses. Bass, Hester Thompson. 2007. (Rookie Reader Repetitive Text Ser.). 32p. (gr. k-2). 14.95 *(978-0-7569-8049-8(6))* Perfection Learning Corp.

—So Many Houses. Bass, Hester Thompson & Thompson-Bass, Hester. 2006. (Rookie Reader Skill Set Ser.). (ENG.). 32p. (J). (gr. k-2). pap. 4.95 *(978-0-516-24999-5(1))* Scholastic Library Publishing.

—Tunjur! Tunjur! Tunjur! A Palestinian Folktale, 0 vols. MacDonald, Margaret Read. 2012. (ENG.). 32p. (J). (gr. -1-3). pap. 9.99 *(978-0-7614-6312-2(7)*, 9780761463122, Two Lions) Amazon Publishing.

Asamiya, Kia. Dark Angel: The Path to Destiny, 5 bks., Bk. 1. Asamiya, Kia. rev. ed. 2003. 200p. pap. 9.99 *(978-1-58664-899-2(3)*, CMX 62301MM, CPM Manga) Central Park Media Corp.

—Nadesico, 4 vols., Vol. 1. Asamiya, Kia. rev. ed. 2003. Orig. Title: Meteor Schlachtschiff Nadesico. 192p. pap. 9.99 *(978-1-56219-901-2(3)*, CMX 62401MM, CPM Manga) Central Park Media Corp.

—Nadesico, 4 vols., Vol. 3. Asamiya, Kia. Cebulski, C. B. & Furuhata, Noriko, trs. from JPN. 2004. Orig. Title: Meteor Schlachtschiff Nadesico. 168p. 9.99 *(978-1-58664-940-1(X)*, CMX 62403MM, CPM Manga) Central Park Media Corp.

—Silent Mobius. Asamiya, Kia. 2003. (Silent Mobius Ser.: Vol. 10). (ENG.). Vol. 10. 184p. pap. 12.95 *(978-1-56931-891-1(3))*; Vol. 11. 176p. pap. 12.95 *(978-1-59116-070-0(7))* Viz Media.

—Steam Detectives. Asamiya, Kia. (Steam Detectives Ser.). (ENG.). Vol. 6. 2003. 192p. pap. 12.95 *(978-1-56931-892-8(1))*; Vol. 7. 2004. 184p. pap. 12.95 *(978-1-59116-208-7(4))* Viz Media.

Asanovic, Vesna. Teen Trailblazers: 30 Fearless Girls Who Changed the World Before They Were 20. Calvert, Jennifer. 2018. (ENG.). 128p. (YA). 16.99 *(978-1-250-20020-4(2)*, 900195895) St. Martin's Pr.

Asare, Meshack. Sosu's Call. Asare, Meshack. 2006. (ENG.). 40p. (J). (gr. k-4). 11.99 *(978-1-929132-21-8(2))* Kane Miller.

Asaro, Massimo, et al. Champions: I Am Legendary. Marz, Ron & Rodriguez, David A. 2018. (Skylanders Ser.). (ENG.). 24p. (J). (gr. 1-5). lib. bdg. 27.07 *(978-1-5321-4245-1(5)*, 28573, Graphic Novels) Spotlight.

Asaro, Massimo. Disney Mickey: No Nap for Pluto. Parent, Nancy. 2020. (Disney Classic 8 X 8 Ser.). (ENG.). 24p. (J). (gr. -1-k). pap. 4.99 ***(978-0-7944-4526-3(8)***, Studio Fun International) Printers Row Publishing Group.

Asbill, Annette. Mouse's Forever Christmas. Asbill, Annette. 2012. 34p. pap. *(978-0-9860247-3-3(2))* Roxby Media Ltd.

Asbjørnsen, Peter Christen, jt. illus. see Arenson, Roberta.

Asch, Devin. Mr. Maxwell's Mouse, 0 vols. Asch, Frank. 2014. (ENG.). 32p. (J). (gr. k-4). pap. 8.95 *(978-1-77138-117-8(5))* Kids Can Pr., Ltd. CAN. Dist: Hachette Bk. Group.

Asch, Devin, jt. illus. see Asch, Frank.

Asch, Frank. Happy Birthday, Moon. Asch, Frank. 2014. (Moonbear Ser.). (ENG.). 32p. (J). (gr. -1-3). 8.99 *(978-1-4424-9400-8(X)*, Aladdin) Simon & Schuster Children's Publishing.

—Just Like Daddy. Asch, Frank. 2015. (Frank Asch Bear Book Ser.). (ENG.). 32p. (J). (gr. -1-3). 7.99 *(978-1-4814-2207-9(3)*, Aladdin) Simon & Schuster Children's Publishing.

—The Lending Zoo. Asch, Frank. 2016. (ENG.). 32p. (J). (gr. -1-3). 16.99 *(978-1-4424-6678-4(2)*, Aladdin) Simon & Schuster Children's Publishing.

—Milk & Cookies. Asch, Frank. 2015. (Frank Asch Bear Book Ser.). (ENG.). 40p. (J). (gr. -1-3). 17.99 *(978-1-4424-6672-2(3)*, Aladdin) Simon & Schuster Children's Publishing.

Asch, Frank. Moonbear. Asch, Frank. 2020. (Moonbear Ser.). (ENG.). 32p. (J). (gr. -1-3). 17.99 ***(978-1-4814-8063-5(4)***, Aladdin) Simon & Schuster Children's Publishing.

Asch, Frank. Moonbear's Bargain. Asch, Frank. 2014. (Moonbear Ser.). (ENG.). 32p. (J). (gr. -1-3). 17.99 *(978-1-4424-9436-7(0)*, Aladdin) Simon & Schuster Children's Publishing.

—Moonbear's Pet. Asch, Frank. 2014. (Moonbear Ser.). (ENG.). 32p. (J). (gr. -1-3). 17.99 *(978-1-4424-9430-5(1)*, Simon & Schuster/Paula Wiseman Bks.) Simon & Schuster/Paula Wiseman Bks.

—Moonbear's Shadow. Asch, Frank. 2014. (Moonbear Ser.). (ENG.). 32p. (J). (gr. -1-3). 8.99 *(978-1-4424-9426-8(3)*, Aladdin) Simon & Schuster Children's Publishing.

—Moonbear's Skyfire. Asch, Frank. 2014. (Moonbear Ser.). (ENG.). 32p. (J). (gr. -1-3). 7.99 *(978-1-4424-9409-1(3)*, Aladdin) Simon & Schuster Children's Publishing.

—Moonbear's Sunrise. Asch, Frank. (Moonbear Ser.). (ENG.). 32p. (J). (gr. -1-3). 2016. 7.99 *(978-1-4424-6648-7(0))*; 2014. 16.99 *(978-1-4424-6647-0(2))* Simon & Schuster Children's Publishing. (Aladdin).

—Mooncake. Asch, Frank. 2014. (Moonbear Ser.). (ENG.). 32p. (J). (gr. -1-3). 7.99 *(978-1-4424-9403-9(4)*, Aladdin) Simon & Schuster Children's Publishing.

—Moondance. Asch, Frank. 2014. (Moonbear Ser.). (ENG.). 32p. (J). (gr. -1-3). 17.99 *(978-1-4424-6659-3(6)*, Aladdin) Simon & Schuster Children's Publishing.

—Moongame. Asch, Frank. 2014. (Moonbear Ser.). (ENG.). 32p. (J). (gr. -1-3). 7.99 *(978-1-4424-9406-0(9)*, Aladdin) Simon & Schuster Children's Publishing.

—Pancakes in Pajamas. Asch, Frank. (Frank Asch Bear Book Ser.). (ENG.). 32p. (J). (gr. -1-3). 2019. 7.99 *(978-1-4814-8061-1(8))*; 2018. 17.99 *(978-1-4814-8060-4(X))* Simon & Schuster Children's Publishing. (Aladdin).

—Pizza. Asch, Frank. (Frank Asch Bear Book Ser.). (ENG.). 32p. (J). (gr. -1-3). 2016. 7.99 *(978-1-4424-6676-0(6))*; 2015. 16.99 *(978-1-4424-6675-3(8))* Simon & Schuster Children's Publishing. (Aladdin).

—Popcorn. Asch, Frank. 2015. (Frank Asch Bear Book Ser.). (ENG.). 40p. (J). (gr. -1-3). 18.99 *(978-1-4424-6662-3(6)*, Aladdin) Simon & Schuster Children's Publishing.

—Star Jumper: Journal of a Cardboard Genius. Asch, Frank. 2006. (ENG.). 128p. (J). (gr. 2-5). 14.95 *(978-1-55337-886-0(5))*; pap. 7.95 *(978-1-55337-887-7(3))* Kids Can Pr., Ltd. CAN. Dist: Hachette Bk. Group.

Asch, Frank & Asch, Devin. The Daily Comet: Boy Saves Earth from Giant Octopus! Asch, Frank & Asch, Devin. 2010. 32p. (J). (gr. k-4). 16.95 *(978-1-55453-281-0(7))* Kids Can Pr., Ltd. CAN. Dist: Hachette Bk. Group.

Asch, Frank & Asch, Frank. Happy Birthday, Moon. Asch, Frank & Asch, Frank. 2005. (Stories to Go! Ser.). (ENG.). 32p. (J). 4.99 *(978-1-4169-0307-9(0)*, Simon & Schuster/Paula Wiseman Bks.) Simon & Schuster/Paula Wiseman Bks.

Asch, Frank, jt. illus. see Asch, Frank.

Asen, LIV-Sissel Kvarstein. Olga the Snowplow & the Disappearance. Moe, Anette. 2019. (ENG.). 42p. (J). (gr. k-4). *(978-82-690877-1-0(8))* Drøm forlag.

Asensio, Agusti. Tranquila Tragaleguas: La Tortuga Cabezota. Ende, Michael. 2003.Tr. of Tranquila Trampeltreu. (SPA.). 42p. (J). (gr. k-3). pap. 8.95 *(978-84-204-3709-5(3))* Santillana USA Publishing Co., Inc.

Ash. Imagine Travelling to the Most Mysterious & Unusual Places! Praveeta. 2011. (ENG.). 146p. (J). pap. *(978-0-9872096-0-3(4)*, Travel Tales of Elves) Praveeta Kumar.

Ashby, Chris. Chocolate Milk Likes Me. Albrecht, John, Jr. 2006. 16p. (J). pap. 8.99 *(978-0-9778586-3-7(4)*, CRP004); pap. 8.99 *(978-0-9778586-2-0(6)*, CRP0003) Crooked River Pr. (Blue Jay Bks.).

Ashcraft Jr, D. C. Charlie Chicken Hawk, 1 vol. Hayes, Beverly. 2009. 20p. pap. 24.95 *(978-1-60836-673-6(1))* America Star Bks.

Ashcroft, Colin Michael, et al. A Field Guide to Dragons, Trolls, & Other Dangerous Monsters, 1 vol. Sautter, A. J. 2014. (Fantasy Field Guides). (ENG.). 32p. (J). (gr. 3-9). lib. bdg. 28.65 *(978-1-4914-0691-5(7)*, Capstone Pr.) Capstone.

—A Field Guide to Elves, Dwarves, & Other Magical Folk, 1 vol. Sautter, A. J. 2014. (Fantasy Field Guides). (ENG.). 32p. (J). (gr. 3-9). lib. bdg. 28.65 *(978-1-4914-0692-2(5)*, Capstone Pr.) Capstone.

—A Field Guide to Goblins, Gremlins, & Other Wicked Creatures, 1 vol. Sautter, A. J. 2014. (Fantasy Field Guides). (ENG.). 32p. (J). (gr. 3-9). lib. bdg. 28.65 *(978-1-4914-0689-2(5)*, Capstone Pr.) Capstone.

Ashcroft, Yoko. Ellie Goes to Japan with Baba. Ashcroft, Yoko. 2019. (ENG.). 60p. (J). pap. 12.99 ***(978-0-9993077-2-4(X))*** Ashcroft, Yoko.

Ashdown, Rebecca. Even Fairies Fart. Stinson, Jennifer. 2017. (ENG.). 32p. (J). (gr. -1-3). 17.99 *(978-0-06-243623-8(6))* HarperCollins Pubs.

—Kugel for Hanukkah? Everin, Gretchen M. 2019. (ENG.). 32p. (J). (gr. -1-3). 8.99 *(978-1-5415-3471-1(9)*, Kar-Ben Publishing) Lerner Publishing Group.

—Wally Wants to Hug. Joosse, Barbara. 2017. (ENG.). 32p. (J). (gr. -1-3). 16.99 *(978-1-4998-0404-1(0))* Little Bee Books Inc.

Ashe, E. Happy Horse: A Children's Book of Horses. Ashe, E. 2003. 18p. (J). bds. 12.95 *(978-0-9727849-0-0(X)*, 0-9727849-0-X) Happy Horse Publishing, Ltd.

Asher, James. The Adoption. Florence, Leigh Anne. 2003. (Woody: the Kentucky Wiener Ser.). 32p. (J). (gr. -1-3). per. 12.95 *(978-0-9741417-0-1(4))* HotDiggetyDog Pr.

—Kentucky's Boone: The Pioneer Spirit. Burton, K. Melissa. 2008. 30p. (J). (gr. 4-7). pap. 14.95 *(978-1-934898-03-1(1))* McClanahan Publishing Hse., Inc.

—Mr. Dogwood Goes to Washington. Florence, Leigh Anne. 2008. (Woody the Kentucky Wiener Ser.). 56p. (J). (gr. 2-8). pap. 12.95 *(978-0-9741417-5-6(5))* HotDiggetyDog Pr.

—Welcomes a Dad, Vol. 2. Florence, Leigh Anne. 2004. (Woody: the Kentucky Wiener Ser.). 32p. (J). (gr. -1-3). per. 12.95 *(978-0-9741417-1-8(2))* HotDiggetyDog Pr.

Asher, James, photos by. Now That's Interesting Kentucky's Capitol. Burton, K. Melissa. 2007. 40p. (J). per. 14.95 *(978-0-913383-96-4(1))* McClanahan Publishing Hse., Inc.

Ashford, Sylvie. A Huntsman Spider in My House: Little Aussie Critters. Ray, Michelle. 2014. (ENG.). 34p. pap. 8.95 *(978-1-61448-842-2(8)*, 9781614488422) Morgan James Publishing.

Ashford, Theodore. Nothing Everything Nothing. Schreyer, Casia. 2019. (ENG.). 250p. (J). pap. ***(978-1-988853-43-7(5))*** Schreyer Ink Publishing.

Ashihara, Hinako. Sos. Ashihara, Hinako. 2005. (Sos Ser.). (ENG.). 192p. (YA). pap. 9.99 *(978-1-59116-735-8(3))* Viz Media.

Ashjaee, Nusha. Don't Stop: A Children's Picture Book. McVie, Christine. 2020. (LyricPop Ser.). 24p. (J). 16.95 *(978-1-61775-805-8(1))* Akashic Bks.

Ashley Comeaux-Foret. The Day Frasier the Frog Jumped High. Guillot, Angela K. 2011. 20p. pap. 24.95 *(978-1-4626-2312-9(3))* PublishAmerica, Inc.

Ashley, Elana, photos by. Splunkunio Splunkey Detective & Peacemaker Detective y Pacificador: Case One: The Missing Friendship Bracelet Caso Primero: El Brazalete de la Amistad Desaparecido. Ashley, Elana. Nikolov, Stefan V., tr. 2005. (SPA & ENG., 32p. (J). (gr. k-3). 17.95 *(978-0-9744812-1-0(1))* Dream Image Pr., LLC.

Ashley, Jonathan. Lily & Kosmo in Outer Outer Space. Ashley, Jonathan. 2018. (ENG.). 208p. (J). (gr. 2-5). 16.99 *(978-1-5344-1364-1(2)*, Simon & Schuster Bks. For Young Readers) Simon & Schuster Bks. For Young Readers.

Ashlock, Lisel. Sing a Season Song. Yolen, Jane. 2015. (ENG.). 48p. (J). (gr. 1-3). 19.99 *(978-1-56846-255-4(7)*, Creative Editions) Creative Co., The.

Ashlock, Lisel Jane. Egg. Koster, Amy Sky. 2020. (ENG.). 14p. (J). (gr. -1 — 1). bds. 9.99 *(978-1-56846-351-3(0)*, Creative Editions) Creative Co., The.

Ashman, Iain. How to Draw Buildings. Beasant, Pam. Tatchell, Judy, ed. 2006. (Young Artist Ser.). 32p. (J). (gr. 4-7). pap. 5.99 *(978-0-7945-1371-9(9)*, Usborne) EDC Publishing.

Ashraf, Aneeza. Father Joe's Six Golden Seeds. Cloward, Kathryn. 2020. (Kathryn the Grape Let's Read Together Ser.: Vol. 12). (ENG.). 72p. (J). pap. 19.99 ***(978-1-970163-27-8(5))*** Kandon UnLtd., Inc.

Ashraf, Aneeza. God's Report Card. Bowe, Maedene S. 2018. (ENG.). 32p. (J). (gr. k-3). pap. 9.99 *(978-1-7323126-1-6(3))* DOMINIONHOUSE Publishing & Design.

—Little Chevoney Bakes a Dream. McMillian, April Chevon. 2019. (Chevoney's Kitchen Catastrophes Ser.: Vol. 1). (ENG.). 28p. (J). pap. 10.00 *(978-1-7216-8050-4(0))* CreateSpace Independent Publishing Platform.

Ashton-Briggs, Shelley. Gale's Gold Ring: The Legend of Lincoln's Lost Gold. Ashton, Kenneth. 2012. (ENG.). 198p. pap. 14.95 *(978-1-4327-8224-5(X))* Outskirts Pr., Inc.

Ashton, John. Chevy: The Big Blue Truck. Bentley, Ann Elizabeth. 2019. (ENG.). 60p. (J). (gr. k-3). pap. *(978-1-912358-04-5(2))* Stellium Ltd.

Ashworth, Nichol, jt. illus. see Cook, Katie.

Aska. My Storee: Just Because You Can't Spell Doesn't Mean You Can't Write! Russell, Paul. 2018. (ENG.). 32p. (J). (gr. -1-3). 17.99 *(978-1-925335-77-4(1)*, 321970, EK Bks.) Exisle Publishing Pty Ltd. AUS. Dist: Hachette Bk. Group.

Aska, Warabe. Luli, el Iceberg. Takamado, Hisako de. (SPA.). 42p. (J). (gr. k-2). *(978-84-8418-039-5(5)*, ZZ5903) Zendrera Zariquiey, Editorial ESP. Dist: Lectorum Pubns., Inc.

Asker, Niklas. The City of Ember: The Graphic Novel. DuPrau, Jeanne. 2012. (City of Ember Ser.: 1). (ENG.). 144p. (J). (gr. 3-7). pap. 9.99 *(978-0-375-86793-4(7)*, Random Hse. Bks. for Young Readers) Random Hse. Children's Bks.

Askin, Corrina & Byrne, Bob. The Supermarket Ghost. Snell, Gordon. 2007. (ENG.). 80p. (J). pap. 10.95 *(978-1-84717-049-1(8))* O'Brien Pr., Ltd., The IRL. Dist: Dufour Editions, Inc.

Askin, Corrina & Clarke, Alan. Something Beginning with P: New Poems from Irish Poets. Cashman, Seamus. 2004. (ENG.). 160p. *(978-0-86278-868-1(4))* O'Brien Pr., Ltd., The.

Asmoro, Antomius Setyo. Happy Birthday to Me & You. Johnson, Jokeeta. 2016. (ENG.). (J). 22.99 *(978-1-4984-9089-4(1))*; pap. 11.99 *(978-1-4984-9088-7(3))* Salem Author Services.

Asmoro, Antonius. No Matter What. Bonner, Jasmine L. 2016. (ENG.). (J). pap. 13.50 *(978-1-366-84809-3(8))* Blurb, Inc.

Asmoro, Dodot. The Curious Bat & the Rainbow. Laughner, Sherri. 2018. (ENG.). 44p. (J). (gr. 2-6). pap. 8.99 *(978-0-692-85016-9(3))* Stardust Bks.

Asmorot, Dodot. Woman in the Mirror. Rap, John. 2017. (ENG.). (J). (gr. 3-6). 19.99 *(978-1-945582-07-3(3))* Annadale Comics.

—Woman in the Mirror: Halloween in the Machine. Rap, John. 2016. (ENG.). (J). (gr. 3-6). 19.99 *(978-1-945582-05-9(7))*; pap. 9.99 *(978-1-945582-04-2(9))* Annadale Comics.

Asner, Anne-Marie. Klutzy Boy. Asner, Anne-Marie. l.t. ed. 2007. (ENG.). 32p. (J). (gr. -1-2). per. 6.95 *(978-0-9753629-4-5(1))* Matzah Ball Bks.

—Kvetchy Boy. Asner, Anne-Marie. l.t. ed. 2006. (ENG.). 32p. (J). per. 6.95 *(978-0-9753629-3-8(3))* Matzah Ball Bks.

—Noshy Boy. Asner, Anne-Marie. l.t. ed. 2004. (ENG.). 32p. (J). (gr. -1-3). per. 6.95 *(978-0-9753629-1-4(7))* Matzah Ball Bks.

—Shluffy Girl. Asner, Anne-Marie. l.t. ed. 2005. (ENG.). 32p. (J). (gr. -1-3). per. 6.95 *(978-0-9753629-2-1(5))* Matzah Ball Bks.

—Shmutzy Girl. Asner, Anne-Marie. l.t. ed. 2004. (ENG.). 32p. (J). (gr. -1-3). per. 6.95 *(978-0-9753629-0-7(9))* Matzah Ball Bks.

Asnong, Jocey. Nuptse & Lhotse Go to the Rockies. rev. ed. 2016. 40p. (J). (gr. k-4). 18.00 *(978-1-77160-152-8(3))* Rocky Mountain Bks.

Asphyxia. The Grimstones Collection. Asphyxia. ed. 2015. (Grimstones Ser.). (ENG.). 488p. (J). (gr. 3-7). pap. 17.99 *(978-1-76011-391-9(3))* Allen & Unwin AUS. Dist: Independent Pubs. Group.

Aspinall, Neal. National Parks: A Kid's Guide to America's Parks, Monuments, & Landmarks, Revised & Updated. McHugh, Erin. 2019. 128p. (J). (gr. 3-7). 19.99 *(978-0-7624-9470-5(0)*, Black Dog & Leventhal Pubs. Inc.) Running Pr.

Aspinall, Sarah. Penguins Love Their ABC's. Aspinall, Sarah. 2017. (ENG.). 40p. (J). (gr. -1-k). 17.99 *(978-1-338-13420-9(5)*, Blue Sky Pr., The) Scholastic, Inc.

Asquith, Elise. The Hippo Who Was Afraid of Water. Asquith, Elise. 2018. (ENG.). 30p. (J). (gr. k-2). pap. *(978-0-6481402-2-1(9))* Budgie Bks.

Asquith, Ros. Can It Be about Me? Moskowitz, Cheryl. 2013. (ENG.). 96p. (J). (gr. 2-5). pap. 8.99 *(978-1-84780-340-5(7)*, Frances Lincoln Children's Bks.) Quarto Publishing Group UK GBR. Dist: Hachette Bk. Group.

—The Great Big Book of Families. Hoffman, Mary. 2011. (ENG.). 40p. (J). (gr. k-3). 17.99 *(978-0-8037-3516-3(2)*, Dial Bks) Penguin Young Readers Group.

—Max the Champion. Stockdale, Sean & Strick, Alex. 2014. (ENG.). 32p. (J). pap. 8.99 *(978-1-84780-519-5(1)*, White Lion Publishing) Quarto Publishing Group UK GBR. Dist: Littlehampton Bk Services, Ltd.

—Pirate Baby. Hoffman, Mary. 2017. (ENG.). 32p. (J). (gr. -1-1). 17.99 *(978-1-910959-95-4(2))* Otter-Barry Bks. GBR. Dist: Independent Pubs. Group.

Asrar, Mahmud & Land, Greg. Weapon X Vol. 1: Weapons of Mutant Destruction Prelude. 2017. (ENG.). 136p. (YA). (gr. 8-17). pap. 15.99 *(978-1-302-90734-1(4))* Marvel Worldwide, Inc.

Asrar, Mahmud, jt. illus. see Gill, Robert.

Assad, Angelique. A True Princess: The Life of St Demiana. Fanous, Sherry. l.t. ed. 2018. (ENG.). 24p. (J). pap. *(978-0-6482814-4-3(2))* St. Shenouda Monastery.

Assadova, Karolina. Clara the Heavy-Hearted Pug. Chaitman, Darren. 2018. (ENG.). 28p. (J). (gr. k-1). *(978-0-6483762-2-4(2))*; pap. *(978-0-6483762-0-0(6))* Dragon King's Daughter, The.

Assanelli, Victoria. Abby Visits the Big City: The City Mouse & the Country Mouse Remixed. Miller, Connie Colwell & Aesop, Aesop. 2016. (Aesop's Fables Remixed Ser.). (ENG.). 24p. (J). (gr. k-3). 20.95 *(978-1-60753-952-0(7))* Amicus Publishing.

—Aladdin & the Genies: Band 14/Ruby (Collins Big Cat) French, Vivian. 2016. (Collins Big Cat Ser.). (ENG.). 48p. (J). pap. 9.95 *(978-0-00-814720-4(5))* HarperCollins Pubs. Ltd. GBR. Dist: Independent Pubs. Group.

—Andrew & the Birthday Surprise: The Boy Who Cried Wolf Remixed. Miller, Connie Colwell & Aesop, Aesop. 2016. (Aesop's Fables Remixed Ser.). (ENG.). 24p. (J). (gr. k-3). 20.95 *(978-1-60753-951-3(9))* Amicus Publishing.

—Henry's Track & Field Day: The Tortoise & the Hare Remixed. Miller, Connie Colwell & Aesop, Aesop. 2016. (Aesop's Fables Remixed Ser.). (ENG.). 24p. (J). (gr. k-3). 20.95 *(978-1-60753-950-6(0))* Amicus Publishing.

—James & the Kindergartener: The Lion & the Mouse Remixed. Miller, Connie Colwell & Aesop, Aesop. 2016. (Aesop's Fables Remixed Ser.). (ENG.). 24p. (J). (gr. k-3). 20.95 *(978-1-60753-954-4(3))* Amicus Publishing.

—Mary, Anna, & the Little Brother: The Lion, the Bear, & the Fox Remixed. Miller, Connie Colwell. 2016. (Aesop's Fables Remixed Ser.). (ENG.). 24p. (J). (gr. k-3). 20.95 *(978-1-60753-955-1(1)*, Amicus Illustrated) Amicus Publishing.

—Rosie's Special Gift: The Goose Who Laid the Golden Eggs Remixed. Miller, Connie Colwell. 2016. (Aesop's Fables Remixed Ser.). (ENG.). 24p. (J). (gr. k-3). 20.95 *(978-1-60753-953-7(5)*, Amicus Illustrated) Amicus Publishing.

Assanelli, Victoria. You Can Be Helpful: Step Aside or Pitch In? Colwell Miller, Connie. 2020. (Making Good Choices Ser.). (ENG.). 24p. (J). (gr. 1-3). pap. 9.99 ***(978-1-68152-632-4(8))*** Amicus.

Assanelli, Victoria. You Can Be Responsible: Do It Now or Put It Off? Miller, Connie Colwell. 2020. (J). lib. bdg. *(978-1-68151-688-2(8))* Amicus Publishing.

—You Can Encourage Others: Tease or Inspire? Miller, Connie Colwell. 2019. (Making Good Choices Ser.). (ENG.). 24p. (J). (gr. 1-3). pap. 9.99 *(978-1-68152-475-7(9))* Amicus.

—You Can Follow the Rules: Cheat or Play Fair? Miller, Connie Colwell. 2019. (Making Good Choices Ser.). (ENG.). 24p. (J). (gr. 1-3). pap. 9.99 *(978-1-68152-476-4(7))* Amicus.

—You Can Make Changes: Ask or Ignore? Miller, Connie Colwell. 2019. (J). *(978-1-68151-691-2(8))* Amicus Publishing.

—You Can Make Changes: Ask or Ignore? Miller, Connie Colwell. 2019. (Making Good Choices Ser.). (ENG.). 24p. (J). (gr. 1-3). pap. 9.99 *(978-1-68152-477-1(5))* Amicus.

—You Can Respect Differences: Assume or Find Out? Miller, Connie Colwell. 2019. (Making Good Choices Ser.). (ENG.). 24p. (J). (gr. 1-3). pap. 9.99 *(978-1-68152-478-8(3))* Amicus.

—You Can Stop Bullying: Stand by or Stand Up? Miller, Connie Colwell. 2019. (J). *(978-1-68151-693-6(4))* Amicus Publishing.

—You Can Stop Bullying: Stand by or Stand Up? Miller, Connie Colwell. 2019. (Making Good Choices Ser.). (ENG.). 24p. (J). (gr. 1-3). pap. 9.99 *(978-1-68152-479-5(1))* Amicus.

Assanelli, Victoria. You Can Use Money Wisely: Spend or Save? Colwell Miller, Connie. 2020. (Making Good Choices Ser.). (ENG.). 24p. (J). (gr. 1-3). pap. 9.99 ***(978-1-68152-635-5(2))*** Amicus.

Assirelli, Francesca. Talia & the Haman-Tushies. Marshall, Linda Elovitz. 2017. (ENG.). 24p. (J). (gr. -1-2). 17.99 *(978-1-5124-0825-6(5)*, 9781512408256, Kar-Ben Publishing) Lerner Publishing Group.

—Talia & the Rude Vegetables, Vol. Marshall, Linda Elovitz. 2011. (ENG.). 24p. (J). (gr. k-3). pap. 6.95 *(978-0-7613-5218-1(X)*, 9780761352181, Kar-Ben Publishing) Lerner Publishing Group.

—Talia & the Very YUM Kippur. Marshall, Linda Elovitz. 2015. (ENG.). 24p. (J). (gr. -1-2). 17.99 *(978-1-4677-5236-7(3))*; Vol. pap. 7.99 *(978-1-4677-5240-4(1)*, 9781467752404) Lerner Publishing Group. (Kar-Ben Publishing).

Assis Brasil, Bruna. Let's Play Yoga! How to Grow Calm Like a Mountain, Strong Like a Warrior, & Joyful Like the Sun. Barros, Lúcia & De Luca, Márcia. 2018. 80p. 14.95 *(978-1-61519-493-3(2)*, 779493) Experiment LLC, The.

Astacio, Mrinali Alvarez. Pon, Pon: A Jugar con el Bebé! 2007. (SPA.). 28p. 14.95 *(978-0-8477-1575-6(2))* Univ. of Puerto Rico Pr.

Astacio, Mrinali Álvarez. Qué crees? Rivera-Lassen, Carmen Leonor. 2009. (SPA.). 30p. (J). 11.95 *(978-0-8477-1581-7(7))* Univ. of Puerto Rico Pr.

Astrella, Mark. Hello Ocean. Ryan, Pam Muñoz. 2014. 32p. pap. 8.00 *(978-1-61003-319-0(1))* Center for the Collaborative Classroom.

—Hello Ocean/Hola Mar. Ryan, Pam Muñoz. ed. 2003. (Charlesbridge Bilingual Bks.). 32p. (J). (gr. -1-2). pap. 7.95 *(978-1-57091-372-3(2))* Charlesbridge Publishing, Inc.

Asuao, Kelcey. Being a Boy in Samoa in the 1950s. Lesa, Ropeti F. 2003. (Polynesian Literature Ser.: Vol. 1). xiii, 197p. (J). pap. 19.95 *(978-0-9728126-3-4(6))* Isles of the Sea Pubs.

A

Atanas. The Lost Island. Johnson, E. Pauline. 2010. (ENG.). 40p. (J). (gr. -1-3). pap. 9.95 *(978-1-897476-44-4(2))* Simply Read Bks. CAN. Dist: Ingram Publisher Services.

Atchley, Kendra. Barley & Betsy: Journey #1 A cat & dog's great adventure to the Mall. Johnson, Michael E. 2011. 36p. pap. 24.95 *(978-1-4560-4077-2(4))* America Star Bks.

Athanassiadis, Kiki. Averses et Réglisses Noires. David, Carole. 2004. (Poetry Ser.). (FRE.). 36p. (J). (gr. 7). pap. *(978-2-89021-674-7(8))* Diffusion du livre Mirabel (DLM).

Atherton, Jim. Lucky the Rubber Ducky. London, Adam. 2009. 14p. (J). pap. 14.95 *(978-0-578-00865-3(3))* AthertonCustoms.

Atiyeh, Michael & Borkowski, Michael. High-Stakes Heist! Carbone, Courtney. 2016. (Little Golden Book Ser.). (ENG.). 24p. (J). (-k). 4.99 *(978-0-385-37426-2(7)*, Golden Bks.) Random Hse. Children's Bks.

—Rocket to the Rescue! Sazaklis, John. 2017. (Little Golden Book Ser.). (ENG.). 24p. (J). (-k). 4.99 *(978-0-399-55849-8(7)*, Golden Bks.) Random Hse. Children's Bks.

Atiyeh, Michael, jt. illus. see Borkowski, Michael.

Atiyeh, Michael, jt. illus. see Lolos, Vasilis.

Atiyen, Michael, jt. illus. see Borkowski, Michael.

Atkin, S. Beth. Gunstories: Life-Changing Experiences with Guns. Atkin, S. Beth. 2007. (ENG.). 256p. (YA). (gr. 8-12). per. 8.99 *(978-0-06-052661-0(0)*, Tegen, Katherine Bks) HarperCollins Pubs.

Atkins, Alison. Humpty Dumpty & Friends. 2005. 10p. bds. *(978-1-84510-767-3(5))* Top That! Publishing PLC.

—Incy Wincy Spider & Friends. 2005. 10p. bds. *(978-1-84510-768-0(3))* Top That! Publishing PLC.

—The Magical Mermaids. Hogg, James. 2007. (Sparkling Jigsaw Book Ser.). 10p. (J). (gr. k-3). *(978-1-84666-373-4(3)*, Tide Mill Pr.) Top That! Publishing PLC.

—The Midnight Fairies. Top That Publishing Staff, ed. 2007. (Sparkling Jigsaw Book Ser.). 10p. (J). (gr. -1). bds. *(978-1-84666-278-2(8)*, Tide Mill Pr.) Top That! Publishing PLC.

—Ten Little Bears. Ranson, Erin. 2017. (Counting to Ten Bks.). (ENG.). 22p. (J). (gr. -1-1). 9.99 *(978-1-78700-250-0(0))* Top That! Publishing PLC GBR. Dist: Independent Pubs. Group.

—There Were Ten Bears in a Bed: A Count-and-Feel Book. Top That Publishing Staff, ed. 2007. (Story Book Ser.). 22p. (J). (gr. -1). bds. *(978-1-84666-130-3(7)*, Tide Mill Pr.) Top That! Publishing PLC.

Atkins, Andy. Invisible Lizard. Cyrus, Kurt. 2017. (ENG.). 32p. (J). (gr. k-2). 16.99 *(978-1-58536-378-0(2)*, 204320) Sleeping Bear Pr.

Atkins, Nancy Taylor, jt. illus. see Boggs, Button.

Atkinson, Bex, jt. illus. see Atkinson, Rebecca.

Atkinson, Brett, jt. illus. see Atkinson, Ruth.

Atkinson, Cale. The Day Santa Stopped Believing in Harold. Fergus, Maureen. 2016. (ENG.). 32p. (J). (gr. -1-3). 16.99 *(978-1-77049-824-2(9)*, Tundra Bks. CAN. Dist: Penguin Random Hse. LLC.

—First Day of Groot! Deneen, Brendan. 2019. (ENG.). 32p. (J). (gr. -1-k). 12.99 *(978-1-368-00069-7(X)*, Marvel Pr.) Disney Publishing Worldwide.

—Harrison P. Spader, Personal Space Invader. Jones, Christianne C. 2018. (Little Boost Ser.). (ENG.). 32p. (J). (gr. -1-2). lib. bdg. 23.99 *(978-1-5158-2722-1(4)*, 137920, Picture Window Bks.) Capstone.

—I Got You a Present! McLennan, Susan & Erskine-Kellie, Mike. 2020. (ENG.). 32p. (J). (gr. -1-2). 16.99 *(978-1-5253-0009-7(1))* Kids Can Pr., Ltd. CAN. Dist: Hachette Bk. Group.

—If I Had a Gryphon. VanSickle, Vikki. (ENG.). 32p. (J). 2018. (— 1). bds. 9.99 *(978-0-7352-6465-6(1))*; 2016. (gr. -1-2). 16.99 *(978-1-77049-809-9(5))* Tundra Bks. CAN. (Tundra Bks.). Dist: Penguin Random Hse. LLC.

—Let's Meet a Veterinarian. Bellisario, Gina. 2013. (Cloverleaf Books (tm) — Community Helpers Ser.). (ENG.). 24p. (J). (gr. k-2). pap. 8.99 *(978-1-4677-0806-7(2)*, 9781467708067, Millbrook Pr.) Lerner Publishing Group.

—Little Red Riding Sheep. Lodding, Linda Ravin. 2017. (ENG.). 40p. (J). (gr. -1-3). 17.99 *(978-1-4814-5748-4(9))* Simon & Schuster Children's Publishing.

—Muddy, Mud, Bud. Lakin, Patricia. 2014. (Penguin Young Readers, Level 1 Ser.). 32p. (J). (gr. k-1). pap. 4.99 *(978-0-448-47989-7(3)*, Penguin Young Readers) Penguin Young Readers Group.

—Night Night, Groot. Deneen, Brendan. 2018. (ENG.). 30p. (J). (gr. -1-k). bds. 7.99 *(978-1-4847-8765-6(X)*, Marvel Pr.) Disney Publishing Worldwide.

—Night Night, Groot. Deneen, Brendan. 2017. (ENG.). 32p. (J). (gr. -1-k). 12.99 *(978-1-4847-3282-3(0)*, Marvel Pr.) Disney Publishing Worldwide.

Atkinson, Cale. Peter & the Tree Children. Wohlleben, Peter. 2020. (ENG.). 40p. (J). (gr. k-3). 17.95 ***(978-1-77164-457-0(5)***, Greystone Bks.) Greystone Books Ltd. CAN. Dist: Publishers Group West (PGW).

Atkinson, Cale. Police Officers in My Community. Bellisario, Gina. 2018. (Meet a Community Helper (Early Bird Stories (tm)) Ser.). (ENG.). 24p. (J). (gr. k-2). 27.99 *(978-1-5415-2020-2(3)*, Lerner Pubns.) Lerner Publishing Group.

Atkinson, Cale. Snow Day for Groot! Deneen, Brendan. 2020. (ENG.). 32p. (J). (gr. -1-k). 12.99 ***(978-1-368-00070-3(3)***, Marvel Pr.) Disney Publishing Worldwide.

Atkinson, Cale. La Tormenta. Schmauss, Judy Kentor. 2016. (Early Rising Readers Ser.). (SPA.). 16p. (J). (gr. 1-1). 6.67 *(978-1-4788-3747-3(0))* Newmark Learning LLC.

—Vroom, Zoom, Bud. Lakin, Patricia & Bader, Bonnie. 2016. (Penguin Young Readers, Level 1 Ser.). 32p. (J). (gr. k-1).

3.99 *(978-0-448-48832-5(9)*, Penguin Young Readers) Penguin Young Readers Group.

Atkinson, Cale. Explorers of the Wild. Atkinson, Cale. 2016. (ENG.). 40p. (J). (gr. -1-3). 16.99 ***(978-1-4847-2340-1(6))*** Little, Brown Bks. for Young Readers.

Atkinson, Katie. Hazel's Adventures Living with Grandma. Stanchfield, Joni. 2017. (ENG.). (J). 22.95 *(978-1-64079-416-0(6))*; pap. 13.95 *(978-1-64079-414-6(X))* Christian Faith Publishing.

Atkinson, Rebecca & Atkinson, Bex. Run for the Hills. McCaughren, Tom. 2016. (Run with the Wind Ser.). (ENG.). 256p. (J). 15.00 *(978-1-84717-876-3(6))* O'Brien Pr., Ltd., The IRL. Dist: Casemate Pubs. & Bk. Distributors, LLC.

—Run with the Wind. McCaughren, Tom. 2016. (Run with the Wind Ser.). (ENG.). 208p. (J). 15.00 *(978-1-84717-837-4(5))* O'Brien Pr., Ltd., The IRL. Dist: Casemate Pubs. & Bk. Distributors, LLC.

Atkinson, Ruth & Atkinson, Brett. Christmas Cutouts. Atkinson, Ruth & Atkinson, Brett. (J). (gr. k-2). pap. *(978-1-876367-20-6(2))* Wizard Bks.

—Rhyme Templates. Atkinson, Ruth & Atkinson, Brett. (J). (gr. k-2). pap. *(978-1-875739-74-5(2))* Wizard Bks.

—Stick Puppet Templates. Atkinson, Ruth & Atkinson, Brett. (J). (gr. k-2). pap. *(978-1-875739-72-1(6))* Wizard Bks.

—Story Templates. Atkinson, Ruth & Atkinson, Brett. (J). (gr. k-2). pap. *(978-1-875739-73-8(4))* Wizard Bks.

—Traditional Rhyme Templates. Atkinson, Ruth & Atkinson, Brett. (J). (gr. k-2). pap. *(978-1-875739-94-3(7))* Wizard Bks.

Atlas, Anderson. The Little Red Schoolhouse. Jessup, Angie Soto. 2019. (Carmelita Ser.: Vol. 1). (ENG.). 26p. (J). pap. 9.99 ***(978-1-0779-7903-1(7))*** Independently Published.

Aton, Barbara. Sailwind the Seabird. Knight, Betty. 2005. (J). per. 19.95 *(978-1-59858-017-4(5))* Dog Ear Publishing, LLC.

Attanasio, Fabiana. Alice in Wonderland Puzzle Book. 2020. (ENG.). 12p. (J). (gr. k). 14.95 ***(978-88-544-1699-4(1))*** White Star ITA. Dist: Sterling Publishing Co., Inc.

—The Wizard of Oz Puzzle Book. 2020. (ENG.). 12p. (J). (gr. k). 14.95 ***(978-88-544-1702-1(5))*** White Star ITA. Dist: Sterling Publishing Co., Inc.

Attansia, Fabiana. Peter Pan Coloring Book. 2016. (ENG.). 80p. (J). (gr. k). pap. 9.95 *(978-1-4549-2090-8(4))* Sterling Publishing Co., Inc.

Attard, Enebor. Samira's Eid. Aktar, Nasreen. 2004. 24p. (J). *(978-1-85269-538-5(2))*; *(978-1-85269-539-2(0))*; *(978-1-85269-540-8(4))*; (ENG & ARA.). pap. *(978-1-85269-122-6(0))*; (ENG & BEN.). pap. *(978-1-85269-131-8(X))*; (ENG & GUJ.). pap. *(978-1-85269-132-5(8))*; (ENG & SOM.). pap. *(978-1-85269-133-2(6))*; (ENG & TUR.). pap. *(978-1-85269-134-9(4))*; (ENG & URD.). pap. *(978-1-85269-135-6(2))*; (ENG & PAN.). pap. *(978-1-85269-183-7(2))*; (ENG & FRE.). pap. *(978-1-85269-502-6(1))*; (ENG & PER.). pap. *(978-1-85269-503-3(X))*; (ENG & ALB.). pap. *(978-1-85269-572-9(2))* Mantra Lingua.

Atteberry, Kevan. Boogie Monster. Bissett, Josie. 2011. 36p. (J). (gr. -1-3). 16.95 *(978-1-935414-10-0(0))* Compendium, Inc., Publishing & Communications.

—Dear Beast. Butler, Dori Hillestad. 2020. (Dear Beast Ser.: 1). 80p. (J). (gr. 1-4). 15.99 *(978-0-8234-4492-2(9))* Holiday Hse., Inc.

—Frankie Stein, 0 vols. Schaefer, Lola M. 2009. (ENG.). 34p. (J). (gr. k-3). pap. 6.99 *(978-0-7614-5608-7(2)*, 9780761456087, Two Lions) Amazon Publishing.

—Frankie Stein Starts School. Schaefer, Lola M. (ENG.). (J). (gr. 1-3). 2018. 34p. pap. 7.99 *(978-1-4778-1049-1(8)*, 9781477810491); 2010. 32p. 15.99 *(978-0-7614-5656-8(2)*, 9780761456568) Amazon Publishing. (Two Lions).

—Halloween Hustle, 0 vols. Gunnufson, Charlotte. 2013. (ENG.). 32p. (J). (gr. -1-2). 16.99 *(978-1-4778-1723-0(9)*, 9781477817230, Two Lions) Amazon Publishing.

—Lunchbox & the Aliens. Fields, Bryan W. 2009. (Froonga Ser.: 1). (ENG.). 208p. (J). (gr. 4-6). pap. 21.19 *(978-0-312-56115-4(6)*, 900058845) Square Fish.

Atteberry, Kevan. Bunnies!!! Atteberry, Kevan. 2015. (ENG.). 32p. (J). (gr. -1-3). 12.99 *(978-0-06-230783-5(5))* HarperCollins Pubs.

—Bunnies!!! Board Book. Atteberry, Kevan. 2018. (ENG.). 34p. (J). (gr. -1 — 1). bds. 7.99 *(978-0-06-274141-7(1)*, HarperFestival) HarperCollins Pubs.

—I Love You More Than the Smell of Swamp Gas. Atteberry, Kevan. 2017. (ENG.). 40p. (J). (gr. -1-3). 17.99 *(978-0-06-240871-6(2))* HarperCollins Pubs.

—Puddles!!! Atteberry, Kevan. 2016. (ENG.). 32p. (J). (gr. -1-3). 14.99 *(978-0-06-230784-2(3)*, Tegen, Katherine Bks) HarperCollins Pubs.

Attia, Caroline. The Big Book of Treasures: The Most Amazing Discoveries Ever Made & Still to Be Made. 2017. (ENG.). 96p. (J). (gr. 3-7). 29.99 *(978-3-89955-797-8(2))* Die Gestalten Verlag DEU. Dist: Ingram Publisher Services.

—David & the Worry Beast: Helping Children Cope with Anxiety. Guanci, Anne Marie. 2007. 48p. (J). (gr. -1-4). pap. 9.95 *(978-0-88282-275-4(6))* New Horizon Pr. Pubs., Inc.

—If You Were a Kid During the California Gold Rush. Gregory, Josh. 2018. (If You Were a Kid Ser.). (ENG.). 32p. (J). (gr. 2-4). lib. bdg. 26.00 *(978-0-531-23214-9(X)*, Children's Pr.) Scholastic Library Publishing.

—The Three Little Pugs & the Big Bad Cat. Davies, Becky. 2017. (ENG.). 32p. (J). pap. *(978-1-84869-576-4(4))* Tiger Tales.

—Three Little Pugs & the Big, Bad Cat. Davies, Becky. 2017. (ENG.). 32p. (J). (gr. -1-2). 16.99 *(978-1-68010-043-3(2))* Tiger Tales.

Attinger, Billy. Baby's First Little Book of Prayers. gif. ed. 2003. (Wee Witness Ser.). 32p. (J). 7.99 *(978-0-7369-1185-6(5))* Harvest Hse. Pubs.

Attiogbe, Magali. Ladybug. Attiogbe, Magali. 2019. (Tales from Nature Ser.). (ENG.). 18p. (J). (gr. -1 — 1). bds. 9.95 ***(978-1-78603-656-8(8)***, Words & Pictures) Quarto Publishing Group UK GBR. Dist: Hachette Bk. Group.

Attwell, Mabel Lucie. Peter Pan & Wendy. Barrie, J. M. 2019. (ENG.). 240p. (J). (gr. 2-7). pap. 9.99 *(978-1-5098-6995-4(6))* Pan Macmillan GBR. Dist: Independent Pubs. Group.

—The Water-Babies. Kingsley, Charles. 2019. (ENG.). 240p. (J). (gr. 2). pap. 9.99 *(978-1-5098-6996-1(4))* Pan Macmillan GBR. Dist: Independent Pubs. Group.

Atwell, Debby. Miss Moore Thought Otherwise: How Anne Carroll Moore Created Libraries for Children. Pinborough, Jan. 2013. (ENG.). 40p. (J). (gr. 1-4). 18.99 *(978-0-547-47105-1(X)*, 1437999) Houghton Mifflin Harcourt Publishing Co.

Atwood, Clara E. Children's Classic in Dramatic Form - Book Four. Stevenson, Augusta. 2019. (ENG.). 222p. (J). pap. 8.95 ***(978-1-6938-5148-3(2))*** Independently Published.

—Children's Classic in Dramatic Form - Book One. Stevenson, Augusta. 2019. (ENG.). 128p. (J). pap. 6.95 ***(978-1-6938-2986-4(X))*** Independently Published.

Atwood, Scott. How Many Sleeps till Disneyland? Atwood, Michele. Hamel, Sharon, ed. 2019. (ENG.). 40p. (J). pap. 12.50 ***(978-1-6720-6089-9(3))*** Independently Published.

Atze, Dave. The Power of Me. Brown, Andrea. 2020. (ENG.). 106p. (J). (gr. 1-6). pap. 10.99 ***(978-0-6487450-0-6(7)***, PowerKids Pr.) Rosen Publishing Group, Inc., The.

Atze, Dave. Selfie Search, 1 vol. Macintosh, Cameron. 2019. (Max Booth: Future Sleuth Ser.). (ENG.). 128p. (J). (gr. 4-4). 19.95 *(978-1-5383-8464-0(7))*; pap. 12.90 *(978-1-5383-8465-7(5))* Enslow Publishing, LLC. (West 44 Bks.).

—Stamp Safari, 1 vol. Macintosh, Cameron. 2019. (Max Booth: Future Sleuth Ser.). (ENG.). 144p. (J). (gr. 4-4). 19.95 *(978-1-5383-8467-1(1))*; pap. 12.90 *(978-1-5383-8468-8(X))* Enslow Publishing, LLC. (West 44 Bks.).

—Tape Escape, 1 vol. Macintosh, Cameron. 2019. (Max Booth: Future Sleuth Ser.). (ENG.). 144p. (J). (gr. 4-4). 19.95 *(978-1-5383-8461-9(2))*; pap. 12.90 *(978-1-5383-8462-6(0))* Enslow Publishing, LLC. (West 44 Bks.).

Atzmon, Shany. Or's Journey. Arison, Shari. 2019. (ENG.). 62p. (J). pap. 21.95 ***(978-1-937505-03-5(0))*** Worthy Shorts.

Aubert, Elena G. Mis 365 Mejores Adivinanzas. Editorial, Equipo. 2003. (SPA.). *(978-84-7630-904-9(X)*, LA30439) Editorial Libsa, S.A. ESP. Dist: Lectorum Pubns., Inc.

Aubin, Antoine, jt. illus. see Shreder, Etienne.

Aubitz, Ashley, jt. illus. see Montano, Andrea.

Aubrey, Meg Kelleher, jt. illus. see Beckett, Andrew.

Auch, Herm. I Was a Third Grade Spy. Auch, Mary Jane. 2004. 86p. (gr. 2-5). 16.00 *(978-0-7569-4138-3(5))* Perfection Learning Corp.

—The Princess & the Pizza. Auch, Mary Jane. 2003. (ENG.). 32p. (J). (gr. -1-3). 7.99 *(978-0-8234-1798-8(0))* Holiday Hse., Inc.

Auch, Herm, jt. illus. see Auch, Mary Jane.

Auch, Mary Jane & Auch, Herm. The Plot Chickens. Auch, Mary Jane. (ENG.). 32p. (J). (gr. -1-3). 2010. pap. 7.99 *(978-0-8234-2307-1(7))*; 2009. 17.99 *(978-0-8234-2087-2(6))* Holiday Hse., Inc.

Auchter, Chris. Jenneli's Dance, 1 vol. Denny, Elizabeth. ed. 2008. (Schchechmala Children's Ser.). (ENG.). 44p. (J). (gr. 1-3). pap. 12.95 *(978-1-894778-61-9(8))* Theytus Bks., Ltd. CAN. Dist: Orca Bk. Pubs. USA.

Auchter, Christopher. Chuck in the City, 1 vol. Wheeler, Jordan. rev. ed. 2009. (ENG.). 32p. (J). (gr. 1-3). pap. 8.95 *(978-1-894778-81-7(2))* Theytus Bks., Ltd. CAN. Dist: Orca Bk. Pubs. USA.

Auclair, Joan. A Leer y Jugar! con Bebés y Niños Pequeños. Oppenheim, Joanne F. & Oppenheim, Stephanie. 2006.Tr. of Read It! Play It! with Babies & Toddlers. (SPA.). 102p. pap. 10.00 *(978-0-9721050-5-7(0))* Oppenheim Toy Portfolio, Inc.

—Read It! Play It! Oppenheim, Joanne F. & Oppenheim, Stephanie. 2005. 176p. pap. 10.00 *(978-0-9721050-1-9(8))* Oppenheim Toy Portfolio, Inc.

Aucoin, Derec, et al. Adventures of the X-Men: Rites of Passage. 2019. (ENG.). 256p. (J). (gr. 5-17). pap. 12.99 *(978-1-302-91985-6(7))* Marvel Worldwide, Inc.

Aucoin, Matt. Explore Atoms & Molecules! With 25 Great Projects. Slingerland, Janet. 2017. (Explore Your World Ser.). 96p. (J). (gr. 1-5). 19.95 *(978-1-61930-491-8(0)*, 2bc680a0-88af-4acf-a4b1-b81e5e2a5532) Nomad Pr.

—Explore Makerspace! With 25 Great Projects. Klepeis, Alicia. 2017. (Explore Your World Ser.). 96p. (J). (gr. 3-4). pap. 14.95 *(978-1-61930-566-3(6)*, b6f96e35-946c-463f-b8e0-f7094ab373ce) Nomad Pr.

—Explore Makerspace! With 25 Great Projects. Klepeis, Alicia. 2017. (Explore Your World Ser.). 96p. (J). (gr. 3-4). 19.95 *(978-1-61930-562-5(3)*, 43cafb55-c10e-40af-b1fa-8d38381a67e2) Nomad Pr.

—Explore Predators & Prey! With 25 Great Projects. Blobaum, Cindy. 2016. (Explore Your World Ser.). 96p. (J). (gr. 1-5). 19.95 *(978-1-61930-456-7(2)*, 940ecaa8-2026-4dcd-babb-0d5c4e95a446) Nomad Pr.

—Explore Shapes & Angles! With 25 Great Projects. Moore, Jeanette. 2017. (Explore Your World Ser.). 96p. (J). (gr. 3-4). 19.95 *(978-1-61930-582-3(8)*, ae5e46ba-eed8-4295-b6e9-47a4d3c5cfc7); pap. 14.95 *(978-1-61930-586-1(0)*, 2e706ef9-3ce0-47b3-80bb-712b81fe8ec4) Nomad Pr.

Audibert, Tara. Moonbeam. Francis, Gail. 2019. (ENG.). 28p. (J). pap. 10.60 ***(978-1-0863-4808-8(7))*** Independently Published.

Audouin, Laurent. Diego from Madrid. Gamonal, Dulce. 2014. (AV2 Fiction Readalong Ser.: Vol. 124). (ENG.). 32p. (J). (gr. -1-3). lib. bdg. 34.28 *(978-1-4896-2280-8(2)*, AV2 by Weigl) Weigl Pubs., Inc.

—Keeping It Green! 2009. (Taking Action for My Planet Ser.). 32p. (YA). (gr. 3-6). lib. bdg. 25.60 *(978-1-60754-797-6(X))* Windmill Bks.

Audrey, Crosby. View from the Middle of the Road: Where the Greenest Grass Grows, 3 vols., volume I. Clark, Lucinda. Brenda, Baratto, ed. 2004. 55p. per. 9.00 *(978-0-9727703-1-6(3)*, 706 855-6173) P.R.A. Publishing.

Auer, Lois. Lucy & the Red-Tailed Hawk. Cerone, Diane. 2007. 32p. (J). pap. 17.00 *(978-0-8059-7565-9(9))* Dorrance Publishing Co., Inc.

Auerbach, Adam. Monkey Brother. Auerbach, Adam. 2017. (ENG.). 40p. (J). 17.99 *(978-1-62779-600-2(2)*, 9781627796002, Holt, Henry & Co. Bks. For Young Readers) Holt, Henry & Co.

—Three Vikings. Auerbach, Adam. 2019. (ENG.). 40p. (J). 17.99 *(978-1-62779-601-9(0)*, 900156502, Holt, Henry & Co. Bks. For Young Readers) Holt, Henry & Co.

Auerbach, Annie. At the Beach. 2018. (Little Bath Bks.). (ENG.). 8p. (J). (gr. -1 — 1). 6.99 *(978-1-4380-7862-5(5)*, B.E.S. Publishing) Peterson's.

—In the Ocean. 2018. (Little Bath Bks.). (ENG.). 8p. (J). (gr. -1 — 1). 6.99 *(978-1-4380-7863-2(3)*, B.E.S. Publishing) Peterson's.

Auerbach, Joshua. Baby Shadows, 1. Auerbach, Joshua. 2003. 8p. (J). bds. 10.00 *(978-0-9744928-0-3(9))* Baby Shadows.

Augarde, Steve. Garage: A Pop-up Book. Augarde, Steve. 2005. 10p. (J). (gr. k-4). reprint ed. 15.00 *(978-0-7567-9299-2(1))* DIANE Publishing Co.

Auger, Dale. Mwâkwa Talks to the Loon: A Cree Story for Children, 1 vol. Auger, Dale. 2007. (ENG.). 32p. (J). (gr. 1-3). pap. 12.95 *(978-1-894974-32-5(8))* Heritage Hse. CAN. Dist: Orca Bk. Pubs. USA.

Auger, Neepin. Discovering Animals: English * French * Cree, 1 vol. 2017. (ENG.). 28p. (J). bds. 12.00 *(978-1-77160-234-1(1))* RMB Rocky Mountain Bks. CAN. Dist: Publishers Group West (PGW).

—Discovering Numbers: English * French * Cree — Updated Edition, 1 vol. 2nd ed. 2019. (ENG.). 30p. (J). bds. 12.00 *(978-1-77160-331-7(3))* RMB Rocky Mountain Bks. CAN. Dist: Publishers Group West (PGW).

—Discovering People: English * French * Cree, 1 vol. 2019. (ENG.). 30p. (J). bds. 12.00 *(978-1-77160-327-0(5))* RMB Rocky Mountain Bks. CAN. Dist: Publishers Group West (PGW).

—Discovering Words: English * French * Cree — Updated Edition, 1 vol. 2nd ed. 2019. (ENG.). 32p. (J). bds. 12.00 *(978-1-77160-329-4(1))* RMB Rocky Mountain Bks. CAN. Dist: Publishers Group West (PGW).

Aughe, Roger. Fun Lovin' Delanie Jo. Hildreth, Ruth Erixon. 2012. 36p. pap. 24.95 *(978-1-4626-7851-8(3))* America Star Bks.

—Nicholas James & Missy. Hildreth, Joann R. 2011. 28p. pap. 24.95 *(978-1-4626-0041-0(7))* America Star Bks.

Augst, Christie. The Goodnight Stone. Ball, Jared. 2019. (ENG.). 42p. (J). pap. 20.45 *(978-1-9736-5977-8(8)*, WestBow Pr.) Author Solutions, Inc.

Augusseau, Stphanie. Celia. Vallat, Christelle. 2014. 36p. pap. 16.99 *(978-1-4413-1536-6(5))* Peter Pauper Pr. Inc.

Auh, Yoonil. A Guide to Practicing Repertoire: Level 1, 11 vols. Auh, Yoonil, photos by. 2003. 85p. (gr. k-12). pap. 135.00 *(978-1-882858-61-3(1))* Yoon-il Auh/Intrepid Pixels.

—A Guide to Practicing Repertoire: Level 2, 11 vols. Auh, Yoonil, photos by. 2003. 85p. (gr. k-12). pap. 135.00 *(978-1-882858-62-0(X))* Yoon-il Auh/Intrepid Pixels.

—Representation Music. Auh, Yoonil, photos by. 2003. 28p. (gr. k-12). pap., instr.'s gde. ed. 25.00 *(978-1-882858-55-2(7))* Yoon-il Auh/Intrepid Pixels.

—Representation Music: A New Approch to Creating Sound & Representing Music. Auh, Yoonil, photos by. 2003. 45p. (gr. k-12). pap. 17.00 *(978-1-882858-54-5(9))* Yoon-il Auh/Intrepid Pixels.

—Singing Hand: Study of Vibrato. Auh, Yoonil, photos by. 2003. (gr. k-12). 50p. pap. 16.00 *(978-1-882858-59-0(X))*; 45p. pap. 16.00 *(978-1-882858-60-6(3))* Yoon-il Auh/Intrepid Pixels.

Aukerman, Robert J. Dream Machine: A Growing Field Adventure. Hoog, Mark E. 2007. (Growing Field Adventure Ser.). (ENG.). 35p. (J). (gr. -1-3). 16.95 *(978-0-9770391-1-1(0)*, 5000) Growing Field Bks.

—Your Song: A Growing Field Adventure. Hoog, Mark. 2007. (ENG.). 43p. (J). (gr. -1-3). 16.95 *(978-0-9770391-2-8(9))* Growing Field Bks.

Auml, Ana. Thanksgiving Day in Canada. Lewicki, Krys Val. Date not set. 48p. (J). *(978-0-929141-42-8(3)*, Napoleon & Co.) Dundurn.

Aunt Judy. Chickens in the Know! Chickens of Different Occupations. Aunt Judy. 2007. 40p. (J). pap. 7.00 *(978-0-9780693-1-5(5))* McEwen, Judith A.

—Chickens on the Go! Chickens from different locations around the World. Aunt Judy. 2nd ed. 2006. 40p. (J). pap. 7.00 *(978-0-9780693-0-8(7))* McEwen, Judith A.

Aureliani, Franco. Aw Yeah Comics Volume 2: Time for.... Adventure! Vol. 2. Baltazar, Art. 2015. (Aw Yeah Comics Ser.: 2). (ENG.). 168p. (J). (gr. 3-7). pap. 12.99 *(978-1-61655-689-1(7))* Dark Horse Comics.

—Dino-Mike & the Museum Mayhem. 2015. (J). lib. bdg. *(978-1-4062-9391-3(1)*, Stone Arch Bks.) Capstone.

Aureliani, Franco. Dino-Mike & the Dinosaur Cove. Aureliani, Franco. 2016. (Dino-Mike! Ser.). (ENG.). 128p. (J). (gr. 2-3). lib. bdg. 25.32 *(978-1-4965-2490-4(X)*, 130422, Stone Arch Bks.) Capstone.

—Dino-Mike & the Jurassic Portal. Aureliani, Franco. 2015. (Dino-Mike! Ser.). (ENG.). 128p. (J). (gr. 2-3). lib. bdg. 25.32 *(978-1-4342-9630-6(X)*, Stone Arch Bks.) Capstone.

—Dino-Mike & the Living Fossils. Aureliani, Franco. 2016. (Dino-Mike! Ser.). (ENG.). 128p. (J). (gr. 2-3). lib. bdg. 25.32 *(978-1-4965-2489-8(6)*, Stone Arch Bks.) Capstone.

—Dino-Mike & the T. Rex Attack. Aureliani, Franco. 2015. (Dino-Mike! Ser.). (ENG.). 128p. (J). (gr. 2-3). lib. bdg. 25.32 *(978-1-4342-9627-6(X)*, Stone Arch Bks.) Capstone.

—Dino-Mike & the Underwater Dinosaurs. Aureliani, Franco. 2015. (Dino-Mike! Ser.). (ENG.). 128p. (J). (gr. 2-3). lib. bdg. 25.32 *(978-1-4342-9629-0(6)*, Stone Arch Bks.) Capstone.

—Superman of Smallville. Aureliani, Franco. Baltazar, Art. 2019. 128p. (J). (gr. 2). pap. 9.99 *(978-1-4012-8392-6(6)*, DC Zoom) DC Comics.

Aureliani, Franco & Garcia, Eduardo. Dino-Mike & Dinosaur Doomsday. Aureliani, Franco. 2016. (Dino-Mike! Ser.). (ENG.). 128p. (J). (gr. 2-3). lib. bdg. 25.32 *(978-1-4965-2491-1(8)*, Stone Arch Bks.) Capstone.

Aureliani, Franco, jt. illus. see Baltazar, Art.

Auriemma, Monica. Collins Big Cat Phonics for Letters & Sounds - the Elf & the Bootmaker: Band 05/Green, Bd. 5. Milford, Alison. 2018. (Collins Big Cat Phonics Ser.). (ENG.). 24p. (J). (gr. k-1). pap. 8.99 *(978-0-00-825166-6(5))* HarperCollins Pubs. Ltd. GBR. Dist: Independent Pubs. Group.

Aussel, Jean-Paul. Oh la la! Level 2 Workbook: 2 Cahier D'Exercises. Favret, Catherine et al. 2004. (FRE.). (J). (gr. 4-7). pap. *(978-2-09-033626-9(9))* Creations loisirs enseignement International.

Austen, Chuck, jt. illus. see Hernandez, Lea.

Austen, Terry. Finn Saves the Day Orange Band. Bodman, Sue & Franklin, Glen F. 2017. (Cambridge Reading Adventures Ser.). (ENG.). 16p. (J). pap. 5.62 *(978-1-108-43977-0(2))* Cambridge Univ. Pr.

Austin, Antoinette & Wooten, Neal. The Little Lobo Who Lost His Howl. Austin, Antoinette & Austin, John. 2008.Tr. of lobito Que. (ENG & SPA.). 32p. (J). pap. 8.99 *(978-0-9817521-6-7(0))* Mirror Publishing.

Austin, Cassie Rita. Peppermint. Austin, Cassie Rita. 2011. 53p. 15.95 *(978-0-9846151-1-7(3))* Paintbrush Tales Publishing, LLC.

Austin, Heather. Many Hands: A Penobscot Indian Story. Perrow, Angeli. 2011. (ENG.). 32p. (J). (gr. -1-3). pap. 10.95 *(978-1-60893-014-2(9))* Down East Bks.

Austin, Heather. Boatyard Ducklings. Austin, Heather. ed. 2008. (ENG.). 32p. (J). (gr. -1-3). 15.95 *(978-0-89272-663-9(6))* Down East Bks.

Austin, Michael. Horned Toad Prince. Hopkins, Jackie Mims. 2010. (ENG.). (J). (gr. k-3). lib. bdg. 18.55 *(978-1-61383-069-7(6))* Perfection Learning Corp.

—Martina the Beautiful Cockroach: A Cuban Folktale, 1 vol. Deedy, Carmen Agra. (ENG.). 32p. (J). 2014. (gr. -1-3). pap. 8.95 *(978-1-56145-787-8(6))*; 2007. (gr. k-3). 16.95 *(978-1-56145-399-3(4))* Peachtree Publishing Co. Inc.

—Martina una Cucarachita Muy Linda: Un Cuento Cubano, 1 vol. Deedy, Carmen Agra. (SPA.). 32p. (J). 2010. pap. 8.95 *(978-1-56145-532-4(6))*; 2007. 17.95 *(978-1-56145-425-9(7))* Peachtree Publishing Co. Inc.

—Railroad John & the Red Rock Run, 1 vol. Crunk, Tony. 2006. (ENG.). 32p. (J). (gr. k-3). 16.95 *(978-1-56145-363-4(3))* Peachtree Publishing Co. Inc.

Austin, Michael Allen. Cowpoke Clyde & Dirty Dawg. Mortensen, Lori. 2013. (ENG.). 32p. (J). (gr. -1-3). 16.99 *(978-0-547-23993-4(9)*, 1098579) Houghton Mifflin Harcourt Publishing Co.

—Cowpoke Clyde Rides the Range. Mortensen, Lori. 2016. (ENG.). 32p. (J). (gr. -1-3). 16.99 *(978-0-544-37030-2(9)*, 1596763) Houghton Mifflin Harcourt Publishing Co.

—Hissy Fitz. Jennings, Patrick. (ENG.). 128p. (J). (gr. 2-4). 2017. 7.99 *(978-1-5124-4145-1(7)*, 9781512441451); 2015. E-Book 27.99 *(978-1-5124-0137-0(4))* Lerner Publishing Group. (Carolrhoda Bks.).

—Seven Rules You Absolutely Must Not Break If You Want to Survive the Cafeteria. Grandits, John. 2017. (ENG.). 32p. (J). (gr. 1-4). 16.99 *(978-0-544-69951-9(3)*, 1627721, Clarion Bks.) Houghton Mifflin Harcourt Trade & Reference Pubs.

—Ten Rules You Absolutely Must Not Break If You Want to Survive the School Bus. Grandits, John. 2018. (ENG.). 32p. (J). (gr. 1-4). pap. 7.99 *(978-1-328-50017-5(9)*, 1717896, HMH Books For Young Readers) Houghton Mifflin Harcourt Publishing Co.

Austin, Mike. Henny, Penny, Lenny, Denny, & Mike. Rylant, Cynthia. 2017. (ENG.). 40p. (J). (gr. -1-4). 17.99 *(978-1-4814-4523-8(5)*, Beach Lane Bks.) Beach Lane Bks.

—The Hidden: A Compendium of Arctic Giants, Dwarves, Gnomes, Trolls, Faeries & Other Strange Beings from Inuit Oral History, 1 vol. Christopher, Neil. 2014. (ENG.). 194p. (YA). (gr. 7). 29.95 *(978-1-927095-59-1(X))* Inhabit Media Inc. CAN. Dist: Consortium Bk. Sales & Distribution.

—Nellie Belle. Fox, Mem. 2015. (ENG.). 32p. (J). (gr. -1-3). 17.99 *(978-1-4169-9005-5(4)*, Beach Lane Bks.) Beach Lane Bks.

—Summer Supper. Pfeffer, Rubin. 2018. 40p. (J). (gr. -1-2). 17.99 *(978-1-5247-1464-2(X))*; (ENG.). lib. bdg. 20.99 *(978-1-5247-1465-9(8))* Random Hse. Children's Bks. (Random Hse. Bks. for Young Readers).

Austin, Mike. Junkyard. Austin, Mike. 2014. (ENG.). 40p. (J). (gr. -1-3). 16.99 *(978-1-4424-5961-8(1)*, Beach Lane Bks.) Beach Lane Bks.

—Monsters Love Colors. Austin, Mike. 2013. (ENG.). 40p. (J). (gr. -1-3). 15.99 *(978-0-06-212594-1(X))* HarperCollins Pubs.

—Monsters Love School. Austin, Mike. 2014. (ENG.). 40p. (J). (gr. -1-3). 15.99 *(978-0-06-228618-5(8))* HarperCollins Pubs.

Austin, Nan. Back in My Day. Austin, Nan. 2019. (ENG.). 26p. (J). pap. 9.49 *(978-0-9600409-2-6(7))* Austin, Nanette.

—The Gingerbread Man: The Adventures of a Remarkable Cookie. Austin, Nan. 2018. (ENG.). 26p. (J). pap. 9.22 *(978-0-9600409-0-2(0))* Austin, Nanette.

Austin, Nan. Origami Salami Goes to School. Austin, Nan. 2020. (ENG.). 28p. (J). pap. 9.33 ***(978-0-9600409-4-0(3))*** Austin, Nanette.

Austin, Richard, photos by. Pocket Piggies Colors! Featuring the Teacup Pigs of Pennywell Farm. 2014. (ENG., 22p. (J). bds. 5.95 *(978-0-7611-7980-1(1)*, 17980) Workman Publishing Co., Inc.

—Pocket Piggies Numbers! Featuring the Teacup Pigs of Pennywell Farm. 2014. (ENG., 22p. (J). bds. 5.95 *(978-0-7611-7979-5(8)*, 17979) Workman Publishing Co., Inc.

—Pocket Piggies Opposites! Featuring the Teacup Pigs of Pennywell Farm. 2016. (ENG., 22p. (J). (gr. -1 — 1). bds. 5.95 *(978-0-7611-8548-2(8)*, 18548) Workman Publishing Co., Inc.

Austin, Tereasa. Grandpa's Woods. McDaniel, Paula. 2008. 44p. pap. 24.95 *(978-1-60474-465-1(0))* America Star Bks.

Austin, Terry & Blevins, Bret. Balance of Power, 1 vol. McCLOUD, Scott. 2013. (Superman Adventures Ser.). (ENG.). 32p. (J). (gr. 2-5). lib. bdg. 22.60 *(978-1-4342-4710-0(4)*, Stone Arch Bks.) Capstone.

Austin, Terry & Burchett, Rick. A Big Problem!, 1 vol. McCLOUD, Scott. 2013. (Superman Adventures Ser.). (ENG.). 32p. (J). (gr. 2-5). lib. bdg. 22.60 *(978-1-4342-4709-4(0)*, Stone Arch Bks.) Capstone.

—Seonimod, 1 vol. McCLOUD, Scott. 2013. (Superman Adventures Ser.). (ENG.). 32p. (J). (gr. 2-5). lib. bdg. 22.60 *(978-1-4342-4711-7(2)*, Stone Arch Bks.) Capstone.

Austin, Terry, jt. illus. see Burchett, Rick.

Austrew, Neva. Daddy's Girl. Jacobs, Breena. ed. 2006. 32p. (J). (gr. -1-k). 15.95 *(978-0-9749423-2-2(4))* Bookworm Bks.

Auth, Dennis. Remember This. Riggs, Jenny Oates. 2017. (ENG.). 34p. (J). (gr. -1-3). 20.95 *(978-1-947860-01-8(1)*, Belle Isle Bks.) Brandylane Pubs., Inc.

—Remembering for Both of Us: A Child Learns about Alzheimer's. Wood, Charlotte B. 2014. 32p. (J). (gr. k-3). 18.95 *(978-1-939930-38-5(3))* Brandylane Pubs., Inc.

Auth, Tony. The Hoboken Chicken Emergency. Pinkwater, Daniel M. 2007. (ENG.). 112p. (J). (gr. 2-4). 17.44 *(978-1-4169-2809-6(X))* Simon & Schuster, Inc.

—The Hoboken Chicken Emergency. Pinkwater, Daniel M. 2007. (ENG.). 112p. (J). (gr. 1-4). pap. 6.99 *(978-1-4169-2810-2(3)*, Aladdin) Simon & Schuster Children's Publishing.

—Uncle Pirate. Rees, Douglas. (ENG.). 112p. (J). (gr. 2-5). 2009. pap. 6.99 *(978-1-4169-4763-9(9))*; 2008. 15.99 *(978-1-4169-4762-2(0))* McElderry, Margaret K. Bks. (McElderry, Margaret K. Bks.).

—Uncle Pirate to the Rescue. Rees, Douglas. 2010. (ENG.). 112p. (J). (gr. 2-5). pap. 6.99 *(978-1-4169-7505-2(5)*, McElderry, Margaret K. Bks.) McElderry, Margaret K. Bks.

Autumn Publishing Staff. ABC Learning. 2004. (Wall Charts Ser.). (J). pap. 4.99 *(978-1-85997-302-8(7))* Byeway Bks.

—Adding Up. 2004. (Wall Charts Ser.). (J). pap. 4.99 *(978-1-85997-319-6(1))* Byeway Bks.

—Counting to 20. Byeway Wall Charts Staff. 2004. (Wall Charts Ser.). (J). pap. 4.99 *(978-1-85997-282-3(9))* Byeway Bks.

—Learn the Alphabet. 2004. (Wall Charts Ser.). (J). pap. 4.99 *(978-1-85997-290-8(X))* Byeway Bks.

—My Skeleton. 2004. (Wall Charts Ser.). (J). pap. 4.99 *(978-1-85997-268-7(3))* Byeway Bks.

—Numbers 1-100. 2004. (Wall Charts Ser.). (J). pap. 4.99 *(978-1-85997-285-4(3))* Byeway Bks.

—Solar System. 2004. (Wall Charts Ser.). (J). pap. 4.99 *(978-1-85997-257-1(8))* Byeway Bks.

—Times Table Wall Chart. 2004. (Wall Charts Ser.). (J). pap. 4.99 *(978-1-85997-114-7(8))* Byeway Bks.

—World Map. 2004. (Wall Charts Ser.). (J). pap. 4.99 *(978-1-85997-235-9(7))* Byeway Bks.

—World of Flags. 2004. (Wall Charts Ser.). (J). pap. 4.99 *(978-1-85997-277-9(2))* Byeway Bks.

Auzary-Luton, Sylvie. Going Batty! Special Glow-in-the-Dark Surprise Pictures. Auzary-Luton, Sylvie. Pottie, Marjolein. 2005. 32p. (J). 15.95 *(978-0-689-04635-3(9)*, Milk & Cookies) ibooks, Inc.

Avakyan, Tatevik. Battle of the Best Friends. Dadey, Debbie. 2012. (Mermaid Tales Ser.: 2). (ENG.). 112p. (J). (gr. 1-4). 18.99 *(978-1-4424-4979-4(9))*; pap. 5.99 *(978-1-4424-2982-6(8))* Simon & Schuster Children's Publishing. (Aladdin).

—Battle of the Best Friends, Bk. 2. Dadey, Debby & Dadey, Debbie. 2015. (Mermaid Tales Ser.). (ENG.). 104p. (J). (gr. 1-4). 27.07 *(978-1-61479-323-6(9)*, 17145, Chapter Bks.) Spotlight.

—Believe Me, Goldilocks Rocks! The Story of the Three Bears As Told by Baby Bear. Loewen, Nancy. (Other Side of the Story Ser.). (ENG.). 24p. (J). (gr. -1-3). 2013. 9.95 *(978-1-4795-1939-2(1))*; 2011. pap. 6.95 *(978-1-4048-7044-4(X))* Capstone. (Picture Window Bks.).

—Believe Me, Goldilocks Rocks! The Story of the Three Bears as Told by Baby Bear. Loewen, Nancy. 2011. (Other Side of the Story Ser.). (ENG.). 24p. (J). (gr. -1-3). lib. bdg. 27.99 *(978-1-4048-6672-0(8)*, Picture Window Bks.) Capstone.

—Books vs. Looks. Dadey, Debbie. 2016. (Mermaid Tales Ser.: 15). (ENG.). 128p. (J). (gr. 1-4). pap. 5.99 *(978-1-4814-4081-3(0)*, Aladdin) Simon & Schuster Children's Publishing.

—Books vs. Looks. Dadey, Debbie. 2016. (Mermaid Tales Ser.: 15). (ENG.). 128p. (J). (gr. 1-4). 16.99 *(978-1-4814-4082-0(9)*, Simon & Schuster/Paula Wiseman Bks.) Simon & Schuster/Paula Wiseman Bks.

—Créeme, ¡Ricitos Es Genial! El Cuento de Los Tres Osos Contado Por Bebé Oso. Loewen, Nancy. (Otro Lado Del Cuento Ser.).Tr. of Believe Me, Goldilocks Rocks!. (SPA.). 24p. (J). (gr. -1-3). 2020. pap. 6.95 *(978-1-5158-6089-1(2)*, 142363); 2019. lib. bdg. 27.99 *(978-1-5158-4650-5(4)*, 141251) Capstone. (Picture Window Bks.).

—The Crook & the Crown. Dadey, Debbie. 2015. (Mermaid Tales Ser.: 13). (ENG.). 128p. (J). (gr. 1-4). pap. 5.99 *(978-1-4814-4075-2(6)*, Aladdin) Simon & Schuster Children's Publishing.

—The Crook & the Crown: Book 13. Dadey, Debbie. 2018. (Mermaid Tales Ser.). (ENG.). 120p. (J). (gr. 1-4). lib. bdg. 27.07 *(978-1-5321-4210-9(2)*, 31086, Chapter Bks.) Spotlight.

—Danger in the Deep Blue Sea. Dadey, Debbie. 2013. (Mermaid Tales Ser.: 4). (ENG.). 112p. (J). (gr. 1-4). 17.99 *(978-1-4424-5319-7(2))*; pap. 5.99 *(978-1-4424-2986-4(0))* Simon & Schuster Children's Publishing. (Aladdin).

—Danger in the Deep Blue Sea, Bk. 4. Dadey, Debby & Dadey, Debbie. 2015. (Mermaid Tales Ser.). (ENG.). 104p. (J). (gr. 1-4). 27.07 *(978-1-61479-325-0(5)*, 17147, Chapter Bks.) Spotlight.

—Dream of the Blue Turtle. Dadey, Debbie. 2014. (Mermaid Tales Ser.: 7). (ENG.). 128p. (J). (gr. 1-4). 16.99 *(978-1-4424-8264-7(8))*; pap. 5.99 *(978-1-4424-8263-0(X))* Simon & Schuster Children's Publishing. (Aladdin).

—Dream of the Blue Turtle, Bk. 7. Dadey, Debby & Dadey, Debbie. 2015. (Mermaid Tales Ser.). (ENG.). 112p. (J). (gr. 1-4). 27.07 *(978-1-61479-328-1(X)*, 17150, Chapter Bks.) Spotlight.

—Eat a Rainbow: Healthy Foods, 1 vol. Kesselring, Susan. 2012. (Move & Get Healthy! Ser.). (ENG.). 32p. (J). (gr. k-4). 28.50 *(978-1-61641-858-8(3)*, 11647, Looking Glass Library) Magic Wagon.

—Fairy Chase. Dadey, Debbie. 2018. (Mermaid Tales Ser.: 18). (ENG.). 112p. (J). (gr. 1-4). 17.99 *(978-1-4814-8712-2(4))*; pap. 5.99 *(978-1-4814-8711-5(6))* Simon & Schuster Children's Publishing. (Aladdin).

—Flower Girl Dreams. Dadey, Debbie. 2017. (Mermaid Tales Ser.: 16). (ENG.). 128p. (J). (gr. 1-4). pap. 5.99 *(978-1-4814-4084-4(5)*, Simon & Schuster/Paula Wiseman Bks.) Simon & Schuster/Paula Wiseman Bks.

—Get Moving in the City, 1 vol. Heron, Jackie. 2012. (Move & Get Healthy! Ser.). (ENG.). 32p. (J). (gr. k-4). 28.50 *(978-1-61641-859-5(1)*, 11649, Looking Glass Library) Magic Wagon.

—Get Moving with Friends & Family, 1 vol. Higgins, Nadia. 2012. (Move & Get Healthy! Ser.). (ENG.). 32p. (J). (gr. k-4). 28.50 *(978-1-61641-860-1(5)*, 11651, Looking Glass Library) Magic Wagon.

—Grow a Garden: Sustainable Foods, 1 vol. Kesselring, Susan. 2012. (Move & Get Healthy! Ser.). (ENG.). 32p. (J). (gr. k-4). 28.50 *(978-1-61641-861-8(3)*, 11653, Looking Glass Library) Magic Wagon.

—Let's Move in the Outdoors, 1 vol. Heron, Jackie. 2012. (Move & Get Healthy! Ser.). (ENG.). 32p. (J). (gr. k-4). 28.50 *(978-1-61641-862-5(1)*, 11655, Looking Glass Library) Magic Wagon.

—The Lost Princess. Dadey, Debbie. 2013. (Mermaid Tales Ser.: 5). (ENG.). 128p. (J). (gr. 1-4). 17.99 *(978-1-4424-8258-6(3))*; pap. 5.99 *(978-1-4424-8257-9(5))* Simon & Schuster Children's Publishing. (Aladdin).

—Lost Princess, Bk. 5. Dadey, Debbie. 2015. (Mermaid Tales Ser.). (ENG.). 120p. (J). (gr. 1-4). 27.07 *(978-1-61479-326-7(3)*, 17148, Chapter Bks.) Spotlight.

—Mermaid Tales, 8 vols., Set. Dadey, Debbie. 2015. (Mermaid Tales Ser.: Vol. 8). (ENG.). 96p. (J). (gr. 1-4). 216.56 *(978-1-61479-321-2(2)*, 17143, Chapter Bks.) Spotlight.

—Mermaid Tales 4-Books-In-1! Trouble at Trident Academy; Battle of the Best Friends; a Whale of a Tale; Danger in the Deep Blue Sea. Dadey, Debbie. 2016. (Mermaid Tales Ser.). (ENG.). 416p. (J). (gr. 1-4). 14.99 *(978-1-4814-7592-1(4)*, Aladdin) Simon & Schuster Children's Publishing.

—Mermaid Tales Sea-Tacular Collection Books 1-10: Trouble at Trident Academy; Battle of the Best Friends; a Whale of a Tale; Danger in the Deep Blue Sea; the Lost Princess; the Secret Sea Horse; Dream of the Blue Turtle; Treasure in Trident City; a Royal Tea; a Tale of Two Sisters. Dadey, Debbie. ed. 2019. (Mermaid Tales Ser.). (ENG.). 1200p. (J). (gr. 1-4). pap. 59.99 *(978-1-5344-5580-1(9)*, Aladdin) Simon & Schuster Children's Publishing.

—A Mermaid Tales Sparkling Collection: Trouble at Trident Academy; Battle of the Best Friends; a Whale of a Tale; Danger in the Deep Blue Sea; the Lost Princess. Dadey, Debbie. ed. 2013. (Mermaid Tales Ser.). (ENG.). 592p. (J). (gr. 1-4). pap. 29.99 *(978-1-4814-0055-8(X)*, Aladdin) Simon & Schuster Children's Publishing.

—The Narwhal Problem. Dadey, Debbie. 2019. (Mermaid Tales Ser.: 19). (ENG.). 112p. (J). (gr. 1-4). 17.99 *(978-1-4814-8715-3(9))*; pap. 5.99 *(978-1-4814-8714-6(0))* Simon & Schuster Children's Publishing. (Aladdin).

Avakyan, Tatevik, et al. The Other Side of the Story. Loewen, Nancy et al. 2013. (Other Side of the Story Ser.). (ENG.). 24p. (J). (gr. -1-3). 99.50 *(978-1-4795-2007-7(1)*, Picture Window Bks.) Capstone.

Avakyan, Tatevik. El Otro Lado Del Cuento. Loewen, Nancy. 2019. (Otro Lado Del Cuento Ser.).Tr. of Other Side of the Story. (SPA.). (J). (gr. -1-3). 111.96 *(978-1-5158-4688-8(1)*, 29724); pap., pap., pap. 27.80 ***(978-1-5158-6113-3(9)***, 30110) Capstone. (Picture Window Bks.).

—The Polar Bear Express. Dadey, Debbie. 2015. (Mermaid Tales Ser.: 11). (ENG.). 128p. (J). (gr. 1-4). pap. 5.99 *(978-1-4814-0260-6(9)*, Aladdin) Simon & Schuster Children's Publishing.

—The Polar Bear Express: Book 11. Dadey, Debbie. 2018. (Mermaid Tales Ser.). (ENG.). 112p. (J). (gr. 1-4). lib. bdg. 27.07 *(978-1-5321-4208-6(0)*, 31084, Chapter Bks.) Spotlight.

—Ready, Set, Goal! Dadey, Debbie. 2017. (Mermaid Tales Ser.: 17). (ENG.). 112p. (J). (gr. 1-4). 16.99 *(978-1-4814-8709-2(4))*; pap. 5.99 *(978-1-4814-8708-5(6))* Simon & Schuster Children's Publishing. (Aladdin).

—A Royal Tea: Book 9. Dadey, Debbie. 2018. (Mermaid Tales Ser.). (ENG.). 104p. (J). (gr. 1-4). lib. bdg. 27.07 *(978-1-5321-4206-2(4)*, 31082, Chapter Bks.) Spotlight.

—The Secret Sea Horse. Dadey, Debbie. 2013. (Mermaid Tales Ser.: 6). (ENG.). 112p. (J). (gr. 1-4). 15.99 *(978-1-4424-8261-6(3))*; pap. 5.99 *(978-1-4424-8260-9(5))* Simon & Schuster Children's Publishing. (Aladdin).

—Secret Sea Horse, Bk. 6. Dadey, Debby & Dadey, Debbie. 2015. (Mermaid Tales Ser.). (ENG.). 96p. (J). (gr. 1-4). 27.07 *(978-1-61479-327-4(1)*, 17149, Chapter Bks.) Spotlight.

—A Tale of Two Sisters. Dadey, Debbie. 2015. (Mermaid Tales Ser.: 10). (ENG.). 128p. (J). (gr. 1-4). 17.99 *(978-1-4814-0258-3(7))*; pap. 5.99 *(978-1-4814-0257-6(9))* Simon & Schuster Children's Publishing. (Aladdin).

—A Tale of Two Sisters: Book 10. Dadey, Debbie. 2018. (Mermaid Tales Ser.). (ENG.). 112p. (J). (gr. 1-4). lib. bdg. 27.07 *(978-1-5321-4207-9(2)*, 31083, Chapter Bks.) Spotlight.

—Treasure in Trident City. Dadey, Debbie. 2014. (Mermaid Tales Ser.: 8). (ENG.). 128p. (J). (gr. 1-4). pap. 5.99 *(978-1-4424-8266-1(4)*, Aladdin) Simon & Schuster Children's Publishing.

—Treasure in Trident City, Bk. 8. Dadey, Debby & Dadey, Debbie. 2015. (Mermaid Tales Ser.). (ENG.). 120p. (J). (gr. 1-4). 27.07 *(978-1-61479-329-8(8)*, 17151, Chapter Bks.) Spotlight.

—Trouble at Trident Academy. Dadey, Debbie. 2012. (Mermaid Tales Ser.: 1). (ENG.). 112p. (J). (gr. 1-4). 17.99 *(978-1-4424-4978-7(0))*; pap. 5.99 *(978-1-4424-2980-2(1))* Simon & Schuster Children's Publishing. (Aladdin).

—Trouble at Trident Academy, Bk. 1. Dadey, Debby & Dadey, Debbie. 2015. (Mermaid Tales Ser.). (ENG.). 104p. (J). (gr. 1-4). 27.07 *(978-1-61479-322-9(0)*, 17144, Chapter Bks.) Spotlight.

—Trouble at Trident Academy/Battle of the Best Friends: Mermaid Tales Flip Book #1-2. Dadey, Debbie. 2018. (Mermaid Tales Ser.). (ENG.). 208p. (J). (gr. 1-4). pap. 7.99 *(978-1-5344-2857-7(7)*, Aladdin) Simon & Schuster Children's Publishing.

—Twist & Shout. Dadey, Debbie. 2016. (Mermaid Tales Ser.: 14). (ENG.). 112p. (J). (gr. 1-4). pap. 5.99 *(978-1-4814-4078-3(0)*, Aladdin) Simon & Schuster Children's Publishing.

—Twist & Shout: Book 14. Dadey, Debbie. 2018. (Mermaid Tales Ser.). (ENG.). 96p. (J). (gr. 1-4). lib. bdg. 27.07 *(978-1-5321-4211-6(0)*, 31087, Chapter Bks.) Spotlight.

—A Whale of a Tale. Dadey, Debbie. 2012. (Mermaid Tales Ser.: 3). (ENG.). 128p. (J). (gr. 1-4). 14.99 *(978-1-4424-5318-0(4))*; pap. 5.99 *(978-1-4424-2984-0(4))* Simon & Schuster Children's Publishing. (Aladdin).

—Whale of a Tale, Bk. 3. Dadey, Debby & Dadey, Debbie. 2015. (Mermaid Tales Ser.). (ENG.). 120p. (J). (gr. 1-4). 27.07 *(978-1-61479-324-3(7)*, 17146, Chapter Bks.) Spotlight.

Avakyan, Tatevik. The Winter Princess. Dadey, Debbie. 2020. (Mermaid Tales Ser.: 20). (ENG.). 112p. (J). (gr. 1-4). 17.99 ***(978-1-4814-8718-4(3))***; pap. 5.99 ***(978-1-4814-8717-7(5))*** Simon & Schuster Children's Publishing. (Aladdin).

Avakyan, Tatevik. Wish upon a Starfish. Dadey, Debbie. 2015. (Mermaid Tales Ser.: 12). (ENG.). 128p. (J). (gr. 1-4). pap. 5.99 *(978-1-4814-0263-7(3)*, Aladdin) Simon & Schuster Children's Publishing.

—Wish upon a Starfish: Book 12. Dadey, Debbie. 2018. (Mermaid Tales Ser.). (ENG.). 112p. (J). (gr. 1-4). lib. bdg. 27.07 *(978-1-5321-4209-3(9)*, 31085, Chapter Bks.) Spotlight.

Avalon, Sherilyn Bridget. The Big We: We Are One Big Family. Avalon, Sherilyn Bridget. 2019. (ENG.). 34p. (J). (gr. k-6). pap. 12.00 *(978-0-9915700-5-8(7))* Place 33 Presses.

Avant, Matthew. Diamond & the Fosters. Weis, Michael David. 2013. 64p. 21.95 *(978-1-59663-635-4(1)*, Castle Keep Pr.) Rock, James A. & Co. Pubs.

Avash, Golam Ashfiqur Rahman. Zach's Train Adventure. Cassita, Z. Jay. 2019. (ENG.). 38p. (J). pap. 9.99 ***(978-1-6901-8918-3(5))*** Independently Published.

Avata, Tania. Hugs, Santa. Subbot, Nadia. 2018. (ENG.). 34p. (J). pap. 10.00 *(978-1-7904-0388-2(X))* Independently Published.

Aveira, Harry. Mimi's Adventure. Wheeler, Keith. 2nd ed. 2019. (Mimi's Adventure Ser.: Vol. 1). (ENG.). 28p. (J). pap. 12.99 *(978-1-950454-25-9(8))* Pen It! Pubns., LLC.

Avelino, Joelle. Dream a Rainbow. Penn, Carlotta. 2017. (ENG.). 30p. (J). pap. 12.00 *(978-0-9996613-0-7(2)*, Daydreamers Pr.) Penn, Carlotta.

Avellis, Adriana. The Umbilical Family: Start a Loving Conversation about Adoption, Egg Donation, Step-Parenting, Same Sex Parenting, & More. Sawyer, Cate. 2018. (ENG.). 30p. (J). pap. *(978-0-9871909-7-0(0))* Hawkeye Publishing Pty. Ltd.

Aven, Jamie H. Saints for Young Readers for Every Day, 2 vols., Vol. 1. Wallace, Susan F. S. P. & Wright, Melissa. 3rd ed. 2005. (J). pap. 15.95 *(978-0-8198-7081-0(1)*, 332-377) Pauline Bks. & Media.

—Saints for Young Readers for Every Day, 2 vols, Vol. 2. Wallace, Susan Helen & Wright, Melissa. 3rd ed. 2005. (J). pap. 15.95 *(978-0-8198-7082-7(X)*, 332-378) Pauline Bks. & Media.

Avendano, Dolores. The Joy of Giving. Testino, Mario et al, photos by. Farina von Buchwald, Martin & Prado Farina, Gabriela. 2005. 89p. (J). 18.00 *(978-0-9777266-0-8(6))* von Buchwald, Martin Farina.

Averbeck, Jim. Except If. Averbeck, Jim. 2011. (ENG.). 40p. (J). (gr. -1-3). 14.99 *(978-1-4169-9544-9(7)*, Atheneum Bks. for Young Readers) Simon & Schuster Children's Publishing.

—The Market Bowl. Averbeck, Jim. 2013. 32p. (J). (gr. -1-3). lib. bdg. 16.95 *(978-1-58089-368-8(6))* Charlesbridge Publishing, Inc.

—Oh No, Little Dragon! Averbeck, Jim. 2012. (ENG.). 40p. (J). (gr. -1-1). 14.99 *(978-1-4169-9545-6(5)*, Atheneum Bks. for Young Readers) Simon & Schuster Children's Publishing.

Averill, Esther. Captains of the City Streets. Averill, Esther. 2005. 164p. (J). (gr. 4-7). 18.95 *(978-1-59017-174-5(8)*, NYR Children's Collection) New York Review of Bks., Inc., The.

—The Hotel Cat. Averill, Esther. 2005. (Jenny's Cat Club Ser.). 180p. (J). (gr. k-4). 17.95 *(978-1-59017-159-2(4)*, NYR Children's Collection) New York Review of Bks., Inc., The.

—Jenny Goes to Sea. Averill, Esther. 2005. (Jenny's Cat Club Ser.). (ENG.). 140p. (J). (gr. k-4). reprint ed. 17.95 *(978-1-59017-155-4(1)*, NYR Children's Collection) New York Review of Bks., Inc., The.

—Jenny's Birthday Book. Averill, Esther. 2005. (Jenny's Cat Club Ser.). (ENG.). 44p. (J). (gr. -1-2). reprint ed. 16.95 *(978-1-59017-154-7(3)*, NYR Children's Collection) New York Review of Bks., Inc., The.

—Jenny's Moonlight Adventure: A Jenny's Cat Club Book. Averill, Esther. 2005. (Jenny's Cat Club Ser.). 32p. (J). (gr. -1-2). 14.95 *(978-1-59017-160-8(8)*, NYR Children's Collection) New York Review of Bks., Inc., The.

—The School for Cats. Averill, Esther. 2005. (Jenny's Cat Club Ser.). 32p. (J). (gr. -1-2). 14.95 *(978-1-59017-173-8(X)*, NYR Children's Collection) New York Review of Bks., Inc., The.

Averill, Esther H. Jenny & the Cat Club: A Collection of Favorite Stories about Jenny Linsky. Averill, Esther H. 2003. (Jenny's Cat Club Ser.). 176p. (J). (gr. k-4). 16.95 *(978-1-59017-047-2(4)*, NYR Children's Collection) New York Review of Bks., Inc., The.

Avery-Parkman, Grace. Spirits of the Northern Lights. Durocher, Skye. 2018. (ENG.). 44p. (J). *(978-1-5255-3236-8(7))*; pap. *(978-1-5255-3237-5(5))* FriesenPress.

Avery, Terry. Who Will Save Mr Squeaky? 2004. 29p. (J). *(978-1-929115-11-2(3))* Azro Pr., Inc.

Avi. Doña Flautina Resuelvelotodo. Avi, tr. Canetti, Yanitzia. (SPA.). 127p. (J). (gr. 2-3). 7.60 *(978-84-236-6130-5(X)*, ED31838) Edebé ESP. Dist: Lectorum Pubns., Inc.

Aviee, Laura. Top-Secret Grandad & Me: Death by Soup, 30 vols. MacPhail, David. 2018. (ENG.). 192p. (J). 9.95 *(978-1-78250-516-7(4)*, Kelpies) Floris Bks. GBR. Dist: Consortium Bk. Sales & Distribution.

—Top-Secret Grandad & Me: Death by Tumble Dryer, 28 vols. MacPhail, David. 2017. (ENG.). 176p. (J). 9.95 *(978-1-78250-426-9(5)*, Kelpies) Floris Bks. GBR. Dist: Consortium Bk. Sales & Distribution.

Avila, Jesus Villicana. A Thankful Day. Cerullo, Claudio V. 2008. 25p. pap. 24.95 *(978-1-60672-599-3(8))* America Star Bks.

Avila, Jorge, jt. illus. see Castro, Patricia.

Avilés Junco, Martha. Stones for Grandpa. Londner, Renee. 2013. 24p. (J). (gr. k-3). lib. bdg. 17.95 *(978-0-7613-7495-4(7)*, Kar-Ben Publishing) Lerner Publishing Group.

Avilés, Martha. Abuelita Full of Life: Abuelita llena de Vida. Costales, Amy. 2007. (ENG, SPA & MUL.). 32p. (J). (gr. -1-3). 14.95 *(978-0-87358-914-7(9))* Cooper Square Publishing Llc.

Aviles, Martha. The Fiesta Dress: A Quinceanera Tale, 0 vols. McCormack, Caren McNelly. 2012. (ENG.). 42p. (J). (gr. k-4). pap. 9.99 *(978-0-7614-6236-1(8)*, 9780761462361, Two Lions) Amazon Publishing.

Avilés, Martha. Nonna's Hanukkah Surprise. Fisman, Karen. 2015. (ENG.). 32p. (J). (gr. -1-3). 17.99 *(978-1-4677-3476-9(4)*, Kar-Ben Publishing) Lerner Publishing Group.

—Say Hello, Lily. Lakritz, Deborah. 2010. (Jewish Identity Ser.). 32p. (J). (gr. -1-3). lib. bdg. 17.95 *(978-0-7613-4511-4(6)*, Kar-Ben Publishing) Lerner Publishing Group.

Aviles, Martha, jt. illus. see McCool, Lindsay Sarles.

Avilés, Martha Graciela. Don't Sneeze at the Wedding. Mayer, Pamela. ed. 2013. (ENG.). 32p. (J). (gr. k-3). E-Book 23.99 *(978-1-4677-1641-3(3)*, Kar-Ben Publishing) Lerner Publishing Group.

—The Shabbat Princess, Vol. Meltzer, Amy. 2011. (ENG.). 32p. (J). (gr. -1-2). pap. 7.95 *(978-0-7613-5106-1(X)*, 9780761351061, Kar-Ben Publishing) Lerner Publishing Group.

—Stones for Grandpa, Vol. Londner, Renee. 2013. (ENG.). 24p. (J). (gr. k-3). pap. 7.95 *(978-0-7613-7496-1(5)*, 9780761374961, Kar-Ben Publishing) Lerner Publishing Group.

Avison, Al, et al. Marvel Visionaries: Stan Lee. 2019. (ENG.). 336p. (YA). (gr. -1-17). pap. 34.99 *(978-1-302-91839-2(7))* Marvel Worldwide, Inc.

Avoltha. Marty's Crazy Adventures Galaxy Zone. Harrison, Christy. 2018. (Marty's Crazy Adventures Ser.: Vol. 2). (ENG.). 100p. (J). pap. 7.95 *(978-1-9840-0349-2(6))* CreateSpace Independent Publishing Platform.

Avril, Adeline. Peter, Apostle of Jesus: The Life of a Saint. Grebille, Boris. 2014. (ENG.). 36p. (J). (gr. 1-7). 14.99 *(978-1-58617-922-9(5))* Ignatius Pr.

—Who Is Jesus? His Life, His Land, His Time. Tertrais, Gaelle. 2018. (ENG.). 96p. (J). (gr. -1-4). pap. 16.99 *(978-1-62164-235-0(6))* Ignatius Pr.

Avril, Francois & Duffour, Jean-Pierre. Half & Half-People of the Caves. Surget, Alain & Hirsinger, Julien. 2008. 48p. (J). 9.95 *(978-1-60115-205-3(1))*; pap. 4.99 *(978-1-60115-206-0(X))* Treasure Bay, Inc.

Avril, Lynne. Amelia Bedelia 12-Book Boxed Set: Amelia Bedelia by the Dozen. Parish, Herman. 2019. (Amelia Bedelia Ser.). (ENG.). 1920p. (J). (gr. 1-5). pap. 59.99 *(978-0-06-293520-5(8)*, Greenwillow Bks.) HarperCollins Pubs.

—Amelia Bedelia 5-Minute Stories. Parish, Herman. 2020. (Amelia Bedelia Ser.). (ENG.). 192p. (J). (gr. -1-3). 12.99 *(978-0-06-296195-2(0)*, Greenwillow Bks.) HarperCollins Pubs.

—Amelia Bedelia & Friends #1: Amelia Bedelia & Friends Beat the Clock. Parish, Herman. 2019. (Amelia Bedelia & Friends Ser.: 1). (ENG.). 160p. (J). (gr. 1-5). 15.99 *(978-0-06-293518-2(6))*; 12.99 *(978-0-06-296181-5(0))*; pap. 5.99 *(978-0-06-293517-5(8))* HarperCollins Pubs. (Greenwillow Bks.).

—Amelia Bedelia & Friends #2: Amelia Bedelia & Friends the Cat's Meow. Parish, Herman. 2019. (Amelia Bedelia & Friends Ser.: 2). (ENG.). 160p. (J). (gr. 1-5). 15.99 *(978-0-06-293522-9(4))*; 12.99 *(978-0-06-296182-2(9))*;

A

pap. 5.99 (978-0-06-293521-2(6)) HarperCollins Pubs. (Greenwillow Bks.).

—Amelia Bedelia & Friends #3: Amelia Bedelia & Friends Arise & Shine. Parish, Herman. 2020. (Amelia Bedelia & Friends Ser.: 3). (ENG.). 160p. (J). (gr. 1-5). 15.99 (978-0-06-296184-6(5)); pap. 5.99 (978-0-06-296183-9(7)) HarperCollins Pubs. (Greenwillow Bks.).

Avril, Lynne. Amelia Bedelia & Friends #4: Amelia Bedelia & Friends Paint the Town. Parish, Herman. 2020. (Amelia Bedelia & Friends Ser.: 4). 160p. (J). (gr. 1-5). 15.99 **(978-0-06-296187-7(X))**; pap. 5.99 **(978-0-06-296186-0(1))** HarperCollins Pubs. (Greenwillow Bks.).

—Amelia Bedelia & Friends Chapter Book Boxed Set #1: All Boxed In [Books 1-4]. Parish, Herman. 2020. (Amelia Bedelia & Friends Ser.). 640p. (J). (gr. 1-5). pap. 23.96 **(978-0-06-302319-2(9)**, Greenwillow Bks.) HarperCollins Pubs.

Avril, Lynne. Amelia Bedelia Bind-Up: Books 1 And 2: Amelia Bedelia Means Business; Amelia Bedelia Unleashed. Parish, Herman. 2015. (Amelia Bedelia Ser.). (ENG.). 320p. (J). (gr. 1-5). 12.99 (978-0-06-240367-4(2), Greenwillow Bks.) HarperCollins Pubs.

—Amelia Bedelia by the Yard. Parish, Herman. 2016. (I Can Read Level 1 Ser.). (ENG.). 32p. (J). (gr. -1-3). pap. 4.99 (978-0-06-233427-5(1), Greenwillow Bks.) HarperCollins Pubs.

—Amelia Bedelia Chalks One Up. Parish, Herman. 2014. (I Can Read Level 1 Ser.). (ENG.). 32p. (J). (gr. -1-3). 16.99 (978-0-06-233422-0(0)); pap. 4.99 (978-0-06-233421-3(2)) HarperCollins Pubs. (Greenwillow Bks.).

—Amelia Bedelia Chapter Book #1: Amelia Bedelia Means Business. Parish, Herman. 2013. (Amelia Bedelia Ser.: No. 1). (ENG.). 160p. (J). (gr. 1-5). 15.99 (978-0-06-209497-1(1)); pap. 5.99 (978-0-06-209496-4(3)) HarperCollins Pubs. (Greenwillow Bks.).

—Amelia Bedelia Chapter Book #10: Amelia Bedelia Ties the Knot. Parish, Herman. 2016. (Amelia Bedelia Ser.). (ENG.). 160p. (J). (gr. 1-5). pap. 5.99 (978-0-06-233416-9(6), Greenwillow Bks.) HarperCollins Pubs.

—Amelia Bedelia Chapter Book 10-Book Box Set. Set. Parish, Herman. 2016. (Amelia Bedelia Ser.). (ENG.). 1600p. (J). (gr. 1-5). pap. 49.99 (978-0-06-256981-3(3), Greenwillow Bks.) HarperCollins Pubs.

—Amelia Bedelia Chapter Book #11: Amelia Bedelia Makes a Splash. Parish, Herman. 2017. (Amelia Bedelia Ser.). (ENG.). 160p. (J). (gr. 1-5). pap. 4.99 (978-0-06-265839-5(5), Greenwillow Bks.) HarperCollins Pubs.

—Amelia Bedelia Chapter Book #2: Amelia Bedelia Unleashed. Parish, Herman. 2013. (Amelia Bedelia Ser.: No. 2). (ENG.). 160p. (J). (gr. 1-5). pap. 5.99 (978-0-06-209499-5(8)); 2nd ed. 15.99 (978-0-06-209500-8(5)) HarperCollins Pubs. (Greenwillow Bks.).

—Amelia Bedelia Chapter Book #3: Amelia Bedelia Road Trip! Parish, Herman. 2013. (Amelia Bedelia Ser.: No. 3). (ENG.). 160p. (J). (gr. 1-5). 15.99 (978-0-06-209503-9(X)); pap. 5.99 (978-0-06-209502-2(1)) HarperCollins Pubs. (Greenwillow Bks.).

—Amelia Bedelia Chapter Book #4: Amelia Bedelia Goes Wild! Parish, Herman. 2014. (Amelia Bedelia Ser.: No. 4). (ENG.). 160p. (J). (gr. 1-5). 15.99 (978-0-06-209507-7(2)); pap. 5.99 (978-0-06-209506-0(4)) HarperCollins Pubs. (Greenwillow Bks.).

—Amelia Bedelia Chapter Book #5. Parish, Herman. 2014. (Amelia Bedelia Ser.). (ENG.). 160p. (J). (gr. 1-5). 9.99 (978-0-06-233399-5(2), Greenwillow Bks.) HarperCollins Pubs.

—Amelia Bedelia Chapter Book #5: Amelia Bedelia Shapes Up. Parish, Herman. 2014. (Amelia Bedelia Ser.). (ENG.). 160p. (J). (gr. 1-5). pap. 5.99 (978-0-06-233396-4(8), Greenwillow Bks.) HarperCollins Pubs.

—Amelia Bedelia Chapter Book #6: Amelia Bedelia Cleans Up. Parish, Herman. 2015. (Amelia Bedelia Ser.). (ENG.). 160p. (J). (gr. 1-5). pap. 5.99 (978-0-06-233400-8(X), Greenwillow Bks.) HarperCollins Pubs.

—Amelia Bedelia Chapter Book #6: Amelia Bedelia Cleans Up (POB) Parish, Herman. 2015. (Amelia Bedelia Ser.). (ENG.). 160p. (J). (gr. 1-5). 9.99 (978-0-06-233403-9(4), Greenwillow Bks.) HarperCollins Pubs.

—Amelia Bedelia Chapter Book #7: Amelia Bedelia Sets Sail. Parish, Herman. 2015. (Amelia Bedelia Ser.). (ENG.). 160p. (J). (gr. 1-5). 15.99 (978-0-06-233405-3(0)); pap. 5.99 (978-0-06-233404-6(2)) HarperCollins Pubs. (Greenwillow Bks.).

—Amelia Bedelia Chapter Book #8: Amelia Bedelia Dances Off. Parish, Herman. 2015. (Amelia Bedelia Ser.). (ENG.). 160p. (J). (gr. 1-5). 15.99 (978-0-06-233409-1(3)); pap. 5.99 (978-0-06-233408-4(5)) HarperCollins Pubs. (Greenwillow Bks.).

—Amelia Bedelia Chapter Book #9: Amelia Bedelia on the Job. Parish, Herman. 2016. (Amelia Bedelia Ser.). (ENG.). 160p. (J). (gr. 1-5). pap. 5.99 (978-0-06-233412-1(3), Greenwillow Bks.) HarperCollins Pubs.

—Amelia Bedelia Gets a Break. Parish, Herman. 2018. (I Can Read Level 1 Ser.). (ENG.). 32p. (J). (gr. -1-3). 16.99 (978-0-06-265889-0(1)); pap. 4.99 (978-0-06-265888-3(3)) HarperCollins Pubs. (Greenwillow Bks.).

—Amelia Bedelia Gets the Picture. Parish, Herman. 2019. (I Can Read Level 1 Ser.). (ENG.). 32p. (J). (gr. -1-3). 16.99 (978-0-06-293525-0(9)); pap. 4.99 (978-0-06-293524-3(0)) HarperCollins Pubs. (Greenwillow Bks.).

—Amelia Bedelia Hits the Trail. Parish, Herman. 2013. (I Can Read Level 1 Ser.). (ENG.). 32p. (J). (gr. -1-3). 16.99 (978-0-06-209527-5(7), Greenwillow Bks.) HarperCollins Pubs.

—Amelia Bedelia I Can Read Box Set #2: Books Are a Ball. Parish, Herman. 2017. (I Can Read Level 1 Ser.). (ENG.). 160p. (J). (gr. -1-3). pap. 19.99 (978-0-06-244357-1(7), Greenwillow Bks.) HarperCollins Pubs.

—Amelia Bedelia Is for the Birds. Parish, Herman. 2015. (I Can Read Level 1 Ser.). (ENG.). 32p. (J). (gr. -1-3). pap. 4.99 (978-0-06-233424-4(7), Greenwillow Bks.) HarperCollins Pubs.

—Amelia Bedelia Joins the Club. Parish, Herman. 2014. (I Can Read Level 1 Ser.). (ENG.). 32p. (J). (gr. -1-3). 16.99 (978-0-06-222131-5(0)); pap. 4.99 (978-0-06-222130-8(2)) HarperCollins Pubs. (Greenwillow Bks.).

—Amelia Bedelia Joins the Club. Parish, Herman. 2014. (I Can Read! - Level 1 (Quality) Ser.). (ENG.). (J). (gr. -1-3). lib. bdg. 14.60 (978-1-62765-422-7(4)) Perfection Learning Corp.

—Amelia Bedelia Makes a Friend. Parish, Herman. 2011. (I Can Read Level 1 Ser.). (ENG.). 32p. (J). (gr. k-3). 16.99 (978-0-06-207516-1(0)); pap. 4.99 (978-0-06-207515-4(2)) HarperCollins Pubs. (Greenwillow Bks.).

—Amelia Bedelia Means Business. Parish, Herman. ed. 2013. (Amelia Bedelia Chapter Book Ser.: 1). (J). lib. bdg. 14.75 (978-0-606-27137-0(6)) Turtleback.

—Amelia Bedelia on the Move. Parish, Herman. 2017. (I Can Read Level 1 Ser.). (ENG.). 32p. (J). (gr. -1-3). 16.99 (978-0-06-265886-9(7)); pap. 4.99 (978-0-06-265885-2(9)) HarperCollins Pubs. (Greenwillow Bks.).

—Amelia Bedelia Sleeps Over. Parish, Herman. 2012. (I Can Read Level 1 Ser.). (ENG.). 32p. (J). (gr. -1-3). 16.99 (978-0-06-209524-4(2)); pap. 4.99 (978-0-06-209523-7(4)) HarperCollins Pubs. (Greenwillow Bks.).

Avril, Lynne. Amelia Bedelia Special Edition Holiday Chapter Book #1: Amelia Bedelia Wraps It Up. Parish, Herman. 2020. (Amelia Bedelia Special Edition Holiday Ser.: 1). (ENG.). 160p. (J). (gr. 1-5). 15.99 **(978-0-06-296204-1(3)**, Greenwillow Bks.) HarperCollins Pubs.

Avril, Lynne. Amelia Bedelia Storybook Favorites: Includes 5 Stories Plus Stickers! Parish, Herman. 2019. (Amelia Bedelia Ser.). (ENG.). 192p. (J). (gr. -1-3). 13.99 (978-0-06-288301-8(1), Greenwillow Bks.) HarperCollins Pubs.

—Amelia Bedelia Storybook Treasury: Amelia Bedelia's First Day of School; Amelia Bedelia's First Field Trip; Amelia Bedelia Makes a Friend; Amelia Bedelia Sleeps over; Amelia Bedelia Hits the Trail. Parish, Herman. 2013. (ENG.). 192p. (J). (gr. -1-3). 11.99 (978-0-06-228714-4(1), Greenwillow Bks.) HarperCollins Pubs.

—Amelia Bedelia Takes the Cake. Parish, Herman. 2016. (I Can Read Level 1 Ser.). (ENG.). 32p. (J). (gr. -1-3). pap. 4.99 (978-0-06-233430-5(1), Greenwillow Bks.) HarperCollins Pubs.

—Amelia Bedelia Tries Her Luck. Parish, Herman. 2013. (I Can Read Level 1 Ser.). (ENG.). 32p. (J). (gr. -1-3). 16.99 (978-0-06-222128-5(0)); pap. 4.99 (978-0-06-222127-8(2)) HarperCollins Pubs. (Greenwillow Bks.).

—Amelia Bedelia under the Weather. Parish, Herman. 2018. (I Can Read Level 1 Ser.). (ENG.). 32p. (J). (gr. -1-3). 16.99 (978-0-06-265892-0(1)); pap. 4.99 (978-0-06-265891-3(3)) HarperCollins Pubs. (Greenwillow Bks.).

—Amelia Bedelia Unleashed. Parish, Herman. ed. 2013. (Amelia Bedelia Chapter Book Ser.: 2). (J). lib. bdg. 14.75 (978-0-606-27138-7(4)) Turtleback.

—Amelia Bedelia's First Apple Pie. Parish, Herman. (Amelia Bedelia Ser.). (ENG.). 32p. (J). (gr. -1-3). 2012. pap. 7.99 (978-0-06-196411-4(5)); 2010. 16.99 (978-0-06-196409-1(3)); 2010. lib. bdg. 17.89 (978-0-06-196410-7(7)) HarperCollins Pubs. (Greenwillow Bks.).

—Amelia Bedelia's First Day of School. Parish, Herman. (Amelia Bedelia Ser.). (ENG.). 32p. (J). (gr. -1-3). 2015. pap. 7.99 (978-0-06-154457-6(4)); 2011. 9.99 (978-0-06-203274-4(7)); 2009. 16.99 (978-0-06-154455-2(8)) HarperCollins Pubs. (Greenwillow Bks.).

—Amelia Bedelia's First Day of School Holiday. Parish, Herman. 2020. (Amelia Bedelia Ser.). 32p. (J). (gr. -1-3). 10.99 (978-0-06-298487-6(X), Greenwillow Bks.) HarperCollins Pubs.

—Amelia Bedelia's First Field Trip. Parish, Herman. (Amelia Bedelia Ser.). (ENG.). 32p. (J). (gr. -1-3). 2013. pap. 6.99 (978-0-06-196415-2(8)); 2011. 16.99 (978-0-06-196413-8(1)) HarperCollins Pubs. (Greenwillow Bks.).

—Amelia Bedelia's First Library Card. Parish, Herman. 2013. (Amelia Bedelia Ser.). (ENG.). 32p. (J). (gr. -1-3). 17.99 (978-0-06-209512-1(9), Greenwillow Bks.) HarperCollins Pubs.

—Amelia Bedelia's First Valentine. Parish, Herman. (Amelia Bedelia Ser.). (ENG.). 32p. (J). (gr. -1-3). 2014. pap. 7.99 (978-0-06-154460-6(4)); 2011. 9.99 (978-0-06-203275-1(5)); 2009. 16.99 (978-0-06-154458-3(2)) HarperCollins Pubs. (Greenwillow Bks.).

—Amelia Bedelia's First Vote. Parish, Herman. (Amelia Bedelia Ser.). 32p. (J). (gr. -1-3). 2020. pap. 6.99 (978-0-06-209407-0(6)); 2012. (ENG.). 16.99 (978-0-06-209405-6(X)); 2012. (ENG.). lib. bdg. 17.89 (978-0-06-209406-3(8)) HarperCollins Pubs. (Greenwillow Bks.).

—Every Cowgirl Loves a Rodeo. Janni, Rebecca. 2012. (Every Cowgirl Ser.). (ENG.). 32p. (J). (gr. -1-k). 17.99 (978-0-8037-3734-1(3), Dial Bks) Penguin Young Readers Group.

—Every Cowgirl Needs a Horse. Janni, Rebecca. 2010. (Every Cowgirl Ser.). 32p. (J). (gr. -1-k). 17.99 (978-0-525-42164-1(5), Dutton Books for Young Readers) Penguin Young Readers Group.

—Every Cowgirl Needs Dancing Boots. Janni, Rebecca. 2011. (Every Cowgirl Ser.). 32p. (J). (gr. -1-k). 17.99 (978-0-525-42341-6(9), Dutton Books for Young Readers) Penguin Young Readers Group.

—If I Ran for President. Stier, Catherine. 2007. (Albert Whitman Prairie Books Ser.). (ENG.). 32p. (J). (gr. 1-4). 18.80 (978-1-5311-7682-2(8)) Perfection Learning Corp.

—If I Ran for President. Stier, Catherine. 2012. (J). 34.28 (978-1-61913-115-6(3)) Weigl Pubs., Inc.

—If I Ran for President. Stier, Catherine. 2007. (ENG.). 32p. (J). (gr. -1-3). pap. 7.99 (978-0-8075-3544-8(3), 807535443) Whitman, Albert & Co.

—Love, Ruby Valentine. Friedman, Laurie. 2006. (Ruby Valentine Ser.). (ENG.). 32p. (J). (gr. k-3). lib. bdg. 16.95 (978-1-57505-899-3(5), Carolrhoda Bks.) Lerner Publishing Group.

—The No-Good Do-Good Pirates. Kraft, Jim. 2013. (AV2 Fiction Readalong Ser.). (ENG.). (J). (gr. k-3). 34.28 (978-1-62127-896-2(4), AV2 by Weigl) Weigl Pubs., Inc.

—The Pirate of Kindergarten. Lyon, George Ella. 2010. (ENG.). 40p. (J). (gr. -1-3). 18.99 (978-1-4169-5024-0(9), Atheneum/Richard Jackson Bks.) Simon & Schuster Children's Publishing.

—Ruby Valentine & the Sweet Surprise. Friedman, Laurie. 2014. (Ruby Valentine Ser.). (ENG.). 32p. (J). (gr. k-3). 16.95 (978-0-7613-8873-9(7), 9780761388739, Carolrhoda Bks.) Lerner Publishing Group.

—Ruby Valentine Saves the Day. Friedman, Laurie. 2010. (Ruby Valentine Ser.). (ENG.). 32p. (J). (gr. k-3). lib. bdg. 16.95 (978-0-7613-4213-7(3), 9780761342137, Carolrhoda Bks.) Lerner Publishing Group.

—Snowball Run: Pulleys. Harkrader, Lisa. 2018. (Science Solves It! ® Ser.). (ENG.). 32p. (J). (gr. 1-3). pap. 5.95 (978-1-63592-003-1(5)) Astra Publishing Hse.

—The Twelve Days of Christmas in Arizona. Stewart, Jennifer J. (Twelve Days of Christmas in America Ser.). (J). (-k). 2018. 22p. bds. 7.95 (978-1-4549-2994-9(4)); 2010. 40p. 12.95 (978-1-4027-7036-4(7)) Sterling Publishing Co., Inc.

—The Twelve Days of Christmas in Louisiana. Cassels, Jean. 2018. (Twelve Days of Christmas in America Ser.). 22p. (J). (-k). bds. 7.95 (978-1-4549-2964-2(2)) Sterling Publishing Co., Inc.

—Wagons Ho! Hallowell, George & Holub, Joan. 2014. (AV2 Fiction Readalong Ser.: Vol. 153). (ENG.). 32p. (J). (gr. -1-3). lib. bdg. 34.28 (978-1-4896-2389-8(2), AV2 by Weigl) Weigl Pubs., Inc.

—Wagons Ho! Hallowell, George & Holub, Joan. 2019. (ENG.). 32p. (J). (gr. -1-k). pap. 7.99 (978-0-8075-8613-6(7), 807586137) Whitman, Albert & Co.

Avril, Lynne, jt. illus. see Cravath, Lynne Avril.

Awadh, Shaila. Zara Likes To... Singh, Josynta. 2018. (ENG.). 20p. (J). pap. (978-0-646-59848-2(1)) Singh, Josynta.

Awes, Jennifer. It Takes a Lot of Love. Ambrosio, Michael. 2007. 32p. (J). 14.95 (978-0-9716085-4-2(7)) LionX Publishing.

Axelsen, Stephen. The Crown Affair. Ransom, Jeanie Franz. 2015. (Nursery-Rhyme Mysteries Ser.: 2). 32p. (J). (gr. 1-4). lib. bdg. 16.95 (978-1-58089-552-1(2)) Charlesbridge Publishing, Inc.

—What Really Happened to Humpty? Ransom, Jeanie Franz. 2010. (Nursery-Rhyme Mysteries Ser.: 1). (ENG.). 40p. (J). (gr. 1-4). pap. 7.95 (978-1-58089-391-6(0)) Charlesbridge Publishing, Inc.

Axelsen, Stephen, jt. illus. see Gamble, Kim.

Axt, Katie. Ant Farmers. Byerly, Wendy. 2016. (1B Bugs Ser.). (ENG.). 24p. (J). pap. 8.00 (978-1-61406-545-6(4)) American Reading Co.

Axtell, David. We're Going on a Lion Hunt. Axtell, David. 2007. (ENG.). 32p. (J). (gr. -1-1). 9.99 (978-0-8050-8219-7(0), 900041018) Square Fish.

Axworthy, Ani. Butterflies & Caterpillars. Ganeri, Anita. 2010. (Animal Families Ser.). (ENG.). 14p. (J). bds. 10.99 (978-1-84089-641-1(8)) Evans Brothers, Ltd. GBR. Dist: Independent Pubs. Group.

Axworthy, Ann. Butterflies & Caterpillars. Ganeri, Anita. 2012. (Animal Families Ser.). 24p. (J). (gr. -1-k). 12.79 (978-1-60753-097-8(X)) Amicus Publishing.

Axworthy, Anni. Frogs & Tadpoles. Ganeri, Anita. 2010. (Animal Families Ser.). (ENG.). 14p. (J). bds. 10.99 (978-1-84089-642-8(6)) Evans Brothers, Ltd. GBR. Dist: Independent Pubs. Group.

—An Old Red Hat. Langford, Jane. 2004. (ENG.). 24p. (J). lib. bdg. 23.65 (978-1-59646-676-0(6)) Dingles & Co.

—Sammy's Secret. Nash, Margaret. 2008. (Tadpoles Ser.). (ENG.). 24p. (J). (gr. -1-3). pap. (978-0-7787-3894-7(9)); lib. bdg. (978-0-7787-3863-3(9)) Crabtree Publishing Co.

Axworthy, Anni. The Dragon Who Couldn't Do Sporty Things. Axworthy, Anni. 2008. (Little Dragon Ser.). (ENG.). 32p. (J). (gr. -1-k). (978-1-84089-533-9(0)) Zero to Ten, Ltd.

—Dragon Who Couldn't Do Sporty Things. Axworthy, Anni. 2010. (Little Dragon Ser.). (ENG.). 32p. (J). (gr. -1-k). pap. (978-1-84089-556-8(X)) Zero to Ten, Ltd.

Axworthy, Anni & Miller, Mike. Madcap Book of Brain Teasers. Brandreth, Gyles. 288p. (J). pap. 6.95 (978-0-233-99568-7(4)) Andre Deutsch GBR. Dist: Trafalgar Square Publishing.

Aya, Choco. Dragon Goes House-Hunting Vol. 1. Tanuki, Kawo. 2018. (Dragon Goes House-Hunting Ser.: 1). (ENG.). 180p. (YA). pap. 12.99 (978-1-62692-885-5(1), 900195570) Seven Seas Entertainment, LLC.

—Dragon Goes House-Hunting Vol. 2. Tanuki, Kawo. 2019. (Dragon Goes House-Hunting Ser.: 2). (ENG.). 180p. (YA). pap. 12.99 (978-1-62692-979-1(3), 900197850) Seven Seas Entertainment, LLC.

Ayache, Avraham. Maharal to the Rescue. Mindel, Nissan. 2010. 67p. (YA). 10.95 (978-0-8266-0032-5(8)) Kehot Pubn. Society.

Ayagalria, Julia, et al. Animals of the River. Ayagalria, Julia et al. 2006. (Animal Story Collection Ser.). 24p. (J). (gr. 2-6). pap. 9.00 (978-1-58084-236-5(4)) Lower Kuskokwim Schl. District.

Ayala, Joseph. Little Cloud Upset. Hertkorn, Michaela C. 2010. 28p. pap. 14.95 (978-1-4389-9837-4(6)) AuthorHouse.

Ayalomeh, Shedrach. The Adventures of Nihu. Uwuigiaren, Omoruyi. 2007. 158p. (J). (gr. 2-8). 16.95 (978-1-934138-15-1(0)) Bouncing Ball Bks., Inc.

—A Visit to Grandad: an African ABC. Fadipe, Sade. 2019. (ENG.). 32p. (J). 16.95 (978-1-911115-81-6(2)) Cassava Republic Pr. GBR. Dist: Consortium Bk. Sales & Distribution.

Aycock, Daniel, et al. Undercover Operations. Mauro, Paul & Melton, H. Keith. 2004. (Detective Academy Ser.). 48p. (J). (978-0-439-57183-8(9)) Scholastic, Inc.

Aye, Nila. Drawing School: Learn to Draw More Than 250 Things! 2017. (ENG.). 256p. (J). (gr. 1-3). pap. 19.99 (978-1-63322-379-0(5), 225468, Walter Foster Jr) Quarto Publishing Group USA.

—Drawing School — Volume 1: Learn to Draw More Than 50 Cool Animals, Objects, People, & Figures! 2018. (Drawing School Ser.). (ENG.). 64p. (J). (gr. 2-5). lib. bdg. 33.32 (978-1-942875-65-9(7), Walter Foster Jr) Quarto Publishing Group USA.

—Drawing School — Volume 2: Learn to Draw More Than 50 Cool Animals, Objects, People, & Figures! 2018. (Drawing School Ser.). (ENG.). 64p. (J). (gr. 2-5). lib. bdg. 33.32 (978-1-942875-66-6(5), Walter Foster Jr) Quarto Publishing Group USA.

—Drawing School — Volume 3: Learn to Draw More Than 50 Cool Animals, Objects, People, & Figures! 2018. (Drawing School Ser.). (ENG.). 64p. (J). (gr. 2-5). lib. bdg. 33.32 (978-1-942875-67-3(3), Walter Foster Jr) Quarto Publishing Group USA.

—Drawing School — Volume 4: Learn to Draw More Than 50 Cool Animals, Objects, People, & Figures! 2018. (Drawing School Ser.). (ENG.). 64p. (J). (gr. 2-5). lib. bdg. 33.32 (978-1-942875-68-0(1), Walter Foster Jr) Quarto Publishing Group USA.

—Fearless Mirabelle & Meg. Haworth, Katie. 2019. (ENG.). 40p. (J). (gr. -1-2). 16.99 (978-1-5362-0811-5(6), Templar) Candlewick Pr.

Aye, Nila. Let's Go Apple Picking! Houran, Lori Haskins. 2020. (Little Golden Book Ser.). 24p. (J). (-k). 4.99 **(978-0-593-12325-6(5)**, Golden Bks.) Random Hse. Children's Bks.

Aye, Nila. Starry Skies: Learn about the Constellations above Us. Chagollan, Samantha. 2018. (ENG.). 32p. (J). (gr. -1-1). 17.95 (978-1-63322-509-1(7), Walter Foster Jr) Quarto Publishing Group USA.

—Sticker Stories: at the Zoo: Includes Stickers, Drawing Steps, & Scenes to Decorate! over 150 Stickers. 2019. (Sticker Stories Ser.). (ENG.). 24p. (J). (gr. -1-3). pap. 7.99 (978-1-63322-708-8(1), 307809, Walter Foster Jr) Quarto Publishing Group USA.

—Sticker Stories: in the Garden: Includes Stickers, Drawing Steps, & Scenes to Decorate! over 150 Stickers. 2019. (Sticker Stories Ser.). (ENG.). 24p. (J). (gr. -1-3). pap. 7.99 (978-1-63322-707-1(3), 307818, Walter Foster Jr) Quarto Publishing Group USA.

—Sticker Stories: under the Sea Escapades: Includes Stickers, Drawing Steps, & Scenes to Decorate! 2018. (Sticker Stories Ser.). (ENG.). 24p. (J). (gr. -1-3). pap. 8.95 (978-1-63322-669-2(7), Walter Foster Jr) Quarto Publishing Group USA.

—What Is a Family? Hames, Cassandra. Cottage Door Press, ed. 2019. (Love You Always Ser.). (ENG.). 18p. (J). (gr. -1-1). bds. 9.99 (978-1-68052-628-8(6), 1004210) Cottage Door Pr.

—What's for Lunch? Thomson, Sarah L. 2016. (Let's-Read-And-Find-Out Science 1 Ser.). (ENG.). 40p. (J). (gr. -1-3). pap. 6.99 (978-0-06-233137-3(X)) HarperCollins Pubs.

Ayers, Dick, et al. Marvel Universe by Chris Claremont Omnibus. 2017. (ENG.). 1144p. (YA). (gr. 8-17). 125.00 (978-1-302-90715-0(8)) Marvel Worldwide, Inc.

Ayers, Linda. My Pet Mosquito. Ayers, Linda. 2004. 45p. (J). per. 6.95 (978-0-9760505-1-3(X)) Blue Thistle Pr.

Ayers, Ryan. The Time Bridge Travelers, 3 bks., Bk. 1. Ayers, Linda. 56p. (J). 2006. 13.95 (978-0-9760505-8-2(7)); 2004. per. 7.95 (978-0-9760505-0-6(1)) Blue Thistle Pr.

—The Time Bridge Travelers & the Mysterious Map, 3 bks., Bk. 2. Ayers, Linda. l.t. ed. (Time Bridge Travelers Ser.: 2). 80p. (J). 2006. 13.95 (978-0-9760505-6-8(0)); 2005. per. 7.95 (978-0-9760505-3-7(6)) Blue Thistle Pr.

—The Time Bridge Travelers & the Time Travel Station, 3 bks., Bk. 3. Ayers, Linda. l.t. ed. 2007. (Time Bridge Travelers Ser.: 3). 140p. (J). lib. bdg. 16.95 (978-0-9786302-8-7(9)); per. 7.95 (978-0-9786302-7-0(0)) Blue Thistle Pr.

Ayesenberg, Nina. Emma's Airport Adventure. Ehlin, Gina. l.t. ed. 2005. (Emma & Friends Ser.). 34p. (J). 15.99 (978-1-59879-015-3(3)) Lifevest Publishing, Inc.

Aylesworth, Laurel. The Clues to Kusachuma. Ford, Adam B. 2018. (ENG.). 176p. (J). (gr. 4-6). 17.99 (978-1-7324594-0-3(1)); pap. 9.99 (978-1-7324594-1-0(X)) H Bar Pr.

Ayliffe, Alex. Dig Dig Digging. Mayo, Margaret. 2006. (ENG.). 24p. (J). (gr. -1-k). bds. 8.99 (978-0-8050-7985-2(8), 900034558, Holt, Henry & Co. Bks. For Young Readers) Holt, Henry & Co.

—Dig Dig Digging ABC. Mayo, Margaret. 2017. (ENG.). 32p. (J). 16.99 (978-1-62779-516-6(2), 900153368, Holt, Henry & Co. Bks. For Young Readers) Holt, Henry & Co.

—Emergency! Mayo, Margaret. 2003. 32p. (J). (gr. -1-1). 14.95 (978-0-87614-922-5(0), Carolrhoda Bks.) Lerner Publishing Group.

—Faraway Farm. Whybrow, Ian. 2006. (ENG.). 32p. (J). (gr. -1-2). lib. bdg. 15.95 (978-1-57505-938-9(X), Carolrhoda Bks.) Lerner Publishing Group.

—Looking High & Low for One Lost Sheep. Goodings, Christina. 2003. 32p. (J). pap. 9.99 (978-0-7459-4524-8(4), Lion Books) Lion Hudson PLC GBR. Dist: Trafalgar Square Publishing.

—Mini Tab: Dig Dig Digging. Mayo, Margaret. 2017. (ENG.). 14p. (J). bds. 6.99 (978-1-62779-714-6(9), 900158593, Holt, Henry & Co. Bks. For Young Readers) Holt, Henry & Co.

—My Very First Bible & Prayers, 2 vols. Rock, Lois. ed. 2011. (My Very First Ser.). (ENG.). 416p. (J). (gr. -1-k). 12.99

(978-0-7459-6186-6(X)) Lion Hudson PLC GBR. Dist: Independent Pubs. Group.

—My Very First Bible Stories Bumper Sticker Book, 1 vol. Rock, Lois. ed. 2013. (My Very First Sticker Bks.). (ENG.). 96p. (J). (gr. -1-k). 13.99 *(978-0-7459-6410-2(9))* Lion Hudson PLC GBR. Dist: Independent Pubs. Group.

—My Very First Nativity Story. Rock, Lois. 2015. (My Very First Ser.). (ENG.). 48p. (J). (gr. -1-k). 7.99 *(978-0-7459-6911-4(9))* Lion Hudson PLC GBR. Dist: Independent Pubs. Group.

—Roar! Mayo, Margaret. 2007. (Carolrhoda Picture Bks.). 32p. (J). (gr. -1-3). 15.95 *(978-0-7613-9473-0(7),* Carolrhoda Bks.) Lerner Publishing Group.

Aymez, Carla. Las Medidas del Tiempo. Kraselsky, Rebeca. rev. ed. 2006. (Otra Escalera Ser.). (ENG.). 48p. (J). (gr. 4). pap. 10.95 *(978-968-5920-80-3(X))* Castillo, Ediciones, S. A. de C. V. MEX. Dist: Macmillan.

Ayonayon, Noreen. Zoo-Sa-Palooza Time with ESA! ESA-Bella That Is! Johnson-McCurdy, Audrey C. 2016. (ENG.). (J). 22.99 *(978-0-9896211-2-0(X))* AJM Bks.

Ayoob, Hana. Here Come the Numbers. Evans, Kyle D. 2019. (ENG.). 42p. (J). pap. *(978-0-9954750-7-6(5))* Explaining Science Publishing.

Ayotte, Andie C. Molly B. Golly's Wonderful Dancing Debut. Hoppe, Bethany A. 2013. 32p. 28.00 *(978-1-937763-85-5(4))* Published by Westview, Inc.

Ayoub, Hamid. One Lost Boy. Hahn, Nancy. 2012. pap. 19.95 *(978-1-4276-5351-2(8))* Aardvark Global Publishing.

Ayoub, Jenna. The Amazing World of Gumball Original Graphic Novel: Midsummer Nightmare: Midsummer Nightmare. Brennan, Meg. 2019. (Amazing World of Gumball Ser.: 6). (ENG.). 144p. (J). (gr. 4-7). pap. 14.99 *(978-1-68415-294-0(1))* Boom! Studios.

Ayres, Honor. A Child's Book of Prayers. Wright, Sally Ann. 2009. 96p. (J). (gr. -1). 10.99 *(978-0-7586-1662-3(7))* Concordia Publishing Hse.

—My Keepsake Bible. Wright, Sally Ann & Wright, Lesley. 2015. (ENG.). 144p. (J). 14.99 *(978-1-4143-9867-9(0),* 4608857) Tyndale Hse. Pubs.

—Ten Christmas Sheep. Godfrey, Jan. 2010. 28p. (J). (gr. -1-k). 12.95 *(978-0-8198-7432-0(9))* Pauline Bks. & Media.

—Where Did Grandad Go? House, Catherine. 2007. (J). 9.95 *(978-0-8198-8312-4(3))* Pauline Bks. & Media.

—Where Do Babies Come From? Wright, Sally Ann. 2007. 29p. (J). 9.95 *(978-0-8198-8311-7(5))* Pauline Bks. & Media.

—Who Made the Morning? Godfrey, Jan. ed. 2008. (ENG.). 28p. (J). (gr. -1-3). 9.99 *(978-0-9798247-0-8(2))* New Day Publishing, Inc.

Ayriss, Linda Holt. S Is for Save the Planet: A How-to-Be Green Alphabet. Herzog, Brad. 2009. (Science Ser.). (ENG.). 40p. (J). (gr. 1-5). 17.95 *(978-1-58536-428-2(2),* 1291948) Sleeping Bear Pr.

Ayto, Russell. Are the Dinosaurs Dead, Dad?, 1 vol. Middleton, Julie. 2013. (ENG.). 32p. (J). (gr. -1-3). 16.95 *(978-1-56145-690-1(X))* Peachtree Publishing Co. Inc.

—Captain Flinn & the Pirate Dinosaurs. Andreae, Giles. 2005. (Captain Flinn & the Pirate Dinosaurs Ser.). (ENG.). 32p. (J). (gr. -1-1). 19.99 *(978-1-4169-0713-8(0),* McElderry, Margaret K. Bks.) McElderry, Margaret K. Bks.

—The Cow That Laid an Egg. Cutbill, Andy. 2008. (ENG.). 32p. (J). (gr. -1-3). 17.99 *(978-0-06-137295-7(1))* HarperCollins Pubs.

—Dustbin Dad. Bently, Peter. (ENG.). 32p. (J). 2014. 15.99 *(978-1-84738-873-5(6));* 2013. pap. 8.99 *(978-1-84738-874-2(4),* Simon & Schuster Children's) Simon & Schuster, Ltd. GBR. Dist: Simon & Schuster, Inc.

—Missing Treasure! Andreae, Giles. 2008. (Captain Flinn & the Pirate Dinosaurs Ser.). (ENG.). 32p. (J). (gr. -1-3). 17.99 *(978-1-4169-6745-3(1),* McElderry, Margaret K. Bks.) McElderry, Margaret K. Bks.

—Old Misery. Sage, James. 2018. (ENG.). 40p. (J). (gr. k-4). 16.99 *(978-1-77138-823-8(4))* Kids Can Pr., Ltd. CAN. Dist: Hachette Bk. Group.

—One More Sheep. Kelly, Mij. 2006. (ENG.). 32p. (J). (gr. k-3). 16.95 *(978-1-56145-378-8(1))* Peachtree Publishing Co. Inc.

—The Somethingosaur. Mitton, Tony. 2014. (ENG.). 32p. (J). 17.99 *(978-0-00-758395-9(8),* HarperCollins Children's Bks.) HarperCollins Pubs. Ltd. GBR. Dist: HarperCollins Pubs.

—Tim, Ted & the Pirates. Whybrow, Ian. 2014. (ENG.). 32p. (J). 17.99 *(978-0-00-755930-5(5),* HarperCollins Children's Bks.) HarperCollins Pubs. Ltd. GBR. Dist: HarperCollins Pubs.

—A Very Pirate Christmas. Knapman, Timothy. 2015. (ENG.). 32p. (J). (gr. -1-k). pap. 11.99 *(978-1-4052-6504-1(3))* Egmont Bks., Ltd. GBR. Dist: Independent Pubs. Group.

—Where Teddy Bears Come From. Burgess, Mark. 2009. (ENG.). 32p. (J). (gr. -1-3). 16.95 *(978-1-56145-487-7(7))* Peachtree Publishing Co. Inc.

—Where's Tim's Ted? It's Time for Bed! Whybrow, Ian. 2014. (ENG.). 32p. (J). 17.99 *(978-0-00-755929-9(1),* HarperCollins Children's Bks.) HarperCollins Pubs. Ltd. GBR. Dist: HarperCollins Pubs.

—Whoops! Moore, Suzi. 2016. (ENG.). 32p. (J). (gr. -1-2). 16.99 *(978-0-7636-8180-7(6),* Templar) Candlewick Pr.

Ayto, Russell. Henry & the Yeti. Ayto, Russell. 2018. (ENG.). 32p. (J). 16.99 *(978-1-68119-683-1(2),* 900181197, Bloomsbury Children's Bks.) Bloomsbury Publishing USA.

Ayuni, Christian. El Oc�ano Interior. Cavero, Juan Jose. 2019. (Torre Amarilla Ser.). (SPA.). 160p. (J). pap. ***(978-958-00-0271-0(1))*** Norma Ediciones, S.A.

—Que Pase el Rey. Maria Izurieta, Ana. 2019. (Torre Roja Ser.). (SPA.). 72p. (J). pap. ***(978-958-776-015-6(8))*** Norma Ediciones, S.A.

Ayzenberg, Nina. Emma & Friends: Emma's Airport Adventure. Ehlin, Gina. l.t. ed. 2005. 32p. (J). per. 10.99 *(978-1-59879-014-6(5))* Lifevest Publishing, Inc.

—Emma & Friends; Emma Rescues Cali. Ehlin, Gina. l.t. ed. 2006. 24p. (J). 17.99 *(978-1-59879-113-6(3));* per. 10.99 *(978-1-59879-112-9(5))* Lifevest Publishing, Inc.

—The Story of Rap & Tap. Byrd, Bill Scott. 2006. 9.95 *(978-0-9776805-0-4(9))* Byrd, Fay T.

AZ. La Piedra de la Felicidad. Reyes, Carlos Jose. 2004. (Primer Acto: Teatro Infantil y Juvenil Ser.). (SPA.). 63p. (J). (gr. -1-7). pap. *(978-958-30-0318-9(2))* Panamericana Editorial.

Azabal, Mar. Ayobami & the Names of the Animals. Lopez Avila, Pilar. 2018. (ENG.). 30p. (J). 16.95 *(978-84-16733-42-2(2))* Cuento de Luz SL ESP. Dist: Publishers Group West (PGW).

Azaceta, Paul & Chee. Talent, Vol. 1. Golden, Christopher et al. 2007. (ENG.). 128p. per. 14.99 *(978-1-934506-05-9(2))* Boom! Studios.

Azaceta, Paul, jt. illus. see Ryan, Michael.

Azam, Jacques. The Book of How. Laffon, Martine. 2007. (ENG.). 90p. (J). (gr. 4-6). 17.95 *(978-0-8109-0716-4(X),* Abrams Bks. for Young Readers) Abrams, Inc.

Azarian, Mary. The Hound Dog's Haiku: And Other Poems for Dog Lovers. Rosen, Michael J. 2011. 56p. (J). (gr. 1-4). 17.99 *(978-0-7636-4499-4(4))* Candlewick Pr.

—Miss Bridie Chose a Shovel. Connor, Leslie. unabr. ed. 2005. (J). (gr. k-3). 27.95 incl. audio *(978-0-8045-6936-1(3),* SAC6936); 29.95 incl. audio compact disk *(978-0-8045-4135-0(3),* SACD4135) Spoken Arts, Inc.

—The Race of the Birkebeiners. Lunge-Larsen, Lise. 2007. (ENG.). 32p. (J). (gr. k — 1). 7.99 *(978-0-618-91599-6(0),* 1014894) Houghton Mifflin Harcourt Publishing Co.

—Snowflake Bentley. Martin, Jacqueline Briggs. 2009. (ENG.). 32p. (J). (gr. -1-3). pap. 8.99 *(978-0-547-24829-5(6),* 1100744) Houghton Mifflin Harcourt Publishing Co.

Azarian, Mary. Farmers Alphabet. Azarian, Mary. 2012. (ENG.). 64p. (gr. -1-2). pap. 15.95 *(978-0-87923-397-6(4))* Godine, David R. Pub.

Azarpay, Kathryn. Castle of the Skull. Fenwick, Richard. 2017. (ENG.). 144p. (J). pap. *(978-0-9935355-8-1(5))* RedSox Pr.

Azeveo, Lafayette. Alex & Her Clubhouse Friends. Simmons, Laura and Roshonda. 2016. (ENG.). (J). 20.99 *(978-1-4984-9086-3(7));* pap. 9.99 *(978-1-4984-9085-6(9))* Salem Author Services.

Azhar, Brian. Declan Likes Sharing. Faulkner, H. B. 2018. (ENG.). 24p. (J). pap. 10.95 *(978-1-7928-0095-5(9))* Independently Published.

Azhderian, Cecelia. Why Is the Sea Salty? And Other Questions about the Ocean. Richmond, Benjamin. 2014. (Good Question! Ser.). 32p. (J). (gr. 1). pap. 5.95 *(978-1-4549-0677-3(4))* Sterling Publishing Co., Inc.

Azinga, Neatra. King Rules for Children: 10 Rules to Bless Your Life. King, Alveda C. Johnson, Deitra P., ed. 2019. (ENG.). 40p. (J). pap. 14.99 *(978-1-0806-4130-7(0))* Independently Published.

Aziz, Lamia. Baby Whale's Mistake, 6 pack. Holden, Pam. 2009. (Red Rocket Readers Ser.). 16p. (gr. 2-2). pap. *(978-1-877363-87-0(1))* Flying Start Bks.

—Watch Out for Whales, 6 pack. Holden, Pam. 2009. (Red Rocket Readers Ser.). 23p. (gr. 2-2). pap. *(978-1-877363-63-4(4),* Red Rocket Readers) Flying Start Bks.

—Whale Rescue, 6 pack. Holden, Pam. 2009. (Red Rocket Readers Ser.). 23p. (gr. 2-2). pap. *(978-1-877363-79-5(0))* Flying Start Bks.

Azizi, Z., photos by. I Belong to the Muslim Faith. Dicker, K. 2009. 24p. (YA). pap. 8.25 *(978-1-4358-8624-7(0))* Rosen Publishing Group, Inc., The.

Azm, Mohsen Abou El. Muhammad: The Life of the Prophet - Based on Original Sources. adapted ed. 2014. (ENG.). 64p. pap. 6.95 *(978-1-906230-62-3(5))* Real Reads Ltd. GBR. Dist: Casemate Pubs. & Bk. Distributors, LLC.

Aznar, Caridad Perez. Un Agujero en el Ala. Anastasio, Antonio. Garcia de la Viuda, Miriam, tr. 2008. (SPA.). (J). (gr. 2-5). *(978-84-7490-950-0(3))* Encuentro Ediciones, S.A.

Azri, Sid. Healthy Mindsets for Little Kids: A Resilience Programme to Help Children Aged 5 - 9 with Anger, Anxiety, Attachment, Body Image, Conflict, Discipline, Empathy & Self-Esteem. Azri, Stephanie. ed. 2019. (ENG.). 160p. 27.95 ***(978-1-78592-865-9(1),*** 697059) Kingsley, Jessica Pubs. GBR. Dist: Hachette UK Distribution.

Azuelo, John Robert. Laki My Smart Dog. Nollis, Norman. 2019. (ENG.). 28p. (J). pap. *(978-1-925960-69-3(2))* Library For All Limited.

Azzalin, Stefano. Draw Scary Monster Mash-Ups. Bolte, Mari. 2017. (Drawing Mash-Ups Ser.). (ENG.). 32p. (J). (gr. 3-9). lib. bdg. 28.65 *(978-1-5157-6935-4(6),* 135414, Capstone Pr.) Capstone.

—Drawing Your Pets. Colich, Abby. 2015. (Drawing Amazing Animals Ser.). (ENG.). 32p. (J). (gr. 3-9). 28.65 *(978-1-4914-2134-5(7),* Capstone Pr.) Capstone.

—The Epic Adventures of Odysseus: An Interactive Mythological Adventure. Hoena, Blake. 2016. (You Choose: Ancient Greek Myths Ser.). (ENG.). 112p. (J). (gr. 3-7). lib. bdg. 32.65 *(978-1-4914-8114-1(5),* Capstone Pr.) Capstone.

Azzalin, Stefano, et al. How to Draw Elves, Dwarves, & Other Magical Folk. Sautter, A. J. 2016. (Drawing Fantasy Creatures Ser.). (ENG.). 32p. (J). (gr. 3-9). lib. bdg. 28.65 *(978-1-4914-8027-4(0),* Capstone Pr.) Capstone.

—How to Draw Orcs, Goblins, & Other Wicked Creatures. Sautter, A. J. 2016. (Drawing Fantasy Creatures Ser.). (ENG.). 32p. (J). (gr. 3-9). lib. bdg. 28.65 *(978-1-4914-8024-3(6),* Capstone Pr.) Capstone.

B

B, B. T., jt. illus. see Blackwood, Basil Temple.

B., Blair. Star Cross'd Destiny: The Fated, 5 vols., Vol. 1. B., Blair. 2005. (YA). per. 14.95 *(978-0-9767540-0-8(2),* 121001, Star Cross'd Destiny) Bohemian Trash Studios.

B. T. B. More Beasts for Worse Children. Belloc, Hilaire. 2008. 48p. pap. *(978-1-4099-1329-0(5))* Dodo Pr.

Baas, Thomas. Aïe ! J'Ai Mal ! Piccolophilo. Piquemal, Michel. 2010. (A. M. Docus Ser.). (FRE.). 32p. (J). *(978-2-226-20965-8(4))* Albin-Michel, Editions.

—C'Est À Moi ! Piccolophilo. Piquemal, Michel. 2010. (A. M. Docus Ser.). (FRE.). 32p. (J). *(978-2-226-20964-1(6))* Albin-Michel, Editions.

—The Pied Piper of Hamelin. 2016. (ENG.). 48p. (J). (gr. -1-3). 19.95 *(978-3-89955-767-1(0))* Die Gestalten Verlag DEU. Dist: Ingram Publisher Services.

Babajanyan, Sona. Bringing down the Wall. Reiter, David P. 2012. 38p. (J). pap. 18.00 *(978-1-922120-19-9(7),* IP Kidz) Interactive Pubns. Pty, Ltd. AUS. Dist: Ingram Content Group.

—Die Mauer Zu Fall Bringen. Reiter, David P. Beer, Michele, tr. from ENG. 2013.Tr. of Bringing down the Wall. (GER.). 38p. pap. *(978-1-922120-52-6(9),* IP Kidz) Interactive Pubns. Pty, Ltd.

Babbitt, Natalie. The Devil's Storybooks: 20 Delightfully Wicked Stories. Babbitt, Natalie. 2012. (ENG.). 224p. (J). (gr. 3-7). pap. 16.99 *(978-0-312-64158-0(3),* 9780312641580) Square Fish.

—Elsie Times Eight. Babbitt, Natalie. 2005. 26p. (J). (gr. k-4). reprint ed. 16.00 *(978-0-7567-9640-2(7))* DIANE Publishing Co.

—Goody Hall. Babbitt, Natalie. 2007. (ENG.). 192p. (J). (gr. 3-7). per. 8.99 *(978-0-312-36983-5(2),* 900044327) Square Fish.

—Kneeknock Rise. Babbitt, Natalie. 2007. (ENG.). 144p. (J). (gr. 3-7). per. 7.99 *(978-0-312-37009-1(1),* 900044346) Square Fish.

—The Search for Delicious. Babbitt, Natalie. 2007. (ENG.). 192p. (J). (gr. 3-7). per. 8.99 *(978-0-312-36982-8(4),* 900044326) Square Fish.

Babcock, Jeff. Bingo Bear Was Here: A Toy Bear's Climb to the Top of Africa's Highest Mountain. Newman, Gwill York. 2003. 48p. (J). pap. 8.95 *(978-0-86534-395-5(0))* Sunstone Pr.

Babeaux, Dennis, jt. photos by see Hall, Terri L.

Babel-Worth, Joyce. Let's Get Ready for Kindergarten! Spanish/English Edition. Kannenberg, Stacey. Sin Fronteras (Without Borders) et al, trs. 2008. (Let's Get Ready Ser.).Tr. of IA prepararse para Kindergarten!. (SPA & ENG.). 32p. (J). lib. bdg. 21.00 *(978-1-933476-05-6(2))* Cedar Valley Publishing.

Babineaux, Jim. Cody Cottontail Makes a Wise Choice! Babineaux, Jim. l.t. ed. 2005. 18p. (J). *(978-0-9769769-0-5(0))* ALCAPS, LLC.

Babinski, Michael. Bobby Bear Learns to Be a Cowboy. Draper, Tricia. 2004. 36p. (gr. -1-3). per. 14.95 *(978-1-58961-246-4(9))* PageFree Publishing, Inc.

Baboni, Elena. Angels among Us. Lane, Leena. 2007. 29p. (J). (gr. k-5). 17.00 *(978-0-8028-5321-9(8),* Eerdmans Bks For Young Readers) Eerdmans, William B. Publishing Co.

Babooram, Aasha. Poco & His Missing Puppy. Babooram, Vima. 2012. 24p. pap. *(978-1-4602-0296-8(1))* FriesenPress.

Babra, Neil. Hamlet. SparkNotes Staff. 2008. (No Fear Shakespeare Illustrated Ser.: 1). 216p. (gr. 5-7). per. 9.95 *(978-1-4114-9873-0(9),* Spark Notes) Sterling Publishing Co., Inc.

Babson, Jane F. A Story of Us: The Dolls' History of People of the United States. Babson, Jane F. 2003. 56p. (J). (gr. 4-5). 10.95 *(978-0-940787-03-2(2))* Winstead Pr., Ltd.

Baccala, Gladys. It's Holiday Time! Woodhouse, Emma. 2012. (ENG.). 18p. (J). bds. *(978-1-58925-640-8(9))* Tiger Tales.

—It's Spring Time! Woodhouse, Emma. 2013. (ENG.). 16p. (gr. -1). bds. 8.95 *(978-1-58925-639-2(5))* Tiger Tales.

Baccaro, Ana. O Menino, o Gnomo e a Floresta Destruida. Vasconcelos, Sandra. 2019. (POR.). 46p. (J). pap. 13.00 ***(978-1-6994-7988-9(7))*** Independently Published.

Bacchin, Giorgio. Blood Cave: Band 10 White/Band 16 Sapphire (Collins Big Cat Progress) Mayhew, Jon. 2014. (Collins Big Cat Progress Ser.). (ENG.). 32p. (J). (gr. 4-5). pap. 9.99 *(978-0-00-751921-7(4))* HarperCollins Pubs. Ltd. GBR. Dist: Independent Pubs. Group.

—Collins Big Cat Phonics for Letters & Sounds - Maps: Band 04/Blue, Bd. 4. Wallace, Karen. 2018. (Collins Big Cat Phonics Ser.). (ENG.). 16p. (J). (gr. k-1). pap. 6.99 *(978-0-00-825165-9(7))* HarperCollins Pubs. Ltd. GBR. Dist: Independent Pubs. Group.

—Hunters of the Sea 3 Explorers. Bradman, Tony. 2017. (Cambridge Reading Adventures Ser.). (ENG.). 40p. pap. 8.99 *(978-1-108-40099-2(X))* Cambridge Univ. Pr.

—Lost at Sea. Millett, Peter. 2016. (Cambridge Reading Adventures Ser.). (ENG.). 26p. pap. 8.08 *(978-1-316-50344-7(5))* Cambridge Univ. Pr.

—The Mountain of Fire 1 Pathfinders. Millett, Peter. 2017. (Cambridge Reading Adventures Ser.). (ENG.). 24p. pap. 7.87 *(978-1-108-40074-9(4))* Cambridge Univ. Pr.

—Sandstorm Purple Band. Millett, Peter. 2016. (Cambridge Reading Adventures Ser.). (ENG.). 24p. pap. 8.08 *(978-1-107-57607-0(5))* Cambridge Univ. Pr.

Bacera, Mami. A Day with Mae. Bacera, Mark. 2019. (Amekoro Ser.: Vol. 1). (ENG.). 34p. (J). pap. 9.29 ***(978-1-6706-7466-1(5))*** Independently Published.

Bach, Annie. Buenas Noches, Mi Querido Bebé (Good Night, My Darling Baby) Capucilli, Alyssa Satin. Romay, Alexis, tr. 2019. (New Books for Newborns Ser.). (SPA.). 16p. (J). (— 1). bds. 7.99 *(978-1-5344-4289-4(8),* Libros Para Ninos) Libros Para Ninos.

—Good Night, My Darling Baby. Capucilli, Alyssa Satin. 2017. (New Books for Newborns Ser.). (ENG.). 16p. (J). (gr. -1 — 1). bds. 7.99 *(978-1-4814-8119-9(3),* Little Simon) Little Simon.

Bach, Annie. Night-Night, Forest Friends. Bach, Annie. 2013. 24p. (J). (gr. -1-k). bds. 9.99 *(978-0-8431-7278-2(9),* Grosset & Dunlap) Penguin Young Readers Group.

Bachalo, Chris. Doctor Strange Vol. 1. 2017. (ENG.). 280p. (YA). (gr. 8-17). 34.99 *(978-1-302-90432-6(9))* Marvel Worldwide, Inc.

Bachalo, Chris, et al. Doctor Strange Vol. 2: The Last Days of Magic. 2017. (ENG.). 168p. (YA). (gr. 8-17). pap. 19.99 *(978-0-7851-9933-5(0))* Marvel Worldwide, Inc.

—Doctor Strange Vol. 4: Mr. Misery. 2017. (ENG.). 136p. (YA). (gr. 8-17). 24.99 *(978-1-302-90586-6(4))* Marvel Worldwide, Inc.

Bachalo, Chris. Marvel Monograph: the Art of Chris Bachalo. 2020. (ENG.). 112p. (YA). (gr. 8-17). pap. 19.99 *(978-1-302-92405-8(2))* Marvel Worldwide, Inc.

—Ultimate X-Men - Volume 5: Ultimate War, 6 vols., Vol. 5. 2006. (ENG.). 112p. (YA). (gr. 8-17). pap. 10.99 *(978-0-7851-1129-0(8))* Marvel Worldwide, Inc.

Bachalo, Chris, et al. Ultimate X-Men Ultimate Collection - Book 3, Bk. 3. 2009. (ENG.). 304p. (YA). (gr. 8-17). pap. 29.99 *(978-0-7851-4187-7(1))* Marvel Worldwide, Inc.

—X-Men Milestones: Operation Zero Tolerance. 2020. (ENG.). 448p. (YA). (gr. 4-17). pap. 39.99 *(978-1-302-92396-9(X))* Marvel Worldwide, Inc.

Bachan. Rocket Salvage, Vol. 1. Mercado, Yehudi. 2018. (ENG.). 152p. (YA). pap. 14.99 *(978-1-941302-52-1(1),* f2d11501-bdcd-4e54-9a9b-fc1fa7beb0bb, Lion Forge) Oni Pr., Inc.

Bachan, Krystal Ann. The Adventures of Fox Brown. Atwarie, Rossi. 2011. 62p. pap. 19.00 *(978-1-60911-845-7(6),* Eloquent Bks.) Strategic Book Publishing & Rights Agency (SBPRA).

Bachelet, Gilles. A Story That Grows. 2019. (ENG.). 32p. (J). *(978-0-8028-5512-1(1),* Eerdmans Bks For Young Readers) Eerdmans, William B. Publishing Co.

Bachelier, Anne. Alice's Adventures in Wonderland, & Through the Looking Glass, 1bk. Carroll, Lewis. 2005. (J). *(978-0-9728620-8-0(0)); (978-0-9769071-0-7(0));* per. *(978-0-9769071-1-4(9));* im. lthr. *(978-0-9728620-9-7(9))* CFM.

Bachem, Paul. Anna's Blizzard, 1 vol. Hart, Alison. 2017. (ENG.). 176p. (J). (gr. 2-4). pap. 7.95 *(978-1-68263-002-0(1))* Peachtree Publishing Co. Inc.

—Emma's River, 1 vol. Hart, Alison. 2010. (ENG.). 160p. (J). (gr. 2-5). 12.95 *(978-1-56145-524-9(5),* Peachtree Junior) Peachtree Publishing Co. Inc.

Bachmann, B. L. Fairy Friends. Howell, Ruth. 2013. 28p. 12.95 *(978-0-9899275-2-9(0))* Ravenwood Publishing.

Bachoc, Patricia. God's Garden: A story about What Happens When We Die. Morrison, Kevin. 2009. 32p. (J). pap. 9.95 *(978-0-8091-6741-8(7),* Ambassador Bks.) Paulist Pr.

Bachs, Ramon & Beaulieu, Jean-François. Disney Kingdoms: Figment Set 2 (Set), 5 vols. Zub, Jim. 2016. (Disney Kingdoms: Figment Set 2 Ser.). (ENG.). 24p. (J). (gr. k-5). lib. bdg. 135.35 *(978-1-61479-580-3(0),* 24361, Graphic Novels) Spotlight.

—Figment 2: the Legacy of Imagination: Volume 1. Zub, Jim. 2016. (Disney Kingdoms: Figment Set 2 Ser.). (ENG.). 24p. (J). (gr. k-5). lib. bdg. 27.07 *(978-1-61479-581-0(9),* 24362, Graphic Novels) Spotlight.

—Figment 2: the Legacy of Imagination: Volume 2. Zub, Jim. 2016. (Disney Kingdoms: Figment Set 2 Ser.). (ENG.). 24p. (J). (gr. k-5). lib. bdg. 27.07 *(978-1-61479-582-7(7),* 24363, Graphic Novels) Spotlight.

—Figment 2: the Legacy of Imagination: Volume 3. Zub, Jim. 2016. (Disney Kingdoms: Figment Set 2 Ser.). (ENG.). 24p. (J). (gr. k-5). lib. bdg. 27.07 *(978-1-61479-583-4(5),* 24364, Graphic Novels) Spotlight.

—Figment 2: the Legacy of Imagination: Volume 4. Zub, Jim. 2016. (Disney Kingdoms: Figment Set 2 Ser.). (ENG.). 24p. (J). (gr. k-5). lib. bdg. 27.07 *(978-1-61479-584-1(3),* 24365, Graphic Novels) Spotlight.

—Figment 2: the Legacy of Imagination: Volume 5. Zub, Jim. 2016. (Disney Kingdoms: Figment Set 2 Ser.). (ENG.). 24p. (J). (gr. k-5). lib. bdg. 27.07 *(978-1-61479-585-8(1),* 24366, Graphic Novels) Spotlight.

Back, Francis. Champlain. Moore, Christopher. 2004. 56p. (J). (gr. 3-7). 18.95 *(978-0-88776-657-2(9),* Tundra Bks.) Tundra Bks. CAN. Dist: Penguin Random Hse. LLC.

Back, Joann & Gary. Monkey Mischief. Hall, Joan. 2015. (ENG.). 34p. (J). pap. 9.99 *(978-0-9819815-9-8(3))* Lamplight Pubns.

Back, Samee. Korean Folks Songs: Stars in the Sky & Dreams in Our Hearts. Choi, Robert. 2014. 32p. (J). (gr. -1-3). pap. 15.95 *(978-0-8048-4468-0(2))* Tuttle Publishing.

Backer, Marni. How Did You Grow So Big, So Soon? Bowen, Anne. 2003. 32p. (J). (gr. -1-1). 15.95 *(978-0-87614-024-6(X),* Carolrhoda Bks.) Lerner Publishing Group.

Backes, Nick. Molly Story Collection. Tripp, Valerie. 2004. (ENG.). 388p. 29.95 *(978-1-59369-458-6(X))* American Girl Publishing, Inc.

—Molly's Cooking Studio. American Girl Editors. 2004. 54p. (gr. 3-18). 15.95 *(978-1-59369-265-0(X))* American Girl Publishing, Inc.

—Samantha's Cooking Studio. American Girl Editors. 2005. 54p. (gr. 3-18). 15.95 *(978-1-59369-268-1(4))* American Girl Publishing, Inc.

Backman, Aidel. Shimmee & the Taste-Me Tree. Weinbach, Shaindel. Date not set. (J). (gr. -1-2). 2.95 *(978-0-87306-305-0(8))* Feldheim Pubs.

Backman, Aidel. The Money in the Honey. Backman, Aidel, adapted by. 2003. 32p. (J). 13.95 *(978-0-8266-0030-1(1))* Merkos L'Inyonei Chinuch.

Bac'ko, Milena. Book of Ju'Anne: Over the High Sea. Ruffins Msl, Joan E. 2019. (Journey Around the World Ser.: Vol. 2). (ENG.). 44p. (J). pap. 19.99 *(978-1-0995-3249-8(3))* Independently Published.

Backshall, Rachel. L' Aventure Magique: Kris et Kate Construisent un Bateau. Finnegan, Ruth. Thio, Gwendolyne, tr. 2019. (FRE.). 30p. (J). (gr. k-3). pap. *(978-1-911221-90-6(6))* Balestier Pr.

Backus, Amber N. Behold: The Birth of Jesus. Backus, Amber N. 2019. (Biblically Based Children's Stories Ser.: Vol. 1). (ENG.). 34p. (J). (gr. -1-3). 17.99 ***(978-1-64669-704-5(9))*** Primedia eLaunch LLC.

Backus, Carole. The Know It All Kitty & the Peanut Butter Factory. Jernigan, Kathy. 2007. (ENG.). 24p. (J). pap. 10.00 ***(978-1-4251-0488-7(6))*** Trafford Publishing.

Backus, Nancy. A Bayou Home: The Adventure of Swampmaster Bejeaux, 1 vol. Backus, Nancy. 2019. (ENG.). 108p. (gr. 3-7). 19.99 *(978-0-578-17393-1(X),* Pelican Publishing) Arcadia Publishing.

B

Bacon, Beth. I Hate Reading: How to Read When You'd Rather Not. Bacon, Beth. 2020. (ENG.). 112p. (J). (gr. 1-5). 12.99 *(978-0-06-296252-2(3),* HarperCollins) HarperCollins Pubs. Ltd. GBR. Dist: HarperCollins Pubs.

Bacon, Greer Alexis. A Very Snowy Night: A Simple Entertaining Winter Theme Story with Pictures for Your Toddler. Bacon, Greer Alexis. 2018. (ENG.). 26p. (J). pap. 9.99 *(978-1-7273-9273-9(6))* CreateSpace Independent Publishing Platform.

Bacon, Irving R. You & the Ten Commandments. Cameron, William J. 2011. 210p. 44.95 *(978-1-258-08112-6(1))* Literary Licensing, LLC.

Bacon, Paul, jt. illus. see O'Sullivan, Tom.

Baczynski, Kristyna. The Book of Terrifyingly Awesome Technology: 27 Experiments for Young Scientists. Connolly, Sean. 2019. (Irresponsible Science Ser.). (ENG.). 240p. (J). (gr. 4-8). 15.95 *(978-1-5235-0494-7(3),* 100494) Workman Publishing Co., Inc.

Badalian, Lucy. George the Dragonslayer & His Friends: On Earth. Badalian, Lucy. 2003. 312p. (YA). per. 18.95 *(978-0-9725344-0-6(7),* 9725344) Millennium Workshop Production.

Badari, Marcelo. Time Atlas: An Interactive Timeline of History. Hegarty, Robert. 2017. (ENG.). 18p. (J). (gr. 1-4). 22.99 *(978-1-944530-09-9(6),* 360 Degrees) Tiger Tales.

Baddeley, Elizabeth. Billie Jean! How Tennis Star Billie Jean King Changed Women's Sports. Rockliff, Mara. 2019. 40p. (J). (gr. -1-3). 17.99 *(978-0-525-51779-5(0),* G.P. Putnam's Sons Books for Young Readers) Penguin Young Readers Group.

—The Cat Who Lived with Anne Frank. Miller, David Lee & Rubin, Steven Jay. 2019. 40p. (J). (gr. -1-3). 17.99 *(978-1-5247-4150-1(7),* Philomel Bks.) Penguin Young Readers Group.

—I Dissent: Ruth Bader Ginsburg Makes Her Mark. Levy, Debbie. 2016. (ENG.). 40p. (J). (gr. -1-3). 18.99 *(978-1-4814-6559-5(7),* Simon & Schuster Bks. For Young Readers) Simon & Schuster Bks. For Young Readers.

—An Inconvenient Alphabet: Ben Franklin & Noah Webster's Spelling Revolution. Anderson, Beth. 2018. (ENG.). 48p. (J). (gr. -1-3). 17.99 *(978-1-5344-0555-4(0),* Simon & Schuster/Paula Wiseman Bks.) Simon & Schuster/Paula Wiseman Bks.

—Leave It to Abigail! The Revolutionary Life of Abigail Adams. Rosenstock, Barb. 2020. 40p. (J). (gr. -1-3). 18.99 *(978-0-316-41571-2(5))* Little, Brown Bks. for Young Readers.

Baddely, Elizabeth. Woman in the House (and Senate) (Revised & Updated) How Women Came to Washington & Changed the Nation. Cooper, Ilene. 2020. (ENG.). 160p. (J). (gr. 3-7). 19.99 *(978-1-4197-4266-8(3),* 1681701, Abrams Bks. for Young Readers) Abrams, Inc.

Baddorf, Robert. Latin for Children. Baddorf, Robert. Perrin, Christopher. 2006. (Latin for Childred Ser.). (ENG.). 162p. (J). (gr. 4-7). pap., act. bk. ed. 16.95 *(978-1-60051-017-5(5))* Classical Academic Pr.

—Latin for Children, Primer B Activity Book! Baddorf, Robert. Perrin, Christopher. 2005. (Latin for Childred Ser.). (ENG.). 196p. (J). (gr. 4-7). pap., act. bk. ed. 16.95 *(978-1-60051-011-3(6))* Classical Academic Pr.

Badel, Ronan. Dragons: Father & Son. Lacroix, Alexandre. 2017. (Drake the Dragon Ser.). (ENG.). 32p. (J). (gr. -1-3). 17.95 *(978-1-910277-25-6(8))* QEB Publishing Inc.

—Dragons in Love. Lacroix, Alexandre. 2019. (Drake the Dragon Ser.). (ENG.). 32p. (J). (gr. -1-1). 17.95 *(978-1-78603-362-8(3),* Words & Pictures) Quarto Publishing Group UK GBR. Dist: Hachette Bk. Group.

—The Wolf Will Not Come, 1 vol. Ouyessad, Myriam. 2019. (ENG.). 32p. (J). 16.99 *(978-0-7643-5780-0(8),* 16320); pap. 9.99 *(978-0-7643-5876-0(6),* 20587) Schiffer Publishing, Ltd.

Badenhorst, Corinne. Blink Blinkers Blinkerboom: 'n Saam-Speel-Storie Met 'n Blink Plan. Badenhorst, Corinne. 2019. (AFR.). 48p. (J). pap. *(978-0-6399842-7-8(4))* Seraph Creative.

—Twinkle-Tree: A Play-A-Long Story for His Glory. Badenhorst, Corinne. 2019. (ENG.). 48p. (J). pap. *(978-0-620-83263-2(0))* Seraph Creative.

Badgero, Amanda. Princess of Boring. McGilvery, Alex. 2nd ed. 2017. (ENG.). 48p. (J). pap. ***(978-0-9959926-3-4(0))*** Celticfrog Publishing.

Badolisani, Noemi. Goccia. Badolisani, Luisio Luciano. 2019. (Ragazzi... e Genitori Ser.: Vol. 10). (ITA.). 104p. (J). pap. *(978-88-6690-490-8(2))* EEE - Edizioni Esordienti E-Bk.

Badulina, Olya. God's Blessings of Fall. Hall, Jean Matthew. 2019. (Bountiful Blessings Ser.). (ENG.). 34p. (J). (gr. k-4). 16.99 ***(978-1-7332828-5-7(8))***; pap. 11.99 ***(978-1-7332828-0-2(7))*** Little Lamb Bks.

Baechle, Austin. Keep Smiling. Meier, Jenny. 2019. (ENG.). 24p. (J). (gr. -1-3). 10.95 ***(978-1-4808-8272-0(0))*** Archway Publishing.

Baek, Gina. The Classic Collection of Mother Goose Nursery Rhymes (Hardcover) Over 101 Cherished Poems (the Classic Edition) 2018. (Classic Edition Ser.: 12). (ENG.). 128p. (J). 19.95 *(978-1-60433-745-7(1),* Applesauce Pr.) Cider Mill Pr. Bk. Pubs., LLC.

—The Classic Collection of Mother Goose Nursery Rhymes (Oversized Padded Board Book) The Classic Edition. 2018. (ENG.). 24p. (J). bds. 12.95 *(978-1-60433-790-7(7),* Applesauce Pr.) Cider Mill Pr. Bk. Pubs., LLC.

—Classic Mother Goose Nursery Rhymes (Board Book) The Classic Edition. 2019. (ENG.). 24p. (J). bds. 8.95 *(978-1-60433-861-4(X),* Applesauce Pr.) Cider Mill Pr. Bk. Pubs., LLC.

Baek, Gina. Classic Nursery Rhymes Oversized Padded Board Book. 2020. (ENG.). 24p. (J). bds. 12.95 ***(978-1-60433-981-9(0),*** Applesauce Pr.) Cider Mill Pr. Bk. Pubs., LLC.

Baek, Gina. Mother Goose Nursery Rhymes: A Little Apple Classic. 2019. (Little Apple Bks.). (ENG.). 28p. (J). 4.99 *(978-1-60433-925-3(X),* Applesauce Pr.) Cider Mill Pr. Bk. Pubs., LLC.

Baek, Matthew J. In God's Hands. Kushner, Lawrence & Schmidt, Gary. 2005. (ENG.). 32p. (gr. k-3). 16.99 *(978-1-58023-224-1(8),* a1cc0a97-7f67-4181-af6c-a32ed0d50d1e, Jewish Lights Publishing) LongHill Partners, Inc.

Baele, Frederic. What on Earth Is That? Savory, Sarah. 2018. (ENG.). pap. 7.50 *(978-1-4323-0869-8(6))* Penguin Random House Grupo Editorial ESP. Dist: Casemate Pubs. & Bk. Distributors, LLC.

Baen, Noah. A Tree Lives. Lewis, Richard. 2006. (ENG.). 48p. per. 12.00 *(978-1-929299-04-1(4))* Touchstone Ctr. Pubns.

Baer, Brian. Gravelle's Land of Horror. O'Coyne, James. Whispering Pine Press International, Inc. Staff, ed. 2007. (ENG.). 120p. (J). per. 9.95 *(978-1-59649-604-0(5))* Whispering Pine Pr. International, Inc.

Baer, Julie. I Only Like What I Like. Baer, Julie, text. 2003. 32p. (J). 15.99 *(978-1-932188-00-4(2))* Bollix Bks.

Baez, Marcelo. The Amazing Work of Scientists with Max Axiom, Super Scientist, 1 vol. Biskup, Agnieszka. 2013. (Graphic Science & Engineering in Action Ser.). (ENG.). 32p. (J). (gr. 3-9). pap. 8.10 *(978-1-62065-701-0(5))*; lib. bdg. 31.32 *(978-1-4296-9936-5(1))* Capstone.

—Epic Athletes: Kevin Durant. Wetzel, Dan. 2020. (Epic Athletes Ser.: 8). (ENG.). 176p. (J). 16.99 *(978-1-250-29583-5(1),* 900195523, Holt, Henry & Co. Bks. For Young Readers) Holt, Henry & Co.

Baez, Marcelo. Epic Athletes: Patrick Mahomes. Wetzel, Dan. 2020. (Epic Athletes Ser.: 9). (ENG.). 160p. (J). 16.99 ***(978-1-250-76231-3(6),*** 900231783, Holt, Henry & Co. Bks. For Young Readers) Holt, Henry & Co.

Baez, Marcelo. Epic Athletes: Simone Biles. Wetzel, Dan. 2020. (Epic Athletes Ser.: 7). (ENG.). 160p. (J). 16.99 *(978-1-250-29582-8(3),* 900195521, Holt, Henry & Co. Bks. For Young Readers) Holt, Henry & Co.

—Graphic Science & Engineering in Action. Enz, Tammy et al. 2013. (Graphic Science & Engineering in Action Ser.). (ENG.). 32p. (gr. 3-4). pap. 190.80 *(978-1-62065-708-9(2))*; (J). pap., pap., pap. 31.80 *(978-1-62065-707-2(4))* Capstone. (Capstone Pr.).

—Graphic Science & Engineering in Action. Biskup, Agnieszka et al. 2013. (Graphic Science & Engineering in Action Ser.). (ENG.). 32p. (J). (gr. 3-9). lib. bdg., lib. bdg., lib. bdg. 125.28 *(978-1-4296-9938-9(8),* Capstone Pr.) Capstone.

—The Incredible Work of Engineers with Max Axiom, Super Scientist, 1 vol. Biskup, Agnieszka. 2013. (Graphic Science & Engineering in Action Ser.). (ENG.). 32p. (J). (gr. 3-9). pap. 8.10 *(978-1-62065-705-8(8))*; lib. bdg. 31.32 *(978-1-4296-9937-2(X))* Capstone. (Capstone Pr.).

—Max Axiom Science & Engineering Activities. Biskup, Agnieszka & Enz, Tammy. 2015. (Max Axiom Science & Engineering Activities Ser.). (ENG.). 32p. (J). (gr. 3-9). pap., pap., pap. 31.80 *(978-1-4914-2536-7(9),* Capstone Pr.) Capstone.

—Max Axiom Science & Engineering Activities. Enz, Tammy & Biskup, Agnieszka. 2015. (Max Axiom Science & Engineering Activities Ser.). (ENG.). 32p. (J). (gr. 3-9). lib. bdg., lib. bdg., lib. bdg. 125.28 *(978-1-4914-2535-0(0),* Capstone Pr.) Capstone.

—Super Cool Chemical Reaction Activities with Max Axiom. Biskup, Agnieszka. 2015. (Max Axiom Science & Engineering Activities Ser.). (ENG.). 32p. (J). (gr. 3-9). lib. bdg. 31.32 *(978-1-4914-2077-5(4),* Capstone Pr.) Capstone.

—Super Cool Construction Activities with Max Axiom. Enz, Tammy. 2015. (Max Axiom Science & Engineering Activities Ser.). (ENG.). 32p. (J). (gr. 3-9). lib. bdg. 31.32 *(978-1-4914-2078-2(2),* Capstone Pr.) Capstone.

—Super Cool Forces & Motion Activities with Max Axiom. Biskup, Agnieszka. 2015. (Max Axiom Science & Engineering Activities Ser.). (ENG.). 32p. (J). (gr. 3-9). lib. bdg. 31.32 *(978-1-4914-2079-9(0),* Capstone Pr.) Capstone.

—Super Cool Mechanical Activities with Max Axiom. Enz, Tammy. 2015. (Max Axiom Science & Engineering Activities Ser.). (ENG.). 32p. (J). (gr. 3-9). lib. bdg. 31.32 *(978-1-4914-2080-5(4),* Capstone Pr.) Capstone.

Bagby, Chris, photos by. Ode to the Appalachian Trail. Bagby, Chris, ed. 2007. 55p. (YA). pap. 16.95 *(978-0-9795659-1-5(X))* Shaffer, Earl Foundation, Inc.

Bagby, Jeffrey K. What's Wrong with Grandma? A Family's Experience with Alzheimer's. Vol. Shawver, Margaret. 2003. (ENG.). 62p. (gr. -1-3). pap. 16.99 *(978-1-59102-174-2(X))* Prometheus Bks., Pubs.

Bagdi, Anita. The Clown's Clothes. Molnar, Eszter. 2016. (ENG.). (J). pap. *(978-1-5262-0423-3(1))* Cambrian Way Trust.

Bagdi, Anita. The Cow Who Didn't Like the View. Molnar, Eszter. 2020. (ENG.). 36p. (J). pap. ***(978-1-9998906-0-5(4))*** Cambrian Way Trust.

Baggetta, Maria. Alphathoughts. Hopkins, Lee Bennett. 2015. (ENG.). 32p. (J). (gr. k-2). 6.95 *(978-1-62091-792-3(0),* Wordsong) Boyds Mills Pr.

—Alphathoughts: Alphabet Poems. Hopkins, Lee Bennett & Boyds Mills Press Staff. 2003. (ENG.). 32p. (J). (gr. k-2). 16.95 *(978-1-56397-979-8(9),* Wordsong) Boyds Mills Pr.

Baggot, Stella. Baby's Very First Fire Truck. 2019. (Baby's Very First Rolling Bks.). (ENG.). 8ppp. (J). 8.99 *(978-0-7945-4730-1(3),* Usborne) EDC Publishing.

Baggott, Stella. Advent Calendar to Color. ed. 2011. (Coloring Bks). (J). ring bd. 7.99 *(978-0-7945-3136-2(9),* Usborne) EDC Publishing.

—Baby's Very First Colors Book. 2009. (Baby Board Bks). 10p. (J). bds. 6.99 *(978-0-7945-2467-8(2),* Usborne) EDC Publishing.

—Baby's Very First Noisy Book Farm. 2013. (Baby's Very First Noisy Book Ser.). (ENG.). 10p. (gr. -1). 15.99 *(978-0-7945-2703-7(5),* Usborne) EDC Publishing.

—Baby's Very First Noisy Christmas. ed. 2019. (Baby's Very First Noisy Bks.). (ENG.). 10ppp. (J). pap. 15.99 *(978-0-7945-3128-7(8),* Usborne) EDC Publishing.

—Baby's Very First Outdoors Book. 2009. (Baby Board Bks). 10p. (J). bds. 6.99 *(978-0-7945-2468-5(0),* Usborne) EDC Publishing.

—Baby's Very First Play Book Garden Words. 2019. (Baby's Very First Board Bks.). (ENG.). 10ppp. (J). 11.99 *(978-0-7945-4425-6(8),* Usborne) EDC Publishing.

—Baby's Very First Slide & See Christmas. 2017. (Baby's Very First Slide & See Board Bks.). (ENG.). 10p. (J). 14.99 *(978-0-7945-4134-7(8),* Usborne) EDC Publishing.

—Baby's Very First Stroller Book Animals. 2015. (Baby's Very First Stroller Bks.). (ENG.). 8p. (J). 7.99 *(978-0-7945-3535-3(6),* Usborne) EDC Publishing.

—Baby's Very First Stroller Book Jungle. 2015. (Baby's Very First Stroller Bks.). (ENG.). 8p. (J). 7.99 *(978-0-7945-3533-9(X),* Usborne) EDC Publishing.

—Baby's Very First Toys Book. 2009. (Baby Board Bks). 10p. (J). bds. 6.99 *(978-0-7945-2466-1(4),* Usborne) EDC Publishing.

—Baby's Very First Tractor Book. 2018. (Baby's Very First Rolling Bks.). (ENG.). 8p. (J). 8.99 *(978-0-7945-4198-9(4),* Usborne) EDC Publishing.

—Baby's Very First Truck Book. 2019. (Baby's Very First Rolling Bks.). (ENG.). 8ppp. (J). 8.99 *(978-0-7945-4462-1(2),* Usborne) EDC Publishing.

—El Bebé Descubre... Mi Biblioteca Baby's Very First Little Library (Baby's Very First Little Library) 2019. (Baby's Very First Bks.). (SPA.). 10p. (J). 7.99 *(978-0-7945-4588-8(2),* Usborne) EDC Publishing.

—Farm Stroller Book. Watt, Fiona. 2010. 8p. (J). 7.99 *(978-0-7945-2811-9(2),* Usborne) EDC Publishing.

—Fold-Out Animals Book. 2017. (Fold-Out Board Bks.). (ENG.). 12p. (J). 7.99 *(978-0-7945-4008-1(2),* Usborne) EDC Publishing.

—Fold-Out Farm Book. 2017. (Fold-Out Board Bks.). (ENG.). 12p. (J). 7.99 *(978-0-7945-4009-8(0),* Usborne) EDC Publishing.

—How to Knit. Allman, Howard, photos by. Watt, Fiona. 2007. (Art Ideas Ser.). 64p. (J). (gr. 4-7). pap. 14.99 *(978-0-7945-1577-5(0),* Usborne) EDC Publishing.

—Lots of Things to Find & Color in Fairyland. 2015. (Lots of Things to Find & Color Ser.). (ENG.). 96p. (J). (gr. k-5). pap. 12.99 *(978-0-7945-3329-8(9),* Usborne) EDC Publishing.

—Rainy Day Stroller Book. Watt, Fiona. 2010. 8p. (J). 7.99 *(978-0-7945-2850-8(3),* Usborne) EDC Publishing.

—Seaside Stroller Book. Watt, Fiona. 2010. 8p. (J). 7.99 *(978-0-7945-2810-2(4),* Usborne) EDC Publishing.

—Sticker Dolly Dressing Dancers. Watt, Fiona. ed. 2011. (Sticker Dolly Dressing Ser.). 24p. (J). pap. 8.99 *(978-0-7945-2931-4(3),* Usborne) EDC Publishing.

—Sticker Dolly Dressing Fashion Long Ago. Bowman, Lucy. 2010. (Sticker Dolly Dressing Ser.). 24p. (J). pap. 8.99 *(978-0-7945-2547-7(4),* Usborne) EDC Publishing.

—Sticker Dolly Dressing Weddings. Watt, Fiona. ed. 2011. (Usborne Activities Ser.). 24p. (J). 8.99 *(978-0-7945-3105-8(9),* Usborne) EDC Publishing.

—Usborne 100 Science Experiments: Internet-Linked. Allman, Howard, photos by. Andrews, Georgina & Knighton, Kate. Chisholm, Jane, ed. 2006. 96p. (J). (gr. 4-7). 15.99 *(978-0-7945-1076-3(0))* EDC Publishing.

—The Usborne Big Book of Vacation Things to Make & Do. Watt, Fiona et al. 2006. 96p. (J). (gr. 1-4). pap. 14.99 *(978-0-7945-1317-7(4),* Usborne) EDC Publishing.

Baggott, Stella. Baby's Very First 123 Book. Baggott, Stella. 2010. (Baby's Very First Board Bks). 10p. (J). bds. 6.99 *(978-0-7945-2606-1(3),* Usborne) EDC Publishing.

—Baby's Very First Noisy Book. Baggott, Stella. 2010. 10p. (J). bds. 14.99 *(978-0-7945-2653-5(5),* Usborne) EDC Publishing.

—Baby's Very First Touchy-Feely Christmas Book. Baggott, Stella. 2010. (Baby's Very First Board Bks). 10p. (J). bds. 6.99 *(978-0-7945-2852-2(X),* Usborne) EDC Publishing.

Baggott, Stella & Leyhane, Vici. Sticker Dolly Dressing Ballerinas. Pratt, Leonie. 2007. (Usborne Activities Ser.). 24p. (J). (gr. -1-3). pap. 8.99 *(978-0-7945-1392-4(1),* Usborne) EDC Publishing.

—Sticker Dolly Dressing Fairies. Pratt, Leonie. 2007. (Usborne Activities Ser.). 24p. (J). (gr. -1-3). pap. 8.99 *(978-0-7945-1391-7(3),* Usborne) EDC Publishing.

Baggott, Stella & Miller, Antonia. Fashion Designer Summer Collection. Watt, Fiona. 2013. (Sticker Dolly Dressing Ser.). (ENG.). 24p. (J). (gr. -1-3). 8.99 *(978-0-7945-3008-2(7),* Usborne) EDC Publishing.

Baggott, Stella, jt. illus. see Leyhane, Vici.

Bagieu, Pénélope. The Witches. Dahl, Roald. 2020. (ENG.). 304p. (J). (gr. 3-7). pap. 14.99 ***(978-1-338-67743-0(8),*** Graphix) Scholastic, Inc.

Bagley, Jessixa. Curious EnCOUNTers: 1 to 13 Forest Friends. Clanton, Ben. 2020. (ENG.). 32p. (J). (gr. -1-2). 17.99 ***(978-1-63217-274-7(7),*** Little Bigfoot) Sasquatch Bks.

Bagley, Jessixa. A Girl, a Raccoon, & the Midnight Moon: (Juvenile Fiction, Mystery, Young Reader Detective Story, Light Fantasy for Kids) Young, Karen Romano. 2020. (ENG.). 392p. (J). (gr. 5-9). 16.99 *(978-1-4521-6952-1(7))* Chronicle Bks. LLC.

Bagley, Jessixa Bagley,Aaron. Vincent Comes Home. Bagley, Aaron & Bagley, Jessixa. 2018. (ENG.). 32p. (J). 17.99 *(978-1-62672-780-9(5),* 900173152) Roaring Brook Pr.

Bagley, Mark. All-New X-Men: Inevitable Vol. 4: IvX. 2017. (ENG.). 128p. (YA). (gr. 8-17). pap. 17.99 *(978-1-302-90523-1(6))* Marvel Worldwide, Inc.

Bagley, Mark, et al. Amazing Spider-Man Epic Collection: Maximum Carnage. 2020. 432p. (YA). (gr. 8-17). pap. 39.99 *(978-1-302-92190-3(8))* Marvel Worldwide, Inc.

Bagley, Mark. Ben Reilly: Scarlet Spider Vol. 2: Death's Sting. 2018. 112p. (YA). (gr. 8-17). pap. 15.99 *(978-0-7851-9459-0(2))* Marvel Worldwide, Inc.

Bagley, Mark, et al. Legends of Marvel: Spider-Man. 2020. (ENG.). 224p. (YA). (gr. 8-17). pap. 15.99 *(978-1-302-91954-2(7))* Marvel Worldwide, Inc.

Bagley, Mark. Spider-Man: Life Story. 2019. (ENG.). 200p. (YA). (gr. 4-17). pap. 24.99 *(978-1-302-91733-3(1))* Marvel Worldwide, Inc.

Bagley, Mark, et al. Spider-Man: the Many Hosts of Carnage. 2019. (ENG.). 480p. (YA). (gr. 8-17). pap. 39.99 *(978-1-302-91964-1(4))* Marvel Worldwide, Inc.

Bagley, Mark. Ultimate Spider-Man - Volume 12 Vol. 12: Superstars. 2007. (ENG.). 144p. (J). (gr. -1-17). pap. 12.99 *(978-0-7851-1629-5(X))* Marvel Worldwide, Inc.

—Ultimate Spider-Man - Volume 5: Public Scrutiny, 5, Vol. 5. 2007. (ENG.). 120p. (J). (gr. 4-17). pap. 11.99 *(978-0-7851-1087-3(9))* Marvel Worldwide, Inc.

—Ultimate Spider-Man - Volume 6: Venom, 8 vols., Vol. 6. 2006. (ENG.). 168p. (J). (gr. 4-17). pap. 15.99 *(978-0-7851-1094-1(1))* Marvel Worldwide, Inc.

—Ultimate Spider-Man - Volume 7: Irresponsible, 8 vols., Vol. 7. 2006. (ENG.). 144p. (J). (gr. -1-17). pap. 12.99 *(978-0-7851-1092-7(5))* Marvel Worldwide, Inc.

—Ultimate Spider-Man: Power & Responsibility Marvel Select Edition. 2019. (ENG.). 200p. (YA). (gr. 4-17). 24.99 *(978-1-302-91886-6(9))* Marvel Worldwide, Inc.

Bagley, Mark. Venom by Donny Cates Vol. 4: Venom Island. 2020. (ENG.). 136p. (YA). (gr. 8-17). pap. 17.99 ***(978-1-302-92020-3(0))*** Marvel Worldwide, Inc.

Bagley, Mark. Venom: First Host. 2018. (Venom: First Host Ser.: 1). (ENG.). 112p. (YA). (gr. 8-17). pap. 15.99 *(978-1-302-91344-1(1))* Marvel Worldwide, Inc.

Bagley, Mark, et al. Venomnibus Vol. 1. 2018. 1096p. (J). (gr. 4-17). pap. 100.00 *(978-1-302-91244-4(5))* Marvel Worldwide, Inc.

Bagley, Mark & Lim, Ron. Venom: Lethal Protector. 2018. (ENG.). 144p. (J). (gr. 4-17). pap. 16.99 *(978-1-302-91176-8(7))* Marvel Worldwide, Inc.

Bagley, Mark, jt. illus. see Deodato, Mike.

Bagley, Mark, jt. illus. see Marquez, David.

Bagley, Mark, jt. illus. see Walker, Tigh.

Bagley, Pat. Fit Kids Cookbook. Duffy, Kate & McRedmond, Sarah. 2004. 94p. (J). (gr. 4-7). spiral bd. 19.95 *(978-0-9709301-6-3(X))* Fit Kids.

—Kirby Soup for the Soul. Kirby, Robert. 2003. 127p. per. 9.95 *(978-0-9744860-2-4(7))* White Horse Bks.

Bagley, Rebecca. Armadillo & Hare: Tales from the Forest. Strong, Jeremy. 2020. (ENG.). 160p. (J). (gr. 2-5). 16.99 *(978-1-338-54059-8(9))* Scholastic, Inc.

Bagley, Tom. Canadian Boys Who Rocked the World, 1 vol. Kyi, Tanya Lloyd. 2007. (ENG.). 126p. (J). (gr. 3-2). pap. 12.95 *(978-1-55285-799-1(9),* 752fb294-f123-4fcc-9c21-a051168dad07) Whitecap Bks., Ltd. CAN. Dist: Firefly Bks., Ltd.

—Canadian Girls Who Rocked the World, 1 vol. Kyi, Tanya Lloyd. 2nd rev. ed. 2009. (ENG.). 128p. (J). (gr. 3-7). pap. 12.95 *(978-1-55285-986-5(X),* a553f2eb-f570-4a50-acb2-3a3a26e9fb7d) Whitecap Bks., Ltd. CAN. Dist: Firefly Bks., Ltd.

Bagley, Val Chadwick. I Will Follow God's Plan for Me. 2004. (J). *(978-1-59156-579-6(0))* Covenant Communications.

—I Will Trust in Heavenly Father & Jesus. 2006. (J). *(978-1-59811-056-2(X))* Covenant Communications.

—I'm Reverent When- Mullins, Amy. 2005. ("Move-About" Book Ser.). (J). *(978-1-59156-951-0(6))* Covenant Communications.

Bagley, Val Chadwick. My Little Book about Prayer. Bagley, Val Chadwick, tr. Beckstrand, Tamara, tr. 2004. (J). bds. 10.95 *(978-1-59156-096-8(9))* Covenant Communications, Inc.

Bagnell Grant, Julie. Annapolis Valley Bound. Newcomb, Joan. 4 Paws Games and Publishing, ed. 2017. (ENG.). (J). pap. *(978-1-988345-51-2(0))* Caswell, Vickianne.

Bagnoli, Gabriele. Disney Snow White & the Seven Dwarfs. Disney & Castellucci, Cecil. 2019. (ENG.). 72p. (J). (gr. 3-7). pap. 12.99 *(978-1-5067-1462-2(5))* Dark Horse Comics.

Bagnoli, Gabriele & Bovo, Beatrice. Disney: Where's Donald? Salati, Giorgio. 2019. (Look & Find Ser.). (ENG.). 48p. (J). *(978-1-5037-5206-1(2),* 4a4058a5-61f0-4477-af08-0b83a97ae4f4, p i kids) Phoenix International Publications, Inc.

Bahia, Elsa. Animal Asanas: Yoga for Children. Oostendorp, Leila Kadri. 2017. (ENG.). 64p. (J). (gr. k-4). 16.95 *(978-3-7913-7275-4(0))* Prestel Verlag GmbH & Co KG. DEU. Dist: Penguin Random Hse. LLC.

Bahng, Jeong-hwa. King Waste & King Save: An Energy Story. Jang, Hye-Kyeong. 2020. (Green Earth Tales Ser.). (ENG.). 32p. (J). (gr. k-4). pap. 8.99 ***(978-1-925235-59-3(9))***; lib. bdg. 27.99 ***(978-1-925235-63-0(7))*** ChoiceMaker Pty. Ltd., The AUS. (Big and SMALL). Dist: Lerner Publishing Group.

Bai, Durga. The Old Animals' Forest Band. Rao, Sirish. 2008. 40p. (J). (gr. -1-3). *(978-81-86211-41-0(1))* Tara Publishing.

Bai, Jenny. The Adventures of Banter & Jafar: Spoiled Rotten, 1 vol. Byrd, Michael. 2009. 36p. pap. 24.95 *(978-1-60836-131-1(4))* America Star Bks.

Baicker-McKee, Carol. An Apple Pie for Dinner, 0 vols. VanHecke, Susan. 2009. (ENG.). 32p. (J). (gr. k-3). 17.99 *(978-0-7614-5452-6(7),* 9780761454526, Two Lions) Amazon Publishing.

Baifus, Rut. Watching My Words: An Illustrated Children's Guide to the Laws of Shemiras Halashon. Grinvald, Zeev & Zryl, Laya. 2013. 63p. (J). *(978-1-56871-539-1(0))* Menucha Pubs. Inc.

Baik, Ji-Won. Let's Go for a Picnic: The Art of Millet. Jo, Seon-Hak. 2017. (Stories of Art Ser.). (ENG.). 36p. (J). (gr. 3-5). lib. bdg. 29.32 *(978-1-925235-27-2(0),* Big and SMALL) ChoiceMaker Pty. Ltd., The AUS. Dist: Lerner Publishing Group.

Baikie, Constance N., jt. illus. see Fulleylove, John.

Bailey, Court. The Homeless Christmas Tree. Gordon, Leslie M. 2005. 48p. (J). 19.95 *(978-1-933285-09-2(5))* Brown Books Publishing Group.

—The Homeless Christmas Tree. Gordon, Leslie M. 2008. (ENG.). 42p. (J). 19.95 *(978-0-87565-384-6(7))* Texas Christian Univ. Pr.

Bailey, Ella. I Don't Know What to Call My Cat. Philip, Simon. 2017. (ENG.). 32p. (J). (gr. -1-3). 16.99 *(978-0-544-97143-1(4),* 1662675, HMH Books For Young Readers) Houghton Mifflin Harcourt Publishing Co.

—One Day in Antarctica. 2016. (One Day on Our Blue Planet Ser.). 32p. (J). (gr. -1-2). 16.95 *(978-1-909263-67-3(2))* Flying Eye Bks. GBR. Dist: Penguin Random Hse. LLC.

—The Porridge Plot. Golden, Che. 2017. (ENG.). 256p. (J). pap. 9.99 *(978-1-84688-414-6(4)*, 351544) Alma Bks. GBR. Dist: Bloomsbury Publishing Plc.

Bailey, Frank. Hockey Canada's Learn All about Hockey: Color & Activity. Huberts, Al. 2012. (Rule 1, Sports Color & Activity Bks.). 188p. (J). (gr. -1-3). pap. 9.99 *(978-1-77049-436-7(7)*, Fenn-Tundra) Tundra Bks. CAN. Dist: Penguin Random Hse. LLC.

Bailey, Hannah. When We Became Humans: Our Incredible Evolutionary Journey. Bright, Michael. 2019. (Incredible Evolution Ser.). (ENG.). 64p. (J). (gr. 2-6). 19.95 ***(978-1-78603-887-6(0)***, Words & Pictures) Quarto Publishing Group UK GBR. Dist: Hachette Bk. Group.

Bailey, Hannah. 100 Greatest Moments in Irish History. Gallagher, Tara. 2011. (ENG.). 64p. (J). 24.00 *(978-0-7171-4970-4(6))* Gill Bks. IRL. Dist: Casemate Pubs. & Bk. Distributors, LLC.

Bailey, Lindsey. Peace People. Short, Robyn & Williams, Nanon McKewn. 2013. 38p. 18.95 *(978-0-9911148-2-5(5))* Goodmedia Communications, LLC.

—The Runaway Train: A Metaphor of the Plight of African American Children. Thompson, James M. Thompson, Danna H., ed. 2018. (ENG.). 32p. (YA). (gr. 7-12). 15.00 *(978-0-692-17501-9(6))* James Matthew Thompson.

Bailey, Lisa. Secret of Bete Grise Bay: A Michigan Lighthouse Adventure. Tillson, M. C. 2008. (ENG.). (J). (gr. 1-5). pap. 9.95 *(978-0-9764824-2-0(8))* A & M Writing and Publishing,.

Bailey, Loretta Dovell. I Saw a White Horse Today. Black, Janet, photos by. McMahon, V. Karen. 2011. 28p. pap. 24.95 *(978-1-4626-0282-7(7))* America Star Bks.

Bailey, Martha. New Mexico: Uno de muchos, de muchos Uno, 1. Bailey, Martha. l.t. ed. 2006. (SPA.). 96p. (J). per. *(978-0-9786448-0-2(8))* Bailey, Martha.

Bailey, Martin. Cornelius. 2020. (ENG.). 32p. (J). (gr. -1-k). 17.99 *(978-0-9951093-7-7(0))* Black Chook Bks. NZL. Dist: Independent Pubs. Group.

—Grandpa's Farm, 1 vol. Giulieri, Anne. 2012. (Engage Literacy Blue Ser.). (ENG.). 32p. (gr. k-2). pap. 5.99 *(978-1-4296-8988-5(9)*, Capstone Pr.) Capstone.

—The Lost Sock, 1 vol. Giulieri, Anne. 2012. (Engage Literacy Red Ser.). (ENG.). 32p. (gr. k-2). pap. 5.99 *(978-1-4296-8940-3(4)*, Capstone Pr.) Capstone.

—Max & the Balloons, 1 vol. Giulieri, Anne. 2012. (Engage Literacy Yellow Ser.). (ENG.). 32p. (gr. k-2). pap. 5.99 *(978-1-4296-8960-1(9)*, Capstone Pr.) Capstone.

—Up & Down, 1 vol. Dale, Jay. 2012. (Engage Literacy Magenta Ser.). (ENG.). 32p. (gr. k-2). pap. 5.99 *(978-1-4296-8878-9(5)*, Capstone Pr.) Capstone.

Bailey, Melissa. Broc & Cara's Gut Book. Wilson, Dave a. 2018. (Broc & Cara's Gut Book Ser.: Vol. 2). (ENG.). 36p. (J). pap. *(978-0-9919411-4-8(4))* Wilson, Dave Publishing.

—Broc & Cara's Picnic Party. Wilson, Dave a. 2014. (Broc & Cara Presents Ser.: Vol. 1). (ENG.). 32p. (J). pap. *(978-0-9919411-2-4(8))* Wilson, Dave Publishing.

—How to Be a Heroine-For Girls: Inspiration from Classic Heroines. Schuller, Kathleen. 2013. 68p. 19.95 *(978-1-4575-1649-8(7))* Dog Ear Publishing, LLC.

—Jamie's Journey: Cancer from the Voice of a Sibling. Wozny, Sharon. 2016. (ENG.). 64p. (J). (gr. 3). pap. 14.95 *(978-1-58985-234-1(6)*, Story Monsters Pr.) Story Monsters LLC.

Bailey, Peter. The Girl with the Broken Wing. Dyer, Heather. 2005. 147p. (J). *(978-1-4156-3468-4(8))* Scholastic, Inc.

—I, Jack. Finney, Patricia. 2004. 192p. (J). 15.99 *(978-0-06-052207-0(0))*; lib. bdg. 16.89 *(978-0-06-052208-7(9))* HarperCollins Pubs.

—The Ice Child. Ward, Nick. 2004. 32p. (J). *(978-1-84458-038-5(5)*, Pavilion Children's Books) Pavilion Bks.

—Jack & Rebel, the Police Dog. 2007. 183p. (J). (gr. 3-7). 15.99 *(978-0-06-088049-1(X))* HarperCollins Pubs.

—The Scarecrow & His Servant. Pullman, Philip. (ENG.). 240p. (J). (gr. 3-7). 2007. 7.99 *(978-0-440-42130-6(6)*, Yearling); 2005. 15.95 *(978-0-375-81531-7(7)*, Knopf Bks. for Young Readers) Random Hse. Children's Bks.

—The Silver Skates. Dodge, Mary Mapes. 2018. (Alma Junior Classics Ser.). 352p. (J). pap. 11.00 *(978-1-84749-720-8(9)*, 382471) Alma Classics GBR. Dist: Bloomsbury Publishing Plc.

—Song of the Dolphin Boy. Laird, Elizabeth. 2019. (ENG.). 224p. (J). (gr. 2-4). 9.99 *(978-1-5098-2823-4(0))* Pan Macmillan GBR. Dist: Independent Pubs. Group.

Bailey, Peter. The Ice Child. Bailey, Peter, tr. Ward, Nick. 2003. 32p. (YA). *(978-1-84365-004-1(5)*, Pavilion Children's Books) Pavilion Bks.

Bailey, Sally. A is for Astoria. Leedom, Karen L. 2010. 32p. 15.00 *(978-0-9826252-0-0(0))* Rivertide Publishing.

Bailey, Sheila. Alligator Jazz, 1 vol. Pittman, Samuel, II. 2018. (ENG.). 32p. (J). (gr. -1-3). 16.99 *(978-1-4556-2422-5(5)*, Pelican Publishing) Arcadia Publishing.

—Carla's Sandwich. Herman, Debbie. 2004. 32p. (J). (gr. k-3). 17.95 *(978-0-9729225-2-4(0))* Flashlight Pr.

—Sweetest Story Bible: Sweet Thoughts & Sweet Words for Little Girls, 1 vol. Stortz, Diane M. 2010. (ENG.). 224p. (J). 16.99 *(978-0-310-71673-0(X))* Zonderkidz.

—Sweetest Story Bible for Toddlers, 1 vol. Stortz, Diane M. 2014. (ENG.). 32p. (J). bds. 9.99 *(978-0-310-74630-0(2))* Zonderkidz.

Bailey, Sian. Grandfather Mountain: Stories of Gods & Heroes from Many Cultures. Muten, Burleigh. 2004. (ENG.). 80p. (J). (gr. 3-6). 19.99 *(978-1-84148-789-2(9))* Barefoot Bks., Inc.

—A Treasury of Fairy Tales. Cresswell, Helen. 2013. (ENG.). 96p. (J). *(978-0-00-754651-0(3)*, HarperCollins Children's Bks.) HarperCollins Pubs. Ltd. GBR. Dist: HarperCollins Pubs.

Bailey, Siân. My Fairytale Princess Mini Jigsaw Book. Bailey, Siân. 2009. (ENG.). 12p. (J). (gr. k-2). bds. 10.99 *(978-0-230-70710-8(6))* Pan Macmillan GBR. Dist: Independent Pubs. Group.

Bailey, Sidney. Grandma & Me Oh What Do We See When We Go to the Zoo? Ray, Sandra. 2011. 32p. 14.99 *(978-1-4520-8133-5(6))* AuthorHouse.

Bailey, Terri L. Minnow Kisses. Shank, Diane S. 2011. 34p. pap. 12.95 *(978-1-936343-60-7(6))* Peppertree Pr., The.

Bailly, Simon. The Book in the Book in the Book. Baer, Julien. 2019. 56p. (J). (gr. -1-3). 18.99 *(978-0-8234-4243-0(8))* Holiday Hse., Inc.

Bailly, Vincent. A Bag of Marbles: The Graphic Novel. Joffo, Joseph. 2013. (ENG.). 128p. (YA). (gr. 7-12). pap. 9.99 *(978-1-4677-1516-4(6)*, 9781467715164); E-Book 43.99 *(978-1-4677-1651-2(0))* Lerner Publishing Group. (Graphic Universe™).

Bain, Murray. Santa Never Brings Me a Banjo, 1 vol. Myles, David. 2018. (ENG.). 32p. (J). (gr. -1-k). 22.95 *(978-1-77108-627-1(0)*, df7b2317-30af-4786-add9-addbea601993) Nimbus Publishing, Ltd. CAN. Dist: Baker & Taylor Publisher Services (BTPS).

Bain, Tris. If We Could Find Another Way. Defossez, Hélène. 2018. (ENG.). 40p. (J). (gr. k-6). pap. 12.95 *(978-1-4218-3806-9(0))* 1st World Publishing, Inc.

Bainbridge, Bob, jt. illus. see Bainbridge, Shane.

Bainbridge, Shane & Bainbridge, Bob. The Hen That Couldn't Lay an Egg. Smith, Clyde. 2011. 32p. pap. 24.95 *(978-1-4626-3796-6(5))* America Star Bks.

Baines, Nigel. Alien Attack! MacDonald, Alan. 2015. 192p. (J). (gr. 2-4). pap. 9.99 *(978-1-4088-2524-2(4)*, 900146259, Bloomsbury Children's Bks.) Bloomsbury Publishing USA.

—All Things Weird & Wonderful. Henderson, Stewart. 2003. (ENG.). 96p. (J). (gr. 2-4). 19.99 *(978-0-7459-4678-8(X))* Lion Hudson PLC GBR. Dist: Independent Pubs. Group.

—The Funniest Animal Joke Book Ever. King, Joe. 2015. 96p. (J). pap. 9.99 *(978-1-78344-233-1(6))* Andersen Pr. GBR. Dist: Independent Pubs. Group.

—The Funniest Dinosaur Joke Book Ever. King, Joe. 2018. 64p. (J). (gr. 2-4). pap. 8.99 *(978-1-78344-648-3(X))* Andersen Pr. GBR. Dist: Independent Pubs. Group.

—The Little Book of Christmas Jokes. King, Joe. 2016. 128p. (J). (gr. k-2). pap. 6.95 *(978-1-78344-487-8(8))* Andersen Pr. GBR. Dist: Independent Pubs. Group.

—The Little Book of Football Jokes. King, Joe. 2018. 128p. (J). (gr. 2-4). pap. 8.99 *(978-1-78344-672-8(2))* Andersen Pr. GBR. Dist: Independent Pubs. Group.

—The Little Book of Spooky Jokes. King, Joe. 2018. 128p. (J). (gr. 2-4). pap. 8.99 *(978-1-78344-572-1(6))* Andersen Pr. GBR. Dist: Independent Pubs. Group.

—Supercool Snotman, No. 8. Dave, Matt. (ENG.). 112p. pap. *(978-1-84738-288-7(6))* Simon & Schuster, Ltd.

—Yuck's Amazing Underpants. Matt and Dave, Matt and. 2012. (Yuck Ser.). (ENG.). 112p. (J). (gr. 2-5). pap. 4.99 *(978-1-4424-5122-3(X)*, Simon & Schuster/Paula Wiseman Bks.) Simon & Schuster/Paula Wiseman Bks.

—Yuck's Big Booger Challenge. Matt & Dave. 2013. (Yuck Ser.). (ENG.). 112p. (J). (gr. 2-5). 15.99 *(978-1-4424-8311-8(3)*, Simon & Schuster/Paula Wiseman Bks.) Simon & Schuster/Paula Wiseman Bks.

—Yuck's Big Booger Challenge. Matt and Dave, Matt and. 2013. (Yuck Ser.). (ENG.). 112p. (J). (gr. 2-5). pap. 4.99 *(978-1-4424-8312-5(1)*, Simon & Schuster/Paula Wiseman Bks.) Simon & Schuster/Paula Wiseman Bks.

—Yuck's Fart Club. Matt and Dave, Matt and. 2013. (Yuck Ser.). (ENG.). 112p. (J). (gr. 2-5). pap. 6.99 *(978-1-4424-8152-7(8)*, Simon & Schuster/Paula Wiseman Bks.) Simon & Schuster/Paula Wiseman Bks.

—Yuck's Mega Magic Wand. Dave, Matt. 9th ed. (ENG.). 112p. pap. *(978-1-84738-298-6(3))* Simon & Schuster, Ltd.

—Yuck's Pet Worm. Matt and Dave, Matt and. 2013. (Yuck Ser.). (ENG.). 112p. (J). (gr. 2-5). pap. 6.99 *(978-1-4424-8149-7(8)*, Simon & Schuster/Paula Wiseman Bks.) Simon & Schuster/Paula Wiseman Bks.

—Yuck's Robotic Butt Blast. Matthews, Morgan & Sinden, David. 2013. (Yuck Ser.). (ENG.). 112p. (J). (gr. 2-5). 15.99 *(978-1-4424-8308-8(3)*, Simon & Schuster/Paula Wiseman Bks.) Simon & Schuster/Paula Wiseman Bks.

—Yuck's Robotic Butt Blast. Matt and Dave, Matt and. 2013. (Yuck Ser.). (ENG.). 112p. (J). (gr. 2-5). pap. 4.99 *(978-1-4424-8309-5(1)*, Simon & Schuster/Paula Wiseman Bks.) Simon & Schuster/Paula Wiseman Bks.

—Yuck's Slime Monster. Matt & Dave. 2012. (Yuck Ser.). (ENG.). 112p. (J). (gr. 2-5). 14.99 *(978-1-4424-5124-7(6)*, Simon & Schuster/Paula Wiseman Bks.) Simon & Schuster/Paula Wiseman Bks.

—Yuck's Slime Monster. Matt and Dave, Matt and. 2012. (Yuck Ser.). (ENG.). 112p. (J). (gr. 2-5). pap. 5.99 *(978-1-4424-5126-1(2)*, Simon & Schuster/Paula Wiseman Bks.) Simon & Schuster/Paula Wiseman Bks.

Baines, Rachel. Shelby Finds Her Family. Groendyk, Barbara. 2019. (ENG.). 34p. (J). pap. 12.99 *(978-1-62586-099-6(4))* Credo Hse. Pubs.

—The Tasty Thumb. Berry, Kelly. 2018. (ENG.). 32p. (J). 13.99 *(978-1-945507-71-7(3))* Carpenter's Son Publishing.

Bair, Michael. Identity Crisis. Meltzer, Brad. rev. ed. 2005. (ENG.). 264p. (YA). 24.99 *(978-1-4012-0688-8(3))* DC Comics.

Baird, Roberta. El Barco Amarillo. Hillert, Margaret. 2020. (Beginning-To-Read: Spanish Easy Stories Ser.). (SPA.). 32p. (J). (-2). 22.60 ***(978-1-68450-887-7(8))***; pap. 11.94 ***(978-1-68404-527-3(4))*** Norwood Hse. Pr.

Baird, Roberta. The Runaway Pumpkin Pie Man, 1 vol. Town, Vicky. 2015. (ENG.). 32p. (J). (gr. k-3). 16.99 *(978-1-4556-2025-8(4)*, Pelican Publishing) Arcadia Publishing.

—The Swamp Where Gator Hides, 1 vol. Berkes, Marianne. 2014. (ENG.). 32p. (J). (gr. k-4). 16.95 *(978-1-58469-470-0(X))*; pap. 8.95 *(978-1-58469-471-7(8))* Sourcebooks, Inc. (Dawn Pubns.).

—The Yellow Boat. Hillert, Margaret. 2016. (BeginningtoRead Ser.). (ENG.). 32p. (J). (gr. -1-2). 22.60 *(978-1-59953-811-2(3))*; pap. 11.94 *(978-1-60357-952-0(4))* Norwood Hse. Pr.

Baisley, Maryann Leake. Madison's Mixed-up Flower Girl Magic & Aiden's Amazing Ring Bearer Act Aiden's Amazing Ring Bearer Act. Beach, Kathleen H. & Weeber, Stephanie B. 2009. 32p. pap. 19.95 *(978-1-4251-7059-2(5))* Trafford Publishing.

Baisley, Stephen, jt. illus. see Comfort, Mike.

Baity, Susan. Celebrations! Anderson, Gennifer. 2013. 38p. pap. 16.95 *(978-1-57258-905-6(1))* TEACH Services, Inc.

Baizer, Gayle Susan. Miss Donna's Mulberry Acres Farm. Douglas, Donna. 2011. (Mulberry Acres Farm Ser.). (ENG.). 24p. (J). (gr. -1-3). pap. 10.99 *(978-1-61036-098-2(2))* Bridge-Logos, Inc.

Bajaj, Subash. The Three Little Pigs. 2010. (J). *(978-1-60617-135-6(6))* Teaching Strategies, LLC.

Bajet, John John. Baby Shark: Doo Doo Doo Doo Doo Doo. 2018. 24p. (J). (gr. -1-k). pap. 6.99 *(978-1-338-55605-6(3)*, Cartwheel Bks.) Scholastic, Inc.

—Bunny & Chick. Skwish, Emily. 2020. (ENG.). 20p. (J). bds. *(978-1-5037-5229-0(1)*, 4e850a18-1362-48e9-896c-e44546d621c6, p i kids) Phoenix International Publications, Inc.

—Hide-And-Seek, Baby Shark! 2019. (ENG.). 12p. (J). (gr. -1 — 1). 8.99 *(978-1-338-60500-6(3)*, Cartwheel Bks.) Scholastic, Inc.

—I Love You, Baby Shark! 2019. (ENG.). 24p. (J). (gr. -1-k). pap. 6.99 *(978-1-338-60634-8(4)*, Cartwheel Bks.) Scholastic, Inc.

Bajet, John John. Time for School, Baby Shark: Doo Doo Doo Doo Doo. 2020. (Baby Shark Ser.). (ENG.). 24p. (J). (gr. -1-k). pap. 6.99 ***(978-1-338-66528-4(6)***, Cartwheel Bks.) Scholastic, Inc.

Bajtlik, Jan. Our Car. Brum, J. M. 2018. (ENG.). 32p. (J). (gr. -1-1). 16.99 *(978-1-62672-246-0(3)*, 900146855) Roaring Brook Pr.

Bajtlik, Jan. Greek Myths & Labyrinths. Bajtlik, Jan. 2019. (ENG.). 80p. (J). (gr. 5). 35.00 *(978-1-5362-0964-8(3))* Candlewick Pr.

Baker, Addison. The Animals Next Door. Baker, Addison. 2019. (Animals Next Door Ser.: Vol. 1). (ENG.). 202p. (J). pap. 14.97 *(978-0-9998358-6-9(6))* Tribute Publishing.

Baker, Alan. Animal Homes. Martin, Debbie. 2004. (Luxury Lift-the-Flap Ser.). 16p. (J). (gr. 1-18). 11.95 *(978-0-7945-0715-2(8)*, Usborne) EDC Publishing.

—Odyssey. 2004. (Kingfisher Epics Ser.). (ENG.). 176p. (YA). (gr. 3-7). pap. 8.99 *(978-0-7534-5723-8(7)*, 900052605, Kingfisher) Roaring Brook Pr.

—Two Tiny Mice: A Mouse-Eye Exploration of Nature. rev. ed. 2014. (ENG.). 40p. (J). (gr. -1-3). 16.95 *(978-1-62914-627-0(7)*, Sky Pony Pr.) Skyhorse Publishing Co., Inc.

Baker, Amanda. The Cheesehead Night Before Christmas. 2007. 40p. (J). per. 19.95 *(978-0-9797781-0-0(7))* Dreams 2 Wings LLC.

—Zack's Zany Zucchiniland. 2012. 32p. (J). 17.95 *(978-0-9832383-1-7(6))* Black Garnet Pr.

Baker, Baygent. One Bad Day. Macdaniels, Adam & Macdaniels, Candice. 2019. (ENG.). 30p. (J). pap. 9.13 ***(978-1-7904-5317-7(8))*** Independently Published.

Baker, Celia M. My Tooth Fell in My Soup: And Other Poems. Korhel, Erik. 2009. 26p. (J). 14.95 *(978-1-935359-02-9(9))* Bk. Pubs. Network.

Baker, Celia Marie. This Is Ella. Ewert, Krista. 2017. (ENG.). (J). *(978-1-5255-1360-2(5))*; (gr. -1-k). *(978-1-5255-1361-9(3))* FriesenPress.

Baker, Darrell. Aladdin. Kreider, Karen. 2015. (Little Golden Book Ser.). (ENG.). 24p. (J). (gr. -1-2). 4.99 *(978-0-7364-2259-8(5)*, Golden/Disney) Random Hse. Children's Bks.

Baker, David. The Adventures of Sugar the Pup. T. 2011. 36p. pap. 24.95 *(978-1-4560-5724-4(3))* America Star Bks.

—The Amazing Chickens at Cliff House. Atkinson, Linda. 2011. 28p. pap. 24.95 *(978-1-4560-7744-0(9))* America Star Bks.

—Baby Dario Eats His First Carrot. Loccisano, Rina. 2012. 48p. pap. 24.95 *(978-1-4560-6100-5(3))* America Star Bks.

—Baby Dario Is Born. Loccisano, Rina. 2012. 36p. pap. 24.95 *(978-1-4560-6099-2(6))* America Star Bks.

—Blackberry Junction. Scott, Gwen. 2011. 28p. pap. 24.95 *(978-1-4560-0951-9(6))* America Star Bks.

—The Blue & Purple Egg. Smith, J. L. 2012. 28p. pap. 24.95 *(978-1-4626-6789-5(9))* America Star Bks.

—Broken Bones Are No Fun, but Broken Bones Won't Stop My Play! Scott, Molly. 2012. 32p. pap. 24.95 *(978-1-4626-7424-4(0))* America Star Bks.

—The Candy Bandit Strikes Again! Coné, Robert. 2011. 28p. pap. 24.95 *(978-1-4560-8019-8(9))* America Star Bks.

—Christmas Island. Norman, Travis D. 2011. 28p. pap. 24.95 *(978-1-4560-9800-1(4))* America Star Bks.

—Claude's Shrinking Shell. Maranhas, Jayne Ellen. 2011. 28p. pap. 24.95 *(978-1-4512-8144-6(7))* America Star Bks.

—Cooldog's Holiday Adventures. Belanger, Kathleen. 2012. 48p. 24.95 *(978-1-4626-3045-5(6))* America Star Bks.

—Dogfish on the Moon: Santa Claus & the Flying Carpet 2. Du Lac, Leo J. 2012. 26p. 24.95 *(978-1-4560-1036-2(0))* America Star Bks.

—Frankie. Phanton, Richard G. 2012. 40p. 24.95 *(978-1-4560-3509-9(6))* America Star Bks.

—Handy Sandy. Carol Hersh. 2011. 28p. pap. 24.95 *(978-1-4560-8991-7(9))* America Star Bks.

—Haylie's Haunted Hamper. Caligiuri, Susan. 2011. 28p. pap. 24.95 *(978-1-4560-0909-0(5))* America Star Bks.

—Kelli, God & New York. Dubrule, Jackie. 2013. 28p. pap. 24.95 *(978-1-4560-0969-4(9))* America Star Bks.

—The Little Mouse on the Prairie. Camp, V. Ray. 2011. 28p. pap. 24.95 *(978-1-4560-1028-7(X))* America Star Bks.

—The Loneliest Leaf. Barry, Debra R. 2011. 28p. pap. 24.95 *(978-1-4560-1002-7(6))* America Star Bks.

—Moon Fruit & the Dragons: Santa Claus & the Flying Carpet 3. Du Lac, Leo J. Washington, Victoria, ed. 2012. 26p. 24.95 *(978-1-4560-1037-9(9))* America Star Bks.

—Our New Addition. Headrick, Julianna. 2011. 28p. pap. 24.95 *(978-1-4560-0933-5(8))* America Star Bks.

—Pigeon Toed. Moore, Tijon Adamson. 2011. 28p. pap. 24.95 *(978-1-4560-0607-5(X))* America Star Bks.

—Playdance Studio. Gaulkin, Marianne Quigley. 2011. 28p. pap. 24.95 *(978-1-4560-2163-4(X))* America Star Bks.

—Rollie & Mollie: Disappearing Act. Swenson, Lynn. 2012. 26p. 24.95 *(978-1-4626-5277-8(8))* America Star Bks.

—Sam & the Tale of the Dragon Prints. Moore, Shawn. 2011. 28p. pap. 24.95 *(978-1-4560-7724-2(4))* America Star Bks.

—The Same As James. Jubilee Jr., Thomas. 2011. 28p. pap. 24.95 *(978-1-4626-0288-9(6))* America Star Bks.

—The Teddy That Went to Iraq. Sarah Taylor. 2011. 28p. pap. 24.95 *(978-1-4560-8382-3(1))* America Star Bks.

—Thunderburps. Spear, Lisa D. 2012. 26p. 24.95 *(978-1-4626-0793-8(4))* America Star Bks.

—The Travels of Chikippo. Padua, Grace. 2012. 26p. 24.95 *(978-1-4626-9782-3(8))* America Star Bks.

—While You Sleep. Dalton, Sommer. 2011. 28p. pap. 24.95 *(978-1-4560-2360-7(8))* America Star Bks.

—You're the Same As Me. Narr, Rachel K. 2012. 26p. 24.95 *(978-1-60749-472-0(8))* America Star Bks.

Baker, David A. My Favorite Sport Is? Wilson, Chloe. 2017. (ENG.). (J). pap. 19.95 *(978-1-63448-571-5(8))* America Star Bks.

Baker, Deborah Ann. Charlie's Dream. Baker, Deborah Ann. 2019. (ENG.). 44p. (J). pap. 19.95 ***(978-1-5210-4214-4(4))*** Independently Published.

Baker, Don, jt. illus. see Armstrong, Bev.

Baker, Ed. The Story of Kitten Cuckoo. Baker, Ed. 2007. (ENG.). 32p. (J). (gr. -1-17). 15.95 *(978-1-933572-04-8(3))* Centro Bks., LLC.

Baker, Edmund. Another Dolphin's Tale, a Love Story. Harpan, Gaile & DiMarcello, Pete. 2012. 16p. pap. 12.95 *(978-1-61493-057-0(0))* Peppertree Pr., The.

—Panic at the Pool. Dimarcello, Pete. Harpan, Gaile, ed. 2013. 20p. pap. 12.95 *(978-1-61493-169-0(0))* Peppertree Pr., The.

Baker-Gusman, Cynthia. A Big Change for Daisy. Collins, Keri T. 2020. (ENG.). 42p. (J). pap. 12.99 ***(978-1-948604-42-0(6))*** Networlding.

Baker, Ian. Codes: How to Make Them & Break Them! Poskitt, Kjartan. 2017. (ENG.). 160p. (J). (gr. 2-7). pap. 6.99 *(978-1-63158-127-4(9)*, Racehorse Publishing) Skyhorse Publishing Co., Inc.

—Growing up Is Hard to Do: Reflections on Your Earliest Beginnings to Your Late Teenage Years. Spence, Jay. 2017. (ENG.). (J). *(978-1-5255-1177-6(7))* FriesenPress.

Baker, Jaana. Aloha Santa. Taylor, Dana. 2019. (ENG.). 28p. (J). pap. 10.99 ***(978-1-7066-1500-2(0))*** Independently Published.

Baker, Janet. Living Things. Chesire, Gerald. 2008. (World of Wonder Ser.). (ENG.). 32p. (J). (gr. 1-4). pap. 9.95 *(978-0-531-23822-6(9)*, Children's Pr.) Scholastic Library Publishing.

Baker, Janet, et al. Living World. Chesire, Gerald. 2008. (World of Wonder Ser.). (ENG.). 32p. (J). (gr. 1-4). 29.00 *(978-0-531-24026-7(6)*, Children's Pr.) Scholastic Library Publishing.

—Scary Creatures of the City. Clarke, Penny. 2009. (Scary Creatures Ser.). (ENG.). 32p. (J). (gr. 2-4). 27.00 *(978-0-531-21820-4(1)*, Watts, Franklin); pap. 8.95 *(978-0-531-22225-6(X)*, Children's Pr.) Scholastic Library Publishing.

Baker, Jeannie. Belonging. Baker, Jeannie. 2004. 32p. (J). *(978-0-7445-9227-6(5))* Walker Bks., Ltd.

—Circle. Baker, Jeannie. 2020. (ENG.). 48p. (J). (gr. k-3). 9.99 *(978-1-5362-1057-6(9))* Candlewick Pr.

—Home. Baker, Jeannie. 2004. (ENG.). 32p. (J). (gr. k-5). 16.99 *(978-0-06-623935-4(4)*, Greenwillow Bks.) HarperCollins Pubs.

—Mirror. Baker, Jeannie. 2010. (ENG.). 48p. (J). (gr. k-4). 19.99 *(978-0-7636-4848-0(5))* Candlewick Pr.

—Playing with Collage. Baker, Jeannie. 2019. (ENG.). 40p. (J). (gr. 3-7). 16.00 *(978-1-5362-0539-8(7))* Candlewick Pr.

Baker, Jennifer. Merlin's Island. Mann, Margaret. 2003. 147p. (gr. 4-7). pap. *(978-0-9538685-2-0(4))* Tayar Books.

Baker, Joanna. Moggies. Stennett, Jayne. 2016. (ENG.). 25p. (J). pap. *(978-1-910223-79-6(4))* UK Bk. Publishing.

—The Moggies' Big Adventure. Stennett, Jayne. 2016. (ENG.). 40p. (J). pap. *(978-1-910223-80-2(8))* UK Bk. Publishing.

Baker, Joe. The Dragon Cant. Dongweck, James. 2004. 32p. (J). per. 16.95 *(978-0-9719632-0-7(7))* Golden Monkey Publishing, LLC.

Baker, Jonathan. The Ultimate Heart. Written By Doretta Elaine Wilson; Illust. 2011. 32p. pap. 24.95 *(978-1-4626-0684-9(9))* America Star Bks.

Baker, Keith. Six Silly Foxes. Moran, Alex. 2003. (Green Light Readers Level 1 Ser.). (ENG.). 24p. (J). (gr. -1-3). pap. 4.99 *(978-0-15-204863-1(4)*, 1194686) Houghton Mifflin Harcourt Publishing Co.

—Six Silly Foxes. Moran, Alex. ed. 2003. (Green Light Readers Level 1 Ser.). (gr. -1-3). lib. bdg. 13.50 *(978-0-613-64595-9(2))* Turtleback.

Baker, Keith. Hap-Pea All Year. Baker, Keith. 2016. (Peas Ser.). (ENG.). 40p. (J). (gr. -1-3). 18.99 *(978-1-4814-5854-2(X)*, Beach Lane Bks.) Beach Lane Bks.

—Hap-Pea All Year. Baker, Keith. 2019. (Peas Ser.). (ENG.). 36p. (J). (gr. -1 — 1). bds. 7.99 *(978-1-5344-5657-0(0)*, Little Simon) Little Simon.

—Hap-Pea All Year: Book & CD. Baker, Keith. 2019. (Peas Ser.). (ENG.). 40p. (J). (gr. -1-3). pap. 9.99 *(978-1-5344-1843-1(1)*, Little Simon) Little Simon.

—Little Green Peas. Baker, Keith. 2016. (Peas Ser.). (ENG.). 36p. (J). (gr. -1 — 1). bds. 7.99 *(978-1-4814-6248-8(2)*, Little Simon) Little Simon.

—Little Green Peas: A Big Book of Colors. Baker, Keith. 2014. (Peas Ser.). (ENG.). 40p. (J). (gr. -1-3). 18.99 *(978-1-4424-7660-8(5)*, Beach Lane Bks.) Beach Lane Bks.

—Little Green Peas: Book & CD. Baker, Keith. 2019. (Peas Ser.). (ENG.). 40p. (J). (gr. -1-3). pap. 9.99 *(978-1-5344-1846-2(6)*, Little Simon) Little Simon.

B

—LMNO Pea-Quel. Baker, Keith. (Peas Ser.). (ENG.). 40p. (J). (gr. -1-3). 2019. 7.99 *(978-1-5344-6669-2(X))*; 2017. 17.99 *(978-1-4814-5856-6(6))* Beach Lane Bks. (Beach Lane Bks.).

Baker, Keith. LMNO Pea-Quel: Book & CD. Baker, Keith. 2020. (Peas Ser.). (ENG.). 40p. (J). (gr. -1-3). pap. 9.99 ***(978-1-5344-1847-9(4)***, Little Simon) Little Simon.

Baker, Keith. LMNO Peas. Baker, Keith. 2010. (Peas Ser.). (ENG.). 40p. (J). (gr. -1-3). 17.99 *(978-1-4169-9141-0(7)*, Beach Lane Bks.) Beach Lane Bks.

—LMNO Peas. Baker, Keith. 2014. (Peas Ser.). (ENG.). 36p. (J). (gr. -1-k). bds. 7.99 *(978-1-4424-8978-3(2)*, Little Simon) Little Simon.

—LMNO Peas: Book & CD. Baker, Keith. 2018. (Peas Ser.). (ENG.). 40p. (J). (gr. -1-3). pap. 9.99 *(978-1-5344-1844-8(X)*, Little Simon) Little Simon.

—Lucky Days with Mr. & Mrs. Green, 1 vol. Baker, Keith. 2007. (Mr. & Mrs. Green Ser.). (ENG.). 72p. (J). (gr. 2-4). 29.93 *(978-1-59961-300-0(X)*, 11674) Spotlight.

—Meet Mr. & Mrs. Green, 1 vol. Baker, Keith. 2007. (Mr. & Mrs. Green Ser.). (ENG.). 71p. (J). (gr. 2-4). 29.93 *(978-1-59961-301-7(8)*, 11675) Spotlight.

—More Mr. & Mrs. Green, 1 vol. Baker, Keith. 2007. (Mr. & Mrs. Green Ser.). (ENG.). 68p. (J). (gr. 2-4). 29.93 *(978-1-59961-302-4(6)*, 11676) Spotlight.

—My Octopus Arms. Baker, Keith. 2013. (ENG.). 40p. (J). (gr. -1-3). 16.99 *(978-1-4424-5843-7(7)*, Beach Lane Bks.) Beach Lane Bks.

—No Two Alike. Baker, Keith. 2011. (ENG.). 40p. (J). (gr. -1-2). 16.99 *(978-1-4424-1742-7(0)*, Beach Lane Bks.) Beach Lane Bks.

—On the Go with Mr. & Mrs. Green, 1 vol. Baker, Keith. 2007. (Mr. & Mrs. Green Ser.). (ENG.). 72p. (J). (gr. 2-4). 29.93 *(978-1-59961-303-1(4)*, 11677) Spotlight.

—1-2-3 Peas. Baker, Keith. 2012. (Peas Ser.). (ENG.). 40p. (J). (gr. -1-3). 17.99 *(978-1-4424-4551-2(3)*, Beach Lane Bks.) Beach Lane Bks.

—1-2-3 Peas. Baker, Keith. 2014. (Peas Ser.). (ENG.). 36p. (J). (gr. -1 — 1). bds. 8.99 *(978-1-4424-9928-7(1)*, Little Simon) Little Simon.

—1-2-3 Peas: Book & CD. Baker, Keith. 2019. (Peas Ser.). (ENG.). 40p. (J). (gr. -1-3). pap. 9.99 *(978-1-5344-1845-5(8)*, Little Simon) Little Simon.

—2 Peas in a Pod! LMNO Peas; 1-2-3 Peas. Baker, Keith. ed. 2013. (ENG.). 80p. (J). (gr. -1-3). 33.99 *(978-1-4424-9991-1(5)*, Beach Lane Bks.) Beach Lane Bks.

—4 Titles, 4 vols. Baker, Keith. ABDO Publishing Company Staff. 2007. (Mr. & Mrs. Green Ser.). (ENG.). 72p. (J). (gr. 2-4). lib. bdg. 119.72 *(978-1-59961-299-7(2)*, 11673) Spotlight.

—5 Peas in a Pod! LMNO Peas; 1-2-3 Peas; Little Green Peas; Hap-Pea All Year; LMNO Pea-Quel. Baker, Keith. ed. 2017. (Peas Ser.). (ENG.). 200p. (J). (-3). 89.99 *(978-1-5344-0379-6(5)*, Beach Lane Bks.) Beach Lane Bks.

Baker, Kyle. Truth: Red, White & Black. Morales, Robert. 2004. 168p. (YA). pap. 14.99 *(978-0-7851-1072-9(0))* Marvel Worldwide, Inc.

Baker, Leslie. A Song for Lena. Hippely, Hilary Horder. 2011. (ENG.). 40p. (J). (gr. -1-3). 19.99 *(978-1-4424-2946-8(1)*, Simon & Schuster Bks. For Young Readers) Simon & Schuster Bks. For Young Readers.

Baker, Markus. Dogs R Amazing! Galvin, Adam & Baker, Mark. 2019. (ENG.). 46p. (J). pap. ***(978-1-9161450-6-1(X))*** R-and-Q.com.

Baker, Megan. My Food Allergy Book. Baker, Eastin. 2019. (ENG.). 26p. (J). pap. 9.99 *(978-1-0770-7388-3(7))* Independently Published.

Baker, Penny. Big Purple Undies. Kelman, Louise & Kelman, Suzanne. Dowling, Jane, ed. 2004. 64p. (J). pap. *(978-0-9580869-6-7(6))* Inhoa Publishing.

Baker, Sara. The Adventures of Armadillo Baby & Annabelli. Zamenhof, Robert. 2013. 56p. pap. 9.29 *(978-0-615-80196-4(X))* RGZ Consulting.

—Do You Do a Didgeridoo. Page, Nick. 2008. 40p. (J). (gr. -1-3). bds. 15.99 *(978-1-84610-571-5(4))* Make Believe Ideas GBR. Dist: Nelson, Thomas Inc.

—Giant Sticker Activity Story Book. Page, Nick & Page, Claire. 2006. (Giant Sticker Bks.). 144p. (J). (gr. -1-k). pap. *(978-1-84610-303-2(7))* Make Believe Ideas.

—Read with Me Gingerbread Fred: Sticker Activity Book. Page, Nick & Page, Claire. 2006. (Read with Me (Make Believe Ideas) Ser.). 12p. (J). (gr. k-2). pap. *(978-1-84610-178-6(6))* Make Believe Ideas.

—Read with Me Rumpelstiltskin: Sticker Activity Book. Page, Nick & Page, Claire. 2006. (Read with Me (Make Believe Ideas) Ser.). 12p. (J). (gr. k-2). pap. *(978-1-84610-182-3(4))* Make Believe Ideas.

—Read with Me the Elves & the Shoemaker: Sticker Activity Book. Page, Nick & Page, Claire. 2006. (Read with Me (Make Believe Ideas) Ser.). 12p. (J). (gr. k-2). pap. *(978-1-84610-177-9(8))* Make Believe Ideas.

—Ready to Read Goldilocks & the Three Bears. 2007. (Ready to Read Ser.). 31p. (J). (gr. k-2). *(978-1-84610-440-4(8))* Make Believe Ideas.

—Ready to Read Sleeping Beauty. 2007. (Ready to Read Ser.). 31p. (J). (gr. k-2). *(978-1-84610-441-1(6))* Make Believe Ideas.

—The Runaway Son. Page, Nick & Page, Claire. 2006. (Read with Me Ser.). 31p. (J). (gr. k-2). *(978-1-84610-176-2(X))* Make Believe Ideas.

—Tales of Irish Enchantment. Lynch, Patricia. 2nd ed. 2010. (ENG.). 208p. (J). (gr. 3-8). 10.99 *(978-1-85635-681-7(7))* Mercier Pr., Ltd., The IRL. Dist: Casemate Pubs. & Bk. Distributors, LLC.

Baker, Sherri. The Adventures of Drew & Ellie: The Magical Dress. Noland, Charles. 2006. (J). *(978-0-9789297-1-8(3))*; 2nd rev. ed. 84p. per. 7.95 *(978-0-9789297-0-1(5))* TMD Enterprises.

Baker-Smith, Grahame. Life: the First Four Billion Years: The Story of Life from the Big Bang to the Evolution of Humans. Jenkins, Martin. 2019. (ENG.). 80p. (J). (gr. 5-9). 24.99 *(978-1-5362-0420-9(X))* Candlewick Pr.

—Robin Hood. Calcutt, David. 2012. (J). 112p. 24.99 *(978-1-84686-357-8(0))*; 176p. (gr. 4-6). pap. 12.99 *(978-1-84686-799-6(1))* Barefoot Bks., Inc.

—Winter's Child. McAllister, Angela. 2015. (ENG.). 40p. (J). (gr. -1-2). 16.99 *(978-0-7636-7964-4(X)*, Templar) Candlewick Pr.

Baker-Smith, Grahame. The Rhythm of the Rain. Baker-Smith, Grahame. 2019. (ENG.). 40p. (J). (gr. -1-3). 17.99 *(978-1-5362-0575-6(3)*, Templar) Candlewick Pr.

—The Twelve Days of Christmas: Panorama Pops. Baker-Smith, Grahame. 2017. (Panorama Pops Ser.). (ENG.). 30p. (J). (gr. k-4). 8.99 *(978-0-7636-9485-2(1))* Candlewick Pr.

Baker, Syd & Gombinski, Rita. Gombinski's Colors in Spanish, French, & German. Winitz, Harris et al. 2004. (J). audio compact disk 14.95 *(978-1-887371-92-6(3)*, 328C) International Linguistics Corp.

Baker, Thea. Love, Agnes: Postcards from an Octopus. Latham, Irene. 2018. (ENG.). 32p. (J). (gr. k-3). 19.99 *(978-1-5124-3993-9(2)*, Millbrook Pr.) Lerner Publishing Group.

Baker, Thea. No Ordinary Jacket. Pashley, Sue-Ellen. 2020. (ENG.). 32p. (J). (gr. -1-2). 17.99 ***(978-1-5362-0966-2(X))*** Candlewick Pr.

Baker, Tom. Finn the Fortunate Tiger Shark & His Fantastic Friends: Learn How to Protect Our Oceans with Finn. Stevens, Georgina. 2nd ed. 2017. (Be the Change Bks.: Vol. 1). (ENG.). (J). (gr. k-2). 32p. *(978-0-9957745-5-1(2))*; 30p. pap. *(978-0-9957745-4-4(4))* Be the Change Bks.

Baker, Zoe. Sophie, the Seagull Who Was Afraid to Fly. Bird, Rosita. 2018. (ENG.). 32p. (J). (gr. k-4). pap. 9.99 *(978-1-68160-527-2(9))* Crimson Cloak Publishing.

Bakker, Jenny. Get Well Soon, Grandpa. Swerts, An. 2013. (ENG.). 32p. (J). (gr. k-2). 15.95 *(978-1-60537-155-9(6))* Clavis Publishing.

Bakos, Barbara. Froggy Day. Pindar, Heather. 2019. (ENG.). 32p. (J). (gr. -1-3). 17.99 *(978-1-84886-411-5(6))* Maverick Arts Publishing GBR. Dist: Lerner Publishing Group.

—Here Come the Helpers. Kimmelman, Leslie. 2018. (ENG.). 14p. (J). (gr. -1). bds. 7.99 *(978-1-5344-0599-8(2)*, Little Simon) Little Simon.

—Leap, Frog, Leap! Florian, Douglas. 2016. (Animals Play Ser.). (ENG.). 18p. (J). (gr. -1-1). bds. 6.99 *(978-1-4998-0142-2(4))* Little Bee Books Inc.

Bakos, Barbara. The MOOsic Makers. Pindar, Heather. 2020. (ENG.). 32p. (J). (gr. -1-3). 17.99 ***(978-1-84886-649-2(6))*** Maverick Arts Publishing GBR. Dist: Lerner Publishing Group.

Bakos, Barbara. National Regular Average Ordinary Day. Katzenberger, Lisa. 2020. 32p. (J). (gr. -1-2). 17.99 *(978-1-5247-9240-4(3)*, Penguin Workshop) Penguin Young Readers Group.

—Once I Was a Pollywog. Florian, Douglas. 2016. (Animals Play Ser.). (ENG.). 18p. (J). (gr. -1-1). bds. 6.99 *(978-1-4998-0141-5(6))* Little Bee Books Inc.

—Rooster Wore Skinny Jeans. Miller, Jessie. 2018. (ENG.). 32p. (J). (gr. -1-3). 17.99 *(978-1-84886-313-2(6))* Maverick Arts Publishing GBR. Dist: Lerner Publishing Group.

Bakos, Barbara. Stegosaurus: The Thoughtful Surprise, 1 vol. Veitch, Catherine. 2020. (Dinosaur Adventures Ser.). (ENG.). 24p. (gr. 1-2). pap. 8.25 ***(978-1-4994-8505-9(0))***; lib. bdg. 24.60 ***(978-1-4994-8507-3(7))*** Rosen Publishing Group, Inc., The. (Windmill Bks.).

Bakshi, Kelly. The First Americans. Bakshi, Kelly. 2012. 16p. pap. 9.95 *(978-1-61633-278-5(6))* Guardian Angel Publishing, Inc.

Balance, Millie. Black Dog Dream Dog, 1 vol. Superle, Michelle. 2011. (ENG.). 126p. (J). (gr. 4-7). pap. 12.95 *(978-1-896580-34-0(3))* Tradewind Bks. CAN. Dist: Orca Bk. Pubs. USA.

Balarinji. Splosh for the Billabong. Moriarty, Ros. 2015. (ENG.). 24p. (J). (— 1). 10.99 *(978-1-76011-212-7(7))* Allen & Unwin AUS. Dist: Independent Pubs. Group.

—Who Saw Turtle? Moriarty, Ros. 2019. (ENG.). 24p. (J). (gr. -1-k). pap. 9.99 *(978-1-76029-780-0(1))* Allen & Unwin AUS. Dist: Independent Pubs. Group.

Balbusso, Anna & Balbusso, Elena. Make the Earth Your Companion. Lewis, J. Patrick. 2017. (ENG.). 32p. (J). (gr. 1-3). pap. 18.99 *(978-1-56846-269-1(7)*, Creative Education) Creative Co., The.

Balbusso, Elena, jt. illus. see Balbusso, Anna.

Balcan, Andreea. Pierre & the Case of the Missing Croissants. Amazing, Rosie. 2020. (Rosie & Pierre Ser.: Vol. 4). (ENG.). 28p. (J). pap. ***(978-1-9992475-7-7(4))*** Annelid Pr.

—Pierre & the Cr�pe Monster: Rosie & Pierre. Amazing, Rosie. 2019. (ENG.). 28p. (J). pap. ***(978-1-9992475-5-3(8))*** Annelid Pr.

—Pierre in Paris. Amazing, Rosie. 2019. (Rosie & Pierre Ser.: Vol. 2). (ENG.). 28p. (J). pap. ***(978-1-9992475-3-9(1))*** Annelid Pr.

—Pierre's Adventure in the Desert. Amazing, Rosie. 2020. (Rosie & Pierre Ser.: Vol. 6). (ENG.). 28p. (J). pap. ***(978-1-7771360-2-4(4))*** Annelid Pr.

—Pierre's Adventure in the Swamp. Amazing, Rosie. 2020. (Rosie & Pierre Ser.: Vol. 5). (ENG.). 28p. (J). pap. ***(978-1-9992475-8-4(2))*** Annelid Pr.

—Pierre's Shop. Amazing, Rosie. 2019. (ENG.). 28p. (J). pap. ***(978-1-9992475-0-8(7))*** Annelid Pr.

Balcan, Ioana. Cheese & Quackers. Ghervase, Alina & Amazing, Rosie. 2020. (ENG.). 28p. (J). pap. ***(978-1-7771360-0-0(8))*** Annelid Pr.

Balcan, Ioana, jt. illus. see Ghervase, Alina.

Balcazar, Abraham. Nina Complot. Chacek, Karen. 2009. (SPA.). 72p. (J). (gr. 3-5). pap. *(978-607-411-017-3(4))* Editorial Almadia.

Balch, Betty Neff. Tales of the Cinnamon Dragon Book I: Adventures in Farr Elvenhome. Balch, Betty Neff. Poythress, Jean Hill. 2004. 152p. (J). lib. bdg. 16.95 *(978-1-930580-46-6(0)*, Luminary Media Group) Pine Orchard, Inc.

Bald, Anna. Morgan's Boat Ride, 1 vol. MacDonald, Hugh. 2014. (ENG.). 24p. (J). (gr. 1-3). pap. 12.95 *(978-1-894838-96-2(3)*, ed381f24-4bf2-437b-8a41-188a706b51b1) Acorn Pr., The CAN. Dist: Baker & Taylor Publisher Services (BTPS).

Baldanzi, Alessandro. The Age of the Book. Rossi, Renzo & Pauli, Erika. 2009. (Reading & Writing Ser.). 32p. (gr. 4-4). 29.50 *(978-0-7614-4321-6(5))* Cavendish Square Publishing LLC.

—A Day with Homo Erectus: Life 400,000 Years Ago. Facchini, Fiorenzo. 2003. (Early Humans Ser.). 48p. (gr. 6-18). lib. bdg. 23.90 *(978-0-7613-2766-0(5)*, Twenty-First Century Bks.) Lerner Publishing Group.

—A Day with Neanderthal Man: Life 70,000 Years Ago. Facchini, Fiorenzo. 2003. (Early Humans Ser.). 48p. (gr. 6-18). lib. bdg. 23.90 *(978-0-7613-2767-7(3)*, Twenty-First Century Bks.) Lerner Publishing Group.

—A Gift from the Gods. Rossi, Renzo. 2009. (Reading & Writing Ser.). 32p. (gr. 4-4). 29.50 *(978-0-7614-4318-6(5))* Cavendish Square Publishing LLC.

—How Writing Began. Rossi, Renzo & Pauli, Erika. 2009. (Reading & Writing Ser.). 32p. (gr. 4-4). 29.50 *(978-0-7614-4317-9(7))* Cavendish Square Publishing LLC.

—In Nineteenth-Century London with Dickens. Rossi, Renzo & Bredeson, Carmen. 2009. (Come See My City Ser.). 48p. (gr. 4-4). lib. bdg. 29.50 *(978-0-7614-4333-9(9))* Cavendish Square Publishing LLC.

—In Renaissance Florence with Leonardo. Rossi, Renzo. 2009. (Come See My City Ser.). 48p. (gr. 4-4). lib. bdg. 29.50 *(978-0-7614-4329-2(0))* Cavendish Square Publishing LLC.

—In the Sun King's Paris with Molière. Rossi, Renzo. 2009. (Come See My City Ser.). 48p. (gr. 4-4). lib. bdg. 29.50 *(978-0-7614-4332-2(0))* Cavendish Square Publishing LLC.

—Modern Times. Silva, Patricia & Pauli, Erika. 2009. (Reading & Writing Ser.). 32p. (gr. 4-4). 29.50 *(978-0-7614-4322-3(3))* Cavendish Square Publishing LLC.

—Reading & Writing Today. Silva, Patricia. 2009. (Reading & Writing Ser.). 32p. (gr. 4-4). 29.50 *(978-0-7614-4324-7(X))* Cavendish Square Publishing LLC.

—The Revolution of the Alphabet. Rossi, Renzo. 2009. (Reading & Writing Ser.). 32p. (gr. 4-4). 29.50 *(978-0-7614-4320-9(7))* Cavendish Square Publishing LLC.

Baldari, Nicoletta. Disney·PIXAR the Incredibles 2: Heroes at Home (Younger Readers Graphic Novel) Marsham, Liz. ed. 2018. (ENG.). 48p. (J). (gr. k-3). 7.99 *(978-1-5067-0943-7(5)*, Dark Horse Books) Dark Horse Comics.

—Rose & Paige. Dawson, Delilah S. 2018. (Star Wars: Forces of Destiny Ser.). (ENG.). 24p. (J). (gr. 4-9). lib. bdg. 27.07 *(978-1-5321-4296-3(X)*, 31122, Graphic Novels) Spotlight.

Baldari, Nicoletta, jt. illus. see Mebberson, Amy.

Baldassarra, Tomaso & Cavada, Dario. Donnie & Dr. Hotchkiss: Monsterinmypocket. Andrucci, John. 2019. (ENG.). 100p. (J). pap. 9.99 *(978-1-7206-0058-9(9))* CreateSpace Independent Publishing Platform.

Baldassi, Deborah. A Cake on a Plate. Weber, K. E. 2004. 16p. (J). *(978-1-86374-325-9(1))* Era Pubns.

Baldeon, David. Gwenpool Strikes Back. 2020. (ENG.). 112p. (YA). (gr. 8-17). pap. 15.99 *(978-1-302-91923-8(7))* Marvel Worldwide, Inc.

—Monsters Unleashed Vol. 1: Monster Mash. 2017. (ENG.). 136p. (J). (gr. 4-17). pap. 15.99 *(978-0-7851-9636-5(6))* Marvel Worldwide, Inc.

—Spirits of Vengeance: War at the Gates of Hell. 2018. (ENG.). 112p. (YA). (gr. 8-17). pap. 15.99 *(978-1-302-91051-8(5))* Marvel Worldwide, Inc.

Baldetti, Laurence. The Quest of Ewilan, Vol. 1: from One World to Another. Bottero, Pierre. 2018. (Quest of Ewilan Ser.: 1). (ENG.). 68p. (YA). (gr. 8-12). 14.99 *(978-1-68405-325-4(0))* Idea & Design Works, LLC.

—The Quest of Ewilan, Vol. 2: Akiro. Lylian. 2019. (Quest of Ewilan Ser.: 2). 68p. (YA). (gr. 8-12). 14.99 *(978-1-68405-543-2(1))* Idea & Design Works, LLC.

Baldursson, Halldór. Egil's Saga: The Story of Egil Skallagrimsson: an Icelandic Classic. 2016. (ENG.). 64p. pap. 6.95 *(978-1-906230-87-6(0))* Real Reads Ltd. GBR. Dist: Casemate Pubs. & Bk. Distributors, LLC.

Baldwin, Alisa. Hip Hop from A to Z: A Fresh Look at the Music, the Culture, & the Message. Dagnino, Michelle. 2007. 192p. (J). (gr. 8-12). pap. *(978-1-897073-36-0(4))* Lobster Pr.

Baldwin, Christopher. Freehand: A Young Boy's Adventures in the War Of 1812. Peterson, Mike. 2012. (ENG.). 44p. (J). pap. 6.95 *(978-1-938384-03-5(2))* Baldwin, Christopher John.

—In the Love of Animals. Geltrich, Brigitta, ed. Date not set. (Animals Ser.). 96p. (J). pap. 6.00 *(978-0-936945-64-4(8))* Creative with Words Pubns.

Baldwin, Cristal. Charlotte. Sherry, Kathryn. 2017. (ENG.). (J). pap. 9.99 *(978-0-692-85277-4(8))* Old Scout Pr.

—Charlotte Learns to Write. Sherry, Kathryn. 2018. (ENG.). 28p. (J). pap. 9.99 *(978-0-692-11902-0(7))* Old Scout Pr.

Baldwin, Cristal. It's GREAT to Be LOVED! Gonzalez, Courtney & Karczmarczyk, Diana. 2020. (ENG.). 32p. (J). ***(978-1-5255-7600-3(3))***; pap. ***(978-1-5255-7601-0(1))*** FriesenPress.

Baldwin, Cristal. It's Great to Be You! Gonzalez, Courtney & Karczmarczyk, Diana. 2018. (ENG.). 24p. (J). *(978-1-5255-2898-9(X))*; pap. *(978-1-5255-2899-6(8))* FriesenPress.

Baldwin, Cristal. The Talent Show. Pfaff, Ellen L. 2019. (Adventures of Ava & Addison Ser.: Vol. 3). (ENG.). 38p. (J). 16.99 ***(978-1-946702-26-5(9))*** Freeze Time Media.

Balek, Dayna Courtney. Simon's Big Move. Reynolds Jr., R. A. 2008. 19p. pap. 24.95 *(978-1-60672-676-1(5))* America Star Bks.

Balholm, Peter. Andy's Pocketknife. Mast, Dorcas R. 2018. (J). pap. *(978-0-7399-2581-2(4))* Rod & Staff Pubs., Inc.

Balian, Lecia. The Sweet Touch, 1 vol. Balian, Lorna. 2005. (ENG.). 32p. (J). (gr. -1-3). 16.95 *(978-1-59572-017-7(0))* Star Bright Bks., Inc.

Balian, Lecia & Balian, Lorna. Where in the World Is Henry?, 1 vol. Balian, Lorna. 2005. (ENG.). 32p. (J). (gr. -1-2). *(978-1-59572-035-1(9))* Star Bright Bks., Inc.

Balian, Lecia, jt. illus. see Balian, Lorna.

Balian, Lorna. Un Fiasco de Bruja, 1 vol. Balian, Lorna. 2003.Tr. of Humbug Witch. (SPA & ENG.). 32p. (J). 12.95 *(978-1-59572-010-8(3))* Star Bright Bks., Inc.

—A Garden for a Groundhog, 1 vol. Balian, Lorna. 2011. (ENG.). 32p. (J). pap. 6.95 *(978-1-59572-296-6(3))* Star Bright Bks., Inc.

—Humbug Witch, 1 vol. Balian, Lorna. 2003. (ENG.). 32p. (J). 12.95 *(978-1-932065-32-9(6)*, 1-718-784-9112) Star Bright Bks., Inc.

—Leprechauns Never Lie, 1 vol. Balian, Lorna. 2004. (ENG.). 32p. (J). 14.95 *(978-1-932065-37-4(7))* Star Bright Bks., Inc.

—A Sweetheart for Valentine, 1 vol. Balian, Lorna. 2005. (ENG.). 32p. (J). 15.95 *(978-1-932065-14-5(8))* Star Bright Bks., Inc.

Balian, Lorna & Balian, Lecia. The Aminal, 1 vol. Balian, Lorna. 2005. (ENG.). 48p. (J). 17.95 *(978-1-59572-006-1(5))* Star Bright Bks., Inc.

Balian, Lorna, jt. illus. see Balian, Lecia.

Balian, Nick & Disney Storybook Art Team, Disney Storybook. Onward Little Golden Book (Disney/Pixar Onward) 2020. (Little Golden Book Ser.). (ENG.). 24p. (J). (-k). 4.99 *(978-0-7364-3929-9(3)*, Golden/Disney) Random Hse. Children's Bks.

Balicevic, Didier. Pirates: 45 Magnetic Pieces. Adam, Ines. 2019. (Magnetology Ser.: 6). (ENG.). 12p. (J). (gr. -1-k). 21.99 Éditions Tourbillon FRA. Dist: Hachette Bk. Group.

Balistreri, Ben. Bad Moooove! #3. Krulik, Nancy. 2018. (Princess Pulverizer Ser.: 3). 144p. (J). (gr. 1-3). 6.99 *(978-0-515-15837-3(2)*, Penguin Workshop) Penguin Young Readers Group.

—Grilled Cheese & Dragons #1. Krulik, Nancy. 2018. (Princess Pulverizer Ser.: 1). 144p. (J). (gr. 1-3). 6.99 *(978-0-515-15831-1(3))*; (ENG.). 15.99 *(978-0-515-15832-8(1))* Penguin Young Readers Group. (Penguin Workshop).

—Quit Buggin' Me! #4. Krulik, Nancy. 2018. (Princess Pulverizer Ser.: 4). 144p. (J). (gr. 1-3). 6.99 *(978-0-515-15840-3(2))*; 15.99 *(978-0-515-15841-0(0))* Penguin Young Readers Group. (Penguin Workshop).

—Worse, Worser, Wurst. Krulik, Nancy. 2018. (Princess Pulverizer Ser.: 2). 144p. (J). (gr. 1-3). 6.99 *(978-0-515-15834-2(8)*, Penguin Workshop) Penguin Young Readers Group.

Balit, Christina. The Adventures of Odysseus. Lupton, Hugh & Morden, Daniel. 2012. 96p. (J). 23.99 *(978-1-84686-703-3(7))* Barefoot Bks., Inc.

—Adventures of Odysseus. Morden, Daniel & Lupton, Hugh. 2017. (ENG.). 96p. (J). (gr. 1-4). pap. 16.99 *(978-1-78285-356-5(1))* Barefoot Bks., Inc.

—Saintly Tales & Legends. Rock, Lois. 2004. 100p. (J). 15.95 *(978-0-8198-7083-4(8)*, 332-379) Pauline Bks. & Media.

Balit, Christina. Treasury of Greek Mythology: Classic Stories of Gods, Goddesses, Heroes & Monsters. Napoli, Donna Jo. 2011. (ENG.). 192p. (J). (gr. 3-7). 24.95 ***(978-1-4263-0892-5(2))***; 24.95 ***(978-1-4263-0893-2(0))*** National Geographic Society.

Balit, Christina. Women of Camelot: Queens & Enchantresses at the Court of King Arthur. Hoffman, Mary. 2006. 69p. (YA). (gr. 5-9). 20.00 *(978-1-4223-5260-1(9))* DIANE Publishing Co.

Balita, Mark Nino. Are You Scared? Help Your Children Overcome Fears & Anxieties. Blum, Ingo. 2019. (ENG.). 36p. (J). pap. 11.95 ***(978-1-9832-7348-3(1))*** Independently Published.

Balita, Mark Nino. Doctor Potty (Hebrew Edition) Kaplan, Hadas. 2019. (HEB.). 24p. (J). 16.00 *(978-0-578-47442-7(5))* Kaplan, Hadas.

Balita, Niño. Kane's Room: A Strange World. Wedderburn Jr, Andrew. 2020. (ENG.). 24p. pap. 10.99 ***(978-1-7960-9396-4(3))*** Xlibris Corp.

Balkovek, James. Makoy, the Apache Boy. Cohen, Rafael. 2013. (ENG.). (J). 14.95 *(978-1-62086-340-4(5))* Mascot Bks., Inc.

—Willa Cather. Cather, Willa. 2004. (Great American Short Stories Ser.). 80p. (gr. 4-7). lib. bdg. 25.00 *(978-0-8368-4251-7(0)*, Gareth Stevens Learning Library) Stevens, Gareth Publishing LLLP.

Balkovek, Jim. Shanaya & Friends: Litter Bugs Turn Eco H. E. R. O. S. Daughtrey, Patricia & Benson, Gary. 2011. 40p. pap. 14.95 *(978-1-60911-475-6(2)*, Eloquent Bks.) Strategic Book Publishing & Rights Agency (SBPRA).

Ball, Alexandra. Care for Our World. Robbins, Karen. 2012. (ENG.). 36p. (J). (gr. -1-3). 16.95 *(978-1-935414-61-2(5))* Compendium, Inc., Publishing & Communications.

Ball, Barbara. Ty the Quiet Giraffe. Hasler, Carrie. 2019. (ENG.). 32p. (J). 16.95 ***(978-1-943198-08-5(X))*** Southwestern Publishing Hse., Inc.

Ball, Bill D., Jr., jt. illus. see Ball, Skyler E.

Ball, Geoff. Trouble in Space: A First Reading Adventure Book. Baxter, Nicola. 2015. 24p. pap. 6.99 *(978-1-86147-491-9(1)*, Armadillo) Anness Publishing GBR. Dist: National Bk. Network.

—Trouble in the Jungle: A First Reading Adventure Book. Baxter, Nicola. 2015. 24p. pap. 6.99 *(978-1-86147-494-0(6)*, Armadillo) Anness Publishing GBR. Dist: National Bk. Network.

—Trouble on the Ice: First Reading Books for 3-5 Year Olds. Baxter, Nicola. 2015. (ENG.). 24p. pap. 6.99 *(978-1-86147-492-6(X)*, Armadillo) Anness Publishing GBR. Dist: National Bk. Network.

—Trouble under the Ocean: First Reading Books for 3-5 Year Olds. Baxter, Nicola. 2015. (ENG.). 24p. pap. 6.99 *(978-1-86147-493-3(8)*, Armadillo) Anness Publishing GBR. Dist: National Bk. Network.

—The Trouble with Tippers. Baxter, Nicola. 2012. (ENG.). 24p. (J). (gr. -1-k). pap. 6.99 *(978-1-84322-783-0(5)*, Armadillo) Anness Publishing GBR. Dist: National Bk. Network.

—The Trouble with Trains. Baxter, Nicola. 2012. (ENG.). 24p. (J). (gr. -1-k). pap. 6.99 *(978-1-84322-785-4(1),* Armadillo) Anness Publishing GBR. Dist: National Bk. Network.
—The Trouble with Trucks. Baxter, Nicola. 2012. (ENG.). 24p. (J). (gr. -1-k). pap. 6.99 *(978-1-84322-786-1(X),* Armadillo) Anness Publishing GBR. Dist: National Bk. Network.
Ball, Geoff, jt. illus. see Riley, Terry.
Ball, Lauren. Sam & Skully. Badeaux, Dewey. 2013. 126p. pap. 12.99 *(978-0-9884057-4-5(1))* Alligator Pr.
Ball, Liz. Bible Stories: Find-the-Picture Puzzles. 2004. (Find-the-Picture Puzzle Ser.: 1). 24p. (J). pap. 2.95 *(978-0-8198-1163-9(7),* 332-026) Pauline Bks. & Media.
—Calling All Animals: The First Book of PunOETRY. Nathan, Jeff. 2003. 96p. per. 9.95 *(978-0-9702730-1-7(0))* Chucklebks. Publishing.
—Miracles & Parables of Jesus: Find-the-Picture Puzzles. 2004. (Find-the-Picture Puzzle Ser.: 2). 24p. (J). pap. 2.95 *(978-0-8198-4830-7(1),* 332-221) Pauline Bks. & Media.
—A Standardbred Star: Learn about Harness Racing with Star & Friends. 2007. (YA). 3.95 *(978-0-9793891-0-8(0))* United States Trotting Association.
—Stories Jesus Told 6pk: Hidden Pictures. Warner Press. 2013. (ENG.). 16p. (J). pap. 13.74 *(978-1-59317-475-0(6))* Warner Pr., Inc.
Ball, Liz. Frog Fun Hidden Treasures: Hidden Picture Puzzles, Vol. 8. Ball, Liz. 2008. (Hidden Treasures Ser.: Vol. 8). 56p. (YA). pap. 6.95 *(978-0-9678159-8-5(3))* Hidden Pictures.
Ball, Natalie. Can You See It?, 1 vol. Dale, Jay. 2012. (Engage Literacy Yellow Ser.). (ENG.). 32p. (gr. k-2). pap. 5.99 *(978-1-4296-8954-0(4),* Capstone Pr.) Capstone.
Ball, Robert. The Fierce 44: Black Americans Who Shook up Our World. The Staff of The Undefeated, The Staff. 2019. (ENG.). 96p. (J). (gr. 5-7). 17.99 *(978-1-328-94062-9(4),* 1704629, HMH Books For Young Readers) Houghton Mifflin Harcourt Publishing Co.
Ball, Ryan. Freddie the Clever Fox. Ogunjobi, Rotimi. 2019. (ENG.). 26p. (J). pap. 9.95 ***(978-1-7128-5829-5(7))*** Independently Published.
—Snotty Mcgrotty. Holland, Matt. 2020. (ENG.). 52p. (J). pap. ***(978-1-83975-081-6(2))*** Grosvenor Hse. Publishing Ltd.
Ball, Ryan. Here I Come... (Ready or Not) Ball, Ryan. 2020. (ENG.). 76p. (J). pap. ***(978-0-9957323-9-1(6))*** SRL Publishing Ltd.
Ball, Sara. Flip-O-storic. 2011. (ENG.). 11p. (J). (gr. -1-k). bds. 16.95 *(978-0-7892-1099-9(1),* 791099, Abbeville Kids) Abbeville Pr., Inc.
Ball, Skyler E. & Ball, Bill D., Jr. Let's Green Things Up! Ball, Skyler E. & Ball, Bill D., Jr. 2011. (ENG.). 30p. (J). 21.00 *(978-0-9834112-0-8(4))* Practical Green Pr.
Ball, Victoria. Phonics Comics: Spooky Sara - Level 3, Level 3. Marks, Melanie. 2006. (ENG.). 24p. (J). (gr. 1-17). per. 3.99 *(978-1-58476-473-1(2),* IKIDS) Innovative Kids.
Balla, Trace. Shine: A Story about Saying Goodbye. Balla, Trace. 2016. (ENG.). 24p. (J). (gr. -1-1). 15.99 *(978-1-74331-634-4(8))* Allen & Unwin AUS. Dist: Independent Pubs. Group.
Ballance, Millie. The Eco-Diary of Kiran Singer, 1 vol. Alderson, Sue Ann. 2007. (ENG.). 64p. (YA). (gr. 4-7). 15.95 *(978-1-896580-47-0(5))* Tradewind Bks. CAN. Dist: Orca Bk. Pubs. USA.
Ballantyne, Robert Michael. The Battery & the Boiler. Adventures in Laying of Submarine Electric Cables (1883) Ballantyne, Robert Michael. 2018. (ENG.). 170p. (J). pap. 9.50 *(978-1-7309-4411-6(6))* Independently Published.
Ballard, Ben. The Be Good Fairy. Wallen-Nichols, Missy. 2013. (ENG.). 32p. (J). 16.95 *(978-0-9853523-0-1(2))* Mawco, Inc.
Ballard, George Anne & Bolton, Georgia Helen. Flowers along the Way. Ballard, George Anne. 2012. 26p. pap. 12.00 *(978-0-9855312-2-5(3))* Bolton Publishing LLC.
Ballard, Merry. Pity's Porch. Crawford, Deborah & Crawford, Ryan. 2012. 24p. pap. 11.50 *(978-1-60976-796-9(9),* Strategic Bk. Publishing) Strategic Book Publishing & Rights Agency (SBPRA).
Balleello, Chiara, jt. illus. see Pellizzari, Barbara.
Ballester, Arnal. Chamario. Polo, Eduardo. 2005. (SPA.). 48p. (J). 8.99 *(978-980-257-278-6(0))* Ekare, Ediciones VEN. Dist: Iaconi, Mariuccia Bk. Imports.
Ballesteros, Carles. Busy Builders: Farm: Build a 37-Inch 3D Farm Play Set - Includes: 32-Page Book - over 100 Press-Out Pieces - 3D Fold-Out Play Set. Knapman, Timothy. 2019. (ENG.). 32p. (J). (gr. k-2). pap. 22.95 ***(978-1-78603-909-5(5))*** QEB Publishing Inc.
Ballesteros, Carles. Changing Faces: Meet Happy Bear. Quarto Children's Books. 2017. (ENG.). 16p. (J). (gr. -1 — 1). bds. 7.95 *(978-1-4197-2474-9(6),* Abrams Appleseed) Abrams, Inc.
Ballesteros, Carles. Dia de Los Muertos. Thong, Roseanne Greenfield. 2020. (ENG.). 32p. (J). (gr. -1-3). pap. 7.99 ***(978-0-8075-1577-8(9),*** 0807515779) Whitman, Albert & Co.
Ballesteros, Carles. Dia de los Muertos. Thong, Roseanne Greenfield. 2015. (ENG.). 32p. (J). (gr. -1-3). 16.99 *(978-0-8075-1566-2(3),* 807515663) Whitman, Albert & Co.
—Is That Your Dad? (a Changing Faces Book) 2019. (Changing Faces Ser.). (ENG.). 18p. (J). (gr. -1 — 1). bds. 7.99 *(978-1-4197-3629-2(9),* Abrams Appleseed) Abrams, Inc.
—My First Art Sticker Book. Dickens, Rosie. ed. 2013. (Art Ser.). 23p. (J). pap. 8.99 *(978-0-7945-3202-4(0),* Usborne) EDC Publishing.
Ballesteros, Carles. Poop! Giménez de Ory, Beatriz. 2020. (ENG.). 28p. (J). bds. ***(978-1-64686-091-3(8))*** Barefoot Bks., Inc.
Ballesteros, Carles. Space Machines: Build Your Own Working Machines! Graham, Ian. 2017. (ENG.). 24p. (J). (gr. k-3). 17.95 *(978-1-68297-212-0(7))* QEB Publishing Inc.
—Wacky Things about Animals — Volume 1: Weird & Amazing Animal Facts! Wagner, Tricia Martineau. 2018. (Wacky Things Ser.). (ENG.). 32p. (J). (gr. 3-5). lib. bdg. 27.99 *(978-1-942875-69-7(X),* Walter Foster Jr) Quarto Publishing Group USA.
—Wacky Things about Animals — Volume 2: Weird & Amazing Animal Facts! Wagner, Tricia Martineau. 2018. (Wacky Things Ser.). (ENG.). 32p. (J). (gr. 3-5). lib. bdg. 27.99 *(978-1-942875-70-3(3),* Walter Foster Jr) Quarto Publishing Group USA.
Ballesteros, Patrick. When Martin Luther King Jr. Wore Roller Skates. Weakland, Mark. (J). 2017. 31p. *(978-1-5158-0141-2(1));* 2016. (ENG.). 32p. (gr. 1-4). pap. 7.95 *(978-1-5158-0137-5(3));* 2016. (ENG.). 32p. (gr. 1-4). lib. bdg. 28.65 *(978-1-4795-9685-0(X))* Capstone. (Picture Window Bks.).
Ballestros, Carles. Building Machines: An Interactive Guide to Construction Machines. Graham, Ian. 2016. (ENG.). 24p. (J). (gr. k-2). 17.95 *(978-1-4197-2109-0(7),* Abrams Bks. for Young Readers) Abrams, Inc.
Balletto, Jim. Daddy's Pot. Curry, Nakeisha M. 2018. (ENG.). 24p. (J). pap. 13.95 *(978-0-9799896-7-4(1))* VLChilds Publishing.
Balleza, Vanessa. But There Are No Palm Trees Here. Antigua, Kianny. Polli, Elizabeth, tr. 2020. (ENG.). 34p. (J). pap. 14.99 ***(978-1-949299-13-7(9))*** Jade Publishing.
—But There Are No Palm Trees Here! Antigua, Kianny. Polli, Elizabeth, tr. 2020. (ENG.). 34p. (J). 18.99 ***(978-1-949299-14-4(7))*** Jade Publishing.
Ballhaus, Verena. David's World: A Picture Book about Living with Autism. Mueller, Dagmar H. 2012. 28p. (J). (gr. -1-k). 16.95 *(978-1-61608-962-7(8),* 608962, Sky Pony Pr.) Skyhorse Publishing Co., Inc.
Ballinger, Bryan. God Loves You Very Much!, 1 vol. Big Idea, Inc. Staff & Kenney, Cindy. 2003. (Big Idea Books / VeggieTales Ser.). (ENG.). 18p. (J). bds. 7.99 *(978-0-310-70623-6(8))* Zonderkidz.
Ballinger, Carolyn. The UFB's of Bugsville, Florida USA, 1 vol. Zinner, Gennieve. 2010. 48p. pap. 24.95 *(978-1-4489-7977-6(3))* PublishAmerica, Inc.
Balmet, Jean-Paul. Star Wars Rebels Servants of the Empire: Edge of the Galaxy. Fry, Jason. 2014. (ENG.). 176p. (J). (gr. 3-7). pap. 6.99 *(978-1-4847-0485-1(1))* Disney Pr.
Balog, Kristine. A Pirate, I Be! Martinez, Richard Anthony. 2018. (ENG.). 28p. (J). (gr. k-5). pap. 12.99 *(978-1-7329511-1-2(X));* 16.99 *(978-1-7329511-0-5(1))* Martinez, Richard A.
Balogh, Andras. Bubba & the Sweet Pea. Boutros, Gladys. 2013. 86p. (J). pap. *(978-0-9873334-7-6(X))* Enlife Pty, Limited.
—Bubba & the Sweet Pea: US English Edition. Boutros, Gladys. 2012. 86p. (J). pap. *(978-0-9873334-1-4(0))* Enlife Pty, Limited.
—Love You Back Grandma. Shukla, Umesh. 2020. 40p. (J). 15.95 *(978-0-9963756-5-8(1))* All About Kids Publishing.
Balogh, Jared. The Adventures of Kirby. Rhodes, Jennifer. 2012. 46p. 24.95 *(978-1-4626-9473-0(X))* America Star Bks.
—Breakfast for Two. Murray, Rosalie. 2013. 32p. pap. 24.95 *(978-1-4560-7051-9(7))* America Star Bks.
—Mama Bird & Her Baby. Begum, Dilara. 2011. 28p. pap. 24.95 *(978-1-4560-6924-7(1))* America Star Bks.
—Pokey's Promise: A Charming Tale of Telling Time. Vadney, Jackie. 2011. 28p. pap. 24.95 *(978-1-4560-2850-3(2))* America Star Bks.
—What Would I Do If I Had a Zoo? McNeal, Cari. 2012. 36p. 24.95 *(978-1-4560-4006-2(5))* America Star Bks.
Balogh, Jared, jt. illus. see Jones, Tina C.
Balouch, Kristen. The Ghost Catcher: A Bengali Folktale. Hamilton, Martha & Weiss, Mitch. 2007. (ENG.). 32p. (J). (gr. -1-3). 16.95 *(978-0-87483-835-0(5))* August Hse. Pubs., Inc.
—Thank You, Trees!, Vol. Langer Karwoski, Gail & Gootman, Marilyn. 2013. (ENG.). 12p. (J). (gr. -1 — 1). bds. 5.95 *(978-1-58013-973-1(6),* 9781580139731, Kar-Ben Publishing) Lerner Publishing Group.
Balouch, Kristen. The Little Little Girl with the Big Big Voice. Balouch, Kristen. 2011. (ENG.). 32p. (J). (gr. -1-k). 12.99 *(978-1-4424-0808-1(1),* Little Simon) Little Simon.
Balsaitis, Rachael. Kimmy's Marvelous Wind-Catching Wonder. Glaser, Linda. 2017. (ENG.). 32p. (J). (gr. -1-k). 16.95 *(978-1-60554-436-6(1))* Redleaf Pr.
Balsano, Sean. Edison the Firefly & the Invention of the Light Bulb. Raye, Donna. 2012. (POR, SPA & ENG.). 28p. pap. 9.99 *(978-0-9836771-0-9(7))* Mindstir Media.
Balsara, Andrea Torrey. Mouse Pet. Roy, Philip. 2015. (ENG.). 32p. 12.95 *(978-1-55380-443-7(0))* Ronsdale Pr. CAN. Dist: SPD-Small Pr. Distribution.
Balta Parks, Elif. Our Values: Champion Gran: Kara Learns about Respect. Chancellor, Deborah. ed. 2019. (British Values Ser.). 32p. (J). (gr. k-2). pap. 10.99 *(978-1-4451-5651-4(2),* Franklin Watts) Hachette Children's Group GBR. Dist: Hachette Bk. Group.
—Our Values: the Red Flag: Josh Learns How Rules Keep Us Safe. Chancellor, Deborah. ed. 2019. (British Values Ser.). 32p. (J). (gr. k-2). pap. 10.99 *(978-1-4451-5653-8(9),* Franklin Watts) Hachette Children's Group GBR. Dist: Hachette Bk. Group.
—Our Values: the Town Makeover: Noah Learns about Community Pride. Chancellor, Deborah. ed. 2020. (British Values Ser.). 32p. (J). (gr. k-2). pap. 10.99 *(978-1-4451-5649-1(0),* Franklin Watts) Hachette Children's Group GBR. Dist: Hachette Bk. Group.
—Our Values: Who Did That? Sasha Learns about Taking Responsibility. Chancellor, Deborah. ed. 2019. (British Values Ser.). 32p. (J). (gr. k-2). pap. 10.99 *(978-1-4451-5655-2(5),* Franklin Watts) Hachette Children's Group GBR. Dist: Hachette Bk. Group.
Baltazar, Armand. Timeless: Diego & the Rangers of the Vastlantic. Baltazar, Armand. (Timeless Ser.: 1). (ENG.). 624p. (J). (gr. 3-7). 2019. pap. 12.99 *(978-0-06-240237-0(4));* 2017. 19.99 *(978-0-06-240236-3(6))* HarperCollins Pubs. (Tegen, Katherine Bks).
Baltazar, Art. Ace: The Origin of Batman's Dog. Korte, Steve. 2017. (DC Super-Pets Origin Stories Ser.). (ENG.). 48p. (J). (gr. 1-3). lib. bdg. 23.99 *(978-1-4965-5138-2(9),* 136162, Stone Arch Bks.) Capstone.
Baltazar, Art. The Amazing Adventures of the DC Super-Pets. Korte, Steve. 2020. (Amazing Adventures of the DC Super-Pets Ser.). (ENG.). (J). (gr. k-2). 85.28 ***(978-1-5158-7207-8(6),*** 200758); pap., pap., pap. 27.80 ***(978-1-5158-7336-5(6),*** 201793) Capstone. (Picture Window Bks.).
Baltazar, Art. The Amazing Mini-Mutts, 1 vol. Lemke, Donald B. 2012. (DC Super-Pets Ser.). (ENG.). 56p. (J). (gr. 1-3). pap. 4.95 *(978-1-4048-7218-9(3));* lib. bdg. 23.99 *(978-1-4048-6488-7(1))* Capstone. (Stone Arch Bks.).
—Attack of the Invisible Cats, 1 vol. Sonnebom, Scott. 2011. (DC Super-Pets Ser.). (ENG.). 56p. (J). (gr. 1-3). pap. 4.95 *(978-1-4048-6847-2(X));* lib. bdg. 23.99 *(978-1-4048-6481-8(4))* Capstone. (Stone Arch Bks.).
—Backward Bowwow, 1 vol. Stephens, Sarah Hines. 2011. (DC Super-Pets Ser.). (ENG.). 56p. (J). (gr. 1-3). pap. 4.95 *(978-1-4048-6845-8(3));* lib. bdg. 23.99 *(978-1-4048-6480-1(6))* Capstone. (Stone Arch Bks.).
—Barnyard Brainwash, 1 vol. Sazaklis, John. 2012. (DC Super-Pets Ser.). (ENG.). 56p. (J). (gr. 1-3). pap. 4.95 *(978-1-4048-7213-4(2));* lib. bdg. 23.99 *(978-1-4048-6483-2(0))* Capstone. (Stone Arch Bks.).
—Battle Bugs of Outer Space, 1 vol. Mason, Jane B. 2011. (DC Super-Pets Ser.). (ENG.). 56p. (J). (gr. 1-3). pap. 4.95 *(978-1-4048-6848-9(8));* lib. bdg. 23.99 *(978-1-4048-6482-5(2))* Capstone. (Stone Arch Bks.).
—The Biggest Little Hero, 1 vol. Sazaklis, John. 2012. (DC Super-Pets Ser.). (ENG.). 56p. (J). (gr. 1-3). pap. 4.95 *(978-1-4048-7664-4(2));* lib. bdg. 23.99 *(978-1-4048-6490-0(3))* Capstone. (Stone Arch Bks.).
—Candy Store Caper, 1 vol. Sazaklis, John. 2012. (DC Super-Pets Ser.). (ENG.). 56p. (J). (gr. 1-3). pap. 4.95 *(978-1-4048-7214-1(0));* lib. bdg. 23.99 *(978-1-4048-6484-9(9))* Capstone. (Stone Arch Bks.).
—The Cat Crime Club, 1 vol. Korte, Steve. 2012. (DC Super-Pets Ser.). (ENG.). 56p. (J). (gr. 1-3). pap. 4.95 *(978-1-4048-7665-1(0));* 23.99 *(978-1-4048-6493-1(8))* Capstone. (Stone Arch Bks.).
Baltazar, Art. Cave of Kryptonite. Korte, Steve. 2020. (Amazing Adventures of the DC Super-Pets Ser.). (ENG.). 32p. (J). (gr. k-2). pap. 6.95 ***(978-1-5158-7321-1(8),*** 201626); lib. bdg. 21.32 ***(978-1-5158-7176-7(2),*** 200566) Capstone. (Picture Window Bks.).
—Crime-Fighting Cat. Korte, Steve. 2020. (Amazing Adventures of the DC Super-Pets Ser.). (ENG.). 32p. (J). (gr. k-2). pap. 6.95 ***(978-1-5158-7322-8(6),*** 201627); lib. bdg. 21.32 ***(978-1-5158-7177-4(0),*** 200567) Capstone. (Picture Window Bks.).
Baltazar, Art. DC Super-Pets Character Encyclopedia, 1 vol. Korte, Steve. 2013. (DC Super-Pets Ser.). (ENG.). 128p. (J). (gr. 1-3). pap. 7.95 *(978-1-4048-8297-3(9));* 26.60 *(978-1-4795-2030-5(6))* Capstone. (Stone Arch Bks.).
—Deep-Sea Duel, 1 vol. Sazaklis, John. 2012. (DC Super-Pets Ser.). (ENG.). 56p. (J). (gr. 1-3). pap. 4.95 *(978-1-4048-7662-0(6));* lib. bdg. 23.99 *(978-1-4048-6489-4(X))* Capstone. (Stone Arch Bks.).
—The Fantastic Flexy Frog, 1 vol. Dahl, Michael. 2012. (DC Super-Pets Ser.). (ENG.). 56p. (J). (gr. 1-3). pap. 4.95 *(978-1-4048-7666-8(9));* 23.99 *(978-1-4048-6494-8(6))* Capstone. (Stone Arch Bks.).
—The Fastest Pet on Earth, 1 vol. Bright, J. E. 2011. (DC Super-Pets Ser.). (ENG.). 56p. (J). (gr. 1-3). pap. 4.95 *(978-1-4048-6623-2(X));* lib. bdg. 23.99 *(978-1-4048-6264-7(1))* Capstone. (Stone Arch Bks.).
—Heroes of the High Seas, 1 vol. Bright, J. E. 2011. (DC Super-Pets Ser.). (ENG.). 56p. (J). (gr. 1-3). 23.99 *(978-1-4048-6263-0(3),* Stone Arch Bks.) Capstone.
—The Hopping Hero, 1 vol. Sazaklis, John. 2011. (DC Super-Pets Ser.). (ENG.). 56p. (J). (gr. 1-3). pap. 4.95 *(978-1-4048-6843-4(7));* lib. bdg. 23.99 *(978-1-4048-6477-1(6))* Capstone. (Stone Arch Bks.).
Baltazar, Art. The Ice Cream Caper. Korte, Steve. 2020. (Amazing Adventures of the DC Super-Pets Ser.). (ENG.). 32p. (J). (gr. k-2). pap. 6.95 ***(978-1-5158-7323-5(4),*** 201628); lib. bdg. 21.32 ***(978-1-5158-7178-1(9),*** 200568) Capstone. (Picture Window Bks.).
Baltazar, Art. Itty Bitty Comics: Grimmiss Island. Aureliani, Franco. 2015. (Itty Bitty Comics Ser.). (ENG.). 104p. (J). (gr. 3-7). pap. 12.99 *(978-1-61655-768-3(0))* Dark Horse Comics.
—Krypto: The Origin of Superman's Dog. Dahl, Michael. 2017. (DC Super-Pets Origin Stories Ser.). (ENG.). 48p. (J). (gr. 1-3). lib. bdg. 23.99 *(978-1-4965-5139-9(7),* 136163, Stone Arch Bks.) Capstone.
—Midway Monkey Madness, 1 vol. Stephens, Sarah. 2011. (DC Super-Pets Ser.). (ENG.). 56p. (J). (gr. 1-3). lib. bdg. 23.99 *(978-1-4048-6305-7(2),* Stone Arch Bks.) Capstone.
—Night of the Scaredy Crows, 1 vol. Stephens, Sarah Hines. 2012. (DC Super-Pets Ser.). (ENG.). 56p. (J). (gr. 1-3). pap. 4.95 *(978-1-4048-7663-7(4));* lib. bdg. 23.99 *(978-1-4048-6492-4(X))* Capstone. (Stone Arch Bks.).
—Pooches of Power!, 1 vol. Stephens, Sarah. 2011. (DC Super-Pets Ser.). (ENG.). 56p. (J). (gr. 1-3). pap. 4.95 *(978-1-4048-6620-1(5));* lib. bdg. 23.99 *(978-1-4048-6306-4(0))* Capstone. (Stone Arch Bks.).
—Royal Rodent Rescue, 1 vol. Sazaklis, John. 2011. (DC Super-Pets Ser.). (ENG.). 56p. (J). (gr. 1-3). pap. 4.95 *(978-1-4048-6622-5(1));* lib. bdg. 23.99 *(978-1-4048-6307-1(9))* Capstone. (Stone Arch Bks.).
—Salamander Smackdown. Sazaklis, John. 2011. (DC Super-Pets Ser.). (ENG.). 56p. (J). (gr. 1-3). pap. 4.95 *(978-1-4048-6844-1(5),* Stone Arch Bks.) Capstone.
—Salamander Smackdown!, 1 vol. Sazaklis, John. 2011. (DC Super-Pets Ser.). (ENG.). 56p. (J). (gr. 1-3). lib. bdg. 23.99 *(978-1-4048-6478-8(4),* Stone Arch Bks.) Capstone.
—Sleepy Time Crime, 1 vol. Stephens, Sarah Hines. 2012. (DC Super-Pets Ser.). (ENG.). 56p. (J). (gr. 1-3). pap. 4.95 *(978-1-4048-7215-8(9));* lib. bdg. 23.99 *(978-1-4048-6485-6(7))* Capstone. (Stone Arch Bks.).
—Streaky: The Origin of Supergirl's Cat. Korte, Steve. 2017. (DC Super-Pets Origin Stories Ser.). (ENG.). 48p. (J). (gr. 1-3). lib. bdg. 23.99 *(978-1-4965-5137-5(0),* 136161, Stone Arch Bks.) Capstone.
—Super Hero Splash Down, 1 vol. Mason, Jane B. 2011. (DC Super-Pets Ser.). (ENG.). 56p. (J). (gr. 1-3). pap. 4.95 *(978-1-4048-6624-9(8));* lib. bdg. 23.99 *(978-1-4048-6357-6(5))* Capstone. (Stone Arch Bks.).
—Super-Pets Showdown, 1 vol. Stephens, Sarah Hines. 2012. (DC Super-Pets Ser.). (ENG.). 56p. (J). (gr. 1-3). pap. 4.95 *(978-1-4048-7216-5(7));* lib. bdg. 23.99 *(978-1-4048-6486-3(5))* Capstone. (Stone Arch Bks.).
—Superpowered Pony, 1 vol. Stephens, Sarah Hines. 2011. (DC Super-Pets Ser.). (ENG.). 56p. (J). (gr. 1-3). pap. 4.95 *(978-1-4048-6846-5(1));* lib. bdg. 23.99 *(978-1-4048-6479-5(2))* Capstone. (Stone Arch Bks.).
—Swamp Thing vs the Zombie Pets, 1 vol. Sazaklis, John. 2012. (DC Super-Pets Ser.). (ENG.). 56p. (J). (gr. 1-3). pap. 4.95 *(978-1-4048-7667-5(7));* lib. bdg. 23.99 *(978-1-4048-6491-7(1))* Capstone. (Stone Arch Bks.).
Baltazar, Art. Trouble on Paradise Island. Korte, Steve. 2020. (Amazing Adventures of the DC Super-Pets Ser.). (ENG.). 32p. (J). (gr. k-2). pap. 6.95 ***(978-1-5158-7324-2(2),*** 201629); lib. bdg. 21.32 ***(978-1-5158-7179-8(7),*** 200569) Capstone. (Picture Window Bks.).
Baltazar, Art. When Migo Met Smallfoot. 2018. (Smallfoot Ser.). (ENG.). 32p. (J). (gr. k-2). 17.99 *(978-1-5344-3173-7(X));* pap. 4.99 *(978-1-5344-3172-0(1))* Simon Spotlight. (Simon Spotlight).
Baltazar, Art. Adventures Begin! Baltazar, Art. Aureliani, Franco. 2013. (Superman Family Adventures Ser.). (ENG.). 32p. (J). (gr. 1-3). 22.60 *(978-1-4342-4786-5(4),* Stone Arch Bks.) Capstone.
—Aw Yeah Comics! and. . Action!, Vol. 1. Baltazar, Art. Aureliani, Franco. 2014. (ENG.). 152p. (J). (gr. 3-7). pap. 12.99 *(978-1-61655-558-0(0))* Dark Horse Comics.
—Itty Bitty Hellboy. Baltazar, Art. Franco. Allie, Scott, ed. 2014. (Itty Bitty Comics Ser.). (ENG.). 128p. (J). (gr. 3-7). pap. 9.99 *(978-1-61655-414-9(2))* Dark Horse Comics.
—Menace of Metallo! Baltazar, Art. Aureliani, Franco. 2013. (Superman Family Adventures Ser.). (ENG.). 32p. (J). (gr. 1-3). 22.60 *(978-1-4342-4794-0(5),* Stone Arch Bks.) Capstone.
—Monkey Metropolis!, 1 vol. Baltazar, Art. Aureliani, Franco. 2013. (Superman Family Adventures Ser.). (ENG.). 32p. (J). (gr. 1-3). 22.60 *(978-1-4342-4791-9(0),* Stone Arch Bks.) Capstone.
—Starro & the Space Dolphins, 1 vol. Baltazar, Art. 2012. (DC Super-Pets Ser.). (ENG.). 56p. (J). (gr. 1-3). pap. 4.95 *(978-1-4048-7217-2(5));* lib. bdg. 23.99 *(978-1-4048-6487-0(3))* Capstone. (Stone Arch Bks.).
—Super-Pets!, 1 vol. Baltazar, Art. Aureliani, Franco. 2013. (Superman Family Adventures Ser.). (ENG.). 32p. (J). (gr. 1-3). 22.60 *(978-1-4342-4792-6(9),* Stone Arch Bks.) Capstone.
—Who Is the Purple Superman?, 1 vol. Baltazar, Art. Aureliani, Franco. 2013. (Superman Family Adventures Ser.). (ENG.). 32p. (J). (gr. 1-3). 22.60 *(978-1-4342-4793-3(7),* Stone Arch Bks.) Capstone.
Baltazar, Art & Aureliani, Franco. Enter - Nightwing! Baltazar, Art & Aureliani, Franco. 2012. (Tiny Titans Ser.). (ENG.). 32p. (J). (gr. 1-3). lib. bdg. 22.60 *(978-1-4342-4540-3(3),* Stone Arch Bks.) Capstone.
—Penguins in the Batcave!, 1 vol. Baltazar, Art & Aureliani, Franco. 2012. (Tiny Titans Ser.). (ENG.). 32p. (J). (gr. 1-3). 22.60 *(978-1-4342-4539-7(X),* Stone Arch Bks.) Capstone.
—Report Card Pickup!, 1 vol. Baltazar, Art & Aureliani, Franco. 2013. (Tiny Titans Ser.). (ENG.). 32p. (J). (gr. 1-3). lib. bdg. 22.60 *(978-1-4342-4699-8(X),* Stone Arch Bks.) Capstone.
—Tiny Titans. Baltazar, Art & Aureliani, Franco. 2013. (Tiny Titans Ser.). (ENG.). 32p. (J). (gr. 1-3). lib. bdg., lib. bdg., lib. bdg. 67.80 *(978-1-4342-4854-1(2),* Stone Arch Bks.) Capstone.
Baltazar, Art & Vecchio, Luciano. Batman: An Origin Story. Sazaklis, John. 2015. (DC Super Heroes Origins Ser.). (ENG.). 48p. (J). (gr. k-2). lib. bdg. 23.99 *(978-1-4342-9727-3(6),* Stone Arch Bks.) Capstone.
—Green Lantern: An Origin Story. Manning, Matthew K. 2015. (DC Super Heroes Origins Ser.). (ENG.). 48p. (J). (gr. k-2). lib. bdg. 23.99 *(978-1-4342-9730-3(6),* Stone Arch Bks.) Capstone.
—Superman: An Origin Story. Manning, Matthew K. 2015. (DC Super Heroes Origins Ser.). (ENG.). 48p. (J). (gr. k-2). lib. bdg. 23.99 *(978-1-4342-9728-0(4),* Stone Arch Bks.) Capstone.
—Wonder Woman: An Origin Story. Sazaklis, John. 2015. (DC Super Heroes Origins Ser.). (ENG.). 48p. (J). (gr. k-2). lib. bdg. 23.99 *(978-1-4342-9729-7(2),* Stone Arch Bks.) Capstone.
Baltazar, Arthur, et al. Aw Yeah Comics! Volume 3: Make Way... for Awesome!, Vol. 3. Baltazar, Arthur & Aureliani, Franco. 2016. (Aw Yeah Comics Ser.: 3). (ENG.). 144p. (J). (gr. 3-7). pap. 12.99 *(978-1-5067-0045-8(4))* Dark Horse Comics.
Balthazar, Flore. Freedom! Le Gall, Frank. 2012. (Miss Annie Ser.). 48p. (J). (gr. 2-4). pap. 39.62 *(978-0-7613-9281-1(5),* Graphic Universe™) Lerner Publishing Group.
—Freedom! Le Gall, Frank & Doo, Robin. 2012. (Miss Annie Ser.: 1). 48p. (J). (gr. 2-4). pap. 6.95 *(978-0-7613-8546-2(0),* Graphic Universe™) Lerner Publishing Group.
—Freedom! Le Gall, Frank. 2012. (Miss Annie Ser.: 1). (ENG.). 48p. (J). (gr. 2-4). lib. bdg. 29.27 *(978-0-7613-7884-6(7),* Graphic Universe™) Lerner Publishing Group.
—Miss Annie. Le Gall, Frank. 2012. (Miss Annie Ser.). 48p. (J). (gr. 2-4). lib. bdg. 58.54 *(978-0-7613-8902-6(4),* Graphic Universe™) Lerner Publishing Group.
—Miss Annie: 6Pack Set. Le Gall, Frank. 2012. (Miss Annie Ser.). 48p. (J). (gr. 2-4). pap. 79.23 *(978-0-7613-9284-2(X),* Graphic Universe™) Lerner Publishing Group.

B

—Miss Annie: Single Copy Set. Le Gall, Frank. 2012. (Miss Annie Ser.). 48p. (J). (gr. 2-4). pap. 13.21 *(978-0-7613-9283-5(1),* Graphic Universe™) Lerner Publishing Group.

—Rooftop Cat. Le Gall, Frank. 2012. (Miss Annie Ser.). 48p. (J). (gr. 2-4). pap. 39.62 *(978-0-7613-9282-8(3));* (ENG.). pap. 6.95 *(978-0-7613-8547-9(9))* Lerner Publishing Group. (Graphic Universe™).

Balus, Connor. Caveman Jimmy from the Future 2: A New Adventure Begins! Ique, Sawyer. 2019. (ENG.). 26p. (J). pap. 9.25 *(978-1-0989-2905-3(5))* Independently Published.

Baluschek, Hans. Peter & Anneli's Journey to the Moon, 1 vol. von Bassewitz, Gerdt. 2007. (ENG.). 110p. (J). (gr. 3-7). *(978-0-88010-584-2(4),* Bell Pond Bks.) SteinerBooks, Inc.

Balvanz, Gwynessa. No Cookies for Christmas: The Story of Grandma's Missing Package. delMazo, Deborah. Horsfall, Jacqueline, ed. 2010. 32p. (J). pap. 9.95 *(978-0-615-32691-7(9))* Zoombird Bks.

Balyeat, Nancy. Emma on a Trip. Stover, Maryanna. 2019. (ENG.). 26p. (J). pap. 12.00 *(978-1-7946-8968-8(0))* Independently Published.

Balzer, Erin. God's Animals, 1 vol. 2018. 10p. (J). bds. 6.99 *(978-0-8254-4550-7(7))* Kregel Pubns.

—God's Families, 1 vol. 2018. 10p. (J). bds. 6.99 *(978-0-8254-4551-4(5))* Kregel Pubns.

Balzer, Jeremy. Tyler the Turtle Is Afraid of the Dark. Crawford, Deborah. 2006. 32p. (J). 14.95 *(978-0-9770516-1-8(7))* Laffin Minor Pr.

Balzola, Asun. El Arbol de Mi Patio. Xirinacs, Olga. 3rd ed. (SPA.). 32p. (J). (gr. 1-3). *(978-84-236-3391-3(8))* Edebé ESP. Dist: Lectorum Pubns., Inc.

—Paloma, Llegaste Por el Aire. Zubizarreta, Patxi. 2003. (SPA.). 24p. *(978-84-246-5913-4(9),* GL3212) La Galera, S.A. Editorial ESP. Dist: Lectorum Pubns., Inc.

Balzola, Sofia. Rosalinde Tiene Ideas en la Cabeza. Nöstlinger, Christine. 2003. (SPA.). 80p. (J). (gr. 3-5). 11.95 *(978-84-204-4804-6(4))* Ediciones Alfaguara ESP. Dist: Santillana USA Publishing Co., Inc.

Bampton, Bob. Animals in the Wild. 2004. (Look & Learn about Ser.). 18p. (J). bds. 5.99 *(978-1-85854-351-2(7))* Brimax Books Ltd. GBR. Dist: Byeway Bks.

—Animals on the Farm. 2004. (Look & Learn about Ser.). 18p. (J). bds. 5.99 *(978-1-85854-319-2(3))* Brimax Books Ltd. GBR. Dist: Byeway Bks.

—Ocean Animals. Goldsack, Gaby. (J). *(978-1-57755-508-7(2))* Flying Frog Publishing, Inc.

Banchini, Giampaolo. Escursione Su Marte. Zapata Banchini, Bruno. 2019. (Viaggi Alieni Ser.: Vol. 1). (ITA.). 32p. (J). pap. 9.50 ***(978-1-6723-6824-7(3))*** Independently Published.

—Excursi� a Mart. Zapata Banchini, Bruno. 2019. (Viatges Allenigenes Ser.: Vol. 1). (CAT.). 32p. (J). pap. 9.50 ***(978-1-6722-0564-1(6))*** Independently Published.

—Excursi�n a Marte. Zapata Banchini, Bruno. 2019. (Viajes Alienigenas Ser.: Vol. 1). (SPA.). 32p. (J). pap. 9.50 ***(978-1-6723-7784-3(6))*** Independently Published.

Bancroft, Bronwyn. The Amazing A-Z Thing. Morgan, Sally. 2015. (ENG.). 32p. (J). (-k). 16.99 *(978-1-921894-19-0(9))* Little Hare Bks. AUS. Dist: Independent Pubs. Group.

—The Eagle Inside. Manning Bancroft, Jack. 2019. (ENG.). 32p. (J). (— 1). pap. 11.99 *(978-1-76012-527-1(X))* Little Hare Bks. AUS. Dist: Independent Pubs. Group.

—Malu Kangaroo. Morecroft, Judith. 2008. (ENG.). 40p. (J). (gr. k-2). pap. 11.95 *(978-1-921272-51-6(1))* Little Hare Bks. AUS. Dist: Independent Pubs. Group.

—The Outback. Porter, Annaliese. 2nd ed. 2008. 28p. (J). (gr. -1-7). pap. 14.95 *(978-1-921248-04-7(1))* Magabala Bks. AUS. Dist: Independent Pubs. Group.

—Sam's Bush Journey. Morgan, Sally & Kwaymullina, Ezekiel. 2011. (ENG.). 32p. (J). (gr. k-1). pap. 8.99 *(978-1-921541-72-8(5))* Little Hare Bks. AUS. Dist: Independent Pubs. Group.

Bancroft, Bronwyn. An Australian 1, 2, 3 of Animals. Bancroft, Bronwyn. 2010. (ENG.). 32p. (J). (gr. -1-k). pap. 8.99 *(978-1-921272-85-1(6))* Little Hare Bks. AUS. Dist: Independent Pubs. Group.

—An Australian ABC of Animals. Bancroft, Bronwyn. 2005. (ENG.). 24p. (J). (gr. -1-k). pap. 17.95 *(978-1-877003-97-4(2))* Little Hare Bks. AUS. Dist: Independent Pubs. Group.

—Patterns of Australia. Bancroft, Bronwyn. 2005. 24p. *(978-1-877003-96-7(4))* Little Hare Bks. AUS. Dist: HarperCollins Pubs. Australia.

—Possum & Wattle: My Big Book of Australian Words. Bancroft, Bronwyn. 2010. (ENG.). 48p. (J). (gr. -1-1). pap. 12.99 *(978-1-921541-67-4(9))* Little Hare Bks. AUS. Dist: Independent Pubs. Group.

—Why I Love Australia. Bancroft, Bronwyn. 2016. (ENG.). 32p. (J). (gr. -1-k). 13.99 *(978-1-76012-512-7(1))* Little Hare Bks. AUS. Dist: Independent Pubs. Group.

Bancroft, Tom & Corley, Rob. Florence Fiasco. Sorrells, W. A. 2007. 136p. (J). *(978-0-9792912-2-7(4))* KidsGive, LLC.

—Nairobi Nightmare. Sorrells, W. A. 2007. 144p. (J). *(978-0-9792912-1-0(6))* KidsGive, LLC.

Bancroft, Tom, jt. illus. see Corley, Rob.

Bancroft, Tom, jt. illus. see Rousseau, Craig.

Band, Debra. All the World Praises You: An Illuminated Aleph-Bet Book. Band, Debra. Band, Arnold J., tr. 2018. (ENG.). 32p. (gr. -1). 19.99 *(978-0-9857996-7-0(6))* Honeybee in the Garden, LLC.

Bandelin, Debra, et al. What's the Difference Between a Turtle & a Tortoise?, 1 vol. Shaskan, Trisha Speed. 2010. (What's the Difference? Ser.). (ENG.). 24p. (J). (gr. k-3). lib. bdg. 27.32 *(978-1-4048-5546-5(7),* Picture Window Bks.) Capstone.

Bandelin, Debra & Dacey, Bob. Abigail Adams: First Lady of the American Revolution. Lakin, Patricia. 2006. 48p. (J). lib. bdg. 15.00 *(978-1-4242-1560-7(9))* Fitzgerald Bks.

—Davy Crockett: A Life on the Frontier. Krensky, Stephen. 2004. (Ready-To-Read Level 3 Ser.). (ENG.). 48p. (J). (gr. 1-3). 16.19 *(978-0-689-85944-1(9),* Simon Spotlight) Simon & Schuster Children's Publishing.

Bandelin, Debra, jt. illus. see Dacey, Bob.

Bandini, Michele. Marvel's Spider-Man: City at War. 2019. (ENG.). 144p. (YA). (gr. 4-17). pap. 19.99 *(978-1-302-91901-6(6))* Marvel Worldwide, Inc.

Bandt, Molly. Loki Out & About. Bandt, Molly. Murua, Tina. 2017. (ENG.). (J). (gr. k-2). 18.99 *(978-1-943331-84-0(7))* Orange Hat Publishing.

Bane, Jeff. Abraham Lincoln. Haldy, Emma E. 2016. (My Early Library: My Itty-Bitty Bio Ser.). (ENG.). 24p. (J). (gr. k-1). 28.50 *(978-1-63470-476-2(2),* 207635) Cherry Lake Publishing.

—Ada Lovelace. Loh-Hagan, Virginia. 2018. (Mi Mini Biografía (My Itty-Bitty Bio): My Early Library). (ENG.). 24p. (J). (gr. k-1). pap. 12.79 *(978-1-5341-0815-8(7),* 210624); lib. bdg. 28.50 *(978-1-5341-0716-8(9),* 210623) Cherry Lake Publishing.

—Amelia Earhart. Haldy, Emma E. 2016. (My Early Library: My Itty-Bitty Bio Ser.). (ENG.). 24p. (J). (gr. k-1). 28.50 *(978-1-63470-480-9(0),* 207651) Cherry Lake Publishing.

—Ayah Bdeir. Sarantou, Katlin. 2019. (My Early Library: My Itty-Bitty Bio Ser.). (ENG.). 24p. (J). (gr. k-1). pap. 12.79 *(978-1-5341-4984-7(8),* 213243); lib. bdg. 28.50 *(978-1-5341-4698-3(9),* 213242) Cherry Lake Publishing.

—Being Present. Marsico, Katie. 2019. (My Early Library: My Mindful Day Ser.). (ENG.). 24p. (J). (gr. k-1). pap. 12.79 *(978-1-5341-4998-4(8),* 213299); lib. bdg. 28.50 *(978-1-5341-4712-6(8),* 213298) Cherry Lake Publishing.

—Benjamin Franklin. Haldy, Emma E. 2016. (My Early Library: My Itty-Bitty Bio Ser.). (ENG.). 24p. (J). (gr. k-1). 28.50 *(978-1-63470-478-6(9),* 207643) Cherry Lake Publishing.

—Booker T. Washington. Haldy, Emma E. 2016. (My Early Library: My Itty-Bitty Bio Ser.). (ENG.). 24p. (J). (gr. k-1). 28.50 *(978-1-63471-018-3(5),* 208152) Cherry Lake Publishing.

—Brush Your Teeth! Marsico, Katie. 2019. (My Early Library: My Healthy Habits Ser.). (ENG.). 24p. (J). (gr. k-1). pap. 12.79 *(978-1-5341-3930-5(3),* 212549); lib. bdg. 28.50 *(978-1-5341-4274-9(6),* 212548) Cherry Lake Publishing.

—Building a Lava Lamp. Rowe, Brooke. 2016. (My Early Library: My Science Fun Ser.). (ENG.). 24p. (J). (gr. k-1). 28.50 *(978-1-63471-026-8(6),* 208184) Cherry Lake Publishing.

—Building a Volcano. Rowe, Brooke. 2016. (My Early Library: My Science Fun Ser.). (ENG.). 24p. (J). (gr. k-1). 28.50 *(978-1-63471-025-1(8),* 208180) Cherry Lake Publishing.

—Chimamanda Ngozi Adichie. Sarantou, Katlin. 2019. (My Early Library: My Itty-Bitty Bio Ser.). (ENG.). 24p. (J). (gr. k-1). pap. 12.79 *(978-1-5341-4983-0(X),* 213239); lib. bdg. 28.50 *(978-1-5341-4697-6(0),* 213238) Cherry Lake Publishing.

—Color & Wavelengths. Bell, Samantha. 2018. (Mi Mini Biografía (My Itty-Bitty Bio): My Early Library). (ENG.). 24p. (J). (gr. k-1). pap. 12.79 *(978-1-5341-0826-4(2),* 210668); lib. bdg. 28.50 *(978-1-5341-0727-4(4),* 210667) Cherry Lake Publishing.

—Compassion. Marsico, Katie. 2019. (My Early Library: My Mindful Day Ser.). (ENG.). 24p. (J). (gr. k-1). pap. 12.79 *(978-1-5341-5000-3(5),* 213307); lib. bdg. 28.50 *(978-1-5341-4714-0(4),* 213306) Cherry Lake Publishing.

—Connection. Marsico, Katie. 2019. (My Early Library: My Mindful Day Ser.). (ENG.). 24p. (J). (gr. k-1). pap. 12.79 *(978-1-5341-4997-7(X),* 213295); lib. bdg. 28.50 *(978-1-5341-4711-9(X),* 213294) Cherry Lake Publishing.

—Coretta Scott King. Spiller, Sara. 2019. (My Early Library: My Itty-Bitty Bio Ser.). (ENG.). 24p. (J). (gr. k-1). pap. 12.79 *(978-1-5341-3924-4(9),* 212525); lib. bdg. 28.50 *(978-1-5341-4268-8(1),* 212524) Cherry Lake Publishing.

—Creating Rain. Rowe, Brooke. 2016. (My Early Library: My Science Fun Ser.). (ENG.). 24p. (J). (gr. k-1). 28.50 *(978-1-63471-027-5(4),* 208188) Cherry Lake Publishing.

—Davy Crockett. Haldy, Emma E. 2017. (My Early Library: My Itty-Bitty Bio Ser.). (ENG.). 24p. (J). (gr. k-1). lib. bdg. 28.50 *(978-1-63472-151-6(9),* 209176) Cherry Lake Publishing.

—Dorothy Vaughan. Loh-Hagan, Virginia. 2018. (Mi Mini Biografía (My Itty-Bitty Bio): My Early Library). (ENG.). 24p. (J). (gr. k-1). pap. 12.79 *(978-1-5341-0810-3(6),* 210604); lib. bdg. 28.50 *(978-1-5341-0711-3(8),* 210603) Cherry Lake Publishing.

—Earth. Devera, Czeena. 2020. (My Early Library: My Guide to the Planets Ser.). (ENG.). 24p. (J). (gr. k-1). pap. 12.79 *(978-1-5341-6111-5(2),* 214444); lib. bdg. 28.50 *(978-1-5341-5881-8(2),* 214443) Cherry Lake Publishing.

—Earth's Structure. Bell, Samantha. 2018. (Mi Mini Biografía (My Itty-Bitty Bio): My Early Library). (ENG.). 24p. (J). (gr. k-1). pap. 12.79 *(978-1-5341-0825-7(4),* 210664); lib. bdg. 28.50 *(978-1-5341-0726-7(6),* 210663) Cherry Lake Publishing.

—Eat Healthy Foods! Marsico, Katie. 2019. (My Early Library: My Healthy Habits Ser.). (ENG.). 24p. (J). (gr. k-1). pap. 12.79 *(978-1-5341-3934-3(6),* 212565); lib. bdg. 28.50 *(978-1-5341-4278-7(9),* 212564) Cherry Lake Publishing.

—Eleanor Roosevelt. Haldy, Emma E. 2016. (My Early Library: My Itty-Bitty Bio Ser.). (ENG.). 24p. (J). (gr. k-1). 28.50 *(978-1-63470-483-0(5),* 207663) Cherry Lake Publishing.

—Empathy. Marsico, Katie. 2019. (My Early Library: My Mindful Day Ser.). (ENG.). 24p. (J). (gr. k-1). pap. 12.79 *(978-1-5341-4995-3(3),* 213287); lib. bdg. 28.50 *(978-1-5341-4709-6(8),* 213286) Cherry Lake Publishing.

—Farmer. Devera, Czeena. 2018. (Mi Mini Biografía (My Itty-Bitty Bio): My Early Library). (ENG.). 24p. (J). (gr. k-1). pap. 12.79 *(978-1-5341-0819-6(X),* 210640); lib. bdg. 28.50 *(978-1-5341-0720-5(7),* 210639) Cherry Lake Publishing.

—Floating a Paper Clip. Rowe, Brooke. 2016. (My Early Library: My Science Fun Ser.). (ENG.). 24p. (J). (gr. k-1). 28.50 *(978-1-63471-032-9(0),* 208208) Cherry Lake Publishing.

—Florence Griffith Joyner. Haldy, Emma E. 2016. (My Early Library: My Itty-Bitty Bio Ser.). (ENG.). 24p. (J). (gr. k-1). 28.50 *(978-1-63471-019-0(3),* 208156) Cherry Lake Publishing.

—Floss Your Teeth! Marsico, Katie. 2019. (My Early Library: My Healthy Habits Ser.). (ENG.). 24p. (J). (gr. k-1). pap. 12.79 *(978-1-5341-3933-6(8),* 212561); lib. bdg. 28.50 *(978-1-5341-4277-0(0),* 212560) Cherry Lake Publishing.

—Frederick Douglass. Haldy, Emma E. 2016. (My Early Library: My Itty-Bitty Bio Ser.). (ENG.). 24p. (J). (gr. k-1). 28.50 *(978-1-63470-479-3(7),* 207647) Cherry Lake Publishing.

—George H. W. Bush. Sarantou, Katlin. 2019. (My Early Library: My Itty-Bitty Bio Ser.). (ENG.). 24p. (J). (gr. k-1). pap. 12.79 *(978-1-5341-4992-2(9),* 213275); lib. bdg. 28.50 *(978-1-5341-4706-5(3),* 213274) Cherry Lake Publishing.

—George Washington. Haldy, Emma E. 2017. (My Early Library: My Itty-Bitty Bio Ser.). (ENG.). 24p. (J). (gr. k-1). lib. bdg. 28.50 *(978-1-63472-152-3(7),* 209180) Cherry Lake Publishing.

—Get Your Exercise! Marsico, Katie. 2019. (My Early Library: My Healthy Habits Ser.). (ENG.). 24p. (J). (gr. k-1). pap. 12.79 *(978-1-5341-3935-0(4),* 212569); lib. bdg. 28.50 *(978-1-5341-4279-4(7),* 212568) Cherry Lake Publishing.

—Gwen Frostic. Sarantou, Katlin. 2019. (My Early Library: My Itty-Bitty Bio Ser.). (ENG.). 24p. (J). (gr. k-1). pap. 12.79 *(978-1-5341-4987-8(2),* 213255); lib. bdg. 28.50 *(978-1-5341-4701-0(2),* 213254) Cherry Lake Publishing.

—Helen Keller. Haldy, Emma E. 2016. (My Early Library: My Itty-Bitty Bio Ser.). (ENG.). 24p. (J). (gr. k-1). 28.50 *(978-1-63471-020-6(7),* 208160) Cherry Lake Publishing.

—Ida B. Wells. Spiller, Sara. 2019. (My Early Library: My Itty-Bitty Bio Ser.). (ENG.). 24p. (J). (gr. k-1). pap. 12.79 *(978-1-5341-3928-2(1),* 212541); lib. bdg. 28.50 *(978-1-5341-4272-5(X),* 212540) Cherry Lake Publishing.

—J. J. Watt. Sarantou, Katlin. 2020. (My Early Library: My Itty-Bitty Bio Ser.). (ENG.). 24p. (J). (gr. k-1). pap. 12.79 *(978-1-5341-6108-5(2),* 214432); lib. bdg. 28.50 *(978-1-5341-5878-8(2),* 214431) Cherry Lake Publishing.

—Jackie Robinson. Haldy, Emma E. 2016. (My Early Library: My Itty-Bitty Bio Ser.). (ENG.). 24p. (J). (gr. k-1). 28.50 *(978-1-63471-021-3(5),* 208164) Cherry Lake Publishing.

—James Bowie. Sarantou, Katlin. 2019. (My Early Library: My Itty-Bitty Bio Ser.). (ENG.). 24p. (J). (gr. k-1). pap. 12.79 *(978-1-5341-4991-5(0),* 213271); lib. bdg. 28.50 *(978-1-5341-4705-8(5),* 213270) Cherry Lake Publishing.

—Jane Goodall. Haldy, Emma E. 2016. (My Early Library: My Itty-Bitty Bio Ser.). (ENG.). 24p. (J). (gr. k-1). 28.50 *(978-1-63471-022-0(3),* 208168) Cherry Lake Publishing.

—Jimmy Carter. Haldy, Emma E. 2016. (My Early Library: My Itty-Bitty Bio Ser.). (ENG.). 24p. (J). (gr. k-1). 28.50 *(978-1-63471-014-5(2),* 208006) Cherry Lake Publishing.

—Jupiter. Devera, Czeena. 2020. (My Early Library: My Guide to the Planets Ser.). (ENG.). 24p. (J). (gr. k-1). pap. 12.79 *(978-1-5341-6118-4(X),* 214472); lib. bdg. 28.50 *(978-1-5341-5888-7(X),* 214471) Cherry Lake Publishing.

—Katherine Johnson. Loh-Hagan, Virginia. 2018. (Mi Mini Biografía (My Itty-Bitty Bio): My Early Library). (ENG.). 24p. (J). (gr. k-1). pap. 12.79 *(978-1-5341-0809-7(2),* 210600); lib. bdg. 28.50 *(978-1-5341-0710-6(X),* 210599) Cherry Lake Publishing.

—Look Out for Germs! Marsico, Katie. 2019. (My Early Library: My Healthy Habits Ser.). (ENG.). 24p. (J). (gr. k-1). lib. bdg. 28.50 *(978-1-5341-4281-7(9),* 212576) Cherry Lake Publishing.

—Lookout for Germs! Marsico, Katie. 2019. (My Early Library: My Healthy Habits Ser.). (ENG.). 24p. (J). (gr. k-1). pap. 12.79 *(978-1-5341-3937-4(0),* 212577) Cherry Lake Publishing.

—Madeleine Albright. Sarantou, Katlin. 2019. (My Early Library: My Itty-Bitty Bio Ser.). (ENG.). 24p. (J). (gr. k-1). pap. 12.79 *(978-1-5341-4986-1(4),* 213251); lib. bdg. 28.50 *(978-1-5341-4700-3(4),* 213250) Cherry Lake Publishing.

—Mail Carrier. Devera, Czeena. 2018. (Mi Mini Biografía (My Itty-Bitty Bio): My Early Library). (ENG.). 24p. (J). (gr. k-1). pap. 12.79 *(978-1-5341-0816-5(5),* 210628); lib. bdg. 28.50 *(978-1-5341-0717-5(7),* 210627) Cherry Lake Publishing.

—Making a Telephone. Rowe, Brooke. 2016. (My Early Library: My Science Fun Ser.). (ENG.). 24p. (J). (gr. k-1). 28.50 *(978-1-63471-029-9(0),* 208196) Cherry Lake Publishing.

—Malala Yousafzai. Spiller, Sara. 2019. (My Early Library: My Itty-Bitty Bio Ser.). (ENG.). 24p. (J). (gr. k-1). pap. 12.79 *(978-1-5341-3927-5(3),* 212537); lib. bdg. 28.50 *(978-1-5341-4271-8(1),* 212536) Cherry Lake Publishing.

—Marian Anderson. Haldy, Emma E. 2016. (My Early Library: My Itty-Bitty Bio Ser.). (ENG.). 24p. (J). (gr. k-1). 28.50 *(978-1-63471-023-7(1),* 208172) Cherry Lake Publishing.

—Marie Curie. Loh-Hagan, Virginia. 2018. (Mi Mini Biografía (My Itty-Bitty Bio): My Early Library). (ENG.). 24p. (J). (gr. k-1). pap. 12.79 *(978-1-5341-0814-1(9),* 210620); lib. bdg. 28.50 *(978-1-5341-0715-1(0),* 210619) Cherry Lake Publishing.

—Mars. Devera, Czeena. 2020. (My Early Library: My Guide to the Planets Ser.). (ENG.). 24p. (J). (gr. k-1). pap. 12.79 *(978-1-5341-6112-2(0),* 214448); lib. bdg. 28.50 *(978-1-5341-5882-5(0),* 214447) Cherry Lake Publishing.

—Martin Luther King, Jr. Haldy, Emma E. 2016. (My Early Library: My Itty-Bitty Bio Ser.). (ENG.). 24p. (J). (gr. k-1). 28.50 *(978-1-63470-477-9(0),* 207639) Cherry Lake Publishing.

—Mary Jackson. Loh-Hagan, Virginia. 2018. (Mi Mini Biografía (My Itty-Bitty Bio): My Early Library). (ENG.). 24p. (J). (gr. k-1). pap. 12.79 *(978-1-5341-0811-0(4),* 210608); lib. bdg. 28.50 *(978-1-5341-0712-0(6),* 210607) Cherry Lake Publishing.

—Maya Angelou. Haldy, Emma E. 2017. (My Early Library: My Itty-Bitty Bio Ser.). (ENG.). 24p. (J). (gr. k-1). lib. bdg. 28.50 *(978-1-63472-153-0(5),* 209184) Cherry Lake Publishing.

—Maya Lin. Spiller, Sara. 2019. (My Early Library: My Itty-Bitty Bio Ser.). (ENG.). 24p. (J). (gr. k-1). pap. 12.79 *(978-1-5341-3926-8(5),* 212533); lib. bdg. 28.50 *(978-1-5341-4270-1(3),* 212532) Cherry Lake Publishing.

—Meditation. Marsico, Katie. 2019. (My Early Library: My Mindful Day Ser.). (ENG.). 24p. (J). (gr. k-1). pap. 12.79 *(978-1-5341-4993-9(7),* 213279); lib. bdg. 28.50 *(978-1-5341-4707-2(1),* 213278) Cherry Lake Publishing.

—Mercury. Devera, Czeena. 2020. (My Early Library: My Guide to the Planets Ser.). (ENG.). 24p. (J). (gr. k-1). pap. 12.79 *(978-1-5341-6116-0(3),* 214464); lib. bdg. 28.50 *(978-1-5341-5886-3(3),* 214463) Cherry Lake Publishing.

—Michelle Obama. Sarantou, Katlin. 2020. (My Early Library: My Itty-Bitty Bio Ser.). (ENG.). 24p. (J). (gr. k-1). pap. 12.79 *(978-1-5341-6104-7(X),* 214416); lib. bdg. 28.50 *(978-1-5341-5874-0(X),* 214415) Cherry Lake Publishing.

—Misty Copeland. Sarantou, Katlin. 2020. (My Early Library: My Itty-Bitty Bio Ser.). (ENG.). 24p. (J). (gr. k-1). pap. 12.79 *(978-1-5341-6105-4(8),* 214420); lib. bdg. 28.50 *(978-1-5341-5875-7(8),* 214419) Cherry Lake Publishing.

—Mother Teresa. Haldy, Emma E. 2017. (My Early Library: My Itty-Bitty Bio Ser.). (ENG.). 24p. (J). (gr. k-1). lib. bdg. 28.50 *(978-1-63472-154-7(3),* 209188) Cherry Lake Publishing.

—Nellie Bly. Spiller, Sara. 2019. (My Early Library: My Itty-Bitty Bio Ser.). (ENG.). 24p. (J). (gr. k-1). pap. 12.79 *(978-1-5341-3929-9(X),* 212545); lib. bdg. 28.50 *(978-1-5341-4273-2(8),* 212544) Cherry Lake Publishing.

—Neptune. Devera, Czeena. 2020. (My Early Library: My Guide to the Planets Ser.). (ENG.). 24p. (J). (gr. k-1). pap. 12.79 *(978-1-5341-6113-9(9),* 214452); lib. bdg. 28.50 *(978-1-5341-5883-2(9),* 214451) Cherry Lake Publishing.

—Openness. Marsico, Katie. 2019. (My Early Library: My Mindful Day Ser.). (ENG.). 24p. (J). (gr. k-1). pap. 12.79 *(978-1-5341-4999-1(6),* 213303); lib. bdg. 28.50 *(978-1-5341-4713-3(6),* 213302) Cherry Lake Publishing.

—Oprah Winfrey. Sarantou, Katlin. 2020. (My Early Library: My Itty-Bitty Bio Ser.). (ENG.). 24p. (J). (gr. k-1). pap. 12.79 *(978-1-5341-6106-1(6),* 214424); lib. bdg. 28.50 *(978-1-5341-5876-4(6),* 214423) Cherry Lake Publishing.

—Peace. Marsico, Katie. 2019. (My Early Library: My Mindful Day Ser.). (ENG.). 24p. (J). (gr. k-1). pap. 12.79 *(978-1-5341-4996-0(1),* 213291); lib. bdg. 28.50 *(978-1-5341-4710-2(1),* 213290) Cherry Lake Publishing.

—Plant Cycle. Bell, Samantha. 2018. (Mi Mini Biografía (My Itty-Bitty Bio): My Early Library). (ENG.). 24p. (J). (gr. k-1). pap. 12.79 *(978-1-5341-0823-3(8),* 210656); lib. bdg. 28.50 *(978-1-5341-0724-3(X),* 210655) Cherry Lake Publishing.

—Playing Musical Bottles. Rowe, Brooke. 2016. (My Early Library: My Science Fun Ser.). (ENG.). 24p. (J). (gr. k-1). 28.50 *(978-1-63471-028-2(2),* 208192) Cherry Lake Publishing.

—Playing with Solar Heat. Rowe, Brooke. 2016. (My Early Library: My Science Fun Ser.). (ENG.). 24p. (J). (gr. k-1). 28.50 *(978-1-63471-031-2(2),* 208204) Cherry Lake Publishing.

—Principal. Devera, Czeena. 2018. (Mi Mini Biografía (My Itty-Bitty Bio): My Early Library). (ENG.). 24p. (J). (gr. k-1). pap. 12.79 *(978-1-5341-0817-2(3),* 210632); lib. bdg. 28.50 *(978-1-5341-0718-2(5),* 210631) Cherry Lake Publishing.

—Pushing & Pulling. Bell, Samantha. 2018. (Mi Mini Biografía (My Itty-Bitty Bio): My Early Library). (ENG.). 24p. (J). (gr. k-1). pap. 12.79 *(978-1-5341-0820-2(3),* 210644); lib. bdg. 28.50 *(978-1-5341-0721-2(5),* 210643) Cherry Lake Publishing.

—Reshma Saujani. Sarantou, Katlin. 2019. (My Early Library: My Itty-Bitty Bio Ser.). (ENG.). 24p. (J). (gr. k-1). pap. 12.79 *(978-1-5341-4985-4(6),* 213247); lib. bdg. 28.50 *(978-1-5341-4699-0(7),* 213246) Cherry Lake Publishing.

—Rosa Parks. Haldy, Emma E. 2016. (My Early Library: My Itty-Bitty Bio Ser.). (ENG.). 24p. (J). (gr. k-1). 28.50 *(978-1-63470-481-6(9),* 207655) Cherry Lake Publishing.

—Rosalyn Sussman Yalow. Loh-Hagan, Virginia. 2018. (Mi Mini Biografía (My Itty-Bitty Bio): My Early Library). (ENG.). 24p. (J). (gr. k-1). pap. 12.79 *(978-1-5341-0813-4(0),* 210616); lib. bdg. 28.50 *(978-1-5341-0714-4(2),* 210615) Cherry Lake Publishing.

—Ruth Bader Ginsburg. Spiller, Sara. 2019. (My Early Library: My Itty-Bitty Bio Ser.). (ENG.). 24p. (J). (gr. k-1). pap. 12.79 *(978-1-5341-3925-1(7),* 212529); lib. bdg. 28.50 *(978-1-5341-4269-5(X),* 212528) Cherry Lake Publishing.

—Sacagawea. Haldy, Emma E. 2016. (My Early Library: My Itty-Bitty Bio Ser.). (ENG.). 24p. (J). (gr. k-1). 28.50 *(978-1-63470-482-3(7),* 207659) Cherry Lake Publishing.

—Sally Ride. Loh-Hagan, Virginia. 2018. (Mi Mini Biografía (My Itty-Bitty Bio): My Early Library). (ENG.). 24p. (J). (gr. k-1). pap. 12.79 *(978-1-5341-0808-0(4),* 210596); lib. bdg. 28.50 *(978-1-5341-0709-0(6),* 210595) Cherry Lake Publishing.

—Saturn. Devera, Czeena. 2020. (My Early Library: My Guide to the Planets Ser.). (ENG.). 24p. (J). (gr. k-1). pap. 12.79 *(978-1-5341-6114-6(7),* 214456); lib. bdg. 28.50 *(978-1-5341-5884-9(7),* 214455) Cherry Lake Publishing.

—Selena Quintanilla-Pérez. Sarantou, Katlin. 2020. (My Early Library: My Itty-Bitty Bio Ser.). (ENG.). 24p. (J). (gr. k-1). pap. 12.79 *(978-1-5341-6103-0(1),* 214412); lib. bdg. 28.50 *(978-1-5341-5873-3(1),* 214411) Cherry Lake Publishing.

—Serena Williams. Sarantou, Katlin. 2020. (My Early Library: My Itty-Bitty Bio Ser.). (ENG.). 24p. (J). (gr. k-1). pap. 12.79 *(978-1-5341-6109-2(0),* 214436); lib. bdg. 28.50 *(978-1-5341-5879-5(0),* 214435) Cherry Lake Publishing.

—Shining a Penny. Rowe, Brooke. 2016. (My Early Library: My Science Fun Ser.). (ENG.). 24p. (J). (gr. k-1). 28.50 *(978-1-63471-030-5(4),* 208200) Cherry Lake Publishing.

—Shirley Ann Jackson. Loh-Hagan, Virginia. 2018. (Mi Mini Biografía (My Itty-Bitty Bio): My Early Library). (ENG.). 24p. (J). (gr. k-1). pap. 12.79 *(978-1-5341-0812-7(2),* 210612); lib. bdg. 28.50 *(978-1-5341-0713-7(4),* 210611) Cherry Lake Publishing.

—Simone Biles. Sarantou, Katlin. 2020. (My Early Library: My Itty-Bitty Bio Ser.). (ENG.). 24p. (J). (gr. k-1). pap. 12.79 *(978-1-5341-6107-8(4),* 214428); lib. bdg. 28.50 *(978-1-5341-5877-1(4),* 214427) Cherry Lake Publishing.

—Sleep Well! Marsico, Katie. 2019. (My Early Library: My Healthy Habits Ser.). (ENG.). 24p. (J). (gr. k-1). pap. 12.79 *(978-1-5341-3936-7(2),* 212573); lib. bdg. 28.50 *(978-1-5341-4280-0(0),* 212572) Cherry Lake Publishing.

—Solar System. Bell, Samantha. 2018. (Mi Mini Biografía (My Itty-Bitty Bio): My Early Library). (ENG.). 24p. (J). (gr. k-1). pap. 12.79 *(978-1-5341-0821-9(1),* 210648); lib. bdg.

28.50 *(978-1-5341-0722-9(3)*, 210647) Cherry Lake Publishing.

—States of Matter. Bell, Samantha. 2018. (Mi Mini Biografía (My Itty-Bitty Bio): My Early Library). (ENG.). 24p. (J). (gr. k-1). pap. 12.79 *(978-1-5341-0824-0(6)*, 210660); lib. bdg. 28.50 *(978-1-5341-0725-0(8)*, 210659) Cherry Lake Publishing.

—Stephen Curry. Sarantou, Katlin. 2020. (My Early Library: My Itty-Bitty Bio Ser.). (ENG.). 24p. (J). (gr. k-1). pap. 12.79 *(978-1-5341-6110-8(4)*, 214440); lib. bdg. 28.50 *(978-1-5341-5880-1(4)*, 214439) Cherry Lake Publishing.

—Stephen Hawking. Sarantou, Katlin. 2019. (My Early Library: My Itty-Bitty Bio Ser.). (ENG.). 24p. (J). (gr. k-1). pap. 12.79 *(978-1-5341-4989-2(9)*, 213263); lib. bdg. 28.50 *(978-1-5341-4703-4(9)*, 213262) Cherry Lake Publishing.

—Stevie Wonder. Sarantou, Katlin. 2019. (My Early Library: My Itty-Bitty Bio Ser.). (ENG.). 24p. (J). (gr. k-1). pap. 12.79 *(978-1-5341-4988-5(0)*, 213259); lib. bdg. 28.50 *(978-1-5341-4702-7(0)*, 213258) Cherry Lake Publishing.

—Sunlight. Bell, Samantha. 2018. (Mi Mini Biografía (My Itty-Bitty Bio): My Early Library). (ENG.). 24p. (J). (gr. k-1). pap. 12.79 *(978-1-5341-0827-1(0)*, 210672); lib. bdg. 28.50 *(978-1-5341-0728-1(2)*, 210671) Cherry Lake Publishing.

—Susan B. Anthony. Spiller, Sara. 2019. (My Early Library: My Itty-Bitty Bio Ser.). (ENG.). 24p. (J). (gr. k-1). pap. 12.79 *(978-1-5341-3923-7(0)*, 212521); lib. bdg. 28.50 *(978-1-5341-4267-1(3)*, 212520) Cherry Lake Publishing.

—Tammy Duckworth. Sarantou, Katlin. 2019. (My Early Library: My Itty-Bitty Bio Ser.). (ENG.). 24p. (J). (gr. k-1). pap. 12.79 *(978-1-5341-4990-8(2)*, 213267); lib. bdg. 28.50 *(978-1-5341-4704-1(7)*, 213266) Cherry Lake Publishing.

—Uranus. Devera, Czeena. 2020. (My Early Library: My Guide to the Planets Ser.). (ENG.). 24p. (J). (gr. k-1). pap. 12.79 *(978-1-5341-6117-7(1)*, 214468); lib. bdg. 28.50 *(978-1-5341-5887-0(1)*, 214467) Cherry Lake Publishing.

—Use a Tissue! Marsico, Katie. 2019. (My Early Library: My Healthy Habits Ser.). (ENG.). 24p. (J). (gr. k-1). pap. 12.79 *(978-1-5341-3932-9(X)*, 212557); lib. bdg. 28.50 *(978-1-5341-4276-3(2)*, 212556) Cherry Lake Publishing.

—Venus. Devera, Czeena. 2020. (My Early Library: My Guide to the Planets Ser.). (ENG.). 24p. (J). (gr. k-1). pap. 12.79 *(978-1-5341-6115-3(5)*, 214460); lib. bdg. 28.50 *(978-1-5341-5885-6(5)*, 214459) Cherry Lake Publishing.

—Walt Disney. Haldy, Emma E. 2016. (My Early Library: My Itty-Bitty Bio Ser.). (ENG.). 24p. (J). (gr. k-1). 28.50 *(978-1-63471-024-4(X)*, 208176) Cherry Lake Publishing.

—Wash Your Hands! Marsico, Katie. 2019. (My Early Library: My Healthy Habits Ser.). (ENG.). 24p. (J). (gr. k-1). pap. 12.79 *(978-1-5341-3931-2(1)*, 212553); lib. bdg. 28.50 *(978-1-5341-4275-6(4)*, 212552) Cherry Lake Publishing.

—Waste & Recycling Collector. Devera, Czeena. 2018. (Mi Mini Biografía (My Itty-Bitty Bio): My Early Library). (ENG.). 24p. (J). (gr. k-1). pap. 12.79 *(978-1-5341-0818-9(1)*, 210636); lib. bdg. 28.50 *(978-1-5341-0719-9(3)*, 210635) Cherry Lake Publishing.

—Weather. Bell, Samantha. 2018. (Mi Mini Biografía (My Itty-Bitty Bio): My Early Library). (ENG.). 24p. (J). (gr. k-1). pap. 12.79 *(978-1-5341-0822-6(X)*, 210652); lib. bdg. 28.50 *(978-1-5341-0723-6(1)*, 210651) Cherry Lake Publishing.

—Yoga. Marsico, Katie. 2019. (My Early Library: My Mindful Day Ser.). (ENG.). 24p. (J). (gr. k-1). pap. 12.79 *(978-1-5341-4994-6(5)*, 213283); lib. bdg. 28.50 *(978-1-5341-4708-9(X)*, 213282) Cherry Lake Publishing.

Bane, T. Glenn. Doodey the Combat Camel. Wardell, Joe. 2012. 20p. pap. 12.95 *(978-0-615-58866-7(2))* Little Clive Pr.

Banek, Yvette. Writing Makeovers 3-4: Improving Skills - Adding Style. Hults, Alaska. Rous, Sheri, ed. 2003. 96p. (J). (gr. 3-5). pap. 11.99 *(978-1-57471-956-7(4)*, 2261) Creative Teaching Pr., Inc.

Banerjee, Mousam. The Adventure Friends: Ski Day. Duhon, Brian. 2020. (Adventure Friends Ser.: Vol. 1). (ENG.). 28p. (J). pap. 14.99 ***(978-1-6728-4682-0(X))*** Independently Published.

—Quint the Bookmobile: Barnabus Rides in Style. Quinton, Kathleen. 2019. (Quint the Bookmobile Ser.: Vol. 2). (ENG.). 32p. (J). (gr. k-3). 16.99 ***(978-1-7337067-0-4(4))***; pap. 8.99 ***(978-1-7337067-1-1(2))*** Quintessential Productions.

Banerjee, Sankha. Martin Luther King. Helfand, Lewis & Teitelbaum, Michael. 2013. (Campfire Graphic Novels Ser.). (ENG.). 88p. (YA). (gr. 5). pap. 11.99 *(978-93-80028-69-9(5)*, Campfire) Steerforth Pr.

—Stolen Hearts: The Love of Eros & Psyche. Foley, Ryan. 2011. (Campfire Graphic Novels Ser.). (ENG.). 88p. (YA). (gr. 5-12). pap. 11.99 *(978-93-80028-48-4(2)*, Campfire) Steerforth Pr.

—The Wright Brothers. Helfand, Lewis. 2011. (Campfire Graphic Novels Ser.). (ENG.). 72p. (YA). (gr. 5-9). pap. 9.99 *(978-93-80028-46-0(6)*, Campfire) Steerforth Pr.

Banerjee, Sunandini. Delhi Thaatha: A Great Grand Story. Viraraghavan, Chitra. 2018. (India List Ser.). (ENG.). 48p. (J). 19.00 *(978-0-85742-549-2(8))* Seagull Bks. IND. Dist: Chicago Distribution Ctr.

Banfield, Beverly. The Emerald Isle Princess & the Silver Tiara. Banfield, Beverly. 2016. (ENG.). (J). pap. *(978-0-9951611-0-8(0))* Copper Tree Publishing.

Bang, Molly. Buried Sunlight: How Fossil Fuels Have Changed the Earth. Bang, Molly. Chisholm, Penny. 2014. (ENG.). 48p. (J). (gr. -1-3). 18.99 *(978-0-545-57785-4(3))* Scholastic, Inc.

—Living Sunlight: How Plants Bring the Earth to Life. Bang, Molly. Chisholm, Penny. 2009. (ENG.). 40p. (J). (gr. -1-3). 18.99 *(978-0-545-04422-6(7)*, Blue Sky Pr., The) Scholastic, Inc.

—My Light. Bang, Molly. 2004. (ENG.). 40p. (J). (gr. -1-3). 18.99 *(978-0-439-48961-4(X))* Scholastic, Inc.

—Ocean Sunlight: How Tiny Plants Feed the Seas. Bang, Molly. Chisholm, Penny. 2012. (ENG.). 48p. (J). (gr. -1-3). 18.99 *(978-0-545-27322-0(6)*, Blue Sky Pr., The) Scholastic, Inc.

—Rivers of Sunlight: How the Sun Moves Water Around the Earth. Bang, Molly. Chisholm, Penny. 2017. (ENG.). 48p. (J). (gr. -1-3). 18.99 *(978-0-545-80541-4(4)*, Blue Sky Pr., The) Scholastic, Inc.

—Ten, Nine, Eight. Bang, Molly. 2003. (ENG.). 24p. (J). (gr. -1-3). reprint ed. pap. 7.99 *(978-0-688-10480-1(0))*; 20th ed. 16.99 *(978-0-688-00906-9(9))* HarperCollins Pubs. (Greenwillow Bks.).

—When Sophie Gets Angry - Really, Really Angry. Bang, Molly. 2004. (Scholastic Bookshelf Ser.). (ENG.). 40p. (J). (gr. -1-3). reprint ed. pap. 7.99 *(978-0-439-59845-3(1)*, Scholastic Paperbacks) Scholastic, Inc.

—When Sophie Thinks She Can't... Bang, Molly. 2018. (When Sophie Ser.). (ENG.). 40p. (J). (gr. -1-3). 17.99 *(978-1-338-15298-2(X)*, Blue Sky Pr., The) Scholastic, Inc.

—When Sophie's Feelings Are Really, Really Hurt. Bang, Molly. 2015. (When Sophie Ser.). (ENG.). 40p. (J). (gr. -1-3). 17.99 *(978-0-545-78831-1(5)*, Blue Sky Pr., The) Scholastic, Inc.

—Wiley & the Hairy Man: Adapted from an American Folk Tale. Bang, Molly. 2009. (ENG.). 66p. (J). (gr. k-2). pap. 10.99 *(978-1-4169-9843-3(8)*, Simon Spotlight) Simon Spotlight.

Bangson Books Inc., Staff & Dupuis, Karina. Memory Match: in the Garden: A Lift-The-Flap Book. 2019. 12p. (J). (— 1). bds. 9.99 *(978-2-89802-017-9(6)*, CrackBoom! Bks.) Chouette Publishing CAN. Dist: Publishers Group West (PGW).

—Memory Match: under the Sea: A Lift-The-Flap Book. 2019. 12p. (J). (— 1). bds. 9.99 *(978-2-89802-018-6(4)*, CrackBoom! Bks.) Chouette Publishing CAN. Dist: Publishers Group West (PGW).

Bania, Michael. Wiggle-Waggle Woof: Counting Sled Dogs in Alaska. Stihler, Chérie B. & Stihler, Chérie B. 2009. (Paws IV Ser.). 32p. (J). (gr. -1-2). pap. 10.99 *(978-1-57061-559-7(4)*, Little Bigfoot) Sasquatch Bks.

—Wiggle-Waggle Woof 1, 2, 3: A Counting Book. Stihler, Chérie B. & Stihler, Chérie B. 2015. (Paws IV Ser.). 11p. (J). (— 1). bds. 8.99 *(978-1-57061-978-6(6)*, Little Bigfoot) Sasquatch Bks.

Banigan, Chris. The Robber Chief: A Tale of Vengeance & Compassion. Rowe, W. W. 2003. (ENG.). 48p. (gr. 1-18). 12.95 *(978-1-55939-186-3(3)*, Snow Lion Publications, Inc.) Shambhala Pubns., Inc.

Banis, Bud. Me & My Shadows -Shadow Puppet Fun ForKids of All Ages: Enhanced with Practical Paper Pastimes. Banis, Bud. 2012. 122p. (J). pap. 14.95 *(978-1-59630-076-7(0)*, BeachHouse Bks.) Science & Humanities Pr.

Bankenaar, Dale. Animal Tales, Vol. 1. Von Wielligh, G. R. 2012. (ENG.). 93p. pap. 12.00 *(978-1-86919-433-8(0))* Protea Boekhuis ZAF. Dist: Casemate Pubs. & Bk. Distributors, LLC.

—Animal Tales, Vol. 2. Von Wielligh, G. R. 2012. (ENG.). 93p. pap. 12.00 *(978-1-86919-504-5(3))* Protea Boekhuis ZAF. Dist: Casemate Pubs. & Bk. Distributors, LLC.

Banki, Caspian & Banki, Damian. What Autism Means to Me. Banki, Caspian & Banki, Lynne. 2003. (ENG.). 40p. (J). per. 12.95 *(978-0-9743801-0-0(5))* Lifelight Bks.

Banki, Damian, jt. illus. see Banki, Caspian.

Banks, Ara Grace. Princess Alexia & the Dragon. Meador, K. 2014. (ENG.). 32p. (J). pap. 14.99 *(978-1-7290-0964-2(6))* Independently Published.

Banks, Erin. The First Music. Pritchett, Dylan. 2006. (ENG.). 32p. (J). (gr. -1-3). 16.95 *(978-0-87483-776-6(6))* August Hse. Pubs., Inc.

—Hush Harbor: Praying in Secret. Evans, Freddi Williams. 2008. (ENG.). 32p. (J). (gr. k-3). 16.95 *(978-0-8225-7965-6(0)*, Carolrhoda Bks.) Lerner Publishing Group.

Banks, Erin Bennett. Change of Heart, 1 vol. Walsh, Alice. 2016. (ENG.). 32p. (J). (gr. 1-3). 19.95 *(978-1-77108-371-3(9)*, bf41c532-3b91-4a41-8bd3-30704366c336) Nimbus Publishing, Ltd. CAN. Dist: Baker & Taylor Publisher Services (BTPS).

—The Walking Bathroom, 1 vol. Grant, Shauntay. 2017. (ENG.). 32p. (J). (gr. -1-k). 22.95 *(978-1-77108-556-4(8)*, 1cf2dcec-0088-424e-90ab-73533cb1a833) Nimbus Publishing, Ltd. CAN. Dist: Baker & Taylor Publisher Services (BTPS).

Banks, Pat. A Is for Appalachia! The Alphabet Book of Appalachian Heritage. Pack, Linda Hager. 2009. (ENG.). 44p. 16.95 *(978-0-8131-2556-5(1))* Univ. Pr. of Kentucky.

—Appalachian Toys & Games from a to Z. Pack, Linda Hager. 2013. (ENG.). 56p. 17.95 *(978-0-8131-4104-6(4))* Univ. Pr. of Kentucky.

Banks, Sandra. The Adventures of Didi & Mr Taco. Schult, Sherry. 2011. 16p. pap. 24.95 *(978-1-4560-8083-9(0))* America Star Bks.

Banks, Timothy. ABCs. Wittrock, Jeni. 2013. (Wizard of Oz Ser.). (ENG.). 24p. (J). (gr. -1-2). 28.65 *(978-1-4765-3765-8(8))* Capstone.

—Bird Boy: A Grimm & Gross Retelling. Harper, Benjamin. 2018. (Michael Dahl Presents: Grimm & Gross Ser.). (ENG.). 64p. (J). (gr. 3-5). lib. bdg. 21.99 *(978-1-4965-7317-9(X)*, 138921, Stone Arch Bks.) Capstone.

—The Brave Little Tailor: A Grimm & Gross Retelling. Bright, J. E. 2018. (Michael Dahl Presents: Grimm & Gross Ser.). (ENG.). 64p. (J). (gr. 3-5). lib. bdg. 21.99 *(978-1-4965-7315-5(3)*, 138919, Stone Arch Bks.) Capstone.

—Feet First. Sonnebom, Scott. 2014. (Frankenstein Journals). (ENG.). 80p. (J). (gr. 2-4). 22.65 *(978-1-4342-8999-5(0)*, Stone Arch Bks.) Capstone.

—The Frankenstein Journals, 1 vol. Sonnebom, Scott. 2014. (Frankenstein Journals). (ENG.). 160p. (J). (gr. 2-4). 9.95 *(978-1-4342-9130-1(8)*, Stone Arch Bks.) Capstone.

—The Frankenstein Journals: Guts or Bust. Sonnebom, Scott. 2015. (Frankenstein Journals). (ENG.). 160p. (J). (gr. 2-4). 9.95 *(978-1-4965-0223-0(X)*, Stone Arch Bks.) Capstone.

—Hans in Luck: A Grimm & Gross Retelling. Bright, J. E. 2018. (Michael Dahl Presents: Grimm & Gross Ser.). (ENG.). 64p. (J). (gr. 3-5). pap. 4.95 *(978-1-4965-7320-9(X)*, 138924); lib. bdg. 21.99 *(978-1-4965-7316-2(1)*, 138920) Capstone. (Stone Arch Bks.).

—I for an Eye. Sonnebom, Scott. 2014. (Frankenstein Journals). (ENG.). 80p. (J). (gr. 2-4). 22.65 *(978-1-4342-9000-7(X)*, Stone Arch Bks.) Capstone.

—The Land of Caring Bou. Coles, Michael Joseph et al. 2006. (J). *(978-0-87483-814-5(2))* August Hse. Pubs., Inc.

—Los Tres Chivos. Hillert, Margaret. 2018. (BeginningtoRead Ser.). (SPA.). 32p. (J). (gr. -1-2). pap. 11.94 *(978-1-68404-241-8(0))* Norwood Hse. Pr.

—Nian: The Chinese New Year Dragon. Loh-Hagan, Virginia. 2019. (ENG.). 32p. (J). (gr. 1-3). 16.99 *(978-1-58536-413-8(4)*, 204755) Sleeping Bear Pr.

—No Guts, No Gloria. Sonnebom, Scott. 2015. (Frankenstein Journals). (ENG.). 80p. (J). (gr. 2-4). 22.65 *(978-1-4965-0221-6(3)*, Stone Arch Bks.) Capstone.

—A Pain in the Butt. Sonnebom, Scott. 2015. (Frankenstein Journals). (ENG.). 80p. (J). (gr. 2-4). 22.65 *(978-1-4965-0222-3(1)*, Stone Arch Bks.) Capstone.

—The Three Goats. Hillert, Margaret & Asbjørnsen, Peter Christen. 2016. (BeginningtoRead Ser.). (ENG.). 32p. (J). (-2). lib. bdg. 22.60 *(978-1-59953-788-7(5))* Norwood Hse. Pr.

—The Three Goats. Hillert, Margaret. 2016. (BeginningtoRead Ser.). (ENG.). 32p. (J). (gr. -1-2). pap. 11.94 *(978-1-60357-914-8(1))* Norwood Hse. Pr.

—A Valentine for Frankenstein. Kimmelman, Leslie. 2018. (ENG.). 32p. (J). (gr. k-3). 17.99 *(978-1-5124-3129-2(X)*, Carolrhoda Bks.) Lerner Publishing Group.

—The Wolf & the Seven Kids: A Grimm & Gross Retelling. Harper, Benjamin. 2018. (Michael Dahl Presents: Grimm & Gross Ser.). (ENG.). 64p. (J). (gr. 3-5). lib. bdg. 21.99 *(978-1-4965-7314-8(5)*, 138918, Stone Arch Bks.) Capstone.

Banks, Timothy. Los Tres Chivos. Banks, Timothy. Hillert, Margaret et al. 2018. (BeginningtoRead Ser.). (SPA.). 32p. (J). (gr. -1-2). lib. bdg. 22.60 *(978-1-59953-957-7(8))* Norwood Hse. Pr.

Banks, Timothy, jt. illus. see Jack Pullan.

Banning, Greg. Wendel & the Great One. Leonetti, Mike. 2008. 383p. *(978-1-55192-812-8(4))* Raincoast Bk. Distribution.

Bannish, Liz. Noodles & Albie. Bennett, Eric. 2014. (ENG.). (J). 17.95 *(978-1-937650-40-7(5))* Small Batch Bks.

Bannister. Book Five: the Parting, Bk. 5. Nykko. 2011. (ElseWhere Chronicles Ser.: 5). (ENG.). 48p. (J). (gr. 4-8). pap. 10.99 *(978-0-7613-7524-1(4)*, Graphic Universe™) Lerner Publishing Group.

—Book Four: the Calling, Bk. 4. Nykko. 2010. (ElseWhere Chronicles Ser.: Bk. 4). (ENG.). 48p. (J). (gr. 4-8). pap. 10.99 *(978-0-7613-6069-8(7)*, Graphic Universe™) Lerner Publishing Group.

—Book One: the Shadow Door, Bk. 1. Nykko. 2009. (ElseWhere Chronicles Ser.: Bk. 1). (ENG.). 48p. (J). (gr. 4-8). pap. 10.99 *(978-0-7613-3963-2(9)*, Graphic Universe™) Lerner Publishing Group.

—Book Six: the Tower of Shadows, Bk. 6. Nykko. 2013. (ElseWhere Chronicles Ser.: 6). (ENG.). 48p. (J). (gr. 4-8). pap. 10.99 *(978-1-4677-1517-1(4)*, Graphic Universe™) Lerner Publishing Group.

—Book Two: the Shadow Spies, Bk. 2. Nykko. 2009. (ElseWhere Chronicles Ser.: Bk. 2). (ENG.). 48p. (J). (gr. 4-8). pap. 10.99 *(978-0-7613-3964-9(7)*, Graphic Universe™) Lerner Publishing Group.

—The Calling. 2010. (Elsewhere Chronicles Ser.: Bk. 4). 48p. (J). (gr. 2-5). lib. bdg. 27.93 *(978-0-7613-6068-1(9)*, Graphic Universe™) Lerner Publishing Group.

—Welcome to the Tribe!, No. 1. Grimaldi. 2013. (Tib & Tumtum Ser.: 1). (ENG.). 48p. (J). (gr. 2-5). lib. bdg. 26.65 *(978-1-4677-1297-2(3)*, 9781467712972, Graphic Universe™) Lerner Publishing Group.

—Welcome to the Tribe! Book 1. Grimaldi, Flora. ed. 2013. (Tib & Tumtum Ser.). (ENG.). 48p. (J). (gr. 2-5). 1. E-Book 39.99 *(978-1-4677-1656-7(1))*; No. 1. pap. 7.99 *(978-1-4677-1522-5(0)*, 9781467715225) Lerner Publishing Group. (Graphic Universe™).

Bannister, A. Book One: The Shadow Door. Nykko. 2009. (Elsewhere Chronicles Ser.). (ENG.). (J). (gr. 4-8). pap. 39.62 *(978-0-7613-4904-4(9))* Lerner Publishing Group.

—Book Three: The Master of Shadows. Nykko. 2009. (Elsewhere Chronicles Ser.). (ENG.). (J). (gr. 4-8). pap. 39.62 *(978-0-7613-5087-3(X))* Lerner Publishing Group.

Bannister, Emily. Hey Diddle Diddle. 2020. (Touch & Trace Nursery Rhymes Ser.). (ENG.). 10p. (J). (— 1). bds. 7.99 *(978-1-68412-959-1(1)*, Silver Dolphin Bks.) Printers Row Publishing Group.

—Itsy Bitsy Spider. 2016. (ENG.). 10p. (J). (gr. -1 — 1). bds. 7.99 *(978-1-62686-764-2(X)*, Silver Dolphin Bks.) Printers Row Publishing Group.

—This Little Piggy. 2018. (Touch & Trace Nursery Rhymes Ser.). (ENG.). 10p. (J). (— 1). bds. 7.99 *(978-1-68412-187-8(6)*, Silver Dolphin Bks.) Printers Row Publishing Group.

—Twinkle, Twinkle Little Star. 2018. (ENG.). 12p. (J). (— 1). 12.99 *(978-1-68412-188-5(4)*, Silver Dolphin Bks.) Printers Row Publishing Group.

Bannister, Philip. Against the Odds: Band 18/Pearl (Collins Big Cat) Reid, Stef. 2014. (Collins Big Cat Ser.). (ENG.). 80p. (J). (gr. 5). pap. 11.99 *(978-0-00-753015-1(3))* HarperCollins Pubs. Ltd. GBR. Dist: Independent Pubs. Group.

Bannon, Laura. Pecos Bill: The Greatest Cowboy of All Time. Bowman, James Cloyd. 2017. (ENG.). 384p. (J). (gr. 4-7). pap. 9.99 *(978-0-8075-6376-2(5)*, 807563765) Whitman, Albert & Co.

—Tales from a Finnish Tupa. Bowman, James Cloyd et al. Kolehmainen, Aili, tr. 2009. 288p. pap. 15.95 *(978-0-8166-6768-0(3))* Univ. of Minnesota Pr.

Banos, Carizza Los. Briana & the Bully Buster Brigade: A Tale about Bully Busting & Empathy. Sorrell Ed D, Deidra a. 2019. (ENG.). 26p. (J). pap. 11.99 ***(978-1-6907-7348-1(0))*** Independently Published.

Bansal, Sujata. Kikli. Sandhu, Rupi K. 2007. (ENG.). 24p. pap. 10.86 *(978-1-4120-6968-7(8))* Trafford Publishing.

Bansch, Helga. En Casa. Janisch, Heinz. Rodriguez Aguilar, Christina, tr. 2009. (SPA.). 32p. (J). (gr. -1-1). *(978-84-263-6857-7(3))* Vives, Luis Editorial (Edelvives).

—Good Night Giants. Janisch, Heinz. 2011. 32p. (J). (gr. -1-3). pap. 14.95 *(978-1-4338-0950-7(8))*; pap. 9.95 *(978-1-4338-0951-4(6))* American Psychological Assn. (Magination Pr.).

Bansch, Helga. I Want a Dog! Bansch, Helga. 2009. 32p. (J). (gr. -1-3). 17.95 *(978-0-7358-2255-9(7))* North-South Bks., Inc.

Banta, Susan. Bubble & Squeak, 1 vol. Bonnett-Rampersaud, Louise. 2006. (ENG.). 24p. (J). (gr. -1-2). 14.99 *(978-0-7614-5310-9(5))* Marshall Cavendish Corp.

—Good Morning, Little Polar Bear. Votaw, Carol J. 2005. (ENG.). 32p. (J). (gr. k-3). 15.95 *(978-1-55971-932-2(X))* Cooper Square Publishing Llc.

—Here Comes Coco. Williams, Rozanne Lanczak. 2005. (Reading for Fluency Ser.). 8p. (J). pap. 3.49 *(978-1-59198-145-9(X)*, 4245) Creative Teaching Pr., Inc.

—La Leyenda del Coqui. 2005. (SPA.). 29p. (J). (gr. k-12). 12.95 *(978-1-58173-256-6(2))* Sweetwater Pr.

—My Friends. Williams, Rozanne Lanczak. Hamaguchi, Carla, ed. 2003. (Sight Word Readers Ser.). 16p. (J). (gr. k-2). pap. 3.49 *(978-1-57471-963-5(7)*, 3585) Creative Teaching Pr., Inc.

—Peeper Has a Fever. Cowan, Charlotte. 2007. (ENG.). 32p. (J). (gr. 3-7). 17.95 *(978-0-9753516-2-8(1))* Hippocratic Pr., The.

—Waking up down Under. Votaw, Carol. 2007. (ENG.). 32p. (J). (gr. k-3). 15.95 *(978-1-55971-976-6(1))* Cooper Square Publishing Llc.

—With All My Heart. Rock, Brian. 2012. (ENG.). 24p. (J). *(978-1-58925-648-4(4))* Tiger Tales.

Banton, Amy Renee. Bob Tales. Morgan, Robert. 2003. 216p. (J). pap. 15.00 *(978-1-888562-06-4(4))* booksonnet.com.

Banyai, Istvan. Tap Dancing on the Roof: Sijo (Poems) Park, Linda Sue. 2015. (ENG.). 48p. (J). (gr. -1-3). 6.99 *(978-0-544-55551-8(1)*, 1610458, HMH Books For Young Readers) Houghton Mifflin Harcourt Publishing Co.

Banyai, Istvan. The Other Side. Banyai, Istvan. 2005. (ENG.). 44p. (J). (gr. k-2). 18.69 *(978-0-8118-4608-0(3)*, Chronicle Bks.) Chronicle Bks. LLC.

Baptiste, Annette Green. In the Shade of the Spade: This Tale in a Poetry Format Takes Us on a Journey. the Illustrations Are Bright & Whimsical. You Can Almost Hear Music. Lee, Deborah Baptiste & Atcheson-Melton, Patty. 2013. 48p. pap. 14.95 *(978-0-9858839-1-1(X))* Lee, Deborah I.

Bar, Thea, jt. illus. see Bar, Yoni.

Bar, Yoni & Bar, Thea. Blake the Snake. Bar, Veronika. l.t. ed. 2016. (ENG.). (J). pap. *(978-4-908892-00-4(8))* BarBar Bks.

Barajas, Sal & Vélez, Gabriel J. La Calaca Review: Un Bilingual Journal of Pensamiento & Palabra. alurista et al. Vélez, Manuel J., ed. 2003. (SPA & ENG.). 152p. per. 15.00 *(978-0-9660773-9-1(3))* Calaca Pr.

Barasch, Lynne. First Come the Zebra. Barasch, Lynne. (ENG.). 40p. (J). 2009. (gr. 1-6). 18.95 *(978-1-60060-365-5(3))*; 2005. pap. 11.95 *(978-1-62014-029-1(2))* Lee & Low Bks., Inc.

—Hiromi's Hands, 1 vol. Barasch, Lynne. 2007. (ENG.). 40p. (J). (gr. k-6). 18.95 *(978-1-58430-275-9(5))* Lee & Low Bks., Inc.

Barasch, Lynne & McCue, Lisa. Part-Time Dog. Thayer, Jane. 2004. (ENG.). 32p. (J). (gr. -1-3). 14.99 *(978-0-06-029693-3(3))* HarperCollins Pubs.

Barba, Ale. The Crankypants Tea Party. Bottner, Barbara. 2020. (ENG.). 40p. (J). (gr. -1-2). 17.99 ***(978-1-4814-5900-6(7))***, Atheneum/Caitlyn Dlouhy Books) Simon & Schuster Children's Publishing.

Barba, Alejandra. Invisible. Baranda, Maria. 2019. (Torre Amarilla Ser.). (SPA.). 152p. (J). pap. ***(978-958-776-499-4(4))*** Norma Ediciones, S.A.

Barbanègre, Raphaëlle. Cinderella & the Furry Slippers. Calì, Davide. 2017. 32p. (J). (gr. -1-2). 17.99 *(978-1-101-91898-2(5)*, Tundra Bks.) Tundra Bks. CAN. Dist: Penguin Random Hse. LLC.

Barbanegre, Raphaelle. Snow White & the 77 Dwarfs. Calì, Davide. 2015. (ENG.). 36p. (J). (gr. -1-2). 17.99 *(978-1-77049-763-4(3)*, Tundra Bks.) Tundra Bks. CAN. Dist: Penguin Random Hse. LLC.

Barbar, Mary. The Attic Treasure. Compton, Lauren Johanna Caitlin. 2015. (ENG.). 36p. (J). pap. ***(978-0-9942139-3-8(X))*** Long Gully Pr.

Barbaresi, Nina. The Tale of Tom Kitten: A Story about Good Behavior. 2006. (J). 6.99 *(978-1-59939-002-4(7))* Cornerstone Pr.

Barbaro, Graziano, jt. illus. see Usai, Luca.

Barbas, Kerren. The Hero Book: Learning Lessons from the People You Admire. Sabin, Ellen. 2005. 64p. 19.95 *(978-0-9759868-1-3(3))* Watering Can.

—The Night Before Christmas dot.com. Gandolfi, Claudine. 2005. (Charming Petites Ser.). 80p. 4.95 *(978-0-88088-844-8(X))* Peter Pauper Pr. Inc.

—Princess Bella: An Art Activity Story Book for Princesses of All Ages. Peter Pauper Press Staff & Zschock, Heather. 2005. (Activity Journal Ser.). 64p. (J). (gr. -1-7). 14.99 *(978-1-59359-972-0(2))* Peter Pauper Pr. Inc.

—Super Scratch & Sketch: A Cool Art Activity Book for Budding Artists of All Ages. 2005. (Activity Journals Ser.). 60p. 12.99 *(978-0-88088-286-6(7))* Peter Pauper Pr. Inc.

—Wild Safari: An Art Activity Book for Imaginative Artists of All Ages. Zschock, Heather. 2005. (Activity Journal Ser.). 64p. (J). (gr. -1-7). 12.99 *(978-1-59359-971-3(4))* Peter Pauper Pr. Inc.

Barbas Steckler, Kerren. Knights Scratch & Sketch: For Brave Artists & Loyal Subjects of All Ages. Nemmers, Tom. 2007. (Scratch & Sketch sER.). 80p. (J). 12.99 *(978-1-59359-877-8(7))* Peter Pauper Pr. Inc.

Barbaso-Crall, Mary Monette. Charlene the Mean Queen. Clarke, Aubrey. 2018. (ENG.). 32p. (J). (gr. k-6). *(978-1-988785-07-3(3))*; pap. *(978-1-988785-06-6(5))* Envision Urban.

—Fly Little Blackbird Fly! Clarke, Aubrey G. 2013. (Fly Little Blackbird Fly! Ser.: Vol. 1). (ENG.). 26p. (J). (gr. k-6). pap. *(978-1-988785-04-2(9))* Envision Urban.

—I Remember Me. Clarke, Aubrey. 2018. (Fly Little Blackbird Fly Ser.: Vol. 3). (ENG.). 26p. (J). (gr. k-6). pap. *(978-1-988785-02-8(2))* Envision Urban.

—It's Not over until It's Over! Clarke, Aubrey G. 3rd ed. 2014. (Fly Little Blackbird Fly Ser.: Vol. 2). (ENG.). 34p. (J). (gr. k-6). pap. *(978-1-988785-03-5(0))* Envision Urban.

Barbelle. Children's Cowboy Songs for Piano. Spivak, Samuel. 2011. 28p. 35.95 *(978-1-258-06408-2(1))* Literary Licensing, LLC.

Barber, Brian. My Favorite Places from a to Z. Snow, Peggy. 2007. (My Favorites Ser.). (ENG.). 32p. (J). (gr. -1). lib. bdg. 15.99 *(978-1-934277-03-4(7))* Mam Green Publishing, Inc.

Barber, Carol. Naya & Nathan. Fripp, Deborah & Fripp, Michael. Fripp, Jean, ed. 2003. (Dolphin Watch Ser.). 32p. (J). (gr. k-4). pap. 5.99 *(978-0-9701008-4-9(1))* Bicast, Inc.

Barber, David L. Custody Battle: A Workbook for Children. Martin-Finks, Nancy. 2005. 68p. per. 19.95 *(978-1-931636-42-1(7))* National Ctr. For Youth Issues.

—Tales of Temper: Grades 3-6. Sartori, Rosanne Sheritz. 2005. 128p. per. 21.95 *(978-1-931636-48-3(6))* National Ctr. For Youth Issues.

Barber, Julia. Colors Around Us. Wilcox, Michael. 2004. 32p. (J). per. 19.95 *(978-1-931780-32-2(3))* School of Color Publishing.

Barber, Shirley. The Fairies Alphabet Puzzle Tray: With Five 6-Piece Jigsaw Puzzles. 2004. 10p. (J). *(978-1-74124-437-3(4))* Five Mile Australia.

Barber, Shirley. The Seventh Unicorn. Barber, Shirley. ed. 32p. (J). *(978-1-74124-399-4(8))* Five Mile Australia.

—Spellbound & the Fairy Book: Packed with 3-D Pictures. Barber, Shirley. 2005. 64p. (J). incl. audio compact disk *(978-1-74124-486-1(2))* Five Mile Australia.

—Tales from Martha B. Rabbit. Barber, Shirley. 2005. 70p. (J). incl. audio compact disk *(978-1-86503-740-0(0))* Five Mile Australia.

Barbera, Michelle. Meerkat's Safari. Graziano, Claudia. 2007. 36p. (J). 15.99 *(978-0-9778072-0-8(7))* Meerkat's Adventures Bks.

Barbera, Tony, et al. The Chronicles of Narnia. Barbera, Tony et al, photos by. Peacock, Ann & Lewis, C. S. 2005. (Chronicles of Narnia Ser.). 64p. (J). *(978-1-4156-3678-7(8))* HarperCollins Pubs.

Barberi, Carlo. Hulk: World War Hulk II. 2018. (Totally Awesome Hulk (2016) Ser.: 6). (ENG.). 112p. (J). (gr. 4-17). pap. 17.99 *(978-1-302-90997-0(5))* Marvel Worldwide, Inc.

—In the Dimming Light, 1 vol. Beechen, Adam & Wong, Walden. 2013. (Justice League Unlimited Ser.). (ENG.). 32p. (J). (gr. 3-6). 22.60 *(978-1-4342-6042-0(9)*, Stone Arch Bks.) Capstone.

—Marvel Heros: Mix & Match Storybook. Meredith, Randy. 2006. 8p. (J). 8.95 *(978-1-57791-299-6(3)*, Penny Candy Pr.) Brighter Minds Children's Publishing.

—Monitor Duty, 1 vol. Beechen, Adam & Wong, Walden. 2013. (Justice League Unlimited Ser.). (ENG.). 32p. (J). (gr. 3-6). 22.60 *(978-1-4342-6041-3(0)*, Stone Arch Bks.) Capstone.

—Ororo: Before the Storm. Sumerak, Marc. 2012. (Ororo: Before the Storm Ser.). (ENG.). 24p. (J). (gr. 2-6). lib. bdg. 27.07 *(978-1-61479-025-9(6)*, 11961);4. lib. bdg. 27.07 *(978-1-61479-027-3(2)*, 11963);Pt. 3. lib. bdg. 27.07 *(978-1-61479-026-6(4)*, 11962) Spotlight. (Marvel Age).

—Who Is the Question?, 1 vol. Beechen, Adam & Wong, Walden. 2013. (Justice League Unlimited Ser.). (ENG.). 32p. (J). (gr. 3-6). 22.60 *(978-1-4342-6044-4(5)*, Stone Arch Bks.) Capstone.

Barberi, Carlo & Beatty, Terry. Batman Versus the Yeti!, 1 vol. Torres, J. 2013. (Batman: the Brave & the Bold Ser.). (ENG.). 32p. (J). (gr. 2-5). 22.60 *(978-1-4342-4708-7(2)*, Stone Arch Bks.) Capstone.

Barberi, Carlo & Wong, Walden. Divide & Conquer, 1 vol. Beechen, Adam. 2013. (Justice League Unlimited Ser.). (ENG.). 32p. (J). (gr. 3-6). lib. bdg. 22.60 *(978-1-4342-4713-1(9)*, Stone Arch Bks.) Capstone.

—Local Hero, 1 vol. Beechen, Adam. 2013. (Justice League Unlimited Ser.). (ENG.). 32p. (J). (gr. 3-6). 22.60 *(978-1-4342-4716-2(3)*, Stone Arch Bks.) Capstone.

—Small Time, 1 vol. Beechen, Adam. 2013. (Justice League Unlimited Ser.). (ENG.). 32p. (J). (gr. 3-6). 22.60 *(978-1-4342-4715-5(5)*, Stone Arch Bks.) Capstone.

Barberis, Franco. Would You Like a Parrot? Barberis, France. 32p. (J). (gr. -1). 16.95 *(978-0-87592-060-3(8))* Scroll Pr., Inc.

Barbieri, Pamela. Happy Halloween: Chunky Peek a Flap Board Book. VonFeder, Rosa. Cottage Door Press, ed. 2018. (Flip a Flap Ser.). (ENG.). 10p. (J). (gr. -1-k). bds. 8.99 *(978-1-68052-341-6(4)*, 1003130) Cottage Door Pr.

Barbieri, Pamela. I'm Not Scared! Dragon, Octavia. 2020. (ENG.). 20p. (J). bds. ***(978-1-5037-5465-2(0)***, ae55e952-530b-42fa-9e33-5279adb40e02, p i kids) Phoenix International Publications, Inc.

Barbieri, Pamela. What Are Little Boys Made Of: Keepsake Greeting Card Board Book. Birdsong, Minnie. ed. 2017. (Little Bird Greetings Ser.). (ENG.). 8p. (J). (gr. -1-k). bds. 6.99 *(978-1-68052-210-5(8)*, 1000571) Cottage Door Pr.

—What Are Little Girls Made Of: Keepsake Greeting Card Board Book. Birdsong, Minnie. ed. 2017. (Little Bird Greetings Ser.). (ENG.). 8p. (J). (gr. -1-k). bds. 6.99 *(978-1-68052-211-2(6)*, 1000581) Cottage Door Pr.

Barbor, Carol. Naya & the Haunted Shipwreck. Fripp, Deborah & Fripp, Michael. Fripp, Jean, ed. 2004. 32p. (J). (gr. k-4). pap. 5.99 *(978-0-9701008-7-0(6))* Bicast, Inc.

Barbosa, Diego. Toby the Sloth Makes Lovely Lemonade. Chan, Christina. 2020. (ENG.). 28p. (J). pap. ***(978-1-922374-89-9(X))*** Library For All Limited.

Barbour, H. S. Pee-Wee Harris on the Briny Deep. Fitzhugh, Percy Keese. 2011. 264p. 47.95 *(978-1-258-09985-5(3))* Literary Licensing, LLC.

—Polly in Egypt: The Polly Brewster Series. Roy, Lillian Elizabeth. 2011. 226p. 44.95 *(978-1-258-09808-7(3))* Literary Licensing, LLC.

—Polly in New York. Roy, Lillian Elizabeth. 2004. reprint ed. pap. 28.95 *(978-1-4179-0068-8(7))* Kessinger Publishing, LLC.

—Polly's Southern Cruise: The Polly Brewster Series. Roy, Lillian Elizabeth. 2011. 294p. 48.95 *(978-1-258-10514-3(4))* Literary Licensing, LLC.

—The Woodcraft Girls at Camp. Roy, Lillian Elizabeth. 2011. 348p. 51.95 *(978-1-258-10242-5(0))* Literary Licensing, LLC.

Barbour, Karen. Let's Talk about Race. Lester, Julius. 2008. (ENG.). 32p. (J). (gr. -1-3). pap. 7.99 *(978-0-06-446226-6(9))* HarperCollins Pubs.

—Princess Scargo & the Birthday Pumpkin. Metaxas, Eric. 2004. (Rabbit Ears-A Classic Tale Ser.). (ENG.). 40p. (J). (gr. 2-6). 28.50 *(978-1-59197-769-8(X)*, 12927, Picture Bk.) Spotlight.

—Wonderful Words: Poems about Reading, Writing, Speaking, & Listening. 2004. (ENG.). 32p. (J). (gr. 1-6). 19.99 *(978-0-689-83588-9(4)*, Simon & Schuster Bks. For Young Readers) Simon & Schuster Bks. For Young Readers.

—You Were Loved Before You Were Born. Bunting, Eve. 2008. (J). pap. *(978-0-439-04062-4(0)*, Blue Sky Pr., The) Scholastic, Inc.

Barbour, Karen. Mr. Williams. Barbour, Karen. rev. ed. 2005. (ENG.). 32p. (J). (gr. 1-5). 19.99 *(978-0-8050-6773-6(6)*, 900030584, Holt, Henry & Co. Bks. For Young Readers) Holt, Henry & Co.

Barbour Publishing Staff. Choosing Thankfulness. 2005. 94p. (J). (gr. k-5). pap. 7.99 *(978-0-9703069-5-1(4))* Train-Up A Child, LLC.

Barbra K. Mudd. The Grey Ghost of the Pharaoh. Vail, Emily Blake. 2004. 176p. (YA). per. 8.99 *(978-0-935087-27-7(3))* Wright Publishing, Inc.

Barchowsky, Damien. Teens Ask Deepak: All the Right Questions. Chopra, Deepak. 2006. (ENG.). 208p. (YA). (gr. 7). pap. 17.99 *(978-0-689-86218-2(0)*, Simon Pulse) Simon Pulse.

Barcilon, Marianne. El Chupete de Gina. Naumann-villemin, Christine & Naumann. 2004. (SPA.). 28p. (J). (gr. -1-k). 14.99 *(978-84-8470-184-2(0)*, COR33211) Corimbo, Editorial S.L. ESP. Dist: Lectorum Pubns., Inc.

Barcita, Pamela. The Little Weed Flower. Whipple, Vicky. 2010. (ENG.). 32p. (J). (gr. -1-12). lib. bdg. 16.95 *(978-1-936299-34-8(8)*, Raven Tree Pr.,Csi) Continental Sales, Inc.

—The Little Weed Flower/La Florecita de la Maleza. Whipple, Vicky. 2010. (ENG & SPA.). 32p. (J). (gr. -1-12). lib. bdg. 16.95 *(978-1-936299-32-4(1)*, Raven Tree Pr.,Csi) Continental Sales, Inc.

—Pardon Me, It's Ham, Not Turkey. Suhay, Lisa. 2007. (J). (gr. -1-3). 17.95 *(978-1-933982-01-4(2))* Bumble Bee Publishing.

—Ruby Lee the Bumble Bee: A Bee of Possibility. Matheson, Dawn. 2006. 40p. (J). (gr. -1-3). lib. bdg. *(978-0-9754342-6-0(8))* Bumble Bee Publishing.

—Ruby Lee the Bumble Bee: A Bee's Bit of Wisdom. Matheson, Dawn. 2005. 34p. (J). (gr. -1-3). 17.95 *(978-0-9754342-1-5(7))* Bumble Bee Publishing.

—Ruby Lee the Bumble Bee: A Bee's Bit of Wisdom. Matheson, Dawn. Cindy, Huffman, ed. 2004. 40p. (J). 17.95 *(978-0-9754342-0-8(9))* Bumble Bee Publishing.

—Ruby Lee the Bumble Bee Critter Count Search & Find Game. Matheson, Dawn. Huffman, Cindy, ed. 2005. 6p. (J). 4.95 *(978-0-9754342-4-6(1))* Bumble Bee Publishing.

—Ruby Lee the Bumble Bee Promotional Coloring Book. 2005. 16p. (J). 4.95 *(978-0-9754342-3-9(3))* Bumble Bee Publishing.

—Seed Was Planted. Palazetti, Toulla. 2010. (ENG.). 32p. (J). (gr. -1-3). pap. 7.95 *(978-1-934960-10-3(1)*, Raven Tree Pr.,Csi) Continental Sales, Inc.

—A Seed Was Planted/Sembré una Semilla. Palazeti, Toulla. 2009. (ENG & SPA.). 32p. (J). (gr. -1-3). 16.95 *(978-1-932748-89-5(X)*, Raven Tree Pr.,Csi) Continental Sales, Inc.

—A Walk with Grandpa. Solomon, Sharon K. (ENG.). 32p. (J). 2010. (gr. 4-7). pap. 7.95 *(978-1-934960-12-7(8))*; 2009. (gr. -1-3). 16.95 *(978-1-934960-11-0(X))* Continental Sales, Inc. (Raven Tree Pr.,Csi).

—A Walk With Grandpa/Un Paseo con el Abuelo. Solomon, Sharon. Del Risco, Eida, tr. 2009. (ENG & SPA.). 32p. (J). (gr. -1-3). 16.95 *(978-1-932748-91-8(1)*, Raven Tree Pr.,Csi) Continental Sales, Inc.

Barclay, Alexandra. Pirates & Parrots. Bodner, Bradford. 2020. (Adventures of Kip MacWhiskers Ser.: 2). (ENG.). 44p. (J). 29.99 ***(978-1-0983-1096-7(9))*** BookBaby.

Barclay, Eric. My Pet Wants a Pet. Broach, Elise. 2018. (ENG.). 40p. (J). 16.99 *(978-1-250-10927-9(2)*, 900165514, Holt, Henry & Co. Bks. For Young Readers) Holt, Henry & Co.

—Once upon a Goat. Richards, Dan. 2019. 40p. (J). (gr. -1-2). 17.99 *(978-1-5247-7374-8(3))*; (ENG.). lib. bdg. 20.99 *(978-1-5247-7375-5(1))* Random Hse. Children's Bks. (Knopf Bks. for Young Readers).

Barclay, Eric. Counting Dogs. Barclay, Eric. 2015. (ENG.). 16p. (J). (gr. -1-k). 10.99 *(978-0-545-78392-7(5)*, Cartwheel Bks.) Scholastic, Inc.

—Sheep Dog & Sheep Sheep. Barclay, Eric. 2019. (ENG.). 40p. (J). (gr. -1-3). 17.99 *(978-0-06-267738-9(1))* HarperCollins Pubs.

—Sheep Dog & Sheep Sheep: Baaad Hair Day. Barclay, Eric. 2020. 40p. (J). (gr. -1-3). 17.99 *(978-0-06-267739-6(X)*, HarperCollins) HarperCollins Pubs. Ltd. GBR. Dist: HarperCollins Pubs.

Barclay, Katerina. The Hand of Zeus. Barclay, Katerina. Barclay, Aegea. 2004. (J). 24.95 *(978-0-9758803-0-2(6)*, 206.612.9698); 29.95 *(978-0-9758803-1-9(4)*, 206 234 2572) Aegean Design.

Bard, Breena. Trespassers. Bard, Breena. 2020. (ENG.). 256p. (J). (gr. 3-7). 24.99 *(978-1-338-26423-4(0))*; pap. 14.99 *(978-1-338-26421-0(4))* Scholastic, Inc. (Graphix).

Barden, Amy-Clare. Spot the Dinosaurs. American Museum of Natural History. 2020. 16p. (J). (gr. -1-2). bds. 8.95 *(978-1-4549-3230-7(9))* Sterling Publishing Co., Inc.

—1-2-3 Predators Bite! An Animal Counting Book. American Museum of Natural History. 2019. 18p. (J). (gr. -1-2). bds. 8.95 *(978-1-4549-3075-4(6))* Sterling Publishing Co., Inc.

Bardin, Dave. Beet Juice Buddies. Hoena, Blake. 2018. (Monster Heroes Ser.). (ENG.). 32p. (J). (gr. k-2). lib. bdg. 21.32 *(978-1-4965-6416-0(2)*, 138263, Stone Arch Bks.) Capstone.

—Boy under the Bed. Hoena, Blake. 2018. (Monster Heroes Ser.). (ENG.). 32p. (J). (gr. k-2). lib. bdg. 21.32 *(978-1-4965-6414-6(6)*, 138261, Stone Arch Bks.) Capstone.

—The Curse of Time. Lay, Kathryn. 2016. (Time Twisters Ser.). (ENG.). 112p. (J). (gr. 2-5). lib. bdg. 29.93 *(978-1-62402-179-4(4)*, 24537, Calico Chapter Bks.) ABDO Publishing Co.

—The Ghost Trap. Hoena, Blake & Hoena, Blake A. 2016. (Monster Heroes Ser.). (ENG.). 32p. (J). (gr. k-2). lib. bdg. 21.32 *(978-1-4965-3757-7(2)*, Stone Arch Bks.) Capstone.

—Haunted Time. Lay, Kathryn. 2016. (Time Twisters Ser.). (ENG.). 112p. (J). (gr. 2-5). lib. bdg. 29.93 *(978-1-62402-178-7(6)*, 24535, Calico Chapter Bks.) ABDO Publishing Co.

—The Horrible Hex. Hoena, Blake. 2018. (Monster Heroes Ser.). (ENG.). 32p. (J). (gr. k-2). lib. bdg. 21.32 *(978-1-4965-6413-9(8)*, 138260, Stone Arch Bks.) Capstone.

—Monster Heroes. Hoena, Blake. ed. 2017. (ENG.). 96p. (J). (gr. k-2). pap. 5.95 *(978-1-62370-783-5(8)*, 133089, Capstone Young Readers) Capstone.

—Peter Powers & His Not-So-Super Powers! Clark, Kent & Snider, Brandon T. (Peter Powers Ser.: 1). 128p. (J). (gr. 1-5). 2017. pap. 5.99 *(978-0-316-35934-4(3))*; 2016. 15.99 *(978-0-316-35932-0(7))* Little, Brown Bks. for Young Readers.

—Peter Powers & the Itchy Insect Invasion! Clark, Kent & Snider, Brandon T. 2017. (Peter Powers Ser.: 3). 128p. (J). (gr. 1-5). 15.99 *(978-0-316-35947-4(5))* Little, Brown Bks. for Young Readers.

—Peter Powers & the League of Lying Lizards! Clark, Kent & Snider, Brandon T. 2017. (Peter Powers Ser.: 4). 128p. (J). (gr. 1-5). pap. 5.99 *(978-0-316-54636-2(4))* Little, Brown Bks. for Young Readers.

—Peter Powers & the Rowdy Robot Raiders! Clark, Kent & Snider, Brandon T. (Peter Powers Ser.: 2). 128p. (J). (gr. 1-5). 2017. pap. 5.99 *(978-0-316-35938-2(6))*; 2016. 15.99 *(978-0-316-35941-2(6))* Little, Brown Bks. for Young Readers.

—Peter Powers & the Sinister Snowman Showdown! Clark, Kent & Snider, Brandon T. 2017. (Peter Powers Ser.: 5). (ENG.). 128p. (J). (gr. 1-5). pap. 5.99 *(978-0-316-54628-7(3))* Little, Brown Bks. for Young Readers.

—Peter Powers & the Swashbuckling Sky Pirates! Clark, Kent. 2017. (Peter Powers Ser.: 6). 128p. (J). (gr. 1-5). pap. 5.99 *(978-0-316-43793-6(X))* Little, Brown Bks. for Young Readers.

—Time & Space. Lay, Kathryn. 2016. (Time Twisters Ser.). (ENG.). 112p. (J). (gr. 2-5). lib. bdg. 29.93 *(978-1-62402-177-0(8)*, 24533, Calico Chapter Bks.) ABDO Publishing Co.

—Time Twisters (Set), 4 vols. Lay, Kathryn. 2016. (Time Twisters Ser.). 112p. (J). (gr. 2-5). lib. bdg. 114.00 *(978-1-62402-176-3(X)*, 24531, Calico Chapter Bks.) ABDO Publishing Co.

—Time Under the Sea. Lay, Kathryn. 2016. (Time Twisters Ser.). (ENG.). 112p. (J). (gr. 2-5). lib. bdg. 29.93 *(978-1-62402-180-0(8)*, 24539, Calico Chapter Bks.) ABDO Publishing Co.

—Vampires & Veggies. Hoena, Blake & Hoena, Blake A. 2016. (Monster Heroes Ser.). (ENG.). 32p. (J). (gr. k-2). lib. bdg. 21.32 *(978-1-4965-3755-3(6)*, Stone Arch Bks.) Capstone.

—The Werewolf Bully. Hoena, Blake. 2018. (Monster Heroes Ser.). (ENG.). 32p. (J). (gr. k-2). lib. bdg. 21.32 *(978-1-4965-6415-3(4)*, 138262, Stone Arch Bks.) Capstone.

—Witch's Brew. Hoena, Blake. 2016. (Monster Heroes Ser.). (ENG.). 32p. (J). (gr. k-2). lib. bdg. 21.32 *(978-1-4965-3756-0(4)*, Stone Arch Bks.) Capstone.

—Zombies & Meatballs. Hoena, Blake & Hoena, Blake A. 2016. (Monster Heroes Ser.). (ENG.). 32p. (J). (gr. k-2). lib. bdg. 21.32 *(978-1-4965-3754-6(8)*, Stone Arch Bks.) Capstone.

Bardo, Yuyun. A, B, C Awal. Hoover, Nadine. 2013. 36p. (J). pap. 12.00 *(978-0-9828492-1-7(4))* Conscience Studio.

Bardoff, Naomi. A House for Everyone: A Story to Help Children Learn about Gender Identity & Gender Expression. Hirst, Jo. 2018. (ENG.). 32p. (J). 16.95 *(978-1-78592-448-4(6)*, 696700) Kingsley, Jessica Pubs. GBR. Dist: Hachette UK Distribution.

—Who Are You? The Kid's Guide to Gender & Identity. Pessin-Whedbee, Brook. 2016. (ENG.). 40p. (J). 18.95 *(978-1-78592-728-7(0)*, 696300) Kingsley, Jessica Pubs. GBR. Dist: Hachette UK Distribution.

Bardoff, Naomi, jt. illus. see Risling-Sholl, Oona.

Bardugo, Miriam. Tales of Tzaddikim. Matov, G. Weinbach, Shaindel, tr. (J). pap. 56.99 *(978-0-89906-842-8(1))* Mesorah Pubns., Ltd.

Barela-Di Bisceglie, Monica. Growing up on the Playground / Nuestro Patio de Recreo. Luna, James. 2018. (ENG & SPA.). 32p. (J). (gr. -1-3). 17.95 *(978-1-55885-871-8(7)*, Piñata Books) Arte Publico Pr.

Barella, Laura. The Brave Little Tailor. 2014. (Flip-Up Fairy Tales Ser.). 24p. (J). *(978-1-84643-654-3(0))* Child's Play International Ltd.

—Donkey Skin. 2011. (Flip-Up Fairy Tales Ser.). 24p. (J). *(978-1-84643-410-5(6))*; (gr. 2-2). *(978-1-84643-371-9(1))* Child's Play International Ltd.

—The Little Mermaid. (Flip-Up Fairy Tales Ser.). 24p. (J). (gr. -1-2). 2010. *(978-1-84643-331-3(2))*; 2009. pap. *(978-1-84643-325-2(8))* Child's Play International Ltd.

—Sleeping Beauty. 2009. (Flip-Up Fairy Tales Ser.). 24p. (J). (gr. -1-2). *(978-1-84643-295-8(2))*; pap. *(978-1-84643-252-1(9))* Child's Play International Ltd.

—The Stonecutter. 2012. (Flip-Up Fairy Tales Ser.). 24p. (J). *(978-1-84643-478-5(5))* Child's Play International Ltd.

Barenbaum, Elena. Captain Billy Finds a Friend. Voitsehovskiy, Boris et al. 2020. (Clever Storytime Ser.). (ENG.). 32p. (J). (gr. -1-17). 10.99 *(978-1-951100-02-5(6))* Clever Media Group.

Baretti, Sonia. Little Explorers: Exploring Space: A Lift-The-Flap Book. Rossini, Delphine, tr. 2019. (Little Explorers Ser.). 10p. (J). (gr. -1). bds. 6.99 *(978-2-89802-128-2(8)*, CrackBoom! Bks.) Chouette Publishing CAN. Dist: Publishers Group West (PGW).

—Little Explorers: Things That Go! A Lift-The-Flap Book. 2019. (Little Explorers Ser.). 10p. (J). (gr. -1). bds. 6.99 *(978-2-89802-126-8(1)*, CrackBoom! Bks.) Chouette Publishing CAN. Dist: Publishers Group West (PGW).

—Never-Ending Activity Book: Amazing Mazes. Acampora, Courtney. 2018. (ENG.). 30p. (J). (gr. -1-k). 14.99 *(978-1-68412-321-6(6)*, Silver Dolphin Bks.) Printers Row Publishing Group.

Baretti, Sonia & Dupuis, Karina. Exploring the Farm. Chouette Publishing Staff, tr. 2018. 10p. (J). (gr. -1). bds. 6.99 *(978-2-924786-18-5(5)*, CrackBoom! Bks.) Chouette Publishing CAN. Dist: Publishers Group West (PGW).

—Exploring the Sea. Chouette Publishing Staff, tr. 2018. 10p. (J). (gr. -1). bds. 6.99 *(978-2-924786-17-8(7)*, CrackBoom! Bks.) Chouette Publishing CAN. Dist: Publishers Group West (PGW).

Baretti, Sonia & Legdani, Sanaa. Around the World: Look & Find Book. ed. 2019. 14p. (J). (gr. -1-1). bds. 8.99 *(978-2-89802-009-4(5)*, CrackBoom! Bks.) Chouette Publishing CAN. Dist: Publishers Group West (PGW).

—Little Detectives at Home: A Look & Find Book. Chouette Publishing Staff, tr. 2017. (ENG.). 14p. (J). (gr. -1-1). bds. 8.99 *(978-2-9815807-9-5(5)*, CrackBoom! Bks.) Chouette Publishing CAN. Dist: Publishers Group West (PGW).

—Little Detectives at School: A Look & Find Book. Chouette Publishing Staff, tr. ed. 2017. (ENG.). 14p. (J). (gr. -1-1). bds. 8.99 *(978-2-924786-00-0(2)*, CrackBoom! Bks.) Chouette Publishing CAN. Dist: Publishers Group West (PGW).

—Little Detectives at the Farm. ed. 2018. (ENG.). 14p. (J). (gr. -1-1). bds. 8.99 *(978-2-924786-56-7(8)*, CrackBoom! Bks.) Chouette Publishing CAN. Dist: Publishers Group West (PGW).

Barg, Soosoonam. All about Korea: Stories, Songs, Crafts & Games for Kids. Bowler, Ann Martin. 2018. 64p. (J). (gr. 3-6). 14.99 *(978-0-8048-4938-8(2))* Tuttle Publishing.

—All about Korea: Stories, Songs, Crafts & More. Bowler, Ann Martin. 2011. (ENG.). 64p. (J). (gr. k-4). 16.95 *(978-0-8048-4012-5(1))* Tuttle Publishing.

Barge III, John. My Hat! My Hat! Where Is My Hat? Olive, Gloria D. 2011. 28p. pap. 24.95 *(978-1-4626-0730-3(6))* America Star Bks.

Barge III, John S. I Can Choose to Be Happy. Constantine, Cara J. 2012. 32p. 24.95 *(978-1-4626-4731-6(6))* America Star Bks.

Barge III, John. The Shoes & the Laces. Dtpolk. 2011. 32p. pap. 24.95 *(978-1-4560-3141-1(4))* America Star Bks.

Barger Cohen, Jan. Lanterns & Firecrackers: A Chinese New Year Story. Zucker, Jonny. 2014. (Festival Time Ser.). (ENG.). 24p. (J). (gr. -1-k). pap. 8.99 *(978-1-84507-076-2(3)*, Frances Lincoln Children's Bks.) Quarto Publishing Group UK GBR. Dist: Hachette Bk. Group.

Barger, Jan. Community Workers. Ross, Kathy. 2005. (Crafts for Kids Who Are Learning about Ser.). (ENG.). 48p. (J). (gr. k-3). lib. bdg., tchr. ed. 26.60 *(978-0-7613-2743-1(6))* Lerner Publishing Group.

—Crafts for Kids Who Are Learning about Dinosaurs. Ross, Kathy. 2008. (Crafts for Kids Who Are Learning about Ser.). (ENG.). 48p. (J). (gr. k-3). lib. bdg. 26.60 *(978-0-8225-6809-4(8))* Lerner Publishing Group.

—Crafts for Kids Who Are Learning about Farm Animals. Ross, Kathy. 2007. (Crafts for Kids Who Are Learning about Ser.). (ENG.). 48p. (J). (gr. k-3). lib. bdg. 26.60 *(978-0-8225-6366-2(5))* Lerner Publishing Group.

—Crafts for Kids Who Are Learning about Insects. Ross, Kathy. 2008. (Crafts for Kids Who Are Learning about Ser.). (ENG.). 48p. (J). (gr. k-3). 26.60 *(978-0-8225-7591-7(4))* Lerner Publishing Group.

—Crafts for Kids Who Are Learning about Transportation. Ross, Kathy. 2006. (Crafts for Kids Who Are Learning about Ser.). 48p. (J). (gr. 3-6). lib. bdg. 25.26 *(978-0-7613-9464-8(8))* Lerner Publishing Group.

—Crafts for Kids Who Are Learning about Weather. Ross, Kathy. 2006. (Crafts for Kids Who Are Learning about Ser.). 47p. (J). (gr. 3-6). lib. bdg. 25.26 *(978-0-7613-2796-7(7))* Lerner Publishing Group.

—Kathy Ross Crafts Colors. Ross, Kathy. 2003. (Crafts from Kathy Ross Ser.). 48p. (J). lib. bdg. 23.93 *(978-0-7613-2651-9(0)*, Millbrook Pr.) Lerner Publishing Group.

—Kathy Ross Crafts Numbers. Ross, Kathy. 2003. 48p. (J). lib. bdg. 23.90 *(978-0-7613-2105-7(5)*, Millbrook Pr.) Lerner Publishing Group.

Barghigiani, Anita. Allegro: A Musical Journey Through 11 Musical Masterpieces. Miles, David W. 2018. (ENG.). 32p. (J). (gr. k-3). 24.99 *(978-1-64170-038-2(6)*, 550038) Familius LLC.

Barham, Timothy E. Pippi's Silent Message: Adventures of Suzy Q & You Too. Cloyd, Suzy. 2012. 24p. 24.95 *(978-1-4512-7832-3(2))* America Star Bks.

Barham, Timothy E. Blonds Blending: The Adventures of Suzy Q & You Too. Barham, Timothy E. 2011. 20p. pap. 24.95 *(978-1-4626-4458-2(9))* America Star Bks.

Barinova, Olga. Buckle Up: A Children's Imaginary Journey about Self-Control. Scott, Stephanie. 2020. (ENG.). 40p. (J). ***(978-1-5255-4721-8(6))***; pap. ***(978-1-5255-4722-5(4))*** FriesenPress.

Barinova, Olga. Mikey Discovers His Super Power. Dolinar, Lorena. 2019. (ENG.). 44p. (J). *(978-1-5255-3611-3(7))*; pap. *(978-1-5255-3612-0(5))* FriesenPress.

Barker, Charles Ferguson. Under Michigan: The Story of Michigan's Rocks & Fossils. Barker, Charles Ferguson. 2005. (Great Lakes Books Ser.). (ENG.). 56p. (J). (gr. 1-4). 18.99 *(978-0-8143-3088-3(6)*, 1092, Great Lakes Bks.) Wayne State Univ. Pr.

—Under New England: The Story of New England's Rocks & Fossils. Barker, Charles Ferguson. 2008. (ENG.). 72p. (J). (gr. 2-7). 12.95 *(978-1-58465-696-8(4))* Univ. Pr. of New England.

—Under Ohio: The Story of Ohio's Rocks & Fossils. Barker, Charles Ferguson. 2007. (ENG.). 56p. (J). (gr. 3-7). 34.95 *(978-0-8214-1755-3(X))* Ohio Univ. Pr.

Barker, Cicely Mary. Flower Fairies Sticker Storybook. 2011. (Flower Fairies Ser.). (ENG.). 16p. (J). (gr. -1-k). pap. 6.99 *(978-0-7232-6697-6(2)*, Warne) Penguin Young Readers Group.

Barker, Clive. Abarat. Barker, Clive. (Abarat Ser.: 1). (ENG.). (YA). (gr. 8). 2011. 528p. pap. 10.99 *(978-0-06-209410-0(6))*; 2004. 496p. reprint ed. pap. 9.99 *(978-0-06-059637-8(6))* HarperCollins Pubs.

—Abarat: Days of Magic, Nights of War, 4 vols., Vol. 2. Barker, Clive. ltd. num. aut. ed. 2004. 493p. 175.00 *(978-1-890885-17-5(7))* Trice, B.E. Publishing.

—Abarat: Absolute Midnight. Barker, Clive. 2013. (Abarat Ser.: 3). (ENG.). 640p. (YA). (gr. 8). pap. 10.99 *(978-0-06-440933-9(3))* HarperCollins Pubs.

—Abarat: Days of Magic, Nights of War. Barker, Clive. (Abarat Ser.: 2). (ENG.). (YA). (gr. 8). 2011. 624p. pap. 9.99 *(978-0-06-209411-7(4))*; 2006. 576p. reprint ed. pap. 9.99 *(978-0-06-059638-5(4))* HarperCollins Pubs.

Barker, Dee Dee, et al. The Stick Lizards: Mystical, Magical, & Legendary Adventure Series. 2019. (Book Ser.: Vol. 1). (ENG.). 172p. (J). pap. 15.00 ***(978-0-9998833-9-6(9))*** MAKE BELIEVE PUBLISHING.

Barker, Erin. What Is Soft? Kantor, Susan. 2018. (ENG.). 14p. (J). (— 1). bds. 7.99 *(978-1-936669-63-9(3))* Blue Manatee Press.

Barker, Gary. Garfield Vol. 3. Evanier, Mark. 2014. (Garfield Ser.: 3). (ENG.). 112p. (J). (gr. 1-3). pap. 13.99 *(978-1-60886-348-8(4))* Boom! Studios.

Barker, James, et al. Minecraft Construction Handbook. Needler, Matthew & Southam, Phil. 2015. 87p. (J). *(978-0-545-82321-0(8))* Scholastic, Inc.

Barker, Lauren. The Littlest Vampire. Hasemore, Thomas. 2018. (ENG.). 28p. (J). pap. 9.13 *(978-1-9999892-0-0(1))* TDH Publishing.

Barker, Lori, jt. illus. see Fentz, Mike.

Barker, Scott. My Crocodile Is... Pink & Fluffy. Make Believe Ideas Ltd. 2020. (ENG.). 10p. (J). bds. ***(978-1-78947-727-6(1))*** Make Believe Ideas.

—On the Farm. Make Believe Ideas Ltd. 2020. (ENG.). 10p. (J). bds. ***(978-1-78947-859-4(6))*** Make Believe Ideas.

—Would You Rather. Make Believe Ideas Ltd. 2020. (ENG.). 12p. (J). bds. ***(978-1-78947-729-0(8))*** Make Believe Ideas.

Barker, Stephen. Chalkboard Alphabet: Learn the ABCs with Chalkboard Pages! 2018. (Chalkboard Concepts Ser.). (ENG.). 14p. (J). (gr. -1-1). bds. 9.95 *(978-1-63322-386-8(8)*, 225485, Walter Foster Jr) Quarto Publishing Group USA.

—Chalkboard Numbers: Learn Numbers with Chalkboard Pages! 2018. (Chalkboard Concepts Ser.). (ENG.). 14p. (J). (gr. -1-1). bds. 9.95 *(978-1-63322-389-9(2)*, Walter Foster Jr) Quarto Publishing Group USA.

—Chalkboard Shapes: Learn Shapes with Chalkboard Pages! 2018. (Chalkboard Concepts Ser.). (ENG.). 14p. (J). (gr. -1-1). bds. 9.95 *(978-1-63322-391-2(4)*, Walter Foster Jr) Quarto Publishing Group USA.

—Hello You. 2017. (Baby's First Peekabook Ser.). (ENG.). 12p. (J). (— 1). bds. 10.99 *(978-1-5098-2891-3(5)*, Campbell Bks.) Pan Macmillan GBR. Dist: Independent Pubs. Group.

—Little Friends. 2017. (Baby's First Peekabook Ser.). (ENG.). 12p. (J). (— 1). bds. 10.99 *(978-1-5098-2892-0(3)*, Campbell Bks.) Pan Macmillan GBR. Dist: Independent Pubs. Group.

—Noah's Ark. 2016. (ENG.). 12p. (J). (gr. -1 — 1). bds. 9.99 *(978-1-62686-814-4(X)*, Silver Dolphin Bks.) Printers Row Publishing Group.

Barker, Tyleen. The Grumpy Little Fox. Barker, Tyleen, ed. Morgan, Karen. 2018. (ENG.). 26p. (J). pap. *(978-1-7752861-0-3(X))* Morgan, Tyleen.

—The Grumpy Little Fox. Barker, Tyleen, ed. Morgan, Karen. 2018. (ENG.). 26p. (J). *(978-1-7752861-1-0(8))* Morgan, Tyleen.

Barker, Vicky. Animals: The Illustrated Geography of Our World. Martineau, Susan. 2019. (Geographics Geography for Kids Ser.). (ENG.). 24p. (J). (gr. 1-5). pap. 6.99 *(978-1-63158-490-9(1)*, Racehorse Publishing) Skyhorse Publishing Co., Inc.

—Darcy Dolphin Is a Little Bit Magic! Watkins, Sam. 2017. (Darcy Dolphin Ser.). (ENG.). 144p. (J). (gr. 1-3). pap. 9.99 *(978-1-4052-8423-3(4))* Egmont Bks., Ltd. GBR. Dist: Independent Pubs. Group.

—Earth: The Illustrated Geography of Our World. Martineau, Susan. 2019. (Geographics Geography for Kids Ser.). (ENG.). 24p. (J). (gr. 1-5). pap. 6.99 *(978-1-63158-489-3(8)*, Racehorse Publishing) Skyhorse Publishing Co., Inc.

—Humanity: The Illustrated Geography of Our World. Martineau, Susan. 2019. (Geographics Geography for Kids Ser.). (ENG.). 24p. (J). (gr. 1-5). pap. 6.99 *(978-1-63158-488-6(X)*, Racehorse Publishing) Skyhorse Publishing Co., Inc.

—Infographics for Kids. Martineau, Susan. 2016. (ENG.). 48p. (J). (gr. 2-5). pap. 7.95 *(978-1-58089-723-5(1))* Charlesbridge Publishing, Inc.

—The Order & Chaos Colouring Book. Haig, Rudi. 2017. (ENG.). 128p. (J). (gr. 3). pap. 9.99 *(978-1-909767-83-6(2))* B Small Publishing GBR. Dist: Independent Pubs. Group.

—STEM Activity Book: Science Technology Engineering Math: Packed with Activities & Facts. Bruzzone, Catherine et al. 2018. (STEM Starters for Kids Ser.). (ENG.). 128p. (J). pap. 14.99 *(978-1-63158-264-6(X)*, Racehorse Publishing) Skyhorse Publishing Co., Inc.

—STEM Starters for Kids Art Activity Book: Packed with Activities & Art Facts. Jacoby, Jenny. 2018. (STEM Starters for Kids Ser.). (ENG.). 32p. (J). 6.99 *(978-1-63158-266-0(6)*, Racehorse Publishing) Skyhorse Publishing Co., Inc.

—STEM Starters for Kids Biology Activity Book: Packed with Activities & Biology Facts. Jacoby, Jenny. 2020. (STEM Starters for Kids Ser.). (ENG.). 32p. (J). (gr. 1-4). pap. 6.99 *(978-1-63158-586-9(X)*, Racehorse Publishing) Skyhorse Publishing Co., Inc.

Barker, Vicky. STEM Starters for Kids Chemistry Activity Book: Packed with Activities & Chemistry Facts. Jacoby, Jenny. 2020. (STEM Starters for Kids Ser.). (ENG.). 32p. (J). (gr. 1-4). pap. 6.99 ***(978-1-63158-641-5(6)***, Racehorse Publishing) Skyhorse Publishing Co., Inc.

Barker, Vicky. STEM Starters for Kids Geology Activity Book: Packed with Activities & Geology Facts. Jacoby, Jenny. 2019. (STEM Starters for Kids Ser.). (ENG.). 32p. (J). (gr. 1-4). pap. 6.99 *(978-1-63158-427-5(8)*, Racehorse Publishing) Skyhorse Publishing Co., Inc.

—STEM Starters for Kids Meteorology Activity Book: Packed with Activities & Meteorology Facts. Jacoby, Jenny. 2019. (STEM Starters for Kids Ser.). (ENG.). 32p. (J). (gr. 1-4). pap. 6.99 *(978-1-63158-428-2(6)*, Racehorse Publishing) Skyhorse Publishing Co., Inc.

—STEM Starters for Kids Physics Activity Book: Packed with Activities & Physics Facts. Jacoby, Jenny. 2018. (STEM Starters for Kids Ser.). (ENG.). 32p. (J). 6.99 *(978-1-63158-265-3(8)*, Racehorse Publishing) Skyhorse Publishing Co., Inc.

—STEM Starters for Kids Robotics Activity Book: Packed with Activities & Robotics Facts. Jacoby, Jenny. 2020. (STEM Starters for Kids Ser.). (ENG.). 32p. (J). (gr. 1-4). pap. 6.99 *(978-1-63158-585-2(1)*, Racehorse Publishing) Skyhorse Publishing Co., Inc.

Barker, Vicky, jt. illus. see Horne, Sarah.

Barklem, Jill. Autumn Story (Brambly Hedge) Barklem, Jill. 2011. (Brambly Hedge Ser.). (ENG.). 32p. (J). 9.99 *(978-0-00-183739-3(7)*, HarperCollins Children's Bks.) HarperCollins Pubs. Ltd. GBR. Dist: HarperCollins Pubs.

—The High Hills (Brambly Hedge) Barklem, Jill. 2018. (Brambly Hedge Ser.). (ENG.). 32p. (J). 9.99 *(978-0-00-825266-3(1)*, HarperCollins Children's Bks.) HarperCollins Pubs. Ltd. GBR. Dist: HarperCollins Pubs.

—Poppy's Babies (Brambly Hedge) Barklem, Jill. 2018. (Brambly Hedge Ser.). (ENG.). 32p. (J). 9.99 *(978-0-00-828281-3(1)*, HarperCollins Children's Bks.) HarperCollins Pubs. Ltd. GBR. Dist: HarperCollins Pubs.

—Sea Story (Brambly Hedge) Barklem, Jill. 2018. (Brambly Hedge Ser.). (ENG.). 32p. (J). 9.99 *(978-0-00-825267-0(X)*, HarperCollins Children's Bks.) HarperCollins Pubs. Ltd. GBR. Dist: HarperCollins Pubs.

—The Secret Staircase (Brambly Hedge) Barklem, Jill. 2018. (Brambly Hedge Ser.). (ENG.). 32p. (J). 9.99 *(978-0-00-826914-2(9)*, HarperCollins Children's Bks.) HarperCollins Pubs. Ltd. GBR. Dist: HarperCollins Pubs.

—Spring Story (Brambly Hedge) Barklem, Jill. 2011. (Brambly Hedge Ser.). (ENG.). 32p. (J). 9.99 *(978-0-00-183922-9(5)*, HarperCollins Children's Bks.) HarperCollins Pubs. Ltd. GBR. Dist: HarperCollins Pubs.

—Summer Story (Brambly Hedge) Barklem, Jill. 2011. (Brambly Hedge Ser.). (ENG.). 32p. (J). 9.99 *(978-0-00-183923-6(3)*, HarperCollins Children's Bks.) HarperCollins Pubs. Ltd. GBR. Dist: HarperCollins Pubs.

—Winter Story (Brambly Hedge) Barklem, Jill. 2017. (Brambly Hedge Ser.). (ENG.). 32p. (J). 9.99 *(978-0-00-824118-6(X)*, HarperCollins Children's Bks.) HarperCollins Pubs. Ltd. GBR. Dist: HarperCollins Pubs.

—A Year in Brambly Hedge. Barklem, Jill. 2017. (ENG.). 128p. (J). 29.99 *(978-0-00-824117-9(1)*, HarperCollins Children's Bks.) HarperCollins Pubs. Ltd. GBR. Dist: HarperCollins Pubs.

Barkley, James. Sounder. Armstrong, William H. 2019. (Trophy Bk.). (ENG.). 128p. (J). (gr. 3-7). reprint ed. pap. 6.99 *(978-0-06-440020-6(4)*, HarperCollins) HarperCollins Pubs. Ltd. GBR. Dist: HarperCollins Pubs.

Barkow, Henriette. That's My Mum: Voici Ma Mere. Brazell, Derek. 2004. (ENG & FRE.). 28p. (J). pap. *(978-1-85269-600-9(1))* Mantra Lingua.

Barkow, Henriette & Johnson, Richard. Don't Cry, Sly! Mos Qaj Dhelperush! 2004. (ENG & ALB.). 32p. (J). pap. *(978-1-85269-648-1(6))* Mantra Lingua.

—The Giant Turnip: Rrepa Gjigante. 2004. 24p. (J). *(978-1-85269-732-7(6))* Mantra Lingua.

Barkow, Henriette & Reed, Nathan. The Buskers of Bremen: Kengetaret Endacak Te Bremenit. 2004. (ALB & ENG.). 24p. (J). pap. *(978-1-85269-764-8(4))* Mantra Lingua.

—The Buskers of Bremen: Les Chanteurs de Rues de Bremen. 2004. (FRE & ENG.). 24p. (J). pap. *(978-1-85269-769-3(5))* Mantra Lingua.

Barks, Carl, jt. illus. see Luthi, Morgan.

Barkus, Mariona. The Flower & the Butterfly. Barkus, Mariona. 250th ed. 2003. *(978-1-932629-00-2(9))* Litkus Pr.

—Illustrated History No. 13, Vol. 13. Barkus, Mariona. 2004. 8p. 20.00 *(978-1-932629-15-6(7))* Litkus Pr.

Barley-Cohrs, Dayna. Uncle Rocky, Fireman: Fire! Brewster, James Burd. 2013. 34p. pap. 11.49 *(978-0-9911994-1-9(3))* J2B Publishing LLC.

—Uncle Rocky, Fireman: Something's Missing. Brewster, James Burd. 2013. 34p. pap. 11.49 *(978-0-9911994-2-6(1))* J2B Publishing LLC.

—Uncle Rocky, Fireman: Sparky Protects. Brewster, James Burd. 2013. (ENG.). (J). pap. 9.99 *(978-0-9911994-4-0(8))* J2B Publishing LLC.

—Uncle Rocky, Fireman: Sparky's Rescue. Brewster, James Burd. 2013. (ENG.). (J). pap. 9.99 *(978-0-9911994-3-3(X))* J2B Publishing LLC.

Barlow, Amanda. I Can Draw People. Gibson, Ray. Watt, Fiona, ed. 2004. (Usborne Playtime Ser.). (SPA.). (J). (gr. -1-18). 32p. lib. bdg., act. bk. ed. 12.95 *(978-1-58086-223-3(3))*; 1p. pap., act. bk. ed. 4.95 *(978-0-7460-3704-1(X))* EDC Publishing.

—Mini Art Ideas. Watt, Fiona. 2004. 96p. (J). 7.95 *(978-0-7945-0842-5(1)*, Usborne) EDC Publishing.

—The Usborne Book of Art Ideas. Watt, Fiona. rev. ed. 2006. (Art Ideas Ser.). 96p. (J). pap. 14.99 *(978-0-7945-0893-7(6)*, Usborne) EDC Publishing.

Barlow, Andrew. Jellytoes Misses the Bus. Barlow, Andrew. 2005. (Jellytoes Ser.). (ENG.). 32p. (J). per. 8.95 *(978-0-9764336-0-6(5))* MJS Publishing Group LLC.

Barlow, Charnelle Pinkney. Just Like a Mama. Duncan, Alice Faye. 2020. (ENG.). 40p. (J). (gr. -1-3). 17.99 *(978-1-5344-6183-3(3))* Simon & Schuster, Inc.

Barlow, Damien, jt. illus. see Barlow, Lisa.

Barlow, Dave. Long Long Time. Bland, Ralph. 2014. 251p. 13.50 *(978-1-933300-00-9(0))* Wandering Sage Pubns., LLC.

Barlow, Donell. Bigfoot & Lightning Bug. Barlow, Donell. 2019. (ENG.). 38p. (J). (gr. k-1). 14.99 ***(978-0-578-54972-9(7))*** Barlow, Donell.

Barlow, Lisa & Barlow, Damien. Ten Little Dinosaurs. Tiger Tales. 2018. (ENG.). 10p. (J). (gr. -1-k). bds. 10.99 *(978-1-68010-534-6(5))* Tiger Tales.

Barlowe, Wayne D. & Meaker, Michael. An Alphabet of Dinosaurs. Dodson, Peter. 2016. (ENG.). 66p. (gr. k-5). 29.95 *(978-1-59687-512-8(7)*, ipicturebooks) ibooks, Inc.

Barlup, Jessica. Who Could You Be at the Zoo? Zaring, Laurie. 2013. 24p. pap. 12.95 *(978-1-61244-175-7(0))* Halo Publishing International.

Barman, Adrienne. Creaturepedia Activity Book: With 30 Drawing Activities, 50 Stickers & a Fold-Out Scene to Color In! 2016. (Creaturepedia Ser.). (ENG.). 40p. (J). (gr. k-3). pap. 9.99 *(978-1-84780-835-6(2)*, Wide Eyed Editions) Quarto Publishing Group UK GBR. Dist: Hachette Bk. Group.

Barmashi, Ani. Great Railroad Series: Laying New Tracks. Levi, Isaac Ben. 2019. (Great Railroad Ser.: Vol. 5). (ENG.). 30p. (J). pap. 9.95 ***(978-1-7330477-1-5(9))*** Living Tree Pr.

Barnard, Bryn. Dinosaurs. Nash, Dylan M. 2007. (ENG.). 24p. (J). (gr. 1-18). 19.95 *(978-1-58117-580-6(9)*, Intervisual/Piggy Toes) Bendon, Inc.

—Discovery in the Cave. Dubowski, Mark. 2010. (Step into Reading Ser.). 48p. (J). (gr. 2-4). pap. 4.99 *(978-0-375-85893-2(8)*, Random Hse. Bks. for Young Readers) Random Hse. Children's Bks.

—Sir Henry, the Polite Knight. Rovetch, L. Bob & Whitman, Emily. 2006. (J). *(978-1-58987-204-2(5))* Kindermusik International.

—Tentacles! Tales of the Giant Squid. Redmond, Shirley Raye. 2003. (Step into Reading Ser.). 48p. (J). (gr. k-3). pap. 4.99 *(978-0-375-81307-8(1)*, Random Hse. Bks. for Young Readers) Random Hse. Children's Bks.

—Tentacles! Tales of the Giant Squid. Redmond, Shirley Raye. 2005. (Step into Reading Ser.). (gr. k-2). 14.00 *(978-0-7569-5576-2(9))* Perfection Learning Corp.

Barnard, Bryn. Quinn's Search for the Samurai. Barnard, Bryn. Rotberg, Gene & Rotberg, Iris. 2012. 48p. (J). pap. *(978-0-615-67490-2(9))* Tower Pr.

Barnard, Frederick & Linton, J. D. The Pilgrim's Progress from This World to That Which Is to Come;Delivered under the Similitude of a Dream. Bunyan, John. 2012. 316p. *(978-1-78139-097-9(5))* Benediction Classics.

Barnard, Lucy. The Christmas Story, 1 vol. Williamson, Karen. ed. 2016. (Bible Mini-Pops Ser.). (ENG.). 12p. (J). 9.99 *(978-1-78128-284-7(6)*, Candle Bks.) Lion Hudson PLC GBR. Dist: Kregel Pubns.

—Do Touch! Don't Touch! Hodgman, Ann. 2012. (ENG.). 18p. (J). bds. *(978-1-58925-867-9(3))* Tiger Tales.

Barnard, Lucy. Frog's Summer Journey (Lerner Edition) Loughrey, Anita. 2020. (Year in Nature Ser.). (ENG.). 24p. (J). (gr. -1-1). 27.99 ***(978-0-7112-5079-6(0))*** QEB Publishing Inc.

Barnard, Lucy. The Helpful Donkey, 1 vol. Edwards, Josh & David, Juliet. ed. 2015. (Bible Animals Ser.). (ENG.). 14p. (J). bds. 9.99 *(978-1-78128-180-2(7)*, Candle Bks.) Lion Hudson PLC GBR. Dist: Kregel Pubns.

—Little Lost Sheep, 1 vol. Edwards, Josh & David, Juliet. ed. 2015. (Bible Animals Ser.). (ENG.). 14p. (J). bds. 9.99 *(978-1-78128-179-6(3)*, Candle Bks.) Lion Hudson PLC GBR. Dist: Kregel Pubns.

Barnard, Lucy. My Bible Stories Colouring & Sticker Book. David, Juliet. ed. 2019. (ENG.). 48p. (J). (gr. k). pap. 8.99 ***(978-1-78128-373-8(7)***, Candle Bks.) Lion Hudson PLC GBR. Dist: Independent Pubs. Group.

Barnard, Lucy. My Little Promise Bible, 1 vol. David, Juliet. ed. 2016. (ENG.). 96p. (J). 9.99 *(978-1-78128-257-1(9)*, Candle Bks.) Lion Hudson PLC GBR. Dist: Independent Pubs. Group.

—My Little Promise Bible Colouring Book, 1 vol. David, Juliet. 2016. 48p. (J). pap. 6.99 *(978-1-78128-307-3(9)*, Candle Bks.) Lion Hudson PLC GBR. Dist: Kregel Pubns.

—Noah & Other Stories, 1 vol. Williamson, Karen. ed. 2015. (Bible Mini-Pops Ser.). (ENG.). 12p. (J). (gr. -1-k). 9.99 *(978-1-78128-149-9(1)*, Candle Bks.) Lion Hudson PLC GBR. Dist: Kregel Pubns.

—A Princess's Crown: A Magnetic Storybook. Lawrence, Trisha. 2008. 6p. (J). (gr. -1-1). bds. 10.99 *(978-2-7641-2186-3(5))* Gardner Pubns.

—Rabbit's Spring Gift (Lerner Edition) Loughrey, Anita. 2020. (Year in Nature Ser.). (ENG.). 24p. (J). (gr. -1-1). 27.99 *(978-0-7112-5083-3(9))* QEB Publishing Inc.

—Squirrel's Busy Day. 2014. 24p. (J). *(978-1-4351-5602-9(1))* Barnes & Noble, Inc.

—Uh-Oh! Oh No! Hodgman, Ann. 2012. (Into-Everything Baby Stages Ser.). (ENG.). 18p. (gr. -1). bds. 7.95 *(978-1-58925-866-2(5))* Tiger Tales.

—The Wise Men's Story, 1 vol. Williamson, Karen. ed. 2016. (Bible Mini-Pops Ser.). (ENG.). 12p. (J). 9.99 *(978-1-78128-283-0(8)*, Candle Bks.) Lion Hudson PLC GBR. Dist: Kregel Pubns.

Barnard, Lucy. Archie's Bag of Treasures. Barnard, Lucy. 2017. (Story Corner Ser.). (ENG.). 24p. (J). (gr. -1-k). lib. bdg. 19.99 *(978-1-68297-192-5(9))* QEB Publishing Inc.

Barnard, Lucy. Hurry Home, Harriet: A Birthday Story. Barnard, Lucy. 2020. (Storytime Ser.). (ENG.). 24p. (J). (gr. -1-1). 17.95 ***(978-0-7112-5115-1(0))*** QEB Publishing Inc.

Barnard, Lucy. I'm Bigger Than You. Barnard, Lucy. 2018. (Story Corner Ser.). (ENG.). 24p. (J). (gr. -1-k). lib. bdg. 19.99 *(978-1-68297-316-5(6))* QEB Publishing Inc.

Barneda, David. Pirates vs. Cowboys. Reynolds, Aaron. 2013. 40p. (J). (gr. k-3). 16.99 *(978-0-375-85874-1(1)*, Knopf Bks. for Young Readers) Random Hse. Children's Bks.

Barner, Bob. Sharks Have Six Senses. Waters, John F. 2015. (Let's-Read-And-Find-Out Science 2 Ser.). (ENG.). 40p. (J). (gr. -1-3). 17.99 *(978-0-06-028140-3(5))* HarperCollins Pubs.

—Wiggle Waggle Bee. Todd, Traci N. 2013. (J). *(978-1-58987-327-8(0))* Kindermusik International.

—Wiggle, Waggle, Loop-De-Loo! Todd, Traci N. 2006. (J). *(978-1-58987-009-3(3))* Kindermusik International.

Barner, Bob. Dinosaur Bones. Barner, Bob. unabr. ed. 2006. (J). (gr. -1-2). 29.95 *(978-0-439-90580-0(X))* Weston Woods Studios, Inc.

Barnes, Bridget. Making Friends Is an Art! Cook, Julia. 2012. (ENG.). 32p. (J). pap. 10.95 *(978-1-934490-30-3(X))* Boys Town Pr.

Barnes, Bridget. Making Friends Is an Art! 2nd Ed. Cook, Julia. 2nd ed. 2020. (Building Relationships Ser.). (ENG.). 32p. (J). (gr. k-5). pap. 10.95 ***(978-1-944882-56-3(1))*** Boys Town Pr.

Barnes, Cheryl Shaw. House Mouse, Senate Mouse. Barnes, Peter W. 2012. (ENG.). 40p. (J). (gr. k-3). 16.99 *(978-1-59698-790-6(1)*, Little Patriot Pr.) Regnery Publishing, Inc., An Eagle Publishing Co.

—Little Miss Patriot. Barnes, Peter W. ed. 2007. 32p. (J). lib. bdg. 17.95 *(978-1-893622-20-3(7)*, VSP Bks.) Vacation Spot Publishing.

—Maestro Mouse: And the Mystery of the Missing Baton. Barnes, Peter W. 2013. (ENG.). 40p. (J). (gr. k-5). 16.95 *(978-1-62157-036-3(3)*, Little Patriot Pr.) Regnery Publishing, Inc., An Eagle Publishing Co.

—Maestro Mouse: And the Mystery of the Missing Baton. Barnes, Peter W. 2005. 32p. (J). 16.95 *(978-1-893622-17-3(7)*, VSP Bks.) Vacation Spot Publishing.

—Marshall, the Courthouse Mouse: A Tail of the U. S. Supreme Court. Barnes, Peter W. 2012. (ENG.). 40p. (J). (gr. k). 18.99 *(978-1-59698-789-0(8)*, Little Patriot Pr.) Regnery Publishing, Inc., An Eagle Publishing Co.

—President Adams' Alligator: And Other White House Pets. Barnes, Peter W. 2003. 32p. (J). 16.95 *(978-1-893622-13-5(4)*, VSP Bks.) Vacation Spot Publishing.

—Woodrow, the White House Mouse. Barnes, Peter W. 2012. (ENG.). 40p. (J). (gr. k-3). 16.95 *(978-1-59698-788-3(X)*, Little Patriot Pr.) Regnery Publishing, Inc., An Eagle Publishing Co.

Barnes, Cheryl Shaw & Barnes, Peter W. Liberty Lee's Tail of Independence. 2012. (ENG.). 36p. (J). (gr. k-3). 16.95 *(978-1-59698-792-0(8)*, Little Patriot Pr.) Regnery Publishing, Inc., An Eagle Publishing Co.

Barnes, Cheryl Shaw, jt. illus. see Barnes, Peter W.

Barnes, Garry. A Tractor Green Day. Stone, Connie. 2008. 36p. pap. 24.95 *(978-1-60474-948-9(2))* PublishAmerica, Inc.

Barnes, Jessica L. DIY Dog Portraits. Gilbert, Elizabeth T. et al. 2016. (DIY Ser.). (ENG.). 128p. (J). (gr. 3-8). 34.65 *(978-1-942875-13-0(4)*, Walter Foster Jr) Quarto Publishing Group USA.

Barnes, Kim. Ajay's Big Move. Grudzina, Rebecca. 2017. (Text Connections Guided Close Reading Ser.). (J). (gr. k-1). *(978-1-4900-1786-0(0))* Benchmark Education Co.

—Treat or Trick? Skwish, Emily. 2019. (ENG.). 20p. (J). bds. *(978-1-5037-4670-1(4)*, aadc2e72-c5c7-4b02-b873-369f42f58140, p i kids) Phoenix International Publications, Inc.

Barnes, Kim & Llewhellin, Gareth. Dear Molly, Dear Olive. Atwood, Megan. 2018. (Dear Molly, Dear Olive Ser.). (ENG.). 96p. (J). (gr. 1-3). 131.94 *(978-1-5158-2925-6(1)*, 28406, Picture Window Bks.) Capstone.

—Molly Gets a Goat: (And Wants to Give It Back) Atwood, Megan. 2018. (Dear Molly, Dear Olive Ser.). (ENG.). 96p. (J). (gr. 1-3). lib. bdg. 21.99 *(978-1-5158-2921-8(9)*, 138457, Picture Window Bks.) Capstone.

—Olive Becomes Famous: (And Hopes She Can Become Un-Famous) Atwood, Megan. 2018. (Dear Molly, Dear Olive Ser.). (ENG.). 96p. (J). (gr. 1-3). lib. bdg. 21.99 *(978-1-5158-2922-5(7)*, 138458, Picture Window Bks.) Capstone.

Barnes, Kimberley. The First Easter Day. Lord, Jill Roman. 2020. 20p. (J). (gr. -1 — 1). bds. 6.99 *(978-1-5460-1435-5(7)*, Worthy Kids/Ideals) Worthy Publishing.

—When I Pray for You. Turner, Matthew Paul. 2019. (ENG.). 48p. (J). (gr. -1-2). 11.99 *(978-0-525-65058-4(X)*, Convergent Bks.) Crown Publishing Group, The.

Barnes, Kimberly. Dream You'll Be. Garcia, Joseph T. 2018. (ENG.). 40p. (J). 16.99 ***(978-1-926444-85-7(X))*** Rainstorm Pr.

Barnes, Meegan. I Wish. Guettier, Nancy. 2015. (ENG.). 32p. (J). pap. 9.95 *(978-1-63047-512-3(2))* Morgan James Publishing.

Barnes-Murphy, Rowan. All Together. Kemp, Marion et al. Date not set. (Whizz Bang Bumper Bk.). 63p. (J). 129.15 *(978-0-582-18259-2(X))*; pap. 129.15 *(978-0-582-18258-5(1))* Addison-Wesley Longman, Ltd. GBR. Dist: Trans-Atlantic Pubns., Inc.

—Mother Goose: Treasury of Favourite Rhymes. Blyton, Enid. 2012. 160p. 24.95 *(978-1-84135-591-7(7))* Award Pubns. Ltd. GBR. Dist: Parkwest Pubns., Inc.

Barnes, Page. Don't Eat My Garden. Barnes, Ben. 2007. 28p. per. 24.95 *(978-1-4241-8964-9(0))* America Star Bks.

Barnes, Peter W. & Barnes, Cheryl Shaw. President Adams' Alligator: And Other White House Pets. 2013. (ENG.). 40p. (J). (gr. k-5). 16.95 *(978-1-62157-035-6(5)*, Little Patriot Pr.) Regnery Publishing, Inc., An Eagle Publishing Co.

Barnes, Peter W., jt. illus. see Barnes, Cheryl Shaw.

Barnes, Sarah. Nine Things Nathan Noticed at Night. Baldwin, Christy. 2005. 24p. (J). per. 13.00 *(978-0-9765072-1-5(8))* Tribute Bks.

—Remembering Wilma. Baldwin, Christy. l.t. ed. 2005. 22p. (J). per. 9.95 (978-0-9765072-0-8(X)) Tribute Bks.

Barnes, Teal. Atheism for Kids. Thorpe, Jessica. 2016. (ENG.). 28p. (J). (gr. 3-6). pap. (978-1-911560-00-5(X)) No Lines Publishing.

Barnes, Tom, photos by. Chicken Run: Action-Packed Storybook. David, Lawrence, ed. 2005. 48p. (gr. k-4). reprint ed. pap. 8.00 (978-0-7567-9472-9(2)) DIANE Publishing Co.

Barnes, Trisha. Once upon A Night. Keyser, William. 2011. (J). pap. 8.99 (978-0-9827531-1-8(X)) River Canyon Pr.

Barnes, William. A Place for All of Us. Hile, Doretta. 2007. 36p. per. 14.94 (978-1-59858-421-9(9)) Dog Ear Publishing, LLC.

Barnet, Nancy. In the Spell of an Ibis: The Education of Minemheb the Scribe. Buchanan, Penelope. 2004. 80p. pap. (978-0-940717-82-4(4)) Cleveland Museum of Art.

Barnett, Charles, et al. The Battle of the Alamo, 1 vol. Doeden, Matt. 2005. (Graphic History Ser.). (ENG.). 32p. (J). (gr. 3-9). 31.32 (978-0-7368-3832-0(5), Capstone Pr.) Capstone.

Barnett, Charles, III, et al. Levi Strauss & Blue Jeans. Olson, Nathan. 2006. (Inventions & Discovery Ser.). (ENG.). 32p. (J). (gr. 3-9). pap. 8.10 (978-0-7368-9646-7(5), Capstone Pr.) Capstone.

Barnett, Charles, III. Political Elections, 1 vol. Miller, Davis Worth & Brevard, Katherine M. 2008. (Cartoon Nation Ser.). (ENG.). 32p. (J). (gr. 3-9). 31.32 (978-1-4296-1333-0(5), Capstone Pr.) Capstone.

Barnett, Charles, et al. Political Parties, 1 vol. Burgan, Michael & Hoena, Blake A. 2008. (Cartoon Nation Ser.). (ENG.). 32p. (J). (gr. 3-9). lib. bdg. 31.32 (978-1-4296-1334-7(3), Capstone Pr.) Capstone.

Barnett, Charles, III, et al. The Sinking of the Titanic, 1 vol. Doeden, Matt. 2005. (Graphic History Ser.). (ENG.). 32p. (J). (gr. 3-9). 31.32 (978-0-7368-3834-4(1), Capstone Pr.) Capstone.

Barnett, Charles. U. S. Immigration. O'Donnell, Liam. 2008. (Cartoon Nation Ser.). (ENG.). 32p. (J). (gr. 3-9). 31.32 (978-1-4296-1983-7(X), Capstone Pr.) Capstone.

Barnett, Charles, III & Hoover, Dave. The Boston Tea Party, 1 vol. Doeden, Matt. 2005. (Graphic History Ser.). (ENG.). 32p. (J). (gr. 3-9). per. 8.10 (978-0-7368-5243-2(3), Capstone Pr.) Capstone.

Barnett, Charles, III & Miller, Phil. The Battle of the Alamo, 1 vol. Doeden, Matt. 2005. (Graphic History Ser.). (ENG.). 32p. (J). (gr. 3-9). per. 8.10 (978-0-7368-5242-5(5), Capstone Pr.) Capstone.

—The Sinking of the Titanic, 1 vol. Doeden, Matt. 2005. (Graphic History Ser.). (ENG.). 32p. (J). (gr. 3-9). per. 8.10 (978-0-7368-5247-0(6), Capstone Pr.) Capstone.

Barnett, Charles, jt. illus. see Dominguez, Richard.

Barnett, Charles, III, jt. illus. see Erwin, Steve.

Barnett, Charles, III, jt. illus. see Miller, Phil.

Barnett, Charles, III, jt. illus. see Whigham, Rod.

Barnett III, Charles, jt. illus. see Miller, Phil.

Barnett, Isa. One World, Many People: Anthropology Made Fun for Kids. Barnett, Annette. 2006. 80p. (J). pap. 19.95 (978-0-9787138-0-5(X)) Young Scholars Pr.

Barnett, Janet. An Adventure in Looking & Listening: Exploring Masterworks at the Albright-Knox Art Gallery. Bayles, Jennifer L. 2003. (J). (978-1-887457-01-9(1)) Buffalo Fine Arts/Albright-Knox Art Gallery.

Barnett, John L. D. The Legend of Tim Turpin. Bernfeld, Peter N. 2017. (ENG.). 100p. (J). (gr. 1-6). pap. 12.99 (978-1-68160-388-9(8)) Crimson Cloak Publishing.

Barnett, Linda. Dottie the Bus Driver in Bicycle Safety. Toombs, Robert. 2013. 24p. pap. 9.99 (978-0-9885180-6-3(6)) Mindstir Media.

Barnett, Michelle. The Courageous Chiropractor & the Night Mare. Gillham, Jennie Lynn & Kingdon DC, Samantha. 2018. (Courageous Chiropractor Ser.: Vol. 1). (ENG.). 34p. (J). (gr. 2-3). pap. 12.99 (978-0-9995191-0-3(7)) Phoenix Cry Publishing.

Barnett, Russell. Secrets of the Oak. Taylor, Alice. (ENG.). 30p. 4.99 (978-0-86322-138-5(6)) Penguin Publishing Group.

Barnett, Sarah. Charlie the Chicken: Fowl Language. Scheufele, Chris "shoof". 2020. (School House Heroes Ser.: Vol. 5). (ENG.). 26p. (J). pap. 10.00 (978-1-6538-4476-0(0)) Independently Published.

Barnett, Thora. Sally Salli & the Case of the Tic Monster: A Book for Kids Who Tic. LeBow, Michael. 2013. 75p. (J). pap. 18.95 (978-1-59630-060-6(4)) Science & Humanities Pr.

Barnhart, Nancy. The Wind in the Willows. Grahame, Kenneth. 2004. reprint ed. pap. 33.95 (978-1-4179-1206-3(5)) Kessinger Publishing, LLC.

Barnhill, Carla. Rufus & the Very Special Baby: A Frolic Christmas Story, Vol. Barnhill, Carla. Rimmington, Natasha. 2016. (Frolic First Faith Ser.). (ENG.). 32p. (J). (gr. -1-3). 12.99 (978-1-5064-1762-2(0), Sparkhouse Family) Augsburg Fortress, Pubs.

Barnhurst, Noel, photos by. Macaroni & Cheese. Spieler, Marlena. 2005. (ENG., 132p. (gr. 8-17). pap. 16.95 (978-0-8118-4962-3(7)) Chronicle Bks. LLC.

—Modern Asian Flavors: A Taste of Shanghai. Wong, Richard. 2006. (ENG., 144p. (gr. 8-17). 18.95 (978-0-8118-5110-7(9)) Chronicle Bks. LLC.

Barnish, Zoe. World in Danger: Tomorrow Could Be a Very Different Day. Morland, Frankie. 2020. (ENG.). 32p. (J). (gr. k-4). pap. 9.99 (978-0-7440-2443-2(9), DK Children) Dorling Kindersley Publishing, Inc.

Barnoski, Karel. Melissa & the Magic Pen. Figueroa, M. A. & Figueroa, P. A. 2004. 36p. pap. 24.95 (978-1-4137-3441-6(3)) PublishAmerica, Inc.

Barnum-Newman, Winifred. Ana & Adam Build & Acrostic. Peterson-Hilleque, Victoria. 2011. (Poetry Builders Ser.). 32p. (J). (gr. 2-4). lib. bdg. 25.27 (978-1-59953-433-6(9)) Norwood Hse. Pr.

—Caperucita Roja. Hillert, Margaret. 2018. (BeginningtoRead Ser.).Tr. of Little Red Riding Hood. (SPA.). 32p. (J). (gr. -1-2). pap. 11.94 (978-1-68404-232-6(1)) Norwood Hse. Pr.

—Little Red Riding Hood. Hillert, Margaret. 2016. (BeginningtoRead Ser.). (ENG.). 32p. (J). (-2). pap. 11.94 (978-1-60357-909-4(5)); lib. bdg. 22.60 (978-1-59953-783-2(4)) Norwood Hse. Pr.

Barnum-Newman, Winifred. Caperucita Roja. Barnum-Newman, Winifred. Hillert, Margaret & Del Risco, Eida. 2018. (BeginningtoRead Ser.).Tr. of Little Red Riding Hood. (SPA.). 32p. (J). (gr. -1-2). lib. bdg. 22.60 (978-1-59953-948-5(9)) Norwood Hse. Pr.

Barnum-Newman, Winifred, jt. illus. see Jack Pullan.

Barnum, Tabatha. The Greatest Mousemas Ever! Quintanilla, Billie. 2012. 36p. 24.95 (978-1-4626-9725-0(9)); pap. 24.95 (978-1-4626-5236-5(0)) America Star Bks.

Baro, Gerardo. Cuentos para Salir Al Recreo. Maine, Margarita. 2019. (Torre Roja Ser.). (SPA.). 60p. (J). (gr. -1-7). pap. (978-958-776-020-0(4)) Norma Ediciones, S.A.

Baron, Andrew. The Adventures of Octopus Rex. 2003. (J). per. 17.95 (978-0-9760348-0-3(8)) Bh Pubns.

—The Adventures of Octopus Rex. Hart, Barbara. 2003. (SPA.). (J). 18.95 (978-0-9760348-1-0(6)) Bh Pubns.

Baron, Cheri Ann. Angelita's Song. Guiffre, William A. 2008. 32p. (J). (gr. -1-3). lib. bdg. 17.95 (978-1-931650-30-4(6)) Guiffre Bk. Publishing.

—Angelita's Song. Guiffre, William. 2008. 32p. (J). (gr. -1-3). pap. 9.95 (978-1-931650-36-6(5)) Guiffre Bk. Publishing.

—The First Gift of Christmas. Guiffre, William A. 2003. 36p. (J). (gr. -1-3). lib. bdg. 17.95 (978-1-931650-21-2(7)) Guiffre Bk. Publishing.

—The First Gift of Christmas. Guiffre, William. 2008. 32p. (J). (gr. -1-3). pap. 9.95 (978-1-931650-33-5(0)) Guiffre Bk. Publishing.

—The Wrong Side of the Bed. Guiffre, William A. 2003. 36p. (J). (gr. -1-3). lib. bdg. 17.95 (978-1-931650-20-5(9)) Guiffre Bk. Publishing.

—The Wrong Side of the Bed. Guiffre, William. 2008. 32p. (J). (gr. -1-3). pap. 9.95 (978-1-931650-34-2(9)) Guiffre Bk. Publishing.

Baron, Kathy. Possum's Three Fine Friends. Bannister, Barbara. 2006. (ENG.). 32p. (gr. 1-3). pap. 9.95 (978-1-57874-096-3(7), Kaeden Bks.) Kaeden Corp.

Barón, Lara & Torres, German. Hero City, No. 22. Tsang, Evonne & Jimenez, Adan. 2012. (Twisted Journeys ® Ser.: 22). (ENG.). 112p. (J). (gr. 4-7). lib. bdg. 27.99 (978-0-7613-4595-4(7), 9780761345954, Graphic Universe™) Lerner Publishing Group.

Baron, Michelle. Lovely Amelia Travels. Salazar Nelson, Stephany. 2017. (ENG.). (J). (gr. k-6). (Costa Rica Ser.: Vol. 1). pap. 16.99 (978-0-9990974-1-0(5)); 38p. 24.99 (978-0-9990974-0-3(7)) Nelson, Tracy C.

Baroncelli, Silvia. Be Safe Around Fire. Heos, Bridget. 2015. (Be Safe! Ser.). 24p. (J). 25.65 (978-1-60753-444-0(4)) Amicus Publishing.

—Be Safe Around Water. Heos, Bridget. 2015. (Be Safe! Ser.). 24p. (J). 25.65 (978-1-60753-448-8(7)) Amicus Publishing.

—Be Safe on the Internet. Heos, Bridget. 2015. (Be Safe! Ser.). 24p. (J). 25.65 (978-1-60753-445-7(2)) Amicus Publishing.

—Be Safe on the Playground. Heos, Bridget. 2015. (Be Safe! Ser.). 24p. (J). 25.65 (978-1-60753-446-4(0)) Amicus Publishing.

—Be Safe on Your Bike. Heos, Bridget. 2015. (Be Safe! Ser.). 24p. (J). 25.65 (978-1-60753-443-3(6)) Amicus Publishing.

—I'll Be a Carpenter. Miller, Connie Colwell. 2019. (J). lib. bdg. (978-1-68151-396-6(X)) Amicus Publishing.

—I'll Be a Chef. Miller, Connie Colwell. 2016. (When I Grow Up Ser.). (ENG.). 24p. (J). (gr. k-3). 20.95 (978-1-60753-759-5(1)) Amicus Publishing.

—I'll Be a Doctor. Miller, Connie Colwell. 2016. (When I Grow Up Ser.). (ENG.). 24p. (J). (gr. k-3). 20.95 (978-1-60753-760-1(5)) Amicus Publishing.

—I'll Be a Firefighter. Miller, Connie Colwell. 2016. (When I Grow Up Ser.). (ENG.). 24p. (J). (gr. k-3). 20.95 (978-1-60753-761-8(3)) Amicus Publishing.

—I'll Be a Librarian. Miller, Connie Colwell. 2019. (J). lib. bdg. (978-1-68151-397-3(8)) Amicus Publishing.

—I'll Be a Musician. Miller, Connie Colwell. 2016. (When I Grow Up Ser.). (ENG.). 24p. (J). (gr. k-3). 20.95 (978-1-60753-762-5(1)) Amicus Publishing.

—I'll Be a Paleontologist. Miller, Connie Colwell. 2016. (When I Grow Up Ser.). (ENG.). 24p. (J). (gr. k-3). 20.95 (978-1-60753-763-2(X)) Amicus Publishing.

—I'll Be a Police Officer. Miller, Connie Colwell. 2019. (J). (978-1-68151-398-0(6), Amicus Readers) Amicus Publishing.

—I'll Be a Teacher. Miller, Connie Colwell. 2019. (J). lib. bdg. (978-1-68151-399-7(4)) Amicus Publishing.

—I'll Be a Truck Driver. Miller, Connie Colwell. 2019. (J). lib. bdg. (978-1-68151-400-0(1)) Amicus Publishing.

—I'll Be a Veterinarian. Miller, Connie Colwell. 2016. (When I Grow Up Ser.). (ENG.). 24p. (J). (gr. k-3). 20.95 (978-1-60753-764-9(8)) Amicus Publishing.

—I'll Be an Engineer. Miller, Connie Colwell. 2019. (J). lib. bdg. (978-1-68151-401-7(X)) Amicus Publishing.

Barone, Bendetta. Regal Academy #1: A School for Fairy Tales. Vergari, Luana. 2018. (Regal Academy Ser.: 1). (ENG.). 96p. (J). 14.99 (978-1-62991-884-6(9), 9781629918846); pap. 9.99 (978-1-62991-883-9(0), 9781629918839) Papercutz.

—Regal Academy #2: Happily Ever After. Vergari, Luana. 2018. (Regal Academy Ser.: 2). (ENG.). 96p. (J). 14.99 (978-1-62991-886-0(5), 9781629918860); pap. 9.99 (978-1-62991-885-3(7), 9781629918853) Papercutz.

Barone, Logan. Dogs Don't Belong at School. Morin, Christina. 2019. (ENG.). 46p. (J). pap. 10.83 (978-1-6778-4762-4(X)) Independently Published.

Barone, Mark. Christ's Passion: The Way of the Cross; A Guide to Understanding Your Path. Young, Mary Beth. 2004. 100p. per. 14.00 (978-0-9760180-1-8(2)) Young, Beth.

Barozzi, Danilo. The Amazing Voyage. Stilton, Geronimo. 2011. (Geronimo Stilton & the Kingdom of Fantasy Ser.: 3). 320p. (J). (gr. 2-5). 14.99 (978-0-545-30771-0(6)) Scholastic, Inc.

—The Enchanted Charms: The Seventh Adventure in the Kingdom of Fantasy. Stilton, Geronimo & Dami, Elisabetta. 2015. 324p. (J). (gr. 2-5). 14.99 (978-0-545-74615-1(9)) Scholastic, Inc.

Barr, Bailey. Diogo the Little Dinosaur. Skwara, Maike Lena. 2013. 28p. (J). (978-0-89985-475-5(3)) R. H. Publishing.

Barr, Kristen. Creative Movement for 3-5 Year Olds: A Complete Curriculum Including 35 Lesson Plans, Dance Notations, Illustrations, Music & Poetry Suggestions Plus Detailed Prop Designs. Forbes, Ross E., photos by. Forbes, Harriet H. 2003. 241p. (J). pap., tchr. ed. 50.00 (978-0-9659944-1-5(4)) First Steps Pr.

Barr, Kristin. Joe Boat. Riggs, Sandy. 2006. (Reader's Clubhouse Level 2 Reader Ser.). (ENG.). 24p. (J). (gr. k-1). pap. 3.99 (978-0-7641-3296-4(2), B.E.S. Publishing) Peterson's.

Barr, Loel. How & Why: A Kids' Book about the Body. Grace, Catherine O'Neill. 2011. (J). (978-0-89043-231-0(7)) Consumers Union of U. S., Inc.

—My Dad Wears Polka-Dotted Socks! Humes, Kristin Joy. 2005. 32p. (J). (gr. -1-7). 15.95 (978-0-9744307-2-0(2)) Merry Lane Pr.

—While You're at School. Weisberg, Edmund M. 2016. (ENG.). (J). (gr. k-3). pap. 9.99 (978-0-9978943-0-1(X)) Putschakap?n Pr.

Barr, Marilyn. A Child's Garden of Bible Stories. Gross, Arthur. 2005. 144p. (J). 10.49 (978-0-7586-0858-1(6)) Concordia Publishing Hse.

Barr, Marilynn G. & Jeffery, Megan E. Hope Finders. Lingo, Susan L. 2006. (Power Builders Curriculum Ser.). 128p. (J). (gr. 1-5). 15.99 (978-0-7847-1235-1(2), 42118) Standard Publishing.

—Joy Builders. Lingo, Susan L. 2006. (Power Builders Curriculum Ser.). 128p. (J). (gr. 1-5). 15.99 (978-0-7847-1234-4(4), 42117) Standard Publishing.

—Peace Makers. Lingo, Susan L. 2006. (Power Builders Curriculum Ser.). 128p. (J). (gr. 1-5). 15.99 (978-0-7847-1233-7(6), 42116) Standard Publishing.

—Power Boosters. Lingo, Susan L. 2006. (Power Builders Curriculum Ser.). 128p. (J). (gr. 1-5). 15.99 (978-0-7847-1232-0(8), 42115) Standard Publishing.

Barr, Steve. The Helping, Caring, & Sharing. Schab, Lisa & Gardner, Richard. Schader, Karen, ed. 2003. (J). per., wbk. ed. 19.95 (978-1-58815-058-5(5), 67238) Childswork/Childsplay.

Barraclough, Emma. Little Lisa's Lonely Lunch. Barraclough, Julius. 2019. (Little Lisa Ser.: Vol. 1). (ENG.). 28p. (J). pap. 9.75 (978-1-9818-8975-4(2)) CreateSpace Independent Publishing Platform.

Barradas, Leticia. Santiago & the Fox of Hatsune. Defosse, Rosana Curiel. (SPA.). 32p. (J). (gr. 3-5). pap. 7.95 (978-970-29-0134-1(0)) Santillana USA Publishing Co., Inc.

—Santiago en el Mundo de me de la Gana. Defosse, Rosana Curiel. (SPA.). 38p. (J). (gr. 3-5). pap. 7.95 (978-970-29-0136-5(7)) Santillana USA Publishing Co., Inc.

—Santiago en el Pantano. Defosse, Rosana Curiel. (Santiago Y Los Valores Ser.). (SPA.). 32p. (J). (gr. 3-5). pap. 7.95 (978-970-29-0133-4(2)) Santillana USA Publishing Co., Inc.

—Santiago y el talisman de la Luz. Defosse, Rosana Curiel. (Santiago Y Los Valores Ser.). (SPA.). 32p. (J). (gr. 3-5). pap. 7.95 (978-970-29-0131-0(6)) Santillana USA Publishing Co., Inc.

—Santiago y los Dobraks. Defosse, Rosana Curiel. (SPA.). 32p. (J). (gr. 3-5). pap. 7.95 (978-970-29-0111-2(1)) Santillana USA Publishing Co., Inc.

Barragán, Paula. Cool Cats Counting. Shahan, Sherry. 2016. (ENG.). 28p. (J). (gr. -1-2). pap. 8.95 (978-1-941460-42-9(9)) August Hse. Pubs., Inc.

—Fiesta! A Celebration of Latino Festivals. Shahan, Sherry. 2008. (ENG.). 32p. (J). (gr. -1-3). 16.95 (978-0-87483-861-9(4)) August Hse. Pubs., Inc.

—Poems to Dream Together: Poemas para Soñar Juntos. Alarcón, Francisco X. 2005. (ENG & SPA.). 32p. (J). (gr. 2-5). 16.95 (978-1-58430-233-9(X)) Lee & Low Bks., Inc.

Barrager, Brigette. Bevan vs. Evan: (and Other School Rivalries), 4. Evans, Zoe. 2012. (Cheer! Ser.: 4). (ENG.). 224p. (J). (gr. 3-7). pap. 6.99 (978-1-4424-3364-9(7), Simon Spotlight) Simon & Schuster Children's Publishing.

—Confessions of a Wannabe Cheerleader. Evans, Zoe. 2011. (Cheer! Ser.: 1). (ENG.). 240p. (J). (gr. 3-7). pap. 6.99 (978-1-4424-2241-4(6), Simon Spotlight) Simon Spotlight.

—Frances Hodgson Burnett's the Secret Garden. Burnett, Frances Hodgson. 2017. (J). (978-1-5182-2305-1(2), Golden Bks.) Random Hse. Children's Bks.

—Fred's Big Feelings: The Life & Legacy of Mister Rogers. Renaud, Laura. 2020. (ENG.). 40p. (J). (gr. -1-3). 17.99 (978-1-5344-4122-4(0), Atheneum Bks. for Young Readers) Simon & Schuster Children's Publishing.

—Holiday Spirit, 3. Evans, Zoe. 2012. (Cheer! Ser.: 3). (ENG.). 224p. (J). (gr. 4-6). 21.19 (978-1-4424-3362-5(0), Simon Spotlight) Simon & Schuster Children's Publishing.

—How to Be a Pirate. Fitzgerald, Isaac. 2020. 40p. (J). 17.99 (978-1-68119-778-4(2), 900186166, Bloomsbury Children's Bks.) Bloomsbury Publishing USA.

—Louise Trapeze Can SO Save the Day. Ostow, Micol. 2016. (Louise Trapeze Ser.: 3). 112p. (J). (gr. 1-4). 14.99 (978-0-553-49747-2(2), Random Hse. Bks. for Young Readers) Random Hse. Children's Bks.

—Louise Trapeze Can So Save the Day. Ostow, Micol. 2016. (Louise Trapeze Ser.: 3). 112p. (J). (gr. 1-4). 5.99 (978-0-553-49750-2(2), Random Hse. Bks. for Young Readers) Random Hse. Children's Bks.

—Louise Trapeze Did NOT Lose the Juggling Chickens. Ostow, Micol. 2016. (Louise Trapeze Ser.: 2). (ENG.). 112p. (J). (gr. 1-4). lib. bdg. 17.99 (978-0-553-49744-1(8), Random Hse. Bks. for Young Readers) Random Hse. Children's Bks.

—Louise Trapeze Is Totally 100% Fearless. Ostow, Micol. 2015. (Louise Trapeze Ser.: 1). 112p. (J). (gr. 1-4). 14.99 (978-0-553-49739-7(1), Random Hse. Bks. for Young Readers) Random Hse. Children's Bks.

—Louise Trapeze Will Not Lose a Tooth. Ostow, Micol. 2017. (Louise Trapeze Ser.: 4). 112p. (J). (gr. 1-4). 14.99 (978-0-553-49751-9(0), Random Hse. Bks. for Young Readers) Random Hse. Children's Bks.

—My Wish for You: Lessons from My Six-Year-Old Daughter. Hahn, Kathryn. 2018. (ENG.). 40p. (J). (gr. -1-3). 17.99 (978-1-338-15040-7(5), Orchard Bks.) Scholastic, Inc.

—Pocket Full of Colors: The Magical World of Mary Blair, Disney Artist Extraordinaire. Tourville, Jacqueline & Guglielmo, Amy. 2017. (ENG.). 48p. (J). (gr. -1-3). 17.99 (978-1-4814-6131-3(1)) Simon & Schuster Children's Publishing.

—Pyramid of One, 2. Evans, Zoe. 2011. (Cheer! Ser.: 2). (ENG.). 240p. (J). (gr. 3-7). pap. 6.99 (978-1-4424-2239-1(4), Simon Spotlight) Simon & Schuster Children's Publishing.

—Revenge of the Titan. Evans, Zoe. 2012. (Cheer! Ser.: 5). (ENG.). 224p. (J). (gr. 3-7). pap. 6.99 (978-1-4424-4634-2(X), Simon Spotlight) Simon Spotlight.

—The Secret Garden. Gilbert, Frances & Burnett, Frances Hodgson. 2017. (Little Golden Book Ser.). 24p. (J). (-k). 4.99 (978-0-399-55225-0(1), Golden Bks.) Random Hse. Children's Bks.

—Sleeping Cinderella & Other Princess Mix-Ups. Clarkson, Stephanie. 2015. (ENG.). 40p. (J). (gr. -1-3). 17.99 (978-0-545-56564-6(2), Orchard Bks.) Scholastic, Inc.

—The Twelve Dancing Princesses: (Books about Princess Dancing, Unicorn Books for Girls & Kids) 2011. (ENG.). 40p. (J). (gr. -1-3). 16.99 (978-0-8118-7696-4(9)) Chronicle Bks. LLC.

—Uni the Unicorn. Rosenthal, Amy Krouse. (Uni the Unicorn Ser.). (ENG.). (J). 2017. 36p. (— 1). bds. 8.99 (978-1-5247-6616-0(X)); 2014. 48p. (gr. -1-3). 17.99 (978-0-385-37555-9(7)) Random Hse. Children's Bks.

—Uni the Unicorn & the Dream Come True. Rosenthal, Amy Krouse. (Uni the Unicorn Ser.). (J). 2019. 36p. (— 1). bds. 8.99 (978-1-9848-4821-5(6)); 2017. (ENG.). 40p. (gr. -1-2). 17.99 (978-1-101-93659-7(2)); 2017. (ENG.). 40p. (gr. -1-2). lib. bdg. 20.99 (978-1-101-93660-3(6)) Random Hse. Children's Bks. (Random Hse. Bks. for Young Readers).

—Uni the Unicorn Dream & Draw Activity Book. Chlebowski, Rachel & Rosenthal, Amy Krouse. 2019. (Uni the Unicorn Ser.). (ENG.). 48p. (J). (gr. -1-2). pap. 12.99 (978-0-593-12304-1(2), Random Hse. Bks. for Young Readers) Random Hse. Children's Bks.

—Uni the Unicorn Uni's First Sleepover. Rosenthal, Amy Krouse. 2019. (Step into Reading Ser.). (ENG.). 32p. (J). (gr. -1-1). pap. 4.99 (978-1-9848-5023-2(7)); lib. bdg. 12.99 (978-1-9848-5024-9(5)) Random Hse. Children's Bks. (Random Hse. Bks. for Young Readers).

—Uni's Land of Unicorns Board Book Boxed Set: Uni the Unicorn; Uni the Unicorn & the Dream Come True. Rosenthal, Amy Krouse. 2019. (Uni the Unicorn Ser.). 36p. (J). (— 1). bds. 17.98 (978-1-9848-9313-0(0), Random Hse. Bks. for Young Readers) Random Hse. Children's Bks.

Barrager, Brigette & Tcherevkoff, Michel. Florabelle. Quinton, Sasha. 2015. (ENG.). 40p. (J). (gr. -1-3). 15.99 (978-0-06-229182-0(3)) HarperCollins Pubs.

Barrameda, Nicklaus. Lino the Lamp Is Afraid of the Dark. Wong, Sunshine. 2016. (ENG.). (J). pap. (978-981-09-9807-3(4)) KREATIF HANDS AND ASSOCIATES.

Barrance, Reuben & Whatmore, Candice. Birthday. 2008. (Usborne Look & Say Ser.). 12p. (J). (gr. -1-3). bds. 7.99 (978-0-7945-1988-9(1), Usborne) EDC Publishing.

Barrance, Reuben, jt. illus. see Whatmore, Candice.

Barreira, Santiago. Snow White & the Seven Dwarfs. Maine, Régis. 2020. (Disney Princesses Ser.). (ENG.). 48p. (J). (gr. 2-6). lib. bdg. 28.50 (978-1-5321-4568-1(3), 35215, Graphic Novels) Spotlight.

Barreiro, Mike, jt. illus. see Eaton, Scot.

Barren, Mel. Sally. Stelzer, Greg. 2020. (ENG.). 36p. (J). 25.95 (978-1-4808-8808-1(7)); pap. 16.95 (978-1-4808-8807-4(9)) Archway Publishing.

Barreto, Andre. The Childhood of Walter Elias Disney. S Santa Rosa, Nereide. 2018. (ENG.). 82p. (J). pap. 18.00 (978-1-949868-00-5(1)) Underline Publishing LLC.

Barreto, Eduardo. Episode IV: A New Hope, 1. Jones, Bruce. 2009. (Star Wars Ser.: No. 2). (ENG.). 24p. (J). (gr. 6-12). 27.07 (978-1-59961-621-6(1), 13777, Graphic Novels) Spotlight.

—Episode IV A New Hope, Vol. 2. Jones, Bruce. 2009. (Star Wars Ser.: No. 2). (ENG.). 24p. (J). (gr. 6-12). 27.07 (978-1-59961-622-3(X), 13778, Graphic Novels) Spotlight.

—Episode IV: A New Hope, 1 vol. Jones, Bruce. 2009. (Star Wars Ser.: No. 2). (ENG.). 24p. (J). (gr. 6-12). Vol. 3. 27.07 (978-1-59961-623-0(8), 13779); Vol. 4. 27.07 (978-1-59961-624-7(6), 13780) Spotlight. (Graphic Novels).

Barrett, Angela. Ana Frank. Poole, Josephine. 2005. (SPA.). 32p. (J). (gr. 3-4). 17.99 (978-1-930332-87-4(4)) Lectorum Pubns., Inc.

—The Most Wonderful Thing in the World. French, Vivian. 2015. (ENG.). 32p. (J). (gr. -1-3). 18.99 (978-0-7636-7501-1(6)) Candlewick Pr.

—The Night Before Christmas. Moore, Clement C. 2012. 30p. (J). (978-1-4351-4416-3(3)) Barnes & Noble, Inc.

—The Night Fairy. Schlitz, Laura Amy. 2011. (ENG.). 128p. (J). (gr. 2-5). pap. 7.99 (978-0-7636-5295-1(4)) Candlewick Pr.

—The Restless Girls. Burton, Jessie. 2019. (ENG.). 160p. (J). 19.99 (978-1-5476-0072-4(1), 900197347, Bloomsbury Children's Bks.) Bloomsbury Publishing USA.

Barrett, Annabelle. Shrinking the Worry Monster: A Kids Guide for Saying Goodbye to Worries. Baird, Sally & Galbraith, Kathryn O. 2019. (ENG.). 48p. (J). (gr. 1-6). 22.95 (978-0-578-51840-4(6)) McMillan, Carol.

Barrett, Basil. His Story Through a Window Told, Su Historia Narrada a Traves de una Ventana: In Pictures & in Rhymes, en Imagenes y en Rimas. Arroyo, Aristeo & Arroyo, Pamela. 2018. (MUL.). 68p. (J). 26.95 (978-1-64003-694-9(6)); pap. 16.95 (978-1-64003-693-2(8)) Covenant Bks.

Barrett, Casey. Coco & Pebbles: Bath Night. Wenning, Jeremy. 2013. 20p. pap. 6.99 *(978-1-938768-16-3(7))* Gypsy Pubns.
—Coco & Pebbles: That's My Duck! Wenning, Jeremy. 2012. 16p. pap. 6.99 *(978-1-938768-04-0(3))* Gypsy Pubns.
—Tommy Fakes the Flu. Kerns, Kristen. 2013. 24p. pap. 8.99 *(978-1-938768-28-6(0))* Gypsy Pubns.
Barrett, Cayla Justine. Just Like Caesar. Grant, Gloria. 2019. (ENG.). 32p. (J). pap. ***(978-0-9879634-6-8(5))*** BODA reLEAF Consulting.
Barrett, Ciara. The Freakalogue. Macken, Dee. 2018. (ENG.). 228p. (J). pap. 11.60 *(978-1-7270-5866-6(6))* CreateSpace Independent Publishing Platform.
Barrett, Diana. Giuseppe's Famous Pizza Pies. Fisher, Meaghan. 2013. 24p. 17.99 *(978-1-938768-34-7(5))*; pap. 8.99 *(978-1-938768-20-0(5))* Gypsy Pubns.
Barrett, Jennifer. The Seven Treasure Hunts. Byars, Betsy. 2020. (ENG.). 80p. (J). (gr. 1-5). pap. 5.99 *(978-0-06-293554-0(2),* HarperCollins) HarperCollins Pubs. Ltd. GBR. Dist: HarperCollins Pubs.
Barrett, Karlish. Mary Loves Butterflies. Jonas, Gennevive. 2012. 40p. pap. 24.95 *(978-1-62709-061-2(4))* America Star Bks.
Barrett, Laura. The Snow Queen. McCaughrean, Geraldine & Andersen, Hans Christian. 2020. 32p. (J). (gr. -1-k). 18.99 *(978-1-4083-5234-2(6),* Orchard Bks.) Hachette Children's Group GBR. Dist: Hachette Bk. Group.
Barrett, Peter. Day & Night in Forest. Barrett, Susan. 2009. 38p. (J). (gr. 2-5). 14.99 *(978-0-8437-0943-8(X))* Hammond World Atlas Corp.
—Dinosaur Babies. Penner, Lucille Recht. 2015. 32p. pap. 5.00 *(978-1-61003-602-3(6))* Center for the Collaborative Classroom.
—A Forest Tree House. Reda, Sheryl A. 2004. (Treasure Tree Ser.). 32p. (J). *(978-0-7166-1606-1(8))* World Bk., Inc.
Barrett, Peter, jt. illus. see Brown, Ruth.
Barrett, Phillip. Where's Larry? 2012. (ENG.). 32p. (J). pap. 15.00 *(978-1-84717-276-1(8))* O'Brien Pr., Ltd., The IRL. Dist: Casemate Pubs. & Bk. Distributors, LLC.
Barrett, Rebecca. Christie Plays Softball. O'Hara, Susan. 2013. 48p. pap. 15.97 *(978-1-62516-519-0(6),* Strategic Bk. Publishing) Strategic Book Publishing & Rights Agency (SBPRA).
—Tim's First Soccer Game. O'Hara, Susan. 2012. 38p. pap. 14.97 *(978-1-61897-199-9(9),* Strategic Bk. Publishing) Strategic Book Publishing & Rights Agency (SBPRA).
Barrett, Robert. The Other Wise Man. 32p. (J). pap. 6.95 *(978-0-8249-5348-5(7),* Ideal Pubns.) Worthy Publishing.
—The Real Story of the Flood. Maier, Paul. 2008. 32p. (J). (gr. 4-7). 16.99 *(978-0-7586-1267-0(2))* Concordia Publishing Hse.
—Why Did the Whole World Go to War? And Other Questions about... World War II. Sandler, Martin W. 2013. (Good Question! Ser.). 32p. (J). (gr. 2). pap. 5.95 *(978-1-4027-9044-7(9))* Sterling Publishing Co., Inc.
Barrett, Robert T. The Real Story of the Creation. Maier, Paul L. 2007. 28p. (J). (gr. -1-18). 16.99 *(978-0-7586-1265-6(6))* Concordia Publishing Hse.
Barrett, Ron. Animals Series, 2 bks., Set. Barrett, Judi. (J). (gr. k-3). pap. 29.95 incl. audio *(978-0-87499-470-4(5))* Live Oak Media.
—Animals Should Definitely Not Act Like People. Barrett, Judi. pap. 35.95 incl. audio compact disk *(978-1-59112-827-4(7))*; (J). pap. 33.95 incl. audio *(978-0-87499-232-8(X))* Live Oak Media.
—Animals Should Definitely Not Wear Clothing. Barrett, Judi. 2012. (Classic Board Bks.). (ENG.). 36p. (J). (gr. -1 — 1). bds. 8.99 *(978-1-4424-3334-2(5),* Little Simon) Little Simon.
—Cloudy with a Chance of Meatballs. Barrett, Judi. (ENG.). (J). (gr. -1-3). 2012. 32p. pap. 9.99 *(978-1-4424-4337-2(5))*; 2011. 34p. bds. 7.99 *(978-1-4424-3023-5(0))* Little Simon. (Little Simon).
—Cloudy with a Chance of Meatballs. Barrett, Judi. ed. 2009. 9.00 *(978-1-55744-455-4(2),* Everbind) Marco Bk. Co.
—An Excessive Alphabet: Avalanches of As to Zillions of Zs. Barrett, Judi. 2016. (ENG.). 40p. (J). (gr. -1-3). 17.99 *(978-1-4814-3986-2(3),* Atheneum/Caitlyn Dlouhy Books) Simon & Schuster Children's Publishing.
Barrett, Ron. The Invisible Alphabet. Stein, Joshua David. 2020. (ENG.). 40p. (J). (-k). 17.99 ***(978-0-593-22277-5(6))*** Penguin Young Readers Group.
Barrett, Ron. Look What I See. Barrett, Judi. 2019. (ENG.). 32p. (J). (gr. -1-k). bds. 8.99 *(978-1-5344-3073-0(3),* Little Simon) Little Simon.
—Lots More Animals Should Definitely Not Wear Clothing. Barrett, Judi. (ENG.). 40p. (J). (gr. -1-3). 2019. 7.99 *(978-1-5344-6667-8(3))*; 2018. 17.99 *(978-1-4814-8866-2(X))* Simon & Schuster Children's Publishing. (Atheneum/Caitlyn Dlouhy Books).
—Pickles to Pittsburgh: Cloudy with a Chance of Meatballs 2. Barrett, Judi. 2012. (ENG.). 32p. (J). (gr. -1-3). pap. 9.99 *(978-1-4424-4459-1(2),* Little Simon) Little Simon.
—Pickles to Pittsburgh: The Sequel to Cloudy with a Chance of Meatballs. Barrett, Judi. 2004. 26p. (gr. -1-3). 17.00 *(978-0-7569-4215-1(2))* Perfection Learning Corp.
—Superhero Joe. Weitzman, Jacqueline Preiss. 2011. (ENG.). 32p. (J). (gr. -1-3). 16.99 *(978-1-4169-9157-1(3),* Simon & Schuster/Paula Wiseman Bks.) Simon & Schuster/Paula Wiseman Bks.
—Superhero Joe & the Creature Next Door. Weitzman, Jacqueline Preiss. 2013. (ENG.). 32p. (J). (gr. -1-3). 16.99 *(978-1-4424-1268-2(2),* Simon & Schuster Bks. For Young Readers) Simon & Schuster Bks. For Young Readers.
Barrett, Ron. Cats Get Famous. Barrett, Ron. 2015. (ENG.). 32p. (J). (gr. -1-3). 17.99 *(978-1-4424-9453-4(0),* Simon & Schuster Bks. For Young Readers) Simon & Schuster Bks. For Young Readers.
—The Marshmallow Incident. Barrett, Ron. Barrett, Judi. 2009. (J). pap. *(978-0-545-04654-1(8),* Scholastic Pr.) Scholastic, Inc.
Barrett, Ronald. Grandpa's Cloudy with a Chance of Meatballs Cookbook. Barrett, Judi. 2013. (ENG.). 64p. (J). (gr. -1-3). spiral bd. 17.99 *(978-1-4424-4475-1(4),* Atheneum Bks. for Young Readers) Simon & Schuster Children's Publishing.
—Pickles to Pittsburgh: Cloudy with a Chance of Meatballs 2. Barrett, Judi. 2013. (Classic Board Bks.). (ENG.). 34p. (J). (gr. -1-k). bds. 7.99 *(978-1-4424-6493-3(3),* Little Simon) Little Simon.
Barrett, Virginia. Shadows. Stott-Thornton, Janet. 2007. (Literacy 2000 Satellites: Stage 2 Ser.). 8p. (J). (gr. -1-3). pap. *(978-0-7327-1173-3(8),* Rigby) Pearson Education Australia.
Barretta, Gene. Conrad & the Cowgirl Next Door, 1 vol. Fretz, Denette. 2014. (Next Door Ser.). (ENG.). 40p. (J). 12.99 *(978-0-310-72349-3(3))* Zonderkidz.
—Monster Trucks. Matthies, Janna. 2009. (ENG.). 14p. (J). (gr. -1-k). 9.95 *(978-1-58117-853-1(0),* Intervisual/Piggy Toes) Bendon, Inc.
—On Top of Spaghetti: A Silly Song Book. 2005. 12p. (J). 12.95 *(978-1-58117-331-4(8),* Intervisual/Piggy Toes) Bendon, Inc.
—Sky High: George Ferris's Big Wheel. Kulling, Monica. 2016. (Step into Reading Ser.). (ENG.). 48p. (J). (gr. k-3). pap. 3.99 *(978-1-101-93452-4(2),* Random Hse. Bks. for Young Readers) Random Hse. Children's Bks.
Barretta, Gene. The Bass Plays the Bass & Other Homographs. Barretta, Gene. 2018. (ENG.). 40p. (J). 18.99 *(978-1-250-17507-6(0),* 900189298, Holt, Henry & Co. Bks. For Young Readers) Holt, Henry & Co.
—The Bat Can Bat: a Book of True Homonyms. Barretta, Gene. 2018. (ENG.). 40p. (J). 17.99 *(978-0-8050-9946-1(8),* 900127127, Holt, Henry & Co. Bks. For Young Readers) Holt, Henry & Co.
—Dear Deer: A Book of Homophones. Barretta, Gene. 2010. (ENG.). 40p. (J). (gr. -1-2). pap. 7.99 *(978-0-312-62899-4(4),* 900066866) Square Fish.
—Lincoln & Kennedy: A Pair to Compare. Barretta, Gene. 2016. (ENG.). 40p. (J). 17.99 *(978-0-8050-9945-4(X),* 900127126, Holt, Henry & Co. Bks. For Young Readers) Holt, Henry & Co.
—Now & Ben: The Modern Inventions of Benjamin Franklin. Barretta, Gene. 2008. (ENG.). 40p. (J). (gr. k-4). pap. 8.99 *(978-0-312-53569-8(4),* 900054750) Square Fish.
—Timeless Thomas: How Thomas Edison Changed Our Lives. Barretta, Gene. 2012. (ENG.). 40p. (J). (gr. 1-5). 18.99 *(978-0-8050-9108-3(4),* 9780805091083, Holt, Henry & Co. Bks. For Young Readers) Holt, Henry & Co.
—Timeless Thomas: How Thomas Edison Changed Our Lives. Barretta, Gene. 2017. (ENG.). 40p. (J). pap. 8.99 *(978-1-250-11478-5(0),* 900171563) Square Fish.
Barrette, Doris. The Christmas Song: Chestnuts Roasting on an Open Fire. Torme, Mel. 2007. 32p. (J). (gr. -1-2). lib. bdg. 17.89 *(978-0-06-072226-5(6))* HarperCollins Pubs.
—The Christmas Song: Chestnuts Roasting on an Open Fire. Tormé, Mel. 2007. (J). lib. bdg. 6.99 *(978-0-06-072227-2(4))* HarperCollins Pubs.
—Never Ask a Bear. Bonnett-Rampersaud, Louise. 2009. (ENG.). 32p. (J). (gr. -1-1). 16.99 *(978-0-06-112876-9(7))* HarperCollins Pubs.
—Thanks for Thanksgiving. Markes, Julie. (ENG.). 32p. (J). (gr. -1-3). 2008. pap. 7.99 *(978-0-06-051098-5(6))*; 2004. 12.99 *(978-0-06-051096-1(X))* HarperCollins Pubs.
—Thanks for Thanksgiving Board Book. Markes, Julie. 2017. (ENG.). 32p. (J). (gr. -1 — 1). bds. 7.99 *(978-0-06-264331-5(2),* HarperFestival) HarperCollins Pubs.
Barrie, J. M., et al. Peter Pan. Barrie, J. M. 2009. (ENG.). 287p. *(978-1-905716-40-1(0),* Collector's Library, The) Pan Macmillan.
Barrie, J. M. Peter Pan: Complete & Unabridged. Barrie, J. M. 2005. 176p. reprint ed. pap. 17.00 *(978-0-7567-9445-3(5))* DIANE Publishing Co.
Barringer, J. M. The Treetop Bird Family. Magden, Loretta. 2007. 28p. (J). 15.95 *(978-0-9788771-0-1(1))* Level Green Bks.
Barrington, Christine. In the Garden: Cat & Claire's Quiet Morning. Barrington, Christine. 2019. (ENG.). 28p. (J). pap. 9.99 ***(978-1-6749-5548-3(0))*** Independently Published.
Barrio, Blanca. Paco. Carballeira, Paula. 2003. 32p. (J). 14.95 *(978-84-95730-38-1(3))* Kalandraka Catalunya, Edicions, S.L. ESP. Dist: Independent Pubs. Group.
Barrionuevo, Al & Mhan, Pop. Astonisher Vol. 2: All the Nightmares. de Campi, Alex. 2018. (ENG.). 144p. (YA). pap. 14.99 *(978-1-941302-80-4(7),* de975e51-91a8-4354-be54-053b8fdb98ce, Lion Forge) Oni Pr., Inc.
Barritt, Carolyn Reed. The Day the Dragon Danced. Haugaard, Kay. 2004. (Day the Dragon Danced Ser.). 32p. (J). (gr. -1-3). 16.95 *(978-1-885008-30-5(9),* Shen's Bks.) Lee & Low Bks., Inc.
Barron, Ann. Maggie's Golden Moment. Profilet, Cynthia. 2005. (J). *(978-0-9637735-1-7(8))* Sterling Pr., Inc.
Barron, Ashley. Birthdays Around the World. Ruurs, Margriet. 2017. (Around the World Ser.). (ENG.). 40p. (J). (gr. -1-2). 18.99 *(978-1-77138-624-1(X))* Kids Can Pr., Ltd. CAN. Dist: Hachette Bk. Group.
—Counting on Fall. Flatt, Lizann. 2017. (Math in Nature Ser.: 1). (ENG.). 32p. (J). (gr. k-2). pap. 7.95 *(978-1-77147-310-1(X))* Owlkids Bks. Inc. CAN. Dist: Publishers Group West (PGW).
—Kyle Goes Alone. Thornhill, Jan. 2015. (ENG.). 32p. (J). (gr. -1-3). 17.95 *(978-1-77147-075-9(5),* Owlkids) Owlkids Bks. Inc. CAN. Dist: Publishers Group West (PGW).
—My Forest Is Green. Lebeuf, Darren. 2019. (ENG.). 32p. (J). (gr. -1-2). 16.99 *(978-1-77138-930-3(3))* Kids Can Pr., Ltd. CAN. Dist: Hachette Bk. Group.
—My Ocean Is Blue. Lebeuf, Darren. 2020. (ENG.). 32p. (J). (gr. -1-2). 17.99 *(978-1-5253-0143-8(8))* Kids Can Pr., Ltd. CAN. Dist: Hachette Bk. Group.
Barron, Ashley. Pretty Tricky: The Sneaky Ways Plants Survive. Kaner, Etta. 2020. (ENG.). 48p. (J). (gr. 2-5). 18.95 ***(978-1-77147-369-9(X))*** Owlkids Bks. Inc. CAN. Dist: Publishers Group West (PGW).
Barron, Ashley. Shaping up Summer. Flatt, Lizann. 2018. (Math in Nature Ser.: 4). (ENG.). 32p. (J). (gr. k-4). pap. 7.95 *(978-1-77147-163-3(8))* Owlkids Bks. Inc. CAN. Dist: Publishers Group West (PGW).
—Sizing up Winter. Flatt, Lizann. 2018. (Math in Nature Ser.: 3). (ENG.). 32p. (J). (gr. k-3). pap. 7.95 *(978-1-77147-339-2(8))* Owlkids Bks. Inc. CAN. Dist: Publishers Group West (PGW).
—Sorting Through Spring. Flatt, Lizann. 2018. (Math in Nature Ser.: 2). (ENG.). 32p. (J). (gr. 1-4). pap. 7.95 *(978-1-77147-153-4(0))* Owlkids Bks. Inc. CAN. Dist: Publishers Group West (PGW).
—Up! How Families Around the World Carry Their Little Ones. Hughes, Susan. 2017. (ENG.). 24p. (J). (gr. -1-2). 15.95 *(978-1-77147-176-3(X))* Owlkids Bks. Inc. CAN. Dist: Publishers Group West (PGW).
—Upsy-Daisy, Baby! Hughes, Susan. 2019. (ENG.). 24p. (J). (gr. -1-1). bds. 9.95 *(978-1-77147-387-3(8))* Owlkids Bks. Inc. CAN. Dist: Publishers Group West (PGW).
Barron, Billy. Chicken Britches! Kruse, Donald W. 2016. (ENG.). (J). (gr. k-6). pap. 12.95 *(978-0-9969964-6-4(X))* Zaccheus Entertainment Co.
Barron, Robert, photos by. Meet Judge Patricia Barron. Barron, Patricia. 2006. 40p. per. 14.95 *(978-1-59858-301-4(8))* Dog Ear Publishing, LLC.
Barron's Educational Series Staff & Rigo, L. Off to School. 2010. (ENG.). 10p. (J). (gr. -1-1). bds. 7.99 *(978-0-7641-6363-0(9),* B.E.S. Publishing) Peterson's.
Barroux. Counting Kindness: Ten Ways to Welcome Refugee Children. Kurman, Hollis. 2020. (ENG.). 32p. (J). (-k). 16.99 ***(978-1-62354-229-0(4))*** Charlesbridge Publishing, Inc.
Barroux. I Could Be- Owen, Karen. 2009. (J). *(978-1-84686-289-2(2))* Barefoot Bks., Inc.
—I Could Be, You Could Be. Owen, Karen. 2010. (ENG.). 32p. (J). (gr. 1-3). 16.99 *(978-1-84686-405-6(4))* Barefoot Bks., Inc.
Barroux. My Panda Sweater. Baum, Gillies. 2020. (ENG.). 24p. (J). pap. ***(978-1-78285-980-2(2))*** Barefoot Bks., Inc.
—My Panda Sweater. Baum & Rosinsky, Lisa. 2020. (J). ***(978-1-78285-979-6(9))*** Barefoot Bks., Inc.
Barroux. The Run. Barroux. 2020. (ENG.). 40p. (J). (gr. -1-3). 17.99 ***(978-1-5344-0886-9(X),*** Aladdin) Simon & Schuster Children's Publishing.
Barroux. Where's the Elephant? Barroux. 2016. (ENG.). 32p. (J). (gr. -1-2). 14.99 *(978-0-7636-8110-4(5))* Candlewick Pr.
Barroux, Sophie, jt. illus. see Derenne, Juliette.
Barroux, Stephane. Mega Bunny. Vidal, Séverine. 2015. (Mega Hero Bks.). (ENG.). 28p. (J). (gr. k-2). 12.95 *(978-1-77085-638-7(2),* 3facd104-00df-4e61-888c-587268579d7c); pap. 6.95 *(978-1-77085-654-7(4),* faaf04b5-3e86-4563-901c-fbd9b3078fbd) Firefly Bks., Ltd.
—Mega Mouse. Vidal, Séverine. 2015. (Mega Hero Bks.). (ENG.). 28p. (J). (gr. k-2). 12.95 *(978-1-77085-639-4(0),* 11a432f2-c844-4943-a955-9a0ab2047791); pap. 6.95 *(978-1-77085-655-4(2),* c0a81080-be44-468c-a108-e5beee05078a) Firefly Bks., Ltd.
—Mega Pig. Vidal, Séverine. 2015. (Mega Hero Bks.). (ENG.). 28p. (J). (gr. k-2). 12.95 *(978-1-77085-636-3(6),* 81923779-b926-4839-8f64-c61338a9da47); pap. 6.95 *(978-1-77085-652-3(8),* 0c39e732-d95b-477a-9839-0386b1f9d09d) Firefly Bks., Ltd.
—Mega Wolf. Vidal, Séverine. 2015. (Mega Hero Bks.). (ENG.). 28p. (J). (gr. k-2). 12.95 *(978-1-77085-637-0(4),* 9dc2edcf-dd2f-44fe-a65b-29051c97782d); pap. 6.95 *(978-1-77085-653-0(6),* 7e4bee25-925e-4ad8-b973-cacb1a9d158a) Firefly Bks., Ltd.
—My Goldfish. 2009. 36p. (J). (gr. -1-2). 15.00 *(978-0-8028-5334-9(X),* Eerdmans Bks For Young Readers) Eerdmans, William B. Publishing Co.
Barroux, Stéphane ("Barroux"). Tickly Toes. Hood, Susan. 2014. (ENG.). 24p. (J). (gr. -1 — 1). bds. 9.95 *(978-1-894786-52-2(1))* Kids Can Pr., Ltd. CAN. Dist: Hachette Bk. Group.
Barrow, Alex. A House for Mouse. Dawnay, Gabby. 2018. (ENG.). 32p. (J). (gr. -1-2). 16.95 *(978-0-500-65137-7(X),* 565137) Thames & Hudson.
—London Calls. Dawnay, Gabby. 2015. (ENG.). 40p. (J). (gr. -1-2). 13.95 *(978-1-84976-230-4(9))* Tate Publishing, Ltd. GBR. Dist: Hachette Bk. Group.
—London Calls Sticker Book. Dawnay, Gabby. 2017. (ENG.). 20p. (J). (gr. k-17). pap. 11.95 *(978-1-84976-384-4(4))* Tate Publishing, Ltd. GBR. Dist: Hachette Bk. Group.
Barrow, Alex. A Roller-Coaster Ride Around the Body. Dawnay, Gabby. (ENG.). 32p. (J). 2018. (gr. k-2). 16.99 ***(978-1-4451-5202-8(9))***; 2019. (gr. 1-5). pap. 11.99 *(978-1-4451-5203-5(7))* Hachette Children's Group GBR. (Franklin Watts). Dist: Hachette Bk. Group.
Barrow, Alex. A Song for Bear. Dawnay, Gabby. 2019. (ENG.). 32p. (J). (gr. -1-2). 14.95 *(978-0-500-65181-0(7),* 565181) Thames & Hudson.
Barrow, Ann. Big Blue. Gill, Shelley. 2005. 32p. (J). (gr. k-3). 7.95 *(978-1-57091-667-0(5))* Charlesbridge Publishing, Inc.
—Doris Free. Brookins, Cara. 2006. 127p. (J). pap. *(978-1-59336-333-8(8))* Mondo Publishing.
Barrow, David. The Best Kind of Bear. Gormley, Greg. 2019. (ENG.). 32p. (J). (-k). 16.99 *(978-1-5362-0823-8(X),* Nosy Crow) Candlewick Pr.
Barrow, David. Good Dog! Taylor, Sean. 2020. (ENG.). 40p. (J). (gr. -1-1). pap. 10.99 ***(978-1-78603-726-8(2),*** 304516); 17.99 ***(978-1-78603-725-1(4),*** 304514) Quarto Publishing Group UK GBR. (Frances Lincoln Children's Bks.). Dist: Hachette UK Distribution.
—My Mom Always Looks after Me So Much! Taylor, Sean. 2019. (ENG.). 32p. (J). (gr. -1-k). ***(978-1-78603-182-2(5))*** Frances Lincoln Childrens Bks.
Barrow, David. Too Many Things! Bryan, Tracy. 2017. (ENG.). (J). (gr. k-3). 19.00 *(978-0-692-83014-7(6))*; pap. 9.99 *(978-0-692-81614-1(3))* Bryan, Tracy Publishing.
Barrow, David. Have You Seen Elephant? Barrow, David. 2016. (ENG.). 32p. (J). (gr. -1-1). 16.99 *(978-1-77657-008-9(1),* 9781776570089) Gecko Pr. NZL. Dist: Lerner Publishing Group.
Barrow, Evie. Howl. Patrick, Kat. 2020. (ENG.). 32p. (J). (gr. -1-3). 16.99 ***(978-1-950354-45-0(8))*** Scribe Pubns. AUS. Dist: Consortium Bk. Sales & Distribution.
Barrows, Laurie. The Comebacks: Coloring Book. Clark, Eli & Boylan, Gerry. 2018. (ENG.). 70p. (J). pap. 9.99 *(978-1-7313-4844-9(4))* Independently Published.
—The Magical, Marvelous Megan G. Beamer: A Day in the Life of A Dreamer. Burnett, Karen Gedig. 2003. (J). pap. 8.95 *(978-0-9668530-6-3(7))* G R Publishing.
—To Bee or Not to Bee: A Book for Beeings Who Feel there's More to Life than Just Making Honey. Penberthy, John. rev. l.t. ed. 2005. 112p. (J). pap. 14.95 *(978-0-9768642-0-2(7))* Panorama Pr., Inc.
Barrows, Mary. From a Tree to a Chair. McDonald, Roseanne. 2019. (ENG.). 36p. (J). (gr. k-6). 22.95 ***(978-1-947860-76-6(3))***; pap. 14.95 ***(978-1-947860-81-0(X))*** Brandylane Pubs., Inc. (Belle Isle Bks.).
Barrows, Mary. Officer Jack - Book 1 - Lost Lady. Brewster, James Burd. 2016. (ENG.). (J). (gr. k-3). 14.99 *(978-1-941927-42-7(4))* J2B Publishing LLC.
—Officer Jack - Book 2 - Underwater. Brewster, James Burd. 2016. (Officer Jack Ser.: Vol. 2). (ENG.). (J). (gr. k-3). 19.99 *(978-1-941927-40-3(8))* J2B Publishing LLC.
—Officer Jack - Book 3 - Rapid Response. Brewster, James Burd. 2016. (ENG.). (J). pap. 11.49 *(978-1-941927-43-4(2))*; (Officer Jack Ser.: Vol. 3). 19.99 *(978-1-941927-44-1(0))* J2B Publishing LLC.
—Officer Jack - Book 4 - Stolen Puppy. Brewster, James Burd. 2016. (ENG.). (J). pap. 9.99 *(978-1-941927-46-5(7))*; (Officer Jack Ser.: Vol. 4). (gr. 3-6). 18.99 *(978-1-941927-47-2(5))* J2B Publishing LLC.
Barrows, Mary. Pete & Petey - Kite Flying. Brewster, James Burd. 2019. (Pete & Petey Ser.: Vol. 3). (ENG.). 36p. (J). pap. 9.99 ***(978-1-948747-55-4(3))*** J2B Publishing LLC.
Barrows, Mary. Pete & Petey - Knight in Shining Armor. Brewster, James Burd. 2019. (Pete & Petey Ser.: Vol. 2). (ENG.). 38p. (J). pap. 10.00 *(978-1-948747-29-5(4))* J2B Publishing LLC.
—Uncle Rocky, Fireman #8 - Fast Action. Brewster, James Burd. 2017. (Uncle Rocky, Fireman Ser.: Vol. 8). (ENG.). 36p. (J). (gr. k-3). 19.99 *(978-1-941927-62-5(9))* J2B Publishing LLC.
Barrows, Mary. Uncle Rocky, Fireman #9 Helping Out. Brewster, James Burd. 2019. (Uncle Rocky, Fireman Ser.: Vol. 9). (ENG.). 34p. (J). pap. 9.99 ***(978-1-941927-69-4(6))*** J2B Publishing LLC.
Barry, Etheldred B. The Giant Scissors. Johnston, Annie Fellows. 2005. reprint ed. pap. 22.95 *(978-1-4179-0341-2(4))* Kessinger Publishing, LLC.
—The Little Colonel's Hero. Johnston, Annie Fellows. 2007. 180p. per. *(978-1-4065-3513-6(3))* Dodo Pr.
—Mary Ware, the Little Colonel's Chum, 1 vol. Johnston, Annie. 2005. (Little Colonel Ser.). (ENG.). 336p. (YA). (gr. 3-6). pap. 19.95 *(978-1-56554-813-8(2),* Pelican Publishing) Arcadia Publishing.
—Mary Ware the Little Colonel's Chum. Johnston, Annie Fellows. 2004. reprint ed. pap. 30.95 *(978-1-4179-1704-4(0))* Kessinger Publishing, LLC.
Barry, Frances. Caterpillar to Butterfly. Barry, Frances. 2019. (Fold Out & Find Out Ser.). (ENG.). 32p. (J). (gr. -1-2). 11.99 *(978-0-7636-4261-7(4))* Candlewick Pr.
Barry, James L. Warriors: Graystripe's Adventure: The Lost Warrior, Warrior's Refuge, Warrior's Return. Hunter, Erin. 2017. (Warriors Graphic Novel Ser.). (ENG.). 272p. (J). (gr. 3-7). pap. 12.99 *(978-0-06-257300-1(4))* HarperCollins Pubs.
—Warriors Manga Box Set: Graystripe's Adventure, 3 vols., Set. Hunter, Erin. 2009. (Warriors Manga Ser.). (ENG.). 336p. (J). (gr. 3-7). pap. 23.97 *(978-0-06-178228-2(9))* HarperCollins Pubs.
—Warriors: Ravenpaw's Path: Shattered Peace, a Clan in Need, the Heart of a Warrior. Hunter, Erin. 2018. (Warriors Graphic Novel Ser.). (ENG.). 272p. (J). (gr. 3-7). pap. 12.99 *(978-0-06-274824-9(6))* HarperCollins Pubs.
—Warriors: Ravenpaw's Path #1: Shattered Peace. Hunter, Erin. 2009. (Warriors Graphic Novel Ser.: 1). (ENG.). 112p. (J). (gr. 3-7). pap. 6.99 *(978-0-06-168865-2(7))* HarperCollins Pubs.
—Warriors: Ravenpaw's Path #2: a Clan in Need. Hunter, Erin. 2010. (Warriors Graphic Novel Ser.: 2). (ENG.). 112p. (J). (gr. 3-7). pap. 7.99 *(978-0-06-168866-9(5))* HarperCollins Pubs.
—Warriors: Ravenpaw's Path #3: the Heart of a Warrior. Hunter, Erin. 2010. (Warriors Graphic Novel Ser.: 3). (ENG.). 112p. (J). (gr. 3-7). pap. 7.99 *(978-0-06-168867-6(3))* HarperCollins Pubs.
—Warriors: SkyClan & the Stranger: 3 Full-Color Warriors Manga Books In 1! Hunter, Erin. 2019. (Warriors Graphic Novel Ser.). (ENG.). 272p. (J). (gr. 3-7). pap. 12.99 *(978-0-06-285737-8(1))* HarperCollins Pubs.
—Warriors: SkyClan & the Stranger #1: the Rescue. Hunter, Erin. 2011. (Warriors Graphic Novel Ser.: 1). (ENG.). 112p. (J). (gr. 3-7). pap. 7.99 *(978-0-06-200836-7(6))* HarperCollins Pubs.
—Warriors: SkyClan & the Stranger #2: Beyond the Code. Hunter, Erin. 2011. (Warriors Graphic Novel Ser.: 2). (ENG.). 112p. (J). (gr. 3-7). pap. 6.99 *(978-0-06-200837-4(4))* HarperCollins Pubs.
—Warriors Super Edition: Hawkwing's Journey. Hunter, Erin. (Warriors Super Edition Ser.: 9). (ENG.). 480p. (J). (gr. 3-7). 2017. pap. 7.99 *(978-0-06-246770-6(0))*; 2016. 18.99 *(978-0-06-246768-3(9))* HarperCollins Pubs.
—Warriors Super Edition: Tallstar's Revenge. Hunter, Erin. 2013. (Warriors Super Edition Ser.: 6). (ENG.). 544p. (J). (gr. 3-7). 18.99 *(978-0-06-221804-9(2))*; lib. bdg. 19.89 *(978-0-06-221805-6(0))* HarperCollins Pubs.

B

—Warriors Super Edition: Tallstar's Revenge. Hunter, Erin. 2020. (Warriors Super Edition Ser.: 6). (ENG.). 560p. (J). (gr. 3-7). pap. 8.99 *(978-0-06-221806-3(9)*, HarperCollins) HarperCollins Pubs. Ltd. GBR. Dist: HarperCollins Pubs.

—Warriors Super Edition: Tigerheart's Shadow. Hunter, Erin. (Warriors Super Edition Ser.: 10). (ENG.). 464p. (J). (gr. 3-7). 2018. pap. 7.99 *(978-0-06-246774-4(3))*; 2017. 18.99 *(978-0-06-246772-0(7))*; 2017. lib. bdg. 19.89 *(978-0-06-246773-7(5))* HarperCollins Pubs.

—Warriors Super Edition: Yellowfang's Secret. Hunter, Erin. (Warriors Super Edition Ser.: 5). (ENG.). (J). (gr. 3-7). 2014. 544p. pap. 7.99 *(978-0-06-208216-9(7))*; 2012. 528p. 18.99 *(978-0-06-208214-5(0))*; 2012. 528p. lib. bdg. 19.89 *(978-0-06-208215-2(9))* HarperCollins Pubs.

—Warriors: Warrior's Refuge, 3 vols. Hunter, Erin. 2007. (Warriors Graphic Novel Ser.: No. 2). (ENG.). 112p. (J). (gr. 3-7). pap. 7.99 *(978-0-06-125231-0(X))* HarperCollins Pubs.

—Warriors: Warrior's Return, 3 vols. Hunter, Erin. 2008. (Warriors Graphic Novel Ser.: No. 3). (ENG.). 112p. (J). (gr. 3-7). pap. 7.99 *(978-0-06-125233-4(6))* HarperCollins Pubs.

Barry, James L. & Hunt, John. Warriors: SkyClan & the Stranger #3: after the Flood. Hunter, Erin. 2012. (Warriors Graphic Novel Ser.: 3). (ENG.). 112p. (J). (gr. 3-7). pap. 7.99 *(978-0-06-200838-1(2))* HarperCollins Pubs.

Barry, James L. & Richardson, Owen. Warriors Super Edition: Moth Flight's Vision. Hunter, Erin. (Warriors Super Edition Ser.: 8). (ENG.). (J). (gr. 3-7). 2016. 544p. pap. 7.99 *(978-0-06-229149-3(1))*; 2015. 528p. 18.99 *(978-0-06-229147-9(5))* HarperCollins Pubs.

Barry, Kevin. Halfway Wild, 1 vol. Freudig, Laura. 2016. (ENG.). 32p. (J). 17.95 *(978-1-934031-48-3(8)*, fd9e6185-4790-4c85-86f5-0482ea0683d1) Islandport Pr., Inc.

—Schnitzel: A Cautionary Tale for Lazy Louts. Shaw, Stephanie. 2016. (ENG.). 32p. (J). (gr. k-3). 16.99 *(978-1-58536-957-7(8)*, 204104) Sleeping Bear Pr.

Barry, Kevin M. Ghost Cat. Bunting, Eve. 2017. (ENG.). 32p. (J). (gr. k-2). 16.99 *(978-1-58536-993-5(4)*, 204323) Sleeping Bear Pr.

—Kindergarrrten Bus. Ornstein, Mike. 2018. (ENG.). 32p. (J). (gr. -1-2). 16.99 *(978-1-58536-398-8(7)*, 204578) Sleeping Bear Pr.

Barry, Matt. Today Jack Is Going to Be... Barry, Stephanie. 2018. (ENG.). 30p. (J). pap. *(978-1-9996129-8-6(1))* Cambria Bks.

Barshaw, Ruth McNally. Leopold the Lion. Brennan-Nelson, Denise. 2015. (ENG.). 32p. (J). (gr. 1-3). 16.99 *(978-1-58536-828-0(8)*, 203951) Sleeping Bear Pr.

Barshaw, Ruth McNally. Best Friends Fur-Ever. Barshaw, Ruth McNally. 2013. (Ellie Mcdoodle Diaries). (ENG.). 192p. (YA). (gr. 3-6). 13.99 *(978-1-61963-175-5(X)*, 900123475, Bloomsbury USA Childrens) Bloomsbury Publishing USA.

—Ellie McDoodle: Have Pen, Will Travel. Barshaw, Ruth McNally. 2nd ed. 2011. (Ellie Mcdoodle Ser.). 192p. (YA). (gr. 3-6). pap. 7.99 *(978-1-59990-715-4(1)*, 900076590, Bloomsbury USA Childrens) Bloomsbury Publishing USA.

—Have Pen, Will Travel. Barshaw, Ruth McNally. 2013. (Ellie Mcdoodle Diaries). (ENG.). 192p. (J). (gr. 3-6). 13.99 *(978-1-61963-173-1(3)*, 900123476, Bloomsbury USA Childrens) Bloomsbury Publishing USA.

—New Kid in School. Barshaw, Ruth McNally. 2013. (Ellie Mcdoodle Diaries). 192p. (J). (gr. 3-6). 12.99 *(978-1-61963-174-8(1)*, 900123470, Bloomsbury USA Childrens) Bloomsbury Publishing USA.

Barshishat, Malka Michaela. How Butterflies Got Colored Wings. Berkove, Lawrence I. 2017. (J). pap. *(978-1-5011-4872-9(9))* Meadowbrook Pr.

Barstow, Montagu. Old Hungarian Fairy Tales: (Illustrated & Unabridged Classic Edition) Orczy, Baroness. 2019. (ENG.). 158p. (J). (gr. k-5). ***(978-625-7959-43-8(8))*** Uhrayoglu, Murat E Kitap Projesi.

Bart, Kathleen. Town Teddy & Country Bear Go Global. Bart, Kathleen. 2011. (J). (gr. k-3). 16.95 *(978-1-932485-60-8(0))* Reverie Publishing Co.

—Town Teddy & Country Bear Tour the USA. Bart, Kathleen. 2008. 32p. (J). (gr. -1-3). pap. 16.95 *(978-1-932485-50-9(3))* Reverie Publishing Co.

Bart, Kathleen & Hofmann, Ginnie. Doll & Teddy Bear Activity Book. Dracker, Pune. 2005. 96p. (J). pap. *(978-1-932485-24-0(4))* Reverie Publishing Co.

Bartczak, Peter. A Voice for the Redwoods. Halter, Loretta. 2010. (ENG.). 64p. (J). 18.95 *(978-0-9822942-0-8(4))* Nature's Hopes & Heroes.

Bartel, Kourtney. Mama Bear's Lullaby. Nelson, Loretta a. 2016. (ENG.). (J). pap. *(978-1-4602-9700-1(8))* FriesenPress.

Bartels, Mark. Little Robert: A True Story. Bartels, Lowell. 2011. 36p. pap. 19.95 *(978-1-4137-7171-8(8))* America Star Bks.

Barth, Alexandra. Teddy Visits the Dentist. Mahadeo Rdh, Elizabeth. 2012. 40p. pap. *(978-0-9569438-0-4(2))* Mahadeo Movement, The.

—Teddy Visits the Dentist: Teddy Gets a Filling. Mahadeo Rdh, Elizabeth. 2012. 42p. (-18). pap. *(978-0-9569438-2-8(9))* Mahadeo Movement, The.

Barth, D. S. Puddle Jumpers. Allen, D. L. 2017. (ENG.). (J). pap. 9.95 *(978-1-947825-64-2(X))* Yorkshire Publishing Group.

Barthelmes, Andrew. If My Mom Were a Platypus: Mammal Babies & Their Mothers, Vol. Michels, Dia L. 4th ed. 2014. (ENG.). 64p. pap. 12.95 *(978-1-938492-11-2(0))* Science, Naturally!.

—If My Mom Were A Platypus- Hebrew Language Edition. Michels, Dia L. 2006. Orig. Title: #1488;#1501; #1488;#1502;#1497; #1492;#1497;#1514;#1492; #1508;#1500;#1496;#1497;#1508;#1493;#1505;. 64p. (J). 29.95 *(978-0-9678020-9-1(1))* Science, Naturally!.

—If My Mom Were a Platypus- Hebrew Language Edition. Michels, Dia L. 2006. Orig. Title: #1488;#1501; #1488;#1502;#1497; #1492;#1497;#1514;#1492; #1508;#1500;#1496;#1497;#1508;#1493;#1505;. (HEB.). 64p. (J). 19.95 *(978-0-9678020-8-4(3))* Science, Naturally!.

Bartholomew. A Fun & Easy Way to Do Your Homework. Berry, Joy. 2010. (Fun & Easy Way Ser.). (ENG.). 48p. (J). (gr. 1-5). pap. 7.95 *(978-1-60577-320-9(4))* Berry, Joy Enterprises.

—A Fun & Easy Way to Get Good Grades. Berry, Joy. 2010. (Fun & Easy Way Ser.). (ENG.). 48p. (J). (gr. 1-5). pap. 7.95 *(978-1-60577-321-6(2))* Berry, Joy Enterprises.

—Good Answers to Tough Questions Disasters. Berry, Joy. 2010. (Good Answers to Tough Questions Ser.). (ENG.). 48p. (J). (gr. k-7). pap. 7.99 *(978-1-60577-510-4(X))* Berry, Joy Enterprises.

—Good Answers to Tough Questions Divorce. Berry, Joy. 2010. (Good Answers to Tough Questions Ser.). (ENG.). 48p. (J). (gr. k-7). pap. 7.99 *(978-1-60577-509-8(6))* Berry, Joy Enterprises.

—Good Answers to Tough Questions Moving. Berry, Joy. 2010. (Good Answers to Tough Questions Ser.). (ENG.). 48p. (J). (gr. k-7). pap. 7.99 *(978-1-60577-508-1(8))* Berry, Joy Enterprises.

—Good Answers to Tough Questions Trauma. Berry, Joy. 2010. (Good Answers to Tough Questions Ser.). (ENG.). 48p. (J). (gr. k-7). pap. 7.99 *(978-1-60577-507-4(X))* Berry, Joy Enterprises.

—Help Me Be Good Being a Bad Sport. Berry, Joy. 2010. (Help Me Be Good Ser.). (ENG.). 32p. (J). (gr. -1-2). pap. 4.99 *(978-1-60577-139-7(2))* Berry, Joy Enterprises.

—Help Me Be Good Being Mean. Berry, Joy. 2010. (Help Me Be Good Ser.). (ENG.). 32p. (J). (gr. -1-2). pap. 4.99 *(978-1-60577-142-7(2))* Berry, Joy Enterprises.

—Help Me Be Good Being Rude. Berry, Joy. 2010. (Help Me Be Good Ser.). (ENG.). 32p. (J). (gr. -1-2). pap. 4.99 *(978-1-60577-138-0(4))* Berry, Joy Enterprises.

—Help Me Be Good Being Selfish. Berry, Joy. 2010. (Help Me Be Good Ser.). (ENG.). 32p. (J). (gr. -1-2). pap. 4.99 *(978-1-60577-133-5(3))* Berry, Joy Enterprises.

—Help Me Be Good Bullying. Berry, Joy. 2010. (Help Me Be Good Ser.). (ENG.). 32p. (J). (gr. -1-2). pap. 4.99 *(978-1-60577-140-3(6))* Berry, Joy Enterprises.

—Help Me Be Good Disobeying. Berry, Joy. 2010. (Help Me Be Good Ser.). (ENG.). 32p. (J). (gr. -1-2). pap. 4.99 *(978-1-60577-137-3(6))* Berry, Joy Enterprises.

—Help Me Be Good Fighting. Berry, Joy. 2010. (Help Me Be Good Ser.). (ENG.). 32p. (J). (gr. -1-2). pap. 4.99 *(978-1-60577-135-9(X))* Berry, Joy Enterprises.

—Help Me Be Good Showing Off. Berry, Joy. 2010. (Help Me Be Good Ser.). (ENG.). 32p. (J). (gr. -1-2). pap. 4.99 *(978-1-60577-143-4(0))* Berry, Joy Enterprises.

—Help Me Be Good Tattling. Berry, Joy. 2010. (Help Me Be Good Ser.). (ENG.). 32p. (J). (gr. -1-2). pap. 4.99 *(978-1-60577-136-6(8))* Berry, Joy Enterprises.

—Help Me Be Good Teasing. Berry, Joy. 2010. (Help Me Be Good Ser.). (ENG.). 32p. (J). (gr. -1-2). pap. 4.99 *(978-1-60577-141-0(4))* Berry, Joy Enterprises.

—Help Me Be Good Whining. Berry, Joy. 2010. (Help Me Be Good Ser.). (ENG.). 32p. (J). (gr. -1-2). pap. 4.99 *(978-1-60577-134-2(1))* Berry, Joy Enterprises.

—I Feel Angry. Leonard, Marcia. 2003. 24p. (J). bds. 2.95 *(978-0-8249-6526-6(4)*, Ideal Pubns.) Worthy Publishing.

—I Feel Happy. Leonard, Marcia. 2003. 24p. (J). bds. 2.95 *(978-0-8249-6523-5(X)*, Ideal Pubns.) Worthy Publishing.

—I Feel Sad. Leonard, Marcia. 2003. 24p. (J). bds. 2.95 *(978-0-8249-6524-2(8)*, Ideal Pubns.) Worthy Publishing.

—I Feel Scared. Leonard, Marcia. 2003. 24p. (J). bds. 2.95 *(978-0-8249-6525-9(6)*, Ideal Pubns.) Worthy Publishing.

—The Smart Kids Allowance System: Step-by-Step Money Management Guidebook. Berry, Rob & Duey, Kathleen. Date not set. (Family Skill Builders Ser.). (J). (gr. k-6). pap. 9.95 *(978-1-883761-34-9(4))* Family Life Productions.

—Winning Skills You Can Work It! an Anthology of Six Books. Berry, Joy. 2010. (Winning Skills Ser.). (ENG.). 304p. (J). (gr. 5-7). pap. 9.95 *(978-1-60577-604-0(1))* Berry, Joy Enterprises.

Bartholomew, Al, jt. photos by see Bartholomew, Linda.

Bartholomew, Erin. Midget: The Story of a Boy Who Was Always Goin' Alone. O'Brien, Msgr Raymond J. 2016. (ENG.). (J). (gr. 4-6). pap. 12.95 *(978-1-936639-70-0(X))* St. Augustine Academy Pr.

—Nice Going, Red: The Story of a Boy Who Couldn't Take It. O'Brien, Msgr Raymond J. 2016. (ENG.). (YA). (gr. 7-12). pap. 14.95 *(978-1-936639-71-7(8))* St. Augustine Academy Pr.

Bartholomew, Linda & Bartholomew, Al, photos by. Adventures in the Tropics. Bartholomew, Linda & Bartholomew, Al. 2005. 76p. (J). 15.00 *(978-0-9764802-1-1(2))* Solutions for Human Services, LLC.

—The Rain Forest Book for Kids. Bartholomew, Linda & Bartholomew, Al. 2005. 32p. (J). 9.00 *(978-0-9764802-0-4(4))* Solutions for Human Services, LLC.

Bartkowiak, Richele, photos by. Sing a Song of Opposites. Schiller, Pamela Byrne. 2014. 24p. (J). *(978-1-60128-859-2(X))* Frog Street Pr.

Bartlett, Alison. Can I Play? Thomas, Janet. 2005. 32p. (J). 8.99 *(978-1-4052-0597-9(0))* Egmont Bks., Ltd. GBR. Dist: Trafalgar Square Publishing.

—Growing Frogs. French, Vivian. 2003. (Read & Wonder Ser.). (ENG.). 32p. (J). (gr. -1-3). pap. 7.99 *(978-0-7636-2052-3(1))* Candlewick Pr.

—Growing Frogs Big Book: Read & Wonder Big Book. French, Vivian. 2003. (Read & Wonder Ser.). (ENG.). 32p. (J). (gr. k-3). pap. 24.99 *(978-0-7636-2232-9(X))* Candlewick Pr.

—T. Rex: Read & Wonder. French, Vivian. 2006. (Read & Wonder Ser.). (ENG.). 32p. (J). (gr. -1-3). reprint ed. pap. 6.99 *(978-0-7636-3177-2(9))* Candlewick Pr.

Bartlett, Alyssa Joy. Boo Boo Kisses from the Littlest Angel, 1 vol. Penley, Janet. 2010. 34p. 24.95 *(978-1-4489-4539-9(9))* PublishAmerica, Inc.

Bartlett, Bella. And If You Can't. Hatcher, Sydney N. 2020. (ENG.). 38p. (J). pap. ***(978-1-64921-972-5(5))*** Yildiz Ilkin.

Bartlett, Rebecca. Disappearing Diamonds: An Upton Charles Adventure. Stern, D. G. 2008. (ENG.). 126p. (J). pap. 9.99 *(978-0-9754676-9-5(7))* Yeoman Hse.

Barto, Linda "iLham". Where the Ghost Camel Grins: Muslim Fables for Families of All Faiths. 2009. (ENG.). 119p. (gr. 5). 19.95 *(978-1-879402-24-9(6))* Tahrike Tarsile Quran, Inc.

Bartók, Mira. The Wonderling. Bartók, Mira. 2017. (ENG.). 464p. (J). (gr. 5-9). 21.99 *(978-0-7636-9121-9(6))* Candlewick Pr.

Bartok, Mira. The Wonderling. Bartok, Mira. 2019. (ENG.). 464p. (J). (gr. 5-9). pap. 9.99 *(978-1-5362-0890-0(6))* Candlewick Pr.

Bartolini, Egle. The Haunted Mansion: Frights of Fancy. Grace, Sina. 2020. (ENG.). 72p. (J). (gr. 4-7). pap. 9.99 *(978-1-68405-607-1(1))* Idea & Design Works, LLC.

—Penguins of Madagascar Vol. 2: Operation Heist. Scott, Cavan et al. 2015. (Penguins of Madagascar Ser.: 2). 64p. (J). (gr. 1-4). pap. 6.99 *(978-1-78276-252-2(3))* Titan Bks. Ltd. GBR. Dist: Penguin Random Hse. LLC.

Bartolini, Egle & Alvarez, Dave. Cat about Town. Davison, Max & Cooper, Chris. 2016. (Adventures of Puss in Boots Ser.: 2). 64p. (J). (gr. 1-4). pap. 6.99 *(978-1-78585-332-6(5))* Titan Bks. Ltd. GBR. Dist: Penguin Random Hse. LLC.

—Puss in Boots Collection - Amazing Tales!, Vol. 1. Davison, Max & Cooper, Chris. 2016. 112p. (J). (gr. 1-4). pap. 12.99 *(978-1-78585-318-0(X))* Titan Bks. Ltd. GBR. Dist: Penguin Random Hse. LLC.

Bartolini, Egle, jt. illus. see Cattish, Anna.

Bartolini, Federica. Lucy's Blue Day - My Diary: For Older Children & Teenagers. Duke, Lisa & Duke, Christopher. 2019. (ENG.). 98p. (J). pap. 14.99 ***(978-1-0859-4133-4(7))*** Independently Published.

Bartolo, Michael, jt. illus. see Tortosa, Wilson.

Bartolomé, Soraya. Hello. O'Neill, Juliana. 2019. (Reading Stars Ser.). (ENG.). 24p. (J). (gr. -1-2). pap. 9.99 *(978-1-5324-1261-5(4))* Xist Publishing.

—Piggy in Heaven. Johnson, Melinda. 2019. (ENG.). 24p. (J). (gr. -1-1). bds. 9.99 *(978-1-64060-165-9(1))* Paraclete Pr., Inc.

Bartolomé, Soraya Pérez. My First Heaven Book. Paraclete Press, Paraclete. 2019. (ENG.). 9p. (J). (gr. -1-k). bds. 8.99 *(978-1-64060-088-1(4))* Paraclete Pr., Inc.

Barton, Annamarie. Sam & Tam in Tam Learns to Walk. Barton, Christine. 2018. (Sam & Tam Ser.: Vol. 1). (ENG.). 28p. (J). pap. 9.99 *(978-1-7286-6087-5(4))* Independently Published.

Barton, Bethany. Give Bees a Chance. Barton, Bethany. 40p. (J). (gr. -1-3). 2019. pap. 8.99 *(978-0-593-11372-1(1)*, Puffin Books); 2017. 17.99 *(978-0-670-01694-5(2)*, Viking Books for Young Readers) Penguin Young Readers Group.

—I'm Trying to Love Math. Barton, Bethany. 2019. (ENG.). 40p. (J). (gr. -1-3). 17.99 *(978-0-451-48090-3(2)*, Viking Books for Young Readers) Penguin Young Readers Group.

—I'm Trying to Love Spiders. Barton, Bethany. (J). (gr. -1-3). 2019. 40p. pap. 8.99 *(978-0-593-11371-4(3)*, Puffin Books); 2015. 34p. 17.99 *(978-0-670-01693-8(4)*, Viking Books for Young Readers) Penguin Young Readers Group.

Barton, Byron. Jump, Frog, Jump! Kalan, Robert. 2004.Tr. of Salta, Ranita, Salta!. (J). (gr. -1-2). 28.95 incl. audio compact disk *(978-1-59112-728-4(9))* Live Oak Media.

—Jump, Frog, Jump! Board Book. Kalan, Robert. 2003.Tr. of Salta, Ranita, Salta!. (ENG.). 34p. (J). (gr. -1-3). bds. 8.99 *(978-0-06-008819-4(2)*, Greenwillow Bks.) HarperCollins Pubs.

Barton, Byron. Boats. Barton, Byron. 2006. 34p. (J). (gr. -1-2). 12.99 *(978-0-06-115017-3(7)*, HarperFestival) HarperCollins Pubs.

—My Bike. Barton, Byron. 2015. (ENG.). 40p. (J). (gr. -1-3). 16.99 *(978-0-06-233699-6(1)*, Greenwillow Bks.) HarperCollins Pubs.

—My Bike Board Book. Barton, Byron. 2016. (ENG.). 40p. (J). (gr. -1-3). bds. 8.99 *(978-0-06-233701-6(7)*, Greenwillow Bks.) HarperCollins Pubs.

—My Bike Lap Book. Barton, Byron. 2016. 40p. (J). (gr. -1-3). bds. 12.99 *(978-0-06-233702-3(5)*, Greenwillow Bks.) HarperCollins Pubs.

—My Bus. Barton, Byron. 2014. (ENG.). 40p. (J). (gr. -1-3). 16.99 *(978-0-06-228736-6(2)*, Greenwillow Bks.) HarperCollins Pubs.

—My Bus Board Book. Barton, Byron. 2015. (ENG.). 38p. (J). (gr. -1 — 1). bds. 8.99 *(978-0-06-228738-0(9)*, Greenwillow Bks.) HarperCollins Pubs.

—My Car. Barton, Byron. (ENG.). 40p. (J). (gr. -1-3). 2016. pap. 7.99 *(978-0-06-239960-1(8))*; 2004. reprint ed. pap. 7.99 *(978-0-06-058940-0(X))* HarperCollins Pubs. (Greenwillow Bks.).

—My Car Board Book. Barton, Byron. 2003. (ENG.). 36p. (J). (gr. -1-3). bds. 7.99 *(978-0-06-056045-4(2)*, Greenwillow Bks.) HarperCollins Pubs.

—My Car/Mi Carro: Bilingual Spanish-English Children's Book. Barton, Byron. 2016. (ENG.). 40p. (J). (gr. -1-3). 17.99 *(978-0-06-245545-1(1))*; pap. 7.99 *(978-0-06-245544-4(3))* HarperCollins Pubs. (Greenwillow Bks.).

—My House. Barton, Byron. 2016. (ENG.). 40p. (J). (gr. -1-3). 16.99 *(978-0-06-233703-0(3)*, Greenwillow Bks.) HarperCollins Pubs.

—My House Board Book. Barton, Byron. 2017. (ENG.). 44p. (J). (gr. -1-3). bds. 8.99 *(978-0-06-233705-4(X)*, Greenwillow Bks.) HarperCollins Pubs.

Barton, Harry. Saint Louis & the Last Crusade. Hubbard, Margaret Ann. 2013. (ENG.). 165p. pap. 11.95 *(978-1-58617-647-1(1))* Ignatius Pr.

Barton, Jill. Lady Lollipop. King-Smith, Dick. (ENG.). 128p. (J). (gr. 2-4). 2011. 18.69 *(978-0-7636-1269-6(3))*; 2003. pap. 7.99 *(978-0-7636-2181-0(1))* Candlewick Pr.

—Little Mouse & the Big Cupcake. Taylor, Thomas. 2017. (ENG.). 24p. (J). (— 1). bds. 6.95 *(978-1-910716-32-8(4))* Boxer Bks., Ltd. GBR. Dist: Sterling Publishing Co., Inc.

—Rattletrap Car. Root, Phyllis. 2006. 40p. (gr. -1-3). reprint ed. pap. 7.99 *(978-0-7636-2007-3(6))* Candlewick Pr.

—Rattletrap Car Big Book. Root, Phyllis. 2009. 40p. (J). (gr. -1-3). pap. 27.99 *(978-0-7636-4139-9(1))* Candlewick Pr.

—Two Little Monkeys. Fox, Mem. 2012. (ENG.). 32p. (J). (gr. -1-3). 16.99 *(978-1-4169-8687-4(1)*, Beach Lane Bks.) Beach Lane Bks.

Barton, Kent. William Shakespeare's Much Ado about Mean Girls. Doescher, Ian. 2019. (Pop Shakespeare Ser.: 1). (ENG.). 176p. (J). (gr. 9). pap. 12.99 *(978-1-68369-117-4(2))* Quirk Bks.

—William Shakespeare's the Taming of the Clueless. Doescher, Ian. 2020. (Pop Shakespeare Ser.: 3). (ENG.). 192p. (YA). (gr. 9). pap. 14.99 *(978-1-68369-175-4(X))* Quirk Bks.

Barton, Patrice. Did You Hear What I Heard? Poems about School. Winters, Kay. 2018. 40p. (J). (gr. k-1). 16.99 *(978-0-399-53898-8(4)*, Dial Bks) Penguin Young Readers Group.

—Hello Goodbye Dog. Gianferrari, Maria. 2017. (ENG.). 40p. (J). 17.99 *(978-1-62672-177-7(7)*, 900141433) Roaring Brook Pr.

—I Like Old Clothes. Hoberman, Mary Ann. 2012. 32p. (J). (gr. k-3). 16.99 *(978-0-375-86951-8(4)*, Knopf Bks. for Young Readers) Random Hse. Children's Bks.

—I Pledge Allegiance. Mora, Pat & Martinez, Libby. 2014. (ENG.). 40p. (J). (gr. -1-2). 16.99 *(978-0-307-93181-8(1)*, Knopf Bks. for Young Readers) Random Hse. Children's Bks.

—The Invisible Boy. Ludwig, Trudy. 2013. (ENG.). 40p. (J). (gr. 1-4). 17.99 *(978-1-58246-450-3(2)*, Knopf Bks. for Young Readers) Random Hse. Children's Bks.

—Jessica Mcbean, Tap Dance Queen. Gerber, Carole. 2006. 144p. (J). 13.95 *(978-0-9718348-7-3(3))* Blooming Tree Pr.

—Jessica McBean, Tap Dance Queen. Gerber, Carole. 2007. (ENG.). 144p. (J). (gr. 1-5). pap. 6.95 *(978-0-9718348-9-7(X))* Blooming Tree Pr.

—The Looking Book. Hallinan, P. K. (ENG.). (J). (gr. -1-1). 2019. 26p. bds. 7.99 *(978-0-8249-1698-5(0)*, Worthy Kids/Ideals); 2009. 32p. 16.99 *(978-0-8249-5607-3(9)*, Ideal Pubns.) Worthy Publishing.

—Oh My! Ginny Fry! Shaw, Gina. 2010. 48p. (J). *(978-0-545-24384-1(X))* Scholastic, Inc.

—Quiet Please, Owen McPhee! Ludwig, Trudy. 2018. (ENG.). 40p. (J). (gr. k-3). lib. bdg. 20.99 *(978-0-399-55714-9(8)*, Knopf Bks. for Young Readers) Random Hse. Children's Bks.

—Remarkably You. Miller, Pat Zietlow. 2019. (ENG.). 32p. (J). (gr. -1-3). 17.99 *(978-0-06-242758-8(X))* HarperCollins Pubs.

—Rosie Sprout's Time to Shine. Wortche, Allison. 2011. 40p. (J). (gr. -1-2). 17.99 *(978-0-375-86721-7(X)*, Knopf Bks. for Young Readers) Random Hse. Children's Bks.

—Waiting for Snow. Shaw, Gina. 2010. 48p. (J). pap. *(978-0-545-24385-8(8))* Scholastic, Inc.

—The Year of the Baby. Cheng, Andrea. 2014. (Anna Wang Novel Ser.: 2). (ENG.). 176p. (J). (gr. 1-4). pap. 6.99 *(978-0-544-22525-1(2)*, 1563367, HMH Books For Young Readers) Houghton Mifflin Harcourt Publishing Co.

—The Year of the Garden. Cheng, Andrea. 2018. (Anna Wang Novel Ser.: 5). (ENG.). 128p. (J). (gr. 1-4). pap. 6.99 *(978-1-328-90017-3(7)*, 1700051, HMH Books For Young Readers) Houghton Mifflin Harcourt Publishing Co.

—The Year of the Three Sisters. Cheng, Andrea. 2016. (Anna Wang Novel Ser.: 4). (ENG.). 160p. (J). (gr. 1-4). pap. 6.99 *(978-0-544-66849-2(9)*, 1625470, HMH Books For Young Readers) Houghton Mifflin Harcourt Publishing Co.

—Yo Prometo Lealtad. Mora, Pat & Martinez, Libby. Dominguez, Adriana, tr. 2020. (SPA.). 40p. (J). (gr. -1-2). 7.99 *(978-0-593-12574-8(6)*, Dragonfly Bks.) Random Hse. Children's Bks.

Barton, Renee. Amagestic: A Caterpillar's Journey. 2005. Orig. Title: Amagestic. (J). per. 7.99 *(978-0-9741864-2-9(2)*, 1) NT Publishing, L.L.C.

Barton, Renee L. ABC Story: Featuring: William. 2003. (J). per. 7.99 *(978-0-9741864-1-2(4)*, 1) NT Publishing, L.L.C.

Barton, Sally. Fairy House. Barton, Sally. 2016. 24p. (J). (gr. -1-1). pap. 9.99 *(978-1-907432-19-4(1))* Hogs Back Bks. GBR. Dist: Independent Pubs. Group.

Bartram, Bob & Eggers, James. Gene Autry & the Ghost Riders. Patten, Lewis B. 2011. 280p. 47.95 *(978-1-258-02621-9(X))* Literary Licensing, LLC.

Bartram, Simon. Once upon a Tomb: A Collection of Gravely Humorous Verses. Lewis, J. Patrick. 2006. (ENG.). 32p. (J). (gr. 1-4). 16.99 *(978-0-7636-1837-7(3))* Candlewick Pr.

Baruffi, Andrea. I Won't Go to Bed! Linn, Margot. 2005. (I'm Going to Read® Ser.: Level 3). 32p. (J). (gr. 1-2). pap. 3.95 *(978-1-4027-2104-5(8))* Sterling Publishing Co., Inc.

Baruzzi, Agnese. Alice's Mazes: A Counting Adventure in Wonderland. 2019. (Search, Find, & Count Ser.). (ENG.). 56p. (J). (gr. 1). pap. 9.95 *(978-88-544-1524-9(3))* White Star ITA. Dist: Sterling Publishing Co., Inc.

Baruzzi, Agnese. Dino Faces/Caras de Dinosaurios. 2020. (My First Puzzle Book Ser.). (ENG.). 14p. (J). (— 1). bds. 8.95 ***(978-88-544-1597-3(9))*** White Star ITA. Dist: Sterling Publishing Co., Inc.

—Dinoland: A Prehistoric Counting Book. 2020. (Search, Find, & Count Ser.). (ENG.). 56p. (J). (gr. 1). pap. 9.95 ***(978-88-544-1626-0(6))*** White Star ITA. Dist: Sterling Publishing Co., Inc.

—Farm Faces/Caras de Granja. 2020. (My First Puzzle Book Ser.). (ENG.). 14p. (J). (— 1). bds. 8.95 ***(978-88-544-1596-6(0))*** White Star ITA. Dist: Sterling Publishing Co., Inc.

Baruzzi, Agnese. Hidden Animals. Blake, Carly. 2018. (ENG.). 28p. (J). (— 1). bds. 8.99 *(978-1-68412-175-5(2)*, Silver Dolphin Bks.) Printers Row Publishing Group.

—I Will Eat You! Francia, Giada. 2018. 32p. (J). (gr. -1-2). 14.99 *(978-0-8234-4031-3(1))* Holiday Hse., Inc.

—Just Like My Mommy. Ikids Staff. 2009. (ENG.). 20p. (J). (gr. 1-17). 19.99 *(978-1-58476-664-3(6))* Innovative Kids.

—Mad for Math, Grade 2. Bertola, Linda, ed. 2018. (Math Adventures Ser.). (ENG.). 72p. (J). (gr. 2). pap. 9.95

(978-1-4114-7906-7(8), Spark Publishing Group) Sterling Publishing Co., Inc.

—Mad for Math, Grade 3. Bertola, Linda, ed. 2018. (Math Adventures Ser.). (ENG.). 72p. (J). (gr. 3). pap. 9.95 *(978-1-4114-7907-4(6)*, Spark Publishing Group) Sterling Publishing Co., Inc.

—Mad for Math, Grade 4. Bertola, Linda, ed. 2018. (Math Adventures Ser.). (ENG.). 72p. (J). (gr. 4). pap. 9.95 *(978-1-4114-7908-1(4)*, Spark Publishing Group) Sterling Publishing Co., Inc.

—Mad for Math, Grade 5. Bertola, Linda, ed. 2018. (Math Adventures Ser.). (ENG.). 72p. (J). (gr. 5). pap. 9.95 *(978-1-4114-7909-8(2)*, Spark Publishing Group) Sterling Publishing Co., Inc.

—Monsterland: A Scary Counting Book. 2019. (Search, Find, & Count Ser.). (ENG.). 56p. (J). (gr. 1). pap. 9.95 *(978-88-544-1525-6(1))* White Star ITA. Dist: Sterling Publishing Co., Inc.

—My Circle Book. 2018. (My First Book Ser.). (ENG.). 20p. (J). (— 1). bds. 6.95 *(978-88-544-1225-5(2))* White Star ITA. Dist: Sterling Publishing Co., Inc.

—My Rectangle Book. 2018. (My First Book Ser.). (ENG.). 20p. (J). (— 1). bds. 6.95 *(978-88-544-1226-2(0))* White Star ITA. Dist: Sterling Publishing Co., Inc.

—My Square Book. 2018. (My First Book Ser.). (ENG.). 20p. (J). (— 1). bds. 6.95 *(978-88-544-1227-9(9))* White Star ITA. Dist: Sterling Publishing Co., Inc.

—My Triangle Book. 2018. (My First Book Ser.). (ENG.). 20p. (J). (— 1). bds. 6.95 *(978-88-544-1228-6(7))* White Star ITA. Dist: Sterling Publishing Co., Inc.

Baruzzi, Agnese. Pet Faces/Caras de Mascotas. 2020. (My First Puzzle Book Ser.). (ENG.). 14p. (J). (— 1). bds. 8.95 ***(978-88-544-1598-0(7))*** White Star ITA. Dist: Sterling Publishing Co., Inc.

Baruzzi, Agnese. Preschool Practice: A Collection of Skill-Building Activities. Piroddi, Chiara. 2018. (Montessori Method Ser.: 12). (ENG.). 128p. (J). (gr. -1-k). pap. 19.95 *(978-1-4549-3180-5(9))* Sterling Publishing Co., Inc.

—Tales of Mystery & Magic. Lupton, Hugh & Barefoot Books. 2015. 64p. (J). (gr. -1-2). 16.99 *(978-1-78285-254-4(9))* Barefoot Bks., Inc.

—Tales of Mystery & Magic. Lupton, Hugh. 2010. (ENG.). 64p. (J). (gr. 3-18). 19.99 *(978-1-84686-258-8(2))* Barefoot Bks., Inc.

—Who's Hiding? Little Bee Books. 2015. (ENG.). 16p. (J). (gr. -1-1). 9.99 *(978-1-4998-0168-2(8))* Little Bee Books Inc.

Baruzzi, Agnese. Wild Faces/Caras Salvajes. 2020. (My First Puzzle Book Ser.). (ENG.). 14p. (J). (— 1). bds. 8.95 ***(978-88-544-1599-7(5))*** White Star ITA. Dist: Sterling Publishing Co., Inc.

Baruzzi, Agnese. Big Size Surprise. Baruzzi, Agnese. 2017. (ENG.). 20p. (J). (-k). bds. 12.99 *(978-988-8341-50-4(2)*, Minedition) Neugebauer, Michael (Publishing) Limited HKG. Dist: Penguin Random Hse. LLC.

—Dinosaur Surprise. Baruzzi, Agnese. 2020. (Yonezu Board Book Ser.). 20p. (J). (gr. -1-k). bds. 11.99 *(978-988-8341-95-5(2)*, Minedition) Neugebauer, Michael (Publishing) Limited HKG. Dist: Penguin Random Hse. LLC.

—Opposites: A Cut-Paper Book. Baruzzi, Agnese. 2013. (ENG.). 10p. (J). (— 1). 15.99 *(978-1-85707-803-9(9))* Tango Bks. GBR. Dist: Independent Pubs. Group.

—Play with Me. Baruzzi, Agnese. 2019. (ENG.). 24p. (J). (gr. -1-k). pap. 9.99 *(978-988-8341-71-9(5)*, Minedition) Neugebauer, Michael (Publishing) Limited HKG. Dist: Penguin Random Hse. LLC.

—Turnabout Shapes. Baruzzi, Agnese. 2019. 30p. (J). (gr. k-1). bds. 11.99 *(978-988-8341-82-5(0)*, Minedition) Neugebauer, Michael (Publishing) Limited HKG. Dist: Penguin Random Hse. LLC.

Baruzzi, Agnese, jt. illus. see Natalini, Sandro.

Basaluzzo, Constanza. The Baby Bible ABCs, 1 vol. Currie, Robin. ed. 2009. (Baby Bible Ser.). (ENG.). 48p. (J). bds. 12.99 *(978-1-4347-6542-0(3)*, 106166) Cook, David C.

—The Baby Bible Storybook for Boys. Currie, Robin. ed. 2008. (Baby Bible Ser.). (ENG.). 46p. (J). bds. 12.99 *(978-0-7814-3501-7(3)*, 105593) Cook, David C.

—The Baby Bible Storybook for Girls. David C. Cook Publishing Company Staff & Currie, Robin. ed. 2008. (Baby Bible Ser.). (ENG.). 46p. (J). bds. 12.99 *(978-1-4347-6783-7(3)*, 106062) Cook, David C.

—Caleb's Hanukkah. Bullard, Lisa. 2012. (Cloverleaf Books (tm) — Fall & Winter Holidays Ser.). (ENG.). 24p. (J). (gr. k-2). lib. bdg. 25.32 *(978-0-7613-5077-4(2)*, 9780761350774, Millbrook Pr.) Lerner Publishing Group.

—Emma's Easter. Bullard, Lisa. 2012. (Holidays & Special Days Ser.). 24p. (J). (gr. k-2). pap. 39.62 *(978-0-7613-9248-4(3)*, Millbrook Pr.) Lerner Publishing Group.

—Kevin's Kwanzaa. Bullard, Lisa. 2012. (Cloverleaf Books (tm) — Fall & Winter Holidays Ser.). (ENG.). 24p. (J). (gr. k-2). 7.99 *(978-0-7613-8588-2(6)*, 9780761385882, Millbrook Pr.) Lerner Publishing Group.

—My Family Celebrates Hanukkah. Bullard, Lisa. 2018. (Holiday Time (Early Bird Stories (tm)) Ser.). (ENG.). 24p. (J). (gr. k-2). 27.99 *(978-1-5415-2006-6(8)*, Lerner Pubns.) Lerner Publishing Group.

—My Family Celebrates Kwanzaa. Bullard, Lisa. 2018. (Holiday Time (Early Bird Stories (tm)) Ser.). (ENG.). 24p. (J). (gr. k-2). 27.99 *(978-1-5415-2011-0(4)*, Lerner Pubns.) Lerner Publishing Group.

—Old MacDonald. 2019. (Nursery Rhyme Board Bks.). (ENG.). 10p. bds. 5.99 *(978-1-68446-114-1(6)*, 141956, Capstone Editions) Capstone.

—Sarah's Passover. Bullard, Lisa. 2012. (Holidays & Special Days Ser.). 24p. (J). (gr. k-2). pap. 39.62 *(978-0-7613-9245-3(9))*; (ENG.). lib. bdg. 25.32 *(978-0-7613-5081-1(0)*, 9780761350811); Vol. (ENG.). pap. 8.99 *(978-0-7613-8582-0(7)*, 9780761385820) Lerner Publishing Group. (Millbrook Pr.).

—Wheels on the Bus. 2019. (Nursery Rhyme Board Bks.). (ENG.). 10p. bds. 5.99 *(978-1-68446-115-8(4)*, 141958, Capstone Editions) Capstone.

Bascle, Brian. The Adventures of Marco Polo, 1 vol. Smalley, Roger. 2005. (Graphic History Ser.). (ENG.). 32p. (J). (gr. 3-9). per. 8.10 *(978-0-7368-5240-1(9)*, Capstone Pr.) Capstone.

—Las Aventuras de Marco Polo. Smalley, Roger. 2006. (Historia Gráficas Ser.). (SPA.). 32p. (J). (gr. 3-9). 31.32 *(978-0-7368-6054-3(1))* Capstone.

—How to Draw Incredible Cars, 1 vol. Sautter, Aaron. 2007. (Drawing Cool Stuff Ser.). (ENG.). 32p. (J). (gr. 3-9). 28.65 *(978-1-4296-0077-4(2)*, Capstone Pr.) Capstone.

—John F. Kennedy: American Visionary, 1 vol. Olson, Nathan. 2007. (Graphic Biographies Ser.). (ENG.). 32p. (J). (gr. 3-9). per. 8.10 *(978-0-7368-7904-0(8)*, 1264943) Capstone.

—Liberty, 1 vol. Collins, Terry. 2009. (Cartoon Nation Ser.). (ENG.). 32p. (J). (gr. 3-9). lib. bdg. 31.32 *(978-1-4296-2340-7(3)*, Capstone Pr.) Capstone.

—Muhammad Ali: American Champion, 1 vol. Burgan, Michael. 2008. (Graphic Biographies Ser.). (ENG.). 32p. (J). (gr. 3-9). per. 8.10 *(978-1-4296-1771-0(3)*, Capstone Pr.) Capstone.

—Paul Revere's Ride. Niz, Xavier & Niz, Xavier W. 2005. (Graphic History Ser.). (ENG.). 32p. (J). (gr. 3-9). 31.32 *(978-0-7368-4965-4(3))* Capstone.

—The Salem Witch Trials, 1 vol. Martin, Michael. 2005. (Graphic History Ser.). (ENG.). 32p. (J). (gr. 3-9). per. 8.10 *(978-0-7368-5246-3(8)*, Capstone Pr.) Capstone.

—Women's Right to Vote, 1 vol. Collins, Terry. 2009. (Cartoon Nation Ser.). (ENG.). 32p. (J). (gr. 3-9). lib. bdg. 31.32 *(978-1-4296-2341-4(1)*, Capstone Pr.) Capstone.

Bascle, Brian, jt. illus. see Carter, Greg.

Bascle, Brian, jt. illus. see Kamerer, Justin.

Bascon, Pedro. Ruby-Rose: Band 14/Ruby (Collins Big Cat), Bd. 14. Foxley, Janet. 2015. (Collins Big Cat Ser.). (ENG.). 48p. (J). (gr. 3-4). pap. 11.99 *(978-0-00-812779-4(4))* HarperCollins Pubs. Ltd. GBR. Dist: Independent Pubs. Group.

Base, Graeme. Eye to Eye. Base, Graeme. 2015. 42p. (J). (gr. -1-1). 24.99 *(978-0-670-07859-2(X))* Random Hse. Australia AUS. Dist: Independent Pubs. Group.

Baseman, Gary. Strong Stuff: Herakles & His Labors. Harris, John. 2005. (ENG.). 32p. (J). (gr. 3-7). 16.95 *(978-0-89236-784-9(9))* Oxford Univ. Pr., Inc.

Basford, Johanna. The Jungle Book. Kipling, Rudyard. 2013. (Vintage Children's Classics Ser.). (ENG.). 256p. (J). (gr. 4-7). pap. 10.99 *(978-0-09-957302-9(4))* Penguin Random Hse. GBR. Dist: Independent Pubs. Group.

Bash, Barbara. Shadows of Night: The Hidden World of the Little Brown Bat, 1 vol. Bash, Barbara. ed. 2004. (ENG.). 32p. (J). (gr. -1-3). pap. 7.95 *(978-0-87156-440-5(8))* Sierra Club Bks. for Children.

Basher, Simon. Basher Civics: Democracy Rules! Weber, Shannon. 2020. (ENG.). 96p. (J). 14.99 *(978-0-7534-7627-7(4)*, 900226417); pap. 9.99 *(978-0-7534-7626-0(6)*, 900226418) Roaring Brook Pr. (Kingfisher).

—Basher Geography: Countries of the World: An Atlas with Attitude. Budzik, Mary. 2018. (Basher Ser.). (ENG.). 200p. (J). 16.99 *(978-0-7534-7378-8(X)*, 900183603); pap. 11.99 *(978-0-7534-7379-5(8)*, 900183604) Roaring Brook Pr. (Kingfisher).

—Basher STEM Junior: Engineering. O'Callaghan, Jonathan. 2020. (Basher Ser.). (ENG.). 96p. (J). 14.99 *(978-0-7534-7560-7(X)*, 900214720); pap. 8.99 *(978-0-7534-7556-0(1)*, 900211741) Roaring Brook Pr. (Kingfisher).

—Basher STEM Junior: Math. O'Callaghan, Jonathan. 2020. (ENG.). 96p. (J). 14.99 *(978-0-7534-7561-4(8)*, 900214718); pap. 8.99 *(978-0-7534-7557-7(X)*, 900211742) Roaring Brook Pr. (Kingfisher).

—Basher STEM Junior: Science. O'Callaghan, Jonathan. 2020. (Basher Ser.). (ENG.). 96p. (J). 14.99 *(978-0-7534-7558-4(8)*, 900214719); pap. 8.99 *(978-0-7534-7554-6(5)*, 900211739) Roaring Brook Pr. (Kingfisher).

—Basher STEM Junior: Technology. O'Callaghan, Jonathan. 2020. (Basher Ser.). (ENG.). 96p. (J). 14.99 *(978-0-7534-7559-1(6)*, 900214716); pap. 8.99 *(978-0-7534-7555-3(3)*, 900211740) Roaring Brook Pr. (Kingfisher).

—Coding with Basher: Code Your Own Website. The Coder School. 2019. (ENG.). 96p. (J). 14.99 *(978-0-7534-7511-9(1)*, 900207864); pap. 9.99 *(978-0-7534-7512-6(X)*, 900207865) Roaring Brook Pr. (Kingfisher).

—Coding with Basher: Coding with Scratch. The Coder School. 2019. (ENG.). 96p. (J). 14.99 *(978-0-7534-7509-6(X)*, 900207862); pap. 9.99 *(978-0-7534-7510-2(3)*, 900207863) Roaring Brook Pr. (Kingfisher).

—Superstars of History. Field, Jacob & Grant, R. J. 2014. (ENG.). 96p. (J). (gr. 3-7). pap. 7.99 *(978-0-545-68024-0(7)*, Scholastic Paperbacks) Scholastic, Inc.

—Superstars of Science. Grant, R. G. 2015. (ENG.). 96p. (J). (gr. 3-7). pap. 7.99 *(978-0-545-82627-3(6)*, Scholastic Paperbacks) Scholastic, Inc.

Basher, Simon. Algebra & Geometry: Anything but Square! Basher, Simon. 2011. (Basher Science Ser.). (ENG.). 128p. (J). (gr. 5-9). pap. 8.99 *(978-0-7534-6597-4(3)*, 900074679, Kingfisher) Roaring Brook Pr.

—Astronomy: Out of This World! Basher, Simon. Green, Dan. 2009. (Basher Science Ser.). (ENG.). 128p. (J). (gr. 5-9). pap. 9.99 *(978-0-7534-6290-4(7)*, 900056024, Kingfisher) Roaring Brook Pr.

—Basher Basics: Creative Writing. Basher, Simon. Budzik, Mary. 2013. (Basher Basics Ser.). (ENG.). 64p. (J). (gr. 3-7). pap. 8.99 *(978-0-7534-7055-8(1)*, 9780753470558, Kingfisher) Roaring Brook Pr.

—Basher Basics: Grammar. Basher, Simon. Budzik, Mary. 2011. (Basher Basics Ser.). (ENG.). 64p. (J). (gr. 3-7). pap. 8.99 *(978-0-7534-6596-7(5)*, 900074678, Kingfisher) Roaring Brook Pr.

—Basher Basics: Space Exploration. Basher, Simon. 2019. (Basher Basics Ser.). (ENG.). 64p. (J). 12.99 *(978-0-7534-7507-2(3)*, 900201812); pap. 8.99 *(978-0-7534-7506-5(5)*, 900201771) Roaring Brook Pr. (Kingfisher).

—Basher Basics: Weather: Whipping up a Storm! Basher, Simon. Green, Dan. 2012. (Basher Basics Ser.). (ENG.). 64p. (J). (gr. 3-7). pap. 8.99 *(978-0-7534-6826-5(3)*, 900081920, Kingfisher) Roaring Brook Pr.

—Basher Science: Extreme Biology: From Superbugs to Clones ... Get to the Edge of Science. Basher, Simon. 2013. (Basher Science Ser.). (ENG.). 64p. (J). (gr. 5-9). pap. 9.99 *(978-0-7534-7050-3(0)*, 900118213, Kingfisher) Roaring Brook Pr.

—Basher Science: Extreme Physics. Basher, Simon. 2013. (Basher Science Ser.). (ENG.). 64p. (J). (gr. 5-9). pap. 9.99 *(978-0-7534-6956-9(1)*, 900088071, Kingfisher) Roaring Brook Pr.

—Basher Science: Microbiology. Basher, Simon. Green, Dan. 2015. (Basher Science Ser.). (ENG.). 128p. (J). (gr. 5-9). pap. 9.99 *(978-0-7534-7194-4(9)*, 900146975, Kingfisher) Roaring Brook Pr.

—Basher Science: the Complete Periodic Table: All the Elements with Style! Basher, Simon. Dingle, Adrian & Green, Dan. 2015. (Basher Science Ser.). (ENG.). 192p. (J). (gr. 5-9). pap. 11.99 *(978-0-7534-7197-5(3)*, 900139963, Kingfisher) Roaring Brook Pr.

—Basher Science: the Complete Periodic Table: All the Elements with Style. Basher, Simon. Dingle, Adrian & Green, Dan. 2015. (Basher Science Ser.). (ENG.). 192p. (J). (gr. 5-9). 16.99 *(978-0-7534-7196-8(5)*, 9780753471968, Kingfisher) Roaring Brook Pr.

—Biology: Life as We Know It! Basher, Simon. Green, Dan. 2008. (Basher Science Ser.). (ENG.). 128p. (J). (gr. 5-9). pap. 8.99 *(978-0-7534-6253-9(2)*, 900054393, Kingfisher) Roaring Brook Pr.

—Chemistry: Getting a Big Reaction! Basher, Simon. Green, Dan. 2010. (Basher Science Ser.). (ENG.). 128p. (J). (gr. 5-9). pap. 8.99 *(978-0-7534-6413-7(6)*, 900066947, Kingfisher) Roaring Brook Pr.

—Dinosaurs: The Bare Bones! Basher, Simon. Green, Dan. 2012. (Basher Basics Ser.). (ENG.). 64p. (J). (gr. 3-7). 12.99 *(978-0-7534-6823-4(9)*, 9780753468234); pap. 8.99 *(978-0-7534-6824-1(7)*, 900081852) Roaring Brook Pr. (Kingfisher).

—Human Body: A Book with Guts! Basher, Simon. Green, Dan. 2011. (Basher Science Ser.). (ENG.). 128p. (J). (gr. 5-10). pap. 8.99 *(978-0-7534-6501-1(9)*, 9780753465011, Kingfisher) Roaring Brook Pr.

—Math: A Book You Can Count On! Basher, Simon. Green, Dan. 2010. (Basher Basics Ser.). (ENG.). 64p. (J). (gr. 3-7). pap. 8.99 *(978-0-7534-6419-9(5)*, 900066948, Kingfisher) Roaring Brook Pr.

—Oceans: Making Waves! Basher, Simon. Green, Dan. 2012. (Basher Science Ser.). (ENG.). 128p. (J). (gr. 5-9). pap. 9.99 *(978-0-7534-6822-7(0)*, 900081821, Kingfisher) Roaring Brook Pr.

—The Periodic Table: Elements with Style! Basher, Simon. Dingle, Adrian. 2007. (Basher Science Ser.). (ENG.). 128p. (J). (gr. 5-9). pap. 8.99 *(978-0-7534-6085-6(8)*, 9780753460856, Kingfisher) Roaring Brook Pr.

—Physics: Why Matter Matters! Basher, Simon. Green, Dan. 2008. (Basher Science Ser.). (ENG.). 128p. (J). (gr. 5-9). pap. 9.99 *(978-0-7534-6214-0(1)*, 900053352, Kingfisher) Roaring Brook Pr.

—Planet Earth: What Planet Are You On? Basher, Simon. Gilpin, Daniel. 2010. (Basher Science Ser.). (ENG.). 128p. (J). (gr. 5-9). pap. 9.99 *(978-0-7534-6412-0(8)*, 900066946, Kingfisher) Roaring Brook Pr.

—Punctuation: The Write Stuff! Basher, Simon. Budzik, Mary. 2010. (Basher Basics Ser.). (ENG.). 64p. (J). (gr. 3-7). pap. 7.99 *(978-0-7534-6420-5(9)*, 900066949, Kingfisher) Roaring Brook Pr.

—Rocks & Minerals: A Gem of a Book! Basher, Simon. Green, Dan. 2009. (Basher Science Ser.). (ENG.). 128p. (J). (gr. 5-9). pap. 9.99 *(978-0-7534-6314-7(8)*, 900059036, Kingfisher) Roaring Brook Pr.

—Technology: A Byte-Sized World! Basher, Simon. Green, Dan. 2012. (Basher Science Ser.). (ENG.). 128p. (J). (gr. 5-9). pap. 8.99 *(978-0-7534-6820-3(4)*, 900081818, Kingfisher) Roaring Brook Pr.

Basic, Zdenko. Steampunk: Charles Dickens a Christmas Carol. 2014. 204p. (gr. 7). 18.95 *(978-0-7624-5090-9(8)*, Running Pr.) Running Pr.

—Steampunk: H. G. Wells. 2013. 408p. (YA). (gr. 7-17). 18.95 *(978-0-7624-4444-1(4)*, Running Pr. Kids) Running Pr.

Basic, Zdenko & Sumberac, Manuel. The Night Before Christmas. Moore, Clement C. 2014. (J). *(978-1-4351-6188-7(2))* Barnes & Noble, Inc.

Basil, Aviel. Being Me from a to Z, Vol. Kukla, Lauren. 2019. (ENG.). 32p. (J). (gr. -1-3). 17.99 *(978-1-5064-5259-3(0)*, Beaming Books) Augsburg Fortress, Pubs.

—Long-Haired Cat-Boy Cub. Keret, Etgar. Silverston, Sondra, tr. 2020. 32p. (J). (gr. -1-1). 18.95 *(978-1-60980-931-7(9)*, Triangle Square) Seven Stories Pr.

—Sticker World - Museum, 1 vol. Wilson, Becky & Lonely Planet Kids. 2018. (Sticker World Ser.). (ENG.). 40p. (J). (gr. 1-3). pap. 6.99 *(978-1-78701-135-9(6)*, 5697) Lonely Planet Global Ltd. IRL. Dist: Hachette Bk. Group.

—Sticker World - Theme Park, 1 vol. Wilson, Becky & Lonely Planet Kids. 2018. (Sticker World Ser.). (ENG.). 40p. (J). (gr. 1-3). pap. 6.99 *(978-1-78701-137-3(2)*, 5699) Lonely Planet Global Ltd. IRL. Dist: Hachette Bk. Group.

—Sticker World - Zoo, 1 vol. Wilson, Becky & Lonely Planet Kids. 2018. (Sticker World Ser.). (ENG.). 40p. (J). (gr. 1-3). pap. 6.99 *(978-1-78701-139-7(9)*, 5701) Lonely Planet Global Ltd. IRL. Dist: Hachette Bk. Group.

Basil, Cory. The Orchard of Hope. Neftzger, Amy. 2017. (J). 29.99 *(978-1-940894-22-5(0)*, Fog Ink) Fields of Gold Publishing, Inc.

—The War of Words. Neftzger, Amy. 2017. 320p. (J). pap. 19.99 *(978-1-940894-26-3(3)*, Fog Ink) Fields of Gold Publishing, Inc.

Basil, Edward. My Mama's Milk. Brown, Kawani Aj. 2016. (ENG.). (J). pap. 12.95 *(978-0-9971763-1-5(8))* Brown, Kawani.

Basile, Javier. El Cine No Fue Siempre Asi. Cerda, Marcelo. 2006. (Cosas No Fueron Siempre Asi Ser.). (SPA.). 38p. (J). pap. *(978-987-1217-10-6(2))* lamique, Ediciones.

—Preguntas que Ponen los Pelos de Punta: Sobre el Aqua y el Fuego. Baredes, Carla & Lotersztain, Ileana. 2004. (SPA.). pap. *(978-987-98042-1-6(X))* lamique, Ediciones.

—Preguntas que Ponen los Pelos de Punta: Sobre la Tierra y el Sol. Baredes, Carla & Lotersztain, Ileana. 2004. (SPA.). pap. *(978-987-98042-0-9(1))* lamique, Ediciones.

Baskey, Kim. Wispy Willy. Hanny, Diane. 2011. 24p. pap. 12.00 *(978-1-4520-9975-0(8))* AuthorHouse.

Baskin, Lyle. The Christmas Bus. Inman, Robert. 2006. 77p. 19.95 *(978-0-9760963-6-8(6))* Novello Festival Pr.

Basova, Xenia. Amo a Mi Papá. Zapple, Elias. Terán, Camila Ayala, tr. 2020. (Cuentos para Dormir Ser.: Vol. 4). (SPA.). 32p. (J). pap. ***(978-1-912704-49-1(8))*** Heads or Tales Pr.

—I Love My Daddy. Zapple, Elias. 2020. (I Love Bedtime Stories Ser.: Vol. 4). (ENG.). 32p. (J). pap. ***(978-1-912704-47-7(1))*** Heads or Tales Pr.

—J'aime Mon Papa. Zapple, Elias. Blanchet, Jean-François, tr. 2020. (J'Aime les Contes du Soir Ser.: Vol. 4). (FRE.). 32p. (J). pap. ***(978-1-912704-48-4(X))*** Heads or Tales Pr.

—わたしはおとうさんがすき Zapple, Elias. Kondo, Katsunori, tr. 2020. (JPN.). 32p. (J). pap. ***(978-1-912704-51-4(X))*** Heads or Tales Pr.

—我爱我的爸爸 Zapple, Elias. 刘全国, tr. 2020. (CHI.). 32p. (J). pap. ***(978-1-912704-71-2(4))*** Heads or Tales Pr.

Bass, Jennifer Vogel, photos by. Edible Colors: See, Learn, Eat. Bass, Jennifer Vogel. (ENG.). (J). 2016. 30p. bds. 8.99 *(978-1-62672-284-2(6)*, 900148613); 2014. 32p. (gr. -1-k). 12.99 *(978-1-62672-002-2(9)*, 900129637) Roaring Brook Pr.

Bass, Milton. Magical Days of Fairies & Friendship. Foland, M. S. Pamela. 2017. (ENG.). (J). pap. 10.89 *(978-0-9990745-4-1(7))* Sonny's Legacy Publishing.

Bass, Patricia A. Adalyn & Elliott Solve the Mystery of the Blue Ghosts. Bass, Robert D. 2018. (Adventures of Adalyn & Elliott Ser.: Vol. 1). (ENG.). 26p. (J). (gr. 1-4). pap. 9.68 *(978-0-692-09813-4(5))* Bass, Robert Enterprises.

—Adalyn y Elliott Resuelven el Misterio de Los Fantasmas Azules. Bass, Robert D. 2019. (SPA.). 26p. (J). (gr. 1-4). pap. 9.68 *(978-0-578-52952-3(1))* Bass, Robert Enterprises.

Bass, Rachel. Pamela's Plan. Noble, Kate. (Zoo Stories Ser.). 32p. (J). (gr. -1-4). 15.95 *(978-0-9631798-4-5(5))* Salmon Run Pr.

Bass, Saul. Henri's Walk to Paris. 2012. (ENG.). 48p. (J). (gr. k-4). 19.95 *(978-0-7893-2263-0(3))* Universe Publishing.

Bassa. El Saltamontes y Las Hormigas. Bailer, Darice et al. 2007. (SPA & ENG.). 28p. (J). *(978-0-545-02965-0(1))* Scholastic, Inc.

Bassani, Srimalie. Amira's Family. Riley, Elliot. 2017. (All Kinds of Families Ser.). (ENG.). 24p. (gr. -1-2). 29.93 *(978-1-68342-318-8(6)*, 9781683423188) Rourke Educational Media.

—Beauregard in a Box. Hutchings, Jessica Lee. 2018. (ENG.). 32p. (J). (gr. 1-3). 16.99 *(978-1-4867-1384-4(X)*, 3e771763-6589-4070-bc69-15b95416f5a2) Flowerpot Pr.

Bassani, Srimalie. Being Like Bella: (Frankie & Peaches: Tales of Total Kindness Book 4) French, Lisa S. 2019. (Frankie & Peaches: Tales of Total Kindness Ser.: Vol. 4). (ENG.). 36p. (J). (gr. k-4). 17.95 ***(978-1-948751-02-5(X))***; pap. 10.95 ***(978-1-948751-03-2(8))*** Favorite World Pr. LLC.

Bassani, Srimalie. Ben's Family. Riley, Elliot. 2017. (All Kinds of Families Ser.). (ENG.). 24p. (gr. -1-2). 29.93 *(978-1-68342-316-4(X)*, 9781683423164); pap. 8.95 *(978-1-68342-412-3(3)*, 9781683424123) Rourke Educational Media.

—The Clean-Up Crew. Coyle, Finn. (Finn's Fun Trucks Ser.). (ENG.). (J). (gr. k-2). 2019. 32p. 6.99 *(978-1-4867-1575-6(3)*, 11689a3c-a1d6-430c-9960-9f6f2a6689c9); 2018. 14p. bds. 8.99 *(978-1-4867-1388-2(2)*, 305b5676-a4e7-43c9-a673-f4800cdb98a1) Flowerpot Pr.

—The Construction Crew. Coyle, Finn. (Finn's Fun Trucks Ser.). (ENG.). (J). (gr. k-2). 2019. 32p. 6.99 *(978-1-4867-1574-9(5)*, 0df351b8-54e2-4e07-a879-927350afa4b6); 2018. 14p. bds. 8.99 *(978-1-4867-1387-5(4)*, 2b01608c-f9fe-4171-8e9e-69f0e0cc3bd5) Flowerpot Pr.

—The Dinosaur Museum. Rosen, Robert. 2017. (Field Trip Fun Ser.). (ENG.). 24p. (gr. -1-2). 29.93 *(978-1-68342-736-0(X)*, 9781683427360); pap. 8.95 *(978-1-68342-788-9(2)*, 9781683427889) Rourke Educational Media.

—Farm Fleet. Coyle, Finn. (Finn's Fun Trucks Ser.). (ENG.). (J). (gr. k-2). 2019. 32p. 6.99 *(978-1-4867-1577-0(X)*, d4dd16ed-56cb-4bb1-9509-7f49276d8fd4); 2018. 14p. bds. 8.99 *(978-1-4867-1488-9(9)*, c9521355-98b5-4239-91e6-4bcf303a2462) Flowerpot Pr.

—Friendly Fliers. Coyle, Finn. 2019. (Finn's Fun Trucks Ser.). (ENG.). (J). (gr. k-2). 32p. 6.99 *(978-1-4867-1580-0(X)*, d4535e9b-21c8-464b-b7d0-3eb68817c1c3); 14p. bds. 8.99 *(978-1-4867-1548-0(6)*, 6579cfb0-c857-445c-afbc-e2aea2123355) Flowerpot Pr.

—Heavy Haulers. Coyle, Finn. 2019. (Finn's Fun Trucks Ser.). (ENG.). (J). (gr. k-2). 32p. 6.99 *(978-1-4867-1789-7(6)*, f50e1f6b-c692-497b-b3fa-16114cb02831); 14p. bds. 8.99 *(978-1-4867-1647-0(4)*, 0370b7e1-3e90-4615-8fa1-d358a2efba7b) Flowerpot Pr.

—How Do Bridges Not Fall Down? A Book about Architecture & Engineering. Shand, Jennifer. (How Do? Ser.). (ENG.). 32p. (J). (gr. 2-5). 2019. 6.99 *(978-1-4867-1469-8(2)*, 676ec9e8-90e7-41e1-897a-e85cf42b5d7d); 2018. 9.99 *(978-1-4867-1485-8(4)*, 312ea465-065d-4415-9912-b7f4eb59a93b) Flowerpot Pr.

—How Do Computers Follow Instructions? A Book about Programming. Liso, J. T. 2019. (How Do? Ser.). (ENG.). 32p. (J). (gr. 1-3). 9.99 *(978-1-4867-1652-4(0)*, 1402c9e0-6f4b-463f-8671-414963b499f6); 6.99

B

(978-1-4867-1791-0(8), de2ed72d-4a8b-43eb-86bf-abcc9b10c7eb) Flowerpot Pr.

—How Do Molecules Stay Together? Hayes, Madeline J. 2019. (How Do? Ser.). (ENG.). 32p. (J). (gr. 1-3). 6.99 *(978-1-4867-1790-3(X),* 9830eef0-8ac1-43fc-a863-c62b26155cd2) Flowerpot Pr.

—How Do Molecules Stay Together? Hayes, Madeline J. 2019. (How Do? Ser.). (ENG.). 32p. (J). (gr. 1-3). 9.99 *(978-1-4867-1651-7(2),* 4cce5a80-962d-4dbd-aad6-482b7cf8f4a0) Flowerpot Pr.

—How Do Seesaws Go up & Down? A Book about Simple Machines. Shand, Jennifer. (How Do? Ser.). (ENG.). 32p. (J). (gr. 1-3). 2019. 6.99 *(978-1-4867-1468-1(4),* 677e47a4-c3f5-4b39-8694-ccbd3c8b8058); 2018. 9.99 *(978-1-4867-1486-5(2),* cf3adfe6-5c21-4be0-954a-ecc9c4e58132) Flowerpot Pr.

Bassani, Srimalie. How Does Soap Clean Your Hands? The Science Behind Healthy Habits. Hayes, Madeline J. 2020. (How Do Ser.). (ENG.). 32p. (J). (gr. 1-3). 6.99 ***(978-1-4867-2074-3(9),*** d878c169-816b-4968-b9e0-aaeebc6f8c6e); 9.99 ***(978-1-4867-2073-6(0),*** 0580dd5a-1131-4d54-9f08-e3eea6960fbc) Flowerpot Pr.

Bassani, Srimalie. I Saw Santa in Albuquerque. Green, J. D. 2018. (I Saw Santa Ser.). (ENG.). 32p. (J). (-3). 12.99 *(978-1-4926-6830-5(3),* Sourcebooks Jabberwocky) Sourcebooks, Inc.

—I Saw Santa in Arizona. Green, J. D. 2018. (I Saw Santa Ser.). (ENG.). 32p. (J). (-3). 12.99 *(978-1-4926-6831-2(1),* Sourcebooks Jabberwocky) Sourcebooks, Inc.

—I Saw Santa in California. Green, J. D. 2018. (I Saw Santa Ser.). (ENG.). 32p. (J). (-3). 12.99 *(978-1-4926-6835-0(4),* Sourcebooks Jabberwocky) Sourcebooks, Inc.

—I Saw Santa in Georgia. Green, J. D. 2018. (I Saw Santa Ser.). (ENG.). 32p. (J). (-3). 12.99 *(978-1-4926-6844-2(3),* Sourcebooks Jabberwocky) Sourcebooks, Inc.

—I Saw Santa in Los Angeles. Green, J. D. 2018. (I Saw Santa Ser.). (ENG.). 32p. (J). (-3). 12.99 *(978-1-4926-6854-1(0),* Sourcebooks Jabberwocky) Sourcebooks, Inc.

—I Saw Santa in Maryland. Green, J. D. 2018. (I Saw Santa Ser.). (ENG.). 32p. (J). (-3). 12.99 *(978-1-4926-6857-2(5),* Sourcebooks Jabberwocky) Sourcebooks, Inc.

—I Saw Santa in New England. Green, J. D. 2018. (I Saw Santa Ser.). (ENG.). 32p. (J). (-3). 12.99 *(978-1-4926-6867-1(2),* Sourcebooks Jabberwocky) Sourcebooks, Inc.

—Jing's Family. Riley, Elliot. 2017. (All Kinds of Families Ser.). (ENG.). 24p. (gr. -1-1). 29.93 *(978-1-68342-145-0(0),* 9781683421450); pap. 8.95 *(978-1-68342-187-0(6),* 9781683421870) Rourke Educational Media.

—Kindergarten Seasons. James, Lauren & Kisloski, Carolyn. 2017. (School Days Ser.). (ENG.). 24p. (gr. -1-2). pap. 8.95 *(978-1-68342-786-5(6),* 9781683427865) Rourke Educational Media.

—Levi's Family. Riley, Elliot. 2017. (All Kinds of Families Ser.). (ENG.). 24p. (gr. -1-2). 29.93 *(978-1-68342-317-1(8),* 9781683423171); pap. 8.95 *(978-1-68342-413-0(1),* 9781683424130) Rourke Educational Media.

—Mail Movers. Coyle, Finn. 2019. (Finn's Fun Trucks Ser.). (ENG.). (J). (gr. k-2). 32p. 6.99 *(978-1-4867-1788-0(8),* 86ad5257-dc70-4d53-a12f-f471201bd1b5); 14p. bds. 8.99 *(978-1-4867-1648-7(2),* f66e7626-55a1-463e-8e4f-7d0c61de496f) Flowerpot Pr.

—MIA's Family. Riley, Elliot. 2017. (All Kinds of Families Ser.). (ENG.). 24p. (gr. -1-2). 29.93 *(978-1-68342-315-7(1),* 9781683423157) Rourke Educational Media.

—Miguel's Family. Riley, Elliot. 2017. (All Kinds of Families Ser.). (ENG.). 24p. (gr. -1-1). 29.93 *(978-1-68342-147-4(7),* 9781683421474) Rourke Educational Media.

—Owen's Family. Riley, Elliot. 2017. (All Kinds of Families Ser.). (ENG.). 24p. (gr. -1-1). pap. 8.95 *(978-1-68342-190-0(6),* 9781683421900) Rourke Educational Media.

Bassani, Srimalie. The Pancake Girl: (Frankie & Peaches: Tales of Total Kindness Book 1) French, Lisa S. 2019. (Frankie & Peaches: Tales of Total Kindness Ser.: Vol. 1). (ENG.). 34p. (J). (gr. k-4). 17.95 ***(978-1-948751-00-1(3));*** pap. 10.95 ***(978-1-948751-01-8(1))*** Favorite World Pr. LLC.

—A Place Made for We: (Frankie & Peaches: Tales of Total Kindness Book 5) French, Lisa S. 2019. (Frankie & Peaches: Tales of Total Kindness Ser.: Vol. 5). (ENG.). 36p. (J). (gr. k-4). 17.95 ***(978-1-948751-08-7(9));*** pap. 10.95 ***(978-1-948751-09-4(7))*** Favorite World Pr. LLC.

Bassani, Srimalie. Rapid Responders. Coyle, Finn. (Finn's Fun Trucks Ser.). (ENG.). (J). (gr. k-2). 2019. 32p. 6.99 *(978-1-4867-1576-3(1),* 6030ab36-e024-4944-8184-e0873e840f71); 2018. 14p. bds. 8.99 *(978-1-4867-1487-2(0),* e2233484-2b5b-4799-a8c9-1d979dd03740) Flowerpot Pr.

—Red Light, Green Light. Taylor, Michael. 2017. (I Help My Friends Ser.). (ENG.). 24p. (gr. -1-2). pap. 8.95 *(978-1-68342-767-4(X),* 9781683427674) Rourke Educational Media.

Bassani, Srimalie. The Smile Machine: (Frankie & Peaches: Tales of Total Kindness Book 3) French, Lisa S. 2019. (Frankie & Peaches: Tales of Total Kindness Ser.: Vol. 3). (ENG.). 36p. (J). (gr. k-4). 17.95 ***(978-1-948751-06-3(2));*** pap. 10.95 ***(978-1-948751-07-0(0))*** Favorite World Pr. LLC.

Bassani, Srimalie. Sonya's Family. Riley, Elliot. 2017. (All Kinds of Families Ser.). (ENG.). 24p. (gr. -1-1). 29.93 *(978-1-68342-146-7(9),* 9781683421467) Rourke Educational Media.

—Space Squad. Coyle, Finn. 2019. (Finn's Fun Trucks Ser.). (ENG.). (J). (gr. k-2). 32p. 6.99 *(978-1-4867-1579-4(6),* 12eddd4b-3ed8-447e-8d82-eb83a195cadb); 14p. bds. 8.99 *(978-1-4867-1549-7(4),* 4d65684a-0566-4bfa-a625-cd268403da62) Flowerpot Pr.

—This Raindrop: Has a Billion Stories to Tell. Ragsdale, Linda. 2020. (ENG.). 40p. (J). (gr. k-2). 16.99 *(978-1-4867-1817-7(5),* b413b74d-cd5f-4134-88be-532752086c7b) Flowerpot Pr.

—Treasure Hunt. James, Lauren & Kisloski, Carolyn. 2017. (Field Trip Fun Ser.). (ENG.). 24p. (gr. -1-2). pap. 8.95 *(978-1-68342-791-9(2),* 9781683427919) Rourke Educational Media.

—A Trip to Grandma's House. Wallace, John & Kisloski, Carolyn. 2017. (Family Time Ser.). (ENG.). 24p. (gr. -1-2). pap. 8.95 *(978-1-68342-756-8(4),* 9781683427568) Rourke Educational Media.

Bassani, Srimalie. The Upside-Down Boys: (Frankie & Peaches: Tales of Total Kindness Book 2) French, Lisa S. 2019. (Frankie & Peaches: Tales of Total Kindness Ser.: Vol. 2). (ENG.). 34p. (J). (gr. k-4). 17.95 ***(978-1-948751-04-9(6));*** pap. 10.95 ***(978-1-948751-05-6(4))*** Favorite World Pr. LLC.

—Waiting Together. Dufayet, Danielle. 2020. (ENG.). 32p. (J). (gr. -1-4). 16.99 ***(978-0-8075-0279-2(0),*** 0807502790) Whitman, Albert & Co.

Bassani, Srimalie. Wally & Molly Go to the Beach. Rosen, Robert. 2017. (I Help My Friends Ser.). (ENG.). 24p. (gr. -1-2). pap. 8.95 *(978-1-68342-779-7(3),* 9781683427797) Rourke Educational Media.

—What Can I Make? Wallace, John & Kisloski, Carolyn. 2017. (Play Time Ser.). (ENG.). 24p. (gr. -1-2). 29.93 *(978-1-68342-706-3(8),* 9781683427063); pap. 8.95 *(978-1-68342-758-2(0),* 9781683427582) Rourke Educational Media.

—Where Is Santa? Wells, Robin. 2017. (My Adventures Ser.). (ENG.). 24p. (gr. -1-2). 29.93 *(978-1-68342-719-3(X),* 9781683427193); pap. 8.95 *(978-1-68342-771-1(8),* 9781683427711) Rourke Educational Media.

Bassani, Srimalie & Sarell, Nadja. I Saw Santa. Green, J. D. 2018. (I Saw Santa Ser.). (ENG.). 32p. (J). (-3). 12.99 *(978-1-4926-6827-5(3),* Sourcebooks Jabberwocky) Sourcebooks, Inc.

—I Saw Santa in Alabama. Green, J. D. 2018. (I Saw Santa Ser.). (ENG.). 32p. (J). (-3). 12.99 *(978-1-4926-6828-2(1),* Sourcebooks Jabberwocky) Sourcebooks, Inc.

—I Saw Santa in Alaska. Green, J. D. 2018. (I Saw Santa Ser.). (ENG.). 32p. (J). (-3). 12.99 *(978-1-4926-6829-9(X),* Sourcebooks Jabberwocky) Sourcebooks, Inc.

—I Saw Santa in Arkansas. Green, J. D. 2018. (I Saw Santa Ser.). (ENG.). 32p. (J). (-3). 12.99 *(978-1-4926-6832-9(X),* Sourcebooks Jabberwocky) Sourcebooks, Inc.

—I Saw Santa in Boston. Green, J. D. 2018. (I Saw Santa Ser.). (ENG.). 32p. (J). (-3). 12.99 *(978-1-4926-6833-6(8),* Sourcebooks Jabberwocky) Sourcebooks, Inc.

—I Saw Santa in Buffalo. Green, J. D. 2018. (I Saw Santa Ser.). (ENG.). 32p. (J). (-3). 12.99 *(978-1-4926-7244-9(0),* Sourcebooks Jabberwocky) Sourcebooks, Inc.

—I Saw Santa in Calgary. Green, J. D. 2018. (I Saw Santa Ser.). (ENG.). 32p. (J). (-3). 12.99 *(978-1-4926-6834-3(6),* Sourcebooks Jabberwocky) Sourcebooks, Inc.

—I Saw Santa in Canada. Green, J. D. 2018. (I Saw Santa Ser.). (ENG.). 32p. (J). (-3). 12.99 *(978-1-4926-6836-7(2),* Sourcebooks Jabberwocky) Sourcebooks, Inc.

—I Saw Santa in Chicago. Green, J. D. 2018. (I Saw Santa Ser.). (ENG.). 32p. (J). (-3). 12.99 *(978-1-4926-6837-4(0),* Sourcebooks Jabberwocky) Sourcebooks, Inc.

—I Saw Santa in Colorado. Green, J. D. 2018. (I Saw Santa Ser.). (ENG.). 32p. (J). (-3). 12.99 *(978-1-4926-6839-8(7),* Sourcebooks Jabberwocky) Sourcebooks, Inc.

—I Saw Santa in Connecticut. Green, J. D. 2018. (I Saw Santa Ser.). (ENG.). 32p. (J). (-3). 12.99 *(978-1-4926-6840-4(0),* Sourcebooks Jabberwocky) Sourcebooks, Inc.

—I Saw Santa in Delaware. Green, J. D. 2018. (I Saw Santa Ser.). (ENG.). 32p. (J). (-3). 12.99 *(978-1-4926-6841-1(9),* Sourcebooks Jabberwocky) Sourcebooks, Inc.

—I Saw Santa in Edmonton. Green, J. D. 2018. (I Saw Santa Ser.). (ENG.). 32p. (J). (-3). 12.99 *(978-1-4926-6842-8(7),* Sourcebooks Jabberwocky) Sourcebooks, Inc.

—I Saw Santa in Florida. Green, J. D. 2018. (I Saw Santa Ser.). (ENG.). 32p. (J). (-3). 12.99 *(978-1-4926-6843-5(5),* Sourcebooks Jabberwocky) Sourcebooks, Inc.

—I Saw Santa in Hawaii. Green, J. D. 2018. (I Saw Santa Ser.). (ENG.). 32p. (J). (-3). 12.99 *(978-1-4926-6845-9(1),* Sourcebooks Jabberwocky) Sourcebooks, Inc.

—I Saw Santa in Idaho. Green, J. D. 2018. (I Saw Santa Ser.). (ENG.). 32p. (J). (-3). 12.99 *(978-1-4926-6846-6(X),* Sourcebooks Jabberwocky) Sourcebooks, Inc.

—I Saw Santa in Illinois. Green, J. D. 2018. (I Saw Santa Ser.). (ENG.). 32p. (J). (-3). 12.99 *(978-1-4926-6847-3(8),* Sourcebooks Jabberwocky) Sourcebooks, Inc.

—I Saw Santa in Indiana. Green, J. D. 2018. (I Saw Santa Ser.). (ENG.). 32p. (J). (-3). 12.99 *(978-1-4926-6848-0(6),* Sourcebooks Jabberwocky) Sourcebooks, Inc.

—I Saw Santa in Iowa. Green, J. D. 2018. (I Saw Santa Ser.). (ENG.). 32p. (J). (-3). 12.99 *(978-1-4926-6849-7(4),* Sourcebooks Jabberwocky) Sourcebooks, Inc.

—I Saw Santa in Kansas. Green, J. D. 2018. (I Saw Santa Ser.). (ENG.). 32p. (J). (-3). 12.99 *(978-1-4926-6850-3(8),* Sourcebooks Jabberwocky) Sourcebooks, Inc.

—I Saw Santa in Kansas City. Green, J. D. 2018. (I Saw Santa Ser.). (ENG.). 32p. (J). (-3). 12.99 *(978-1-4926-6851-0(6),* Sourcebooks Jabberwocky) Sourcebooks, Inc.

—I Saw Santa in Kentucky. Green, J. D. 2018. (I Saw Santa Ser.). (ENG.). 32p. (J). (-3). 12.99 *(978-1-4926-6852-7(4),* Sourcebooks Jabberwocky) Sourcebooks, Inc.

—I Saw Santa in Las Vegas. Green, J. D. 2018. (I Saw Santa Ser.). (ENG.). 32p. (J). (-3). 12.99 *(978-1-4926-6853-4(2),* Sourcebooks Jabberwocky) Sourcebooks, Inc.

—I Saw Santa in Louisiana. Green, J. D. 2018. (I Saw Santa Ser.). (ENG.). 32p. (J). (-3). 12.99 *(978-1-4926-6855-8(9),* Sourcebooks Jabberwocky) Sourcebooks, Inc.

—I Saw Santa in Maine. Green, J. D. 2018. (I Saw Santa Ser.). (ENG.). 32p. (J). (-3). 12.99 *(978-1-4926-6856-5(7),* Sourcebooks Jabberwocky) Sourcebooks, Inc.

—I Saw Santa in Massachusetts. Green, J. D. 2018. (I Saw Santa Ser.). (ENG.). 32p. (J). (-3). 12.99 *(978-1-4926-6858-9(3),* Sourcebooks Jabberwocky) Sourcebooks, Inc.

—I Saw Santa in Michigan. Green, J. D. 2018. (I Saw Santa Ser.). (ENG.). 32p. (J). (-3). 12.99 *(978-1-4926-6859-6(1),* Sourcebooks Jabberwocky) Sourcebooks, Inc.

—I Saw Santa in Minnesota. Green, J. D. 2018. (I Saw Santa Ser.). (ENG.). 32p. (J). (-3). 12.99 *(978-1-4926-6860-2(5),* Sourcebooks Jabberwocky) Sourcebooks, Inc.

—I Saw Santa in Mississippi. Green, J. D. 2018. (I Saw Santa Ser.). (ENG.). 32p. (J). (-3). 12.99 *(978-1-4926-6861-9(3),* Sourcebooks Jabberwocky) Sourcebooks, Inc.

—I Saw Santa in Missouri. Green, J. D. 2018. (I Saw Santa Ser.). (ENG.). 32p. (J). (-3). 12.99 *(978-1-4926-6862-6(1),* Sourcebooks Jabberwocky) Sourcebooks, Inc.

—I Saw Santa in Montana. Green, J. D. 2018. (I Saw Santa Ser.). (ENG.). 32p. (J). (-3). 12.99 *(978-1-4926-6863-3(X),* Sourcebooks Jabberwocky) Sourcebooks, Inc.

—I Saw Santa in Nebraska. Green, J. D. 2018. (I Saw Santa Ser.). (ENG.). 32p. (J). (-3). 12.99 *(978-1-4926-6864-0(8),* Sourcebooks Jabberwocky) Sourcebooks, Inc.

—I Saw Santa in Nevada. Green, J. D. 2018. (I Saw Santa Ser.). (ENG.). 32p. (J). (-3). 12.99 *(978-1-4926-6865-7(6),* Sourcebooks Jabberwocky) Sourcebooks, Inc.

—I Saw Santa in New Jersey. Green, J. D. 2018. (I Saw Santa Ser.). (ENG.). 32p. (J). (-3). 12.99 *(978-1-4926-6869-5(9),* Sourcebooks Jabberwocky) Sourcebooks, Inc.

—I Saw Santa in New Mexico. Green, J. D. 2018. (I Saw Santa Ser.). (ENG.). 32p. (J). (-3). 12.99 *(978-1-4926-6870-1(2),* Sourcebooks Jabberwocky) Sourcebooks, Inc.

—I Saw Santa in New York. Green, J. D. 2018. (I Saw Santa Ser.). (ENG.). 32p. (J). (-3). 12.99 *(978-1-4926-6871-8(0),* Sourcebooks Jabberwocky) Sourcebooks, Inc.

—I Saw Santa in New York City. Green, J. D. 2018. (I Saw Santa Ser.). (ENG.). 32p. (J). (-3). 12.99 *(978-1-4926-6872-5(9),* Sourcebooks Jabberwocky) Sourcebooks, Inc.

—I Saw Santa in Newfoundland. Green, J. D. 2018. (I Saw Santa Ser.). (ENG.). 32p. (J). (-3). 12.99 *(978-1-4926-6866-4(4),* Sourcebooks Jabberwocky) Sourcebooks, Inc.

—I Saw Santa in North Carolina. Green, J. D. 2018. (I Saw Santa Ser.). (ENG.). 32p. (J). (-3). 12.99 *(978-1-4926-6873-2(7),* Sourcebooks Jabberwocky) Sourcebooks, Inc.

—I Saw Santa in North Dakota. Green, J. D. 2018. (I Saw Santa Ser.). (ENG.). 32p. (J). (-3). 12.99 *(978-1-4926-6874-9(5),* Sourcebooks Jabberwocky) Sourcebooks, Inc.

—I Saw Santa in Nova Scotia. Green, J. D. 2018. (I Saw Santa Ser.). (ENG.). 32p. (J). (-3). 12.99 *(978-1-4926-6875-6(3),* Sourcebooks Jabberwocky) Sourcebooks, Inc.

—I Saw Santa in Ohio. Green, J. D. 2018. (I Saw Santa Ser.). (ENG.). 32p. (J). (-3). 12.99 *(978-1-4926-6876-3(1),* Sourcebooks Jabberwocky) Sourcebooks, Inc.

—I Saw Santa in Oklahoma. Green, J. D. 2018. (I Saw Santa Ser.). (ENG.). 32p. (J). (-3). 12.99 *(978-1-4926-6877-0(X),* Sourcebooks Jabberwocky) Sourcebooks, Inc.

—I Saw Santa in Oregon. Green, J. D. 2018. (I Saw Santa Ser.). (ENG.). 32p. (J). (-3). 12.99 *(978-1-4926-6878-7(8),* Sourcebooks Jabberwocky) Sourcebooks, Inc.

—I Saw Santa in Ottawa. Green, J. D. 2018. (I Saw Santa Ser.). (ENG.). 32p. (J). (-3). 12.99 *(978-1-4926-6879-4(6),* Sourcebooks Jabberwocky) Sourcebooks, Inc.

—I Saw Santa in Pennsylvania. Green, J. D. 2018. (I Saw Santa Ser.). (ENG.). 32p. (J). (-3). 12.99 *(978-1-4926-6880-0(X),* Sourcebooks Jabberwocky) Sourcebooks, Inc.

—I Saw Santa in Pittsburgh. Green, J. D. 2018. (I Saw Santa Ser.). (ENG.). 32p. (J). (-3). 12.99 *(978-1-4926-6882-4(6),* Sourcebooks Jabberwocky) Sourcebooks, Inc.

—I Saw Santa in San Francisco. Green, J. D. 2018. (I Saw Santa Ser.). (ENG.). 32p. (J). (-3). 12.99 *(978-1-4926-6884-8(2),* Sourcebooks Jabberwocky) Sourcebooks, Inc.

—I Saw Santa in South Dakota. Green, J. D. 2018. (I Saw Santa Ser.). (ENG.). 32p. (J). (-3). 12.99 *(978-1-4926-6886-2(9),* Sourcebooks Jabberwocky) Sourcebooks, Inc.

—I Saw Santa in St. Louis. Green, J. D. 2018. (I Saw Santa Ser.). (ENG.). 32p. (J). (-3). 12.99 *(978-1-4926-6887-9(7),* Sourcebooks Jabberwocky) Sourcebooks, Inc.

—I Saw Santa in Toronto. Green, J. D. 2018. (I Saw Santa Ser.). (ENG.). 32p. (J). (-3). 12.99 *(978-1-4926-6890-9(7),* Sourcebooks Jabberwocky) Sourcebooks, Inc.

—I Saw Santa in Utah. Green, J. D. 2018. (I Saw Santa Ser.). (ENG.). 32p. (J). (-3). 12.99 *(978-1-4926-6891-6(5),* Sourcebooks Jabberwocky) Sourcebooks, Inc.

—I Saw Santa in Vancouver. Green, J. D. 2018. (I Saw Santa Ser.). (ENG.). 32p. (J). (-3). 12.99 *(978-1-4926-6892-3(3),* Sourcebooks Jabberwocky) Sourcebooks, Inc.

—I Saw Santa in Vermont. Green, J. D. 2018. (I Saw Santa Ser.). (ENG.). 32p. (J). (-3). 12.99 *(978-1-4926-6893-0(1),* Sourcebooks Jabberwocky) Sourcebooks, Inc.

—I Saw Santa in Virginia. Green, J. D. 2018. (I Saw Santa Ser.). (ENG.). 32p. (J). (-3). 12.99 *(978-1-4926-6894-7(X),* Sourcebooks Jabberwocky) Sourcebooks, Inc.

—I Saw Santa in Washington. Green, J. D. 2018. (I Saw Santa Ser.). (ENG.). 32p. (J). (-3). 12.99 *(978-1-4926-6895-4(8),* Sourcebooks Jabberwocky) Sourcebooks, Inc.

—I Saw Santa in Washington DC. Green, J. D. 2018. (I Saw Santa Ser.). (ENG.). 32p. (J). (-3). 12.99 *(978-1-4926-6896-1(6),* Sourcebooks Jabberwocky) Sourcebooks, Inc.

—I Saw Santa in West Virginia. Green, J. D. 2018. (I Saw Santa Ser.). (ENG.). 32p. (J). (-3). 12.99 *(978-1-4926-6897-8(4),* Sourcebooks Jabberwocky) Sourcebooks, Inc.

—I Saw Santa in Wisconsin. Green, J. D. 2018. (I Saw Santa Ser.). (ENG.). 32p. (J). (-3). 12.99 *(978-1-4926-6898-5(2),* Sourcebooks Jabberwocky) Sourcebooks, Inc.

—I Saw Santa in Wyoming. Green, J. D. 2018. (I Saw Santa Ser.). (ENG.). 32p. (J). (-3). 12.99 *(978-1-4926-6899-2(0),* Sourcebooks Jabberwocky) Sourcebooks, Inc.

Bassani, Srimalle. Monsters. Ahmed, Suhel. 2015. (Doodle Magic Ser.). (ENG.). 64p. (J). (gr. k). spiral bd. 14.95 *(978-1-62686-478-8(0),* Silver Dolphin Bks.) Readerlink Distribution Services, LLC.

—Princesses. Ahmed, Suhel. Silver Dolphin Staff, ed. 2015. (Doodle Magic Ser.). (ENG.). 64p. (J). (gr. k). spiral bd. 14.95 *(978-1-62686-479-5(9),* Silver Dolphin Bks.) Readerlink Distribution Services, LLC.

Basseches, K. B., photos by. ABeCedarios: Mexican Folk Art ABCs in English & Spanish. Weill, Cynthia. 2008. (First Concepts in Mexican Folk Art Ser.). (ENG., 32p. (J). (gr. k — 1). 14.95 *(978-1-933693-13-2(4))* Cinco Puntos Pr.

Bassett, Jeni. The Biggest Christmas Tree Ever. Kroll, Steven. (StoryPlay Ser.). (ENG.). (J). (gr. -1-k). 2017. 40p. 5.99 *(978-1-338-18735-9(X));* 2009. 32p. pap. 4.99 *(978-0-545-12119-4(1))* Scholastic, Inc. (Cartwheel Bks.).

—The Biggest Pumpkin Ever. Kroll, Steven. 2007. (ENG.). 32p. (J). (gr. -1-k). pap. 4.99 *(978-0-439-92946-2(6))* Scholastic, Inc.

—The Biggest Pumpkin Surprise Ever. Kroll, Steven. 2012. (ENG.). 10p. (J). (gr. -1-k). 6.99 *(978-0-545-40285-9(9),* Cartwheel Bks.) Scholastic, Inc.

—The Biggest Snowman Ever. Kroll, Steven. 2005. (ENG.). 32p. (J). (gr. -1-3). 4.99 *(978-0-439-62768-9(0),* Cartwheel Bks.) Scholastic, Inc.

—The Biggest Valentine Ever. Kroll, Steven. 2006. (ENG.). 32p. (J). (gr. -1-k). pap. 3.99 *(978-0-439-76419-3(X))* Scholastic, Inc.

Bassett, Madge A. At Bumblebee Farm. Bassett, Madge A. 2009. 20p. pap. 13.46 *(978-1-4251-9230-3(0))* Trafford Publishing.

Basso, Bill. Beware! It's Friday the 13th. McMullan, Kate. 2005. (Dragon Slayers' Academy Ser.: 13). 112p. (J). (gr. 2-5). pap. 5.99 *(978-0-448-43531-2(4),* Grosset & Dunlap) Penguin Young Readers Group.

—Class Trip to the Cave of Doom, 3 vols. McMullan, Kate. 2003. (Dragon Slayers' Academy Ser.: 3). (ENG.). 112p. (J). (gr. 2-5). pap. 5.99 *(978-0-448-43110-9(6),* Grosset & Dunlap) Penguin Young Readers Group.

—Class Trip to the Cave of Doom, 1 vol. McMullan, Kate. 2006. (Dragon Slayers' Academy Ser.: No. 3). (ENG.). 112p. (J). (gr. 2-6). 27.07 *(978-1-59961-123-5(6),* 5426, Chapter Bks.) Spotlight.

—Countdown to the Year 1000. McMullan, Kate. 2003. (Dragon Slayers' Academy Ser.: 8). 112p. (J). (gr. 2-5). pap. 5.99 *(978-0-448-43508-4(X),* Grosset & Dunlap) Penguin Young Readers Group.

—Countdown to the Year 1000, 1 vol. McMullan, Kate. 2007. (Dragon Slayers' Academy Ser.: No. 8). (ENG.). 107p. (J). (gr. 2-6). 27.07 *(978-1-59961-376-5(X),* 5432, Chapter Bks.) Spotlight.

—Danger! Wizard at Work, No. 11. McMullan, Kate. 2004. (Dragon Slayers' Academy Ser.: 11). 112p. (J). (gr. 2-5). pap. 5.99 *(978-0-448-43529-9(2),* Grosset & Dunlap) Penguin Young Readers Group.

—Double Dragon Trouble. McMullan, Kate. 2005. (Dragon Slayers' Academy Ser.: 15). 112p. (J). (gr. 2-5). pap. 5.99 *(978-0-448-43821-4(6),* Grosset & Dunlap) Penguin Young Readers Group.

—The Ghost of Sir Herbert Dungeonstone, 1 vol. McMullan, Kate. 2006. (Dragon Slayers' Academy Ser.: No. 12). (ENG.). 112p. (J). (gr. 2-6). 27.07 *(978-1-59961-124-2(4),* 5427, Chapter Bks.) Spotlight.

—The Ghost of Sir Herbert Dungeonstone #12. McMullan, Kate. 2004. (Dragon Slayers' Academy Ser.: 12). (ENG.). 112p. (J). (gr. 2-5). pap. 5.99 *(978-0-448-43530-5(6),* Grosset & Dunlap) Penguin Young Readers Group.

—Hail! Hail! Camp Dragononka! McMullan, Kate. 2006. (Dragon Slayers' Academy Ser.: 17). 224p. (J). (gr. 2-5). pap. 6.99 *(978-0-448-44124-5(1),* Grosset & Dunlap) Penguin Young Readers Group.

—Help! It's Parent's Day at DSA. McMullan, Kate. 2004. (Dragon Slayers' Academy Ser.: 10). 112p. (J). (gr. 2-5). pap. 5.99 *(978-0-448-43220-5(X),* Grosset & Dunlap) Penguin Young Readers Group.

—Help! It's Parent's Day at DSA, 1 vol. McMullan, Kate. 2006. (Dragon Slayers' Academy Ser.: No. 10). (ENG.). 112p. (J). (gr. 2-6). 27.07 *(978-1-59961-125-9(2),* 5428, Chapter Bks.) Spotlight.

—Knight for a Day, 5. McMullan, Kate. 2003. (Dragon Slayer's Academy Ser.: 5). (ENG.). 109p. (J). (gr. 2-4). 17.44 *(978-0-448-43277-9(3))* Penguin Young Readers Group.

—Knight for a Day, 1 vol. McMullan, Kate. 2007. (Dragon Slayers' Academy Ser.: No. 5). (ENG.). 109p. (J). (gr. 2-6). 27.07 *(978-1-59961-377-2(8),* 5433, Chapter Bks.) Spotlight.

—Little Giant-Big Trouble. McMullan, Kate. 2007. (Dragon Slayers' Academy Ser.: 19). 112p. (J). (gr. 2-5). pap. 5.99 *(978-0-448-44448-2(8),* Grosset & Dunlap) Penguin Young Readers Group.

—Never Trust a Troll!, 18. McMullan, Kate. 2006. (Dragon Slayer's Academy Ser.: 18). 112p. (J). (gr. 2-4). 17.44 *(978-0-448-44393-5(7))* Penguin Young Readers Group.

—The New Kid at School, 1 vol. McMullan, Kate. 2006. (Dragon Slayers' Academy Ser.: No. 1). (ENG.). 112p. (J). (gr. 2-6). 27.07 *(978-1-59961-126-6(0),* 5429, Chapter Bks.) Spotlight.

—The New Kid at School #1. McMullan, Kate. 2003. (Dragon Slayers' Academy Ser.: 1). (ENG.). 112p. (J). (gr. 2-5). mass mkt. 5.99 *(978-0-448-43108-6(4),* Grosset & Dunlap) Penguin Young Readers Group.

—Pig Latin - Not Just for Pigs! McMullan, Kate. 2005. (Dragon Slayers' Academy Ser.: 14). 112p. (J). (gr. 2-5). pap. 5.99 *(978-0-448-43820-7(8),* Grosset & Dunlap) Penguin Young Readers Group.

—Pig Latin - Not Just for Pigs! McMullan, Kate. 2006. (Dragon Slayers' Academy Ser.: No. 14). (ENG.). 112p. (J). (gr. 2-6). 27.07 *(978-1-59961-127-3(9),* 5430, Chapter Bks.) Spotlight.

—Revenge of the Dragon Lady, 2 vols. McMullan, Kate. 2003. (Dragon Slayers' Academy Ser.: 2). (ENG.). 112p. (J). (gr. 2-5). mass mkt. 5.99 *(978-0-448-43109-3(2),* Grosset & Dunlap) Penguin Young Readers Group.

—Revenge of the Dragon Lady, 1 vol. McMullan, Kate. 2007. (Dragon Slayers' Academy Ser.: No. 2). (ENG.). 109p. (J). (gr. 2-6). 27.07 *(978-1-59961-378-9(6)*, 5434, Chapter Bks.) Spotlight.

—Sir Lancelot, Where Are You?, 1 vol. McMullan, Kate. 2007. (Dragon Slayers' Academy Ser.: No. 6). (ENG.). 109p. (J). (gr. 2-6). 27.07 *(978-1-59961-379-6(4)*, 5435, Chapter Bks.) Spotlight.

—Sir Lancelot, Where Are You? #6, 6. McMullan, Kate. 2003. (Dragon Slayers' Academy Ser.: 6). (ENG.). 112p. (J). (gr. 2-5). 5.99 *(978-0-448-43278-6(1)*, Grosset & Dunlap) Penguin Young Readers Group.

—Slime Time. Dadey, Debbie & Dadey, Nathan. 2004. 58p. (J). *(978-0-439-64362-7(7))* Scholastic, Inc.

—A Wedding for Wiglaf? McMullan, Kate. 2007. (Dragon Slayers' Academy Ser.: No. 4). (ENG.). 109p. (J). (gr. 2-6). 27.07 *(978-1-59961-380-2(8)*, 5436, Chapter Bks.) Spotlight.

—A Wedding for Wiglaf? #4, 4. McMullan, Kate. 2003. (Dragon Slayer's Academy Ser.: 4). 112p. (J). (gr. 2-4). 17.44 *(978-0-448-43111-6(4))* Penguin Young Readers Group.

—Wheel of Misfortune. McMullan, Kate. 2003. (Dragon Slayers' Academy Ser.: 7). 112p. (J). (gr. 2-5). pap. 5.99 *(978-0-448-43507-7(1)*, Grosset & Dunlap) Penguin Young Readers Group.

—Wheel of Misfortune, 1 vol. McMullan, Kate. 2007. (Dragon Slayers' Academy Ser.: No. 7). (ENG.). 109p. (J). (gr. 2-6). 27.07 *(978-1-59961-381-9(6)*, 5437, Chapter Bks.) Spotlight.

—World's Oldest Living Dragon. McMullan, Kate. 2006. (Dragon Slayers' Academy Ser.: 16). 112p. (J). (gr. 2-5). pap. 5.99 *(978-0-448-44112-2(8)*, Grosset & Dunlap) Penguin Young Readers Group.

—97 Ways to Train a Dragon. McMullan, Kate. 2003. (Dragon Slayers' Academy Ser.: 9). 112p. (J). (gr. 2-5). pap. 5.99 *(978-0-448-43177-2(7)*, Grosset & Dunlap) Penguin Young Readers Group.

Basta, Mary, jt. illus. see Liddell, Daniel.

Basta, Stormie. Grandma's Traditions. Wilson, Angela. 2012. 24p. pap. 24.95 *(978-1-4626-9410-5(1))* America Star Bks.

—My Aunt & Me. Wilson, Angela. 2012. 26p. 24.95 *(978-1-4626-6630-0(2))* America Star Bks.

—Tara the Terrified Turtle. Wilson, Angela. 2012. 28p. pap. 24.95 *(978-1-4626-7454-1(2))* America Star Bks.

Bastien, Valerie. Sing Out Loud Book II: Developing Your Voice. Hoops, Kevin, photos by. Vendera, Jaime & McGee, Anne Loader. 2012. 52p. (YA). pap. 7.99 *(978-1-936307-09-8(X))* Vendera Publishing.

—Sing Out Loud Book III: Owning Your Voice. Hoops, Kevin, photos by. Vendera, Jaime & McGee, Anne Loader. 2012. 44p. (YA). pap. 7.99 *(978-1-936307-10-4(3))* Vendera Publishing.

Bastien, Valerie & Bingham, Jerry. Sing Out Loud Book I: Discovering Your Voice. Hoops, Kevin, photos by. Vendera, Jaime & McGee, Anne Loader. 2012. 52p. (YA). pap. 7.99 *(978-1-936307-08-1(1))* Vendera Publishing.

Bastrykin, Viktor. Russkii Les: Roman. Sokolov-Mikitov, I. S. 2017. (RUS.). 94p. (J). *(978-5-699-69219-4(3))* EKSMO, Izdatel'stvo.

Basu, Suddhasattwa. Ka, the Story of Garuda: Based on the English Translation by Tim Parks of the Italian Original by Roberto Calasso. Calasso, Roberto & Parks, Tim. 2004. (J). *(978-81-89020-04-0(8))* Katha.

Basu, Sudipta & Roy, Avijit. Brayden's Birthday at the Ballpark. West, Jessica Marie. 2019. (Alliterative Alphabet Ser.: Vol. 2). (ENG.). 34p. (J). pap. 11.35 *(978-1-7292-8613-5(5))* Independently Published.

Basulto, Rita. De carta en Carta. MacHado, Ana Maria. 2004. (SPA.). 44p. (gr. 3-5). pap. 7.95 *(978-968-19-1483-7(X))* Santillana USA Publishing Co., Inc.

Bate, Helen. The Creature. Bate, Helen. 2017. (ENG.). 32p. (J). (gr. -1-k). 17.99 *(978-1-910959-14-5(6))* Otter-Barry Bks. GBR. Dist: Independent Pubs. Group.

Bates, Amy. Adventure: Lonely Leader. Stern, Ricki & Worcester, Heidi P. 2003. (Beryl E. Bean Ser.: No. 3). 64p. (J). lib. bdg. 16.89 *(978-0-06-028774-0(8))* HarperCollins Pubs.

—Donavan's Double Trouble. DeGross, Monalisa. 192p. (J). (gr. 2-5). 2008. lib. bdg. 16.89 *(978-0-06-077294-9(8))*; 2007. (ENG.). 16.99 *(978-0-06-077293-2(X))* HarperCollins Pubs. (Amistad).

—Minette's Feast: The Delicious Story of Julia Child & Her Cat. Reich, Susanna. 2012. (ENG.). 40p. (J). (gr. -1-2). 17.95 *(978-1-4197-0177-1(0)*, Abrams Bks. for Young Readers) Abrams, Inc.

—My Puppy's First Year. 2007. (ENG.). 24p. (gr. k-3). pap. 12.99 *(978-0-8249-5571-7(4)*, Ideal Pubns.) Worthy Publishing.

—Pumpkin Cat. Turner, Ann Warren. 2004. (ENG.). 32p. (gr. -1-2). 15.99 *(978-0-7868-0494-8(7))* Hyperion Pr.

—Rock-A-Bye Room. Meyers, Susan. 2013. (ENG.). 32p. (J). (gr. -1-k). 17.95 *(978-1-4197-0537-3(7)*, Abrams Bks. for Young Readers) Abrams, Inc.

—A Song for Aunt Polly. Twain, Mark. 2004. (Adventures of Tom Sawyer Ser.: Vol. 1). 32p. (J). *(978-0-7607-3963-1(3))* Barnes & Noble, Inc.

—The Story of Barbie (Barbie) Eagan, Cindy. 2017. (ENG.). 40p. (J). (gr. -1-3). lib. bdg. 20.99 *(978-1-5247-7058-7(2)*, Random Hse. Bks. for Young Readers) Random Hse. Children's Bks.

—Susan B. Anthony: Fighter for Women's Rights. Hopkinson, Deborah. 2005. 32p. (J). lib. bdg. 15.00 *(978-1-4242-1563-8(3))* Fitzgerald Bks.

Bates, Amy June. The Adventures of Tom Sawyer: A Song for Aunt Polly. Twain, Mark. 2007. (Easy Reader Classics Ser.). (ENG.). 32p. (J). (gr. k-3). lib. bdg. 27.07 *(978-1-59961-334-5(4)*, 6211) Spotlight.

—Applesauce Weather. Frost, Helen. 2016. 112p. (J). (gr. 3-7). 14.99 *(978-0-7636-7576-9(8))* Candlewick Pr.

—Applesauce Weather. Frost, Helen. 2018. 112p. (J). (gr. 3-7). pap. 6.99 *(978-1-5362-0361-5(0))* Candlewick Pr.

—The Brothers Kennedy: John, Robert, Edward. Krull, Kathleen. 2010. (ENG.). 40p. (J). (gr. -1-3). 16.99 *(978-1-4169-9158-8(1)*, Simon & Schuster Bks. For Young Readers) Simon & Schuster Bks. For Young Readers.

—Christian, the Hugging Lion. Richardson, Justin & Parnell, Peter. 2010. (ENG.). 32p. (J). (gr. -1-3). 16.99 *(978-1-4169-8662-1(6)*, Simon & Schuster Bks. For Young Readers) Simon & Schuster Bks. For Young Readers.

—Hillary Rodham Clinton: Dreams Taking Flight. Krull, Kathleen. 2015. (ENG.). 48p. (J). (gr. k-5). 17.99 *(978-1-4814-5113-0(8)*, Simon & Schuster Bks. For Young Readers) Simon & Schuster Bks. For Young Readers.

—I Will Rejoice: Celebrating Psalm 118. Wilson, Karma. 2007. (ENG.). 32p. (J). (gr. -1-3). 14.99 *(978-0-310-71117-9(7))* Zonderkidz.

Bates, Amy June. Joey: The Story of Joe Biden. Biden, Jill. 2020. (ENG.). 48p. (J). (gr. -1-3). 19.99 ***(978-1-5344-8053-7(6)***, Simon & Schuster/Paula Wiseman Bks.) Simon & Schuster/Paula Wiseman Bks.

Bates, Amy June. Ketzel, the Cat Who Composed. Newman, Lesléa. 2015. 40p. (J). (gr. k-3). 16.99 *(978-0-7636-6555-5(X))* Candlewick Pr.

—Loving Hands. Johnston, Tony. 2018. 32p. (J). (gr. -1-1). 16.99 *(978-0-7636-7993-4(3))* Candlewick Pr.

—Martin's Dream. Kurtz, Jane. 2008. (Ready-To-Read Level 1 Ser.). (ENG.). 32p. (J). (gr. -1-1). 16.19 *(978-1-4169-2774-7(3)*, Aladdin) Simon & Schuster Children's Publishing.

—Red Butterfly. Sonnichsen, A. L. 2015. (ENG.). 400p. (J). (gr. 3-7). 17.99 *(978-1-4814-1109-7(8))* Simon & Schuster, Inc.

—Sam the Man & the Cell Phone Plan. Dowell, Frances O'Roark. 2019. (Sam the Man Ser.: 5). (ENG.). 176p. (J). (gr. 1-4). 16.99 *(978-1-5344-1261-3(1))* Simon & Schuster Children's Publishing.

—Sam the Man & the Chicken Plan. Dowell, Frances O'Roark. (Sam the Man Ser.: 1). (ENG.). (J). (gr. 1-4). 2017. 144p. pap. 7.99 *(978-1-4814-4067-7(5))*; 2016. 128p. 16.99 *(978-1-4814-4066-0(7))* Simon & Schuster Children's Publishing.

—Sam the Man & the Dragon Van Plan. Dowell, Frances O'Roark. 2018. (Sam the Man Ser.: 3). (ENG.). 160p. (J). (gr. 1-4). 16.99 *(978-1-4814-4072-1(1)*, Atheneum/Caitlyn Dlouhy Books) Simon & Schuster Children's Publishing.

—Sam the Man & the Rutabaga Plan. Dowell, Frances O'Roark. (Sam the Man Ser.: 2). (ENG.). (J). (gr. 1-4). 2018. 144p. pap. 6.99 *(978-1-4814-4070-7(5)*, Atheneum Bks. for Young Readers); 2017. 128p. 16.99 *(978-1-4814-4069-1(1)*, Atheneum/Caitlyn Dlouhy Books) Simon & Schuster Children's Publishing.

—Sam the Man & the Secret Detective Club Plan. Dowell, Frances O'Roark. 2018. (Sam the Man Ser.: 4). (ENG.). 192p. (J). (gr. 1-4). 16.99 *(978-1-5344-1258-3(1)*, Atheneum/Caitlyn Dlouhy Books) Simon & Schuster Children's Publishing.

—The Story of Barbie & the Woman Who Created Her. Eagan, Cindy. 2017. (ENG.). 40p. (J). (gr. -1-3). 17.99 *(978-0-399-55378-3(9)*, Random Hse. Bks. for Young Readers) Random Hse. Children's Bks.

—Susan B. Anthony: Fighter for Women's Rights. Hopkinson, Deborah. 2005. (Ready-to-read SOFA Ser.). (ENG.). 32p. (J). (gr. 1-3). pap. 4.99 *(978-0-689-86909-9(6)*, Simon Spotlight) Simon Spotlight.

—Sweet Dreams. Jewel. 2013. (ENG.). 32p. (J). (gr. -1-k). 17.99 *(978-1-4424-8931-8(6)*, Simon & Schuster/Paula Wiseman Bks.) Simon & Schuster/Paula Wiseman Bks.

—That's What I'd Do. Jewel. 2012. (ENG.). 32p. (J). (gr. -1-k). 17.99 *(978-1-4424-5813-0(5)*, Simon & Schuster/Paula Wiseman Bks.) Simon & Schuster/Paula Wiseman Bks.

—Waiting for the Magic. MacLachlan, Patricia. (ENG.). (J). (gr. 3-7). 2012. 176p. pap. 6.99 *(978-1-4169-2746-4(8))*; 2011. 160p. 16.99 *(978-1-4169-2745-7(X))* Simon & Schuster Children's Publishing. (Atheneum Bks. for Young Readers).

—Wishworks, Inc. Tolan, Stephanie S. 2011. (ENG.). (J). (gr. 2-5). lib. bdg. 16.60 *(978-1-61383-361-2(X))* Perfection Learning Corp.

—Wishworks, Inc. Tolan, Stephanie S. 2011. (ENG.). 160p. (J). (gr. 2-5). pap. 5.99 *(978-0-545-03155-4(9)*, Levine, Arthur A. Bks.) Scholastic, Inc.

—You Can Do It! Dungy, Tony. 2008. (ENG.). 32p. (J). (gr. -1-2). 19.99 *(978-1-4169-5461-3(9)*, Little Simon Inspirations) Little Simon Inspirations.

Bates, Amy June. The Big Umbrella. Bates, Amy June. Bates, Juniper. 2018. (ENG.). 40p. (J). (gr. -1-3). 17.99 *(978-1-5344-0658-2(1)*, Simon & Schuster/Paula Wiseman Bks.) Simon & Schuster/Paula Wiseman Bks.

Bates, Amy June. La Sombrilla Grande (the Big Umbrella) Bates, Amy June. Bates, Juniper. Romay, Alexis, tr. 2020. (SPA.). 40p. (J). (gr. -1-3). 7.99 ***(978-1-5344-6844-3(7))***; 17.99 ***(978-1-5344-6843-6(9))*** Simon & Schuster/Paula Wiseman Bks. (Simon & Schuster/Paula Wiseman Bks.).

—When I Draw a Panda. Bates, Amy June. 2020. (ENG.). 40p. (J). (gr. -1-3). 17.99 ***(978-1-4814-5148-2(0)***, Simon & Schuster/Paula Wiseman Bks.) Simon & Schuster/Paula Wiseman Bks.

Bates, Ben, et al. DC Teen Titans Go! Fisch, Sholly et al. 2020. (DC Teen Titans Go! Ser.). (ENG.). (J). (gr. 2-6). 263.16 ***(978-1-4965-9951-3(9)***, 201392, Stone Arch Bks.) Capstone.

Bates, Ben. Mega Man 3: Return of Dr. Wily. Flynn, Ian. 2012. (Mega Man Ser.: 3). (ENG.). 112p. (J). (gr. 4-7). pap. 11.99 *(978-1-936975-11-2(4))* Archie Comic Pubns., Inc.

—Pinkie Pie, 1 vol. Anderson, Ted. 2015. (My Little Pony Ser.). (ENG.). 24p. (J). (gr. 1-8). 27.07 *(978-1-61479-333-5(6)*, 17155, Graphic Novels) Spotlight.

—Teenage Mutant Ninja Turtles Volume 5: Krang War, Vol. 5. Waltz, Tom & Eastman, Kevin B. 2013. (Teenage Mutant Ninja Turtles Ser.: 5). (ENG.). 104p. pap. 17.99 *(978-1-61377-640-7(3)*, 9781613776407) Idea & Design Works, LLC.

Bates, Ben & Corona, Jorge. Food Fright & Par for the Course. Fisch, Sholly & Hagan, Merrill. 2019. (DC Teen Titans Go! Ser.). (ENG.). 32p. (J). (gr. 2-6). lib. bdg. 21.93 *(978-1-4965-7993-5(3)*, 139824, Stone Arch Bks.) Capstone.

Bates, Ben, jt. illus. see Corona, Jorge.

Bates, Bill. Guide Me Home, Sunny. Written By Pamela McFarland; Illustrated. 2011. 44p. pap. 24.95 *(978-1-4560-8890-3(4))* America Star Bks.

Bates, Bob. Anna's Home by the River: A Children's History of Anaheim. Eastman, Gail. 2007. 199p. (J). pap. *(978-0-9797419-0-6(4))* Tesoro Publishing.

Bates, Brenda J., et al. My Little Pinto, 1 vol. Tessin, Kit Elaine. 2010. 26p. pap. 24.95 *(978-1-4489-9173-0(0))* PublishAmerica, Inc.

Bates, Delphine Branon & EsDesignStudio. Help Me Remember the Days of Creation. Bates, Delphine Branon. 2010. 24p. (J). 11.95 *(978-0-9799116-3-7(X))* LifeSong Pubs.

Bates, George. On a Windy Night. Day, Nancy Raines. 2010. (ENG.). 40p. (J). (gr. -1-3). 16.95 *(978-0-8109-3900-4(2)*, Abrams Bks. for Young Readers) Abrams, Inc.

Bates, Ivan. Coconut Comes to School. Doherty, Berlie. 2004. (ENG.). 32p. (J). (gr. k-2). 18.00 *(978-0-00-710433-8(2)*, HarperCollins Children's Bks.) HarperCollins Pubs. Ltd. GBR. Dist: Independent Pubs. Group.

—Do Like a Duck Does! Hindley, Judy. 2007. 40p. (J). (gr. -1-2). 4.99 *(978-0-7636-3284-7(8))* Candlewick Pr.

—Do Like a Duck Does! Hindley, Judy. 2007. (gr. -1-k). 15.00 *(978-0-7569-8127-3(1))* Perfection Learning Corp.

—Farmer Dale's Red Pickup Truck. Wheeler, Lisa. 2014. (ENG.). 32p. (J). (— 1). bds. 7.99 *(978-0-544-24765-9(5)*, 1566128, HMH Books For Young Readers) Houghton Mifflin Harcourt Publishing Co.

—Grandma Elephant's in Charge. Jenkins, Martin. 2014. (Read & Wonder Ser.). (ENG.). 32p. (J). (gr. k-3). 7.99 *(978-0-7636-7381-9(1))* Candlewick Pr.

—Grandma Elephant's in Charge. Jenkins, Martin. 2014. (ENG.). (J). (gr. k-3). lib. bdg. 17.60 *(978-1-62765-722-8(3))* Perfection Learning Corp.

—How Many Kisses Do You Want Tonight? Bajaj, Varsha. 2007. 32p. (J). (gr. -1 — 1). 6.99 *(978-0-316-06735-5(0))* Little, Brown Bks. for Young Readers.

—One Dark Night. Wheeler, Lisa. 2006. (ENG.). 32p. (J). (gr. -1-3). reprint ed. pap. 6.99 *(978-0-15-205888-3(5)*, 1197678) Houghton Mifflin Harcourt Publishing Co.

—There, There. McBratney, Sam. (ENG.). (J). 2015. 32p. (-k). bds. 7.99 *(978-0-7636-7565-3(2))*; 2013. 40p. (gr. -1-2). 15.99 *(978-0-7636-6702-3(1))* Candlewick Pr. (Templar).

Bates, Jean, jt. illus. see Martin, Marilyn.

Bates, Jeffrey. The Little Bucket: Deep Space Meeting. Bates, Jeffrey. 2015. (Full-Fillment Ser.: Vol. 2). (ENG.). 42p. (J). pap. 11.95 ***(978-1-7075-5762-2(4))*** Independently Published.

Bates, Lindsey E. & Wiggan, Desmond. Oh! I Wish. Roberts, Pauline. 2012. 24p. pap. 9.95 *(978-0-9848243-3-5(2))* Beckham Pubns. Co.

Batori, Susan. Beware the Mighty Bitey. Pindar, Heather. 2019. (ENG.). 32p. (J). (gr. -1-3). 17.99 *(978-1-84886-361-3(6))* Maverick Arts Publishing GBR. Dist: Lerner Publishing Group.

—Little Fennec Fox & Jerboa Turquoise Band. Whybrow, Ian. 2017. (Cambridge Reading Adventures Ser.). (ENG.). 16p. pap. 5.62 *(978-1-108-43092-0(9))* Cambridge Univ. Pr.

—Strictly No Crocs. Pindar, Heather. 2019. (Early Bird Readers — Blue (Early Bird Stories (tm)) Ser.). (ENG.). 32p. (J). (gr. -1-2). pap. 7.99 *(978-1-5415-4618-9(0))* Lerner Publishing Group.

—There Was a Black Hole That Swallowed the Universe. Ferrie, Chris. 2019. 40p. (J). (-3). 17.99 *(978-1-4926-8077-2(X)*, Sourcebooks Jabberwocky) Sourcebooks, Inc.

—Wanted! Criminals of the Animal Kingdom. Tekavec, Heather. 2020. (ENG.). 32p. (J). (gr. 1-4). 18.99 *(978-1-5253-0024-0(5))* Kids Can Pr., Ltd. CAN. Dist: Hachette Bk. Group.

Batori, Susan. Wild Symphony. Brown, Dan. 2020. (ENG.). 44p. (J). (gr. -1-2). 18.99 ***(978-0-593-12384-3(0))***; lib. bdg. 21.99 ***(978-0-593-12385-0(9))*** Random Hse. Children's Bks. (Rodale Kids).

Batra, Nancy. The Question Is Why? Yager, Jeff. 2016. (ENG.). (J). 24.95 *(978-1-938998-68-3(5))*; 38p. pap. 14.95 *(978-1-938998-69-0(3))* Hannacroix Creek Bks., Inc.

—Toys, Tools, Guns & Rules: A Children's Book about Gun Safety. Golob, Julie. 2018. (ENG.). 40p. (J). pap. 9.99 *(978-0-9996456-0-4(9))* Golob, Julie.

Batsel, Hannah. A Is for Another Rabbit. Batsel, Hannah. 2020. (ENG.). 32p. (J). (gr. -1-2). 17.99 *(978-1-5415-2950-2(2)*, Carolrhoda Bks.) Lerner Publishing Group.

Batson, Alan, et al. Ariel & the Big Baby: Rapunzel Finds a Friend. Koster, Amy Sky. 2017. (J). *(978-1-5379-1732-0(3))* Random Hse., Inc.

Batson, Alan. Baby Mcstuffins (Disney Junior: Doc Mcstuffins) Liberts, Jennifer. 2017. (Little Golden Book Ser.). (ENG.). 24p. (J). (-k). 4.99 *(978-0-7364-3567-3(0)*, Golden/Disney) Random Hse. Children's Bks.

—Branch's Bunker Birthday. Lewman, David. 2018. (J). *(978-1-5444-0208-6(2)*, Golden Bks.) Random Hse. Children's Bks.

—Doc Mcstuffins: Caught Blue-Handed. Higginson, Sheila Sweeny & Redeker, Kent. 2018. (World of Reading Level Pre-1 Ser.). (ENG.). 32p. (J). (gr. -1-2). lib. bdg. 27.07 *(978-1-5321-4177-5(7)*, 31059) Spotlight.

Batson, Alan. Dungeon Crawl! (Minecraft Woodsword Chronicles #5) Eliopulos, Nick. 2020. (Stepping Stone Book(TM) Ser.). (ENG.). 144p. (J). (gr. 1-4). 9.99 ***(978-1-9848-5065-2(2))***; 12.99 ***(978-1-9848-5066-9(0))*** Random Hse. Children's Bks. (Random Hse. Bks. for Young Readers).

Batson, Alan. Feels Like a Party! (DreamWorks Trolls) Random House & Layman, Barbara. 2019. 10p. (J). (— 1). 12.99 *(978-1-9848-5061-4(X)*, Random Hse. Bks. for Young Readers) Random Hse. Children's Bks.

—Ghast in the Machine! (Minecraft Woodsword Chronicles #4) Eliopulos, Nick. 2020. (Stepping Stone Book(TM) Ser.). (ENG.). 144p. (J). (gr. 1-4). 9.99 *(978-1-9848-5062-1(8)*, Random Hse. Bks. for Young Readers) Random Hse. Children's Bks.

—Ghostbusters (Ghostbusters) Sazaklis, John. 2016. (Little Golden Book Ser.). (ENG.). 24p. (J). (gr. -1-2). 4.99 *(978-1-5247-1489-5(5)*, Golden Bks.) Random Hse. Children's Bks.

—I Am a Pilot (Star Wars) Golden Books Staff. 2016. (Little Golden Book Ser.). (ENG.). 24p. (J). (-k). 4.99 *(978-0-7364-3621-2(9)*, Golden Bks.) Random Hse. Children's Bks.

—I Am Anna (Disney Frozen) Webster, Christy. 2020. (Little Golden Book Ser.). (ENG.). 24p. (J). (-k). 4.99 *(978-0-7364-4018-9(6)*, Golden/Disney) Random Hse. Children's Bks.

—I Am Dumbo (Disney Classic) Jordan, Apple. 2019. (Little Golden Book Ser.). (ENG.). 24p. (J). (-k). 4.99 *(978-0-7364-3933-6(1)*, Golden/Disney) Random Hse. Children's Bks.

—I Am Elsa (Disney Frozen) Webster, Christy. 2020. (Little Golden Book Ser.). (ENG.). 24p. (J). (-k). 4.99 *(978-0-7364-4016-5(X)*, Golden/Disney) Random Hse. Children's Bks.

—I Am Mulan (Disney Princess) Carbone, Courtney. 2020. (Little Golden Book Ser.). (ENG.). 24p. (J). (-k). 4.99 *(978-0-7364-4044-8(5)*, Golden/Disney) Random Hse. Children's Bks.

Batson, Alan. I Am Olaf (Disney Frozen) Webster, Christy. 2020. (Little Golden Book Ser.). (ENG.). 24p. (J). (-k). 5.99 ***(978-0-7364-4128-5(X)***, Golden/Disney) Random Hse. Children's Bks.

Batson, Alan. I Am Simba (Disney the Lion King) Sazaklis, John. 2019. (Little Golden Book Ser.). (ENG.). 24p. (J). (-k). 4.99 *(978-0-7364-3970-1(6)*, Golden/Disney) Random Hse. Children's Bks.

—I Am the Genie (Disney Aladdin) Sazaklis, John. 2019. (Little Golden Book Ser.). (ENG.). 24p. (J). (-k). 4.99 *(978-0-7364-3866-7(1)*, Golden/Disney) Random Hse. Children's Bks.

—Inside Out (Disney/Pixar Inside Out) Random House Disney Staff. 2016. (Little Golden Book Ser.). (ENG.). 24p. (J). (-k). 4.99 *(978-0-7364-3629-8(4)*, Golden/Disney) Random Hse. Children's Bks.

—Jake & the Neverland Pirates: X Marks the Croc! La Rose, Melinda. 2014. (World of Reading Level Pre-1 Ser.). (ENG.). 32p. (J). (gr. -1-2). lib. bdg. 27.07 *(978-1-61479-247-5(X)*, 1761) Spotlight.

—Star Wars: the Last Jedi (Star Wars) Schaefer, Elizabeth. 2018. (Little Golden Book Ser.). (ENG.). 24p. (J). (-k). 4.99 *(978-0-7364-3586-4(7)*, Golden Bks.) Random Hse. Children's Bks.

—We Are the Resistance (Star Wars) Schaefer, Elizabeth. 2019. (Little Golden Book Ser.). (ENG.). 24p. (J). (-k). 4.99 *(978-0-593-11836-8(7)*, Golden Bks.) Random Hse. Children's Bks.

Batson, Alan & Disney Storybook Artists Staff. Disney Princess: Dazzling Adventures. Acampora, Courtney. 2018. (ENG.). 16p. (J). (gr. -1-k). bds. 12.99 *(978-0-7944-4127-2(0))* Studio Fun International.

Batson, Alan & Laguna, Fabio. Trolls World Tour Big Golden Book (DreamWorks Trolls World Tour) Lewman, David. 2020. (Big Golden Book Ser.). (ENG.). 48p. (J). (gr. -1-2). 10.99 *(978-0-593-12791-9(9)*, Golden Bks.) Random Hse. Children's Bks.

Batson, Alan, jt. illus. see Disney Storybook Art Team.

Batson, Alan, jt. illus. see Golden Books.

Batson, Alan, jt. illus. see Kennett, Chris.

Batson, Alan, jt. illus. see Laguna, Fabio.

Batson, Alan, jt. illus. see Random House.

Batson, Alan, jt. illus. see RH Disney Staff.

Batson, Susann. Rachel Serves a Stew. Kirkle, Diane Luise. 2009. 28p. pap. 10.95 *(978-1-935137-59-7(X))* Guardian Angel Publishing, Inc.

Batson, Susann. Sparkie: A Star Afraid of the Dark. Batson, Susann. 2008. 16p. pap. 7.95 *(978-1-935137-01-6(8))* Guardian Angel Publishing, Inc.

Battaglia, Aurelius. Animal Sounds. Golden Books Staff. 2005. (Golden Sturdy Book Ser.). 26p. (J). (gr. k — 1). bds. 7.99 *(978-0-375-83278-9(5)*, Golden Bks.) Random Hse. Children's Bks.

—Pets for Peter Book & Puzzle. Watson, Jane Werner. 2017. (Little Golden Book Ser.). 22p. (J). (gr. -1-2). 5.99 *(978-0-399-55363-9(0)*, Golden Bks.) Random Hse. Children's Bks.

Batten, John D. Europa's Fairy Book. Jacobs, Joseph, ed. 2013. 330p. pap. *(978-1-909302-35-8(X))* Abela Publishing.

Batten, John D. Europa's Fairy Book. Jacobs, Joseph. 2019. (ENG.). 244p. (J). (gr. k-4). ***(978-605-7748-68-3(9))***; pap. *(978-605-7876-72-0(5))* Uhrayoglu, Murat E Kitap Projesi.

Batten, John D. Indian Fairy Tales. Jacobs, Joseph. 2011. (Dover Children's Classics Ser.). (ENG.). 255p. (J). (gr. 2-5). reprint ed. pap. 19.95 *(978-0-486-21828-1(7))* Dover Pubns., Inc.

—More Celtic Fairy Tales: [illustrated Edition]. Vairous. Jacobs, Joseph, ed. 2019. (ENG.). 262p. (J). (gr. k-4). pap. *(978-605-7876-75-1(X))* Uhrayoglu, Murat E Kitap Projesi.

Batten, John D. More Celtic Fairy Tales: [Illustrated Edition]. Vairous. Jacobs, Joseph, ed. 2019. (ENG.). 262p. (J). (gr. k-4). ***(978-605-7748-74-4(3))*** Uhrayoglu, Murat E Kitap Projesi.

Batten, John D. & Cardew, Gloria. Indian Fairy Tales. Jacobs, Joseph. 2019. (ENG.). 312p. (J). (gr. k-6). ***(978-605-7748-72-0(7))***; pap. *(978-605-7876-73-7(3))* Uhrayoglu, Murat E Kitap Projesi.

Battersby, Katherine. You're Five! Unwin, Shelly. 2018. (ENG.). 32p. (J). (-k). 9.99 *(978-1-76029-131-0(5))* Allen & Unwin AUS. Dist: Independent Pubs. Group.

B

—You're Four! Unwin, Shelly. 2018. (ENG.). 32p. (J). (-k). 9.99 *(978-1-76029-130-3(7))* Allen & Unwin AUS. Dist: Independent Pubs. Group.

—You're One! Unwin, Shelly. 2019. (ENG.). 26p. (J). (— 1). bds. 7.99 *(978-1-9848-9245-4(2))*, Doubleday Bks. for Young Readers) Random Hse. Children's Bks.

—You're Three! Unwin, Shelly. 2018. (ENG.). 32p. (J). (-k). 9.99 *(978-1-76029-129-7(3))* Allen & Unwin AUS. Dist: Independent Pubs. Group.

—You're Two! Unwin, Shelly. 2019. (ENG.). 26p. (J). (— 1). bds. 7.99 *(978-1-9848-9247-8(9))*, Doubleday Bks. for Young Readers) Random Hse. Children's Bks.

Batti, Kimberly Rose. Charlotte Bakeman Has Her Say. Finger, Mary E. 2007. 96p. (J). 16.00 *(978-0-9746911-2-1(7))* Little Pear Pr.

—Mumsi Meets a Lion. Stegall, Kim. 2008. (gr. -1-1). pap. 7.99 *(978-1-59166-871-8(9))* BJU Pr.

Battis, Gwen. Dawn of Day. McPhail, J. A. 2012. 200p. 17.99 *(978-0-9851196-2-1(4))*; pap. 10.99 *(978-0-9851196-1-4(6))* Rowe Publishing.

—Hark! I Hear a Meadowlark! Bird, Roy & Harp, Kim. 2013. 34p. 16.99 *(978-1-939054-08-1(7))*; 36p. pap. 10.99 *(978-1-939054-07-4(9))* Rowe Publishing.

Battistel, Cinzia. A Dolphin's Wish: How You Can Help Make a Difference & Save Our Oceans. Sourcebooks Jabberwocky & McCurdie, Trevor. 2020. (ENG.). 32p. (J). (-3). 17.99 *(978-1-7282-0522-9(0))* Sourcebooks, Inc.

Battle, Ryan. Kenny's Favorite Things. Rochon, Ken. 2018. (ENG.). 28p. (J). pap. 19.95 *(978-1-942688-63-1(6))* Perfect Publishing.

Battut, Éric. The Little Pea. Battut, Éric. 2011. 28p. (J). (gr. -1-k). 16.95 *(978-1-61608-482-0(0)*, 608482, Sky Pony Pr.) Skyhorse Publishing Co., Inc.

Battuz, Christine. Bath Time! Walters, Eric. 2020. (ENG.). 20p. (J). (gr. -1 — 1). bds. 10.95 ***(978-1-4598-2130-9(0))*** Orca Bk. Pubs. USA.

Battuz, Christine. Candace Center Stage, 1 vol. Cameron Bure, Candace. 2018. (ENG.). 32p. (J). 17.99 *(978-0-310-76287-4(1))* Zonderkidz.

—Five Busy Beavers. Partheniou Grasso, Stella. 2018. (ENG.). 32p. (J). (gr. -1-2). 14.99 *(978-1-5107-2145-6(2)*, Sky Pony Pr.) Skyhorse Publishing Co., Inc.

—Goodnight, Arctic Animals: A Nightlight Book. 2019. (Nightlight Book Ser.). 14p. (J). (gr. -1-k). 12.99 *(978-2-89802-058-2(3)*, CrackBoom! Bks.) Chouette Publishing CAN. Dist: Publishers Group West (PGW).

—Goodnight, Farm Animals. Chouette Publishing Staff, tr. 2017. (Nightlight Book Ser.). 14p. (J). (gr. -1-k). 12.99 *(978-2-9815807-7-1(9)*, CrackBoom! Bks.) Chouette Publishing CAN. Dist: Publishers Group West (PGW).

—Grow, Candace, Grow. Bure, Candace Cameron. 2020. (ENG.). 32p. (J). (gr. -1-3). E-Book *(978-0-310-76275-1(8))* Zonderkidz.

—Hello, Goodbye, & a Very Little Lie. Jones, Christianne C. 2010. (Little Boost Ser.). (ENG.). 32p. (J). (gr. -1-1). lib. bdg. 23.99 *(978-1-4048-6167-1(X)*, Picture Window Bks.) Capstone.

—Jackie & Jesse & Joni & Jae: A Rosh Hashanah Story. Barash, Chris. 2019. (J). *(978-1-68115-550-0(8)*, Apples & Honey Pr.) Behrman Hse., Inc.

Battuz, Christine, et al. Little Boost. Bracken, Beth et al. 2019. (Little Boost Ser.). (ENG.). (J). (gr. -1-2). 352.81 *(978-1-5158-4592-8(3)*, 29432, Picture Window Bks.) Capstone.

Battuz, Christine. Little Red Riding Hood. Channing, Margot. ed. 2017. (Scribblers Look & Say Ser.). 18p. (J). (gr. -1-1). bds. 9.95 *(978-1-912006-23-6(5)*, Scribblers) Book Hse. GBR. Dist: Sterling Publishing Co., Inc.

—Little Red Riding Hood & the Big Bad Wolf Sticker Book. Channing, Margot. ed. 2019. (Scribblers Fun Activity Ser.). 32p. (J). (gr. -1). pap. 5.95 *(978-1-912904-51-8(9)*, Scribblers) Book Hse. GBR. Dist: Sterling Publishing Co., Inc.

—Marvelous Maravilloso: Me & My Beautiful Family. Lara, Carrie. 2018. 32p. (J). *(978-1-4338-2856-0(1)*, Magination Pr.) American Psychological Assn.

—Munching Millie. Parkes, Brenda. 2015. (Shared Reading Contemporary Tales Ser.). (J). (gr. k-1). *(978-1-4900-2117-1(5))* Benchmark Education Co.

—Munching Millie: Big Book Edition. Parkes, Brenda. 2015. (Shared Reading Contemporary Tales Ser.). (J). (gr. k-1). *(978-1-4900-2112-6(4))* Benchmark Education Co.

—My Sister Beth's Pink Birthday. Szymona, Marlene L. 2014. 32p. (J). *(978-1-4338-1654-3(7))*; pap. *(978-1-4338-1655-0(5))* American Psychological Assn. (Magination Pr.).

—My Teacher's Not Here! Button, Lana. 2018. (ENG.). 32p. (J). (gr. -1-2). 16.99 *(978-1-77138-356-1(9))* Kids Can Pr., Ltd. CAN. Dist: Hachette Bk. Group.

—Shy Spaghetti & Excited Eggs: A Kid's Menu of Feelings. Nemiroff, Marc A. & Annunziata, Jane. 2011. 48p. (J). (gr. -1-3). 15.95 *(978-1-4338-0956-9(7))*; pap. 10.95 *(978-1-4338-0957-6(5))* American Psychological Assn. (Magination Pr.).

—What If Bunny's NOT a Bully? Button, Lana. 2020. (ENG.). 32p. (J). (gr. -1-2). 17.99 *(978-1-5253-0055-4(5))* Kids Can Pr., Ltd. CAN. Dist: Hachette Bk. Group.

Battuz, Christine, jt. illus. see Chambers, Nick.

Battuz, Christine, jt. illus. see Jenkins, Ellie.

Battuz, Christine, jt. illus. see Palacios, Sara.

Bauer, Betsy. My Little Golden Book about Jackie Robinson. Berrios, Frank J. 2018. (Little Golden Book Ser.). 24p. (J). (-k). 4.99 *(978-0-525-57868-0(4)*, Golden Bks.) Random Hse. Children's Bks.

Bauer, Charlene. Adventures of Toy Boy & the New Kid at School. Lewis, J., ed. 2019. (Adventures of Toy Boy Ser.: Vol. 2). (ENG.). 66p. (J). pap. 6.99 *(978-1-9732-2736-6(3))* Independently Published.

Bauer, Dana. An Almost True Horse Tale. Layos, Alexandra. l.t. ed. 2003. 20p. (J). (gr. 1-5). pap. 8.95 *(978-0-9655501-3-0(3))* Saddle & Bridle, Inc.

—Two Miniature Horses. Carpenter Czerw, Nancy. 2006. (Itty & Bitty Ser.). (ENG.). 32p. (J). (gr. -1-3). 15.95 *(978-0-9755618-2-9(0))* McWitty Pr., Inc.

Bauer, Dana, jt. illus. see Berlin, Rose Mary.

Bauer, Joe. Epic Fail. Bauer, Michael Gerard. 2012. 192p. *(978-1-86291-992-1(5))* Scholastic Australia.

Bauer, John. An Illustrated Treasury of Swedish Folk & Fairy Tales, 5 vols. 2019. (ENG.). 256p. (J). 24.95 *(978-1-78250-593-8(8))* Floris Bks. GBR. Dist: Consortium Bk. Sales & Distribution.

—Lucifer: Good Angel Gone Bad. Wilde, Gloria. 2007. 36p. 14.95 *(978-1-57258-462-4(9)*, 945-6323) TEACH Services, Inc.

Bauer, Jutta. Grandpa's Angel. Bauer, Jutta. 2005. (ENG.). 48p. (J). (gr. k-12). 12.99 *(978-0-7636-2743-0(7))* Candlewick Pr.

Bauer, Larry. Activités de Noël. Hanegar, Renee. (FRE.). 16p. pap. *(978-0-590-16904-2(1))* Scholastic Canada, Ltd.

—Activités d'Halloween. Friedman, Pamela. (FRE.). 16p. pap. *(978-0-439-00533-3(7))* Scholastic Canada, Ltd.

Bauer, Stephanie. Alligator Alphabet. Blackstone, Stella. (J). (gr. -1-k). 2007. 32p. bds. 8.99 *(978-1-84686-073-7(3))*; 2005. (ENG.). 48p. 16.99 *(978-1-84148-494-5(6))* Barefoot Bks., Inc.

—Autumn. Hedlund, Stephanie. 2013. (Seasons Ser.). (ENG.). 24p. (J). (gr. -1-3). lib. bdg. 27.07 *(978-1-61641-992-9(X)*, 13258, Looking Glass Library) Magic Wagon.

—Counting Cockatoos. Blackstone, Stella. 2007. (ENG.). 32p. (J). (gr. -1-k). bds. 8.99 *(978-1-84686-061-4(X))* Barefoot Bks., Inc.

—Riddle Diddle Farm. Shore, Diane Z. & Calvert, Deanna. 2018. (ENG.). 10p. (J). (gr. -1-1). bds. 9.99 *(978-1-68152-406-1(6))* Amicus.

—Riddle Diddle Ocean. Shore, Diane Z. & Calvert, Deanna. 2019. (Riddle Diddle Dumplings Ser.). 10p. (J). (gr. -1-1). bds. 9.99 *(978-1-68152-499-3(6))* Amicus.

—Riddle Diddle Rainforest. Shore, Diane Z. & Calvert, Deanna. 2019. (Riddle Diddle Dumplings Ser.). (ENG.). 10p. (J). (gr. -1-1). bds. 9.99 *(978-1-68152-500-6(3))* Amicus.

—Riddle Diddle Safari. Shore, Diane Z. & Calvert, Deanna. 2018. (ENG.). 10p. (J). (gr. -1-1). bds. 9.99 *(978-1-68152-407-8(4))* Amicus.

—Seasons, 4 vols. Hedlund, Stephanie. 2013. (Seasons Ser.: 4). (ENG.). 24p. (J). (gr. -1-3). lib. bdg. 108.28 *(978-1-61641-991-2(1)*, 13256, Looking Glass Library) Magic Wagon.

—Spring. Hedlund, Stephanie. 2013. (Seasons Ser.). (ENG.). 24p. (J). (gr. -1-3). lib. bdg. 27.07 *(978-1-61641-993-6(8)*, 13260, Looking Glass Library) Magic Wagon.

—Summer. Hedlund, Stephanie. 2013. (Seasons Ser.). (ENG.). 24p. (J). (gr. -1-3). lib. bdg. 27.07 *(978-1-61641-994-3(6)*, 13262, Looking Glass Library) Magic Wagon.

—Winter. Hedlund, Stephanie. 2013. (Seasons Ser.). (ENG.). 24p. (J). (gr. -1-3). lib. bdg. 27.07 *(978-1-61641-995-0(4)*, 13264, Looking Glass Library) Magic Wagon.

Bauer, Stephanie. Octopus Opposites. Bauer, Stephanie. Blackstone, Stella. 32p. (J). (gr. -1-k). 2011. bds. 8.99 *(978-1-84686-591-6(3))*; 2010. 16.99 *(978-1-84686-328-8(7))* Barefoot Bks., Inc.

Bauerle, Tanja. The Park Our Town Built. Bertrand, Diane Gonzalez. 2011. (ENG & SPA.). 32p. (gr. -1-3). lib. bdg. 16.95 *(978-1-936299-14-0(3)*, Raven Tree Pr.,Csi) Continental Sales, Inc.

—Wright on Time: Collection 1. Cottrell-Bentley, Lisa M. 2012. 376p. pap. 19.99 *(978-1-937848-00-2(0))* Do Life Right, Inc.

—Wright on Time: Iowa. Cottrell-Bentley, Lisa M. 2013. 164p. pap. 12.99 *(978-1-937848-06-4(X))* Do Life Right, Inc.

—Wright on Time: Minnesota. Cottrell-Bentley, Lisa M. 2012. 126p. pap. 12.99 *(978-1-937848-02-6(7))* Do Life Right, Inc.

Baughman, Lee, jt. illus. see Clark College Economic and Community Dev.

Baughman, Lee, jt. illus. see Mitsein, Rebekah.

Bauknecht, Julie. Garda Gaby: The Danger of Playing Truant. McCann, David. Brundige, Britt, ed. l.t. ed. 2003. 14p. (J). (gr. k-5). spiral bd. 5.99 *(978-1-929063-92-5(X)*, 324) Moons & Stars Publishing For Children.

—My Grandma Rides a Harley: She's Cool! Davidson, Jean. 2007. (J). *(978-1-930596-79-5(0))* Amherst Pr.

Bauknight, Wilfred, jt. illus. see Blanc, Mike.

Baum, Ann. Bunny in a Basket. Baglio, Ben M. 2005. 142p. (J). *(978-0-439-68761-4(6))* Scholastic, Inc.

—Collie with a Card. Baglio, Ben M. 2004. 136p. (J). pap. *(978-0-439-68760-7(8))* Scholastic, Inc.

—Corgi in the Cupcakes. Baglio, Ben M. 2008. 142p. (J). pap. *(978-0-439-02533-1(8))* Scholastic, Inc.

—Tabby under the Tree. Baglio, Ben M. & Lasher, Mary Ann. 2007. 145p. (J). *(978-0-439-02532-4(X))* Scholastic, Inc.

Baum, Ann & Lasher, Mary Ann. Colt on Christmas Eve. Baglio, Ben M. 2005. 142p. (J). pap. *(978-0-439-77522-9(1))* Scholastic, Inc.

—Dalmatian in the Daisies. Baglio, Ben M. 2007. 154p. (J). *(978-0-439-87120-4(4))* Scholastic, Inc.

Baum, Hélène. Meet the Artist: Frank Bowling. Whitley, Zoe. 2019. (ENG.). 32p. (J). (gr. k-2). pap. 12.95 *(978-1-84976-630-2(4))* Tate Publishing, Ltd. GBR. Dist: Hachette Bk. Group.

Baum, Juli. Toinette & the Elves: Illustrated Edition. Coolidge, Susan. 2019. (ENG.). 36p. (J). pap. 9.40 ***(978-1-7095-9782-4(8))*** Independently Published.

Baum, Kipley, jt. photos by see Oudinot, Wanda.

Baum, L. Frank & McKowen, Scott. The Wonderful Wizard of Oz. Baum, L. Frank. 2005. (Sterling Unabridged Classics Ser.). 176p. (J). (gr. 5). 9.95 *(978-1-4027-2504-3(3))* Sterling Publishing Co., Inc.

Baum, L. Frank & Neill, John R. The Emerald City of Oz: Novels 6 Through 10 of the Oz Series. 2014. viii, 791p. (J). *(978-1-4351-5615-9(3))* Barnes & Noble, Inc.

Bauman, Jill. The Tale of Squirrel Nutkin. 2006. (J). 6.99 *(978-1-59939-017-8(5))* Cornerstone Pr.

Bauman, Todd. Absurd Alphabedtime Stories. Hunter, Julius K. 2nd rev. l.t. ed. 2004. 32p. (J). 16.95 *(978-0-9761422-0-1(1))* J.K.H. Enterprises.

Baumann, Marty. Phonics Comics. Katschke, Judy. 2006. (ENG.). 24p. (J). (gr. 1-17). per. 3.99 *(978-1-58476-411-3(2)*, IKIDS) Innovative Kids.

Baumert, Olga. For Spacious Skies: Katharine Lee Bates & the Inspiration for America the Beautiful. Churnin, Nancy. 2020. (She Made History Ser.). (ENG.). 32p. (J). (gr. -1-3). 16.99 ***(978-0-8075-2530-2(8)***, 807525308) Whitman, Albert & Co.

—The Little Witch's Book of Spells. Kusby, Ariel. 2020. (ENG.). 144p. (J). (gr. 3-7). 16.99 ***(978-1-4521-8361-9(9))*** Chronicle Bks. LLC.

Baumgardner, Julie. Crow 2. Cope, Steven R. 2012. 158p. pap. 16.00 *(978-1-936138-49-4(2))* Wind Pubns.

Baumgardner, Mary Alice. A Job for Arabella. Carolina Canines for Service & Nowak, Pat. 2007. 56p. (J). per. *(978-0-9800070-0-8(3))* Carolina Canines for Service Inc.

Baumgartner-Cohen, Beatrice. Parker et le Beurre de Cacahu�te. Lewis, Dana M. Azzaz, Karim, tr. 2019. (FRE.). 26p. (J). pap. 9.89 ***(978-1-7059-1906-4(5))*** Independently Published.

Baur, Cati. Four Sisters, Vol. 1: Enid. Ferdjoukh, Malika. 2018. (Four Sisters Ser.: 1). 160p. (YA). (gr. 8-12). 19.99 *(978-1-68405-196-0(7))* Idea & Design Works, LLC.

—Four Sisters, Vol. 2: Hortense. Ferdjoukh, Malika. 2019. (Four Sisters Ser.: 2). 160p. (YA). (gr. 8-12). pap. 19.99 *(978-1-68405-433-6(8))* Idea & Design Works, LLC.

Baur, Laura. The Riverbank. 2012. (ENG.). 24p. (J). (gr. -1-k). spiral bd. 14.99 *(978-1-85103-393-5(9))* Moonlight Publishing, Ltd. GBR. Dist: Independent Pubs. Group.

Bausman, Mary. Chrissie's Shell. Keith, Brooke. 2010. 32p. (J). 14.99 *(978-1-59317-398-2(9))* Warner Pr., Inc.

—God Loves Me Coloring Pages: For Toddlers & 2s. Standard Publishing Staff. 2016. (ENG.). 192p. (J). 16.99 *(978-0-7847-1796-7(6)*, 140203) Standard Publishing.

—The Green Ribbon Day. Jones, Colleen E. 2016. (ENG.). (J). 21.95 *(978-1-63525-049-7(8))*; pap. 12.95 *(978-1-63525-047-3(1))* Christian Faith Publishing.

Bautista, Cisar Evangelis. Círculos y Calendarios. Mariscal, Libia E. Barajas. rev. ed. 2006. (Otra Escalera Ser.). (SPA & ENG.). 24p. (J). (gr. 2-4). pap. 9.95 *(978-968-5920-71-1(0))* Castillo, Ediciones, S. A. de C. V. MEX. Dist: Macmillan.

Bautista Jaun Oliver, Juan. Ungalala. Parkes, Brenda. 2015. (Shared Reading Classics Ser.). (J). (gr. k-1). *(978-1-4900-2107-2(8))* Benchmark Education Co.

—Ungalala: Big Book Edition. Parkes, Brenda. 2015. (Shared Reading Classics Ser.). (J). (gr. k-1). *(978-1-4900-2103-4(5))* Benchmark Education Co.

Bautista, Juan. Miss Mary Mack. Everett, Melissa. 2017. (ENG.). 20p. (J). (gr. -1-2). bds. *(978-1-4867-1240-3(1))* Flowerpot Children's Pr. Inc.

Bautista, Juan & Oliver, Juan. Las Gotas de Agua. Schmauss, Judy Kentor. 2016. (Early Rising Readers Ser.). (SPA.). (J). (gr. -1). 6.67 *(978-1-4788-3665-0(2))* Newmark Learning LLC.

—Yo Soy una Rana. Lindeen, Mary. 2016. (Early Rising Readers Ser.). (SPA.). (J). (gr. -1). 6.67 *(978-1-4788-3713-8(6))* Newmark Learning LLC.

Bautista Juan Oliver, Juan. I Am a Frog. Lindeen, Mary. 2015. (Early Rising Readers Ser.). (J). (gr. -1-k). 5.83 *(978-1-4788-1701-7(1))* Newmark Learning LLC.

—Raindrops. Schmauss, Judy Kentor. 2015. (Early Rising Readers Ser.). (J). (gr. -1-k). 5.83 *(978-1-4788-1594-5(9))* Newmark Learning LLC.

—The Surprise. Koons, Linda. 2015. (Early Rising Readers Ser.). (J). (gr. -1-k). 5.83 *(978-1-4788-2140-3(X))* Newmark Learning LLC.

Bave, Terry, et al. How to Draw Cartoons & Caricatures. Tatchell, Judy. rev. ed. 2006. (How to Draw Ser.). 40p. (J). (gr. 4-7). pap. 5.99 *(978-0-7945-1374-0(3)*, Usborne) EDC Publishing.

Baviera, Rocco. Earth Day: An Alphabet Book. Kowalski, Gary. 2009. (ENG.). 32p. (J). (gr. -1-4). 12.00 *(978-1-55896-542-3(4)*, 1297770, Skinner Hse. Bks.) Unitarian Universalist Assn.

Baviere, Vanessa. Le C�leri R�moulade: Une Histoire � Vomir. Folliet, Delphine. 2019. (FRE.). 26p. (J). pap. 9.13 ***(978-1-6737-4373-9(0))*** Independently Published.

—Le Petit Trou des Fesses du Loup: Une Histoire Dangereuse. Folliet, Delphine. 2019. (FRE.). 24p. (J). pap. 9.13 ***(978-1-6737-9188-4(3))*** Independently Published.

Baxter, Leon. The Lion First Bible. Alexander, Pat. ed. 2014. (ENG.). 480p. (J). pap. 12.99 *(978-0-7459-6484-3(2))* Lion Hudson PLC GBR. Dist: Independent Pubs. Group.

—Lion First Bible. Alexander, Pat. ed. 2008. (ENG.). 480p. (J). (gr. k-2). 12.99 *(978-0-7459-6103-3(7))* Lion Hudson PLC GBR. Dist: Independent Pubs. Group.

—The Lion First Bible & Prayers, 1 vol. Alexander, Pat & Box, Su. ed. 2014. (ENG.). 608p. (J). (gr. k-3). 16.99 *(978-0-7459-6493-5(1))* Lion Hudson PLC GBR. Dist: Independent Pubs. Group.

Baxter, Mia. Ana's Story: A Journey of Hope. Bush Hager, Jenna. 2008. (ENG.). 304p. (YA). (gr. 9-12). pap. 9.99 *(978-0-06-137909-3(3))* HarperCollins Pubs.

Baxter, Rhea. Growing Up: Home & School. Zorro, Sephone. 2017. 144p. pap. 7.99 *(978-1-941429-55-6(6))* Handersen Publishing.

Baxter, Shelby. Ethan's Talent Search. Jones, Sharonda & Woodyard, Eric. 2019. (ENG.). 32p. (J). pap. 15.00 *(978-1-7188-3022-6(X))* CreateSpace Independent Publishing Platform.

Baxter, Stephen. Matilda: Be Outrageous: Big Ideas from a Small Girl. Dahl, Roald. 2019. (ENG.). 32p. (J). (gr. 3-7). 9.99 *(978-1-5247-9361-6(2)*, Grosset & Dunlap) Penguin Young Readers Group.

Bayard, Janie Domengeaux. Ferdinand the Frog. Borland, Jerre Shadrick. 2011. 32p. pap. 24.95 *(978-1-4560-6116-6(X))* America Star Bks.

Bayarri, Jordi. Albert Einstein & the Theory of Relativity. Bayarri, Jordi. 2020. (Graphic Science Biographies Ser.). 40p. (J). (gr. 5-8). 29.32 *(978-1-5415-7823-4(6))*; (ENG.). pap. 8.99 *(978-1-5415-8696-3(4))* Lerner Publishing Group. (Graphic Universe™).

—Charles Darwin & the Theory of Evolution. Bayarri, Jordi. 2020. (Graphic Science Biographies Ser.). 40p. (J). (gr. 5-8). 29.32 *(978-1-5415-7822-7(8))*; (ENG.). pap. 8.99 *(978-1-5415-8697-0(2))* Lerner Publishing Group. (Graphic Universe™).

—Isaac Newton & the Laws of Motion. Bayarri, Jordi. 2020. (Graphic Science Biographies Ser.). 40p. (J). (gr. 5-8). 29.32 *(978-1-5415-7824-1(4)*, Graphic Universe™) Lerner Publishing Group.

—Marie Curie & Radioactivity. Bayarri, Jordi. 2020. (Graphic Science Biographies Ser.). 40p. (J). (gr. 5-8). 29.32 *(978-1-5415-7821-0(X))*; (ENG.). pap. 8.99 *(978-1-5415-8699-4(9))* Lerner Publishing Group. (Graphic Universe™).

Bayer, Florian. Animal Allstars: African Animals Facts & Folklore. Klepeis, Alicia. 2017. (ENG.). 64p. (J). (gr. 1-4). 24.95 *(978-3-89955-782-4(4))* Die Gestalten Verlag DEU. Dist: Ingram Publisher Services.

Baykovska, Ira. Habu & the Lost Zebra. Solomon, Beth. 2020. (ENG.). 32p. (J). (gr. k-1). ***(978-1-9163239-1-9(X))*** Novewell Publishing.

Baykovska, Ira. The Nasty Princess. Cabot, Maxi Blue. 2018. (ENG.). 50p. (J). pap. 10.75 *(978-1-7286-7239-7(2))* Independently Published.

Bayless, Julie. Crawly School for Bugs: Poems to Drive You Buggy. Harrison, David. 2018. 32p. (J). (gr. k-4). 17.95 *(978-1-62979-204-0(7)*, Wordsong) Boyds Mills Pr.

Bayley, Nicola. Can I Come Too? Patten, Brian. 2020. (ENG.). 32p. (J). (gr. -1-3). 7.99 ***(978-1-68263-218-5(0))*** Peachtree Publishing Co. Inc.

Bayley, Nicola. The Tyger Voyage. Adams, Richard. 2013. (ENG.). 32p. (J). 15.95 *(978-1-56792-491-6(3))* Godine, David R. Pub.

—Yo Subía la Escalera y Otras Rimas Infantiles. Puncel, María. 2003. (SPA.). 24p. 4.95 *(978-84-372-8015-8(X))* Altea, Ediciones, S.A. - Grupo Santillana ESP. Dist: Santillana USA Publishing Co., Inc.

Baylis, Asia. No! Stop! Tell! Copeland, Latasha. 2019. (ENG.). 30p. (J). pap. 9.99 ***(978-1-0745-6678-4(5))*** Independently Published.

Bayne, Alexis. A Lady's Cage. Lane, Mandy & The Author Studio, Blaire, eds. 2019. (ENG.). 124p. (J). pap. 6.99 *(978-1-7941-9994-1(2))* Independently Published.

Baynes, Pauline. Le Cheval et Son Ecuyer. Morgaut, Philippe, tr. 2005. (Chronicles of Narnia Ser.). (FRE.). 234p. (J). per. 21.95 *(978-2-07-054644-2(6))* Gallimard, Editions FRA. Dist: Distribooks, Inc.

—The Chronicles of Narnia: 7 Books in 1 Hardcover. Lewis, C. S. ed. 2004. (Chronicles of Narnia Ser.). (ENG.). 784p. (J). (gr. 5). 32.99 *(978-0-06-059824-2(7))* HarperCollins Pubs.

—The Chronicles of Narnia Box Set: 7 Books in 1 Box Set, Bks. 1 to 7, Set. Lewis, C. S. rev. ed. 2007. (Chronicles of Narnia Ser.). (ENG.). (J). (gr. 3-18). 120.00 *(978-0-06-024488-0(7)*, HarperCollins) HarperCollins Pubs. Ltd. GBR. Dist: HarperCollins Pubs.

—The Coat of Many Colors. Koralek, Jenny. 2004. 32p. (J). 16.00 *(978-0-8028-5277-9(7))* Eerdmans, William B. Publishing Co.

—The Horse & His Boy. Lewis, C. S. (Chronicles of Narnia Ser.: 3). (ENG.). 240p. (J). (gr. 3-18). 2008. pap. 8.99 *(978-0-06-440501-0(X))*; 2007. 17.99 *(978-0-06-023488-1(1))* HarperCollins Pubs. Ltd. GBR. (HarperCollins). Dist: HarperCollins Pubs.

—I Believe: The Nicene Creed. 2004. 32p. (YA). (gr. 3-18). 16.00 *(978-0-8028-5258-8(0))* Eerdmans, William B. Publishing Co.

—The Last Battle. Lewis, C. S. (Chronicles of Narnia Ser.: 7). (ENG.). 224p. (J). (gr. 3-18). 2008. pap. 8.99 *(978-0-06-440503-4(6))*; 2007. 17.99 *(978-0-06-023493-5(8))* HarperCollins Pubs. Ltd. GBR. (HarperCollins). Dist: HarperCollins Pubs.

—The Lion, the Witch & the Wardrobe. Lewis, C. S. abr. ed. (Chronicles of Narnia Ser.: 2). (ENG.). 208p. (J). (gr. 3-18). 2008. pap. 8.99 *(978-0-06-440499-0(4))*; 2007. 17.99 *(978-0-06-023481-2(4))*; 2007. lib. bdg. 18.89 *(978-0-06-023482-9(2))* HarperCollins Pubs. Ltd. GBR. (HarperCollins). Dist: HarperCollins Pubs.

—The Lion, the Witch & the Wardrobe Movie Tie-In Edition. Lewis, C. S. movie tie-in ed. 2005. (Chronicles of Narnia Ser.: 2). (ENG.). 224p. (J). (gr. 3-7). pap. 7.99 *(978-0-06-076548-4(8)*, HarperFestival) HarperCollins Pubs.

—The Magician's Nephew. Lewis, C. S. (Chronicles of Narnia Ser.: 1). (ENG.). 208p. (J). (gr. 3-18). 2008. pap. 8.99 *(978-0-06-440505-8(2))*; 2007. 17.99 *(978-0-06-023497-3(0))* HarperCollins Pubs. Ltd. GBR. (HarperCollins). Dist: HarperCollins Pubs.

—The Moses Basket. Koralek, Jenny. 2004. 32p. (J). 16.00 *(978-0-8028-5251-9(3))* Eerdmans, William B. Publishing Co.

—Prince Caspian: The Return to Narnia. Lewis, C. S. (Chronicles of Narnia Ser.: 4). (ENG.). 240p. (J). (gr. 3-18). 2008. pap. 8.99 *(978-0-06-440500-3(1))*; 2007. 17.99 *(978-0-06-023483-6(0))* HarperCollins Pubs. Ltd. GBR. (HarperCollins). Dist: HarperCollins Pubs.

—The Silver Chair. Lewis, C. S. (Chronicles of Narnia Ser.: 6). (ENG.). 256p. (J). (gr. 3-18). 2008. pap. 8.99 *(978-0-06-440504-1(4))*; 2007. 17.99 *(978-0-06-023495-9(4))* HarperCollins Pubs. Ltd. GBR. (HarperCollins). Dist: HarperCollins Pubs.

—The Voyage of the Dawn Treader. Lewis, C. S. (Chronicles of Narnia Ser.: 5). (ENG.). 256p. (J). (gr. 3-18). 2008. pap. 8.99 *(978-0-06-440502-7(8))*; 2007. 17.99 *(978-0-06-023486-7(5))* HarperCollins Pubs. Ltd. GBR. (HarperCollins). Dist: HarperCollins Pubs.

Baynes, Pauline. Prince Caspian, Bk. 7. Baynes, Pauline. Lewis, C. S. 2008. (Chronicles of Narnia Ser.). 768p. (J). (gr. 3). pap. 99.99 *(978-0-06-076552-1(6))* HarperCollins Pubs.

—Questionable Creatures: A Bestiary. Baynes, Pauline. 2006. (ENG.). 48p. (J). (gr. 5-18). 18.00 *(978-0-8028-5284-7(X))* Eerdmans, William B. Publishing Co.

Baynton, Terri Rose. Gwendolyn! MacIver, Juliette. 2018. 32p. pap. 6.99 *(978-0-7333-3518-1(7))* ABC Bks. AUS. Dist: HarperCollins Pubs.

—Room on Our Rock. Temple, Kate. 2019. (J). 12.99 *(978-1-61067-902-2(4))* Kane Miller.

Bayoc, Cbabi. Young Cornrows Callin Out the Moon. Forman, Ruth. 2007. (ENG.). 24p. (J). (gr. -1-3). lib. bdg. 16.95 *(978-0-89239-218-6(5))* Lee & Low Bks., Inc.

Bayramoglu, Hatice. How My Brother Saved Christmas. Green-Warren, Loretta M. 2018. (ENG.). 26p. (J). pap. 12.00 *(978-1-7309-2249-7(X))* Independently Published.

Bayramoglu, Hatice. It's a Basketball Birthday Party! Drummer Jr, Brian C. 2019. (ENG.). 34p. (J). pap. 15.00 ***(978-1-6975-0503-0(1))*** Independently Published.

—Kaleb's Voice. Simmons-Perry, Shonda. 2019. (ENG.). 26p. (J). pap. 9.95 ***(978-1-7082-3894-0(8))*** Independently Published.

Bayramoglu, Hatice. Nia's Dream the Talking Tulips. Baniti, Nailah. 2nd ed. 2013. 24p. pap. 7.99 *(978-0-9853574-5-0(2))* Mountan Creek Pubns.

—Tip & Ben Find a Friend. Champeau, Brandy. 2018. (ENG.). 40p. (J). pap. 10.00 *(978-0-692-10412-5(7))* Exploring ExPr.ion LLC.

Bayramoglu, Hatice. Nia's Dream. Bayramoglu, Hatice. Baniti, Nailah. 2012. 26p. pap. 7.99 *(978-0-9853574-4-3(4))* Mountan Creek Pubns.

Bays, Gail, jt. illus. see Rothenberger, Boyd.

Bayu, Fabianus. Uwayan Nenkosi Yofudu: Wayan & the Turtle King. Bezuidenhout, Yvette. Dlamini, Mpho, tr. 2018. (ZUL.). 30p. (J). pap. *(978-1-7750990-9-3(1))* Fshbks.

Bayu, Fabianus. Wayan en Die Skilpad Koning: Wayan & the Turtle King. Bezuidenhout, Yvette. 2020. (AFR.). 30p. (J). (gr. 3-6). pap. ***(978-1-9990012-3-0(0))*** Fshbks.

Bayu, Fabianus. Wayan et le Roi Tortue: Wayan & the Turtle King. Bezuidenhout, Yvette. Hulin, Jerome, tr. from ENG. 2017. (978-1-7750990-3-1 Ser.). (FRE & ENG.). 28p. (J). (gr. 3-6). pap. *(978-1-7750990-3-1(2))* Fshbks.

Bayu, Fabianus. Wayan et le Roi Tortue: Wayan Sy Ilay Mpanjaka Sokatra. Bezuidenhout, Yvette. Harvel-Randrenjatovo, Aina, tr. 2020. (MLG.). 34p. (J). (gr. 3-6). pap. ***(978-1-9990012-4-7(9))*** Fshbks.

—Wayan to Kame No ōsama: ワヤンとカメの王さま; Bezuidenhout, Yvette. Terado, Yuki, tr. 2020. (JPN.). 30p. (J). (gr. 3-6). pap. ***(978-1-9990012-1-6(4))*** Fshbks.

Bayu, Fabianus. Wayan y el Rey de Las Tortugas: Wayan & the Turtle King. Bezuidenhout, Yvette. Garcia Benito, Diana, tr. 2018. (SPA.). 28p. (J). (gr. 3-6). pap. *(978-1-7750990-8-6(3))* Fshbks.

—韋恩與烏龜國王 Wayan & the Turtle King. Bezuidenhout, Yvette. Lai, Wendy, tr. 2018. (CHI.). 30p. (J). (gr. 3-6). pap. *(978-1-7750990-6-2(7))* Fshbks.

Bazaldua, Oscar. Loki: the God Who Fell to Earth. 2020. 128p. (YA). (gr. 8-17). pap. 17.99 *(978-1-302-92031-9(6))* Marvel Worldwide, Inc.

Bazaldua, Oscar, jt. illus. see Gleason, Patrick.

Bazyl, Anna. Ohio Wildlife: A Coloring Field Guide. Fernand, Amalia Celeste. 2019. (ENG.). 120p. (J). pap. 14.99 *(978-1-7339923-0-5(8))* Horn, Jonathan.

Bazzoni, Lainie M. A. Windsock Wesley & His Wild & Wonderful Weather MacHine, Living in Cloud. Fox, Alex. 2010. 48p. pap. 16.50 *(978-1-60911-873-0(1),* Eloquent Bks.) Strategic Book Publishing & Rights Agency (SBPRA).

Be-Papas. Revolutionary Girl Utena. Saito, Chiho. 2003. (Revolutionary Girl Utena Ser.: 3). (ENG.). 200p. pap. 9.95 *(978-1-56931-812-6(3))* Viz Media.

Beable, Georgie. Where the Cat Led. Stuart, Hazel. 2020. (ENG.). 46p. (J). pap. ***(978-1-83975-011-3(1))*** Grosvenor Hse. Publishing Ltd.

Beach, Bryan. The Science of Flying Reptiles. Woolf, Alex. 2017. (ENG.). 32p. (J). (gr. 3). pap. 9.95 *(978-0-531-26900-8(0),* Watts, Franklin) Scholastic Library Publishing.

—The Science of Flying Reptiles: The Terrifying Truth about the Pterosaurs. Woolf, Alex. 2017. (Science of Dinosaurs Ser.). (ENG.). 32p. (J). (gr. 3). lib. bdg. 29.00 *(978-0-531-25830-9(0),* Watts, Franklin) Scholastic Library Publishing.

—The Science of Oceans: The Watery Truth about 72 Percent of Our Planet's Surface. MacDonald, Fiona. 2018. (Science of the Earth Ser.). (ENG.). 32p. (J). (gr. 3-7). lib. bdg. 29.00 *(978-0-531-22767-1(7),* Watts, Franklin) Scholastic Library Publishing.

—The Science of Oceans: The Watery Truth about 72 Percent of Our Planet's Surface. Macdonald, Fiona. 2018. (Science of the Earth Ser.). (ENG.). 40p. (J). (gr. 3-7). pap. 9.95 *(978-0-531-23077-0(5),* Watts, Franklin) Scholastic Library Publishing.

—Yogi Bear's Guide to Bugs. Weakland, Mark. 2015. (Yogi Bear's Guide to the Great Outdoors Ser.). (ENG.). 32p. (J). (gr. k-2). lib. bdg. 28.65 *(978-1-4914-6546-2(8))* Capstone.

—Yogi Bear's Guide to Rocks. Weakland, Mark. 2015. (Yogi Bear's Guide to the Great Outdoors Ser.). (ENG.). 32p. (J). (gr. k-2). lib. bdg. 28.65 *(978-1-4914-6548-6(4))* Capstone.

Beach, Bryan & Cornia, Christian. Yogi Bear's Guide to the Great Outdoors. Weakland, Mark. 2015. (Yogi Bear's Guide to the Great Outdoors Ser.). (ENG.). 32p. (gr. 1-2). 114.60 *(978-1-4914-6967-5(6))* Capstone.

Beach, Bryan & Lundie, Isobel. The Science of Vehicles: The Turbo-Charged Truth about Trucks & Cars. Canavan, Roger. 2019. (Science of Engineering Ser.). (ENG.). 32p. (J). (gr. 3-3). lib. bdg. 29.00 *(978-0-531-13198-5(X),* Watts, Franklin) Scholastic Library Publishing.

Beach, Bryan, jt. illus. see Affonso, Alexandre.

Beach, Bryan, jt. illus. see Lundie, Isobel.

Beach, Bryan, jt. illus. see Myer, Ed.

Beach, Bryan, jt. illus. see Vaisberg, Diego.

Beach, Joshua, jt. illus. see Hobson, Ryan.

Beach, Mary FitzGerald. The Black Sheep, Harper, Stephan J. I.t. ed. 2005. 32p. (J). lib. bdg. 16.95 *(978-0-9741800-1-4(7))* Inspire Press, Inc.

Beachamp, Afiyah. The Queen of IT. Bush, Vicki-Ann. 2011. 60p. (J). pap. 9.98 *(978-0-9816949-7-9(7))* Salt of the Earth Pr.

Beachum, Mark, et al. Iron Man 2020. 2018. (ENG.). 304p. (J). (gr. 4-17). pap. 34.99 *(978-1-302-91390-8(5))* Marvel Worldwide, Inc.

Beacon, Dawn. Action! Writing Your Own Play, 1 vol. Loewen, Nancy. 2010. (Writer's Toolbox Ser.). (ENG.). 32p. (J). (gr. 2-4). pap. 8.95 *(978-1-4048-6392-7(3));* lib. bdg. 27.99 *(978-1-4048-6017-9(7))* Capstone. (Picture Window Bks.).

—Animal Fairy Tales, 1 vol. Guillain, Charlotte. (Animal Fairy Tales Ser.). (ENG.). 24p. 2014. (gr. 1-2). lib. bdg. 119.95 *(978-1-4109-6116-7(8));* 2013. (gr. -1-2). pap. 324.70 *(978-1-4109-5527-2(3));* 2013. (gr. -1-2). lib. bdg. 95.96 *(978-1-4109-5027-7(1))* Capstone. (Raintree).

—Animal Fairy Tales Big Book Collection. Guillain, Charlotte. 2013. (Animal Fairy Tales Ser.). (ENG.). 24p. (J). (gr. -1-2). 130.00 *(978-1-4109-5045-1(X),* NA-r) Heinemann-Raintree.

—Cat & the Beanstalk, 1 vol. Guillain, Charlotte. 2014. (Animal Fairy Tales Ser.). (ENG.). 24p. (J). (gr. -1-2). lib. bdg. 23.99 *(978-1-4109-6113-6(3),* Raintree) Capstone.

—The Emperor Penguin's New Clothes, 1 vol. Guillain, Charlotte. 2014. (Animal Fairy Tales Ser.). (ENG.). 24p. (J). (gr. -1-2). pap. 6.49 *(978-1-4109-6121-1(4));* 26.00 *(978-1-4109-6134-1(6));* lib. bdg. 23.99 *(978-1-4109-6114-3(1))* Capstone. (Raintree).

—Goldiclucks & the Three Bears, 1 vol. Guillain, Charlotte. 2013. (Animal Fairy Tales Ser.). (ENG.). 24p. (J). (gr. -1-2). pap. 6.49 *(978-1-4109-5028-4(X),* Raintree); 26.00 *(978-1-4109-5040-6(9),* NA-r) Capstone.

—Just the Facts [Scholastic]: Writing Your Own Research Report. Loewen, Nancy. 2010. (Writer's Toolbox Ser.). 32p. pap. 0.50 *(978-1-4048-6171-8(8),* Picture Window Bks.) Capstone.

—The Kitten Who Cried Dog, 1 vol. Guillain, Charlotte. 2013. (Animal Fairy Tales Ser.). (ENG.). 24p. (J). (gr. -1-2). pap. 6.49 *(978-1-4109-5029-1(8),* Raintree) Capstone.

—The Kitten Who Cried Dog. Guillain, Charlotte & Aesop, Aesop. 2013. (Animal Fairy Tales Ser.). (ENG.). 24p. (J). (gr. -1-2). 26.00 *(978-1-4109-5041-3(7),* NA-r) Capstone.

—The Kitten Who Cried Dog, 1 vol. Guillain, Charlotte. 2013. (Animal Fairy Tales Ser.). (ENG.). 24p. (J). (gr. -1-2). lib. bdg. 23.99 *(978-1-4109-5023-9(9),* Raintree) Capstone.

—Little Red Riding Duck, 1 vol. Guillain, Charlotte. 2013. (Animal Fairy Tales Ser.). (ENG.). 24p. (J). (gr. -1-2). pap. 6.49 *(978-1-4109-5030-7(1),* Raintree); 26.00 *(978-1-4109-5042-0(5),* NA-r); lib. bdg. 23.99 *(978-1-4109-5024-6(7),* Raintree) Capstone.

—Pandarella, 1 vol. Guillain, Charlotte. 2013. (Animal Fairy Tales Ser.). (ENG.). 24p. (J). (gr. -1-2). pap. 6.49 *(978-1-4109-5031-4(X),* Raintree) Capstone.

—Pandarella. Guillain, Charlotte & Perrault, Charles. 2013. (Animal Fairy Tales Ser.). (ENG.). 24p. (J). (gr. -1-2). 26.00 *(978-1-4109-5043-7(3),* NA-r) Capstone.

—Pandarella, 1 vol. Guillain, Charlotte. 2013. (Animal Fairy Tales Ser.). (ENG.). 24p. (J). (gr. -1-2). lib. bdg. 23.99 *(978-1-4109-5025-3(5),* Raintree) Capstone.

—The Poodle & the Pea, 1 vol. Guillain, Charlotte. 2013. (Animal Fairy Tales Ser.). (ENG.). 24p. (J). (gr. -1-2). pap. 6.49 *(978-1-4109-5032-1(8),* Raintree) Capstone.

—The Poodle & the Pea. Guillain, Charlotte & Andersen, Hans. 2013. (Animal Fairy Tales Ser.). (ENG.). 24p. (J). (gr. -1-2). 26.00 *(978-1-4109-5044-4(1),* NA-r) Capstone.

—The Poodle & the Pea, 1 vol. Guillain, Charlotte. 2013. (Animal Fairy Tales Ser.). (ENG.). 24p. (J). (gr. -1-2). lib. bdg. 23.99 *(978-1-4109-5026-0(3),* Raintree) Capstone.

—Ratpunzel, 1 vol. Guillain, Charlotte. 2014. (Animal Fairy Tales Ser.). (ENG.). 24p. (J). (gr. -1-2). lib. bdg. 23.99 *(978-1-4109-6112-9(5),* Raintree) Capstone.

—Rumplesnakeskin, 1 vol. Guillain, Charlotte. 2014. (Animal Fairy Tales Ser.). (ENG.). 24p. (J). (gr. -1-2). lib. bdg. 23.99 *(978-1-4109-6111-2(7),* Raintree) Capstone.

—Sleeping Badger, 1 vol. Guillain, Charlotte. 2014. (Animal Fairy Tales Ser.). (ENG.). 24p. (J). (gr. -1-2). lib. bdg. 23.99 *(978-1-4109-6115-0(X),* Raintree) Capstone.

—The Twelve Days of Christmas in Colorado. Ashman, Linda. 2018. (Twelve Days of Christmas in America Ser.). 22p. (J). (-k). bds. 7.95 *(978-1-4549-2927-7(8))* Sterling Publishing Co., Inc.

Beacon, Dawn. Peter Piper. Beacon, Dawn. 2011. (Favorite Mother Goose Rhymes Ser.). (ENG.). 16p. (J). (gr. -1-2). lib. bdg. 14.21 *(978-1-60954-282-5(7),* 200234) Child's World, Inc., The.

Beacon, Dawn & Lyles, Christopher. Just the Facts: Writing Your Own Research Report, 1 vol. Loewen, Nancy. 2009. (Writer's Toolbox Ser.). (ENG.). 32p. (J). (gr. 2-4). pap. 8.95 *(978-1-4048-5702-5(8),* Picture Window Bks.) Capstone.

Beakakchush. Seven Boys Who Turned into Geese: A Chumash Story about the Big Dipper. Ikba, Taloa. 2019. (ENG.). 34p. (J). pap. 5.50 ***(978-1-7034-4823-8(5))*** Independently Published.

Beaky, Suzanne. The Busy Life of Ernestine Buckmeister. Lodding, Linda Ravin. 2011. (ENG.). 32p. (J). (gr. -1-1). 16.95 *(978-0-9799746-9-4(0))* Flashlight Pr.

—Hailey Twitch & the Campground Itch. Barnholdt, Lauren. 2011. (Hailey Twitch Ser.: 3). (ENG.). 144p. (J). (gr. 2-4). pap. 8.99 *(978-1-4022-2446-1(X),* Sourcebooks Jabberwocky) Sourcebooks, Inc.

—Hailey Twitch & the Great Teacher Switch. Barnholdt, Lauren. 2010. (Hailey Twitch Ser.: 2). (ENG.). 176p. (J). (gr. 2-4). pap. 10.99 *(978-1-4022-2445-4(1),* Sourcebooks Jabberwocky) Sourcebooks, Inc.

—Hailey Twitch & the Wedding Glitch. Barnholdt, Lauren. 2011. (Hailey Twitch Ser.: 4). (ENG.). 144p. (J). (gr. 2-4). pap. 6.99 *(978-1-4022-2447-8(8),* Sourcebooks Jabberwocky) Sourcebooks, Inc.

—Hailey Twitch Is Not a Snitch. Barnholdt, Lauren. 2010. (Hailey Twitch Ser.: 1). (ENG.). 160p. (J). (gr. 2-4). pap. 6.99 *(978-1-4022-2444-7(3))* Sourcebooks, Inc.

—The Original Cowgirl: The Wild Adventures of Lucille Mulhall. Lang, Heather. 2015. (ENG.). 32p. (J). (gr. -1-3). 16.99 *(978-0-8075-2931-7(1),* 807529311) Whitman, Albert & Co.

—Rupert the Wrong-Word Pirate. Owens, Greg. 2006. (J). *(978-1-58987-143-4(X))* Kindermusik International.

—She'll Be Comin' Round the Mountain. Schwaeber, Barbie H., ed. 2007. (American Favorites Ser.). (ENG.). 32p. (J). (gr. -1-3). 14.95 *(978-1-59249-687-7(3))* Soundprints.

—She'll Be Comin Round the Mountain. Schwaeber, Barbie H. 2007. (American Favorites Ser.). (ENG.). 32p. (J). (gr. -1-3). 9.85 *(978-1-59249-688-4(1))* Soundprints.

—She'll Be Comin' Round the Mountain. rev. ed. 2007. (ENG.). 24p. (J). (gr. -1-k). 4.99 *(978-1-59069-604-0(2))* Studio Mouse LLC.

—What's Bugging Nurse Penny? A Story about Lice. Stier, Catherine. 2013. (ENG.). 32p. (J). (gr. -1-3). 16.99 *(978-0-8075-8803-1(2),* 807588032) Whitman, Albert & Co.

Beals, Cam. Apodaca: Battle for Bowen. Beals, Rodger. 2019. (ENG.). 84p. (J). (gr. 4-6). *(978-1-9990625-4-5(X))* Beals, Cam.

Beals, Cam. Tiffany the Impaler: Dragons vs Donuts. Beals, Cam. 2019. (Tiffany the Impaler Ser.: Vol. 1). (ENG.). 116p. (J). (gr. 1-5). *(978-1-9990625-2-1(3))* Beals, Cam.

Beals, Kaela. Mais Que Vas-Tu Faire de Tes Cheveux? Anderson-Yantha, Ndija. Biwole, Nathalie Michele, tr. 2018. (FRE.). 56p. (J). pap. *(978-0-9958577-2-8(5))* Anderson-Yantha, Ndija.

—What Are You Gonna Do with That Hair? Anderson-Yantha, Ndija. Garnsworthy, Mario, ed. 2016. (ENG.). (J). (gr. 3-7). pap. *(978-0-9958577-0-4(9))* Anderson-Yantha, Ndija.

Beam, Burgandy & Han, Yu-Mei. Tom Thumb. Hillert, Margaret. 2016. (BeginningtoRead Ser.). (ENG.). 32p. (J). (-2). lib. bdg. 22.60 *(978-1-59953-790-0(7))* Norwood Hse. Pr.

Beam, Matt. City Alphabet, 1 vol. Schwartz, Joanne. 2009. (ENG.). 60p. (gr. -1-4). 18.95 *(978-0-88899-928-3(3))* Groundwood Bks. CAN. Dist: Publishers Group West (PGW).

Bean, Brett. Centaur School #5. Coats, Lucy. 2016. (Beasts of Olympus Ser.: 5). (ENG.). 144p. (J). (gr. 2-4). 6.99 *(978-1-101-99505-1(X),* Grosset & Dunlap) Penguin Young Readers Group.

—Dragon Healer. Coats, Lucy. 2015. 136p. (J). *(978-1-4806-8442-3(2),* Grosset & Dunlap) Penguin Publishing Group.

—Dragon Healer #4. Coats, Lucy. 2015. (Beasts of Olympus Ser.: 4). (ENG.). 144p. (J). (gr. 2-4). 6.99 *(978-0-448-46196-0(X),* Grosset & Dunlap) Penguin Young Readers Group.

—Gods of the North #7. Coats, Lucy. 2017. (Beasts of Olympus Ser.: 7). (ENG.). 144p. (J). (gr. 2-4). 6.99 *(978-0-451-53433-0(6),* Grosset & Dunlap) Penguin Young Readers Group.

—Hound of Hades #2. Coats, Lucy. 2015. (Beasts of Olympus Ser.: 2). (ENG.). 144p. (J). (gr. 2-4). 6.99 *(978-0-448-46194-6(3),* Penguin Workshop) Penguin Young Readers Group.

—The Lizard War. Patton, Jack. 2015. 123p. (J). *(978-0-545-81265-8(8))* Scholastic, Inc.

—Steeds of the Gods #3. Coats, Lucy. 2015. (Beasts of Olympus Ser.: 3). (ENG.). 144p. (J). (gr. 2-4). 6.99 *(978-0-448-46195-3(1),* Penguin Workshop) Penguin Young Readers Group.

—The Unicorn Emergency #8. Owen, Lucy Margaret & Coats, Lucy. 2018. (Beasts of Olympus Ser.: 8). (ENG.). 144p. (J). (gr. 2-4). 6.99 *(978-0-515-15952-3(2),* Penguin Workshop) Penguin Young Readers Group.

—Zeus's Eagle. Coats, Lucy. 2016. 135p. (J). *(978-1-5182-1746-3(X),* Grosset & Dunlap) Penguin Publishing Group.

—Zeus's Eagle #6. Coats, Lucy. 2016. (Beasts of Olympus Ser.: 6). (ENG.). 144p. (J). (gr. 2-4). 6.99 *(978-1-101-99552-5(1),* Grosset & Dunlap) Penguin Young Readers Group.

Bean, Brett. Kingdom Caper #1. Bean, Brett. 2020. (Zoo Patrol Squad Ser.: 1). (ENG.). 80p. (J). (gr. 3-7). 12.99 ***(978-0-593-09370-2(4),*** Penguin Workshop) Penguin Young Readers Group.

Bean, Izzy. Armored Armadillo to Zippy Zebra: An Alliterative Anthology of Animals. Baker, Carol Robinson. 2018. (ENG.). 62p. (J). (gr. k-6). 24.99 *(978-0-692-07967-6(X));* (gr. 1-6). pap. 14.95 *(978-0-692-07947-8(5))* Baker, Carol Robinson.

—Kit Kitten & the Topsy-Turvy Feelings: A Story about Parents Who Aren't Always Able to Care. Evans, Jane. 2015. (ENG.). 32p. (C). 16.95 *(978-1-84905-602-1(1),* 693040) Kingsley, Jessica Pubs. GBR. Dist: Hachette UK Distribution.

—Little Charlotte & the Piano. Holliday, Charlotte Tacy. 2018. (ENG.). 42p. (J). pap. 12.95 *(978-1-64191-743-8(1))* Christian Faith Publishing.

—Little Meerkat's Big Panic: A Story about Learning New Ways to Feel Calm. Evans, Jane. 2016. (ENG.). 48p. 16.95 *(978-1-78592-703-4(5),* 693957) Kingsley, Jessica Pubs. GBR. Dist: Hachette UK Distribution.

—St Viper's School for Super Villains. the Big Bank Burglary. Donovan, Kim. 2013. 160p. pap. *(978-0-9571300-2-9(3))* Squawk Bks.

Bean, Jonathan. The Apple Pie That Papa Baked. Thompson, Lauren. 2007. (ENG.). 32p. (J). (gr. k-3). 18.99 *(978-1-4169-1240-8(1),* Simon & Schuster Bks. For Young Readers) Simon & Schuster Bks. For Young Readers.

—Bad Bye, Good Bye. Underwood, Deborah. 2014. (ENG.). 32p. (J). (gr. -1-3). 16.99 *(978-0-547-92852-4(1),* 1515634, HMH Books For Young Readers) Houghton Mifflin Harcourt Publishing Co.

—Emmy & the Home for Troubled Girls. Jonell, Lynne. 2010. (Emmy & the Rat Ser.: 2). (ENG.). 384p. (J). (gr. 4-7). pap. 13.99 *(978-0-312-60873-6(X),* 900065172) Square Fish.

—Emmy & the Incredible Shrinking Rat, 1. Jonell, Lynne. 2008. (Emmy & the Rat Ser.: 1). (ENG.). 368p. (J). (gr. 4-6). pap. 8.99 *(978-0-312-38460-9(2),* 900053524) Square Fish.

—One Starry Night. Thompson, Lauren. (ENG.). 32p. (J). 2011. (gr. -1-3). lib. bdg. 17.99 *(978-0-689-82851-5(9));* 2003. 6.99 *(978-0-689-84215-3(5))* McElderry, Margaret K. Bks. (McElderry, Margaret K. Bks.).

—Real Cowboys. Hoefler, Kate. 2016. (ENG.). 32p. (J). (gr. -1-3). 17.99 *(978-0-544-14892-5(4),* 1547831, HMH Books For Young Readers) Houghton Mifflin Harcourt Publishing Co.

Bean, Jonathan. Big Snow. Bean, Jonathan. 2013. (ENG.). 32p. (J). (gr. -1-1). 17.99 *(978-0-374-30696-0(6),* 900087739, Farrar, Straus & Giroux (BYR)) Farrar, Straus & Giroux.

—Building Our House. Bean, Jonathan. 2013. (ENG.). 48p. (J). (gr. -1-1). 19.99 *(978-0-374-38023-6(6),* 900038444, Farrar, Straus & Giroux (BYR)) Farrar, Straus & Giroux.

Bean, Rani. It's Called Fishing, Not Catching. Heywood, Joseph Keith. 2017. (ENG.). (J). (gr. k-3). pap. 12.99 *(978-0-692-82719-2(6))* Heywood, Joseph.

Bear, Andrea. We Are the People of This World: Book One. Santana, Sr. Stella. 2011. 40p. pap. 14.95 *(978-1-61204-643-3(6),* Eloquent Bks.) Strategic Book Publishing & Rights Agency (SBPRA).

Beard, Lauren. The Fairytale Hairdresser & Cinderella. Longstaff, Abie. 2014. (Fairytale Hairdresser Ser.: 2). (ENG.). 32p. (J). (-k). pap. 13.99 *(978-0-552-56535-6(0))* Transworld Publishers Ltd. GBR. Dist: Independent Pubs. Group.

—The Fairytale Hairdresser & Father Christmas. 2014. (Fairytale Hairdresser Ser.: 5). (ENG.). 32p. (J). (-k). pap. 12.99 *(978-0-552-57052-7(4))* Transworld Publishers Ltd. GBR. Dist: Independent Pubs. Group.

—The Fairytale Hairdresser & Rapunzel. Longstaff, Abie. 2014. (Fairytale Hairdresser Ser.: 1). (ENG.). 32p. (J). (-k). pap. 12.99 *(978-0-552-56186-0(X))* Transworld Publishers Ltd. GBR. Dist: Independent Pubs. Group.

—The Fairytale Hairdresser & Sleeping Beauty. Longstaff, Abie. 2014. (Fairytale Hairdresser Ser.: 3). (ENG.). 32p. (J). (-k). pap. 12.99 *(978-0-552-56755-8(8))* Transworld Publishers Ltd. GBR. Dist: Independent Pubs. Group.

—The Fairytale Hairdresser & Snow White. Longstaff, Abie. 2015. (Fairytale Hairdresser Ser.: 4). (ENG.). 32p. (J). (-k). pap. 12.99 *(978-0-552-56777-0(9))* Transworld Publishers Ltd. GBR. Dist: Independent Pubs. Group.

—The Fairytale Hairdresser & the Little Mermaid. Longstaff, Abie. 2015. (Fairytale Hairdresser Ser.). (ENG.). 32p. (J). (-k). pap. 12.99 *(978-0-552-57054-1(0))* Transworld Publishers Ltd. GBR. Dist: Independent Pubs. Group.

Bearden, Romare. Li'l Dan the Drummer Boy: A Civil War Story. Bearden, Romare. 2003. (ENG.). 40p. (J). (gr. -1-3). 24.99 *(978-0-689-86237-3(7),* Simon & Schuster Bks. For Young Readers) Simon & Schuster Bks. For Young Readers.

Beardshaw, Ros. My Pet Star. Averiss, Corrinne. 2020. 32p. (J). (gr. -1-k). (ENG.). pap. 10.99 *(978-1-4083-5366-0(0));* 18.99 *(978-1-4083-5363-9(6))* Hachette Children's Group GBR. (Orchard Bks.). Dist: Hachette Bk. Group.

Beardshaw, Rosalind. Box. Flyte, Min. 2016. (ENG.). 26p. (J). (gr. -1-2). 15.99 *(978-0-7636-8939-1(4),* Nosy Crow) Candlewick Pr.

—The Christmas Fairy. Booth, Anne. 2017. (ENG.). 32p. (J). (gr. -1-2). 15.99 *(978-0-7636-9629-0(3),* Nosy Crow) Candlewick Pr.

—The Fairiest Fairy. Booth, Anne. 2016. (ENG.). 32p. (J). (gr. -1-2). 15.99 *(978-0-7636-8659-8(X),* Nosy Crow) Candlewick Pr.

—Funny Face, Sunny Face. Symes, Sally. 2015. (ENG.). 32p. (J). (-k). 14.99 *(978-0-7636-7606-3(3),* Nosy Crow) Candlewick Pr.

—I See the Moon: Rhymes for Bedtime. Nosy Crow. 2019. (ENG.). 24p. (J). (-k). 16.99 *(978-1-5362-0579-4(6),* Nosy Crow) Candlewick Pr.

—Jack's Bed. Rickards, Lynne. 2006. (Green Bananas Ser.). (ENG.). 48p. (J). (gr. -1-k). *(978-0-7787-1044-8(0));* lib. bdg. *(978-0-7787-1028-8(9))* Crabtree Publishing Co.

—Just Right for Christmas. Black, Birdie. 2014. (ENG.). 24p. (J). (-k). bds. 6.99 *(978-0-7636-7563-9(6),* Nosy Crow) Candlewick Pr.

—Just Right for Two. Corderoy, Tracey. 2014. (ENG.). 32p. (J). (gr. -1-2). 15.99 *(978-0-7636-7344-4(7),* Nosy Crow) Candlewick Pr.

—Lola at the Library. McQuinn, Anna. 2006. (Lola Reads Ser.). (ENG.). 32p. (J). (gr. -1 — 1). 16.99 *(978-1-58089-113-4(6));* 7.99 *(978-1-58089-142-4(X))* Charlesbridge Publishing, Inc.

—Lola at the Library. McQuinn, Anna. 2007. 22p. (gr. -1). 16.95 *(978-0-7569-7931-7(5))* Perfection Learning Corp.

—Lola Gets a Cat. McQuinn, Anna. (Lola Reads Ser.). (ENG.). 28p. (J). (-k). 2018. pap. 6.99 *(978-1-58089-845-4(9));* 2017. lib. bdg. 15.99 *(978-1-58089-736-5(3))* Charlesbridge Publishing, Inc.

—Lola Goes to School. McQuinn, Anna. (Lola Reads Ser.). (ENG.). 32p. (J). (-k). 2020. pap. 7.99 *(978-1-62354-171-2(9));* 2019. lib. bdg. 16.99 *(978-1-58089-938-3(2))* Charlesbridge Publishing, Inc.

—Lola le Lee Al Pequeno Leo. McQuinn, Anna. 2013. (Lola Reads Ser.). (ENG.). 28p. (J). (-k). pap. 7.99 *(978-1-58089-599-6(9))* Charlesbridge Publishing, Inc.

—Lola Loves Stories. McQuinn, Anna. 2010. (Lola Reads Ser.). (ENG.). 28p. (J). (gr. k — 1). pap. 7.99 *(978-1-58089-259-9(0))* Charlesbridge Publishing, Inc.

—Lola Planta un Jardín. McQuinn, Anna. 2017. (Lola Reads Ser.). (SPA.). 28p. (J). (-k). 16.99 *(978-1-58089-797-6(5));* pap. 7.99 *(978-1-58089-786-0(X))* Charlesbridge Publishing, Inc.

—Lola Plants a Garden. McQuinn, Anna. (Lola Reads Ser.). (ENG.). 28p. (J). (-k). 2017. pap. 7.99 *(978-1-58089-695-5(2));* 2014. 16.99 *(978-1-58089-694-8(4))* Charlesbridge Publishing, Inc.

—Lola Quiere un Gato. McQuinn, Anna. 2019. (Lola Reads Ser.). (SPA.). 28p. (J). (-k). 16.99 *(978-1-58089-670-2(7));* pap. 7.99 *(978-1-58089-988-8(9))* Charlesbridge Publishing, Inc.

—Lola Reads to Leo. McQuinn, Anna. 2012. (Lola Reads Ser.). (ENG.). 28p. (J). (-k). 16.99 *(978-1-58089-403-6(8));* pap. 7.99 *(978-1-58089-404-3(6))* Charlesbridge Publishing, Inc.

—Lola Va a la Escuela. McQuinn, Anna. 2020. (Lola Reads Ser.). (SPA.). 32p. (J). (-k). pap. 7.99 *(978-1-62354-172-9(7))* Charlesbridge Publishing, Inc.

B

—Mole's Babies. Bedford, David. 2012. (ENG.). 32p. (J). *(978-1-58925-108-3(3))*; pap. *(978-1-58925-435-0(X))* Tiger Tales.
—Mole's in Love. Bedford, David. 2009. 32p. (J). (gr. -1-1). (ENG.). 21.19 *(978-1-58925-084-0(2))*; pap. 6.95 *(978-1-58925-417-6(1))* Tiger Tales.
—Walk & See: 123. Nosy Crow. 2018. (Walk & See Ser.). (ENG.). 26p. (J). (— 1). bds. 7.99 *(978-0-7636-9338-1(3))*, Nosy Crow) Candlewick Pr.
—Walk & See: ABC. Nosy Crow. 2018. (Walk & See Ser.). (ENG.). 26p. (J). (— 1). bds. 7.99 *(978-0-7636-9623-8(4))*, Nosy Crow) Candlewick Pr.
—Walk & See: Colors. Nosy Crow. 2018. (Walk & See Ser.). (ENG.). 26p. (J). (— 1). bds. 7.99 *(978-0-7636-9917-8(9))*, Nosy Crow) Candlewick Pr.
—Walk & See: Opposites. Nosy Crow. 2018. (Walk & See Ser.). (ENG.). 26p. (J). (— 1). bds. 7.99 *(978-1-5362-0248-9(7))*, Nosy Crow) Candlewick Pr.
—Warthog: A Counting Adventure. Black, Birdie. 2017. (ENG.). 24p. (J). (gr. -1-2). 14.99 *(978-0-7636-9323-7(5))*, Nosy Crow) Candlewick Pr.
Beardshaw, Rosalind. A Lola le Encantan Los Cuentos. Beardshaw, Rosalind. McQuinn, Anna. Canetti, Yanitzia, tr. 2012. (Lola Reads Ser.). (SPA.). 28p. (J). (-k). pap. 7.99 *(978-1-58089-444-9(5))* Charlesbridge Publishing, Inc.
—Lola Plants a Garden: Lola Planta un Jardín. Beardshaw, Rosalind. McQuinn, Anna & Calvo, Carlos E. 2017. (SPA & ENG.). (J). pap. *(978-1-63289-027-6(5))* Charlesbridge Publishing, Inc.
—Lola Reads to Leo: Lola le Lee Al Pequeño Leo. Beardshaw, Rosalind. McQuinn, Anna & Canetti, Yanitzia. 2017. (SPA & ENG.). (J). pap. *(978-1-63289-028-3(3))* Charlesbridge Publishing, Inc.
Bearss, Patricia. The Adventures of Forealdo. Paul J McSorley; Illustrated By Patricia. 2011. 36p. pap. 24.95 *(978-1-4560-8429-5(1))* America Star Bks.
Beasley, Dion. Cheeky Dogs: To Lake Nash & Back. Bell, Johanna. 2019. (ENG.). 128p. (J). (gr. 3-5). 22.99 ***(978-1-76052-811-9(0)***, A&U Children's) Allen & Unwin AUS. Dist: Independent Pubs. Group.
Beasley, Dion. Go Home, Cheeky Animals! Bell, Johanna. 2016. (ENG.). 32p. (J). (-1). 18.99 *(978-1-76029-165-5(X))* Allen & Unwin AUS. Dist: Independent Pubs. Group.
Beasley, Jessalyn Claire. Little Birder: A Field Guide to Birds of the Alphabet. Beasley, Jessalyn Claire. 2018. (ENG.). 60p. (J). (gr. k-2). 25.99 *(978-0-578-40036-5(7))* One Odd Duck Bks.
Beaton, Alyson. Grow: An Environmentally Friendly Book. Beaton, Alyson. Bradley, K. J. 2009. (ENG.). 23p. (J). (gr. k-k). 16.95 *(978-0-9771992-6-6(6))* Featherproof Bks.
Beaton, Clare. Cerdota Grandota. Blackstone, Stella. 2003.Tr. of How Big Is a Pig. 24p. (J). (gr. k-2). pap. 6.99 *(978-1-84148-926-1(3))* Barefoot Bks., Inc.
—Clare Beaton's Action Rhymes. 2010. 14p. (J). (gr. -1-k). bds. 6.99 *(978-1-84686-473-5(9))* Barefoot Bks., Inc.
—Clare Beaton's Animal Rhymes. Books, Barefoot. 2014. 14p. (J). (gr. -1-k). bds. 6.99 *(978-1-78285-080-9(5))* Barefoot Bks., Inc.
—Clare Beaton's Garden Rhymes. Books, Barefoot. 2014. 14p. (J). (gr. -1-k). bds. 6.99 *(978-1-78285-081-6(3))* Barefoot Bks., Inc.
—Clare Beaton's Nursery Rhymes. 2010. 14p. (J). (gr. -1-k). bds. 6.99 *(978-1-84686-472-8(0))* Barefoot Bks., Inc.
—La Comida/Food. 2003. (Bilingual First Books/English-Spanish Ser.). (ENG.). 24p. (J). (gr. -1-2). pap. 4.95 *(978-0-7641-2609-3(1))*, B.E.S. Publishing) Peterson's.
—Daisy Gets Dressed. 2005. 24p. (J). 15.99 *(978-1-84148-794-6(5))* Barefoot Bks., Inc.
—Elusive Moose. Gannij, Joan. (J). (gr. -1-k). 2011. 32p. pap. 7.99 *(978-1-84686-075-1(X))*; 2007. 24p. bds. 7.99 *(978-1-84686-001-0(6))* Barefoot Bks., Inc.
—English-Spanish Bilingual First Books, 6 bks. (J). lib. bdg. 86.70 *(978-1-56674-944-2(1))* Forest Hse. Publishing Co., Inc.
—Hay una Vaca Entre las Coles. Blackstone, Stella & Bass, Jules. 2003.Tr. of There's a Cow in the Cabbage Patch. (SPA.). 32p. (J). (gr. k-2). pap. 6.99 *(978-1-84148-965-0(4))* Barefoot Bks., Inc.
—Hidden Hippo. Gannij, Joan. (J). (gr. -1-2). 2011. 32p. pap. 6.99 *(978-1-84686-533-6(6))*; 2009. (ENG.). 24p. bds. 7.99 *(978-1-84686-329-5(5))* Barefoot Bks., Inc.
—I Dreamt I Was a Dinosaur. Blackstone, Stella. (J). (gr. -1-k). 2006. 24p. bds. 7.99 *(978-1-84686-015-7(6))*; 2005. (ENG.). 32p. 15.99 *(978-1-84148-238-5(2))* Barefoot Bks., Inc.
—Lucy the Cat at the Farm: Lucie le Chat a la Ferme. Bruzzone, Catherine. 2005. (Lucy Cat Ser.). (ENG & FRE.). 24p. (J). (gr. -1-1). pap. 7.99 *(978-1-902915-11-1(9))* B Small Publishing GBR. Dist: Independent Pubs. Group.
—Mrs. Moon: Lullabies for Bedtime. 2003. 48p. (J). 19.99 incl. audio compact disk *(978-1-84148-176-0(9))* Barefoot Bks., Inc.
—Read, Learn & Create: The nature craft book. 2019. (ENG.). 32p. (J). (gr. 1-4). lib. bdg. 17.99 *(978-1-58089-843-0(2))* Charlesbridge Publishing, Inc.
—Secret Seahorse. Blackstone, Stella. 2005. (J). (gr. -1-2). 24p. bds. 7.99 *(978-1-905236-15-2(8))*; 24p. 15.99 *(978-1-84148-704-5(X))*; 32p. pap. 7.99 *(978-1-84148-937-7(9))* Barefoot Bks., Inc.
—There's a Billy Goat in the Garden. Gugler, Laurel Dee. 2003. 32p. (J). (gr. -1-2). 14.99 *(978-1-84148-089-3(4))* Barefoot Bks., Inc.
—Who Are You, Baby Kangaroo? Blackstone, Stella. (J). 2005. 24p. (gr. -1-2). bds. 6.99 *(978-1-905236-19-0(0))*; 2004. 32p. 14.99 *(978-1-84148-217-0(X))* Barefoot Bks., Inc.
—Who Are You Baby Kangaroo? Blackstone, Stella. 2011. (ENG.). 32p. (J). (gr. -1-2). pap. 6.99 *(978-1-84686-190-1(X))* Barefoot Bks., Inc.
—Zoe & Her Zebra. Blackstone, Stella. 2011. 32p. (J). (gr. -1-2). pap. 6.99 *(978-1-84686-536-7(0))* Barefoot Bks., Inc.
Beaton, Clare. Un Alce, Veinte Ratones. Beaton, Clare. Blackstone, Stella. 2006.Tr. of One Moose, Twenty Mice. 32p. (J). (gr. -1-k). bds. 6.99 *(978-1-84686-019-5(9))* Barefoot Bks., Inc.
—Cerdota Grandota. Beaton, Clare. Blackstone, Stella. 2006.Tr. of How Big Is a Pig. 24p. (J). (gr. -1-k). bds. 6.99 *(978-1-84686-018-8(0))* Barefoot Bks., Inc.
—Clare Beaton's Bedtime Rhymes. Beaton, Clare. Books, Barefoot. 2012. 14p. (J). (gr. -1-k). bds. 6.99 *(978-1-84686-737-8(1))* Barefoot Bks., Inc.
—Clare Beaton's Farmyard Rhymes. Beaton, Clare. 2012. 14p. (J). (gr. -1-k). bds. 6.99 *(978-1-84686-736-1(3))* Barefoot Bks., Inc.
—How Big Is a Pig? Beaton, Clare. Blackstone, Stella. 2004. 24p. (J). (gr. -1-k). pap. 6.99 *(978-1-84148-702-1(3))* Barefoot Bks., Inc.
—How Loud Is a Lion? Beaton, Clare. Blackstone, Stella. 2007. 24p. (J). (gr. -1-k). bds. 7.99 *(978-1-84686-000-3(8))* Barefoot Bks., Inc.
—How Loud Is a Lion? Beaton, Clare. Blackstone, Stella. 2011. 24p. (J). (gr. -1-2). pap. 6.99 *(978-1-84686-534-3(4))* Barefoot Bks., Inc.
—I Dreamt I Was a Dinosaur. Beaton, Clare. Blackstone, Stella. 2011. 32p. (J). (gr. -1-k). pap. 7.99 *(978-1-84686-025-6(3))* Barefoot Bks., Inc.
—Make & Colour Paper Planes. Beaton, Clare. 2004. (ENG.). 24p. (J). (gr. 1-4). pap. 8.99 *(978-1-874735-94-6(8))* B Small Publishing GBR. Dist: Independent Pubs. Group.
—Make Your Own Noah's Ark. Beaton, Clare. 2007. (J). (gr. k-3). 9.95 *(978-0-8198-4862-8(X))* Pauline Bks. & Media.
—Ocean Craft Book. Beaton, Clare. Haig, Rudi. 2019. (ENG.). 32p. (J). (gr. 1-4). 17.99 *(978-1-58089-941-3(2))* Charlesbridge Publishing, Inc.
Beaton, Clare, jt. illus. see Harter, Debbie.
Beaton, Jill, jt. illus. see Or, Elbert.
Beatrice, Chris. The Book of Beeing: Moral Tails in an Immoral World. Friedman, J. S. 2017. (Maurice's Valises Ser.). (ENG.). 50p. (J). (gr. k-4). 7.99 *(978-94-91613-22-7(7))* Mouse Prints Pr. NLD. Dist: Ingram Publisher Services.
—Casablanca. Friedman, J. S. 2013. (Maurice's Valises Ser.: Vol. 3). (ENG.). 53p. (J). (gr. k-4). 16.95 *(978-94-91613-09-8(X))* Mouse Prints Pr. NLD. Dist: Ingram Publisher Services.
—In the Beginning. Friedman, J. S. 2013. (Maurice's Valises Ser.: Vol. 1). (ENG.). 45p. (J). (gr. k-4). 16.95 *(978-94-91613-03-6(0))* Mouse Prints Pr. NLD. Dist: Ingram Publisher Services.
—The Micetro of Moscow. Friedman, J. S. 2013. (Maurice's Valises Ser.: Vol. 2). (ENG.). 44p. (J). (gr. k-4). 16.95 *(978-94-91613-06-7(5))* Mouse Prints Pr. NLD. Dist: Ingram Publisher Services.
Beatrix, Potter. The Tale of Mrs. Tittlemouse. Potter, Beatrix. 2016. (Beatrix Potter Classics Ser.). (ENG.). 54p. (J). (gr. k-3). pap. 12.99 *(978-1-5324-0024-7(1))* Xist Publishing.
—The Tale of Peter Rabbit. Potter, Beatrix. 2016. (Beatrix Potter Classics Ser.). (ENG.). 54p. (J). (gr. k-3). pap. 12.99 *(978-1-5324-0014-8(4))* Xist Publishing.
—The Tale of Squirrel Nutkin. Potter, Beatrix. 2016. (Beatrix Potter Classics Ser.). (ENG.). 54p. (J). (gr. k-3). pap. 12.99 *(978-1-5324-0015-5(2))* Xist Publishing.
—The Tale of Tom Kitten. Potter, Beatrix. 2016. (Beatrix Potter Classics Ser.). (ENG.). 54p. (J). (gr. k-3). pap. 12.99 *(978-1-5324-0018-6(7))* Xist Publishing.
Beattie, Steven M., II. These Are My Sensors. Beattie, Steven M., II. 2007. 32p. (gr. -1-k). 19.99 *(978-1-59879-310-9(1))*; (J). 13.99 *(978-1-59879-363-5(2))* Lifevest Publishing, Inc.
Beatty-Anderson, Annika. Eat Rutabagas. Apps, Jerry. 2016. (ENG.). 28p. (J). (gr. 1-6). 10.00 *(978-1-930596-08-5(1))* Guest Cottage, Incorporated, The.
—Stormy. Apps, Jerry. 2016. (ENG.). 32p. (J). (gr. 1-6). 10.00 *(978-1-930596-09-2(X))* Guest Cottage, Incorporated, The.
Beatty, Connie & Phillippi, Faith. Why Owls Say Who. Beatty, Connie. 2008. 20p. per. 24.95 *(978-1-4137-6715-5(X))* America Star Bks.
Beatty, Terry, et al. Batman: the Brave & the Bold. Torres, J. 2013. (Batman: the Brave & the Bold Ser.). (ENG.). 32p. (J). (gr. 2-5). lib. bdg., lib. bdg., lib. bdg. 135.60 *(978-1-4342-4858-9(5))*, Stone Arch Bks.) Capstone.
Beatty, Terry. Benedict Arnold: American Hero & Traitor, 1 vol. Burgan, Michael. 2007. (Graphic Biographies Ser.). (ENG.). 32p. (J). (gr. 3-9). per. 8.10 *(978-0-7368-7906-4(4))*, Capstone Pr.) Capstone.
Beatty, Terry & Purcell, Gordon. The U. S. Constitution. Burgan, Michael. 2011. (Cornerstones of Freedom: Third Ser.). (ENG.). 64p. (J). (gr. 4-6). pap. 8.95 *(978-0-531-26567-3(6))*, Children's Pr.) Scholastic Library Publishing.
Beatty, Terry, jt. illus. see Barberi, Carlo.
Beatty, Terry, jt. illus. see Martin, Cynthia.
Beatty, Terry, jt. illus. see Purcell, Gordon.
Beaty, Janice J. & Beaty, Lillian C. Jarod & the Mystery of the Utah Arches: A National Park Adventure Series Book. 2016. 118p. (J). pap. *(978-1-63293-122-1(2))* Sunstone Pr.
Beaty, Lillian C. Jarod & the Mystery of the Petroglyphs: A National Park Adventure Series Book. Beaty, Janice J. 2015. 118p. (J). pap. *(978-1-63293-071-2(4))* Sunstone Pr.
Beaty, Lillian C., jt. illus. see Beaty, Janice J.
Beaty, Olivia. My Super Hero. Hemann, Jill Schroeder. 2020. (ENG.). 28p. (J). pap. 11.60 ***(978-1-0983-0831-5(X))*** BookBaby.
Beauchamp, Paris. Flossie's Beauty Shop. Lancaster, Camille. 2020. (ENG.). 28p. (J). (gr. k-3). pap. 8.99 ***(978-1-0878-7122-6(0))*** Lancaster, Camille.
Beaucher, Aleksandra. The Adventures of Blue Ocean Bob: Blue Ocean Bob Discovers His Purpose. Olbrys, Brooks. Hamilton, Emma Walton, ed. 2010. (Adventures of Blue Ocean Bob Ser.: Vol. 1). 32p. (J). (gr. -1-5). 16.99 *(978-0-9829613-0-8(8))* Children's Success Unlimited LLC.
Beaudesson, Emmanuel. Junipero Serra: Founder of the California Missions. Gondosch, Linda. 2015. (ENG.). 36p. (J). (gr. -1-7). 14.99 *(978-1-62164-062-2(0))* Ignatius Pr.
—Let's Pray the Rosary. Vial-Andru, Mauricette. 2015. (ENG.). 32p. (J). (gr. 1-6). 14.99 *(978-1-62164-034-9(5))* Ignatius Pr.
—Our Holy Father, the Pope: The Papacy from Saint Peter to the Present. Caffery, Don R. 2013. (ENG.). 48p. (J). (gr. 2-8). 14.95 *(978-1-58617-921-2(7))* Ignatius Pr.
Beaudette, Michelle. The Boss of Me. Beaudette, Cathy. 2011. 32p. pap. *(978-1-77067-350-2(4))* FriesenPress.
Beaudoin, Beau. Boetry. Beaudoin, Beau. 2007. 40p. (J). per. 15.95 *(978-0-9788401-1-2(9))* Red Ink Pr.
Beaulieu, Jean-François, jt. illus. see Bachs, Ramon.
Beaulieu, Jean-François, jt. illus. see Coelho, Jorge.
Beaulieu, Jean-François, jt. illus. see Ruiz, Felix.
Beaulieu, Jean-François, jt. illus. see Walker, Tigh.
Beaulieu, Jean-François, jt. illus. see Young, Skottie.
Beaulieu, Jimméy. L' Evasion d'Alfred le Dindon. Langlois, Annie. 2004. (Roman Jeunesse Ser.). (FRE.). 96p. (J). (gr. 4-7). pap. *(978-2-89021-687-7(X))* Diffusion du livre Mirabel (DLM).
Beaulieu, Jimmy. Mia, Matt & the Lazy Gator, 1 vol. Langlois, Annie. Cummins, Sarah, tr. (Formac First Novels Ser.). (ENG.). 64p. (J). (gr. 1-5). 2016. pap. 5.95 *(978-0-88780-936-1(7))*, 8039c1d4-41d2-4b4c-ac25-385e6b6a7787); 2010. 14.95 *(978-0-88780-938-5(3))*, 938) Formac Publishing Co., Ltd. CAN. Dist: Lerner Publishing Group, Formac Lorimer Bks. Ltd.
—Mia, Matt & the Turkey Chase, 1 vol. Langlois, Annie. Cummins, Sarah, tr. 2008. (Formac First Novels Ser.). (ENG.). 64p. (J). (gr. 2-5). 5.95 *(978-0-88780-763-3(1))*, 763) Formac Publishing Co., Ltd. CAN. Dist: Formac Lorimer Bks. Ltd.
—Mia, Matt & the Turkey Chase. Langlois, Suzanne. Cummins, Sarah, tr. 2008. (Formac First Novels Ser.). (ENG.). 64p. (J). (gr. 2-5). 14.95 *(978-0-88780-765-7(8))*, 765) Formac Publishing Co., Ltd. CAN. Dist: Formac Lorimer Bks. Ltd.
Beaumont, Peter. The Three Little Girls & the Giant Sea Turtle. Lowe, Lana. 2006. (J). *(978-0-9777274-0-7(8))* Lone Star Publishing Co.
Beautyman, Kirsti. The Lost Homework. O'Neill, Richard. 2019. (Child's Play Library). 32p. (J). (gr. k-4). (ENG.). pap. *(978-1-78628-345-0(X))*; *(978-1-78628-346-7(8))* Child's Play International Ltd.
Beauvais, Gailanna. How Are We Blessed? Beauvais, Gailanna. 2012. 40p. pap. 9.95 *(978-0-9884679-0-3(9))* Visual Velocity.
Beauvisage, Alice. My Blankie. Beauvisage, Alice. 2013. (ENG.). 12p. (J). (gr. -1-k). bds. 6.95 *(978-1-927018-08-8(0))* Simply Read Bks. CAN. Dist: Ingram Publisher Services.
Beavan, Elliott. The Mysterious Corridor. Zapple, Elias. 2018. (Duke & Michel American-English Edition Ser.: Vol. 1). (ENG.). 236p. (J). (gr. 4-6). pap. *(978-1-912704-00-2(5))* Heads or Tales Pr.
Beaver, Moses. An Aboriginal Carol, 1 vol. Bouchard, David & Aglukark, Susan. 2007. (ENG.). 32p. (J). (gr. 2-5). 24.95 *(978-0-88995-406-9(2))*, dc5a150f-80c9-4c33-a2ab-4c184b5b2d34) Trifolium Bks., Inc. CAN. Dist: Firefly Bks., Ltd.
—An Aboriginal Carol: French Edition, 1 vol. Bouchard, David. 2007. (FRE.). 32p. (J). (gr. 3-18). 24.95 *(978-0-88995-413-7(5))*, 02e2f111-4d71-484c-92fa-1a7cb7a7a160) Fitzhenry & Whiteside, Ltd. CAN. Dist: Firefly Bks., Ltd.
Beaverho, Archie. The Old Man with the Otter Medicine. Blondin, John. Sundberg, Mary Rose, tr. ed. 2007. (Old Man with the Otter Medicine Ser.). (ENG, DOI & DGR.). 40p. 22.95 *(978-1-894778-49-7(9))* Theytus Bks., Ltd. CAN. Dist: Univ. of Toronto Pr.
Beavers, Ethen. Aquaman! (DC Super Friends) Berrios, Frank. 2018. (Little Golden Book Ser.). (ENG.). 24p. (J). (-k). 4.99 *(978-0-525-58224-3(X))*, Golden Bks.) Random Hse. Children's Bks.
—Ara's Rocky Road to White Belt. Lee, Master Taekwon & Nodelman, Jeffrey. 2017. (Team Taekwondo Ser.: 1). 108p. (J). (gr. 1-4). pap. 9.99 *(978-1-62336-880-7(4))*, 9781623368807, Rodale Kids) Random Hse. Children's Bks.
—Attack of the Deadly Diapers. Atwood, Megan. 2020. (Michael Dahl Presents: Side-Splitting Stories Ser.). (ENG.). 72p. (J). (gr. 3-6). pap. 5.95 *(978-1-4965-9209-5(3))*, 142237); lib. bdg. 25.32 *(978-1-4965-8705-3(7))*, 141439) Capstone. (Stone Arch Bks.).
—Bad Weather! (DC Super Friends) Berrios, Frank. 2014. (Little Golden Book Ser.). (ENG.). 24p. (J). (-k). 4.99 *(978-0-385-38440-7(8))*, Golden Bks.) Random Hse. Children's Bks.
—Baeoh & the Bully: Team Taekwondo #2. Lee, Master Taekwon & Nodelman, Jeffrey. 2018. (Team Taekwondo Ser.: 2). 96p. (J). (gr. 1-4). pap. 9.99 *(978-1-62336-945-3(2))*, 9781623369453, Rodale Kids) Random Hse. Children's Bks.
—Batman! (DC Super Friends) Wrecks, Billy. 2012. (Little Golden Book Ser.). (ENG.). 24p. (J). (-k). 4.99 *(978-0-307-93103-0(X))*, Golden Bks.) Random Hse. Children's Bks.
—Batman Tangles with Terror. Manning, Matthew K. 2017. (DC Super Hero Stories Ser.). (ENG.). 56p. (J). (gr. 1-3). lib. bdg. 25.32 *(978-1-4965-4632-6(6))*, Stone Arch Bks.) Capstone.
—Be Brave Like Batman! (DC Super Friends) Hitchcock, Laura. 2019. (ENG.). 40p. (J). (gr. -1-2). 9.99 *(978-1-5247-6915-4(0))*, Random Hse. Bks. for Young Readers) Random Hse. Children's Bks.
—Bedtime for Batman. Dahl, Michael. (DC Super Heroes Ser.). (ENG.). (J). (gr. -1-2). 2017. 30p. bds. 7.99 *(978-1-62370-921-1(0))*, 136564); 2016. 32p. 15.95 *(978-1-62370-732-3(3))*; 2016. 32p. lib. bdg. 22.65 *(978-1-5158-0652-3(9))* Capstone. (Stone Arch Bks.).
—Bug Brigade. Manning, Matthew K. 2020. (Michael Dahl Presents: Side-Splitting Stories Ser.). (ENG.). 72p. (J). (gr. 3-6). pap. 5.95 *(978-1-4965-9207-1(7))*, 142235); lib. bdg. 25.32 *(978-1-4965-8703-9(0))*, 141437) Capstone. (Stone Arch Bks.).
—The Cheerleaders of Doom. Buckley, Michael. 2011. (Nerds Ser.). (ENG.). 288p. (J). (gr. 3-7). pap. 7.95 *(978-1-4197-0124-5(X))* Abrams, Inc.
—Clayface Returns. Sazaklis, John. 2016. (You Choose Stories: Batman Ser.). (ENG.). 112p. (J). (gr. 2-6). lib. bdg. 32.65 *(978-1-4965-3089-9(6))*, Stone Arch Bks.) Capstone.
—DC Super Hero Stories. Manning, Matthew K. 2017. (DC Super Hero Stories Ser.). (ENG.). 56p. (J). (gr. 1-3). 101.28 *(978-1-4965-4636-4(9))*, 26180, Stone Arch Bks.) Capstone.
—The Flash! (DC Super Friends) Berrios, Frank. 2018. (Little Golden Book Ser.). (ENG.). 24p. (J). (-k). 4.99 *(978-1-5247-6858-4(8))*, Golden Bks.) Random Hse. Children's Bks.
—The Flash Races the Rogues. Manning, Matthew K. 2017. (DC Super Hero Stories Ser.). (ENG.). 56p. (J). (gr. 1-3). lib. bdg. 25.32 *(978-1-4965-4633-3(4))*, Stone Arch Bks.) Capstone.
—How to Be Cheeri: Team Taekwondo #3. Lee, Master Taekwon & Nodelman, Jeffrey. 2019. (Team Taekwondo Ser.: 3). 108p. (J). (gr. 1-4). 14.99 *(978-1-62336-950-7(9))*, 9781623369507); pap. 9.99 *(978-1-62336-948-4(7))*, 9781623369484) Random Hse. Children's Bks. (Rodale Kids).
—I Am Captain Kirk. Berrios, Frank. 2019. (Little Golden Book Ser.). 24p. (J). (-k). 4.99 *(978-1-9848-2973-3(4))*, Golden Bks.) Random Hse. Children's Bks.
—I Am Mr. Spock. Schaefer, Elizabeth. 2019. (Little Golden Book Ser.). 24p. (J). (-k). 4.99 *(978-1-9848-2975-7(0))*, Golden Bks.) Random Hse. Children's Bks.
—The Joker's Dozen. Sutton, Laurie S. 2015. (You Choose Stories: Batman Ser.). (ENG.). 112p. (J). (gr. 2-6). lib. bdg. 32.65 *(978-1-4342-9707-5(1))*, Stone Arch Bks.) Capstone.
—The Lazarus Plan. Sazaklis, John. 2016. (You Choose Stories: Batman Ser.). (ENG.). 112p. (J). (gr. 2-6). lib. bdg. 32.65 *(978-1-4965-3088-2(8))*, Stone Arch Bks.) Capstone.
—M Is for Mama's Boy. Buckley, Michael. 2010. (ENG.). 288p. (J). (gr. 3-7). pap. 6.95 *(978-0-8109-9674-8(X))*, Amulet Bks.) Abrams, Inc.
—Poker Face, 1 vol. Beechen, Adam. 2013. (Justice League Unlimited Ser.). (ENG.). 32p. (J). (gr. 3-6). lib. bdg. 22.60 *(978-1-4342-4714-8(7))*, Stone Arch Bks.) Capstone.
—The Riddler's Ransom. Hoena, Blake. 2015. (You Choose Stories: Batman Ser.). (ENG.). 112p. (J). (gr. 2-6). lib. bdg. 32.65 *(978-1-4342-9706-8(3))*, Stone Arch Bks.) Capstone.
—Seed Bank Heist. Bright, J. E. 2015. (You Choose Stories: Batman Ser.). (ENG.). 112p. (J). (gr. 2-6). pap. 6.95 *(978-1-4342-9709-9(8))*, Stone Arch Bks.) Capstone.
Beavers, Ethen. Star Trek Alphabet Book (Star Trek) Golden Books. 2020. (Little Golden Book Ser.). 24p. (J). (-k). 4.99 ***(978-0-593-12187-0(2)***, Golden Bks.) Random Hse. Children's Bks.
Beavers, Ethen. Star Wars: Attack of the Clones (Star Wars) Golden Books. 2015. (Little Golden Book Ser.). (ENG.). 24p. (J). (-k). 4.99 *(978-0-7364-3546-8(8))*, Golden Bks.) Random Hse. Children's Bks.
—Summer Freeze! Terrell, Brandon. 2015. (You Choose Stories: Batman Ser.). (ENG.). 112p. (J). (gr. 2-6). lib. bdg. 32.65 *(978-1-4342-9708-2(X))*, Stone Arch Bks.) Capstone.
—Super-Pets! (DC Super Friends) Wrecks, Billy. 2016. (Little Golden Book Ser.). (ENG.). 24p. (J). (gr. -1-k). 4.99 *(978-0-553-53923-3(X))*, Golden Bks.) Random Hse. Children's Bks.
—Super-Villain Smackdown! Sazaklis, John. 2015. (You Choose Stories: Batman Ser.). (ENG.). 112p. (J). (gr. 2-6). lib. bdg. 32.65 *(978-1-4965-0528-6(X))*, Stone Arch Bks.) Capstone.
—Superman Battles the Billionaire Bully. Manning, Matthew K. 2017. (DC Super Hero Stories Ser.). (ENG.). 56p. (J). (gr. 1-3). lib. bdg. 25.32 *(978-1-4965-4634-0(2))*, Stone Arch Bks.) Capstone.
—Superman! (DC Super Friends) Wrecks, Billy. 2013. (Little Golden Book Ser.). (ENG.). 24p. (J). (-k). 4.99 *(978-0-307-93195-5(1))*, Golden Bks.) Random Hse. Children's Bks.
—The Terrible Trio. Sutton, Laurie S. 2015. (You Choose Stories: Batman Ser.). (ENG.). 112p. (J). (gr. 2-6). lib. bdg. 32.65 *(978-1-4965-0529-3(8))*, Stone Arch Bks.) Capstone.
—Too Many Tribbles! Berrios, Frank & Random House Staff. 2019. (Little Golden Book Ser.). 24p. (J). (-k). 4.99 *(978-1-9848-4800-0(3))*, Golden Bks.) Random Hse. Children's Bks.
—A Topps League Story: Book Six: Batter Up! Scaletta, Kurtis. 2013. (ENG.). 112p. (J). (gr. 2-4). pap. 5.95 *(978-1-4197-0727-8(2))*, Amulet Bks.) Abrams, Inc.
—Wonder Woman Wrestles Circe's Sorcery. Manning, Matthew K. 2017. (DC Super Hero Stories Ser.). (ENG.). 56p. (J). (gr. 1-3). lib. bdg. 25.32 *(978-1-4965-4635-7(0))*, Stone Arch Bks.) Capstone.
—You Choose Stories: Batman. Sazaklis, John. 2016. (You Choose Stories: Batman Ser.). (ENG.). 112p. (gr. 2-3). 261.20 *(978-1-4965-3100-1(0))*, Stone Arch Bks.) Capstone.
Beavers, Ethen & Cornia, Christian. Michael Dahl Presents: Side-Splitting Stories. Atwood, Megan et al. 2020. (Michael Dahl Presents: Side-Splitting Stories Ser.). (ENG.). (J). (gr. 3-6). 101.28 *(978-1-4965-8707-7(3))*, 29779); pap., pap., pap. 23.80 *(978-1-4965-9219-4(0))*, 29948) Capstone. (Stone Arch Bks.).
Beavers, Melinda. I Want to Be a Lion. Troupe, Thomas Kingsley. 2015. (I Want to Be... Ser.). (ENG.). 24p. (J). (gr. k-3). lib. bdg. 27.32 *(978-1-4795-6860-4(0))*, Picture Window Bks.) Capstone.

—The Zoo's Annual Piggyback Race. Harrigan, Matt. 2013. 32p. (J). pap. 6.99 *(978-0-9873437-0-3(X))* Hedgebury AUS. Dist: New Shelves Distribution.

Beavis, Paul. I'm Joking: 500+ Original Jokes for Kids. Moffatt, Tom E. 2020. (ENG.). 236p. (J). (gr. 3-6). pap. ***(978-0-9951210-2-7(8))*** Write Laugh.

Bebirian, Helena. Good Night God, Love Olivia. Mammola-Koravos, Beth A. l.t. ed. 2006. 32p. (J). (gr. -1-1). 15.95 *(978-1-59879-110-5(9))* Lifevest Publishing, Inc.

Beccard, Helen L. Saint Catherine of Siena: The Story of the Girl Who Saw Saints in the Sky. Windeatt, Mary F. 2009. (ENG.). 65p. (J). (gr. 3-7). reprint ed. pap. 7.95 *(978-0-89555-421-5(6))* TAN Bks.

Beccia, Carlyn. Monstrous: The Lore, Gore, & Science Behind Your Favorite Monsters. Beccia, Carlyn. 2019. (ENG.). 148p. (J). (gr. 4-8). lib. bdg. 19.99 *(978-1-5124-4916-7(4),* Carolrhoda Bks.) Lerner Publishing Group.

Becher, Arthur E. A Little Book of Christmas. Bangs, John Kendrick. 2019. (ENG.). 114p. (J). (gr. k-6). pap. ***(978-625-7959-13-1(6))*** Uhrayoglu, Murat E Kitap Projesi.

Beck, Andrea. Elliot's Fire Truck, 1 vol. Beck, Andrea. 2018. (ENG.). 32p. (J). (gr. -1-k). 13.95 *(978-1-4598-2249-8(8))* Orca Bk. Pubs. USA.

—Pierre in the Air!, 1 vol. Beck, Andrea. 2011. (Pierre le Poof Ser.: 3). (ENG.). 32p. (J). (gr. -1-k). 19.95 *(978-1-55469-032-9(3))* Orca Bk. Pubs. USA.

—Pierre le Poof!, 1 vol. Beck, Andrea. 2009. (Pierre le Poof Ser.: 1). (ENG.). 32p. (J). (gr. -1-k). 19.95 *(978-1-55469-028-2(5))* Orca Bk. Pubs. USA.

Beck, Blaze. Skinni Mini & Friends in the Valley of Hope. Beck, Ernie. 2012. 74p. pap. 13.99 *(978-0-9858398-5-7(6))* Mindstir Media.

Beck, Charles. Admiral Richard E Byrd. Steinberg, Alfred. 2011. 128p. 40.95 *(978-1-258-01853-5(5))* Literary Licensing, LLC.

Beck, David Michael. Ilfanti & the Orb of Prophecy. Bowyer, Clifford B. 2009. (Imperium Saga: 1). (ENG.). 416p. 19.95 *(978-0-9787782-7-9(8))* Silver Leaf Bks., LLC.

—Swords for Hire: Two of the Most Unlikely Heroes You'll Ever Meet. Allen, Will. 2003. 168p. (gr. 3-18). pap. 6.95 *(978-0-9724882-0-4(0))* Centerpunch Pr.

Beck, Ian. White Fang. London, Jack. 2019. 288p. (J). pap. 10.00 *(978-1-84749-801-4(9),* 900210529, Alma Classics) Bloomsbury Publishing USA.

Beck, Robert. Soccerland, 0 vols. Choat, Beth. 2012. (International Sports Academy Ser.: 0). (ENG.). 242p. (YA). (gr. 7-9). pap. 8.99 *(978-0-7614-6249-1(X),* 9780761462491, Skyscape) Amazon Publishing.

Beck, Sam. The Very Short, Entirely True History of Unicorns. Laskow, Sarah. 2019. 96p. (J). (gr. 3-7). 12.99 *(978-1-5247-9273-2(X),* Penguin Workshop) Penguin Young Readers Group.

Beck, Thomas. Fiona the Frivolous Firefly & Her BFF Fernando the Flatulent. McLaughlin, Janice. 2019. (ENG.). 26p. (J). pap. 9.15 *(978-1-0923-6571-0(0))* Independently Published.

—Gavin the Gregarious Grasshopper. McLaughlin, Janice. 2019. (ENG.). 28p. (J). pap. 9.13 *(978-1-0722-3499-9(8))* Independently Published.

—Grasshopper Coloring / Activity Book. McLaughlin, Janice. 2019. (ENG.). 40p. (J). pap. 5.38 *(978-1-0722-3358-9(4))* Independently Published.

Becker, Aaron. Journey. Becker, Aaron. 2013. 40p. (J). (gr. -1-3). 16.99 *(978-0-7636-6053-6(1))* Candlewick Pr.

—The Journey Trilogy. Becker, Aaron. 2017. 120p. (J). (gr. -1-3). 49.99 *(978-0-7636-9537-8(8))* Candlewick Pr.

Becker, Aaron. My Favorite Color: I Can Only Pick One? Becker, Aaron. 2020. (ENG.). 16p. (J). (gr. -1-3). bds. 15.99 ***(978-1-5362-1474-1(4))*** Candlewick Pr.

Becker, Aaron. Return. Becker, Aaron. 2016. 40p. (J). (gr. -1-3). 16.99 *(978-0-7636-7730-5(2))* Candlewick Pr.

—A Stone for Sascha. Becker, Aaron. 2018. 48p. (J). (gr. k-4). 17.99 *(978-0-7636-6596-8(7))* Candlewick Pr.

—You Are Light. Becker, Aaron. 2019. (ENG.). 16p. (J). (gr. -1-3). 15.99 *(978-1-5362-0115-4(4))* Candlewick Pr.

Becker, Baruch. The Aleph Bias Ship on the Aleph Bias Trip. Altein, Chani. Rosenfeld, D. L. & Leverton, Yossi, eds. 2009. 30p. (J). 10.95 *(978-1-929628-25-4(0))* Hachai Publishing.

—Olf der Aleph Bais Shif. Altein, Chani. Brod, Chani, tr. from ENG. 2014.Tr. of Aleph Bais Trip on the Aleph Bais Ship. 32p. (J). 10.95 *(978-1-929628-77-3(3))* Hachai Publishing.

Becker, Bill. Jose & Mariano Meet Taotaomon'a, l.t. ed. 2004. 112p. (YA). per. 5.00 *(978-0-9761366-0-6(0))* Cebrano Publishing.

Becker, Boruch. Touch of Chanukah: A Touch & Feel Book. Rouss, Sylvia. 2011. (J). bds. 9.95 *(978-0-8266-0013-4(1))* Kehot Pubn. Society.

—A Touch of Passover: A Touch & Feel Book. Sollish, Ari. 2006. 12p. (J). bds. 7.95 *(978-0-8266-0021-9(2))* Merkos L'Inyonei Chinuch.

—Touch of Shabbat: A Touch & Feel Book. Krinsky, Rivkah. 2011. (J). bds. 9.95 *(978-0-8266-0019-6(0))* Kehot Pubn. Society.

Becker, Charlotte, jt. illus. see Richardson, Frederick.

Becker, Charlotte, jt. illus. see Winter, Milo.

Becker, Frank. You Can TRIUMPH over TERROR: 7 Steps to Plan, Prepare, & Persevere. Becker, Frank. 2005. 230p. per. 24.95 *(978-0-9766720-0-5(6),* 92868) Greenbush Pr.

Becker, Joseph. Annabelle & Aiden in the Story of Life. Becker, Joseph. 2016. 20p. pap. 9.95 *(978-0-9978066-0-1(5))* Imaginarium Pr.

Becker, Joseph Raphael. Annabelle & Aiden-Story of Life: The Story of Life. Becker, Joseph Raphael. 2016. (ENG.). (J). 15.95 *(978-0-9978066-1-8(3))* Imaginarium Pr.

Becker, Lisa E., jt. illus. see Becker, LuAnne E.

Becker, LuAnne E. Thunder on the Reservation. Winderman, Jay B. 2007. 147p. (J). (gr. 3-7). per. 13.95 *(978-0-9761623-2-2(6))* Pill Bug Pr.

Becker, LuAnne E. & Becker, Lisa E. Thunder on the Desert. Winderman, Jay B. 2005. 152p. (J). (gr. 3-7). per. 13.95 *(978-0-9761623-1-5(8))* Pill Bug Pr.

Becker, Pamela. Oil Paints, 1 vol. Bolte, Mari. 2013. (Paint It Ser.). (ENG.). 32p. (J). (gr. 3-9). 28.65 *(978-1-4765-3110-6(2))* Capstone.

—Pastels, 1 vol. Bolte, Mari. 2013. (Paint It Ser.). (ENG.). 32p. (J). (gr. 3-9). 28.65 *(978-1-4765-3111-3(0))* Capstone.

Becker, Paula. Here's the Reason God Made Me. Keefer, Mikal. 2017. (Best of Li'l Buddies Ser.). (ENG.). 16p. (J). bds. 6.99 *(978-1-4707-4860-9(6))* Group Publishing, Inc.

—Mad, Glad, or Sad, God Is for Me. Keefer, Mikal. 2017. (Best of Li'l Buddies Ser.). (ENG.). 16p. (J). bds. 6.99 *(978-1-4707-4856-2(8))* Group Publishing, Inc.

—Michael Makes Friends at School. Rustad, Martha. 2017. (Cloverleaf Books (tm) — off to School Ser.). (ENG.). 24p. (J). (gr. k-2). pap. 8.99 *(978-1-5124-5577-9(6),* 9781512455779); lib. bdg. 25.32 *(978-1-5124-3937-3(1))* Lerner Publishing Group. (Millbrook Pr.).

—Tanya Takes the School Bus. Rustad, Martha. 2017. (Cloverleaf Books (tm) — off to School Ser.). (ENG.). 24p. (J). (gr. k-2). pap. 8.99 *(978-1-5124-5580-9(6),* Millbrook Pr.) Lerner Publishing Group.

—This Is My Continent. Bullard, Lisa. 2016. (Cloverleaf Books (tm) — Where I Live Ser.). (ENG.). 24p. (J). (gr. k-2). 25.32 *(978-1-4677-9525-8(9),* 9781467795258, Millbrook Pr.) Lerner Publishing Group.

—To Planet Earth! Bellisario, Gina. 2017. (Cloverleaf Books (tm) — Space Adventures Ser.). (ENG.). 24p. (J). (gr. k-2). 25.32 *(978-1-5124-2535-2(4),* 9781512425352, Millbrook Pr.) Lerner Publishing Group.

—Who Works at Hannah's School? Bullard, Lisa. 2017. (Cloverleaf Books (tm) — off to School Ser.). (ENG.). 24p. (J). (gr. k-2). pap. 8.99 *(978-1-5124-5581-6(4),* Millbrook Pr.) Lerner Publishing Group.

Becker, Paula J. Journey to the Sun. Shepherd, Jodie. 2017. (Cloverleaf Books (tm) — Space Adventures Ser.). (ENG.). 24p. (J). (gr. k-2). 25.32 *(978-1-5124-2538-3(9),* 9781512425383, Millbrook Pr.) Lerner Publishing Group.

—My Home, Your Home. Bullard, Lisa. 2015. (Cloverleaf Books (tm) — Alike & Different Ser.). (ENG.). 24p. (J). (gr. k-2). lib. bdg. 25.32 *(978-1-4677-4904-6(4),* 9781467749046, Millbrook Pr.) Lerner Publishing Group.

—My Language, Your Language. Bullard, Lisa. 2015. (Cloverleaf Books (tm) — Alike & Different Ser.). (ENG.). 24p. (J). (gr. k-2). pap. 8.99 *(978-1-4677-6034-8(X),* 9781467760348); lib. bdg. 25.32 *(978-1-4677-4906-0(0),* 9781467749060) Lerner Publishing Group. (Millbrook Pr.).

—Tanya Takes the School Bus. Rustad, Martha E. H. 2017. (Cloverleaf Books (tm) — off to School Ser.). (ENG.). 24p. (J). (gr. k-2). 25.32 *(978-1-5124-3939-7(8),* 9781512439397, Millbrook Pr.) Lerner Publishing Group.

—This Is My Town. Bullard, Lisa. 2016. (Cloverleaf Books (tm) — Where I Live Ser.). (ENG.). 24p. (J). (gr. k-2). 25.32 *(978-1-4677-9522-7(4),* 9781467795227, Millbrook Pr.) Lerner Publishing Group.

—To Planet Earth! Bellisario, Gina. ed. 2017. (Cloverleaf Books (tm) — Space Adventures Ser.). (ENG.). 24p. (J). (gr. k-2). E-Book 38.65 *(978-1-5124-3890-1(1),* 9781512438901); E-Book 38.65 *(978-1-5124-2831-5(0));* E-Book 4.99 *(978-1-5124-3891-8(X),* 9781512438918) Lerner Publishing Group. (Millbrook Pr.).

—To the Sun! Shepherd, Jodie. ed. 2017. (Cloverleaf Books (tm) — Space Adventures Ser.). (ENG.). 24p. (J). (gr. k-2). E-Book 4.99 *(978-1-5124-3900-7(2),* 9781512439007); E-Book 38.65 *(978-1-5124-2835-3(3));* E-Book 38.65 *(978-1-5124-3899-4(5),* 9781512438994) Lerner Publishing Group. (Millbrook Pr.).

—Who Works at Hannah's School? Bullard, Lisa. 2017. (Cloverleaf Books (tm) — off to School Ser.). (ENG.). 24p. (J). (gr. k-2). 25.32 *(978-1-5124-3940-3(1),* 9781512439403, Millbrook Pr.) Lerner Publishing Group.

Becker, Rebecca J. Grobar & the Mind Control Potion. Cox, Joseph J. 2005. 168p. (J). per. 9.95 *(978-0-9764659-3-5(0))* Suckerfish Bks.

Becker, Suzy. Bud & Scooter. Becker, Suzy. Date not set. 48p. (J). (gr. k-3). 15.99 *(978-0-06-028970-6(8));* 16.89 *(978-0-06-028971-3(6))* HarperCollins Pubs.

—Kate the Great Except When She's Not. Becker, Suzy. 2014. (Kate the Great Ser.: 1). 272p. (J). (gr. 3-7). 12.99 *(978-0-385-38742-2(3),* Crown Books For Young Readers) Random Hse. Children's Bks.

—Kate the Great, Except When She's Not. Becker, Suzy. 2014. (Kate the Great Ser.: 1). (ENG.). 272p. (J). (gr. 3-7). lib. bdg. 15.99 *(978-0-385-38743-9(1),* Crown Books For Young Readers) Random Hse. Children's Bks.

—Kate the Great Winner Takes All. Becker, Suzy. 2016. (Kate the Great Ser.: 2). 256p. (J). (gr. 3-7). 12.99 *(978-0-385-38880-1(2),* Crown Books For Young Readers) Random Hse. Children's Bks.

Becker, Toni. Sonny - the Spectacular. Keaster, Diane W. l.t. ed. 2006. (ZC Horses: Vol. 9). (ENG.). 80p. (J). per. 7.95 *(978-0-9721496-9-3(4))* ZC Horses Series of Children's Bks.

Becker, Wayne. Laugh Out Loud Jokes. Namm, Diane. 2004. (Laugh-A-Long Readers Ser.). (J). *(978-0-7607-5281-4(8))* Barnes & Noble, Inc.

—My House. Jensen, Patricia. 2003. (My First Reader Ser.). (ENG.). 32p. (J). 18.50 *(978-0-516-22934-8(6),* Children's Pr.) Scholastic Library Publishing.

—Slithery Squirmy Jokes. Namm, Diane. 2004. (Laugh-A-Long Readers Ser.). (J). *(978-0-7607-5282-1(6))* Barnes & Noble, Inc.

—Who Says? Flaxman, Jessica & Hall, Kirsten. 2003. (My First Reader Ser.). (ENG.). 32p. (J). 18.50 *(978-0-516-22958-4(3),* Children's Pr.) Scholastic Library Publishing.

Beckerman, Chad. Frannie in Pieces. Ephron, Delia. 2007. 374p. (YA). (gr. 7-12). lib. bdg. 17.89 *(978-0-06-074717-6(X),* HarperTeen) HarperCollins Pubs.

Beckes, Shirley. Abigail's Ballet Class. James, Annabelle. 2004. 10p. (J). (gr. -1-k). 12.49 *(978-1-883043-54-4(9))* Straight Edge Pr., The.

—Abigail's Bedtime. James, Annabelle. 2004. (J). bds. 12.99 *(978-1-883043-53-7(0),* 6022) Straight Edge Pr., The.

—The Day I Followed the Pickle. Pugliano-Martin, Carol. ed. 2004. (Reader's Theater Ser.). (J). pap. *(978-1-4108-2297-0(4),* A22974) Benchmark Education Co.

—The Frog Prince: Imagination in a Box. Brandon, Wendy. 2004. 10p. (J). bds. 17.99 *(978-1-883043-49-0(2))* Straight Edge Pr., The.

—Halloween Math. Crawley, Brian. ed. 2004. (Reader's Theater Ser.). (J). pap. *(978-1-4108-2300-7(8),* A23008) Benchmark Education Co.

Beckes, Shirley V. The Frog Prince: Board Book & Puppet Theater. Brandon, Wendy. 2004. (J). *(978-1-883043-46-9(8))* Straight Edge Pr., The.

Becket, Nancy. No Ordinary Cat. Sermons, Faye. 2009. 40p. pap. 16.99 *(978-1-4389-6242-9(8))* AuthorHouse.

Beckett, Andrew & Aubrey, Meg Kelleher. Searching for Sunshine. Baglio, Ben M. 2005. 158p. (J). *(978-0-439-79249-3(5))* Scholastic, Inc.

Beckett, Garner. The Cats of Grand Central. Archibald, Laura. 2004. 30p. 16.95 *(978-0-9730951-0-4(5))* Solomon's Signature CAN. Dist: Hushion Hse. Publishing, Ltd.

Beckett, Kinsey. When Mommy Is Home with Me. Moulton, Alison. 2017. (J). 14.99 *(978-1-4622-0093-1(1),* Horizon Pubs.) Cedar Fort, Inc./CFI Distribution.

Beckett, Kyle. How to Build a Haunted House. Tupta, Frank. 2020. (ENG.). 40p. (J). (gr. -1-2). 17.99 *(978-1-5420-0543-2(4),* 9781542005432, Two Lions) Amazon Publishing.

Beckett, Sheilah. The Nutcracker. Balducci, Rita. 2014. (Little Golden Book Ser.). 24p. (J). (-k). 4.99 *(978-0-385-36993-0(X),* Golden Bks.) Random Hse. Children's Bks.

—The Twelve Days of Christmas. 2015. (Little Golden Book Ser.). 24p. (J). (gr. k-k). 4.99 *(978-0-307-00149-8(0),* Golden Bks.) Random Hse. Children's Bks.

Beckman, Jeff & Aguirre, Diego. Amos the Elf & His Magical Pajamas. Joyce, Kelley A. 2012. 38p. pap. 9.95 *(978-0-9881822-0-2(3))* Elf Garb.

Beckman, Olivia. Around the World Right Now. Cascone, Gina & Sheppard, Bryony Williams. 2017. (ENG.). 32p. (J). (gr. k-3). 16.99 *(978-1-58536-976-8(4),* 204230) Sleeping Bear Pr.

—Dear Santa, I Know It Looks Bad, but It Wasn't My Fault. Lewis, Norma. 2018. (J). *(978-1-4413-2421-4(6))* Peter Pauper Pr. Inc.

Beckstead, Lene. Color Me Baptized. 2009. 32p. pap. 6.95 *(978-0-88494-335-8(6))* Deseret Bk. Co.

Beckstrand, Jared. Baby Gets a Cake. Harris, Brooke. 2009. (Reader's Theater Nursery Rhymes & Songs Set B Ser.). 48p. (J). pap. *(978-1-60859-150-3(6))* Benchmark Education Co.

—A Fly on the Wall Street. Nelson, Sandi. 2013. 23p. (J). 19.99 *(978-1-938690-29-7(X))* Salem Author Services.

Beckstrand, Karl. Crumbs on the Stairs - Migas en Las Escaleras: A Mystery. Beckstrand, Karl. ed. (Mini-Mysteries for Minors Ser.: 2).Tr. of Migas en Las Escaleras. (ENG & SPA.). 24p. 2011. (J). pap. 14.95 *(978-0-9776065-9-7(7),* Gozo Bks.); 2007. 14.95 *(978-0-9776065-0-4(3))* Premio Publishing & Gozo Bks., LLC.

Becq, Cécile. Puss in Boots. 2016. (Once upon a Timeless Tale Ser.). (ENG.). 32p. (J). (gr. k-2). 9.99 *(978-1-74297-536-8(4))* Little Hare Bks. AUS. Dist: Independent Pubs. Group.

Becton, Daniel Walker. Wormy Worm. Becton, Daniel Walker. Becton, Sarah Walker & Becton, Franklyn Hall. 2007. 88p. (J). 19.95 *(978-1-878398-59-8(8),* Blue Note Bks.) Blue Note Pubns.

Becue, Benjamin. Touch & Explore Construction. Babin, Stephanie. 2019. (Touch & Explore Ser.: 8). (ENG.). 16p. (J). (gr. -1-k). 14.99 *(978-2-408-00794-2(1))* Editions Tourbillon FRA. Dist: Hachette Bk. Group.

Beddia, Maria. P Is for Pterodactyl: The Worst Alphabet Book Ever. Haldar, Raj & Carpenter, Chris. 2018. 40p. (J). (-3). 17.99 *(978-1-4926-7431-3(1),* Sourcebooks Jabberwocky) Sourcebooks, Inc.

Beddows, Eric. Joyful Noise: Poems for Two Voices. Fleischman, Paul. rev. ed. 2019. (Charlotte Zolotow Bk.). (ENG.). 64p. (J). (gr. 3-7). pap. 6.99 *(978-0-06-446093-4(2),* HarperCollins) HarperCollins Pubs. Ltd. GBR. Dist: HarperCollins Pubs.

—Night Cars, 1 vol. Jam, Teddy. 2006. (ENG.). 32p. (J). (gr. k — 1). bds. 11.95 *(978-0-88899-748-7(5))* Groundwood Bks. CAN. Dist: Publishers Group West (PGW).

—Toes. Seidler, Tor. 2004. 176p. (J). (gr. 3-18). (ENG.). 15.99 *(978-0-06-054099-9(0));* lib. bdg. 16.89 *(978-0-06-054100-2(8))* HarperCollins Pubs. (Geringer, Laura Book).

—Zoom, 1 vol. Wynne-Jones, Tim. 2009. (ENG.). 96p. (J). (gr. -1-2). 25.00 *(978-0-88899-936-8(4))* Groundwood Bks. CAN. Dist: Publishers Group West (PGW).

—Zoom at Sea, 1 vol. Wynne-Jones, Tim. 2013. (ENG.). 32p. (J). (gr. -1-2). 14.95 *(978-1-55498-391-9(6))* Groundwood Bks. CAN. Dist: Publishers Group West (PGW).

Bedell, Barbara. El Ciclo de Vida del Arbol. Kalman, Bobbie & Smithyman, Kathryn. 2005. (Serie Ciclos de Vida Ser.). (SPA.). 32p. (J). (gr. 1-4). pap. *(978-0-7787-8711-2(7))* Crabtree Publishing Co.

—The Life Cycle of a Raccoon. Kalman, Bobbie & Crossingham, John. 2003. (Life Cycle Ser.). (ENG.). 32p. (J). (gr. 3-4). pap. *(978-0-7787-0691-5(5));* lib. bdg. *(978-0-7787-0661-8(3))* Crabtree Publishing Co.

—Refugee Child: My Memories of the 1956 Hungarian Revolution. Kalman, Bobbie. 2006. (ENG.). 224p. (J). (gr. 3-7). lib. bdg. *(978-0-7787-2760-6(2))* Crabtree Publishing Co.

Beder, John. Click!, 1 vol. Crum, Shutta. 2004. (ENG.). 24p. (J). (gr. -1-1). pap. 3.95 *(978-1-55005-079-0(6),* 592d7306-8e34-4a21-8444-be8a4f3b235e) Clockwise Pr. CAN. Dist: Firefly Bks., Ltd.

Bedford, F. D. Peter & Wendy: The Restored Text. Barrie, J. M. Jones, Andrea, ed. 2015. 216p. (J). pap. 8.95 *(978-0-9823714-8-0(9))* Reginetta Pr., LLC.

—Peter Pan. Barrie, J. M. 2005. (Barnes & Noble Classics Ser.). 208p. per. 7.95 *(978-1-59308-213-0(4))* Barnes & Noble, Inc.

—Peter Pan, Vol. Barrie, J. M. 2004. (Modern Library Classics Ser.). (ENG.). 192p. (J). (gr. 3-7). pap. 10.95 *(978-0-8129-7297-9(X),* Modern Library) Random House Publishing Group.

Bedford, F. D., jt. illus. see Rackham, Arthur.

Bedford, Francis Donkin & Rackham, Arthur. Peter Pan. Barrie, J. M. 2015. (Word Cloud Classics Ser.). (ENG.). 272p. pap. 14.99 *(978-1-62686-392-7(X),* Canterbury Classics) Printers Row Publishing Group.

Bedford, Sabrina. How to Eat a Rainbow: Magical Raw Vegan Recipes for Kids!, 26 vols. Bedford, Ellie. 2nd rev. ed. 2015. (ENG.). 64p. (J). pap. 17.99 *(978-1-940184-22-7(3))* Vegan Pubs.

Bednarczyk, Samanta. Chat Pas Moi Qu'est un Menteur. Mouillot, Sophie. 2019. (FRE.). 36p. (J). pap. *(978-2-917822-65-4(1))* Pgcom Editions.

—Mamounette. Mouillot, Sophie. 2017. (FRE.). (J). pap. *(978-2-917822-49-4(X))* Pgcom Editions.

Bednorz, Brett. It's a Wonderful Life in the Garden. Kuepper, T. A. 2018. (Adventures of Archie Artichoke: Vol. 3). (ENG.). 64p. (J). (gr. k-4). 25.95 *(978-0-9977327-6-4(8));* pap. 15.95 *(978-0-9977327-5-7(X))* TK Enterprises.

Bednorz, Brett. There's a Circus at Farmer Frank's. Kuepper, T. A. 2019. (Adventures of Archie Artichoke Ser.: Vol. 4). (ENG.). 80p. (J). (gr. k-4). pap. 15.95 ***(978-1-7324354-1-4(3))*** TK Enterprises.

Bedoni, Lillian. Brother Bobcat & His Journey to Health: The Right Diet Helps Control Diabetes. Schwartz, Anna L. et al. 2018. (J). pap. *(978-1-63293-214-3(8))* Sunstone Pr.

Bedouet, Thierry. Baby Animals. Babin, Stephanie. 2019. (PlayTabs Ser.). (ENG.). 12p. (J). (gr. -1 — 1). bds. 12.99 *(978-2-408-00793-5(3))* Éditions Tourbillon FRA. Dist: Hachette Bk. Group.

—Bathtime: A Pull-The-Tab Book. Le Henand, Alice. 2019. (Pull & Play Ser.: 5). (ENG.). 14p. (J). (gr. -1 — 1). bds. 12.99 *(978-2-408-01282-3(1))* Éditions Tourbillon FRA. Dist: Hachette Bk. Group.

—Brothers & Sisters: A Pull-The-Tab Book. Le Henand, Alice. 2020. (Pull & Play Ser.: 7). (ENG.). 14p. (J). (gr. -1 — 1). bds. 12.99 *(978-2-408-01595-4(2))* Éditions Tourbillon FRA. Dist: Hachette Bk. Group.

—Feelings: A Pull-The-Tab Book. Le Henand, Alice. 2019. (Pull & Play Ser.: 4). (ENG.). 14p. (J). (gr. -1 — 1). bds. 12.99 *(978-2-408-00792-8(5))* Éditions Tourbillon FRA. Dist: Hachette Bk. Group.

—Mealtime: A Pull-The-Tab Book. Le Henand, Alice. 2020. (Pull & Play Ser.: 6). (ENG.). 14p. (J). (gr. -1 — 1). bds. 12.99 *(978-2-408-01594-7(4))* Éditions Tourbillon FRA. Dist: Hachette Bk. Group.

Bedouet, Thierry. Patience: A Pull-The-Tab Book. Le Henand, Alice. 2020. (Pull & Play Ser.: 8). (ENG.). 14p. (J). (gr. -1 — 1). bds. 12.99 ***(978-2-408-01994-5(X))*** Éditions Tourbillon FRA. Dist: Hachette Bk. Group.

Bedouet, Thierry. Please & Thank You: A Pull-The-Tab Book. 2017. (Pull & Play Ser.: 2). (ENG.). 14p. (J). (gr. -1 — 1). bds. 12.99 *(978-2-7459-9076-1(4))* Éditions Tourbillon FRA. Dist: Hachette Bk. Group.

Bedrick, Jeff. Madison Meets the Minister. Emm, David. 2010. (ENG.). 48p. (J). 12.95 *(978-1-889658-42-1(1))* New Canaan Publishing Co. LLC.

Bee, William. Stanley the Mailman. 2016. (J). pap. *(978-1-56145-946-9(1),* Peachtree Junior) Peachtree Publishing Co. Inc.

Bee, William. And the Cars Go... Bee, William. 2013. (ENG.). 32p. (J). (-k). 15.99 *(978-0-7636-6580-7(0))* Candlewick Pr.

—Migloo's Day. Bee, William. 2015. (ENG.). (J). (gr. -1-2). 14.99 *(978-0-7636-7374-1(9))* Candlewick Pr.

Bee, William. Stanley el Constructor. Bee, William. 2020. (Stanley Picture Bks.: 10). (SPA.). 32p. (J). (gr. -1-2). 8.99 ***(978-1-68263-223-9(7))*** Peachtree Publishing Co. Inc.

Bee, William. Stanley the Farmer, 1 vol. Bee, William. 2015. (Stanley Picture Bks.: 3). (ENG.). 32p. (J). (gr. 1-2). 14.95 *(978-1-56145-803-5(1))* Peachtree Publishing Co. Inc.

—Stanley the Mailman, 1 vol. Bee, William. 2016. (Stanley Picture Bks.: 5). (ENG.). 32p. (J). (gr. -1-2). 14.95 *(978-1-56145-867-7(8))* Peachtree Publishing Co. Inc.

Bee, William. Stanley y Su Escuela. Bee, William. 2020. (Stanley Picture Bks.: 11). (SPA.). 32p. (J). (gr. -1-2). 8.99 ***(978-1-68263-224-6(5))*** Peachtree Publishing Co. Inc.

Bee, William. Stanley's Colors, 1 vol. Bee, William. 2016. (Stanley Board Bks.: 1). (ENG.). 20p. (J). (gr. -1-k). bds. 6.95 *(978-1-56145-948-3(8),* Freestone) Peachtree Publishing Co. Inc.

—Stanley's Diner, 1 vol. Bee, William. 2015. (Stanley Picture Bks.: 4). (ENG.). 32p. (J). (gr. -1-2). 14.99 *(978-1-56145-802-8(3))* Peachtree Publishing Co. Inc.

Bee, William. Stanley's Fire Engine. Bee, William. 2020. (Stanley Picture Bks.: 9). (ENG.). 32p. (J). (gr. -1-2). 14.99 ***(978-1-68263-214-7(8))*** Peachtree Publishing Co. Inc.

Bee, William. Stanley's Numbers, 1 vol. Bee, William. 2017. (Stanley Board Bks.: 3). (ENG.). 20p. (J). (gr. -1 — 1). bds. 6.95 *(978-1-56145-976-6(3))* Peachtree Publishing Co. Inc.

—Stanley's Opposites, 1 vol. Bee, William. 2017. (Stanley Board Bks.: 4). (ENG.). 20p. (J). (gr. -1 — 1). bds. 6.95 *(978-1-56145-977-3(1))* Peachtree Publishing Co. Inc.

—Stanley's Paint Box. Bee, William. 2020. (Stanley Board Bks.: 5). (ENG.). 18p. (J). (gr. -1-1). bds. 6.99 *(978-1-68263-186-7(9))* Peachtree Publishing Co. Inc.

—Stanley's School. Bee, William. 2018. (Stanley Picture Bks.: 7). (ENG.). 32p. (J). (gr. -1-2). 14.95 *(978-1-68263-070-9(6))* Peachtree Publishing Co. Inc.

—Stanley's Shapes, 1 vol. Bee, William. 2016. (Stanley Board Bks.: 2). (ENG.). 20p. (J). (gr. -1-k). bds. 6.95 *(978-1-56145-949-0(6),* Freestone) Peachtree Publishing Co. Inc.

—Stanley's Store, 1 vol. Bee, William. 2017. (Stanley Picture Bks.: 6). (ENG.). 32p. (J). (gr. -1-2). 14.95 *(978-1-56145-868-4(6))* Peachtree Publishing Co. Inc.

—Stanley's Toolbox. Bee, William. 2020. (Stanley Board Bks.: 6). (ENG.). 18p. (J). (gr. -1-1). bds. 6.99 *(978-1-68263-187-4(7))* Peachtree Publishing Co. Inc.

B

—Stanley's Train, 1 vol. Bee, William. 2019. (Stanley Picture Bks.: 8). (ENG.). 32p. (J). (gr. -1-2). 14.95 *(978-1-68263-108-9(7))* Peachtree Publishing Co. Inc.

Beebe, Elecia. High on the Saddle: An Intergenerational Adventure into the Mountains of Oregon. Shumaker, Bonnie. 2018. (ENG.). 48p. (J). pap. 12.95 *(978-1-55571-923-4(6)*, Grid Pr.) L & R Publishing, LLC.

Beebe, Garrett. If You Give a Cactus a Hug. Prather, Anastasia. 2018. (ENG.). 36p. (J). (gr. 2-6). pap. 9.95 *(978-0-692-09851-6(8))* Prather, Anastasia.

Beebe, Robb. Judy: A Story of Divine Corners. Baldwin, Faith. 2011. 264p. 47.95 *(978-1-258-08877-4(0))* Literary Licensing, LLC.

—Tailspin Tommy: The Mystery of the Midnight Patrol. Stevens, Mark. 2011. 226p. 44.95 *(978-1-258-10164-0(5))* Literary Licensing, LLC.

Beebe, Susan. The Get Well Soon... Balloon. Parker, Vicki Sue. 2005. 16p. (J). 15.00 *(978-1-931117-35-7(7)*, BALL) Lash & Assocs. Publishing/Training, Inc.

Beech, Bryan. Follow the Prophet: A Flashlight Discovery Book. Gibby, Shauna. 2019. (J). 16.99 *(978-1-62972-576-5(5))* Deseret Bk. Co.

Beech, Mark. Being a Leader, 1 vol. Mayer, Cassie. 2007. (Citizenship Ser.). (ENG.). 24p. (J). (gr. -1-1). pap. 6.29 *(978-1-4034-9494-8(0)*, Heinemann) Capstone.

—Being Fair, 1 vol. Mayer, Cassie. 2007. (Citizenship Ser.). (ENG.). 24p. (J). (gr. -1-1). pap. 6.29 *(978-1-4034-9491-7(6)*, Heinemann) Capstone.

—Being Helpful, 1 vol. Mayer, Cassie. 2007. (Citizenship Ser.). (ENG.). 24p. (J). (gr. -1-1). pap. 6.29 *(978-1-4034-9493-1(2)*, Heinemann) Capstone.

—Being Honest, 1 vol. Mayer, Cassie. 2007. (Citizenship Ser.). (ENG.). 24p. (J). (gr. -1-1). pap. 6.29 *(978-1-4034-9492-4(4)*, Heinemann) Capstone.

—Being Responsible, 1 vol. Mayer, Cassie. 2007. (Citizenship Ser.). (ENG.). 24p. (J). (gr. -1-1). pap. 6.29 *(978-1-4034-9497-9(5)*, Heinemann) Capstone.

—Billy Plonka & the Grot Laboratory. Billings, Ian. 2016. (ENG.). (J). pap. *(978-0-9933456-1-6(1))* Pom, Tiddley.

—Country Money. Whitehead, William. 2015. (How Money Works). (ENG.). 64p. (J). (gr. 4-6). pap. 15.93 *(978-1-68404-069-8(8))* Norwood Hse. Pr.

—Country Money. Whitehead, William et al. 2015. (How Money Works). (ENG.). 64p. (J). (gr. 4-6). lib. bdg. 29.27 *(978-1-59953-719-1(2))* Norwood Hse. Pr.

—Do You Remember? Docherty, Helen. 2018. (ENG.). 32p. pap. 8.95 *(978-0-571-32114-8(3)*, Faber & Faber Children's Bks.) Faber & Faber, Inc.

—Dragons at Crumbling Castle: And Other Tales. Pratchett, Terry. (ENG.). 352p. (J). (gr. 5-7). 2016. pap. 8.99 *(978-0-544-81313-7(8)*, 1641909, HMH Books For Young Readers); 2015. 17.99 *(978-0-544-46659-3(4)*, 1600657) Houghton Mifflin Harcourt Publishing Co.

—Family Money. Whitehead, William. 2015. (How Money Works). (ENG.). 64p. (J). (gr. 4-6). pap. 15.93 *(978-1-68404-070-4(1))*; lib. bdg. 29.27 *(978-1-59953-717-7(6))* Norwood Hse. Pr.

—Following Rules, 1 vol. Mayer, Cassie. 2007. (Citizenship Ser.). (ENG.). 24p. (J). (gr. -1-1). pap. 6.29 *(978-1-4034-9495-5(9)*, Heinemann) Capstone.

—A Funeral in the Bathroom: And Other School Poems. Dakos, Kalli. 2017. (ENG.). 48p. (J). (gr. -1-3). pap. 7.99 *(978-0-8075-2676-7(2)*, 807526762) Whitman, Albert & Co.

—Hans in Luck. Hughes, Mónica. 2014. (Traditional Tales Ser.). (ENG.). 16p. (J). (gr. k-1). pap. 6.95 *(978-1-62521-564-2(9)*, Capstone Classroom) Capstone.

—My Dad, the Earth Warrior. Haq, Gary. 2018. (ENG.). 276p. (J). (gr. k-6). pap. *(978-1-9999337-9-1(6))* Gazzimodo.

—Wilfred the (Un)Wise. Lester, Cas. 2016. (ENG.). 288p. (J). (gr. k-3). pap. 8.99 *(978-1-84812-464-6(3))* Bonnier Publishing GBR. Dist: Independent Pubs. Group.

—World Money. Bailey, Gerry. 2015. (How Money Works). (ENG.). 64p. (J). (gr. 4-6). pap. 15.93 *(978-1-68404-071-1(X))* Norwood Hse. Pr.

—World Money. Bailey, Gerry & Law, Felicia. 2015. (How Money Works). (ENG.). 64p. (J). (gr. 4-6). lib. bdg. 29.27 *(978-1-59953-720-7(6))* Norwood Hse. Pr.

—Your Money. Bailey, Gerry. 2015. (How Money Works). (ENG.). 64p. (J). (gr. 4-6). pap. 15.93 *(978-1-68404-072-8(8))* Norwood Hse. Pr.

—Your Money. Bailey, Gerry & Law, Felicia. 2015. (How Money Works). (ENG.). 64p. (J). (gr. 4-6). lib. bdg. 29.27 *(978-1-59953-718-4(4))* Norwood Hse. Pr.

Beedie, Duncan. Get Coding 2! Build Five Computer Games Using HTML & JavaScript. Whitney, David. 2019. (ENG.). 224p. (J). (gr. 4-7). 18.99 *(978-1-5362-1030-9(7))*; pap. 12.99 *(978-1-5362-0541-1(9))* Candlewick Pr.

—Monsters' Nonsense: the Grumpy Guest: Level 5. Bently, Peter. 2018. (Monsters' Nonsense Ser.). (ENG.). 24p. (J). (gr. k-2). 14.95 *(978-1-68297-304-2(2))* QEB Publishing Inc.

—Monsters' Nonsense: the Wizard of Poob. Bently, Peter. 2018. (Monsters' Nonsense Ser.). (ENG.). 24p. (J). (gr. k-2). 14.95 *(978-1-68297-303-5(4))* QEB Publishing Inc.

—Pirates Don't Drive Diggers. English, Alex. 2019. (Early Bird Readers — Orange (Early Bird Stories (tm)) Ser.). (ENG.). 32p. (J). (gr. k-3). 27.99 *(978-1-5415-4221-1(5)*, 9781541542211); pap. 7.99 *(978-1-5415-7414-4(1)*, 9781541574144) Lerner Publishing Group. (Lerner Pubns.).

—Remember 10 with Explorer Ben. Veitch, Catherine. 2017. (ENG.). 48p. (J). (gr. k-4). 16.95 *(978-1-68297-206-9(2))* QEB Publishing Inc.

Beedie, Duncan. The Lumberjack's Beard. Beedie, Duncan. 2017. (ENG.). 40p. (J). (gr. k-3). 16.99 *(978-0-7636-9649-8(8)*, Templar) Candlewick Pr.

—Molly's Moon Mission. Beedie, Duncan. 2020. (ENG.). 40p. (J). (gr. -1-1). 17.99 *(978-1-5362-1016-3(1)*, Templar) Candlewick Pr.

Beeke, Tiphanie. Fast Asleep in a Little Village in Israel. MacLeod, Jennifer Tzivia. 2018. (J). *(978-1-68115-539-5(7)*, Apples & Honey Pr.) Behrman Hse., Inc.

—Fletcher & the Falling Leaves. Rawlinson, Julia. (ENG.). 32p. (J). (gr. -1-2). 2008. pap. 7.99 *(978-0-06-157397-2(3))*; 2006. 17.99 *(978-0-06-113401-2(5))* HarperCollins Pubs. (Greenwillow Bks.).

—Fletcher & the Snowflake Christmas. Rawlinson, Julia. 2010. (ENG.). 32p. (J). (gr. -1-2). 16.99 *(978-0-06-199033-5(7)*, Greenwillow Bks.) HarperCollins Pubs.

—Fletcher & the Springtime Blossoms. Rawlinson, Julia. 2009. (ENG.). 32p. (J). (gr. -1-2). 17.99 *(978-0-06-168855-3(X)*, Greenwillow Bks.) HarperCollins Pubs.

Beeke, Tiphanie. Fletcher & the Summer Show. Rawlinson, Julia. 2020. (ENG.). 32p. (J). (gr. 2-4). 21.99 ***(978-1-913134-63-1(6))*** Graffeg Limited GBR. Dist: Independent Pubs. Group.

Beeke, Tiphanie. Latke, the Lucky Dog. Fischer, Ellen. 2014. (ENG.). 24p. (J). (gr. -1-2). 17.95 *(978-0-7613-9038-1(3)*, 9780761390381, Kar-Ben Publishing) Lerner Publishing Group.

—Some Bunny to Talk To: A Story for Children about Going to Therapy. Conte, Paola et al. 2014. 32p. (J). *(978-1-4338-1649-9(0))*; pap. *(978-1-4338-1650-5(4))* American Psychological Assn. (Magination Pr.).

—The Stars Will Still Shine. Rylant, Cynthia. 2005. 40p. (J). lib. bdg. 17.89 *(978-0-06-054640-3(9))* HarperCollins Pubs.

—The Stars Will Still Shine. Rylant, Cynthia. 2005. (ENG.). 40p. (J). (gr. -1-3). 17.99 *(978-0-06-054639-7(5)*, HarperCollins) HarperCollins Pubs. Ltd. GBR. Dist: HarperCollins Pubs.

—That's How Much I Love You. Rudi, Julie A. 2013. (ENG.). 20p. (gr. -1). bds. 8.95 *(978-1-58925-644-6(1))* Tiger Tales.

Beeke, Tiphanie. The Noisy Way to Bed. Beeke, Tiphanie, tr. Whybrow, Ian. 2004. (J). *(978-0-439-55690-3(2)*, Levine, Arthur A. Bks.) Scholastic, Inc.

Beeler, Joe. The Secret of Fort Pioneer: A Bret King Mystery. Scott, Dan. 2011. 190p. 42.95 *(978-1-258-09951-0(9))* Literary Licensing, LLC.

Beeman, Kate. Charlie's Magic Glasses. Beeman, Kate. 2016. (ENG.). (J). pap. 11.95 *(978-0-692-78475-4(6))* Salty Sea Publishing.

Beene, Jason. Operation Fireball. Farber, Erica. 2014. (Fish Finelli Ser.). (ENG.). 172p. (J). (gr. 3-7). 15.99 *(978-1-4521-1083-7(2))* Chronicle Bks. LLC.

—Operation Fireball, Bk. 2. Farber, E. S. 2015. (Fish Finelli Ser.). (ENG.). 184p. (J). (gr. 3-7). pap. 6.99 *(978-1-4521-2875-7(8))* Chronicle Bks. LLC.

—Sophie Simon Solves Them All. Graff, Lisa. 2012. (ENG.). 112p. (J). (gr. 3-5). pap. 7.99 *(978-1-250-02898-3(1)*, 900118313) Square Fish.

—The Wednesdays. Bourbeau, Julie. (ENG.). 256p. (J). (gr. 2-5). 2013. pap. 7.99 *(978-0-375-87286-0(8)*, Yearling); 2012. 16.99 *(978-0-375-86890-0(9)*, Knopf Bks. for Young Readers) Random Hse. Children's Bks.

Beer, Sophie. Christmas in 100 Words. words&pictures. 2019. (My World in 100 Words Ser.). (ENG.). 20p. (J). (gr. -1 — 1). bds. 9.95 ***(978-0-7112-4263-0(1)***, Words & Pictures) Quarto Publishing Group UK GBR. Dist: Hachette Bk. Group.

—Elton John. Sanchez Vegara, Maria Isabel. 2020. (Little People, BIG DREAMS Ser.: 50). (ENG.). 32p. (J). (gr. -1-2). 15.99 ***(978-0-7112-5840-2(6)***, Frances Lincoln Children's Bks.) Quarto Publishing Group UK GBR. Dist: Hachette Bk. Group.

Beer, Sophie. Go, Grandma, Go! Plourde, Lynn. 2020. (ENG.). 20p. (J). (— 1). bds. 7.99 *(978-1-5344-5222-0(2)*, Little Simon) Little Simon.

—Go, Grandpa, Go! Plourde, Lynn. 2020. (ENG.). 20p. (J). (— 1). bds. 7.99 *(978-1-5344-5224-4(9)*, Little Simon) Little Simon.

—Izzy & Frank. Lehman, Katrina. 2020. (ENG.). 32p. (J). (gr. -1-2). 16.99 *(978-1-950354-23-8(7))* Scribe Pubns. AUS. Dist: Consortium Bk. Sales & Distribution.

Beers, Robert Lee. The Batty Bat. Freeman, David. 2012. 24p. pap. 24.95 *(978-1-4241-0177-1(8))* PublishAmerica, Inc.

—Hidden Treasure. Miller, Judith J. 2013. 24p. pap. 10.95 *(978-1-61633-419-2(3))* Guardian Angel Publishing, Inc.

—The Scarecrow. Freeman, David. 2012. 24p. 24.95 *(978-1-4626-9609-3(0))*; 20p. pap. 24.95 *(978-1-4137-9543-1(9))* PublishAmerica, Inc.

—The Whispery Witch. Freeman, David. 2012. 24p. pap. 24.95 *(978-1-4137-9620-9(6))* PublishAmerica, Inc.

Beeson, Jan. Mako in My Backyard. Paul & Lady Jan. 2013. 34p. pap. 12.99 *(978-0-9890482-3-1(3))* Beeson, Jan.

—Wesley the Wobbly Bear. Paul & Lady Jan. 2013. 38p. pap. 12.99 *(978-0-9890482-4-8(1))* Beeson, Jan.

—Zeela the Zebra of a Different Color. Beeson, Paul & Beeson, Lady Jan. 2013. 38p. pap. 12.99 *(978-0-9890482-5-5(X))* Beeson, Jan.

Beeuwsaert, Matt. I Got Game. Beeuwsaert, Matt. 2003. 176p. per. 14.95 *(978-0-9724358-0-2(8))* Beex Art Bks.

Beezley, Edwina. The Happy Tree Book of Children's Verse. Varella, Leonor. 2018. (ENG.). 90p. (J). pap. *(978-1-84897-931-4(2))* Olympia Publishers.

BEFEC Mulguin and Associates Staff. Tres Cabezas y un Volcan. Hernandez, Alejandro. rev. ed. 2006. (Castillo de la Lectura Blanca Ser.). (SPA & ENG.). 56p. (J). (gr. k). pap. 6.95 *(978-968-5920-88-9(5))* Castillo, Ediciones, S. A. de C. V. MEX. Dist: Macmillan.

Befort, Oana. Backpack Explorer: Bird Watch: What Will You Find? Editors of Storey Publishing. 2020. (Backpack Explorer Ser.). (ENG.). 48p. (J). 12.95 *(978-1-63586-251-5(5)*, 626251) Storey Publishing, LLC.

Begay, Patrick. What Does 'died' Mean? Halishá óolyé Daaztsâa? Thomas, Marjorie & Ruffenach, Jessie. 2005. (ENG & NAV.). 32p. (J). (gr. 4-7). pap. 9.00 *(978-1-893354-56-2(3))* Salina Bookshelf Inc.

Begay, Shonto. Soldier Sister, Fly Home. Flood, Nancy Bo. 2016. 176p. (J). (gr. 5). lib. bdg. 16.95 *(978-1-58089-702-0(9))* Charlesbridge Publishing, Inc.

Beghelli, Annalisa. Home for a Penguin, Home for a Whale. Williams, Brenda. 2019. (ENG.). 32p. (J). (gr. -1-4). *(978-1-78285-743-3(5))* Barefoot Bks., Ltd.

—The Illustrated Encyclopedia of Outer Space: An a to Z Guide to Facts & Figures. Mattarelli, Diego & Pagliari, Emanuela. 2020. (ENG.). 64p. (J). (gr. 1-5). 9.99 *(978-1-63158-591-3(6)*, Racehorse Publishing) Skyhorse Publishing Co., Inc.

—Marie Curie & the Power of Persistence. Valenti, Karla. 2020. (My Super Science Heroes Ser.). 48p. (J). (-3). 17.99 *(978-1-7282-1356-9(8))* Sourcebooks, Inc.

Begin, Jean-Guy. Chapeau, Camomille! Richard, Martine. 2004. (Des 6 Ans Ser.). (FRE.). 64p. 7.95 *(978-2-922565-96-6(3))* Editions de la Paix CAN. Dist: World of Reading, Ltd.

—Des Legumes Pour Frank Einstein. Lavoie, Rejean. 2004. (Des 9 Ans. Ser.: Vol. 44). (FRE.). 120p. (J). 8.95 *(978-2-89599-006-2(9))* Editions de la Paix CAN. Dist: World of Reading, Ltd.

—Disparition Chez les Lutins. Mallet, C. Claire. 2003. (Collection des 6 Ans: Vol. 21). (FRE.). 64p. (J). 7.95 *(978-2-922565-64-5(5))* Editions de la Paix CAN. Dist: World of Reading, Ltd.

—La Fee Dentiste. Deslauriers, Anne. 2004. (Collection des 6 Ans). (FRE.). 64p. (J). 7.95 *(978-2-922565-99-7(8))* Editions de la Paix CAN. Dist: World of Reading, Ltd.

—OGM et Chant de Mais. Cotes, Gilles. 2004. (FRE.). 112p. (J). *(978-2-89599-002-4(6))* Editions de la Paix CAN. Dist: World of Reading, Ltd.

Begin, Mary Jane. Before I Go to Sleep / Traditional Chinese Edition: Babl Children's Books in Chinese & English. Hood, Thomas. l.t. ed. 2016. (ENG.). (J). 14.99 *(978-1-68304-192-4(5))* Babl Books, Incorporated.

—R Is for Rhode Island Red: A Rhode Island Alphabet. Allio, Mark R. 2005. (Discover America State by State Ser.). (ENG.). 40p. (J). (gr. k-5). 17.95 *(978-1-58536-149-6(6))* Sleeping Bear Pr.

Begley, Amy. Mouse & the Midnight Visitor. Heffernan, Marion. 2019. (ENG.). 42p. (J). pap. 21.61 ***(978-1-7283-9410-7(4))*** AuthorHouse.

Begonia, Ruby. Don't Be a Chicken. Binks. 2013. 32p. 15.95 *(978-1-935448-22-8(6))* Lost Coast Pr.

—The Girl with Chipmunk Hands. Binks. 2013. 24p. (J). 15.95 *(978-1-935448-20-4(X))* Lost Coast Pr.

Beha, Philippe. The Best Time. Poulin, Andree. 2009. (My First Stories Ser.). 24p. (J). (gr. -1-3). 25.60 *(978-1-60754-350-3(8))*; pap. 8.15 *(978-1-60754-351-0(6))* Windmill Bks.

Béha, Philippe. Fairy Tale Breakfasts: A Cookbook for Young Readers & Eaters. Yolen, Jane. 2009. (Fairy Tale Cookbooks Ser.). 32p. (J). (gr. 2-5). 25.60 *(978-1-60754-573-6(X))*; pap. 10.55 *(978-1-60754-574-3(8))* Windmill Bks.

—Fairy Tale Desserts: A Cookbook for Young Readers & Eaters. Yolen, Jane. 2009. (Fairy Tale Cookbooks Ser.). 32p. (J). (gr. 2-5). 25.60 *(978-1-60754-583-5(7))*; pap. 10.55 *(978-1-60754-584-2(5))* Windmill Bks.

—Fairy Tale Dinners: A Cookbook for Young Readers & Eaters. Yolen, Jane. 2009. (Fairy Tale Cookbooks Ser.). 32p. (J). (gr. 2-5). 25.60 *(978-1-60754-580-4(2))*; pap. 10.55 *(978-1-60754-582-8(9))* Windmill Bks.

Beha, Philippe. Fairy Tale Feasts: A Literary Cookbook for Young Readers & Eaters. Yolen, Jane & Stemple, Heidi E. Y. (ENG.). 264p. (J). 2009. (gr. -1-3). pap. 20.00 *(978-1-56656-751-0(3)*, Crocodile Bks.); 2006. (gr. 4-7). 24.95 *(978-1-56656-643-8(6))* Interlink Publishing Group, Inc.

Béha, Philippe. Fairy Tale Lunches: A Cookbook for Young Readers & Eaters. Yolen, Jane. 2009. (Fairy Tale Cookbooks Ser.). 32p. (J). (gr. 2-5). 25.60 *(978-1-60754-576-7(4))*; pap. 10.55 *(978-1-60754-577-4(2))* Windmill Bks.

Beha, Philippe. The King Has Goat Ears, 1 vol. Jovanovic, Katarina. 2008. (ENG.). 32p. (J). (gr. -1-k). 16.95 *(978-1-896580-22-7(X))* Tradewind Bks. CAN. Dist: Orca Bk. Pubs. USA.

Béha, Philippe. The Prairie Dogs, 1 vol. Goertzen, Glenda. 2004. (ENG.). 164p. pap. *(978-1-55005-113-1(X))* Fitzhenry & Whiteside, Ltd.

Beha, Philippe. The Undesirables. Briere, Paule. 2009. (ENG.). 32p. (J). (gr. -1-3). 16.95 *(978-1-894965-88-0(4))* Simply Read Bks. CAN. Dist: Ingram Publisher Services.

—The Worst Time. Poulin, Andrée. 2009. (My First Stories Ser.). 24p. (J). (gr. -1-3). 25.60 *(978-1-60754-367-1(2))*; pap. 8.15 *(978-1-60754-368-8(0))* Windmill Bks.

Beha, Philippe. City Kids: Street & Skyscraper Rhymes, 1 vol. Kennedy, X. J. 2010. (ENG.). 86p. (J). (gr. 1-3). 17.95 *(978-1-896580-44-9(0))* Tradewind Bks. CAN. Dist: Orca Bk. Pubs. USA.

Béha, Philippe. The Golden Touch, 1 vol. Huser, Glen. 2015. (ENG.). 64p. (J). (gr. 1-3). 18.00 *(978-1-896580-73-9(4))* Tradewind Bks. CAN. Dist: Orca Bk. Pubs. USA.

Behan, Rachel A. Finding Jesus: Contemporary Children's Story. Sellers, Amy C., ed. l.t. ed. 2006. 19p. (J). 24.95 *(978-1-934194-00-3(X))* Olmstead Publishing LLC.

Behe, Cheri. When Jake Grows Up! Kershaw, Dorcas. 2018. (ENG.). 38p. (J). 22.99 *(978-1-5456-4762-2(3))*; pap. 12.49 *(978-1-5456-4761-5(5))* Salem Author Services.

Behl, Anne-Kathrin. Help, I Don't Want a Babysitter! Wagner, Anke. 2015. 32p. (J). 17.95 *(978-0-7358-4214-4(0))* North-South Bks., Inc.

—My Amazing Mozart Sound Book (Provisional) Godeau, Natacha. 2017. 10p. (J). (gr. -1-2). bds. 14.95 *(978-2-7338-5067-1(9))* Auzou, Philippe Editions FRA. Dist: Consortium Bk. Sales & Distribution.

Behr, Joyce. Funny Skits & Sketches. Halligan, Terry. unabr. ed. 2003. 128p. (YA). (gr. 4-12). pap. 15.00 *(978-0-88734-688-0(X))* Players Pr., Inc.

—Humorous Monologues. Bolton, Martha. 2003. 128p. (J). (gr. 2-7). 19.00 *(978-0-8069-6750-9(1))* Sterling Publishing Co., Inc.

Behr, Robbi. Babies Ruin Everything. Swanson, Matthew. 2016. (ENG.). 40p. (J). 16.99 *(978-1-250-08057-8(6)*, 900154883) Imprint IND. Dist: Macmillan.

—Everywhere, Wonder. Swanson, Matthew. 2017. (ENG.). 48p. (J). 17.99 *(978-1-250-08795-9(3)*, 900158205) Imprint IND. Dist: Macmillan.

—The Real Mccoys. Swanson, Matthew. 2017. (Real Mccoys Ser.: 1). (ENG.). 336p. (J). 16.99 *(978-1-250-09852-8(1)*, 900161848) Imprint IND. Dist: Macmillan.

—The Real Mccoys. Swanson, Matthew. 2018. (Real Mccoys Ser.: 1). (ENG.). 352p. (J). pap. 7.99 *(978-1-250-09853-5(X)*, 900161849) Square Fish.

—The Real Mccoys: Two's a Crowd. Swanson, Matthew. 2018. (Real Mccoys Ser.: 2). (ENG.). 336p. (J). 16.99 *(978-1-250-09855-9(6)*, 900161851) Imprint IND. Dist: Macmillan.

—The Real Mccoys: Two's a Crowd. Swanson, Matthew. 2019. (Real Mccoys Ser.: 2). (ENG.). 352p. (J). pap. 7.99 *(978-1-250-09857-3(2)*, 900161852) Square Fish.

—The Real Mccoys: Wonder Undercover. Swanson, Matthew. 2019. (Real Mccoys Ser.: 3). (ENG.). 352p. (J). 16.99 *(978-1-250-30782-8(1)*, 900198140) Imprint IND. Dist: Macmillan.

Beier, Ellen. Albert Einstein, Creative Genius. Mattern, Joanne & Santrey, Laurence. 2005. 45p. (J). pap. *(978-0-439-80152-2(4))* Scholastic, Inc.

—Anne of Green Gables. Helldorfer, M. C. 2003. 40p. (J). (gr. -1-2). pap. 7.99 *(978-0-440-41614-2(0)*, Dragonfly Bks.) Random Hse. Children's Bks.

—Brave Norman. Clements, Andrew. 2015. 32p. pap. 4.00 *(978-1-61003-600-9(X))* Center for the Collaborative Classroom.

—Centerfield Ballhawk. Christopher, Matt. 2009. (New Peach Street Mudders Sports Library). 64p. (J). (gr. 2-4). lib. bdg. 23.93 *(978-1-59953-317-9(0))* Norwood Hse. Pr.

—Dolores & the Big Fire: Dolores & the Big Fire. Clements, Andrew. 2003. (Pets to the Rescue Ser.). (ENG.). 32p. (J). (gr. -1-1). pap. 4.99 *(978-0-689-83440-0(3)*, Simon Spotlight) Simon Spotlight.

—Un Genio Creativo. Santrey, Laurence & Mattern, Joanne. 2007.Tr. of Albert Einstein. (ENG.). 48p. (J). (gr. k-2). pap. 4.99 *(978-0-439-87479-3(3)*, Scholastic en Espanol) Scholastic, Inc.

—Man Out at First. Christopher, Matt. 2009. (New Peach Street Mudders Sports Library). 64p. (J). (gr. 2-4). lib. bdg. 23.93 *(978-1-59953-319-3(7))* Norwood Hse. Pr.

—Mrs. Peachtree & the Eighth Avenue Cat. Silverman, Erica. 2011. (ENG.). 32p. (J). (gr. -1-3). pap. 16.99 *(978-1-4424-4340-2(5)*, Simon & Schuster Bks. For Young Readers) Simon & Schuster Bks. For Young Readers.

—Tara & Tiree, Fearless Friends: A True Story. Clements, Andrew. 2003. (Pets to the Rescue Ser.). (ENG.). 32p. (J). (gr. -1-2). pap. 4.99 *(978-0-689-83441-7(1)*, Simon Spotlight) Simon Spotlight.

Beifus, Ruth. Round & Round the Jewish Year Vol. 1: Elul-Tishrei. Rosenberg, Tziporah. 2009. 67p. (J). (gr. 3-6). 19.99 *(978-1-59826-376-3(5))* Feldheim Pubs.

—Round & Round the Jewish Year Vol. 2: Cheshvan-Shevat. Rosenberg, Tziporah. Gross, Sherie, tr. 2008. 68p. (J). (gr. 3-6). 19.99 *(978-1-59826-281-0(5))* Feldheim Pubs.

Beighley, Marci, et al. Adventures of Strawberry Shortcake! Harimann, Sierra et al. 2016. 126p. (J). *(978-1-101-95018-0(8))* Penguin Random Hse. LLC.

Beighton, Matt. Spot the Dot. Beighton, Matt. 2018. (ENG.). 34p. (J). pap. 9.99 *(978-1-9997244-8-1(8)*, Green Monkey Bks.) Purple Sword Pubns., LLC.

Beingessner, Laura. Rachel Carson & Her Book That Changed the World. Lawlor, Laurie. 2014. (ENG.). 32p. (J). (gr. 1-4). 7.99 *(978-0-8234-3193-9(2))* Holiday Hse., Inc.

—Sail Away with Me. Collins-Philippe, Jane. 2010. 32p. (J). (gr. -1-2). 15.95 *(978-0-88776-842-2(3)*, Tundra Bks.) Tundra Bks. CAN. Dist: Penguin Random Hse. LLC.

Beinicke, Steve. The Heat Is On. Tanaka, Shelley. (J). pap. 4.99 *(978-1-55054-200-4(1)*, Da Capo Pr. Inc.) Hachette Bks.

Beisch, Leigh, photos by. Ice Cream Treats: Easy Ways to Transform Your Favorite Ice Cream into Spectacular Desserts. Ferreira, Charity. 2004. (ENG., 96p. (gr. 8-17). pap. 16.95 *(978-0-8118-4102-3(2))* Chronicle Bks. LLC.

Beise, Sarah. Calling All Cars. Fliess, Sue. 2016. 32p. (J). (-3). 14.99 *(978-1-4926-1881-2(0)*, 9781492618812, Sourcebooks Jabberwocky) Sourcebooks, Inc.

Beitchman, Daniel. Boy Versus Fly: A Dean Bean Adventure. Beitchman, Daniel. 2018. (ENG.). 36p. (J). (gr. k-4). pap. *(978-1-7751796-2-7(1))* Beitchman, Daniel.

Beith, Laura Huliska. Five Little Ladybugs with Hand Puppet. Gerth, Melanie. 2009. (ENG.). 12p. 12.95 *(978-1-58117-889-0(1)*, Intervisual/Piggy Toes) Bendon, Inc.

Beitia, Maria. La Pluma. Satz, Mario. 2019. (SPA.). 40p. (J). (gr. 2-4). pap. 17.95 *(978-84-17440-07-7(0))* Akiara Bks. ESP. Dist: Independent Pubs. Group.

Beitz-Grant, Heather. The Magic Tree House, 1 vol. Shoesmith-Bateman, Amanda. 2010. 22p. 24.95 *(978-1-4489-3866-7(X))* PublishAmerica, Inc.

Belzym, Kateryna. What Are Dads Afraid Of? Children's Book about Overcoming Fears [Illustrated Bedtime Story Age 3-5]. Shvets, Hanna & Malenar, Oscar. 2019. (ENG.). 26p. (J). pap. 9.99 ***(978-1-6512-6972-5(6))*** Independently Published.

Belanger, Andy. Kill Shakespeare, 2 vols. McCreery, Conor & Del Sol, Anthony. 2011. (Kill Shakespeare Ser.: 2). 148p. pap. 19.99 *(978-1-61377-025-2(1)*, 9781613770252) Idea & Design Works, LLC.

Belanger, Damon. Costi & the Raindrop Adventure. Khamis, Johnny. 2007. 32p. (J). (gr. -1-3). 6.95 *(978-1-60005-029-9(8))* Happy About.

Belcher, Andy, photos by. Crabs Blue Band. Hall, Ralph. 2017. (Cambridge Reading Adventures Ser.). (ENG., 16p. pap. 5.62 *(978-1-108-43537-6(8))* Cambridge Univ. Pr.

—In the Sea Red Band. Llewellyn, Claire. 2016. (Cambridge Reading Adventures Ser.). (ENG., 16p. pap. 7.37 *(978-1-107-57578-3(8))* Cambridge Univ. Pr.

Belcher, Andy & Belcher, Angie, photos by. Rally Challenge: Band 10/White (Collins Big Cat) Belcher, Andy & Belcher, Angie. 2005. (Collins Big Cat Ser.). (ENG., 32p. (J). (gr. 1-3). pap. 9.99 *(978-0-00-718632-7(0))* HarperCollins Pubs. Ltd. GBR. Dist: Independent Pubs. Group.

Belcher, Angie. Oceans Alive: Band 14/Ruby (Collins Big Cat) Belcher, Angie. 2007. (Collins Big Cat Ser.). (ENG.). 48p. (J). (gr. 3-4). pap. 12.99 *(978-0-00-723092-1(3))* HarperCollins Pubs. Ltd. GBR. Dist: Independent Pubs. Group.

Belcher, Angie, jt. photos by see Belcher, Andy.

Belcher, Mary. Lilies for Looper. Stuart, Rachel Foster. 2017. (ENG.). (J). (gr. k-4). pap. 14.99 *(978-0-9973805-0-7(0)*, Kaleidoscope Bks.) I Am My Life Publishing, LLC.

Belden, Georgie. Charlie the Sailor. Belden, Georgie. 2018. (ENG.). 42p. (J). pap. 10.00 *(978-1-7268-4265-5(7))* Independently Published.

—The Four Fuzzy Wuzzy Amigos. Belden, Georgie. 2018. (ENG.). 34p. (J). pap. 10.00 *(978-1-7311-8196-1(5))* Independently Published.

Belden, Georgie. Giada. Belden, Georgie. 2019. (Lost Mermaids of Coral City Ser.: Vol. 2). (ENG.). 44p. (J). pap. 10.00 ***(978-1-7040-6200-6(4))*** Independently Published.

Belden, Georgie. King Louie & Queen Pixie Doodle Book Two. Belden, Georgie. 2018. (Adventures of King Louie & Queen Pixie Doodle Ser.: Vol. 2). (ENG.). 32p. (J). pap. 10.00 *(978-1-7199-0680-7(7))* Independently Published.

—The Kingdom of King Louie & Queen Pixie Doodle. Belden, Georgie. 2018. (Adventures of King Louie & Queen Pixie Doodle Ser.: Vol. 1). (ENG.). 114p. (J). pap. 22.00 *(978-1-7241-6415-5(5))* Independently Published.

Belgradi, Facundo. Las Aventuras de Robin Hood. 2019. (Brújula y la Veleta Ser.). (SPA.). 64p. (J). (gr. 4-7). pap. 5.95 *(978-987-718-549-2(0))* Ediciones Lea S.A. ARG. Dist: Independent Pubs. Group.

—Sandokan: El Tigre de la Malasia. 2019. (Brújula y la Veleta Ser.). (SPA.). 64p. (J). (gr. 4-7). pap. 5.95 *(978-987-718-558-4(X))* Ediciones Lea S.A. ARG. Dist: Independent Pubs. Group.

Belgrave, T. Tobias & the Super Scary Science Teacher. Din, R. 2019. (Super Scary Science Teacher Ser.: Vol. 1). (ENG.). 50p. (J). pap. 5.38 *(978-1-0722-9104-6(5))* Independently Published.

Belik, Anastasia. Piper's Christmas Adventure. Adam, Lia. 2018. (ENG.). 32p. (J). pap. 9.99 *(978-1-7907-0778-2(1))* Independently Published.

Belisle, John. In God's Kitchen. Kavanagh, James. 2004. 32p. (J). 15.95 *(978-1-58355-241-4(3))* Western National Parks Assn.

Belkholm, Erica. The Case of the Florida Freeze, 1 vol. Jacobson, Ryan. l.t. ed. 2005. (Santa Claus: Super Spy Ser.). (ENG.). 80p. (J). per. 4.99 *(978-0-9774122-0-4(2)*, Getchu Bks.) Lake 7 Creative, LLC.

Belknap, Barbara. An Anasazi Welcome. Matthews, Kay. 2004. 40p. (gr. 4-7). pap. 6.95 *(978-1-878610-27-0(9))* Red Crane Bks., Inc.

Bell, Andrea. The Bucks Bandit (Diary of a 5th Grade Outlaw Book 3) Loveless, Gina. 2020. (Diary of a 5th Grade Outlaw Ser.: 3). (ENG.). 192p. (J). 13.99 ***(978-1-5248-6089-9(1))*** Andrews McMeel Publishing.

Bell, Andrea. Diary of a 5th Grade Outlaw (Diary of a 5th Grade Outlaw Book 1) Loveless, Gina. 2019. (Diary of a 5th Grade Outlaw Ser.). (ENG.). 240p. (J). 13.99 *(978-1-5248-5548-2(0))* Andrews McMeel Publishing.

—The Friend Thief (Diary of a 5th Grade Outlaw Book 2) Loveless, Gina. 2020. (Diary of a 5th Grade Outlaw Ser.). (ENG.). 224p. (J). 13.99 *(978-1-5248-5574-1(X))* Andrews McMeel Publishing.

Bell, Bill. The Night Before Christmas. Moore, Clement C. 2011. (ENG.). 32p. (J). (gr. k-2). 6.95 *(978-1-61608-470-7(7)*, 608470, Sky Pony Pr.) Skyhorse Publishing Co., Inc.

—Oscar Wilde's the Selfish Giant. Wilde, Oscar & Hollingsworth, Mary. 2013. (ENG.). 40p. (J). (gr. -1-1). 14.95 *(978-1-62087-540-7(3)*, 620540, Sky Pony Pr.) Skyhorse Publishing Co., Inc.

Bell, Bill. Noah: The Incredible Voyager. Bell, Bill. 2004. 48p. (J). (gr. -1-3). per. 14.99 *(978-0-88092-801-4(8))* Royal Fireworks Publishing Co.

Bell, Bill, jt. illus. see Brack, Amanda.

Bell, Cece. Bug Patrol. Mortensen, Denise Dowling. 2013. (ENG.). 32p. (J). (gr. -1-3). 16.99 *(978-0-618-79024-1(1)*, 100547) Houghton Mifflin Harcourt Publishing Co.

—Crankee Doodle. Angleberger, Tom. (ENG.). 32p. (J). (gr. -1-3). 2018. pap. 7.99 *(978-1-328-86928-9(8)*, 1696689, HMH Books For Young Readers); 2013. 16.99 *(978-0-547-81854-2(8)*, 1496644) Houghton Mifflin Harcourt Publishing Co.

—Inspector Flytrap in the Goat Who Chewed Too Much (Inspector Flytrap #3) Angleberger, Tom. 2017. (ENG.). 112p. (J). (gr. 1-4). 14.95 *(978-1-4197-0956-2(9)*, 1065101, Amulet Bks.) Abrams, Inc.

—Inspector Flytrap in the President's Mane Is Missing (Inspector Flytrap #2). 2. Angleberger, Tom. 2016. (Inspector Flytrap Ser.). (ENG.). 112p. (J). (gr. 1-4). 14.95 *(978-1-4197-0955-5(0)*, 1065001, Amulet Bks.) Abrams, Inc.

—Inspector Flytrap (Inspector Flytrap #1) Angleberger, Tom. 2016. (Inspector Flytrap Ser.). (ENG.). 112p. (J). (gr. 1-4). 14.95 *(978-1-4197-0948-7(8)*, 1064901); pap. 5.95 *(978-1-4197-0965-4(8)*, 1064903) Abrams, Inc. (Amulet Bks.).

Bell, Cece. Bee-Wigged. Bell, Cece. 2017. 40p. (J). (gr. -1-3). 6.99 *(978-0-7636-9312-1(X))* Candlewick Pr.

—Chick & Brain: Egg or Eyeball? Bell, Cece. 2020. (Chick & Brain Ser.). 72p. (J). (gr. -1-3). 12.99 *(978-1-5362-0439-1(0))* Candlewick Pr.

—Chick & Brain: Smell My Foot! Bell, Cece. 2019. (Chick & Brain Ser.). (ENG.). 72p. (J). (gr. -1-3). 12.99 *(978-0-7636-7936-1(4))* Candlewick Pr.

—Chuck & Woodchuck. Bell, Cece. 2016. 32p. (J). (gr. -1-3). 15.99 *(978-0-7636-7524-0(5))* Candlewick Pr.

—I Yam a Donkey! Bell, Cece. 2015. (Yam & Donkey Book Ser.). (ENG.). 32p. (J). (gr. -1-3). 17.99 *(978-0-544-08720-0(8)*, 1538104) Houghton Mifflin Harcourt Publishing Co.

—Itty Bitty. Bell, Cece. (J). (gr. -1-2). 2017. 24p. bds. 6.99 *(978-0-7636-9313-8(8))*; 2009. (ENG.). 32p. 9.99 *(978-0-7636-3616-6(9))* Candlewick Pr.

—Rabbit & Robot: The Sleepover. Bell, Cece. (Candlewick Sparks Ser.). 56p. (J). (gr. k-4). 2014. pap. 4.99 *(978-0-7636-6875-4(3))*; 2012. 14.99 *(978-0-7636-5475-7(2))* Candlewick Pr.

—Rabbit & Robot & Ribbit. Bell, Cece. (Candlewick Sparks Ser.). 48p. (J). (gr. k-4). 2017. pap. 4.99 *(978-0-7636-9782-2(6))*; 2016. 14.99 *(978-0-7636-7935-4(6))* Candlewick Pr.

—Sock Monkey Boogie-Woogie. Bell, Cece. 2015. (Cece Bell's Sock Monkey Ser.). 32p. (J). (gr. -1-3). 14.00 *(978-0-7636-7758-9(2))* Candlewick Pr.

—Sock Monkey Rides Again. Bell, Cece. 2015. (Cece Bell's Sock Monkey Ser.). 32p. (J). (gr. -1-3). 14.00 *(978-0-7636-7760-2(4))* Candlewick Pr.

—Sock Monkey Takes a Bath. Bell, Cece. 2015. (Cece Bell's Sock Monkey Ser.). 32p. (J). (gr. -1-3). 14.00 *(978-0-7636-7759-6(0))* Candlewick Pr.

Bell, Corydon, jt. illus. see Diggins, Julia E.

Bell, Don. Favorite Scary Stories of American Children. Young, Richard & Dockrey Young, Judy. rev. ed. 2005. (ENG.). 128p. (J). (gr. 3-6). pap. 8.95 *(978-0-87483-563-2(1))* August Hse. Pubs., Inc.

—Tales of Heroes, Vol. 4. DeSpain, Pleasant. 2005. (Books of Nine Lives: Vol. 4). (ENG.). 80p. (J). (gr. 3-6). 14.95 *(978-0-87483-666-0(2))* August Hse. Pubs., Inc.

—Tales of Holidays, Vol. 5. DeSpain, Pleasant. 2005. (Books of Nine Lives: Vol. 5). (ENG.). 80p. (J). (gr. 3-6). 14.95 *(978-0-87483-667-7(0))* August Hse. Pubs., Inc.

—Tales of Insects, Vol. 6. DeSpain, Pleasant. 2005. (Books of Nine Lives: Vol. 6). (ENG.). 80p. (J). (gr. 3-6). 14.95 *(978-0-87483-668-4(9))* August Hse. Pubs., Inc.

—Tales of Nonsense & Tomfoolery. DeSpain, Pleasant. (ENG.). 80p. (J). (gr. 3-6). 2006. pap. 9.95 *(978-0-87483-645-5(X))*; Vol. 2. 2005. (Books of Nine Lives: Vol. 2). 14.95 *(978-0-87483-670-7(0))* August Hse. Pubs., Inc.

—Tales of Tricksters. DeSpain, Pleasant. 2005. (Books of Nine Lives: Vol. 1). (ENG.). 80p. (J). (gr. -1-12). 14.95 *(978-0-87483-669-1(7))* August Hse. Pubs., Inc.

—Tales of Tricksters: Books of Nine Lives, Vol. 1. DeSpain, Pleasant. 2006. (ENG.). 80p. (J). (gr. 3-6). pap. 9.95 *(978-0-87483-644-8(1))* August Hse. Pubs., Inc.

—Tales of Wisdom & Justice, Vol. 3. DeSpain, Pleasant. 2005. (Books of Nine Lives: Vol. 3). (ENG.). 80p. (J). (gr. 3-6). 14.95 *(978-0-87483-671-4(9))* August Hse. Pubs., Inc.

—Tales of Wisdom & Justice: Books of Nine Lives. DeSpain, Pleasant. 2006. (Books of Nine Lives: Vol. 3). (ENG.). 80p. (J). (gr. 3-6). pap. 9.95 *(978-0-87483-646-2(8))* August Hse. Pubs., Inc.

Bell, Don. Tales of Cats, Vol. 9. Bell, Don, tr. DeSpain, Pleasant. 2005. (ENG.). 80p. (J). (gr. 3-6). 14.95 *(978-0-87483-713-1(8))* August Hse. Pubs., Inc.

—Tales of Enchantment, Vol. 7. Bell, Don, tr. DeSpain, Pleasant. 2005. (ENG.). 80p. (J). (gr. 3-6). 14.95 *(978-0-87483-711-7(1))* August Hse. Pubs., Inc.

—Tales to Frighten & Delight, Vol. 8. Bell, Don, tr. DeSpain, Pleasant. 2005. (ENG.). 80p. (J). (gr. -1-12). 14.95 *(978-0-87483-712-4(X))* August Hse. Pubs., Inc.

Bell, Eden. The Day of the Backyard Dragon Adventure. Bell, Kevin. 2019. (ENG.). 52p. (J). pap. 15.95 *(978-1-64471-358-7(6))* Covenant Bks.

Bell, Eleanor. Jack & Boo's Dinosaur Island. Bell, Philip. 2013. 32p. pap. *(978-0-9562980-3-4(6))* Beachy Bks.

Bell, Fred. Zack in the Middle. Michels, Dia L. 2005. (Newly Independent Reader Ser.). (ENG.). 48p. (J). (gr. -1-3). 9.95 *(978-1-930775-01-5(6))* Platypus Media, L.L.C.

Bell, Greg, jt. illus. see Rosen, Barry.

Bell, Hope. Money Mike Wants a Brand New Bike. Bell, Hope. Bell, Mariah, ed. 2018. (Youth Entrepreneur Ser.: Vol. 1). (ENG.). 30p. (J). (gr. k-5). pap. 8.99 *(978-0-692-16751-9(X))* Hope Belle LLC.

Bell, Jennifer. Safe in a Storm. Swinburne, Stephen R. 2016. (J). *(978-0-545-66987-0(1))* Scholastic, Inc.

Bell, Jennifer A. The Adventures of Sophie Mouse Collection: A New Friend; the Emerald Berries; Forget-Me-Not Lake; Looking for Winston. Green, Poppy. ed. 2018. (Adventures of Sophie Mouse Ser.). (ENG.). 512p. (J). (gr. k-4). pap. 23.99 *(978-1-5344-2908-6(5)*, Little Simon) Little Simon.

—The Adventures of Sophie Mouse Collection #2: The Maple Festival; Winter's No Time to Sleep!; the Clover Curse; a Surprise Visitor. Green, Poppy. ed. 2019. (Adventures of Sophie Mouse Ser.). (ENG.). 512p. (J). (gr. k-4). pap. 23.99 *(978-1-5344-4641-0(9)*, Little Simon) Little Simon.

—Big or Little? Stinson, Kathy. 2nd ed. 2014. (ENG.). 24p. (J). (gr. -1 — 1). bds. 6.95 *(978-1-55451-610-0(2)*, 9781554516100) Annick Pr., Ltd. CAN. Dist: Publishers Group West (PGW).

—Broken Birthday. Sheinmel, Courtney. 2017. (Stella Batts Ser.). (ENG.). 160p. (J). (gr. 2-3). 9.99 *(978-1-58536-921-8(7)*, 204228) Sleeping Bear Pr.

—The Clover Curse. Green, Poppy. 2016. (Adventures of Sophie Mouse Ser.: 7). (ENG.). 128p. (J). (gr. k-4). 17.99 *(978-1-4814-5184-0(7)*, Little Simon) Little Simon.

—The Clover Curse. Green, Poppy. 2017. (Adventures of Sophie Mouse Ser.). (ENG.). 128p. (J). (gr. k-4). lib. bdg. 27.07 *(978-1-5321-4116-4(5)*, 26989, Chapter Bks.) Spotlight.

—The Emerald Berries. Green, Poppy. 2015. (Adventures of Sophie Mouse Ser.: 2). (ENG.). 128p. (J). (gr. k-4). pap. 5.99 *(978-1-4814-2835-4(7)*, Little Simon) Little Simon.

—The Emerald Berries. Green, Poppy. 2017. (Adventures of Sophie Mouse Ser.). (ENG.). 128p. (J). (gr. k-4). lib. bdg. 27.07 *(978-1-5321-4111-9(4)*, 26984, Chapter Bks.) Spotlight.

—Forget-Me-Not Lake. Green, Poppy. 2015. (Adventures of Sophie Mouse Ser.: 3). (ENG.). 128p. (J). (gr. k-4). 16.99 *(978-1-4814-3000-5(9)*, Little Simon) Little Simon.

—Forget-Me-Not Lake. Green, Poppy. 2017. (Adventures of Sophie Mouse Ser.). (ENG.). 128p. (J). (gr. k-4). lib. bdg. 27.07 *(978-1-5321-4112-6(2)*, 26985, Chapter Bks.) Spotlight.

—Grandma's Christmas Wish. Berry Byrd, Holly. Cottage Door Press, ed. 2019. (Love You Always Ser.). (ENG.). 18p. (J). (gr. -1-1). bds. 9.99 *(978-1-68052-704-9(5)*, 1004370) Cottage Door Pr.

—The Great Bake Off. Green, Poppy. 2019. (Adventures of Sophie Mouse Ser.: 14). (ENG.). 128p. (J). (gr. k-4). 16.99 *(978-1-5344-3301-4(5))*; pap. 5.99 *(978-1-5344-3300-7(7))* Little Simon. (Little Simon).

—The Great Big Paw Print. Green, Poppy. 2016. (Adventures of Sophie Mouse Ser.: 9). (ENG.). 128p. (J). (gr. k-4). 16.99 *(978-1-4814-7149-7(X)*, Little Simon) Little Simon.

—The Great Big Paw Print. Green, Poppy. 2017. (Adventures of Sophie Mouse Ser.). (ENG.). 128p. (J). (gr. k-4). lib. bdg. 27.07 *(978-1-5321-4118-8(1)*, 26991, Chapter Bks.) Spotlight.

—Hattie in the Spotlight. Green, Poppy. 2020. (Adventures of Sophie Mouse Ser.: 16). (ENG.). 128p. (J). (gr. k-4). 16.99 *(978-1-5344-6019-5(5))*; pap. 5.99 *(978-1-5344-6018-8(7))* Little Simon. (Little Simon).

—It's Raining, It's Pouring. Green, Poppy. 2017. (Adventures of Sophie Mouse Ser.: 10). (ENG.). 128p. (J). (gr. k-4). 16.99 *(978-1-4814-8590-6(3)*, Little Simon) Little Simon.

—Journey to the Crystal Cave. Green, Poppy. 2017. (Adventures of Sophie Mouse Ser.: 12). (ENG.). 128p. (J). (gr. k-4). 16.99 *(978-1-4814-9986-6(6))*; pap. 5.99 *(978-1-4814-9985-9(8))* Little Simon. (Little Simon).

—The Little Bully, 1 vol. Bracken, Beth. 2012. (Little Boost Ser.). (ENG.). 32p. (J). (gr. -1-1). lib. bdg. 23.99 *(978-1-4048-6795-6(3)*, Picture Window Bks.) Capstone.

—Little Cat's Luck. Bauer, Marion Dane. 2016. (ENG.). 224p. (J). (gr. 3-7). 17.99 *(978-1-4814-2488-2(2)*, Simon & Schuster Bks. For Young Readers) Simon & Schuster Bks. For Young Readers.

—Little Dog, Lost. Bauer, Marion Dane. 2013. (ENG.). 208p. (J). (gr. 3-7). pap. 7.99 *(978-1-4424-3424-0(4)*, Atheneum Bks. for Young Readers) Simon & Schuster Children's Publishing.

—Little Wing Learns to Fly. Brill, Calista. 2016. (Little Wing Ser.). (ENG.). 32p. (J). (gr. -1-3). 17.99 *(978-0-06-236033-5(7)*, HarperCollins) HarperCollins Pubs. Ltd. GBR. Dist: HarperCollins Pubs.

—Looking for Winston. Green, Poppy. 2015. (Adventures of Sophie Mouse Ser.: 4). (ENG.). 128p. (J). (gr. k-4). pap. 5.99 *(978-1-4814-3003-6(3)*, Little Simon) Little Simon.

—Looking for Winston. Green, Poppy. 2017. (Adventures of Sophie Mouse Ser.). (ENG.). 128p. (J). (gr. k-4). lib. bdg. 27.07 *(978-1-5321-4113-3(0)*, 26986, Chapter Bks.) Spotlight.

—Love You More. Urda, Gary. 2018. (ENG.). 40p. (J). (gr. -1-3). 17.99 *(978-1-4998-0652-6(3))* Little Bee Books Inc.

—The Maple Festival. Green, Poppy. 2015. (Adventures of Sophie Mouse Ser.: 5). (ENG.). 128p. (J). (gr. k-4). pap. 5.99 *(978-1-4814-4196-4(5)*, Little Simon) Little Simon.

—The Maple Festival. Green, Poppy. 2017. (Adventures of Sophie Mouse Ser.). (ENG.). 128p. (J). (gr. k-4). lib. bdg. 27.07 *(978-1-5321-4114-0(9)*, 26987, Chapter Bks.) Spotlight.

—The Missing Tooth Fairy. Green, Poppy. 2019. (Adventures of Sophie Mouse Ser.: 15). (ENG.). 128p. (J). (gr. k-4). 16.99 *(978-1-5344-4949-7(3))*; pap. 5.99 *(978-1-5344-4948-0(5))* Little Simon. (Little Simon).

—The Mouse House. Green, Poppy. 2017. (Adventures of Sophie Mouse Ser.: 11). (ENG.). 128p. (J). (gr. k-4). pap. 5.99 *(978-1-4814-9435-9(X)*, Little Simon) Little Simon.

—My Pen Pal, Santa. Stanton, Melissa. 2013. 32p. (J). (gr. -1-2). 9.99 *(978-0-375-86992-1(1)*, Random Hse. Bks. for Young Readers) Random Hse. Children's Bks.

—A New Friend. Green, Poppy. 2015. (Adventures of Sophie Mouse Ser.: 1). (ENG.). 128p. (J). (gr. k-4). pap. 5.99 *(978-1-4814-2832-3(2)*, Little Simon) Little Simon.

—A New Friend. Green, Poppy. 2017. (Adventures of Sophie Mouse Ser.). (ENG.). 128p. (J). (gr. k-4). lib. bdg. 27.07 *(978-1-5321-4110-2(6)*, 26983, Chapter Bks.) Spotlight.

—Nothing Is Scary with Harry: Tall Trade Format. McElligott, Katie. 2019. (ENG.). 24p. (J). (gr. -1-3). 14.99 *(978-1-68052-386-7(4)*, 1003510) Cottage Door Pr.

—Safe in a Storm. Swinburne, Stephen R. 2016. (ENG.). 32p. (J). (gr. -1-k). 10.99 *(978-0-545-86792-4(4))* Scholastic, Inc.

—Scaredy Cat. Sheinmel, Courtney. 2016. (Stella Batts Ser.). (ENG.). 160p. (J). (gr. 1-3). 9.99 *(978-1-58536-919-5(5)*, 204026) Sleeping Bear Pr.

—Silverlake Art Show. Green, Poppy. 2018. (Adventures of Sophie Mouse Ser.: 13). (ENG.). 128p. (J). (gr. k-4). 16.99 *(978-1-5344-1725-0(7))*; pap. 5.99 *(978-1-5344-1724-3(9))* Little Simon. (Little Simon).

—Stella Batts: A Case of the Meanies. Sheinmel, Courtney. 2012. (Stella Batts Ser.: 4). (ENG.). (J). (gr. 1-3). 168p. pap. 5.99 *(978-1-58536-199-1(2)*, 202257);4. 144p. 18.69 *(978-1-58536-198-4(4)*, 202252) Sleeping Bear Pr.

—Stella Batts: None of Your Beeswax. Sheinmel, Courtney. 2014. (Stella Batts Ser.). (ENG.). 184p. (J). (gr. 1-3). 9.99 *(978-1-58536-853-2(9)*, 203677) Sleeping Bear Pr.

—Stella Batts: Pardon Me. Sheinmel, Courtney. 2012. (Stella Batts Ser.: 3). (ENG.). 160p. (J). (gr. 1-3). 11.99 *(978-1-58536-193-9(3)*, 202270); pap. 5.99 *(978-1-58536-194-6(1)*, 202271) Sleeping Bear Pr.

—Stella Batts - Who's in Charge? Sheinmel, Courtney. 2013. (Stella Batts Ser.). (ENG.). 152p. (J). (gr. 1-3). 9.99 *(978-1-58536-849-5(0)*, 202888) Sleeping Bear Pr.

—Stella Batts Something Blue. Sheinmel, Courtney. 2014. (Stella Batts Ser.). (ENG.). 176p. (J). (gr. 1-3). 11.99 *(978-1-58536-851-8(2)*, 203016) Sleeping Bear Pr.

—Superstar. Sheinmel, Courtney. 2015. (Stella Batts Ser.). (ENG.). 184p. (J). (gr. 1-3). pap. 5.99 *(978-1-58536-856-3(3)*, 203956) Sleeping Bear Pr.

—A Surprise Visitor. Green, Poppy. 2016. (Adventures of Sophie Mouse Ser.: 8). (ENG.). 128p. (J). (gr. k-4). pap. 5.99 *(978-1-4814-6698-1(4)*, Little Simon) Little Simon.

—A Surprise Visitor. Green, Poppy. 2017. (Adventures of Sophie Mouse Ser.). (ENG.). 128p. (J). (gr. k-4). lib. bdg. 27.07 *(978-1-5321-4117-1(3)*, 26990, Chapter Bks.) Spotlight.

—Third Grade Angels. Spinelli, Jerry. 2014. (ENG.). 160p. (J). (gr. 2-5). pap. 6.99 *(978-0-545-38773-6(6)*, Levine, Arthur A. Bks.) Scholastic, Inc.

—Too Shy for Show-And-Tell, 1 vol. Bracken, Beth. 2012. (Little Boost Ser.). (ENG.). 32p. (J). (gr. -1-1). 7.95 *(978-1-4048-7418-3(6)*, Picture Window Bks.) Capstone.

—Too Shy for Show-and-Tell. Bracken, Beth. 2011. (Little Boost Ser.). (ENG.). 32p. (J). (gr. -1-1). lib. bdg. 23.99 *(978-1-4048-6654-6(X)*, Picture Window Bks.) Capstone.

—Twinsanity. Sheinmel, Courtney. 2017. (Zacktastic Ser.). (ENG.). 272p. (J). (gr. 2-4). 11.99 *(978-1-58536-936-2(5)*, 204319); pap. 6.99 *(978-1-58536-937-9(3)*, 204333) Sleeping Bear Pr.

—When a Dad Says "I Love You" Wood, Douglas. 2013. (ENG.). 32p. (J). (gr. -1-3). 17.99 *(978-0-689-87532-8(0)*, Simon & Schuster Bks. For Young Readers) Simon & Schuster Bks. For Young Readers.

—When a Grandpa Says I Love You Wood, Douglas. 2014. (ENG.). 32p. (J). (gr. -1-3). 16.99 *(978-0-689-81512-6(3)*, Simon & Schuster Bks. For Young Readers) Simon & Schuster Bks. For Young Readers.

—Winter's No Time to Sleep! Green, Poppy. 2015. (Adventures of Sophie Mouse Ser.: 6). (ENG.). 128p. (J). (gr. k-4). pap. 5.99 *(978-1-4814-4199-5(X)*, Little Simon) Little Simon.

—Winter's No Time to Sleep! Green, Poppy. 2017. (Adventures of Sophie Mouse Ser.). (ENG.). 128p. (J). (gr. k-4). lib. bdg. 27.07 *(978-1-5321-4115-7(7)*, 26988, Chapter Bks.) Spotlight.

Bell, Jonas. Hark the Herald Angels Sing. Flowerpot Press, ed. 2019. (ENG.). 16p. (J). (gr. k-2). bds. 5.99 *(978-1-4867-1820-7(5)*, 2439a44c-8443-4bb4-900f-b4643dc09d3b) Flowerpot Pr.

Bell, Kerry. Wonder Walk. Alam, Ilham. 2019. (ENG.). 20p. (J). *(978-1-77180-323-6(1))*; pap. *(978-1-77180-307-6(X))* Iguana Bks.

Bell, Liesl. Babytionary. Rokhsar, Lillian. 2012. (ENG.). 40p. 17.99 *(978-0-9884922-0-2(2))* Begoo Bks., LLC.

Bell, Loman. Old Glory. Bell, Loman. 2012. 40p. pap. *(978-0-9866065-8-8(8))* Wood Islands Prints.

—Old Glory Faces the Hurricane. Bell, Loman. 2013. 46p. pap. *(978-0-9918033-2-3(9))* Wood Islands Prints.

Bell-Myers, Darcy. Animal Alphabet. Mischel, Jenny Ann. 2006. (J). bds. *(978-0-9769239-0-9(4))* Perfect 4 Preschool.

—Higgledy-Piggledy: Mabel's World. D'Amico, Christine. 2005. (ENG.). 32p. (J). 16.95 *(978-0-9716631-1-4(4))* Attitude Pr. Inc.

Bell, Nick. Mary the Tooth Fairy. Bell, Nick. 32p. (J). 2008. pap. 6.95 *(978-1-60108-025-7(5))*; 2007. (gr. -1-2). 15.95 *(978-1-60108-015-8(8))* Red Cygnet Pr.

Bell, Owain. Thomas & the Hide & Seek Animals. Awdry, Wilbert V. & Awdry, W. 2007. (Thomas & Friends Ser.). (ENG.). 24p. (J). (gr. -1-k). 5.99 *(978-0-375-84173-6(3)*, Random Hse. Bks. for Young Readers) Random Hse. Children's Bks.

Bell, Rahele Jomepour. Our Favorite Day of the Year. Ali, A. E. 2020. (ENG.). 40p. (J). (gr. -1-3). 17.99 *(978-1-4814-8563-0(6)*, Salaam Reads) Simon & Schuster Bks. For Young Readers.

Bell, Rebecca. Capitano Ricco. Bell, Rebecca. 2005. 36p. (J). 9.95 *(978-1-934138-06-9(1))* Bouncing Ball Bks., Inc.

—Message from Miami: The Adventures of Sharp-Eye, Book 2. Bell, Rebecca. 2005. (Adventures of Sharp-Eye). 30p. (J). 9.95 *(978-1-934138-09-0(6))* Bouncing Ball Bks., Inc.

—Princess Sara. Bell, Rebecca. 2005. 34p. (J). 9.95 *(978-1-934138-07-6(X))* Bouncing Ball Bks., Inc.

—A Regular Bug: The Adventures of Sharp-Eye, Book 1. Bell, Rebecca. 2005. (Adventures of Sharp-Eye: Bk. 1). 25p. (J). 9.95 *(978-1-934138-08-3(8))* Bouncing Ball Bks., Inc.

Bell, Samantha. Angel Donor. Gladen, Jennifer. 2012. 24p. pap. 10.95 *(978-1-61633-274-7(3))* Guardian Angel Publishing, Inc.

—Bella Saves the Beach. Stewart, Nancy. 2013. 24p. 19.95 *(978-1-61633-370-6(7))*; pap. 11.95 *(978-1-61633-371-3(5))* Guardian Angel Publishing, Inc.

—Burgher & the Woebegone. Chatel, Kim. 2010. 102p. pap. 8.95 *(978-1-61633-061-3(9))* Guardian Angel Publishing, Inc.

—Butterfly Colors. Varner, Michelle P. l.t. ed. 2017. (ENG.). 16p. (J). (gr. -1-5). 9.95 *(978-1-61633-903-6(9))* Guardian Angel Publishing, Inc.

—Cathy's Animal Garden: Enter at Your Own Risk. Tomio, Stacy. 2010. (ENG.). 32p. (J). 16.95 *(978-1-934617-04-5(0)*, Alma Little) Elva Resa Publishing, LLC.

—G Is for Groundhog. Butler, Kristi M. l.t. ed. 2018. (ENG.). 24p. (J). (gr. k-3). pap. 10.95 *(978-1-61633-940-1(3))* Guardian Angel Publishing, Inc.

Bell, Samantha. Gracie & Grover Go to the Beach. Butler, Kristi M. l.t. ed. 2019. (Amazing Grace Acres Ser.: Vol. 5). (ENG.). 24p. (J). (gr. k-3). pap. 10.95 ***(978-1-61633-989-0(6))*** Guardian Angel Publishing, Inc.

Bell, Samantha. Growing up Dreams. Berger, Susan J. 2010. 24p. pap. 10.95 *(978-1-61633-029-3(5))* Guardian Angel Publishing, Inc.

—One Pelican at a Time: A Story of the Gulf Oil Spill. Stewart, Nancy. 2011. 26p. (J). 19.95 *(978-1-61633-138-2(0))*; pap. 11.95 *(978-1-61633-139-9(9))* Guardian Angel Publishing, Inc.

—Shaping up the Year. Cox, Tracey M. 2009. 24p. pap. 10.95 *(978-1-935137-73-3(5))* Guardian Angel Publishing, Inc.

Bell, Siobhan. Hip Shapes. Blackstone, Stella. 2012. 24p. (J). (gr. -1-1). pap. 18.69 *(978-1-84686-762-0(2))* Barefoot Bks., Ltd. GBR. Dist: Children's Plus, Inc.

—Ship Shapes. Blackstone, Stella. (J). 2008. 24p. (gr. -1-k). bds. 7.99 *(978-1-84686-157-4(8))*; 2006. 0024p. 15.99 *(978-1-905236-34-3(4))*; 2006. *(978-1-4156-6474-2(9))* Barefoot Bks., Inc.

—We All Go Traveling By. Roberts, Sheena. 24p. (J). 2011. (gr. -1-2). 9.99 *(978-1-84686-655-5(3))*; 2004. (ENG.). pap. 9.99 *(978-1-84148-410-5(5))*; 2003. (ENG.). 17.99 *(978-1-84148-168-5(8))* Barefoot Bks., Inc.

B

Bell, Siobhan & Fatus, Sophie. Babushka. Roberts, Sheena et al. 2013. 32p. (J). (gr. k-3). pap. 7.99 *(978-1-84148-411-2(3))* Barefoot Bks., Inc.

Bell, Susan. My Name Is Jake. Turner, Jennifer. 2012. 32p. (J). 14.99 *(978-1-938032-04-2(7))*; pap. 7.99 *(978-1-938032-05-9(5))* Peaks Pr. LLC.

Bellamy, Marian Meredith. Goldie & Androcles — A Fable for the 21st Century. Bellamy, Marian Meredith. 2005. 91p. (YA). per. 20.00 *(978-0-9765341-0-5(X))* Meredith Group Ltd., The.

Bellemare, Josee. The Fragrant Garden. Lee, Day's. 2005. (ENG.). 32p. (J). (gr. -1-7). per. 11.95 *(978-1-894917-26-1(X)*, Napoleon & Co.) Dundurn CAN. Dist: Ingram Publisher Services.

Bellemare, Paule Trudel. Being Cool: Band 10 White/Band 17 Diamond (Collins Big Cat Progress) Zephaniah, Benjamin. 2014. (Collins Big Cat Progress Ser.). (ENG.). 32p. (J). (gr. 5-6). pap. 9.99 *(978-0-00-751929-3(X))* HarperCollins Pubs. Ltd. GBR. Dist: Independent Pubs. Group.

Belley, Nikola. The History of God's World. Emery, R. Meredith. 2018. (ENG.). 48p. (J). (gr. k-6). pap. 14.00 *(978-0-9991835-0-2(8))*; 24.00 *(978-0-9991835-2-6(4))* By His Grace Publishing.

Belli, Alfredo. The Great Escape White Band. Millett, Peter. 2016. (Cambridge Reading Adventures Ser.). (ENG.). 24p. pap. 8.08 *(978-1-107-55158-9(7))* Cambridge Univ. Pr.

—Oliver Twist. Dickens, Charles. 2008. (Green Apple Step Two Ser.). (ENG.). 96p. (J). (gr. 5). pap. incl. audio compact disk *(978-88-530-0580-9(7))* Cideb.

—Speed Bonnie Boat: A Tale from Scottish History Inspired by the Skye Boat Song, 45 vols. 2017. (Traditional Scottish Tales Ser.). (ENG.). 24p. (J). 11.95 *(978-1-78250-367-5(6)*, Kelpies) Floris Bks. GBR. Dist: Consortium Bk. Sales & Distribution.

Bellinger, Marie. Pick-a-WooWoo - Wizards Words of Wisdom, 16 vols., Vol. 7. Harper, Julie Ann. 2009. 32p. pap. *(978-0-9803669-6-9(8))* Pick-a-Woo Woo Pubs.

—Pick-a-WooWoo - Yep I See Spirit: The Gift of Sight, 16 vols., Vol. 6. Harper, Julie Ann. 2009. 32p. pap. *(978-0-9803669-5-2(X))* Pick-a-Woo Woo Pubs.

Bellini, Dan. Mystekos Spring. Klco, Amy. 2020. (Lake of Two Worlds - Book 4 Ser.: Vol. 4). (ENG.). 178p. (J). pap. 9.49 ***(978-0-9979511-4-1(1))*** Enchantment Pr.

Bellini, Dan. Mystekos Summer. Klco, Amy. 2019. (Lake of Two Worlds Ser.: Vol. 1). (ENG.). 172p. (J). pap. 9.49 *(978-0-9979511-1-0(7))* Enchantment Pr.

Belliveau, Kate. Harriet & Corbin Meet at Kitsilano Beach: Two Very Different Birds Teach Each Other about Meditation & Conversation. Patterson, Kathryn. 2019. (ENG.). 32p. (J). pap. 10.00 *(978-1-7203-3646-4(6))* CreateSpace Independent Publishing Platform.

Bello, Thiago Dal, jt. illus. see Lima, Rico.

Bellomy, Gail. Fun O' Licious. Clawson, Kimberly. 2007. (ENG.). 56p. per. 16.95 *(978-1-4241-5556-9(8))* America Star Bks.

Bellon, Teresa. Baby Loves Earth: An ABC of Our Planet. Eckford, Jennifer. ed. 2020. (Baby Loves Ser.). (ENG.). 30p. (J). (gr. -1 — 1). bds. 12.99 ***(978-0-7112-5319-3(6)***, 334929, Frances Lincoln Children's Bks.) Quarto Publishing Group UK GBR. Dist: Hachette UK Distribution.

Bellon, Teresa. Farm Animals. words&pictures. 2020. (Little Hands Stroller Bks.). (ENG.). 14p. (J). (gr. -1 — 1). bds. 8.99 *(978-0-7112-5055-0(3)*, 332669, Words & Pictures) Quarto Publishing Group UK GBR. Dist: Hachette UK Distribution.

—Ocean Adventures: A Magic Bath Book. words&pictures. 2020. (Little Hands Bath Bks.). (ENG.). 8p. (J). (gr. -1 — 1). 9.99 *(978-0-7112-5056-7(1)*, 331083, Words & Pictures) Quarto Publishing Group UK GBR. Dist: Hachette UK Distribution.

—Pond Pals: A Magic Bath Book. words&pictures. 2020. (Little Hands Bath Bks.). (ENG.). 8p. (J). (gr. -1 — 1). 9.99 *(978-0-7112-5057-4(X)*, 331084, Words & Pictures) Quarto Publishing Group UK GBR. Dist: Hachette UK Distribution.

Bellón, Teresa. Speak up, Mouse! 2018. (J). bds. 7.99 *(978-1-61067-779-0(X))* Kane Miller.

—Splish Splash, Seahorse! 2018. (J). bds. 7.99 *(978-1-61067-780-6(3))* Kane Miller.

—Time for Bed, Hippo! 2018. (J). bds. 7.99 *(978-1-61067-781-3(1))* Kane Miller.

Bellon, Teresa. Toys. words&pictures. 2020. (Little Hands Stroller Bks.). (ENG.). 14p. (J). (gr. -1 — 1). bds. 8.99 *(978-0-7112-5054-3(5)*, 331437, Words & Pictures) Quarto Publishing Group UK GBR. Dist: Hachette Bk. Group.

Belloni, Valentina, et al. Blancanieves: 4 Cuentos Predilectos de Alrededor Del Mundo. Gunderson, Jessica. 2020. (Cuentos Multiculturales Ser.).Tr. of Snow White Stories Around the World. (SPA.). 32p. (J). (gr. k-2). pap. 6.95 *(978-1-5158-6069-3(8)*, 142290); lib. bdg. 27.99 *(978-1-5158-5711-2(5)*, 142071) Capstone. (Picture Window Bks.).

—Cenicienta: 4 Cuentos Predilectos de Alrededor Del Mundo. Meister, Cari. 2020. (Cuentos Multiculturales Ser.).Tr. of Cinderella Stories Around the World. (SPA.). 32p. (J). (gr. k-2). pap. 6.95 *(978-1-5158-6068-6(X)*, 142289); lib. bdg. 27.99 *(978-1-5158-5710-5(7)*, 142072) Capstone. (Picture Window Bks.).

—Cinderella Stories Around the World: 4 Beloved Tales, 1 vol. Meister, Cari. 2014. (Multicultural Fairy Tales Ser.). (ENG.). 32p. (J). (gr. k-2). lib. bdg. 27.99 *(978-1-4795-5433-1(2)*, Picture Window Bks.) Capstone.

—Cuentos Multiculturales. Meister, Cari. 2020. (Cuentos Multiculturales Ser.).Tr. of Multicultural Fairy Tales. (SPA.). (J). (gr. k-2). 167.94 *(978-1-5158-5752-5(2)*, 29931, Picture Window Bks.) Capstone.

Belloni, Valentina. How Kate Warne Saved President Lincoln. Van Steenwyk, Elizabeth. 2016. (ENG.). 32p. (J). (gr. -1-3). 16.99 *(978-0-8075-4117-3(6)*, 807541176) Whitman, Albert & Co.

—A Persian Princess: By Barbara Diamond Goldin: Illustrated by Valentina Belloni. Goldin, Barbara Diamond. 2020. (J). *(978-1-68115-553-1(2)*, Apples & Honey Pr.) Behrman Hse., Inc.

Belloni, Valentina. Playdate in Outer Space. Foote, Michele. 2020. (ENG.). 44p. (J). 29.99 ***(978-1-7283-5154-4(5))***; pap. 20.99 ***(978-1-7283-5152-0(9))*** AuthorHouse.

Belloni, Valentina, et al. Rapunzel: 3 Cuentos Predilectos de Alrededor Del Mundo. Meister, Cari. 2020. (Cuentos Multiculturales Ser.).Tr. of Rapunzel Stories Around the World. (SPA.). 32p. (J). (gr. k-2). pap. 6.95 *(978-1-5158-6071-6(X)*, 142293); lib. bdg. 27.99 *(978-1-5158-5713-6(1)*, 142074) Capstone. (Picture Window Bks.).

—Rapunzel Stories Around the World: 3 Beloved Tales, 1 vol. Meister, Cari. 2014. (Multicultural Fairy Tales Ser.). (ENG.). 32p. (J). (gr. k-2). lib. bdg. 27.99 *(978-1-4795-5436-2(7)*, Picture Window Bks.) Capstone.

—Snow White Stories Around the World: 4 Beloved Tales, 1 vol. Gunderson, Jessica. 2014. (Multicultural Fairy Tales Ser.). (ENG.). 32p. (J). (gr. k-2). lib. bdg. 27.99 *(978-1-4795-5434-8(0)*, Picture Window Bks.) Capstone.

Belloni, Valentina. Where Is Owl's Scarf? A Lift-The-Flap Book. Cooke, Brandy. 2016. (ENG.). 16p. (J). (gr. -1-1). bds. 6.99 *(978-1-4998-0176-7(9))* Little Bee Books Inc.

Bellucci, Arianna. The Blue Carbuncle. adapted abr. ed. 2019. (Sweet Cherry Easy Classics Ser.: 3). (ENG.). 112p. (J). (gr. 4-8). *(978-1-78226-577-1(5)*, b4dda4d1-c22e-4801-8c9a-b70d477f2496) Sweet Cherry Publishing.

—Charles Augustus Milverton. Doyle, A. Conan. adapted abr. ed. 2020. (Sweet Cherry Easy Classics Ser.: 16). (ENG.). 112p. (J). 6.95 *(978-1-78226-655-6(0)*, f311537d-d9eb-474b-a96d-a9ae9ed45fbd) Sweet Cherry Publishing GBR. Dist: Baker & Taylor Publisher Services (BTPS).

—The Copper Beeches. Doyle, A. Conan. adapted abr. ed. 2020. (Sweet Cherry Easy Classics Ser.: 13). (ENG.). 112p. (J). 6.95 *(978-1-78226-652-5(6)*, a46b836d-d608-407b-b3ba-3386b5930c53) Sweet Cherry Publishing GBR. Dist: Baker & Taylor Publisher Services (BTPS).

—The Engineer's Thumb. Doyle, A. Conan. adapted abr. ed. 2020. (Sweet Cherry Easy Classics Ser.: 15). (ENG.). 112p. (J). 6.95 *(978-1-78226-654-9(2)*, 8dd2dbc1-e8a1-4b6c-acf0-6dc453325131) Sweet Cherry Publishing GBR. Dist: Baker & Taylor Publisher Services (BTPS).

—The Naval Treaty. adapted abr. ed. 2019. (Sweet Cherry Easy Classics Ser.: 7). (ENG.). 152p. (J). (gr. 4-8). *(978-1-78226-581-8(3)*, 5319b2ed-9cca-4dbf-9a13-65d5b5814ec1) Sweet Cherry Publishing.

—The Red-Headed League. adapted abr. ed. 2019. (Sweet Cherry Easy Classics Ser.: 5). (ENG.). 120p. (J). (gr. 4-8). *(978-1-78226-579-5(1)*, 8802296f-45d6-4d21-bb57-5b84530dad6a) Sweet Cherry Publishing.

—The Reigate Squires. adapted abr. ed. 2019. (Sweet Cherry Easy Classics Ser.: 6). (ENG.). 112p. (J). (gr. 4-8). pap. *(978-1-78226-580-1(5)*, f2aef2c7-b916-41d7-a70a-a741b8c8cd77) Sweet Cherry Publishing.

—A Scandal in Bohemia. Doyle, A. Conan & Baudet, Stephanie. adapted abr. ed. 2020. (Sweet Cherry Easy Classics Ser.: 11). (ENG.). 120p. (J). (gr. 4-8). 6.95 *(978-1-78226-651-8(8)*, 14b0d276-5aad-4c19-ac63-3fb8d15a3a5f) Sweet Cherry Publishing GBR. Dist: Baker & Taylor Publisher Services (BTPS).

—The Sign of the Four. adapted abr. ed. 2019. (Sweet Cherry Easy Classics Ser.: 2). (ENG.). 256p. (J). (gr. 4-8). *(978-1-78226-576-4(7)*, a59ae9f3-662c-4ad2-8068-e48a5d55406b) Sweet Cherry Publishing.

—Silver Blaze. Doyle, A. Conan. adapted abr. ed. 2020. (Sweet Cherry Easy Classics Ser.: 12). (ENG.). 120p. (J). 6.95 *(978-1-78226-656-3(9)*, 59e7dcaa-e5a7-4908-a832-e6c9adc0a1a5) Sweet Cherry Publishing GBR. Dist: Baker & Taylor Publisher Services (BTPS).

—The Six Napoleons. Doyle, A. Conan. adapted abr. ed. 2020. (Sweet Cherry Easy Classics Ser.: 14). (ENG.). 112p. (J). 6.95 *(978-1-78226-653-2(4)*, 8937b286-2fc9-4761-8fa0-8d91c4cd624f) Sweet Cherry Publishing GBR. Dist: Baker & Taylor Publisher Services (BTPS).

—The Speckled Band. adapted abr. ed. 2019. (Sweet Cherry Easy Classics Ser.: 4). (ENG.). 128p. (J). (gr. 4-8). *(978-1-78226-578-8(3)*, e6f85ac9-ed40-4ed8-92ff-8089425cfbd2) Sweet Cherry Publishing.

—A Study in Scarlet. adapted abr. ed. 2019. (Sweet Cherry Easy Classics Ser.: 1). (ENG.). 216p. (J). (gr. 4-8). *(978-1-78226-575-7(9)*, 3f1d7187-0469-49ca-bf2a-83f6d6418a6f) Sweet Cherry Publishing.

—The Sussex Vampire, 1 vol. adapted abr. ed. 2019. (Sweet Cherry Easy Classics Ser.: 8). (ENG.). 112p. (J). (gr. 5-8). *(978-1-78226-582-5(1)*, 2e9ec927-6a77-450d-9f8d-481abeb9e5e4) Sweet Cherry Publishing.

—The Three Students. adapted abr. ed. 2019. (Sweet Cherry Easy Classics Ser.: 10). (ENG.). 120p. (J). (gr. 4-8). *(978-1-78226-584-9(8)*, acab3781-169d-4353-a9cb-666b020fed62) Sweet Cherry Publishing.

—The Veiled Lodger. adapted abr. ed. 2019. (Sweet Cherry Easy Classics Ser.: 9). (ENG.). 104p. (J). (gr. 4-8). *(978-1-78226-583-2(X)*, 5540f1cd-f25e-432d-ba19-300c496969d1) Sweet Cherry Publishing.

Belmont, Dennis. Cubby Goes to the Playroom: A Book about Play Therapy. Canfield, Cathy. 2016. (ENG.). (J). (gr. k-4). pap. 9.99 *(978-0-68418-880-2(6))* Primedia eLaunch LLC.

Belmonte, David. John Cook's Civil War Story. Marsico, Katie. 2018. (Narrative Nonfiction: Kids in War Ser.). (ENG.). 32p. (J). (gr. 2-4). 27.99 *(978-1-5124-5680-6(2)*, Lerner Pubns.); pap. 9.99 *(978-1-5415-1191-0(3))* Lerner Publishing Group.

Belomlinsky, Alex. Tommy the Fishboy. Kurlander, Keith. 2012. 34p. 24.95 *(978-1-4626-4527-5(5))* America Star Bks.

Belomlinsky, M., jt. illus. see Synepolsky, I.

Below, Halina. Chestnut Dreams, 1 vol. Below, Halina. 2003. (ENG.). 40p. (J). (gr. -1-2). pap. 5.95 *(978-1-55041-690-9(1)*, 4cc85dad-60ec-42a1-8cce-6eb02c85b388) Clockwise Pr. CAN. Dist: Firefly Bks., Ltd.

Belser, Maud Corier. Grace & Marie's Little Farm on the Hill. 2007. 32p. (J). bds. 18.00 *(978-0-9791076-0-3(1))* WebbWorks.

Belsvik, Inger Lise. Hannah, Blue Magic & the Foxes. Barton, Grete Belinda. 2018. (ENG.). 54p. (YA). *(978-82-999555-2-2(1))* Bien Forlag.

Belton, Robyn. Farmer John's Tractor. Sutton, Sally. 2012. (ENG.). 32p. (J). *(978-1-921150-94-4(7))* Walker Bks. Australia Pty, Ltd.

—Farmer John's Tractor. Sutton, Sally. 2013. (ENG.). 32p. (J). (gr. -1-2). 15.99 *(978-0-7636-6430-5(8))* Candlewick Pr.

Belyaev, Roman. How Does a Lighthouse Work? Belyaev, Roman. 2018. (How It Works). (ENG.). 48p. (J). (gr. 1-4). 16.99 *(978-1-911509-24-0(1))* B Small Publishing GBR. Dist: Independent Pubs. Group.

Bembry, Shanylah & Renee, Ashley. No Bullying. Bembry, Shanylah. 2016. (ENG.). (J). pap. 10.95 *(978-1-942022-75-6(1))* Butterfly Typeface, The.

Bemelmans, Ludwig. Noodle. Leaf, Munro. 2006. 56p. (J). 15.99 *(978-0-590-04310-6(2)*, Levine, Arthur A. Bks.) Scholastic, Inc.

Bemporad, Alex, jt. photos by see Pervan, Ivo.

Ben-Ami, Doron. Autumn Journey, 1 vol. Cummings, Priscilla. 2009. (ENG.). 120p. (gr. 3-6). pap. 12.95 *(978-0-87033-606-5(1)*, 9780870336065, Cornell Maritime Pr./Tidewater Pubs.) Schiffer Publishing, Ltd.

—Nicki, 1. Creel, Ann Howard. 2007. (American Girl: Nicki Ser.). (ENG.). 136p. (J). (gr. 3-6). pap. 21.19 *(978-1-59369-259-9(5))* American Girl Publishing, Inc.

—Tornado. Byars, Betsy. 2020. (Trophy Chapter Bks.). (ENG.). 64p. (J). (gr. 1-5). pap. 4.99 *(978-0-06-442063-1(9)*, HarperCollins) HarperCollins Pubs. Ltd. GBR. Dist: HarperCollins Pubs.

Ben, Ereddia. The Dragon Quest: A Music Composition Adventure. Ben, Ereddia. 2018. (Music Composition Adventures Ser.: Vol. 1). (ENG.). 92p. (J). (gr. 1-6). pap. 12.95 *(978-0-9998338-0-3(4))* Bonsai Bks.

Ben Lulu, Coral. The Small Flower: A Story about the Struggle to Fulfill Yourself. Turm, Dror. 2020. (ENG.). 30p. (J). pap. 15.00 ***(978-1-7192-0022-6(X))*** CreateSpace Independent Publishing Platform.

Ben-Moshe, Jana. Hebrew Through Prayer, Bk. 1. Kaye, Terry et al. Siegel, Adam, ed. 96p. (J). (gr. 4-5). pap. 6.95 *(978-0-87441-563-6(2))* Behrman Hse., Inc.

—Learn & Do Bible Book. Gurvis, Laura K. 64p. (J). (gr. k-2). pap. 4.95 *(978-0-87441-530-8(6))* Behrman Hse., Inc.

Ben-Yosef, Yoni, photos by. Edmond Lachenal & His Legacy. Eidelberg, Martin & Cass, Claire. 2009. 208p. 95.00 *(978-0-9788371-3-6(4))* Jason Jacques Gallery Pr. The.

Ben�tez, Miguel. Freddie Ramos Tracks down a Drone. Jules, Jacqueline. 2020. (Zapato Power Ser.). (ENG.). 96p. (J). (gr. 1-5). pap. 5.99 ***(978-0-8075-9563-3(2)***, 0807595632) Whitman, Albert & Co.

Benaglia, Fred. Hug This Book! Saltzberg, Barney. 2016. (ENG.). 32p. (gr. -1-k). 16.95 *(978-0-7148-7284-1(9))* Phaidon Pr., Inc.

—Twinkle, Twinkle, ABC: A Mixed-Up, Mashed-up Melody. Saltzberg, Barney. 2017. (ENG.). 32p. (gr. -1 — 1). bds. 12.95 *(978-0-7148-7507-1(4))* Phaidon Pr., Inc.

Benally, Kendrick. Ch'at to Yinilo'/Frog Brings Rain. Powell, Patricia Hruby. Thomas, Peter A., tr. 2006. (NAV & ENG.). 32p. (J). (gr. 4-7). 17.95 *(978-1-893354-08-1(3))* Salina Bookshelf Inc.

—Zinnia: How the Corn Was Saved. Powell, Patricia Hruby. Ruffenach, Jessie, ed. Thomas, Peter, tr. from NAV. 2004. (ENG & NAV.). 32p. (J). (gr. -1-3). 17.95 *(978-1-893354-38-8(5))* Salina Bookshelf Inc.

Benas, Jeanne. More Spooky Texas Tales. Tingle, Tim & Moore, Doc. 2010. (ENG.). 104p. (gr. 4-6). lib. bdg. 18.95 *(978-0-89672-700-7(9))* Texas Tech Univ. Pr.

Benatar, Raquel & Rubio, Adrian. Go, Milka, Go! The Life of Milka Duno. Benatar, Raquel & Rubio, Adrian. 2008.Tr. of Corre, Milka, Corre!. (SPA & ENG.). 32p. (J). 19.95 *(978-1-56492-360-8(6))* Laredo Publishing Co., Inc.

Benatar, Raquel & Torrecilla, Pablo. Isabel Allende: Recuerdos para un Cuento. Benatar, Raquel & Torrecilla, Pablo. Petersen, Patricia, tr. 2004. (ENG & SPA.). (J). 14.95 *(978-1-56492-341-7(X)*, Piñata Books) Arte Publico Pr.

Benator, Seth. A Ballet for Bobcat. Benator, Eileen B. l.t. ed. 2005. 32p. (J). (gr. -1-2). 15.95 *(978-0-9748478-7-0(9))* Lion's Tale Pr., LLC.

—A Marching Band for Bears. Benator, Eileen. 2004. 32p. (J). lib. bdg. 15.95 *(978-0-9748478-5-6(2))* Lion's Tale Pr., LLC.

Benbassat, Julie. The Screaming Hairy Armadillo & 76 Other Animals with Weird, Wild Names. Murrie, Matthew & Murrie, Steve. 2020. (ENG.). 176p. (J). (gr. 1-5). pap. 14.95 *(978-1-5235-0811-2(6)*, 100811) Workman Publishing Co., Inc.

Benchimol, Brigitte & Zima, Siegfried. Jadyn & the Magic Bubble: Discovering India. Benchimol, Brigitte. 2007. 58p. (J). (gr. 3-4). 19.95 *(978-0-9701654-9-7(8))* East West Discovery Pr.

Bencivenni, Beatrice. Collins Big Cat Phonics for Letters & Sounds - the Foolish, Timid Rabbit: Band 03/Yellow, Bd. 3. Kuenzler, Lou. 2018. (Collins Big Cat Phonics Ser.). (ENG.). 16p. (J). (gr. k-1). pap. 6.99 *(978-0-00-825155-0(X))* HarperCollins Pubs. Ltd. GBR. Dist: Independent Pubs. Group.

Benda, Wladyslaw T. A Girl of the Limberlost. Stratton-Porter, Gene. 2005. reprint ed. pap. 38.95 *(978-0-7661-9424-3(8))* Kessinger Publishing, LLC.

Bendall-Brunello, John. Big Pig. Doyle, Malachy. 2006. (ENG.). 32p. (J). (gr. -1-k). pap. 9.99 *(978-0-689-87485-7(5))* Simon & Schuster, Ltd. GBR. Dist: Simon & Schuster, Inc.

—Dinosnore! 2016. (J). *(978-1-4351-6490-1(3))* Barnes & Noble, Inc.

—I Love You This Much, 1 vol. Hodges, Lynn & Buchanan, Sue. (ENG.). (J). 2010. 36p. pap. 6.99 *(978-0-310-72265-6(9))*; 2005. 16p. (gr. -1). bds. 6.99 *(978-0-310-70961-9(X))* Zonderkidz.

—Moose on the Loose. Wargin, Kathy-jo. 2009. (ENG.). 32p. (J). (gr. k-6). 15.95 *(978-1-58536-427-5(4))* Sleeping Bear Pr.

—My Barnyard! A Read & Play Book! Schwartz, Betty Ann & Seresin, Lynn. 2015. (ENG.). 10p. (J). (gr. -1-k). 7.99 *(978-0-545-69077-5(3)*, Cartwheel Bks.) Scholastic, Inc.

—Otter Out of Water. Wargin, Kathy-jo. 2014. (ENG.). 32p. (J). (gr. k-3). 15.95 *(978-1-58536-431-2(2)*, 203005) Sleeping Bear Pr.

—Peep Leap, 0 vols. Verdick, Elizabeth. 2013. (ENG.). 32p. (J). (gr. -1-2). 16.99 *(978-1-4778-1640-0(2)*, 9781477816400, Two Lions) Amazon Publishing.

—Peter & the Wolf: Band 09/Gold (Collins Big Cat) Redmond, Diane. 2007. (Collins Big Cat Ser.). (ENG.). 24p. (J). (gr. 1-2). pap. 8.99 *(978-0-00-718674-7(6))* HarperCollins Pubs. Ltd. GBR. Dist: Independent Pubs. Group.

—100 Days of Cool. Murphy, Stuart J. 2003. (MathStart 2 Ser.). (ENG.). 40p. (J). (gr. 1-18). pap. 6.99 *(978-0-06-000123-0(2))* HarperCollins Pubs.

Bendall-Brunello, John. Archie's Amazing Adventure. Bendall-Brunello, John, tr. Grindley, Sally. 2003. 32p. (YA). *(978-1-84365-026-3(6)*, Pavilion Children's Books) Pavilion Bks.

Bendall-Brunello, John, jt. illus. see Wargin, Kathy-jo.

Bendell, Norm. Autism & You. Gerber, Lauren. 2015. (ENG.). 56p. (J). pap. 19.95 net. *(978-1-61254-223-2(9))* Brown Books Publishing Group.

Bender, Rebecca. Duck Days. Leach, Sara. 2020. (Slug Days Stories Ser.: 3). 120p. (J). (gr. 2-4). 17.95 ***(978-1-77278-148-9(7))*** Pajama Pr. CAN. Dist: Ingram Publisher Services.

Bender, Rebecca. Penguin Days. Leach, Sara. 2019. (Slug Days Stories Ser.: 2). (ENG.). 104p. (J). (gr. 2-5). 15.95 *(978-1-77278-053-6(7))* Pajama Pr. CAN. Dist: Ingram Publisher Services.

—Slug Days. Leach, Sara. (Slug Days Stories Ser.: 1). 120p. (J). (gr. 2-4). 2020. pap. 12.95 *(978-1-77278-032-1(4))*; 2017. (ENG.). 16.95 *(978-1-77278-022-2(7))* Pajama Pr. CAN. Dist: Ingram Publisher Services.

Bender, Rebecca. Giraffe & Bird. Bender, Rebecca. 2017. (Giraffe & Bird Ser.: 2). (ENG.). 32p. (J). (gr. -1-2). 17.95 *(978-1-77278-025-3(1))* Pajama Pr. CAN. Dist: Ingram Publisher Services.

—Giraffe & Bird Together Again. Bender, Rebecca. 2018. (Giraffe & Bird Ser.: 4). (ENG.). 32p. (J). (gr. k-2). 17.95 *(978-1-77278-051-2(0))* Pajama Pr. CAN. Dist: Ingram Publisher Services.

Bender, Robert. Alphabet Movers. Benzwie, Teresa. (ENG.). 30p. (J). (gr. -1-6). pap. *(978-1-930798-08-3(3))* National Dance Education Organization.

—By the Baobab Tree. Archambault, John. 2005. (J). *(978-1-58669-164-6(3))* Childcraft Education Corp.

—Mail Monkeys. Greene, Rhonda Gowler. 2006. (J). pap. *(978-1-58669-217-9(8))* Childcraft Education Corp.

Bendick, Jeanne. After the Sun Goes Down: The Story of Animals at Night. Blough, Glenn O. 2011. 50p. (gr. 1). 35.95 *(978-1-258-09913-8(6))* Literary Licensing, LLC.

Bendick, Jeanne. Herodotus & the Road to History. Bendick, Jeanne. 2009. (ENG.). 79p. (J). (gr. 4-6). pap. 13.95 *(978-1-932350-20-3(9))* Ignatius Pr.

Bendis, Keith. Calvin Can't Fly: The Story of a Bookworm Birdie. Berne, Jennifer. 2015. 40p. (J). (gr. -1-2). pap. 8.95 *(978-1-4549-1575-1(7))* Sterling Publishing Co., Inc.

Bendoly, Lynne. What Do You Do on a Rainy Day? Farrell, Steve. 2013. 48p. pap. 24.95 *(978-1-4626-9685-7(6))* America Star Bks.

Benedetto, Anthony M. Emblems of the Infinite King: Enter the Knowledge of the Living God. Lister, J. Ryan. 2019. (ENG.). 184p. 24.99 *(978-1-4335-6338-6(X))* Crossway.

Benenfeld, Rikki. I Go to the Ohel. Hodakov, Levi. Rosenfeld, D. L. & Leverton, Yossi, eds. 2011. (Toddler Experience Ser.). 32p. (J). 10.95 *(978-1-929628-61-2(7))* Hachai Publishing.

Benenfeld, Rikki. I Go to Eretz Yisroel. Benenfeld, Rikki. 2017. (Toddler Experience Ser.). (ENG.). 28p. (J). 10.95 *(978-1-929628-92-6(7))* Hachai Publishing.

—I Go to the Doctor. Benenfeld, Rikki. 2004. (Toddler Experience Ser.). (J). lib. bdg. 10.95 *(978-1-929628-15-5(3))* Hachai Publishing.

—Let's Go Shopping. Benenfeld, Rikki. 2005. (Toddler Experience Ser.). 24p. (J). 10.95 *(978-1-929628-20-9(X))* Hachai Publishing.

—Let's Meet Community Helpers. Benenfeld, Rikki. 2013. 32p. (J). 10.95 *(978-1-929628-75-9(7))* Hachai Publishing.

Benevenia, Rose. Dolly & Babe. Benevenia, Rose. l.t. ed. 2004. 9p. (J). (gr. k-2). pap. 9.00 *(978-0-9729044-0-7(9))* Cabbage Patch Pr.

Benfold Haywood, Ian P. The Rule of Claw. Brindley, John. 2009. (Exceptional Reading & Language Arts Titles for Intermediate Grades Ser.). (ENG.). 408p. (YA). (gr. 7-12). 18.95 *(978-1-58013-608-2(7))* Lerner Publishing Group.

Benger, Chelsi L. The Daily Adventures of Ruckus & Otis. Zabriskie, Cindy. 2008. 24p. pap. 24.95 *(978-1-60672-829-1(6))* America Star Bks.

Bengtz, Ture. White Squaw: The True Story of Jennie Wiley. Wheeler, Arville. 2011. 178p. (gr. 4-7). 42.95 *(978-1-258-05911-8(8))* Literary Licensing, LLC.

Benham, Tors. Cheeky Frog. Wolfe, Jane. 2016. 8p. (J). (gr. -1-12). bds. 6.99 *(978-1-84322-718-2(5),* Armadillo) Anness Publishing GBR. Dist: National Bk. Network.

—Crazy Cow. Wolfe, Jane. 2013. (ENG.). 8p. (J). (gr. -1-k). bds. 6.99 *(978-1-84322-775-5(4),* Armadillo) Anness Publishing GBR. Dist: National Bk. Network.

—Dizzy Duck. Wolfe, Jane. 2016. 8p. (J). (gr. -1-12). bds. 6.99 *(978-1-84322-719-9(3),* Armadillo) Anness Publishing GBR. Dist: National Bk. Network.

—Happy Cat. Wolfe, Jane. 2016. 8p. bds. 6.99 *(978-1-84322-720-5(7),* Armadillo) Anness Publishing GBR. Dist: National Bk. Network.

—Hungry Horse. Wolfe, Jane. 2016. (ENG.). 8p. bds. 6.99 *(978-1-84322-721-2(5),* Armadillo) Anness Publishing GBR. Dist: National Bk. Network.

—Messy Pig. Wolfe, Jane. 2013. 8p. (J). (gr. -1-k). bds. 6.99 *(978-1-84322-777-9(0),* Armadillo) Anness Publishing GBR. Dist: National Bk. Network.

—Noisy Dog. Wolfe, Jane. 2013. 8p. (J). (gr. -1-k). bds. 6.99 *(978-1-84322-779-3(7),* Armadillo) Anness Publishing GBR. Dist: National Bk. Network.

—Pull the Lever: Who Does What? Wolfe, Jane. 2014. (ENG.). 8p. (J). (gr. -1-2). bds. 6.99 *(978-1-86147-392-9(3),* Armadillo) Anness Publishing GBR. Dist: National Bk. Network.

—Pull the Lever: Who's in Here? Wolfe, Jane. 2014. (ENG.). 8p. (J). (gr. -1-2). bds. 6.99 *(978-1-86147-394-3(X),* Armadillo) Anness Publishing GBR. Dist: National Bk. Network.

—Sleepy Sheep. Wolfe, Jane. 2013. 8p. (J). (gr. -1-k). bds. 6.99 *(978-1-84322-778-6(9),* Armadillo) Anness Publishing GBR. Dist: National Bk. Network.

Beniamino Brady. The Symph - in Search of Harmony. George Trad. 2012. 38p. 30.50 *(978-1-61897-519-5(6),* Strategic Bk. Publishing) Strategic Book Publishing & Rights Agency (SBPRA).

Benicio, Angelique. Sarah's Waterfall: A Healing Story about Sexual Abuse. Akers, Ellery. 2009. (J). *(978-1-884444-79-1(2))* Safer Society Pr.

Beningo, Mary. One Hungry Dragon. Wenzlick, Julie J. 2017. (ENG.). 30p. (J). pap. 10.99 *(978-0-9978925-6-7(0))* Wordmeister Pr.

Benioff, Carol. Big Night for Salamanders. Lamstein, Sarah Marwil. 2010. (ENG.). 40p. (J). (gr. 3-k). 17.95 *(978-1-932425-98-7(5))* Boyds Mills Pr.

—Preacher's Night Before Christmas, 1 vol. Layne, Steven L. 2006. (Night Before Christmas Ser.). (ENG.). 32p. (J). (gr. k-3). 16.99 *(978-1-58980-321-3(3),* Pelican Publishing) Arcadia Publishing.

Benítez, Miguel. Freddie Ramos Adds It All Up. Jules, Jacqueline. 2019. (Zapato Power Ser.: 8). (ENG.). 96p. (J). (gr. 1-5). 14.99 *(978-0-8075-9539-8(X),* 080759539X) Whitman, Albert & Co.

Benítez, Miguel. Freddie Ramos Adds It All Up. Jules, Jacqueline. 2020. (Zapato Power Ser.). (ENG.). 96p. (J). (gr. 1-5). pap. 5.99 ***(978-0-8075-9559-6(4),*** 807595594) Whitman, Albert & Co.

Benítez, Miguel. Freddie Ramos Hears It All. Jules, Jacqueline. (Zapato Power Ser.: 7). (ENG.). 96p. (J). (gr. 1-5). 2019. pap. 5.99 *(978-0-8075-9542-8(X),* 080759542X); 2018. 14.99 *(978-0-8075-9500-8(4),* 807595004) Whitman, Albert & Co.

Benítez, Miguel. Freddie Ramos Makes a Splash. Jules, Jacqueline. 2013. (Zapato Power Ser.: Book 4). (ENG.). 96p. (J). (gr. 1-5). pap. 5.99 *(978-0-8075-9486-5(5),* 807594865) Whitman, Albert & Co.

Benítez, Miguel. Freddie Ramos Makes a Splash Bk. 4. Jules, Jacqueline. 2012. (Zapato Power Ser.: Book 4). (ENG.). 96p. (J). (gr. 1-5). 14.99 *(978-0-8075-9485-8(7),* 807594857) Whitman, Albert & Co.

—Freddie Ramos Rules New York. Jules, Jacqueline. 2016. (Zapato Power Ser.: 6). (ENG.). 96p. (J). (gr. 1-5). 14.99 *(978-0-8075-9497-1(0),* 807594970) Whitman, Albert & Co.

Benítez, Miguel. Freddie Ramos Rules New York. Jules, Jacqueline. 2017. (Zapato Power Ser.). (ENG.). 96p. (J). (gr. 1-5). pap. 5.99 *(978-0-8075-9499-5(7),* 807594997) Whitman, Albert & Co.

—Freddie Ramos Springs into Action. Jules, Jacqueline. 2011. (Zapato Power Ser.: Book 2). (ENG.). 96p. (J). (gr. 1-5). pap. 5.99 *(978-0-8075-9483-4(0),* 807594830) Whitman, Albert & Co.

—Freddie Ramos Stomps the Snow. Jules, Jacqueline. 2014. (Zapato Power Ser.: Book 5). (ENG.). 96p. (J). (gr. 1-5). 14.99 *(978-0-8075-9487-2(3),* 807594873) Whitman, Albert & Co.

—Freddie Ramos Takes Off, Bk. 1. Jules, Jacqueline. 2011. (Zapato Power Ser.: Book 1). (ENG.). 88p. (J). (gr. 1-5). pap. 5.99 *(978-0-8075-9479-7(2),* 807594792) Whitman, Albert & Co.

Benítez, Miguel. Freddie Ramos Tracks down a Drone. Jules, Jacqueline. 2020. (Zapato Power Ser.). (ENG.). 96p. (J). (gr. 1-5). 14.99 ***(978-0-8075-9544-2(6),*** 807595446) Whitman, Albert & Co.

Benítez, Miguel. Freddie Ramos Zooms to the Rescue. Jules, Jacqueline. 2012. (Zapato Power Ser.: Book 3). (ENG.). 96p. (J). (gr. 1-5). pap. 5.99 *(978-0-8075-9484-1(9),* 807594849) Whitman, Albert & Co.

Benito, Lucia. He's Not Like Us! Ooli & Tooli When Life Is Unrooly. Pollak, Ora. 2018. (Ooli & Tooli When Life Is Unrooly Ser.: Vol. 2). (ENG.). 38p. (J). (gr. k-2). 21.49 *(978-0-9987126-8-0(X));* pap. 11.99 *(978-0-9987126-7-3(1))* ooli & tooli llc.

Benjamin, Christina. What Is This? Williams, Rozanne Lanczak. Hamaguchi, Carla, ed. 2003. 16p. (J). (gr. k-2). pap. 3.49 *(978-1-57471-965-9(3),* 3587) Creative Teaching Pr., Inc.

Benjamin-Farren, Joan. Shuli & Me: From Slavery to Freedom A Storybook Omer Calendar. Benjamin-Farren, Joan. 2006. (J). 19.95 *(978-0-9788802-0-0(X))* Black Jasmine.

Benjamin, Ryan. Return of the Jedi. Gallardo, Adam. 2011. (Star Wars: Infinites Ser.). (ENG.). 24p. (J). (gr. 6-12). 27.07 *(978-1-59961-853-1(2),* 13819); Vol. 2. 27.07 *(978-1-59961-854-8(0),* 13820); Vol. 3. 27.07 *(978-1-59961-855-5(9),* 13821); Vol. 4. 27.07 *(978-1-59961-856-2(7),* 13822) Spotlight. (Graphic Novels).

Benji, Brianna. Dinosaurs: And Other Poems. Barnes, Edward. 2018. (ENG.). 36p. (J). pap. 13.99 *(978-4-527-89300-0(9))* BCB Productions.

Bennenfeld, Rikki. I Go to the Dentist. Benenfeld, Rikki. Rosenfeld, Dina & Leverton, Yossi, eds. 2011. (Toddler Experience Ser.). (ENG.). 32p. (J). 10.95 *(978-1-929628-60-5(9))* Hachai Publishing.

Bennett, Andy. Feeling Happy: A Turn-and-Learn Emotions Book. Weiss, Ellen. 2006. (PBS Kids Ser.). 10p. (J). bds. 6.95 *(978-1-57791-311-5(6))* Brighter Minds Children's Publishing.

—Fruit Salad: A Touch-and-Learn Book. Weiss, Ellen. 2006. (PBS Kids Ser.). 8p. (J). (gr. -1-k). bds. 6.95 *(978-1-57791-314-6(0))* Brighter Minds Children's Publishing.

—The Great Cake. Gerstein, Sherry. 2006. 14p. (J). (gr. -1-3). bds. 6.95 *(978-1-57791-260-6(8))* Brighter Minds Children's Publishing.

—Hide & Peek: A Lift-A-Flap Letters Book. Gerstein, Sherry. 2006. 14p. (J). (gr. -1-3). bds. 6.95 *(978-1-57791-259-0(4))* Brighter Minds Children's Publishing.

—I Don't Want to Go to School! A Fold-Out Surprise Book. Weiss, Ellen. 2006. (PBS Kids Ser.). 12p. (J). 6.95 *(978-1-57791-313-9(2))* Brighter Minds Children's Publishing.

—Imagination Vacation: A Color-Foil Shapes Book. Gerstein, Sherry. 2006. 14p. (J). (gr. -1-3). bds. 6.95 *(978-1-57791-261-3(6))* Brighter Minds Children's Publishing.

—Moo, Moo Who Are You? Gerstein, Sherry. 2006. 14p. (J). (gr. -1-k). bds. 7.95 *(978-1-57791-258-3(6))* Brighter Minds Children's Publishing.

—Winter Spring Summer Fall: A Touch-and-Feel Seasons Book. Weiss, Ellen. 2006. (PBS Kids Ser.). 8p. (J). (gr. -1-k). bds. 6.95 *(978-1-57791-312-2(4))* Brighter Minds Children's Publishing.

Bennett, Brent. The Day Papa Came Home, Justus, Barbara & Starbird, Caroline. Newman, Timothy, ed. 2004. 20p. (YA). *(978-0-9755996-0-0(7))* Heifer Project International.

Bennett, Cameron. A CatFish Tale. Brodsky, Kathy. 2012. (ENG.). (J). 19.99 *(978-0-9828529-3-4(2))* Helpingwords.

—El Cuento de Don Gato Pez: Ligeramente Basado en una Historia Real. Brodsky, Kathy. 2016.Tr. of CatFish Tale. (SPA.). (J). (gr. 3-7). 19.99 *(978-0-9828529-7-2(5))* Helpingwords.

—Just Sniffing Around. Brodsky, Kathy. 2009. (ENG.). 40p. 19.99 *(978-0-578-03620-5(7))* Helpingwords.

—Mi Árbol Doblado. Brodsky, Kathy. ed. 2017.Tr. of My Bent Tree. (SPA & ENG.). (J). (gr. -1-4). 1995.00 *(978-0-9977922-0-1(5))* Helpingwords.

—My Bent Tree. Brodsky, Kathy. 2008. (ENG.). 44p. (J). 19.95 *(978-0-615-16066-5(2))* Helpingwords.

Bennett, Carl A., jt. illus. see Bennett, James.

Bennett, Davis, jt. illus. see Raney, Tom.

Bennett, Elizabeth. The Peanuts Guide to the Seasons: A Jumbo Activity Book. Schulz, Charles. 2003. (Peanuts Club with Charlie Brown & Friends Ser.). 144p. (J). *(978-0-439-46826-8(4))* Scholastic, Inc.

Bennett, Erin Susanne. The Patchwork Path: A Quilt Map to Freedom. Stroud, Bettye. 2007. 32p. (J). (gr. k-3). pap. 7.99 *(978-0-7636-3519-0(7))* Candlewick Pr.

Bennett, Felix. The Lost World. Brenchley, Chaz & Doyle, A. Conan. 2009. (Real Reads Ser.). 64p. (J). (gr. 4-8). pap. 13.55 *(978-1-60754-395-4(8));* lib. bdg. 32.25 *(978-1-60754-394-7(X))* Windmill Bks.

—War of the Worlds. Wells, H. G. 2013. (Classics of Science Fiction Ser.). (ENG.). 64p. pap. 6.95 *(978-1-906230-12-8(9))* Real Reads Ltd. GBR. Dist: Casemate Pubs. & Bk. Distributors, LLC.

Bennett, Harry, Jr. Purple pup girls are grape Jelly. Bumbalough, Jerry. 2007. 16p. (J). 8.95 *(978-0-9797960-0-5(8))* Thirsty Sponge Publishing Co.

Bennett, James. Tell Me a Silly Story. Reiner, Carl. 2010. 32p. (J). (gr. -1). 16.95 *(978-1-60747-713-6(0),* Pickwick Pr.) Phoenix Bks., Inc.

—The 2000 Year Old Man Goes to School. Brooks, Mel & Reiner, Carl. 2006. 32p. (J). (gr. 4-8). reprint ed. 18.00 *(978-1-4223-5622-7(1))* DIANE Publishing Co.

—The 2000 Year Old Man Goes to School. Brooks, Mel & Reiner, Carl. 2005. (ENG.). 40p. (J). (gr. -1-3). 17.99 *(978-0-06-076676-4(X))* HarperCollins Pubs.

Bennett, James & Bennett, Carl A. Tell Me Another Scary Story... but Not Too Scary! Reiner, Carl. 2009. (ENG.). 32p. (J). (gr. 4-7). 16.95 *(978-1-59777-630-1(0))* Phoenix Bks., Inc.

Bennett, Jax. Extraordinary Military Kids: A Workbook for & about Military Kids. Numbers, Megan. 2017. (ENG.). (J). pap. 14.95 *(978-1-55571-892-3(2),* Hellgate Pr.) L & R Publishing, LLC.

Bennett, Jerry. I Walk for Water. Andrews, Lindsey. 2012. (ENG.). 43p. (J). 16.95 *(978-0-615-49668-9(7))* Hilarity Waters Pr.

Bennett, Jill, jt. illus. see Watts, Marjorie Anne.

Bennett, Joe. Crew: Big Trouble in Little Mogadishu. Priest, Christopher. 2004. (Marvel Heroes Ser.). 160p. (YA). pap. 16.99 *(978-0-7851-1307-2(X))* Marvel Worldwide, Inc.

Bennett, Joe, et al. Heroes Reborn: Captain America. 2020. (ENG.). 488p. (J). (gr. 4-17). pap. 44.99 ***(978-1-302-92345-7(5))*** Marvel Worldwide, Inc.

Bennett, Joe, et al. Immortal Hulk Vol. 1. 2019. (Immortal Hulk HC Ser.: 1). 248p. (YA). (gr. 8-17). 34.99 *(978-1-302-91965-8(2))* Marvel Worldwide, Inc.

Bennett, Joe. Immortal Hulk Vol. 1: Or Is He Both? 2018. (Immortal Hulk Ser.: 1). 128p. (YA). (gr. 8-17). pap. 15.99 *(978-1-302-91255-0(0))* Marvel Worldwide, Inc.

Bennett, Joe. Immortal Hulk Vol. 2. 2020. 224p. (YA). (gr. 8-17). 34.99 ***(978-1-302-92347-1(1))*** Marvel Worldwide, Inc.

Bennett, Joe. Immortal Hulk Vol. 3: Hulk in Hell. 2019. 112p. (YA). pap. 15.99 *(978-1-302-91506-3(1))* Marvel Worldwide, Inc.

—Immortal Hulk Vol. 4: Abomination. 2019. (Immortal Hulk Ser.: 4). (ENG.). 112p. (YA). (gr. 8-17). pap. 15.99 *(978-1-302-91667-1(X))* Marvel Worldwide, Inc.

Bennett, Joe. Immortal Hulk Vol. 7: Hulk Is Hulk. 2020. (ENG.). 112p. (YA). (gr. 8-17). pap. 15.99 ***(978-1-302-92051-7(0))*** Marvel Worldwide, Inc.

Bennett, Joey. Immortal Hulk Vol. 5: Breaker of Worlds. 2019. (Immortal Hulk Ser.: 5). 112p. (YA). (gr. 8-17). pap. 15.99 *(978-1-302-91668-8(8))* Marvel Worldwide, Inc.

Bennett, John. Gatita Va Rápido. Pugliano-Martin, Carol. 2015. (Early Connections Ser.). (SPA.). (J). (gr. k-1). *(978-1-4900-3455-3(2))* Benchmark Education Co.

—Little Cat Goes Fast - 6 Pack: Set of 6 with Teacher Materials Common Core Edition. Pugliano-Martin, Carol. 2015. (Early Connections Ser.). (J). (gr. k-1). 37.00 *(978-1-5021-4705-9(X))* Benchmark Education Co.

—Old Macdonald on His Farm. Andrews, Jackie. 2012. (ENG.). 32p. pap. 6.50 *(978-1-84135-195-7(4))* Award Pubns. Ltd. GBR. Dist: Parkwest Pubns., Inc.

—Three Billy-Goats Gruff. Andrews, Jackie. 2012. (ENG.). 32p. pap. 6.50 *(978-1-84135-196-4(2))* Award Pubns. Ltd. GBR. Dist: Parkwest Pubns., Inc.

Bennett, Lorna. C Is for Chinook: An Alberta Alphabet. Welykochy, Dawn. rev. ed. 2004. (Discover Canada Province by Province Ser.). (ENG.). 40p. (J). (gr. 1-3). 19.99 *(978-1-58536-223-3(9),* 202053) Sleeping Bear Pr.

—L Is for Land of Living Skies: A Saskatchewan Alphabet. Aksomitis, Linda. 2010. (Discover Canada Province by Province Ser.). (ENG.). 32p. (J). (gr. 1-3). 17.95 *(978-1-58536-490-9(8),* 202194) Sleeping Bear Pr.

—Sandwiches for Duke, 1 vol. Sadler, Judy Ann. 2007. (ENG.). 32p. (J). (gr. 1-3). 8.95 *(978-1-55005-062-2(1),* 267905f8-5c12-436f-b32c-b3b66c51113b) Fitzhenry & Whiteside, Ltd. CAN. Dist: Firefly Bks., Ltd.

—Stories of the Aurora: The Myths & Facts of the Northern Lights, 1 vol. Galat, Joan Marie. 2016. (Dot to Dot in the Sky Ser.). (ENG.). 68p. (J). (gr. 6-8). pap. 16.95 *(978-1-77050-210-9(6),* 047efdad-4568-432b-abe4-a0b8f055d028) Whitecap Bks., Ltd. CAN. Dist: Firefly Bks., Ltd.

—Stories of the Moon. Galat, Joan. 2004. (Dot to Dot in the Sky Ser.: 0). (ENG.). 64p. (J). (gr. 6-8). pap. 12.95 *(978-1-55285-610-9(0),* ce2944fd-71ac-49da-be71-f792cc696a3e) Whitecap Bks., Ltd. CAN. Dist: Firefly Bks., Ltd.

—True Story. Chan, Marty. 2009. (ENG.). 32p. (J). 9.95 *(978-0-9810449-0-3(5))* Ink Jockey, Inc. CAN. Dist: Univ. of Toronto Pr.

Bennett, Lorna & Yu, Chao. Stories of the Planets. Galat, Joan. 2003. (Dot to Dot in the Sky Ser.: 0). (ENG.). 64p. (J). (gr. 6-8). pap. 12.95 *(978-1-55285-392-4(6),* 92a3548d-a226-43b7-b584-596f3d3b1e35) Whitecap Bks., Ltd. CAN. Dist: Firefly Bks., Ltd.

Bennett, Michele & Dunlap, Joan. Backpack Cat. Bennett, Marcia. 2004. 124p. 19.95 *(978-1-932196-50-4(1))* WordWright.biz, Inc.

Bennett-Minnerly, Denise. The Color Tree. Bennett-Minnerly, Denise. 2005. (J). 14.95 *(978-1-56290-328-2(4))* Crystal Productions.

Bennett, Nneka. Vision of Beauty: The Story of Sarah Breedlove Walker. Lasky, Kathryn. 2012. (Candlewick Biographies Ser.). (ENG.). 56p. (J). (gr. 3-7). 14.99 *(978-0-7636-6428-2(6));* pap. 4.99 *(978-0-7636-6092-5(2))* Candlewick Pr.

Bennett, Scott. Battle of the Dinosaurs: An Antiwar Children's Fable. Poppel, George. 2016. (Pandamonium Bks.). (ENG.). (J). (gr. k-4). pap. 12.95 *(978-0-9973316-4-6(X))* Inprint Bks.

Bennett, Stephanie. Tiny Tito & Gigantic Jerome. Grebing, Debra. Powderly, Shawn, ed. 2019. (Tiny Tito & Gigantic Jerome Ser.: Vol. 1). (ENG.). 30p. (J). pap. 10.00 ***(978-1-0820-3930-0(6))*** Independently Published.

Bennington, Mark. Young Romans, Vol. Williams, Rose. 2004. (ENG.). 176p. pap., tchr. ed. 39.00 *(978-1-84331-081-5(3))* Bolchazy-Carducci Pubs.

Bennion, Anneliese. A Paper Hug. Skolmoski, Stephanie. 2006. 36p. (J). 6.95 *(978-0-9786425-0-1(3))* DesignAbility.

Benny, Mike. Just as Good: How Larry Doby Changed America's Game. Crowe, Chris. 2012. (ENG.). 32p. (J). (gr. 1-4). 16.99 *(978-0-7636-5026-1(9))* Candlewick Pr.

—The Listeners. Whelan, Gloria. 2009. (Tales of Young Americans Ser.). (ENG.). 40p. (J). (gr. 1-4). 17.95 *(978-1-58536-419-0(3),* 202154) Sleeping Bear Pr.

Benny, Mike, jt. illus. see Ellison, Chris.

Benoit, Jérôme, jt. illus. see Fayolle, Diane.

Benoit, Renne. Baby Cakes. Heras, Theo. 2017. (ENG.). 24p. (J). (gr. -1-k). 13.95 *(978-1-77278-030-7(8))* Pajama Pr. CAN. Dist: Ingram Publisher Services.

—Big City Bees, 1 vol. de Vries, Maggie. 2013. 48p. (J). (gr. k-3). 17.95 *(978-1-55365-906-8(6))* Greystone Books Ltd. CAN. Dist: Publishers Group West (PGW).

—Boy in Motion: Rick Hansen's Story. Manson, Ainslie. 2009. (ENG.). 48p. (J). (gr. k-3). pap. 12.00 *(978-1-55365-427-8(7))* Greystone Books Ltd. CAN. Dist: Publishers Group West (PGW).

Benoit, Renné. Clean Sweep! Frank Zamboni's Ice Machine: Great Idea Series. Kulling, Monica. (Great Idea Ser.: 8). (ENG.). 32p. (J). (gr. k-3). 2017. pap. 6.99 *(978-1-77049-796-2(X));* 2016. 17.99 *(978-1-77049-795-5(1))* Tundra Bks. CAN. (Tundra Bks.). Dist: Penguin Random Hse. LLC.

Benoit, Renne. F Is for French: Un Livre d'Alphabet Sur le Quebec - A Quebec Alphabet. Arsenault, Elaine. 2013. (Discover Canada Province by Province Ser.). (ENG.). 40p. (J). (gr. 1-4). 17.95 *(978-1-58536-435-0(5),* 202351) Sleeping Bear Pr.

Benoit, Renné. Fraser Bear: A Cub's Life. de Vries, Maggie. 2012. 48p. (J). (gr. k-4). pap. 10.95 *(978-1-926812-95-3(6))* Greystone Books Ltd. CAN. Dist: Publishers Group West (PGW).

Benoit, Renne. John F. Kennedy & the Stormy Sea. Goldsmith, Howard. 2006. (Ready-To-read COFA Ser.). (ENG.). 32p. (J). (gr. k-2). pap. 4.99 *(978-0-689-86816-0(2),* Simon Spotlight) Simon Spotlight.

Benoit, Renné. John F. Kennedy & the Stormy Sea. Goldsmith, Howard. 2006. 32p. (J). lib. bdg. 15.00 *(978-1-4242-0958-3(7))* Fitzgerald Bks.

—Little Dance. Sleeping Bear Press. 2013. (ENG.). 20p. (J). (gr. -1-k). 8.99 *(978-1-58536-884-6(9),* 202899) Sleeping Bear Pr.

—PoPo's Lucky Chinese New Year. Loh-Hagan, Virginia. 2016. (ENG.). 32p. (J). (gr. 1-4). 16.99 *(978-1-58536-978-2(0),* 204113) Sleeping Bear Pr.

Benoit, Renne. The Secret of the Village Fool, 1 vol. Upjohn, Rebecca. 2012. (ENG.). 32p. (J). (gr. 1-3). lib. bdg. 18.95 *(978-1-926920-75-7(9))* Second Story Pr. CAN. Dist: Orca Bk. Pubs. USA.

—Tale of a Great White Fish: A Sturgeon Story. de Vries, Maggie. 2010. (ENG.). 48p. (J). (gr. k-4). pap. 10.95 *(978-1-55365-303-5(3))* Greystone Books Ltd. CAN. Dist: Publishers Group West (PGW).

—Thanksgiving: A Harvest Celebration. Stiegemeyer, Julie. 32p. (J). 2006. (gr. -1-3). per. 7.49 *(978-0-7586-0916-8(7));* 2003. 13.49 *(978-0-7586-0530-6(7))* Concordia Publishing Hse.

—Tooling Around: Crafty Creatures & the Tools They Use. Jackson, Ellen. 2014. (ENG.). 32p. (J). (gr. -1-3). 17.95 *(978-1-58089-564-4(6))* Charlesbridge Publishing, Inc.

—When-I-Was-a-Little-Girl, 1 vol. Gilmore, Rachna. 2007. (ENG.). 24p. (J). (gr. 1-3). 14.95 *(978-1-897187-12-8(2))* Second Story Pr. CAN. Dist: Orca Bk. Pubs. USA.

—Where's Bunny? Heras, Theo. 2018. (ENG.). 24p. (J). (gr. -1-k). 13.95 *(978-1-77278-043-7(X))* Pajama Pr. CAN. Dist: Ingram Publisher Services.

—A Year of Borrowed Men. Barker, Michelle. 2016. (ENG.). 40p. (J). (gr. 1-4). 18.95 *(978-1-927485-83-5(5))* Pajama Pr. CAN. Dist: Ingram Publisher Services.

Benoit, Renné & Lyons, Chris. S Is for the Stanley Cup: A Hockey Championship Alphabet. Ulmer, Michael. 2017. (ENG.). 32p. (J). (gr. 1-4). 16.99 *(978-1-58536-972-0(1),* 204226) Sleeping Bear Pr.

Benoit, Renne & Second Story Press Staff. Lily & the Paper Man, 1 vol. Upjohn, Rebecca. 2007. (ENG.). 24p. (J). (gr. 1-3). 15.95 *(978-1-897187-19-7(X))* Second Story Pr. CAN. Dist: Orca Bk. Pubs. USA.

Bensch, April. Billy the Bully Two. David, Patricia. 2019. (ENG.). 50p. (J). (gr. k-6). 18.95 ***(978-1-950768-02-8(3));*** pap. 12.95 ***(978-1-950768-01-1(5))*** ProsePress.

Bensch, April. Madeline Becomes a Star. Wheeler-Cribb, Peggy. 2013. 50p. 29.95 *(978-0-9886194-1-8(5))* ProsePress.

Bensley, Ann. Lola & Crow. Bensley, Ann. 2017. (ENG.). (J). 16.99 *(978-0-9995242-1-3(6))* Bensley, Ann-Mari.

—Taco & Squirrel. Bensley, Ann. 2017. (ENG.). (J). 16.99 *(978-0-9995242-0-6(8))* Bensley, Ann-Mari.

Benson, Barbara. One. Kellbart, L. S. 2007. (ENG.). 76p. (J). (gr. k-k). per. *(978-1-85756-610-9(6))* Janus Publishing Co.

Benson, Daryl, photos by. Alberta: Images, 1 vol. Benson, Daryl. rev. ed. 2004. (ENG., 120p. 49.95 *(978-0-9684576-2-7(2),* ac6bb226-73cc-4d2d-899b-0786ba39bc4a) Cullor Bks. CAN. Dist: Lone Pine Publishing USA.

Benson, Patrick. Christopher Mouse: The Tale of a Small Traveler. Wise, William. 2006. (ENG.). 160p. (YA). (gr. 2-5). per. 8.99 *(978-1-58234-708-0(5),* 9781582347080, Bloomsbury USA Childrens) Bloomsbury Publishing USA.

—North: The Amazing Story of Arctic Migration. Dowson, Nick. 2013. (ENG.). 56p. (J). (gr. 2-5). 7.99 *(978-0-7636-6663-7(7))* Candlewick Pr.

—Owl Babies. Waddell, Martin. (ENG.). (J). 2019. 24p. (— 1). bds. 9.99 *(978-1-5362-0963-1(5));* 2017. 32p. (gr. -1-2). 16.99 *(978-0-7636-9519-4(X));* 2015. 22p. (— 1). bds. 7.99 *(978-0-7636-7961-3(5))* Candlewick Pr.

—Owl Babies Book & Toy Gift Set. Waddell, Martin. 2016. (ENG.). (J). (-k). bds. 15.99 *(978-0-7636-8898-1(3))* Candlewick Pr.

—Owl Babies Lap-Size Board Book. Waddell, Martin. 2018. (ENG.). 22p. (J). (— 1). bds. 12.99 *(978-0-7636-9520-0(3))* Candlewick Pr.

—Snow Leopard: Ghost of the Mountains. Anderson, Justin. 2019. (ENG.). 32p. (J). (gr. k-3). 16.99 *(978-1-5362-0540-4(0))* Candlewick Pr.

—Soon. Knapman, Timothy. 2015. (ENG.). 33p. (J). (-k). 16.99 *(978-0-7636-7478-6(8))* Candlewick Pr.

—The Stone Bird. McCartney, Jenny. 2018. (ENG.). 32p. (J). (gr. -1-3). 17.99 *(978-1-5415-1455-3(6))* Lerner Publishing Group.

—The Wind in the Willows. Grahame, Kenneth. 2009. (ENG.). 304p. (J). pap. 11.99 *(978-0-00-647926-0(X))* HarperCollins Pubs.

Benson, Patrick, jt. illus. see Allibone, Judith.

Bentley, Amelia. Sid the Wizard. Bentley, Amelia. Flanagan, Moya. 2020. (Sid's Adventures Ser.: Vol. 1). (ENG.). 36p. (J). pap. 9.99 ***(978-1-6794-9751-3(0))*** Independently Published.

Bentley, Anita. Zoey & Bel, 1 vol. Casebolt, Christan. 2009. 14p. pap. 24.95 *(978-1-60813-220-1(X))* America Star Bks.

Bentley, James. Amazing Atlantic Canadian Kids: Awesome Stories of Bravery & Adventure, 1 vol. Boileau, John. 2019. (ENG.). 160p. (J). pap. 19.95 *(978-1-77108-797-1(8),* dceb7e36-3ffb-4586-b4c1-3571f96edb6a) Nimbus Publishing, Ltd. CAN. Dist: Baker & Taylor Publisher Services (BTPS).

Bentley, Jonathan. Audrey's Tree House. Hughes, Jenny. 2015. (J). pap. *(978-0-545-81405-8(7),* Scholastic Pr.) Scholastic, Inc.

—Check on Me. Daddo, Andrew. 2015. 32p. 17.99 *(978-0-7333-2419-2(3))* ABC Bks. AUS. Dist: HarperCollins Pubs.

—Daddy Kiss. Allum, Margaret. 2010. (ENG.). 24p. (J). (gr. -1). *(978-1-921541-30-8(X))* Little Hare Bks.

B

—First Day. Daddo, Andrew. 2017. 32p. (J). pap. 6.99 *(978-0-7333-3271-5(4))* ABC Bks. AUS. Dist: HarperCollins Pubs.

—From Me to You. Bertini, Anthony. 2019. (ENG.). 32p. (J). 12.99 *(978-1-61067-903-9(2))* Kane Miller.

—I Do It. Daddo, Andrew. 2017. 32p. pap. 6.99 *(978-0-7333-2851-0(2))* ABC Bks. AUS. Dist: HarperCollins Pubs.

—The Lilac Ladies. Hughes, Jenny. 2014. (ENG.). 32p. (J). (gr. -1-k). 17.99 *(978-1-921894-23-7(7))* Little Hare Bks. AUS. Dist: Independent Pubs. Group.

—Little Big. 2015. (ENG.). 32p. (J). 16.00 *(978-0-8028-5462-9(1))*, Eerdmans Bks For Young Readers) Eerdmans, William B. Publishing Co.

—Pink. Holmes, Janet A. 2013. (ENG.). 32p. (J). (gr. -1-k). pap. 9.99 *(978-1-921894-10-7(5))* Little Hare Bks. AUS. Dist: Independent Pubs. Group.

—The Second Sky. Guest, Patrick. 2019. (ENG.). 32p. (J). *(978-0-8028-5520-6(2))*, Eerdmans Bks For Young Readers) Eerdmans, William B. Publishing Co.

—Swim, Duck, Swim! Nilsen, Anna. 2014. (Flippety-Flaps Ser.). (ENG.). 8p. (J). (— 1). bds. 6.99 *(978-1-877003-19-6(0))* Little Hare Bks. AUS. Dist: Independent Pubs. Group.

—Tales from a Tall Forest. Micaleff, Shaun. 2019. (ENG.). 224p. (J). (gr. 2-4). 21.99 *(978-1-76012-959-0(3))* Hardie Grant Egmont Pty, Ltd. AUS. Dist: Independent Pubs. Group.

—When I Grow Up. Daddo, Andrew. 2017. 32p. 17.99 *(978-0-7333-3341-5(9))* ABC Bks. AUS. Dist: HarperCollins Pubs.

—Where Is Bear? 2017. (ENG.). 32p. (J). (gr. -1-2). 16.99 *(978-0-399-55593-0(5))*, Doubleday Bks. for Young Readers) Random Hse. Children's Bks.

Bentley, Julia Faye. What Will It Take for a Toad to Kiss a Monkey: The Adventures of Princess Gracie & Prince Wallaby. Bentley, Douglas W. 2008. 52p. per. 24.95 *(978-1-4137-8849-5(1))* America Star Bks.

Bentley, Nicolas. The Wind on the Moon. Linklater, Eric. 2017. (ENG.). 376p. (YA). (gr. 7). pap. 12.99 *(978-1-68137-103-0(0))*, NYRB Kids) New York Review of Bks., Inc., The.

Bentley, Tadgh. Dragons Eat Noodles on Tuesdays. Stahl, Jon. 2019. (ENG.). 40p. (J). (gr. -1-3). 17.99 *(978-1-338-12551-1(6))*, Scholastic Pr.) Scholastic, Inc.

Bentley, Tadgh. Little Penguin & the Lollipop. Bentley, Tadgh. 2017. (ENG.). 40p. (J). (gr. -1-3). 17.99 *(978-0-06-256078-0(6))* HarperCollins Pubs.

Bentley, Tadgh. Little Penguin & the Mysterious Object. Bentley, Tadgh. 2020. (I Can Read Level 1 Ser.). (ENG.). 32p. (J). (gr. -1-3). 16.99 ***(978-0-06-269998-5(9))***; pap. 4.99 ***(978-0-06-269997-8(0))*** HarperCollins Pubs. (Balzer & Bray).

Bentley, Tadgh. Little Penguin Gets the Hiccups. Bentley, Tadgh. 2015. (ENG.). 40p. (J). (gr. -1-3). 17.99 *(978-0-06-233536-4(7))* HarperCollins Pubs.

—Little Penguin Gets the Hiccups Board Book. Bentley, Tadgh. 2016. (ENG.). 34p. (J). (gr. -1 — 1). bds. 8.99 *(978-0-06-265224-9(9))*, Balzer & Bray) HarperCollins Pubs.

—Little Penguin Stays Awake. Bentley, Tadgh. 2018. (ENG.). 40p. (J). (gr. -1-3). 17.99 *(978-0-06-268977-1(0))*, Balzer & Bray) HarperCollins Pubs.

—Little Penguin's New Friend. Bentley, Tadgh. 2019. (I Can Read Level 1 Ser.). (ENG.). 32p. (J). (gr. -1-3). 16.99 *(978-0-06-269995-4(4))*; pap. 4.99 *(978-0-06-269994-7(6))* HarperCollins Pubs. (Balzer & Bray).

—Samson: the Piranha Who Went to Dinner. Bentley, Tadgh. 2017. (ENG.). 40p. (J). (gr. -1-3). 17.99 *(978-0-06-233537-1(5))* HarperCollins Pubs.

Bently, Peter. Blackthorn Winter. Wilson, Douglas. 2003. 141p. (J). per. 12.00 *(978-1-932168-10-5(9))* Veritas Pr., Inc.

Bently, Renee. Kate Kate & the Bizzy Girls: The Queen. Kanafani, Deborah. Anderson, Kirsten, ed. 2016. (ENG.). (J). pap. 10.00 *(978-0-9833532-6-3(3))* Bizzy Girls Publishing.

—My Mother's Mummy: Kate Kate & the Bizzy Girls. Kanafani, Deborah. 2018. (Kate Kate & the Bizzy Girls Ser.: Vol. 3). (ENG.). 122p. (J). pap. 7.99 *(978-0-9833532-7-0(1))* Bizzy Girls Publishing.

Benton, Jim. Am I the Princess or the Frog? Benton, Jim. 2005. (Dear Dumb Diary Ser.: 3). (ENG.). 160p. (J). (gr. 3-7). pap. 6.99 *(978-0-439-62907-2(1))* Scholastic, Inc.

—Attack of the 50-Ft. Cupid. Benton, Jim. (Franny K. Stein, Mad Scientist Ser.: 2). (ENG.). 112p. (J). (gr. 2-5). 2005. pap. 6.99 *(978-0-689-86296-0(2))*; 2004. 17.99 *(978-0-689-86292-2(X))* Simon & Schuster Bks. For Young Readers. (Simon & Schuster Bks. For Young Readers).

—Attack of the 50-Ft. Cupid. Benton, Jim. 2011. (Franny K. Stein, Mad Scientist Ser.). (ENG.). 112p. (J). (gr. 2-6). 27.07 *(978-1-59961-818-0(4))*, 7828, Chapter Bks.) Spotlight.

—Bad Hair Day. Benton, Jim. 2019. (Franny K. Stein, Mad Scientist Ser.: 8). (ENG.). 112p. (J). (gr. 1-5). 15.99 *(978-1-5344-1337-5(5))*, Simon & Schuster Bks. For Young Readers) Simon & Schuster Bks. For Young Readers.

—Can Adults Become Human? Benton, Jim. 2006. (Dear Dumb Diary Ser.: 5). (ENG.). 144p. (J). (gr. 3-7). 6.99 *(978-0-439-79621-7(0))*, Scholastic Paperbacks) Scholastic, Inc.

—Catwad #3. Benton, Jim. 2020. (Catwad Ser.: 3). (ENG.). 128p. (J). (gr. 3-7). pap. 8.99 *(978-1-338-61628-6(5))*, Graphix) Scholastic, Inc.

—The Complete Franny K. Stein, Mad Scientist: Lunch Walks among Us; Attack of the 50-Ft. Cupid; the Invisible Fran; the Fran That Time Forgot; Frantastic Voyage; the Fran with Four Brains; the Frandidate. Benton, Jim. ed. 2012. (Franny K. Stein, Mad Scientist Ser.). (ENG.). 784p. (J). (gr. 2-5). pap. 44.99 *(978-1-4424-7424-6(6))*, Simon & Schuster Bks. For Young Readers) Simon & Schuster Bks. For Young Readers.

—Dumbness Is a Dish Best Served Cold. Benton, Jim. 2016. (Dear Dumb Diary Ser.). 224p. (J). (gr. 3-7). 12.99 *(978-0-545-93228-8(9))*, Scholastic Pr.) Scholastic, Inc.

—The Fran That Time Forgot. Benton, Jim. 4th ed. 2005. (Franny K. Stein, Mad Scientist Ser.: 4). (ENG.). 112p. (J). (gr. 2-5). mass mkt. 6.99 *(978-0-689-86298-4(9))*; 17.99 *(978-0-689-86294-6(6))* Simon & Schuster Bks. For Young Readers. (Simon & Schuster Bks. For Young Readers).

—The Fran That Time Forgot. Benton, Jim. 2011. (Franny K. Stein, Mad Scientist Ser.). (ENG.). 112p. (J). (gr. 2-6). 27.07 *(978-1-59961-820-3(6))*, 7830, Chapter Bks.) Spotlight.

—The Fran with Four Brains. Benton, Jim. (Franny K. Stein, Mad Scientist Ser.: 6). (ENG.). 112p. (J). (gr. 2-5). 2007. pap. 6.99 *(978-1-4169-0232-4(5))*; 2006. 17.99 *(978-1-4169-0231-7(7))* Simon & Schuster Bks. For Young Readers. (Simon & Schuster Bks. For Young Readers).

—The Fran with Four Brains. Benton, Jim. 2011. (Franny K. Stein, Mad Scientist Ser.). (ENG.). 112p. (J). (gr. 2-6). 27.07 *(978-1-59961-822-7(2))*, 7832, Chapter Bks.) Spotlight.

—The Frandidate. Benton, Jim. (Franny K. Stein, Mad Scientist Ser.: 7). (ENG.). (J). (gr. 2-5). 2009. 112p. pap. 6.99 *(978-1-4169-0234-8(1))*; No. 7. 2008. 128p. 17.99 *(978-1-4169-0233-1(3))* Simon & Schuster Bks. For Young Readers. (Simon & Schuster Bks. For Young Readers).

—The Frandidate. Benton, Jim. 2011. (Franny K. Stein, Mad Scientist Ser.). (ENG.). 128p. (J). (gr. 2-6). 27.07 *(978-1-59961-823-4(0))*, 7833, Chapter Bks.) Spotlight.

—Frantastic Voyage. Benton, Jim. 2006. (Franny K. Stein, Mad Scientist Ser.: 5). (ENG.). 112p. (J). (gr. 2-5). pap. 6.99 *(978-1-4169-0230-0(9))*; 17.99 *(978-1-4169-0229-4(5))* Simon & Schuster Bks. For Young Readers. (Simon & Schuster Bks. For Young Readers).

—Frantastic Voyage. Benton, Jim. 2011. (Franny K. Stein, Mad Scientist Ser.). (ENG.). 112p. (J). (gr. 2-6). 27.07 *(978-1-59961-821-0(4))*, 7831, Chapter Bks.) Spotlight.

—The Handbook. Benton, Jim. 2017. 240p. (J). (gr. 3-7). 12.99 *(978-0-545-94240-9(3))*, Scholastic Pr.) Scholastic, Inc.

—The Invisible Fran. Benton, Jim. (Franny K. Stein, Mad Scientist Ser.: 3). (ENG.). 112p. (J). (gr. 2-5). 2005. pap. 6.99 *(978-0-689-86297-7(0))*; 2004. 17.99 *(978-0-689-86293-9(8))* Simon & Schuster Bks. For Young Readers. (Simon & Schuster Bks. For Young Readers).

—The Invisible Fran. Benton, Jim. 2011. (Franny K. Stein, Mad Scientist Ser.). (ENG.). 112p. (J). (gr. 2-6). 27.07 *(978-1-59961-819-7(2))*, 7829, Chapter Bks.) Spotlight.

—It's Me. Benton, Jim. 2019. (Catwad Ser.: 1). 112p. (J). (gr. 3-7). pap. 8.99 *(978-1-338-32602-4(3))* Scholastic, Inc.

—It's Not My Fault! I Know Everything. Benton, Jim. 2009. (Dear Dumb Diary Ser.: 8). (ENG.). 144p. (J). (gr. 3-7). 6.99 *(978-0-439-82597-9(0))*, Scholastic Paperbacks) Scholastic, Inc.

—Let's Do a Thing! Benton, Jim. 2017. (Victor Shmud, Total Expert Ser.: 1). (ENG.). 128p. (J). (gr. 2-5). pap. 5.99 *(978-0-545-93229-5(7))*, Scholastic Paperbacks) Scholastic, Inc.

—Let's Pretend This Never Happened. Benton, Jim. 2004. (Dear Dumb Diary Ser.: 1). 112p. (J). (gr. 4-7). pap. 6.99 *(978-0-439-62904-1(7))*, Scholastic Paperbacks) Scholastic, Inc.

—Let's Pretend This Never Happened. Benton, Jim. ed. 2004. (Dear Dumb Diary Ser.: 1). 95p. (gr. -1-2). 17.20 *(978-1-4176-3050-9(7))* Turtleback.

—Lunch Walks among Us. Benton, Jim. 2004. (Franny K. Stein, Mad Scientist Ser.: 1). (ENG.). 112p. (J). (gr. 2-5). mass mkt. 6.99 *(978-0-689-86295-3(4))*, Simon & Schuster Bks. For Young Readers) Simon & Schuster Bks. For Young Readers.

—Lunch Walks among Us. Benton, Jim. 2011. (Franny K. Stein, Mad Scientist Ser.). (ENG.). 112p. (J). (gr. 2-6). 27.07 *(978-1-59961-817-3(6))*, 7827, Chapter Bks.) Spotlight.

—Lunch Walks among Us. Benton, Jim. ed. 2004. (Franny K. Stein, Mad Scientist Ser.: 1). 102p. (gr. 2-5). lib. bdg. 16.00 *(978-1-4176-4054-6(5))* Turtleback.

—Lunch Walks among Us novel. Benton, Jim. 2003. (Franny K. Stein, Mad Scientist Ser.: 1). (ENG.). 112p. (J). (gr. 2-5). 17.99 *(978-0-689-86291-5(1))*, Simon & Schuster Bks. For Young Readers) Simon & Schuster Bks. For Young Readers.

—Me (Just Like You, Only Better) Benton, Jim. 2011. (Dear Dumb Diary Ser.: 12). (ENG.). 160p. (J). (gr. 3-7). pap. 6.99 *(978-0-545-11616-9(3))*, Scholastic Paperbacks) Scholastic, Inc.

—My Pants Are Haunted! Benton, Jim. 2004. (Dear Dumb Diary Ser.: 2). (ENG.). 144p. (J). (gr. 2-5). mass mkt. 6.99 *(978-0-439-62905-8(5))*, Scholastic Paperbacks) Scholastic, Inc.

—Never Do Anything, Ever. Benton, Jim. 2005. (Dear Dumb Diary Ser.: 4). (ENG.). 144p. (J). (gr. 3-7). pap. 6.99 *(978-0-439-62908-9(X))*, Scholastic Paperbacks) Scholastic, Inc.

—Never Underestimate Your Dumbness. Benton, Jim. 2008. (Dear Dumb Diary Ser.: 7). (ENG.). 160p. (J). (gr. 3-7). 6.99 *(978-0-439-82596-2(2))* Scholastic, Inc.

—Night of the Living Things (Victor Shmud, Total Expert #2) Benton, Jim. 2017. (Victor Shmud, Total Expert Ser.: 2). (ENG.). 112p. (J). (gr. 2-5). pap. 5.99 *(978-0-545-93234-9(3))*; lib. bdg. 16.99 *(978-0-545-93235-6(1))* Scholastic, Inc. (Scholastic Paperbacks).

—Nobody's Perfect. I'm As Close As It Gets. Benton, Jim. 2013. (Dear Dumb Diary Year Two Ser.: 3). 144p. (J). (gr. 3-7). pap. 6.99 *(978-0-545-37764-5(1))*, Scholastic Paperbacks) Scholastic, Inc.

—Okay, So Maybe I Do Have Superpowers. Benton, Jim. 2011. (Dear Dumb Diary Ser.: 11). (ENG.). 160p. (J). (gr. 3-7). pap. 6.99 *(978-0-545-11615-2(5))*, Scholastic Paperbacks) Scholastic, Inc.

—The Problem with Here Is That It's Where I'm From. Benton, Jim. 2007. (Dear Dumb Diary Ser.: 6). (ENG.). 128p. (J). (gr. 3-7). 6.99 *(978-0-439-79622-4(9))*, Scholastic Paperbacks) Scholastic, Inc.

Benton, Jim. Recipe for Disaster. Benton, Jim. 2020. (Franny K. Stein, Mad Scientist Ser.: 9). (ENG.). 128p. (J). (gr. 1-5). 15.99 ***(978-1-5344-1340-5(5))***, Simon & Schuster Bks. For Young Readers) Simon & Schuster Bks. For Young Readers.

Benton, Jim. Soy Yo, DOS. Benton, Jim. 2019. (Pangato Ser.: 2). (SPA.). 128p. (J). (gr. 3-7). pap. 8.99 *(978-1-338-60119-0(9))*, Scholastic en Espanol) Scholastic, Inc.

—That's What Friends Aren't For. Benton, Jim. 2010. (Dear Dumb Diary Ser.: 9). 144p. (J). (gr. 3-7). 6.99 *(978-0-545-11612-1(0))*, Scholastic Paperbacks) Scholastic, Inc.

—What I Don't Know Might Hurt Me. Benton, Jim. 2013. (Dear Dumb Diary Year Two Ser.: 4). (ENG.). 144p. (J). (gr. 3-7). pap. 6.99 *(978-0-545-37765-2(X))*, Scholastic Paperbacks) Scholastic, Inc.

—The Worst Things in Life Are Also Free. Benton, Jim. 2010. (Dear Dumb Diary Ser.: 10). 160p. (J). (gr. 3-7). pap. 6.99 *(978-0-545-11614-5(7))*, Scholastic Paperbacks) Scholastic, Inc.

—You Can Bet on That. Benton, Jim. 2014. (Dear Dumb Diary Year Two Ser.: 5). 160p. (J). (gr. 3-7). pap. 6.99 *(978-0-545-64257-6(4))*, Scholastic Paperbacks) Scholastic, Inc.

Benton, Lynne & Ursell, Martin. Chariot Race/La Carrera de Carrozas. Benton, Lynne. 2009. (Let's Read! Spanish-English Ser.). (ENG.). 32p. (J). (gr. k-3). 17.44 *(978-0-7641-4364-9(6))*, B.E.S. Publishing) Peterson's.

Benton, Marilyn. Bubba, the Busy Beaver. Folmsbee, Judi. 2013. (ENG.). 48p. (J). 20.00 *(978-1-886068-68-1(2))* Fruitbearer Publishing, LLC.

Benton, Matthew. Ella & the Potty. Venters, Wanda J. 2019. (Unicorns Ser.: Vol. 6). (ENG.). 34p. (J). pap. 9.45 ***(978-1-6744-5040-7(0))*** Independently Published.

Benton, Tim. Dancing Forever. Bryant, Ann. 2006. (Ballerina Dreams Ser.). 105p. (J). lib. bdg. 4.99 *(978-0-7945-1299-6(2))*, Usborne) EDC Publishing.

—Dancing Princess. Bryant, Ann. 2006. (Ballerina Dreams Ser.). 102p. (J). per. 4.99 *(978-0-7945-1297-2(6))*, Usborne) EDC Publishing.

—Dancing with the Stars. Bryant, Ann. 2006. (Ballerina Dreams Ser.). 107p. (J). per. 4.99 *(978-0-7945-1298-9(4))*, Usborne) EDC Publishing.

—Jasmine's Lucky Star. Bryant, Ann. 2006. (Ballerina Dreams Ser.). 104p. (J). per. 4.99 *(978-0-7945-1295-8(X))*, Usborne) EDC Publishing.

—Poppy's Secret Wish. Bryant, Ann. 2006. (Ballerina Dreams Ser.). 105p. (J). per. 4.99 *(978-0-7945-1294-1(1))*, Usborne) EDC Publishing.

—Rose's Big Decision. Bryant, Ann. 2006. (Ballerina Dreams Ser.). 102p. (J). per. 4.99 *(978-0-7945-1296-5(8))*, Usborne) EDC Publishing.

Bentsen, Erika. The Adventures of Captain Stinky & Sailor Puss: Captain Stinky & Sailor Puss Meet the Magicals. Fisher, Colin. 2019. (Adventures of Captain Stinky & Sailor Puss Ser.: Vol. 3). (ENG.). 56p. (J). pap. ***(978-0-9951295-0-4(9))*** Fisher, Colin.

Bentsen, Erika. The Adventures of Captain Stinky & Sailor Puss: Captain Stinky & Sailor Puss Rescue a Pirate. Fisher, Colin. 2nd ed. 2019. (Adventures of Captain Stinky & Sailor Puss Ser.: Vol. 2). (ENG.). 46p. (J). pap. *(978-0-473-47133-0(7))* Fisher, Colin.

Bentulan, Christian. Such Exquisite Calamity. Beaupré, Sydnie. 2020. (Such Exquisite Calamity Ser.: Vol. 1). (ENG.). 346p. (J). pap. ***(978-0-9952642-0-5(1))*** Beaupré, Sydnie.

Beop-Ryong, Yuy. Chronicles of the Cursed Sword, 10 vols. Hui-Jin, Park. rev. ed. 2004. 176p. Vol. 6. pap. 9.99 *(978-1-59182-423-7(0))*; Vol. 7. pap. 9.99 *(978-1-59182-424-4(9))* TOKYOPOP, Inc.

Bera, Aparna. Nelly & I: Bilingual Story. Sabbagh, Zakaria. Vale, Valentina, ed. 2019. (ENG.). 88p. (J). pap. 17.99 *(978-1-0958-8492-8(1))* Independently Published.

Bera, Aparna & Kvirikashvili, Lika. Peace Plan. Pratten, Julie. 2018. (ENG.). 40p. (J). pap. 9.99 *(978-1-7291-9644-1(6))* Independently Published.

Beranek, Carlo. Baby Shark. Puffinton, Brick. Cottage Door Press, ed. 2019. (Finger Puppet Board Book Ser.). (ENG.). 12p. (J). (gr. -1 — 1). bds. 6.99 *(978-1-68052-711-7(8))*, 1004440) Cottage Door Pr.

—Touch-And-Feel Tower Animals. Hegarty, Patricia. 2019. (ENG.). 14p. (J). (gr. 2-k). bds. 10.99 *(978-1-68010-595-7(7))* Tiger Tales.

—Touch-And-Feel Tower: Dinos. Hegarty, Patricia. 2020. (ENG.). 14p. (J). (-k). bds. 10.99 *(978-1-68010-609-1(0))* Tiger Tales.

Berard, Real. The Foot of the River, 1 vol. Lalor, George. 2015. (ENG.). 32p. (J). (gr. 8-12). pap. 9.95 *(978-0-919143-43-2(1))*, 5658be9b-2452-4d82-9221-2507f7cf1583) Pemmican Pubns., Inc. CAN. Dist: Firefly Bks., Ltd.

Bercasio, Edgar B. Tom's Secret: A Child's Search. Bercasio Pascal, Patty. Bercasio, Siegfredo Belbes, ed. 2016. (ENG.). (J). pap. *(978-1-4602-8325-7(2))* FriesenPress.

Berchtold, Lauren. Tortoise & Hare Run a Race: Lap Book Edition. Smith, Carrie. 2016. (My First Reader's Theater Tales Ser.). (J). (gr. k). *(978-1-5021-5509-2(5))* Benchmark Education Co.

—Tortoise & Hare Run a Race: Small Book Edition. Smith, Carrie. 2016. (My First Reader's Theater Tales Ser.). (J). (gr. k). *(978-1-5021-5514-6(1))* Benchmark Education Co.

Berchtold, Lauren Marie. Parade Feathers. Schmauss, Judy Kentor. 2015. (Early Rising Readers Ser.). (J). (gr. -1-k). 5.83 *(978-1-4788-2141-0(8))* Newmark Learning LLC.

—Pi, Pi! Chucu Chucu! Koons, Linda. 2016. (Early Rising Readers Ser.). (SPA.). 16p. (J). (gr. 1-1). 29.00 *(978-1-4788-3890-6(6))* Newmark Learning LLC.

—Plumas para Desfilar. Schmauss, Judy Kentor. 2016. (Early Rising Readers Ser.). (SPA.). 16p. (J). (gr. 1-1). 6.67 *(978-1-4788-4168-5(0))* Newmark Learning LLC.

Bercier, Dominic. Hold My Hand: A Father & Son Book. Poulin, Bernard A. 2018. (ENG.). 32p. (J). pap. *(978-0-9920538-8-8(9))* Mirror Comics Studios.

Berck, Jessica. Animal Countdown. Robbins, Lisa. 2016. (ENG.). (J). pap. 11.99 *(978-0-9862331-9-7(6))* Hear My Heart Publishing.

Berdugina, Tatyana. Animals. Clever Publishing. 2019. (Look & Find, Clever Baby Ser.). (ENG.). 22p. (J). (gr. -1 — 1). bds. 7.99 *(978-1-948418-16-4(9))* Clever Media Group.

Bereal, JaeMe. In Her Hands: The Story of Sculptor Augusta Savage, 1 vol. Schroeder, Alan & National Geographic Learning Staff. 2009. (ENG.). 48p. (J). (gr. 1-5). pap. 12.95 *(978-1-60060-989-3(9))*, 37ac47ed-6365-4c71-9202-1a8dbf60025f) Lee & Low Bks., Inc.

—In Her Hands: The Story of Sculptor Augusta Savage. Schroeder, Alan. 2009. (ENG.). 48p. (J). (gr. 1-6). 19.95 *(978-1-60060-332-7(7))* Lee & Low Bks., Inc.

Bereciartu, Julia. The Duchess & Guy: A Rescue-To-Riches Puppy Love Story. Furstinger, Nancy. 2019. (ENG.). 32p. (J). (gr. -1-3). 17.99 *(978-0-358-02304-3(1))*, 1738855, HMH Books For Young Readers) Houghton Mifflin Harcourt Publishing Co.

Bereciartu, Julia. High-Five to the Hero: 15 Favorite Fairytales Retold with Boy Power. Murrow, Vita. ed. 2019. (ENG.). 96p. (J). (gr. -1-3). 19.99 ***(978-1-78603-782-4(3))***, Frances Lincoln Children's Bks.) Quarto Publishing Group UK GBR. Dist: Hachette Bk. Group.

—Power to the Princess: 15 Favorite Fairytales Retold with Girl Power. Murrow, Vita. 2018. (ENG.). 96p. (J). (gr. k-3). 19.99 ***(978-1-78603-203-4(1))***, Frances Lincoln Children's Bks.) Quarto Publishing Group UK GBR. Dist: Hachette Bk. Group.

—Welcome to Ballet School: Written by a Professional Ballerina. Bouder, Ashley. 2020. (ENG.). 64p. (J). (gr. -1-2). 19.99 ***(978-0-7112-5128-1(2))***, Frances Lincoln Children's Bks.) Quarto Publishing Group UK GBR. Dist: Hachette Bk. Group.

Berends, Jenny. Bearen Bear & the Bunbury Tales. Due, Kirsten L. 2013. 194p. pap. *(978-0-9884916-3-2(X))* Roxby Media Ltd.

Berendsen, Bailey. Lost in the Woods: A Bigfoot Story. Berendsen, Bailey. 2019. (Cryptid Adventures Ser.: Vol. 1). (ENG.). 38p. (J). pap. 14.50 *(978-1-0972-0756-5(0))* Independently Published.

Berenger, Al. Abraham Lincoln. Berenger, Al. 2018. (Pocket Bios Ser.). (ENG.). 32p. (J). 14.99 *(978-1-250-16611-1(X))*, 900187188) Roaring Brook Pr.

—Albert Einstein. Berenger, Al. 2018. (Pocket Bios Ser.). (ENG.). 32p. (J). 14.99 *(978-1-250-16609-8(8))*, 900187186) Roaring Brook Pr.

—Anne Frank. Berenger, Al. 2018. (Pocket Bios Ser.). (ENG.). 32p. (J). 14.99 *(978-1-250-16877-1(5))*, 900187748) Roaring Brook Pr.

—Coco Chanel. Berenger, Al. 2018. (Pocket Bios Ser.). (ENG.). 32p. (J). 14.99 *(978-1-250-16625-8(X))*, 900187202) Roaring Brook Pr.

—Frida Kahlo. Berenger, Al. 2018. (Pocket Bios Ser.). (ENG.). 32p. (J). 14.99 *(978-1-250-16875-7(9))*, 900187746) Roaring Brook Pr.

—Muhammad Ali. Berenger, Al. 2018. (Pocket Bios Ser.). (ENG.). 32p. (J). 14.99 *(978-1-250-16874-0(0))*, 900187743) Roaring Brook Pr.

—Neil Armstrong. Berenger, Al. 2018. (Pocket Bios Ser.). (ENG.). 32p. (J). 14.99 *(978-1-250-16619-7(5))*, 900187196) Roaring Brook Pr.

—Nelson Mandela. Berenger, Al. 2018. (Pocket Bios Ser.). (ENG.). 32p. (J). 14.99 *(978-1-250-16613-5(6))*, 900187190) Roaring Brook Pr.

—Pocket Bios: Buddha. Berenger, Al. 2019. (Pocket Bios Ser.). (ENG.). 32p. (J). 14.99 *(978-1-250-16888-7(0))*, 900187758) Roaring Brook Pr.

—Pocket Bios: Charlie Chaplin. Berenger, Al. 2018. (Pocket Bios Ser.). (ENG.). 32p. (J). 14.99 *(978-1-250-16623-4(3))*, 900187200) Roaring Brook Pr.

—Pocket Bios: Isaac Newton. Berenger, Al. 2018. (Pocket Bios Ser.). (ENG.). 32p. (J). 14.99 *(978-1-250-16879-5(1))*, 900187750) Roaring Brook Pr.

—Pocket Bios: Joan of Arc. Berenger, Al. 2019. (Pocket Bios Ser.). (ENG.). 32p. (J). 14.99 *(978-1-250-16892-4(9))*, 900187762) Roaring Brook Pr.

—Pocket Bios: John F. Kennedy. Berenger, Al. 2019. (Pocket Bios Ser.). (ENG.). 32p. (J). 14.99 *(978-1-250-16894-8(5))*, 900187764) Roaring Brook Pr.

—Pocket Bios: Marie Antoinette. Berenger, Al. 2019. (Pocket Bios Ser.). (ENG.). 32p. (J). 14.99 *(978-1-250-16882-5(1))*, 900187752) Roaring Brook Pr.

—Pocket Bios: Pablo Picasso. Berenger, Al. 2019. (Pocket Bios Ser.). (ENG.). 32p. (J). 14.99 *(978-1-250-16898-6(8))*, 900187766) Roaring Brook Pr.

—Pocket Bios: Pocahontas. Berenger, Al. 2019. (Pocket Bios Ser.). (ENG.). 32p. (J). 14.99 *(978-1-250-16884-9(8))*, 900187754) Roaring Brook Pr.

—Pocket Bios: Princess Diana. Berenger, Al. 2019. (Pocket Bios Ser.). (ENG.). 32p. (J). 14.99 *(978-1-250-16890-0(2))*, 900187760) Roaring Brook Pr.

—Pocket Bios: Vincent Van Gogh. Berenger, Al. 2019. (Pocket Bios Ser.). (ENG.). 32p. (J). 14.99 *(978-1-250-16886-3(4))*, 900187756) Roaring Brook Pr.

—Rosa Parks. Berenger, Al. 2018. (Pocket Bios Ser.). (ENG.). 32p. (J). 14.99 *(978-1-250-16617-3(9))*, 900187194) Roaring Brook Pr.

Berenger, Al, jt. illus. see Unique Heritage Media.

Berenschot, Myriam. Ella the Swinging Duck. Overmeer, Suzan. 2020. (ENG.). 32p. (J). (gr. -1). 9.95 *(978-1-60537-517-5(9))*; 17.95 *(978-1-60537-498-7(9))* Clavis Publishing.

Berenstain, Jan. The Berenstain Bears & the Baby Chipmunk. Berenstain, Jan. Berenstain, Stan. 2005. (I Can Read Level 1 Ser.). (ENG.). 32p. (J). (gr. k-3). pap. 4.99 *(978-0-06-058413-9(0))* HarperCollins Pubs.

—The Berenstain Bears & the Big Spelling Bee, No. 6. Berenstain, Jan. Berenstain, Stan & Berenstain, Mike. 2007. (Berenstain Bears Ser.). (ENG.). 32p. (J). (gr. -1-2). pap. 3.99 *(978-0-06-057386-7(4),* HarperFestival) HarperCollins Pubs.

—The Berenstain Bears & the Trouble with Chores. Berenstain, Jan. Berenstain, Stan. 2005. (Berenstain Bears Ser.). (ENG.). 32p. (J). (gr. -1-3). pap. 3.99 *(978-0-06-057382-9(1),* HarperFestival) HarperCollins Pubs.

—The Berenstain Bears & the Trouble with Commercials. Berenstain, Jan. Berenstain, Stan & Berenstain, Mike. 2007. (Berenstain Bears Ser.). (ENG.). 32p. (J). (gr. -1-2). pap. 3.99 *(978-0-06-057387-4(2),* HarperFestival) HarperCollins Pubs.

—The Berenstain Bears & the Wishing Star. Berenstain, Jan. Berenstain, Stan. 2005. (I Can Read Level 1 Ser.). (ENG.). 32p. (J). (gr. k-3). pap. 4.99 *(978-0-06-058347-7(9))* HarperCollins Pubs.

—The Berenstain Bears & Too Much Car Trip. Berenstain, Jan. Berenstain, Stan. 2006. (Berenstain Bears Ser.). (ENG.). 32p. (J). (gr. -1-2). pap. 3.99 *(978-0-06-057384-3(8),* HarperFestival) HarperCollins Pubs.

—The Berenstain Bears' Bedtime Battle. Berenstain, Jan. Berenstain, Stan. 2004. (Berenstain Bears Ser.). (ENG.). 32p. (J). (gr. -1-3). pap. 4.99 *(978-0-06-057381-2(3),* HarperFestival) HarperCollins Pubs.

—The Berenstain Bears Clean House. Berenstain, Jan. Berenstain, Stan. 2004. (I Can Read Level 1 Ser.). (ENG.). 32p. (J). (gr. k-3). pap. 4.99 *(978-0-06-058335-4(5))* HarperCollins Pubs.

—The Berenstain Bears down on the Farm. Berenstain, Jan. Berenstain, Stan. 2006. (I Can Read Level 1 Ser.). (ENG.). 32p. (J). (gr. k-3). pap. 4.99 *(978-0-06-058351-4(7))* HarperCollins Pubs.

—The Berenstain Bears Go on a Ghost Walk. Berenstain, Jan. Berenstain, Stan. 2005. (Berenstain Bears Ser.). (ENG.). 32p. (J). (gr. -1-2). 10.99 *(978-0-06-057399-7(6));* pap. 3.99 *(978-0-06-057383-6(X))* HarperCollins Pubs. (HarperFestival).

—The Berenstain Bears Go on Vacation. Berenstain, Jan. Berenstain, Stan & Berenstain, Mike. 2010. (Berenstain Bears Ser.). (ENG.). 32p. (J). (gr. -1-3). pap. 7.99 *(978-0-06-057433-8(X))* HarperCollins Pubs.

—The Berenstain Bears Hug & Make Up. Berenstain, Jan. Berenstain, Stan. 2006. (Berenstain Bears Ser.). (ENG.). 32p. (J). (gr. -1-2). pap. 3.99 *(978-0-06-057385-0(6),* HarperFestival) HarperCollins Pubs.

—The Berenstain Bears Lose a Friend. Berenstain, Jan. Berenstain, Stan & Berenstain, Mike. 2007. (Berenstain Bears Ser.). (ENG.). 32p. (J). (gr. -1-2). pap. 3.99 *(978-0-06-057389-8(9),* HarperFestival) HarperCollins Pubs.

—The Berenstain Bears' New Kitten. Berenstain, Jan. Berenstain, Stan & Berenstain, Mike. 2007. (I Can Read Level 1 Ser.). (ENG.). 32p. (J). (gr. k-3). 16.99 *(978-0-06-058356-9(8));* pap. 4.99 *(978-0-06-058357-6(6))* HarperCollins Pubs.

—The Berenstain Bears' New Pup. Berenstain, Jan. Berenstain, Stan. 2005. (I Can Read Level 1 Ser.). (ENG.). 32p. (J). (gr. k-3). pap. 4.99 *(978-0-06-058344-6(4))* HarperCollins Pubs.

—The Berenstain Bears' New Pup. Berenstain, Jan. Berenstain, Stan. 2017. (I Can Read Level 1 Ser.). (ENG.). 40p. (J). (gr. -1-3). 9.99 *(978-0-06-257272-1(5))* HarperCollins Pubs.

—The Berenstain Bears' Old-Fashioned Christmas. Berenstain, Jan. Berenstain, Mike. 2012. (Berenstain Bears Ser.). (ENG.). 32p. (J). (gr. -1-3). 12.99 *(978-0-06-057443-7(7))* HarperCollins Pubs.

—The Berenstain Bears Out West. Berenstain, Jan. Berenstain, Stan. 2006. (I Can Read Level 1 Ser.). (ENG.). 32p. (J). (gr. k-3). pap. 4.99 *(978-0-06-058354-5(1))* HarperCollins Pubs.

—The Berenstain Bears Play T-Ball. Berenstain, Jan. Berenstain, Stan. (I Can Read Level 1 Ser.). (ENG.). 32p. (J). (gr. k-3). 2005. 16.99 *(978-0-06-058337-8(1));* 2004. pap. 4.99 *(978-0-06-058338-5(X))* HarperCollins Pubs.

—The Berenstain Bears Say Please & Thank You. Berenstain, Jan. Berenstain, Mike. 2011. (Berenstain Bears Ser.). (ENG.). 32p. (J). (gr. -1-3). 12.99 *(978-0-06-057437-6(2))* HarperCollins Pubs.

—The Berenstain Bears' Seashore Treasure. Berenstain, Jan. Berenstain, Stan. 2005. (I Can Read Level 1 Ser.). (ENG.). 32p. (J). (gr. k-3). pap. 4.99 *(978-0-06-058341-5(X))* HarperCollins Pubs.

—The Berenstain Bears Trim the Tree. Berenstain, Jan. Berenstain, Mike. 2007. (Berenstain Bears Ser.). (ENG.). 16p. (J). (gr. -1-1). pap. 6.99 *(978-0-06-057417-8(8),* HarperFestival) HarperCollins Pubs.

Berenstain, Jan & Berenstain, Mike. The Berenstain Bears: All Aboard! Berenstain, Jan & Berenstain, Mike. 2010. (I Can Read Level 1 Ser.). (ENG.). 32p. (J). (gr. k-3). 16.99 *(978-0-06-168971-0(8))* HarperCollins Pubs.

—The Berenstain Bears: All Aboard! Berenstain, Jan & Berenstain, Mike. 2010. (I Can Read Level 1 Ser.). (ENG.). 32p. (J). (gr. k-3). pap. 4.99 *(978-0-06-057418-5(6),* HarperCollins) HarperCollins Pubs. Ltd. GBR. Dist: HarperCollins Pubs.

—The Berenstain Bears & Mama for Mayor! Berenstain, Jan & Berenstain, Mike. 2012. (I Can Read Level 1 Ser.). (ENG.). 32p. (J). (gr. k-3). 16.99 *(978-0-06-207528-4(4));* pap. 4.99 *(978-0-06-207527-7(6))* HarperCollins Pubs.

—The Berenstain Bears & the Nutcracker. Berenstain, Jan & Berenstain, Mike. 2011. (Berenstain Bears Ser.). (ENG.). 32p. (J). (gr. -1-3). pap. 3.99 *(978-0-06-057396-6(1),* HarperFestival) HarperCollins Pubs.

—The Berenstain Bears & the Shaggy Little Pony. Berenstain, Jan & Berenstain, Mike. 2011. (I Can Read Level 1 Ser.). (ENG.). 32p. (J). (gr. k-3). 16.99 *(978-0-06-168972-7(6));* pap. 4.99 *(978-0-06-057419-2(4))* HarperCollins Pubs.

—The Berenstain Bears & the Tooth Fairy. Berenstain, Jan & Berenstain, Mike. 2012. (Berenstain Bears Ser.). (ENG.). 24p. (J). (gr. -1-3). pap. 3.99 *(978-0-06-207549-9(7),* HarperFestival) HarperCollins Pubs.

—The Berenstain Bears at the Aquarium. Berenstain, Jan & Berenstain, Mike. 2012. (I Can Read Level 1 Ser.). (ENG.). 32p. (J). (gr. k-3). 16.99 *(978-0-06-207525-3(X));* pap. 4.99 *(978-0-06-207524-6(1))* HarperCollins Pubs.

—The Berenstain Bears' Baby Easter Bunny. Berenstain, Jan & Berenstain, Mike. 2008. (Berenstain Bears Ser.). (ENG.). 16p. (J). (gr. -1-1). pap. 6.99 *(978-0-06-057420-8(8),* HarperFestival) HarperCollins Pubs.

—The Berenstain Bears' Big Bedtime Book. Berenstain, Stan & Berenstain, Jan. Berenstain, Mike. 2008. (Berenstain Bears Ser.). 48p. (J). (gr. -1-3). 13.89 *(978-0-06-057435-2(6))* HarperCollins Pubs.

—The Berenstain Bears' Class Trip. Berenstain, Jan & Berenstain, Mike. 2009. (I Can Read Level 1 Ser.). (ENG.). 32p. (J). (gr. k-3). 16.99 *(978-0-06-168973-4(4));*No. 4. pap., act. bk. ed. 4.99 *(978-0-06-057416-1(X))* HarperCollins Pubs.

—The Berenstain Bears Come Clean for School. Berenstain, Jan & Berenstain, Mike. 2011. (Berenstain Bears Ser.). (ENG.). 32p. (J). (gr. -1-3). pap. 3.99 *(978-0-06-057395-9(3),* HarperFestival) HarperCollins Pubs.

—The Berenstain Bears' Computer Trouble. Berenstain, Jan & Berenstain, Mike. 2010. (Berenstain Bears Ser.). (ENG.). 32p. (J). (gr. -1-3). 10.99 *(978-0-06-057410-9(0));* pap. 3.99 *(978-0-06-057394-2(5))* HarperCollins Pubs. (HarperFestival).

—The Berenstain Bears' Dinosaur Dig. Berenstain, Jan & Berenstain, Mike. 2012. (Berenstain Bears Ser.). (ENG.). 24p. (J). (gr. -1-3). pap. 3.99 *(978-0-06-207548-2(9),* HarperFestival) HarperCollins Pubs.

—The Berenstain Bears' Family Reunion. Berenstain, Jan et al. 2009. (I Can Read Level 1 Ser.). (ENG.). 32p. (J). (gr. k-3). pap. 4.99 *(978-0-06-058360-6(6))* HarperCollins Pubs.

—The Berenstain Bears Go Out to Eat. Berenstain, Jan & Berenstain, Mike. 2009. (Berenstain Bears Ser.). (ENG.). 32p. (J). (gr. -1-2). pap. 3.99 *(978-0-06-057393-5(7),* HarperFestival) HarperCollins Pubs.

—The Berenstain Bears' Really Big Pet Show. Berenstain, Jan & Berenstain, Mike. 2008. (Berenstain Bears Ser.). 32p. (J). (gr. -1-2). 8.99 *(978-0-06-057406-2(2),* HarperFestival) HarperCollins Pubs.

—The Berenstain Bears: Safe & Sound! Berenstain, Jan & Berenstain, Mike. 2009. (Berenstain Bears Ser.). (ENG.). 32p. (J). (gr. -1-3). pap. 3.99 *(978-0-06-057391-1(0),* HarperFestival) HarperCollins Pubs.

—The Berenstain Bears: Sick Days. Berenstain, Jan & Berenstain, Mike. 2009. (Berenstain Bears Ser.). (ENG.). 32p. (J). (gr. -1-3). pap. 3.99 *(978-0-06-057392-8(9),* HarperFestival) HarperCollins Pubs.

—The Berenstain Bears' Sleepover. Berenstain, Jan & Berenstain, Mike. 2008. (I Can Read Level 1 Ser.). (ENG.). 32p. (J). (gr. k-3). 16.99 *(978-0-06-168974-1(2));* Vol. 3. pap., act. bk. ed. 4.99 *(978-0-06-057415-4(1))* HarperCollins Pubs.

—The Berenstain Bears: We Love Our Dad! Berenstain, Jan & Berenstain, Mike. 2013. (Berenstain Bears Ser.). (ENG.). 24p. (J). (gr. -1-3). pap. 3.99 *(978-0-06-207551-2(9),* HarperFestival) HarperCollins Pubs.

—The Berenstain Bears: We Love Our Mom! Berenstain, Jan & Berenstain, Mike. 2012. (Berenstain Bears Ser.). (ENG.). 24p. (J). (gr. -1-3). pap. 3.99 *(978-0-06-207547-5(0),* HarperFestival) HarperCollins Pubs.

—The Berenstain Bears: We Love Trucks! Berenstain, Jan & Berenstain, Mike. 2013. (I Can Read Level 1 Ser.). (ENG.). 32p. (J). (gr. -1-3). 16.99 *(978-0-06-207536-9(5));* pap. 4.99 *(978-0-06-207535-2(7))* HarperCollins Pubs.

—The Berenstain Bears' Winter Wonderland. Berenstain, Jan & Berenstain, Mike. 2011. (Berenstain Bears Ser.). (ENG.). 16p. (J). (gr. -1-1). pap. 6.99 *(978-0-06-057427-7(5),* HarperFestival) HarperCollins Pubs.

—Nothing Ever Happens at the South Pole. Berenstain, Stan & Berenstain, Jan. 2012. (ENG.). 40p. (J). (gr. -1-3). 10.99 *(978-0-06-207532-1(2))* HarperCollins Pubs.

Berenstain, Jan, jt. illus. see Berenstain, Mike.

Berenstain, Jan, jt. illus. see Berenstain, Stan.

Berenstain, Jan & Mike. The Berenstain Bears & the Haunted House. Berenstain, Jan et al. 2010. (Berenstain Bears Ser.). (ENG.). 16p. (J). (gr. -1-1). pap. 6.99 *(978-0-06-057426-0(7),* HarperFestival) HarperCollins Pubs.

—The Berenstain Bears' Really Big Pet Show. Berenstain, Mike & Berenstain, Jan. 2008. (Berenstain Bears Ser.). (ENG.). 32p. (J). (gr. -1-2). pap. 3.99 *(978-0-06-057390-4(2),* HarperFestival) HarperCollins Pubs.

—The Berenstain Bears' Valentine Party. Berenstain, Jan & Berenstain, Mike. 2008. (Berenstain Bears Ser.). (ENG.). 16p. (J). (gr. -1-3). pap. 6.99 *(978-0-06-057425-3(9),* HarperFestival) HarperCollins Pubs.

Berenstain, Mike. The Berenstain Bears & the Ducklings. Berenstain, Stan & Berenstain, Jan. 2018. 30p. (J). *(978-1-5444-0097-6(7),* BRO-adap20180125-161) Harper & Row Ltd.

—The Berenstain Bears Christmas Fun Sticker & Activity Book, 1 vol. Berenstain, Jan. 2016. (Berenstain Bears/Living Lights: a Faith Story Ser.). (ENG.). 32p. (J). pap. 6.99 *(978-0-310-75384-1(8))* Zonderkidz.

—The Berenstain Bears Easter Fun Sticker & Activity Book, 1 vol. Berenstain, Jan. 2017. (Berenstain Bears/Living Lights: a Faith Story Ser.). (ENG.). 32p. (J). pap. 7.99 *(978-0-310-75381-0(3))* Zonderkidz.

—The Berenstain Bears' Holiday Cookbook: Cub-Friendly Cooking with an Adult, 1 vol. 2016. (Berenstain Bears/Living Lights: a Faith Story Ser.). (ENG.). 96p. (J). 12.99 *(978-0-310-75399-5(6))* Zonderkidz.

—The Berenstain Bears Hugs & Kisses Sticker & Activity Book, 1 vol. Berenstain, Jan. 2016. (Berenstain Bears/Living Lights: a Faith Story Ser.). (ENG.). 32p. (J). pap. 6.99 *(978-0-310-75382-7(1))* Zonderkidz.

—The Berenstain Bears Save Christmas. Berenstain, Stan & Berenstain, Jan. 2005. (Berenstain Bears Ser.). 48p. (J). (gr. -1-3). pap. 6.99 *(978-0-06-052672-6(6),* HarperFestival) HarperCollins Pubs.

—The Berenstain Bears Spring Storybook Favorites: Includes 7 Stories Plus Stickers! Berenstain, Jan & Mike. 2019. (Berenstain Bears Ser.). (ENG.). 192p. (J). (gr. -1-3). 13.99 *(978-0-06-288310-0(0))* HarperCollins Pubs.

Berenstain, Mike, et al. My Favorite Berenstain Bears Stories: Learning to Read Box Set. Berenstain, Mike et al. 2018. (I Can Read Level 1 Ser.). (ENG.). 160p. (J). (gr. -1-3). pap. 19.99 *(978-0-06-265459-5(4))* HarperCollins Pubs.

Berenstain, Mike. The Berenstain Bears 12-Book Phonics Fun! Includes 12 Mini-Books Featuring Short & Long Vowel Sounds. Berenstain, Mike. 2013. (My First I Can Read Ser.). (ENG.). 100p. (J). (gr. -1-3). pap. 14.99 *(978-0-06-222346-3(1))* HarperCollins Pubs.

—Berenstain Bears: 5-Minute Berenstain Bears Stories. Berenstain, Mike. Berenstain, Jan & Berenstain, Stan. 2015. (Berenstain Bears Ser.). (ENG.). 192p. (J). (gr. -1-3). 12.99 *(978-0-06-236018-2(3),* HarperFestival) HarperCollins Pubs.

—The Berenstain Bears & the Ducklings. Berenstain, Mike. 2018. (I Can Read Level 1 Ser.). (ENG.). 32p. (J). (gr. -1-3). 16.99 *(978-0-06-265456-4(X),* BRO-adap20180125-161); pap. 4.99 *(978-0-06-265455-7(1),* BRO-adap20180125-161) HarperCollins Pubs.

Berenstain, Mike. The Berenstain Bears & the Ghost of the Theater. Berenstain, Mike. 2020. (I Can Read Level 1 Ser.). (ENG.). 32p. (J). (gr. -1-3). 16.99 ***(978-0-06-265475-5(6))**;* pap. 4.99 ***(978-0-06-265474-8(8))*** HarperCollins Pubs. Ltd. GBR. (HarperCollins). Dist: HarperCollins Pubs.

Berenstain, Mike. The Berenstain Bears Are SuperBears! Berenstain, Mike. 2015. (I Can Read Level 1 Ser.). (ENG.). 32p. (J). (gr. -1-3). pap. 4.99 *(978-0-06-235008-4(0))* HarperCollins Pubs.

—The Berenstain Bears Around the World. Berenstain, Mike. 2016. (I Can Read Level 1 Ser.). (ENG.). 32p. (J). (gr. -1-3). pap. 4.99 *(978-0-06-235023-7(4))* HarperCollins Pubs.

—The Berenstain Bears' Big Family Album. Berenstain, Mike. 2019. (Berenstain Bears Ser.). (ENG.). 24p. (J). (gr. -1-3). pap. 3.99 *(978-0-06-265467-0(5),* HarperFestival) HarperCollins Pubs.

—The Berenstain Bears' Big Machines. Berenstain, Mike. 2017. (I Can Read Level 1 Ser.). (ENG.). 32p. (J). (gr. -1-3). 16.99 *(978-0-06-235039-8(0));* pap. 4.99 *(978-0-06-235038-1(2))* HarperCollins Pubs.

—The Berenstain Bears' Big Track Meet. Berenstain, Mike. 2020. (I Can Read Level 1 Ser.). (ENG.). 32p. (J). (gr. -1-3). 16.99 *(978-0-06-265472-4(1));* pap. 4.99 *(978-0-06-265471-7(3))* HarperCollins Pubs. Ltd. GBR. (HarperCollins). Dist: HarperCollins Pubs.

—The Berenstain Bears' Easter Parade. Berenstain, Mike. 2014. (Berenstain Bears Ser.). (ENG.). 24p. (J). (gr. -1-3). pap. 3.99 *(978-0-06-207554-3(3),* HarperFestival) HarperCollins Pubs.

—The Berenstain Bears Get Ready for Bed. Berenstain, Mike. 2018. (Berenstain Bears Ser.). (ENG.). 16p. (J). (gr. -1-3). pap. 6.99 *(978-0-06-265465-6(9),* HarperFestival) HarperCollins Pubs.

—The Berenstain Bears Get Ready for School. Berenstain, Mike. 2015. (Berenstain Bears Ser.). (ENG.). 16p. (J). (gr. -1-1). pap. 6.99 *(978-0-06-207552-9(7),* HarperFestival) HarperCollins Pubs.

—The Berenstain Bears Go Back to School. Berenstain, Mike. Berenstain, Stan & Berenstain, Jan. (Berenstain Bears Ser.). (ENG.). 32p. (J). (gr. -1-3). 2009. pap. 6.99 *(978-0-06-052675-7(0));* 2005. 15.99 *(978-0-06-052673-3(4))* HarperCollins Pubs. (HarperFestival).

—The Berenstain Bears: Gone Fishin'! Berenstain, Mike. 2014. (I Can Read Level 1 Ser.). (ENG.). 32p. (J). (gr. -1-3). 16.99 *(978-0-06-207560-4(8));* pap. 4.99 *(978-0-06-207559-8(4))* HarperCollins Pubs.

—The Berenstain Bears' Graduation Day. Berenstain, Mike. 2014. (Berenstain Bears Ser.). (ENG.). 24p. (J). (gr. -1-3). pap. 3.99 *(978-0-06-207555-0(1),* HarperFestival) HarperCollins Pubs.

—The Berenstain Bears: Hospital Friends. Berenstain, Mike. 2015. (Berenstain Bears Ser.). (ENG.). 24p. (J). (gr. -1-3). pap. 3.99 *(978-0-06-207541-3(1),* HarperFestival) HarperCollins Pubs.

—The Berenstain Bears Just Grin & Bear It! Wisdom from Bear Country. Berenstain, Mike. 2018. (Berenstain Bears Ser.). (ENG.). 96p. (J). (gr. -1-3). 9.99 *(978-0-06-274133-2(0))* HarperCollins Pubs.

—The Berenstain Bears' Lemonade Stand. Berenstain, Mike. 2014. (I Can Read Level 1 Ser.). (ENG.). 32p. (J). (gr. -1-3). 16.99 *(978-0-06-207545-1(4));* pap. 4.99 *(978-0-06-207544-4(6))* HarperCollins Pubs.

—The Berenstain Bears: Long, Long Ago. Berenstain, Mike. 2018. (Berenstain Bears Ser.). (ENG.). 24p. (J). (gr. -1-3). pap. 3.99 *(978-0-06-265462-5(4),* HarperFestival) HarperCollins Pubs.

—The Berenstain Bears' Night Before Christmas. Berenstain, Mike. 2013. (Berenstain Bears Ser.). (ENG.). 24p. (J). (gr. -1-3). pap. 3.99 *(978-0-06-207553-6(5),* HarperFestival) HarperCollins Pubs.

—The Berenstain Bears' Pet Rescue. Berenstain, Mike. 2018. (Berenstain Bears Ser.). (ENG.). 24p. (J). (gr. -1-3). pap. 3.99 *(978-0-06-265464-9(0),* HarperFestival) HarperCollins Pubs.

—The Berenstain Bears Pirate Adventure. Berenstain, Mike. 2016. (Berenstain Bears Ser.). (ENG.). 24p. (J). (gr. -1-3). pap. 3.99 *(978-0-06-235021-3(8),* HarperFestival) HarperCollins Pubs.

—The Berenstain Bears Play Football! Berenstain, Mike. 2017. (I Can Read Level 1 Ser.). (ENG.). 32p. (J). (gr. -1-3). pap. 4.99 *(978-0-06-235033-6(1))* HarperCollins Pubs.

—The Berenstain Bears Save Christmas. Berenstain, Mike. Berenstain, Jan et al. 2003. (Berenstain Bears Ser.). (ENG.). 48p. (J). (gr. -1-3). 14.99 *(978-0-06-052670-2(X),* HarperFestival) HarperCollins Pubs.

—The Berenstain Bears' Show-And-Tell. Berenstain, Mike. 2017. (Berenstain Bears Ser.). (ENG.). 24p. (J). (gr. -1-3). pap. 3.99 *(978-0-06-235031-2(5),* HarperFestival) HarperCollins Pubs.

—The Berenstain Bears Storybook Favorites: Includes 6 Stories Plus Stickers! Berenstain, Mike. Berenstain, Stan & Jan. 2020. (Berenstain Bears Ser.). (ENG.). 192p. (J). (gr. -1-3). 13.99 *(978-0-06-293002-6(8),* HarperCollins) HarperCollins Pubs. Ltd. GBR. Dist: HarperCollins Pubs.

—The Berenstain Bears Take-Along Storybook Set: Dinosaur Dig, Go Green, When I Grow up, under the Sea, the Tooth Fairy. Berenstain, Mike. Berenstain, Jan. 2016. (Berenstain Bears Ser.). (ENG.). 120p. (J). (gr. -1-3). pap. 11.99 *(978-0-06-241155-6(1),* HarperFestival) HarperCollins Pubs.

—The Berenstain Bears Take Off! Berenstain, Mike. 2016. (I Can Read Level 1 Ser.). (ENG.). 32p. (J). (gr. -1-3). pap. 4.99 *(978-0-06-235018-3(8))* HarperCollins Pubs.

—The Berenstain Bears: That's So Rude! Berenstain, Mike. 2019. (Berenstain Bears Ser.). (ENG.). 24p. (J). (gr. -1-3). pap. 3.99 *(978-0-06-265469-4(1))* HarperCollins Pubs.

—The Berenstain Bears under the Sea. Berenstain, Mike. 2016. (Berenstain Bears Ser.). (ENG.). 24p. (J). (gr. -1-3). pap. 3.99 *(978-0-06-235011-4(0),* HarperFestival) HarperCollins Pubs.

—The Berenstain Bears' Valentine Love Bug. Berenstain, Mike. 2014. (Berenstain Bears Ser.). (ENG.). 24p. (J). (gr. -1-3). pap. 6.99 *(978-0-06-207562-8(4),* HarperFestival) HarperCollins Pubs.

Berenstain, Mike. The Berenstain Bears Visit Big Bear City. Berenstain, Mike. 2020. (Berenstain Bears Ser.). (ENG.). 24p. (J). (gr. -1-3). pap. 3.99 ***(978-0-06-265477-9(2),*** HarperFestival) HarperCollins Pubs.

Berenstain, Mike. The Berenstain Bears Visit Grizzlyland. Berenstain, Mike. 2018. (Berenstain Bears Ser.). (ENG.). 24p. (J). (gr. -1-3). pap. 3.99 *(978-0-06-265463-2(2),* HarperFestival) HarperCollins Pubs.

—The Berenstain Bears Visit the Farm. Berenstain, Mike. 2020. (Berenstain Bears Ser.). (ENG.). 16p. (J). (gr. -1-3). 6.99 *(978-0-06-265470-0(5),* HarperFestival) HarperCollins Pubs.

—The Berenstain Bears Visit the Firehouse. Berenstain, Mike. 2016. (Berenstain Bears Ser.). (ENG.). 24p. (J). (gr. -1-3). pap. 3.99 *(978-0-06-235016-9(1),* HarperFestival) HarperCollins Pubs.

—The Berenstain Bears: We Love Baseball! Berenstain, Mike. 2017. (I Can Read Level 1 Ser.). (ENG.). 32p. (J). (gr. -1-3). pap. 4.99 *(978-0-06-235028-2(5))* HarperCollins Pubs.

—The Berenstain Bears: We Love Soccer! Berenstain, Mike. 2016. (I Can Read Level 1 Ser.). (ENG.). 32p. (J). (gr. -1-3). pap. 4.99 *(978-0-06-235013-8(7))* HarperCollins Pubs.

—The Berenstain Bears: We Love the Library. Berenstain, Mike. 2017. (Berenstain Bears Ser.). (ENG.). 24p. (J). (gr. -1-3). pap. 3.99 *(978-0-06-235036-7(6),* HarperFestival) HarperCollins Pubs.

—The Berenstain Bears: Welcome to Bear Country. Berenstain, Mike. 2017. (Berenstain Bears Ser.). (ENG.). 24p. (J). (gr. -1-3). pap. 3.99 *(978-0-06-235026-8(9),* HarperFestival) HarperCollins Pubs.

—The Berenstain Bears: When I Grow Up. Berenstain, Mike. 2015. (Berenstain Bears Ser.). (ENG.). 24p. (J). (gr. -1-3). pap. 3.99 *(978-0-06-235005-3(6),* HarperFestival) HarperCollins Pubs.

Berenstain, Mike & Berenstain, Jan. The Berenstain Bears Lose a Friend. Berenstain, Mike & Berenstain, Jan. 2007. (Berenstain Bears Ser.). 32p. (J). (gr. -1-1). 8.99 *(978-0-06-057405-5(4),* HarperFestival) HarperCollins Pubs.

—The Berenstain Bears: We Love Our Dad!/We Love Our Mom! Berenstain, Mike & Berenstain, Jan. 2018. (Berenstain Bears Ser.). (ENG.). 48p. (J). (gr. -1-3). pap. 4.99 *(978-0-06-269718-9(8),* HarperFestival) HarperCollins Pubs.

Berenstain, Mike & Berenstain, Stan & Jan. The Berenstain Bears & the Bad Influence. Berenstain, Mike et al. 2008. (Berenstain Bears Ser.). (ENG.). 32p. (J). (gr. -1-3). pap. 3.99 *(978-0-06-057388-1(0),* HarperFestival) HarperCollins Pubs.

Berenstain, Mike, jt. illus. see Berenstain, Jan.

Berenstain, Stan. The Berenstain Bears & a Job Well Done, 1 vol. Berenstain, Jan & Berenstain, Mike. 2010. (Berenstain Bears/Living Lights: a Faith Story Ser.). (ENG.). 32p. (J). (gr. -1-2). pap. 3.99 *(978-0-310-71254-1(8))* Zonderkidz.

Berenstain, Stan, et al. The Berenstain Bears & the Bad Influence. Berenstain, Stan et al. 2008. (Berenstain Bears Ser.). 32p. (J). (gr. -1-2). 8.99 *(978-0-06-057404-8(6),* HarperFestival) HarperCollins Pubs.

Berenstain, Stan. Berenstain Bears & the Gift of Courage, 1 vol. Berenstain, Jan & Berenstain, Mike. 2010. (Berenstain Bears/Living Lights: a Faith Story Ser.). (ENG.). 32p. (J). (gr. -1-2). pap. 3.99 *(978-0-310-71256-5(4))* Zonderkidz.

Berenstain, Stan, et al. The Berenstain Bears Save Christmas. Berenstain, Stan et al. 2003. (Berenstain Bears Ser.). (J). (gr. k-3). 129.90 *(978-0-06-056995-2(6))* HarperCollins Pubs.

Berenstain, Stan. The Berenstain Bears Give Thanks, 1 vol. Berenstain, Stan. Berenstain, Mike et al. 2009. (Berenstain Bears/Living Lights: a Faith Story Ser.). (ENG.). 32p. (J). (gr. -1-2). pap. 3.99 *(978-0-310-71251-0(3))* Zonderkidz.

—Berenstain Bears Love Their Neighbors, 1 vol. Berenstain, Stan. Berenstain, Jan et al. 2009. (Berenstain Bears/Living Lights: a Faith Story Ser.). (ENG.). 32p. (J). (gr. -1-2). pap. 3.99 *(978-0-310-71249-7(1))* Zonderkidz.

B

—Faithful Friends, 1 vol. Berenstain, Stan. Berenstain, Mike et al. 2009. (Berenstain Bears/Living Lights: a Faith Story Ser.). (ENG.). 32p. (J). (gr. -1-2). pap. 3.99 (978-0-310-71253-4(X)) Zonderkidz.

Berenstain, Stan & Berenstain, Jan. The Berenstain Bears & Too Much Car Trip. Berenstain, Stan & Berenstain, Jan. 2006. (Berenstain Bears Ser.). 32p. (J). (gr. -1-2). 10.99 (978-0-06-057400-0(3), HarperFestival) HarperCollins Pubs.

—The Berenstain Bears God Shows the Way, 1 vol. Berenstain, Stan & Berenstain, Jan. Berenstain, Mike. 2014. (I Can Read! / Berenstain Bears / Living Lights Ser.). (ENG.). 96p. (J). 9.99 (978-0-310-74211-1(0)) Zonderkidz.

—The Berenstain Bears Trouble With Pets. Berenstain, Stan & Berenstain, Jan. 2012. (Berenstain First Time Chapter Bks.). 32p. (J). (gr. -1-3). pap. 3.99 (978-0-679-80848-0(5), Random Hse. Bks. for Young Readers) Random Hse. Children's Bks.

Berenstain, Stan & Jan. The Berenstain Bears' Big Bedtime Book. Berenstain, Mike et al. (Berenstain Bears Ser.). (ENG.). 48p. (J). (gr. -1-3). 2011. pap. 7.99 (978-0-06-057436-9(4)); 2008. 12.99 (978-0-06-057434-5(8), HarperFestival) HarperCollins Pubs.

—The Berenstain Bears Storybook Treasury. Berenstain, Mike et al. 2012. (Berenstain Bears Ser.). (ENG.). 192p. (J). (gr. -1-3). 11.99 (978-0-06-212014-4(X), HarperFestival) HarperCollins Pubs.

Berenstain, Stan & Jan, jt. illus. see Berenstain, Mike.

Berenzy, Alix. Into the Sea. Guiberson, Brenda Z. 2014. 32p. pap. 9.00 (978-1-61003-227-8(6)) Center for the Collaborative Classroom.

Berenzy, Alix. Sammy: The Classroom Guinea Pig. Berenzy, Alix. 2008. (ENG.). 32p. (J). (gr. k-3). pap. 9.99 (978-0-312-37964-3(1), 900050314) Square Fish.

Berg, Curt. The Parable of the Plant. Berg, Ben. 2017. (ENG.). 26p. (J). 21.95 (978-1-64028-838-6(4)); pap. 12.95 (978-1-64028-528-6(8)) Christian Faith Publishing.

Berg, Deva Jean. A Tail of Two Sisters. Berg, Deva Jean. 2013. 26p. pap. 9.95 (978-1-939790-07-1(7)) Lorian Assn., The.

Berg, Elizabeth. Little Joe's Christmas. Conroy, James F. 2012. (ENG.). 44p. (J). pap. 17.95 (978-1-59299-846-3(1)) Inkwater Pr.

Berg, Jessica. The Unstoppable Jimmy. O'Brien, Liam & O'Brien, Noreen. 2020. (ENG.). 40p. (J). (gr. k-6). 22.95 **(978-1-951565-06-0(1))**; pap. 14.95 **(978-1-951565-07-7(X))** Brandylane Pubs., Inc. (Belle Isle Bks.).

Berg, Kelly. Cassie's Creepy Candy Store. Sauvageau-Smestad, Sheila. 2006. 35p. (J). per. 17.95 (978-0-9767732-2-1(8)) W & B Pubs.

Berg, Maria. The Velveteen Rabbit. Williams, Margery. 2018. (ENG.). 36p. (J). (gr. k-5). 24.95 (978-1-60025-124-5(2)) Bassett, Maurice.

Berg, Michelle. Dive In! Prince, April Jones. 2013. (ENG.). 14p. (J). (gr. -1 — 1). bds. 7.95 (978-1-4197-0523-6(7)) Abrams, Inc.

—First Foil Poetry Love, 2 vols. Feldman, Thea. 2005. (First Foil Poetry Haikus Ser.). 10p. (J). 6.95 (978-1-58117-189-1(7), Intervisual/Piggy Toes) Bendon, Inc.

—First Foil Poetry Seasons, 2 vols. Ageledis, Ida. 2005. (First Foil Poetry Haikus Ser.). 10p. (J). 6.95 (978-1-58117-188-4(9), Intervisual/Piggy Toes) Bendon, Inc.

—Noah's Ark. Karr, Lily. 2007. (ENG.). 6p. (J). (gr. -1). bds. 12.99 (978-0-439-86396-4(1)) Scholastic, Inc.

—Old MacDonald: A Hand-Puppet Board Book. Ackerman, Jill. 2007. (Little Scholastic Ser.). 6p. (J). (gr. -1 — 1). bds. 12.99 (978-0-545-02603-1(2)) Scholastic, Inc.

—This Little Piggy: A Hand-Puppet Board Book. Ackerman, Jill. 2007. (Little Scholastic Ser.). 6p. (J). (gr. -1 — 1). bds. 12.99 (978-0-545-03038-0(2)) Scholastic, Inc.

Berg, Ron. Magic Pony Carousel #1: Sparkle the Circus Pony. Shire, Poppy. 2007. (Magic Pony Carousel Ser.: 1). (ENG.). 96p. (J). (gr. 2-5). pap. 3.99 (978-0-06-083779-2(9)) HarperCollins Pubs.

—Magic Pony Carousel #3: Star the Western Pony. Shire, Poppy. 2007. (Magic Pony Carousel Ser.: 3). (ENG.). 96p. (J). (gr. 2-5). pap. 3.99 (978-0-06-083785-3(3)) HarperCollins Pubs.

—Magic Pony Carousel #4: Jewel the Midnight Pony. Shire, Poppy. 2008. (Magic Pony Carousel Ser.: 4). (ENG.). 96p. (J). (gr. 2-5). pap. 4.99 (978-0-06-083788-4(8)) HarperCollins Pubs.

—Magic Pony Carousel #5: Flame the Desert Pony. Shire, Poppy. 2008. (Magic Pony Carousel Ser.: 5). (ENG.). 96p. (J). (gr. 2-5). pap. 3.99 (978-0-06-083794-5(2)) HarperCollins Pubs.

Berganza, Carlos. Daddy Loves You. Lazar, Mark. 2015. (ENG.). (J). (978-0-9949915-0-8(9)) Lazcan Publishing.

Berge, Erlend. Ethiopian Voices: Tsion's Life. Bellward, Stacy. 2008. 32p. (J). (gr. 4-7). 19.99 (978-0-9797481-1-0(9)) Amharic Kids.

Bergen, Brenda. Journey of the Phoenix. Singh, Rajinder. 2011. 24p. (J). (gr. -1-3). 10.00 (978-0-918224-83-5(7)) Radiance Pubs.

Berger, Carin. Are We Pears Yet? Paul, Miranda. 2017. (ENG.). 40p. (J). 17.99 (978-1-62672-351-1(6), 900153624) Roaring Brook Pr.

—Behold the Bold Umbrellaphant: And Other Poems. Prelutsky, Jack. 2006. (ENG.). 40p. (J). (gr. -1-4). 16.99 (978-0-06-054317-4(5), Greenwillow Bks.) HarperCollins Pubs.

—Stardines Swim High Across the Sky: And Other Poems. Prelutsky, Jack. 2013. (ENG.). 40p. (J). (gr. -1-3). 17.99 (978-0-06-201464-1(1), Greenwillow Bks.) HarperCollins Pubs.

Berger, Carin. All of Us. Berger, Carin. 2018. (ENG.). 40p. (J). (gr. -1-3). 17.99 (978-0-06-269413-3(8), Greenwillow Bks.) HarperCollins Pubs.

—A Curious Menagerie: Of Herds, Flocks, Leaps, Gaggles, Scurries, & More! Berger, Carin. 2019. (ENG.). 40p. (J). (gr. -1-3). 17.99 (978-0-06-264457-2(2), Greenwillow Bks.) HarperCollins Pubs.

—Finding Spring. Berger, Carin. 2015. (ENG.). 40p. (J). (gr. -1-3). 17.99 (978-0-06-225019-3(1), Greenwillow Bks.) HarperCollins Pubs.

—Forever Friends. Berger, Carin. 2010. (ENG.). 40p. (J). (gr. -1-1). 16.99 (978-0-06-191528-4(9), Greenwillow Bks.) HarperCollins Pubs.

—Good Night! Good Night! Berger, Carin. 2017. (ENG.). 40p. (J). (gr. -1-3). 17.99 (978-0-06-240884-6(4), Greenwillow Bks.) HarperCollins Pubs.

—The Little Yellow Leaf. Berger, Carin. 2008. (ENG.). 40p. (J). (gr. -1-3). 16.99 (978-0-06-145223-9(8), Greenwillow Bks.) HarperCollins Pubs.

—A Perfect Day. Berger, Carin. 2012. (ENG.). 40p. (J). (gr. -1-3). 16.99 (978-0-06-201580-8(X), Greenwillow Bks.) HarperCollins Pubs.

Berger, Joe. Chitty Chitty Bang Bang. Fleming, Ian. 2013. (Chitty Chitty Bang Bang Ser.: 1). (ENG.). 160p. (J). (gr. 4-7). pap. 7.99 (978-0-7636-6666-8(1)) Candlewick Pr.

—Chitty Chitty Bang Bang & the Race Against Time. Boyce, Frank Cottrell. (Chitty Chitty Bang Bang Ser.: 3). (ENG.). 240p. (J). (gr. 4-7). 2014. pap. 6.99 (978-0-7636-6931-7(8)); 2013. 15.99 (978-0-7636-5982-0(7)) Candlewick Pr.

—Chitty Chitty Bang Bang Flies Again. Boyce, Frank Cottrell. (Chitty Chitty Bang Bang Ser.: 2). (ENG.). (J). (gr. 4-7). 2013. 224p. pap. 6.99 (978-0-7636-6353-7(0)); 2012. 192p. 15.99 (978-0-7636-5957-8(6)) Candlewick Pr.

—Chitty Chitty Bang Bang over the Moon. Boyce, Frank Cottrell. (Chitty Chitty Bang Bang Ser.: 4). (ENG.). (J). (gr. 4-7). 2015. 304p. pap. 6.99 (978-0-7636-7666-7(7)); 2014. 240p. 15.99 (978-0-7636-5983-7(5)) Candlewick Pr.

—Dot. Zuckerberg, Randi. 2013. (ENG.). 32p. (J). (gr. -1-3). 17.99 (978-0-06-228751-9(6)) HarperCollins Pubs.

—Girl & Gorilla: Out & About. Walton, Rick. 2016. (ENG.). 32p. (J). (gr. -1-3). 17.99 (978-0-06-227891-3(6)) HarperCollins Pubs.

—The Great Granny Cake Contest! Hubble Bubble. Corderoy, Tracey. 2017. (Hubble Bubble Ser.). (ENG.). 128p. (J). (gr. 1-4). pap. 6.99 (978-0-7636-8849-3(5), Nosy Crow) Candlewick Pr.

—Hubble Bubble, Granny Trouble. Corderoy, Tracey. 2012. (Hubble Bubble Ser.). (ENG.). 32p. (J). (gr. -1-2). 14.99 (978-0-7636-5904-2(5), Nosy Crow) Candlewick Pr.

—Princess in Training. Sauer, Tammi. (ENG.). 40p. (J). (gr. -1-3). 2015. 7.99 (978-0-544-45609-9(2), 1599394, HMH Books For Young Readers); 2012. 16.99 (978-0-15-206599-7(7), 1199626) Houghton Mifflin Harcourt Publishing Co.

—The Super-Spooky Fright Night! Hubble Bubble. Corderoy, Tracey. (Hubble Bubble Ser.). (ENG.). 128p. (J). (gr. 1-4). 2017. 14.99 (978-0-7636-9502-6(5)); 2016. pap. 6.99 (978-0-7636-8653-6(0)) Candlewick Pr. (Nosy Crow).

—Superhero Dad. Knapman, Timothy. (ENG.). (J). 2018. 26p. (-k). bds. 8.99 (978-0-7636-9951-2(9)); 2016. 30p. (gr. -1-2). 15.99 (978-0-7636-8657-4(3)) Candlewick Pr. (Nosy Crow).

Berger, Joe. Superhero Gran. Knapman, Timothy. 2020. (ENG.). 32p. (J). (gr. -1-2). 15.99 **(978-1-5362-1442-0(6)**, Nosy Crow) Candlewick Pr.

Berger, Joe. Superhero Mom. Knapman, Timothy. (ENG.). (J). 2020. 26p. (-k). bds. 8.99 (978-1-5362-1215-0(6)); 2019. 32p. (gr. -1-2). 15.99 (978-1-5362-0567-1(2)) Candlewick Pr. (Nosy Crow).

—The Wacky Winter Wonderland! Hubble Bubble. Corderoy, Tracey. 2017. (Hubble Bubble Ser.). (ENG.). 128p. (J). (gr. 1-4). 14.99 (978-0-7636-9624-5(2)); pap. 6.99 (978-0-7636-9625-2(0)) Candlewick Pr. (Nosy Crow).

—Whizz! Pop! Granny, Stop! Corderoy, Tracey. 2013. (ENG.). 32p. (J). (gr. -1-2). 14.99 (978-0-7636-6551-7(7), Nosy Crow) Candlewick Pr.

Berger, Joe. The Pudding Problem. Berger, Joe. 2017. (Lyttle Lies Ser.: 1). (ENG.). 240p. (J). (gr. 3-7). 13.99 (978-1-4814-7083-4(3), McElderry, Margaret K. Bks.) McElderry, Margaret K. Bks.

—The Stinky Truth. Berger, Joe. 2018. (Lyttle Lies Ser.: 2). (ENG.). 240p. (J). (gr. 3-7). 13.99 (978-1-4814-7086-5(8), McElderry, Margaret K. Bks.) McElderry, Margaret K. Bks.

Bergeron, Jerry J. & Bergeron, Jerry L. Not Far from You. Daniel, Barbara Beck. 2019. (ENG.). 50p. (J). (gr. k-3). pap. 12.99 (978-1-7336241-3-8(9)) Yellow City Publishing.

Bergeron, Jerry L., jt. illus. see Bergeron, Jerry J.

Bergeron, John W. Jean-Paul Hébert Was There/Jean-Paul Hébert Etait Là, 1 vol. Hébert-Collins, Sheila. 2004. (FRE.). 32p. (J). (gr. k-3). 16.99 (978-1-56554-928-9(7), Pelican Publishing) Arcadia Publishing.

Berggren, Jeff. Chicken Cherries. Berggren, Jeff. Hansen, Tammy A., ed. l.t. ed. 2005. 32p. (J). per. 14.95 (978-0-9755033-0-0(8)) Deep Dish Design.

—My Moon Lagoon. Berggren, Jeff. Hansen, Tammy A., ed. 2007. (J). per. 14.95 (978-0-9755033-1-7(6)) Deep Dish Design.

Berghausen, Nina. Jamison! a Shark Returns. Berghausen, Consie. 2018. (ENG.). 42p. (J). (gr. k-6). 22.99 (978-0-9988773-6-5(0)) Richer Life, LLC.

Bergier, Vincent. New York Day & Night. Pollet, Aurelie. 2019. (ENG.). 30p. (J). (-k). 16.95 (978-3-7913-7378-2(1)) Prestel Verlag GmbH & Co KG. DEU. Dist: Penguin Random Hse. LLC.

Bergin, Mark. The Adventures of Perseus. Hepplewhite, Peter & Salariya, David. 2013. 32p. (J). (978-1-4351-5119-2(4)) Barnes & Noble, Inc.

Bergin, Mark. A Cow Goes Moo! Channing, Margot. ed. 2020. (Creature Features Ser.). 10p. (J). (— 1). bds. 8.95 **(978-1-912904-99-0(3)**, Scribblers) Book Hse. GBR. Dist: Sterling Publishing Co., Inc.

Bergin, Mark. Extreme Comparisons: Fastest, Tallest, Strongest, Biggest Record Breakers. Graham, Ian. 2014. (Big Book Of... Ser.). 64p. (gr. 3-6). 37.10 (978-1-907184-91-8(0)) Book Hse. GBR. Dist: Black Rabbit Bks.

Bergin, Mark. A Fish Goes Splash! Channing, Margot. ed. 2020. (Creature Features Ser.). 10p. (J). (— 1). bds. 8.95 **(978-1-913337-01-8(4)**, Scribblers) Book Hse. GBR. Dist: Sterling Publishing Co., Inc.

Bergin, Mark. Inside the Beagle with Charles Darwin. Macdonald, Fiona. 2005. (ENG.). 48p. (J). (gr. 3-6). 19.95 (978-1-59270-041-7(1)) Enchanted Lion Bks., LLC.

—It's Fun to Draw Cars, Planes, & Trains. 2015. (It's Fun to Draw Ser.). (ENG.). 32p. (J). (gr. -1-3). 5.99 (978-1-63220-410-3(X), Sky Pony Pr.) Skyhorse Publishing Co., Inc.

—It's Fun to Draw Creepy-Crawlies. 2015. (It's Fun to Draw Ser.). (ENG.). 32p. (J). (gr. -1-3). 5.99 (978-1-63220-406-6(1), Sky Pony Pr.) Skyhorse Publishing Co., Inc.

—It's Fun to Draw Ponies & Horses. 2015. (It's Fun to Draw Ser.). (ENG.). 32p. (J). (gr. -1-3). 5.99 (978-1-63220-415-8(0), Sky Pony Pr.) Skyhorse Publishing Co., Inc.

Bergin, Mark. A Lion Goes Roar! Channing, Margot. ed. 2020. (Creature Features Ser.). 10p. (J). (— 1). bds. 8.95 **(978-1-913337-00-1(6)**, Scribblers) Book Hse. GBR. Dist: Sterling Publishing Co., Inc.

Bergin, Mark. The Migration of a Whale. Kant, Tanya. 2008. (Amaze Ser.). (ENG.). 32p. (J). (gr. k-3). 27.00 (978-0-531-24049-6(5)); pap. 8.95 (978-0-531-23803-5(2)) Scholastic Library Publishing. (Children's Pr.).

Bergin, Mark. An Owl Goes Hoot! Channing, Margot. ed. 2020. (Creature Features Ser.). 10p. (J). (— 1). bds. 8.95 **(978-1-912904-98-3(5)**, Scribblers) Book Hse. GBR. Dist: Sterling Publishing Co., Inc.

Bergin, Mark, et al. Scary Creatures of the Deep. Pipe, Jim. 2009. (Scary Creatures Ser.). (ENG.). 32p. (J). (gr. k-3). 24.94 (978-0-531-21822-8(8)) Scholastic Library Publishing.

Bergin, Mark. You Wouldn't Want to Be a Chicago Gangster! Some Dangerous Characters You'd Better Avoid. Matthews, Rupert. 2010. (ENG.). 32p. (J). (gr. 3-3). pap. 9.95 (978-0-531-22825-8(8), Watts, Franklin) Scholastic Library Publishing.

—You Wouldn't Want to Be a Chicago Gangster! Some Dangerous Characters You'd Better Avoid. Matthews, Rupert & Salariya, David. 2010. (You Wouldn't Want To... Ser.). (ENG.). 32p. (J). (gr. 4-6). 26.19 (978-0-531-20470-2(7), Watts, Franklin) Scholastic Library Publishing.

—You Wouldn't Want to Be a Crusader! Macdonald, Fiona. 2017. (ENG.). 32p. (J). (gr. 3). lib. bdg. 29.00 (978-0-531-23831-8(8), Watts, Franklin) Scholastic Library Publishing.

—You Wouldn't Want to Be a Crusader! A War You'd Rather Not Fight. MacDonald, Fiona. 2005. (You Wouldn't Want to... Ser.). (ENG.). 32p. (J). (gr. 2-5). 29.00 (978-0-531-12412-3(6)); pap. 9.95 (978-0-531-12392-8(8)) Scholastic Library Publishing. (Watts, Franklin).

—You Wouldn't Want to Be a Pony Express Rider! A Dusty, Thankless Job You'd Rather Not Do. Ratliff, Thomas. 2012. (ENG.). 32p. (J). lib. bdg. 29.00 (978-0-531-20872-4(9)) Scholastic Library Publishing.

—You Wouldn't Want to Explore with Lewis & Clark! An Epic Journey You'd Rather Not Make. Morley, Jacqueline. 2013. (ENG.). 32p. (J). (gr. 3). pap. 9.95 (978-0-531-23039-8(2)); 29.00 (978-0-531-25942-9(0)) Scholastic Library Publishing. (Watts, Franklin).

—You Wouldn't Want to Live Without Bacteria! Canavan, Roger. 2015. (You Wouldn't Want to Live Without... Ser.). (ENG.). 32p. (J). (gr. 3). lib. bdg. 29.00 (978-0-531-21363-6(3), Watts, Franklin) Scholastic Library Publishing.

—You Wouldn't Want to Live Without Dirt! Graham, Ian. 2016. (You Wouldn't Want to Live Without... Ser.). (ENG.). 32p. (J). (gr. 3). lib. bdg. 29.00 (978-0-531-21488-6(5), Watts, Franklin) Scholastic Library Publishing.

—You Wouldn't Want to Live Without Extreme Weather! Canavan, Roger. 2015. (You Wouldn't Want to Live Without... Ser.). (ENG.). 32p. (J). (gr. 3). pap. 9.95 (978-0-531-21408-4(7)); lib. bdg. 29.00 (978-0-531-21365-0(X)) Scholastic Library Publishing. (Watts, Franklin).

—You Wouldn't Want to Live Without Glass! Graham, Ian. 2016. (You Wouldn't Want to Live Without... Ser.). (ENG.). 32p. (J). (gr. 3). lib. bdg. 29.00 (978-0-531-22460-1(0), Watts, Franklin) Scholastic Library Publishing.

—You Wouldn't Want to Live Without Gravity! Rooney, Anne. 2016. (You Wouldn't Want to Live Without... Ser.). (ENG.). 32p. (J). (gr. 3). lib. bdg. 29.00 (978-0-531-21487-9(7), Watts, Franklin) Scholastic Library Publishing.

—You Wouldn't Want to Live Without Libraries! Macdonald, Fiona. 2018. (You Wouldn't Want to Live Without... Ser.). (ENG.). (J). (gr. 3). 40p. pap. 9.95 (978-0-531-19358-7(6)); 32p. lib. bdg. 29.00 (978-0-531-12811-4(3)) Scholastic Library Publishing. (Watts, Franklin).

—You Wouldn't Want to Live Without Math! Rooney, Anne. 2016. (You Wouldn't Want to Live Without... Ser.). (ENG.). 32p. (J). (gr. 3-6). lib. bdg. 29.00 (978-0-531-22461-8(9), Watts, Franklin) Scholastic Library Publishing.

—You Wouldn't Want to Live Without Simple Machines! Rooney, Anne. 2018. (You Wouldn't Want to Live Without... Ser.). (ENG.). 32p. (J). (gr. 3). lib. bdg. 29.00 (978-0-531-12815-2(6), Watts, Franklin) Scholastic Library Publishing.

—You Wouldn't Want to Live Without Sleep! Pipe, Jim. 2016. (You Wouldn't Want to Live Without... Ser.). (ENG.). 32p. (J). (gr. 3). lib. bdg. 29.00 (978-0-531-21492-3(3), Watts, Franklin) Scholastic Library Publishing.

—You Wouldn't Want to Live Without Soap! Woolf, Alex. 2015. (You Wouldn't Want to Live Without... Ser.). (ENG.). 32p. (J). (gr. 3). lib. bdg. 29.00 (978-0-531-21927-0(5), Watts, Franklin) Scholastic Library Publishing.

—You Wouldn't Want to Live Without the Internet! Rooney, Anne. 2015. (You Wouldn't Want to Live Without... Ser.). (ENG.). 32p. (J). (gr. 3). lib. bdg. 29.00 (978-0-531-21931-7(3), Watts, Franklin) Scholastic Library Publishing.

—You Wouldn't Want to Live Without the Writing! Canavan, Roger. 2015. (You Wouldn't Want to Live Without... Ser.). (ENG.). 32p. (J). (gr. 3). lib. bdg. 29.00 (978-0-531-21930-0(5), Watts, Franklin) Scholastic Library Publishing.

—You Wouldn't Want to Live Without Trees! Pipe, Jim. 2016. (You Wouldn't Want to Live Without... Ser.). (ENG.). 32p. (J). (gr. 3-6). lib. bdg. 29.00 (978-0-531-22463-2(5), Watts, Franklin) Scholastic Library Publishing.

—You Wouldn't Want to Work on the Brooklyn Bridge! An Enormous Project That Seemed Impossible. Ratliff, Thomas. 2009. (ENG.). 32p. (J). (gr. 3-18). pap. 9.95 (978-0-531-20519-8(3), Watts, Franklin) Scholastic Library Publishing.

—You Wouldn't Want to Work on the Brooklyn Bridge! An Enormous Project That Seemed Impossible. Ratliff, Tom. 2009. (You Wouldn't Want to Ser.). (ENG.). 32p. (J). (gr. 3-12). 29.00 (978-0-531-21328-5(5)) Scholastic Library Publishing.

Bergin, Mark & Hewetson, N. J. Super Trucks. Graham, Ian. 2014. (Time Shift Speed Ser.). 32p. (gr. 3-6). 31.35 (978-1-908973-97-9(8)) Book Hse. GBR. Dist: Black Rabbit Bks.

Bergin, Molly. I Love You, Michigan Baby. Vernick, Shirley. 2018. (ENG.). 22p. (J). (gr. -1-k). bds. 8.95 (978-1-946064-96-7(3), 806496, Duo Pr. Llc (US)) Duo Pr. LLC.

Bergman, Shannon, jt. illus. see Ross, Sharon.

Bergmann, Andy. The Starry Giraffe. Bergmann, Andy. 2017. (ENG.). 40p. (J). (gr. -1-3). 15.99 (978-1-4814-9100-6(8), Aladdin) Simon & Schuster Children's Publishing.

Bergmann, Sarah. Potty Palooza: A Step-By-Step Guide to Using a Potty. Gordon, Rachel & Gold, Claudia. 2013. (ENG.). 32p. (J). (gr. k — 1). bds. 9.95 (978-0-7611-7485-1(0), 17485) Workman Publishing Co., Inc.

Bergna, Monica. Juguemos en el Bosque. Anónimo. 2004. (SPA.). 28p. (J). (gr. k-18). pap. 6.50 (978-980-257-282-3(9)) Ekare, Ediciones VEN. Dist: Iaconi, Mariuccia Bk. Imports.

Bergner, Bobby. Why kitty Is afraid of Poo: A cautionary Tale. Bergner, Bobby. 2008. 20p. 12.99 (978-0-615-21301-9(4)) Bergner, Bobby.

Bergsma, Laura. Full Steam Ahead: A Pug Boat Family. Bergsma, Laura. 2019. (ENG.). 50p. (J). pap. 14.95 **(978-1-0791-3223-6(6))** Independently Published.

Bergström, Gunilla. Good Night, Alfie Atkins. Bergstrom, Gunilla. Dyssegaard, Elisabeth Kallick, tr. from SWE. 2005. 32p. (J). 15.00 (978-91-29-66154-5(4)) R & S Bks. SWE. Dist: Macmillan.

Bergting, Peter & Renta, Kathryn. We'll Soon Be Home Again. Bab Bonde, Jessica. Barbito, Sunshine, tr. from SWE. 2020. (ENG.). 104p. (YA). (gr. 9). pap. 14.99 (978-1-5067-1549-0(4), Dark Horse Books) Dark Horse Comics.

Bergum, Constance. Under the Snow, 1 vol. Stewart, Melissa. 2019. (ENG.). 32p. (J). (gr. -1-3). pap. 7.95 (978-1-68263-125-6(7)) Peachtree Publishing Co. Inc.

Bergum, Constance R. Beneath the Sun. Stewart, Melissa. (ENG.). 32p. (J). (gr. -1-3). 2020. pap. 7.99 (978-1-68263-159-1(1)); 2014. 16.95 (978-1-56145-733-5(7)) Peachtree Publishing Co. Inc.

—Dancing with Katya, 1 vol. Chaconas, Dori. 2007. (ENG.). 32p. (J). (gr. k-3). 16.95 (978-1-56145-376-4(5)) Peachtree Publishing Co. Inc.

—The Sunsets of Miss Olivia Wiggins, 1 vol. Laminack, Lester L. rev. ed. 2018. (ENG.). 32p. (J). (gr. 1-5). pap. 8.95 (978-1-68263-063-1(3)) Peachtree Publishing Co. Inc.

—Under the Snow, 1 vol. Stewart, Melissa. 2009. (ENG.). 32p. (J). (gr. -1-3). 16.95 (978-1-56145-493-8(1)) Peachtree Publishing Co. Inc.

—When Rain Falls, 1 vol. Stewart, Melissa. (ENG.). 32p. (J). (gr. k-3). 2019. pap. 7.95 (978-1-68263-100-3(1)); 2013. 16.95 (978-1-56145-438-9(9)) Peachtree Publishing Co. Inc.

Bergum, Constance Rummel. Who's Faster? Animals on the Move. Meyer, Eileen R. 2012. (J). (978-0-87842-592-1(6)) Mountain Pr. Publishing Co., Inc.

Bergwerf, Barbara J. A Butterfly Called Hope, 1 vol. Monroe, Mary Alice. 2013. (ENG.). 32p. (J). (gr. -1-4). 17.95 (978-1-60718-854-4(6)); pap. 9.95 (978-1-60718-856-8(2)) Arbordale Publishing.

—Carolina's Story: Sea Turtles Get Sick Too!, 1 vol. Rathmell, Donna. 2005. (ENG.). 32p. (J). (gr. -1-3). 15.95 (978-0-9764943-0-0(2)) Arbordale Publishing.

—Turtle Summer: A Journal for My Daughter, 1 vol. Monroe, Mary Alice. 2007. (ENG.). 32p. (J). (gr. k-4). 16.95 (978-0-9777423-5-6(0)) Arbordale Publishing.

Bergwerf, Barbara J. A Butterfly Called Hope. Bergwerf, Barbara J., photos by. Monroe, Mary Alice. 2013. (ENG.). (J). (gr. -1-2). lib. bdg. 20.55 (978-1-62765-424-1(0)) Perfection Learning Corp.

—Carolina's Story: Sea Turtles Get Sick Too!, 1 vol. Bergwerf, Barbara J., photos by. Rathmell, Donna. 2005. (ENG.). 32p. (J). (gr. -1-3). pap. 8.95 (978-1-934359-00-6(9)) Arbordale Publishing.

Berkeley, Jon. Tooth Fairy's First Night. Bowen, Anne. 2005. (Carolrhoda Picture Bks.). 32p. (J). (gr. -1-3). 15.95 (978-1-57505-753-8(0)) Lerner Publishing Group.

Berkson, Suzanne Raphael. The Parakeet Named Dreidel. Singer, Isaac Bashevis. 2015. (J). pap. (978-0-374-30096-8(8)); (ENG.). 32p. 17.99 (978-0-374-30094-4(1), 9780374300944, Farrar, Straus & Giroux (BYR)) Farrar, Straus & Giroux.

Berley, Brian. Molly Rides. Ford, Adam B. 2016. (ENG.). (J). pap. 12.95 (978-0-9893092-3-3(1)) H Bar Pr.

Berlin, Rose Mary. Itty & Bitty - On the Road. Czerw, Nancy Carpenter. 2008. (Itty & Bitty Ser.: 3). (ENG.). 32p. (J). (gr. -1-3). 16.95 (978-0-9755618-4-3(7)) McWitty Pr., Inc.

—Storytime Stickers: Baby Animals at Play. Ryals, Katherine. 2010. (Storytime Stickers Ser.). 16p. (J). (gr. k-2). pap. 5.95 (978-1-4027-5933-8(9)) Sterling Publishing Co., Inc.

Berlin, Rose Mary & Bauer, Dana. Friends on the Farm. Carpenter Czerw, Nancy. 2006. (Itty & Bitty Ser.). (ENG.). 32p. (J). (gr. -1-3). 15.95 *(978-0-9755618-3-6(9))* McWitty Pr., Inc.

Berlin, Rose Mary, jt. illus. see Schories, Pat.

Berlinger, Nancy A. Mother's Surprise. Templeton, Donna L. 2009. (ENG.). 32p. (J). pap. 9.99 *(978-0-9764336-6-8(4))* MJS Publishing Group LLC.

Berman, Linda. San Diego Activity & Coloring Book for All Ages. Penix, Sherry. Date not set. (J). pap. *(978-0-9670612-0-7(2))*; pap. *(978-0-9670612-1-4(0))* Sher-A-Craft.

Berman, Rachel. Bradley Mcgogg: The Very Fine Frog. Beiser, Tim. 2011. (ENG.). 24p. (J). (gr. k-k). pap. 7.95 *(978-1-77049-276-9(3)*, Tundra Bks.) Tundra Bks. CAN. Dist: Penguin Random Hse. LLC.

—Bradley McGogg: The Very Fine Frog. Beiser, Tim. 2009. (ENG.). 24p. (J). (gr. k-k). 17.95 *(978-0-88776-864-4(4)*, Tundra Bks.) Tundra Bks. CAN. Dist: Penguin Random Hse. LLC.

—Miss Mousie's Blind Date. Beiser, Tim. 2012. 24p. (J). (gr. -1-2). 17.95 *(978-1-77049-251-6(8)*, Tundra Bks.) Tundra Bks. CAN. Dist: Penguin Random Hse. LLC.

Bermejo, Ana. Drawing Animals with Crayola! Allen, Kathy. 2018. (Let's Draw with Crayola ®! Ser.). (ENG.). 32p. (J). (gr. -1-3). 27.99 *(978-1-5124-3295-4(4)*, Lerner Pubns.) Lerner Publishing Group.

—I Like to Read. Charlesworth, Liza. 2017. 16p. (J). *(978-1-338-18030-5(4))* Scholastic, Inc.

—Kindergarten, Here We Come! Lee, Quinlan B. 2016. 32p. (J). *(978-0-545-94860-9(6))* Scholastic, Inc.

—Let's Draw Vehicles with Crayola! Allen, Kathy. 2018. (Let's Draw with Crayola ®! Ser.). (ENG.). 32p. (J). (gr. -1-3). lib. bdg. 27.99 *(978-1-5124-3297-8(0)*, Lerner Pubns.) Lerner Publishing Group.

—There Was an Old Lady Who Gobbled a Skink. Wissinger, Tamera Will. 2016. 36p. (J). (gr. -1-k). 16.99 *(978-1-63220-428-8(2)*, Sky Pony Pr.) Skyhorse Publishing Co., Inc.

Bermejo, Hilbert. The Ramblings of Clyde Frog & Jasmine. Smith, Mary L. 2013. 30p. pap. 11.99 *(978-1-61286-156-2(3))* Avid Readers Publishing Group.

—Robin's New Attitude. Elliott, Dawn. Harrell, Dori, ed. 2019. (ENG.). 42p. (J). pap. 9.99 *(978-1-0906-4610-1(0))* Independently Published.

Bermudez, Alyssa. Amelia Chamelia & the Birthday Party. Sieveking, Laura. 2019. (Amelia Chamelia Ser.). 96p. (J). (gr. k). 9.99 ***(978-0-14-379166-9(4)***, Puffin) Penguin Random Hse. AUS. Dist: Independent Pubs. Group.

—Amelia Chamelia & the Farm Adventure. Sieveking, Laura. 2019. (Amelia Chamelia Ser.). 96p. (J). (gr. k). 9.99 ***(978-0-14-379164-5(8)***, Puffin) Penguin Random Hse. AUS. Dist: Independent Pubs. Group.

—Amelia Chamelia & the Gelato Surprise. Sieveking, Laura. 2019. (Amelia Chamelia Ser.). 96p. (J). (gr. k). 9.99 ***(978-0-14-379160-7(5)***, Puffin) Penguin Random Hse. AUS. Dist: Independent Pubs. Group.

—Amelia Chamelia & the School Play: Amelia Chamelia 3. Sieveking, Laura. 2019. (Amelia Chamelia Ser.). 96p. (J). (gr. k). 9.99 ***(978-0-14-379162-1(1)***, Puffin) Penguin Random Hse. AUS. Dist: Independent Pubs. Group.

Bermudez, Alyssa. Lucia the Luchadora. Garza, Cynthia Leonor. 2017. (ENG.). 32p. (J). (gr. -1-2). 16.99 *(978-1-57687-827-9(9)*, powerHouse Bks.) powerHse. Bks.

—Lucia the Luchadora & the Million Masks. Garza, Cynthia Leonor. 2018. (ENG.). 32p. (J). (gr. -1-2). 16.99 *(978-1-57687-894-1(5)*, powerHouse Bks.) powerHse. Bks.

—My Singing Nana. Mora, Pat. 2019. 32p. (J). *(978-1-4338-3021-1(3)*, Magination Pr.) American Psychological Assn.

Bermudez, Donald. Martin Luther King: The Peaceful Warrior. Clayton, Ed. 2017. 128p. (J). (gr. 3-7). 16.99 *(978-0-7636-7471-7(0))* Candlewick Pr.

Bermudez, Raymund. Depth Charge, 1 vol. Sherman, M. Zachary & Lee, Raymund. 2012. (Bloodlines Ser.). (ENG.). 88p. (J). (gr. 4-8). pap. 6.95 *(978-1-4342-3876-4(8)*, Stone Arch Bks.) Capstone.

—Depth Charge, 1 vol. Sherman, M. Zachary. 2012. (Bloodlines Ser.). (ENG.). 88p. (J). (gr. 4-8). lib. bdg. 26.65 *(978-1-4342-3764-4(8)*, Stone Arch Bks.) Capstone.

—Emergency Ops, 1 vol. Sherman, M. Zachary & Lee, Raymund. 2012. (Bloodlines Ser.). (ENG.). 88p. (J). (gr. 4-8). lib. bdg. 26.65 *(978-1-4342-3766-8(4)*, Stone Arch Bks.) Capstone.

Bermudez, Raymund, et al. The Heart of War. Sherman, M. Zachary. 2013. (Bloodlines Ser.). (ENG.). 240p. (J). (gr. 4-8). pap. 7.95 *(978-1-62370-002-7(7)*, Capstone Young Readers) Capstone.

Bermundo, Michael. Sir Princess Petra's Mission: The Pen Pieyu Adventures. Robinson, Diane Mae. 2nd ed. 2017. (Pen Pieyu Adventures Ser.: Vol. 3). (ENG.). 106p. (J). (gr. 1-5). *(978-0-9952482-1-2(4))* Robinson, Diane Mae.

Bernabe, Tabitha Victoria. What to Be When I Grow Up. Bernabe, Victor. 2008. 28p. pap. 24.95 *(978-1-60703-696-8(7))* America Star Bks.

Bernadin, James. Encyclopedia Brown & the Case of the Soccer Scheme. Sobol, Donald J. 2013. (Encyclopedia Brown Ser.: 29). (ENG.). 96p. (J). (gr. 3-7). pap. 5.99 *(978-0-14-242288-5(6)*, Puffin Books) Penguin Young Readers Group.

Bernal, Mitchell. Skelanimals: Dead Animals Need Love Too, Bernal, Mitchell. l.t. ed. 2005. 22p. (J). per. 12.95 *(978-0-9766621-0-5(8)*, 818 554-8965) Kreations.

Bernal, Rafael. El Hombre de la Arena. Hoffmann, E. T. A. Toro, Jorge & Gonzalez, Carlos Mario, trs. 2004. (Cajon de Cuentos Ser.). (SPA.). 220p. (J). (gr. 4-7). *(978-958-30-0724-8(2))* Panamericana Editorial.

Bernal, Victor Garcia. Vida y Fortuna de un Muchacho Inquieto Que Se Convirtió en Científico. Barajas Mariscal, Libia E. & Mariscal, Libia Barajas. rev. ed. 2009. (Otra Escalera Ser.). (SPA & ENG.). 24p. (gr. 4-6). pap. 17.99 *(978-968-5920-61-2(3))* Castillo, Ediciones, S. A. de C. V. MEX. Dist: Lectorum Pubns., Inc.

Bernard, C. E. B. Tales of an Old Lumber Camp: A Story of Early Days in A Great Industry. Hamlin, John. 2011. 188p. 42.95 *(978-1-258-04052-9(2))* Literary Licensing, LLC.

Bernard, Camille. ABC Prayers. Baudic, Myriam. ed. 2020. (ENG.). 64p. (J). (gr. -1-k). 8.99 *(978-0-7459-7879-6(7)*, Lion Children's) Lion Hudson PLC GBR. Dist: Independent Pubs. Group.

Bernard, Courtney. Get Ella to the Apollo, 1 vol. Mullarkey, Lisa & Mullarkey, John. 2015. (Art of Time Travel Ser.). (ENG.). 128p. (J). (gr. 2-5). 29.93 *(978-1-62402-087-2(9)*, 16790, Calico Chapter Bks.) ABDO Publishing Co.

—Mary Molds a Monster, 1 vol. Mullarkey, Lisa & Mullarkey, John. 2015. (Art of Time Travel Ser.). (ENG.). 128p. (J). (gr. 2-5). 29.93 *(978-1-62402-088-9(7)*, 16792, Calico Chapter Bks.) ABDO Publishing Co.

—Monet Changes Mediums, 1 vol. Mullarkey, Lisa & Mullarkey, John. 2015. (Art of Time Travel Ser.). (ENG.). 128p. (J). (gr. 2-5). 29.93 *(978-1-62402-089-6(5)*, 16794, Calico Chapter Bks.) ABDO Publishing Co.

—Shakespeare Saves the Globe, 1 vol. Mullarkey, Lisa & Mullarkey, John. 2015. (Art of Time Travel Ser.). (ENG.). 128p. (J). (gr. 2-5). 29.93 *(978-1-62402-090-2(9)*, 16796, Calico Chapter Bks.) ABDO Publishing Co.

Bernard, Danielle Yvette. Kisses in My Pocket. Bernard, Danielle Yvette. 2020. (ENG.). 26p. (J). pap. 12.50 ***(978-1-0997-5079-3(2))*** Independently Published.

Bernard, Donna. Word Skills in Rhythm & Rhyme Level 1. Sitton, Rebecca. 2004. 122p. (gr. 1-18). spiral bd. 59.95 *(978-1-886050-62-4(7))* Egger Publishing, Inc.

—Word Skills in Rhythm & Rhyme Level 2. Sitton, Rebecca. 2004. 118p. (gr. 2-18). spiral bd. 59.95 *(978-1-886050-63-1(5))* Egger Publishing, Inc.

—Word Skills in Rhythm & Rhyme Level 3. Sitton, Rebecca. 2004. 112p. (gr. 3-18). spiral bd. 59.95 *(978-1-886050-64-8(3))* Egger Publishing, Inc.

Bernard Westcott, Nadine. Comin' down to Storytime. Reid, Rob. 2009. (J). (gr. -1-3). 17.95 *(978-1-60213-039-5(6)*, Upstart Bks.) Highsmith Inc.

—We're Going on a Book Hunt. Miller, Pat. 2008. (J). (gr. -1). 17.95 *(978-1-60213-034-0(5)*, Upstart Bks.) Highsmith Inc.

—What's in There? All about Before You Were Born. Harris, Robie H. 2013. (Let's Talk about You & Me Ser.). (ENG.). 40p. (J). (-k). 16.99 *(978-0-7636-3630-2(4))* Candlewick Pr.

—Ziggy McFinster's Nantucket Adventure. Bagley, Conor. 2008. (ENG.). 40p. (J). (gr. -1-3). 16.95 *(978-1-56625-315-4(2))* Bonus Bks., Inc.

Bernardin, James. Case of the Kidnapped Cupid. Star, Nancy. 2005. (Calendar Club Mysteries Ser.). 79p. (J). *(978-0-439-67263-4(5))* Scholastic, Inc.

—The Case of the Thanksgiving Thief. Star, Nancy. 2004. 79p. (J). *(978-0-439-67261-0(9))* Scholastic, Inc.

—Go Back to Bed! Guy, Ginger Foglesong. 2006. (ENG.). 32p. (J). (gr. k-3). 16.95 *(978-1-57505-750-7(6)*, Carolrhoda Bks.) Lerner Publishing Group.

—Great Escapes #1: Nazi Prison Camp Escape. Burgan, Michael. 2020. (Great Escapes Ser.: 1). (ENG.). 128p. (J). (gr. 3-7). 16.99 *(978-0-06-286036-1(4))*; pap. 4.99 *(978-0-06-286035-4(6))* HarperCollins Pubs. Ltd. GBR. (HarperCollins). Dist: HarperCollins Pubs.

—Great Escapes #2: Journey to Freedom 1838. Winston, Sherri. 2020. (Great Escapes Ser.: 2). (ENG.). 128p. (J). (gr. 3-7). 16.99 *(978-0-06-286039-2(9))*; pap. 4.99 *(978-0-06-286038-5(0))* HarperCollins Pubs. Ltd. GBR. (HarperCollins). Dist: HarperCollins Pubs.

—A Horn for Louis. Kimmel, Eric A. 2006. (Stepping Stone Book(TM) Ser.). 96p. (J). (gr. 2-5). per. 4.99 *(978-0-375-84005-0(2)*, Random Hse. Bks. for Young Readers) Random Hse. Children's Bks.

—I Know Who Likes You. Cooney, Doug. 2005. (ENG.). 224p. (J). (gr. 3-7). pap. 10.99 *(978-1-4169-0261-4(9)*, Simon & Schuster Bks. For Young Readers) Simon & Schuster Bks. For Young Readers.

—Lumber Camp Library. Kinsey-Warnock, Natalie. 2003. (ENG.). 96p. (J). (gr. 2-5). pap. 4.99 *(978-0-06-444292-3(6))* HarperCollins Pubs.

—Michelle Obama: First Lady, Going Higher. Corey, Shana. 2018. (Step into Reading Ser.). (ENG.). 48p. (J). (gr. k-3). pap. 4.99 *(978-1-5247-7229-1(1)*, Random Hse. Bks. for Young Readers) Random Hse. Children's Bks.

—Mystery of the Snow Day Bigfoot. Star, Nancy. 2005. (Calendar Club Mysteries Ser.: Vol. 3). 77p. (J). pap. 3.95 *(978-0-439-67262-7(7))* Scholastic, Inc.

—Say What? Haddix, Margaret Peterson. 2005. 91p. (J). 11.65 *(978-0-7569-5465-9(7))* Perfection Learning Corp.

—Say What? Haddix, Margaret Peterson. 2005. (ENG.). 96p. (J). (gr. 1-5). pap. 5.99 *(978-0-689-86256-4(3)*, Simon & Schuster Bks. For Young Readers) Simon & Schuster Bks. For Young Readers.

—The Twelve Prayers of Christmas, Vol. Chand, Candy. 2009. (HarperBlessings Ser.). (ENG.). 32p. (J). (gr. -1-2). 16.99 *(978-0-06-077636-7(6))* HarperCollins Pubs.

—Would I Trade My Parents? Numeroff, Laura. 2009. (ENG.). 32p. (J). (gr. -1-3). 16.95 *(978-0-8109-0637-2(6)*, Abrams Bks. for Young Readers) Abrams, Inc.

—Yes, Virginia: There Is a Santa Claus. Piehal, Chris. 2010. (ENG.). 32p. (J). (gr. -1-2). 16.99 *(978-0-06-200173-3(6))* HarperCollins Pubs.

Bernardin, James & Cowdrey, Richard. The Legend of the Candy Cane: The Inspirational Story of Our Favorite Christmas Candy, 1 vol. Walburg, Lori. ed. 2012. (ENG.). 32p. (J). 15.99 *(978-0-310-73012-5(0))* Zonderkidz.

Bernardini, Cristian. Believe Me, I Never Felt a Pea! The Story of the Princess & the Pea As Told by the Princess. Loewen, Nancy. 2016. (Other Side of the Story Ser.). (ENG.). 24p. (J). (gr. -1-3). lib. bdg. 27.99 *(978-1-4795-8622-6(6)*, Picture Window Bks.) Capstone.

—Gertrude & Reginald the Monsters Talk about Living & Nonliving, 1 vol. Braun, Eric. 2012. (In the Science Lab Ser.). (ENG.). 24p. (J). (gr. k-3). pap. 9.95 *(978-1-4048-7237-0(X)*, Picture Window Bks.) Capstone.

Bernardini, Cristian. Honestly, Our Music Stole the Show! The Story of the Bremen Town Musicians As Told by the Donkey. Gunderson, Jessica. 2018. (Other Side of the Story Ser.). (ENG.). (J). pap. 41.70 ***(978-1-5158-2329-2(6)***, 27519); 24p. (gr. -1-3). lib. bdg. 27.99 *(978-1-5158-2296-7(6)*, 137005) Capstone. (Picture Window Bks.).

Bernardini, Cristian. The Lion & the Mouse, Narrated by the Timid but Truthful Mouse. Loewen, Nancy. 2018. (Other Side of the Fable Ser.). (ENG.). 24p. (J). (gr. -1-3). lib. bdg. 27.99 *(978-1-5158-2866-2(2)*, 138404, Picture Window Bks.) Capstone.

Bernardini, Cristian. Listen, My Bridge Is SO Cool! The Story of the Three Billy Goats Gruff As Told by the Troll. Loewen, Nancy. 2018. (Other Side of the Story Ser.). (ENG.). (J). pap. 41.70 ***(978-1-5158-2333-9(4)***, 27521); 24p. (gr. -1-3). lib. bdg. 27.99 *(978-1-5158-2297-4(4)*, 137006) Capstone. (Picture Window Bks.).

Bernardini, Cristian. No Lie, I Acted Like a Beast! The Story of Beauty & the Beast As Told by the Beast, 1 vol. Loewen, Nancy. 2013. (Other Side of the Story Ser.). (ENG.). 24p. (J). (gr. -1-3). pap. 6.95 *(978-1-4048-8083-2(6))*; lib. bdg. 27.99 *(978-1-4048-7938-6(2))* Capstone. (Picture Window Bks.).

—No Lie, I Acted Like a Beast: The Story of Beauty & the Beast as Told by the Beast. Loewen, Nancy. 2013. (Other Side of the Story Ser.). (ENG.). 24p. (J). (gr. -1-3). 9.95 *(978-1-4795-1944-6(8)*, Picture Window Bks.) Capstone.

—No Lie, Pigs (And Their Houses) Can Fly! The Story of the Three Little Pigs As Told by the Wolf. Gunderson, Jessica. 2016. (Other Side of the Story Ser.). (ENG.). 24p. (J). (gr. -1-3). lib. bdg. 27.99 *(978-1-4795-8621-9(8)*, Picture Window Bks.) Capstone.

—Trust Me, Jack's Beanstalk Stinks! The Story of Jack & the Beanstalk as Told by the Giant. Braun, Eric. 2011. (Other Side of the Story Ser.). (ENG.). 24p. (J). (gr. -1-3). pap. 6.95 *(978-1-4048-7050-5(4))*; lib. bdg. 27.99 *(978-1-4048-6675-1(2))* Capstone. (Picture Window Bks.).

Bernardini, Cristian & Guerlais, Gérald. The Other Side of the Story Classroom Collection. Loewen, Nancy & Gunderson, Jessica. 2018. (Other Side of the Story Ser.). (ENG.). (J). pap., pap., pap. 750.60 ***(978-1-5158-2325-4(3)***, 27516, Picture Window Bks.) Capstone.

Bernardini, Cristian, jt. illus. see Guerlais, Gérald.

Bernardini, Cristian Luis. En Serio, ¡Juan y Sus Frijoles Son unos Horrores! El Cuento de Juan y Los Frijoles Contado Por el Gigante. Braun, Eric Mark. 2019. (Otro Lado Del Cuento Ser.).Tr. of Trust Me, Jack's Beanstalk Stinks!. (SPA.). 24p. (J). (gr. -1-3). lib. bdg. 27.99 *(978-1-5158-4653-6(9)*, 141253); pap. 6.95 *(978-1-5158-6088-4(4)*, 142365) Capstone. (Picture Window Bks.).

Bernasconi, Pablo. Pumpkin Town! or, Nothing Is Better & Worse Than Pumpkins. McKy, Katie. 2008. (ENG.). 32p. (J). (gr. -1-3). pap. 7.99 *(978-0-547-18193-6(0)*, 1055964) Houghton Mifflin Harcourt Publishing Co.

Bernatene, Poly. The Adventures of Lettie Peppercorn. Gayton, Sam. 2016. (ENG.). 304p. (J). (gr. 3-7). 16.99 *(978-1-4814-4769-0(6)*, McElderry, Margaret K. Bks.) McElderry, Margaret K. Bks.

Bernatene, Poly. The Bookshop Girl. Bishop, Sylvia. (ENG.). (J). (gr. 3-7). 2020. 144p. pap. 8.99 ***(978-1-68263-199-7(0))***; 2018. 135p. 17.99 *(978-1-68263-045-7(5))* Peachtree Publishing Co. Inc.

Bernatene, Poly. I'm a Gnome! Peill-Meininghaus, Jessica. 2019. 40p. (J). (gr. -1-2). 17.99 *(978-1-5247-1984-5(6)*, Crown Books For Young Readers) Random Hse. Children's Bks.

—I'm a Gnome! Peill-Meininghaus, Jessica. 2019. (ENG.). 40p. (J). (gr. -1-2). lib. bdg. 20.99 *(978-1-5247-1985-2(4)*, Crown Books For Young Readers) Random Hse. Children's Bks.

—Prince Ribbit, 1 vol. Emmett, Jonathan. 2017. (ENG.). 32p. (J). (gr. -1-2). 16.95 *(978-1-56145-761-8(2))* Peachtree Publishing Co. Inc.

—The Princess & the Pig. Emmett, Jonathan. 2011. (ENG.). 32p. (J). (gr. k-8). 17.99 *(978-0-8027-2334-5(9)*, 900076370, Bloomsbury USA Childrens) Bloomsbury Publishing USA.

—Ribbit! Folgueira, Rodrigo. (ENG.). (J). 2016. 34p. (-k). bds. 8.99 *(978-0-553-53721-5(0))*; 2013. 40p. (gr. -1-k). 16.99 *(978-0-307-98146-2(0))* Random Hse. Children's Bks. (Knopf Bks. for Young Readers).

—The Santa Trap, 1 vol. Emmett, Jonathan. 2012. (ENG.). 32p. (J). 15.95 *(978-1-56145-670-3(5))* Peachtree Publishing Co. Inc.

—Skyfishing: (a Grand Tale with Grandpa) Sterer, Gideon. 2017. (ENG.). 40p. (J). (gr. -1-3). 17.95 *(978-1-4197-1911-0(4)*, Abrams Bks. for Young Readers) Abrams, Inc.

—The Sorcerer's Apprentice. 2007. (Usborne Young Reading: Series One Ser.). 47p. (J). (gr. -1-3). 8.99 *(978-0-7945-1589-8(4)*, Usborne) EDC Publishing.

—Still Life. West, Jacqueline. 2015. (Books of Elsewhere Ser.: 5). (ENG.). 352p. (J). (gr. 5). 8.99 *(978-0-14-242297-7(5)*, Puffin Books) Penguin Young Readers Group.

—The Strangers. West, Jacqueline. 2014. (Books of Elsewhere Ser.: 4). (ENG.). 336p. (J). (gr. 5). pap. 8.99 *(978-0-14-242575-6(3)*, Puffin Books) Penguin Young Readers Group.

—The Tickle Tree. Strathie, Chae. 2008. 24p. (J). (gr. -1-1). *(978-1-84539-344-1(9))*; *(978-1-84539-345-8(7))* Meadowside Children's Bks.

—Who Did This? Hao, K. T. 2008. (ENG.). 32p. (J). (gr. -1). lib. bdg. 16.50 *(978-1-933327-33-4(2))* Purple Bear Bks., Inc.

—Who Did This? Hao, K. T. 2008. (ENG.). 32p. (J). (gr. -1). 15.95 *(978-1-933327-32-7(4))* Purple Bear Bks., Inc.

Bernatene, Poly. The Monster Diaries. Bernatene, Poly. Saracino, Luciano. 2009. 32p. (J). 15.99 *(978-1-60010-502-9(5)*, Worthwhile Bks.) Idea & Design Works, LLC.

Berner, Alan. Rescuing Rialto: a Baby Sea Otter's Story. Mapes, Lynda V. 2019. (ENG.). 40p. (J). 18.99 *(978-1-250-14764-6(6)*, 900181793) Roaring Brook Pr.

Berner, Paulette L. The Cottontails & the Jackrabbits. Berner, R. Thomas. 2008. 22p. (J). per. 19.95 *(978-0-922993-06-2(8))* Marquette Bks.

Berner, Rotraut Susanne. The Cat: Or, How I Lost Eternity. Richter, Jutta. Brailovsky, Anna, tr. 2007. (ENG.). 80p. (J). (gr. 1-6). 14.00 *(978-1-57131-676-9(0))* Milkweed Editions.

Berneri, Camilo. Awesome Riddles for Awesome Kids: Trick Questions, Riddles & Brain Teasers for Kids Age 8-12. O'Smiles, Myles. 2018. (ENG.). 90p. (J). (gr. 4-6). *(978-1-988650-66-1(6))* Crimson Hill Bks.

Berneri, Camilo Luis. Awesome Riddles for Awesome Kids: Trick Questions, Riddles & Brain Teasers for Kids Age 8-12. O'Smiles, Myles. 2018. (ENG.). 90p. (J). (gr. 4-6). pap. *(978-1-988650-65-4(8))* Crimson Hill Bks.

—Clever Scenarios for Clever Kids: Thinking Questions for Kids, a Would You Rather Children's Game Book for Kids 8-12. O'Smiles, Myles. 2018. (ENG.). 94p. (J). (gr. 4-6). *(978-1-988650-61-6(5))*; pap. *(978-1-988650-60-9(7))* Crimson Hill Bks.

—Fun Jokes for Funny Kids: Jokes, Riddles & Brain-Teasers for Kids 6-10. O'Smiles, Myles. 2018. (ENG.). (J). 90p. (gr. 4-6). *(978-1-988650-62-3(3))*; 90p. (gr. 4-6). pap. *(978-1-988650-63-0(1))*; 106p. (gr. 3-6). pap. *(978-1-988650-51-7(8))* Crimson Hill Bks.

—More Jokes, Riddles & Scenarios for Happy Kids: A Children's Activity Book for Kids 8-12. O'Smiles, Myles. 2018. (ENG.). 90p. (J). (gr. 4-6). *(978-1-988650-69-2(0))* Crimson Hill Bks.

—Myles & the Telling Bee. O'Smiles, Myles. 2019. (ENG.). 88p. (J). pap. *(978-1-988650-99-9(2))* Crimson Hill Bks.

—Myles & the Telling Bee. O'Smiles, Myles. 2019. (ENG.). 88p. (J). (gr. 4-6). *(978-1-989595-01-5(4))*; pap. *(978-1-989595-00-8(6))* Crimson Hill Bks.

—Stinky Facts for Stinky Kids: Smelly, Stinky & Silly Facts for Kids 8 To 12. O'Smiles, Myles. 2019. (ENG.). 90p. (J). (gr. 4-6). pap. *(978-1-988650-95-1(X))* Crimson Hill Bks.

—Would You Rather? Silly, Challenging & Hilarious Questions for Kids 8-12. O'Smiles, Myles. 2019. (ENG.). 98p. (J). pap. *(978-1-989595-03-9(0))* Crimson Hill Bks.

—Would You Rather? Silly, Challenging & Hilarious Questions for Kids 8-12. O'Smiles, Myles. 2019. (ENG.). 98p. (J). (gr. 4-6). *(978-1-989595-05-3(7))*; pap. *(978-1-989595-04-6(9))* Crimson Hill Bks.

Bernhard, Durga. While You Are Sleeping. Bernhard, Durga. 2011. 24p. (J). (gr. k-3). 14.95 *(978-1-57091-473-7(7))* Charlesbridge Publishing, Inc.

Bernhard, Durga Yael. The Dreidel That Wouldn't Spin: A Toyshop Tale of Hanukkah, Vol. Simpson, Martha Seif. 2014. (ENG.). 32p. (J). (gr. -1-2). 16.95 *(978-1-937786-28-1(5)*, Wisdom Tales) World Wisdom, Inc.

—Green Bible Stories for Children. Lehman-Wilzig, Tami. 2011. (ENG.). 48p. (J). (gr. 3-5). lib. bdg. 10.99 *(978-0-7613-5135-1(3)*, 9780761351351, Kar-Ben Publishing) Lerner Publishing Group.

—Never Say a Mean Word Again: A Tale from Medieval Spain, Vol. Jules, Jacqueline. 2014. 32p. (J). (gr. -1-3). 16.95 *(978-1-937786-20-5(X)*, Wisdom Tales) World Wisdom, Inc.

Bernhard, Durga Yael. Yaya, Come Here! A Day in the Life of a Boy in West Africa: in English & Amharic. Eshetie, Amlaku B., tr. 2019. (ENG.). 48p. (J). pap. 11.99 ***(978-1-6944-0063-5(8))*** Independently Published.

Berning, Natalia. Mr. Bugabug's Journey. Cartales, Jewell. 2017. (ENG.). (J). 23.99 *(978-1-4984-9398-7(X))*; pap. 12.99 *(978-1-4984-9397-0(1))* Salem Author Services.

Berns, Jane M. Allergy Busters: A Story for Children with Autism or Related Spectrum Disorders Struggling with Allergies. Chara, Kathleen A. & Chara, Paul J. 2004. (ENG.). 48p. pap. 18.95 *(978-1-84310-782-8(1)*, 691986) Kingsley, Jessica Pubs. GBR. Dist: Hachette UK Distribution.

—Amy Elizabeth Goes to Play Therapy. Chara, Kathleen A. et al. 2004. (ENG.). 64p. (C). pap. 18.95 *(978-1-84310-775-0(9)*, 692177) Kingsley, Jessica Pubs. GBR. Dist: Hachette UK Distribution.

Bernstein, Gabo León. The Legend of Black Bart, 1 vol. Guerra, Elisa Puricelli. Pernigotti, Chiara, tr. 2014. (Minerva Mint Ser.). (ENG.). 160p. (J). (gr. 2-4). 25.32 *(978-1-4342-6512-8(9))*; pap. 7.99 *(978-1-4342-6515-9(3))* Capstone. (Stone Arch Bks.).

—Merlin's Island, 1 vol. Guerra, Elisa Puricelli. Pernigotti, Chiara, tr. 2014. (Minerva Mint Ser.). (ENG.). 160p. (J). (gr. 2-4). 25.32 *(978-1-4342-6511-1(0))*; pap. 7.99 *(978-1-4342-6514-2(5))* Capstone. (Stone Arch Bks.).

Bernstein, Galia. Veterans Day. Morey, Allan. 2018. (Holidays in Rhythm & Rhyme Ser.). (ENG.). 24p. (J). (gr. -1-3). lib. bdg. 33.99 *(978-1-68410-393-5(2)*, 140355) Cantata Learning.

Bernstein, Galia. Cinderella. Jarman, Julia. 2014. (Traditional Tales Ser.). (ENG.). 32p. (J). (gr. 1-2). pap. 7.95 *(978-1-62521-546-8(0)*, Capstone Classroom) Capstone.

—The Eight Knights of Hanukkah. Kimmelman, Leslie. 2020. (ENG.). 48p. (J). (gr. -1-3). 17.99 *(978-0-8234-3958-4(5))* Holiday Hse., Inc.

—Four Clever Brothers 1 Pathfinders. Rickards, Lynne. 2017. (Cambridge Reading Adventures Ser.). (ENG.). 24p. pap. 6.74 *(978-1-108-41081-6(2))* Cambridge Univ. Pr.

—The Jungle Book. Kipling, Rudyard & Ladybird Books Staff. 2015. (Ladybird Classics Ser.). 72p. (J). (gr. 3-7). 10.99 *(978-1-4093-1358-8(1))* Penguin Bks., Ltd. GBR. Dist: Independent Pubs. Group.

—King Fox Purple Band. Bradman, Tom. 2016. (Cambridge Reading Adventures Ser.). (ENG.). 24p. pap. 8.08 *(978-1-107-56215-8(5))* Cambridge Univ. Pr.

—Monkey & Elephant: Candlewick Sparks. Schaefer, Carole Lexa. 2013. (Candlewick Sparks Ser.). 48p. (J). (gr. k-4). pap. 4.99 *(978-0-7636-6261-5(5))* Candlewick Pr.

—Monkey & Elephant & a Secret Birthday Surprise. Schaefer, Carole Lexa. (Candlewick Sparks Ser.). 48p. (J). (gr. k-4).

B

2016. pap. 4.99 *(978-0-7636-8744-1(8))*; 2015. 14.99 *(978-0-7636-6131-1(7))* Candlewick Pr.

—Monkey & Elephant & the Babysitting Adventure. Schaefer, Carole Lexa. (Candlewick Sparks Ser.). 48p. (J). (gr. k-4). 2017. pap. 4.99 *(978-0-7636-9781-5(8))*; 2016. 14.99 *(978-0-7636-6535-7(5))* Candlewick Pr.

—Monkey & Elephant Get Better. Schaefer, Carole Lexa. (Candlewick Sparks Ser.). 48p. (J). (gr. k-4). 2014. pap. 4.99 *(978-0-7636-7180-8(0))*; 2013. 14.99 *(978-0-7636-4841-1(8))* Candlewick Pr.

—Monkey & Elephant Go Gadding. Schaefer, Carole Lexa. 2015. (Candlewick Sparks Ser.). 48p. (J). (gr. k-4). pap. 4.99 *(978-0-7636-8030-5(3))* Candlewick Pr.

—Princess Frog. Richemont, Enid. 2014. (Tadpoles: Fairytale Twists Ser.). (ENG.). 32p. (J). (gr. 1-2). *(978-0-7787-0443-0(2))*; pap. *(978-0-7787-0452-2(1))* Crabtree Publishing Co.

—Veterans Day. Morey, Allan. 2017. (Holidays in Rhythm & Rhyme Ser.). (ENG.). 24p. (J). (gr. -1-3). lib. bdg. 33.99 incl. audio compact disk *(978-1-68410-059-0(3)*, 31522) Cantata Learning.

Bernstein, Galia & Giovine, Sergio. The Hidden Gold. Buckey, Sarah M. 2012. (American Girl Mysteries Ser.). (ENG.). 150p. (J). (gr. 4-6). pap. 21.19 *(978-1-59369-902-4(6))* American Girl Publishing, Inc.

Bernstein, Galia & Ruffle, Mark. Build the Human Body. Walker, Richard. 2013. (Build It Ser.). (ENG.). 32p. (J). (gr. 1-1). pap. 19.95 *(978-1-60710-413-1(X)*, Silver Dolphin Bks.) Printers Row Publishing Group.

—Build the T. Rex. Naish, Darren. 2013. (Build It Ser.). (ENG.). 32p. (J). (gr. 1-1). pap. 19.95 *(978-1-60710-415-5(6)*, Silver Dolphin Bks.) Printers Row Publishing Group.

Berrett, Pat, photos by. A More Abundant Life: New Deal Artists & Public Art in New Mexico. Hoefer, Jacqueline, ed. 2003. 196p. 60.00 *(978-0-86534-305-4(5))* Sunstone Pr.

Berrie, Christine. Bird Bingo. 2012. (ENG.). 160p. (gr. 1-17). 29.95 *(978-1-85669-917-4(X)*, King, Laurence Publishing) Orion Publishing Group, Ltd. GBR. Dist: Hachette Bk. Group.

Berringer, Nick. The Super Joke Book. Brandreth, Gyles. 2009. (ENG.). 112p. (J). (gr. 2-7). pap. 5.95 *(978-1-4027-4713-7(6))* Sterling Publishing Co., Inc.

Berrios, Nancy M. When DREAMS Come True... Berrios, Nancy M. 2019. (ENG.). 34p. (J). pap. 9.99 ***(978-1-5484-7385-3(5))*** CreateSpace Independent Publishing Platform.

Berry, Alicia. In a Belly, Stinky & Smelly. Lehr, Kristin. 2020. (Heaven's Heroes Ser.: 3). (ENG.). 40p. (J). (gr. k-2). 16.99 ***(978-1-951970-00-0(4))*** Elk Lake Publishing, Inc.

Berry, Bob. How to Draw Steampunk: Discover the Secrets to Drawing, Painting, & Illustrating the Curious World of Science Fiction in the Victorian Age. Marsocci, Joey & DeBlasio, Allison. 2014. (Fantasy Underground Ser.). (ENG.). 128p. (YA). (gr. 8-12). lib. bdg. 37.32 *(978-1-939581-22-8(2)*, Walter Foster Jr) Quarto Publishing Group USA.

—Learn to Draw Ancient Times. Phan, Sandy & Walter Foster Jr. Creative Team. 2014. (Learn to Draw Ser.). (ENG.). 40p. (J). (gr. 3-5). lib. bdg. 33.32 *(978-1-939581-26-6(5)*, Walter Foster Jr) Quarto Publishing Group USA.

Berry, Bob, et al. My First Library Sesame Street: 12 Board Books. Brian Warling Photography (Firm) Staff et al, photos by. Sesame Workshop Staff, ed. 2010. (ENG.). 120p. (J). bds. *(978-1-4127-0515-8(0)*, 550309c1-9a37-4382-af9d-de3107985300) Phoenix International Publications, Inc.

—Sesame Street: 3-Book Potty Set. Houlihan, Brian & Brooke, Susan Rich. Broderick, Kathy, ed. 2016. (Read, Look, & Play Ser.). (ENG.). 50p. (J). *(978-1-5037-1068-9(8)*, 8969fb5f-e456-4b34-8eb5-525726ec805a, p i kids) Phoenix International Publications, Inc.

Berry, Bob, et al. Sesame Street: Busy Monsters. PI Kids. 2020. (ENG.). 80p. (J). ***(978-1-5037-5454-6(5)***, 599cc070-5652-4fbe-bc46-59a0823194df, p i kids) Phoenix International Publications, Inc.

Berry, Bob, et al. Sesame Street: Explore with Elmo. Houlihan, Brian. 2016. (Play-A-Sound Ser.). (ENG.). 14p. (J). bds. *(978-1-5037-1056-6(4)*, 3baed545-05b1-4128-84c2-0448a102fbad, p i kids) Phoenix International Publications, Inc.

—Sesame Street: Potty Time Songs. Publications International Ltd. Staff, ed. 2010. (Play-A-Song Ser.). (ENG.). 12p. (J). 4.69 net. *(978-1-4508-0365-6(2)*, 0844334c-2821-4b21-84c9-c2e96cc0b080) Phoenix International Publications, Inc.

Berry, Bob, jt. illus. see Brannon, Tom.

Berry, Holly. Frog Went A-Dancing. Rovetch, L. Bob. 2006. (J). *(978-1-58987-008-6(5))* Kindermusik International.

—The Gingerbread Cowboy. Squires, Janet. 2006. (ENG.). 32p. (J). (gr. -1-3). 17.99 *(978-0-06-077863-7(6))*; lib. bdg. 18.89 *(978-0-06-077864-4(4))* HarperCollins Pubs.

—I'm a Pig. Weeks, Sarah. 2005. 32p. (J). (gr. -1-2). lib. bdg. 16.89 *(978-0-06-074344-4(1)*, Geringer, Laura Book) HarperCollins Pubs.

—Long May She Wave. Fulton, Kristen. 2017. (ENG.). 40p. (J). (gr. -1-3). 17.99 *(978-1-4814-6096-5(X)*, McElderry, Margaret K. Bks.) McElderry, Margaret K. Bks.

—Thanksgiving on Plymouth Plantation. Stanley, Diane. 2004. (Time-Traveling Twins Ser.). (ENG.). 48p. (J). (gr. k-5). 16.99 *(978-0-06-027069-8(1))* HarperCollins Pubs.

—Woof: a Love Story. Weeks, Sarah. 2009. (ENG.). 32p. (J). (gr. -1-3). 16.99 *(978-0-06-025007-2(0))* HarperCollins Pubs.

Berry, Kathy. April in Paris. Matisse, Lauri Anne. 2020. (April in Paris Ser.: Vol. 1). (ENG.). 34p. (J). pap. 12.00 ***(978-0-9630069-7-4(5))*** Matisse Studios.

Berry, Max. Meet the ANZACs. Saxby, Claire. 2015. 36p. (J). (gr. k-3). 14.99 *(978-0-85798-193-6(5))* Random Hse. Australia AUS. Dist: Independent Pubs. Group.

Berry, VacieAnna. Dandylion. Laible, Steve William, ed. ed. 2012. (ENG.). 38p. (J). pap. 9.95 *(978-0-9844784-6-0(9)*, Empire Holdins - Literary Division for Young Readers) Kodel Group, LLC, The.

Bersanetti, Sandra. El Pueblo de los Silencios. Brignole, Giancarla, tr. (Fabulas De Familia Ser.). (SPA.). 32p. *(978-970-20-0271-0(0))* Castillo, Ediciones, S. A. de C. V.

—Los Regalos de Tia Terciopelina. Bresanetti, Sandra & Bresanetti, S. Brignole, Giancarla, tr. rev. ed. 2006. (Fabulas De Familia Ser.). (SPA & ENG.). 32p. (J). (gr. k-4). pap. 6.95 *(978-970-20-0253-6(2))* Castillo, Ediciones, S. A. de C. V. MEX. Dist: Macmillan.

Bersani, Shennen. Animais Parceiros (Animal Partners in Portuguese), 1 vol. Cohn, Scotti. Sacciotto, Adriana & Wiedemann, Tatiana, trs. 2019. (POR.). 32p. (J). 11.95 *(978-1-64351-405-5(9))* Arbordale Publishing.

—Animal Partners, 1 vol. Cohn, Scotti. 2015. (ENG.). 32p. (J). (gr. 2-5). 17.95 *(978-1-62855-448-9(7))* Arbordale Publishing.

—Astro: The Steller Sea Lion, 1 vol. Harvey, Jeanne Walker. 2010. (ENG.). 32p. (J). (gr. -1-4). pap. 9.95 *(978-1-60718-874-2(0))* Arbordale Publishing.

—Beginnings. Watson, Lori Ann. 2009. 32p. (J). (gr. -1-1). 12.95 *(978-0-8198-1172-1(6))* Pauline Bks. & Media.

—Butterfly Colors & Counting. Pallotta, Jerry. 2013. (Jerry Pallotta's Counting Bks.). 10p. (J). (— 1). bds. 5.95 *(978-1-57091-899-5(6))* Charlesbridge Publishing, Inc.

—Butterfly Counting. Pallotta, Jerry. 2015. (Jerry Pallotta's Counting Bks.). 32p. (J). (gr. -1-2). 17.95 *(978-1-57091-414-0(1))* Charlesbridge Publishing, Inc.

—Un Case con Sentido Común. Daemicke, Songju Ma. 2016. (SPA.). 32p. (J). (gr. k-3). pap. 9.95 *(978-1-62855-854-8(7))* Arbordale Publishing.

—A Case of Sense, 1 vol. Daemicke, Songju Ma. 2016. (ENG & SPA.). 32p. (J). (gr. k-3). 17.95 *(978-1-62855-852-4(0))* Arbordale Publishing.

—Erase un Elefante, 1 vol. Stanek, Linda. 2016. (SPA.). 32p. (J). (gr. k-3). pap. 11.95 *(978-1-62855-745-9(1))* Arbordale Publishing.

—Eyeball Alphabet Book. Pallotta, Jerry. 2015. (J). pap. *(978-0-545-74731-8(7))* Scholastic, Inc.

—The Glaciers Are Melting!, 1 vol. Love, Donna. 2011. (ENG.). 32p. (J). (gr. -1-4). 16.95 *(978-1-60718-126-2(6))*; pap. 8.95 *(978-1-60718-136-1(3))* Arbordale Publishing.

—Home in the Cave, 1 vol. Halfmann, Janet. 2012. (ENG.). 32p. (J). (gr. -1-4). 17.95 *(978-1-60718-522-2(9))*; pap. 9.95 *(978-1-60718-531-4(8))* Arbordale Publishing.

—Honey Girl: The Hawaiian Monk Seal. Harvey, Jeanne Walker. 2017. (ENG.). 32p. (J). (gr. k-3). pap. 9.95 *(978-1-62855-922-4(5))* Arbordale Publishing.

—Honey Girl: The Hawaiian Monk Seal. Walker, Harvey Jeanne. 2017. (ENG.). 32p. (J). (gr. k-3). 17.95 *(978-1-62855-921-7(7))* Arbordale Publishing.

—The Long & the Short of It: A Tale about Hair. Meyers, Barbara & Mays, Lydia. 2011. (ENG.). 48p. (J). (gr. 2-4). 14.95 *(978-1-60443-017-2(6))* American Cancer Society, Inc.

—My Sister, Alicia May. Tupper Ling, Nancy. 2009. (ENG.). 32p. (J). (gr. k-2). 16.95 *(978-0-9792035-9-6(7))* Pleasant St. Pr.

—Nana, What's Cancer? Fead, Beverlye Hyman et al. 2009. (ENG.). 64p. (J). (gr. -1-7). 14.95 *(978-1-60443-010-3(9)*, 1604430109) American Cancer Society, Inc.

—Ocean Counting: Odd Numbers. Pallotta, Jerry. 2005. (Jerry Pallotta's Counting Bks.). 32p. (J). (gr. -1-3). pap. 7.95 *(978-0-88106-150-5(6))* Charlesbridge Publishing, Inc.

—Once upon an Elephant, 1 vol. Stanek, Linda. 2016. (ENG.). 32p. (J). (gr. k-3). 17.95 *(978-1-62855-731-2(1))* Arbordale Publishing.

—Rêves de Guépard. Stanek, Linda. Troff, Sophie, tr. 2019. (FRE.). 32p. (J). 11.95 *(978-1-64351-589-2(6))* Arbordale Publishing.

—Salamander Season, 1 vol. Curtis, Jennifer Keats & Frederick, J. Adam. 2015. (ENG.). 32p. (J). (gr. 1-4). 17.95 *(978-1-62855-556-1(4))* Arbordale Publishing.

—Sea Slime. Prager, Ellen J. 2014. (ENG.). (J). (gr. -1-3). lib. bdg. 20.55 *(978-1-62765-774-7(6))* Perfection Learning Corp.

—Sea Slime: It's Eeuwy, Gooey & under the Sea, 1 vol. Prager, Ellen. 2014. (ENG.). 32p. (J). (gr. 1-4). 17.95 *(978-1-62855-210-2(7))* Arbordale Publishing.

—Sea Slime: It's Eeuwy, Gooey & under the Sea, 1 vol. Prager, Ellen. 2014. (SPA.). 32p. (J). (gr. 1-4). pap. 9.95 *(978-1-62855-228-7(X))* Arbordale Publishing.

—The Shape Family Babies, 1 vol. Haas, Kristin. 2014. (ENG.). 32p. (J). (gr. -1-3). 17.95 *(978-1-62855-211-9(5))* Arbordale Publishing.

—Shark Baby, 1 vol. Downer, Ann. 2013. (SPA & ENG.). 32p. (J). (gr. -1-3). 17.95 *(978-1-60718-622-9(5))*; pap. 9.95 *(978-1-60718-634-2(9))* Arbordale Publishing.

—Temporada de Salamandras. Curtis, Jennifer Keats & Frederick, J. Adam. 2015. (SPA.). 32p. (J). (gr. 1-4). pap. 9.95 *(978-1-62855-574-5(2))* Arbordale Publishing.

—Tiburoncito, 1 vol. Downer, Ann. 2013. (SPA.). 32p. (J). (gr. -1-3). 17.95 *(978-1-60718-709-7(4))*; pap. 11.95 *(978-1-62855-351-2(0))* Arbordale Publishing.

Bersani, Shennen. Let My Colors Out. Bersani, Shennen. Filigenzi, Courtney. 2009. (ENG.). 16p. (J). (gr. -1-k). 11.95 *(978-1-60443-011-0(7)*, 1604430117) American Cancer Society, Inc.

—Los Bebés de la Familia Geométrica, 1 vol. Bersani, Shennen. Haas, Kristin & Toth, Rosalyna. 2014.Tr. of Shape Family Babies. (SPA.). 32p. (J). (gr. -1-3). pap. 11.95 *(978-1-62855-229-4(8))* Arbordale Publishing.

—Sueño con Chitas. Bersani, Shennen. Stanek, Linda. 2018. (SPA.). 32p. (J). (gr. 2-3). pap. 11.95 *(978-1-60718-747-9(7)*, 9781607187479) Arbordale Publishing.

Berserik, Teun. Blake & Mortimer Vol. 26: The Valley of the Immortals Part 2 - the Thousandth Arm of the Mekong. 2020. (Blake & Mortimer Ser.: 26). (ENG.). 64p. pap. 15.95 *(978-1-84918-437-3(2))* CineBook GBR. Dist: National Bk. Network.

—The Valley of the Immortals. 2019. (Blake & Mortimer Ser.: 25). (ENG.). 64p. pap. 15.95 *(978-1-84918-428-1(3))* CineBook GBR. Dist: National Bk. Network.

Berson, Harold. Loretta Mason Potts. Chase, Mary. (ENG.). 224p. (J). (gr. 3-7). 2020. pap. 11.99 ***(978-1-68137-506-9(0)***, NYRB Kids); 2014. 16.95 *(978-1-59017-757-0(6)*, NYR Children's Collection) New York Review of Bks., Inc., The.

Bersson, Robert & Trobaugh, Scott. Stripes & Stars. Bersson, Robert & Shoup, Dolores. l.t. ed. 2003. 40p. (J). (gr. 1-4). per. 16.95 *(978-0-9740585-0-4(5))* Legacy Group Productions, LLC.

Bertagnolli, Daniel. Whooo Turned Out the Lights? Bertagnolli, Daniel. 2009. (ENG.). 24p. (J). pap. 9.14 *(978-1-4269-0590-2(4))* Trafford Publishing.

Bertelè, Luca, jt. illus. see Lorenzo, Veronica Di.

Bertelle, Nicoletta. Abracadabra! The Magic of Trying. Giraldo, Maria Loretta & Hagen, Katie ten. 2018. 32p. (J). *(978-1-4338-2874-4(X)*, Magination Pr.) American Psychological Assn.

—Saints & Their Stories. Giraldo, Maria Loretta. Moran, Margaret Edward, tr. 2010.Tr. of I Santi: i miei primi Amici. 168p. (J). (gr. 2-5). 19.95 *(978-0-8198-7134-3(6))* Pauline Bks. & Media.

Bertholf, Bret. Leon & the Champion Chip. Kurzweil, Allen. 2005. 352p. (J). 15.99 *(978-0-06-053933-7(X))*; lib. bdg. 16.89 *(978-0-06-053934-4(8))* HarperCollins Pubs.

—Leon & the Spitting Image. Kurzweil, Allen. (ENG.). 320p. (J). (gr. 3-18). 2005. pap. 7.99 *(978-0-06-053932-0(1)*, Greenwillow Bks.); 2003. 16.99 *(978-0-06-053930-6(5))* HarperCollins Pubs.

Bertino, Mike, jt. illus. see Althea, Erin.

Bertolami, Vince. Kristie's Excellent Adventures: A Visit to the Fridge. McNeely Schultz, Geri. 2013. (ENG.). 40p. (J). pap. 9.99 *(978-1-935766-88-9(0))* Windy City Pubs.

Bertolucci, Federico. Desert Adventure. Bordiglioni, Stephen & Bordiglioni, Stefano. 2009. (Dinodino's Dinosaur Adventures Ser.). 56p. (J). (gr. k-4). 30.95 *(978-1-60754-714-3(7))*; pap. 12.85 *(978-1-60754-721-1(X))* Windmill Bks.

—Earthquake! Bordiglioni, Stephen & Bordiglioni, Stefano. 2009. (Dinodino's Dinosaur Adventures Ser.). 56p. (J). (gr. k-4). 30.95 *(978-1-60754-713-6(9))*; pap. 12.85 *(978-1-60754-719-8(8))* Windmill Bks.

—Volcano! Bordiglioni, Stephen & Bordiglioni, Stefano. 2009. (Dinodino's Dinosaur Adventures Ser.). 56p. (J). (gr. k-4). 30.95 *(978-1-60754-712-9(0))*; pap. 12.85 *(978-1-60754-717-4(1))* Windmill Bks.

Berton, Charles. The Ladybug & the Bully Frog. Rice, Caroleann. 2018. (ENG.). 48p. (J). pap. 13.49 *(978-1-5456-3499-8(8))* Salem Author Services.

Bertoni, Oliver. The Coconut Tree. Rochelin, Ghyslaine. 2010. (HAT.). 32p. (J). pap. 14.95 *(978-1-60195-319-3(4))* International Step by Step Assn.

Bertozzi, Nick. Diabetes & Me: An Essential Guide for Kids & Parents. 2013. (ENG.). 176p. pap. 15.00 *(978-0-8090-3871-8(4)*, 900078404, Hill & Wang) Farrar, Straus & Giroux.

—A Hitch at the Fairmont. Averbeck, Jim. (ENG.). 416p. (J). (gr. 3-7). 2015. pap. 9.99 *(978-1-4424-9448-0(4))*; 2014. 16.99 *(978-1-4424-9447-3(6)*, Atheneum Bks. for Young Readers) Simon & Schuster Children's Publishing.

Bertozzi, Nick. Houdini: The Handcuff King. Lutes, Jason. 2019. (Center for Cartoon Studies Presents Ser.). (ENG.). 96p. (J). (gr. 5-9). pap. 12.99 ***(978-1-368-04288-8(0))*** Little, Brown Bks. for Young Readers.

Bertozzi, Nick. Lewis & Clark. Bertozzi, Nick. 2011. (ENG.). 144p. (YA). (gr. 7-18). pap. 19.99 *(978-1-59643-450-9(3)*, 900054959, First Second Bks.) Roaring Brook Pr.

—Shackleton: Antarctic Odyssey. Bertozzi, Nick. 2014. (ENG.). 128p. (YA). (gr. 7-12). pap. 17.99 *(978-1-59643-451-6(1)*, 900054960, First Second Bks.) Roaring Brook Pr.

Bertran, Nuria. Sabelotodo: 1000 Desafíos para Tu Inteligencia. Barberi, Marco et al, trs. 2003. (SPA.). 384p. 35.00 *(978-84-494-2372-7(4)*, GML07104-192209) Oceano Grupo Editoria, S.A. ESP. Dist: Cengage Gale.

Bertrand, Cécile & Bertrand, Cécile. Stand Up! (Sunscreen) Laouénan, Christine & Laouénan, Christine. Moloney, Kate, ed. 2012. (ENG.). 80p. (YA). (gr. 5-9). pap. 12.95 *(978-1-4197-0198-6(3)*, Amulet Bks.) Abrams, Inc.

Bertrand, Cécile, jt. illus. see Bertrand, Cécile.

Bertrand, Frederique. New York in Pajamarama. Leblond, Michaël. 2013. (ENG.). 32p. (J). (gr. -1-2). 15.99 *(978-1-907912-23-8(1))* Phoenix Yard Bks. GBR. Dist: Independent Pubs. Group.

Berube, Kate. The Sandcastle That Lola Built. Maynor, Megan. 2018. 40p. (J). (-k). 17.99 *(978-1-5247-1615-8(4)*, Knopf Bks. for Young Readers) Random Hse. Children's Bks.

Berube, Kate. Second Banana. Thornburgh, Blair. 2020. (ENG.). 32p. (J). (gr. -1-3). 16.99 ***(978-1-4197-4234-7(5)***, 1680701, Abrams Bks. for Young Readers) Abrams, Inc.

Berube, Kate. The Summer Nick Taught His Cats to Read. Manley, Curtis. 2016. (ENG.). 32p. (J). (gr. -1-3). 17.99 *(978-1-4814-3569-7(8)*, Simon & Schuster Bks. For Young Readers) Simon & Schuster Bks. For Young Readers.

Besco, Stacy Rose. It Was an Accident. Borden, Joy. 2020. (ENG.). 18p. (J). pap. 12.49 ***(978-1-63050-806-7(3))*** Salem Author Services.

Beshwaty, Steve. Adam et le Raton Dessinateur. Decary, Marie. 2004. (Premier Roman Ser.). (FRE.). 64p. (J). (gr. 1-4). pap. *(978-2-89021-643-3(8))* Diffusion du livre Mirabel (DLM).

Beshwaty, Steve. Adam's Tropical Adventure. Decary, Marie. 2005. 54p. (J). lib. bdg. 12.00 *(978-1-4242-1202-6(2))* Fitzgerald Bks.

—Adam's Tropical Adventure. Décary, Marie. Cummins, Sarah, tr. 2005. (Formac First Novels Ser.: 56). (ENG.). 64p. (gr. 2-5). 14.95 *(978-0-88780-687-2(2)*, 687); (J). 4.95 *(978-0-88780-686-5(4)*, 686) Formac Publishing Co., Ltd. CAN. Dist: Formac Lorimer Bks. Ltd.

—Floop Does the Laundry. Tremblay, Carole. 2009. (Floop Ser.). 24p. (J). (gr. -1-k). 25.60 *(978-1-60754-333-6(8))*; pap. 8.15 *(978-1-60754-334-3(6))* Windmill Bks.

—Floop in the Dark. Tremblay, Carole. 2009. (Floop Ser.). 24p. (J). (gr. -1-k). 25.60 *(978-1-60754-341-1(9))*; pap. 8.15 *(978-1-60754-342-8(7))* Windmill Bks.

—Floop's Flowers. Tremblay, Carole. 2009. (Floop Ser.). 24p. (J). (gr. -1-k). 25.60 *(978-1-60754-344-2(3))*; pap. 8.15 *(978-1-60754-346-6(X))* Windmill Bks.

—Floop's New Umbrella. Tremblay, Carole. 2009. (Floop Ser.). 24p. (J). (gr. -1-k). 25.60 *(978-1-60754-347-3(8))*; pap. 8.15 *(978-1-60754-348-0(6))* Windmill Bks.

Beskow, Elsa. Thumbelina, 30 vols. Andersen, Hans Christian. 2016.Tr. of Tommelise. (ENG.). 32p. (J). 17.95 *(978-1-78250-245-6(9))* Floris Bks. GBR. Dist: Consortium Bk. Sales & Distribution.

Besom, Mae. What Do You Do with a Chance. Yamada, Kobi. 2017. (ENG.). (J). 16.95 *(978-1-943200-73-3(4))* Compendium, Inc., Publishing & Communications.

—What Do You Do with a Problem? Yamada, Kobi. 2016. (ENG.). 36p. (J). (gr. -1-3). 16.95 *(978-1-943200-00-9(9))* Compendium, Inc., Publishing & Communications.

—What Do You Do with an Idea? Yamada, Kobi. 2014. (ENG.). 36p. (J). (gr. -1-3). 16.95 *(978-1-938298-07-3(1))* Compendium, Inc., Publishing & Communications.

Bessey, Brandan. Peanut the Tiny Horse. Havice, L. K. 2012. 50p. *(978-1-4602-0956-1(7))*; pap. *(978-1-4602-0954-7(0))* FriesenPress.

Bessey, Vance. Fanciful Tales & Poems: For Grandchildren of Any Age. Heymann, Irene Rommel. Heyman, Frank J., ed. 2012. 102p. (-18). pap. 14.95 *(978-1-934949-63-4(9))* Just Write Bks.

Best, Cathy. Daniel's World. DeLoach, Kathleen. 2004. (J). pap. 15.95 *(978-0-9747440-5-6(0))* Three Moons Media.

—Le Monde de Daniel: Un livre sur les enfants Handicapés. DeLoach, Kathleen. 2005. (FRE.). (J). pap. 15.95 *(978-1-933514-01-7(9))* Three Moons Media.

—El Mundo de Daniel: Un libro sobre niños Minusválidos. DeLoach, Kathleen. 2005. (SPA.). 20p. (J). pap. 15.95 *(978-1-933514-00-0(0))* Three Moons Media.

Best, Virginia. Pansy in London: The Mystery of the Missing Pup, vol. 5. Bardes, Cynthia. 2017. (Pansy the Poodle Mystery Ser.: 5th book in the series). (ENG.). 32p. (J). (gr. -1-2). 21.95 *(978-0-692-82604-1(1))* Octobre Pr.

Bester, Shayle. The Cool Nguni. Bester, Maryanne. 2007. (Cool Nguni Ser.). (ENG.). 24p. (J). (gr. k-2). 12.00 *(978-1-77009-264-8(1))* Jacana Media ZAF. Dist: Independent Pubs. Group.

—I Know That! Bester, Maryanne. 2015. (ENG.). 32p. (J). (gr. -1-k). pap. 9.95 *(978-1-4314-0491-9(8))* Jacana Media ZAF. Dist: Independent Pubs. Group.

—The Long Trousers. Bester, Maryanne. 2009. (Cool Nguni Ser.). (ENG.). 32p. (J). (gr. 2-4). pap. 12.00 *(978-1-77009-499-4(7))* Jacana Media ZAF. Dist: Independent Pubs. Group.

—The Missing Ball. Bester, Maryanne. 2010. (Cool Nguni Ser.: 4). (ENG.). 32p. (J). (gr. k-2). pap. 12.00 *(978-1-77009-704-9(X))* Jacana Media ZAF. Dist: Independent Pubs. Group.

—The Three Billy Goats Gruff. Bloch, Carole. 2011. (Best Loved Tales for Africa Ser.). (ENG.). 32p. (J). (gr. k-2). pap. 10.95 *(978-1-77009-765-0(1))* Jacana Media ZAF. Dist: Independent Pubs. Group.

—Three Friends & a Taxi. Bester, Maryanne. 2007. (Cool Nguni Ser.: 1). (ENG.). 24p. (J). (gr. k-2). 12.00 *(978-1-77009-265-5(X))* Jacana Media ZAF. Dist: Independent Pubs. Group.

—Why Dog Is Afraid of Storms. Clegg, Maryanne & Bester, Maryanne. 2012. 32p. (J). (gr. -1-k). pap. 12.95 *(978-1-4314-0219-9(2))* Jacana Media ZAF. Dist: Independent Pubs. Group.

Betancourt, Raymond. Everywhere Coquis. Hooper, Nancy. Quinones, Jacqueline, tr. 2003.Tr. of En Dondequiera Coquies. (ENG.). 48p. (J). 13.95 *(978-0-942929-14-0(4)*, Omni Arts Publishing) Read Street Publishing, Inc.

Betanzos, Sue. My New Backyard Garden. 2006.Tr. of Mi Nuevo Jardin del Traspatio. (SPA & ENG.). (J). *(978-0-9792253-0-7(2))* Tucson Botanical Gardens.

Beth, Sara. I Couldn't Wait to Meet You. Love, Jessica. 2019. (ENG.). 32p. (J). pap. 15.00 *(978-1-5454-8701-3(4))* CreateSpace Independent Publishing Platform.

Beth, Shannon. One Blue Shoe. Conti, Alexis. 2013. (ENG.). (J). (gr. -1-3). 14.95 *(978-1-937406-11-0(3))* Mascot Bks., Inc.

Bethards, David. Meditation for Little People. Langford, Anne. 2003. 40p. (gr. k-4). reprint ed. 8.95 *(978-0-87516-211-9(8)*, Devorss Pubns.) DeVorss & Co.

Betiku, Olatukunbo. Gerald, Fish of the Spirit! A Caribbean Tale of Fortune & Greed. Amon, Ras Ran. ed. 2006. Orig. Title: Gerald, Fish of the Spirit! A Caribbean Tale of Fortune & Greed. (ENG.). (J). 7.99 *(978-0-9776603-0-8(3))* One Love Assn. Bks.

Betowers. Where Are My ABCs: Lift a Flap Pop up Board Book. Finch, Rusty. 2017. (Lift a Pop Ser.). (ENG.). 12p. (J). (gr. -1-k). bds. 8.99 *(978-1-68052-177-1(2)*, 1001750) Cottage Door Pr.

—Where Are My Colors: Lift a Flap Pop up Board Book. Finch, Rusty. 2017. (Lift a Pop Ser.). (ENG.). 12p. (J). (gr. -1-k). bds. 8.99 *(978-1-68052-178-8(0)*, 1001760) Cottage Door Pr.

Betowers, jt. illus. see Crisp, Dan.

Betteo, Patricio. Soy el Robot. Fernández, Bernardo. 2010. (SPA.). 47p. (J). (gr. 2-4). pap. *(978-607-411-031-9(X))* Editorial Almadia.

—Un Tutu Muy Apretado. Clark, Sherryl. rev. ed. 2006. (Castillo de la Lectura Verde Ser.). (ENG.). 88p. (J). (gr. 2-4). pap. 7.95 *(978-970-20-0851-4(4))* Castillo, Ediciones, S. A. de C. V. MEX. Dist: Macmillan.

Bettio, Jennifer. Dragon Disarray. 2019. (ENG.). 34p. (J). pap. *(978-1-989027-12-7(1))* Cavern of Dreams Publishing Hse.

Bettio, Jennifer. TYLER the Painted Turtle: Adventures Around a Creek. Misiak, Zig. 2020. (Clan Animals Ser.: Vol. 2). (ENG.). 28p. (J). pap. 9.25 ***(978-1-7072-2482-1(X))*** Independently Published.

Bettoli, Delana. This Is the Stable. Cotten, Cynthia. 2008. (ENG.). 32p. (J). (gr. -1-3). pap. 7.99 *(978-0-312-38421-0(1)*, 900053322) Square Fish.

Betton, Jen. Twilight Chant. Thompson, Holly. 2018. (ENG.). 32p. (J). (gr. -1-3). 17.99 *(978-0-544-58648-2(4)*, 1614141, Clarion Bks.) Houghton Mifflin Harcourt Trade & Reference Pubs.

Betton, Jen. Hedgehog Needs a Hug. Betton, Jen. 2018. 32p. (J). (gr. -1-3). 17.99 *(978-1-5247-3712-2(7)*, G.P. Putnam's Sons Books for Young Readers) Penguin Young Readers Group.

Betts, Anni. Breathe Like a Bear: 30 Mindful Moments for Kids to Feel Calm & Focused Anytime, Anywhere. Willey, Kira. 2017. (ENG.). 96p. (J). (gr. -1-3). pap. 15.99 *(978-1-62336-883-8(9)*, 9781623368838, Rodale Kids) Random Hse. Children's Bks.

—Mindfulness Moments for Kids: Breathe Like a Bear. Willey, Kira. 2019. (Mindfulness Moments for Kids Ser.). (ENG.). 26p. (J). (— 1). bds. 7.99 *(978-1-9848-9411-3(0)*, Rodale Kids) Random Hse. Children's Bks.

—Mindfulness Moments for Kids: Bunny Breaths. Willey, Kira. 2020. (Mindfulness Moments for Kids Ser.). (ENG.). 26p. (J). (— 1). bds. 7.99 *(978-0-593-11985-3(1)*, Rodale Kids) Random Hse. Children's Bks.

—Mindfulness Moments for Kids: Listen Like an Elephant. Willey, Kira. 2019. (Mindfulness Moments for Kids Ser.). (ENG.). 26p. (J). (— 1). bds. 7.99 *(978-1-9848-9410-6(2)*, Rodale Kids) Random Hse. Children's Bks.

Betts, Jan Yalich. All about Children. Saul, Robert A. 2018. (ENG.). 34p. (J). pap. 12.95 *(978-0-692-15368-0(3))* Saul, Robert.

Betts, Louis. Swift Fawn the Little Foundling. Wade, Mary H. 2005. reprint ed. pap. 15.95 *(978-1-4179-1811-9(X))* Kessinger Publishing, LLC.

Betz, Katy. Grit & Grace, Vol. Rivadeneira, Caryn. 2017. (ENG.). 144p. (J). (gr. 4-6). pap. 9.99 *(978-1-5064-2495-8(3)*, Sparkhouse Family) Augsburg Fortress, Pubs.

—I Forgive You: Love We Can Hear, Ask for, & Give. Lataif, Nicole. 2014. (ENG.). 40p. (J). 10.95 *(978-0-8198-3726-4(1))* Pauline Bks. & Media.

Beus, Bryan. The Hunt for Dark Infinity. Dashner, James. 2009. (13th Reality Ser.: Bk. 2). 446p. (J). 18.95 *(978-1-60641-034-9(2)*, Shadow Mountain) Shadow Mountain Publishing.

—The Hunt for Dark Infinity. Dashner, James. 2010. (13th Reality Ser.: 2). (ENG.). 544p. (J). (gr. 3-7). pap. 9.99 *(978-1-4169-9153-3(0)*, Aladdin) Simon & Schuster Children's Publishing.

—The Journal of Curious Letters. Dashner, James. 2008. (13th Reality Ser.: Bk. 1). 434p. (J). (gr. 4-7). 17.95 *(978-1-59038-831-0(3)*, Shadow Mountain) Shadow Mountain Publishing.

—The Journal of Curious Letters. Dashner, James. 2009. (13th Reality Ser.: 1). (ENG.). 528p. (J). (gr. 3-7). pap. 9.99 *(978-1-4169-9152-6(2)*, Aladdin) Simon & Schuster Children's Publishing.

Beus, Bryan. Westly: A Spider's Tale. Beus, Bryan. 2015. (ENG.). 176p. (J). (gr. 4-6). 15.99 *(978-1-62972-068-5(2)*, Shadow Mountain) Shadow Mountain Publishing.

Bevan, Mandi. Perry Peanut Goes to the Seaside: The Adventures of Perry Peanut. Beal, Mandy. 2019. (ENG.). 24p. (J). pap. 12.45 *(978-1-9822-0969-8(0)*, Balboa Pr.) Author Solutions, Inc.

Bevans Marks And Barrow. Danny Kaye's Stories from Far Away Places. Kaye, Danny. 2011. 30p. 35.95 *(978-1-258-00232-9(9))* Literary Licensing, LLC.

Beveridge, Jim, photos by. Belize Living Alphabet. Beveridge, Dorothy. 2013. 38p. pap. *(978-976-8142-51-1(0))* Producciones de la Hamaca.

—Birding in Belize with Colours. Beveridge, Dorothy. 2013. 32p. pap. *(978-976-8142-55-9(3))* Producciones de la Hamaca.

—Counting Belize Frogs & Toads. Beveridge, Dorothy. 2012. 26p. pap. *(978-976-8142-47-4(2))* Producciones de la Hamaca.

Beverley, Virginia. The Criminal Life of Effie O. An Entertainment. Savage, Sam. 2005. 216p. (YA). per. 15.00 *(978-0-9719925-6-6(8))* Papas & Nellie Pr.

Bevilacqua, Carol. Animal Defenses. Hoyt, Richard, photos by. Echols, Jean C. 2003. (Great Explorations in Math & Science Ser.). 40p. (Orig.). (J). reprint ed. pap., tchr. ed. 9.00 *(978-0-924886-88-1(9)*, GEMS) Univ. of California, Berkeley, Lawrence Hall of Science.

Bevilacqua, Carol & Klofkorn, Lisa. Fingerprinting. Hoyt, Richard, photos by. Ahouse, Jeremy John & Barber, Jacqueline. 2006. (Great Explorations in Math & Science Ser.). 72p. (J). 10.50 *(978-1-931542-06-7(6)*, GEMS) Univ. of California, Berkeley, Lawrence Hall of Science.

—Of Cabbages & Chemistry. Hoyt, Richard, photos by. Barber, Jacqueline. Bergman Publishing Co. Staff & Fairwell, Kay, eds. rev. ed. 2003. (Great Explorations in Math & Science Ser.). 80p. (J). (gr. 4-8). pap., tchr. ed. 10.50 *(978-0-924886-28-7(5)*, GEMS) Univ. of California, Berkeley, Lawrence Hall of Science.

Bevilacqua, Silvana. Rosie's Dream Cape. Freedman, Zelda. 2005. (ENG.). 116p. (J). pap. 6.95 *(978-1-55380-025-5(7))* Ronsdale Pr. CAN. Dist: Literary Pr. Group of Canada.

Bevington, Nancy. Bruno Dreams of Ice Cream. Whitfield, Peter. 2005. 28p. (J). (gr. k-3). 15.95 *(978-1-894965-21-7(3))* Simply Read Bks. CAN. Dist: Ingram Publisher Services.

—Zen Tails No Presents Please. Whitfield, Peter. 2005. (ENG.). 28p. (J). (gr. -1-3). 15.95 *(978-1-894965-23-1(X))* Simply Read Bks. CAN. Dist: Ingram Publisher Services.

—Zen Tails up & Down. Whitfield, Peter. 2005. (ENG.). 28p. (J). (gr. -1-3). 15.95 *(978-1-894965-22-4(1))* Simply Read Bks. CAN. Dist: Ingram Publisher Services.

Bevis, Mary & Powell, Consie. Old Woman Winter. Bevis, Mary. 2010. 32p. (J). (gr. 1-2). 16.95 *(978-0-9819307-7-0(8))* Raven Productions, Inc.

Bevis, Vivian. Dream Helmet. New, William. 2005. (ENG.). 32p. (J). 11.95 *(978-1-55380-021-7(4))* Ronsdale Pr. CAN. Dist: Literary Pr. Group of Canada.

—Llamas in the Laundry. New, William. 2005. (ENG.). 32p. (J). 12.95 *(978-0-921870-97-5(3))* Ronsdale Pr. CAN. Dist: Literary Pr. Group of Canada.

Bewley, Kaye & Ĉernic, Adrijana. Ami in the Malverns: Swanny Pond. Bewley, Kaye. 2017. (Ami in the Malverns Ser.: Vol. 1). (ENG.). 50p. (J). pap. ***(978-1-909426-59-7(8))*** Bewley Bks.

Bey, Charles. Rhyming on Time. Mac, Cola. 2011. 20p. pap. 24.95 *(978-1-4560-6940-7(3))* America Star Bks.

Bey, Elihu "Adofo", jt. illus. see Kuumba, Mshindo.

Bey, Saleam. Muffy's First Day of School. McKay-Omar, Amabel. 2019. (ENG.). 48p. (J). pap. ***(978-1-5255-6215-0(0))***; ***(978-1-5255-6214-3(2))*** FriesenPress.

Beyer, David. The Crying Christmas Tree, 1 vol. Crow, Allan. 2015. (ENG.). 32p. (J). pap. 10.95 *(978-0-921827-13-9(X)*, eee32616-0b17-4cf7-9e42-ef24232cdcd4) Pemmican Pubns., Inc. CAN. Dist: Firefly Bks., Ltd.

Beyer, Ramsey. The Next Big Thing: A History of the Boom-Or-Bust Moments That Shaped the Modern World. Faulk, Richard. 2015. (ENG.). 224p. (YA). (gr. 9-12). pap. 12.99 *(978-1-936976-67-6(6)*, Zest Bks.) Lerner Publishing Group.

Beyl, Charles. Annie's Plan: Taking Charge of Schoolwork & Homework. Kraus, Jeanne R. 2006. 48p. (J). (gr. 2-5). 14.95 *(978-1-59147-481-4(7))*; pap. 9.95 *(978-1-59147-482-1(5))* American Psychological Assn. (Magination Pr.).

—Learning to Plan & Be Organized: Enhancing Executive Function Skills in Kids with AD/HD. Nadeau, Kathleen G. 2016. 128p. (J). pap. *(978-1-4338-2213-1(X)*, Magination Pr.) American Psychological Assn.

—Learning to Slow Down & Pay Attention: A Book for Kids about ADHD. Nadeau, Kathleen G. & Dixon, Ellen B. 3rd ed. 2004. 96p. (J). 14.95 *(978-1-59147-149-3(4))*; pap. 12.95 *(978-1-59147-155-4(9))* American Psychological Assn. (Magination Pr.).

—Mind over Basketball: Coach Yourself to Handle Stress. Weierbach, Jane & Phillips-Hershey, Elizabeth. 2007. (Coach Yourself to Handle Stress Ser.). 48p. (J). (gr. 3-7). 14.95 *(978-1-4338-0135-8(3)*, 4418006); per. 9.95 *(978-1-4338-0136-5(1)*, 4418007) American Psychological Assn. (Magination Pr.).

—My Parents Are Divorced Too: A Book for Kids by Kids. 2nd ed. 2006. 64p. (J). (gr. 3-7). 14.95 *(978-1-59147-241-4(5))*; per. 9.95 *(978-1-59147-242-1(3))* American Psychological Assn. (Magination Pr.).

Beyl, Charles. Scout the Mighty Tugboat. Beyl, Charles. 2020. (ENG.). 32p. (J). (gr. -1-3). 16.99 ***(978-0-8075-7264-1(0)***, 0807572640) Whitman, Albert & Co.

Beyruth, Danilo. Ghost Rider: Four on the Floor, Vol. 1. 2017. (ENG.). 144p. (YA). (gr. 8-17). pap. 15.99 *(978-0-7851-9664-8(1))* Marvel Worldwide, Inc.

—Man Without Fear: the Death of Daredevil. 2019. 112p. (YA). (gr. -1-17). pap. 15.99 *(978-1-302-91748-7(X))* Marvel Worldwide, Inc.

Beyruth, Danilo, jt. illus. see Coello, Iban.

Bezak, Klaudia. Ang Mananambal Nga Iring: Cebuano Edition of the Healer Cat. Pere, Tuula. Recina, Kris, tr. 2019. (CEB.). 40p. (J). (gr. k-4). ***(978-952-357-157-0(5))***; pap. ***(978-952-357-158-7(3))*** Wickwick oy.

—Ang Manggagamot Na Pusa: Tagalog Edition of the Healer Cat. Pere, Tuula. Azarcon, Raymond, tr. 2019. (TGL.). 40p. (J). (gr. k-4). ***(978-952-357-271-3(7))***; pap. ***(978-952-357-272-0(5))*** Wickwick oy.

—Arxa &#65533;zdəki Mətn: Azeri Edition of the Healer Cat. Pere, Tuula. Kərimov, Taleh, tr. 2019. (AZE.). 40p. (J). (gr. k-4). ***(978-952-325-039-0(6))*** Wickwick oy.

Bezak, Klaudia. Arxa üzdəki Mətn: Azeri Edition of the Healer Cat. Pere, Tuula. Kərimov, Taleh, tr. 2019. (AZE.). 40p. (J). (gr. k-4). pap. *(978-952-357-127-3(3))* Wickwick oy.

Bezak, Klaudia. Bisad Bogsan: Somali Edition of the Healer Cat. Pere, Tuula. Iman, Noor, tr. 2019. (SOM.). 40p. (J). (gr. k-4). ***(978-952-357-277-5(6))***; pap. ***(978-952-357-278-2(4))*** Wickwick oy.

—C&#65533; M&#65533;o Thần Y: Vietnamese Edition of the Healer Cat. Pere, Tuula. Dinh, Julie, tr. 2019. (VIE.). 40p. (J). (gr. k-4). ***(978-952-325-038-3(8))*** Wickwick oy.

—Chat Geris&#65533; A: Haitian Creole Edition of the Healer Cat. Pere, Tuula. Desir, Joel Thony, tr. 2019. (HAT.). 40p. (J). (gr. k-4). ***(978-952-357-217-1(2))***; pap. ***(978-952-357-218-8(0))*** Wickwick oy.

Bezak, Klaudia. Cô Mèo Thần Y: Vietnamese Edition of the Healer Cat. Pere, Tuula. Dinh, Julie, tr. 2019. (VIE.). 40p. (J). (gr. k-4). pap. *(978-952-357-144-0(3))* Wickwick oy.

—De Geneeskat: Dutch Edition of the Healer Cat. Pere, Tuula. Van Eekelen, Mariken, tr. 2019. (DUT.). 40p. (J). (gr. k-4). *(978-952-325-006-2(X))*; pap. *(978-952-357-092-4(7))* Wickwick oy.

—Den Helbredende Kat: Danish Edition of the Healer Cat. Pere, Tuula. Agerskov Christensen, Lisbeth, tr. 2019. (DAN.). 40p. (J). (gr. k-4). *(978-952-325-007-9(8))*; pap. *(978-952-357-093-1(5))* Wickwick oy.

—Die Geneser Kat: Afrikaans Edition of the Healer Cat. Pere, Tuula. Stols, Victor, tr. 2019. (AFR.). 40p. (J). (gr. k-4). *(978-952-357-099-3(4))*; pap. *(978-952-357-100-6(1))* Wickwick oy.

—Die Gesundmacherkatze: German Edition of the Healer Cat. Pere, Tuula. Wenzel, Werner, tr. 2019. (GER.). 40p. (J). (gr. k-4). *(978-952-325-001-7(9))*; pap. *(978-952-357-087-0(0))* Wickwick oy.

—Dziedējosā Kaķene: Latvian Edition of the Healer Cat. Pere, Tuula. Vernera, Justīne, tr. 2019. (LAV.). 40p. (J). (gr. k-4). pap. *(978-952-357-137-2(0))*; ***(978-952-325-009-3(4))*** Wickwick oy.

Bezak, Klaudia. Et Medicus Cattus: Latin Edition of the Healer Cat. Pere, Tuula. Udraoni, Rose, tr. 2019. (LAT.). 40p. (J). (gr. k-4). ***(978-952-357-187-7(7))***; pap. ***(978-952-357-188-4(5))*** Wickwick oy.

Bezak, Klaudia. A Gata Curadora: Galician Edition of the Healer Cat. Pere, Tuula. Guede, Damian, tr. 2019. (GLG.). 40p. (J). (gr. k-4). *(978-952-357-108-2(7))*; pap. *(978-952-357-109-9(5))* Wickwick oy.

—A Gata Que Curava: Portuguese Edition of the Healer Cat. Pere, Tuula. Jagnow, Dieter, tr. 2019. (POR.). 40p. (J). (gr. k-4). *(978-952-325-013-0(2))*; pap. *(978-952-357-095-5(1))* Wickwick oy.

—La Gata Sanadora: Catalan Edition of the Healer Cat. Pere, Tuula. Displas, Mireia, tr. 2019. (CAT.). 40p. (J). (gr. k-4). *(978-952-357-105-1(2))*; pap. *(978-952-357-106-8(0))* Wickwick oy.

—La Gata Sanadora: Spanish Edition of the Healer Cat. Pere, Tuula. Fuentes, María, tr. 2019. (SPA.). 40p. (J). (gr. k-4). *(978-952-325-003-1(5))*; pap. *(978-952-357-089-4(7))* Wickwick oy.

—Græðikisan: Icelandic Edition of the Healer Cat. Pere, Tuula. Baroason, Helgi Mar, tr. 2019. (ICE.). 40p. (J). (gr. k-4). *(978-952-357-117-4(6))*; pap. *(978-952-357-118-1(4))* Wickwick oy.

Bezak, Klaudia. A Gy&#65533;gy&#65533;t&#65533; Macska: Hungarian Edition of the Healer Cat. Pere, Tuula. Czuczor, Tamas, tr. 2019. (HUN.). 40p. (J). (gr. k-4). ***(978-952-357-114-3(1))*** Wickwick oy.

Bezak, Klaudia. A Gyógyító Macska: Hungarian Edition of the Healer Cat. Pere, Tuula. Czuczor, Tamas, tr. 2019. (HUN.). 40p. (J). (gr. k-4). pap. *(978-952-357-115-0(X))* Wickwick oy.

Bezak, Klaudia. Hadurree Fayyistuu: Oromo Edition of the Healer Cat. Pere, Tuula. Fayyistuu, Hadurree, tr. 2019. (ORM.). 40p. (J). (gr. k-4). ***(978-952-357-229-4(6))***; pap. ***(978-952-357-230-0(X))*** Wickwick oy.

Bezak, Klaudia. The Healer Cat. Pere, Tuula. Korman, Susan, ed. 2018. (ENG.). 40p. (J). (gr. k-4). pap. *(978-952-7107-57-7(1))* Wickwick oy.

—The Healer Cat: Greek Edition of the Healer Cat. Pere, Tuula. Papakosta, Irene, tr. 2018. (GRE.). 40p. (J). (gr. k-4). pap. *(978-952-7107-81-2(4))* Wickwick oy.

Bezak, Klaudia. The Healer Cat (Oriya) Oriya Edition of the Healer Cat. Pere, Tuula. Mahapatro, Gouri Sankar, tr. 2019. (ORI.). 40p. (J). (gr. k-4). ***(978-952-357-280-5(6))***; pap. ***(978-952-357-281-2(4))*** Wickwick oy.

—The Healer Cat (Sinhala) Sinhala Edition of the Healer Cat. Pere, Tuula. Jayasinghe, L. Sankha, ed. 2019. (SIN.). 40p. (J). (gr. k-4). ***(978-952-357-283-6(0))***; pap. ***(978-952-357-284-3(9))*** Wickwick oy.

Bezak, Klaudia. Helbrederkatten Heka: Norwegian Edition of the Healer Cat. Pere, Tuula. Dore, Lisbeth, tr. 2019. (NOR.). 40p. (J). (gr. k-4). *(978-952-325-008-6(6))*; pap. *(978-952-357-094-8(3))* Wickwick oy.

—I Gcás Cneisil Cit: Irish Edition of the Healer Cat. Pere, Tuula. Stanler, Marina, tr. 2019. (GLE.). 40p. (J). (gr. k-4). *(978-952-357-145-7(1))*; pap. *(978-952-357-146-4(X))* Wickwick oy.

Bezak, Klaudia. IKati Eyayinothando: Xhosa Edition of the Healer Cat. Pere, Tuula. Matyobeni, Sindiswa Gloria, tr. 2019. (XHO.). 40p. (J). (gr. k-4). pap. ***(978-952-357-248-5(2))*** Wickwick oy.

—IKati Eyayinothando: XhosaEdition of the Healer Cat. Pere, Tuula. Matyobeni, Sindiswa Gloria, tr. 2019. (XHO.). 40p. (J). (gr. k-4). ***(978-952-357-247-8(4))*** Wickwick oy.

—Ilay Saka Mpanasitrana: Malagasy Edition of the Healer Cat. Pere, Tuula. Ralaivao, Zafimamy Gabriella, tr. 2019. (MLG.). 40p. (J). (gr. k-4). ***(978-952-357-193-8(1))***; pap. ***(978-952-357-194-5(X))*** Wickwick oy.

Bezak, Klaudia. Kate Gydytoja: Lithuanian Edition of the Healer Cat. Pere, Tuula. Bučys, Vaidas, tr. 2019. (LIT.). 40p. (J). (gr. k-4). pap. *(978-952-357-138-9(9))*; ***(978-952-325-010-9(8))*** Wickwick oy.

—Katten Gottis: Swedish Edition of the Healer Cat. Pere, Tuula. Nikolowski-Bogomoloff, Angelika, tr. 2018. (SWE.). 40p. (J). (gr. k-4). pap. *(978-952-7107-59-1(8))* Wickwick oy.

—Katu Sendatzailea: Basque Edition of the Healer Cat. Pere, Tuula. Ibarra, Galder, tr. 2019. (BAQ.). 40p. (J). (gr. k-4). *(978-952-357-148-8(6))*; pap. *(978-952-357-149-5(4))* Wickwick oy.

Bezak, Klaudia. Kočka L&#65533;čitelka: Czech Edition of the Healer Cat. Pere, Tuula. Cap, Michal, tr. 2019. (CZE.). 40p. (J). (gr. k-4). ***(978-952-325-011-6(6))*** Wickwick oy.

Bezak, Klaudia. Kočka Léčitelka: Czech Edition of the Healer Cat. Pere, Tuula. Cap, Michal, tr. 2019. (CZE.). 40p. (J). (gr. k-4). pap. *(978-952-357-132-7(X))* Wickwick oy.

—Kotka Uzdrowicielka: Polish Edition of the Healer Cat. Pere, Tuula. Podstawsk, Bożena, tr. 2019. (POL.). 40p. (J). (gr. k-4). *(978-952-325-012-3(4))*; pap. *(978-952-357-139-6(7))* Wickwick oy.

Bezak, Klaudia. Kucing Penyembuh Ajaib: Malay Edition of the Healer Cat. Pere, Tuula. 2019. (MAY.). 40p. (J). (gr. k-4). ***(978-952-357-196-9(6))***; pap. ***(978-952-357-197-6(4))*** Wickwick oy.

Bezak, Klaudia. Kucing Tukang Tamba: Javanese Edition of the Healer Cat. Pere, Tuula. Anggarini, Dyah D., tr. 2019. (JAV.). 40p. (J). (gr. k-4). *(978-952-325-029-1(9))*; pap. *(978-952-357-135-8(4))* Wickwick oy.

Bezak, Klaudia. La Kuracanto Kato: Esperanto Edition of the Healer Cat. Pere, Tuula. Kiyani, Usman, tr. 2019. (EPO.). 40p. (J). (gr. k-4). ***(978-952-357-169-3(9))***; pap. ***(978-952-357-170-9(2))*** Wickwick oy.

Bezak, Klaudia. Labarin Magen Waraka: Hausa Edition of the Healer Cat. Pere, Tuula. Abubakar, Mansur, tr. 2019. (HAU.). 40p. (J). (gr. k-4). *(978-952-357-111-2(7))*; pap. *(978-952-357-112-9(5))* Wickwick oy.

Bezak, Klaudia. Lub Kho Neeg Lub Siab Miv: Hmong Edition of the Healer Cat. Pere, Tuula. Eldorka, Thainas, tr. 2019. (SIT.). 40p. (J). (gr. k-4). ***(978-952-357-172-3(9))***; pap. ***(978-952-357-173-0(7))*** Wickwick oy.

Bezak, Klaudia. Mačka Vidarka: Serbian Edition of the Healer Cat. Pere, Tuula. 2019. (SRP.). 40p. (J). (gr. k-4). pap. *(978-952-357-141-9(9))*; ***(978-952-325-021-5(3))*** Wickwick oy.

Bezak, Klaudia. Mačka Zdravilka: Slovenian Edition of the Healer Cat. Pere, Tuula. VIDIC, Bostjan, tr. 2019. (SLV.). 40p. (J). (gr. k-4). ***(978-952-357-238-6(5))***; pap. ***(978-952-357-239-3(3))*** Wickwick oy.

Bezak, Klaudia. Maca Iscjeliteljka: Bosnian Edition of the Healer Cat. Pere, Tuula. Karamustafic, Irma, tr. 2019. (BOS.). 40p. (J). (gr. k-4). *(978-952-325-015-4(9))*; pap. *(978-952-357-128-0(1))* Wickwick oy.

—Maca Iscjeljiteljka: Croatian Edition of the Healer Cat. Pere, Tuula. Karamustafic, Irma, tr. 2019. (HRV.). 40p. (J). (gr. k-4). *(978-952-325-016-1(7))*; pap. *(978-952-357-131-0(1))* Wickwick oy.

Bezak, Klaudia. Macja Sh&#65533;ruese: Albanian Edition of the Healer Cat. Pere, Tuula. Tagani, Iliriana Bisha, tr. 2019. (ALB.). 40p. (J). (gr. k-4). ***(978-952-325-059-8(0))*** Wickwick oy.

Bezak, Klaudia. Macja Shëruese: Albanian Edition of the Healer Cat. Pere, Tuula. Tagani, Iliriana Bisha, tr. 2019. (ALB.). 40p. (J). (gr. k-4). pap. *(978-952-357-126-6(5))* Wickwick oy.

Bezak, Klaudia. Mphaka Wamphamvu Zochiritsa: Chicheva Edition of the Healer Cat. Pere, Tuula. Symon Simbotah, Symon, tr. 2019. (NYA.). 40p. (J). (gr. k-4). ***(978-952-357-160-0(5))*** Wickwick oy.

—Mphaka Wamphamvu Zochiritsa: Chicheva Edition of the Healer Cat. Pere, Tuula. Simbotah, Symon, tr. 2019. (NYA.). 40p. (J). (gr. k-4). pap. ***(978-952-357-161-7(3))*** Wickwick oy.

—Nwa Mba Ogworia: Igbo Edition of the Healer Cat. Pere, Tuula. Nwakpu, Ikechukwu John, tr. 2019. (IBO.). 40p. (J). (gr. k-4). ***(978-952-357-211-9(3))***; pap. ***(978-952-357-212-6(1))*** Wickwick oy.

—Ológbò Olùwòsàn Náà Yor&#65533;b&#65533; Edition of the Healer Cat. Pere, Tuula. Agboọla ́, Ṣọlá, tr. 2019. (YOR.). 40p. (J). (gr. k-4). ***(978-952-357-123-5(0))*** Wickwick oy.

Bezak, Klaudia. Ológbò Olùwòsàn Náà Yorùbá Edition of the Healer Cat. Pere, Tuula. Agboọla ́, Ṣọlá, tr. 2019. (YOR.). 40p. (J). (gr. k-4). pap. *(978-952-357-124-2(9))* Wickwick oy.

Bezak, Klaudia. Paka Tabibu: Swahili Edition of the Healer Cat. Pere, Tuula. Njogu, Alphan, tr. 2019. (SWA.). 40p. (J). (gr. k-4). ***(978-952-357-241-6(5))***; pap. ***(978-952-357-242-3(3))*** Wickwick oy.

Bezak, Klaudia. Parantajakissa: Finnish Edition of the Healer Cat. Pere, Tuula. 2018. (FIN.). 40p. (J). (gr. k-4). pap. *(978-952-7107-58-4(X))* Wickwick oy.

—Pisica Tămăduitoare: Romanian Edition of the Healer Cat. Pere, Tuula. Hubati, Laura, tr. 2019. (RUM.). 40p. (J). (gr. k-4). pap. *(978-952-357-140-2(0))*; ***(978-952-325-014-7(0))*** Wickwick oy.

—Les Pouvoirs de Céleste le Chat: French Edition of the Healer Cat. Pere, Tuula. Gozen, Natacha, tr. 2019. (FRE.). 40p. (J). (gr. k-4). *(978-952-325-004-8(3))*; pap. *(978-952-357-090-0(0))* Wickwick oy.

—Sang Kucing Penyembuh: Indonesian Edition of the Healer Cat. Pere, Tuula. Anggarini, Dyah D., tr. 2019. (IND.). 40p. (J). (gr. k-4). *(978-952-325-025-3(6))*; pap. *(978-952-357-133-4(8))* Wickwick oy.

—Seren y Gath Hud: Welsh Edition of the Healer Cat. Pere, Tuula. Robinson, Evic, tr. 2019. (WEL.). 40p. (J). (gr. k-4). *(978-952-357-120-4(6))*; pap. *(978-952-357-121-1(4))* Wickwick oy.

—Tabib Mushuk: Uzbek Edition of the Healer Cat. Pere, Tuula. Xushvaqov, Akmal, tr. 2019. (UZB.). 40p. (J). (gr. k-4). *(978-952-357-151-8(6))*; pap. *(978-952-357-152-5(4))* Wickwick oy.

—Tebip Pişik: Turkmen Edition of the Healer Cat. Pere, Tuula. Kos, Jahan, tr. 2019. (TUK.). 40p. (J). (gr. k-4). *(978-952-357-154-9(0))*; pap. *(978-952-357-155-6(9))* Wickwick oy.

—Tervendaja Kass: Estonian Edition of the Healer Cat. Pere, Tuula. Laansoo-Hamarik, Helen, tr. 2019. (EST.). 40p. (J). (gr. k-4). *(978-952-325-005-5(1))*; pap. *(978-952-357-091-7(9))* Wickwick oy.

Bezak, Klaudia. The Umelaphi Ikati: Zulu Edition of the Healer Cat. Pere, Tuula. Ibilibo, Maybelle, tr. 2019. (ZUL.). 40p. (J). (gr. k-4). ***(978-952-357-214-0(8))***; pap. ***(978-952-357-215-7(6))*** Wickwick oy.

—Şifacı Kedi: Turkish Edition of the Healer Cat. Pere, Tuula. Ayan, Nesli, tr. 2019. (TUR.). 40p. (J). (gr. k-4). ***(978-952-325-020-8(5))***; pap. ***(978-952-357-142-6(7))*** Wickwick oy.

—ΗΓάτα-Θεραπεύτρια Greek Edition of the Healer Cat. Pere, Tuula. Papakosta, Irene, tr. 2018. (GRE.). 40p. (J). (gr. k-4). ***(978-952-7107-82-9(2))*** Wickwick oy.

—Айыктырумышык Kyrgyz Edition of the Healer Cat. Pere, Tuula. Anarkulov, Nazgul, tr. 2019. (KIR.). 40p. (J). (gr. k-4). ***(978-952-357-184-6(2))***; pap. ***(978-952-357-185-3(0))*** Wickwick oy.

—Дәвачыпеси Tatar Edition of the Healer Cat. Pere, Tuula. Zakiyev, Ilgizar, tr. 2019. (TAT.). 40p. (J). (gr. k-4). ***(978-952-357-244-7(X))***; pap. ***(978-952-357-245-4(8))*** Wickwick oy.

—Д&#65533;сныг&#65533;ды Ossetian Edition of the Healer Cat. Pere, Tuula. Kokaytı, Fatimae, tr. 2019. (OSS.). 40p. (J). (gr. k-4). ***(978-952-357-205-8(9))***; pap. ***(978-952-357-206-5(7))*** Wickwick oy.

—Емшімысық Kazakh Edition of the Healer Cat. Pere, Tuula. Kusmanova, Assel, tr. 2019. (KAZ.). 40p. (J). (gr. k-4). ***(978-952-357-181-5(8))***; pap. ***(978-952-357-182-2(6))*** Wickwick oy.

Bezak, Klaudia. КОТКАТАЛЕЧИТЕЛК Bulgarian Edition of the Healer Cat. Pere, Tuula. Santana, Pavlina, tr. 2019. (BUL.). 40p. (J). (gr. k-4). *(978-952-325-051-2(5))*; pap. ***(978-952-357-129-7(X))*** Wickwick oy.

B

Bezak, Klaudia. Кошка-лекарка Belarusian Edition of the Healer Cat. Pere, Tuula. Akishyna, Diana, tr. 2019. (RUS.). 40p. (J). (gr. k-4). ***(978-952-357-253-9(9))***; pap. ***(978-952-357-254-6(7))*** Wickwick oy.

Bezak, Klaudia. Кошка-целитель; Russian Edition of the Healer Cat. Pere, Tuula. Chernikova, Yulia, tr. 2018. (RUS.). 40p. (J). (gr. k-4). pap. *(978-952-7107-83-6(0))* Wickwick oy.

Bezak, Klaudia. Кошка-целительница Russian Edition of the Healer Cat. Pere, Tuula. Chernikova, Yulia, tr. 2018. (RUS.). 40p. (J). (gr. k-4). ***(978-952-7107-84-3(9))*** Wickwick oy.

Bezak, Klaudia. Кішка-цілитель; Ukrainian Edition of the Healer Cat. Pere, Tuula. Lutska, Yulia, tr. 2019. (UKR.). 40p. (J). (gr. k-4). *(978-952-325-026-0(4))*; pap. *(978-952-357-143-3(5))* Wickwick oy.

Bezak, Klaudia. Мачката; Исцелите; Macedonian Edition of the Healer Cat. Pere, Tuula. Markovska, Martina, tr. 2019. (MAC.). 40p. (J). (gr. k-4). ***(978-952-357-190-7(7))***; pap. ***(978-952-357-191-4(5))*** Wickwick oy.

—Циск -дарбанхо; Ingush Edition of the Healer Cat. Pere, Tuula. Zarema, Hanieva, tr. 2019. (INH.). 40p. (J). (gr. k-4). ***(978-952-357-175-4(3))***; pap. ***(978-952-357-176-1(1))*** Wickwick oy.

—Цициг-дарбанча; Селена; Chechen Edition of the Healer Cat. Pere, Tuula. Akhmadov, Lida, tr. 2019. (CHE.). 40p. (J). (gr. k-4). ***(978-952-357-256-0(3))***; pap. ***(978-952-357-257-7(1))*** Wickwick oy.

—Բուժող; Կատուն; Armenian Edition of the Healer Cat. Pere, Tuula. Baghdasaryan, Lilith, tr. 2019. (ARM.). 40p. (J). (gr. k-4). ***(978-952-357-102-0(8))***; pap. ***(978-952-357-103-7(6))*** Wickwick oy.

—चमत्कारी; बिलैया; Bhojpuri Edition of the Healer Cat. Pere, Tuula. Khan, Roohi, tr. 2019. (BHO.). 40p. (J). (gr. k-4). ***(978-952-357-268-3(7))***; pap. ***(978-952-357-269-0(5))*** Wickwick oy.

—बिरामीला; निको; पार्ने; बिराली; Nepalese Edition of the Healer Cat. Pere, Tuula. Ghimire, Sandeep, tr. 2019. (NEP.). 40p. (J). (gr. k-4). ***(978-952-357-202-7(4))***; pap. ***(978-952-357-203-4(2))*** Wickwick oy.

—रोग; बराकरणारे; मांजर; Marathi Edition of the Healer Cat. Pere, Tuula. Desouza, Evelyn, tr. 2019. (MAR.). 40p. (J). (gr. k-4). ***(978-952-357-265-2(2))***; pap. ***(978-952-357-266-9(0))*** Wickwick oy.

—रोगहरबिल्ली; Hindi Edition of the Healer Cat. Pere, Tuula. Khan, Roohi, tr. 2019. (HIN.). 40p. (J). (gr. k-4). ***(978-952-357-220-1(2))***; pap. ***(978-952-357-221-8(0))*** Wickwick oy.

—আৰোগ্যকা; মেকুৰীটো; Assamese Edition of the Healer Cat. Pere, Tuula. Assam, Biki, tr. 2019. (ASM.). 40p. (J). (gr. k-4). ***(978-952-357-163-1(X))***; pap. ***(978-952-357-164-8(8))*** Wickwick oy.

—রোগ; উপশমকারী; বিড়াল; Bengali Edition of the Healer Cat. Pere, Tuula. Hossain, Masud, tr. 2019. (BEN.). 40p. (J). (gr. k-4). ***(978-952-357-166-2(4))***; pap. ***(978-952-357-167-9(2))*** Wickwick oy.

—ਰੋਗ; ਦੂਰ; ਕਰਨ; ਵਾਲੀ; ਬਿੱਲੀ; Punjabi Edition of the Healer Cat. Pere, Tuula. Khan, Abid, tr. 2019. (PAN.). 40p. (J). (gr. k-4). ***(978-952-357-232-4(6))***; pap. ***(978-952-357-233-1(4))*** Wickwick oy.

—ધ હિલર; કેટ; Gujarati Edition of the Healer Cat. Pere, Tuula. Prajapati, Hardik, ed. 2019. (GUJ.). 40p. (J). (gr. k-4). ***(978-952-357-259-1(8))***; pap. ***(978-952-357-260-7(1))*** Wickwick oy.

—குணப்படு பூனை Tamil Edition of the Healer Cat. Pere, Tuula. Chokkanathan, Naga, tr. 2019. (TAM.). 40p. (J). (gr. k-4). ***(978-952-357-250-8(4))***; pap. ***(978-952-357-251-5(2))*** Wickwick oy.

—దివ్య; మార్జాలం Telugu Edition of the Healer Cat. Pere, Tuula. Rao, N. Rajasekhar, tr. 2019. (TEL.). 40p. (J). (gr. k-4). ***(978-952-357-235-5(0))***; pap. ***(978-952-357-236-2(9))*** Wickwick oy.

—ವೈದ್ಯ; ಬೆಕ್ಕು Kannada Edition of the Healer Cat. Pere, Tuula. Kattakkal, Tomsan, tr. 2019. (KAN.). 40p. (J). (gr. k-4). ***(978-952-357-178-5(8))***; pap. ***(978-952-357-179-2(6))*** Wickwick oy.

—വൈദ്യത്ത! Malayalam Edition of the Healer Cat. Pere, Tuula. Kattakkal, Tomsan, tr. 2019. (MAL.). 40p. (J). (gr. k-4). ***(978-952-357-199-0(0))***; pap. ***(978-952-357-200-3(8))*** Wickwick oy.

—แมวผู้เย$ Thai Edition of the Healer Cat. Pere, Tuula. Phan Ngoen, Suwattana, tr. 2019. (THA.). 40p. (J). (gr. k-4). ***(978-952-357-208-9(3))***; pap. ***(978-952-357-209-6(1))*** Wickwick oy.

—ການ; ມັດ້າຣະ; ການປິ່ນປ% Lao Edition of the Healer Cat. Pere, Tuula. Markozi, Peter, tr. 2019. (LAO.). 40p. (J). (gr. k-4). ***(978-952-357-226-3(1))***; pap. ***(978-952-357-227-0(X))*** Wickwick oy.

Bezak, Klaudia. მკურნალი კატა Georgian Edition of the Healer Cat. Pere, Tuula. Patarava, Tamar, tr. 2019. (GEO.). 40p. (J). (gr. k-4). *(978-952-325-444-2(8))*; pap. *(978-952-357-098-6(6))* Wickwick oy.

—እታ; እትፍውስ; ድሙ Tigrinya Edition of the Healer Cat. Pere, Tuula. 2019. (TIR.). 40p. (J). (gr. k-4). *(978-952-325-443-5(X))*; pap. *(978-952-357-097-9(8))* Wickwick oy.

—ፈዋሿ ድመት Amharic Edition of the Healer Cat. Pere, Tuula. 2019. (AMH.). 40p. (J). (gr. k-4). *(978-952-325-429-9(4))*; pap. *(978-952-357-096-2(X))* Wickwick oy.

Bezak, Klaudia. សត្វឆ្មា<D Khmer Edition of the Healer Cat. Pere, Tuula. Hoeun, So, tr. 2019. (CAM.). 40p. (J). ***(978-952-357-223-2(7))***; pap. ***(978-952-357-224-9(5))*** Wickwick oy.

Bezak, Klaudia. いやしねこ Japanese Edition of the Healer Cat. Pere, Tuula. Kodaira, Kaori, tr. 2019. (JPN.). 40p. (J). (gr. k-4). *(978-952-325-043-7(4))*; pap. *(978-952-357-134-1(6))* Wickwick oy.

—会治病的猫 Chinese Edition of the Healer Cat. Pere, Tuula. Sun, Wei, tr. 2019. (CHI.). 40p. (J). (gr. k-4). *(978-952-325-044-4(2))*; pap. *(978-952-357-130-3(3))* Wickwick oy.

Bezak, Klaudia. 약손 고양이 Korean Edition of the Healer Cat. Pere, Tuula. Lee, Myoungsang, tr. 2019. (KOR.). 40p. (J). (gr. k-4). ***(978-952-325-042-0(6))***; pap. ***(978-952-357-136-5(2))*** Wickwick oy.

Bezesky, Tracy. David's Journey: The Story of David Jal, One of the Lost Boys of Sudan. Jal, David & Jacobs, Laura K. 2012. (ENG.). 32p. 20.00 *(978-1-934478-30-1(X))* Sunray Publishing.

Bhabha, Shiraaz. The Closet Ghosts. Bhabha, Shiraaz. Krishnaswami, Uma. 2013. (ENG.). 32p. (J). (gr. 2). 16.95 *(978-0-89239-208-7(8))* Lee & Low Bks., Inc.

Bhachu, Verinder. The Usborne Science Encyclopedia: Internet-Linked. Rogers, Kirsteen et al. 2009. (Usborne Internet-Linked Encyclopedia Ser.). 448p. (J). (gr. 4-7). 19.99 *(978-0-7945-2629-0(2),* Usborne) EDC Publishing.

Bhachu, Verindr. Science Encyclopedia. Wilkes, Angela. 2009. (Library of Science Ser Ser.). 448p. (J). 39.99 *(978-0-7945-2527-9(X),* Usborne) EDC Publishing.

Bhargav, Manoj. The Adventures of Caroline: And the Emerald Dragon. Oberst, Eric R. 2018. (Adventures of Caroline Ser.: Vol. 2). (ENG.). 156p. (J). (gr. 4-6). 24.99 *(978-0-692-16754-0(4))* Painted Leaf Publishing.

Bhargav, Manoj. Las Aventuras de Carolina: Y el Drag�n Esmeralda. Oberst, Elena Kristin. Arguindegui, Lucia, tr. 2019. (Las Aventuras de Carolina Ser.: Vol. 2). (SPA.). 216p. (J). pap. 8.99 ***(978-1-0726-5972-3(7))*** Independently Published.

Bhargava, Neirah & Dave, Vijay, photos by. What You Will See Inside a Hindu Temple. Jani, Vandana & Jani, Mehendra. 2005. (What You Will See Inside ... Ser.). (ENG., 32p. (J). (gr. 3-7). 17.99 *(978-1-59473-116-7(0),* 08eb9a41-a019-4d4a-a3a6-430015c2e2c1, Skylight Paths Publishing) LongHill Partners, Inc.

Bhatnagar, Gaurav. I Want to Be Like: A Story of Family Love. Houston, Skyler. 2019. (ENG.). 20p. (J). (gr. k-4). pap. 10.00 ***(978-0-578-55574-4(3))*** Houston, Skyler.

Bhatnagar, Gaurav. Super Duper Darien! Inspired by the Imagination of Darien X. Perkins. Perkins, Darien Xavier & Perkins III M Ed, Howard Carroll. 2019. (Super Super Darien Ser.: Vol. 1). (ENG.). 26p. (J). pap. 15.00 *(978-1-7976-6635-8(5))* Independently Published.

Bhend, Käthi. Henrietta & the Golden Eggs. Johansen, Hanna. Barrett, John S., tr. 2004. (ENG.). 64p. (J). pap. 9.95 *(978-1-56792-288-2(0))* Godine, David R. Pub.

Bhowmick, Avijit. What's That Weed? Hudson, Russ. 2017. (ENG.). (J). (gr. k-6). 25.00 *(978-0-692-96385-2(5))* Hudson, Russ.

Bhuiyan, Julia. Mickey the Monarch. Sommers, Audrey. Mattie, Dugan, ed. 2013. 42p. pap. 14.95 *(978-0-9851996-2-3(8))* HMSI, Inc.

Bhushan, Rahul. Taj Mahal. Arnold, Caroline & Comora, Madeleine. 2007. (ENG.). 32p. (J). (gr. k-12). lib. bdg. 17.95 *(978-0-7613-2609-0(X),* Millbrook Pr.) Lerner Publishing Group.

Bia, Elena. Greyfriars Bobby: a Puppy's Tale, 30 vols. Sloan, Michelle. 2019. (Traditional Scottish Tales Ser.). (ENG.). 32p. (J). 11.95 *(978-1-78250-590-7(3),* Kelpies) Floris Bks. GBR. Dist: Consortium Bk. Sales & Distribution.

Biagiotti, Aldo, photos by. Escape from Death Valley: A Tale of Two Burros. Biagiotti, Aldo. 2003. (Books for Young Learners). (ENG., 16p. (J). 5.75 net. *(978-1-57274-661-9(0),* 2737, Bks. for Young Learners) Owen, Richard C. Pubs., Inc.

Bialk, Andy. Break Out! 2017. 32p. (J). *(978-1-5182-4734-7(2),* Simon Spotlight) Simon Spotlight.

Bianca & Annie West. Dogs Don't Wear Underwear. Carmen & Thane Johnson. 2009. 20p. pap. 12.99 *(978-1-4389-4128-8(5))* AuthorHouse.

Bianchi, Ana. The Sailor Who Loved to Draw. Bianchi, Ms. 2018. (ENG.). 32p. (J). (gr. -1-8). 15.95 *(978-1-58423-711-2(2),* aa39c005-d909-4f65-825b-bd674742aeea, Gingko Pr.) Gingko Pr., Inc.

Bianchi, Fausto. The Battle of Kupe & Te Wheke: a Maori Tale: Band 13/Topaz (Collins Big Cat) Agnew, Leoni. 2016. (Collins Big Cat Ser.). (ENG.). 32p. (J). (gr. 2-3). pap. 9.99 *(978-0-00-814716-7(7))* HarperCollins Pubs. Ltd. GBR. Dist: Independent Pubs. Group.

—The Story for Children, 1 vol. Lucado, Max et al. 2011. (Story Ser.). (ENG.). 288p. (J). (gr. -1-3). 19.99 *(978-0-310-71975-5(5))* Zonderkidz.

—The Story for Children: A Storybook Bible. Lucado, Max et al. 2011. 287p. (J). *(978-0-310-73211-2(5))* Zonderkidz.

Bianchi, John. ¡Arriba! Pitt, Marilyn & Sánchez, Lucía M. 2010. (1G Libros Papas Fritas Ser.).Tr. of Get Up. (SPA & ENG.). 12p. (J). (gr. k-1). pap. 8.00 *(978-1-61541-084-2(8))* American Reading Co.

—Bear Gets a Hat. 2017. (Bird, Bunny, & Bear Ser.). (ENG.). 12p. (J). pap. 9.60 *(978-1-61406-305-6(2))* American Reading Co.

—Come with Me. Hileman, Jane & Pitt, Marilyn. (1G Potato Chip Bks.). 12p. (gr. k-1). 2016. (ENG.). (J). pap. 8.00 *(978-1-61541-162-7(3))*; 2011. pap. 33.92 *(978-1-61541-163-4(1))* American Reading Co.

—Dinosaur Party. Rieger, Linda. 2007. 20p. (J). *(978-0-9779427-2-5(4))* Pathways into Science.

—Flying Animals. Rieger, Linda. ed. 2006. 20p. (J). *(978-0-9779427-1-8(6))* Pathways into Science.

—Home Alone. Hileman, Jane & Pitt, Marilyn. (Power 50 - Potato Chip Bks). 12p. 2011. pap. 33.92 *(978-1-61541-408-6(8))*; 2010. (ENG.). (J). pap. 9.60 *(978-1-61541-407-9(X))* American Reading Co.

—How Are We Alike? Rieger, Linda. ed. 2006. 20p. (J). *(978-0-9779427-0-1(8))* Pathways into Science.

—I Like My Stuff. Pitt, Marilyn & Hileman, Jane. 2013. (1G Potato Chip Bks.). (ENG.). 12p. (J). (gr. k-1). pap. 8.00 *(978-1-59301-769-9(3))* American Reading Co.

—I Love to Sleep. Hileman, Jane & Pitt, Marilyn. 2013. (1G Potato Chip Bks.). (ENG.). 12p. (J). (gr. k-1). pap. 8.00 *(978-1-59301-797-2(9))* American Reading Co.

—I Want a Dog. Hileman, Jane & Pitt, Marilyn. 2013. (1G Potato Chip Bks.). (ENG.). 12p. (J). (gr. k-1). pap. 8.00 *(978-1-59301-768-2(5))* American Reading Co.

—Let Me In. Pitt, Marilyn & Hileman, Jane. 2016. (1G Potato Chip Bks.). (ENG.). 12p. (J). (gr. k-1). pap. 8.00 *(978-1-61541-168-9(2))* American Reading Co.

—Let Me In. Hileman, Jane & Pitt, Marilyn. 2011. (Power 50 - Potato Chip Bks). 12p. pap. 33.92 *(978-1-61541-169-6(0))* American Reading Co.

—My Babies. Pitt, Marilyn & Hileman, Jane. 2016. (1G Potato Chip Bks.). (ENG.). 12p. (J). (gr. k-1). pap. 8.00 *(978-1-61541-065-1(1))* American Reading Co.

—La Nevada: Snow Dog. Pitt, Marilyn & Sanchez, Lucia M. 2011. (poder de 50 - Libros papas fritas Ser.). (SPA.). 12p. pap. 33.92 *(978-1-61541-439-0(8))* American Reading Co.

—Perro en Apuros: Let Me In. Pitt, Marilyn & Sanchez, Lucia M. 2011. (poder de 50 - Libros papas fritas Ser.). (SPA.). 12p. pap. 33.92 *(978-1-61541-165-8(8))* American Reading Co.

—Pretty Cat. Pitt, Marilyn & Hileman, Jane. 2017. (1G Potato Chip Bks.). (ENG.). 12p. (J). (gr. k-1). pap. 8.00 *(978-1-61541-067-5(8))* American Reading Co.

—Smelling Good. Pitt, Marilyn. 2016. (1B Potato Chip Bks.). (ENG.). 16p. (J). pap. 8.00 *(978-1-61406-685-9(X))* American Reading Co.

—Snow Dog. Hileman, Jane & Pitt, Marilyn. (1G Potato Chip Bks.). 12p. (gr. k-1). 2014. (ENG.). (J). pap. 9.60 *(978-1-61541-297-6(2))*; 2011. pap. 33.92 *(978-1-61541-298-3(0))* American Reading Co.

—Solos en Casa. Pitt, Marilyn & Sánchez, Lucía M. 2010. (1G Libros Papas Fritas Ser.).Tr. of Home Alone. (SPA.). 12p. (J). (gr. k-1). pap. 9.60 *(978-1-61541-409-3(6))* American Reading Co.

—Start the Clean Up. Rieger, Linda. 2008. 20p. (J). *(978-0-9779427-5-6(9))* Pathways into Science.

—The Storm. Pitt, Marilyn & Hileman, Jane. 2017. (1G Potato Chip Bks.). (ENG.). 12p. (J). (gr. k-1). pap. 9.60 *(978-1-61541-232-7(8))* American Reading Co.

—The Storm. Hileman, Jane & Pitt, Marilyn. 2011. (Power 50 - Potato Chip Bks). 12p. pap. 33.92 *(978-1-61541-233-4(6))* American Reading Co.

—Time for a Bath. Hileman, Jane & Pitt, Marilyn. 2013. (1G Potato Chip Bks.). (ENG.). 12p. (J). (gr. k-1). pap. 8.00 *(978-1-59301-772-9(3))* American Reading Co.

—La Tormenta: The Storm. Pitt, Marilyn & Sanchez, Lucia M. 2011. (poder de 50 - Libros papas fritas Ser.). (SPA.). 12p. pap. 33.92 *(978-1-61541-441-3(X))* American Reading Co.

—Up Here. Pitt, Marilyn & Hileman, Jane. 2016. (1G Potato Chip Bks.). (ENG.). 12p. (J). (gr. k-1). pap. 8.00 *(978-1-61541-015-6(5))* American Reading Co.

—Water in Our House. Rieger, Linda. 2008. 20p. (J). *(978-0-9779427-6-3(7))* Pathways into Science.

—Water Party. Rieger, Linda. 2008. 20p. (J). *(978-0-9779427-3-2(2))* Pathways into Science.

—Where Is Here? 2016. (1G Bird, Bunny, & Bear Ser.). (ENG.). 12p. (J). pap. 8.00 *(978-1-61406-592-0(6))* American Reading Co.

—Where Is My Boy? Pitt, Marilyn & Hileman, Jane. 2012. (1G Potato Chip Bks.). (ENG.). 12p. (J). (gr. k-1). pap. 8.00 *(978-1-59301-766-8(9))* American Reading Co.

—Where Is That Dog? Pitt, Marilyn & Hileman, Jane. 2013. (1G Potato Chip Bks.). (ENG.). 12p. (J). (gr. k-1). pap. 8.00 *(978-1-59301-770-5(7))* American Reading Co.

—Will You Go? Hileman, Jane. 2016. (2G Potato Chip Bks.). (ENG.). 12p. (J). pap. 8.00 *(978-1-61406-684-2(1))* American Reading Co.

—You Can't Have It! Hileman, Jane & Pitt, Marilyn. 2012. (1G Potato Chip Bks.). (ENG.). 12p. (J). (gr. k-1). pap. 8.00 *(978-1-59301-767-5(7))* American Reading Co.

Bianchi, John. My Ride. Bianchi, John. 2006. (2G Potato Chip Bks.). (ENG.). 12p. (J). pap. 8.00 *(978-1-61406-682-8(5))* American Reading Co.

—Over & Under. Bianchi, John. 2011. (2G Bird, Bunny & Bear Ser.). (ENG.). 16p. (J). pap. 8.00 *(978-1-61406-686-6(8))* American Reading Co.

—The Sun. Bianchi, John. 2010. (2G Bird, Bunny & Bear Ser.). (ENG.). 16p. (J). pap. 8.00 *(978-1-61406-688-0(4))* American Reading Co.

—What Can You Do? Bianchi, John. 2017. (2G Bird. Bunny & Bear Ser.). (ENG.). 16p. (J). pap. 8.00 *(978-1-61406-681-1(7))* American Reading Co.

Bianchi, John & Taylor, Trace. Perro en Apuros: Let Me In. Pitt, Marilyn et al. 2010. (1G Our World Ser.). (ENG.). 24p. (J). pap. 9.60 *(978-1-61541-170-2(4))* American Reading Co.

Bianchi, Simone, et al. Star Wars: Showdown on the Smuggler's Moon (Set), 6 vols. Aaron, Jason. 2016. (Star Wars: Showdown on the Smuggler's Moon Ser.). (ENG.). 24p. (J). (gr. 6-12). lib. bdg. 162.42 *(978-1-61479-553-7(3),* 24387, Graphic Novels) Spotlight.

Bianchi, Simone. Thanos Rising Marvel Select Edition. 2019. (ENG.). 120p. (YA). (gr. 8-17). 24.99 *(978-1-302-91883-5(4))* Marvel Worldwide, Inc.

Bianchi, Simone & Ponsor, Justin. Showdown on the Smuggler's Moon: Volume 1. Aaron, Jason. 2016. (Star Wars: Showdown on the Smuggler's Moon Ser.). (ENG.). 24p. (J). (gr. 6-12). lib. bdg. 27.07 *(978-1-61479-554-4(1),* 24388, Graphic Novels) Spotlight.

Bianco, Francesca. St. Francis & the Christmas Miracle of Greccio. Campbell, Jeffrey. 2014. (ENG.). 28p. (J). 14.95 *(978-0-9796766-3-5(0),* Tau Publishing) Vesuvius Pr. Inc.

Bianco, Mike, jt. illus. see Larter, John.

Bianda, Junissa. Ana & Andrew Set 2 (Set), 4 vols. Platt, Christine. 2019. (Ana & Andrew Ser.). (ENG.). 32p. (J). (gr. -1-3). lib. bdg. 114.00 *(978-1-5321-3635-1(8),* 33716, Calico Chapter Bks) Magic Wagon.

—The Christmas Tree. Acampora, Courtney. 2018. (Christmas Gift Tags Ser.). (ENG.). 12p. (J). (— 1). bds. 4.99 *(978-1-68412-385-8(2),* Silver Dolphin Bks.) Printers Row Publishing Group.

—Counting Dinos. Pinder, Eric. 2018. (ENG.). 32p. (J). 16.99 *(978-0-8075-1281-4(8),* 807512818) Whitman, Albert & Co.

—Going to Ghana. Platt, Christine. 2019. (Ana & Andrew Ser.). (ENG.). 32p. (J). (gr. -1-3). lib. bdg. 28.50 *(978-1-5321-3636-8(6),* 33718, Calico Chapter Bks) Magic Wagon.

—The Magic Violin. Platt, Christine. 2019. (Ana & Andrew Ser.). (ENG.). 32p. (J). (gr. -1-3). lib. bdg. 28.50 *(978-1-5321-3637-5(4),* 33720, Calico Chapter Bks) Magic Wagon.

—The New Baby. Platt, Christine. 2019. (Ana & Andrew Ser.). (ENG.). 32p. (J). (gr. -1-3). lib. bdg. 28.50 *(978-1-5321-3638-2(2),* 33722, Calico Chapter Bks) Magic Wagon.

—The Perfect Pet. Platt, Christine. 2019. (Ana & Andrew Ser.). (ENG.). 32p. (J). (gr. -1-3). lib. bdg. 28.50 *(978-1-5321-3639-9(0),* 33724, Calico Chapter Bks) Magic Wagon.

—Ready to Learn. Winget, Rosie. 2018. (Think & Find Pull Tab Book Ser.). (ENG.). 18p. (J). (gr. -1-2). bds. 9.99 *(978-1-68052-322-5(8),* 1002980) Cottage Door Pr.

Biasin, Elena. Maya & Gaia, un Compleanno Speciale / a Special Birthday: Libro Illustrato per Bambini: Italiano-Inglese (Edizione Bilingue) Biasin, Elena. 2016. (ITA.). (J). (gr. k). *(978-90-824948-2-2(5))* Biasin, Elena.

Biasotto, Natalia. Joanabelha. Dowgan, S. 2019. (POR.). 32p. (J). pap. 9.99 ***(978-1-6882-9996-2(3))*** Independently Published.

Bibb, Tatjana. Reggie & Mrs Crumble's Cookery Lesson. MacKie, Sarah. 2018. (Reggie the Reading Dog Ser.: Vol. 4). (ENG.). 22p. (J). (gr. 1-2). pap. *(978-0-9957738-2-0(3))* Bell, Caxton Publishing.

Bibb, Tatjana. Reggie the Reading Dog. MacKie, Sarah Louise. 2nd ed. 2020. (Reggie the Reading Dog Ser.: Vol. 1). (ENG.). 26p. (J). (gr. k-2). pap. ***(978-1-9161737-1-2(3))*** Bell, Caxton Publishing.

Bichman, David. Adventures with Rebbe Mendel. Sternfeld, Nathan. Pomerantz, Riva, tr. 230p. 21.99 *(978-1-58330-550-8(5))* Feldheim Pubs.

—All about Motti & His Adventures with Rebbe Mendel. Sternfeld, Nathan. 2004. 220p. (J). 20.99 *(978-1-58330-669-7(2))* Feldheim Pubs.

Bickel, Karla. The Animals' Debate. Bickel, Karla. I.t. ed. 2004. 16p. (J). (gr. -1-6). pap. 5.00 *(978-1-891452-16-1(9),* 10) Heart Arbor Bks.

—Easter Lights. Bickel, Karla. I.t. ed. 2004. 16p. (J). (gr. -1-6). pap. 5.00 *(978-1-891452-14-7(2),* 7) Heart Arbor Bks.

—Fishnet Valentine. Bickel, Karla. I.t. ed. 2004. 16p. (J). (gr. -1-5). pap. 5.00 *(978-1-891452-13-0(4),* 4) Heart Arbor Bks.

—Handmade Necklace. Bickel, Karla. I.t. ed. 2004. 16p. (J). (gr. -1-6). pap. 5.00 *(978-1-891452-11-6(8),* 1) Heart Arbor Bks.

—Heart Petals on the Hearth: A Collection of Children's Stories. Bickel, Karla. 2004. 64p. (J). (gr. -1-6). 20.00 *(978-1-891452-00-0(2))* Heart Arbor Bks.

—The Kite Who Was Afraid to Fly. Bickel, Karla. I.t. ed. 2004. 16p. (J). (gr. -1-6). pap. 5.00 *(978-1-891452-08-6(8),* 6) Heart Arbor Bks.

—Lilac Rose: A Flower's Lifetime. Bickel, Karla. l.t. ed. 2004. 16p. (J). (gr. -1-6). pap. 5.00 *(978-1-891452-10-9(X)*, 8) Heart Arbor Bks.

—The Reading Machine. Bickel, Karla. l.t. ed. 2004. 16p. (J). (gr. -1-6). pap. 5.00 *(978-1-891452-15-4(0)*, 9) Heart Arbor Bks.

—Surprise Christmas Birthday Party. Bickel, Karla. l.t. ed. 2004. 16p. (J). (gr. -1-6). pap. 5.00 *(978-1-891452-12-3(6)*, 3) Heart Arbor Bks.

—Teacher's Remarkable Secret. Bickel, Karla. l.t. ed. 2004. 16p. (J). (gr. -1-6). pap. 5.00 *(978-1-891452-09-3(6)*, 2) Heart Arbor Bks.

Bickell, Joy. Anna & the Christmas Tree. Hrehirchuk, Stephanie. 2018. (Anna's Angels Ser.: Vol. 4). (ENG.). 38p. (J). (gr. 3-5). pap. *(978-0-9958839-8-7(X))* Anna's Angels Pr.

Bickford-Smith, Coralie, jt. illus. see Tenniel, John.

Bicking, Judith. Anton Finds a Treasure. Margaret I. Pascuzzo. 2008. (ENG.). 18p. pap. 12.00 *(978-1-4251-8683-8(1))* Trafford Publishing.

—Anton Loses a Friend. Pascuzzo, Margaret I. 2009. (ENG.). 22p. pap. 12.00 *(978-1-4269-0650-3(1))* Trafford Publishing.

—Es Mi Hora de Dormir... pero Estoy Sediento! Benish, Shannon. 2019. (It's Time Ser.: Vol. 1). (SPA.). 50p. (J). pap. 10.99 *(978-0-9984228-7-9(8))* Rebel Redd Bks.

—My Toys. Mullican, Judy. l.t. ed. 2005. (HRL Board Book Ser.). (J). (gr. -1-k). pap. 10.95 *(978-1-57332-307-9(1)*, HighReach Learning, Incorporated) Carson-Dellosa Publishing, LLC.

—Tayla Takes a Trip. Zadunajsky, Donna M. 2013. (ENG.). 40p. pap. 9.99 *(978-1-938037-36-8(7))* Zadunajsky, Donna M.

—Tayla's Day at the Beach. Zadunajsky, Donna M. 2013. (ENG.). 26p. pap. 6.99 *(978-1-938037-34-4(0))* Zadunajsky, Donna M.

—Tayla's First Day of School. Zadunajsky, Donna M. 2013. (ENG.). 26p. pap. 9.15 *(978-1-938037-35-1(9))* Zadunajsky, Donna M.

Bicking, Judy. A Pond Full of Feelings. Bicking, Judy. Fogle, Llynda & González, Althea. 2005. (SPA.). (J). *(978-0-9760282-9-1(8))* RAPC - Sparkle & Shine Project.

Bicklmeier, Dakota. Ruby's Bubble. Lindsay, Lisele. 2020. (ENG.). 48p. (J). ***(978-1-5255-5496-4(4))***; pap. ***(978-1-5255-5497-1(2))*** FriesenPress.

Bicknelle, Millie. The Princess & Her King. Townsend, Will. 2019. (ENG.). 30p. (J). 20.00 ***(978-0-578-56601-6(X))*** Man's Chief End.

Biddle, Bruce. At the Park. Hoenecke, Karen. 2003. (Bridging School to Home Series B). (ENG.). 8p. (gr. k-1). pap. 7.95 *(978-1-879835-37-5(1)*, Kaeden Bks.) Kaeden Corp.

—Camping. Hooker, Karen. l.t. ed. 2003. (ENG.). 16p. (gr. k-1). pap. 7.95 *(978-1-879835-32-0(0)*, Kaeden Bks.) Kaeden Corp.

—What's for Dinner? Hoenecke, Karen. 2006. (Bridging School to Home Series B). (ENG.). 8p. (gr. k-1). pap. 7.95 *(978-1-879835-36-8(3)*, Kaeden Bks.) Kaeden Corp.

—What's Inside? Hoenecke, Karen. l.t. ed. 2005. (ENG.). 16p. (gr. k-1). pap. 7.95 *(978-1-57874-009-3(6)*, Kaeden Bks.) Kaeden Corp.

Biddle, Buffie. Ally's Scoliosis Adventure: A Story for Young Girls with Scoliosis. Yang, Bridget. 2019. (ENG.). 26p. (J). pap. 9.50 ***(978-1-6996-3318-2(5))*** Independently Published.

Biddlespacher, Tara. Goblinheart: A Fairy Tale. Axel, Brett. 2012. (J). 15.00 *(978-0-9769771-2-4(5))* Eastwaterfront Pr.

Biddulph, Rob. Blown Away. Biddulph, Rob. 2015. (ENG.). 40p. (J). (gr. -1-3). 17.99 *(978-0-06-236724-2(2))* HarperCollins Pubs.

—The Grizzly Bear Who Lost His GRRRRR! Biddulph, Rob. 2016. (ENG.). 40p. (J). (gr. -1-3). 17.99 *(978-0-06-236725-9(0))* HarperCollins Pubs.

—Odd Dog Out. Biddulph, Rob. 2019. (ENG.). 32p. (J). (gr. -1-3). 17.99 *(978-0-06-236726-6(9)*, HarperCollins) HarperCollins Pubs. Ltd. GBR. Dist: HarperCollins Pubs.

Biedrzycki, David. The Beetle Alphabet Book. Pallotta, Jerry. 2004. (Jerry Pallotta's Alphabet Bks.). 32p. (J). (gr. -1-3). (ENG.). 17.95 *(978-1-57091-551-2(2))*; pap. 7.95 *(978-1-57091-552-9(0))* Charlesbridge Publishing, Inc.

—Dory Story. Pallotta, Jerry. 2006. 32p. (J). (gr. -1-3). pap. 7.95 *(978-0-88106-076-8(3))* Charlesbridge Publishing, Inc.

—How Will I Get to School This Year? Pallotta, Jerry. 2011. (J). *(978-0-545-26659-8(9))* Scholastic, Inc.

Biedrzycki, David. Bad Bugs Are My Business. Biedrzycki, David. (Ace Lacewing, Bug Detective Ser.). 44p. (J). (gr. k-4). 2011. pap. 8.95 *(978-1-57091-693-9(4))*; 2009. 16.95 *(978-1-57091-692-2(6))* Charlesbridge Publishing, Inc.

—Bear Alert. Biedrzycki, David. (Breaking News Ser.: 1). 32p. (J). (gr. -1-3). 2018. 8.99 *(978-1-58089-664-1(2))*; 2016. lib. bdg. 17.95 *(978-1-58089-624-5(3))* Charlesbridge Publishing, Inc.

—The Big Swat. Biedrzycki, David. 2010. (Ace Lacewing, Bug Detective Ser.). 44p. (J). (gr. k-4). 16.95 *(978-1-57091-747-9(7))* Charlesbridge Publishing, Inc.

—Big Swat. Biedrzycki, David. 2012. (Ace Lacewing, Bug Detective Ser.). 44p. (J). (gr. k-4). pap. 8.95 *(978-1-57091-748-6(5))* Charlesbridge Publishing, Inc.

—Breaking News: Bear Alert. Biedrzycki, David. 2014. (Breaking News Ser.: 1). 32p. (J). (gr. -1-3). 17.95 *(978-1-58089-663-4(4))* Charlesbridge Publishing, Inc.

—Bug Detective. Biedrzycki, David. 2008. (Ace Lacewing, Bug Detective Ser.). 40p. (J). (gr. k-4). pap. 8.95 *(978-1-57091-684-7(5))* Charlesbridge Publishing, Inc.

—Groundhog's Runaway Shadow. Biedrzycki, David. 32p. (J). (gr. -1-3). 2019. pap. 8.99 *(978-1-62354-112-5(3))*; 2016. 17.99 *(978-1-58089-734-1(7))* Charlesbridge Publishing, Inc.

—Me & My Dragon. Biedrzycki, David. 2011. (Me & My Dragon Ser.). 40p. (J). (gr. -1-3). 17.95 *(978-1-58089-278-0(7))*; (ENG.). pap. 7.95 *(978-1-58089-279-7(5))* Charlesbridge Publishing, Inc.

—Me & My Dragon: Christmas Spirit. Biedrzycki, David. 2015. (Me & My Dragon Ser.). 40p. (J). (gr. -1-3). lib. bdg. 17.95 *(978-1-58089-622-1(7))* Charlesbridge Publishing, Inc.

—Mi Dragón y Yo. Biedrzycki, David. 2014. 32p. (J). (gr. -1-3). (SPA.). pap. 7.95 *(978-1-58089-574-3(3))*; lib. bdg. 17.95 *(978-1-58089-693-1(6))* Charlesbridge Publishing, Inc.

—Santa Retires. Biedrzycki, David. 2012. (ENG.). 32p. (J). (gr. -1-3). pap. 7.95 *(978-1-58089-294-0(9))* Charlesbridge Publishing, Inc.

—Scared of Halloween. Biedrzycki, David. 2013. (Me & My Dragon Ser.). 32p. (J). (gr. -1-3). pap. 7.99 *(978-1-58089-659-7(6))* Charlesbridge Publishing, Inc.

Biedrzycki, David & Bonnet, Rosalinde. Santa's New Jet. Biedrzycki, David. 2011. 32p. (J). (gr. -1-2). 16.95 *(978-1-58089-291-9(4))*; pap. 7.95 *(978-1-58089-292-6(2))* Charlesbridge Publishing, Inc.

Biehn, Curt & Rai, Rachel. The Adventures of Sunny the Mouse: Sunny Finds a New Home & Home Alone. Vest, Terri L. 2019. (Adventures of Sunny the Mouse Ser.: Vol. 1). (ENG.). 46p. (J). pap. 10.00 *(978-1-0902-5564-8(0))* Independently Published.

Bielecki, Jan. Freaky & Fearless: Bazookas for Beginners. Etherington, Robin. 2017. (Freaky & Fearless Ser.: 3). (ENG.). 304p. (J). (gr. 4-7). pap. 8.99 *(978-1-84812-584-1(4))* Bonnier Publishing GBR. Dist: Independent Pubs. Group.

—Freaky & Fearless: How to Tell a Tall Tale. Etherington, Robin. 2016. (Freaky & Fearless Ser.: 1). (ENG.). 240p. (J). (gr. 4-7). pap. 8.99 *(978-1-84812-510-0(0))* Bonnier Publishing GBR. Dist: Independent Pubs. Group.

—Freaky & Fearless: The Art of Being a Freak. Etherington, Robin. 2017. (Freaky & Fearless Ser.: 2). (ENG.). 288p. (J). (gr. 4-7). pap. 8.99 *(978-1-84812-512-4(7))* Bonnier Publishing GBR. Dist: Independent Pubs. Group.

—Jack Versus Veto. Eldridge, Jim. 2016. (Wrestling Trolls Ser.: 5). (ENG.). 176p. (YA). (gr. k-3). pap. 9.99 *(978-1-4714-0267-8(3))* Bonnier Publishing GBR. Dist: Independent Pubs. Group.

Bienfait, Andree. The Catholic Bible for Children. Amiot, Karine-Marie et al. 2011. (ENG.). 238p. (gr. -1-3). pap. 16.99 *(978-1-58617-659-4(5))* Ignatius Pr.

Bier, Donna. I Wish I Could Fly. Bier, Andreas. 2009. 20p. pap. 9.14 *(978-1-4269-0271-0(9))* Trafford Publishing.

Biesty, Stephen. Emergency Vehicles. Green, Rod. 2015. (Inside Vehicles Ser.). (ENG.). 16p. (J). (gr. k-4). 15.99 *(978-0-7636-7959-0(3)*, Templar) Candlewick Pr.

—Exploring Space: from Galileo to the Mars Rover & Beyond. Jenkins, Martin. 2017. (ENG.). 64p. (J). (gr. 3-7). 17.99 *(978-0-7636-8931-5(9))* Candlewick Pr.

—Flying Machines. Graham, Ian. 2018. (Inside Vehicles Ser.). (ENG.). 16p. (J). (gr. k-3). 17.99 *(978-1-5362-0281-6(9)*, Templar) Candlewick Pr.

—Giant Vehicles. Green, Rod. 2014. (Inside Vehicles Ser.). (ENG.). 16p. (J). (gr. k-4). 15.99 *(978-0-7636-7404-5(4)*, Templar) Candlewick Pr.

—Into the Unknown: How Great Explorers Found Their Way by Land, Sea, & Air. Ross, Stewart. (ENG.). 96p. (J). (gr. 3-7). 2014. pap. 15.99 *(978-0-7636-6992-8(X))*; 2011. 19.99 *(978-0-7636-4948-7(1))* Candlewick Pr.

—Stephen Biesty's Cross-Sections Castle. Platt, Richard. 2019. (Stephen Biesty Cross Sections Ser.). (ENG.). 32p. (J). (gr. 4-7). 19.99 *(978-1-4654-8470-3(1)*, DK Children) Dorling Kindersley Publishing, Inc.

—Stephen Biesty's Cross-Sections Man-Of-War. Platt, Richard. 2019. (Stephen Biesty Cross Sections Ser.). (ENG.). 32p. (J). (gr. 4-7). 19.99 *(978-1-4654-8471-0(X)*, DK Children) Dorling Kindersley Publishing, Inc.

Biesty, Stephen. Stephen Biesty's Incredible Body Cross-Sections. Platt, Richard. 2020. (Stephen Biesty Cross Sections Ser.). (ENG.). 32p. (J). (gr. 4-7). 19.99 ***(978-1-4654-9145-9(7)***, DK Children) Dorling Kindersley Publishing, Inc.

Biesty, Stephen. Stephen Biesty's Incredible Cross Sections of Everything. Platt, Richard. rev. ed. 2020. (Stephen Biesty Cross Sections Ser.). (ENG.). 32p. (J). (gr. 4-7). 19.99 *(978-1-4654-9000-1(0)*, DK Children) Dorling Kindersley Publishing, Inc.

—Stephen Biesty's Incredible Explosions: Exploded Views of Astonishing Things. Platt, Richard. 2004. 32p. (J). (gr. 2-8). reprint ed. 20.00 *(978-0-7567-7680-0(5))* DIANE Publishing Co.

—Stephen Biesty's More Incredible Cross-Sections. Platt, Richard. 25th ed. 2019. (Stephen Biesty Cross Sections Ser.). (ENG.). 32p. (J). (gr. 4-7). 19.99 *(978-1-4654-8573-1(2)*, DK Children) Dorling Kindersley Publishing, Inc.

—The Story of Buildings: From the Pyramids to the Sydney Opera House & Beyond. Dillon, Patrick. 2014. (ENG.). 96p. (J). (gr. 4-7). 19.99 *(978-0-7636-6990-4(3))* Candlewick Pr.

—Trains. Graham, Ian. 2017. (Inside Vehicles Ser.). (ENG.). 16p. (J). (gr. k-3). 15.99 *(978-0-7636-9647-4(1)*, Templar) Candlewick Pr.

Biet, Pascal. Leo & Lester. Bloom, Becky. 2003. (J). 32p. 15.95 *(978-1-59034-582-5(7))*; 33p. pap. *(978-1-59034-583-2(5))* Mondo Publishing.

Bifano, Laura. Le Canot Rouge. Davidson, Leslie A. Martinez, Rachel, tr. from ENG. 2020. (FRE.). 32p. (J). (gr. -1-k). pap. 12.95 *(978-1-4598-2448-5(2))* Orca Bk. Pubs. USA.

—In the Red Canoe. Davidson, Leslie A. 2020. (ENG.). 32p. (J). (gr. -1-k). 12.95 *(978-1-4598-2447-8(4))* Orca Bk. Pubs. USA.

Big Idea Productions Staff. Lost in Place: A Lesson in Overcoming Fear, 1 vol. Peterson, Doug & Kenney, Cindy. 2005. (Big Idea Books / VeggieTown Values Ser.: Bk. 4). (ENG.). 32p. (J). pap. 3.99 *(978-0-310-70629-8(7))* Zonderkidz.

Bigbee, Linda. I'd Like a Cat Like That: Coloring Book. Allen, John. 2018. (ENG.). 38p. (J). pap. 8.99 *(978-1-7237-5839-3(6))* Independently Published.

Bigda, Diane. Fashion Astrology. Zenkel, Suzanne Siegel. 2005. (Charming Petites Ser.). 80p. 4.95 *(978-0-88088-842-4(3))* Peter Pauper Pr. Inc.

Bigelow, Holly. Greek Roots J-Ology. Duncan, Leonard C. Date not set. 140p. (J). (gr. 6-12). spiral bd. 25.00 *(978-0-941414-01-2(9))* L. C. D.

Biggar, Breanne. Different Kinds of Special. Koffman, Donna Carol. 2011. 36p. pap. *(978-1-55483-897-4(5))* Insomniac Pr.

Biggers, Liza. Danny Yukon & the Secrets of the Amazing Lamp — Elementary Edition. Daniels Jr, Prince & Nettleton, Pamela Hill. 2016. (ENG.). (J). pap. 14.95 *(978-0-9964901-8-4(3))* Sager Group, The.

—Our Daddy Is Invincible! Maxwell, Shannon. 40p. (J). 2011. 15.95 *(978-1-61751-003-8(3))*; 2010. pap. 9.95 *(978-1-61751-002-1(5))* Kurdyla, E L Publishing LLC. (4th Division Pr.).

Biggin, Gary & Lipscombe, Nick. Space. Butterfield, Moira. 32p. (J). mass mkt. 8.99 *(978-0-590-24424-4(8))* Scholastic, Inc.

Biggin, Gary, jt. illus. see Lyon, Chris.

Biggs, Brian. Attack of the Tagger. Van Draanen, Wendelin. unabr. ed. 2006. (Shredderman Ser.: Bk. 2). (J). (gr. 3-6). audio 24.95 *(978-1-59519-758-0(3))* Live Oak Media.

—Attack of the Tagger. Van Draanen, Wendelin. 2008. (Shredderman Ser.: 2). (ENG.). 176p. (gr. 1-4). 7.99 *(978-0-440-41913-6(1))* Perfection Learning Corp.

Biggs, Brian. Bike & Trike. Verdick, Elizabeth. 2020. (ENG.). 48p. (J). (gr. -1-3). 7.99 ***(978-1-5344-8043-8(9))***; 17.99 *(978-1-5344-1517-1(3))* Simon & Schuster/Paula Wiseman Bks. (Simon & Schuster/Paula Wiseman Bks.).

Biggs, Brian. Brownie & Pearl Get Dolled Up. Rylant, Cynthia. 2010. (Brownie & Pearl Ser.). (ENG.). 24p. (J). (gr. -1-3). 15.99 *(978-1-4169-8631-7(6)*, Beach Lane Bks.) Beach Lane Bks.

—Brownie & Pearl Get Dolled Up. Rylant, Cynthia. 2014. (Brownie & Pearl Ser.). (ENG.). 24p. (J). (gr. -1-k). 16.99 *(978-1-4424-9568-5(5))*; pap. 4.99 *(978-1-4424-9567-8(7))* Simon Spotlight. (Simon Spotlight).

—Brownie & Pearl Go for a Spin. Rylant, Cynthia. 2012. (Brownie & Pearl Ser.). (ENG.). 24p. (J). (gr. -1-3). 14.99 *(978-1-4169-8633-1(2)*, Beach Lane Bks.) Beach Lane Bks.

—Brownie & Pearl Go for a Spin. Rylant, Cynthia. 2015. (Brownie & Pearl Ser.). (ENG.). 24p. (J). (gr. -1-k). pap. 3.99 *(978-1-4814-2570-4(6)*, Simon Spotlight) Simon Spotlight.

—Brownie & Pearl Grab a Bite. Rylant, Cynthia. 2011. (Brownie & Pearl Ser.). (ENG.). 24p. (J). (gr. -1-k). 13.99 *(978-1-4169-8634-8(0)*, Beach Lane Bks.) Beach Lane Bks.

—Brownie & Pearl Grab a Bite. Rylant, Cynthia. 2014. (Brownie & Pearl Ser.). (ENG.). 24p. (J). (gr. -1-k). 16.99 *(978-1-4814-1717-4(7))*; pap. 4.99 *(978-1-4814-1715-0(0))* Simon Spotlight. (Simon Spotlight).

—Brownie & Pearl Hit the Hay. Rylant, Cynthia. 2011. (Brownie & Pearl Ser.). (ENG.). 24p. (J). (gr. -1-k). 13.99 *(978-1-4169-8635-5(9)*, Beach Lane Bks.) Beach Lane Bks.

—Brownie & Pearl Hit the Hay. Rylant, Cynthia. 2013. (Brownie & Pearl Ser.). (ENG.). 24p. (J). (gr. -1-k). 17.99 *(978-1-4424-8742-0(9))*; pap. 3.99 *(978-1-4424-8741-3(0))* Simon Spotlight. (Simon Spotlight).

—Brownie & Pearl Make Good. Rylant, Cynthia. 2012. (Brownie & Pearl Ser.). (ENG.). 24p. (J). (gr. -1-k). 16.99 *(978-1-4169-8636-2(7)*, Beach Lane Bks.) Beach Lane Bks.

—The Brownie & Pearl Ready-to-Read Collection: Brownie & Pearl Step Out; Brownie & Pearl Get Dolled Up; Brownie & Pearl Grab a Bite; Brownie & Pearl See the Sights; Brownie & Pearl Go for a Spin; Brownie & Pearl Hit the Hay. Rylant, Cynthia. 2016. (Brownie & Pearl Ser.). (ENG.). 144p. (J). (gr. -1-k). 12.99 *(978-1-4814-8653-8(5)*, Simon Spotlight) Simon Spotlight.

—Brownie & Pearl See the Sights. Rylant, Cynthia. 2010. (Brownie & Pearl Ser.). (ENG.). 24p. (J). (gr. -1-k). 14.99 *(978-1-4169-8637-9(5)*, Beach Lane Bks.) Beach Lane Bks.

—Brownie & Pearl See the Sights. Rylant, Cynthia. 2013. (Brownie & Pearl Ser.). (ENG.). 24p. (J). (gr. -1-k). 17.99 *(978-1-4424-8744-4(5))*; pap. 4.99 *(978-1-4424-8743-7(7))* Simon Spotlight. (Simon Spotlight).

—Brownie & Pearl Step Out. Rylant, Cynthia. 2009. (Brownie & Pearl Ser.). (ENG.). 24p. (J). (gr. -1-3). 16.99 *(978-1-4169-8632-4(4)*, Beach Lane Bks.) Beach Lane Bks.

—Brownie & Pearl Step Out. Rylant, Cynthia. 2014. (Brownie & Pearl Ser.). (ENG.). 24p. (J). (gr. -1-k). 16.99 *(978-1-4814-0314-6(1))*; pap. 4.99 *(978-1-4814-0313-9(3))* Simon Spotlight. (Simon Spotlight).

—Brownie & Pearl Take a Dip. Rylant, Cynthia. 2011. (Brownie & Pearl Ser.). (ENG.). 24p. (J). (gr. -1-3). 16.99 *(978-1-4169-8638-6(3)*, Beach Lane Bks.) Beach Lane Bks.

—Don't Swap Your Sweater for a Dog. Applegate, Katherine. 2008. (Roscoe Riley Rules Ser.: 3). (ENG.). 96p. (J). (gr. 1-5). pap. 4.99 *(978-0-06-114885-9(7))* HarperCollins Pubs.

—Don't Tap-Dance on Your Teacher. Applegate, Katherine. 2009. (Roscoe Riley Rules Ser.: 5). (ENG.). 96p. (J). (gr. 1-5). pap. 4.99 *(978-0-06-114889-7(X))* HarperCollins Pubs.

—Don't Tap-Dance on Your Teacher. Applegate, Katherine. ed. 2016. (Roscoe Riley Rules Ser.: 5). (ENG.). 112p. (J). (gr. 1-5). 14.75 *(978-0-606-39252-5(1))* Turtleback.

—EllRay Jakes & the Beanstalk. Warner, Sally. 2013. (EllRay Jakes Ser.: 5). (ENG.). 144p. (J). (gr. 1-3). pap. 5.99 *(978-0-14-242359-2(9)*, Puffin Books) Penguin Young Readers Group.

—EllRay Jakes Is Magic. Warner, Sally. 2014. (EllRay Jakes Ser.: 6). (ENG.). 176p. (J). (gr. 1-3). pap. 5.99 *(978-0-14-242360-8(2)*, Puffin Books) Penguin Young Readers Group.

—EllRay Jakes Stands Tall. Warner, Sally. 2016. (EllRay Jakes Ser.: 9). (ENG.). (J). (gr. 1-3). 176p. 5.99 *(978-0-14-751253-6(0)*, Puffin Books); 160p. 14.99 *(978-0-451-46913-7(5)*, Viking Books for Young Readers) Penguin Young Readers Group.

—Ellray Jakes the Dragon Slayer, No. 4. Warner, Sally. 2013. (EllRay Jakes Ser.: 4). (ENG.). 144p. (J). (gr. 1-3). pap. 5.99 *(978-0-14-242358-5(0)*, Puffin Books) Penguin Young Readers Group.

—EllRay Jakes the Recess King! Warner, Sally. 2015. (EllRay Jakes Ser.: 8). (ENG.). 176p. (J). (gr. 1-3). 5.99 *(978-0-14-751252-9(2)*, Puffin Books); 14.99 *(978-0-451-46911-3(9)*, Viking Books for Young Readers) Penguin Young Readers Group.

—Enemy Spy. Van Draanen, Wendelin. 2006. (Shredderman Ser.: 4). (ENG.). 192p. (J). (gr. 1-4). 7.99 *(978-0-440-41915-0(8)*, Yearling) Random Hse. Children's Bks.

—Football with Dad. Berrios, Frank. 2015. (Little Golden Book Ser.). 24p. (J). (-k). 4.99 *(978-0-385-37925-0(0)*, Golden Bks.) Random Hse. Children's Bks.

—Frank Einstein & the Antimatter Motor. Scieszka, Jon. 2014. (Frank Einstein Ser.). 192p. (J). (gr. 3-7). pap. 7.95 *(978-1-4197-1506-8(2))* Abrams, Inc.

—Frank Einstein & the Antimatter Motor (Frank Einstein Series #1) Book One. Scieszka, Jon. (ENG.). (J). 2017. 208p. (gr. 3-7). pap. 7.95 *(978-1-4197-2492-3(4))*; 2014. 192p. (gr. 3-7). 13.95 *(978-1-4197-1601-0(8))*; 2014. 192p. (gr. 2-6). 13.95 *(978-1-4197-1218-0(7))* Abrams, Inc. (Amulet Bks.).

—Frank Einstein & the Bio-Action Gizmo (Frank Einstein Series #5) Book Five. Scieszka, Jon. (ENG.). (J). (gr. 3-7). 2018. (Frank Einstein Ser.: 5). 192p. pap. 7.99 *(978-1-4197-3125-9(4))*; 2017. 176p. 13.99 *(978-1-4197-2297-4(2))* Abrams, Inc. (Amulet Bks.).

—Frank Einstein & the BrainTurbo. Scieszka, Jon. 2015. (Frank Einstein Ser.). (ENG.). 192p. (J). (gr. 3-7). pap. 8.95 *(978-1-4197-1924-0(6))* Abrams, Inc.

—Frank Einstein & the BrainTurbo (Frank Einstein Series #3), 3. Scieszka, Jon. 2015. (ENG.). 192p. (J). (gr. 3-7). 13.95 *(978-1-4197-1643-0(3)*, Amulet Bks.) Abrams, Inc.

—Frank Einstein & the BrainTurbo (Frank Einstein Series #3) Book Three. Scieszka, Jon. 2017. (Frank Einstein Ser.). (ENG.). 208p. (J). (gr. 3-7). pap. 7.99 *(978-1-4197-2735-1(4)*, Amulet Bks.) Abrams, Inc.

—Frank Einstein & the Electro-Finger. Scieszka, Jon. 2015. (Frank Einstein Ser.). (ENG.). 176p. (YA). (gr. 3-7). pap. 7.95 *(978-1-4197-1666-9(2))* Abrams, Inc.

—Frank Einstein & the Electro-Finger (Frank Einstein Series #2) Book Two. Scieszka, Jon. 2017. (ENG.). 192p. (J). (gr. 3-7). pap. 7.95 *(978-1-4197-2493-0(2)*, Amulet Bks.) Abrams, Inc.

—Frank Einstein & the Evoblaster Belt, Bk. 4. Scieszka, Jon. 2016. (Frank Einstein Ser.). (ENG.). 208p. (J). (gr. 3-7). pap. 7.95 *(978-1-4197-2379-7(0))* Abrams, Inc.

—Frank Einstein & the EvoBlaster Belt (Frank Einstein Series #4) Book Four. Scieszka, Jon. (Frank Einstein Ser.). (ENG.). (J). (gr. 3-7). 2017. 224p. pap. 7.99 *(978-1-4197-2736-8(2))*; 2016. 208p. 13.95 *(978-1-4197-1887-8(8))* Abrams, Inc. (Amulet Bks.).

—Frank Einstein & the Space-Time Zipper (Frank Einstein Series #6) Scieszka, Jon. 2018. (Frank Einstein Ser.). (ENG.). 176p. (J). (gr. 3-7). 13.99 *(978-1-4197-2547-0(5)*, Amulet Bks.) Abrams, Inc.

—Frank Einstein & the Space-Time Zipper (Frank Einstein Series #6) Book Six. Scieszka, Jon. 2019. (Frank Einstein Ser.). (ENG.). 176p. (J). (gr. 3-7). pap. 7.99 *(978-1-4197-3384-0(2)*, Amulet Bks.) Abrams, Inc.

—I'm a T. Rex! Shealy, Dennis R. 2010. (Little Golden Book Ser.). 32p. (J). (gr. -1-2). 4.99 *(978-0-375-85806-2(7)*, Golden Bks.) Random Hse. Children's Bks.

—Meet the Gecko, 3. Van Draanen, Wendelin. 2005. (Shredderman Ser.: 3). (ENG.). 169p. (J). (gr. 3-6). 17.44 *(978-0-440-41914-3(X))* Random House Publishing Group.

—Never Glue Your Friends to Chairs. Applegate, Katherine. 2008. (Roscoe Riley Rules Ser.: 1). (ENG.). 96p. (J). (gr. 1-5). pap. 4.99 *(978-0-06-114881-1(4))* HarperCollins Pubs.

—Never Race a Runaway Pumpkin. Applegate, Katherine. 2009. (Roscoe Riley Rules Ser.: 7). (ENG.). 96p. (J). (gr. 1-5). pap. 4.99 *(978-0-06-178370-8(6))* HarperCollins Pubs.

—Never Swim in Applesauce. Applegate, Katherine. 2008. (Roscoe Riley Rules Ser.: 4). (ENG.). 96p. (J). (gr. 1-5). pap. 4.99 *(978-0-06-114887-3(3))* HarperCollins Pubs.

—Never Swipe a Bully's Bear. Applegate, Katherine. 2008. (Roscoe Riley Rules Ser.: 2). (ENG.). 96p. (J). (gr. 1-5). pap. 4.99 *(978-0-06-114883-5(0))* HarperCollins Pubs.

—Never Walk in Shoes That Talk. Applegate, Katherine. 2009. (Roscoe Riley Rules Ser.: 6). (ENG.). 96p. (J). (gr. 1-5). pap. 4.99 *(978-0-06-114891-0(1))* HarperCollins Pubs.

—Noisy Night. Barnett, Mac. 2017. (ENG.). 32p. (J). 16.99 *(978-1-59643-967-2(X)*, 900126272) Roaring Brook Pr.

—One Beastly Beast: Two Aliens, Three Inventors, Four Fantastic Tales. Nix, Garth. 2007. 176p. (J). (gr. 2-6). lib. bdg. 16.89 *(978-0-06-084320-5(9)*, Eos) HarperCollins Pubs.

—Roscoe Riley Rules #1: Never Glue Your Friends to Chairs. Applegate, Katherine. (Roscoe Riley Rules Ser.: 1). (ENG.). (J). (gr. 1-5). 2016. 128p. pap. 4.99 *(978-0-06-239248-0(4))*; 2008. 96p. 15.99 *(978-0-06-114882-8(2))* HarperCollins Pubs. Ltd. GBR. (HarperCollins). Dist: HarperCollins Pubs.

—Roscoe Riley Rules #2: Never Swipe a Bully's Bear. Applegate, Katherine. 2008. (Roscoe Riley Rules Ser.: 2). (ENG.). 96p. (J). (gr. 1-5). 15.99 *(978-0-06-114884-2(9)*, HarperCollins) HarperCollins Pubs. Ltd. GBR. Dist: HarperCollins Pubs.

—Roscoe Riley Rules #3: Don't Swap Your Sweater for a Dog. Applegate, Katherine. (Roscoe Riley Rules Ser.: 3). (ENG.). (J). (gr. 1-5). 2016. 128p. pap. 4.99 *(978-0-06-239250-3(6))*; 2008. 96p. 15.99 *(978-0-06-114886-6(5))* HarperCollins Pubs. Ltd. GBR. (HarperCollins). Dist: HarperCollins Pubs.

—Roscoe Riley Rules 4 Books In 1! Never Glue Your Friends to Chairs; Never Swipe a Bully's Bear; Don't Swap Your Sweater for a Dog; Never Swim in Applesauce. Applegate, Katherine. 2016. (Roscoe Riley Rules Ser.). (ENG.). 448p. (J). (gr. 1-5). 16.99 *(978-0-06-256427-6(7),* HarperCollins) HarperCollins Pubs. Ltd. GBR. Dist: HarperCollins Pubs.

—Roscoe Riley Rules #4: Never Swim in Applesauce. Applegate, Katherine. (Roscoe Riley Rules Ser.: 4). (ENG.). (J). (gr. 1-5). 2016. 128p. pap. 4.99 *(978-0-06-239251-0(4));* 2008. 96p. 15.99 *(978-0-06-114888-0(1))* HarperCollins Pubs. Ltd. GBR. (HarperCollins). Dist: HarperCollins Pubs.

—Roscoe Riley Rules #6: Never Walk in Shoes That Talk. Applegate, Katherine. 2009. (Roscoe Riley Rules Ser.: 6). (ENG.). 96p. (J). (gr. 1-5). 14.99 *(978-0-06-114892-7(X),* HarperCollins) HarperCollins Pubs. Ltd. GBR. Dist: HarperCollins Pubs.

—Roscoe Riley Rules #7: Never Race a Runaway Pumpkin. Applegate, Katherine. 2009. (Roscoe Riley Rules Ser.: 7). (ENG.). 96p. (J). (gr. 1-5). 15.99 *(978-0-06-178372-2(2),* HarperCollins) HarperCollins Pubs. Ltd. GBR. Dist: HarperCollins Pubs.

—Sammy Keyes & the Wild Things. Van Draanen, Wendelin. 2008. (Sammy Keyes Ser.: 11). (ENG.). 320p. (J). (gr. 5-7). 7.99 *(978-0-440-42112-2(8),* Yearling) Random Hse. Children's Bks.

—Secret Identity, 1. Van Draanen, Wendelin. 2006. (Shredderman Ser.: 1).Tr. of Al Haqiqa Wara ¿Al Fatak¿. (ENG.). 144p. (J). (gr. 3-6). reprint ed. 16.19 *(978-0-440-41912-9(3))* Random House Publishing Group.

—Shredderman: Secret Identity. Van Draanen, Wendelin. unabr. ed. 2006. (Shredderman Ser.: Bk. 1).Tr. of Shredderman - Al Haqiqa Wara ¿Al Fatak¿. (J). (gr. 2-4). audio 24.95 *(978-1-59519-762-7(1))* Live Oak Media.

—This Is Not a Normal Animal Book. Segal-Walters, Julie. 2017. (ENG.). 48p. (J). (gr. -1-3). 17.99 *(978-1-4814-3922-0(7),* Simon & Schuster/Paula Wiseman Bks.) Simon & Schuster/Paula Wiseman Bks.

—What Kind of Car Does a T. Rex Drive? Lee, Mark. 2019. 40p. (J). (gr. -1-2). 17.99 *(978-1-5247-4123-5(X),* G.P. Putnam's Sons Books for Young Readers) Penguin Young Readers Group.

Biggs, Brian. Everything Goes: 123 Beep Beep Beep!: a Counting Book. Biggs, Brian. 2012. (ENG.). 24p. (J). (gr. -1 — 1). bds. 7.99 *(978-0-06-195812-0(3))* HarperCollins Pubs.

—Everything Goes: Blue Bus, Red Balloon: a Book of Colors. Biggs, Brian. 2013. (ENG.). 24p. (J). (gr. -1 — 1). bds. 7.99 *(978-0-06-195814-4(X))* HarperCollins Pubs.

—Everything Goes: by Sea. Biggs, Brian. 2013. (ENG.). 56p. (J). (gr. -1-3). 14.99 *(978-0-06-195811-3(5))* HarperCollins Pubs.

—Everything Goes: Good Night, Trucks: a Bedtime Book. Biggs, Brian. 2013. (ENG.). 24p. (J). (gr. -1 — 1). bds. 7.99 *(978-0-06-195815-1(8))* HarperCollins Pubs.

—Everything Goes: in the Air. Biggs, Brian. 2012. (ENG.). 56p. (J). (gr. -1-3). 16.99 *(978-0-06-195810-6(7),* Balzer & Bray) HarperCollins Pubs.

—Everything Goes: on Land. Biggs, Brian. 2011. (ENG.). 56p. (J). (gr. -1-3). 14.99 *(978-0-06-195809-0(3))* HarperCollins Pubs.

—Everything Goes: Santa Goes Everywhere! Biggs, Brian. 2013. (ENG.). 24p. (J). (gr. -1 — 1). bds. 7.99 *(978-0-06-195817-5(4))* HarperCollins Pubs.

—Everything Goes: Stop! Go!: a Book of Opposites. Biggs, Brian. 2012. (ENG.). 24p. (J). (gr. -1 — 1). bds. 7.99 *(978-0-06-195813-7(1))* HarperCollins Pubs.

—Everything Goes: What Flies in the Air? Biggs, Brian. 2013. (ENG.). 24p. (J). (gr. -1 — 1). bds. 7.99 *(978-0-06-195816-8(6))* HarperCollins Pubs.

—The Space Walk. Biggs, Brian. 2019. 40p. (J). (gr. -1-2). 17.99 *(978-0-525-55337-3(1),* Dial Bks) Penguin Young Readers Group.

Biggs, Brian & Abbott, Simon. Everything Goes: Henry Goes Skating. Biggs, Brian. 2012. (My First I Can Read Ser.). (ENG.). 32p. (J). (gr. -1-3). 16.99 *(978-0-06-195821-2(2));* pap. 4.99 *(978-0-06-195820-5(4))* HarperCollins Pubs.

—Everything Goes: Henry in a Jam. Biggs, Brian. 2012. (My First I Can Read Ser.). (ENG.). 32p. (J). (gr. -1-3). pap. 4.99 *(978-0-06-195818-2(2))* HarperCollins Pubs.

—Everything Goes: Henry on Wheels. Biggs, Brian. 2013. (My First I Can Read Ser.). (ENG.). 32p. (J). (gr. -1-3). 16.99 *(978-0-06-195823-6(9))* HarperCollins Pubs.

Biggs, Gene. A First Dictionary. Wittels, Harriet & Greisman, Joan. 2004. 239p. (J). (gr. 4-8). reprint ed. pap. 15.00 *(978-0-7567-8422-5(0))* DIANE Publishing Co.

Bigham, Sean. Arctic Wolf. Flaherty, William. 2018. (Animals Illustrated Ser.). (ENG.). 24p. (J). (gr. k-2). 12.95 *(978-1-77227-213-0(2))* Inhabit Media Inc. CAN. Dist: Consortium Bk. Sales & Distribution.

Bigham, Sean. Journey to the Winter Camp, 1 vol. MacDonald, Caleb. 2017. (Nunavummi Ser.). (ENG.). 48p. (gr. 3-3). 7.95 ***(978-1-77266-572-7(X))*** Inhabit Education CAN. Dist: Consortium Bk. Sales & Distribution.

Bigham, Sean, jt. illus. see Qitsualik-Tinsley, Sean.

Bigly, Ashley D., jt. illus. see Bratton, Deborah B.

Bigwood, John. Colour Away Your Worries. Buster Books et al. 2017. (ENG.). 112p. (J). (gr. 1-6). pap. 13.99 *(978-1-78055-309-2(9))* O'Mara, Michael Bks., Ltd. GBR. Dist: Independent Pubs. Group.

Bigwood, John, jt. illus. see Dreidemy, Joëlle.

Bihun, Robb. Edison's Frankenstein 1910. Yambar, Chris, ed. 2003. (YA). mass mkt. 7.95 *(978-1-929515-27-1(8))* Comic Library International.

Bijan, Samaddar. Hakims Big Imagination. Mabrey, Chris. 2019. (ENG.). 36p. (J). (gr. k-2). 18.99 *(978-0-9979042-9-1(1))* Mabrey, Chris.

Bijloo, Adrian. Hungry Tiger & Clever Rabbit: A Tale from Korea. Samson, Lucretia. 2016. 24p. (J). pap. 9.95 *(978-1-927244-58-6(7))* Clean Slate Pr. Ltd. NZL. Dist: Flying Start Bks.

—Hungry Tiger & Clever Rabbit (Big Book Edition) A Tale from Korea. Samson, Lucretia. 2016. 24p. (J). pap. *(978-1-927244-68-5(4))* Flying Start Bks.

Bikadoroff, Roxanna. The Alphabet Thief, 1 vol. Richardson, Bill. 2017. (ENG.). 40p. (J). (gr. k-4). 16.95 *(978-1-55498-877-8(2))* Groundwood Bks. CAN. Dist: Publishers Group West (PGW).

—The Bunny Band, 1 vol. Richardson, Bill. 2018. (ENG.). 32p. (J). (gr. k-2). 16.95 *(978-1-77306-093-4(7))* Groundwood Bks. CAN. Dist: Publishers Group West (PGW).

—The Man Who Knew Everything: The Strange Life of Athanasius Kircher. Peters, Marilee. 2017. (ENG.). 60p. (J). (gr. 5-8). 19.95 *(978-1-55451-974-3(8));* pap. 12.95 *(978-1-55451-973-6(X))* Annick Pr., Ltd. CAN. Dist: Publishers Group West (PGW).

Bila Mobe, Manzana (cassy). Kabuika Wants to Make New Friends. Kamunga, Kabuika. 2020. (ENG.). 46p. (J). pap. 12.95 ***(978-1-4218-3659-1(9))*** 1st World Publishing, Inc.

Bilal, Nabeeh. Callaloo: The Trickster & the Magic Quilt. Canady, Marjuan T. 2018. (ENG.). 54p. (J). pap. 7.99 *(978-0-692-13045-2(4))* Bilal, Nabeeh.

Bilan, Edgar. Mommy Works. Bilan Hochenberg, Nerissa. 2013. 24p. pap. *(978-1-4602-2602-5(X))* FriesenPress.

Bileck, Marvin. Nobody's Birthday. Colver, Anne. 2012. 44p. 35.95 *(978-1-258-23347-1(9));* pap. 20.95 *(978-1-258-24718-8(6))* Literary Licensing, LLC.

—Rain Makes Applesauce (Restored Edition) Scheer, Julian. 2019. 32p. (J). (gr. -1-3). 18.99 *(978-0-8234-4361-1(2))* Holiday Hse., Inc.

Bilen, Danielle. The Legend of Cypress River. Gellert, Adam. 2017. (ENG.). (J). (gr. 1-6). pap. 9.99 *(978-0-692-90901-0(X))* Cypress River Publishing.

—La Leyenda Del Rio Cipres. Gellert, Adam. 2017. (SPA.). 44p. (J). (gr. 2-6). pap. 9.99 *(978-0-692-98702-5(9))* Cypress River Publishing.

Bilgihan, Evren. To Beg Our Cousin — The King. Garfield, M. 2018. (ENG.). 344p. (J). pap. 14.99 *(978-0-9964136-4-0(2),* Pennaeth Publishing) Garfield, M.

Bilibin, Ivan. Cuentos y Leyendas Populares Rusos: Edición Juvenil Ilustrada. Afanasiev, Aleksander. 2019. (SPA.). 220p. (J). pap. 11.30 *(978-1-7178-3144-6(3))* Independently Published.

—Russian Fairy Tales. Afanasyev, Alexander. 2013. 80p. *(978-1-909115-59-0(2));* 2012. 90p. pap. *(978-1-908478-68-9(3))* Planet, The.

—Russian Folk Tales - Russkie Narodnye Skazki. Afanasyev, Alexander. 2013. 94p. *(978-1-909115-32-3(0))* Planet, The.

—Skazki Pushkina - Fairy Tales. Pushkin, Alexander. 2013. 48p. *(978-1-909115-58-3(4))* Planet, The.

—The Tale of Tsarevich Ivan, the Firebird, & the Grey Wolf. Afanasyev, Alexander. 2013. 28p. pap. *(978-1-909115-50-7(9))* Planet, The.

Bilik-Franklin, MidiAna & Griffith, Indigo, photos by. The Carseat Tourist. 2006. (J). bds. 7.95 *(978-0-9772825-0-0(3))* Critter Camp Inc.

Bill, Graf. Nacho Money. Sparks, Candi et al. 2012. (Can I Have Some Money? Ser.). 36p. pap. 11.99 *(978-0-9789445-6-8(9))* Sparks Fly.

Billen-Frye, Paige, et al. Best-Loved Parables of Jesus. Burgdorf, Larry et al. 2014. (ENG.). 101p. (J). 9.99 *(978-0-7586-4662-0(3))* Concordia Publishing Hse.

Billen-Frye, Paige. The Wise & Foolish Builders: A Parable of Jesus, Matthew 7:24-27 & Luke 6:47-49 for Children. Burgdorf, Larry. 2007. (Arch Bks.). 16p. (J). 2.49 *(978-0-7586-1263-2(X))* Concordia Publishing Hse.

Billet, Marion. Busy London. 2018. (ENG.). 10p. (J). (-k). bds. 8.99 *(978-1-5098-5144-7(5))* Pan Macmillan GBR. Dist: Independent Pubs. Group.

—Busy London at Christmas. 2017. (ENG.). 10p. (J). (-k). bds. 8.99 *(978-1-5098-5151-5(8),* Campbell Bks.) Pan Macmillan GBR. Dist: Independent Pubs. Group.

—Hello! London. 3rd ed. 2014. (Hello! Ser.). (ENG.). 10p. (J). (-k). bds. 19.99 *(978-1-4472-4682-4(9))* Pan Macmillan GBR. Dist: Independent Pubs. Group.

—I Love Classical Music. 2019. (ENG.). 16p. (J). (gr. -1 — 1). 9.99 *(978-1-338-26721-1(3),* Cartwheel Bks.) Scholastic, Inc.

—I Love the Nutcracker. 2018. (ENG.). 16p. (J). (gr. -1 — 1). bds. 9.99 *(978-1-338-26720-4(5),* Cartwheel Bks.) Scholastic, Inc.

—London. 2019. (My First Touch & Find Ser.). (ENG.). 10p. (J). (gr. -1-k). bds. 9.99 *(978-1-5098-8368-4(1))* Pan Macmillan GBR. Dist: Independent Pubs. Group.

—The London Noisy Book: A Press-The-page Sound Book. 2019. (Campbell London Range Ser.). (ENG.). 10p. (J). (gr. -1-k). bds. 23.99 *(978-1-5290-0955-2(3))* Pan Macmillan GBR. Dist: Independent Pubs. Group.

—The London Noisy Bus. 2nd ed. 2018. (ENG.). 10p. (J). (— 1). bds. 12.99 *(978-1-5098-2904-0(0))* Pan Macmillan GBR. Dist: Independent Pubs. Group.

—My First London Bus. ed. 2015. (Whizzy Wheels Ser.). (ENG.). 10p. (J). (-k). bds. 9.99 *(978-0-230-76057-8(0))* Pan Macmillan GBR. Dist: Independent Pubs. Group.

—My First London Bus Cloth Book. 2018. (Campbell London Range Ser.). (ENG.). 8p. (J). (— 1). 15.99 *(978-1-5098-8193-2(X),* Campbell Bks.) Pan Macmillan GBR. Dist: Independent Pubs. Group.

—My First London Taxi. ed. 2015. (Whizzy Wheels Ser.). (ENG.). 10p. (J). (-k). bds. 11.99 *(978-0-230-76103-2(8))* Pan Macmillan GBR. Dist: Independent Pubs. Group.

—Noisy Farm: My First Sound Book. 2017. (ENG.). 16p. (J). (gr. -1 — 1). 9.99 *(978-1-338-13220-5(2),* Cartwheel Bks.) Scholastic, Inc.

—Noodle Loves the Beach. Nosy Crow Staff. 2012. (Noodle Ser.). (ENG.). 10p. (J). (gr. k — 1). bds. 8.99 *(978-0-7636-5898-4(7),* Nosy Crow) Candlewick Pr.

Billet, Marion. There Are 101 Things to Find in London. 2020. (ENG.). 16p. (J). (gr. -1-k). bds. 15.99 ***(978-1-5290-2329-9(7),*** Campbell Bks.) Pan Macmillan GBR. Dist: Independent Pubs. Group.

Billet, Marion. I Love Music: My First Sound Book. Billet, Marion. 2016. (ENG.). 16p. (J). (gr. -1 — 1). 9.99 *(978-1-338-03261-1(5),* Cartwheel Bks.) Scholastic, Inc.

—Littleland. Billet, Marion. 2013. (ENG.). 32p. (J). (gr. k-k). 14.99 *(978-0-7636-6550-0(9),* Nosy Crow) Candlewick Pr.

—Littleland Around the World. Billet, Marion. 2014. (ENG.). 32p. (J). (-k). 14.99 *(978-0-7636-7579-0(2),* Nosy Crow) Candlewick Pr.

—My Big London Play Set, 2 vols. Billet, Marion. 2017. (ENG.). 1p. (J). (gr. -1-1). pap. 26.99 *(978-1-5098-1548-7(1))* Pan Macmillan GBR. Dist: Independent Pubs. Group.

Billiau, Loic. Clang! Wile E. Coyote Experiments with Magnetism. Weakland, Mark. 2017. (Wile E. Coyote, Physical Science Genius Ser.). (ENG.). 32p. (J). (gr. 3-5). lib. bdg. 31.32 *(978-1-5157-3731-5(4),* Capstone Pr.) Capstone.

—Fred Flintstone's Adventures with Screws: Righty Tighty, Lefty Loosey. Weakland, Mark. 2016. (Flintstones Explain Simple Machines Ser.). (ENG.). 24p. (J). (gr. k-2). lib. bdg. 27.99 *(978-1-4914-8478-4(0))* Capstone.

—Kaboom! Wile E. Coyote Experiments with Chemical Reactions. Weakland, Mark. 2017. (Wile E. Coyote, Physical Science Genius Ser.). (ENG.). 32p. (J). (gr. 3-5). lib. bdg. 31.32 *(978-1-5157-3733-9(0),* Capstone Pr.) Capstone.

—The Loch Ness Monster. Chambers, Catherine. 2015. (Autobiographies You Never Thought You'd Read! Ser.). (ENG.). 32p. (J). (gr. 3-5). 30.65 *(978-1-4109-7962-9(8),* Raintree) Capstone.

—The Tooth Fairy. Chambers, Catherine. 2015. (Autobiographies You Never Thought You'd Read! Ser.). (ENG.). 32p. (J). (gr. 3-5). pap. 7.99 *(978-1-4109-7969-8(5),* Raintree) Capstone.

Billin-Fry, Paige. The Ball Book. Hillert, Margaret. 2016. (BeginningtoRead Ser.). (ENG.). 32p. (J). (gr. -1-2). pap. 11.94 *(978-1-60357-935-3(4));* (gr. k-2). 22.60 *(978-1-59953-794-8(X))* Norwood Hse. Pr.

Billin-Frye, Paige. ¡a Limpiar el Campamento! (Clean-Sweep Campers) Fractions. Penner, Lucille Recht. 2007. (Math Matters en Español Ser.). (SPA.). 32p. (J). (gr. 1-3). pap. 5.95 *(978-1-57565-253-5(6))* Astra Publishing Hse.

—Butterfly Express: A Book about Life Cycles. Moncure, Jane Belk. 2013. (Magic Castle Readers Ser.). (ENG.). 32p. (J). (gr. -1-2). 14.21 *(978-1-62323-588-8(X),* 206323) Child's World, Inc., The.

—Clean-Sweep Campers: Fractions. Penner, Lucille Recht. 2006. (Math Matters ® Ser.). (ENG.). 32p. (J). (gr. k-3). pap. 5.95 *(978-1-57565-096-8(7))* Astra Publishing Hse.

—Clever Trevor. Levers. Albee, Sarah. 2006. (Science Solves It! ® Ser.). (ENG.). 32p. (J). (gr. 1-3). pap. 5.95 *(978-1-57565-123-1(8))* Astra Publishing Hse.

—December, 1 vol. Kesselring, Mari. 2009. (Months of the Year Ser.). (ENG.). 24p. (J). (gr. k-2). 27.07 *(978-1-60270-639-2(5),* 11585, Looking Glass Library) Magic Wagon.

—The Easter Victory. Rottmann, Erik. 2006. (Arch Bks.). (ENG.). 16p. (J). (gr. -1-3). 2.49 *(978-0-7586-0869-7(1))* Concordia Publishing Hse.

—Everybody Wins! Division. Bruce, Sheila. 2006. (Math Matters ® Ser.). (ENG.). 32p. (J). (gr. k-3). pap. 5.95 *(978-1-57565-101-9(7))* Astra Publishing Hse.

—February, 1 vol. Kesselring, Mari. 2009. (Months of the Year Ser.). (ENG.). 24p. (J). (gr. k-2). 27.07 *(978-1-60270-629-3(8),* 11565, Looking Glass Library) Magic Wagon.

—Flower Girl. Herman, Gail. 2012. (Penguin Young Readers, L3 Ser.). (ENG.). 32p. (J). (gr. 1-4). 3.99 *(978-0-448-49487-6(6),* Grosset & Dunlap) Penguin Publishing Group.

—Flower Girl. Herman, Gail. 2012. (Penguin Young Readers: Level 3 Ser.: Level 2). (ENG.). 48p. (J). (gr. 1-3). 16.19 *(978-0-448-41108-8(3))* Penguin Young Readers Group.

—The Giant Jelly Bean Jar. Aboff, Marcie. 2013. (Puffin Young Readers, L3 Ser.). (ENG.). 32p. (J). (gr. -1-3). pap. 3.99 *(978-0-448-46624-8(4),* Puffin) Penguin Publishing Group.

—The Giant Jelly Bean Jar. Aboff, Marcie et al. 2004. (Puffin Easy-to-Read Ser.). 32p. (gr. k-3). 14.00 *(978-0-7569-2824-7(9))* Perfection Learning Corp.

—Here We Go 'Round the Year: A Book about the Months. Moncure, Jane Belk. 2013. (Magic Castle Readers Ser.). (ENG.). 32p. (J). (gr. -1-2). 14.21 *(978-1-62323-582-6(0),* 206318) Child's World, Inc., The.

—The House in the Meadow, 1 vol. Crum, Shutta. 2008. (ENG.). 32p. (J). pap. 9.95 *(978-1-55455-091-3(2),* 736d3047-5c4e-47db-a346-12421e8aab85) Fitzhenry & Whiteside, Ltd. CAN. Dist: Firefly Bks., Ltd.

—Ice Cream Cows & Mitten Sheep: A Book about Farm Animals. Moncure, Jane Belk. 2013. (Magic Castle Readers Ser.). (ENG.). 32p. (J). (gr. -1-2). 14.21 *(978-1-62323-583-3(9),* 206319) Child's World, Inc., The.

—January, 1 vol. Kesselring, Mari. 2009. (Months of the Year Ser.). (ENG.). 24p. (J). (gr. k-2). 27.07 *(978-1-60270-628-6(X),* 11563, Looking Glass Library) Magic Wagon.

—Lulu's Lemonade: Liquid Measure. deRubertis, Barbara. 2006. (Math Matters ® Ser.). (ENG.). 32p. (J). (gr. k-2). pap. 5.95 *(978-1-57565-093-7(2))* Astra Publishing Hse.

—Patty's Pictures. Janovich, Leah. 2010. 16p. (J). *(978-0-545-24820-4(5))* Scholastic, Inc.

—A Pocketful of Pets: A Search-and-Count Adventure. Moncure, Jane Belk. 2013. (Magic Castle Readers Ser.). (ENG.). 32p. (J). (gr. -1-2). 14.21 *(978-1-62323-584-0(7),* 206317) Child's World, Inc., The.

—A Slimy Story. Knudsen, Michelle. 2004. 32p. (J). lib. bdg. 20.00 *(978-1-4242-1150-0(6))* Fitzgerald Bks.

—A Slimy Story: Earthworms. Knudsen, Michelle. 2006. (Science Solves It! ® Ser.). (ENG.). 32p. (J). (gr. k-2). pap. 5.95 *(978-1-57565-144-6(0))* Astra Publishing Hse.

—Tara Pays Up! Taxes. Larsen, Kirsten. 2006. (Social Studies Connects ® Ser.). (ENG.). 32p. (J). (gr. 1-3). pap. 5.95 *(978-1-57565-187-3(4))* Astra Publishing Hse.

—This Is the Dreidel. Levine, Abby. 2012. (J). 34.28 *(978-1-61913-134-7(X))* Weigl Pubs., Inc.

—¡Todos Ganan! (Everybody Wins!) Division. Bruce, Sheila. 2006. (Math Matters en Español Ser.). (SPA.). 32p. (J). (gr. 1-3). pap. 5.95 *(978-1-57565-162-0(9))* Astra Publishing Hse.

—Trevor el Ingenioso (Clever Trevor) Albee, Sarah. 2008. (Science Solves It! ® en Español Ser.).Tr. of Clever Trevor. (SPA.). 32p. (J). (gr. 1-3). pap. 5.95 *(978-1-57565-263-4(3))* Astra Publishing Hse.

—The Way We Do It in Japan. Iijima, Geneva Cobb. 2013. (AV2 Fiction Readalong Ser.). (ENG.). (J). (gr. -1-3). 34.28 *(978-1-62127-899-3(9),* AV2 by Weigl) Weigl Pubs., Inc.

—Where Is Baby Bear? A Book about Animal Homes. Moncure, Jane Belk. 2013. (Magic Castle Readers Ser.). (ENG.). 32p. (J). (gr. -1-2). 14.21 *(978-1-62323-585-7(5),* 206320) Child's World, Inc., The.

Billings, David Joseph. Road Trip with Rabbit & Squash. Billings, David Joseph. 2006. 48p. (J). per. *(978-0-9789036-0-2(9))* Billings, David J.

Billings, Hammatt. Uncle Tom's Cabin: With Original 1852 Illustrations by Hammett Billings. Stowe, Harriet Beecher. 2019. (ENG.). 416p. (J). 19.95 *(978-1-64594-007-4(1))* Athanatos Publishing Group.

Billmaier, Elise M. Mr. Grudge. Plettner, Edith D. 2020. (ENG.). 30p. (J). pap. 9.99 ***(978-1-7271-3113-0(4))*** CreateSpace Independent Publishing Platform.

Billman, Dave, et al. Phonics. Thompson, Kim & Carder, Ken. 2009. 96p. (J). (gr. -1-3). pap. 10.99 incl. audio compact disk *(978-1-57583-820-5(6))* Twin Sisters IP, LLC.

Billout, Guy. All the World's a Stage. Hopkins, Lee Bennett. 2013. (ENG.). 40p. (J). (gr. 4-7). 19.99 *(978-1-56846-218-9(2),* Creative Editions) Creative Co., The.

Bills, Taylor. Goldilocks & the Three Bears. 2009. 24p. 12.95 *(978-0-9776845-2-6(0))* 3D Alley, Inc.

—Jack & the Beanstalk. 2009. 24p. 12.95 *(978-0-9776845-3-3(9))* 3D Alley, Inc.

—Tear Soup: A Recipe for Healing after Loss. Schwiebert, Pat & DeKlyen, Chuck. 2nd rev. l.t. ed. 2004. (ENG.). 56p. (gr. -1-12). reprint ed. 19.95 *(978-0-9615197-6-6(2),* 798) Grief Watch.

—Three Little Pigs. 2009. 24p. (J). 12.95 *(978-0-9776845-0-2(4))* 3D Alley, Inc.

—Twas the Night before Christmas. 2009. 24p. 12.95 *(978-0-9776845-4-0(7))* 3D Alley, Inc.

—The Ugly Duckling. 2009. 24p. 12.95 *(978-0-9776845-1-9(2))* 3D Alley, Inc.

—We Were Gonna Have a Baby, but We Had an Angel Instead. Schwiebert, Pat. 2004. 24p. pap. 7.95 *(978-0-9724241-1-0(3),* 717) Grief Watch.

Billups, Takarais & Horwitz, Suzanne. Not Without Him! Black Inventors. Hardy, C. Ch�rie. 2020. (ENG.). 34p. (J). pap. 12.95 ***(978-1-946753-46-5(7))*** Avant-garde Bks.

Bilyeu, Dan. Weird Rocks, 1 vol. Corriel, Michele. 2013. (ENG.). 36p. (J). 12.00 *(978-0-87842-597-6(7))* Mountain Pr. Publishing Co., Inc.

Binch, Caroline. Look Back! Cooke, Trish. (ENG.). 32p. (J). 2019. pap. 8.95 *(978-1-56656-099-3(3));* 2014. 17.95 *(978-1-56656-980-4(X))* Interlink Publishing Group, Inc. (Crocodile Bks.).

Binch, Caroline. The Princess & the Castle. Binch, Caroline. 2005. (ENG.). 32p. (J). (gr. k-2). 8.99 *(978-0-09-943236-4(6),* Red Fox) Random House Children's Books GBR. Dist: Independent Pubs. Group.

Binder, Lenore. Bananas & Bears, 1 vol. Binder, Anita. 2010. 24p. 24.95 *(978-1-4489-5946-4(2))* PublishAmerica, Inc.

Binder, Pat. Bluebonnet at the State Fair of Texas, 1 vol. Casad, Mary Brooke. 2010. (Bluebonnet Ser.). (ENG.). 40p. (J). (gr. k-3). pap. 8.95 *(978-1-58980-830-0(4),* Pelican Publishing) Arcadia Publishing.

Bindon, John. Armored Dinosaurs. Lessem, Don. 2004. (Meet the Dinosaurs Ser.). 32p. (gr. 2-5). (J). per. 6.95 *(978-0-8225-2570-7(4));* (ENG.). lib. bdg. 23.93 *(978-0-8225-1374-2(9))* Lerner Publishing Group.

—Carnivoros Gigantes. Lessem, Don. 2005.Tr. of Giant Meat-Eating Dinosaurs. (SPA.). 32p. (J). (gr. 2-4). pap. 6.95 *(978-0-8225-2963-7(7))* Lerner Publishing Group.

—The Deadliest Dinosaurs. Lessem, Don. (Meet the Dinosaurs Ser.). 32p. (gr. 2-4). 2005. (ENG.). lib. bdg. 23.93 *(978-0-8225-1421-3(4));* 2004. (J). per. 6.95 *(978-0-8225-2619-3(0))* Lerner Publishing Group.

—Dinosaurios Acorazados. Lessem, Don. 2005. (Meet the Dinosaurs Ser.).Tr. of Armored Dinosaurs. (SPA.). 32p. (J). (gr. 2-4). per. 6.95 *(978-0-8225-2958-3(0))* Lerner Publishing Group.

—Dinosaurios Con Plumas. Lessem, Don. Translations.com Staff, tr. from ENG. 2006. (Conoce A Los Dinosaurios (Meet the Dinosaurs) Ser.).Tr. of Feathered Dinosaurs. (SPA.). 32p. (gr. 2-4). lib. bdg. 23.93 *(978-0-8225-6242-9(1))* Lerner Publishing Group.

—Dinosaurios Cornudos. Lessem, Don. 2005. (Meet the Dinosaurs Ser.).Tr. of Horned Dinosaurs. (SPA.). 32p. (J). (gr. 2-4). per. 6.95 *(978-0-8225-2967-5(X));* (gr. 3-7). lib. bdg. 23.93 *(978-0-8225-2966-8(1),* Ediciones Lerner) Lerner Publishing Group.

—Los Dinosaurios Mas Mortiferos. Lessem, Don. 2006. (Conoce A los Dinosaurios Ser.). 32p. (J). (gr. 3-7). lib. bdg. 23.93 *(978-0-8225-6240-5(5),* Ediciones Lerner) Lerner Publishing Group.

—Los Dinosaurios Mas Pequenos. Lessem, Don. 2005. (Meet the Dinosaurs Ser.).Tr. of Smallest Dinosaurs. (SPA.). 32p. (J). (gr. 2-4). per. 6.95 *(978-0-8225-2969-9(6))* Lerner Publishing Group.

—Dinosaurios Pico de Pato. Lessem, Don. 2005. (Meet the Dinosaurs Ser.).Tr. of Duck-Billed Dinosaurs. (SPA.). 32p. (J). (gr. 2-4). per. 6.95 *(978-0-8225-2961-3(0))* Lerner Publishing Group.

—Dinosaurios Pico de Pato. Lessem, Don. Translations.com Staff, tr. 2005. (Conoce A Los Dinosaurios (Meet the Dinosaurs) Ser.).Tr. of Duck-Billed Dinosaurs. (SPA.). 32p. (gr. 2-4). lib. bdg. 23.93 *(978-0-8225-2959-0(9))* Lerner Publishing Group.

—Duck-Billed Dinosaurs. Lessem, Don. (Meet the Dinosaurs Ser.). 32p. (J). 2005. (gr. 2-5). per. 6.95 *(978-0-8225-2571-4(2));* 2004. (gr. 3-7). lib. bdg. 23.93 *(978-0-8225-1369-8(2))* Lerner Publishing Group.

—The Fastest Dinosaurs. Lessem, Don. 2005. 32p. (gr. 2-4). (J). pap. 6.95 *(978-0-8225-2620-9(4))*; (ENG.). lib. bdg. 23.93 *(978-0-8225-1422-0(2))* Lerner Publishing Group.
—Feathered Dinosaurs. Lessem, Don. 2005. 32p. (J). (gr. 2-4). pap. 6.95 *(978-0-8225-2621-6(2))* Lerner Publishing Group.
—Flying Giants of Dinosaur Time. Lessem, Don. 2005. (Meet the Dinosaurs Ser.). 32p. (J). (gr. 3-7). lib. bdg. 23.93 *(978-0-8225-1424-4(9))* Lerner Publishing Group.
—Flying Giants of Dinosaur Time. Lessem, Dino Don. 2005. (Meet the Dinosaurs Ser.). 32p. (J). (gr. 2-5). pap. 6.95 *(978-0-8225-2622-3(0))* Lerner Publishing Group.
—Giant Meat-Eating Dinosaurs. Lessem, Don. 2004. (Meet the Dinosaurs Ser.). (J). 32p. (gr. 4-7). lib. bdg. 23.93 *(978-0-8225-3925-4(X))*; pap. 7.95 *(978-0-8225-5326-7(0)*, Lerner Pubns.) Lerner Publishing Group.
—Giant Plant-Eating Dinosaurs. Lessem, Don. 2004. (Meet the Dinosaurs Ser.). 32p. (J). (gr. 3-7). lib. bdg. 23.93 *(978-0-8225-1371-1(4))* Lerner Publishing Group.
—Gigantes Marinos de la Época de los Dinosaurios. Lessem, Don. Translations.com Staff, tr. from ENG. 2006. (Conoce A Los Dinosaurios (Meet the Dinosaurs) Ser.). (SPA.). 32p. (gr. 2-4). lib. bdg. 23.93 *(978-0-8225-6244-3(8))* Lerner Publishing Group.
—Gigantes Voladores de la Epoca de los Dinosaurios. Lessem, Don. Translations.com Staff, tr. from ENG. 2006. (Conoce A Los Dinosaurios (Meet the Dinosaurs) Ser.).Tr. of Flying Giants of Dinosaur Time. (SPA.). 32p. (gr. 2-4). lib. bdg. 23.93 *(978-0-8225-6243-6(X))* Lerner Publishing Group.
—Herbívoros Gigantes. Lessem, Don. 2005. (Meet the Dinosaurs Ser.).Tr. of Giant Plant-Eating Dinosaurs. (SPA.). 32p. (J). (gr. 2-4). per. 6.95 *(978-0-8225-2965-1(3))* Lerner Publishing Group.
—Herbívoros Gigantes. Lessem, Don. Translations.com Staff, tr. 2005. (Conoce A Los Dinosaurios (Meet the Dinosaurs) Ser.). (SPA.). 32p. (gr. 2-4). lib. bdg. 23.93 *(978-0-8225-2964-4(5))* Lerner Publishing Group.
—Horned Dinosaurs. Lessem, Don. (Meet the Dinosaurs Ser.). 32p. (gr. 2-5). 2005. (J). per. 6.95 *(978-0-8225-2574-5(7))*; 2004. (ENG.). lib. bdg. 23.93 *(978-0-8225-1370-4(6))* Lerner Publishing Group.
—Los Dinosaurios Más Inteligentes. Lessem, Don. Translations.com Staff, tr. from ENG. 2006. (Conoce A Los Dinosaurios (Meet the Dinosaurs) Ser.). (SPA.). 32p. (gr. 2-4). lib. bdg. 23.93 *(978-0-8225-6245-0(6))* Lerner Publishing Group.
—Los Dinosaurios Más Pequeños. Lessem, Don. Translations.com Staff, tr. 2005. (Conoce A Los Dinosaurios (Meet the Dinosaurs) Ser.).Tr. of Smallest Dinosaurs. (SPA.). 32p. (gr. 2-4). lib. bdg. 23.93 *(978-0-8225-2968-2(8))* Lerner Publishing Group.
—Megabugs: And Other Prehistoric Critters That Roamed the Planet. Becker, Helaine. 2019. (ENG.). 32p. (J). (gr. 3-7). 17.99 *(978-1-77138-811-5(0))* Kids Can Pr., Ltd. CAN. Dist: Hachette Bk. Group.
—Pterosaurs up Close: Flying Reptiles. Dodson, Peter. 2011. (Zoom in on Dinosaurs! Ser.). 24p. (gr. k-2). 23.95 *(978-0-7660-3332-0(5))* Enslow Publishing, LLC.
—Sea Giants of Dinosaur Time. Lessem, Don. 2005. 32p. (J). (gr. 2-5). pap. 6.95 *(978-0-8225-2623-0(9))*; (gr. 3-7). lib. bdg. 23.93 *(978-0-8225-1425-1(7))* Lerner Publishing Group.
—The Smallest Dinosaurs. Lessem, Don. 2004. (Meet the Dinosaurs Ser.). 32p. (J). (gr. -1-3). lib. bdg. 23.93 *(978-0-8225-1372-8(2))*; (gr. 2-5). per. 6.95 *(978-0-8225-2575-2(5))* Lerner Publishing Group.
—The Smartest Dinosaurs. Lessem, Don. (Meet the Dinosaurs Ser.). 32p. (gr. 2-4). 2005. (ENG.). lib. bdg. 23.93 *(978-0-8225-1373-5(0))*; 2004. (J). pap. 6.95 *(978-0-8225-2618-6(2))* Lerner Publishing Group.
Bindon, John, jt. illus. see Marshall, Todd.
Bines, Gary & Boller, Gary. Freaky Facts about Natural Disasters. Fecher, Sarah & Oliver, Clare. Anderson, Jill, ed. 2006. (Freaky Facts Ser.). (ENG.). 32p. (J). (gr. 2-5). pap. 8.95 *(978-1-58728-542-4(8))* Cooper Square Publishing Llc.
Bines, Gary & Hancock, David. The Usborne Little Encyclopedia of Space. Dowswell, Paul. 2005. 64p. (J). (gr. -1-3). 6.95 *(978-0-7945-1091-6(4)*, Usborne) EDC Publishing.
Bing, Christopher. Lincoln Shot: A President's Life Remembered. Denenberg, Barry. 2011. (ENG.). 96p. (J). (gr. 5-9). pap. 14.99 *(978-0-312-60442-4(4)*, 900076473) Square Fish.
Bingham, Jerry, et al. Black Panther Epic Collection: Revenge of the Black Panther. 2019. (ENG.). 456p. (J). (gr. 4-17). pap. 39.99 *(978-1-302-91542-1(8))* Marvel Worldwide, Inc.
Bingham, Jerry. Sing Out Loud Book IV: Owning the Stage. Hoops, Kevin, photos by. Vendera, Jaime & McGee, Anne Loader. 2012. 36p. (YA). pap. 7.99 *(978-1-936307-11-1(1))* Vendera Publishing.
Bingham, Jerry, V, et al. Taskmaster: Anything You Can Do... 2020. (ENG.). 352p. (YA). (gr. 4-17). pap. 34.99 *(978-1-302-92131-6(2))* Marvel Worldwide, Inc.
Bingham, Jerry, jt. illus. see Bastien, Valerie.
Bingham, Nelly. Friendship Is the True Treasure. Gomez, Vicky. 2016. (MUL.). (J). pap. 12.95 *(978-1-63525-362-7(4))* Christian Faith Publishing.
Bingham, Pamela E. A Thought for Thanksgiving. Stilwell, Norma Mintum. 2011. 24p. pap. 14.95 *(978-1-936343-93-5(2))* Peppertree Pr., The.
Bingmer, Zehra. How to Fulfill Wishes: A Bedtime Story. Wolf, Sascha. Hat, Hyper, tr. 2019. (ENG.). 26p. (J). pap. 9.99 ***(978-1-0884-7867-7(0))*** Independently Published.
Binus, Ari. Around the Shabbos Table. Berman, Seryl. 2008. 40p. (J). (gr. -1-k). pap. 10.95 *(978-1-929628-44-5(7))* Hachai Publishing.
—Hayyim's Ghost. Kimmel, Eric A. 2005. 40p. (J). 16.95 *(978-1-932687-02-6(5)*, Devora Publishing) Simcha Media Group.
—Izzy Hagbah. 2005. 37p. (J). (gr. 1-4). 16.95 *(978-1-932687-38-5(6))*; per. 9.95 *(978-1-932687-39-2(4))* Simcha Media Group. (Devora Publishing).
—Littlest Tree. Rouss, Sylvia. 2005. 32p. (J). pap. 9.95 *(978-1-932687-26-2(2)*, Devora Publishing) Simcha Media Group.
—The Littlest Tree. Rouss, Sylvia. 2005. 32p. (J). 16.95 *(978-1-932687-25-5(4)*, Devora Publishing) Simcha Media Group.
Bios Agency, photos by. The Shark: Silent Hunter. Le Bloas-Julienne, Renee. 2007. (Animal Close-Ups Ser.). 26p. (J). (gr. 1-4). pap. 6.95 *(978-1-57091-631-1(4))* Charlesbridge Publishing, Inc.
Birch, Linda. Start Here. Lane, Sheila Mary & Kemp, Marion. Date not set. (Whizz Bang Bumper Bk.). 64p. (J). pap. 129.15 *(978-0-582-19331-4(1))* Addison-Wesley Longman, Ltd. GBR. Dist: Trans-Atlantic Pubns., Inc.
Birch, Reginal. The Christmas Angel. Brown, Abbie Farwell. 2019. (ENG.). 96p. (J). (gr. k-4). pap. ***(978-625-7959-24-7(1))*** Urhayoglu, Murat E Kitap Projesi.
Birch, Reginald. Little Lord Fauntleroy. Burnett, Frances Hodgson. 2004. reprint ed. pap. 27.95 *(978-1-4179-4302-9(5))* Kessinger Publishing, LLC.
Birchall, Mark. Be Gentle, Python! Willis, Jeanne. 2005. (Picture Bks.). 28p. (J). (gr. k-2). 7.95 *(978-1-57505-508-4(2))* Lerner Publishing Group.
—Be Quiet, Parrot! Willis, Jeanne. 2005. (Picture Bks.). 32p. (J). (gr. k-2). 7.25 *(978-1-57505-492-6(2))* Lerner Publishing Group.
—No Biting, Puma! Willis, Jeanne. 2005. (Picture Bks.). 28p. (J). (gr. k-2). 7.25 *(978-1-57505-509-1(0))* Lerner Publishing Group.
—Take Turns, Penguin! Willis, Jeanne. 2003. (Picture Bks.). 32p. (J). (gr. -1-3). 7.95 *(978-1-57505-493-3(0)*, Carolrhoda Bks.) Lerner Publishing Group.
Birchall, Mark. Rabbit's Birthday Surprise. Birchall, Mark. 2003. 32p. (J). (gr. -1-3). 15.95 *(978-0-87614-910-2(7)*, Carolrhoda Bks.) Lerner Publishing Group.
—Rabbit's Wooly Sweater. Birchall, Mark. 2003. (Picture Bks.). 32p. (J). (gr. -1-3). 15.95 *(978-1-57505-465-0(5)*, Carolrhoda Bks.) Lerner Publishing Group.
Birck, Jan. The Wild Soccer Bunch, Book 2, Diego the Tornado: Diego the Tornado. Masannak, Joachim. Part, Michael, ed. Schler, Helga, tr. 2011. (ENG.). 148p. (J). (gr. 4-7). 12.95 *(978-0-9844257-1-6(3))* Sole Bks.
Bird, Bob. Photo Firsts. Dorman, Meg. 2020. (ENG.). 28p. (J). pap. ***(978-1-922331-48-9(1))*** Library For All Limited.
Bird, Glen. Dinosaur Jigsaw Atlas. Pearcey, Alice, ed. 2004. 20p. (J). 14.95 *(978-0-7945-0913-2(4)*, Usborne) EDC Publishing.
Bird, Glen, jt. illus. see Cartwright, Stephen.
Bird, Jemima. Our Cat Henry Comes to the Swings. Clanchy, Kate. 2007. 32p. (J). (gr. -1-1). 16.00 *(978-1-56148-563-5(2)*, Good Bks.) Skyhorse Publishing Co., Inc.
Bird, Matthew. Crown & Covenant, 3 bks. Bond, Doug. 2004. (Crown & Covenant Ser.). (J). per. 26.99 *(978-0-87552-671-3(3))* P & R Publishing.
—First Son & President: A Story about John Quincy Adams. Gherman, Beverly. 2005. (Creative Minds Biographies Ser.). (ENG.). 64p. (gr. 4-8). lib. bdg. 22.60 *(978-1-57505-756-9(5)*, Carolrhoda Bks.) Lerner Publishing Group.
—King's Arrow. Bond, Douglas. 2003. (Crown & Covenant Ser.). 208p. (J). per. 10.99 *(978-0-87552-743-7(4))* P & R Publishing.
—Rebel's Keep. Bond, Douglas. 2004. (Crown & Covenant Ser.). 285p. (J). per. 9.99 *(978-0-87552-744-4(2))* P & R Publishing.
Bird, Nikolai. Dear Principal Petunia: Word Processing. Zocchi, Judy. 2005. (Click & Squeak Ser.). 32p. (J). pap. 9.95 *(978-1-59646-111-6(X))* Dingles & Co.
Bird, Richard E., photos by. Freddy in the City: Center City Sites. Bird, Janice W. Date not set. 32p. (J). (gr. 2-5). pap. 5.95 *(978-0-9710071-1-6(X))* JFW, Ltd.
Birdi, Amrit. Ark Angel: an Alex Rider Graphic Novel. Horowitz, Anthony & Johnston, Antony. 2020. (ENG.). 176p. (J). (gr. 4-7). pap. 14.99 ***(978-1-5362-0733-0(0))*** Candlewick Pr.
Birdsong, Keith. Voice of the Paiutes: A Story about Sarah Winnemucca. Shull, Jodie A. 2007. (Creative Minds Biography Ser.). 64p. (J). (gr. 3-7). lib. bdg. 22.60 *(978-0-8225-5990-0(0))* Lerner Publishing Group.
Birdy, Miss, jt. illus. see Slusser, Lauren.
Birgele, Laura. Sarah & the Sock Revolution. Petrilli, Laura. 2018. (ENG.). 50p. (J). pap. *(978-1-9999606-1-2(0))* Lapet Publishing.
Birkett, Georgie. Clean It! 2009. (Helping Hands Ser.). 24p. (J). (gr. -1-k). *(978-1-84643-283-5(9))* Child's Play International Ltd.
—Clean It!/¡a Limpiar! ed. 2009. (Helping Hands English/Spanish Edition Ser.). (SPA.). 24p. (J). (gr. -1-k). pap. *(978-1-84643-569-0(2))* Child's Play International Ltd.
—Cook It! 2009. (Helping Hands Ser.). 24p. (J). (gr. -1-k). *(978-1-84643-284-2(7))* Child's Play International Ltd.
—Cook It!/¡a Cocinar! ed. 2009. (Helping Hands English/Spanish Edition Ser.). (SPA.). 24p. (J). (gr. -1-k). pap. *(978-1-84643-568-3(4))* Child's Play International Ltd.
—Fix It! 2009. (Helping Hands Ser.). 24p. (J). (gr. -1-k). *(978-1-84643-286-6(3))* Child's Play International Ltd.
—Fix It!/¡a Reparar! ed. 2009. (Helping Hands English/Spanish Edition Ser.). (ENG.). 24p. (J). (gr. -1-k). pap. *(978-1-84643-571-3(4))* Child's Play International Ltd.
—Grow It! 2009. (Helping Hands Ser.). 24p. (J). (gr. -1-k). *(978-1-84643-285-9(5))* Child's Play International Ltd.
—Grow It!/¡a Sembrar! ed. 2009. (Helping Hands English/Spanish Edition Ser.). (ENG.). 24p. (J). (gr. -1-k). pap. *(978-1-84643-570-6(6))* Child's Play International Ltd.
—Ha Ha, Baby! Petty, Kate. 2008. (ENG.). 32p. (J). (gr. -1-k). 14.95 *(978-1-905417-12-4(8))* Boxer Bks., Ltd. GBR. Dist: Sterling Publishing Co., Inc.
—Hoppy Birthday, Jo-Jo! Goodhart, Pippa. 2005. (Green Bananas Ser.). (ENG.). 48p. (J). lib. bdg. *(978-0-7787-1025-7(4))* Crabtree Publishing Co.
—How to Bathe Your Little Dino. Clarke, Jane. 2017. 16p. (J). bds. 8.99 *(978-1-61067-495-9(2))* Kane Miller.
—How to Brush Your Teeth with Snappy Crocodile. Clarke, Jane. 2017. 16p. (J). bds. 8.99 *(978-1-61067-494-2(4))* Kane Miller.
—How to Feed Your Cheeky Monkey. Clarke, Jane. 2017. 16p. (J). bds. 8.99 *(978-1-61067-497-3(9))* Kane Miller.
—How to Tuck in Your Sleepy Lion. Clarke, Jane. 2017. 16p. (J). bds. 8.99 *(978-1-61067-496-6(0))* Kane Miller.
—I'm Big Now! Simmons, Anthea. 2017. (ENG.). 32p. (J). (gr. -1-3). 17.99 *(978-1-5124-3947-2(9))* Lerner Publishing Group.
—A Is for Apple. Tiger Tales. 2011. (ENG.). 26p. (J). (-k). bds. 7.95 *(978-1-58925-872-3(X))* Tiger Tales.
—123 Count with Me. Tiger Tales. 2011. (ENG.). 26p. (J). (-k). bds. 7.95 *(978-1-58925-873-0(8))* Tiger Tales.
Birkett, Georgie & Stockham, Jess. Helping Hands Board Book Set Of 6. 2020. (Social & Emotional Learning Sets Ser.). (ENG.). 144p. (J). pap., pap., pap. ***(978-1-78628-530-0(4))*** Child's Play International Ltd.
Birky, Rachael. The Lone, Lone Cloud. Shifler, Ann. 2012. 28p. pap. 16.00 *(978-1-58158-133-1(5))* McDougal Publishing Co.
Birmingham, Chi. The Mortification of Fovea Munson. Heider, Mary Winn. 2018. (ENG.). 336p. (J). (gr. 3-7). E-Book *(978-1-4847-8107-4(4))* Little, Brown Bks. for Young Readers.
Birmingham, Christian. Black Beauty. Sewell, Anna. 2019. (ENG.). 240p. (J). (gr. 5). 24.99 *(978-1-5362-1124-5(9))* Candlewick Pr.
—Dear Olly. Morpurgo, Michael. 2007. (ENG.). 128p. (J). (gr. 4-7). mass mkt. 7.99 *(978-0-00-675333-9(7)*, HarperCollins Children's Bks.) HarperCollins Pubs. Ltd. GBR. Dist: HarperCollins Pubs.
Birmingham, Christian. The Legend of Sleepy Hollow. Irving, Washington. 2020. (ENG.). 128p. (J). (gr. 4-7). 16.99 ***(978-1-78675-098-3(8))*** Palazzo Editions, Ltd. GBR. Dist: Independent Pubs. Group.
Birmingham, Christian. The Night Before Christmas. Moore, Clement C. (J). (gr. -1 — 1). 2007. 26p. 5.95 *(978-0-7624-3014-7(1))*; 10th anniv. ed. 2005. 48p. 9.95 *(978-0-7624-2416-0(8))* Running Pr. (Running Pr. Kids).
—The Story of Holly & Ivy. Godden, Rumer. 2017. (ENG.). 80p. (J). (gr. 2-4). pap. 8.99 *(978-1-5098-0505-1(2))* Pan Macmillan GBR. Dist: Independent Pubs. Group.
—Thief Lord. Funke, Cornelia. 2010. (ENG.). 368p. (J). (gr. 4-7). pap. 7.99 *(978-0-545-22770-4(4))* Scholastic, Inc.
Birnbach, Alece. Rise of the Undead Redhead. Dougherty, Meghan. 2014. (Dorothy's Derby Chronicles Ser.: 1). (ENG.). 256p. (J). (gr. 3-6). pap. 10.99 *(978-1-4022-9535-5(9)*, Sourcebooks Jabberwocky) Sourcebooks, Inc.
—Woe of Jade Doe. Dougherty, Meghan. 2015. (Dorothy's Derby Chronicles Ser.: 2). (ENG.). 288p. (J). (gr. 4-7). pap. 6.99 *(978-1-4926-0147-0(0)*, Sourcebooks Jabberwocky) Sourcebooks, Inc.
Birnbaum, A. Little World, Hello! Savo, Jimmy. 2012. 194p. 42.95 *(978-1-258-23434-8(3))*; pap. 27.95 *(978-1-258-24665-5(1))* Literary Licensing, LLC.
Birnbaum, A. Green Eyes. Birnbaum, A. 2011. (Family Storytime Ser.). 48p. (J). (gr. -1-2). pap. 7.99 *(978-0-375-86201-4(3)*, Dragonfly Bks.) Random Hse. Children's Bks.
Biro, Val. Animal Tales for Bedtime. Jennings, Linda. 2013. (ENG.). 96p. (J). 16.50 *(978-1-84135-932-8(7))* Award Pubns. Ltd. GBR. Dist: Parkwest Pubns., Inc.
—The Bible for Children. Fiona Fox Staff, ed. 2015. (ENG.). 280p. 33.00 *(978-1-84135-827-7(4))* Award Pubns. Ltd. GBR. Dist: Parkwest Pubns., Inc.
—The Donkey & the Lapdog with the Lion & the Mouse. Award, Anna & Aesop, Aesop. 2014. (ENG.). 24p. (J). pap. 6.95 *(978-1-84135-953-3(X))* Award Pubns. Ltd. GBR. Dist: Parkwest Pubns., Inc.
—How to Draw Dinosaurs & Prehistoric Life. Claridge, Marit. Tatchell, Judy, ed. 2006. (Young Artist Ser.). 32p. (J). (gr. 4-7). pap. 5.99 *(978-0-7945-1372-6(7)*, Usborne) EDC Publishing.
—The Secret of the Lost Necklace: 3 Great Adventure Stories. Blyton, Enid. 2013. (ENG.). 272p. (J). 16.50 *(978-1-84135-587-0(9))* Award Pubns. Ltd. GBR. Dist: Parkwest Pubns., Inc.
—100 Bible Stories for Children. Andrews, Jackie. 2012. (ENG.). 208p. (J). 21.50 *(978-1-84135-105-6(9))* Award Pubns. Ltd. GBR. Dist: Parkwest Pubns., Inc.
Biro, Val. Gumdrop & the Elephant. Biro, Val. 2015. (ENG.). 32p. (J). pap. 9.99 *(978-1-78270-049-4(8))* Award Pubns. Ltd. GBR. Dist: Parkwest Pubns., Inc.
Birth, Ryan. What Do Monsters Look Like? Tayler, Amber. 2009. 36p. pap. 11.25 *(978-1-935125-51-8(6))* Robertson Publishing.
Bisacco, Stefania. Las Hojas. Linden, Mary. 2016. (Early Rising Readers Ser.). (SPA.). (J). (gr. -1). 6.67 *(978-1-4788-3655-1(5))* Newmark Learning LLC.
—Las Nubes. Schmauss, Judy Kentor. 2016. (Early Rising Readers Ser.). (SPA.). 16p. (J). (gr. 1-1). 6.67 *(978-1-4788-4218-7(0))* Newmark Learning LLC.
Bisacco, Stephania. Leaves. Lindeen, Mary. 2015. (Early Rising Readers Ser.). (J). (gr. -1-k). 5.83 *(978-1-4788-1593-8(0))* Newmark Learning LLC.
Bisaillon, Josée. Bedtime 123, 1 vol. Walters, Eric. 2017. (ENG.). 26p. (J). (gr. -1 — 1). bds. 10.95 *(978-1-4598-1073-0(2))* Orca Bk. Pubs. USA.
—Benno & the Night of Broken Glass. Wiviott, Meg. 2010. (ENG.). 32p. (J). (gr. 2-5). lib. bdg. 17.95 *(978-0-8225-9929-6(5)*, Kar-Ben Publishing) Lerner Publishing Group.
—The Blue Vase, 1 vol. Jovanovic, Katerina. 2015. (ENG.). 120p. (J). (gr. 1-3). pap. 10.95 *(978-1-896580-91-3(2))* Tradewind Bks. CAN. Dist: Orca Bk. Pubs. USA.
—BookSpeak! Poems About Books. Salas, Laura Purdie. 2011. (ENG.). 32p. (J). (gr. -1-3). 17.99 *(978-0-547-22300-1(5)*, 1061778) Houghton Mifflin Harcourt Publishing Co.
—The Boreal Forest: A Year in the World's Largest Land Biome. Carmichael, L. E. 2020. (ENG.). 48p. (J). (gr. 3-7). 18.99 *(978-1-5253-0044-8(X))* Kids Can Pr., Ltd. CAN. Dist: Hachette Bk. Group.
Bisaillon, Josée. Dancing with Daisy, 1 vol. Coates, Jan. 2019. (ENG.). 44p. (J). (gr. -1-3). pap. 12.95 ***(978-1-927917-20-6(4))*** Running the Goat, Bks. & Broadsides CAN. Dist: Orca Bk. Pubs. USA.
Bisaillon, Josee. A Fish Named Glub, 0 vols. Bar-el, Dan. 2014. (ENG.). 32p. (J). (gr. -1-3). 16.95 *(978-1-55453-812-6(2))* Kids Can Pr., Ltd. CAN. Dist: Hachette Bk. Group.
Bisaillon, Josée. A Great Big Night, 1 vol. Inglis, Kate. 2020. (ENG.). 32p. (J). 17.95 ***(978-1-77108-908-1(3)***, 6f2732c5-cd16-4ba4-a1fc-07904d37063e) Nimbus Publishing, Ltd. CAN. Dist: Baker & Taylor Publisher Services (BTPS).
Bisaillon, Josée. The Great Moon Hoax. Krensky, Stephen. 2011. (Carolrhoda Picture Bks.). (ENG.). 32p. (J). (gr. 2-5). lib. bdg. 16.95 *(978-0-7613-5110-8(8))* Lerner Publishing Group.
—I Can't Sleep: Imagination - Bedtime. Kim, Cecil. Cowley, Joy, ed. 2015. (Step up — Creative Thinking Ser.). (ENG.). 32p. (J). (gr. -1-2). 10.00 *(978-1-925186-41-3(5)*, Big and SMALL) ChoiceMaker Pty. Ltd., The AUS. Dist: Lerner Publishing Group.
Bisaillon, Josee. I Can't Sleep: Imagination - Bedtime. Kim, Cecil. Cowley, Joy, ed. 2015. (Step up - Creative Thinking Ser.). (ENG.). 32p. (gr. -1-2). 26.65 *(978-1-925246-13-1(2))*; 7.99 *(978-1-925246-65-0(5))*; 26.65 *(978-1-925246-39-1(6))* ChoiceMaker Pty. Ltd., The AUS. (Big and SMALL). Dist: Lerner Publishing Group.
Bisaillon, Josée. Leap! Lawson, JonArno. 2017. (ENG.). 32p. (J). (gr. -1-2). 16.99 *(978-1-77138-678-4(9))* Kids Can Pr., Ltd. CAN. Dist: Hachette Bk. Group.
Bisaillon, Josée. La Lune Est un �tang D'Argent. Cassidy, Sara. Martinez, Rachel, tr. from ENG. 2020. (FRE.). 32p. (J). (gr. -1-k). 19.95 ***(978-1-4598-2452-2(0))*** Orca Bk. Pubs. USA.
Bisaillon, Josée. Milo & Georgie. Galbraith, Bree. 2017. (ENG.). 32p. (J). (gr. -1-3). 16.95 *(978-1-77147-170-1(0))* Owlkids Bks. Inc. CAN. Dist: Publishers Group West (PGW).
—The Moon Is a Silver Pond, 1 vol. Cassidy, Sara. 2019. (ENG.). 24p. (J). (gr. -1 — 1). bds. 10.95 *(978-1-4598-1864-4(4))* Orca Bk. Pubs. USA.
—My Head in the Clouds, 1 vol. Chaperon, Danielle. 2019. Orig. Title: Ma Tête en L'air. (ENG.). 32p. (J). (gr. -1-k). 19.95 *(978-1-4598-2178-1(5))* Orca Bk. Pubs. USA.
—Oh No, School! Chang, Hae-Kyung. 2014. 32p. (J). *(978-1-4338-1333-7(5)*, Magination Pr.) American Psychological Assn.
—The Snow Knows, 1 vol. McGrath, Jennifer. 2016. (ENG.). 32p. (J). (gr. -1-k). 22.95 *(978-1-77108-441-3(3)*, 297c65cc-a5e0-45d4-a41c-24c56cf21f37) Nimbus Publishing, Ltd. CAN. Dist: Baker & Taylor Publisher Services (BTPS).
Bisaillon, Josée. Le Soleil Est une P�che. Cassidy, Sara. Martinez, Rachel, tr. from ENG. 2020. (FRE.). 32p. (J). (gr. -1-k). 19.95 ***(978-1-4598-2455-3(5))*** Orca Bk. Pubs. USA.
Bisaillon, Josée. Ten Cents a Pound, 1 vol. Tran-Davies, Nhung N. 2018. (ENG.). 24p. (J). (gr. 1-3). 18.95 *(978-1-77260-056-8(3))* Second Story Pr. CAN. Dist: Orca Bk. Pubs. USA.
—Usha & the Stolen Sun. Galbraith, Bree. 2020. (ENG.). 32p. (J). (gr. -1-4). 17.95 *(978-1-77147-276-0(6))* Owlkids Bks. Inc. CAN. Dist: Publishers Group West (PGW).
Bisaillon, Josée & Bisaillon, Josée. Benno & the Night of Broken Glass. Vol. Wiviott, Meg. 2010. (ENG.). 32p. (J). (gr. 2-5). pap. 8.99 *(978-0-8225-9975-3(9)*, Kar-Ben Publishing) Lerner Publishing Group.
—Mom, Dad, Our Books, & Me. Marcotte, Danielle. 2016. (ENG.). 32p. (J). (gr. -1-3). 16.95 *(978-1-77147-201-2(4)*, Owlkids) Owlkids Bks. Inc. CAN. Dist: Publishers Group West (PGW).
—Winter's Coming: A Story of Seasonal Change. Thornhill, Jan. 2014. (ENG.). 32p. (J). (gr. 3-3). 16.95 *(978-1-77147-002-5(X)*, Owlkids) Owlkids Bks. Inc. CAN. Dist: Publishers Group West (PGW).
Bisaillon, Josée, jt. illus. see Bisaillon, Josée.
Bischoff, Hailey. The Littlest Angel. Parks, Brooklyn. 2019. (ENG.). 32p. (J). 15.99 *(978-1-4621-2316-2(3))* Cedar Fort, Inc./CFI Distribution.
Biscoe, Cee. God Is Always with Me: Psalm 139. Mackall, Dandi Daley. 2019. (Child's First Bible Ser.). (ENG.). 16p. (J). bds. 7.99 *(978-1-4964-3277-3(0)*, 20_31604, Tyndale Kids) Tyndale Hse. Pubs.
—God Takes Care of Me: Psalm 23. Mackall, Dandi Daley. 2019. (Child's First Bible Ser.). (ENG.). 16p. (J). bds. 7.99 *(978-1-4964-3276-6(2)*, 20_31601, Tyndale Kids) Tyndale Hse. Pubs.
—Grandma Cuddles: With Touch-And-Feel Animals!, 1 vol. 2020. (ENG.). 12p. (J). bds. 9.99 *(978-1-4002-1459-4(9))* Nelson, Thomas Inc.
—Psalms for Little Hearts: 25 Psalms for Joy, Hope, & Praise. Mackall, Dandi Daley. 2019. (Child's First Bible Ser.). (ENG.). 112p. (J). 12.99 *(978-1-4964-3275-9(4)*, 20_31281, Tyndale Kids) Tyndale Hse. Pubs.
—Snuggle Time Bible Stories, 1 vol. Nellist, Glenys. 2019. (Snuggle Time Padded Board Book Ser.). (ENG.). 26p. (J). bds. 9.99 *(978-0-310-76625-4(7))* Zonderkidz.
—Snuggle Time Christmas Stories, 1 vol. Nellist, Glenys. 2017. (Snuggle Time Padded Board Book Ser.). (ENG.). 26p. (J). bds. 9.99 *(978-0-310-76132-7(8))* Zonderkidz.
—Snuggle Time Fall Blessings, 1 vol. Nellist, Glenys. 2019. (Snuggle Time Padded Board Book Ser.). (ENG.). 24p. (J). bds. 9.99 *(978-0-310-76751-0(2))* Zonderkidz.
—Snuggle Time Psalms, 1 vol. Nellist, Glenys. 2016. (Snuggle Time Padded Board Book Ser.). (ENG.). 30p. (J). bds. 9.99 *(978-0-310-74925-7(5))* Zonderkidz.

Biscoe, Cee. You & Me. Bradshaw, Sarah. 2018. (Tender Moments Ser.). (ENG.). 20p. (J). bds. 8.99 (978-1-926444-45-1(0)) Rainstorm Pr.

—You Are the Love in My Heart. Bradshaw, Sarah. 2018. (Tender Moments Ser.). (ENG.). 20p. (J). bds. 8.99 (978-1-926444-40-6(X)) Rainstorm Pr.

Biser, Dee. Forest House Firsts: Supplemental Selected Early Childhood Stories, 2 bks. Glyman, Caroline A. (J). (gr. k-3). lib. bdg. 29.90 (978-1-56674-910-7(7)) Forest Hse. Publishing Co., Inc.

Bishop, Barbara L. Children Today Around the U S A. Bishop, Barbara L. 2008. 40p. pap. 13.95 (978-1-934246-25-2(5)) Peppertree Pr., The.

Bishop, Ben. Lost Trail: Nine Days Alone in the Wilderness, 1 vol., Vol. Fendler, Donn & Plourde, Lynn. 2011. (ENG.). 72p. (J). (gr. 4-7). pap. 14.95 (978-0-89272-945-6(7)) Down East Bks.

Bishop, Christina. Enchanted Fairyland: A Sphinx & Trevi Adventure. Adam's Creations Publishing. 2007. (ENG.). 30p. (J). 19.95 (978-0-9785695-0-1(4)) Adam's Creations Publishing, LLC.

—The Puzzle Box of Nefertiti: A Sphinx & Trevi Adventure. Hayes, Celeste. 2011. 42p. (J). pap. 19.95 (978-0-9785695-3-2(9)) Adam's Creations Publishing, LLC.

Bishop, Craig. My Friend with Autism: Enhanced Edition. Bishop, Beverly. 3rd ed. 2020. (ENG.). 38p. (J). (gr. -1-1). pap. 14.95 (978-1-949177-50-3(5)) Future Horizons, Inc.

Bishop, Franklin, jt. illus. see **Bishop, Helena Edwards.**

Bishop, Gavin. Cook's Cook: The Cook Who Cooked for Captain Cook. Bishop, Gavin. 2018. (ENG.). 40p. (J). (gr. 2-5). 17.99 (978-1-77657-204-5(1)) Gecko Pr. NZL. Dist: Lerner Publishing Group.

Bishop, Helena Edwards & Bishop, Franklin. The Wayward Haggis. 2012. 40p. pap. 18.95 (978-1-4477-6514-1(1)) Lulu Pr., Inc.

Bishop, John E. Robber Raccoon, 1 vol. Bottiglieri, Tim. 2009. 16p. pap. 24.95 (978-1-61546-432-6(8)) America Star Bks.

Bishop, Kathleen Wong. Celebrating Holidays in Hawaii. Hayashi, Leslie Ann. 2010. (ENG.). 36p. (J). 14.95 (978-1-56647-914-1(2)) Mutual Publishing LLC.

—Fables Beneath the Rainbow. Hayashi, Leslie Ann. 2005. 32p. (J). 14.95 (978-1-56647-741-3(7), 477417) Mutual Publishing LLC.

—A Fishy Alphabet in Hawaii. Hayashi, Leslie Ann. 2007. (J). 13.95 (978-1-56647-830-4(8)) Mutual Publishing LLC.

Bishop, Louise. What Does God Look Like? Bradley, Pamela J. 2019. (ENG.). 38p. (J). (gr. -1-3). pap. 14.99 (978-1-950034-60-4(7)) Yorkshire Publishing Group.

Bishop, Megan. The Stories of Christmas: As Told by a Little Lamb. Blackburn, C. Edward. l.t. ed. 2005. 24p. (J). 9.95 (978-0-9727440-3-4(7)) Redline Bks.

Bishop, Mike. Oliver's Adventure, a First Visit to the Eye Doctor. Nicksich, Karen Marie. 2019. (ENG.). 60p. (J). (gr. k-4). pap. 18.00 (978-1-7337159-2-8(4)) Nicksich, Karen M.

Bishop, Monica. Lily the Lark: Flight School. Bishop, Monica. 2016. (Lily the Lark Ser.: Vol. 2). (ENG.). (J). pap. 9.99 (978-0-9895101-6-5(6)) CoreyJF Publishing.

Bishop, Nic. Chasing Cheetahs: The Race to Save Africa's Fastest Cat. Montgomery, Sy. 2017. (Scientists in the Field Ser.). (ENG.). 80p. (J). (gr. 5-7). pap. 9.99 (978-1-328-74089-2(7), 1677129, HMH Books For Young Readers) Houghton Mifflin Harcourt Publishing Co.

Bishop, Nic. Big Cats. Bishop, Nic. 2019. (Nic Bishop Ser.). (ENG.). 48p. (J). (gr. -1-3). 17.99 (978-0-545-60577-9(6), Scholastic Pr.) Scholastic, Inc.

—Snakes. Bishop, Nic. 2012. (Nic Bishop Ser.). (ENG.). 48p. (J). (gr. -1-3). 17.99 (978-0-545-20638-9(3), Scholastic Nonfiction) Scholastic, Inc.

—Weird Little Monsters: Band 12/Copper (Collins Big Cat) Bishop, Nic. 2007. (Collins Big Cat Ser.). (ENG.). 32p. (J). (gr. 2-4). pap. 9.99 (978-0-00-723080-8(X)) HarperCollins Pubs. Ltd. GBR. Dist: Independent Pubs. Group.

Bishop, Nic. Chameleon! Bishop, Nic, photos by. 2005. (J). pap. (978-0-439-78111-4(6), Scholastic Pr.) Scholastic, Inc.

—Chameleon Chameleon. Bishop, Nic, photos by. Cowley, Joy. 2005. (ENG.). 32p. (J). (gr. -1-3). 18.99 (978-0-439-66653-4(8), Scholastic Pr.) Scholastic, Inc.

—Chasing Cheetahs: The Race to Save Africa's Fastest Cats. Bishop, Nic, photos by. Montgomery, Sy. 2014. (Scientists in the Field Ser.). (ENG.). 80p. (J). (gr. 5-7). 18.99 (978-0-547-81549-7(2), 1496216, HMH Books For Young Readers) Houghton Mifflin Harcourt Publishing Co.

—Kakapo Rescue: Saving the World's Strangest Parrot. Bishop, Nic, photos by. Montgomery, Sy. 2010. (Scientists in the Field Ser.). (ENG.). 80p. (J). (gr. 5-7). 18.00 (978-0-618-49417-0(0), 591725) Houghton Mifflin Harcourt Publishing Co.

—Red-Eyed Tree Frog. Bishop, Nic, photos by. Cowley, Joy. 2006. (Scholastic Bookshelf Ser.). (ENG.). 32p. (J). (gr. -1-3). mass mkt. 6.99 (978-0-439-78221-0(X), Scholastic Paperbacks) Scholastic, Inc.

Bishop, Nic, photos by. Quest for the Tree Kangaroo: An Expedition to the Cloud Forest of New Guinea. Montgomery, Sy & National Geographic Learning Staff. 2009. (Scientists in the Field Ser.). (ENG., 80p. (J). (gr. 5-7). pap. 9.99 (978-0-547-24892-9(X), 1100904) Houghton Mifflin Harcourt Publishing Co.

—Quest for the Tree Kangaroo: An Expedition to the Cloud Forest of New Guinea. Montgomery, Sy. 2006. (Scientists in the Field Ser.). (ENG., 80p. (J). (gr. 5-7). 18.99 (978-0-618-49641-9(6), 591726) Houghton Mifflin Harcourt Publishing Co.

—The Tarantula Scientist. Montgomery, Sy. 2007. (Scientists in the Field Ser.). (ENG., 80p. (J). (gr. 5-7). pap. 9.99 (978-0-618-91577-4(X), 1014892) Houghton Mifflin Harcourt Publishing Co.

Bishop, Nic, photos by. Butterflies & Moths. Bishop, Nic. 2009. (Nic Bishop Ser.). (ENG., 48p. (J). (gr. -1-3). 17.99 (978-0-439-87757-2(1)) Scholastic, Inc.

—The Cloud Forest: Band 11/Lime (Collins Big Cat) Bishop, Nic. 2005. (Collins Big Cat Ser.). (ENG., 32p. (J). (gr. 2-3). pap. 9.99 (978-0-00-718641-9(X)) HarperCollins Pubs. Ltd. GBR. Dist: Independent Pubs. Group.

—Frogs. Bishop, Nic. 2008. (Nic Bishop Ser.). (ENG., 48p. (J). (gr. -1-3). 18.99 (978-0-439-87755-8(5)) Scholastic, Inc.

—Is There Anyone Out There?: Band 10/White (Collins Big Cat) Bishop, Nic. 2005. (Collins Big Cat Ser.). (ENG., 32p. (J). (gr. 2-3). pap. 10.99 (978-0-00-718635-8(5)) HarperCollins Pubs. Ltd. GBR. Dist: Independent Pubs. Group.

—Marsupials. Bishop, Nic. 2009. (Nic Bishop Ser.). (ENG., 48p. (J). (gr. -1-3). 17.99 (978-0-439-87758-9(X)) Scholastic, Inc.

—NIC Bishop - Spiders. Bishop, Nic. 2012. (Scholastic Reader Level 2 Ser.). (ENG., 32p. (J). (gr. k-2). pap. 3.99 (978-0-545-23757-4(2), Scholastic Paperbacks) Scholastic, Inc.

—Spiders. Bishop, Nic. 2007. (Nic Bishop Ser.). (ENG., 48p. (J). (gr. -1-3). 17.99 (978-0-439-87756-5(3), Scholastic Nonfiction) Scholastic, Inc.

Bishop, Roma. Christmas Fun: Bible Activity Book. Lane, Leena. 2015. (J). pap. 9.95 (978-0-8198-1651-1(5)) Pauline Bks. & Media.

—Christmas Fun: My First Bible Activity BK. Lane, Leena. 2004. 32p. pap. 6.95 (978-1-59325-043-0(6)) Word Among Us Pr.

—Friends of God: My First Bible Activity BK. Lane, Leena. 2004. 32p. pap. 6.95 (978-1-59325-042-3(8)) Word Among Us Pr.

Bishop, Tracey. One Love, Two Worlds. Howard, Ian T. 2010. 36p. pap. 14.75 (978-1-60911-771-9(9), Eloquent Bks.) Strategic Book Publishing & Rights Agency (SBPRA).

Bishop, Tracy. Alexis's Half-Baked Idea. Simon, Coco. 2019. (Cupcake Diaries: 32). (ENG.). 160p. (J). (gr. 3-7). 17.99 (978-1-5344-4067-8(4)); pap. 6.99 (978-1-5344-4066-1(6)) Simon Spotlight. (Simon Spotlight).

—Amy Is a Little Bit Chicken. Barkley, Callie. 2015. (Critter Club Ser.: 13). (ENG.). 128p. (J). (gr. k-4). pap. 5.99 (978-1-4814-5174-1(X), Little Simon) Little Simon.

—Amy on Park Patrol. Barkley, Callie. 2017. (Critter Club Ser.: 17). (ENG.). 128p. (J). (gr. k-3). pap. 5.99 (978-1-4814-9432-8(5), Little Simon) Little Simon.

Bishop, Tracy. Amy the Puppy Whisperer. Barkley, Callie. 2020. (Critter Club Ser.: 21). (ENG.). 128p. (J). (gr. k-4). 17.99 (978-1-5344-6622-7(3)); pap. 5.99 (978-1-5344-6621-0(5)) Little Simon. (Little Simon).

Bishop, Tracy. Ellie Steps up to the Plate. Barkley, Callie. 2018. (Critter Club Ser.: 18). (ENG.). 128p. (J). (gr. k-4). 17.99 (978-1-5344-1179-1(8)); pap. 5.99 (978-1-5344-1178-4(X)) Little Simon. (Little Simon).

—Ellie the Flower Girl. Barkley, Callie. 2016. (Critter Club Ser.: 14). (ENG.). 128p. (J). (gr. k-4). pap. 5.99 (978-1-4814-6718-6(2), Little Simon) Little Simon.

—First Grade, Here I Come! Steinberg, D. J. 2016. (Here I Come! Ser.). (ENG.). 32p. (J). (gr. -1-1). pap. 5.99 (978-0-448-48920-9(1), Grosset & Dunlap) Penguin Young Readers Group.

—Goodbye, School. Lippert, Tonya K. 2019. (J). (978-1-4338-3029-7(9), Magination Pr.) American Psychological Assn.

—Liz & the Nosy Neighbor. Barkley, Callie. 2018. (Critter Club Ser.: 19). (ENG.). 128p. (J). (gr. k-4). 16.99 (978-1-5344-2969-7(7)); pap. 5.99 (978-1-5344-2968-0(9)) Little Simon. (Little Simon).

—Liz's Night at the Museum. Barkley, Callie. 2016. (Critter Club Ser.: 15). (ENG.). 128p. (J). (gr. k-4). pap. 5.99 (978-1-4814-7164-0(3), Little Simon) Little Simon.

—Marion & the Girls' Getaway. Barkley, Callie. 2019. (Critter Club Ser.: 20). (ENG.). 128p. (J). (gr. k-4). 16.99 (978-1-5344-4870-4(5)); pap. 5.99 (978-1-5344-4869-8(1)) Little Simon. (Little Simon).

—Marion & the Secret Letter. Barkley, Callie. 2017. (Critter Club Ser.: 16). (ENG.). 128p. (J). (gr. k-4). pap. 5.99 (978-1-4814-8702-3(7), Little Simon) Little Simon.

—Not the Quitting Kind. Roth, Sarra J. 2014. 32p. (J). pap. 16.99 (978-1-4413-1415-4(6)) Peter Pauper Pr. Inc.

—Pipsie, Nature Detective: the Lunchnapper: The Lunchnapper, 0 vols. DeDonato, Rick. 2016. (Pipsie, Nature Detective Ser.). (ENG.). 40p. (J). (gr. -1-2). 17.99 (978-1-5039-5061-0(1), 9781503950610, Two Lions) Amazon Publishing.

—Remembering Ethan. Newman, Lesléa. 2020. (J). (978-1-4338-3113-3(9), Magination Pr.) American Psychological Assn.

—Snowball Moon. Slayton, Fran Cannon. (ENG.). (J). (gr. -1-k). 2019. 26p. bds. 7.99 (978-1-4998-0991-6(3)); 2017. 32p. 16.99 (978-1-4998-0495-9(4)) Little Bee Books Inc.

Bishop, Tracy Nishimura. Pop Flies, Robo-Pets, & Other Disasters. Kamata, Suzanne. 2020. (ENG.). 208p. (J). (gr. 4-8). 16.99 (978-1-947159-36-5(4), One Elm Books) Red Chair Pr.

Bissell, Robert. Robert Bissell's Rabbits & Bears. 2013. (ENG.). (J). 7.95 (978-0-7649-6476-3(3)) Pomegranate Communications, Inc.

Bist, Vandana. The Princess with the Longest Hair. Raote, Komilla. 26p. (J). (978-81-85586-78-6(0)) Katha.

Bistricean, Claudius. The Adventures of Fergus & Lady: Home Sweet Home. Bistricean, Karen. 2006. (J). (978-0-9786975-1-8(0)) Fergus & Lady Publishing.

—The Adventures of Fergus & Lady: The Beginning. Bistricean, Karen. 2006. (J). (978-0-9786975-0-1(2)) Fergus & Lady Publishing.

Biswas, Pulak. Catch That Crocodile! Ravishankar, Anushka. collector's ed. 2007. 40p. (J). (gr. -1-2). 25.00 (978-81-86211-94-6(2)) Tara Publishing IND. Dist: Consortium Bk. Sales & Distribution.

—The Flute, 1 vol. Gilmore, Rachna. 2012. (ENG.). 32p. (J). (gr. -1-k). 16.95 (978-1-896580-57-9(2)) Tradewind Bks. CAN. Dist: Orca Bk. Pubs. USA.

Bitetto, Marco A. V. Journal of Amateur Computing: Spring/Summer 2003 Issue. Bitetto, Marco A. V. l.t. ed. 2003. 120p. (YA). (gr. 9-12). pap. 22.00 (978-1-58578-482-0(6)) Institute of Cybernetics Research, Inc.

Bitskoff, Aleksei. My Rotten Stepbrother Ruined Cinderella. Mahoney, Jerry. 2017. (My Rotten Stepbrother Ruined Fairy Tales Ser.). (ENG.). 160p. (J). (gr. 3-6). lib. bdg. 26.65 (978-1-4965-4466-7(8), 134771, Stone Arch Bks.) Capstone.

—My Rotten Stepbrother Ruined Snow White. Mahoney, Jerry. 2017. (My Rotten Stepbrother Ruined Fairy Tales Ser.). (ENG.). 160p. (J). (gr. 3-6). pap. 8.95 (978-1-4965-4467-4(6), 134772); lib. bdg. 26.65 (978-1-4965-4463-6(3), 134768) Capstone. (Stone Arch Bks.).

—My Stupid Stepbrother Ruined Aladdin. Mahoney, Jerry. 2017. (My Rotten Stepbrother Ruined Fairy Tales Ser.). (ENG.). 160p. (J). (gr. 3-6). lib. bdg. 26.65 (978-1-4965-4464-3(1), 134769, Stone Arch Bks.) Capstone.

—My Stupid Stepbrother Ruined Beauty & the Beast. Mahoney, Jerry. 2017. (My Rotten Stepbrother Ruined Fairy Tales Ser.). (ENG.). 160p. (J). (gr. 3-6). lib. bdg. 26.65 (978-1-4965-4465-0(X), 134770, Stone Arch Bks.) Capstone.

Bitskoff, Aleksei & Knight, Tom. Who Will Marry Prince Harry? Bradman, Tony. 2016. (Reading Ladder Ser.). (ENG.). 48p. (J). (gr. k-2). pap. 7.99 (978-1-4052-7824-9(2)) Egmont Bks., Ltd. GBR. Dist: Independent Pubs. Group.

Bivins, Christopher. Bears Barge In. Sensel, Joni. 2003. 32p. (J). (gr. -1-18). 14.95 (978-0-9701195-0-6(X)) Dream Factory Bks.

—The Garbage Monster. Sensel, Joni. 2003. 24p. (J). (gr. -1-18). 14.95 (978-0-9701195-2-0(6)) Dream Factory Bks.

Bixby, Sean. The Goblin's Story. Dongweck, James. 2013. (J). (978-0-9719632-2-1(3)) Golden Monkey Publishing, LLC.

Bixler, Bunny. The Banyan Chronicles. McClayton, Raleigh. 2018. (ENG.). 26p. (J). pap. 9.99 (978-1-9830-9353-1(X)) Independently Published.

Bixley, Donovan. The Great Kiwi 123 Book. 2018. 32p. (J). (gr. -1-k). pap. 9.99 (978-1-988516-07-3(2)) Upstart Pr. NZL. Dist: Independent Pubs. Group.

—The Great Kiwi ABC Book. 2017. 24p. (J). (gr. -1-k). pap. 9.99 (978-1-927262-71-9(2)) Upstart Pr. NZL. Dist: Independent Pubs. Group.

—Little Bo Peep & More ... Favourite Nursery Rhymes. 2015. 24p. (J). (— 1). 9.99 (978-1-927262-08-5(9)) Upstart Pr. NZL. Dist: Independent Pubs. Group.

—Maddy West & the Tongue Taker, 1 vol. Falkner, Brian. 2014. (ENG.). 256p. (J). (gr. 4-8). 12.95 (978-1-62370-084-3(1), Capstone Young Readers) Capstone.

—Maddy West & the Tongue Taker. Falkner, Brian. 2018. (ENG.). 236p. (J). pap. 12.95 (978-0-6482879-0-2(4)) Lulu Pr., Inc.

—Pussycat, Pussycat: Purrfect Nursery Rhymes. 2016. 24p. (J). (— 1). pap. 9.99 (978-1-927262-28-3(3)) Upstart Pr. NZL. Dist: Independent Pubs. Group.

—Unmasked. 2018. (Flying Furballs Ser.: 3). 112p. (J). (gr. 2-4). pap. 8.99 (978-1-927262-93-1(3)) Upstart Pr. NZL. Dist: Independent Pubs. Group.

Bixley, Donovan. Great Kiwi 123 Book. Bixley, Donovan. 2019. 24p. (J). (gr. -1-k). 16.99 (978-1-988516-23-3(4)) Upstart Pr. NZL. Dist: Independent Pubs. Group.

—Hot Air. Bixley, Donovan. 2017. (Flying Furballs Ser.: 2). 112p. (J). (gr. 2-4). pap. 8.99 (978-1-927262-54-2(2)) Upstart Pr. NZL. Dist: Independent Pubs. Group.

—Kit-Napped. Bixley, Donovan. 2019. (Flying Furballs Ser.: 5). 112p. (J). (gr. 4-7). pap. 8.99 (978-1-988516-16-5(1)) Upstart Pr. NZL. Dist: Independent Pubs. Group.

—Most Wanted. Bixley, Donovan. 2018. (Flying Furballs Ser.: 4). 112p. (J). (gr. 2-4). pap. 8.99 (978-1-927262-99-3(2)) Upstart Pr. NZL. Dist: Independent Pubs. Group.

Bizjak, Donna. Gator & Pete - More Alike Than It Seems. McGovern, Suzanne. 2007. (J). 13.99 (978-0-9792558-0-9(5)) Hatch Ideas, Inc.

Bjarkadottir, Bjork. Your Body Is Awesome: Body Respect for Children. Danielsdottir, Sigrun. 2014. (ENG.). 36p. (J). 17.95 (978-1-84819-228-7(2), 694244, Singing Dragon) Kingsley, Jessica Pubs. GBR. Dist: Hachette UK Distribution.

Bjarnason, Bjarni Thor. Raphael: The Angel Who Decided to Visit Earth. Snorradottir, Asthildur Bj. 2011. 74p. pap. 21.50 (978-1-60976-683-2(0), Strategic Bk. Publishing) Strategic Book Publishing & Rights Agency (SBPRA).

Bjelica, Alex. Aaliyah's Dress. Morris, Hannah. Duncan, Kit, ed. 2017. (Adventures of the Four Bankieteers Ser.: Vol. 3). (ENG.). 42p. (J). pap. (978-1-912274-06-2(X)) ActiveMindCare Publishing.

—Ahmad's Pockets. Morris, Hannah. Duncan, Kit, ed. 2017. (Adventures of the Four Bankieteers Ser.: Vol. 1). (ENG.). 54p. (J). pap. (978-1-912274-00-0(0)) ActiveMindCare Publishing.

—Alligator Daddy: Holistic Thinking Kids. Hoeschele, Micah R. 2018. (ENG.). 30p. (J). pap. (978-1-7751638-3-1(0)) Hammill, Kristy.

—Ibrahim's Apple. Morris, Hannah. Duncan, Kit, ed. 2017. (Adventures of the Four Bankieteers Ser.: Vol. 2). (ENG.). 38p. (J). pap. (978-1-912274-03-1(5)) ActiveMindCare Publishing.

—Ja'far Escapes. Morris, Hannah. Duncan, Kit, ed. 2017. (Adventures of the Four Bankieteers Ser.: Vol. 4). (ENG.). 38p. (J). pap. (978-1-912274-09-3(4)) ActiveMindCare Publishing.

—Looking at the Big Picture: Holistic Thinking Kids. Hammill, Kristy. 2019. (ENG.). 36p. (J). pap. (978-1-7751638-7-9(3)) Hammill, Kristy.

—The Lost Elves: The Magical Elf Adventures of Zippy, Bippy, & Toppy. Simeon, Phil. 2018. (ENG.). 36p. (J). pap. 11.95 (978-1-7256-9391-3(7)) CreateSpace Independent Publishing Platform.

—Think for Myself at School: Holistic Thinking Kids. Hammill, Kristy. 2018. (ENG.). 30p. (J). pap. (978-1-7751638-2-4(2)) Hammill, Kristy.

—Think for Myself at the Park: Holistic Thinking Kids. Hammill, Kristy. 2018. (Think for Myself Ser.: Vol. 3). (ENG.). 32p. (J). pap. (978-1-7751638-5-5(7)) Hammill, Kristy.

—We Are What We Think: Holistic Thinking Kids. Hammill, Kristy. 2018. (ENG.). 32p. (J). pap. (978-1-7751638-6-2(5)) Hammill, Kristy.

Bjork, Sarah. The Alphabet Battle. Jensen, Melanie Bjork. 2019. (ENG.). 48p. (J). pap. 12.00 (978-1-0712-4183-7(4)) Independently Published.

Bjorklund, L. F. Captured Words: The Story of A Great Indian. Browin, Frances Williams. 2011. 192p. 42.95 (978-1-258-09914-5(4)) Literary Licensing, LLC.

Bjorklund, Lorence. Stubby Pringle's Christmas. Schaefer, Jack. 2017. (ENG.). 48p. pap. 16.95 (978-0-8263-5865-3(9)) Univ. of New Mexico Pr.

Bjorklung, Lorence. Boy Scout Pioneer. Seibert, Jerry. 2012. 192p. 42.95 (978-1-258-25301-1(1)); pap. 27.95 (978-1-258-25517-6(0)) Literary Licensing, LLC.

Björkman, Steve. After-School Sports Club Adventures. Heller, Alyson. 2016. (J). (978-1-4814-7741-3(2)) Simon & Schuster Children's Publishing.

—The Best Boat Ever Built. Larcombe, Jennifer Rees. 2004. (Best Bible Stories Ser.). 24p. (gr. -1-3). pap. 2.99 (978-1-58134-148-5(2)) Crossway.

Bjorkman, Steve. Coyotes All Around. Murphy, Stuart J. 2003. (MathStart 2 Ser.). (ENG.). 40p. (J). (gr. 1-18). pap. 5.99 (978-0-06-051531-7(7)) HarperCollins Pubs.

Björkman, Steve. Coyotes All Around. Murphy, Stuart J. ed. 2003. (Mathstart: Level 2 Ser.). 32p. (J). (gr. -1-3). 16.00 (978-0-613-68415-6(X)) Turtleback.

—Danger on the Lonely Road. Larcombe, Jennifer Rees. 2004. (Best Bible Stories Ser.). 24p. (gr. -1-3). pap. 2.99 (978-1-58134-149-2(0)) Crossway.

—Dirt on My Shirt. Foxworthy, Jeff. 2008. 32p. (J). (gr. -1-2). lib. bdg. 17.89 (978-0-06-120847-8(7)) HarperCollins Pubs.

Bjorkman, Steve. Dirt on My Shirt. Foxworthy, Jeff. 2008. (ENG.). 32p. (J). (gr. -1-3). 17.99 (978-0-06-120846-1(9), HarperFestival) HarperCollins Pubs.

Björkman, Steve. Dirt on My Shirt. Foxworthy, Jeff. 2009. (I Can Read Book 2 Ser.). 32p. (J). (gr. -1-3). 16.99 (978-0-06-176525-4(2)) HarperCollins Pubs.

Bjorkman, Steve. Dirt on My Shirt. Foxworthy, Jeff. 2013. (ENG.). 32p. (J). (gr. -1-3). 9.99 (978-0-06-223191-8(X), HarperFestival) HarperCollins Pubs.

—Dirt on My Shirt: Selected Poems. Foxworthy, Jeff. 2009. (I Can Read Level 2 Ser.). (ENG.). 32p. (J). (gr. k-3). pap. 4.99 (978-0-06-176524-7(4)) HarperCollins Pubs.

—The Dog That Pitched a No-Hitter. Christopher, Matt. 2013. (Passport to Reading Ser.). (ENG.). 48p. (J). (gr. 1-4). 4.99 (978-0-316-21848-1(0)) Little, Brown Bks. for Young Readers.

—The Dog That Pitched a No-Hitter. Christopher, Matt. 2018. (Matt Christopher Sports Readers Ser.). (ENG.). 48p. (J). (gr. 1-4). lib. bdg. 27.07 (978-1-5321-4255-0(2), 31055) Spotlight.

—The Dog That Stole Football Plays. Christopher, Matt. 2013. (Harry the Dog Ser.: 1). (ENG.). 32p. (J). (gr. 1-4). pap. 4.99 (978-0-316-21849-8(9)) Little, Brown Bks. for Young Readers.

—The Dog That Stole Football Plays. Christopher, Matt. 2018. (Matt Christopher Sports Readers Ser.). (ENG.). 32p. (J). (gr. 1-4). lib. bdg. 27.07 (978-1-5321-4256-7(0), 31056) Spotlight.

—Emily Post's the Guide to Good Manners for Kids. Senning, Cindy P. & Post, Peggy. 2004. (ENG.). 144p. (J). (gr. 3-7). 16.99 (978-0-06-057196-2(9)) HarperCollins Pubs.

—Emily's Everyday Manners. Post, Peggy & Senning, Cindy P. 2006. (ENG.). 32p. (J). (gr. -1-2). 16.99 (978-0-06-076174-5(1)); lib. bdg. 17.89 (978-0-06-076177-6(6)) HarperCollins Pubs. (Collins).

Björkman, Steve. Farmer Brown's Field Trip. Carlson, Melody. 2004. 40p. (gr. -1-3). 9.99 (978-1-58134-142-3(3)) Crossway.

—The Guide to Good Manners for Kids. Post, Peggy & Senning, Cindy Post. 2006. 144p. (J). (gr. 4-8). reprint ed. 16.00 (978-1-4223-5621-0(3)) DIANE Publishing Co.

—Hide!!! Foxworthy, Jeff. 2010. (ENG.). 32p. (J). (gr. -1-2). 17.99 (978-0-8253-0554-2(3)) Beaufort Bks., Inc.

Bjorkman, Steve. In the Waves. Stella, Lennon & Stella, Maisy. 2015. (ENG.). 40p. (J). (gr. -1-3). 17.99 (978-0-06-235939-1(8)) HarperCollins Pubs.

Björkman, Steve. Lost in Jerusalem! Larcombe, Jennifer Rees. 2004. (Best Bible Stories Ser.). 24p. (gr. -1-3). pap. 2.99 (978-1-58134-150-8(4)) Crossway.

—My Parents Are Divorced My Elbows Have Nicknames & Other Fact. Cochran, Bill. 2009. (ENG.). 32p. (J). (gr. -1-3). 17.99 (978-0-06-053942-9(9)) HarperCollins Pubs.

—The Other Brother. Carlson, Melody. 2004. 40p. (gr. -1-3). 9.99 (978-1-58134-122-5(9)) Crossway.

—Same Old Horse. Murphy, Stuart J. 2005. (MathStart Ser.). 40p. (J). 15.99 (978-0-06-055770-6(2)) HarperCollins Pubs.

Bjorkman, Steve. Same Old Horse. Murphy, Stuart J. 2005. (MathStart 2 Ser.). (ENG.). 40p. (J). (gr. 1). pap. 5.99 (978-0-06-055771-3(0)) HarperCollins Pubs.

Björkman, Steve. Silly Street. Foxworthy, Jeff. 2009. 32p. (J). (ENG.). (gr. -1-2). 17.99 (978-0-06-171918-9(8)); (gr. k-2). lib. bdg. 18.89 (978-0-06-171919-6(6)) HarperCollins Pubs.

Bjorkman, Steve. Silly Street: Selected Poems. Foxworthy, Jeff. 2010. (I Can Read Level 2 Ser.). (ENG.). 32p. (J). (gr. k-3). pap. 4.99 (978-0-06-176528-5(7)) HarperCollins Pubs.

—Sometimes You Win — Sometimes You Learn for Kids. Maxwell, John C. 2016. 32p. (J). (gr. -1-3). 18.99 (978-0-316-28408-0(4)) Little, Brown Bks. for Young Readers.

Björkman, Steve. Squirrel in the House. Vande Velde, Vivian. 2017. (Twitch the Squirrel Ser.: 2). (ENG.). 80p. (J). (gr. 1-4). pap. 6.99 (978-0-8234-3877-8(5)) Holiday Hse., Inc.

—Squirrel in the Museum. Vande Velde, Vivian. (Twitch the Squirrel Ser.). (ENG.). 112p. (J). (gr. 1-4). 2020. pap. 7.99 (978-0-8234-4680-3(8)); 2019. 15.99 (978-0-8234-4167-9(9)) Holiday Hse., Inc.

Bjorkman, Steve. Sticky, Sticky, Stuck! Gutch, Michael. 2013. (ENG.). 32p. (J). (gr. -1-3). 17.99 (978-0-06-199818-8(4)) HarperCollins Pubs.

Björkman, Steve. The Terrible Giant. Larcombe, Jennifer Rees. 2004. (Best Bible Stories Ser.). 24p. (gr. -1-3). 2.99 *(978-1-58134-054-9(0))* Crossway.

—Time for T-Ball. Heller, Alyson. 2010. (After-School Sports Club Ser.). (ENG.). 32p. (J). (gr. -1-1). pap. 4.99 *(978-1-4169-9412-1(2)*, Simon Spotlight) Simon Spotlight.

—Touchdown! Heller, Alyson. 2010. (After-School Sports Club Ser.). (ENG.). 32p. (J). (gr. -1-1). pap. 3.99 *(978-1-4169-9413-8(0)*, Simon Spotlight) Simon Spotlight.

—The Walls That Fell down Flat. Larcombe, Jennifer Rees. 2004. (Best Bible Stories Ser.). 24p. (gr. -1-3). pap. 2.99 *(978-1-58134-151-5(2))* Crossway.

—Your Amazing Digestion from Mouth Through Intestine. Settel, Joanne. 2019. (Your Amazing Body Bks.). (ENG.). 112p. (J). (gr. 3). 19.99 *(978-1-4814-8688-0(8))* Simon & Schuster Children's Publishing.

Björkman, Steve & Björkman, Steve. Jay Mcgraw's Life Strategies for Dealing with Bullies. McGraw, Jay. 2008. (ENG.). 192p. (J). (gr. 4-8). 17.99 *(978-1-4169-7473-4(3)*, Aladdin) Simon & Schuster Children's Publishing.

—Let's Go Skating! Heller, Alyson. 2009. (After-School Sports Club Ser.). (ENG.). 32p. (J). (gr. -1-1). pap. 3.99 *(978-1-4169-9411-4(4)*, Simon Spotlight) Simon Spotlight.

—Soccer Day. Heller, Alyson. 2009. (After-School Sports Club Ser.). (ENG.). 32p. (J). (gr. -1-1). pap. 4.99 *(978-1-4169-9410-7(6)*, Simon Spotlight) Simon Spotlight.

—Squirrel in the House. Vande Velde, Vivian. 2016. (Twitch the Squirrel Ser.: 2). (ENG.). 80p. (J). (gr. 1-4). 15.95 *(978-0-8234-3633-0(0))* Holiday Hse., Inc.

—8 Class Pets + 1 Squirrel ÷ 1 Dog = Chaos. Vande Velde, Vivian. (Twitch the Squirrel Ser.: 1). (ENG.). 80p. (J). (gr. 1-4). 2012. pap. 6.99 *(978-0-8234-2594-5(0))*; 2011. 15.95 *(978-0-8234-2364-4(6))* Holiday Hse., Inc.

Björkman, Steve, jt. illus. see Björkman, Steve.

Bjorkman, Steve, jt. illus. see Murphy, Stuart J.

Bjornsen, Holly. A Children's Adventure Duo: Thad the Sailor & Little Miss Lavendar. White, Elga Haymon. Freudiger, Victoria, ed. 2007. 130p. (J). per. 13.95 *(978-0-9785728-2-2(3))* Digi-Tall Media.

Björnson, Barbara. A Grandma Like Yours: A Grandpa Like Yours. Rosenbaum, Andria Warmflash. 2006. 32p. (J). 16.95 *(978-1-58013-167-4(0)*, Kar-Ben Publishing) Lerner Publishing Group.

Bjornson, Barbara. Hope-So. Hills, Jodi. 2004. (ENG.). 36p. (J). 16.95 *(978-0-9726504-2-7(3))* TRISTAN Publishing, Inc.

Bk, Blanca. Hoky the Caring Wolf. Blanco, César. Brokenbrow, Jon, tr. 2013. (ENG.). 32p. (J). (gr. k-2). 15.95 *(978-84-15241-92-8(5))* Cuento de Luz SL ESP. Dist: Publishers Group West (PGW).

Blabey, Aaron. The Bad Guys in Attack of the Zittens. 2017. 139p. (J). *(978-1-5379-5580-3(2))* Scholastic, Inc.

—The Bad Guys in Intergalactic Gas, 5. 2017. (Bad Guys Ser.). (ENG.). 144p. (J). (gr. 2-4). 18.69 *(978-1-5364-2908-4(2))* Scholastic, Inc.

—I Need a Hug. 2018. (ENG.). 32p. (J). (gr. -1-k). 14.99 *(978-1-338-29710-2(4)*, Scholastic Pr.) Scholastic, Inc.

—Pig the Elf. 2017. 24p. (J). pap. *(978-1-338-23004-8(2)*, Scholastic Pr.) Scholastic, Inc.

Blabey, Aaron. The Bad Guys. Blabey, Aaron. (Bad Guys Ser.: 4). (ENG.). 144p. (J). (gr. 2-5). 2017. pap. 5.99 *(978-1-338-08753-6(3)*, Scholastic Paperbacks); 2017. pap. 5.99 *(978-1-338-08749-9(5)*, Scholastic Paperbacks); 2016. pap. 5.99 *(978-0-545-91240-2(7)*, Scholastic Pr.) Scholastic, Inc.

—The Bad Guys Box Set: Books 1-5. Blabey, Aaron. 2018. (Bad Guys Ser.). (ENG.). (J). (gr. 2-5). 29.95 *(978-1-338-26722-8(1)*, Scholastic Paperbacks) Scholastic, Inc.

—The Bad Guys in Mission Unpluckable. Blabey, Aaron. 2017. (Bad Guys Ser.: 2). (ENG.). 144p. (J). (gr. 2-5). pap. 5.99 *(978-0-545-91241-9(5)*, Scholastic Pr.) Scholastic, Inc.

—The Brothers Quibble. Blabey, Aaron. 2015. 32p. (J). (gr. k-3). 16.99 *(978-0-14-350706-2(0))* Random Hse. Australia AUS. Dist: Independent Pubs. Group.

—Chancho el Campeón. Blabey, Aaron. 2018. (Chancho el Pug Ser.). (SPA.). 32p. (J). (gr. -1-k). pap. 4.99 *(978-1-338-32967-4(7)*, Scholastic en Espanol) Scholastic, Inc.

—Chancho el Pug. Blabey, Aaron. 2018. (Pig the Pug Ser.). (SPA.). 32p. (J). (gr. -1-k). pap. 4.99 *(978-1-338-29953-3(0)*, Scholastic en Espanol) Scholastic, Inc.

—Chancho la Estrella. Blabey, Aaron. 2019. (Chancho el Pug Ser.). (SPA.). 32p. (J). (gr. -1-k). pap. 4.99 *(978-1-338-35909-1(6)*, Scholastic en Espanol) Scholastic, Inc.

—Don't Call Me Bear! Blabey, Aaron. 2019. (ENG.). 32p. (J). (gr. -1-k). 14.99 *(978-1-338-36002-8(7)*, Scholastic Pr.) Scholastic, Inc.

—I Need a Hug. Blabey, Aaron. 2019. (SPA.). 32p. (J). (gr. -1-k). pap. 4.99 *(978-1-338-56595-9(8)*, Scholastic en Espanol) Scholastic, Inc.

Blabey, Aaron. Pig the Slob. Blabey, Aaron. 2020. (ENG.). 24p. (J). ***(978-1-4431-8281-2(8)***, Scholastic Pr.) Scholastic, Inc.

Blabey, Aaron. Pig the Tourist. Blabey, Aaron. 2020. (Pig the Pug Ser.). (ENG.). 32p. (J). (gr. -1-k). 14.99 *(978-1-338-59339-6(0)*, Scholastic Pr.) Scholastic, Inc.

—The Return of Thelma the Unicorn. Blabey, Aaron. 2019. (ENG.). 36p. (J). (gr. -1-k). 14.99 *(978-1-338-60889-2(4)*, Scholastic Pr.) Scholastic, Inc.

—Los Tipos Malos. Blabey, Aaron. 2018. (Los Tipos Malos Ser.: 1).Tr. of Bad Guys. (SPA.). 144p. (J). (gr. 2-5). pap. 5.99 *(978-1-338-13896-2(0)*, Scholastic en Espanol) Scholastic, Inc.

—Los Tipos Malos en el Conejillo Contraataca. Blabey, Aaron. 2019. (Los Tipos Malos Ser.: 3). (SPA.). 144p. (J). (gr. 2-5). pap. 5.99 *(978-1-338-30010-9(5)*, Scholastic en Espanol) Scholastic, Inc.

—Los Tipos Malos en Misión Improbable. Blabey, Aaron. 2018. (Los Tipos Malos Ser.: 2). (SPA.). 144p. (J). (gr. 2-5). pap. 5.99 *(978-1-338-15550-1(4))* Scholastic, Inc.

Black, Abby N. The Antediluvians 2: Multiple Targets. Black, Abby N. 2019. (ENG.). 516p. (YA). (gr. 7-12). pap. 19.95 ***(978-0-9909737-4-4(3))*** South Main Media by Mindwatering.

Black, Allison. Barnyard Boogie! McCanna, Tim. 2017. (ENG.). 24p. (J). (gr. -1-k). 12.95 *(978-1-4197-2346-9(4)*, Abrams Appleseed) Abrams, Inc.

—Future Astronaut. Alexander, Lori. 2019. (Future Baby Ser.). (ENG.). 24p. (J). (gr. -1 — 1). bds. 8.99 *(978-1-338-31222-5(7)*, Cartwheel Bks.) Scholastic, Inc.

—Future President (Future Baby) Alexander, Lori. 2019. (Future Baby Ser.: 3). (ENG.). 24p. (J). (gr. -1 — 1). bds. 8.99 *(978-1-338-31224-9(3)*, Cartwheel Bks.) Scholastic, Inc.

—Go, Girls, Go! Gilbert, Frances. 2019. (ENG.). 40p. (J). (gr. -1-3). 17.99 *(978-1-5344-2482-1(2)*, Beach Lane Bks.) Beach Lane Bks.

—Poop or Get off the Potty! McNamara, Margaret. 2019. (ENG.). 32p. (J). 16.99 *(978-1-250-12440-1(9)*, 900174402, Holt, Henry & Co. Bks. For Young Readers) Holt, Henry & Co.

—Sea. 2018. (My First Touch & Find Ser.). (ENG.). 12p. (J). (— 1). bds. 8.95 *(978-1-4549-2947-5(2))* Sterling Publishing Co., Inc.

—Space Cat Glow-In-the-Dark Locked Diary. Mudpuppy. 2017. (ENG.). 192p. (J). (gr. -1-7). 10.99 *(978-0-7353-5212-4(7))* Mudpuppy Pr.

Black, Allison. Unicorn Munch. Little Bee Books. 2020. (Crunchy Board Bks.). (ENG.). 12p. (J). (gr. -1-1). bds. 9.99 ***(978-1-4998-1103-2(9))*** Little Bee Books Inc.

Black, Allison. What Do They Do with All That Poo? Kurtz, Jane. 2018. (ENG.). 40p. (J). (gr. -1-3). 17.99 *(978-1-4814-7986-8(5)*, Beach Lane Bks.) Beach Lane Bks.

—Wise Owl Playing Cards to Go. Mudpuppy. 2019. (ENG.). (J). (gr. -1-5). 7.99 *(978-0-7353-5812-6(5))* Mudpuppy Pr.

—Zoo. 2018. (My First Touch & Find Ser.). (ENG.). 12p. (J). (— 1). bds. 8.95 *(978-1-4549-2945-1(6))* Sterling Publishing Co., Inc.

Black, Andrew. Critter's Day Out. Luehrs, Rachel. 2019. (ENG.). 46p. (J). pap. 14.99 ***(978-1-6925-2230-8(2))*** Independently Published.

Black, Bronze. What's So Hot about Volcanoes? Duffield, Wendell A. 2011. 96p. (J). pap. 16.00 *(978-0-87842-574-7(8))* Mountain Pr. Publishing Co., Inc.

Black, Elisheva. The Search Is On! Can You Find the Ten Pieces of Chametz? Ribowsky, Helene & Zlotowitz, Rachel. 2017. 31p. (J). *(978-1-4226-1870-7(6)*, ArtScroll Series) Mesorah Pubns., Ltd.

Black, Ilene. Emma Mcdougal & the Quest for Father Time. Cowden, Matt. 2008. 190p. (J). 24.95 *(978-0-9799189-0-2(1))* His Work Christian Publishing.

Black, Joanna & Carter, Lydia. Mermaid of Doom Bar. Maxwell, Keith. 2019. (ENG.). 48p. (J). pap. *(978-1-912601-97-4(4))* Mirador Publishing.

Black, Kieron. The Incredible Sister Brigid. Carville, Declan. 29p. pap. 7.95 *(978-0-9538222-2-5(2))* Discovery Pubns. GBR. Dist: Irish Bks. & Media, Inc.

Black, Pam. Candee Bar. 42p. (J). 2007. spiral bd. *(978-0-9800791-2-8(8))*; 2nd rev. ed. 2008. spiral bd. 18.95 *(978-0-9800791-3-5(6))* Moore Publishing.

Black, Theo. The Poison Eaters: And Other Stories. Black, Holly. 2011. (ENG.). 224p. (YA). (gr. 9). pap. 9.99 *(978-1-4424-1232-3(1)*, McElderry, Margaret K. Bks.) McElderry, Margaret K. Bks.

Blackall, Sophie. The All Powerful Ring. Marciano, John Bemelmans. 2016. (Witches of Benevento Ser.: 2). (ENG.). 144p. (J). (gr. 2-5). 13.99 *(978-0-451-47180-2(6)*, Viking Books for Young Readers) Penguin Young Readers Group.

—Big Red Lollipop. Khan, Rukhsana. 2010. 40p. (J). (gr. -1-3). 17.99 *(978-0-670-06287-4(1)*, Viking Books for Young Readers) Penguin Young Readers Group.

—Finding Winnie: The True Story of the World's Most Famous Bear. Mattick, Lindsay. 2015. (ENG.). 56p. (J). (gr. -1-3). 18.99 *(978-0-316-32490-8(6))* Little Brown & Co.

—A Fine Dessert: Four Centuries, Four Families, One Delicious Treat. Jenkins, Emily. 2015. (ENG.). 44p. (J). (gr. -1-3). 20.99 *(978-0-375-96832-7(6)*, Schwartz & Wade Bks.) Random Hse. Children's Bks.

—A Fine Dessert: Four Centuries, Four Families, One Delicious Treat. Jenkins, Emily. 2015. 40p. (J). (gr. -1-3). 17.99 *(978-0-375-86832-0(1)*, Schwartz & Wade Bks.) Random Hse. Children's Bks.

—Ivy + Bean. Barrows, Annie. 2007. (Ivy & Bean Ser.: Bk. 1). 120p. (gr. 1-5). 16.00 *(978-0-7569-8142-6(5))* Perfection Learning Corp.

—Ivy + Bean. Barrows, Annie. ed. 2007. (Ivy & Bean Ser.: 1). (J). lib. bdg. 16.00 *(978-1-4177-7972-7(1))* Turtleback.

—Ivy + Bean - Book 2. Barrows, Annie. 2007. (Ivy & Bean Ser.: IVYB). (ENG.). 136p. (J). (gr. 1-5). pap. 5.99 *(978-0-8118-4911-1(2))* Chronicle Bks. LLC.

—Ivy + Bean - Book 3. Barrows, Annie. 2007. (Ivy & Bean Ser.: IVYB). (ENG.). 124p. (J). (gr. 1-5). pap. 5.99 *(978-0-8118-6250-9(X))* Chronicle Bks. LLC.

—Ivy + Bean - Make the Rules. Barrows, Annie. 2012. (Ivy & Bean Ser.). (ENG.). 127p. (J). (gr. 1-5). 14.99 *(978-1-4521-0295-5(3))* Chronicle Bks. LLC.

—Ivy + Bean - No News Is Good News. Barrows, Annie. 2012. (Ivy & Bean Ser.). (ENG.). 144p. (J). (gr. 1-5). pap. 5.99 *(978-1-4521-0781-3(5))* Chronicle Bks. LLC.

—Ivy + Bean - No News Is Good News. Barrows, Annie. ed. 2012. (Ivy & Bean Ser.: 8). (J). lib. bdg. 16.00 *(978-0-606-26950-6(9))* Turtleback.

—Ivy + Bean + Me: A Fill-in-the-Blank Book. Barrows, Annie. 2014. (ENG.). 104p. (J). (gr. 3-9). 10.99 *(978-1-4521-3729-2(3))* Chronicle Bks. LLC.

—Ivy + Bean Take Care of the Babysitter. Barrows, Annie. 2007. (Ivy & Bean Ser.: Bk. 4). (ENG.). pap., tchr. ed. *(978-0-8118-8667-3(0))* Chronicle Bks. LLC.

—Ivy + Bean Take the Case. Barrows, Annie. 2013. (Ivy & Bean Ser.). (ENG.). 128p. (J). (gr. 1-5). 14.99 *(978-1-4521-0699-1(1))* Chronicle Bks. LLC.

—Ivy & Bean - Book 1 (Ivy & Bean Books, Books for Elementary School), Volume 1. Barrows, Annie. 2007. (Ivy & Bean Ser.: IVYB). (ENG.). 120p. (J). (gr. 1-5). pap. 5.99 *(978-0-8118-4909-8(0))* Chronicle Bks. LLC.

—Ivy & Bean - Book 5. Barrows, Annie. 2008. (Ivy & Bean Ser.: IVYB). (ENG.). 124p. (J). (gr. 1-5). 14.99 *(978-0-8118-6265-3(8))* Chronicle Bks. LLC.

—Ivy & Bean - Book 6. Barrows, Annie. 2009. (Ivy & Bean Ser.: IVYB). (ENG.). 136p. (J). (gr. 1-5). 14.99 *(978-0-8118-6266-0(6))* Chronicle Bks. LLC.

—Ivy & Bean #5: Bound to Be Bad. Barrows, Annie. 2009. (Ivy & Bean Ser.: IVYB). (ENG.). 128p. (J). (gr. 1-5). pap. 5.99 *(978-0-8118-6857-0(5))* Chronicle Bks. LLC.

—Ivy & Bean & the Ghost That Had to Go. Barrows, Annie. ed. 2007. (Ivy & Bean Ser.: 2). (J). lib. bdg. 16.00 *(978-1-4177-9273-3(6))* Turtleback.

—Ivy & Bean & the Ghost That Had to Go (Book 2), Bk. 2. Barrows, Annie. 2006. (Ivy & Bean Ser.: IVYB). (ENG.). 136p. (J). (gr. 1-5). 14.99 *(978-0-8118-4910-4(4))* Chronicle Bks. LLC.

—Ivy & Bean Book 1, Bk. 1. Barrows, Annie. 2006. (Ivy & Bean Ser.: IVYB). (ENG.). 120p. (J). (gr. 1-5). 14.99 *(978-0-8118-4903-6(1))* Chronicle Bks. LLC.

—Ivy & Bean Boxed Set: Books 7-9 (Books about Friendship, Gifts for Young Girls) Barrows, Annie. 2013. (Ivy & Bean Ser.). (ENG.). 428p. (J). (gr. 1-5). 19.99 *(978-1-4521-1732-4(2))* Chronicle Bks. LLC.

—Ivy & Bean: Break the Fossil Record - Book 3. Barrows, Annie. 2007. (Ivy & Bean Ser.: IVYB). (ENG.). 132p. (J). (gr. 1-5). 14.99 *(978-0-8118-5683-6(6))* Chronicle Bks. LLC.

—Ivy & Bean Doomed to Dance (Book 6) Barrows, Annie. 2010. (ENG.). 136p. (J). (gr. 1-5). pap. 5.99 *(978-0-8118-7666-7(7))* Chronicle Bks. LLC.

—Ivy & Bean Make the Rules, Bk. 9. Barrows, Annie. 2013. (Ivy & Bean Ser.: 9). (ENG.). 144p. (J). (gr. 1-5). pap. 5.99 *(978-1-4521-1148-3(0))* Chronicle Bks. LLC.

Blackall, Sophie. Ivy & Bean Make the Rules: #9. Barrows, Annie. 2020. (Ivy & Bean Ser.). (ENG.). 128p. (J). (gr. 1-4). lib. bdg. 27.07 ***(978-1-5321-4485-1(7)***, 35175, Chapter Bks.) Spotlight.

—Ivy & Bean: No News Is Good News: #8. Barrows, Annie. 2020. (Ivy & Bean Ser.). (ENG.). 128p. (J). (gr. 1-4). lib. bdg. 27.07 ***(978-1-5321-4484-4(9)***, 35174, Chapter Bks.) Spotlight.

Blackall, Sophie. Ivy & Bean No News Is Good News (Book 8) Barrows, Annie. 2011. (Ivy & Bean Ser.: IVYB). (ENG.). 128p. (J). (gr. 1-5). 14.99 *(978-0-8118-6693-4(9))* Chronicle Bks. LLC.

Blackall, Sophie. Ivy & Bean: One Big Happy Family: #11. Barrows, Annie. 2020. (Ivy & Bean Ser.). (ENG.). 128p. (J). (gr. 1-4). lib. bdg. 27.07 ***(978-1-5321-4487-5(3)***, 35177, Chapter Bks.) Spotlight.

Blackall, Sophie. Ivy & Bean One Big Happy Family (Book 11) Barrows, Annie. (ENG.). (J). (gr. 1-4). 2020. 128p. pap. 5.99 *(978-1-4521-6910-1(1))*; 2018. (Ivy & Bean Ser.: 11). 124p. 14.99 *(978-1-4521-6400-7(2))* Chronicle Bks. LLC.

Blackall, Sophie. Ivy & Bean Set 2 (Set), 4 vols. Barrows, Annie. 2020. (Ivy & Bean Ser.). (ENG.). 128p. (J). (gr. 1-4). lib. bdg. 108.28 ***(978-1-5321-4483-7(0)***, 35173, Chapter Bks.) Spotlight.

Blackall, Sophie. Ivy & Bean: Take Care of the Babysitter - Book 4. Barrows, Annie. 2008. (Ivy & Bean Ser.: IVYB). (ENG.). 144p. (J). (gr. 1-5). 14.99 *(978-0-8118-5685-0(2))* Chronicle Bks. LLC.

—Ivy & Bean Take Care of the Babysitter: Book 4. Barrows, Annie. 2008. (Ivy & Bean Ser.: IVYB). (ENG.). 128p. (J). (gr. 1-5). pap. 5.99 *(978-0-8118-6584-5(3))* Chronicle Bks. LLC.

Blackall, Sophie. Ivy & Bean Take the Case: #10. Barrows, Annie. 2020. (Ivy & Bean Ser.). (ENG.). 128p. (J). (gr. 1-4). lib. bdg. 27.07 ***(978-1-5321-4486-8(5)***, 35176, Chapter Bks.) Spotlight.

Blackall, Sophie. Ivy & Bean Take the Case (Book 10), Volume 10. Barrows, Annie. 2014. (ENG.). 136p. (J). (gr. 1-4). pap. 5.99 *(978-1-4521-2871-9(5))* Chronicle Bks. LLC.

—Ivy & Bean What's the Big Idea? (Book 7) Barrows, Annie. 2011. (ENG.). 132p. (J). (gr. 1-5). pap. 5.99 *(978-1-4521-0236-8(8))* Chronicle Bks. LLC.

—Ivy & Bean What's the Big Idea? (Book 7) Barrows, Annie et al. 2010. (ENG.). 128p. (J). (gr. 1-5). 14.99 *(978-0-8118-6692-7(0))* Chronicle Bks. LLC.

—Lord & Lady Bunny — Almost Royalty! Horvath, Polly. 2016. (Mr. & Mrs. Bunny Ser.: 2). (ENG.). 304p. (J). (gr. 3-7). pap. 8.99 *(978-0-307-98068-7(5)*, Yearling) Random Hse. Children's Bks.

—Meet Wild Boars. Rosoff, Meg. 2005. (Wild Boars Ser.). (ENG.). 40p. (J). (gr. -1-1). pap. 21.19 *(978-0-312-37963-6(3)*, 900050313) Square Fish.

—The Mighty Lalouche. Olshan, Matthew. 2013. 40p. (J). (gr. -1-3). 17.99 *(978-0-375-86225-0(0)*, Schwartz & Wade Bks.) Random Hse. Children's Bks.

—Mischief Season. Marciano, John Bemelmans. 2016. (Witches of Benevento Ser.: 1). 128p. (J). (gr. 2-5). 13.99 *(978-0-451-47181-9(4)*, Viking Books for Young Readers) Penguin Young Readers Group.

—Mr. & Mrs. Bunny — Detectives Extraordinaire! Horvath, Polly. (Mr. & Mrs. Bunny Ser.: 1). (J). (gr. 3-7). 2014. 272p. pap. 8.99 *(978-0-375-86530-5(6))*; 2012. 256p. 16.99 *(978-0-375-86755-2(4))* Random Hse. Children's Bks. (Schwartz & Wade Bks.).

—The Nine Lives of Alexander Baddenfield. Marciano, John Bemelmans. 2013. (ENG.). 144p. (J). (gr. 5). 16.99 *(978-0-670-01406-4(0)*, Viking Books for Young Readers) Penguin Young Readers Group.

—Pecan Pie Baby. Woodson, Jacqueline. (ENG.). 32p. (J). (gr. k-3). 2013. 7.99 *(978-0-14-751128-7(3)*, Puffin Books); 2010. 16.99 *(978-0-399-23987-8(1)*, G.P. Putnam's Sons Books for Young Readers) Penguin Young Readers Group.

—Red Butterfly: How a Princess Smuggled the Secret of Silk Out of China. Noyes, Deborah. 2019. 32p. (J). (gr. 1-4). 7.99 *(978-1-5362-0376-9(9))* Candlewick Pr.

—Ruby's Wish. Bridges, Shirin Yim. 2015. (ENG.). 36p. (J). (gr. 3-7). pap. 7.99 *(978-1-4521-4569-3(5))* Chronicle Bks. LLC.

—Runaway Rosa. Marciano, John Bemelmans. 2018. (Witches of Benevento Ser.: 5). 96p. (J). (gr. 2-5). 13.99 *(978-0-425-29151-1(0)*, Viking Books for Young Readers) Penguin Young Readers Group.

—The Secret Janara. Marciano, John Bemelmans. 2019. (Witches of Benevento Ser.: 6). 144p. (J). (gr. 3-7). 13.99 *(978-0-425-29154-2(5)*, Viking Books for Young Readers) Penguin Young Readers Group.

—Spinster Goose: Twisted Rhymes for Naughty Children. Wheeler, Lisa. 2011. (ENG.). 48p. (J). (gr. k-5). 19.99 *(978-1-4169-2541-5(4)*, Atheneum Bks. for Young Readers) Simon & Schuster Children's Publishing.

—Take Two! A Celebration of Twins. Lewis, J. Patrick & Yolen, Jane. 2012. (ENG.). 72p. (J). (gr. -1-3). 18.99 *(978-0-7636-3702-6(5))* Candlewick Pr.

—A Voyage in the Clouds: The (Mostly) True Story of the First International Flight by Balloon In 1785. Olshan, Matthew. 2016. (ENG.). 40p. (J). 17.99 *(978-0-374-32954-9(0)*, 900079051, Farrar, Straus & Giroux (BYR)) Farrar, Straus & Giroux.

—Winnie's Great War. Mattick, Lindsay & Greenhut, Josh. (ENG.). 256p. (J). (gr. 3-7). 2019. pap. 7.99 *(978-0-316-44709-6(9))*; 2018. 16.99 *(978-0-316-44712-6(9))* Little, Brown Bks. for Young Readers.

—Wombat Walkabout. Shields, Carol Diggory. 2009. (ENG.). 32p. (J). (gr. -1-k). 17.99 *(978-0-525-47865-2(5)*, Dutton Books for Young Readers) Penguin Young Readers Group.

Blackall, Sophie. The Baby Tree. Blackall, Sophie. 2014. 32p. (J). (gr. k-3). 17.99 *(978-0-399-25718-6(7)*, Nancy Paulsen Books) Penguin Young Readers Group.

Blackbird. Mr. Hookworm. Blackbird. 2006. (J). per. 18.00 *(978-0-9789798-6-7(9)*, 978-0-9789798-6-7) Blackbird's World Publishing Co.

Blacker, Elizabeth A. Adventures on Amelia Island: A Pirate, a Princess, & Buried Treasure. Wood, Jane R., photos by. Wood, Jane R. ed. 2007. (ENG.). 132p. (J). (gr. 3-8). pap. 8.99 *(978-0-9792304-0-0(3))* Florida Kids Pr., Inc.

Blackery, Evgeniia. Lily the Limpet Gets Lost. Rosen, Emma. 2019. (Seaside Stories Ser.: Vol. 1). (ENG.). 28p. (J). (gr. k-2). pap. ***(978-1-9996292-2-9(1))*** Sartain Publishing Ltd.

Blackford, Ami. Quest for the Dragon Stone: A Duncan Family Adventure. Blackford, Ami. 2006. 48p. (J). (gr. 3-7). 16.95 *(978-1-60108-008-0(5))* Red Cygnet Pr.

—Quest for the Elfin Elixir: A Duncan Family Adventure Book 2. Blackford, Ami. 2007. 79p. (J). (gr. 3-7). 16.95 *(978-1-60108-021-9(2))* Red Cygnet Pr.

Blackford, Jessica. Bully, Bully, Back off Me. Bender, Lora. 2017. (ENG.). (J). pap. 12.95 *(978-1-63525-231-6(8))* Christian Faith Publishing.

Blackford, John. The Secret of Willow Ridge: Gabe's Dad Finds Recovery. Moore, Helen H. 2010. (ENG.). 128p. (J). (gr. 3-7). pap. 12.95 *(978-0-9818482-0-4(6))* Central Recovery Pr.

Blackham, Tessa. From a Small Seed - the Story of Eliza Hamilton. Andros, Camille. 2019. (ENG.). 40p. (J). 18.99 *(978-1-250-29742-6(7)*, 900195928, Holt, Henry & Co. Bks. For Young Readers) Holt, Henry & Co.

Blackler, B�;. The Big Magical Cloud. Blackler, Dep. 2020. (ENG.). 42p. (J). ***(978-1-7771044-0-5(8))***; pap. ***(978-1-7771044-1-2(6))*** Honu World Publishing.

Blackley, Mary Beth. Thank You, Peter. Lundy, Charlotte. Waldrep, Evelyn L., ed. 2003. 32p. (gr. k-3). 15.95 *(978-0-9670280-8-8(6))* Bay Light Publishing.

Blackman, N. S. The Secret Dinosaur #2: Hunters Attack! Blackman, N. S. 2014. (Dinotek Adventures Ser.). (ENG.). 99p. (J). pap. *(978-0-9927525-1-4(5))* Dinosaur Books Ltd.

—The Secret Dinosaur #3: Jurassic Adventure. Blackman, N. S. 2014. (Dinotek Adventures Ser.). (ENG.). 128p. (J). pap. *(978-0-9927525-2-1(3))* Dinosaur Books Ltd.

Blackmon, Kim. Glorious Praise. Wilkinson, William L. 2012. 32p. pap. 10.00 *(978-1-62050-019-4(1))* Angels of Agape.

Blackmond, David. Jeremiah's Mighty Big to-Do List. Mukherjee, Wanda. 2018. (ENG.). 76p. (J). (gr. 2-6). pap. 16.95 *(978-0-9824741-1-2(3))* Sojourner Publishing, Inc.

Blackmore, Katherine. Because of You, Mom. 2019. (J). 13.99 *(978-1-62972-520-8(X))* Deseret Bk. Co.

—Betsy's Day at the Game. Bancroft, Greg. 2013. (ENG.). 40p. (gr. k-5). pap. 13.95 *(978-1-938063-01-5(5)*, Mighty Media Kids) Mighty Media Pr.

—Good Night Bears. Gamble, Adam & Jasper, Mark. 2018. (Good Night Our World Ser.). 20p. (J). (— 1). bds. 9.95 *(978-1-60219-515-8(3))* Good Night Bks.

—Good Night Bedtime. Gamble, Adam & Jasper, Mark. 2018. (Good Night Our World Ser.). 20p. (J). (— 1). bds. 9.95 *(978-1-60219-471-7(8))* Good Night Bks.

—Good Night Cape Cod National Seashore. Gamble, Adam & Jasper, Mark. 2020. (Good Night Our World Ser.). 20p. (J). (— 1). bds. 9.95 *(978-1-60219-793-0(8))* Good Night Bks.

—Good Night Dancers. Gamble, Adam & Jasper, Mark. 2017. (Good Night Our World Ser.). 20p. (J). (gr. -1 — 1). bds. 9.95 *(978-1-60219-427-4(0))* Good Night Bks.

—Good Night Love. Gamble, Adam & Jasper, Mark. 2018. (Good Night Our World Ser.). (ENG.). 20p. (J). (— 1). bds. 9.95 *(978-1-60219-775-6(X))* Good Night Bks.

—Good Night Maui. Gamble, Adam & Jasper, Mark. 2018. (Good Night Our World Ser.). 20p. (J). (— 1). bds. 9.95 *(978-1-60219-681-0(8))* Good Night Bks.

—Good Night Summer. Gamble, Adam & Jasper, Mark. 2017. (Good Night Our World Ser.). 20p. (J). (— 1). bds. 9.95 *(978-1-60219-440-3(8))* Good Night Bks.

—Good Night Turtles. Gamble, Adam & Jasper, Mark. 2020. (Good Night Our World Ser.). (ENG.). 20p. (J). (— 1). bds. 9.95 *(978-1-60219-877-7(2))* Good Night Bks.

—How Many? A Counting Book. Panec, D. J. 2016. 41p. (J). *(978-1-4844-8056-4(2))* Treasure Bay, Inc.

—How Many? Cuantos Hay? A Counting Book: Spanish/English Bilingual Edition (We Both Read - Level Pk-K) Panec, D. J. 2016. (We Both Read - Level Pk -K

Ser.). (ENG & SPA.). 41p. (J). pap. 4.99 *(978-1-60115-074-5(1))* Treasure Bay, Inc.

—How Many? (We Both Read - Level Pk-K) A Counting Book. Panec, D. J. 2016. (We Both Read - Level Pk -K Ser.). (ENG.). 41p. (J). 9.95 *(978-1-60115-291-6(4))* Treasure Bay, Inc.

Blackmore, Katherine & Wiltse, Kris. A Kiss on the Keppie, 0 vols. Newman, Lesléa. 2012. (ENG.). 24p. (J). (gr. -1-2). 12.99 *(978-0-7614-6241-5(4),* 9780761462415, Two Lions) Amazon Publishing.

Blackmore, Katherine, jt. illus. see Chan, Suwin.

Blackshear, Sue. Tuskaloosa Tales: Stories of Tuscaloosa & Its People. 2011. 95p. (J). *(978-0-9801113-2-3(3))* Look Again Pr., LLC.

Blacksheep, Beverly. Baby Learns about Animals. Ruffenach, Jessie, ed. Thomas, Peter, tr. from NAV. 2004. (ENG & NAV.). 16p. (J). (gr. -1-12). 7.95 *(978-1-893354-49-4(0))* Salina Bookshelf Inc.

—Baby Learns about Colors. Ruffenach, Jessie, ed. Thomas, Peter, tr. from NAV. 2004. (ENG & NAV.). 16p. (J). (gr. -1-12). 7.95 *(978-1-893354-48-7(2))* Salina Bookshelf Inc.

—Baby Learns about Seasons. Ruffenach, Jessie, ed. Thomas, Peter, tr. from ENG. 2005. (NAV & ENG.). 16p. (J). (gr. 4-7). 7.95 *(978-1-893354-61-6(X))* Salina Bookshelf Inc.

—Baby Learns about Senses. Ruffenach, Jessie, ed. Thomas, Peter, tr. from ENG. 2005. (NAV & ENG.). 16p. (J). (gr. 4-7). 7.95 *(978-1-893354-63-0(6))* Salina Bookshelf Inc.

—Baby Learns about Time. Ruffenach, Jessie, ed. Thomas, Peter, tr. from ENG. 2005. (NAV & ENG.). 16p. (J). (gr. 4-7). 7.95 *(978-1-893354-64-7(4))* Salina Bookshelf Inc.

—Baby Learns about Weather. Ruffenach, Jessie, ed. Thomas, Peter, tr. from ENG. 2005. (NAV & ENG.). 16p. (J). (gr. 4-7). 7.95 *(978-1-893354-62-3(8))* Salina Bookshelf Inc.

—Baby Learns to Count. Ruffenach, Jessie, ed. Thomas, Peter, tr. l.t. ed. 2003. (NAV & ENG.). 16p. (J). (gr. -1-12). 7.95 *(978-1-893354-47-0(4))* Salina Bookshelf Inc.

—Baby's First Laugh. Ruffenach, Jessie, ed. Thomas, Peter, tr. from ENG. 2003. (NAV & ENG.). 100p. (J). (gr. -1-12). 7.95 *(978-1-893354-39-5(3))* Salina Bookshelf Inc.

Blackstone, Stella. The Animal Boogie. Harter, Debbie. 2005. 32p. (J). (gr. -1-1). 14.99 *(978-1-84148-094-7(0))* Barefoot Bks., Inc.

Blackwell, Amy. Aretha Franklin. Sanchez Vegara, Maria Isabel. 2020. (Little People, BIG DREAMS Ser.: 44). (ENG.). 32p. (J). (gr. -1-2). 15.99 ***(978-0-7112-4686-7(6),*** Frances Lincoln Children's Bks.) Quarto Publishing Group UK GBR. Dist: Hachette Bk. Group.

Blackwell, Amy. Rise Up: Ordinary Kids with Extraordinary Stories. Li, Amanda. 2020. (ENG.). 120p. (J). 16.99 *(978-1-5248-5529-1(4))* Andrews McMeel Publishing.

Blackwell, David. Escape from the Forbidden Planet. Grasso, Julie Anne. 2012. 172p. (J). pap. *(978-0-9873725-0-5(5))* Grasso, Julie Anne AUS. Dist: INT Bks.

—Return to Cardamom. Grasso, Julie A. 2013. (Cardamom Ser.: Bk. 2). (ENG.). 136p. (J). pap. *(978-0-9873725-2-9(1))* Grasso, Julie Anne AUS. Dist: INT Bks.

Blackwood, Basil Temple & B, B. T. Cautionary Tales for Children: Designed for the Admonition of Children Between the Ages of Eight & Fourteen Years. Belloc, Hilaire. 2018. (ENG.). 80p. (J). (gr. 3-6). pap. 6.95 *(978-1-68422-284-1(2))* Martino Fine Bks.

Blackwood, Freya. Baby Day. Godwin, Jane & Bell, Davina. 2019. (ENG.). 40p. (J). (gr. -1-3). 17.99 *(978-1-4814-7034-6(5))* Simon & Schuster Children's Publishing.

—Banjo & Ruby Red. Gleeson, Libby. 2018. (ENG.). 30p. (J). (gr. -1-k). bds. 11.99 *(978-1-76012-965-1(8))* Little Hare Bks. AUS. Dist: Independent Pubs. Group.

—The Bike Ride. Ormerod, Jan. 2017. (Maudie & Bear Stories Ser.). (ENG.). 10p. (J). (gr. -1-k). bds. 9.99 *(978-1-76012-898-2(8))* Little Hare Bks. AUS. Dist: Independent Pubs. Group.

Blackwood, Freya. The Feather. Wild, Margaret. 2020. (ENG.). 32p. (J). (gr. -1-k). pap. 12.99 ***(978-1-76050-635-3(4))*** Little Hare Bks. AUS. Dist: Independent Pubs. Group.

Blackwood, Freya. Go to Sleep, Jessie. Gleeson, Libby. 2018. (ENG.). 32p. (J). (gr. -1-k). 11.95 *(978-1-76050-124-2(7))* Little Hare Bks. AUS. Dist: Independent Pubs. Group.

—Half a World Away. Gleeson, Libby. 2007. (J). pap. *(978-0-439-88978-0(2),* Levine, Arthur A. Bks.) Scholastic, Inc.

—Hattie Helps Out. Godwin, Jane & Bell, Davina. 2016. (ENG.). 32p. (J). (gr. -1-k). 19.99 *(978-1-74343-543-4(6))* Allen & Unwin AUS. Dist: Independent Pubs. Group.

—Her Mother's Face. Doyle, Roddy. 2008. (J). pap. *(978-0-439-81502-4(9),* Levine, Arthur A. Bks.) Scholastic, Inc.

—Making Up. Ormerod, Jan. 2017. (Maudie & Bear Stories Ser.). (ENG.). 10p. (J). (gr. -1-k). bds. 9.99 *(978-1-76012-899-9(6))* Little Hare Bks. AUS. Dist: Independent Pubs. Group.

—Molly & Mae: A Friendship Journey. Parker, Danny & Bodman, Charlotte. 2017. (ENG.). 32p. (J). (gr. -1-3). 16.99 *(978-1-328-71543-2(4),* 1674164, HMH Books For Young Readers) Houghton Mifflin Harcourt Publishing Co.

—My Two Blankets. Kobald, Irena. 2015. (ENG.). 32p. (J). (gr. 1-4). 17.99 *(978-0-544-43228-4(2),* 1595822, HMH Books For Young Readers) Houghton Mifflin Harcourt Publishing Co.

—Perfect. Parker, Danny. 32p. (J). 2018. (ENG.). (gr. -1-k). 10.99 *(978-1-76050-140-2(9));* 2017. (— 1). 16.99 *(978-1-921894-84-8(9))* Little Hare Bks. AUS. Dist: Independent Pubs. Group.

—The Runaway Hug. Bland, Nick. 2013. (ENG.). 32p. (J). (gr. -1-2). 16.99 *(978-0-449-81825-1(X),* Random Hse. Bks. for Young Readers) Random Hse. Children's Bks.

—The Snack. Ormerod, Jan. 2018. (Maudie & Bear Stories Ser.). (ENG.). 10p. (J). (— 1). bds. 9.99 *(978-1-76050-038-2(0))* Little Hare Bks. AUS. Dist: Independent Pubs. Group.

—The Treasure Box. Wild, Margaret. 2017. (ENG.). 40p. (J). (gr. k-3). 16.99 *(978-0-7636-9084-7(8))* Candlewick Pr.

Blackwood, Freyda. Impressionists. Dickens, Rosie. 2009. (Young Reading Ser.). 64p. (J). 6.99 *(978-0-7945-2154-7(1),* Usborne) EDC Publishing.

Blackwood, Kristin. Big Blue. Oelschlager, Vanita. 2008. (ENG.). 32p. (J). (gr. -1-3). 17.95 *(978-0-9800162-5-3(8))* VanitaBooks.

—Carrot. Oelschlager, Vanita. 2011. (ENG.). 44p. (gr. -1-3). (J). pap. 8.95 *(978-0-9826366-0-2(1));* 15.95 *(978-0-9819714-9-0(0))* VanitaBooks.

—Elefante. Oelschlager, Vanita. 2011. 20p. (J). (gr. k-k). (SPA.). bds. 6.95 *(978-0-9826366-5-7(2));* (ENG.). bds. 6.95 *(978-0-9826366-4-0(4))* VanitaBooks.

—Farfalla: A Story of Loss & Hope. Oelschlager, Vanita. 2012. (ENG.). 40p. (J). (gr. -1-3). 15.95 *(978-0-9832904-0-7(7))* VanitaBooks.

—Ivan's Great Fall: Poetry for Summer & Autumn from Great Poets & Writers of the Past. Oelschlager, Vanita. 2009. (ENG.). 44p. (J). (gr. -1-3). 15.95 *(978-0-9819714-1-4(5));* pap. 8.95 *(978-0-9819714-2-1(3))* VanitaBooks.

—Ivy in Bloom: The Poetry of Spring from Great Poets & Writers from the Past. Oelschlager, Vanita. 2009. (ENG.). 40p. (J). (gr. -1-3). 17.95 *(978-0-9800162-7-7(4))* VanitaBooks.

—Let Me Bee. Oelschlager, Vanita. 2008. (ENG.). 42p. (J). (gr. -1-3). 17.95 *(978-0-9800162-1-5(5))* VanitaBooks.

—Made in China: A Story of Adoption. Oelschlager, Vanita. 2008. (ENG.). 32p. (J). (gr. -1-3). 17.95 *(978-0-9800162-3-9(1))* VanitaBooks.

—A Tale of Two Daddies. Oelschlager, Vanita. 2010. (ENG.). 42p. (J). (gr. -1-3). 15.95 *(978-0-9819714-5-2(8));* pap. 8.95 *(978-0-9819714-6-9(6))* VanitaBooks.

—What Pet Will I Get? Oelschlager, Vanita. 2008. (ENG.). 38p. (J). (gr. -1-3). 17.95 *(978-0-9800162-2-2(3),* 991700007) VanitaBooks.

Blackwood, Kristin & Blanc, Mike. Bonyo Bonyo. Oelschlager, Vanita. 2010. (ENG.). 42p. (J). (gr. -1-3). pap. 8.95 *(978-0-9819714-4-5(X));* 15.95 *(978-0-9819714-3-8(1))* VanitaBooks.

Blackwood, Kristin, jt. illus. see Hegan, Robin.

Blades, Ann. A Candle for Christmas, 1 vol. Speare, Jean. (ENG.). 32p. (J). pap. 4.95 *(978-0-88899-149-2(5))* Groundwood Bks. CAN. Dist: Publishers Group West (PGW).

—A Salmon for Simon, 1 vol. Waterton, Betty. 35th ed. 2013. (ENG.). 32p. (J). (gr. -1-k). 14.95 *(978-1-55498-392-6(4))* Groundwood Bks. CAN. Dist: Publishers Group West (PGW).

—Six Darn Cows, 1 vol. Laurence, Margaret & James Lorimer and Company Ltd. Staff. 2nd rev. ed. 2011. (Kids of Canada Ser.). (ENG.). 32p. (J). (gr. k-3). 14.95 *(978-1-55277-719-0(7),* 719) James Lorimer & Co. Ltd., Pubs. CAN. Dist: Formac Lorimer Bks. Ltd.

Blades, Ann, jt. illus. see Waterton, Betty.

Bladholm, Cheri. Fear Not, Joseph. Stiegemeyer, Julie. 2008. 32p. (J). (gr. -1-3). 13.49 *(978-0-7586-1498-8(5))* Concordia Publishing Hse.

Bladimir, Trejo. Ecuador. Sojos, Catalina. 2015. 24p. (J). (gr. -1-2). pap. 12.95 *(978-9978-07-415-2(5),* Alfaguara Infantil) Santillana Ecuador ECU. Dist: Santillana USA Publishing Co., Inc.

Blain, Theresa A. Visualize World Geography in 7 Minutes a Day: Let Pictography Take You from Clueless to Knowing the World. Blain, Theresa A. 2003. 302p. per. 19.95 *(978-0-9741401-0-0(4))* Tender Heart Pr.

Blaine, Janice. Skookum Sal, Birling Gal. Kellerhals-Stewart, Heather. unabr. ed. 2003. (ENG.). 32p. (J). 18.95 *(978-1-55017-285-0(9))* Harbour Publishing Co., Ltd. CAN. Dist: Publishers Group West (PGW).

Blair, Beth L. Five Kids & a Monkey, 3 vols., Set. Riccio, Nina M. (J). (gr. 2-6). 23.85 *(978-0-9653955-3-3(7))* Creative Attic, Inc., The.

Blair, Culverson & Simpson, Howard. Afro-Bets Book of Shapes. Brown, Margery W. 2nd ed. 2004. (Afro-Bets Ser.). 24p. (J). (gr. -1-1). pap. 3.95 *(978-0-940975-58-3(0),* Sankofa Bks.) Just Us Bks., Inc.

—Book of Colors: Meet the Color Family. Brown, Margery W. 2nd ed. 2004. (Afro-Bets Ser.). 24p. (J). (gr. -1-1). pap. 3.95 *(978-0-940975-57-6(2),* Sankofa Bks.) Just Us Bks., Inc.

Blair, Jocelyn. Little Dutch Girl in World War II. Harkes, Willy. l.t. ed. 2004. 22p. (J). pap. 13.95 *(978-0-9741627-1-3(X))* PricePoint+Publications.

Blair, June H. Totally Trouble. Krapp, JoAnn Vergona. 2017. (J). (gr. 3-5). pap. 12.95 *(978-0-9722576-5-7(9))* JoAnn Vergona Krapp & Gene Zaner.

—Trouble Times Three. Krapp, JoAnn Vergona. 2015. 64p. (J). (gr. 3-5). pap. 12.95 *(978-0-9722576-4-0(0))* JoAnn Vergona Krapp & Gene Zaner.

Blair, Karen. Puddle Hunters. Murray, Kirsty. 2019. (ENG.). 32p. (J). (gr. -1-1). 16.99 *(978-1-76029-674-2(0))* Allen & Unwin AUS. Dist: Independent Pubs. Group.

—Something Wonderful. Caisley, Raewyn. 2018. 32p. (J). (gr. -1-3). 13.99 *(978-0-14-350666-9(8),* Puffin) Penguin Random Hse. AUS. Dist: Independent Pubs. Group.

Blair, Karen. Baby Animal Farm. Blair, Karen. 2014. (ENG.). 16p. (J). (— 1). bds. 6.99 *(978-0-7636-7069-6(3))* Candlewick Pr.

Blair, Mary. I Can Fly. Krauss, Ruth. 2003. (Little Golden Book Ser.). (ENG.). 24p. (J). (gr. -1-2). 4.99 *(978-0-307-00146-7(6),* 312-12, Golden Bks.) Random Hse. Children's Bks.

Blair, Richard P., photos by. Point Reyes Visions Guidebook: Where to go, What to Do. Goodwin, Kathleen P. 2004. 80p. 21.95 *(978-0-9671527-0-7(4))* Color & Light Editions.

Blair, Tim. If You Ask a Scientist a Question. Small, Adrienne H. 2019. (ENG.). 20p. (J). (gr. k-4). pap. 12.99 ***(978-1-63132-076-7(9))*** Advanced Publishing LLC.

Blaisdell, Elinore. Rhymes & Verses: Collected Poems for Young People. de la Mare, Walter. 2005. 351p. (J). (gr. 4-8). reprint ed. 19.00 *(978-0-7567-8944-2(3))* DIANE Publishing Co.

Blaise, Aaron & Larsson, Therese. Lion King (2019) Picture Book, the: Hakuna Matata. Rubiano, Brittany. 2019. (ENG.). 40p. (J). (gr. -1-k). 17.99 *(978-1-368-03927-7(8))* Disney Pr.

Blake, Anne Catharine. Child's Guide to Baptism. Stanton, Sue. 2006. (Child's Guide Ser.). (ENG.). 32p. (J). (gr. 3-7). 9.95 *(978-0-8091-6728-9(X),* 6728-x) Paulist Pr.

—Child's Guide to First Holy Communion. Ficocelli, Elizabeth. 2003. 32p. 10.95 *(978-0-8091-6708-1(5),* 3708-5) Paulist Pr.

—Child's Guide to the Rosary. Ficocelli, Elizabeth. 2009. (J). 10.95 *(978-0-8091-6736-4(0))* Paulist Pr.

—Child's Guide to the Seven Sacraments. Ficocelli, Elizabeth. 2005. 32p. (J). *(978-0-8091-6723-4(9),* 6723-9) Paulist Pr.

—Child's Guide to the Stations of the Cross. Stanton, Sue. (J). 2018. (ENG.). pap. 12.95 *(978-0-8091-6786-9(7));* 2008. 32p. 10.95 *(978-0-8091-6739-5(5),* 6739-5) Paulist Pr.

—Josh's Smiley Faces: A Story about Anger. Ditta-Donahue, Gina. 2003. 32p. (J). pap. 9.95 *(978-1-59147-001-4(3));* 14.95 *(978-1-59147-000-7(5))* American Psychological Assn. (Magination Pr.).

—Katie's Premature Brother = el Hermano Prematuro de Katie. Hawkins-Walsh, Elizabeth & Pierson-Solis, Lennard. 2006. (J). *(978-1-56123-197-3(5))* Centering Corp.

—Tinkle, Tinkle, Little Tot: Songs & Rhymes for Toilet Training. Lansky, Bruce & Pottle, Robert. 2005. 32p. (J). 8.95 *(978-0-88166-492-8(8),* 1182) Meadowbrook Pr.

Blake, Anne Catharine. Child's Guide to Reconciliation. Blake, Anne Catharine, tr. Ficocelli, Elizabeth. 2004. 32p. 9.95 *(978-0-8091-6709-8(3),* 6709-3) Paulist Pr.

Blake, Beccy. Clown School. Shipton, Paul. 2005. (ENG.). 24p. (J). lib. bdg. 23.65 *(978-1-59646-752-1(5))* Dingles & Co.

—Collins Big Cat Phonics for Letters & Sounds - Pat It: Band 01A/Pink A, Bd. 1A. Raby, Charlotte. 2018. (Collins Big Cat Phonics Ser.). (ENG.). 16p. (J). (gr. -1-k). pap. 6.99 *(978-0-00-825129-1(0))* HarperCollins Pubs. Ltd. GBR. Dist: Independent Pubs. Group.

—Detective Derek. Wallace, Karen. 2009. (Go! Readers Ser.). 48p. (J). (gr. 2-5). pap. 12.85 *(978-1-60754-276-6(5));* lib. bdg. 32.25 *(978-1-60754-275-9(7))* Windmill Bks.

—Ghost Mouse. Wallace, Karen. 2009. (Go! Readers Ser.). 48p. (J). (gr. 2-5). pap. 12.85 *(978-1-60754-273-5(0));* lib. bdg. 32.25 *(978-1-60754-272-8(2))* Windmill Bks.

—My Big, New Bed. Nash, Margaret. 2008. (Tadpoles Ser.). (ENG.). 24p. (J). (gr. -1-2). lib. bdg. *(978-0-7787-3859-6(0));* pap. *(978-0-7787-3890-9(6))* Crabtree Publishing Co.

—Tortoise Races Home. Atkins, Jill. 2009. (Tadpoles Ser.). (ENG.). (J). (gr. k-k). lib. bdg. 17.55 *(978-1-61383-950-8(2))* Perfection Learning Corp.

—Tortoise Races Home. Atkins, Jill. 2009. (Tadpoles Ser.). (ENG.). 24p. (J). (gr. -1-2). pap. *(978-0-7787-3902-9(3))* Crabtree Publishing Co.

—What Am I?: Band 00/Lilac (Collins Big Cat) Kelly, Maoliosa. 2007. (Collins Big Cat Ser.). (ENG.). 16p. (J). (gr. -1-k). pap. 7.99 *(978-0-00-718679-2(7))* HarperCollins Pubs. Ltd. GBR. Dist: Independent Pubs. Group.

Blake, Carol. Yang the Dragon Tells His Story, Halloween Train. Wilkinson, James H. 2013. 32p. pap. 15.99 *(978-0-9886360-0-2(X))* Kids At Heart Publishing, LLC.

Blake, Cecil J. Sammy's Saturdays: The Pie Contest. Petrone-Brown, Barbara. 2019. (ENG.). 30p. (J). pap. 14.95 ***(978-1-6970-1664-2(2))*** Independently Published.

Blake, Edward, jt. illus. see Millingen, Stephen.

Blake, Elinor. We're Going to Be Friends. White, Jack. 2017. 32p. (J). (gr. 1-5). 16.95 *(978-0-9964016-9-2(5))* Third Man Books.

Blake, Francis. The A to Z of Everyday Things. Weaver, Janice. 2004. 128p. (J). (gr. 5). pap. 8.95 *(978-0-88776-671-8(4),* Tundra Bks.) Tundra Bks. CAN. Dist: Penguin Random Hse. LLC.

—From Head to Toe: Bound Feet, Bathing Suits, & Other Bizarre & Beautiful Things. Weaver, Janice. 2003. 80p. (J). (gr. 5-9). pap. 16.95 *(978-0-88776-654-1(4),* Tundra Bks.) Tundra Bks. CAN. Dist: Penguin Random Hse. LLC.

—Nibbling on Einstein's Brain: The Good, the Bad & the Bogus in Science. Swanson, Diane. 2nd rev. ed. 2009. (ENG.). 160p. (J). (gr. 1-12). 24.95 *(978-1-55451-187-7(9),* 9781554511877) Annick Pr., Ltd. CAN. Dist: Publishers Group West (PGW).

—Rude Stories. Andrews, Jan. 2010. 88p. (J). (gr. 1-4). 19.95 *(978-0-88776-921-4(7),* Tundra Bks.) Tundra Bks. CAN. Dist: Penguin Random Hse. LLC.

Blake, Hayley. The Nugget Peak Crew. Lake, Susan. 2019. (ENG.). 46p. (J). pap. 12.99 ***(978-1-0891-4434-2(2))*** Independently Published.

Blake, Jenn, et al. Diamond Tiara & Silver Spoon. Whitley, Jeremy. 2018. (My Little Pony: Friends Forever Ser.). (ENG.). 24p. (J). (gr. 1-8). lib. bdg. 27.07 *(978-1-5321-4235-2(8),* 28563, Graphic Novels) Spotlight.

Blake, Jocelyn. Mama Is on an Airplane. Blake, Jocelyn. ed. 2006. (J). per. 9.99 *(978-0-9790572-0-5(5))* Kreativ Kaos.

Blake, Joshua, jt. illus. see Stites, Theresa.

Blake, Joshua Aaron. Just A Little Child. Wood, Debra. l.t. ed. 2006. 33p. (J). per. 12.95 *(978-1-59879-087-0(0))* Lifevest Publishing, Inc.

—William Warrior Bear. Wood, Debra. l.t. ed. 2005. 30p. (J). per. 12.95 *(978-1-59879-001-6(3))* Lifevest Publishing, Inc.

Blake, Judith. Grandma Brown's Three Fine Pigs. Griffiths, Neil. 2015. (ENG.). 32p. (J). pap. 9.99 *(978-0-9537099-7-7(3),* Red Robin Bks.) Corner To Learn Ltd. GBR. Dist: Parkwest Pubns., Inc.

Blake, Mike. Blades of Green: Adventures in Backyard Habitats. Prokos, Anna. 2017. (Imagine That! Ser.). (ENG.). 32p. (J). (gr. 2-4). lib. bdg. 26.65 *(978-1-63440-147-0(6));* E-Book 39.99 *(978-1-63440-159-3(X))* Red Chair Pr.

—Let It Rain: Exploring the Amazon Rain Forest. Boynton, Alice & Blevins, Wiley. 2017. (Imagine That! Ser.). (ENG.). 32p. (J). (gr. 2-4). lib. bdg. 26.65 *(978-1-63440-273-6(1))* Red Chair Pr.

Blake, Nelson. Luke Cage Vol. 1: Sins of the Father. 2017. (ENG.). 112p. (YA). (gr. 8-17). pap. 15.99 *(978-1-302-90778-5(6))* Marvel Worldwide, Inc.

Blake, Nelson & Sanna, Guillermo. Luke Cage Vol. 2: Caged! 2018. (ENG.). 112p. (YA). (gr. 8-17). pap. 15.99 *(978-1-302-90779-2(4))* Marvel Worldwide, Inc.

Blake, Quentin. Ace Dragon Ltd. Hoban, Russell. 2015. (ENG.). 48p. (J). (gr. k-3). 16.99 *(978-0-7636-7482-3(6))* Candlewick Pr.

—Agu Trot. Dahl, Roald. 2003.Tr. of Esio Trot. (SPA.). 64p. (J). (gr. 3-5). pap. 9.95 *(978-84-204-4436-9(7))* Santillana USA Publishing Co., Inc.

—All the Year Round. Yeoman, John. 2019. (ENG.). 32p. (J). (gr. k-2). 16.99 *(978-1-78344-613-1(7))* Andersen Pr. GBR. Dist: Independent Pubs. Group.

—Arabel's Raven. Aiken, Joan. 2007. (ENG.). 160p. (J). (gr. 3-7). pap. 11.95 *(978-0-15-206094-7(4),* 1198305) Houghton Mifflin Harcourt Publishing Co.

—Bananas in My Ears: A Collection of Nonsense Stories, Poems, Riddles, & Rhymes. Rosen, Michael. 2012. (ENG.). 96p. (J). (gr. k-12). 15.99 *(978-0-7636-6248-6(8))* Candlewick Pr.

—The Bear's Water Picnic. Yeoman, John. 2011. 40p. (J). (gr. k-k). pap. 12.99 *(978-1-84939-004-0(5))* Andersen Pr. GBR. Dist: Independent Pubs. Group.

—The Bear's Winter House. Yeoman, John. 2012. (J). *(978-1-4351-4374-6(4))* Barnes & Noble, Inc.

—The Bear's Winter House. Yeoman, John. 2010. 32p. (J). (gr. k-k). pap. 12.99 *(978-1-84270-916-0(X))* Andersen Pr. GBR. Dist: Independent Pubs. Group.

—Billy & the Minpins. Dahl, Roald. 2019. (ENG.). 128p. (J). (gr. 2-4). 7.99 *(978-0-593-11342-4(X),* Puffin Books) Penguin Young Readers Group.

—Boy & Going Solo. Dahl, Roald. 2010. (ENG.). 400p. (J). (gr. 3-7). 10.99 *(978-0-14-241741-6(6),* Puffin Books) Penguin Young Readers Group.

—Las Brujas. Dahl, Roald.Tr. of Witches. (SPA.). 200p. (gr. 5-8). (J). pap. 9.95 *(978-84-204-4815-2(X));* 2003. (YA). pap. 12.95 *(978-958-24-0100-9(1))* Santillana USA Publishing Co., Inc.

—Charlie & the Chocolate Factory. Dahl, Roald. 2007. 17.00 *(978-0-7569-8213-3(8))* Penguin Publishing Group.

—Charlie & the Chocolate Factory. Dahl, Roald. (ENG.). (J). (gr. 3-7). 2011. 160p. 16.99 *(978-0-14-241821-5(8));* 2007. 192p. 7.99 *(978-0-14-241031-8(4));* 2004. 176p. pap. 7.99 *(978-0-14-240108-8(0))* Penguin Young Readers Group. (Puffin Books).

—Charlie & the Great Glass Elevator. Dahl, Roald. 2007. (ENG.). 192p. (J). (gr. 3-7). 7.99 *(978-0-14-241032-5(2),* Puffin Books) Penguin Young Readers Group.

—Charlie & the Great Glass Elevator. Dahl, Roald. 2005. (Puffin Modern Classics Ser.). (ENG.). 176p. (J). (gr. 3-7). pap. 7.99 *(978-0-14-240412-6(8),* Puffin Books) Penguin Young Readers Group.

—Charlie's Gobstoppingly Great Sticker Activity Book. Dahl, Roald. 2018. (ENG.). 32p. (J). (gr. 3-7). pap. 7.99 *(978-1-5247-8622-9(5),* Grosset & Dunlap) Penguin Young Readers Group.

—A Christmas Carol. Dickens, Charles. unabr. ed. 2004. (Chrysalis Childrens Classics Ser.). 190p. (Orig.). (YA). pap. *(978-1-84365-063-8(0),* Pavilion Children's Books) Pavilion Bks.

—Collins Musicals - Roald Dahl's the Three Little Pigs (Book + CD/CD-ROM): a Tail-Twistingly Treacherous Musical. White, Matthew et al. 2007. (and C Black Musicals Ser.). (ENG.). 64p. (J). (gr. 2-6). pap. 42.95 incl. cd-rom *(978-0-7136-8202-1(7))* HarperCollins Pubs. Ltd. GBR. Dist: Independent Pubs. Group.

—The Complete Adventures of Charlie & Mr. Willy Wonka. Dahl, Roald. 2010. (ENG.). 336p. (J). (gr. 3-7). 10.99 *(978-0-14-241740-9(8),* Puffin Books) Penguin Young Readers Group.

—Los Cretinos. Dahl, Roald. 2005. (Infantil Ser.).Tr. of Twist. (SPA.). 106p. (gr. 3-5). per. 9.95 *(978-968-19-0559-0(8))* Santillana USA Publishing Co., Inc.

—Cuentos en Verso para Niños Perversos. Dahl, Roald. 3rd ed.Tr. of Revolting Rhymes. (SPA.). 32p. (J). (gr. 5-8). pap. 10.95 *(978-84-372-2183-0(8))* Santillana USA Publishing Co., Inc.

—Danny el Campeon del Mundo. Dahl, Roald. 2003.Tr. of Danny the Champion of the World. (SPA.). 200p. (YA). (gr. 5-8). 9.95 *(978-84-204-4431-4(6))* Ediciones Alfaguara ESP. Dist: Santillana USA Publishing Co., Inc.

—Danny the Champion of the World. Dahl, Roald. ed. 2007. 205p. (gr. 4-7). 18.40 *(978-1-4177-8611-4(6))* Turtleback.

—Dream Big & Other Life Lessons from the Enormous Crocodile. Dahl, Roald. 2019. (ENG.). 32p. (J). (gr. -1-2). 8.99 *(978-1-5247-9209-1(8),* Grosset & Dunlap) Penguin Young Readers Group.

—The Eejits. Dahl, Roald & Fitt, Matthew. 2006. 96p. (J). (gr. 1-7). pap. 9.99 *(978-1-84502-097-2(9))* Black and White Publishing Ltd. GBR. Dist: Independent Pubs. Group.

—Enormous Crocodile. Dahl, Roald. 2009. (ENG.). (J). (gr. 2-4). lib. bdg. 18.60 *(978-1-61383-187-8(0))* Perfection Learning Corp.

—Esio Trot. Dahl, Roald. 2009. (ENG.). 96p. (J). (gr. 3-7). 7.99 *(978-0-14-241382-1(8),* Puffin Books) Penguin Young Readers Group.

—Fantastic Mr. Dahl. Rosen, Michael. 2012. 166p. (J). (gr. 3-6). 21.19 *(978-0-14-132213-1(6))* Penguin Young Readers Group.

—Fantastic Mr. Fox. Dahl, Roald. 2007. 17.00 *(978-0-7569-8286-7(3))* Penguin Publishing Group.

—Fantastic Mr. Fox. Dahl, Roald. 2007. (ENG.). 112p. (J). (gr. 3-7). 7.99 *(978-0-14-241034-9(9),* Puffin Books) Penguin Young Readers Group.

—Gabriel-Ernest & Other Tales. Saki. 2015. (Alma Junior Classics Ser.). 128p. (J). pap. 9.99 *(978-1-84749-592-1(3),* 333177) Alma Classics GBR. Dist: Bloomsbury Publishing Plc.

—George's Marvelous Medicine. Dahl, Roald. 2007. (ENG.). 112p. (J). (gr. 3-7). 7.99 *(978-0-14-241035-6(7),* Puffin Books) Penguin Young Readers Group.

—George's Marvelous Medicine. Dahl, Roald. 2008. 88p. (gr. 4-7). 18.00 *(978-0-7569-8777-0(6))* Perfection Learning Corp.

—The Giraffe & the Pelly & Me. Dahl, Roald. 2009. (ENG.). 96p. (Orig.). (J). (gr. 3-7). 7.99 *(978-0-14-241384-5(4)*, Puffin Books) Penguin Young Readers Group.

—The Great Piratical Rumbustification & the Librarian & the Robbers. Mahy, Margaret. 2013. (ENG.). 64p. (J). pap. 8.95 *(978-1-56792-169-4(8))* Godine, David R. Pub.

—The Heron & the Crane. Yeoman, John. 2011. 32p. (J). (gr. -1-k). pap. 13.99 *(978-1-84939-200-6(5))* Andersen Pr. GBR. Dist: Independent Pubs. Group.

—The House in the Tree. Pitzorno, Bianca. Parkin, Stephen, tr. 2017. 128p. (J). pap. 10.99 *(978-1-84688-410-8(1)*, 351541) Alma Bks. GBR. Dist: Bloomsbury Publishing Plc.

—How Tom Beat Captain Najork & His Hired Sportsmen. Hoban, Russell. 2006. (ENG.). 32p. (J). (gr. k-4). pap. 7.95 *(978-1-56792-322-3(4))* Godine, David R. Pub.

—James & the Giant Peach. Dahl, Roald. (ENG.). (J). (gr. 3-7). 2016. 176p. 17.99 *(978-0-425-28765-1(3))*; 2011. 128p. pap. 15.99 *(978-0-14-241823-9(4))*; 2007. 176p. 7.99 *(978-0-14-241036-3(5))* Penguin Young Readers Group. (Puffin Books).

—James & the Giant Peach. Dahl, Roald. ed. 2007. 146p. (gr. 4-7). 18.40 *(978-1-4177-8608-4(6))* Turtleback.

—James & the Giant Peach: The Scented Peach Edition. Dahl, Roald. 2018. (ENG.). 176p. (J). (gr. 3-7). 7.99 *(978-0-451-48079-8(1)*, Puffin Books) Penguin Young Readers Group.

—James y el Melocoton Gigante. Dahl, Roald. 2003.Tr. of James & the Giant Peach. (SPA.). 184p. pap. 9.95 *(978-968-19-0625-2(X))* Aguilar, Altea, Taurus, Alfaguara, S.A. de C.V MEX. Dist: Santillana USA Publishing Co., Inc.

—The Magic Finger. Dahl, Roald. 2009. (ENG.). 96p. (J). (gr. 3-7). 7.99 *(978-0-14-241385-2(2)*, Puffin Books) Penguin Young Readers Group.

—The Magic Finger. Dahl, Roald. 2003. (CHI.). 133p. (J). pap. 11.70 *(978-957-574-476-2(4))* Youth Cultural Publishing Co. CHN. Dist: Chinasprout, Inc.

—La Maravillosa Granja de McBroom. Fleischman, Sid. 13th ed. 2003.Tr. of McBroom's Wonderful One-Acre Farm. (SPA.). 96p. (J). (gr. 3-5). 7.95 *(978-84-204-4885-5(0))* Ediciones Alfaguara ESP. Dist: Santillana USA Publishing Co., Inc.

—La Maravillosa Medicina de Jorge. Dahl, Roald. (Serie Naranja Ser.).Tr. of George's Marvelous Medicine Spanish. (SPA.). 118p. 2014. (J). pap. 11.95 *(978-1-64101-232-4(3))*; 2005. (gr. 3-5). per. 11.95 *(978-968-19-0547-7(4))* Santillana USA Publishing Co., Inc.

—The Marzipan Pig. Hoban, Russell. 2016. (ENG.). 48p. (J). (gr. 1-4). 15.95 *(978-1-59017-999-4(4)*, NYR Children's Collection) New York Review of Bks., Inc., The.

—Matilda. Dahl, Roald. 2007.Tr. of Matilda. (ENG.). 256p. (J). (gr. 3-7). 7.99 *(978-0-14-241037-0(3)*, Puffin Books) Penguin Young Readers Group.

—Matilda: Broadway Tie-In. Dahl, Roald. ed. 2013.Tr. of Matilda. (ENG.). 256p. (J). (gr. 3-7). pap. 7.99 *(978-0-14-242538-1(9)*, Puffin Books) Penguin Young Readers Group.

—Matilda: The Chocolate Cake Edition. Dahl, Roald. 2019.Tr. of Matilda. (ENG.). 256p. (J). (gr. 3-7). 7.99 *(978-1-9848-3620-5(X)*, Puffin Books) Penguin Young Readers Group.

—Matilda (Puffin Modern Classics) Dahl, Roald. 2004. (Puffin Modern Classics Ser.).Tr. of Matilda. (ENG.). 240p. (J). (gr. 3-7). pap. 7.99 *(978-0-14-240253-5(2)*, Puffin Books) Penguin Young Readers Group.

—Meet Monster: The First Big Monster Book. Blance, Ellen & Cook, Ann. 2020. (ENG.). 160p. (J). (gr. -1-3). 19.95 *(978-1-68137-428-4(5)*, NYR Children's Collection) New York Review of Bks., Inc., The.

—Michael Rosen's Sad Book. Rosen, Michael. 2005. (ENG.). 34p. (J). (gr. 1-3). 21.19 *(978-0-7636-2597-9(3))* Candlewick Pr.

—The Missing Golden Ticket & Other Splendiferous Secrets. Dahl, Roald. 2010. (ENG.). 128p. (J). (gr. 3-7). 7.99 *(978-0-14-241742-3(4)*, Puffin Books) Penguin Young Readers Group.

—Mouse Trouble. Yeoman, John. 2011. 32p. (J). (gr. -1-k). pap. 12.99 *(978-1-84939-201-3(3))* Andersen Pr. GBR. Dist: Independent Pubs. Group.

—Mr. Nodd's Ark. Yeoman, John. ed. 2016. 32p. (J). (-k). pap. 13.99 *(978-1-78344-374-1(X))* Andersen Pr. GBR. Dist: Independent Pubs. Group.

—A Near Thing for Captain Najork. Hoban, Russell. 2006. (ENG.). 32p. (J). (gr. -1-3). pap. 7.95 *(978-1-56792-323-0(2))* Godine, David R. Pub.

—Quentin Blake's the Seven Voyages of Sinbad the Sailor. Yeoman, John. 2012. (ENG.). 120p. (J). (gr. 2-4). 19.99 *(978-1-84365-129-1(7)*, Pavilion Children's Books) Pavilion Bks. GBR. Dist: Penguin Random Hse. LLC.

—Reekin Rhymes: Revolting Rhymes in Scots. Dahl, Roald. Fitt, Matthew, tr. 2018. 52p. (J). (gr. 4-7). pap. 13.99 *(978-1-78530-183-4(7))* Black and White Publishing Ltd. GBR. Dist: Independent Pubs. Group.

—The Rights of the Reader. Pennac, Daniel. Adams, Sarah, tr. 2008.Tr. of Comme un roman.. (ENG.). 176p. (YA). (gr. 9). 16.99 *(978-0-7636-3801-6(3))* Candlewick Pr.

—Roald Dahl's Revolting Recipes. Baldwin, Jan, photos by. Dahl, Felicity et al. 2003. (ENG.). 32p. (gr. 3-7). 9.99 *(978-0-14-037827-0(0))* Perfection Learning Corp.

—Santa's Last Present. Murail, Elvire & Murail, Marie-aude. 2004. (ENG.). 32p. (J). (gr. 3-7). 12.95 *(978-1-56145-319-1(6))* Peachtree Publishing Co. Inc.

—The Seven Voyages of Sinbad the Sailor. Yeoman, John. 2003. (Chrysalis Childrens Classics Ser.). (YA). pap. *(978-1-84365-040-9(1)*, Pavilion Children's Books) Pavilion Bks.

—Sixes & Sevens. Yeoman, John. 2012. 32p. (J). (gr. -1-k). pap. 11.99 *(978-1-84939-308-9(7))* Andersen Pr. GBR. Dist: Independent Pubs. Group.

—The Tale of Kitty in Boots. Potter, Beatrix. 2016. (Peter Rabbit Ser.). (ENG.). 72p. (J). (gr. -1-2). 20.00 *(978-0-241-24944-4(9)*, Warne) Penguin Young Readers Group.

—The Twits. Dahl, Roald. (ENG.). 112p. (J). (gr. 3-7). 2017. 17.99 *(978-0-425-29009-5(3))*; 2007. 7.99 *(978-0-14-241039-4(X))* Penguin Young Readers Group. (Puffin Books).

—The Twits. Dahl, Roald. 2007. 76p. (gr. 4-7). 18.00 *(978-0-7569-8234-8(0))* Perfection Learning Corp.

—Uncle. Martin, J. P. 2017. (Uncle Ser.). (ENG.). 176p. (J). (gr. 4-7). pap. 9.99 *(978-1-68137-185-6(5)*, NYRB Kids) New York Review of Bks., Inc., The.

—Uncle Cleans Up. Martin, J. P. 2008. (Uncle Ser.). (ENG.). 184p. (J). (gr. 4-7). 17.95 *(978-1-59017-276-6(0)*, NYR Children's Collection) New York Review of Bks., Inc., The.

—The Wild Washerwomen. Yeoman, John. 2009. (Andersen Press Picture Bks). (ENG.). 32p. (J). (gr. k-3). 16.95 *(978-0-7613-5152-8(3))* Lerner Publishing Group.

—The Witches. Dahl, Roald. 2007. (ENG.). 224p. (J). (gr. 3-7). 7.99 *(978-0-14-241011-0(X)*, Puffin Books) Penguin Young Readers Group.

—Wizzil. Steig, William. 2014. 32p. pap. 8.00 *(978-1-61003-221-6(7))* Center for the Collaborative Classroom.

—The Young Performing Horse. Yeoman, John. 2016. 32p. (J). (-k). pap. 13.99 *(978-1-78344-375-8(8))* Andersen Pr. GBR. Dist: Independent Pubs. Group.

Blake, Quentin. Loveykins. Blake, Quentin. (ENG.). 32p. (J). 2016. (gr. -1-3). pap. 8.99 *(978-1-56145-760-1(4))*; 2003. (gr. k-3). 15.95 *(978-1-56145-282-8(3))* Peachtree Publishing Co. Inc.

—Mrs. Armitage, Queen of the Road. Blake, Quentin. 2003. (ENG.). 32p. (J). (gr. k-3). 15.95 *(978-1-56145-287-3(4))* Peachtree Publishing Co. Inc.

—Tell Me a Picture. Blake, Quentin. 2003. (Single Titles Ser.). 128p. lib. bdg. 29.90 *(978-0-7613-2748-6(7)*, Millbrook Pr.) Lerner Publishing Group.

Blake, Quentin & Terrazzini, Daniela Jaglenka. Matilda. Dahl, Roald. 2013.Tr. of Matilda. (ENG.). 240p. (J). (gr. 3-7). 17.99 *(978-0-14-242427-8(7)*, Puffin Books) Penguin Young Readers Group.

Blake, Quentin, jt. illus. see Eccles, Jane.

Blake, Robert J. Akiak: A Tale from the Iditarod. Blake, Robert J. 2004. (ENG.). 40p. (J). (gr. k-3). reprint ed. pap. 7.99 *(978-0-14-240185-9(4)*, Puffin Books) Penguin Young Readers Group.

Blake, Rose. A History of Pictures for Children: From Cave Paintings to Computer Drawings. Hockney, David & Gayford, Martin. 2018. (ENG.). 128p. (J). (gr. 5-9). 24.99 *(978-1-4197-3211-9(0)*, Abrams Bks. for Young Readers) Abrams, Inc.

Blake, Spencer, et al. Spyology. Blake, Spencer. Steer, Dugald A., ed. 2008. (Ologies Ser.: 7). (ENG.). 32p. (J). (gr. 3-7). 25.99 *(978-0-7636-4048-4(4))* Candlewick Pr.

Blake, Stephanie. Poo Bum. Blake, Stephanie. 2020. (ENG.). 32p. (J). (gr. -1-1). 17.99 *(978-1-877467-96-7(0))* Gecko Pr. NZL. Dist: Lerner Publishing Group.

—Super Bunny. Blake, Stephanie. 2015. (ENG.). 38p. (J). 15.95 *(978-0-7358-4223-6(X))* North-South Bks., Inc.

Blakemore, Jamie. Up in the Clouds. Grace, Laura. 2020. (ENG.). 32p. (J). pap. ***(978-1-83975-126-4(6))*** Grosvenor Hse. Publishing Ltd.

Blakeslee, Lys. Heroes A2Z #1: (Heroes a to Z): Alien Ice Cream. Anthony, David & David, Charles. 2007. 128p. (J). pap. 4.99 *(978-0-9728461-8-9(2))* Sigil Publishing.

—Heroes A2Z #13: (Heroes a to Z): Monkey Monster Truck. Anthony, David & Clasman, Charles David. 2012. 128p. (J). mass mkt. 4.99 *(978-0-9846528-1-5(7))* Sigil Publishing.

—Heroes A2Z #2: (Heroes a to Z): Bowling over Halloween: Bowling over Halloween. Anthony, David & David, Charles. 2007. (Heroes A2Z Ser.). 128p. (J). pap. 4.99 *(978-0-9728461-9-6(0))* Sigil Publishing.

—Natalie: School's First Day of Me, 1 vol. Mackall, Dandi Daley. 2009. (That's Nat! Ser.: 3). (ENG.). 96p. (J). (gr. 1-4). pap. 4.99 *(978-0-310-71568-9(7))* Zonderkidz.

—Natalie & the Bestest Friend Race, 1 vol. Mackall, Dandi Daley. 2009. (That's Nat! Ser.: 5). (ENG.). 96p. (J). (gr. 1-4). pap. 4.99 *(978-0-310-71570-2(9))* Zonderkidz.

—Natalie & the Downside-Up Birthday, 1 vol. Mackall, Dandi Daley. 2009. (That's Nat! Ser.: 4). (ENG.). 96p. (J). (gr. 1-4). pap. 4.99 *(978-0-310-71569-6(5))* Zonderkidz.

—Natalie & the One-of-a-Kind Wonderful Day!, 1 vol. Mackall, Dandi Daley. 2009. (That's Nat! Ser.: 1). (ENG.). 96p. (J). (gr. 1-4). pap. 4.99 *(978-0-310-71566-5(0))* Zonderkidz.

—Natalie Really Very Much Wants to Be a Star, 1 vol. Mackall, Dandi Daley. 2009. (That's Nat! Ser.: 2). (ENG.). 96p. (J). (gr. 1-4). pap. 4.99 *(978-0-310-71567-2(9))* Zonderkidz.

—Natalie Wants a Puppy, 1 vol. Mackall, Dandi Daley. 2009. (That's Nat! Ser.: 6). (ENG.). 96p. (J). (gr. 1-4). pap. 4.99 *(978-0-310-71571-9(7))* Zonderkidz.

Blakeslee, S. E. Once upon a Blue Moon: The Chronicles of the Blue Moon. Blakeslee, S. E. 2007. (ENG.). 32p. (J). 17.95 *(978-0-9789031-0-7(2))* Blaumond Pr.

Blakeslee, Susan. Jungle Walk. Deaton, L. Ray. 2018. (ENG.). 28p. (J). pap. 12.95 *(978-1-64349-383-1(3))* Christian Faith Publishing.

Blanc, Katherine. No Dogs, Please! Blanc, Katherine. 2013. (ENG.). (J). (gr. -1-3). 14.95 *(978-1-62086-388-6(X))* Mascot Bks., Inc.

Blanc, Mike. Fish-Boy: An Inuit Folk Tale. 2018. (ENG.). 42p. (J). (gr. 1-4). 8.95 *(978-1-938164-21-7(0))*; 15.95 *(978-1-938164-20-0(2))* VanitaBooks.

—Francesca. Oelschlager, Vanita. 2008. (ENG.). 32p. (J). (gr. -1-3). 17.95 *(978-0-9800162-4-6(X))* VanitaBooks.

—I Came from the Water: One Haitian Boy's Incredible Tale of Survival. Oelschlager, Vanita. 2012. (ENG.). 40p. (J). (gr. -1-3). 15.95 *(978-0-9832904-4-5(X))* VanitaBooks.

—Magic Words: From the Ancient Oral Tradition of the Inuit. Oelschlager, Vanita. 2013. (ENG.). 24p. (J). (gr. -1-3). 15.95 *(978-0-9832904-6-9(6))* VanitaBooks.

—Magic Words: From the Ancient Oral Tradition of the Inuit. 2013. (ENG.). 24p. (J). (gr. -1-3). pap. 8.95 *(978-0-9832904-7-6(4))* VanitaBooks.

—Porcupette Finds a Family. Oelschlager, Vanita. 2010. (ENG.). 44p. (gr. -1-3). 15.95 *(978-0-9819714-7-6(4))*; pap. 8.95 *(978-0-9819714-8-3(2))* VanitaBooks.

—A Tale of Two Mommies. Oelschlager, Vanita. 2011. (ENG.). 40p. (J). (gr. -1-3). 15.95 *(978-0-9826366-6-4(0))*; pap. 8.95 *(978-0-9826366-7-1(9))* VanitaBooks.

Blanc, Mike & Bauknight, Wilfred. Postcards from a War. Oelschlager, Vanita. 2009. (ENG.). 40p. (J). (gr. 1-4). 15.95 *(978-0-9800162-9-1(0))*; pap. 8.95 *(978-0-9819714-0-7(7))* VanitaBooks.

Blanc, Mike, jt. illus. see Blackwood, Kristin.

Blancbec, Alain. !الغراب المشاكس يحاول تغيير سلوكه The Cheeky Crow Tries to Be Good! Davis, Mandie. Davis, Badger, ed. 2019. (Cheeky Crow Ser.: Vol. 3). (ARA.). 72p. (J). pap. *(978-1-9164839-2-7(5))* Davis, Mandie.

Blanchard, Eliana. The Easter Chicken. Blanchard, Eliana. 2018. (ENG.). 24p. (J). 20.00 *(978-0-692-07621-7(2))* KidsCanPublish.Org.

Blanchard, Sue. Kids' Whodunits: Catch the Clues!, 1. Conrad, Hy. 2007. (Jonah Bixby Mystery: Kid Detective! Ser.). (ENG.). 90p. (J). (gr. 2-4). 18.69 *(978-1-4027-3966-8(4))* Sterling Publishing Co., Inc.

—Kids' Whodunits Vol. 2: Crack the Cases!, 2. Conrad, Hy. 2009. (Jonah Bixby Mystery: Kid Detective! Ser.). (ENG.). 96p. (J). (gr. 2-4). 21.19 *(978-1-4027-5398-5(5))* Sterling Publishing Co., Inc.

Blanchart, Stephanie. Mama Bear. Quintart, Natalie. 2005. (Tiger Tales Ser.). 32p. (J). (gr. -1-2). 6.95 *(978-1-58925-394-0(9))* Tiger Tales.

Blanchet, Pascal. Marguerite's Christmas. Desjardins, India. 2015. (ENG.). 72p. (J). (gr. 2). 19.95 *(978-1-59270-178-0(7))* Enchanted Lion Bks., LLC.

Blanchin, Matthieu, jt. illus. see Moutarde.

Blanco, German. When Pencil Met Eraser. Kilpatrick, Karen & Ramos, Luis O., Jr. 2019. (When Pencil Met Eraser Ser.). (ENG.). 40p. (J). 17.99 *(978-1-250-30939-6(5)*, 900198485) Imprint IND. Dist: Macmillan.

—When Pencil Met the Markers. Kilpatrick, Karen & Ramos, Luis O., Jr. 2020. (When Pencil Met Eraser Ser.). (ENG.). 288p. (J). 18.99 *(978-1-250-30940-2(9)*, 900198486) Imprint IND. Dist: Macmillan.

Blanco, Mar. Dorothy: A Different Kind of Friend. Aliaga, Roberto. Brokenbrow, Jon, tr. 2013. 28p. (J). (gr. -1-k). 16.95 *(978-84-15619-81-9(2))* Cuento de Luz SL ESP. Dist: Publishers Group West (PGW).

Blanco, Martin. El Ataque de Los Murciélagos. Dahl, Michael. 2019. (Biblioteca Maldita Ser.). (SPA.). 40p. (J). (gr. 4-8). lib. bdg. 23.99 *(978-1-4965-8538-7(0)*, 141287, Stone Arch Bks.) Capstone.

—Attack of the Paper Bats: 10th Anniversary Edition. Dahl, Michael. 10th ed. 2017. (Library of Doom Ser.). (ENG.). 48p. (J). (gr. 4-8). pap. 6.25 *(978-1-4965-5537-3(6)*, 136561); lib. bdg. 23.99 *(978-1-4965-5531-1(7)*, 136555) Capstone. (Stone Arch Bks.).

—La Biblioteca Maldita. Dahl, Michael. 2019. (Biblioteca Maldita Ser.).Tr. of Library of Doom. (SPA.). (J). (gr. 4-8). 143.94 *(978-1-4965-8573-8(9)*, 29722, Stone Arch Bks.) Capstone.

Blanco, Martin, et al. Library of Doom: Complete Series. Dahl, Michael. ed. 2017. (Library of Doom Ser.). (ENG.). 48p. (J). (gr. 4-8). 287.88 *(978-1-4965-5783-4(2)*, 27424, Stone Arch Bks.) Capstone.

Blanco, Martin. Páginas Envenenadas. Dahl, Michael. 2019. (Biblioteca Maldita Ser.). (SPA.). 40p. (J). (gr. 4-8). lib. bdg. 23.99 *(978-1-4965-8534-9(8)*, 141283, Stone Arch Bks.) Capstone.

—Poison Pages: 10th Anniversary Edition. Dahl, Michael. 10th ed. 2017. (Library of Doom Ser.). (ENG.). 48p. (J). (gr. 4-8). pap. 6.25 *(978-1-4965-5533-5(3)*, 136557); lib. bdg. 23.99 *(978-1-4965-5527-4(9)*, 136551) Capstone. (Stone Arch Bks.).

Blanco, Migy. Cinderella's Stepsister & the Big Bad Wolf. Carey, Lorraine. 2015. (ENG.). 32p. (J). (gr. -1-2). 15.99 *(978-0-7636-8005-3(2)*, Nosy Crow) Candlewick Pr.

—Fairy Floss: The Sweet Story of Cotton Candy. Ingalls, Ann. 2017. (ENG.). 40p. (J). (gr. -1-3). 17.99 *(978-1-4998-0238-2(2))* Little Bee Books Inc.

Blanco, Migy. Little Owl's Bedtime. Newson, Karl. 2020. (ENG.). 24p. (J). (— 1). bds. 9.99 ***(978-1-5362-1446-8(9)***, Nosy Crow) Candlewick Pr.

Blanco, Migy. Love You Always. Stickley, Frances. 2019. (ENG.). 32p. (J). (gr. -1-2). 17.99 *(978-0-593-12400-0(6)*, Random Hse. Bks. for Young Readers) Random Hse. Children's Bks.

—Old MacDonald's Things That Go. Clarke, Jane. 2017. (ENG.). 32p. (J). (-k). 15.99 *(978-0-7636-9326-8(X)*, Nosy Crow) Candlewick Pr.

—This Little Snowman. Fronis, Aly. 2018. (ENG.). 16p. (J). (gr. -1-k). bds. 5.99 *(978-1-4998-0716-5(3))* Little Bee Books Inc.

—This Little Turkey. Fronis, Aly. 2016. (ENG.). 16p. (J). (gr. -1-k). bds. 5.99 *(978-1-4998-0302-0(8))* Little Bee Books Inc.

—Under the Sea. Fry, Sonali. 2014. (Dream Doodle Draw! Ser.). (ENG.). 96p. (J). (gr. -1-2). pap. 7.99 *(978-1-4814-0453-2(9)*, Little Simon) Little Simon.

Bland, Barry, jt. illus. see Antle, Bhagavan.

Bland, Nick. King Pig. 2013. (J). pap. *(978-0-545-67013-5(6))* Scholastic, Inc.

Bland, Nick. The Very Cranky Bear. Bland, Nick. 2014. (ENG.). 32p. (J). (gr. -1-k). 17.99 *(978-0-545-61269-2(1)*, Orchard Bks.) Scholastic, Inc.

Blanden, Neale, jt. illus. see Sta.Maria, Ian.

Blander, Katy. Pride & Joy: African-American Baby Celebrations. Shepherd, Paul, photos by. Robinson, Janice. 2005. 188p. (YA). reprint ed. pap. 17.00 *(978-0-7567-9320-3(3))* DIANE Publishing Co.

Blanding, Allison. Sweet Dreams for Scotty. McKechnie, Edward. 2007. 14p. (J). spiral bd. 14.95 *(978-0-9785302-0-4(9))* Beanstalk Pubns.

Blanding, Dexter. My Life As a Third Grade Werewolf. Longmeyer, C. M. 2014. (ENG.). (J). (gr. 2-3). pap. 7.99 *(978-0-635-11144-9(6))* Gallopade International.

—My Life As a Third Grade Zombie. Longmeyer, C. M. 2013. (My Life As a Third Grade... Ser.). (ENG.). (J). (gr. -1-3). pap. 7.99 *(978-0-635-11131-9(4))* Gallopade International.

Blank, Michael. The School for Good & Evil: the Ever Never Handbook. Chainani, Soman. 2016. (School for Good & Evil Ser.). (ENG.). 304p. (J). (gr. 3-7). 17.99 *(978-0-06-242305-4(3))* HarperCollins Pubs.

Blanks, Natascha Alex. Vietnam ABCs: A Book about the People & Places of Vietnam, 1 vol. Alberti, Theresa. 2007. (Country ABCs Ser.). (ENG.). 32p. (J). (gr. k-5). lib. bdg. 28.65 *(978-1-4048-2251-1(8)*, Picture Window Bks.) Capstone.

Blanski, Maribeth. Would You Invite a Skunk to Your Wedding? Pate, Ginger. 2009. 32p. (J). 16.95 *(978-1-880851-73-9(3))* Greene Bark Pr., Inc.

Blanz, Aurélie. Just Like Brothers. Baguley, Elizabeth. 2018. 32p. (J). (gr. -1-2). 16.99 *(978-1-78285-345-9(6))* Barefoot Bks., Inc.

—Moi, Je Sais Tout Sur la Maitresse. Delebarre, Nathalie. 2008. (Albums Gautier-Languereau Ser.: Vol. 3929791). (FRE.). (J). *(978-2-01-392979-0(X))* Gautier-Languereau.

—Moi Je Sais Tout Sur les Princesses (Pg 72) Delebarre, Nathalie. 2011. (Petits Gautier Ser.: Vol. 3934833). (FRE.). (J). pap. *(978-2-01-393483-1(1))* Gautier-Languereau.

—The Wonder That Is You, 1 vol. Nellist, Glenys. 2019. (ENG.). 32p. (J). 17.99 *(978-0-310-76669-8(9))* Zonderkidz.

Blard-Quintard, Aurélie. The Heat Is On! Harper, Charise Mericle. 2018. (Next Best Junior Chef Ser.: 2). (ENG.). 192p. (J). (gr. 3-7). 12.99 *(978-0-544-98028-0(X)*, 1664276, HMH Books For Young Readers) Houghton Mifflin Harcourt Publishing Co.

—The Heat Is On. Harper, Charise Mericle. 2019. (Next Best Junior Chef Ser.: 2). (ENG.). 192p. (J). (gr. 3-7). pap. 7.99 *(978-1-328-56139-8(9)*, 1725608, HMH Books For Young Readers) Houghton Mifflin Harcourt Publishing Co.

—Lights, Camera, Cook! Harper, Charise Mericle. (Next Best Junior Chef Ser.: 1). (ENG.). 192p. (J). (gr. 3-7). 2018. pap. 7.99 *(978-1-328-50701-3(7)*, 1719056); 2017. 12.99 *(978-0-544-91260-1(8)*, 1655497) Houghton Mifflin Harcourt Publishing Co. (HMH Books For Young Readers).

—The Winner Is ... Harper, Charise Mericle. 2019. (Next Best Junior Chef Ser.: 3). (ENG.). 192p. (J). (gr. 3-7). pap. 7.99 *(978-1-328-55902-9(5)*, 1725609, HMH Books For Young Readers) Houghton Mifflin Harcourt Publishing Co.

Blasco, Julio Antonio. Animal Musicians. Alcade, Pedro. 2019. (ENG.). 56p. (J). (gr. 2-3). 14.95 *(978-2-924774-54-0(3))* La Montagne Secrete CAN. Dist: Independent Pubs. Group.

—Animaux Musiciens. Alcalde, Pedro. 2020. (ENG.). 64p. (J). (gr. 2-4). 14.95 *(978-2-924774-58-8(6))* Secret Mountain CAN. Dist: Independent Pubs. Group.

Blaskovich, Dominique. Three Little Words. Langley, Karen. 2003. 146p. (YA). 17.95 *(978-0-9745990-0-7(X)*, 100) In Cahoots.

Blass, Tatiana. A Familia Mobilia. 2014. (POR.). (J). *(978-85-405-0456-1(1))* APC/Cosac Naify.

Blassingame, Calvin. Chinqua Where? The Spirit of Rural America, 1947-1955. McKinley, Fred B. 2003. 319p. 24.95 *(978-0-9729655-0-7(5))* Willow Creel Publishing Co.

Blasutta, Mary Lynn. Instant Wedding Planner: Get from 'Will You?' to 'I Do!' in Record Time. Shawne, Jennifer L. 2005. (ENG.). 148p. (gr. 8-17). 16.95 *(978-0-8118-4854-1(X))* Chronicle Bks. LLC.

—School & Earth Smarts Planner. Falligant, Erin, ed. 2006. (ENG.). 112p. spiral bd. 9.95 *(978-1-59369-484-5(9))* American Girl Publishing, Inc.

Blathwayt, Benedict. Great Big Train. 2015. (J). *(978-0-553-51289-2(7))* Knopf, Alfred A. Inc.

Blattman, Julia. The Mess That We Made. Lord, Michelle. 2020. 32p. (J). (gr. k-2). 18.95 *(978-1-947277-14-4(6))* Flashlight Pr.

Blatz-Harvey, Elizabeth. The Windows of My World. Blatz-Harvey, Elizabeth. 2011. 32p. *(978-0-9868730-3-4(9))* Cheaper Cheeper Copy.

Blau, Aljoscha. The Fantastic Adventures of Baron Munchausen. Janisch, Heinz. 2010. (ENG.). 32p. (J). (gr. -1-3). 17.95 *(978-1-59270-091-2(8))* Enchanted Lion Bks., LLC.

Blau, Aljosha. The Jungle Books: The Mowgli Stories. Kipling, Rudyard. 2015. 240p. (J). 26.95 *(978-0-7358-4226-7(4))* North-South Bks., Inc.

Blau, Nicole. Bedtime. Adelman, Nechama Dina. 2003. 30p. (J). 10.95 *(978-1-929628-12-4(9))* Hachai Publishing.

Blay, Amy. Brush, Flush, Wash: 5 Color Lift a Flap. Wing, Scarlett. Cottage Door Press, ed. 2018. (Busy & Bright Baby Ser.). (ENG.). 12p. (J). (gr. -1-k). bds. 7.99 *(978-1-68052-281-5(7)*, 1002660) Cottage Door Pr.

—Hat, Socks, Shoes: 5 Color Lift a Flap. Wing, Scarlett. Cottage Door Press, ed. 2018. (Busy & Bright Baby Ser.). (ENG.). 12p. (J). (gr. -1-k). bds. 7.99 *(978-1-68052-283-9(3)*, 1002680) Cottage Door Pr.

—Hug, Kiss, Love: 5 Color Lift a Flap. Wing, Scarlett. Cottage Door Press, ed. 2018. (Busy & Bright Baby Ser.). (ENG.). 12p. (J). (gr. -1-k). bds. 7.99 *(978-1-68052-273-0(6)*, 1002580) Cottage Door Pr.

—Let's Care for Baby! Krasinski, Géraldine. 2017. (Play*Learn*Do Ser.). (ENG.). 10p. (J). (gr. -1 — 1). bds. 14.99 Éditions Tourbillon FRA. Dist: Hachette Bk. Group.

—Little Red Riding Hood. 2018. (ENG.). 10p. (J). bds. 10.99 *(978-2-7338-5625-3(1))* Auzou, Philippe Editions FRA. Dist: Consortium Bk. Sales & Distribution.

—Sip, Chew, Yum: 5 Color Lift a Flap. Wing, Scarlett. Cottage Door Press, ed. 2018. (Busy & Bright Baby Ser.). (ENG.). 12p. (J). (gr. -1-k). bds. 7.99 *(978-1-68052-282-2(5)*, 1002670) Cottage Door Pr.

—Taco Tuesday. Puffinton, Brick. Cottage Door Press, ed. 2019. (Finger Puppet Board Book Ser.). (ENG.). 12p. (J).

B

(gr. -1 — 1). bds. 6.99 *(978-1-68052-712-4(6)*, 1004450) Cottage Door Pr.

Blazek, Scott R. Clovis Crawfish & Bertile's Bon Voyage, 1 vol. Fontenot, Mary Alice. 2008. (Clovis Crawfish Ser.). (ENG.). 32p. (J). (gr. k-3). 16.99 *(978-1-58980-541-5(0)*, Pelican Publishing) Arcadia Publishing.

—Clovis Crawfish & Michelle Mantis, 1 vol. Fontenot, Mary Alice. 2008. (Clovis Crawfish Ser.). (ENG.). 32p. (J). (gr. k-3). 16.99 *(978-1-58980-540-8(2)*, Pelican Publishing) Arcadia Publishing.

Blazquez, Lydia. The Bath. Koons, Linda. 2015. (Early Rising Readers Ser.). (J). (gr. -1-k). 5.83 *(978-1-4788-1586-0(8))* Newmark Learning LLC.

Blázquez, Lydia Mba. El Baño. Koons, Linda. 2016. (Early Rising Readers Ser.). (SPA.). (J). (gr. -1). 6.67 *(978-1-4788-3703-9(9))* Newmark Learning LLC.

Blazquez, Lydia Mba. El Cinturon. Lindeen, Mary. 2016. (Early Rising Readers Ser.). (SPA.). 16p. (J). (gr. 1-1). 6.67 *(978-1-4788-3728-2(4))* Newmark Learning LLC.

—El Dia Del Color Morado. Corriols, Carmen. 2016. (Early Rising Readers Ser.). (SPA.). 16p. (J). (gr. 1-1). 6.67 *(978-1-4788-4169-2(9))* Newmark Learning LLC.

—Purple Day. Corriols, Carmen. 2015. (Early Rising Readers Ser.). (J). (gr. -1-k). 5.83 *(978-1-4788-2138-0(8))* Newmark Learning LLC.

—El Semáforo. Linden, Mary. 2016. (Early Rising Readers Ser.). (SPA.). (J). (gr. -1). 6.67 *(978-1-4788-3652-0(0))* Newmark Learning LLC.

—This Belt. Lindeen, Mary. 2015. (Early Rising Readers Ser.). (J). (gr. -1-k). 5.83 *(978-1-4788-1687-4(2))* Newmark Learning LLC.

Blecha, Aaron. Attack of the Tighty Whities! Krulik, Nancy. 2012. (George Brown, Class Clown Ser.: 7). 128p. (J). (gr. 2-4). pap. 5.99 *(978-0-448-45575-4(7)*, Grosset & Dunlap) Penguin Young Readers Group.

—The Boy Who Cried Shark. Ocean, Davy. 2015. (Shark School Ser.: 4). (ENG.). 144p. (J). (gr. 1-4). 16.99 *(978-1-4814-0689-5(2)*, Aladdin) Simon & Schuster Children's Publishing.

—Burp or Treat ... Smell My Feet! Super Special. Krulik, Nancy. 2014. (George Brown, Class Clown Ser.: No. 3). 208p. (J). (gr. 2-4). 6.99 *(978-0-448-46115-1(3)*, Grosset & Dunlap) Penguin Young Readers Group.

—Dance Your Pants Off!, No. 9. Krulik, Nancy. 2013. (George Brown, Class Clown Ser.: 9). 128p. (J). (gr. 2-4). pap. 5.99 *(978-0-448-45679-9(6)*, Grosset & Dunlap) Penguin Young Readers Group.

—Deep-Sea Disaster. Ocean, Davy. 2014. (Shark School Ser.: 1). (ENG.). 128p. (J). (gr. 1-4). 17.99 *(978-1-4814-0679-6(5)*, Aladdin) Simon & Schuster Children's Publishing.

—Deep-Sea Treasury: Deep-Sea Disaster; Lights! Camera! Hammerhead!; Squid-Napped; the Boy Who Cried Shark. Ocean, Davy. 2015. (Shark School Ser.). (ENG.). 528p. (J). (gr. 1-4). 14.99 *(978-1-4814-5115-4(4)*, Aladdin) Simon & Schuster Children's Publishing.

Blecha, Aaron. Dinomighty! (graphic Novel) Trine, Greg. 2020. (Dinomighty! Ser.: 1). (ENG.). 224p. (J). (gr. 3-7). 13.99 ***(978-0-358-33156-8(0)***, 1780200, Etch) Houghton Mifflin Harcourt Publishing Co.

Blecha, Aaron. Dribble, Dribble, Drool! Krulik, Nancy. ed. 2016. (George Brown, Class Clown Ser.: 18). (ENG.). 128p. (J). (gr. 2-4). 14.75 *(978-0-606-39308-9(0))* Turtleback.

—Dribble, Dribble, Drool! #18. Krulik, Nancy. 2016. (George Brown, Class Clown Ser.: 18). 128p. (J). (gr. 2-4). 5.99 *(978-0-448-48286-6(X)*, Grosset & Dunlap) Penguin Young Readers Group.

—Eww! What's on My Shoe? #11. Krulik, Nancy. 2013. (George Brown, Class Clown Ser.: 11). 128p. (J). (gr. 2-4). 5.99 *(978-0-448-46114-4(5)*, Grosset & Dunlap) Penguin Young Readers Group.

—Fishin' Impossible, 8. Ocean, Davy. 2017. (Shark School Ser.). (ENG.). 144p. (J). (gr. 1-3). 18.69 *(978-1-5364-1675-6(4)*, Aladdin) Simon & Schuster Children's Publishing.

—Fishin': Impossible. Ocean, Davy. 2017. (Shark School Ser.: 8). (ENG.). 144p. (J). (gr. 1-4). pap. 5.99 *(978-1-4814-6549-6(X)*, Aladdin) Simon & Schuster Children's Publishing.

—Hey! Who Stole the Toilet?, 8 vols. Krulik, Nancy. 2012. (George Brown, Class Clown Ser.: 8). 128p. (J). (gr. 2-4). pap. 5.99 *(978-0-448-45576-1(5)*, Grosset & Dunlap) Penguin Young Readers Group.

—How Do You Pee in Space? #13. Krulik, Nancy. 2014. (George Brown, Class Clown Ser.: 13). 128p. (J). (gr. 2-4). pap. 5.99 *(978-0-448-46113-7(7)*, Grosset & Dunlap) Penguin Young Readers Group.

—It's a Bird, It's a Plane, It's Toiletman! #17. Krulik, Nancy & dePaola, Tomie. 2016. (George Brown, Class Clown Ser.: 17). 128p. (J). (gr. 1-3). bds. 5.99 *(978-0-448-48285-9(1)*, Grosset & Dunlap) Penguin Young Readers Group.

—Lice Check, 12. Krulik, Nancy E. 2014. (George Brown, Class Clown Ser.). (ENG.). 128p. (J). (gr. 2-4). 17.44 *(978-1-4844-2140-6(X))* Penguin Young Readers Group.

—Lice Check, No. 12. Krulik, Nancy. 2014. (George Brown, Class Clown Ser.: 12). 128p. (J). (gr. 2-4). 4.99 *(978-0-448-46112-0(9)*, Grosset & Dunlap) Penguin Young Readers Group.

—Long Fin Silver. Ocean, Davy. 2018. (Shark School Ser.: 9). (ENG.). 144p. (J). (gr. 1-4). 16.99 *(978-1-4814-6553-3(8))*; pap. 5.99 *(978-1-4814-6552-6(X))* Simon & Schuster Children's Publishing. (Aladdin).

—More Bible Tales, 1 vol. Hartman, Bob. ed. 2013. (ENG.). 96p. (J). (gr. 2-4). 8.99 *(978-0-7459-6435-5(4))* Lion Hudson PLC GBR. Dist: Independent Pubs. Group.

—Our Principal Breaks a Spell! Calmenson, Stephanie. 2019. (Quix Ser.). (ENG.). 64p. (J). (gr. k-3). 16.99 *(978-1-4814-6675-2(5))*; pap. 5.99 *(978-1-4814-6674-5(7))* Simon & Schuster Children's Publishing. (Aladdin).

—Our Principal Is a Frog! Calmenson, Stephanie. 2018. (Quix Ser.). (ENG.). 64p. (J). (gr. k-3). 16.99 *(978-1-4814-6667-7(4))*; pap. 5.99 *(978-1-4814-6665-3(8))* Simon & Schuster Children's Publishing. (Aladdin).

—Our Principal Is a Wolf! Calmenson, Stephanie. 2018. (Quix Ser.). (ENG.). 64p. (J). (gr. k-3). 16.99 *(978-1-4814-6669-1(0))*; pap. 5.99 *(978-1-4814-6668-4(2))* Simon & Schuster Children's Publishing. (Aladdin).

—Our Principal's in His Underwear! Calmenson, Stephanie. 2019. (Quix Ser.). (ENG.). 64p. (J). (gr. k-3). 16.99 *(978-1-4814-6672-1(0))*; pap. 5.99 *(978-1-4814-6671-4(2))* Simon & Schuster Children's Publishing. (Aladdin).

Blecha, Aaron. Our Principal's Wacky Wishes! Calmenson, Stephanie. 2020. (Quix Ser.). (ENG.). 64p. (J). (gr. k-3). 17.99 ***(978-1-5344-5756-0(9))***; pap. 5.99 ***(978-1-5344-5755-3(0))*** Simon & Schuster Children's Publishing. (Aladdin).

Blecha, Aaron. Return to the Scene of the Burp #19. Krulik, Nancy. 2017. (George Brown, Class Clown Ser.: 19). (ENG.). 128p. (J). (gr. 1-3). 5.99 *(978-0-448-48287-3(8)*, Grosset & Dunlap) Penguin Young Readers Group.

—Revenge of the Killer Worms #16. Krulik, Nancy & dePaola, Tomie. 2015. (George Brown, Class Clown Ser.: 16). 128p. (J). (gr. 1-3). bds. 5.99 *(978-0-448-48284-2(3)*, Grosset & Dunlap) Penguin Young Readers Group.

—A Royal Pain in the Burp, No. 15A. Krulik, Nancy & dePaola, Tomie. 2015. (George Brown, Class Clown Ser.: 15). 128p. (J). (gr. 1-3). bds. 4.99 *(978-0-448-48283-5(5)*, Grosset & Dunlap) Penguin Young Readers Group.

—Shark Party. Ocean, Davy. 2014. (ENG.). 128p. (J). pap. *(978-1-84877-926-6(7))* Templar Publishing.

—Shark School 3-Books-In-1! #2: The Boy Who Cried Shark; a Fin-Tastic Finish; Splash Dance. Ocean, Davy. 2019. (Shark School Ser.). (ENG.). 416p. (J). (gr. 1-4). pap. 8.99 *(978-1-5344-3329-8(5)*, Aladdin) Simon & Schuster Children's Publishing.

—Shark School Fin-Tastic Collection Books 1-10: Deep-Sea Disaster; Lights! Camera! Hammerhead!; Squid-Napped!; the Boy Who Cried Shark; a Fin-tastic Finish; Splash Dance; Tooth or Dare; Fishin': Impossible; Long Fin Silver; Space Invaders. Ocean, Davy. ed. 2019. (Shark School Ser.). (ENG.). 1376p. (J). (gr. 1-4). pap. 59.99 *(978-1-5344-1873-8(3)*, Aladdin) Simon & Schuster Children's Publishing.

—Shark School Shark-Tacular Collection Books 1-8: Deep-Sea Disaster; Lights! Camera! Hammerhead!; Squid-Napped!; the Boy Who Cried Shark; a Fin-tastic Finish; Splash Dance; Tooth or Dare; Fishin': Impossible. Ocean, Davy. ed. 2017. (Shark School Ser.). (ENG.). 1104p. (J). (gr. 1-4). pap. 47.99 *(978-1-5344-0239-3(X)*, Aladdin) Simon & Schuster Children's Publishing.

—'Snot Funny! Krulik, Nancy & dePaola, Tomie. 2015. (George Brown, Class Clown Ser.: 14). 128p. (J). (gr. 2-4). bds. 5.99 *(978-0-448-48282-8(7)*, Grosset & Dunlap) Penguin Young Readers Group.

—Space Invaders. Ocean, Davy. 2019. (Shark School Ser.: 10). (ENG.). 128p. (J). (gr. 1-4). 16.99 *(978-1-4814-6556-4(2))*; pap. 5.99 *(978-1-4814-6555-7(4))* Simon & Schuster Children's Publishing. (Aladdin).

—Splash Dance. Ocean, Davy. 2015. (Shark School Ser.: 6). (ENG.). 128p. (J). (gr. 1-4). pap. 5.99 *(978-1-4814-0694-9(9)*, Aladdin) Simon & Schuster Children's Publishing.

—Super Burp! #1, No. 1. Krulik, Nancy. 2010. (George Brown, Class Clown Ser.: 1). 128p. (J). (gr. 2-4). pap. 5.99 *(978-0-448-45367-5(3)*, Grosset & Dunlap) Penguin Young Readers Group.

—The Tall Tale of Paul Bunyan. Stone Arch Books Staff. 2010. (Graphic Spin Ser.). (ENG.). 40p. (J). (gr. 3-6). pap. 5.95 *(978-1-4342-2268-8(3)*, Stone Arch Bks.) Capstone.

—Ten Monsters in the Bed. Cotton, Katie. 2015. (ENG.). 24p. (J). (gr. -1-1). 12.99 *(978-1-4998-0067-8(3))* Little Bee Books Inc.

—The Three Little Pigs. Capstone Press Staff. 2010. (Graphic Spin Ser.). (ENG.). 40p. (J). (gr. 3-6). pap. 5.95 *(978-1-4342-1395-2(1)*, Stone Arch Bks.) Capstone.

—Tooth or Dare. Ocean, Davy. 2016. (Shark School Ser.: 7). (ENG.). 128p. (J). (gr. 1-4). pap. 5.99 *(978-1-4814-6546-5(5)*, Aladdin) Simon & Schuster Children's Publishing.

—Trouble Magnet #2. Krulik, Nancy. 2010. (George Brown, Class Clown Ser.: 2). (ENG.). 128p. (J). (gr. 2-4). pap. 5.99 *(978-0-448-45368-2(1)*, Grosset & Dunlap) Penguin Young Readers Group.

—The Ugly Duckling: The Graphic Novel, 1 vol. Andersen, Hans. 2009. (Graphic Spin Ser.). (ENG.). 40p. (J). (gr. 3-6). pap. 5.95 *(978-1-4342-1742-4(6)*, Stone Arch Bks.) Capstone.

—Wet & Wild! #5, 5 vols. Krulik, Nancy. 2011. (George Brown, Class Clown Ser.: 5). 128p. (J). (gr. 2-4). pap. 5.99 *(978-0-448-45570-9(6)*, Grosset & Dunlap) Penguin Young Readers Group.

—What's Black & White & Stinks All Over? Krulik, Nancy. 2011. (George Brown, Class Clown Ser.: 4). 128p. (J). (gr. 2-4). pap. 5.99 *(978-0-448-45370-5(3)*, Grosset & Dunlap) Penguin Young Readers Group.

—World's Worst Wedgie #3, 3. Krulik, Nancy. 2010. (George Brown, Class Clown Ser.: 3). (ENG.). 128p. (J). (gr. 2-4). 5.99 *(978-0-448-45369-9(X)*, Grosset & Dunlap) Penguin Young Readers Group.

—Zombiekins 2. Bolger, Kevin. 2011. (J). 10.99 *(978-1-59514-432-4(3)*, Razorbill) Penguin Publishing Group.

Blecha, Aaron. Good Morning, Grizzle Grump! Blecha, Aaron. 2017. (ENG.). 32p. (J). (gr. -1-3). 17.99 *(978-0-06-229749-5(X))* HarperCollins Pubs.

—Goodnight, Grizzle Grump! Blecha, Aaron. 2015. (ENG.). 32p. (J). (gr. -1-3). 17.99 *(978-0-06-229746-4(5))* HarperCollins Pubs.

Blechman, Nicholas. Information Graphics: Animal Kingdom. Rogers, Simon. 2014. (ENG.). 80p. (J). (gr. 1-4). 17.99 *(978-0-7636-7122-8(3)*, Big Picture Press) Candlewick Pr.

Blechmann, R. O. The One & Only 1, 2, 3 Book. Blechmann, R. O. 2013. (ENG.). 24p. (J). (gr. -1-k). 15.99 *(978-1-56846-245-5(X)*, Creative Editions) Creative Co., The.

Bleck, Linda. A Children's Treasury of Mother Goose. 2015. 32p. (J). (-k). pap. 6.95 *(978-1-4549-1473-0(4))* Sterling Publishing Co., Inc.

—Tickly Spider. Brown, Margaret Wise. 2019. (Margaret Wise Brown Classics Ser.). (ENG.). 32p. (J). (gr. -1-k). 12.99 *(978-1-68412-749-8(1)*, Silver Dolphin Bks.) Printers Row Publishing Group.

—We Gather Together: Celebrating the Harvest Season. Pfeffer, Wendy. 2014. 32p. (J). (gr. 1-4). 8.99 *(978-0-14-751282-6(4)*, Puffin Books) Penguin Young Readers Group.

Blecker, Lisa. The Good in Me from a to Z by Dottie. Blecker, Lisa. 2006. bds. 20.00 *(978-1-931492-21-8(2))* Discover Writing Pr.

Bledsoe, William B. Everyone Has a Story to Tell. Isbell, Rebecca & Buchanan, Marilyn. 2004. (J). 14.95 *(978-0-9755906-0-7(X))* Olde Town Publishing.

Blefari, Roberto. I Like Animals: What Jobs Are There? Martin, Steve. 2020. (That's a Job? Ser.). (ENG.). 48p. (J). 16.99 ***(978-1-78240-897-0(5)***, 324274, Ivy Kids) Ivy Group, The GBR. Dist: Hachette UK Distribution.

Blegvad, Erik. Ana Banana y Yo. Blegvad, Lenore. 14th ed. 2003.Tr. of Anna Banana & Me. (SPA.). 56p. (gr. k-3). pap. 10.95 *(978-84-204-0083-9(1)*, Alfaguara) Santillana USA Publishing Co., Inc.

—The Diamond in the Window. Langton, Jane. 2018. (Hall Family Chronicles). (J). pap. *(978-1-930900-93-6(7))* Purple Hse. Pr.

—Elephi: The Cat with the High IQ. Stafford, Jean. 2017. (ENG.). 80p. (gr. 1-3). pap. 6.95 *(978-0-486-81426-1(2))* Dover Pubns., Inc.

—Mud Pies & Other Recipes: A Cookbook for Dolls. Winslow, Marjorie. 2010. 56p. (J). (gr. k-4). 15.95 *(978-1-59017-368-8(6)*, NYR Children's Collection) New York Review of Bks., Inc., The.

—Sea Clocks: The Story of Longitude. Borden, Louise. 2004. (ENG.). 48p. (J). (gr. 2-5). 19.99 *(978-0-689-84216-0(3)*, McElderry, Margaret K. Bks.) McElderry, Margaret K. Bks.

—The Young Hans Christian Andersen. Hesse, Karen. 2005. (ENG.). 48p. (J). (gr. 2-5). 16.99 *(978-0-439-67990-9(7))* Scholastic, Inc.

Blegvad, Erik. Ana Banana y Yo. Blegvad, Erik, tr. Blegvad, Lenore. Puncel, María, tr. 2003.Tr. of Anna Banana & Me. (SPA.). 56p. (J). (gr. k-3). pap. 9.95 *(978-84-204-4375-1(1))* Santillana USA Publishing Co., Inc.

Blegvad, Erik & Starr, Branka. The Mushroom Center Disaster. Bodecker, N. M. 2004. (ENG.). 48p. (J). reprint ed. *(978-1-931561-98-3(2))* MacAdam/Cage Publishing, Inc.

Bleicher, David. I Can Celebrate the Jewish Holidays. Grishaver, Joel Lurie. 2010. 96p. (J). pap. 14.95 *(978-1-934527-33-7(5))* Torah Aura Productions.

Blevins, Bret, jt. illus. see Austin, Terry.

Bliss, Bob. The Hardest Lessons: The Lost Babies Series #3. 2007. 118p. (J). per. 5.99 *(978-0-9792499-2-1(9))* Eagle Tree Pr.

—The Ruby Hind: The Lost Babies Series #1. 2007. 116p. (J). per. 5.99 *(978-0-9792499-0-7(2))* Eagle Tree Pr.

—Too Many Parents: The Lost Babies Series #2. 2007. 109p. (J). per. 5.99 *(978-0-9792499-1-4(0))* Eagle Tree Pr.

Bliss, Harry. Countdown to Kindergarten. Mcghee, Alison. 2006. (ENG.). 32p. (J). (gr. -1-3). reprint ed. pap. 7.99 *(978-0-15-205586-8(X)*, 1196800) Houghton Mifflin Harcourt Publishing Co.

—Countdown to Kindergarten. Mcghee, Alison. pap. incl. audio compact disk *(978-1-59112-469-6(7))*; pap. 39.95 incl. audio *(978-1-59112-929-5(X))*; 2004. (J). 28.95 incl. audio compact disk *(978-1-59112-928-8(1))* Live Oak Media.

—Diary of a Fly. Cronin, Doreen. (ENG.). 40p. (J). (gr. -1-3). 2013. 9.99 *(978-0-06-223298-4(3))*; 2007. 16.99 *(978-0-06-000156-8(9))* HarperCollins Pubs.

—Diary of a Fly. Cronin, Doreen. 2008. (J). (gr. -1-3). 25.95 incl. audio *(978-1-4301-0404-9(X))*; 28.95 incl. audio compact disk *(978-1-4301-0407-0(4))* Live Oak Media.

—Diary of a Spider. Cronin, Doreen. (ENG.). 40p. (J). (gr. -1-3). 2013. 9.99 *(978-0-06-223300-4(9))*; 2005. 16.99 *(978-0-06-000153-7(4))* HarperCollins Pubs.

—Diary of a Spider. Cronin, Doreen. unabr. ed. 2006. (Picture Book Readalong Ser.). (J). (gr. -1-2). 28.95 incl. audio compact disk *(978-1-59519-486-2(X))* Live Oak Media.

—Diary of a Spider. Cronin, Doreen. unabr. ed. 2006. (J). (gr. -1-3). 29.95 *(978-0-439-90579-4(6))* Weston Woods Studios, Inc.

—Diary of a Worm. Cronin, Doreen. 2003. (ENG.). 40p. (J). (gr. -1-3). 17.99 *(978-0-06-000150-6(X))*; lib. bdg. 18.89 *(978-0-06-000151-3(8))* HarperCollins Pubs.

—Diary of a Worm. Cronin, Doreen. pap. 16.95 incl. audio *(978-1-59112-867-0(6))*; pap. incl. audio *(978-1-59112-869-4(2))*; pap. 18.95 incl. audio compact disk *(978-1-59112-871-7(4))*; pap. incl. audio compact disk *(978-1-59112-873-1(0))* Live Oak Media.

—Diary of a Worm: Nat the Gnat. Cronin, Doreen. 2014. (I Can Read Level 1 Ser.). (ENG.). 32p. (J). (gr. -1-3). pap. 4.99 *(978-0-06-208707-2(X))* HarperCollins Pubs.

—Diary of a Worm: Teacher's Pet. Cronin, Doreen. 2013. (I Can Read Level 1 Ser.). (ENG.). 32p. (J). (gr. -1-3). 16.99 *(978-0-06-208705-8(3))*; pap. 4.99 *(978-0-06-208704-1(5))* HarperCollins Pubs.

—A Fine, Fine School. Creech, Sharon. ed. 2004. (J). (gr. k-3). spiral bd. *(978-0-616-11106-2(1))* Canadian National Institute for the Blind/Institut National Canadien pour les Aveugles.

—A Fine, Fine School. Creech, Sharon. 2003. (ENG.). 32p. (J). (gr. -1-3). pap. 7.99 *(978-0-06-000728-7(1))* HarperCollins Pubs.

—A Fine, Fine School. Creech, Sharon. 2003. pap. 37.95 incl. audio *(978-1-59112-222-7(8))*; pap. 39.95 incl. audio compact disk *(978-1-59112-555-6(3))* Live Oak Media.

—A Fine, Fine School. Creech, Sharon. 2004. (J). (gr. -1-3). 14.65 *(978-0-7569-3179-7(7))* Perfection Learning Corp.

—Good Rosie! Dicamillo, Kate. 2018. (J). (gr. k-3). (ENG.). 32p. 16.99 *(978-0-7636-8979-7(3))*; 40p. ***(978-1-4063-8357-7(0))*** Candlewick Pr.

—Grandma in Blue with Red Hat. Menchin, Scott. 2015. (ENG.). 32p. (J). (gr. -1-3). 16.95 *(978-1-4197-1484-9(8)*, Abrams Bks. for Young Readers) Abrams, Inc.

—Invisible Inkling. Jenkins, Emily. 2012. (Invisible Inkling Ser.: 1). (ENG.). 176p. (J). (gr. 1-5). pap. 5.99 *(978-0-06-180222-5(0))* HarperCollins Pubs.

—Invisible Inkling: Dangerous Pumpkins. Jenkins, Emily. 2012. (Invisible Inkling Ser.: 2). (ENG.). 160p. (J). (gr. 1-5). 14.99 *(978-0-06-180223-2(9)*, Balzer & Bray) HarperCollins Pubs.

—Louise, the Adventures of a Chicken. Dicamillo, Kate. 2009. (J). (gr. -1-2). 29.95 incl. audio compact disk *(978-1-4301-0688-3(3))* Live Oak Media.

—Louise, the Adventures of a Chicken. DiCamillo, Kate. 2008. (ENG.). 56p. (J). (gr. -1-3). 17.99 *(978-0-06-075554-6(7))* HarperCollins Pubs.

—Mrs. Watson Wants Your Teeth. Mcghee, Alison. 2007. 32p. (J). reprint ed. 16.00 *(978-1-4223-6777-3(0))* DIANE Publishing Co.

—Mrs. Watson Wants Your Teeth. Mcghee, Alison. 2008. (ENG.). 36p. (J). (gr. -1-3). pap. 7.99 *(978-0-15-206348-1(X)*, 1199013) Houghton Mifflin Harcourt Publishing Co.

—Mrs. Watson Wants Your Teeth. Mcghee, Alison. unabr. ed. 2007. (Picture Book Readalong Ser.). (J). (gr. -1-2). 28.95 incl. audio compact disk *(978-1-59519-902-7(0))* Live Oak Media.

—My Favorite Pets: By Gus W. for Ms. Smolinski's Class. Birdsall, Jeanne. 2016. (ENG.). 40p. (J). (gr. -1-2). 16.99 *(978-0-385-75570-2(8)*, Knopf Bks. for Young Readers) Random Hse. Children's Bks.

—Sorry (Really Sorry) Cotler, Joanna. 2020. 32p. (J). (gr. -1-3). 17.99 *(978-1-9848-1247-6(5)*, Philomel Bks.) Penguin Young Readers Group.

—The Sweetest Witch Around. McGhee, Alison. 2014. (ENG.). 32p. (J). (gr. -1-3). 15.99 *(978-1-4424-7833-6(0)*, Simon & Schuster/Paula Wiseman Bks.) Simon & Schuster/Paula Wiseman Bks.

—A Very Brave Witch. Mcghee, Alison. 2007. (J). (gr. -1-3). 24.95 incl. audio *(978-0-545-04268-0(2))* Scholastic, Inc.

—A Very Brave Witch. McGhee, Alison. (ENG.). 32p. (J). (gr. -1-3). 2011. 7.99 *(978-0-689-86731-6(X))*; 2009. 9.99 *(978-1-4169-8670-6(7))*; 2006. 19.99 *(978-0-689-86730-9(1))* Simon & Schuster/Paula Wiseman Bks. (Simon & Schuster/Paula Wiseman Bks.).

—Which Would You Rather Be? Steig, William. 2005. (ENG.). 32p. (J). (gr. -1-3). reprint ed. pap. 8.99 *(978-0-06-443792-9(2))* HarperCollins Pubs.

Bliss, Harry. Grace for Gus. Bliss, Harry. 2018. (ENG.). 40p. (J). (gr. -1-3). 17.99 *(978-0-06-264410-7(6)*, Tegen, Katherine Bks) HarperCollins Pubs.

Bliss, Penelopy. Pompo the Monkey - Adventures in Africa. Bliss, Penelopy. 2020. (Adventures in Africa Ser.). (ENG.). 32p. (J). (gr. 1-2). 21.99 ***(978-1-64826-905-9(2))*** Bliss Publishing.

Bliss, Ryan T. Mooseclumps. Bliss, Ryan T. 2013. 58p. 15.99 *(978-0-615-75521-2(6))* Artsy Bee, LLC.

Blitt, Barry. The Adventures of Mark Twain by Huckleberry Finn. Burleigh, Robert. 2011. (ENG.). 48p. (J). (gr. 2-5). 19.99 *(978-0-689-83041-9(6)*, Atheneum Bks. for Young Readers) Simon & Schuster Children's Publishing.

—The Founding Fathers! Those Horse-Ridin', Fiddle-Playin', Book-Readin', Gun-Totin' Gentlemen Who Started America. Winter, Jonah. 2015. (ENG.). 48p. (J). (gr. k-3). 18.99 *(978-1-4424-4274-0(3))* Simon & Schuster Children's Publishing.

—George Washington's Birthday: A Mostly True Tale. McNamara, Margaret. 2012. (ENG.). 40p. (J). (gr. -1-3). 17.99 *(978-0-375-84499-7(6)*, Schwartz & Wade Bks.) Random Hse. Children's Bks.

—Once upon a Time, the End: Asleep in 60 Seconds. Kloske, Geoffrey. 2005. (ENG.). 40p. (J). (gr. -1-3). 18.99 *(978-0-689-86619-7(4)*, Atheneum Bks. for Young Readers) Simon & Schuster Children's Publishing.

—What's the Weather Inside? Wilson, Karma. 2009. (ENG.). 176p. (J). (gr. 1-5). 17.99 *(978-1-4169-0092-4(6)*, McElderry, Margaret K. Bks.) McElderry, Margaret K. Bks.

—You Never Heard of Casey Stengel?! Winter, Jonah. 2016. 40p. (J). (gr. -1-3). 17.99 *(978-0-375-87013-2(X))*; (ENG.). 20.99 *(978-0-375-97013-9(4))* Random Hse. Children's Bks. (Schwartz & Wade Bks.).

Bloch, Beth. My Oh My Sweet Potato Pie. Bloch, Beth. 2005. 32p. (J). 16.00 *(978-0-9771515-0-9(6))* Dream Creek Pr.

Bloch, Serge. A Bunch of Punctuation. Hopkins, Lee Bennett. 2018. (ENG.). 32p. (J). (gr. 3-7). 17.95 *(978-1-59078-994-0(6)*, Wordsong) Boyds Mills Pr.

—George & His Shadow. Cali, Davide. 2017. (ENG.). 40p. (J). (gr. -1-3). 17.99 *(978-0-06-256830-4(2))* HarperCollins Pubs.

—I Dare You Not to Yawn. Boudreau, Helene. (J). 2017. 28p. (— 1). bds. 8.99 *(978-0-7636-9307-7(3))*; 2013. (ENG.). 32p. (gr. -1-3). 15.99 *(978-0-7636-5070-4(6))* Candlewick Pr.

—I Voted: Making a Choice Makes a Difference. Shulman, Mark. 2020. 40p. (J). (gr. -1-3). 18.99 *(978-0-8234-4561-5(5)*, Neal Porter Bks) Holiday Hse., Inc.

—One Proud Penny. Siegel, Randy. 2017. (ENG.). 32p. (J). 17.99 *(978-1-62672-235-4(8)*, 9781626722354) Roaring Brook Pr.

—Toby Goes Bananas. Girard, Franck. 2017. (ENG.). 96p. (J). (gr. 2-5). pap. 9.99 *(978-0-545-85283-8(8)*, Graphix) Scholastic, Inc.

—The Underwear Salesman: And Other Jobs for Better or Verse. Lewis, J. Patrick. 2009. (ENG.). 64p. (J). (gr. 2-5). 19.99 *(978-0-689-85325-8(4)*, Atheneum Bks. for Young Readers) Simon & Schuster Children's Publishing.

—What If Soldiers Fought with Pillows? True Stories of Imagination & Courage. Camlot, Heather. 2020. (ENG.).

40p. (J). (gr. 4). 18.95 *(978-1-77147-362-0(2))* Owlkids Bks. Inc. CAN. Dist: Publishers Group West (PGW).

—3, 2, 1, Draw! Reimagine Your World with 50 Drawing Activities from Serge Bloch. 2016. (ENG.). 80p. (J). (gr. k-3). pap. 12.99 *(978-1-84780-774-8(7)*, Wide Eyed Editions) Quarto Publishing Group UK GBR. Dist: Hachette Bk. Group.

Blocker, Simini. My So-Called Superpowers. Nuhfer, Heather. 2019. (My So-Called Superpowers Ser.: 1). (ENG.). 272p. (J). pap. 7.99 *(978-1-250-29421-0(5)*, 900179186) Square Fish.

—My So-Called Superpowers: All the Feels. Nuhfer, Heather. 2020. (My So-Called Superpowers Ser.: 3). (ENG.). 40p. (J). 14.99 *(978-1-250-13864-4(7)*, 900179135) Imprint IND. Dist: Macmillan.

—My So-Called Superpowers: Mixed Emotions. Nuhfer, Heather. 2019. (My So-Called Superpowers Ser.: 2). (ENG.). 256p. (J). 14.99 *(978-1-250-13862-0(0)*, 900179133) Imprint IND. Dist: Macmillan.

—The Singing Rock & Other Brand-New Fairy Tales. Lachenmeyer, Nathaniel. 2019. (ENG.). 112p. (J). 17.99 *(978-1-59643-750-0(2)*, 900078772, First Second Bks.) Roaring Brook Pr.

Blocksma, Mary. What's on the Beach? A Great Lakes Treasure Hunt. Blocksma, Mary. 2003. (Great Lakes Treasure Hunts Ser.: No. 1). 48p. (J). pap. 9.95 *(978-0-9708575-1-4(9))* Beaver Island Arts.

Blodau, Peter. Tina & the Tooth Fairy. Snell, Gordon. 2005. (Pandas Ser.: 31). (ENG.). 64p. (J). pap. 9.95 *(978-0-86278-601-4(0))* O'Brien Pr., Ltd., The IRL. Dist: Dufour Editions, Inc.

Bloggs, Josy. Let's Play Chess! Includes Chessboard & Full Set of Chess Pieces. Bloggs, Josy. 2019. (ENG.). 8p. (J). bds. 12.99 *(978-1-78950-599-3(2)*, 6b3d5064-ce03-4080-a5ee-397a4e013dcd) Arcturus Publishing GBR. Dist: Baker & Taylor Publisher Services (BTPS).

Blondahl, Samuel. The Outdoor Adventures of Charlie & Kaylee: Hunting Fear (book 1) Callsen, Terri. Lignor, Amy, ed. 2012. 156p. pap. 9.85 *(978-1-938634-10-9(1))* Freedom of Speech Publishing, Inc.

Blondon, Herve. The Miracle of the Myrrh. Alborghetti, Marci. 2003. (J). 16.95 *(978-0-87946-249-9(3)*, 708) ACTA Pubns.

Bloodworth, Mark. The Ants & the Grasshopper. Worley, Rob M. & Aesop, Aesop. 2010. (Short Tales Fables Ser.). (ENG.). 32p. (J). (gr. 1-4). 27.07 *(978-1-60270-551-7(8)*, 13403, Short Tales) Magic Wagon.

—Beauty & the Beast. Long, Christopher E. 2008. (Short Tales Fairy Tales Ser.). (ENG.). 32p. (J). (gr. 2-5). 27.07 *(978-1-60270-127-4(X)*, 592, Short Tales) Magic Wagon.

—The Haunted Cabin Mystery, 1 vol. Warner, Gertrude Chandler. 2010. (Boxcar Children Graphic Novels Ser.). (ENG.). 32p. (J). (gr. 3-8). 29.93 *(978-1-60270-717-7(0)*, 3678, Graphic Planet - Fiction) Magic Wagon.

—The Town Mouse & the Country Mouse. Long, Christopher E. & Aesop, Aesop. 2010. (Short Tales Fables Ser.). (ENG.). 32p. (J). (gr. 1-4). 27.07 *(978-1-60270-556-2(9)*, 13413, Short Tales) Magic Wagon.

—Tree House Mystery, 1 vol. Long, Christopher E. & Warner, Gertrude Chandler. 2010. (Boxcar Children Graphic Novels Ser.). (ENG.). 32p. (J). (gr. 3-8). 29.93 *(978-1-60270-716-0(2)*, 3677, Graphic Planet - Fiction) Magic Wagon.

Bloom, Harry. Egypt Magnified: With a 3x Magnifying Glass. Long, David. 2018. (Magnified Ser.). (ENG.). 48p. (J). (gr. k-3). 22.99 ***(978-1-78603-097-9(7)***, Wide Eyed Editions) Quarto Publishing Group UK GBR. Dist: Hachette Bk. Group.

Bloom, Lloyd. The Green Book. Walsh, Jill Paton & Paton Walsh, Jill. 2012. (ENG.). 80p. (J). (gr. 4-6). pap. 6.99 *(978-0-312-64122-1(2)*, 900077672) Square Fish.

Bloom, Suzanne. Girls A to Z. Bunting, Eve. 2013. (ENG.). 32p. (gr. k-2). 21.19 *(978-1-56397-147-1(X))* Boyds Mills Pr.

—Girls a to Z. Bunting, Eve. 2013. (ENG.). 32p. (J). (gr. k-2). pap. 7.95 *(978-1-62091-028-3(4))* Boyds Mills Pr.

—Melissa Parkington's Beautiful, Beautiful Hair. Brisson, Pat. 2006. (ENG.). 32p. (J). (gr. 1-k). 16.95 *(978-1-59078-409-9(X))* Boyds Mills Pr.

—My Special Day at Third Street School. Bunting, Eve. 2009. (ENG.). 32p. (J). (gr. k-2). pap. 10.95 *(978-1-59078-745-8(5))* Boyds Mills Pr.

Bloom, Tom. Pocketdoodles for Young Artists, 1 vol. Zimmerman, Bill. 2010. (ENG.). 272p. (J). (gr. 1). 9.99 *(978-1-4236-0466-2(0))* Gibbs Smith, Publisher.

Bloomfield, Kevin. Mr. Biggs in the City. Bloomfield, Kevin. 2011. (ENG & SPA.). 32p. (gr. -1-3). lib. bdg. 16.95 *(978-1-936299-26-3(7)*, Raven Tree Pr.,Csi) Continental Sales, Inc.

Blotnick, Elihu. Glimmins: Children of the Western Woods. Blotnick, Elihu. 2009. 72p. (J). (gr. 1-18). pap. 14.50 *(978-0-915090-18-1(X)*, California Street) Firefall Editions.

Blowars, Ryan, jt. illus. see Smale, Denise L.

Blowers, Lisa. A Cricket's Carol. Moulton, Mark Kimball. 2004. 32p. (J). 14.95 *(978-0-8249-5488-8(2)*, Ideal Pubns.) Worthy Publishing.

Bloye, Susan y. Herman Takes a Walk. Huhn, Kim M. 2018. (ENG.). 32p. (J). 22.00 *(978-0-692-07421-3(X))* Sacred Structure Pr.

Bludworth, Brent. I Wonder What It's Like to Be a Raindrop: The Rainmaking Bacteria. Bell, Keith. 2018. (ENG.). 28p. (J). (gr. k-6). 14.99 *(978-0-9995720-0-9(8))* Bell, Keith.

Blue, Beatrice. Cog. van Eekhout, Greg. 2019. (ENG.). 208p. (J). (gr. 3-7). 16.99 *(978-0-06-268607-7(0))* HarperCollins Pubs.

Blue, Buster. I Know a Rhino. Harrison, Kevin. 2nd rev. ed. 2006. 37p. (J). (gr. -1-3). per. 10.99 *(978-1-59092-223-1(9))* Blue Forge Pr.

—Maxwell Dreams of Trains. Anna, Jennifer. 2009. (ENG.). 88p. (J). 10.99 *(978-1-883573-05-8(X))* Blue Forge Pr.

Blue, Dima. The Celebration Series Presents: Celebrating Judaism. Smith, Alison K. 2020. (Celebration Ser.: Vol. 2). (ENG.). 32p. (J). pap. 9.99 ***(978-1-5031-3993-0(X))*** CreateSpace Independent Publishing Platform.

Blue, Duck Egg, et al. 1 2 3: Touch & Trace Early Learning Fun! 2014. (ENG.). 26p. (J). bds. 13.50 *(978-1-84135-943-4(2))* Award Pubns. Ltd. GBR. Dist: Parkwest Pubns., Inc.

Blue, Melissa. Edison the Christmas Elf & the Imperfect Perfect Toy. Vaitonis, Steven. 2014. 32p. (J). (gr. -1-1). pap. 12.95 *(978-1-939930-33-0(2)*, Belle Isle Bks.) Brandylane Pubs., Inc.

Bluecheese, Wally. The Little Book of Happiness. Heim, Julia & Dami, Elisabetta. 2013. 42p. (J). pap. *(978-0-545-48255-4(0))* Scholastic, Inc.

Bluedorn, Johannah. Bless the Lord: The 103rd Psalm. 2005. 32p. (J). 13.00 *(978-1-933228-02-0(4)*, 3000) Trivium Pursuit.

—The Lord Builds the House: The 127th Psalm. 2004. 32p. (J). 10.00 *(978-0-9743616-1-1(5))* Trivium Pursuit.

Bluedorn, Johannah. Little Bitty Baby Learns Greek. Bluedorn, Johannah. 2006. (GRE & ENG.). 30p. (J). bds. *(978-1-933228-06-8(7))* Trivium Pursuit.

—Little Bitty Baby Learns Hebrew. Bluedorn, Johannah. 2005. 26p. (J). bds. 12.00 *(978-1-933228-00-6(8))* Trivium Pursuit.

—The Story of Mr. Pippin. Bluedorn, Johannah. 2004. 32p. (J). 12.00 *(978-0-9743616-8-0(2))* Trivium Pursuit.

Bluhm, Joe. Dear Sister. McGhee, Alison. 2019. (ENG.). 192p. (J). (gr. 5). pap. 7.99 *(978-1-4814-5143-7(X)*, Atheneum Bks. for Young Readers) Simon & Schuster Children's Publishing.

—The Magician's Secret. Hyman, Zachary. 2018. (ENG.). 40p. (J). (gr. k-3). 17.99 *(978-1-77049-894-5(X)*, Tundra Bks.) Tundra Bks. CAN. Dist: Penguin Random Hse. LLC.

Bluhm, Joe, jt. illus. see Joyce, William.

Blum, Alex A. Treasure Island. Brooks, Jon & Stevenson, Robert Louis. 2015. (Classics Illustrated Ser.: 21). 48p. pap. 9.95 *(978-1-906814-47-2(3))* Classic Comic Store, Ltd. GBR. Dist: Casemate Pubs. & Bk. Distributors, LLC.

Blum, Julia C. What the Sea Wants. Banghart, Tracy E. 2006. 64p. (YA). kivar 16.00 *(978-0-9779753-0-3(4))* LizStar Bks.

Blume, Rebecca. Baby Whales. Blume, Rebecca. 2007. 8p. (J). 5.00 *(978-0-9785427-2-6(X))* Liberty Artists Management.

—When the World Was Green! Blume, Rebecca. 2007. 32p. (J). per. 14.00 *(978-0-9785427-1-9(1))* Liberty Artists Management.

Blumen, Paula. Home Sweet Home. Cassany, Mia. 2017. (ENG.). 40p. (J). (gr. k-3). 16.99 *(978-1-78603-113-6(2)*, Frances Lincoln Children's Bks.) Quarto Publishing Group UK GBR. Dist: Hachette UK Distribution.

Blumenfeld, Tamar. Journey Through Jerusalem. Benjamin, Amanda. 2016. (J). *(978-1-68115-531-9(1))* Behrman Hse., Inc.

—Yosef's Dream, Vol. Rouss, Sylvia A. 2015. (ENG.). (J). *(978-1-68115-506-7(0))* Behrman Hse., Inc.

Blundell, Kim, jt. illus. see Cartwright, Stephen.

Blundell, Tony. Chicken Licken: Band 08/Purple (Collins Big Cat) Strong, Jeremy. 2007. (Collins Big Cat Ser.). (ENG.). 24p. (J). (gr. 1-2). pap. 8.99 *(978-0-00-718672-3(X))* HarperCollins Pubs. Ltd. GBR. Dist: Independent Pubs. Group.

—Samosa Thief. Dhami, Narinder. 2005. (ENG.). 24p. (J). lib. bdg. 23.65 *(978-1-59646-708-8(8))* Dingles & Co.

—The Sneezles: Band 10/White (Collins Big Cat) Strong, Jeremy. 2005. (Collins Big Cat Ser.). (ENG.). 32p. (J). (gr. 1-3). pap. 9.99 *(978-0-00-718628-0(2))* HarperCollins Pubs. Ltd. GBR. Dist: Independent Pubs. Group.

Blunt, Fred. Cat Has a Plan. Gehl, Laura. 2020. (Ready-To-Reads Ser.). (ENG.). 32p. (J). (gr. -1-k). 17.99 ***(978-1-5344-5411-8(X))***; pap. 4.99 ***(978-1-5344-5410-1(1))*** Simon Spotlight. (Simon Spotlight).

Blunt, Fred. Cow Takes a Bow. Punter, Russell. 2014. (Usborne Phonics Readers Ser.). (ENG.). (J). pap. 6.99 *(978-0-7945-3368-7(X)*, Usborne) EDC Publishing.

—Croc Gets a Shock. MacKinnon, Mairi. 2014. (Usborne Phonics Readers Ser.). (ENG.). (J). (gr. -1-3). pap. 6.99 *(978-0-7945-3395-3(7)*, Usborne) EDC Publishing.

—The Rabbit's Tale. 2013. (Usborne First Reading: Level 1 Ser.). (ENG.). 32p. (J). (gr. -1-3). 6.99 *(978-0-7945-3346-5(9)*, Usborne) EDC Publishing.

—Snail Brings the Mail. Punter, Russell & MacKinnon, Mairi. 2014. (Usborne Phonics Readers Ser.). (ENG.). (J). pap. 6.99 *(978-0-7945-3369-4(8)*, Usborne) EDC Publishing.

—Underpants for Ants. Punter, Russell. 2014. (Usborne Phonics Readers Ser.). (ENG.). (J). (gr. -1-3). pap. 6.99 *(978-0-7945-3396-0(5)*, Usborne) EDC Publishing.

Blunt, Fred. Gnome. Blunt, Fred. 2020. (ENG.). 32p. (J). (gr. -1-3). 17.99 *(978-1-5415-9624-5(2))* Lerner Publishing Group.

Bluth, Don. Dragon's Lair, Vol. 1. Mangels, Andy et al. O'Reilly, Sean Patrick, ed. 2008. 164p. (YA). 19.95 *(978-0-9763095-5-0(6))* Arcana Studio, Inc.

Bluthenthal, Diana Cain. I'm a Kid. You're a Baby. 2020. (J). *(978-0-689-85470-5(6))* Simon & Schuster Children's Publishing.

—Just in Case. Viorst, Judith. 2010. (ENG.). 40p. (J). (gr. -1-2). 6.99 *(978-1-4424-1282-8(8)*, Atheneum Bks. for Young Readers) Simon & Schuster Children's Publishing.

Bluthenthal, Diana Cain. I'm Not Invited? Bluthenthal, Diana Cain. 2008. (ENG.). 32p. (J). (gr. -1-2). 10.99 *(978-1-4169-7141-2(6)*, Aladdin) Simon & Schuster Children's Publishing.

Bluze, April, jt. illus. see Bluze, Donna.

Bluze, Donna & Bluze, April. Whiskers. Bluze, Donna. 2017. (ENG.). (J). 18.99 *(978-1-946989-03-1(7))* Full Court Pr.

Blye, Steven G. The Dangerous Pet. Siems, Thomas F. 2009. (ENG.). 46p. pap. 21.99 *(978-1-4415-3454-5(7))* Xlibris Corp.

Blyth, Eileen. Healthy Air: Book C of Healthy Me, 3 books. Hawthorne, Grace. 2004. 48p. (J). pap. 73.75 *(978-0-944235-49-2(2))* American Cancer Society, Inc.

—Healthy Bodies: Book A of Healthy Me, 3 books. Hawthorne, Grace. 2004. 48p. (J). pap. 73.75 *(978-0-944235-47-8(6))* American Cancer Society, Inc.

—Healthy Food: Book B of Healthy Me, 3 bks. Hawthorne, Grace. 2004. 48p. (J). pap. 73.75 *(978-0-944235-48-5(4))* American Cancer Society, Inc.

—To Whom the Angel Spoke: A Story of the Christmas, 1 vol. Kay, Terry. 2nd rev. ed. 2009. (ENG.). 32p. (J). (gr. k-4). 14.95 *(978-1-56145-502-7(4))* Peachtree Publishing Co. Inc.

Blythe, Ainsley, jt. illus. see Blythe, Dana.

Blythe, Dana & Blythe, Ainsley. Masterpiece. Goettsche, Bruce. 2019. (ENG.). 36p. (J). pap. 9.99 ***(978-1-6990-3778-2(7))*** Independently Published.

Blythe, Gary. Beauty & the Beast. McCaughrean, Geraldine. 2003. (Picture Bks.). 32p. (J). (gr. -1-3). 15.95 *(978-1-57505-491-9(4)*, Carolrhoda Bks.) Lerner Publishing Group.

—Ice Bear: Read & Wonder: in the Steps of the Polar Bear. Davies, Nicola. 2008. (Read & Wonder Ser.). (ENG.). 32p. (J). (gr. -1-3). pap. 7.99 *(978-0-7636-4149-8(9))* Candlewick Pr.

—Ice Bear with Audio, Peggable: Read, Listen, & Wonder: in the Steps of the Polar Bear. Davies, Nicola. 2009. (Read, Listen, & Wonder Ser.). (ENG.). 32p. (J). (gr. -1-3). pap. 9.99 *(978-0-7636-4441-3(2))* Candlewick Pr.

—Little Plum. Godden, Rumer. 2016. (ENG.). 112p. (J). (gr. k-2). pap. 10.99 *(978-1-4472-9276-0(6))* Pan Macmillan GBR. Dist: Independent Pubs. Group.

—Miss Happiness & Miss Flower. Godden, Rumer. 2016. (ENG.). 128p. (J). (gr. k-2). pap. 9.99 *(978-1-4472-9274-6(X))* Pan Macmillan GBR. Dist: Independent Pubs. Group.

—The Moon Dragons. Sheldon, Dyan. 2015. (ENG.). 32p. (J). (gr. -1-3). 16.95 *(978-1-4677-6314-1(4)*, 9781467763141); E-Book 27.99 *(978-1-4677-6318-9(7))* Lerner Publishing Group.

—The Perfect Bear. Shields, Gillian. 2008. (ENG.). 32p. (J). (gr. -1-3). 16.99 *(978-1-4169-5363-0(9)*, Simon & Schuster Bks. For Young Readers) Simon & Schuster Bks. For Young Readers.

—A Treasury of Princess Stories. 2009. (ENG.). 80p. (J). (gr. 2-5). 19.99 *(978-0-7636-4478-9(1))* Candlewick Pr.

—The Whales' Song. Sheldon, Dyan. 2016. (ENG.). 32p. (J). (gr. k-2). pap. 15.95 *(978-0-09-973760-5(4)*, Red Fox) Random House Children's Books GBR. Dist: Independent Pubs. Group.

Blythe, Philip. Nature Hunt! Bewildering Puzzles of the Animal Kingdom. Blythe, Philip. 2005. (ENG.). 32p. pap., act. bk. ed. *(978-1-877003-82-0(4))* Little Hare Bks. AUS. Dist: HarperCollins Pubs. Australia.

Boake, Kathy. Chitchat: Celebrating the World's Languages. Isabella, Jude. 2013. (ENG.). 44p. (J). (gr. 3-7). 17.95 *(978-1-55453-787-7(8))* Kids Can Pr., Ltd. CAN. Dist: Hachette Bk. Group.

—Worms for Breakfast: How to Feed a Zoo. Becker, Helaine. 2016. (ENG.). 40p. (J). (gr. 2-5). 16.95 *(978-1-77147-105-3(0)*, Owlkids) Owlkids Bks. Inc. CAN. Dist: Publishers Group West (PGW).

—You Are Weird: Your Body's Peculiar Parts & Funny Functions. Swanson, Diane. 2009. (ENG.). 40p. (J). (gr. 3-7). pap. 7.95 *(978-1-55453-283-4(3))* Kids Can Pr., Ltd. CAN. Dist: Hachette Bk. Group.

Board, Perry. Thomas's Sheep & the Spectacular Science Project, 1 vol. Layne, Steven L. 2004. (ENG.). 32p. (J). (gr. k-3). 16.99 *(978-1-58980-210-0(1)*, Pelican Publishing) Arcadia Publishing.

Boast, James. Once upon a Jungle. Knowles, Laura. 2017. (ENG.). 32p. (J). (gr. k-3). 18.95 *(978-1-77085-971-5(3)*, a254489b-12f9-443c-af01-452b62486c39) Firefly Bks., Ltd.

Boatright, Emily Belle, jt. illus. see Lynch, Timothy.

Bobak, Cathy. Poetry from A to Z: A Guide for Young Writers. Janeczko, Paul B. 2012. (ENG.). 144p. (J). (gr. 4-7). pap. 8.99 *(978-1-4424-6061-4(X)*, Simon & Schuster Bks. For Young Readers) Simon & Schuster Bks. For Young Readers.

Bobbiesi, Laura. Grandma's Girl. Hill, Susanna Leonard. 2020. 40p. (J). (-3). 17.99 *(978-1-7282-0623-3(5))* Sourcebooks, Inc.

—Shine. Griffin, Dagny. 2020. (ENG.). 40p. (J). 14.99 *(978-1-4964-3749-5(7)*, 20_32293) Tyndale Hse. Pubs.

Bobbish, John. Trail Fever: The Life of a Texas Cowboy. Lightfoot, D. J. exp. ed. 2003. 88p. (J). (gr. 3-18). pap. 12.95 *(978-0-9728768-0-3(4))* Seven Rivers Publishing.

Bober, Michael, jt. illus. see Buettner, Bernie.

Bobillo, Juan. Bird. Trillo, Carlos. 2003. 48p. (YA). (gr. 11-18). 12.95 *(978-1-931724-22-7(9))* Diamond Select Toys & Collectibles.

Bobo, Keturah A. I Am Enough. Byers, Grace. 2018. (ENG.). 32p. (J). (gr. -1-3). 18.99 *(978-0-06-266712-0(2)*, Balzer & Bray) HarperCollins Pubs.

—I Believe I Can. Byers, Grace. 2020. (ENG.). 32p. (J). (gr. -1-3). 18.99 *(978-0-06-266713-7(0)*, Balzer & Bray) HarperCollins Pubs.

—A Is for All the Things You Are: A Joyful ABC Book. Hindley, Anna Forgerson & Nat'l Mus Afr Am Hist Culture, Nat'l Mus. 2019. (ENG.). 26p. (J). (— 1). bds. 9.95 *(978-1-58834-650-6(1)*, Smithsonian Bks.) Smithsonian Institution Scholarly Pr.

—The Night Is Yours. Zachariah, Abdul-Razak. 2019. (ENG.). 32p. (J). (gr. -1-2). 17.99 *(978-0-525-55271-0(5)*, Dial Bks) Penguin Young Readers Group.

Bobooks, Bob and Ed. Amy Throw's a Line... A Fishing Adventure. Belinda, Haley. 2018. (Wiggly Road Trilogy Ser.: Vol. 1). (ENG.). 38p. (J). (gr. 1-3). pap. *(978-1-9998344-9-4(6))* Norton's Independent Publishing.

Bobrek, Aleksandra. Carter Crow & Friends: A Children's Story from the Old Oak Kingdom. Morgan, David C. 2018. (Old Oak Kingdom Ser.: Vol. 1). (ENG.). 34p. (J). pap. *(978-1-9164767-0-7(8))* Morgan, David C.

—Nick. Lau, Sherman. 2018. (ENG.). 40p. (J). (gr. k-4). *(978-1-7329410-0-7(9))* Alpine Studios.

Bobri, Vladimir. N Is for Nursery, 1 vol. Budney, Blossom. 2018. (ENG.). 32p. (J). 20.00 *(978-1-85124-482-9(4))* Bodleian Library GBR. Dist: Chicago Distribution Ctr.

—Sleepy Book. Zolotow, Charlotte. 2016. (ENG.). 36p. (J). 20.00 *(978-1-85124-457-7(3))* Bodleian Library GBR. Dist: Chicago Distribution Ctr.

—What Is Red? Gottlieb, Suzanne. 2016. (ENG.). 24p. (J). 20.00 *(978-1-85124-458-4(1))* Bodleian Library GBR. Dist: Chicago Distribution Ctr.

Bobrizky, George. Steps in Ballet: Basic Exercises at the Barre, Basic Center Exercises, Basic Allegro Steps. Mara, Thalia. 2004. (ENG.). 192p. pap. 24.95 *(978-0-87127-262-1(8)*, Elysian Editions) Princeton Bk. Co. Pubs.

Bobzin, Liz. At the Shore. Doughty, Carole. l.t. ed. 2019. (My Family & Me Ser.: Vol. 3). (ENG.). 20p. (J). (gr. k-6). pap. 11.99 *(978-1-63073-282-0(6))* Faithful Life Pubs.

Boccanfuso, Emanuele. The Gold Rush. Jeffrey, Gary. 2012. (Graphic History of the American West Ser.). (ENG.). 24p. (J). (gr. 3-8). pap. 8.15 *(978-1-4339-6741-2(3)*, Gareth Stevens Learning Library) Stevens, Gareth Publishing LLLP.

—Mermaids. Jeffrey, Gary. 2012. (Graphic Mythical Creatures Ser.). (ENG.). 24p. (J). (gr. 3-5). pap. 8.15 *(978-1-4339-6765-8(0))*; lib. bdg. 24.95 *(978-1-4339-6763-4(4))* Stevens, Gareth Publishing LLLP. (Gareth Stevens Learning Library).

Boccardo, Johanna. Sam's Sunflower. Powell, Jillian. 2008. (Tadpoles Ser.). (ENG.). 24p. (J). (gr. -1-3). pap. *(978-0-7787-3895-4(7))*; lib. bdg. *(978-0-7787-3864-0(7))* Crabtree Publishing Co.

Bocchino, Serena. What Am I? the Story of an Abstract Painting. Bocchino, Serena. l.t. ed. 2005. 32p. (J). per. 19.95 *(978-0-9767674-0-4(6))* Serena Bocchino/In His Perfect Time Collection.

Bocik, Adam. Twelve upon a Time. Galluzzi, Edward. 3rd ed. 2009. 298p. (J). pap. *(978-1-926585-69-7(0))* CCB Publishing.

Bock, Janna. For the Right to Learn. Langston-George, Rebecca. 2015. (Encounter: Narrative Nonfiction Picture Bks.). (ENG.). 40p. (J). (gr. 3-6). 15.95 *(978-1-62370-426-1(X)*, Capstone Pr.) Capstone.

—For the Right to Learn: Malala Yousafzai's Story. Langston-George, Rebecca. (Encounter: Narrative Nonfiction Picture Bks.). (ENG.). 40p. (J). (gr. 3-6). 2016. pap. 7.95 *(978-1-4914-6556-1(5))*; 2015. lib. bdg. 29.32 *(978-1-4914-6071-9(7))* Capstone. (Capstone Pr.).

—Frankly, I'd Rather Spin Myself a New Name! The Story of Rumpelstiltskin As Told by Rumpelstiltskin. Gunderson, Jessica. 2016. (Other Side of the Story Ser.). (ENG.). 24p. (J). (gr. -1-3). lib. bdg. 27.99 *(978-1-4795-8624-0(2)*, Picture Window Bks.) Capstone.

—Gustave Eiffel's Spectacular Idea: The Eiffel Tower. Cooper, Sharon Katz. 2015. (Story Behind the Name Ser.). (ENG.). 32p. (J). (gr. 2-4). lib. bdg. 29.32 *(978-1-4795-7136-9(9)*, Picture Window Bks.) Capstone.

—Trust Me, Hansel & Gretel Are SWEET! The Story of Hansel & Gretel As Told by the Witch. Loewen, Nancy. 2016. (Other Side of the Story Ser.). (ENG.). 24p. (J). (gr. -1-3). lib. bdg. 27.99 *(978-1-4795-8623-3(4)*, Picture Window Bks.) Capstone.

Bock, Janna Rose. Por el Derecho a Estudiar: La Historia de Malala Yousafzai. Langston-George, Rebecca Ann. 2019. (Encuentros: Narrativa de No Ficción Ser.). (SPA.). 40p. (J). (gr. 3-6). lib. bdg. 29.32 *(978-1-5435-8268-0(0)*, 141301) Capstone.

Bock, Janna Rose & Moors, Steve. Encounter en Espanol. Gassman, Julie & Langston-George, Rebecca Ann. 2019. (Encuentros: Narrativa de No Ficción Ser.). (SPA.). (J). (gr. 3-6). 57.31 *(978-1-5435-8289-5(3)*, 29728) Capstone.

Bock, Suzanne. In the Beginning: Angels with Attitudes, 2004. 32p. (J). 12.99 *(978-0-9758709-0-7(4)*, 11412) Journey Stone Creations, LLC.

—Meet the Angels, l.t. ed. 2004. 10p. (J). bds. 12.99 *(978-0-9758709-4-5(7)*, 13401) Journey Stone Creations, LLC.

—A Place for the King: Christmas from the Angels Point of View. Stimkorb, Patricia. 2004. 48p. (J). 15.99 *(978-0-9758709-6-9(3)*, 12420) Journey Stone Creations, LLC.

Bock, William Sauts. African Mythology Rocks! Altman, Linda Jacobs. 2011. (Mythology Rocks! Ser.). 112p. (gr. 6-7). pap. 12.88 *(978-1-59845-328-7(9))*; lib. bdg. 34.27 *(978-0-7660-3896-7(3))* Enslow Publishing, LLC.

—Celtic Mythology Rocks! Bernard, Catherine. 2011. (Mythology Rocks! Ser.). 104p. (gr. 6-7). pap. 12.88 *(978-1-59845-326-3(2))*; lib. bdg. 34.27 *(978-0-7660-3895-0(5))* Enslow Publishing, LLC.

—Chinese Mythology Rocks! Collier, Irene Dea. 2011. (Mythology Rocks! Ser.). 128p. (gr. 6-7). pap. 12.88 *(978-1-59845-330-0(0))*; lib. bdg. 34.27 *(978-0-7660-3898-1(X))* Enslow Publishing, LLC.

—Gods & Goddesses in Greek Mythology Rock! Houle, Michelle M. 2011. (Mythology Rocks! Ser.). 128p. (gr. 6-7). lib. bdg. 34.27 *(978-0-7660-3897-4(1))* Enslow Publishing, LLC.

—Heroes in Greek Mythology Rock! Spies, Karen Bornemann. 2011. (Mythology Rocks! Ser.). 128p. (gr. 6-7). pap. 12.88 *(978-1-59845-331-7(9))*; lib. bdg. 34.27 *(978-0-7660-3900-1(5))* Enslow Publishing, LLC.

—Maya & Aztec Mythology Rocks! Schuman, Michael A. 2011. (Mythology Rocks! Ser.). 128p. (gr. 6-7). lib. bdg. 34.27 *(978-0-7660-3899-8(8))* Enslow Publishing, LLC.

—The Shore Ghosts & Other Stories of New Jersey. Homer, Larona. 2005. 154p. (J). (gr. 4-8). pap. *(978-0-912608-82-2(X))* Middle Atlantic Pr.

Bocquet, Fanny. Mes Emotions Ok ! Mais J'en Fais Quoi ? Bande Dessinée Educative Pour Enfants. Calderon, Anne. 2018. (FRE.). 48p. (J). pap. 22.00 *(978-2-9701219-1-6(3))* Trono-Calderon, Anne.

—My Emotions Ok, but What Do I Do with Them ? An Educational Comic Book for Children. Calderon, Anne. 2018. (ENG.). 48p. (J). pap. 22.00 *(978-2-9701219-0-9(5))* Trono-Calderon, Anne.

B

Bodart, Denis. Green Manor: The Inconvenience of Being Dead. Vehlmann, Fabien. 2008. (Expresso Collection). (ENG.). 96p. pap. 19.95 *(978-1-905460-64-9(3))* CineBook GBR. Dist: National Bk. Network.

—Green Manor Pt. 1: Assassins & Gentleman. Vehlmann, Fabien. 2008. (Expresso Collection). (ENG.). 56p. pap. 13.95 *(978-1-905460-53-3(8))* CineBook GBR. Dist: National Bk. Network.

Boddington's Studio. Mr. Boddington's Studio: Washington, DC ABCs. Boddington's Studio LLC. 2020. 28p. (J). (-k). bds. 9.99 *(978-1-5247-9351-7(5)*, Penguin Workshop) Penguin Young Readers Group.

Boddington's Studio. Mr. Boddington's Studio: NYC ABCs. Boddington's Studio. 2019. 28p. (J). (-k). bds. 9.99 *(978-1-5247-9203-9(9)*, Penguin Workshop) Penguin Young Readers Group.

Boddy, James & Moon, Paul. Joni-Pip. King, Carrie. 2010. 476p. pap. *(978-0-9555246-9-1(5))* Bothy Bks., Corwall, A Div. of Grace & Patrick Pubs., Ltd.

Boddy, Joe. Hidden Picture Mania. Daste, Larry et al. 2006. (Dover Children's Activity Bks.). (ENG.). 96p. (J). (gr. 3-6). per. 7.95 *(978-0-486-45911-0(X))* Dover Pubns., Inc.

—Lucy Goose Goes to Texas. Bea, Holly. 2005. (ENG.). 32p. (J). (gr. -1-5). 15.95 *(978-1-932073-15-7(9))* New World Library.

Bodecker, N. M. Magic by the Lake. Eager, Edward. 2016. (Tales of Magic Ser.: 2). (ENG.). 224p. (J). (gr. 3-7). pap. 7.99 *(978-0-544-67170-6(8)*, 1625816, HMH Books For Young Readers) Houghton Mifflin Harcourt Publishing Co.

—The Well-Wishers. Eager, Edward. 2016. (Tales of Magic Ser.: 6). (ENG.). 240p. (J). (gr. 3-7). pap. 7.99 *(978-0-544-67167-6(8)*, 1625810, HMH Books For Young Readers) Houghton Mifflin Harcourt Publishing Co.

Bodeker, Brian. The Little Crescent Moon & the Bright Evening Star. Humann, Walter J. 2nd ed. (J). (gr. -1-5). pap. 9.95 *(978-0-9674864-1-3(6))* WJH Publishing.

Bodel, Itai, photos by. The Amazing Fishing Rod. Herzog, Pearl. 2013. 34p. (J). *(978-1-4226-1436-5(0))* Mesorah Pubns., Ltd.

Boden, Lucy. Christmas Bear. Archer, Mandy. 2019. (ENG.). 20p. (J). 16.99 ***(978-1-989219-54-6(3))*** Rainstorm Pr.

Boden, Lucy. Look! It's Baby Duck Red Band. Pritchard, Gabby. 2016. (Cambridge Reading Adventures Ser.). (ENG.). 16p. pap. 7.37 *(978-1-107-54957-9(4))* Cambridge Univ. Pr.

Bodett, Tom. My Farm Friends. Minor, Wendell. 2012. 29.95 *(978-1-4301-1096-5(1))* Live Oak Media.

Bodily, Michael. The Smart Way to Be. Knudsen, Sherilyn. 2005. 32p. (J). per. 9.95 *(978-0-9768451-0-2(5))* HPN Publishing.

Bodnaruk, Iryna. Ella & Owen 1: the Cave of Aaaaah! Doom! Kent, Jaden. 2017. (Ella & Owen Ser.: 1). (ENG.). 112p. (J). (gr. k-3). pap. 5.99 *(978-1-4998-0368-6(0))* Little Bee Books Inc.

—Ella & Owen 10: the Dragon Games! Kent, Jaden. 2018. (Ella & Owen Ser.: 10). (ENG.). 112p. (J). (gr. k-3). 16.99 *(978-1-4998-0617-5(5))*; pap. 5.99 *(978-1-4998-0616-8(7))* Little Bee Books Inc.

—Ella & Owen 2: Attack of the Stinky Fish Monster! Kent, Jaden. 2017. (Ella & Owen Ser.: 2). (ENG.). 112p. (J). (gr. k-3). pap. 5.99 *(978-1-4998-0369-3(9))* Little Bee Books Inc.

—Ella & Owen: 4 Books In 1! Kent, Jaden. 2019. (Ella & Owen Ser.: 1). (ENG.). 416p. (J). (gr. k-3). 14.99 *(978-1-4998-0998-5(0))* Little Bee Books Inc.

—Ella & Owen 5: the Great Troll Quest. Kent, Jaden. 2017. (Ella & Owen Ser.: 5). (ENG.). 112p. (J). (gr. k-3). 16.99 *(978-1-4998-0474-4(1))*; pap. 5.99 *(978-1-4998-0473-7(3))* Little Bee Books Inc.

—Ella & Owen 6: Dragon Spies! Kent, Jaden. 2017. (Ella & Owen Ser.: 6). (ENG.). 112p. (J). (gr. k-3). 16.99 *(978-1-4998-0476-8(8))*; pap. 5.99 *(978-1-4998-0475-1(X))* Little Bee Books Inc.

—Ella & Owen 7: Twin Trouble. Kent, Jaden. 2018. (Ella & Owen Ser.: 7). (ENG.). 112p. (J). (gr. k-3). 16.99 *(978-1-4998-0611-3(6))*; pap. 5.99 *(978-1-4998-0610-6(8))* Little Bee Books Inc.

—Ella & Owen 8: the Worst Pet. Kent, Jaden. 2018. (Ella & Owen Ser.: 8). (ENG.). 112p. (J). (gr. k-3). 16.99 *(978-1-4998-0613-7(2))*; pap. 5.99 *(978-1-4998-0612-0(4))* Little Bee Books Inc.

—Ella & Owen 9: Grumpy Goblins. Kent, Jaden. 2018. (Ella & Owen Ser.: 9). (ENG.). 112p. (J). (gr. k-3). 16.99 *(978-1-4998-0615-1(9))*; pap. 5.99 *(978-1-4998-0614-4(0))* Little Bee Books Inc.

—The Missing Letters: A Dreidel Story. Londner, Renee. 2017. (ENG.). 32p. (J). (gr. -1-3). 17.99 *(978-1-4677-8933-2(X)*, 9781467789332, Kar-Ben Publishing) Lerner Publishing Group.

Bodoff, Janet. Eat Your Vegetables. Toscano, Leesa. 2012. 24p. pap. 24.95 *(978-1-4626-5278-5(6))* America Star Bks.

Body, Adrienne. Granddad's Fish Tank. Body, Adrienne. 2019. (ENG.). 28p. (J). pap. 9.99 ***(978-1-7110-4983-0(2))*** Independently Published.

Boedoe, Geefwee. Arrowville. Boedoe, Geefwee. 2004. 40p. (J). (gr. -1-2). 16.89 *(978-0-06-055599-3(8)*, Geringer, Laura Book) HarperCollins Pubs.

Boehm Sr, William Michel, jt. illus. see Lynch, Tim.

Boelke, David, jt. illus. see Pyle, Howard.

Boelter, Ashaki. Diaries of the Doomed. Boelter, Ashaki. 2004. 88p. (YA). per. 6.95 *(978-0-9721067-4-0(X)*, Writing Wild & Crazy) Shakalot High Entertainment.

Boemmels, Kayleigh. I Hear a Red Crayon: A Child's Perspective of Her Brother's Autism. Feuer, Bonnie. I.t. ed. 2015. (ENG.). 36p. (gr. 3-12). 19.95 *(978-0-9825468-9-5(0))* Connecticut Pr., The.

Boer, E. A. J. Het Boek Met Alle Verhalen: De Avonturen Van Kaboutertje Klok. Henkelman, Mechtild. 2018. (DUT.). 108p. (J). pap. *(978-90-829370-0-8(X))* Henkelman, Mechtild.

—Kaboutertje Klok Vertelt 24 Verhaaltjes. Henkelman, Mechtild. 2018. (DUT.). 164p. (J). pap. *(978-90-824973-9-7(5))* Henkelman, Mechtild.

Boerger, Andy. The Adventures of Sherlock Ferret. Ashton, Hugh. 2018. (Sherlock Ferret Ser.). (ENG.). 222p. (J). *(978-1-912605-40-8(6))* j-views.

—Sherlock Ferret & the Missing Necklace. Ashton, Hugh. 2018. (ENG.). 50p. (J). pap. *(978-1-912605-32-3(5))* j-views.

—Sherlock Ferret & the Multiplying Masterpieces. Ashton, Hugh. 2018. (Sherlock Ferret Ser.: Vol. 2). (ENG.). 56p. (J). pap. *(978-1-912605-36-1(8))* j-views.

—Sherlock Ferret & the Phantom Photographer. Ashton, Hugh. 2017. (ENG.). (J). pap. 5.99 *(978-0-9979336-5-9(8))* Inknbeans Pr.

—Sherlock Ferret & the Phantom Photographer. Ashton, Hugh. 2018. (Sherlock Ferret Ser.: Vol. 4). (ENG.). 46p. (J). pap. *(978-1-912605-38-5(4))* j-views.

—Sherlock Ferret & the Poisoned Pond. Ashton, Hugh. 2018. (Sherlock Ferret Ser.: Vol. 3). (ENG.). 56p. (J). pap. *(978-1-912605-37-8(6))* j-views.

—What Does the Tooth Fairy Do with Our Teeth? Barry, Denise. 2014. (ENG.). 34p. (J). (gr. -1-2). 14.95 *(978-1-62086-841-6(5))* Mascot Bks., Inc.

Boeri, Irene & Spagarino, Cristina. Cristalli Di Neve: Fiabe Della Buonanotte. Buttini, Barbara. 2018. (ITA.). 136p. (J). pap. 11.90 *(978-1-7903-9784-6(7))* Independently Published.

Boerio, Carrie Lacey. Tired of Naps! Davis, Mary (Molly) C. 2019. (ENG.). 24p. (J). (gr. k-2). 9.99 ***(978-0-578-51894-7(5))*** Readitagain LLC.

Boersma, Alex. Crispr: A Powerful Way to Change DNA. Ridge, Yolanda. 2020. 116p. (YA). (gr. 9-9). pap. 14.95 ***(978-1-77321-423-8(3))*** Annick Pr., Ltd. CAN. Dist: Publishers Group West (PGW).

Boetger, Nikki. In the Wild. Rainstorm Publishing, ed. 2019. (Playful Shapes Ser.). (ENG.). 16p. (J). 8.99 ***(978-1-926444-69-7(8))*** Rainstorm Pr.

—Peek a Boo Halloween. Rainstorm Publishing, ed. 2019. (ENG.). 14p. (J). (gr. -1-1). 7.99 ***(978-1-77402-115-6(3))*** Rainstorm Pr.

Boey, Stephanie. I Want to Be a Great White Shark. Troupe, Thomas Kingsley. 2015. (I Want to Be... Ser.). (ENG.). 24p. (J). (gr. k-3). lib. bdg. 27.32 *(978-1-4795-6859-8(7)*, Picture Window Bks.) Capstone.

—The Little Beaver. Jordan, Christopher. 2008. (ENG.). 24p. (J). (gr. k-3). *(978-1-55168-249-5(4))* Magma.

—Little Lamb to the Rescue. Briers, Erica. 2004. (ENG.). 24p. (J). *(978-1-55168-257-0(5))* Fenn, H. B. & Co., Ltd.

—The Little Moose. Martin, Ruth. 2008. (ENG.). 35p. (J). *(978-1-55168-332-4(6))* Fenn, H. B. & Co., Ltd.

—Little Seal Finds a Friend. Harris, Sue. 2007. (ENG.). 24p. (J). *(978-1-55168-295-2(8))* Fenn, H. B. & Co., Ltd.

—Runaway Chick. Briers, Erica. 2006. (ENG.). 24p. (J). *(978-1-55168-314-0(8))* Fenn, H. B. & Co., Ltd.

Bogacki, Tomasz. When You Visit Grandma & Grandpa. Bogacki, Tomasz, tr. Bowen, Anne. 2004. (Carolrhoda Picture Books Ser.). 32p. (J). (gr. -1-3). 15.95 *(978-1-57505-610-4(0))* Lerner Publishing Group.

Bogacki, Tomek. Big Box for Ben, 1 vol. Bruss, Deborah. 2011. (ENG.). 16p. (J). (gr. -1-k). bds. 6.95 *(978-1-59572-265-2(3))* Star Bright Bks., Inc.

—Christmas Is Coming. Bowen, Anne. 2007. (Carolrhoda Picture Bks.). 28p. (J). (gr. -1-3). 16.95 *(978-1-57505-934-1(7)*, Carolrhoda Bks.) Lerner Publishing Group.

—Cinco Criaturas. Jenkins, Emily. Cortes, Eunice, tr. 2003. (Picture Bks.).Tr. of Five Creatures. (SPA.). (J). *(978-970-690-648-9(7))* Planeta Mexicana Editorial S. A. de C. V.

—Five Creatures. Jenkins, Emily. 2005. (ENG.). 32p. (J). (gr. -1-1). reprint ed. per. 8.99 *(978-0-374-42328-5(8)*, 900028272) Square Fish.

—Mole Catches the Sky. Tarlow, Ellen. 2014. (ENG.). (J). 16.99 *(978-1-59572-656-8(X))* Star Bright Bks., Inc.

—El Pajaro, el Mono y la Serpiente en la Selva. Banks, Kate. (SPA.). 24p. (J). (gr. k-2). *(978-84-261-3129-4(8)*, JV2823) Juventud, Editorial ESP. Dist: Lectorum Pubns., Inc.

—Small, Medium, Large, 1 vol. Jenkins, Emily. 2011. (ENG.). 32p. (J). 19.95 *(978-1-59572-278-2(5))* Star Bright Bks., Inc.

—Small Medium Large, 1 vol. Jenkins, Emily. 2011. (ENG.). 32p. (J). pap. 12.95 *(978-1-59572-299-7(8))* Star Bright Bks., Inc.

Bogade, Maria. Ben's Flying Flowers. Maier, Inger M. 2012. 32p. (J). 14.95 *(978-1-4338-1133-3(2))*; pap. 9.95 *(978-1-4338-1132-6(4))* American Psychological Assn. (Magination Pr.).

—Healing Days: A Guide for Kids Who Have Experienced Trauma. Straus, Susan Farber. 2013. 32p. (J). *(978-1-4338-1292-7(4))*; pap. *(978-1-4338-1293-4(2))* American Psychological Assn.

—Jamie Is Jamie: A Book about Being Yourself & Playing Your Way. Moradian, Afsaneh. 2018. (ENG.). 32p. (J). (gr. -1-3). 12.99 *(978-1-63198-139-5(0)*, 81395) Free Spirit Publishing, Inc.

—The Lost (and Found) Balloon. Jenkins, Celeste. 2013. (ENG.). 32p. (J). (gr. -1-3). 18.99 *(978-1-4424-6697-5(9)*, Aladdin) Simon & Schuster Children's Publishing.

Bogade, Maria. Wee Granny's Magic Bag & the Ceilidh, 30 vols. McKay, Elizabeth. 2nd rev. ed. 2020. (ENG.). 32p. (J). 11.95 ***(978-1-78250-652-2(7)***, Kelpies) Floris Bks. GBR. Dist: Consortium Bk. Sales & Distribution.

Bogade, Maria. Wee Granny's Magic Bag & the Pirates, 30 vols. McKay, Elizabeth. 2018. (ENG.). 32p. (J). 11.95 *(978-1-78250-475-7(3)*, Kelpies) Floris Bks. GBR. Dist: Consortium Bk. Sales & Distribution.

Bogan, Lyuba. What God Wants for Christmas: Read along, Sing Along. Bradford, Amy L. 2006. 20p. (J). (gr. 4-7). 14.99 incl. audio compact disk *(978-1-57229-914-6(2))* FamilyLife.

Bogan, Paulette. Chicks & Salsa. Reynolds, Aaron. 2007. (ENG.). 32p. (J). (gr. 1-3). pap. 7.99 *(978-1-59990-099-5(8)*, 900044569, Bloomsbury USA Childrens) Bloomsbury Publishing USA.

Bogan, Paulette. Bossy Flossy. Bogan, Paulette. 2016. (ENG.). 32p. (J). 16.99 *(978-1-62779-358-2(5)*, 900147468, Holt, Henry & Co. Bks. For Young Readers) Holt, Henry & Co.

—Virgil & Owen Stick Together. Bogan, Paulette. 2016. 32p. (J). 16.99 *(978-1-61963-373-5(6)*, 900135294, Bloomsbury USA Childrens) Bloomsbury Publishing USA.

Bogatch, Yana. Grimoire Noir. Greentea, Vera. 2019. (ENG.). 288p. (YA). 24.99 *(978-1-250-30573-2(X)*, 900197572); pap. 17.99 *(978-1-62672-598-0(5)*, 900162654) Roaring Brook Pr. (First Second Bks.).

Bogdan, Enache. The Boy Who Cried Wolf. Sommer, Carl. 2014. (Sommer-Time Story Classics Ser.). (ENG.). 32p. (J). (gr. k-4). 16.95 *(978-1-57537-079-8(4))* Advance Publishing, Inc.

—The Silent Scream. Sommer, Carl & Aesop, Aesop. 2009. (Quest for Success Ser.). (ENG.). 40p. (YA). pap. 4.95 *(978-1-57537-285-3(1))*; lib. bdg. 12.95 *(978-1-57537-260-0(6))* Advance Publishing, Inc.

—The Silent Scream(El Grito Silencioso) Sommer, Carl & Aesop, Aesop. ed. 2009. (Quest for Success Bilingual Ser.). (SPA & ENG.). 72p. (YA). lib. bdg. 14.95 *(978-1-57537-235-8(5))* Advance Publishing, Inc.

Bogdanovic, Toma. The Snow Queen. Andersen, Hans. adapted ed. 32p. (J). (gr. -1-5). 16.95 *(978-0-87592-048-1(9))* Scroll Pr., Inc.

Bogdanovic, Toma, jt. illus. see Van Nutt, Robert.

Bogdanska, Kasia. Seagulls Soar. Sayre, April Pulley. 2020. (ENG.). 32p. (J). (gr. -1-3). 17.99 *(978-1-68437-197-6(X))* Boyds Mills Pr.

Boger-Bass, Vallerie. The Mustard Seed: A Christian Promise. Boger-Bass, Vallerie. 2003. 40p. pap. 10.00 *(978-0-8059-5640-5(9))* Dorrance Publishing Co., Inc.

Bogert, Beth. The Goblins of Knottingham: A History of Challah. Klein, Zoë. 2017. (J). *(978-1-68115-526-5(5))* Behrman Hse., Inc.

Boggelen-Heutink, Ellen van. The Incredible Adventures of Captain Cameron MacDuddyfunk in Cuggermuggerland. Simons, Alan L. 2013. 98p. pap. *(978-0-9877503-8-9(0))* Baronel Bks.

Boggs, Button & Atkins, Nancy Taylor. The Woods of Wicomico (2nd Ed.) Galbari, Nuala C. 2020. (ENG.). 166p. (J). (gr. 4-6). pap. 19.95 ***(978-1-951565-26-8(6)***, Belle Isle Bks.); 2nd ed. 30.95 ***(978-1-951565-17-6(7))*** Brandylane Pubs., Inc.

Boggs II, Kenny. King Cake for Cassius: A Mardi Gras Story. Boyle, Diane R. 2004. (ENG.). 26p. pap. 13.50 *(978-1-4120-2256-9(8))* Trafford Publishing.

Bognadove, Jon, et al. New Mutants Epic Collection: Curse of the Valkyries. 2018. 496p. (J). (gr. 4-17). pap. 39.99 *(978-1-302-91017-4(5))* Marvel Worldwide, Inc.

—X-Men Milestones: Inferno. 2019. 496p. (YA). (gr. 4-17). pap. 34.99 *(978-1-302-91970-2(9))* Marvel Worldwide, Inc.

Bogosian, Harry. Topside. Monk, J. N. 2019. 200p. (YA). (gr. 7-12). (ENG.). pap. 14.99 *(978-1-5415-7285-0(8))*; lib. bdg. 33.32 *(978-1-5124-4589-3(4))* Lerner Publishing Group. (Graphic Universe™).

Bohart, Lisa. The Blue Lobster. Taylor-Chiarello, Robin. 2011. 36p. pap. 15.95 *(978-1-936343-84-3(3))* Peppertree Pr., The.

—The Blue Lobster's Holiday! Chiarello, Robin Taylor. 2012. 40p. pap. 16.95 *(978-1-61493-053-2(8))* Peppertree Pr., The.

—The Christmas Horse. Cooper, Margaret. 2008. 32p. pap. 12.95 *(978-0-9821654-9-2(8))* Peppertree Pr., The.

—Christmas on the Internet. Bizzarro, Grace. 2013. 20p. pap. 12.95 *(978-1-61493-197-3(6))* Peppertree Pr., The.

—The Clam Diggers Ball. Chiarello, Robin Taylor. 2011. 40p. pap. 15.95 *(978-1-61493-013-6(9))* Peppertree Pr., The.

—The Croaker Sack Bunny. Harris, Dee. 2012. 24p. pap. 12.95 *(978-1-61493-043-3(0))* Peppertree Pr., The.

—Donkeys Are Special & So Are You! Krueger, T. W. 2013. (ENG.). 46p. (J). 12.99 *(978-0-9887454-0-7(2))* Donkey Publishing.

Bohart, Lisa. I Am Not a Hippopotamus, I Am a Little Girl. Harris, Dee. 2020. (ENG.). 24p. (J). 22.95 ***(978-1-61493-708-1(7))*** Peppertree Pr., The.

Bohart, Lisa. I Am Not a Hippopotamus, I Am a Little Girl, Book. Harris, Dee. 2011. 24p. pap. 12.95 *(978-1-61493-005-1(8))* Peppertree Pr., The.

—The Magic Blue Bike. Harris, Dee. 2018. (ENG.). 40p. (J). (gr. k-6). 26.95 *(978-1-61493-588-9(2))* Peppertree Pr., The.

—Murky, Quirky, Beserky Math. Desjardins, Margaret M. 2013. 24p. pap. 13.95 *(978-1-61493-210-9(7))* Peppertree Pr., The.

—A Ribbon for Diego. Miranda, Edward. 2008. 28p. pap. 12.95 *(978-0-9821654-5-4(5))* Peppertree Pr., The.

—Sadie the Ladybug. Cross, Jenny. 2009. 44p. pap. 14.95 *(978-1-936051-39-7(7))* Peppertree Pr., The.

—Signs of Love. Nelson, Jan. 2009. 24p. pap. 12.95 *(978-1-936051-54-0(0))* Peppertree Pr., The.

Bohl, Al. Zaanan: The Mermen of Immersia. Bohl, Al. 2019. (Zaanan Ser.: Vol. 5). (ENG.). 246p. (J). (gr. 4-8). pap. 20.00 ***(978-1-6704-3604-7(7))*** Independently Published.

Bohlmann, Siegfried. Dr. Rabbit. Hare, Eric B. fac. ed. 2010. 127p. per. 11.95 *(978-1-57258-278-1(2)*, 945-6131) TEACH Services, Inc.

Bohman, Jennifer White. Snowy Owls: Whoo Are They?, 1 vol. Ford, Ansley Watson & Holt, Denver W. 2008. (ENG.). 64p. (J). (gr. 3-7). pap. 12.00 *(978-0-87842-543-3(8))* Mountain Pr. Publishing Co., Inc.

Bohman, Natasha. David's Big Break. Loever, Charmaine. 2008. 52p. pap. 22.99 *(978-1-4389-3173-9(5))* AuthorHouse.

Bohn, Ken & Garrison, Ron. San Diego Zoo. Bohn, Ken & Garrison, Ron, photos by. Pearce, Claudia & Worley, Karen E. 2003. (Great Zoos of the United States Ser.). 24p. (J). lib. bdg. 24.60 *(978-0-8239-6321-8(7)*, PowerKids Pr.) Rosen Publishing Group, Inc., The.

Bohn, Kendall. The Original Abstract Adventure. 2009. 54p. pap. 8.95 *(978-0-929636-99-3(6))* Syren Bk. Co.

Bohn, Klaus. Healthy Me: I Love Fruit, I Love Veggies. Bohn, Klaus. 2012. (ENG.). 44p. (J). pap. *(978-1-77143-034-0(6)*, CCB Publishing) CCB Publishing.

Bohnet, Christopher, jt. illus. see VanDeWeghe, Lindsay.

Bohrer, Joe. Red & Slim: One Hot Day. Stamp, Jeffrey. 2008. 40p. (J). 16.99 *(978-0-9794543-0-1(1))* Syllabets, LLC.

Boiger, Alexandra. Doctor All-Knowing: A Folk Tale from the Brothers Grimm. 2018. (ENG.). 40p. (J). (gr. -1-1). 11.99 *(978-1-5344-3370-0(8)*, Atheneum Bks. for Young Readers) Simon & Schuster Children's Publishing.

—Ella Persistió: 13 Mujeres Americanas Que Cambiaron el Mundo. Clinton, Chelsea. 2017. (SPA.). 32p. (J). (gr. -1-3). 17.99 *(978-0-525-51494-7(5)*, Philomel Bks.) Penguin Young Readers Group.

—Ella Persistió Alrededor Del Mundo: 13 Mujeres Que Cambiaron la Historia. Clinton, Chelsea. 2018. (SPA.). 32p. (J). (gr. -1-3). 17.99 *(978-0-525-51702-3(2)*, Philomel Bks.) Penguin Young Readers Group.

Boiger, Alexandra. Ella Persistió en el Deporte: Americanas Olímpicas Que Revolucionaron el Juego. Clinton, Chelsea. 2020. (SPA.). 32p. (J). (gr. -1-3). 17.99 ***(978-0-593-20478-8(6)***, Philomel Bks.) Penguin Young Readers Group.

Boiger, Alexandra. Happy Birthday, Mrs. Piggle-Wiggle. MacDonald, Betty Bard. 2007. (Mrs. Piggle-Wiggle Ser.). 193p. (J). (gr. 3-7). lib. bdg. 16.89 *(978-0-06-072813-7(2))* HarperCollins Pubs.

—Happy Birthday, Mrs. Piggle-Wiggle. Canham, Anne MacDonald & MacDonald, Betty. (ENG.). 208p. (J). (gr. 3-7). 2008. pap. 7.99 *(978-0-06-072814-4(0))*; 2007. 16.99 *(978-0-06-072812-0(4))* HarperCollins Pubs.

—Hello, Mrs. Piggle Wiggle. MacDonald, Betty. 2007. (ENG.). 176p. (J). (gr. 3-7). 16.99 *(978-0-397-31715-8(8)*, HarperCollins) HarperCollins Pubs. Ltd. GBR. Dist: HarperCollins Pubs.

—Hello, Mrs. Piggle-Wiggle. MacDonald, Betty. 2007. (Trophy Bk.). (ENG.). 176p. (J). (gr. 3-7). pap. 7.99 *(978-0-06-440149-4(9)*, HarperCollins) HarperCollins Pubs. Ltd. GBR. Dist: HarperCollins Pubs.

—The Little Bit Scary People. Jenkins, Emily. 2008. (ENG.). 32p. (gr. -1-1). 16.99 *(978-1-4231-0075-1(1))* Hyperion Pr.

—The Monster Princess. MacHale, D. J. 2010. (ENG.). 40p. (J). (gr. -1-1). 17.99 *(978-1-4169-4809-4(0)*, Aladdin) Simon & Schuster Children's Publishing.

—Mrs. Piggle-Wiggle. MacDonald, Betty. rev. ed. 2007. (ENG.). 144p. (J). (gr. 3-7). 16.99 *(978-0-397-31712-7(3))*; pap. 5.99 *(978-0-06-440148-7(0))* HarperCollins Pubs. Ltd. GBR. (HarperCollins). Dist: HarperCollins Pubs.

—Mrs. Piggle-Wiggle's Magic. MacDonald, Betty. 2007. (Trophy Bk.). (ENG.). 192p. (J). (gr. 3-7). pap. 6.99 *(978-0-06-440151-7(0)*, HarperCollins) HarperCollins Pubs. Ltd. GBR. Dist: HarperCollins Pubs.

—Poor Doreen: a Fishy Tale. Lloyd-Jones, Sally. 2014. (ENG.). 40p. (J). (gr. -1-3). 17.99 *(978-0-375-86918-1(2)*, Schwartz & Wade Bks.) Random Hse. Children's Bks.

—Roxie & the Hooligans. Naylor, Phyllis Reynolds. 2007. 115p. (gr. 2-5). 16.00 *(978-0-7569-8284-3(7))* Perfection Learning Corp.

—Roxie & the Hooligans. Naylor, Phyllis Reynolds. 2007. (ENG.). 128p. (J). (gr. 3-5). pap. 7.99 *(978-1-4169-0244-7(9)*, Simon & Schuster/Paula Wiseman Bks.) Simon & Schuster Children's Publishing.

—Roxie & the Hooligans, 1. Naylor, Phyllis Reynolds. 2006. (ENG.). 128p. (J). (gr. 2-5). 17.99 *(978-1-4169-0243-0(0))* Simon & Schuster, Inc.

—Roxie & the Hooligans at Buzzard's Roost. Naylor, Phyllis Reynolds. (ENG.). 208p. (J). (gr. 2-5). 2019. pap. 7.99 *(978-1-4814-3783-7(6))*; 2018. 16.99 *(978-1-4814-3782-0(8))* Simon & Schuster Children's Publishing. (Atheneum Bks. for Young Readers).

—She Persisted. Clinton, Chelsea. 2019. (ENG.). 32p. (J). (—1). bds. 9.99 *(978-0-593-11758-3(1)*, Philomel Bks.) Penguin Young Readers Group.

—She Persisted: 13 American Women Who Changed the World. Clinton, Chelsea. 2017. (ENG.). 32p. (J). (gr. -1-3). 17.99 *(978-1-5247-4172-3(8)*, Philomel Bks.) Penguin Young Readers Group.

—She Persisted Around the World: 13 Women Who Changed History. Clinton, Chelsea. 2018. 32p. (J). (gr. -1-3). 17.99 *(978-0-525-51699-6(9)*, Philomel Bks.) Penguin Young Readers Group.

—She Persisted Boxed Set, 2 vols. Clinton, Chelsea. 2018. 64p. (J). (gr. -1-3). 35.98 *(978-1-9848-1219-3(X)*, Philomel Bks.) Penguin Young Readers Group.

Boiger, Alexandra. She Persisted in Sports: American Olympians Who Changed the Game. Clinton, Chelsea. 2020. (ENG.). 32p. (J). (gr. -1-3). 17.99 ***(978-0-593-11454-4(X)***, Philomel Bks.) Penguin Young Readers Group.

Boiger, Alexandra. Take Your Mama to Work Today. Reichert, Amy. 2012. (ENG.). 40p. (J). (gr. -1-8). 16.99 *(978-1-4169-7095-8(9)*, Atheneum Bks. for Young Readers) Simon & Schuster Children's Publishing.

—Tallulah's Ice Skates. Singer, Marilyn. 2018. (Tallulah Ser.). (ENG.). 48p. (J). (gr. -1-3). 17.99 *(978-0-544-59692-4(7)*, 1615570, Clarion Bks.) Houghton Mifflin Harcourt Trade & Reference Pubs.

—Tallulah's Nutcracker. Singer, Marilyn. 2013. (Tallulah Ser.). (ENG.). 48p. (J). (gr. -1-3). 17.99 *(978-0-547-84557-9(X)*, 1500234) Houghton Mifflin Harcourt Publishing Co.

—Tallulah's Solo. Singer, Marilyn. 2012. (Tallulah Ser.). (ENG.). 40p. (J). (gr. -1-3). 17.99 *(978-0-547-33004-4(9)*, 1417225) Houghton Mifflin Harcourt Publishing Co.

—Tallulah's Tap Shoes. Singer, Marilyn. 2015. (ENG.). 48p. (J). (gr. -1-3). 16.99 *(978-0-544-23687-5(4)*, 1564710) Houghton Mifflin Harcourt Publishing Co.

—Tallulah's Toe Shoes. Singer, Marilyn. 2013. (ENG.). 48p. (J). (gr. -1-3). 16.99 *(978-0-547-48223-1(X)*, 1439652) Houghton Mifflin Harcourt Publishing Co.

—Tallulah's Tutu. Singer, Marilyn. 2011. (Tallulah Ser.). (ENG.). 40p. (J). (gr. -1-3). 17.99 *(978-0-547-17353-5(9)*, 1054629) Houghton Mifflin Harcourt Publishing Co.

—When Jackie Saved Grand Central. Wing, Natasha. 2017. (ENG.). 48p. (J). (gr. 1-4). 17.99 *(978-0-547-44921-0(6)*, 1435124, HMH Books For Young Readers) Houghton Mifflin Harcourt Publishing Co.

—While Mama Had a Quick Little Chat. Reichert, Amy. 2005. (ENG.). 40p. (J). (gr. -1-2). 16.99 *(978-0-689-85170-4(7)*,

Atheneum/Richard Jackson Bks.) Simon & Schuster Children's Publishing.

Boiger, Alexandra. Max & Marla. Boiger, Alexandra. 2015. (ENG.). 32p. (J). (-k). 17.99 *(978-0-399-17504-6(0)*, G.P. Putnam's Sons Books for Young Readers) Penguin Young Readers Group.

—Max & Marla Are Flying Together. Boiger, Alexandra. 2019. (ENG.). 32p. (J). (-k). 17.99 *(978-0-525-51566-1(6)*, Philomel Bks.) Penguin Young Readers Group.

—Max & Marla Are Going on a Trip. Boiger, Alexandra. 2020. (ENG.). 32p. (J). (-k). 17.99 *(978-0-525-51570-8(4)*, Philomel Bks.) Penguin Young Readers Group.

Boivin, Valérie. Walking in the City with Jane: A Story of Jane Jacobs. Hughes, Susan. 2018. (ENG.). 36p. (J). (gr. 1-4). 18.99 *(978-1-77138-653-1(3))* Kids Can Pr., Ltd. CAN. Dist: Hachette Bk. Group.

Bojesen, Niels Bo. Vitello Becomes a Businessman. Aakeson, Kim Fupz & Garde, Ruth. 2014. (Vitello Ser.). (ENG.). 32p. (J). (gr. k-3). pap. 9.99 *(978-1-78269-001-6(8)*, Pushkin Children's Bks.) Steerforth Pr.

—Vitello Carries a Knife. Aakeson, Kim Fupz & Garde, Ruth. 2014. (Vitello Ser.). (ENG.). 32p. (J). (gr. k-3). pap. 9.99 *(978-1-78269-005-4(0)*, Pushkin Children's Bks.) Steerforth Pr.

—Vitello Gets a Yucky Girlfriend. Aakeson, Kim Fupz & Garde, Ruth. 2014. (Vitello Ser.). (ENG.). 32p. (J). (gr. k-3). pap. 9.99 *(978-1-78269-003-0(4)*, Pushkin Children's Bks.) Steerforth Pr.

—Vitello Scratches a Car. Aakeson, Kim Fupz & Garde, Ruth. 2014. (Vitello Ser.). (ENG.). 32p. (J). (gr. k-3). pap. 9.99 *(978-1-78269-002-3(6)*, Pushkin Children's Bks.) Steerforth Pr.

—Vitello Wants a Dad. Aakeson, Kim Fupz & Garde, Ruth. 2014. (Vitello Ser.). (ENG.). 32p. (J). (gr. k-3). pap. 9.99 *(978-1-78269-004-7(2)*, Pushkin Children's Bks.) Steerforth Pr.

Bolam, Emily. Bumpy Books - Colors. 2019. (ENG.). 10p. (J). (— 1). bds. 8.99 *(978-1-68412-358-2(5)*, Silver Dolphin Bks.) Printers Row Publishing Group.

—Bumpy Books - Patterns. 2018. (ENG.). 10p. (J). (— 1). bds. 8.99 *(978-1-68412-356-8(9)*, Silver Dolphin Bks.) Printers Row Publishing Group.

—Bumpy Books: 1, 2, 3. 2018. (ENG.). 10p. (J). (— 1). bds. 8.99 *(978-1-68412-357-5(7)*, Silver Dolphin Bks.) Printers Row Publishing Group.

—Can You Play?, Linn, Margot. 2005. (I'm Going to Read® Ser.: Level 1). 28p. (J). (gr. -1-k). pap. 3.95 *(978-1-4027-2094-9(7))* Sterling Publishing Co., Inc.

—Colors. 2009. 10p. (J). (gr. -1-k). 5.95 *(978-1-58925-845-7(2))* Tiger Tales.

—The Copy Crocs, 1 vol. Bedford, David. (ENG.). 32p. (J). 2015. (gr. -1-3). pap. 7.95 *(978-1-56145-885-1(6))*; 2004. (gr. k-3). 15.95 *(978-1-56145-304-7(8))* Peachtree Publishing Co. Inc.

—Counting. 2009. 10p. (J). (gr. -1-k). 5.95 *(978-1-58925-846-4(0))* Tiger Tales.

—Farm Babies. Keast, Jennifer H. 2014. (ENG.). 12p. (J). bds. *(978-1-4508-9224-7(8)*, 37e56bc1-b08d-4e3a-a9d5-249c12262e9a, p i kids) Phoenix International Publications, Inc.

—Hello, Animals! Prasadam, Smriti. 2010. (ENG.). 10p. (J). (gr. -1-k). bds. 6.99 *(978-1-58925-861-7(4))* Tiger Tales.

—Hello, Bugs! Prasadam, Smriti. 2010. (ENG.). 10p. (J). (gr. -1-k). bds. 6.99 *(978-1-58925-862-4(2))* Tiger Tales.

—In the Beginning: Bible Stories for Little Hands, 1 vol. Rock, Lois. ed. 2014. (Bible Stories for Little Hands Ser.). (ENG.). 8p. (J). (gr. -1 — 1). bds. 8.99 *(978-0-7459-6449-2(4))* Lion Hudson PLC GBR. Dist: Independent Pubs. Group.

—In the Jungle. 2013. (Peekabooks Ser.). (ENG.). 8p. (J). (gr. -1 — 1). bds. 5.99 *(978-0-7641-6629-7(8)*, B.E.S. Publishing) Peterson's.

—Jesus Is Born: A Spot-the-Difference Jigsaw Book, 1 vol. Rock, Lois. ed. 2014. (Bible Stories for Little Hands Ser.). (ENG.). 8p. (J). (gr. -1 — 1). bds. 8.99 *(978-0-7459-6450-8(8))* Lion Hudson PLC GBR. Dist: Independent Pubs. Group.

—Jesus, the Good Shepherd. St. Pierre, Stephanie. 2003. 14p. (J). bds. 7.99 *(978-0-7847-1272-6(7)*, 04032) Standard Publishing.

—The Lost Sheep: A Spot-the-Difference Jigsaw Book, 1 vol. Rock, Lois. ed. 2014. (Bible Stories for Little Hands Ser.). (ENG.). 8p. (J). (gr. -1 — 1). bds. 8.99 *(978-0-7459-6451-5(6))* Lion Hudson PLC GBR. Dist: Independent Pubs. Group.

—Mi Primera Biblia Ilustrada / My First Picture Bible. Piper, Sophie. 2018. (SPA.). 224p. (J). (-k). 15.95 *(978-1-945540-50-9(8))* Penguin Random House Grupo Editorial ESP. Dist: Penguin Random Hse. LLC.

—Noah's Ark: A Spot-the-Difference Jigsaw Book, 1 vol. Rock, Lois. ed. 2014. (Bible Stories for Little Hands Ser.). (ENG.). 8p. (J). (gr. -1 — 1). bds. 8.99 *(978-0-7459-6442-3(7))* Lion Hudson PLC GBR. Dist: Independent Pubs. Group.

Bolan, Cassandre. El Camion de Navidad. Blankenship, J. B. Salgado, Adela, tr. 2016. (SPA.). (J). pap. 10.95 *(978-0-9907434-5-3(4))* NarraGarden LLC.

—Le Camion de Noel. Blankenship, J. B. Monserrat, Delphine, tr. 2015. (FRE.). 48p. (J). pap. 10.95 *(978-0-9907434-6-0(2))* NarraGarden LLC.

—Not Today, Aliens! Blankenship, J. B. 2018. (ENG.). 38p. (J). (gr. 1-3). pap. 9.95 *(978-0-9970312-1-8(2))* SitStayRead.

Bolan, Michael. Stella Eats Out. Stephens, Ann Marie. 2004. 32p. (J). per. 12.95 *(978-0-9729285-2-6(9)*, 2-9) Kinkachoo Pr., The.

Bolan, Michael P. Christmas for Bly & Ray. Stephens, Ann Marie. 2003. 45p. (J). per. 11.95 *(978-0-9729285-0-2(2)*, 0-9729285-0-2) Kinkachoo Pr., The.

—A Surprise for Ray. Stephens, Ann Marie. 2003. 47p. (J). per. 11.95 *(978-0-9729285-1-9(0)*, 0-9729285-1-0) Kinkachoo Pr., The.

Bolder, Joe, jt. illus. see Cordner, Theo.

Boldi, Florina. Pug in Boots. 2013. 42p. pap. 9.99 *(978-0-9829132-6-0(5))* Left Paw Pr.

Boldrin, Elisa. Scared of the Dark. Thornton, Caroline L. 2nd ed. 2018. (ENG.). 32p. (J). (gr. k-3). pap. *(978-1-78926-482-1(0))* Independent Publishing Network.

Boldrin, Elisa & Naik, Neha. The Adventures of Mrs Ribozome. Inic, Elle. 2019. (ENG.). 42p. (J). (gr. 1-3). ***(978-1-925934-03-8(9))***; pap. ***(978-1-925934-00-7(4))*** Elle Inic.

Boldt, Claudia. Animalicious: A Quirky ABC Book. Dewdney, Anna & Duncan, Reed. 2019. 32p. (J). (gr. -1-1). 14.99 *(978-1-5247-9205-3(5)*, Penguin Workshop) Penguin Young Readers Group.

—Lots of Frogs. Calvert, Howard. 2020. 32p. (J). (gr. -1-k). pap. 10.99 *(978-1-4449-3965-1(3))* Hachette Children's Group GBR. Dist: Hachette Bk. Group.

Boldt, Claudia. Star Gazers, Skyscrapers & Extraordinary Sausages. Boldt, Claudia. 2010. (Child's Play Library). 32p. (J). (gr. 1-2). pap. *(978-1-84643-344-3(4))* Child's Play International Ltd.

—Uugghh! Boldt, Claudia. 2011. (Child's Play Library). 32p. (J). (gr. 2-2). *(978-1-84643-372-6(X))* Child's Play International Ltd.

Boldt, Claudia H. The Ghosts Go Marching. 2020. (ENG.). 30p. (J). (— 1). bds. 7.99 ***(978-0-593-11874-0(X)***, Random Hse. Bks. for Young Readers) Random Hse. Children's Bks.

Boldt, Fabienne & Wensell, Ulises. In the Meadow. Linke, Uwe. 2007. (Moving Book Ser.). (ENG.). 20p. (J). bds. 11.95 *(978-0-7358-2126-2(7))* North-South Bks., Inc.

Boldt, Mike. The Dino Files #2: Too Big to Hide. McAnulty, Stacy. 2017. (Dino Files Ser.: 2). (ENG.). 128p. (J). (gr. 2-5). 5.99 *(978-1-5247-0151-2(3)*, Random Hse. Bks. for Young Readers) Random Hse. Children's Bks.

—The Duck Says. Wilson, Troy. 2016. 29p. (J). *(978-1-338-03466-0(9))* Scholastic, Inc.

—How to Grow a Dinosaur. Esbaum, Jill. 2018. 40p. (J). (-k). 17.99 *(978-0-399-53910-7(7)*, Dial Bks) Penguin Young Readers Group.

—I Don't Want to Be a Frog. Petty, Dev. (ENG.). (J). 2018. 32p. (gr. -1-2). pap. 7.99 *(978-1-9848-5208-3(6)*, Dragonfly Bks.); 2018. 26p. (— 1). bds. 8.99 *(978-0-525-57950-2(8)*, Doubleday Bks. for Young Readers); 2015. 32p. (gr. -1-2). lib. bdg. 19.99 *(978-0-375-97334-5(6)*, Doubleday Bks. for Young Readers) Random Hse. Children's Bks.

—I Don't Want to Be Big. Petty, Dev. 2016. 32p. (J). (gr. -1-2). 16.99 *(978-1-101-93920-8(6)*, Doubleday Bks. for Young Readers) Random Hse. Children's Bks.

—I Don't Want to Go to Sleep. Petty, Dev. 2018. 32p. (J). (gr. -1-2). 16.99 *(978-1-5247-6896-6(0)*, Doubleday Bks. for Young Readers) Random Hse. Children's Bks.

—It's Not a Dinosaur! McAnulty, Stacy. 2016. (Dino Files Ser.: 3). 128p. (J). (gr. 2-5). 9.99 *(978-0-553-52197-9(7)*, Random Hse. Bks. for Young Readers) Random Hse. Children's Bks.

—Loud Lula. 0 vols. Duffield, Katy S. 2015. (ENG.). 32p. (J). (gr. k-2). 17.99 *(978-1-4778-2776-5(5)*, 9781477827765, Two Lions) Amazon Publishing.

—Loud Lula. Duffield, Katy. 2015. 32p. (J). *(978-1-4778-2785-7(4))* Amazon Publishing.

—A Mysterious Egg. McAnulty, Stacy. (Dino Files Ser.: 1). 128p. (J). (gr. 2-5). 2017. 5.99 *(978-1-5247-0150-5(5))*; 2016. 9.99 *(978-0-553-52191-7(8))* Random Hse. Children's Bks. (Random Hse. Bks. for Young Readers).

—There's Nothing to Do! Petty, Dev. (ENG.). 32p. (J). (gr. -1-2). 2019. pap. 7.99 *(978-0-593-11897-9(9)*, Dragonfly Bks.); 2017. 16.99 *(978-0-399-55803-0(9)*, Doubleday Bks. for Young Readers); 2017. lib. bdg. 19.99 *(978-0-399-55804-7(7)*, Doubleday Bks. for Young Readers) Random Hse. Children's Bks.

—Tiara Saurus Rex. Sayres, Brianna Caplan. 2015. 32p. (J). (gr. -1-1). 16.99 *(978-1-61963-263-9(2)*, 9781619632639, Bloomsbury USA Childrens) Bloomsbury Publishing USA.

—Too Big to Hide. McAnulty, Stacy. 2016. (Dino Files Ser.: 2). 96p. (J). (gr. 2-5). 9.99 *(978-0-553-52194-8(2)*, Random Hse. Bks. for Young Readers) Random Hse. Children's Bks.

Boldt, Mike. Attack of the 50-Foot Fluffy. Boldt, Mike. 2018. (ENG.). 32p. (J). (gr. -1-3). 17.99 *(978-1-4814-4887-1(0)*, McElderry, Margaret K. Bks.) McElderry, Margaret K. Bks.

—Colors Versus Shapes. Boldt, Mike. 2014. (ENG.). 40p. (J). (gr. -1-3). 16.99 *(978-0-06-210303-1(2))* HarperCollins Pubs.

—A Tiger Tail: (or What Happened to Anya on Her First Day of School) Boldt, Mike. 2016. (ENG.). 40p. (J). (gr. -1-3). 17.99 *(978-1-4814-4885-7(4))* Simon & Schuster, Inc.

—123 Versus ABC. Boldt, Mike. 2013. (ENG.). 32p. (J). (gr. -1-3). 17.99 *(978-0-06-210299-7(0))* HarperCollins Pubs.

Boles, Diana. Mr. Bear Goes Nowhere. Garcia, Linda Jenkins. 2020. (ENG.). 24p. (J). pap. 13.95 ***(978-1-64531-734-0(X))*** Newman Springs Publishing, Inc.

Boles, Terry. I Can Do It! I Can Bowl!/I Can Ski!/I Can Do It All. Johns, Linda & Jones, Melanie Davis. 2006. (ENG.). 93p. (J). (gr. k-2). pap. 9.95 *(978-0-531-16923-0(5)*, Children's Pr.) Scholastic Library Publishing.

—I Can Ski! Jones, Melanie Davis. 2003. (Rookie Readers Ser.). 32p. (J). 19.50 *(978-0-516-22878-5(1)*, Children's Pr.) Scholastic Library Publishing.

Bolick, Brian. So, Where do all the teeth Go? Saunders, Helen. 2006. (J). *(978-0-9763143-3-2(9))* Happy Heart Kids Publishing.

Bolick Smith, Pamela. The Little Girl Who Saved the World. Lupton, Richard Gregg. 2019. (ENG.). 48p. (J). 25.95 ***(978-1-64569-141-9(1))***; pap. 15.95 ***(978-1-64349-715-0(4))*** Christian Faith Publishing.

Bolle, Frank. My Cat Merigold. Joy, Angelica. 2008. 56p. pap. 19.95 *(978-1-59858-591-9(6))* Dog Ear Publishing, LLC.

Bolle, Frank & Wilson, George. Man of the Atom. Newman, Paul S. 2005. (Doctor Solar Ser.: Vol. 3). (ENG.). 200p. 49.95 *(978-1-59307-374-9(7))* Dark Horse Comics.

Bollen, Roger. Honey Bunny's Honey Bear. Sadler, Marilyn. 2007. (Step into Reading Ser.). (ENG.). 32p. (J). (gr. -1-1). per. 4.99 *(978-0-375-84326-6(4)*, Random Hse. Bks. for Young Readers) Random Hse. Children's Bks.

—It's Not Easy Being a Bunny. Sadler, Marilyn. 2020. (ENG.). 26p. (J). (— 1). bds. 8.99 *(978-1-9848-9510-3(9)*, Random Hse. Bks. for Young Readers) Random Hse. Children's Bks.

—P. J. Funnybunny's Bag of Tricks. Sadler, Marilyn. 2005. (Step into Reading Ser.). 32p. 14.00 *(978-0-7569-5405-5(3))* Perfection Learning Corp.

—P. J. Funnybunny's Bag of Tricks. Sadler, Marilyn. 2004. (Step into Reading Ser.). 32p. (J). (gr. -1-1). pap. 4.99 *(978-0-375-82444-9(8)*, Random Hse. Bks. for Young Readers) Random Hse. Children's Bks.

Boller, David. Jared: Boy from the Bottom. Wallace, Patrick. 2003. 153p. (J). per. *(978-0-9740753-0-3(2))* Heritage Youth, Inc.

Boller, Gary. The Asteroid Excursion. Foxe, Steve. 2020. (Mr. Kazarian, Alien Librarian Ser.). (ENG.). 64p. (J). (gr. 3-5). lib. bdg. 21.99 ***(978-1-4965-8368-0(X)***, 140652, Stone Arch Bks.) Capstone.

Boller, Gary. The Black Hole Bandits. Foxe, Steve. 2020. (Mr. Kazarian, Alien Librarian Ser.). (ENG.). 64p. (J). (gr. 3-5). lib. bdg. 21.99 *(978-1-4965-8367-3(1)*, 140651, Stone Arch Bks.) Capstone.

Boller, Gary. Mr. Kazarian, Alien Librarian. Foxe, Steve. (Mr. Kazarian, Alien Librarian Ser.). (ENG.). (J). (gr. 3-5). 2020. 65.97 ***(978-1-5158-7353-2(6)***, 201810); 2020. pap., pap. 13.90 ***(978-1-5158-7352-5(8)***, 201809); 2020. 64p. pap. 6.95 *(978-1-4965-9341-2(3)*, 142359); 2019. 64p. 21.99 *(978-1-4965-8366-6(3)*, 140650) Capstone. (Stone Arch Bks.).

—Mr. Kazarian, Alien Librarian. 2020. (Mr. Kazarian, Alien Librarian Ser.). (ENG.). (J). (gr. 3-5). 43.98 ***(978-1-4965-8370-3(1)***, 177323, Stone Arch Bks.) Capstone.

Boller, Gary, jt. illus. see Bines, Gary.

Bolling, Vickey. Jesus Is My Special Friend. Balika, Susan S. 2013. (Happy Day Ser.). (ENG.). 16p. (J). pap. 2.49 *(978-1-4143-9294-3(X)*, 4608284) Tyndale Hse. Pubs.

—Jesus Is My Special Friend. Balika, Susan. 2003. 24p. (J). 2.49 *(978-0-7847-1270-2(0))* Standard Publishing.

Bollinger, Carol. The Misadventures of Our Son Henry. Owens, Robert & Owens, Donna. 2007. 52p. per. 16.95 *(978-1-4241-8721-8(4))* America Star Bks.

Bollinger, Peter. Basilosaurus. Zabludoff, Marc. 2010. (Prehistoric Beasts Ser.). 32p. (gr. 2-2). 30.93 *(978-0-7614-3999-8(4))* Cavendish Square Publishing LLC.

—Dire Wolf. Zabludoff, Marc. 2010. (Prehistoric Beasts Ser.). 32p. (gr. 2-2). 30.93 *(978-0-7614-3998-1(6))* Cavendish Square Publishing LLC.

—Doedicurus. Zabludoff, Marc. 2011. (Prehistoric Beasts Ser.). 32p. (gr. 2-2). 30.93 *(978-1-60870-033-2(X))* Cavendish Square Publishing LLC.

—Gastornis. Zabludoff, Marc. 2010. (Prehistoric Beasts Ser.). 32p. (gr. 2-2). 30.93 *(978-0-7614-4000-0(3))* Cavendish Square Publishing LLC.

—Giant Ground Sloth. Zabludoff, Marc. 2010. (Prehistoric Beasts Ser.). 32p. (gr. 2-2). 30.93 *(978-0-7614-3997-4(8))* Cavendish Square Publishing LLC.

—Hyracotherium. Zabludoff, Marc. 2011. (Prehistoric Beasts Ser.). 32p. (gr. 2-2). 30.93 *(978-1-60870-034-9(8))* Cavendish Square Publishing LLC.

—Kronosaurus. Zabludoff, Marc. 2011. (Prehistoric Beasts Ser.). 32p. (gr. 2-2). 30.93 *(978-1-60870-035-6(6))* Cavendish Square Publishing LLC.

—Mastodon. Zabludoff, Marc. 2011. (Prehistoric Beasts Ser.). 32p. (gr. 2-2). 30.93 *(978-1-60870-036-3(4))* Cavendish Square Publishing LLC.

—Saber-Toothed Cat. Zabludoff, Marc. 2011. (Prehistoric Beasts Ser.). 32p. (gr. 2-2). 30.93 *(978-1-60870-037-0(2))* Cavendish Square Publishing LLC.

—Space & the Planets. Hirschmann, Kris. 2003. (Magic School Bus Science Fact Finder Ser.). (ENG.). 96p. (J). (gr. 3-6). 16.19 *(978-0-439-38175-8(4))* Scholastic, Inc.

—Woolly Mammoth. Zabludoff, Marc. 2010. (Prehistoric Beasts Ser.). 32p. (gr. 2-2). 30.93 *(978-0-7614-3996-7(X))* Cavendish Square Publishing LLC.

Bollinger, Peter. Algernon Graeves Is Scary Enough. Bollinger, Peter. 2005. 32p. (J). (gr. -1-3). lib. bdg. 15.89 *(978-0-06-052269-8(0)*, Geringer, Laura Book) HarperCollins Pubs.

Bollinger/Papp. King Kong: Meet Kong & Ann. 2005. 32p. (J). lib. bdg. 13.85 *(978-1-4242-0615-5(4))* Fitzgerald Bks.

Bolliot, Joanna. Pompon. Elschner, Géraldine. 2017. (ENG.). 32p. (J). (gr. k-2). 17.99 *(978-988-8341-43-6(X)*, Minedition) Neugebauer, Michael (Publishing) Limited HKG. Dist: Penguin Random Hse. LLC.

Bolognese, Don. Dinosaur Hunter. Alphin, Elaine Marie. 2003. (I Can Read Bks.). (J). 48p. 15.99 *(978-0-06-028303-2(3))*; 64p. (gr. 2-3). 16.89 *(978-0-06-028304-9(1))* HarperCollins Pubs.

—Dinosaur Hunter. Alphin, Elaine Marie. 2004. (I Can Read Bks.). 48p. (gr. 2-4). 14.00 *(978-0-7569-3241-1(6))* Perfection Learning Corp.

—Dinosaur Hunter: I Can Read Level 4. Alphin, Elaine Marie. 2004. 48p. (J). pap. 3.99 *(978-1-68432-078-3(X)*, HarperCollins) HarperCollins Pubs.

Bolognese, Don. First Flight: The Story of Tom Tate & the Wright Brothers. Shea, George. 2003. (I Can Read Level 4 Ser.). (ENG.). 48p. (J). (gr. k-3). pap. 4.99 ***(978-0-06-444215-2(2))*** HarperCollins Pubs.

Bolognese, Don. The Warhorse. Bolognese, Don. 2010. (ENG.). 176p. (J). (gr. 5-9). pap. 9.99 *(978-1-4424-2942-0(9)*, Simon & Schuster Bks. For Young Readers) Simon & Schuster Bks. For Young Readers.

Bolshakov, Mary Jane. Frankenslime. Buras, Shelle. 2018. (ENG.). 38p. (J). pap. 12.00 *(978-1-7295-1811-3(7))* CreateSpace Independent Publishing Platform.

Bolster, Rob. The Addition Book. Pallotta, Jerry. 2006. 32p. (J). *(978-0-439-89637-5(1))* Scholastic, Inc.

—The Construction Alphabet Book. Pallotta, Jerry. 2006. (Jerry Pallotta's Alphabet Bks.). 32p. (J). (gr. -1-3). lib. bdg. 17.95 *(978-1-57091-437-9(0))*; per. 7.95 *(978-1-57091-438-6(9))* Charlesbridge Publishing, Inc.

—Count by Fives. Pallotta, Jerry. 2008. 32p. (J). *(978-0-545-00245-5(1))* Scholastic, Inc.

—Count by Tens. Pallotta, Jerry. 2008. 32p. (J). *(978-0-545-07068-3(6))* Scholastic, Inc.

—Going Lobstering. Pallotta, Jerry. 2008. 20p. (J). (gr. -1-3). bds. 7.95 *(978-1-57091-623-6(3))* Charlesbridge Publishing, Inc.

—Hammerhead vs. Bull Shark. Pallotta, Jerry. 2016. (Who Would Win? Ser.). (ENG.). 32p. (J). (gr. 1-3). pap. 3.99 *(978-0-545-30170-1(X))* Scholastic, Inc.

—Hershey's Weights & Measures. Pallotta, Jerry. 2003. (Hershey's Ser.). (ENG.). 32p. (J). 16.99 *(978-0-439-38876-4(7)*, Cartwheel Bks.) Scholastic, Inc.

—Jaguar vs. Skunk. Pallotta, Jerry. 2017. 32p. (J). *(978-1-338-20629-6(X))* Scholastic, Inc.

—Killer Whale vs. Great White Shark. Pallotta, Jerry. 2016. (Who Would Win? Ser.). (ENG.). 32p. (J). (gr. 2-5). pap. 3.99 *(978-0-545-16075-9(8))* Scholastic, Inc.

—Komodo Dragon vs. King Cobra. Pallotta, Jerry. 2016. (Who Would Win? Ser.). (ENG.). 32p. (J). (gr. 1-3). pap. 3.99 *(978-0-545-30171-8(8))* Scholastic, Inc.

—Lion vs. Tiger. Pallotta, Jerry. 2016. (Who Would Win? Ser.). (ENG.). 32p. (J). (gr. 2-5). pap. 3.99 *(978-0-545-17571-5(2))* Scholastic, Inc.

—Multiplication. Pallotta, Jerry. 2008. 32p. (J). *(978-0-545-00686-6(4))* Scholastic, Inc.

—Pizza Fractions. Pallotta, Jerry. 2007. 32p. (J). pap. *(978-0-545-00687-3(2))* Scholastic, Inc.

—Polar Bear vs. Grizzly Bear. Pallotta, Jerry. 2015. (Who Would Win? Ser.). (ENG.). (J). (gr. 1-3). pap. 3.99 *(978-0-545-17572-2(0))* Scholastic, Inc.

—The Subtraction Book. Pallotta, Jerry. 2007. 32p. (J). *(978-0-439-89638-2(X))* Scholastic, Inc.

—Tarantula vs. Scorpion. Pallotta, Jerry. 2016. (Who Would Win? Ser.). (ENG.). 32p. (J). (gr. 1-3). pap. 3.99 *(978-0-545-30172-5(6))* Scholastic, Inc.

—Tyrannosaurus Rex vs. Velociraptor. Pallotta, Jerry. 2016. (Who Would Win? Ser.). (ENG.). 32p. (J). (gr. 1-3). pap. 3.99 *(978-0-545-17573-9(9))* Scholastic, Inc.

—U. S. Navy Alphabet Book. Garnett, Sammie & Pallotta, Jerry. 2004. (Jerry Pallotta's Alphabet Bks.). 32p. (J). (gr. -1-3). pap. 7.95 *(978-1-57091-587-1(3))* Charlesbridge Publishing, Inc.

—Weights & Measures. Pallotta, Jerry. 2008. 32p. (J). pap. *(978-0-545-06448-4(1))* Scholastic, Inc.

—Whale vs. Giant Squid. Pallotta, Jerry. 2016. (Who Would Win? Ser.). (ENG.). 32p. (J). (gr. 1-3). pap. 3.99 *(978-0-545-30173-2(4))* Scholastic, Inc.

—Who Would Win?: Battle Royale. Pallotta, Jerry. 2018. (ENG.). 160p. (J). (gr. 1-3). 9.99 *(978-1-338-20677-7(X))* Scholastic, Inc.

Bolt, Susan Collier. Gadoo the Cat: An Armenian Folktale. Gopigian, Susan Kadian. 2008. 39p. 16.95 *(978-0-9801453-0-4(9))* Wayne State Univ. Pr.

Bolton, Bill. How Heavy? Wacky Ways to Compare Weight, 1 vol. Weakland, Mark. 2013. (Wacky Comparisons Ser.). (ENG.). 24p. (J). (gr. -1-2). 28.65 *(978-1-4048-8322-2(3))*; pap. 8.95 *(978-1-4795-1912-5(X))* Capstone. (Picture Window Bks.).

—It Only Takes a Minute. Goetz, Bracha. 2017. (ENG.). 22p. (J). 10.95 *(978-1-945560-02-6(9))* Hachai Publishing.

—My Magnetic Counting Book: Ten Dancing Dinosaurs. 2006. (Magnix Learning Fun Ser.). 12p. (J). (gr. -1-3). 9.95 *(978-1-932915-16-7(8))* Sandvik Innovations, LLC.

—Santa's Christmas Train. James, Helen Foster. 2019. (ENG.). 26p. (J). (gr. -1-1). bds. 7.99 *(978-1-5460-1434-8(9)*, Worthy Kids/Ideals) Worthy Publishing.

Bolton-Eells, Sharon. Amelia, A to Z. Hicks, Rob & Hicks, Kim. 2011. (J). *(978-0-9829908-0-3(4))* Island Media Publishing, LLC.

Bolton, Georgia Helen, jt. illus. see Ballard, George Anne.

Bolton, John, et al. X-Men Classic: the Complete Collection Vol. 2. 2019. (ENG.). 520p. (YA). (gr. 4-17). pap. 39.99 *(978-1-302-92058-6(8))* Marvel Worldwide, Inc.

Bolton, Kyle. SMASH 2: Fearless. Bolton, Chris A. 2018. 160p. (J). (gr. 4-7). 18.99 *(978-0-7636-8118-0(0))*; pap. 11.99 *(978-1-5362-0035-5(2))* Candlewick Pr.

—SMASH: Trial by Fire. Bolton, Chris A. 2018. 160p. (J). (gr. 4-7). pap. 11.99 *(978-0-7636-5406-1(X))* Candlewick Pr.

—Trial by Fire. Bolton, Chris A. 2013. 160p. (J). (gr. 4-7). 18.99 *(978-0-7636-5596-9(1))* Candlewick Pr.

Bolton, Marie. The Teeth Thief. Mallender, Mark. 2017. (ENG.). (J). pap. *(978-1-911589-38-9(5)*, Choir Pr., The) Action Publishing Technology Ltd.

Bolund, Inna. Amanda the Panda, 1 vol. Finch, Donna. 2009. (ENG.). 27p. pap. 24.95 *(978-1-61546-797-6(1))* America Star Bks.

Boman, Erik, photos by. Blahnik by Boman: Shoes, Photographs, Conversation. Blahnik, Manolo. 2005. (ENG., 224p. (gr. 8-17). 85.00 *(978-0-8118-5116-9(8))* Chronicle Bks. LLC.

Bomboland. Paper World: Planet Earth. Bomboland. 2019. (ENG.). 30p. (J). (gr. 3-7). 24.99 *(978-1-5362-0854-2(X)*, Big Picture Press) Candlewick Pr.

Bonadonna, Davide & Keitzmueller, Christian. Uncover a T. Rex. Schatz, Dennis. 2020. (Uncover Ser.). (ENG.). 16p. (J). (gr. 3-7). 22.99 *(978-1-68412-551-7(0)*, Silver Dolphin Bks.) Printers Row Publishing Group.

Bonadonna, Davide & Kitzmüller, Christian. Uncover a Shark. Gordon, David George. 2020. (Uncover Ser.). (ENG.). 16p. (J). (gr. 3-7). 22.99 *(978-1-68412-550-0(2)*, Silver Dolphin Bks.) Printers Row Publishing Group.

Bonatti, Marco. Pink. Doering, Amanda. 2018. (Sing Your Colors! Ser.). (ENG.). 24p. (J). (gr. -1-2). 33.99 *(978-1-68410-315-7(0)*, 140700); lib. bdg. 33.99 incl. audio compact disk *(978-1-68410-140-5(9)*, 31849) Cantata Learning.

Bonatti, Marco, et al. Sing Your Colors! Doering, Amanda & Hoena, Blake. 2018. (Sing Your Colors! Ser.). (ENG.). (J). (gr. -1-2). 271.92 *(978-1-68410-439-0(4)*, 29690) Cantata Learning.

Bonavita, Madison M. Theo's Special Gift. Martin, Candice J. l.t. ed. 2006. 12p. (J). per. 12.99 *(978-1-59879-190-7(7))* Lifevest Publishing, Inc.

B

Bond, Anna. Alice's Adventures in Wonderland. Carroll, Lewis. 150th anniv. ed. 2015. 192p. (J). (gr. 5). 30.00 *(978-0-14-751587-2(4),* Puffin Books) Penguin Young Readers Group.

Bond, Bob. President Lincoln Listened: A Story of Compassion. Moody, Dwight Lyman. 2006. (Story Time Ser.). (ENG.). 24p. (J). (gr. -1-4). 7.99 *(978-1-84550-115-0(2),* c185cb21-b466-47e7-9535-8abc701d88be) Christian Focus Pubns. GBR. Dist: Baker & Taylor Publisher Services (BTPS).

Bond, Brooke. The World Caught a Germ. Goldspink, Hannah. 2020. (ENG.). 40p. (J). ***(978-0-2288-3216-4(0));*** pap. ***(978-0-2288-3215-7(2))*** Tellwell Talent.

Bond, Clint & Clark, Andy. The Great Snail Race. Ostrow, Kim. ed. 2005. (SpongeBob SquarePants Ser.: No. 6). 22p. (J). lib. bdg. 15.00 *(978-1-59054-830-1(2))* Fitzgerald Bks.

—The Great Snail Race. 2005. (SpongeBob SquarePants Ser.). (ENG.). 24p. (J). pap. 3.99 *(978-0-689-87313-3(1),* Simon Spotlight/Nickelodeon) Simon Spotlight/Nickelodeon.

Bond, Denny. The Baby Bunny. Hillert, Margaret. 2016. (BeginningtoRead Ser.). (ENG.). 32p. (J). (gr. -1-2). pap. 11.94 *(978-1-60357-934-6(6));* (gr. k-2). 22.60 *(978-1-59953-793-1(1))* Norwood Hse. Pr.

—Mary, Did You Know? Lowry, Mark & Greene, Buddy. 2005. 24p. (J). (gr. -1-k). bds. 9.99 incl. audio compact disk *(978-1-57791-176-0(8))* Brighter Minds Children's Publishing.

Bond, Felicia. The Best Mouse Cookie. Numeroff, Laura. 2006. (If You Give... Ser.). (ENG.). 32p. (J). (gr. -1-2). 9.99 *(978-0-06-113760-0(X))* HarperCollins Pubs.

—The Best Mouse Cookie Board Book. Numeroff, Laura. 2019. (If You Give... Ser.). (ENG.). 24p. (J). (gr. -1 — 1). bds. 7.99 *(978-0-694-01270-1(X),* HarperCollins) HarperCollins Pubs. Ltd. GBR. Dist: HarperCollins Pubs.

—The Best Mouse Cookie Padded Board Book. Numeroff, Laura. 2018. (If You Give... Ser.). (ENG.). 24p. (J). (gr. -1 — 1). bds. 9.99 *(978-0-06-284483-5(0))* HarperCollins Pubs.

—Christmas in the Manger Padded Board Book. Buck, Nola. 2018. (ENG.). 18p. (J). (gr. -1 — 1). bds. 9.99 *(978-0-06-286347-8(9))* HarperCollins Pubs.

—El Gran Granero Rojo: Big Red Barn Board Book (Spanish Edition), 1 vol. Brown, Margaret Wise. 2003.Tr. of Big Red Barn. (SPA.). 34p. (J). (gr. -1-3). bds. 7.99 *(978-0-06-009107-1(X),* HarperCollins Español) HarperCollins Christian Publishing.

—Happy Birthday, Mouse! Numeroff, Laura. 2020. (If You Give... Ser.). (ENG.). 24p. (J). (gr. -1 — 1). bds. 7.99 *(978-0-694-01425-5(7),* Balzer & Bray) HarperCollins Pubs.

—Happy Easter, Mouse! Numeroff, Laura. 2019. (If You Give... Ser.). (ENG.). 24p. (J). (gr. -1 — 1). bds. 7.99 *(978-0-694-01422-4(2),* Balzer & Bray) HarperCollins Pubs.

—Happy Valentine's Day, Mouse! Numeroff, Laura. 2019. (If You Give... Ser.). (ENG.). 24p. (J). (gr. -1 — 1). bds. 7.99 *(978-0-06-180432-8(0),* Balzer & Bray) HarperCollins Pubs.

—Happy Valentine's Day, Mouse! Lap Edition. Numeroff, Laura. 2015. (If You Give... Ser.). (ENG.). 24p. (J). (gr. -1-3). bds. 12.99 *(978-0-06-242740-3(7))* HarperCollins Pubs.

—If You Give a Bear a Brownie: Book & Doll. Numeroff, Laura Joffe. Date not set. (J). 19.99 *(978-0-694-01423-1(0))* HarperCollins Pubs.

—If You Give a Bear a Brownie Recipes. Numeroff, Laura Joffe. Date not set. 32p. (J). (gr. -1-2). 12.99 *(978-0-06-028559-3(1))* HarperCollins Pubs.

—If You Give a Cat a Cupcake. Numeroff, Laura Joffe. 2008. (If You Give... Ser.). 32p. (J). (gr. -1-3). lib. bdg. 17.89 *(978-0-06-028325-4(4))* HarperCollins Pubs.

—If You Give a Cat a Cupcake. Numeroff, Laura. 2008. (If You Give... Ser.). (ENG.). 32p. (J). (gr. -1-3). 17.99 *(978-0-06-028324-7(6))* HarperCollins Pubs.

—If You Give a Cat a Cupcake: Book & Doll. Numeroff, Laura Joffe. Date not set. (If You Give... Ser.). (J). 19.99 *(978-0-694-01431-6(1))* HarperCollins Pubs.

—If You Give a Cat a Cupcake Recipes. Numeroff, Laura Joffe. Date not set. 32p. (J). (gr. -1-2). 12.99 *(978-0-06-028560-9(5))* HarperCollins Pubs.

—If You Give a Dog a Donut. Numeroff, Laura. 2011. (If You Give... Ser.). (ENG.). 32p. (J). (gr. -1-3). 17.99 *(978-0-06-026683-7(X));* 17.89 *(978-0-06-026684-4(8))* HarperCollins Pubs.

—If You Give a Moose a Muffin. Numeroff, Laura Joffe. Date not set. (J). bds. 6.99 *(978-0-694-01426-2(5))* HarperCollins Pubs.

—If You Give a Moose a Muffin: Book & Doll. Numeroff, Laura Joffe. Date not set. (J). 19.99 *(978-0-694-01421-7(4))* HarperCollins Pubs.

—If You Give a Moose a Muffin Recipe Book. Numeroff, Laura Joffe. Date not set. 32p. (J). (gr. -1-2). 12.99 *(978-0-06-028562-3(1))* HarperCollins Pubs.

—If You Give a Mouse a Brownie. Numeroff, Laura. 2016. (If You Give... Ser.). (ENG.). 32p. (J). (gr. -1-3). 17.99 *(978-0-06-027571-6(5));* lib. bdg. 18.89 *(978-0-06-027572-3(3))* HarperCollins Pubs.

—If You Give a Mouse a Cookie. Numeroff, Laura Joffe. Date not set. 32p. (J). (gr. -1-2). 4.95 *(978-0-06-443166-8(5))* HarperCollins Pubs.

—If You Give a Mouse a Cookie. Numeroff, Laura Joffe. 25th anniv. ed. 2015. (If You Give... Ser.). (ENG.). 40p. (J). (gr. -1-3). 17.99 *(978-0-06-024586-3(7),* HarperCollins) HarperCollins Pubs. Ltd. GBR. Dist: HarperCollins Pubs.

—If You Give a Pig a Pancake. Numeroff, Laura Joffe. Date not set. (J). 6.99 *(978-0-694-01430-9(3))* HarperCollins Pubs.

—If You Give a Pig a Party. Numeroff, Laura. 2005. (If You Give... Ser.). (ENG.). 32p. (J). (gr. -1-2). lib. bdg. 17.89 *(978-0-06-028327-8(0))* HarperCollins Pubs.

—If You Give a Pig a Party. Numeroff, Laura. 2005. (If You Give... Ser.). (ENG.). 32p. (J). (gr. -1-2). 17.99 *(978-0-06-028326-1(2),* HarperCollins) HarperCollins Pubs. Ltd. GBR. Dist: HarperCollins Pubs.

—If You Give a Pig a Pumpkin: Book & Doll. Numeroff, Laura Joffe. Date not set. (J). 19.99 *(978-0-694-01432-3(X))* HarperCollins Pubs.

—If You Take a Mouse to the Movies: a Special Christmas Edition. Numeroff, Laura. ed. 2009. (If You Give... Ser.). (ENG.). 72p. (J). (gr. -1-3). 18.99 *(978-0-06-176280-2(6))* HarperCollins Pubs.

—It's Pumpkin Day, Mouse! Numeroff, Laura. 2019. (If You Give... Ser.). (ENG.). 24p. (J). (gr. -1 — 1). bds. 7.99 *(978-0-694-01429-3(X),* Balzer & Bray) HarperCollins Pubs.

—Merry Christmas, Mouse! Numeroff, Laura. 2019. (If You Give... Ser.). (ENG.). 24p. (J). (gr. -1 — 1). bds. 7.99 *(978-0-06-134499-2(0),* HarperCollins) HarperCollins Pubs. Ltd. GBR. Dist: HarperCollins Pubs.

—Moose Stroller Songs. Numeroff, Laura Joffe. Date not set. (J). 9.99 *(978-0-694-01424-8(9))* HarperCollins Pubs.

—Mouse Cookie Delights: 3 Board Book Bites: The Best Mouse Cookie; Happy Birthday, Mouse!; Time for School, Mouse! Numeroff, Laura. 2020. (If You Give... Ser.). (ENG.). 72p. (J). (gr. -1 — 1). pap. 22.97 *(978-0-06-298394-7(6),* Balzer & Bray) HarperCollins Pubs.

—A Mouse Cookie First Library. Numeroff, Laura. 2007. (If You Give... Ser.). (ENG.). 100p. (J). (gr. -1-2). bds. 15.99 *(978-0-06-117479-7(3),* HarperFestival) HarperCollins Pubs.

—Mouse Cookies & More: A Treasury. Numeroff, Laura. 2015. (If You Give... Ser.). (ENG.). 224p. (J). (gr. -1-3). 24.99 *(978-0-06-113763-1(4),* HarperCollins) HarperCollins Pubs. Ltd. GBR. Dist: HarperCollins Pubs.

—Pig Pancakes. Numeroff, Laura Joffe. Date not set. 32p. (J). (gr. -1-2). 1.00 *(978-0-06-028563-0(X))* HarperCollins Pubs.

—Pig Stroller Songs. Numeroff, Laura Joffe. Date not set. (J). 10.99 *(978-0-694-01428-6(1))* HarperCollins Pubs.

—Si le das un Pastelito a un Gato: If You Give a Cat a Cupcake (Spanish Edition), 1 vol. Numeroff, Laura. 2010. (If You Give... Ser.). (SPA.). 32p. (J). (gr. -1-3). 16.99 *(978-0-06-180431-1(2),* HarperCollins Español) HarperCollins Christian Publishing.

—Si le Haces una Fiesta a una Cerdita: If You Give a Pig a Party (Spanish Edition), 1 vol. Numeroff, Laura. 2006. (If You Give... Ser.).Tr. of If You Give a Pig a Party. (SPA.). 32p. (J). (gr. -1-3). 16.99 *(978-0-06-081532-5(9),* HarperCollins Español) HarperCollins Christian Publishing.

—Si Llevas un Ratón a la Escuela: If You Take a Mouse to School (Spanish Edition), 1 vol. Numeroff, Laura. 2003. (If You Give... Ser.).Tr. of If You Take a Mouse to School. (SPA.). 32p. (J). (gr. -1-3). 17.99 *(978-0-06-052340-4(9),* HarperCollins Español) HarperCollins Christian Publishing.

—Time for School, Mouse! Numeroff, Laura. 2019. (If You Give... Ser.). (ENG.). 24p. (J). (gr. -1 — 1). bds. 7.99 *(978-0-06-143307-8(1),* HarperCollins) HarperCollins Pubs. Ltd. GBR. Dist: HarperCollins Pubs.

—Time for School, Mouse! Lap Edition. Numeroff, Laura. 2016. (If You Give... Ser.). (ENG.). 24p. (J). (gr. -1-3). bds. 12.99 *(978-0-06-242741-0(5))* HarperCollins Pubs.

Bond, Felicia. Big Hugs Little Hugs. Bond, Felicia. 2013. 30p. (J). (gr. -1-k). bds. 7.99 *(978-0-399-16206-0(2),* Philomel Bks.) Penguin Young Readers Group.

—Day It Rained Hearts. Bond, Felicia. 2006. (ENG.). 36p. (J). (gr. -1-3). pap. 7.99 *(978-0-06-073123-6(0))* HarperCollins Pubs.

—The Halloween Play. Bond, Felicia. Orig. Title: The Halloween Performance. 32p. (J). (gr. -1-1). 2008. (ENG.). pap. 7.99 *(978-0-06-135796-1(0));* 2003. 6.99 *(978-0-06-054443-0(0))* HarperCollins Pubs.

—Poinsettia & the Firefighters. Bond, Felicia. 2003. (J). *(978-0-06-056871-9(2))* HarperCollins Pubs.

Bond, Felicia, jt. illus. see Cole, Henry.

Bond, Ganna. The Super Cute Activity Book for Girls: Join the Dots - Mazes - Coloring - Word Search - Spot the Difference - Ages 4-8. Meane, Jinarta. 2019. (Super Cute Activity Bks.: Vol. 1). (ENG.). 78p. (J). pap. 6.99 *(978-1-0807-5196-9(3))* Independently Published.

Bond, Higgins. Alphabet of Space. Galvin, Laura Gates. (ENG.). 40p. 2009. 9.95 *(978-1-59249-990-8(2));* 2007. (J). (gr. -1-k). 15.95 *(978-1-59249-656-3(3))* Soundprints.

—Groundhog at Evergreen Road. Korman, Susan. 2003. (Smithsonian's Backyard (PB) Ser.). (ENG.). (J). (gr. -1-2). lib. bdg. 17.55 *(978-0-7569-3496-5(6))* Perfection Learning Corp.

—Groundhog at Evergreen Road. Korman, Susan. (Smithsonian's Backyard Ser.). (ENG.). 32p. (J). (gr. -1-2). 2005. 15.95 *(978-1-59249-022-6(0),* BA5024); 2003. 19.95 *(978-1-59249-025-7(5),* BC5024); 2003. 8.95 *(978-1-59249-061-5(1),* SC5024); 2003. 4.95 *(978-1-59249-023-3(9),* BB5074); 2003. 6.95 *(978-1-59249-024-0(7),* S5024) Soundprints.

—Handshake in Space: The Apollo-Soyuz Test Project. Tan, Sheri. 2009. 32p. (J). (gr. 1-5). pap. 9.95 incl. audio *(978-1-60727-104-8(4));* (ENG.). 9.95 *(978-1-60727-115-4(X));* (ENG.). 17.95 *(978-1-60727-114-7(1));* pap. 9.95 incl. reel tape *(978-1-59249-203-9(7))* Soundprints.

—Lorraine. Secor, Ketch. 2018. 32p. (J). (-4). 17.99 *(978-1-4926-1692-4(3))* Sourcebooks, Inc.

—The Mighty Mississippi: The Life & Times of America's Greatest River. Vieira, Linda. 2005. (J). *(978-7-80802-789-7(8))* Walker & Co.

—A Place for Bats, 1 vol. Stewart, Melissa. (ENG.). 32p. (J). 2012. 16.95 *(978-1-56145-624-6(1));* 2017. (Place For... Ser.: 5). (gr. 1-5). 16.95 *(978-1-56145-762-5(0))* Peachtree Publishing Co. Inc.

—A Place for Birds, 1 vol. Stewart, Melissa. (ENG.). 32p. (J). (gr. 1-5). 2009. 16.95 *(978-1-56145-474-7(5));* 2015. (Place For... Ser.: 2). 16.95 *(978-1-56145-839-4(2))* Peachtree Publishing Co. Inc.

—A Place for Butterflies, 1 vol. Stewart, Melissa. (ENG.). 32p. (J). (gr. 1-5). 2006. 16.95 *(978-1-56145-357-3(9));* 2nd rev. ed. 2014. (Place For... Ser.: 1). pap. 7.99 *(978-1-56145-784-7(1))* Peachtree Publishing Co. Inc.

—A Place for Fish, 1 vol. Stewart, Melissa. (ENG.). 32p. (J). (gr. 1-5). 2011. 16.95 *(978-1-56145-562-1(8));* 2018. (Place For Ser.: 4). 16.95 *(978-1-68263-011-2(0));* 2018. (Place For Ser.: 4). pap. 7.95 *(978-1-68263-012-9(9))* Peachtree Publishing Co. Inc.

—A Place for Frogs, 1 vol. Stewart, Melissa. rev. ed. 2016. (Place For... Ser.: 3). (ENG.). 32p. (J). (gr. 1-5). 16.95 *(978-1-56145-901-8(1))* Peachtree Publishing Co. Inc.

—A Place for Turtles. Stewart, Melissa. rev. ed. 2019. (Place For... Ser.: 6). (ENG.). 32p. (J). (gr. 1-5). 16.95 *(978-1-68263-096-9(X));* pap. 7.95 *(978-1-68263-097-6(8))* Peachtree Publishing Co. Inc.

—Please Don't Wake the Animals: A Book about Sleep, 1 vol. Batten, Mary. 2008. (ENG.). 32p. (J). (gr. k-3). 16.95 *(978-1-56145-393-1(5))* Peachtree Publishing Co. Inc.

—Trails above the Tree Line: A Story of a Rocky Mountain Meadow. Fraggalosch, Audrey. 2005. (Soundprints' Wild Habitats Ser.). (ENG.). (J). (gr. 1-4). 36p. 15.95 *(978-1-56899-941-8(0),* B7021); 32p. pap. 6.95 *(978-1-56899-942-5(9),* S7021) Soundprints.

—Who Has a Belly Button?, 1 vol. Batten, Mary. 2003. (ENG.). 32p. (J). (gr. 1-5). 15.95 *(978-1-56145-235-4(1))* Peachtree Publishing Co. Inc.

Bond, Nancy. Career Ideas for Kids Who Like Animals & Nature. Reeves, Diane Lindsey. 2nd rev. ed. 2007. (Career Ideas for Kids Ser.). 208p. (gr. 4-9). 32.95 *(978-0-8160-6539-4(X),* Ferguson Publishing Co.) Facts On File, Inc.

—Career Ideas for Kids Who Like Art. Reeves, Diane Lindsey. 2nd rev. ed. 2007. (Career Ideas for Kids Ser.). 208p. (gr. 4-9). 32.95 *(978-0-8160-6541-7(1),* Ferguson Publishing Co.) Facts On File, Inc.

—Career Ideas for Kids Who Like Math & Money. Reeves, Diane Lindsey. 2nd rev. ed. 2007. (Career Ideas for Kids Ser.). 208p. (gr. 4-9). 32.95 *(978-0-8160-6545-5(4),* Ferguson Publishing Co.); per. 16.95 *(978-0-8160-6546-2(2),* Checkmark Bks.) Facts On File, Inc.

—Career Ideas for Kids Who Like Science. Reeves, Diane Lindsey. 2nd rev. ed. 2007. (Career Ideas for Kids Ser.). 208p. (gr. 4-9). 32.95 *(978-0-8160-6549-3(7),* Checkmark Bks.) Facts On File, Inc.

—Career Ideas for Kids Who Like Sports. Reeves, Diane Lindsey. 2nd rev. ed. 2007. (Career Ideas for Kids Ser.). 208p. (gr. 4-9). lib. bdg. 32.95 *(978-0-8160-6551-6(9),* Checkmark Bks.) Facts On File, Inc.

—Career Ideas for Kids Who Like Talking. Reeves, Diane Lindsey. 2nd rev. ed. 2007. (Career Ideas for Kids Ser.). 208p. (gr. 4-9). 32.95 *(978-0-8160-6553-0(5),* Checkmark Bks.) Facts On File, Inc.

—Career Ideas for Kids Who Like Writing. Reeves, Diane Lindsey & Clasen, Lindsey. 2nd rev. ed. 2007. (Career Ideas for Kids Ser.). 208p. (gr. 4-9). 32.95 *(978-0-8160-6555-4(1),* Ferguson Publishing Co.) Facts On File, Inc.

Bond, Nancy. Career Ideas for Kids Who Like Computers. Bond, Nancy. Reeves, Diane Lindsey & Clasen, Lindsey. 2nd rev. ed. 2007. (Career Ideas for Kids Ser.). 208p. (gr. 4-9). 32.95 *(978-0-8160-6543-1(8),* Ferguson Publishing Co.) Facts On File, Inc.

Bond, Rebecca. The House That George Built. Slade, Suzanne. 32p. (J). (gr. 1-4). 2015. pap. 7.95 *(978-1-58089-263-6(9));* 2012. 16.95 *(978-1-58089-262-9(0))* Charlesbridge Publishing, Inc.

Bond, Rebecca. Escape from Baxters' Barn. Bond, Rebecca. 2017. (ENG.). 256p. (J). (gr. 3-7). pap. 7.99 *(978-1-328-74093-9(5),* 1677137, HMH Books For Young Readers) Houghton Mifflin Harcourt Publishing Co.

—Pig & Goose & the First Day of Spring. Bond, Rebecca. 2017. 48p. (J). (gr. k-3). lib. bdg. 12.99 *(978-1-58089-594-1(8))* Charlesbridge Publishing, Inc.

Bonder, Dianna. Black & White Blanche, 1 vol. Toews, Marj. 2006. (ENG.). 32p. (J). (gr. -1-3). 9.95 *(978-1-55005-132-2(6),* 5af68e02-0985-4617-b463-aaeed8f0f093) Trifolium Bks., Inc. CAN. Dist: Firefly Bks., Ltd.

—Digging Canadian Dinosaurs, 1 vol. Grambo, Rebecca L. 2004. (ENG.). 64p. (J). (gr. 2-6). pap. 16.95 *(978-1-55285-395-5(0),* b53753ea-3f24-4f72-b028-28421c051e7d) Whitecap Bks., Ltd. CAN. Dist: Firefly Bks., Ltd.

—Leon's Song, 1 vol. McLellan, Stephanie Simpson. 2004. (ENG.). 32p. (J). (gr. -1-3). *(978-1-55041-813-2(0))* Fitzhenry & Whiteside, Ltd.

—Leon's Song, 1 vol. Simpson McLellan, Stephanie. 2005. (ENG.). 32p. (J). (gr. -1-2). pap. 7.95 *(978-1-55041-815-6(7),* cf755b5b-6ddf-41c8-b526-ec23d03a8e69) Fitzhenry & Whiteside, Ltd. CAN. Dist: Firefly Bks., Ltd.

—A Pacific Alphabet, 1 vol. Ruurs, Margriet. 2004. (ENG.). 32p. (J). (gr. -1-2). 9.95 *(978-1-55285-264-4(4),* d7c2886c-39f9-4bd7-bd97-eaa6c73e7668) Whitecap Bks., Ltd. CAN. Dist: Firefly Bks., Ltd.

—Pedro, the Pirate. Hoppey, Tim. 2012. (ENG & SPA.). 32p. (J). lib. bdg. 16.95 *(978-1-936299-18-8(6),* Raven Tree Pr.,Csi) Continental Sales, Inc.

—The Pied Piper of Hamelin: A German Folktale. StJohn, Amanda. 2011. (Folktales from Around the World Ser.). (ENG.). 24p. (J). (gr. k-3). 28.50 *(978-1-60973-142-7(5),* 201146) Child's World, Inc., The.

Bonder, Dianna. Accidental Alphabet, 1 vol. Bonder, Dianna. 2nd ed. 2004. (ENG.). 32p. (J). (gr. -1-2). pap. 8.95 *(978-1-55285-596-6(1),* 5d84bdad-e4ee-42e5-bdd5-e16039147aa4) Whitecap Bks., Ltd. CAN. Dist: Firefly Bks., Ltd.

—Dogabet, 1 vol. Bonder, Dianna. (ENG.). 32p. (J). 2011. (gr. k-2). pap. 8.95 *(978-1-55285-940-7(1),* aef92a0f-1b42-4f2b-9fd7-7169bc81c401); 2007. (gr. -1-2). 19.95 *(978-1-55285-797-7(2),* 4eb9088e-6708-4ee4-b2f8-bf52682e23e5, Walrus Bks.) Whitecap Bks., Ltd. CAN. Dist: Firefly Bks., Ltd.

Bondestam, Linda. My Little Small. 2018. (ENG.). 52p. (J). (gr. -1-3). 15.95 *(978-1-59270-209-1(0))* Enchanted Lion Bks., LLC.

Bondoc, Elmo, et al. Ms. Marvel: Metamorphosis. 2019. 232p. (J). (gr. 4-7). pap. 12.99 *(978-1-302-91808-8(7))* Marvel Worldwide, Inc.

Bondoc, Elmo, jt. illus. see Greene, Sanford.

Bondy, Jeremy. The Secret to Clara's Calm. Levitt, Tamara. 2017. (ENG.). 36p. (J). 15.95 *(978-1-61429-390-3(2))* Wisdom Pubns.

Bone, J. The Collected Alison Dare Little Miss Adventures. Torres, J. 2005. (J). *(978-1-4156-1359-7(1))* Oni Pr., Inc.

Boné, Thomas H. The Teacher Who Would Not Retire Becomes a Movie Star. 2012. (J). *(978-0-9792918-6-9(0))* Blue Marlin Pubns.

—The Teacher Who Would Not Retire Discovers a New Planet. 2009. (J). 17.95 *(978-0-9792918-3-8(6))* Blue Marlin Pubns.

—The Teacher Who Would Not Retire Goes to Camp. 2005. (J). *(978-0-9674602-7-7(1))* Blue Marlin Pubns.

—The Teacher Who Would Not Retire Retires. 2017. (J). *(978-0-9885295-7-1(2))* Blue Marlin Pubns.

Bone, Thomas H. & LeTourneau, Anthony Alex. Mama, Can Armadillos Swim? 2004. (J). 17.00 *(978-0-9674602-6-0(3))* Blue Marlin Pubns.

Bonet, Roger, jt. illus. see Sandoval, Rafa.

Bonet, Xavier. The Boy Who Was It: And Other Scary Tales. Dahl, Michael. 2016. (Michael Dahl's Really Scary Stories Ser.). (ENG.). 72p. (J). (gr. 1-3). lib. bdg. 25.32 *(978-1-4965-3772-0(6),* Stone Arch Bks.) Capstone.

Bonet, Xavier. Cuentos Escalofriantes de Michael Dahl. Dahl, Michael. 2020. (Cuentos Escalofriantes de Michael Dahl Ser.).Tr. of Michael Dahl's Really Scary Stories. (SPA.). (J). (gr. 1-3). 101.28 ***(978-1-4965-9830-1(X),*** 200730, Stone Arch Bks.) Capstone.

—Un Desconocido en Las Escaleras y Otros Cuentos de Miedo. Dahl, Michael. 2020. (Cuentos Escalofriantes de Michael Dahl Ser.).Tr. of Stranger on the Stairs & Other Scary Tales. (SPA.). 72p. (J). (gr. 1-3). lib. bdg. 25.32 ***(978-1-4965-9822-6(9),*** 200710, Stone Arch Bks.) Capstone.

Bonet, Xavier. The Doll That Waved Goodbye: And Other Scary Tales. Dahl, Michael. 2015. (Michael Dahl's Really Scary Stories Ser.). (ENG.). 72p. (J). (gr. 1-3). lib. bdg. 25.32 *(978-1-4965-0595-8(6),* Stone Arch Bks.) Capstone.

Bonet, Xavier. El Fantasma Del Teléfono y Otros Cuentos de Miedo. Dahl, Michael. 2020. (Cuentos Escalofriantes de Michael Dahl Ser.).Tr. of Phantom on the Phone & Other Scary Tales. (SPA.). 72p. (J). (gr. 1-3). lib. bdg. 25.32 ***(978-1-4965-9821-9(0),*** 200709, Stone Arch Bks.) Capstone.

Bonet, Xavier. The Final Frankenstein. Troupe, Thomas Kingsley. 2019. (Michael Dahl Presents: Midnight Library 4D Ser.). (ENG.). 80p. (J). (gr. 4-6). lib. bdg. 25.32 *(978-1-4965-7896-9(1),* 139611, Stone Arch Bks.) Capstone.

—Frightmares: A Creepy Collection of Scary Stories. Dahl, Michael. 2015. (Michael Dahl's Really Scary Stories Ser.). (ENG.). 224p. (J). (gr. 1-3). pap. 8.95 *(978-1-4965-0598-9(0),* Stone Arch Bks.) Capstone.

—Frightmares 2: More Scary Stories for the Fearless Reader. Dahl, Michael. 2016. (Michael Dahl's Really Scary Stories Ser.). (ENG.). 224p. (J). (gr. 1-3). pap. 8.95 *(978-1-4965-4136-9(7),* Stone Arch Bks.) Capstone.

—Frightmares 3: Even More Scary Stories to Read If You Dare. Dahl, Michael. ed. 2017. (Michael Dahl's Really Scary Stories Ser.). (ENG.). 224p. (J). (gr. 1-3). pap. 8.95 *(978-1-4965-4915-0(5),* 135655, Stone Arch Bks.) Capstone.

—The Girl in the Graveyard: And Other Scary Tales. Dahl, Michael. 2017. (Michael Dahl's Really Scary Stories Ser.). (ENG.). 72p. (J). (gr. 1-3). lib. bdg. 25.32 *(978-1-4965-4901-3(5),* 135653, Stone Arch Bks.) Capstone.

—The Goblin in the Grass: And Other Scary Tales. Dahl, Michael. 2016. (Michael Dahl's Really Scary Stories Ser.). (ENG.). 72p. (J). (gr. 1-3). lib. bdg. 25.32 *(978-1-4965-3773-7(4),* Stone Arch Bks.) Capstone.

—The Gulliver Giant. Troupe, Thomas Kingsley. 2019. (Michael Dahl Presents: Midnight Library 4D Ser.). (ENG.). 80p. (J). (gr. 4-6). lib. bdg. 25.32 *(978-1-4965-7894-5(5),* 139609, Stone Arch Bks.) Capstone.

—The Library Claw: And Other Scary Tales. Dahl, Michael. 2017. (Michael Dahl's Really Scary Stories Ser.). (ENG.). 72p. (J). (gr. 1-3). lib. bdg. 25.32 *(978-1-4965-4902-0(3),* 135654, Stone Arch Bks.) Capstone.

Bonet, Xavier. La Mano de la Muñeca Dice Adiós: Y Otros Cuentos de Miedo. Dahl, Michael. 2020. (Cuentos Escalofriantes de Michael Dahl Ser.).Tr. of Doll That Waved Goodbye & Other Scary Tales. (SPA.). 72p. (J). (gr. 1-3). lib. bdg. 25.32 ***(978-1-4965-9820-2(2),*** 200708, Stone Arch Bks.) Capstone.

Bonet, Xavier. Medieval Times: A Handbook for Time Travelers. Stokes, Jonathan W. 2019. (Thrifty Guides). 160p. (J). (gr. 3-7). pap. 8.99 *(978-0-451-48028-6(7),* Puffin Books) Penguin Young Readers Group.

—Mermaids. Meister, Cari. 2019. (Mythical Creatures Ser.). (ENG.). 32p. (J). (gr. k-2). lib. bdg. 27.99 *(978-1-5158-4442-6(0),* 140562, Picture Window Bks.) Capstone.

Bonet, Xavier. Midnight at the Barclay Hotel. Bradley, Fleur. 2020. 320p. (J). (gr. 3-7). 17.99 ***(978-0-593-20290-6(2),*** Viking Books for Young Readers) Penguin Young Readers Group.

Bonet, Xavier. The Minotaur Maze. Troupe, Thomas Kingsley. 2019. (Michael Dahl Presents: Midnight Library 4D Ser.). (ENG.). 80p. (J). (gr. 4-6). lib. bdg. 25.32 *(978-1-4965-7895-2(3),* 139610, Stone Arch Bks.) Capstone.

—The Monster in the Mailbox: And Other Scary Tales. Dahl, Michael. 2016. (Michael Dahl's Really Scary Stories Ser.). (ENG.). 72p. (J). (gr. 1-3). lib. bdg. 25.32 *(978-1-4965-3771-3(8),* Stone Arch Bks.) Capstone.

—The Mystery of Sol 2 Wayfarers. Kubuitsile, Lauri. 2017. (Cambridge Reading Adventures Ser.). (ENG.). 32p. pap. 7.87 *(978-1-108-43672-4(2))* Cambridge Univ. Pr.

Bonet, Xavier, et al. Mythical Creatures. Doeden, Matt & Meister, Cari. 2019. (Mythical Creatures Ser.). (ENG.). (J). (gr. k-2). 111.96 *(978-1-5158-4449-5(8)*, 29329, Picture Window Bks.) Capstone.

Bonet, Xavier. The Night Octopus: And Other Scary Tales. Dahl, Michael. 2017. (Michael Dahl's Really Scary Stories Ser.). (ENG.). 72p. (J). (gr. 1-3). lib. bdg. 25.32 *(978-1-4965-4899-3(X)*, 135651, Stone Arch Bks.) Capstone.

—Oscar & the Amazing Gravity Repellent. Peterson, Tina L. 2015. (Middle-Grade Novels Ser.). (ENG.). 224p. (J). (gr. 3-4). lib. bdg. 26.65 *(978-1-4965-0000-7(8)*, Stone Arch Bks.) Capstone.

—The Phantom on the Phone & Other Scary Tales. Dahl, Michael. 2015. (Michael Dahl's Really Scary Stories Ser.). (ENG.). 72p. (J). (gr. 1-3). lib. bdg. 25.32 *(978-1-4965-0597-2(2)*, Stone Arch Bks.) Capstone.

—Radio Delley. Martinez, Alex. 2019. 64p. (J). (gr. 4-7). pap. 9.99 *(978-1-68405-448-0(6))* Idea & Design Works, LLC.

—Shadow Shoes: And Other Scary Tales. Dahl, Michael. 2017. (Michael Dahl's Really Scary Stories Ser.). (ENG.). 72p. (J). (gr. 1-3). lib. bdg. 25.32 *(978-1-4965-4900-6(7)*, 135652, Stone Arch Bks.) Capstone.

—The Stranger on the Stairs: And Other Scary Tales. Dahl, Michael. 2015. (Michael Dahl's Really Scary Stories Ser.). (ENG.). 72p. (J). (gr. 1-3). lib. bdg. 25.32 *(978-1-4965-0594-1(8)*, Stone Arch Bks.) Capstone.

—The Thrifty Guide to Ancient Greece: A Handbook for Time Travelers. Stokes, Jonathan W. (Thrifty Guides: 3). (J). (gr. 3-7). 2019. 144p. pap. 8.99 *(978-1-101-99816-8(4)*, Puffin Books); 2018. 150p. 13.99 *(978-0-451-48027-9(9)*, Viking Books for Young Readers) Penguin Young Readers Group.

—Unbelievably Boring Bart. Patterson, James. 2018. (ENG.). 272p. (J). (gr. 3-7). 13.99 *(978-0-316-41153-0(1)*, Jimmy Patterson) Little Brown & Co.

—The Voice in the Boys' Room & Other Scary Tales. Dahl, Michael. 2015. (Michael Dahl's Really Scary Stories Ser.). (ENG.). 72p. (J). (gr. 1-3). lib. bdg. 25.32 *(978-1-4965-0596-5(4)*, Stone Arch Bks.) Capstone.

Bonet, Xavier. La Voz en el Baño de Los niños y Otros Cuentos de Miedo. Dahl, Michael. 2020. (Cuentos Escalofriantes de Michael Dahl Ser.).Tr. of Voice in the Boys' Room & Other Scary Tales. (SPA.). 72p. (J). (gr. 1-3). lib. bdg. 25.32 ***(978-1-4965-9823-3(7)***, 200711, Stone Arch Bks.) Capstone.

Bonet, Xavier. Zombie Cupcakes: And Other Scary Tales. Dahl, Michael. 2016. (Michael Dahl's Really Scary Stories Ser.). (ENG.). 72p. (J). (gr. 1-3). lib. bdg. 25.32 *(978-1-4965-3774-4(2)*, Stone Arch Bks.) Capstone.

Bonforte, Lisa. Ponies, Vol. 2. Pollack, Pam & Belviso, Meg. 2003. (Penguin Young Readers, Level 2 Ser.: Vol. 2). 48p. (J). (gr. 1-2). mass mkt. 4.99 *(978-0-448-42524-5(6)*, Penguin Young Readers) Penguin Young Readers Group.

—Rainforest Animals. Smith, Kathie Billingslea. 2005. 12p. (J). (gr. k-3). 6.99 *(978-1-57755-509-4(0))* Flying Frog Publishing, Inc.

—Seal Pup Grows Up: The Story of a Harbor Seal. Zoehfeld, Kathleen Weidner. 2011. (Smithsonian Oceanic Collection Ser.). (ENG.). 32p. (J). (gr. -1-3). 19.95 *(978-1-60727-663-0(1))* Soundprints.

Bongini, Barbara. The Lost & Found Weekend. Thorpe, Kiki. 2019. (Makers Make It Work Ser.). (ENG.). 32p. (J). (gr. k-3). 25.32 *(978-1-63592-115-1(5))* Astra Publishing Hse.

Bonham, Bob. Book of Mormon Numbers. Daybell, Chad. 2004. (J). bds. 8.95 *(978-1-55517-755-3(7)*, 77557) Cedar Fort, Inc./CFI Distribution.

—Sariah Mcduff: Book Three of the Sariah Mcduff Series: Valentine's Day Scrooge. Setzer, Lee Ann. 2005. (J). per. 5.95 *(978-1-55517-841-3(3))* Cedar Fort, Inc./CFI Distribution.

Bonhomme, Matthieu. William & the Lost Spirit. Bonneval, Gwen de & Smith, Owen. Smith, Anne Collins, tr. 2013. (ENG.). 160p. (YA). (gr. 8-12). lib. bdg. 30.65 *(978-0-7613-8567-7(3)*, 9780761385677, Graphic Universe™) Lerner Publishing Group.

Boni, Simone. Sword Quest. Dixon, Andy. Brooks, Felicity, ed. rev. ed. 2005. (Usborne Fantasy Puzzle Bks.). 31p. (J). (gr. 3-7). pap., pap. 7.95 *(978-0-7945-1096-1(5)*, Usborne) EDC Publishing.

Bonilla Raya, Rocio. Vamos a la cama. 2018. (SPA.). 22p. (J). bds. 15.99 *(978-84-947835-1-7(3))* Editorial Flamboyant ESP. Dist: Lectorum Pubns., Inc.

Bonilla, Rocío. The Big Book of Superpowers. Isern, Susanna. 2020. (ENG.). 40p. (J). (gr. k-3). 18.99 *(978-1-5064-6319-3(3)*, Beaming Books) Augsburg Fortress, Pubs.

—The Highest Mountain of Books in the World. Lethem, Mara. 2016. (J). *(978-1-4413-1999-9(9))* Peter Pauper Pr. Inc.

Bonilla, Rocio. Mi Oso Grande, Mi Oso Pequeño, y Yo. del Mazo, Margarita. 2019. (ENG.). 36p. (J). 16.95 *(978-84-17123-49-0(0))* NubeOcho Ediciones ESP. Dist: Consortium Bk. Sales & Distribution.

—My Big Bear, My Small Bear & Me. Ediz. A Colori. del Mazo, Margarita. 2019. (ENG.). 36p. (J). 16.95 *(978-84-17123-50-5(4))* NubeOcho Ediciones ESP. Dist: Consortium Bk. Sales & Distribution.

Bonilla, Rocío. What Colour Is a Kiss? 2016. (ENG.). 32p. (J). (-k). lib. bdg. 16.95 *(978-1-58089-739-6(8))* Charlesbridge Publishing, Inc.

Bonilla, Rocío & Malet, Oriol. Max & the Superheroes. Bonilla, Rocío & Lethem, Mara. 2018. (ENG.). 48p. (J). (gr. -1-3). lib. bdg. 14.99 *(978-1-58089-844-7(0))* Charlesbridge Publishing, Inc.

Bonita, Raquel. I'll Believe You When ... Unbelievable Idioms from Around the World. Schubert, Susan. 2020. 32p. (J). (gr. k-2). 17.99 *(978-1-911373-49-0(8))* Lantana Publishing GBR. Dist: Lerner Publishing Group.

Bonita, Todd. Tae Kwon Do! Pierce, Terry. 2006. (Step into Reading: Step 1 Ser.). (ENG.). 32p. (J). (gr. -1-1). lib. bdg. 16.19 *(978-0-375-93448-3(0))* Random House Publishing Group.

—Tae Kwon Do! Pierce, Terry. 2006. (Step into Reading Ser.). 32p. (J). (gr. -1-1). per. 4.99 *(978-0-375-83448-6(6)*, Random Hse. Bks. for Young Readers) Random Hse. Children's Bks.

Bonne-Müller, Caroline. Portrait of an Artist: Claude Monet: Discover the Artist Behind the Masterpieces. Brownridge, Lucy. 2020. (Portrait of an Artist Ser.). (ENG.). 32p. (J). (gr. 2-5). 16.99 ***(978-0-7112-4877-9(X)***, Wide Eyed Editions) Quarto Publishing Group UK GBR. Dist: Hachette Bk. Group.

Bonnell, B. T. The Little Loony Tales: Hatched. Jack, Lizzie. 2011. 34p. 19.95 *(978-1-4575-0665-9(3))*; pap. 14.95 *(978-1-4575-0520-1(7))* Dog Ear Publishing, LLC.

Bonnell, Mary Ann. Trees Are Made of Gas: The Story of Carbon & Climate. Johnson, Kirk. 2020. 40p. (J). (gr. 2-4). pap. 18.95 ***(978-1-68275-274-6(7))*** Fulcrum Publishing.

Bonner, Will. Five Enormous Dinosaurs. (Classic Books with Holes 8x8 Ser.). 16p. (J). 2019. (ENG.). pap. *(978-1-78628-213-2(5))*; 2019. bds. *(978-1-78628-218-7(6))*; 2018. pap. *(978-1-78628-177-5(5))*; 2018. (ENG.). pap. incl. audio compact disk *(978-1-78628-230-9(5))*; 2018. (ENG.). pap. incl. audio compact disk *(978-1-78628-234-7(8))* Child's Play International Ltd.

Bonnet, Rosalinde. Alphabet Picture Book. ed. 2011. (Alphabet Picture Book Ser.). 26p. (J). ring bd. 11.99 *(978-0-7945-2954-3(2)*, Usborne) EDC Publishing.

—The Art Collector. Wahl, Jan. 2011. 32p. (J). (gr. k-3). 15.95 *(978-1-58089-270-4(1))* Charlesbridge Publishing, Inc.

—Ella & Penguin: a Perfect Match. Maynor, Megan. 2017. (ENG.). 32p. (J). (gr. -1-3). 17.99 *(978-0-06-233089-5(6))* HarperCollins Pubs.

—Ella & Penguin Stick Together. Maynor, Megan. 2016. (ENG.). 32p. (J). (gr. -1-3). 17.99 *(978-0-06-233088-8(8))* HarperCollins Pubs.

—Fold-Out Nursery Rhymes. 2018. (Fold-Out Board Bks.). (ENG.). 12p. (J). 7.99 *(978-0-7945-4196-5(8)*, Usborne) EDC Publishing.

Bonnet, Rosalinde. God Loves You, Little Peanut, 1 vol. Bourland, Annette. 2020. (ENG.). 32p. (J). 15.99 ***(978-0-310-76888-3(8))*** Zonderkidz.

Bonnet, Rosalinde. The Little Red Elf. McGrath, Barbara Barbieri. 32p. (J). 2010. (gr. -1-2). pap. 7.95 *(978-1-58089-237-7(X))*; 2009. (gr. k-2). 22.44 *(978-1-58089-236-0(1))* Charlesbridge Publishing, Inc.

—Love Is Kind, 1 vol. Sassi, Laura. 2018. (ENG.). 32p. (J). 16.99 *(978-0-310-75489-3(5))* Zonderkidz.

—My First Word Book. Brooks, Felicity. 2014. (ENG.). (J). 9.99 *(978-0-7945-3381-6(7)*, Usborne) EDC Publishing.

—Pablo in the Snow. Sloat, Teri. 2017. (ENG.). 40p. (J). 16.99 *(978-1-62779-412-1(3)*, 9781627794121, Holt, Henry & Co. Bks. For Young Readers) Holt, Henry & Co.

—Poppy's Best Babies. Eaddy, Susan. 2018. 40p. (J). (gr. k-3). 15.99 *(978-1-58089-770-9(3))* Charlesbridge Publishing, Inc.

—Poppy's Best Paper. Eaddy, Susan. 2015. 40p. (J). (gr. k-3). lib. bdg. 15.95 *(978-1-58089-614-6(6))* Charlesbridge Publishing, Inc.

—Poppy's Best Paper (1 Hardcover/1 CD) Eaddy, Susan. 2016. (ENG.). (J). (gr. 1-4). audio compact disk 29.95 *(978-1-4301-2187-9(4))* Live Oak Media.

—Sing-Along Christmas Carols. Watt, Fiona. 2010. (Baby Board Books with CD Ser.). 10p. (J). bds. 14.99 incl. audio compact disk *(978-0-7945-2660-3(8)*, Usborne) EDC Publishing.

—Zip! Zoom! on a Broom. Sloat, Teri. 2017. 40p. (J). (gr. -1-3). 16.99 *(978-0-316-25673-5(0))* Little Brown & Co.

—Zip! Zoom! on a Broom. Sloat, Teri. 2019. 24p. (J). (gr. -1 — 1). bds. 7.99 *(978-0-316-25672-8(2))* Little, Brown Bks. for Young Readers.

Bonnet, Rosalinde, jt. illus. see Biedrzycki, David.

Bonnet, Rosaline. Very First Nursery Rhymes. Bonnet, Rosaline. 2010. (Very First Words Board Bks). 12p. (J). bds. 6.99 *(978-0-7945-2723-5(X)*, Usborne) EDC Publishing.

Bonnett, Rosalind. Santa Flap Book. Taplin, Sam. ed. 2019. (Flap Bks.). (ENG.). 10ppp. (J). 7.99 *(978-0-7945-3316-8(7)*, Usborne) EDC Publishing.

Bonney, Joan, jt. illus. see Gauthier, Elizabeth.

Bonnice, Lindsey. Libby & Pearl: The Best of Friends. Bonnice, Lindsey. 2016. (ENG.). 32p. (J). (gr. -1-3). 14.99 *(978-0-06-245927-5(9))* HarperCollins Pubs.

Bonnie, Spino. Wild about Manners. Lorraine, Loria. 2013. 36p. 17.99 *(978-0-9881889-1-4(0))* Piccolo Tales.

Bono, Elena. El Sombrero de Ramito. Bono, Elena. Bono, E. Brignole, Giancarla, tr. rev. ed. 2006. (Fabulas De Familia Ser.). (SPA & ENG.). 32p. (J). (gr. k-4). pap. 6.95 *(978-970-20-0261-1(3))* Castillo, Ediciones, S. A. de C. V. MEX. Dist: Macmillan.

Bonotaux, Gilles. Dirty Rotten Bugs? Arthropods Unite to Tell Their Side of the Story. Bonotaux, Gilles. 2007. (ENG.). 48p. (J). (gr. 3-6). 14.95 *(978-1-58728-593-6(2)*, 1267604) Cooper Square Publishing Llc.

Bonson, Tom. The Marvelous Monsters Talent Show. Regan, Patrick. 2014. (J). *(978-1-4351-5617-3(X)*, Blackbirch Pr., Inc.) Barnes & Noble, Inc.

Bonte, Therese. Sami et Julie - Sami a des Poux Niveau 2. Lamarche, Léo. 2015. (J'Apprends Avec Sami et Julie Ser.). (FRE.). (J). *(978-2-01-270619-4(3))* Hachette Education.

Bonvillain, Tamra, jt. illus. see Bustos, Natacha.

Boo, Binny. Got Brains? Graves, Emma T. 2018. (My Undead Life Ser.). (ENG.). 112p. (J). (gr. 3-6). pap. 7.95 *(978-1-4965-6451-1(0)*, 138363); lib. bdg. 25.99 *(978-1-4965-6447-4(2)*, 138359) Capstone. (Stone Arch Bks.).

—OMG, Zombie! Graves, Emma T. 2018. (My Undead Life Ser.). (ENG.). 112p. (J). (gr. 3-6). pap. 7.95 *(978-1-4965-6448-1(0)*, 138360); lib. bdg. 25.99 *(978-1-4965-6444-3(8)*, 138356) Capstone. (Stone Arch Bks.).

—Really Rotten Drama. Graves, Emma T. 2018. (My Undead Life Ser.). (ENG.). 112p. (J). (gr. 3-6). pap. 7.95 *(978-1-4965-6449-8(9)*, 138361); lib. bdg. 25.99 *(978-1-4965-6445-0(6)*, 138357) Capstone. (Stone Arch Bks.).

—Total FREAK-Out. Graves, Emma T. 2018. (My Undead Life Ser.). (ENG.). 112p. (J). (gr. 3-6). lib. bdg. 25.99 *(978-1-4965-6446-7(4)*, 138358, Stone Arch Bks.) Capstone.

Boo, Sweeney. Marvel Action: Captain Marvel: A. I. M. Small (Book Two) Maggs, Sam. 2020. 72p. (J). (gr. 4-7). pap. 9.99 ***(978-1-68405-684-2(5))*** Idea & Design Works, LLC.

Boo, Sweeney. Marvel Action: Captain Marvel: Cosmic CAT-Tastrophe (Book One) Maggs, Sam. 2020. (Marvel Action: Captain Marvel Ser.: 1). 72p. (J). (gr. 4-7). pap. 9.99 *(978-1-68405-624-8(1))* Idea & Design Works, LLC.

Boog, Carl Michael. A Child's Garden of Religion Stories. Matimore, Rev Patrick Henry. 2018. (Madonna Ser.: Vol. 1). (ENG.). 294p. (J). (gr. 3-4). pap. 14.95 *(978-1-64051-071-5(0))* St. Augustine Academy Pr.

Boog, Carle Michel. Heroes of God's Church. Matimore, Rev Patrick Henry. 2018. (Madonna Ser.: Vol. 3). (ENG.). 304p. (J). (gr. 4-6). pap. 14.95 *(978-1-64051-073-9(7))* St. Augustine Academy Pr.

Booher-Jones, Penny. Miracle Miles & His Buddy Bunch - the Best Day Ever! Bengco, Paras. 2019. (ENG.). 60p. (J). pap. 12.99 ***(978-0-578-41435-5(X))*** Independent Pub.

Booher Jones, Penny a. Here Comes Fall! Redimere, Cassia T. 2019. (ENG.). 36p. (J). pap. 10.00 ***(978-1-0730-2360-8(5))*** Independently Published.

Booher Jones, Penny a. To Swim with Dolphins. Booher Jones, Penny a. 2014. (ENG.). 52p. (J). pap. 5.99 ***(978-1-6992-3262-0(8))*** Independently Published.

Books, Appleknobb. Charlie's Monster. Books, Appleknobb. 2013. 26p. (J). pap. 13.95 *(978-0-9890903-0-8(2))* Happy Apple Bks.

Books, Kitanie. My Invisible Cosmic Zebra Has a Concussion - Now What? Riley, Jessie. 2016. (ENG.). (YA). (gr. 7-12). pap. 16.99 *(978-1-935734-70-3(9))* Kitanie Bks.

—My Invisible Cosmic Zebra Has a Vestibular Disorder - Now What? Riley, Jessie. 2016. (ENG.). (YA). (gr. 7-12). pap. 16.99 *(978-1-935734-83-3(0))* Kitanie Bks.

—My Invisible Cosmic Zebra Has Allergies - Now What? Riley, Jessie. 2016. (ENG.). (YA). (gr. 7-12). pap. 16.99 *(978-1-935734-95-6(4))* Kitanie Bks.

—My Invisible Cosmic Zebra Has Celiac Disease - Now What? Riley, Jessie. 2016. (ENG.). (YA). (gr. 7-12). pap. 16.99 *(978-1-935734-74-1(1))* Kitanie Bks.

—My Invisible Cosmic Zebra Has Crohn's Disease - Now What? Riley, Jessie. 2016. (ENG.). (YA). (gr. 7-12). pap. 16.99 *(978-1-935734-84-0(9))* Kitanie Bks.

—My Invisible Cosmic Zebra Has Diabetes - Now What? Riley, Jessie. 2016. (ENG.). (YA). (gr. 7-12). pap. 16.99 *(978-1-935734-76-5(8))* Kitanie Bks.

—My Invisible Cosmic Zebra Has Ehlers-Danlos Syndrome - Now What? Riley, Jessie. 2016. (ENG.). (YA). (gr. 7-12). pap. 16.99 *(978-1-935734-75-8(X))* Kitanie Bks.

—My Invisible Cosmic Zebra Has Fibromyalgia - Now What? Riley, Jessie. 2016. (ENG.). (YA). (gr. 7-12). pap. 16.99 *(978-1-935734-78-9(4))* Kitanie Bks.

—My Invisible Cosmic Zebra Has Hashimoto's Disease - Now What? Riley, Jessie. 2016. (ENG.). (YA). (gr. 7-12). pap. 16.99 *(978-1-935734-90-1(3))* Kitanie Bks.

—My Invisible Cosmic Zebra Has Lupus - Now What? Riley, Jessie. 2016. (ENG.). (YA). (gr. 7-12). pap. 16.99 *(978-1-935734-71-0(7))* Kitanie Bks.

—My Invisible Cosmic Zebra Has Lyme Disease - Now What? Riley, Jessie. 2016. (ENG.). (YA). (gr. 7-12). pap. 16.99 *(978-1-935734-73-4(3))* Kitanie Bks.

—My Invisible Cosmic Zebra Has Migraines - Now What? Riley, Jessie. 2016. (ENG.). (YA). (gr. 7-12). pap. 16.99 *(978-1-935734-72-7(5))* Kitanie Bks.

—My Invisible Cosmic Zebra Has Multiple Sclerosis - Now What? Riley, Jessie. 2016. (ENG.). (YA). (gr. 7-12). pap. 16.99 *(978-1-935734-93-2(8))* Kitanie Bks.

—My Invisible Cosmic Zebra Has Pots - Now What? Riley, Jessie. 2016. (ENG.). (YA). (gr. 7-12). pap. 16.99 *(978-1-935734-81-9(4))* Kitanie Bks.

—My Invisible Cosmic Zebra Has Ptsd - Now What? Riley, Jessie. 2016. (ENG.). (YA). (gr. 7-12). pap. 16.99 *(978-1-935734-86-4(5))* Kitanie Bks.

—My Invisible Cosmic Zebra Has Rheumatoid Arthritis - Now What? Riley, Jessie. 2016. (ENG.). (YA). (gr. 7-12). pap. 16.99 *(978-1-935734-94-9(6))* Kitanie Bks.

—My Invisible Cosmic Zebra Has Sjogren's Syndrome - Now What? Riley, Jessie. 2016. (ENG.). (YA). (gr. 7-12). pap. 16.99 *(978-1-935734-82-6(2))* Kitanie Bks.

Books, Om Art and. Vacation at the Beach: World of Cats. Skrypnyk-Harnagea, Anastasia & Harnagea Theophilus, Suzana. 2019. (ENG.). 32p. (J). pap. 9.99 *(978-1-0928-7215-7(9))* Independently Published.

BOOM! Studios, jt. illus. see Allen, Brooklyn.

BOOM! Studios, jt. illus. see Sygh, Rian.

Boon, Debbie. If You Go Walking in Tiger Wood. Durant, Alan. 2005. (ENG.). 24p. (J). (gr. -1-k). pap. 9.99 *(978-0-00-710390-4(5)*, HarperSport) HarperCollins Pubs. Ltd. GBR. Dist: Independent Pubs. Group.

—Tiger's Tales: Band 10/White (Collins Big Cat) Morgan, Michaela. 2005. (Collins Big Cat Ser.). (ENG.). 32p. (J). (gr. 1-3). pap. 9.99 *(978-0-00-718631-0(2))* HarperCollins Pubs. Ltd. GBR. Dist: Independent Pubs. Group.

Boon, Emilie. Ella & Monkey at Sea. Boon, Emilie. 2018. 32p. (J). (gr. -1-2). 16.99 *(978-0-7636-9233-9(6))* Candlewick Pr.

Boone, Patti. To Be a Frog. Devol, Laura. 2010. 20p. pap. 12.95 *(978-1-60910-278-4(9))* Booklocker.com, Inc.

Boos, Andre. Amazing Animal Puzzle Stickers, 1 vol., Vol. 2. Teora. 2005. (Amazing Animal Puzzle Stickers Ser.). (ENG.). 8p. (J). pap. 5.99 *(978-1-59496-064-2(X))* Teora USA LLC.

—Amazing Animal Puzzle Stickers: #1, 1 vol. 2005. (Amazing Animal Puzzle Stickers Ser.). (ENG.). 8p. (J). pap. 5.99 *(978-1-59496-063-5(1))* Teora USA LLC.

—Amazing Animal Puzzle Stickers: #3, 1 vol., Vol. 3. 2005. (Amazing Animal Puzzle Stickers Ser.). (ENG.). 8p. (J). pap. 5.99 *(978-1-59496-065-9(8))* Teora USA LLC.

—Hi! Read, Stick & Learn about Animals. Little Bears are Brown, 1 vol. 2004. (ENG.). 20p. (J). pap. 6.99 *(978-1-59496-003-1(8))* Teora USA LLC.

—Hi! Read, Stick & Learn about Animals. Little rabbits have Fur, 1 vol. 2004. (ENG.). 20p. (J). pap. 6.99 *(978-1-59496-002-4(X))* Teora USA LLC.

Boos, Ben. Fantasy: An Artist's Realm. Boos, Ben. 2010. 96p. (J). (gr. 5-9). 19.99 *(978-0-7636-4056-9(5))* Candlewick Pr.

—Swords: An Artist's Devotion. Boos, Ben. 2008. 96p. (J). (gr. 5-9). 24.99 *(978-0-7636-3148-2(5))* Candlewick Pr.

Boos, Ben & Ford, A. G. What Color Is My World? The Lost History of African-American Inventors. Abdul-Jabbar, Kareem & Obstfeld, Raymond. (J). (gr. 3-7). 2013. 96p. pap. 7.99 *(978-0-7636-6442-8(1))*; 2012. 44p. 17.99 *(978-0-7636-4564-9(8))* Candlewick Pr.

Boot, Maaike. Search & Find Animals. Taylor, Georgie. 2020. (Water Painting Search & Find Ser.). (ENG.). 10p. (J). (gr. -1-k). bds. 10.99 *(978-1-78958-321-2(7))* Top That! Publishing PLC GBR. Dist: Independent Pubs. Group.

—Search & Find Dinosaurs. Taylor, Georgie. 2020. (Water Painting Search & Find Ser.). (ENG.). 10p. (J). (gr. -1-k). bds. 10.99 *(978-1-78958-322-9(5))* Top That! Publishing PLC GBR. Dist: Independent Pubs. Group.

—Search & Find under the Sea. Taylor, Georgie. 2020. (Water Painting Search & Find Ser.). (ENG.). 10p. (J). (gr. -1-k). bds. 10.99 *(978-1-78958-323-6(3))* Top That! Publishing PLC GBR. Dist: Independent Pubs. Group.

—Search & Find Unicorns. Taylor, Georgie. 2020. (Water Painting Search & Find Ser.). (ENG.). 10p. (J). (gr. -1-k). bds. 10.99 *(978-1-78958-324-3(1))* Top That! Publishing PLC GBR. Dist: Independent Pubs. Group.

Booth, Anita K. Squirrels!!! An Informative & Entertaining Book about Our Favorite Mountain Mammal. Booth, Anita K., photos by. 2nd ed. 2004. 76p. 12.95 *(978-0-9748702-1-2(8))* AKB Design.

Booth, George. Here, George! Boynton, Sandra. 2018. (ENG.). 32p. (J). (gr. -1-k). bds. 7.99 *(978-1-5344-2964-2(6)*, Little Simon) Little Simon.

—Never Tease a Weasel. Soule, Jean Conder. 2011. 40p. (J). (gr. -1-2). pap. 7.99 *(978-0-375-87285-3(X)*, Dragonfly Bks.) Random Hse. Children's Bks.

—School! Adventures at the Harvey N. Trouble Elementary School. McMullan, Kate. 2012. (ENG.). 176p. (J). (gr. 1-4). pap. 8.99 *(978-0-312-55595-5(4)*, 900074611) Square Fish.

—Who Invited You? Fleming, Candace. 2009. (ENG.). 36p. (J). (gr. -1-3). 10.99 *(978-1-4424-0219-5(9)*, Atheneum Bks. for Young Readers) Simon & Schuster Children's Publishing.

Booth, Graham. Henry Explores the Jungle. Taylor, Mark. 2012. (ENG.). 48p. (J). (gr. -1-3). 18.95 *(978-1-930900-56-1(2))* Purple Hse. Pr.

—Henry the Castaway. Taylor, Mark. 2010. 48p. (J). (gr. -1-3). 18.95 *(978-1-930900-47-9(3))* Purple Hse. Pr.

—Henry the Explorer. Taylor, Mark. 2011. (J). 18.95 *(978-1-930900-48-6(1))* Purple Hse. Pr.

Booth, Scott. How to Draw Superheroes & Super Villains. 2003. 64p. (J). *(978-0-439-55133-5(1))* Scholastic, Inc.

Booth, Tom. Derek Jeter Presents Night at the Stadium. Bildner, Phil. 2016. (Jeter Publishing Ser.). (ENG.). 32p. (J). (gr. -1-3). 18.99 *(978-1-4814-2655-8(9)*, Aladdin) Simon & Schuster Children's Publishing.

—Gargantis. Taylor, Thomas. 2020. (ENG.). 352p. (J). (gr. 3-7). 16.99 *(978-1-5362-0859-7(0))* Candlewick Pr.

Booth, Tom. Malamander. Taylor, Thomas. (Legends of Eerie-On-Sea Ser.). (ENG.). (J). (gr. 3-7). 2020. 320p. pap. 7.99 ***(978-1-5362-1515-1(5))***; 2019. 304p. 16.99 *(978-1-5362-0722-4(5))* Candlewick Pr.

Booth, Tom. Who Wins? 100 Historical Figures Go Head-To-Head & You Decide the Winner! Swartz, Clay. 2016. (Who Wins? Ser.). (ENG.). 104p. (J). (gr. 3-6). spiral bd. 14.95 *(978-0-7611-8544-4(5)*, 18544) Workman Publishing Co., Inc.

Booth, Tom. Day at the Beach. Booth, Tom. 2018. (Jeter Publishing Ser.). (ENG.). 40p. (J). (gr. -1-3). 18.99 *(978-1-5344-1105-0(4)*, Aladdin) Simon & Schuster Children's Publishing.

—This Is Christmas. Booth, Tom. 2018. (Jeter Publishing Ser.). (ENG.). 40p. (J). (gr. -1-3). 17.99 *(978-1-5344-1090-9(2)*, Aladdin) Simon & Schuster Children's Publishing.

Boothroyd, Sa. Before the World Was Ready: Stories of Daring Genius in Science. Eamer, Claire. 2013. (ENG.). 128p. (J). (gr. 4-7). pap. 14.95 *(978-1-55451-535-6(1)*, 9781554515356) Annick Pr., Ltd. CAN. Dist: Publishers Group West (PGW).

—The World in Your Lunch Box: The Wacky History & Weird Science of Everyday Foods. Eamer, Claire. 2012. (ENG.). 128p. (J). (gr. 2-18). 3rd ed. 22.95 *(978-1-55451-393-2(6)*, 9781554513932); 4th ed. pap. 14.95 *(978-1-55451-392-5(8)*, 9781554513925) Annick Pr., Ltd. CAN. Dist: Publishers Group West (PGW).

Bootman, Colin. Almost to Freedom. Nelson, Vaunda Micheaux. 2003. (ENG.). 40p. (J). (gr. k-3). 17.99 *(978-1-57505-342-4(X)*, Carolrhoda Bks.) Lerner Publishing Group.

—Climbing Lincoln's Steps. Slade, Suzanne. 2016. (ENG.). 32p. (J). (gr. -1-3). pap. 6.99 *(978-0-8075-1205-0(2)*, 807512052) Whitman, Albert & Co.

—Dad, Jackie, & Me, 1 vol. Uhlberg, Myron. (ENG.). 32p. (J). 2010. pap. 8.95 *(978-1-56145-531-7(8))*; 2007. 16.95 *(978-1-56145-329-0(3))* Peachtree Publishing Co. Inc.

—Finding Lincoln. Malaspina, Ann. 2009. (ENG.). 32p. (J). (gr. 2-3). 16.99 *(978-0-8075-2435-0(2)*, 807524352) Whitman, Albert & Co.

—Grandmama's Pride. Birtha, Becky. 2016. (ENG.). 32p. (J). (gr. -1-3). pap. 6.99 *(978-0-8075-3022-1(0)*, 807530220) Whitman, Albert & Co.

—Hey, Charleston! The True Story of the Jenkins Orphanage Band. Rockwell, Anne. ed. 2013. (ENG.). 32p. E-Book 16.95 *(978-0-7613-8843-2(5))* Lerner Publishing Group.

B

—Love Twelve Miles Long. Armand, Glenda. (ENG.). 32p. (J). 2015. pap. 9.95 *(978-1-62014-254-7(6))*; 2013. 17.95 *(978-1-60060-245-0(2))* Lee & Low Bks., Inc.

—The Steel Pan Man of Harlem. 2009. (Carolrhoda Picture Bks.). 32p. (J). (gr. 1-3). 16.95 *(978-0-8225-9026-2(3))* Lerner Publishing Group.

—A Storm Called Katrina, 1 vol. Uhlberg, Myron. (ENG.). 40p. (J). (gr. 2-4). 2015. pap. 8.95 *(978-1-56145-887-5(2))*; 2011. 17.95 *(978-1-56145-591-1(1))* Peachtree Publishing Co. Inc.

—Sunday Best. Scholastic, Inc. Staff et al. 2004. (Just for You Ser.). (ENG.). 32p. pap. 3.99 *(978-0-439-56854-8(4))*, Teaching Resources) Scholastic, Inc.

—Tiny Stitches: The Life of Medical Pioneer Vivien Thomas, 1 vol. Hooks, Gwendolyn. 2016. (ENG.). 32p. (J). (gr. 2-8). 18.95 *(978-1-62014-156-4(6))*, 8e427ebb-289c-4659-b228-222befcc15a3) Lee & Low Bks., Inc.

Borando, Silvia. The Cat Book: A Minibombo Book. Borando, Silvia. 2017. (Minibombo Ser.). (ENG.). 32p. (J). (-k). 9.99 *(978-0-7636-9472-2(X))* Candlewick Pr.

—Near, Far: A Minibombo Book. Borando, Silvia. 2016. (Minibombo Ser.). (ENG.). 48p. (J). (-k). 14.00 *(978-0-7636-8783-0(9))* Candlewick Pr.

—Now You See Me, Now You Don't: A Minibombo Book. Borando, Silvia. 2016. (Minibombo Ser.). (ENG.). 28p. (J). (-k). 14.00 *(978-0-7636-8782-3(0))* Candlewick Pr.

—Shapes at Play: A Minibombo Book. Borando, Silvia. 2016. (Minibombo Ser.). (ENG.). 48p. (J). (-k). 14.00 *(978-0-7636-9038-0(4))* Candlewick Pr.

—Shapes, Reshape! A Minibombo Book. Borando, Silvia. 2016. (Minibombo Ser.). (ENG.). 48p. (J). (-k). 14.00 *(978-0-7636-9039-7(2))* Candlewick Pr.

Borchedt, Fred. Zombies Ate My Homework: Redstone Junior High #1. Stevens, Cara J. 2017. (Redstone Junior High Ser.: 1). (ENG.). 192p. (J). (gr. 3-7). pap. 11.99 *(978-1-5107-2232-3(7))*, Sky Pony Pr.) Skyhorse Publishing Co., Inc.

Borday, Irene. Mi Calle. Parramón, José María. (Coleccion Estoy En...).Tr. of My Street. (SPA.). 32p. (J). (gr. k-3). 6.36 *(978-84-342-1003-5(7))* Parramon Ediciones S.A. ESP. Dist: Lectorum Pubns., Inc.

—Mi Casa. Parramón, José María. (Coleccion Estoy En...).Tr. of My House. (SPA.). 32p. (J). (gr. k-3). 6.36 *(978-84-342-1002-8(9))* Parramon Ediciones S.A. ESP. Dist: Lectorum Pubns., Inc.

—Mi Escuela. Parramón, José María. (Coleccion Estoy En...).Tr. of My School. (SPA.). 32p. (J). (gr. k-3). 6.36 *(978-84-342-1004-2(5))* Parramon Ediciones S.A. ESP. Dist: Lectorum Pubns., Inc.

—Mi Jardin. Parramón, José María. (Coleccion Estoy En...).Tr. of My Garden. (SPA.). 32p. (J). (gr. k-3). 6.36 *(978-84-342-1005-9(3))* Parramon Ediciones S.A. ESP. Dist: Lectorum Pubns., Inc.

Bordelois, Augusto. Sunflower Promise. Hemery, Kathleen Maresh. 2005. (J). *(978-1-56123-188-1(6))* Centering Corp.

Border, Terry. Big Brother Peanut Butter. Border, Terry. 2018. (ENG.). 32p. (J). (gr. -1-2). 17.99 *(978-1-5247-4006-1(3))*, Philomel Bks.) Penguin Young Readers Group.

—Happy Birthday, Cupcake! Border, Terry. Mack, Jeff. 2015. 32p. (J). (gr. k-3). bds. 17.99 *(978-0-399-17160-4(6))*, Philomel Bks.) Penguin Young Readers Group.

—Merry Christmas, Peanut! Border, Terry. 2017. (ENG.). 32p. (J). (gr. -1-2). 17.99 *(978-0-399-17621-0(7))*, Philomel Bks.) Penguin Young Readers Group.

—Peanut Butter & Cupcake. Border, Terry. 2014. 32p. (J). (gr. -1-2). 17.99 *(978-0-399-16773-7(0))*, Philomel Bks.) Penguin Publishing Group.

—Peanut Butter's Delicious Colors. Border, Terry. 2017. (ENG.). 20p. (J). (— 1). bds. 6.99 *(978-0-399-54883-3(1))*, Philomel Bks.) Penguin Young Readers Group.

Border, Terry. Scaredy Snacks! Border, Terry. 2020. 32p. (J). (gr. -1-2). 17.99 ***(978-1-5247-4016-0(0))***, Philomel Bks.) Penguin Young Readers Group.

Border, Terry. Snack Attack! Border, Terry. 2019. (ENG.). 32p. (J). (gr. -1-2). 17.99 *(978-1-5247-4011-5(X))*, Philomel Bks.) Penguin Young Readers Group.

Bordicchia, Gaia. The Amazing Animal Atlas. Crumpton, Nick. 2017. 52p. (J). (gr. 1-3). 28.95 *(978-1-909263-11-6(7))* Flying Eye Bks. GBR. Dist: Penguin Random Hse. LLC.

—Miss Doll & Friends: A Surprise for Miss Doll. Cowley, Joy. 2014. (ENG.). 8p. pap. *(978-0-927244-52-7(7))*, Joy Cowley Club) Flying Start Bks.

—Miss Doll & Friends: Old Jokes. Cowley, Joy. 2014. (ENG.). 8p. pap. *(978-0-927244-60-2(8))*, Joy Cowley Club) Flying Start Bks.

—Miss Doll & Friends: Red Lipstick. Cowley, Joy. 2014. (ENG.). 8p. pap. *(978-0-927244-78-7(0))*, Joy Cowley Club) Flying Start Bks.

—Miss Doll & Friends: Rocking Race. Cowley, Joy. 2014. (ENG.). 8p. pap. *(978-0-927244-64-0(0))*, Joy Cowley Club) Flying Start Bks.

—Miss Doll & Friends: The Rainbow Bird. Cowley, Joy. 2014. (ENG.). 8p. pap. *(978-0-927244-65-7(9))*, Joy Cowley Club) Flying Start Bks.

—Miss Doll & Friends: Tin Clown. Cowley, Joy. 2014. (ENG.). 8p. pap. *(978-0-927244-55-8(1))*, Joy Cowley Club) Flying Start Bks.

—Miss Doll & Friends: Tin Clown¿s Hat. Cowley, Joy. 2014. (ENG.). 8p. pap. *(978-0-927244-79-4(9))*, Joy Cowley Club) Flying Start Bks.

—Miss Doll & Friends: Toy Music. Cowley, Joy. 2014. (ENG.). 8p. pap. *(978-0-927244-59-6(4))*, Joy Cowley Club) Flying Start Bks.

—Miss Doll & Friends: Where Is Fire Engine? Cowley, Joy. 2014. (ENG.). 8p. pap. *(978-0-927244-57-2(8))*, Joy Cowley Club) Flying Start Bks.

—Miss Doll & Friends: Yellow Duck. Cowley, Joy. 2014. (ENG.). 8p. pap. *(978-0-927244-62-6(4))*, Joy Cowley Club) Flying Start Bks.

Bordin, Claudia. The Atlas of Classic Tales. 2019. (ENG.). 48p. (J). (gr. k). 14.95 *(978-88-544-1301-6(1))* White Star ITA. Dist: Sterling Publishing Co., Inc.

—The Atlas of Fairy Tales: Flying over Enchanted Worlds. 2017. (ENG.). 48p. (J). (gr. k). 16.95 *(978-88-544-1187-6(6))* White Star ITA. Dist: Sterling Publishing Co., Inc.

Bordoni, Chiara. Sing-along Nursery Rhymes. Watt, Fiona. 2009. (Baby Board Books w/CD Ser.). 12p. (J). (gr. -1). bds. 15.99 *(978-0-7945-2351-0(X))*, Usborne) EDC Publishing.

Bordoy, Irene. El Patito Feo. Orihuela, Luz. Sarfatti, Esther, tr. 2006. (Bilingual Tales Ser.). (SPA & ENG.). 24p. (J). (gr. -1-3). pap. 3.99 *(978-0-439-77376-8(8))*, Scholastic en Espanol) Scholastic, Inc.

Boren, Deborah. Easter LILLI & the Mystery of the Bunny Eggs. Hendley, LaDann. 2017. (ENG.). (J). (gr. k-5). 20.00 *(978-1-941516-28-7(9))*; pap. 11.00 *(978-1-941516-27-0(0))* Franklin Scribes.

Boretzki, Anja. Animal Pants. Moses, Brian. 2018. (ENG.). 24p. (J). (gr. -1-k). pap. 9.99 *(978-1-5098-5243-7(3))* Pan Macmillan GBR. Dist: Independent Pubs. Group.

Borg, Jay. Arctic Alan: Space Adventure. Rathmill, Vanessa. 2019. (Arctic Alan Ser.: Vol. 2). (ENG.). 26p. (J). pap. 9.13 ***(978-1-6869-9241-4(6))*** Independently Published.

Borgatti, Katherine. Damien of Molokai: Builder of Community. Yoffie, Barbara. 2013. (Saints & Me! Ser.). (ENG.). (J). pap. 4.99 *(978-0-7648-2242-1(X))* Liguori Pubns.

—Mary & Joseph: Models of Faith. Yoffie, Barbara. 2013. (Saints & Me! Ser.). (ENG.). (J). pap. 4.99 *(978-0-7648-2335-0(3))* Liguori Pubns.

—Saints of North America Activity Book. 2013. (Saints & Me! Ser.). (ENG.). (J). pap. 12.49 *(978-0-7648-2243-8(8))* Liguori Pubns.

Borgella, Marjorie. Never Finished, Never Done! Scholastic, Inc. Staff & Brooks, Regina. 2004. (Just for You Ser.). (ENG.). 32p. pap. 3.99 *(978-0-439-56863-0(3))*, Teaching Resources) Scholastic, Inc.

Borges, J. The Lizard. Saramago, José. Caistor, Lucia & Caistor, Nick, trs. 2019. 24p. (J). (gr. 1-4). 17.95 *(978-1-60980-933-1(5))*, Triangle Square) Seven Stories Pr.

Borges, M. L. Milo & Chico: Two Friends That Love Cupcakes. Borges, M. L. 2019. (ENG.). 28p. (J). pap. 10.94 *(978-1-0979-8813-6(9))* Independently Published.

Borgions, Mark. How Airplanes Get from Here ... to There! Brown, Jordan D. 2016. (Science of Fun Stuff Ser.). (ENG.). 48p. (J). (gr. 1-3). pap. 3.99 *(978-1-4814-6164-1(8))*, Simon Spotlight) Simon Spotlight.

—How Airplanes Get from Here... to There! Brown, Jordan. 2016. 48p. (J). *(978-1-5182-1871-2(7))*, Simon Spotlight) Simon Spotlight.

—Looking Up! The Science of Stargazing. Rao, Joe. 2017. (Science of Fun Stuff Ser.). (ENG.). 48p. (J). (gr. 1-3). pap. 4.99 *(978-1-4814-7917-2(2))*, Simon Spotlight) Simon Spotlight.

—The Thrills & Chills of Amusement Parks. Brown, Jordan D. 2015. (Science of Fun Stuff Ser.). (ENG.). 48p. (J). (gr. 1-3). pap. 3.99 *(978-1-4814-2858-3(6))*, Simon Spotlight) Simon Spotlight.

—The 4-1-1 on Phones! Einhorn, Kama. 2015. (History of Fun Stuff Ser.). (ENG.). 48p. (J). (gr. 1-3). pap. 4.99 *(978-1-4814-4404-0(2))*, Simon Spotlight) Simon Spotlight.

Borgman, Jim. Zits: Chillax, 1. Scott, Jerry. 2013. (Zits Ser.: 1). (ENG.). 256p. (YA). (gr. 8-12). pap. 9.99 *(978-0-06-222851-2(X))* HarperCollins Pubs.

—Zits: Shredded. Scott, Jerry. 2014. (Zits Ser.: 2). (ENG.). 224p. (YA). (gr. 8). pap. 9.99 *(978-0-06-222853-6(6))*, HarperTeen) HarperCollins Pubs.

Borin, Magharita. A Frog's Life. Kelly, Irene. 2018. (ENG.). 40p. (J). (gr. -1-3). 17.99 *(978-0-8234-2601-0(7))* Holiday Hse., Inc.

Borin, Margherita. Who Lives in the Ocean? The Secret Life of the Depths. 2017. (ENG.). 16p. (J). (gr. 1). 16.95 *(978-88-544-1201-9(5))* White Star ITA. Dist: Sterling Publishing Co., Inc.

Boring, Wayne. Superman: The Atomic Age Superman, 1953-1956, Vol. 2. Schwartz, Alvin. 2016. (Superman Atomic Age Sundays Ser.: 2). 180p. 49.99 *(978-1-63140-537-2(3))*, 9781631405372) Idea & Design Works, LLC.

Borinsky Editing and Design. I Can't Eat That! A Story about Food Allergies & Anaphylaxis. Pal, Sunita. 2019. (ENG.). 26p. (J). pap. 12.99 *(978-1-7228-9155-8(6))* CreateSpace Independent Publishing Platform.

Borisova, Rinna. Santa Says. Aigil, Nathalie. 2019. (ENG.). 26p. (J). pap. *(978-1-925960-55-6(2))* Library For All Limited.

Borja, Robert. Heroes of American Explorations: Frontiers of America Series. McCall, Edith. 2011. 124p. 40.95 *(978-1-258-03255-5(4))* Literary Licensing, LLC.

—Stories of American Steamboats. McCall, Edith. 2011. 126p. 40.95 *(978-1-258-10111-4(4))* Literary Licensing, LLC.

Borkowski, Michael. I Am Captain Snowball! (the Secret Life of Pets 2) Shealy, Dennis R. 2019. (Step into Reading Ser.). (ENG.). 24p. (J). (gr. -1-1). 12.99 *(978-1-9848-4983-0(2))*, Random Hse. Bks. for Young Readers) Random Hse. Children's Bks.

—Secret Life of Pets 2 Deluxe Step into Reading (Secret Life of Pets 2) Random House. 2019. (Step into Reading Ser.). (ENG.). 24p. (J). (gr. -1-1). pap. 5.99 *(978-1-9848-4982-3(4))*, Random Hse. Bks. for Young Readers) Random Hse. Children's Bks.

—X-Ray Vision! (DC Super Friends) Wrecks, Billy. 2014. (Pictureback(R) Ser.). (ENG.). 16p. (J). (gr. -1-2). 4.99 *(978-0-385-38718-7(0))*, Random Hse. Bks. for Young Readers) Random Hse. Children's Bks.

Borkowski, Michael & Atiyeh, Michael. Guardians of the Galaxy (Marvel: Guardians of the Galaxy) Sazaklis, John. 2016. (Little Golden Book Ser.). (ENG.). 24p. (J). (-k). 4.99 *(978-0-399-55096-6(8))*, Golden Bks.) Random Hse. Children's Bks.

Borkowski, Michael & Atiyen, Michael. The Big Freeze (Marvel) Wrecks, Billy. 2016. (Little Golden Book Ser.). (ENG.). 24p. (J). (-k). 4.99 *(978-0-307-97656-7(4))*, Golden Bks.) Random Hse. Children's Bks.

Borkowski, Michael, jt. illus. see Atiyeh, Michael.

Borlasca, Hector. Big Kid Shoes. Kosara, Tori. 2011. (J). *(978-0-545-36967-1(3))* Scholastic, Inc.

—Halloween Hide & Seek: Hidden Picture Puzzles, 1 vol. Kalz, Jill. 2012. (Seek It Out Ser.). (ENG.). 32p. (J). (gr. k-3). 9.95 *(978-1-4048-7728-3(2))*; lib. bdg. 27.32 *(978-1-4048-7495-4(X))* Capstone. (Picture Window Bks.).

—I Am Smart. Taylor-Butler, Christine. (My First Reader Ser.). (ENG.). 32p. (J). (gr. k-1). 2006. per. 3.95 *(978-0-516-24971-1(1))*; 2005. lib. bdg. 18.50 *(978-0-516-25176-9(7))* Scholastic Library Publishing. (Children's Pr.).

—It's Too Crowded in Here! And Other Jewish Folktales, Vol. 2010. (ENG.). 64p. (J). pap. 7.95 *(978-0-87441-850-7(X))* Behrman Hse., Inc.

—Jesus Loves Me, 1 vol. Zondervan Staff. 2008. (I Can Read! / Song Ser.). (ENG.). 32p. (J). (gr. -1-3). pap. 4.99 *(978-0-310-71619-8(5))* Zonderkidz.

—The Little Cookie Girl. Williams, Rozanne Lanczak. Hamaguchi, Carla, ed. 2003. (Sight Word Readers Ser.). 16p. (J). (gr. k-2). pap. 3.49 *(978-1-57471-967-3(X))*, 3589) Creative Teaching Pr., Inc.

Borlasca, Hector. Los Meteoritos Odiaban a Los Dinosaurios. Accame, Jorge. 2019. (Torre Azul Ser.). (SPA.). 112p. (J). pap. ***(978-987-545-629-7(2))*** Norma Ediciones, S.A.

Borlasca, Hector. My House/Mi Casa. Rosa-Mendoza, Gladys. (English Spanish Foundations Ser.). (gr. -1-1). 2007. per. 19.95 *(978-1-931398-84-8(4))*; 2006. (ENG & SPA.). 20p. (J). bds. 6.95 *(978-1-931398-18-3(6))* Me+Mi Publishing.

—Pretend & Play Kitty: With Real Crown You Can Wear! Hapka, Cathy. 2004. (Role Play Ser.). 10p. (J). (gr. -1-18). bds. 6.99 *(978-1-57151-742-5(1))* Playhouse Publishing.

—Yiddish Saves the Day! Levy, Debbie. 2019. (J). *(978-1-68115-544-9(3))*, Apples & Honey Pr.) Behrman Hse., Inc.

—30 Mice Are Very Nice. Fleming, Maria & Scholastic Canada Ltd. Staff. 2005. (ENG.). 16p. (J). (gr. -1-1). pap. 2.99 *(978-0-439-69026-3(9))* Scholastic, Inc.

Bornoff, Emily. Snuggle down Deep. Ohanesian, Diane. 2018. (ENG.). 32p. (J). (gr. -1-3). 16.99 *(978-1-4998-0651-9(5))* Little Bee Books Inc.

—Where Did They Go? Big Picture Press, Big Picture. 2016. (ENG.). 32p. (J). (-k). 14.99 *(978-0-7636-8920-9(3))*, Big Picture Press) Candlewick Pr.

Boroff, Ariel. Aliana Reaches for the Moon. Roettiger, Laura. 2019. (ENG.). 34p. (J). (gr. k-5). pap. 9.99 ***(978-1-63233-196-0(9))*** Elfrig Publishing.

Borowski, Maripat. Generous Jennifer: Sharing Is Contagious. Snow, Carleena. 2018. (ENG.). 30p. (J). pap. 9.95 *(978-1-7323592-0-8(2))* Periwinkle Pr.

Borrajero, Judy. Snowflake's Vacation. Sprague, Howard Lee. 2011. 40p. pap. 9.95 *(978-1-881276-16-6(3))* Serey/Jones Pubs.

Borrero, Justo. Christmas Reindeer Food Mishap. Antoinette, Nicole. 2018. (ENG.). 48p. (J). 19.99 *(978-1-939761-05-7(0))* Faith Bks. & MORE.

Borrero, Justo. Percance en la Cena de Navidad de Los Renos. Antoinette, Nicole. Tellez, Martha Cecilia, tr. 2019. (SPA.). 48p. (J). 19.99 ***(978-1-939761-56-9(5))*** Faith Bks. & MORE.

Borrero, Justo. El Reno y la Cena de Navidad. Antoinette, Nicole. 2016. (SPA.). (J). pap. 14.99 *(978-1-939761-49-1(2))* Faith Bks. & MORE.

Borromeo, Mike. Clemens, Rusty, & Tomato Juice. Odom, Sarah B. 2018. (ENG.). 64p. (J). pap. 14.00 *(978-1-7921-1149-5(5))* Independently Published.

—Mimsy's Bible Mystery Tales. Odom, Sarah B. 2019. (ENG.). 72p. (J). pap. 15.00 *(978-1-0706-4346-5(7))* Independently Published.

—Mimsy's Tales of Giants, Lions, & Whales. Odom, Sarah B. 2019. (ENG.). 90p. (J). pap. 18.00 *(978-1-0918-7274-5(0))* Independently Published.

—Splashes & Splishes. Hatt, Pat. 2019. (ENG.). 26p. (J). pap. 9.99 *(978-1-7952-6490-7(X))* Independently Published.

Borsan, Luis. Freaky Foods from Around the World: Platillos Sorprendentes de todo el Mundo. Winner, Ramana Moreno. Haake, Susana, tr. 2004. (ENG & SPA.). (J). (gr. 1-5). pap. 15.95 *(978-0-9651174-2-5(1))* BrainStorm 3000.

Borsboom, Tjarda. Let's Go! Crowe, Carmen. Cottage Door Press, ed. 2019. (Lift-A-Sound Board Book Ser.). (ENG.). 12p. (J). (gr. -1-k). bds. 12.99 *(978-1-68052-529-8(8))*, 1004120) Cottage Door Pr.

Borsch, Kim. Cookie's Colorful World. Kline, Joel. 2011. 32p. pap. 24.95 *(978-1-4560-7578-1(0))* America Star Bks.

Borstel, Ian von. Friends Forever: A Rachel Beth Tale, 1 vol. Marin, Dale Diane. 2009. 31p. pap. 24.95 *(978-1-61546-149-3(3))* America Star Bks.

Borstelmann, Marc. Weapon X Vol. 2: The Search for Weapon H. 2018. (ENG.). 136p. (YA). (gr. 8-17). pap. 15.99 *(978-1-302-90735-8(2))* Marvel Worldwide, Inc.

Borten, Helen. The Jungle. 2018. (ENG.). 40p. (J). (gr. -1-4). 16.95 *(978-1-59270-230-5(9))* Enchanted Lion Bks., LLC.

Bortz, Nathan. Little Joey Goes to Camp. Savalle, Joseph. 2019. (ENG.). 32p. (J). 19.99 *(978-1-7327194-4-6(6))* UNITED Hse. Publishing.

Bos, Elaheh. Le Grand Secret de Sam: Surmonter la Peur. Margolese, Stephanie. Beaulieu, Maroussia, tr. 2019. (FRE.). 48p. (J). pap. 15.50 *(978-1-0797-9573-8(1))* Independently Published.

—Sam's Big Secret. Margolese, Stephanie. 2016. (ENG.). 48p. (J). pap. *(978-0-9810556-0-2(5))* Bos, Ela.

Bos, Hilbrand. Illumination Presents the Secret Life of Pets 2: Little Dog in the Big City. 2019. (Play-A-Sound Ser.). (ENG.). 12p. (J). bds. *(978-1-5037-4565-0(1))*, f63f3a80-ba62-4ce5-a375-aa30de26cab4, p i kids) Phoenix International Publications, Inc.

Bos, Miriam. Jingle Bells: 3 Button Handle Book. Berry Byrd, Holly. Cottage Door Press, ed. 2017. (Early Bird Sound Bks.). (ENG.). 12p. (J). (gr. -1-k). bds. 9.99 *(978-1-68052-230-3(2))*, 1002160) Cottage Door Pr.

Bosa, Subi. A Piece of Black Cake for Santa. Marshall, Yolanda T. 2019. (ENG.). 32p. (J). pap. ***(978-1-9991155-4-8(6))*** Gamalma Pr.

Bosa, Subi. Talks with Liyah: Conquering Bullies. Griffin, Aujah. 2018. (Talks with Liyah Ser.: Vol. 1). (ENG.). 34p. (J). pap. 11.99 *(978-1-7287-3194-0(1))* Independently Published.

—Talks with Liyah: Good Touches Bad Touches. Griffin, Aujah. 2018. (ENG.). 36p. (J). pap. 11.99 *(978-1-7287-3177-3(1))* Independently Published.

—Talks with Liyah: How to Be Happy. Griffin, Aujah. 2018. (Talks with Liyah Ser.: Vol. 1). (ENG.). 28p. (J). pap. 11.99 *(978-1-7287-3204-6(2))* Independently Published.

—Talks with Liyah: The Art of Being a Girl. Griffin, Aujah. 2018. (Talks with Liyah Ser.: Vol. 1). (ENG.). 36p. (J). pap. 11.99 *(978-1-7287-3221-3(2))* Independently Published.

Bosak, Virginia. Rachel & the Magic Beads. Buchanan, Johnny & Conway, Beth. 2007. 16p. (YA). pap. 7.99 *(978-0-9768772-9-5(5))* Wise Guides, LLC.

Bosch, David. Mommy Always Comes Back. Schnee-Bosch, Penny. 2013. 40p. pap. 13.95 *(978-0-9727993-6-2(2))* Athanata Arts, Ltd.

Bosch, Meritxell. FishFishFish. Nordling, Lee. 2015. (Three-Story Bks.). (ENG.). 32p. (J). (gr. k-3). pap. 6.95 *(978-1-4677-4576-5(6))*, 9781467745765, Graphic Universe™) Lerner Publishing Group.

Bosch, Nicole. One-of-a-Kind Stamps & Crafts. Ross, Kathy. 2010. (Girl Crafts Ser.). (ENG.). 48p. (gr. 2-5). pap. 7.95 *(978-1-58013-885-7(3))* Lerner Publishing Group.

Bosch, Nicole in den. Beautiful Beads. Ross, Kathy. 2009. (Girl Crafts Ser.). (ENG.). 48p. (gr. 2-5). 26.60 *(978-0-8225-9214-3(2))*, Millbrook Pr.) Lerner Publishing Group.

—Bedroom Makeover Crafts. Ross, Kathy. 2008. (Girl Crafts Ser.). (ENG.). 48p. (gr. 2-5). (J). 26.60 *(978-0-8225-7593-1(0))*, Millbrook Pr.); pap. 7.95 *(978-1-58013-823-9(3))*, First Avenue Editions) Lerner Publishing Group.

—Creative Kitchen Crafts. Ross, Kathy. 2010. (Girl Crafts Ser.). (ENG.). 48p. (gr. 2-5). lib. bdg. 26.60 *(978-0-8225-9217-4(7))*, Millbrook Pr.) Lerner Publishing Group.

—Fairy World Crafts. Ross, Kathy. 2008. (Girl Crafts Ser.). (ENG.). 48p. (J). (gr. 2-5). lib. bdg. 26.60 *(978-0-8225-7509-2(4))*, Millbrook Pr.) Lerner Publishing Group.

—Girlfriends' Get-Together Craft Book. Ross, Kathy. 2007. (Girl Crafts Ser.). (ENG.). 48p. (gr. 2-5). pap. 7.95 *(978-0-7613-9465-5(6))*, First Avenue Editions) Lerner Publishing Group.

—Jazzy Jewelry, Pretty Purses, & More! Ross, Kathy. 2009. (Girl Crafts Ser.). (ENG.). 48p. (gr. 2-5). 26.60 *(978-0-8225-9212-9(6))*; pap. 7.95 *(978-1-58013-883-3(7))*, Millbrook Pr.) Lerner Publishing Group.

—One-of-a-Kind Stamps & Crafts. Ross, Kathy. 2010. (Girl Crafts Ser.). (ENG.). 48p. (gr. 2-5). lib. bdg. 26.60 *(978-0-8225-9216-7(9))*, Millbrook Pr.) Lerner Publishing Group.

—The Scrapbooker's Idea Book. Ross, Kathy. 2006. (Girl Crafts Ser.). 48p. (J). (gr. 3-7). per. 7.95 *(978-0-8225-6511-6(0))*, First Avenue Editions) Lerner Publishing Group.

Boschi, Roland, et al. Ghost Rider Vol. 2: Hearts of Darkness II. 2020. (ENG.). 136p. (YA). (gr. 8-17). pap. 17.99 ***(978-1-302-92006-7(5))*** Marvel Worldwide, Inc.

Bosgra, Johann. Diving for Colors in Hawaii: A Color Identification Book for Keiki. Hopkins, Jane. 2003. (ENG.). 18p. (J). (gr. -1-1). bds. 7.95 *(978-0-9729905-1-6(8))* Beachhouse Publishing, LLC.

—Diving for Numbers in Hawaii. Hopkins, Jane. 2003. (ENG.). 20p. (J). (gr. -1-k). bds. 7.95 *(978-0-9729905-0-9(X))* Beachhouse Publishing, LLC.

—Diving for Shapes in Hawaii: An Identification Book for Keiki. Gillespie, Jane. 2004. (ENG.). 20p. (J). bds. 8.95 *(978-1-933067-04-9(7))* Beachhouse Publishing, LLC.

Boskovic, Sanja. My Feet Go Together Click! Click! Click! Foresta, David Samuel. 2018. (Go Together Ser.: Vol. 1). (ENG.). 26p. (J). pap. 12.99 *(978-0-578-42370-8(7))* Foresta, David Samuel.

Bosley, Andrew. Silent Journey. Watson, Carl. 2020. (ENG.). 176p. (J). (gr. 4-8). 16.99 ***(978-1-947159-30-3(5))***, One Elm Books) Red Chair Pr.

Bosma, Sam. Attack of the 50 Foot Wallflower. Heidicker, Christian McKay. (ENG.). 320p. (YA). (gr. 9). 2019. pap. 11.99 *(978-1-4814-9914-9(9))*; 2018. 18.99 *(978-1-4814-9913-2(0))* Simon & Schuster Bks. For Young Readers. (Simon & Schuster Bks. For Young Readers).

—Fantasy Sports, No. 1. 2015. (Fantasy Sports Ser.: 1). (ENG.). 56p. (J). (gr. 5-9). 19.95 *(978-1-907704-80-2(9))* Nobrow Ltd. GBR. Dist: Penguin Random Hse. LLC.

—Stand-Off. Smith, Andrew. 2016. (ENG.). 432p. (YA). (gr. 7). pap. 12.99 *(978-1-4814-1830-0(0))*, Simon & Schuster Bks. For Young Readers) Simon & Schuster Bks. For Young Readers.

—Thisby Thestoop & the Black Mountain. Gorman, Zac. (ENG.). 336p. (J). (gr. 3-7). 2019. pap. 6.99 *(978-0-06-249568-6(2))*; 2018. 16.99 *(978-0-06-249567-9(4))* HarperCollins Pubs.

—Thisby Thestoop & the Wretched Scrattle. Gorman, Zac. 2019. (ENG.). 384p. (J). (gr. 3-7). 16.99 *(978-0-06-249574-7(7))* HarperCollins Pubs.

—Winger. Smith, Andrew. (ENG.). (YA). (gr. 7). 2014. 464p. pap. 12.99 *(978-1-4424-4493-5(2))*; 2013. 448p. 18.99 *(978-1-4424-4492-8(4))* Simon & Schuster Bks. For Young Readers. (Simon & Schuster Bks. For Young Readers).

Bosnia, Nella. Arturo y Clementina. Turin, Adela. (SPA.). 40p. (J). (gr. 3-5). *(978-84-264-3801-0(6))* Editorial Lumen ESP. Dist: Lectorum Pubns., Inc.

—La Herencia del Hada. Turin, Adela. (SPA.). 40p. (J). (gr. 3-5). *(978-84-264-3556-9(4))* Editorial Lumen ESP. Dist: Lectorum Pubns., Inc.

—Rosa Caramelo. Turin, Adela. (SPA.). 40p. (J). (gr. 2-4). *(978-84-264-3800-3(8))* Editorial Lumen ESP. Dist: Lectorum Pubns., Inc.

Bosschaert, Greet. Totally Lisa. Boonen, Stefan. 2008. (ENG.). 118p. (J). (gr. 4-7). 15.95 *(978-1-60537-005-7(3))* Clavis Publishing.

Bossi, Lisa Burnett. The Happiness Tree: Celebrating the Gifts of Trees We Treasure. Gosline, Andrea Alban. 2008. (ENG.). 40p. (J). (gr. k-3). 18.99 *(978-0-312-37017-6(2),* 900044354) Feiwel & Friends.

—Ten Little Wishes: A Baby Animal Counting Book. Gosline, Andrea Alban. 2007. 40p. (J). (gr. -1-k). 16.89 *(978-0-06-053411-0(7))* HarperCollins Pubs.

Bostanic, Ashley D. Angels, Angels Everywhere. Branz, Susan M. 2017. (ENG.). (J). 19.95 *(978-1-68197-856-7(3));* (gr. -1-3). 12.95 *(978-1-68197-854-3(7))* Christian Faith Publishing.

Bostian, Laurie. Appalachian State, A to Z. Webb, Anne Aldridge. 2010. (J). 18.95 *(978-1-933251-69-1(7))* Parkway Pubs., Inc.

Bostic, Alex. Man of Destiny: The Life of Leopold Sedar Senghor. Collin, Grace. 2006. 32p. (J). lib. bdg. 16.95 *(978-1-886366-15-2(2))* Sights Productions.

Bostock, Mike. Think of an Eel. Wallace, Karen. 2009. (Read, Listen, & Wonder Ser.). (ENG.). 32p. (J). (gr. -1-3). pap. 8.99 *(978-0-7636-3994-5(X))* Candlewick Pr.

—Think of an Eel Big Book. Wallace, Karen. 2004. (Read & Wonder Ser.). (ENG.). 32p. (J). (gr. -1-2). pap. 24.99 *(978-0-7636-2470-5(5))* Candlewick Pr.

Boston, David. The Dancing Turtle: A Folktale from Brazil. DeSpain, Pleasant. 2019. (ENG.). 32p. (J). (gr. -1-4). pap. 8.95 *(978-1-941460-46-7(1))* August Hse. Pubs., Inc.

—Wonder Tales from Around the World. 2006. (World Storytelling from August House Ser.). (ENG.). 158p. (J). (gr. 3-7). pap. 19.95 *(978-0-87483-422-2(8),* AH228) August Hse. Pubs., Inc.

Boston, Paul. The Book of Comparisons. Gifford, Clive. 2018. (ENG.). 96p. (J). 17.99 *(978-1-61067-667-0(X))* Kane Miller.

—Find Your Way in Space. 2017. (Find Your Way Ser.). (ENG.). 32p. (J). (gr. 1-4). 14.95 *(978-1-68297-047-8(7),* QED Publishing) Quarto Publishing Group UK GBR. Dist: Hachette Bk. Group.

—The United States in 100 Words. Dickmann, Nancy. 2019. (In a Nutshell Ser.). (ENG.). 112p. (J). (gr. 2-6). 19.95 *(978-0-7112-4243-2(7),* Words & Pictures) Quarto Publishing Group UK GBR. Dist: Hachette Bk. Group.

Boston, Paul. Map Your Way. Boston, Paul. 2018. (ENG.). 128p. (J). (gr. -1-2). pap. 14.95 ***(978-1-68297-307-3(7))*** QEB Publishing Inc.

Boston, Peter. The Stones of Green Knowe. Boston, L. M. 2006. (Green Knowe Ser.: 6). (ENG.). 144p. (J). (gr. 3-7). pap. 10.95 *(978-0-15-205566-0(5),* 1196740) Houghton Mifflin Harcourt Publishing Co.

Bostrom, Christopher. The Secret of the Twelve Days of Christmas. Bostrom, Kathleen. 2005. 68p. (gr. -1-7). per. 10.95 *(978-1-931195-74-4(9))* KiwE Publishing, Ltd.

Bostrom, Laura. I Am. Propes, Chrysti Carol. 3rd ed. 2013. 40p. 24.95 *(978-0-9790791-8-4(7))* Fig & The Vine, LLC, The.

—I Am Here. Propes, Chrysti Carol. 3rd ed. 2013. 32p. 24.95 *(978-0-9790791-9-1(5))* Fig & The Vine, LLC, The.

Bostrom, Sally. The Magic Apple Tree. Kendall, Jack. I.t. ed. 2006. (ENG.). 48p. (J). per. 9.95 *(978-0-9787740-4-2(3))* Peppertree Pr., The.

Bosworth, David. Song of the Jackalope. Campbell, Roy. 2nd ed. 2006. 140p. (YA). pap. 12.95 *(978-1-933538-04-4(X))* Bridgeway Bks.

Botman, Loes. Hello Animals, What Makes You Special?, 65 vols. 2015. (Hello Animals Ser.). (ENG.). 12p. (J). 9.95 *(978-1-78250-218-0(1))* Floris Bks. GBR. Dist: Consortium Bk. Sales & Distribution.

—Hello Animals, Where Do You Live?, 65 vols. 2015. (Hello Animals Ser.). (ENG.). 12p. (J). 9.95 *(978-1-78250-219-7(X))* Floris Bks. GBR. Dist: Consortium Bk. Sales & Distribution.

—Hello Birds, What Do You Say?, 30 vols. 2018. (Hello Animals Ser.). Orig. Title: Klein Vogelboek. (ENG.). 12p. (J). 9.95 *(978-1-78250-488-7(5))* Floris Bks. GBR. Dist: Consortium Bk. Sales & Distribution.

—Hello Bugs, What Do You Do?, 30 vols. 2017. (Hello Animals Ser.). Orig. Title: Klein Insectenboek. (ENG.). 12p. (J). 9.95 *(978-1-78250-383-5(8))* Floris Bks. GBR. Dist: Consortium Bk. Sales & Distribution.

—Hello Farm, How Do You Do?, 80 vols. Thiebout, Marjolein. (Hello Animals Ser.). Orig. Title: Weet Je, Weet Je Wat... de Dieren Zeggen?. (ENG.). 14p. (J). 2013. 9.95 *(978-0-86315-962-6(1));* 2nd rev. ed. 2019. 9.95 *(978-1-78250-588-4(1))* Floris Bks. GBR. Dist: Consortium Bk. Sales & Distribution.

Bottini, William. The Other Side of the Bridge. Nesamoney, Sophia. 2018. (ENG.). 212p. (YA). pap. 16.99 *(978-0-9981849-3-7(4))* Society of Young Inklings.

Bottino, Dean. The Sacred Stone. Kim, David. 2018. (ENG.). 172p. (J). pap. 12.95 *(978-1-7286-5309-9(6))* Independently Published.

Bottner, Barbara. Pish & Posh. Bottner, Barbara. Kruglik, Gerald. 2004. (I Can Read Bks.). 48p. (J). (gr. k-3). pap. 15.99 *(978-0-06-051416-7(7))* HarperCollins Pubs.

—Pish & Posh Wish for Fairy Wings. Bottner, Barbara. Kruglik, Gerald. (I Can Read Level 2 Ser.). 48p. (J). 2007. (ENG.). (gr. k-3). pap. 4.99 *(978-0-06-051421-1(3),* Tegen, Katherine Bks); 2006. (gr. -1-3). lib. bdg. 16.89 *(978-0-06-051420-4(5))* HarperCollins Pubs.

Bou, David. Snow Pants in April. Duckering, Tobi. 2020. (ENG.). 32p. (J). ***(978-1-5255-5862-7(5))***; pap. ***(978-1-5255-5863-4(3))*** FriesenPress.

Bouchain, Nava. Los Diminutos. Suarez de la Prida, Isabel. 2003. (SPA.). 32p. (J). (gr. k-3). pap. 6.95 *(978-968-19-0631-3(4))* Santillana USA Publishing Co., Inc.

Bouchal, Renee'. The World Will Never Forget. Baurys, Tamra. 2011. 34p. pap. 12.95 *(978-0-9833354-2-9(7))* Amira Rock Publishing.

Bouchard, Amy. Alphabet Zwoop: Poemlets for Young Children. Holzer, Madeleine. 2018. (ENG.). 32p. (J). (gr. k-4). 16.99 *(978-0-942942-31-6(0))* Emu Editions.

Bouchelion, Anastasia & Enright, Kameron. God Made Me Too. Pace, Eugenia Ann. 2011. (ENG.). 26p. (J). pap. 15.99 ***(978-1-4653-6240-7(1))*** Xlibris Corp.

Boucher, Jason. Allergy Avengers: Knowledge Is Our Super Power. Civin, Todd & Keen, Tammi. 2019. (ENG.). 44p. (J). pap. 14.95 *(978-1-7933-1410-9(1))* Independently Published.

Boucher, Jerry. Raccoons. Boucher, Jerry, photos by. Kite, L. Patricia. 2004. (Early Bird Nature Bks.). 47p. (J). 25.26 *(978-0-8225-3049-7(X),* Lerner Pubns.) Lerner Publishing Group.

Boucher, Joelle. Las Ballenas y Otros Mamíferos Marinos / Whales & Other Sea Mammals. Geistdoerfer, Patrick. 2018. (Altea Benjamín Ser.). (SPA.). 32p. (J). (gr. 3-7). pap. 10.99 *(978-1-947783-60-7(2),* Altea) Penguin Random House Grupo Editorial ESP. Dist: Penguin Random Hse. LLC.

Boucher, Julie. The Little Tree That Would Be Great. Desrochers, Diane O. 2009. 36p. pap. 14.95 *(978-0-9819727-7-0(2))* Fiction Publishing, Inc.

Boudreau, Chantale, jt. illus. see Dupuis, Karina.

Boudreau, Iris. Odd One Out (Provisional Title) Chaperon, Danielle. 2017. 40p. (J). (gr. -1). 12.95 *(978-2-7338-5066-4(0))* Auzou, Philippe Editions FRA. Dist: Consortium Bk. Sales & Distribution.

Boudreau, Paulette. God Is in Everything: A Bedtime Story for Little Ears. Calderon, Marcia. 2018. (ENG.). 32p. (J). pap. 10.99 *(978-1-7259-0492-7(6))* CreateSpace Independent Publishing Platform.

Boufantino, Simone, et al. Black Panther: This Is Black Panther. West, Alexandra. 2019. (World of Reading Level 1 Ser.). (ENG.). 32p. (J). (gr. -1-3). lib. bdg. 27.07 *(978-1-5321-4397-7(4),* 33802) Spotlight.

Bougaeva, Sonja. The Story of Crime & Punishment. Yehoshua, A. B. & Dostoevsky, Fyodor. Schoffman, Stuart, tr. 2016. (Save the Story Ser.: 4). (ENG.). 104p. (J). (gr. 3-7). 19.95 *(978-1-78269-014-6(X),* Pushkin Children's Bks.) Steerforth Pr.

Bouganim, Revital. The Great Adventures of Bottom the Bassett Hound. Ryshpan-Harris, Joanne. 2008. 60p. (J). pap. 5.95 *(978-1-4259-8558-5(0))* AuthorHouse.

Boughton, Sam. Hello, Dinosaurs! Boughton, Sam. 2019. (Animal Facts & Flaps Ser.). (ENG.). 16p. (J). (-k). bds. 12.99 *(978-1-5362-0809-2(4),* Templar) Candlewick Pr.

—Hello, Elephant! Boughton, Sam. 2020. (ENG.). 16p. (J). (-k). bds. 12.99 *(978-1-5362-1021-7(8),* Templar) Candlewick Pr.

Boulanger, Annie. Lili Macaroni. Testa, Nicole. 2019. (ENG.). 32p. (J). (gr. k-2). 17.95 *(978-1-77278-093-2(6))* Pajama Pr. CAN. Dist: Ingram Publisher Services.

Boulanger, Linda. Finding a Leprechaun. DuBois, Diana Marie. 2019. (Clover Chronicles Ser.: Vol. 1). (ENG.). 148p. (J). pap. 10.00 *(978-0-9983036-6-6(6))* Three Danes Publishing LLC.

Bouloubasis, Petros. Little Red Rhyming Hood. Fliess, Sue. 2019. (ENG.). 32p. (J). (gr. -1-3). 16.99 *(978-0-8075-4597-3(X),* 080754597X) Whitman, Albert & Co.

—Mary Had a Little Lab. Fliess, Sue. 2018. (ENG.). 32p. (J). (gr. -1-3). 16.99 *(978-0-8075-4982-7(7),* 807549827) Whitman, Albert & Co.

Bouloubasis, Petros. Mary Had a Little Lab. Fliess, Sue. 2020. (ENG.). 32p. (J). (gr. -1-3). pap. 7.99 ***(978-0-8075-4986-5(X)***, 080754986X) Whitman, Albert & Co.

—The Princess & the Petri Dish. Fliess, Sue. 2020. (ENG.). 32p. (J). (gr. -1-3). 16.99 ***(978-0-8075-6644-2(6)***, 807566446) Whitman, Albert & Co.

Bouma, Donna Mae. Hit the Ball, Joe! Hoops, Tanner. 2019. (ENG.). 64p. (J). 27.95 ***(978-1-64559-571-7(4))***; pap. 17.95 ***(978-1-64559-569-4(2))*** Covenant Bks.

Bouma, Donna Mae. Maggie & the Big Move. Haveman, Patricia Ann. 2018. (ENG.). 82p. (J). pap. 15.95 *(978-1-64300-158-6(2))* Covenant Bks.

Bouma, Xanthe. Little Sid: The Tiny Prince Who Became Buddha. Lendler, Ian. 2018. (ENG.). 40p. (J). 17.99 *(978-1-62672-636-9(1),* 9781626726369, First Second Bks.) Roaring Brook Pr.

Bouma, Xanthe, et al. Red Maze. Siegel, Mark & Siegel, Alexis. 2019. (5 Worlds Ser.: 3). 256p. (J). (gr. 3-7). 20.99 *(978-1-101-93592-7(8),* Random Hse. Bks. for Young Readers) Random Hse. Children's Bks.

—The Sand Warrior. Siegel, Mark & Siegel, Alexis. 2017. (5 Worlds Ser.: 1). (ENG.). 256p. (J). (gr. 3-7). lib. bdg. 21.99 *(978-1-101-93587-3(1),* Random Hse. Bks. for Young Readers) Random Hse. Children's Bks.

—Sand Warrior. Siegel, Mark & Siegel, Alexis. 2017. (5 Worlds Ser.: 1). 256p. (J). (gr. 3-7). pap. 12.99 *(978-1-101-93588-0(X),* Random Hse. Bks. for Young Readers) Random Hse. Children's Bks.

—The Sand Warrior. Siegel, Mark & Siegel, Alexis. ed. 2017. (5 Worlds Ser.: 1). lib. bdg. 24.50 *(978-0-606-40243-9(8))* Turtleback.

—5 Worlds Book 1: the Sand Warrior. Siegel, Mark & Siegel, Alexis. 2017. (5 Worlds Ser.: 1). 256p. (J). (gr. 3-7). 18.99 *(978-1-101-93586-6(3),* Random Hse. Bks. for Young Readers) Random Hse. Children's Bks.

—5 Worlds Book 3: the Red Maze. Siegel, Mark & Siegel, Alexis. 2019. (5 Worlds Ser.: 3). (ENG.). 256p. (J). (gr. 3-7). pap. 12.99 *(978-1-101-93594-1(4));* lib. bdg. 23.99 *(978-1-101-93593-4(6))* Random Hse. Children's Bks. (Random Hse. Bks. for Young Readers).

Bounds, Jessica. Winston Loves Wind. Harrison, Karin. 2016. (ENG.). (J). pap. *(978-1-4602-9424-6(6))* FriesenPress.

Bour-Chollet, Céline, et al. La Hora. Bour-Chollet, Céline et al. (Coleccion Mundo Maravilloso). (SPA.). 48p. (J). (gr. 2-4). *(978-84-348-4485-8(0),* SM1439) SM Ediciones ESP. Dist: Lectorum Pubns., Inc.

Bour, Laura, jt. illus. see de Hugo, Pierre.

Bourbonnière, Sylvie. Dream Songs Night Songs: From China to Senegal. Lacoursiere, Patrick. 2006. (ENG.). 36p. (J). (gr. -1-2). 16.95 *(978-2-923163-24-6(9))* La Montagne Secrete CAN. Dist: Independent Pubs. Group.

—Dream Songs Night Songs: From Mali to Louisiana. Lacoursiere, Patrick. 2006. (ENG.). 36p. (J). (gr. -1-2). 16.95 *(978-2-923163-06-2(0))* La Montagne Secrete CAN. Dist: Independent Pubs. Group.

Boureau, Silvere. A Bully Grows Up: Erik Meets the Wizard: Adult Guide Edition, 1. Hacker, Caryn Sabes. 2006. 34p. (J). tchr. ed. 15.95 *(978-0-9791046-0-2(2))* Caryn Solutions, LLC.

Bourgeau, Vincent. Shhh! This Book Is Sleeping. Ramadier, Cédric. 2016. (ENG.). 20p. (J). (gr. -1 — 1). bds. 8.99 *(978-0-553-53875-5(6),* Random Hse. Bks. for Young Readers) Random Hse. Children's Bks.

Bourgeois, Anne Marie. Song on the Wind, 1 vol. Everson, Caroline. 2018. (ENG.). 32p. (J). (gr. -1-2). 18.95 *(978-1-927083-30-7(3),* 827f38d4-93f8-4ca8-8e9c-cc1bad0d687f) Fifth Hse. Pubs. CAN. Dist: Firefly Bks., Ltd.

Bourgonje, Chantal. Harry's Midnight Adventure. Campbell, Catherine. 2018. (Bad Cat Club Ser.: Vol. 1). (ENG.). 82p. (J). (gr. 1-2). pap. *(978-1-9164538-0-7(5))* Campbell, Catherine.

—The Lucky, Lucky Leaf: A Horace & Nim Story. Hoskins, David. 2018. (Horace & Nim Story Ser.). (ENG.). 32p. (J). (gr. -1-k). 9.99 *(978-1-78711-306-0(X),* Hubble & Hattie) Veloce Publishing Ltd. GBR. Dist: Hachette Bk. Group.

—Worzel Goes for a Walk! Will You Come, Too? Pickles, Catherine. 2018. (ENG.). 32p. (J). (gr. -1-k). 9.99 *(978-1-78711-292-6(6),* Hubble & Hattie) Veloce Publishing Ltd. GBR. Dist: Hachette Bk. Group.

Bourke, John-Francis. Hands Can. Hudson, Cheryl Willis. 2013. 32p. (J). (-k). 4.99 *(978-0-7636-6336-0(0))* Candlewick Pr.

—Las Manos. Hudson, Cheryl Willis. 2014. 32p. (J). (-k). pap. 4.99 *(978-0-7636-7392-5(7))* Candlewick Pr.

Bourke, John-Francis. Hands Can. Bourke, John-Francis, photos by. Hudson, Cheryl Willis. 2013. (ENG.). 32p. (J). (gr. -1-1). 17.44 *(978-0-7636-1667-0(2))* Candlewick Pr.

Bourke, John-Francis, photos by. Hands Can. Hudson, Cheryl Willis. (J). (gr. k-k). 2012. 32p. pap. 24.99 *(978-0-7636-5819-9(7));* 2007. 24p. bds. 7.99 *(978-0-7636-3292-2(9))* Candlewick Pr.

Bournakis, Maria. Everlasting Truth. Vardamaskos, Angela. 2008. 48p. pap. 24.95 *(978-1-60610-950-2(2))* America Star Bks.

Bourne, C. L. Sam the Big Blue Bear, Vol. 1. Bourne, C. L. Date not set. 24p. (J). (gr. k-4). pap. *(978-0-9651281-4-8(8))* Beach Front Bks.

Bourrouet, Jonathan. Alphabet Fun, Book 1: Coloring & Activity Book. Bumpers, Katrina B. Lopez, Eddie, ed. 2008. 64p. pap. 10.95 *(978-0-9797208-0-2(X))* K's Kids Publishing.

Bourseiller, Philippe, photos by. 50 Ways to Save the Earth. Jankéliowitch, Anne & Jankéliowitch, Anne. 2008. (ENG.). 128p. (J). (gr. 3-7). 19.95 *(978-0-8109-7239-1(5),* Abrams Bks. for Young Readers) Abrams, Inc.

Boushee, Luke. The Young Adventurer's Guide to (Almost) Everything: Build a Fort, Camp Like a Champ, Poop in the Woods-45 Action-Packed Outdoor Activities. Hewitt, Ben. 2019. (ENG.). 208p. (J). (gr. 3-7). 16.95 *(978-1-61180-594-9(5),* Roost Books) Shambhala Pubns., Inc.

Bousidan, Inbal Gigi. French Toast Sundays. Spielman, Gloria. 2018. (J). *(978-1-68115-529-6(X),* Apples & Honey Pr.) Behrman Hse., Inc.

Bousum, Julie. The Mouse Family Christmas, 1 vol. Johnson, Gerald J. J. 2009. 26p. pap. 24.95 *(978-1-61546-536-1(7))* America Star Bks.

Boutavant, Marc. All Aboard Train Matching Game. 2016. (ENG.). 36p. (J). (gr. -1-17). 14.99 *(978-1-4521-4861-8(9))* Chronicle Bks. LLC.

—Around the World with Mouk. 2009. (ENG.). 32p. (J). (gr. 3-17). 17.99 *(978-0-8118-6926-3(1))* Chronicle Bks. LLC.

—Barkus. Maclachlan, Patricia. 2017. (Barkus Ser.: 1). (ENG.). 56p. (J). (gr. 1-4). 14.99 *(978-1-4521-1182-7(0))* Chronicle Bks. LLC.

—Barkus: Book 1. Maclachlan, Patricia. 2018. (Barkus Ser.: 1). (ENG.). 56p. (J). (gr. 1-4). pap. 6.99 *(978-1-4521-7262-0(5))* Chronicle Bks. LLC.

—Barkus Dog Dreams: Book 2. Maclachlan, Patricia. 2018. (Barkus Ser.: 2). (ENG.). 52p. (J). (gr. 1-4). 14.99 *(978-1-4521-1676-1(8))* Chronicle Bks. LLC.

—Barkus Dog Dreams: Book 2 (Barkus Book 2, Dog Book for Children) MacLachlan, Patricia. 2020. (ENG.). 56p. (J). (gr. 1-4). pap. 6.99 *(978-1-4521-8080-9(6))* Chronicle Bks. LLC.

—Dumpster Dog! Gutman, Colas. 2019. (Adventures of Dumpster Dog Ser.). 64p. (J). 8.95 *(978-1-59270-252-7(X))* Enchanted Lion Bks., LLC.

—Dumpster Dog! Gutman, Colas. Charette, Allison M., tr. from FRE. 2019. (Adventures of Dumpster Dog Ser.). (ENG.). 64p. (J). 14.95 *(978-1-59270-235-0(X))* Enchanted Lion Bks., LLC.

—Edmond, the Moonlit Party. Desbordes, Astrid. 2015. (ENG.). 32p. (J). (gr. -1-3). 17.95 *(978-1-59270-174-2(4))* Enchanted Lion Bks., LLC.

—Ghosts. Goldie, Sonia. 2013. 40p. (J). (gr. -1-3). 16.95 *(978-1-59270-142-1(6))* Enchanted Lion Bks., LLC.

—Merry Christmas, Dumpster Dog! Gutman, Colas. Charette, Allison M., tr. 2019. (Adventures of Dumpster Dog Ser.). 72p. (J). (ENG.). 14.95 *(978-1-59270-271-8(6));* 8.95 *(978-1-59270-273-2(2))* Enchanted Lion Bks., LLC.

Boutavant, Marc. Not an Alphabet Book: the Case of the Missing Cake. McLaughlin, Eoin. 2020. (ENG.). 40p. (J). (-k). 16.99 ***(978-1-5362-1267-9(9))*** Candlewick Pr.

Boutavant, Marc. Sitting Still Like a Frog Activity Book: 75 Mindfulness Games for Kids. Snel, Eline. 2019. 100p. (J). (gr. -1-3). pap. 16.95 *(978-1-61180-588-8(0),* Bala Kids) Shambhala Pubns., Inc.

—The Thing. Desbordes, Astrid. 2017. (ENG.). 32p. (J). (gr. -1-3). 17.95 *(978-1-59270-217-6(1))* Enchanted Lion Bks., LLC.

—What Happens Next? Davies, Nicola. 2012. (Flip the Flap & Find Out Ser.). (ENG.). 24p. (J). (gr. -1-2). 9.99 *(978-0-7636-6264-6(X))* Candlewick Pr.

—Who Lives Here? Davies, Nicola. 2012. (Flip the Flap & Find Out Ser.). (ENG.). 24p. (J). (gr. -1-2). 9.99 *(978-0-7636-6263-9(1))* Candlewick Pr.

Boutheyette, Valerie. After the Ark: Eli & Ella the Little Elephants - Children of the King! Teis, Sean P. 2013. 32p. pap. 14.99 *(978-1-937129-84-2(5))* Faithful Life Pubs.

Bouthyette, Valerie. Al the Magic Elephant. Warugaba, Christine. 2015. (ENG.). 30p. (J). pap. *(978-99977-770-2-7(6))* FURAHA Pubs. Ltd.

—Alice l'Hôte des Gorilles. Warugaba, Christine. 2018. (FRE.). 38p. (J). pap. *(978-99977-773-7-9(9))* FURAHA Pubs. Ltd.

—Beauty, the Donkey-Mooing Beltie. Lindemer, C. R. 2008. 32p. (J). pap. *(978-0-9821058-2-5(7))* Shapato Publishing, LLC.

—Bella Devient la Princesse Girafe. Warugaba, Christine. 2019. (FRE.). 28p. (J). pap. *(978-99977-774-6-1(8))* FURAHA Pubs. Ltd.

—The Blackboard in the Sky. Warugaba, Christine. 2014. (ENG.). 34p. (J). pap. *(978-99977-770-3-4(4))* FURAHA Pubs. Ltd.

—A Change of Hats. Dowling, Iris Gray. 2012. 28p. pap. 14.99 *(978-1-937129-36-1(5))* Faithful Life Pubs.

—Dr. Dee Dee Dynamo's Beemore Breakthru. Williams, Oneeka. 2017. (ENG.). (J). (gr. -1-3). 14.95 *(978-1-68401-016-5(0))* Mascot Bks., Inc.

—Gertrude & the Creature. Costello, Judi. 2008. 28p. pap. 24.95 *(978-1-60672-737-9(0))* America Star Bks.

—Isla Saves Egypt. Dewees-Gilger, Connie. 2013. (ENG.). (J). 14.95 *(978-1-62086-375-6(8))* Mascot Bks., Inc.

—The Leprechaun Trap. 2008. 40p. (J). pap. 10.95 *(978-0-9800835-0-7(8))* Clinch Media.

—Old Mean Molly, 1 vol. Arline-Hicks, Patience & Hicks, Wendi N. 2009. 38p. pap. 24.95 *(978-1-60749-678-6(X))* America Star Bks.

—A Pony for My Birthday. Dowling, Iris Gray. 2012. 36p. pap. 10.99 *(978-1-937129-50-7(0))* Faithful Life Pubs.

—Timid Timmy the Brave. Hladik, Terry L. 2008. 28p. pap. 12.95 *(978-0-9822540-5-9(9))* Peppertree Pr., The.

—The 4 Police Soaps. Warugaba, Christine. 2016. (ENG.). 24p. (J). pap. *(978-99977-770-7-2(7))* FURAHA Pubs. Ltd.

Bouttell, Robin & Hawke, Richard. Creepy Critters: A Pop-Up Book of Creatures That Jump, Crawl, & Fly. 2012. (ENG.). 14p. (J). (gr. -1-3). 15.95 *(978-0-8109-8942-9(5),* Abrams Bks. for Young Readers) Abrams, Inc.

Bouxom, Sophie. Una Ola de Alegria para Jose Maria. Kochka. 2020. (SPA.). 32p. (J). (gr. -1-2). 12.95 ***(978-84-9145-333-8(4)***, Picarona Editorial) Ediciones Obelisco ESP. Dist: Spanish Pubs., LLC.

Bove, Lorelay. Disney Frozen 2: Touch & Feel Forest. Editors of Studio Fun International. 2019. (ENG.). 10p. (J). (— 1). bds. 9.99 *(978-0-7944-4444-0(X),* Studio Fun International) Printers Row Publishing Group.

—Pencils, Pens & Brushes: a Great Girls' Guide to Disney Animation. Johnson, Mindy. 2019. (ENG.). 80p. (J). (gr. 3-7). 18.99 *(978-1-368-02868-4(3))* Disney Pr.

Bovo, Beatrice, jt. illus. see Bagnoli, Gabriele.

Bowater, Charlie. Scrap City. Thornton, D. S. 2015. (Middle-Grade Novels Ser.). (ENG.). 352p. (J). (gr. 4-8). lib. bdg. 27.99 *(978-1-4965-0475-3(5),* Stone Arch Bks.) Capstone.

Bowden, Cecelia. Peggy Sue & the Pepper Patch. Hopper, Missy. 2010. 32p. (J). *(978-1-57736-430-6(9))* Providence Hse Pubs.

Bowden, Rob, photos by. Sydney. Mason, Paul. 2007. (Global Cities Ser.). 64p. (gr. 5-8). lib. bdg. 30.00 *(978-0-7910-8849-4(9),* Chelsea Hse.) Facts On File, Inc.

—Tokyo. Barber, Nicola. 2006. (Global Cities Ser.). 61p. (gr. 5-8). 30.00 *(978-0-7910-8855-5(3),* Chelsea Hse.) Facts On File, Inc.

Bowden, Rob & Cooper, Adrian, photos by. London. Mason, Paul. 2006. (Global Cities Ser.). 61p. (gr. 5-8). 30.00 *(978-0-7910-8852-4(9),* Chelsea Hse.) Facts On File, Inc.

Bowen, Betsy. Big Belching Bog. Root, Phyllis. 2010. (ENG.). 40p. (gr. 2-3). 15.95 *(978-0-8166-3359-3(2))* Univ. of Minnesota Pr.

—Dhegdheer: A Scary Somali Folktale. 2007. (SOM & ENG.). *(978-1-931016-18-6(6)); (978-1-931016-19-3(4))* Minnesota Humanities Ctr.

—Great Wolf & the Good Woodsman. Hoover, Helen. 2005. (Fesler-Lampert Minnesota Heritage Ser.). 40p. (J). (gr. -1-7). 14.95 *(978-0-8166-4445-2(4))* Univ. of Minnesota Pr.

—The Lost Forest. Root, Phyllis. 2019. (ENG.). 40p. (J). 17.95 *(978-0-8166-9796-0(5))* Univ. of Minnesota Pr.

—Plant a Pocket of Prairie. Root, Phyllis. 2014. (ENG.). 40p. 14.95 *(978-0-8166-7980-5(0))* Univ. of Minnesota Pr.

Bowen, Betsy, jt. illus. see Prange, Beckie.

Bowen-Simms, Paula. Animals at Night. Garnett, Jaye. Parragon Books, ed. 2020. (Pbs Kids Ser.). (ENG.). 14p. (J). (gr. -1-k). bds. 10.99 ***(978-1-68052-932-6(3)***, 1005740, Parragon Books) Cottage Door Pr.

—Ask a Firefighter. Garnett, Jaye. Cottage Door Press, ed. 2020. (Pbs Kids Ser.). (ENG.). 12p. (J). (gr. -1-k). bds. 6.99 ***(978-1-68052-800-8(9)***, 1005130) Cottage Door Pr.

—Ask a Veterinarian. Garnett, Jaye. Cottage Door Press, ed. 2020. (Pbs Kids Ser.). (ENG.). 12p. (J). (gr. -1-k). bds. 6.99 ***(978-1-68052-801-5(7)***, 1005140) Cottage Door Pr.

—Big, Busy Airport. Garnett, Jaye. Parragon Books, ed. 2020. (Pbs Kids Ser.). (ENG.). 14p. (J). (gr. -1-k). bds. 10.99 ***(978-1-68052-931-9(5)***, 1005730, Parragon Books) Cottage Door Pr.

—Bugs! Garnett, Jaye. Cottage Door Press, ed. 2020. (PBS KIDS Chunky Lift-A-Flap Board Book Ser.). (ENG.). 12p. (J). (gr. -1-k). bds. 7.99 ***(978-1-68052-935-7(8)***, 1005780) Cottage Door Pr.

—Fish! Garnett, Jaye. Parragon Books, ed. 2020. (PBS KIDS Chunky Lift-A-Flap Board Book Ser.). (ENG.). 12p. (J). (gr. -1-k). bds. 7.99 ***(978-1-68052-936-4(6)***, 1005790) Cottage Door Pr.

—Scales & Tails. Garnett, Jaye. Cottage Door Press, ed. 2020. (PBS Kids Touch & Feel Board Book Ser.). (ENG.). 10p. (J). (gr. -1-k). bds. 9.99 ***(978-1-68052-950-0(1)***, 1005930) Cottage Door Pr.

Bower, Brittany, jt. illus. see Bower, Jan.

B

Bower, Jan. Cody's Castle: Encouraging Others. Bower, Gary. l.t. ed. 2004. (Thinking of Others: Vol. 4). 32p. (J). 16.95 (978-0-9704621-3-8(1)) Storybook Meadow Publishing.

—The Garden Where I Grow: And Other Poems for Cultivating a Happy Family. Bower, Gary. 2012. (Bright Future Bks.). (ENG.). 32p. (J). 11.99 (978-0-9845236-2-7(6)) Storybook Meadow Publishing.

—I'm a Michigan Kid! Bower, Gary. 2005. 48p. (J). 17.99 (978-0-9704621-6-9(6)) Storybook Meadow Publishing.

—Jingle in My Pocket. Bower, Gary. 2009. 32p. 11.99 (978-0-9704621-9-0(0)) Storybook Meadow Publishing.

—Mommy Love. Bower, Gary. 2012. (Little Lovable Board Bks.). (ENG.). 16p. (J). bds. 8.50 (978-0-9845236-0-3(X)) Storybook Meadow Publishing.

—One Amazing Night: A Christmas Story. Porter, Beverly J. 2019. (ENG.). 34p. (J). pap. 11.99 (978-1-62586-143-6(5)) Credo Hse. Pubs.

—Over Land & Sea: The Story of International Adoption, 1 vol. Layne, Steven L. 2005. (ENG.). 32p. (J). (gr. k-3). 16.99 (978-1-58980-182-0(2), Pelican Publishing) Arcadia Publishing.

—The Person I Marry. Bower, Gary. 2008. 32p. (J). pap. 11.99 (978-0-9704621-7-6(4)) Storybook Meadow Publishing.

—There's a Party in Heaven! A Joyful Peek at the Land of Surprises. Bower, Gary. 2007. (ENG.). 32p. (J). 11.99 (978-0-9704621-8-3(2)) Storybook Meadow Publishing.

Bower, Jan & Bower, Brittany. I'm a Michigan Kid Coloring & Activity Book. Bower, Gary. 2006. 48p. (J). pap. 7.95 (978-0-9704621-5-2(8), Bower Bks.) Storybook Meadow Publishing.

Bower, Jenn. Strangers at the Manger. Hendey, Lisa M. 2016. (Chime Travelers Ser.: 5). (ENG.). 144p. (gr. 2-5). pap. 8.99 (978-1-63253-100-1(3), B53100, Servant Bks.) Franciscan Media.

—The Whisper in the Ruins. Hendey, Lisa M. 2016. (Chime Travelers Ser.: 3). (ENG.). 128p. (gr. 2-5). pap. 8.99 (978-1-63253-036-3(8), B53036, Servant Bks.) Franciscan Media.

Bower, Jennifer. A Dime. Morey, Allan. 2018. (Money Values Ser.). (ENG.). 24p. (J). (gr. 1-3). lib. bdg. 33.99 incl. audio compact disk (978-1-68410-126-9(3), 31845) Cantata Learning.

—The Funniest Man in Baseball: The True Story of Max Patkin. Vernick, Audrey. 2018. (ENG.). 40p. (J). (gr. 1-4). 17.99 (978-0-544-81377-9(4), 1642034, Clarion Bks.) Houghton Mifflin Harcourt Trade & Reference Pubs.

—A Nickel. Morey, Allan. 2018. (Money Values Ser.). (ENG.). 24p. (J). (gr. 1-3). lib. bdg. 33.99 incl. audio compact disk (978-1-68410-133-7(6), 31846) Cantata Learning.

—A Penny. Morey, Allan. 2018. (Money Values Ser.). (ENG.). 24p. (J). (gr. 1-3). lib. bdg. 33.99 incl. audio compact disk (978-1-68410-120-7(4), 31844) Cantata Learning.

—A Quarter. Morey, Allan. 2018. (Money Values Ser.). (ENG.). 24p. (J). (gr. 1-3). lib. bdg. 33.99 incl. audio compact disk (978-1-68410-138-2(7), 31847) Cantata Learning.

Bower, Ling Lou. Leilani Keeps Hawaii Beautiful. Nicksich, Karen. 2020. (ENG.). 32p. (J). (gr. k-3). pap. 12.00 (978-1-0878-6320-7(1)) Nicksich, Karen M.

Bower, Tamara. How the Amazon Queen Fought the Prince of Egypt. Bower, Tamara. 2014. (ENG.). 36p. (J). (gr. 2-6). 16.99 (978-1-4814-2526-1(9), Atheneum Bks. for Young Readers) Simon & Schuster Children's Publishing.

—The Shipwrecked Sailor: An Egyptian Tale with Hieroglyphs. Bower, Tamara. 2014. (ENG.). 32p. (J). (gr. 2-5). 16.99 (978-1-4814-2525-4(0), Atheneum Bks. for Young Readers) Simon & Schuster Children's Publishing.

Bowering, Carson, et al. Rory's Helpers. 2017. (ENG.). 36p. (J). pap. (978-1-7751115-0-4(4)) Monaghan, Sue.

Bowerman, Cody. Silly Dog & a Cat. Caylor, Larry. 2016. (ENG.). (J). (gr. 1-6). 19.95 (978-1-939930-84-2(7), Belle Isle Bks.) Brandylane Pubs., Inc.

Bowers, Geneva. Beyoncé: Shine Your Light. Warren, Sarah. 2019. (ENG.). 32p. (J). (gr. -1-3). 16.99 (978-1-328-58516-5(6), 1729453, HMH Books For Young Readers) Houghton Mifflin Harcourt Publishing Co.

Bowers, Jenny. Little Pear Tree. Williams, Rachel. 2014. (ENG.). 12p. (J). (-k). bds. 14.99 (978-0-7636-7126-6(6), Big Picture Press) Candlewick Pr.

—Sticker Style: Shop. Big Picture Press, Big Picture. 2015. (ENG.). 12p. (J). (gr. k-3). pap. 12.99 (978-0-7636-7770-1(1), Big Picture Press) Candlewick Pr.

Bowers, Jenny. Sticker Style: House. Bowers, Jenny. 2015. (ENG.). 12p. (J). (gr. k-3). pap. 12.99 (978-0-7636-7983-5(6), Big Picture Press) Candlewick Pr.

Bowers, Tim. Acoustic Rooster & His Barnyard Band. Alexander, Kwame. 2011. (ENG.). 32p. (gr. k-5). lib. bdg. 15.95 (978-1-58536-688-0(9)) Sleeping Bear Pr.

—Cool Dog, School Dog, 0 vols. Heiligman, Deborah. 2013. (ENG.). 32p. (J). (gr. -1-3). pap. 9.99 (978-1-4778-1670-7(4), 9781477816707, Two Lions) Amazon Publishing.

—Dinosaur Pet. Greenfield, Howard. 2012. (ENG.). 28p. (J). (gr. -1-3). 17.95 (978-1-936140-36-7(5)) Charlesbridge Publishing, Inc.

—Dogku. Clements, Andrew. 2007. (ENG.). 40p. (J). (gr. -1-3). 18.99 (978-0-689-85823-9(X), Atheneum Bks. for Young Readers) Simon & Schuster Children's Publishing.

—Dream Big, Little Pig! Yamaguchi, Kristi. 2011. (ENG.). 32p. (J). (gr. -1-3). 16.99 (978-1-4022-5275-4(7), Sourcebooks Jabberwocky) Sourcebooks, Inc.

—First Dog. Lewis, J. Patrick & Zappitello, Beth. 2009. (ENG.). 32p. (J). (gr. k-6). 15.95 (978-1-58536-467-1(3)) Sleeping Bear Pr.

—Fun Dog, Sun Dog, 0 vols. Heiligman, Deborah. 2011. (ENG.). 34p. (J). (gr. -1-2). pap. 7.99 (978-0-7614-5836-4(0), 9780761458364, Two Lions) Amazon Publishing.

—Gorgonzola: A Very Stinkysaurus. Palatini, Margie. 2008. (ENG.). 32p. (J). (gr. -1-2). 17.99 (978-0-06-073897-6(9), Tegen, Katherine Bks) HarperCollins Pubs.

—It's a Big World, Little Pig! Yamaguchi, Kristi. 2012. (ENG.). 32p. (J). (gr. k-3). 16.99 (978-1-4022-6644-7(8), Sourcebooks Jabberwocky) Sourcebooks, Inc.

—Memoirs of a Goldfish. Scillian, Devin. 2010. (ENG.). 32p. (J). (gr. 1-4). 15.95 (978-1-58536-507-4(6), 202200) Sleeping Bear Pr.

—Memoirs of a Hamster. Scillian, Devin. 2013. (ENG.). 32p. (J). (gr. -1-2). 15.99 (978-1-58536-831-0(8), 202365) Sleeping Bear Pr.

—Memoirs of a Parrot. Scillian, Devin. 2016. (ENG.). 32p. (J). (gr. k-3). 16.99 (978-1-58536-962-1(4), 204036) Sleeping Bear Pr.

—Memoirs of an Elf. Scillian, Devin. 2014. (ENG.). 32p. (J). (gr. 1-4). 16.99 (978-1-58536-910-2(1), 203676) Sleeping Bear Pr.

—Not Your Typical Dragon. Bar-el, Dan. 2013. (ENG.). 40p. (J). (gr. -1-k). 17.99 (978-0-670-01402-6(8), Viking Books for Young Readers) Penguin Young Readers Group.

—Puss in Boots. Findlay, Lisa. 2008. (Step into Reading: Step 3 Ser.). (ENG.). 48p. (J). (gr. k-2). lib. bdg. 16.19 (978-0-375-94671-4(3)) Random Hse. Bks. for Young Readers.

—Puss in Boots. Findlay, Lisa. 2008. (Step into Reading Ser.). 48p. (J). (gr. k-3). pap. 4.99 (978-0-375-84671-7(9), Random Hse. Bks. for Young Readers) Random Hse. Children's Bks.

—Rappy & His Favorite Things. Gutman, Dan. 2019. (I Can Read Level 2 Ser.). (ENG.). 32p. (J). (gr. -1-3). 16.99 (978-0-06-225272-2(0)); pap. 4.99 (978-0-06-225271-5(2)) HarperCollins Pubs.

—Rappy Goes to Mars. Gutman, Dan. 2017. (I Can Read Level 2 Ser.). (ENG.). 32p. (J). (gr. -1-3). 16.99 (978-0-06-225269-2(0)); pap. 4.99 (978-0-06-225268-5(2)) HarperCollins Pubs.

—Rappy Goes to School. Gutman, Dan. 2016. (ENG.). 40p. (J). (gr. -1-3). 17.99 (978-0-06-229181-3(5)) HarperCollins Pubs.

—Rappy Goes to the Library. Gutman, Dan. 2017. (I Can Read Level 2 Ser.). (ENG.). 32p. (J). (gr. -1-3). pap. 4.99 (978-0-06-225265-4(8)) HarperCollins Pubs.

—Rappy Goes to the Supermarket. Gutman, Dan. 2017. (I Can Read Level 2 Ser.). (ENG.). 32p. (J). (gr. -1-3). 4.99 (978-0-06-225262-3(3)) HarperCollins Pubs.

—Rappy the Raptor. Gutman, Dan. 2015. (ENG.). 40p. (J). (gr. -1-3). 17.99 (978-0-06-229180-6(7)) HarperCollins Pubs.

—Sam & Jack: Three Stories. Moran, Alex. ed. 2003. (Green Light Readers Level 1 Ser.). (ENG.). 24p. (J). (gr. -1-3). pap. 4.99 (978-0-15-204862-4(6), 1194682) Houghton Mifflin Harcourt Publishing Co.

—Shampoodle. Holub, Joan. 2009. (Step into Reading Ser.). 32p. (J). (gr. -1-1). pap. 4.99 (978-0-375-85576-4(9), Random Hse. Bks. for Young Readers) Random Hse. Children's Bks.

—Snow Dog, Go Dog, 0 vols. Heiligman, Deborah. 2013. (ENG.). 32p. (J). (gr. -1-2). 15.99 (978-1-4778-1724-7(7), 9781477817247, Two Lions) Amazon Publishing.

—Sorry, Grown-Ups, You Can't Go to School! Geist, Christina. 2019. (ENG.). 40p. (J). (gr. -1-2). 17.99 (978-1-5247-7084-6(1)); lib. bdg. 20.99 (978-1-5247-7085-3(X)) Random Hse. Children's Bks. (Random Hse. Bks. for Young Readers).

—Suppose You Meet a Dinosaur: a First Book of Manners. Sierra, Judy. 2016. 40p. (J). (gr. -1-2). 7.99 (978-1-101-93250-6(3), Dragonfly Bks.) Random Hse. Children's Bks.

—10 Hungry Rabbits: Counting & Color Concepts. Lobel, Anita. 2012. 24p. (J). (gr. k-k). 9.99 (978-0-375-86864-1(X), Knopf Bks. for Young Readers) Random Hse. Children's Bks.

Bowers, Tim. First Dog's White House Christmas. Bowers, Tim. Lewis, J. Patrick & Zappitello, Beth. 2010. (ENG.). 32p. (J). (gr. 1-4). 15.95 (978-1-58536-503-6(3), 202197) Sleeping Bear Pr.

Bowes, Anne. The Adventures of Cedric the Bear. Wilson, Lucia. 2019. (ENG.). 112p. (J). pap. (978-94-93056-16-9(3)) Amsterdam Publishers.

Bowes, Brian. The Hole Story of Kirby the Sneak & Arlo the True, Vol. Williamson, Greg. 2015. (ENG.). 128p. pap. 15.00 (978-1-904130-83-3(6)) Waywiser Pr., The GBR. Dist: SPD-Small Pr. Distribution.

—Ivy, Homeless in San Francisco. Brenner, Summer. 2nd ed. 2011. (ENG.). 176p. (J). (gr. 4-7). pap. 15.00 (978-1-60486-317-8(X)) PM Pr.

Bowie, Maliana. Majesta the Monarch Butterfly. Ortega, Hilary. 2017. (ENG.). 48p. (J). pap. 12.95 (978-1-63575-905-1(6)) Christian Faith Publishing.

Bowie, Sarah. Let's See Ireland! Bowie, Sarah. (ENG.). 32p. 2019. pap. 15.00 (978-1-78849-132-7(7)); 2016. (J). 21.00 (978-1-84717-731-5(X)) O'Brien Pr., Ltd., The IRL. Dist: Casemate Pubs. & Bk. Distributors, LLC.

Bowker, Margie. The Adventures of Clever Kitty. Rouse, Walt. 2013. 56p. pap. (978-1-4602-1254-7(1)) FriesenPress.

Bowler, Colin. The Big Posh Yacht. Volke, Gordon. 2004. 24p. pap. 7.00 (978-1-84161-116-7(6)) Ravette Publishing, Ltd. GBR. Dist: Parkwest Pubns., Inc.

—The Little Lost Whale. Volke, Gordon. 2004. 24p. pap. 7.00 (978-1-84161-118-1(2)) Ravette Publishing, Ltd. GBR. Dist: Parkwest Pubns., Inc.

—Louis the Lifeboat Activity Sticker Book. Volke, Gordon. 2004. 16p. pap. 6.00 (978-1-84161-120-4(4)) Ravette Publishing, Ltd. GBR. Dist: Parkwest Pubns., Inc.

—The Nasty Black Stuff. Volke, Gordon. 2004. 24p. pap. 7.00 (978-1-84161-119-8(0)) Ravette Publishing, Ltd. GBR. Dist: Parkwest Pubns., Inc.

—The Pirate's Gold. Volke, Gordon. 2004. 24p. pap. 7.00 (978-1-84161-117-4(4)) Ravette Publishing, Ltd. GBR. Dist: Parkwest Pubns., Inc.

Bowler, Gareth. Sally B & Me. Beerling, F. J. 2017. 28p. (J). 9.99 (978-1-9997520-7-1(4)) Fairy Faye Pubns. GBR. Dist: Independent Pubs. Group.

Bowler, Kristin. She Represents: Women Who Are Changing the Game ... & the World. Donohue, Caitlin. 2020. (ENG.). 216p. (YA). (gr. 8-12). 37.32 (978-1-5415-7900-2(3), Zest Bks.) Lerner Publishing Group.

Bowles, Carol. Saving the Rain Forest with Cammie & Cooper. Albert, Toni Diana. l.t. ed. 2003. 32p. (J). pap. 7.95 (978-1-929432-02-8(X), 800-353-2791) Trickle Creek Bks.

Bowles, Cindy M. Twin Tails: Journey to Oceanus... the Coloring Book: the TWIN TAILS: Journey to Oceanus Coloring Book. Bowles, Cindy M. 2019. (Twin Tails Coloring Book Series by Cillyart Ser.: Vol. 3). (ENG.). 60p. (J). pap. 8.00 (978-1-0892-2623-9(3)) Independently Published.

Bowles, Doug. G Is for Gold Medal: An Olympics Alphabet. Herzog, Brad. 2015. (Av2 Fiction Readalong 2016 Ser.). (ENG.). (J). (gr. 1-4). lib. bdg. 34.28 (978-1-4896-3738-3(9), AV2 by Weigl) Weigl Pubs., Inc.

—The Gingerbread Man (El Hombre de Pan de Jengibre), Grades PK - 3. McCafferty, Catherine. 2007. (Keepsake Stories Ser.). (ENG.). 32p. (gr. -1-3). pap. 3.99 (978-0-7696-5415-7(0), 0769654150, Brighter Child) Carson-Dellosa Publishing, LLC.

—Johnny Moore & the Wright Brothers' Flying Machine. Schulz, Walter A. 2011. (History Speaks: Picture Books Plus Reader's Theater Ser.). 48p. pap. 56.72 (978-0-7613-7633-0(X)) Lerner Publishing Group.

—Johnny Moore & the Wright Brothers' Flying Machine. Schulz, Walter A. & Schultz, Walter A. 2011. (History Speaks: Picture Books Plus Reader's Theater Ser.). (ENG.). 48p. (gr. 2-4). pap. 9.95 (978-0-7613-7117-5(6)) Lerner Publishing Group.

—Little Baseball. Herzog, Brad. 2011. (Little Sports Ser.). (ENG.). 22p. (J). 7.95 (978-1-58536-547-0(5)) Sleeping Bear Pr.

—Little Basketball. Herzog, Brad. 2011. (Little Sports Ser.). (ENG.). 22p. 9.95 (978-1-58536-181-6(X)) Sleeping Bear Pr.

—Little Football. Herzog, Brad. 2011. (Little Sports Ser.). (ENG.). 22p. (J). 7.95 (978-1-58536-546-3(7)) Sleeping Bear Pr.

—Little Soccer. Herzog, Brad. 2011. (Little Sports Ser.). (ENG.). 22p. 9.95 (978-1-58536-197-7(6)) Sleeping Bear Pr.

—One Kansas Farmer: A Kansas Number Book. Scillian, Devin & Scillian, Corey. 2009. (America by the Numbers Ser.). (ENG.). 40p. (J). (gr. 1-3). 19.99 (978-1-58536-182-3(8), 202031) Sleeping Bear Pr.

—P Is for Prairie Dog: A Prairie Alphabet. Fredericks, Anthony D. 2011. (Sleeping Bear Alphabets Ser.). (ENG.). 32p. (J). (gr. k-6). 16.95 (978-1-58536-508-1(4)) Sleeping Bear Pr.

—S Is for Sunflower: A Kansas Alphabet. Scillian, Devin & Scillian, Corey. 2004. (State Ser.). (ENG.). 40p. (J). 17.95 (978-1-58536-061-1(9), 1235980) Sleeping Bear Pr.

Bowles, Doug. G Is for Gold Medal: An Olympics Alphabet. Bowles, Doug. Herzog, Brad. rev. ed. 2011. (Sports Alphabet Ser.). (ENG.). 32p. (J). (gr. 1-4). 15.95 (978-1-58536-462-6(2), 202184) Sleeping Bear Pr.

Bowles, Janice. El primer día de escuela de Katy: Fiction-tp-Fact Big Book. Jones, Tammy & Smith, Carrie. enl. ed. 2004. (SPA.). (J). pap. 26.00 (978-1-4108-2365-6(2), 23652) Benchmark Education Co.

Bowles, Jennifer. Alexander & the Great Vegetable Feud. Hawkins, Linda J. 2004. 40p. (J). (gr. k-5). 19.99 (978-0-9742806-1-5(5)) Heart to Heart Publishing, Inc.

Bowles, Michael J. N. In the Neighborhood. Michels, Dia L. 2005. (Look What I See! Where Can I Be? Ser.: 1). (ENG.). 32p. (J). (gr. -1-12). 9.95 (978-1-930775-00-8(8)) Platypus Media, L.L.C.

Bowles, Michael J. N., photos by. At Home: Look What I See! Where Can I Be? Michels, Dia L. 2005. (Look What I See! Where Can I Be? Ser.). (ENG., 32p. (J). (gr. -1-12). 9.95 (978-1-930775-06-0(7)) Platypus Media, L.L.C.

—Look What I See! Where Can I Be? At the Synagogue. Michels, Dia L. 2005. (Look What I See! Where Can I Be? Ser.). (ENG., 32p. (J). (gr. -1-3). 9.95 (978-1-930775-16-9(4)) Platypus Media, L.L.C.

—Look What I See! Where Can I Be? With My Animal Friends. Michels, Dia L. l.t. ed. 2005. (Look What I See! Where Can I Be? Ser.: 3). (ENG., 32p. (J). (gr. -1-12). 9.95 (978-1-930775-07-7(5)) Platypus Media, L.L.C.

—Visiting China. Michels, Dia L. 2005. (Look What I See! Where Can I Be? Ser.: 5). (ENG., 32p. (J). (gr. -1-3). 9.95 (978-1-930775-15-2(6)) Platypus Media, L.L.C.

Bowles, Michael J. N. & Bowles, Michael J. N., photos by. Look What I See! Where Can I Be? With My Animal Friends. Michels, Dia. 2007. (ENG., 32p. (J). 9.95 (978-1-930775-08-4(3)) Platypus Media, L.L.C.

Bowles, Michael J. N., jt. photos by see Bowles, Michael J. N.

Bowles, Nan. Onion, a North Carolina Dolphin. Taylor, Jessica Sarah. 2019. (ENG.). 26p. (J). (gr. k-5). pap. 14.99 (978-0-578-47208-9(2)) Outer Banks Ctr. for Dolphin Research.

Bowles, Paula. My Tail's Not Tired. Novotny-Hunter, Jana. 2017. (Child's Play Library). 32p. (J). (ENG.). (978-1-84643-985-8(X)); pap. (978-1-84643-986-5(8)) Child's Play International Ltd.

—Sammy Claws: the Christmas Cat. Rowland, Lucy. 2019. (ENG.). 32p. (J). (gr. -1-3). 10.99 (978-0-06-295911-9(5)) HarperCollins Pubs.

—What Little Kitten Wants Red Band. Harper, Kathryn. 2017. (Cambridge Reading Adventures Ser.). (ENG.). 16p. pap. 5.62 (978-1-108-40569-0(X)) Cambridge Univ. Pr.

Bowles, Paula. Messy Jesse. Bowles, Paula. 2015. (ENG.). 32p. (J). (gr. -1-2). 16.99 (978-1-58925-133-5(4)) Tiger Tales.

—Scary Mary. Bowles, Paula. 2012. (ENG.). 24p. (J). (gr. -1-2). 12.95 (978-1-58925-110-6(5)) Tiger Tales.

—What Goes Up. Bowles, Paula. 2013. (ENG.). 32p. (J). (gr. -1-1). 12.95 (978-1-58925-119-9(9)) Tiger Tales.

Bowlsby, Tina Marie. The Adventures of LC, the Lucky Calf. Pereira, William. 2005. (J). 18.95 (978-0-9773133-0-3(1)) Little Tule Bks.

Bowman, Alexandra. Milton Saves the Bakery. Hickman, Karen M. 2018. (ENG.). 48p. (J). pap. 12.95 (978-1-939535-75-7(1)) Deep Sea Publishing.

Bowman, Brent. Kim the Frog. Fox, Stephen. 2003. (Little Lagoon Ser.). 22p. (J). bds. 6.95 (978-0-9729197-0-8(8), Gom Foxtail) Gom Publishing, LLC.

Bowman, David. Beyond Bethlehem: A Book of Mormon Christmas. 2008. 32p. (J). pap. 11.95 (978-1-59038-991-1(3)) Deseret Bk. Co.

—Who's Your Greatest Hero? A Book of Mormon Story Applied to Children. 2009. (J). (978-1-60641-153-7(5)) Deseret Bk. Co.

Bowman, David. Who's Your Hero? Vol. 2: Book of Mormon Stories Applied to Children. Bowman, David. 2006. 80p. (J). pap. 14.95 (978-1-59038-691-0(4)) Deseret Bk. Co.

Bowman, Hootie. Go Hokies Go: An Interactive Book Featuring Virginia Tech University. Jones, Bryan. 2012. 12p. 19.95 (978-0-9836211-0-2(1)) Collegiate Kids Bks., LLC.

Bowman, Jeanne. The Selfish Giant. Wilde, Oscar. 2019. (ENG.). 32p. (J). 17.99 (978-1-64170-126-6(9), 550126) Familius LLC.

Bowman, Leslie. La Dama de Cobre. Ross, Alice & Ross, Kent. 2006. (Yo Solo - Historia (on My Own - History) Ser.). (SPA.). 48p. (gr. 2-4). lib. bdg. 25.26 (978-0-8225-6262-7(6)) Lerner Publishing Group.

Bowman, Leslie W. A Name of Honor. Blasi, Kathleen McAlpin. 2006. (J). (978-1-59336-692-6(2)) Mondo Publishing.

Bowman, Patti. Jeanna Giraffe Explores Snow. Bowman, Patti. 2019. (Journaling Giraffes Ser.). (ENG.). 76p. (J). (gr. 1-3). pap. 10.99 (978-0-9981354-7-2(X)) Silver Linden Pr.

Bowman, Patti. Jenny Giraffe Visits the Beach: A Drawing, Coloring, Writing Journal for Kids. Bowman, Patti. 2016. (J). (gr. 2-3). pap. 11.95 (978-0-9981354-2-7(9)) Silver Linden Pr.

—Jeremiah Giraffe Explores Art: A Drawing, Coloring, Writing Journal for Kids. Bowman, Patti. 2016. (Journaling Giraffes Ser.). (J). (gr. 2-3). pap. 11.95 (978-0-9981354-0-3(2)) Silver Linden Pr.

—Jonathan Giraffe Visits a Pumpkin Farm: A Drawing, Coloring, Writing Journal for Kids. Bowman, Patti. 2016. 76p. (J). (gr. 2-3). pap. 11.95 (978-0-9981354-1-0(0)) Silver Linden Pr.

—Joshua Giraffe Goes Camping: A Drawing, Coloring, Writing Journal for Kids. Bowman, Patti. 2016. (J). (gr. 2-3). pap. 11.95 (978-0-9981354-3-4(7)) Silver Linden Pr.

Bowman, Shawna. The Bat House Bag. Flowers, Dawna. 2019. (Horror Shorts Ser.: Vol. 8). (ENG.). 50p. (J). pap. 5.99 (978-1-7189-1399-8(0)) CreateSpace Independent Publishing Platform.

—Sally Scratch & the Squirrel. Flowers, Dawna. 2019. (Horror Shorts Ser.: Vol. 7). (ENG.). 28p. (J). pap. 5.95 (978-1-7189-1356-1(7)) CreateSpace Independent Publishing Platform.

Bowman, Todd A. Jay's Friend Kitty Brew. Davis, Bertha M. 2013. 28p. pap. 14.99 (978-0-9886360-5-7(0)) Kids At Heart Publishing, LLC.

—Jay's Friend Kitty Brew Jumbo Coloring & Activity Book. Davis, Bertha. 2013. 26p. pap. 9.99 (978-0-9899472-1-3(1)) Kids At Heart Publishing, LLC.

Bowser, Katya. Everyday Things with Morgan. Massey, K. J. 2013. 24p. 19.99 (978-0-9910489-4-6(6)) Create & Blossom, LLC.

Bowser, Ken. All about Systems. Ball, Jacqueline A. 2017. (Space Cat Explores STEM Ser.). (ENG.). 24p. (J). (gr. 1-3). pap. 4.99 (978-1-63440-199-9(9)); lib. bdg. 19.99 (978-1-63440-195-1(6), 9781634401951) Red Chair Pr.

—We Use Tools All Day. Ball, Jacqueline A. 2017. (Space Cat Explores STEM Ser.). (ENG.). 24p. (J). (gr. 1-3). pap. 4.99 (978-1-63440-200-2(6), 9781634402002); lib. bdg. 19.99 (978-1-63440-196-8(4)) Red Chair Pr.

—What Makes a Building Strong? Ball, Jacqueline A. 2017. (Space Cat Explores STEM Ser.). (ENG.). 24p. (J). (gr. 1-3). pap. 4.99 (978-1-63440-201-9(4)); lib. bdg. 19.99 (978-1-63440-197-5(2), 9781634401975) Red Chair Pr.

—The World Humans Made. Ball, Jacqueline A. 2017. (Space Cat Explores STEM Ser.). (ENG.). 24p. (J). (gr. 1-3). pap. 4.99 (978-1-63440-198-2(0)); lib. bdg. 19.99 (978-1-63440-194-4(8), 9781634401944) Red Chair Pr.

Bowser, Ken. Bobbi's Big Brake: Self-Confidence. Bowser, Ken. ed. 2016. (Funny Bone Readers (tm) — Truck Pals on the Job Ser.). (ENG.). 24p. (J). (gr. k-2). E-Book 30.65 (978-1-63440-064-0(X)) Red Chair Pr.

Bowser, Ken. The Case of the Clicking Clock: Solving Mysteries Through Science, Technology, Engineering, Art & Math. Bowser, Ken. 2020. (Jesse Steam Mysteries Ser.). (ENG.). 64p. (J). (gr. 2-5). pap. 8.99 (978-1-63440-946-9(9)); lib. bdg. 26.65 (978-1-63440-945-2(0)) Red Chair Pr.

—The Clue in the Painted Pattern: Solving Mysteries Through Science, Technology, Engineering, Art & Math. Bowser, Ken. 2020. (Jesse Steam Mysteries Ser.). (ENG.). 64p. (J). (gr. 2-5). pap. 8.99 (978-1-63440-952-0(3)); lib. bdg. 26.65 (978-1-63440-951-3(5)) Red Chair Pr.

—The Conundrum of the Crooked Crayon: Solving Mysteries Through Science, Technology, Engineering, Art & Math. Bowser, Ken. 2020. (Jesse Steam Mysteries Ser.). (ENG.). 64p. (J). (gr. 2-5). pap. 8.99 (978-1-63440-934-6(5)); lib. bdg. 26.65 (978-1-63440-933-9(7)) Red Chair Pr.

Bowser, Ken. Gus & the Mighty Mess: Helping Others. Bowser, Ken. ed. 2016. (Funny Bone Readers (tm) — Truck Pals on the Job Ser.). (ENG.). 24p. (J). (gr. k-2). E-Book 30.65 (978-1-63440-067-1(4)) Red Chair Pr.

—Hal & Al: Self-Esteem. Bowser, Ken. ed. 2016. (Funny Bone Readers (tm) — Truck Pals on the Job Ser.). (ENG.). 24p. (J). (gr. k-2). E-Book 30.65 (978-1-63440-070-1(4)) Red Chair Pr.

—Hitch Takes Off: Perseverance. Bowser, Ken. ed. 2016. (Funny Bone Readers (tm) — Truck Pals on the Job Ser.). (ENG.). 24p. (J). (gr. k-2). E-Book 30.65 (978-1-63440-073-2(9)) Red Chair Pr.

—Lawni Takes the Field: Teamwork. Bowser, Ken. ed. 2016. (Funny Bone Readers (tm) — Truck Pals on the Job Ser.). (ENG.). 24p. (J). (gr. k-2). E-Book 30.65 (978-1-63440-076-3(3)) Red Chair Pr.

—One Wrong Turn: Helping Those in Need. Bowser, Ken. ed. 2016. (Funny Bone Readers (tm) — Truck Pals on the

Job Ser.). (ENG.). 24p. (J). (gr. k-2). E-Book 30.65 *(978-1-63440-079-4(8))* Red Chair Pr.

Bowser, Ken. The Riddle of the Spinning Sycamore Seed: Solving Mysteries Through Science, Technology, Engineering, Art & Math. Bowser, Ken. 2020. (Jesse Steam Mysteries Ser.). (ENG.). 64p. (J). (gr. 2-5). pap. 8.99 ***(978-1-63440-940-7(X))***; lib. bdg. 26.65 ***(978-1-63440-939-1(6))*** Red Chair Pr.

—The Secret in the Jelly Bean Jar: Solving Mysteries Through Science, Technology, Engineering, Art & Math. Bowser, Ken. 2020. (Jesse Steam Mysteries Ser.). (ENG.). 64p. (J). (gr. 2-5). pap. 8.99 ***(978-1-63440-958-2(2))***; lib. bdg. 26.65 ***(978-1-63440-957-5(4))*** Red Chair Pr.

Bowser, Milton. Cartoon Stories from the Teachings of Buddha. l.t. ed. 2003. (Cartoon Ser.). (JPN & SPA.). 72p. (YA). 10.00 *(978-0-940178-34-2(6)*, Buddha 1) Sitare, Ltd.

Bowser, Sean T. Pear-A-Dise. Keefer, Nick T. 2013. 28p. pap. 12.95 *(978-0-9894814-6-5(8))* Warren Publishing, Inc.

Box, Marty. The Little Red Beetle Goes Shopping. Box, Marty. McKenna, Allen. 2005. (ENG.). 40p. pap. *(978-1-84401-521-4(1))* Athena Pr.

Box, Paul. Stubborn & Disobedient, 1 vol. Guinn, Dolores Hollyfield. 2009. 19p. pap. 24.95 *(978-1-4489-0902-5(3))* America Star Bks.

Boxell, Pat. The Littlest Tree. Marlow, Michael. 2019. (ENG.). 36p. (J). pap. 12.95 *(978-1-64096-778-6(8))* Newman Springs Publishing, Inc.

Boyajian, Ann. Journey to the Heart: Centering Prayer for Children. Jelenek, Frank X. 2007. (ENG.). 32p. (J). (gr. -1-3). pap. 18.99 *(978-1-55725-482-5(6)*, 4826) Paraclete Pr., Inc.

—Look! A Child's Guide to Advent & Christmas. Alary, Laura. 2017. (ENG.). 32p. (J). pap. 16.99 *(978-1-61261-866-1(9))* Paraclete Pr., Inc.

—Make Room: A Child's Guide to Lent & Easter. Alary, Laura. 2016. (ENG.). 32p. (J). pap. 15.99 *(978-1-61261-659-9(3))* Paraclete Pr., Inc.

—O, Say Can You See? America's Symbols, Landmarks, & Important Words. Scholastic, Inc. Staff & Keenan, Sheila. 2007. (ENG.). 64p. (J). (gr. -1-3). pap. 7.99 *(978-0-439-59360-1(3)*, Scholastic Nonfiction) Scholastic, Inc.

Boyce, Sarah. The Little Bakery. Knowlman, Andrew. 2017. (ENG.). (YA). (gr. 7-10). pap. *(978-1-911589-32-7(6)*, Choir Pr., The) Action Publishing Technology Ltd.

Boyce, Tami. Grandee & Her Silly Birds. Dunst, Dede. 2020. (ENG.). 26p. (J). 21.95 ***(978-1-0983-3126-9(5))*** BookBaby.

Boyce, Tami. Harry & the Pelican. Leaf, Amy. 2019. (ENG.). 30p. (J). (gr. k-3). 19.99 *(978-0-578-44020-0(2))* Leaf Publishing, LLC.

—Harry & the Pelican. Leaf, Amy. 2019. (ENG.). 30p. (J). pap. 9.99 *(978-0-692-19308-2(1))* Leaf Publishing, LLC.

—Harry & the Pelican Coloring Book. Leaf, Amy. 2019. (ENG.). 30p. (J). pap. 5.99 *(978-0-578-49097-7(8))* Leaf Publishing, LLC.

—If I Take My Horse to School. Roberson, Karen L. 2018. (ENG.). 32p. (J). pap. 14.95 *(978-0-578-42605-1(6))* Roberson, Karen.

—Night Night Hamlet. Plyler, Clint D. 2018. (Bear Ridge Ser.: Vol. 1). (ENG.). 24p. (J). (gr. k-4). pap. 7.50 *(978-0-692-18569-8(0))* Plyler, Clint.

—Pipsqueak the Puppy. Webber, Lissa. 2018. (Pipsqueak Ser.). (ENG.). 40p. (J). (gr. k-2). 18.95 *(978-0-692-18284-0(5))* Argonne Bks. LLC.

—While Mommy Is Out. Griffis, Teri Errico. 2017. (ENG.). 40p. (J). pap. 20.00 *(978-0-692-88542-0(0))* Griffis, Teri Errico.

Boyd, Aaron. Babu's Song. Stuve-Bodeen, Stephanie. 2003. (ENG.). 32p. (J). 16.95 *(978-1-58430-058-8(2))*; (gr. -1-3). pap. 10.95 *(978-1-60060-275-7(4))* Lee & Low Bks., Inc.

—Calling the Water Drum, 1 vol. Redding, LaTisha. 2016. (ENG.). 32p. (J). (gr. 1-4). 17.95 *(978-1-62014-194-6(9))* Lee & Low Bks., Inc.

—Low-Down Bad-Day Blues. Scholastic, Inc. Staff & Barnes, Derrick. 2004. (Just for You Ser.). (ENG.). 32p. (gr. k-1). pap. 3.99 *(978-0-439-56867-8(6)*, Teaching Resources) Scholastic, Inc.

—Ned Redd, World Traveler: A Search-And-Find Adventure. Kaufmann, Kelli. 2005. (J). *(978-1-58987-135-9(9))* Kindermusik International.

—The Story of Civil Rights Hero John Lewis, 1 vol. Haskins, Jim & Benson, Kathleen. 2019. (Story Of Ser.). (ENG.). 64p. (J). (gr. 4-8). pap. 9.95 *(978-1-62014-854-9(4)*, b2edfbfc-cf83-4dab-b586-56fec5f3e22e) Lee & Low Bks., Inc.

Boyd, Brian. Full Mouse, Empty Mouse: A Tale of Food & Feelings. Zeckhausen, Dina. 2007. 40p. (J). (gr. 2-7). 14.95 *(978-1-4338-0132-7(9)*, 4418003); pap. 9.95 *(978-1-4338-0133-4(7)*, 4418004) American Psychological Assn. (Magination Pr.).

Boyd, Chie. Diamond's Dream (Lucky Bunnies #3) Coe, Catherine. 2020. (Lucky Bunnies Ser.: 3). (ENG.). 128p. (J). (gr. 2-5). pap. 5.99 *(978-1-338-61099-4(6)*, Scholastic Paperbacks) Scholastic, Inc.

—Petal's Party (Lucky Bunnies #2) Coe, Catherine. 2020. (ENG.). 128p. (J). (gr. 2-5). pap. 5.99 *(978-1-338-58913-9(X)*, Scholastic Paperbacks) Scholastic, Inc.

—Rock-A-Bye, Dino. Eliot, Hannah. 2019. (ENG.). 20p. (J). (gr. -1). bds. 9.99 *(978-1-5344-5640-2(6)*, Little Simon) Little Simon.

—Sky's Surprise (Lucky Bunnies #1) Coe, Catherine. 2020. (ENG.). 128p. (J). (gr. 2-5). pap. 5.99 *(978-1-338-58911-5(3)*, Scholastic Paperbacks) Scholastic, Inc.

Boyd, Chie Y., et al. Animal Babies: Slipcase 4-Pack Including Babies in the Wild, Babies in the Forest, Babies in the Snow, & Babies on the Farm. Swift, Ginger. Cottage Door Press, ed. 2018. (ENG.). 48p. (J). (gr. -1-2). bds., bds., bds. 24.99 *(978-1-68052-338-6(4)*, 9001180) Cottage Door Pr.

Boyd, Chie Y. Babies on the Farm: Chunky Lift a Flap Board Book. Swift, Ginger. Cottage Door Press, ed. 2016. (Lift a Flap Ser.). (ENG.). 12p. (J). (gr. -1-k). bds. 7.99 *(978-1-68052-150-4(0)*, 1001440) Cottage Door Pr.

—Campfire Songs. Wing, Scarlett. Cottage Door Press, ed. 2019. (Early Bird Song Ser.). (ENG.). 10p. (J). (gr. -1-4). bds. 18.99 *(978-1-68052-372-0(4)*, 1003370) Cottage Door Pr.

Boyd, Lizi. I Love Daddy: Super Sturdy Picture Books. Boyd, Lizi. 2004. (Super Sturdy Picture Bks.). (ENG.). 24p. (J). (gr. -1 — 1). 8.99 *(978-0-7636-2217-6(6))* Candlewick Pr.

—I Love Grandma. Boyd, Lizi. 2009. (Super Sturdy Picture Bks.). 24p. (J). (gr. -1-k). 8.99 *(978-0-7636-3728-6(9))* Candlewick Pr.

—I Love Grandpa. Boyd, Lizi. 2009. (Super Sturdy Picture Bks.). 24p. (J). (gr. -1-k). 8.99 *(978-0-7636-3727-9(0))* Candlewick Pr.

Boyd, Patti. Magical Circus Train. Kidd, Ron. 16p. (J). (gr. -1-18). 19.95 *(978-0-9627001-5-6(0))* Futech Educational Products, Inc.

Boyd, Shelby. Run, Girl, Run! Breshears, Alyce Park. 2013. 36p. pap. 7.95 *(978-1-60414-742-1(3))* Fideli Publishing, Inc.

Boyd, Sheree. El Aire: Afuera, Adentro y en Todos Lados, 1 vol. Stille, Darlene R. Robledo, Sol, tr. 2007. (Ciencia Asombrosa Ser.). (SPA.). 24p. (J). (gr. k-4). lib. bdg. 27.32 *(978-1-4048-3209-1(2)*, Picture Window Bks.) Capstone.

—Electricity: Bulbs, Batteries, & Sparks. Stille, Darlene R. 2004. (Amazing Science Ser.). (ENG.). 24p. (J). (gr. k-4). 27.32 *(978-1-4048-0245-2(2)*, Picture Window Bks.) Capstone.

—La Energía: Calor, Luz y Combustible. Stille, Darlene R. & Picture Window Books Staff. Robledo, Sol, tr. 2007. (Ciencia Asombrosa Ser.). (SPA.). 24p. (J). (gr. k-4). 27.32 *(978-1-4048-3213-8(0)*, Picture Window Bks.) Capstone.

—Imanes: Atraen y Rechazan, 1 vol. Rosinsky, Natalie M. & Picture Window Books Staff. Robledo, Sol, tr. 2007. (Ciencia Asombrosa Ser.).Tr. of Magnets: Pulling Together & Pushing Apart. (SPA.). 24p. (J). (gr. k-4). 27.32 *(978-1-4048-3220-6(3)*, Picture Window Bks.) Capstone.

—Imanes: Atraen y Rechazan, 1 vol. Rosinsky, Natalie M. Robledo, Sol, tr. 2007. (Ciencia Asombrosa Ser.).Tr. of Magnets: Pulling Together & Pushing Apart. (SPA.). 24p. (J). (gr. k-4). per. 8.19 *(978-1-4048-2497-3(9)*, Picture Window Bks.) Capstone.

—La Materia: Mira, Toca, Prueba, Huele, 1 vol. Stille, Darlene R. & Picture Window Books Staff. Robledo, Sol, tr. 2007. (Ciencia Asombrosa Ser.). (SPA.). 24p. (J). (gr. k-4). 27.32 *(978-1-4048-3221-3(1)*, Picture Window Bks.) Capstone.

—Matter: See It, Touch It, Taste It, Smell It, 1 vol. Stille, Darlene R. 2004. (Amazing Science Ser.). (ENG.). 24p. (J). (gr. k-4). per. 8.95 *(978-1-4048-0344-2(0)*, Picture Window Bks.) Capstone.

—El Movimiento: Tira y Empuja, Rápido y Despacio. Stille, Darlene R. Robledo, Sol, tr. 2007. (Ciencia Asombrosa Ser.). (SPA.). 24p. (J). (gr. k-4). lib. bdg. 27.32 *(978-1-4048-3222-0(X)*, Picture Window Bks.) Capstone.

—El Papa Francisco Dice... Pope Francis, Pope. 2019. (SPA.). 32p. (J). bds. 8.95 *(978-0-8294-4655-5(9))* Loyola Pr.

—Pope Francis Says... Pope Francis, Pope. 2019. (ENG.). 32p. (J). bds. 8.95 *(978-0-8294-4653-1(2))* Loyola Pr.

—El Suelo: Tierra y Arena, 1 vol. Rosinsky, Natalie M. Robledo, Sol, tr. 2007. (Ciencia Asombrosa Ser.). (SPA.). 24p. (J). (gr. k-4). lib. bdg. 27.32 *(978-1-4048-3211-4(4)*, Picture Window Bks.) Capstone.

—Tag along Books Set: Tag along Ring 3 Book Set. Edited. 2015. (Tag Along Ser.). (ENG.). (J). (gr. -1-k). 19.99 *(978-1-68052-051-4(2)*, 1000520) Cottage Door Pr.

—La Temperatura: Caliente y Frío. Stille, Darlene R. & Picture Window Books Staff. Robledo, Sol, tr. 2007. (Ciencia Asombrosa Ser.). (SPA.). 24p. (J). (gr. k-4). 27.32 *(978-1-4048-3234-3(3)*, Picture Window Bks.) Capstone.

—Temperature: Heating up & Cooling Down, 1 vol. Stille, Darlene R. 2004. (Amazing Science Ser.). (ENG.). 24p. (J). (gr. k-4). per. 8.95 *(978-1-4048-0345-9(9)*, Picture Window Bks.) Capstone.

Boyd, Sheree. Motion: Push & Pull, Fast & Slow. Boyd, Sheree, tr. Stille, Darlene R. 2004. (Amazing Science Ser.). (ENG.). 24p. (J). (gr. k-4). 27.32 *(978-1-4048-0250-6(9)*, Picture Window Bks.) Capstone.

Boyd, T. C. The Night Before Christmas: A Visit from St. Nicholas. Moore, Clement C. 2018. (ENG.). 42p. (J). (gr. k-6). 15.99 *(978-1-945934-40-7(9))*; pap. 4.99 *(978-1-945934-42-1(5))* Cosimo, Inc. (Cosimo Classics).

Boyd, Tamra. Beautiful You. Cast, Leah. 2017. (ENG.). 23p. (J). 20.95 *(978-1-4787-8693-1(0))* Outskirts Pr., Inc.

Boyden, Robin. Ghostly Whispers: Book 10. Specter, Baron. 2018. (Graveyard Diaries). (ENG.). 112p. (J). (gr. 2-5). lib. bdg. 29.93 *(978-1-5321-3181-3(X)*, 28457, Calico Chapter Bks.) ABDO Publishing Co.

—Ghosts of Pheasant Hill: Book 7. Specter, Baron. 2018. (Graveyard Diaries). (ENG.). 112p. (J). (gr. 2-5). lib. bdg. 29.93 *(978-1-5321-3178-3(X)*, 28451, Calico Chapter Bks.) ABDO Publishing Co.

—Graveyard Diaries Set 2 (Set), 4 vols. Specter, Baron. 2018. (Graveyard Diaries). 112p. (J). (gr. 2-5). lib. bdg. 114.00 *(978-1-5321-3177-6(1)*, 28449, Calico Chapter Bks.) ABDO Publishing Co.

—Hobgoblins Just Wanna Have Fun: Book 8. Specter, Baron. 2018. (Graveyard Diaries). (ENG.). 112p. (J). (gr. 2-5). lib. bdg. 29.93 *(978-1-5321-3179-0(8)*, 28453, Calico Chapter Bks.) ABDO Publishing Co.

—The Hole Nine Yards. Deutsch, Stacia. 2017. (Mysterious Makers of Shaker Street Ser.). (ENG.). 112p. (J). (gr. 2-4). pap. 6.95 *(978-1-4965-4683-8(0)*, 135213); lib. bdg. 22.65 *(978-1-4965-4679-1(2)*, 135204) Capstone. (Stone Arch Bks.).

—Joe-Joe the Wizard Brews up Solids, Liquids, & Gases, 1 vol. Braun, Eric. 2012. (In the Science Lab Ser.). (ENG.). 24p. (J). (gr. k-3). pap. 9.95 *(978-1-4048-7238-7(8)*, Picture Window Bks.) Capstone.

—Mad Margaret Experiments with the Scientific Method, 1 vol. Braun, Eric. 2012. (In the Science Lab Ser.). (ENG.). 24p. (J). (gr. k-3). pap. 9.95 *(978-1-4048-7710-8(X))*; lib. bdg. 27.32 *(978-1-4048-7373-5(2))* Capstone. (Picture Window Bks.).

—The Mysterious Makers of Shaker Street, 4 vols. Deutsch, Stacia. 2017. (Mysterious Makers of Shaker Street Ser.). (ENG.). 112p. (J). (gr. 2-4). 87.96 *(978-1-4965-4701-9(2)*, 26519); pap., pap., pap. 27.80 *(978-1-4965-4702-6(0)*, 26520) Capstone. (Stone Arch Bks.).

—A Picture's Worth a Thousand Clues. Deutsch, Stacia. 2017. (Mysterious Makers of Shaker Street Ser.). (ENG.). 112p. (J). (gr. 2-4). pap. 6.95 *(978-1-4965-4681-4(4)*, 135210); lib. bdg. 22.65 *(978-1-4965-4677-7(6)*, 135202) Capstone. (Stone Arch Bks.).

—Sounds Like Trouble. Deutsch, Stacia. 2017. (Mysterious Makers of Shaker Street Ser.). (ENG.). 112p. (J). (gr. 2-4). pap. 6.95 *(978-1-4965-4680-7(6)*, 135211); lib. bdg. 22.65 *(978-1-4965-4676-0(8)*, 135201) Capstone. (Stone Arch Bks.).

—That's the Spirit! Deutsch, Stacia. 2017. (Mysterious Makers of Shaker Street Ser.). (ENG.). 112p. (J). (gr. 2-4). pap. 6.95 *(978-1-4965-4682-1(2)*, 135212); lib. bdg. 22.65 *(978-1-4965-4678-4(4)*, 135203) Capstone. (Stone Arch Bks.).

—Zombies Revisited: Book 9. Specter, Baron. 2018. (Graveyard Diaries). (ENG.). 112p. (J). (gr. 2-5). lib. bdg. 29.93 *(978-1-5321-3180-6(1)*, 28455, Calico Chapter Bks.) ABDO Publishing Co.

Boye, B. D. Easy As 1, 2, 3. Boye, B. D. l.t. ed. 2005. 22p. (J). per. 4.99 *(978-0-9768078-0-3(7))* Innerchild Publishing, Inc.

—The Look Book. Boye, B. D. l.t. ed. 2004. 20p. (J). per. 4.99 *(978-0-9768078-1-0(5)*, 100001) Innerchild Publishing, Inc.

—Our New Home. Boye, B. D. l.t. ed. 2005. 18p. (J). per. 4.99 *(978-0-9768078-2-7(3))* Innerchild Publishing, Inc.

Boyer, Cécile. Woof Meow Tweet-Tweet. 2011. (ENG.). 48p. (J). (gr. -1). 15.95 *(978-1-934734-60-5(8))* Seven Footer Pr.

Boyer, Christine M. Sweetest Joy, 1 vol. Middleton, Leeanne. 2010. 18p. pap. 24.95 *(978-1-4489-8068-0(2))* PublishAmerica, Inc.

Boyer, Lyn. Baby Bumblebee. Grudzina, Rebecca. 2010. (Rising Readers Ser.). (J). 3.49 *(978-1-60719-688-4(3))* Newmark Learning LLC.

—A Baby Bumblebee for Mommy. Grudzina, Rebecca. 2009. (Reader's Theater Nursery Rhymes & Songs Set B Ser.). 48p. (J). pap. *(978-1-60859-149-7(2))* Benchmark Education Co.

—London Bridge. Harris, Brooke. 2010. (Rising Readers Ser.). (J). 3.49 *(978-1-60719-702-7(2))* Newmark Learning LLC.

—London Bridge Has Fallen Down. Harris, Brooke. 2009. (Reader's Theater Nursery Rhymes & Songs Set B Ser.). 48p. (J). pap. *(978-1-60859-159-6(X))* Benchmark Education Co.

—My Day at the Beach. Moses, Jessie. 2017. (Text Connections Guided Close Reading Ser.). (J). (gr. k). *(978-1-4900-1769-3(0))* Benchmark Education Co.

—Zachary's Zoo, 1 vol. Nappa, Mike & Nappa, Amy. 2007. (I Can Read! Ser.). (ENG.). 32p. (J). (gr. -1-1). pap. 4.99 *(978-0-310-71466-8(4))* Zonderkidz.

Boyer, Lyn, jt. illus. see Hierstein, Judy.

Boyer, Mitch. Vivian the Dog Moves to the Big City. Boyer, Mitch. 2017. (ENG.). 40p. (J). (gr. -1-3). 17.99 *(978-0-06-267327-5(0))* HarperCollins Pubs.

Boyer, Robin. Alphabet Stickers. Hoffman, Joan. 2006. (ENG.). 64p. (J). (gr. -1-k). 7.99 *(978-1-58947-746-9(4))* School Zone Publishing Co.

—Andrew & Allen Learn about Adverbs. Robinson, Joanna Jarc. 2014. (Language Builders Ser.). (ENG.). 32p. (J). (gr. 2-4). pap. 11.94 *(978-1-60357-704-5(1))*; lib. bdg. 25.27 *(978-1-59953-669-9(2))* Norwood Hse. Pr.

Boyer, Robin, et al. Brain Games: Amazing Activity Book. 2019. (ENG.). 40p. (J). *(978-1-5037-4926-9(6)*, 397f8bcd-13ff-40ea-a942-fc43a40c602f, p i kids) Phoenix International Publications, Inc.

—Brain Games: Awesome Activity Book. 2019. (ENG.). 40p. (J). *(978-1-5037-4925-2(8)*, 1b4e65ee-cfcd-4d77-b272-ebd74167059b, p i kids) Phoenix International Publications, Inc.

Boyer, Robin. Dot-to-Dots. School Zone Interactive Staff. 2006. (ENG.). 64p. (J). (gr. 1-2). 7.99 *(978-1-58947-302-7(7))* School Zone Publishing Co.

—First Grade Scholar. Hall, M. C. 2004. (ENG.). 32p. (J). pap. 2.99 *(978-1-58947-456-7(2))* School Zone Publishing Co.

—Kindergarten Basics. Hoffman, Joan. 2004. (ENG.). 32p. (J). pap. 2.99 *(978-1-58947-436-9(8))* School Zone Publishing Co.

—Kindergarten Scholar. Burton, Marilee R. 2004. (ENG.). 32p. (J). pap. 2.99 *(978-1-58947-455-0(4))* School Zone Publishing Co.

—Manuscript Writing K-2. Veinje, Marie. 2005. (ENG.). 64p. (J). (gr. k-2). pap. 3.99 *(978-1-58947-397-3(3))* School Zone Publishing Co.

—Multiplication Facts Made Easy 3-4. Irvin, Barbara Bando. 2005. (ENG.). 64p. (J). (gr. 3-4). pap. 3.99 *(978-1-58947-328-7(0)*, 02214) School Zone Publishing Co.

—Second Grade Scholar. Hall, M. C. 2005. (ENG.). 32p. (J). pap., wbk. ed. 2.99 *(978-1-58947-457-4(0))* School Zone Publishing Co.

—Third Grade Scholar. Giglio, Judy. 2005. (ENG.). 32p. (J). pap. 2.99 *(978-1-58947-458-1(9))* School Zone Publishing Co.

Boyer, Susy. Gone Fishing. Arena, Felice & Kettle, Phil. 2004. (J). pap. *(978-1-59336-359-8(1))* Mondo Publishing.

—Look at Me, 1 vol. Giulieri, Anne. 2012. (Engage Literacy Magenta Ser.). (ENG.). 32p. (gr. k-2). pap. 5.99 *(978-1-4296-8856-7(4)*, Capstone Pr.) Capstone.

—My Big Sandcastle, 1 vol. Giulieri, Anne. 2012. (Engage Literacy Magenta Ser.). (ENG.). 32p. (gr. k-2). pap. 5.99 *(978-1-4296-8870-3(X)*, Capstone Pr.) Capstone.

—On the Farm/By Felice Arena & Phil Kettle; Illustrated by Susy Boyer. Arena, Felice & Kettle, Phil. 2004. (J). pap. *(978-1-59336-363-5(X))* Mondo Publishing.

—Pirate Ship: By Felice Arena & Phil Kettle: Illustrated by Susy Boyer. Arena, Felice & Kettle, Phil. 2004. (J). pap. *(978-1-59336-362-8(1))* Mondo Publishing.

—The Secret Tree House, 1 vol. Giulieri, Anne. 2012. (Engage Literacy Green Ser.). (ENG.). 32p. (gr. k-2). pap. 5.99 *(978-1-4296-8999-1(4)*, Capstone Pr.) Capstone.

—Surprise Pancakes for Mom, 1 vol. Giulieri, Anne. 2012. (Engage Literacy Red Ser.). (ENG.). 32p. (gr. k-2). pap. 5.99 *(978-1-4296-8948-9(X)*, Capstone Pr.) Capstone.

—Tennis Ace. Arena, Felice & Kettle, Phil. 2004. (J). pap. *(978-1-59336-360-4(5))* Mondo Publishing.

—The Volcano Sand Hill, 1 vol. Giulieri, Anne. 2012. (Engage Literacy Blue Ser.). (ENG.). 32p. (gr. k-2). pap. 5.99 *(978-1-4296-8976-2(5)*, Capstone Pr.) Capstone.

Boyette, Judy Siler. The Borrowed Princess: The Daughters of the Lost King Series. Underwood, Steve. Ashby, Amy, ed. 2017. (Daughters of the Lost King Ser.: Vol. 1). (ENG.). (J). (gr. 4-6). pap. 14.95 *(978-1-943258-55-0(4))* Warren Publishing, Inc.

Boykin, Brian, jt. illus. see Lane, Queen.

Boyle, Bob. Rosie & Rex: A Nose for Fun! Boyle, Bob. 2014. (ENG.). 40p. (J). (gr. -1-3). 15.99 *(978-0-06-221131-6(5))* HarperCollins Pubs.

Boyle, David. The Lovely Duckling. Dolan, Penny. 2014. (Tadpoles: Fairytale Twists Ser.). (ENG.). 32p. (J). (gr. 1-2). *(978-0-7787-0445-4(9))*; pap. *(978-0-7787-0480-5(7))* Crabtree Publishing Co.

Boyles, Renee. Belle-Duck at the Peabody. Wells, Dean Faulkner. 2015. (ENG.). 56p. (J). pap. 14.95 ***(978-0-916242-80-0(3))*** Yoknapatawpha Pr.

Boyles, Shawn. Cavern of Babel. Packard, Albert. 2006. (J). per. 14.95 *(978-0-9790652-0-0(8))* Diamond Triple C Ranch.

Boyne, Linda. The Apple Tree. White, Cal. 2008. 48p. pap. 24.95 *(978-1-4241-8636-5(6))* America Star Bks.

Boynton-Hughes, Brooke. Baby Love. DiTerlizzi, Angela. 2015. (ENG.). 32p. (J). (gr. -1-3). 17.99 *(978-1-4424-3392-2(2)*, Beach Lane Bks.) Beach Lane Bks.

—Baby Love. DiTerlizzi, Angela. 2018. (Classic Board Bks.). (ENG.). 36p. (J). (gr. -1 — 1). bds. 7.99 *(978-1-5344-2035-9(5)*, Little Simon) Little Simon.

—Bark Park! Krisher, Trudy. 2018. (ENG.). 40p. (J). (-3). 17.99 *(978-1-4814-3075-3(0)*, Beach Lane Bks.) Beach Lane Bks.

—Blanket of Love. Capucilli, Alyssa Satin. 2017. (New Books for Newborns Ser.). (ENG.). 16p. (J). (gr. -1 — 1). bds. 7.99 *(978-1-4814-8972-0(0)*, Little Simon) Little Simon.

—Manta de Amor (Blanket of Love) Capucilli, Alyssa Satin. Romay, Alexis, tr. 2019. (New Books for Newborns Ser.). (SPA.). 16p. (J). (— 1). bds. 7.99 *(978-1-5344-5077-6(7)*, Libros Para Ninos) Libros Para Ninos.

Boynton, Jeannette & Holdeen, Bonnie. God Loves Variety. Boynton, Jeannette. 2007. (J). per. 10.99 *(978-1-59879-264-5(4))* Lifevest Publishing, Inc.

Boynton, Sandra. Are You a Cow? Boynton, Sandra. 2012. (ENG.). 16p. (J). (gr. -1-k). bds. 5.99 *(978-1-4424-1733-5(1)*, Little Simon) Little Simon.

—Azul el Sombrero, Verde el Sombrero. Boynton, Sandra. 2003.Tr. of Blue Hat, Green Hat. (SPA.). 14p. (J). (gr. -1 — 1). bds. 5.99 *(978-0-689-86304-2(7)*, Libros Para Ninos) Libros Para Ninos.

—Big Box of Little Pookie: Little Pookie; What's Wrong, Little Pookie?; Night-Night, Little Pookie; Happy Birthday, Little Pookie; Let's Dance, Little Pookie; Spooky Pookie. Boynton, Sandra. ed. 2017. (Little Pookie Ser.). (ENG.). 108p. (J). (gr. -1-k). bds. 35.99 *(978-1-5344-0477-9(5)*, Little Simon) Little Simon.

—Boynton's Greatest Hits the Big Green Box: Happy Hippo, Angry Duck; but Not the Armadillo; Dinosaur Dance!; Are You a Cow? Boynton, Sandra. ed. 2018. (ENG.). 64p. (J). (gr. -1-k). bds. 23.99 *(978-1-5344-3353-3(8)*, Little Simon) Little Simon.

—Buenas Noches a Todos (Going to Bed Book) Boynton, Sandra. 2004.Tr. of Going to Bed Book. (SPA.). 14p. (J). (gr. -1 — 1). bds. 5.99 *(978-0-689-86652-4(6)*, Libros Para Ninos) Libros Para Ninos.

—But Not the Armadillo. Boynton, Sandra. 2018. (ENG.). 16p. (J). (gr. -1-k). bds. 5.99 *(978-1-4814-8100-7(2)*, Little Simon) Little Simon.

Boynton, Sandra. Christmas Parade. Boynton, Sandra. (ENG.). 32p. (J). (gr. -1-1). 2020. bds. 7.99 ***(978-1-5344-7806-0(X))***; 2012. 14.99 *(978-1-4424-6813-9(0))* Little Simon. (Little Simon).

Boynton, Sandra. Consider Love. Boynton, Sandra. 2013. (ENG.). 32p. (J). (gr. -1-3). 14.99 *(978-1-4424-9465-7(4)*, Little Simon) Little Simon.

—Dinosaur Dance! Boynton, Sandra. 2016. (ENG.). 16p. (J). (gr. -1-k). bds. 5.99 *(978-1-4814-8099-4(5)*, Little Simon) Little Simon.

—The Going to Bed Book. Boynton, Sandra. 2006. (ENG.). 14p. (J). bds. 12.95 *(978-1-4169-2794-5(8)*, Little Simon) Little Simon.

—The Going to Bed Book: Lap Edition. Boynton, Sandra. 2004. (ENG.). 14p. (J). (gr. -1-k). bds. 9.99 *(978-0-689-87028-6(0)*, Little Simon) Little Simon.

—Happy Birthday, Little Pookie. Boynton, Sandra. 2017. (Little Pookie Ser.). (ENG.). 18p. (J). (gr. -1-k). bds. 5.99 *(978-1-4814-9770-1(7)*, Little Simon) Little Simon.

—Happy Hippo, Angry Duck: A Book of Moods. Boynton, Sandra. 2011. (ENG.). 16p. (J). (gr. -1-k). bds. 5.99 *(978-1-4424-1731-1(5)*, Little Simon) Little Simon.

—Hippos Go Berserk! Boynton, Sandra. 2009. (ENG.). 32p. (J). 9.99 *(978-1-4169-9619-4(2)*, Little Simon) Little Simon.

Boynton, Sandra. How Big Is Zagnodd? Boynton, Sandra. 2020. (ENG.). 16p. (J). (gr. -1). bds. 7.99 ***(978-1-5344-8256-2(3))***, Little Simon) Little Simon.

Boynton, Sandra. I Love You, Little Pookie. Boynton, Sandra. 2018. (Little Pookie Ser.). (ENG.). 18p. (J). (-k). bds. 5.99 *(978-1-5344-3723-4(1)*, Little Simon) Little Simon.

—Let's Dance, Little Pookie. Boynton, Sandra. 2017. (Little Pookie Ser.). (ENG.). 18p. (J). (gr. -1-k). bds. 5.99 *(978-1-4814-9772-5(3)*, Little Simon) Little Simon.

—Little Pookie. Boynton, Sandra. 2017. (Little Pookie Ser.). (ENG.). 18p. (J). (gr. -1-k). bds. 5.99 *(978-1-4814-9768-8(5)*, Little Simon) Little Simon.

B

—Merry Christmas, Little Pookie. Boynton, Sandra. 2018. (Little Pookie Ser.). (ENG.). 18p. (J). (-k). bds. 5.99 *(978-1-5344-3724-1(X)*, Little Simon) Little Simon.
—Moo, Baa, la la La! Special 30th Anniversary Edition! Boynton, Sandra. ed. 2012. (ENG.). 18p. (J). (gr. -1 — 1). bds. 8.99 *(978-1-4424-5410-1(5)*, Little Simon) Little Simon.
—Muu - Beee - ¡Asi Fue! Boynton, Sandra. 2003. (SPA.). 14p. (J). (gr. -1 — 1). bds. 5.99 *(978-0-689-86302-8(0)*, Libros Para Ninos) Libros Para Ninos.
—Night-Night, Little Pookie. Boynton, Sandra. 2017. (Little Pookie Ser.). (ENG.). 18p. (J). (gr. -1-k). bds. 5.99 *(978-1-4814-9771-8(5)*, Little Simon) Little Simon.
—Opuestos. Boynton, Sandra. Ziegler, Argentina Palacios, tr. 2004.Tr. of Opposites. (SPA.). 16p. (J). (gr. -1 — 1). bds. 5.99 *(978-0-689-86978-5(9)*, Libros Para Ninos) Libros Para Ninos.
—Perritos: Un Libro para Contar y Ladrar. Boynton, Sandra. 2004.Tr. of Doggies. (SPA.). 14p. (J). (gr. -1 — 1). bds. 5.99 *(978-0-689-86303-5(9)*, Libros Para Ninos) Libros Para Ninos.
—Sandra Boynton's Moo, Baa, la la La! Boynton, Sandra. ed. 2009. (ENG.). 16p. (J). bds. 16.99 *(978-1-4169-5035-6(4)*, Little Simon) Little Simon.
—Silly Lullaby. Boynton, Sandra. 2019. (ENG.). 16p. (J). (-k). bds. 5.99 *(978-1-5344-5282-4(6)*, Little Simon) Little Simon.
—What's Wrong, Little Pookie? Boynton, Sandra. 2017. (Little Pookie Ser.). (ENG.). 18p. (J). (gr. -1-k). bds. 5.99 *(978-1-4814-9769-5(3)*, Little Simon) Little Simon.
Boynton, Suki. The Hunter Maiden: Feminist Folktales from Around the World. Phelps, Ethel Johnston. 2017. (Feminist Folktales Ser.: 4). (ENG.). 176p. (J). (gr. 2-7). 14.95 *(978-1-55861-434-5(6))* Feminist Pr. at The City Univ. of New York.
—Kamala: Feminist Folktales from Around the World. Phelps, Ethel Johnston, ed. 2016. (Feminist Folktales Ser.: 2). (ENG.). 120p. (J). (gr. 2-7). pap. 14.95 *(978-1-55861-940-1(2))* Feminist Pr. at The City Univ. of New York.
—Sea Girl: Feminist Folktales from Around the World. Phelps, Ethel Johnston, ed. 2017. (Feminist Folktales Ser.: 3). (ENG.). 200p. (J). (gr. 2-7). pap. 14.95 *(978-1-55861-418-5(4))* Feminist Pr. at The City Univ. of New York.
—Tatterhood: Feminist Folktales from Around the World. Phelps, Ethel Johnston, ed. 2016. (Feminist Folktales Ser.: 1). 120p. (J). (gr. k). pap. 14.95 *(978-1-55861-929-6(1))* Feminist Pr. at The City Univ. of New York.
Bozak, Jon. Marc's Mission: Way of the Warrior Kid (a Novel) Willink, Jocko. 2018. (Way of the Warrior Kid Ser.: 2). (ENG.). 160p. (J). 13.99 *(978-1-250-15679-2(3)*, 900185103) Feiwel & Friends.
—Marc's Mission: Way of the Warrior Kid (a Novel) Willink, Jocko. 2019. (Way of the Warrior Kid Ser.: 2). (ENG.). 224p. (J). pap. 8.99 *(978-1-250-29443-2(6)*, 900195076) Square Fish.
—Way of the Warrior Kid: From Wimpy to Warrior the Navy SEAL Way: a Novel. Willink, Jocko. 2017. (Way of the Warrior Kid Ser.: 1). (ENG.). 192p. (J). 13.99 *(978-1-250-15107-0(4)*, 900182685) Feiwel & Friends.
—Way of the Warrior Kid: From Wimpy to Warrior the Navy SEAL Way: a Novel. Willink, Jocko. 2018. (Way of the Warrior Kid Ser.: 1). (ENG.). 192p. (J). pap. 7.99 *(978-1-250-15861-1(3)*, 900182686) Square Fish.
Bozarth, Mollie. Oak Street Tree House: The Day They Messaged God. Daniels, Dick. 2019. (Oak Street Tree House Ser.: Vol. 1). (ENG.). 36p. (J). (gr. k-3). 17.95 *(978-0-578-44950-0(1))* Leadership Development Group, The.
Bozeman, Gary. The Broccoli Bush. Sawyer, J. Scott. 2012. 36p. pap. 24.95 *(978-1-4626-2501-7(0))* America Star Bks.
Bozer, Chris. 10 Things You Should Know about Dinosaurs. Parker, Steve. Gallagher, Belinda & Borton, Paula, eds. 2004. (10 Things You Should Know Ser.). 24p. (J). 6.99 *(978-1-84236-120-7(1))* Miles Kelly Publishing, Ltd. GBR. Dist: Independent Pubs. Group.
Braasch, Gary. How We Know What We Know about Our Changing Climate: Scientists & Kids Explore Global Warming, 1 vol. Braasch, Gary. Cherry, Lynne. 2010. (ENG.). 66p. (J). (gr. 5-8). 18.95 *(978-1-58469-103-7(4)*, Dawn Pubns.) Sourcebooks, Inc.
Braasch, Gary, photos by. How We Know What We Know about Our Changing Climate: Scientists & Kids Explore Global Warming. Cherry, Lynne. 2008. (J). pap. *(978-1-58469-104-4(2))* Dawn Pubns.
Braasch, Gary, photos by. How We Know What We Know about Our Changing Climate: Scientists & Kids Explore Global Warming. Braasch, Gary. Cherry, Lynne. 2010. (ENG., 66p. (J). (gr. 5-8). pap. 11.95 *(978-1-58469-130-3(1)*, Dawn Pubns.) Sourcebooks, Inc.
Brace, Eric. Please Write in This Book. Amato, Mary. (ENG.). (J). (gr. 2-5). 2008. 97p. pap. 7.99 *(978-0-8234-2138-1(4))*; 2006. 112p. 16.95 *(978-0-8234-1932-6(0))* Holiday Hse., Inc.
Brace, Eric. You're Pulling My Leg! 400 Human-Body Sayings from Head to Toe. Brace, Eric. Street, Pat. (ENG.). 48p. (J). (gr. 1-4). 2017. 8.99 *(978-0-8234-3772-6(8))*; 2016. 18.95 *(978-0-8234-2135-0(X))* Holiday Hse., Inc.
Brack, Amanda. The Best & Biggest Fun Workbook for Minecrafters Grades 1 And 2: An Unofficial Learning Adventure for Minecrafters. Sky Pony Press. 2019. 356p. (J). (gr. 1-2). pap. 15.99 *(978-1-5107-4496-7(7)*, Sky Pony Pr.) Skyhorse Publishing Co., Inc.
—The Best & Biggest Fun Workbook for Minecrafters Grades 3 And 4: An Unofficial Learning Adventure for Minecrafters. Sky Pony Press. 2019. (ENG.). 356p. (J). (gr. 3-4). pap. 15.99 *(978-1-5107-4497-4(5)*, Sky Pony Pr.) Skyhorse Publishing Co., Inc.
—The Big Book of Math for Minecrafters: Adventures in Addition, Subtraction, Multiplication, & Division. Sky Pony Press. 2018. (Math for Minecrafters Ser.). 384p. (J). (gr. 1-4). pap. 19.99 *(978-1-5107-3759-4(6)*, Sky Pony Pr.) Skyhorse Publishing Co., Inc.
—A Creeper Camps Out: The Creeper Diaries, an Unofficial Minecrafters Novel, Book Eleven. Mann, Greyson. 2019. (Creeper Diaries: 11). 192p. (J). (gr. 3-7). 12.99 *(978-1-5107-4105-8(4)*, Sky Pony Pr.) Skyhorse Publishing Co., Inc.
—Creeper Family Vacation: The Creeper Diaries, an Unofficial Minecrafter's Novel, Book Five. Mann, Greyson. 2018. (Creeper Diaries: 5). (ENG.). 216p. (J). (gr. 3-7). 12.99 *(978-1-5107-3115-8(6)*, Sky Pony Pr.) Skyhorse Publishing Co., Inc.
—Creeper on the Case: The Creeper Diaries, an Unofficial Minecrafters Novel, Book Six. Mann, Greyson. 2018. (Creeper Diaries: 6). (ENG.). 192p. (J). (gr. 3-7). 12.99 *(978-1-5107-3749-5(9)*, Sky Pony Pr.) Skyhorse Publishing Co., Inc.
—Creeper's Got Talent: The Creeper Diaries, an Unofficial Minecrafter's Novel, Book Two. Mann, Greyson. 2017. (Creeper Diaries: 2). (ENG.). 192p. (J). (gr. 2-7). 12.99 *(978-1-5107-1821-0(4)*, Sky Pony Pr.) Skyhorse Publishing Co., Inc.
—Creepin' Through the Snow: The Creeper Diaries, an Unofficial Minecrafter's Novel, Special Edition. Mann, Greyson. 2017. (Creeper Diaries: 6). (ENG.). 176p. (J). (gr. 3-7). 12.99 *(978-1-5107-2734-2(5)*, Sky Pony Pr.) Skyhorse Publishing Co., Inc.
—The Enchanted Creeper: The Creeper Diaries, an Unofficial Minecrafters Novel, Book Seven. Mann, Greyson. 2018. (Creeper Diaries: 7). (ENG.). 192p. (J). (gr. 3-7). 12.99 *(978-1-5107-3750-1(2)*, Sky Pony Pr.) Skyhorse Publishing Co., Inc.
—The Enchanted Creeper Box Set: Six Unofficial Adventures for Minecrafters! Mann, Greyson. 2019. (Creeper Diaries). 1152p. (J). (gr. 4-6). pap. 29.99 *(978-1-5107-4735-7(4)*, Sky Pony Pr.) Skyhorse Publishing Co., Inc.
—Field Trip to the Taiga: The Creeper Diaries, an Unofficial Minecrafters Novel, Book Nine. Mann, Greyson. 2019. (Creeper Diaries: 9). (ENG.). 192p. (J). (gr. 3-7). 12.99 *(978-1-5107-4103-4(8)*, Sky Pony Pr.) Skyhorse Publishing Co., Inc.
—Get a Job, Creep: The Creeper Diaries, an Unofficial Minecrafters Novel, Book Ten. Mann, Greyson. 2019. (Creeper Diaries: 10). 192p. (J). (gr. 3-7). 12.99 *(978-1-5107-4104-1(6)*, Sky Pony Pr.) Skyhorse Publishing Co., Inc.
—The Great Big Fun Workbook for Minecrafters: Grades 1 And 2: An Unofficial Workbook. Sky Pony Press. 2018. 356p. (J). (gr. 1-2). pap. 15.99 *(978-1-5107-3986-4(6)*, Sky Pony Pr.) Skyhorse Publishing Co., Inc.
—The Great Big Fun Workbook for Minecrafters: Grades 3 And 4: An Unofficial Workbook. Sky Pony Press. 2018. 356p. (J). (gr. 3-4). pap. 15.99 *(978-1-5107-3985-7(8)*, Sky Pony Pr.) Skyhorse Publishing Co., Inc.
—Handwriting for Minecrafters: Cursive. Sky Pony Press. 2018. (ENG.). 64p. (J). 7.99 *(978-1-5107-3254-4(3)*, Sky Pony Pr.) Skyhorse Publishing Co., Inc.
—Handwriting for Minecrafters: Printing. Sky Pony Press. 2018. (ENG.). 64p. (J). pap. 7.99 *(978-1-5107-3253-7(5)*, Sky Pony Pr.) Skyhorse Publishing Co., Inc.
—The Jokiest Joking Bathroom Joke Book Ever Written ... No Joke! 1,001 Hilarious Potty Jokes to Make You Laugh While You Go. Roche, May. 2018. (Jokiest Joking Joke Bks.). (ENG.). 224p. (J). pap. 9.99 *(978-1-250-19003-1(7)*, 900192349) St. Martin's Pr.
—The Jokiest Joking Knock-Knock Joke Book Ever Written... No Joke! 1,001 Brand-New Knee-Slappers That Will Keep You Laughing Out Loud. Boone, Brian. 2018. (Jokiest Joking Joke Bks.). (ENG.). 256p. (J). pap. 9.99 *(978-1-250-16346-2(3)*, 900186524) St. Martin's Pr.
—The Jokiest Joking Puns Book Ever Written ... No Joke! 1,001 Brand-New Wisecracks That Will Keep You Laughing Out Loud. Boone, Brian. 2019. (Jokiest Joking Joke Bks.). (ENG.). 256p. (J). pap. 9.99 *(978-1-250-20199-7(3)*, 900193005) St. Martin's Pr.
—The Jokiest Joking Riddles Book Ever Written ... No Joke! 1,001 All-New Brain Teasers That Will Keep You Laughing Out Loud. Boone, Brian. 2020. (Jokiest Joking Joke Bks.: 4). (ENG.). 240p. (J). pap. 9.99 *(978-1-250-24047-7(6)*, 900211550) St. Martin's Pr.
—The Jokiest Joking Trivia Book Ever Written ... No Joke! 1,001 Surprising Facts to Amaze Your Friends. Boone, Brian. 2018. (Jokiest Joking Joke Bks.). (ENG.). 272p. (J). pap. 9.99 *(978-1-250-19976-8(X)*, 900195020) St. Martin's Pr.
—Know-It-All Trivia Book for Minecrafters: Over 800 Amazing Facts & Insider Secrets. Boone, Brian. 2017. 176p. (J). pap. 12.99 *(978-1-5107-3090-8(7)*, Sky Pony Pr.) Skyhorse Publishing Co., Inc.
—Math Facts for Minecrafters: Addition & Subtraction. Sky Pony Press. 2017. (Math for Minecrafters Ser.). 64p. (J). pap. 7.99 *(978-1-5107-3093-9(1)*, Sky Pony Pr.) Skyhorse Publishing Co., Inc.
—Math Facts for Minecrafters: Multiplication & Division. Sky Pony Press. 2017. (Math for Minecrafters Ser.). (ENG.). 64p. (J). 7.99 *(978-1-5107-3092-2(3)*, Sky Pony Pr.) Skyhorse Publishing Co., Inc.
—Math for Minecrafters Word Problems: Grades 1-2. Sky Pony Press. 2017. (Math for Minecrafters Ser.). 64p. (J). pap. 7.99 *(978-1-5107-3085-4(0)*, Sky Pony Pr.) Skyhorse Publishing Co., Inc.
—Math for Minecrafters Word Problems: Grades 3-4. Sky Pony Press. 2017. (Math for Minecrafters Ser.). 64p. (J). pap. 7.99 *(978-1-5107-3086-1(9)*, Sky Pony Pr.) Skyhorse Publishing Co., Inc.
—Math Fun for Minecrafters: Grades 1-2. Sky Pony Press. 2018. (Math for Minecrafters Ser.). (ENG.). 64p. (J). (gr. 1-2). pap. 7.99 *(978-1-5107-3760-0(X)*, Sky Pony Pr.) Skyhorse Publishing Co., Inc.
—Math Fun for Minecrafters: Grades 3-4. Sky Pony Press. 2018. (Math for Minecrafters Ser.). (ENG.). 64p. (J). (gr. 3-4). pap. 7.99 *(978-1-5107-3761-7(8)*, Sky Pony Pr.) Skyhorse Publishing Co., Inc.
—The Mini Jokiest Joke Book: Side-Splitters That Will Keep You Laughing Out Loud. Wagner, Kathi. 2020. (Jokiest Joking Joke Bks.: 1). (ENG.). 128p. (J). pap. 4.99 *(978-1-250-27033-7(2)*, 900223331) St. Martin's Pr.
—The Mini Jokiest Knock-Knock Joke Book: Knee-Slappers That Will Keep You Laughing Out Loud. Boone, Brian. 2020. (Jokiest Joking Joke Bks.: 3). (ENG.). 128p. (J). pap. 4.99 *(978-1-250-27037-5(5)*, 900223335) St. Martin's Pr.
—The Mini Jokiest Puns Book: Wisecracks That Will Keep You Laughing Out Loud. Boone, Brian. 2020. (Jokiest Joking Joke Bks.: 2). (ENG.). 128p. (J). pap. 4.99 *(978-1-250-27035-1(9)*, 900223333) St. Martin's Pr.
—Mob School Survivor: The Creeper Diaries, an Unofficial Minecrafter's Novel, Book One. Mann, Greyson. 2017. (Creeper Diaries: 1). (ENG.). 180p. (J). (gr. 2-7). 12.99 *(978-1-5107-1814-2(1)*, Sky Pony Pr.) Skyhorse Publishing Co., Inc.
—Mob School Swap: The Creeper Diaries, an Unofficial Minecrafters Novel, Book Eight. Mann, Greyson. 2019. (Creeper Diaries: 8). (ENG.). 192p. (J). (gr. 3-7). 12.99 *(978-1-5107-3751-8(0)*, Sky Pony Pr.) Skyhorse Publishing Co., Inc.
—New Creep at School: The Creeper Diaries, an Unofficial Minecrafter's Novel, Book Three. Mann, Greyson. 2017. (Creeper Diaries: 3). (ENG.). 184p. (J). (gr. 3-7). 12.99 *(978-1-5107-3112-7(1)*, Sky Pony Pr.) Skyhorse Publishing Co., Inc.
—The Overworld Games: The Creeper Diaries, an Unofficial Minecrafter's Novel, Book Four. Mann, Greyson. 2018. (Creeper Diaries: 4). (ENG.). 200p. (J). (gr. 3-7). 12.99 *(978-1-5107-3114-1(8)*, Sky Pony Pr.) Skyhorse Publishing Co., Inc.
—Pop, Sizzle, Boom! 101 Science Experiments for the Mad Scientist in Every Kid. Oyler, Amy. 2017. (ENG.). 224p. (J). pap. 14.99 *(978-1-250-09282-3(5)*, 900159756) St. Martin's Pr.
—Reading Success for Minecrafters: Grades 1-2. Sky Pony Press. 2017. (ENG.). 64p. (J). pap. 7.99 *(978-1-5107-3088-5(5)*, Sky Pony Pr.) Skyhorse Publishing Co., Inc.
—Reading Success for Minecrafters: Grades 3-4. Sky Pony Press. 2017. 64p. (J). pap. 7.99 *(978-1-5107-3089-2(3)*, Sky Pony Pr.) Skyhorse Publishing Co., Inc.
Brack, Amanda. Spectacular Science for Smart Kids: Clever Experiments & STEM Activities for Hours of Screen-Free Fun at Home. Oyler, Amy. 2020. (ENG.). 256p. (J). pap. 16.99 ***(978-1-250-27378-9(1)***, 900236339) St. Martin's Pr.
Brack, Amanda. Spelling for Minecrafters: Grade 1. Sky Pony Press. 2019. (Spelling for Minecrafters Ser.). 64p. (J). (gr. 1-1). pap. 7.99 *(978-1-5107-3762-4(6)*, Sky Pony Pr.) Skyhorse Publishing Co., Inc.
—Spelling for Minecrafters: Grade 2. Sky Pony Press. 2019. 64p. (J). (gr. 2-2). pap. 7.99 *(978-1-5107-3766-2(9)*, Sky Pony Pr.) Skyhorse Publishing Co., Inc.
—Spelling for Minecrafters: Grade 3. Sky Pony Press. 2019. (Spelling for Minecrafters Ser.). 64p. (J). (gr. 3-3). pap. 7.99 *(978-1-5107-4111-9(9)*, Sky Pony Pr.) Skyhorse Publishing Co., Inc.
—Spelling for Minecrafters: Grade 4. Sky Pony Press. 2019. (Spelling for Minecrafters Ser.). (ENG.). 64p. (J). (gr. 4-4). pap. 7.99 *(978-1-5107-4112-6(7)*, Sky Pony Pr.) Skyhorse Publishing Co., Inc.
—Superheroes of the Bible: Action & Adventure Stories about Real-Life Heroes. Stevens, Cara J. 2018. 112p. (J). (gr. -1-7). pap. 9.99 *(978-1-68099-322-6(4)*, Good Bks.) Skyhorse Publishing Co., Inc.
—The Ultimate Jokiest Joking Joke Book Ever Written ... No Joke! The Hugest Pile of Jokes, Knock-Knocks, Puns, & Knee-Slappers That Will Keep You Laughing Out Loud. Boone, Brian et al. 2019. (Jokiest Joking Joke Bks.). (ENG.). 496p. (J). pap. 14.99 *(978-1-250-23870-2(6)*, 900211021) St. Martin's Pr.
—The Unofficial Harry Potter Joke Book 4-Book Box Set: Includes Great Guffaws for Gryffindor, Stupefying Shenanigans for Slytherin, Howling Hilarity for Hufflepuff, and Raucous Jokes & Riddikulus Riddles for Ravenclaw! Boone, Brian. 2019. (Unofficial Harry Potter Joke Book Ser.). 704p. (J). (gr. 2-2). pap. 19.99 *(978-1-5107-4816-3(4)*, Sky Pony Pr.) Skyhorse Publishing Co., Inc.
—The Unofficial Harry Potter Joke Book: Howling Hilarity for Hufflepuff. Boone, Brian. 2019. (Unofficial Harry Potter Joke Book Ser.). 176p. (J). (gr. 2-2). pap. 7.99 *(978-1-5107-4093-8(7)*, Sky Pony Pr.) Skyhorse Publishing Co., Inc.
—The Unofficial Harry Potter Joke Book: Raucous Jokes & Riddikulus Riddles for Ravenclaw. Boone, Brian. 2019. (Unofficial Harry Potter Joke Book Ser.). 176p. (J). (gr. 2-2). pap. 7.99 *(978-1-5107-4094-5(5)*, Sky Pony Pr.) Skyhorse Publishing Co., Inc.
—The Unofficial Harry Potter Joke Book: Stupefying Shenanigans for Slytherin. Boone, Brian. 2018. (Unofficial Harry Potter Joke Book Ser.). 176p. (J). (gr. 2-2). pap. 7.99 *(978-1-5107-3768-6(5)*, Sky Pony Pr.) Skyhorse Publishing Co., Inc.
—An Unofficial Joke Book for Fortniters: Sidesplitting Jokes & Shenanigans from Salty Springs. Boone, Brian. 2019. (ENG.). 176p. (J). (gr. 3-3). pap. 7.99 *(978-1-5107-4807-1(5)*, Sky Pony Pr.) Skyhorse Publishing Co., Inc.
Brack, Amanda. Unofficial Math Adventures for Harry Potter Fans: Addition & Subtraction: Grades 1-2. 2020. 64p. (J). (gr. 1-2). pap. 7.99 ***(978-1-5107-6026-4(1)***, Sky Pony Pr.) Skyhorse Publishing Co., Inc.
—Unofficial Math Adventures for Harry Potter Fans: Multiplication & Division: Grades 3-4. 2020. 64p. (J). (gr. 3-4). pap. 7.99 ***(978-1-5107-6027-1(X)***, Sky Pony Pr.) Skyhorse Publishing Co., Inc.
Brack, Amanda. Unofficial STEM Challenges for Minecrafters: Grades 1-2. Sky Pony Press. 2018. (STEM for Minecrafters Ser.). (ENG.). 64p. (J). (gr. 1-2). pap. 7.99 *(978-1-5107-3757-0(X)*, Sky Pony Pr.) Skyhorse Publishing Co., Inc.
—Unofficial STEM Challenges for Minecrafters: Grades 3-4. Sky Pony Press. 2018. (STEM for Minecrafters Ser.). (ENG.). 64p. (J). (gr. 1-2). pap. 7.99 *(978-1-5107-3758-7(8)*, Sky Pony Pr.) Skyhorse Publishing Co., Inc.
—Uproarious Riddles for Minecrafters: Mobs, Ghasts, Biomes, & More. Boone, Brian. 2018. (Jokes for Minecrafters Ser.). (ENG.). 184p. (J). (gr. 1-6). pap. 7.99 *(978-1-5107-2717-5(5)*, Sky Pony Pr.) Skyhorse Publishing Co., Inc.
—Writing for Minecrafters: Grade 1. Sky Pony Press. 2019. 64p. (J). (gr. 1-1). pap. 7.99 *(978-1-5107-3763-1(4)*, Sky Pony Pr.) Skyhorse Publishing Co., Inc.
—Writing for Minecrafters: Grade 2. Sky Pony Press. 2019. (Writing for Minecrafters Ser.). (ENG.). 64p. (J). (gr. 2-2). pap. 7.99 *(978-1-5107-3767-9(7)*, Sky Pony Pr.) Skyhorse Publishing Co., Inc.
—Writing for Minecrafters: Grade 3. Sky Pony Press. 2019. (Writing for Minecrafters Ser.). 64p. (J). (gr. 3-3). pap. 7.99 *(978-1-5107-4120-1(8)*, Sky Pony Pr.) Skyhorse Publishing Co., Inc.
—Writing for Minecrafters: Grade 4. Sky Pony Press. 2019. (Writing for Minecrafters Ser.). 64p. (J). (gr. 4-4). pap. 7.99 *(978-1-5107-4121-8(6)*, Sky Pony Pr.) Skyhorse Publishing Co., Inc.
Brack, Amanda & Bell, Bill. The Night Before Christmas: A Brick Story. Moore, Clement C. 2015. (ENG.). 32p. (J). (gr. -1). 12.99 *(978-1-63450-179-8(9)*, Sky Pony Pr.) Skyhorse Publishing Co., Inc.
Bracken, Carolyn. Dinosaurs: A Nonfiction Companion to the Original Magic School Bus Series. Jackson, Tom. 2014. (Magic School Bus Presents Ser.). (ENG.). 32p. (J). (gr. 1-3). pap. 6.99 *(978-0-545-68583-2(4)*, Scholastic Paperbacks) Scholastic, Inc.
—Eloise Takes a Trip. Fry, Sonali. 2007. (Eloise Ser.). (ENG.). 16p. (J). (gr. -1-1). 7.99 *(978-1-4169-3343-4(3)*, Little Simon) Little Simon.
—Henry & Mudge & Mrs. Hopper's House. Rylant, Cynthia. 2004. (Ready-to-Read Ser.). 40p. (gr. k-2). 14.00 *(978-0-7569-2200-9(3))* Perfection Learning Corp.
—Henry & Mudge & Mrs. Hopper's House. Rylant, Cynthia. (Henry & Mudge Ser.: 22). (ENG.). 40p. (J). (gr. k-2). 2004. pap. 4.99 *(978-0-689-83446-2(2))*; 2003. 17.99 *(978-0-689-81153-1(5))* Simon Spotlight. (Simon Spotlight).
—Henry & Mudge & Mrs. Hopper's House. Rylant, Cynthia. ed. 2004. (Henry & Mudge Ready-To-Read Ser.: 22). 40p. (gr. k-2). lib. bdg. 13.55 *(978-0-613-90376-9(5))* Turtleback.
—Henry & Mudge & the Funny Lunch. Rylant, Cynthia. 2005. (Henry & Mudge Ser.: 24). (ENG.). 40p. (J). (gr. k-2). pap. 4.99 *(978-0-689-83444-8(6)*, Simon Spotlight) Simon Spotlight.
—Henry & Mudge & the Funny Lunch. Rylant, Cynthia. ed. 2005. (Henry & Mudge Ready-To-Read Ser.: 24). 40p. (gr. k-2). lib. bdg. 13.55 *(978-1-4176-7107-6(6))* Turtleback.
—Henry & Mudge & the Tall Tree House. Rylant, Cynthia. 2003. (Henry & Mudge Ser.). (ENG.). 40p. (J). (gr. k-2). pap. 4.99 *(978-0-689-83445-5(4)*, Simon Spotlight) Simon Spotlight.
—Henry & Mudge & the Tumbling Trip. Rylant, Cynthia. 2006. (Henry & Mudge Ser.). 40p. (gr. k-3). 14.00 *(978-0-7569-6904-2(2))* Perfection Learning Corp.
—Henry & Mudge & the Tumbling Trip. Rylant, Cynthia. (Henry & Mudge Ser.: 27). (ENG.). 40p. (J). (gr. k-2). 2006. pap. 4.99 *(978-0-689-83452-3(7))*; 2005. 16.99 *(978-0-689-81180-7(2))* Simon Spotlight. (Simon Spotlight).
—Henry & Mudge & the Wild Goose Chase. Rylant, Cynthia. ed. 2005. (Henry & Mudge Ser.). 40p. (J). lib. bdg. 15.00 *(978-1-59054-946-9(5))* Fitzgerald Bks.
—Henry & Mudge & the Wild Goose Chase. Rylant, Cynthia. 2004. (Henry & Mudge Ser.). 40p. (gr. k-2). 14.00 *(978-0-7569-3366-1(8))* Perfection Learning Corp.
—Henry & Mudge & the Wild Goose Chase. Rylant, Cynthia. 2003. (Henry & Mudge Ser.: 23). (ENG.). 40p. (J). (gr. k-2). 17.99 *(978-0-689-81172-2(1)*, Simon Spotlight) Simon Spotlight.
—Henry & Mudge & the Wild Goose Chase. Rylant, Cynthia. ed. 2004. (Henry & Mudge Ready-To-Read Ser.: 26). 40p. (gr. k-2). lib. bdg. 13.55 *(978-1-4176-4340-0(4))* Turtleback.
—The Magic School Bus & the Butterfly Bunch. Earhart, Kristin et al. 2010. 32p. (J). *(978-0-545-16727-7(2))* Scholastic, Inc.
—The Magic School Bus & the Shark Adventure. Smith, Elizabeth. 2007. (Scholastic Reader Ser.). (J). *(978-0-545-03464-7(7))* Scholastic, Inc.
—The Magic School Bus at the First Thanksgiving. Cole, Joanna. 2006. (J). pap. *(978-0-439-89935-2(4))* Scholastic, Inc.
—The Magic School Bus Fights Germs. Egan, Kate & Cole, Joanna. 2008. pap. *(978-0-545-03465-4(5)*, Scholastic, Inc.) Scholastic, Inc.
—The Magic School Bus Fixes a Bone. Earhart, Kristin. 2010. 32p. (J). pap. *(978-0-545-23950-9(8)*, Cartwheel Bks.) Scholastic, Inc.
—The Magic School Bus Inside a Volcano. Earhart, Kristin et al. 2012. 32p. (J). *(978-0-545-35685-5(7))* Scholastic, Inc.
—The Magic School Bus Rides the Wind, Level 2. Capeci, Anne & Cole, Joanna. 2007. (Magic School Bus Science Reader Ser.). (ENG.). 32p. (J). (gr. -1-3). pap. 4.99 *(978-0-439-80108-9(7)*, Cartwheel Bks.) Scholastic, Inc.
—Merry Christmas, Eloise! Cheshire, Marc. 2006. (Eloise Ser.). (ENG.). 18p. (J). (gr. -1-1). pap. 7.99 *(978-0-689-87155-9(4)*, Little Simon) Little Simon.
—Our Solar System. Jackson, Tom. 2014. (Magic School Bus Presents Ser.). (ENG.). 32p. (J). (gr. 1-3). pap. 6.99 *(978-0-545-68365-4(3)*, Scholastic Paperbacks) Scholastic, Inc.
—Planet Earth. Jackson, Tom. 2014. (Magic School Bus Presents Ser.). (ENG.). 32p. (J). (gr. 1-3). pap. 6.99 *(978-0-545-68012-7(3))* Scholastic, Inc.
—Polar Animals. O'Brien, Cynthia. 2014. (Magic School Bus Presents Ser.). (ENG.). 32p. (J). (gr. 1-3). pap. 6.99 *(978-0-545-68586-3(9)*, Scholastic Paperbacks) Scholastic, Inc.

—The Rainforest. Jackson, Tom. 2014. (Magic School Bus Presents Ser.). (ENG.). 32p. (J). (gr. 1-3). pap. 6.99 *(978-0-545-68585-6(0)*, Scholastic Paperbacks) Scholastic, Inc.
—Sea Creatures. Jackson, Tom. 2014. (Magic School Bus Presents Ser.). (ENG.). 32p. (J). (gr. -1-3). pap. 6.99 *(978-0-545-68366-1(1)*, Scholastic Paperbacks) Scholastic, Inc.
—Volcanoes & Earthquakes: A Nonfiction Companion to the Original Magic School Bus Series. Jackson, Tom. 2014. (Magic School Bus Presents Ser.). (ENG.). 32p. (J). (gr. 1-3). pap. 6.99 *(978-0-545-68584-9(2)*, Scholastic Paperbacks) Scholastic, Inc.
—Wild Weather. Callery, Sean. 2014. (Magic School Bus Presents Ser.). (ENG.). 32p. (J). (gr. -1-3). pap. 6.99 *(978-0-545-68367-8(X))* Scholastic, Inc.
Bracken, Carolyn. Henry & Mudge & the Funny Lunch. Bracken, Carolyn. Rylant, Cynthia. 2004. (Henry & Mudge Ser.: 24). (ENG.). 40p. (J). (gr. k-2). 16.99 *(978-0-689-81178-4(0)*, Simon Spotlight) Simon Spotlight.
Bracken, Carolyn, jt. illus. see Degen, Bruce.
Bracken, Carolyn, jt. illus. see Glasser, Robin Preiss.
Brackett, Mike. Clawde: The Far-Fetched Tale of a Maine Lobster. Brackett, Mike. 2019. (ENG.). 38p. (J). pap. 14.62 *(978-1-0990-7270-3(0))* Independently Published.
Bradbrooke, Floyd. Catch Caisie's Smile. Langford, Thea. l.t. ed. 2019. (ENG.). 26p. (J). *(978-1-910301-69-2(8))* AESOP Pubns.
Bradburn, Ryan. Conditional Following Directions Fun Deck: Fd68. 2003. (J). 11.95 *(978-1-58650-290-4(5))* Super Duper Pubns.
—Using I & Me Fun Deck: Fd61. Webber, Thomas. 2003. (J). 11.95 *(978-1-58650-292-8(1))* Super Duper Pubns.
Bradbury, Ray & Mugnaini, Joe. The Halloween Tree. Bradbury, Ray. Eller, Jon, ed. 2005. 494p. (J). (gr. 4-12). per. 75.00 *(978-1-887368-80-3(9))* Gauntlet, Inc.
Braddock, Paige. It's Tokyo, Charlie Brown! Schulz, Charles M. & Scott, Vicki. 2012. (Peanuts Ser.). (ENG.). 96p. (J). (gr. 2). pap. 9.99 *(978-1-60886-270-2(4))* Boom! Studios.
—Peanuts, Vol. 2. Schulz, Charles M. & Houghton, Shane. 2013. (Peanuts Ser.). (ENG.). 112p. (J). (gr. 1-3). pap. 13.99 *(978-1-60886-299-3(2))* Boom! Studios.
Braddock, Paige & Scott, Vicki. Charles M. Schulz's Lucy. Cooper, Jason. 2019. (Peanuts Ser.). (ENG.). 96p. (J). 14.99 *(978-1-68415-296-4(8))* Boom! Studios.
—Peanuts Vol. 10. Schulz, Charles M. & Cooper, Jason. 2018. (Peanuts Ser.: 10). (ENG.). 128p. (J). (gr. 1-3). pap. 13.99 *(978-1-68415-220-9(8))* Boom! Studios.
Braddock, Paige, jt. illus. see Scott, Vicki.
Bradfield, Jolly Roger. Benjamin Dilley's Thirsty Camel. Bradfield, Jolly Roger. 2012. (ENG.). 64p. (J). (gr. 4-7). 18.95 *(978-1-930900-60-8(0))* Purple Hse. Pr.
—Un Perfecto Caballero para Dragones. Bradfield, Jolly Roger. 2009. (SPA.). 64p. (J). (gr. 1-3). *(978-84-7490-974-6(0))* Encuentro Ediciones, S.A.
Bradfield, Roger. Alvin Fernald's Incredible Buried Treasure. Hicks, Clifford B. 2009. (J). 17.95 *(978-1-930900-43-1(0))* Purple Hse. Pr.
—The Pickle-Chiffon Pie Olympics. 2011. 64p. (J). (gr. -1-3). 18.95 *(978-1-930900-52-3(X))* Purple Hse. Pr.
—The Together Book (Sesame Street) Dwight, Revena. 2017. (Little Golden Book Ser.). 24p. (J). (-k). 4.99 *(978-1-5247-1978-4(1)*, Golden Bks.) Random Hse. Children's Bks.
Bradford, June. Chock Full of Chocolate. MacLeod, Elizabeth. 2005. (Kids Can Do It Ser.). 40p. (J). (gr. 3-7). 6.95 *(978-1-55337-763-4(X))* Kids Can Pr., Ltd. CAN. Dist: Hachette Bk. Group.
—Embroidery. Sadler, Judy Ann. 2006. 40p. (J). pap. *(978-0-439-89943-7(5))* Scholastic, Inc.
—Hemp Jewelry. Sadler, Judy Ann & Sadler, Judy. 2005. (Kids Can Do It Ser.). 40p. (J). (gr. 3-7). 6.95 *(978-1-55337-775-7(3))* Kids Can Pr., Ltd. CAN. Dist: Hachette Bk. Group.
—Hemp Jewelry. Sadler, Judy Ann. 2005. (Kids Can Do It Ser.). (ENG.). 40p. (YA). (gr. 3-6). 18.69 *(978-1-55337-774-0(5))* Kids Can Pr., Ltd. CAN. Dist: Children's Plus, Inc.
Bradford, Tim. Raise the Flag: Terrific Flag Facts, Stories, & Trivia! Gifford, Clive. 2018. (ENG.). 96p. (J). (gr. 2-5). pap. 14.95 ***(978-1-68297-338-7(7))*** QEB Publishing Inc.
Bradley, Amy. The Magic Within. Armstrong, Paightyn. 2019. (ENG.). 138p. (J). ***(978-1-5255-3914-5(0))***; pap. ***(978-1-5255-3915-2(9))*** FriesenPress.
Bradley, Arianne. Little Girl's Pencil. Roberts, Brittney. 2020. (ENG.). 26p. (J). pap. 10.00 ***(978-1-7004-6579-5(1))*** Independently Published.
Bradley, Cindy. Whose Moose Am I? Guthrie, Arlo. 2014. (ENG.). (J). 15.00 *(978-0-9915370-3-7(3))* Rising Son International, Ltd.
Bradley, Jeanette. When the Babies Came to Stay. McDonnell, Christine. 2020. 36p. (J). (-k). 16.99 *(978-1-9848-3545-1(9)*, Viking Books for Young Readers) Penguin Young Readers Group.
Bradley, Jeanette. Love, Mama. Bradley, Jeanette. 2019. (ENG.). 28p. (J). bds. 7.99 *(978-1-250-24035-4(2)*, 900211506) Roaring Brook Pr.
Bradley, Jennie. Alphabet. Rainstorm Publishing, ed. 2019. (Handle Board Ser.). (ENG.). 20p. (J). bds. 7.99 ***(978-1-926444-48-2(5))*** Rainstorm Pr.
Bradley, Jennie. Animals. Ackland, Nick. 2017. (Busy Baby Ser.). (ENG.). 10p. (J). (gr. -1 — 1). bds. 6.99 *(978-0-7641-6892-5(4)*, B.E.S. Publishing) Peterson's.
Bradley, Jennie. Build Your Own Play Train. Boultwood, Ellie et al. 2019. (J). ***(978-0-312-52957-4(0))*** St. Martin's Pr.
—Numbers. Rainstorm Publishing, ed. 2019. (Handle Board Ser.). (ENG.). 20p. (J). bds. 7.99 ***(978-1-926444-49-9(3))*** Rainstorm Pr.
Bradley, Jennie. Out & About. Ackland, Nick. 2017. (Busy Baby Ser.). (ENG.). 10p. (J). (gr. -1 — 1). bds. 6.99 *(978-0-7641-6893-2(2)*, B.E.S. Publishing) Peterson's.
Bradley, Jess. Agent Moose. O'Hara, Mo. 2020. (Agent Moose Ser.: 1). (ENG.). 128p. (J). 10.99 *(978-1-250-22221-3(4)*, 900207972) Feiwel & Friends.
Bradley, Jess. Draw Kawaii in 5 Simple Steps. 2020. (ENG.). 80p. (J). (gr. 1-3). pap. 9.95 ***(978-1-4549-4283-2(5))*** Sterling Publishing Co., Inc.
Bradley, Jess. I Know Sasquatch. 2015. (Fiction Picture Bks.). (ENG.). 32p. (J). (gr. -1-2). lib. bdg. 22.60 *(978-1-4795-6481-1(8)*, Picture Window Bks.) Capstone.
Bradley, Jessica. Blastoff to the Secret Side of the Moon!, 1 vol. Nickel, Scott. 2013. (Comics Land Ser.). (ENG.). 32p. (J). (gr. k-2). 7.95 *(978-1-4342-4273-0(0))*; lib. bdg. 25.32 *(978-1-4342-4031-6(2))* Capstone. (Stone Arch Bks.).
—Comics Land. 2013. (Comics Land Ser.). (ENG.). 32p. (J). (gr. k-2). 63.60 *(978-1-4342-8516-4(2))*; lib. bdg., lib. bdg., lib. bdg. 202.56 *(978-1-4342-6063-5(1))* Capstone. (Stone Arch Bks.).
—Dinosaurs for Breakfast, 1 vol. Lemke, Amy J. 2013. (Comics Land Ser.). (ENG.). 32p. (J). (gr. k-2). 7.95 *(978-1-4342-4270-9(6))*; lib. bdg. 25.32 *(978-1-4342-4029-3(0))* Capstone. (Stone Arch Bks.).
—Frank 'n' Beans, 1 vol. Lemke, Amy J. & Lemke, Donald B. 2013. (Comics Land Ser.). (ENG.). 32p. (J). (gr. k-2). 7.95 *(978-1-4342-6284-4(7))*; lib. bdg. 25.32 *(978-1-4342-4988-3(3))* Capstone. (Stone Arch Bks.).
—Goat on a Boat, 1 vol. Sazaklis, John. 2013. (Comics Land Ser.). (ENG.). 32p. (J). (gr. k-2). 7.95 *(978-1-4342-6282-0(0))*; lib. bdg. 25.32 *(978-1-4342-4944-9(1))* Capstone. (Stone Arch Bks.).
—The Good, the Bad, & the Monkeys, 1 vol. Sonneborn, Scott. 2013. (Comics Land Ser.). (ENG.). 32p. (J). (gr. k-2). 7.95 *(978-1-4342-6283-7(9))*; lib. bdg. 25.32 *(978-1-4342-4945-6(X))* Capstone. (Stone Arch Bks.).
—My Little Bro-Bot, 1 vol. Lemke, Amy J. & Lemke, Donald B. 2013. (Comics Land Ser.). (ENG.). 32p. (J). (gr. k-2). 7.95 *(978-1-4342-6285-1(5))*; lib. bdg. 25.32 *(978-1-4342-4989-0(1))* Capstone. (Stone Arch Bks.).
—The New Kid from Planet Glorf, 1 vol. Kaplan, Arie. 2013. (Comics Land Ser.). (ENG.). 32p. (J). (gr. k-2). 7.95 *(978-1-4342-4272-3(2))*; lib. bdg. 25.32 *(978-1-4342-4032-3(0))* Capstone. (Stone Arch Bks.).
—Snorkeling with Sea-Bots, 1 vol. Lemke, Amy J. 2013. (Comics Land Ser.). (ENG.). 32p. (J). (gr. k-2). 7.95 *(978-1-4342-4271-6(4))*; lib. bdg. 25.32 *(978-1-4342-4030-9(4))* Capstone. (Stone Arch Bks.).
Bradley, Katie. The Runaway Injera: In English & Amharic. Ready Set Go Books. Eshetie, Amlaku B., tr. 2019. (ENG.). 40p. (J). pap. 11.99 *(978-1-0991-8381-2(2))* Independently Published.
Bradley, Katie & Nordeen, Sandra. Beautiful Hair: Celebrating Ethiopian Hairstyles in English & Amharic. Ready Set Go Books. 2019. (ENG.). 34p. (J). pap. 9.99 ***(978-1-7037-8223-3(2))*** Independently Published.
Bradley, Katie & Students from Riverview Elementary Schoo. Fire: A Good Servant but a Bad Master, in English & Amharic. Ready Set Go Books. 2020. (ENG.). 36p. (J). pap. 9.99 ***(978-1-6588-6197-7(3))*** Independently Published.
—Fire: In English & Afaan Oromo. Ready Set Go Books. 2019. (ENG.). 36p. (J). pap. 9.99 ***(978-1-6774-1555-7(X))*** Independently Published.
Bradley, Katie, jt. illus. see Instructors from Clark College Economic.
Bradley, Lois. Blind Tom: The Horse Who Helped Build the Great Railroad. Redmond, Shirley Raye. 2009. (J). pap. 10.00 *(978-0-87842-558-7(6))* Mountain Pr. Publishing Co., Inc.
—Eyes of Pharaoh. Eboch, Chris. 2017. (ENG.). (J). (gr. 3-6). 22.99 *(978-1-945017-27-8(9))* Spellbound River Pr.
Bradley, Pat, jt. illus. see Calhoun, Brian.
Bradley, Sandy. The Crows of Hidden Creek. Niemela, JoAnn Huston. 2003. 109p. (YA). 20.00 *(978-0-9716786-0-6(X))* Ten Minas Publishing.
Bradley, Timothy J. Infestation. Bradley, Timothy J. 2013. (ENG.). 192p. (J). (gr. 3-7). pap. 5.99 *(978-0-545-45904-4(4))* Scholastic, Inc.
Bradley, Vanessa. Daisy Street. Chase, Diana. 2005. 128p. (Orig.). (J). pap. 13.50 *(978-1-920731-11-3(3))* Fremantle Pr. AUS. Dist: Independent Pubs. Group.
Bradshaw, Carrie Anne. Nathan Saves Summer. Renert, Gerry. 2010. (ENG.). 32p. (J). (gr. -1-3). 16.95 *(978-1-934960-76-9(4)*, Raven Tree Pr.,Csi) Continental Sales, Inc.
—Nathan Saves Summer/Nathan Rescata el Verano. Renert, Gerry. 2010. (ENG & SPA.). 32p. (J). (gr. -1-3). 16.95 *(978-1-934960-74-5(8)*, Raven Tree Pr.,Csi) Continental Sales, Inc.
Bradshaw, Jim. Suddenly Alligator: Adventures in Adverbs, 1 vol. Walton, Rick. 2011. (ENG.). 36p. (J). (gr. 2-3). pap. 7.99 *(978-1-4236-2087-7(9))* Gibbs Smith, Publisher.
Bradshaw, Nick. Spidey: Freshman Year. 2019. 272p. (J). (gr. 4-7). pap. 12.99 *(978-1-302-91655-8(6))* Marvel Worldwide, Inc.
Bradshaw, Nick, et al. Spidey (Set), 6 vols. Thompson, Robbie. 2016. (Spidey Ser.). (ENG.). 24p. (J). (gr. 2-8). lib. bdg. 162.42 *(978-1-61479-592-6(4)*, 24373, Marvel Age) Spotlight.
Bradshaw, Nick & Campbell, Jim. Spidey #1. Thompson, Robbie. 2016. (Spidey Ser.). (ENG.). 24p. (J). (gr. 2-8). lib. bdg. 27.07 *(978-1-61479-593-3(2)*, 24374, Marvel Age) Spotlight.
—Spidey #2. Thompson, Robbie. 2016. (Spidey Ser.). (ENG.). 24p. (J). (gr. 2-8). lib. bdg. 27.07 *(978-1-61479-594-0(0)*, 24375, Marvel Age) Spotlight.
—Spidey #3. Thompson, Robbie. 2016. (Spidey Ser.). (ENG.). 24p. (J). (gr. 2-8). lib. bdg. 27.07 *(978-1-61479-595-7(9)*, 24376, Marvel Age) Spotlight.
Brady, Annie. Shackleton - the Boss: The Remarkable Adventures of Ernest Shackleton. Smith, Michael. 2nd rev. ed. 2010. (ENG.). 128p. (J). pap. 15.95 *(978-1-905172-27-6(3))* Collins Pr., The IRL. Dist: Dufour Editions, Inc.
Brady, D. The Betty & Barney Hill Alien Abduction. Bowman, Chris. 2019. (Paranormal Mysteries Ser.). (ENG.). 24p. (J). (gr. 3-8). lib. bdg. 22.95 *(978-1-64487-093-8(2)*, Black Sheep) Bellwether Media.
Brady, Irene. Illustrating Nature: Right-brain Art in a Left-Brain World. Brady, Irene. 2004. spiral bd. 25.95 *(978-0-915965-09-0(7))* Nature Works Press.
Brady, Jesse. Trapped in a Video Game (Book 1) Brady, Dustin. 2018. (Trapped in a Video Game Ser.: 1). (ENG.). 144p. (J). pap. 9.99 *(978-1-4494-9486-5(2))* Andrews McMeel Publishing.
—Trapped in a Video Game (Book 2) The Invisible Invasion. Brady, Dustin. 2018. (Trapped in a Video Game Ser.: 2). (ENG.). 160p. (J). 13.99 *(978-1-4494-9617-3(2))*; pap. 9.99 *(978-1-4494-9489-6(7))* Andrews McMeel Publishing.
—Trapped in a Video Game (Book 3) Robots Revolt. Brady, Dustin. 2018. (Trapped in a Video Game Ser.: 3). (ENG.). 176p. (J). pap. 9.99 *(978-1-4494-9515-2(X))* Andrews McMeel Publishing.
—Trapped in a Video Game (Book 4) Return to Doom Island. Brady, Dustin. 2018. (Trapped in a Video Game Ser.: 4). (ENG.). 168p. (J). 13.99 *(978-1-4494-9625-8(3))*; pap. 9.99 *(978-1-4494-9518-3(4))* Andrews McMeel Publishing.
Brady, Laurie. A Charm for Jo. Brady, Bill. l.t. ed. 2005. (Turtle Books). 32p. (J). (gr. 2-5). lib. bdg. 15.95 *(978-0-944727-48-5(4))* Jason & Nordic Pubs.
Brady, Lisa. Here, There, & Everywhere: The Story of Sreeeeeeeet the Lorikeett. Tweti, Mira. 2008. 47p. (J). (gr. 4-7). *(978-0-615-17122-7(2))* Parrot Pr.
Braffet, Holly. If You Were a Dinosaur in Hawaii. BeachHouse Publishing. 2010. 22p. (J). (gr. -1-1). bds. 7.95 *(978-1-933067-39-1(X))* Beachhouse Publishing, LLC.
—Kekoa & the Egg Mystery. 2010. (ENG.). 32p. (J). (gr. -1-2). 14.95 *(978-1-933067-35-3(7))* Beachhouse Publishing, LLC.
—Little Mouse's Hawaiian Christmas Present. Ebie, Mora. 2011. 28p. (J). *(978-1-56647-956-1(8))* Mutual Publishing LLC.
—Maile & the Huli Hula Chicken. Braffet, Mary. 2010. 32p. (J). 12.95 *(978-1-56647-925-7(8))* Mutual Publishing LLC.
Braga, Humberto. The Girl from Atlantis. Schenkman, Richard. 2010. 144p. (J). (gr. 2-7). 16.99 *(978-0-9841809-0-5(7))* GMI Bks.
Bragadottir, Hrefna. Don't Go There! Willis, Jeanne. 2019. (ENG.). 32p. (J). (gr. -1-k). 17.99 *(978-1-5415-5508-2(2))* Lerner Publishing Group.
Braginetz, Donna. Real Live Monsters: Level 2. Schecter, Barbara. 2020. (Bank Street Ready-To-Read Ser.). (ENG.). 50p. (J). pap. 9.95 ***(978-1-876966-26-3(2))*** ibooks, Inc.
Brailsford, Jill. Ellabeth's Light. Darlison, Aleesah. 2017. (Unicorn Riders Ser.). (ENG.). 112p. (J). (gr. 3-5). pap. 5.95 *(978-1-4795-6559-7(8)*, 128549); lib. bdg. 22.65 *(978-1-4795-6551-1(2)*, 128541) Capstone. (Picture Window Bks.).
—Ellabeth's Test. Darlison, Aleesah. (Unicorn Riders Ser.). (ENG.). 112p. (J). (gr. 3-5). 2017. pap. 5.95 *(978-1-4795-6555-9(5)*, 128545); 2016. lib. bdg. 22.65 *(978-1-4795-6547-4(4))* Capstone. (Picture Window Bks.).
—Krystal's Charge. Darlison, Aleesah. 2017. (Unicorn Riders Ser.). (ENG.). 112p. (J). (gr. 3-5). pap. 5.95 *(978-1-4795-6558-0(X)*, 128548); lib. bdg. 22.65 *(978-1-4795-6550-4(4)*, 128540) Capstone. (Picture Window Bks.).
—Krystal's Choice. Darlison, Aleesah. (Unicorn Riders Ser.). (ENG.). 112p. (J). (gr. 3-5). 2017. pap. 5.95 *(978-1-4795-6554-2(7)*, 128544); 2016. lib. bdg. 22.65 *(978-1-4795-6546-7(6))* Capstone. (Picture Window Bks.).
—Quinn's Riddles. Darlison, Aleesah. (Unicorn Riders Ser.). (ENG.). 112p. (J). (gr. 3-5). 2017. pap. 5.95 *(978-1-4795-6552-8(0)*, 128542); 2016. lib. bdg. 22.65 *(978-1-4795-6544-3(X))* Capstone. (Picture Window Bks.).
—Quinn's Truth. Darlison, Aleesah. 2017. (Unicorn Riders Ser.). (ENG.). 112p. (J). (gr. 3-5). pap. 5.95 *(978-1-4795-6556-6(3)*, 128546); lib. bdg. 22.65 *(978-1-4795-6548-1(2)*, 128538) Capstone. (Picture Window Bks.).
—Unicorn Riders. Darlison, Aleesah. 2017. (Unicorn Riders Ser.). (ENG.). 112p. (J). (gr. 3-5). 181.20 *(978-1-5158-0821-3(1)*, 25856, Picture Window Bks.) Capstone.
—Willow's Challenge. Darlison, Aleesah. 2017. (Unicorn Riders Ser.). (ENG.). 112p. (J). (gr. 3-5). 2017. pap. 5.95 *(978-1-4795-6553-5(9)*, 128543); 2016. lib. bdg. 22.65 *(978-1-4795-6545-0(8))* Capstone. (Picture Window Bks.).
—Willow's Victory. Darlison, Aleesah. 2017. (Unicorn Riders Ser.). (ENG.). 112p. (J). (gr. 3-5). pap. 5.95 *(978-1-4795-6557-3(1)*, 128547); lib. bdg. 22.65 *(978-1-4795-6549-8(0)*, 128539) Capstone. (Picture Window Bks.).
Braithwaite, Doug, et al. Excalibur Epic Collection: Curiouser & Curiouser. 2020. (ENG.). 472p. (YA). (gr. 8-17). pap. 39.99 *(978-1-302-92276-4(9))* Marvel Worldwide, Inc.
Braithwaite, Doug, jt. illus. see Ross, Alex.
Braithwaite, Barrington. A Man Called Garvey: The Life & Times of the Great Leader Marcus Garvey. Mohamed, Paloma. l.t. ed. 2004. (Majority Press Inc., Wisdom for Children Ser.: No. 1). (ENG.). 36p. (J). 12.95 *(978-0-912469-40-9(4))* Majority Pr., The.
Braithwaite, Barry. Caribbean Mythology & Modern Life: 5 Plays for Young People. Mohamed, Paloma. 2004. (Majority Press Inc., Wisdom for Children Ser.: Vol. 2). (ENG.). 216p. (J). per. 19.95 *(978-0-912469-42-3(0))* Majority Pr., The.
Braley, Carolyn. Ginny the Giraffe. Robbins, Carole. 2019. (ENG.). 58p. (J). pap. 13.95 *(978-1-64492-197-5(9))* Christian Faith Publishing.
Braley, Shawn. Great Medieval Projects. Bordessa, Kris. 2008. (Build It Yourself Ser.). 128p. (J). (gr. 3-7). 21.95 *(978-1-934670-26-2(X)*, c01acd21-51be-4922-9e96-f7c34fb94e6f) Nomad Pr.
—Great Medieval Projects: You Can Build Yourself. Bordessa, Kris. 2008. (Build It Yourself Ser.). 128p. (J). (gr. 3-7). pap. 15.95 *(978-0-9792268-0-9(5)*, 9f62be38-bea5-46a0-b1cc-6ca745f298ca) Nomad Pr.
—Great Pioneer Projects. Dickinson, Rachel. 2007. (Build It Yourself Ser.: 1). 128p. (J). (gr. 3-7). pap. 15.95 *(978-0-9785037-6-5(7)*, 9bd20233-c0be-4643-bc99-e228b41a5b46) Nomad Pr.
—World Myths & Legends: 25 Projects You Can Build Yourself. Ceceri, Kathy. 2010. (Build It Yourself Ser.). 128p. (J). (gr. 3-7). 21.95 *(978-1-934670-44-6(8)*, b9cfa0c8-9109-42ac-8d51-8082405d7645); pap. 15.95 *(978-1-934670-43-9(X)*, c88946ec-1513-49b3-bad6-35b192bf1c15) Nomad Pr.
Brallier, Christine. The Night Before Christmas. 2013. (ENG.). 32p. (J). 16.99 *(978-0-9789688-2-3(4))* Brownian Bee Pr.
Bramall, Dan. The Awesome Book of Awesomeness. Frost, Adam. 2015. (ENG.). 112p. (J). (gr. 2-4). pap. 9.99 *(978-1-61963-793-1(6)*, 900148771, Bloomsbury Activity Bks.) Bloomsbury Publishing USA.
Bramer, Christopher. Tale of the Rainbird. Owens, Robin Bee. 2019. (ENG.). 44p. (J). pap. 10.99 *(978-1-949350-09-8(6))* BOCH Publishing, L.L.C.
Bramer, Christopher. The Wand. Owens, Robin Bee. 2019. (ENG.). 60p. (J). pap. 9.95 ***(978-1-949350-07-4(X))*** BOCH Publishing, L.L.C.
Bramlett, Jarob. There's Always Room at Our Table. Farmer, Jill. 2020. (ENG.). 20p. (J). pap. 12.49 ***(978-1-63129-475-4(X))*** Salem Author Services.
Bramsen, Carin. The Yellow Tutu. Bramsen, Kirsten. 2013. (ENG.). 40p. (J). (gr. -1-1). 22.44 *(978-0-375-85168-1(2))* Random House Publishing Group.
—The Yellow Tutu. Bramsen, Kirsten. 2013. (ENG.). 40p. (J). (-k). pap. 7.99 *(978-0-375-84393-8(0)*, Dragonfly Bks.) Random Hse. Children's Bks.
Bramsen, Carin. Sleepover Duck! Bramsen, Carin. 2018. 40p. (J). (gr. -1-2). 17.99 *(978-0-385-38417-9(3)*, Random Hse. Bks. for Young Readers) Random Hse. Children's Bks.
Branam, Sandy. Kiki & the Red Shoes. Chappas, Bess. 2007. (J). 17.99 *(978-1-60131-012-5(9))* Big Tent Bks.
Branca, Daniel, jt. illus. see Heymans, Mau.
Branca, Valeria. Santa's Elves Save Christmas. 2019. (Lift-The-Flap Book Ser.). 10p. (J). (gr. -1). bds. 7.99 *(978-2-89802-130-5(X)*, CrackBoom! Bks.) Chouette Publishing CAN. Dist: Publishers Group West (PGW).
Branch, Beverly. The Miller & the Donkey: A Tale about Thinking for Yourself. Aesop, Aesop. 2006. (J). *(978-1-59939-087-1(6)*, Reader's Digest Young Families, Inc.) Studio Fun International.
—The Nightingale. 2006. (J). 6.99 *(978-1-59939-020-8(5))* Cornerstone Pr.
—Thumbelina: A Tale about Being Nice. 2006. (J). 6.99 *(978-1-59939-024-6(8))* Cornerstone Pr.
Branch, Erica. Whitlee's Magical Adventure. Watson, Corinda. 2019. (ENG.). 36p. (J). (gr. k-6). pap. 9.99 ***(978-1-7336121-1-1(4))*** Watson, Corinda.
Branch Jr., Robert F. Loving Danger. Williams, Eula. 2012. 20p. pap. 24.95 *(978-1-4626-6954-7(9))* America Star Bks.
Brand, Anton. Gamenite Episode #03: A Litfps Battle Royale Gaming Adventure. Cassyjosh & Smith, Bec J. 2018. (Gamenite Ser.: Vol. 3). (ENG.). 92p. (J). pap. 7.99 *(978-1-7915-7286-0(3))* Independently Published.
Brandao, Lucia. From Another World, 1 vol. MacHado, Ana Maria & Machado, Ana Maria. Baeta, Luisa, tr. 2005. (ENG.). 136p. (J). (gr. 3-7). pap. 9.95 *(978-0-88899-641-1(1))* Groundwood Bks. CAN. Dist: Publishers Group West (PGW).
Brandenburg, Claire. The Saint & His Bees. Jackson, Dessi. 2013. (ENG.). 28p. (J). (gr. -1-3). pap. 9.99 *(978-1-62395-487-1(8))* Xist Publishing.
Brandenburg, Claire. The Cow Jumped over the Moon. Brandenburg, Claire. 2017. (ENG.). 28p. (J). (gr. -1-k). pap. 9.99 *(978-1-5324-0172-5(8))* Xist Publishing.
—The Monk Who Grew Prayer. Brandenburg, Claire. 2003. (ENG.). 32p. (J). pap. 11.95 *(978-1-888212-66-2(7))* Ancient Faith Publishing.
Brandenburg, Lisa. Maybe Dying Is Like Becoming a Butterfly. van Hest, Pimm. 2019. 32p. (J). (ENG.). 9.95 *(978-1-60537-505-2(5))*; 17.95 *(978-1-60537-494-9(6))* Clavis Publishing.
—That's for Babies. Kramer, Jackie Az-a. 2019. (ENG.). 32p. (J). 17.95 *(978-1-60537-455-0(5))*; 9.95 *(978-1-60537-456-7(3))* Clavis Publishing.
Brandi, Lillian & Shortall, Leonard. Encyclopedia Brown & the Case of the Midnight Visitor, 1 vol. Sobol, Donald J. 2015. (Encyclopedia Brown Ser.). (ENG.). 96p. (J). (gr. 2-6). 27.07 *(978-1-61479-309-0(3)*, 16935, Chapter Bks.) Spotlight.
Brandon, Dan & Weaver, Brandon. Before You Meet Prince Charming: A Guide to Radiant Purity. Mally, Sarah. 2006. (ENG.). 272p. (YA). pap. 14.00 *(978-0-9719405-4-3(1))* Tomorrow's Forefathers, Inc.
Brandon, Theresa. Year of the Dragon: The Complete Story Experience Edition. Anna, Jennifer. 2nd exp. ed. 2005. (Turtle's Back Bks.). 100p. (J). (gr. -1-6). pap. 14.99 *(978-1-883573-18-8(1))* Blue Forge Pr.
Brandon, Vicky. The Wren & the Groundhog. Mcwherter, Barbara. 2011. 40p. pap. 24.95 *(978-1-4560-5512-7(7))* America Star Bks.
Brandt, Kim Wilson. Trust Your Instincts: The Bully. McCook-Blackburn, Brenda & Blackburn, Natalie. 2019. (ENG.). 28p. (J). pap. 11.95 ***(978-1-9772-0554-4(2))*** Outskirts Pr., Inc.
Brandt, Linda M. Henry's Life As a Tulip Bulb: Developing an Attitude of Gratitude (Book 1) Brandt, Linda M. 2013. 24p. pap. 15.95 *(978-1-61314-084-0(3))* Innovo Publishing, LLC.
Brandt, Michael. The Bunny, the Bear, the Bug & the Bee. Brandt-Taylor, Diane. 2005. (J). cd-rom 9.88 *(978-0-9773236-0-9(9))* TaySysCo Publishing.
Brandt, Susan. What Am I? A Hawai'i Animal Guessing Game. Harrington, Daniel. 2006. (J). *(978-1-56647-813-7(8))* Mutual Publishing LLC.
Branman, Liz. Twins. Friday, Anita. 2013. 34p. pap. 11.99 *(978-0-9899544-0-2(4))* Two Chicks.

B

Brannen, Sarah. The Ugly Duckling. Namm, Diane. 2012. (Silver Penny Stories Ser.). 48p. (J). (gr. -1-1). 4.95 *(978-1-4027-8437-8(6))* Sterling Publishing Co., Inc.

Brannen, Sarah S. All Kinds of Families. Simon, Norma. 40th anniv. ed. 2016. (ENG.). 32p. (J). (gr. -1-3). 16.99 *(978-0-8075-0286-0(3)*, 807502863) Whitman, Albert & Co.

—At Home in Her Tomb: Lady Dai & the Ancient Chinese Treasures of Mawangdui. Liu-Perkins, Christine. 2014. 80p. (J). (gr. 4-7). lib. bdg. 19.95 *(978-1-58089-370-1(8))* Charlesbridge Publishing, Inc.

—Digging for Troy: From Homer to Hisarlik. Cline, Eric H. & Rubalcaba, Jill. 2011. 80p. (J). (gr. 4-7). 17.95 *(978-1-58089-326-8(0))* Charlesbridge Publishing, Inc.

—Feathers: Not Just for Flying. Stewart, Melissa. 2014. (ENG.). 32p. (J). (gr. 1-4). pap. 7.95 *(978-1-58089-431-9(3))* Charlesbridge Publishing, Inc.

—The Fox & the Grapes. Olmstead, Kathleen. 2014. (Silver Penny Stories Ser.). 48p. (J). (gr. -1-1). 4.95 *(978-1-4027-8345-6(0))* Sterling Publishing Co., Inc.

—Madame Martine. 2015. 32p. (J). *(978-1-4896-3864-9(4))* Weigl Pubs., Inc.

—The Pied Piper of Hamelin. Olmstead, Kathleen. 2014. (Silver Penny Stories Ser.). 48p. (J). (gr. -1-1). 4.95 *(978-1-4027-8349-4(3))* Sterling Publishing Co., Inc.

—The Pig Scramble, 1 vol. Kinney, Jessica. 2011. (ENG.). 36p. (J). 17.95 *(978-1-934031-61-2(5)*, 712b9809-b0b0-4e47-ac60-66ebbf11fc6e) Islandport Pr., Inc.

—Seashells: More Than a Home. Stewart, Melissa. 32p. (J). (gr. 1-4). 2020. pap. 7.99 *(978-1-62354-173-6(5))*; 2019. lib. bdg. 16.99 *(978-1-58089-810-2(6))* Charlesbridge Publishing, Inc.

—The Very Beary Tooth Fairy. Levine, Arthur A. 2013. (J). *(978-0-439-47404-7(3)*, Scholastic Pr.) Scholastic, Inc.

Brannen, Sarah S. Bear Needs Help. Brannen, Sarah S. 2019. (ENG.). 32p. (J). (gr. -1-2). 16.99 *(978-0-525-51650-7(6)*, Philomel Bks.) Penguin Young Readers Group.

—Madame Martine. Brannen, Sarah S. 2014. (ENG.). 32p. (J). (gr. -1-3). 16.99 *(978-0-8075-4905-6(3)*, 807549053) Whitman, Albert & Co.

Brannen, Sarah S. A Perfect Day. Brannen, Sarah S. 2020. (ENG.). 32p. (J). (gr. -1-2). 17.99 ***(978-1-9848-1284-1(X)***, Philomel Bks.) Penguin Young Readers Group.

Brannon, Tom. Abby's Pink Party (Sesame Street) Kleinberg, Naomi. 2011. (ENG.). 12p. (J). (gr. k — 1). bds. 5.99 *(978-0-307-92956-3(6)*, Random Hse. Bks. for Young Readers) Random Hse. Children's Bks.

—B Is for Bedtime! (Sesame Street) Kleinberg, Naomi. 2017. (ENG.). 12p. (J). (— 1). bds. 6.99 *(978-0-399-55812-2(8)*, Random Hse. Bks. for Young Readers) Random Hse. Children's Bks.

—Circle of Friends (Sesame Street) Kleinberg, Naomi. 2012. (ENG.). 12p. (J). (gr. k-k). bds. 5.99 *(978-0-307-93185-6(4)*, Random Hse. Bks. for Young Readers) Random Hse. Children's Bks.

—Cooking with Sam-I-Am. Carbone, Courtney. 2018. (Step into Reading Ser.). (ENG.). 32p. (J). (gr. -1-1). pap. 4.99 *(978-1-5247-7088-4(4)*, Random Hse. Bks. for Young Readers) Random Hse. Children's Bks.

—Cooking with the Grinch (Dr. Seuss) Rabe, Tish. 2017. (Step into Reading Ser.). (ENG.). 32p. (J). (gr. -1-1). pap. 4.99 *(978-1-5247-1462-8(3))*; lib. bdg. 12.99 *(978-1-5247-1463-5(1))* Random Hse. Children's Bks. (Random Hse. Bks. for Young Readers).

—Dr. Seuss's Lovey Things. Seuss. 2019. (Dr. Seuss's Things Board Bks.). (ENG.). 26p. (J). (— 1). bds. 8.99 *(978-1-9848-5188-8(8)*, Random Hse. Bks. for Young Readers) Random Hse. Children's Bks.

Brannon, Tom. Dr. Seuss's School Things. Seuss. 2020. (Dr. Seuss's Things Board Bks.). (ENG.). 26p. (J). (— 1). bds. 8.99 ***(978-0-593-17396-1(1)***, Random Hse. Bks. for Young Readers) Random Hse. Children's Bks.

Brannon, Tom. Dr. Seuss's Spooky Things. Seuss. 2019. (Dr. Seuss's Things Board Bks.). (ENG.). 26p. (J). (— 1). bds. 8.99 *(978-1-9848-5097-3(0)*, Random Hse. Bks. for Young Readers) Random Hse. Children's Bks.

—Dr. Seuss's Spring Things. Seuss. 2020. (Dr. Seuss's Things Board Bks.). (ENG.). 26p. (J). (— 1). bds. 8.99 *(978-1-9848-9509-7(5)*, Random Hse. Bks. for Young Readers) Random Hse. Children's Bks.

—Elmo's Christmas Snowman (Sesame Street) Kleinberg, Naomi. 2013. (ENG.). 12p. (J). (— 1). bds. 6.99 *(978-0-449-81257-0(X)*, Random Hse. Bks. for Young Readers) Random Hse. Children's Bks.

—Elmo's Countdown to Christmas (Sesame Street) Kleinberg, Naomi. 2016. (Lift-The-Flap Ser.). (ENG.). 12p. (J). (-k). bds. 6.99 *(978-0-399-55213-7(8)*, Random Hse. Bks. for Young Readers) Random Hse. Children's Bks.

—Elmo's Easter Egg Surprises (Sesame Street) Webster, Christy. 2020. (Little Golden Book Ser.). (ENG.). 24p. (J). (-k). 4.99 *(978-0-593-12251-8(8)*, Golden Bks.) Random Hse. Children's Bks.

—Halloween Fun for Everyone! (Dr. Seuss/Cat in the Hat) Rabe, Tish. 2016. (ENG.). 12p. (J). (— 1). bds. 9.99 *(978-1-101-93495-1(6)*, Random Hse. Bks. for Young Readers) Random Hse. Children's Bks.

—Happy & Sad, Grouchy & Glad (Sesame Street) Allen, Constance. 2017. (Little Golden Book Ser.). 24p. (J). (-k). 4.99 *(978-1-5247-1576-2(X)*, Golden Bks.) Random Hse. Children's Bks.

—Have No Fear! Halloween Is Here! (Dr. Seuss/the Cat in the Hat Knows a Lot About. Rabe, Tish. 2016. (Step into Reading Ser.). (ENG.). 24p. (J). (gr. -1-1). 4.99 *(978-1-101-93492-0(1)*, Random Hse. Bks. for Young Readers) Random Hse. Children's Bks.

—Hic! Albee, Sarah. 2006. (Step-By-Step Readers Ser.). (J). pap. *(978-1-59939-061-1(2)*, Reader's Digest Young Families, Inc.) Studio Fun International.

—Hokey Pokey Elmo (Sesame Street) Tabby, Abigail. 2016. (Little Golden Book Ser.). 24p. (J). (-k). 4.99 *(978-1-101-93725-9(4)*, Golden Bks.) Random Hse. Children's Bks.

—Hooray for Hair! (Dr. Seuss/Cat in the Hat) Rabe, Tish. 2013. (Step into Reading Ser.). (ENG.). 48p. (J). (gr. k-3). pap. 4.99 *(978-0-375-87048-4(2)*, Random Hse. Bks. for Young Readers) Random Hse. Children's Bks.

Brannon, Tom. Hooray for Our Heroes! (Sesame Street) Albee, Sarah. 2020. (ENG.). 32p. (J). (gr. -1-1). 10.99 ***(978-0-593-37319-4(7)***, Random Hse. Bks. for Young Readers) Random Hse. Children's Bks.

Brannon, Tom. I Am Sam-I-Am. Rabe, Tish. 2019. (Dr. Seuss's I Am Board Bks.). (ENG.). 26p. (J). (— 1). bds. 7.99 *(978-0-525-57958-8(3)*, Random Hse. Bks. for Young Readers) Random Hse. Children's Bks.

—I Am the Lorax. Carbone, Courtney. 2020. (Dr. Seuss's I Am Board Bks.). (ENG.). 26p. (J). (— 1). bds. 7.99 *(978-0-593-11914-3(2)*, Random Hse. Bks. for Young Readers) Random Hse. Children's Bks.

—I Love You Valentine Songs. 2012. (J). *(978-1-4508-3303-5(9))* Phoenix International Publications, Inc.

Brannon, Tom. If I Had Your Vote — By the Cat in the Hat. Random House. 2020. (Beginner Books(R) Ser.). (ENG.). 48p. (J). (gr. -1-2). 9.99 ***(978-0-593-12797-1(8))***; lib. bdg. 12.99 ***(978-0-593-12798-8(6))*** Random Hse. Children's Bks. (Random Hse. Bks. for Young Readers).

Brannon, Tom. K Is for Kindness (Sesame Street) Shepherd, Jodie. 2018. (Big Golden Book Ser.). (ENG.). 32p. (J). (-k). 10.99 *(978-1-5247-6415-9(9)*, Golden Bks.) Random Hse. Children's Bks.

—Let's Help the Earth. Reader's Digest Staff. 2008. (Sesame Street Ser.). (ENG.). 12p. (J). (gr. -1-k). bds. 12.99 *(978-0-7944-1696-6(9))* Reader's Digest Assn., Inc., The.

—My First Songs (Sesame Street) Random House. 2017. (ENG.). 26p. (J). (-k). bds. 8.99 *(978-1-5247-1770-4(3)*, Random Hse. Bks. for Young Readers) Random Hse. Children's Bks.

—Once upon a Sesame Street Christmas. Cole, Geri. 2017. (ENG.). 48p. (J). (gr. -1-3). 14.99 *(978-0-7624-6162-2(4)*, Running Pr. Kids) Running Pr.

—Peanuts: Snoopy Goes to Space. Broderick, Kathy. 2020. (Play-A-Sound Ser.). (ENG.). 10p. (J). *(978-1-5037-5256-6(9)*, 3e026f8c-6d8b-4d87-836c-68b7e20a2eee, p i kids) Phoenix International Publications, Inc.

—Phonics Fun! (Sesame Street) Kimmelman, Leslie & Shepherd, Jodie. 2017. (ENG.). 144p. (J). (gr. -1-2). pap. 12.99 *(978-1-101-93755-6(6)*, Random Hse. Bks. for Young Readers) Random Hse. Children's Bks.

Brannon, Tom. S Is for School! (Sesame Street) A Lift-The-Flap Board Book. Posner-Sanchez, Andrea. 2020. (ENG.). 12p. (J). (— 1). bds. 7.99 ***(978-0-593-17376-3(7)***, Random Hse. Bks. for Young Readers) Random Hse. Children's Bks.

Brannon, Tom. Sesame: Elmo's Noisy Farm. Brooke, Susan Rich. 2019. (Look & Find Ser.). (ENG.). 16p. (J). bds. *(978-1-5037-4655-8(0)*, 4463d15b-b563-4579-a91a-e3e73331cf36, p i kids) Phoenix International Publications, Inc.

—Sesame: Elmo's Potty Book. 2019. (Look & Find Ser.). (ENG.). 16p. (J). bds. *(978-1-5037-4656-5(9)*, b434cb2d-778f-44f6-8cba-0ff222d5db41, p i kids) Phoenix International Publications, Inc.

—Sesame: Sing & Play!: Cookie Monster & You. Beck, Riley. 2019. (Play-A-Song Ser.). (ENG.). 8p. (J). bds. *(978-1-5037-4653-4(4)*, 5a243908-5620-4374-ab66-24d93e0e1ee5, p i kids) Phoenix International Publications, Inc.

—Sesame: Sing & Play!: Elmo Is My Friend! Wage, Erin Rose. 2019. (Play-A-Song Ser.). (ENG.). 8p. (J). bds. *(978-1-5037-4654-1(2)*, 3d10b559-14e1-4552-8b74-af2539d9ad16, p i kids) Phoenix International Publications, Inc.

Brannon, Tom, et al. Sesame Street. 2016. (Me Reader Ser.). (ENG.). 192p. (J). *(978-1-5037-0702-3(4)*, f40622c4-fabe-4baa-aac4-aaf17eca632f, p i kids) Phoenix International Publications, Inc.

Brannon, Tom. Sesame Street: ABCs with Elmo! Winslow, Claire. 2019. (Play-A-Sound Ser.). (ENG.). 24p. (J). *(978-1-5037-4568-1(6)*, a8d035ba-4ef6-470e-b421-61f812d2b18a, p i kids) Phoenix International Publications, Inc.

—Sesame Street: Elmo's Potty Book. Kids, Pi. 2019. (Look & Find Ser.). (ENG.). 18p. (J). *(978-1-5037-4627-5(5)*, 736f8c70-f54c-4798-9cac-542a9a802387, p i kids) Phoenix International Publications, Inc.

—Sesame Street: It's Cool to Be Kind. Wage, Erin Rose. 2019. (Play-A-Sound Ser.). (ENG.). 12p. (J). bds. *(978-1-5037-4912-2(6)*, 07783d68-82d9-428d-bd67-6a75ef9df5a9, p i kids) Phoenix International Publications, Inc.

—Sesame Street: Moo! Moo! Cock-A-Doodle-Doo!... & Elmo Too! Brooke, Susan Rich. 2016. (Look & Find Ser.). (ENG.). 24p. (J). *(978-1-5037-1381-9(4)*, 98a0b660-9d5c-40aa-800a-1a450ef8b09c, p i kids) Phoenix International Publications, Inc.

Brannon, Tom, et al. Sesame Street: My First Manners. Albee, Sarah et al. 2018. (ENG.). 96p. (J). pap., pap. *(978-1-5037-4029-7(3)*, df033525-f8cd-4aae-bee6-96a8a136582b, p i kids) Phoenix International Publications, Inc.

Brannon, Tom. Sesame Street: 5 Little Rubber Duckies. Mitter, Matt. 2018. (ENG.). 12p. (J). (gr. -1-k). bds. 11.99 *(978-0-7944-4119-7(X)*, Reader's Digest Children's Bks.) Studio Fun International.

—Sesame Street: 5 Patitos de Hule. Mitter, Matt. 2018. (SPA.). 12p. (J). (gr. -1-k). bds. 11.99 *(978-0-7944-4178-4(5)*, Reader's Digest Children's Bks.) Studio Fun International.

Brannon, Tom. Sesame Street: Elmo's Lift & Slide ABC. Heath, Autumn B. 2nd ed. 2020. (Lift & Slide Ser.). (ENG.). 10p. (J). (— 1). bds. 11.99 ***(978-0-7944-4694-9(9)***, Studio Fun International) Printers Row Publishing Group.

Brannon, Tom. A Sweet Christmas on Sesame Street (Sesame Street) A Scratch & Sniff Story. Shepherd, Jodie. 2018. (ENG.). 24p. (J). (gr. -1-2). 9.99 *(978-0-525-58133-8(2)*, Random Hse. Bks. for Young Readers) Random Hse. Children's Bks.

—Take Us Out to the Ball Game (Sesame Street) Allen, Constance. 2017. (Pictureback(R) Ser.). (ENG.). 24p. (J). (gr. -1-2). pap. 6.99 *(978-1-5247-6824-9(3)*, Random Hse. Bks. for Young Readers) Random Hse. Children's Bks.

—A Tale about Tails (Dr. Seuss/the Cat in the Hat Knows a Lot about That!) Rabe, Tish. 2014. (Step into Reading Ser.). (ENG.). 48p. (J). (gr. k-3). 4.99 *(978-0-385-37117-9(9)*, Random Hse. Bks. for Young Readers) Random Hse. Children's Bks.

Brannon, Tom & Berry, Bob. Sesame: On the Farm. Wage, Erin Rose. 2017. (ENG.). 120p. (J). *(978-1-5037-1687-2(2)*, 668a012f-93a4-44d9-a02e-d994b4fc0afc, p i kids) Phoenix International Publications, Inc.

—Sesame Street: Explore & Play with Sesame Friends. Brooke, Susan Rich. 2018. (Look & Find Ser.). (ENG.). 18p. (J). *(978-1-5037-2165-4(5)*, ea0f43c3-3c09-45fa-83c2-8bf2142c11ae, p i kids) Phoenix International Publications, Inc.

Brannon, Tom & Sesame Workshop. Sesame Street: Sound Storybook Treasury. Brooke, Susan Rich. 2019. (Play-A-Sound Ser.). (ENG.). 36p. (J). bds. *(978-1-5037-5308-2(5)*, 9f9e0942-06cb-4689-9e08-6cf247cb2324, p i kids) Phoenix International Publications, Inc.

Brannon, Tom, jt. illus. see Cooke, Tom.

Bransom, Paul. The Wind in the Willows. Grahame, Kenneth. 2013. 176p. pap. 35.00 *(978-1-927558-25-6(5))* Birch Tree Publishing.

Bransom, Paul & Gleeson, J. M. Just So Stories. Kipling, Rudyard. 2016. 256p. (J). (gr. 1-1). 16.99 *(978-1-944686-44-4(4)*, Racehorse Publishing) Skyhorse Publishing Co., Inc.

Bransom, Paul, jt. illus. see Gleeson, J. M.

Brant, Shelley. God Made You. Froeb, Lori C. 2019. (ENG.). 6p. (J). (— 1). 12.99 *(978-0-7944-4214-9(5)*, Studio Fun International) Printers Row Publishing Group.

Brantley-Newton, Vanessa. Class Act #2. Starling Lyons, Kelly. 2017. (Jada Jones Ser.: 2). 96p. (J). (gr. 1-3). (ENG.). 6.99 *(978-0-451-53427-9(1))*; lib. bdg. 15.99 *(978-0-451-53428-6(X))* Penguin Young Readers Group. (Penguin Workshop).

—Drum City. Guidone, Thea. 2015. (ENG.). 32p. (J). (gr. -1-2). 7.99 *(978-0-553-52350-8(3)*, Dragonfly Bks.) Random Hse. Children's Bks.

Brantley-Newton, Vanessa. Early Sunday Morning. Millner, Denene. 2020. (ENG.). 40p. (J). (gr. -1-3). 17.99 ***(978-1-5344-7653-0(9))*** Simon & Schuster, Inc.

Brantley-Newton, Vanessa. Every Little Thing: Based on the Song 'Three Little Birds' by Bob Marley (Music Books for Children, African American Baby Books, Bob Marley Books for Kids) Marley, Cedella & Marley, Bob. 2012. (ENG.). 32p. (J). (gr. -1-1). 16.99 *(978-1-4521-0697-7(5))* Chronicle Bks. LLC.

—Every Little Thing: Based on the Song 'Three Little Birds' by Bob Marley (Preschool Music Books, Children Song Books, Reggae for Kids) Marley, Cedella & Marley, Bob. 2015. (ENG.). 24p. (J). (gr. -1-k). bds. 7.99 *(978-1-4521-4290-6(4))* Chronicle Bks. LLC.

—Go, Jade, Go! Dungy, Tony & Dungy, Lauren. 2013. (Tony & Lauren Dungy Ready-To-Reads Ser.). (ENG.). 32p. (J). (gr. k-2). pap. 3.99 *(978-1-4424-5466-8(0)*, Simon Spotlight) Simon Spotlight.

Brantley Newton, Vanessa. Go, Jade, Go! Dungy, Tony & Dungy, Lauren. 2013. (Tony & Lauren Dungy Ready-To-Reads Ser.). (ENG.). 32p. (J). (gr. k-2). 16.99 *(978-1-4424-5467-5(9)*, Simon Spotlight) Simon Spotlight.

Brantley-Newton, Vanessa. Hannah Sparkles: a Friend Through Rain or Shine. Mellom, Robin. 2017. (ENG.). 32p. (J). (gr. -1-3). 17.99 *(978-0-06-232233-3(8))* HarperCollins Pubs.

—Hannah Sparkles: Hooray for the First Day of School! Mellom, Robin. 2019. (ENG.). 32p. (J). (gr. -1-3). 17.99 *(978-0-06-232234-0(6))* HarperCollins Pubs.

—Here Comes the Parade! Dungy, Tony & Dungy, Lauren. 2014. (Tony & Lauren Dungy Ready-To-Reads Ser.). (ENG.). 32p. (J). (gr. k-2). pap. 4.99 *(978-1-4424-5469-9(5)*, Simon Spotlight) Simon Spotlight.

Brantley Newton, Vanessa. Hula-Hoopin' Queen. Godin, Thelma Lynne. 2014. (ENG.). 40p. (J). 18.95 *(978-1-60060-846-9(9))* Lee & Low Bks., Inc.

—I Can Do It! Holland, Trish. 2014. (Little Golden Book Ser.). 24p. (J). (-k). 4.99 *(978-0-449-81310-2(X)*, Golden Bks.) Random Hse. Children's Bks.

—Justin & the Bully. Dungy, Tony & Dungy, Lauren. 2012. (Tony & Lauren Dungy Ready-To-Reads Ser.). (ENG.). 32p. (J). (gr. k-2). pap. 4.99 *(978-1-4424-5718-8(X)*, Simon Spotlight) Simon Spotlight.

Brantley-Newton, Vanessa. The King of Kindergarten. Barnes, Derrick. 2019. (ENG.). 32p. (J). (-k). 17.99 *(978-1-5247-4074-0(8)*, Nancy Paulsen Books) Penguin Young Readers Group.

—Like Vanessa. Charles, Tami. 2018. 288p. (J). (gr. 5). 16.99 *(978-1-58089-777-8(0))* Charlesbridge Publishing, Inc.

—Magic Trash: A Story of Tyree Guyton & His Art. Shapiro, J. H. 2015. (ENG.). 32p. (J). (gr. k-3). pap. 7.95 *(978-1-58089-386-2(4))* Charlesbridge Publishing, Inc.

—Mama's Work Shoes. Levis, Caron. 2019. (ENG.). 40p. (J). (gr. -1-2). 16.99 *(978-1-4197-2554-8(8)*, Abrams Bks. for Young Readers) Abrams, Inc.

Brantley Newton, Vanessa. Mary Had a Little Glam. Sauer, Tammi. 2016. (Mary Had a Little Glam Ser.: 1). 32p. (J). (gr. -1-2). 16.95 *(978-1-4549-1393-1(2))* Sterling Publishing Co., Inc.

Brantley-Newton, Vanessa. Mary Had a Little Glam. Sauer, Tammi. 2018. (Mary Had a Little Glam Ser.: 1). 24p. (J). (— 1). bds. 8.95 *(978-1-4549-3285-7(6))* Sterling Publishing Co., Inc.

—The Missing Cupcake Mystery. Dungy, Tony & Dungy, Lauren. 2013. (Tony & Lauren Dungy Ready-To-Reads Ser.). (ENG.). 32p. (J). (gr. k-2). pap. 4.99 *(978-1-4424-5463-7(6)*, Simon Spotlight) Simon Spotlight.

Brantley Newton, Vanessa. The Missing Fox. Cox, Katherine. 2015. 32p. (J). *(978-1-4806-8800-1(2))* Scholastic, Inc.

—Mister & Lady Day: Billie Holiday & the Dog Who Loved Her. Novesky, Amy. (ENG.). 32p. (J). (gr. -1-3). 2017. 7.99 *(978-0-544-80905-5(X)*, 1641354, HMH Books For Young Readers); 2013. 16.99 *(978-0-15-205806-7(0)*, 1197445) Houghton Mifflin Harcourt Publishing Co.

Brantley-Newton, Vanessa. My Three Best Friends & Me, Zulay. Best, Cari. 2015. (ENG.). 40p. (J). (gr. -1-3). 18.99 *(978-0-374-38819-5(9)*, 900031513, Farrar, Straus & Giroux (BYR)) Farrar, Straus & Giroux.

Brantley Newton, Vanessa. A Night Out with Mama. Wallis, Quvenzhané. 2017. (ENG.). 40p. (J). (gr. -1-3). 17.99 *(978-1-4814-5880-1(9)*, Simon & Schuster Bks. For Young Readers) Simon & Schuster Bks. For Young Readers.

Brantley-Newton, Vanessa. One Love (Music Books for Children, African American Baby Books, Bob Marley Book for Kids) Marley, Cedella. 2014. (ENG.). 24p. (J). (gr. -1-k). bds. 7.99 *(978-1-4521-3855-8(9))* Chronicle Bks. LLC.

Brantley Newton, Vanessa. The Plans I Have for You Journal, 1 vol. Parker, Amy. 2015. (ENG.). 208p. (J). pap. 12.99 *(978-0-310-72523-7(2))* Zonderkidz.

Brantley-Newton, Vanessa. Rock Star #1. Lyons, Kelly Starling. 2017. (Jada Jones Ser.: 1). (ENG.). 96p. (J). (gr. 1-3). 6.99 *(978-0-448-48751-9(9))*; lib. bdg. 15.99 *(978-0-448-48752-6(7))* Penguin Young Readers Group. (Penguin Workshop).

—Ruby Goldberg's Bright Idea. Humphrey, Anna. 2013. (ENG.). 144p. (J). (gr. 3-7). 17.99 *(978-1-4424-8027-8(0)*, Simon & Schuster Bks. For Young Readers) Simon & Schuster Bks. For Young Readers.

Brantley Newton, Vanessa. Ruby's New Home. Dungy, Tony & Dungy, Lauren. 2011. (Ready-To-Read Level 2 Ser.). (ENG.). 32p. (J). (gr. k-2). lib. bdg. 17.44 *(978-1-4424-2948-2(8)*, Simon Spotlight) Simon & Schuster Children's Publishing.

Brantley-Newton, Vanessa. Ruby's New Home. Dungy, Tony & Dungy, Lauren. 2011. (Tony & Lauren Dungy Ready-To-Reads Ser.). (ENG.). 32p. (J). (gr. k-2). pap. 4.99 *(978-1-4169-9784-9(9)*, Simon Spotlight) Simon Spotlight.

Brantley Newton, Vanessa. Scholastic Reader Level 2: Katie Fry, Private Eye #1: the Lost Kitten. Cox, Katherine. 2015. (Scholastic Reader Level 2 Ser.). (ENG.). 32p. (J). (gr. 1-3). pap. 3.99 *(978-0-545-66672-5(4))* Scholastic, Inc.

Brantley-Newton, Vanessa. Sewing Stories: Harriet Powers' Journey from Slave to Artist. Herkert, Barbara. 2015. 40p. (J). (gr. -1-3). 17.99 *(978-0-385-75462-0(0)*, Knopf Bks. for Young Readers) Random Hse. Children's Bks.

Brantley Newton, Vanessa. A Team Stays Together! Dungy, Tony & Dungy, Lauren. 2011. (Tony & Lauren Dungy Ready-To-Reads Ser.). (ENG.). 32p. (J). (gr. k-2). pap. 4.99 *(978-1-4424-3539-1(9)*, Simon Spotlight) Simon Spotlight.

Brantley-Newton, Vanessa. We Shall Overcome: The Story of a Song. Levy, Debbie. 2013. 32p. (J). (gr. -1-3). 17.99 *(978-1-4231-1954-8(1))* Hyperion Bks. for Children.

—The Youngest Marcher: The Story of Audrey Faye Hendricks, a Young Civil Rights Activist. Levinson, Cynthia. 2017. (ENG.). 40p. (J). (gr. k-5). 17.99 *(978-1-4814-0070-1(3))* Simon & Schuster, Inc.

Brantley-Newton, Vanessa, jt. illus. see Myers, Nneka.

Brantley Newton, Vanessa, jt. illus. see Newton, Vanessa.

Branton, Molly. The Enchanted Lizard: La Lagartijita Mágica. Carter, Aubrey Smith. Nelson, Esther Whitt, ed. 2006. (ENG & SPA.). 96p. (J). 18.95 *(978-1-893271-38-8(2)*, Maverick Bks.) Trinity Univ. Pr.

Brantz, Loryn. Kindergarten Sight Word Reader. Rebboah, Julie A. 2008. (ENG.). 156p. (J). pap. 19.99 *(978-0-9817826-0-7(4))* Lightning Bug Learning Pr.

—Not Just a Dot. 2014. 32p. (J). (-k). 16.95 *(978-1-62914-622-5(6)*, Sky Pony Pr.) Skyhorse Publishing Co., Inc.

—Reproducible Kindergarten Sight Word Reader. Rebboah, Julie A. 2008. (ENG.). 156p. (J). ring bd. 39.99 *(978-0-9817826-3-8(9))* Lightning Bug Learning Pr.

Brantz, Loryn. Feminist Baby. Brantz, Loryn. 2017. (Feminist Baby Ser.). 22p. (J). (gr. -1 — 1). bds. 12.99 ***(978-1-4847-7858-6(8))*** Little, Brown Bks. for Young Readers.

—Feminist Baby Finds Her Voice! Brantz, Loryn. 2018. (Feminist Baby Ser.). 22p. (J). (gr. -1 — 1). bds. 9.99 ***(978-1-368-02279-8(0))*** Little, Brown Bks. for Young Readers.

—Feminist Baby! He's a Feminist Too! Brantz, Loryn. 2019. (Feminist Baby Ser.). 22p. (J). (gr. -1 — 1). 9.99 ***(978-1-368-02299-6(5))*** Little, Brown Bks. for Young Readers.

Brascaglia, Vincent. Pelé: The King of Soccer. Simon, Eddy. 2017. (ENG.). 144p. (J). 19.99 *(978-1-62672-979-7(4)*, 9781626729797); pap. 15.99 *(978-1-62672-755-7(4)*, 900172778) Roaring Brook Pr. (First Second Bks.).

Brasil, Bruna Assis. No! I Won't Go to School, 1 vol. Núñez, Alonso. Morrison, Dave, tr. from SPA. 2018. (ENG.). 32p. (J). (gr. -1-1). 16.95 *(978-0-88448-646-6(X)*, 884646) Tilbury Hse. Pubs.

Braslavskii, Felix. Prilaskaite L'va: Amerikanskiye i Angliiskiye Stikhi Dlya Detei. Kovner, Vladimir, tr. from ENG. 2010. (RUS.). 110p. (J). pap. *(978-1-934881-43-9(0)*, M-Graphics) M-Graphics Publishing.

Brassard, France. Curtain Up! A Book for Young Performers. McLean, Dirk. 2010. (ENG.). 40p. (J). (gr. 1-4). 17.95 *(978-0-88776-899-6(7)*, Tundra Bks.) Tundra Bks. CAN. Dist: Penguin Random Hse. LLC.

—Lily & the Mixed-Up Letters. Hodge, Deborah. 2007. 32p. (J). (gr. 1-4). 18.95 *(978-0-88776-757-9(5)*, Tundra Bks.) Tundra Bks. CAN. Dist: Penguin Random Hse. LLC.

Brassard, Joyce. Meet Self-Control. Brassard, Len. 2019. (Black Belt Character Development Ser.: Vol. 5). (ENG.). 26p. (J). pap. 9.99 *(978-1-7943-0320-1(0))* Independently Published.

Brassel, Sondra. The Friendship Puzzle: Helping Kids Learn about Accepting & Including Kids with Autism. Coe, Julie L. 2009. 24p. (J). (gr. k-2). 14.95 *(978-0-9789182-4-8(X))* Larstan Publishing, Inc.

Brassey, Richard. George & the Dragon & Other Saintly Stories. 2003. (ENG.). 40p. *(978-1-84255-019-9(5),* Orion Children's Bks.) Hachette Children's Group.

—Ghosts, Rogues & Highwaymen: 20 Stories from British History. McCaughrean, Geraldine. 2003. (ENG.). 128p. (J). pap. 9.99 *(978-1-85881-894-8(X),* Orion) Orion Publishing Group, Ltd. GBR. Dist: Trafalgar Square Publishing.

—Rebels & Royals: 20 Stories from British History. McCaughrean, Geraldine. 2003. (Britannia Ser.). (ENG.). 128p. (J). pap. 9.99 *(978-1-85881-852-8(4),* Orion) Orion Publishing Group, Ltd. GBR. Dist: Trafalgar Square Publishing.

Bratton, Ashley A., jt. illus. see Bratton, Deboral B.

Bratton, Ashley D., jt. illus. see Bratton, Deboral B.

Bratton, Deboral B. & Bigly, Ashley D. Record-a-Sport Golf Organizer. Bratton, Deboral B. & Bigly, Ashley D. Bigly, Ashley D., ed. 2003. (gr. 1-18). 18.95 *(978-1-931746-00-7(1))* Sport Your Stuff Corp.

Bratton, Deboral B. & Bratton, Ashley A. Record-a-Sport Football Sport Organizer. Bratton, Deboral B. & Bratton, Ashley A. Bratton, Ashley A., ed. 2003. (gr. 1-18). 18.95 *(978-1-931746-05-2(2))* Sport Your Stuff Corp.

Bratton, Deboral B. & Bratton, Ashley D. Record-a-Sport Baseball & Softball Organizer. Bratton, Deboral B. & Bratton, Ashley D. Bratton, Deboral B. & Bratton, Ashley D., eds. 2003. (gr. 1-18). 18.95 *(978-1-931746-03-8(6))* Sport Your Stuff Corp.

—Record-a-Sport Basketball Sport Organizer. Bratton, Deboral B. & Bratton, Ashley D. 2003. (gr. 1-18). 18.95 *(978-1-931746-02-1(8))* Sport Your Stuff Corp.

—Record-a-Sport Soccer Sport Organizer. Bratton, Deboral B. & Bratton, Ashley D. 2003. (gr. 1-18). 18.95 *(978-1-931746-04-5(4))* Sport Your Stuff Corp.

—Record-a-Sport Tennis Organizer. Bratton, Deboral B. & Bratton, Ashley D. 2003. (gr. 1-18). 18.95 *(978-1-931746-06-9(0))* Sport Your Stuff Corp.

Bratun, Katy. All Aboard Noah's Ark! Josephs, Mary. 2007. (Chunky Book(R) Ser.). 22p. (J). (— 1). bds. 3.99 *(978-0-679-86054-9(1),* Golden Inspirational) Random Hse. Children's Bks.

Bratun, Katy, et al. Alphabet of Insects. Schwaeber, Barbie Heit. 2007. (ENG.). 40p. (J). (gr. -1-3). 15.95 *(978-1-59249-725-6(X))* Soundprints.

Bratun, Katy. Josh's Halloween Pumpkin, 1 vol. Lay, Kathryn. 2008. (ENG.). 32p. (J). (gr. k-3). 16.99 *(978-1-58980-595-8(X),* Pelican Publishing) Arcadia Publishing.

—Just Mommy & Me. Morrow, Tara Jaye. 2004. 32p. (J). 13.89 *(978-0-06-000725-6(7))* HarperCollins Pubs.

—Katie Caught a Cold. Cowan, Charlotte. 2007. (ENG.). 32p. (J). (gr. 3-7). 17.95 *(978-0-9753516-3-5(X))* Hippocratic Pr., The.

—Sadie's Sore Throat. Cowan, Charlotte. 2007. (Dr. Hippo Ser.). (ENG.). 32p. (J). (gr. 3-7). 17.95 *(978-0-9753516-4-2(8))* Hippocratic Pr., The.

Bratun, Katy. Gingerbread Mouse. Bratun, Katy. 32p. (J). (gr. -1-2). 2003. lib. bdg. 13.89 *(978-0-06-009081-4(2));* Vol. 2007. (ENG.). per. 7.99 *(978-0-06-009082-1(0))* HarperCollins Pubs.

Brauckman-Towns, Krista. Buffalo Prairie. Lee, Evelyn. (Amazing Animal Adventures Ser.). (ENG.). 32p. (J). (gr. -1-2). 19.95 *(978-1-59249-435-4(8),* BC7110) Soundprints.

Brauckmann-Towns, Krista. Bluestem Horizon: A Story of a Tallgrass Prairie. Lee, Evelyn. 2005. (Soundprints' Wild Habitats Ser.). (ENG.). 32p. (J). (gr. 1-4). 8.95 *(978-1-59249-098-1(0))* Soundprints.

—Buffalo Prairie. Lee, Evelyn. 2005. (Amazing Animal Adventures Ser.). (ENG.). 36p. (J). (gr. -1-2). 2.95 *(978-1-59249-434-7(X),* S7160); 15.95 *(978-1-59249-432-3(3),* B7110); pap. 6.95 *(978-1-59249-433-0(1),* S7110) Soundprints.

Braught, Mark. Cosmo's Moon. Scillian, Devin. 2003. (ENG.). 40p. (J). (gr. 1-4). 15.95 *(978-1-58536-123-6(2),* 201986) Sleeping Bear Pr.

—Ellen Craft's Escape from Slavery. Moore, Cathy. 2010. (History Speaks: Picture Books Plus Reader's Theater Ser.). (ENG.). 48p. (gr. 2-4). pap. 9.95 *(978-0-7613-6672-0(5));* lib. bdg. 27.93 *(978-0-7613-5875-6(7),* Millbrook Pr.) Lerner Publishing Group.

—J Is for Jump Shot: A Basketball Alphabet. Ulmer, Michael. 2005. (Sports Alphabet Ser.). (ENG.). 40p. (J). (gr. -1-5). 16.95 *(978-1-58536-229-5(8))* Sleeping Bear Pr.

—J Is for Jump Shot: A Basketball Alphabet. Ulmer, Michael. 2015. (Av2 Fiction Readalong 2016 Ser.). (ENG.). (J). (gr. 1-4). lib. bdg. 34.28 *(978-1-4896-3753-6(2),* AV2 by Weigl) Weigl Pubs., Inc.

—J Is for Jump Shot: A Basketball Alphabet. Ulmer, Mike. rev. ed. 2006. (Sports Ser.). (ENG.). 40p. (J). (gr. k-5). pap. 7.95 *(978-1-58536-338-4(3))* Sleeping Bear Pr.

—A Peck of Peaches: A Georgia Number Book. Crane, Carol. rev. ed. 2007. (State Counting Ser.). (ENG.). 40p. (J). (gr. 1-3). 17.95 *(978-1-58536-177-9(1))* Sleeping Bear Pr.

—T Is for Touchdown: A Football Alphabet. Herzog, Brad. 2006. (Sports Alphabet Ser.). (ENG.). 40p. (J). (gr. 1-4). pap. 7.95 *(978-1-58536-337-7(5),* 202300) Sleeping Bear Pr.

—T Is for Touchdown: A Football Alphabet. Herzog, Brad. 2015. (Av2 Fiction Readalong 2016 Ser.). (ENG.). (J). (gr. 1-4). lib. bdg. 34.28 *(978-1-4896-3765-9(6),* AV2 by Weigl) Weigl Pubs., Inc.

Braught, Mark, jt. illus. see Stacy, Alan.

Brault, Christopher. Raceboy & Super Qwok Adventures. Winkel, Andrew. 2012. (ENG.). 356p. (J). pap. 16.00 *(978-0-9837905-1-8(5))* Hierophantasm.

Braun, Chris. Galactic Treasure Hunt: Lost City of Atlantis. Childress, Jamie. 2015. (ENG.). 100p. (J). pap. 4.99 *(978-1-931882-62-0(2))* Adventures Unlimited Pr.

—Galactic Treasure Hunt #4: Lost in Time. Childress, Jamie. 2008. (Galactic Treasure Hunt Ser.). (ENG.). 176p. (J). pap. 5.99 *(978-1-931882-89-7(4))* Adventures Unlimited Pr.

—Galactic Treasure Hunt 5: Lost Fortress of Light. Childress, Jamie. 2010. (Galactic Treasure Hunt Ser.). (ENG.). 230p. (J). pap. 6.99 *(978-1-935487-06-7(X))* Adventures Unlimited Pr.

—Lost City of the Moon. Childress, Jamie. 2005. (ENG.). 115p. (J). (gr. -1-7). per. 4.99 *(978-1-931882-45-3(2))* Adventures Unlimited Pr.

—Lost Universe. Childress, Jamie. 2007. (ENG.). 162p. (J). (gr. 4-7). per. 4.99 *(978-1-931882-74-3(6))* Adventures Unlimited Pr.

Braun, Chuck. How & Why Folktales: From Around the World. Egelberg, Arlene & Clark, Raymond C. 2004. 106p. (gr. 6-12). pap., stu. ed. 15.00 *(978-0-86647-180-0(4))* Pro Lingua Assocs., Inc.

Braun, Dieter. Wild Animals of the South. Calleja, Jen, tr. 2017. 152p. (J). (gr. 2-3). 35.00 *(978-1-909263-97-0(4))* Flying Eye Bks. GBR. Dist: Penguin Random Hse. LLC.

Braun, Eric. Taking Care of Your Centaur. 2020. 24p. (J). lib. bdg. *(978-1-68072-909-2(8))* Black Rabbit Bks.

—Taking Care of Your Dragon. 2020. 24p. (J). lib. bdg. *(978-1-68072-910-8(1))* Black Rabbit Bks.

—Taking Care of Your Griffin. 2020. 24p. (J). lib. bdg. *(978-1-68072-911-5(X))* Black Rabbit Bks.

—Taking Care of Your Phoenix. 2020. 24p. (J). lib. bdg. *(978-1-68072-912-2(8))* Black Rabbit Bks.

—Taking Care of Your Sea Monster. 2020. 24p. (J). lib. bdg. *(978-1-68072-914-6(4))* Black Rabbit Bks.

—Taking Care of Your Unicorn. 2020. 24p. (J). lib. bdg. *(978-1-68072-913-9(6))* Black Rabbit Bks.

Braun, Lisa. The Special Women We Call Grandmom, 1 vol. McDermott, Mary. 2010. 20p. pap. 24.95 *(978-1-4489-9749-7(6))* PublishAmerica, Inc.

Braun, Mina. Mindful Kids: 50 Activities for Calm, Focus & Peace. Stewart, Whitney. 2017. (ENG.). 50p. (J). (gr. -1-4). 14.99 *(978-1-78285-327-5(8))* Barefoot Bks., Inc.

Braun, Seb. Bat & Sloth Hang Around (Bat & Sloth: Time to Read, Level 2) Kimmelman, Leslie. 2020. (Time to Read Ser.). (ENG.). 32p. (J). (gr. k-2). 12.99 ***(978-0-8075-0580-9(3),*** 0807505803); 12.99 ***(978-0-8075-0585-4(4),*** 807505854) Whitman, Albert & Co.

—Bat & Sloth: Lost & Found. Kimmelman, Leslie. 2020. (Time to Read Ser.). (ENG.). 32p. (J). (gr. k-2). pap. 3.99 ***(978-0-8075-0579-3(X),*** 080750579X) Whitman, Albert & Co.

—Bat & Sloth Lost & Found (Bat & Sloth: Time to Read, Level 2) Kimmelman, Leslie. 2020. (Time to Read Ser.). (ENG.). 32p. (J). (gr. k-2). 12.99 ***(978-0-8075-0586-1(2),*** 807505862) Whitman, Albert & Co.

Braun, Seb. Pancakes with Grandma. Smith, Kathryn. 2020. (ENG.). 12p. (J). (-k). bds. 9.99 *(978-1-68010-623-7(6))* Tiger Tales.

—Picnic with Mommy. Smith, Kathryn. 2020. (ENG.). 12p. (J). (-k). bds. 9.99 *(978-1-68010-622-0(8))* Tiger Tales.

Braun, Sebastian. I'm a Clown! 2012. (Look at Me Ser.). 12p. (J). spiral bd. *(978-1-84643-472-3(6))* Child's Play International Ltd.

—I'm a Monster! 2012. (Look at Me Ser.). (ENG.). 12p. (J). bds. *(978-1-84643-470-9(X))* Child's Play International Ltd.

—I'm a Robot! 2012. (Look at Me Ser.). 12p. (J). spiral bd. *(978-1-84643-469-3(6))* Child's Play International Ltd.

—I'm an Alien! 2012. (Look at Me Ser.). 12p. (J). spiral bd. *(978-1-84643-471-6(8))* Child's Play International Ltd.

Braun, Sebastian. Peekaboo Baby. Braun, Sebastian. 2012. (ENG.). 16p. (J). (gr. -1 — 1). bds. 6.99 *(978-0-7636-5933-2(9))* Candlewick Pr.

Braun, Sébastien. Babi Bag Siwgwr. Gates, Susan & Ceredigion, Cymdeithas Lyfrau. Williams, Dylan, tr. 2005. (WEL.). 80p. pap. *(978-1-902416-96-0(1))* Cymdeithas Lyfrau Ceredigion.

Braun, Sebastien. Be Careful What You Sniff For #1, No. 1. Krulik, Nancy. 2013. (Magic Bone Ser.: 1). (ENG.). 128p. (J). (gr. 1-3). pap. 5.99 *(978-0-448-46399-5(7),* Grosset & Dunlap) Penguin Young Readers Group.

—The Best Mom in the World! Clever Publishing & Reider, Katja. 2020. (Clever Family Stories Ser.). (ENG.). 18p. (J). (gr. -1 — 1). bds. 5.99 *(978-1-949998-92-4(4))* Clever Media Group.

Braun, Sebastien. Big Bug Log. Nosy Crow Staff. 2017. (ENG.). 18p. (J). (gr. -1-2). bds. 9.99 *(978-0-7636-9322-0(7),* Nosy Crow) Candlewick Pr.

Braun, Sebastien. Broadway Doggie #10. Krulik, Nancy. 2016. (Magic Bone Ser.: 10). (ENG.). 128p. (J). (gr. 1-3). 5.99 *(978-0-448-48875-2(2),* Grosset & Dunlap) Penguin Young Readers Group.

Braun, Sébastien. Can You Say It, Too? Brrr! Brrr! Nosy Crow Staff. 2017. (Can You Say It, Too? Ser.). (ENG.). 10p. (J). (— 1). bds. 8.99 *(978-0-7636-9622-1(6),* Nosy Crow) Candlewick Pr.

Braun, Sebastien. Can You Say It, Too? Cheep! Cheep! Nosy Crow. 2017. (Can You Say It, Too? Ser.). (ENG.). 10p. (J). (— 1). bds. 8.99 *(978-0-7636-9329-9(4),* Nosy Crow) Candlewick Pr.

Braun, Sébastien. Can You Say It, Too? Growl! Growl! Nosy Crow Staff. 2014. (Can You Say It, Too? Ser.). (ENG.). 10p. (J). (— 1). bds. 8.99 *(978-0-7636-7396-3(X),* Nosy Crow) Candlewick Pr.

—Can You Say It, Too? Hoot! Hoot! Nosy Crow Staff. 2015. (Can You Say It, Too? Ser.). (ENG.). 10p. (J). (— 1). bds. 8.99 *(978-0-7636-7588-2(1),* Nosy Crow) Candlewick Pr.

—Can You Say It, Too? Jingle! Jingle! Nosy Crow Staff. 2015. (Can You Say It, Too? Ser.). (ENG.). 10p. (J). (— 1). bds. 8.99 *(978-0-7636-8002-2(8),* Nosy Crow) Candlewick Pr.

Braun, Sebastien. Can You Say It, Too? Moo! Moo! Nosy Crow. 2014. (Can You Say It, Too? Ser.). (ENG.). 10p. (J). (— 1). bds. 8.99 *(978-0-7636-7066-5(9),* Nosy Crow) Candlewick Pr.

Braun, Sébastien. Can You Say It, Too? Quack! Quack! Nosy Crow Staff. 2015. (Can You Say It, Too? Ser.). (ENG.). 10p. (J). (— 1). bds. 8.99 *(978-0-7636-7589-9(X),* Nosy Crow) Candlewick Pr.

—Can You Say It, Too? Roar! Roar! Nosy Crow Staff. 2014. (Can You Say It, Too? Ser.). (ENG.). 10p. (J). (— 1). bds. 8.99 *(978-0-7636-7397-0(8),* Nosy Crow) Candlewick Pr.

—Can You Say It, Too? Stomp! Stomp! Nosy Crow. 2018. (Can You Say It, Too? Ser.). (ENG.). 10p. (J). (— 1). bds. 8.99 *(978-0-7636-9934-5(9),* Nosy Crow) Candlewick Pr.

Braun, Sebastien. Can You Say It, Too? Tweet! Tweet! Nosy Crow. 2019. (Can You Say It, Too? Ser.). (ENG.). 10p. (J). (— 1). bds. 8.99 *(978-1-5362-0556-5(7),* Nosy Crow) Candlewick Pr.

Braun, Sébastien. Can You Say It, Too? Woof! Woof! Crow, Nosy. 2014. (Can You Say It, Too? Ser.). (ENG.). 10p. (J). (— 1). bds. 8.99 *(978-0-7636-6605-7(X),* Nosy Crow) Candlewick Pr.

—Catch That Wave. Krulik, Nancy. 2013. (Magic Bone Ser.: 2). 128p. (J). (gr. 1-3). pap. 5.99 *(978-0-448-46444-2(6),* Grosset & Dunlap) Penguin Young Readers Group.

Braun, Sebastien. A Day with Dad. Clever Publishing & Reider, Katja. 2020. (Clever Family Stories Ser.). (ENG.). 18p. (J). (gr. -1 — 1). bds. 5.99 *(978-1-949998-93-1(2))* Clever Media Group.

Braun, Sébastien. Dog on His Bus. Seltzer, Eric & Hall, Kirsten. 2012. (Penguin Young Readers, Level 2 Ser.). 32p. (J). (gr. 1-2). pap. 4.99 *(978-0-448-45904-2(3),* Penguin Young Readers) Penguin Young Readers Group.

—Dog on His Bus. Seltzer, Eric & Hall, Kirsten. ed. 2012. (Penguin Young Readers Level 2 Ser.). lib. bdg. 13.55 *(978-0-606-25815-9(9))* Turtleback.

Braun, Sebastien. Dogs Don't Have Webbed Feet #7. Krulik, Nancy. 2015. (Magic Bone Ser.: 7). (ENG.). 128p. (J). (gr. 1-3). 5.99 *(978-0-448-48096-1(4),* Grosset & Dunlap) Penguin Young Readers Group.

Braun, Sébastien. Don't Mess with the Ninja Puppy!, No. 6. Krulik, Nancy. 2014. (Magic Bone Ser.: 6). 128p. (J). (gr. 1-3). 5.99 *(978-0-448-48095-4(6),* Grosset & Dunlap) Penguin Young Readers Group.

—First Snow. Ford, Bernette G. 2005. 32p. (J). *(978-0-9547373-3-7(4))* Boxer Bks., Ltd.

—First Snow. Ford, Bernette. 2018. (ENG.). 28p. (J). (gr. -1-1). bds. 7.95 *(978-1-910716-63-2(4))* Boxer Bks., Ltd. GBR. Dist: Sterling Publishing Co., Inc.

—Follow That Furball. Krulik, Nancy. 2013. (Magic Bone Ser.: 3). 128p. (J). (gr. 1-3). 5.99 *(978-0-448-46445-9(4),* Grosset & Dunlap) Penguin Young Readers Group.

Braun, Sebastien. Fox & Crow Are Not Friends. Wiley, Melissa. 2012. (Step into Reading Ser.). 48p. (J). (gr. k-3). pap. 4.99 *(978-0-375-86982-2(4),* Random Hse. Bks. for Young Readers) Random Hse. Children's Bks.

Braun, Sébastien. Go Fetch! Krulik, Nancy. 2014. (Magic Bone Ser.: 5). 128p. (J). (gr. 1-3). 5.99 *(978-0-448-48094-7(8),* Grosset & Dunlap) Penguin Young Readers Group.

Braun, Sebastien. How Many Sleeps 'til Christmas? Sperring, Mark. 2014. (ENG.). 32p. (J). (gr. -1-2). 16.99 *(978-1-58925-160-1(1))* Tiger Tales.

—How Many Sleeps 'Til My Birthday? Sperring, Mark. 2016. (ENG.). 32p. (J). (gr. -1-2). 16.99 *(978-1-68010-009-9(2))* Tiger Tales.

—Learn to Read with Tug the Pup & Friends! Box Set 1: Levels Included: A-C, Set. Wood, Julie M. 2014. (My Very First I Can Read Ser.). (ENG.). 132p. (J). (gr. -1-3). pap. 14.99 *(978-0-06-226689-7(6))* HarperCollins Pubs.

Braun, Sébastien. Magic Bone: Two Tales, One Dog. Krulik, Nancy. 2016. (Magic Bone Ser.: 12). 192p. (J). (gr. 1-3). 6.99 *(978-0-448-48877-6(9),* Grosset & Dunlap) Penguin Young Readers Group.

Braun, Sebastien. My Love Is All Around. McLean, Danielle. 2020. (ENG.). 32p. (J). (gr. -1-2). 17.99 *(978-1-68010-194-2(3))* Tiger Tales.

—Never Box with a Kangaroo #11. Krulik, Nancy. 2016. (Magic Bone Ser.: 11). 128p. (J). (gr. 1-3). 5.99 *(978-0-448-48876-9(0),* Grosset & Dunlap) Penguin Young Readers Group.

—A New Baby for Birdie. Clever Publishing & Reider, Katja. 2020. (Clever Family Stories Ser.). (ENG.). 18p. (J). (gr. -1 — 1). bds. 5.99 *(978-1-949998-94-8(0))* Clever Media Group.

Braun, Sebastien. Nice Snowing You! Krulik, Nancy. 2014. (Magic Bone Ser.: 4). 128p. (J). (gr. 1-3). 5.99 *(978-0-448-46446-6(2),* Grosset & Dunlap) Penguin Young Readers Group.

—Nice Snowing You! Krulik, Nancy E. 2014. 108p. (J). *(978-1-62565-236-2(4),* Grosset & Dunlap) Penguin Publishing Group.

Braun, Sebastien. Pup Art #9. Krulik, Nancy. 2015. (Magic Bone Ser.: 9). 128p. (J). (gr. 1-3). bds. 5.99 *(978-0-448-48749-6(7),* Grosset & Dunlap) Penguin Young Readers Group.

Braun, Sébastien. Rootin' Tootin' Cow Dog #8. Krulik, Nancy & dePaola, Tomie. 2015. (Magic Bone Ser.: 8). 128p. (J). (gr. 1-3). bds. 5.99 *(978-0-448-48097-8(2),* Grosset & Dunlap) Penguin Young Readers Group.

—Shapes & Colors. 2012. (J). *(978-1-58865-852-4(X))* Kidsbooks, LLC.

Braun, Sebastien. Spinderella. Donaldson, Julia. 2017. (ENG.). 32p. (J). (gr. -1-k). pap. 10.99 *(978-1-4052-8272-7(X))* Egmont Bks., Ltd. GBR. Dist: Independent Pubs. Group.

Braun, Sebastien. Spinderella Book & Plush Set. Donaldson, Julia. 2018. (ENG.). 32p. (J). (gr. -1-k). 19.99 *(978-1-4052-9156-9(7))* Egmont Bks., Ltd. GBR. Dist: Independent Pubs. Group.

—Super Special: Two Tales, One Dog. Krulik, Nancy. ed. 2016. (Magic Bone Ser.: Vol. 12). (ENG.). 192p. (J). (gr. 1-3). 17.20 *(978-0-606-39309-6(9))* Turtleback.

—The Tiger Prowls: A Pop-Up Book of Wild Animals. 2016. (ENG.). 12p. (J). 16.99 *(978-1-4711-2215-6(8),* Simon & Schuster Children's) Simon & Schuster, Ltd. GBR. Dist: Simon & Schuster, Inc.

Braun, Sebastien. Back to Bed, Ed!, 1 vol. Braun, Sebastien. (ENG.). 32p. (J). (gr. -1-3). 2014. pap. 7.95 *(978-1-56145-775-5(2));* 2010. 15.95 *(978-1-56145-518-8(0))* Peachtree Publishing Co. Inc.

—Digger & Tom! Braun, Sebastien. 2013. (ENG.). 32p. (J). (gr. -1-3). 16.99 *(978-0-06-207752-3(X))* HarperCollins Pubs.

—I Love My Daddy. Braun, Sebastien. 2004. (ENG.). 32p. (J). (gr. -1-2). 12.99 *(978-0-06-054311-2(6))* HarperCollins Pubs.

—I Love My Daddy Board Book. Braun, Sebastien. 2017. (ENG.). 32p. (J). (gr. -1 — 1). bds. 8.99 *(978-0-06-256425-2(0),* Tegen, Katherine Bks) HarperCollins Pubs.

—I Love My Mommy Board Book. Braun, Sebastien. 2017. (ENG.). 26p. (J). (gr. -1 — 1). bds. 7.99 *(978-0-06-256424-5(2),* Tegen, Katherine Bks) HarperCollins Pubs.

—I Love You More. Braun, Sebastien. 2013. (ENG.). 20p. (J). (gr. -1-k). bds. 8.95 *(978-1-58925-620-0(4))* Tiger Tales.

—Mayday Mouse. Braun, Sebastien. 2017. (Child's Play Library). 32p. (J). pap. *(978-1-84643-758-8(X));* (ENG.). *(978-1-84643-759-5(8))* Child's Play International Ltd.

—One Sleepy Night. Braun, Sebastien. 2013. (ENG.). 20p. (J). (-k). bds. 8.95 *(978-1-58925-619-4(0))* Tiger Tales.

—Raj & the Best Day Ever. Braun, Sebastien. 2019. (ENG.). 40p. (J). (gr. -1-2). 16.99 *(978-1-5362-0570-1(2),* Templar) Candlewick Pr.

—Toot & Pop! Braun, Sebastien. 2012. (ENG.). 32p. (J). (gr. -1-2). 12.99 *(978-0-06-207750-9(3))* HarperCollins Pubs.

Braun, Sébastien. Who Can Swim? Braun, Sébastien. 2014. (ENG.). 14p. (J). (— 1). bds. 6.99 *(978-0-7636-6752-8(8))* Candlewick Pr.

Braun, Sebastien. Whoosh & Chug! Braun, Sebastien. 2014. (ENG.). 32p. (J). (gr. -1-3). 16.99 *(978-0-06-207754-7(6))* HarperCollins Pubs.

Braun, Sebastien & Evans, Lisa. A Little Help from My Friends! Book Set Of 4. Birchall, Mark et al. 2020. (Social & Emotional Learning Sets Ser.). (ENG.). 144p. (J). pap., pap., pap. ***(978-1-78628-539-3(8))*** Child's Play International Ltd.

Bravi, Soledad. Good Night! Marchon, Benoit. 2013. (ENG.). 40p. (J). (gr. k — 1). bds. 8.99 *(978-0-547-89314-3(0),* 1508644) Houghton Mifflin Harcourt Publishing Co.

—Spoonful: A Peek-A-Boo Book. Marchon, Benoit. 2013. (ENG.). 38p. (J). (gr. k — 1). bds. 7.99 *(978-0-547-89313-6(2),* 1508643) Houghton Mifflin Harcourt Publishing Co.

Bravi, Soledad. The Noisy Book. Bravi, Soledad. 2013. (ENG.). 116p. (J). (gr. -1-3). bds. 16.95 *(978-1-877467-52-3(9))* Gecko Pr. NZL. Dist: Lerner Publishing Group.

Bravo, Constanza. El Libro de Oro de las Fabulas. Uribe, Veronica & Espoo. 2004. (SPA.). 126p. (J). (gr. -1-3). 9.99 *(978-980-257-209-0(8))* Ekare, Ediciones VEN. Dist: Lectorum Pubns., Inc.

Bravo, Constanza, photos by. Don Quijote de la Mancha (Edición Adaptada y Anotada) Cervantes, Miguel de. 2016. (Serie Naranja Ser.). (SPA., 304p. (J). (gr. 5-8). pap. 11.95 *(978-958-9002-27-8(7),* Loqueleo) Santillana USA Publishing Co., Inc.

Bravo, Fran, jt. illus. see Bravo, Juan.

Bravo, Juan & Bravo, Fran. Un Dragon a Dieta. Cano, Carles & Carles, Cano. 2006. (Montana Encantada Ser.). (SPA.). 36p. (J). (gr. 1-2). pap. 8.50 *(978-84-241-8747-7(4))* Everest Editora ESP. Dist: Lectorum Pubns., Inc.

Bray, Pamela. Ayiana & the Hurricane Katrina Classmate. Powell, GinaMarie. 2008. 28p. pap. 24.95 *(978-1-60441-965-8(2))* America Star Bks.

Brayton, Julie. You Will Be My Baby Even When. Becker, Christie. 2003. 32p. (J). (gr. -1-1). 14.95 *(978-0-9728116-0-6(5))* Becker, Christie.

Brazell, Derek. Ali Baba & the Forty Thieves. Barkow, Henriette. 2004. 28p. (J). (ENG & SWE.). pap. *(978-1-84444-539-4(9));* (ENG, RUS, SWE & SOM.). pap. *(978-1-84444-540-0(2));* (POL & ENG.). pap. *(978-1-84444-545-5(3))* Mantra Lingua.

—Lima's Red Hot Chilli. Mills, David. 2004. (J). 24p. *(978-1-85269-505-7(6));* 24p. *(978-1-85269-504-0(8));* 24p. *(978-1-85269-429-6(7));* 24p. *(978-1-85269-534-7(X));* 24p. *(978-1-85269-467-8(X));* 24p. *(978-1-85269-468-5(8));* (ENG & SPA.). 32p. pap. *(978-1-85269-942-0(6));* (ENG & KHM.). 32p. pap. *(978-1-85269-542-2(0));* (ENG & KOR.). 32p. pap. *(978-1-85269-543-9(9));* (ENG & FRE.). 32p. pap. *(978-1-85269-533-0(1));* (ENG & PER.). 32p. pap. *(978-1-85269-506-4(4));* (ENG & TAM.). 32p. pap. *(978-1-85269-469-2(6));* (ENG & GRE.). 32p. pap. *(978-1-85269-466-1(1));* (ENG & ALB.). 32p. pap. *(978-1-85269-465-4(3));* (ENG & URD.). 32p. pap. *(978-1-85269-427-2(0));* (ENG & TUR.). 32p. pap. *(978-1-85269-426-5(2));* (ENG & SOM.). 32p. pap. *(978-1-85269-425-8(4));* (ENG & POR.). 32p. pap. *(978-1-85269-424-1(6));* (ENG & GUJ.). 32p. pap. *(978-1-85269-423-4(8));* (ENG & BEN.). 32p. pap. *(978-1-85269-421-0(1));* (ENG & ARA.). 32p. pap. *(978-1-85269-420-3(3))* Mantra Lingua.

—Mei Ling's Hiccups. Mills, David. 2004. (J). 24p. *(978-1-85269-559-0(5));* (CHI & ENG.). 32p. pap. *(978-1-85269-703-7(2));* (ENG & CHI.). 32p. pap. *(978-1-85269-555-2(2));* (ENG & ARA.). 32p. pap. *(978-1-85269-553-8(6));* (ENG & CZE.). 32p. pap. *(978-1-85269-682-5(6));* (ENG & POL.). 32p. pap. *(978-1-85269-626-9(5));* (ENG & SPA.). 32p. pap. *(978-1-85269-565-1(X));* (ENG & POR.). 32p. pap. *(978-1-85269-562-0(5));* (ENG & JPN.). 32p. pap. *(978-1-85269-560-6(9));* (ENG & URD.). 32p. pap. *(978-1-85269-568-2(4));* (ENG.). 32p. pap. *(978-1-85269-563-7(3));* (ENG & PAN.). 32p. pap. *(978-1-85269-561-3(7));* (ENG & GUJ.). 32p. pap. *(978-1-85269-558-3(7));* (ENG & KOR.). 32p. pap. *(978-1-85269-704-4(0));* (ENG & VIE.). 32p. pap. *(978-1-85269-569-9(2));* (ENG & TUR.). 32p. pap. *(978-1-85269-567-5(6));* (ENG & TAM.). 32p. pap. *(978-1-85269-566-8(8));* (ENG & FRE.). 32p. pap.

(978-1-85269-557-6(9)); (ENG & PER.). 32p. pap. *(978-1-85269-556-9(0))*; (ENG & BEN.). 32p. pap. *(978-1-85269-554-5(4))*; (ENG & ALB.). 32p. pap. *(978-1-85269-552-1(8))* Mantra Lingua.

—Mei Ling's Hiccups: Higgadii Mii Linig. Mills, David. 2004. (ENG & SOM.). 32p. (J). pap. *(978-1-85269-564-4(1))* Mantra Lingua.

—That's My Mum. Barkow, Henriette. 2004. (J). 24p. *(978-1-85269-604-7(4))*; (ENG & YOR.). 28p. pap. *(978-1-84444-381-9(7))*; (ALB & ENG.). 28p. pap. *(978-1-85269-595-8(1))*; (ENG & ITA.). 28p. pap. *(978-1-85269-804-1(7))*; (GER & ENG.). 28p. pap. *(978-1-85269-803-4(9))*; (ENG & VIE.). 28p. pap. *(978-1-85269-802-7(0))*; (ENG & CZE.). 28p. pap. *(978-1-85269-628-3(1))*; (ENG & URD.). 28p. pap. *(978-1-85269-609-2(5))*; (ENG & TUR.). 28p. pap. *(978-1-85269-608-5(7))*; (ENG & SPA.). 28p. pap. *(978-1-85269-606-1(0))*; (ENG & SOM.). 28p. pap. *(978-1-85269-605-4(2))*; (ENG & POR.). 28p. pap. *(978-1-85269-603-0(6))*; (ENG & PAN.). 28p. pap. *(978-1-85269-602-3(8))*; (ENG & GUJ.). 28p. pap. *(978-1-85269-601-6(X))*; (ENG & PER.). 28p. pap. *(978-1-85269-599-6(4))*; (ENG & CHI.). 28p. pap. *(978-1-85269-598-9(6))*; (ENG & BEN.). 28p. pap. *(978-1-85269-597-2(8))* Mantra Lingua.

—That's My Mum: Ajo Eshte Nena Ime. Barkow, Henriette. 2004. (ENG & ARA.). 28p. (J). pap. *(978-1-85269-596-5(X))* Mantra Lingua.

—Welcome to the World Baby. Robert, Na'ima Bint & Petrova-Browning, Nina. 2005. (ENG & BUL.). 32p. (J). pap. *(978-1-84444-721-3(9))* Mantra Lingua.

—Welcome to the World Baby. Robert, Na'ima Bint. 2005. 32p. (J). (WEL, ENG, KOR & KUR.). pap. *(978-1-84444-633-9(6))*; (ENG & SNA.). pap. *(978-1-84444-450-2(3))*; (YOR & ENG.). pap. *(978-1-84444-297-3(7))*; (ENG & VIE.). pap. *(978-1-84444-296-6(9))*; (ENG & URD.). pap. *(978-1-84444-295-9(0))*; (TUR & ENG.). pap. *(978-1-84444-293-5(4))*; (ENG & SWA.). pap. *(978-1-84444-290-4(X))*; (SPA & ENG.). pap. *(978-1-84444-289-8(6))*; (ENG & SOM.). pap. *(978-1-84444-288-1(8))*; (ENG & RUS.). pap. *(978-1-84444-287-4(X))*; (ENG & RUM.). pap. *(978-1-84444-286-7(1))*; (ENG & POR.). pap. *(978-1-84444-285-0(3))*; (POL & ENG.). pap. *(978-1-84444-284-3(5))*; (ENG & PAN.). pap. *(978-1-84444-283-6(7))*; (ENG & KOR.). pap. *(978-1-84444-282-9(9))*; (JPN & ENG.). pap. *(978-1-84444-281-2(0))*; (ENG & ITA.). pap. *(978-1-84444-280-5(2))*; (ENG & HIN.). pap. *(978-1-84444-279-9(9))*; (ENG & GUJ.). pap. *(978-1-84444-278-2(0))*; (ENG & GER.). pap. *(978-1-84444-276-8(4))*; (FRE & ENG.). pap. *(978-1-84444-275-1(6))*; (ENG & PER.). pap. *(978-1-84444-274-4(8))*; (ENG, HRV & SER.). pap. *(978-1-84444-273-7(X))*; (ENG & CHI.). pap. *(978-1-84444-272-0(1))*; (ENG & CHI.). pap. *(978-1-84444-271-3(3))*; (ENG & BEN.). pap. *(978-1-84444-270-6(5))*; (ENG & ARA.). pap. *(978-1-84444-269-0(1))*; (ENG & ALB.). pap. *(978-1-84444-268-3(3))* Mantra Lingua.

Breadcrumbs, Ink. The Dragon Grammar Book: Grammar for Kids, Dragons, & the Whole Kingdom. Robinson, Diane Mae. 2017. (ENG.). 140p. (YA). (gr. 7-12). *(978-1-988714-04-2(4))* Robinson, Diane Mae.

Bready, Jane Gilltrap. R Is for Race: A Stock Car Alphabet. Herzog, Brad. 2006. (Sports Ser.). (ENG.). 40p. (J). (gr. -1-5). 16.95 *(978-1-58536-272-1(7))* Sleeping Bear Pr.

—R Is for Race: A Stock Car Alphabet. Herzog, Brad. 2015. (Av2 Fiction Readalong 2016 Ser.). (ENG.). (J). (gr. 1-4). lib. bdg. 34.28 *(978-1-4896-3762-8(1)*, AV2 by Weigl) Weigl Pubs., Inc.

Breakespeare, Andrew. Mole Who was Scared of the Dark. Gates, Susan. 2005. (ENG.). 24p. (J). lib. bdg. 23.65 *(978-1-59646-710-1(X))* Dingles & Co.

Breathed, Berkeley. The Bill the Cat Story: A Bloom County Epic. Breathed, Berkeley. 2016. (ENG.). 40p. (J). (gr. -1-3). 18.99 *(978-0-399-54662-4(6)*, Philomel Bks.) Penguin Young Readers Group.

—Mars Needs Moms! Breathed, Berkeley. 2007. (ENG.). 40p. (J). (gr. k-3). 17.99 *(978-0-399-24736-1(X)*, Philomel Bks.) Penguin Young Readers Group.

—Pete & Pickles. Breathed, Berkeley. 2008. (ENG.). 48p. (J). (gr. -1-k). 17.99 *(978-0-399-25082-8(4)*, Philomel Bks.) Penguin Young Readers Group.

Breaux, Joe Ann. Confederate Coloring & Learning Book. Walker, Gary C. 2004. 41p. (J). (gr. 1-7). pap. 4.95 *(978-0-9617898-5-5(9))* A & W Enterprises.

Breaux, Wayne, Jr., et al. Rifts Adventure Guide. Siembieda, Kevin. 2006. (Rifts RPG Ser.). (YA). pap. 22.95 *(978-1-57457-072-4(2))* Palladium Bks., Inc.

Brech, Nora. Cornelia & the Jungle Machine. Brech, Nora. 2019. (ENG.). 32p. (J). (gr. k-2). 17.99 *(978-1-77657-259-5(9))* Gecko Pr. NZL. Dist: Lerner Publishing Group.

Brechner, Katrina. Eskimo Kids: Fire & Ice. Brechner, Ron. 2018. (ENG.). 50p. (J). pap. 6.99 *(978-1-7255-2284-8(5))* CreateSpace Independent Publishing Platform.

Brecke, Nicole. Airplanes & Ships You Can Draw. Brecke, Nicole. Stockland, Patricia M. 2010. (Ready, Set, Draw! Ser.). (ENG.). 32p. (gr. 2-4). lib. bdg. 25.26 *(978-0-7613-4166-6(8)*, Millbrook Pr.) Lerner Publishing Group.

—Cars, Trucks, & Motorcycles You Can Draw. Brecke, Nicole. Stockland, Patricia M. 2009. (Ready, Set, Draw! Ser.). (ENG.). 32p. (gr. 2-4). lib. bdg. 25.26 *(978-0-7613-4162-8(5)*, Millbrook Pr.) Lerner Publishing Group.

—Cats You Can Draw. Brecke, Nicole. Stockland, Patricia M. 2009. (Ready, Set, Draw! Ser.). (ENG.). 32p. (gr. 2-4). lib. bdg. 25.26 *(978-0-7613-4161-1(7)*, Millbrook Pr.) Lerner Publishing Group.

—Cool Boy Stuff You Can Draw. Brecke, Nicole. Stockland, Patricia M. 2009. (Ready, Set, Draw! Ser.). (ENG.). 32p. (gr. 2-4). lib. bdg. 25.26 *(978-0-7613-4163-5(3)*, Millbrook Pr.) Lerner Publishing Group.

—Cool Girl Stuff You Can Draw. Brecke, Nicole. Stockland, Patricia M. 2009. (Ready, Set, Draw! Ser.). (ENG.). 32p. (gr. 2-4). lib. bdg. 25.26 *(978-0-7613-4164-2(1)*, Millbrook Pr.) Lerner Publishing Group.

—Dinosaurs & Other Prehistoric Creatures You Can Draw. Brecke, Nicole. Stockland, Patricia M. 2010. (Ready, Set, Draw! Ser.). (ENG.). 32p. (gr. 2-4). lib. bdg. 25.26 *(978-0-7613-4169-7(2)*, Millbrook Pr.) Lerner Publishing Group.

—Dogs You Can Draw. Brecke, Nicole. Stockland, Patricia M. 2009. (Ready, Set, Draw! Ser.). (ENG.). 32p. (gr. 2-4). lib. bdg. 25.26 *(978-0-7613-4159-8(5)*, Millbrook Pr.) Lerner Publishing Group.

—Extinct & Endangered Animals You Can Draw. Brecke, Nicole. Stockland, Patricia M. 2010. (Ready, Set, Draw! Ser.). (ENG.). 32p. (gr. 2-4). lib. bdg. 25.26 *(978-0-7613-4165-9(X)*, Millbrook Pr.) Lerner Publishing Group.

—Horses You Can Draw. Brecke, Nicole. Stockland, Patricia M. 2009. (Ready, Set, Draw! Ser.). (ENG.). 32p. (gr. 2-4). lib. bdg. 25.26 *(978-0-7613-4160-4(9)*, Millbrook Pr.) Lerner Publishing Group.

—Insects You Can Draw. Brecke, Nicole. Stockland, Patricia M. 2010. (Ready, Set, Draw! Ser.). (ENG.). 32p. (J). (gr. 2-4). lib. bdg. 25.26 *(978-0-7613-4170-3(6)*, Millbrook Pr.) Lerner Publishing Group.

—Sea Creatures You Can Draw. Brecke, Nicole. Stockland, Patricia M. 2010. (Ready, Set, Draw! Ser.). (ENG.). 32p. (gr. 2-4). lib. bdg. 25.26 *(978-0-7613-4168-0(4)*, Millbrook Pr.) Lerner Publishing Group.

—Spaceships, Aliens, & Robots You Can Draw. Brecke, Nicole. Stockland, Patricia M. 2010. (Ready, Set, Draw! Ser.). (ENG.). 32p. (gr. 2-4). lib. bdg. 25.26 *(978-0-7613-4167-3(6)*, Millbrook Pr.) Lerner Publishing Group.

Breckel, Heather, et al. My Little Pony: Friendship Is Magic, 8 vols. Abdo Publishing et al. 2015. (My Little Pony: Friendship Is Magic Ser.: Vol. 8). (ENG.). 24p. (J). (gr. 2-5). 216.56 *(978-1-61479-375-5(1)*, 18206, Graphic Novels) Spotlight.

—My Little Pony: Friendship Is Magic. Cook, Katie. 2015. (My Little Pony: Friendship Is Magic Ser.). (ENG.). 24p. (J). (gr. 2-5). lib. bdg. 27.07 *(978-1-61479-377-9(8)*, 18208);3. lib. bdg. 27.07 *(978-1-61479-378-6(6)*, 18209) Spotlight. (Graphic Novels).

—Plants vs. Zombies Volume 11: War & Peas. Tobin, Paul. 2018. (ENG.). 88p. (J). (gr. 3-7). 9.99 *(978-1-5067-0677-1(0)*, Dark Horse Books) Dark Horse Comics.

Breckel, Heather, jt. illus. see Hernandez, Jennifer.

Breckel, Heather, jt. illus. see Uyetake, Neil.

Breckenridge, Scott, jt. illus. see Breckenridge, Trula.

Breckenridge, Trula & Breckenridge, Scott. Squiggly the Roach. Breckenridge, Trula & Breckenridge, Scott. 2004. (J). per. *(978-0-9749480-6-5(3)*, MSPpress) Mama Specific Productions.

Breckenridge, Trula & Lynch, Todd. Ricca the Ladybug. Breckenridge, Trula & Lynch, Todd. 2004. (J). per. *(978-0-9749480-8-9(X)*, MSPpress) Mama Specific Productions.

Breckenridge, Trula & Palmore, Iyende. FiFi the Leaf. Breckenridge, Trula & Palmore, Iyende. 2004. (J). per. *(978-0-9749480-7-2(1)*, MSPpress) Mama Specific Productions.

Brecknell, Annie. A Day to Remember. Medina, Sarah. 48p. pap. 8.99 *(978-0-7459-4770-9(0)*, Lion Books) Lion Hudson PLC GBR. Dist: Trafalgar Square Publishing.

Breckon, Brett. Dragon Days. 2004. (ENG.). 82p. 17.95 *(978-1-84323-301-5(0))* Beekman Bks., Inc.

Brecon, Connah. Allergic Alpaca. Thomas, Kiah. 2019. (ENG.). 32p. (J). (gr. -1-k). 15.99 ***(978-1-76050-343-7(6))*** Little Hare Bks. AUS. Dist: Independent Pubs. Group.

Brecon, Connah. Blue. Hoena, Blake. 2018. (Sing Your Colors! Ser.). (ENG.). 24p. (J). (gr. -1-2). lib. bdg. 33.99 *(978-1-68410-316-4(9)*, 140862); lib. bdg. 33.99 incl. audio compact disk *(978-1-68410-116-0(6)*, 31850) Cantata Learning.

Brecon, Connah. Foothand, Elbownose. Thomas, Kiah. 2019. (ENG.). 24p. (J). (gr. -1-k). 15.99 ***(978-1-76050-202-7(2))*** Little Hare Bks. AUS. Dist: Independent Pubs. Group.

Brecon, Connah. Paws Mcdraw. Brecon, Connah. 2016. (ENG.). 32p. (J). (gr. -1-2). 16.99 *(978-1-68010-035-8(1))* Tiger Tales.

Brecon, Connah & Painter, Andrew. You & Me 2 Wayfarers. Rickards, Lynne. 2017. (Cambridge Reading Adventures Ser.). (ENG.). 24p. pap. 6.74 *(978-1-108-41083-0(9))* Cambridge Univ. Pr.

Bredius, Rein. Little Stories. Franco, Eloise. 2003. 66p. (gr. k-5). 5.95 *(978-0-87516-384-0(X)*, Devorss Pubns.) DeVorss & Co.

Bree, Marlin. Kids' Magic Secrets: Simple Magic Tricks & Why They Work. Bree, Loris. 2003. (ENG.). 112p. (J). (gr. 2-6). pap. 10.99 *(978-1-892147-08-0(4))* Marlor Pr., Inc.

Breeden, Don. A Mako Meets a Puffer: A Reel Fish Story. Swift, Austin Christopher. 2004. (J). per. 10.95 *(978-0-9764208-0-4(5))* Austin Christopher Swift.

Breedlove, Bonnie. Footsteps. Leadens, Todd. 2019. (ENG.). 40p. (J). pap. 12.99 ***(978-1-7079-0992-6(X))*** Independently Published.

Breemer, Kelly. The Great Farmapalooza. Lord, Jill Roman. 2020. (ENG.). 22p. (J). (-k). bds. 9.99 ***(978-1-0877-0616-0(5)***, 005824877, B&H Kids) B&H Publishing Group.

Breemer, Kelly. The Silent Noisy Night (padded) Lord, Jill Roman. 2018. (ENG.). 24p. (J). (— 1). bds. 12.99 *(978-1-5359-2373-6(3)*, 005806930, B&H Kids) B&H Publishing Group.

Breems, Beau. The Promise. Breems, Beau. 2006. (YA). 10.00 *(978-0-9768680-9-5(1))*; 20.00 *(978-0-9768680-8-8(3))* Burning Bush Creation.

Breems, Beau A. La Gran Historia: The Illustrated Gospel from Creation to Resurrection. Breems, Beau A. 2005.Tr. of His Story. (SPA.). (J). 10.99 *(978-0-9768680-5-7(9))*; 50p. 19.95 *(978-0-9768680-1-9(6)*, 1000); 50p. per. 14.95 *(978-0-9768680-3-3(2)*, 3000) Burning Bush Creation.

—His Story: The Illustrated Gospel from Creation to Resurrection. Breems, Beau A. l.t. ed. 2005.Tr. of Gran Historia. 50p. (J). 19.95 *(978-0-9768680-0-2(8)*, 0-9768680-0-8) Burning Bush Creation.

Breems, Beau Alan. His Story: The Illustrated Gospel from Creation to Resurrection. Breems, Beau Alan. 2005. (J). per. 14.95 *(978-0-9768680-2-6(4))* Burning Bush Creation.

Breen, Steve. Woodpecker Wants a Waffle. Breen, Steve. 2016. (ENG.). 32p. (J). (gr. -1-3). 17.99 *(978-0-06-234257-7(6))* HarperCollins Pubs.

Breen Withrow, Lesley. Bunny Bus. Paquette, Ammi-Joan. 2017. (ENG.). 32p. (J). 16.99 *(978-0-374-30225-2(1)*, 900145607, Farrar, Straus & Giroux (BYR)) Farrar, Straus & Giroux.

Breener, Kelly. Sweet Dreams Moonbeams. Conway, Sara. 2019. (ENG.). 20p. (J). bds. 7.99 ***(978-1-926444-92-5(2))*** Rainstorm Pr.

Breeze. The Adventures of Maxima & Coustaud: In Search of a Global Solution. Al Nahyan, Sheikha Shamma Bint Sultan. 2nd ed. 2020. (Adventures of Maxima & Coustaud Ser.: Vol. 2). (ENG.). 52p. (J). ***(978-1-912513-74-1(9))*** Silver Quill Publishing.

Breeze, Julia. Petey, the Bird Who Loved to Sing. Leder, Barbara Turner. Ransone, Rob, ed. 2019. (ENG.). 38p. (J). pap. 10.00 *(978-1-0962-8157-3(0))* Independently Published.

Bregoli, Jane. The Goat Lady. Bregoli, Jane. 2008. (ENG.). 32p. (J). (gr. 2-6). pap. 8.95 *(978-0-88448-309-0(6)*, 884309) Tilbury Hse. Pubs.

Breidenthal, Kathryn. Gordon Parks: No Excuses, 1 vol. Parks, Gordon, Jr., photos by. Parr, Ann. 2006. (ENG.). 32p. (J). (gr. k-3). 16.99 *(978-1-58980-411-1(2)*, Pelican Publishing) Arcadia Publishing.

Breiehagen, Per. The Brave Little Puppy. Evert, Lori. 2016. 28p. (J). (-k). bds. 8.99 *(978-0-399-54945-8(5)*, Random Hse. Bks. for Young Readers) Random Hse. Children's Bks.

—The Christmas Wish. Evert, Lori. 2013. (ENG.). 48p. (J). (gr. -1-2). 17.99 *(978-0-449-81681-3(8)*, Random Hse. Bks. for Young Readers) Random Hse. Children's Bks.

—The Christmas Wish: Read & Listen Edition. Evert, Lori. ed. 2013. (ENG.). 48p. (J). (gr. -1-2). E-Book *(978-0-449-81942-5(6)*, Random Hse. Bks. for Young Readers) Random Hse. Children's Bks.

—The Puppy's Wish (a Wish Book) Evert, Lori. 2017. 28p. (J). (-k). bds. 8.99 *(978-0-399-55054-6(2)*, Random Hse. Bks. for Young Readers) Random Hse. Children's Bks.

—The Tiny Wish. Evert, Lori. 2015. (ENG.). 48p. (J). (gr. -1-2). lib. bdg. 20.99 *(978-0-375-97336-9(2)*, Random Hse. Bks. for Young Readers) Random Hse. Children's Bks.

Breiehagen, Per. The Polar Bear Wish. Breiehagen, Per, photos by. Evert, Lori. 2018. 48p. (J). (gr. -1-2). 17.99 *(978-1-5247-6566-8(X)*, Random Hse. Bks. for Young Readers) Random Hse. Children's Bks.

Breithaupt, Andrew. How to Build an Iglu & a Qamutiik, 1 vol. Awa, Solomon. ed. 2013. (ENG.). 32p. (J). (gr. 3-6). 9.95 *(978-1-927095-31-7(X))* Inhabit Media Inc. CAN. Dist: Consortium Bk. Sales & Distribution.

Breitweiser, Mitch, et al. Annihilation: the Complete Collection Vol. 1. 2018. 472p. (YA). (gr. 8-17). pap. 34.99 *(978-1-302-91286-4(0))* Marvel Worldwide, Inc.

Bremer, Amanda. Runaway at Sea. McInnis, Margreit. Brittenham, Noreen, ed. 2020. (ENG.). 314p. (J). (gr. 3-6). pap. 12.95 ***(978-1-949864-84-7(7))*** Red Penguin Bks.

Brenden, Stefanie. Matthew's Very Happy Day. Brenden, Sally. 2018. (ENG.). 36p. (J). pap. 5.38 *(978-0-9972957-3-3(2))* Brenden, Sally.

Brenier, Claire, jt. illus. see Fortier, Natali.

Brenlla, Laura. The Case of the Missing Train: The Owl & Officer Smitty. Heflin, Carrie. Cottage Door Press, ed. 2020. (Smithsonian Kids the Owl & Officer Smitty Ser.). (ENG.). 32p. (J). (gr. -1-2). 9.99 ***(978-1-68052-943-2(9)***, 1005860) Cottage Door Pr.

—Don't Be Cross, Goldilocks! A Story about Forgiveness. Nicholson, Sue. 2020. (Fairytale Friends Ser.). (ENG.). 24p. (J). (gr. -1-k). lib. bdg. 27.99 ***(978-0-7112-4476-4(6))*** QEB Publishing Inc.

Brenlla, Laura. Gods, Goddesses, & Heroes, 1 vol. Lonely Planet Kids & Accatino, Marzia. 2020. (ENG.). 80p. (J). (gr. 4-7). 17.99 *(978-1-83869-061-8(1)*, Lonely Planet Kids) Lonely Planet Global Ltd. IRL. Dist: Hachette Bk. Group.

Brenlla, Laura. Hansel & Gretel's Gingerbread House: A Story about Hope. Nicholson, Sue. 2020. (Fairytale Friends Ser.). (ENG.). 24p. (J). (gr. -1-k). lib. bdg. 27.99 ***(978-0-7112-4479-5(0))*** QEB Publishing Inc.

Brenlla, Laura. Hibernation Hotel. Kelly, John. 2017. (ENG.). 32p. (J). *(978-1-84869-675-4(2))* Tiger Tales.

Brenlla, Laura. The Princess's Survival Guide. 2020. (ENG.). 80p. (J). (gr. 3). 16.95 ***(978-88-544-1668-0(1))*** White Star ITA. Dist: Sterling Publishing Co., Inc.

Brenn, Lisa. The Trilogy: Three Adventures of the Müsh-Mice. Grandpa Casey. 2012. 46p. 24.95 *(978-1-4626-9378-8(4))* America Star Bks.

Brennan, Anthony. Miracle Men. Downey, Glen. 2007. (Timeline Ser.). 48p. pap. 8.99 *(978-1-4190-4410-6(9))* Steck-Vaughn.

—Tales from the Tundra: A Collection of Inuit Stories, 1 vol. Kaslik, Ibi. 2018. (ENG.). 58p. (J). (gr. 4-7). pap. 11.95 *(978-1-77227-184-3(5))* Inhabit Media Inc. CAN. Dist: Consortium Bk. Sales & Distribution.

Brennan, Cait. The Virginia Giant: The True Story of Peter Francisco. Norfolk, Sherry & Norfolk, Bobby. 2014. (ENG.). 160p. (J). (gr. 4-7). 16.99 *(978-1-62619-117-4(4)*, History Pr., The) Arcadia Publishing.

Brennan, Carla. El asma en un Minuto: Lo que usted necesita Saber. Plaut, Thomas F. Velez, Stacey, ed. Biaggi, Maria Elena, tr. 8th ed. 2008.Tr. of One Minute Asthma: What You Need to Know. (SPA & ENG.). 80p. (YA). pap. 6.00 *(978-0-914625-31-5(4))* Pedipress, Inc.

—One Minute Asthma: What You Need to Know. Plaut, Thomas F. Velez, Stacey, ed. 8th ed. 2008.Tr. of asma en un minuto: lo que usted necesita Saber. (ENG & SPA.). 80p. (YA). pap. 6.00 *(978-0-914625-30-8(6))* Pedipress, Inc.

Brennan, Craig. Mommy, Where Does Everything Come From? Samuels, Gregory Robert. 2008. 11p. pap. 24.95 *(978-1-60610-437-8(3))* America Star Bks.

Brennan, Lisa. Another Müsh-Mice Adventure. Grandpa Casey. 2012. 48p. 24.95 *(978-1-4626-9379-5(2))* America Star Bks.

—Another Müsh-Mice Adventure: Florida Vacation, 1 vol. Grandpa Casey. 2009. 45p. pap. 24.95 *(978-1-60813-329-1(X))* America Star Bks.

Brennan, Lisa. God's Great Idea. Phipps, Lisa. 2019. (ENG.). 46p. (J). pap. ***(978-981-14-3667-3(3))*** Brindal Bks.

Brennan, Lisa. Going Green: Another Mush-Mice Adventure, 1 vol. Grandpa Casey. 2010. 34p. pap. 24.95 *(978-1-4489-7375-0(9))* America Star Bks.

—I Didn't Do Nuthin' McGlotham, L. R. E. Bailin, Jill, ed. 2013. 42p. 18.99 *(978-0-9892711-5-8(3))* Mindstir Media.

—Meet the Müsh-Mice. Grandpa Casey. 2012. 28p. 24.95 *(978-1-4626-9380-1(6))* America Star Bks.

—The Trilogy: Three adventures of the Müsh-Mice. Casey, Grandpa. 2011. 48p. pap. 24.95 *(978-1-4626-2095-1(7))* America Star Bks.

Brennan, Morgaine. The Talent Show Tail. Lubbers, Megan. 2019. (Fairy Pact School of Magic Ser.: Vol. 2). (ENG.). 82p. (J). pap. 5.99 ***(978-1-0810-4405-3(5))*** Independently Published.

Brennan, Neil. River Friendly, River Wild. Kurtz, Jane. 2007. (ENG.). 40p. (J). (gr. -1-3). 8.99 *(978-1-4169-3487-5(1)*, Simon & Schuster/Paula Wiseman Bks.) Simon & Schuster/Paula Wiseman Bks.

Brennan, Tim, jt. illus. see Turner, Dona.

Brenneman, Lynette Leaman, photos by. Susanna's Surprise: A Day at the Hans Herr House. 2012. 32p. (J). *(978-0-9859737-0-4(6))* Brenneman, Lynette.

Brent, Isabelle. Fairy Tales of the Brothers Grimm: Twenty Classic Stories Including Rumpelstiltskin, Rapunzel, Snow White, & the Golden Goose. 2020. 144p. (J). (gr. -1-12). 16.00 *(978-1-86147-867-2(4)*, Armadillo) Anness Publishing GBR. Dist: National Bk. Network.

—The Little Mermaid & Other Tales from Hans Christian Andersen. Andersen, Hans. 2019. 144p. (J). (gr. -1-12). 16.00 *(978-1-86147-862-7(3)*, Armadillo) Anness Publishing GBR. Dist: National Bk. Network.

—Saint Anthony the Great. Vol. Chryssavgis, John & Rouvelas, Marilyn. 2015. 28p. (J). (gr. k-2). 17.95 *(978-1-937786-46-5(3)*, Wisdom Tales) World Wisdom, Inc.

Brenton Mckenna. Aussie Kids: Meet Sam at the Mangrove Creek. Seden, Paul. 2020. (Aussie Kids Ser.). 64p. (J). (gr. k-2). 12.99 ***(978-1-76089-412-2(5)***, Puffin) Penguin Random Hse. AUS. Dist: Independent Pubs. Group.

Brereton, Alice. Frankenbunny. Esbaum, Jill. 2017. 40p. (J). (gr. -1-2). 16.95 *(978-1-4549-2172-1(2))* Sterling Publishing Co., Inc.

—Glacier on the Move. Rusch, Elizabeth. 2019. (ENG.). 32p. (J). (gr. 1-4). 17.99 *(978-1-5132-6230-7(0)*, Graphic Arts Bks.) West Margin Pr.

—Joan & the Secrets of the Universe. MacLeod, Jennifer Tzivia. 2018. (J). *(978-1-5124-4437-7(5)*, Kar-Ben Publishing) Lerner Publishing Group.

—Meet My Monsters. Sarac, Annie. 2020. 40p. (J). (-3). 17.99 *(978-1-4926-9367-3(7)*, Sourcebooks Jabberwocky) Sourcebooks, Inc.

—Nightlights. Paolilli, Paul & Brewer, Dan. 2017. (ENG.). 32p. (J). (gr. -1-3). 16.99 *(978-0-8075-5622-1(X)*, 080755622X) Whitman, Albert & Co.

—This Book Is Spineless. Leslie, Lindsay. 2019. (ENG.). 32p. (J). 17.99 *(978-1-62414-658-9(9)*, 900196535) Page Street Publishing Co.

Bresnahan, Patrick. The Puddinhead Story. DiBattista, Mary Ann & Finn, Sandra J. 2010. (ENG.). 34p. 19.95 *(978-0-615-24552-2(8)*, 9780615245522) Puddinhead LLC.

Breton, Katia. The Mysterious Case of the Iws: A Story to Help Children Cope with Death. Danesh, H. B. 2012. 48p. pap. *(978-0-9782845-9-6(3))* International Education for Peace Institute (Canada).

Breton, Michel. Le Pere Noel a Rambouillet. Barbotin, Veronique. 2018. (FRE.). 44p. (J). pap. *(978-2-917822-60-9(0))* Pgcom Editions.

Brett, Cathy. Boys! Orme, Helen. 2007. (Siti's Sisters Ser.). (ENG.). 36p. (J). per. *(978-1-84167-600-5(4))* Ransom Publishing Ltd.

—Electrigirl. Cotterill, Jo. 2017. (Electrigirl Ser.). (ENG.). 240p. (J). (gr. 4-8). pap. 8.95 *(978-1-4965-5654-7(2)*, 136670); pap., pap., pap. 26.85 *(978-1-4965-5646-2(1)*, 27371); 75.96 *(978-1-4965-5651-6(8)*, 27370); lib. bdg. 25.32 *(978-1-4965-5650-9(X)*, 136667) Capstone. (Stone Arch Bks.).

—Electrigirl & the Deadly Swarm. Cotterill, Jo. 2017. (Electrigirl Ser.). (ENG.). 240p. (J). (gr. 4-8). pap. 8.95 *(978-1-4965-5661-5(5)*, 136671); lib. bdg. 25.32 *(978-1-4965-5662-2(3)*, 136668) Capstone. (Stone Arch Bks.).

—Electrigirl & the Invisible Thieves. Cotterill, Jo. 2017. (Electrigirl Ser.). (ENG.). 240p. (J). (gr. 4-8). pap. 8.95 *(978-1-4965-5669-1(0)*, 136672); lib. bdg. 25.32 *(978-1-4965-5670-7(4)*, 136669) Capstone. (Stone Arch Bks.).

—Lost! Orme, Helen. 2007. (Siti's Sisters Ser.). (ENG.). 36p. (J). per. *(978-1-84167-598-5(9))* Ransom Publishing Ltd.

—Odd One Out. Orme, Helen. 2007. (Siti's Sisters Ser.). (ENG.). 36p. (J). per. *(978-1-84167-597-8(0))* Ransom Publishing Ltd.

—Stalker. Orme, Helen. 2007. (Siti's Sisters Ser.). (ENG.). 36p. (J). per. *(978-1-84167-595-4(4))* Ransom Publishing Ltd.

—Taken for a Ride. Orme, Helen. 2007. (Siti's Sisters Ser.). (ENG.). 36p. (J). per. *(978-1-84167-596-1(2))* Ransom Publishing Ltd.

—Trouble with Teachers. Orme, Helen. 2007. (Siti's Sisters Ser.). (ENG.). 36p. (J). per. *(978-1-84167-599-2(7))* Ransom Publishing Ltd.

Brett, Emily. Marcus' Last Stand. Zonneveld, Brianna. 2018. (ENG.). 96p. (J). pap. *(978-0-9958021-2-4(2))* Cascia Bks.

Brett, Harold M. The Peterkin Papers. Hale, Lucretia. 2005. reprint ed. pap. 24.95 *(978-1-4179-3265-8(1))* Kessinger Publishing, LLC.

Brett, Jan. The Mother's Day Mice. Bunting, Eve. 2017. (Holiday Classics Ser.). (ENG.). 40p. (J). (gr. -1-3). 8.99 *(978-0-544-88033-7(1),* 1651181, HMH Books For Young Readers) Houghton Mifflin Harcourt Publishing Co.

—Noelle of the Nutcracker. Jane, Pamela. 2003. (ENG.). 64p. (J). (gr. 5-7). pap. 8.95 *(978-0-618-36922-5(8),* 488685) Houghton Mifflin Harcourt Publishing Co.

—Scary, Scary Halloween Gift Edition. Bunting, Eve. 2017. (ENG.). 40p. (J). (gr. -1-3). 8.99 *(978-0-544-88034-4(X),* 1651183, HMH Books For Young Readers) Houghton Mifflin Harcourt Publishing Co.

—The Secret Clocks: Time Senses of Living Things. Simon, Seymour. 2012. (Dover Children's Science Bks.). (ENG.). 80p. (J). (gr. 3-5). pap. 5.99 *(978-0-486-48866-0(7),* 488667) Dover Pubns., Inc.

Brett, Jan. The Animals' Santa. Brett, Jan. 2014. 40p. (J). (gr. -1-k). 17.99 *(978-0-399-25784-1(5),* G.P. Putnam's Sons Books for Young Readers) Penguin Young Readers Group.

—Annie & the Wild Animals. Brett, Jan. 2012. 32p. (J). (gr. -1-k). 17.99 *(978-0-399-16104-9(X),* G.P. Putnam's Sons Books for Young Readers) Penguin Young Readers Group.

—Armadillo Rodeo. Brett, Jan. 2004. 32p. (J). (gr. -1-3). pap. 8.99 *(978-0-14-240125-5(0),* Puffin Books) Penguin Young Readers Group.

—Beauty & the Beast. Brett, Jan. 2011. (ENG.). 32p. (J). (gr. k-3). 17.99 *(978-0-399-25731-5(4),* G.P. Putnam's Sons Books for Young Readers) Penguin Young Readers Group.

—Cinders: A Chicken Cinderella. Brett, Jan. 2013. (ENG.). 32p. (J). (gr. k). 18.99 *(978-0-399-25783-4(7),* G.P. Putnam's Sons Books for Young Readers) Penguin Publishing Group.

—Daisy Comes Home. Brett, Jan. 2005. 32p. (J). (gr. k-3). reprint ed. pap. 7.99 *(978-0-14-240270-2(2),* Puffin Books) Penguin Young Readers Group.

—The Easter Egg. Brett, Jan. 32p. (J). 2017. (-k). bds. 9.99 *(978-0-399-54733-1(9));* 2010. (ENG.). (gr. -1-k). 18.99 *(978-0-399-25238-9(X))* Penguin Young Readers Group. (G.P. Putnam's Sons Books for Young Readers).

—The First Dog. Brett, Jan. 2015. (ENG.). 32p. (J). (gr. -1-k). 17.99 *(978-0-399-17270-0(X),* G.P. Putnam's Sons Books for Young Readers) Penguin Young Readers Group.

—Fritz & the Beautiful Horses. Brett, Jan. 2016. 32p. (J). (-k). 17.99 *(978-0-399-17458-2(3),* G.P. Putnam's Sons Books for Young Readers) Penguin Young Readers Group.

—Gingerbread Baby. Brett, Jan. 2003. 32p. (J). (gr. -1 — 1). bds. 7.99 *(978-0-399-24166-6(3),* G.P. Putnam's Sons Books for Young Readers) Penguin Young Readers Group.

—Gingerbread Christmas. Brett, Jan. 32p. (J). (-k). 2019. bds. 8.99 *(978-1-9848-1246-9(7));* 2016. (ENG.). 18.99 *(978-0-399-17071-3(5))* Penguin Young Readers Group. (G.P. Putnam's Sons Books for Young Readers).

—Gingerbread Friends. Brett, Jan. 32p. (J). 2017. (-k). bds. 8.99 *(978-1-5247-3942-3(1));* 2008. (gr. -1-k). 18.99 *(978-0-399-25161-0(8))* Penguin Young Readers Group. (G.P. Putnam's Sons Books for Young Readers).

—Hedgie Blasts Off! Brett, Jan. 2006. 32p. (J). (gr. -1-3). 17.99 *(978-0-399-24621-0(5),* G.P. Putnam's Sons Books for Young Readers) Penguin Young Readers Group.

—Home for Christmas. Brett, Jan. 2011. 32p. (J). (gr. -1-k). 18.99 *(978-0-399-25653-0(9),* G.P. Putnam's Sons Books for Young Readers) Penguin Young Readers Group.

—Honey... Honey... Lion! Brett, Jan. (J). (gr. -1-3). 2014. (ENG.). 40p. 7.99 *(978-0-14-751352-6(9),* Puffin Books); 2005. 32p. 18.99 *(978-0-399-24463-6(8),* G.P. Putnam's Sons Books for Young Readers) Penguin Young Readers Group.

—Jan Brett's Animal Treasury. Brett, Jan. 2017. 144p. (J). (gr. -1-3). 29.99 *(978-1-5247-3802-0(6),* G.P. Putnam's Sons Books for Young Readers) Penguin Young Readers Group.

—Jan Brett's Christmas Treasury. Brett, Jan. 2018. (ENG.). 256p. (J). (gr. -1-3). 40.00 *(978-0-525-51718-4(9),* G.P. Putnam's Sons Books for Young Readers) Penguin Young Readers Group.

—Little Library, 3 vols. Brett, Jan. 2003. 36p. (J). (gr. -1 — 1). bds. 23.99 *(978-0-399-24183-3(3),* G.P. Putnam's Sons Books for Young Readers) Penguin Young Readers Group.

—The Mermaid. Brett, Jan. 2017. 32p. (J). (gr. -1-3). 18.99 *(978-0-399-17072-0(3),* G.P. Putnam's Sons Books for Young Readers) Penguin Young Readers Group.

—El Mitón. Brett, Jan. 2017.Tr. of Mitten. 32p. (J). (gr. -1-3). pap. 9.99 *(978-0-425-29170-2(7),* Puffin Books) Penguin Young Readers Group.

—The Mitten. Brett, Jan. 20th anniv. ed. 2009. (ENG.). 32p. (J). (gr. -1-k). 18.99 *(978-0-399-25296-9(7),* G.P. Putnam's Sons Books for Young Readers) Penguin Young Readers Group.

—The Mitten: Oversized Board Book. Brett, Jan. 2014. (ENG.). 32p. (J). (gr. -1 — 1). bds. 14.99 *(978-0-399-16981-6(4),* G.P. Putnam's Sons Books for Young Readers) Penguin Young Readers Group.

—Mossy. Brett, Jan. 2012. 32p. (J). (gr. -1-k). 18.99 *(978-0-399-25782-7(9),* G.P. Putnam's Sons Books for Young Readers) Penguin Young Readers Group.

—The Night Before Christmas: Book & DVD. Brett, Jan. Moore, Clement Clarke. 2011. (ENG.). 32p. (J). (gr. -1-k). 20.00 *(978-0-399-25670-7(9),* G.P. Putnam's Sons Books for Young Readers) Penguin Young Readers Group.

—On Noah's Ark. Brett, Jan. 32p. (J). (gr. -1 — 1). 2009. bds. 7.99 *(978-0-399-25220-4(7));* 2003. 18.99 *(978-0-399-24028-7(4))* Penguin Young Readers Group. (G.P. Putnam's Sons Books for Young Readers).

—The Snowy Nap. Brett, Jan. 2018. (ENG.). 32p. (J). (gr. -1-3). 18.99 *(978-0-399-17073-7(1),* G.P. Putnam's Sons Books for Young Readers) Penguin Young Readers Group.

—The Tale of the Tiger Slippers. Brett, Jan. 2019. (ENG.). 32p. (J). (gr. -1-3). 18.99 *(978-0-399-17074-4(X),* G.P. Putnam's Sons Books for Young Readers) Penguin Young Readers Group.

—The Three Snow Bears. Brett, Jan. (J). (gr. -1 — 1). 2013. 32p. bds. 14.99 *(978-0-399-16326-5(3));* 2012. (ENG.). 34p. bds. 8.99 *(978-0-399-26009-4(9));* 2007. 40p. 18.99 *(978-0-399-24792-7(0))* Penguin Young Readers Group. (G.P. Putnam's Sons Books for Young Readers).

—Town Mouse, Country Mouse. Brett, Jan. 2003. 32p. (J). (gr. -1-3). pap. 7.99 *(978-0-698-11986-4(X),* Puffin Books) Penguin Young Readers Group.

—The Turnip. Brett, Jan. 2015. (ENG.). 32p. (J). (-k). 18.99 *(978-0-399-17070-6(7),* G.P. Putnam's Sons Books for Young Readers) Penguin Young Readers Group.

—The Twelve Days of Christmas. Brett, Jan. (J). 2019. 30p. (— 1). bds. 14.99 *(978-1-9848-1657-3(8));* 2004. (ENG.). 32p. (gr. -1 — 1). bds. 7.99 *(978-0-399-24329-5(1))* Penguin Young Readers Group. (G.P. Putnam's Sons Books for Young Readers).

—The Umbrella. Brett, Jan. (J). (gr. -1 — 1). 2011. 36p. bds. 7.99 *(978-0-399-25540-3(0));* 2004. 32p. 18.99 *(978-0-399-24215-1(5))* Penguin Young Readers Group. (G.P. Putnam's Sons Books for Young Readers).

—The Wild Christmas Reindeer. Brett, Jan. 2018. (ENG.). 32p. (J). (-k). bds. 8.99 *(978-0-525-51579-1(8),* G.P. Putnam's Sons Books for Young Readers) Penguin Young Readers Group.

—The 3 Little Dassies. Brett, Jan. 2010. (ENG.). 32p. (J). (gr. -1-k). 18.99 *(978-0-399-25499-4(4),* G.P. Putnam's Sons Books for Young Readers) Penguin Young Readers Group.

Brett, Jeannie. Decorated Horses. Patent, Dorothy Hinshaw. 2015. 48p. (J). (gr. 3-7). 17.95 *(978-1-58089-362-6(7))* Charlesbridge Publishing, Inc.

—Fishing for Numbers: A Maine Number Book. Reynolds, Cynthia Furlong. 2005. (America by the Numbers Ser.). (ENG.). 40p. (J). (gr. 1-3). 19.99 *(978-1-58536-035-2(X),* 201953) Sleeping Bear Pr.

—Little Massachusetts. Hale, Kate. 2016. (Little State Ser.). (ENG.). 20p. (J). (gr. -1-k). 9.95 *(978-1-58536-949-2(7),* 204035) Sleeping Bear Pr.

—Little New Jersey. Noble, Trinka Hakes. 2012. (My Little State Ser.). (ENG.). 20p. (J). bds. 9.95 *(978-1-58536-786-3(9))* Sleeping Bear Pr.

—Little New York. Wilbur, Helen. 2010. (My Little State Ser.). (ENG.). 22p. (J). 9.95 *(978-1-58536-491-6(6))* Sleeping Bear Pr.

—Little North Carolina. Crane, Carol. 2011. (My Little State Ser.). (ENG.). 20p. 9.95 *(978-1-58536-545-6(9))* Sleeping Bear Pr.

—Little Pennsylvania Board Book. Noble, Trinka Hakes. 2010. (My Little State Ser.). (ENG.). 22p. (J). 9.95 *(978-1-58536-506-7(8))* Sleeping Bear Pr.

—My Cat, Coon Cat, 1 vol. Fuller, Sandy Ferguson. (ENG.). (J). 2017. 32p. pap. 12.95 *(978-1-944762-13-1(2),* b2906ff5-ebae-49b4-b6c3-8331c1153946); 2011. 36p. 17.95 *(978-1-934031-32-2(1),* 10d80457-0774-47e5-868a-a3327e46f398) Islandport Pr., Inc.

—One If by Land: A Massachusetts Number Book. Stemple, Heidi E. Y. 2006. (Count Your Way Across the U. S. A. Ser.). (ENG.). 40p. (J). 17.95 *(978-1-58536-186-1(0))* Sleeping Bear Pr.

Brett, Jeannie. Little Maine. Brett, Jeannie. 2010. (My Little State Ser.). (ENG.). 22p. (J). 9.95 *(978-1-58536-497-8(5))* Sleeping Bear Pr.

—Wild about Bears. Brett, Jeannie. 2014. 240p. (J). (gr. 1-4). pap. 7.95 *(978-1-58089-419-7(4))* Charlesbridge Publishing, Inc.

Brett, Tyler & Romano, Tony. False Creek. 2010. (ENG.). 22p. bds. 9.95 *(978-1-897476-66-6(3))* Simply Read Bks. CAN. Dist: Ingram Publisher Services.

Breuer, Paul. The Coaster Cats Go to the Amusement Park. Jack Stanley. 2006. 19p. (J). pap. 5.99 *(978-0-9776284-0-7(X))* Forbes Literary Ltd. Inc.

Brevannes, Maurice. Lafayette: French-American Hero. Bishop, Claire Huchet. 2011. 82p. 37.95 *(978-1-258-03539-6(1))* Literary Licensing, LLC.

—Red Falcons of Tremoine. Peart, Hendry. 2007. (ENG.). 256p. (J). (gr. 4-6). pap. 13.95 *(978-1-932350-15-9(2))* Ignatius Pr.

Brever, Amy. I'm So Angry. Mosby, Pamela. 2013. 28p. pap. 7.99 *(978-0-9886272-4-6(8))* Brothers N Publishing Corp.

Brewer, Dean, jt. illus. see Brewer, Sarah.

Brewer, Jenny. Happy Birthday, Tulip & Violet! McKay, Antoinetta. 2018. (ENG.). 32p. (J). pap. 15.00 *(978-1-7321045-0-1(6))* I Follow the Leader, LLC.

Brewer, Kathaleen. A Researcher or a Sleuth. Cruzan, Patricia. 2019. (ENG.). 176p. (J). pap. 17.00 *(978-0-9975839-2-2(4))* Clear Creek Pubs.

—The Wonder in the Woods. Cruzan, Patricia. 2013. 250p. pap. 15.00 *(978-0-9653543-7-0(7))* Clear Creek Pubs.

Brewer, Norma P. We Go to Mass. Hyland, Maura. 2017. (ENG.). 40p. (J). pap. 8.00 *(978-1-84730-780-4(9))* Veritas Pubns. IRL. Dist: Casemate Pubs. & Bk. Distributors, LLC.

Brewer, Paul. How to Trick or Treat in Outer Space. Krull, Kathleen. 2004. (ENG.). 32p. (J). (gr. k-3). tchr. ed. 16.95 *(978-0-8234-1844-2(8))* Holiday Hse., Inc.

—Robert & the Attack of the Giant Tarantula. Seuling, Barbara. 2003. (Oh No, It's Robert Ser.). (ENG.). 64p. (J). pap. 3.99 *(978-0-439-23545-7(6),* Scholastic Paperbacks) Scholastic, Inc.

—Robert & the Great Escape. Seuling, Barbara. 2003. (Robert Bks.). (ENG.). 120p. (J). 15.95 *(978-0-8126-2700-8(8))* Cricket Bks.

—Robert & the Happy Endings. Seuling, Barbara. 2007. (Robert Bks.). (ENG.). 160p. (J). (gr. 1-4). 16.95 *(978-0-8126-2748-0(2))* Cricket Bks.

—Robert & the Lemming Problem. Seuling, Barbara. 2003. (Robert Bks.). (ENG.). 120p. (J). 15.95 *(978-0-8126-2686-5(9))* Cricket Bks.

—Robert & the Practical Jokes. Seuling, Barbara. 2006. (Robert Bks.). (ENG.). 150p. (J). (gr. k-4). 16.95 *(978-0-8126-2741-1(5))* Cricket Bks.

—Robert Goes to Camp. Seuling, Barbara. 2007. (Robert Bks.). (ENG.). 160p. (J). (gr. k-4). 16.95 *(978-0-8126-2753-4(9))* Cricket Bks.

—Robert Takes a Stand. Seuling, Barbara. 2004. (Robert Bks.). (ENG.). 120p. (J). 15.95 *(978-0-8126-2712-1(1))* Cricket Bks.

—You Must Be Joking, Two! Even Cooler Jokes, Plus 11 1/2 Tips for Laughing Yourself into Your Own Stand-Up Comedy Routine. 2007. (ENG.). 128p. (J). (gr. k-5). 17.95 *(978-0-8126-2752-7(0))* Cricket Bks.

Brewer, Sarah & Brewer, Dean. Our New Garden. Brewer, Sarah. 2013. 20p. pap. 24.95 *(978-1-63004-768-9(6))* America Star Bks.

Brewer, Terry. The Monster Stick & Other Appalachian Tall Tales. Lepp, Paul & Lepp, Bil. 2006. (ENG.). 160p. (gr. 10-18). pap. 9.95 *(978-0-87483-577-9(1))* August Hse. Pubs., Inc.

Brewer, Trish, jt. illus. see Milner, Fran.

Brewis, Megan. Henry & Boo. Brewis, Megan. 2017. (Child's Play Library). 32p. (J). *(978-1-84643-999-5(X));* pap. *(978-1-84643-998-8(1))* Child's Play International Ltd.

Brewster, Jane. Sarah Boone: A Lowcountry Girl, 1 vol. Adams, Michelle. 2009. (ENG.). 152p. (J). (gr. 3-6). 15.95 *(978-1-58980-657-3(3),* Pelican Publishing) Arcadia Publishing.

Brewster, Sam. Book of Bones: 10 Record-Breaking Animals. Balkan, Gabrielle. 2017. (ENG.). 48p. (gr. -1-4). 19.95 *(978-0-7148-7512-5(0))* Phaidon Pr., Inc.

—Walk This Underground World. Baker, Kate. 2019. (ENG.). 24p. (J). (gr. k-3). 19.99 *(978-1-5362-0856-6(6),* Big Picture Press) Candlewick Pr.

—Walk This Wild World. Baker, Kate. 2018. (ENG.). 24p. (J). (gr. k-3). 19.99 *(978-0-7636-9899-7(7),* Big Picture Press) Candlewick Pr.

Breyfogle, Norm. Goodbye Forever. Morgan, Melanie J. 2011. (Archie New Look Ser.). (ENG.). 112p. (J). (gr. 5). pap. 10.95 *(978-1-879794-63-4(2))* Archie Comic Pubns., Inc.

Brezzi, Sara. The Farm. 2020. (World Around Me Ser.). (ENG.). 16p. (J). (— 1). bds. 7.95 ***(978-88-544-1695-6(9))*** White Star ITA. Dist: Sterling Publishing Co., Inc.

Brezzi, Sara. Nita's First Signs. MacMillan, Kathy. 2018. (Little Hands Signing Ser.: 1). (ENG.). 12p. (J). bds. 14.99 *(978-1-945547-67-6(7),* 554767) Familius LLC.

Brezzi, Sara. The Sea. 2020. (World Around Me Ser.). (ENG.). 16p. (J). (— 1). bds. 7.95 ***(978-88-544-1696-3(7))*** White Star ITA. Dist: Sterling Publishing Co., Inc.

—Toys. 2020. (World Around Me Ser.). (ENG.). 16p. (J). (— 1). bds. 7.95 ***(978-88-544-1697-0(5))*** White Star ITA. Dist: Sterling Publishing Co., Inc.

—Vehicles. 2020. (World Around Me Ser.). (ENG.). 16p. (J). (— 1). bds. 7.95 ***(978-88-544-1698-7(3))*** White Star ITA. Dist: Sterling Publishing Co., Inc.

Brian, Harrold. Ingrown Tyrone. Thompson, Tolya L. 2004. (Smarties Ser.: 4). 33p. (J). 16.00 *(978-0-9708296-2-7(0))* Savor Publishing Hse., Inc.

Briant, Ed. Petal & Poppy. Clough, Lisa. 2014. (Green Light Readers Level 2 Ser.). (ENG.). 32p. (J). (gr. -1-3). pap. 4.99 *(978-0-544-11380-0(2),* 1541816, HMH Books For Young Readers) Houghton Mifflin Harcourt Publishing Co.

—Petal & Poppy & the Penguin. Clough, Lisa. 2014. (Green Light Readers Level 2 Ser.). (ENG.). 32p. (J). (gr. -1-3). pap. 3.99 *(978-0-544-13330-3(7),* 1544663, HMH Books For Young Readers) Houghton Mifflin Harcourt Publishing Co.

—Petal & Poppy & the Spooky Halloween! Clough, Lisa. 2014. (Green Light Readers Level 2 Ser.). (ENG.). 32p. (J). (gr. -1-3). 12.99 *(978-0-544-33602-5(X),* 1584098, HMH Books For Young Readers) Houghton Mifflin Harcourt Publishing Co.

Briant, Ed. A Day at the Beach, No. 1. Briant, Ed. 2006. 32p. (J). (gr. -1). 17.89 *(978-0-06-079982-3(X))* HarperCollins Pubs.

—Petal & Poppy & the Mystery Valentine. Briant, Ed. Jahn-Clough, Lisa & Clough, Lisa. 2015. (Green Light Readers Level 2 Ser.). (ENG.). 32p. (J). (gr. 1-4). pap. 4.99 *(978-0-544-55549-5(X),* 1610456, HMH Books For Young Readers) Houghton Mifflin Harcourt Publishing Co.

Brickell, Shanna. Keller's Heart. Gray, John. 2019. (ENG.). 40p. (J). (gr. -1). 12.99 *(978-1-64060-174-1(0))* Paraclete Pr., Inc.

Bricking, Jennifer. An Egg-Stra Special Easter. Rusu, Meredith. 2018. (Beanie Boos Ser.). (ENG.). 24p. (J). (gr. -1-k). pap. 4.99 *(978-1-338-30756-6(8))* Scholastic, Inc.

—Molly's Pilgrim. Cohen, Barbara. 2018. (ENG.). 48p. (J). (gr. 1-5). pap. 4.99 *(978-0-06-287094-0(7))* HarperCollins Pubs.

—Ten Magic Butterflies. McKellar, Danica. (J). 2019. 38p. (— 1). bds. 8.99 *(978-1-101-93385-5(2));* 2018. (ENG.). 40p. (gr. -1-1). 17.99 *(978-1-101-93382-4(8));* 2018. (ENG.). 40p. (gr. -1-1). lib. bdg. 20.99 *(978-1-101-93383-1(6))* Random Hse. Children's Bks. (Crown Books For Young Readers).

—Unicorn Treasure Hunt. Rusu, Meredith. 2019. (Beanie Boos Ser.). (ENG.). 24p. (J). (gr. -1-3). pap. 4.99 *(978-1-338-34458-5(7))* Scholastic, Inc.

Brickman, Robin. Leaflets Three, Let It Be! The Story of Poison Ivy. Sanchez, Anita. 2015. (ENG.). 32p. (J). (gr. -1-3). 16.95 *(978-1-62091-445-8(X))* Boyds Mills Pr.

—A Log's Life. Pfeffer, Wendy. 2007. (ENG.). 32p. (J). (gr. -1-3). 7.99 *(978-1-4169-3483-7(9),* Aladdin) Simon & Schuster Children's Publishing.

—One Night in the Coral Sea. Collard, Sneed B., III. 2006. 32p. (J). (gr. 1-4). pap. 7.95 *(978-1-57091-390-7(0))* Charlesbridge Publishing, Inc.

—One Night in the Coral Sea. Collard, Sneed B., III. 2006. 32p. (gr. 3-7). 17.95 *(978-0-7569-6969-1(7))* Perfection Learning Corp.

Brickner, Marian. I'm Lucy: A Day in the Life of a Young Bonobo. Levine, Mathea. 2008. 32p. (gr. -1-3). 19.95 *(978-0-615-18110-3(4))* Blue Bark Pr.

Bridge, Sam. Roll On. Tate, Connie. 2017. (ENG.). (J). pap. 9.56 *(978-0-9847982-8-5(5))* Lucky Jenny Publishing.

—Scooter Boy. Tate, Connie. 2018. (ENG.). 32p. (J). pap. 11.25 *(978-1-7323301-0-8(7))* Lucky Jenny Publishing.

—Sylvester's Cat-Astrophic Tale. Tate, Connie. 2018. (ENG.). 60p. (J). (gr. 2-6). 17.50 *(978-1-7323301-9-1(0))* Lucky Jenny Publishing.

—Sylvester's CAT-Astropic Tale. Tate, Connie. 2019. (ENG.). 60p. (J). (gr. 2-6). pap. 19.95 *(978-1-7323301-7-7(4))* Lucky Jenny Publishing.

Bridgeman, Kristi. A Carnival of Cats, 1 vol. Ghigna, Charles. 2015. (ENG.). 26p. (J). (gr. -1 — 1). bds. 9.95 *(978-1-4598-0686-3(7))* Orca Bk. Pubs. USA.

—The Knot Fairy. Hinman, Bobbie. ed. 2010. (ENG.). 32p. (J). (gr. -1-1). 16.95 *(978-0-9786791-0-1(5))* Best Fairy Bks.

—A Parade of Puppies, 1 vol. Ghigna, Charles. 2016. (ENG.). 26p. (J). (gr. -1 — 1). bds. 9.95 *(978-1-4598-0963-5(7))* Orca Bk. Pubs. USA.

—The Sock Fairy. Hinman, Bobbie. 2008. (ENG.). 32p. (J). (gr. -1-1). 16.95 *(978-0-9786791-1-8(3))* Best Fairy Bks.

Bridgen, Rachel Annie. Serious Sas & Messy Magda. Pierres, Marianne De. 2013. 32p. pap. *(978-1-909423-04-6(1))* Bks. to Treasure.

B

Bridges, Jeanne Rorex. Crossing Bok Chitto: A Choctaw Tale of Friendship & Freedom. Tingle, Tim. (ENG.). 40p. (J). 2008. (gr. 2-7). pap. 8.95 *(978-1-933693-20-0(7));* 2006. (gr. 1-8). 17.95 *(978-0-938317-77-7(6))* Cinco Puntos Pr.

Bridges, John, et al. D6 Adventure. Vrtis, Nikola, ed. 2004. (ENG.). 144p. 19.99 *(978-1-932867-00-8(7),* weg 51011, West End Games) Purgatory Publishing, Inc.

Bridges, Moire. Hermanita y el Rey: Una Parabola. Bridges, Moire. 2007. 28p. (J). (gr. -1-3). 13.99 *(978-1-59879-427-4(2))* Lifevest Publishing, Inc.

—Sissy & the King: A Parable. Bridges, Moire. 2007. (J). (gr. -1-3). 26p. 13.99 *(978-1-59879-425-0(6));* 32p. 19.99 *(978-1-59879-403-8(5))* Lifevest Publishing, Inc.

Bridgman, L. J. The Young Puritans in King Philip's War. Smith, Mary P. Wells. 2011. 396p. 54.95 *(978-1-258-05550-9(3))* Literary Licensing, LLC.

Bridgman, L. T. Finger Plays for Nursery & Kindergarten. Poulsson, Emilie. 70th ed. 2011. (Dover Children's Activity Bks.). (ENG.). 80p. (J). (gr. 4-7). reprint ed. pap. 8.95 *(978-0-486-22588-3(7))* Dover Pubns., Inc.

Bridwell, Norman. Clifford Takes a Swim. 2016. (J). *(978-1-338-08716-1(9))* Scholastic, Inc.

Bridwell, Norman. Clifford at the Circus. Bridwell, Norman. 2010. (Clifford 8x8 Ser.). (ENG.). 32p. (J). (gr. -1-3). pap. 3.99 *(978-0-545-21584-8(6),* Cartwheel Bks.) Scholastic, Inc.

—Clifford Collection. Bridwell, Norman. 2012. (ENG.). 192p. (J). (gr. -1-k). 12.99 *(978-0-545-45013-3(6))* Scholastic, Inc.

—Clifford Goes to Kindergarten. Bridwell, Norman. 2015. (Clifford Ser.). (ENG.). 32p. (J). (gr. -1-k). pap. 3.99 *(978-0-545-82335-7(8))* Scholastic, Inc.

—Clifford Makes the Team. Bridwell, Norman. 2011. (Scholastic Reader Level 1 Ser.). (ENG.). 32p. (J). (gr. -1-2). pap. 3.99 *(978-0-545-23141-1(8))* Scholastic, Inc.

—Clifford Takes a Trip. Bridwell, Norman. 2011. (Clifford Ser.). (ENG.). 32p. (J). (gr. -1-k). pap. 3.99 *(978-0-545-21591-6(9),* Cartwheel Bks.) Scholastic, Inc.

—Clifford the Big Red Dog. Bridwell, Norman. (Clifford Ser.). (ENG.). 32p. (J). (gr. -1-k). 2018. 16.99 *(978-1-338-30473-2(9));* 2010. pap. 3.99 *(978-0-545-21578-7(1),* Cartwheel Bks.) Scholastic, Inc.

—Clifford the Big Red Dog. Bridwell, Norman. Scholastic, Inc. Staff. unabr. ed. 2006. (Clifford Ser.). (ENG.). (J). (gr. -1-3). audio compact disk 10.99 *(978-0-439-87587-5(0))* Scholastic, Inc.

—Clifford the Big Red Dog: Color Facsimile of 1963 First Edition. Bridwell, Norman. 2019. (ENG.). 46p. (J). (gr. -1-k). pap. 3.95 *(978-1-68422-347-3(4))* Martino Fine Bks.

—Clifford the Firehouse Dog. Bridwell, Norman. 2010. (Clifford Ser.).Tr. of Clifford the Firehouse Dog. (ENG.). 32p. (J). (gr. -1-3). pap. 3.99 *(978-0-545-21580-0(3),* Cartwheel Bks.) Scholastic, Inc.

—Clifford Va a Kindergarten. Bridwell, Norman. 2017. (Clifford Ser.). (SPA.). 32p. (J). (gr. -1-1). 3.99 *(978-1-338-04504-8(0),* Scholastic en Espanol) Scholastic, Inc.

—Clifford Visits the Zoo. Bridwell, Norman. 2014. (ENG.). 40p. (J). (— 1). 12.99 *(978-0-545-66896-5(4))* Scholastic, Inc.

—Clifford y la Hora de Dormir. Bridwell, Norman. ed. 2003. (Clifford Ser.).Tr. of Clifford's Bedtime. (SPA & ENG.). 7p. (J). (gr. -1 — 1). bds. 4.99 *(978-0-439-54568-6(4),* Scholastic en Espanol) Scholastic, Inc.

—Clifford y la Hora del Bano. Bridwell, Norman. ed. 2003. (Clifford Ser.).Tr. of Clifford's Bathtime. (SPA & ENG.). 16p. (J). (gr. -1 — 1). bds. 4.99 *(978-0-439-54567-9(6),* Scholastic en Espanol) Scholastic, Inc.

—Clifford's Bedtime Story. Bridwell, Norman. 2013. (Clifford Ser.). (ENG.). 20p. (J). (gr. -1-k). bds. 8.99 *(978-0-545-49577-6(6))* Scholastic, Inc.

—Clifford's Bedtime Story Box. Bridwell, Norman. 2013. (Clifford Ser.). (ENG.). 32p. (J). (gr. -1-k). 10.99 *(978-0-545-61521-1(6))* Scholastic, Inc.

—Clifford's Birthday Party. Bridwell, Norman. 50th anniv. ed. 2013. (Clifford Ser.). (ENG.). 32p. (J). (gr. -1-3). pap. 4.99 *(978-0-545-47956-1(8))* Scholastic, Inc.

—Clifford's Christmas. Bridwell, Norman. 2011. (Clifford Ser.). (ENG.). 32p. (J). (gr. -1-k). pap. 3.99 *(978-0-545-21596-1(X),* Cartwheel Bks.) Scholastic, Inc.

—Clifford's Day with Dad. Bridwell, Norman. 2011. (Clifford Ser.). (ENG.). 32p. (J). (gr. -1-k). pap. 3.99 *(978-0-545-21593-0(5),* Cartwheel Bks.) Scholastic, Inc.

—Clifford's Family. Bridwell, Norman. 2010. (Clifford Ser.). (ENG.). 32p. (J). (gr. -1-2). pap. 3.99 *(978-0-545-21585-5(4),* Cartwheel Bks.) Scholastic, Inc.

—Clifford's First Christmas. Bridwell, Norman. 2010. (Clifford Ser.). (ENG.). 20p. (J). (gr. -1 — 1). bds. 6.99 *(978-0-545-21773-6(3)*, Cartwheel Bks.) Scholastic, Inc.
—Clifford's First Easter. Bridwell, Norman. 2010. (Clifford Ser.). (ENG.). 14p. (J). (gr. -1 — 1). bds. 6.99 *(978-0-545-20010-3(5)*, Cartwheel Bks.) Scholastic, Inc.
—Clifford's First Halloween. Bridwell, Norman. 2010. (Clifford Ser.). (ENG.). 20p. (J). (gr. k — 1). bds. 6.99 *(978-0-545-21774-3(1)*, Cartwheel Bks.) Scholastic, Inc.
—Clifford's Good Deeds. Bridwell, Norman. (Clifford Ser.). (ENG.). (J). (gr. -1-3). 2010. 32p. pap. 4.99 *(978-0-545-21579-4(X)*, Cartwheel Bks.); 2007. audio compact disk 9.99 *(978-0-545-01483-0(2))* Scholastic, Inc.
—Clifford's Halloween. Bridwell, Norman. 2011. (Clifford Ser.). (ENG.). 32p. (J). (gr. -1-k). pap. 3.99 *(978-0-545-21595-4(1)*, Cartwheel Bks.) Scholastic, Inc.
—Clifford's Happy Easter. Bridwell, Norman. 2011. (Clifford Ser.). (ENG.). 32p. (J). (gr. -1-k). pap. 3.99 *(978-0-545-21587-9(0)*, Cartwheel Bks.) Scholastic, Inc.
—Clifford's Manners. Bridwell, Norman. 2010. (Clifford Ser.). (ENG.). 32p. (J). (gr. -1-2). pap. 3.99 *(978-0-545-21586-2(2)*, Cartwheel Bks.) Scholastic, Inc.
—La Colección. Bridwell, Norman. 2012. (Clifford Ser.). (SPA.). 192p. (J). (gr. -1-k). 12.99 *(978-0-545-45692-0(4)*, Scholastic en Espanol) Scholastic, Inc.
—Halloween. Bridwell, Norman. 2017. (Clifford Ser.). (ENG.). 48p. (J). (gr. -1-k). 8.99 *(978-1-338-18831-8(3))* Scholastic, Inc.
—La Primera Navidad. Bridwell, Norman. 2010. (Clifford Ser.). (SPA.). 20p. (J). (gr. -1 — 1). bds. 6.99 *(978-0-545-23847-2(1)*, Scholastic en Espanol) Scholastic, Inc.
Brieger, Ms. Kirsten. Jacob's Journey, Living with Type 1 Diabetes. Kleiman, Deanna. 2012. 28p. pap. 9.95 *(978-0-615-60112-0(X))* TwinsBooks.
Briel, Elizabeth. H Is for Hong Kong: A Primer in Pictures. Morrissey, Tricia. 2009. (Alphabetical World Ser.). (ENG.). 36p. (J). (gr. k-4). 12.95 *(978-1-934159-13-2(1))* ThingsAsian Pr.
Brien, Audrey. Vehicles. Clever Publishing. 2019. (My First Words Ser.). (ENG.). 192p. (J). (gr. -1 — 1). pap. 7.99 *(978-1-948418-65-2(7))* Clever Media Group.
—45 Games... School Days. Auzou Publishing Staff, ed. 2018. 52p. (J). 6.99 *(978-2-7338-5621-5(9))* Auzou, Philippe Editions FRA. Dist: Consortium Bk. Sales & Distribution.
Briere, Charity. Garden Bugs of Alberta: Gardening to Attract, Repel & Control, 1 vol. Macaulay, Doug et al. rev. ed. 2008. (ENG.). 224p. pap. 21.95 *(978-1-55105-586-2(4)*, 98a26786-da07-4767-9d8e-60e27a38fcff) Lone Pine Publishing USA.
Brierley, Louise. When the World Was Young: Creation & Pourquoi Tales. Mayo, Margaret. 2017. (ENG.). 80p. (J). (gr. 2-5). 33.99 *(978-1-5344-2236-0(6)*, Simon & Schuster Bks. For Young Readers) Simon & Schuster Bks. For Young Readers.
Briggs, Alice. Bo Goes to Hawaii. Simmons, Lisa. 2017. (ENG.). 30p. (J). 18.99 *(978-0-9996717-3-3(1))* Simbosa Publishing.
Briggs, Alice a. Sadie Sees Paris. Simmons, Lisa. 2017. (Sadie Sees... Ser.: Vol. 1). (ENG.). 24p. (J). 18.99 *(978-0-9996717-1-9(5))* Simbosa Publishing.
Briggs, Antony. Complicated Dragons - Adult Coloring Book: Black Line Edition. Coloring, Complicated. 2016. (ENG.). 54p. (J). pap. *(978-1-911302-25-4(6))* Complicated Coloring.
Briggs, Antony. Mermaid Cursive Handwriting Workbook for Kids - Lowercase Words & Letters: Joined-Up Handwriting Practice. with Jokes, Practice Sheets, Coloring Pages & More. Workbooks, Little Learner. 2019. (Little Learner Workbooks Ser.: Vol. 6). (ENG.). 120p. (J). pap. 7.99 ***(978-1-7017-9401-6(2))*** Independently Published.
Briggs, Charlotte. Sarah's Happy Harvest Time, 1 vol. Bush, Leanne. 2009. 32p. pap. 24.95 *(978-1-60813-818-0(6))* America Star Bks.
Briggs, Eleanor, photos by. The Man-Eating Tigers of Sundarbans. Montgomery, Sy. 2004. (ENG., 64p. (J). (gr. 5-7). pap. 7.99 *(978-0-618-49490-3(1)*, 491721) Houghton Mifflin Harcourt Publishing Co.
—The Man-Eating Tigers of Sundarbans. Montgomery, Sy. 2004. 57p. (J). 14.60 *(978-0-7569-5180-1(1))* Perfection Learning Corp.
Briggs-Greenberg, Ruthie. Dan the Biggest Dump Truck, Vol. Adams, Chris. 2017. (ENG.). 40p. (J). (gr. -1-2). 15.95 *(978-1-63076-056-4(0))* Muddy Boots Pr.
Briggs, Harry. Come una y Cuenta Veinte. Tang, Greg & Greg, Tang. 2003.Tr. of Grapes of Math. (SPA.). 40p. (J). (gr. 3-4). 14.99 *(978-84-241-8075-1(5))* Everest Editora ESP. Dist: Lectorum Pubns., Inc.
—The Grapes of Math. Tang, Greg. 2004. (Scholastic Bookshelf Ser.). (ENG.). 40p. (J). (gr. 2-5). pap. 7.99 *(978-0-439-59840-8(0)*, Scholastic Paperbacks) Scholastic, Inc.
—The Grapes of Math: Mind-Stretching Math Riddles. Tang, Greg. 2004. (Scholastic Bookshelf Ser.). (gr. 2-5). 17.00 *(978-0-7569-3195-7(9))* Perfection Learning Corp.
—Math for All Seasons. Tang, Greg. 2005. (Scholastic Bookshelf Ser.). (ENG.). 40p. (J). (gr. -1-3). pap. 6.99 *(978-0-439-75537-5(9)*, Scholastic Paperbacks) Scholastic, Inc.
—Math Potatoes: Mind-Stretching Brain Food. Tang, Greg. 2005. (Math Potatoes Ser.). (ENG.). 40p. (J). (gr. 2-5). 18.99 *(978-0-439-44390-6(3)*, Scholastic Pr.) Scholastic, Inc.
—Un, Dos, Tres, el Ano Se Fue. Tang, Greg & Greg, Tang. 2003.Tr. of Math for All Seasons. (SPA.). 40p. (J). (gr. 2-3). 14.99 *(978-84-241-8074-4(7))* Everest Editora ESP. Dist: Lectorum Pubns., Inc.
Briggs Johnson, Chloe. Big Dog, Little Dog, Fish. Sexton, Bethany. 2015. (ENG.). 17.95 *(978-1-59298-862-4(8))* Beaver's Pond Pr., Inc.
Briggs, Karen. The Rain Flower. Duroux, Mary. 2005. 22p. (J). pap. 13.45 *(978-0-85575-467-9(2))* Aboriginal Studies Pr. AUS. Dist: Independent Pubs. Group.
Briggs, Korwin. Baby Geek. Mazzenga, Mark. 2019. (ENG.). 20p. (J). (gr. -1 — 1). bds. 10.99 *(978-1-941367-63-6(1))* Downtown Bookworks.
—Dung for Dinner: A Stomach-Churning Look at the Animal Poop, Pee, Vomit, & Secretions That People Have Eaten (and Often Still Do!) Virnig, Christine. 2020. (ENG.). 176p. (J). 19.99 *(978-1-250-24679-0(2)*, 900214489, Holt, Henry & Co. Bks. For Young Readers) Holt, Henry & Co.
—The Invention Hunters Discover How Electricity Works. 2019. (ENG.). 48p. (J). E-Book *(978-0-316-43686-1(0))* Little Brown & Co.
Briggs, Mayke Beckmann. Here You Are. Briggs, Mayke Beckmann. 2007. 44p. (J). 16.95 *(978-0-9776469-1-3(2))* BoathouseBooks.
Briggs, Paige. Trinity: Cleric. Lee, Maria. 2019. (Trinity Ser.: Vol. 2). (ENG.). 270p. (J). pap. 12.50 *(978-1-0811-3911-7(0))* Independently Published.
—Trinity: Dragon. Lee, Maria. 2018. (ENG.). 356p. (J). pap. 13.50 *(978-1-7199-5294-1(9))* Independently Published.
Briggs, Paul. Catch My Breath: Walt Disney Animation Studios Artist Showcase. Briggs, Paul. 2017. (Walt Disney Animation Studios Artist Showcase Ser.). (ENG.). 48p. (J). (gr. 1-3). 16.99 *(978-1-4847-2837-6(8))* Hyperion Bks. for Children.
Briggs, Scott, photos by. Mighty Stallion 5 A Stallion's Heart. Kasten, Victoria. 2007. (J). per. 8.95 *(978-0-9788850-5-2(8))* Victoria Tecken.
Brigham, Anthea. Henrietta, World War II Hen: This Is a True Story. Brigham, Anthea. 2008. (ENG.). 28p. (J). 7.00 *(978-0-9740778-2-6(8))* Whale's Jaw Publishing.
Bright, Alasdair. Bears Beware. Giff, Patricia Reilly. 2012. (Zigzag Kids Ser.: 5). (ENG.). 80p. (J). (gr. 1-4). pap. 4.99 *(978-0-375-85913-7(6)*, Yearling) Random Hse. Children's Bks.
—Big Whopper. Giff, Patricia Reilly. 2010. (Zigzag Kids Ser.: 2). (ENG.). 80p. (J). (gr. 1-4). pap. 4.99 *(978-0-553-49469-3(4)*, Yearling) Random Hse. Children's Bks.
—The Big Whopper, 2. Giff, Patricia Reilly. 2010. (Zigzag Kids Ser.). (ENG.). 80p. (gr. 1-4). lib. bdg. 17.44 *(978-0-385-90926-6(8)*, Lamb, Wendy Bks.) Random Hse. Children's Bks.
—Flying Feet. Giff, Patricia Reilly. 2011. (Zigzag Kids Ser.: 3). (ENG.). 80p. (J). (gr. 1-4). 4.99 *(978-0-375-85911-3(X)*, Yearling);3. lib. bdg. 17.44 *(978-0-385-90754-5(0)*, Lamb, Wendy Bks.) Random Hse. Children's Bks.
—Number One Kid. Giff, Patricia Reilly. 2010. (Zigzag Kids Ser.: 1). (ENG.). 80p. (J). (gr. 1-4). pap. 4.99 *(978-0-553-49468-6(6)*, Yearling) Random Hse. Children's Bks.
—Star Time. Giff, Patricia Reilly. 2011. (Zigzag Kids Ser.: 4). (ENG.). 80p. (J). (gr. 1-4). 4.99 *(978-0-375-85912-0(8)*, Yearling) Random Hse. Children's Bks.
—Super Surprise. Giff, Patricia Reilly. 2012. (Zigzag Kids Ser.: 6). (ENG.). 80p. (J). (gr. 1-4). pap. 4.99 *(978-0-375-85914-4(4)*, Yearling) Random Hse. Children's Bks.
—Zigzag Zoom. Giff, Patricia Reilly. 2013. (Zigzag Kids Ser.: 8). (ENG.). 80p. (J). (gr. 1-4). pap. 4.99 *(978-0-307-97703-8(X)*, Yearling) Random Hse. Children's Bks.
Bright, Bonnie. I Want to Make Friends: A Story for Kids in Preschool & Kindergarten & a Guidance Section for Parents. Rothenberg, B. Annye. 2012. 48p. (J). pap. 9.95 *(978-0-9790420-4-1(6))* Perfecting Parenting Pr.
Bright, Bonnie. Peli Can Surf. Munoz, Eric Noel. 2019. (ENG.). 42p. (J). pap. 12.00 ***(978-1-0937-5886-3(4))*** Independently Published.
Bright, Bonnie. The Tangle Tower. Bright, Bonnie. Elin Hirschman, Jessica. 2006. 32p. (J). (gr. k-2). 14.95 *(978-0-9701155-6-0(3))* Cookie Bear Pr., Inc.
Bright, Bonnie04. I'm Getting Ready for Kindergarten. Rothenberg, B. Annye. 2012. 48p. (J). pap. 9.95 *(978-0-9790420-5-8(4))* Perfecting Parenting Pr.
Bright, Mark, et al. Avengers West Coast Epic Collection: Lost in Space-Time. 2019. (ENG.). 488p. (YA). (gr. 4-17). pap. 39.99 *(978-1-302-91971-9(7))* Marvel Worldwide, Inc.
Bright, Mark, jt. illus. see Windsor-Smith, Barry.
Bright, Michael. Crash, Bang, Boom, Zing. Bright, Belle. 2009. 12p. pap. 24.95 *(978-1-60749-383-9(7))* America Star Bks.
Bright, Phyllis. Tayance, a Young Sioux Indian. Nichele, Neika. 2008. 47p. pap. 24.95 *(978-1-60703-606-7(1))* America Star Bks.
Bright, Todd. Taste Your Words. Clark, Bonnie. 2020. 32p. (J). (gr. -1-3). 17.99 *(978-1-5460-1517-8(5)*, Worthy Kids/Ideals) Worthy Publishing.
Brightling, Geoff, jt. illus. see Anderson, Peter.
Brighton, Catherine. My Tour of Europe: By Teddy Roosevelt, Age 10. Jackson, Ellen, ed. 2003. 40p. 14.95 *(978-0-7613-1998-6(0)*, Millbrook Pr.) Lerner Publishing Group.
Brighton, Catherine. My Napoleon. Brighton, Catherine. 2005. 26p. (J). (gr. k-4). reprint ed. 17.00 *(978-0-7567-8931-2(1))* DIANE Publishing Co.
Brightwell, Charlotte. Jungle Show. Brightwell, Charlotte. 2017. (ENG.). 28p. (J). pap. *(978-0-9956006-9-0(4))* Blossom Spring Publishing.
Brightwood, Laura. The House That Talked to Itself. 2006. (J). *(978-0-9779290-3-0(5))* 3-C Institute for Social Development.
Brightwood, Laura. Anansi & the Turtle. Brightwood, Laura, . 2006. (J). *(978-0-9779290-0-9(0))* 3-C Institute for Social Development.
—Bully Goat Grim. Brightwood, Laura, . 2006. (J). *(978-0-9779290-2-3(7))* 3-C Institute for Social Development.
—Debate in Sign Language. Brightwood, Laura, . 2006. (J). *(978-0-9779290-6-1(X))* 3-C Institute for Social Development.
—The Ghost House. Brightwood, Laura, . 2006. (J). *(978-0-9779290-1-6(9))* 3-C Institute for Social Development.
—Growing up in East L. A. Brightwood, Laura, . 2006. (J). *(978-0-9779290-8-5(6))* 3-C Institute for Social Development.
—I Am A Frog. Brightwood, Laura, . 2007. (J). DVD *(978-1-934409-02-2(2))* 3-C Institute for Social Development.
—Ka-ulu the Strong. Brightwood, Laura, . 2006. (J). *(978-0-9789871-3-8(6))* 3-C Institute for Social Development.
—King Zargon Rules. Brightwood, Laura, . 2006. (J). *(978-0-9789871-0-7(1))* 3-C Institute for Social Development.
—King's New Suit. Brightwood, Laura, . 2007. (J). DVD *(978-1-934409-05-3(7))* 3-C Institute for Social Development.
—Left Out. Brightwood, Laura, . 2006. (J). *(978-0-9779290-7-8(8))* 3-C Institute for Social Development.
—Lion & Mousie. Brightwood, Laura, . 2007. (J). DVD *(978-1-934409-00-8(6))* 3-C Institute for Social Development.
—Little Freddie & His Whistle. Brightwood, Laura, . 2007. (J). DVD *(978-1-934409-01-5(4))* 3-C Institute for Social Development.
—Look What You've Done. Brightwood, Laura, . 2007. (J). DVD *(978-1-934409-03-9(0))* 3-C Institute for Social Development.
—Mousanga Bira Mousa. Brightwood, Laura, . 2006. (J). *(978-0-9789871-1-4(X))* 3-C Institute for Social Development.
—Red Hat / Blue Hat. Brightwood, Laura, . 2006. (J). *(978-0-9779290-5-4(1))* 3-C Institute for Social Development.
—Wise People of Helm. Brightwood, Laura, . 2006. (J). *(978-0-9779290-4-7(3))* 3-C Institute for Social Development.
—Wolf under the Bed. Brightwood, Laura, . 2007. (J). DVD *(978-1-934409-04-6(9))* 3-C Institute for Social Development.
—The Woodsman & His Ax. Brightwood, Laura, . 2007. (J). DVD *(978-1-934409-07-7(3))* 3-C Institute for Social Development.
Brightwood, Laura. The Banana Fairy Fuss. Brightwood, Laura. Pifer, Kimberly, ed. 2012. (J). *(978-1-934409-34-3(0))* 3-C Institute for Social Development.
—Bee Is for Bold. Brightwood, Laura. Pifer, Kimberly, ed. 2012. (J). *(978-1-934409-40-4(5))* 3-C Institute for Social Development.
—Buzz off, Bee! Brightwood, Laura. Pifer, Kimberly, ed. 2012. (J). *(978-1-934409-45-9(6))* 3-C Institute for Social Development.
—The Cheery Garden. Brightwood, Laura. Pifer, Kimberly, ed. 2012. (J). *(978-1-934409-38-1(3))* 3-C Institute for Social Development.
—Elephant's Trunk of Confidence. Brightwood, Laura. Pifer, Kimberly, ed. 2012. (J). *(978-1-934409-33-6(2))* 3-C Institute for Social Development.
—Giraffe's Shocking Surprise. Brightwood, Laura. Pifer, Kimberly, ed. 2012. (J). *(978-1-934409-30-5(8))* 3-C Institute for Social Development.
—Knot for Singing Parrot. Brightwood, Laura. Pifer, Kimberly, ed. 2012. (J). *(978-1-934409-23-7(5))* 3-C Institute for Social Development.
—LifeStories for Kids K-2: Grades K-2. Brightwood, Laura. DeRosier, Melissa. 2007. Orig. Title: Life Skills & Character Education Through Storytelling. ring bd. incl. DVD *(978-0-9789871-8-3(7))* 3-C Institute for Social Development.
—Parrot's Winter Blues. Brightwood, Laura. Pifer, Kimberly, ed. 2012. (J). *(978-1-934409-21-3(9))* 3-C Institute for Social Development.
—Poodle's Broken E. Brightwood, Laura. Pifer, Kimberly, ed. 2012. (J). *(978-1-934409-28-2(6))* 3-C Institute for Social Development.
Briglia, Anthony. Lance Dragon Defends His Castle with Simple Machines, 1 vol. Braun, Eric. 2012. (In the Science Lab Ser.). (ENG.). 24p. (J). (gr. k-3). pap. 9.95 *(978-1-4048-7708-5(8)*, Picture Window Bks.) Capstone.
Brigman, June. The Apprentice of Zoldex: The Imperium Saga: the Adventures of Kyria, 12 vols., Vol. 8. Bowyer, Clifford B. 2008. (Imperium Saga: 8). (ENG.). 208p. (J). 5.99 *(978-0-9787782-2-4(7)*, BK0023) Silver Leaf Bks., LLC.
—The Awakening: The Imperium Saga: the Adventures of Kyria, 12 vols., Vol. 2. Bowyer, Clifford B. 2004. (Imperium Saga: 2). (ENG.). 182p. (J). 5.99 *(978-0-9744354-1-1(4)*, BK0004) Silver Leaf Bks., LLC.
—The Child of Prophecy: The Imperium Saga: the Adventures of Kyria, 12 vols., Vol. 1. Bowyer, Clifford B. 2004. (Imperium Saga: 1). (ENG.). 182p. (J). 5.99 *(978-0-9744354-0-4(6)*, BK0002) Silver Leaf Bks., LLC.
—The Darkness Within: The Imperium Saga: the Adventures of Kyria, 12 vols., Vol. 9. Bowyer, Clifford B. 2009. (Imperium Saga: 9). (ENG.). (J). 5.99 *(978-0-9787782-4-8(3))* Silver Leaf Bks., LLC.
—The Mage's Council: The Imperium Saga: the Adventures of Kyria, 12 vols., Vol. 3. Bowyer, Clifford B. 2005. (Imperium Saga: 3). (ENG.). 182p. (J). 5.99 *(978-0-9744354-2-8(2)*, BK0006) Silver Leaf Bks., LLC.
—Puffin Graphics: Black Beauty. Sewell, Anna. 2005. (ENG.). 176p. (J). (gr. 3-7). 10.99 *(978-0-14-240408-9(X)*, Puffin Books) Penguin Young Readers Group.
—Quest for the Shard: The Imperium Saga: the Adventures of Kyria, 12 vols., Vol. 6. Bowyer, Clifford B. 2007. (Imperium Saga: 6). (ENG.). 166p. (J). 5.99 *(978-0-9744354-8-0(1)*, BK0020) Silver Leaf Bks., LLC.
—The Rescue of Nezbith: The Imperium Saga: the Adventures of Kyria, 12 vols., Vol. 10. Bowyer, Clifford B. 2009. (Imperium Saga: 10). (ENG.). 176p. (J). 7.99 *(978-0-9787782-5-5(1))* Silver Leaf Bks., LLC.
—The Shard of Time: The Imperium Saga: the Adventures of Kyria, 12 vols., Vol. 4. Bowyer, Clifford B. 2005. (Imperium Saga: 4). (ENG.). 182p. (J). 5.99 *(978-0-9744354-3-5(0)*, BK0007) Silver Leaf Bks., LLC.
—The Spread of Darkness: The Imperium Saga: the Adventures of Kyria, 12 vols., Vol. 7. Bowyer, Clifford B. 2007. (Imperium Saga: 7). (ENG.). 158p. (J). 5.99 *(978-0-9787782-1-7(9)*, BK0022) Silver Leaf Bks., LLC.
Brigman, June, et al. Star Wars Legends Epic Collection: the Rebellion Vol. 3. 2019. (ENG.). 488p. (YA). (gr. -1-17). pap. 39.99 *(978-1-302-91814-9(1))* Marvel Worldwide, Inc.
Brigman, June. Trapped in Time: The Imperium Saga: the Adventures of Kyria, 12 vols., Vol. 5. Bowyer, Clifford B. 2006. (Imperium Saga: 5). (ENG.). 150p. (J). 5.99 *(978-0-9744354-7-3(3)*, BK0008) Silver Leaf Bks., LLC.
Brignaud, Pierre. Baby Caillou, Bathtime. ed. 2016. (ENG.). 6p. (J). (— 1). 6.99 *(978-2-89718-225-0(3))* Caillouet, Gerry.
—Baby Caillou: Good Morning! Chouette Publishing Staff. 2013. (Baby Caillou Ser.). (ENG.). 10p. (J). (gr. -1 — 1). 9.99 *(978-2-89718-098-0(6))* Caillouet, Gerry.
—Caillou: I Love You. L'Heureux, Christine. 2012. (Hand in Hand Ser.). (ENG.). 24p. (J). (gr. -1-k). 5.95 *(978-2-89450-860-2(3))* Caillouet, Gerry.
—Caillou: I'm Not Hungry! Nadeau, Nicole. 2011. (Hand in Hand Ser.). (ENG.). 24p. (J). (gr. -1-k). 5.95 *(978-2-89450-829-9(8))* Caillouet, Gerry.
—Caillou: No More Diapers. L'Heureux, Christine. 2011. (Hand in Hand Ser.). (ENG.). 24p. (J). (gr. -1-k). 5.95 *(978-2-89450-840-4(9))* Caillouet, Gerry.
—Caillou: Sometimes Moms Get Angry. Egar, Joann. 2014. (Hand in Hand Ser.). (ENG.). 24p. (J). (gr. -1-k). 5.99 *(978-2-89718-116-1(8))* Caillouet, Gerry.
—Caillou: The Broken Castle. Sanschagrin, Joceline. 2nd ed. 2011. (Clubhouse Ser.). (ENG.). 24p. (J). (gr. -1-k). pap. 3.95 *(978-2-89450-764-3(X))* Caillouet, Gerry.
—Caillou - A Day at the Farm. Sanschagrin, Joceline. 2016. (Step by Step Ser.). (ENG.). 24p. (J). (gr. k-k). bds. 5.99 *(978-2-89718-254-0(7))* Caillouet, Gerry.
—Caillou - My First Dictionary. rev. ed. 2007. (Dictionaries Ser.). (ENG.). 16p. (J). (gr. -1-k). bds. 12.95 *(978-2-89450-627-1(9))* Caillouet, Gerry.
—Caillou - The Shopping Trip. Nadeau, Nicole. 2010. (Big Dipper Ser.). (ENG.). 24p. (J). (gr. -1-k). pap. 3.95 *(978-2-89450-718-6(6))* Caillouet, Gerry.
—Caillou - Toddler Essentials: 5 Books about Growing. 2015. (ENG.). 120p. (J). (gr. -1-k). 12.99 *(978-2-89718-171-0(0))* Caillouet, Gerry.
—Caillou & the Big Bully. L'Heureux, Christine. 2015. (Hand in Hand Ser.). (ENG.). 24p. (J). (gr. -1-k). 5.95 *(978-2-89718-199-4(0))* Caillouet, Gerry.
—Caillou Asks Nicely. 2015. (Step by Step Ser.). (ENG.). 24p. (J). (gr. k-k). bds. 5.99 *(978-2-89718-175-8(3))* Caillouet, Gerry.
—Caillou at the Doctor. Sanschagrin, Joceline. 3rd ed. 2013. (Step by Step Ser.). (ENG.). 24p. (J). (gr. -1-k). bds. 5.99 *(978-2-89718-058-4(7))* Caillouet, Gerry.
—Caillou Goes to Day Care. 2019. (Caillou's Essentials Ser.). (ENG.). 24p. (J). (gr. -1-k). bds. 7.99 *(978-2-89718-490-2(6))* Caillouet, Gerry.
—Caillou: Good Night! Sleep Well: Nighttime. ed. 2017. (Caillou's Essentials Ser.). (ENG.). 24p. (J). (gr. -1-k). bds. 7.99 *(978-2-89718-357-8(8))* Caillouet, Gerry.
—Caillou: Happy Easter! Rudel-Tessier, Melanie. 2012. (Confetti Ser.). (ENG.). 24p. (J). (gr. -1-1). pap. 4.99 *(978-2-89450-947-0(2))* Caillouet, Gerry.
—Caillou: I Can Brush My Teeth: Healthy Toddler. ed. 2017. (Caillou's Essentials Ser.). (ENG.). 24p. (J). (gr. -1-k). bds. 7.99 *(978-2-89718-356-1(X))* Caillouet, Gerry.
—Caillou: It's Mine! Sanschagrin, Joceline. 3rd ed. 2013. (Step by Step Ser.). (ENG.). 24p. (J). (gr. -1-k). bds. 5.99 *(978-2-89718-059-1(5))* Caillouet, Gerry.
—Caillou: Jobs People Do. 2011. (Dictionaries Ser.). (ENG.). 16p. (J). (gr. -1-k). bds. 12.95 *(978-2-89450-831-2(X))* Caillouet, Gerry.
—Caillou Loves His Daddy. L'Heureux, Christine. ed. 2018. (Caillou's Essentials Ser.). (ENG.). 24p. (J). (gr. -1-k). bds. 7.99 *(978-2-89718-440-7(X))* Caillouet, Gerry.
—Caillou Loves His Mommy. L'Heureux, Christine. ed. 2018. (Caillou's Essentials Ser.). (ENG.). 24p. (J). (gr. -1-k). bds. 7.99 *(978-2-89718-441-4(8))* Caillouet, Gerry.
—Caillou Meets a Princess. L'Heureux, Christine. 2014. (Hand in Hand Ser.). (ENG.). 24p. (J). (gr. -1-k). 5.99 *(978-2-89718-114-7(1))* Caillouet, Gerry.
—Caillou, My First ABC: The Alphabet Soup. Publishing, Chouette. 2015. (ENG.). 32p. (J). (gr. -1-k). 9.99 *(978-2-89718-201-4(6))* Caillouet, Gerry.
—Caillou, My House: Includes 4 Chunky Board Books. Paradis, Anne. 2015. (ENG.). 40p. (J). (gr. -1-k). bds. 16.99 *(978-2-89718-224-3(5))* Caillouet, Gerry.
—Caillou, No More Diapers. L'Heureux, Christine. 2016. (Hand in Hand Ser.: 2). (ENG.). 24p. (J). (gr. -1-k). bds. 7.99 *(978-2-89718-296-0(2))* Caillouet, Gerry.
—Caillou, Potty Time. Sanschagrin, Joceline. 2016. (Hand in Hand Ser.: 1). (ENG.). 24p. (J). (gr. -1-k). bds. 7.99 *(978-2-89718-295-3(4))* Caillouet, Gerry.
—Caillou Takes a Bath. 2014. (Step by Step Ser.). (ENG.). 24p. (J). (gr. -1 — 1). bds. 5.99 *(978-2-89718-138-3(9))* Caillouet, Gerry.
—Caillou Takes a Nap. 2014. (Step by Step Ser.). (ENG.). 24p. (J). (gr. -1 — 1). bds. 5.99 *(978-2-89718-147-5(8))* Caillouet, Gerry.
—Caillou: What Should I Wear? 2010. (Interactive Bks.). (ENG.). 10p. (J). (gr. -1-1). bds. 12.95 *(978-2-89450-767-4(4))* Caillouet, Gerry.
—Caillou: Where Is Teddy? 2015. (Step by Step Ser.). (ENG.). 24p. (J). (gr. k-k). bds. 5.99 *(978-2-89718-173-4(7))* Caillouet, Gerry.
—Le Combats des Chocolats. Decary, Marie. 2003. (Roman Jeunesse Ser.). (FRE.). 96p. (J). (gr. 4-7). pap. *(978-2-89021-611-2(X))* Diffusion du livre Mirabel (DLM).
—Good Night! Légaré, Gisèle & L'Heureux, Christine. 2006. (Hand in Hand Ser.). (ENG.). 24p. (J). (gr. -1-k). 5.95 *(978-2-89450-588-5(4))* Caillouet, Gerry.

—Play with Me! L'Heureux, Christine. 2009. (Big Dipper Ser.). (ENG.). 24p. (J). (gr. -1-k). pap. 3.95 *(978-2-89450-679-0(1))* Caillouet, Gerry.

—Rose Neon Series. Decary, Marie. 2004. 96p. (J). (gr. 4-7). pap. *(978-2-89021-700-3(0))* Diffusion du livre Mirabel (DLM).

—Le Visage Masqué. Sanschagrin, Joceline. 2004. (Mon Roman Ser.). (FRE.). 160p. (J). (gr. 2). pap. *(978-2-89021-651-8(9))* Diffusion du livre Mirabel (DLM).

Brignaud, Pierre & Depratto, Marcel. Day Care. Légaré, Gisèle & L'Heureux, Christine. 2008. (Big Dipper Ser.). (ENG.). 24p. (J). (gr. -1-k). pap. 3.95 *(978-2-89450-657-8(0))* Caillouet, Gerry.

Brignaud, Pierre & Legdani, Sanaa. Caillou - My Little Library. ed. 2017. (ENG.). 72p. (J). (gr. -1-k). bds. 9.99 *(978-2-89718-359-2(4))* Caillouet, Gerry.

Brignaud, Pierre & Sévigny, Eric. Caillou - Learning for Fun - Ages 3-4. 2013. (Activity Bks.). (ENG.). 64p. (J). (gr. -1-1). 6.99 *(978-2-89718-049-2(8))* Caillouet, Gerry.

—Caillou - Learning for Fun!, Ages 4-5. 2013. (Activity Bks.). (ENG.). 64p. (J). (gr. -1-1). 6.99 *(978-2-89718-050-8(1))* Caillouet, Gerry.

Brignaud, Pierre & Sévigny, Éric. Caillou, My First French Word Book: Learn a New Language with Caillou! Paradis, Anne. 2016. (ENG.). 32p. (J). (gr. -1-k). 9.99 *(978-2-89718-305-9(5))* Caillouet, Gerry.

—Caillou, My First Spanish Word Book. Paradis, Anne. 2016. (ENG.). 32p. (J). (gr. -1-k). 9.99 *(978-2-89718-306-6(3))* Caillouet, Gerry.

Briles, Patti. My Loose Tooth. Williams, Rozanne Lanczak. Hamaguchi, Carla, ed. 2003. (Sight Word Readers Ser.). 16p. (J). (gr. k-2). pap. 3.49 *(978-1-57471-972-7(6)*, 3594) Creative Teaching Pr., Inc.

Briles, Patty. Grandma's Lists. Williams, Rozanne Lanczak. 2006. (Learn to Write Ser.). 8p. (J). (gr. k-2). pap. 3.49 *(978-1-59198-284-5(7)*, 6178) Creative Teaching Pr., Inc.

—Grandma's Lists. Williams, Rozanne Lanczak. Maio, Barbara & Faulkner, Stacey, eds. 2006. (J). per. 6.99 *(978-1-59198-335-4(5))* Creative Teaching Pr., Inc.

—What Is the Best Pet?, Vol. 4258. Williams, Rozanne Lanczak. 2005. 16p. (J). pap. 3.49 *(978-1-59198-160-2(3)*, 4258) Creative Teaching Pr., Inc.

—When You Go Walking. Williams, Rozanne Lanczak. 2006. (Learn to Write Ser.). 16p. (J). (gr. k-2). pap. 3.49 *(978-1-59198-292-0(8)*, 6188) Creative Teaching Pr., Inc.

—When You Go Walking. Williams, Rozanne Lanczak. Maio, Barbara, ed. 2006. (J). per. 8.99 *(978-1-59198-345-3(2))* Creative Teaching Pr., Inc.

Brim, Warren & Eglitis, Anna. Creatures of the Rainforest: Two Artists Explore Djabugay Country. Brim, Warren & Eglitis, Anna. 2005. (ENG.). 64p. (J). (gr. k). 19.95 *(978-1-875641-99-4(8))* Magabala Bks. AUS. Dist: Independent Pubs. Group.

Brinesh, Heather Jane. Renewable Energy: Discover the Fuel of the Future. Sneideman, Joshua & Twamley, Erin. 2016. (Build It Yourself Ser.). 128p. (J). (gr. 3-7). 22.95 *(978-1-61930-356-0(6)*, 13d5d6c8-114e-42b6-bc5b-6aa89e4349ce) Nomad Pr.

Bringer Deik, Julien. La Farfalla Di Velluto, l'Aquilone e L'Americano. Ferre, Gil. 2014. (ENG & ITA.). (J). pap. *(978-2-89687-517-7(4))* chouetteditions.com.

Bringle, Beverly. Rising Fawn & the Fire Mystery. Awiakta, Marilou. 2007. (ENG.). 96p. (J). (gr. 4-7). pap. 14.95 *(978-1-55591-600-8(7))* Fulcrum Publishing.

Brinkman, Paula. Yoga Bear: Yoga for Youngsters, Vol. Pierce, Karen F. 2004. (ENG.). 48p. (J). (gr. -1-1). 15.95 *(978-1-55971-897-4(8))* Cooper Square Publishing Llc.

Brinkmann, Barbara. Dormi Bene, Piccolo Lupo - Priyatnykh Snov, Malen'kiy Volchyonok (Italiano - Russo) Libro per Bambini Bilingue Da 2-4 Anni, con Audiolibro MP3 Da Scaricare. Renz, Ulrich. Haase, Margherita, tr. 2018. (Sefa Libri Illustrati in Due Lingue Ser.). (ITA.). 28p. (J). pap. *(978-3-7399-0612-6(X))* Boedeker, Kirsten. Sefa Verlag.

—Dormi Bene, Piccolo Lupo - Schlaf Gut, Kleiner Wolf (Italiano - Tedesco) Libro per Bambini Bilingue Da 2-4 Anni, con Audiolibro MP3 Da Scaricare. Renz, Ulrich. Haase, Margherita, tr. 2018. (Sefa Libri Illustrati in Due Lingue Ser.). (ITA.). 28p. (J). pap. *(978-3-7399-0605-8(7))* Boedeker, Kirsten. Sefa Verlag.

—Dormi Bene, Piccolo Lupo - Sleep Tight, Little Wolf (Italiano - Inglese) Libro per Bambini Bilingue Da 2-4 Anni, con Audiolibro MP3 Da Scaricare. Renz, Ulrich. Haase, Margherita, tr. 2018. (Sefa Libri Illustrati in Due Lingue Ser.). (ITA.). 28p. (J). pap. *(978-3-7399-0623-2(5))* Boedeker, Kirsten. Sefa Verlag.

—Dors Bien, Petit Loup - Dormi Bene, Piccolo Lupo (Français - Italien) Livre Bilingue Pour Enfants À Partir de 2-4 Ans, Avec Livre Audio MP3 À Télécharger. Renz, Ulrich. Lottigier, Celeste, tr. 2018. (Sefa Albums Illustrés en Deux Langues Ser.). (FRE.). 28p. (J). pap. *(978-3-7399-0601-0(4))* Boedeker, Kirsten. Sefa Verlag.

Brinkmann, Barbara. Dors Bien, Petit Loup - Gjumin e �mb�l, Ujku I Vog�l (fran�ais - Albanais) Livre Bilingue Pour Enfants, Avec Livre Audio � T�l�charger. Lottigier, Celeste & Gashi, Jeta Abazi, trs. 2019. (FRE.). 42p. (J). pap. ***(978-3-7399-0947-9(1))*** Boedeker, Kirsten. Sefa Verlag.

—Dors Bien, Petit Loup - Head ��d, V�ike Hundu (fran�ais - Estonien) Livre Bilingue Pour Enfants � Partir de 2-4 Ans, Avec Livre Audio MP3 � T�l�charger. Lottigier, Celeste & Magi, Liisi, trs. 2018. (FRE.). 42p. (J). pap. ***(978-3-7399-0676-8(6))*** Boedeker, Kirsten. Sefa Verlag.

Brinkmann, Barbara. Dors Bien, Petit Loup - Lala Salama, Mbwa Mwitu Mdogo (français - Swahili) Livre Bilingue Pour Enfants à Partir de 2-4 Ans, Avec Livre Audio MP3 à Télécharger. Lottigier, Celeste & Makasi, George Aclay, trs. 2018. (FRE.). 42p. (J). pap. *(978-3-7399-0632-4(4))* Boedeker, Kirsten. Sefa Verlag.

—Dors Bien, Petit Loup - Nam Jayyidan Ayyuha Adh-Dhaib As-Sagir (Français - Arabe) Livre Bilingue Pour Enfants À Partir de 2-4 Ans, Avec Livre Audio MP3 À Télécharger. Renz, Ulrich. Boussayer, Abdelaaziz, tr. 2018. (Sefa Albums Illustrés en Deux Langues Ser.). (FRE.). 28p. (J). pap. *(978-3-7399-0621-8(9))* Boedeker, Kirsten. Sefa Verlag.

—Dors Bien, Petit Loup - Nuku Hyvin, Pieni Susi (français - Finlandais) Livre Bilingue Pour Enfants à Partir de 2-4 Ans, Avec Livre Audio MP3 à Télécharger. Lottigier, Celeste & Hach, Virpi, trs. 2018. (FRE.). 42p. (J). pap. *(978-3-7399-0695-9(2))* Boedeker, Kirsten. Sefa Verlag.

Brinkmann, Barbara. Dors Bien, Petit Loup - Qongchu', Ngavyaw' Mach (fran�ais - Klingon) Livre Bilingue Pour Enfants, Avec Livre Audio � T�l�charger. Lottigier, Celeste & Litaer, Lieven L., trs. 2019. (FRE.). 42p. (J). pap. ***(978-3-7399-1082-6(8))*** Boedeker, Kirsten. Sefa Verlag.

Brinkmann, Barbara. Dors Bien, Petit Loup - Que Duermas Bien, Pequeño Lobo (Français - Espagnol) Livre Bilingue Pour Enfants À Partir de 2-4 Ans, Avec Livre Audio MP3 À Télécharger. Renz, Ulrich. Landmesser, Anneli, tr. 2018. (Sefa Albums Illustrés en Deux Langues Ser.). (FRE.). 28p. (J). pap. *(978-3-7399-0616-4(2))* Boedeker, Kirsten. Sefa Verlag.

—Dors Bien, Petit Loup - Shpi Dobshe, Mawi Vilku (Français - Polonais) Livre Bilingue Pour Enfants À Partir de 2-4 Ans, Avec Livre Audio MP3 À Télécharger. Renz, Ulrich. Lottigier, Celeste, tr. 2018. (Sefa Albums Illustrés en Deux Langues Ser.). (FRE.). 28p. (J). pap. *(978-3-7399-0620-1(0))* Boedeker, Kirsten. Sefa Verlag.

—Dors Bien, Petit Loup - Slaap Lekker, Kleine Wolf (Français - Néerlandais) Livre Bilingue Pour Enfants À Partir de 2-4 Ans, Avec Livre Audio MP3 À Télécharger. Lottigier, Celeste & Van Den Berg, Jonathan, trs. 2018. (FRE.). 42p. (J). pap. *(978-3-7399-0646-1(4))* Boedeker, Kirsten. Sefa Verlag.

—Dors Bien, Petit Loup - Sleep Tight, Little Wolf (Français - Anglais) Livre Bilingue Pour Enfants À Partir de 2-4 Ans, Avec Livre Audio MP3 À Télécharger. Renz, Ulrich. Lottigier, Celeste, tr. 2018. (Sefa Albums Illustrés en Deux Langues Ser.). (FRE.). 28p. (J). pap. *(978-3-7399-0602-7(2))* Boedeker, Kirsten. Sefa Verlag.

—Dors Bien, Petit Loup - Sov Godt, Lille Ulv (français - Norvégien) Livre Bilingue Pour Enfants, Avec Livre Audio à Télécharger. Lottigier, Celeste & Glathe, David Immanuel, trs. 2019. (FRE.). 42p. (J). pap. *(978-3-7399-0923-3(4))* Boedeker, Kirsten. Sefa Verlag.

—Dors Bien, Petit Loup - Sov Gott, Lilla Vargen (français - Suédois) Livre Bilingue Pour Enfants à Partir de 2-4 Ans, Avec Livre Audio MP3 à Télécharger. Lottigier, Celeste & Bienzle Arruda, Katrin, trs. 2018. (FRE.). 42p. (J). pap. *(978-3-7399-0693-5(6))* Boedeker, Kirsten. Sefa Verlag.

—Nam Jayyidan Ayyuha Adh-Dhaib As-Sagir - Sleep Tight, Little Wolf (Arabic - English) Bilingual Children's Book with MP3 Audiobook for Download, Age 2-4 & Up. Renz, Ulrich. Boussayer, Abdelaaziz, tr. 2018. (Sefa Picture Books in Two Languages Ser.). (ARA.). 28p. (J). pap. *(978-3-7399-0609-6(X))* Boedeker, Kirsten. Sefa Verlag.

Brinkmann, Barbara. Que Duermas Bien, Peque�o Lobo - Qongchu', Ngavyaw' Mach (espa�ol - Klingon) Libro Infantil Biling�e, con Audiolibro Descargable. Litaer, Lieven L. & Landmesser, Anneli, trs. 2019. (SPA.). 42p. (J). pap. ***(978-3-7399-1070-3(4))*** Boedeker, Kirsten. Sefa Verlag.

Brinkmann, Barbara. Que Duermas Bien, Pequeño Lobo - Sov Gott, Lilla Vargen (español - Sueco) Libro Infantil Bilingüe con Audiolibro Mp3 Descargable, a Partir de 2-4 Años. Landmesser, Anneli & Bienzle Arruda, Katrin, trs. 2018. (SPA.). 42p. (J). pap. *(978-3-7399-0681-2(2))* Boedeker, Kirsten. Sefa Verlag.

—Schlaf Gut, Kleiner Wolf - Dors Bien, Petit Loup (Deutsch - Französisch) Zweisprachiges Kinderbuch Mit MP3 Hörbuch Zum Herunterladen, AB 2-4 Jahren. Renz, Ulrich. Lottigier, Celeste, tr. 2018. (Sefa Bilinguale Bilderbücher Ser.). (GER.). 28p. (J). pap. *(978-3-7399-0618-8(9))* Boedeker, Kirsten. Sefa Verlag.

—Schlaf Gut, Kleiner Wolf - Gjumin e ëmbël, Ujku I Vogël (Deutsch - Albanisch) Zweisprachiges Kinderbuch, Mit Hörbuch Zum Herunterladen. Gashi, Jeta Abazi & Gashi, Qendrim R., trs. 2019. (GER.). 42p. (J). pap. *(978-3-7399-0948-6(X))* Boedeker, Kirsten. Sefa Verlag.

Brinkmann, Barbara. Schlaf Gut, Kleiner Wolf - Hǎo M�ng, Xiǎo L�ng Zǎi (Deutsch - Chinesisch) Zweisprachiges Kinderbuch Mit H�rbuch Zum Herunterladen. Wu, Li, tr. 2019. (GER.). 42p. (J). pap. ***(978-3-7399-1018-5(6))*** Boedeker, Kirsten. Sefa Verlag.

—Schlaf Gut, Kleiner Wolf - Head ��d, V�ike Hundu (Deutsch - Estnisch) Zweisprachiges Kinderbuch Mit Mp3 H�rbuch Zum Herunterladen, Ab 2-4 Jahren. Magi, Liisi, tr. 2018. (GER.). 42p. (J). pap. ***(978-3-7399-0652-2(9))*** Boedeker, Kirsten. Sefa Verlag.

Brinkmann, Barbara. Schlaf Gut, Kleiner Wolf - Lala Salama, Mbwa Mwitu Mdogo (Deutsch - Swahili) Zweisprachiges Kinderbuch Mit Mp3 Hörbuch Zum Herunterladen, Ab 2-4 Jahren. Makasi, George Aclay, tr. 2018. (GER.). 42p. (J). pap. *(978-3-7399-0630-0(8))* Boedeker, Kirsten. Sefa Verlag.

—Schlaf Gut, Kleiner Wolf - Nuku Hyvin, Pieni Susi (Deutsch - Finnisch) Zweisprachiges Kinderbuch Mit MP3 Hörbuch Zum Herunterladen, AB 2-4 Jahren. Renz, Ulrich. Hach, Virpi, tr. 2018. (Sefa Bilinguale Bilderbücher Ser.). (GER.). 28p. (J). pap. *(978-3-7399-0617-1(0))* Boedeker, Kirsten. Sefa Verlag.

—Schlaf Gut, Kleiner Wolf - Priyatnykh Snov, Malen'kiy Volchyonok (Deutsch - Russisch) Zweisprachiges Kinderbuch Mit MP3 Hörbuch Zum Herunterladen, AB 2-4 Jahren. Renz, Ulrich. Hordiyenko, Svetlana, tr. 2018. (Sefa Bilinguale Bilderbücher Ser.). (GER.). 28p. (J). pap. *(978-3-7399-0615-7(4))* Boedeker, Kirsten. Sefa Verlag.

Brinkmann, Barbara. Schlaf Gut, Kleiner Wolf - Qongchu', Ngavyaw' Mach (Deutsch - Klingonisch) Zweisprachiges Kinderbuch, Mit H�rbuch Zum Herunterladen. Renz, Ulrich. Litaer, Lieven L., tr. 2019. (GER.). 42p. (J). pap. ***(978-3-7399-1062-8(3))*** Boedeker, Kirsten. Sefa Verlag.

Brinkmann, Barbara. Schlaf Gut, Kleiner Wolf - Schlof Guad, Gloana Wolf (Deutsch - Bairisch) Zweisprachiges Kinderbuch Mit Mp3 Hörbuch Zum Herunterladen, Ab 2-4 Jahren Zum Herunterladen, Ab 2-4 Jahren. Winterholler, Elisabeth, tr. 2018. (GER.). 42p. (J). pap. *(978-3-7399-0650-8(2))* Boedeker, Kirsten. Sefa Verlag.

—Schlaf Gut, Kleiner Wolf - Slaap Lekker, Kleine Wolf (Deutsch - Holländisch) Zweisprachiges Kinderbuch Mit Mp3 Hörbuch Zum Herunterladen, Ab 2-4 Jahren. Van Den Berg, Jonathan, tr. 2018. (GER.). 42p. (J). pap. *(978-3-7399-0649-2(9))* Boedeker, Kirsten. Sefa Verlag.

—Schlaf Gut, Kleiner Wolf - Sov Godt, Lille Ulv (Deutsch - Norwegisch) Zweisprachiges Kinderbuch, Mit Hörbuch Zum Herunterladen. Glathe, David Emmanuel, tr. 2019. (GER.). 42p. (J). pap. *(978-3-7399-0924-0(2))* Boedeker, Kirsten. Sefa Verlag.

—Schlaf Gut, Kleiner Wolf - Sov Gott, Lilla Vargen (Deutsch - Schwedisch) Zweisprachiges Kinderbuch, Ab 2-4 Jahren, Mit Mp3-Hörbuch Zum Herunterladen. Bienzle Arruda, Katrin, tr. 2018. (GER.). 42p. (J). pap. *(978-3-7399-0526-6(3))* Boedeker, Kirsten. Sefa Verlag.

—Sleep Tight, Little Wolf - Dormi Bene, Piccolo Lupo (English - Italian) Bilingual Children's Book with Mp3 Audiobook for Download, Age 2-4 & Up. Savill, Pete & Haase, Margherita, trs. 2018. (ENG.). 42p. (J). pap. *(978-3-7399-0648-5(0))* Boedeker, Kirsten. Sefa Verlag.

—Sleep Tight, Little Wolf - Dors Bien, Petit Loup (English - French) Bilingual Children's Book with MP3 Audiobook for Download, Age 2-4 & Up. Renz, Ulrich. Savill, Pete, tr. 2018. (Sefa Picture Books in Two Languages Ser.). (ENG.). 28p. (J). pap. *(978-3-7399-0608-9(1))* Boedeker, Kirsten. Sefa Verlag.

—Sleep Tight, Little Wolf - Gjumin e ëmbël, Ujku I Vogël (English - Albanian) Bilingual Children's Book, with Audiobook for Download. Savill, Pete & Gashi, Jeta Abazi, trs. 2019. (ENG.). 42p. (J). pap. *(978-3-7399-0912-7(9))* Boedeker, Kirsten. Sefa Verlag.

—Sleep Tight, Little Wolf - Head ööd, Väike Hundu (English - Estonian) Bilingual Children's Book with Mp3 Audiobook for Download, Age 2-4 & Up. Savill, Pete & Magi, Liisi, trs. 2018. (ENG.). 42p. (J). pap. *(978-3-7399-0653-9(7))* Boedeker, Kirsten. Sefa Verlag.

—Sleep Tight, Little Wolf - Lala Salama, Mbwa Mwitu Mdogo (English - Swahili) Bilingual Children's Book, Age 2-4 & up, with Mp3 Audiobook for Download. Makasi, George Aclay & Savill, Pete, trs. 2018. (ENG.). 42p. (J). pap. *(978-3-7399-0633-1(2))* Boedeker, Kirsten. Sefa Verlag.

—Sleep Tight, Little Wolf - Nuku Hyvin, Pieni Susi (English - Finnish) Bilingual Children's Book with Mp3 Audiobook for Download, Age 2-4 & Up. Savill, Pete & Hach, Virpi, trs. 2018. (ENG.). 42p. (J). pap. *(978-3-7399-0638-6(3))* Boedeker, Kirsten. Sefa Verlag.

Brinkmann, Barbara. Sleep Tight, Little Wolf - Qongchu', Ngavyaw' Mach (English - Klingon) Bilingual Children's Book, with Audiobook for Download. Litaer, Lieven L. & Savill, Pete, trs. 2019. (ENG.). 42p. (J). pap. ***(978-3-7399-1069-7(0))*** Boedeker, Kirsten. Sefa Verlag.

Brinkmann, Barbara. Sleep Tight, Little Wolf - Que Duermas Bien, Pequeño Lobo (English - Spanish) Bilingual Children's Book with MP3 Audiobook for Download, Age 2 & Up. Renz, Ulrich. Landmesser, Anneli, tr. 2018. (Sefa Picture Books in Two Languages Ser.). (ENG.). 28p. (J). pap. *(978-3-7399-0622-5(7))* Boedeker, Kirsten. Sefa Verlag.

—Sleep Tight, Little Wolf - Schlaf Gut, Kleiner Wolf (English - German) Bilingual Children's Book with MP3 Audiobook for Download, Age 2-4 & Up. Renz, Ulrich. Savill, Pete, tr. 2018. (Sefa Picture Books in Two Languages Ser.). (ENG.). 28p. (J). pap. *(978-3-7399-0604-1(9))* Boedeker, Kirsten. Sefa Verlag.

—Sleep Tight, Little Wolf - Slaap Lekker, Kleine Wolf (English - Dutch) Bilingual Children's Book with MP3 Audiobook for Download, Age 2-4 & Up. Renz, Ulrich. Van Den Berg, Jonathan, tr. 2018. (Sefa Picture Books in Two Languages Ser.). (ENG.). 28p. (J). pap. *(978-3-7399-0606-5(5))* Boedeker, Kirsten. Sefa Verlag.

—Sleep Tight, Little Wolf - Somn Ushor, Mikule Lup (English - Romanian) Bilingual Children's Book with Mp3 Audiobook for Download, Age 2-4 & Up. Savill, Pete & Gitman, Stefan, trs. 2018. (ENG.). 42p. (J). pap. *(978-3-7399-0746-8(0))* Boedeker, Kirsten. Sefa Verlag.

—Sleep Tight, Little Wolf - Sov Gott, Lilla Vargen (English - Swedish) Bilingual Children's Book with MP3 Audiobook for Download, Age 2-4 & Up. Renz, Ulrich. Thordsen, Narona, tr. 2018. (Sefa Picture Books in Two Languages Ser.). (ENG.). 28p. (J). pap. *(978-3-7399-0603-4(0))* Boedeker, Kirsten. Sefa Verlag.

—Sleep Tight, Little Wolf (Arabic Edition) A Bedtime Story for Sleepy (and Not So Sleepy) Children. Renz, Ulrich. 2016. (ARA.). (J). pap. *(978-3-7399-0117-6(9))* Boedeker, Kirsten. Sefa Verlag.

Brinkmann, Barbara. Sleep Tight, Little Wolf (English - Persian, Farsi, Dari) Bilingual Children's Book, with Audiobook for Download. Savill, Pete & Mortezai, Jahan, trs. 2019. (ENG.). 42p. (J). pap. ***(978-3-7399-0961-5(7))*** Boedeker, Kirsten. Sefa Verlag.

Brinkmann, Barbara. Sleep Tight, Little Wolf (French Edition) Renz, Ulrich. 2016. (FRE.). (J). pap. *(978-3-7399-0127-5(6))* Boedeker, Kirsten. Sefa Verlag.

—Sleep Tight, Little Wolf (Italian Edition) A Bedtime Story for Sleepy (and Not So Sleepy) Children. Renz, Ulrich. 2016. (ITA.). (J). pap. *(978-3-7399-0126-8(8))* Boedeker, Kirsten. Sefa Verlag.

—Sleep Tight, Little Wolf (Russian Edition) A Bedtime Story for Sleepy (and Not So Sleepy) Children. Renz, Ulrich. 2016. (RUS.). (J). pap. *(978-3-7399-0119-0(5))* Boedeker, Kirsten. Sefa Verlag.

—Sleep Tight, Little Wolf (Spanish Edition) A Bedtime Story for Sleepy (and Not So Sleepy) Children. Renz, Ulrich. 2016. (SPA.). (J). pap. *(978-3-7399-0118-3(7))* Boedeker, Kirsten. Sefa Verlag.

Brinkmann, Barbara. Sov Gott, Lilla Vargen - Qongchu', Ngavyaw' Mach (svenska - Klingon) Tv�spr�kig Barnbok, Med Ljudbok Som Nedladdning. Litaer, Lieven L. & Bienzle Arruda, Katrin, trs. 2019. (SWE.). 42p. (J). pap. ***(978-3-7399-1071-0(2))*** Boedeker, Kirsten. Sefa Verlag.

Brinkmann, Barbara. Sov Gott, Lilla Vargen - Que Duermas Bien, Pequeño Lobo (Svenska - Spanska) Tvåspråkig Barnbok Med Ljudbok SOM Mp3-Nedladdning, Från 2-4 År. Renz, Ulrich. Bienzle Arruda, Katrin, tr. 2018. (Sefa Bilderböcker På Två Språk Ser.). (SWE.). 28p. (J). pap. *(978-3-7399-0619-5(7))* Boedeker, Kirsten. Sefa Verlag.

—Sov Gott, Lilla Vargen - Sleep Tight, Little Wolf (Svenska - Engelska) Tvåspråkig Barnbok Med Ljudbok SOM Mp3-Nedladdning, Från 2-4 År. Renz, Ulrich. Thordsen, Narona, tr. 2018. (Sefa Bilderböcker På Två Språk Ser.). (SWE.). 28p. (J). pap. *(978-3-7399-0614-0(6))* Boedeker, Kirsten. Sefa Verlag.

Brinley, Natalie Totire. Pip's Ridiculous Road Trip. Brannon, Pat. 2019. (ENG.). 38p. (J). pap. 11.99 *(978-1-0916-9939-7(9))* Independently Published.

Brinson, Connor J. Princess Olivia & the Leap Frog, 1 vol. Brinson, Julie L. 2009. 22p. pap. 24.95 *(978-1-60813-802-9(X))* America Star Bks.

Brislane, Niche. Paula & the Parrot. Vaughn, J. D. 2009. 16p. pap. 8.49 *(978-1-4389-8634-0(3))* AuthorHouse.

Brisley, Joyce Lankester. Adventures of the Little Wooden Horse. Williams, Ursula Moray. 2015. (Macmillan Classics Ser.). (ENG.). 272p. (J). (gr. k-2). 16.99 *(978-1-4472-7304-2(4))* Pan Macmillan GBR. Dist: Independent Pubs. Group.

Brisley, Joyce Lankester. The Milly-Molly-Mandy Storybook. Brisley, Joyce Lankester. 2019. (ENG.). 224p. (J). 13.99 *(978-0-7534-7471-6(9)*, 900196716, Kingfisher) Roaring Brook Pr.

Brissard, Cecile. Tabouli: The Story of a Heart-Driven Diabetes Alert Dog. Pelicano, Matt. 2019. (ENG.). 308p. (J). (gr. 4-6). pap. 16.95 ***(978-0-578-53203-5(4))*** April Fool Publishing.

Bristol, Chloe. Nonsense! The Curious Story of Edward Gorey. Mortensen, Lori. 2020. (ENG.). 40p. (J). (gr. -1-3). 17.99 *(978-0-358-03368-4(3)*, 1740073, Versify) Houghton Mifflin Harcourt Publishing Co.

—The Secrets of Winterhouse. Guterson, Ben. 2018. (Winterhouse Ser.: 2). (ENG.). 384p. (J). 16.99 *(978-1-250-12390-9(9)*, 900174323, Holt, Henry & Co. Bks. For Young Readers) Holt, Henry & Co.

—The Secrets of Winterhouse. Guterson, Ben. 2019. (Winterhouse Ser.: 2). (ENG.). 400p. (J). pap. 7.99 *(978-1-250-23352-3(6)*, 900174324) Square Fish.

—Winterhouse, Bk. 1. Guterson, Ben. 2018. (Winterhouse Ser.: 1). (ENG.). 384p. (J). 16.99 *(978-1-250-12388-6(7)*, 900174320, Holt, Henry & Co. Bks. For Young Readers) Holt, Henry & Co.

—Winterhouse. Guterson, Ben. 2018. (Winterhouse Ser.: 1). (ENG.). 400p. (J). pap. 8.99 *(978-1-250-29419-7(3)*, 900174321) Square Fish.

—The Winterhouse Mysteries. Guterson, Ben. 2019. (Winterhouse Ser.: 3). (ENG.). 384p. (J). 16.99 *(978-1-250-12392-3(5)*, 900174326, Holt, Henry & Co. Bks. For Young Readers) Holt, Henry & Co.

Bristol, Mark. Simply Social 7 at School. Neal, Angie & Kjesbo, Rynette. 2011. 216p. (J). spiral bd. 34.95 net. *(978-1-60723-005-2(4))* Super Duper Pubns.

Bristow, Ian. Secret Supers: What Happens When 'differently-Abled' People Become 'super-Abled'? McKee, Leslie & Hall, Rik, eds. 2019. (Secret Supers Ser.: Vol. 1). (ENG.). 110p. (J). pap. 6.95 *(978-0-9978234-3-1(7))* Hom, Jonathan.

Bristow, Ian C. Frank Has the Sniffles. Riggs, Jonny. 2018. (ENG.). 28p. (J). pap. 9.99 *(978-0-692-06813-7(9))* Riggs, Jon.

Briswalter, Maren. The King & the Gifts of Gold, 24 vols. Dreissig, Georg. Drake, Jonathan, tr. 2019. (ENG.). 32p. (J). 19.95 *(978-1-78250-601-0(2))* Floris Bks. GBR. Dist: Consortium Bk. Sales & Distribution.

—The Pied Piper of Hamelin, 40 vols. 2014. Orig. Title: Rattenfänger Von Hameln. (ENG.). 32p. (J). 17.95 *(978-1-78250-035-3(9))* Floris Bks. GBR. Dist: Consortium Bk. Sales & Distribution.

Brito, Carlos. Zoey's Web World. Rosenberg, Harvey. 2014. (ENG.). (J). pap. 9.13 *(978-0-9822824-9-6(4))* Go Jolly Bks.

Britt, Joanna & Edwards, Laurie J. Island Sting, Book 1. Doerr, Bonnie J. 2010. 282p. (YA). (gr. 5-11). pap. 11.99 *(978-1-61603-002-5(X))* Leap Bks.

Britt, Joanna, jt. illus. see Edwards, Laurie J.

Britt, Rachel. Good Manners for Very Young Children with Rio the Rat. Lister, John C. 2005. (J). 18.00 *(978-0-8059-6913-9(6))* Dorrance Publishing Co., Inc.

Britt, Stephan. School Years: A Family Keepsake of School Memories (Journal for Kids, Journal for Teens, High School Journal) 2006. (ENG.). (gr. 8-17). 16.95 *(978-0-8118-5153-4(2))* Chronicle Bks. LLC.

Britt, Stephanie. The Story of Aloha Bear. Adair, Dick. 2008. 24p. (J). 12.95 *(978-1-59700-492-3(8))* Island Heritage Publishing.

—The Story of George Washington. Pingry, Patricia A. 2015. (ENG.). 24p. (J). bds. 6.99 *(978-0-8249-1973-3(4)*, Ideal Pubns.) Worthy Publishing.

—The Story of Gettysburg. Pingry, Patricia A. 2003. (ENG.). 26p. (J). (gr. -1-k). bds. 7.69 *(978-0-8249-6503-7(5)*, Ideal Pubns.) Worthy Publishing.

—The Story of Ulysses S. Grant. Smith, Tamara. 2005. 26p. (J). bds. 7.69 *(978-0-8249-6565-5(5)*, Ideal Pubns.) Worthy Publishing.

Britt, Stephanie M. Writing Makeovers 1-2: Improving Skills - Adding Style. Hults, Alaska. Rous, Sheri, ed. 2003. 96p. (J). (gr. 1-3). pap. 11.99 *(978-1-57471-955-0(6)*, 2260) Creative Teaching Pr., Inc.

Britt, Stephanie McFetridge. I May Be Little. Lashbrook, Marilyn. 2012. 32p. (J). pap. 8.00 *(978-1-935014-41-6(2))* Hutchings, John Pubs.

—Out on a Limb. Lashbrook, Marilyn. 2012. 32p. (J). pap. 8.00 *(978-1-935014-37-9(4))* Hutchings, John Pubs.

B

—The Story of Passover. Silberg, Francis Barry. 2017. (ENG.). 24p. (J). (gr. -1-k). bds. 6.99 *(978-0-8249-1652-7(2))* Worthy Publishing.
—Who Needs a Boat? Lashbrook, Marilyn. 2012. 32p. (J). pap. 8.00 *(978-1-935014-39-3(0))* Hutchings, John Pubs.
Brittany, Jackson. Keira & Me: Homonyms & Homophones. Wells-Strozier, Marsay Latrice. 2016. (ENG.). (J). (gr. 2-6). 20.95 *(978-0-692-79807-2(2))* Yasram Global Industries, LLC.
Brittany's Books. I Can Too! African American Girls. Brittany's Books, creator. 2006. 44p. (J). lib. bdg. 9.95 *(978-0-9778796-8-7(2))* Brittany's Bks.
Brittingham, Geoffrey. Peter Cottontail & the Easter Bunny Imposter. Smith, Suzanne C. 24p. (J). pap. 3.25 *(978-0-8249-5372-0(X),* Ideal Pubns.) Worthy Publishing.
Brittingham, Jennifer. Emily I Think I Saw Heaven. Holbrook, James. 2007. 40p. per. 14.95 *(978-1-934246-56-6(5))* Peppertree Pr., The.
Britto, Romero. Color Play! An Interactive Pop Art Book. Britto, Romero. 2011. (ENG.). 12p. (J). (gr. -1-k). 10.99 *(978-1-4169-9622-4(2),* Little Simon) Little Simon.
—Where Is Friendship Bear? Britto, Romero. 2010. (ENG.). 16p. (J). (gr. -1-k). 12.99 *(978-1-4169-9623-1(0),* Little Simon) Little Simon.
Britton, Stephen. Normal Norman. Lazar, Tara. 2016. 40p. (J). (gr. -1). 14.95 *(978-1-4549-1321-4(5))* Sterling Publishing Co., Inc.
Britton, Terre. Shelly & the Bee. Forrest Hankins, Rochelle. 2018. (Shelly Shines Ser.: Vol. 4). (ENG.). 34p. (J). pap. 9.99 *(978-0-9993131-1-4(8))* ShellyShines Bks.
—Shelly Shines Activity Book: Teacher's Guide. Forrest Hankins, Rochelle. 2018. (ENG.). 36p. (J). pap. 14.99 *(978-0-9993131-3-8(4))* ShellyShines Bks.
Brizuela, Dario. Apokolips Invasion. Manning, Matthew K. 2018. (You Choose Stories: Superman Ser.). (ENG.). 112p. (J). (gr. 2-6). lib. bdg. 32.65 *(978-1-4965-5825-1(1),* 136913, Stone Arch Bks.) Capstone.
—April Fools, 1 vol. Fisch, Sholly. 2012. (DC Super Friends Ser.). (ENG.). 32p. (J). (gr. 2-3). lib. bdg. 22.60 *(978-1-4342-4544-1(6),* Stone Arch Bks.) Capstone.
—Blossom Battle! Sutton, Laurie S. 2019. (Amazing Adventures of Batman! Ser.). (ENG.). 32p. (J). (gr. k-2). lib. bdg. 25.32 *(978-1-5158-3980-4(X),* 139706, Stone Arch Bks.) Capstone.
—Coding in Scratch for Beginners: 4D an Augmented Reality Experience. Ziter, Rachel. 2018. (Junior Makers 4D Ser.). (ENG.). 48p. (J). (gr. 3-9). lib. bdg. 31.99 *(978-1-5157-9490-5(3),* 136715, Capstone Classroom) Capstone.
—Doll Winners Squad. Tobin, Paul. 2010. (Avengers Ser.: No. 2). (ENG.). 24p. (J). (gr. 2-6). 27.07 *(978-1-59961-766-4(8),* 28, Marvel Age) Spotlight.
—The Felon's Fowl Flames: Batman & Robin Use Fire Investigation to Crack the Case. Korte, Steve. 2017. (Batman & Robin Crime Scene Investigations Ser.). (ENG.). 32p. (J). (gr. 4-8). lib. bdg. 28.65 *(978-1-5157-6852-4(X),* 135371, Stone Arch Bks.) Capstone.
—Hungry for Power, 1 vol. Fisch, Sholly. 2012. (DC Super Friends Ser.). (ENG.). 32p. (J). (gr. 2-3). lib. bdg. 22.60 *(978-1-4342-4541-0(1),* Stone Arch Bks.) Capstone.
—Invisible Destroyer. Baltazar, Art & Aureliani, Franco. 2013. (Green Lantern: the Animated Ser.). (ENG.). 32p. (J). (gr. 2-5). 22.60 *(978-1-4342-4796-4(1),* Stone Arch Bks.) Capstone.
—Just My Luck, 1 vol. Fisch, Sholly. 2013. (DC Super Friends Ser.). (ENG.). 32p. (J). (gr. 2-3). lib. bdg. 22.60 *(978-1-4342-4702-5(3),* Stone Arch Bks.) Capstone.
—Marvel Super Hero Adventures: Meet Ant-Man & the Wasp. West, Alexandra. 2019. (World of Reading Level 1 Ser.). (ENG.). 32p. (J). (gr. -1-3). lib. bdg. 27.07 *(978-1-5321-4401-1(6),* 33806) Spotlight.
—Marvel Super Hero Adventures: Thwip! You Are It! West, Alexandra. 2019. (World of Reading Level Pre-1 Ser.). (ENG.). 32p. (J). (gr. -1-2). lib. bdg. 27.07 *(978-1-5321-4392-2(3),* 33797) Spotlight.
—Marvel Super Hero Adventures: Tricky Trouble! West, Alexandra. 2019. (World of Reading Level Pre-1 Ser.). (ENG.). 32p. (J). (gr. -1-2). lib. bdg. 27.07 *(978-1-5321-4393-9(1),* 33798) Spotlight.
—Marvel's Super Hero Adventures: Flying Super Heroes. Little, Sally. 2019. (ENG.). 10p. (J). (gr. -1-k). bds. 8.99 *(978-0-7944-4407-5(5),* Studio Fun International) Printers Row Publishing Group.
—Metallo Attacks! Steele, Michael Anthony. 2018. (You Choose Stories: Superman Ser.). (ENG.). 112p. (J). (gr. 2-6). lib. bdg. 32.65 *(978-1-4965-5826-8(X),* 136914, Stone Arch Bks.) Capstone.
—Metropolis Mayhem. Stephens, Sarah Hines. 2018. (You Choose Stories: Superman Ser.). (ENG.). 112p. (J). (gr. 2-6). lib. bdg. 32.65 *(978-1-4965-5827-5(8),* 136915, Stone Arch Bks.) Capstone.
—Mud Menace! Sutton, Laurie S. 2019. (Amazing Adventures of Batman! Ser.). (ENG.). 32p. (J). (gr. k-2). lib. bdg. 25.32 *(978-1-5158-3979-8(6),* 139705, Stone Arch Bks.) Capstone.
—The Prints of Thieves: Batman & Robin Use Fingerprint Analysis to Crack the Case. Korte, Steve. 2017. (Batman & Robin Crime Scene Investigations Ser.). (ENG.). 32p. (J). (gr. 4-8). lib. bdg. 28.65 *(978-1-5157-6859-3(7),* 135374, Stone Arch Bks.) Capstone.
—Rain of Fear! Snider, Brandon T. 2019. (Amazing Adventures of Batman! Ser.). (ENG.). 32p. (J). (gr. k-2). lib. bdg. 25.32 *(978-1-5158-3981-1(8),* 139707, Stone Arch Bks.) Capstone.
—Reptile Raid. Sutton, Laurie S. 2020. (Amazing Adventures of Batman! Ser.). (ENG.). 32p. (J). (gr. k-2). pap. 5.95 *(978-1-5158-5881-2(2),* 142137); lib. bdg. 25.32 *(978-1-5158-4822-6(1),* 141604) Capstone. (Picture Window Bks.).
—The Rule of Three. Manning, Matthew K. et al. 2015. (Beware the Batman Ser.). (ENG.). 32p. (J). (gr. 3-6). lib. bdg. 22.60 *(978-1-4342-9739-6(X),* Stone Arch Bks.) Capstone.
—Sand Trap! Cadenhead, MacKenzie & Ryan, Sean. 2019. (Marvel Super Hero Adventures Ser.). (ENG.). 80p. (J). (gr. 1-5). lib. bdg. 27.07 *(978-1-5321-4315-1(X),* 31845, Chapter Bks.) Spotlight.
—Scooby-Doo! a Science of Chemical Reactions Mystery: The over-Reacting Ghost. Peterson, Megan Cooley. 2017. (Scooby-Doo Solves It with S. T. E. M. Ser.). (ENG.). 32p. (J). (gr. 3-6). pap. 7.95 *(978-1-5157-3701-8(2));* lib. bdg. 28.65 *(978-1-5157-3697-4(0))* Capstone. (Capstone Pr.).
—Scooby-Doo! a Science of Light Mystery: The Angry Alien. Peterson, Megan Cooley. 2017. (Scooby-Doo Solves It with S. T. E. M. Ser.). (ENG.). 32p. (J). (gr. 3-6). pap. 7.95 *(978-1-5157-3704-9(7));* lib. bdg. 28.65 *(978-1-5157-3700-1(4))* Capstone. (Capstone Pr.).
—Scooby-Doo! & the Pyramids of Giza: The Phantom Pharaohs. Weakland, Mark. 2018. (Unearthing Ancient Civilizations with Scooby-Doo! Ser.). (ENG.). 32p. (J). (gr. 3-6). lib. bdg. 27.99 *(978-1-5157-7513-3(5),* 135893, Capstone Pr.) Capstone.
—Scooby-Doo! & the Pyramids of Giza: The Phantom Pharaohs. Weakland, Mark. 2018. (Unearthing Ancient Civilizations with Scooby-Doo! Ser.). (ENG.). 32p. (J). (gr. 3-6). pap. 8.95 *(978-1-5157-7517-1(8),* 135897, Capstone Pr.) Capstone.
—Scooby-Doo! & the Ruins of Machu Picchu: The Hidden City Howler. Weakland, Mark. 2018. (Unearthing Ancient Civilizations with Scooby-Doo! Ser.). (ENG.). 32p. (J). (gr. 3-6). pap. 8.95 *(978-1-5157-7518-8(6),* 135898, Capstone Pr.) Capstone.
—Scooby-Doo! & the Ruins of Machu Picchu: The Hidden City Howler. Weakland, Mark. 2018. (Unearthing Ancient Civilizations with Scooby-Doo! Ser.). (ENG.). 32p. (J). (gr. 3-6). lib. bdg. 27.99 *(978-1-5157-7514-0(3),* 135894, Capstone Pr.) Capstone.
—Scooby-Doo Solves It with S. T. E. M. Peterson, Megan Cooley. 2017. (Scooby-Doo Solves It with S. T. E. M. Ser.). (ENG.). 32p. (J). (gr. 3-6). 229.20 *(978-1-5157-3717-9(9),* 25460, Capstone Pr.) Capstone.
—Scooby-Doo! Team-Up - Doomed!, Vol. 7. Fisch, Sholly. 2019. 128p. (J). (gr. 2). pap. 12.99 *(978-1-4012-9233-1(X))* DC Comics.
—The Spider-Doctor. McCann, Jim. 2019. (Marvel Super Hero Adventures Graphic Novels Ser.). (ENG.). 24p. (J). (gr. 1-5). lib. bdg. 27.07 *(978-1-5321-4451-6(2),* 33856, Marvel Age) Spotlight.
—Spider-Man & the Stolen Vibranium. McCann, Jim. 2019. (Marvel Super Hero Adventures Graphic Novels Ser.). (ENG.). 24p. (J). (gr. 1-5). lib. bdg. 27.07 *(978-1-5321-4452-3(0),* 33857, Marvel Age) Spotlight.
—The Spitting Image: Batman & Robin Use DNA Analysis to Crack the Case. Korte, Steve. 2017. (Batman & Robin Crime Scene Investigations Ser.). (ENG.). 32p. (J). (gr. 4-8). lib. bdg. 28.65 *(978-1-5157-6858-6(9),* 135373, Stone Arch Bks.) Capstone.
—Superman & the Menace on Mercury: A Solar System Adventure. Korte, Steve. 2018. (Superman Solar System Adventures Ser.). (ENG.). 32p. (J). (gr. 4-8). lib. bdg. 27.99 *(978-1-5435-1567-1(3),* 137925, Capstone Pr.) Capstone.
—Superman & the Nightmare on Neptune: A Solar System Adventure. Korte, Steve. 2018. (Superman Solar System Adventures Ser.). (ENG.). 32p. (J). (gr. 4-8). lib. bdg. 27.99 *(978-1-5435-1574-9(6),* 137929, Capstone Pr.) Capstone.
—Superman & the Utopia on Uranus: A Solar System Adventure. Korte, Steve. 2018. (Superman Solar System Adventures Ser.). (ENG.). 32p. (J). (gr. 4-8). lib. bdg. 27.99 *(978-1-5435-1573-2(8),* 137928, Capstone Pr.) Capstone.
—Superman & the Villains on Venus: A Solar System Adventure. Korte, Steve. 2018. (Superman Solar System Adventures Ser.). (ENG.). 32p. (J). (gr. 4-8). lib. bdg. 27.99 *(978-1-5435-1566-4(5),* 137924, Capstone Pr.) Capstone.
—Superman Day Disaster. Korte, Steve. 2018. (You Choose Stories: Superman Ser.). (ENG.). 112p. (J). (gr. 2-6). lib. bdg. 32.65 *(978-1-4965-5824-4(3),* 136912, Stone Arch Bks.) Capstone.
—Superman Solar System Adventures. Korte, Steve. 2018. (Superman Solar System Adventures Ser.). (ENG.). 32p. (J). (gr. 4-8). 223.92 *(978-1-5435-1607-4(6),* 28051, Stone Arch Bks.) Capstone.
—Teenage Mutant Ninja Turtles: New Animated Adventures. Byerly, Kenny. 2015. (Teenage Mutant Ninja Turtles: New Animated Adventures Ser.). (ENG.). 24p. (J). (gr. 1-5). lib. bdg. 27.07 *(978-1-61479-460-8(X),* 19557); lib. bdg. 27.07 *(978-1-61479-459-2(6),* 19556) Spotlight. (Graphic Novels).
—Teenage Mutant Ninja Turtles: New Animated Adventures, 3. Tipton, Scott. 2015. (Teenage Mutant Ninja Turtles: New Animated Adventures Ser.). (ENG.). 24p. (J). (gr. 1-5). lib. bdg. 27.07 *(978-1-61479-461-5(8),* 19558, Graphic Novels) Spotlight.
—Teenage Mutant Ninja Turtles: New Animated Adventures, 4. Burnham, Erik. 2015. (Teenage Mutant Ninja Turtles: New Animated Adventures Ser.). (ENG.). 24p. (J). (gr. 1-5). lib. bdg. 27.07 *(978-1-61479-462-2(6),* 19559, Graphic Novels) Spotlight.
—Thwip! You Are It! West, Alexandra. 2017. (J). *(978-1-5182-2667-0(1))* Disney Pr.
—The Trail of Tricks: Batman & Robin Use Footwear & Tire Tread Analysis to Crack the Case. Korte, Steve. 2017. (Batman & Robin Crime Scene Investigations Ser.). (ENG.). 32p. (J). (gr. 4-8). lib. bdg. 28.65 *(978-1-5157-6857-9(0),* 135372, Stone Arch Bks.) Capstone.
—Tricks & Treats! Snider, Brandon T. 2019. (Amazing Adventures of Batman! Ser.). (ENG.). 32p. (J). (gr. k-2). lib. bdg. 25.32 *(978-1-5158-3982-8(6),* 139708, Stone Arch Bks.) Capstone.
—Tricky Trouble! West, Alexandra. 2017. (J). *(978-1-5182-2668-7(X))* Disney Pr.
—True Colors, 1 vol. Baltazar, Art et al. 2013. (Green Lantern: the Animated Ser.). (ENG.). 32p. (J). (gr. 2-5). 22.60 *(978-1-4342-4795-7(3),* Stone Arch Bks.) Capstone.
—Welcome to Super Hero High! (DC Super Hero Girls) Carbone, Courtney. 2017. (Step into Reading Ser.). (ENG.). 32p. (J). (gr. k-3). pap. 4.99 *(978-1-5247-6611-5(9),* Random Hse. Bks. for Young Readers) Random Hse. Children's Bks.
—Wonder Woman for President/Rule the School! (DC Super Hero Girls) Fontana, Shea. 2018. (Step into Reading Ser.). (ENG.). 48p. (J). (gr. k-4). pap. 5.99 *(978-0-525-57809-3(9));* lib. bdg. 12.99 *(978-0-525-57810-9(2))* Random Hse. Children's Bks. (Random Hse. Bks. for Young Readers).
—You Choose Stories: Superman. Manning, Matthew K. et al. 2018. (You Choose Stories: Superman Ser.). (ENG.). 112p. (J). (gr. 2-6). 130.60 *(978-1-4965-5828-2(6),* 27469, Stone Arch Bks.) Capstone.
Brizuela, Dario & Corona, Jorge. May I Have This Trance? and Last Pizza. Fisch, Sholly & Wolfram, Amy. 2020. (DC Teen Titans Go! Ser.). (ENG.). 32p. (J). (gr. 2-6). lib. bdg. 21.93 ***(978-1-4965-9942-1(X),*** 201383, Stone Arch Bks.) Capstone.
Brizuela, Dario & Hernandez, Lea. Save the Date and Opposite Day! Fisch, Sholly. 2020. (DC Teen Titans Go! Ser.). (ENG.). 32p. (J). (gr. 2-6). lib. bdg. 21.93 ***(978-1-4965-9944-5(6),*** 201385, Stone Arch Bks.) Capstone.
Brizuela, Dario & Lawson, Jeremy. My Little Mustache & Family Plan. Fisch, Sholly & Hagan, Merrill. 2020. (DC Teen Titans Go! Ser.). (ENG.). 32p. (J). (gr. 2-6). lib. bdg. 21.93 ***(978-1-4965-9943-8(8),*** 201384, Stone Arch Bks.) Capstone.
Brizuela, Dario & Lozano, Omar. The Big Freeze. Sutton, Laurie S. 2020. (Amazing Adventures of Batman! Ser.). (ENG.). 32p. (J). (gr. k-2). pap. 5.95 *(978-1-5158-5883-6(9),* 142139); lib. bdg. 25.32 *(978-1-5158-4824-0(8),* 141606) Capstone. (Picture Window Bks.).
Brizuela, Dario & Staton, Joe. Dinosaur Round-Up, 1 vol. Fisch, Sholly & Ottolini, Horacio. 2012. (DC Super Friends Ser.). (ENG.). 32p. (J). (gr. 2-3). lib. bdg. 22.60 *(978-1-4342-4542-7(X),* Stone Arch Bks.) Capstone.
Brizuela, Dario, jt. illus. see Cornia, Christian.
Brizuela, Dario, jt. illus. see Laufman, Derek.
Brizuela, Dario, jt. illus. see Lozano, Omar.
Brizuela, Dario, jt. illus. see Random House.
Brizuela, Dario, jt. illus. see Vecchio, Luciano.
Brizzi, Liz. Baby Alpaca's Adventure. Rivera, Ann. 2020. (ENG.). 48p. (J). pap. 15.00 ***(978-1-0983-0697-7(X))*** BookBaby.
Broad, Keith F. Peregrine's Christmas Adventure, 2nd Edition: Book I the Pottontot Chronicles. Broad, Keith F. 2012. (ENG.). 120p. (J). pap. *(978-0-9949551-5-9(4))* Whimsey River Productions, Inc.
Broad, Michael. Ghost Diamond!, No. 1. Broad, Michael. 2011. (Agent Amelia Ser.: 1). (ENG.). 144p. (J). (gr. 2-5). lib. bdg. 22.60 *(978-0-7613-8056-6(6))* Lerner Publishing Group.
—Zombie Cows!, No. 2. Broad, Michael. 2011. (Agent Amelia Ser.: 2). (ENG.). 144p. (J). (gr. 2-5). pap. 5.95 *(978-0-7613-8066-5(3),* 9780761380665); lib. bdg. 22.65 *(978-0-7613-8057-3(4),* 9780761380573) Lerner Publishing Group. (Darby Creek).
Broadbent, Eli. Castle in the Sky. Jayne, Stacey. 2019. (ENG.). 30p. (J). pap. *(978-0-473-46963-4(4))* Broadbent, Stacey.
—A Friend Like Frank. Broadbent, Stacey. 2017. (ENG.). (J). pap. *(978-0-473-41588-4(7))* Broadbent, Stacey.
—A Friend Like Frank. Jayne, Stacey. 2019. (ENG.). 38p. (J). pap. *(978-0-473-46964-1(2))* Broadbent, Stacey.
Broadbent, Eli. I'm Feeling Angry. Jayne, Stacey. 2019. (ENG.). 44p. (J). pap. ***(978-0-473-49644-9(5))*** Broadbent, Stacey.
Broadhurst, Colin. Bella's Adventures: Bella in the City. Broadhurst, Sherree. 2010. 38p. pap. 14.50 *(978-1-60976-179-0(0),* Eloquent Bks.) Strategic Book Publishing & Rights Agency (SBPRA).
Broadley, Leo. The Boy Who Cried Wolf: Band 01B/Pink B (Collins Big Cat), Bk. 2. Jenkins, Saffy. 2013. (Collins Big Cat Ser.). (ENG.). 16p. (J). (gr. -1-k). pap. 6.99 *(978-0-00-751267-6(8))* HarperCollins Pubs. Ltd. GBR. Dist: Independent Pubs. Group.
—The Friendly Witch. Elliot, Rachel. 2015. (ENG.). 28p. (J). (gr. -1-3). 7.99 *(978-1-85733-725-9(5))* Lerner Publishing Group.
—The Goat Cafe. Simon, Francesca. 2019. (ENG.). 32p. 16.95 *(978-0-571-32867-3(9),* Faber & Faber Children's Bks.) Faber & Faber, Inc.
Broadnax, Charles. Time for Bed: Andrew & April's Adventures. Kearney Cooper, Nicole. 2005. (J). 7.00 *(978-0-9766086-7-7(7))* nVision Publishing.
Broadway, Hannah. In the Snow. Hayes, Felix. 2014. (Monkey & Robot Ser.). 32p. (J). (gr. -1-k). pap. 10.99 *(978-1-4088-0656-2(8),* 900126953, Bloomsbury Children's Bks.) Bloomsbury Publishing USA.
Broccardo, Andrea & Unzueta, Ángel. Star Wars Vol. 11: The Scourging of Shu-Torun. 2019. 144p. (YA). (gr. 4-17). pap. 17.99 *(978-1-302-91450-9(2))* Marvel Worldwide, Inc.
Broccardo, Andrea, jt. illus. see Gaston, Francesco.
Broccardo, Andrea, jt. illus. see Muhr, Jason.
Brochard, Philippe. Le Tombeau en Peril, Vol. 56. Leblanc, Louise. 2003. (Premier Roman Ser.). (FRE.). 64p. (J). (gr. 2-5). pap. *(978-2-89021-282-4(3))* Diffusion du livre Mirabel (DLM).
Brochard, Philippe, jt. illus. see Casson, Sophie.
Brock, Annie. The Ultimate Teacher Appreciation Gift Book: Create, Color, & Fill in a Year of Classroom Memories with the Best Teacher Ever. 2020. (Books for Teachers Ser.). (ENG.). 64p. (J). pap. 10.00 *(978-1-64604-026-1(0))* Ulysses Pr.
Brock, C. E. Persuasion. Austen, Jane. 2019. (ENG.). 398p. (J). (gr. 4-6). pap. 17.00 *(978-1-0735-1641-4(5))* Independently Published.
—Persuasion: Illustrated & Annotated. Austen, Jane. 2019. (ENG.). 210p. (J). (gr. 4-6). pap. 8.99 *(978-1-0815-2219-3(4))* Independently Published.
—The Railway Children. Nesbit, E. (YA). 14.95 *(978-0-8118-4933-3(3))* Chronicle Bks. LLC.
—The Railway Children. Nesbit, E. 2008. (ENG.). 248p. per. *(978-1-4065-9815-5(1))* Dodo Pr.
—Tales of the Norse Warrior Gods: The Heroes of Asgard. Keary, Annie & Keary, Eliza. 2005. (ENG.). 272p. (gr. 3-7). per. 9.95 *(978-0-486-44053-8(2))* Dover Pubns., Inc.
Brock, Charles Edmund. Flehes an Hens Horn. Nesbit, E. Williams, Nicholas, tr. from ENG. 2012. (COR.). 260p. pap. *(978-1-78201-003-6(3))* Evertype.
—The Railway Children. Nesbit, E. 2012. 232p. pap. *(978-1-78201-004-3(1))* Evertype.
Brock, Emma. Merrimeg (Illustrated Edition) Bowen, William. 2019. (ENG.). 84p. (J). pap. ***(978-1-4068-9805-7(8))*** Echo Library.
Brock, George Ann. Eagle Rock: The Memoirs of a Little Girl, 1941-1945. Monhollon, Lake Pylant. 2003. 137p. (J). 14.95 *(978-0-9712142-1-7(2))* Reflection Publishing Co.
Brock, H. M. Beauty & the Beast. 2012. (ENG.). 48p. (J). 12.95 *(978-1-59583-460-7(5),* 9781595834607, Green Tiger Pr.) Laughing Elephant.
Brock, Jason S. Homecoming: Shafer's Tale of Lost & Found. Tillinger, Theresa D. & Freeman, Patti Bowman. 2018. (Homecoming Ser.: Vol. 1). (ENG.). 48p. (J). (gr. 1-4). 20.00 *(978-0-692-93617-7(3))* Tillinger, Theresa D.
Brocket, Jane, photos by. Spotty, Stripy, Swirly: What Are Patterns? 2012. (Jane Brocket's Clever Concepts Ser.). (ENG., 32p. (J). (gr. -1-2). lib. bdg. 26.65 *(978-0-7613-4613-5(9),* Millbrook Pr.) Lerner Publishing Group.
Brocket, Jane, photos by. Circles, Stars, & Squares: Looking for Shapes. Brocket, Jane. 2012. (Jane Brocket's Clever Concepts Ser.). (ENG., 32p. (J). (gr. -1-2). lib. bdg. 26.65 *(978-0-7613-4611-1(2),* Millbrook Pr.) Lerner Publishing Group.
—Cold, Crunchy, Colorful: Using Our Senses. Brocket, Jane. 2014. (Jane Brocket's Clever Concepts Ser.). (ENG., 32p. (J). (gr. -1-2). lib. bdg. 26.65 *(978-1-4677-0233-1(1),* Millbrook Pr.) Lerner Publishing Group.
—Rainy, Sunny, Blowy, Snowy - What Are Seasons? Brocket, Jane. 2014. (Jane Brocket's Clever Concepts Ser.). (ENG., 32p. (J). (gr. -1-2). lib. bdg. 26.65 *(978-1-4677-0231-7(5),* Millbrook Pr.) Lerner Publishing Group.
—Spiky, Slimy, Smooth: What Is Texture? Brocket, Jane. 2011. (Jane Brocket's Clever Concepts Ser.). (ENG., 32p. (J). (gr. -1-2). 26.65 *(978-0-7613-4614-2(7),* Millbrook Pr.) Lerner Publishing Group.
—Stickiest, Fluffiest, Crunchiest: Super Superlatives. Brocket, Jane. ed. 2015. (Jane Brocket's Clever Concepts Ser.). (ENG., 32p. (J). (gr. -1-2). E-Book 39.99 *(978-1-4677-9268-4(3),* Millbrook Pr.) Lerner Publishing Group.
—1 Cookie, 2 Chairs, 3 Pears: Numbers Everywhere. Brocket, Jane. 2013. (Jane Brocket's Clever Concepts Ser.). (ENG., 32p. (J). (gr. -1-2). lib. bdg. 26.65 *(978-1-4677-0232-4(3));* E-Book 39.99 *(978-1-4677-1702-1(9))* Lerner Publishing Group. (Millbrook Pr.).
Brockington, Saif. I Can. Miller-Joseph, Jennifer. 2019. (ENG.). 38p. (J). (gr. 1-5). 14.99 *(978-1-947928-61-9(9));* (gr. 2-5). pap. 12.99 *(978-1-947928-60-2(0))* VMH Publishing.
Brockschmidt, Kev. Pocketdoodles for Christmas, 1 vol. Wood, Anita. 2015. 240p. pap. 9.99 *(978-1-4236-4115-5(9))* Gibbs Smith, Publisher.
Brocoli, Steffie. Number Circus. Misslin, Sylvie. 2019. (ENG.). 22p. (J). (gr. -1-2). *(978-1-78285-765-5(6))* Barefoot Bks., Ltd.
Broda, Ron. In My Backyard. Ruurs, Margriet. 2007. 32p. (J). (gr. -1-3). 18.95 *(978-0-88776-775-3(3),* Tundra Bks.) Tundra Bks. CAN. Dist: Penguin Random Hse. LLC.
Broderick, Al R. Muffy, Fluffy, & Dexter In. Broderick, Lonia R. 2013. 20p. 20.99 *(978-1-62839-255-5(X))* Salem Author Services.
Broderick, Gardner. Simeon the Snail & the Stained Glass Butterfly. McKelvey, T. L. 2020. (ENG.). 40p. (J). 22.99 ***(978-1-951263-08-9(1))*** Pen It! Pubns., LLC.
Broderick, Setsu. Japanese Traditions: Rice Cakes, Cherry Blossoms & Matsuri - A Year of Seasonal Japanese Festivities. Broderick, Setsu. Moore, Willamarie. 2010. 48p. (J). (gr. 2-6). 16.95 *(978-4-8053-1089-2(8))* Tuttle Publishing.
Broders, Roger & Le Coultre, Marcel. Le Formidable Événement (1921) LeBlanc, Maurice. 2019. (FRE.). 244p. (J). pap. 22.99 *(978-1-0811-0772-7(3))* Independently Published.
Brodie, N. eale. In Vietnam/en Vietnam. Zocchi, Judy. 2005. (Global Adventures II Ser.).Tr. of En Vietnam. (ENG & SPA.). 32p. (J). pap. 10.95 *(978-1-59646-166-6(7))* Dingles & Co.
Brodie, Neal. Seaside Circles/Círculos a la orilla del Mar. Dingles, Molly. 2006. (Community of Shapes Ser.).Tr. of Círculos a la orilla del Mar. (ENG & SPA.). 32p. (J). per. 10.95 *(978-1-59646-259-5(0))* Dingles & Co.
Brodie, Neale. Crescent Kitchen. Dingles, Molly. 2006. (Community of Shapes Ser.). (J). *(978-1-59646-049-2(0))* Dingles & Co.
—Crescent Kitchen: Cocina de Medialuna. Dingles, Molly. 2006. (ENG & SPA.). (J). 21.65 *(978-1-59646-050-8(4))* Dingles & Co.
—In Canada. Zocchi, Judy. 2005. (Global Adventures II Ser.). 32p. (J). pap. 10.95 *(978-1-59646-168-0(3));* lib. bdg. 21.65 *(978-1-59646-083-6(0));* per. 10.95 *(978-1-59646-169-7(1))* Dingles & Co.
—In Canada/en Canada. Zocchi, Judy. 2005. (Global Adventures II Ser.).Tr. of En Canada. (ENG & SPA.). 32p. (J). pap. 10.95 *(978-1-59646-170-3(5));* lib. bdg. 21.65 *(978-1-59646-084-3(9));* per. 10.95 *(978-1-59646-171-0(3))* Dingles & Co.
—In Cuba. Zocchi, Judy. 2005. (Global Adventures II Ser.). 32p. (J). pap. 10.95 *(978-1-59646-160-4(8));* lib. bdg.

21.65 *(978-1-59646-079-9(2))*; per. 10.95 *(978-1-59646-161-1(6))* Dingles & Co.

—In Cuba/en Cuba. Zocchi, Judy. 2005. (Global Adventures II Ser.).Tr. of En Cuba. (ENG & SPA.). 32p. (J). pap. 10.95 *(978-1-59646-162-8(4))*; lib. bdg. 21.65 *(978-1-59646-080-5(6))*; per. 10.95 *(978-1-59646-163-5(2))* Dingles & Co.

—In Germany. Zocchi, Judy. 2005. (Global Adventures II Ser.). 32p. (J). pap. 10.95 *(978-1-59646-180-2(2))*; lib. bdg. 21.65 *(978-1-59646-089-8(X))*; per. 10.95 *(978-1-59646-181-9(0))* Dingles & Co.

—In Germany/en Alemania. Zocchi, Judy. 2005. (Global Adventures II Ser.).Tr. of En Alemania. (ENG & SPA.). (J). 32p. pap. 10.95 *(978-1-59646-182-6(9))*; 28p. lib. bdg. 21.65 *(978-1-59646-090-4(3))*; 32p. per. 10.95 *(978-1-59646-183-3(7))* Dingles & Co.

—In Japan. Zocchi, Judy. 2005. (Global Adventures I Ser.). 32p. (J). pap. 10.95 *(978-1-59646-139-0(X))*; lib. bdg. 21.65 *(978-1-59646-004-1(0))*; per. 10.95 *(978-1-59646-140-6(3))* Dingles & Co.

—In Japan/en Japón. Zocchi, Judy. 2005. (Global Adventures I Ser.).Tr. of En Japón. (ENG & SPA.). 32p. (J). pap. 10.95 *(978-1-59646-141-3(1))*; lib. bdg. 21.65 *(978-1-59646-005-8(9))*; per. 10.95 *(978-1-59646-142-0(X))* Dingles & Co.

—In Mexico. Zocchi, Judy. 2005. (Global Adventures I Ser.). 32p. (J). pap. 10.95 *(978-1-59646-135-2(7))*; lib. bdg. 21.65 *(978-1-59646-002-7(4))*; per. 10.95 *(978-1-59646-136-9(5))* Dingles & Co.

—In Mexico/en México. Zocchi, Judy. 2005. (Global Adventures I Ser.).Tr. of En México. (ENG & SPA.). 32p. (J). pap. 10.95 *(978-1-59646-137-6(3))*; lib. bdg. 21.65 *(978-1-59646-003-4(2))*; per. 10.95 *(978-1-59646-138-3(1))* Dingles & Co.

—In Nigeria. Zocchi, Judy. 2005. (Global Adventures I Ser.). 32p. (J). pap. 10.95 *(978-1-59646-143-7(8))*; lib. bdg. 21.65 *(978-1-59646-010-2(5))*; per. 10.95 *(978-1-59646-144-4(6))* Dingles & Co.

—In Nigeria/en Nigeria. Zocchi, Judy. 2005. (Global Adventures I Ser.).Tr. of En Nigeria. (ENG & SPA.). 32p. (J). pap. 10.95 *(978-1-59646-145-1(4))*; lib. bdg. 21.65 *(978-1-59646-011-9(3))*; per. 10.95 *(978-1-59646-146-8(2))* Dingles & Co.

—In Scotland. Zocchi, Judy. 2005. (Global Adventures I Ser.). 32p. (J). pap. 10.95 *(978-1-59646-147-5(0))*; lib. bdg. 21.65 *(978-1-59646-012-6(1))*; per. 10.95 *(978-1-59646-149-9(7))* Dingles & Co.

—In Scotland/en Escocia. Zocchi, Judy. 2005. (Global Adventures I Ser.).Tr. of En Escocia. (ENG & SPA.). 32p. (J). pap. 10.95 *(978-1-59646-150-5(0))*; lib. bdg. *(978-1-59646-013-3(X))*; per. 10.95 *(978-1-59646-151-2(9))* Dingles & Co.

—In South Africa. Zocchi, Judith Mazzeo. 2008. (J). *(978-1-59646-642-5(1))*; pap. *(978-1-59646-643-2(X))* Dingles & Co.

—In Spain. James, Yolanda. 2008. (J). *(978-1-59646-772-9(X))* Dingles & Co.

—In Sweden. Zocchi, Judy. 2005. (Global Adventures II Ser.). 32p. (J). pap. 10.95 *(978-1-59646-176-5(4))*; lib. bdg. 21.65 *(978-1-59646-087-4(3))*; per. 10.95 *(978-1-59646-177-2(2))* Dingles & Co.

—In Sweden/en Suecia. Zocchi, Judy. 2005. (Global Adventures I Ser.).Tr. of En Japón. (ENG & SPA.). 32p. (J). pap. 10.95 *(978-1-59646-178-9(0))*; lib. bdg. 21.65 *(978-1-59646-088-1(1))*; per. 10.95 *(978-1-59646-179-6(9))* Dingles & Co.

—In Switzerland. Zocchi, Judy. 2005. (Global Adventures I Ser.). 32p. (J). pap. 10.95 *(978-1-59646-156-7(X))*; lib. bdg. 21.65 *(978-1-59646-006-5(7))*; per. 10.95 *(978-1-59646-157-4(8))* Dingles & Co.

—In Switzerland/en Suiza. Zocchi, Judy. 2005. (Global Adventures I Ser.).Tr. of En Suiza. (ENG & SPA.). 32p. (J). pap. 10.95 *(978-1-59646-158-1(6))*; lib. bdg. 21.65 *(978-1-59646-007-2(5))*; per. 10.95 *(978-1-59646-159-8(4))* Dingles & Co.

—In the United States. Zocchi, Judy. 2005. (Global Adventures II Ser.). 32p. (J). pap. 10.95 *(978-1-59646-172-7(1))*; lib. bdg. 21.65 *(978-1-59646-085-0(7))*; per. 9.95 *(978-1-59646-173-4(X))* Dingles & Co.

—In the United States/en los Estados Unidos. Zocchi, Judy. 2005. (Global Adventures II Ser.).Tr. of En los Estados Unidos. (ENG & SPA.). 32p. (J). pap. 10.95 *(978-1-59646-174-1(8))*; lib. bdg. 21.65 *(978-1-59646-086-7(5))*; per. 10.95 *(978-1-59646-175-8(6))* Dingles & Co.

—In Turkey. Zocchi, Judy. 2005. (Global Adventures I Ser.). 32p. (J). pap. 10.95 *(978-1-59646-152-9(7))*; lib. bdg. 21.65 *(978-1-59646-031-7(8))*; per. 10.95 *(978-1-59646-153-6(5))* Dingles & Co.

—In Turkey/en Turquía. Zocchi, Judy. 2005. (Global Adventures I Ser.).Tr. of En Turquía. (ENG & SPA.). 32p. (J). pap. 10.95 *(978-1-59646-154-3(3))*; lib. bdg. 21.65 *(978-1-59646-032-4(6))*; per. 10.95 *(978-1-59646-155-0(1))* Dingles & Co.

—In Vietnam. Zocchi, Judy. 2005. (Global Adventures II Ser.). 32p. (J). pap. 10.95 *(978-1-59646-164-2(0))*; lib. bdg. 21.65 *(978-1-59646-081-2(4))*; per. 10.95 *(978-1-59646-165-9(9))* Dingles & Co.

—In Vietnam/en Vietnam. Zocchi, Judy. 2005. (Global Adventures II Ser.).Tr. of En Vietnam. (ENG & SPA.). 32p. (J). lib. bdg. 21.65 *(978-1-59646-082-9(2))*; per. 10.95 *(978-1-59646-167-3(5))* Dingles & Co.

—Oval Opera. Dingles, Molly. 2006. (Community of Shapes Ser.). 29p. (J). *(978-1-59646-047-8(4))* Dingles & Co.

—Oval Opera: Ópera de óvalos. Dingles, Molly. 2006. (SPA & ENG.). (J). *(978-1-59646-048-5(2))* Dingles & Co.

—Seaside Circles. Dingles, Molly. 2006. (Community of Shapes Ser.). 32p. (J). pap. 10.95 *(978-1-59646-256-4(6))*; lib. bdg. 21.65 *(978-1-59646-033-1(4))*; per. 10.95 *(978-1-59646-257-1(4))* Dingles & Co.

—Seaside Circles/Círculos a la orilla del Mar. Dingles, Molly. 2006. (Community of Shapes Ser.).Tr. of Círculos a la orilla del Mar. (ENG & SPA.). 32p. (J). pap. 10.95 *(978-1-59646-258-8(2))*; lib. bdg. 21.65 *(978-1-59646-034-8(2))* Dingles & Co.

—Star Ship. Dingles, Molly. 2006. (Community of Shapes Ser.). 29p. (J). *(978-1-59646-039-3(3))* Dingles & Co.

—Star Ship: Barco de Estrellas. Dingles, Molly. 2006. (SPA & ENG.). (J). *(978-1-59646-040-9(7))* Dingles & Co.

—Sweet Hearts. Dingles, Molly. 2006. (Community of Shapes Ser.). (J). *(978-1-59646-037-9(7))* Dingles & Co.

—Sweet Hearts: Dulce Corazón. Dingles, Molly. 2006. (SPA & ENG.). (J). *(978-1-59646-038-6(5))* Dingles & Co.

—Town Squares. Dingles, Molly. 2006. (Community of Shapes Ser.). 32p. (J). pap. 10.95 *(978-1-59646-264-9(7))*; lib. bdg. 21.65 *(978-1-59646-041-6(5))*; per. 10.95 *(978-1-59646-265-6(5))* Dingles & Co.

—Town Squares/Cuadrados en la Plaza. Dingles, Molly. 2006. (Community of Shapes Ser.).Tr. of Cuadrados en la Plaza. (ENG & SPA.). 32p. (J). pap. 10.95 *(978-1-59646-266-3(3))*; lib. bdg. 21.65 *(978-1-59646-042-3(3))*; per. 10.95 *(978-1-59646-267-0(1))* Dingles & Co.

Brodie, Neale & McCarthy, Pat. Bertie Wiggins' Amazing Ears. James, Yolanda et al. 2008. (ENG & SPA.). 32p. (J). lib. bdg. 23.65 *(978-1-59646-774-3(6))* Dingles & Co.

Brodner, Steve. Davy Crockett. Kunstler, James Howard. 2004. (Rabbit Ears-A Classic Tale Ser.). (ENG.). 36p. (J). (gr. 2-6). 28.50 *(978-1-59197-762-9(2)*, 12923, Picture Bk.) Spotlight.

Brodner, Terry. Vinny Gets a Job. Brodner, Terry. 2020. (ENG.). 40p. (J). (gr. -1-3). 17.99 ***(978-1-5344-1356-6(1)***, Aladdin) Simon & Schuster Children's Publishing.

Brody, Joyce. Cora the Caterpillar. Mann, Gerre. 2012. 20p. pap. 14.99 *(978-1-61170-088-6(4))* Robertson Publishing.

Brody, Rachel. Mr. Rick: The Fix-It Bee. Jones, Sheryl. 2018. (ENG.). 52p. (J). pap. 10.95 *(978-1-55571-924-1(4)*, Grid Pr.) L & R Publishing, LLC.

Broeck, Fabricio Vanden. Chico Rey. Bergna, Monica. rev. ed. 2006. (Otra Escalera Ser.). (ENG.). 24p. (J). (gr. -1-k). pap. 8.95 *(978-970-20-0830-9(1))* Castillo, Ediciones, S. A. de C. V. MEX. Dist: Macmillan.

—En la Ultima Frontera. Ortiz, Gilberto Rendon & Rendon, Gilberto. rev. ed. 2006. (SPA & ENG.). 268p. (YA). (gr. 8-12). pap. 8.95 *(978-970-20-0134-8(X))* Castillo, Ediciones, S. A. de C. V. MEX. Dist: Macmillan.

—Under the Breadfruit Tree: Island Poems. Gunning, Monica. 2004. (ENG.). 48p. (J). (gr. 2-k). pap. 9.95 *(978-1-59078-258-3(5))* Boyds Mills Pr.

Broeck, Fabricio Vanden, jt. illus. see Vigil, Luis Gerardo Sanchez.

Broecker, Randy. Terrifying Tales to Tell at Night: 10 Scary Stories to Give You Nightmares! 2019. 240p. (J). (gr. 2-6). pap. 7.99 *(978-1-5107-5124-8(6)*, Sky Pony Pr.) Skyhorse Publishing Co., Inc.

Broekstra, Lorette. Baby Bear Goes to the Zoo. 2004. (Baby Bear Ser.). 32p. (J). pap. 4.99 *(978-1-85854-711-4(3))* Brimax Books Ltd. GBR. Dist: Byeway Bks.

Broesch, Valerie, jt. illus. see Zabel, Randy.

Brokenshire, Nick. Amelia Cole Omnibus. Kirkbride, D. J. & Knave, Adam P. 2017. (Amelia Cole Ser.). 500p. (YA). (gr. 8-12). pap. 39.99 *(978-1-63140-899-1(2))* Idea & Design Works, LLC.

Brol, Magda. Pirates Don't Go to School! Macdonald, Alan. 2019. (ENG.). 32p. (J). (gr. -1-2). 17.99 *(978-1-68010-156-0(0))* Tiger Tales.

Brolin, Carol. Money...Cool! Fabris, Judith. l.t. ed. 2003. 155p. (YA). pap. 9.95 *(978-1-893335-12-7(7))* Archipelago Pr.

Bromley Bartram, Jessica. Summer North Coming-Winter North Coming, 1 vol. Bentley, Dorothy. 2019. (ENG.). 32p. (J). (gr. 1-3). 19.95 *(978-1-55455-465-2(9)*, 92cd5703-8790-4b9c-b2c9-145a4d670b73) Fitzhenry & Whiteside, Ltd. CAN. Dist: Firefly Bks., Ltd.

Bron, Anna. Salma the Syrian Chef. Ramadan, Danny. 2020. (ENG.). 40p. (J). (gr. -1-2). 18.95 *(978-1-77321-375-0(X))* Annick Pr., Ltd. CAN. Dist: Publishers Group West (PGW).

Bronfeyn, Lily. Cheese Please, Chimpanzees: Fun with Spelling. Traynor, Tracy. 2008. (Milet Wordwise Ser.). (ENG.). 28p. (J). (gr. k-2). pap. 6.95 *(978-1-84059-511-6(6))* Milet Publishing.

Bronowski, Karen Kmetz. The Golden Leaf. Rendina, Donna Rae. 2011. 24p. 20.00 *(978-1-61170-014-5(0))* Robertson Publishing.

Bronson, Jody. Fox Talk. Carmichael, L. E. 2013. 62p. *(978-0-9881638-5-0(3))*; pap. *(978-0-9881638-6-7(1))* Ashby-BP Publishing.

Bronson, Linda. All Year Long. Deady, Kathleen W. 2004. (Carolrhoda Picture Books Ser.). 32p. (J). (gr. -1-3). 15.95 *(978-1-57505-537-4(6))* Lerner Publishing Group.

—Gorp's Secret: An Empowering Tale in Pumpernickel Park. Chessen, Sherri. 2008. (ENG.). 36p. (J). 16.95 *(978-0-9724249-3-6(8))* Gorp Group Pr., The.

—The Story of Halloween. Greene, Carol. 2004. 40p. (J). 15.99 *(978-0-06-027946-2(X))*; lib. bdg. 16.89 *(978-0-06-029560-8(0))* HarperCollins Pubs.

—The Three Funny Friends. Zolotow, Charlotte. 2006. 27p. (J). (gr. k-4). reprint ed. 16.00 *(978-0-7567-9860-4(4))* DIANE Publishing Co.

Bronson, Tammy Carter. Kaleidonotes & the Mixed-up Orchestra. Bronson, Tammy Carter. Bronson, Matthew Shane. 2nd rev. ed. 2003. 24p. (J). lib. bdg. 12.99 *(978-0-9678167-6-0(9))* Bookaroos Publishing, Inc.

—Polliwog. Bronson, Tammy Carter. 2006. (ENG & SPA.). (J). 7.99 *(978-0-9678167-5-3(0))* Bookaroos Publishing, Inc.

—Polliwog. Bronson, Tammy Carter. Davi, Annou, tr. 2004. (SPA & ENG.). 32p. (J). lib. bdg. 17.00 *(978-0-9678167-4-6(2))* Bookaroos Publishing, Inc.

Bronson, Wilfrid S. Cats. 2008. 84p. (J). per. 18.95 *(978-0-86534-645-1(3))* Sunstone Pr.

—The Grasshopper Book. 2009. 136p. (J). pap. 22.95 *(978-0-86534-690-1(9))* Sunstone Pr.

—Starlings. 2008. 84p. (J). pap. 18.95 *(978-0-86534-649-9(6))* Sunstone Pr.

—Stooping Hawk & Stranded Whale, Sons of Liberty. 2009. 236p. (J). pap. 22.95 *(978-0-86534-715-1(8))* Sunstone Pr.

—Turtles. 2008. 68p. (J). pap. 18.95 *(978-0-86534-651-2(8))* Sunstone Pr.

—The Wonder World of Ants. 2009. 96p. (J). pap. 19.95 *(978-0-86534-691-8(7))* Sunstone Pr.

Bronte, Jules & Oapos, Jem. The Castle Adventure. 2013. 171p. pap. *(978-1-908804-08-2(4))* Bingham Mayne & Smith, Ltd.

Brook, Autumn. Moving Day. Perry, Barbara. 2019. (ENG.). 34p. (J). (gr. -1-3). pap. 11.99 ***(978-1-61254-383-3(9))*** Brown Books Publishing Group.

—A Perfect Puddle. Perry, Barbara. 2019. (ENG.). 34p. (J). (gr. -1-3). pap. 11.99 ***(978-1-61254-382-6(0))*** Brown Books Publishing Group.

—Ted the Friendly Frog & the Race at Golden Lake. McCall, Scott. 2019. (ENG.). 34p. (J). (gr. -1-2). pap. 11.99 ***(978-1-61254-381-9(2))*** Brown Books Publishing Group.

—Ted the Friendly Frog & the Tale of the Diamond. McCall, Scott. 2019. (ENG.). 34p. (J). (gr. -1-2). pap. 11.99 ***(978-1-61254-380-2(4))*** Brown Books Publishing Group.

Brooke, Iris. A Pageant of Kings & Queens. Matthews, C. M. et al. 2011. (ENG.). 98p. pap. 20.95 *(978-0-521-23596-9(0))* Cambridge Univ. Pr.

Brooke, Janet. Mishan's Garden. Vollbracht, James. 2013. (ENG.). 32p. (J). (gr. k-9). 16.95 *(978-1-61429-112-1(8))* Wisdom Pubns.

—Prince Siddhartha: The Story of Buddha. Landaw, Jonathan. 2nd rev. ed. 2011. (ENG.). 144p. (J). (gr. 2-7). pap. 22.95 *(978-0-86171-653-1(1))* Wisdom Pubns.

Brooke, L. Leslie. Ring o' Roses, a Nursery Rhyme Picture Book. Brooke, L. Leslie. 2012. 102p. pap. 9.99 *(978-1-61720-438-8(2))* Wilder Pubns., Corp.

Brooker Brooker, Kyrsten. Bitter & Sweet, 1 vol. Feder, Sandra V. 2018. (ENG.). 32p. (J). (gr. k-2). 17.95 *(978-1-55498-995-9(7))* Groundwood Bks. CAN. Dist: Publishers Group West (PGW).

Brooker, Kyrsten. Chik Chak Shabbat. Rockliff, Mara. 32p. (J). (gr. -1-2). 2016. 7.99 *(978-0-7636-8895-0(9))*; 2014. 15.99 *(978-0-7636-5528-0(7))* Candlewick Pr.

—Dinner with the Highbrows. Holt, Kimberly Willis. 2014. (ENG.). 36p. (J). (gr. -1-2). 17.99 *(978-0-8050-8088-9(0)*, 900039274, Holt, Henry & Co. Bks. For Young Readers) Holt, Henry & Co.

—The Honeybee Man. Nargi, Lela. 2011. 40p. (J). (gr. -1-3). 17.99 *(978-0-375-84980-0(7)*, Schwartz & Wade Bks.) Random Hse. Children's Bks.

—Nothing Ever Happens on 90th Street. Schotter, Roni. 2014. 32p. pap. 7.00 *(978-1-61003-316-9(7))* Center for the Collaborative Classroom.

—The Passover Parrot, 2nd Edition. Zusman, Evelyn. rev. ed. 2018. (ENG.). 32p. (J). (gr. -1-3). 17.99 *(978-1-5124-2882-7(5)*, 9781512428827, Kar-Ben Publishing) Lerner Publishing Group.

—Precious & the Boo Hag. McKissack, Patricia C. & Moss, Onawumi Jean. 2005. (ENG.). 40p. (J). (gr. -1-3). 19.99 *(978-0-689-85194-0(4)*, Atheneum Bks. for Young Readers) Simon & Schuster Children's Publishing.

—Tadeo's Search for Circles, 1 vol. Brooker, Marion. 2011. (ENG.). 32p. (J). (gr. k-1). 18.95 *(978-1-55455-173-6(0)*, 3bc3c943-3cb6-4137-b088-6ef6ef59ce4d) éditeur, Annika Parance CAN. Dist: Firefly Bks., Ltd.

—They Saw the Future: Oracles, Psychics, Scientists, Great Thinkers, & Pretty Good Guessers. Krull, Kathleen. 2014. (ENG.). 112p. (J). (gr. -1-3). pap. 45.99 *(978-1-4814-3623-6(6)*, Atheneum Bks. for Young Readers) Simon & Schuster Children's Publishing.

—When We Go Walking, 0 vols. Best, Cari. 2013. (ENG.). 32p. (J). (gr. -1-3). 17.99 *(978-1-4778-1648-6(8)*, 9781477816486, Two Lions) Amazon Publishing.

Brookes, Debbie Joy. The Secret Wave. Brookes, Debbie Joy. 2019. (ENG.). 90p. (J). pap. ***(978-1-78132-893-4(5))*** SilverWood Bks.

Brookes, Katie. Flutterby the Knitted Butterfly. McRoy, Miss Rachel. 2017. (ENG.). 30p. (J). pap. *(978-1-9999243-0-0(4))* B is for Bks.

Brookes, Rob. Under the Oaken Bough: Folk & Fairy Tales. Brooks, Simon. 2018. (ENG.). 160p. (J). (gr. -1-6). pap. 12.95 *(978-1-62491-110-1(2))* Parkhurst Brothers, Inc., Pubs.

Brookfield, Maureen. E Is for Empire: A New York State Alphabet. Burg, Ann. 2003. (Discover America State by State Ser.). (ENG.). 40p. (J). 17.95 *(978-1-58536-113-7(5))* Sleeping Bear Pr.

—N Is for Nutmeg: A Connecticut Alphabet. Elissa, Grodin. 2003. (Discover America State by State Ser.). (ENG.). 40p. (J). 17.95 *(978-1-58536-124-3(0))* Sleeping Bear Pr.

Brookfield, Maureen K. Times Square: A New York State Number Book. Burg, Ann E. 2005. (Count Your Way Across the USA Ser.). (ENG.). 40p. (J). (gr. k-6). 16.95 *(978-1-58536-195-3(X))* Sleeping Bear Pr.

—Yankee Doodle Numbers: A Connecticut Number Book. Grodin, Elissa D. rev. ed. 2007. (Count Your Way Across the U. S. A. Ser.). (ENG.). 40p. (J). (gr. 3-7). 17.95 *(978-1-58536-175-5(5))* Sleeping Bear Pr.

Brooks, Brett. Winston & Bentley: Best Friends. Peppler, Mark W. 2019. (Winston & Bentley Ser.: Vol. 1). (ENG.). 34p. (J). pap. 9.98 ***(978-1-7228-3523-1(0))*** CreateSpace Independent Publishing Platform.

Brooks, Brian. Oopsy Daisy's Bad Day. Brooks, Brian. 2007. 62p. (J). reprint ed. 13.00 *(978-1-4223-9004-7(7))* DIANE Publishing Co.

Brooks, Brian, jt. illus. see Reger, Rob.

Brooks, David. A Is for Airplane. Howell, Theresa. 2003. (MUL.). 28p. (J). (gr. -1-k). bds. 6.95 *(978-0-87358-831-7(2))* Cooper Square Publishing Llc.

—Animals. 2005. (My First Book Ser.). 9p. (J). (gr. -1-1). bds. 3.95 *(978-1-933050-09-6(8))* Sweetwater Pr.

—Awesome Animals ABC. Biskup, Agnieszka. 2005. (J). *(978-1-58987-095-6(6))* Kindermusik International.

—Mi Primer Libro Alfabeto. Alvarez, Lourdes M. 2005. (Mi primer libro Ser.). (SPA.). 9p. (J). (gr. -1 — 1). bds. 3.95 *(978-1-933050-02-7(0))* Sweetwater Pr.

—Mi Primer Libro Animales. Alvarez, Lourdes M. 2005. (Mi primer libro Ser.). (SPA.). 9p. (J). (gr. -1 — 1). bds. 3.95 *(978-1-933050-04-1(7))* Sweetwater Pr.

—Mi Primer Libro Cosas. Alvarez, Lourdes M. 2005. (Mi primer libro Ser.). (SPA.). 9p. (J). (gr. -1 — 1). bds. 3.95 *(978-1-933050-03-4(9))* Sweetwater Pr.

—Mi Primer Libro Formas. Alvarez, Lourdes M. 2005. (Mi primer libro Ser.). (SPA.). 9p. (J). (gr. -1 — 1). bds. 3.95 *(978-1-933050-05-8(5))* Sweetwater Pr.

—Mi Primer Libro Numeros. Alvarez, Lourdes M. 2005. (Mi primer libro Ser.). (SPA.). 9p. (J). (gr. -1 — 1). bds. 3.95 *(978-1-933050-00-3(4))* Sweetwater Pr.

—The Mountain Pine Beetle: Tiny but Mighty. Turnbaugh, Kay. 2011. (Pruett Ser.). (ENG.). 48p. (J). pap. 14.95 *(978-0-87108-958-8(0)*, West Winds Pr.) West Margin Pr.

—My First Book Alphabet. Alvarez, Lourdes M. 2005. (My First Book Ser.). 9p. (J). (gr. -1-17). bds. 3.95 *(978-1-933050-08-9(X))* Sweetwater Pr.

—My First Book Colors. Alvarez, Lourdes M. 2005. (My First Book Ser.). 9p. (J). (gr. -1-1). bds. 3.95 *(978-1-933050-07-2(1))* Sweetwater Pr.

—My First Book Numbers. Alvarez, Lourdes M. 2005. (My First Book Ser.). 9p. (J). (gr. -1-1). bds. 3.95 *(978-1-933050-06-5(3))* Sweetwater Pr.

—My First Book Shapes. Alvarez, Lourdes M. 2005. (My First Book Ser.). 9p. (J). (gr. -1-1). bds. 3.95 *(978-1-933050-11-9(X))* Sweetwater Pr.

—My First Book Things. Alvarez, Lourdes M. 2005. (My First Book Ser.). 9p. (J). (gr. -1-1). bds. 3.95 *(978-1-933050-10-2(1))* Sweetwater Pr.

Brooks, David. You Can Count in the Desert, Vol. Brooks, David. 2005. (You Can Count Ser.). (ENG.). 24p. (J). (gr. -1 — 1). 7.95 *(978-1-55971-910-0(9))* Cooper Square Publishing Llc.

Brooks, Dennis. Rusty Hooks & the Great Sailboat Race. Colvin, Joshua C. 2018. (ENG.). 36p. (J). (gr. k-3). 19.95 *(978-0-692-17283-4(1))* Jib & Jigger, Inc.

Brooks, Dominic. Is It My Turn Yet? 2008. 30p. (J). per. *(978-0-9795768-2-9(2))* Better Tomorrow Publishing, A.

Brooks, Elizabeth, et al. How to Make Historic American Costumes. Evans, Mary & Landes, William-Alan. rev. ed. 2003. 180p. (J). (gr. 8-12). pap. 22.00 *(978-0-88734-636-1(7))* Players Pr., Inc.

Brooks, Erik. Beluga Whales, Grizzly Tales, & More Alaska Kidsnacks: Fun Recipes for Cooking with Kids. Bugni, Alice. 2016. (Paws IV Ser.). 32p. (J). (gr. -1-2). pap. 10.99 *(978-1-57061-999-1(9)*, Little Bigfoot) Sasquatch Bks.

—If I Were a Bear. Gill, Shelley. 2019. (If I Were Ser.). 22p. (J). (— 1). bds. 9.99 *(978-1-63217-196-2(1)*, Little Bigfoot) Sasquatch Bks.

—If I Were a Bird. Gill, Shelley. 2019. (If I Were Ser.). 22p. (J). (— 1). bds. 9.99 *(978-1-63217-211-2(9)*, Little Bigfoot) Sasquatch Bks.

—If I Were a Whale. Gill, Shelley. 2017. (If I Were Ser.). 20p. (J). (— 1). bds. 9.99 *(978-1-63217-104-7(X)*, Little Bigfoot) Sasquatch Bks.

—Polar Polka: Counting Polar Bears in Alaska. Stihler, Cherie B. 2008. (Paws IV Ser.). 32p. (J). (gr. -1-2). pap. 10.95 *(978-1-57061-520-7(9)*, Little Bigfoot) Sasquatch Bks.

—The Runaway Tortilla. Kimmel, Eric A. 2016. (ENG.). 32p. (J). (gr. k-3). pap. 10.99 *(978-1-943328-70-3(6)*, West Winds Pr.) West Margin Pr.

—The Runaway Tortilla. Kimmel, Eric A. 2017. (ENG.). 32p. (J). (gr. k-3). 26.99 *(978-1-5132-6079-2(0)*, West Winds Pr.) West Margin Pr.

—Sea Star Wishes. Ode, Eric. 2018. 32p. (J). (gr. -1-3). pap. 10.99 *(978-1-63217-154-2(6)*, Little Bigfoot) Sasquatch Bks.

—Sea Star Wishes: Poems from the Coast. Ode, Eric. 2013. 32p. (J). (gr. -1-3). 16.99 *(978-1-57061-790-4(2)*, Little Bigfoot) Sasquatch Bks.

—Totem Tale: A Tall Story from Alaska. Vanasse, Deb. 2006. (Paws IV Ser.). 32p. (J). (gr. -1-2). pap. 10.99 *(978-1-57061-439-2(3)*, Little Bigfoot) Sasquatch Bks.

—What Are You Hungry For? Feed Your Tummy & Your Heart. Aronson, Emme & Aronson, Phillip. 2007. 32p. (J). (gr. -1-3). lib. bdg. 16.89 *(978-0-06-054308-2(6))* HarperCollins Pubs.

—Who Has These Feet? Hulbert, Laura. 2011. (ENG.). 44p. (J). (gr. -1-2). 18.99 *(978-0-8050-8907-3(1)*, 900054728, Holt, Henry & Co. Bks. For Young Readers) Holt, Henry & Co.

Brooks, Kaarina. Peikko, the Foolish Ogre. Brooks, Kaarina, tr. 2003. (Aspasia Children's Bks.). (ENG.). 61p. pap. 12.00 *(978-0-9731053-2-2(1))* Aspasia Bks. CAN. Dist: Univ. of Toronto Pr.

Brooks, Karen Stormer. The Magic Box: When Parents Can't Be There to Tuck You In. Sederman, Marty & Epstein, Seymour. 2003. 32p. (J). (gr. -1-3). 14.95 *(978-1-55798-807-2(2)*, Magination Pr.) American Psychological Assn.

—Sister for Sale!, 1 vol. Adams, Michelle Medlock & Adams, Michelle M. 2007. (I Can Read! Ser.). (ENG.). 32p. (J). (gr. -1-1). pap. 4.99 *(978-0-310-71469-9(9))* Zonderkidz.

Brooks, Mark, et al. Amazing Spider-Man by J. Michael Straczynski Omnibus Vol. 2. 2020. 1136p. (YA). (gr. 8-17). 125.00 *(978-1-302-92313-6(7))* Marvel Worldwide, Inc.

—Han Solo: Volume 4. Liu, Marjorie. 2017. (Star Wars: Han Solo Ser.). (ENG.). 24p. (J). (gr. 6-12). lib. bdg. 27.07 *(978-1-5321-4018-1(5)*, 25451, Graphic Novels) Spotlight.

Brooks, Mark & Oback, Sonia. Han Solo: Volume 1. Liu, Marjorie. 2017. (Star Wars: Han Solo Ser.). (ENG.). 24p. (J). (gr. 6-12). lib. bdg. 27.07 *(978-1-5321-4015-0(0)*, 25448, Graphic Novels) Spotlight.

—Han Solo: Volume 2. Liu, Marjorie. 2017. (Star Wars: Han Solo Ser.). (ENG.). 24p. (J). (gr. 6-12). lib. bdg. 27.07 *(978-1-5321-4016-7(9)*, 25449, Graphic Novels) Spotlight.

—Han Solo: Volume 3. Liu, Marjorie. 2017. (Star Wars: Han Solo Ser.). (ENG.). 24p. (J). (gr. 6-12). lib. bdg. 27.07 *(978-1-5321-4017-4(7)*, 25450, Graphic Novels) Spotlight.

—Han Solo: Volume 5. Liu, Marjorie. 2017. (Star Wars: Han Solo Ser.). (ENG.). 24p. (J). (gr. 6-12). lib. bdg. 27.07 *(978-1-5321-4019-8(3)*, 25452, Graphic Novels) Spotlight.

Brooks, Molly. Science Comics: Flying Machines: How the Wright Brothers Soared. Wilgus, Alison. 2017. (Science Comics Ser.). (ENG.). 128p. (J). pap. 12.99 *(978-1-62672-139-5(4)*, 900140349, First Second Bks.) Roaring Brook Pr.

Brooks, Molly. Field Trip. Brooks, Molly. 2019. (Sanity & Tallulah Ser.: 2). (ENG.). 240p. (J). (gr. 3-7). pap. 12.99 *(978-1-368-02377-1(0))* Disney Pr.

B

—Sanity & Tallulah. Brooks, Molly. 2018. (Sanity & Tallulah Ser.: 1). (ENG.). 240p. (J). (gr. 3-7). 21.99 *(978-1-368-00844-0(5))*; pap. 12.99 *(978-1-368-02280-4(4))* Hyperion Bks. for Children.

Brooks, Nan. Go Back to Bed! Williams, Tracey V. 2018. (ENG.). 30p. (J). pap. 10.99 *(978-1-7198-6277-6(X))* Independently Published.

—The Little Reindeer. Tyrell, Melissa. enl. ed. 2005. (ENG.). 10p. (J). (gr. -1-3). 4.95 *(978-1-58117-119-8(6))*, Intervisual/Piggy Toes) Bendon, Inc.

—Make New Friends. Schwaeber, Barbie. (American Favorites Ser.). (ENG.). 32p. (J). (gr. -1-3). 2008. 14.95 *(978-1-59249-728-7(4))*; 2007. 8.95 *(978-1-59249-729-4(2))* Soundprints.

—Make New Friends. Soundprints Staff. Schwaeber, Barbie Heit & Williams, Tracee, eds. 2008. (ENG.). 24p. (J). (gr. -1). 4.99 *(978-1-59069-651-4(4))* Studio Mouse LLC.

—Making Minestrone. Blackstone, Stella. 2006. 32p. (J). (gr. k-4). reprint ed. 16.00 *(978-0-7567-9926-7(0))* DIANE Publishing Co.

—This Little Piggy. 2004. (J). 11.99 *(978-1-890647-10-0(1))* TOMY International, Inc.

Brooks, Nan & Grayson, Rick. Science Tub Topics: Approaching Science Through Discovery. Morton, Debra & Stover, Elizabeth. Jennett, Pamela, ed. 2003. 128p. (J). (gr. k-3). pap. 13.99 *(978-1-57471-953-6(X)*, 2811) Creative Teaching Pr., Inc.

Brooks, P. S. Positively Purple. Ragsdale, Linda. 2019. (ENG.). 32p. (J). (gr. k-2). 16.99 *(978-1-4867-1467-4(6)*, 47fb56e2-afb3-4249-b682-d08ada47d7ce) Flowerpot Pr.

Brooks, Patrick & Lombardo, Serena. Roman Myths: Volume Two. Macdonald, Fiona. ed. 2020. 88p. (J). (gr. 2). 12.95 *(978-1-912904-83-9(7)*, Scribblers) Book Hse. GBR. Dist: Sterling Publishing Co., Inc.

Brooks, Ron. The Dream of the Thylacine. Wild, Margaret. 2013. (ENG.). 32p. (J). (gr. 3-5). 23.99 *(978-1-74237-383-6(6))* Allen & Unwin AUS. Dist: Independent Pubs. Group.

—Old Pig. Wild, Margaret. 2017. (ENG.). 32p. (J). (gr. -1-1). 17.99 *(978-1-76029-389-5(X))* Allen & Unwin AUS. Dist: Independent Pubs. Group.

Brooks, S. G. The Three Armadillies Tuff, 1 vol. Hopkins, Jackie Mims. 2011. (ENG.). 32p. (J). pap. 7.95 *(978-1-56145-598-0(9)*, Peachtree Junior) Peachtree Publishing Co. Inc.

—Westley the Wicked & the Rascally Ring Bear. Slater, David Michael. 2012. 36p. pap. 10.95 *(978-1-61413-028-4(0))* Puddletown Publishing Group, Inc.

Brooks, Scott. Shark Attack! Mad Libs. Matheis, Mickie. 2018. (Mad Libs Ser.). 48p. (J). (gr. 3-7). pap. 4.99 *(978-1-5247-8819-3(8)*, Mad Libs) Penguin Young Readers Group.

Brooks, Scott R. Benedict Arnold: Hero or Enemy Spy? Derr, Aaron. 2018. (Hidden History — Spies Ser.). (ENG.). 32p. (J). (gr. 2-5). pap. 8.99 *(978-1-63440-293-4(6))*; lib. bdg. 26.65 *(978-1-63440-279-8(0))* Red Chair Pr.

Brooks, Scott R. Daniel Inouye: World War II Hero & Senator. Walters, Jennifer Marino. 2020. (Beginner Biography (LOOK! Books (tm)) Ser.). (ENG.). 24p. (J). (gr. k-2). pap. 6.99 ***(978-1-63440-896-7(9))***; lib. bdg. 25.32 ***(978-1-63440-729-8(6))*** Red Chair Pr.

Brooks, Scott R. Elizabeth Cady Stanton: Fighter for Women's Rights. Cipriano, Jeri. 2020. (Beginner Biography (LOOK! Books (tm)) Ser.). (ENG.). 24p. (J). (gr. k-2). pap. 6.99 *(978-1-63440-988-9(4))*; lib. bdg. 25.32 *(978-1-63440-987-2(6))* Red Chair Pr.

—Harriet Tubman: Union Spy. Cipriano, Jeri. 2018. (Hidden History — Spies Ser.). (ENG.). 32p. (J). (gr. 2-5). pap. 8.99 *(978-1-63440-297-2(9))*; lib. bdg. 26.65 *(978-1-63440-284-2(7))* Red Chair Pr.

—Moe Berg: Spy Catcher. Cipriano, Jeri. 2018. (Hidden History — Spies Ser.). (ENG.). 32p. (J). (gr. 2-5). pap. 8.99 *(978-1-63440-294-1(4))*; lib. bdg. 26.65 *(978-1-63440-280-4(4))* Red Chair Pr.

—Rose Greenhow: Confederate Spy. Mattern, Joanne. 2018. (Hidden History — Spies Ser.). (ENG.). 32p. (J). (gr. 2-5). pap. 8.99 *(978-1-63440-295-8(2))*; lib. bdg. 26.65 *(978-1-63440-281-1(2))* Red Chair Pr.

—Ruby Bridges: A Brave Child Who Made History. Cipriano, Jeri. 2020. (Beginner Biography (LOOK! Books (tm)) Ser.). (ENG.). 24p. (J). (gr. k-2). pap. 6.99 *(978-1-63440-964-3(7))*; lib. bdg. 25.32 *(978-1-63440-963-6(9))* Red Chair Pr.

Brooks, Scott R. Sequoyah: Man of Many Words. Cipriano, Jeri. 2020. (Beginner Biography (LOOK! Books (tm)) Ser.). (ENG.). 24p. (J). (gr. k-2). pap. 6.99 ***(978-1-63440-982-7(5))***; lib. bdg. 25.32 ***(978-1-63440-981-0(7))*** Red Chair Pr.

Brooks, Scott R. Sojourner Truth: Fighting for Freedom. Cipriano, Jeri. 2020. (Beginner Biography (LOOK! Books (tm)) Ser.). (ENG.). 24p. (J). (gr. k-2). pap. 6.99 *(978-1-63440-994-0(9))*; lib. bdg. 25.32 *(978-1-63440-993-3(0))* Red Chair Pr.

—Wilma Rudolph: Fastest Woman on Earth. Cipriano, Jeri. 2020. (Beginner Biography (LOOK! Books (tm)) Ser.). (ENG.). 24p. (J). (gr. k-2). pap. 6.99 *(978-1-63440-976-6(0))*; lib. bdg. 25.32 *(978-1-63440-975-9(2))* Red Chair Pr.

Brooks, Sonya L. Betsy's Blessing: Daddy, My Piggy Bank Is Not Empty. Brooks, Sonya L. 2019. (ENG.). 26p. (J). pap. 15.95 *(978-1-0720-3587-9(1))* Independently Published.

Brooks, Timothy. No Bees, Please! Dennis, Nicole S. 2018. (Little Scary Mouse Ser.: Vol. 1). (ENG.). 28p. (J). (gr. k-2). 14.88 *(978-1-7326042-0-9(7))* Little Scary Mouse.

Brooksbank, Angela. B Is for Baby. Atinuke. 2019. (ENG.). 40p. (J). (gr. -1-2). 16.99 *(978-1-5362-0166-6(9))* Candlewick Pr.

—Baby Goes to Market. Atinuke. (ENG.). (J). 2019. 26p. (-k). bds. 8.99 *(978-1-5362-0552-7(4))*; 2017. 32p. (gr. -1-2). 16.99 *(978-0-7636-9570-5(X)*, 40028171753) Candlewick Pr.

Brooksbank, Angela. Catch That Chicken! Atinuke. 2020. (ENG.). 32p. (J). (-k). 16.99 ***(978-1-5362-1268-6(7))*** Candlewick Pr.

Brookshire, Breezy. Empowered: How God Shaped 11 Women's Lives (and Can Shape Yours Too) Parks, Catherine. 2019. (ENG.). 208p. (J). (gr. 2-8). pap. 14.99 *(978-1-5359-3455-8(7)*, 005809927, B&H Kids) B&H Publishing Group.

—For Such a Time As This: Stories of Women from the Bible, Retold for Girls. Smith, Angie. 2014. (ENG.). 256p. (gr. 1-5). 14.99 *(978-1-4336-8046-5(7)*, 005559503, B&H Kids) B&H Publishing Group.

—How Big Is Love? (padded Board Book) Parker, Amy. 2016. (Faith, Hope, Love Ser.). (ENG.). 24p. (J). (gr. -1-k). bds. 9.99 *(978-1-4336-9042-6(X)*, 005778804, B&H Kids) B&H Publishing Group.

—How Far Is Faith? (padded Board Book) Parker, Amy. 2016. (Faith, Hope, Love Ser.). (ENG.). 24p. (J). (gr. -1-k). bds. 9.99 *(978-1-4336-9040-2(3)*, 005778802, B&H Kids) B&H Publishing Group.

—How High Is Hope? (padded Board Book) Parker, Amy. 2016. (Faith, Hope, Love Ser.). (ENG.). 24p. (J). (gr. -1-k). bds. 9.99 *(978-1-4336-9041-9(1)*, 005778803, B&H Kids) B&H Publishing Group.

Brophy, Brian, photos by. From My Eyes: Life from a Ten Year Old Boy's Perspective. Brophy, Brian. Brophy, Doris, ed. 2003. per. *(978-0-9745232-0-0(8))* Brophy, Doris Anne.

Brophy, Nannette. The Color of My Fur. Brophy, Nannette. 2019. (ENG.). 34p. (J). (gr. k-4). 16.99 *(978-1-7336564-0-5(5))* Major Masterpieces Ltd.

Broseghini, Giorgia. Have You Ever Heard a Dragon's Song? Lift & Listen Adventure. Birdsong, Minnie. Cottage Door Press, ed. 2018. (ENG.). 12p. (J). (gr. -1-2). bds. 16.99 *(978-1-68052-326-3(0)*, 1003020) Cottage Door Pr.

—Wild Bios: Yakkie Robinson. Acampora, Courtney & Fischer, Maggie. 2020. (Wild Bios Ser.). (ENG.). 16p. (J). (— 1). bds. 7.99 *(978-1-68412-913-3(3)*, Silver Dolphin Bks.) Printers Row Publishing Group.

Brosgol, Vera. Lyric McKerrigan, Secret Librarian. Weinstein, Jacob Sager. 2018. (ENG.). 48p. (J). (gr. -1-3). 17.99 *(978-0-544-80122-6(9)*, 1640248, Clarion Bks.) Houghton Mifflin Harcourt Trade & Reference Pubs.

Brosgol, Vera. Anya's Ghost. Brosgol, Vera. 2011. (ENG.). 224p. (YA). (gr. 7-12). 22.99 *(978-1-59643-713-5(8)*, 900075181); pap. 17.99 *(978-1-59643-552-0(6)*, 900062110) Roaring Brook Pr. (First Second Bks.).

—Be Prepared. Brosgol, Vera. 2018. (ENG.). 256p. (J). pap. 12.99 *(978-1-62672-445-7(8)*, 900157564, First Second Bks.) Roaring Brook Pr.

—Leave Me Alone! Brosgol, Vera. 2016. (ENG.). 40p. (J). 17.99 *(978-1-62672-441-9(5)*, 900157394) Roaring Brook Pr.

Brosnan, Katie. Keith among the Pigeons. Brosnan, Katie. 2020. (Child's Play Library). 32p. (J). *(978-1-78628-344-3(1))*; pap. *(978-1-78628-343-6(3))* Child's Play International Ltd.

Brosseau, Pat, jt. illus. see McCaig, Dave.

Brothers, Fillbach. Clone Wars Adventures. Blackman, Haden & The Fillbach Brothers. 2011. (Star Wars Digests Ser.). (ENG.). 96p. (J). (gr. 3-8). 29.93 *(978-1-59961-906-4(7)*, 13754, Graphic Novels) Spotlight.

—Star Wars: Clone Wars Adventures. Blackman, Haden. 2011. (Star Wars Digests Ser.). (ENG.). 96p. (J). (gr. 3-8). 29.93 *(978-1-59961-905-7(9)*, 13753, Graphic Novels) Spotlight.

Brough, Hazel. The Charm of the Bearclaw Necklace. Searcy, Margaret Zehmer. 80p. (J). (gr. 3-7). pap. 7.95 *(978-1-56554-777-3(2)*, Pelican Publishing) Arcadia Publishing.

Brough, Karen. Lighting the Earth. Hoffman, Diana / Lynne. 2014. 34p. (J). 23.95 *(978-0-9891296-4-0(0)*, Aurora Books) Eco-Justice Pr., LLC.

Broughton, Ilona & Szijgyarto, Cynthia. Goats in Coats. Nagy, Jennifer. 2009. 20p. pap. 12.99 *(978-1-4389-6586-4(9))* AuthorHouse.

Brouhard, Crary & Carrol, Patrick. Sounds of HU. Klemp, Joan & Moore, Anthony N. 2013. (J). pap. *(978-1-57043-363-4(1))* Eckankar.

Brouillard, Anne. The Bathtub Prima Donna. Brouillard, Anne. 2004. 24p. (J). (gr. k-4). reprint ed. 13.00 *(978-0-7567-7755-5(0))* DIANE Publishing Co.

Broussalian, Maureen. Lady Louise, Adventures at the North Pole. Petit, Karen. 2nd ed. 2018. (Lady Louise Ser.: Vol. 3). (ENG.). 70p. (J). (gr. k-3). 24.99 *(978-1-68454-984-9(1))* Primedia eLaunch LLC.

Broutin, Chistian. Trees. 2012. (ENG.). 38p. (J). (gr. -1-k). spiral bd. 14.99 *(978-1-85103-401-7(3))* Moonlight Publishing, Ltd. GBR. Dist: Independent Pubs. Group.

Broutin, Christian. El Barco. (Coleccion Mundo Maravilloso). (SPA.). 40p. (J). (gr. 2-4). *(978-84-348-3810-9(9)*, BA9293) SM Ediciones.

Broutin, Christian. Boats. Broutin, Christian. Matthews, Sarah, tr. from FRE. ed. 2019. (My First Discoveries Ser.). (ENG.). 36p. (J). (gr. -1-k). spiral bd. 16.99 *(978-1-85103-471-0(4))* Moonlight Publishing, Ltd. GBR. Dist: Independent Pubs. Group.

—In the Jungle. Broutin, Christian. Delafosse, Claude. 2013. (ENG.). 36p. (J). (gr. -1-k). spiral bd. 13.99 *(978-1-85103-417-8(X))* Moonlight Publishing, Ltd. GBR. Dist: Independent Pubs. Group.

—Let's Look at the Jungle. Broutin, Christian. Delafosse, Claude. 2012. (ENG.). 38p. (J). (gr. k-3). spiral bd. 11.99 *(978-1-85103-332-4(7))* Moonlight Publishing, Ltd. GBR. Dist: Independent Pubs. Group.

—The Town. Broutin, Christian. 2012. (ENG.). 36p. (J). (gr. -1-k). spiral bd. 13.99 *(978-1-85103-395-9(5))* Moonlight Publishing, Ltd. GBR. Dist: Independent Pubs. Group.

Brouwer, Aafke. Ginny's Egg. Goodhart, Pippa. 142p. (J). pap. 7.50 *(978-0-7497-4557-8(6))* Egmont Bks., Ltd. GBR. Dist: Trafalgar Square Publishing.

Brouwer, James. The Deep. Taylor, Tom. 2017. (ENG.). 160p. (J). (gr. 3). pap. 14.99 *(978-1-68415-200-1(3))* Boom! Studios.

Brower, William. Why be Normal? From Soup to Nuts, Mostly Nuts. Puscheck, Herbert Charles. 2005. 212p. (YA). per. 12.95 *(978-0-9707976-1-2(3))* Rose River Publishing Co.

Brown, Adrienne. Jimmy & Jane & the Tale of the Yellow Moon. Sadler, Ian. 2017. (Rhyme, Laugh & Learn Ser.: 3). (ENG.). 32p. (J). (gr. -1-2). 16.95 *(978-0-9964157-6-7(9))* Gelos Pubns.

—Juan Castell & Aunt Sofia's Book of Please, Thank You, Welcome. Sadler, Ian. 2018. (Rhyme, Laugh & Learn Ser.: 4). (ENG.). 32p. (J). (gr. -1-2). 15.95 *(978-0-9964157-8-1(5))* Gelos Pubns.

Brown, Adrienne, et al. Silvermist & the Ladybug Curse. Herman, Gail. 2008. (Disney Fairies Chapters Ser.). (ENG.). 117p. (J). (gr. 1-4). 18.69 *(978-0-7364-2508-7(X))* Random House Publishing Group.

Brown, Adrienne, jt. illus. see Disney Book Group.

Brown, Alan. Adventures in Makerspace, 4 vols. McClintock Miller, Shannon & Hoena, Blake. 2018. (Adventures in Makerspace Ser.). (ENG.). 32p. (J). (gr. 3-5). 122.60 *(978-1-4965-7759-7(0)*, 28597); pap., pap., pap. 31.80 *(978-1-4965-7760-3(4)*, 28700) Capstone. (Stone Arch Bks.).

Brown, Alan. Beach Nightmare. Foxe, Steve. 2020. (Scary Graphics Ser.). (ENG.). 40p. (J). (gr. 3-5). lib. bdg. 25.32 ***(978-1-4965-9796-0(6))***, 200590, Stone Arch Bks.) Capstone.

Brown, Alan. A Building Mission. McClintock Miller, Shannon & Hoena, Blake. 2019. (Adventures in Makerspace Ser.). (ENG.). 32p. (J). (gr. 3-5). lib. bdg. 30.65 *(978-1-4965-7948-5(8)*, 139757, Stone Arch Bks.) Capstone.

—A Coding Mission. Miller, Shannon & Hoena, B. A. 2018. (Adventures in Makerspace Ser.). (ENG.). 32p. (J). (gr. 3-5). 30.65 *(978-1-4965-7743-6(4)*, 138429, Stone Arch Bks.) Capstone.

—Draw Amazing Animal Mash-Ups. Bolte, Mari. 2017. (Drawing Mash-Ups Ser.). (ENG.). 32p. (J). (gr. 3-9). lib. bdg. 28.65 *(978-1-5157-6936-1(4)*, 135415, Capstone Pr.) Capstone.

—Fantastic Forces & Motion: Discover the Science Behind Superpowers & Become Supersmart. Lin, Joy. 2019. (Superpower Science Ser.). (ENG.). 32p. (J). (gr. 4-9). pap. 8.99 *(978-1-4380-1265-0(9))*, B.E.S. Publishing) Peterson's.

—Fred Flintstone's Adventures with Inclined Planes: A Rampin' Good Time. Weakland, Mark. 2016. (Flintstones Explain Simple Machines Ser.). (ENG.). 24p. (J). (gr. k-2). lib. bdg. 27.99 *(978-1-4914-8476-0(4))* Capstone.

—Fred Flintstone's Adventures with Wheels & Axles: Bedrock & Roll! Weakland, Mark. 2016. (Flintstones Explain Simple Machines Ser.). (ENG.). 24p. (J). (gr. k-2). lib. bdg. 27.99 *(978-1-4914-8474-6(8))* Capstone.

—Heroes of Light & Sound: Discover the Science Behind Superpowers & Become Supersmart. Lin, Joy. 2019. (Superpower Science Ser.). (ENG.). 32p. (J). (gr. 4-9). pap. 8.99 *(978-1-4380-1266-7(7))*, B.E.S. Publishing) Peterson's.

—Jonny Jakes Investigates the Hamburgers of Doom. Judge, Malcolm. 2016. (Middle-Grade Novels Ser.). (ENG.). 240p. (J). (gr. 4-7). lib. bdg. 26.65 *(978-1-4965-2678-6(3)*, Stone Arch Bks.) Capstone.

—Jonny Jakes Investigates the Old School Ghoul. Judge, Malcolm. 2016. (Middle-Grade Novels Ser.). (ENG.). 240p. (J). (gr. 4-7). lib. bdg. 25.99 *(978-1-4965-2829-2(8)*, Stone Arch Bks.) Capstone.

—A Low-Tech Mission. McClintock Miller, Shannon & Hoena, Blake. 2018. (Adventures in Makerspace Ser.). (ENG.). 32p. (J). (gr. 3-5). 30.65 *(978-1-4965-7744-3(2)*, 138430); pap. 7.95 *(978-1-4965-7748-1(5)*, 139047) Capstone. (Stone Arch Bks.).

—Magnetic Mess. Anderson, J. L. 2016. (Paisley Atoms Ser.). (ENG.). 64p. (gr. 2-5). 28.50 *(978-1-68191-717-7(3)*, 9781681917177) Rourke Educational Media.

—Make Your Own Paper Projects. Pierce, Nick. 2017. (ENG.). 48p. (J). (gr. 2). pap. 8.95 *(978-1-911242-92-5(X)*, Scribo) Book Hse. GBR. Dist: Sterling Publishing Co., Inc.

—Masters of Matter: Discover the Science Behind Superpowers & Become Supersmart. Lin, Joy. 2019. (Superpower Science Ser.). (ENG.). 32p. (J). (gr. 4-9). pap. 8.99 *(978-1-4380-1267-4(5))*, B.E.S. Publishing) Peterson's.

—Mystery at Camp Kookaburra. Steinkraus, Kyla. 2016. (Paisley Atoms Ser.). (ENG.). 64p. (gr. 2-5). 28.50 *(978-1-68191-712-2(2)*, 9781681917122) Rourke Educational Media.

—A Photo Journal Mission. McClintock Miller, Shannon & Hoena, Blake. 2019. (Adventures in Makerspace Ser.). (ENG.). 32p. (J). (gr. 3-5). lib. bdg. 30.65 *(978-1-4965-7950-8(X)*, 139759, Stone Arch Bks.) Capstone.

—Power Play. Steinkraus, Kyla. 2016. (Paisley Atoms Ser.). (ENG.). 64p. (gr. 2-5). 28.50 *(978-1-68191-715-3(7)*, 9781681917153) Rourke Educational Media.

—A Recycled-Art Mission. McClintock Miller, Shannon & Hoena, Blake. 2019. (Adventures in Makerspace Ser.). (ENG.). 32p. (J). (gr. 3-5). lib. bdg. 30.65 *(978-1-4965-7949-2(6)*, 139758, Stone Arch Bks.) Capstone.

—A Robotics Mission. McClintock Miller, Shannon & Hoena, Blake. 2018. (Adventures in Makerspace Ser.). (ENG.). 32p. (J). (gr. 3-5). 30.65 *(978-1-4965-7746-7(9)*, 138431); pap. 7.95 *(978-1-4965-7750-4(7)*, 139048) Capstone. (Stone Arch Bks.).

—Rumpelstiltskin: An Interactive Fairy Tale Adventure. Braun, Eric. 2017. (You Choose: Fractured Fairy Tales Ser.). (ENG.). 112p. (J). (gr. 3-7). pap. 6.95 *(978-1-5157-8777-8(X)*, 136328); lib. bdg. 32.65 *(978-1-5157-8775-4(3)*, 136326) Capstone. (Capstone Pr.).

—Runaway Robot. Anderson, J. L. 2016. (Paisley Atoms Ser.). (ENG.). 64p. (gr. 2-5). 28.50 *(978-1-68191-716-0(5)*, 9781681917160) Rourke Educational Media.

Brown, Alan, et al. Scary Graphics. Foxe, Steve et al. 2020. (Scary Graphics Ser.). (ENG.). (J). (gr. 3-5). 101.28 ***(978-1-4965-9832-5(6))***, 200761, Stone Arch Bks.) Capstone.

Brown, Alan. Sounds Like Fun. Anderson, J. L. 2016. (Paisley Atoms Ser.). (ENG.). 64p. (gr. 2-5). 28.50 *(978-1-68191-718-4(1)*, 9781681917184) Rourke Educational Media.

—A Stop-Motion Animation Mission. McClintock Miller, Shannon & Hoena, Blake. 2019. (Adventures in Makerspace Ser.). (ENG.). 32p. (J). (gr. 3-5). lib. bdg. 30.65 *(978-1-4965-7951-5(8)*, 139760, Stone Arch Bks.) Capstone.

—Storm Warning: Unofficial Graphic Novel #3 for Fortniters. Meyer, Nathan. 2020. (Storm Shield Ser.: 3). 160p. (J). (gr. 2-8). pap. 11.99 *(978-1-5107-5716-5(3)*, Sky Pony Pr.) Skyhorse Publishing Co., Inc.

—The Super Human Body: Discover the Science Behind Superpowers & Become Supersmart. Lin, Joy. 2019. (Superpower Science Ser.). (ENG.). 32p. (J). (gr. 4-9). pap. 8.99 *(978-1-4380-1268-1(3)*, B.E.S. Publishing) Peterson's.

—Twist in Time. Anderson, J. L. 2016. (Paisley Atoms Ser.). (ENG.). 64p. (gr. 2-5). 28.50 *(978-1-68191-720-7(3)*, 9781681917207) Rourke Educational Media.

—Under the Sea. Steinkraus, Kyla. 2016. (Paisley Atoms Ser.). (ENG.). 64p. (gr. 2-5). 28.50 *(978-1-68191-713-9(0)*, 9781681917139) Rourke Educational Media.

Brown, Alan. What's in the Woods? Foxe, Steve. 2020. (Scary Graphics Ser.). (ENG.). 40p. (J). (gr. 3-5). lib. bdg. 25.32 ***(978-1-4965-9799-1(0))***, 200593, Stone Arch Bks.) Capstone.

Brown, Alan. Whoosh! Wile E. Coyote Experiments with Flight & Gravity. Weakland, Mark. 2017. (Wile E. Coyote, Physical Science Genius Ser.). (ENG.). 32p. (J). (gr. 3-5). lib. bdg. 31.32 *(978-1-5157-3732-2(2)*, Capstone Pr.) Capstone.

—A 3-D Printing Mission. McClintock Miller, Shannon & Hoena, Blake. 2018. (Adventures in Makerspace Ser.). (ENG.). 32p. (J). (gr. 3-5). 30.65 *(978-1-4965-7745-0(0)*, 138428); pap. 7.95 *(978-1-4965-7749-8(3)*, 139045) Capstone. (Stone Arch Bks.).

Brown, Alan, jt. illus. see Pota, Giovanni.

Brown, Alison. I Love You Night & Day. Prasadam-Halls, Smriti. 2014. (ENG.). 32p. (J). (gr. -1-1). 16.99 *(978-1-61963-222-6(5)*, 900127512, Bloomsbury USA Childrens) Bloomsbury Publishing USA.

—I'll Love You Always. Sperring, Mark. (ENG.). (J). 2017. 26p. bds. 7.99 *(978-1-68119-598-8(4)*, 900179023); 2016. 32p. 16.99 *(978-1-68119-345-8(0)*, 900170374) Bloomsbury Publishing USA. (Bloomsbury USA Childrens).

—I'll Love You Always (padded Board Book) Sperring, Mark. 2017. 26p. (J). bds. 9.99 *(978-1-68119-847-7(9)*, 900189033, Bloomsbury USA Childrens) Bloomsbury Publishing USA.

—I'll Never Let You Go. Prasadam-Halls, Smriti. 2015. (ENG.). 32p. (J). 16.99 *(978-1-61963-922-5(X)*, 900152078, Bloomsbury USA Childrens) Bloomsbury Publishing USA.

—Little Owl's Egg. Gliori, Debi. (ENG.). 32p. (J). 2018. bds. 7.99 *(978-1-68119-893-4(2)*, 900191670, Bloomsbury Children's Bks.); 2017. 16.99 *(978-1-68119-324-3(8)*, 900170041, Bloomsbury USA Childrens) Bloomsbury Publishing USA.

—Love You, Love You, 1 vol. Zondervan, G. J. 2020. 20p. (J). bds. 9.99 *(978-0-310-76841-8(1))* Zonderkidz.

—Snowy Bear. Mitton, Tony. (ENG.). (J). 2016. 26p. bds. 7.99 *(978-1-68119-084-6(2)*, 900158411); 2015. 32p. (gr. -1-1). 16.99 *(978-1-61963-905-8(X)*, 900151395) Bloomsbury Publishing USA. (Bloomsbury USA Childrens).

—The Wheels on the Dump Truck. Burton, Jeffrey. 2020. (Wheels on The... Ser.). (ENG.). 16p. (J). (gr. -1-k). bds. 5.99 *(978-1-5344-4248-1(0)*, Little Simon) Little Simon.

—The Wheels on the Fire Truck. Burton, Jeffrey. 2019. (Wheels on The... Ser.). (ENG.). 16p. (J). (gr. -1-k). bds. 5.99 *(978-1-5344-4244-3(8)*, Little Simon) Little Simon.

—The Wheels on the Garbage Truck. Burton, Jeffrey. 2019. (Wheels on The... Ser.). (ENG.). 16p. (J). (gr. -1-k). bds. 5.99 *(978-1-5344-4246-7(4)*, Little Simon) Little Simon.

Brown, Alison. The Wheels on the Trucks: The Wheels on the Fire Truck; the Wheels on the Garbage Truck; the Wheels on the Dump Truck. Burton, Jeffrey. ed. 2020. (Wheels on The... Ser.). (ENG.). 48p. (J). (gr. -1-k). bds. 17.99 ***(978-1-5344-6977-8(X)***, Little Simon) Little Simon.

Brown, Amanda, jt. illus. see Ambler, Laura.

Brown, Anna. Love Is Real. Lawler, Janet. 2013. (ENG.). 32p. (J). (gr. -1-3). 15.99 *(978-0-06-224170-2(2))* HarperCollins Pubs.

Brown, Bill. Mabel on the Move, 6. Mazer, Anne. 2009. (Sister Magic Ser.: 6). (ENG.). 128p. (J). (gr. 3-6). pap. 16.19 *(978-0-439-87251-5(0))* Scholastic, Inc.

—Mabel Strikes a Chord, 4. Mazer, Anne. 2008. (Sister Magic Ser.). (ENG.). 86p. (J). (gr. 3-6). 17.44 *(978-0-439-87249-2(9))* Scholastic, Inc.

Brown, Bob, et al. Black Widow: Marvel Team-Up. 2020. (ENG.). 208p. (YA). (gr. 4-17). pap. 29.99 *(978-1-302-92278-8(5))* Marvel Worldwide, Inc.

Brown, Bob & Buscema, Sal. Avengers/Defenders War. 2019. (ENG.). 136p. (J). (gr. 4-17). pap. 19.99 *(978-1-302-92317-4(X))* Marvel Worldwide, Inc.

Brown, Bobby. A Midnight's Lullaby: Volume One. Hogan, Micki. 2011. 40p. pap. 24.95 *(978-1-4560-2090-3(0))* America Star Bks.

Brown, Brenda. The Pocket Guide to Mischief, 1 vol. King, Bart. 2008. (ENG.). 208p. (J). (gr. 5-6). pap. 9.99 *(978-1-4236-0366-5(4))* Gibbs Smith, Publisher.

Brown, Calef. Gertrude Is Gertrude Is Gertrude Is Gertrude. Winter, Jonah. 2009. (ENG.). 40p. (J). (gr. -1-3). 19.99 *(978-1-4169-4088-3(X)*, Atheneum Bks. for Young Readers) Simon & Schuster Children's Publishing.

—Pop-Up Aesop. Harris, John. 2005. (ENG.). 10p. (gr. -1-7). 19.95 *(978-0-89236-814-3(4))* Oxford Univ. Pr., Inc.

—The Yggyssey: How Iggy Wondered What Happened to All the Ghosts, Found Out Where They Went, & Went There. Pinkwater, Daniel M. 2009. 12p. (J). (gr. 4-6). 18.69 *(978-0-618-59445-0(0))* Houghton Mifflin Harcourt Publishing Co.

Brown, Calef. Boy Wonders. Brown, Calef. 2011. (ENG.). 40p. (J). (gr. -1-3). 16.99 *(978-1-4169-7877-0(1),* Atheneum Bks. for Young Readers) Simon & Schuster Children's Publishing.
—The Ghostly Carousel: Delightfully Frightful Poems. Brown, Calef. 2018. (ENG.). 32p. (J). (gr. 1-4). 17.99 *(978-1-5124-2661-8(X),* Carolrhoda Bks.) Lerner Publishing Group.
—Hypnotize a Tiger: Poems about Just about Everything. Brown, Calef. 2015. (ENG.). 144p. (J). (gr. 3-7). 18.99 *(978-0-8050-9928-7(X),* 900126307, Holt, Henry & Co. Bks. For Young Readers) Holt, Henry & Co.
—Pirateria: The Wonderful Plunderful Pirate Emporium. Brown, Calef. 2012. (ENG.). 40p. (J). (gr. -1-3). 16.99 *(978-1-4169-7878-7(X),* Atheneum Bks. for Young Readers) Simon & Schuster Children's Publishing.
—Up Verses Down: Poems, Paintings, & Serious Nonsense. Brown, Calef. 2019. (ENG.). 80p. (J). 19.99 *(978-0-8050-9929-4(8),* 900126308, Holt, Henry & Co. Bks. For Young Readers) Holt, Henry & Co.
Brown, Chris. Chief Hawah's Book of Native American Indians. 2006. (ENG.). 32p. (J). (gr. -1-3). 14.99 *(978-0-7145-3308-7(4))* Boyars, Marion Pubs., Inc.
Brown, Chris L. My Aunt & Me. Parker, Ms. Alichia R. 2013. 24p. pap. 9.99 *(978-0-578-12712-5(1))* A PAR Educational, LLC.
Brown, Christina. Mark-Napped!, 1 vol. Sipila, Ellie. 2019. (ENG.). 64p. (gr. 2-7). 9.95 *(978-1-4556-2463-8(2),* Pelican Publishing) Arcadia Publishing.
—SHARE This Book. Hutton, John. 2018. (ENG.). 14p. (J). (— 1). bds. 7.99 *(978-1-936669-67-7(6))* Blue Manatee Press.
Brown, Christopher. The Treehouse Adventure. Jack, David M. 2017. (Furnace Room Ser.: 2). (ENG.). 36p. (J). (gr. k-3). 21.33 *(978-0-692-81087-3(0))* BookBaby.
Brown, Clarence. Reeses' BIG DAY at the PARK. Clark, Sharita, ed. 2018. (ENG.). 30p. (J). pap. 10.99 ***(978-0-9997551-0-5(2))*** CBJ Entertainment.
Brown, Clovis. Anancy & Friends: A Grandmother's Anancy Stories for Her Grandchildren. Richmond, Beulah. 2004. (ENG.). 52p. pap. 5.99 *(978-976-8184-48-1(5))* Penguin Publishing Group.
—Naughty Eddie Larue. Wohlt, Julia. 27p. *(978-976-610-173-2(6))* Creative Links.
Brown, Craig. How Do You Raise a Raisin? Ryan, Pam Muñoz. 32p. (J). 2004. (ENG.). (gr. 3-6). 22.44 *(978-1-57091-397-6(8))*; 2003. (gr. k-3). pap. 7.95 *(978-1-57091-398-3(6))* Charlesbridge Publishing, Inc.
Brown, Craig. Mule Train Mail. Brown, Craig. 2009. 36p. (J). (gr. -1-3). pap. 7.95 *(978-1-58089-188-2(8))* Charlesbridge Publishing, Inc.
Brown, Dan. Books for Oliver. Larkin, Jim & Rambo, Lee Elliot. 2006. (J). *(978-1-59336-336-9(2))*; pap. *(978-1-59336-337-6(0))* Mondo Publishing.
—Impatient Pamela Asks: Why Are My Feet So Huge? Koski, Mary B. 2003. (Impatient Pamela Ser.). 32p. (J). (gr. -1-3). pap. 4.95 *(978-1-930650-02-2(7))* mTrellis Publishing, Inc.
—Impatient Pamela Calls 9-1-1. Koski, Mary B. (Impatient Pamela Ser.). 32p. (J). 2003. (gr. -1-3). 15.95 *(978-0-9663281-9-6(1))*; 2nd ed. 2004. (ENG.). (gr. 1-3). 14.95 *(978-1-930650-09-1(4))* mTrellis Publishing, Inc.
—I've Been Working on the Railroad. Galvin, Laura Gates. 2008. (ENG.). 32p. (J). (gr. k-2). 14.95 *(978-1-59249-771-3(3))*; 8.95 *(978-1-59249-772-0(1))* Soundprints.
—Learn to Call 911. Collins, Lori & Koski, Mary. 2007. (ENG.). 16p. (J). (gr. k-2). pap. 2.95 *(978-1-930650-05-3(1))* mTrellis Publishing, Inc.
—A Picture Book of George Washington Carver. Adler, David A. 2008. (Picture Book Biography Ser.). (J). (gr. -1-2). 28.95 incl. audio compact disk *(978-1-4301-0348-6(5))* Live Oak Media.
Brown, Daniel J. Billy Brown's Cat, 1 vol. Pulford, Elizabeth. 2012. (Engage Literacy Green Ser.). (ENG.). 32p. (gr. k-2). pap. 5.99 *(978-1-4296-8838-3(6),* Capstone Pr.) Capstone.
Brown, Danny R. There's a Swimming Pool in My Desk! Chanan, Hallie Sophie & Chanan, Michael Craig. 2018. (ENG.). 32p. (J). pap. 6.99 *(978-1-7268-8428-0(7))* Independently Published.
Brown, Dennis L. A Gullah Alphabet. Clary, Margie Willis. 2007. (J). *(978-0-87844-184-6(0))* Sandlapper Publishing Co., Inc.
Brown, Diane. A Baby Doll from Santy Claus. Zabel, Vivian. 2017. (ENG.). (J). (gr. k-3). 21.99 *(978-1-940310-71-8(7))*; pap. 17.99 *(978-1-940310-72-5(5))* 4RV Pub.
Brown, Don. A Kid's Guide to Chicago. Bartlett, Karen T. 2010. 64p. pap. 16.95 *(978-1-934907-03-0(0))* Twin Lights Pubs., Inc.
Brown, Don. All Stations! Distress! April 15, 1912: the Day the Titanic Sank. Brown, Don. 2010. (Actual Times Ser.: 2). (ENG.). 64p. (J). (gr. 1-5). pap. 8.99 *(978-1-59643-644-2(1),* 900068840) Square Fish.
—Gold! Gold from the American River! January 24, 1848: the Day the Gold Rush Began. Brown, Don. 2014. (Actual Times Ser.: 3). (ENG.). 64p. (J). (gr. 1-5). 9.99 *(978-1-250-04060-2(4),* 900124081) Square Fish.
—The Great American Dust Bowl. Brown, Don. 2013. (ENG.). 80p. (YA). (gr. 7). 18.99 *(978-0-547-81550-3(6),* 1496217) Houghton Mifflin Harcourt Publishing Co.
—He Has Shot the President! April 14, 1865: the Day John Wilkes Booth Killed President Lincoln. Brown, Don. 2014. (Actual Times Ser.: 5). (ENG.). 64p. (J). (gr. 1-5). 17.99 *(978-1-59643-224-6(1),* 900041130) Roaring Brook Pr.
—Mack Made Movies. Brown, Don. 2008. (J). (gr. 2-5). 25.95 incl. audio compact disk *(978-1-4301-0432-2(5))*; pap. 16.95 incl. audio *(978-1-4301-0431-5(7))*; pap. 39.95 incl. audio compact disk *(978-1-4301-0436-0(8))*;Set. pap. 37.95 incl. audio *(978-1-4301-0433-9(3))* Live Oak Media.
—Up & Down: The Adventures of John Jeffries, First American to Fly. Brown, Don. 2018. 40p. (J). (gr. 1-4). 16.99 *(978-1-58089-812-6(2))* Charlesbridge Publishing, Inc.
—A Wizard from the Start: The Incredible Boyhood & Amazing Inventions of Thomas Edison. Brown, Don. 2010. (ENG.). 32p. (J). (gr. -1-3). 17.99 *(978-0-547-19487-5(0),* 1057822) Houghton Mifflin Harcourt Publishing Co.
Brown, Douglas. My Mommy's a Trucker. Mitchell, Robyn. 2017. (ENG.). 36p. (J). 24.95 *(978-0-9972129-8-3(5))*; pap. 12.95 *(978-0-9972129-7-6(7))* CRLE Publishing.
Brown, E. Jackie. The Adventures of Fujimori-San. Kline, Spencer. 2010. 20p. 12.99 *(978-1-4520-6275-4(7))* AuthorHouse.
Brown, Elbrite. Cinnamon Brown & the Seven Dwarfs. Jackson, Ellen B. 2006. (J). *(978-0-670-06106-8(9),* Viking Adult) Penguin Publishing Group.
Brown, Eliot R. Baby Don't Smoke. Jaime, Everett. 2012. (ENG.). 40p. (YA). pap. 9.95 *(978-1-935826-20-0(4))* Kalindi Pr.
—Official Handbook of the Marvel Universe Omnibus. 2019. (ENG.). 576p. (YA). (gr. 4-17). 75.00 *(978-1-302-92060-9(X))* Marvel Worldwide, Inc.
Brown, Erin O'Leary. En Mi Patio. Curry, Don L. 2011. (Rookie Ready to Learn Español Ser.). (SPA.). 32p. (J). pap. 5.95 *(978-0-531-26784-4(9),* Children's Pr.) Scholastic Library Publishing.
Brown, Fiona. How to Draw Lettering. Tatchell, Judy & Varley, Carol. 2006. (Young Artist Ser.). 32p. (J). (gr. 4-7). pap. 5.99 *(978-0-7945-1379-5(4),* Usborne) EDC Publishing.
Brown, Garry, jt. illus. see Manna, Francesco.
Brown, Gloria. What Sea Creature Is This? Allen, Nancy Kelly. 2012. (J). *(978-1-933176-41-3(5))* Red Rock Pr., Inc.
Brown, Gloria Dean. Shanleya's Quest: A Botany Adventure for Kids Ages 9 - 99, 1 vol. Elpel, Thomas J. 32p. 12.50 *(978-1-892784-16-2(5),* 1511) HOPS Pr., LLC.
Brown, Hazel. Prince Henry St. Clair Earl of Orkney. Brown, Hazel. Bramadat, Dawn, ed. 2013. 106p. pap. 25.95 *(978-1-935786-57-3(1))* St. Clair Pubns.
Brown, Heather. Hugs for You. Hannigan, Paula. 2012. (J). (-k). (ENG.). 10p. bds. 7.99 *(978-1-4494-2192-2(X))*; *(978-1-4351-5022-5(8))* Andrews McMeel Publishing.
—Today I'll Be a Princess. Croyle, Paula. 2015. (ENG.). 12p. (J). bds. 5.99 *(978-1-4494-6057-0(7))* Andrews McMeel Publishing.
—Under Construction. Hannigan, Paula & Accord Publishing Staff. 2012. (ENG.). 12p. (J). bds. 14.99 *(978-1-4494-0498-7(7))* Andrews McMeel Publishing.
—Under Construction. Hannigan, Paula. 2013. (ENG.). 18p. (J). bds. 5.99 *(978-1-4494-3556-1(4))* Andrews McMeel Publishing.
Brown, Heather. The Robot Book. Brown, Heather. 2010. (ENG.). 12p. (J). bds. 16.99 *(978-0-7407-9725-5(5))* Andrews McMeel Publishing.
Brown, Jahla. My Friend Is Deaf. Pride, Dana. 2018. (ENG.). 28p. (Orig.). (J). pap. 9.95 *(978-0-9983858-3-9(2))* Everlasting Publishing.
Brown, James. The Trapdoor Mysteries: the Scent of Danger: Book 2, Bk. 2. Longstaff, Abie & Longstaff, Abie. 2020. (Trapdoor Mysteries Ser.: 2). 192p. (J). (gr. 2-4). pap. 9.99 *(978-1-5102-0022-7(3))* Little, Brown Bks. for Young Readers.
—A World of Discovery. Platt, Richard. 2019. (World Of Ser.). (ENG.). 64p. (J). (gr. 2-5). 25.00 *(978-1-5362-0766-8(7))* Candlewick Pr.
—A World of Information. Platt, Richard. 2017. (World Of Ser.). (ENG.). 64p. (J). (gr. k-12). 25.00 *(978-0-7636-9348-0(0))* Candlewick Pr.
Brown, James. Farm. Brown, James. 2013. (ENG.). 16p. (J). (gr. -1 — 1). bds. 6.99 *(978-0-7636-5931-8(2))* Candlewick Pr.
—A World of Cities. Brown, James. 2018. (World Of Ser.). (ENG.). 64p. (J). (gr. 2-5). 25.00 *(978-0-7636-9879-9(2))* Candlewick Pr.
Brown, Jane Clark. Marvin One Too Many. Paterson, Katherine. 2003. (I Can Read Bks.). 48p. (J). (gr. k-3). pap. 3.99 *(978-0-06-444279-4(9))* HarperCollins Pubs.
Brown, Jason. Hanner & the Bullies. Curtiss, A. B. & Curtiss, A. B. 2012. 140p. pap. 9.99 *(978-0-932529-63-3(1))* Oldcastle Publishing.
Brown, Jeffrey. Jedi Academy. Brown, Jeffrey. 2013. (Star Wars Ser.: Bk. 1). 160p. (J). (ENG.). (gr. 3-7). 12.99 *(978-0-545-50517-8(8))*; pap. *(978-0-545-60999-9(2))* Scholastic, Inc.
—Lucy & Andy Neanderthal. Brown, Jeffrey. 2016. (Lucy & Andy Neanderthal Ser.: 1). 224p. (J). (gr. 3-7). 12.99 *(978-0-385-38835-1(7),* Crown Books For Young Readers) Random Hse. Children's Bks.
—The Phantom Bully. Brown, Jeffrey. 2015. (Star Wars: Jedi Academy Ser.: 3). (ENG.). 176p. (J). (gr. 3-7). 12.99 *(978-0-545-62126-7(7))* Scholastic, Inc.
—Return of the Padawan. Brown, Jeffrey. 2014. (Star Wars: Jedi Academy Ser.: Bk. 2). (ENG.). 176p. (J). (gr. 3-7). 12.99 *(978-0-545-62125-0(9))* Scholastic, Inc.
Brown, Jessica. Shine. Dee, Sherree. 2019. (ENG.). 28p. (J). pap. *(978-1-5255-4121-6(8))* FriesenPress.
Brown, Jo. Andy Alligator. Albee, Sarah. 2009. (Snappy Fun Bks.). (ENG.). 10p. (J). (gr. -1 — 1). bds. 7.99 *(978-0-7944-1908-0(9),* Reader's Digest Children's Bks.) Studio Fun International.
—Hootenanny! A Festive Counting Book. Ainsworth, Kimberly. 2011. (ENG.). 32p. (J). (gr. -1-k). 12.99 *(978-1-4424-2273-5(4),* Little Simon) Little Simon.
—My Rainbow Book of Bedtime Prayers, 1 vol. Box, Su. 2009. 16p. (J). bds. 9.99 *(978-0-8254-7917-5(7),* Lion Children's) Lion Hudson PLC GBR. Dist: Kregel Pubns.
—My Rainbow Book of Everyday Prayers, 1 vol. Box, Su. 2009. (ENG.). 16p. (J). bds. 9.99 *(978-0-8254-7918-2(5),* Lion Children's) Lion Hudson PLC GBR. Dist: Kregel Pubns.
—Penny Penguin. Mitter, Matt. 2010. (Snappy Fun Ser.). (ENG.). 10p. (J). bds. 7.99 *(978-0-7944-2014-7(1))* Reader's Digest Assn., Inc., The.
—Snappy Heads Tommy T Rex. Albee, Sarah & Hood, Susan. 2009. (New Snappy Fun Ser.). (ENG.). 10p. (J). (gr. -1-k). bds. 7.99 *(978-0-7944-1907-3(0))* Reader's Digest Assn., Inc., The.
—This Is Our World: A Story about Taking Care of the Earth. Sollinger, Emily. 2010. (Little Green Bks.). (ENG.). 12p. (J). (gr. -1-1). bds. 8.99 *(978-1-4169-7821-3(6),* Little Simon) Little Simon.
Brown, Jo. Where's My Mommy? Brown, Jo. 2006. (Storytime Board Bks.). 18p. (J). (gr. -1-3). bds. 6.95 *(978-1-58925-795-5(2))* Tiger Tales.
Brown, Jonathan. Madison & the New Neighbors, 1 vol. Braver, Vanita. 2014. (ENG.). 32p. (J). 15.99 *(978-1-59572-686-5(1))* Star Bright Bks., Inc.
Brown Jr., David F. Tabby Goes to School: The First in the Tabatha Adventures Series, 1 vol. Brown Sr., David F. 2009. 20p. pap. 24.95 *(978-1-60836-181-6(0))* America Star Bks.
Brown, Judy. Collins Big Cat Phonics for Letters & Sounds - Mog & Mim: Band 01B/Pink B, Bd. 1B. Coe, Catherine. 2018. (Collins Big Cat Phonics Ser.). (ENG.). 16p. (J). (gr. -1-k). pap. 6.99 *(978-0-00-825139-0(8))* HarperCollins Pubs. Ltd. GBR. Dist: Independent Pubs. Group.
—Creep from the Deep. Burchett, Janet & Vogler, Sara. 10th ed. (ENG.). 96p. (J). pap. *(978-0-330-37607-5(1),* Pan) Pan Macmillan.
—No Problem! Bennett, Leonie. 2004. (ENG.). 16p. (J). lib. bdg. 23.65 *(978-1-59646-680-7(4))* Dingles & Co.
—Shiver & Deliver. Burchett, Janet & Vogler, Sara. 7th ed. 2003. (ENG.). 87p. (J). pap. *(978-0-330-37604-4(7),* Pan) Pan Macmillan.
Brown, Kait. Tiberius Goes to School. Harvey, Keith. 2010. (Tiberius Tales Ser.). 24p. (J). (gr. -1-2). pap. 8.15 *(978-1-60754-837-9(2))*; lib. bdg. 25.60 *(978-1-60754-833-1(X))* Windmill Bks.
Brown, Karen. Jessica the Furry Baroo. Moore, Judith. 2007. 44p. per. 14.95 *(978-1-59858-364-9(6))* Dog Ear Publishing, LLC.
Brown, Kate & Hickman, Paula. Tiberius Goes to School. Harvey, Keith. 2014. (ENG.). 24p. pap. 8.95 *(978-1-84135-919-9(X))* Award Pubns. Ltd. GBR. Dist: Parkwest Pubns., Inc.
Brown, Kate, jt. illus. see Vieceli, Emma.
Brown, Kathryn. The House That Jane Built: A Story about Jane Addams. Stone, Tanya Lee. 2015. (ENG.). 32p. (J). (gr. 1-4). 18.99 *(978-0-8050-9049-9(5),* 900060591, Holt, Henry & Co. Bks. For Young Readers) Holt, Henry & Co.
—The Inside Tree. Smith, Linda. Date not set. 32p. (J). (gr. -1-3). 5.99 *(978-0-06-443542-0(3))* HarperCollins Pubs.
—Kisses on the Wind. Moser, Lisa. 2009. 32p. (J). (gr. -1-2). 16.99 *(978-0-7636-3110-9(8))* Candlewick Pr.
—Mama Loves. Dotlich, Rebecca Kai. 2004. 32p. (J). (gr. -1-2). lib. bdg. 15.89 *(978-0-06-029408-3(6))* HarperCollins Pubs.
—My Little Grandmother Often Forgets. Lindbergh, Reeve. 2007. (ENG.). 32p. (J). (gr. -1-1). 16.99 *(978-0-7636-1989-3(2))* Candlewick Pr.
—Nora's Chicks. Maclachlan, Patricia. 2013. 40p. (J). (gr. -1-2). 15.99 *(978-0-7636-4753-7(5))* Candlewick Pr.
—The Old Woman Who Named Things. Rylant, Cynthia. 2015. 32p. pap. 7.00 *(978-1-61003-498-2(8))* Center for the Collaborative Classroom.
—The Old Woman Who Named Things. Rylant, Cynthia. 2004. (gr. -1-3). 17.00 *(978-0-7569-4204-5(7))* Perfection Learning Corp.
—The Quite Contrary Man: A True American Tale. Hyatt, Patricia Rusch. 2011. (ENG.). 32p. (J). (gr. k-4). 16.95 *(978-0-8109-4065-9(5),* Abrams Bks. for Young Readers) Abrams, Inc.
Brown, Keith Henry. Birth of the Cool: How Jazz Great Miles Davis Found His Sound. Berman, Kathleen Cornell. 2019. (ENG.). 40p. (J). 17.99 *(978-1-62414-690-9(2),* 900197958) Page Street Publishing Co.
Brown, Kelly. Citizenship, 1 vol. Skog, Jason. 2008. (Cartoon Nation Ser.). (ENG.). 32p. (J). (gr. 3-9). 31.32 *(978-1-4296-1331-6(9),* Capstone Pr.) Capstone.
—The FBI. Collins, Terry. 2008. (Cartoon Nation Ser.). (ENG.). 32p. (J). (gr. 3-9). 31.32 *(978-1-4296-1982-0(1),* Capstone Pr.) Capstone.
Brown, Ken. El Rey de los Bosques. Day, David. (SPA.). 27p. (J). *(978-84-236-4737-8(4))* Edebé ESP. Dist: Lectorum Pubns., Inc.
Brown, Ken. Mucky Pup. Brown, Ken. 2007. (ENG.). 32p. (J). (gr. k-2). 11.99 *(978-1-84270-652-7(7))* Andersen Pr. GBR. Dist: Independent Pubs. Group.
—The Scarecrow's Hat, 1 vol. Brown, Ken. 2011. (ENG.). 32p. (J). (gr. -1-1). pap. 7.95 *(978-1-56145-570-6(9))* Peachtree Publishing Co. Inc.
—What's the Time, Grandma Wolf?, 1 vol. Brown, Ken. 2015. (ENG.). 32p. (J). (gr. -1-2). pap. 7.95 *(978-1-56145-891-2(0))* Peachtree Publishing Co. Inc.
Brown, Kevin. Can a Hippo Hop? Tidd, Louise Vitellaro. 2006. (ENG.). 24p. (gr. k-2). pap. 8.95 *(978-1-57874-043-7(6),* Kaeden Bks.) Kaeden Corp.
—Come on Down. Knowlton, Laurie Lazzaro. 2005. (J). *(978-1-933248-07-3(6))* World Quest Learning.
—God Thought of Everything Strange & Slimy. Bruno, Bonnie. 2006. 128p. (YA). (gr. 3-6). pap. 8.99 *(978-0-7847-1448-5(7),* 04084) Standard Publishing.
—God Thought of Everything Weird & Wacky. Bruno, Bonnie. 2006. 128p. (J). (gr. 3-6). pap. 8.99 *(978-0-7847-1447-8(9),* 04083) Standard Publishing.
—Smile & Say Cheetah! Hamilton, Linda. 2005. *(978-1-933248-00-4(9))* World Quest Learning.
Brown, Kevin Christian. The Mustard Seed Prayer. Vera, J. 2012. 24p. 24.95 *(978-1-4626-5848-0(2))* America Star Bks.
Brown, Kristen Leigh. Toe Beans. Foreman, Steven Miles. 2019. (Lee Lee's Big Adventures Ser.: Vol. 1). (ENG.). 26p. (J). pap. 12.99 *(978-1-7933-1126-9(9))* Independently Published.
Brown, Kwan. Pitty the Bully: Compassion over Reaction. Brown, Jessica. 2020. (ENG.). 28p. (J). pap. 16.99 ***(978-1-7283-6316-5(0))*** AuthorHouse.
Brown, Lillie Wyatt. Do I Have to Clean My Room? Rome, Jacqueline Thomas. 2011. 36p. pap. 9.95 *(978-1-936513-24-6(2))* PearlStone Publishing, Inc.
Brown, Linnea. This Is BRIEF! Or Starting Preschool & Homeschool Children Reading Naturally - at Once. Briefing Associates Staff. Khaiphus, Kosta Demetrius, ed. 2004. 136p. (gr. -1-1). pap. 24.95 *(978-0-9706105-0-8(5))* BR:IEFing Assocs. of New England.
Brown, Lisa. Emily's Blue Period. Daly, Cathleen. 2014. (ENG.). 56p. (J). (gr. -1-2). 17.99 *(978-1-59643-469-1(4),* 900055551) Roaring Brook Pr.
—Goldfish Ghost. Snicket, Lemony. 2017. (ENG.). 40p. (J). 17.99 *(978-1-62672-507-2(1),* 9781626725072) Roaring Brook Pr.
—Mummy Cat. Ewert, Marcus. 2015. (ENG.). 48p. (J). (gr. 1-4). 16.99 *(978-0-544-34082-4(5),* 1584824, Clarion Bks.) Houghton Mifflin Harcourt Trade & Reference Pubs.
—My First Holy Communion. Ascough, Deirdre Mary. 2013. (ENG.). 72p. (J). (gr. 1-7). pap. 17.95 *(978-1-58617-708-9(7))* Ignatius Pr.
—Sometimes You Get What You Want. Gary, Meredith. 2008. (ENG.). 32p. (J). (gr. -1 — 1). 16.99 *(978-0-06-114015-0(5))* HarperCollins Pubs.
—The Two Mutch Sisters. Brendler, Carol. 2018. (ENG.). 40p. (J). (gr. -1-3). 17.99 *(978-0-544-43074-7(3),* 1595749, Clarion Bks.) Houghton Mifflin Harcourt Trade & Reference Pubs.
Brown, Lisa. How to Be. Brown, Lisa. 2006. (ENG.). 32p. (J). (gr. -1 — 1). 17.99 *(978-0-06-054635-9(2))* HarperCollins Pubs.
—Vampire Boy's Good Night. Brown, Lisa. 2010. (ENG.). 32p. (J). (gr. -1-2). 16.99 *(978-0-06-114011-2(2))* HarperCollins Pubs.
Brown, Lise C. Sammy's Broken Leg (Oh, No!) & the Amazing Cast That Fixed It. Mandell, Judith Wolf. (ENG.). (J). 2017. 18.99 *(978-0-9974449-0-2(8))*; 2016. pap. 13.99 *(978-0-9974449-1-9(6))* Harpeth Ridge Pr.
Brown, Marc. The Banza: A Haitian Story. Wolkstein, Diane. 33p. (J). (gr. k-2). pap. 5.99 *(978-0-8072-1268-4(7),* Listening Library) Random Hse. Audio Publishing Group.
—Born to Read. Sierra, Judy. 2008. (ENG.). 40p. (J). (gr. -1-2). 16.99 *(978-0-375-84687-8(5),* Knopf Bks. for Young Readers) Random Hse. Children's Bks.
—Dancing Feet! Craig, Lindsey. 2010. 40p. (J). (gr. -1-2). 16.99 *(978-0-375-86181-9(5),* Knopf Bks. for Young Readers) Random Hse. Children's Bks.
—Dancing Feet! Craig, Lindsey. 2012. 32p. (J). (gr. k-k). 6.99 *(978-0-307-93081-1(5),* Knopf Bks. for Young Readers) Random Hse. Children's Bks.
—Everyone Counts. Sierra, Judy. 2019. 40p. (J). (gr. -1-2). 17.99 *(978-0-525-64620-4(5),* Knopf Bks. for Young Readers) Random Hse. Children's Bks.
—Farmyard Beat. Craig, Lindsey. 2012. 32p. (J). (gr. k-k). 6.99 *(978-0-307-93082-8(3),* Knopf Bks. for Young Readers) Random Hse. Children's Bks.
—How to Be a Friend. Brown, Laurie Krasny. 2014. 32p. pap. 7.00 *(978-1-61003-381-7(7))* Center for the Collaborative Classroom.
—If All the Animals Came Inside. Pinder, Eric. 2012. (ENG.). 40p. (J). (gr. -1-3). 17.99 *(978-0-316-09883-0(3))* Little Brown & Co.
—The Little Shop of Monsters. Stine, R. L. 2015. 48p. (J). (gr. -1-3). 17.00 *(978-0-316-36983-1(7))* Little Brown & Co.
—Mary Mcscary. Stine, R. L. 2017. (ENG.). 40p. (J). (gr. 2-5). 16.99 *(978-1-338-03856-9(7),* Orchard Bks.) Scholastic, Inc.
—Monkey: Not Ready for Bedtime. 2017. (J). pap. *(978-0-399-55782-8(2))* Knopf, Alfred A. Inc.
—Read-Aloud Rhymes for the Very Young. 2016. (ENG.). 112p. (J). (gr. -1-2). 15.99 *(978-0-399-55357-8(6),* Dragonfly Bks.) Random Hse. Children's Bks.
—Swamp Monsters. Christian, Mary Blount. 48p. (J). (gr. 1-2). pap. 3.99 *(978-0-8072-1355-1(1),* Listening Library) Random Hse. Audio Publishing Group.
—Wild about Books. Sierra, Judy. 2004. (ENG.). 40p. (J). (gr. -1-2). 17.99 *(978-0-375-82538-5(X),* Knopf Bks. for Young Readers) Random Hse. Children's Bks.
Brown, Marc. Arthur & the 1,001 Dads, Bk. 28. Brown, Marc. 2003. (ENG.). 64p. (J). (gr. 1-4). pap. 4.25 *(978-0-316-12280-1(7))* Little, Brown Bks. for Young Readers.
—Arthur & the Big Snow. Brown, Marc. 2005. (ENG.). 32p. (J). (gr. -1-1). per. 3.99 *(978-0-316-05770-7(3))* Little, Brown Bks. for Young Readers.
—Arthur's Heart Mix-Up. Brown, Marc. 2018. (Arthur Ser.). (ENG.). 24p. (J). (gr. -1-k). pap. 4.99 *(978-1-338-27760-9(X),* Cartwheel Bks.) Scholastic, Inc.
—Arthur's Jelly Beans. Brown, Marc. 2018. (Arthur Ser.). (ENG.). 24p. (J). (gr. -1-k). pap. 4.99 *(978-1-338-27762-3(6),* Cartwheel Bks.) Scholastic, Inc.
—Arthur's Mystery Babysitter. Brown, Marc. 2004. (ENG.). 24p. (J). (gr. -1-1). pap. 3.99 *(978-0-316-73394-6(6),* Tingley, Megan Bks.) Little, Brown Bks. for Young Readers.
—Arthur's off to School. Brown, Marc. 2019. (Arthur [Brown] Ser.). (ENG.). 24p. (J). (gr. -1-k). pap. 4.99 *(978-1-338-27761-6(8),* Cartwheel Bks.) Scholastic, Inc.
—Arthur's Tooth. Brown, Marc. 2005. (ENG.). 32p. (J). (gr. -1-3). pap. 10.99 *(978-0-316-05960-2(9))* Little, Brown Bks. for Young Readers.
—D. W.'s Perfect Present. Brown, Marc. 2004. (ENG.). 32p. (J). (gr. -1-1). pap. 3.99 *(978-0-316-73386-1(5),* Tingley, Megan Bks.) Little, Brown Bks. for Young Readers.
—Good Night, D. W. Brown, Marc. 2004. (ENG.). 24p. (J). (gr. -1-1). pap. 3.99 *(978-0-316-73385-4(7))* Little, Brown Bks. for Young Readers.
Brown, Marcia. Stone Soup: Classroom Edition. Brown, Marcia. 2020. (ENG.). 48p. (J). (gr. -1-3). 29.99 ***(978-1-5344-5712-6(7),*** Atheneum Bks. for Young Readers) Simon & Schuster Children's Publishing.
Brown, Margaret. Little Raindrop. Schoeningh, Debby. 2012. 24p. pap. 9.95 *(978-0-9746360-7-8(X))* Country Side Pr., The.
Brown, Mari. Catching Boo. Rowlinson, Joanne. 2008. 24p. (J). (gr. -1-3). *(978-0-9739962-2-7(6))* Wuehr, Tina.
—Field Dance. Wuehr, Tina L. 2005. 18p. (J). (gr. -1-3). *(978-0-9739962-0-3(X))* Wuehr, Tina.
—Neela Potts Has Lots of Knots. Wuehr, Tina L. 2008. 30p. (J). (gr. -1-3). *(978-0-9739962-3-4(4))* Wuehr, Tina.
—Why Can't I Have Glue? Wuehr, Tina L. 2007. 20p. (J). (gr. -1-3). *(978-0-9739962-1-0(8))* Wuehr, Tina.

Brown, Marilyn. Girls Can! Make it Happen. Kupchella, Rick. 2004. (ENG.). 40p. (J). 16.95 *(978-0-9726504-3-4(1))* TRISTAN Publishing, Inc.

Brown, Marion, jt. illus. see McDonald, Marion.

Brown, Mark. Arthur & the Big Snow. Brown, Mark. 2018. (Arthur Ser.). (ENG.). 24p. (J). (gr. -1-k). pap. 4.99 *(978-1-338-27759-3(6)*, Cartwheel Bks.) Scholastic, Inc.

—Arthur Jumps into Fall. Brown, Mark. 2018. (Arthur Ser.). (ENG.). 24p. (J). (gr. -1-k). pap. 4.99 *(978-1-338-27758-6(8)*, Cartwheel Bks.) Scholastic, Inc.

Brown, Martin. Blood-Curdling Box, 20 vols. Deary, Terry. 2008. 2880p. pap. *(978-1-4071-0815-5(8)*, Scholastic) Scholastic, Inc.

Brown, Martin. Lesser Spotted Animals. Brown, Martin. 2016. (ENG.). 56p. (J). (gr. 2-5). 18.99 *(978-1-338-08934-9(X))* Scholastic, Inc.

Brown, Mary Barrett. Playful Slider: The North American River Otter. Esbensen, Barbara Juster. 2011. (Fesler-Lampert Minnesota Heritage Ser.). (ENG.). 32p. pap. 11.95 *(978-0-8166-7765-8(4))* Univ. of Minnesota Pr.

Brown, Matt, photos by. Amigos en la Escuela, 1 vol. Bunnett, Rochelle. Muñoz, Yenny, tr. from ENG. 2007.Tr. of Friends at School. (SPA., 32p. (J). (gr. -1). pap. 5.95 *(978-1-59572-041-2(3))* Star Bright Bks., Inc.

Brown, Merrilees. Caspian Finds a Friend. Veissid, Jacqueline. 2019. (ENG.). 36p. (J). (gr. k-3). 17.99 *(978-1-4521-3780-3(3))* Chronicle Bks. LLC.

Brown, Michael D. Tanker's Adventures in Monterey. Brown, Maureen E. 2007. 24p. (J). 13.95 *(978-0-615-16200-3(2))* TankerToys.

Brown, Michelle. Harbour Tales: Book 1. Hobson, David. 2018. (ENG.). 48p. (J). pap. 12.95 *(978-1-4566-3181-9(0))* eBookit.com.

Brown, Nick. The Watermelon Story. Miro. 2003. 103p. (J). pap. *(978-1-84426-258-8(8))* Upfront Publishing Ltd.

Brown, Palmer. Beyond the Pawpaw Trees. Brown, Palmer. 2011. (Anna Lavinia Ser.). (ENG.). 136p. (J). (gr. k-4). 17.95 *(978-1-59017-461-6(5)*, NYR Children's Collection) New York Review of Bks., Inc., The.

—Hickory. Brown, Palmer. 2013. (ENG.). 56p. (J). (gr. -1-2). 16.95 *(978-1-59017-627-6(8)*, NYR Children's Collection) New York Review of Bks., Inc., The.

—The Silver Nutmeg. Brown, Palmer. 2012. (Anna Lavinia Ser.). (ENG.). 152p. (J). (gr. k-4). 15.95 *(978-1-59017-500-2(X)*, NYR Children's Collection) New York Review of Bks., Inc., The.

—Something for Christmas. Brown, Palmer. 2011. (ENG.). 40p. (J). (gr. -1-2). 12.95 *(978-1-59017-462-3(3)*, NYR Children's Collection) New York Review of Bks., Inc., The.

Brown, Peter. Creepy Carrots! Reynolds, Aaron. 2012. (ENG.). 40p. (J). (gr. -1-3). 17.99 *(978-1-4424-0297-3(0)*, Simon & Schuster Bks. For Young Readers) Simon & Schuster Bks. For Young Readers.

—Creepy Pair of Underwear! Reynolds, Aaron. 2017. (ENG.). 48p. (J). (gr. -1-3). 17.99 *(978-1-4424-0298-0(9)*, Simon & Schuster Bks. For Young Readers) Simon & Schuster Bks. For Young Readers.

—Kaline Klattermaster's Tree House. Kimmel, Haven. 2010. (ENG.). 160p. (J). (gr. 2-7). pap. 7.99 *(978-0-689-87403-1(0)*, Atheneum Bks. for Young Readers) Simon & Schuster Children's Publishing.

—Kaline Klattermaster's Tree House. Kimmel, Haven. 2008. (ENG.). 152p. (J). (gr. 4-6). 18.69 *(978-0-689-87402-4(2))* Simon & Schuster, Inc.

—The Purple Kangaroo. Black, Michael Ian. 2009. (ENG.). 32p. (J). (gr. -1-3). 17.99 *(978-1-4169-5771-3(5)*, Simon & Schuster Bks. For Young Readers) Simon & Schuster Bks. For Young Readers.

—The Wild Robot Escapes. 2018. 279p. (J). *(978-0-316-45375-2(7))* Little Brown & Co.

Brown, Petra. Auntie Loves You. James, Helen Foster. 2018. (ENG.). 32p. (J). (gr. -1-1). 15.99 *(978-1-5341-1011-3(9)*, 204589) Sleeping Bear Pr.

—The Big City. Gilmore, Grace. 2015. (Tales from Maple Ridge Ser.: 3). (ENG.). 128p. (J). (gr. k-4). pap. 5.99 *(978-1-4814-3006-7(8)*, Little Simon) Little Simon.

—Conker. Morpurgo, Michael. 2016. (Reading Ladder Ser.). (ENG.). 48p. (J). (gr. k-2). pap. 7.99 *(978-1-4052-8254-3(1))* Egmont Bks., Ltd. GBR. Dist: Independent Pubs. Group.

—The Ghost of Juniper Creek. Gilmore, Grace. 2015. (Tales from Maple Ridge Ser.: 4). (ENG.). 128p. (J). (gr. k-4). pap. 5.99 *(978-1-4814-3009-8(2)*, Little Simon) Little Simon.

—Grandma Loves You! James, Helen Foster. 2013. (ENG.). 32p. (J). (gr. -1 — 1). 14.99 *(978-1-58536-836-5(9)*, 202884) Sleeping Bear Pr.

—Grandma's Christmas Wish. James, Helen Foster. (ENG.). (J). (gr. -1-1). 2019. 18p. bds. 8.99 *(978-1-5341-1064-9(X)*, 204835); 2015. 32p. 15.99 *(978-1-58536-918-8(7)*, 203955) Sleeping Bear Pr.

—Grandpa Loves You! James, Helen Foster. 2016. (ENG.). 32p. (J). (gr. -1-1). 15.99 *(978-1-58536-940-9(3)*, 204032) Sleeping Bear Pr.

—A Horse Named Jack. Heyden, Linda Vander. 2018. (ENG.). 32p. (J). (gr. -1-2). 16.99 *(978-1-58536-395-7(2)*, 204411) Sleeping Bear Pr.

—Hush, Little Baby. 2007. (Padded Hardcover Ser.). 18p. (J). 8.95 *(978-1-58925-819-8(3))* Tiger Tales.

—I Will Keep You Safe & Sound. Houran, Lori Haskins. 2013. (J). *(978-0-545-19752-6(X)*, Scholastic Pr.) Scholastic, Inc.

—Logan Pryce Makes a Mess. Gilmore, Grace. 2015. (Tales from Maple Ridge Ser.: 1). (ENG.). 128p. (J). (gr. k-4). pap. 5.99 *(978-1-4814-2624-4(9)*, Little Simon) Little Simon.

—Lost in the Blizzard. Gilmore, Grace. 2015. (Tales from Maple Ridge Ser.: 5). (ENG.). 128p. (J). (gr. k-4). pap. 5.99 *(978-1-4814-4749-2(1)*, Little Simon) Little Simon.

—The Lucky Wheel. Gilmore, Grace. 2015. (Tales from Maple Ridge Ser.: 2). (ENG.). 128p. (J). (gr. k-4). pap. 5.99 *(978-1-4814-2627-5(3)*, Little Simon) Little Simon.

—Mommy Loves You. James, Helen Foster. 2017. (ENG.). 32p. (J). (gr. -1-k). 15.99 *(978-1-58536-941-6(1)*, 204232) Sleeping Bear Pr.

—The New Kid. Gilmore, Grace. 2016. (Tales from Maple Ridge Ser.: 6). (ENG.). 128p. (J). (gr. k-4). pap. 5.99 *(978-1-4814-4746-1(7)*, Little Simon) Little Simon.

—Rags Hero Dog of WWI: A True Story. Raven, Margot Theis. 2014. (ENG.). 32p. (J). (gr. 2-5). 16.99 *(978-1-58536-258-5(1)*, 203672) Sleeping Bear Pr.

—With Love, Grandma. James, Helen Foster. 2018. (ENG.). 32p. (J). (gr. k-2). 15.99 *(978-1-58536-942-3(X)*, 204330) Sleeping Bear Pr.

Brown, Petra. When the Wind Blew. Brown, Petra. 2017. (ENG.). 32p. (J). (gr. k-3). 16.99 *(978-1-58536-969-0(1)*, 204234) Sleeping Bear Pr.

Brown, Priscella. Little Charlie & the Christmas Tree: Little Charlie & His Awesome Adventures. Richardson, Kimberlie D. 2016. (ENG.). 42p. (J). pap. 19.95 *(978-1-4787-8076-2(2))* Outskirts Pr., Inc.

Brown, R. Where Is My Bunny? My Fun Backyard on the East Coast of Florida. Brown, A. 2019. (ENG.). 28p. (J). pap. 9.99 *(978-1-0713-0803-5(3))* Independently Published.

Brown, Reggie. The Magnificent Makers #1: How to Test a Friendship. Griffith, Theanne. 2020. (Magnificent Makers Ser.: 1). (ENG.). 112p. (J). (gr. 2-5). 5.99 ***(978-0-593-12298-3(4))***; lib. bdg. 12.99 ***(978-0-593-12299-0(2))*** Random Hse. Children's Bks. (Random Hse. Bks. for Young Readers).

—The Magnificent Makers #2: Brain Trouble. Griffith, Theanne. 2020. (Magnificent Makers Ser.: 2). 112p. (J). (gr. 2-5). 5.99 ***(978-0-593-12301-0(8))***; (ENG.). lib. bdg. 12.99 ***(978-0-593-12302-7(6))*** Random Hse. Children's Bks. (Random Hse. Bks. for Young Readers).

Brown, Reilly, et al. Agents of Atlas: the Complete Collection Vol. 2. 2020. (ENG.). 448p. (YA). (gr. 8-17). pap. 39.99 *(978-1-302-92272-6(6))* Marvel Worldwide, Inc.

—Spider-Man/Deadpool Vol. 2: Side Pieces. 2017. 120p. (YA). (gr. 8-17). pap. 16.99 *(978-0-7851-9992-2(6))* Marvel Worldwide, Inc.

Brown, Richard. A Kid's Guide to Washington, D. C. Clark, Diane C. et al. rev. ed. 2008. (ENG.). 160p. (J). (gr. 1-4). pap. 15.99 *(978-0-15-206125-8(8)*, 1198393) Houghton Mifflin Harcourt Publishing Co.

Brown, Richard, jt. illus. see Cordell, Matthew.

Brown, Rick. Boker Tov! Good Morning!, Vol. Black, Joe. 2009. (Kar-Ben Favorites Ser.). (ENG.). 24p. (J). (gr. -1 — 1). pap. 8.95 *(978-0-7613-3951-9(5)*, Kar-Ben Publishing) Lerner Publishing Group.

Brown, Robert & Paultyn, Tony. Magic Islands. Edwards, Irene. 2019. (ENG.). 206p. (J). pap. ***(978-1-9161619-4-8(4))*** Cambria Bks.

Brown, Rod. Freedom's a-Callin Me. Shange, Ntozake. 2012. (ENG.). 32p. (J). (gr. 3-7). 16.99 *(978-0-06-133741-3(2)*, Collins) HarperCollins Pubs.

—Grandpa Stops a War: A Paul Robeson Story. Robeson, Susan. 2019. 32p. (J). (gr. k-4). 17.95 *(978-1-60980-882-2(7)*, Triangle Square) Seven Stories Pr.

—We Troubled the Waters. Shange, Ntozake. 2009. (ENG.). 32p. (J). (gr. 4-18). 16.99 *(978-0-06-133735-2(8)*, Collins) HarperCollins Pubs.

Brown, Ron. Holy Hum. Hauser, Sheri. aut. ed. 2005. 42p. (YA). per. 12.50 *(978-0-9766718-8-6(3))* Glorybound Publishing.

Brown, Ruth. Black Beauty. Sewell, Anna. 2019. 32p. (J). (-k). pap. 14.99 *(978-1-78344-216-4(6))* Andersen Pr. GBR. Dist: Independent Pubs. Group.

—The Christmas Mouse. 2013. (J). *(978-1-4351-5021-8(X))* Barnes & Noble, Inc.

—The Quayside Cat. Forward, Toby. 2014. (ENG.). 32p. (J). (gr. -1-3). 16.95 *(978-1-4677-3452-3(7)*, 9781467734523) Lerner Publishing Group.

Brown, Ruth. Black Beauty. Brown, Ruth. Sewell, Anna. 2016. (ENG.). 32p. (J). (gr. -1-3). 17.99 *(978-1-5124-1619-0(3)*, 9781512416190) Lerner Publishing Group.

—Gracie, the Lighthouse Cat. Brown, Ruth. 2011. (Andersen Press Picture Bks). (ENG.). 32p. (J). (gr. -1-3). 16.95 *(978-0-7613-7454-1(X))* Lerner Publishing Group.

—Greyfriars Bobby. Brown, Ruth. 2013. 32p. (J). (gr. -1-k). pap. 12.99 *(978-1-84939-632-5(9))* Andersen Pr. GBR. Dist: Independent Pubs. Group.

—Night-Time Tale. Brown, Ruth. 2007. (ENG.). 32p. (J). (gr. -1-k). pap. 10.99 *(978-1-84270-475-2(3))* Andersen Pr. GBR. Dist: Independent Pubs. Group.

—Snail Trail. Brown, Ruth. 2013. 24p. (J). (gr. -1-k). 12.99 *(978-1-84939-252-5(8))* Andersen Pr. GBR. Dist: Independent Pubs. Group.

Brown, Ruth & Barrett, Peter. James Herriot's Treasury for Children: Warm & Joyful Tales by the Author of All Creatures Great & Small. Herriot, James. ed. 2014. (ENG.). 272p. (J). (gr. -1-3). 25.99 *(978-1-250-05813-3(9)*, 900139655, St. Martin's Griffin) St. Martin's Pr.

Brown, Scott. The Curse of the Werepenguin. Woodrow, Allan. (Werepenguin Ser.). (ENG.). 352p. (J). (gr. 3-7). 2020. 8.99 ***(978-0-451-48046-0(5)***, Puffin Books); 2019. 17.99 *(978-0-451-48044-6(9)*, Viking Books for Young Readers) Penguin Young Readers Group.

—The Revenge of the Werepenguin. Woodrow, Allan. 2020. (Werepenguin Ser.). 384p. (J). (gr. 3-7). 17.99 ***(978-0-593-11423-0(X)***, Viking Books for Young Readers) Penguin Young Readers Group.

Brown, Stephen. Flowers in the Sun. Gates, Margo. 2020. (Plant Life Cycles (Pull Ahead Readers — Fiction) Ser.). (ENG.). 16p. (J). (gr. -1-1). pap. 6.99 ***(978-1-7284-0310-6(3))***; lib. bdg. 22.65 ***(978-1-5415-9028-1(7))*** Lerner Publishing Group. (Lerner Pubns.).

—Pumpkin Seeds. Gates, Margo. 2020. (Plant Life Cycles (Pull Ahead Readers — Fiction) Ser.). (ENG.). 16p. (J). (gr. -1-1). pap. 6.99 ***(978-1-7284-0308-3(1))***; lib. bdg. 22.65 ***(978-1-5415-9027-4(9))*** Lerner Publishing Group. (Lerner Pubns.).

Brown, Steve. Allosaurus: The Troublesome Tooth, 1 vol. Veitch, Catherine. 2020. (Dinosaur Adventures Ser.). (ENG.). 24p. (gr. 1-2). pap. 8.25 ***(978-1-4994-8485-4(2)***, Windmill Bks.) Rosen Publishing Group, Inc., The.

Brown, Steve. Collins Big Cat Phonics for Letters & Sounds - Monster Treat: Band 05/Green, Bd. 5. Sparkes, Amy. 2018. (Collins Big Cat Phonics Ser.). (ENG.). 24p. (J). (gr. k-1). pap. 6.99 *(978-0-00-825167-3(3))* HarperCollins Pubs. Ltd. GBR. Dist: Independent Pubs. Group.

—Epple the Elephant (Who Was Allergic to Peanuts) Crouse, Livingstone. 2018. (ENG.). 40p. (J). (gr. 1-3). 17.99 *(978-1-68412-377-3(1)*, Silver Dolphin Bks.) Printers Row Publishing Group.

—Oh Bella! Yellow Band. Kubuitsile, Lauri. 2016. (Cambridge Reading Adventures Ser.). (ENG.). 15p. pap. 7.37 *(978-1-107-55070-4(X))* Cambridge Univ. Pr.

—Right Side Up! Adventures in Chelm. Kimmel, Eric A. 2019. (J). *(978-1-68115-548-7(6)*, Apples & Honey Pr.) Behrman Hse., Inc.

—The Wondrous Dinosaurium. Condon, John. 2020. (ENG.). 32p. (J). (gr. -1-3). 17.99 *(978-1-84886-474-0(4))* Maverick Arts Publishing GBR. Dist: Lerner Publishing Group.

Brown, Stevi. Glory Gone Forgotten: The Untold Story of the 12th Kentucky Cavalry. Goodall, Barry, Jr. Embry, Eugene, ed. 2nd rev. ed. 2005. 182p. *(978-0-9763932-1-4(2)*, 500) Goodall, Barry.

Brown, Suzy. There's a Beetle in My Bed. Kirk, Bill. 2009. 16p. pap. 9.95 *(978-1-61633-005-7(8))* Guardian Angel Publishing, Inc.

—There's a Spider in My Sink! Kirk, Bill. 2008. 16p. pap. 9.95 *(978-1-935137-25-2(5))* Guardian Angel Publishing, Inc.

Brown, Tempe. The Little Dirt People. Brown, Tempe. 2013. 50p. pap. 14.95 *(978-1-4507-3904-7(0))* Bush Publishing Inc.

Brown, Tim. Bark & Tim: A True Story of Friendship. Vernick, Audrey Glassman & Gidaro, Ellen Glassman. 2003. 32p. (J). 14.95 *(978-1-57072-271-4(4))* Overmountain Pr.

Brown, Toni Sorenson, photos by. Heroes of the Bible. 2004. 32p. (J). 17.95 *(978-1-59156-097-5(7))* Covenant Communications, Inc.

Browne, Anita. Cycle, Children's Games & Other Songs. Rice, Ruth Mason & Villar, Rose. 2012. 56p. 36.95 *(978-1-258-23019-7(4))*; pap. 21.95 *(978-1-258-24214-5(1))* Literary Licensing, LLC.

Browne, Anthony. Hide & Seek. Browne, Anthony. 2018. (ENG.). 32p. (J). (gr. -1-2). 17.99 *(978-1-5362-0260-1(6))* Candlewick Pr.

—How Do You Feel? Browne, Anthony. 2012. (ENG.). 32p. (J). (gr. -1-2). 16.99 *(978-0-7636-5862-5(6))* Candlewick Pr.

—The Little Bear Book. Browne, Anthony. 2014. (ENG.). 24p. (J). (gr. -1-2). 15.99 *(978-0-7636-7007-8(3))* Candlewick Pr.

—Little Beauty. Browne, Anthony. (ENG.). 32p. (J). (gr. -1-2). 2010. pap. 6.99 *(978-0-7636-4967-8(8))*; 2008. 16.99 *(978-0-7636-3959-4(1))* Candlewick Pr.

—Little Frida. Browne, Anthony. 2019. (ENG.). 32p. (J). (gr. -1-1). 16.99 *(978-1-5362-0933-4(3))* Candlewick Pr.

—Mi Mama. Browne, Anthony. Fuentes Silva, Andrea, tr. 2005. (Los Especiales de A la Orilla del Viento Ser.). (SPA.). 28p. (J). *(978-968-16-7375-8(1))* Fondo de Cultura Economica.

—My Mom. Browne, Anthony. 2009. (ENG.). 32p. (J). (gr. k-3). pap. 8.99 *(978-0-374-40026-2(1)*, 900058756) Square Fish.

—One Gorilla: a Counting Book. Browne, Anthony. (ENG.). (J). 2015. 26p. (— 1). bds. 7.99 *(978-0-7636-7915-6(1))*; 2013. 32p. (gr. -1-2). 17.99 *(978-0-7636-6352-0(2))* Candlewick Pr.

—Willy & the Cloud. Browne, Anthony. 2017. (ENG.). 32p. (J). (gr. -1-2). 16.99 *(978-0-7636-9498-2(3))* Candlewick Pr.

—Willy's Stories. Browne, Anthony. 2015. (ENG.). 32p. (J). (gr. k-3). 16.99 *(978-0-7636-7761-9(2))* Candlewick Pr.

Browne, Christopher. Marlo. Browne, Christopher. 2017. (ENG.). 40p. (J). (gr. -1-3). 17.99 *(978-0-06-244113-3(2))* HarperCollins Pubs.

—Marlo & the Dinosaurs. Browne, Christopher. 2018. (ENG.). 40p. (J). (gr. -1-3). 17.99 *(978-0-06-244115-7(9)*, Balzer & Bray) HarperCollins Pubs.

Browne, Eileen. Handa's Hen. Browne, Eileen. 2004. (ENG & PAN.). 32p. (J). bds. *(978-1-84444-194-5(6))* Mantra Lingua.

—Handa's Noisy Night. Browne, Eileen. 2020. (ENG.). 32p. (J). (gr. -1-2). 16.99 *(978-1-5362-1489-5(2))*; 7.99 *(978-1-5362-1109-2(5))* Candlewick Pr.

—Handa's Surprise. Browne, Eileen. 2011. (Read & Share Ser.). (ENG.). 32p. (J). (gr. -1-2). pap. 24.99 *(978-0-7636-5385-9(3))* Candlewick Pr.

—Handa's Surprise: Read & Share. Browne, Eileen. 2013. (Read & Share Ser.). (ENG.). 32p. (J). (gr. k-2). 16.19 *(978-0-7636-0863-7(7))* Candlewick Pr.

—Handa's Surprise: Read & Share. Browne, Eileen. 2004. (ENG & BEN.). 32p. (J). pap. *(978-1-85269-472-2(6))*; pap. *(978-1-85269-473-9(4))*; pap. *(978-1-85269-474-6(2))*; pap. *(978-1-85269-475-3(0))*; pap. *(978-1-85269-477-7(7))*; pap. *(978-1-85269-478-4(5))*; pap. *(978-1-85269-507-1(2))*; pap. *(978-1-85269-508-8(0))*; pap. *(978-1-85269-509-5(9))*; pap. *(978-1-85269-510-1(2))*; pap. *(978-1-85269-512-5(9))*; pap. *(978-1-85269-513-2(7))*; pap. *(978-1-85269-515-6(3))*; pap. *(978-1-85269-476-0(9))*; pap. *(978-1-85269-514-9(5))* Mantra Lingua.

Browne, Francis, photos by. Father Browne's Galway. O'Donnell, E. E. 2007. (ENG., 112p. 21.99 *(978-1-85607-938-9(4))* Currach Pr. IRL. Dist: Casemate Pubs. & Bk. Distributors, LLC.

Browne, Gordon. Down the Snow Stairs: Or, from Goodnight to Goodmorning. Corkran, Alice. 2012. 278p. pap. 14.95 *(978-1-934671-12-2(6))* Salem Ridge Press LLC.

—Fairy Tales from Hans Andersen (Illustrated) Barry, ed. Paull, Susannah Mary, tr. 2018. (ENG.). 804p. (J). pap. 49.90 *(978-1-7928-6385-1(3))* Independently Published.

Browne, James. Return of Chancellor Paddywack: A Sequel to Magic Marmalade, A Tale of the Moonlight Fairies. Licht, Sharon. 2012. 112p. (J). pap. *(978-1-927360-69-9(2))* CCB Publishing.

Browne, Paula. El Cumpleanos de la Mona. Browne, Paula. Isabel, Isaias, tr. 2004. (Paca, la Macaca Ser.). (SPA.). 20p. pap. 4.95 *(978-85-7416-214-0(0))* Callis Editora Ltda BRA. Dist: Independent Pubs. Group.

—Paca, la macaca en la Cocina. Browne, Paula. Isabel, Isaias, tr. 2004. (Paca, la Macaca Ser.). (SPA.). 20p. pap. 4.95 *(978-85-7416-210-2(8))* Callis Editora Ltda BRA. Dist: Independent Pubs. Group.

—Paca, la Macaca va al Mercado. Browne, Paula. Isabel, Isaias, tr. 2004. (Paca, la Macaca Ser.). 20p. pap. 4.95 *(978-85-7416-215-7(9))* Callis Editora Ltda BRA. Dist: Independent Pubs. Group.

—Que Desbarajuste, Paca. Browne, Paula. Isabel, Isaias, tr. 2004. (Paca, la Macaca Ser.). 20p. pap. 6.95 *(978-85-7416-211-9(6))* Callis Editora Ltda BRA. Dist: Independent Pubs. Group.

Browne, Stephanie. Gumbo the Bayou Dog. Thrasher, Jeanni. 2020. (ENG.). 26p. (J). pap. 12.99 ***(978-1-952011-14-6(0))*** Pen It! Pubns., LLC.

Browning, Diane. Signed, Abiah Rose. Browning, Diane. 2010. (ENG.). 32p. (J). (gr. -1-2). 15.99 *(978-1-58246-311-7(5)*, Tricycle Pr.) Random Hse. Children's Bks.

Browning, Kurt. T Is for Tutu: A Ballet Alphabet. Rodriguez, Sonia. 2015. (Av2 Fiction Readalong 2016 Ser.). (ENG.). (J). (gr. 1-4). lib. bdg. 34.28 *(978-1-4896-3768-0(0)*, AV2 by Weigl) Weigl Pubs., Inc.

Browning, Lisa Marie. His Little Princess: Treasured Letters from Your King a Devotional for Children. Shepherd, Sheri Rose. 2006. (His Princess Ser.). (ENG.). 128p. (J). (gr. 4-7). 15.99 *(978-1-59052-601-9(5)*, Multnomah Bks.) Crown Publishing Group, The.

Browning, Suzan. Dinosaur George Pre-hysterical Adventures: What Color Were Dinosaurs? Quisenberry, Stacey. 2007. (J). 3.95 *(978-0-9797304-3-6(0))* Raining Popcorn Media.

Brownjohn, Emma. Yes I Can! Be Healthy. Brownjohn, Emma. 2011. (Yes I Can! Ser.). (ENG.). 18p. (J). (gr. -1-k). 12.99 *(978-1-85707-734-6(2))* Tango Bks. GBR. Dist: Independent Pubs. Group.

Brownlee, Karen. The Sakura Tree, 1 vol. McTighe, Carolyn. 2007. (ENG.). 32p. (J). (gr. k-3). 15.95 *(978-0-88995-354-3(6)*, e343120d-f345-4018-a057-25b04d214bff) Red Deer Pr. CAN. Dist: Firefly Bks., Ltd.

Brownlee, Kelly Jackson. The Boy Who Wanted to be a Dancer. Gambassi, Rod. 2007. 22p. (J). 23.95 *(978-1-889829-18-0(8))* Window Bks.

Brownlee, Sunny. Ida Claire Decorates with Flair. Rowles, Louis. 2004. 24p. (J). pap. *(978-0-9708748-1-8(2))* Rowles, Louis.

Brownlie, Ian, jt. illus. see McInturff, Linda.

Brownlie, Ian D. Until the Letter Came. St. John, Patricia. 2004. 44p. (J). pap. *(978-1-932381-14-6(7)*, 5580) Bible Visuals International, Inc.

Brownlow, Mike. Dinosaurs of Doom! 2011. (Time Pirates Ser.). (ENG.). 12p. (J). (gr. k-2). bds. 24.99 *(978-0-230-74179-9(7))* Pan Macmillan GBR. Dist: Independent Pubs. Group.

—Rocky & Daisy at the Park, 1 vol. Crow, Melinda Melton. 2013. (My Two Dogs Ser.). (ENG.). 32p. (J). (gr. 2-3). pap. 5.95 *(978-1-4342-6118-2(2))*; lib. bdg. 22.65 *(978-1-4342-4163-4(7))* Capstone. (Stone Arch Bks.).

—Rocky & Daisy Get Trained, 1 vol. Crow, Melinda Melton. 2013. (My Two Dogs Ser.). (ENG.). 32p. (J). (gr. 2-3). pap. 5.95 *(978-1-4342-6116-8(6))*; lib. bdg. 22.65 *(978-1-4342-4161-0(0))* Capstone. (Stone Arch Bks.).

—Rocky & Daisy Go Camping, 1 vol. Crow, Melinda Melton. 2013. (My Two Dogs Ser.). (ENG.). 32p. (J). (gr. 2-3). pap. 5.95 *(978-1-4342-6117-5(4))*; lib. bdg. 22.65 *(978-1-4342-4162-7(9))* Capstone. (Stone Arch Bks.).

—Rocky & Daisy Go Home, 1 vol. Crow, Melinda Melton. 2013. (My Two Dogs Ser.). (ENG.). 32p. (J). (gr. 2-3). pap. 5.95 *(978-1-4342-6115-1(8))*; lib. bdg. 22.65 *(978-1-4342-4160-3(2))* Capstone. (Stone Arch Bks.).

Brownlow, Mike. The Elves & the Shoemaker. Brownlow, Mike. 2014. (Traditional Tales Ser.). (ENG.). 12p. (J). (gr. -1-k). pap. 5.95 *(978-1-62521-554-3(1)*, Capstone Classroom) Capstone.

Broxon, Janet. Every Orchard Tree. Hubbell, Patricia. 2008. (J). *(978-1-55971-986-5(9)*, NorthWord Bks. for Young Readers) T&N Children's Publishing.

Broyles, Beverly Ashley. Germs on Their Fingers! Ferrin, Wendy Wakefield. Tono, Lucia, tr. 2003.Tr. of Gernenes en Tus Manos!. (SPA & ENG.). 64p. (J). (gr. 1-7). 17.95 *(978-0-9703632-1-3(4))*; pap. 12.95 *(978-0-9703632-0-6(6))* Wakefield Connection, The.

—Grandmother's Alligator: Burukenge Wa Nyanya. Ferrin, Wendy Wakefield. Mwangi, Simmon, tr. 2003. (SWA & ENG.). 56p. (J). (gr. 1-18). 17.95 *(978-0-9703632-3-7(0))* Wakefield Connection, The.

—Grandmother's Alligator/Burukenge Wa Nyanya Activity Guide. 2005. (ENG & SWA.). (J). 12.95 *(978-0-9703632-7-5(3))* Wakefield Connection, The.

Brozman, Owen. Seriously, You Have to Eat. Mansbach, Adam. 2015. 32p. (J). 15.95 *(978-1-61775-408-1(0))* Akashic Bks.

Brozyna, Andrew. A Young Scientist's Guide to Defying Disasters with Skill & Daring: Includes 20 Experiments for the Sink, Bathtub & Backyard, 1 vol. Doyle, James. 2012. (ENG.). 160p. (J). (gr. 5-6). 14.99 *(978-1-4236-2440-0(8))* Gibbs Smith, Publisher.

—A Young Scientist's Guide to Faulty Freaks of Nature, 1 vol. Doyle, James. 2013. 160p. (J). (gr. 5-6). 14.99 *(978-1-4236-2455-4(6))* Gibbs Smith, Publisher.

Brubacher, Marilyn. Don't Call Me Different. Martin, Mary S. 2016. (ENG.). 190p. (J). pap. 8.25 *(978-0-7399-2539-3(3))* Rod & Staff Pubs., Inc.

Bruce, Allison. Engineering: Cool Women Who Design. May, Vicki V. 2016. (Girls in Science Ser.). 112p. (J). (gr. 3-7). 19.95 *(978-1-61930-341-6(8)*, e1753766-ba47-49df-8ef4-0de97ba40e73); (ENG.). 26.19 *(978-1-4844-8450-0(9)*, 1401403) Nomad Pr.

—Forensics: Cool Women Who Investigate. Yasuda, Anita. 2016. (Girls in Science Ser.). 112p. (J). (gr. 3-7). 19.95

(978-1-61930-346-1(9), c10728d7-4a96-4ec9-802a-a6e1837c0a47) Nomad Pr.

Bruce, Cindy, jt. illus. see Robertson, Elysia Hill.

Bruce, Dwayne. That Curious Sign on Aisle Nine. Morey, Kyle Lb. 2017. (ENG.). (J). pap. 9.99 *(978-0-9979656-2-9(2))* C Turtle Publishing.

Bruchnalski, Marcin. The Four Little Pigs. Nye, Kimara. 2019. (Early Bird Readers — Purple (Early Bird Stories (tm)) Ser.). (ENG.). 32p. (J). (gr. k-3). 27.99 *(978-1-5415-4227-3(4),* 9781541542273); pap. 7.99 *(978-1-5415-7422-9(2),* 9781541574229) Lerner Publishing Group. (Lerner Pubns.).

Brucker, Glenn. Ice Journey. Downey, Glen. 2007. 48p. (J). lib. bdg. 23.08 *(978-1-4242-1618-5(4))* Fitzgerald Bks.

Bruckner, Wes. Lemon Path Encounter, 1 vol. Bruckner, Tai. 2009. 15p. pap. 24.95 *(978-1-60836-407-7(0))* America Star Bks.

Brudlos, Joseph. Alpha Shade Chapter One. Brudlos, Christopher. 2005. (YA). per. 24.95 net. *(978-0-9768705-0-0(9))* Alpha Shade, Inc.

Brudos, Susan E. Will You Be My Friend? — We Really Are No Different. Downey, Joni J. 2004. (J). pap. *(978-0-932991-34-8(3))* Place In The Woods, The.

Brudos, Susan E. & Rubino, Alisa A. Wayne's Trail. 2004. (J). pap. *(978-0-932991-62-1(9))* Place In The Woods, The.

Brueggeman, Bryan. Fruzzle's Mystery Talent: A Bed Time Fantasy Story for Children Ages 3-10. Brueggeman, Karen & Paddock, Briana. 2013. 48p. pap. 10.99 *(978-0-9892565-0-6(2))* Dolphins Publishing.

Brueggemann, Mindy, photos by. Who Is Lilly? Brueggemann, Mindy. 2013. 44p. pap. 9.95 *(978-0-9855676-1-3(9))* Dankworth Publishing.

Bruel, Nick. Dinosaur Trouble. King-Smith, Dick. 2012. (ENG.). 128p. (J). (gr. 2-5). pap. 16.99 *(978-1-59643-935-1(1),* 9781596439351) Roaring Brook Pr.

Bruel, Nick. Bad Kitty. Bruel, Nick. (Bad Kitty Ser.). (ENG.). 40p. (J). (gr. -1-3). 2nd ed. 2007. 18.99 *(978-1-59643-299-4(3),* 900044918); 10th anniv. ed. 2015. 17.99 *(978-1-62672-245-3(5),* 900146688) Roaring Brook Pr.

—A Bad Kitty Christmas: Includes Three Ready-To-Hang Ornaments! Bruel, Nick. 2011. (Bad Kitty Ser.). (ENG.). 40p. (J). (gr. -1-3). 17.99 *(978-1-59643-668-8(9),* 900070722) Roaring Brook Pr.

—Bad Kitty Does Not Like Thanksgiving. Bruel, Nick. 2019. (Bad Kitty Ser.). (ENG.). 24p. (J). 5.99 *(978-1-250-19842-6(9),* 900194593) Roaring Brook Pr.

—Bad Kitty Gets a Bath. Bruel, Nick. 2008. (Bad Kitty Ser.). (ENG.). 128p. (J). (gr. 2-5). 15.99 *(978-1-59643-341-0(8),* 900048537) Roaring Brook Pr.

—Bad Kitty Gets a Bath. Bruel, Nick. 2009. (Bad Kitty Ser.). (ENG.). 144p. (J). (gr. 2-5). pap. 6.99 *(978-0-312-58138-1(6),* 900061992) Square Fish.

—Bad Kitty: Kitten Trouble. Bruel, Nick. 2018. (Bad Kitty Ser.). (ENG.). 160p. (J). 13.99 *(978-1-250-18208-1(5),* 900190504) Roaring Brook Pr.

—Bad Kitty: Kitten Trouble. Bruel, Nick. 2019. (Bad Kitty Ser.). (ENG.). 160p. (J). pap. 6.99 *(978-1-250-23328-8(3),* 900190505) Square Fish.

—Bad Kitty Meets the Baby. Bruel, Nick. 2011. (Bad Kitty Ser.). (ENG.). 144p. (J). (gr. 2-5). 15.99 *(978-1-59643-597-1(6),* 900065553) Roaring Brook Pr.

—Bad Kitty Meets the Baby. Bruel, Nick. 2012. (Bad Kitty Ser.). (ENG.). 160p. (J). (gr. 2-5). pap. 6.99 *(978-0-312-64121-4(4),* 9780312641214) Square Fish.

—Bad Kitty: Searching for Santa. Bruel, Nick. 2019. (Bad Kitty Ser.). (ENG.). 24p. (J). 9.99 *(978-1-250-19843-3(7),* 900194594) Roaring Brook Pr.

—Bad Kitty vs Uncle Murray: The Uproar at the Front Door. Bruel, Nick. 2010. (Bad Kitty Ser.). (ENG.). 160p. (J). (gr. 2-5). 15.99 *(978-1-59643-596-4(8),* 900065551) Roaring Brook Pr.

—Bad Kitty vs Uncle Murray: The Uproar at the Front Door. Bruel, Nick. 2011. (Bad Kitty Ser.). (ENG.). 176p. (J). (gr. 2-5). pap. 6.99 *(978-0-312-67483-0(X),* 900072896) Square Fish.

—Happy Birthday, Bad Kitty. Bruel, Nick. 2009. (Bad Kitty Ser.). (ENG.). 160p. (J). (gr. 2-5). 16.99 *(978-1-59643-342-7(6),* 900048539) Roaring Brook Pr.

—Happy Birthday, Bad Kitty. Bruel, Nick. 2010. (Bad Kitty Ser.). (ENG.). 176p. (J). (gr. 2-5). pap. 6.99 *(978-0-312-62902-1(8),* 9780312629021) Square Fish.

—Poor Puppy & Bad Kitty. Bruel, Nick. ed. 2012. (Bad Kitty Ser.). (ENG.). 40p. (J). (gr. -1-3). 18.99 *(978-1-59643-844-6(4),* 900095970) Roaring Brook Pr.

—Who Is Melvin Bubble? Bruel, Nick. 2006. (ENG.). 32p. (J). (gr. -1-3). 18.99 *(978-1-59643-116-4(4),* 900031725) Roaring Brook Pr.

—A Wonderful Year. Bruel, Nick. 2015. (ENG.). 40p. (J). (gr. -1-1). 17.99 *(978-1-59643-611-4(5),* 900065924) Roaring Brook Pr.

Bruff, Alex & Taylor, Matt. City Trails - Rome, 1 vol. Lonely Planet Kids & Butterfield, Moira. 2017. (City Trails Ser.). (ENG.). 104p. (J). (gr. 4-7). pap. 12.99 *(978-1-78657-964-5(2),* 5660) Lonely Planet Global Ltd. IRL. Dist: Hachette Bk. Group.

—City Trails - Sydney, 1 vol. Lonely Planet Kids & Greathead, Helen. 2017. (City Trails Ser.). (ENG.). 104p. (J). (gr. 4-7). pap. 12.99 *(978-1-78657-966-9(9),* 5663) Lonely Planet Global Ltd. IRL. Dist: Hachette Bk. Group.

—City Trails - Tokyo, 1 vol. Lonely Planet Kids & Claybourne, Anna. 2017. (City Trails Ser.). (ENG.). 104p. (J). (gr. 4-7). pap. 12.99 *(978-1-78657-726-9(7),* 5656) Lonely Planet Global Ltd. IRL. Dist: Hachette Bk. Group.

—City Trails - Washington DC, 1 vol. Lonely Planet Kids & Butterfield, Moira. 2017. (City Trails Ser.). (ENG.). 104p. (J). (gr. 4-7). pap. 12.99 *(978-1-78657-962-1(6),* 5658) Lonely Planet Global Ltd. IRL. Dist: Hachette Bk. Group.

Brughera, Pamela, jt. illus. see Pisapia, Blasco.

Bruha, Victor, jt. illus. see Therian, Francis Patrick.

Bruhl, Heather M. The Elephant Who Snored. Bruhl, Heather M. 2018. (ENG.). 38p. (J). pap. 14.95 *(978-1-7324181-0-3(1))* Longwood Publishing.

—Mommy, Where Are We Going? Bruhl, Heather M. 2019. (ENG.). 40p. (J). pap. 14.95 *(978-1-7324181-1-0(X))* Longwood Publishing.

Bruhn, Joan Z. Children's Chillers & Thrillers. Johnson, Liliane & Dufton, Jo S. 136p. (Orig.). (J). pap. 10.00 *(978-0-930069-04-9(8))* Jasmine Pr.

Bruijn, Charlotte. Are You Eating Candy Without Me? Malesevic, Draga Jenny. 2020. 32p. (J). (-k). 17.99 *(978-1-5247-9201-5(2),* Penguin Workshop) Penguin Young Readers Group.

Brulot, Heleen. Elephants at the Airport. Wolfson, Steve. 2013. 32p. pap. 11.95 *(978-0-9798324-5-1(4))* Argami Productions, LLC.

Brummer Everett, Michéle. My First Book of Feminism (for Boys) Merberg, Julie. 2018. (ENG.). 20p. (J). bds. 10.99 *(978-1-941367-62-9(3))* Downtown Bookworks.

Brumpton, Keith. Soccer Camp. Bedford, David. 3rd ed. 2004. 80p. *(978-1-877003-45-5(X))* Little Hare Bks. AUS. Dist: HarperCollins Pubs. Australia.

—The Soccer Machine, 1. Bedford, David. 2006. (Team Ser.). (ENG.). 68p. (J). (gr. 3-6). 17.44 *(978-1-933605-00-5(6))* Kane Miller.

—The Soccer Machine. Bedford, David. 2003. 80p. *(978-1-877003-26-4(3))* Little Hare Bks. AUS. Dist: HarperCollins Pubs. Australia.

—Top of the League. Bedford, David. 2nd ed. 2003. 80p. *(978-1-877003-30-1(1))* Little Hare Bks. AUS. Dist: HarperCollins Pubs. Australia.

Brun, Charles. Carnet Blanc St Valery en Caux. 2016. (Bnf Monuments Ser.). (FRE.). (J). pap. *(978-2-01-116970-9(4))* Hachette Groupe Livre.

—Carnet Ligne St Valery en Caux. 2016. (Bnf Monuments Ser.). (FRE.). (J). pap. *(978-2-01-116945-7(3))* Hachette Groupe Livre.

Bruna, Dick. Sweet Dreams, Miffy. Bruna, Dick. 2019. (Miffy Ser.). (ENG.). 24p. (J). (gr. -1-2). 9.99 *(978-1-5344-3317-5(1),* Simon Spotlight) Simon Spotlight.

Brundage, Frances. Cinderella: A Fairy Story. 2004. reprint ed. pap. 15.95 *(978-1-4179-8713-9(8))* Kessinger Publishing, LLC.

—The Three Bears. 2004. (Shape Bks.). (ENG.). 16p. (J). (gr. -1-3). 9.95 *(978-1-883211-94-3(8),* 9781883211943) Laughing Elephant.

Brundage, Scott. A Is for Astronaut: Blasting Through the Alphabet. Anderson, Clayton. 2018. (ENG.). 32p. (J). (gr. 1-4). 16.99 *(978-1-58536-396-4(0),* 204409) Sleeping Bear Pr.

—The Basketball Blowout: MVP#4. Kelly, David A. 2017. (Most Valuable Players Ser.: 4). 128p. (J). (gr. 1-4). 5.99 *(978-0-553-51328-8(1),* Random Hse. Bks. for Young Readers) Random Hse. Children's Bks.

—Chase the Chupacabra, 1 vol. Fields, Jan. 2014. (Monster Hunters Ser.). (ENG.). 80p. (J). (gr. 2-5). 29.93 *(978-1-62402-044-5(5),* 1523, Calico Chapter Bks.) ABDO Publishing Co.

—Confront the Goat Man. Fields, Jan. 2018. (Monster Hunters Ser.). (ENG.). 80p. (J). (gr. 2-5). lib. bdg. 29.93 *(978-1-5321-3366-4(9),* 31155, Calico Chapter Bks.) ABDO Publishing Co.

—Discover the Thunderbird. Fields, Jan. 2018. (Monster Hunters Ser.). (ENG.). 80p. (J). (gr. 2-5). lib. bdg. 29.93 *(978-1-5321-3367-1(7),* 31157, Calico Chapter Bks.) ABDO Publishing Co.

—The First Men Who Went to the Moon. Greene, Rhonda Gowler. 2019. (ENG.). 32p. (J). (gr. 1-4). 16.99 *(978-1-58536-412-1(6),* 204650) Sleeping Bear Pr.

—Football Fumble. Kelly, David A. 2016. (Most Valuable Players Ser.: 3). 128p. (J). (gr. 1-4). 5.99 *(978-0-553-51325-7(7),* Random Hse. Bks. for Young Readers) Random Hse. Children's Bks.

—The Gold Medal Mess: Mvp #1. Kelly, David A. 2016. (Most Valuable Players Ser.: 1). 128p. (J). (gr. 1-4). 5.99 *(978-0-553-51319-6(2),* Random Hse. Bks. for Young Readers) Random Hse. Children's Bks.

—Hunt for Sewer Gators, 1 vol. Fields, Jan. 2014. (Monster Hunters Ser.). (ENG.). 80p. (J). (gr. 2-5). 29.93 *(978-1-62402-045-2(3),* 1525, Calico Chapter Bks.) ABDO Publishing Co.

—Hunt the Ozark Howler, 1 vol. Fields, Jan. 2016. (Monster Hunters Ser.). (ENG.). 80p. (J). (gr. 2-5). lib. bdg. 29.93 *(978-1-62402-152-7(2),* 21531, Calico Chapter Bks.) ABDO Publishing Co.

—Meet the Mothman, 1 vol. Fields, Jan. 2016. (Monster Hunters Ser.). (ENG.). 80p. (J). (gr. 2-5). lib. bdg. 29.93 *(978-1-62402-153-4(0),* 21533, Calico Chapter Bks.) ABDO Publishing Co.

—Monster Hunters, 4 vols. ABDO Publishing Company Staff & Fields, Jan. 2014. (Monster Hunters Ser.: 4). 80p. (J). (gr. 2-5). lib. bdg. 114.00 *(978-1-62402-043-8(7),* 1521, Calico Chapter Bks.) ABDO Publishing Co.

—Monster Hunters Set 2, 4 vols. Fields, Jan & ABDO Publishing Company Staff. 2016. (Monster Hunters Ser.). (ENG.). 80p. (J). (gr. 2-5). lib. bdg. 114.00 *(978-1-62402-151-0(4),* 21529, Calico Chapter Bks.) ABDO Publishing Co.

—MVP #2: the Soccer Surprise. Kelly, David A. 2016. (Most Valuable Players Ser.: 2). 128p. (J). (gr. 1-4). 4.99 *(978-0-553-51322-6(2),* Random Hse. Bks. for Young Readers) Random Hse. Children's Bks.

—The Night the Lights Went Out on Christmas. Paul, Ellis. 2015. (ENG.). 32p. (J). (gr. -1-3). 16.99 *(978-0-8075-4543-0(0),* 807545430) Whitman, Albert & Co.

—Search for Bigfoot, 1 vol. Fields, Jan. 2014. (Monster Hunters Ser.). (ENG.). 80p. (J). (gr. 2-5). 29.93 *(978-1-62402-046-9(1),* 1527, Calico Chapter Bks.) ABDO Publishing Co.

—Seek the Mogollon Monster. Fields, Jan. 2018. (Monster Hunters Ser.). (ENG.). 80p. (J). (gr. 2-5). lib. bdg. 29.93 *(978-1-5321-3368-8(5),* 31159, Calico Chapter Bks.) ABDO Publishing Co.

—Spot the Loveland Frog. Fields, Jan. 2018. (Monster Hunters Ser.). (ENG.). 80p. (J). (gr. 2-5). lib. bdg. 29.93 *(978-1-5321-3369-5(3),* 31161, Calico Chapter Bks.) ABDO Publishing Co.

—Spot the Swamp Lizard Man, 1 vol. Fields, Jan. 2016. (Monster Hunters Ser.). (ENG.). 80p. (J). (gr. 2-5). lib. bdg. 29.93 *(978-1-62402-154-1(9),* 21535, Calico Chapter Bks.) ABDO Publishing Co.

—Tame Tahoe Tessie, 1 vol. Fields, Jan. 2014. (Monster Hunters Ser.). (ENG.). 80p. (J). (gr. 2-5). 29.93 *(978-1-62402-047-6(X),* 1529, Calico Chapter Bks.) ABDO Publishing Co.

—Track the Turtle Lake Monster, 1 vol. Fields, Jan. 2016. (Monster Hunters Ser.). (ENG.). 80p. (J). (gr. 2-5). lib. bdg. 29.93 *(978-1-62402-155-8(7),* 21537, Calico Chapter Bks.) ABDO Publishing Co.

Brundige, Britt. Legend of the Blue Unicorn. Durant, Sybrina. Johnson, Sandi, ed. 2019. (ENG.). 42p. (J). (gr. 4-6). pap. 12.99 ***(978-1-6794-2932-3(9))*** Independently Published.

Brundige, Britt & Sturgeon, Bobbi. Cats on Vacation. Johnson, Sandi. Durant, Sybrina, ed. 2014. (ENG.). 12p. (J). (gr. -1-6). pap. 12.99 *(978-1-929063-46-8(6),* 146) Moons & Stars Publishing For Children.

Brundige, Britt, jt. illus. see Johnson, Jim.

Brundige, Britt, jt. illus. see Sturgeon, Bobbi.

Brunelet, Madeleine, et al. Angel Stories from the Bible. Grossetête, Charlotte. 2017. (ENG.). 48p. (J). (gr. k-4). 15.99 *(978-1-62164-207-7(0))* Ignatius Pr.

Brunelet, Madeleine. Love Is. Amiot, Karine-Marie. 2019. (ENG.). 32p. (J). (gr. k-3). 16.99 *(978-1-5064-5208-1(6),* Beaming Books) Augsburg Fortress, Pubs.

Brunellière, Lucie. Deep in the Forest: A Seek-And-Find Adventure. Antòn, Josef. 2017. (ENG.). 14p. (J). (gr. -1-k). bds. 17.95 *(978-1-4197-2351-3(0),* Abrams Appleseed) Abrams, Inc.

Bruner, Garth. Flying High with Butterflies: A Pre-K/ K Complete Supplemental Unit. Bair, Heather. 2004. per. 9.95 *(978-1-891541-03-2(X))* Insect Lore.

—I Spy a Butterfly: A Second Grade Complete Supplemental Unit. Bair, Heather. 2005. per. 9.95 *(978-1-891541-05-6(6))* Insect Lore.

—Michael's Superheroes. Meyers, Carly J. J. 2013. 28p. (J). pap. *(978-0-8425-2845-0(8),* BYU Creative Works) Brigham Young Univ.

—O'H Me O'H My A Butterfly: A First Grade Complete Supplemental Unit. Bair, Heather. 2005. per. 9.95 *(978-1-891541-04-9(8))* Insect Lore.

—Only YOU Can Save Christmas! A Help-The-Elf Adventure. Wallace, Adam. 2017. 40p. (J). (gr. 1-5). 16.99 *(978-1-4926-4136-0(7),* Sourcebooks Jabberwocky) Sourcebooks, Inc.

—Soccer Roy: First Team. Curneen, Gary & Curneen, Erin. 2016. (ENG.). (J). pap. *(978-1-910515-62-4(0))* Bennion Kearny, Ltd.

Bruner, Justine. Imagination Rocks. Edwards, Cindi. 2009. 28p. pap. 13.99 *(978-1-4490-0386-9(9))* AuthorHouse.

Bruner, Tammy. Grandad's Book. Snyder, Jennifer. (J). 2005. 8.99 *(978-1-4183-0079-1(9));* 2004. bds. 9.99 *(978-1-4183-0015-9(2))* Christ Inspired, Inc.

Brunet, Joshua S. I'm in Love with a Big Blue Frog. Peter, Paul et al. 2013. 28p. (J). (gr. -1-3). 17.95 *(978-1-936140-37-4(3))* Charlesbridge Publishing, Inc.

—When Butterflies Cross the Sky: The Monarch Butterfly Migration. Cooper, Sharon Katz. 2015. (Extraordinary Migrations Ser.). (ENG.). 24p. (J). (gr. k-3). pap. 8.95 *(978-1-4795-6100-1(2));* lib. bdg. 27.32 *(978-1-4795-6076-9(6))* Capstone. (Picture Window Bks.).

Brunetti, Ivan & Schindelman, Joseph. Charlie & the Chocolate Factory: (Penguin Classics Deluxe Edition) Dahl, Roald. 2011. (Penguin Classics Deluxe Edition Ser.). 168p. (gr. 5). 16.00 *(978-0-14-310633-3(3),* Penguin Classics) Penguin Publishing Group.

Brunk, Carol Lee. Cartoon Mouse: PreReader 22. Brunk, Carol Lee. 2019. (Prereader Ser.: Vol. 22). (ENG.). 84p. (J). pap. 17.00 *(978-1-7229-6766-6(8))* CreateSpace Independent Publishing Platform.

—Castle: PreReader 23. Brunk, Carol Lee. 2019. (Prereader Ser.: Vol. 23). (ENG.). 64p. (J). pap. 13.00 *(978-1-7229-6773-4(0))* CreateSpace Independent Publishing Platform.

Brunk, Carol Lee. Cloud: PreReader 25. Brunk, Carol Lee. 2020. (Prereader Ser.: Vol. 25). (ENG.). 76p. (J). pap. 15.65 ***(978-1-7229-6803-8(6))*** CreateSpace Independent Publishing Platform.

Brunk, Carol Lee. Danced: Prereader 21. Brunk, Carol Lee. 2019. (Prereader Ser.: Vol. 21). (ENG.). 52p. (J). pap. 12.00 *(978-1-7229-6757-4(9))* CreateSpace Independent Publishing Platform.

Brunk, Carol Lee. The Elf: PreReader Volume 27. Brunk, Carol Lee. 2020. (Prereader Ser.: Vol. 27). (ENG.). 80p. (J). pap. 15.78 ***(978-1-7229-6839-7(7))*** CreateSpace Independent Publishing Platform.

—Point: PreReader Volume 26. Brunk, Carol Lee. 2020. (Prereader Ser.: Vol. 26). (ENG.). 50p. (J). pap. 10.60 ***(978-1-7229-6813-7(3))*** CreateSpace Independent Publishing Platform.

Brunk, Carol Lee. Pumpkin: PreReader 24. Brunk, Carol Lee. 2019. (Prereader Ser.: Vol. 24). (ENG.). 70p. (J). pap. 15.00 *(978-1-7229-6795-6(1))* CreateSpace Independent Publishing Platform.

Brunkus, Denise. Aloha-Ha-Ha! Park, Barbara. 2006. (Junie B. Jones Ser.: 26). (ENG.). 128p. (J). (gr. 1-4). lib. bdg. 13.95 *(978-0-375-93403-2(0),* Random Hse. Bks. for Young Readers) Random Hse. Children's Bks.

—Boo... & I Mean It! Park, Barbara. 2005. (Junie B. Jones Ser.: Bk. 7). 86p. (gr. 1-4). 15.00 *(978-0-7569-4783-5(9))* Perfection Learning Corp.

—Boo... & I Mean It! Park, Barbara. 2004. (Junie B. Jones Ser.: 24). (ENG.). 96p. (J). (gr. 1-4). lib. bdg. 13.99 *(978-0-375-92806-2(5),* Random Hse. Bks. for Young Readers) Random Hse. Children's Bks.

—Charlie Hits It Big. Blumenthal, Deborah. 2008. 32p. (J). (gr. -1). lib. bdg. 17.89 *(978-0-06-056354-7(0))* HarperCollins Pubs.

—Dumb Bunny. Park, Barbara. 2007. (Junie B. Jones Ser.: 27). (ENG.). 128p. (J). (gr. 1-4). lib. bdg. 14.99 *(978-0-375-93809-2(5),* Random Hse. Bks. for Young Readers) Random Hse. Children's Bks.

—The Frog Principal. Calmenson, Stephanie. 2006. (ENG.). 32p. (J). pap. 5.99 *(978-0-439-81217-7(8),* Scholastic Paperbacks) Scholastic, Inc.

—The Green Toenails Gang. Sharmat, Marjorie Weinman & Sharmat, Mitchell. 2nd ed. 2005. (Olivia Sharp: Agent for Secrets Ser.). 80p. (J). (gr. 3-7). per. 5.99 *(978-0-440-42063-7(6),* Yearling) Random Hse. Children's Bks.

—Junie B., First Grader: Cheater Pants. Park, Barbara. 2003. (Junie B. Jones Ser.: 21). (ENG.). 96p. (J). (gr. 1-4). lib. bdg. 13.99 *(978-0-375-92301-2(2),* Random Hse. Bks. for Young Readers) Random Hse. Children's Bks.

—Junie B., First Grader - Aloha-Ha-Ha! Park, Barbara. 2007. (Junie B. Jones Ser.). 119p. (gr. 1-4). 15.00 *(978-0-7569-8085-6(2))* Perfection Learning Corp.

—Junie B., First Grader - Boss of Lunch. Park, Barbara. 2003. (Junie B., First Grader Ser.: No. 2). 96p. (J). (gr. k-3). lib. bdg. 11.99 *(978-0-375-90294-9(5),* Golden Bks.) Random Hse. Children's Bks.

—Junie B. Jones #19: Boss of Lunch. Park, Barbara. 2003. (Junie B. Jones Ser.: 19). 96p. (J). (gr. 1-4). 4.99 *(978-0-375-80294-2(0),* Random Hse. Bks. for Young Readers) Random Hse. Children's Bks.

—Junie B. Jones #20: Toothless Wonder. Park, Barbara. 2003. (Junie B. Jones Ser.: 20). (ENG.). 96p. (J). (gr. 1-4). pap. 4.99 *(978-0-375-82223-0(2),* Random Hse. Bks. for Young Readers) Random Hse. Children's Bks.

—Junie B. Jones #21: Cheater Pants. Park, Barbara. 2004. (Junie B. Jones Ser.: 21). 96p. (J). (gr. 1-4). 4.99 *(978-0-375-82302-2(6),* Random Hse. Bks. for Young Readers) Random Hse. Children's Bks.

—Junie B. Jones #22: One-Man Band. Park, Barbara. 2004. (Junie B. Jones Ser.: 22). 96p. (J). (gr. 1-4). 4.99 *(978-0-375-82536-1(3),* Random Hse. Bks. for Young Readers) Random Hse. Children's Bks.

—Junie B. Jones #23: Shipwrecked, No. 23. Park, Barbara. 2005. (Junie B. Jones Ser.: 23). (ENG.). 96p. (J). (gr. 1-4). mass mkt. 4.99 *(978-0-375-82805-8(2),* Random Hse. Bks. for Young Readers) Random Hse. Children's Bks.

—Junie B. Jones #24: BOO... & I MEAN It! Park, Barbara. 2005. (Junie B. Jones Ser.: 24). (ENG.). 96p. (J). (gr. 1-4). 4.99 *(978-0-375-82807-2(9),* Random Hse. Bks. for Young Readers) Random Hse. Children's Bks.

—Junie B. Jones #25: Jingle Bells, Batman Smells! (P. S. So Does May.) Park, Barbara. 2009. (Junie B. Jones Ser.: 25). (ENG.). 128p. (J). (gr. 1-4). 4.99 *(978-0-375-82809-6(5),* Random Hse. Bks. for Young Readers) Random Hse. Children's Bks.

—Junie B. Jones #26: Aloha-Ha-Ha! Park, Barbara. 2007. (Junie B. Jones Ser.: 26). (ENG.). 128p. (J). (gr. 1-4). per. 4.99 *(978-0-375-83404-2(4),* Random Hse. Bks. for Young Readers) Random Hse. Children's Bks.

—Junie B. Jones #27: Dumb Bunny. Park, Barbara. 2009. (Junie B. Jones Ser.: 27). (ENG.). 128p. (J). (gr. 1-4). 4.99 *(978-0-375-83810-1(4),* Random Hse. Bks. for Young Readers) Random Hse. Children's Bks.

—Junie B. Jones #28: Turkeys We Have Loved & Eaten (and Other Thankful Stuff) Park, Barbara. (Junie B. Jones Ser.: 28). (ENG.). 144p. (J). (gr. 1-4). 2014. 4.99 *(978-0-375-87115-3(2));* No. 28. 2012. 11.99 *(978-0-375-87063-7(6))* Random Hse. Children's Bks. (Random Hse. Bks. for Young Readers).

—Junie B. Jones Books in a Bus: Books 1-28, 28 vols. Park, Barbara. 2015. (Junie B. Jones Ser.). (ENG.). (J). (gr. 1-4). 139.72 *(978-1-101-93859-1(5),* Random Hse. Bks. for Young Readers) Random Hse. Children's Bks.

—Junie B. Jones Complete Kindergarten Collection: Books 1-17 with Paper Dolls in Boxed Set, 17 vols. Park, Barbara. 2014. (Junie B. Jones Ser.). (ENG.). 96p. (J). (gr. 1-4). 84.83 *(978-0-385-37694-5(4),* Random Hse. Bks. for Young Readers) Random Hse. Children's Bks.

—Junie B. Jones Deluxe Holiday Edition: Jingle Bells, Batman Smells! (P. S. So Does May.) Park, Barbara. 2019. (Junie B. Jones Ser.: 25). 144p. (J). (gr. 1-4). 18.99 *(978-1-9848-9269-0(X));* (ENG.). lib. bdg. 21.99 *(978-1-9848-9370-3(X))* Random Hse. Children's Bks. (Random Hse. Bks. for Young Readers).

—Junie B. Jones Fifth Boxed Set Ever! Books 17-20, 4 vols. Park, Barbara. 2008. (Junie B. Jones Ser.). (ENG.). (J). (gr. 1-4). 19.96 *(978-0-375-85570-2(X),* Random Hse. Bks. for Young Readers) Random Hse. Children's Bks.

—Junie B. Jones Fourth Boxed Set Ever! Books 13-16, 4 vols. Park, Barbara. 2004. (Junie B. Jones Ser.). (ENG.). (J). (gr. 1-4). 19.96 *(978-0-375-82829-4(X),* Random Hse. Bks. for Young Readers) Random Hse. Children's Bks.

—Junie B. Jones Third Boxed Set Ever! Books 9-12, 4 vols., Bks. 9-12. Park, Barbara. 2003. (Junie B. Jones Ser.). (ENG.). (J). (gr. 1-4). 19.96 *(978-0-375-82552-1(5),* Random Hse. Bks. for Young Readers) Random Hse. Children's Bks.

—Junie B. Jones y Su Gran Bocota. Park, Barbara. 2005. (Junie B. Jones Ser.).Tr. of Junie B. Jones & Her Big Fat Mouth. (SPA.). 80p. (J). (gr. 2-5). pap. 4.99 *(978-0-439-42516-2(6),* Scholastic en Espanol) Scholastic, Inc.

—Junie B. My Valentime. Park, Barbara. 2013. (Junie B. Jones Ser.). (ENG.). 12p. (J). (gr. -1-2). pap. 5.99 *(978-0-385-37302-9(3),* Random Hse. Bks. for Young Readers) Random Hse. Children's Bks.

—Junie B. 's Essential Survival Guide to School (Junie B. Jones) Park, Barbara. 2013. (Junie B. Jones Ser.). (ENG.). 144p. (J). (gr. 1-4). 12.99 *(978-0-449-81783-4(0),* Random Hse. Bks. for Young Readers) Random Hse. Children's Bks.

—Junie B.'s These Puzzles Hurt My Brain! Park, Barbara. 2011. (Junie B. Jones Ser.). (ENG.). 240p. (J). (gr. 1-4). 5.99 *(978-0-375-87123-8(3),* Random Hse. Bks. for Young Readers) Random Hse. Children's Bks.

—My Teacher for President. Winters, Kay. 2008. (ENG.). 32p. (J). (gr. k-3). pap. 7.99 *(978-0-14-241170-4(1),* Puffin Books) Penguin Young Readers Group.

—My Teacher for President. Winters, Kay. 2008. (gr. -1-k). 17.00 *(978-0-7569-8925-5(6))* Perfection Learning Corp.

—One-Man Band. Park, Barbara. 2003. (Junie B. Jones Ser.: 22). (ENG.). 96p. (J). (gr. 1-4). lib. bdg. 13.99

B

(978-0-375-92522-1(8), Random Hse. Bks. for Young Readers) Random Hse. Children's Bks.

—The Pizza Monster. Sharmat, Marjorie Weinman & Sharmat, Mitchell. 2nd ed. 2005. (Olivia Sharp: Agent for Secrets Ser.: 1). 80p. (J). (gr. 3-7). reprint ed. 5.99 *(978-0-440-42059-0(8)*, Yearling) Random Hse. Children's Bks.

—The Princess of the Fillmore Street School. Sharmat, Marjorie Weinman & Sharmat, Mitchell. 2005. (Olivia Sharp: Agent for Secrets Ser.). 80p. (J). (gr. 3-7). 5.99 *(978-0-440-42060-6(1)*, Yearling) Random Hse. Children's Bks.

—Read All about It! Bush, Laura & Hager, Jenna Bush. (ENG.). 32p. (J). (gr. -1-3). 2010. pap. 7.99 *(978-0-06-156077-4(4))*; 2008. 17.99 *(978-0-06-156075-0(8))*; 2008. lib. bdg. 18.89 *(978-0-06-156076-7(6))* HarperCollins Pubs.

—Sloppy Joe. Keane, Dave. 2009. (ENG.). 32p. (J). (gr. -1-2). 16.99 *(978-0-06-171020-9(2))* HarperCollins Pubs.

—The Sly Spy. Sharmat, Marjorie Weinman & Sharmat, Mitchell. 2005. (Olivia Sharp: Agent for Secrets Ser.). 80p. (J). (gr. 3-7). per. 5.99 *(978-0-440-42062-0(8)*, Yearling) Random Hse. Children's Bks.

—Toothless Wonder. Park, Barbara. 2003. (Junie B. Jones Ser.: Bk. 3). 80p. (gr. 1-4). 15.00 *(978-0-7569-1621-3(6))* Perfection Learning Corp.

Brunner, Terry. Where Is Cecil? McCoy, M. M. Maximilian Press Publishers Staff, ed. unabr. l.t. ed. 2005. 28p. (J). lib. bdg. 12.50 *(978-1-930211-68-1(6))* Maximilian Pr. Pubs.

Bruno, Carey. Dinky Goes to the Hamptons. Kil, Emily. 2019. (ENG.). 41p. (J). 24.95 ***(978-1-9772-1393-8(6))***; pap. 16.95 ***(978-1-9772-1392-1(8))*** Outskirts Pr., Inc.

Bruno, Iacopo. The Ability. Vaughan, M. M. (Ability Ser.). (ENG.). (YA). (gr. 3-7). 2014. 352p. pap. 8.99 *(978-1-4424-5201-5(3))*; 2013. 336p. 15.99 *(978-1-4424-5200-8(5))* McElderry, Margaret K. Bks. (McElderry, Margaret K. Bks.).

—The Actual & Truthful Adventures of Becky Thatcher. Lawson, Jessica. 2014. (ENG.). 224p. (J). (gr. 3-7). 18.99 *(978-1-4814-0150-0(5)*, Simon & Schuster Bks. For Young Readers) Simon & Schuster Bks. For Young Readers.

—Anything but Ordinary Addie: The True Story of Adelaide Herrmann, Queen of Magic. Rockliff, Mara. 2016. 48p. (J). (gr. 1-4). 17.99 *(978-0-7636-6841-9(9))* Candlewick Pr.

—The Box & the Dragonfly. Sanders, Ted. 2015. (Keepers Ser.: No. 1). 534p. (J). *(978-0-06-239019-6(8))* Harper & Row Ltd.

—Brother from a Box. Kuhlman, Evan. 2013. (ENG.). 288p. (J). (gr. 4-7). pap. 6.99 *(978-1-4424-2659-7(4)*, Atheneum Bks. for Young Readers) Simon & Schuster Children's Publishing.

—Brother from a Box. Kuhlman, Evan. 2012. (ENG.). 288p. (J). (gr. 4-6). 21.19 *(978-1-4424-2658-0(6))* Simon & Schuster, Inc.

—The Cathedral of Fear. Adler, Irene. McGuinness, Nanette, tr. 2015. (Sherlock, Lupin, & Me Ser.). (ENG.). 256p. (J). (gr. 4-8). lib. bdg. 26.65 *(978-1-4965-0490-6(9)*, Stone Arch Bks.) Capstone.

—Compass of Dreams, 1 vol. Baccalario, Pierdomenico. Pernigotti, Chiara, tr. 2014. (Enchanted Emporium Ser.). (ENG.). 240p. (J). (gr. 4-8). 26.65 *(978-1-4342-6517-3(X)*, Stone Arch Bks.) Capstone.

—A Crystal of Time. Chainani, Soman. 2019. 624p. (J). *(978-0-06-288641-5(X))*; *(978-0-06-290697-7(6))*; *(978-0-06-289559-2(1))*; *(978-0-06-290764-6(6))* Harper & Row Ltd.

—The Dark Lady, 1 vol. Adler, Irene. 2014. (Sherlock, Lupin, & Me Ser.). (ENG.). 240p. (J). (gr. 4-8). 12.95 *(978-1-62370-040-9(X)*, Capstone Young Readers) Capstone.

—Good Night, Zombie. Preller, James. 2013. (Scary Tales Ser.: 3). (ENG.). 112p. (J). (gr. 2-5). pap. 7.99 *(978-1-250-01891-5(9)*, 900087728) Feiwel & Friends.

—Home Sweet Horror. Preller, James. 2013. (Scary Tales Ser.: 1). (ENG.). 112p. (J). (gr. 2-5). pap. 6.99 *(978-1-250-01887-8(0)*, 900087724) Feiwel & Friends.

—I Scream, You Scream! Preller, James. 2013. (Scary Tales Ser.: 2). (ENG.). 112p. (J). (gr. 2-5). 14.99 *(978-1-250-01888-5(9)*, 9781250018885); pap. 6.99 *(978-1-250-01889-2(7)*, 900087726) Feiwel & Friends.

—Iron Hearted Violet. Barnhill, Kelly. 2014. (ENG.). 448p. (J). (gr. 3-7). pap. 8.99 *(978-0-316-05675-5(8))* Little, Brown Bks. for Young Readers.

—The Keepers #2: the Harp & the Ravenvine. Sanders, Ted. (Keepers Ser.: 2). (ENG.). (J). (gr. 3-7). 2017. 688p. pap. 7.99 *(978-0-06-227586-8(0))*; 2016. 672p. 16.99 *(978-0-06-227585-1(2))* HarperCollins Pubs.

—The Keepers #3: the Portal & the Veil. Sanders, Ted. (Keepers Ser.: 3). (ENG.). (J). (gr. 3-7). 2018. 608p. pap. 7.99 *(978-0-06-227589-9(5))*; 2017. 592p. 16.99 *(978-0-06-227588-2(7))* HarperCollins Pubs.

—The Keepers #4: the Starlit Loom. Sanders, Ted. (Keepers Ser.: 4). (ENG.). 448p. (J). (gr. 3-7). 2019. pap. 7.99 *(978-0-06-227592-9(5))*; 2018. 16.99 *(978-0-06-227591-2(7))* HarperCollins Pubs.

—The Keepers: the Box & the Dragonfly. Sanders, Ted. (Keepers Ser.: 1). (ENG.). (J). (gr. 3-7). 2016. 560p. pap. 7.99 *(978-0-06-227583-7(6))*; 2015. 544p. 16.99 *(978-0-06-227582-0(8))* HarperCollins Pubs.

—The Last Ever After. Chainani, Soman. 2015. 655p. (J). *(978-0-06-241756-5(8))* Harper & Row Ltd.

—Map of the Passages. Baccalario, Pierdomenico. McGuinness, Nanette, tr. 2015. (Enchanted Emporium Ser.). (ENG.). 240p. (J). (gr. 4-8). 12.95 *(978-1-62370-204-5(6)*, Capstone Young Readers) Capstone.

—Mesmerized: How Ben Franklin Solved a Mystery That Baffled All of France. Rockliff, Mara. 48p. (J). (gr. 1-4). 2017. (ENG.). 7.99 *(978-0-7636-9515-6(7))*; 2015. 17.99 *(978-0-7636-6351-3(4))* Candlewick Pr.

—Mindscape. Vaughan, M. M. 2015. (Ability Ser.). (ENG.). 336p. (YA). (gr. 3-7). pap. 7.99 *(978-1-4424-5205-3(6)*, McElderry, Margaret K. Bks.) McElderry, Margaret K. Bks.

—Mister Max: the Book of Kings: Mister Max 3. Voigt, Cynthia. 2016. (Mister Max Ser.: 3). (ENG.). 352p. (J). (gr. 3-7). 7.99 *(978-0-307-97688-8(2)*, Yearling) Random Hse. Children's Bks.

—Mister Max: the Book of Lost Things: Mister Max 1. Voigt, Cynthia. 2014. (Mister Max Ser.: 1). (ENG.). 400p. (J). (gr. 3-7). 8.99 *(978-0-307-97682-6(3)*, Yearling) Random Hse. Children's Bks.

—Mister Max: the Book of Secrets: Mister Max 2. Voigt, Cynthia. 2015. (Mister Max Ser.: 2). (ENG.). 384p. (J). (gr. 3-7). 6.99 *(978-0-307-97685-7(8)*, Yearling) Random Hse. Children's Bks.

—The Mystery of the Scarlet Rose. Adler, Irene. McGuinness, Nanette, tr. 2015. (Sherlock, Lupin, & Me Ser.). (ENG.). 256p. (J). (gr. 4-8). lib. bdg. 26.65 *(978-1-4342-6524-1(2)*, Stone Arch Bks.) Capstone.

—Nightmareland. Preller, James. 2014. (Scary Tales Ser.: 4). (ENG.). 112p. (J). (gr. 2-5). 15.99 *(978-1-250-01892-2(7)*, 9781250018922) Feiwel & Friends.

—The School for Good & Evil. Chainani, Soman. 2013. (School for Good & Evil Ser.: 1). (ENG.). 496p. (J). (gr. 3-7). 17.99 *(978-0-06-210489-2(6))* HarperCollins Pubs.

—The School for Good & Evil. Chainani, Soman. 2018. (School for Good & Evil Ser.: 1). (ENG.). 544p. (J). (gr. 3-7). pap. 8.99 *(978-0-06-210490-8(X)*, HarperCollins) HarperCollins Pubs. Ltd. GBR. Dist: HarperCollins Pubs.

—The School for Good & Evil. Chainani, Soman. ed. 2014. (School for Good & Evil Ser.: 1). 496p. (J). lib. bdg. 17.20 *(978-0-606-36513-0(3))* Turtleback.

—The School for Good & Evil #2: a World Without Princes. Chainani, Soman. 2014. (School for Good & Evil Ser.: 2). (ENG.). 448p. (J). (gr. 3-7). 17.99 *(978-0-06-210492-2(6))* HarperCollins Pubs.

—The School for Good & Evil #2: a World Without Princes. Chainani, Soman. 2018. (School for Good & Evil Ser.: 2). (ENG.). 512p. (J). (gr. 3-7). pap. 8.99 *(978-0-06-210493-9(4)*, HarperCollins) HarperCollins Pubs. Ltd. GBR. Dist: HarperCollins Pubs.

—Sergeant Reckless: The True Story of the Little Horse Who Became a Hero. McCormick, Patricia. 2017. (ENG.). 40p. (J). (gr. 1-5). 17.99 *(978-0-06-229259-9(5)*, Balzer & Bray) HarperCollins Pubs.

Bruno, Iacopo. Sergeant Reckless: the True Story of the Little Horse Who Became a Hero. McCormick, Patricia. 2020. 40p. (J). (gr. 1-5). pap. 8.99 ***(978-0-06-229260-5(9)***, Balzer & Bray) HarperCollins Pubs.

Bruno, Iacopo. The Spindlers. Oliver, Lauren. (ENG.). (J). (gr. 3-7). 2013. 272p. pap. 8.99 *(978-0-06-197809-8(4))*; 2012. 256p. 16.99 *(978-0-06-197808-1(6))* HarperCollins Pubs.

—Star of Stone, 2. Baccalario, Pierdomenico. Janeczko, Leah D., tr. 2012. (Century Quartet Ser.). (ENG.). 304p. (J). (gr. 6-8). lib. bdg. 22.44 *(978-0-375-95896-0(7))* Random House Publishing Group.

—The Story Collector: A New York Public Library Book. Tubb, Kristin O'Donnell. 2018. (Story Collector Ser.: 1). (ENG.). 272p. (J). 16.99 *(978-1-250-14380-8(2)*, 900180568, Holt, Henry & Co. Bks. For Young Readers) Holt, Henry & Co.

—The Story Collector: A New York Public Library Book. Tubb, Kristin O'Donnell. 2020. (Story Collector Ser.: 1). (ENG.). 272p. (J). pap. 7.99 *(978-1-250-21144-6(1)*, 900180569) Square Fish.

—The Story Seeker: A New York Public Library Book. Tubb, Kristin O'Donnell. 2020. (Story Collector Ser.: 2). (ENG.). 48p. (J). 16.99 *(978-1-250-30109-3(2)*, 900196578, Holt, Henry & Co. Bks. For Young Readers) Holt, Henry & Co.

—Suitcase of Stars, 1 vol. Baccalario, P. D. 2014. (Enchanted Emporium Ser.). (ENG.). 240p. (J). (gr. 4-8). pap. 9.25 *(978-1-4342-6519-7(6)*, Stone Arch Bks.) Capstone.

—Suitcase of Stars, 1 vol. Baccalario, P. D. Pernigotti, Chiara, tr. 2014. (Enchanted Emporium Ser.). (ENG.). 240p. (J). (gr. 4-8). 26.65 *(978-1-4342-6516-6(1)*, Stone Arch Bks.) Capstone.

—The Book of Kings. Voigt, Cynthia. 2015. (Mister Max Ser.: 3). (ENG.). 352p. (J). (gr. 3-7). 16.99 *(978-0-307-97687-1(4)*, Knopf Bks. for Young Readers) Random Hse. Children's Bks.

—The Thief of Mirrors. Baccalario, Pierdomenico & McGuinness, Nanette. Pernigotti, Chiara, tr. 2015. (Enchanted Emporium Ser.). (ENG.). 240p. (J). (gr. 4-8). lib. bdg. 26.65 *(978-1-4965-0516-3(6)*, Stone Arch Bks.) Capstone.

—The Tom Sawyer Collection: The Adventures of Tom Sawyer; the Adventures of Huckleberry Finn; the Actual & Truthful Adventures of Becky Thatcher. Lawson, Jessica & Twain, Mark. ed. 2014. (ENG.). 944p. (J). (gr. 3-7). 52.99 *(978-1-4814-0536-2(5)*, Simon & Schuster Bks. For Young Readers) Simon & Schuster Bks. For Young Readers.

—A World Without Princes. Chainani, Soman. 2014. (School for Good & Evil Trilogy: No. 2). (ENG.). 400p. (J). *(978-0-06-234072-6(7))* Harper & Row Ltd.

Bruno, Iacopo, jt. illus. see Iacopo, Bruno.

Bruno, Margaret Farrell. My Little Friend Goes to the Zoo. Finnegan, Evelyn M. 2006. 32p. (J). (gr. -1-3). reprint ed. pap. 7.00 *(978-1-4223-5402-5(4))* DIANE Publishing Co.

Brunot, Katerina. Story Time with Princess Dorothy. Scretching, Dorothy/Janis. Walters, Steve, ed. 2012. 32p. (J). 20.00 *(978-0-9719767-4-0(0)*, Crowned Warrior Publishing) Walters, Steve Ministries.

Bruns, Scott. Demo: The Story of a Junkyard Dog. Bozak, Jon. 2008. (ENG.). 56p. (J). (gr. 2-4). 16.95 *(978-0-9816188-0-7(4))* Jocko Publishing.

Brunson, Rachael. Think Farm Animals: A Lift-The-Flap Guessing Book, 1 vol. Robbins, Karen S. 2018. (ENG.). 24p. (J). bds. 12.99 *(978-0-7643-5582-0(1)*, 9907) Schiffer Publishing, Ltd.

—Think Zoo Animals: A Lift-The-Flap Guessing Book, 1 vol. Robbins, Karen S. 2018. (ENG.). 24p. (J). bds. 12.99 *(978-0-7643-5583-7(X)*, 9908) Schiffer Publishing, Ltd.

Brunson, Stephanie. The Chocolate Kingdom Caper. Ballman, Swanee. 2003. 32p. (J). per. 6.95 *(978-1-59094-025-9(3)*, 1590940253) Jawbone Publishing Corp.

Brus, Mischa. Little Full Stop: English, bks. 8, bk. 2. Brus, Mischa. Schlitz, Matt. 2019.Tr. of French, Chinese, Japanese. (ENG.). 34p. (J). (gr. k-2). *(978-0-9751837-1-7(0))* Mambooks AUS. Dist: Ingram Content Group.

Brusch, Beat. La Historia de la Hoja de Papel / the History of the Sheet of Paper. Limousin, Odile. 2018. (Altea Benjamín Ser.). (SPA.). 32p. (J). (gr. 3-7). pap. 10.99 *(978-1-947783-58-4(0)*, Altea) Penguin Random House Grupo Editorial ESP. Dist: Penguin Random Hse. LLC.

Bruschetti-Weiss, Janet. A Starfish Called Rhonda. Bruschetti-Weiss, Janet. 2003. 28p. (J). *(978-0-9747716-0-1(0))* Weiss, Janet Bruschetti.

Brush, Joan. Our House Is Round: A Kid's Book about Why Protecting Our Earth Matters. Kondonassis, Yolanda. 2012. 48p. (J). (gr. -1-k). 16.95 *(978-1-61608-588-9(6)*, 608588, Sky Pony Pr.) Skyhorse Publishing Co., Inc.

Brush, Mark. My World of Dreams. Morgan, David. 2017. (ENG.). 65p. (J). pap. *(978-1-911113-96-6(8))* Spiderwize.

Bryan, Ashley. All Things Bright & Beautiful. Alexander, Cecil F. 2010. (ENG.). 40p. (J). (gr. -1-3). 18.99 *(978-1-4169-8939-4(0)*, Atheneum Bks. for Young Readers) Simon & Schuster Children's Publishing.

—Blooming Beneath the Sun. Rossetti, Christina. 2019. (ENG.). 40p. (J). (gr. -1-3). 17.99 *(978-1-5344-4092-0(5)*, Atheneum/Caitlyn Dlouhy Books) Simon & Schuster Children's Publishing.

—I Am Loved. Giovanni, Nikki. 2018. (ENG.). 32p. (J). (gr. -1-3). 17.99 *(978-1-5344-0492-2(9)*, Atheneum/Caitlyn Dlouhy Books) Simon & Schuster Children's Publishing.

—A Nest Full of Stars. Berry, James. 2004. 104p. (J). (gr. 2-18). 16.89 *(978-0-06-052748-8(X))* HarperCollins Pubs.

—Sail Away. Hughes, Langston. 2015. (ENG.). 40p. (J). (gr. -1-3). 17.99 *(978-1-4814-3085-2(8))* Simon & Schuster Children's Publishing.

—The Sun Is So Quiet. Giovanni, Nikki. 2014. (ENG.). 32p. (J). (gr. -1-3). 8.99 *(978-1-250-04669-7(6)*, 900131698) Square Fish.

Bryan, Ashley. Ashley Bryan: Words to My Life's Song. Bryan, Ashley. 2009. (ENG.). 64p. (J). (gr. -1-18). 19.99 *(978-1-4169-0541-7(3)*, Atheneum Bks. for Young Readers) Simon & Schuster Children's Publishing.

—Ashley Bryan's Puppets: Making Something from Everything. Bryan, Ashley. 2014. (ENG.). 80p. (J). (gr. -1). 19.99 *(978-1-4424-8728-4(3)*, Atheneum Bks. for Young Readers) Simon & Schuster Children's Publishing.

—Beautiful Blackbird. Bryan, Ashley. 2003. (ENG.). 40p. (J). (gr. -1-3). 19.99 *(978-0-689-84731-8(9)*, Atheneum Bks. for Young Readers) Simon & Schuster Children's Publishing.

—Can't Scare Me! Bryan, Ashley. 2013. (ENG.). 40p. (J). (gr. -1-3). 16.99 *(978-1-4424-7657-8(5)*, Atheneum Bks. for Young Readers) Simon & Schuster Children's Publishing.

—Freedom over Me: Eleven Slaves, Their Lives & Dreams Brought to Life by Ashley Bryan. Bryan, Ashley. 2016. (ENG.). 56p. (J). (gr. 4-6). 17.99 *(978-1-4814-5690-6(3)*, Atheneum/Caitlyn Dlouhy Books) Simon & Schuster Children's Publishing.

—Infinite Hope: A Black Artist's Journey from World War II to Peace. Bryan, Ashley. 2019. (ENG.). 112p. (J). (gr. 5). 21.99 *(978-1-5344-0490-8(2)*, Atheneum/Caitlyn Dlouhy Books) Simon & Schuster Children's Publishing.

—Who Built the Stable? A Nativity Poem. Bryan, Ashley. 2012. (ENG.). 40p. (J). (gr. -1-3). 16.99 *(978-1-4424-0934-7(7)*, Atheneum Bks. for Young Readers) Simon & Schuster Children's Publishing.

Bryan, Ashley. All Night, All Day: A Child's First Book of African-American Spirituals. Bryan, Ashley, selected by. 2004. (ENG.). 48p. (J). (gr. -1-3). 7.99 *(978-0-689-86786-6(7)*, Atheneum Bks. for Young Readers) Simon & Schuster Children's Publishing.

Bryan, Diana. The Fisherman & His Wife, 1 vol. Grimm, Jacob & Grimm, Wilhelm K. 2005. (Rabbit Ears-A Classic Tale Ser.). (ENG.). 32p. (J). (gr. 2-6). 28.50 *(978-1-59197-747-6(9)*, 12938, Picture Bk.) Spotlight.

—The Monkey People: A Columbian Folktale. Metaxas, Eric. 2005. (Rabbit Ears-A Classic Tale Ser.). (ENG.). 36p. (J). (gr. 2-6). 28.50 *(978-1-59679-226-5(4)*, 12934, Picture Bk.) Spotlight.

Bryan, Ed. Cinderella: A Nosy Crow Fairy Tale. Nosy Crow Staff. 2016. (ENG.). (J). (gr. -1-2). 9.99 *(978-0-7636-8654-3(9)*, Nosy Crow) Candlewick Pr.

—Jack & the Beanstalk: a Nosy Crow Fairy Tale. Nosy Crow Staff. 2017. (ENG.). 32p. (J). (gr. -1-2). 9.99 *(978-0-7636-9332-9(4)*, Nosy Crow) Candlewick Pr.

—Little Red Riding Hood: a Nosy Crow Fairy Tale. Nosy Crow Staff. 2017. (ENG.). 32p. (J). (gr. -1-2). 9.99 *(978-0-7636-9331-2(6)*, Nosy Crow) Candlewick Pr.

—The Three Little Pigs: A Nosy Crow Fairy Tale. Nosy Crow Staff. 2016. (ENG.). (J). (gr. -1-2). 9.99 *(978-0-7636-8655-0(7)*, Nosy Crow) Candlewick Pr.

Bryan, Hintz. Mr. Blue a Job for You. Donahue, Laurie. 2010. 32p. (J). 15.95 *(978-0-9799116-2-0(1))* LifeSong Pubs.

Bryan-Hunt, Jan. J Is for Jesus: An Easter Alphabet & Activity Book, Vol. O'Neal, Debbie Trafton. 2005. (ENG.). 32p. (J). (gr. 3-7). per., act. bk. ed. 11.99 *(978-0-8066-5123-1(7)*, Augsburg Bks.) Augsburg Fortress, Pubs.

—Pumpkin Fever. Simon, Charnan. 2011. (Rookie Ready to Learn Ser.). 40p. (J). (ENG.). pap. 5.95 *(978-0-531-26803-2(9))*; (gr. -1-k). lib. bdg. 23.00 *(978-0-531-25643-5(X))* Scholastic Library Publishing. (Children's Pr.).

Bryan, Jade. Dragon Girl. Bryan, Jade. 2018. (ENG.). 30p. (J). pap. 9.99 *(978-1-7901-9296-0(X))* Independently Published.

Bryan, Tara Tidwell. To See the Stars, 1 vol. Andrews, Jan. 2019. (ENG.). 160p. (YA). (gr. 8-12). pap. 13.95 ***(978-1-927917-17-6(4))*** Running the Goat, Bks. & Broadsides CAN. Dist: Orca Bk. Pubs. USA.

Bryant, Bill. The Little Mermaid. Reed, Gary. 2008. (Short Tales Fairy Tales Ser.). (ENG.). 32p. (J). (gr. 2-5). 27.07 *(978-1-60270-129-8(6)*, 596, Short Tales) Magic Wagon.

Bryant, Carol W. & Klug, Leigh A. Hamilton Troll Cookbook: Easy to Make Recipes for Children. Shields, Kathleen J. 2016. (Hamilton Troll Adventures Ser.). (ENG.). (J). (gr. 2-5). pap. 14.95 *(978-1-941345-29-0(8))* Erin Go Bragh Publishing.

Bryant, Carol W. & Klug, Leigh A. Hamilton Troll Cookbook: Easy to Make Recipes for Children. 2017. (Hamilton Troll Adventures Ser.: Vol. 15). (ENG.). 88p. (J). pap. 19.95 ***(978-1-941345-59-7(X))*** Erin Go Bragh Publishing.

Bryant, Carol W., jt. illus. see Klug, Leigh A.

Bryant, Jacquelyn. The Twin's Adventures: A Race with an Officer Friendly. Tate, Hakim. 2018. (ENG.). 24p. (J). (gr. k-3). pap. 9.99 *(978-0-692-15282-9(2))* Tate, Hakim.

Bryant, Julie. Right Where You Need Me. Grant, Rose. 2012. 16p. pap. 15.99 *(978-1-4685-6856-1(6))* AuthorHouse.

Bryant, Kerry. Freddie & Mee. Wales, Sid. 2013. 28p. pap. *(978-1-78222-097-8(6))* Paragon Publishing, Rothersthorpe.

Bryant, Kristin. Seeing with Your Eyes Closed: Energy's Magic Book One. Kiss, D. R. 2018. (ENG.). 228p. (J). pap. 13.95 *(978-1-7321763-0-0(2))* Psychedelic Otter Publishing.

Bryant, Laura. Five Little Penguins Slipping on the Ice. Metzger, Steve. 2008. (ENG.). (J). (gr. -1-3). audio compact disk 18.95 *(978-0-545-07408-7(8))* Scholastic, Inc.

—Five Little Sharks Swimming in the Sea. Metzger, Steve. 2004. (J). *(978-0-439-66139-3(0))*; pap. *(978-0-439-59228-4(3))* Scholastic, Inc.

Bryant, Laura J. Eres un Regalo de Dios. Bergren, Lisa Tawn. 2018. (SPA.). 40p. (J). (gr. -1-2). 9.95 *(978-1-947783-03-4(3))* Penguin Random House Grupo Editorial ESP. Dist: Penguin Random Hse. LLC.

—A Fairy in a Dairy, 0 vols. Nolan, Lucy. 2013. (ENG.). 33p. (J). (gr. -1-2). pap. 9.99 *(978-1-4778-1678-3(X)*, 9781477816783, Two Lions) Amazon Publishing.

—God Found Us You. Bergren, Lisa Tawn. 2009. (J). lib. bdg. 3.99 *(978-0-06-113177-6(6))* HarperCollins Pubs.

—God Found Us You. Bergren, Lisa Tawn. 2009. (HarperBlessings Ser.). (ENG.). 40p. (J). (gr. -1-2). 10.99 *(978-0-06-113176-9(8))* HarperCollins Pubs.

—God Gave Us Angels: A Picture Book. Bergren, Lisa Tawn. 2014. (ENG.). 40p. (J). (gr. -1-2). 10.99 *(978-1-60142-661-1(5)*, WaterBrook Pr.) Crown Publishing Group, The.

—God Gave Us Easter. Bergren, Lisa Tawn. 2020. (God Gave Us Ser.). (ENG.). 30p. (J). (gr. -1 — 1). bds. 6.99 *(978-0-525-65444-5(5)*, WaterBrook Pr.) Crown Publishing Group, The.

—God Gave Us Love. Bergren, Lisa Tawn. 2011. (God Gave Us Ser.). (ENG.). 22p. (J). (gr. k — 1). bds. 6.99 *(978-0-307-73027-5(1)*, WaterBrook Pr.) Crown Publishing Group, The.

—God Gave Us Sleep. Bergren, Lisa Tawn. 2015. (ENG.). 40p. (J). (gr. -1-2). 10.99 *(978-1-60142-663-5(1)*, WaterBrook Pr.) Crown Publishing Group, The.

—God Gave Us So Much: A Limited-Edition Three-Book Treasury. Bergren, Lisa Tawn. 2010. (ENG.). 112p. 19.99 *(978-0-307-44629-9(8)*, WaterBrook Pr.) Crown Publishing Group, The.

—God Gave Us the World: A Picture Book. Bergren, Lisa Tawn. 2011. (God Gave Us Ser.). (ENG.). 40p. (gr. -1-2). 10.99 *(978-1-4000-7448-8(7)*, WaterBrook Pr.) Crown Publishing Group, The.

—God's Light, Shining Bright. Nolan, Allia Zobel. 2006. 8p. (J). 12.99 *(978-0-8254-5527-8(8))* Kregel Pubns.

—Heaven God's Promise for Me, 1 vol. Lotz, Anne Graham & Graham Lotz, Anne. 2011. (ENG.). 40p. (J). 16.99 *(978-0-310-71601-3(2))* Zondervan.

—How Big Is God? Bergren, Lisa Tawn. 2008. (HarperBlessings Ser.). (ENG.). 32p. (J). (gr. -1-2). 10.99 *(978-0-06-113174-5(1))* HarperCollins Pubs.

—I Need You. Murphy, Patricia J. 2003. (Rookie Readers Ser.). 31p. (J). (gr. 1-2). 12.60 *(978-0-7569-2065-4(5))* Perfection Learning Corp.

—I Need You. Murphy, Patricia J. 2003. (Rookie Reader Español Ser.). (ENG.). (J). (gr. k-2). pap. 4.95 *(978-0-516-26966-5(6)*, Children's Pr.) Scholastic Library Publishing.

—If You Were My Baby: A Wildlife Lullaby. Hodgkins, Fran. (ENG.). (J). (gr. -1-3). 2007. 26p. bds. 7.95 *(978-1-58469-090-0(9))*; 2005. 32p. 16.95 *(978-1-58469-074-0(7))*; 2005. 32p. pap. 8.95 *(978-1-58469-075-7(5))* Sourcebooks, Inc. (Dawn Pubns.).

—Jam & Honey. Morales, Melita. 2011. 32p. (J). (gr. -1-2). 15.99 *(978-1-58246-299-8(2)*, Tricycle Pr.) Random Hse. Children's Bks.

—Jo MacDonald Had a Garden. Quattlebaum, Mary. 2013. (ENG.). 26p. (J). (gr. -1-3). bds. 7.95 *(978-1-58469-225-6(1)*, Dawn Pubns.) Sourcebooks, Inc.

—Jo MacDonald Hiked in the Woods. Quattlebaum, Mary. 2013. (ENG.). 32p. (J). (gr. -1-3). 16.95 *(978-1-58469-334-5(7))*; pap. 8.95 *(978-1-58469-335-2(5))* Sourcebooks, Inc. (Dawn Pubns.).

—Jo MacDonald Saw a Pond. Quattlebaum, Mary. (ENG.). (J). 2013. 26p. (gr. -1 — 1). bds. 7.95 *(978-1-58469-224-9(3))*; 2011. 32p. 16.95 *(978-1-58469-150-1(6))*; 2011. 32p. pap. 8.95 *(978-1-58469-151-8(4))* Sourcebooks, Inc. (Dawn Pubns.).

—Kitty Cat, Kitty Cat, Are You Going to School?, 0 vols. Martin, Bill, Jr. et al. 2013. (ENG.). 24p. (J). (gr. -1-2). 16.99 *(978-1-4778-1722-3(0)*, 9781477817223, Two Lions) Amazon Publishing.

Bryant, Laura J. Kitty Cat, Kitty Cat, Are You Going to Sleep? Martin, Bill, Jr. et al. 2020. (ENG.). 26p. (J). (gr. -1-3). pap. 9.99 ***(978-1-4778-4734-3(0)***, 9781477847343, Two Lions) Amazon Publishing.

Bryant, Laura J. Kitty Cat, Kitty Cat, Are You Waking Up?, 0 vols. Martin, Bill, Jr. & Sampson, Michael. 2011. (ENG.). 26p. (J). (gr. -1-1). pap. 6.99 *(978-0-7614-5841-8(7),* 9780761458418, Two Lions) Amazon Publishing.

—Little Fox Goes to the End of the World, 0 vols. Tompert, Ann. 2010. (ENG.). 32p. (J). (gr. 1-3). 16.99 *(978-0-7614-5703-9(8),* 9780761457039, Two Lions) Amazon Publishing.

—M Is for Mountain State: A West Virginia Alphabet. Riehle, Mary Ann McCabe. 2004. (State Ser.). (ENG.). 40p. (J). 17.95 *(978-1-58536-151-9(8))* Sleeping Bear Pr.

—Only God Can Make a Kitten, 1 vol. Greene, Rhonda Gowler. 2016. (ENG.). 28p. (J). bds. 9.99 *(978-0-310-75008-6(3))* Zonderkidz.

—La Pascua Es un Regalo de Dios. Bergren, Lisa Tawn. 2018. (SPA.). 40p. (J). (gr. -1-2). 9.95 *(978-1-947783-04-1(1))* Penguin Random House Grupo Editorial ESP. Dist: Penguin Random Hse. LLC.

—Seven Little Bunnies, 0 vols. Stiegemeyer, Julie. 2010. (ENG.). 24p. (J). (gr. -1-3). 15.99 *(978-0-7614-5600-1(7),* 9780761456001, Two Lions) Amazon Publishing.

Bryant, Laura J. This Little Pup. Bryant, Laura J. 2020. (ENG.). 32p. (J). (gr. -1-3). 16.99 ***(978-0-8075-7865-0(7),*** 807578657) Whitman, Albert & Co.

Bryant, Michael. Bein' with You This Way. Nikola-Lisa, W. 97th ed. 2013. (ENG.). 32p. (J). (gr. -1-3). 10.95 *(978-1-880000-26-7(1))* Lee & Low Bks., Inc.

Bryant, Ray. The Book of Space: 50 Questions & All the Answers. 2013. (Questions Ser.). (ENG.). 64p. (J). (gr. k-3). 7.99 *(978-0-7534-7099-2(3),* 900118769, Kingfisher) Roaring Brook Pr.

Bryant, Remi. Color with Speedy & Friends. Arnold, William. 2019. (ENG.). 32p. (J). (gr. k-6). pap. 3.95 incl. audio compact disk ***(978-0-9701239-2-3(2))*** Rhette Enterprises, Inc.

Bryant, Ron. London & Sydney Explorent le Monde: Texas. Coleman, Kellen M. & Coleman, Berthina. 2018. (FRE.). 26p. (J). pap. 10.00 *(978-0-9988929-7-9(1))* Fomenky Publishing.

Bryars, Bart. The Tales of Ittybittyville. Bryars, Dianne Smith. 2017. (ENG.). (J). (gr. k-3). 25.00 *(978-0-692-82963-9(6))* Bryars, Bart.

Brycelea, Clifford & Yazzie, Johnson. The Stone Cutter & the Navajo Maiden. Browne, Vee. Manavi, Lorraine Begay, tr. from ENG. 2008. (NAV & ENG.). 32p. (J). (gr. -1-3). 17.95 *(978-1-893354-92-0(X))* Salina Bookshelf Inc.

Brychta, Alex. Camping Adventure. Hunt, Roderick. 2003. (ENG.). 24p. pap. *(978-0-19-845203-4(9))* Oxford Univ. Pr., Inc.

Bryer, Tom. Fun Poems for Kids. Bryer, Tom. 2012. 26p. *(978-1-908341-74-7(2))* Paragon Publishing, Rothersthorpe.

Bryksenkova, Yelena. Elizabeth & Zenobia: The Walls of Withering House. Miller, Jessica. 2019. (ENG.). 224p. (J). (gr. 4-8). pap. 8.99 *(978-1-4197-3378-9(8),* Amulet Bks.) Abrams, Inc.

—Light Filters In: Poems. Kaufman, Caroline. 2018. (ENG.). 224p. (YA). (gr. 8). 14.99 *(978-0-06-284468-2(7))* HarperCollins Pubs.

—When the World Didn't End: Poems. Kaufman, Caroline. 2019. (ENG.). 192p. (YA). (gr. 8). 14.99 *(978-0-06-291038-7(8))* HarperCollins Pubs.

Bryne, Kelly. The Three Little Pigs: A Wheel-Y Silly Fairy Tale. Gallo, Tina. 2011. (Little Simon Sillies Ser.). (ENG.). 14p. (J). (gr. -1-1). 6.99 *(978-1-4424-2107-3(X),* Little Simon) Little Simon.

Brynestad, Lea. S Is for Stillwater. Brynestad, Lea. 2018. (ENG.). 32p. (J). (gr. k-6). 18.99 *(978-0-692-10001-1(6))* Brynestad, Lea.

Brynjolson, Rhian. Goose Girl, 1 vol. Mclellan, Joe & McLellan, Matrine. 2015. (ENG.). 32p. (J). (gr. 2-4). mass mkt. 10.95 *(978-1-894717-44-1(9),* f5ea4a33-20b4-4b30-b17d-f553fd040ed4) Pemmican Pubns., Inc. CAN. Dist: Firefly Bks., Ltd.

—How the Turtle Got Its Shell: A Nanabosho Legend. McLellan, Joseph. 2015. (ENG.). 32p. (J). mass mkt. 10.95 *(978-0-921827-40-5(7),* ae600540-de47-46be-be3d-c8478474bf69) Pemmican Pubns., Inc. CAN. Dist: Firefly Bks., Ltd.

—Jen & the Great One, 1 vol. Evyindson, Peter. 2015. (ENG.). 32p. (J). (gr. k-4). mass mkt. 10.95 *(978-0-921827-19-1(9),* 51e37bea-0bcb-45c0-b2b8-9f90475be003) Pemmican Pubns., Inc. CAN. Dist: Firefly Bks., Ltd.

—Nanabosho & the Woodpecker, 1 vol. McLellan, Joe. 2015. (ENG.). 32p. (Orig.). (J). mass mkt. 10.95 *(978-0-921827-49-8(0),* ff39bd2e-bb8b-45cb-b7d2-1860a55f54ae) Pemmican Pubns., Inc. CAN. Dist: Firefly Bks., Ltd.

—Nanabosho Dances, 1 vol. McLellan, Joe. 2015. (ENG.). 32p. (J). (gr. -1-2). pap. 10.95 *(978-0-921827-14-6(8),* ca4b755c-3c71-4d82-90f4-2f7dc376ce8d) Pemmican Pubns., Inc. CAN. Dist: Firefly Bks., Ltd.

—Nanabosho, Soaring Eagle & the Great Sturgeon, 1 vol. McLellan, Joe. 2015. (ENG.). 52p. (J). (gr. -1-2). mass mkt. 10.95 *(978-0-921827-23-8(7),* e4378877-28b4-43de-af2e-f362ebf05572) Pemmican Pubns., Inc. CAN. Dist: Firefly Bks., Ltd.

—The Night Rebecca Stayed Too Late, 1 vol. Eyvindson, Peter. 2015. (ENG.). 32p. (J). mass mkt. 10.95 *(978-0-921827-39-9(3),* 78572c41-d72d-4046-87cc-382c6af1574c) Pemmican Pubns., Inc. CAN. Dist: Firefly Bks., Ltd.

—Red Parka Mary, 1 vol. Eyvindson, Peter. 2015. (ENG.). 32p. (Orig.). (J). mass mkt. 10.95 *(978-0-921827-50-4(4),* 7b59caf0-dd9b-4b37-8bbb-dcb209a88b30) Pemmican Pubns., Inc. CAN. Dist: Firefly Bks., Ltd.

Bryson, Rob. Nora & the Worry Zoot. Gordon. 2019. (ENG.). 26p. (J). (gr. -1-3). ***(978-0-2288-1838-0(9));*** ***(978-0-2288-1839-7(7))*** Tellwell Talent.

Brzozowski, Christina. Sniffle, Sneeze, Cough Back Off! Grimshaw, Luke. 2008. 24p. pap. 24.95 *(978-1-60703-607-4(X))* America Star Bks.

—Sniffle, Sneeze, Cough... Back Off!, 1 vol. Grimshaw, Luke. 2010. 22p. 24.95 *(978-1-4512-1034-7(5))* America Star Bks.

Btween Animation. The Most Forgetful Rabbit Ever. Woods, Candace. 2019. (Most Forgetful Rabbit Ever Ser.: Vol. 1). (ENG.). 50p. (J). (gr. k-3). pap. 16.99 ***(978-0-578-55878-3(5))*** Woods, Candace E.

Buba, Joy. Lyrico: The Only Horse of His Kind. Foster, Elizabeth Vincent. 2nd ed. 2004. 230p. (gr. 6-8). reprint ed. 8.95 *(978-0-930407-21-6(0))* Parabola Bks.

Bubar, Lorraine. Lullaby. Friedman, Debbie. 2014. (ENG.). 32p. (J). 18.99 *(978-1-58023-807-6(6),* d9c32597-badd-475b-8a24-b8382e4bea2d, Jewish Lights Publishing) LongHill Partners, Inc.

Bubbeo, Philip. Little & Big: A Bigfoot Story. Fouch, Robert L. 2017. (ENG.). (J). pap. 8.99 *(978-0-9907913-2-4(7))* Fouch, Robert L.

Bubp, Jennifer. The Lizard Who Wanted to Be a Mouse. Russell, Allyson. 2009. 28p. pap. 12.95 *(978-1-59858-938-2(5))* Dog Ear Publishing, LLC.

Buccheri, Chiara. I'll Haunt You! Meet a Ghost. Knudsen, Shannon. 2014. (Monster Buddies Ser.). (ENG.). 24p. (J). (gr. k-2). lib. bdg. 23.99 *(978-0-7613-9186-9(X),* 9780761391869, Millbrook Pr.) Lerner Publishing Group.

Bucci, Gino. No More Peanut Butter, Daniel! Ciccone, Tiziana & Linardi, Franca. 2012. 36p. pap. 13.95 *(978-1-61897-718-2(0),* Strategic Bk. Publishing) Strategic Book Publishing & Rights Agency (SBPRA).

—The Pancake Princess. Ciccone, Tizania & Linardi, Franca. 2012. 36p. pap. 13.95 *(978-1-61897-720-5(2),* Strategic Bk. Publishing) Strategic Book Publishing & Rights Agency (SBPRA).

Bucci, Marco. Good Night, Forest. Brennan-Nelson, Denise. 2018. (ENG.). 32p. (J). (gr. -1-2). 16.99 *(978-1-58536-388-9(X),* 204410) Sleeping Bear Pr.

—Good Night, Reindeer. Nelson, Denise Brennan. 2017. (ENG.). 32p. (J). (gr. -1-2). 16.99 *(978-1-58536-370-4(7),* 204329) Sleeping Bear Pr.

—Norbert's Big Dream. Degman, Lori. 2016. (ENG.). 32p. (J). (gr. k-3). 16.99 *(978-1-58536-959-1(4),* 204108) Sleeping Bear Pr.

—The Nutcracker & the Four Realms: the Dance of the Realms. Glass, Calliope. 2018. (ENG.). 40p. (J). (gr. -1-k). 16.99 *(978-1-368-02036-7(4))* Disney Pr.

—Sheriff Callie's Wild West: Callie Asks for Help. Auerbach, Annie & Kramer, Mike. 2018. (World of Reading Level Pre-1 Ser.). (ENG.). 32p. (J). (gr. -1-2). lib. bdg. 27.07 *(978-1-5321-4184-3(X),* 28529) Spotlight.

—Sheriff Callie's Wild West: Peck's Trail Mix Mix-Up. Auerbach, Annie & Kramer, Mike. 2018. (World of Reading Level Pre-1 Ser.). (ENG.). 32p. (J). (gr. -1-2). lib. bdg. 27.07 *(978-1-5321-4185-0(8),* 31063) Spotlight.

Bucco, Joe. Everyman: Be the People. Goldman, Steven & Goldman, Dan. 2004. 96p. per. 6.00 *(978-0-9759152-0-2(7))* KINJIN Global.

Buchanan, Alexander "lex". Bonnie B-One's Supersonic Move. Ross, Liesl. 2018. (ENG.). 34p. (J). 24.95 *(978-0-578-42456-9(8))* Ross, Liesl.

Buchanan, Diane. Please Don't Say Fart. Samuels, Josh. Buchanan, Samuel, ed. 2019. (ENG.). 46p. (J). pap. 6.99 ***(978-1-7339436-0-4(9))*** Jakki Joy Publishing.

Buchanan, James & Buchanan, Melissa. Studio: a Place for Art to Start. Arrow, Emily. 2020. (ENG.). 40p. (J). (gr. -1-2). 17.99 *(978-0-7352-6445-4(6),* Tundra Bks.) Tundra Bks. CAN. Dist: Penguin Random Hse. LLC.

Buchanan, Jessie, jt. illus. see Thoraval, Carly.

Buchanan, Melissa, jt. illus. see Buchanan, James.

Buchanan, Yvonne. Celebremos Juneteenth! Weatherford, Carole Boston. de La Vega, Eida, tr. from ENG. 2007. (SPA.). 32p. (J). (gr. -1-3). pap. 7.95 *(978-1-60060-247-4(9))* Lee & Low Bks., Inc.

Bucher, Barbara Latini. Three Young Wild Cats. Evans, Betty J. 2008. 20p. pap. 24.95 *(978-1-60610-809-3(3))* America Star Bks.

Bucher, Cecile. Ben, the Bells & the Peacocks. Trooboff, Rhoda. 2006. (ENG.). 36p. (J). per. 15.00 *(978-0-9773536-0-6(5))* Tenley Circle Pr.

Buchheim, Su Jen. Just As You Are: The Story of Leon & Sam. Marks, Nancy Freeman. 2003. 32p. (J). 15.00 *(978-0-9722430-1-8(1))* Wave Publishing.

Buchheit, Barbie. How Do I Know God Loves Me? Rechenberg, Mary Koeberl. 2018. (ENG.). 48p. (J). (gr. k-6). pap. 10.95 *(978-1-7328384-0-6(2))* Farmer Valley Publishing.

Buchholc, Ada. Bad Girls of Fashion: Style Rebels Through the Ages. Croll, Jennifer. 2016. (ENG.). 208p. (J). pap. 14.95 *(978-1-55451-785-5(0))* Annick Pr., Ltd. CAN. Dist: Publishers Group West (PGW).

Buchholz, Quint. The Summer of the Pike. Richter, Jutta. Brailovsky, Anna, tr. 2006. (ENG.). 132p. (J). (gr. 2-8). 16.95 *(978-1-57131-671-4(X));* (gr. 8-12). per. 6.95 *(978-1-57131-672-1(8))* Milkweed Editions.

Buchs, Thomas. Alphabet of Dinosaurs. Schwaeber, Barbie Heit. (ENG.). 40p. 2009. 9.95 *(978-1-59249-993-9(7));* 2007. (J). (gr. -1-2). 15.95 *(978-1-59249-724-9(1))* Soundprints.

Buchs, Thomas, et al. Alphabet of Dinosaurs. Schwaeber, Barbie Heit. 2011. (Alphabet Bks.). (ENG.). 40p. (J). (gr. -1-3). 17.95 *(978-1-60727-671-5(2));* 9.95 *(978-1-60727-444-5(2))* Soundprints.

Buchs, Thomas. Alphabet of Insects. Schwaeber, Barbie Heit. 2009. (ENG.). 40p. 9.95 *(978-1-59249-992-2(9))* Soundprints.

—Moon Walk. Rau, Dana Meachen. 2004. (Soundprints' Read-and-Discover Ser.). 48p. (gr. -1-3). 13.95 *(978-0-7569-3370-8(6))* Perfection Learning Corp.

—Moon Walk. Rau, Dana. 3rd ed. 2003. (Soundprints' Read-and-Discover Ser.). (ENG.). 48p. (J). (gr. -1-3). pap. 4.35 *(978-1-59249-015-8(8),* S2006) Soundprints.

—Red Bat at Sleep Hollow Lane. Halfmann, Janet. 2004. (ENG.). 32p. (J). (gr. -1-2). 9.95 *(978-1-59249-345-6(9),* PB5027) Soundprints.

Bucker, Jutta. Wiley & Jasper. Bucker, Jutta, tr. Moss, Miriam. 2003. (J). 25p. pap. *(978-1-59336-061-0(4));* 32p. 15.95 *(978-1-59336-060-3(6))* Mondo Publishing.

Buckett, George. Never Talk to Strangers. Joyce, Irma. 2009. 32p. (J). (gr. -1-2). 9.99 *(978-0-375-84964-0(5),* Golden Bks.) Random Hse. Children's Bks.

Buckingham, Caz. Little Book of Woodland Bird Songs. Pinnington, Andrea. 2018. (ENG.). 26p. (J). (gr. k-4). 19.95 *(978-0-2281-0031-7(3),* feb6b5d2-3078-4bf5-b86a-cc98300643d1) Firefly Bks., Ltd.

Buckingham, Faye. My First Unicorn Dot-To-Dot: Over 50 Fantastic Puzzles. Potter, Joe & Golding, Elizabeth. 2019. (My First Activity Bks.). (ENG.). 64p. (J). (gr. -1-2). pap. 6.99 *(978-1-4380-1272-8(1),* B.E.S. Publishing) Peterson's.

Buckingham, Gabriella. The Wheels on the Bus & Other Action Rhymes. 2013. (ENG.). 16p. (J). (gr. -1-12). bds. 7.99 *(978-1-84322-830-1(0),* Armadillo) Anness Publishing GBR. Dist: National Bk. Network.

Buckingham, Mark. Fables Vol. 4: March of the Wooden Soldiers, Vol. 4. Willingham, Bill. rev. ed. 2004. (ENG.). 240p. pap. 17.99 *(978-1-4012-0222-4(5),* Vertigo) DC Comics.

Buckingham, Mark, et al. Spider-Man: Light in the Darkness. 2019. (ENG.). 432p. (YA). (gr. -1-17). pap. 39.99 *(978-1-302-91863-7(X))* Marvel Worldwide, Inc.

Buckingham, Matt. Bible People Factfile. Martin, Peter. ed. 2014. (ENG.). 48p. (J). (gr. 2-4). 14.99 *(978-0-7459-6388-4(9))* Lion Hudson PLC GBR. Dist: Independent Pubs. Group.

Buckland, Arthur H. The Lost Explorers (Illustrated Edition) MacDonald, Alexander. 2018. (ENG.). 220p. (J). pap. *(978-1-4068-1744-7(9))* Echo Library.

Buckler, Rich, et al. What If? Classic: the Complete Collection Vol. 3. 2020. (ENG.). 488p. (YA). (gr. 4-17). pap. 39.99 *(978-1-302-92274-0(2))* Marvel Worldwide, Inc.

Buckley, Annie. The Kids' Yoga Deck: 50 Poses & Games. Buckley, Annie. 2003. (ENG.). 50p. (gr. 8-17). 14.95 *(978-0-8118-3698-2(3))* Chronicle Bks. LLC.

Buckley, Barbara, photos by. The World Around My House: A Book of Discovery! Buckley, Barbara. 2017. (ENG., (J). (gr. k-3). pap. 13.99 *(978-0-692-89591-7(4))* Buckley, Barbara.

Buckley, Carol, photos by. Tarra & Bella: The Elephant & Dog Who Became Best Friends. Buckley, Carol. 2009. 32p. (J). (gr. -1-k). 17.99 *(978-0-399-25443-7(9),* G.P. Putnam's Sons Books for Young Readers) Penguin Young Readers Group.

Buckley, Jaime. The Day Annabelle Was Bitten by a Doodlebug. Wenzlick, Julie. 2018. (ENG.). 32p. (J). (gr. k-3). 20.00 *(978-0-9978925-9-8(5))* Wordmeister Pr.

—The Day Maise Picked a Daisy. Wenzlick, Julie. 2017. (ENG.). 50p. (J). pap. 13.99 *(978-0-9978925-4-3(4))* Wordmeister Pr.

—The Day Maisie & Annabelle Got the Giggles. Wenzlick, Julie. 2018. (ENG.). 50p. (J). 21.99 *(978-0-9978925-7-4(9))* Wordmeister Pr.

—The Day Maisie & Annabelle Got the Giggles. Wenzlick, Julie. 2018. (ENG.). 50p. (J). pap. 13.99 *(978-0-9978925-8-1(7))* Wordmeister Pr.

—The Day Maisie Picked a Daisy. Wenzlick, Julie J. 2018. (ENG.). 50p. (J). 20.00 *(978-0-9978925-1-2(X))* Wordmeister Pr.

Buckley, Jaime. The Dream War: Annabelle vs. Maisie. Wenzlick, Julie. 2020. (ENG.). 50p. (J). pap. 15.00 ***(978-1-7351213-0-7(4))*** Wordmeister Pr.

Buckley, Jaime. #theyusedto: A Short Story about Empathy, Inspiration & Strength. Dimitrievski, Stephanie. 2018. (ENG.). 30p. (YA). *(978-1-5255-3290-0(1));* pap. *(978-1-5255-3291-7(X))* FriesenPress.

Buckley, Joel. Adam & the Tattooed Angel. Butler, Heather. 2004. 64p. pap. *(978-1-84427-043-9(2))* Scripture Union.

—Ellie & the Clown Crisis. Butler, Heather. 2004. 64p. pap. *(978-1-84427-023-1(8))* Scripture Union.

—Peter Goes Feet First! Willoughby, R. 2004. 64p. pap. *(978-1-85999-766-6(X))* Scripture Union.

—Peter Puts His Foot in It! Willoughby, R. 2004. 64p. pap. *(978-1-85999-765-9(1))* Scripture Union.

—Peter Strides Out. Willoughby, R. 2004. 64p. pap. *(978-1-84427-022-4(X))* Scripture Union.

Buckley, Linda. Six Colorful Annies: A Pre-School Edition. Costa, Bernardette. 2018. (ENG.). 36p. (J). pap. 9.95 *(978-1-7219-2476-9(0))* CreateSpace Independent Publishing Platform.

Buckner, David. Even Scary Things Get the Blues. Buckner, David. 2018. (ENG.). 38p. (J). pap. 12.95 *(978-1-7264-5011-9(2))* CreateSpace Independent Publishing Platform.

Buckner, Jon. Gilbert Grump & the Search for the Lost Smile, 1 vol. Lamb, Kenny. 2017. (Gilbert Grump Ser.: 2). (ENG.). 36p. (J). (gr. -1-2). 15.95 *(978-1-943978-21-2(2),* d8717614-d2e8-4862-b57c-fdd02759ca2f) WunderMill, Inc.

Buckner, Julie. Jubilee!, 1 vol. Tunks, Karyn. 2012. (ENG.). 32p. (J). (gr. k-3). 16.99 *(978-1-58980-880-5(0),* Pelican Publishing) Arcadia Publishing.

Buckner, Julie Dupre. Clovis Crawfish & Echo Gecko, 1 vol. Fontenot, Mary Alice. 2003. (Clovis Crawfish Ser.). (ENG.). 32p. (J). (gr. k-3). 16.99 *(978-1-56554-708-7(X),* Pelican Publishing) Arcadia Publishing.

—Clovis Crawfish & Silvie Sulphur, 1 vol. Fontenot, Mary Alice. 2004. (Clovis Crawfish Ser.). (ENG.). 32p. (J). (gr. k-3). 16.99 *(978-1-56554-864-0(7),* Pelican Publishing) Arcadia Publishing.

—Voices of the Western Frontier, 1 vol. Garland, Sherry. 2016. (Voices of History Ser.). (ENG.). 40p. (J). (gr. -1-6). 17.99 *(978-1-4556-1961-0(2),* Pelican Publishing) Arcadia Publishing.

Buckner, Julie Dupre, jt. illus. see Butler, Julie Dupre.

Bucs, David. Sleepover at the Museum. LeFrak, Karen. 2019. 40p. (J). (gr. -1-2). 17.99 *(978-1-5247-7140-9(6));* (ENG.). lib. bdg. 20.99 *(978-1-5247-7141-6(4))* Random Hse. Children's Bks. (Crown Books For Young Readers).

Buczek, Sarah. The Long Journey: A Tale of Friendship. Pickering, Jeannine. 2020. (ENG.). 24p. (J). pap. 10.95 ***(978-1-9822-5072-0(0),*** Balboa Pr.) Author Solutions, Inc.

Budd, Jordan. Outback Bob: And the 20-Foot Purple Ape. Remien, Robert. 2020. (Adventures of Outback Bob Ser.: Vol. 1). (ENG.). 32p. (J). ***(978-0-2288-2974-4(7));*** pap. ***(978-0-2288-2973-7(9))*** Tellwell Talent.

Budgen, Tim. Big Cats, Little Cats. Weaver, A. J. 2013. 32p. pap. *(978-1-909423-03-9(3))* Bks. to Treasure.

—Big Shark, Little Shark. Membrino, Anna. 32p. (J). 2020. (— 1). bds. 7.99 *(978-1-9848-9514-1(1));* 2017. (ENG.). (gr. -1-1). pap. 4.99 *(978-0-399-55728-6(8))* Random Hse. Children's Bks. (Random Hse. Bks. for Young Readers).

—Big Shark, Little Shark Go to School. Membrino, Anna. 2019. (Step into Reading Ser.). 32p. (J). (gr. -1-1). (ENG.). pap. 4.99 *(978-1-9848-9349-9(1));* lib. bdg. 12.99 *(978-1-9848-9350-5(5))* Random Hse. Children's Bks. (Random Hse. Bks. for Young Readers).

—I Think My Grandpa Might Be Santa: Padded Board Book. Berry Byrd, Holly. Cottage Door Press, ed. 2017. (Love You Always Ser.). (ENG.). 18p. (J). (gr. -1-1). bds. 9.99 *(978-1-68052-045-3(8),* 1000460) Cottage Door Pr.

Budgen, Tim. When You Adopt a ... Starwhal. Rose, Matilda. 2020. (When You Adopt Ser.). (ENG.). 32p. (J). (gr. -1-3). 12.99 ***(978-1-4197-4723-6(1),*** 1702001, Abrams Appleseed) Abrams, Inc.

Budig, Greg. Still: A Winter's Journey. Budig, Greg. 2009. 32p. (J). (gr. 3-18). pap. 16.95 *(978-0-916144-87-6(9))* Stemmer Hse. Pubs.

Budwine, Greg. Benjamin Franklin: You Know What to Say. Uglow, Loyd. 2003. (J). lib. bdg. 23.95 incl. audio *(978-1-57537-791-9(8))* Advance Publishing, Inc.

—Can You Help Me Find My Smile? Sommer, Carl. 2003. (Another Sommer-Time Story Ser.). (ENG.). 48p. (J). (gr. k-4). lib. bdg. 23.95 incl. audio compact disk *(978-1-57537-707-0(1));* (gr. 1-4). 16.95 incl. audio compact disk *(978-1-57537-507-6(9))* Advance Publishing, Inc.

—Can You Help Me Find My Smile? Me Puedes Ayudar a Encontrar Mi Sonrisa? Sommer, Carl. ed. 2009. (Another Sommer-Time Story Bilingual Ser.). (SPA & ENG.). 48p. (J). lib. bdg. 16.95 *(978-1-57537-150-4(2))* Advance Publishing, Inc.

—Fast Forward. Sommer, Carl. 2009. (Quest for Success Ser.). (ENG.). 56p. (YA). pap. 4.95 *(978-1-57537-277-8(0));* lib. bdg. 12.95 *(978-1-57537-252-5(5))* Advance Publishing, Inc.

—Fast Forward(Avance Acelarado) Sommer, Carl. ed. 2009. (Quest for Success Bilingual Ser.). (SPA & ENG.). 104p. (YA). lib. bdg. 14.95 *(978-1-57537-227-3(4))* Advance Publishing, Inc.

—I Am a Lion! Sommer, Carl. (J). 2014. *(978-1-57537-403-1(X));* 2003. (ENG.). 48p. (gr. k-4). lib. bdg. 23.95 incl. audio compact disk *(978-1-57537-709-4(8));* 2003. (ENG.). 48p. (gr. 1-4). 16.95 incl. audio compact disk *(978-1-57537-509-0(5))* Advance Publishing, Inc.

—I Am a Lion!(Yo Soy un León!) Sommer, Carl. ed. 2009. (Another Sommer-Time Story Bilingual Ser.). (SPA & ENG.). 48p. (J). lib. bdg. 16.95 *(978-1-57537-153-5(7))* Advance Publishing, Inc.

—It's Not Fair! Sommer, Carl. (J). 2014. pap. *(978-1-57537-955-5(4));* 2003. (ENG.). 48p. 9.95 *(978-1-57537-021-7(2));* 2003. (ENG.). 48p. lib. bdg. 16.95 *(978-1-57537-070-5(0));* 2003. (ENG.). 48p. (gr. k-4). lib. bdg. 23.95 incl. audio compact disk *(978-1-57537-720-9(9));* 2003. (ENG.). 48p. (gr. 1-4). 16.95 incl. audio compact disk *(978-1-57537-520-5(6))* Advance Publishing, Inc.

—It's Not Fair!(No Es Justo) ! Sommer, Carl. ed. 2009. (Another Sommer-Time Story Bilingual Ser.). (SPA & ENG.). 48p. (J). lib. bdg. 16.95 *(978-1-57537-155-9(3))* Advance Publishing, Inc.

—King of the Pond. Sommer, Carl. (J). 2014. pap. *(978-1-57537-956-2(2));* 2003. (ENG.). 48p. (gr. k-4). lib. bdg. 23.95 incl. audio compact disk *(978-1-57537-716-2(0));* 2003. (ENG.). 48p. (gr. 1-4). 16.95 incl. audio compact disk *(978-1-57537-516-8(8))* Advance Publishing, Inc.

—King of the Pond(El Rey Del Estanque) Sommer, Carl. ed. 2009. (Another Sommer-Time Story Bilingual Ser.). (SPA & ENG.). 48p. (J). lib. bdg. 16.95 *(978-1-57537-156-6(1))* Advance Publishing, Inc.

—Lost & Found. Sommer, Carl. 2009. (Quest for Success Ser.). 56p. (YA). pap. 4.95 *(978-1-57537-280-8(0));* lib. bdg. 12.95 *(978-1-57537-255-6(X))* Advance Publishing, Inc.

—Lost & Found(Perdida y Encontrada) Sommer, Carl. ed. 2009. (Quest for Success Bilingual Ser.). (ENG & SPA.). 96p. (YA). lib. bdg. 14.95 *(978-1-57537-229-7(0))* Advance Publishing, Inc.

—No One Will Ever Know. Sommer, Carl. 2014. (J). pap. *(978-1-57537-962-3(7))* Advance Publishing, Inc.

—Proud Rooster & Little Hen. Sommer, Carl. (J). 2014. pap. *(978-1-57537-964-7(3));* 2003. (ENG.). 48p. lib. bdg. 23.95 incl. audio compact disk *(978-1-57537-710-0(1));* 2003. (ENG.). 48p. (gr. 1-4). 16.95 incl. audio compact disk *(978-1-57537-510-6(9))* Advance Publishing, Inc.

—Proud Rooster & Little Hen(Gallito Orgulloso y Gallinita) Sommer, Carl. ed. 2009. (Another Sommer-Time Story Bilingual Ser.). (SPA & ENG.). 48p. (J). 16.95 *(978-1-57537-164-1(2))* Advance Publishing, Inc.

—The Race. Sommer, Carl. 2009. (Quest for Success Ser.). (ENG.). 56p. (YA). lib. bdg. 12.95 *(978-1-57537-256-3(8))* Advance Publishing, Inc.

—The Race(La Carrera) Sommer, Carl. ed. 2009. (Quest for Success Bilingual Ser.). (SPA & ENG.). 104p. (YA). lib. bdg. 14.95 *(978-1-57537-230-3(4))* Advance Publishing, Inc.

—The Racing Fools. Sommer, Carl. 2009. (Quest for Success Ser.). (ENG.). 56p. (YA). pap. 4.95 *(978-1-57537-281-5(9))* Advance Publishing, Inc.

—The Revolt. Sommer, Carl. 2009. (Quest for Success Ser.). (ENG.). 56p. (YA). pap. 4.95 *(978-1-57537-283-9(5));* lib. bdg. 12.95 *(978-1-57537-258-7(4))* Advance Publishing, Inc.

—The Revolt(La Revuelta) Sommer, Carl. ed. 2009. (Quest for Success Bilingual Ser.). (SPA & ENG.). 104p. (YA). lib.

B

bdg. 14.95 *(978-1-57537-232-7(0))* Advance Publishing, Inc.
—The Roar. Sommer, Carl. 2009. (Quest for Success Ser.). (ENG.). 56p. (YA). pap. 4.95 *(978-1-57537-284-6(3))*; lib. bdg. 12.95 *(978-1-57537-259-4(2))* Advance Publishing, Inc.
—The Roar(El Rugido) Sommer, Carl. ed. 2009. (Quest for Success Bilingual Ser.). (SPA & ENG.). 96p. (YA). lib. bdg. 14.95 *(978-1-57537-233-4(9))* Advance Publishing, Inc.
—Three Little Pigs. Sommer, Carl. 2014. (J). pap. *(978-1-57537-968-5(6))* Advance Publishing, Inc.
—Tied up in Knots. Sommer, Carl. 2003. (Another Sommer-Time Story Ser.). (ENG.). 48p. (J). 16.95 incl. audio compact disk *(978-1-57537-503-8(6))* Advance Publishing, Inc.
—Tied up in Knots Read-along. Sommer, Carl. 2003. (Another Sommer-Time Story Ser.). (ENG.). 48p. (J). lib. bdg. 23.95 incl. audio compact disk *(978-1-57537-703-2(9))* Advance Publishing, Inc.
—Tied up in Knots(Enredados) Sommer, Carl. ed. 2009. (Another Sommer-Time Story Bilingual Ser.). (SPA & ENG.). 48p. (J). lib. bdg. 16.95 *(978-1-57537-169-6(3))* Advance Publishing, Inc.
—Time Remote! Sommer, Carl. (J). 2014. pap. *(978-1-57537-970-8(8))*; 2003. (ENG.). 48p. (gr. 1-4). 16.95 incl. audio compact disk *(978-1-57537-512-0(5))* Advance Publishing, Inc.
—Time Remote! Read-along. Sommer, Carl. 2003. (Another Sommer-Time Story Ser.). (ENG.). 48p. (J). lib. bdg. 23.95 incl. audio compact disk *(978-1-57537-712-4(8))* Advance Publishing, Inc.
—Time Remote!(El Control Del Tiempo!) Sommer, Carl. ed. 2009. (Another Sommer-Time Story Bilingual Ser.). (SPA & ENG.). 48p. (J). lib. bdg. 16.95 *(978-1-57537-170-2(7))* Advance Publishing, Inc.
—The Ugly Caterpillar. Sommer, Carl. (J). 2014. pap. *(978-1-57537-971-5(6))*; 2003. 48p. (gr. 1-4). 16.95 incl. audio compact disk *(978-1-57537-515-1(X))* Advance Publishing, Inc.
—The Ugly Caterpillar Read-along. Sommer, Carl. 2003. (Another Sommer-Time Story Ser.). (ENG.). 48p. (J). lib. bdg. 23.95 incl. audio compact disk *(978-1-57537-715-5(2))* Advance Publishing, Inc.
—The Ugly Caterpillar(La Oruga Fea) Sommer, Carl. ed. 2009. (Another Sommer-Time Story Bilingual Ser.). (SPA & ENG.). 48p. (J). (gr. k-3). lib. bdg. 16.95 *(978-1-57537-171-9(5))* Advance Publishing, Inc.
Budwine, Greg & Vignolo, Enrique. Three Little Pigs(Los Tres Cerditos) Sommer, Carl. ed. 2009. (Another Sommer-Time Story Bilingual Ser.). (SPA & ENG.). 48p. (J). lib. bdg. 16.95 *(978-1-57537-168-9(5))* Advance Publishing, Inc.
Buehner, Caralyn & Buehner, Mark. Fanny's Dream. Buehner, Caralyn & Buehner, Mark. 2003. (ENG.). 32p. (J). (gr. k-3). 7.99 *(978-0-14-250060-6(7)*, Puffin Books) Penguin Young Readers Group.
Buehner, Mark. Dex: the Heart of a Hero. Buehner, Caralyn. 2007. (ENG.). 32p. (J). (gr. -1-3). pap. 7.99 *(978-0-06-443845-2(7))* HarperCollins Pubs.
—Goldilocks & the Three Bears. Buehner, Caralyn. 2009. 32p. (J). (gr. -1-k). pap. 7.99 *(978-0-14-241275-6(9)*, Puffin Books) Penguin Young Readers Group.
—Merry Christmas, Mr. Mouse. Buehner, Caralyn. 2015. 40p. (J). (gr. -1-k). 17.99 *(978-0-8037-4010-5(7)*, Dial Bks) Penguin Young Readers Group.
—My Life with the Wave. 2004. (ENG.). (J). (gr. -1-3). lib. bdg. 8.84 *(978-0-7569-3200-8(9))* Perfection Learning Corp.
—My Life with the Wave. Cowan, Catherine. ed. 2004. (J). (gr. k-3). spiral bd. *(978-0-616-11863-4(5))* Canadian National Institute for the Blind/Institut National Canadien pour les Aveugles.
—My Life with the Wave. Cowan, Catherine. 2004. (ENG.). 32p. (J). (gr. -1-3). reprint ed. pap. 7.99 *(978-0-06-056200-7(5))* HarperCollins Pubs.
—Snowmen All Year. Buehner, Caralyn. 2010. (ENG.). 32p. (J). (gr. -1-2). 17.99 *(978-0-8037-3383-1(6)*, Dial Bks) Penguin Young Readers Group.
—Snowmen All Year Board Book. Buehner, Caralyn. 2012. 28p. (J). (gr. -1-k). bds. 6.99 *(978-0-8037-3905-5(2)*, Dial Bks) Penguin Young Readers Group.
—Snowmen at Christmas. Buehner, Caralyn. (J). (gr. -1-k). 2010. (ENG.). 28p. bds. 7.99 *(978-0-8037-3551-4(0))*; 2005. 32p. 17.99 *(978-0-8037-2995-7(2))* Penguin Young Readers Group. (Dial Bks).
—Snowmen at Play. Buehner, Caralyn. 2013. (ENG.). 16p. (J). (gr. -1-k). 7.99 *(978-0-448-47782-4(3)*, Grosset & Dunlap) Penguin Young Readers Group.
—Snowmen at Work. Buehner, Caralyn. 2012. 32p. (J). (gr. -1-2). 17.99 *(978-0-8037-3579-8(0)*, Dial Bks) Penguin Young Readers Group.
—Snowmen Galore. Buehner, Caralyn. 2017. (ENG.). 32p. (J). (gr. -1-2). 23.99 *(978-0-7352-3016-3(1)*, Dial Bks) Penguin Young Readers Group.
—Superdog: The Heart of a Hero. Buehner, Caralyn. 2004. 32p. (J). (gr. -1-3). lib. bdg. 17.89 *(978-0-06-623621-6(5))* HarperCollins Pubs.
—This First Thanksgiving Day. Melmed, Laura Krauss. 2003. (ENG.). 22p. (J). (gr. -1-3). 18.80 *(978-1-5311-8696-8(3))* Perfection Learning Corp.
—This First Thanksgiving Day: A Counting Story. Melmed, Laura Krauss. 2003. (ENG.). 32p. (J). (gr. -1-3). pap. 7.99 *(978-0-06-054184-2(9))* HarperCollins Pubs.
Buehner, Mark. Mi Vida con la Ola. Buehner, Mark. Cowan, Catherine. Rubio, Esther, tr. 2004. (SPA.). 29p. (J). 19.99 *(978-84-88342-45-4(4))* S.A. Kokinos ESP. Dist: Lectorum Pubns., Inc.
Buehner, Mark, jt. illus. see Buehner, Caralyn.
Buehner, Mark E. Snowmen at Halloween. Buehner, Caralyn M. 2019. 32p. (J). (gr. -1-2). 17.99 *(978-0-525-55468-4(8)*, Dial Bks) Penguin Young Readers Group.
Buehr, Walter. The First Book of Machines. Buehr, Walter. 2017. (ENG.). (J). (gr. 4-6). pap. 12.95 *(978-0-692-97395-0(8))* Living Library Pr.
Buehrle, Jackie. Sage & the Peacock. Knesek, Marian. 2011. 28p. pap. 24.95 *(978-1-4512-2211-1(4))* America Star Bks.
Buehrle, Jacquelyn. The Adventures of Hooch & Mile-A-Minute-Freebee. Signor, Priscilla M. 2011. 28p. pap. 24.95 *(978-1-4560-0936-6(2))* America Star Bks.
—A Bunny Named Apple. Tardif, Elizabeth. 2011. 28p. pap. 24.95 *(978-1-4560-0946-5(X))* America Star Bks.
—My Seeing Eye Glasses. Glass, Alberta. 2011. 28p. pap. 24.95 *(978-1-4560-2829-9(4))* PublishAmerica, Inc.
—The Rainbow in My Pocket. Hazekamp, Michelle R. 2011. 28p. pap. 24.95 *(978-1-4560-0927-4(3))* America Star Bks.
—The Story of Ocos: King of the Sky, Master of the Water. Trimoglie, Mario. 2011. 28p. pap. 24.95 *(978-1-4560-2015-6(3))* America Star Bks.
—Sylvester the One-Legged Seagull. Horstmann, Deborah McFillin. 2012. 28p. 24.95 *(978-1-4560-2308-9(X))* America Star Bks.
—Winky Sue's Peppermint Birthday. Bocanegra, Deborah. 2012. 26p. 24.95 *(978-1-4560-7282-7(X))* America Star Bks.
Buel, Hubert. The Shy Stegosaurus of Cricket Creek. Lampman, Evelyn Sibley. 2007. 218p. (J). (gr. 4-7). per. 12.00 *(978-1-930900-37-0(6))* Purple Hse. Pr.
Buell, Carl Dennis. Stickeen. Muir, John. Date not set. 94p. (J). 16.95 *(978-0-8488-2803-5(8))* Amereon Ltd.
—Stickeen. Muir, John. 2008. (ENG.). 96p. (J). (gr. 3-5). reprint ed. pap. 10.00 *(978-0-930588-48-9(7))* Heyday.
Buelt, Laura. Langur Monkey's Day. Hammerslough, Jane. 2005. (Wild Reading Adventures! Ser.). (ENG.). (J). (gr. -1-2). 36p. 2.95 *(978-1-59249-143-8(X)*, S7156); 36p. 9.95 *(978-1-59249-144-5(8)*, PS7156); 32p. 19.95 *(978-1-59249-221-3(5)*, BC7106); 32p. 8.95 *(978-1-59249-222-0(3)*, SC7106) Soundprints.
—Langur Monkey's Day. Hammerslough, Jane & Smithsonian Institution Staff. rev. ed. 2008. (ENG.). 24p. (J). (gr. -1-3). 4.99 *(978-1-59249-706-5(3)*, Little Soundprints) Soundprints.
Buelt, Laura. Langur Monkey's Day. Buelt, Laura, tr. Hammerslough, Jane. 2005. (Wild Reading Adventures! Ser.). (ENG.). 36p. (J). (gr. -1-2). 15.95 *(978-1-59249-141-4(3)*, B7106); pap. 6.95 *(978-1-59249-142-1(1)*, S7106) Soundprints.
Bueno, Fran. The Haunted High-Tops. Knight, Rosie. 2020. (Scary Graphics Ser.). (ENG.). 40p. (J). (gr. 3-5). lib. bdg. 25.32 ***(978-1-4965-9797-7(4)***, 200591, Stone Arch Bks.) Capstone.
Buettner, Bernie & Bober, Michael. Saidy Stories Two. Buettner, Barbara. 2016. (ENG.). (J). pap. 15.95 *(978-0-9962857-2-8(5))* Northshire Pr.
Buevara, Isaias. Revelation: A Visual Journey. 2005. 96p. per. 41.99 *(978-0-9763800-3-0(X)*, 10) Orison Pubs.
Buffagni, Matteo. Asgardians of the Galaxy Vol. 2: War of the Realms. 2019. (ENG.). 112p. (YA). (gr. 8-17). pap. 15.99 *(978-1-302-91692-3(0))* Marvel Worldwide, Inc.
Buffagni, Matteo, et al. Captain America & the Avengers: the Complete Collection. 2017. 296p. (J). (gr. 4-17). pap. 34.99 *(978-1-302-90858-4(8))* Marvel Worldwide, Inc.
Buffalohead, Julie. Sacagawea. 2005. (Libros Ilustrados (Picture Bks.)). (SPA & ENG.). 40p. (J). (gr. 3-6). 16.95 *(978-0-8225-3191-3(7)*, Ediciones Lerner) Lerner Publishing Group.
—Sacagawea. Erdrich, Liselotte. 2003. (ENG.). 40p. (J). (gr. 3-6). 19.99 *(978-0-87614-646-0(9)*, Carolrhoda Bks.) Lerner Publishing Group.
Buffinet, Jacqueline. I Go Exploring. Payne, Gaynell. 2012. 34p. 21.99 *(978-0-9884657-0-1(1))* DreamLand Mediaworks LLC.
Bug, Dream. Perfect Pests. Krzak, Jennifer. 2018. (ENG.). 40p. (J). pap. 10.99 *(978-0-9998819-0-3(6))* Zion Publishing.
Buggs, Michael A. Tabard. Buggs, Michael A. 64p. (Orig.). (J). (gr. 2-6). pap. 15.00 *(978-0-9657723-0-3(6))* Mogul Comics.
Buhagiar, Jason. Freddie Learns to Behave. Fynn, Pauline. 2017. (ENG.). (J). (gr. 1-3). *(978-0-9955093-9-9(5))* Perfect Pubs.
Bui, Cat-Tuong. The Night Our Parents Went Out. Goodman, Katie & Kisiel, Soren. 2015. (ENG.). 32p. (J). (gr. -1-2). 16.95 *(978-1-57687-747-0(7)*, powerHouse Bks.) powerHse. Bks.
Bui, Thi. Chicken of the Sea. Nguyen, Viet Thanh. 2019. (J). 18.99 *(978-1-944211-73-8(X)*, 24ecb176-e51c-4100-8bb6-a7e1f8f9baef) McSweeney's Publishing.
—A Different Pond. Phi, Bao. 2017. (Fiction Picture Bks.). (ENG.). 32p. (J). (gr. k-4). lib. bdg. 23.32 *(978-1-4795-9746-8(5)*, 133351, Picture Window Bks.) Capstone.
Buisán, David, jt. illus. see Cummins, Lucy Ruth.
Bukala, Stephanie. What's That Smell? Kruse, Donald W. 2017. (ENG.). (J). (gr. k-5). pap. 14.95 *(978-0-9985191-2-8(X))* Zaccheus Entertainment Co.
Bukiert, Katarzyna. Little Women. 2017. (ENG.). 32p. (J). (gr. -1-3). *(978-1-4867-1268-7(1))* Flowerpot Children's Pr. Inc.
Bukowski, Katie. Goodnight Sleep Tight, No More Books Tonight. Bukowski, Katie. 2017. (ENG.). (J). (gr. -1-3). 7.99 *(978-0-692-98878-7(5))* Bukowski, Katie Lynn.
Bulankina, Alexandra. The Fairies of Frost. Nystrom, Hayley. 2019. (ENG.). 40p. (J). 17.99 *(978-1-948256-23-0(1))* Willow Moon Publishing.
Bulankina, Alexandra. The Fairies of Frost. Nystrom, Hayley. 2019. (ENG.). 40p. (J). pap. 13.99 ***(978-1-948256-25-4(8))*** Willow Moon Publishing.
Bulens, John. Doggie Investigation Gang, (Dig) Series: Book Four: the Case of the Missing Tutu. Katsos, Shara Puglisi. 2018. (ENG.). 78p. (J). (gr. k-4). pap. 7.95 *(978-0-578-40341-0(2))* Independent Pub.
Bulgaru, Irina. Peety & Poncho Visit Austria. Dreis, Jim. 2018. (Peety & Poncho Ser.: Vol. 6). (ENG.). 80p. (J). pap. 15.99 *(978-1-7237-3557-8(4))* Independently Published.
Bull, Andrea & Bull, Robert J. Animal Appetites: A Book of Unusual ABCs. Bull, Andrea & Bull, Robert J. 2015. (ENG.). 40p. (J). pap. 10.95 *(978-0-9948622-0-4(2))* BookBaby.
Bull, Carolyn. Los Tres Osos. Boase, Wendy. (Primeros Cuentos Ser.). (SPA.). 28p. (J). (gr. k-3). pap. 7.95 *(978-1-56014-475-5(0))* Santillana USA Publishing Co., Inc.
Bull, Peter. A Cool Kid's Field Guide to Space. Regan, Lisa. 2009. (Cool Kid's Field Guide Ser.). 26p. (J). (gr. 1-3). spiral bd. 6.99 *(978-0-8416-7142-3(7))* Hammond World Atlas Corp.
—Coral Reefs: in Danger: In Danger. Brooke, Samantha. 2008. (Penguin Young Readers, Level 3 Ser.). 48p. (J). (gr. 1-3). mass mkt. 4.99 *(978-0-448-44872-5(6)*, Penguin Young Readers) Penguin Young Readers Group.
—Horses. Date not set. (Old MacDonald Stickers Ser.). 16p. (J). 2.98 *(978-0-7525-7060-0(9))* Parragon, Inc.
—How Is My Brain Like a Supercomputer? And Other Questions about the Human Body. Stewart, Melissa. 2014. (Good Question! Ser.). 32p. (J). (gr. 1). pap. 5.95 *(978-1-4549-0681-0(2))* Sterling Publishing Co., Inc.
—Transport. (Music about Us Ser.). 64p. 9.95 *(978-1-85909-294-1(2)*, Warner Bros. Pubns.) Alfred Publishing Co., Inc.
—Under the Sea. 2004. (Out & about Ser.). 12p. (J). bds. 4.99 *(978-1-85997-806-1(1))* Byeway Bks.
—Under the Sea. (J). 2.29 *(978-1-59445-061-7(7))* Dogs in Hats Children's Publishing Co.
—Under the Sea. (Puzzle Shapes Ser.). (J). 10p. bds. *(978-2-89393-938-4(4))*; 8p. bds. *(978-2-7643-0146-3(4))* Phidal Publishing, Inc./Editions Phidal, Inc.
Bull, Robert J., jt. illus. see Bull, Andrea.
Bull Teilman, Gunvor. Sigurd & His Brave Companions: A Tale of Medieval Norway. Undset, Sigrid. 2013. (ENG.). 152p. pap. 16.95 *(978-0-8166-7826-6(X))* Univ. of Minnesota Pr.
Bulla, Randy. Father, Ford, $5 a Day: The Mullers from Missouri. Wells, Sherry A. 2003. 128p. lib. bdg. 14.00 *(978-0-934981-11-8(6))* Lawells Publishing.
Bullard, Joyce. Patience, 1 vol. Price, J. M. 2010. 16p. pap. 24.95 *(978-1-4489-6233-4(1))* PublishAmerica, Inc.
Bullas, Will. M Is for Masterpiece: An Art Alphabet. Domeniconi, David. rev. ed. 2006. (Art & Culture Ser.). (ENG.). 48p. (J). (gr. -1-3). 17.95 *(978-1-58536-276-9(X))* Sleeping Bear Pr.
Bullen, Marjorie. Silly Frog. Carsonie, Diane Lynn. 2008. 16p. per. 24.95 *(978-1-4241-9253-3(6))* America Star Bks.
Bullen, Marjorie J. Little Red Chicken, 1 vol. Carsonie, Diane Lynn. 2009. 17p. pap. 24.95 *(978-1-60813-495-3(4))* America Star Bks.
Buller, Jon. Simon's Dream. Schade, Susan. 2009. (Fog Mound Ser.: 3). (ENG.). 208p. (J). (gr. 3-7). pap. 12.99 *(978-0-689-87689-9(0)*, Aladdin) Simon & Schuster Children's Publishing.
—Travels of Thelonious. Schade, Susan. 2007. (Fog Mound Ser.: 1). (ENG.). 224p. (J). (gr. 3-7). pap. 11.99 *(978-0-689-87685-1(8)*, Aladdin) Simon & Schuster Children's Publishing.
Bullock, Brad. When I Grow Up. Jasper, J. J. 2003. 16p. (J). *(978-0-9727279-8-3(1))* Pine Hill Graphics.
Bullock, Demitrius. Ballardine. Carr, Aj. 2018. (ENG.). 38p. (J). pap. 10.15 *(978-1-7290-1022-8(9))* Independently Published.
Bullock Jr., Michael A. Christmas & the Little Dolls. Jones, Debra. 2011. 24p. pap. 24.95 *(978-1-4560-6679-6(X))* America Star Bks.
Bullock, Kathleen. Alphonso's Little Reward. Karwatowicz, Patricia. l.t. ed. 2017. (ENG.). (J). pap. 10.95 *(978-1-61633-829-6(5))* Guardian Angel Publishing, Inc.
—Clip-Clop, Tippity-Tap French Vocabulary on the Farm. Chatel, Kim. 2011. 24p. pap. 10.95 *(978-1-61633-136-8(4))* Guardian Angel Publishing, Inc.
—Nina's Best New Christmas Tradition. Karwatowicz, Patricia. l.t. ed. 2018. (ENG.). 20p. (J). (gr. k-5). pap. 10.95 *(978-1-61633-953-1(5))* Guardian Angel Publishing, Inc.
—Once Twice Thrice. Chatel, Kim. l.t. ed. 2016. (ENG.). (J). (gr. k-2). pap. 9.95 *(978-1-61633-802-2(4))* Guardian Angel Publishing, Inc.
Bullock, Kathleen. The Clown-Around Kids. Bullock, Kathleen. 2012. (ENG.). (J). pap. 10.95 *(978-1-61633-223-5(9))* Guardian Angel Publishing, Inc.
—Li-Li. Bullock, Kathleen. l.t. ed. 2019. (ENG.). 28p. (J). (gr. 1-5). pap. 10.95 *(978-1-61633-965-4(9))* Guardian Angel Publishing, Inc.
Bullon-Fernandez, Maria. One Haunted House. Lee, Calee M. 2017. (ENG.). 32p. (J). (gr. -1-k). pap. 9.99 *(978-1-5324-0199-2(X))* Xist Publishing.
Bullshields, Charles. The Legend of the Buffalo Stone, 1 vol. 2015. (ENG.). 32p. (J). (gr. 1-3). 19.95 *(978-1-927527-41-2(4))* Heritage Hse. CAN. Dist: Orca Bk. Pubs. USA.
Bulmer, Tim. Brilliant Baxter at the Fun Fair. Cordrey, Carol. 2020. (ENG.). 20p. (J). pap. ***(978-1-912850-58-7(3))*** Clink Street Publishing.
Bulpin, Chloe. The Thrilling Voyage. Hecht, Tracey & Fieber, Sarah. 2019. (Nocturnals Ser.: 4). (J). (gr. 1-7). 15.99 *(978-1-944020-21-7(7)*, Fabled Films Pr. LLC) Fabled Films LLC.
Bultje, Jan Willem, photos by. Estonia. Hiisjärv, Piret & Hiiepuu, Ene. 2006. (Looking at Europe Ser.). 48p. (YA). (gr. 5-8). 22.95 *(978-1-881508-32-8(3))* Oliver Pr., Inc.
—Latvia. Aizpuriete, Amanda. Hartgers, Katarina, tr. 2006. (Looking at Europe Ser.). 48p. (YA). (gr. 5-8). 22.95 *(978-1-881508-37-3(4))* Oliver Pr., Inc.
Bumstead, Debbie. Dientecito y la Placa Peligros. Nelson, James Gary. 2011. 16p. pap. 9.95 *(978-1-61633-132-0(1))* Guardian Angel Publishing, Inc.
—Smileytooth & Bushwack Plaque. Nelson, James Gary. 2009. 16p. pap. 9.95 *(978-1-61633-009-5(0))* Guardian Angel Publishing, Inc.
—Smileytooth & the Castle Hassle. Nelson, James Gary. 2008. 24p. pap. 10.95 *(978-1-933090-95-5(2))* Guardian Angel Publishing, Inc.
—Smileytooth & the Plaque Attack. Nelson, James Gary. 2008. 20p. pap. 10.95 *(978-1-935137-48-1(4))* Guardian Angel Publishing, Inc.
Bumstead, Heather L. Why Mama Wasn't Worried. Kudagammana, Bhante Sila. 2019. (ENG.). 42p. (J). 28.95 ***(978-1-64801-116-0(0))***; pap. 18.95 ***(978-1-64531-600-8(9))*** Newman Springs Publishing, Inc.
Bunch, Paul. Just an Ordinary Little Dog: Barnaby's Story. Mason, Alexis. 2010. (J). *(978-0-9755280-4-4(1))* Insight Technical Education.
Bundad, Mike. Earth Day. Berne, Emma Carlson. 2018. (Holidays in Rhythm & Rhyme Ser.). (ENG.). 24p. (C). (gr. k-2). lib. bdg. 33.99 *(978-1-68410-378-2(9)*, 140362); pap. 7.95 *(978-1-68410-191-7(3)*, 137466) Cantata Learning.
—Green. Doering, Amanda. 2018. (Sing Your Colors! Ser.). (ENG.). 24p. (J). (gr. -1-2). 33.99 *(978-1-68410-311-9(8)*, 140698); lib. bdg. 33.99 incl. audio compact disk *(978-1-68410-117-7(4)*, 31851) Cantata Learning.
Bundoc, Oliver Kryzz. Alex Cavey: Woodcutting Adventure. Kamen, Bruce. 2018. (ENG.). 30p. (J). pap. *(978-1-9164474-0-0(6))* Mila-K Publishing.
—Misty Blue: Kloudsville Series. Marie, K. 2018. (Kloudsville Ser.: 1). (ENG.). 36p. 21.99 *(978-0-9989541-1-0(X))* BookBaby.
Bunk, Tomas. Quantoons: MetaphysicalIllustrations by Tomas Bunk. Eisenkraft, Arthur & Kirkpatrick, Larry D. 2005. (ENG.). 174p. (YA). pap. 27.95 *(978-0-87355-265-3(2))* National Science Teachers Assn.
Bunker, Natalie. When I Grow Up. Evans, Melissa. 2018. (ENG.). 24p. (J). pap. 12.95 *(978-1-64300-317-7(8))* Covenant Bks.
Bunker, Thomas. The Doctor Said I Have Leukemi. Bryant, Cathy. 2012. 24p. pap. 24.95 *(978-1-4560-6929-2(2))* America Star Bks.
—Eric & Wrinkles Meet the Bunnyworms. Bradford, Danette J. 2012. 28p. pap. 24.95 *(978-1-4560-4261-5(0))* America Star Bks.
—Ritzi's Bath. Goodman, Peggy. 2012. 28p. 24.95 *(978-1-4560-4138-0(X))* America Star Bks.
Bunker, Tom. Trinity Goes to Soccer Camp. Myers, Bob. 2012. 36p. 24.95 *(978-1-4560-2906-7(1))* America Star Bks.
Bunkus, Denise. Groundhog Gets a Say. Swallow, Pamela Curtis & Swallow, Pamela C. 2007. (ENG.). 40p. (J). (gr. k-3). pap. 7.99 *(978-0-14-240896-4(4)*, Puffin Books) Penguin Young Readers Group.
Bunster-Elsesser, Alejandra. The Bird That Forgot How to Fly Goes to the Everglades: Fairytales from Historic Florida. Bunster-Esesser, Alejandra. 2016. (Fairytales from Historic Florida Ser.: Vol. 2). (ENG.). (J). (gr. k-6). pap. 15.00 *(978-0-692-73515-2(1))* Bunster, Alejandra.
Bunting, Matt, jt. illus. see Faulkner, Matt.
Burach, Ross. Billy Bloo Is Stuck in Goo. Hamburg, Jennifer. 2017. 32p. (J). (gr. -1-3). 16.99 *(978-0-545-88015-2(7)*, Scholastic Pr.) Scholastic, Inc.
—Snowman's Magic Hat: A Lift-The-Flap Book. Burton, Jeffrey. 2019. (ENG.). 14p. (J). (-k). bds. 7.99 *(978-1-5344-5325-8(3)*, Little Simon) Little Simon.
Burach, Ross. Hi-Five Animals! Burach, Ross. 2018. (ENG.). 20p. (J). (gr. -1 — 1). bds. 6.99 *(978-1-338-24567-7(8)*, Scholastic Pr.) Scholastic, Inc.
—I Am Not a Chair! Burach, Ross. 2017. (ENG.). 40p. (J). (gr. -1-3). 17.99 *(978-0-06-236016-8(7))* HarperCollins Pubs.
—Let's Play Make Bee-Lieve. Burach, Ross. 2020. (Bumble & Bee Ser.: 2). (ENG.). 48p. (J). (gr. -1-1). lib. bdg. 23.99 *(978-1-338-50526-9(2))* Scholastic, Inc.
—Let's Play Make Bee-Lieve - An Acorn Book. Burach, Ross. 2020. (Bumble & Bee Ser.: 2). (ENG.). 48p. (J). (gr. -1-1). pap. 4.99 *(978-1-338-50525-2(4))* Scholastic, Inc.
—Pine & Boof: Blast Off! Burach, Ross. 2018. (ENG.). 32p. (J). (gr. -1-3). 17.99 *(978-0-06-241852-4(1))* HarperCollins Pubs.
—Pine & Boof: the Lucky Leaf. Burach, Ross. 2017. (ENG.). 40p. (J). (gr. -1-3). 17.99 *(978-0-06-241850-0(5))* HarperCollins Pubs.
—There's a Giraffe in My Soup. Burach, Ross. 2016. (ENG.). 32p. (J). (gr. -1-3). 17.99 *(978-0-06-236014-4(0))* HarperCollins Pubs.
Buran, Jon, jt. illus. see Di Vito, Andrea.
Burbank, Addison. Know Your Mass. Manousos, Demetrius. 2006. 96p. (YA). per. 14.95 *(978-1-892331-44-1(6))* Angelus Pr.
Burbridge, William J. Animals, Animals Everywhere. Murphy, D. Cathy. 2013. 16p. pap. 24.95 *(978-1-4626-2414-0(6))* America Star Bks.
Burch, Benjamin. Bouncy Tires! (Blaze & the Monster Machines) Tillworth, Mary. 2016. (Little Golden Book Ser.). (ENG.). 24p. (J). (gr. -1-k). 4.99 *(978-0-553-53891-5(8)*, Golden Bks.) Random Hse. Children's Bks.
—Dragon Hiccups. Depken, Kristen L. 2015. (Little Golden Book Ser.). (ENG.). 24p. (J). (-k). 4.99 *(978-0-553-52310-2(4)*, Golden Bks.) Random Hse. Children's Bks.
—Mighty Troll & Wonder Dragon. Depken, Kristen L. 2016. (Little Golden Book Ser.). (ENG.). 24p. (J). (gr. -1-k). 4.99 *(978-1-101-93149-3(3)*, Golden Bks.) Random Hse. Children's Bks.
Burch, Benjamin. Time to Be Kind! (Corn & Peg) Cooke, Annie. 2020. (Little Golden Book Ser.). (ENG.). 24p. (J). (-k). 4.99 ***(978-0-593-12394-2(8)***, Golden Bks.) Random Hse. Children's Bks.
Burch, Benjamin. Wind Power! (Blaze & the Monster Machines) Golden Books. 2016. (Little Golden Book Ser.). (ENG.). 24p. (J). (-k). 4.99 *(978-1-101-93682-5(7)*, Golden Bks.) Random Hse. Children's Bks.
Burch, Deborah. God's Greatest Gift. 2007. 32p. (J). lib. bdg. 17.95 *(978-0-9796477-7-2(0))* God's Greatest Gift, LLC.
Burch, Deborah. God's Greatest Gift. Burch, Deborah. l.t. ed. 2006. (ENG.). 32p. (J). lib. bdg. *(978-0-9779445-3-8(0))* Zoe Life Publishing.
Burch, Ellen. Potcakes. Rybak, B. E. 2019. (Potcakes Ser.: Vol. 1). (FRE.). 34p. (J). ***(978-1-7752110-2-0(9))*** Tellwell Talent.

Burch, Lynda S., photos by. Meet Me at the Park! Burch, Lynda S. 2005. 64p. (J). E-Book 6.00 incl. cd-rom *(978-1-933090-15-3(4))* Guardian Angel Publishing, Inc.
—Wicky wacky Things that Go! Boats 1. Burch, Lynda S. 2004. 28p. (J). E-Book 9.95 incl. cd-rom *(978-1-933090-03-0(0))* Guardian Angel Publishing, Inc.
—Wicky Wacky Things that Go! Busses. Burch, Lynda S. 2004. 28p. (J). E-Book 9.95 incl. cd-rom *(978-1-933090-06-1(5))* Guardian Angel Publishing, Inc.
—Wicky Wacky Things that Go! Emergency Vehicles. Burch, Lynda S. 2004. 30p. (J). E-Book 9.95 incl. cd-rom *(978-1-933090-13-9(8))* Guardian Angel Publishing, Inc.
—Wicky Wacky Things that Go! Tractors. Burch, Lynda S. 2004. 28p. (J). E-Book 9.95 incl. cd-rom *(978-1-933090-09-2(X))* Guardian Angel Publishing, Inc.
—Wicky Wacky Things that Go! Trains 1. Burch, Lynda S. 2004. 16p. (J). E-Book 9.95 incl. cd-rom *(978-1-933090-02-3(2))* Guardian Angel Publishing, Inc.
—Wicky Wacky Things That Go! Trucks. Burch, Lynda S. 2004. 28p. (J). E-Book 9.95 incl. cd-rom *(978-1-933090-11-5(1))* Guardian Angel Publishing, Inc.
—Zoom Zoom Zoom Come Count with Me! Burch, Lynda S. 2005. 20p. (J). E-Book 6.00 incl. cd-rom *(978-1-933090-14-6(6))* Guardian Angel Publishing, Inc.
Burch, Lynda S. & Roberts, MarySue, photos by. I SEE Seaside Birds! 2006. 32p. (J). 16.99 *(978-1-933090-16-0(2))* Guardian Angel Publishing, Inc.
—I SEE Seaside Birds! Burch, Lynda S. 2004. 52p. (J). E-Book 9.95 incl. cd-rom *(978-1-933090-05-4(7))* Guardian Angel Publishing, Inc.
—Wicky Wacky Things that Go! Automobiles 1. Burch, Lynda S. 2004. 30p. (J). E-Book 9.95 incl. cd-rom *(978-1-933090-12-2(X))* Guardian Angel Publishing, Inc.
Burchak, Evgenija. The Year after Christmas. James, Michael. 2018. (ENG.). 32p. (J). pap. 9.90 *(978-1-7309-0978-8(7))* Independently Published.
Burcham, David. Joseph & Snowy Joe Blue, 1 vol. Ross, Patrick. 2009. 25p. pap. 24.95 *(978-1-61582-314-7(X))* PublishAmerica, Inc.
—Oliver: The Great Escape. Ross, Patrick. 2009. 34p. pap. 24.95 *(978-1-60749-151-4(6))* America Star Bks.
—Runt River Rat's Wild Ride, 1 vol. Ross, Patrick. 2010. 24p. 24.95 *(978-1-4512-0067-6(6))* PublishAmerica, Inc.
Burchartz, Roxanne. Shamrock Sean & the Bird's Nest. Gogarty, Brian. 2007. (ENG.). 12p. (J). pap. 7.95 *(978-0-86278-969-5(9))* O'Brien Pr., Ltd., The IRL. Dist: Dufour Editions, Inc.
—Shamrock Sean & the Wishing Well. Gogarty, Brian. 2007. (ENG.). 12p. (J). pap. 7.95 *(978-0-86278-967-1(2))* O'Brien Pr., Ltd., The IRL. Dist: Dufour Editions, Inc.
—Shamrock Sean Goes Fishing. Gogarty, Brian. 2007. (ENG.). 12p. (J). pap. 7.95 *(978-0-86278-968-8(0))* O'Brien Pr., Ltd., The IRL. Dist: Dufour Editions, Inc.
Burchell, Scott, jt. illus. see Watson, Mia.
Burchett, Rick. Cosmic Bounty Hunter, 1 vol. Hoena, Blake A. & Loughridge, Lee. 2010. (Superman Ser.). (ENG.). 56p. (J). (gr. 3-6). lib. bdg. 26.65 *(978-1-4342-2133-9(4)*, Stone Arch Bks.) Capstone.
—Cosmic Bounty Hunter, 1 vol. Loughridge, Lee & Hoena, Blake A. 2014. (Superman Ser.). (ENG.). 56p. (J). (gr. 3-6). pap. 4.95 *(978-1-4342-2769-0(3)*, Stone Arch Bks.) Capstone.
—Phantasm Strikes!, 1 vol. Slott, Dan et al. 2013. (Batman Adventures Ser.). (ENG.). 32p. (J). (gr. 3-6). 22.60 *(978-1-4342-6035-2(6)*, Stone Arch Bks.) Capstone.
—Prankster of Prime Time, 1 vol. Pasko, Martin & Loughridge, Lee. 2014. (Superman Ser.). (ENG.). 56p. (J). (gr. 3-6). pap. 4.95 *(978-1-4342-2763-8(4)*, Stone Arch Bks.) Capstone.
—The Puppet Master's Revenge, 1 vol. Lemke, Donald B. 2009. (Batman Ser.). (ENG.). 56p. (J). (gr. 3-6). 26.65 *(978-1-4342-1560-4(1)*, Stone Arch Bks.) Capstone.
—Puppet Master's Revenge. Lemke, Donald. 2013. (Batman Ser.). (ENG.). 56p. (J). (gr. 3-6). pap. 4.95 *(978-1-4342-1727-1(2)*, Stone Arch Bks.) Capstone.
—The Shadow Masters. Kupperberg, Paul. (Superman Ser.). (ENG.). 56p. (J). (gr. 3-6). 2014. pap. 4.95 *(978-1-4342-2768-3(5))*; 2010. lib. bdg. 26.65 *(978-1-4342-2079-0(6))* Capstone. (Stone Arch Bks.)
Burchett, Rick & Austin, Terry. Be Careful What You Wish For... McCLOUD, Scott. 2012. (Superman Adventures Ser.). (ENG.). 32p. (J). (gr. 2-5). lib. bdg. 22.60 *(978-1-4342-4550-2(0)*, Stone Arch Bks.) Capstone.
—Distant Thunder, 1 vol. McCLOUD, Scott. 2012. (Superman Adventures Ser.). (ENG.). 32p. (J). (gr. 2-5). 22.60 *(978-1-4342-4551-9(9)*, Stone Arch Bks.) Capstone.
—Eye to Eye, 1 vol. McCLOUD, Scott. 2012. (Superman Adventures Ser.). (ENG.). 32p. (J). (gr. 2-5). lib. bdg. 22.60 *(978-1-4342-4552-6(7)*, Stone Arch Bks.) Capstone.
—Jinx - Little Miss Steps. Torres, J. 2013. (Jinx Ser.: 2). (ENG.). 112p. (YA). (gr. 5). pap. 9.99 *(978-1-936975-41-9(6))* Archie Comic Pubns., Inc.
—Little Miss Steps. Torres, J. 2013. (Jinx Ser.: 2). (ENG.). 114p. (YA). (gr. 5). 16.99 *(978-1-936975-42-6(4))* Archie Comic Pubns., Inc.
—Men of Steel, 1 vol. Dini, Paul. 2012. (Superman Adventures Ser.). (ENG.). 32p. (J). (gr. 2-5). lib. bdg. 22.60 *(978-1-4342-4549-6(7)*, Stone Arch Bks.) Capstone.
Burchett, Rick, jt. illus. see Austin, Terry.
Burchfield, Cindy. Gimme, Gimme Moocher Marmots. Burchfield, Cindy. 2007. 48p. per. 18.95 *(978-1-59858-457-8(X))* Dog Ear Publishing, LLC.
Burchwell, Erin. Harriett's Homecoming: A High-Flying Tour of Cincinnati. Levine, Susan Sachs. 2012. (ENG.). 32p. (J). (gr. -1-3). 19.95 *(978-1-933197-97-5(8))* Orange Frazer Pr.
Burchwell, Erin McCauley. Packard Takes Flight: A Bird's-Eye View of Columbus, Ohio. Levine, Susan Sachs. 2010. (ENG.). 32p. 17.99 *(978-1-60949-051-5(7)*, History Pr., The) Arcadia Publishing.
Burckhardt, Marc. Chasing Redbird. Creech, Sharon. 2012. (ENG.). 272p. (J). (gr. 4-18). pap. 7.99 *(978-0-06-440696-3(2)*, HarperCollins) HarperCollins Pubs. Ltd. GBR. Dist: HarperCollins Pubs.
—Daddy Loves His Little Girl. Cash, John Carter. 2010. (ENG.). 32p. (J). (gr. -1-3). 16.99 *(978-1-4169-7482-6(2)*, Little Simon Inspirations) Little Simon Inspirations.
—A Drive in the Country. Rosen, Michael J. 2007. (ENG.). 32p. (J). (gr. k-4). 16.99 *(978-0-7636-2140-7(4))* Candlewick Pr.
—Spring, Summer, Autumn, Winter. Siebert, Diane. 2005. (J). *(978-1-59336-299-7(4))*; pap. *(978-1-59336-300-0(1))* Mondo Publishing.
—When Bob Met Woody: The Story of the Young Bob Dylan. Golio, Gary. 2011. (ENG.). 40p. (J). (gr. 3-7). 17.99 *(978-0-316-11299-4(2))* Little, Brown Bks. for Young Readers.
Burd, Clara M. Stories of Great Adventures. Bailey, Carolyn Sherwin. 2005. reprint ed. pap. 24.95 *(978-1-4179-0215-6(9))* Kessinger Publishing, LLC.
Burda, Alexandra. Du Kan Flyga, Lilla Fågel: You Can Fly, Little Bird, Swedish Edition. Pere, Tuula. Torstensson, Elisabeth, tr. 2018. (SWE.). 36p. (J). (gr. k-4). *(978-952-7107-08-9(3))*; pap. *(978-952-5878-46-2(5))* Wickwick oy.
Burda, Alexandra. I Need a Pet! Smith, Robin J. 2016. (ENG.). 40p. (J). pap. 12.00 ***(978-1-5376-1335-2(9))*** CreateSpace Independent Publishing Platform.
Burda, Alexandra. Osaat Lentää, Lintu Pieni: Finnish Edition of You Can Fly, Little Bird. Pere, Tuula. 2018. (FIN.). 36p. (J). (gr. k-4). *(978-952-7107-07-2(5))*; pap. *(978-952-5878-96-7(1))* Wickwick oy.
—You Can Fly, Little Bird. Pere, Tuula. Korman, Susan, ed. 2018. (ENG.). 36p. (J). (gr. k-4). *(978-952-7107-06-5(7))*; pap. *(978-952-5878-26-4(0))* Wickwick oy.
Burden, Andrea. Kerka's Book. Bozarth, Jan. 2010. (Fairy Godmother Academy Ser.: 2). (ENG.). 224p. (J). (gr. 3-7). pap. 6.99 *(978-0-375-85183-4(6)*, Yearling) Random Hse. Children's Bks.
—Zally's Book, 3. Bozarth, Jan. 2010. (Fairy Godmother Academy Ser.: No. 3). (ENG.). 208p. (J). (gr. 4-6). lib. bdg. 22.44 *(978-0-375-95185-5(7))* Random House Publishing Group.
—Zally's Book. Bozarth, Jan. 2010. (Fairy Godmother Academy Ser.: 3). (ENG.). 208p. (J). (gr. 3-7). pap. 6.99 *(978-0-375-85185-8(2)*, Yearling) Random Hse. Children's Bks.
Burden, P. John. Mendel Rosenbusch: Tales for Jewish Children. Weber, Ilse. Fisher, Hans, tr. from GER. 2006. Orig. Title: Mendel Rosenbusch: Geschichen Fur Jud Kinder. 128p. (J). pap. 18.00 *(978-1-933480-05-3(X))* Bunim and Bannigan Ltd.
—Mendel Rosenbusch: Tales for Jewish Children, 1 vol. Weber, Ilse. Fisher, Hans & Fisher, Ruth, trs. ed. 2006. Orig. Title: Mendel Rosenbusch: Geschichen Fur Jud Kinder. (ENG.). 58p. (J). lib. bdg. 18.95 *(978-1-933480-04-6(1))* Bunim and Bannigan Ltd.
Burfoot, Ella. Bear & Me. 2013. (J). *(978-1-4351-4753-9(7))* Barnes & Noble, Inc.
—Don't Kiss the Frog! Princess Stories with Attitude. 2013. (ENG.). 80p. (YA). (gr. 1-5). pap. 8.99 *(978-0-7534-6946-0(4)*, 9780753469460, Kingfisher) Roaring Brook Pr.
Burfoot, Ella. Louie & the Monsters. Burfoot, Ella. 2005. 32p. (J). (gr. -1-2). 6.95 *(978-1-58925-395-7(7))* Tiger Tales.
Burg, Donna. Cow Moooves Through the Books of the Bible: Genesis. Alsbrooks, Stephanie. 2004. (J). bds. 9.99 *(978-1-4183-0002-9(0))* Christ Inspired, Inc.
—Cow Moooves Through the Books of the Bible: Job. Alsbrooks, Stephanie. 2004. (J). bds. 9.99 *(978-1-4183-0006-7(3))* Christ Inspired, Inc.
—Cow Moooves Through the Books of the Bible - Exodus. Alsbrooks, Stephanie. 2004. (J). bds. 9.99 *(978-1-4183-0007-4(1))* Christ Inspired, Inc.
—Cow Moooves Through the Books of the Bible - Joshua. Alsbrooks, Stephanie. 2004. (J). bds. 9.99 *(978-1-4183-0017-3(9))* Christ Inspired, Inc.
Burgerman, Jon. Splat! Burgerman, Jon. 2017. (ENG.). 32p. (J). (-k). 16.99 *(978-0-7352-2876-4(0)*, Dial Bks) Penguin Young Readers Group.
Burgess, Dan. Aquaman: Undertow. Behling, Steve. 2018. (Aquaman Ser.). (ENG.). 224p. (J). (gr. 3-7). 12.99 *(978-0-06-287419-1(5)*, HarperFestival) HarperCollins Pubs.
Burgess, Daniel. What Happened in Tutterhelm. Slater, Melissa. 2018. (ENG.). 28p. (J). (gr. k-6). pap. 11.50 *(978-1-63135-777-0(8))* Strategic Book Publishing & Rights Agency (SBPRA).
Burgess, Don & Schalkwijk, Bob, photos by. Could You Live Like a Tarahumara? Podrías Vivir Como un Tarahumara? Bilingual English & Spanish. Burgess, Don. 2017. (Kids' Books from Here & There Ser.). (ENG., (J). (gr. 4-6). 24.95 *(978-1-939604-19-4(2))* Barranca Pr.
Burgess, Dyan. Crashing into a Police Car. Burgess, Lily. 2016. (ENG.). (J). pap. *(978-1-925181-18-0(9))* D & M Fancy Pastry.
Burgess, Gina. Luckie's Ocean Adventure. Martin, Terri. Welwood, Margaret, ed. 2019. (ENG.). 34p. (J). pap. 9.75 ***(978-1-0754-8140-6(6))*** Independently Published.
Burgess, H. & Fitterling, Michael A. A Victorious Union. Optic, Oliver. 2005. (Blue & Gray Ser.). (ENG.). 369p. (J). (gr. -1-12). reprint ed. pap. 19.99 *(978-1-890623-13-5(X))* Lost Classic Bks.
Burgess, Mark. The Best Bear in All the World. Willis, Jeanne et al. 2016. (Winnie-The-Pooh Ser.). (ENG.). 128p. (J). (gr. 3-7). 21.99 *(978-0-399-18747-6(2)*, Dutton Books for Young Readers) Penguin Young Readers Group.
—Return to the Hundred Acre Wood. Benedictus, David. 2009. (Winnie-The-Pooh Ser.). (ENG.). 216p. (J). (gr. 3-7). 21.99 *(978-0-525-42160-3(2)*, Dutton Books for Young Readers) Penguin Young Readers Group.
Burgess, Mark. Mutiny at Crossbones Bay. Burgess, Mark. Cox, Phil Roxbee, ed. 2006. (Usborne Puzzle Adventures Ser.). 48p. (J). (gr. 3-7). pap. 4.99 *(978-0-7945-1407-5(3)*, Usborne) EDC Publishing.
Burgess, Omar. Hassan & Aneesa Celebrate Eid. Rahim, Yasmeen. 2018. (Hassan & Aneesa Ser.). (ENG.). 24p. (J). pap. 5.99 *(978-0-86037-698-9(2))* Kube Publishing Ltd. GBR. Dist: Consortium Bk. Sales & Distribution.
—Hassan & Aneesa Go to Masjid. Rahim, Yasmeen. 2016. (Hassan & Aneesa Ser.). (ENG.). 28p. (J). pap. 5.99 *(978-0-86037-521-0(8))* Kube Publishing Ltd. GBR. Dist: Consortium Bk. Sales & Distribution.
—Hassan & Aneesa Love Ramadan. Rahim, Yasmeen. 2017. (Hassan & Aneesa Ser.). (ENG.). 24p. (J). pap. 5.99 *(978-0-86037-642-2(7))* Kube Publishing Ltd. GBR. Dist: Consortium Bk. Sales & Distribution.
—Hassan & Aneesah Go to Madrasa. Rahim, Yasmeen. 2016. (Hassan & Aneesa Ser.). (ENG.). 16p. (J). pap. 5.99 *(978-0-86037-459-6(9))* Kube Publishing Ltd. GBR. Dist: Consortium Bk. Sales & Distribution.
—My Special Angels: Two Noble Scribes. Noor, Razana. 2017. (ENG.). 24p. (J). (gr. -1-2). 8.95 *(978-0-86037-645-3(1))* Kube Publishing Ltd. GBR. Dist: Consortium Bk. Sales & Distribution.
—Zak & His Little Lies. Mair, J. Samia. 2018. (ENG.). 32p. (J). (gr. -1-2). 12.95 *(978-0-86037-627-9(3))* Kube Publishing Ltd. GBR. Dist: Consortium Bk. Sales & Distribution.
Burgin, Norma. La Pequena Tortuga y la Cancion del Mar. Cain, Sheridan. 2003. (SPA.). 24p. (J). (gr. k-2). *(978-84-8418-037-1(9)*, ZZ30445) Zendrera Zariquiey, Editorial ESP. Dist: Lectorum Pubns., Inc.
Burgin, Roger. Legendary 12: Valy Tiger Vol. 3: the Wild One. Ngo, Son Bac. 2017. (Legendary 12 Ser.: Vol. 3). (ENG.). (J). (gr. 2-6). pap. *(978-0-9944947-6-4(9))* Jaguar Ngo Investment Pty Ltd.
Burgler, Nathalie. Little Pro Skater. Michel, Henry. 2019. (ENG.). 26p. (J). pap. 18.95 *(978-1-0769-5190-8(2))* Independently Published.
Burgting, Peter. Dungeons & Dragons: Dark Sun - Ianto's Tomb. Irvine, Alex. 2011. (Dungeons & Dragons Ser.). (ENG.). 132p. 24.99 *(978-1-60010-996-6(9)*, 9781600109966) Idea & Design Works, LLC.
Burick Jr., Michael, jt. illus. see Burick, Rebecca.
Burick, Rebecca & Burick Jr., Michael. Little Daisy Tutu. Burick, Rebecca. 2012. 28p. pap. 24.95 *(978-1-4560-6883-7(0))* America Star Bks.
Burk, Penny Ross. The Glass Bottle. Burk, Penny Ross. 2019. (ENG.). 74p. (J). (gr. 1-3). pap. 18.00 *(978-0-9966940-8-7(0))* Penzart.
Burke, Chris, et al. Silent Forest, 1. Beranek, Adam et al. 2004. 136p. per. 11.95 *(978-0-9752582-0-0(6))* Silent Devil Productions.
Burke, Daniel. Of Wolves & Lambs & Others. Tsaliovich, Anatoly. 2005. 73p. (YA). pap. 12.99 *(978-0-9773816-0-9(9))* ATInternational Pubs.
Burke, Erin & Torche, Jen. Merriam-Webster Kids: Words All Around! 2019. (ENG.). 192p. (J). spiral bd. *(978-1-5037-4577-3(5)*, 73055fc1-0edd-406e-afce-9524228b51f0, p i kids) Phoenix International Publications, Inc.
Burke, Fatti. I Look up to... Malala Yousafzai. Membrino, Anna. 2019. 22p. (J). (— 1). bds. 7.99 *(978-0-525-64440-8(7)*, Random Hse. Bks. for Young Readers) Random Hse. Children's Bks.
—I Look up to... Michelle Obama. Membrino, Anna. 2018. (ENG.). 22p. (J). (— 1). bds. 7.99 *(978-0-525-57954-0(0)*, Random Hse. Bks. for Young Readers) Random Hse. Children's Bks.
—I Look up to... Misty Copeland. Membrino, Anna. 2019. (ENG.). 22p. (J). (— 1). bds. 7.99 *(978-1-9848-5214-4(0)*, Random Hse. Bks. for Young Readers) Random Hse. Children's Bks.
—I Look up to... Oprah Winfrey. Membrino, Anna. 2019. (ENG.). 22p. (J). (— 1). bds. 7.99 *(978-1-9848-5212-0(4)*, Random Hse. Bks. for Young Readers) Random Hse. Children's Bks.
—I Look up to... Ruth Bader Ginsburg. Membrino, Anna. 2018. (ENG.). 22p. (J). (— 1). bds. 7.99 *(978-0-525-57952-6(4)*, Random Hse. Bks. for Young Readers) Random Hse. Children's Bks.
—I Look up to... Serena Williams. Membrino, Anna. 2019. 22p. (J). (— 1). bds. 7.99 *(978-0-525-64442-2(3)*, Random Hse. Bks. for Young Readers) Random Hse. Children's Bks.
—Wheels: Cars, Cogs, Carousels, & Other Things That Spin. Turner, Tracey. (Wheels Ser.). (ENG.). 48p. (J). 2020. pap. 10.99 ***(978-0-7534-7532-4(4)***, 900208201); 2019. 16.99 *(978-0-7534-7531-7(6)*, 900208200) Roaring Brook Pr. (Kingfisher).
Burke, Frank. Animal Antics. Burke, Frank. (Orig.). (J). pap. 3.59 *(978-0-927206-05-1(6))* Author's Connection Pr.
Burke, Jacquie. A Rainbow of Rabbits. Burke, Jacquie. Sames, Sandra, ed. 2019. (ENG.). 44p. (J). pap. *(978-0-473-47336-5(4))* Tinker & Tiger.
Burke, Jim. A Christmas Gift for Mama. Thompson, Lauren. 2003. (J). pap. 16.95 *(978-0-590-30726-0(6))* Scholastic, Inc.
—Johnny Appleseed: The Legend & the Truth. Yolen, Jane. (ENG.). 32p. (J). (gr. 1-4). 2011. pap. 7.99 *(978-0-06-059137-3(4))*; 2008. 16.99 *(978-0-06-059135-9(8))* HarperCollins Pubs.
—Miss Little's Gift. Wood, Douglas. 2017. 32p. (J). (gr. k-4). 6.99 *(978-0-7636-9837-9(7))* Candlewick Pr.
—Walt Whitman. Levin, Jonathan, ed. 2008. (Poetry for Young People Ser.: 6). 48p. (J). (gr. 3-7). pap. 6.95 *(978-1-4027-5477-7(9))* Sterling Publishing Co., Inc.
Burke, Kathryn Schaar. Mule Boy. Gilbert, Joan. 2004. 248p. (YA). per. 12.95 *(978-0-930973-30-8(5))* Delaware &Lehigh National Heritage Corridor, Inc.
Burke, Randy Du. Yummy: The Last Days of a Southside Shorty, 1 vol. Neri, G. 2010. (ENG.). 94p. (J). (gr. 5-12). pap. 16.95 *(978-1-58430-267-4(4)*, 13e4424e-a7d8-4c18-a663-e37931d0485b) Lee & Low Bks., Inc.
Burke, Ruth Anne. Cat Tales. Brown, Pauline A. 2013. 146p. (J). pap. 9.99 *(978-0-9838653-2-2(9))* Doorlight Pubns.
—Mama's Books: An Oregon Trail Story. Nash, Nancy. 2013. (J). pap. 9.95 *(978-0-9838653-6-0(1))* Doorlight Pubns.
Burke, Shane. Tube World. Swanson, David. 2012. 158p. pap. 10.00 *(978-0-9830830-4-7(5))* Swanson, David.
—Tube World. Swanson, David C. N. 2012. 158p. pap. 25.00 *(978-0-9830830-2-3(9))* Swanson, David.
Burke, Steven. The Little House That Didn't Have a Home. Sullivan, Neil. 2018. (ENG.). 36p. (J). (gr. -1-k). 10.99 *(978-1-78711-307-7(8)*, Hubble & Hattie) Veloce Publishing Ltd. GBR. Dist: Hachette Bk. Group.
—My Grandad Can Draw Anything: But, He Can't Draw Hands! Sullivan, Neil. 2020. (ENG.). 36p. (J). (gr. -1-3). 10.99 *(978-1-78711-515-6(1)*, Hubble & Hattie) Veloce Publishing Ltd. GBR. Dist: Hachette Bk. Group.
Burke, Susan S. Venus & Serena Williams. Swanson, June. 2003. (You Must Be Joking! Riddle Bks.). 32p. (J). (gr. 2-5). pap. 5.95 *(978-0-8225-9842-8(6))* Lerner Publishing Group.
Burke, Tina. My First Kitten. Chimes, Lisa. 2016. (ENG.). 32p. (J). 10.99 *(978-1-61067-517-8(7))* Kane Miller.
—My First Puppy. Chimes, Lisa. 2016. (ENG.). 32p. (J). 10.99 *(978-1-61067-516-1(9))* Kane Miller.
Burkert, Howard, photos by. Love You, Teddy - a Tail of Loss & Hope. Ulch, Virginia. 2007. 32p. per. 18.95 *(978-1-59858-354-0(9))* Dog Ear Publishing, LLC.
Burkert, Nancy Ekholm. Mouse & Lion. Burkert, Rand. 2011. 32p. (J). (gr. -1-3). 18.99 *(978-0-545-10147-9(6)*, Di Capua, Michael) Scholastic, Inc.
Burkert, Nancy Ekholm, jt. illus. see Crane, Jordan.
Burkes-Larrañaga, Dustin. Johnny Appleseed Plants Trees Across the Land, 1 vol. 2014. (American Folk Legends Ser.). (ENG.). 32p. (J). (gr. k-2). lib. bdg. 27.99 *(978-1-4795-5428-7(6)*, Picture Window Bks.) Capstone.
Burkes-Larrañaga, Dustin, et al. Thorns, Horns, & Crescent Moons: Reading & Writing Nature Poems, 1 vol. Fandel, Jennifer & Miller, Connie Colwell. 2014. (Poet in You Ser.). (ENG.). 32p. (J). (gr. 2-4). lib. bdg. 27.99 *(978-1-4795-2197-5(3)*, Picture Window Bks.) Capstone.
Burket, Shelia. Wollie the Wheelbarrow. Hunt, Debbie Colleen. 24p. 2012. 24.95 *(978-1-4626-9969-8(3))*; 2011. pap. 24.95 *(978-1-4626-2980-0(6))* America Star Bks.
Burkett, D. Brent. Dream-of-Jade: The Emperor's Cat. Alexander, Lloyd. 2005. (ENG.). 48p. (J). (gr. 3-7). 17.95 *(978-0-8126-2736-7(9))* Cricket Bks.
—Reggie. Bunting, Eve. 2006. (ENG.). 112p. (J). (gr. 1-4). 16.95 *(978-0-8126-2746-6(6))* Cricket Bks.
Burkholder, Andrew. Qviet. 2015. (ENG.). 248p. pap. 22.95 *(978-1-937541-11-8(8))* 2dcloud.
Burkholder, Edith. Growing with the Millers. Martin, Mildred A. 2012. 144p. (J). *(978-1-884377-23-5(8))* Green Pastures Pr.
—Missionary Stories with the Millers. Martin, Mildred A. 2009. 208p. (J). *(978-1-884377-17-4(3))*; pap. *(978-1-884377-16-7(5))* Green Pastures Pr.
—Wisdom & the Millers: Proverbs for Children. Martin, Mildred A. 2009. 159p. (J). *(978-1-884377-15-0(7))*; pap. *(978-1-884377-14-3(9))* Green Pastures Pr.
Burks, James. All Paws on Deck. Young, Jessica. 2016. (Haggis & Tank Unleashed Ser.: 1). (ENG.). 80p. (J). (gr. k-2). pap. 4.99 *(978-0-545-81886-5(9))* Scholastic, Inc.
—The Best Friend Plan: The Adventures of Allie & Amy 1. Calmenson, Stephanie & Cole, Joanna. 2020. (Quix Ser.). (ENG.). 96p. (J). (gr. k-3). 16.99 *(978-1-5344-5251-0(6))*; pap. 5.99 *(978-1-5344-5250-3(8))* Simon & Schuster Children's Publishing. (Aladdin).
—Digging for Dinos. Young, Jessica. 2016. (Haggis & Tank Unleashed Ser.: 2). (ENG.). 80p. (J). (gr. k-2). 15.99 *(978-0-545-81889-6(3))* Scholastic, Inc.
—Howl at the Moon: a Branches Book (Haggis & Tank Unleashed #3) Young, Jessica. 2017. (Haggis & Tank Unleashed Ser.: 3). (ENG.). 80p. (J). (gr. k-2). pap. 4.99 *(978-1-338-04525-3(3))* Scholastic, Inc.
—Itty Bitty Kitty. Holub, Joan. 2015. (ENG.). 32p. (J). (gr. -1-3). 17.99 *(978-0-06-232219-7(2))* HarperCollins Pubs.
—Itty Bitty Kitty: Firehouse Fun. Holub, Joan. 2016. 32p. (J). *(978-1-5182-1953-5(5))* Harper & Row Ltd.
—Itty Bitty Kitty & the Rainy Play Day. Holub, Joan. 2016. (ENG.). 32p. (J). (gr. -1-3). 17.99 *(978-0-06-232220-3(6))* HarperCollins Pubs.
—Itty Bitty Kitty: Firehouse Fun. Holub, Joan. 2016. (My First I Can Read Ser.). (ENG.). 32p. (J). (gr. -1-3). pap. 4.99 *(978-0-06-232221-0(4))* HarperCollins Pubs.
—The Monstore. Lazar, Tara. 2013. (ENG.). 32p. (J). (gr. -1-2). 17.99 *(978-1-4424-2017-5(0)*, Aladdin) Simon & Schuster Children's Publishing.
—Open Wide! Krensky, Stephen. 2014. (ENG.). 14p. (J). (— 1). 6.99 *(978-0-545-53368-3(6)*, Cartwheel Bks.) Scholastic, Inc.
Burks, James. Rockin' Rockets: The Adventures of Allie & Amy 2. Calmenson, Stephanie & Cole, Joanna. 2020. (Quix Ser.). (ENG.). 96p. (J). (gr. k-3). 17.99 ***(978-1-5344-5254-1(0))***; pap. 5.99 ***(978-1-5344-5253-4(2))*** Simon & Schuster Children's Publishing. (Aladdin).
Burks, James. Willy Maykit in Space. Trine, Greg. (ENG.). 208p. (J). (gr. 3-7). 2016. pap. 7.99 *(978-0-544-66848-5(0)*, 1625468); 2015. 14.99 *(978-0-544-31351-4(8)*, 1581676) Houghton Mifflin Harcourt Publishing Co. (HMH Books For Young Readers).
Burks, Justin Fox, photos by. Sewing School ® Quilts: 15 Projects Kids Will Love to Make; Stitch up a Patchwork Pet, Scrappy Journal, T-Shirt Quilt, & More. Plumley, Amie Petronis & Lisle, Andria. 2018. (Sewing School Ser.). (ENG., 160p. (J). spiral bd. 18.95 *(978-1-61212-859-7(9)*, 622859) Storey Publishing, LLC.
Burling, Jeff & Swampy, Lloyd. Nanabosho & Kitchie Odjig, 1 vol. McLellan, Joseph et al. 2015. (ENG.). 32p. (J). mass mkt. 10.95 *(978-0-921827-58-0(X)*, aa03fcc5-804c-49c7-8585-035afdd3fd0d) Pemmican Pubns., Inc. CAN. Dist: Firefly Bks., Ltd.
Burlinson, James, et al. Minecraft Redstone Handbook. Farwell, Nick & Steer, Don. 2015. 93p. (J). *(978-0-545-82320-3(X))* Scholastic, Inc.
Burlinson, James & Cordner, Theo. Minecraft. Farwell, Nick. 2014. 79p. (J). *(978-0-545-68575-7(3))* Scholastic, Inc.

B

Burma, Willingham. Clang Went the Cymbals: An Onomatopoeia Alphabet Book. Jordan, Dana Hall. 2008. 32p. (J). 15.99 *(978-0-9798664-0-1(5))* Capture Bks.

Burn, Doris. Andrew Henry's Meadow. Burn, Doris. 2012. 48p. (J). (gr. 1-4). 16.99 *(978-0-399-25608-0(3),* Philomel Bks.) Penguin Young Readers Group.

Burn, Ted. Y Is for Yellowhammer: An Alabama Alphabet. Crane, Carol. 2003. (Discover America State by State Ser.). (ENG.). 40p. (J). 17.95 *(978-1-58536-118-2(6))* Sleeping Bear Pr.

Burnard-Fullington, Shelby. Huzzah- a Pool Mouse. Watling, Missy. 2019. (ENG.). 26p. (J). pap. 9.99 *(978-1-0916-9942-7(9))* Independently Published.

Burnell Walsh, Avenda. Loophole Forest Tells Its Tale of Enchantment. Smith, Roy. Magpie, ed. 2012. 38p. *(978-1-908000-18-7(X))* Pyjama Pr.

Burnett, Anne. The Passion for Children: Bilingual (English & Spanish) Guide to the Passion of Christ, 1 bk. Turton, Karalynn Teresa. Ruiz, Jeanette, tr. 2005. (J). 3.00 *(978-0-9765180-0-6(7))* Catholic World Mission.

Burnett, Dylan. Ant-Man: Worldhive Tpb. 2020. 112p. (YA). (gr. 8-17). pap. 15.99 ***(978-1-302-92258-0(0))*** Marvel Worldwide, Inc.

Burnett, Dylan. Cosmic Ghost Rider: Baby Thanos Must Die. 2019. (Cosmic Ghost Rider Ser.: 1). (ENG.). 112p. (YA). (gr. 8-17). pap. 15.99 *(978-1-302-91353-3(0))* Marvel Worldwide, Inc.

—X-Force Vol. 1: Sins of the Past, Vol. 1. 2019. (ENG.). 112p. pap. 15.99 *(978-1-302-91573-5(8))* Marvel Worldwide, Inc.

Burnett, Jenifer. My Jungle Quilt. Burnett, Jenifer. 2006. 32p. (J). 19.99 *(978-0-9777570-0-8(5))* Summerside Lane.

Burnett, Lindy. The Big Sled Race. Hall, Kirsten. 2003. (Hello Reader! Ser.). (J). pap. 3.99 *(978-0-439-32104-4(2))* Scholastic, Inc.

—The Book of Wizard Craft: In Which the Apprentice Finds Spells, Potions, Fantastic Tales & 50 Enchanting Things to Make. Kilby, Janice Eaton et al. 2019. (Books of Wizard Craft Ser.: 1). 144p. (J). (gr. 3-7). lthr. 19.95 *(978-1-4549-3547-6(2))* Sterling Publishing Co., Inc.

—The Book of Wizard Magic: In Which the Apprentice Finds Marvelous Magic Tricks, Mystifying Illusions & Astonishing Tales. Kilby, Janice Eaton et al. 2019. (Books of Wizard Craft Ser.: 3). 144p. (J). (gr. 3-7). lthr. 19.95 *(978-1-4549-3548-3(0))* Sterling Publishing Co., Inc.

—I Live Here! 2010. (My World Ser.).Tr. of Yo Vivo Aqui!. (ENG.). 24p. (J). (gr. -1-1). pap. 8.15 *(978-1-61533-033-1(X));* lib. bdg. 25.60 *(978-1-60754-950-5(6))* Windmill Bks.

—I Live Here!/Yo Vivo Aqui! Rosa-Mendoza, Gladys. Gonzalez, Margarita E. & Weber, Amy, eds. 2007. (# 1 Bilingual Board Book Ser.). (ENG & SPA.). 20p. (J). (gr. -1-k). bds. 6.95 *(978-1-931398-19-0(4))* Me+Mi Publishing.

—Space Trip. Williams, Rozanne Lanczak. 2005. (Reading for Fluency Ser.). 80p. (J). pap. 32.49 *(978-1-59198-142-8(5),* 4242) Creative Teaching Pr., Inc.

—The Sunset Switch. Kudlinski, Kathleen V. 2005. (Picture Book Ser.). (ENG.). 32p. (J). (gr. k-3). 15.95 *(978-1-55971-916-2(8))* Cooper Square Publishing Llc.

Burnett, Seb. Aliens Sticker Book. Robson, Kirsteen. 2014. (Usborne Activities Ser.). (ENG.). 22p. (J). 8.99 *(978-0-7945-3101-0(6),* Usborne) EDC Publishing.

—The Footballing Frog: Band 14/Ruby (Collins Big Cat) Jungman, Ann. 2007. (Collins Big Cat Ser.). (ENG.). 48p. (J). (gr. 3-4). pap. 11.99 *(978-0-00-723087-7(7))* HarperCollins Pubs. Ltd. GBR. Dist: Independent Pubs. Group.

Burnette, Emily. What Is a Temple? Wright, Briana. 2016. (ENG.). (J). 14.99 *(978-1-4621-1748-2(1))* Cedar Fort, Inc./CFI Distribution.

Burney, Laura & Sawyer, Peter. The Outside Play & Learning Book: Activities for Young Children. Miller, Karen. Charner, Kathleen, ed. 2004. 253p. (Orig.). (gr. -1-k). pap. 24.95 *(978-0-87659-117-8(9),* 10009) Gryphon Hse., Inc.

Burney, Ryan. Real-Life Sea Monsters. Jango-Cohen, Judith. 2007. (On My Own Science Ser.). 48p. (J). (gr. 3-7). lib. bdg. 25.26 *(978-0-8225-6747-9(4),* Millbrook Pr.) Lerner Publishing Group.

Burnham, Janet Hayward. Jeremy the Puny. Burnham, Janet Hayward. 2003. (J). (gr. 3-6). pap. 14.95 *(978-0-9740743-0-6(6))* My Little Jessie Pr.

Burningham, John. Wind in the Willows. Grahame, Kenneth. 2019. (ENG.). 240p. (J). (gr. 2-6). 26.99 *(978-0-241-35343-1(2))* Penguin Random Hse. AUS. Dist: Independent Pubs. Group.

Burningham, John. Borka: The Adventures of a Goose with No Feathers. Burningham, John. 2018. (ENG.). 32p. (J). (gr. -1-2). 16.99 *(978-1-5362-0040-9(9))* Candlewick Pr.

—Granpa. Burningham, John. 2003. 32p. (J). (gr. -1-2). pap. 14.99 *(978-0-09-943408-5(3),* Red Fox) Random House Children's Books GBR. Dist: Independent Pubs. Group.

—It's a Secret! Burningham, John. 2009. (ENG.). 56p. (J). (gr. -1-2). 17.99 *(978-0-7636-4275-4(4))* Candlewick Pr.

—John Burningham. Burningham, John. ltd. ed. 2009. (ENG.). 224p. (gr. k-12). 70.00 *(978-0-7636-4434-5(X))* Candlewick Pr.

—Motor Miles. Burningham, John. 2016. (ENG.). 32p. (J). (gr. -1-2). 16.99 *(978-0-7636-9064-9(3))* Candlewick Pr.

—Mouse House. Burningham, John. 2018. (ENG.). 32p. (J). (gr. -1-2). 16.99 *(978-1-5362-0039-3(5))* Candlewick Pr.

—Picnic. Burningham, John. 2014. (ENG.). 32p. (J). (-k). 17.99 *(978-0-7636-6945-4(8))* Candlewick Pr.

—Tug of War. Burningham, John. 2013. (ENG.). 32p. (J). (gr. k-3). 16.99 *(978-0-7636-6575-3(4))* Candlewick Pr.

—The Way to the Zoo. Burningham, John. 2014. (ENG.). 40p. (J). (gr. -1-2). 15.99 *(978-0-7636-7317-8(X))* Candlewick Pr.

Burns, Brigette. Don't Eat That, Nonsense. Perry, Raney. 2019. (ENG.). 40p. (J). pap. 9.99 ***(978-1-7027-8722-2(2))*** Independently Published.

Burns, Cara. Mia's Wish. Landis, J. J. 2018. (ENG.). 34p. (J). pap. 9.95 *(978-1-7320463-0-6(1))* Three Chucks.

Burns, Charles. The Jungle. Sinclair, Upton. deluxe ed. 2006. (Penguin Classics Deluxe Edition Ser.). (ENG.). 432p. (gr. 12-18). 19.00 *(978-0-14-303958-7(X),* Penguin Classics) Penguin Publishing Group.

Burns, Donna. Forever Buster: What a Name! What a Dog, We Exclaim! Rabbett, Martin. 2007. (J). 13.95 *(978-0-9794649-0-4(0))* Hula Moon Pr.

—Pono the Dog That Dreams. Fujii, Jocelyn. 2008. (ENG.). 40p. (YA). 14.95 *(978-0-9794649-2-8(7))* Hula Moon Pr.

Burns, Doris. Christina Katerina & the Box. Gauch, Patricia Lee. 2012. (ENG.). 32p. (J). (gr. -1-3). 8.95 *(978-1-59078-915-5(6))* Boyds Mills Pr.

Burns, Heather. All That Glitters. Scott, Lisa Ann. 2017. 117p. (J). pap. *(978-1-338-13559-6(7))* Scholastic, Inc.

—Clover Fields Fiasco: A 4D Book. Meister, Cari. 2018. (Three Horses Ser.). (ENG.). 56p. (J). (gr. k-2). pap. 4.95 *(978-1-5158-2951-5(0),* 138498); lib. bdg. 22.65 *(978-1-5158-2947-8(2),* 138486) Capstone. (Picture Window Bks.).

Burns, Heather. Clueless: a Totally Classic Picture Book. Heckerling, Amy. 2020. (ENG.). 32p. (J). (gr. -1-3). 17.99 ***(978-0-7624-7058-7(5),*** Running Pr. Kids) Running Pr.

Burns, Heather. Dreams That Sparkle, 4. Scott, Lisa Ann. 2017. (Enchanted Pony Academy Ser.). (ENG.). 128p. (J). (gr. 1-4). 17.44 *(978-1-5364-0219-3(2))* Scholastic, Inc.

—Dreamy Dress-Up. Downy, Rufus. Cottage Door Press, ed. 2019. (Colorforms Activity Bks.). (ENG.). 12p. (J). (gr. -1-2). bds. 9.99 *(978-1-68052-740-7(1),* 1004610) Cottage Door Pr.

—Let It Glow, 3. Scott, Lisa Ann. 2017. (Enchanted Pony Academy Ser.). (ENG.). 128p. (J). (gr. 1-4). 17.44 *(978-1-5364-0218-6(4))* Scholastic, Inc.

—Movie Madness: A 4D Book. Meister, Cari. 2018. (Three Horses Ser.). (ENG.). 56p. (J). (gr. k-2). pap. 4.95 *(978-1-5158-2954-6(5),* 138501); lib. bdg. 22.65 *(978-1-5158-2950-8(2),* 138497) Capstone. (Picture Window Bks.).

—The Princess Without a Crown. Ellis, Nicole. 2019. (ENG.). 32p. (J). 15.99 *(978-1-4621-3572-1(2),* Sweetwater Bks.) Cedar Fort, Inc./CFI Distribution.

—Roller Coaster Ride: A 4D Book. Meister, Cari. 2018. (Three Horses Ser.). (ENG.). 56p. (J). (gr. k-2). pap. 4.95 *(978-1-5158-2952-2(9),* 138499); lib. bdg. 22.65 *(978-1-5158-2948-5(0),* 138495) Capstone. (Picture Window Bks.).

—Seaside Escape: A 4D Book. Meister, Cari. 2018. (Three Horses Ser.). (ENG.). 56p. (J). (gr. k-2). pap. 4.95 *(978-1-5158-2953-9(7),* 138500); lib. bdg. 22.65 *(978-1-5158-2949-2(9),* 138496) Capstone. (Picture Window Bks.).

—Wings That Shine, 2. Scott, Lisa Ann. 2017. (Enchanted Pony Academy Ser.). (ENG.). 128p. (J). (gr. 1-4). 17.44 *(978-1-5364-0217-9(6))* Scholastic, Inc.

Burns, Howard M. The Boy Who Saved the Town, 1 vol. Seabrooke, Brenda. 2009. (ENG.). 30p. (J). (gr. 2-5). 8.95 *(978-0-87033-405-4(0),* 9780870334054, Cornell Maritime Pr./Tidewater Pubs.) Schiffer Publishing, Ltd.

—Captain Tugalong, 1 vol. Cache, Dee. 2009. (ENG.). 30p. (J). (gr. -1-3). 12.95 *(978-0-87033-515-0(4),* 9780870335150, Cornell Maritime Pr./Tidewater Pubs.) Schiffer Publishing, Ltd.

Burns, John M. Wuthering Heights. Bronte, Emily. 2011. (ENG.). 160p. lib. bdg. 24.95 *(978-1-907127-80-9(1))* Classical Comics GBR. Dist: Publishers Group West (PGW).

Burns, Mike. Your Life as a Cabin Boy on a Pirate Ship. Gunderson, Jessica. 2012. (Way It Was Ser.). (ENG.). 32p. (J). (gr. 2-5). pap. 8.95 *(978-1-4048-7249-3(3));* lib. bdg. 27.32 *(978-1-4048-7159-5(4))* Capstone. (Picture Window Bks.).

Burns, Oliver. The Anxiety Workbook for Kids: Take Charge of Fears & Worries Using the Gift of Imagination. Alter, Robin & Clarke, Crystal. 2016. (ENG.). 136p. (J). (gr. k-5). pap. 18.95 *(978-1-62625-477-0(X),* 34770) New Harbinger Pubns.

Burns, Raymond. The Secret of the Stone Frog. Snow, Dorothea J. 2011. 214p. 44.95 *(978-1-258-08002-0(8))* Literary Licensing, LLC.

Burns, Sandra. The Great Horned Owl. Bingamon-Haller, Mary. 2013. 28p. pap. 8.99 *(978-1-938768-12-5(4))* Gypsy Pubns.

—If You Could See Her Smile. Burkhart, Alma J. 2013. 24p. pap. 8.99 *(978-1-938768-32-3(9))* Gypsy Pubns.

—Leafy Finds a Home. Alders, Willa. 2013. 24p. pap. 8.99 *(978-1-938768-13-2(2))* Gypsy Pubns.

—Roscoe the Volunteer Emt. Wenning, Jeremy. 2013. 24p. pap. 8.99 *(978-1-938768-19-4(1))* Gypsy Pubns.

—The Stillwater River. Bingamon-Haller, Mary. 2013. 24p. pap. 8.99 *(978-1-938768-30-9(2))* Gypsy Pubns.

Burns, Taurus. Kyle Jeffries, Pilgrim. Radley, Gail. 2010. (J). pap. *(978-0-87743-712-3(2))* Baha'i Publishing Trust, U.S.

Burns, Theresa. Sly Fly & the Gray Mare. Hoffman, Terri. 2013. 26p. (J). 15.95 *(978-1-940224-15-2(2))* Taylor and Seale Publishing.

—Through the Magic Shed: A Grand Adventure Lies Ahead! Phillips, Denine W. 2019. (ENG.). 52p. (J). (gr. 2-6). 16.95 *(978-0-9851799-2-2(9))* Stoneledge Pr.

—Through the Magic Shed: A Grand Adventure Lies Ahead! Phillips, Denine. 2018. (ENG.). 34p. (J). pap. 12.95 *(978-0-9851799-1-5(0))* Stoneledge Pr.

—The Underwater Orchestra. Gantry, Chris. 2013. 38p. (J). 16.98 *(978-1-940224-19-0(5))* Taylor and Seale Publishing.

Burns, Theresa. Queen Emileen. Burns, Theresa. 2013. 36p. 15.50 *(978-1-949224-23-8(6))* Taylor and Seale Publishing.

Burns Yu, Brenna. Hazel & Twig: the Lost Egg. Yu, Brenna Burns. 2020. 40p. (J). (gr. -1-2). 16.99 *(978-1-5362-0492-6(7))* Candlewick Pr.

Burr, Dan. Book of Mormon Family Reader. McKellar, Tyler. 2017. viii, 292p. 24.99 *(978-1-62972-334-1(7))* Deseret Bk. Co.

—The Book of Mormon Family Reader: Spanish Edition. McKellar, Tyler. 2019. (SPA.). viii, 292p. pap. 19.99 *(978-1-62972-624-3(9))* Deseret Bk. Co.

—Easter Walk: A Treasure Hunt for the Real Meaning of Easter. Rowley, Deborah Pace. 2010. (J). *(978-1-60641-055-4(5))* Deseret Bk. Co.

—The Enchanted Tunnel Vol. 3: Journey to Jerusalem. Monson, Marianne. 2011. (J). (gr. 3-6). pap. 7.99 *(978-1-60908-068-6(8))* Deseret Bk. Co.

—The Enchanted Tunnel Vol. 4: Wandering in the Wilderness. Monson, Marianne. 2011. 85p. (YA). (gr. 3-6). pap. 7.99 *(978-1-60908-069-3(6))* Deseret Bk. Co.

—God Bless Your Way: A Christmas Journey. Freeman, Emily. 2007. 32p. (J). (gr. -1-3). 19.95 incl. audio compact disk *(978-1-59038-806-8(2))* Deseret Bk. Co.

—My Home Can Be a Holy Place. Oaks, Kristen M. 2015. (J). 18.99 *(978-1-62972-099-9(2))* Deseret Bk. Co.

—The New Testament Family Reader. McKellar, Tyler, ed. 2019. 210p. 24.99 *(978-1-62972-571-0(4))* Deseret Bk. Co.

—One Little Match. Monson, Thomas S. 2014. (J). 17.99 *(978-1-60907-868-3(3))* Deseret Bk. Co.

—Sam's Christmas Wish. Durrant, George D. 2014. (ENG.). 32p. (J). (gr. 3). 17.99 *(978-1-60907-606-1(0),* Shadow Mountain) Shadow Mountain Publishing.

—The Testimony Glove. Oaks, Kristen M. & Phillips, JoAnn. 2010. (J). (gr. -1-4). 17.99 *(978-1-60641-151-3(9))* Deseret Bk. Co.

Burran, Debbie. Kevin Is a Smart Cookie. Reichman, Beverley. 2020. (ENG.). 40p. (J). pap. 15.95 ***(978-1-64531-953-5(9))*** Newman Springs Publishing, Inc.

Burrier, Sara. Nurses When the Sun Shines: A Little Book on Night Weaning. Havener, Katherine. 2nd ed. 2013. 20p. (J). pap. 9.99 *(978-0-615-75642-4(5))* Elea Pr.

Burril, April. Being Creepy. Burril, JimmyO. 2019. (Adventures of Creepy & Boo Ser.: Vol. 2). (ENG.). 34p. (J). pap. 9.99 *(978-1-9812-4658-8(4))* CreateSpace Independent Publishing Platform.

Burrington, Stasia. Mae among the Stars. Ahmed, Roda. 2018. (ENG.). 40p. (J). (gr. -1-3). 17.99 *(978-0-06-265173-0(0))* HarperCollins Pubs.

Burris, Andrea. A Dog Lover's Alphabet Book. Burris, Andrea. Schad, Anna. 2007. (ENG.). 32p. (J). (gr. k-2). 14.95 *(978-0-9743294-1-3(X))* A & D Bks.

Burris, Andrea M. The Kitty Cat Alphabet Book. Burris, Andrea M. Schad, Anna M. 2004. (ENG.). 32p. (J). 14.95 *(978-0-9743294-0-6(1),* 1230444) A & D Bks.

Burris, Priscilla. Aloha for Carol Ann. Sorenson, Margo. 2011. 32p. (J). (gr. -1-3). pap. 8.95 *(978-1-60349-027-6(2),* Marimba Bks.) Just Us Bks., Inc.

—Dad School. Van Slyke, Rebecca. 2016. (ENG.). 32p. (J). (gr. -1-2). 19.99 *(978-0-385-38896-2(9),* Doubleday Bks. for Young Readers) Random Hse. Children's Bks.

—Edgar's Second Word. Vernick, Audrey. 2014. (ENG.). 32p. (J). (gr. -1-3). 16.99 *(978-0-547-68462-8(2),* 1476531, Clarion Bks.) Houghton Mifflin Harcourt Trade & Reference Pubs.

—Emily Santos, Star of the Week. Williams, Rozanne Lanczak. 2006. (Learn to Write Ser.). 16p. (J). (gr. k-2). pap. 2.99 *(978-1-59198-298-2(7),* 6194) Creative Teaching Pr., Inc.

—Emily Santos, Star of the Week. Williams, Rozanne Lanczak. Maio, Barbara, ed. 2006. (J). per. 8.99 *(978-1-59198-358-3(4))* Creative Teaching Pr., Inc.

—Fear the Bunny. Morris, Richard T. 2019. (ENG.). 40p. (J). (gr. -1-3). 17.99 *(978-1-4814-7800-7(1))* Simon & Schuster Children's Publishing.

—Games Galore for Children's Parties & More: 80 Fun Games & Activities for Parties, Classroom, Youth Groups, Carnivals, Company Picnics, Rainy Days & Special Occasions. Pence, Shari A. Stearns, Debra & Kohout, Rosemary, eds. 2nd rev. ed. 2005. (ENG.). 121p. (J). (gr. -1-7). pap. 12.00 *(978-0-9645771-4-(9))* Funcastle Pubns.

—Grandma's Tiny House. Brown-Wood, Janay. 2017. 32p. (J). (-k). lib. bdg. 16.99 *(978-1-58089-712-9(6))* Charlesbridge Publishing, Inc.

—Heidi Heckelbeck 3 Books In 1! Heidi Heckelbeck Has a Secret; Heidi Heckelbeck Casts a Spell; Heidi Heckelbeck & the Cookie Contest. Coven, Wanda. 2014. (Heidi Heckelbeck Ser.). (ENG.). 384p. (J). (gr. k-4). pap. 8.99 *(978-1-4814-2771-5(7),* Little Simon) Little Simon.

—Heidi Heckelbeck & the Big Mix-Up. Coven, Wanda. 2016. (Heidi Heckelbeck Ser.: 18). (ENG.). 128p. (J). (gr. k-4). pap. 5.99 *(978-1-4814-7169-5(4),* Little Simon) Little Simon.

—Heidi Heckelbeck & the Christmas Surprise. Coven, Wanda. 2013. (Heidi Heckelbeck Ser.: 9). (ENG.). 128p. (J). (gr. k-2). 17.99 *(978-1-4424-8125-1(0));* pap. 5.99 *(978-1-4424-8124-4(2))* Little Simon. (Little Simon).

—Heidi Heckelbeck & the Cookie Contest. Coven, Wanda. 2012. (Heidi Heckelbeck Ser.: 3). (ENG.). 128p. (J). (gr. k-2). 16.99 *(978-1-4424-4166-8(6));* pap. 5.99 *(978-1-4424-4165-1(8))* Little Simon. (Little Simon).

—Heidi Heckelbeck & the Magic Puppy. Coven, Wanda. 2017. (Heidi Heckelbeck Ser.: 20). (ENG.). 128p. (J). (gr. k-4). pap. 5.99 *(978-1-4814-9521-9(6),* Little Simon) Little Simon.

—Heidi Heckelbeck & the Never-Ending Day. Coven, Wanda. 2017. (Heidi Heckelbeck Ser.: 21). (ENG.). 128p. (J). (gr. k-4). 16.99 *(978-1-4814-9525-7(9));* pap. 5.99 *(978-1-4814-9524-0(0))* Little Simon. (Little Simon).

—Heidi Heckelbeck & the Secret Admirer. Coven, Wanda. 2012. (Heidi Heckelbeck Ser.: 6). (ENG.). 128p. (J). (gr. k-4). 16.99 *(978-1-4424-4175-0(5));* pap. 5.99 *(978-1-4424-4174-3(7))* Little Simon. (Little Simon).

—Heidi Heckelbeck & the Snoopy Spy. Coven, Wanda. 2018. (Heidi Heckelbeck Ser.: 23). (ENG.). 128p. (J). (gr. k-4). 16.99 *(978-1-5344-1111-1(9));* pap. 5.99 *(978-1-5344-1110-4(0))* Little Simon. (Little Simon).

—Heidi Heckelbeck & the Wacky Tacky Spirit Week. Coven, Wanda. 2019. (Heidi Heckelbeck Ser.: 27). (ENG.). 128p. (J). (gr. k-4). 16.99 *(978-1-5344-4636-6(2),* Little Simon) Little Simon.

—Heidi Heckelbeck Casts a Spell. Coven, Wanda. 2012. (Heidi Heckelbeck Ser.: 2). (ENG.). 128p. (J). (gr. k-4). 16.99 *(978-1-4424-4088-3(0));* pap. 5.99 *(978-1-4424-3567-4(4))* Little Simon. (Little Simon).

—The Heidi Heckelbeck Collection: A Bewitching Four-Book Boxed Set: Heidi Hecklebeck Has a Secret; Heidi Hecklebeck Casts a Spell; Heidi Hecklebeck & the Cookie Contest; Heidi Hecklebeck in Disguise. Coven, Wanda. ed. 2013. (Heidi Heckelbeck Ser.). (ENG.). 512p. (J). (gr. k-4). pap. 23.99 *(978-1-4424-8976-9(6),* Little Simon) Little Simon.

Burris, Priscilla. Heidi Heckelbeck for Class President. Coven, Wanda. 2020. (Heidi Heckelbeck Ser.: 30). (ENG.). 128p. (J). (gr. k-4). 17.99 ***(978-1-5344-6131-4(0));*** pap. 5.99 ***(978-1-5344-6130-7(2))*** Little Simon. (Little Simon).

Burris, Priscilla. Heidi Heckelbeck Gets Glasses. Coven, Wanda. 2012. (Heidi Heckelbeck Ser.: 5). (ENG.). 128p. (J). (gr. k-2). pap. 5.99 *(978-1-4424-4171-2(2));* 15.99 *(978-1-4424-4172-9(0))* Little Simon. (Little Simon).

—Heidi Heckelbeck Goes to Camp! Coven, Wanda. 2013. (Heidi Heckelbeck Ser.: 8). (ENG.). 128p. (J). (gr. k-2). 16.99 *(978-1-4424-6481-0(X));* pap. 5.99 *(978-1-4424-6480-3(1))* Little Simon. (Little Simon).

—Heidi Heckelbeck Has a New Best Friend. Coven, Wanda. 2018. (Heidi Heckelbeck Ser.: 22). (ENG.). 128p. (J). (gr. k-4). 16.99 *(978-1-5344-1108-1(9));* pap. 5.99 *(978-1-5344-1107-4(0))* Little Simon. (Little Simon).

—Heidi Heckelbeck Has a Secret. Coven, Wanda. 2012. (Heidi Heckelbeck Ser.: 1). (ENG.). 128p. (J). (gr. k-4). 17.99 *(978-1-4424-4087-6(2));* pap. 5.99 *(978-1-4424-3565-0(8))* Little Simon. (Little Simon).

—Heidi Heckelbeck in Disguise. Coven, Wanda. 2012. (Heidi Heckelbeck Ser.: 4). (ENG.). 128p. (J). (gr. k-2). 17.99 *(978-1-4424-4169-9(0));* pap. 5.99 *(978-1-4424-4168-2(2))* Little Simon. (Little Simon).

—Heidi Heckelbeck Is a Flower Girl. Coven, Wanda. 2014. (Heidi Heckelbeck Ser.: 11). (ENG.). 128p. (J). (gr. k-4). pap. 5.99 *(978-1-4814-0498-3(9),* Little Simon) Little Simon.

—Heidi Heckelbeck Is Not a Thief! Coven, Wanda. 2015. (Heidi Heckelbeck Ser.: 13). (ENG.). 128p. (J). (gr. k-4). pap. 5.99 *(978-1-4814-2324-3(X),* Little Simon) Little Simon.

—Heidi Heckelbeck Is Ready to Dance! Coven, Wanda. 2013. (Heidi Heckelbeck Ser.: 7). (ENG.). 128p. (J). (gr. k-2). pap. 5.99 *(978-1-4424-5191-9(2));* 17.99 *(978-1-4424-5192-6(0))* Little Simon. (Little Simon).

—Heidi Heckelbeck Is So Totally Grounded! Coven, Wanda. 2018. (Heidi Heckelbeck Ser.: 24). (ENG.). 128p. (J). (gr. k-4). 16.99 *(978-1-5344-2645-0(0));* pap. 5.99 *(978-1-5344-2644-3(2))* Little Simon. (Little Simon).

—Heidi Heckelbeck Is the Bestest Babysitter! Coven, Wanda. 2015. (Heidi Heckelbeck Ser.: 16). (ENG.). 128p. (J). (gr. k-4). pap. 5.99 *(978-1-4814-4630-3(4),* Little Simon) Little Simon.

—Heidi Heckelbeck Lends a Helping Hand. Coven, Wanda. 2019. (Heidi Heckelbeck Ser.: 26). (ENG.). 128p. (J). (gr. k-4). pap. 5.99 *(978-1-5344-4529-1(3),* Little Simon) Little Simon.

—Heidi Heckelbeck Lights! Camera! Awesome! Coven, Wanda. 2018. (Heidi Heckelbeck Ser.: 25). (ENG.). 128p. (J). (gr. k-4). 16.99 *(978-1-5344-2648-1(5));* pap. 5.99 *(978-1-5344-2647-4(7))* Little Simon. (Little Simon).

—Heidi Heckelbeck Makes a Wish: Super Special! Coven, Wanda. 2016. (Heidi Heckelbeck Ser.: 17). (ENG.). 160p. (J). (gr. k-4). pap. 5.99 *(978-1-4814-6613-4(5),* Little Simon) Little Simon.

—Heidi Heckelbeck Might Be Afraid of the Dark. Coven, Wanda. 2015. (Heidi Heckelbeck Ser.: 15). (ENG.). 128p. (J). (gr. k-4). pap. 5.99 *(978-1-4814-4627-3(4),* Little Simon) Little Simon.

Burris, Priscilla. Heidi Heckelbeck Pool Party! Coven, Wanda. 2020. (Heidi Heckelbeck Ser.: 29). (ENG.). 128p. (J). (gr. k-4). 17.99 ***(978-1-5344-6128-4(0));*** pap. 5.99 ***(978-1-5344-6127-7(2))*** Little Simon. (Little Simon).

Burris, Priscilla. Heidi Heckelbeck Says Cheese! Coven, Wanda. 2015. (Heidi Heckelbeck Ser.: 14). (ENG.). 128p. (J). (gr. k-4). pap. 5.99 *(978-1-4814-2327-4(4),* Little Simon) Little Simon.

—Heidi Heckelbeck Takes the Cake. Coven, Wanda. 2020. (Heidi Heckelbeck Ser.: 28). (ENG.). 128p. (J). (gr. k-4). 16.99 *(978-1-5344-6114-7(0));* pap. 5.99 *(978-1-5344-6113-0(2))* Little Simon. (Little Simon).

—Heidi Heckelbeck Tries Out for the Team. Coven, Wanda. 2017. (Heidi Heckelbeck Ser.: 19). (ENG.). 128p. (J). (gr. k-4). pap. 5.99 *(978-1-4814-7172-5(4),* Little Simon) Little Simon.

Burris, Priscilla. Henry Heckelbeck & the Haunted Hideout. Coven, Wanda. 2020. (Henry Heckelbeck Ser.: 3). (ENG.). 128p. (J). (gr. k-4). 17.99 ***(978-1-5344-6117-8(5));*** pap. 5.99 ***(978-1-5344-6116-1(7))*** Little Simon. (Little Simon).

Burris, Priscilla. Henry Heckelbeck Gets a Dragon. Coven, Wanda. 2019. (Henry Heckelbeck Ser.: 1). (ENG.). 128p. (J). (gr. k-4). 16.99 *(978-1-5344-6104-8(3));* pap. 5.99 *(978-1-5344-6103-1(5))* Little Simon. (Little Simon).

—Henry Heckelbeck Never Cheats. Coven, Wanda. 2019. (Henry Heckelbeck Ser.: 2). (ENG.). 128p. (J). (gr. k-4). 16.99 *(978-1-5344-6107-9(8));* pap. 5.99 *(978-1-5344-6106-2(X))* Little Simon. (Little Simon).

Burris, Priscilla. Henry Heckelbeck Spells Trouble. Coven, Wanda. 2020. (Henry Heckelbeck Ser.: 4). (ENG.). 128p. (J). (gr. k-4). 17.99 ***(978-1-5344-6120-8(5));*** pap. 5.99 ***(978-1-5344-6119-2(1))*** Little Simon. (Little Simon).

Burris, Priscilla. Humphrey's Big Birthday Bash. Birney, Betty G. 2018. (Humphrey's Tiny Tales Ser.: 8). (ENG.). 96p. (J). (gr. k-3). 5.99 *(978-1-5247-3721-4(6),* Puffin Books) Penguin Young Readers Group.

—Humphrey's Creepy-Crawly Camping Adventure. Birney, Betty G. 2015. (Humphrey's Tiny Tales Ser.: 3). (ENG.). 96p. (J). (gr. k-3). 5.99 *(978-0-14-751459-2(2),* Puffin Books); 15.99 *(978-0-399-17227-4(0),* G.P. Putnam's Sons Books for Young Readers) Penguin Young Readers Group.

—Humphrey's Mixed-Up Magic Trick. Birney, Betty G. 2016. (Humphrey's Tiny Tales Ser.: 5). (ENG.). 96p. (J). (gr. k-3). 5.99 *(978-0-14-751461-5(4)*, Puffin Books) Penguin Young Readers Group.
—Humphrey's Pet Show Panic. Birney, Betty G. 2018. (Humphrey's Tiny Tales Ser.: 7). (ENG.). 96p. (J). (gr. k-3). 4.99 *(978-1-5247-3718-4(6)*, Puffin Books) Penguin Young Readers Group.
—Humphrey's Playful Puppy Problem. Birney, Betty G. 2014. (Humphrey's Tiny Tales Ser.: 2). (ENG.). 96p. (J). (gr. k-3). pap. 4.99 *(978-0-14-751484-4(3)*, Puffin Books) Penguin Young Readers Group.
—Humphrey's Really Wheely Racing Day. Birney, Betty G. 2014. (Humphrey's Tiny Tales Ser.: 1). (ENG.). 96p. (J). (gr. k-3). pap. 5.99 *(978-0-14-751485-1(1)*, Puffin Books) Penguin Young Readers Group.
—Humphrey's Treasure Hunt Trouble. Birney, Betty G. 2017. (Humphrey's Tiny Tales Ser.: 6). (ENG.). 96p. (J). (gr. k-3). 5.99 *(978-0-14-751462-2(2)*, Puffin Books) Penguin Young Readers Group.
—I Can Be Responsible. Burch, Regina G. & Donovan Guntly, Jenette. 2004. (Doing the Right Thing Ser.). 16p. (gr. -1-2). lib. bdg. 21.00 *(978-0-8368-4245-6(6)*, Gareth Stevens Learning Library) Stevens, Gareth Publishing LLLP.
—I Love You All Day Long. Rusackas, Francesca. 2004. (ENG.). 32p. (J). (gr. -1-k). reprint ed. pap. 7.99 *(978-0-06-050278-2(9))* HarperCollins Pubs.
—Isabelle & Isabella's Little Book of Rules. Busath, Isabelle & Thordsen, Isabella. 2013. (ENG.). 120p. (J). (gr. -1-7). 12.99 *(978-1-4424-9980-5(X)*, Simon Spotlight) Simon Spotlight.
—It's Good to Have a Grandma. Macdonald, Maryann. 2019. (ENG.). 32p. (J). (gr. -1-3). 16.99 *(978-0-8075-3676-6(8)*, 807536768) Whitman, Albert & Co.
—It's Good to Have a Grandpa. Macdonald, Maryann. 2019. (ENG.). 32p. (J). (gr. -1-3). 16.99 *(978-0-8075-3675-9(X)*, 080753675X) Whitman, Albert & Co.
—Natsumi! Lendroth, Susan. 2018. (ENG.). 32p. (J). (gr. -1-3). 16.99 *(978-0-399-17090-4(1)*, G.P. Putnam's Sons Books for Young Readers) Penguin Young Readers Group.
—The Swim Lesson. Williams, Rozanne Lanczak. 2005. (Reading for Fluency Ser.). 8p. (J). pap. 3.49 *(978-1-59198-148-0(4)*, 4248) Creative Teaching Pr., Inc.
—This Is My Story. Williams, Rozanne Lanczak. 2006. (Learn to Write Ser.). 8p. (J). (gr. k-2). pap. 3.49 *(978-1-59198-280-7(4)*, 6174) Creative Teaching Pr., Inc.
—This Is My Story. Williams, Rozanne Lanczak. Maio, Barbara & Faulkner, Stacey, eds. 2006. (J). per. 6.99 *(978-1-59198-331-6(2))* Creative Teaching Pr., Inc.
—Where Have You Been? Williams, Rozanne Lanczak. Hamaguchi, Carla, ed. 2003. (Sight Word Readers Ser.). 16p. (J). (gr. k-2). pap. 3.49 *(978-1-57471-970-3(X)*, 3592) Creative Teaching Pr., Inc.
—1-2-3, My Feelings & Me. Millar, Goldie & Berger, Lisa A. 2019. (ENG.). 40p. (J). 15.99 *(978-1-63198-362-7(8))* Free Spirit Publishing, Inc.
Burris, Priscilla. The Ants Go Marching: Count-and-Sing. Burris, Priscilla. 2016. (ENG.). 16p. (J). (— 1). bds. 6.99 *(978-0-545-82504-7(0)*, Cartwheel Bks.) Scholastic, Inc.
—Hello School! Burris, Priscilla. 2018. 32p. (J). (-k). 16.99 *(978-0-399-17202-1(5)*, Nancy Paulsen Books) Penguin Young Readers Group.
Burris, Priscilla. Daddy All Day Long. Burris, Priscilla, tr. Rusackas, Francesca. 2004. 32p. (J). (gr. -1-k). lib. bdg. 13.89 *(978-0-06-050285-0(1))* HarperCollins Pubs.
Burris, Shiloh. Bloo the Bear: In the City. Gollman, Jen Whitney. 2018. (Bloo the Bear Ser.: Vol. 1). (ENG.). 38p. (J). pap. 12.99 *(978-1-7915-5289-3(7))* Independently Published.
Burroughs, Derrie. Baby Love. Tika. Standish, Joyce, ed. I.t. ed. 2006. 18p. (J). (gr. 1-5). pap. 15.00 *(978-0-9716244-1-2(0))* TLS Publishing.
Burroughs, Scott. Balloon Blow-Up. 2013. (Hardy Boys: the Secret Files Ser.: 13). (ENG.). 112p. (J). (gr. 1-4). pap. 5.99 *(978-1-4424-5371-5(0)*, Aladdin) Simon & Schuster Children's Publishing.
—The Bicycle Thief. Dixon, Franklin W. 2011. (Hardy Boys: the Secret Files Ser.: 6). (ENG.). 96p. (J). (gr. 1-4). pap. 5.99 *(978-1-4169-9396-4(7)*, Aladdin) Simon & Schuster Children's Publishing.
—The Disappearing Dog. 2011. (Hardy Boys: the Secret Files Ser.: 7). (ENG.). 96p. (J). (gr. 1-4). pap. 5.99 *(978-1-4424-2314-5(5)*, Aladdin) Simon & Schuster Children's Publishing.
—Fossil Frenzy. 2014. (Hardy Boys: the Secret Files Ser.: 14). (ENG.). 96p. (J). (gr. 1-4). pap. 5.99 *(978-1-4424-9043-7(8)*, Aladdin) Simon & Schuster Children's Publishing.
—God's Armor for Me. Shearer, Amelia. 2014. (Happy Day Ser.). (ENG.). 16p. (J). pap. 2.49 *(978-1-4143-9480-0(2)*, 4608470) Tyndale Hse. Pubs.
—God's Special Rule. Redford, Marjorie & Rice, Courtney. 2013. (Happy Day Ser.). (ENG.). 16p. (J). pap. 2.49 *(978-1-4143-9300-1(8)*, 4608290) Tyndale Hse. Pubs.
—The Great American Story of Charlie Brown, Snoopy, & the Peanuts Gang! Perkins, Chloe. 2017. (History of Fun Stuff Ser.). (ENG.). 48p. (J). (gr. 1-3). pap. 4.99 *(978-1-4814-9553-0(4)*, Simon Spotlight) Simon Spotlight.
—The Great Coaster Caper. 2012. (Hardy Boys: the Secret Files Ser.: 9). (ENG.). 112p. (J). (gr. 1-4). pap. 5.99 *(978-1-4424-1669-7(6)*, Aladdin) Simon & Schuster Children's Publishing.
—The Great Escape. Dixon, Franklin W. 2015. (Hardy Boys: the Secret Files Ser.: 17). (ENG.). 112p. (J). (gr. 1-4). pap. 5.99 *(978-1-4814-2267-3(7)*, Aladdin) Simon & Schuster Children's Publishing.
—The Hardy Boys Secret Files Collection Books 1-5: Trouble at the Arcade; the Missing Mitt; Mystery Map; Hopping Mad; a Monster of a Mystery. ed. 2014. (Hardy Boys: the Secret Files Ser.). (ENG.). 496p. (J). (gr. 1-4). pap. 29.99 *(978-1-4814-1473-9(9)*, Aladdin) Simon & Schuster Children's Publishing.
—The Harlem Globetrotters Present the Points Behind Basketball. Dobrow, Larry. 2018. (Science of Fun Stuff Ser.). (ENG.). 40p. (J). (gr. 1-3). 17.99 *(978-1-4814-8752-8(3))*; pap. 4.99 *(978-1-4814-8751-1(5))* Simon Spotlight. (Simon Spotlight).
—The High Score & Lowdown on Video Games! Krensky, Stephen. 2015. (History of Fun Stuff Ser.). (ENG.). 48p. (J). (gr. 1-3). 16.99 *(978-1-4814-2916-0(7))*; pap. 3.99 *(978-1-4814-2915-3(9))* Simon Spotlight. (Simon Spotlight).
—Hopping Mad, 4. 2010. (Hardy Boys: the Secret Files Ser.: 4). (ENG.). 96p. (J). (gr. 1-4). pap. 5.99 *(978-1-4169-9395-7(9))* Simon & Schuster, Inc.
—Lights, Camera ... Zombies! 2013. (Hardy Boys: the Secret Files Ser.: 12). (ENG.). 96p. (J). (gr. 1-4). pap. 5.99 *(978-1-4424-5369-2(9)*, Aladdin) Simon & Schuster Children's Publishing.
—Medieval Upheaval. Dixon, Franklin W. 2015. (Hardy Boys: the Secret Files Ser.: 18). (ENG.). 96p. (J). (gr. 1-4). pap. 5.99 *(978-1-4814-2269-7(3)*, Aladdin) Simon & Schuster Children's Publishing.
—The Missing Mitt. 2010. (Hardy Boys: the Secret Files Ser.: 2). (ENG.). 112p. (J). (gr. 1-4). pap. 5.99 *(978-1-4169-9394-0(0)*, Aladdin) Simon & Schuster Children's Publishing.
—A Monster of a Mystery. 2011. (Hardy Boys: the Secret Files Ser.: 5). (ENG.). 96p. (J). (gr. 1-4). pap. 5.99 *(978-1-4169-9166-3(2)*, Aladdin) Simon & Schuster Children's Publishing.
—Mystery Map, 3. 2010. (Hardy Boys: the Secret Files Ser.: 3). (ENG.). 96p. (J). (gr. 1-4). pap. 5.99 *(978-1-4169-9165-6(4)*, Aladdin) Simon & Schuster Children's Publishing.
—The Race Is On. Dixon, Franklin W. 2015. (Hardy Boys: the Secret Files Ser.: 19). (ENG.). 96p. (J). (gr. 1-4). pap. 5.99 *(978-1-4814-2271-0(5)*, Aladdin) Simon & Schuster Children's Publishing.
—Robot Rumble, 11. 2013. (Hardy Boys: the Secret Files Ser.: 11). (ENG.). 96p. (J). (gr. 1-4). pap. 5.99 *(978-1-4424-5367-8(2)*, Aladdin) Simon & Schuster Children's Publishing.
—A Rockin' Mystery. 2012. (Hardy Boys: the Secret Files Ser.: 10). (ENG.). 96p. (J). (gr. 1-4). pap. 5.99 *(978-1-4424-1671-0(8)*, Aladdin) Simon & Schuster Children's Publishing.
—The Scoop on Ice Cream! Williams, Bonnie. 2014. (History of Fun Stuff Ser.). (ENG.). 48p. (J). (gr. 1-3). pap. 4.99 *(978-1-4814-0981-0(6)*, Simon Spotlight) Simon Spotlight.
—Sports Sabotage, 8. 2012. (Hardy Boys: the Secret Files Ser.: 8). (ENG.). 112p. (J). (gr. 1-4). pap. 5.99 *(978-1-4424-2316-9(1)*, Aladdin) Simon & Schuster Children's Publishing.
—The Stellar Story of Space Travel. Lakin, Patricia. 2016. (History of Fun Stuff Ser.). (ENG.). 48p. (J). (gr. 1-3). pap. 4.99 *(978-1-4814-5623-4(7)*, Simon Spotlight) Simon Spotlight.
—The Superstar Story of the Harlem Globetrotters: History of Fun Stuff. Dobrow, Larry. 2017. (History of Fun Stuff Ser.). (ENG.). 40p. (J). (gr. 1-3). 16.99 *(978-1-4814-8749-8(3))*; pap. 4.99 *(978-1-4814-8748-1(5))* Simon Spotlight. (Simon Spotlight).
—Trouble at the Arcade, 1. 2010. (Hardy Boys: the Secret Files Ser.: 1). (ENG.). 96p. (J). (gr. 1-4). pap. 5.99 *(978-1-4169-9164-9(6)*, Aladdin) Simon & Schuster Children's Publishing.
—True Colors! the Story of Crayola. Burton, Jesse. 2018. (History of Fun Stuff Ser.). (ENG.). 40p. (J). (gr. 1-3). 17.99 *(978-1-5344-2567-5(5))*; pap. 4.99 *(978-1-5344-2566-8(7))* Simon Spotlight. (Simon Spotlight).
—Unmasking the Science of Superpowers! Brown, Jordan. 2016. (Science of Fun Stuff Ser.). (ENG.). 48p. (J). (gr. 1-3). pap. 3.99 *(978-1-4814-6778-0(6)*, Simon Spotlight) Simon Spotlight.
Burroughs, Scott. The Super Short, Amazing Story of David & Goliath. Burroughs, Scott. Burroughs, Chrysti. 2005. 32p. (J). (gr. -1-3). 10.99 *(978-0-8254-2412-0(7))* Kregel Pubns.
Burroughs, Scott & Harrison, Nancy. The Who Was? Activity Book. London, Jordan & Who HQ. 2018. (Who Was? Ser.). 112p. (J). (gr. 3-7). act. bk. ed. 7.99 *(978-1-5247-8997-8(6)*, Penguin Workshop) Penguin Young Readers Group.
Burrowes, Adjoa J. Mi Escalera, 1 vol. Derby, Sally. de la Vega, Eida, tr. 2005. (SPA.). 32p. (J). (gr. k-2). pap. 10.95 *(978-1-880000-75-5(X)*, 0fdcdb5d-0522-4d60-92ff-59e840c7442a) Lee & Low Bks., Inc.
Burrows, Ailsa. The Jar of Happiness. Burrows, Ailsa. (Child's Play Library). 32p. (J). 2016. *(978-1-84643-729-8(6))*; 2015. pap. *(978-1-84643-728-1(8))* Child's Play International Ltd.
Burrows, Dana. The Big School. Brown, Bennique Inderria. 2018. (ENG.). 46p. (J). pap. 10.00 *(978-1-7916-9126-4(9))* Independently Published.
Burrows, Jacen, et al. Black Panther Vol. 2: Avengers of the New World. 2018. (Black Panther by Ta-Nehisi Coates (2016) HC Ser.: 2). (ENG.). 264p. (J). (gr. 4-17). 34.99 *(978-1-302-90895-9(2))* Marvel Worldwide, Inc.
Burrows, Jacen. Moon Knight: Legacy Vol. 1: Crazy Runs in the Family. 2018. (ENG.). 136p. (YA). (gr. 8-17). pap. 17.99 *(978-1-302-90937-6(1))* Marvel Worldwide, Inc.
Burrows, Jeffrey Scott. Keri Tarr - Cat Detective. Lement, Wendy. 2004. (ENG.). 80p. (J). pap. 9.95 *(978-1-891369-52-0(0))* Breakaway Bks.
Burrows, Sophie. Yann's Hajj Trip: The Journey of a Lifetime. Gilani, Fawzia. 2018. (ENG.). 32p. (J). 8.95 *(978-0-86037-623-1(0))* Kube Publishing Ltd. GBR. Dist: Consortium Bk. Sales & Distribution.
Burruss, Melissa, jt. illus. see Castillo, Cesar.
Bursi, Simona. Bible Stories for Boys, 1 vol. Martin, Peter. ed. 2014. (ENG.). 48p. (J). (gr. k-4). 14.99 *(978-0-7459-6370-9(6))* Lion Hudson PLC GBR. Dist: Kregel Pubns.
—Bible Stories for Girls. Goodings, Christina & Martin, Peter. ed. 2014. (ENG.). 48p. (J). (gr. k-4). 11.99 *(978-0-7459-6371-6(4))* Lion Hudson PLC GBR. Dist: Independent Pubs. Group.
Bursi, Simona, et al. The Usborne Book of Greek Myths. Milbourne, Anna & Stowell, Louie. Brocklehurst, Ruth, ed. 2014. (ENG.). 301p. (J). (gr. 4-7). pap. 22.99 *(978-0-7945-2130-1(4)*, Usborne) EDC Publishing.
Burstein, Anna. The Way to Cat Tail Pond. Burstein, Fred. 2017. (ENG.). 62p. (J). (gr. k-4). 21.00 *(978-1-5154-3893-9(7))* Wilder Pubns., Corp.
—The Way to Cattail Pond. Burstein, Fred. 2017. (ENG.). 62p. (J). (gr. k-4). pap. 14.95 *(978-1-5154-1713-2(1))* Wilder Pubns., Corp.
Bursztyn, Dina. The Land of Lost Things: El País de las Cosas Perdidas. Bursztyn, Dina. 2011. (SPA & ENG.). 32p. (J). (gr. -1-3). 16.95 *(978-1-55885-690-5(0)*, Piñata Books) Arte Publico Pr.
Burt, Emily. Jeremy Steadfast Told a Lie. Ralph, Rachel. 2020. (ENG.). 34p. (J). pap. 13.99 ***(978-1-952894-90-9(5))*** Pen It! Pubns., LLC.
Burt, Kelly. Animalimericks! Henderson, Kris. 2009. 32p. pap. 14.99 *(978-1-4389-4333-6(4))* AuthorHouse.
Burt, Mary Alice. Beginning the Walk: A Tool for Developing A Preschooler's Faith. Burt, Mary Alice. 2004. 164p. (J). cd-rom 19.95 *(978-0-9641134-2-8(2))* Products With A Purpose.
Burt-Sullivan, Neallia. Tino Turtle Travels to Beijing, China. Ahern, Carolyn L. 2011. (ENG.). 56p. (J). (gr. -1-4). 19.95 incl. audio compact disk *(978-0-9793158-4-8(0))* Tino Turtle Travels, LLC.
Burt Sullivan, Neallia. Tino Turtle Travels to Kenya - the Great Safari. Ahern, Carolyn L. 2009. (ENG & SWA.). 32p. (J). (gr. -1-4). 19.95 incl. audio compact disk *(978-0-9793158-3-1(2))* Tino Turtle Travels, LLC.
—Tino Turtle Travels to London, England. Ahern, Carolyn L. (J). 2007. 36p. 17.95 incl. audio compact disk *(978-0-9793158-0-0(8))*; 2008. (ENG.). 32p. 19.95 incl. audio compact disk *(978-0-9816297-0-4(9))* Tino Turtle Travels, LLC.
—Tino Turtle Travels to Mexico City, Mexico. Ahern, Carolyn L. 2008. (ENG & SPA.). 32p. (J). (gr. -1-4). 19.95 incl. audio compact disk *(978-0-9793158-2-4(4))* Tino Turtle Travels, LLC.
—Tino Turtle Travels to Paris, France. Ahern, Carolyn L. 2007. 36p. (J). (gr. -1-4). 17.95 incl. audio compact disk *(978-0-9793158-1-7(6))* Tino Turtle Travels, LLC.
Burton, Carl, jt. illus. see Burton, Linda.
Burton, Claudia. The Adventures of Remmington the Dog: An Unexpected Friend. Redfern, Holly. 2007. 28p. (gr. -1-3). per. 14.95 *(978-1-59858-317-5(4))* Dog Ear Publishing, LLC.
Burton, Izzy. Do Not Go in There. Horn, Ariel. 2020. (ENG.). 32p. (J). 18.99 *(978-1-250-18949-3(7)*, 900192254) Imprint IND. Dist: Macmillan.
Burton, Jane & Greenaway, Frank, photos by. Cat. Rayner, Matthew & BVetMed MRCVS Staff. 2004. (I Am Your Pet Ser.). 32p. (gr. k-4). lib. bdg. 27.00 *(978-0-8368-4102-2(6)*, Gareth Stevens Learning Library) Stevens, Gareth Publishing LLLP.
—Dog. Rayner, Matthew & BVetMed MRCVS Staff. 2004. (I Am Your Pet Ser.). 32p. (gr. k-4). lib. bdg. 27.00 *(978-0-8368-4103-9(4)*, Gareth Stevens Learning Library) Stevens, Gareth Publishing LLLP.
—Rabbit. Rayner, Matthew & BVetMed MRCVS Staff. 2004. (I Am Your Pet Ser.). 32p. (gr. k-4). lib. bdg. 27.00 *(978-0-8368-4105-3(0)*, Gareth Stevens Learning Library) Stevens, Gareth Publishing LLLP.
Burton, Jane & King, Dave, photos by. Mammal: Eyewitness Books. Parker, Steve. 2004. 63p. (gr. 4-8). reprint ed. 16.00 *(978-0-7567-7286-4(9))* DIANE Publishing Co.
Burton, Jane, jt. photos by see Greenaway, Frank.
Burton, Jessie S. Lessons in Courage: A Square Books Adventure. Hughes, Julie B. 2019. (Square Books Adventure Ser.: Vol. 1). (ENG.). 66p. (J). (gr. 3-6). pap. 7.95 ***(978-1-0878-1366-0(2))*** SDC Publishing, LLC.
Burton, John J. Spikez: Titanium Edition. Mayers, Richard a. 2019. (Spikez Ser.: Vol. 1). (ENG.). 318p. (J). (gr. 6). pap. ***(978-1-9162126-0-2(3))*** Burton Mayers Bks.
Burton, Linda & Burton, Carl. Pay Attention, Emily Brown! Burton, Linda & Burton, Carl. 2011. 32p. (J). *(978-1-60613-027-8(7))* Woodbine Hse.
Burton, Terry. English. Award, Anna. 2012. (ENG.). 36p. (J). pap. 8.25 *(978-1-84135-801-7(0))* Award Pubns. Ltd. GBR. Dist: Parkwest Pubns., Inc.
—English/French. Award, Anna. 2012. (J). 96p. 11.50 *(978-1-84135-798-6(7))*; (ENG.). 36p. pap. 8.25 *(978-1-84135-802-4(9))* Award Pubns. Ltd. GBR. Dist: Parkwest Pubns., Inc.
—Gingerbread Man. Andrews, Jackie. 2012. (ENG.). 32p. pap. 6.50 *(978-1-84135-193-3(8))* Award Pubns. Ltd. GBR. Dist: Parkwest Pubns., Inc.
Burton, Terry. English. Burton, Terry. Ward, Anna. 2012. (ENG.). 96p. (J). 11.50 *(978-1-84135-797-3(9))* Award Pubns. Ltd. GBR. Dist: Parkwest Pubns., Inc.
Burton, Terry & Hicks, Angela. My First Picture Dictionary. Giles, Sophie et al. 2014. (ENG.). 125p. 17.50 *(978-1-84135-873-4(8))* Award Pubns. Ltd. GBR. Dist: Parkwest Pubns., Inc.
Burton, Tim. The Nightmare Before Christmas: 20th Anniversary Edition. Burton, Tim. 20th anniv. ed. 2013. (ENG.). 40p. (J). (gr. 1-3). 17.99 *(978-1-4231-7869-9(6))* Disney Pr.
Burton, Virginia Lee. The Emperor's New Clothes. Andersen, Hans & Starbright Foundation Staff. (Folk Tale Classics Ser.). (ENG.). 48p. (J). (gr. -1-3). 2014. 8.99 *(978-0-544-15952-5(7)*, 1550259, HMH Books For Young Readers); 2004. pap. 7.99 *(978-0-618-34420-8(9)*, 480621) Houghton Mifflin Harcourt Publishing Co.
Burton, Virginia Lee. The Little House. Burton, Virginia Lee. 2009. (ENG.). 42p. (J). (gr. -1 — 1). bds. 7.99 *(978-0-547-13104-7(6)*, 1048359) Houghton Mifflin Harcourt Publishing Co.
—Mike Mulligan & His Steam Shovel, 1 vol. Burton, Virginia Lee. 2006. (ENG.). 48p. (J). (gr. -1-3). 10.99 *(978-0-618-73756-7(1)*, 482681) Houghton Mifflin Harcourt Publishing Co.
Burtseva, Irina. Performing Poodles. Crisp, Maureen. 2019. (Circus Quest Ser.: Vol. 3). (ENG.). 112p. (J). (gr. 1-5). pap. *(978-0-473-47472-0(7))* Marmac Media.
Burtseva, Irina. Tumbling Town. Crisp, Maureen. 2020. (Circus Quest Ser.: Vol. 4). (ENG.). 104p. (J). (gr. 1-5). pap. ***(978-0-473-50734-3(X))*** Marmac Media.
Busaluzzo, Constanza. The Baby Bible Sing & Pray. David C. Cook Publishing Company Staff & Currie, Robin. ed. 2008. (Baby Bible Ser.). (ENG.). 46p. (J). bds. 12.99 *(978-0-7814-4893-2(X)*, 105653) Cook, David C.
—Stories about Jesus. David C. Cook Publishing Company Staff & Currie, Robin. ed. 2008. (Baby Bible Ser.). (ENG.). 46p. (J). bds. 12.99 *(978-0-7814-4889-5(1)*, 105652) Cook, David C.
Busby, Ailie. Eating Well!/¡Comer Bien! Mlawer, Teresa, tr. 2020. (Just Like Me/¡Igual Que Yo! (English/Spanish Bilingual) Ser.: 4). (ENG.). 12p. (J). bds. ***(978-1-78628-448-8(0))*** Child's Play International Ltd.
Busby, Ailie. Elephant's Birthday Bells: Jump up & Join In. Grant, Carrie and David. 2013. 32p. (J). pap. 7.99 *(978-1-61067-181-1(3))* Kane Miller.
—Fall. Child's Play. 2015. (Seasons Ser.: 4). (ENG.). 12p. (J). (gr. 1-1). bds. *(978-1-84643-744-1(X))* Child's Play International Ltd.
Busby, Ailie. Feeling Great!/¡Sentirse Bien! Mlawer, Teresa, tr. 2020. (Just Like Me/¡Igual Que Yo! (English/Spanish Bilingual) Ser.: 4). (ENG.). 12p. (J). bds. ***(978-1-78628-451-8(0))*** Child's Play International Ltd.
—Five Little Ducks - First Book of Nursery Games. 2020. (Nursery Time Ser.: 3). (ENG.). 26p. (J). bds. ***(978-1-78628-410-5(3))*** Child's Play International Ltd.
Busby, Ailie. Henry Helps Clean His Room, 1 vol. Bracken, Beth. 2012. (Henry Helps Ser.). (ENG.). 24p. (J). (gr. -1 — 1). pap. 5.95 *(978-1-4048-7668-2(5))*; lib. bdg. 22.65 *(978-1-4048-7306-3(6))* Capstone. (Picture Window Bks.).
—Henry Helps Make Cookies, 1 vol. Bracken, Beth. 2012. (Henry Helps Ser.). (ENG.). 24p. (J). (gr. -1 — 1). pap. 5.95 *(978-1-4048-7669-9(3))*; lib. bdg. 22.65 *(978-1-4048-7303-2(1))* Capstone. (Picture Window Bks.).
—Henry Helps Plant a Garden, 1 vol. Bracken, Beth. 2012. (Henry Helps Ser.). (ENG.). 24p. (J). (gr. -1 — 1). pap. 5.95 *(978-1-4048-7670-5(7))*; lib. bdg. 22.65 *(978-1-4048-7305-6(8))* Capstone. (Picture Window Bks.).
—Henry Helps Wash the Car, 1 vol. Bracken, Beth. 2012. (Henry Helps Ser.). (ENG.). 24p. (J). (gr. -1 — 1). pap. 5.95 *(978-1-4048-7671-2(5))*; lib. bdg. 22.65 *(978-1-4048-7304-9(X))* Capstone. (Picture Window Bks.).
—Henry Helps with Dinner, 1 vol. Bracken, Beth. 2012. (Henry Helps Ser.). (ENG.). 32p. (J). (gr. -1 — 1). pap. 5.95 *(978-1-4048-7675-0(8)*, Picture Window Bks.) Capstone.
—Henry Helps with Laundry, 1 vol. Bracken, Beth. (Henry Helps Ser.). (ENG.). 24p. (J). (gr. -1 — 1). 2012. pap. 5.95 *(978-1-4048-7674-3(X))*; 2011. lib. bdg. 22.65 *(978-1-4048-6772-7(4))* Capstone. (Picture Window Bks.).
—Henry Helps with the Baby, 1 vol. Bracken, Beth. (Henry Helps Ser.). (ENG.). 24p. (J). (gr. -1 — 1). 2012. pap. 5.95 *(978-1-4048-7672-9(3))*; 2011. lib. bdg. 22.65 *(978-1-4048-6770-3(8))* Capstone. (Picture Window Bks.).
—Henry Helps with the Dog, 1 vol. Bracken, Beth. (Henry Helps Ser.). (ENG.). 24p. (J). (gr. -1 — 1). 2012. pap. 5.95 *(978-1-4048-7673-6(1))*; 2011. lib. bdg. 22.65 *(978-1-4048-6771-0(6))* Capstone. (Picture Window Bks.).
—Imani's Library Book Red Band. Hawes, Alison. 2017. (Cambridge Reading Adventures Ser.). (ENG.). 16p. pap. 5.62 *(978-1-108-40072-5(8))* Cambridge Univ. Pr.
—Invierno/Winter. Child's Play. Mlawer, Teresa, tr. ed. 2019. (Spanish/English Bilingual Editions Ser.). (ENG & SPA.). 12p. (J). (gr. 1-1). bds. *(978-1-78628-306-1(9))* Child's Play International Ltd.
Busby, Ailie. Just Like Me! Board Book Set Of 4. 2020. (Social & Emotional Learning Sets Ser.). (ENG.). 48p. (J). bds., bds., bds. ***(978-1-78628-528-7(2))*** Child's Play International Ltd.
Busby, Ailie. Lion's Speedy Sauce: Jump up & Join In. Grant, Carrie and David. 2013. 32p. (J). pap. 7.99 *(978-1-61067-180-4(5))* Kane Miller.
Busby, Ailie. Looking Good!/¡Lucir Bien! Mlawer, Teresa, tr. 2020. (Just Like Me/¡Igual Que Yo! (English/Spanish Bilingual) Ser.: 4). (ENG.). 12p. (J). bds. ***(978-1-78628-450-1(2))*** Child's Play International Ltd.
Busby, Ailie. Lulu & the Noisy Baby. Reid, Camilla. 2016. (Lulu Ser.). 32p. (J). (gr. -1-k). *(978-1-4088-2818-2(9)*, 142105, Bloomsbury Children's Bks.) Bloomsbury Publishing Plc.
—Lulu Loves Colours. Reid, Camilla. 2015. 12p. (J). (gr. -1-k). bds. 8.99 *(978-1-4088-4964-4(X)*, 900146185, Bloomsbury Children's Bks.) Bloomsbury Publishing USA.
—Lulu Loves Numbers. Reid, Camilla. 2015. 12p. (J). (gr. -1-1). bds. 8.99 *(978-1-4088-4957-6(7)*, 900143539, Bloomsbury Children's Bks.) Bloomsbury Publishing USA.
—Lulu Loves Shapes. Reid, Camilla. 2015. (Lulu Ser.). 12p. (J). (gr. -1-1). bds. 8.99 *(978-1-4088-4958-3(5)*, 900143491, Bloomsbury Children's Bks.) Bloomsbury Publishing USA.
Busby, Ailie. On the Go!/¡a Moverse! Mlawer, Teresa, tr. 2020. (Just Like Me/¡Igual Que Yo! (English/Spanish Bilingual) Ser.: 4). (ENG.). 12p. (J). bds. ***(978-1-78628-449-5(9))*** Child's Play International Ltd.
Busby, Ailie. Otoño/Fall. Child's Play. Mlawer, Teresa, tr. ed. 2019. (Spanish/English Bilingual Editions Ser.). (ENG.). 12p. (J). (gr. 1-1). bds. *(978-1-78628-305-4(0))* Child's Play International Ltd.
Busby, Ailie. Pat-A-Cake! - First Book of Nursery Rhymes. 2020. (Nursery Time Ser.: 3). (ENG.). 26p. (J). bds. ***(978-1-78628-411-2(1))*** Child's Play International Ltd.

B

Busby, Ailie. Primavera/Spring. Child's Play. Mlawer, Teresa, tr. ed. 2019. (Spanish/English Bilingual Editions Ser.). (ENG & SPA.). 12p. (J). (gr. 1-1). bds. (978-1-78628-303-0(4)) Child's Play International Ltd.

Busby, Ailie. See-Saw! - First Book of Nursery Songs. 2020. (Nursery Time Ser.: 3). (ENG.). 26p. (J). bds. **(978-1-78628-409-9(X))** Child's Play International Ltd.

Busby, Ailie. Spring. Child's Play. 2015. (Seasons Ser.: 4). 12p. (J). (gr. 1-1). spiral bd. (978-1-84643-741-0(5)) Child's Play International Ltd.

—Summer. Child's Play. 2015. (Seasons Ser.: 4). 12p. (J). (gr. 1-1). spiral bd. (978-1-84643-742-7(3)) Child's Play International Ltd.

—Verano/Summer. Child's Play. Mlawer, Teresa, tr. ed. 2019. (Spanish/English Bilingual Editions Ser.). (ENG & SPA.). 12p. (J). (gr. 1-1). bds. (978-1-78628-304-7(2)) Child's Play International Ltd.

—Where Are My Shoes? Yellow Band. Bodman, Sue & Franklin, Glen. 2017. (Cambridge Reading Adventures Ser.). (ENG.). 16p. (J). pap. 5.62 (978-1-108-43964-0(0)) Cambridge Univ. Pr.

—Who's the Boss Rhinoceros? Puttock, Simon. 32p. (J). pap. 8.99 (978-0-7497-4354-3(9)) Egmont Bks., Ltd. GBR. Dist: Trafalgar Square Publishing.

—Winter. Child's Play. 2015. (Seasons Ser.: 4). 12p. (J). (gr. 1-1). spiral bd. (978-1-84643-745-8(8)) Child's Play International Ltd.

Busby, Ailie, jt. illus. see Anderson, Laura Ellen.

Buscema, John, et al. Amazing Spider-Man Epic Collection: the Secret of the Petrified Tablet. 2020. (ENG.). 456p. (YA). (gr. 4-17). pap. 39.99 (978-1-302-92196-5(7)) Marvel Worldwide, Inc.

Buscema, John, et al. Avengers Epic Collection: This Beachhead Earth. 2020. (ENG.). 504p. (J). (gr. 4-17). pap. 39.99 **(978-1-302-92197-2(5))** Marvel Worldwide, Inc.

Buscema, John, et al. The Avengers Omnibus Vol. 3. 2018. (ENG.). 760p. (J). (gr. 4-17). 100.00 (978-1-302-91020-4(5)) Marvel Worldwide, Inc.

—Black Widow Epic Collection: Beware the Black Widow. 2020. (ENG.). 424p. (J). (gr. 4-17). pap. 39.99 (978-1-302-92126-2(6)) Marvel Worldwide, Inc.

—Captain Marvel: Starforce. 2019. (ENG.). 184p. (YA). (gr. -1-17). pap. 19.99 (978-1-302-91797-5(8)) Marvel Worldwide, Inc.

—Conan the Barbarian: the Original Marvel Years Omnibus Vol. 2. 2019. 856p. (gr. 10-17). 125.00 (978-1-302-91514-8(2)) Marvel Worldwide, Inc.

Buscema, John. Conan the Barbarian: the Original Marvel Years Omnibus Vol. 3. 2020. (ENG.). 824p. (YA). (gr. 8-17). 125.00 (978-1-302-91783-8(8)) Marvel Worldwide, Inc.

—Marvel Visionaries: John Buscema. 2019. (ENG.). 352p. (YA). (gr. 8-17). pap. 34.99 (978-1-302-91781-4(1)) Marvel Worldwide, Inc.

Buscema, John, et al. The Mighty Thor Omnibus Vol. 3. 2017. (ENG.). 1000p. (J). (gr. 4-17). 125.00 (978-1-302-90381-7(0)) Marvel Worldwide, Inc.

Buscema, John. The Shadow in the Tomb & Other Stories. Thomas, Roy. 2004. (Conan Ser.: Vol. 5). (ENG.). 160p. pap. 15.95 (978-1-59307-175-2(2)) Dark Horse Comics.

Buscema, John, et al. Silver Surfer Omnibus Vol. 1. 2020. 576p. (J). (gr. 4-17). 100.00 **(978-1-302-92269-6(6))** Marvel Worldwide, Inc.

Buscema, John, et al. The Thanos Wars: Infinity Origin Omnibus. 2019. (ENG.). 800p. (J). (gr. 4-17). 100.00 (978-1-302-91530-8(4)) Marvel Worldwide, Inc.

—What If? Classic: the Complete Collection Vol. 2. 2019. (ENG.). 376p. (YA). (gr. 4-17). pap. 39.99 (978-1-302-92059-3(6)) Marvel Worldwide, Inc.

Buscema, John & Buscema, Sal. Thor Epic Collection: into the Dark Nebula. 2020. (ENG.). 480p. (YA). (gr. 4-17). pap. 39.99 (978-1-302-92248-1(3)) Marvel Worldwide, Inc.

Buscema, John, jt. illus. see Kirby, Jack.

Buscema, Sal, et al. Marvel Masterworks: Marvel Team-Up Vol. 5. 2020. (ENG.). 304p. (J). (gr. 4-17). 75.00 **(978-1-302-92218-4(1))** Marvel Worldwide, Inc.

Buscema, Sal, et al. Marvel Masterworks: the Incredible Hulk Vol. 13. 2019. (Marvel Masterworks: the Incredible Hulk Ser.: 13). (ENG.). 288p. (YA). (gr. 4-17). 75.00 (978-1-302-91926-9(1)) Marvel Worldwide, Inc.

Buscema, Sal. The Mighty Thor by Walter Simonson Vol. 3. 2018. (ENG.). 264p. (J). (gr. 4-17). pap. 29.99 (978-1-302-90901-7(0)) Marvel Worldwide, Inc.

Buscema, Sal, et al. Thing: Project Pegasus. 2018. (ENG.). 160p. (J). (gr. 4-17). pap. 24.99 (978-1-302-91149-2(X)) Marvel Worldwide, Inc.

Buscema, Sal. Thor by Walter Simonson Vol. 2. 2018. (ENG.). 240p. (J). (gr. 4-17). pap. 24.99 (978-1-302-90902-4(9)) Marvel Worldwide, Inc.

Buscema, Sal, et al. Thor vs. Hulk. 2017. (ENG.). 336p. (YA). (gr. 8-17). pap. 29.99 (978-0-7851-8515-4(1)) Marvel Worldwide, Inc.

Buscema, Sal, jt. illus. see Brown, Bob.

Buscema, Sal, jt. illus. see Buscema, John.

Buscema, Sal, jt. illus. see Frenz, Ron.

Buscema, Sal, jt. illus. see Trimpe, Herb.

Busch, Isabelle V. Theoretical Dragon Anatomy: Structure & Function. Busch, Isabelle V. 2019. (ENG.). 50p. (YA). (gr. 7-12). 25.95 (978-0-9986610-9-4(0)) Episode.Media.

Busch, Wilhelm. Max & Moritz. Busch, Wilhelm. Ledsom, Mark, tr. 2020. (ENG.). 64p. (J). (gr. 1-4). pap. 9.99 (978-1-78269-253-9(3), Pushkin Children's Bks.) Steerforth Pr.

Bush, John. Mr Crookodile. Paul, Korky. 2016. (Reading Ladder Ser.). (ENG.). 48p. (J). (gr. k-2). pap. 7.99 (978-1-4052-8204-8(5)) Egmont Bks., Ltd. GBR. Dist: Independent Pubs. Group.

Bush, Robert Quacken. The Return of Pete Pack Rat. Bush, Robert Quacken, photos by. rev. deluxe ed. 2005. 64p. (J). (gr. 2-4). reprint ed. 12.95 (978-0-9712757-1-3(8)) Quackenbush, Robert Studios.

—The Return of Pete Pack Rat. Bush, Robert Quacken, photos by. Bush, Robert Quacken. Bush, Robert Quacken, ed. rev. deluxe ed. 2005. 64p. (J). (gr. 2-4). reprint ed. pap. 6.95 (978-0-9712757-2-0(6)) Quackenbush, Robert Studios.

Bush, Timothy. All in Just One Cookie. Goodman, Susan. 2006. (ENG.). 32p. (J). (gr. -1-4). 17.99 (978-0-06-009092-0(8), Greenwillow Bks.) HarperCollins Pubs.

—Capital Mysteries #12: the Ghost at Camp David. Roy, Ron. 2010. (Capital Mysteries Ser.: 12). (ENG.). 96p. (J). (gr. 1-4). pap. 4.99 (978-0-375-85925-0(X), Random Hse. Bks. for Young Readers) Random Hse. Children's Bks.

—Capital Mysteries #14: Turkey Trouble on the National Mall, 14. Roy, Ronald. 2012. (Capital Mysteries Ser.). (ENG.). 96p. (J). (gr. 1-4). lib. bdg. 17.44 (978-0-375-87004-0(0)) Random House Publishing Group.

—Capital Mysteries #14: Turkey Trouble on the National Mall. Roy, Ron. 2012. (Capital Mysteries Ser.: 14). (ENG.). 96p. (J). (gr. 1-4). 4.99 (978-0-307-93220-4(6), Random Hse. Bks. for Young Readers) Random Hse. Children's Bks.

—Capital Mysteries #3: the Skeleton in the Smithsonian. Roy, Ron. 2003. (Capital Mysteries Ser.: 3). (ENG.). 96p. (J). (gr. 1-4). 5.99 (978-0-307-26517-3(X), Random Hse. Bks. for Young Readers) Random Hse. Children's Bks.

—Capital Mysteries #5: Who Broke Lincoln's Thumb? Roy, Ron. 2005. (Capital Mysteries Ser.: 5). 96p. (J). (gr. 1-4). per. 5.99 (978-0-375-82558-3(4), Random Hse. Bks. for Young Readers) Random Hse. Children's Bks.

—Capital Mysteries #7: Trouble at the Treasury. Roy, Ron. 2006. (Capital Mysteries Ser.: 7). 96p. (J). (gr. 1-4). per. 5.99 (978-0-375-83969-6(0), Random Hse. Bks. for Young Readers) Random Hse. Children's Bks.

—The Election-Day Disaster. Roy, Ron. 2008. (Capital Mysteries Ser.: No. 10). 87p. (gr. 1-4). 15.00 (978-0-7569-8802-9(0)) Perfection Learning Corp.

—The Election-Day Disaster. Roy, Ron. 2008. (Capital Mysteries Ser.: 10). (ENG.). 96p. (J). (gr. 1-4). 5.99 (978-0-375-84805-6(3), Random Hse. Bks. for Young Readers) Random Hse. Children's Bks.

—Fireworks at the FBI. Roy, Ron. 2006. (Capital Mysteries Ser.: 6). 96p. (J). (gr. 1-4). per. 5.99 (978-0-375-87527-4(1), Random Hse. Bks. for Young Readers) Random Hse. Children's Bks.

—Mystery at the Washington Monument. Roy, Ron. 2007. (Capital Mysteries Ser.: No. 8). 87p. (gr. 1-4). 15.00 (978-0-7569-7845-7(9)) Perfection Learning Corp.

—Mystery at the Washington Monument, 8. Roy, Ron. 2007. (Capital Mysteries Ser.: No. 8). (ENG.). 87p. (J). (gr. 3-6). lib. bdg. 17.44 (978-0-375-93970-9(9)) Random House Publishing Group.

—Mystery at the Washington Monument. Roy, Ron. 2007. (Capital Mysteries Ser.: 8). (ENG.). 96p. (J). (gr. 1-4). per. 5.99 (978-0-375-83970-2(4), Random Hse. Bks. for Young Readers) Random Hse. Children's Bks.

—The Secret at Jefferson's Mansion. Roy, Ron. 2009. (Capital Mysteries Ser.: 11). (ENG.). 96p. (J). (gr. 1-4). 5.99 (978-0-375-84533-8(X), Random Hse. Bks. for Young Readers) Random Hse. Children's Bks.

—Teddy Bear, Teddy Bear: A Traditional Rhyme. 2005. 32p. (J). 14.99 (978-0-06-057835-0(1)); (gr. -1 — 1). lib. bdg. 15.89 (978-0-06-057836-7(X)) HarperCollins Pubs.

—A Thief at the National Zoo. Roy, Ron. 2008. (Capital Mysteries Ser.: No. 9). 87p. (gr. k-3). 15.00 (978-0-7569-8329-1(0)) Perfection Learning Corp.

—A Thief at the National Zoo, 9. Roy, Ron. 2007. (Capital Mysteries Ser.: No. 9). (ENG.). 87p. (J). (gr. 2-4). lib. bdg. 17.44 (978-0-375-94804-6(X)) Random House Publishing Group.

—A Thief at the National Zoo. Roy, Ron. 2007. (Capital Mysteries Ser.: 9). 96p. (J). (gr. 1-4). per. 5.99 (978-0-375-84804-9(5), Random Hse. Bks. for Young Readers) Random Hse. Children's Bks.

—Trapped on the D. C. Train! Capital Mysteries #13. Roy, Ron. 2011. (Capital Mysteries Ser.: 13). 96p. (J). (gr. 1-4). 5.99 (978-0-375-85926-7(8), Random Hse. Bks. for Young Readers) Random Hse. Children's Bks.

—Trouble at the Treasury, 7. Roy, Ron. 2003. (Capital Mysteries Ser.: No. 7). (ENG.). 86p. (J). (gr. 2-4). lib. bdg. 17.44 (978-0-375-93969-3(5)) Random House Publishing Group.

—Who Broke Lincoln's Thumb?, 5. Roy, Ron. 2005. (Capital Mysteries Ser.: No. 5). (ENG.). 86p. (J). (gr. 2-4). lib. bdg. 17.44 (978-0-375-92558-0(9)) Random House Publishing Group.

Bush, Timothy. Capital Mysteries #4: a Spy in the White House. Bush, Timothy, tr. Roy, Ron. 2004. (Capital Mysteries Ser.: 4). 96p. (J). (gr. 1-4). 5.99 (978-0-375-82557-6(6), Random Hse. Bks. for Young Readers) Random Hse. Children's Bks.

—A Spy in the White House, 4. Bush, Timothy, tr. Roy, Ron. 2004. (Capital Mysteries Ser.: No. 4). (ENG.). 86p. (J). (gr. 2-4). lib. bdg. 17.44 (978-0-375-92557-3(0)) Random House Publishing Group.

Bushell, William. My Hearing Loss & Me: We Get along Most of the Time. Anderson Jr., John F. 2004. (ENG.). 44p. pap. 24.00 (978-1-4120-0308-7(3)) Trafford Publishing.

Bushnaq, Saba. The Coffee Monster & the Land of Coffee. Friedman, Nate. 2020. (Coffee Monster Ser.: Vol. 2). (ENG.). 40p. (J). pap. **(978-1-987976-60-1(6))** Mirror World Publishing.

Bushnell, Holly. Lamby & Flossie's Tales from the Travel Pouch. Lennon, Jude. 2018. (ENG.). 78p. (J). (gr. 1-3). pap. (978-1-9997959-3-1(8)) Little Lamb Publishing.

—Lamby Goes Camping. Lennon, Jude. 2018. (ENG.). 24p. (J). (gr. k-2). pap. (978-1-9997959-2-4(X)) Little Lamb Publishing.

—Oluby-Loon Travels in Her Balloon: Oluby Visits Kenya. Tanner, Suzanne. 2017. (ENG.). (J). pap. (978-1-9998036-0-5(4)) Tanner, Suzanne.

Bushnell, Holly Faith. MR Crocodile Adventures: Magenta the Witch Works Her Magic on a Bored MR Crocodile. Tapia-Bowes, Sally-Anne. 2016. (ENG.). (J). pap. (978-0-9931919-4-7(0)) PurplePenguinPublishing.

Busike, Jim. Sophia the Bionic Cat. Smith, Karolyn. 2016. (ENG.). (J). 19.99 (978-1-68419-345-5(1)) Primedia eLaunch LLC.

Buske Thomas, Natalie. Fred: The Real Life Adventures of a Little Girl with a Big Imagination. Buske Thomas, Natalie. 2016. (ENG.). (J). (gr. k-6). 18.99 (978-0-9666919-4-8(6)) Independent Spirit Publishing.

Busko, Anastasia. The Mouse Who Wanted Some Cheese. Lindsey, Era Cathlean. 2019. (ENG.). 34p. (J). 16.99 **(978-1-0878-1193-2(7))** Sing Creative Consulting.

Busquets, Carlos. Los Animales Cuentan 365 Historias. 2nd ed. 2004. (SPA.). 193p. (J). (gr. -1-7). 14.50 (978-970-22-0445-9(3)) Larousse, Ediciones, S. A. de C. V. MEX. Dist: Giron Bks.

Bussard, Frances Mae. Baron. Bussard, Frances Mae. 2020. (Coastal Dune Lake Critters Ser.: Vol. 3). (ENG.). 34p. (J). (gr. k-5). pap. 14.95 **(978-0-578-65018-0(5))** Bussard, Frances.

Busse, Alyssa. Chickenfriend. Roth, Penny S. 2018. (ENG.). 32p. (J). (gr. -1). pap. 12.95 (978-1-943027-27-9(7), 164283) Electric Moon Publishing.

Busse, Diana. Imagine If ... Benger, Lisa. 2016. (Imagine If ... Ser.: Vol. 1). (ENG.). (J). (gr. 1-6). 19.99 (978-0-9980893-1-7(1)) Young Createers.

—Imagine If... Farm Animals Talked. Benger, Lisa. 2016. (ENG.). (J). pap. 9.99 (978-0-9980893-0-0(3)) Young Createers.

Bustamante, Frank, et al. The Testimony of Jacob Hollow. Bustamante, Frank & Gray, Dan, eds. alt. ed. 2003. (YA). bds. 19.95 (978-0-9728526-0-9(3)) Third World Games, Inc.

Bustamante, Martin. Copernicus, Galileo & Newton: Band 18/Pearl (Collins Big Cat) Nelson, Jo. 2014. (Collins Big Cat Ser.). (ENG.). 80p. (J). (gr. 5). pap. 10.99 (978-0-00-753017-5(X)) HarperCollins Pubs. Ltd. GBR. Dist: Independent Pubs. Group.

—The Journey of Odysseus: Band 15/Emerald (Collins Big Cat) Morgan, Hawys. 2017. (Collins Big Cat Tales Ser.). (ENG.). 48p. (J). (gr. 3-4). pap. 12.99 (978-0-00-817941-0(7)) HarperCollins Pubs. Ltd. GBR. Dist: Independent Pubs. Group.

Bustamante, Martin, et al. The Young Artist's Guide to Drawing Fantasy Creatures. Sautter, Aaron. 2016. (Drawing Fantasy Creatures Ser.). (ENG.). 112p. (J). (gr. 3-9). pap. 9.95 (978-1-4914-8670-2(8), Capstone Pr.) Capstone.

Bustamante, Martín Horacio. Dragons. Doeden, Matt. 2019. (Mythical Creatures Ser.). (ENG.). 32p. (J). (gr. k-2). lib. bdg. 27.99 (978-1-5158-4443-3(9), 140563, Picture Window Bks.) Capstone.

—Griffins. Doeden, Matt. 2019. (Mythical Creatures Ser.). (ENG.). 32p. (J). (gr. k-2). lib. bdg. 27.99 (978-1-5158-4444-0(7), 140564, Picture Window Bks.) Capstone.

Bustard, Ned. Bible History ABCs: God's Story from a to Z. Nichols, Stephen J. 2019. (ENG.). 60p. 16.99 (978-1-4335-6437-6(8)) Crossway.

—Reformation ABCs: The People, Places, & Things of the Reformation-From a to Z. Nichols, Stephen J. 2017. (ENG.). 56p. 16.99 (978-1-4335-5282-3(5)) Crossway.

Bustos, Ignacio. Cuentos ClÁsicos Policiales Contados para NiÑos. 2019. (Brújula y la Veleta Ser.). (SPA.). 64p. (J). (gr. 4-7). pap. 5.95 (978-987-718-559-1(8)) Ediciones Lea S.A. ARG. Dist: Independent Pubs. Group.

Bustos, Ignacio. Fuiste Vos, Robot. Vaccarini, Franco. 2020. (Mis Cuentos Ser.). (SPA.). 24p. (J). (gr. k-2). pap. 4.95 **(978-987-718-633-8(0))** Ediciones Lea S.A. ARG. Dist: Independent Pubs. Group.

Bustos, Miguel. Bruce Lee. Sanchez Vegara, Maria Isabel. 2019. (Little People, Big Dreams Ser.: Vol. 29). (ENG.). 32p. (J). (gr. -1-2). **(978-1-78603-789-3(0))** Frances Lincoln Childrens Bks.

Bustos, Miguel. Bucketloads of Friends. Cassany, Mia. 2018. (ENG.). 44p. (J). (gr. -1-3). 14.95 (978-3-7913-7357-7(9)) Prestel Verlag GmbH & Co KG. DEU. Dist: Penguin Random Hse. LLC.

Bustos, Natacha. Moon Girl & Devil Dinosaur: Full Moon. 2020. 280p. (J). (gr. 4-7). pap. 12.99 (978-1-302-92113-2(4)) Marvel Worldwide, Inc.

—Moon Girl & Devil Dinosaur: in the Beginning. 2019. 272p. (J). (gr. 4-7). pap. 12.99 (978-1-302-91654-1(8)) Marvel Worldwide, Inc.

—Moon Girl & Devil Dinosaur Vol. 3: The Smartest There Is. 2017. (ENG.). 136p. (J). (gr. 4-17). pap. 17.99 (978-1-302-90534-7(1)) Marvel Worldwide, Inc.

—Moon Girl & Devil Dinosaur Vol. 4: Girl-Moon. 2018. (ENG.). 136p. (J). (gr. 4-17). pap. 17.99 (978-1-302-90535-4(X)) Marvel Worldwide, Inc.

—Moon Girl & Devil Dinosaur Vol. 5: Fantastic Three. 2018. (ENG.). 136p. (J). (gr. 4-17). pap. 17.99 (978-1-302-91099-0(X)) Marvel Worldwide, Inc.

—Moon Girl & Devil Dinosaur Vol. 6: Save Our School. 2018. (Moon Girl & Devil Dinosaur Ser.: 6). (ENG.). 112p. (J). (gr. 4-17). pap. 17.99 (978-1-302-91100-3(7)) Marvel Worldwide, Inc.

Bustos, Natacha, et al. Moon Girl & the Marvel Universe. 2018. (Moon Girl & the Marvel Universe Ser.: 1). 112p. (YA). (gr. 8-17). pap. 15.99 (978-1-302-91370-0(0)) Marvel Worldwide, Inc.

Bustos, Natacha & Bonvillain, Tamra. BFF #5: Know How. Reeder, Amy & Montclare, Brandon. 2017. (Moon Girl & Devil Dinosaur Ser.). (ENG.). 24p. (J). (gr. 2-8). lib. bdg. 27.07 (978-1-5321-4012-9(6), 25500, Marvel Age) Spotlight.

—Eureka! Reeder, Amy & Montclare, Brandon. 2017. (Moon Girl & Devil Dinosaur Ser.). (ENG.). 24p. (J). (gr. 2-8). lib. bdg. 27.07 (978-1-5321-4013-6(4), 25501, Marvel Age) Spotlight.

—'Nuff Said. Reeder, Amy & Montclare, Brandon. 2017. (Moon Girl & Devil Dinosaur Ser.). (ENG.). 24p. (J). (gr. 2-8). lib. bdg. 27.07 (978-1-5321-4011-2(8), 25499, Marvel Age) Spotlight.

—Old Dogs & New Tricks. Reeder, Amy & Montclare, Brandon. 2017. (Moon Girl & Devil Dinosaur Ser.). (ENG.). 24p. (J). (gr. 2-8). lib. bdg. 27.07 (978-1-5321-4009-9(6), 25497, Marvel Age) Spotlight.

—Out of the Frying Pan... Reeder, Amy & Montclare, Brandon. 2017. (Moon Girl & Devil Dinosaur Ser.). (ENG.). 24p. (J). (gr. 2-8). lib. bdg. 27.07 (978-1-5321-4010-5(X), 25498, Marvel Age) Spotlight.

—Repeat after Me. Reeder, Amy & Montclare, Brandon. 2017. (Moon Girl & Devil Dinosaur Ser.). (ENG.). 24p. (J). (gr. 2-8). lib. bdg. 27.07 (978-1-5321-4008-2(8), 25496, Marvel Age) Spotlight.

Bustos, Natacha & Duarte, Gustavo. Moon Girl & Devil Dinosaur Vol. 7. 2019. (ENG.). 120p. (YA). pap. 15.99 (978-1-302-91436-3(7)) Marvel Worldwide, Inc.

Bustos, Natacha, jt. illus. see Failla, Marco.

Busuttil, Conor. The Children of Lir: Ireland's Favourite Legend. Maher, Laura Ruth. 2019. (ENG.). 32p. 16.99 (978-1-78849-106-8(8)) O'Brien Pr., Ltd., The IRL. Dist: Casemate Pubs. & Bk. Distributors, LLC.

—The Magic Piano. O'Sullivan, Helen. 2013. 34p. pap. (978-1-908773-36-4(7)) Iponymous Publishing, Ltd.

Butchart, Avalon. Frogs, Snails & Sasquatch Tales. Kerr, Kyersten. 2019. (ENG.). 24p. (J). **(978-0-2288-2281-3(5))**; pap. **(978-0-2288-2279-0(3))** Tellwell Talent.

Butcher, Ben. Toy Story 2, Vol. 2. Nicholas, Christopher. 2006. (Little Golden Book Ser.). (ENG.). 24p. (J). (gr. -1-2). 4.99 (978-0-7364-2394-6(X), Golden/Disney) Random Hse. Children's Bks.

Butcher, Rosie. How Do You Care for a Very Sick Bear? Bayer, Vanessa. 2019. (ENG.). 32p. (J). 16.99 (978-1-250-29843-0(1), 900196186) Feiwel & Friends.

Butcher, Rosie. The Joy in You. Deeley, Cat. 2020. (ENG.). 32p. (J). (gr. -1-3). lib. bdg. 21.99 **(978-0-593-18142-3(5)**, Random Hse. Bks. for Young Readers) Random Hse. Children's Bks.

—The Joy in You. Deeley, Cat. 2020. (ENG.). 32p. (J). (gr. -1-3). 18.99 **(978-0-593-18141-6(7)**, Random Hse. Bks. for Young Readers) Random Hse. Children's Bks.

—The Night Before Christmas, 1 vol. 2020. (Stories of Christmas Ser.). (ENG.). 24p. (J). (gr. 1-2). pap. 8.25 **(978-1-4994-8589-9(1))**; lib. bdg. 24.60 **(978-1-4994-8591-2(3))** Rosen Publishing Group, Inc., The. (Windmill Bks.).

Butcher, Rosie. There's Only One You. Heling, Kathryn & Hembrook, Deborah. 2019. 32p. (J). (gr. -1-2). 16.95 (978-1-4549-2292-6(3)) Sterling Publishing Co., Inc.

—The Wishing Star. Chiew, Suzanne. 2020. (ENG.). 22p. (J). (-k). bds. 9.99 (978-1-68010-620-6(1)) Tiger Tales.

Butcher, Sally K., jt. illus. see Arjas, Pirkko.

Butcher, Sam. The Gospel According to the Apostles, 1 vol. MacArthur, John. 2005. (ENG.). 288p. pap. 15.99 (978-0-7852-7180-2(5)) Nelson, Thomas Inc.

—Precious Moments: Angel Kisses & Snuggle Time Prayers with Dolly. 2003. 8.40 (978-0-7180-0575-7(9)) Nelson, Thomas Inc.

—Precious Moments: Angel Kisses & Snuggle Time Prayers with Teddy Bear. 2003. 8.40 (978-0-7180-0567-2(8)) Nelson, Thomas Inc.

—Precious Moments: Small Hands Bible with Lavender Bible Cover. 2003. 12.84 (978-0-7180-0570-2(8)) Nelson, Thomas Inc.

—Precious Moments: Small Hands Bible with Pink Bible Cover. 2003. 12.84 (978-0-7180-0576-4(7)) Nelson, Thomas Inc.

—Precious Moments: Storybook Bible & Girl Prayer Pal Set. 2003. 14.60 (978-0-7180-0569-6(4)) Nelson, Thomas Inc.

Butenko, Bohdan. Clementine Loves Red. Boglar, Krystyna. Lloyd-Jones, Antonia & Krasodomska-Jones, Zosia, trs. 2017. (ENG.). 120p. (J). (gr. 2-4). pap. 13.95 (978-1-78269-118-1(9), Pushkin Children's Bks.) Steerforth Pr.

Buterbaugh, Aaron. The Evil Pajamas: The Poch Sister Adventures. Buterbaugh, Aaron. 2019. (Poch Sister Adventures Ser.: Vol. 1). (ENG.). 36p. (J). pap. 5.99 **(978-1-5208-7784-6(6))** Independently Published.

Butler, Bryan C. E: A Tale For Everybody. Harvey, Paul, Jr. 2013. (ENG.). 44p. (J). 25.00 (978-0-9887774-0-8(1)) Aurandt, Paul H II.

Butler, Chris. My Body. 2010. (My World Ser.) Tr. of Mi Cuerpo. (ENG.). 24p. (J). (gr. -1-1). pap. 8.15 (978-1-61533-027-0(5)); lib. bdg. 25.60 (978-1-60754-947-5(6)) Windmill Bks.

—My Body/Mi Cuerpo. Rosa-Mendoza, Gladys. 2007. (English Spanish Foundations Ser.). (ENG & SPA.). 20p. (gr. -1-2). pap. 19.95 (978-1-931398-85-5(2)) Me+Mi Publishing.

Butler, Daniel. Henry Loves Hills. Brennan, Patrick E. 2016. (ENG.). 24p. (J). (gr. k-5). pap. 17.99 (978-0-692-76882-2(3)) Olive & Ink.

Butler, Daniel G. Henry Loves Hills. Brennan, Patrick E. 2016. (ENG.). 24p. (J). (gr. k-5). 19.99 (978-0-578-16978-1(9)) Olive & Ink.

Butler, David. Shackleton: A Graphic Account: the Voyage of the James Caird. McCumiskey, Gavin. 2016. (ENG.). 96p. (J). pap. 17.00 (978-1-84889-281-1(0)) Collins Pr., The IRL. Dist: Dufour Editions, Inc.

Butler, Desi. Cluck, Cluck, Cluck. Butler, Desi. 2018. (ENG.). 34p. (J). pap. 9.13 (978-1-7295-6312-0(0)) CreateSpace Independent Publishing Platform.

Butler, Ella. Bear. Butler, Ella. 2010. (Peepo! Ser.). (ENG.). 10p. (J). (— 1). bds. 6.99 (978-0-230-74377-9(3)) Pan Macmillan GBR. Dist: Independent Pubs. Group.

Butler, Geoff. A Gift of Music: Emile Benoit & His Fiddle, 1 vol. Walsh, Alice. 2010. (ENG.). 32p. (J). (gr. k-5). (978-1-897174-52-4(7)) Breakwater Bks., Ltd.

Butler, Jerry. Freedom Train North: Stories of the Underground Railroad in Wisconsin. Pferdehirt, Julia. Date not set. (J). (gr. 3-8). pap. 10.00 (978-0-9664925-0-7(1)) Living History Pr.

Butler, John. Baby Animals Lift-the-Flap. Smith, Alastair. 2005. 16p. (J). (gr. 1-18). 11.95 (978-0-7945-0966-8(5), Usborne) EDC Publishing.

—Familias de Animales Libro Con Paginas Puzzle. Milbourne, Anna. 2004. (Titles in Spanish Ser.). (SPA.). 8p. (J). 8.95 (978-0-7460-6108-4(0), Usborne) EDC Publishing.

—Good Night, Little Bunny: A Changing-Picture Book. Hawkins, Emily. 2011. (ENG.). 14p. (J). (gr. -1-2). 12.99 (978-0-7636-5263-0(6), Templar) Candlewick Pr.

—I Love You, Every Little Bit. Wang, Margaret. 2006. (ENG.). 10p. (gr. -1-k). bds. 9.95 (978-1-58117-482-3(9), Intervisual/Piggy Toes) Bendon, Inc.

—If Your Dreams Take off & Fly. 2013. (J). *(978-1-4351-4769-0(3))* Barnes & Noble, Inc.
—Just One More? Alberts, Nancy Markham. 2007. (ENG.). 24p. (J). (gr. -1-7). 14.95 *(978-1-59354-195-8(3),* Handprint Bks.) Chronicle Bks. LLC.
—Little Bunny. Thompson, Lauren. 2013. (ENG.). 30p. (J). (gr. -1-k). bds. 5.99 *(978-1-4424-5851-2(8),* Little Simon) Little Simon.
—Little Chick. Thompson, Lauren. 2014. (ENG.). 30p. (J). (gr. -1-k). bds. 5.99 *(978-1-4424-9311-7(9),* Little Simon) Little Simon.
—Little Chick. Thompson, Lauren. 2014. (J). *(978-1-4351-5351-6(0),* Simon & Schuster Bks. For Young Readers) Simon & Schuster Bks. For Young Readers.
—Little Chick/Little Bunny Vertical 2-Pack. Thompson, Lauren. ed. 2014. (ENG.). 60p. (J). (gr. -1-k). bds. 11.98 *(978-1-4814-1876-8(9),* Little Simon) Little Simon.
—Little Lamb. Thompson, Lauren. 2014. (J). *(978-1-4351-5352-3(9),* Simon & Schuster Bks. For Young Readers) Simon & Schuster Bks. For Young Readers.
—Mama for Owen. Bauer, Marion Dane. 2007. (ENG.). 32p. (J). (gr. -1-3). 19.99 *(978-0-689-85787-4(X),* Simon & Schuster Bks. For Young Readers) Simon & Schuster Bks. For Young Readers.
—Nighttime Lift-the-flap. Smith, Alastair. 2005. 16p. (J). (gr. 1-18). 11.95 *(978-0-7945-0967-5(3),* Usborne) EDC Publishing.
—Sharks. Parker, Steve. 2010. (I Love Animals Ser.). (ENG.). 24p. (J). (gr. 1-5). 25.60 *(978-1-61533-249-6(9));* pap. 8.15 *(978-1-61533-254-0(5))* Windmill Bks.
—Wee Little Bunny. Thompson, Lauren. 2010. (Wee Little Ser.). (ENG.). 32p. (J). (gr. -1-1). 14.99 *(978-1-4169-7937-1(9),* Simon & Schuster Bks. For Young Readers) Simon & Schuster Bks. For Young Readers.
—Wee Little Chick. Thompson, Lauren. 2008. (Wee Little Ser.). (ENG.). 32p. (J). (gr. -1-1). 17.99 *(978-1-4169-3468-4(5),* Simon & Schuster Bks. For Young Readers) Simon & Schuster Bks. For Young Readers.
—Wee Little Lamb. Thompson, Lauren. 2009. (Wee Little Ser.). (ENG.). 32p. (J). (gr. -1-3). 16.99 *(978-1-4169-3469-1(3),* Simon & Schuster Bks. For Young Readers) Simon & Schuster Bks. For Young Readers.
—When Anju Loved Being an Elephant. Henrichs, Wendy. 2011. (ENG.). 32p. (gr. k-5). lib. bdg. 16.95 *(978-1-58536-533-3(5))* Sleeping Bear Pr.
—Where Is Baby?, 1 vol. Galbraith, Kathryn O. 2013. (ENG.). 32p. (J). (gr. -1-1). 16.95 *(978-1-56145-707-6(8))* Peachtree Publishing Co. Inc.
—10 Things You Should Know about Sharks. Parker, Steve. Gallagher, Belinda & Borton, Paula, eds. 2004. (10 Things You Should Know Ser.). 24p. (J). 6.99 *(978-1-84236-118-4(X))* Miles Kelly Publishing, Ltd. GBR. Dist: Independent Pubs. Group.
Butler, John. Bedtime in the Jungle, 1 vol. Butler, John. 2019. (ENG.). 32p. (J). (gr. -1-2). pap. 7.95 *(978-1-68263-145-4(1))* Peachtree Publishing Co. Inc.
—Can You Cuddle Like a Koala? Butler, John. 2005. (ENG.). 20p. (J). (gr. k-1). bds. 6.99 *(978-1-56145-347-4(1))* Peachtree Publishing Co. Inc.
—Can You Growl Like a Bear? Butler, John. 2012. (ENG.). 20p. (J). bds. 6.99 *(978-1-56145-667-3(5))* Peachtree Publishing Co. Inc.
—Hush, Little Ones. Butler, John. 2003. (ENG.). 24p. (J). (gr. k-k). bds. 6.95 *(978-1-56145-297-2(1))* Peachtree Publishing Co. Inc.
—If You See a Kitten, 1 vol. Butler, John. 2015. (ENG.). 24p. (J). (gr. 1-2). pap. 7.95 *(978-1-56145-838-7(4))* Peachtree Publishing Co. Inc.
—Ten in the Den, 1 vol. Butler, John. 2016. (ENG.). 32p. (J). (gr. -1-1). pap. 7.95 *(978-1-56145-965-0(8))* Peachtree Publishing Co. Inc.
—Ten in the Meadow. Butler, John. 2006. (ENG.). 32p. (J). (gr. k-1). 15.95 *(978-1-56145-372-6(2))* Peachtree Publishing Co. Inc.
Butler, Julie Dupre & Buckner, Julie Dupre. Clovis Crawfish & the Twin Sister, 1 vol. Fontenot, Mary Alice & Fontenot Landry, Julie. 2007. (Clovis Crawfish Ser.). (ENG.). 32p. (J). (gr. k-3). 16.99 *(978-1-58980-467-8(8),* Pelican Publishing) Arcadia Publishing.
Butler, Lindsay L. American History for Young Minds - Volume 1, Looking Towards the Sky, Book 1, the First Airplane. Cudeyro, Erica M. 2008. 20p. pap. 11.95 *(978-1-934925-34-8(9),* Eloquent Bks.) Strategic Book Publishing & Rights Agency (SBPRA).
Butler, Lisa. Adventures That Lead to Home. Hele, Bonita Jewel. 2012. (ENG.). 32p. (J). (gr. -1-3). 12.99 *(978-0-615-50182-6(6))* Hartlyn Kids Media, LLC.
—The Bamboo Dance. Sia, Cress. 2011. (ENG.). 32p. (J). (gr. -1-3). 12.99 *(978-0-615-48984-1(2))* Hartlyn Kids Media, LLC.
Butler, Livie, et al. Believe Big. 2019. (ENG.). 30p. (J). pap. 9.99 ***(978-1-948927-72-7(1))*** Butler, Kate Bks.
Butler, Marybeth. The Animal Pokey. Behrens, Janice. 2019. (Rookie Toddler Ser.). (ENG.). 12p. (J). (gr. -1 — 1). bds. 6.95 *(978-0-531-12926-5(8),* Children's Pr.) Scholastic Library Publishing.
—Can You Make a Happy Face? Behrens, Janice. 2018. (Rookie Toddler Ser.). (ENG.). 12p. (J). (gr. -1 — 1). bds. 6.95 *(978-0-531-22889-0(4),* Children's Pr.) Scholastic Library Publishing.
—Can You Turn the Page? Behrens, Janice. 2018. (Rookie Toddler Ser.). (ENG.). 12p. (J). (gr. -1 — 1). bds. 6.95 *(978-0-531-22891-3(6),* Children's Pr.) Scholastic Library Publishing.
—Find & Point Easter. Chanko, Pamela. 2019. (Rookie Toddler Ser.). (ENG.). 12p. (J). (gr. -1 — 1). bds. 6.95 *(978-0-531-12929-6(2),* Children's Pr.) Scholastic Library Publishing.
—Five Little Pumpkins. 2018. (Rookie Toddler Ser.). (ENG.). 12p. (J). (gr. -1 — 1). bds. 6.95 *(978-0-531-12703-2(6),* Children's Pr.) Scholastic Library Publishing.
—Knock, Knock! Who's There? A Book of Animal Sounds. Chanko, Pamela. 2017. (Rookie Toddler Ser.). (ENG.). 12p. (J). (gr. -1 — 1). bds. 6.95 *(978-0-531-22682-7(4),* Children's Pr.) Scholastic Library Publishing.
—One Potato, Two Potato. Behrens, Janice. 2019. (Rookie Toddler Ser.). (ENG.). 12p. (J). (gr. -1 — 1). bds. 6.95 *(978-0-531-12925-8(X),* Children's Pr.) Scholastic Library Publishing.
Butler, Nicola. Art Treasury. Dickins, Rosie. 2007. (Art Treasury Ser.). 94p. (J). 19.99 *(978-0-7945-1452-5(9),* Usborne) EDC Publishing.
Butler, Ralph M. When Mommy Had a Mastectomy. Greenfield, Nancy Reuben. 2016. (ENG.). 40p. (gr. -1-3). 14.95 *(978-0-910155-60-1(7))* Bartleby Pr.
Butler, Reginald. Connor & Clara Build a Concrete Poem. Atwood, Megan. 2011. (Poetry Builders Ser.). 32p. (J). (gr. 2-4). lib. bdg. 25.27 *(978-1-59953-434-3(7))* Norwood Hse. Pr.
—Inclined Planes. Marsico, Katie. 2012. (Simple Machines Ser.). (ENG.). 24p. (J). (gr. -1-2). 27.07 *(978-1-61473-273-0(6),* 204978) Child's World, Inc., The.
—Levers. Marsico, Katie. 2012. (Simple Machines Ser.). (ENG.). 24p. (J). (gr. -1-2). 27.07 *(978-1-61473-274-7(4),* 204979) Child's World, Inc., The.
—Pulleys. Marsico, Katie. 2012. (Simple Machines Ser.). (ENG.). 24p. (J). (gr. -1-2). 27.07 *(978-1-61473-275-4(2),* 204980) Child's World, Inc., The.
—Screws. Sirota, Lyn. 2012. (Simple Machines Ser.). (ENG.). 24p. (J). (gr. -1-2). 27.07 *(978-1-61473-276-1(0),* 204981) Child's World, Inc., The.
—Wedges. Marsico, Katie. 2012. (Simple Machines Ser.). (ENG.). 24p. (J). (gr. -1-2). 27.07 *(978-1-61473-277-8(9),* 204982) Child's World, Inc., The.
—Wheels. Owings, Lisa. 2012. (Simple Machines Ser.). (ENG.). 24p. (J). (gr. -1-2). 27.07 *(978-1-61473-278-5(7),* 204983) Child's World, Inc., The.
Butler, Rosemary. My Merry Menagerie: Lighthearted Verses & Drawings. Butler, Rosemary. 2013. 144p. 19.99 *(978-1-883378-22-6(2))* Sun on Earth Bks.
Butler, Rosemary. The Mysterious Snippets of Yarn. Butler, Rosemary. 2019. (ENG.). 58p. (J). (gr. k-6). 14.99 ***(978-1-883378-08-0(7))*** Sun on Earth Bks.
Butler, Sharon. Atop the Tree Top: A Christmas Story. Taylor, C. Brian. 2003. (J). 15.95 *(978-0-9747054-0-8(3))* Rilly Silly Bk. Co., The.
Butler-Stoney, T. The Old Man Who Lived in a Wood. Butler-Stoney, T. 2018. (ENG.). 30p. (J). (gr. 1-6). pap. 14.99 *(978-1-944322-20-5(5),* Woks Print) Writers of the Apocalypse, The.
Butler, Tad. Alexander Graham Bell. McPherson, Stephanie Sammartino. 2007. (History Maker Biographies Ser.). (ENG.). 48p. (gr. 3-6). lib. bdg. 27.93 *(978-0-8225-7606-8(6),* Lerner Pubns.) Lerner Publishing Group.
—Don't Sweat It: Ask Art & Pat. Humphrey, Art & Humphrey, Pat. pap. 11.95 *(978-0-9712305-0-7(1))* Heart Path Publishing.
—Florence Nightingale. Aller, Susan Bivin. 2007. (History Maker Biographies Ser.). (ENG.). 48p. (gr. 3-6). lib. bdg. 27.93 *(978-0-8225-7609-9(0),* Lerner Pubns.) Lerner Publishing Group.
—George Washington Carver. Doeden, Matt. 2007. (History Maker Biographies Ser.). 48p. (J). (gr. 3-7). lib. bdg. 26.60 *(978-0-8225-7605-1(8),* Lerner Pubns.) Lerner Publishing Group.
—Jane Goodall. Waxman, Laura Hamilton. 2007. (History Maker Biographies Ser.). (ENG.). 48p. (J). (gr. 3-6). lib. bdg. 27.93 *(978-0-8225-7610-5(4),* Lerner Pubns.) Lerner Publishing Group.
—Louis Braille. Donaldson, Madeline. 2007. (History Maker Biographies Ser.). 48p. (J). lib. bdg. 26.60 *(978-0-8225-7608-2(2),* Lerner Pubns.) Lerner Publishing Group.
Butterfield, Amy. When I'm Asleep, I Can Fly. Ostrowski, Jill. 2017. (ENG.). 24p. (J). (gr. -1-3). *(978-1-5255-1307-7(9))* FriesenPress.
Butterfield, Amy. Where the Rhythm Takes Us. Ostrowski, Jill. 2020. (ENG.). 32p. (J). ***(978-1-5255-6916-6(3));*** pap. ***(978-1-5255-6917-3(1))*** FriesenPress.
Butterfield, Blue. Christmas in Maine. Coffin, Robert Tristram. 2015. (ENG.). 32p. (J). 17.95 *(978-1-939017-76-5(9),* 63243c69-1626-47e1-8f1a-0186c2974f4e) Islandport Pr., Inc.
Butterfield, Cathy. Meerkats Don't Fly. Miller, Mark. 2007. (J). *(978-0-9794393-0-8(2))* Good Turn Publishing.
Butterfield, Ned. The Adventures of Tom Sawyer: With a Discussion of Imagination. Twain, Mark. 2003. (Values in Action Illustrated Classics Ser.). 190p. (J). *(978-1-59203-027-9(0))* Learning Challenge, Inc.
—Dad Still Smiles. Brochu, Lisa. 2003. (Books for Young Learners). (ENG.). 12p. (J). pap. 5.75 net. *(978-1-57274-601-5(7),* 2731, Bks. for Young Learners) Owen, Richard C. Pubs., Inc.
—The Day the Circus Came to Town. Carlson, Melody. 2004. 31p. (gr. -1-3). 14.99 *(978-1-58134-158-4(X))* Crossway.
—Swiss Family Robinson: With a Discussion of Teamwork. Wyss, Johann David. 2003. (Values in Action Illustrated Classics Ser.). 191p. (J). *(978-1-59203-036-1(X))* Learning Challenge, Inc.
Butterfield, Ned. The Adventures of Sherlock Holmes: With a Discussion of Curiosity. Butterfield, Ned, tr. Doyle, A. Conan. 2003. (Values in Action Illustrated Classics Ser.). (J). *(978-1-59203-045-3(9))* Learning Challenge, Inc.
—The Hunchback of Notre Dame: With a Discussion of Compassion. Butterfield, Ned, tr. Hugo, Victor. 2003. (Values in Action Illustrated Classics Ser.). (J). *(978-1-59203-049-1(1))* Learning Challenge, Inc.
Butterly, Mikki. My Little Blessings Bible, 1 vol. David, Juliet. ed. 2015. (ENG.). 224p. (J). (gr. -1-k). 14.99 *(978-1-78128-193-2(9),* Candle Bks.) Lion Hudson PLC GBR. Dist: Kregel Pubns.
Butterworth & Heath, jt. illus. see Felter.
Butterworth and Heath, jt. illus. see Felter and Gunston.
Butterworth, Mary. Rainbow Bikes. Jordan, Evanne. Lorenzo, Gina, ed. 2016. (ENG.). (J). (gr. k-3). pap. 9.99 *(978-0-9911970-1-9(1))* Interdimensional Pr.
Butterworth, Nick. Albert le Blanc. Butterworth, Nick. 2003. (ENG.). 32p. (J). pap. 6.99 ***(978-0-00-711971-4(2),*** HarperCollins Children's Bks.) HarperCollins Pubs. Ltd. GBR. Dist: HarperCollins Pubs.
—Albert le Blanc to the Rescue. Butterworth, Nick. 2008. (ENG.). 32p. (J). pap. 6.99 ***(978-0-00-725068-4(1),*** HarperCollins Children's Bks.) HarperCollins Pubs. Ltd. GBR. Dist: HarperCollins Pubs.
Butterworth, Nick. One Snowy Night. Butterworth, Nick. 2007. (ENG.). 32p. (J). 24.00 *(978-0-00-725942-7(5))* HarperCollins Pubs. Ltd. GBR. Dist: Independent Pubs. Group.
—One Snowy Night (a Percy the Park Keeper Story) Butterworth, Nick. 2019. (Percy the Park Keeper Story Ser.). (ENG.). 32p. (J). pap. 7.99 *(978-0-00-834012-4(9),* HarperCollins Children's Bks.) HarperCollins Pubs. Ltd. GBR. Dist: HarperCollins Pubs.
—Percy's Bumpy Ride (a Percy the Park Keeper Story) Butterworth, Nick. ed. 2019. (Percy the Park Keeper Story Ser.). (ENG.). 32p. (J). pap. 11.00 *(978-0-00-715514-9(X),* HarperCollins Children's Bks.) HarperCollins Pubs. Ltd. GBR. Dist: HarperCollins Pubs.
—Q Pootle 5. Butterworth, Nick. ed. 2009. (ENG.). 32p. (J). (gr. -1-k). pap. 11.95 *(978-0-00-717235-1(4),* HarperCollins Children's Bks.) HarperCollins Pubs. Ltd. GBR. Dist: HarperCollins Pubs.
—The Secret Path (a Percy the Park Keeper Story) Butterworth, Nick. ed. 2011. (Tales from Percy's Park Ser.). (ENG.). 32p. (J). pap. 11.95 *(978-0-00-715518-7(2),* HarperCollins Children's Bks.) HarperCollins Pubs. Ltd. GBR. Dist: HarperCollins Pubs.
—The Treasure Hunt (a Percy the Park Keeper Story) Butterworth, Nick. ed. 2019. (Percy the Park Keeper Story Ser.). (ENG.). 32p. (J). (gr. k-2). pap. 11.00 *(978-0-00-715517-0(4),* HarperCollins Children's Bks.) HarperCollins Pubs. Ltd. GBR. Dist: HarperCollins Pubs.
—The Whisperer. Butterworth, Nick. 2005. (ENG.). 32p. (J). (gr. k-3). pap. 15.95 *(978-0-00-712018-5(4),* HarperCollins Children's Bks.) HarperCollins Pubs. Ltd. GBR. Dist: HarperCollins Pubs.
Butterworth, Nick & Inkpen, Mick. Who Made Me? Doney, Meryl & Doney, Malcolm. 3rd ed. 2014. (ENG.). 32p. (J). (gr. -1). 7.99 *(978-1-78128-138-3(6),* Candle Bks.) Lion Hudson PLC GBR. Dist: Independent Pubs. Group.
Buttler, Elizabeth. Me & Rolly Maloo. Wong, Janet S. 2014. 240p. (J). (gr. 2-5). pap. 7.95 *(978-1-58089-159-2(4))* Charlesbridge Publishing, Inc.
Buttner, Thom. Smoking Stinks!! Gosselin, Kim. 2nd ed. 2009. (Substance Free Kids Ser.). 30p. (J). (gr. -1-3). pap. 16.95 *(978-1-891383-20-5(5))* JayJo Bks., LLC.
Button, Joshua. Joshua & the Two Crabs. Button, Joshua. 2010. 24p. (J). (gr. k-2). pap. 12.95 *(978-1-921248-48-1(3))* Magabala Bks. AUS. Dist: Independent Pubs. Group.
—Steve Goes to Carnival. Button, Joshua. Wells, Robyn. 2019. (ENG.). 56p. (J). (gr. k-3). 17.99 *(978-1-5362-0034-8(4))* Candlewick Pr.
Butzer, C. M. The First Dinosaur: How Science Solved the Greatest Mystery on Earth. Lendler, Ian. 2019. (ENG.). 224p. (J). (gr. 5). 24.99 *(978-1-5344-2700-6(7),* McElderry, Margaret K. Bks.) McElderry, Margaret K. Bks.
—The First Dinosaur: How Science Solved the Greatest Mystery on Earth. Lendler, Ian. 2019. (J). *(978-1-5344-2701-3(5))* Simon & Schuster, Inc.
—Guts & Glory: the American Civil War. Thompson, Ben. 2015. (Guts & Glory Ser.: 1). (ENG.). 352p. (J). (gr. 3-7). pap. 8.99 *(978-0-316-32051-1(X))* Little, Brown Bks. for Young Readers.
—World War II. Thompson, Ben. 2016. (ENG.). 384p. (J). E-Book *(978-0-316-32199-0(0))* Little Brown & Co.
Butzer, C. M. The Gettysburg. Butzer, C. M. 2009. (ENG.). 80p. (YA). (gr. 4-9). pap. 9.99 *(978-0-06-156175-7(4))* HarperCollins Pubs.
—Gettysburg: The Graphic Novel. Butzer, C. M. 2008. (ENG.). 80p. (J). (gr. 5-9). 16.99 *(978-0-06-156176-4(2))* HarperCollins Pubs.
Butzlaff, Hanna. Anthony, the Ant! Hassell, Andrea. 2009. (ENG.). 24p. pap. 15.99 *(978-1-4363-9944-9(0))* Xlibris Corp.
Buurlage, Marijke. Llama Drama Playing Cards to Go. Mudpuppy. 2019. (ENG.). (J). (gr. -1-5). 7.99 *(978-0-7353-5732-7(3))* Mudpuppy Pr.
Buxton, Annabelle. Barefoot Books Solar System. Jankéliowitch, Anne. 2019. (ENG.). 52p. (J). *(978-1-78285-823-2(7))* Barefoot Bks., Inc.
Buxton, Caragh. Freedom's Heart. Conover McKinnis, Sara. 2019. (ENG.). 32p. (J). pap. 12.00 *(978-0-578-45015-5(1))* Mot de Mere Publishing.
—Snow Cones in Heaven. Conover McKinnis, Sara. 2019. (ENG.). 30p. (J). pap. 12.00 *(978-0-578-48293-4(2))* Mot de Mere Publishing.
Buxton, Caragh. Gently Bentley. Buxton, Caragh. 2019. (Child's Play Library). 32p. (J). *(978-1-78628-203-3(8));* pap. *(978-1-78628-202-6(X))* Child's Play International Ltd.
Buxton, Michael. In the Jungle: Create Amazing Pictures, One Sticker at a Time! Seed, Karen Gordon. 2018. (Sticka-Pix Ser.). (ENG.). 36p. (J). (gr. 2-5). pap. 6.99 *(978-1-4380-1138-7(5),* B.E.S. Publishing) Peterson's.
—In the Ocean: Create Amazing Pictures, One Sticker at a Time! Seed, Karen Gordon. 2018. (Sticka-Pix Ser.). (ENG.). 36p. (J). (gr. 2-5). pap. 6.99 *(978-1-4380-1139-4(3),* B.E.S. Publishing) Peterson's.
—In the Wild: Create Amazing Pictures, One Sticker at a Time! Seed, Karen Gordon. 2018. (Sticka-Pix Ser.). (ENG.). 36p. (J). (gr. 2-5). pap. 6.99 *(978-1-4380-1140-0(7),* B.E.S. Publishing) Peterson's.
—On the Move: Create Amazing Pictures, One Sticker at a Time! Seed, Karen Gordon. 2018. (Sticka-Pix Ser.). (ENG.). 36p. (J). (gr. 2-5). pap. 6.99 *(978-1-4380-1141-7(5),* B.E.S. Publishing) Peterson's.
Buzio, Carolina. Babies Can Sleep Anywhere. Wheeler, Lisa. 2017. (ENG.). 32p. (J). (gr. -1-k). 14.95 *(978-1-4197-2536-4(X),* Abrams Appleseed) Abrams, Inc.
Búzio, Carolina. Babies Can Sleep Anywhere. Wheeler, Lisa. 2019. (ENG.). 22p. (J). (gr. -1 — 1). 7.99 *(978-1-4197-3492-2(X),* Abrams Appleseed) Abrams, Inc.
Búzio, Carolina. Indestructibles: All Year Round: A Book of Seasons. Pixton, Amy. 2020. (Indestructibles Ser.). (ENG.). 12p. (J). pap. 5.95 ***(978-1-5235-1113-6(3),*** 101113) Workman Publishing Co., Inc.
—Indestructibles: Big & Little: A Book of Opposites. Pixton, Amy. 2020. (Indestructibles Ser.). (ENG.). 12p. (J). pap. 5.95 ***(978-1-5235-1114-3(1),*** 101114) Workman Publishing Co., Inc.
Búzio, Carolina. Wonderful Me: I Believe in Me. Grover, Lorie Ann. 2020. (ENG.). 24p. (J). (gr. -1 — 1). 9.99 *(978-1-338-28624-3(2),* Cartwheel Bks.) Scholastic, Inc.
By Design, Book Cover. Discipline. May, W. J. 2019. (Omega Queen Ser.: Vol. 1). (ENG.). 216p. (J). pap. 9.99 ***(978-1-6906-2239-0(3))*** Independently Published.
—Limits of Magic. May, W. J. 2019. (Mending Magic Ser.: Vol. 5). (ENG.). 208p. (J). pap. 9.99 ***(978-1-6976-2260-7(7))*** Independently Published.
—The Price for Peace. May, W. J. 2019. (Royal Factions Ser.: Vol. 1). (ENG.). 212p. (J). pap. 9.99 ***(978-1-6867-7294-8(7))*** Independently Published.
By Design, Book Cover. Ticking Clock: Paranormal Fantasy Fae Fairy Young Adult/New Adult Romance. May, W. J. 2018. (ENG.). 258p. (J). pap. 9.99 *(978-1-7913-7128-9(0))* Independently Published.
Byars, Bob M. Ernie Tales. Woody, John. 2012. pap. 13.95 *(978-0-9848019-9-2(5))* Inkwell Books LLC.
Byatt, Jo. Bib on, Bunny! 2019. (Chatterboox Ser.). 10p. (J). bds. *(978-1-78628-207-1(0))* Child's Play International Ltd.
—Dive in, Ducky! 2019. (Chatterboox Ser.). 10p. (J). bds. *(978-1-78628-209-5(7))* Child's Play International Ltd.
—Play Time, Puppy! 2019. (Chatterboox Ser.). 10p. (J). bds. *(978-1-78628-208-8(9))* Child's Play International Ltd.
—Sleep Tight, Teddy! 2019. (Chatterboox Ser.). 10p. (J). bds. *(978-1-78628-210-1(0))* Child's Play International Ltd.
Bybyk, Steven & Khmelovska, Natalie. Chasing the Moon: The Drawing Book. Rodriguez, Josue D. 2016. (ENG.). (J). (gr. 2-6). pap. 15.99 *(978-1-63587-619-2(2))* Rodriguez, Josue D.
Bye, Alexandra. The Only Woman in the Photo: Frances Perkins & Her New Deal for America. Krull, Kathleen. 2020. (ENG.). 48p. (J). (gr. -1-3). 18.99 *(978-1-4814-9151-8(2),* Simon & Schuster Bks. For Young Readers) Simon & Schuster Bks. For Young Readers.
—A Race Around the World: Two Lady Journalists, 75 Days. Rose, Caroline Starr. 2019. (She Made History Ser.). (ENG.). 32p. (J). (gr. -1-3). 16.99 *(978-0-8075-0010-1(0),* 807500100) Whitman, Albert & Co.
Bye, Alexandra & Akia, Kylie. Leading the Way: Women in Power. Howell, Janet & Howell, Theresa. 2019. 144p. (J). (gr. 5). 24.99 *(978-1-5362-0846-7(9))* Candlewick Pr.
Byer, Janice. The Most Unusual Pet Ever, Henry Our Great Blue Heron & His Adventures 2nd Edition. Perry, Sondra. 2014. 49p. 18.95 *(978-1-62652-432-3(7))* Salem Author Services.
Byer, Stacey. Fun, Fun, One Crab on the Run. Picayo, Mario. 2012. (J). *(978-1-934370-27-8(4))* Editorial Campana.
Byerly, Robbie. Ants. Byerly, Robbie. Washington, Joi. 2010. (1-3Y Bugs Ser.). (ENG.). 16p. (J). (gr. k-2). pap. 9.60 *(978-1-61541-359-1(6))* American Reading Co.
—Wasps (1-3Y) Byerly, Robbie. 2016. (1-3Y Bugs Ser.). (ENG.). 20p. (J). pap. 8.00 *(978-1-61406-690-3(6))* American Reading Co.
Byers, Bradley. Don't Let the Bedbugs Bite, 1 vol. Long, Samantha Gail. 2010. 24p. 24.95 *(978-1-4512-8681-6(3))* PublishAmerica, Inc.
Byers, Brian. Noah's Babies Colors & Caring. Mead, David. 2005. 22p. (J). bds. 6.95 *(978-0-9746440-7-3(2))* Virtue Bks.
—Noah's Babies Opposites & Offerings. 2005. 22p. (J). bds. 6.95 *(978-0-9746440-6-6(4))* Virtue Bks.
—Noah's Babies Patterns & Praying. Mead, David. 2005. 22p. (J). bds. 6.95 *(978-0-9746440-4-2(8))* Virtue Bks.
—Noah's Babies Shapes & Sharing. Mead, David. 2005. 22p. (J). bds. 6.95 *(978-0-9746440-5-9(6))* Virtue Bks.
Byers, Helen. Colors of Israel. Grossman, Laurie. (Colors of the World Ser.). 24p. 2005. (gr. 3-6). lib. bdg. 19.93 *(978-1-57505-382-0(9));* 2003. (J). (gr. 1-4). pap. 5.95 *(978-1-57505-523-7(6))* Lerner Publishing Group.
Byers, Helen. Colors of France. Byers, Helen. 2005. (Colors of the World Ser.). 24p. (J). (gr. 3-6). 5.95 *(978-1-57505-565-7(1))* Lerner Publishing Group.
Byers, Leon. Will's Bow Hunting Adventure. Busteed, Kerri J. 2012. 108p. pap. 30.00 *(978-1-61897-207-1(3),* Strategic Bk. Publishing) Strategic Book Publishing & Rights Agency (SBPRA).
—Will's First Hunt. Busteed, Kerri J. 2010. 80p. pap. 21.50 *(978-1-60911-483-1(3),* Eloquent Bks.) Strategic Book Publishing & Rights Agency (SBPRA).
Byers, Michael. Barbara Park, 1 vol. Kolpin, Molly. 2013. (Your Favorite Authors Ser.). (ENG.). 24p. (J). (gr. 1-3). 25.99 *(978-1-4765-0223-6(4));* pap. 7.95 *(978-1-4765-3438-1(1))* Capstone. (Capstone Pr.).
—Dav Pilkey, 1 vol. Hicks, Kelli L. 2013. (Your Favorite Authors Ser.). (ENG.). 24p. (J). (gr. 1-3). 25.99 *(978-1-4765-0221-2(8));* pap. 7.95 *(978-1-4765-3436-7(5))* Capstone. (Capstone Pr.).
—Encountering Bigfoot: Eyewitness Accounts, 1 vol. Krohn, Katherine. 2014. (Eyewitness to the Unexplained Ser.). (ENG.). 32p. (J). (gr. 3-9). 31.32 *(978-1-4914-0243-6(1),* Capstone Pr.) Capstone.
—Grace Lin, 1 vol. Colich, Abby. 2013. (Your Favorite Authors Ser.). (ENG.). 24p. (J). (gr. 1-3). pap. 7.95 *(978-1-4765-3445-9(4),* Capstone Pr.) Capstone.
—Jacqueline Woodson. Simons, Lisa M. B. 2017. (Your Favorite Authors Ser.). (ENG.). 24p. (J). (gr. 1-3). lib. bdg. 25.99 *(978-1-5157-3558-8(3),* Capstone Pr.) Capstone.

—Jackanapes, Daddy Darwin's Dovecot & Other Stories. Ewing, Juliana Horatia. 2007. (ENG.). 112p. (J). (gr. 4-7). per. *(978-1-4065-2527-4(8))* Dodo Pr.

Caldecott, Randolph. Old Christmas: From the Sketch Book of Washington Irving (Illustrated).: Christmas / the Stage-Coach / Christmas Eve / Christmas Day / the Christmas Dinner. Irving, Washington. Barry, ed. 2019. (Christmas Stories Ser.: Vol. 3). (ENG.). 96p. (J). pap. 19.97 ***(978-1-7074-9696-9(X))*** Independently Published.

Caldecott, Randolph. Randolph Caldecott: The Man Who Could Not Stop Drawing. Marcus, Leonard S. 2013. (ENG.). 64p. (J). (gr. 5-9). 24.99 *(978-0-374-31025-7(4),* 900074253, Farrar, Straus & Giroux (BYR)) Farrar, Straus & Giroux.

Caldecott, Randolph. The Babes in the Wood - Illustrated by Randolph Caldecott. Caldecott, Randolph. 2016. (ENG.). (J). *(978-1-4733-3498-4(5))* Read Bks.

—The House That Jack Built - Illustrated by Randolph Caldecott. Caldecott, Randolph. 2016. (ENG.). (J). *(978-1-4733-3497-7(7))* Read Bks.

—R. Caldecott's Picture Book - No. 2 - Containing the Three Jovial Huntsmen, Sing a Song for Sixpence, the Queen of Hearts, the Farmers Boy. Caldecott, Randolph. 2016. (ENG.). (J). *(978-1-4733-3496-0(9))* Read Bks.

—Sing a Song for Sixpence - Illustrated by Randolph Caldecott. Caldecott, Randolph. 2016. (ENG.). (J). *(978-1-4733-3491-5(8))* Read Bks.

Calder, Jill. What Is Poetry?: the Essential Guide to Reading & Writing Poems. Rosen, Michael. 2019. (ENG.). 208p. (J). (gr. 3-7). 15.99 *(978-1-5362-0159-8(6))*; pap. 7.99 *(978-1-5362-0158-1(8))* Candlewick Pr.

Calderas, Gloria. Grandma's House. Hall, Kirsten. 2004. (My First Reader Ser.). (ENG.). 32p. (J). (gr. k-1). pap. 3.95 *(978-0-516-25502-6(9),* Children's Pr.) Scholastic Library Publishing.

Calderas, Gloria, et al. Teatro Del Gato Garabato. Flor Ada, Alma & Campoy, F. Isabel. 2015. (Santillana USA Ser.). (SPA.). 32p. (J). (gr. 6-6). pap. 15.95 *(978-1-63113-551-4(1),* Santillana) Santillana USA Publishing Co., Inc.

Calderon, Gloria. Mambru se fue a la Guerra. Iribarren, Elena, ed. 2005. (SPA.). 27p. (gr. -1-2). reprint ed. pap. 14.00 *(978-0-7567-8948-0(6))* DIANE Publishing Co.

Calderon, Lee. There Was an Odd Princess Who Swallowed a Pea, 0 vols. Ward, Jennifer. 2011. (ENG.). 32p. (J). (gr. -1-3). 16.99 *(978-0-7614-5822-7(0),* 9780761458227, Two Lions) Amazon Publishing.

Calderon, Marcela. Un Dia Sin Tele. White, Amy. Kratky, Lada J., tr. 2009. (Colección Fácil de Leer Ser.). (SPA.). 16p. (gr. k-2). pap. 5.99 *(978-1-60396-409-8(6))* Ediciones Alfaguara ESP. Dist: Santillana USA Publishing Co., Inc.

—Dos Perros y una Abuela. Monkman, Olga. 2003. (SPA.). 31p. (J). (gr. k-3). pap. 9.95 *(978-950-511-642-3(X))* Santillana USA Publishing Co., Inc.

Calderon, Marcela. No TV Day. White, Amy. 2008. (Fácil de Leer / Easy to Read Ser.). (ENG.). 16p. (J). pap. 5.99 ***(978-1-59820-561-9(7),*** Santillana Texto) Santillana USA Publishing Co., Inc.

Calderon, Marcela. Poems by the Sea. 2017. (Poems Just for Me Ser.). 32p. (gr. 7-8). 27.25 *(978-1-4994-8388-8(0),* Windmill Bks.) Rosen Publishing Group, Inc., The.

Calderón, Marcela, jt. illus. see Kosec, Polona.

Calderwood, Damon & Waite, Donald E., photos by. Baby Birds in the Wild, 1 vol. 2015. (ENG., 48p. (J). (gr. -1-k). pap. 6.95 *(978-1-77203-064-8(3))* Heritage Hse. CAN. Dist: Orca Bk. Pubs. USA.

Caldwell, Ben. All-Action Classics: Dracula. Stoker, Bram. 2019. (All-Action Classics Ser.: 1). 128p. (J). (gr. 5-9). pap. 9.95 *(978-1-4549-3500-1(6))* Sterling Publishing Co., Inc.

—All-Action Classics: the Wizard of Oz. Baum, L. Frank. 2019. (All-Action Classics Ser.: 2). 128p. (J). (gr. 5-9). pap. 9.95 *(978-1-4549-3502-5(2))* Sterling Publishing Co., Inc.

Caldwell, Ben. The Royale Treatment, 2 vols. Caldwell, Ben. 2006. (ENG.). 96p. pap. 6.95 *(978-1-59307-340-4(2))* Dark Horse Comics.

Caldwell, Kristy. Away with Words: The Daring Story of Isabella Bird. Mortensen, Lori. 2019. (ENG.). 36p. (J). (gr. 1-5). 17.95 *(978-1-68263-005-1(6))* Peachtree Publishing Co. Inc.

—Flowers for Sarajevo, 1 vol. McCutcheon, John. 2017. (ENG.). 32p. (J). (gr. 2-4). 19.95 *(978-1-56145-943-8(7))* Peachtree Publishing Co. Inc.

—Perfecto Pet Show. Springfield, Pepper. 2017. (Bobs & Tweets Ser.: 2). (ENG.). 80p. (J). (gr. -1-3). 9.99 *(978-0-545-87073-3(9))* Scholastic, Inc.

—Scout Camp (Bobs & Tweets #4) Springfield, Pepper. 2019. (Bobs & Tweets Ser.: 4). (ENG.). 64p. (J). (gr. 1-3). pap. 5.99 *(978-1-338-35540-6(6))* Scholastic, Inc.

Caldwell, Kristy. Thanks to Frances Perkins: Fighter for Workers' Rights. Hopkinson, Deborah. 2020. (ENG.). 36p. (J). (gr. 1-5). 18.99 ***(978-1-68263-136-2(2))*** Peachtree Publishing Co. Inc.

Caldwell, Kristy. Trick or Tweet. Springfield, Pepper. 2018. (Bobs & Tweets Ser.: 3). (ENG.). 64p. (J). (gr. -1-3). pap. 5.99 *(978-1-338-36100-1(7))* Scholastic, Inc.

Calero, Dennis. The Invisible Man. Wells, H. G. (Classic Fiction Ser.). 72p. 2010. pap. 0.60 *(978-1-4342-3208-3(5))*; 2007. (ENG.). (J). (gr. 5-9). lib. bdg. 27.99 *(978-1-59889-831-6(0))* Capstone. (Stone Arch Bks.).

—The Invisible Man, 1 vol. Wells, H. G. 2007. (Classic Fiction Ser.). (ENG.). 72p. (J). (gr. 5-9). per. 7.15 *(978-1-59889-887-3(6),* Stone Arch Bks.) Capstone.

—The Tell-Tale Heart, 1 vol. Harper, Benjamin & Poe, Edgar Allen. 2013. (Edgar Allan Poe Graphic Novels Ser.). (ENG.). 72p. (J). (gr. 5-9). lib. bdg. 27.99 *(978-1-4342-3023-2(6),* Stone Arch Bks.) Capstone.

—The Tell-Tale Heart, 1 vol. Poe, Edgar Allen & Harper, Benjamin. 2013. (Edgar Allan Poe Graphic Novels Ser.). (ENG.). 72p. (J). (gr. 5-9). pap. 6.10 *(978-1-4342-4261-7(7),* Stone Arch Bks.) Capstone.

—The Tell-Tale Heart Package. Poe, Edgar Allen. 2013. (ENG.). 62p. (J). (gr. 5-8). pap. 35.70 *(978-1-4342-4285-3(4),* Stone Arch Bks.) Capstone.

Calero, Dennis, jt. illus. see Dimaya, Emerson.

Calero, Dennis, jt. illus. see Fabul, J. C.

Calero, Dennis, jt. illus. see Jimenz, Jim.

Caley, Isabel W. Ted Gilman. Gilman, Dorothy Foster. 2011. 200p. 44.95 *(978-1-258-06474-7(X))* Literary Licensing, LLC.

—A Yankee Girl at Shiloh. Curtis, Alice Turner. 2018. (ENG.). 96p. (J). (gr. 4-7). pap. *(978-1-4068-8887-4(7))* Echo Library.

Calhoun, Brian & Bradley, Pat. Little Joe Chickapig. Calhoun, Brian. 2020. (ENG.). 32p. (J). (gr. -1-k). 9.99 *(978-0-7944-4452-5(0),* Studio Fun International) Printers Row Publishing Group.

Calico World Entertainment Staff. Luigi & the Lost Wish, 1 vol. Knights, Harry B. 2003. (Nicholas Stories Ser.: 4). (ENG.). 56p. (J). (gr. k-3). 16.95 *(978-1-58980-162-2(8),* Pelican Publishing) Arcadia Publishing.

—The Maiden Voyage of Kris Kringle, 1 vol. Knights, Harry B. 2003. (Nicholas Stories Ser.: 3). (ENG.). 56p. (J). (gr. k-3). 16.95 *(978-1-58980-161-5(X),* Pelican Publishing) Arcadia Publishing.

Calimee, John, et al. Venomnibus Vol. 2. 2019. (Venomnibus Ser.: 2). (ENG.). 1176p. (J). (gr. 4-17). 125.00 *(978-1-302-91653-4(X))* Marvel Worldwide, Inc.

Calindas, Marconi. Of Petals & Hope: Sunny Sunflower Triumphs over Bullying. Cafege, Adam. 2013. 36p. pap. 24.95 *(978-0-9840204-4-7(6))* Pacific Raven Pr.

Calitri, Susan. Let's Go to the Zoo. Harkrader, Lisa. 2020. (ENG.). 18p. (J). bds. ***(978-1-64269-255-6(7),*** b6d121c5-036d-4044-8362-9c5b1a9af5da, Sequoia Publishing & Media LLC) Phoenix International Publications, Inc.

Calitri, Susan. Mommies & Babies on the Farm. Hawksley, Gerald. 2004. (J). bds. 11.99 *(978-1-890647-11-7(X))* TOMY International, Inc.

Calitri, Susan Chapman. What Time Is It? Cifuentes, Carolina, ed. 2010. (My World Ser.).Tr. of Que Hora Es?. (ENG.). 24p. (J). (gr. -1-1). pap. 8.15 *(978-1-61533-041-6(0))* Windmill Bks.

Call, Angela. Hold on to Your Horses. Tayler, Sandra. 2008. 32p. (J). per. 15.00 *(978-0-9779074-8-9(1))* Tayler Corp., The.

Call, Brian. White Shirts: A Baptism Keepsake for Boys. Rowley, Deborah Pace. 2006. 32p. (J). 16.99 *(978-1-59038-633-0(7))* Deseret Bk. Co.

Call, Brian D. Sarah's Cloud. Call, Brian D., tr. 2003. (J). 15.95 *(978-1-57008-955-8(8))* Deseret Bk. Co.

Call, Greg. The Attack of the Frozen Woodchucks. Elish, Dan. 2008. (ENG.). 256p. (J). (gr. 3-7). 16.99 *(978-0-06-113870-6(3),* Geringer, Laura Book) HarperCollins Pubs.

—The Book of Storms. Hatfield, Ruth. ed. 2016. (Book of Storms Trilogy Ser.). (ENG.). 384p. (J). (gr. 5-9). 18.40 *(978-0-606-39364-5(1))* Turtleback.

—House of Secrets. Columbus, Chris & Vizzini, Ned. (House of Secrets Ser.: 1). (J). 2014. (ENG.). 512p. (gr. 3-7). pap. 7.99 *(978-0-06-219247-9(7),* Balzer & Bray); 2013. (ENG.). 496p. (gr. 3-7). 17.99 *(978-0-06-219246-2(9),* Balzer & Bray); 2013. 490p. *(978-0-06-225964-6(4))* HarperCollins Pubs.

—House of Secrets: Battle of the Beasts. Columbus, Chris & Vizzini, Ned. (House of Secrets Ser.: 2). (ENG.). 480p. (J). (gr. 3-7). 2015. pap. 7.99 *(978-0-06-219250-9(7))*; 2014. 17.99 *(978-0-06-219249-3(3))* HarperCollins Pubs.

—The Last Dogs: the Vanishing. Holt, Christopher. 2013. (Last Dogs Ser.: 1). (ENG.). 400p. (J). (gr. 3-7). pap. 8.99 *(978-0-316-20004-2(2))* Little, Brown Bks. for Young Readers.

—Peter & the Shadow Thieves. Barry, Dave & Pearson, Ridley. 2007. (Starcatchers Ser.: Bk. 2). 556p. (gr. 5-9). 19.00 *(978-0-7569-8060-3(7))* Perfection Learning Corp.

—Peter & the Shadow Thieves (Peter & the Starcatchers), 2. Barry, Dave & Pearson, Ridley. rev. ed. 2007. (Peter & the Starcatchers Ser.: 2). (ENG.). 592p. (J). (gr. 5-9). pap. 9.99 *(978-1-4231-0855-9(8))* Hyperion Bks. for Children.

—Peter & the Starcatchers (Peter & the Starcatchers, Book One) Barry, Dave & Pearson, Ridley. rev. ed. 2006. (Peter & the Starcatchers Ser.: 1). (ENG.). 480p. (J). (gr. 5-9). reprint ed. pap. 9.99 *(978-0-7868-4907-9(X),* Disney Editions) Disney Pr.

—Peter & the Sword of Mercy, 4. Barry, Dave & Pearson, Ridley. 2011. (Peter & the Starcatchers Ser.: Bk. 4). (ENG.). 528p. (J). (gr. 5-9). pap. 9.99 *(978-1-4231-3070-3(7))* Hyperion Bks. for Children.

—Phantom Stallion Box Set: The Wild One; Mustang Moon; Dark Sunshine. Farley, Terri. 2004. (Phantom Stallion Ser.). 704p. (J). (gr. 5-18). pap. 14.99 *(978-0-06-059504-3(3),* HarperCollins) HarperCollins Pubs.

—The Pirate's Coin.. Malone, Marianne. 2014. (Sixty-Eight Rooms Adventures Ser.: 3). (ENG.). 240p. (J). (gr. 3-7). 7.99 *(978-0-307-97720-5(X),* Yearling) Random Hse. Children's Bks.

—Stealing Magic. Malone, Marianne. (ENG.). (J). 2012. (Sixty-Eight Rooms Adventures Ser.: 2). 256p. (gr. 3-7). 16.99 *(978-0-375-86819-1(4),* Random Hse. Bks. for Young Readers); 2. 2013. (Sixty-Eight Rooms Adventures Ser.). 272p. (gr. 4-6). lib. bdg. 21.19 *(978-0-375-96819-8(9),* Yearling) Random Hse. Children's Bks.

—Stealing Magic: a Sixty-Eight Rooms Adventure. Malone, Marianne. 2013. (Sixty-Eight Rooms Adventures Ser.: 2). (ENG.). 272p. (J). (gr. 3-7). pap. 7.99 *(978-0-375-86790-3(2),* Yearling) Random Hse. Children's Bks.

—A Tale of Two Castles. Levine, Gail Carson. (ENG.). (J). (gr. 3-7). 2012. 352p. pap. 6.99 *(978-0-06-122967-1(9))*; 2011. 336p. 16.99 *(978-0-06-122965-7(2))* HarperCollins Pubs.

Call, Greg, jt. illus. see Dorman, Brandon.

Call, Greg, jt. illus. see Triplett, Gina.

Call, Ken. Barack Obama: Presidente de Estados Unidos. Edwards, Roberta. 2009.Tr. of Barack Obama: United States President. (SPA.). 64p. (J). (gr. 2-5). pap. 9.99 *(978-1-63113-956-7(8),* Loqueleo) Santillana USA Publishing Co., Inc.

—Michelle Obama: Primera Dama y Primera Mama. Edwards, Roberta. 2010. (SPA.). 48p. (J). (gr. 1-4). pap. 14.95 *(978-1-63113-870-6(7))*; (gr. 3-5). pap. 9.99 *(978-1-60396-946-8(2))* Santillana USA Publishing Co., Inc.

Call, Ken. Michelle Obama: Primera Dama y Primera Mamá. Edwards, Roberta. 2010. (0). (SPA.). 48p. (J). pap. 10.99 ***(978-1-63113-962-8(2))*** Santillana USA Publishing Co., Inc.

Callaghan, Laura. Vivienne Westwood. Vegara, Isabel Sanchez. 2020. (Little People, BIG DREAMS Ser.: 24). (ENG.). 24p. (J). (— 1). bds. 8.99 ***(978-0-7112-4594-5(0),*** 329970, Frances Lincoln Children's Bks.) Quarto Publishing Group UK GBR. Dist: Hachette UK Distribution.

—Vivienne Westwood: My First Vivienne Westwood. Sanchez Vegara, Maria Isabel. 2020. (Little People, Big Dreams Ser.: Vol. 24). (ENG.). 24p. (J). (gr. -1). bds. ***(978-0-7112-4595-2(9))*** Frances Lincoln Childrens Bks.

Callahan, Charlie. Samantha Loses Her Sweet Tooth. Callahan, Charlie. 2004. (J). *(978-0-9754019-0-3(4))* Periscope Pr.

Callan, Clark. Bubbles & the Berry Bush. Mokry, Shannon L. 2018. (ENG.). 34p. (J). (gr. k-2). pap. 11.99 *(978-0-9987112-9-4(2))* Sillygeese Publishing, LLC.

Callan, Clark. Bubbles & the Big Race. Mokry, Shannon L. 2019. (Bubbles the Bubble Blowing Dragon Ser.: Vol. 3). (ENG.). 34p. (J). 18.99 ***(978-1-951521-03-5(X))***; pap. 12.99 ***(978-1-951521-04-2(8))*** Sillygeese Publishing, LLC.

Calle (liberum donum studios), Juan. Alien Lockdown. Collins, Ailynn. 2019. (Michael Dahl Presents: Screams in Space 4D Ser.). (ENG.). 112p. (J). (gr. 3-5). lib. bdg. 26.65 *(978-1-4965-7905-8(4),* 139615, Stone Arch Bks.) Capstone.

—The Final Mission. Brezenoff, Steve. 2019. (Michael Dahl Presents: Screams in Space 4D Ser.). (ENG.). 112p. (J). (gr. 3-5). lib. bdg. 26.65 *(978-1-4965-7902-7(X),* 139612, Stone Arch Bks.) Capstone.

—A Hole in the Dome. Brezenoff, Steve. 2019. (Michael Dahl Presents: Screams in Space 4D Ser.). (ENG.). 112p. (J). (gr. 3-5). lib. bdg. 26.65 *(978-1-4965-7903-4(8),* 139613, Stone Arch Bks.) Capstone.

Calle, Juan. By the Shore. Potter, William. 2018. (All-Action Animal Art Ser.). 32p. (J). (gr. 7-10). 27.50 *(978-1-5383-4726-3(1))*; pap. 11.75 *(978-1-5383-4724-9(5))* Rosen Publishing Group, Inc., The. (PowerKids Pr.).

—Desert Animals. Potter, William. 2018. (All-Action Animal Art Ser.). 32p. (J). (gr. 7-10). 27.50 *(978-1-5383-4730-0(X))*; pap. 11.75 *(978-1-5383-4728-7(8))* Rosen Publishing Group, Inc., The. (PowerKids Pr.).

—The Discovery of Anime & Manga: The Asian Hall of Fame. Amara, Phil & Chin, Oliver. 2019. (Asian Hall of Fame Ser.). (ENG.). 36p. (J). 16.95 *(978-1-59702-146-3(6))* Immedium.

—The Discovery of Fireworks & Gunpowder: The Asian Hall of Fame. Amara, Phil & Chin, Oliver. 2018. (Asian Hall of Fame Ser.). (ENG.). 40p. (J). (gr. -1-3). 16.95 *(978-1-59702-142-5(3))* Immedium.

—Drawing Ocean Animals. Colich, Abby. 2015. (Drawing Amazing Animals Ser.). (ENG.). 32p. (J). (gr. 3-9). 28.65 *(978-1-4914-2131-4(2),* Capstone Pr.) Capstone.

—Epic Adventures, 1 vol. Potter, William. 2019. (Ultimate Fantasy Art Ser.). (ENG.). 32p. (gr. 3-4). 27.50 *(978-1-7253-0340-9(X))*; pap. 11.75 *(978-1-7253-0338-6(8))* Rosen Publishing Group, Inc., The. (PowerKids Pr.).

—Fantastic Monsters, 1 vol. Potter, William. 2019. (Ultimate Fantasy Art Ser.). (ENG.). 32p. (gr. 3-4). 27.50 *(978-1-7253-0332-4(9))*; pap. 11.75 *(978-1-7253-0330-0(2))* Rosen Publishing Group, Inc., The. (PowerKids Pr.).

—Forest Animals. Potter, William. 2018. (All-Action Animal Art Ser.). 32p. (J). (gr. 7-10). 27.50 *(978-1-5383-4754-6(7))*; pap. 11.75 *(978-1-5383-4752-2(0))* Rosen Publishing Group, Inc., The. (PowerKids Pr.).

—Gothic Horror, 1 vol. Potter, William. 2019. (Ultimate Fantasy Art Ser.). (ENG.). 32p. (gr. 3-4). 27.50 *(978-1-7253-0320-1(5))*; pap. 11.75 *(978-1-7253-0318-8(3))* Rosen Publishing Group, Inc., The. (PowerKids Pr.).

—Grassland Animals. Potter, William. 2018. (All-Action Animal Art Ser.). 32p. (J). (gr. 7-10). 27.50 *(978-1-5383-4734-8(2))*; pap. 11.75 *(978-1-5383-4732-4(6))* Rosen Publishing Group, Inc., The. (PowerKids Pr.).

—Heroes of History & Myth, 1 vol. Potter, William. 2019. (Ultimate Fantasy Art Ser.). (ENG.). 32p. (gr. 3-4). 27.50 *(978-1-7253-0324-9(8))*; pap. 11.75 *(978-1-7253-0322-5(1))* Rosen Publishing Group, Inc., The. (PowerKids Pr.).

—How to Create Fantasy Art. Potter, William. 2018. (ENG.). 160p. (J). pap. 12.99 *(978-1-78888-314-6(4),* 071354bb-0ceb-41cd-84e8-bbf826ed92f0) Arcturus Publishing GBR. Dist: Baker & Taylor Publisher Services (BTPS).

—How to Draw Incredible Dinosaurs, 1 vol. McCurry, Kristen. 2012. (Smithsonian Drawing Bks.). (ENG.). 64p. (gr. 3-6). (J). pap. 7.19 *(978-1-4296-9450-6(5),* Capstone Pr.); pap. 41.70 *(978-1-4296-9451-3(3))*; (J). lib. bdg. 34.65 *(978-1-4296-8750-8(9),* Capstone Pr.) Capstone.

—Jungle Animals. Potter, William. 2018. (All-Action Animal Art Ser.). 32p. (J). (gr. 7-10). 27.50 *(978-1-5383-4738-6(5))*; pap. 11.75 *(978-1-5383-4736-2(9))* Rosen Publishing Group, Inc., The. (PowerKids Pr.).

Calle, Juan. My Slime Is Alive! Schenkel, Katie. 2020. (Scary Graphics Ser.). (ENG.). 40p. (J). (gr. 3-5). lib. bdg. 25.32 ***(978-1-4965-9798-4(2),*** 200592, Stone Arch Bks.) Capstone.

Calle, Juan. Open Waters. Potter, William. 2018. (All-Action Animal Art Ser.). 32p. (J). (gr. 7-10). 27.50 *(978-1-5383-4742-3(3))*; pap. 11.75 *(978-1-5383-4740-9(7))* Rosen Publishing Group, Inc., The. (PowerKids Pr.).

—Over the Reef. Potter, William. 2018. (All-Action Animal Art Ser.). 32p. (J). (gr. 7-10). 27.50 *(978-1-5383-4746-1(6))*; pap. 11.75 *(978-1-5383-4744-7(X))* Rosen Publishing Group, Inc., The. (PowerKids Pr.).

—Steampunk World, 1 vol. Potter, William. 2019. (Ultimate Fantasy Art Ser.). (ENG.). 32p. (gr. 3-4). 27.50 *(978-1-7253-0328-7(0))*; pap. 11.75 *(978-1-7253-0326-3(4))* Rosen Publishing Group, Inc., The. (PowerKids Pr.).

—Urban Magic, 1 vol. Potter, William. 2019. (Ultimate Fantasy Art Ser.). (ENG.). 32p. (gr. 3-4). 27.50 *(978-1-7253-0336-2(1))*; pap. 11.75 *(978-1-7253-0334-8(5))* Rosen Publishing Group, Inc., The. (PowerKids Pr.).

—Whales, Sharks, & Dolphins. Potter, William. 2018. (All-Action Animal Art Ser.). 32p. (J). (gr. 7-10). 27.50 *(978-1-5383-4750-8(4))*; pap. 11.75 *(978-1-5383-4748-5(2))* Rosen Publishing Group, Inc., The. (PowerKids Pr.).

—Year of the Rooster. Chin, Oliver. 2016. (Tales from the Chinese Zodiac Ser.: 12). (ENG.). 40p. (J). (gr. -1). 15.95 *(978-1-59702-125-8(3))* Immedium.

Calle, Juan & Howard, Colin. Drawing Amazing Animals. Colich, Abby. 2015. (Drawing Amazing Animals Ser.). (ENG.). 32p. (J). (gr. 3-9). lib. bdg., lib. bdg., lib. bdg. 114.60 *(978-1-4914-2559-6(8),* Capstone Pr.) Capstone.

Calle, Santiago. Brilliant Bugs: Discover the Amazing Talents of Insects, Spiders & More Creepy Crawlies. Turner, Matt. 2020. (ENG.). 96p. (J). (gr. 2-6). 19.99 *(978-1-913077-19-8(5),* f901c7ee-208d-41f5-a6d8-4ce02c01ebc3, Beetle Bks.) Hungry Tomato Ltd. GBR. Dist: Baker & Taylor Publisher Services (BTPS).

—Deadly Spiders. Turner, Matt. 2017. (Crazy Creepy Crawlers Ser.). (ENG.). 32p. (J). (gr. 3-6). 27.99 *(978-1-5124-1553-7(7),* 9781512415537); E-Book 42.65 *(978-1-5124-3596-2(1),* 9781512435962); E-Book 42.65 *(978-1-5124-2713-4(6))*; E-Book 4.99 *(978-1-5124-3597-9(X),* 9781512435979) Lerner Publishing Group. (Hungry Tomato ®).

—Extraordinary Insects. Turner, Matt. 2017. (Crazy Creepy Crawlers Ser.). (ENG.). 32p. (J). (gr. 3-6). 27.99 *(978-1-5124-1556-8(1),* 9781512415568); E-Book 4.99 *(978-1-5124-3600-6(3),* 9781512436006); E-Book 42.65 *(978-1-5124-3599-3(6),* 9781512435993); E-Book 42.65 *(978-1-5124-2716-5(0))* Lerner Publishing Group. (Hungry Tomato ®).

—Flying Creepy Crawlers. Turner, Matt. 2017. (Crazy Creepy Crawlers Ser.). (ENG.). 32p. (J). (gr. 3-6). 27.99 *(978-1-5124-1554-4(5),* 9781512415544); E-Book 42.65 *(978-1-5124-3602-0(X),* 9781512436020); E-Book 4.99 *(978-1-5124-3603-7(8),* 9781512436037); E-Book 42.65 *(978-1-5124-2714-1(4))* Lerner Publishing Group. (Hungry Tomato ®).

—Tiny Creepy Crawlers. Turner, Matt. 2017. (Crazy Creepy Crawlers Ser.). (ENG.). 32p. (J). (gr. 3-6). 27.99 *(978-1-5124-1555-1(3),* 9781512415551); E-Book 42.65 *(978-1-5124-3605-1(4),* 9781512436051); E-Book 42.65 *(978-1-5124-2715-8(2))*; E-Book 4.99 *(978-1-5124-3606-8(2),* 9781512436068) Lerner Publishing Group. (Hungry Tomato ®).

Calle Velez, Juan. Could You Survive the Jurassic Period? An Interactive Prehistoric Adventure. Doeden, Matt. 2020. (You Choose: Prehistoric Survival Ser.). (ENG.). 112p. (J). (gr. 3-7). pap. 6.95 *(978-1-4966-5808-1(6),* 142240); lib. bdg. 32.65 *(978-1-5435-7402-9(5),* 140693) Capstone.

—Could You Survive the New Stone Age? An Interactive Prehistoric Adventure. Troupe, Thomas Kingsley. 2020. (You Choose: Prehistoric Survival Ser.). (ENG.). 112p. (J). (gr. 3-7). pap. 6.95 *(978-1-4966-5810-4(8),* 142242); lib. bdg. 32.65 *(978-1-5435-7405-0(X),* 140697) Capstone.

—End User. Brezenoff, Steve. 2019. (Michael Dahl Presents: Screams in Space 4D Ser.). (ENG.). 112p. (J). (gr. 3-5). lib. bdg. 26.65 *(978-1-4965-8335-2(3),* 140515, Stone Arch Bks.) Capstone.

—Michael Dahl Presents: Screams in Space 4D. Brezenoff, Steve & Collins, Ailynn. 2019. (Michael Dahl Presents: Screams in Space 4D Ser.). (ENG.). (J). (gr. 3-5). 159.90 *(978-1-4965-8338-3(8),* 29321, Stone Arch Bks.) Capstone.

—Vampire Invasion. Collins, Ailynn. 2019. (Michael Dahl Presents: Screams in Space 4D Ser.). (ENG.). 112p. (J). (gr. 3-5). lib. bdg. 26.65 *(978-1-4965-8334-5(5),* 140514, Stone Arch Bks.) Capstone.

Callen, Liz. Pen Pal Penguin. Scraper, Katherine. 2012. 8p. (J). *(978-0-7367-2639-9(X))* Zaner-Bloser, Inc.

—Reading, Rhyming, And 'Rithmetic. Crawley, Dave. 2010. (ENG.). 32p. (J). (gr. 2-k). 17.95 *(978-1-59078-565-2(7),* Wordsong) Boyds Mills Pr.

Calles, Rosa M. Dodo the Bird & Other Stories. De Aragon, Ray J. 105p. (Orig.). (J). (gr. 1-12). pap. 5.95 *(978-0-932906-21-2(4))* Pan-American Publishing Co.

Callias, Aurore. Le Bal D'Automne. Badescu, Ramona. 2010. (A. M. Alb. Ill. C. Ser.). (FRE.). 68p. (J). *(978-2-226-20926-9(3))* Albin-Michel, Editions.

—Tristesse et Chèvrefeuille. Badescu, Ramona. 2010. (A. M. Alb. Ill. C. Ser.). (FRE.). 68p. (J). *(978-2-226-20707-4(4))* Albin-Michel, Editions.

Callicutt, Kenneth. Rodeo Star. Quinton, Sasha. 2018. (ENG.). 32p. (J). (gr. 1-3). 12.99 *(978-1-68412-452-7(2),* Silver Dolphin Bks.) Printers Row Publishing Group.

Callicutt, Kenny, jt. illus. see Joyce, William.

Callie, Kittie. To Obey Is Better: And Other Stories with Life Lessons for Children. Spaulding, David R. 2016. (ENG.). (J). pap. 16.95 *(978-1-4796-0661-0(8))* TEACH Services, Inc.

Callo, Valeria. A Quien le Toca? Peyron, Gabriela. rev. ed. 2006. (Otra Escalera Ser.). (SPA & ENG.). 24p. (J). (gr. 2-4). pap. 9.95 *(978-968-5920-57-5(5))* Castillo, Ediciones, S. A. de C. V. MEX. Dist: Macmillan.

Calo, Marcos. The Ballgame with No One at Bat. Brezenoff, Steve. 2013. (Field Trip Mysteries Ser.). (ENG.). 88p. (J). (gr. 3-6). pap. 5.95 *(978-1-4342-6211-0(1))*; lib. bdg. 25.32 *(978-1-4342-5978-3(1))* Capstone. (Stone Arch Bks.).

—The Bowling Lane Without Any Strikes. Brezenoff, Steve. 2013. (Field Trip Mysteries Ser.). (ENG.). 88p. (J). (gr. 3-6). pap. 5.95 *(978-1-4342-6212-7(X))*; lib. bdg. 25.32 *(978-1-4342-5979-0(X))* Capstone. (Stone Arch Bks.).

—The Carnival Caper: An Interactive Mystery Adventure. Brezenoff, Steve. 2017. (You Choose Stories: Field Trip Mysteries Ser.). (ENG.). 112p. (J). (gr. 3-7). lib. bdg. 32.65 *(978-1-4965-2645-8(7)*, Stone Arch Bks.) Capstone.

—The Cave That Shouldn't Collapse. Brezenoff, Steve. 2011. (Field Trip Mysteries Ser.). (ENG.). 88p. (J). (gr. 3-6). pap. 5.95 *(978-1-4342-3430-8(4))*; lib. bdg. 25.32 *(978-1-4342-3227-4(1))* Capstone. (Stone Arch Bks.).

—The Crook That Made Kids Cry, 1 vol. Brezenoff, Steve. 2013. (Field Trip Mysteries Ser.). (ENG.). 88p. (J). (gr. 3-6). pap. 5.95 *(978-1-4342-6210-3(3))*; lib. bdg. 25.32 *(978-1-4342-5977-6(3))* Capstone. (Stone Arch Bks.).

—Daphne Definitely Doesn't Do Dances. Charles, Tami. 2018. (Daphne, Secret Vlogger Ser.). (ENG.). 96p. (J). (gr. 4-7). pap. 4.95 *(978-1-4965-6301-9(8)*, 138030); lib. bdg. 24.65 *(978-1-4965-6297-5(6)*, 138024) Capstone. (Stone Arch Bks.).

—Daphne Definitely Doesn't Do Drama. Charles, Tami. 2018. (Daphne, Secret Vlogger Ser.). (ENG.). 96p. (J). (gr. 4-7). pap. 4.95 *(978-1-4965-6299-9(2)*, 138029); lib. bdg. 24.65 *(978-1-4965-6295-1(X)*, 138021) Capstone. (Stone Arch Bks.).

—Daphne Definitely Doesn't Do Fashion. Charles, Tami. 2018. (Daphne, Secret Vlogger Ser.). (ENG.). 96p. (J). (gr. 4-7). pap. 4.95 *(978-1-4965-6300-2(X)*, 138031); lib. bdg. 24.65 *(978-1-4965-6296-8(8)*, 138022) Capstone. (Stone Arch Bks.).

—Daphne Definitely Doesn't Do Sports. Charles, Tami. 2018. (Daphne, Secret Vlogger Ser.). (ENG.). 96p. (J). (gr. 4-7). pap. 4.95 *(978-1-4965-6298-2(4)*, 138028); lib. bdg. 24.65 *(978-1-4965-6294-4(1)*, 138020) Capstone. (Stone Arch Bks.).

—Daphne, Secret Vlogger, 4 vols. Charles, Tami. 2018. (Daphne, Secret Vlogger Ser.). (ENG.). 96p. (J). (gr. 4-7). 98.60 *(978-1-4965-6306-4(9)*, 28113); pap., pap., pap. 19.80 *(978-1-4965-6307-1(7)*, 28114) Capstone. (Stone Arch Bks.).

—The Dinosaur That Disappeared, 1 vol. Brezenoff, Steve. 2013. (Field Trip Mysteries Ser.). (ENG.). 88p. (J). (gr. 3-6). pap. 5.95 *(978-1-4342-6213-4(8))*; lib. bdg. 25.32 *(978-1-4342-5980-6(3))* Capstone. (Stone Arch Bks.).

—The Disappearing Fruit: An Interactive Mystery Adventure. Brezenoff, Steve. 2017. (You Choose Stories: Field Trip Mysteries Ser.). (ENG.). 112p. (J). (gr. 3-7). lib. bdg. 32.65 *(978-1-4965-2643-4(0)*, Stone Arch Bks.) Capstone.

—Doom at Grant's Tomb. Wells, Marcia. 2017. (Eddie Red Undercover Ser.: 3). (ENG.). 208p. (J). (gr. 5-7). pap. 7.99 *(978-0-544-93733-8(3)*, 1658347, HMH Books For Young Readers) Houghton Mifflin Harcourt Publishing Co.

—Doom at Grant's Tomb. Wells, Marcia. ed. 2017. (Eddie Red Undercover Ser.: 3). (ENG.). (J). (gr. 5-7). lib. bdg. 17.20 *(978-0-606-39813-8(9))* Turtleback.

—The Elves & the Shoemaker. McFadden, Deanna. 2012. (Silver Penny Stories Ser.). 48p. (J). (gr. -1-1). 4.95 *(978-1-4027-8334-0(5))* Sterling Publishing Co., Inc.

—The Everglades Poacher Who Pretended. Brezenoff, Steve. 2012. (Field Trip Mysteries Ser.). (ENG.). 88p. (J). (gr. 3-6). pap. 5.95 *(978-1-4342-4197-9(1))*; lib. bdg. 25.32 *(978-1-4342-3790-3(7))* Capstone. (Stone Arch Bks.).

—The Grand Canyon Burros That Broke. Brezenoff, Steve. 2012. (Field Trip Mysteries Ser.). (ENG.). 88p. (J). (gr. 3-6). pap. 5.95 *(978-1-4342-4198-6(X))*; lib. bdg. 25.32 *(978-1-4342-3788-0(5))* Capstone. (Stone Arch Bks.).

—King Arthur & His Knights. Namm, Diane. 2014. (Silver Penny Stories Ser.). 48p. (J). (gr. -1-1). 4.95 *(978-1-4027-8432-3(5))* Sterling Publishing Co., Inc.

—The Library Shelves: An Interactive Mystery Adventure. Brezenoff, Steve. 2019. (You Choose Stories: Field Trip Mysteries Ser.). (ENG.). 112p. (J). (gr. 3-7). lib. bdg. 32.65 *(978-1-4965-4860-3(4)*, 135459, Stone Arch Bks.) Capstone.

—The Messed-Up Museum: An Interactive Mystery Adventure. Brezenoff, Steve. 2019. (You Choose Stories: Field Trip Mysteries Ser.). (ENG.). 112p. (J). (gr. 3-7). lib. bdg. 32.65 *(978-1-4965-4859-7(0)*, 135458, Stone Arch Bks.) Capstone.

—The Missing Bully: An Interactive Mystery Adventure. Brezenoff, Steven. 2017. (You Choose Stories: Field Trip Mysteries Ser.). (ENG.). 112p. (J). (gr. 3-7). lib. bdg. 32.65 *(978-1-4965-2642-7(2)*, Stone Arch Bks.) Capstone.

—The Mount Rushmore Face That Couldn't See. Brezenoff, Steve. 2012. (Field Trip Mysteries Ser.). (ENG.). 88p. (J). (gr. 3-6). pap. 5.95 *(978-1-4342-4199-3(8)*, Stone Arch Bks.) Capstone.

—The Mystery Across the Secret Bridge. Paris, Harper. 2015. (Greetings from Somewhere Ser.: 7). (ENG.). 128p. (J). (gr. k-4). pap. 5.99 *(978-1-4814-2367-0(3)*, Little Simon) Little Simon.

—The Mystery at the Coral Reef. Paris, Harper. 2015. (Greetings from Somewhere Ser.: 8). (ENG.). 128p. (J). (gr. k-4). pap. 5.99 *(978-1-4814-2370-0(3)*, Little Simon) Little Simon.

—Mystery in Mayan Mexico. Wells, Marcia. 2016. (Eddie Red Undercover Ser.: 2). (ENG.). 224p. (J). (gr. 5-7). pap. 7.99 *(978-0-544-66850-8(2)*, 1625472, HMH Books For Young Readers) Houghton Mifflin Harcourt Publishing Co.

—The Mystery in the Forbidden City. Paris, Harper. 2014. (Greetings from Somewhere Ser.: 4). (ENG.). 128p. (J). (gr. k-2). pap. 5.99 *(978-1-4814-0299-6(4)*, Little Simon) Little Simon.

—The Mystery of the Gold Coin. Paris, Harper. 2014. (Greetings from Somewhere Ser.: 1). (ENG.). 128p. (J). (gr. k-4). pap. 5.99 *(978-1-4424-9718-4(1)*, Little Simon) Little Simon.

—The Mystery of the Icy Paw Prints. Paris, Harper. 2015. (Greetings from Somewhere Ser.: 9). (ENG.). 128p. (J). (gr. k-4). pap. 5.99 *(978-1-4814-2373-1(8)*, Little Simon) Little Simon.

—The Mystery of the Mosaic. Paris, Harper. 2014. (Greetings from Somewhere Ser.: 2). (ENG.). 128p. (J). (gr. k-2). pap. 5.99 *(978-1-4424-9721-4(1)*, Little Simon) Little Simon.

—The Mystery of the Mosaic. Paris, Harper. 2014. (Greetings from Somewhere Ser.: Vol. 2). (ENG.). 115p. (J). (gr. k-2). lib. bdg. 16.80 *(978-1-62765-837-9(8))* Perfection Learning Corp.

—The Mystery of the Secret Society. Paris, Harper. 2016. (Greetings from Somewhere Ser.: 10). (ENG.). 128p. (J). (gr. k-4). pap. 5.99 *(978-1-4814-5171-0(5)*, Little Simon) Little Simon.

—The Mystery of the Stolen Painting. Paris, Harper. 2014. (Greetings from Somewhere Ser.: 3). (ENG.). 128p. (J). (gr. k-2). pap. 5.99 *(978-1-4814-0296-5(X)*, Little Simon) Little Simon.

—The Mystery of the Suspicious Spices. Paris, Harper. 2014. (Greetings from Somewhere Ser.: 6). (ENG.). 128p. (J). (gr. k-4). pap. 5.99 *(978-1-4814-1467-8(4)*, Little Simon) Little Simon.

—Mystery on Museum Mile. Wells, Marcia. 2015. (Eddie Red Undercover Ser.). (ENG.). 256p. (J). (gr. 5-7). pap. 7.99 *(978-0-544-43940-5(6)*, 1596839, HMH Books For Young Readers) Houghton Mifflin Harcourt Publishing Co.

—The Outlaw from Outer Space: An Interactive Mystery Adventure. Brezenoff, Steve. 2017. (You Choose Stories: Field Trip Mysteries Ser.). (ENG.). 112p. (J). (gr. 3-7). lib. bdg. 32.65 *(978-1-4965-2644-1(9)*, Stone Arch Bks.) Capstone.

—The Ride That Was Really Haunted. Brezenoff, Steve. 2011. (Field Trip Mysteries Ser.). (ENG.). 88p. (J). (gr. 3-6). pap. 5.95 *(978-1-4342-3427-8(4))*; lib. bdg. 25.32 *(978-1-4342-3224-3(7))* Capstone. (Stone Arch Bks.).

—Robin Hood. McFadden, Deanna. 2013. (Silver Penny Stories Ser.). 48p. (J). (gr. -1-1). 4.95 *(978-1-4027-8339-5(6))* Sterling Publishing Co., Inc.

—The Seals That Wouldn't Swim. Brezenoff, Steve. 2011. (Field Trip Mysteries Ser.). (ENG.). 88p. (J). (gr. 3-6). pap. 5.95 *(978-1-4342-3428-5(2))*; lib. bdg. 25.32 *(978-1-4342-3225-0(5))* Capstone. (Stone Arch Bks.).

—The Steadfast Tin Soldier. Olmstead, Kathleen & Andersen, Hans. 2013. (Silver Penny Stories Ser.). 48p. (J). (gr. -1-1). 4.95 *(978-1-4027-8351-7(5))* Sterling Publishing Co., Inc.

—The Substitutes: An Up2U Action Adventure, 1 vol. Lay, Kathryn. 2015. (Up2U Adventures Ser.). (ENG.). 80p. (J). (gr. 2-5). 29.93 *(978-1-62402-095-7(X)*, 17359, Calico Chapter Bks.) ABDO Publishing Co.

—The Symphony That Was Silent. Brezenoff, Steve. 2011. (Field Trip Mysteries Ser.). (ENG.). 88p. (J). (gr. 3-6). pap. 5.95 *(978-1-4342-3429-2(0))*; lib. bdg. 25.32 *(978-1-4342-3226-7(3))* Capstone. (Stone Arch Bks.).

—The Yellowstone Kidnapping That Wasn't. Brezenoff, Steve. 2012. (Field Trip Mysteries Ser.). (ENG.). 88p. (J). (gr. 3-6). pap. 5.95 *(978-1-4342-4200-6(5))*; lib. bdg. 25.32 *(978-1-4342-3789-7(3))* Capstone. (Stone Arch Bks.).

Calo, Marcos, jt. illus. see Kelly, Cooper.

Calouttì, Amy. When the Moon Is a Smile. Raffa-Mulligan, Teena. 2019. (ENG.). 32p. (J). (gr. k-3). *(978-0-6484892-0-7(5))*; pap. *(978-0-6484892-1-4(3))* Daisy Lane Publishing.

Calver, Paul. Colours & Shapes. Giles, Angela & Picthall, Chez. 2015. (ENG.). 6p. (J). 9.99 *(978-1-909763-42-5(X))* Award Pubns. Ltd. GBR. Dist: Parkwest Pubns., Inc.

—123. Giles, Angela & Picthall, Chez. 2015. (ENG.). 6p. (J). 9.99 *(978-1-909763-29-6(2))* Award Pubns. Ltd. GBR. Dist: Parkwest Pubns., Inc.

Calvert, Lissa. Accidental Evie. Basham, Tom. 2012. 120p. *(978-1-77097-373-2(7))*; pap. *(978-1-77097-374-9(5))* FriesenPress.

Calvert, Lissa. Adventures in the High Meadow: With Tiac, Eo, & Wooly. Turner, Allan. 2020. (ENG.). 210p. (J). ***(978-1-5255-5442-1(5))***; pap. ***(978-1-5255-5443-8(3))*** FriesenPress.

Calvert, Lissa. Foxes on the Ridge. Pavlick, Leon E. & PAVLICK, A. N. N. M. 2012. 48p. pap. *(978-1-77097-852-2(6))* FriesenPress.

—Lump Lump & the Blanket of Dreams: Inspired by Navajo Culture & Folklore. Jackson, Gwen. 2016. (ENG.). (J). *(978-1-4602-9929-6(9))* FriesenPress.

—Sailing Home. Basham, Tom. 2012. 168p. *(978-1-77097-370-1(2))* FriesenPress.

Calvert, Steph. An Apatosaurus Would NOT Make a Good Spy. Sadler, Heather. 2018. (Dinosaur Daydreams Ser.). (ENG.). 24p. (J). (gr. -1-2). lib. bdg. 27.99 *(978-1-5158-2128-1(5)*, 136732, Picture Window Bks.) Capstone.

—Dinosaur Daydreams. Sadler, Heather et al. 2018. (Dinosaur Daydreams Ser.). (ENG.). 24p. (J). (gr. -1-2). 111.96 *(978-1-5158-2154-0(4)*, 27391, Picture Window Bks.) Capstone.

—A Stegosaurus Would Not Make a Good Pirate. Troupe, Thomas Kingsley. 2018. (Dinosaur Daydreams Ser.). (ENG.). 24p. (J). (gr. -1-2). lib. bdg. 27.99 *(978-1-5158-2129-8(3)*, 136733, Picture Window Bks.) Capstone.

—A T-Rex Would Not Make a Good Knight. Troupe, Thomas Kingsley. 2018. (Dinosaur Daydreams Ser.). (ENG.). 24p. (J). (gr. -1-2). lib. bdg. 27.99 *(978-1-5158-2126-7(9)*, 136730, Picture Window Bks.) Capstone.

—A Triceratops Would NOT Make a Good Ninja. Katzenberger, Lisa. 2018. (Dinosaur Daydreams Ser.). (ENG.). 24p. (J). (gr. -1-2). pap. 7.95 *(978-1-5158-2131-1(5)*, 136735, Picture Window Bks.) Capstone.

Calvert-Weyant, Linda. Abigail & the Lost Purse. Riggin, Lisa. 2011. 32p. (J). 9.95 *(978-1-59530-359-2(6))* Hallmark Card, Inc.

Calvetti, Leonello & Massini, Luca. Iguanodon. Dalla Vecchia, Fabio Marco. 2007. (Dinosaur Profiles Ser.). (ENG.). 32p. (J). (gr. 3-7). lib. bdg. 25.65 *(978-1-4103-0736-1(0)*, Blackbirch Pr., Inc.) Cengage Gale.

—Meet Brachiosaurus. Cunningham, Mark. 2014. (Age of Dinosaurs Ser.). (ENG.). 32p. (gr. 3-3). lib. bdg. 29.50 *(978-1-62712-601-4(5))* Cavendish Square Publishing LLC.

—Meet Caudipteryx. Knight, Sheryn. 2014. (Age of Dinosaurs Ser.). (ENG.). 32p. (gr. 3-3). lib. bdg. 29.50 *(978-1-62712-610-6(4))* Cavendish Square Publishing LLC.

—Meet Ornitholestes. Raymond, Jayne. 2014. (Age of Dinosaurs Ser.). (ENG.). 32p. (gr. 3-3). lib. bdg. 29.50 *(978-1-62712-613-7(9))* Cavendish Square Publishing LLC.

—Meet Stegosaurus. Miller, Henley. 2014. (Age of Dinosaurs Ser.). (ENG.). 32p. (gr. 3-3). lib. bdg. 29.50 *(978-1-62712-604-5(X))* Cavendish Square Publishing LLC.

—Meet Triceratops. Cunningham, Mark & Vecchia, Fabio Marco Dalla. 2014. (Age of Dinosaurs Ser.). (ENG.). 32p. (gr. 3-3). lib. bdg. 29.50 *(978-1-62712-607-6(4))* Cavendish Square Publishing LLC.

—Meet Tyrannosaurus Rex. Raymond, Jayne. 2014. (Age of Dinosaurs Ser.). (ENG.). 32p. (gr. 3-3). lib. bdg. 29.50 *(978-1-62712-598-7(1))* Cavendish Square Publishing LLC.

Camacho, Edgar. Kiko Robot. Rincón, Valentín. 2019. (SPA.). 120p. (J). (gr. k-2). pap. 7.95 *(978-607-8237-90-6(X))* Nostra Ediciones MEX. Dist: Independent Pubs. Group.

Camacho, Ricardo. Los Bandidos de Rio Frio. Payno, Manuel. 2003. (SPA.). 91p. (J). pap. *(978-970-643-638-2(3))* Selector, S.A. de C.V. MEX. Dist: Spanish Pubs., LLC.

Camagni, Jacopo. Ms. Isaacson's Third Grade Field Trip. Tobin, Paul. 2010. (Avengers Ser.: No. 2). (ENG.). 24p. (J). (gr. 2-6). 27.07 *(978-1-59961-768-8(4)*, 30, Marvel Age) Spotlight.

—Which Wish? Tobin, Paul. 2010. (Avengers Ser.: No. 2). (ENG.). 24p. (J). (gr. 2-6). 27.07 *(978-1-59961-769-5(2)*, 31, Marvel Age) Spotlight.

Camagni, Jacopo & Petit, Cory. Best Story Ever. Seeley, Tim & Brown, Reilly. 2015. (Guardians of the Galaxy Ser.). (ENG.). 24p. (J). (gr. 3-6). 27.07 *(978-1-61479-390-8(5)*, 18221, Marvel Age) Spotlight.

Camarca, Erin. Rattlestiltskin. Kimmel, Eric A. 2016. (ENG.). 32p. (J). (gr. k-3). 16.99 *(978-1-943328-38-3(2)*, West Winds Pr.) West Margin Pr.

Camargo, Nina de, jt. illus. see Neves, Nik.

Camburn, Carol A. Ernest & Elston. Barnes, Laura T. 2005. (Ernest Ser.). 32p. (J). (gr. -1-3). 15.95 *(978-0-9674681-6-7(7))* Barnesyard Bks.

—Ernest's Special Christmas. Barnes, Laura T. 2003. (Ernest Ser.). 36p. (J). (gr. k-3). 17.95 *(978-0-9674681-3-6(2))* Barnesyard Bks.

Camcam, Princesse. Marie from Paris. Sabatier-Morel, Francoise & Pellegrini, Isabelle. 2014. (AV2 Fiction Readalong Ser.: Vol. 131). (ENG.). 32p. (J). (gr. -1-3). lib. bdg. 34.28 *(978-1-4896-2262-4(4)*, AV2 by Weigl) Weigl Pubs., Inc.

—Miyako from Tokyo. Yamada, Miho. 2014. (AV2 Fiction Readalong Ser.: Vol. 132). (ENG.). 32p. (J). (gr. -1-3). lib. bdg. 34.28 *(978-1-4896-2268-6(3)*, AV2 by Weigl) Weigl Pubs., Inc.

Camden, Jean. How to Make a Planet: A Step-By-Step Guide to Building the Earth. Forbes, Scott. 2014. (ENG.). 64p. (J). (gr. 3-7). 17.95 *(978-1-894786-88-1(2))* Kids Can Pr., Ltd. CAN. Dist: Hachette Bk. Group.

Cameron, Chad. A Day with No Crayons. Rusch, Elizabeth. 2007. (ENG.). 32p. (J). (gr. -1-3). 15.95 *(978-0-87358-910-9(6))* Cooper Square Publishing Llc.

—Fall Mixed Up. Raczka, Robert. 2011. (ENG.). 40p. (J). (gr. -1-3). lib. bdg. 19.99 *(978-0-7613-4606-7(6)*, 9780761346067, Carolrhoda Bks.) Lerner Publishing Group.

Cameron, Cheryl. Adventures of a Stuttering Superhero: Adventure #1 Interrupt-Itis. Block, Kim. 2016. (Adventures of a Stuttering Superhero Ser.: Vol. 1). (ENG.). (J). pap. *(978-1-77302-356-4(X))* Tellwell Talent.

—Adventures of a Stuttering Superhero: Adventure #2: Melissa Meets Her Stamily. Block, Kim. 2018. (Adventures of a Stuttering Superhero Ser.: Vol. 2). (ENG.). 26p. (J). (gr. k-4). pap. *(978-1-7750071-2-8(X))* Tellwell Talent.

—Les Aventures d'une Superheroine du Begaiement: 1. L'Interromptite. Block, Kim. Lamoureux, Genevieve, tr. 2017. (Aventures d'une Superheroine du Begaiement Ser.: Vol. 1). (FRE.). 20p. (J). (gr. k-5). pap. *(978-1-7750071-1-1(1))* Tellwell Talent.

Cameron, Craig. Backhoe Joe. Alexander, Lori. 2014. (ENG.). 40p. (J). (gr. -1-3). 15.99 *(978-0-06-225015-5(9))* HarperCollins Pubs.

—The Big Train. Klein, Adria F. 2013. (Train Time Ser.). (ENG.). 32p. (J). (gr. -1-1). pap. 5.95 *(978-1-4342-4886-2(0)*, Stone Arch Bks.) Capstone.

—Big Train Takes a Trip, 1 vol. Klein, Adria F. 2013. (Train Time Ser.). (ENG.). 32p. (gr. -1-1). (J). pap. 5.95 *(978-1-4342-6194-6(8))*; (J). lib. bdg. 22.65 *(978-1-4342-4781-0(3))*; pap. 29.70 *(978-1-4342-6300-1(2))* Capstone. (Stone Arch Bks.).

—Chico Plays Hide & Seek. Adams, Ben. 2013. (Googly Eyes Ser.). (ENG.). 12p. (J). (gr. -1-k). bds. 6.99 *(978-1-84322-280-4(9)*, Armadillo) Anness Publishing GBR. Dist: National Bk. Network.

—Circus Train, 1 vol. Klein, Adria F. 2013. (Train Time Ser.). (ENG.). 32p. (J). (gr. -1-1). pap. 5.95 *(978-1-4342-4883-1(6))*; lib. bdg. 22.65 *(978-1-4342-4188-7(2))* Capstone. (Stone Arch Bks.).

—Circus Train & the Clowns, 1 vol. Klein, Adria F. 2013. (Train Time Ser.). (ENG.). 32p. (gr. -1-1). (J). pap. 5.95 *(978-1-4342-6195-3(6))*; (J). lib. bdg. 22.65 *(978-1-4342-4782-7(1))*; pap. 29.70 *(978-1-4342-6303-2(7))* Capstone. (Stone Arch Bks.).

—City Train, 1 vol. Klein, Adria F. 2013. (Train Time Ser.). (ENG.). 32p. (J). (gr. -1-1). lib. bdg. 22.65 *(978-1-4342-4189-4(0)*, Stone Arch Bks.) Capstone.

—City Train in Trouble, 1 vol. Klein, Adria F. 2013. (Train Time Ser.). (ENG.). 32p. (gr. -1-1). (J). pap. 5.95 *(978-1-4342-6196-0(4))*; (J). lib. bdg. 22.65 *(978-1-4342-4783-4(X))*; pap. 29.70 *(978-1-4342-6302-5(9))* Capstone. (Stone Arch Bks.).

—Freddie the Fish, Star of the Show. Baxter, Nicola & Adams, Ben. 2013. (Googly Eyes Ser.). 12p. (J). (gr. -1-k). bds. 6.99 *(978-1-84322-621-5(9)*, Armadillo) Anness Publishing GBR. Dist: National Bk. Network.

—Freight Train, 1 vol. Klein, Adria F. 2013. (Train Time Ser.). (ENG.). 32p. (J). (gr. -1-1). pap. 5.95 *(978-1-4342-4885-5(2)*, Stone Arch Bks.) Capstone.

—The Full Freight Train, 1 vol. Klein, Adria F. 2013. (Train Time Ser.). (ENG.). 32p. (gr. -1-1). (J). pap. 5.95 *(978-1-4342-6197-7(2))*; pap. 29.70 *(978-1-4342-6301-8(0))* Capstone. (Stone Arch Bks.).

—Happy Birthday. Hewitt, Sally. 2003. 14p. (J). pap. 10.95 *(978-1-57145-735-6(6)*, Silver Dolphin Bks.) Readerlink Distribution Services, LLC.

—Happy Doctor. Hewitt, Sally. 2003. 14p. (J). pap. 10.95 *(978-1-57145-734-9(8)*, Silver Dolphin Bks.) Readerlink Distribution Services, LLC.

—Happy Dresser. Hewitt, Sally. 2003. 14p. (J). pap. 10.95 *(978-1-57145-733-2(X)*, Silver Dolphin Bks.) Readerlink Distribution Services, LLC.

—The Pig with the Curliest Tail. Adams, Ben. 2013. (Googly Eyes Ser.). 12p. (J). (gr. -1-k). bds. 6.99 *(978-1-84322-618-5(9)*, Armadillo) Anness Publishing GBR. Dist: National Bk. Network.

—Polly the Farm Puppy. Adams, Ben. 2013. (Googly Eyes Ser.). 12p. (J). (gr. -1-k). bds. 6.99 *(978-1-84322-319-1(8)*, Armadillo) Anness Publishing GBR. Dist: National Bk. Network.

—A Real Live Pet! Living vs. Nonliving Things. Lukidis, Lydia. 2018. (Science Solves It! ® Ser.). (ENG.). 32p. (J). (gr. k-2). pap. 5.95 *(978-1-63592-009-3(4))* Astra Publishing Hse.

—Train Time. Klein, Adria F. 2013. (Train Time Ser.). (ENG.). 32p. (J). (gr. -1-1). lib. bdg., lib. bdg., lib. bdg. 113.25 *(978-1-4342-6056-7(9)*, Stone Arch Bks.) Capstone.

Cameron, Ed. The Dog That's Not a Poodle. Schultze, Gwendolyn. 2011. 54p. (J). pap. 12.00 *(978-1-892076-97-7(7))* Dancing Moon Pr.

Cameron, Eren. Claudita de San Alfonso. Campana, Carolina. 2020. (SPA.). 104p. (J). pap. 15.00 ***(978-1-7041-1892-5(1))*** Independently Published.

Cameron, Eugenia. The Basket of Seeds. St. Julian, Ska. 2013. 122p. pap. 10.99 *(978-0-9899182-0-6(3))* Chris Six Group, The.

Cameron, Marie. The Barefoot Book of Buddhist Tales. Chodzin, Sherab. 2012. 80p. (J). (gr. 1-5). pap. 14.99 *(978-1-84686-824-5(6))* Barefoot Bks., Inc.

—Clever Katya: A Fairy Tale from Old Russia. Hoffman, Mary. 2005. 32p. (J). (gr. k-3). pap., pap. 6.99 *(978-1-905236-05-3(0))* Barefoot Bks., Inc.

Camia, Nicholas. S Is for Suplex. Schrodt, Ryan L. 2020. (ENG.). 36p. (J). (gr. -1-k). pap. 9.95 ***(978-0-9993886-4-8(9))*** Mrs. Weisz Bks.

Camille, Diana. The Goops Circus: A Whimsical Telling of Do-Good Tales. Ross, Barbara & Beatty, Nicholas. 2010. (Goops Ser.). 58p. (J). 19.95 incl. audio compact disk *(978-0-9712368-4-4(4))* Goops Unlimited.

—A Treasury of Goops: Timeless Manners for Every Generation. 2005. Orig. Title: Goops & How to Be Them. (ENG.). 45p. (J). 19.95 *(978-0-9712368-5-1(2)*, 8006811891) Goops Unlimited.

Camilleri, Michael. One Minute's Silence. Metzenthen, David. 2014. (ENG.). 48p. (J). (gr. k). 24.99 *(978-1-74331-624-5(0))* Allen & Unwin AUS. Dist: Independent Pubs. Group.

Caminador, Juan. Cenicienta en el Baile. Hillert, Margaret. 2018. (BeginningtoRead Ser.).Tr. of Cinderella at the Ball. (SPA.). 32p. (J). (gr. -1-2). pap. 11.94 *(978-1-68404-233-3(X))* Norwood Hse. Pr.

—Cinderella at the Ball. Hillert, Margaret. 2016. (BeginningtoRead Ser.). (ENG.). 32p. (J). (-2). lib. bdg. 22.60 *(978-1-59953-778-8(8))* Norwood Hse. Pr.

Caminador, Juan. Cenicienta en el Baile. Caminador, Juan. Hillert, Margaret & Del Risco, Eida. 2018. (BeginningtoRead Ser.).Tr. of Cinderella at the Ball. (SPA.). 32p. (J). (gr. -1-2). lib. bdg. 22.60 *(978-1-59953-949-2(7))* Norwood Hse. Pr.

Caminador, Juan, jt. illus. see Jack Pullan.

Camling, Candace. North Carolina, the First Golden State, 1 vol. Wagner, Tricia & Wagner, Tricia Martineau. 2017. (ENG.). 32p. (J). (gr. -1-3). 16.99 *(978-1-4556-2273-3(7)*, Pelican Publishing) Arcadia Publishing.

—The Southern Twelve Days of Christmas, 1 vol. Davis, David. 2013. (ENG.). 32p. (J). (gr. k-3). 16.99 *(978-1-4556-1773-9(3)*, Pelican Publishing) Arcadia Publishing.

—The Twelve Days of Christmas — In Texas, That Is, 1 vol. Davis, David. 2011. (ENG.). 32p. (J). (gr. k-3). 16.99 *(978-1-58980-924-6(6)*, Pelican Publishing) Arcadia Publishing.

Camm, Martin. Day & Night in Swamp. Cheshire, Gerard. 2009. 38p. (J). (gr. 2-5). 14.99 *(978-0-8437-0974-2(X))* Hammond World Atlas Corp.

—Meyers Buch der Baeren. (GER.). 48p. *(978-3-411-07461-7(2))* Bibliographisches Institut & F. A. Brockhaus AG DEU. Dist: i. b. d., Ltd.

—Meyers Buch der Wale und Delfine. (GER.). 48p. *(978-3-411-07451-8(5))* Bibliographisches Institut & F. A. Brockhaus AG DEU. Dist: i. b. d., Ltd.

—A Wasp Builds a Nest. Scarborough, Kate. 2016. (ENG.). 24p. (J). (gr. 1-3). 12.95 *(978-1-77085-695-0(1)*, 7e895e4d-f6a2-41ed-a67b-077d31075716) Firefly Bks., Ltd.

Camm, Sue. Baby Animals. 2004. 24p. (J). bds. 6.99 *(978-1-85854-728-2(8))* Brimax Books Ltd. GBR. Dist: Byeway Bks.

Cammarano, Antonella. Kareem's Birthday Ride. Le Gendre, Kimaada. 2019. (Naturebella's Kids Books: Multicultural Ser.: Vol. 3). (ENG.). 36p. (J). pap. 10.99 ***(978-1-7326320-4-2(9))*** Le Gendre, Kimaada.

Cammarano, Antonella. Luis's Lucky Day. Caulfield, Kathleen. 2018. (ENG.). (J). 32p. 19.95 *(978-0-9978732-2-1(1))*; 48p. pap. 14.95 *(978-0-9978732-0-7(5))* Conquistador Pubns.

Cammarano, Antonella. Luis's Visitor. Caulfield, Kathleen. 2018. (ENG.). 48p. (J). pap. 14.95 ***(978-0-9978732-3-8(X))*** Conquistador Pubns.

C

Cammarano, Antonella. Marley's Beach Adventure Coloring Book. Le Gendre, Kimaada. 2019. (Naturebella's Kids Coloring Bks.: Vol. 1). (ENG.). 28p. (J). pap. 6.95 *(978-1-7326320-2-8(2))* Le Gendre, Kimaada.

—My Friend Josh Has Dyspraxia. Draper, Christine R. Williams, Ruth-Abigail, ed. 2018. (ENG.). 44p. (J). pap. *(978-1-909986-19-0(4))* achieve2day.

—Rain's Busy Day at the Farm. Le Gendre, Kimaada. 2018. (Naturebella's Kids Books: Multicultural Ser.: Vol. 2). (ENG.). 30p. (J). pap. 10.95 *(978-1-7326320-1-1(4))* Le Gendre, Kimaada.

Cammarano, Antonella. Rain's Busy Day at the Farm Coloring Book. Le Gendre, Kimaada. 2019. (Naturebella's Kids Multicultural Bks.: Vol. 2). (ENG.). 24p. (J). pap. 6.95 ***(978-1-7326320-3-5(0))*** Le Gendre, Kimaada.

Cammell, Sandra. Big Red Comes to Stay. Eggleton, Jill. 2004. (Rigby Sails Early Ser.). (ENG.). 16p. (gr. 1-2). pap. 6.95 *(978-0-7578-9303-2(1))* Houghton Mifflin Harcourt Publishing Co.

—King of the Zoo, 6 pack. Holden, Pam. 2009. (Red Rocket Readers Ser.). 16p. (gr. -1-1). pap. *(978-1-877363-13-9(8),* Red Rocket Readers) Flying Start Bks.

—Rainy Day, Sunny Day - 6 Pack: Set of 6 with Teacher Materials Common Core Edition. Walker, Nan. 2015. (Early Connections Ser.). (J). (gr. k-1). 37.00 *(978-1-5021-4713-4(0))* Benchmark Education Co.

—Turtle's Trouble. Eggleton, Jill. 2003. (Rigby Sails Early Ser.). (ENG.). 16p. (gr. 1-2). pap. 6.95 *(978-0-7578-8672-0(8))* Houghton Mifflin Harcourt Publishing Co.

Cammuso, Frank. Otto's Orange Day. Lynch, Jay. (Otto the Cat Ser.). (ENG.). 40p. (J). (gr. -1-3). 2013. pap. 6.99 *(978-1-935179-27-6(6));* 2008. 12.95 *(978-0-9799238-2-1(4))* TOON Books / RAW Junior, LLC.

Cammuso, Frank. The Dodgeball Chronicles. Cammuso, Frank. 2008. (Knights of the Lunch Table Ser.: 1). (ENG.). 144p. (J). (gr. 3-5). pap. 10.99 *(978-0-439-90322-6(X),* Graphix) Scholastic, Inc.

Cammuso, Frank & Lynch, Jay. Otto's Orange Day, 1 vol. Lynch, Jay & Cammuso, Frank. Lynch, Jay. 2013. (Toon Bks.). (ENG.). 36p. (J). (gr. 2-3). lib. bdg. 29.93 *(978-1-61479-154-6(6),* 14846) Spotlight.

Camp, Joaquin. Circus Girl. Novotny Hunter, Jana. 2020. (Child's Play Library). 32p. (J). pap. *(978-1-78628-297-2(6));* ***(978-1-78628-298-9(4))*** Child's Play International Ltd.

Campana, Ilaria. Little Red Reading Hood & the Misread Wolf. Wilson, Troy. 2019. 32p. (J). (gr. -1-3). 17.99 *(978-0-7624-9266-4(X),* Running Pr. Kids) Running Pr.

Campana, Michael/ D. The Greedy Racecar Driver. Campana, Michael/ D. 2009. (ENG.). 40p. (J). 16.99 *(978-0-9817791-0-2(7))* Iron Fire Publishng Co.

Campbell, Alex. Horatio: The Tale of a Snail Without a Shell. Lacey, J. J. 2018. (ENG.). 52p. (J). pap. 7.99 *(978-1-7178-0364-1(4))* Independently Published.

Campbell, Alex & Spay, Anthony. Jackie Robinson. Raatma, Lucia & O'Hern, Kerri. (Biografías Gráficas (Graphic Biographies) Ser.). 32p. (gr. 5-8). 2007. (SPA.). pap. 10.50 *(978-0-8368-7889-9(2));* 2007. (SPA.). lib. bdg. 28.00 *(978-0-8368-7882-0(5));* 2006. lib. bdg. 28.00 *(978-0-8368-6198-3(1))* Stevens, Gareth Publishing LLLP.

Campbell, Alex, jt. illus. see Spay, Anthony.

Campbell, Blendon. Father Abraham. Tarbell, Ida M. 2004. reprint ed. pap. 15.95 *(978-1-4179-0070-1(9))* Kessinger Publishing, LLC.

Campbell, Brent. Lobo & the Rabbit Stew. Schwartz, Marcia. 2010. (ENG.). 32p. (J). (gr. -1-12). lib. bdg. 16.95 *(978-1-936299-02-7(X),* Raven Tree Pr.,Csi) Continental Sales, Inc.

—Lobo & the Rabbit Stew/El Lobo y el Caldo de Conejo. Schwartz, Marcia. 2010. (ENG & SPA.). 32p. (J). (gr. -1-12). lib. bdg. 16.95 *(978-1-936299-00-3(3),* Raven Tree Pr.,Csi) Continental Sales, Inc.

Campbell, Bruce, photos by. Buddhism in Thailand. Hawker, Frances & Sunantha Phusomsai. 2009. (ENG., 32p. (J). (gr. 3-6). *(978-0-7787-5006-2(X));* pap. *(978-0-7787-5023-9(X))* Crabtree Publishing Co.

—Christianity in Mexico. Hawker, Frances & Paz, Noemi. 2009. (ENG., 32p. (J). (gr. 3-6). *(978-0-7787-5007-9(8));* pap. *(978-0-7787-5024-6(8))* Crabtree Publishing Co.

—Hinduism in Bali. Hawker, Frances & Resi, Putu. 2009. (ENG., 32p. (J). (gr. 3-6). *(978-0-7787-5008-6(6));* pap. *(978-0-7787-5025-3(6))* Crabtree Publishing Co.

—Islam in Turkey. Hawker, Frances & Alicavusoglu, Leyla. 2009. (ENG., 32p. (J). (gr. 3-6). *(978-0-7787-5009-3(4));* pap. *(978-0-7787-5026-0(4))* Crabtree Publishing Co.

—Judaism in Israel. Hawker, Frances & Taub, Daniel. 2009. (ENG., 32p. (J). (gr. 3-6). *(978-0-7787-5010-9(8));* pap. *(978-0-7787-5027-7(2))* Crabtree Publishing Co.

—Sikhism in India. Hawker, Frances & Bhatia, Mohini. 2009. (ENG., 32p. (J). (gr. 3-6). *(978-0-7787-5011-6(6));* pap. *(978-0-7787-5028-4(0))* Crabtree Publishing Co.

Campbell Campbell, Eva. Africville, 1 vol. Grant, Shauntay. 2018. (ENG.). 32p. (gr. k-2). 18.95 *(978-1-77306-043-9(0))* Groundwood Bks. CAN. Dist: Publishers Group West (PGW).

Campbell, Cathy. Stewart's Tree: A Book for Brothers & Sisters When a Baby Dies Shortly after Birth. Campbell, Cathy. 2018. (ENG.). 40p. 15.95 *(978-1-78592-399-9(4),* 696674) Kingsley, Jessica Pubs. GBR. Dist: Hachette UK Distribution.

Campbell, Celeste Francis. The Heart of a Knight: Written & Illustrated by Celeste Campbell. Campbell, Celeste Francis. 2019. (ENG.). 34p. (J). pap. 13.99 *(978-1-0725-5433-2(X))* Independently Published.

Campbell, D. B. The Cat Wants to Play. Coulton, Mia. 2011. (ENG.). 12p. (J). pap. 5.35 *(978-1-933624-74-7(4))* Maryruth Bks., Inc.

—Lunch for Baby Elephant. Coulton, Mia. 2009. (ENG.). 12p. pap. 5.50 *(978-1-933624-49-5(3));* pap. 5.35 *(978-1-933624-42-6(6))* Maryruth Bks., Inc.

Campbell, Donna P. Pieces of Me. Pierce, AnneMarie. (J). (gr. 1-9). *(978-0-9623937-3-0(8))* Forword.

Campbell, Emily. The Little Boy from Jamaica: A Canadian History Story. Clunis, Devon & Clunis, Pearlene. 2017. (ENG.). (J). pap. *(978-1-4602-9913-5(2))* FriesenPress.

Campbell, Emily. The Little Girl from Osoyoos. Clunis, Pearlene & Clunis, Devon. 2019. (ENG.). 24p. (J). ***(978-1-5255-5039-3(X));*** pap. ***(978-1-5255-5040-9(3))*** FriesenPress.

Campbell, Eva. Light a Candle, 1 vol. Nkongolo, Godfrey & Walters, Eric. ed. 2019. (ENG & SWA.). 32p. (J). (gr. 1-3). 19.95 *(978-1-4598-1700-5(1))* Orca Bk. Pubs. USA.

—The Matatu, 1 vol. Walters, Eric. 2012. (ENG.). 32p. (J). (gr. -1-k). 19.95 *(978-1-55469-301-6(2))* Orca Bk. Pubs. USA.

Campbell-Howes, Andrew. The Dog with the Golden Eyes. Kay, L. M. 2019. (ENG.). 116p. (J). (gr. 2-4). pap. *(978-2-901773-20-7(6))* Tither, Lesley.

Campbell, J. Scott. Marvel Monograph: the Art of J. Scott Campbell - the Complete Covers Vol. 1. 2019. (ENG.). 112p. (YA). (gr. -1-17). pap. 19.99 *(978-1-302-91758-6(7))* Marvel Worldwide, Inc.

Campbell, Jacquie. A Winter Solstice Celebration. Lemay, Didi. 2008. 56p. pap. 23.99 *(978-1-4389-0998-1(5))* AuthorHouse.

Campbell, Jenney. Zachary Z. Packrat & His Amazing Collections. Bessesen, Brooke. 2008. 40p. pap. 19.95 *(978-1-932082-83-8(2))* Arizona Highways.

Campbell, Jenny. Build-a-Skill Instant Books Math Facts To 20. Cernak, Kim & Williams, Rozanne Lanczak. Faulkner, Stacey, ed. 2007. (J). 4.99 *(978-1-59198-418-4(1))* Creative Teaching Pr., Inc.

—Build-a-SKill Instant Books Synonyms & Antonyms. Callella, Kim & Williams, Rozanne Lanczak. Faulkner, Stacey, ed. 2007. (J). 4.99 *(978-1-59198-419-1(X))* Creative Teaching Pr., Inc.

—Forever Home. Philipson, Sandra J. 2007. (ENG.). 89p. (J). (gr. 3-7). bds. 7.95 *(978-1-59624-080-3(6))* Cleveland Clinic Pr.

—Life Cycles. Cernek, Kim. Rous, Sheri, ed. 2003. (Stepping into Standards Theme Ser.). 64p. (J). (gr. 2-4). pap. 10.99 *(978-1-59198-002-5(X),* 2484) Creative Teaching Pr., Inc.

—Mapping. Cernek, Kim & Shiotsu, Vicky. Rous, Sheri, ed. 2003. (Stepping into Standards Theme Ser.). 64p. (J). (gr. 2-4). pap. 10.99 *(978-1-59198-004-9(6),* CTP2486) Creative Teaching Pr., Inc.

—Max's Rules. Philipson, Sandra. 2004. (J). 9.95 *(978-1-929821-10-5(7))* Chagrin River Publishing Co.

—Nutrition. Cernek, Kim et al. Rous, Sheri, ed. 2003. (Stepping into Standards Theme Ser.). 64p. (J). (gr. 2-4). pap. 10.99 *(978-1-59198-000-1(3),* CTP2482) Creative Teaching Pr., Inc.

—Oceans of Fun. Jordano, Kimberly & Corcoran, Tebra. Fisch, Teri L., ed. 2003. (Stepping into Standards Theme Ser.). 64p. (J). (gr. k-2). pap. 10.99 *(978-1-57471-946-8(7),* 2474) Creative Teaching Pr., Inc.

—Ollie's Monsters & Other Stories. Philipson, Sandra J. 2010. 48p. (J). pap. 10.95 *(978-1-929821-09-9(3))* Chagrin River Publishing Co.

—Operation: Reuse It! - Read Think Reuse. Persad, Sabbithry. 2011. (Garbology Kids Ser.). (ENG.). 40p. (J). (gr. k-2). pap. 8.95 *(978-0-9812439-1-7(6))* Firewater Media Group CAN. Dist: Independent Pubs. Group.

—Plants. Lewis, Dawn & Jacks, Cyndie. Jennett, Pamela & Rous, Sheri, eds. 2003. (Stepping into Standards Theme Ser.). 64p. (J). (gr. 2-4). pap. 10.99 *(978-1-59198-006-3(2),* CTP2488) Creative Teaching Pr., Inc.

—Sight Word Puzzles & Activities. Lewis, Sue & Abrams, Suzanne. Rous, Sheri, ed. 2004. 96p. (J). pap. 11.99 *(978-1-59198-052-0(6),* CTP 2239) Creative Teaching Pr., Inc.

—Soaring into Space. Jordano, Kimberly & Corcoran, Tebra. Fisch, Teri L., ed. 2003. (Stepping into Standards Theme Ser.). 64p. (J). (gr. k-2). pap. 10.99 *(978-1-57471-952-9(1),* 2480) Creative Teaching Pr., Inc.

—A Very Special Twin Story. Alt, Susan. 2004. 32p. (J). pap. 15.95 *(978-1-891846-26-7(4),* TBSPECIAL, Twins Bks.) Sterling Investments I, LLC DBA Twins Magazine.

—Weather Wonders. Jordano, Kimberly & Corcoran, Tebra. Fisch, Teri L., ed. 2003. (Stepping into Standards Theme Ser.). 64p. (J). (gr. k-2). pap. 10.99 *(978-1-57471-950-5(5),* 2478) Creative Teaching Pr., Inc.

—Zipping Around the Zoo. Jordano, Kimberly & Corcoran, Tebra. Fisch, Teri L., ed. 2003. (Stepping into Standards Theme Ser.). 64p. (J). (gr. k-2). pap. 10.99 *(978-1-57471-948-2(3),* 2476) Creative Teaching Pr., Inc.

Campbell, Jenny & Grayson, Rick. Consonant Puzzles & Activities, Vol. 2143. Cernek, Kim. Cernek, Kim, ed. 2004. 96p. (J). pap. 12.99 *(978-1-59198-067-4(4),* 2143) Creative Teaching Pr., Inc.

—Vowel Puzzles & Activities, Vol. 2144. Lewis, Sue & Stern, Amy. Cernek, Kim, ed. 2004. 96p. (J). pap. 12.99 *(978-1-59198-068-1(2),* 2144) Creative Teaching Pr., Inc.

—Word Family Puzzles & Activities, Vol. 2145. Lewis, Sue & Stern, Amy. Cernek, Kim, ed. 2004. 96p. (J). pap. 12.99 *(978-1-59198-069-8(0),* 2145) Creative Teaching Pr., Inc.

Campbell, Jenny & Tom, Darcy. Build-a-Skill Instant Books Beginning & Ending Consonant Sounds. Shiotsu, Vicky. Faulkner, Stacey, ed. 2007. (J). 4.99 *(978-1-59198-416-0(5))* Creative Teaching Pr., Inc.

—Build-a-Skill Instant Books Color, Shape & Number Words. Cernek, Kim & Williams, Rozanne Lanczak. Shiotsu, Vicky & Faulkner, Stacey, eds. 2007. (J). 4.99 *(978-1-59198-411-5(4))* Creative Teaching Pr., Inc.

—Build-a-Skill Instant Books Consonant Blends & Digraphs. Cernak, Kim. Shiotsu, Vicky & Faulkner, Stacey, eds. 2007. (J). 4.99 *(978-1-59198-410-8(6))* Creative Teaching Pr., Inc.

—Build-a-Skill Instant Books R-Controled Vowels & Vowel Digraphs. Cernak, Kim. Shiotsu, Vicky & Faulkner, Stacey, eds. 2007. (J). 4.99 *(978-1-59198-413-9(0))* Creative Teaching Pr., Inc.

—Build-a-Skill Instant Books Short & Long Vowels. Callella, Kim. Shiotsu, Vicky & Faulkner, Stacey, eds. 2007. (J). 4.99 *(978-1-59198-412-2(2))* Creative Teaching Pr., Inc.

—Build-a-Skill Instant Books Sight Words, Part 1. Williams, Rozanne Lanczak. Faulkner, Stacey, ed. 2007. (J). 4.99 *(978-1-59198-414-6(9))* Creative Teaching Pr., Inc.

—Build-a-Skill Instant Books Sight Words, Part 2. Williams, Rozanne Lanczak. Faulkner, Stacey, ed. 2007. (J). 4.99 *(978-1-59198-415-3(7))* Creative Teaching Pr., Inc.

—Build-a-Skill Instant Books Time & Money. Cernek, Kim. Faulkner, Stacey, ed. 2007. (J). 4.99 *(978-1-59198-417-7(3))* Creative Teaching Pr., Inc.

—Build-a-Skill Instant Books Word Families-Long Vowels. Lubben, Amy & Williams, Rozanne Lanczak. Shiotsu, Vicky & Faulkner, Stacey, eds. 2007. (J). 4.99 *(978-1-59198-409-2(2))* Creative Teaching Pr., Inc.

—Build-a-Skill Instant Books Word Families-Short Vowels. Lubben, Amy & Williams, Rozanne Lanczak. Shiotsu, Vicky & Faulkner, Stacey, eds. 2007. (J). 4.99 *(978-1-59198-408-5(4))* Creative Teaching Pr., Inc.

Campbell, Jim. Over the Garden Wall Original Graphic Novel: Distillatoria. Case, Jonathan. 2018. (Over the Garden Wall Ser.). (ENG.). 144p. (YA). (gr. 4-7). pap. 14.99 *(978-1-68415-268-1(2))* Boom! Studios.

Campbell, Jim, et al. Over the Garden Wall Vol. 5. Lien-Sjursen, Kiernan. 2018. (Over the Garden Wall Ser.: 5). (ENG.). 112p. (J). (gr. 4-7). pap. 14.99 *(978-1-68415-242-1(9))* Boom! Studios.

Campbell, Jim, jt. illus. see Araujo, Andre Lima.

Campbell, Jim, jt. illus. see Bradshaw, Nick.

Campbell, Jim, jt. illus. see McGee, Cara.

Campbell, K. G. Aliens Get the Sniffles Too! Ahhh-Choo! Duffield, Katy S. 2017. 32p. (J). (gr. -1-2). 16.99 *(978-0-7636-6502-9(9))* Candlewick Pr.

—Dylan the Villain. 2016. (J). *(978-0-698-40517-2(X))* Penguin Bks., Ltd.

—Flora & Ulysses: The Illuminated Adventures. Dicamillo, Kate. 2013. 240p. (J). (gr. 3-7). 18.99 *(978-0-7636-6040-6(X))* Candlewick Pr.

—Flora & Ulysses: The Illuminated Adventures. DiCamillo, Kate. 2016. (ENG.). 231p. (J). (gr. 3-7). pap. 7.99 *(978-0-7636-8764-9(2))* Candlewick Pr.

—Flora & Ulysses: The Illuminated Adventures. Dicamillo, Kate. ed. 2016. (ENG.). 256p. (J). (gr. 3-7). 17.20 *(978-0-606-39100-9(2))* Turtleback.

—Who Wants a Tortoise? Keane, Dave. 2016. 40p. (J). (gr. k-3). 17.99 *(978-0-385-75417-0(5),* Knopf Bks. for Young Readers) Random Hse. Children's Bks.

Campbell, K. G. Dylan the Villain. Campbell, K. G. 2016. 32p. (J). (gr. -1-1). 17.99 *(978-0-451-47642-5(5),* Viking Books for Young Readers) Penguin Young Readers Group.

Campbell, Karen. Great Big Holy Bible: Fall Quarter, Year One. Vineyard Church of Columbus. 2007. (J). ring bd. 19.99 *(978-0-9786394-7-1(2))* Ampelon Publishing, LLC.

Campbell, Keith. Lester's Dreadful Sweaters. Campbell, Keith. 2012. (ENG.). 32p. (J). (gr. -1-3). 16.95 *(978-1-55453-770-9(3))* Kids Can Pr., Ltd. CAN. Dist: Hachette Bk. Group.

Campbell, Ken. Jeff & His Magic Hot Air Balloon. Cliffe, Kara. 2013. 44p. pap. 15.50 *(978-1-62212-186-1(4),* Strategic Bk. Publishing) Strategic Book Publishing & Rights Agency (SBPRA).

Campbell, Lang. The Bunny Rabbit Gentleman Makes a Kite: Uncle Wiggily Goes Swimming. Garis, Howard R. Trust, T'He Gunston Q., ed. 2019. (ENG.). 26p. (J). pap. 6.99 *(978-1-7956-5285-8(3))* Independently Published.

—How Mr. Hedgehog Helped Him Get up the Slippery Hill: Uncle Wiggily's Auto Sled. Garis, Howard R. Trust, The Gunston, ed. 2019. (ENG.). 26p. (J). pap. 6.99 *(978-1-7957-3394-6(2))* Independently Published.

—Uncle Wiggily Distributes Thanksgiving Cakes: Uncle Wiggily Goes Swimming. Garis, Howard R. Trust, The Gunston, ed. 2019. (ENG.). 26p. (J). pap. 6.99 *(978-1-7956-3760-2(9))* Independently Published.

—What Happened in the Snow Fort: Uncle Wiggily's Auto Sled. Garis, Howard R. Trust, The Gunston, ed. 2019. (ENG.). 26p. (J). pap. 6.99 *(978-1-7957-8492-4(X))* Independently Published.

Campbell, Lisa. The Worn-Out Backpack. Romagnoli, L. M. 2008. 15p. pap. 24.95 *(978-1-60563-934-5(6))* America Star Bks.

Campbell, Lizy J. Chrissie & the Crust Monster. Van Duyn, Amy. 2018. (ENG.). 50p. (J). pap. 14.99 *(978-1-949609-41-7(3))* Pen It! Pubns., LLC.

Campbell, Lizy J. Home Tweet Home. Bartzen, Della. 4 Paws Games and Publishing. ed. 2019. (ENG.). 48p. (J). pap. ***(978-1-988345-98-7(7))*** Caswell, Vickianne.

—One Black Bird. Forehand, Terri. 2020. (ENG.). 26p. (J). pap. 12.99 ***(978-1-952011-04-7(3))*** Pen It! Pubns., LLC.

—Pappa Cane. Rahal Ramos Fern�ndez, Aleida. 2020. (ENG.). 38p. (J). pap. 14.99 ***(978-1-952011-55-9(8))*** Pen It! Pubns., LLC.

Campbell, Lorne, photos by. Get Cooking. Stern, Sam & Stern, Susan. 2009. (ENG.). 144p. (J). (gr. 5-18). pap. 17.99 *(978-0-7636-3926-6(5))* Candlewick Pr.

Campbell, Marie L. A Pocketful of Passage. 2007. (Great Lakes Books Ser.). (ENG.). 96p. (J). (gr. 3-7). per. 12.99 *(978-0-8143-3341-9(9),* 2078) Wayne State Univ. Pr.

Campbell-Quillen, Virginia. A Montana Love Affair: Letting Go & Being Free. McIntosh, Anne. 2005. (YA). 16.95 *(978-1-59494-008-8(8))* CPCC Pr.

Campbell, Ray. Landi of Terrebonne Bayou. Charlton, Ella Mae. 2012. 176p. 42.95 *(978-1-258-23763-9(6));* pap. 27.95 *(978-1-258-24653-2(8))* Literary Licensing, LLC.

Campbell, Richard P., photos by. Growing Patterns: Fibonacci Numbers in Nature. Campbell, Sarah C. 2010. (ENG., 32p. (J). (gr. 2-5). 17.99 *(978-1-59078-752-6(8))* Boyds Mills Pr.

—Mysterious Patterns: Finding Fractals in Nature. Campbell, Sarah C. 2014. (ENG.). 32p. (J). (gr. 2-5). 17.99 *(978-1-62091-627-8(4))* Boyds Mills Pr.

—Wolfsnail: A Backyard Predator. Campbell, Sarah C. 2008. (ENG., 32p. (J). (gr. k-2). 17.95 *(978-1-59078-554-6(1))* Boyds Mills Pr.

Campbell, Rod. Dear Zoo. Campbell, Rod. 2004. 16p. (J). (CHI & ENG.). bds. *(978-1-84444-171-6(7));* (RUS & ENG.). bds. *(978-1-84444-178-5(4));* (VIE & ENG.). bds. *(978-1-84444-183-9(0));* (ENG & ALB.). bds. *(978-1-84444-167-9(9));* (ENG & ARA.). bds. *(978-1-84444-168-6(7));* (CHI & ENG.). bds. *(978-1-84444-170-9(9));* (ENG & PER.). bds. *(978-1-84444-172-3(5));* (ENG & FRE.). bds. *(978-1-84444-173-0(3));* (ENG & GUJ.). bds. *(978-1-84444-174-7(1));* (ENG & HIN.). bds. *(978-1-84444-175-4(X));* (ENG & PAN.). bds. *(978-1-84444-176-1(8));* (ENG & POR.). bds. *(978-1-84444-177-8(6));* (ENG & SPA.). bds. *(978-1-84444-179-2(2));* (ENG & SOM.). bds. *(978-1-84444-180-8(6));* (ENG & TUR.). bds. *(978-1-84444-181-5(4));* (URD & ENG.). bds. *(978-1-84444-182-2(2))* Mantra Lingua.

—Dear Zoo. Campbell, Rod. 2019. (Dear Zoo & Friends Ser.). (ENG.). 24p. (J). (— 1). 17.99 *(978-1-5344-6012-6(8),* Little Simon) Little Simon.

—Dear Zoo: From the Zoo. Campbell, Rod. 25th ed. 2007. 18p. (J). (gr. -1 — 1). bds. 6.99 *(978-1-4169-4737-0(X),* Little Simon) Little Simon.

—Dear Zoo Animal Shapes. Campbell, Rod. 2016. (Dear Zoo & Friends Ser.). (ENG.). 20p. (J). (gr. -1 — 1). bds. 6.99 *(978-1-4814-8069-7(3),* Little Simon) Little Simon.

—Dinosaurs. Campbell, Rod. 2015. (Dear Zoo & Friends Ser.). (ENG.). 14p. (J). (gr. -1 — 1). bds. 6.99 *(978-1-4814-4985-4(0),* Little Simon) Little Simon.

—Farm Animals. Campbell, Rod. 2015. (Dear Zoo & Friends Ser.). (ENG.). 14p. (J). (gr. -1 — 1). bds. 6.99 *(978-1-4814-4984-7(2),* Little Simon) Little Simon.

—Oh Dear! A Farm Lift-The-Flap Book. Campbell, Rod. 2019. (Dear Zoo & Friends Ser.). (ENG.). 18p. (J). (— 1). bds. 7.99 *(978-1-5344-4319-8(3),* Little Simon) Little Simon.

Campbell, Ross. Leonardo, 1 vol. Lynch, Brian. 2015. (Teenage Mutant Ninja Turtles Ser.). (ENG.). 24p. (J). (gr. 3-7). 27.07 *(978-1-61479-339-7(5),* 17339, Graphic Novels) Spotlight.

Campbell, Scott. Brobot Bedtime. Bardhan-Quallen, Sudipta. 2017. (ENG.). 32p. (J). (gr. k-2). 16.95 *(978-1-4197-2290-5(5),* Abrams Bks. for Young Readers) Abrams, Inc.

—East Dragon, West Dragon. Eversole, Robyn. 2012. (ENG.). 40p. (J). (gr. -1-2). 17.99 *(978-0-689-85828-4(0),* Atheneum Bks. for Young Readers) Simon & Schuster Children's Publishing.

—If Dogs Run Free. Dylan, Bob. 2013. (ENG.). 40p. (J). (gr. -1-3). 17.99 *(978-1-4516-4879-9(0))* Simon & Schuster Children's Publishing.

—Skulls! Thornburgh, Blair. 2019. (ENG.). 40p. (J). (gr. -1-3). 17.99 *(978-1-5344-1400-6(2))* Simon & Schuster Children's Publishing.

—Xo, Ox: A Love Story. Rex, Adam. 2017. (ENG.). 40p. (J). 17.99 *(978-1-62672-288-0(9),* 900149172) Roaring Brook Pr.

—Zombie in Love 2 + 1. DiPucchio, Kelly. 2014. (ENG.). 32p. (J). (gr. -1-3). 14.99 *(978-1-4424-5937-3(9),* Atheneum Bks. for Young Readers) Simon & Schuster Children's Publishing.

Campbell, Scott. Hug Machine. Campbell, Scott. 2017. (ENG.). 36p. (J). (gr. -1 — 1). bds. 7.99 *(978-1-5344-0026-9(5),* Little Simon) Little Simon.

Campbell, Scott & Thomas, Louis. Ginny Goblin Is Not Allowed to Open This Box. Goodner, David. 2018. (ENG.). 40p. (J). (gr. -1-3). 17.99 *(978-0-544-76415-6(3),* 1635200, HMH Books For Young Readers) Houghton Mifflin Harcourt Publishing Co.

Campbell, Scott, jt. illus. see Joseph, Robin.

Campbell, Tracy. Splish Splash. Affleck, Julie. 2020. (ENG.). 26p. (J). pap. 15.00 ***(978-1-7027-8479-5(7))*** Independently Published.

Campeau, Tamara. In the Sky at Nighttime. Deal, Laura. 2019. (ENG.). 28p. (J). 16.95 *(978-1-77227-238-3(8))* Inhabit Media Inc. CAN. Dist: Consortium Bk. Sales & Distribution.

Campeau, Tamara. Kits, Cubs, & Calves: An Arctic Summer. Napayok-Short, Suzie. 2020. (ENG.). 32p. (J). 17.95 ***(978-1-77227-274-1(4))*** Inhabit Media Inc. CAN. Dist: Consortium Bk. Sales & Distribution.

Campeau, Tamara. The Muskox & the Caribou, 1 vol. Mike, Nadia. 2018. (ENG.). 32p. (J). (gr. -1-k). 16.95 *(978-1-77227-163-8(2))* Inhabit Media Inc. CAN. Dist: Consortium Bk. Sales & Distribution.

Campidelli, Maurizio. The Attack on Pearl Harbor: December 7 1941, 1 vol. Yomtov, Nel. 2014. (24-Hour History Ser.). (ENG.). 48p. (J). (gr. 3-9). pap. 8.95 *(978-1-4329-9299-6(6));* lib. bdg. 33.99 *(978-1-4329-9293-4(7))* Capstone. (Heinemann).

Campidelli, Maurizio, et al. Disney: Where's Mickey? Drage, Emma. 2019. (ENG.). 48p. (J). *(978-1-5037-3935-2(X),* 404a92a0-236a-4275-a7eb-39ebcab97d32, p i kids) Phoenix International Publications, Inc.

Campidelli, Maurizio. Disney*Pixar Onward. 2020. (Look & Find Ser.). (ENG.). 24p. (J). ***(978-1-5037-5252-8(6),*** 91c50d6a-3843-4ac6-9f7a-3b2f14c2f081, p i kids) Phoenix International Publications, Inc.

Campidelli, Maurizio. How to Live Like an Egyptian Mummy Maker. Farndon, John. 2016. (How to Live Like ... Ser.). (ENG.). 32p. (J). (gr. 3-6). 27.99 *(978-1-5124-0629-0(5),* 9781512406290, Hungry Tomato ®) Lerner Publishing Group.

—The Science of Basketball with Max Axiom, Super Scientist. Bethea, Nikole Brooks. 2015. (Science of Sports with Max Axiom Ser.). (ENG.). 32p. (J). (gr. 3-9). lib. bdg. 31.32 *(978-1-4914-6084-9(9),* Capstone Pr.) Capstone.

Campidelli, Maurizio & Viana, Tatio. How to Live Like a Caribbean Pirate. Farndon, John. 2016. (How to Live Like ... Ser.). (ENG.). 32p. (J). (gr. 3-6). 27.99 *(978-1-5124-0631-3(7),* 9781512406313, Hungry Tomato ®) Lerner Publishing Group.

Campidelli, Maurizio, jt. illus. see Aranda, Tomás.

Campidelli, Maurizio, jt. illus. see Aranda, Tom.

Campillo Quiles, Juan Carlos. Las Aventuras de S. Haro Herraiz, Javier. 2018. (S Ser.: Vol. 1). (SPA.). 246p. (J). pap. 12.00 *(978-1-7200-3490-2(7))* Independently Published.

Campillo Quiles, Juan Carlos. Las Aventuras Del Pr�ncipe V�ctor. Haro Herraiz, Javier. 2019. (SPA.). 74p. (J). pap. 15.50 ***(978-1-0999-8184-5(0))*** Independently Published.

Campion, Pascal. Dog Days in the City. Kendall, Jodi. (ENG.). (J). (gr. 3-7). 2019. 336p. pap. 6.99 *(978-0-06-248457-4(5))*; 2018. 320p. 16.99 *(978-0-06-248456-7(7))* HarperCollins Pubs.

—Me & Grandma. Catherine, Maria. 2015. (Time Together Ser.). (ENG.). 32p. (J). (gr. -1-2). 8.95 *(978-1-4795-5795-0(1)*, Picture Window Bks.) Capstone.

—Me & Grandpa. Catherine, Maria. 2015. (Time Together Ser.). (ENG.). 32p. (J). (gr. -1-2). 8.95 *(978-1-4795-5796-7(X)*, Picture Window Bks.) Capstone.

—The Paper Kingdom. Rhee, Helena Ku. 2020. (ENG.). 40p. (J). (gr. -1-2). 17.99 *(978-0-525-64461-3(X))*; lib. bdg. 20.99 *(978-0-525-64462-0(8))* Random Hse. Children's Bks. (Random Hse. Bks. for Young Readers).

—Time Together: Me & Dad, 1 vol. Catherine, Maria. 2014. (Time Together Ser.). (ENG.). 32p. (J). (gr. -1-2). 8.95 *(978-1-4795-2253-8(8)*, Picture Window Bks.) Capstone.

—Time Together: Me & Mom, 1 vol. Catherine, Maria. 2014. (Time Together Ser.). (ENG.). 32p. (J). (gr. -1-2). 8.95 *(978-1-4795-2252-1(X)*, Picture Window Bks.) Capstone.

—The Unlikely Story of a Pig in the City. Kendall, Jodi. 2017. (ENG.). 336p. (J). (gr. 3-7). 16.99 *(978-0-06-248453-6(2))* HarperCollins Pubs.

—The Unlikely Story of a Pig in the City. Kendall, Jodi. 2018. (ENG.). 352p. (J). (gr. 3-7). pap. 7.99 *(978-0-06-248454-3(0)*, HarperCollins) HarperCollins Pubs. Ltd. GBR. Dist: HarperCollins Pubs.

—We Are Twins. Driscoll, Laura. 2012. (Penguin Young Readers, Level 1 Ser.). 32p. (J). (gr. k-1). mass mkt. 4.99 *(978-0-448-46157-1(9)*, Penguin Young Readers) Penguin Young Readers Group.

Campis, Adrian, Jr. A Journey with the Spider & Snake to Arizona. Cook, Beatrice. 2007. (J). 14.95 *(978-0-9795867-0-5(4))* Travel America Bks.

Campos F, Angel. La Conspiracion de Las Tias. Estrada, Gabriela Aguileta. rev. ed. 2007. (Castillo de la Lectura Verde Ser.). (SPA & ENG.). 136p. (J). (gr. 2-4). pap. 7.95 *(978-970-20-0174-4(9))* Castillo, Ediciones, S. A. de C. V. MEX. Dist: Macmillan.

Campos, Leo. Meltdown 4 Voyagers. Millett, Peter. 2017. (Cambridge Reading Adventures Ser.). (ENG.). 32p. pap. 7.87 *(978-1-108-43485-0(1))* Cambridge Univ. Pr.

Campos, Marc & Wyman, M. C. Uncanny Origins: Myths & Magic. 2019. 168p. (J). (gr. 3-7). pap. 12.99 *(978-1-302-92043-2(X))* Marvel Worldwide, Inc.

Camuncoli, Giuseppe, et al. Amazing Spider-Man: the Clone Conspiracy. 2017. (ENG.). 496p. (YA). (gr. 8-17). pap. 39.99 *(978-1-302-90599-6(6))* Marvel Worldwide, Inc.

—Amazing Spider-Man: Worldwide Vol. 2. 2017. (ENG.). 232p. (J). (gr. 4-17). 34.99 *(978-1-302-90842-3(1))* Marvel Worldwide, Inc.

Camuncoli, Giuseppe. Amazing Spider-Man: Worldwide Vol. 5. 2017. 144p. (J). (gr. 4-17). pap. 17.99 *(978-1-302-90238-4(5))* Marvel Worldwide, Inc.

Camuncoli, Giuseppe & Kirk, Leonard. Star Wars: Darth Vader - Dark Lord of the Sith Vol. 2. 2020. (ENG.). 336p. (J). (gr. 4-17). 34.99 ***(978-1-302-92545-1(8))*** Marvel Worldwide, Inc.

Canac, Hélène. Cassandra Steps Out: Book 1. Bottier, Isabelle. 2019. (Cassandra: Animal Psychic Ser.). (ENG.). 56p. (J). (gr. 4-8). pap. 8.99 *(978-1-5415-7283-6(1))*; lib. bdg. 26.65 *(978-1-5415-4397-3(1))* Lerner Publishing Group. (Graphic Universe™).

—Out on a Limb. Bottier, Isabelle & MacTyre, Norwyn. 2020. (Cassandra: Animal Psychic Ser.). 56p. (J). (gr. 4-8). 26.65 *(978-1-5415-4398-0(X)*, Graphic Universe™) Lerner Publishing Group.

—Out on a Limb: Book 2. Bottier, Isabelle. 2020. (Cassandra: Animal Psychic Ser.). (ENG.). 56p. (J). (gr. 4-8). pap. 8.99 *(978-1-5415-8693-2(X)*, Graphic Universe™) Lerner Publishing Group.

Canale, Melina. El Misterio de la Casa Verde. Huidobro, Norma. 2019. (Torre Azul Ser.). (SPA.). 136p. (J). pap. ***(978-958-776-006-4(9))*** Norma Ediciones, S.A.

—El Misterio Del Mayordomo. Huidobro, Norma. 2019. (Torre Azul Ser.). (SPA.). 138p. (J). (gr. -1-7). pap. ***(978-958-776-483-3(8))*** Norma Ediciones, S.A.

Canals, Sonia. What Do Animals Eat for Lunch? Massey, Kay. 2009. (Little Green Footprints Ser.). 12p. (J). (gr. -1-k). bds. 11.40 *(978-1-60754-697-9(3))* Windmill Bks.

—Where Do Animals Hide? Massey, Kay. 2009. (Little Green Footprints Ser.). 12p. (J). (gr. -1-k). bds. 11.40 *(978-1-60754-696-2(5))* Windmill Bks.

Canals, Sonia & O'Toole, Jeanette. What Do You See in the Sea? Massey, Kay. 2009. (Little Green Footprints Ser.). 12p. (J). (gr. -1-k). bds. 11.40 *(978-1-60754-698-6(1))* Windmill Bks.

—What Is a Flower's Special Power? Massey, Kay. 2009. (Little Green Footprints Ser.). 12p. (J). (gr. -1-k). bds. 11.40 *(978-1-60754-695-5(7))* Windmill Bks.

Canas, Alex. Gold & the Settling of the West: Bridges Edition. Harness, Cheryl. 2015. (Prime Plus Ser.). (YA). (gr. 6-8). pap. *(978-1-4900-1946-8(4))* Benchmark Education Co.

—Gold & the Settling of the West: Bridges Edition Set of 6 with Common Core Indicators. Harness, Cheryl. 2015. (Prime Plus Ser.). (YA). (gr. 6-8). 69.00 net. *(978-1-4900-2042-6(X))* Benchmark Education Co.

—Immigration 1850-1925: Bridges Edition. Worth, Richard. 2015. (Prime Plus Ser.). (YA). (gr. 6-8). pap. *(978-1-4900-1947-5(2))* Benchmark Education Co.

—Immigration 1850-1925: Bridges Edition Set of 6 with Common Core Indicators. Worth, Richard. 2015. (Prime Plus Ser.). (YA). (gr. 6-8). 69.00 net. *(978-1-4900-2043-3(8))* Benchmark Education Co.

—The Industrial Revolution: Bridges Edition. Reisfeld, Randi. 2015. (Prime Plus Ser.). (YA). (gr. 6-8). pap. *(978-1-4900-1948-2(0))* Benchmark Education Co.

—The Industrial Revolution: Bridges Edition Set of 6 with Common Core Indicators. Reisfeld, Randi. 2015. (Prime Plus Ser.). (YA). (gr. 6-8). 69.00 net. *(978-1-4900-2044-0(6))* Benchmark Education Co.

—Westward Expansion: Bridges Edition. Harness, Cheryl. 2015. (Prime Plus Ser.). (YA). (gr. 6-8). pap. *(978-1-4900-1945-1(6))* Benchmark Education Co.

—Westward Expansion: Bridges Edition Set of 6 with Common Core Indicators. Harness, Cheryl. 2015. (Prime Plus Ser.). (YA). (gr. 6-8). 69.00 net. *(978-1-4900-2041-9(1))* Benchmark Education Co.

Cañas, Alicia. El Hombre Que Perdió Su Imagen. Cañas, Alicia, tr. Sierra I. Fabra, Jordi & Sierra i Fabra, Jordi. 2nd ed. 2004.Tr. of Man Who Lost His Image. (SPA.). 128p. (J). (gr. 8-12). pap. 12.99 *(978-84-207-4478-0(6))* Grupo Anaya, S.A. ESP. Dist: Lectorum Pubns., Inc.

Canavan, Jean. Stevie Inchworm. Clinton, Ann M. 2009. 24p. (J). 31.99 *(978-1-4363-9471-0(6))* Xlibris Corp.

Canavese, Antonella. Henry & the Super Chillies. Jans, Miriam. 2018. (Animal Alliance Ser.: Vol. 1). (ENG.). 36p. (J). pap. *(978-0-6484063-0-3(X))* Bellybutton Bks.

Canby, Kelly. Fuchsia Fierce. Jones, Christianne C. 2016. (ENG.). 32p. (J). (gr. -1-2). 15.95 *(978-1-62370-786-6(2)*, Capstone Young Readers) Capstone.

—Fuchsia Fierce. Jones, Christianne. 2016. (Fiction Picture Bks.). (ENG.). 32p. (J). (gr. -1-2). lib. bdg. 22.65 *(978-1-5158-0553-0(0)*, Picture Window Bks.) Capstone.

—Just My Style. Shore, Diane Z. & Fairbanks, Jessica Alexander. 2018. (ENG.). 32p. (J). (gr. 1-3). 17.99 *(978-1-68152-202-9(0))* Amicus.

—Phil Pickle. Herzog, Kenny. 2016. (J). *(978-1-4413-1933-3(6))* Peter Pauper Pr. Inc.

Cancio, Damian. Mirando y Mirando: La Gran Aventura. Gonzalez-Villariny, Natali. 2012.Tr. of Great Adventure. (SPA & ENG.). 10p. (J). 8.99 *(978-0-9765007-1-1(X))* Big-head fish.

Cancio Leyva, Rams's. Tao de la Vojagantoj: Dek Ses ĉinaj Legendoj Kaj Infanrakontoj. Nunez Hernandez K a, Mayra. 2018. (Mas-Libro Ser.: Vol. 201). (EPO.). 80p. (YA). pap. *(978-2-36960-118-0(3))* Unesko-Grupo Narbonia.

Candace, Bonnie & Ellen. What to Do When You Worry Too Much: A Kid's Guide to Overcoming Anxiety. Huebner, Dawn. 2005. ("What to Do" Workbooks for Kids). 80p. (J). (gr. 1-7). per. 15.95 *(978-1-59147-314-5(4)*, Magination Pr.) American Psychological Assn.

—Wishing Wellness: A Workbook for Children of Parents with Mental Illness. Clarke, Lisa Anne. 2006. 127p. (J). (gr. 1-7). per. 14.95 *(978-1-59147-313-8(6)*, Magination Pr.) American Psychological Assn.

Candlewick Press Staff. Judy Moody & the Thrill Points Race. Michalak, Jamie. ed. 2011. (Judy Moody Ser.). 48p. (J). (gr. k-3). pap. 3.99 *(978-0-7636-5552-5(X))* Candlewick Pr.

Candlewick Press Staff & Ladybird Books Staff. Peppa Pig & the Busy Day at School. Candlewick Press Staff. 2013. (Peppa Pig Ser.). (ENG.). 32p. (J). (-k). 12.99 *(978-0-7636-6525-8(8)*, Candlewick Entertainment) Candlewick Pr.

Candlewick Press Staff, jt. illus. see Reynolds, Peter H.

Candon, Jennifer. When Fuzzy Was Afraid: Of Losing His Mother. Maier, Inger M. 2004. 32p. (J). 14.95 *(978-1-59147-168-4(0))*; pap. 9.95 *(978-1-59147-169-1(9))* American Psychological Assn. (Magination Pr.).

—When Fuzzy Was Afraid of Big & Loud Things. Maier, Inger M. 2005. (Fuzzy the Little Sheep Ser.). 32p. (J). (gr. -1-3). 14.95 *(978-1-59147-322-0(5))*; per. 9.95 *(978-1-59147-323-7(3))* American Psychological Assn. (Magination Pr.).

—When Lizzie Was Afraid: Of Trying New Things. Maier, Inger M. 2004. 32p. (J). 14.95 *(978-1-59147-170-7(2))*; pap. 9.95 *(978-1-59147-171-4(0))* American Psychological Assn. (Magination Pr.).

Canet Gregori, Juan Simeon. In�s. Canet Gregori, Juan Simeon. 2019. (SPA.). 356p. (J). pap. 16.00 ***(978-1-6710-0095-7(1))*** Independently Published.

Canga, C. B. The Burglar Who Bit the Big Apple. Brezenoff, Steve. 2010. (Field Trip Mysteries Ser.). (ENG.). 88p. (J). (gr. 3-6). 25.32 *(978-1-4342-2139-1(3))*; pap. 5.95 *(978-1-4342-2771-3(5))* Capstone. (Stone Arch Bks.).

—Celebrating California: 50 States to Celebrate. Bauer, Marion Dane & Rucker, Justin. 2013. (Green Light Readers Level 3 Ser.). (ENG.). 40p. (J). (gr. 1-4). 12.99 *(978-0-547-98385-1(9)*, 1524119); pap. 3.99 *(978-0-547-89697-7(2)*, 1509662) Houghton Mifflin Harcourt Publishing Co.

—Celebrating Florida: 50 States to Celebrate. Bauer, Marion Dane. 2013. (Green Light Readers Level 3 Ser.). (ENG.). 40p. (J). (gr. 1-4). 12.99 *(978-0-547-89699-1(9)*, 1509704); pap. 3.99 *(978-0-547-89698-4(0)*, 1509703) Houghton Mifflin Harcourt Publishing Co.

—Celebrating Georgia: 50 States to Celebrate. Kurtz, Jane. 2015. (Green Light Readers Level 3 Ser.). 40p. (J). (gr. 1-4). pap. 3.99 *(978-0-544-41975-9(8)*, 1595310, HMH Books For Young Readers) Houghton Mifflin Harcourt Publishing Co.

—Celebrating Louisiana: 50 States to Celebrate. Kurtz, Jane. 2016. (Green Light Readers Level 3 Ser.). (ENG.). 40p. (J). (gr. 1-4). pap. 4.99 *(978-0-544-51827-8(6)*, 1606225, HMH Books For Young Readers) Houghton Mifflin Harcourt Publishing Co.

—Celebrating New York: 50 States to Celebrate. Bauer, Marion Dane. 2013. (Green Light Readers Level 3 Ser.). (ENG.). 40p. (J). (gr. 1-4). pap. 4.99 *(978-0-547-89781-3(2)*, 1509706) Houghton Mifflin Harcourt Publishing Co.

—Celebrating North Carolina: 50 States to Celebrate. Bauer, Marion Dane. 2014. (Green Light Readers Level 3 Ser.). (ENG.). 40p. (J). (gr. 1-4). 12.99 *(978-0-544-28875-1(0)*, 1572122, HMH Books For Young Readers) Houghton Mifflin Harcourt Publishing Co.

—Celebrating Texas: 50 States to Celebrate. Bauer, Marion Dane. 2013. (Green Light Readers Level 3 Ser.). (ENG.). 40p. (J). (gr. 1-4). pap. 3.99 *(978-0-547-89786-8(3)*, 1509708) Houghton Mifflin Harcourt Publishing Co.

—The Crook Who Crossed the Golden Gate Bridge. Brezenoff, Steve. 2010. (Field Trip Mysteries Ser.). (ENG.). 88p. (J). (gr. 3-6). 25.32 *(978-1-4342-2138-4(5))*; pap. 5.95 *(978-1-4342-2770-6(7))* Capstone. (Stone Arch Bks.).

—The Ghost Who Haunted the Capitol. Brezenoff, Steve. 2010. (Field Trip Mysteries Ser.). (ENG.). 88p. (J). (gr. 3-6). 25.32 *(978-1-4342-2140-7(7))*; pap. 5.95 *(978-1-4342-2772-0(3))* Capstone. (Stone Arch Bks.).

Canga, C. B. Good Night Sydney. Gamble, Adam & Jasper, Mark. 2020. (Good Night Our World Ser.). (ENG.). 20p. (J). (— 1). bds. 9.95 *(978-1-60219-804-3(7))* Good Night Bks.

—Grimm's Fairy Tales, 1 vol. Grimm, Jacob & Grimm, Wilhelm K. 2011. (Calico Illustrated Classics Ser.: No. 3). (ENG.). 112p. (J). (gr. 2-5). 29.93 *(978-1-61641-102-2(3)*, 4011, Calico Chapter Bks.) ABDO Publishing Co.

—Monica & the Bratty Stepsister, 1 vol. Gallagher, Diana G. 2010. (Monica Ser.). (ENG.). 88p. (J). (gr. 4-8). 26.65 *(978-1-4342-1980-0(1)*, Stone Arch Bks.) Capstone.

Canga, C. B. On the Bus, on the Case, 1 vol. Brezenoff, Steve. 2010. (Field Trip Mysteries Ser.). (ENG.). 240p. (J). (gr. 3-6). 12.95 *(978-1-4342-2531-3(3)*, Stone Arch Bks.) Capstone.

—The Painting That Wasn't There. Brezenoff, Steve. 2009. (Field Trip Mysteries Ser.). (ENG.). 88p. (J). (gr. 3-6). lib. bdg. 25.32 *(978-1-4342-1608-3(X)*, Stone Arch Bks.) Capstone.

Canga, C. B. Paul Bunyan vs. Hals Halson: The Giant Lumberjack Challenge! Bateman, Teresa. 2012. (J). 34.28 *(978-1-61913-126-2(9))* Weigl Pubs., Inc.

Canga, C. B. The Red Badge of Courage. Crane, Stephen. 2010. (Calico Illustrated Classics Ser.: No. 1). (ENG.). 112p. (J). (gr. 2-5). 29.93 *(978-1-60270-711-5(1)*, 3975, Calico Chapter Bks.) ABDO Publishing Co.

—The Teacher Who Forgot Too Much. Brezenoff, Steve. 2009. (Field Trip Mysteries Ser.). (ENG.). 88p. (J). (gr. 3-6). lib. bdg. 25.32 *(978-1-4342-1609-0(8)*, Stone Arch Bks.) Capstone.

—The Village That Almost Vanished. Brezenoff, Steve. 2009. (Field Trip Mysteries Ser.). (ENG.). 88p. (J). (gr. 3-6). lib. bdg. 25.32 *(978-1-4342-1611-3(X)*, Stone Arch Bks.) Capstone.

—Your Life as a Settler in Colonial America. Troupe, Thomas Kingsley. 2012. (Way It Was Ser.). (ENG.). 32p. (J). (gr. 2-5). pap. 8.95 *(978-1-4048-7251-6(5))*; lib. bdg. 27.32 *(978-1-4048-7156-4(X))* Capstone. (Picture Window Bks.).

—The Zombie Who Visited New Orleans, 1 vol. Brezenoff, Steve. 2010. (Field Trip Mysteries Ser.). (ENG.). 88p. (J). (gr. 3-6). 25.32 *(978-1-4342-2141-4(5))*; pap. 5.95 *(978-1-4342-2773-7(1))* Capstone. (Stone Arch Bks.).

—The Zoo with the Empty Cage. Brezenoff, Steve. 2009. (Field Trip Mysteries Ser.). (ENG.). 88p. (J). (gr. 3-6). lib. bdg. 25.32 *(978-1-4342-1610-6(1)*, Stone Arch Bks.) Capstone.

Canga, Chris Barnard. El Cuadro Desaparecido. Brezenoff, Steve. 2019. (Misterios de Excursión Ser.). (SPA.). 88p. (J). (gr. 3-6). lib. bdg. 25.32 *(978-1-4965-8539-4(9)*, 141288, Stone Arch Bks.) Capstone.

—El Maestro Que Olvidaba Casi Todo. Brezenoff, Steve. 2019. (Misterios de Excursión Ser.). (SPA.). 88p. (J). (gr. 3-6). lib. bdg. 25.32 *(978-1-4965-8540-0(2)*, 141289, Stone Arch Bks.) Capstone.

—Misterios de Excursión. Brezenoff, Steve. 2019. (Misterios de Excursión Ser.). (SPA.). (J). (gr. 3-6). 101.28 *(978-1-4965-8571-4(2)*, 29720, Stone Arch Bks.) Capstone.

—El Pueblo Que Casi Desapareció. Brezenoff, Steve. 2019. (Misterios de Excursión Ser.). (SPA.). 88p. (J). (gr. 3-6). lib. bdg. 25.32 *(978-1-4965-8542-4(9)*, 141291, Stone Arch Bks.) Capstone.

—El Zoológico con la Jaula Vacía. Brezenoff, Steve. 2019. (Misterios de Excursión Ser.). (SPA.). 88p. (J). (gr. 3-6). lib. bdg. 25.32 *(978-1-4965-8541-7(0)*, 141290, Stone Arch Bks.) Capstone.

Cangialosi, Ciro, et al. Disney Sweet Dreams, Mickey. Parent, Nancy. 2020. (Disney Die-Cut Classics Ser.). (ENG.). 68p. (J). (gr. 1-3). 9.99 *(978-0-7944-4482-2(2)*, Studio Fun International) Printers Row Publishing Group.

—DuckTales: Fowl Play. Ferrari, Alessandro & Behling, Steve. 2019. (Duck Tales Ser.: 4). (ENG.). 72p. (J). (gr. 4-7). pap. 9.99 *(978-1-68405-403-9(6))* Idea & Design Works, LLC.

Cangialosi, Ciro, jt. illus. see Giuliani, Mady.

Caniac, Nina. Baby Pets Play! Caniac, Nina. 2012. (ENG.). 10p. (J). (gr. -1). 12.95 *(978-2-7338-2153-4(9))* Auzou, Philippe Editions FRA. Dist: Consortium Bk. Sales & Distribution.

Caniglia. Fuckin' Lie down Already. Piccirilli, Tom. 73p. (YA). 2005. pap. 11.95 *(978-0-9728656-6-1(7))*; 2003. 45.00 *(978-0-9728656-1-6(6))*; 2003. 100.00 *(978-0-9728656-0-9(8))* Endeavor Pr.

Canizales. Hoy No Juegas. Serrano, Pilar. 2019. (SPA.). 40p. (J). 15.95 *(978-84-17123-45-1(8))* NubeOcho Ediciones ESP. Dist: Consortium Bk. Sales & Distribution.

—Today You Can't Play. Serrano, Pilar. 2019. (ENG.). 40p. (J). 15.95 *(978-84-17123-46-8(6))* NubeOcho Ediciones ESP. Dist: Consortium Bk. Sales & Distribution.

Cann, Helen. The Barefoot Book of Father & Daughter Tales. Evetts-Secker, Josephine. 2012. 96p. (J). 23.99 *(978-1-84686-761-3(4))* Barefoot Bks., Inc.

—Brigid's Cloak: An Ancient Irish Story. Milligan, Bryce. 32p. (J). (gr. k-17). 2005. pap. 9.00 *(978-0-8028-5297-7(1)*, Eerdmans Bks For Young Readers); 2004. 16.00 *(978-0-8028-5224-3(6))* Eerdmans, William B. Publishing Co.

—A Calendar of Festivals. Gilchrist, Cherry. 2006. 79p. (J). (gr. 4-8). reprint ed. pap. 10.00 *(978-1-4223-5551-0(9))* DIANE Publishing Co.

—Dance Stories. Stemple, Heidi E. Y. & Yolen, Jane. 2010. (ENG.). 99p. (J). (gr. 3-18). 21.99 *(978-1-84686-219-9(1))* Barefoot Bks., Inc.

—Feathers for Peacock, Vol. Jules, Jacqueline. 2016. (ENG.). 28p. (J). (gr. -1-3). 16.95 *(978-1-937786-53-3(6)*, Wisdom Tales) World Wisdom, Inc.

—Fireside Stories: Tales for a Winter's Eve. Matthews, Caitlin & Barefoot Books. 2015. 96p. (J). (gr. 2-6). 19.99 *(978-1-78285-251-3(4))* Barefoot Bks., Inc.

—A Forest of Stories. Singh, Rina & Gonzales. 2005. (ENG.). 80p. (J). 12.99 *(978-1-84148-882-0(8))* Barefoot Bks., Inc.

—A Forest of Stories: Magical Tree Tales from Around the World. Singh, Rina. 2003. 64p. (J). 19.99 *(978-1-84148-963-6(8))* Barefoot Bks., Inc.

—The Lion Bible for Children. Watts, Murray. ed. 2008. (ENG.). 352p. (J). 12.99 *(978-0-7459-6095-1(2))* Lion Hudson PLC GBR. Dist: Independent Pubs. Group.

—Little Leap Forward: A Boy in Beijing. Yue, Guo & Farrow, Clare. 2008. (ENG.). 128p. (YA). (gr. 4-7). 16.99 *(978-1-84686-114-7(4))* Barefoot Bks., Inc.

—Little Leap Forward: A Boy in Beijing. Yue, Gui & Farrow, Clare. 2011. 120p. (J). (gr. 3-6). pap. 12.99 *(978-1-84686-539-8(5))* Barefoot Bks., Inc.

—Manger. Hopkins, Lee Bennett. 2014. (ENG.). 34p. (J). 16.00 *(978-0-8028-5419-3(2)*, Eerdmans Bks For Young Readers) Eerdmans, William B. Publishing Co.

—Marauder's Map Guide to Hogwarts (Harry Potter) Pascal, Erinn. 2018. (Harry Potter Ser.). 52p. (J). (gr. 2-2). 14.99 *(978-1-338-25280-4(1))* Scholastic, Inc.

—Mother & Daughter Tales. Evetts-Secker, Josephine. 2011. 40p. (J). 21.99 *(978-1-84686-572-5(7))* Barefoot Bks., Inc.

—The Raiders Vol. 2: The Inuk Quartet. Riel, Jörn & Chodzin, Sherab. 2013. 128p. (J). (gr. 4-6). pap. 9.99 *(978-1-84686-744-6(4))* Barefoot Bks., Inc.

—Riding on a Caravan: A Silk Road Adventure. Krebs, Laurie. 2017. (ENG.). 32p. (J). (gr. -1-4). pap. 8.99 *(978-1-78285-344-2(8))* Barefoot Bks., Inc.

—Snow King. Howell, Gill. 2005. (ENG.). 24p. (J). lib. bdg. 23.65 *(978-1-59646-742-2(8))* Dingles & Co.

—The Snowstorm. Riel, Jørn et al. 2012. 128p. (J). (gr. 4-6). pap. 9.99 *(978-1-84686-797-2(5))* Barefoot Bks., Inc.

—We're Riding on a Caravan: An Adventure on the Silk Road. Krebs, Laurie. 2005. 32p. (J). 16.99 *(978-1-84148-343-6(5))* Barefoot Bks., Inc.

—We're Riding on a Caravan: An Adventure on the Silk Road. Krebs, Laurie. 2007. 32p. (J). (gr. k-3). pap. 24.94 *(978-1-84686-108-6(X))* Barefoot Bks., Ltd. GBR. Dist: Children's Plus, Inc.

Cannavicci, Luigi. Davey the Deer Is Feeling Down. Neal, Rosaleigh & Vitale, Grace. 2018. (ENG.). 38p. (J). (gr. k-6). pap. 11.95 *(978-1-946540-09-6(9))* Strategic Book Publishing & Rights Agency (SBPRA).

Cannavicci, Luigi A. The Christmas Adventure. Moore, Stephen. Moore, Lynne, ed. 2019. (ENG.). 56p. (J). ***(978-0-2288-2195-3(9))***; pap. ***(978-0-2288-2194-6(0))*** Tellwell Talent.

Cannavicci, Luigi A. Lucinda, Queen of Everything. Ciccone, Tiziana & Linardi, Franca. 2012. 36p. pap. 13.95 *(978-1-61897-719-9(9)*, Strategic Bk. Publishing) Strategic Book Publishing & Rights Agency (SBPRA).

—Taylor, Please Stop Talking! Ciccone, Tiziana. 2013. 32p. pap. 12.95 *(978-1-62516-817-7(9)*, Strategic Bk. Publishing) Strategic Book Publishing & Rights Agency (SBPRA).

Cannell, Jon. The Elephant from Baghdad, 0 vols. Holmes, Mary Tavener & Harris, John. 2012. (ENG.). 40p. (J). (gr. k-3). 17.99 *(978-0-7614-6111-1(6)*, 9780761461111, Two Lions) Amazon Publishing.

—A Giraffe Goes to Paris, 0 vols. Holmes, Mary Tavener & Harris, John. 2010. (ENG.). 32p. (J). (gr. 1-4). 17.99 *(978-0-7614-5595-0(7)*, 9780761455950, Two Lions) Amazon Publishing.

—Make It, Shake It, Mix It Up: 44 Bible Stories Brought to Life with Science. Kennedy, Nancy B. 2008. 61p. pap. 10.99 *(978-0-7586-1334-9(2))* Concordia Publishing Hse.

—My Travels with Clara. Holmes, Mary Tavener. 2007. (ENG.). 32p. (J). (gr. 3-7). 17.95 *(978-0-89236-880-8(2))* Oxford Univ. Pr., Inc.

—The Worst Night Ever. Barry, Dave. 2016. (Class Trip Ser.: 2). (ENG.). 256p. (J). (gr. 3-7). 13.99 *(978-1-4847-0850-7(4))* Hyperion Bks. for Children.

Cannella, Marco. Tattoo of Death. Montgomery, R. A. 2007. (Choose Your Own Adventure Ser.: 22). (ENG.). 144p. (J). (gr. 4-8). pap. 7.99 *(978-1-933390-22-2(0))* Chooseco LLC.

Cannella, Marco, jt. illus. see Louie, Wes.

Cannella, Marco, jt. illus. see Semionov, Vladimir.

Canning, Seán. The Cat That Loves to Eat. Canning, Seán. Canning, Erin, ed. 2005. (J). 9.95 *(978-0-9773134-0-2(9))* SP Family Productions, LLC.

Cannon, Annie. Horseshoe Crabs & Shorebirds: The Story of a Food Web, 1 vol. Crenson, Victoria. 2003. (ENG.). 32p. (J). (gr. 3-5). 16.95 *(978-0-7614-5115-0(3))* Marshall Cavendish Corp.

—Horseshoe Crabs & Shorebirds: The Story of a Foodweb, 0 vols. Crenson, Victoria. unabr. ed. 2009. (ENG.). 42p. (J). (gr. 3-5). pap. 9.99 *(978-0-7614-5552-3(3)*, 9780761455523, Two Lions) Amazon Publishing.

Cannon, Janell. Pinduli. Cannon, Janell. 2004. (ENG.). 48p. (J). (gr. -1-3). 17.99 *(978-0-15-204668-2(2)*, 1194069) Houghton Mifflin Harcourt Publishing Co.

Cannon, Kevin & Cannon, Zander. T-Minus: The Race to the Moon. Ottaviani, Jim. 2009. (ENG.). 128p. (J). (gr. 3-7). 36.19 *(978-1-4169-8682-9(0)*, Aladdin) Simon & Schuster Children's Publishing.

Cannon, Kevin, jt. illus. see Cannon, Zander.

Cannon, Lane. A Tale of Tails: A Grand Animal Anthology. Seidel, Charleen. 2020. (ENG.). 24p. (J). 24.99 ***(978-1-947773-73-8(9))*** Yawn's Bks. & More, Inc.

Cannon, Martin. Toad Catchers' Creek. Weiner, Brian. Weintraub, Claudia & Frederick, Robin, eds. 2005. 40p. (J). lib. bdg. 17.99 *(978-1-932949-58-2(5))* Illusion Factory, The.

Cannon, Nick, et al. Neon Aliens Ate My Homework: And Other Poems. Cannon, Nick. 2015. (ENG.). 144p. (J). (gr. 2-5). 14.99 *(978-0-545-72281-0(0))* Scholastic, Inc.

C

Cannon, Zander & Cannon, Kevin. T-Minus: The Race to the Moon. Ottaviani, Jim. 2009. (ENG.). 128p. (J). (gr. 3-7). pap. 17.99 *(978-1-4169-4960-2(7)*, Aladdin) Simon & Schuster Children's Publishing.

Cannon, Zander, jt. illus. see Cannon, Kevin.

Cano, Fern. Colossal Course! A Monster Truck Myth. Hoena, Blake. 2018. (ThunderTrucks! Ser.). (ENG.). 56p. (J). (gr. k-2). lib. bdg. 21.99 *(978-1-4965-5735-3(2)*, 136725, Stone Arch Bks.) Capstone.

—Gas Guzzler! A Monster Truck Myth. Hoena, Blake. 2018. (ThunderTrucks! Ser.). (ENG.). 56p. (J). (gr. k-2). lib. bdg. 21.99 *(978-1-4965-5737-7(9)*, 136727, Stone Arch Bks.) Capstone.

—Hansel & Gretel & Zombies: a Graphic Novel. Harper, Benjamin. 2016. (Far Out Fairy Tales Ser.). (ENG.). 40p. (J). (gr. 3-6). lib. bdg. 25.32 *(978-1-4965-2509-3(4)*, Stone Arch Bks.) Capstone.

—Maximum Horsepower! A Monster Truck Myth. Hoena, Blake. 2018. (ThunderTrucks! Ser.). (ENG.). 56p. (J). (gr. k-2). lib. bdg. 21.99 *(978-1-4965-5738-4(7)*, 136728, Stone Arch Bks.) Capstone.

—Monster Maze! A Monster Truck Myth. Hoena, Blake. 2018. (ThunderTrucks! Ser.). (ENG.). 56p. (J). (gr. k-2). lib. bdg. 21.99 *(978-1-4965-5736-0(0)*, 136726, Stone Arch Bks.) Capstone.

—Pecos Bill, Monster Wrangler: A Graphic Novel. Harper, Benjamin. 2019. (Far Out Folktales Ser.). (ENG.). 40p. (J). (gr. 3-6). lib. bdg. 25.32 *(978-1-4965-7841-9(4)*, 139307, Stone Arch Bks.) Capstone.

—The Robo-Battle of Mega Tortoise vs. Hazard Hare: A Graphic Novel. Peters, Stephanie. 2017. (Far Out Fables Ser.). (ENG.). 40p. (J). (gr. 3-6). pap. 4.95 *(978-1-4965-5424-6(8)*, 136357); lib. bdg. 25.32 *(978-1-4965-5420-8(5)*, 136353) Capstone. (Stone Arch Bks.).

—Thundertrucks!, 4 vols. Hoena, Blake. 2018. (ThunderTrucks! Ser.). (ENG.). 56p. (J). (gr. k-2). 87.96 *(978-1-4965-5751-3(4)*, 27389, Stone Arch Bks.) Capstone.

—ThunderTrucks! Hoena, Blake. 2018. (ThunderTrucks! Ser.). (ENG.). 56p. (J). (gr. k-2). 175.92 *(978-1-4965-6498-6(7)*, 28379, Stone Arch Bks.) Capstone.

—ThunderTrucks! Monster Truck Myths. Hoena, Blake. ed. 2018. (ThunderTrucks! Ser.). (ENG.). 144p. (J). (gr. k-2). pap. 7.95 *(978-1-68436-000-0(5)*, 136729, Stone Arch Bks.) Capstone.

—The Wind in the Willows. Peters, Stephanie True. 2016. (Graphic Revolve: Common Core Editions Ser.). (ENG.). 72p. (J). (gr. 5-9). pap. 6.95 *(978-1-4965-3564-1(2)*, Stone Arch Bks.) Capstone.

—The Wind in the Willows. Peters, Stephanie True. 2016. (Graphic Revolve: Common Core Editions Ser.). (ENG.). 72p. (J). (gr. 5-9). lib. bdg. 27.99 *(978-1-4965-3562-7(6)*, Stone Arch Bks.) Capstone.

Cano, Fern, jt. illus. see Cabrera, Eva.

Cano, Fernando. Above. Terrell, Brandon. 2013. (Tony Hawk: Live2Skate Ser.). (ENG.). 72p. (gr. 3-4). pap. 35.70 *(978-1-4342-6266-0(9)*, Stone Arch Bks.) Capstone.

—Alice, Secret Agent of Wonderland: A Graphic Novel. Schenkel, Katie. 2020. (Far Out Classic Stories Ser.). (ENG.). 40p. (J). (gr. 3-6). pap. 5.95 *(978-1-4965-9192-0(5)*, 142205); lib. bdg. 25.32 *(978-1-4965-8684-1(0)*, 141429) Capstone. (Stone Arch Bks.).

Cano, Fernando. The Dragon & the Swordmaker: A Graphic Novel. Peters, Stephanie. 2020. (Far Out Fairy Tales Ser.). (ENG.). 40p. (J). (gr. 3-6). pap. 5.95 ***(978-1-4965-9907-0(1)***, 201318); lib. bdg. 25.32 ***(978-1-4965-9685-7(4)***, 199252) Capstone. (Stone Arch Bks.).

Cano, Fernando, et al. Far Out Classic Stories. Harper, Benjamin et al. 2020. (Far Out Classic Stories Ser.). (ENG.). (J). (gr. 3-6). 101.28 *(978-1-4965-8693-3(X)*, 29777); pap., pap., pap. 23.80 *(978-1-4965-9275-0(1)*, 29972) Capstone. (Stone Arch Bks.).

Cano, Fernando. Happy Birthday, Batman! Bird, Benjamin. 2019. (DC Super Heroes Ser.). (ENG.). 32p. (J). (gr. -1-1). lib. bdg. 22.65 *(978-1-68446-106-6(5)*, 141346, Capstone Editions) Capstone.

Cano, Fernando. Los Superchivitos Gruff: Una Novela Gráfica. Tulien, Sean. 2020. (Cuentos de Hadas Futuristas Ser.).Tr. of Super Billy Goats Gruff: a Graphic Novel. (SPA.). 40p. (J). (gr. 3-6). pap. 5.95 ***(978-1-4965-9961-2(6)***, 201607); lib. bdg. 25.32 ***(978-1-4965-9815-8(6)***, 200703) Capstone. (Stone Arch Bks.).

Cano, Fernando. Peter Pan. Hoena, B. A. & Barrie, J. M. 2015. (Graphic Revolve: Common Core Editions Ser.). (ENG.). 72p. (J). (gr. 5-9). lib. bdg. 27.99 *(978-1-4965-0372-5(4)*, Stone Arch Bks.) Capstone.

—Peter Pan in Mummy Land: A Graphic Novel. Harper, Benjamin. 2020. (Far Out Classic Stories Ser.). (ENG.). 40p. (J). (gr. 3-6). pap. 5.95 *(978-1-4965-9193-7(3)*, 142206); lib. bdg. 25.32 *(978-1-4965-8686-5(7)*, 141430) Capstone. (Stone Arch Bks.).

—Private Eye Princess & the Emerald Pea: A Graphic Novel. Powell, Martin. 2019. (Far Out Fairy Tales Ser.). (ENG.). 40p. (J). (gr. 3-6). pap. 5.95 *(978-1-4965-8443-4(0)*, 140968); lib. bdg. 25.32 *(978-1-4965-8394-9(9)*, 140685) Capstone. (Stone Arch Bks.).

—Raw. Hoena, Blake A. 2013. (Tony Hawk: Live2Skate Ser.). (ENG.). 72p. (gr. 3-4). pap. 35.70 *(978-1-4342-6268-4(5)*, Stone Arch Bks.) Capstone.

—Super Billy Goats Gruff. Tulien, Sean. 2015. (Far Out Fairy Tales Ser.). (ENG.). 40p. (J). (gr. 3-6). lib. bdg. 25.32 *(978-1-4342-9649-8(0)*, Stone Arch Bks.) Capstone.

Cano, Fernando M., jt. illus. see Aburto, Jesus.

Cantalapiedra, Jose. Plumas en la Pradera. Lopez, Minia. 2006. (SPA.). (J). 10.00 *(978-0-9773531-5-6(X))* Charming Pubns.

Cantell, Brenda. Digging for Buried Treasure. Thompson, Lisa. 2006. (Treasure Trackers Ser.). 80p. (J). (gr. 3-4). lib. bdg. 19.00 *(978-0-7910-8872-2(3)*, Chelsea Hse.) Facts On File, Inc.

—In Search of the Egyptian Queen. Thompson, Lisa. 2006. (Treasure Trackers Ser.). 80p. (J). (gr. 3-4). lib. bdg. 19.00 *(978-0-7910-8874-6(X))* Facts On File, Inc.

Canter, Idalia. Hansi & the Ice Man. Ebel, Julia Taylor, Jr. 2014. 32p. (YA). lib. bdg. 19.95 *(978-1-933251-81-3(6))* Parkway Pubs., Inc.

—The Picture Man. Ebel, Julia Taylor. 2009. (ENG.). 32p. (J). 16.95 *(978-1-933251-63-9(8))* Parkway Pubs., Inc.

Cantini, Barbara. Anyone but Ivy Pocket. Krisp, Caleb. 2015. (Ivy Pocket Ser.: 1). (ENG.). 400p. (J). (gr. 3-7). 17.99 *(978-0-06-236434-0(0)*, Greenwillow Bks.) HarperCollins Pubs.

—Bring Me the Head of Ivy Pocket. Krisp, Caleb. 2018. (Ivy Pocket Ser.: 3). (ENG.). 416p. (J). (gr. 3-7). pap. 6.99 *(978-0-06-236441-8(3)*, Greenwillow Bks.) HarperCollins Pubs.

Cantone, AnnaLaura. Pecorino Plays Ball. Madison, Alan. 2006. (ENG.). 40p. (J). (gr. -1-3). 15.95 *(978-0-689-86522-0(8)*, Atheneum Bks. for Young Readers) Simon & Schuster Children's Publishing.

—Pecorino's First Concert. Madison, Alan. 2010. (ENG.). 40p. (J). (gr. -1-3). 16.99 *(978-1-4424-2191-2(6)*, Atheneum Bks. for Young Readers) Simon & Schuster Children's Publishing.

Cantor, Patricia. Christopher SAT Straight up in Bed. Long, Kathy. 2013. (ENG.). 40p. (J). 16.00 *(978-0-8028-5359-2(5)*, Eerdmans Bks For Young Readers) Eerdmans, William B. Publishing Co.

Cantrell, Anna. Bayou Song. Cancienne, Henry, photos by. Simon, Margaret Gibson. 2018. (J). *(978-1-946160-23-2(7))* Univ. of Louisiana at Lafayette Pr.

Cantrell, Katie. The Magic of Giving, 1 vol. Dunston, Marc. 2010. (ENG.). 32p. (J). (gr. k-3). 16.99 *(978-1-58980-805-8(3)*, Pelican Publishing) Arcadia Publishing.

Cantucci, Alessandro & Morandi, Andrea. Ancient Mesopotamian Civilization. Wildwood, Gretchen. 2009. (Ancient Civilizations & Their Myths & Legends Ser.). (YA). (gr. 5-9). lib. bdg. 32.75 *(978-1-4042-8037-3(5))* Rosen Publishing Group, Inc., The.

Canty, Charlotte. Something So Big. Waddell, Martin. 2004. (ENG.). 24p. (J). lib. bdg. 23.65 *(978-1-59646-706-4(1))* Dingles & Co.

Canty, John. Heads & Tails. Canty, John. 2018. (ENG.). 40p. (J). (-k). 16.99 *(978-1-5362-0033-1(6))* Candlewick Pr.

—Heads & Tails: Insects. Canty, John. 2020. (ENG.). 40p. (J). (-k). 17.99 *(978-1-5362-0784-2(5))* Candlewick Pr.

Canuso, Jackie, jt. illus. see Canuso, Julie.

Canuso, Julie & Canuso, Jackie. All Aboard with Noah: Pop-Up, 1 vol. David, Juliet. ed. 2016. (ENG.). 12p. (J). (gr. -1-k). 9.99 *(978-0-78128-249-6(8)*, Candle Bks.) Lion Hudson PLC GBR. Dist: Independent Pubs. Group.

Canyon, Christopher. Ancient Rhymes, a Dolphin Lullaby, 1 vol. Denver, John. 2004. (ENG.). 36p. (J). (gr. -1-6). pap. 8.95 *(978-1-58469-065-8(8)*, Dawn Pubns.) Sourcebooks, Inc.

—Ancient Rhymes, a Dolphin Lullaby: With Audio CD & Score, 1 vol. Denver, John. 2004. (ENG.). 36p. (J). (gr. -1-6). 19.99 *(978-1-58469-064-1(X)*, Dawn Pubns.) Sourcebooks, Inc.

—Earth & Me, Our Family Tree: Nature's Creatures. Lewis, J. Patrick. 2004. (Sharing Nature with Children Book Ser.). 36p. (J). (gr. -1-5). 16.95 *(978-1-58469-031-3(3))*; pap. 7.95 *(978-1-58469-030-6(5))* Dawn Pubns.

—Earth & Us-Continuous: Earth's Past & Future. Lewis, J. Patrick. 2004. (Sharing Nature with Children Book Ser.). 36p. (J). 16.95 *(978-1-58469-024-5(0))*; pap. 7.95 *(978-1-58469-023-8(2))* Dawn Pubns.

—Earth & You - A Closer View: Nature's Features. Lewis, J. Patrick. 2004. (Sharing Nature with Children Book Ser.). 36p. (J). (gr. -1-3). 16.95 *(978-1-58469-016-0(X))* Dawn Pubns.

—Grandma's Feather Bed, 1 vol. Denver, John. 2007. (ENG.). 36p. (J). (gr. -1-6). pap. 8.95 *(978-1-58469-096-2(8)*, Dawn Pubns.) Sourcebooks, Inc.

—John Denver's Grandma's Feather Bed. Denver, John. 2007. (ENG.). 36p. (J). (gr. -1-6). 19.95 *(978-1-58469-095-5(X)*, Dawn Pubns.) Sourcebooks, Inc.

—John Denver's Sunshine on My Shoulders, 1 vol. Denver, John. 2003. (ENG.). 32p. (J). pap. 8.95 *(978-1-58469-050-4(X)*, Dawn Pubns.) Sourcebooks, Inc.

—John Denver's Take Me Home, Country Roads, 1 vol. 2005. (ENG.). 34p. (J). (gr. -1-6). 8.95 *(978-1-58469-073-3(9)*, Dawn Pubns.) Sourcebooks, Inc.

—Sunshine on My Shoulders, 1 vol. Denver, John. 2003. (ENG.). 32p. 19.99 *(978-1-58469-048-1(8)*, Dawn Pubns.) Sourcebooks, Inc.

—Wonderful Nature, Wonderful You, 1 vol. Ireland, Karin. 2017. (ENG.). 32p. (J). (gr. k-3). 16.95 *(978-1-58469-582-0(X)*, Dawn Pubns.) Sourcebooks, Inc.

Canyon, Christopher. John Denver's Take Me Home, Country Roads, 1 vol. Canyon, Christopher, adapted by. 2005. (ENG.). 34p. (J). (gr. -1-6). 19.95 *(978-1-58469-072-6(0)*, Dawn Pubns.) Sourcebooks, Inc.

Canyon, Christopher & Hovemann, Anisa Claire. Environmentalism & Nature Book Set: Environment Education Books for Kids. Pratt-Serafini, Kristin Joy et al. 2020. (ENG.). (J). (gr. 5-8). pap. 43.80 ***(978-1-7282-4201-9(0)***, Dawn Pubns.) Sourcebooks, Inc.

Canyon, Jeanette. Over in the Jungle: A Rainforest Rhyme. Berkes, Marianne. 2007. (ENG.). 32p. (J). (gr. -1-2). 16.95 *(978-1-58469-091-7(7)*, Dawn Pubns.) Sourcebooks, Inc.

—Over in the Jungle: A Rainforest Rhyme, 1 vol. Berkes, Marianne. 2007. (ENG.). 32p. (J). (gr. -1-3). 8.95 *(978-1-58469-092-4(5)*, Dawn Pubns.) Sourcebooks, Inc.

—Over in the Ocean: In a Coral Reef. Berkes, Marianne. (ENG.). (J). (gr. -1-2). 2006. 26p. bds. 7.95 *(978-1-58469-082-5(8))*; 2004. 32p. 16.99 *(978-1-58469-063-4(1))*; 2004. 32p. pap. 8.95 *(978-1-58469-062-7(3))* Sourcebooks, Inc. (Dawn Pubns.).

Canzi, Nerina. Kaya's Heart Song. Tharan Sanders, Diwa. 2018. 32p. (J). (gr. -1-2). 17.99 *(978-1-911373-22-3(6))* Lantana Publishing GBR. Dist: Lerner Publishing Group.

Canzoneri, Bryant David. So Did I. Canzoneri, David Arden. 2020. (ENG.). 32p. (J). (gr. k-3). 19.99 ***(978-1-7320414-5-5(8))***; pap. 9.99 ***(978-1-7320414-6-2(6))*** Woodfrost Publishing.

Capaldi, Gina. Jobs from A to Z. Mangrum, Allison. 2006. 28p. pap. 9.50 *(978-1-55501-675-3(8))* Ballard & Tighe Pubs.

—Misiones Espanolas (Spanish Missions) Lilly, Melinda. 2005. (Lecturas Historicas Norteamericanas (Reading American Histor Ser.). 24p. (J). (gr. 3-7). lib. bdg. 22.79 *(978-1-59515-638-9(0))* Rourke Educational Media.

—The Passover Cowboy. Goldin, Barbara Diamond. 2016. (J). *(978-1-68115-527-2(3))* Behrman Hse., Inc.

—What Anna Loves. Simmons, Andra. 2006. 24p. (J). (gr. -1-3). 15.95 *(978-1-59714-044-7(9))* Heyday.

Capaldi, Gina. Arts & Crafts Across the USA. Capaldi, Gina. Rife, Douglas M. Mitchell, Judith, ed. 2005. 240p. (J). pap. 19.95 *(978-1-57310-445-6(0))* Teaching & Learning Co.

—A Boy Named Beckoning: The True Story of Dr. Carlos Montezuma, Native American Hero. Capaldi, Gina. (ENG.). 32p. (J). (gr. 3-6). 2019. 9.99 *(978-1-5415-7837-1(6)*, 9781541578371); 2008. lib. bdg. 18.99 *(978-0-8225-7644-0(9))* Lerner Publishing Group. (Carolrhoda Bks.).

—Red Bird Sings: The Story of Zitkala-Sa, Native American Author, Musician, & Activist. Capaldi, Gina. Pearce, Q. L. 2019. (ENG.). 32p. (J). (gr. 3-6). 9.99 *(978-1-5415-7836-4(8)*, 9781541578364, Carolrhoda Bks.) Lerner Publishing Group.

Capaldi, Mario. Odysseus & the Wooden Horse: A Greek Legend. 2003. (Dominie Collection of Myths & Legends). (SPA.). 20p. (J). lib. bdg. *(978-0-7685-2425-3(3))* Dominie Pr., Inc.

—Odysseus & the Wooden Horse: A Greek Legend. 2004. (ENG.). 20p. (J). (gr. 3-3). pap. 6.47 net. *(978-0-7685-2128-3(9)*, Dominie Elementary) Savvas Learning Co.

Capannelli, Natalie. If We Were Gone: Imagining the World Without People. Coy, John. 2020. (ENG.). 32p. (J). (gr. k-4). lib. bdg. 19.99 *(978-1-5415-2357-9(1)*, Millbrook Pr.) Lerner Publishing Group.

Caparo, Antonio. The Secret of Rover. Wildavsky, Rachel. 2015. (ENG.). 360p. (J). (gr. 4-8). pap. 7.95 *(978-1-4197-1968-4(8)*, Amulet Bks.) Abrams, Inc.

Caparo, Antonio Javier. The Adventures of Sherlock Holmes. Doyle, A. Conan. 2011. (Calico Illustrated Classics Ser.: No. 4). (ENG.). 112p. (J). (gr. 2-5). 29.93 *(978-1-61641-610-2(6)*, 4035, Calico Chapter Bks.) ABDO Publishing Co.

Caparó, Antonio Javier. Gulliver in Lilliput. Findlay, Lisa & Swift, Jonathan. 2010. (Step into Reading: Step 3 Ser.). (ENG.). 48p. (J). (gr. k-2). lib. bdg. 16.19 *(978-0-375-96585-2(8))* Random Hse. Bks. for Young Readers.

—Gulliver in Lilliput. Findlay, Lisa & Swift, Jonathan. 2010. (Step into Reading Ser.). 48p. (J). (gr. k-3). pap. 4.99 *(978-0-375-86585-5(3)*, Random Hse. Bks. for Young Readers) Random Hse. Children's Bks.

—The Ice Dragon, 4. Abbott, Tony. 2012. (Underworlds Ser.: 4). (ENG.). 112p. (J). (gr. 2-5). pap. 4.99 *(978-0-545-30834-2(8))* Scholastic, Inc.

Caparo, Antonio Javier. If We Were Giants. Matthews, Dave & Smith, Clete Barrett. 2020. (ENG.). 304p. (J). (gr. 3-7). 16.99 *(978-1-4847-7871-5(5))* Disney Publishing Worldwide.

Caparó, Antonio Javier. Invisible Lines. Amato, Mary. 2011. (ENG.). 336p. (gr. 4-6). lib. bdg. 22.44 *(978-1-60684-043-6(6))* Egmont Bks., Ltd. GBR. Dist: Children's Plus, Inc.

Caparo, Antonio Javier. The Lost Treasure of Tuckernuck. Fairlie, Emily. (Tuckernuck Mysteries Ser.: 1). (ENG.). (J). (gr. 3-7). 2013. 320p. pap. 6.99 *(978-0-06-211891-2(9))*; 2012. 304p. 16.99 *(978-0-06-211890-5(0))* HarperCollins Pubs. (Tegen, Katherine Bks).

—The Magic Thief. Prineas, Sarah. (Magic Thief Ser.: 1). (ENG.). (J). (gr. 5-9). 2008. 432p. 16.99 *(978-0-06-137587-3(X))*; 1. 2009. 448p. pap. 7.99 *(978-0-06-137590-3(X))* HarperCollins Pubs.

—The Magic Thief: Found. Prineas, Sarah. 2011. (Magic Thief Ser.: 3). (ENG.). 384p. (J). (gr. 5). pap. 7.99 *(978-0-06-137595-8(0))* HarperCollins Pubs.

—The Magic Thief: Home. Prineas, Sarah. (Magic Thief Ser.: 4). (ENG.). 416p. (J). (gr. 3-7). 2015. pap. 7.99 *(978-0-06-220956-6(6))*; 2014. 17.99 *(978-0-06-220954-2(X))* HarperCollins Pubs.

—The Magic Thief: Lost. Prineas, Sarah. (Magic Thief Ser.: 2). (ENG.). (J). (gr. 5-18). 2009. 400p. 17.99 *(978-0-06-137589-7(6))*; 2. 2010. 416p. pap. 7.99 *(978-0-06-137592-7(6))* HarperCollins Pubs.

—Magic Tree House Deluxe Holiday Edition: Christmas in Camelot. Osborne, Mary Pope. 2019. (Magic Tree House (R) Merlin Mission Ser.: 1). 144p. (J). (gr. 2-5). 18.99 *(978-1-9848-9519-6(2))*; (ENG.). lib. bdg. 21.99 *(978-1-9848-9520-2(6))* Random Hse. Children's Bks. (Random Hse. Bks. for Young Readers).

—The Magician's Bird. Fairlie, Emily. (Tuckernuck Mysteries Ser.: 2). (ENG.). 288p. (J). (gr. 3-7). 2014. pap. 6.99 *(978-0-06-211894-3(3))*; 2013. 16.99 *(978-0-06-211893-6(5))* HarperCollins Pubs. (Tegen, Katherine Bks).

—Missing on Superstition Mountain, Book 1. Broach, Elise. 2012. (Superstition Mountain Mysteries (Quality) Ser.: Vol. 1). (ENG.). 262p. (J). (gr. 3-7). lib. bdg. 18.00 *(978-1-68065-135-5(8))* Perfection Learning Corp.

—The Night Before Christmas. Moore, Clement C. 2017. (ENG.). 40p. (J). (gr. -1-2). 17.99 *(978-1-5344-0085-6(0)*, Little Simon) Little Simon.

—Rudolph Shines Again. May, Robert L. (Classic Board Bks.). (ENG.). (J). (gr. -1 — 1). 2018. 42p. bds. 7.99 *(978-1-5344-1839-4(3))*; 2015. 40p. 17.99 *(978-1-4424-7498-7(X))* Little Simon. (Little Simon).

—Rudolph the Red-Nosed Reindeer. May, Robert L. 2017. (Classic Board Bks.). (ENG.). 42p. (J). (gr. -1-k). bds. 7.99 *(978-1-5344-0027-6(3)*, Little Simon) Little Simon.

—Rudolph the Red-Nosed Reindeer a Christmas Gift Set: Rudolph the Red-Nosed Reindeer; Rudolph Shines Again. May, Robert L. ed. 2017. (ENG.). 80p. (J). (gr. -1-1). 35.99 *(978-1-5344-0028-3(1)*, Little Simon) Little Simon.

—Rudolph the Red-Nosed Reindeer a Christmas Keepsake Collection: Rudolph the Red-Nosed Reindeer; Rudolph Shines Again. May, Robert L. ed. 2018. (Classic Board Bks.). (ENG.). 84p. (J). (gr. -1-k). bds. 15.99 *(978-1-5344-3229-1(9)*, Little Simon) Little Simon.

—Shakespeare Retold. Nesbit, E. 2016. (ENG.). 128p. (J). (gr. 1-5). 19.99 *(978-0-06-240453-4(9))* HarperCollins Pubs.

—The Shark Rider. Prager, Ellen. 2015. (Tristan Hunt & the Sea Guardians Ser.: 2). (ENG.). 326p. (J). (gr. 3-7). pap. 9.95 *(978-1-938063-51-0(1)*, Mighty Media Junior Readers) Mighty Media Pr.

—The Shark Whisperer. Prager, Ellen. 2014. (Tristan Hunt & the Sea Guardians Ser.). (ENG.). 288p. (J). (gr. 3-7). pap. 9.95 *(978-1-938063-44-2(9)*, Mighty Media Junior Readers) Mighty Media Pr.

Caparó, Antonio Javier. Sherlock Holmes & the Hound of the Baskervilles, 1 vol. Doyle, A. Conan. 2011. (Calico Illustrated Classics Ser.: No. 3). (ENG.). 112p. (J). (gr. 2-5). 29.93 *(978-1-61641-109-1(0)*, 4025, Calico Chapter Bks.) ABDO Publishing Co.

Caparo, Antonio Javier. Stingray City. Prager, Ellen. 2016. (Tristan Hunt & the Sea Guardians Ser.: 3). (ENG.). 292p. (J). (gr. 2-7). pap. 9.95 *(978-1-938063-70-1(8)*, Mighty Media Junior Readers) Mighty Media Pr.

—Treasure on Superstition Mountain. Broach, Elise. 2014. (Superstition Mountain Mysteries Ser.: 2). (ENG.). 304p. (J). (gr. 3-7). pap. 9.99 *(978-1-250-03990-3(8)*, 900123693) Square Fish.

Capdevila (Max), Francesc. The Little Mermaid/la Sirenita. 2003. (Bilingual Fairy Tales Ser.: BILI).Tr. of Sirenita. (ENG.). 32p. (J). (gr. -1-7). pap. 6.99 *(978-0-8118-3911-2(7))* Chronicle Bks. LLC.

—Thumbelina/Pulgarcita. ed. 2004. (Bilingual Fairy Tales Ser.: BILI). (ENG.). 32p. (J). (gr. -1-7). pap. 6.99 *(978-0-8118-3928-0(1))* Chronicle Bks. LLC.

—The Ugly Duckling/el Patito Feo. Escardó i Bas, Mercè. 2004. (Bilingual Fairy Tales Ser.: BILI). (ENG.). 32p. (J). (gr. -1-7). 6.99 *(978-0-8118-4455-0(2))* Chronicle Bks. LLC.

Capdevila, Gemma. Marinero en Tierra Firme. de Ahumada, Laia. Llasat, Isabel, tr. 2020. (SPA.). 64p. (J). (gr. 4-7). pap. 17.95 *(978-84-17440-35-0(6))* Akiara Bks. ESP. Dist: Independent Pubs. Group.

Capdevila, Roser. Aprendamos a Convivir. Ballart, Elisabet.Tr. of Let's Learn to Get Along. (SPA.). 48p. (J). (gr. 3-5). 13.56 *(978-84-233-3109-3(1))* Ediciones Destino ESP. Dist: Lectorum Pubns., Inc.

—Atencion, Bebe Ataca! Joly, Fanny. 2003. (Coleccion Bebe). (SPA.). (J). (gr. 1-3). *(978-84-246-3652-4(X)*, GL30758) La Galera, S.A. Editorial ESP. Dist: Lectorum Pubns., Inc.

—Un Bebe? Que Mala Idea! Joly, Fanny. 2003. (Coleccion Bebe). (SPA.). (J). (gr. 1-3). *(978-84-246-3651-7(1)*, GL30757) La Galera, S.A. Editorial ESP. Dist: Lectorum Pubns., Inc.

Capelle, Joanna. Pumpkin in Hollow Countdown. Evans, Alwyn & Davis, Anne. 16p. (J). pap. 7.49 *(978-1-86368-045-5(4))* Fremantle Pr. AUS. Dist: Independent Pubs. Group.

Capezzali, Shannon. Thursdays for Therapy. Kent-White, Marissa. 2018. (ENG.). 40p. (J). pap. 12.99 *(978-1-7295-2213-4(0))* CreateSpace Independent Publishing Platform.

Capiello, Leonetto. Carnet Blanc Sous-Vetements Hygieniques. 2016. (Bnf Affiches Ser.). (FRE.). (J). pap. *(978-2-01-116954-9(2))* Hachette Groupe Livre.

—Carnet Ligne Sous-Vetements Hygieniques. 2016. (Bnf Affiches Ser.). (FRE.). (J). pap. *(978-2-01-116979-2(8))* Hachette Groupe Livre.

Capizzi, Giusi. Come down, Cat! Koons, Linda. 2015. (Early Rising Readers Ser.). (J). (gr. -1-k). 5.83 *(978-1-4788-1682-9(1))* Newmark Learning LLC.

—Cool Duck & Lots of Hats. Dale, Elizabeth. 2019. (Early Bird Readers — Pink (Early Bird Stories (tm)) Ser.). (ENG.). 32p. (J). (gr. -1-2). 27.99 *(978-1-5415-4157-3(X)*, Lerner Pubns.) Lerner Publishing Group.

—Dog in a Dress & Run, Tom, Run! Dale, Katie. 2019. (Early Bird Readers — Red (Early Bird Stories (tm)) Ser.). (ENG.). 32p. (J). (gr. -1-2). 27.99 *(978-1-5415-4166-5(9)*, Lerner Pubns.) Lerner Publishing Group.

—Hide & Peek Animals. DiPerna, Kaitlyn. 2019. (Hide & Peek Ser.). (ENG.). 16p. (J). (— 1). 8.99 *(978-1-68412-529-6(4)*, Silver Dolphin Bks.) Printers Row Publishing Group.

—Just Like You. Dodd, Sarah J. ed. 2019. (ENG.). 32p. (J). (gr. -1-k). pap. 8.99 *(978-0-7459-7713-3(8))* Lion Hudson PLC GBR. Dist: Independent Pubs. Group.

—Legs. Dodd, Sarah J. ed. 2015. (ENG.). 32p. (J). (gr. -1-k). 12.99 *(978-0-7459-6597-0(0))* Lion Hudson PLC GBR. Dist: Independent Pubs. Group.

—Legs: The Tale of a Meerkat Lost & Found. Dodd, Sarah J. ed. 2016. (ENG.). 32p. (J). (gr. -1-k). pap. 7.99 *(978-0-7459-6598-7(9)*, Lion Books) Lion Hudson PLC GBR. Dist: Independent Pubs. Group.

—El Paseo en Bote. Corriols, Carmen. 2016. (Early Rising Readers Ser.). (SPA.). 16p. (J). (gr. 1-1). 6.67 *(978-1-4788-3727-5(6))* Newmark Learning LLC.

—Porcupine's Picnic: Who Eats What? Rosenthal, Betsy R. 2017. (ENG.). 32p. (J). (gr. -1-2). 19.99 *(978-1-4677-9519-7(4)*, 9781467795197); E-Book 30.65 *(978-1-5124-2840-7(X))* Lerner Publishing Group. (Millbrook Pr.).

—Ven, Gato, Baja. Koons, Linda. 2016. (Early Rising Readers Ser.). (SPA.). 16p. (J). (gr. 1-1). 6.67 *(978-1-4788-3730-5(6))* Newmark Learning LLC.

—Viv the Vet & Top Dog. Dale, Katie. 2020. (Early Bird Readers — Red (Early Bird Stories (tm)) Ser.). (ENG.). 32p. (J). (gr. -1-2). pap. 7.99 *(978-1-5415-8731-1(6)*, Lerner Pubns.) Lerner Publishing Group.

Caple, Kathy. Frog & Ball. 2020. (J). *(978-0-8234-4341-3(8))* Holiday Hse., Inc.

Caple, Kathy. Hillary to the Rescue. Caple, Kathy. 2003. (Picture Bks.). 32p. (J). (gr. -1-3). 15.95 (978-1-57505-420-9(5), Carolrhoda Bks.) Lerner Publishing Group.
—A Night at the Zoo. Caple, Kathy. 2014. (I Like to Read Ser.). (ENG.). 24p. (J). (gr. -1-3). 14.95 (978-0-8234-3044-4(8)) Holiday Hse., Inc.
—Starring Hillary. Caple, Kathy. 2003. (Picture Bks.). 28p. (J). (gr. -1-3). 15.95 (978-1-57505-261-8(X), Carolrhoda Bks.) Lerner Publishing Group.
—Termite Tales: Brand New Readers. Caple, Kathy. 2009. (Brand New Readers Ser.). (ENG.). 48p. (J). (gr. -1-3). pap. 6.99 (978-0-7636-3901-3(X)) Candlewick Pr.
—Termite Trouble: Brand New Readers. Caple, Kathy. 2005. (Brand New Readers Ser.). (ENG.). 32p. (J). (gr. -1-3). pap. 5.99 (978-0-7636-2573-3(6)) Candlewick Pr.
Caple, Laurie. Farm Crossing: The Amazing Adventures of Addie & Zachary. Bushnell, Jack. 2005. (ENG.). 96p. (gr. 3-8). pap. 9.95 (978-0-9636191-5-0(2)) Chippewa Valley Museum.
—The Legend of Old Abe: A Civil War Eagle. Wargin, Kathy-jo. 2006. (Legend (Sleeping Bear) Ser.). (ENG.). 40p. (J). (gr. 3-7). 17.95 (978-1-58536-232-5(8)) Sleeping Bear Pr.
—North Star Numbers: A Minnesota Number Book. Wargin, Kathy-jo. 2008. (Count Your Way Across the U. S. A. Ser.). (ENG.). 40p. (J). (gr. -1-3). 17.95 (978-1-58536-187-8(9)) Sleeping Bear Pr.
Caple, Laurie A. Sweet Dreams, Wild Animals! A Story of Sleep, 1 vol. Meyer, Eileen R. 2015. (ENG.). 32p. (J). pap. (978-0-87842-637-9(X)) Mountain Pr. Publishing Co., Inc.
Capobianco, Danny & Unwin, Dave. Ranger Red Presents: Blossom, the Ringtail Possum. Holland, Bradley R. 2015. (ENG.). (J). pap. (978-0-9943385-1-8(1)) Ranger Red.
Capon, Jenny. A Little Book of Alliterations. Arthur, Felix. 2011. (Inside Pocket Single Titles Ser.). (ENG.). 64p. (J). (gr. k-3). 7.99 (978-0-9562315-5-0(1)) Lerner Publishing Group.
Caponigro, Laureen. Whistling Dixie. Phillips, Dixie. 2012. 16p. pap. 9.95 (978-1-61633-272-3(7)) Guardian Angel Publishing, Inc.
Capotorto, Glenda. The Pickle & the Pepperoni: An Adventure in Making a Pizza Pie. Capotorto, Nick. 2019. (Adventure Ser.: Vol. 2). (ENG.). 34p. (J). pap. 11.99 **(978-1-6947-9939-5(5))** Independently Published.
Cappello, Liam. Economics for Infants. Kates, Steven. 2017. (ENG.). (J). (978-1-925501-43-8(4)) Connor Court Publishing Pty Ltd.
Cappoen, Jennifer T. Rainbow Silk. Hollingsworth, Cindy W. Bemer Coble, Lynn, ed. 2018. (ENG.). 28p. (J). (gr. k-2). pap. 10.99 (978-1-946198-10-5(2)) Paws and Claws Publishing, LLC.
Cappoen, Jennifer Tipton. Anna the Storm-Water Drain Cat. Day, Stella Barton. Bemer Coble, Lynn, ed. 2016. (ENG.). (J). (gr. k-2). pap. 11.99 (978-1-946198-00-6(5)) Paws and Claws Publishing, LLC.
—Anna's Ballet Costume. Hollingsworth, Cindy W. Bemer Coble, Lynn, ed. 2018. (ENG.). 32p. (J). (gr. k-3). pap. 12.99 (978-1-946198-13-6(7)) Paws and Claws Publishing, LLC.
—Boo-Boos & Bandages at School & from Heaven. Johnson, Amy. Coble, Lynn Bemer, ed. 2016. (ENG.). (J). (gr. 1-4). pap. 11.99 (978-1-946198-01-3(3)) Paws and Claws Publishing, LLC.
—Little Boys Run. Little Boys Play. Dixon, Dallas L. Williams, Nancy E., ed. 2013. 44p. (J). pap. 12.98 (978-1-938526-40-4(6)) Laurus Co., Inc., The.
—The Miracle of Susie the Puppy That Changed the Law. Lawrence, Donna. Coble, Lynn Bemer, ed. 2012. 54p. 24.95 (978-0-9846724-2-4(7)) Paws and Claws Publishing, LLC.
—The Next Good Samaritan-It Could Be You! Kids Helping Others. Johnson, Amy. Bemer Coble, Lynn, ed. 2017. (ENG.). (J). (gr. 1-3). pap. 12.99 (978-1-946198-07-5(2)) Paws and Claws Publishing, LLC.
—Shelby's Shoes. Dixon, Dallas L. Williams, Nancy E., ed. 2013. 24p. (J). pap. 12.98 (978-1-938526-33-6(3)) Laurus Co., Inc., The.
—The Shoe, the Necklace, & the Giant. Ghani, Samna. Williams, Nancy E., ed. 2012. 48p. (J). pap. 9.95 (978-1-938526-18-3(X)) Roxby Media Ltd. GBR. Dist: Laurus Co., The.
—The Story about Tigger. Pendergraft, Cameron. Bemer Coble, Lynn, ed. 2017. (ENG.). (J). pap. 12.99 (978-1-946198-02-0(1)) Paws and Claws Publishing, LLC.
—The Story about Tigger & Elsa. Pendergraft, Cameron. Bemer Coble, Lynn, ed. 2019. (ENG.). 50p. (J). (gr. k-3). pap. 12.99 (978-1-946198-15-0(3)) Paws and Claws Publishing, LLC.
—Susie's Tale Hand with Paw We Changed the Law. Lawrence, Donna. Coble, Lynn Bemer, ed. 2012. 64p. 24.95 (978-0-9846724-1-7(9)) Paws and Claws Publishing, LLC.
—The Tooth Fairy Goes to School. Ghani, Samna. Williams, Nancy E., ed. 2013. 44p. (J). pap. 10.98 (978-1-938526-31-2(7)) Laurus Co., Inc., The.
—Twig's Christmas Dream. Hollingsworth, Cindy W. Bemer Coble, Lynn, ed. 2018. (ENG.). 28p. (J). (gr. 1-3). pap. 12.99 (978-1-946198-14-3(5)) Paws and Claws Publishing, LLC.
Cappoli, Sara. Firebirds. Jeffrey, Gary. 2012. (Graphic Mythical Creatures Ser.). (ENG.). 24p. (J). (gr. 3-5). pap. 8.15 (978-1-4339-6757-3(X)); lib. bdg. 24.95 (978-1-4339-6755-9(3)) Stevens, Gareth Publishing LLLP. (Gareth Stevens Learning Library).
Cappon, Manuela, et al. Everyday Life of the Aztecs, Incas & Mayans. Grant, Neil. 2003. (Uncovering History Ser.). 46p. (J). lib. bdg. 28.50 (978-1-58340-253-5(5)) Black Rabbit Bks.
Cappon, Manuela. Everyday Life of the Celts. Grant, Neil. 2004. (Uncovering History Ser.). 46p. (J). (gr. 4-7). lib. bdg. 19.95 (978-1-58340-252-8(7)) Black Rabbit Bks.
—In Caesar's Rome with Cicero. Leoni, Cristiana & Pauli, Erika. 2009. (Come See My City Ser.). 48p. (gr. 4-4). lib. bdg. 29.50 (978-0-7614-4328-5(2)) Cavendish Square Publishing LLC.
—In Pericles' Athens with Socrates. Leoni, Cristiana. 2009. (Come See My City Ser.). 48p. (gr. 4-4). lib. bdg. 29.50 (978-0-7614-4326-1(6)) Cavendish Square Publishing LLC.
—New York in the 1930s with la Guardia. Leoni, Cristiana. 2009. (Come See My City Ser.). 48p. (gr. 4-4). 29.50 (978-0-7614-4336-0(3)) Cavendish Square Publishing LLC.
Cappon, Manuela. Every Day Life in Ancient Rome. Cappon, Manuela, tr. Grant, Neil. 2003. (Uncovering History Ser.). 46p. (J). lib. bdg. 28.50 (978-1-58340-249-8(7)) Black Rabbit Bks.
Capps, Leigh. Mommy's Hat. Samuel, Lynette M. 2005. (J). per. (978-0-9727703-3-0(X)) P.R.A. Publishing.
Caprara, Collette. Sweetpea County's Secret Quilt. Hall, Noelle Chason & Joanne Beeker Clurman. 2011. 28p. pap. 24.95 (978-1-4626-2248-1(8)) America Star Bks.
Caprio, Pattie. The frog in the Well. Lin, Joyce, tr. 2008. (ENG & CHI.). 36p. (J). 14.95 (978-0-9801305-1-5(4)) CE Bilingual Bks. LLC.
Caprio-Scalera, Jill & Edrington, Greg Q. Gramma's 'Jammas. Caprio-Scalera, Jill. 2013. 28p. pap. 12.50 (978-1-60976-464-7(1), Strategic Bk. Publishing) Strategic Book Publishing & Rights Agency (SBPRA).
Capriotti, Benedetta. Collins Big Cat Phonics for Letters & Sounds - in the Frog Bog: Band 03/Yellow, Bd. 3. Ryan, Margaret. 2018. (Collins Big Cat Phonics Ser.). (ENG.). 16p. (J). (gr. k-1). pap. 6.99 (978-0-00-825154-3(1)) HarperCollins Pubs. Ltd. GBR. Dist: Independent Pubs. Group.
—Wild Bios: William Sheepspeare. Acampora, Courtney & Fischer, Maggie. 2019. (Wild Bios Ser.). (ENG.). 16p. (J). (— 1). bds. 7.99 (978-1-68412-619-4(3), Silver Dolphin Bks.) Printers Row Publishing Group.
Capsey, Steve. How to Draw Cool Cars: Start Drawing in Seconds. Capsey, Steve. 2015. (How to Draw Ser.). (ENG.). (J). pap. (978-1-78209-913-0(1)) Miles Kelly Publishing, Ltd.
Caputo, Antonella, et al. Graphic Classics - O. Henry, Vol. 11. Henry, O. et al. Pomplun, Tom, ed. 2005. (ENG.). 144p. pap. 11.95 (978-0-9746648-2-8(0), fbd25b95-87db-4c14-81cb-dea018dfc189) Eureka Productions.
Caputo, Jim. The Animal Zone. Chmielewski, Gary. rev. ed. 2007. (Funny Zone Ser.). (ENG.). 24p. (J). (gr. 2-4). pap. 11.94 (978-1-60357-677-2(0)) Norwood Hse. Pr.
—Animal Zone. Chmielewski, Gary. rev. ed. 2007. (Funny Zone Ser.). (ENG.). 24p. (J). (gr. 2-4). lib. bdg. 22.60 (978-1-59953-139-7(9)) Norwood Hse. Pr.
—The Classroom Zone. Chmielewski, Gary. rev. ed. 2007. (Funny Zone Ser.). (ENG.). 24p. (J). (gr. 2-4). pap. 11.94 (978-1-60357-680-2(0)) Norwood Hse. Pr.
—Classroom Zone. Chmielewski, Gary. rev. ed. 2007. (Funny Zone Ser.). (ENG.). 24p. (J). (gr. 2-4). lib. bdg. 22.60 (978-1-59953-145-8(3)) Norwood Hse. Pr.
—The Computer Zone. Chmielewski, Gary. rev. ed. 2009. (Funny Zone Ser.). (ENG.). 24p. (J). (gr. 2-4). pap. 11.94 (978-1-60357-684-0(3)) Norwood Hse. Pr.
—The Computer Zone: Jokes, Riddles, Tongue Twisters & Daffynitions. Chmielewski, Gary. rev. ed. 2009. (Funny Zone Ser.). (ENG.). 24p. (J). (gr. 2-4). lib. bdg. 22.60 (978-1-59953-300-1(6)) Norwood Hse. Pr.
—Crafts Across America. Littlefield, Cindy A. 2008. (ENG.). 128p. (J). 16.99 (978-0-8249-6809-0(3), Ideal Pubns.) Worthy Publishing.
—The Fright Zone. Chmielewski, Gary. rev. ed. 2009. (Funny Zone Ser.). (ENG.). 24p. (J). (gr. 2-4). pap. 11.94 (978-1-60357-685-7(1)) Norwood Hse. Pr.
—The Fright Zone: Jokes, Riddles, Tongue Twisters & Daffynitions. Chmielewski, Gary. rev. ed. 2009. (Funny Zone Ser.). (ENG.). 24p. (J). (gr. 2-4). lib. bdg. 22.60 (978-1-59953-298-1(0)) Norwood Hse. Pr.
—The Ghost Zone. Chmielewski, Gary. rev. ed. 2009. (Funny Zone Ser.). (ENG.). 24p. (J). (gr. 2-4). pap. 11.94 (978-1-60357-686-4(X)) Norwood Hse. Pr.
—The Ghost Zone: Jokes, Riddles, Tongue Twisters & Daffynitions. Chmielewski, Gary. rev. ed. 2009. (Funny Zone Ser.). (ENG.). 24p. (J). (gr. 2-4). lib. bdg. 22.60 (978-1-59953-297-4(2)) Norwood Hse. Pr.
—The History Zone. Chmielewski, Gary. rev. ed. 2007. (Funny Zone Ser.). (ENG.). 24p. (J). (gr. 2-4). pap. 11.94 (978-1-60357-678-9(9)) Norwood Hse. Pr.
—History Zone. Chmielewski, Gary. rev. ed. 2007. (Funny Zone Ser.). (ENG.). 24p. (J). (gr. 2-4). lib. bdg. 22.60 (978-1-59953-141-0(0)) Norwood Hse. Pr.
—Let's Eat in the Funny Zone. Chmielewski, Gary. rev. ed. 2007. (Funny Zone Ser.). (ENG.). 24p. (J). (gr. 2-4). pap. 11.94 (978-1-60357-681-9(9)) Norwood Hse. Pr.
—Let's Eat in the Funny Zone: Jokes, Riddles, Tongue Twisters & Daffynitions. Chmielewski, Gary. rev. ed. 2007. (Funny Zone Ser.). (ENG.). 24p. (J). (gr. 2-4). lib. bdg. 22.60 (978-1-59953-181-6(X)) Norwood Hse. Pr.
—Let's Go in the Funny Zone. Chmielewski, Gary. rev. ed. 2007. (Funny Zone Ser.). (ENG.). 24p. (J). (gr. 2-4). pap. 11.94 (978-1-60357-682-6(7)) Norwood Hse. Pr.
—Let's Go in the Funny Zone: Jokes, Riddles, Tongue Twisters & Daffynitions. Chmielewski, Gary. rev. ed. 2007. (Funny Zone Ser.). (ENG.). 24p. (J). (gr. 2-4). lib. bdg. 22.60 (978-1-59953-182-3(8)) Norwood Hse. Pr.
—The Medical Zone. Chmielewski, Gary. rev. ed. 2009. (Funny Zone Ser.). (ENG.). 24p. (J). (gr. 2-4). pap. 11.94 (978-1-60357-687-1(8)) Norwood Hse. Pr.
—The Medical Zone: Jokes, Riddles, Tongue Twisters & Daffynitions. Chmielewski, Gary. rev. ed. 2009. (Funny Zone Ser.). (ENG.). 24p. (J). (gr. 2-4). lib. bdg. 22.60 (978-1-59953-299-8(9)) Norwood Hse. Pr.
—The Science Zone. Chmielewski, Gary. rev. ed. 2007. (Funny Zone Ser.). (ENG.). 24p. (J). (gr. 2-4). pap. 11.94 (978-1-60357-683-3(5)) Norwood Hse. Pr.
—The Science Zone: Jokes, Riddles, Tongue Twisters & Daffynitions. Chmielewski, Gary. rev. ed. 2007. (Funny Zone Ser.). (ENG.). 24p. (J). (gr. 2-4). lib. bdg. 22.60 (978-1-59953-183-0(6)) Norwood Hse. Pr.
—The Sports Zone. Chmielewski, Gary. rev. ed. 2007. (Funny Zone Ser.). (ENG.). 24p. (J). (gr. 2-4). pap. 11.94 (978-1-60357-679-6(7)); lib. bdg. 22.60 (978-1-59953-144-1(5)) Norwood Hse. Pr.
Capuyan, Salvador. A Place Called Raindot: Book 2. Mullins, B. D. 2018. (ENG.). 24p. (J). pap. 20.99 (978-1-4907-9209-5(0)) Trafford Publishing.
—Savanna Hannah's Day at the Farm. Phipps, Dorothy J. 2018. (ENG.). 24p. (J). pap. 15.99 (978-1-5434-8485-4(9)) Xlibris Corp.
Caraballo, Samuel & Torrecilla, Pablo. Estrellita in the Big City/Estrellita en la Ciudad Grande. Caraballo, Samuel & Torrecilla, Pablo. 2008. (SPA & ENG.). 32p. (J). (gr. -1-4). 16.95 (978-1-55885-498-7(3), Piñata Books) Arte Publico Pr.
Carabelli, Francesca. The Cats on Ben Yehuda Street, Vol. Stampler, Ann Redisch. 2013. (ENG.). 32p. (J). (gr. -1-2). 7.95 (978-0-7613-8124-2(4), 9780761381242, Kar-Ben Publishing) Lerner Publishing Group.
—Even Princesses Go to the Potty: A Potty Training Life-The-Flap Story. Wax, Naomi & Wax, Wendy. 2014. (ENG.). 22p. (J). (gr. -1 — 1). 7.99 (978-1-4424-8886-1(7), Little Simon) Little Simon.
—If You Were a Circle, 1 vol. Blaisdell, Molly. 2009. (Math Fun Ser.). (ENG.). 24p. (J). (gr. 2-4). lib. bdg. 28.65 (978-1-4048-5514-4(9), Picture Window Bks.) Capstone.
—If You Were a Fraction, 1 vol. Shaskan, Trisha Speed. 2008. (Math Fun Ser.). (ENG.). 24p. (J). (gr. 2-4). pap. 7.95 (978-1-4048-4791-0(X), Picture Window Bks.) Capstone.
—If You Were a Minus Sign, 1 vol. Shaskan, Trisha Speed. 2008. (Math Fun Ser.). (ENG.). 24p. (J). (gr. 2-4). pap. 7.95 (978-1-4048-4788-0(X), Picture Window Bks.) Capstone.
—If You Were a Minus Sign [LTD Commodities]. Shaskan, Trisha Speed. 2010. (Math Fun Ser.). 24p. pap. 3.50 (978-1-4048-6256-2(0), Picture Window Bks.) Capstone.
—If You Were a Minus Sign [Scholastic]. Shaskan, Trisha Speed. 2010. (Math Fun Ser.). 24p. pap. 0.52 (978-1-4048-6173-2(4), Picture Window Bks.) Capstone.
—If You Were a Minute, 1 vol. Shaskan, Trisha Speed. 2009. (Math Fun Ser.). (ENG.). 24p. (J). (gr. 2-4). pap. 7.95 (978-1-4048-5202-0(6)); lib. bdg. 28.65 (978-1-4048-5201-3(8)) Capstone. (Picture Window Bks.).
—If You Were a Plus Sign, 1 vol. Shaskan, Trisha Speed. 2008. (Math Fun Ser.). (ENG.). 24p. (J). (gr. 2-4). pap. 7.95 (978-1-4048-4785-9(5), Picture Window Bks.) Capstone.
—If You Were a Plus Sign [LTD Commodities]. Shaskan, Trisha Speed. 2010. (Math Fun Ser.). 24p. pap. 3.50 (978-1-4048-6257-9(9), Picture Window Bks.) Capstone.
—If You Were a Plus Sign [Scholastic]. Shaskan, Trisha Speed. 2010. (Math Fun Ser.). 24p. pap. 0.52 (978-1-4048-6172-5(6), Picture Window Bks.) Capstone.
—If You Were a Quadrilateral, 1 vol. Blaisdell, Molly. 2009. (Math Fun Ser.). (ENG.). 24p. (J). (gr. 2-4). pap. 7.95 (978-1-4048-5690-5(0), Picture Window Bks.) Capstone.
Carabelli, Francesca & Dillard, Sarah. Math Fun, 1 vol. Aboff, Marcie & Shaskan, Trisha Speed. 2009. (Math Fun Ser.). (ENG.). 192p. (J). (gr. 2-4). pap. 14.95 (978-1-4048-5611-0(0), Picture Window Bks.) Capstone.
Caracino, Leah. Bud the Pup. Wilson, Barbara. 2012. (ENG.). 22p. (gr. k-3). pap. 9.00 (978-1-56778-539-5(5)) Wilson Language Training.
—Jack & His Pal Max. Wilson, Barbara. 2012. (ENG.). 16p. (gr. k-3). pap. 9.00 (978-1-56778-540-1(9)) Wilson Language Training.
—Mrs. Piglin Visits Sick Mr. Fox. Wilson, Barbara. 2012. (ENG.). 16p. (gr. k-3). pap. 9.00 (978-1-56778-541-8(7)) Wilson Language Training.
—Ted & Matt. Wilson, Barbara. 2012. (ENG.). 24p. (gr. k-3). pap. 9.00 (978-1-56778-544-9(1)) Wilson Language Training.
Caralivanos, Leyla. Being Charley: Embracing Differences. Bosch, Morghan & Bosch, Karen. 2019. (ENG.). 54p. (J). (gr. -1-3). 25.95 **(978-1-64559-670-7(2))**; pap. 15.95 **(978-1-64559-669-1(9))** Covenant Bks.
Caramagna, Joe. Spider-Verse #1. Wolff, Danielle. 2019. (Ultimate Spider-Man Web-Warriors Ser.). (ENG.). 24p. (J). (gr. 2-8). lib. bdg. 27.07 (978-1-5321-4459-2(8), 33864, Marvel Age) Spotlight.
—Spider-Verse #2. Dini, Paul. 2019. (Ultimate Spider-Man Web-Warriors Ser.). (ENG.). 24p. (J). (gr. 2-8). lib. bdg. 27.07 (978-1-5321-4460-8(1), 33865, Marvel Age) Spotlight.
—Spider-Verse #3. Burke, Kevin & Wyatt, Chris. 2019. (Ultimate Spider-Man Web-Warriors Ser.). (ENG.). 24p. (J). (gr. 2-8). lib. bdg. 27.07 (978-1-5321-4461-5(X), 33866, Marvel Age) Spotlight.
—Spider-Verse #4. Son, Eugene. 2019. (Ultimate Spider-Man Web-Warriors Ser.). (ENG.). 24p. (J). (gr. 2-8). lib. bdg. 27.07 (978-1-5321-4462-2(8), 33867, Marvel Age) Spotlight.
—Ultimate Spider-Man Web-Warriors (Set), 4 vols. 2019. (Ultimate Spider-Man Web-Warriors Ser.). (ENG.). 24p. (J). (gr. 2-8). lib. bdg. 108.28 (978-1-5321-4458-5(X), 33863, Marvel Age) Spotlight.
Caramia, Palma. Frammenti - Primo Volume. Bianconi, Ilaria Rita. 2020. (ITA.). 114p. (J). pap. 8.69 **(978-1-7992-2285-9(3))** Independently Published.
Caravela, Elena. The Birds of the Harbor. Italia, John. 2006. (ENG.). 32p. (J). (gr. -1-3). 15.95 (978-0-9726614-8-7(6)) Shenanigan Bks.
—A Night of Tamales & Roses. Kraus, Joanna H. 2007. (ENG.). 32p. (J). (gr. -1-3). 15.95 (978-0-9726614-4-7(1)) Shenanigan Bks.
Caraway, Crystal L. They Were the Shoes of ALL Shoes. James, Alva. 2019. (ENG.). 28p. (J). pap. 19.99 **(978-1-5456-7933-3(9))** Salem Author Services.
Caraway, James. Ben Franklin. Friedman, Estelle. 2011. 44p. 35.95 (978-1-258-07275-9(0)) Literary Licensing, LLC.
Carbajal, Diego. Cantemos en Español Song-Book: Spanish Learning Song-Book for Children. Dorn, Susy. 2006. (SPA.). (J). (978-0-9764010-6-3(1)) Susy Dorn Productions, LLC.
—Sal y Pimienta Song-Book: Spanish Learning Song-Book for Children. Dorn, Susy. 2006. (SPA.). (J). (978-0-9764010-7-0(X)) Susy Dorn Productions, LLC.
Carbajal, Richard, jt. illus. see Hammond, Ted.
Carbajal, Richard Pimentel, jt. illus. see Hammond, Ted.
Carballeira, Enrique. Me Pesa Mucho la Cabeza. Frias Conde, Xavier. 2018. (SPA.). 30p. (J). (gr. k-4). pap. 15.00 (978-0-9985390-9-6(0)) Jade Publishing.
Carbaugh, Sam. The Civil War: The Conflict Between the States. Cummings, Judy Dodge. 2017. (Inquire & Investigate Ser.). (ENG.). 128p. (J). (gr. 7-9). pap. 17.95 (978-1-61930-606-6(9), 03584857-960b-4b14-907b-60173d49d00e) Nomad Pr.
—The Civil War: The Conflict Between the States. Cummings, Judy Dodge. 2017. (Inquire & Investigate Ser.). (ENG.). 128p. (J). (gr. 7-9). 22.95 (978-1-61930-602-8(6), b7d9cc80-5314-47c6-98e4-0a182ae23913) Nomad Pr.
—Robotics: Discover the Science & Technology of the Future with 20 Projects. Ceceri, Kathy. 2012. (Build It Yourself Ser.). 128p. (J). (gr. 3-7). 21.95 (978-1-936749-76-8(9), a95a0f70-dc13-4de7-abb2-2ba552970d47) Nomad Pr.
—Timekeeping: Explore the History & Science of Telling Time with 15 Projects. Formichelli, Linda & Martin, W. Eric. 2012. (Build It Yourself Ser.). (ENG.). 128p. (J). (gr. 3-7). 21.95 (978-1-61930-136-8(9), 778ff797-34b5-4fa0-94ee-2bf46802810c) Nomad Pr.
Carbaugh, Samuel. Amazing Math: Projects You Can Build Yourself. Bardos, Laszlo C. 2010. (Build It Yourself Ser.). 128p. (J). (gr. 3-7). 21.95 (978-1-934670-58-3(8), 32c2a8c5-261c-41bb-ae81-5a9aad307c44) Nomad Pr.
—Chemistry: Investigate the Matter That Makes up Your World. Mooney, Carla. 2016. (Inquire & Investigate Ser.). 128p. (J). (gr. 6-10). 22.95 (978-1-61930-361-4(2), 4bd59194-5e46-42e8-b063-cc6d123da866) Nomad Pr.
—Food - 25 Amazing Projects: Investigate the History & Science of What We Eat. Reilly, Kathleen M. 2010. (Build It Yourself Ser.). 128p. (J). (gr. 3-7). 21.95 (978-1-934670-60-6(X), 42316860-17b9-408d-8bf9-2a10bafb88d2) Nomad Pr.
—Forensics: Uncover the Science & Technology of Crime Scene Investigation. Mooney, Carla. 2013. (Inquire & Investigate Ser.). 128p. (J). (gr. 6-10). 21.95 (978-1-61930-188-7(1), 1a52da3c-76f4-491c-851b-2ee54b2c464a); pap. 16.95 (978-1-61930-184-9(9), 7ccc8fe8-3aff-477d-babc-c93bc44592ea) Nomad Pr.
—Genetics: Breaking the Code of Your DNA. Mooney, Carla. 2014. (Inquire & Investigate Ser.). 128p. (J). (gr. 6-10). pap. 16.95 (978-1-61930-212-9(8), f5c30a92-0faf-4cef-acae-14989a7a466d) Nomad Pr.
—George Washington: 25 Great Projects You Can Build Yourself. Mooney, Carla. 2010. (Build It Yourself Ser.). 128p. (J). (gr. 3-7). 21.95 (978-1-934670-64-4(2), c2240798-65fe-48bb-8110-1e09c57d6a3b); pap. 15.95 (978-1-934670-63-7(4), 938cc8c7-d334-4bd7-821c-2736d6b7fefd) Nomad Pr.
—Human Movement: How the Body Walks, Runs, Jumps, & Kicks. Mooney, Carla. 2017. (Inquire & Investigate Ser.). 128p. (J). (gr. 6-10). 22.95 (978-1-61930-481-9(3), e2fcf089-a1cb-4410-8e13-377e7f5ba48b) Nomad Pr.
—Physics: Investigate the Forces of Nature. Gardner, Jane P. 2014. (Inquire & Investigate Ser.). 128p. (J). (gr. 6-10). 21.95 (978-1-61930-227-3(6), 6de1f7ff-e4ca-4080-a624-5481d8697581) Nomad Pr.
—Planetary Science: Explore New Frontiers. Wood, Matthew Brenden. 2017. (Inquire & Investigate Ser.). 128p. (J). (gr. 7-9). pap. 17.95 (978-1-61930-571-7(2), 7bbef0bf-678c-454a-8499-d0cafb035eda) Nomad Pr.
—Planetary Science: Explore New Frontiers. Wood, Matthew Brenden. 2017. (Inquire & Investigate Ser.). 128p. (J). (gr. 7-9). 22.95 (978-1-61930-567-0(4), eba906f5-dc57-46aa-be3d-4e1fb5673987) Nomad Pr.
—Timekeeping: Explore the History & Science of Telling Time with 15 Projects. Formichelli, Linda et al. 2012. (Build It Yourself Ser.). 128p. (J). (gr. 3-7). pap. 15.95 (978-1-61930-033-0(8), b6e3a6df-d8d0-4fb1-b580-48cc69fd7c9a) Nomad Pr.
Carbaugh, Samuel & Rizvi, Farah. Food - 25 Amazing Projects: Investigate the History & Science of What We Eat. Reilly, Kathleen M. 2010. (Build It Yourself Ser.). 128p. (J). (gr. 3-7). pap. 15.95 (978-1-934670-59-0(6), 737d11fc-0386-4fba-950a-6e62cd76f4b9) Nomad Pr.
carciofocontento. My Garden Home. Little Bee Books. 2017. (ENG.). 16p. (J). (gr. -1-k). bds. 7.99 (978-1-4998-0443-0(1)) Little Bee Books Inc.
Card, Vanessa. Christian Church. Brown, Alan & Seaman, Alison. 2004. 32p. pap. (978-0-7136-5497-4(X), A&C Black) Bloomsbury Publishing Plc.
Card, Vanessa, jt. illus. see Mukhida, Zul.
Cardell, David. Kawaii Dolphin Composition Notebook: For Pre-K, Kindergarten, & Elementary Students - College Ruled. David, Designs by. 2019. (Kawaii Sea Friends Composition Notebook Ser.: Vol. 1). (ENG.). 122p. (J). pap. 6.99 (978-1-0772-8208-7(7)) Independently Published.
—Kawaii Dolphin Composition Notebook: Wide Ruled for Pre-K, Kindergarten, & Elementary Students. David, Designs by. 2019. (Kawaii Sea Friends Composition Notebook Ser.: Vol. 3). (ENG.). 122p. (J). pap. 6.99 (978-1-0770-4784-6(3)) Independently Published.
—Kawaii Jellyfish Composition Notebook: For Pre-K, Kindergarten, & Elementary Students - College Ruled. David, Designs by. 2019. (Kawaii Sea Friends Composition Notebook Ser.: Vol. 10). (ENG.). 122p. (J). pap. 6.99 (978-1-0772-8334-3(2)) Independently Published.
—Kawaii Jellyfish Composition Notebook: Wide Ruled for Pre-K, Kindergarten, & Elementary Students. David, Designs by. 2019. (Kawaii Sea Friends Composition Notebook Ser.: Vol. 4). (ENG.). 122p. (J). pap. 6.99 (978-1-0770-4905-5(6)) Independently Published.
—Kawaii Lobster Handwriting Notebook: For Pre-K, Kindergarten, & Elementary Students - Dotted Line Ruled for Handwriting Practice. David, Designs by. 2019. (Kawaii Sea Friends Handwriting Notebook Ser.: Vol. 4).

C

(ENG.). 122p. (J). pap. 5.99 *(978-1-0774-3782-1(X))* Independently Published.

Cardemil, Carmen. Cuentos Ecologicos. Schkolnik, Saul. 2nd ed. 2003. (la Orilla del Viento Ser.).Tr. of Ecological Tales. (SPA.). 56p. (J). (gr. 3-7). per. *(978-968-16-4757-5(2),* FC6400) Fondo de Cultura Economica MEX. Dist: Lectorum Pubns., Inc.

—Gerardo y la Cama. Morábito, Fabio. 2003. (SPA.). *(978-968-494-087-1(4),* CI31141) Centro de Informacion y Desarrollo de la Comunicacion y la Literatura MEX. Dist: Lectorum Pubns., Inc.

—La Historia de Manu (Manu's Story) del Rio, Ana Maria. 2003. (Coleccion Derechos Del Nino Ser.). (SPA.). 32p. (J). (gr. 3-5). pap. 7.95 *(978-84-204-5845-8(7))* Santillana USA Publishing Co., Inc.

—Maritimi Quiere Ser Escritora. Delgado, Luis Cabrera. 2005. (SPA.). 148p. (J). 13.00 *(978-956-239-225-9(2))* Aguilar Chilena de Ediciones, Ltd. CHL. Dist: Ediciones Universal.

Cardenas, Patricia Karla, jt. illus. see Cardenas, Patricia Karla Marquez.

Cardenas, Patricia Karla Marquez & Cardenas, Patricia Karla. La Tinta de Las Moras. Hernandez, Georgina. rev. ed. 2007. (Castillo de la Lectura Roja Ser.). (SPA & ENG.). 144p. (YA). (gr. 7). pap. 8.95 *(978-968-5920-40-7(0))* Castillo, Ediciones, S. A. de C. V. MEX. Dist: Macmillan.

Cardew, Gloria, jt. illus. see Batten, John D.

Cardillo, Linda & Albert, Dar. The Smallest Christmas Tree. Cardillo, Linda. 2013. 42p. pap. 9.49 *(978-0-9910861-0-8(4))* Bellastoria Pr.

Cardinal, Chelsea. Fox 8: A Story. Saunders, George. 2018. (ENG.). 64p. 17.00 *(978-1-9848-1802-7(3),* Random House) Random House Publishing Group.

Cardinal, Isabelle. The Promise, 1 vol. Bat Zvi, Pnina & Wolfe, Margie. 2018. (ENG.). 32p. (J). (gr. 1-3). 18.95 *(978-1-77260-058-2(X))* Second Story Pr. CAN. Dist: Orca Bk. Pubs. USA.

Cardinal, John. I'd Rather Be Riding My Bike. Pinder, Eric. I.t. ed. 2013. 42p. (gr. k-1). pap. 10.95 *(978-1-62253-401-2(8))* Evolved Publishing.

—Sully P. Snooferpoot's Amazing New Christmas Pot. Shaw Ph D, Aaron. Diamond, Lane, ed. 2016. (Sully P. Snooferpoot Ser.: Vol. 4). (ENG.). (J). (gr. k-2). 26.95 *(978-1-62253-633-7(9));* pap. 10.95 *(978-1-62253-632-0(0))* Evolved Publishing.

—Sully P. Snooferpoot's Amazing New Dayswitcher. Shaw Ph D, Aaron. Diamond, Lane, ed. 2016. (Sully P. Snooferpoot Ser.: Vol. 3). (ENG.). (J). (gr. k-3). 26.95 *(978-1-62253-630-6(4));* pap. 10.95 *(978-1-62253-629-0(0))* Evolved Publishing.

Cardinale, Christopher. Which Side Are You On? The Story of a Song. Lyon, George Ella. 2011. (ENG.). 40p. (J). (gr. 2-4). 17.95 *(978-1-933693-96-5(7))* Cinco Puntos Pr.

Cardinali, Diana, jt. illus. see Sisters, Dominican.

Cardon, Laurent. A Poesia Da Primeira Vez. Paiva, Stela Maris Rezende. 2014. (POR.). 30p. (J). *(978-85-250-5613-9(8))* Globo, Editora SA.

Cardona, Dawn M. All the Little Snowflakes. Jin, Cindy. 2020. (ENG.). 18p. (J). (gr. -1-k). bds. 7.99 ***(978-1-5344-7099-6(9),*** Little Simon) Little Simon.

Cardona, Dawn M. Five Little Thank-Yous. Jin, Cindy. 2019. (ENG.). 12p. (J). (-k). bds. 7.99 *(978-1-5344-5139-1(0),* Little Simon) Little Simon.

Cardona, Jose & Williams, Don. Mulan (Disney Princess) 2013. (Little Golden Book Ser.). (ENG.). 24p. (J). (-k). 4.99 *(978-0-7364-3053-1(9),* Golden/Disney) Random Hse. Children's Bks.

Cardona, Jose Maria. Meet Shimmer & Shine! (Shimmer & Shine) Random House. 2016. (Step into Reading Ser.). (ENG.). 24p. (J). (gr. -1-1). 4.99 *(978-0-553-52203-7(5),* Random Hse. Bks. for Young Readers) Random Hse. Children's Bks.

Cardoni, Paolo. Albert. Lebscky, Ibi. (Coleccion Seran Famosos).Tr. of Little Albert Einstein. (SPA.). 28p. (J). (gr. 2-4). 10.36 *(978-84-233-1400-3(6))* Ediciones Destino ESP. Dist: Lectorum Pubns., Inc.

—Amadeus. Lebscky, Ibi. (Coleccion Seran Famosos). (SPA.). 32p. (J). (gr. 2-4). 14.95 *(978-84-233-1262-7(3))* Ediciones Destino ESP. Dist: AIMS International Bks., Inc.

—Leonardo. Lebscky, Ibi. (Coleccion Seran Famosos).Tr. of Little Leonardo de Vinci. (SPA.). 28p. (J). (gr. 2-4). 10.36 *(978-84-233-1399-0(9))* Ediciones Destino ESP. Dist: Lectorum Pubns., Inc.

—Marie. Lebscky, Ibi. (Coleccion Seran Famosos).Tr. of Little Marie Curie. (SPA.). 28p. (J). (gr. 2-4). 14.95 *(978-84-233-2086-8(3))* Ediciones Destino ESP. Dist: AIMS International Bks., Inc.

—Pablito. Lebscky, Ibi. (Coleccion Seran Famosos).Tr. of Little Pablo Picasso. (SPA.). 28p. (J). (gr. 2-4). 14.95 *(978-84-233-1265-8(8))* Ediciones Destino ESP. Dist: AIMS International Bks., Inc.

—William. Lebscky, Ibi. (Coleccion Seran Famosos).Tr. of Little Wm. Shakespeare. (SPA.). 28p. (J). (gr. 2-4). 10.36 *(978-84-233-1663-2(7))* Ediciones Destino ESP. Dist: Lectorum Pubns., Inc.

Cardoso, Sofia. Resilience: A Book to Encourage Resilience, Persistence & to Help Children Bounce Back from Challenges & Adversity. Sanders, Jayneen. 2017. (ENG.). 42p. (J). (gr. k-3). *(978-1-925089-35-6(5));* pap. *(978-1-925089-34-9(7))* UpLoad Publishing Pty, Ltd.

—You, Me & Empathy: Teaching Children about Empathy, Feelings, Kindness, Compassion, Tolerance & Recognising Bullying Behaviours. Sanders, Jayneen. 2017. (J). (gr. k-3). (ENG.). 40p. *(978-1-925089-12-7(6),* Educate2Empower Publishing); (SPA.). 42p. pap. *(978-1-925089-36-3(3))* UpLoad Publishing Pty, Ltd.

Cardwell, Brett. My Name Is Mac. Reynolds, Lori. 2016. (ENG.). (J). *(978-1-925515-56-5(7));* pap. *(978-1-925515-45-9(1))* Vivid Publishing.

Cardy, Jason, jt. illus. see Nicholson, Kat.

Cardy, Jason, jt. illus. see Shalvey, Declan.

Carey, Bob. A Home for Dixie: The True Story of a Rescued Puppy. Jackson, Emma. 40p. (J). (gr. -1-3). 2010. (ENG.). pap. 7.99 *(978-0-06-144964-2(4),* Collins); 2008. lib. bdg. 17.89 *(978-0-06-144963-5(6))* HarperCollins Pubs.

Carey, Joseph. Jack Kat Had a Day, 1 vol. Carey, Kathleen. 2009. 21p. pap. 24.95 *(978-1-60836-314-8(7))* America Star Bks.

Carey, Nicole. Arabella's Purple Sparkly New Shoes. Carey, Nicole. Carey, Ron. 2020. (ENG.). 68p. (J). (gr. k-1). pap. 16.00 ***(978-1-7331945-6-3(8));*** 3rd ed. pap. 15.00 ***(978-1-7331945-7-0(6))*** Carey, Nicole.

Cariello, Sergio. The Action Bible: God's Redemptive Story. Mauss, Doug, ed. ed. 2010. (Action Bible Ser.). (ENG.). 752p. (J). (gr. 3-7). 29.99 *(978-0-7814-4499-6(3),* 105228) Cook, David C.

Cariello, Sergio. The Action Bible: God's Redemptive Story. rev. ed. 2020. (Action Bible Ser.). (ENG.). 832p. (J). 29.99 ***(978-0-8307-7744-0(X),*** 146992) Cook, David C.

Cariello, Sergio. The Action Bible Anytime Devotions: 90 Ways to Help Kids Connect with God Anytime, Anywhere. 2020. (Action Bible Ser.: 1). (ENG.). 200p. (J). pap. 16.99 *(978-0-8307-7898-0(5),* 149325) Cook, David C.

—The Action Bible Coloring Book: 55 Reproducible Pages of Bible Heroes & Devotions. David C Cook. 2019. (Action Bible Ser.). (ENG.). 112p. (J). 14.99 *(978-0-8307-7590-3(0),* 144661) Cook, David C.

—La Biblia en Acción. ed. 2018. (Action Bible Ser.). (SPA.). 752p. (J). 27.99 *(978-0-8307-7316-9(9),* 145144) Cook, David C.

—The Heroes of God, 1 vol. Martin, Gary & Zondervan Staff. 2009. (Z Graphic Novels / Son of Samson Ser.). (ENG.). 160p. (J). pap. 6.99 *(978-0-310-71284-8(X))* Zondervan.

—The NIV Action Study Bible. 2018. (Action Bible Ser.). (ENG.). 1248p. (J). 32.99 *(978-0-8307-7254-4(5),* 144641); im. lthr. 39.99 *(978-0-8307-7255-1(3),* 144643) Cook, David C.

—The Raiders of Joppa, 1 vol. Martin, Gary. 2008. (Z Graphic Novels / Son of Samson Ser.). (ENG.). 160p. (J). (gr. 4-7). pap. 6.99 *(978-0-310-71282-4(3))* Zonderkidz.

Cariello, Sergio, et al. Resurrection, Vol. 5. Dixon, Chuck. 2004. (Crux Ser.: Vol. 5). 160p. (YA). pap. 15.95 *(978-1-59314-053-3(3))* CrossGeneration Comics, Inc.

Cariello, Sergio. The Sword of Revenge, 1 vol. Martin, Gary & Zondervan Bibles Staff. 2009. (Z Graphic Novels / Son of Samson Ser.). (ENG.). 160p. (J). pap. 6.99 *(978-0-310-71285-5(8))* Zondervan.

—The Tears of Jehovah, 1 vol. Martin, Gary. 2012. (Z Graphic Novels / Son of Samson Ser.). (ENG.). 160p. (J). pap. 6.99 *(978-0-310-71286-2(6))* Zondervan.

—Teknon & the Champion Warriors. Sapp, Brent. 2003. 7.99 *(978-1-57229-219-2(9))* FamilyLife.

—The Witch of Endor, 1 vol. Martin, Gary. 2008. (Z Graphic Novels / Son of Samson Ser.). (ENG.). 160p. (J). pap. 6.99 *(978-0-310-71283-1(1))* Zonderkidz.

Cariello, Sergio & Lanphear, Dave. The Maiden of Thunder, 1 vol. Martin, Gary & Zondervan Bibles Staff. 2008. (Z Graphic Novels / Son of Samson Ser.). (ENG.). 160p. (J). (gr. 4-7). pap. 6.99 *(978-0-310-71281-7(5))* Zondervan.

Carigiet, Alois. A Bell for Ursli: A Story from the Engadine in Switzerland, 23 vols. 2007. (ENG.). 44p. (J). *(978-0-86315-614-4(2))* Floris Bks.

Carisse, Carissa. Buddy Boy Brooks Takes the Wheel: A Mile Wide Tale from the Mighty Mississippi. Singleton, Glynn. 2007. 32p. (J). (gr. 2-4). 12.95 *(978-1-57072-320-9(6))* Overmountain Pr.

Carle, Eric. Amor de la Oruga Muy Hambrienta. 2018. (World of Eric Carle Ser.). (SPA.). 32p. (J). (-k). 8.99 *(978-1-5247-9151-3(2))* Penguin Young Readers Group.

—Animal Stories: 8 Animal Stories, over 35 Sounds. Wagner, Veronica. 2014. (Play-A-Sound Ser.). (ENG.). 36p. (J). bds. *(978-1-4508-8529-4(2),* 28e5aba9-efd0-4c96-bb18-a5edae0a62bf, p i kids) Phoenix International Publications, Inc.

Carle, Eric, et al. Artist to Artist: 23 Major Illustrators Talk to Children about Their Art. Eric Carle Museum of Picture Book Art Staff. Gauch, Patricia Lee et al, eds. 2007. 114p. (J). (gr. k-3). 30.00 *(978-0-399-24600-5(2),* Philomel Bks.) Penguin Young Readers Group.

Carle, Eric. Baby Bear, Baby Bear, What Do You See? Martin, Bill, Jr. (Brown Bear & Friends Ser.). (ENG.). (J). (gr. -1-k). 2014. 28p. bds. 12.99 *(978-0-8050-9949-2(2),* 900127480); 2011. 40p. 8.99 *(978-0-8050-9291-2(9),* 900069194); 2007. 32p. 17.99 *(978-0-8050-8336-1(7),* 900044467) Holt, Henry & Co. (Holt, Henry & Co. Bks. For Young Readers).

Carle, Eric. Baby Bear, Baby Bear, What Do You See? / Oso Bebé, Oso Bebé, ¿qué Ves Ahí? (Bilingual Board Book - English / Spanish) Martin, Bill, Jr. 2020. (Brown Bear & Friends Ser.: 1). (ENG.). 13p. (J). bds. 9.99 ***(978-1-250-76607-6(9),*** 900232403, Holt, Henry & Co. Bks. For Young Readers) Holt, Henry & Co.

Carle, Eric. Baby Bear, Baby Bear, What Do You See? 10th Anniversary Edition with Audio CD. Martin, Bill, Jr. 2016. (Brown Bear & Friends Ser.). (ENG.). 32p. (J). 19.99 *(978-1-62779-731-3(9),* 9781627797313, Holt, Henry & Co. Bks. For Young Readers) Holt, Henry & Co.

—Baby Bear, Baby Bear, What Do You See? Big Book. Martin, Bill, Jr. 2011. (Brown Bear & Friends Ser.). (ENG.). 32p. (J). (gr. -1-k). pap. 27.99 *(978-0-8050-9345-2(1),* 9780805093452, Holt, Henry & Co. Bks. For Young Readers) Holt, Henry & Co.

—Baby Bear, Baby Bear, What Do You See? Board Book. Martin, Bill, Jr. 2009. (Brown Bear & Friends Ser.). (ENG.). 28p. (J). (gr. -1-k). bds. 8.99 *(978-0-8050-8990-5(X),* 900058689, Holt, Henry & Co. Bks. For Young Readers) Holt, Henry & Co.

—Brown Bear & Friends. Martin, Bill, Jr. unabr. ed. 2011. (Brown Bear & Friends Ser.). (ENG.). (J). (gr. -1-k). bds. 39.99 *(978-1-4272-1448-5(4),* 900079838) Macmillan Audio.

—Brown Bear Book & CD Storytime Set. Martin, Bill, Jr. unabr. ed. 2013. (Brown Bear & Friends Ser.). (ENG.). (J). (gr. -1-k). 12.99 *(978-1-4272-3510-7(4),* 900126004) Macmillan Audio.

—Brown Bear, Brown Bear, What Do You See? Martin, Bill, Jr. (Brown Bear & Friends Ser.). (J). 2012. (ENG.). 28p. (gr. -1-k). bds. 12.99 *(978-0-8050-9577-7(2),* 900084747); 2007. 32p. pap. 7.95 *(978-0-8050-8797-0(4));* 3rd anniv. ed. 2008. (ENG.). 32p. (gr. -1-k). pap. 27.95 *(978-0-8050-8718-5(4),* 900049190) Holt, Henry & Co. (Holt, Henry & Co. Bks. For Young Readers).

—Brown Bear, Brown Bear, What Do You See? Martin, Bill, Jr. (J). 2004. (SHO.). 27p. pap. *(978-1-84444-165-5(2));* 2004. (ENG & POR.). 32p. pap. *(978-1-84444-159-4(8));* 2004. (KUR & ENG.). 26p. pap. *(978-1-84444-158-7(X));* 2004. (YOR & ENG.). 25p. pap. *(978-1-84444-129-7(6));* 2004. (ENG & TUR.). 27p. pap. *(978-1-84444-127-3(X));* 2004. (TAM & ENG.). 32p. pap. *(978-1-84444-126-6(1));* 2004. (SOM & ENG.). 27p. pap. *(978-1-84444-125-9(3));* 2004. (PAN & ENG.). 32p. pap. *(978-1-84444-123-5(7));* 2004. (ENG & HIN.). 32p. pap. *(978-1-84444-122-8(9));* 2004. (GUJ & ENG.). 32p. pap. *(978-1-84444-121-1(0));* 2004. (PER & ENG.). 32p. pap. *(978-1-84444-120-4(2));* 2004. (ENG & ARA.). 32p. pap. *(978-1-84444-116-7(4));* 2004. (ALB & ENG.). 26p. pap. *(978-1-84444-115-0(6));* 2003. (URD & ENG.). 32p. pap. *(978-1-84444-128-0(8));* 2003. (CHI & ENG.). 32p. pap. *(978-1-84444-118-1(0))* Mantra Lingua.

—Brown Bear, Brown Bear, What Do You See? Martin, Bill, Jr. 2003. (VIE & ENG.). 32p. (J). pap. 12.95 *(978-1-84444-124-2(5))* Mantra Lingua GBR. Dist: Chinasprout, Inc.

—Brown Bear, Brown Bear, What Do You See? / Oso Pardo, Oso Pardo, ¿qué Ves Ahí? (Bilingual Board Book - English / Spanish) Martin, Bill, Jr. 2017. (ENG.). 28p. (J). bds. 9.99 *(978-1-250-15232-9(1),* 900183597, Holt, Henry & Co. Bks. For Young Readers) Holt, Henry & Co.

—Brown Bear, Brown Bear, What Do You See? 50th Anniversary Edition Padded Board Book. Martin, Bill, Jr. 50th anniv. ed. 2016. (Brown Bear & Friends Ser.). (ENG.). 28p. (J). bds. 9.99 *(978-1-62779-722-1(X),* 900158726, Holt, Henry & Co. Bks. For Young Readers) Holt, Henry & Co.

—Brown Bear, Brown Bear, What Do You See? 50th Anniversary Edition with Audio CD. Martin, Bill, Jr. 2016. (Brown Bear & Friends Ser.). (ENG.). 32p. (J). 19.99 *(978-1-62779-721-4(1),* 900158723, Holt, Henry & Co. Bks. For Young Readers) Holt, Henry & Co.

—Brown Bear, Brown Bear, What Do You See? My First Reader. Martin, Bill, Jr. 2010. (My First Reader Ser.). (ENG.). 40p. (J). (gr. -1-2). 8.99 *(978-0-8050-9244-8(7),* 900066982, Holt, Henry & Co. Bks. For Young Readers) Holt, Henry & Co.

—Brown Bear, Brown Bear, What Do You See? Slide & Find. Martin, Bill, Jr. 2010. (Slide & Find Ser.). (ENG.). 22p. (J). (-1). bds. 12.99 *(978-0-312-50926-2(X),* 900070116) St. Martin's Pr.

—Eric Carle: Firefly, Light up the Sky. Wage, Erin Rose. 2015. (Play-A-Sound Ser.). (ENG.). 10p. (J). *(978-1-4508-9779-2(7),* 2a817751-dfe5-43e5-bf5c-af78ec037277, p i kids) Phoenix International Publications, Inc.

—The Foolish Tortoise. Buckley, Richard. (World of Eric Carle Ser.). (ENG.). 24p. (J). (gr. -1-3). 2013. pap. 10.99 *(978-1-4424-6638-8(3));* 2009. bds. 7.99 *(978-1-4169-7916-6(6))* Little Simon. (Little Simon).

—The Foolish Tortoise. Buckley, Richard. 2015. (World of Eric Carle Ser.). (ENG.). 24p. (J). (gr. k-2). pap. 4.99 *(978-1-4814-3577-2(9),* Simon Spotlight) Simon Spotlight.

—The Foolish Tortoise: Lap Edition. Buckley, Richard. 2013. (World of Eric Carle Ser.). (ENG.). 24p. (J). (gr. -1-k). bds. 12.99 *(978-1-4424-8990-5(1),* Little Simon) Little Simon.

—The Greedy Python. Buckley, Richard. 2012. (World of Eric Carle Ser.). (ENG.). 24p. (J). (gr. -1-1). 17.99 *(978-1-4424-4577-2(7));* pap. 4.99 *(978-1-4424-4576-5(9))* Simon Spotlight. (Simon Spotlight).

—The Greedy Python. Buckley, Richard. 2009. (World of Eric Carle Ser.). (ENG.). 24p. (J). (gr. -1-k). bds. 7.99 *(978-1-4169-8290-6(6),* Little Simon) Little Simon.

—The Greedy Python: Lap Edition. Buckley, Richard. 2013. (World of Eric Carle Ser.). (ENG.). 24p. (J). (gr. -1-k). bds. 12.99 *(978-1-4424-8991-2(X),* Little Simon) Little Simon.

—I Love Mom with the Very Hungry Caterpillar. 2017. (World of Eric Carle Ser.). (ENG.). 32p. (J). (-k). 8.99 *(978-0-451-53346-3(1))* Penguin Young Readers Group.

—The Lamb & the Butterfly. Sundgaard, Arnold. 2013. (ENG.). 32p. (J). (gr. -1-k). 17.99 *(978-0-545-44326-5(1),* Orchard Bks.) Scholastic, Inc.

—Lift-the-Tab: Baby Bear, Baby Bear, What Do You See? Martin, Bill, Jr. 2016. (Brown Bear & Friends Ser.). (ENG.). 28p. (J). bds. 6.99 *(978-1-62779-724-5(6),* 9781627797245, Holt, Henry & Co. Bks. For Young Readers) Holt, Henry & Co.

—Lift-The-Tab: Brown Bear, Brown Bear, What Do You See? 50th Anniversary Edition. Martin, Bill & Martin, Bill, Jr. 2016. (Brown Bear & Friends Ser.). (ENG.). 28p. (J). bds. 9.99 *(978-1-62779-723-8(8),* 900158733, Holt, Henry & Co. Bks. For Young Readers) Holt, Henry & Co.

—Oso Panda, Oso Panda, ¿Qué Ves Ahí? Martin, Bill, Jr. Mlawer, Teresa, tr. 2008. (Brown Bear & Friends Ser.).Tr. of Brown Bear, Brown Bear, What Do You See?. (SPA.). 32p. (J). (gr. -1-k). 18.99 *(978-0-8050-8348-4(0),* 900044876, Holt, Henry & Co. Bks. For Young Readers) Holt, Henry & Co.

—Oso Panda, Oso Panda, ¿Qué Ves Ahí? Martin, Bill, Jr. Mlawer, Teresa, tr. ed. 2009. (Brown Bear & Friends Ser.).Tr. of Brown Bear, Brown Bear, What Do You See?. (SPA.). 26p. (J). (gr. -1-k). bds. 9.99 *(978-0-8050-8756-7(7),* 900049804, Holt, Henry & Co. Bks. For Young Readers) Holt, Henry & Co.

—Panda Bear, Panda Bear, What Do You See? Martin, Bill, Jr. (Brown Bear & Friends Ser.). (J). 2014. (ENG.). 28p. (gr. -1-k). bds. 12.99 *(978-0-8050-9950-8(6),* 900127482); 2011. (ENG.). 40p. (gr. -1-2). 8.99 *(978-0-8050-9292-9(7),* 900069195); 2007. 32p. 7.95 *(978-0-8050-8799-4(0));* 2007. (ENG.). 32p. (gr. -1-k). pap. 27.99 *(978-0-8050-8102-2(X),* 900039555); 2006. (ENG.). 28p. (gr. -1-k). bds. 8.99 *(978-0-8050-8078-0(3),* 900038948); 2003. (ENG.). 32p. (gr. -1-k). 18.99 *(978-0-8050-1758-8(5),* 9780805017588) Holt, Henry & Co. (Holt, Henry & Co. Bks. For Young Readers).

—Panda Bear, Panda Bear, What Do You See?, 1 vol. Martin, Bill, Jr. unabr. ed. 2011. (Brown Bear & Friends Ser.). (ENG.). (J). (gr. -1-k). 9.99 *(978-1-4272-1254-2(6),* 900075947) Macmillan Audio.

—Panda Bear, Panda Bear, What Do You See? Martin, Bill, Jr. 2013. (Slide & Find Ser.). (ENG.). 22p. (J). (gr. -1 — 1). bds. 12.99 *(978-0-312-51581-2(2),* 900118540) St. Martin's Pr.

—Panda Bear, Panda Bear, What Do You See? 10th Anniversary Edition. Martin, Bill, Jr. 2013. (Brown Bear & Friends Ser.). (ENG.). 28p. (J). (gr. -1-k). 19.99 *(978-0-8050-9778-8(3),* 900119353, Holt, Henry & Co. Bks. For Young Readers) Holt, Henry & Co.

—Polar Bear Book & CD Storytime Set. Martin, Bill, Jr. unabr. ed. 2012. (Brown Bear & Friends Ser.). (ENG.). (J). (gr. -1-k). 12.99 *(978-1-4272-3256-4(3),* 900122506) Macmillan Audio.

—Polar Bear, Polar Bear, What Do You Hear? Martin, Bill, Jr. (Brown Bear & Friends Ser.). (J). 2012. (ENG.). 28p. (gr. -1-k). bds. 12.99 *(978-0-8050-9095-6(9),* 900062022); 2007. 32p. 7.95 *(978-0-8050-8798-7(2));* 20th anniv. ed. 2011. (ENG.). 32p. (gr. -1-k). 19.99 *(978-0-8050-9066-6(5),* 900061041) Holt, Henry & Co. (Holt, Henry & Co. Bks. For Young Readers).

Carle, Eric. Polar Bear, Polar Bear, What Do You Hear? / Oso Polar, Oso Polar, ¿qué Es Ese Ruido? (Bilingual Board Book - English / Spanish) Martin, Bill, Jr. 2020. (ENG.). 13p. (J). bds. 9.99 ***(978-1-250-76606-9(0),*** 900232401, Holt, Henry & Co. Bks. For Young Readers) Holt, Henry & Co.

Carle, Eric. Polar Bear, Polar Bear, What Do You Hear? My First Reader. Martin, Bill, Jr. 2010. (My First Reader Ser.). (ENG.). 40p. (J). (gr. -1-2). 8.99 *(978-0-8050-9245-5(5),* 900066985, Holt, Henry & Co. Bks. For Young Readers) Holt, Henry & Co.

—Polar Bear, Polar Bear What Do You Hear? Sound Book. Martin, Bill, Jr. 2011. (Brown Bear & Friends Ser.). (ENG.). 24p. (J). (gr. -1-k). bds. 14.95 *(978-0-312-51346-7(1),* 900079163) St. Martin's Pr.

—String-Alongs. Chronicle Books Staff. 2012. (ENG.). 10p. (J). (gr. -1-17). 18.99 *(978-1-4521-0515-4(4))* Chronicle Bks. LLC.

—Why Noah Chose the Dove. Singer, Isaac Bashevis. Shub, Elizabeth, tr. from ENG. 2013. (ENG.). 32p. (J). (gr. k-3). pap. 22.44 *(978-1-250-02199-1(5),* 900096527) Square Fish.

—The World of Eric Carle. p i kids. 2015. (Me Reader Ser.). (ENG.). 192p. (J). *(978-1-4508-9781-5(9),* 62f0c45c-9706-43cc-a943-6b681aa8fa04, p i kids) Phoenix International Publications, Inc.

—World of Eric Carle: First Look & Find Book & Blocks. Wage, Erin Rose. 2019. (Look & Find Ser.). (ENG.). 16p. (J). *(978-1-5037-4779-1(4),* ef27afcc-5a48-425f-8eab-9ce107ad32e9, p i kids) Phoenix International Publications, Inc.

Carle, Eric. World of Eric Carle: Me Reader Jr: 8-Book Library & Electronic Reader. Skwish, Emily. 2016. (Me Reader Jr Ser.). (ENG.). 80p. (J). bds., bds. ***(978-1-5037-0698-9(2),*** eebc24f1-0cbf-4c2e-b57e-23ed130a5f34, p i kids) Phoenix International Publications, Inc.

Carle, Eric. 1, 2, 3, to the Zoo Train Flash Cards. Chronicle Books Staff. 2013. (ENG.). 21p. (J). (gr. -1 — 1). 14.99 *(978-1-4521-1341-8(6))* Chronicle Bks. LLC.

Carle, Eric. All about the Very Hungry Caterpillar. Carle, Eric. 2018. (World of Eric Carle Ser.). (ENG.). 10p. (J). (gr. k-k). bds. 9.99 *(978-1-5247-8588-8(1),* Grosset & Dunlap) Penguin Young Readers Group.

—Amigos. Carle, Eric. 2016. (SPA.). 22p. (J). (— 1). bds. 7.99 *(978-0-399-54506-1(9))* Penguin Young Readers Group.

—La Araña Muy Ocupada. Carle, Eric. 2004.Tr. of Very Busy Spider. (SPA.). 32p. (J). (gr. -1-k). 21.99 *(978-0-399-24241-0(4))* Penguin Young Readers Group.

—The Artist Who Painted a Blue Horse. Carle, Eric. (ENG.). (J). (gr. -1 — 1). 2013. 22p. bds. 7.99 *(978-0-399-16402-6(2));* 2011. 32p. 17.99 *(978-0-399-25713-1(6))* Penguin Young Readers Group.

—Calm with the Very Hungry Caterpillar. Carle, Eric. 2019. (World of Eric Carle Ser.). (ENG.). 32p. (J). (-k). 8.99 *(978-1-5247-9218-3(7))* Penguin Young Readers Group.

—Can a Cat Do That? Carle, Eric. 2018. (World of Eric Carle Ser.). (ENG.). 32p. (J). (gr. -1-k). 17.99 *(978-1-5344-2725-9(2));* pap. 4.99 *(978-1-5344-2724-2(4))* Simon Spotlight. (Simon Spotlight).

—Can You Guess?: Animals with the Very Hungry Caterpillar. Carle, Eric. 2020. (World of Eric Carle Ser.). (ENG.). 14p. (J). (-k). bds. 8.99 *(978-1-5247-8636-6(5))* Penguin Young Readers Group.

—Can You Guess?: Food with the Very Hungry Caterpillar. Carle, Eric. 2020. (World of Eric Carle Ser.). (ENG.). 14p. (J). (-k). bds. 8.99 *(978-1-5247-8637-3(3))* Penguin Young Readers Group.

—Christmas Cheer for the Grouchy Ladybug. Carle, Eric. 2019. (ENG.). 32p. (J). (gr. -1-3). 9.99 *(978-0-06-293226-6(8))* HarperCollins Pubs.

—De la Cabeza a Los Pies: From Head to Toe (Spanish Edition) Carle, Eric.Tr. of From Head to Toe. (SPA.). 32p. (J). (gr. -1-3). 2007. pap. 8.99 *(978-0-06-051313-9(6));* 2003. 17.99 *(978-0-06-051302-3(0))* HarperCollins Christian Publishing. (HarperCollins Español).

—Does a Kangaroo Have a Mother, Too? Carle, Eric. 2005. (ENG.). 32p. (J). (gr. -1-3). reprint ed. pap. 7.99 *(978-0-06-443642-7(X))* HarperCollins Pubs.

—Dream Snow. Carle, Eric. 2015. (ENG.). 22p. (J). (gr. -1 — 1). bds. 9.99 *(978-0-399-17314-1(5))* Penguin Young Readers Group.

—¿el Canguro Tiene Mamá? Does a Kangaroo Have a Mother, Too? (Spanish Edition), 1 vol. Carle, Eric. 2008.Tr. of Does a Kangaroo Have a Mother, Too?. (SPA.). 32p. (J). (gr. -1-3). pap. 7.99 *(978-0-06-001111-6(4),* HarperCollins Español) HarperCollins Christian Publishing.

—Eric Carle Classics: The Tiny Seed; Pancakes, Pancakes!; Walter the Baker. Carle, Eric. 2011. (World of Eric Carle Ser.). (ENG.). 112p. (J). (gr. -1-2). 19.99 *(978-1-4424-3988-7(2),* Simon & Schuster Bks. For

Young Readers) Simon & Schuster Bks. For Young Readers.

—The Eric Carle Gift Set: The Tiny Seed; Pancakes, Pancakes!; a House for Hermit Crab; Rooster's off to See the World. Carle, Eric. ed. 2013. (World of Eric Carle Ser.). (ENG.). 124p. (J). (gr. -1 — 1). bds. 34.99 *(978-1-4424-8885-4(9)*, Little Simon) Little Simon.

—The Eric Carle Mini Library: A Storybook Gift Set. Carle, Eric. ed. 2009. (World of Eric Carle Ser.). (ENG.). 148p. (J). 14.99 *(978-1-4169-8516-7(6)*, Little Simon) Little Simon.

—The Eric Carle Ready-To-Read Collection: Have You Seen My Cat?; the Greedy Python; Pancakes, Pancakes!; Rooster Is off to See the World; a House for Hermit Crab; Walter the Baker. Carle, Eric. ed. 2014. (World of Eric Carle Ser.). (ENG.). 160p. (J). (gr. -1-2). pap. 15.99 *(978-1-4814-1632-0(4)*, Simon Spotlight) Simon Spotlight.

—Eric Carle Six Classic Board Books Box Set. Carle, Eric. 2018. (ENG.). 160p. (J). (gr. -1 — 1). pap. 48.94 *(978-0-06-281568-2(7)*, HarperFestival) HarperCollins Pubs.

—Eric Carle's Book of Many Things. Carle, Eric. 2019. (World of Eric Carle Ser.). (ENG.). 80p. (J). (gr. -1-2). 16.99 *(978-1-5247-8867-4(8))* Penguin Young Readers Group.

—Friends. Carle, Eric. (ENG.). (J). (gr. -1-k). 2015. 24p. bds. 7.99 *(978-0-399-17206-9(8))*; 2013. 32p. 17.99 *(978-0-399-16533-7(9))* Penguin Young Readers Group. (Philomel Bks.).

—From Head to Toe Big Book. Carle, Eric. 2007. (ENG.). 32p. (J). (gr. -1-k). pap. 24.99 *(978-0-06-111972-9(5)*, HarperFestival) HarperCollins Pubs.

—From Head to Toe Padded Board Book. Carle, Eric. 2018. (ENG.). 28p. (J). (gr. -1 — 1). bds. 9.99 *(978-0-06-274766-2(5)*, HarperFestival) HarperCollins Pubs.

—From Head to Toe/de la Cabeza a Los Pies Board Book: Bilingual Edition. Carle, Eric. 2020. (ENG.). 28p. (J). (gr. -1 — 1). bds. 8.99 *(978-0-06-051315-3(2)*, HarperFestival) HarperCollins Pubs.

—El Gallo Sale a Ver el Mundo (Rooster's off to See the World) Carle, Eric. 2018. (World of Eric Carle Ser.). (SPA.). 32p. (J). (gr. k-3). 7.99 *(978-1-5344-2447-0(4)*, Libros Para Ninos) Libros Para Ninos.

—Happy Birthday from the Very Hungry Caterpillar. Carle, Eric. 2019. (World of Eric Carle Ser.). (ENG.). 32p. (J). (gr. -1-2). 8.99 *(978-1-5247-9082-0(6))* Penguin Young Readers Group.

Carle, Eric. Happy Halloween from the Very Busy Spider: A Lift-The-Flap Book. Carle, Eric. 2020. (World of Eric Carle Ser.). (ENG.). 10p. (J). (-k). bds. 12.99 ***(978-0-593-09710-6(6))*** Penguin Young Readers Group.

Carle, Eric. Have You Seen My Cat? Carle, Eric. 2012. (World of Eric Carle Ser.). (ENG.). 24p. (J). (gr. -1-k). 17.99 *(978-1-4424-4575-8(0))*; pap. 4.99 *(978-1-4424-4574-1(2))* Simon Spotlight. (Simon Spotlight).

—Have You Seen My Cat? A Slide-And-Peek Board Book. Carle, Eric. 2009. (World of Eric Carle Ser.). (ENG.). 16p. (J). bds. 8.99 *(978-1-4169-8514-3(X)*, Little Simon) Little Simon.

—House for Hermit Crab. Carle, Eric. 2004. (World of Eric Carle Ser.). (ENG.). 32p. (J). (gr. k-3). bds. 8.99 *(978-0-689-87064-4(7)*, Little Simon) Little Simon.

—A House for Hermit Crab. Carle, Eric. 2013. (World of Eric Carle Ser.). (ENG.). 32p. (J). (gr. -1-2). pap. 9.99 *(978-1-4424-7224-2(3)*, Little Simon) Little Simon.

—A House for Hermit Crab. Carle, Eric. 2014. (World of Eric Carle Ser.). (ENG.). 32p. (J). (gr. k-2). pap. 4.99 *(978-1-4814-0915-5(8)*, Simon Spotlight) Simon Spotlight.

—Hugs & Kisses for the Grouchy Ladybug. Carle, Eric. 2018. (ENG.). 32p. (J). (gr. -1-3). 9.99 *(978-0-06-283568-0(8))* HarperCollins Pubs.

—I Love Dad with the Very Hungry Caterpillar. Carle, Eric. 2018. (World of Eric Carle Ser.). (ENG.). 32p. (J). (-k). 8.99 *(978-1-5247-8589-5(X))* Penguin Young Readers Group.

—La Mariquita Malhumorada: The Grouchy Ladybug Board Book (Spanish Edition) Carle, Eric. 2020. (SPA.). 44p. (J). (gr. -1 — 1). bds. 9.99 *(978-0-06-297350-4(9)*, HarperFestival) HarperCollins Pubs.

—Mister Seahorse. Carle, Eric. 2004. (ENG.). 32p. (J). (gr. -1-k). 18.99 *(978-0-399-24269-4(4))* Penguin Young Readers Group.

—Mister Seahorse: Board Book. Carle, Eric. 2011. (ENG.). 64p. (J). (gr. -1 — 1). bds. 9.99 *(978-0-399-25490-1(0))* Penguin Young Readers Group.

—My First Busy Book. Carle, Eric. 2015. (World of Eric Carle Ser.). (ENG.). 12p. (J). (gr. -1). bds. 14.99 *(978-1-4814-5791-0(8)*, Little Simon) Little Simon.

—My First Busy World. Carle, Eric. 2019. (World of Eric Carle Ser.). (ENG.). 12p. (J). (gr. -1). bds. 14.99 *(978-1-5344-4391-4(6)*, Little Simon) Little Simon.

—My First I See You: A Mirror Book. Carle, Eric. 2018. (World of Eric Carle Ser.). (ENG.). 14p. (J). (gr. -1 — 1). bds. 7.99 *(978-1-5344-2454-8(7)*, Little Simon) Little Simon.

—My First Peek-A-Boo Animals. Carle, Eric. 2017. (World of Eric Carle Ser.). (ENG.). 18p. (J). (gr. -1 — 1). bds. 7.99 *(978-1-5344-0105-1(9)*, Little Simon) Little Simon.

—My Own Very Busy Spider Coloring Book. Carle, Eric. 2004. 32p. (J). (gr. -1-k). 5.99 *(978-0-399-24309-7(7)*, Philomel Bks.) Penguin Young Readers Group.

—My Own Very Hungry Caterpillar Coloring Book. Carle, Eric. 2003. (ENG.). 32p. (J). (gr. -1-k). 6.99 *(978-0-399-24207-6(4))* Penguin Young Readers Group.

—My Own Very Lonely Firefly Coloring Book. Carle, Eric. 2006. (ENG.). 32p. (J). (gr. -1-k). 5.99 *(978-0-399-24646-3(0)*, Philomel Bks.) Penguin Young Readers Group.

—My Own Very Quiet Cricket Coloring Book. Carle, Eric. 2005. (ENG.). 32p. (J). (gr. -1-k). 5.99 *(978-0-399-24475-9(1)*, Philomel Bks.) Penguin Young Readers Group.

—My Very First Book of Animal Homes. Carle, Eric. 2007. (ENG.). 20p. (J). (gr. -1 — 1). bds. 5.99 *(978-0-399-24647-0(9))* Penguin Young Readers Group.

—My Very First Book of Animal Sounds. Carle, Eric. 2007. 40p. (J). (gr. -1 — 1). bds. 5.99 *(978-0-399-24648-7(7)*, Philomel Bks.) Penguin Young Readers Group.

—My Very First Book of Colors. Carle, Eric. 2005. (ENG.). 20p. (J). (gr. -1 — 1). bds. 5.99 *(978-0-399-24386-8(0))* Penguin Young Readers Group.

—My Very First Book of Food. Carle, Eric. 2007. (ENG.). 18p. (J). (gr. -1 — 1). bds. 5.99 *(978-0-399-24747-7(5))* Penguin Young Readers Group.

—My Very First Book of Motion. Carle, Eric. 2007. (ENG.). 18p. (J). (gr. -1 — 1). bds. 5.99 *(978-0-399-24748-4(3))* Penguin Young Readers Group.

—My Very First Book of Numbers. Carle, Eric. 2006. (ENG.). 20p. (J). (gr. -1 — 1). bds. 5.99 *(978-0-399-24509-1(X))* Penguin Young Readers Group.

—My Very First Book of Numbers / Mi Primer Libro de Números: Bilingual Edition. Carle, Eric. 2013. 20p. (J). (gr. -1 — 1). bds. 5.99 *(978-0-399-16141-4(4))* Penguin Young Readers Group.

—My Very First Book of Shapes. Carle, Eric. 2005. (ENG.). 20p. (J). (gr. -1 — 1). bds. 5.99 *(978-0-399-24387-5(9))* Penguin Young Readers Group.

—My Very First Book of Shapes / Mi Primer Libro de Formas: Bilingual Edition. Carle, Eric. 2013. (ENG.). 20p. (J). (gr. -1 — 1). bds. 5.99 *(978-0-399-16142-1(2))* Penguin Young Readers Group.

—My Very First Book of Words. Carle, Eric. 2006. (ENG.). 20p. (J). (gr. -1 — 1). bds. 5.99 *(978-0-399-24510-7(3))* Penguin Young Readers Group.

—The Nonsense Show. Carle, Eric. Mack, Jeff. 2015. (ENG.). 40p. (J). (gr. -1-2). 18.99 *(978-0-399-17687-6(X)*, Philomel Bks.) Penguin Young Readers Group.

—La Oruga Muy Hambrienta/the Very Hungry Caterpillar: Bilingual Board Book. Carle, Eric. 2011. (ENG.). 24p. (J). (gr. -1 — 1). bds. 10.99 *(978-0-399-25605-9(9))* Penguin Young Readers Group.

—Pancakes, Pancakes! Carle, Eric. 2004. (World of Eric Carle Ser.). (ENG.). 32p. (J). (gr. -1-3). bds. 8.99 *(978-0-689-87148-1(1)*, Little Simon) Little Simon.

—Pancakes, Pancakes! Carle, Eric. 2013. (World of Eric Carle Ser.). (ENG.). 24p. (J). (gr. -1-1). 16.99 *(978-1-4424-7275-4(8))*; pap. 3.99 *(978-1-4424-7274-7(X))* Simon Spotlight. (Simon Spotlight).

—¡Panqueques, Panqueques! (Pancakes, Pancakes!) Carle, Eric. 2017. (World of Eric Carle Ser.). (SPA.). 32p. (J). (gr. -1-3). 7.99 *(978-1-5344-0205-8(5)*, Libros Para Ninos) Libros Para Ninos.

—Papá, Por Favor, Bájame la Luna (Papa, Please Get the Moon for Me) Carle, Eric. 2018. (World of Eric Carle Ser.). (SPA.). 32p. (J). (gr. -1-k). bds. 10.99 *(978-1-5344-1327-6(8))*; (gr. k-3). 8.99 *(978-1-5344-1326-9(X))* Libros Para Ninos. (Libros Para Ninos).

—Rooster Is off to See the World. Carle, Eric. 2013. (World of Eric Carle Ser.). (ENG.). 24p. (J). (gr. -1-1). 16.99 *(978-1-4424-7270-9(7))*; pap. 3.99 *(978-1-4424-7269-3(3))* Simon Spotlight. (Simon Spotlight).

—La Semillita (the Tiny Seed) Carle, Eric. Romay, Alexis, tr. 2016. (World of Eric Carle Ser.). (SPA.). 40p. (J). (gr. -1-3). 7.99 *(978-1-4814-7834-2(6)*, Libros Para Ninos) Libros Para Ninos.

Carle, Eric. Sleep Tight with the Very Hungry Caterpillar. Carle, Eric. 2020. (World of Eric Carle Ser.). (ENG.). 10p. (J). (-k). bds. 12.99 ***(978-0-593-22257-7(1))*** Penguin Young Readers Group.

Carle, Eric. "Slowly, Slowly, Slowly," Said the Sloth. Carle, Eric. 2007. (gr. -1-3). 18.00 *(978-0-7569-8002-3(X))* Perfection Learning Corp.

—Slowly, Slowly, Slowly, Said the Sloth. Carle, Eric. 2007. (ENG.). 32p. (J). (gr. -1-2). pap. 7.99 *(978-0-14-240847-6(6))* Penguin Young Readers Group.

—The Tiny Seed. Carle, Eric. (World of Eric Carle Ser.). (ENG.). (J). (gr. -1-3). 2009. 36p. 7.99 *(978-1-4169-7917-3(4))*; 2005. 34p. bds. 8.99 *(978-0-689-87149-8(X))* Little Simon. (Little Simon).

—The Tiny Seed. Carle, Eric. 2015. (World of Eric Carle Ser.). (ENG.). 32p. (J). (gr. k-2). pap. 4.99 *(978-1-4814-3575-8(2)*, Simon Spotlight) Simon Spotlight.

—The Tiny Seed: Book & CD. Carle, Eric. 2018. (World of Eric Carle Ser.). (ENG.). 40p. (J). (gr. -1-3). pap. 9.99 *(978-1-5344-1426-6(6)*, Little Simon) Little Simon.

—The Very Busy Spider. Carle, Eric. (Penguin Young Readers, Level 2 Ser.). (J). 2014. (ENG.). 32p. (gr. 1-2). pap. 4.99 *(978-0-448-48052-7(2)*, Penguin Young Readers); 2011. 24p. (gr. -1 — 1). bds. 15.99 *(978-0-399-25601-1(6)*, Philomel Bks.) Penguin Young Readers Group.

—The Very Eric Carle Treasury. Carle, Eric. 2017. (ENG.). 152p. (J). (-k). 35.00 *(978-1-5247-3992-8(8)*, Philomel Bks.) Penguin Young Readers Group.

—The Very Hungry Caterpillar. Carle, Eric. 2004. 20p. (J). (ENG & BEN.). pap. *(978-1-85269-125-7(5))*; (ENG & URD.). pap. *(978-1-85269-129-5(8))*; (ENG & CHI.). (gr. -1-2). pap. *(978-1-85269-126-4(3))*; (ARA & ENG.). (gr. -1-5). pap. *(978-1-85269-124-0(7))* Mantra Lingua.

—The Very Hungry Caterpillar. Carle, Eric. Mack, Jeff. 2015. 24p. (J). (gr. -1-k). bds. 19.99 *(978-0-399-17317-2(X)*, Philomel Bks.) Penguin Young Readers Group.

—The Very Hungry Caterpillar: 50th Anniversary Golden Edition. Carle, Eric. 50th ed. 2018. (ENG.). 40p. (J). (-k). 22.99 *(978-0-525-51619-4(0)*, Philomel Bks.) Penguin Young Readers Group.

—The Very Hungry Caterpillar: Board Book & CD. Carle, Eric. 2007. (ENG.). 24p. (J). (gr. -1 — 1). bds., bds. 16.99 *(978-0-399-24745-3(9)*, Philomel Bks.) Penguin Young Readers Group.

—The Very Hungry Caterpillar/la Oruga Muy Hambrienta. Carle, Eric. ed. 2011. (ENG.). 32p. (J). (gr. -1-k). 21.99 *(978-0-399-25604-2(0))* Penguin Young Readers Group.

—The Very Hungry Caterpillar's Christmas 123. Carle, Eric. 2015. (World of Eric Carle Ser.). (ENG.). 18p. (J). (— 1). bds. 9.99 *(978-0-448-49009-0(9))* Penguin Young Readers Group.

Carle, Eric. The Very Hungry Caterpillar's Garden Picnic: A Scratch-And-Sniff Book. Carle, Eric. 2020. (World of Eric Carle Ser.). (ENG.). 12p. (J). (-k). bds. 12.99 ***(978-0-593-09704-5(1))*** Penguin Young Readers Group.

Carle, Eric. The Very Quiet Cricket. Carle, Eric. 2014. (Penguin Young Readers, Level 3 Ser.). (ENG.). 32p. (J). (gr. 1-3). pap. 4.99 *(978-0-448-48138-8(3))* Penguin Young Readers Group.

—Walter el Panadero (Walter the Baker) Carle, Eric. 2018. (World of Eric Carle Ser.). (SPA.). 40p. (J). (gr. -1-3). 7.99 *(978-1-5344-3281-9(7)*, Libros Para Ninos) Libros Para Ninos.

—Walter the Baker. Carle, Eric. 2012. (World of Eric Carle Ser.). (ENG.). 34p. (J). (gr. -1 — 1). bds. 7.99 *(978-1-4424-4941-1(1)*, Little Simon) Little Simon.

—Walter the Baker. Carle, Eric. 2014. (World of Eric Carle Ser.). (ENG.). 32p. (J). (gr. -1-2). pap. 4.99 *(978-1-4814-0917-9(4)*, Simon Spotlight) Simon Spotlight.

—Watch Out! a Giant! Carle, Eric. 2017. (World of Eric Carle Ser.). (ENG.). 28p. (J). (gr. -1-k). bds. 9.99 *(978-1-5344-0051-1(6)*, Little Simon) Little Simon.

—What's Your Favorite Animal? Carle, Eric. (Eric Carle & Friends' What's Your Favorite Ser.: 1). (ENG.). (J). (gr. -1-1). 2015. 30p. bds. 8.99 *(978-1-62779-303-2(8)*, 900145986); 2014. 40p. 17.99 *(978-0-8050-9641-5(8)*, 900086971) Holt, Henry & Co. (Holt, Henry & Co. Bks. For Young Readers).

—Where Is the Sun? Carle, Eric. 2019. (World of Eric Carle Ser.). (ENG.). 32p. (J). (gr. -1-k). 17.99 *(978-1-5344-5548-1(5))*; pap. 4.99 *(978-1-5344-5547-4(7))* Simon Spotlight. (Simon Spotlight).

—Where Is the Very Hungry Caterpillar? A Lift-The-Flap Book. Carle, Eric. 2020. (World of Eric Carle Ser.). (ENG.). 10p. (J). (-k). 12.99 *(978-1-5247-8632-8(2))* Penguin Young Readers Group.

—You Are Ready! The World Is Waiting. Carle, Eric. 2020. (ENG.). 32p. (J). (gr. -1-3). 9.99 *(978-0-06-295352-0(4)*, HarperCollins) HarperCollins Pubs. Ltd. GBR. Dist: HarperCollins Pubs.

Carle, Eric. You're My Little Baby: A Touch-And-Feel Book. Carle, Eric. 2020. (World of Eric Carle Ser.). (ENG.). 14p. (J). (gr. -1 — 1). bds. 7.99 ***(978-1-5344-7493-2(5)***, Little Simon) Little Simon.

Carle, Eric. 1, 2, 3 to the Zoo: An Oversized Counting Book. Carle, Eric. 2019. (ENG.). 18p. (J). (— 1). bds. 12.99 *(978-1-9848-1256-8(4))* Penguin Young Readers Group.

—1, 2, 3 with the 10 Little Rubber Ducks: A Spring Counting Book. Carle, Eric. 2019. (ENG.). 22p. (J). (gr. -1 — 1). bds. 8.99 *(978-0-06-288256-1(2)*, HarperFestival) HarperCollins Pubs.

—10 Little Rubber Ducks. Carle, Eric. 2005. (ENG.). 36p. (J). (gr. -1-1). 21.99 *(978-0-06-074075-7(2)*, HarperCollins) HarperCollins Pubs. Ltd. GBR. Dist: HarperCollins Pubs.

—10 Little Rubber Ducks Board Book. Carle, Eric. 2010. (ENG.). 34p. (J). (gr. -1-k). bds. 8.99 *(978-0-06-196428-2(X)*, HarperFestival) HarperCollins Pubs.

Carletta-Vietes, Lisa. And I Thought about You. Kurstedt, Rosanne. 2012. (J). 14.95 *(978-1-937406-65-3(2))* Mascot Bks., Inc.

Carletti, Emanuela. In the Beginning, 1 vol. Goodings, Christina. ed. 2015. (ENG.). 16p. (J). (gr. -1-k). pap. 6.99 *(978-0-7459-6568-0(7))* Lion Hudson PLC GBR. Dist: Independent Pubs. Group.

—Lost Sheep Story, 1 vol. Goodings, Christina. ed. 2015. (ENG.). 16p. (J). (gr. -1-k). pap. 6.99 *(978-0-7459-6571-0(7))* Lion Hudson PLC GBR. Dist: Independent Pubs. Group.

—Noah's Ark, 1 vol. Goodings, Christina. ed. 2015. (ENG.). 16p. (J). (gr. -1-k). pap. 6.99 *(978-0-7459-6569-7(5))* Lion Hudson PLC GBR. Dist: Independent Pubs. Group.

—Water Doodle Bible / Biblia de Pintar con Agua (bilingual / Bilingüe) 2019. 16p. (J). bds. 14.99 *(978-1-4964-3664-1(4)*, 20_32236) Tyndale Hse. Pubs.

Carletti, Emanuela & Guicciardini, Desideria. I Don't Want to Be Nice! A Book about Showing Kindness. Graves, Sue. 2017. (Our Emotions & Behavior Ser.). (ENG.). 28p. (J). (gr. -1-3). 12.99 *(978-1-63198-132-6(3)*, 81326) Free Spirit Publishing, Inc.

—I Don't Want to Wait. Graves, Sue. 2019. (Our Emotions & Behavior Ser.). (ENG.). 28p. (J). (gr. -1-2). 12.99 *(978-1-63198-413-6(6)*, 84136) Free Spirit Publishing, Inc.

—I Want to Win! A Book about Being a Good Sport. Graves, Sue. 2017. (Our Emotions & Behavior Ser.). (ENG.). 28p. (J). (gr. k-4). 12.99 *(978-1-63198-131-9(5))* Free Spirit Publishing, Inc.

—Why Should I? Graves, Sue. 2019. (Our Emotions & Behavior Ser.). (ENG.). 28p. (J). (gr. -1-2). 12.99 *(978-1-63198-412-9(8))* Free Spirit Publishing, Inc.

Carlin, Laura. King of the Sky. Davies, Nicola. 2017. (ENG.). 48p. (J). (gr. -1-3). 17.99 *(978-0-7636-9568-2(8))* Candlewick Pr.

—The Promise. Davies, Nicola. (ENG.). 40p. (J). (gr. k-4). 2017. 8.99 *(978-0-7636-9303-9(0))*; 2014. 16.99 *(978-0-7636-6633-0(5))* Candlewick Pr.

Carlin, Laura. Your Mind Is Like the Sky: A First Book of Mindfulness. Ballard, Bronwen. 2019. (ENG.). 32p. (J). (gr. 2-5). 17.99 ***(978-1-78603-986-6(9)***, Frances Lincoln Children's Bks.) Quarto Publishing Group UK GBR. Dist: Hachette Bk. Group.

Carling, Amelia Lau. Bravo, Chico Canta! Bravo!, 1 vol. Mora, Pat & Martinez, Libby. Iribarren, Elena, tr. 2014. (SPA.). 32p. (J). (gr. -1-2). 8.95 *(978-1-55498-344-5(4))* Groundwood Bks. CAN. Dist: Publishers Group West (PGW).

Carloni, Marco. Electricity & Magnetism: Bridges Edition, Set Of 10. Pelleschi, Andrea. 2013. (Prime Plus Ser.). (J). (gr. 6-8). 99.00 net. *(978-1-4509-9950-2(6))* Benchmark Education Co.

—Electricity & Magnetism: Prime Bridges Edition. Pelleschi, Andrea. 2013. (Prime Ser.). (YA). (gr. 6-8). pap. *(978-1-4509-9701-0(5))* Benchmark Education Co.

—Electricity & Magnetism: Set Of 10. Pelleschi, Andrea. 2013. (Prime Plus Ser.). (J). (gr. 6-8). 99.00 net. *(978-1-4509-9926-7(3))* Benchmark Education Co.

—Light: Bridges Edition, Set Of 10. Worth, Richard. 2013. (Prime Plus Ser.). (J). (gr. 6-8). 99.00 net. *(978-1-4509-9949-6(2))* Benchmark Education Co.

—Light: Prime Bridges Edition. Worth, Richard. 2013. (Prime Ser.). (YA). (gr. 6-8). pap. *(978-1-4509-9700-3(7))* Benchmark Education Co.

—Light: Set Of 10. Worth, Richard. 2013. (Prime Plus Ser.). (J). (gr. 6-8). 99.00 net. *(978-1-4509-9925-0(5))* Benchmark Education Co.

—The Nature of Energy: Bridges Edition, Set Of 10. Kestral, Ted. 2013. (Prime Plus Ser.). (J). (gr. 6-8). 99.00 net. *(978-1-4509-9946-5(8))* Benchmark Education Co.

—The Nature of Energy: Prime Bridges Edition. Kestral, Ted. 2013. (Prime Ser.). (YA). (gr. 6-8). pap. *(978-1-4509-9697-6(3))* Benchmark Education Co.

—The Nature of Energy: Set Of 10. Kestral, Ted. 2013. (Prime Plus Ser.). (J). (gr. 6-8). 99.00 net. *(978-1-4509-9922-9(0))* Benchmark Education Co.

—Sound: Bridges Edition, Set Of 10. Piddock, Charles. 2013. (Prime Plus Ser.). (J). (gr. 6-8). 99.00 net. *(978-1-4509-9948-9(4))* Benchmark Education Co.

—Sound: Prime Bridges Edition. Piddock, Charles. 2013. (Prime Ser.). (YA). (gr. 6-8). pap. *(978-1-4509-9699-0(X))* Benchmark Education Co.

—Sound: Set Of 10. Piddock, Charles. 2013. (Prime Plus Ser.). (J). (gr. 6-8). 99.00 net. *(978-1-4509-9924-3(7))* Benchmark Education Co.

—Thermal Energy: Bridges Edition, Set Of 10. Kestral, Ted. 2013. (Prime Plus Ser.). (J). (gr. 6-8). 99.00 net. *(978-1-4509-9947-2(6))* Benchmark Education Co.

—Thermal Energy: Prime Bridges Edition. Kestral, Ted. 2013. (Prime Ser.). (YA). (gr. 6-8). pap. *(978-1-4509-9698-3(1))* Benchmark Education Co.

—Thermal Energy: Set Of 10. Kestral, Ted. 2013. (Prime Plus Ser.). (J). (gr. 6-8). 99.00 net. *(978-1-4509-9923-6(9))* Benchmark Education Co.

Carlos, Uribe & Lawrence, Tate. Protectors of the Wood #3: The Ghost Girl. Kixmiller, John. 2019. (ENG.). 326p. (YA). pap. 20.00 *(978-0-578-45016-2(X))* Protectors of The Wood.

Carlow, Emma. Flora the Fairy. Bradman, Tony. 2nd ed. 2016. (Reading Ladder Ser.). (ENG.). 48p. (J). (gr. k-2). pap. 7.99 *(978-1-4052-8225-3(8))* Egmont Bks., Ltd. GBR. Dist: Independent Pubs. Group.

—Flora the Fairy's Magic Spells. Bradman, Tony. 2nd ed. 2016. (Reading Ladder Ser.). (ENG.). 48p. (J). (gr. k-2). 7.99 *(978-1-4052-8227-7(4))* Egmont Bks., Ltd. GBR. Dist: Independent Pubs. Group.

Carlow, Emma. Flora the Fairy. Carlow, Emma. Bradman, Tony. 2005. (Green Bananas Ser.). (ENG.). 48p. (J). lib. bdg. *(978-0-7787-1022-6(X))* Crabtree Publishing Co.

Carlson, Al & Nicklaus, Carol. The Human Apes. Carlson, Dale. 2nd ed. 2005. (ENG.). 155p. (gr. 8-12). reprint ed. pap. 14.95 *(978-1-884158-31-5(5))* Bick Publishing Hse.

Carlson, Andy. The Amazing Action Alphabet Activities. Kehl, Esther. 2009. 40p. (J). spiral bd. 12.50 *(978-0-9788089-1-4(6))* SeeHearDo Co., LLC, The.

—American History: Presidents: Grade 4-5. Morris, Deborah & Morris, Larry. 2005. (Skill Builders (Rainbow Bridge Publishing) Ser.). 80p. per. 3.99 *(978-1-59441-267-7(7)*, RB-904000) Carson-Dellosa Publishing, LLC.

Carlson, Andy, et al. Division: Grades 4-6. Breur, Jessica. 2005. (Skill Builders (Rainbow Bridge Publishing) Ser.). 80p. per. 3.99 *(978-1-59441-268-4(5)*, RB-904001) Carson-Dellosa Publishing, LLC.

Carlson, Christine. Kaycee Kangaroo Lost in Alphabet Forest: Adventures of Kaycee Kangaroo. Tonderum, Angela. 2008. 41p. pap. 24.95 *(978-1-60672-601-3(3))* America Star Bks.

Carlson, Claudia. Avi the Ambulance Goes to School, Vol. 2015. (ENG.). (J). pap. *(978-1-68115-503-6(6))* Behrman Hse., Inc.

Carlson, Eric. I Am God's Storyteller. Hendey, Lisa M. 2019. (ENG.). 32p. (J). (gr. -1). 17.99 *(978-1-64060-162-8(7))* Paraclete Pr., Inc.

—The Night the Stars Fell: The Astounding 1833 Leonid Meteor Shower. Crum, Sally. 2018. (ENG.). 48p. (J). (gr. 1-6). pap. 14.95 *(978-1-5154-1716-3(6))* Wilder Pubns., Corp.

Carlson, Eric S. Race to Moonrise Rev. Crum, Sally. 2006. 12.95 *(978-1-932738-31-5(2))* Western Reflections Publishing Co.

Carlson, Josh, jt. illus. see LeTourneau, Anthony.

Carlson Jr, Suzanne. English-Japanese Trouble Children's Bilingual Picture Book. Carlson Jr, Richard. 2018. (ENG.). 24p. (J). pap. 10.99 *(978-1-7315-4825-2(7))* Independently Published.

—English-Uzbek Time/Vaqt Children's Bilingual Picture Book. Carlson Jr, Richard. 2018. (ENG.). 28p. (J). pap. 10.99 *(978-1-7241-5418-7(4))* Independently Published.

Carlson, Kevin. Autism Coloring Book. Carlson, Jr. 2009. 50p. pap. 9.95 *(978-1-60264-383-3(0))* Virtualbookworm.com Publishing, Inc.

Carlson, Kim. Elwood: A Dog with Heart. Schroeder, Frauna. 2006. 32p. (J). per. 9.95 *(978-1-892076-20-5(9))* Dancing Moon Pr.

Carlson, Kirsten. The Giraffe Who Was Afraid of Heights, 1 vol. Ufer, David A. 2006. (ENG.). 32p. (J). (gr. -1-3). 15.95 *(978-0-9768823-0-5(2))* Arbordale Publishing.

—The Giraffe Who Was Afraid of Heights in Chinese. Ufer, David A. Ping, He, tr. 2019. (CHI.). 32p. (J). (gr. -1-2). pap. 11.95 *(978-1-60718-390-7(0))* Arbordale Publishing.

Carlson, Kirsten. Luminous Finds Her Aura. Heine, John. 2019. (ENG.). 122p. (J). (gr. 4-6). pap. 8.99 ***(978-1-947239-18-0(X))*** Best Publishing Co.

Carlson, Kirsten. Ocean Seasons, 1 vol. Hirschi, Ron. 2007. (ENG.). 32p. (J). (gr. k-4). 15.95 *(978-0-9777423-2-5(6))*; pap. 9.95 *(978-1-60718-863-6(5))* Arbordale Publishing.

—Sea Secrets, Vol. Cerullo, Mary M. & Simmons, Beth E. 2015. (Long Term Ecological Research Ser.). (ENG.). 32p. (J). (gr. 1-5). pap. 9.95 *(978-1-63076-075-5(7))* Taylor Trade Publishing.

C

Carlson, Lisa. Calamity Jane. Krensky, Stephen. 2006. (On My Own Folklore Ser.). (ENG.). 48p. (gr. 2-4). lib. bdg. 25.26 *(978-1-57505-886-3(3),* Millbrook Pr.) Lerner Publishing Group.

—Calamity Jane. 2007. (On My Own Folklore Ser.). 48p. (J). (gr. -1-3). per. 6.95 *(978-0-8225-6480-5(7),* First Avenue Editions) Lerner Publishing Group.

Carlson, Mickey. Everyday Virtues: Classic Tales to Read with Kids. Autry, James A. & Autry, Rick. 2017. 195p. (J). pap. *(978-1-57312-971-8(2))* Smyth & Helwys Publishing, Inc.

Carlson, Nancy. Halloween. Kessel, Joyce K. 2007. (Yo Solo - Festividades (on My Own - Holidays) Ser.). (SPA.). (gr. 2-4). pap. 39.62 *(978-0-8225-9676-9(8))* Lerner Publishing Group.

—Halloween. Kessel, Joyce K. Translations.com Staff, tr. from ENG. 2007. (Yo Solo - Festividades (on My Own - Holidays) Ser.). (SPA.). 48p. (gr. 2-4). lib. bdg. 25.26 *(978-0-8225-7790-4(9));* per. 6.95 *(978-0-8225-7793-5(3))* Lerner Publishing Group.

—Zip It! Lindaman, Jane. 2012. (ENG.). 32p. (J). (gr. k-4). lib. bdg. 16.95 *(978-0-7613-5592-2(8),* Carolrhoda Bks.) Lerner Publishing Group.

Carlson, Nancy. Arnie & the Skateboard Gang. Carlson, Nancy. 2012. (Nancy Carlson Picture Bks). 32p. (J). (gr. k-2). 56.72 *(978-0-7613-9303-0(X),* Carolrhoda Bks.) Lerner Publishing Group.

—Arnie Goes to Camp. Carlson, Nancy. 2012. (Nancy Carlson Picture Bks). 32p. (J). (gr. k-2). 56.72 *(978-0-7613-9302-3(1),* Carolrhoda Bks.) Lerner Publishing Group.

—Harriet & George's Christmas Treat. Carlson, Nancy. 2005. (Picture Bks.). 32p. (J). (gr. k-2). 15.95 *(978-1-57505-506-0(6))* Lerner Publishing Group.

—Harriet & the Roller Coaster. Carlson, Nancy. unabr. ed. (J). (gr. k-3). 24.95 incl. audio *(978-0-941078-56-6(6));* pap. 15.95 incl. audio *(978-0-941078-54-2(X));* pap., tchr. ed. 31.95 incl. audio *(978-0-941078-55-9(8))* Live Oak Media.

—Harriet & Walt. Carlson, Nancy. unabr. ed. (J). (gr. k-3). 24.95 incl. audio *(978-0-941078-59-7(0));* pap. 15.95 incl. audio *(978-0-941078-57-3(4));* pap., tchr. ed. 31.95 incl. audio *(978-0-941078-58-0(2))* Live Oak Media.

—Harriet's Halloween Candy. Carlson, Nancy. unabr. ed. (J). pap., tchr. ed. 31.95 incl. audio *(978-0-941078-52-8(3));* 24.95 incl. audio *(978-0-941078-53-5(1));* pap. 15.95 incl. audio *(978-0-941078-51-1(5))* Live Oak Media.

—Henry's 100 Days of Kindergarten. Carlson, Nancy. 2004. (ENG.). 32p. (J). (gr. -1-1). 18.69 *(978-0-670-05977-5(3),* Viking) Penguin Publishing Group.

—Henry's Show & Tell. Carlson, Nancy. 2012. (Nancy Carlson Picture Bks). 32p. (J). (gr. k-2). 56.72 *(978-0-7613-9308-5(0),* Carolrhoda Bks.) Lerner Publishing Group.

—I Don't Like to Read! Carlson, Nancy. (ENG.). 32p. (J). 2009. (gr. k-2). pap. 7.99 *(978-0-14-241451-4(4),* Puffin Books); 2007. (gr. -1-1). 21.19 *(978-0-670-06191-4(3))* Penguin Young Readers Group.

—It's Going to Be Perfect! Carlson, Nancy. 2012. (Nancy Carlson Picture Bks). 32p. (J). (gr. k-2). 56.72 *(978-0-7613-9299-6(8),* Carolrhoda Bks.) Lerner Publishing Group.

—It's Not My Fault! Carlson, Nancy. 2003. 32p. (J). (gr. k-2). 15.95 *(978-1-57505-598-5(8))* Lerner Publishing Group.

—Life Is Fun. Carlson, Nancy. 2012. (Nancy Carlson Picture Bks). 32p. (J). (gr. k-2). 56.72 *(978-0-7613-9300-9(5),* Carolrhoda Bks.) Lerner Publishing Group.

—Look Out, Kindergarten, Here I Come! Carlson, Nancy. Mlawer, Teresa, tr. 2004.Tr. of Preparate, Kindergarten! Alla Voy!. 32p. (J). (gr. -1-k). 16.99 *(978-0-670-03673-8(0),* Viking Books for Young Readers) Penguin Young Readers Group.

—Louanne Pig in Witch Lady, 2nd Edition. Carlson, Nancy. 2nd rev. ed. 2006. (ENG.). 32p. (J). (gr. k-2). per. 9.99 *(978-0-8225-6197-2(2),* Carolrhoda Bks.) Lerner Publishing Group.

—Loudmouth George Earns His Allowance. Carlson, Nancy. 2007. (ENG.). 32p. (J). (gr. k-2). 15.95 *(978-0-8225-6560-4(9),* Carolrhoda Bks.) Lerner Publishing Group.

—My Best Friend Moved Away. Carlson, Nancy. 2012. (Nancy Carlson Picture Bks). 32p. (J). (gr. k-2). 56.72 *(978-0-7613-9309-2(9),* Carolrhoda Bks.) Lerner Publishing Group.

—My Family Is Forever. Carlson, Nancy. 2006. (ENG.). 32p. (J). (gr. -1-k). pap. 6.99 *(978-0-14-240561-1(2),* Puffin Books) Penguin Young Readers Group.

—Poor Carl. Carlson, Nancy. 2012. (Nancy Carlson Picture Bks). 32p. (J). (gr. k-2). 56.72 *(978-0-7613-9305-4(6),* Carolrhoda Bks.) Lerner Publishing Group.

—Sit Still! Carlson, Nancy. 2012. (Nancy Carlson Picture Bks). 32p. (J). (gr. k-2). 56.72 *(978-0-7613-9301-6(3),* Carolrhoda Bks.) Lerner Publishing Group.

—Smile a Lot! Carlson, Nancy. (Nancy Carlson Picture Bks). 32p. (J). (gr. k-2). 2012. 56.72 *(978-0-7613-9310-8(2));* 2012. (ENG.). 9.99 *(978-0-7613-9173-9(8));* 2003. 15.95 *(978-0-87614-869-3(0))* Lerner Publishing Group. (Carolrhoda Bks.).

—Snowden. Carlson, Nancy. 2012. (Nancy Carlson Picture Bks). 32p. (J). (gr. k-2). 56.72 *(978-0-7613-9307-8(2),* Carolrhoda Bks.) Lerner Publishing Group.

—Take Time to Relax! Carlson, Nancy. 2012. (Nancy Carlson Picture Bks). 32p. (J). (gr. k-2). 56.72 *(978-0-7613-9304-7(8),* Carolrhoda Bks.) Lerner Publishing Group.

—Think Happy! Carlson, Nancy. (Nancy Carlson Picture Bks). 32p. (J). (gr. k-3). 2012. 56.72 *(978-0-7613-9312-2(9));* 2009. (ENG.). 16.95 *(978-0-8225-8940-2(0))* Lerner Publishing Group. (Carolrhoda Bks.).

Carlson, Nancy. Harriet & the Garden. Carlson, Nancy, tr. 2nd rev. ed. 2005. (Nancy Carlson's Neighborhood Ser.). 32p. (gr. k-2). 15.95 *(978-1-57505-710-1(7))* Lerner Publishing Group.

Carlson, Nancy Gayle. One, Two, Tie Your Shoes! Gregory, Lorraine NAR NEEDED. 2010. (J). *(978-0-545-26482-2(0))* Scholastic, Inc.

Carlson, Patrick. Abraham Lincoln Says... Don't Give Up! Del Bianco, Lou. 2018. (ENG.). 46p. (J). (gr. k-5). pap. 12.95 *(978-0-9989987-6-3(1))* Niche Content Pr.

—Albert Is Our Mascot. Wells, Jason & Wells, Jeff. 2013. (That's Not Our Mascot Ser.). (ENG.). (J). 14.95 *(978-1-62086-283-4(2))* Mascot Bks., Inc.

—Aubie Is Our Mascot. Wells, Jason & Wells, Jeff. 2013. (That's Not Our Mascot Ser.). (ENG.). (J). 14.95 *(978-1-62086-292-6(1))* Mascot Bks., Inc.

—Awesome Adventures of the Lemonade Boys. Knowles, Jennifer. 2019. (ENG.). 36p. (J). pap. 9.95 *(978-1-0959-0841-9(3))* Independently Published.

—Big Al Is Our Mascot. Wells, Jason & Wells, Jeff. 2013. (That's Not Our Mascot Ser.). (ENG.). (J). 14.95 *(978-1-62086-290-2(5))* Mascot Bks., Inc.

—Big Red Is Our Mascot. Wells, Jason & Wells, Jeff. 2013. (That's Not Our Mascot Ser.). (ENG.). (J). 14.95 *(978-1-62086-291-9(3))* Mascot Bks., Inc.

—Bully Is Our Mascot. Wells, Jason & Wells, Jeff. 2013. (That's Not Our Mascot Ser.). (ENG.). (J). 14.95 *(978-1-62086-294-0(8))* Mascot Bks., Inc.

—Cocky Is Our Mascot. Wells, Jason & Wells, Jeff. 2013. (That's Not Our Mascot Ser.). (ENG.). (J). 14.95 *(978-1-62086-287-2(5))* Mascot Bks., Inc.

Carlson, Patrick. The Curly Twirly Tales of Miss Evelyn. Baharian M Ed, Rebecca. 2019. (Lizard Adventure Ser.: Vol. 2). (ENG.). 26p. (J). pap. 14.99 ***(978-1-7088-7824-5(6))*** Independently Published.

Carlson, Patrick. Hairy Dawg Is Our Mascot. Wells, Jason & Wells, Jeff. 2013. (That's Not Our Mascot Ser.). (ENG.). (J). 14.95 *(978-1-62086-284-1(0))* Mascot Bks., Inc.

—Mike the Tiger Is Our Mascot. Wells, Jason & Wells, Jeff. 2013. (That's Not Our Mascot Ser.). (ENG.). (J). 14.95 *(978-1-62086-293-3(X))* Mascot Bks., Inc.

—Poppin's Pumpkin Patch Parade. Wayne, Richard, ed. 2016. (ENG.). 32p. (J). pap. 12.98 *(978-0-9801692-1-8(6))* Gemstone Literary.

—Reveille Is Our Mascot. Wells, Jason & Wells, Jeff. 2013. (That's Not Our Mascot Ser.). (ENG.). (J). 14.95 *(978-1-62086-296-4(4))* Mascot Bks., Inc.

—Scratch Is Our Mascot. Wells, Jason & Wells, Jeff. 2013. (That's Not Our Mascot Ser.). (ENG.). (J). 14.95 *(978-1-62086-285-8(9))* Mascot Bks., Inc.

—Smokey Is Our Mascot. Wells, Jason & Wells, Jeff. 2013. (That's Not Our Mascot Ser.). (ENG.). (J). 14.95 *(978-1-62086-288-9(3))* Mascot Bks., Inc.

—Truman Is Our Mascot. Wells, Jason & Wells, Jeff. 2013. (That's Not Our Mascot Ser.). (ENG.). (J). 14.95 *(978-1-62086-286-5(7))* Mascot Bks., Inc.

Carlson, Richard. English-Urdu Time Children's Bilingual Picture Book. Carlson Jr, Richard. 2018. (ENG.). 28p. (J). pap. 10.99 *(978-1-7241-5002-8(2))* Independently Published.

—Italiano-Fiammingo (Belga) Veicoli/Voertuigen Dizionario Bilingue Illustrato per Bambini. Carlson Jr, Richard. 2018. (ITA.). 24p. (J). pap. 10.99 *(978-1-7198-9338-1(1))* Independently Published.

Carlson, Suzanne. Deutsch-Afrikaans Ich Wurde in Meinen Gefühlen Verletzt/My Gevoelens Is Gekwets Zweisprachiges Bilderbuch Für Kinder. Carlson, Richard. 2019. (GER.). 24p. (J). pap. 10.99 *(978-1-0816-1527-7(3))* Independently Published.

—Deutsch-Afrikaans Zeit/Tyd Zweisprachiges Bilderbuch Für Kinder. Carlson Jr, Richard. 2018. (GER.). 28p. (J). pap. 10.99 *(978-1-7312-0665-7(8))* Independently Published.

—Deutsch-Albanisch Ich Wurde in Meinen Gefühlen Verletzt/Ndjenjat e Mia Janë Të lënduara Zweisprachiges Bilderbuch Für Kinder. Carlson, Richard. 2019. (GER.). 24p. (J). pap. 10.99 *(978-1-0816-1602-1(4))* Independently Published.

—Deutsch-Albanisch Zeit/Koha Zweisprachiges Bilderbuch Für Kinder. Carlson Jr, Richard. 2018. (GER.). 28p. (J). pap. 10.99 *(978-1-7312-0898-9(7))* Independently Published.

—Deutsch-Amharisch Ich Wurde in Meinen Gefühlen Verletzt/ስሜቴ ተጎድቷል Zweisprachiges Bilderbuch Für Kinder. Carlson, Richard. 2019. (GER.). 24p. (J). pap. 10.99 *(978-1-0816-1898-8(1))* Independently Published.

—Deutsch-Amharisch Zeit Zweisprachiges Bilderbuch Für Kinder. Carlson Jr, Richard. 2018. (GER.). 28p. (J). pap. 10.99 *(978-1-7312-0955-9(X))* Independently Published.

Carlson, Suzanne. Deutsch-Arabisch Ich Wurde in Meinen Gef&#65533;hlen Verletzt Zweisprachiges Bilderbuch F&#65533;r Kinder. Carlson, Richard. 2019. (GER.). 24p. (J). pap. 10.99 ***(978-1-0884-0431-7(6))*** Independently Published.

Carlson, Suzanne. Deutsch-Arabisch Zeit Zweisprachiges Bilderbuch Für Kinder. Carlson Jr, Richard. 2018. (GER.). 28p. (J). pap. 10.99 *(978-1-7312-1024-1(8))* Independently Published.

—Deutsch-Armenisch Ich Wurde in Meinen Gefühlen Verletzt/Ես վիրավորված եմ Zweisprachiges Bilderbuch Für Kinder. Carlson, Richard. 2019. (GER.). 24p. (J). pap. 10.99 *(978-1-0816-2325-8(X))* Independently Published.

—Deutsch-Armenisch Zeit Zweisprachiges Bilderbuch Für Kinder. Carlson Jr, Richard. 2018. (GER.). 28p. (J). pap. 10.99 *(978-1-7902-0023-8(7))* Independently Published.

—Deutsch-Aserbaidschanisch Ich Wurde in Meinen Gefühlen Verletzt/Hisslərim Yaralandı Zweisprachiges Bilderbuch Für Kinder. Carlson, Richard. 2019. (GER.). 24p. (J). pap. 10.99 *(978-1-0816-2622-8(4))* Independently Published.

—Deutsch-Aserbaidschanisch Zeit/Zaman Zweisprachiges Bilderbuch Für Kinder. Carlson Jr, Richard. 2018. (GER.). 28p. (J). pap. 10.99 *(978-1-7902-0045-0(8))* Independently Published.

—Deutsch-Baskisch Ich Wurde in Meinen Gefühlen Verletzt/Nire Sentimenduak Minduta Zweisprachiges Bilderbuch Für Kinder. Carlson, Richard. 2019. (GER.). 24p. (J). pap. 10.99 *(978-1-0816-2950-2(9))* Independently Published.

—Deutsch-Baskisch Zeit/Denbora Zweisprachiges Bilderbuch Für Kinder. Carlson Jr, Richard. 2018. (GER.). 28p. (J). pap. 10.99 *(978-1-7902-0080-1(6))* Independently Published.

—Deutsch-Bengalisch Ich Wurde in Meinen Gefühlen Verletzt Zweisprachiges Bilderbuch Für Kinder. Carlson, Richard. 2019. (GER.). 24p. (J). pap. 10.99 *(978-1-0817-7057-0(0))* Independently Published.

—Deutsch-Bengalisch Zeit Zweisprachiges Bilderbuch Für Kinder. Carlson Jr, Richard. 2018. (GER.). 28p. (J). pap. 10.99 *(978-1-7902-4094-4(8))* Independently Published.

—Deutsch-Birmanisch Ich Wurde in Meinen Gefühlen Verletzt Zweisprachiges Bilderbuch Für Kinder. Carlson, Richard. 2019. (GER.). 24p. (J). pap. 10.99 *(978-1-0817-9104-9(7))* Independently Published.

—Deutsch-Birmanisch Zeit Zweisprachiges Bilderbuch Für Kinder. Carlson Jr, Richard. 2018. (GER.). 28p. (J). pap. 10.99 *(978-1-7903-2878-9(0))* Independently Published.

—Deutsch-Bosnisch Ich Wurde in Meinen Gefühlen Verletzt/Moja Osjecanja Su Povrijeđena Zweisprachiges Bilderbuch Für Kinder. Carlson, Richard. 2019. (GER.). 24p. (J). pap. 10.99 *(978-1-0817-7891-0(1))* Independently Published.

—Deutsch-Bosnisch Zeit/Vrijeme Zweisprachiges Bilderbuch Für Kinder. Carlson Jr, Richard. 2018. (GER.). 28p. (J). pap. 10.99 *(978-1-7903-2471-2(8))* Independently Published.

—Deutsch-Bulgarisch Ich Wurde in Meinen Gefühlen Verletzt/Чувствата ми са наранени Zweisprachiges Bilderbuch Für Kinder. Carlson, Richard. 2019. (GER.). 24p. (J). pap. 10.99 *(978-1-0817-8570-3(5))* Independently Published.

—Deutsch-Bulgarisch Zeit Zweisprachiges Bilderbuch Für Kinder. Carlson Jr, Richard. 2018. (GER.). 28p. (J). pap. 10.99 *(978-1-7903-2720-1(2))* Independently Published.

—Deutsch-Chinesisch Kantonesisch Traditional Ich Wurde in Meinen Gefühlen Verletzt/我的情感受到了傷害 Zweisprachiges Bilderbuch Für Kinder. Carlson, Richard. 2019. (GER.). 24p. (J). pap. 10.99 *(978-1-0828-0859-3(8))* Independently Published.

—Deutsch-Chinesisch Kantonesisch Traditional Zeit Zweisprachiges Bilderbuch Für Kinder. Carlson Jr, Richard. 2018. (GER.). 28p. (J). pap. 10.99 *(978-1-7905-0199-1(7))* Independently Published.

—Deutsch-Chinesisch Traditional Mandarin (Taiwan) Ich Wurde in Meinen Gefühlen Verletzt/我的感覺受傷了Zweisprachiges Bilderbuch Für Kinder. Carlson, Richard. 2019. (GER.). 24p. (J). pap. 10.99 *(978-1-0828-1084-8(3))* Independently Published.

—Deutsch-Chinesisch Traditional Mandarin (Taiwan) Zeit Zweisprachiges Bilderbuch Für Kinder. Carlson Jr, Richard. 2018. (GER.). 28p. (J). pap. 10.99 *(978-1-7905-0309-4(4))* Independently Published.

—Deutsch-Dänisch Ich Wurde in Meinen Gefühlen Verletzt/Mine Følelser Blev Såret Zweisprachiges Bilderbuch Für Kinder. Carlson, Richard. 2019. (GER.). 24p. (J). pap. 10.99 *(978-1-0831-4172-9(4))* Independently Published.

—Deutsch-Dänisch Zeit/Tid Zweisprachiges Bilderbuch Für Kinder. Carlson Jr, Richard. 2018. (GER.). 28p. (J). pap. 10.99 *(978-1-7906-3153-7(X))* Independently Published.

Carlson, Suzanne. Deutsch-Dari Ich Wurde in Meinen Gef&#65533;hlen Verletzt Zweisprachiges Bilderbuch F&#65533;r Kinder. Carlson, Richard. 2019. (GER.). 24p. (J). pap. 10.99 ***(978-1-0885-7681-6(8))*** Independently Published.

Carlson, Suzanne. Deutsch-Dari Zeit Zweisprachiges Bilderbuch Für Kinder. Carlson Jr, Richard. 2018. (GER.). 28p. (J). pap. 10.99 *(978-1-7906-3179-7(3))* Independently Published.

—Deutsch-Englisch Ich Wurde in Meinen Gefühlen Verletzt/My Feelings Are Hurt Zweisprachiges Bilderbuch Für Kinder. Carlson, Richard. 2019. (GER.). 24p. (J). pap. 10.99 *(978-1-0814-3942-2(4))* Independently Published.

—Deutsch-Englisch Zeit/Time Zweisprachiges Bilderbuch Für Kinder. Carlson Jr, Richard. 2018. (GER.). 28p. (J). pap. 10.99 *(978-1-7311-6893-1(4))* Independently Published.

—Deutsch-Estnisch Ich Wurde in Meinen Gefühlen Verletzt/Mu Tunded Said Haavata Zweisprachiges Bilderbuch Für Kinder. Carlson, Richard. 2019. (GER.). 24p. (J). pap. 10.99 *(978-1-0831-5001-1(4))* Independently Published.

—Deutsch-Estnisch Zeit/Aeg Zweisprachiges Bilderbuch Für Kinder. Carlson Jr, Richard. 2018. (GER.). 28p. (J). pap. 10.99 *(978-1-7906-3469-9(5))* Independently Published.

—Deutsch-Finnisch Ich Wurde in Meinen Gefühlen Verletzt/Tunteitani on Loukattu Zweisprachiges Bilderbuch Für Kinder. Carlson, Richard. 2019. (GER.). 24p. (J). pap. 10.99 *(978-1-0831-5854-3(6))* Independently Published.

—Deutsch-Finnisch Zeit/Aika Zweisprachiges Bilderbuch Für Kinder. Carlson Jr, Richard. 2018. (GER.). 28p. (J). pap. 10.99 *(978-1-7906-6999-8(5))* Independently Published.

—Deutsch-Flämisch (Belgisch) Ich Wurde in Meinen Gefühlen Verletzt/Mijn Gevoelens Zijn Gekwetst Zweisprachiges Bilderbuch Für Kinder. Carlson, Richard. 2019. (GER.). 24p. (J). pap. 10.99 *(978-1-0858-1753-0(9))* Independently Published.

—Deutsch-Flämisch (Belgisch) Zeit/de Tijd Zweisprachiges Bilderbuch Für Kinder. Carlson Jr, Richard. 2018. (GER.). 28p. (J). pap. 10.99 *(978-1-7906-7209-7(0))* Independently Published.

—Deutsch-Französisch Ich Wurde in Meinen Gefühlen Verletzt/on a Blessé Mes Sentiments Zweisprachiges Bilderbuch Für Kinder. Carlson, Richard. 2019. (GER.). 24p. (J). pap. 10.99 *(978-1-0858-5324-8(1))* Independently Published.

—Deutsch-Französisch Zeit/le Temps Zweisprachiges Bilderbuch Für Kinder. Carlson Jr, Richard. 2018. (GER.). 28p. (J). pap. 10.99 *(978-1-7906-7279-0(1))* Independently Published.

—Deutsch-Galizisch Ich Wurde in Meinen Gefühlen Verletzt/Os Meus Sentimentos Están Feridos Zweisprachiges Bilderbuch Für Kinder. Carlson, Richard. 2019. (GER.). 24p. (J). pap. 10.99 *(978-1-0858-6941-6(5))* Independently Published.

—Deutsch-Georgisch Ich Wurde in Meinen Gefühlen Verletzt/ჩემიგრძნობებიშეურაცხყოფილია Zweispra. Carlson, Richard. 2019. (GER.). 24p. (J). pap. 10.99 *(978-1-0858-7467-0(2))* Independently Published.

—Deutsch-Georgisch Zeit Zweisprachiges Bilderbuch Für Kinder. Carlson Jr, Richard. 2018. (GER.). 28p. (J). pap. 10.99 *(978-1-7906-7341-4(0))* Independently Published.

—Deutsch-Griechisch Ich Wurde in Meinen Gefühlen Verletzt/Πληγώθηκαν ΤαΣυναισθήματά Μου Zweisprachiges Bilderbuch Für Kin. Carlson, Richard. 2019. (GER.). 24p. (J). pap. 10.99 *(978-1-0858-7776-3(0))* Independently Published.

—Deutsch-Griechisch Zeit Zweisprachiges Bilderbuch Für Kinder. Carlson Jr, Richard. 2018. (GER.). 28p. (J). pap. 10.99 *(978-1-7906-7479-4(4))* Independently Published.

Carlson, Suzanne. Deutsch-Gujarati Ich Wurde in Meinen Gef&#65533;hlen Verletzt Zweisprachiges Bilderbuch F&#65533;r Kinder. Carlson, Richard. 2019. (GER.). 24p. (J). pap. 10.99 ***(978-1-0860-6721-7(5))*** Independently Published.

Carlson, Suzanne. Deutsch-Gujarati Zeit Zweisprachiges Bilderbuch Für Kinder. Carlson Jr, Richard. 2018. (GER.). 28p. (J). pap. 10.99 *(978-1-7907-0077-6(9))* Independently Published.

Carlson, Suzanne. Deutsch-Haitianische Sprache Ich Wurde in Meinen Gef&#65533;hlen Verletzt/Santiman M Blese Zweisprachiges Bilderbuch F&#65533;r Kinder. Carlson, Richard. 2019. (GER.). 24p. (J). pap. 10.99 ***(978-1-0860-6576-3(X))*** Independently Published.

Carlson, Suzanne. Deutsch-Haitianische Sprache Zeit/Tan Zweisprachiges Bilderbuch Für Kinder. Carlson Jr, Richard. 2018. (GER.). 28p. (J). pap. 10.99 *(978-1-7907-3163-3(1))* Independently Published.

Carlson, Suzanne. Deutsch-Hausa Ich Wurde in Meinen Gef&#65533;hlen Verletzt/Na Ji Jikkata Zweisprachiges Bilderbuch F&#65533;r Kinder. Carlson, Richard. 2019. (GER.). 24p. (J). pap. 10.99 ***(978-1-0860-8007-0(6))*** Independently Published.

Carlson, Suzanne. Deutsch-Hausa Zeit/Lokaci Zweisprachiges Bilderbuch Für Kinder. Carlson Jr, Richard. 2018. (GER.). 28p. (J). pap. 10.99 *(978-1-7907-3199-2(2))* Independently Published.

Carlson, Suzanne. Deutsch-Hebr&#65533;isch Ich Wurde in Meinen Gef&#65533;hlen Verletzt Zweisprachiges Bilderbuch F&#65533;r Kinder. Carlson, Richard. 2019. (GER.). 24p. (J). pap. 10.99 ***(978-1-0885-8183-4(8))*** Independently Published.

—Deutsch-Hindi Ich Wurde in Meinen Gef&#65533;hlen Verletzt Zweisprachiges Bilderbuch F&#65533;r Kinder. Carlson, Richard. 2019. (GER.). 24p. (J). pap. 10.99 ***(978-1-0860-8240-1(0))*** Independently Published.

Carlson, Suzanne. Deutsch-Hindi Zeit Zweisprachiges Bilderbuch Für Kinder. Carlson Jr, Richard. 2018. (GER.). 28p. (J). pap. 10.99 *(978-1-7907-3306-4(5))* Independently Published.

Carlson, Suzanne. Deutsch-Indonesisch Ich Wurde in Meinen Gef&#65533;hlen Verletzt/Perasaanku Terluka Zweisprachiges Bilderbuch F&#65533;r Kinder. Carlson, Richard. 2019. (GER.). 24p. (J). pap. 10.99 ***(978-1-0862-8167-5(5))*** Independently Published.

Carlson, Suzanne. Deutsch-Indonesisch Zeit/Waktu Zweisprachiges Bilderbuch Für Kinder. Carlson Jr, Richard. 2018. (GER.). 28p. (J). pap. 10.99 *(978-1-7907-4691-0(4))* Independently Published.

Carlson, Suzanne. Deutsch-Isl&#65533;ndisch Ich Wurde in Meinen Gef&#65533;hlen Verletzt/&#65533;g Er S&#65533;r&#65533;ur Zweisprachiges Bilderbuch F&#65533;r Kinder. Carlson, Richard. 2019. (GER.). 24p. (J). pap. 10.99 ***(978-1-0860-9065-9(9))*** Independently Published.

Carlson, Suzanne. Deutsch-Isländisch Zeit/Tími Zweisprachiges Bilderbuch Für Kinder. Carlson Jr, Richard. 2018. (GER.). 28p. (J). pap. 10.99 *(978-1-7907-4603-3(5))* Independently Published.

Carlson, Suzanne. Deutsch-Italienisch Ich Wurde in Meinen Gef&#65533;hlen Verletzt/Mi Sento Ferito Zweisprachiges Bilderbuch F&#65533;r Kinder. Carlson, Richard. 2019. (GER.). 24p. (J). pap. 10.99 ***(978-1-0862-9666-2(4))*** Independently Published.

Carlson, Suzanne. Deutsch-Italienisch Zeit/Tempo Zweisprachiges Bilderbuch Für Kinder. Carlson Jr, Richard. 2018. (GER.). 28p. (J). pap. 10.99 *(978-1-7909-5140-6(2))* Independently Published.

Carlson, Suzanne. Deutsch-Japanisch Ich Wurde in Meinen Gef&#65533;hlen Verletzt/ぼくは傷ついた Zweisprachiges Bilderbuch F&#65533;r Kinder. Carlson, Richard. 2019. (GER.). 24p. (J). pap. 10.99 ***(978-1-0863-0117-5(X))*** Independently Published.

—Deutsch-Jiddisch Ich Wurde in Meinen Gef&#65533;hlen Verletzt Zweisprachiges Bilderbuch F&#65533;r Kinder. Carlson, Richard. 2019. (GER.). 24p. (J). pap. 10.99 ***(978-1-6942-0568-1(1))*** Independently Published.

—Deutsch-Kannada Ich Wurde in Meinen Gef&#65533;hlen Verletzt Zweisprachiges Bilderbuch F&#65533;r Kinder. Carlson, Richard. 2019. (GER.). 24p. (J). pap. 10.99 ***(978-1-0864-9110-4(6))*** Independently Published.

Carlson, Suzanne. Deutsch-Kannada Zeit Zweisprachiges Bilderbuch Für Kinder. Carlson Jr, Richard. 2018. (GER.). 28p. (J). pap. 10.99 *(978-1-7909-5321-9(9))* Independently Published.

Carlson, Suzanne. Deutsch-Kasachisch Ich Wurde in Meinen Gef�hlen Verletzt/Сезімтал балатуралыоқиға Zweisprachiges Bilderbuch F�r Kind. Carlson, Richard. 2019. (GER.). 24p. (J). pap. 10.99 ***(978-1-0865-0459-0(3))*** Independently Published.

Carlson, Suzanne. Deutsch-Kasachisch Zeit Zweisprachiges Bilderbuch Für Kinder. Carlson Jr, Richard. 2018. (GER.). 28p. (J). pap. 10.99 *(978-1-7909-9253-9(2))* Independently Published.

—Deutsch-Katalanisch Ich Wurde in Meinen Gefühlen Verletzt/M'han Ferit Els Meus Sentiments Zweisprachiges Bilderbuch Für Kinder. Carlson, Richard. 2019. (GER.). 24p. (J). pap. 10.99 *(978-1-0821-2716-8(7))* Independently Published.

—Deutsch-Katalanisch Zeit/el Temps Zweisprachiges Bilderbuch Für Kinder. Carlson Jr, Richard. 2018. (GER.). 28p. (J). pap. 10.99 *(978-1-7904-0911-2(X))* Independently Published.

Carlson, Suzanne. Deutsch-Koreanisch Ich Wurde in Meinen Gef�hlen Verletzt/마음이아팠어요 Zweisprachiges Bilderbuch F�r Kinder. Carlson, Richard. 2019. (GER.). 24p. (J). pap. 10.99 ***(978-1-0869-2249-3(2))*** Independently Published.

Carlson, Suzanne. Deutsch-Koreanisch Zeit Zweisprachiges Bilderbuch Für Kinder. Carlson Jr, Richard. 2018. (GER.). 28p. (J). pap. 10.99 *(978-1-7909-9672-8(4))* Independently Published.

—Deutsch-Kroatisch Ich Wurde in Meinen Gefühlen Verletzt/Moji Osjecaji Su Povrijeđeni Zweisprachiges Bilderbuch Für Kinder. Carlson, Richard. 2019. (GER.). 24p. (J). pap. 10.99 *(978-1-0828-1302-3(8))* Independently Published.

—Deutsch-Kroatisch Zeit/Vrijeme Zweisprachiges Bilderbuch Für Kinder. Carlson Jr, Richard. 2018. (GER.). 28p. (J). pap. 10.99 *(978-1-7905-5441-6(1))* Independently Published.

—Deutsch-Kurdisch Zeit Zweisprachiges Bilderbuch Für Kinder. Carlson Jr, Richard. 2018. (GER.). 28p. (J). pap. 10.99 *(978-1-7909-9868-5(9))* Independently Published.

Carlson, Suzanne. Deutsch-Laotisch Ich Wurde in Meinen Gef�hlen Verletzt Zweisprachiges Bilderbuch F�r Kinder. Carlson, Richard. 2019. (GER.). 24p. (J). pap. 10.99 ***(978-1-0870-9286-7(8))*** Independently Published.

Carlson, Suzanne. Deutsch-Laotisch Zeit Zweisprachiges Bilderbuch Für Kinder. Carlson Jr, Richard. 2018. (GER.). 28p. (J). pap. 10.99 *(978-1-7909-9926-2(X))* Independently Published.

Carlson, Suzanne. Deutsch-Lettisch Ich Wurde in Meinen Gef�hlen Verletzt/Es Esmu Sāpināts Zweisprachiges Bilderbuch F�r Kinder. Carlson, Richard. 2019. (GER.). 24p. (J). pap. 10.99 ***(978-1-0873-0348-2(6))*** Independently Published.

Carlson, Suzanne. Deutsch-Lettisch Zeit/Laiks Zweisprachiges Bilderbuch Für Kinder. Carlson Jr, Richard. 2018. (GER.). 28p. (J). pap. 10.99 *(978-1-7913-3876-3(3))* Independently Published.

Carlson, Suzanne. Deutsch-Litauisch Ich Wurde in Meinen Gef�hlen Verletzt/Mane įskaudino Zweisprachiges Bilderbuch F�r Kinder. Carlson, Richard. 2019. (GER.). 24p. (J). pap. 10.99 ***(978-1-0873-1002-2(4))*** Independently Published.

Carlson, Suzanne. Deutsch-Litauisch Zeit/Laikas Zweisprachiges Bilderbuch Für Kinder. Carlson Jr, Richard. 2018. (GER.). 28p. (J). pap. 10.99 *(978-1-7913-4902-8(1))* Independently Published.

Carlson, Suzanne. Deutsch-Malaiisch Ich Wurde in Meinen Gef�hlen Verletzt/Perasaan Saya Disakiti Zweisprachiges Bilderbuch F�r Kinder. Carlson, Richard. 2019. (GER.). 24p. (J). pap. 10.99 ***(978-1-0873-1125-8(X))*** Independently Published.

Carlson, Suzanne. Deutsch-Malaiisch Zeit/Masa Zweisprachiges Bilderbuch Für Kinder. Carlson Jr, Richard. 2018. (GER.). 28p. (J). pap. 10.99 *(978-1-7913-5248-6(0))* Independently Published.

—Deutsch-Malayalam Zeit Zweisprachiges Bilderbuch Für Kinder. Carlson Jr, Richard. 2018. (GER.). 28p. (J). pap. 10.99 *(978-1-7913-5329-2(0))* Independently Published.

Carlson, Suzanne. Deutsch-Maltesisch Ich Wurde in Meinen Gef�hlen Verletzt/Weġġgħuni Zweisprachiges Bilderbuch F�r Kinder. Carlson, Richard. 2019. (GER.). 24p. (J). pap. 10.99 ***(978-1-0873-1177-7(2))*** Independently Published.

Carlson, Suzanne. Deutsch-Maltesisch Zeit/in Zweisprachiges Bilderbuch Für Kinder. Carlson Jr, Richard. 2018. (GER.). 28p. (J). pap. 10.99 *(978-1-7913-5384-1(3))* Independently Published.

Carlson, Suzanne. Deutsch-Marathi Ich Wurde in Meinen Gef�hlen Verletzt/माझ्या भावनादुखावल्यागेल्याआह&# Carlson, Richard. 2019. (GER.). 24p. (J). pap. 10.99 ***(978-1-0873-1240-8(X))*** Independently Published.

Carlson, Suzanne. Deutsch-Marathi Zeit Zweisprachiges Bilderbuch Für Kinder. Carlson Jr, Richard. 2018. (GER.). 28p. (J). pap. 10.99 *(978-1-7913-5522-7(6))* Independently Published.

Carlson, Suzanne. Deutsch-Mazedonisch Ich Wurde in Meinen Gef�hlen Verletzt/Моитечувства сеповредени Zweisprachiges Bilderbuch F�r Kin. Carlson, Richard. 2019. (GER.). 24p. (J). pap. 10.99 ***(978-1-0873-1049-7(0))*** Independently Published.

Carlson, Suzanne. Deutsch-Mazedonisch Zeit Zweisprachiges Bilderbuch Für Kinder. Carlson Jr, Richard. 2018. (GER.). 28p. (J). pap. 10.99 *(978-1-7913-4989-9(7))* Independently Published.

—Deutsch-Mongolisch Zeit Zweisprachiges Bilderbuch Für Kinder. Carlson Jr, Richard. 2018. (GER.). 28p. (J). pap. 10.99 *(978-1-7913-8142-4(1))* Independently Published.

Carlson, Suzanne. Deutsch-Montenegrinisch Ich Wurde in Meinen Gef�hlen Verletzt/Moja Osjecanja Su Povrijeđena Zweisprachiges Bilderbuch F�r Kinder. Carlson, Richard. 2019. (GER.). 24p. (J). pap. 10.99 ***(978-1-0873-1378-8(3))*** Independently Published.

Carlson, Suzanne. Deutsch-Montenegrinisch Zeit/Vrijeme Zweisprachiges Bilderbuch Für Kinder. Carlson Jr, Richard. 2018. (GER.). 28p. (J). pap. 10.99 *(978-1-7913-8333-6(5))* Independently Published.

Carlson, Suzanne. Deutsch-Nepalesisch Ich Wurde in Meinen Gef�hlen Verletzt Zweisprachiges Bilderbuch F�r Kinder. Carlson, Richard. 2019. (GER.). 24p. (J). pap. 10.99 ***(978-1-6934-5880-4(2))*** Independently Published.

Carlson, Suzanne. Deutsch-Nepalesisch Zeit Zweisprachiges Bilderbuch Für Kinder. Carlson Jr, Richard. 2018. (GER.). 28p. (J). pap. 10.99 *(978-1-7915-1276-7(3))* Independently Published.

—Deutsch-Niederländisch Ich Wurde in Meinen Gefühlen Verletzt/Mijn Gevoelens Zijn Gekwetst Zweisprachiges Bilderbuch Für Kinder. Carlson, Richard. 2019. (GER.). 24p. (J). pap. 10.99 *(978-1-0831-4744-8(7))* Independently Published.

—Deutsch-Niederländisch Zeit/Tijd Zweisprachiges Bilderbuch Für Kinder. Carlson Jr, Richard. 2018. (GER.). 28p. (J). pap. 10.99 *(978-1-7906-3353-1(2))* Independently Published.

Carlson, Suzanne. Deutsch-Norwegisch Ich Wurde in Meinen Gef�hlen Verletzt/F�lelsene Mine Er S�ret Zweisprachiges Bilderbuch F�r Kinder. Carlson, Richard. 2019. (GER.). 24p. (J). pap. 10.99 ***(978-1-0873-1446-4(1))*** Independently Published.

Carlson, Suzanne. Deutsch-Norwegisch Zeit/Tid Zweisprachiges Bilderbuch Für Kinder. Carlson Jr, Richard. 2018. (GER.). 28p. (J). pap. 10.99 *(978-1-7915-5998-4(0))* Independently Published.

Carlson, Suzanne. Deutsch-Pandschabisch Ich Wurde in Meinen Gef�hlen Verletzt Zweisprachiges Bilderbuch F�r Kinder. Carlson, Richard. 2019. (GER.). 24p. (J). pap. 10.99 ***(978-1-0874-7857-9(X))*** Independently Published.

Carlson, Suzanne. Deutsch-Pandschabisch Zeit Zweisprachiges Bilderbuch Für Kinder. Carlson Jr, Richard. 2018. (GER.). 28p. (J). pap. 10.99 *(978-1-7915-6845-0(9))* Independently Published.

Carlson, Suzanne. Deutsch-Paschtu Ich Wurde in Meinen Gef�hlen Verletzt Zweisprachiges Bilderbuch F�r Kinder. Carlson, Richard. 2019. (GER.). 24p. (J). pap. 10.99 ***(978-1-6934-6374-7(1))*** Independently Published.

Carlson, Suzanne. Deutsch-Paschtu Zeit Zweisprachiges Bilderbuch Für Kinder. Carlson Jr, Richard. 2018. (GER.). 28p. (J). pap. 10.99 *(978-1-7915-6152-9(7))* Independently Published.

Carlson, Suzanne. Deutsch-Persisch (Farsi) Ich Wurde in Meinen Gef�hlen Verletzt Zweisprachiges Bilderbuch F�r Kinder. Carlson, Richard. 2019. (GER.). 24p. (J). pap. 10.99 ***(978-1-6934-6708-0(9))*** Independently Published.

Carlson, Suzanne. Deutsch-Persisch (Farsi) Zeit Zweisprachiges Bilderbuch Für Kinder. Carlson Jr, Richard. 2018. (GER.). 28p. (J). pap. 10.99 *(978-1-7915-6233-5(7))* Independently Published.

Carlson, Suzanne. Deutsch-Polnisch Ich Wurde in Meinen Gef�hlen Verletzt/Zranione Uczucia Zweisprachiges Bilderbuch F�r Kinder. Carlson, Richard. 2019. (GER.). 24p. (J). pap. 10.99 ***(978-1-0873-1851-6(3))*** Independently Published.

Carlson, Suzanne. Deutsch-Polnisch Zeit/Czas Zweisprachiges Bilderbuch Für Kinder. Carlson Jr, Richard. 2018. (GER.). 28p. (J). pap. 10.99 *(978-1-7915-6282-3(5))* Independently Published.

Carlson, Suzanne. Deutsch-Portugiesisch (Brasilianisch) Ich Wurde in Meinen Gef�hlen Verletzt/Meus Sentimentos Est�o Feridos Zweisprachiges Bilderbuch F�r Kinder. Carlson, Richard. 2019. (GER.). 24p. (J). pap. 10.99 ***(978-1-0874-7534-9(1))*** Independently Published.

Carlson, Suzanne. Deutsch-Portugiesisch (Brasilianisch) Zeit/Tempo Zweisprachiges Bilderbuch Für Kinder. Carlson Jr, Richard. 2018. (GER.). 28p. (J). pap. 10.99 *(978-1-7915-6345-5(7))* Independently Published.

Carlson, Suzanne. Deutsch-Portugiesisch (Portugal) Ich Wurde in Meinen Gef�hlen Verletzt/Os Meus Sentimentos Est�o Feridos Zweisprachiges Bilderbuch F�r Kinder. Carlson, Richard. 2019. (GER.). 24p. (J). pap. 10.99 ***(978-1-0874-7678-0(X))*** Independently Published.

Carlson, Suzanne. Deutsch-Portugiesisch (Portugal) Zeit/ Tempo Zweisprachiges Bilderbuch Für Kinder. Carlson Jr, Richard. 2018. (GER.). 28p. (J). pap. 10.99 *(978-1-7915-6404-9(6))* Independently Published.

Carlson, Suzanne. Deutsch-Rum�nisch Ich Wurde in Meinen Gef�hlen Verletzt/Sunt Jignit Zweisprachiges Bilderbuch F�r Kinder. Carlson, Richard. 2019. (GER.). 24p. (J). pap. 10.99 ***(978-1-0874-7891-3(X))*** Independently Published.

Carlson, Suzanne. Deutsch-Rumänisch Zeit/Timpul Zweisprachiges Bilderbuch Für Kinder. Carlson Jr, Richard. 2018. (GER.). 28p. (J). pap. 10.99 *(978-1-7915-6905-1(6))* Independently Published.

Carlson, Suzanne. Deutsch-Russisch Ich Wurde in Meinen Gef�hlen Verletzt/Оскорбленныечувства Zweisprachiges Bilderbuch F�r Kinder. Carlson, Richard. 2019. (GER.). 24p. (J). pap. 10.99 ***(978-1-0874-8281-1(X))*** Independently Published.

Carlson, Suzanne. Deutsch-Russisch Zeit/Bpemr Zweisprachiges Bilderbuch Für Kinder. Carlson Jr, Richard. 2018. (GER.). 28p. (J). pap. 10.99 *(978-1-7915-7309-6(6))* Independently Published.

Carlson, Suzanne. Deutsch-Schwedisch Ich Wurde in Meinen Gef�hlen Verletzt/Mina K�nslor �r S�rade Zweisprachiges Bilderbuch F�r Kinder. Carlson, Richard. 2019. (GER.). 24p. (J). pap. 10.99 ***(978-1-6937-4327-6(2))*** Independently Published.

Carlson, Suzanne. Deutsch-Schwedisch Zeit/Tid Zweisprachiges Bilderbuch Für Kinder. Carlson Jr, Richard. 2018. (GER.). 28p. (J). pap. 10.99 *(978-1-7916-9082-3(3))* Independently Published.

Carlson, Suzanne. Deutsch-Serbisch (Kyrillisch) Ich Wurde in Meinen Gef�hlen Verletzt/Мојаосећања суповређена Zweisprachiges Bilderbuch F�r. Carlson, Richard. 2019. (GER.). 24p. (J). pap. 10.99 ***(978-1-6934-7299-2(6))*** Independently Published.

Carlson, Suzanne. Deutsch-Serbisch (Kyrillisch) Zeit Zweisprachiges Bilderbuch Für Kinder. Carlson Jr, Richard. 2018. (GER.). 28p. (J). pap. 10.99 *(978-1-7915-7434-5(3))* Independently Published.

Carlson, Suzanne. Deutsch-Serbisch (Latein) Ich Wurde in Meinen Gef�hlen Verletzt/Osecanja Su Mi Povređena Zweisprachiges Bilderbuch F�r Kinder. Carlson, Richard. 2019. (GER.). 24p. (J). pap. 10.99 ***(978-1-6934-8020-1(4))*** Independently Published.

Carlson, Suzanne. Deutsch-Serbisch (Latein) Zeit/Vreme Zweisprachiges Bilderbuch Für Kinder. Carlson Jr, Richard. 2018. (GER.). 28p. (J). pap. 10.99 *(978-1-7915-7550-2(1))* Independently Published.

Carlson, Suzanne. Deutsch-Singhalesisch Ich Wurde in Meinen Gef�hlen Verletzt Zweisprachiges Bilderbuch F�r Kinder. Carlson, Richard. 2019. (GER.). 24p. (J). pap. 10.99 ***(978-1-6936-3130-6(X))*** Independently Published.

Carlson, Suzanne. Deutsch-Singhalesisch Zeit Zweisprachiges Bilderbuch Für Kinder. Carlson Jr, Richard. 2018. (GER.). 28p. (J). pap. 10.99 *(978-1-7915-7859-6(4))* Independently Published.

Carlson, Suzanne. Deutsch-Slowakisch Ich Wurde in Meinen Gef�hlen Verletzt/Ranili Moje City Zweisprachiges Bilderbuch F�r Kinder. Carlson, Richard. 2019. (GER.). 24p. (J). pap. 10.99 ***(978-1-6937-1900-4(2))*** Independently Published.

Carlson, Suzanne. Deutsch-Slowakisch Zeit/as Zweisprachiges Bilderbuch Für Kinder. Carlson Jr, Richard. 2018. (GER.). 28p. (J). pap. 10.99 *(978-1-7916-3360-8(9))* Independently Published.

Carlson, Suzanne. Deutsch-Slowenisch Ich Wurde in Meinen Gef�hlen Verletzt/Moja Prizadeta čustva Zweisprachiges Bilderbuch F�r Kinder. Carlson, Richard. 2019. (GER.). 24p. (J). pap. 10.99 ***(978-1-6937-2143-4(0))*** Independently Published.

Carlson, Suzanne. Deutsch-Slowenisch Zeit/;as Zweisprachiges Bilderbuch Für Kinder. Carlson Jr, Richard. 2018. (GER.). 28p. (J). pap. 10.99 *(978-1-7916-3413-1(3))* Independently Published.

Carlson, Suzanne. Deutsch-Somalisch Ich Wurde in Meinen Gef�hlen Verletzt/Dareenadayda Ayaa Dhaawacmay Zweisprachiges Bilderbuch F�r Kinder. Carlson, Richard. 2019. (GER.). 24p. (J). pap. 10.99 ***(978-1-6937-2306-3(9))*** Independently Published.

Carlson, Suzanne. Deutsch-Somalisch Zeit/Waqti Zweisprachiges Bilderbuch Für Kinder. Carlson Jr, Richard. 2018. (GER.). 28p. (J). pap. 10.99 *(978-1-7916-3439-1(7))* Independently Published.

Carlson, Suzanne. Deutsch-Suaheli Ich Wurde in Meinen Gef�hlen Verletzt/Hisia Zangu Zinaumia Zweisprachiges Bilderbuch F�r Kinder. Carlson, Richard. 2019. (GER.). 24p. (J). pap. 10.99 ***(978-1-6937-3118-1(5))*** Independently Published.

Carlson, Suzanne. Deutsch-Suaheli Zeit/Muda Zweisprachiges Bilderbuch Für Kinder. Carlson Jr, Richard. 2018. (GER.). 28p. (J). pap. 10.99 *(978-1-7916-9044-1(0))* Independently Published.

Carlson, Suzanne. Deutsch-Tadschikisch Ich Wurde in Meinen Gef�hlen Verletzt/эҳсосотмҷриҳадоршуда Zweisprachiges Bilderbuch F�r Kinder. Carlson, Richard. 2019. (GER.). 24p. (J). pap. 10.99 ***(978-1-6939-5477-1(X))*** Independently Published.

—Deutsch-Tagalog Ich Wurde in Meinen Gef�hlen Verletzt/Nasaktan Ang Aking Damdamin Zweisprachiges Bilderbuch F�r Kinder. Carlson, Richard. 2019. (GER.). 24p. (J). pap. 10.99 ***(978-1-6939-5094-0(4))*** Independently Published.

Carlson, Suzanne. Deutsch-Tagalog Zeit/Oras Zweisprachiges Bilderbuch Für Kinder. Carlson Jr, Richard. 2018. (GER.). 28p. (J). pap. 10.99 *(978-1-7917-4379-6(X))* Independently Published.

Carlson, Suzanne. Deutsch-Tamilisch Ich Wurde in Meinen Gef�hlen Verletzt Zweisprachiges Bilderbuch F�r Kinder. Carlson, Richard. 2019. (GER.). 24p. (J). pap. 10.99 ***(978-1-6939-5822-9(8))*** Independently Published.

Carlson, Suzanne. Deutsch-Tamilisch Zeit Zweisprachiges Bilderbuch Für Kinder. Carlson, Richard. 2018. (GER.). 28p. (J). pap. 10.99 *(978-1-7917-4402-1(8))* Independently Published.

Carlson, Suzanne. Deutsch-T�rkisch Ich Wurde in Meinen Gef�hlen Verletzt/Duygularım İncindi Zweisprachiges Bilderbuch F�r Kinder. Carlson, Richard. 2019. (GER.). 24p. (J). pap. 10.99 ***(978-1-6941-9491-6(4))*** Independently Published.

—Deutsch-Telugu Ich Wurde in Meinen Gef�hlen Verletzt Zweisprachiges Bilderbuch F�r Kinder. Carlson, Richard. 2019. (GER.). 24p. (J). pap. 10.99 ***(978-1-6939-5984-4(4))*** Independently Published.

Carlson, Suzanne. Deutsch-Telugu Zeit Zweisprachiges Bilderbuch Für Kinder. Carlson Jr, Richard. 2018. (GER.). 28p. (J). pap. 10.99 *(978-1-7917-4423-6(0))* Independently Published.

Carlson, Suzanne. Deutsch-Thail�ndisch Ich Wurde in Meinen Gef�hlen Verletzt Zweisprachiges Bilderbuch F�r Kinder. Carlson, Richard. 2019. (GER.). 24p. (J). pap. 10.99 ***(978-1-6939-8095-4(9))*** Independently Published.

Carlson, Suzanne. Deutsch-Thailändisch Zeit Zweisprachiges Bilderbuch Für Kinder. Carlson Jr, Richard. 2018. (GER.). 28p. (J). pap. 10.99 *(978-1-7917-4477-9(X))* Independently Published.

Carlson, Suzanne. Deutsch-Tigrinja Ich Wurde in Meinen Gef�hlen Verletzt/ስምዒተይተጎዲኡ እዩ Zweisprachiges Bilderbuch F�r Kinder. Carlson, Richard. 2019. (GER.). 24p. (J). pap. 10.99 ***(978-1-6939-8763-2(5))*** Independently Published.

Carlson, Suzanne. Deutsch-Tigrinja Zeit Zweisprachiges Bilderbuch Für Kinder. Carlson Jr, Richard. 2018. (GER.). 28p. (J). pap. 10.99 *(978-1-7917-4542-4(3))* Independently Published.

—Deutsch-Traditional Chinesisch Mandarin Ich Wurde in Meinen Gefühlen Verletzt/我的情感受到了傷害 Zweisprachiges Bilderbuch Für Kinder. Carlson, Richard. 2019. (GER.). 24p. (J). pap. 10.99 *(978-1-0823-2449-9(3))* Independently Published.

—Deutsch-Traditional Chinesisch Mandarin Zeit Zweisprachiges Bilderbuch Für Kinder. Carlson Jr, Richard. 2018. (GER.). 28p. (J). pap. 10.99 *(978-1-7904-5681-9(9))* Independently Published.

—Deutsch-Tschechisch Ich Wurde in Meinen Gefühlen Verletzt/Mé City Jsou Zraněny Zweisprachiges Bilderbuch Für Kinder. Carlson, Richard. 2019. (GER.). 24p. (J). pap. 10.99 *(978-1-0828-1517-1(9))* Independently Published.

—Deutsch-Tschechisch Zeit/as Zweisprachiges Bilderbuch Für Kinder. Carlson Jr, Richard. 2018. (GER.). 28p. (J). pap. 10.99 *(978-1-7905-5487-4(X))* Independently Published.

—Deutsch-Türkisch Zeit/Zaman Zweisprachiges Bilderbuch Für Kinder. Carlson Jr, Richard. 2018. (GER.). 28p. (J). pap. 10.99 *(978-1-7917-4565-3(2))* Independently Published.

Carlson, Suzanne. Deutsch-Ukrainisch Ich Wurde in Meinen Gef�hlen Verletzt/Менезачепили заживе Zweisprachiges Bilderbuch F�r Kinder. Carlson, Richard. 2019. (GER.). 24p. (J). pap. 10.99 ***(978-1-6941-9755-9(7))*** Independently Published.

Carlson, Suzanne. Deutsch-Ukrainisch Zeit/ Zweisprachiges Bilderbuch Für Kinder. Carlson Jr, Richard. 2018. (GER.). 28p. (J). pap. 10.99 *(978-1-7917-4619-3(5))* Independently Published.

Carlson, Suzanne. Deutsch-Ungarisch Ich Wurde in Meinen Gef�hlen Verletzt/Megb�nt�dtam Zweisprachiges Bilderbuch F�r Kinder. Carlson, Richard. 2019. (GER.). 24p. (J). pap. 10.99 ***(978-1-0860-8678-2(3))*** Independently Published.

Carlson, Suzanne. Deutsch-Ungarisch Zeit Zweisprachiges Bilderbuch Für Kinder. Carlson Jr, Richard. 2018. (GER.). 28p. (J). pap. 10.99 *(978-1-7907-4536-4(5))* Independently Published.

Carlson, Suzanne. Deutsch-Urdu Ich Wurde in Meinen Gef�hlen Verletzt Zweisprachiges Bilderbuch F�r Kinder. Carlson, Richard. 2019. (GER.). 24p. (J). pap. 10.99 ***(978-1-6941-9892-1(8))*** Independently Published.

Carlson, Suzanne. Deutsch-Urdu Zeit Zweisprachiges Bilderbuch Für Kinder. Carlson Jr, Richard. 2018. (GER.). 28p. (J). pap. 10.99 *(978-1-7917-4648-3(9))* Independently Published.

Carlson, Suzanne. Deutsch-Usbekisch Ich Wurde in Meinen Gef�hlen Verletzt/His-Tuyg'ularim Yaralandi Zweisprachiges Bilderbuch F�r Kinder. Carlson, Richard. 2019. (GER.). 24p. (J). pap. 10.99 ***(978-1-6942-0046-4(9))*** Independently Published.

Carlson, Suzanne. Deutsch-Usbekisch Zeit/Vaqt Zweisprachiges Bilderbuch Für Kinder. Carlson Jr, Richard. 2018. (GER.). 28p. (J). pap. 10.99 *(978-1-7917-4677-3(2))* Independently Published.

—Deutsch-Vereinfachtes Chinesisch Mandarin Ich Wurde in Meinen Gefühlen Verletzt/我的感情受到了伤害 Zweisprachiges Bilderbuch Für Kinder. Carlson, Richard. 2019. (GER.). 24p. (J). pap. 10.99 *(978-1-0825-1477-7(2))* Independently Published.

—Deutsch-Vereinfachtes Chinesisch Mandarin Zeit Zweisprachiges Bilderbuch Für Kinder. Carlson Jr, Richard. 2018. (GER.). 28p. (J). pap. 10.99 *(978-1-7905-0144-1(X))* Independently Published.

Carlson, Suzanne. Deutsch-Vietnamesisch Ich Wurde in Meinen Gef�hlen Verletzt/Cảm X�c Của M�nh Bị Tổn Thương Zweisprachiges Bilderbuch F�r Kinder. Carlson, Richard. 2019. (GER.). 24p. (J). pap. 10.99 ***(978-1-6942-0177-5(5))*** Independently Published.

Carlson, Suzanne. Deutsch-Vietnamesisch Zeit/ Gian Zweisprachiges Bilderbuch Für Kinder. Carlson Jr, Richard. 2018. (GER.). 28p. (J). pap. 10.99 *(978-1-7917-4691-9(8))* Independently Published.

Carlson, Suzanne. Deutsch-Walisisch Ich Wurde in Meinen Gef�hlen Verletzt/Fy Nheimladau Yn Brifo Zweisprachiges Bilderbuch F�r Kinder. Carlson, Richard. 2019. (GER.). 24p. (J). pap. 10.99 ***(978-1-6942-0409-7(X))*** Independently Published.

Carlson, Suzanne. Deutsch-Weißrussisch Ich Wurde in Meinen Gefühlen Verletzt/Абражаныя пачуцці Zweisprachiges Bilderbuch Für Kinder. Carlson, Richard. 2019. (GER.). 24p. (J). pap. 10.99 *(978-1-0817-6887-4(8))* Independently Published.

—Deutsch-Weißrussisch Zeit Zweisprachiges Bilderbuch Für Kinder. Carlson Jr, Richard. 2018. (GER.). 28p. (J). pap. 10.99 *(978-1-7902-4053-1(0))* Independently Published.

—Deutsch-Xhosa Zeit/Ixesha Zweisprachiges Bilderbuch Für Kinder. Carlson Jr, Richard. 2018. (GER.). 28p. (J). pap. 10.99 *(978-1-7917-4721-3(3))* Independently Published.

Carlson, Suzanne. Deutsch-Yoruba Ich Wurde in Meinen Gef�hlen Verletzt/� d�n M� Iọ́k�n Mi Zweisprachiges Bilderbuch F�r Kinder. Carlson, Richard. 2019. (GER.). 24p. (J). pap. 10.99 ***(978-1-6942-0751-7(X))*** Independently Published.

Carlson, Suzanne. Deutsch-Yoruba Zeit/Àkókò Zweisprachiges Bilderbuch Für Kinder. Carlson Jr, Richard. 2018. (GER.). 28p. (J). pap. 10.99 *(978-1-7917-7554-4(3))* Independently Published.

Carlson, Suzanne. Deutsch-Zulu Ich Wurde in Meinen Gef�hlen Verletzt/Ngiphatheke Kabuhlungu Zweisprachiges Bilderbuch F�r Kinder. Carlson, Richard. 2019. (GER.). 24p. (J). pap. 10.99 ***(978-1-6942-0926-9(1))*** Independently Published.

Carlson, Suzanne. Deutsch-Zulu Zeit/Isikhathi Zweisprachiges Bilderbuch Für Kinder. Carlson Jr, Richard. 2018. (GER.). 28p. (J). pap. 10.99 *(978-1-7917-7602-2(7))* Independently Published.

—Deutsch/Irisch-Gälisch Zeit/Am Zweisprachiges Bilderbuch Für Kinder. Carlson Jr, Richard. 2018. (GER.). 28p. (J). pap. 10.99 *(978-1-7907-5515-8(8))* Independently Published.

Carlson, Suzanne. Deutsch/Irisch-G�lisch Ich Wurde in Meinen Gef�hlen Verletzt/T� M� Gortaithe Zweisprachiges Bilderbuch F�r Kinder. Carlson, Richard. 2019. (GER.). 24p. (J). pap. 10.99 ***(978-1-0862-9095-0(X))*** Independently Published.

—Deutsch/Kastilisch-Spanisch Ich Wurde in Meinen Gef�hlen Verletzt/Han Herido Mis Sentimientos Zweisprachiges Bilderbuch F�r Kinder. Carlson, Richard. 2019. (GER.). 24p. (J). pap. 10.99 ***(978-1-6937-2461-9(8))*** Independently Published.

Carlson, Suzanne. Deutsch/Kastilisch-Spanisch Zeit/Tiempo Zweisprachiges Bilderbuch Für Kinder. Carlson Jr, Richard. 2018. (GER.). 28p. (J). pap. 10.99 *(978-1-7916-3496-4(6))* Independently Published.

Carlson, Suzanne. Deutsch/Khmer-Sprache (Kambodschanisch) Ich Wurde in Meinen Gef�hlen Verletzt Zweisprachiges Bilderbuch F�r Kinder. Carlson, Richard. 2019. (GER.). 24p. (J). pap. 10.99 ***(978-1-0867-1789-1(9))*** Independently Published.

Carlson, Suzanne. Deutsch/Khmer-Sprache (Kambodschanisch) Zeit Zweisprachiges Bilderbuch Für Kinder. Carlson Jr, Richard. 2018. (GER.). 28p. (J). pap. 10.99 *(978-1-7909-9593-6(0))* Independently Published.

Carlson, Suzanne. Deutsch/Latein-Amerikanisch Spanisch Ich Wurde in Meinen Gef�hlen Verletzt/Han Herido Mis Sentimientos Zweisprachiges Bilderbuch F�r Kinder. Carlson, Richard. 2019. (GER.). 24p. (J). pap. 10.99 ***(978-1-6937-2817-4(6))*** Independently Published.

Carlson, Suzanne. Deutsch/Latein-Amerikanisch Spanisch Zeit/Tiempo Zweisprachiges Bilderbuch Für Kinder. Carlson Jr, Richard. 2018. (GER.). 28p. (J). pap. 10.99 *(978-1-7916-3541-1(5))* Independently Published.

Carlson, Suzanne. Deutsch/Shanghai-Dialekt Ich Wurde in Meinen Gef�hlen Verletzt/我的感情受到了伤害 Zweisprachiges Bilderbuch F�r Kinder. Carlson, Richard. 2019. (GER.). 24p. (J). pap. 10.99 ***(978-1-6934-8345-5(9))*** Independently Published.

Carlson, Suzanne. Deutsch/Shanghai-Dialekt Zeit Zweisprachiges Bilderbuch Für Kinder. Carlson Jr, Richard. 2018. (GER.). 28p. (J). pap. 10.99 *(978-1-7915-7745-2(8))* Independently Published.

—English-Afrikaans My Feelings Are Hurt/My Gevoelens Is Gekwets Children's Bilingual Picture Book. Carlson, Richard. 2019. (ENG.). 24p. (J). pap. 10.99 *(978-1-0744-4439-6(6))* Independently Published.

Carlson, Suzanne. English-Afrikaans Outdoors/Buitelug Children's Bilingual Picture Dictionary. Carlson, Richard. 2019. (ENG.). 24p. (J). pap. 10.99 ***(978-1-6715-9585-9(8))*** Independently Published.

Carlson, Suzanne. English-Afrikaans Time/Tyd Children's Bilingual Picture Book. Carlson Jr, Richard. 2018. (ITA.). 28p. (J). pap. 10.99 *(978-1-7201-9389-0(4))* Independently Published.

—English-Afrikaans Trouble/Moeilikheid Children's Bilingual Picture Book. Carlson Jr, Richard. 2018. (ENG.). 24p. (J). pap. 10.99 *(978-1-7313-6673-3(6))* Independently Published.

—English-Albanian My Feelings Are Hurt/Ndjenjat e Mia Janë Të lënduara Children's Bilingual Picture Book. Carlson, Richard. 2019. (ENG.). 24p. (J). pap. 10.99 *(978-1-0744-4887-5(1))* Independently Published.

—English-Albanian Time/Koha Children's Bilingual Picture Book. Carlson Jr, Richard. 2018. (ENG.). 28p. (J). pap. 10.99 *(978-1-7201-9400-2(9))* Independently Published.

—English-Albanian Trouble/Shqetësim Children's Bilingual Picture Book. Carlson Jr, Richard. 2018. (ENG.). 24p. (J). pap. 10.99 *(978-1-7313-6723-5(6))* Independently Published.

—English-Amharic My Feelings Are Hurt/ስሜቴ ተጎድቷል Children's Bilingual Picture Book. Carlson, Richard. 2019. (ENG.). 24p. (J). pap. 10.99 *(978-1-0744-5493-7(6))* Independently Published.

—English-Amharic Time Children's Bilingual Picture Book. Carlson Jr, Richard. 2018. (ENG.). 28p. (J). pap. 10.99 *(978-1-7201-9422-4(X))* Independently Published.

—English-Amharic Trouble Children's Bilingual Picture Book. Carlson Jr, Richard. 2018. (ENG.). 24p. (J). pap. 10.99 *(978-1-7313-6799-0(6))* Independently Published.

—English-Arabic My Feelings Are Hurt/جرحت مشاعري Children's Bilingual Picture Book. Carlson, Richard. 2019. (ENG.). 24p. (J). pap. 10.99 *(978-1-0767-8218-2(3))* Independently Published.

—English-Arabic Time Children's Bilingual Picture Book. Carlson Jr, Richard. 2018. (ENG.). 28p. (J). pap. 10.99 *(978-1-7201-9432-3(7))* Independently Published.

—English-Arabic Trouble Children's Bilingual Picture Book. Carlson Jr, Richard. 2018. (ENG.). 24p. (J). pap. 10.99 *(978-1-7312-1301-3(8))* Independently Published.

—English-Armenian My Feelings Are Hurt/Ես վիրավորված եմ Children's Bilingual Picture Book. Carlson, Richard. 2019. (ENG.). 24p. (J). pap. 10.99 *(978-1-0744-5762-4(5))* Independently Published.

—English-Armenian Time Children's Bilingual Picture Book. Carlson Jr, Richard. 2018. (ENG.). 28p. (J). pap. 10.99 *(978-1-7201-9451-4(3))* Independently Published.

—English-Armenian Trouble Children's Bilingual Picture Book. Carlson Jr, Richard. 2018. (ENG.). 24p. (J). pap. 10.99 *(978-1-7314-2168-5(0))* Independently Published.

—English-Azerbaijani My Feelings Are Hurt/Hisslərim Yaralandı Children's Bilingual Picture Book. Carlson, Richard. 2019. (ENG.). 24p. (J). pap. 10.99 *(978-1-0746-2473-6(4))* Independently Published.

—English-Azerbaijani Time/Zaman Children's Bilingual Picture Book. Carlson Jr, Richard. 2018. (ENG.). 28p. (J). pap. 10.99 *(978-1-7201-9754-6(7))* Independently Published.

—English-Azerbaijani Trouble Children's Bilingual Picture Book. Carlson Jr, Richard. 2018. (ENG.). 24p. (J). pap. 10.99 *(978-1-7314-2195-1(8))* Independently Published.

—English-Basque My Feelings Are Hurt/Nire Sentimenduak Minduta Children's Bilingual Picture Book. Carlson, Richard. 2019. (ENG.). 24p. (J). pap. 10.99 *(978-1-0746-6077-2(3))* Independently Published.

—English-Basque Time/Denbora Children's Bilingual Picture Book. Carlson Jr, Richard. 2018. (ENG.). 28p. (J). pap. 10.99 *(978-1-7201-9787-4(3))* Independently Published.

—English-Basque Trouble/Arazoa Children's Bilingual Picture Book. Carlson Jr, Richard. 2018. (ENG.). 24p. (J). pap. 10.99 *(978-1-7314-6671-6(4))* Independently Published.

—English-Belarusian My Feelings Are Hurt/Абражаныя пачуцці Children's Bilingual Picture Book. Carlson, Richard. 2019. (ENG.). 24p. (J). pap. 10.99 *(978-1-0746-6245-5(8))* Independently Published.

—English-Belarusian Time Children's Bilingual Picture Book. Carlson Jr, Richard. 2018. (ENG.). 28p. (J). pap. 10.99 *(978-1-7201-9816-1(0))* Independently Published.

—English-Belarusian Trouble Children's Bilingual Picture Book. Carlson Jr, Richard. 2018. (ENG.). 24p. (J). pap. 10.99 *(978-1-7314-6721-8(4))* Independently Published.

—English-Bengali My Feelings Are Hurt Children's Bilingual Picture Book. Carlson, Richard. 2019. (ENG.). 24p. (J). pap. 10.99 *(978-1-0746-6616-3(X))* Independently Published.

—English-Bengali Time Children's Bilingual Picture Book. Carlson Jr, Richard. 2018. (ENG.). 28p. (J). pap. 10.99 *(978-1-7201-9834-5(9))* Independently Published.

—English-Bengali Trouble Children's Bilingual Picture Book. Carlson Jr, Richard. 2018. (ENG.). 24p. (J). pap. 10.99 *(978-1-7314-6783-6(4))* Independently Published.

—English-Bosnian My Feelings Are Hurt/Moja Osjecanja Su Povrijeđena Children's Bilingual Picture Book. Carlson, Richard. 2019. (ENG.). 24p. (J). pap. 10.99 *(978-1-0746-6985-0(1))* Independently Published.

—English-Bosnian Time/Vrijeme Children's Bilingual Picture Book. Carlson Jr, Richard. 2018. (ENG.). 28p. (J). pap. 10.99 *(978-1-7201-9855-0(1))* Independently Published.

—English-Bosnian Trouble/Problem Children's Bilingual Picture Book. Carlson Jr, Richard. 2018. (ENG.). 24p. (J). pap. 10.99 *(978-1-7314-6859-8(8))* Independently Published.

—English-Bulgarian Time Children's Bilingual Picture Book. Carlson Jr, Richard. 2018. (ENG.). 28p. (J). pap. 10.99 *(978-1-7202-1819-7(6))* Independently Published.

—English-Burmese (Myanmar) My Feelings Are Hurt Children's Bilingual Picture Book. Carlson, Richard. 2019. (ENG.). 24p. (J). pap. 10.99 *(978-1-0746-7734-3(X))* Independently Published.

—English-Burmese (Myanmar) Time Children's Bilingual Picture Book. Carlson Jr, Richard. 2018. (ENG.). 28p. (J). pap. 10.99 *(978-1-7202-2005-3(0))* Independently Published.

—English-Burmese (Myanmar) Trouble Children's Bilingual Picture Book. Carlson Jr, Richard. 2018. (ENG.). 24p. (J). pap. 10.99 *(978-1-7315-0166-0(8))* Independently Published.

—English-Catalan My Feelings Are Hurt/M'han Ferit Els Meus Sentiments Children's Bilingual Picture Book. Carlson, Richard. 2019. (ENG.). 24p. (J). pap. 10.99 *(978-1-0748-8131-3(1))* Independently Published.

—English-Catalan Time/el Temps Children's Bilingual Picture Book. Carlson Jr, Richard. 2018. (ENG.). 28p. (J). pap. 10.99 *(978-1-7202-2300-9(9))* Independently Published.

—English-Catalan Trouble/Problemes Children's Bilingual Picture Book. Carlson Jr, Richard. 2018. (ENG.). 24p. (J). pap. 10.99 *(978-1-7315-0307-7(5))* Independently Published.

—English-Chinese Mandarin Traditional My Feelings Are Hurt/我的情感受到了傷害 Children's Bilingual Picture Book. Carlson, Richard. 2019. (ENG.). 24p. (J). pap. 10.99 *(978-1-0748-8277-8(6))* Independently Published.

—English-Chinese Mandarin Traditional Time Children's Bilingual Picture Book. Carlson Jr, Richard. 2018. (ENG.). 28p. (J). pap. 10.99 *(978-1-7202-2318-4(1))* Independently Published.

—English-Chinese Mandarin Traditional Trouble Children's Bilingual Picture Book. Carlson Jr, Richard. 2018. (ENG.). 24p. (J). pap. 10.99 *(978-1-7312-1329-7(8))* Independently Published.

—English-Chinese Simplified Mandarin My Feelings Are Hurt/我的感情受到了伤害 Children's Bilingual Picture Book. Carlson, Richard. 2019. (ENG.). 24p. (J). pap. 10.99 *(978-1-0749-9867-7(7))* Independently Published.

—English-Chinese Simplified (Mandarin) Time Children's Bilingual Picture Book. Carlson Jr, Richard. 2018. (ENG.). 28p. (J). pap. 10.99 *(978-1-7202-2412-9(9))* Independently Published.

—English-Chinese Simplified (Mandarin) Trouble Children's Bilingual Picture Book. Carlson Jr, Richard. 2018. (ENG.). 24p. (J). pap. 10.99 *(978-1-7315-0376-3(8))* Independently Published.

—English-Chinese Traditional Cantonese My Feelings Are Hurt/我的情感受到了傷害 Children's Bilingual Picture Book. Carlson, Richard. 2019. (ENG.). 24p. (J). pap. 10.99 *(978-1-0750-0370-7(9))* Independently Published.

—English-Chinese Traditional Cantonese Time Children's Bilingual Picture Book. Carlson Jr, Richard. 2018. (ENG.). 28p. (J). pap. 10.99 *(978-1-7202-2443-3(9))* Independently Published.

—English-Chinese Traditional Cantonese Trouble Children's Bilingual Picture Book. Carlson Jr, Richard. 2018. (ENG.). 24p. (J). pap. 10.99 *(978-1-7315-0463-0(2))* Independently Published.

—English-Chinese Traditional Mandarin (Taiwan) My Feelings Are Hurt/我的感覺受傷了 Children's Bilingual Picture Book. Carlson, Richard. 2019. (ENG.). 24p. (J). pap. 10.99 *(978-1-0750-7606-0(4))* Independently Published.

—English-Chinese Traditional Mandarin (Taiwan) Time Children's Bilingual Picture Book. Carlson Jr, Richard. 2018. (ENG.). 28p. (J). pap. 10.99 *(978-1-7202-2542-3(7))* Independently Published.

—English-Chinese Traditional Mandarin (Taiwan) Trouble Children's Bilingual Picture Book. Carlson Jr, Richard. 2018. (ENG.). 24p. (J). pap. 10.99 *(978-1-7315-0504-0(3))* Independently Published.

—English-Croatian My Feelings Are Hurt/Moji Osjecaji Su Povrijeđeni Children's Bilingual Picture Book. Carlson, Richard. 2019. (ENG.). 24p. (J). pap. 10.99 *(978-1-0751-1757-2(7))* Independently Published.

—English-Croatian Time/Vrijeme Children's Bilingual Picture Book. Carlson Jr, Richard. 2018. (ENG.). 28p. (J). pap. 10.99 *(978-1-7201-9888-8(8))* Independently Published.

—English-Croatian Trouble/Nevolja Children's Bilingual Picture Book. Carlson Jr, Richard. 2018. (ENG.). 24p. (J). pap. 10.99 *(978-1-7315-0565-1(5))* Independently Published.

—English-Czech My Feelings Are Hurt/Mé City Jsou Zraněny Children's Bilingual Picture Book. Carlson, Richard. 2019. (ENG.). 24p. (J). pap. 10.99 *(978-1-0751-1926-2(X))* Independently Published.

—English-Czech Time/ as Children's Bilingual Picture Book. Carlson Jr, Richard. 2018. (ENG.). 28p. (J). pap. 10.99 *(978-1-7202-2584-3(2))* Independently Published.

—English-Czech Trouble/Potíz Children's Bilingual Picture Book. Carlson Jr, Richard. 2018. (ENG.). 24p. (J). pap. 10.99 *(978-1-7315-0590-3(6))* Independently Published.

—English-Danish My Feelings Are Hurt/Mine Følelser Blev Såret Children's Bilingual Picture Book. Carlson, Richard. 2019. (ENG.). 24p. (J). pap. 10.99 *(978-1-0751-2094-7(2))* Independently Published.

—English-Danish Time/Tid Children's Bilingual Picture Book. Carlson Jr, Richard. 2018. (ENG.). 28p. (J). pap. 10.99 *(978-1-7202-4923-8(7))* Independently Published.

—English-Danish Trouble/Ballade Children's Bilingual Picture Book. Carlson Jr, Richard. 2018. (ENG.). 24p. (J). pap. 10.99 *(978-1-7315-0612-2(0))* Independently Published.

—English-Dari My Feelings Are Hurt Children's Bilingual Picture Book. Carlson, Richard. 2019. (ENG.). 24p. (J). pap. 10.99 *(978-1-0767-8390-5(2))* Independently Published.

—English-Dari Time Children's Bilingual Picture Book. Carlson Jr, Richard. 2018. (ENG.). 28p. (J). pap. 10.99 *(978-1-7202-5010-4(3))* Independently Published.

—English-Dari Trouble Children's Bilingual Picture Book. Carlson Jr, Richard. 2018. (ENG.). 24p. (J). pap. 10.99 *(978-1-7315-0956-7(1))* Independently Published.

—English-Dutch My Feelings Are Hurt/Mijn Gevoelens Zijn Gekwetst Children's Bilingual Picture Book. Carlson, Richard. 2019. (ENG.). 24p. (J). pap. 10.99 *(978-1-0751-3256-8(8))* Independently Published.

—English-Dutch Time/Tijd Children's Bilingual Picture Book. Carlson Jr, Richard. 2018. (ENG.). 28p. (J). pap. 10.99 *(978-1-7202-6302-9(7))* Independently Published.

—English-Dutch Trouble/Problemen Children's Bilingual Picture Book. Carlson Jr, Richard. 2018. (ENG.). 24p. (J). pap. 10.99 *(978-1-7315-0640-5(6))* Independently Published.

—English-Estonian My Feelings Are Hurt/Mu Tunded Said Haavata Children's Bilingual Picture Book. Carlson, Richard. 2019. (ENG.). 24p. (J). pap. 10.99 *(978-1-0751-3578-1(8))* Independently Published.

—English-Estonian Time/Aeg Children's Bilingual Picture Book. Carlson Jr, Richard. 2018. (ENG.). 28p. (J). pap. 10.99 *(978-1-7202-7494-0(0))* Independently Published.

—English-Estonian Trouble/Pahandus Children's Bilingual Picture Book. Carlson Jr, Richard. 2018. (ENG.). 24p. (J). pap. 10.99 *(978-1-7315-0661-0(9))* Independently Published.

—English-Finnish My Feelings Are Hurt/Tunteitani on Loukattu Children's Bilingual Picture Book. Carlson, Richard. 2019. (ENG.). 24p. (J). pap. 10.99 *(978-1-0753-3203-6(6))* Independently Published.

—English-Finnish Time/Aika Children's Bilingual Picture Book. Carlson Jr, Richard. 2018. (ENG.). 28p. (J). pap. 10.99 *(978-1-7202-7613-5(7))* Independently Published.

—English-Finnish Trouble/Kiusaaminen Children's Bilingual Picture Book. Carlson Jr, Richard. 2018. (ENG.). 24p. (J). pap. 10.99 *(978-1-7315-0979-6(0))* Independently Published.

—English-Flemish (Belgian) My Feelings Are Hurt/Mijn Gevoelens Zijn Gekwetst Children's Bilingual Picture Book. Carlson, Richard. 2019. (ENG.). 24p. (J). pap. 10.99 *(978-1-0753-3500-6(0))* Independently Published.

—English-Flemish (Belgian) Time/de Tijd Children's Bilingual Picture Book. Carlson Jr, Richard. 2018. (ENG.). 28p. (J). pap. 10.99 *(978-1-7202-7657-9(9))* Independently Published.

—English-Flemish (Belgian) Trouble/Problemen Children's Bilingual Picture Book. Carlson Jr, Richard. 2018. (ENG.). 24p. (J). pap. 10.99 *(978-1-7315-1006-8(3))* Independently Published.

—English-Galician My Feelings Are Hurt/Os Meus Sentimentos Están Feridos Children's Bilingual Picture Book. Carlson, Richard. 2019. (ENG.). 24p. (J). pap. 10.99 *(978-1-0753-3623-2(6))* Independently Published.

—English-Georgian My Feelings Are Hurt/ჩემი გრძნობები შეურაცხყოფილია Children's Bilingual Pictu. Carlson, Richard. 2019. (ENG.). 24p. (J). pap. 10.99 *(978-1-0753-3803-8(4))* Independently Published.

—English-Georgian Time Children's Bilingual Picture Book. Carlson Jr, Richard. 2018. (ENG.). 28p. (J). pap. 10.99 *(978-1-7202-7712-5(5))* Independently Published.

—English-Georgian Trouble Children's Bilingual Picture Book. Carlson Jr, Richard. 2018. (ENG.). 24p. (J). pap. 10.99 *(978-1-7315-3595-5(3))* Independently Published.

—English-German My Feelings Are Hurt/Ich Wurde in Meinen Gefühlen Verletzt Children's Bilingual Picture Book. Carlson, Richard. 2019. (ENG.). 24p. (J). pap. 10.99 *(978-1-0753-4080-2(2))* Independently Published.

—English-German Time/Zeit Children's Bilingual Picture Book. Carlson Jr, Richard. 2018. (ENG.). 28p. (J). pap. 10.99 *(978-1-7237-0241-9(2))* Independently Published.

—English-German Trouble. Carlson Jr, Richard. 2018. (ENG.). 24p. (J). pap. 10.99 *(978-1-7312-1351-8(4))* Independently Published.

—English-Greek My Feelings Are Hurt/Πληγώθηκαν Τα Συναισθήματά Μου Children's Bilingual Picture Book. Carlson, Richard. 2019. (ENG.). 24p. (J). pap. 10.99 *(978-1-0753-4622-4(3))* Independently Published.

—English-Greek Time Children's Bilingual Picture Book. Carlson Jr, Richard. 2018. (ENG.). 28p. (J). pap. 10.99 *(978-1-7237-2625-5(7))* Independently Published.

—English-Greek Trouble Children's Bilingual Picture Book. Carlson Jr, Richard. 2018. (ENG.). 24p. (J). pap. 10.99 *(978-1-7315-3682-2(8))* Independently Published.

—English-Gujarati My Feelings Are Hurt Children's Bilingual Picture Book. Carlson, Richard. 2019. (ENG.). 24p. (J). pap. 10.99 *(978-1-0753-4918-8(4))* Independently Published.

—English-Gujarati Time Children's Bilingual Picture Book. Carlson Jr, Richard. 2018. (ENG.). 28p. (J). pap. 10.99 *(978-1-7237-2723-8(7))* Independently Published.

—English-Gujarati Trouble Children's Bilingual Picture Book. Carlson Jr, Richard. 2018. (ENG.). 24p. (J). pap. 10.99 *(978-1-7315-3871-0(5))* Independently Published.

—English-Haitian Creole My Feelings Are Hurt/Santiman M Blese Children's Bilingual Picture Book. Carlson, Richard. 2019. (ENG.). 24p. (J). pap. 10.99 *(978-1-0755-1010-6(4))* Independently Published.

—English-Haitian Creole Time/Tan Children's Bilingual Picture Book. Carlson Jr, Richard. 2018. (ENG.). 28p. (J). pap. 10.99 *(978-1-7237-4162-3(0))* Independently Published.

—English-Haitian Creole Trouble/Dezòd Children's Bilingual Picture Book. Carlson Jr, Richard. 2018. (ENG.). 24p. (J). pap. 10.99 *(978-1-7315-4568-8(1))* Independently Published.

—English-Hausa My Feelings Are Hurt/Na Ji Jikkata Children's Bilingual Picture Book. Carlson, Richard. 2019. (ENG.). 24p. (J). pap. 10.99 *(978-1-0755-1176-9(3))* Independently Published.

—English-Hausa Time/Lokaci Children's Bilingual Picture Book. Carlson Jr, Richard. 2018. (ENG.). 28p. (J). pap. 10.99 *(978-1-7237-5927-7(9))* Independently Published.

—English-Hausa Trouble/Matsala Children's Bilingual Picture Book. Carlson Jr, Richard. 2018. (ENG.). 24p. (J). pap. 10.99 *(978-1-7315-4602-9(5))* Independently Published.

—English-Hebrew My Feelings Are Hurt/אני מרגיש פגוע Children's Bilingual Picture Book. Carlson, Richard. 2019. (ENG.). 24p. (J). pap. 10.99 *(978-1-0767-8822-1(X))* Independently Published.

—English-Hebrew Time Children's Bilingual Picture Book. Carlson Jr, Richard. 2018. (ENG.). 28p. (J). pap. 10.99 *(978-1-7237-5994-9(5))* Independently Published.

—English-Hebrew Trouble Children's Bilingual Picture Book. Carlson Jr, Richard. 2018. (ENG.). 24p. (J). pap. 10.99 *(978-1-7312-1648-9(3))* Independently Published.

—English-Hindi My Feelings Are Hurt/मेरी भावनाओं को ठेस पहुँची है Children's Bilingual Picture Book. Carlson, Richard. 2019. (ENG.). 24p. (J). pap. 10.99 *(978-1-0755-1583-5(1))* Independently Published.

—English-Hindi Time Children's Bilingual Picture Book. Carlson Jr, Richard. 2018. (ENG.). 28p. (J). pap. 10.99 *(978-1-7237-6344-1(6))* Independently Published.

—English-Hindi Trouble Children's Bilingual Picture Book. Carlson Jr, Richard. 2018. (ENG.). 24p. (J). pap. 10.99 *(978-1-7312-1363-1(8))* Independently Published.

—English-Hungarian My Feelings Are Hurt/Megbántódtam Children's Bilingual Picture Book. Carlson, Richard. 2019. (ENG.). 24p. (J). pap. 10.99 *(978-1-0755-1778-5(8))* Independently Published.

—English-Hungarian Time Children's Bilingual Picture Book. Carlson Jr, Richard. 2018. (ENG.). 28p. (J). pap. 10.99 *(978-1-7237-6406-6(X))* Independently Published.

—English-Hungarian Trouble/Baj Children's Bilingual Picture Book. Carlson Jr, Richard. 2018. (ENG.). 24p. (J). pap. 10.99 *(978-1-7315-4628-9(9))* Independently Published.

—English-Icelandic My Feelings Are Hurt/Ég Er Særður Children's Bilingual Picture Book. Carlson, Richard. 2019. (ENG.). 24p. (J). pap. 10.99 *(978-1-0755-1962-8(4))* Independently Published.

—English-Icelandic Time/T. Carlson Jr, Richard. 2018. (ENG.). 28p. (J). pap. 10.99 *(978-1-7238-2528-6(X))* Independently Published.

—English-Icelandic Trouble/Vandræði Children's Bilingual Picture Book. Carlson Jr, Richard. 2018. (ENG.). 24p. (J). pap. 10.99 *(978-1-7315-4717-0(X))* Independently Published.

—English-Indonesian My Feelings Are Hurt/Perasaanku Terluka Children's Bilingual Picture Book. Carlson, Richard. 2019. (ENG.). 24p. (J). pap. 10.99 *(978-1-0755-2089-1(4))* Independently Published.

—English-Indonesian Time/Waktu Children's Bilingual Picture Book. Carlson Jr, Richard. 2018. (ENG.). 28p. (J). pap. 10.99 *(978-1-7238-2581-1(6))* Independently Published.

—English-Indonesian Trouble/Masalah Children's Bilingual Picture Book. Carlson Jr, Richard. 2018. (ENG.). 24p. (J). pap. 10.99 *(978-1-7315-4745-3(5))* Independently Published.

—English-Irish Gaelic My Feelings Are Hurt/Tá Mé Gortaithe Children's Bilingual Picture Book. Carlson, Richard. 2019. (ENG.). 24p. (J). pap. 10.99 *(978-1-0755-2209-3(9))* Independently Published.

—English-Irish Gaelic Time/Am Children's Bilingual Picture Book. Carlson Jr, Richard. 2018. (ENG.). 28p. (J). pap. 10.99 *(978-1-7238-8965-3(2))* Independently Published.

—English-Irish Gaelic Trouble/Triobióid Children's Bilingual Picture Book. Carlson Jr, Richard. 2018. (ENG.). 24p. (J). pap. 10.99 *(978-1-7315-4795-8(1))* Independently Published.

—English-Italian My Feelings Are Hurt/Mi Sento Ferito Children's Bilingual Picture Book. Carlson, Richard. 2019. (ENG.). 24p. (J). pap. 10.99 *(978-1-0756-5061-1(5))* Independently Published.

—English-Italian Time/Tempo Children's Bilingual Picture Book. Carlson Jr, Richard. 2018. (ENG.). 28p. (J). pap. 10.99 *(978-1-7239-0787-6(1))* Independently Published.

—English-Italian Trouble/Guaio Children's Bilingual Picture Book. Carlson Jr, Richard. 2018. (ENG.). 24p. (J). pap. 10.99 *(978-1-7313-1544-1(9))* Independently Published.

—English-Japanese My Feelings Are Hurt/ぼくは傷ついた Children's Bilingual Picture Book. Carlson, Richard. 2019. (ENG.). 24p. (J). pap. 10.99 *(978-1-0756-5126-7(3))* Independently Published.

—English-Japanese Time Children's Bilingual Picture Book. Carlson Jr, Richard. 2018. (ENG.). 28p. (J). pap. 10.99 *(978-1-7239-2096-7(7))* Independently Published.

—English-Kannada My Feelings Are Hurt Children's Bilingual Picture Book. Carlson, Richard. 2019. (ENG.). 24p. (J). pap. 10.99 *(978-1-0756-5253-0(7))* Independently Published.

—English-Kannada Time Children's Bilingual Picture Book. Carlson Jr, Richard. 2018. (ENG.). 28p. (J). pap. 10.99 *(978-1-7239-4295-2(2))* Independently Published.

—English-Kannada Trouble Children's Bilingual Picture Book. Carlson Jr, Richard. 2018. (ENG.). 24p. (J). pap. 10.99 *(978-1-7315-4846-7(X))* Independently Published.

—English-Kazakh My Feelings Are Hurt/Сезімтал бала туралы оқиға Children's Bilingual Picture Book. Carlson, Richard. 2019. (ENG.). 24p. (J). pap. 10.99 *(978-1-0756-5420-6(3))* Independently Published.

—English-Kazakh Time Children's Bilingual Picture Book. Carlson Jr, Richard. 2018. (ENG.). 28p. (J). pap. 10.99 *(978-1-7239-4563-2(3))* Independently Published.

—English-Kazakh Trouble Children's Bilingual Picture Book. Carlson Jr, Richard. 2018. (ENG.). 24p. (J). pap. 10.99 *(978-1-7315-9791-5(6))* Independently Published.

—English-Khmer (Cambodian) My Feelings Are Hurt/ខ្ញុំមានអារម្មណ៍ឈឺចាប់ Children's Bilingual Picture Book. Carlson, Richard. 2019. (ENG.). 24p. (J). pap. 10.99 *(978-1-0756-5915-7(9))* Independently Published.

—English-Khmer (Cambodian) Time Children's Bilingual Picture Book. Carlson Jr, Richard. 2018. (ENG.). 28p. (J). pap. 10.99 *(978-1-7239-4577-9(3))* Independently Published.

—English-Khmer (Cambodian) Trouble Children's Bilingual Picture Book. Carlson Jr, Richard. 2018. (ENG.). 24p. (J). pap. 10.99 *(978-1-7315-9873-8(4))* Independently Published.

—English-Korean My Feelings Are Hurt/마음이 아팠어요 Children's Bilingual Picture Book. Carlson, Richard. 2019. (ENG.). 24p. (J). pap. 10.99 *(978-1-0756-5987-4(6))* Independently Published.

—English-Korean Time Children's Bilingual Picture Book. Carlson Jr, Richard. 2018. (ENG.). 28p. (J). pap. 10.99 *(978-1-7239-4585-4(4))* Independently Published.

—English-Korean Trouble Children's Bilingual Picture Book. Carlson Jr, Richard. 2018. (ENG.). 24p. (J). pap. 10.99 *(978-1-7315-9819-6(X))* Independently Published.

—English-Kurdish Trouble Children's Bilingual Picture Book. Carlson Jr, Richard. 2018. (ENG.). 24p. (J). pap. 10.99 *(978-1-7901-9986-0(7))* Independently Published.

—English-Lao (Laotian) My Feelings Are Hurt Children's Bilingual Picture Book. Carlson, Richard. 2019. (ENG.). 24p. (J). pap. 10.99 *(978-1-0756-6396-3(2))* Independently Published.

—English-Lao (Laotian) Time Children's Bilingual Picture Book. Carlson Jr, Richard. 2018. (ENG.). 28p. (J). pap. 10.99 *(978-1-7239-4856-5(X))* Independently Published.

—English-Lao (Laotian) Trouble Children's Bilingual Picture Book. Carlson Jr, Richard. 2018. (ENG.). 24p. (J). pap. 10.99 *(978-1-7917-7787-6(2))* Independently Published.

—English-Latvian My Feelings Are Hurt/Es Esmu Sāpināts Children's Bilingual Picture Book. Carlson, Richard. 2019. (ENG.). 24p. (J). pap. 10.99 *(978-1-0756-6551-6(5))* Independently Published.

—English-Latvian Time/Laiks Children's Bilingual Picture Book. Carlson Jr, Richard. 2018. (ENG.). 28p. (J). pap. 10.99 *(978-1-7239-4983-8(3))* Independently Published.

—English-Latvian Trouble/Nelgs Notikums Children's Bilingual Picture Book. Carlson Jr, Richard. 2018. (ENG.). 24p. (J). pap. 10.99 *(978-1-7917-8436-2(4))* Independently Published.

—English-Lithuanian My Feelings Are Hurt/Mane įskaudino Children's Bilingual Picture Book. Carlson, Richard. 2019. (ENG.). 24p. (J). pap. 10.99 *(978-1-0756-6990-3(1))* Independently Published.

—English-Lithuanian Time/Laikas Children's Bilingual Picture Book. Carlson Jr, Richard. 2018. (ENG.). 28p. (J). pap. 10.99 *(978-1-7239-4999-9(X))* Independently Published.

—English-Lithuanian Trouble/Beda Children's Bilingual Picture Book. Carlson Jr, Richard. 2018. (ENG.). 24p. (J). pap. 10.99 *(978-1-7917-8459-1(3))* Independently Published.

—English-Macedonian My Feelings Are Hurt/Моите чувства се повредени Children's Bilingual Picture Book. Carlson, Richard. 2019. (ENG.). 24p. (J). pap. 10.99 *(978-1-0756-7174-6(4))* Independently Published.

—English-Macedonian Time Children's Bilingual Picture Book. Carlson Jr, Richard. 2018. (ENG.). 28p. (J). pap. 10.99 *(978-1-7239-7612-4(1))* Independently Published.

—English-Macedonian Trouble/Children's Bilingual Picture Book. Carlson Jr, Richard. 2018. (ENG.). 24p. (J). pap. 10.99 *(978-1-7917-8523-9(9))* Independently Published.

—English-Malay My Feelings Are Hurt/Perasaan Saya Disakiti Children's Bilingual Picture Book. Carlson, Richard. 2019. (ENG.). 24p. (J). pap. 10.99 *(978-1-0756-7370-2(4))* Independently Published.

—English-Malay Time/Masa Children's Bilingual Picture Book. Carlson Jr, Richard. 2018. (ENG.). 28p. (J). pap. 10.99 *(978-1-7239-7623-0(7))* Independently Published.

—English-Malay Trouble/Masalah Children's Bilingual Picture Book. Carlson Jr, Richard. 2018. (ENG.). 24p. (J). pap. 10.99 *(978-1-7917-8551-2(4))* Independently Published.

—English-Malayalam My Feelings Are Hurt Children's Bilingual Picture Book. Carlson, Richard. 2019. (ENG.). 24p. (J). pap. 10.99 *(978-1-0756-7714-4(9))* Independently Published.

—English-Malayalam Trouble Children's Bilingual Picture Book. Carlson Jr, Richard. 2018. (ENG.). 24p. (J). pap. 10.99 *(978-1-7917-8723-3(1))* Independently Published.

—English-Maltese My Feelings Are Hurt/Weġġgħuni Children's Bilingual Picture Book. Carlson, Richard. 2019. (ENG.). 24p. (J). pap. 10.99 *(978-1-0756-8096-0(4))* Independently Published.

—English-Maltese Time Children's Bilingual Picture Book. Carlson Jr, Richard. 2018. (ENG.). 28p. (J). pap. 10.99 *(978-1-7240-0286-0(4))* Independently Published.

—English-Maltese Trouble/Inkwiet Children's Bilingual Picture Book. Carlson Jr, Richard. 2018. (ENG.). 24p. (J). pap. 10.99 *(978-1-7917-8761-5(4))* Independently Published.

—English-Marathi My Feelings Are Hurt/माझ्या भावना दुखावल्या गेल्या आहेत Chil. Carlson, Richard. 2019. (ENG.). 24p. (J). pap. 10.99 *(978-1-0758-1276-7(3))* Independently Published.

—English-Marathi Time Children's Bilingual Picture Book. Carlson Jr, Richard. 2018. (ENG.). 28p. (J). pap. 10.99 *(978-1-7240-0783-4(1))* Independently Published.

—English-Marathi Trouble Children's Bilingual Picture Book. Carlson Jr, Richard. 2018. (ENG.). 24p. (J). pap. 10.99 *(978-1-7917-8964-0(1))* Independently Published.

—English-Mongolian My Feelings Are Hurt/Бигомдож байна Children's Bilingual Picture Book. Carlson, Richard. 2019. (ENG.). 24p. (J). pap. 10.99 *(978-1-0756-8358-9(0))* Independently Published.

—English-Mongolian Time Children's Bilingual Picture Book. Carlson Jr, Richard. 2018. (ENG.). 28p. (J). pap. 10.99 *(978-1-7240-0888-6(9))* Independently Published.

—English-Mongolian Trouble/Children's Bilingual Picture Book. Carlson Jr, Richard. 2018. (ENG.). 24p. (J). pap. 10.99 *(978-1-7917-9098-1(4))* Independently Published.

—English-Montenegrin My Feelings Are Hurt/Moja Osjecanja Su Povrijeđena Children's Bilingual Picture Book. Carlson, Richard. 2019. (ENG.). 24p. (J). pap. 10.99 *(978-1-0758-0947-7(9))* Independently Published.

—English-Montenegrin Time/Vrijeme Children's Bilingual Picture Book. Carlson Jr, Richard. 2018. (ENG.). 28p. (J). pap. 10.99 *(978-1-7240-0926-5(5))* Independently Published.

—English-Montenegrin Trouble/Nevolja Children's Bilingual Picture Book. Carlson Jr, Richard. 2018. (ENG.). 24p. (J). pap. 10.99 *(978-1-7917-9209-1(X))* Independently Published.

—English-Nepali My Feelings Are Hurt/मेरो भावनामा चोट पुगेको छ Children's Bilingual Picture Book. Carlson, Richard. 2019. (ENG.). 24p. (J). pap. 10.99 *(978-1-0767-9113-9(1))* Independently Published.

—English-Nepali Time Children's Bilingual Picture Book. Carlson Jr, Richard. 2018. (ENG.). 28p. (J). pap. 10.99 *(978-1-7240-1327-9(0))* Independently Published.

—English-Nepali Trouble/Children's Bilingual Picture Book. Carlson Jr, Richard. 2018. (ENG.). 24p. (J). pap. 10.99 *(978-1-7917-9299-2(5))* Independently Published.

—English-Norwegian My Feelings Are Hurt/Følelsene Mine Er Såret Children's Bilingual Picture Book. Carlson, Richard. 2019. (ENG.). 24p. (J). pap. 10.99 *(978-1-0758-1572-0(X))* Independently Published.

—English-Norwegian Time/Tid Children's Bilingual Picture Book. Carlson Jr, Richard. 2018. (ENG.). 28p. (J). pap. 10.99 *(978-1-7240-3689-6(0))* Independently Published.

—English-Norwegian Trouble/Trøbbel Children's Bilingual Picture Book. Carlson Jr, Richard. 2018. (ENG.). 24p. (J). pap. 10.99 *(978-1-7917-9379-1(7))* Independently Published.

—English-Pashto My Feelings Are Hurt Children's Bilingual Picture Book. Carlson, Richard. 2019. (ENG.). 24p. (J). pap. 10.99 *(978-1-0767-9343-0(6))* Independently Published.

—English-Pashto Time Children's Bilingual Picture Book. Carlson Jr, Richard. 2018. (ENG.). 28p. (J). pap. 10.99 *(978-1-7240-3953-8(9))* Independently Published.

—English-Pashto Trouble Children's Bilingual Picture Book. Carlson Jr, Richard. 2018. (ENG.). 24p. (J). pap. 10.99 *(978-1-7917-9563-4(3))* Independently Published.

—English-Persian (Farsi) My Feelings Are Hurt Children's Bilingual Picture Book. Carlson, Richard. 2019. (ENG.). 24p. (J). pap. 10.99 *(978-1-0767-9506-9(4))* Independently Published.

—English-Persian (Farsi) Time Children's Bilingual Picture Book. Carlson Jr, Richard. 2018. (ENG.). 28p. (J). pap. 10.99 *(978-1-7240-4926-1(7))* Independently Published.

—English-Persian (Farsi) Trouble Children's Bilingual Picture Book. Carlson Jr, Richard. 2018. (ENG.). 24p. (J). pap. 10.99 *(978-1-7918-2720-5(9))* Independently Published.

—English-Polish My Feelings Are Hurt/Zranione Uczucia Children's Bilingual Picture Book. Carlson, Richard. 2019. (ENG.). 24p. (J). pap. 10.99 *(978-1-0758-1702-1(1))* Independently Published.

—English-Polish Time/Czas Children's Bilingual Picture Book. Carlson Jr, Richard. 2018. (ENG.). 28p. (J). pap. 10.99 *(978-1-7240-4982-7(8))* Independently Published.

—English-Polish Trouble/Klopoty Children's Bilingual Picture Book. Carlson Jr, Richard. 2018. (ENG.). 24p. (J). pap. 10.99 *(978-1-7918-2964-3(3))* Independently Published.

—English-Portuguese (Brazilian) My Feelings Are Hurt/Meus Sentimentos Estão Feridos Children's Bilingual Picture Book. Carlson, Richard. 2019. (ENG.). 24p. (J). pap. 10.99 *(978-1-0758-2303-9(X))* Independently Published.

—English-Portuguese (Brazilian) Time/Tempo Children's Bilingual Picture Book. Carlson Jr, Richard. 2018. (ENG.). 28p. (J). pap. 10.99 *(978-1-7240-7742-4(2))* Independently Published.

—English-Portuguese (Brazilian) Trouble/Encrenca Children's Bilingual Picture Book. Carlson Jr, Richard. 2018. (ENG.). 24p. (J). pap. 10.99 *(978-1-7918-2998-8(8))* Independently Published.

—English-Portuguese (Portugal) My Feelings Are Hurt/Os Meus Sentimentos Estão Feridos Children's Bilingual Picture Book. Carlson, Richard. 2019. (ENG.). 24p. (J). pap. 10.99 *(978-1-0758-2417-3(6))* Independently Published.

—English-Portuguese (Portugal) Time/Tempo Children's Bilingual Picture Book. Carlson Jr, Richard. 2018. (ENG.). 28p. (J). pap. 10.99 *(978-1-7240-7785-1(6))* Independently Published.

—English-Punjabi My Feelings Are Hurt Children's Bilingual Picture Book. Carlson, Richard. 2019. (ENG.). 24p. (J). pap. 10.99 *(978-1-0758-5162-9(9))* Independently Published.

—English-Punjabi Time Children's Bilingual Picture Book. Carlson Jr, Richard. 2018. (ENG.). 28p. (J). pap. 10.99 *(978-1-7240-8866-6(1))* Independently Published.

—English-Punjabi Trouble Children's Bilingual Picture Book. Carlson Jr, Richard. 2018. (ENG.). 24p. (J). pap. 10.99 *(978-1-7918-3087-8(0))* Independently Published.

—English-Romanian My Feelings Are Hurt/Sunt Jignit Children's Bilingual Picture Book. Carlson, Richard. 2019. (ENG.). 24p. (J). pap. 10.99 *(978-1-0758-5373-9(7))* Independently Published.

—English-Romanian Time/Timpul Children's Bilingual Picture Book. Carlson Jr, Richard. 2018. (ENG.). 28p. (J). pap. 10.99 *(978-1-7241-1066-4(7))* Independently Published.

—English-Romanian Trouble/În Încurcatura Children's Bilingual Picture Book. Carlson Jr, Richard. 2018. (ENG.). 24p. (J). pap. 10.99 *(978-1-7918-3153-0(2))* Independently Published.

—English-Russian My Feelings Are Hurt/Оскорбленные чувства Children's Bilingual Picture Book. Carlson, Richard. 2019. (ENG.). 24p. (J). pap. 10.99 *(978-1-0758-5579-5(9))* Independently Published.

—English-Russian Time Children's Bilingual Picture Book. Carlson Jr, Richard. 2018. (ENG.). 28p. (J). pap. 10.99 *(978-1-7241-1145-6(0))* Independently Published.

—English-Russian Trouble/Problem Children's Bilingual Picture Book. Carlson Jr, Richard. 2018. (ENG.). 24p. (J). pap. 10.99 *(978-1-7918-3508-8(2))* Independently Published.

—English-Serbian (Cyrillic) My Feelings Are Hurt/Моја осећања су повређена Children's Bilingual Picture Book. Carlson, Richard. 2019. (ENG.). 24p. (J). pap. 10.99 *(978-1-0758-5828-4(3))* Independently Published.

—English-Serbian (Cyrillic) Time Children's Bilingual Picture Book. Carlson Jr, Richard. 2018. (ENG.). 28p. (J). pap. 10.99 *(978-1-7241-1182-1(5))* Independently Published.

—English-Serbian (Cyrillic) Trouble Children's Bilingual Picture Book. Carlson Jr, Richard. 2018. (ENG.). 24p. (J). pap. 10.99 *(978-1-7918-4048-8(5))* Independently Published.

—English-Serbian (Latin) My Feelings Are Hurt/Osecanja Su Mi Povređena Children's Bilingual Picture Book. Carlson, Richard. 2019. (ENG.). 24p. (J). pap. 10.99 *(978-1-0758-6118-5(7))* Independently Published.

—English-Serbian (Latin) Time/Vreme Children's Bilingual Picture Book. Carlson Jr, Richard. 2018. (ENG.). 28p. (J). pap. 10.99 *(978-1-7241-1219-4(8))* Independently Published.

—English-Serbian (Latin) Trouble/Nevolja Children's Bilingual Picture Book. Carlson Jr, Richard. 2018. (ENG.). 24p. (J). pap. 10.99 *(978-1-7918-4095-2(7))* Independently Published.

—English-Shanghainese My Feelings Are Hurt/我的感情受到了伤害 Children's Bilingual Picture Book. Carlson, Richard. 2019. (ENG.). 24p. (J). pap. 10.99 *(978-1-0758-6534-3(4))* Independently Published.

—English-Shanghainese Trouble Children's Bilingual Picture Book. Carlson Jr, Richard. 2018. (ENG.). 24p. (J). pap. 10.99 *(978-1-7918-4173-7(2))* Independently Published.

—English-Sinhala My Feelings Are Hurt/මගේ හැඟීම් වලට රිදිලා Children's Bilingual Picture Book. Carlson, Richard. 2019. (ENG.). 24p. (J). pap. 10.99 *(978-1-0758-6762-0(2))* Independently Published.

—English-Sinhala Trouble Children's Bilingual Picture Book. Carlson Jr, Richard. 2018. (ENG.). 24p. (J). pap. 10.99 *(978-1-7918-4280-2(1))* Independently Published.

—English-Slovak My Feelings Are Hurt/Ranili Moje City Children's Bilingual Picture Book. Carlson, Richard. 2019. (ENG.). 24p. (J). pap. 10.99 *(978-1-0760-6362-5(4))* Independently Published.

—English-Slovak Time; as Children's Bilingual Picture Book. Carlson Jr, Richard. 2018. (ENG.). 28p. (J). pap. 10.99 *(978-1-7241-1362-7(3))* Independently Published.

—English-Slovak Trouble/Problémy Children's Bilingual Picture Book. Carlson Jr, Richard. 2018. (ENG.). 24p. (J). pap. 10.99 *(978-1-7918-4338-0(7))* Independently Published.

—English-Slovenian (Slovene) My Feelings Are Hurt/Moja Prizadeta čustva Children's Bilingual Picture Book. Carlson, Richard. 2019. (ENG.). 24p. (J). pap. 10.99 *(978-1-0760-6550-6(3))* Independently Published.

—English-Slovenian (Slovene) Time;as Children's Bilingual Picture Book. Carlson Jr, Richard. 2018. (ENG.). 28p. (J). pap. 10.99 *(978-1-7241-1915-5(X))* Independently Published.

—English-Slovenian (Slovene) Trouble/Tezava Children's Bilingual Picture Book. Carlson Jr, Richard. 2018. (ENG.). 24p. (J). pap. 10.99 *(978-1-7918-4364-9(6))* Independently Published.

—English-Somali My Feelings Are Hurt/Dareenadayda Ayaa Dhaawacmay Children's Bilingual Picture Book. Carlson, Richard. 2019. (ENG.). 24p. (J). pap. 10.99 *(978-1-0760-6821-7(9))* Independently Published.

—English-Somali Time/Waqti Children's Bilingual Picture Book. Carlson Jr, Richard. 2018. (ENG.). 28p. (J). pap. 10.99 *(978-1-7241-2020-5(4))* Independently Published.

—English-Somali Trouble/Dhibaato Children's Bilingual Picture Book. Carlson Jr, Richard. 2018. (ENG.). 24p. (J). pap. 10.99 *(978-1-7919-0611-5(7))* Independently Published.

—English-Spanish (Castilian) My Feelings Are Hurt/Han Herido Mis Sentimientos Children's Bilingual Picture Book. Carlson, Richard. 2019. (ENG.). 24p. (J). pap. 10.99 *(978-1-0762-8998-8(3))* Independently Published.

—English-Spanish (Castilian) Trouble/Problema Children's Bilingual Picture Book. Carlson Jr, Richard. 2018. (ENG.). 24p. (J). pap. 10.99 *(978-1-7919-0677-1(X))* Independently Published.

—English-Spanish (Latin-America) My Feelings Are Hurt/Han Herido Mis Sentimientos Children's Bilingual Picture Book. Carlson, Richard. 2019. (ENG.). 24p. (J). pap. 10.99 *(978-1-0762-9194-3(5))* Independently Published.

C

—English-Spanish (Latin-America) Time/Tiempo Children's Bilingual Picture Book. Carlson Jr, Richard. 2018. (ENG.). 28p. (J). pap. 10.99 *(978-1-7241-2101-1(4))* Independently Published.

—English-Spanish (Latin-America) Trouble/Problema Children's Bilingual Picture Book. Carlson Jr, Richard. 2018. (ENG.). 24p. (J). pap. 10.99 *(978-1-7919-0714-3(8))* Independently Published.

—English-Spanish (Mexico) My Feelings Are Hurt/Han Herido Mis Sentimientos Children's Bilingual Picture Book. Carlson, Richard. 2019. (ENG.). 24p. (J). pap. 10.99 *(978-1-0762-9440-1(5))* Independently Published.

—English-Spanish (Mexico) Time/Tiempo Children's Bilingual Picture Book. Carlson Jr, Richard. 2018. (ENG.). 28p. (J). pap. 10.99 *(978-1-7241-2137-0(5))* Independently Published.

—English-Spanish (Mexico) Trouble/Problema Children's Bilingual Picture Book. Carlson Jr, Richard. 2018. (ENG.). 24p. (J). pap. 10.99 *(978-1-7919-0754-9(7))* Independently Published.

—English-Swahili My Feelings Are Hurt/Hisia Zangu Zinaumia Children's Bilingual Picture Book. Carlson, Richard. 2019. (ENG.). 24p. (J). pap. 10.99 *(978-1-0763-0943-3(7))* Independently Published.

—English-Swahili Trouble/Shida Children's Bilingual Picture Book. Carlson Jr, Richard. 2018. (ENG.). 24p. (J). pap. 10.99 *(978-1-7919-0821-8(7))* Independently Published.

—English-Swedish My Feelings Are Hurt/Mina Känslor är Sårade Children's Bilingual Picture Book. Carlson, Richard. 2019. (ENG.). 24p. (J). pap. 10.99 *(978-1-0763-1189-4(X))* Independently Published.

—English-Swedish Time/Tid Children's Bilingual Picture Book. Carlson Jr, Richard. 2018. (ENG.). 28p. (J). pap. 10.99 *(978-1-7241-2210-0(X))* Independently Published.

—English-Swedish Trouble/Trubbel Children's Bilingual Picture Book. Carlson Jr, Richard. 2018. (ENG.). 24p. (J). pap. 10.99 *(978-1-7313-1607-3(0))* Independently Published.

—English-Tagalog My Feelings Are Hurt/Nasaktan Ang Aking Damdamin Children's Bilingual Picture Book. Carlson, Richard. 2019. (ENG.). 24p. (J). pap. 10.99 *(978-1-0763-1625-7(5))* Independently Published.

—English-Tagalog Time/Oras Children's Bilingual Picture Book. Carlson Jr, Richard. 2018. (ENG.). 28p. (J). pap. 10.99 *(978-1-7241-2236-0(3))* Independently Published.

—English-Tagalog Trouble/Gulo Children's Bilingual Picture Book. Carlson Jr, Richard. 2018. (ENG.). 24p. (J). pap. 10.99 *(978-1-7919-0850-8(0))* Independently Published.

—English-Tajik My Feelings Are Hurt/эҳсосотм ҷриҳа дор шуда Children's Bilingual Picture Book. Carlson, Richard. 2019. (ENG.). 24p. (J). pap. 10.99 *(978-1-0763-1883-1(5))* Independently Published.

—English-Tamil My Feelings Are Hurt/எனது உணர்வுகள் காயமாகின Children's Bilingual Picture Book. Carlson, Richard. 2019. (ENG.). 24p. (J). pap. 10.99 *(978-1-0765-0255-1(5))* Independently Published.

—English-Tamil Time Children's Bilingual Picture Book. Carlson Jr, Richard. 2018. (ENG.). 28p. (J). pap. 10.99 *(978-1-7241-4538-3(X))* Independently Published.

—English-Tamil Trouble Children's Bilingual Picture Book. Carlson Jr, Richard. 2018. (ENG.). 24p. (J). pap. 10.99 *(978-1-7919-0897-3(7))* Independently Published.

—English-Telugu My Feelings Are Hurt Children's Bilingual Picture Book. Carlson, Richard. 2019. (ENG.). 24p. (J). pap. 10.99 *(978-1-0765-0621-4(6))* Independently Published.

—English-Telugu Time Children's Bilingual Picture Book. Carlson Jr, Richard. 2018. (ENG.). 28p. (J). pap. 10.99 *(978-1-7241-4893-3(1))* Independently Published.

—English-Telugu Trouble Children's Bilingual Picture Book. Carlson Jr, Richard. 2018. (ENG.). 24p. (J). pap. 10.99 *(978-1-7919-6539-6(3))* Independently Published.

—English-Thai My Feelings Are Hurt/ความรู้สึกของผมคือเสียใจ Children's Bilingual Picture Book. Carlson, Richard. 2019. (ENG.). 24p. (J). pap. 10.99 *(978-1-0765-0888-1(X))* Independently Published.

—English-Thai Time Children's Bilingual Picture Book. Carlson Jr, Richard. 2018. (ENG.). 28p. (J). pap. 10.99 *(978-1-7241-4910-7(5))* Independently Published.

—English-Thai Trouble/Children's Bilingual Picture Book. Carlson Jr, Richard. 2018. (ENG.). 24p. (J). pap. 10.99 *(978-1-7919-6596-9(2))* Independently Published.

—English-Tigrinya My Feelings Are Hurt/ስምዒተይ ተጎዲኡ እዩ Children's Bilingual Picture Book. Carlson, Richard. 2019. (ENG.). 24p. (J). pap. 10.99 *(978-1-0765-1621-3(1))* Independently Published.

—English-Tigrinya Time Children's Bilingual Picture Book. Carlson Jr, Richard. 2018. (ENG.). 28p. (J). pap. 10.99 *(978-1-7241-4930-5(X))* Independently Published.

—English-Tigrinya Trouble Children's Bilingual Picture Book. Carlson Jr, Richard. 2018. (ENG.). 24p. (J). pap. 10.99 *(978-1-7920-2406-1(1))* Independently Published.

—English-Turkish My Feelings Are Hurt/Duygularım İncindi Children's Bilingual Picture Book. Carlson, Richard. 2019. (ENG.). 24p. (J). pap. 10.99 *(978-1-0765-1881-1(8))* Independently Published.

—English-Turkish Time/Zaman Children's Bilingual Picture Book. Carlson Jr, Richard. 2018. (ENG.). 28p. (J). pap. 10.99 *(978-1-7241-4946-6(6))* Independently Published.

—English-Turkish Trouble/Üzüntü Children's Bilingual Picture Book. Carlson Jr, Richard. 2018. (ENG.). 24p. (J). pap. 10.99 *(978-1-7920-2466-5(5))* Independently Published.

—English-Ukrainian My Feelings Are Hurt/Мене зачепили за живе Children's Bilingual Picture Book. Carlson, Richard. 2019. (ENG.). 24p. (J). pap. 10.99 *(978-1-0765-2434-8(6))* Independently Published.

—English-Ukrainian Time Children's Bilingual Picture Book. Carlson Jr, Richard. 2018. (ENG.). 28p. (J). pap. 10.99 *(978-1-7241-4964-0(4))* Independently Published.

—English-Urdu My Feelings Are Hurt Children's Bilingual Picture Book. Carlson, Richard. 2019. (ENG.). 24p. (J). pap. 10.99 *(978-1-0767-9667-7(2))* Independently Published.

—English-Urdu Trouble Children's Bilingual Picture Book. Carlson Jr, Richard. 2018. (ENG.). 24p. (J). pap. 10.99 *(978-1-7920-2525-9(4))* Independently Published.

—English-Uzbek My Feelings Are Hurt/His-Tuyg'ularim Yaralandi Children's Bilingual Picture Book. Carlson, Richard. 2019. (ENG.). 24p. (J). pap. 10.99 *(978-1-0765-2666-3(7))* Independently Published.

—English-Uzbek Trouble/Muammo Children's Bilingual Picture Book. Carlson Jr, Richard. 2018. (ENG.). 24p. (J). pap. 10.99 *(978-1-7920-2765-9(6))* Independently Published.

—English-Vietnamese My Feelings Are Hurt/Cảm Xúc Của Mình Bị Tổn Thương Children's Bilingual Picture Book. Carlson, Richard. 2019. (ENG.). 24p. (J). pap. 10.99 *(978-1-0765-3045-5(1))* Independently Published.

—English-Vietnamese Time Children's Bilingual Picture Book. Carlson Jr, Richard. 2018. (ENG.). 28p. (J). pap. 10.99 *(978-1-7241-5431-6(1))* Independently Published.

—English-Vietnamese Trouble/Children's Bilingual Picture Book. Carlson Jr, Richard. 2018. (ENG.). 24p. (J). pap. 10.99 *(978-1-7920-2802-1(4))* Independently Published.

—English-Welsh My Feelings Are Hurt/Fy Nheimladau Yn Brifo Children's Bilingual Picture Book. Carlson, Richard. 2019. (ENG.). 24p. (J). pap. 10.99 *(978-1-0765-3253-4(5))* Independently Published.

—English-Welsh Numbers/Rhifau Children's Bilingual Picture Dictionary. Carlson Jr, Richard. 2018. (ENG.). 26p. (J). pap. 10.99 *(978-1-7310-3090-0(8))* Independently Published.

—English-Welsh School/Ysgol Children. Carlson Jr, Richard. 2018. (ENG.). 24p. (J). pap. 10.99 *(978-1-7310-6770-8(4))* Independently Published.

—English-Welsh Time/Amser Children's Bilingual Picture Book. Carlson Jr, Richard. 2018. (ENG.). 28p. (J). pap. 10.99 *(978-1-7310-2838-9(5))* Independently Published.

—English-Welsh Tools/Offer Children's Bilingual Picture Dictionary. Carlson Jr, Richard. 2018. (ENG.). 26p. (J). pap. 10.99 *(978-1-7311-1420-4(6))* Independently Published.

—English-Welsh Trouble/Trafferth Children's Bilingual Picture Book. Carlson Jr, Richard. 2018. (ENG.). 24p. (J). pap. 10.99 *(978-1-7920-8695-3(4))* Independently Published.

—English-Welsh Vehicles/Cerbydau Children's Bilingual Picture Dictionary. Carlson Jr, Richard. 2018. (ENG.). 24p. (J). pap. 10.99 *(978-1-7311-1495-2(8))* Independently Published.

—English-Xhosa Time Children's Bilingual Picture Book. Carlson Jr, Richard. 2018. (ENG.). 28p. (J). pap. 10.99 *(978-1-7241-5444-6(3))* Independently Published.

—English-Xhosa Trouble/Ingxaki Children's Bilingual Picture Book. Carlson Jr, Richard. 2018. (ENG.). 24p. (J). pap. 10.99 *(978-1-7920-8329-7(7))* Independently Published.

—English-Yiddish My Feelings Are Hurt Children's Bilingual Picture Book. Carlson, Richard. 2019. (ENG.). 24p. (J). pap. 10.99 *(978-1-0767-9858-9(6))* Independently Published.

—English-Yoruba My Feelings Are Hurt/Ó dùn Mí lọ́kàn Mi Children's Bilingual Picture Book. Carlson, Richard. 2019. (ENG.). 24p. (J). pap. 10.99 *(978-1-0765-3700-3(6))* Independently Published.

—English-Yoruba Time. Carlson Jr, Richard. 2018. (ENG.). 28p. (J). pap. 10.99 *(978-1-7241-5454-5(0))* Independently Published.

—English-Yoruba Trouble/Wàhálà Children's Bilingual Picture Book. Carlson Jr, Richard. 2018. (ENG.). 24p. (J). pap. 10.99 *(978-1-7920-8558-1(3))* Independently Published.

—English-Zulu My Feelings Are Hurt/Ngiphatheke Kabuhlungu Children's Bilingual Picture Book. Carlson, Richard. 2019. (ENG.). 24p. (J). pap. 10.99 *(978-1-0765-3873-4(8))* Independently Published.

—English-Zulu Trouble/Inkinga Children's Bilingual Picture Book. Carlson Jr, Richard. 2018. (ENG.). 24p. (J). pap. 10.99 *(978-1-7920-8628-1(8))* Independently Published.

Carlson, Suzanne. Espa&#65533;ol-Afrik&#65533;ans Herramientas/Gereedskap Diccionario Biling&#65533;e de Im&#65533;genes para Ni&#65533;os. Carlson, Richard. 2019. (SPA.). 26p. (J). pap. 10.99 ***(978-1-6869-0879-8(2))*** Independently Published.

—Espa&#65533;ol-Afrik&#65533;ans Veh&#65533;culos/Voertuie Diccionario Biling&#65533;e de Im&#65533;genes para Ni&#65533;os. Carlson, Richard. 2019. (SPA.). 24p. (J). pap. 10.99 ***(978-1-0887-3451-3(0))*** Independently Published.

—Espa&#65533;ol-Alban&#65533;s Herramientas/Veglat Diccionario Biling&#65533;e de Im&#65533;genes para Ni&#65533;os. Carlson, Richard. 2019. (SPA.). 26p. (J). pap. 10.99 ***(978-1-6869-1014-2(2))*** Independently Published.

—Espa&#65533;ol-Alban&#65533;s Veh&#65533;culos/Automjetet Diccionario Biling&#65533;e de Im&#65533;genes para Ni&#65533;os. Carlson, Richard. 2019. (SPA.). 24p. (J). pap. 10.99 ***(978-1-0887-5458-0(9))*** Independently Published.

—Espa&#65533;ol-Alem&#65533;n Herramientas/Werkzeuge Diccionario Biling&#65533;e de Im&#65533;genes para Ni&#65533;os. Carlson, Richard. 2019. (SPA.). 26p. (J). pap. 10.99 ***(978-1-6872-3842-9(1))*** Independently Published.

—Espa&#65533;ol-Alem&#65533;n Veh&#65533;culos/Fahrzeuge Diccionario Biling&#65533;e de Im&#65533;genes para Ni&#65533;os. Carlson, Richard. 2019. (SPA.). 24p. (J). pap. 10.99 ***(978-1-0894-6879-0(2))*** Independently Published.

—Espa&#65533;ol-Amh&#65533;rico Herramientas/መሳሪያዎች Diccionario Biling&#65533;e de Im&#65533;genes para Ni&#65533;os. Carlson, Richard. 2019. (SPA.). 26p. (J). pap. 10.99 ***(978-1-6869-1209-2(9))*** Independently Published.

—Espa&#65533;ol-Amh&#65533;rico Veh&#65533;culos/ተሽከርካሪዎች Diccionario Biling&#65533;e de Im&#65533;genes para Ni&#65533;os. Carlson, Richard. 2019. (SPA.). 24p. (J). pap. 10.99 ***(978-1-0887-6056-7(2))*** Independently Published.

—Espa&#65533;ol-&#65533;rabe Del Golfo Veh&#65533;culos Diccionario Biling&#65533;e de Im&#65533;genes para Ni&#65533;os. Carlson, Richard. 2019. (SPA.). 24p. (J). pap. 10.99 ***(978-1-0887-9508-8(0))*** Independently Published.

—Espa&#65533;ol-&#65533;rabe Egipcio Veh&#65533;culos Diccionario Biling&#65533;e de Im&#65533;genes para Ni&#65533;os. Carlson, Richard. 2019. (SPA.). 24p. (J). pap. 10.99 ***(978-1-0887-8569-0(7))*** Independently Published.

—Espa&#65533;ol-&#65533;rabe Herramientas Diccionario Biling&#65533;e de Im&#65533;genes para Ni&#65533;os. Carlson, Richard. 2019. (SPA.). 26p. (J). pap. 10.99 ***(978-1-6870-6128-7(9))*** Independently Published.

—Espa&#65533;ol-&#65533;rabe Levantino Veh&#65533;culos Diccionario Biling&#65533;e de Im&#65533;genes para Ni&#65533;os. Carlson, Richard. 2019. (SPA.). 24p. (J). pap. 10.99 ***(978-1-0888-0928-0(6))*** Independently Published.

—Espa&#65533;ol-&#65533;rabe Magreb&#65533; Veh&#65533;culos Diccionario Biling&#65533;e de Im&#65533;genes para Ni&#65533;os. Carlson, Richard. 2019. (SPA.). 24p. (J). pap. 10.99 ***(978-1-0888-1174-0(4))*** Independently Published.

—Espa&#65533;ol-&#65533;rabe Veh&#65533;culos Diccionario Biling&#65533;e de Im&#65533;genes para Ni&#65533;os. Carlson, Richard. 2019. (SPA.). 24p. (J). pap. 10.99 ***(978-1-0887-9302-2(9))*** Independently Published.

—Espa&#65533;ol-Armenio Herramientas/Գործիքներ Diccionario Biling&#65533;e de Im&#65533;genes para Ni&#65533;os. Carlson, Richard. 2019. (SPA.). 26p. (J). pap. 10.99 ***(978-1-6870-6842-2(9))*** Independently Published.

—Espa&#65533;ol-Armenio Veh&#65533;culos/Տրանսպորտային միջոցներ Diccionario Biling&#65533;e de Im&#65533;genes para Ni&#65533;os. Carlson, Richard. 2019. (SPA.). 24p. (J). pap. 10.99 ***(978-1-0888-1953-1(2))*** Independently Published.

—Espa&#65533;ol-Azerbaiyano Herramientas/Alətlər Diccionario Biling&#65533;e de Im&#65533;genes para Ni&#65533;os. Carlson, Richard. 2019. (SPA.). 26p. (J). pap. 10.99 ***(978-1-6870-7571-0(9))*** Independently Published.

—Espa&#65533;ol-Azerbaiyano Veh&#65533;culos/Nəqliyyat Vasitələri Diccionario Biling&#65533;e de Im&#65533;genes para Ni&#65533;os. Carlson, Richard. 2019. (SPA.). 24p. (J). pap. 10.99 ***(978-1-0888-2194-7(4))*** Independently Published.

—Espa&#65533;ol-B&#65533;lgaro Herramientas/Инструменти Diccionario Biling&#65533;e de Im&#65533;genes para Ni&#65533;os. Carlson, Richard. 2019. (SPA.). 26p. (J). pap. 10.99 ***(978-1-6870-8838-3(1))*** Independently Published.

—Espa&#65533;ol-B&#65533;lgaro Veh&#65533;culos/Превозни средства Diccionario Biling&#65533;e de Im&#65533;genes para Ni&#65533;os. Carlson, Richard. 2019. (SPA.). 24p. (J). pap. 10.99 ***(978-1-0890-3660-9(4))*** Independently Published.

—Espa&#65533;ol-Bengal&#65533; Herramientas/যন্ত্রপাতি Diccionario Biling&#65533;e de Im&#65533;genes para Ni&#65533;os. Carlson, Richard. 2019. (SPA.). 26p. (J). pap. 10.99 ***(978-1-6870-8005-9(4))*** Independently Published.

—Espa&#65533;ol-Bengal&#65533; Veh&#65533;culos/যানবাহন Diccionario Biling&#65533;e de Im&#65533;genes para Ni&#65533;os. Carlson, Richard. 2019. (SPA.). 24p. (J). pap. 10.99 ***(978-1-0888-2747-5(0))*** Independently Published.

—Espa&#65533;ol-Bielorruso Herramientas/Інструменты Diccionario Biling&#65533;e de Im&#65533;genes para Ni&#65533;os. Carlson, Richard. 2019. (SPA.). 26p. (J). pap. 10.99 ***(978-1-6870-7897-1(1))*** Independently Published.

—Espa&#65533;ol-Bielorruso Veh&#65533;culos/Транспартныя сродкі Diccionario Biling&#65533;e de Im&#65533;genes para Ni&#65533;os. Carlson, Richard. 2019. (SPA.). 24p. (J). pap. 10.99 ***(978-1-0888-2450-4(1))*** Independently Published.

—Espa&#65533;ol-Birmano Herramientas Diccionario Biling&#65533;e de Im&#65533;genes para Ni&#65533;os. Carlson, Richard. 2019. (SPA.). 26p. (J). pap. 10.99 ***(978-1-6870-8930-4(2))*** Independently Published.

—Espa&#65533;ol-Birmano Veh&#65533;culos Diccionario Biling&#65533;e de Im&#65533;genes para Ni&#65533;os. Carlson, Richard. 2019. (SPA.). 24p. (J). pap. 10.99 ***(978-1-0890-3907-5(7))*** Independently Published.

—Espa&#65533;ol-Bosnio Herramientas/Alati Diccionario Biling&#65533;e de Im&#65533;genes para Ni&#65533;os. Carlson, Richard. 2019. (SPA.). 26p. (J). pap. 10.99 ***(978-1-6870-8164-3(6))*** Independently Published.

—Espa&#65533;ol-Bosnio Veh&#65533;culos/Vozila Diccionario Biling&#65533;e de Im&#65533;genes para Ni&#65533;os. Carlson, Richard. 2019. (SPA.). 24p. (J). pap. 10.99 ***(978-1-0890-3368-4(0))*** Independently Published.

—Espa&#65533;ol-Canar&#65533;s Herramientas Diccionario Biling&#65533;e de Im&#65533;genes para Ni&#65533;os. Carlson, Richard. 2019. (SPA.). 26p. (J). pap. 10.99 ***(978-1-6874-3011-3(X))*** Independently Published.

—Espa&#65533;ol-Canar&#65533;s Veh&#65533;culos Diccionario Biling&#65533;e de Im&#65533;genes para Ni&#65533;os. Carlson, Richard. 2019. (SPA.). 24p. (J). pap. 10.99 ***(978-1-0896-2195-9(7))*** Independently Published.

—Espa&#65533;ol-Catal&#65533;n Herramientas/Eines Diccionario Biling&#65533;e de Im&#65533;genes para Ni&#65533;os. Carlson, Richard. 2019. (SPA.). 26p. (J). pap. 10.99 ***(978-1-6870-9028-7(9))*** Independently Published.

—Espa&#65533;ol-Catal&#65533;n Veh&#65533;culos/Vehicles Diccionario Biling&#65533;e de Im&#65533;genes para Ni&#65533;os. Carlson, Richard. 2019. (SPA.). 24p. (J). pap. 10.99 ***(978-1-0890-4098-9(9))*** Independently Published.

—Espa&#65533;ol-Checo Herramientas/N&#65533;stroje Diccionario Biling&#65533;e de Im&#65533;genes para Ni&#65533;os. Carlson, Richard. 2019. (SPA.). 26p. (J). pap. 10.99 ***(978-1-6870-9694-4(5))*** Independently Published.

—Espa&#65533;ol-Checo Veh&#65533;culos/Dopravn&#65533; Prostředky Diccionario Biling&#65533;e de Im&#65533;genes para Ni&#65533;os. Carlson, Richard. 2019. (SPA.). 24p. (J). pap. 10.99 ***(978-1-0892-4480-6(0))*** Independently Published.

—Espa&#65533;ol-Chino Canton&#65533;s Tradicional Herramientas/工具 Diccionario Biling&#65533;e de Im&#65533;genes para Ni&#65533;os. Carlson, Richard. 2019. (SPA.). 26p. (J). pap. 10.99 ***(978-1-6870-9359-2(8))*** Independently Published.

—Espa&#65533;ol-Chino Canton&#65533;s Tradicional Veh&#65533;culos/交通工具 Diccionario Biling&#65533;e de Im&#65533;genes para Ni&#65533;os. Carlson, Richard. 2019. (SPA.). 24p. (J). pap. 10.99 ***(978-1-0891-5188-3(8))*** Independently Published.

—Espa&#65533;ol-Chino Mandar&#65533;n Simplificado Herramientas/工具 Diccionario Biling&#65533;e de Im&#65533;genes para Ni&#65533;os. Carlson, Richard. 2019. (SPA.). 26p. (J). pap. 10.99 ***(978-1-6870-9251-9(6))*** Independently Published.

—Espa&#65533;ol-Chino Mandar&#65533;n Simplificado Veh&#65533;culos/车辆 Diccionario Biling&#65533;e de Im&#65533;genes para Ni&#65533;os. Carlson, Richard. 2019. (SPA.). 24p. (J). pap. 10.99 ***(978-1-0890-4792-6(4))*** Independently Published.

—Espa&#65533;ol-Chino Mandar&#65533;n Tradicional Herramientas/工具 Diccionario Biling&#65533;e de Im&#65533;genes para Ni&#65533;os. Carlson, Richard. 2019. (SPA.). 26p. (J). pap. 10.99 ***(978-1-6870-9121-5(8))*** Independently Published.

—Espa&#65533;ol-Chino Mandar&#65533;n Tradicional (Taiw&#65533;n) Veh&#65533;culos/載具 Diccionario Biling&#65533;e de Im&#65533;genes para Ni&#65533;os. Carlson, Richard. 2019. (SPA.). 24p. (J). pap. 10.99 ***(978-1-0891-5445-7(3))*** Independently Published.

—Espa&#65533;ol-Chino Mandar&#65533;n Tradicional Veh&#65533;culos/載具 Diccionario Biling&#65533;e de Im&#65533;genes para Ni&#65533;os. Carlson, Richard. 2019. (SPA.). 24p. (J). pap. 10.99 ***(978-1-0890-4339-3(2))*** Independently Published.

—Espa&#65533;ol-Cingal&#65533;s Herramientas/මෙවලම් Diccionario Biling&#65533;e de Im&#65533;genes para Ni&#65533;os. Carlson, Richard. 2019. (SPA.). 26p. (J). pap. 10.99 ***(978-1-6883-2545-6(X))*** Independently Published.

—Espa&#65533;ol-Cingal&#65533;s Veh&#65533;culos Diccionario Biling&#65533;e de Im&#65533;genes para Ni&#65533;os. Carlson, Richard. 2019. (SPA.). 24p. (J). pap. 10.99 ***(978-1-6862-7908-9(6))*** Independently Published.

—Espa&#65533;ol-Coreano Herramientas/공구들 Diccionario

Biling�e de Im�genes para Ni�os. Carlson, Richard. 2019. (SPA.). 26p. (J). pap. 10.99 ***(978-1-6874-4986-3(4))*** Independently Published.

—Espa�ol-Coreano Veh�culos/운송수단 Diccionario Biling�e de Im�genes para Ni�os. Carlson, Richard. 2019. (SPA.). 24p. (J). pap. 10.99 ***(978-1-0897-7268-2(8))*** Independently Published.

—Espa�ol-Criollo Haitiano Herramientas/Zouti Yo Diccionario Biling�e de Im�genes para Ni�os. Carlson, Richard. 2019. (SPA.). 26p. (J). pap. 10.99 ***(978-1-6872-4500-7(2))*** Independently Published.

—Espa�ol-Criollo Haitiano Veh�culos/Machin Yo Diccionario Biling�e de Im�genes para Ni�os. Carlson, Richard. 2019. (SPA.). 24p. (J). pap. 10.99 ***(978-1-0895-9699-8(5))*** Independently Published.

—Espa�ol-Croata Herramientas/Alati Diccionario Biling�e de Im�genes para Ni�os. Carlson, Richard. 2019. (SPA.). 26p. (J). pap. 10.99 ***(978-1-6870-9461-2(6))*** Independently Published.

—Espa�ol-Croata Veh�culos/Vozila Diccionario Biling�e de Im�genes para Ni�os. Carlson, Richard. 2019. (SPA.). 24p. (J). pap. 10.99 ***(978-1-0891-6415-9(7))*** Independently Published.

—Espa�ol-Dan�s Herramientas/V�rkt�j Diccionario Biling�e de Im�genes para Ni�os. Carlson, Richard. 2019. (SPA.). 26p. (J). pap. 10.99 ***(978-1-6871-0170-9(1))*** Independently Published.

—Espa�ol-Dan�s Veh�culos/K�ret�jer Diccionario Biling�e de Im�genes para Ni�os. Carlson, Richard. 2019. (SPA.). 24p. (J). pap. 10.99 ***(978-1-0892-5079-1(7))*** Independently Published.

—Espa�ol-Dar� Herramientas Diccionario Biling�e de Im�genes para Ni�os. Carlson, Richard. 2019. (SPA.). 26p. (J). pap. 10.99 ***(978-1-6871-0341-3(0))*** Independently Published.

—Espa�ol-Dar� Veh�culos Diccionario Biling�e de Im�genes para Ni�os. Carlson, Richard. 2019. (SPA.). 24p. (J). pap. 10.99 ***(978-1-0894-3580-8(0))*** Independently Published.

—Espa�ol-Eslovaco Herramientas/N�stroje Diccionario Biling�e de Im�genes para Ni�os. Carlson, Richard. 2019. (SPA.). 26p. (J). pap. 10.99 ***(978-1-6883-2801-3(7))*** Independently Published.

—Espa�ol-Eslovaco Veh�culos/Vozidl� Diccionario Biling�e de Im�genes para Ni�os. Carlson, Richard. 2019. (SPA.). 24p. (J). pap. 10.99 ***(978-1-6862-8097-9(1))*** Independently Published.

—Espa�ol-Esloveno (Eslovenia) Herramientas/Orodja Diccionario Biling�e de Im�genes para Ni�os. Carlson, Richard. 2019. (SPA.). 26p. (J). pap. 10.99 ***(978-1-6883-3000-9(3))*** Independently Published.

—Espa�ol-Esloveno (Eslovenia) Veh�culos/Vozila Diccionario Biling�e de Im�genes para Ni�os. Carlson, Richard. 2019. (SPA.). 24p. (J). pap. 10.99 ***(978-1-6864-7167-4(X))*** Independently Published.

—Espa�ol-Estonio Herramientas/T��riistad Diccionario Biling�e de Im�genes para Ni�os. Carlson, Richard. 2019. (SPA.). 26p. (J). pap. 10.99 ***(978-1-6871-0789-3(0))*** Independently Published.

—Espa�ol-Estonio Veh�culos/S�idukid Diccionario Biling�e de Im�genes para Ni�os. Carlson, Richard. 2019. (SPA.). 24p. (J). pap. 10.99 ***(978-1-0894-5307-9(8))*** Independently Published.

—Espa�ol-Finland�s Herramientas/Ty�kalut Diccionario Biling�e de Im�genes para Ni�os. Carlson, Richard. 2019. (SPA.). 26p. (J). pap. 10.99 ***(978-1-6872-2187-2(1))*** Independently Published.

—Espa�ol-Finland�s Veh�culos/Kulkuneuvot Diccionario Biling�e de Im�genes para Ni�os. Carlson, Richard. 2019. (SPA.). 24p. (J). pap. 10.99 ***(978-1-0894-5811-1(8))*** Independently Published.

—Espa�ol-Flamenco (belga) Herramientas/Werktuigen Diccionario Biling�e de Im�genes para Ni�os. Carlson, Richard. 2019. (SPA.). 26p. (J). pap. 10.99 ***(978-1-6872-2353-1(X))*** Independently Published.

—Espa�ol-Flamenco (belga) Veh�culos/Voertuigen Diccionario Biling�e de Im�genes para Ni�os. Carlson, Richard. 2019. (SPA.). 24p. (J). pap. 10.99 ***(978-1-0894-6138-8(0))*** Independently Published.

—Espa�ol-Franc�s Herramientas/Outils Diccionario Biling�e de Im�genes para Ni�os. Carlson, Richard. 2019. (SPA.). 26p. (J). pap. 10.99 ***(978-1-6872-2931-1(7))*** Independently Published.

—Espa�ol-Franc�s Veh�culos/V�hicules Diccionario Biling�e de Im�genes para Ni�os. Carlson, Richard. 2019. (SPA.). 24p. (J). pap. 10.99 ***(978-1-0894-6429-7(0))*** Independently Published.

—Espa�ol-Ga�lico Irland�s Herramientas/Uirlis� Diccionario Biling�e de Im�genes para Ni�os. Carlson, Richard. 2019. (SPA.). 26p. (J). pap. 10.99 ***(978-1-6872-6340-7(X))*** Independently Published.

—Espa�ol-Ga�lico Irland�s Veh�culos/Feithicl� Diccionario Biling�e de Im�genes para Ni�os. Carlson, Richard. 2019. (SPA.). 24p. (J). pap. 10.99 ***(978-1-0896-1202-5(8))*** Independently Published.

—Espa�ol-Gal�s Herramientas/Offer Diccionario Biling�e de Im�genes para Ni�os. Carlson, Richard. 2019. (SPA.). 26p. (J). pap. 10.99 ***(978-1-6884-6184-0(1))*** Independently Published.

—Espa�ol-Georgiano Herramientas/სამუშაოიარაღები Diccionario Biling�e de Im�genes para Ni�os. Carlson, Richard. 2019. (SPA.). 26p. (J). pap. 10.99 ***(978-1-6872-3038-6(2))*** Independently Published.

—Espa�ol-Georgiano Veh�culos/სატრანსპორტოსაშუალებები Diccionario Biling�e de Im�genes para Ni�os. Carlson, Richard. 2019. (SPA.). 24p. (J). pap. 10.99 ***(978-1-0894-6691-8(9))*** Independently Published.

—Espa�ol-Griego Herramientas/Εργαλεία Diccionario Biling�e de Im�genes para Ni�os. Carlson, Richard. 2019. (SPA.). 26p. (J). pap. 10.99 ***(978-1-6872-3960-0(6))*** Independently Published.

—Espa�ol-Griego Veh�culos/Οχήματα Diccionario Biling�e de Im�genes para Ni�os. Carlson, Richard. 2019. (SPA.). 24p. (J). pap. 10.99 ***(978-1-0895-9335-5(X))*** Independently Published.

—Espa�ol-Guyarat� Herramientas/સાધનો Diccionario Biling�e de Im�genes para Ni�os. Carlson, Richard. 2019. (SPA.). 26p. (J). pap. 10.99 ***(978-1-6872-4090-3(6))*** Independently Published.

—Espa�ol-Guyarat� Veh�culos/વાહનો Diccionario Biling�e de Im�genes para Ni�os. Carlson, Richard. 2019. (SPA.). 24p. (J). pap. 10.99 ***(978-1-0895-9526-7(3))*** Independently Published.

—Espa�ol-H�ngaro Herramientas/Szersz�mok Diccionario Biling�e de Im�genes para Ni�os. Carlson, Richard. 2019. (SPA.). 26p. (J). pap. 10.99 ***(978-1-6872-5441-2(9))*** Independently Published.

—Espa�ol-H�ngaro Veh�culos/J�rművek Diccionario Biling�e de Im�genes para Ni�os. Carlson, Richard. 2019. (SPA.). 24p. (J). pap. 10.99 ***(978-1-0896-0500-3(5))*** Independently Published.

—Espa�ol-Hausa Herramientas/Kayan Aiki Diccionario Biling�e de Im�genes para Ni�os. Carlson, Richard. 2019. (SPA.). 26p. (J). pap. 10.99 ***(978-1-6872-4614-1(9))*** Independently Published.

—Espa�ol-Hausa Veh�culos-Abin Hawa/Mota Diccionario Biling�e de Im�genes para Ni�os. Carlson, Richard. 2019. (SPA.). 24p. (J). pap. 10.99 ***(978-1-0895-9895-4(5))*** Independently Published.

—Espa�ol-Hebreo Herramientas Diccionario Biling�e de Im�genes para Ni�os. Carlson, Richard. 2019. (SPA.). 26p. (J). pap. 10.99 ***(978-1-6872-4792-6(7))*** Independently Published.

—Espa�ol-Hebreo Veh�culos/כלירכב Diccionario Biling�e de Im�genes para Ni�os. Carlson, Richard. 2019. (SPA.). 24p. (J). pap. 10.99 ***(978-1-0896-0066-4(6))*** Independently Published.

—Espa�ol-Hindi Herramientas/औजार Diccionario Biling�e de Im�genes para Ni�os. Carlson, Richard. 2019. (SPA.). 26p. (J). pap. 10.99 ***(978-1-6872-5333-0(1))*** Independently Published.

—Espa�ol-Hindi Veh�culos/वाहन Diccionario Biling�e de Im�genes para Ni�os. Carlson, Richard. 2019. (SPA.). 24p. (J). pap. 10.99 ***(978-1-0896-0344-3(4))*** Independently Published.

—Espa�ol-Holand�s Herramientas/Gereedschappen Diccionario Biling�e de Im�genes para Ni�os. Carlson, Richard. 2019. (SPA.). 26p. (J). pap. 10.99 ***(978-1-6871-0512-7(X))*** Independently Published.

—Espa�ol-Holand�s Veh�culos/Voertuigen Diccionario Biling�e de Im�genes para Ni�os. Carlson, Richard. 2019. (SPA.). 24p. (J). pap. 10.99 ***(978-1-0894-3847-2(8))*** Independently Published.

—Espa�ol-Indonesio Herramientas/Perkakas Diccionario Biling�e de Im�genes para Ni�os. Carlson, Richard. 2019. (SPA.). 26p. (J). pap. 10.99 ***(978-1-6872-5993-6(3))*** Independently Published.

—Espa�ol-Indonesio Veh�culos/Kendaraan Diccionario Biling�e de Im�genes para Ni�os. Carlson, Richard. 2019. (SPA.). 24p. (J). pap. 10.99 ***(978-1-0896-0836-3(5))*** Independently Published.

—Espa�ol-Ingl�s Herramientas/Tools Diccionario Biling�e de Im�genes para Ni�os. Carlson, Richard. 2019. (SPA.). 26p. (J). pap. 10.99 ***(978-1-6871-0638-4(X))*** Independently Published.

—Espa�ol-Ingl�s Veh�culos/Vehicles Diccionario Biling�e de Im�genes para Ni�os. Carlson, Richard. 2019. (SPA.). 24p. (J). pap. 10.99 ***(978-1-0894-4326-1(9))*** Independently Published.

—Espa�ol-Island�s Herramientas/Verkf�ri Diccionario Biling�e de Im�genes para Ni�os. Carlson, Richard. 2019. (SPA.). 26p. (J). pap. 10.99 ***(978-1-6872-5590-7(3))*** Independently Published.

—Espa�ol-Island�s Veh�culos/Farart�ki Diccionario Biling�e de Im�genes para Ni�os. Carlson, Richard. 2019. (SPA.). 24p. (J). pap. 10.99 ***(978-1-0896-0618-5(4))*** Independently Published.

—Espa�ol-Italiano Herramientas/Attrezzi Diccionario Biling�e de Im�genes para Ni�os. Carlson, Richard. 2019. (SPA.). 26p. (J). pap. 10.99 ***(978-1-6874-2725-0(9))*** Independently Published.

—Espa�ol-Italiano Veh�culos/Veicoli Diccionario Biling�e de Im�genes para Ni�os. Carlson, Richard. 2019. (SPA.). 24p. (J). pap. 10.99 ***(978-1-0896-1854-6(9))*** Independently Published.

—Espa�ol-Japon�s Herramientas/工具 Diccionario Biling�e de Im�genes para Ni�os. Carlson, Richard. 2019. (SPA.). 26p. (J). pap. 10.99 ***(978-1-6874-2847-9(6))*** Independently Published.

—Espa�ol-Japon�s Veh�culos/のりもの Diccionario Biling�e de Im�genes para Ni�os. Carlson, Richard. 2019. (SPA.). 24p. (J). pap. 10.99 ***(978-1-0896-1978-9(2))*** Independently Published.

—Espa�ol-Jemer (camboyano) Herramientas Diccionario Biling�e de Im�genes para Ni�os. Carlson, Richard. 2019. (SPA.). 26p. (J). pap. 10.99 ***(978-1-6874-3282-7(1))*** Independently Published.

—Espa�ol-Jemer (camboyano) Veh�culos Diccionario Biling�e de Im�genes para Ni�os. Carlson, Richard. 2019. (SPA.). 24p. (J). pap. 10.99 ***(978-1-0897-6487-8(1))*** Independently Published.

—Espa�ol-Kazajo Herramientas/Құрал-саймандар Diccionario Biling�e de Im�genes para Ni�os. Carlson, Richard. 2019. (SPA.). 26p. (J). pap. 10.99 ***(978-1-6874-3142-4(6))*** Independently Published.

—Espa�ol-Kazajo Veh�culos/Көліктер Diccionario Biling�e de Im�genes para Ni�os. Carlson, Richard. 2019. (SPA.). 24p. (J). pap. 10.99 ***(978-1-0897-6096-2(5))*** Independently Published.

—Espa�ol-Kurdo Herramientas Diccionario Biling�e de Im�genes para Ni�os. Carlson, Richard. 2019. (SPA.). 26p. (J). pap. 10.99 ***(978-1-6874-5240-5(7))*** Independently Published.

—Espa�ol-Kurdo Veh�culos Diccionario Biling�e de Im�genes para Ni�os. Carlson, Richard. 2019. (SPA.). 24p. (J). pap. 10.99 ***(978-1-0897-8632-0(8))*** Independently Published.

—Espa�ol-Lao (laosiano) Herramientas Diccionario Biling�e de Im�genes para Ni�os. Carlson, Richard. 2019. (SPA.). 26p. (J). pap. 10.99 ***(978-1-6876-3423-8(8))*** Independently Published.

—Espa�ol-Lao (laosiano) Veh�culos Diccionario Biling�e de Im�genes para Ni�os. Carlson, Richard. 2019. (SPA.). 24p. (J). pap. 10.99 ***(978-1-0898-0972-2(7))*** Independently Published.

—Espa�ol-Let�n Herramientas/Darbarīki Diccionario Biling�e de Im�genes para Ni�os. Carlson, Richard. 2019. (SPA.). 26p. (J). pap. 10.99 ***(978-1-6876-3614-0(1))*** Independently Published.

—Espa�ol-Let�n Veh�culos/Transporta līdzekļi Diccionario Biling�e de Im�genes para Ni�os. Carlson, Richard. 2019. (SPA.). 24p. (J). pap. 10.99 ***(978-1-0898-1113-8(6))*** Independently Published.

—Espa�ol-Lituano Herramientas/Įrankiai Diccionario Biling�e de Im�genes para Ni�os. Carlson, Richard. 2019. (SPA.). 26p. (J). pap. 10.99 ***(978-1-6876-3781-9(4))*** Independently Published.

—Espa�ol-Lituano Veh�culos/Transporto Priemones Diccionario Biling�e de Im�genes para Ni�os. Carlson, Richard. 2019. (SPA.). 24p. (J). pap. 10.99 ***(978-1-0898-1510-5(7))*** Independently Published.

—Espa�ol-Macedonio Herramientas/Алати Diccionario Biling�e de Im�genes para Ni�os. Carlson, Richard. 2019. (SPA.). 26p. (J). pap. 10.99 ***(978-1-6876-4035-2(1))*** Independently Published.

—Espa�ol-Macedonio Veh�culos/Возила Diccionario Biling�e de Im�genes para Ni�os. Carlson, Richard. 2019. (SPA.). 24p. (J). pap. 10.99 ***(978-1-0898-1922-6(6))*** Independently Published.

—Espa�ol-Malabar Herramientas Diccionario Biling�e de Im�genes para Ni�os. Carlson, Richard. 2019. (SPA.). 26p. (J). pap. 10.99 ***(978-1-6877-4021-2(6))*** Independently Published.

—Espa�ol-Malabar Veh�culos Diccionario Biling�e de Im�genes para Ni�os. Carlson, Richard. 2019. (SPA.). 24p. (J). pap. 10.99 ***(978-1-0898-2488-6(2))*** Independently Published.

—Espa�ol-Malayo Herramientas/Alat Diccionario Biling�e de Im�genes para Ni�os. Carlson, Richard. 2019. (SPA.). 26p. (J). pap. 10.99 ***(978-1-6876-4744-3(5))*** Independently Published.

—Espa�ol-Malayo Veh�culos/Kenderaan Diccionario Biling�e de Im�genes para Ni�os. Carlson, Richard. 2019. (SPA.). 24p. (J). pap. 10.99 ***(978-1-0898-2253-0(7))*** Independently Published.

—Espa�ol-Malt�s Herramientas/Għodda Diccionario Biling�e de Im�genes para Ni�os. Carlson, Richard. 2019. (SPA.). 26p. (J). pap. 10.99 ***(978-1-6878-1827-0(4))*** Independently Published.

—Espa�ol-Malt�s Veh�culos/Vetturi Diccionario Biling�e de Im�genes para Ni�os. Carlson, Richard. 2019. (SPA.). 24p. (J). pap. 10.99 ***(978-1-0898-2698-9(2))*** Independently Published.

—Espa�ol-Marat� Herramientas/हत्यारे Diccionario Biling�e de Im�genes para Ni�os. Carlson, Richard. 2019. (SPA.). 26p. (J). pap. 10.99 ***(978-1-6878-2035-8(X))*** Independently Published.

—Espa�ol-Mongol Herramientas/Багаж Diccionario Biling�e de Im�genes para Ni�os. Carlson, Richard. 2019. (SPA.). 26p. (J). pap. 10.99 ***(978-1-6878-2211-6(5))*** Independently Published.

—Espa�ol-Mongol Veh�culos/Тээврийнхэрэгсэл Diccionario Biling�e de Im�genes para Ni�os. Carlson, Richard. 2019. (SPA.). 24p. (J). pap. 10.99 ***(978-1-0898-3801-2(8))*** Independently Published.

—Espa�ol-Montenegrino Herramientas/Алати Diccionario Biling�e de Im�genes para Ni�os. Carlson, Richard. 2019. (SPA.). 26p. (J). pap. 10.99 ***(978-1-6878-2528-5(9))*** Independently Published.

—Espa�ol-Montenegrino Veh�culos/Vozila Diccionario Biling�e de Im�genes para Ni�os. Carlson, Richard. 2019. (SPA.). 24p. (J). pap. 10.99 ***(978-1-6860-4631-5(6))*** Independently Published.

—Espa�ol-Nepal� Herramientas Diccionario Biling�e de Im�genes para Ni�os. Carlson, Richard. 2019. (SPA.). 26p. (J). pap. 10.99 ***(978-1-6880-9129-0(7))*** Independently Published.

—Espa�ol-Nepal� Veh�culos/सवारीसाधनहरू Diccionario Biling�e de Im�genes para Ni�os. Carlson, Richard. 2019. (SPA.). 24p. (J). pap. 10.99 ***(978-1-6860-4960-6(9))*** Independently Published.

—Espa�ol-Noruego Herramientas/Verkt�y Diccionario Biling�e de Im�genes para Ni�os. Carlson, Richard. 2019. (SPA.). 26p. (J). pap. 10.99 ***(978-1-6881-3020-3(9))*** Independently Published.

—Espa�ol-Noruego Veh�culos/Kj�ret�yer Diccionario Biling�e de Im�genes para Ni�os. Carlson, Richard. 2019. (SPA.). 24p. (J). pap. 10.99 ***(978-1-6860-5152-4(2))*** Independently Published.

—Espa�ol-Panyab� Herramientas/ਸੰਦ Diccionario Biling�e de Im�genes para Ni�os. Carlson, Richard. 2019. (SPA.). 26p. (J). pap. 10.99 ***(978-1-6883-1574-7(8))*** Independently Published.

C

—Espa&#65533;ol-Panyab&#65533; Veh&#65533;culos/ਸਵਾਰੀ Diccionario Biling&#65533;e de Im&#65533;genes para Ni&#65533;os. Carlson, Richard. 2019. (SPA.). 24p. (J). pap. 10.99 ***(978-1-6862-5610-3(8))*** Independently Published.

—Espa&#65533;ol-Past&#65533;n Herramientas Diccionario Biling&#65533;e de Im&#65533;genes para Ni&#65533;os. Carlson, Richard. 2019. (SPA.). 26p. (J). pap. 10.99 ***(978-1-6881-3323-5(2))*** Independently Published.

—Espa&#65533;ol-Past&#65533;n Veh&#65533;culos Diccionario Biling&#65533;e de Im&#65533;genes para Ni&#65533;os. Carlson, Richard. 2019. (SPA.). 24p. (J). pap. 10.99 ***(978-1-6860-5362-7(2))*** Independently Published.

—Espa&#65533;ol-Persa (farsi) Herramientas Diccionario Biling&#65533;e de Im&#65533;genes para Ni&#65533;os. Carlson, Richard. 2019. (SPA.). 26p. (J). pap. 10.99 ***(978-1-6881-3850-6(1))*** Independently Published.

—Espa&#65533;ol-Persa (farsi) Veh&#65533;culos Diccionario Biling&#65533;e de Im&#65533;genes para Ni&#65533;os. Carlson, Richard. 2019. (SPA.). 24p. (J). pap. 10.99 ***(978-1-6860-5767-0(9))*** Independently Published.

—Espa&#65533;ol-Polaco Herramientas/Narzędzia Diccionario Biling&#65533;e de Im&#65533;genes para Ni&#65533;os. Carlson, Richard. 2019. (SPA.). 26p. (J). pap. 10.99 ***(978-1-6881-4118-6(9))*** Independently Published.

—Espa&#65533;ol-Polaco Veh&#65533;culos/Pojazdy Diccionario Biling&#65533;e de Im&#65533;genes para Ni&#65533;os. Carlson, Richard. 2019. (SPA.). 24p. (J). pap. 10.99 ***(978-1-6862-4566-4(1))*** Independently Published.

—Espa&#65533;ol-Portugu&#65533;s (Brasil) Herramientas/Ferramentas Diccionario Biling&#65533;e de Im&#65533;genes para Ni&#65533;os. Carlson, Richard. 2019. (SPA.). 26p. (J). pap. 10.99 ***(978-1-6881-5054-6(4))*** Independently Published.

—Espa&#65533;ol-Portugu&#65533;s (Brasil) Veh&#65533;culos/Ve&#65533;culos Diccionario Biling&#65533;e de Im&#65533;genes para Ni&#65533;os. Carlson, Richard. 2019. (SPA.). 24p. (J). pap. 10.99 ***(978-1-6862-4824-5(5))*** Independently Published.

—Espa&#65533;ol-Portugu&#65533;s (Portugal) Herramientas/Ferramentas Diccionario Biling&#65533;e de Im&#65533;genes para Ni&#65533;os. Carlson, Richard. 2019. (SPA.). 26p. (J). pap. 10.99 ***(978-1-6881-5259-5(8))*** Independently Published.

—Espa&#65533;ol-Portugu&#65533;s (Portugal) Veh&#65533;culos/Ve&#65533;culos Diccionario Biling&#65533;e de Im&#65533;genes para Ni&#65533;os. Carlson, Richard. 2019. (SPA.). 24p. (J). pap. 10.99 ***(978-1-6862-5112-2(2))*** Independently Published.

—Espa&#65533;ol-Rumano Herramientas/Unelte Diccionario Biling&#65533;e de Im&#65533;genes para Ni&#65533;os. Carlson, Richard. 2019. (SPA.). 26p. (J). pap. 10.99 ***(978-1-6883-1744-4(9))*** Independently Published.

—Espa&#65533;ol-Rumano Veh&#65533;culos/Vehicule Diccionario Biling&#65533;e de Im&#65533;genes para Ni&#65533;os. Carlson, Richard. 2019. (SPA.). 24p. (J). pap. 10.99 ***(978-1-6862-6158-9(6))*** Independently Published.

—Espa&#65533;ol-Ruso Herramientas/Инструменты Diccionario Biling&#65533;e de Im&#65533;genes para Ni&#65533;os. Carlson, Richard. 2019. (SPA.). 26p. (J). pap. 10.99 ***(978-1-6883-1910-3(7))*** Independently Published.

—Espa&#65533;ol-Ruso Veh&#65533;culos/Транспорт Diccionario Biling&#65533;e de Im&#65533;genes para Ni&#65533;os. Carlson, Richard. 2019. (SPA.). 24p. (J). pap. 10.99 ***(978-1-6862-6758-1(4))*** Independently Published.

—Espa&#65533;ol-Serbio (cir&#65533;lico) Herramientas/Алати Diccionario Biling&#65533;e de Im&#65533;genes para Ni&#65533;os. Carlson, Richard. 2019. (SPA.). 26p. (J). pap. 10.99 ***(978-1-6883-2071-0(7))*** Independently Published.

—Espa&#65533;ol-Serbio (cir&#65533;lico) Veh&#65533;culos/Возила Diccionario Biling&#65533;e de Im&#65533;genes para Ni&#65533;os. Carlson, Richard. 2019. (SPA.). 24p. (J). pap. 10.99 ***(978-1-6862-6955-4(2))*** Independently Published.

—Espa&#65533;ol-Serbio (lat&#65533;n) Herramientas/Alati Diccionario Biling&#65533;e de Im&#65533;genes para Ni&#65533;os. Carlson, Richard. 2019. (SPA.). 26p. (J). pap. 10.99 ***(978-1-6883-2192-2(6))*** Independently Published.

—Espa&#65533;ol-Serbio (lat&#65533;n) Veh&#65533;culos/Vozila Diccionario Biling&#65533;e de Im&#65533;genes para Ni&#65533;os. Carlson, Richard. 2019. (SPA.). 24p. (J). pap. 10.99 ***(978-1-6862-7236-3(7))*** Independently Published.

—Espa&#65533;ol-Shanghain&#65533;s Veh&#65533;culos/车辆 Diccionario Biling&#65533;e de Im&#65533;genes para Ni&#65533;os. Carlson, Richard. 2019. (SPA.). 24p. (J). pap. 10.99 ***(978-1-6862-7482-4(3))*** Independently Published.

—Espa&#65533;ol-Somal&#65533; Herramientas/Qalab Diccionario Biling&#65533;e de Im&#65533;genes para Ni&#65533;os. Carlson, Richard. 2019. (SPA.). 26p. (J). pap. 10.99 ***(978-1-6883-3484-7(X))*** Independently Published.

—Espa&#65533;ol-Somal&#65533; Veh&#65533;culos/Gaadiid Diccionario Biling&#65533;e de Im&#65533;genes para Ni&#65533;os. Carlson, Richard. 2019. (SPA.). 24p. (J). pap. 10.99 ***(978-1-6864-7340-1(0))*** Independently Published.

—Espa&#65533;ol-Suajili Herramientas/Zana Diccionario Biling&#65533;e de Im&#65533;genes para Ni&#65533;os. Carlson, Richard. 2019. (SPA.). 26p. (J). pap. 10.99 ***(978-1-6883-3739-8(3))*** Independently Published.

—Espa&#65533;ol-Suajili Veh&#65533;culos/Magari Diccionario Biling&#65533;e de Im&#65533;genes para Ni&#65533;os. Carlson, Richard. 2019. (SPA.). 24p. (J). pap. 10.99 ***(978-1-6864-7470-5(9))*** Independently Published.

—Espa&#65533;ol-Sueco Herramientas/Verktyg Diccionario Biling&#65533;e de Im&#65533;genes para Ni&#65533;os. Carlson, Richard. 2019. (SPA.). 26p. (J). pap. 10.99 ***(978-1-6884-4168-2(9))*** Independently Published.

—Espa&#65533;ol-Sueco Veh&#65533;culos/Fordon Diccionario Biling&#65533;e de Im&#65533;genes para Ni&#65533;os. Carlson, Richard. 2019. (SPA.). 24p. (J). pap. 10.99 ***(978-1-6864-7661-7(2))*** Independently Published.

—Espa&#65533;ol-Tagalo Herramientas/Mga Gamit Diccionario Biling&#65533;e de Im&#65533;genes para Ni&#65533;os. Carlson, Richard. 2019. (SPA.). 26p. (J). pap. 10.99 ***(978-1-6884-4309-9(6))*** Independently Published.

—Espa&#65533;ol-Tagalo Veh&#65533;culos/Mga Sasakyan Diccionario Biling&#65533;e de Im&#65533;genes para Ni&#65533;os. Carlson, Richard. 2019. (SPA.). 24p. (J). pap. 10.99 ***(978-1-6864-8013-3(X))*** Independently Published.

—Espa&#65533;ol-Tailand&#65533;s Herramientas/เครื่องมือ Diccionario Biling&#65533;e de Im&#65533;genes para Ni&#65533;os. Carlson, Richard. 2019. (SPA.). 26p. (J). pap. 10.99 ***(978-1-6884-5064-6(5))*** Independently Published.

—Espa&#65533;ol-Tailand&#65533;s Veh&#65533;culos/ยานพาหนะ Diccionario Biling&#65533;e de Im&#65533;genes para Ni&#65533;os. Carlson, Richard. 2019. (SPA.). 24p. (J). pap. 10.99 ***(978-1-6864-9479-6(3))*** Independently Published.

—Espa&#65533;ol-Tamil Herramientas Diccionario Biling&#65533;e de Im&#65533;genes para Ni&#65533;os. Carlson, Richard. 2019. (SPA.). 26p. (J). pap. 10.99 ***(978-1-6884-4488-1(2))*** Independently Published.

—Espa&#65533;ol-Tamil Veh&#65533;culos/வாகனங்கள் Diccionario Biling&#65533;e de Im&#65533;genes para Ni&#65533;os. Carlson, Richard. 2019. (SPA.). 24p. (J). pap. 10.99 ***(978-1-6864-9141-2(7))*** Independently Published.

—Espa&#65533;ol-T&#65533;lugu Herramientas Diccionario Biling&#65533;e de Im&#65533;genes para Ni&#65533;os. Carlson, Richard. 2019. (SPA.). 26p. (J). pap. 10.99 ***(978-1-6884-4658-8(3))*** Independently Published.

—Espa&#65533;ol-T&#65533;lugu Veh&#65533;culos Diccionario Biling&#65533;e de Im&#65533;genes para Ni&#65533;os. Carlson, Richard. 2019. (SPA.). 24p. (J). pap. 10.99 ***(978-1-6864-9297-6(9))*** Independently Published.

—Espa&#65533;ol-Tigri&#65533;a Herramientas/መሳርሒ Diccionario Biling&#65533;e de Im&#65533;genes para Ni&#65533;os. Carlson, Richard. 2019. (SPA.). 26p. (J). pap. 10.99 ***(978-1-6884-5187-2(0))*** Independently Published.

—Espa&#65533;ol-Tigri&#65533;a Veh&#65533;culos/መጓዓዝያ Diccionario Biling&#65533;e de Im&#65533;genes para Ni&#65533;os. Carlson, Richard. 2019. (SPA.). 24p. (J). pap. 10.99 ***(978-1-6864-9715-5(6))*** Independently Published.

—Espa&#65533;ol-Turco Herramientas/Aletler Diccionario Biling&#65533;e de Im&#65533;genes para Ni&#65533;os. Carlson, Richard. 2019. (SPA.). 26p. (J). pap. 10.99 ***(978-1-6884-5403-3(9))*** Independently Published.

—Espa&#65533;ol-Turco Veh&#65533;culos/Ara&#65533;lar Diccionario Biling&#65533;e de Im&#65533;genes para Ni&#65533;os. Carlson, Richard. 2019. (SPA.). 24p. (J). pap. 10.99 ***(978-1-6864-9870-1(5))*** Independently Published.

—Espa&#65533;ol-Ucraniano Herramientas/Інструменти Diccionario Biling&#65533;e de Im&#65533;genes para Ni&#65533;os. Carlson, Richard. 2019. (SPA.). 26p. (J). pap. 10.99 ***(978-1-6884-5539-9(6))*** Independently Published.

—Espa&#65533;ol-Ucraniano Veh&#65533;culos/Транспортнізасоби Diccionario Biling&#65533;e de Im&#65533;genes para Ni&#65533;os. Carlson, Richard. 2019. (SPA.). 24p. (J). pap. 10.99 ***(978-1-6865-0111-1(0))*** Independently Published.

—Espa&#65533;ol-Urd&#65533; Herramientas Diccionario Biling&#65533;e de Im&#65533;genes para Ni&#65533;os. Carlson, Richard. 2019. (SPA.). 26p. (J). pap. 10.99 ***(978-1-6884-5727-0(5))*** Independently Published.

—Espa&#65533;ol-Urd&#65533; Veh&#65533;culos Diccionario Biling&#65533;e de Im&#65533;genes para Ni&#65533;os. Carlson, Richard. 2019. (SPA.). 24p. (J). pap. 10.99 ***(978-1-6866-8503-3(3))*** Independently Published.

—Espa&#65533;ol-Uzbeko Herramientas/Asboblar Diccionario Biling&#65533;e de Im&#65533;genes para Ni&#65533;os. Carlson, Richard. 2019. (SPA.). 26p. (J). pap. 10.99 ***(978-1-6884-6011-9(X))*** Independently Published.

—Espa&#65533;ol-Uzbeko Veh&#65533;culos/Transport Vositalari Diccionario Biling&#65533;e de Im&#65533;genes para Ni&#65533;os. Carlson, Richard. 2019. (SPA.). 24p. (J). pap. 10.99 ***(978-1-6866-8590-3(4))*** Independently Published.

—Espa&#65533;ol-Vasco Herramientas/Tresnak Diccionario Biling&#65533;e de Im&#65533;genes para Ni&#65533;os. Carlson, Richard. 2019. (SPA.). 26p. (J). pap. 10.99 ***(978-1-6870-7695-3(2))*** Independently Published.

—Espa&#65533;ol-Vasco Veh&#65533;culos/Ibilgailuak Diccionario Biling&#65533;e de Im&#65533;genes para Ni&#65533;os. Carlson, Richard. 2019. (SPA.). 24p. (J). pap. 10.99 ***(978-1-0888-2333-0(5))*** Independently Published.

—Espa&#65533;ol-Vietnamita Herramientas/dụng Cụ Diccionario Biling&#65533;e de Im&#65533;genes para Ni&#65533;os. Carlson, Richard. 2019. (SPA.). 26p. (J). pap. 10.99 ***(978-1-6884-6108-6(6))*** Independently Published.

—Espa&#65533;ol-Vietnamita Veh&#65533;culos/Phương Tiện Diccionario Biling&#65533;e de Im&#65533;genes para Ni&#65533;os. Carlson, Richard. 2019. (SPA.). 24p. (J). pap. 10.99 ***(978-1-6866-8685-6(4))*** Independently Published.

—Espa&#65533;ol-Xhosa Herramientas/Izixhobo Diccionario Biling&#65533;e de Im&#65533;genes para Ni&#65533;os. Carlson, Richard. 2019. (SPA.). 26p. (J). pap. 10.99 ***(978-1-6884-6276-2(7))*** Independently Published.

—Espa&#65533;ol-Xhosa Veh&#65533;culos/Izithuthi Diccionario Biling&#65533;e de Im&#65533;genes para Ni&#65533;os. Carlson, Richard. 2019. (SPA.). 24p. (J). pap. 10.99 ***(978-1-6866-8893-5(8))*** Independently Published.

—Espa&#65533;ol-Y&#65533;dish Herramientas/מכשירים Diccionario Biling&#65533;e de Im&#65533;genes para Ni&#65533;os. Carlson, Richard. 2019. (SPA.). 26p. (J). pap. 10.99 ***(978-1-6884-6782-8(3))*** Independently Published.

—Espa&#65533;ol-Yoruba Herramientas/Awọn Irin Iṣe Diccionario Biling&#65533;e de Im&#65533;genes para Ni&#65533;os. Carlson, Richard. 2019. (SPA.). 26p. (J). pap. 10.99 ***(978-1-6884-6385-1(2))*** Independently Published.

—Espa&#65533;ol-Yoruba Veh&#65533;culos Diccionario Biling&#65533;e de Im&#65533;genes para Ni&#65533;os. Carlson, Richard. 2019. (SPA.). 24p. (J). pap. 10.99 ***(978-1-6866-9415-8(6))*** Independently Published.

—Espa&#65533;ol-Zul&#65533; Herramientas/Amathuluzi Diccionario Biling&#65533;e de Im&#65533;genes para Ni&#65533;os. Carlson, Richard. 2019. (SPA.). 26p. (J). pap. 10.99 ***(978-1-6884-6541-1(3))*** Independently Published.

—Espa&#65533;ol-Zul&#65533; Veh&#65533;culos/Izimoto Diccionario Biling&#65533;e de Im&#65533;genes para Ni&#65533;os. Carlson, Richard. 2019. (SPA.). 24p. (J). pap. 10.99 ***(978-1-6866-9648-0(5))*** Independently Published.

Carlson, Suzanne. Español-Afrikáans Problema/Moeilikheid Libro Bilingüe de Imágenes para Niños. Carlson, Richard. 2019. (SPA.). 24p. (J). pap. 10.99 *(978-1-0703-3885-9(0))* Independently Published.

—Español-Albanés Problema/Shqetësim Libro Bilingüe de Imágenes para Niños. Carlson, Richard. 2019. (SPA.). 24p. (J). pap. 10.99 *(978-1-0703-3962-7(8))* Independently Published.

—Español-Alemán Problema/Ärger Libro Bilingüe de Imágenes para Niños. Carlson, Richard. 2019. (SPA.). 24p. (J). pap. 10.99 *(978-1-0708-8112-6(0))* Independently Published.

—Español-Amhárico Problema/ችግር Libro Bilingüe de Imágenes para Niños. Carlson, Richard. 2019. (SPA.). 24p. (J). pap. 10.99 *(978-1-0703-4164-4(9))* Independently Published.

—Español-Árabe Problema Libro Bilingüe de Imágenes para Niños. Carlson, Richard. 2019. (SPA.). 24p. (J). pap. 10.99 *(978-1-0714-5960-7(0))* Independently Published.

—Español-Armenio Problema/Անախորժություն Libro Bilingüe de Imágenes para Niños. Carlson, Richard. 2019. (SPA.). 24p. (J). pap. 10.99 *(978-1-0704-4195-5(3))* Independently Published.

—Español-Azerbaiyano Problema/Yaramazlıq Libro Bilingüe de Imágenes para Niños. Carlson, Richard. 2019. (SPA.). 24p. (J). pap. 10.99 *(978-1-0704-4299-0(2))* Independently Published.

—Español-Bengalí Problema/বিপদ Libro Bilingüe de Imágenes para Niños. Carlson, Richard. 2019. (SPA.). 24p. (J). pap. 10.99 *(978-1-0704-5237-1(8))* Independently Published.

—Español-Bielorruso Problema/Непрыемнасці Libro Bilingüe de Imágenes para Niños. Carlson, Richard. 2019. (SPA.). 24p. (J). pap. 10.99 *(978-1-0704-4825-1(7))* Independently Published.

—Español-Birmano Problema Bilingüe de Imágenes para Niños. Carlson, Richard. 2019. (SPA.). 24p. (J). pap. 10.99 *(978-1-0704-5544-0(X))* Independently Published.

—Español-Bosnio Problema/Problem Libro Bilingüe de Imágenes para Niños. Carlson, Richard. 2019. (SPA.). 24p. (J). pap. 10.99 *(978-1-0704-5369-9(2))* Independently Published.

—Español-Búlgaro Problema/Неприятности Libro Bilingüe de Imágenes para Niños. Carlson, Richard. 2019. (SPA.). 24p. (J). pap. 10.99 *(978-1-0704-5494-8(X))* Independently Published.

—Español-Canarés Problema/ತೊಂದರೆ Libro Bilingüe de Imágenes para Niños. Carlson, Richard. 2019. (SPA.). 24p. (J). pap. 10.99 *(978-1-0711-6090-9(7))* Independently Published.

—Español-Catalán Problema/Problemes Libro Bilingüe de Imágenes para Niños. Carlson, Richard. 2019. (SPA.). 24p. (J). pap. 10.99 *(978-1-0704-5685-0(3))* Independently Published.

—Español-Checo Problema/Potíz Libro Bilingüe de Imágenes para Niños. Carlson, Richard. 2019. (SPA.). 24p. (J). pap. 10.99 *(978-1-0705-8596-3(3))* Independently Published.

—Español-Chino Cantonés Tradicional Problema/麻煩 Libro Bilingüe de Imágenes para Niños. Carlson, Richard. 2019. (SPA.). 24p. (J). pap. 10.99 *(978-1-0705-8374-7(X))* Independently Published.

—Español-Chino Mandarín Simplificado Problema/麻烦 Libro Bilingüe de Imágenes para Niños. Carlson, Richard. 2019. (SPA.). 24p. (J). pap. 10.99 *(978-1-0704-6278-3(0))* Independently Published.

—Español-Chino Mandarín Tradicional Problema/麻煩 Libro Bilingüe de Imágenes para Niños. Carlson, Richard. 2019. (SPA.). 24p. (J). pap. 10.99 *(978-1-0704-6172-4(5))* Independently Published.

—Español-Chino Mandarín Tradicional (Taiwán) Problema/麻煩 Libro Bilingüe de Imágenes para Niños. Carlson, Richard. 2019. (SPA.). 24p. (J). pap. 10.99 *(978-1-0705-8426-3(6))* Independently Published.

—Español-Cingalés Problema/හිරිහැරය Libro Bilingüe de Imágenes para Niños. Carlson, Richard. 2019. (SPA.). 24p. (J). pap. 10.99 *(978-1-0721-2156-5(5))* Independently Published.

—Español-Coreano Problema/장난 Libro Bilingüe de Imágenes para Niños. Carlson, Richard. 2019. (SPA.). 24p. (J). pap. 10.99 *(978-1-0711-6464-8(3))* Independently Published.

—Español-Criollo Haitiano Problema/Dezòd Libro Bilingüe de Imágenes para Niños. Carlson, Richard. 2019. (SPA.). 24p. (J). pap. 10.99 *(978-1-0708-8692-3(0))* Independently Published.

—Español-Croata Problema/Nevolja Libro Bilingüe de Imágenes para Niños. Carlson, Richard. 2019. (SPA.). 24p. (J). pap. 10.99 *(978-1-0705-8497-3(5))* Independently Published.

—Español-Danés Problema/Ballade Libro Bilingüe de Imágenes para Niños. Carlson, Richard. 2019. (SPA.). 24p. (J). pap. 10.99 *(978-1-0705-8738-7(9))* Independently Published.

—Español-Darí Problema/مشکل Libro Bilingüe de Imágenes para Niños. Carlson, Richard. 2019. (SPA.). 24p. (J). pap. 10.99 *(978-1-0714-6023-8(4))* Independently Published.

—Español-Eslovaco Problema/Problémy Libro Bilingüe de Imágenes para Niños. Carlson, Richard. 2019. (SPA.). 24p. (J). pap. 10.99 *(978-1-0724-3485-6(7))* Independently Published.

—Español-Esloveno (Eslovenia) Problema/Tezava Libro Bilingüe de Imágenes para Niños. Carlson, Richard. 2019. (SPA.). 24p. (J). pap. 10.99 *(978-1-0725-1801-3(5))* Independently Published.

—Español-Estonio Problema/Pahandus Libro Bilingüe de Imágenes para Niños. Carlson, Richard. 2019. (SPA.). 24p. (J). pap. 10.99 *(978-1-0707-3549-8(3))* Independently Published.

—Español-Finlandés Problema/Kiusaaminen Libro Bilingüe de Imágenes para Niños. Carlson, Richard. 2019. (SPA.). 24p. (J). pap. 10.99 *(978-1-0707-3726-3(7))* Independently Published.

—Español-Flamenco (belga) Problema/Problemen Libro Bilingüe de Imágenes para Niños. Carlson, Richard. 2019. (SPA.). 24p. (J). pap. 10.99 *(978-1-0707-4012-6(8))* Independently Published.

—Español-Francés Problema/Problème Libro Bilingüe de Imágenes para Niños. Carlson, Richard. 2019. (SPA.). 24p. (J). pap. 10.99 *(978-1-0708-7879-9(0))* Independently Published.

—Español-Gaélico Irlandés Problema/Trioblóid Libro Bilingüe de Imágenes para Niños. Carlson, Richard. 2019. (SPA.). 24p. (J). pap. 10.99 *(978-1-0711-5835-7(X))* Independently Published.

—Español-Georgiano Problema/უსიამოვნება Libro Bilingüe de Imágenes para Niños. Carlson, Richard. 2019. (SPA.). 24p. (J). pap. 10.99 *(978-1-0708-7981-9(9))* Independently Published.

—Español-Griego Problema/Πρόβλημα Libro Bilingüe de Imágenes para Niños. Carlson, Richard. 2019. (SPA.). 24p. (J). pap. 10.99 *(978-1-0708-8277-2(1))* Independently Published.

—Español-Guyaratí Problema/તકલીફ Libro Bilingüe de Imágenes para Niños. Carlson, Richard. 2019. (SPA.). 24p. (J). pap. 10.99 *(978-1-0708-8463-9(4))* Independently Published.

—Español-Hausa Problema/Matsala Libro Bilingüe de Imágenes para Niños. Carlson, Richard. 2019. (SPA.). 24p. (J). pap. 10.99 *(978-1-0710-1631-2(8))* Independently Published.

—Español-Hebreo Problema/צרהצרורה Libro Bilingüe

de Imágenes para Niños. Carlson, Richard. 2019. (SPA.). 24p. (J). pap. 10.99 *(978-1-0714-6090-0(0))* Independently Published.

—Español-Hindi Problema/शरारत Libro Bilingüe de Imágenes para Niños. Carlson, Richard. 2019. (SPA.). 24p. (J). pap. 10.99 *(978-1-0711-5449-6(4))* Independently Published.

—Español-Holandés Problema/Problemen Libro Bilingüe de Imágenes para Niños. Carlson, Richard. 2019. (SPA.). 24p. (J). pap. 10.99 *(978-1-0705-9106-3(8))* Independently Published.

—Español-Húngaro Problema/Baj Libro Bilingüe de Imágenes para Niños. Carlson, Richard. 2019. (SPA.). 24p. (J). pap. 10.99 *(978-1-0711-5533-2(4))* Independently Published.

—Español-Indonesio Problema/Masalah Libro Bilingüe de Imágenes para Niños. Carlson, Richard. 2019. (SPA.). 24p. (J). pap. 10.99 *(978-1-0711-5738-1(8))* Independently Published.

—Español-Inglés Problema/Trouble Libro Bilingüe de Imágenes para Niños. Carlson, Richard. 2019. (SPA.). 24p. (J). pap. 10.99 *(978-1-0703-3073-0(6))* Independently Published.

—Español-Islandés Problema/Vandræði Libro Bilingüe de Imágenes para Niños. Carlson, Richard. 2019. (SPA.). 24p. (J). pap. 10.99 *(978-1-0711-5645-2(4))* Independently Published.

—Español-Italiano Problema/Guaio Libro Bilingüe de Imágenes para Niños. Carlson, Richard. 2019. (SPA.). 24p. (J). pap. 10.99 *(978-1-0710-1730-2(6))* Independently Published.

—Español-Japonés Problema/トラブル Libro Bilingüe de Imágenes para Niños. Carlson, Richard. 2019. (SPA.). 24p. (J). pap. 10.99 *(978-1-0711-5938-5(0))* Independently Published.

—Español-Jemer (camboyano) Problema/បញ្ហ Libro Bilingüe de Imágenes para Niños. Carlson, Richard. 2019. (SPA.). 24p. (J). pap. 10.99 *(978-1-0711-6319-1(1))* Independently Published.

—Español-Kazajo Problema/Бәлеге қалу Libro Bilingüe de Imágenes para Niños. Carlson, Richard. 2019. (SPA.). 24p. (J). pap. 10.99 *(978-1-0711-6229-3(2))* Independently Published.

—Español-Kurdo Problema/کێشە Libro Bilingüe de Imágenes para Niños. Carlson, Richard. 2019. (SPA.). 24p. (J). pap. 10.99 *(978-1-0714-6194-5(X))* Independently Published.

—Español-Lao (laosiano) Problema Libro Bilingüe de Imágenes para Niños. Carlson, Richard. 2019. (SPA.). 24p. (J). pap. 10.99 *(978-1-0712-8281-6(6))* Independently Published.

—Español-Letón Problema/Nelāgs Notikums Libro Bilingüe de Imágenes para Niños. Carlson, Richard. 2019. (SPA.). 24p. (J). pap. 10.99 *(978-1-0712-8493-3(2))* Independently Published.

—Español-Lituano Problema/Beda Libro Bilingüe de Imágenes para Niños. Carlson, Richard. 2019. (SPA.). 24p. (J). pap. 10.99 *(978-1-0712-8827-6(X))* Independently Published.

—Español-Macedonio Problema/Беља Libro Bilingüe de Imágenes para Niños. Carlson, Richard. 2019. (SPA.). 24p. (J). pap. 10.99 *(978-1-0713-1618-4(4))* Independently Published.

—Español-Malabar Problema/ബുദ്ധിമുട്ടിക്കുക Libro Bilingüe de Imágenes para Niños. Carlson, Richard. 2019. (SPA.). 24p. (J). pap. 10.99 *(978-1-0713-2102-7(1))* Independently Published.

—Español-Malayo Problema/Masalah Libro Bilingüe de Imágenes para Niños. Carlson, Richard. 2019. (SPA.). 24p. (J). pap. 10.99 *(978-1-0713-1807-2(1))* Independently Published.

—Español-Maltés Problema/Inkwiet Libro Bilingüe de Imágenes para Niños. Carlson, Richard. 2019. (SPA.). 24p. (J). pap. 10.99 *(978-1-0713-2236-9(2))* Independently Published.

—Español-Maratí Problema/त्रास Libro Bilingüe de Imágenes para Niños. Carlson, Richard. 2019. (SPA.). 24p. (J). pap. 10.99 *(978-1-0713-2411-0(X))* Independently Published.

—Español-Mongol Problema/Хэрэгт орсон нь Libro Bilingüe de Imágenes para Niños. Carlson, Richard. 2019. (SPA.). 24p. (J). pap. 10.99 *(978-1-0714-4876-2(5))* Independently Published.

—Español-Montenegrino Problema/Nevolja Libro Bilingüe de Imágenes para Niños. Carlson, Richard. 2019. (SPA.). 24p. (J). pap. 10.99 *(978-1-0714-4975-2(3))* Independently Published.

—Español-Nepalí Problema/समस्या Libro Bilingüe de Imágenes para Niños. Carlson, Richard. 2019. (SPA.). 24p. (J). pap. 10.99 *(978-1-0714-5085-7(9))* Independently Published.

—Español-Noruego Problema/Trøbbel Libro Bilingüe de Imágenes para Niños. Carlson, Richard. 2019. (SPA.). 24p. (J). pap. 10.99 *(978-1-0714-5237-0(1))* Independently Published.

—Español-Panyabí Problema Libro Bilingüe de Imágenes para Niños. Carlson, Richard. 2019. (SPA.). 24p. (J). pap. 10.99 *(978-1-0714-7396-2(4))* Independently Published.

—Español-Persa (farsi) Problema/دردسر Libro Bilingüe de Imágenes para Niños. Carlson, Richard. 2019. (SPA.). 24p. (J). pap. 10.99 *(978-1-0714-6438-0(8))* Independently Published.

—Español-Polaco Problema/Klopoty Libro Bilingüe de Imágenes para Niños. Carlson, Richard. 2019. (SPA.). 24p. (J). pap. 10.99 *(978-1-0714-6693-3(3))* Independently Published.

—Español-Portugués (Brasil) Problema/Encrenca Libro Bilingüe de Imágenes para Niños. Carlson, Richard. 2019. (SPA.). 24p. (J). pap. 10.99 *(978-1-0714-7127-2(9))* Independently Published.

—Español-Portugués (Portugal) Problema/Sarilhos Libro Bilingüe de Imágenes para Niños. Carlson, Richard. 2019. (SPA.). 24p. (J). pap. 10.99 *(978-1-0714-7251-4(8))* Independently Published.

—Español-Rumano Problema/În încurcătură Libro Bilingüe de Imágenes para Niños. Carlson, Richard. 2019. (SPA.). 24p. (J). pap. 10.99 *(978-1-0714-7579-9(7))* Independently Published.

—Español-Ruso Problema/Проблема Libro Bilingüe de Imágenes para Niños. Carlson, Richard. 2019. (SPA.). 24p. (J). pap. 10.99 *(978-1-0714-7733-5(1))* Independently Published.

—Español-Serbio (cirílico) Problema/Невоља Libro Bilingüe de Imágenes para Niños. Carlson, Richard. 2019. (SPA.). 24p. (J). pap. 10.99 *(978-1-0721-1753-7(3))* Independently Published.

—Español-Serbio (latín) Problema/Nevolja Libro Bilingüe de Imágenes para Niños. Carlson, Richard. 2019. (SPA.). 24p. (J). pap. 10.99 *(978-1-0721-1852-7(1))* Independently Published.

—Español-Somalí Problema/Dhibaato Libro Bilingüe de Imágenes para Niños. Carlson, Richard. 2019. (SPA.). 24p. (J). pap. 10.99 *(978-1-0725-8270-0(8))* Independently Published.

—Español-Suajili Problema/Shida Libro Bilingüe de Imágenes para Niños. Carlson, Richard. 2019. (SPA.). 24p. (J). pap. 10.99 *(978-1-0725-8670-8(3))* Independently Published.

—Español-Sueco Problema/Trubbel Libro Bilingüe de Imágenes para Niños. Carlson, Richard. 2019. (SPA.). 24p. (J). pap. 10.99 *(978-1-0710-1855-2(8))* Independently Published.

—Español-Tagalo Problema/Gulo Libro Bilingüe de Imágenes para Niños. Carlson, Richard. 2019. (SPA.). 24p. (J). pap. 10.99 *(978-1-0725-8839-9(0))* Independently Published.

—Español-Tailandés Problema/ยุ่งแล้วเชียว Libro Bilingüe de Imágenes para Niños. Carlson, Richard. 2019. (SPA.). 24p. (J). pap. 10.99 *(978-1-0727-3578-6(4))* Independently Published.

—Español-Tamil Problema Libro Bilingüe de Imágenes para Niños. Carlson, Richard. 2019. (SPA.). 24p. (J). pap. 10.99 *(978-1-0725-9204-4(5))* Independently Published.

—Español-Télugu Problema Libro Bilingüe de Imágenes para Niños. Carlson, Richard. 2019. (SPA.). 24p. (J). pap. 10.99 *(978-1-0727-3475-8(3))* Independently Published.

—Español-Tigriña Problema/ፀገም Libro Bilingüe de Imágenes para Niños. Carlson, Richard. 2019. (SPA.). 24p. (J). pap. 10.99 *(978-1-0727-3782-7(5))* Independently Published.

—Español-Turco Problema/Üzüntü Libro Bilingüe de Imágenes para Niños. Carlson, Richard. 2019. (SPA.). 24p. (J). pap. 10.99 *(978-1-0727-3890-9(2))* Independently Published.

—Español-Ucraniano Problema/Проблема Libro Bilingüe de Imágenes para Niños. Carlson, Richard. 2019. (SPA.). 24p. (J). pap. 10.99 *(978-1-0727-4015-5(X))* Independently Published.

—Español-Urdú Problema/پریشانی Libro Bilingüe de Imágenes para Niños. Carlson, Richard. 2019. (SPA.). 24p. (J). pap. 10.99 *(978-1-0727-4118-3(0))* Independently Published.

—Español-Uzbeko Problema/Muammo Libro Bilingüe de Imágenes para Niños. Carlson, Richard. 2019. (SPA.). 24p. (J). pap. 10.99 *(978-1-0727-4414-6(7))* Independently Published.

—Español-Vasco Problema/Arazoa Libro Bilingüe de Imágenes para Niños. Carlson, Richard. 2019. (SPA.). 24p. (J). pap. 10.99 *(978-1-0704-4739-1(0))* Independently Published.

—Español-Vietnamita Problema/Rắc Rối Libro Bilingüe de Imágenes para Niños. Carlson, Richard. 2019. (SPA.). 24p. (J). pap. 10.99 *(978-1-0727-4536-5(4))* Independently Published.

—Español-Xhosa Problema/Ingxaki Libro Bilingüe de Imágenes para Niños. Carlson, Richard. 2019. (SPA.). 24p. (J). pap. 10.99 *(978-1-0727-4703-1(0))* Independently Published.

—Español-Yoruba Problema Libro Bilingüe de Imágenes para Niños. Carlson, Richard. 2019. (SPA.). 24p. (J). pap. 10.99 *(978-1-0727-4808-3(8))* Independently Published.

—Español-Zulú Problema/Inkinga Libro Bilingüe de Imágenes para Niños. Carlson, Richard. 2019. (SPA.). 24p. (J). pap. 10.99 *(978-1-0727-4921-9(1))* Independently Published.

—Français-Afrikaans le Temps/Tyd Livre d'Images Bilingue Pour Enfants. Carlson Jr, Richard. 2018. (FRE.). 28p. (J). pap. 10.99 *(978-1-7266-7939-8(X))* Independently Published.

—Français-Afrikaans on a Blessé Mes Sentiments/My Gevoelens Is Gekwets Livre d'images Bilingue Pour Enfants. Carlson, Richard. 2019. (FRE.). 24p. (J). pap. 10.99 *(978-1-0769-8144-8(5))* Independently Published.

—Français-Albanais le Temps/Koha Livre d'Images Bilingue Pour Enfants. Carlson Jr, Richard. 2018. (FRE.). 28p. (J). pap. 10.99 *(978-1-7241-7801-5(6))* Independently Published.

—Français-Albanais on a Blessé Mes Sentiments/Ndjenjat e Mia Janë Të lënduara Livre d'images Bilingue Pour Enfants. Carlson, Richard. 2019. (FRE.). 24p. (J). pap. 10.99 *(978-1-0771-1879-9(1))* Independently Published.

—Français-Allemand le Temps/Zeit Livre d'Images Bilingue Pour Enfants. Carlson Jr, Richard. 2018. (FRE.). 28p. (J). pap. 10.99 *(978-1-7288-0844-4(8))* Independently Published.

—Français-Allemand on a Blessé Mes Sentiments/Ich Wurde in Meinen Gefühlen Verletzt Livre d'images Bilingue Pour Enfants. Carlson, Richard. 2019. (FRE.). 24p. (J). pap. 10.99 *(978-1-0780-5827-8(X))* Independently Published.

—Français-Amharique le Temps Livre d'Images Bilingue Pour Enfants. Carlson Jr, Richard. 2018. (FRE.). 28p. (J). pap. 10.99 *(978-1-7241-8031-5(2))* Independently Published.

—Français-Amharique on a Blessé Mes Sentiments/ስሜቴ ተጎድቷል Livre d'images Bilingue Pour Enfants. Carlson, Richard. 2019. (FRE.). 24p. (J). pap. 10.99 *(978-1-0771-2132-4(6))* Independently Published.

—Français-Anglais le Temps/Time Livre d'Images Bilingue Pour Enfants. Carlson Jr, Richard. 2018. (FRE.). 28p. (J). pap. 10.99 *(978-1-7287-7720-7(8))* Independently Published.

—Français-Anglais on a Blessé Mes Sentiments/My Feelings Are Hurt Livre d'images Bilingue Pour Enfants. Carlson, Richard. 2019. (FRE.). 24p. (J). pap. 10.99 *(978-1-0769-7972-8(6))* Independently Published.

—Français-Arabe le Temps Livre d'Images Bilingue Pour Enfants. Carlson Jr, Richard. 2018. (FRE.). 28p. (J). pap. 10.99 *(978-1-7241-8132-9(7))* Independently Published.

—Français-Arabe on a Blessé Mes Sentiments/جرحت مشاعري Livre d'images Bilingue Pour Enfants. Carlson, Richard. 2019. (FRE.). 24p. (J). pap. 10.99 *(978-1-0791-8830-1(4))* Independently Published.

—Français-Arménien le Temps Livre d'Images Bilingue Pour Enfants. Carlson Jr, Richard. 2018. (FRE.). 28p. (J). pap. 10.99 *(978-1-7266-8029-5(0))* Independently Published.

—Français-Arménien on a Blessé Mes Sentiments/Ես վիրավորված եմ Livre d'images Bilingue Pour Enfants. Carlson, Richard. 2019. (FRE.). 24p. (J). pap. 10.99 *(978-1-0771-2689-3(1))* Independently Published.

—Français-Azéri le Temps/Zaman Livre d'Images Bilingue Pour Enfants. Carlson Jr, Richard. 2018. (FRE.). 28p. (J). pap. 10.99 *(978-1-7267-1853-0(0))* Independently Published.

—Français-Azéri on a Blessé Mes Sentiments/Hisslərim Yaralandı Livre d'images Bilingue Pour Enfants. Carlson, Richard. 2019. (FRE.). 24p. (J). pap. 10.99 *(978-1-0771-2977-1(7))* Independently Published.

—Français-Basque le Temps/Denbora Livre d'Images Bilingue Pour Enfants. Carlson Jr, Richard. 2018. (FRE.). 28p. (J). pap. 10.99 *(978-1-7268-1196-5(4))* Independently Published.

—Français-Basque on a Blessé Mes Sentiments/Nire Sentimenduak Minduta Livre d'images Bilingue Pour Enfants. Carlson, Richard. 2019. (FRE.). 24p. (J). pap. 10.99 *(978-1-0771-3236-8(0))* Independently Published.

—Français-Bengali le Temps Livre d'Images Bilingue Pour Enfants. Carlson Jr, Richard. 2018. (FRE.). 28p. (J). pap. 10.99 *(978-1-7268-3994-5(X))* Independently Published.

—Français-Bengali on a Blessé Mes Sentiments Livre d'images Bilingue Pour Enfants. Carlson, Richard. 2019. (FRE.). 24p. (J). pap. 10.99 *(978-1-0771-3699-1(4))* Independently Published.

—Français-Biélorusse le Temps Livre d'Images Bilingue Pour Enfants. Carlson Jr, Richard. 2018. (FRE.). 28p. (J). pap. 10.99 *(978-1-7268-1672-4(9))* Independently Published.

—Français-Biélorusse on a Blessé Mes Sentiments/Абражаныя пачуцці Livre d'images Bilingue Pour Enfants. Carlson, Richard. 2019. (FRE.). 24p. (J). pap. 10.99 *(978-1-0771-3522-2(X))* Independently Published.

—Français-Birman le Temps Livre d'Images Bilingue Pour Enfants. Carlson Jr, Richard. 2018. (FRE.). 28p. (J). pap. 10.99 *(978-1-7268-4923-4(6))* Independently Published.

—Français-Birman on a Blessé Mes Sentiments Livre d'images Bilingue Pour Enfants. Carlson, Richard. 2019. (FRE.). 24p. (J). pap. 10.99 *(978-1-0775-6530-2(5))* Independently Published.

—Français-Bosnien le Temps/Vrijeme Livre d'Images Bilingue Pour Enfants. Carlson Jr, Richard. 2018. (FRE.). 28p. (J). pap. 10.99 *(978-1-7268-4058-3(1))* Independently Published.

—Français-Bosnien on a Blessé Mes Sentiments/Moja Osjecanja Su Povrijeđena Livre d'images Bilingue Pour Enfants. Carlson, Richard. 2019. (FRE.). 24p. (J). pap. 10.99 *(978-1-0775-1109-5(4))* Independently Published.

—Français-Bulgare le Temps Livre d'Images Bilingue Pour Enfants. Carlson Jr, Richard. 2018. (FRE.). 28p. (J). pap. 10.99 *(978-1-7268-4682-0(2))* Independently Published.

—Français-Bulgare on a Blessé Mes Sentiments/Чувствата ми са наранени Livre d'images Bilingue Pour Enfants. Carlson, Richard. 2019. (FRE.). 24p. (J). pap. 10.99 *(978-1-0775-6209-7(8))* Independently Published.

—Français-Catalan le Temps/el Temps Livre d'Images Bilingue Pour Enfants. Carlson Jr, Richard. 2018. (FRE.). 28p. (J). pap. 10.99 *(978-1-7268-9647-4(1))* Independently Published.

—Français-Catalan on a Blessé Mes Sentiments/M'han Ferit Els Meus Sentiments Livre d'images Bilingue Pour Enfants. Carlson, Richard. 2019. (FRE.). 24p. (J). pap. 10.99 *(978-1-0775-6804-4(5))* Independently Published.

—Français-Chinois Cantonais Traditionnel le Temps Livre d'Images Bilingue Pour Enfants. Carlson Jr, Richard. 2018. (FRE.). 28p. (J). pap. 10.99 *(978-1-7286-4378-6(3))* Independently Published.

—Français-Chinois Cantonais Traditionnel on a Blessé Mes Sentiments/我的情感受到了傷害 Livre d'images Bilingue Pour Enfants. Carlson, Richard. 2019. (FRE.). 24p. (J). pap. 10.99 *(978-1-0777-8932-6(7))* Independently Published.

—Français-Chinois Mandarin Simplifié le Temps Livre d'Images Bilingue Pour Enfants. Carlson Jr, Richard. 2018. (FRE.). 28p. (J). pap. 10.99 *(978-1-7268-9976-5(4))* Independently Published.

—Français-Chinois Mandarin Simplifié on a Blessé Mes Sentiments/我的感情受到了伤害 Livre d'images Bilingue Pour Enfants. Carlson, Richard. 2019. (FRE.). 24p. (J). pap. 10.99 *(978-1-0777-6869-7(9))* Independently Published.

—Français-Chinois Mandarin Traditionnel le Temps Livre d'Images Bilingue Pour Enfants. Carlson Jr, Richard. 2018. (FRE.). 28p. (J). pap. 10.99 *(978-1-7268-9958-1(6))* Independently Published.

—Français-Chinois Mandarin Traditionnel on a Blessé Mes Sentiments/我的情感受到了傷害 Livre d'images Bilingue Pour Enfants. Carlson, Richard. 2019. (FRE.). 24p. (J). pap. 10.99 *(978-1-0775-7691-9(9))* Independently Published.

—Français-Chinois Mandarin Traditionnel Simplifié (Taiwan) le Temps Livre d'Images Bilingue Pour Enfants. Carlson Jr, Richard. 2018. (FRE.). 28p. (J). pap. 10.99 *(978-1-7286-7865-8(X))* Independently Published.

—Français-Chinois Mandarin Traditionnel Simplifié (Taiwan) on a Blessé Mes Sentiments/我的感覺受傷了 Livre d'images Bilingue Pour Enfants. Carlson, Richard. 2019. (FRE.). 24p. (J). pap. 10.99 *(978-1-0777-9061-2(9))* Independently Published.

—Français-Cingalais le Temps Livre d'Images Bilingue Pour Enfants. Carlson Jr, Richard. 2018. (FRE.). 28p. (J). pap. 10.99 *(978-1-7308-8849-6(6))* Independently Published.

—Français-Cingalais on a Blessé Mes Sentiments/මගේ හැඟීම් වලට රිදිලා Livre d'images Bilingue Pour Enfants. Carlson, Richard. 2019. (FRE.). 24p. (J). pap. 10.99 *(978-1-0806-7012-3(2))* Independently Published.

—Français-Coréen le Temps Livre d'Images Bilingue Pour Enfants. Carlson Jr, Richard. 2018. (FRE.). 28p. (J). pap. 10.99 *(978-1-7292-3536-2(0))* Independently Published.

—Français-Coréen on a Blessé Mes Sentiments/마음이 아팠어요 Livre d'images Bilingue Pour Enfants. Carlson, Richard. 2019. (FRE.). 24p. (J). pap. 10.99 *(978-1-0796-2404-5(X))* Independently Published.

—Français-Créole Haïtien le Temps/Tan Livre d'Images Bilingue Pour Enfants. Carlson Jr, Richard. 2018. (FRE.). 28p. (J). pap. 10.99 *(978-1-7288-0898-7(7))* Independently Published.

—Français-Créole Haïtien on a Blessé Mes Sentiments/Santiman M Blese Livre d'images Bilingue Pour Enfants. Carlson, Richard. 2019. (FRE.). 24p. (J). pap. 10.99 *(978-1-0782-4148-9(1))* Independently Published.

—Français-Croate le Temps/Vrijeme Livre d'Images Bilingue Pour Enfants. Carlson Jr, Richard. 2018. (FRE.). 28p. (J). pap. 10.99 *(978-1-7286-7917-4(6))* Independently Published.

—Français-Croate on a Blessé Mes Sentiments/Moji Osjecaji Su Povrijeđeni Livre d'images Bilingue Pour Enfants. Carlson, Richard. 2019. (FRE.). 24p. (J). pap. 10.99 *(978-1-0777-9278-4(6))* Independently Published.

—Français-Danois le Temps/Tid Livre d'Images Bilingue Pour Enfants. Carlson Jr, Richard. 2018. (FRE.). 28p. (J). pap. 10.99 *(978-1-7287-5154-2(3))* Independently Published.

—Français-Danois on a Blessé Mes Sentiments/Mine Følelser Blev Såret Livre d'images Bilingue Pour Enfants. Carlson, Richard. 2019. (FRE.). 24p. (J). pap. 10.99 *(978-1-0780-4672-5(7))* Independently Published.

—Français-Dari le Temps Livre d'Images Bilingue Pour Enfants. Carlson Jr, Richard. 2018. (FRE.). 28p. (J). pap. 10.99 *(978-1-7287-7274-5(5))* Independently Published.

—Français-Dari on a Blessé Mes Sentiments Livre d'images Bilingue Pour Enfants. Carlson, Richard. 2019. (FRE.). 24p. (J). pap. 10.99 *(978-1-0791-8934-6(3))* Independently Published.

—Français-Espagne d'Amérique Latine le Temps/Tiempo Livre d'Images Bilingue Pour Enfants. Carlson Jr, Richard. 2018. (FRE.). 28p. (J). pap. 10.99 *(978-1-7309-3799-6(3))* Independently Published.

—Français-Espagne d'Amérique Latine on a Blessé Mes Sentiments/Han Herido Mis Sentimientos Livre d'images Bilingue Pour Enfants. Carlson, Richard. 2019. (FRE.). 24p. (J). pap. 10.99 *(978-1-0806-8361-1(5))* Independently Published.

—Français-Espagnol Castilan on a Blessé Mes Sentiments/Han Herido Mis Sentimientos Livre d'images Bilingue Pour Enfants. Carlson, Richard. 2019. (FRE.). 24p. (J). pap. 10.99 *(978-1-0806-8248-5(1))* Independently Published.

—Français-Estonien le Temps/Aeg Livre d'Images Bilingue Pour Enfants. Carlson Jr, Richard. 2018. (FRE.). 28p. (J). pap. 10.99 *(978-1-7287-7761-0(5))* Independently Published.

—Français-Estonien on a Blessé Mes Sentiments/Mu Tunded Said Haavata Livre d'images Bilingue Pour Enfants. Carlson, Richard. 2019. (FRE.). 24p. (J). pap. 10.99 *(978-1-0780-4895-8(9))* Independently Published.

—Français-Finlandais le Temps/Aika Livre d'Images Bilingue Pour Enfants. Carlson Jr, Richard. 2018. (FRE.). 28p. (J). pap. 10.99 *(978-1-7288-0714-0(X))* Independently Published.

—Français-Finlandais on a Blessé Mes Sentiments/Tunteitani on Loukattu Livre d'images Bilingue Pour Enfants.

C

Carlson, Richard. 2019. (FRE.). 24p. (J). pap. 10.99 *(978-1-0780-5022-7(8))* Independently Published.

—Français-Flamand (Belge) le Temps/de Tijd Livre d'Images Bilingue Pour Enfants. Carlson Jr, Richard. 2018. (FRE.). 28p. (J). pap. 10.99 *(978-1-7288-0734-8(4))* Independently Published.

—Français-Flamand (belge) on a Blessé Mes Sentiments/Mijn Gevoelens Zijn Gekwetst Livre d'images Bilingue Pour Enfants. Carlson, Richard. 2019. (FRE.). 24p. (J). pap. 10.99 *(978-1-0780-5139-2(9))* Independently Published.

—Français-Gaélique Irlandais le Temps/Am Livre d'Images Bilingue Pour Enfants. Carlson Jr, Richard. 2018. (FRE.). 28p. (J). pap. 10.99 *(978-1-7290-6197-8(4))* Independently Published.

—Français-Gaélique Irlandais on a Blessé Mes Sentiments/Tá Mé Gortaithe Livre d'images Bilingue Pour Enfants. Carlson, Richard. 2019. (FRE.). 24p. (J). pap. 10.99 *(978-1-0790-0168-6(9))* Independently Published.

—Français-Galicien on a Blessé Mes Sentiments/Os Meus Sentimentos Están Feridos Livre d'images Bilingue Pour Enfants. Carlson, Richard. 2019. (FRE.). 24p. (J). pap. 10.99 *(978-1-0780-5322-8(7))* Independently Published.

—Français-Gallois on a Blessé Mes Sentiments/Fy Nheimladau Yn Brifo Livre d'images Bilingue Pour Enfants. Carlson, Richard. 2019. (FRE.). 24p. (J). pap. 10.99 *(978-1-0810-6225-5(8))* Independently Published.

—Français-Géorgien le Temps Livre d'Images Bilingue Pour Enfants. Carlson Jr, Richard. 2018. (FRE.). 28p. (J). pap. 10.99 *(978-1-7288-0760-7(3))* Independently Published.

—Français-Géorgien on a Blessé Mes Sentiments/ჩემი გრძნობები შეურაცხყოფილია Livre d'images Bili. Carlson, Richard. 2019. (FRE.). 24p. (J). pap. 10.99 *(978-1-0780-5455-3(X))* Independently Published.

—Français-Grec le Temps Livre d'Images Bilingue Pour Enfants. Carlson Jr, Richard. 2018. (FRE.). 28p. (J). pap. 10.99 *(978-1-7288-0865-9(0))* Independently Published.

—Français-Grec on a Blessé Mes Sentiments/Πληγώθηκαν Τα Συναισθήματά Μου Livre d'images Bilingue Pour Enfants. Carlson, Richard. 2019. (FRE.). 24p. (J). pap. 10.99 *(978-1-0782-1429-2(8))* Independently Published.

—Français-Gujarati le Temps Livre d'Images Bilingue Pour Enfants. Carlson Jr, Richard. 2018. (FRE.). 28p. (J). pap. 10.99 *(978-1-7288-0885-7(5))* Independently Published.

—Français-Gujarati on a Blessé Mes Sentiments Livre d'images Bilingue Pour Enfants. Carlson, Richard. 2019. (FRE.). 24p. (J). pap. 10.99 *(978-1-0782-4062-8(0))* Independently Published.

—Français-Hausa le Temps/Lokaci Livre d'Images Bilingue Pour Enfants. Carlson Jr, Richard. 2018. (FRE.). 28p. (J). pap. 10.99 *(978-1-7288-0987-8(8))* Independently Published.

—Français-Hausa on a Blessé Mes Sentiments/Na Ji Jikkata Livre d'images Bilingue Pour Enfants. Carlson, Richard. 2019. (FRE.). 24p. (J). pap. 10.99 *(978-1-0782-4277-6(1))* Independently Published.

—Français-Hébreu le Temps Livre d'Images Bilingue Pour Enfants. Carlson Jr, Richard. 2018. (FRE.). 28p. (J). pap. 10.99 *(978-1-7288-5234-8(X))* Independently Published.

—Français-Hindi le Temps Livre d'Images Bilingue Pour Enfants. Carlson Jr, Richard. 2018. (FRE.). 28p. (J). pap. 10.99 *(978-1-7288-9621-2(5))* Independently Published.

—Français-Hindi on a Blessé Mes Sentiments Livre d'images Bilingue Pour Enfants. Carlson, Richard. 2019. (FRE.). 24p. (J). pap. 10.99 *(978-1-0782-4799-3(4))* Independently Published.

—Français-Hollandais le Temps/Tijd Livre d'Images Bilingue Pour Enfants. Carlson Jr, Richard. 2018. (FRE.). 28p. (J). pap. 10.99 *(978-1-7287-7656-9(2))* Independently Published.

—Français-Hollandais on a Blessé Mes Sentiments/Mijn Gevoelens Zijn Gekwetst Livre d'images Bilingue Pour Enfants. Carlson, Richard. 2019. (FRE.). 24p. (J). pap. 10.99 *(978-1-0780-4793-7(6))* Independently Published.

—Français-Hongrois le Temps Livre d'Images Bilingue Pour Enfants. Carlson Jr, Richard. 2018. (FRE.). 28p. (J). pap. 10.99 *(978-1-7288-9692-2(4))* Independently Published.

—Français-Hongrois on a Blessé Mes Sentiments/Megbántódtam Livre d'images Bilingue Pour Enfants. Carlson, Richard. 2019. (FRE.). 24p. (J). pap. 10.99 *(978-1-0782-4970-6(9))* Independently Published.

—Français-Indonésien le Temps/Waktu Livre d'Images Bilingue Pour Enfants. Carlson Jr, Richard. 2018. (FRE.). 28p. (J). pap. 10.99 *(978-1-7288-9835-3(8))* Independently Published.

—Français-Indonésien on a Blessé Mes Sentiments/Perasaanku Terluka Livre d'images Bilingue Pour Enfants. Carlson, Richard. 2019. (FRE.). 24p. (J). pap. 10.99 *(978-1-0784-9922-4(5))* Independently Published.

—Français-Islandais le Temps/Tími Livre d'Images Bilingue Pour Enfants. Carlson Jr, Richard. 2018. (FRE.). 28p. (J). pap. 10.99 *(978-1-7288-9727-1(0))* Independently Published.

—Français-Islandais on a Blessé Mes Sentiments/Ég Er Særður Livre d'images Bilingue Pour Enfants. Carlson, Richard. 2019. (FRE.). 24p. (J). pap. 10.99 *(978-1-0784-9663-6(3))* Independently Published.

—Français-Italien le Temps/Tempo Livre d'Images Bilingue Pour Enfants. Carlson Jr, Richard. 2018. (FRE.). 28p. (J). pap. 10.99 *(978-1-7290-9130-2(X))* Independently Published.

—Français-Italien on a Blessé Mes Sentiments/Mi Sento Ferito Livre d'images Bilingue Pour Enfants. Carlson, Richard. 2019. (FRE.). 24p. (J). pap. 10.99 *(978-1-0791-5197-8(4))* Independently Published.

—Français-Japonais le Temps Livre d'Images Bilingue Pour Enfants. Carlson Jr, Richard. 2018. (FRE.). 28p. (J). pap. 10.99 *(978-1-7290-9475-4(9))* Independently Published.

—Français-Japonais on a Blessé Mes Sentiments/ぼくは傷ついた Livre d'images Bilingue Pour Enfants. Carlson, Richard. 2019. (FRE.). 24p. (J). pap. 10.99 *(978-1-0793-9926-4(7))* Independently Published.

—Français-Kannada le Temps Livre d'Images Bilingue Pour Enfants. Carlson Jr, Richard. 2018. (FRE.). 28p. (J). pap. 10.99 *(978-1-7290-9537-9(2))* Independently Published.

—Français-Kannada on a Blessé Mes Sentiments Livre d'images Bilingue Pour Enfants. Carlson, Richard. 2019. (FRE.). 24p. (J). pap. 10.99 *(978-1-0794-0347-3(7))* Independently Published.

—Français-Kasakh le Temps Livre d'Images Bilingue Pour Enfants. Carlson Jr, Richard. 2018. (FRE.). 28p. (J). pap. 10.99 *(978-1-7290-9611-6(5))* Independently Published.

—Français-Kasakh on a Blessé Mes Sentiments/Сезімтал балатуралыоқиға Livre d'images Bilingue Pour Enfants. Carlson, Richard. 2019. (FRE.). 24p. (J). pap. 10.99 *(978-1-0794-0927-7(0))* Independently Published.

—Français-Khmer (Cambodgien) le Temps Livre d'Images Bilingue Pour Enfants. Carlson Jr, Richard. 2018. (FRE.). 28p. (J). pap. 10.99 *(978-1-7291-8977-1(6))* Independently Published.

—Français-Khmer (cambodgien) on a Blessé Mes Sentiments Livre d'images Bilingue Pour Enfants. Carlson, Richard. 2019. (FRE.). 24p. (J). pap. 10.99 *(978-1-0796-2146-4(6))* Independently Published.

—Français-Kurde le Temps Livre d'Images Bilingue Pour Enfants. Carlson Jr, Richard. 2018. (FRE.). 28p. (J). pap. 10.99 *(978-1-7292-7999-1(6))* Independently Published.

—Français-Lao (Laotien) le Temps Livre d'Images Bilingue Pour Enfants. Carlson Jr, Richard. 2018. (FRE.). 28p. (J). pap. 10.99 *(978-1-7292-8057-7(9))* Independently Published.

—Français-Lao (laotien) on a Blessé Mes Sentiments Livre d'images Bilingue Pour Enfants. Carlson, Richard. 2019. (FRE.). 24p. (J). pap. 10.99 *(978-1-0796-2687-2(5))* Independently Published.

—Français-Letton le Temps/Laiks Livre d'Images Bilingue Pour Enfants. Carlson Jr, Richard. 2018. (FRE.). 28p. (J). pap. 10.99 *(978-1-7293-2041-9(4))* Independently Published.

—Français-Letton on a Blessé Mes Sentiments/Es Esmu Sāpināts Livre d'images Bilingue Pour Enfants. Carlson, Richard. 2019. (FRE.). 24p. (J). pap. 10.99 *(978-1-0796-2910-1(6))* Independently Published.

—Français-Lithuanien le Temps/Laikas Livre d'Images Bilingue Pour Enfants. Carlson Jr, Richard. 2018. (FRE.). 28p. (J). pap. 10.99 *(978-1-7293-2058-7(9))* Independently Published.

—Français-Lithuanien on a Blessé Mes Sentiments/Mane įskaudino Livre d'images Bilingue Pour Enfants. Carlson, Richard. 2019. (FRE.). 24p. (J). pap. 10.99 *(978-1-0796-3232-3(8))* Independently Published.

—Français-Macédonien le Temps Livre d'Images Bilingue Pour Enfants. Carlson Jr, Richard. 2018. (FRE.). 28p. (J). pap. 10.99 *(978-1-7293-2095-2(3))* Independently Published.

—Français-Macédonien on a Blessé Mes Sentiments/Моите чувства се повредени Livre d'images Bilingue Pour Enfants. Carlson, Richard. 2019. (FRE.). 24p. (J). pap. 10.99 *(978-1-0800-6873-9(2))* Independently Published.

—Français-Malais le Temps/Masa Livre d'Images Bilingue Pour Enfants. Carlson Jr, Richard. 2018. (FRE.). 28p. (J). pap. 10.99 *(978-1-7293-5322-6(3))* Independently Published.

—Français-Malais on a Blessé Mes Sentiments/Perasaan Saya Disakiti Livre d'images Bilingue Pour Enfants. Carlson, Richard. 2019. (FRE.). 24p. (J). pap. 10.99 *(978-1-0800-7214-9(4))* Independently Published.

—Français-Malayalam le Temps Livre d'Images Bilingue Pour Enfants. Carlson Jr, Richard. 2018. (FRE.). 28p. (J). pap. 10.99 *(978-1-7293-5421-6(1))* Independently Published.

—Français-Malayalam on a Blessé Mes Sentiments Livre d'images Bilingue Pour Enfants. Carlson, Richard. 2019. (FRE.). 24p. (J). pap. 10.99 *(978-1-0800-7511-9(9))* Independently Published.

—Français-Maltais le Temps Livre d'Images Bilingue Pour Enfants. Carlson Jr, Richard. 2018. (FRE.). 28p. (J). pap. 10.99 *(978-1-7293-6033-0(5))* Independently Published.

—Français-Maltais on a Blessé Mes Sentiments/Weġġgħuni Livre d'images Bilingue Pour Enfants. Carlson, Richard. 2019. (FRE.). 24p. (J). pap. 10.99 *(978-1-0802-3790-6(9))* Independently Published.

—Français-Marathi le Temps Livre d'Images Bilingue Pour Enfants. Carlson Jr, Richard. 2018. (FRE.). 28p. (J). pap. 10.99 *(978-1-7294-3790-2(7))* Independently Published.

—Français-Marathi on a Blessé Mes Sentiments/माझ्या भावना दुखावल्या गेल्या आहेê. Carlson, Richard. 2019. (FRE.). 24p. (J). pap. 10.99 *(978-1-0802-7168-9(6))* Independently Published.

—Français-Mongol le Temps Livre d'Images Bilingue Pour Enfants. Carlson Jr, Richard. 2018. (FRE.). 28p. (J). pap. 10.99 *(978-1-7294-3905-0(5))* Independently Published.

—Français-Mongol on a Blessé Mes Sentiments/Би гомдож байна Livre d'images Bilingue Pour Enfants. Carlson, Richard. 2019. (FRE.). 24p. (J). pap. 10.99 *(978-1-0802-9368-1(X))* Independently Published.

—Français-Monténégrin le Temps/Vrijeme Livre d'Images Bilingue Pour Enfants. Carlson Jr, Richard. 2018. (FRE.). 28p. (J). pap. 10.99 *(978-1-7294-4049-0(5))* Independently Published.

—Français-Monténégrin on a Blessé Mes Sentiments/Moja Osjecanja Su Povrijeđena Livre d'images Bilingue Pour Enfants. Carlson, Richard. 2019. (FRE.). 24p. (J). pap. 10.99 *(978-1-0802-9615-6(8))* Independently Published.

—Français-Népalais le Temps Livre d'Images Bilingue Pour Enfants. Carlson Jr, Richard. 2018. (FRE.). 28p. (J). pap. 10.99 *(978-1-7294-4108-4(4))* Independently Published.

—Français-Népalais on a Blessé Mes Sentiments/मेरो भावनामा चोट पुगेको छ Livre d'images Bilingue Pour Enfants. Carlson, Richard. 2019. (FRE.). 24p. (J). pap. 10.99 *(978-1-0804-4749-7(0))* Independently Published.

—Français-Norvégien le Temps/Tid Livre d'Images Bilingue Pour Enfants. Carlson Jr, Richard. 2018. (FRE.). 28p. (J). pap. 10.99 *(978-1-7307-2897-6(9))* Independently Published.

—Français-Norvégien on a Blessé Mes Sentiments/Følelsene Mine Er Såret Livre d'images Bilingue Pour Enfants. Carlson, Richard. 2019. (FRE.). 24p. (J). pap. 10.99 *(978-1-0804-4909-5(4))* Independently Published.

—Français-Ourdou le Temps Livre d'Images Bilingue Pour Enfants. Carlson Jr, Richard. 2018. (FRE.). 28p. (J). pap. 10.99 *(978-1-7311-1577-5(6))* Independently Published.

—Français-Ourdou on a Blessé Mes Sentiments Livre d'images Bilingue Pour Enfants. Carlson, Richard. 2019. (FRE.). 24p. (J). pap. 10.99 *(978-1-0810-5769-5(6))* Independently Published.

—Français-Ouzbek le Temps/Vaqt Livre d'Images Bilingue Pour Enfants. Carlson Jr, Richard. 2018. (FRE.). 28p. (J). pap. 10.99 *(978-1-7311-6435-3(1))* Independently Published.

—Français-Ouzbek on a Blessé Mes Sentiments/His-Tuyg'ularim Yaralandi Livre d'images Bilingue Pour Enfants. Carlson, Richard. 2019. (FRE.). 24p. (J). pap. 10.99 *(978-1-0810-5910-1(9))* Independently Published.

—Français-Pashto le Temps Livre d'Images Bilingue Pour Enfants. Carlson Jr, Richard. 2018. (FRE.). 28p. (J). pap. 10.99 *(978-1-7307-2936-2(3))* Independently Published.

—Français-Pashto on a Blessé Mes Sentiments Livre d'images Bilingue Pour Enfants. Carlson, Richard. 2019. (FRE.). 24p. (J). pap. 10.99 *(978-1-0804-5122-7(6))* Independently Published.

—Français-Pendjabi le Temps Livre d'Images Bilingue Pour Enfants. Carlson Jr, Richard. 2018. (FRE.). 28p. (J). pap. 10.99 *(978-1-7308-4710-3(2))* Independently Published.

—Français-Pendjabi on a Blessé Mes Sentiments Livre d'images Bilingue Pour Enfants. Carlson, Richard. 2019. (FRE.). 24p. (J). pap. 10.99 *(978-1-0806-2503-1(8))* Independently Published.

—Français-Perse (Farsi) le Temps Livre d'Images Bilingue Pour Enfants. Carlson Jr, Richard. 2018. (FRE.). 28p. (J). pap. 10.99 *(978-1-7307-3091-7(4))* Independently Published.

—Français-Perse (Farsi) on a Blessé Mes Sentiments Livre d'images Bilingue Pour Enfants. Carlson, Richard. 2019. (FRE.). 24p. (J). pap. 10.99 *(978-1-0804-6034-2(9))* Independently Published.

—Français-Polonais le Temps/Czas Livre d'Images Bilingue Pour Enfants. Carlson Jr, Richard. 2018. (FRE.). 28p. (J). pap. 10.99 *(978-1-7307-6927-6(6))* Independently Published.

—Français-Polonais on a Blessé Mes Sentiments/Zranione Uczucia Livre d'images Bilingue Pour Enfants. Carlson, Richard. 2019. (FRE.). 24p. (J). pap. 10.99 *(978-1-0804-6229-2(5))* Independently Published.

—Français-Portugais (Brésilien) le Temps/Tempo Livre d'Images Bilingue Pour Enfants. Carlson Jr, Richard. 2018. (FRE.). 28p. (J). pap. 10.99 *(978-1-7308-0667-4(8))* Independently Published.

—Français-Portugais (brésilien) on a Blessé Mes Sentiments/Meus Sentimentos Estão Feridos Livre d'images Bilingue Pour Enfants. Carlson, Richard. 2019. (FRE.). 24p. (J). pap. 10.99 *(978-1-0804-6664-1(9))* Independently Published.

—Français-Portugais (Portugal) le Temps/Tempo Livre d'Images Bilingue Pour Enfants. Carlson Jr, Richard. 2018. (FRE.). 28p. (J). pap. 10.99 *(978-1-7308-0695-7(3))* Independently Published.

—Français-Portugais (Portugal) on a Blessé Mes Sentiments/Os Meus Sentimentos Estão Feridos Livre d'images Bilingue Pour Enfants. Carlson, Richard. 2019. (FRE.). 24p. (J). pap. 10.99 *(978-1-0804-6931-4(1))* Independently Published.

—Français-Roumain le Temps/Timpul Livre d'Images Bilingue Pour Enfants. Carlson Jr, Richard. 2018. (FRE.). 28p. (J). pap. 10.99 *(978-1-7308-4799-8(4))* Independently Published.

—Français-Roumain on a Blessé Mes Sentiments/Sunt Jignit Livre d'images Bilingue Pour Enfants. Carlson, Richard. 2019. (FRE.). 24p. (J). pap. 10.99 *(978-1-0806-3344-9(8))* Independently Published.

—Français-Russe le Temps Livre d'Images Bilingue Pour Enfants. Carlson Jr, Richard. 2018. (FRE.). 28p. (J). pap. 10.99 *(978-1-7308-4945-9(8))* Independently Published.

—Français-Russe on a Blessé Mes Sentiments/Оскорбленные чувства; Livre d'images Bilingue Pour Enfants. Carlson, Richard. 2019. (FRE.). 24p. (J). pap. 10.99 *(978-1-0806-3824-6(5))* Independently Published.

—Français-Serbe (Cyrillique) le Temps Livre d'Images Bilingue Pour Enfants. Carlson Jr, Richard. 2018. (FRE.). 28p. (J). pap. 10.99 *(978-1-7308-4975-6(X))* Independently Published.

—Français-Serbe (cyrillique) on a Blessé Mes Sentiments/Моја осећања су повређена Livre d'images Bilingue Pour Enfants. Carlson, Richard. 2019. (FRE.). 24p. (J). pap. 10.99 *(978-1-0806-6609-6(5))* Independently Published.

—Français-Serbe (Latin) le Temps/Vreme Livre d'Images Bilingue Pour Enfants. Carlson Jr, Richard. 2018. (FRE.). 28p. (J). pap. 10.99 *(978-1-7308-8617-1(5))* Independently Published.

—Français-Serbe (latin) on a Blessé Mes Sentiments/Osecanja Su Mi Povređena Livre d'images Bilingue Pour Enfants. Carlson, Richard. 2019. (FRE.). 24p. (J). pap. 10.99 *(978-1-0806-6698-0(2))* Independently Published.

—Français-Shanghaïen le Temps Livre d'Images Bilingue Pour Enfants. Carlson Jr, Richard. 2018. (FRE.). 28p. (J). pap. 10.99 *(978-1-7308-8742-0(2))* Independently Published.

—Français-Shanghaïen on a Blessé Mes Sentiments/我的感情受到了伤害 Livre d'images Bilingue Pour Enfants. Carlson, Richard. 2019. (FRE.). 24p. (J). pap. 10.99 *(978-1-0806-6854-0(3))* Independently Published.

—Français-Slovaque le Temps/as Livre d'Images Bilingue Pour Enfants. Carlson Jr, Richard. 2018. (FRE.). 28p. (J). pap. 10.99 *(978-1-7308-9133-5(0))* Independently Published.

—Français-Slovaque on a Blessé Mes Sentiments/Ranili Moje City Livre d'images Bilingue Pour Enfants. Carlson, Richard. 2019. (FRE.). 24p. (J). pap. 10.99 *(978-1-0806-7351-3(2))* Independently Published.

—Français-Slovène le Temps/ as Livre d'Images Bilingue Pour Enfants. Carlson Jr, Richard. 2018. (FRE.). 28p. (J). pap. 10.99 *(978-1-7309-3663-0(6))* Independently Published.

—Français-Slovène on a Blessé Mes Sentiments/Moja Prizadeta čustva Livre d'images Bilingue Pour Enfants. Carlson, Richard. 2019. (FRE.). 24p. (J). pap. 10.99 *(978-1-0806-7630-9(9))* Independently Published.

—Français-Somali le Temps/Waqti Livre d'Images Bilingue Pour Enfants. Carlson Jr, Richard. 2018. (FRE.). 28p. (J). pap. 10.99 *(978-1-7309-3699-9(7))* Independently Published.

—Français-Somali on a Blessé Mes Sentiments/Dareenadayda Ayaa Dhaawacmay Livre d'images Bilingue Pour Enfants. Carlson, Richard. 2019. (FRE.). 24p. (J). pap. 10.99 *(978-1-0806-7907-2(3))* Independently Published.

—Français-Suédois le Temps/Tid Livre d'Images Bilingue Pour Enfants. Carlson Jr, Richard. 2018. (FRE.). 28p. (J). pap. 10.99 *(978-1-7309-4145-0(1))* Independently Published.

—Français-Suédois on a Blessé Mes Sentiments/Mina Känslor är Sårade Livre d'images Bilingue Pour Enfants. Carlson, Richard. 2019. (FRE.). 24p. (J). pap. 10.99 *(978-1-0806-8960-6(5))* Independently Published.

—Français-Swahili le Temps/Muda Livre d'Images Bilingue Pour Enfants. Carlson Jr, Richard. 2018. (FRE.). 28p. (J). pap. 10.99 *(978-1-7309-4074-3(9))* Independently Published.

—Français-Swahili on a Blessé Mes Sentiments/Hisia Zangu Zinaumia Livre d'images Bilingue Pour Enfants. Carlson, Richard. 2019. (FRE.). 24p. (J). pap. 10.99 *(978-1-0806-8597-4(9))* Independently Published.

—Français-Tadjik on a Blessé Mes Sentiments/эҳсосотм ҷриҳа дор шуда Livre d'images Bilingue Pour Enfants. Carlson, Richard. 2019. (FRE.). 24p. (J). pap. 10.99 *(978-1-0806-9497-6(8))* Independently Published.

—Français-Tagalog le Temps/Oras Livre d'Images Bilingue Pour Enfants. Carlson Jr, Richard. 2018. (FRE.). 28p. (J). pap. 10.99 *(978-1-7309-4172-6(9))* Independently Published.

—Français-Tagalog on a Blessé Mes Sentiments/Nasaktan Ang Aking Damdamin Livre d'images Bilingue Pour Enfants. Carlson, Richard. 2019. (FRE.). 24p. (J). pap. 10.99 *(978-1-0806-9281-1(9))* Independently Published.

—Français-Tamil le Temps Livre d'Images Bilingue Pour Enfants. Carlson Jr, Richard. 2018. (FRE.). 28p. (J). pap. 10.99 *(978-1-7309-4361-4(6))* Independently Published.

—Français-Tamil on a Blessé Mes Sentiments/எனது உணர்வுகள் காயமாகின Livre d'images Bilingue Pour Enfants. Carlson, Richard. 2019. (FRE.). 24p. (J). pap. 10.99 *(978-1-0806-9753-3(5))* Independently Published.

—Français-Tchèque le Temps/as Livre d'Images Bilingue Pour Enfants. Carlson Jr, Richard. 2018. (FRE.). 28p. (J). pap. 10.99 *(978-1-7287-1664-0(0))* Independently Published.

—Français-Tchèque on a Blessé Mes Sentiments/Mé City Jsou Zraněny Livre d'images Bilingue Pour Enfants. Carlson, Richard. 2019. (FRE.). 24p. (J). pap. 10.99 *(978-1-0780-4348-9(5))* Independently Published.

—Français-Télougou le Temps Livre d'Images Bilingue Pour Enfants. Carlson Jr, Richard. 2018. (FRE.). 28p. (J). pap. 10.99 *(978-1-7309-8696-3(X))* Independently Published.

—Français-Télougou on a Blessé Mes Sentiments Livre d'images Bilingue Pour Enfants. Carlson, Richard. 2019. (FRE.). 24p. (J). pap. 10.99 *(978-1-0808-7260-2(4))* Independently Published.

—Français-Thaï le Temps Livre d'Images Bilingue Pour Enfants. Carlson Jr, Richard. 2018. (FRE.). 28p. (J). pap. 10.99 *(978-1-7309-8739-7(7))* Independently Published.

—Français-Thaï on a Blessé Mes Sentiments/ความรู้สึกของผมคือเสียใจ Livre d'images Bilingue Pour Enfants. Carlson, Richard. 2019. (FRE.). 24p. (J). pap. 10.99 *(978-1-0808-7468-2(2))* Independently Published.

—Français-Tigrigna le Temps Livre d'Images Bilingue Pour Enfants. Carlson Jr, Richard. 2018. (FRE.). 28p. (J). pap. 10.99 *(978-1-7309-8789-2(3))* Independently Published.

—Français-Tigrigna on a Blessé Mes Sentiments/ስምዒተይተጎዲኡ እዩ Livre d'images Bilingue Pour Enfants. Carlson, Richard. 2019. (FRE.). 24p. (J). pap. 10.99 *(978-1-0808-7690-7(1))* Independently Published.

—Français-Turc le Temps/Zaman Livre d'Images Bilingue Pour Enfants. Carlson Jr, Richard. 2018. (FRE.). 28p. (J). pap. 10.99 *(978-1-7309-8882-0(2))* Independently Published.

—Français-Turc on a Blessé Mes Sentiments/Duygularım İncindi Livre d'images Bilingue Pour Enfants. Carlson, Richard. 2019. (FRE.). 24p. (J). pap. 10.99 *(978-1-0808-7915-1(3))* Independently Published.

—Français-Ukrainien le Temps Livre d'Images Bilingue Pour Enfants. Carlson Jr, Richard. 2018. (FRE.). 28p. (J). pap. 10.99 *(978-1-7310-7092-0(6))* Independently Published.

—Français-Ukrainien on a Blessé Mes Sentiments/Менезачепили заживе Livre d'images Bilingue Pour Enfants. Carlson, Richard. 2019. (FRE.). 24p. (J). pap. 10.99 *(978-1-0808-8143-7(3))* Independently Published.

—Français-Vietnamien on a Blessé Mes Sentiments/Cảm Xúc Của Mình Bị Tổn Thương Livre d'images Bilingue Pour Enfants. Carlson, Richard. 2019. (FRE.). 24p. (J). pap. 10.99 *(978-1-0810-6041-1(7))* Independently Published.

—Français-Xhosa le Temps Livre d'Images Bilingue Pour Enfants. Carlson Jr, Richard. 2018. (FRE.). 28p. (J). pap. 10.99 *(978-1-7311-6571-8(4))* Independently Published.

—Français-Yiddish on a Blessé Mes Sentiments Livre d'images Bilingue Pour Enfants. Carlson, Richard. 2019. (FRE.). 24p. (J). pap. 10.99 *(978-1-0810-6334-4(3))* Independently Published.

—Français-Yoruba le Temps Livre d'Images Bilingue Pour Enfants. Carlson Jr, Richard. 2018. (FRE.). 28p. (J). pap. 10.99 *(978-1-7311-6582-4(X))* Independently Published.

—Français-Yoruba on a Blessé Mes Sentiments/Ó dùn Mí lọ́kàn Mi Livre d'images Bilingue Pour Enfants. Carlson, Richard. 2019. (FRE.). 24p. (J). pap. 10.99 *(978-1-0810-6476-1(5))* Independently Published.

—Français-Zoulou le Temps/Isikhathi Livre d'Images Bilingue Pour Enfants. Carlson Jr, Richard. 2018. (FRE.). 28p. (J). pap. 10.99 *(978-1-7311-6620-3(6))* Independently Published.

—Français-Zoulou on a Blessé Mes Sentiments/Ngiphatheke Kabuhlungu Livre d'images Bilingue Pour Enfants. Carlson, Richard. 2019. (FRE.). 24p. (J). pap. 10.99 *(978-1-0810-6716-8(0))* Independently Published.

—Italiano-Afrikaans Attrezzi/Gereedskap Dizionario Bilingue Illustrato per Bambini. Carlson Jr, Richard. 2019. (ITA.). 26p. (J). pap. 10.99 *(978-1-7934-5445-4(0))* Independently Published.

Carlson, Suzanne. Italiano-Afrikaans Mi Sento Ferito/My Gevoelens Is Gekwets Libro Illustrato Bilingue per Bambini. Carlson, Richard. 2019. (ITA.). 24p. (J). pap. 10.99 ***(978-1-6944-2628-4(9))*** Independently Published.

Carlson, Suzanne. Italiano-Albanese Attrezzi/Veglat Dizionario Bilingue Illustrato per Bambini. Carlson Jr, Richard. 2019. (ITA.). 26p. (J). pap. 10.99 *(978-1-7934-5904-6(5))* Independently Published.

—Italiano-Albanese Guaio/Shqetësim Libro Illustrato Bilingue per Bambini. Carlson, Richard. 2019. (ITA.). 24p. (J). pap. 10.99 *(978-1-0989-3483-5(0))* Independently Published.

Carlson, Suzanne. Italiano-Albanese Mi Sento Ferito/Ndjenjat e Mia Jan&#65533; T&#65533; l&#65533;nduara Libro Illustrato Bilingue per Bambini. Carlson, Richard. 2019. (ITA.). 24p. (J). pap. 10.99 ***(978-1-6947-0185-5(9))*** Independently Published.

Carlson, Suzanne. Italiano-Amarico Attrezzi/Dizionario Bilingue Illustrato per Bambini. Carlson Jr, Richard. 2019. (ITA.). 26p. (J). pap. 10.99 *(978-1-7934-5950-3(9))* Independently Published.

—Italiano-Amarico Guaio/ችግር Libro Illustrato Bilingue per Bambini. Carlson, Richard. 2019. (ITA.). 24p. (J). pap. 10.99 *(978-1-0989-5280-8(4))* Independently Published.

Carlson, Suzanne. Italiano-Amarico Mi Sento Ferito/ስሜቴተጎድቷል Libro Illustrato Bilingue per Bambini. Carlson, Richard. 2019. (ITA.). 24p. (J). pap. 10.99 ***(978-1-6947-0631-7(1))*** Independently Published.

Carlson, Suzanne. Italiano-Arabo Attrezzi Dizionario Bilingue Illustrato per Bambini. Carlson Jr, Richard. 2019. (ITA.). 26p. (J). pap. 10.99 *(978-1-7934-6422-4(7))* Independently Published.

—Italiano-Arabo Guaio Libro Illustrato Bilingue per Bambini. Carlson, Richard. 2019. (ITA.). 24p. (J). pap. 10.99 *(978-1-0993-9444-7(9))* Independently Published.

Carlson, Suzanne. Italiano-Arabo Mi Sento Ferito Libro Illustrato Bilingue per Bambini. Carlson, Richard. 2019. (ITA.). 24p. (J). pap. 10.99 ***(978-1-6963-1185-4(3))*** Independently Published.

Carlson, Suzanne. Italiano-Armeno Attrezzi/Dizionario IO Bilingue Illustrato per Bambini. Carlson Jr, Richard. 2019. (ITA.). 26p. (J). pap. 10.99 *(978-1-7934-6579-5(7))* Independently Published.

—Italiano-Armeno Guaio/Անախորժություն Libro Illustrato Bilingue per Bambini. Carlson, Richard. 2019. (ITA.). 24p. (J). pap. 10.99 *(978-1-0989-5385-0(1))* Independently Published.

Carlson, Suzanne. Italiano-Armeno Mi Sento Ferito/Եսվիրավորված եմ Libro Illustrato Bilingue per Bambini. Carlson, Richard. 2019. (ITA.). 24p. (J). pap. 10.99 ***(978-1-6948-5269-4(5))*** Independently Published.

Carlson, Suzanne. Italiano-Azero Attrezzi Dizionario Bilingue Illustrato per Bambini. Carlson Jr, Richard. 2019. (ITA.). 26p. (J). pap. 10.99 *(978-1-7934-6600-6(9))* Independently Published.

—Italiano-Azero Guaio/Yaramazlıq Libro Illustrato Bilingue per Bambini. Carlson, Richard. 2019. (ITA.). 24p. (J). pap. 10.99 *(978-1-0989-5464-2(5))* Independently Published.

Carlson, Suzanne. Italiano-Azero Mi Sento Ferito/Hisslərim Yaralandı Libro Illustrato Bilingue per Bambini. Carlson, Richard. 2019. (ITA.). 24p. (J). pap. 10.99 ***(978-1-6948-5533-6(3))*** Independently Published.

Carlson, Suzanne. Italiano-Basco Attrezzi/Tresnak Dizionario Bilingue Illustrato per Bambini. Carlson Jr, Richard. 2019. (ITA.). 26p. (J). pap. 10.99 *(978-1-7934-6671-6(8))* Independently Published.

Carlson, Suzanne. Italiano-Basco Mi Sento Ferito/Nire Sentimenduak Minduta Libro Illustrato Bilingue per Bambini. Carlson, Richard. 2019. (ITA.). 24p. (J). pap. 10.99 ***(978-1-6948-6045-3(0))*** Independently Published.

Carlson, Suzanne. Italiano-Bengalese Attrezzi Dizionario Bilingue Illustrato per Bambini. Carlson Jr, Richard. 2019. (ITA.). 26p. (J). pap. 10.99 *(978-1-7938-1653-5(0))* Independently Published.

—Italiano-Bengalese Guaio/বিপদ Libro Illustrato Bilingue per Bambini. Carlson, Richard. 2019. (ITA.). 24p. (J). pap. 10.99 *(978-1-0989-6039-1(4))* Independently Published.

Carlson, Suzanne. Italiano-Bengalese Mi Sento Ferito Libro Illustrato Bilingue per Bambini. Carlson, Richard. 2019. (ITA.). 24p. (J). pap. 10.99 ***(978-1-6948-6655-4(6))*** Independently Published.

Carlson, Suzanne. Italiano-Bielorusso Attrezzi/Dizionario Bilingue Illustrato per Bambini. Carlson Jr, Richard. 2019. (ITA.). 26p. (J). pap. 10.99 *(978-1-7938-1392-3(2))* Independently Published.

—Italiano-Bielorusso Guaio/Непрыемнасці Libro Illustrato Bilingue per Bambini. Carlson, Richard. 2019. (ITA.). 24p. (J). pap. 10.99 *(978-1-0989-5810-7(1))* Independently Published.

Carlson, Suzanne. Italiano-Bielorusso Mi Sento Ferito/Абражаныяпачуцці Libro Illustrato Bilingue per Bambini. Carlson, Richard. 2019. (ITA.). 24p. (J). pap. 10.99 ***(978-1-6948-6365-2(4))*** Independently Published.

Carlson, Suzanne. Italiano-Bosniaco Attrezzi/Alati Dizionario Bilingue Illustrato per Bambini. Carlson Jr, Richard. 2019. (ITA.). 26p. (J). pap. 10.99 *(978-1-7939-5130-4(6))* Independently Published.

—Italiano-Bosniaco Guaio/Problem Libro Illustrato Bilingue per Bambini. Carlson, Richard. 2019. (ITA.). 24p. (J). pap. 10.99 *(978-1-0990-6241-4(1))* Independently Published.

Carlson, Suzanne. Italiano-Bosniaco Mi Sento Ferito/Moja Osjecanja Su Povrijeđena Libro Illustrato Bilingue per Bambini. Carlson, Richard. 2019. (ITA.). 24p. (J). pap. 10.99 ***(978-1-6948-6796-4(X))*** Independently Published.

Carlson, Suzanne. Italiano-Bulgaro Attrezzi/Dizionario Bilingue Illustrato per Bambini. Carlson Jr, Richard. 2019. (ITA.). 26p. (J). pap. 10.99 *(978-1-7939-5287-5(6))* Independently Published.

—Italiano-Bulgaro Guaio/Неприятност Libro Illustrato Bilingue per Bambini. Carlson, Richard. 2019. (ITA.). 24p. (J). pap. 10.99 *(978-1-0990-8611-3(6))* Independently Published.

Carlson, Suzanne. Italiano-Bulgaro Mi Sento Ferito/Чувствата ми са наранени Libro Illustrato Bilingue per Bambini. Carlson, Richard. 2019. (ITA.). 24p. (J). pap. 10.99 ***(978-1-6948-6924-1(5))*** Independently Published.

Carlson, Suzanne. Italiano-Burmese Attrezzi Dizionario Bilingue Illustrato per Bambini. Carlson Jr, Richard. 2019. (ITA.). 26p. (J). pap. 10.99 *(978-1-7939-5589-0(1))* Independently Published.

—Italiano-Burmese Guaio Libro Illustrato Bilingue per Bambini. Carlson, Richard. 2019. (ITA.). 24p. (J). pap. 10.99 *(978-1-0990-8731-8(7))* Independently Published.

Carlson, Suzanne. Italiano-Burmese Mi Sento Ferito Libro Illustrato Bilingue per Bambini. Carlson, Richard. 2019. (ITA.). 24p. (J). pap. 10.99 ***(978-1-6948-7247-0(5))*** Independently Published.

Carlson, Suzanne. Italiano-Catalano Attrezzi/Eines Dizionario Bilingue Illustrato per Bambini. Carlson Jr, Richard. 2019. (ITA.). 26p. (J). pap. 10.99 *(978-1-7939-6231-7(6))* Independently Published.

—Italiano-Catalano Guaio/Problemes Libro Illustrato Bilingue per Bambini. Carlson, Richard. 2019. (ITA.). 24p. (J). pap. 10.99 *(978-1-0990-9021-9(0))* Independently Published.

Carlson, Suzanne. Italiano-Catalano Mi Sento Ferito/M'han Ferit Els Meus Sentiments Libro Illustrato Bilingue per Bambini. Carlson, Richard. 2019. (ITA.). 24p. (J). pap. 10.99 ***(978-1-6948-7436-8(2))*** Independently Published.

Carlson, Suzanne. Italiano-Ceco Attrezzi/Nástroje Dizionario Bilingue Illustrato per Bambini. Carlson Jr, Richard. 2019. (ITA.). 26p. (J). pap. 10.99 *(978-1-7939-6558-5(7))* Independently Published.

—Italiano-Ceco Guaio/Potíz Libro Illustrato Bilingue per Bambini. Carlson, Richard. 2019. (ITA.). 24p. (J). pap. 10.99 *(978-1-0991-9007-0(X))* Independently Published.

Carlson, Suzanne. Italiano-Ceco Mi Sento Ferito/M&#65533; City Jsou Zraněny Libro Illustrato Bilingue per Bambini. Carlson, Richard. 2019. (ITA.). 24p. (J). pap. 10.99 ***(978-1-6948-9979-8(9))*** Independently Published.

Carlson, Suzanne. Italiano-Ceco Veicoli Dizionario Bilingue Illustrato per Bambini. Carlson Jr, Richard. 2018. (ITA.). 24p. (J). pap. 10.99 *(978-1-7198-7225-6(2))* Independently Published.

—Italiano-Cinese Cantonese Tradizionale Guaio/麻煩 Libro Illustrato Bilingue per Bambini. Carlson, Richard. 2019. (ITA.). 24p. (J). pap. 10.99 *(978-1-0991-8776-6(1))* Independently Published.

Carlson, Suzanne. Italiano-Cinese Cantonese Tradizionale Mi Sento Ferito/我的情感受到了傷害 Libro Illustrato Bilingue per Bambini. Carlson, Richard. 2019. (ITA.). 24p. (J). pap. 10.99 ***(978-1-6948-7710-9(8))*** Independently Published.

Carlson, Suzanne. Italiano-Cinese Cantonese Tradizionale Veicoli Dizionario Bilingue Illustrato per Bambini. Carlson Jr, Richard. 2018. (ITA.). 24p. (J). pap. 10.99 *(978-1-7198-5963-9(9))* Independently Published.

—Italiano-Cinese Mandarino Tradizionale Attrezzi/ Dizionario Bilingue Illustrato per Bambini. Carlson Jr, Richard. 2019. (ITA.). 26p. (J). pap. 10.99 *(978-1-7939-6309-3(6))* Independently Published.

—Italiano-Cinese Mandarino Tradizionale Guaio/麻煩 Libro Illustrato Bilingue per Bambini. Carlson, Richard. 2019. (ITA.). 24p. (J). pap. 10.99 *(978-1-0990-9150-6(0))* Independently Published.

Carlson, Suzanne. Italiano-Cinese Mandarino Tradizionale Mi Sento Ferito/我的情感受到了傷害 Libro Illustrato Bilingue per Bambini. Carlson, Richard. 2019. (ITA.). 24p. (J). pap. 10.99 ***(978-1-6948-7511-2(3))*** Independently Published.

Carlson, Suzanne. Italiano-Cinese Mandarino Tradizionale (Taiwan) Guaio/麻煩 Libro Illustrato Bilingue per Bambini. Carlson, Richard. 2019. (ITA.). 24p. (J). pap. 10.99 *(978-1-0991-8901-2(2))* Independently Published.

Carlson, Suzanne. Italiano-Cinese Mandarino Tradizionale (Taiwan) Mi Sento Ferito/我的感覺受傷了 Libro Illustrato Bilingue per Bambini. Carlson, Richard. 2019. (ITA.). 24p. (J). pap. 10.99 ***(978-1-6948-7840-3(6))*** Independently Published.

Carlson, Suzanne. Italiano-Cinese Mandarino Tradizionale (Taiwan) Veicoli Dizionario Bilingue Illustrato per Bambini. Carlson Jr, Richard. 2018. (ITA.). 24p. (J). pap. 10.99 *(978-1-7198-5996-7(5))* Independently Published.

—Italiano-Cinese Semplificato Tradizionale Attrezzi/ Dizionario Bilingue Illustrato per Bambini. Carlson Jr, Richard. 2019. (ITA.). 26p. (J). pap. 10.99 *(978-1-7939-6386-4(X))* Independently Published.

—Italiano-Cinese Semplificato Tradizionale Guaio/麻烦 Libro Illustrato Bilingue per Bambini. Carlson, Richard. 2019. (ITA.). 24p. (J). pap. 10.99 *(978-1-0990-9533-7(6))* Independently Published.

Carlson, Suzanne. Italiano-Cinese Semplificato Tradizionale Mi Sento Ferito/我的感情受到了伤害 Libro Illustrato Bilingue per Bambini. Carlson, Richard. 2019. (ITA.). 24p. (J). pap. 10.99 ***(978-1-6948-7619-5(5))*** Independently Published.

Carlson, Suzanne. Italiano-Coreano Attrezzi/Dizionario Bilingue Illustrato per Bambini. Carlson Jr, Richard. 2019. (ITA.). 26p. (J). pap. 10.99 *(978-1-7944-4964-0(7))* Independently Published.

—Italiano-Coreano Guaio/장난 Libro Illustrato Bilingue per Bambini. Carlson, Richard. 2019. (ITA.). 24p. (J). pap. 10.99 *(978-1-0993-8693-0(4))* Independently Published.

Carlson, Suzanne. Italiano-Coreano Mi Sento Ferito/마음이 아팠어요 Libro Illustrato Bilingue per Bambini. Carlson, Richard. 2019. (ITA.). 24p. (J). pap. 10.99 ***(978-1-6955-1574-1(9))*** Independently Published.

Carlson, Suzanne. Italiano-Coreano Veicoli Dizionario Bilingue Illustrato per Bambini. Carlson Jr, Richard. 2018. (ITA.). 24p. (J). pap. 10.99 *(978-1-7200-3992-1(5))* Independently Published.

—Italiano-Creolo Haitiano Attrezzi/Zouti Yo Dizionario Bilingue Illustrato per Bambini. Carlson Jr, Richard. 2019. (ITA.). 26p. (J). pap. 10.99 *(978-1-7943-3672-8(9))* Independently Published.

—Italiano-Creolo Haitiano Guaio/Dezòd Libro Illustrato Bilingue per Bambini. Carlson, Richard. 2019. (ITA.). 24p. (J). pap. 10.99 *(978-1-0992-7841-9(4))* Independently Published.

Carlson, Suzanne. Italiano-Creolo Haitiano Mi Sento Ferito/Santiman M Blese Libro Illustrato Bilingue per Bambini. Carlson, Richard. 2019. (ITA.). 24p. (J). pap. 10.99 ***(978-1-6952-7129-6(7))*** Independently Published.

Carlson, Suzanne. Italiano-Creolo Haitiano Veicoli/Machin Yo Dizionario Bilingue Illustrato per Bambini. Carlson Jr, Richard. 2018. (ITA.). 24p. (J). pap. 10.99 *(978-1-7199-0702-6(1))* Independently Published.

—Italiano-Croato Attrezzi/Alati Dizionario Bilingue Illustrato per Bambini. Carlson Jr, Richard. 2019. (ITA.). 26p. (J). pap. 10.99 *(978-1-7939-6457-1(2))* Independently Published.

—Italiano-Croato Guaio/Nevolja Libro Illustrato Bilingue per Bambini. Carlson, Richard. 2019. (ITA.). 24p. (J). pap. 10.99 *(978-1-0991-8954-8(3))* Independently Published.

Carlson, Suzanne. Italiano-Croato Mi Sento Ferito/Moji Osjecaji Su Povrijeđeni Libro Illustrato Bilingue per Bambini. Carlson, Richard. 2019. (ITA.). 24p. (J). pap. 10.99 ***(978-1-6948-9880-7(6))*** Independently Published.

Carlson, Suzanne. Italiano-Croato Veicoli/Vozila Dizionario Bilingue Illustrato per Bambini. Carlson Jr, Richard. 2018. (ITA.). 24p. (J). pap. 10.99 *(978-1-7198-7218-8(X))* Independently Published.

—Italiano-Curdo Guaio/کێشە Libro Illustrato Bilingue per Bambini. Carlson, Richard. 2019. (ITA.). 24p. (J). pap. 10.99 *(978-1-0993-9803-2(7))* Independently Published.

—Italiano-Curdo Veicoli Dizionario Bilingue Illustrato per Bambini. Carlson Jr, Richard. 2018. (ITA.). 24p. (J). pap. 10.99 *(978-1-7200-4016-3(8))* Independently Published.

—Italiano-Danese Attrezzi/Værktøj Dizionario Bilingue Illustrato per Bambini. Carlson Jr, Richard. 2019. (ITA.). 26p. (J). pap. 10.99 *(978-1-7941-3835-3(8))* Independently Published.

—Italiano-Danese Guaio/Ballade Libro Illustrato Bilingue per Bambini. Carlson, Richard. 2019. (ITA.). 24p. (J). pap. 10.99 *(978-1-0991-9063-6(0))* Independently Published.

Carlson, Suzanne. Italiano-Danese Mi Sento Ferito/Mine F&#65533;lelser Blev S&#65533;ret Libro Illustrato Bilingue per Bambini. Carlson, Richard. 2019. (ITA.). 24p. (J). pap. 10.99 ***(978-1-6950-4213-1(1))*** Independently Published.

Carlson, Suzanne. Italiano-Danese Veicoli/K. Carlson Jr, Richard. 2018. (ITA.). 24p. (J). pap. 10.99 *(978-1-7198-7242-3(2))* Independently Published.

—Italiano-Dari Attrezzi Dizionario Bilingue Illustrato per Bambini. Carlson Jr, Richard. 2019. (ITA.). 26p. (J). pap. 10.99 *(978-1-7941-6144-3(9))* Independently Published.

—Italiano-Dari Guaio/مشکل Libro Illustrato Bilingue per Bambini. Carlson, Richard. 2019. (ITA.). 24p. (J). pap. 10.99 *(978-1-0993-9651-9(4))* Independently Published.

Carlson, Suzanne. Italiano-Dari Mi Sento Ferito Libro Illustrato Bilingue per Bambini. Carlson, Richard. 2019. (ITA.). 24p. (J). pap. 10.99 ***(978-1-6963-1252-3(3))*** Independently Published.

Carlson, Suzanne. Italiano-Dari Veicoli Dizionario Bilingue Illustrato per Bambini. Carlson Jr, Richard. 2018. (ITA.). 24p. (J). pap. 10.99 *(978-1-7198-8653-6(9))* Independently Published.

—Italiano-Ebraico Attrezzi/כלים Dizionario Bilingue Illustrato per Bambini. Carlson Jr, Richard. 2019. (ITA.). 26p. (J). pap. 10.99 *(978-1-7944-0123-5(7))* Independently Published.

—Italiano-Ebraico Guaio/צרה+צרורה Libro Illustrato Bilingue per Bambini. Carlson, Richard. 2019. (ITA.). 24p. (J). pap. 10.99 *(978-1-0993-9718-9(9))* Independently Published.

Carlson, Suzanne. Italiano-Ebraico Mi Sento Ferito Libro Illustrato Bilingue per Bambini. Carlson, Richard. 2019. (ITA.). 24p. (J). pap. 10.99 ***(978-1-6963-1377-3(5))*** Independently Published.

Carlson, Suzanne. Italiano-Estone Attrezzi/Tööriistad Dizionario Bilingue Illustrato per Bambini. Carlson Jr, Richard. 2019. (ITA.). 26p. (J). pap. 10.99 *(978-1-7942-0843-8(7))* Independently Published.

—Italiano-Estone Guaio/Pahandus Libro Illustrato Bilingue per Bambini. Carlson, Richard. 2019. (ITA.). 24p. (J). pap. 10.99 *(978-1-0991-9256-2(0))* Independently Published.

Carlson, Suzanne. Italiano-Estone Mi Sento Ferito/Mu Tunded Said Haavata Libro Illustrato Bilingue per Bambini. Carlson, Richard. 2019. (ITA.). 24p. (J). pap. 10.99 ***(978-1-6950-4458-6(4))*** Independently Published.

Carlson, Suzanne. Italiano-Estone Veicoli/S. Carlson Jr, Richard. 2018. (ITA.). 24p. (J). pap. 10.99 *(978-1-7198-9257-5(1))* Independently Published.

—Italiano-Fiammingo (Belga) Attrezzi/Werktuigen Dizionario Bilingue Illustrato per Bambini. Carlson Jr, Richard. 2019. (ITA.). 26p. (J). pap. 10.99 *(978-1-7942-7080-0(9))* Independently Published.

—Italiano-Fiammingo (Belga) Guaio/Problemen Libro Illustrato Bilingue per Bambini. Carlson, Richard. 2019. (ITA.). 24p. (J). pap. 10.99 *(978-1-0992-4242-7(8))* Independently Published.

Carlson, Suzanne. Italiano-Fiammingo (Belga) Mi Sento Ferito/Mijn Gevoelens Zijn Gekwetst Libro Illustrato Bilingue per Bambini. Carlson, Richard. 2019. (ITA.). 24p. (J). pap. 10.99 ***(978-1-6950-4613-9(7))*** Independently Published.

Carlson, Suzanne. Italiano-Finlandese Attrezzi/Työkalut Dizionario Bilingue Illustrato per Bambini. Carlson Jr, Richard. 2019. (ITA.). 26p. (J). pap. 10.99 *(978-1-7942-1028-8(8))* Independently Published.

—Italiano-Finlandese Guaio/Kiusaaminen Libro Illustrato Bilingue per Bambini. Carlson, Richard. 2019. (ITA.). 24p. (J). pap. 10.99 *(978-1-0991-9341-5(9))* Independently Published.

Carlson, Suzanne. Italiano-Finlandese Mi Sento Ferito/Tunteitani on Loukattu Libro Illustrato Bilingue per Bambini. Carlson, Richard. 2019. (ITA.). 24p. (J). pap. 10.99 ***(978-1-6950-4545-3(9))*** Independently Published.

Carlson, Suzanne. Italiano-Finlandese Veicoli/Kulkuneuvot Dizionario Bilingue Illustrato per Bambini. Carlson Jr, Richard. 2018. (ITA.). 24p. (J). pap. 10.99 *(978-1-7198-9325-1(X))* Independently Published.

—Italiano-Francese Attrezzi/Outils Dizionario Bilingue Illustrato per Bambini. Carlson Jr, Richard. 2019. (ITA.). 26p. (J). pap. 10.99 *(978-1-7942-7118-0(X))* Independently Published.

—Italiano-Francese Guaio/Problème Libro Illustrato Bilingue per Bambini. Carlson, Richard. 2019. (ITA.). 24p. (J). pap. 10.99 *(978-1-0992-4530-5(3))* Independently Published.

Carlson, Suzanne. Italiano-Francese Mi Sento Ferito/on a Bless&#65533; Mes Sentiments Libro Illustrato Bilingue per Bambini. Carlson, Richard. 2019. (ITA.). 24p. (J). pap. 10.99 ***(978-1-6950-4756-3(7))*** Independently Published.

Carlson, Suzanne. Italiano-Francese Veicoli/V. Carlson Jr, Richard. 2018. (ITA.). 24p. (J). pap. 10.99 *(978-1-7198-9343-5(8))* Independently Published.

C

—Italiano-Gaelico Irlandese Attrezzi/Uirlisí Dizionario Bilingue Illustrato per Bambini. Carlson Jr, Richard. 2019. (ITA.). 26p. (J). pap. 10.99 *(978-1-7944-0303-1(5))* Independently Published.

—Italiano-Gaelico Irlandese Guaio/Trioblóid Libro Illustrato Bilingue per Bambini. Carlson, Richard. 2019. (ITA.). 24p. (J). pap. 10.99 *(978-1-0992-9576-8(9))* Independently Published.

Carlson, Suzanne. Italiano-Gaelico Irlandese Mi Sento Ferito/T� M� Gortaithe Libro Illustrato Bilingue per Bambini. Carlson, Richard. 2019. (ITA.). 24p. (J). pap. 10.99 ***(978-1-6952-8514-9(X))*** Independently Published.

Carlson, Suzanne. Italiano-Gaelico Irlandese Veicoli/Feithiclí Dizionario Bilingue Illustrato per Bambini. Carlson Jr, Richard. 2018. (ITA.). 24p. (J). pap. 10.99 *(978-1-7200-2135-3(X))* Independently Published.

Carlson, Suzanne. Italiano-Galiziano Mi Sento Ferito/Os Meus Sentimentos Est�n Feridos Libro Illustrato Bilingue per Bambini. Carlson, Richard. 2019. (ITA.). 24p. (J). pap. 10.99 ***(978-1-6950-4911-6(X))*** Independently Published.

Carlson, Suzanne. Italiano-Gallese Attrezzi/Offer Dizionario Bilingue Illustrato per Bambini. Carlson Jr, Richard. 2019. (ITA.). 26p. (J). pap. 10.99 *(978-1-7945-7972-9(9))* Independently Published.

Carlson, Suzanne. Italiano-Gallese Mi Sento Ferito/Fy Nheimladau Yn Brifo Libro Illustrato Bilingue per Bambini. Carlson, Richard. 2019. (ITA.). 24p. (J). pap. 10.99 ***(978-1-6963-4625-2(8))*** Independently Published.

Carlson, Suzanne. Italiano-Georgiano Attrezzi/ Dizionario Bilingue Illustrato per Bambini. Carlson Jr, Richard. 2019. (ITA.). 26p. (J). pap. 10.99 *(978-1-7943-3330-7(4))* Independently Published.

—Italiano-Georgiano Guaio/უსიამოვნება Libro Illustrato Bilingue per Bambini. Carlson, Richard. 2019. (ITA.). 24p. (J). pap. 10.99 *(978-1-0992-6037-7(X))* Independently Published.

Carlson, Suzanne. Italiano-Georgiano Mi Sento Ferito/ჩემი გრძნობები შეურაცხყოფილია Libro Illustrato Bilingue Per. Carlson, Richard. 2019. (ITA.). 24p. (J). pap. 10.99 ***(978-1-6950-5337-3(0))*** Independently Published.

Carlson, Suzanne. Italiano-Georgiano Veicoli Dizionario Bilingue Illustrato per Bambini. Carlson Jr, Richard. 2018. (ITA.). 24p. (J). pap. 10.99 *(978-1-7198-9350-3(0))* Independently Published.

—Italiano-Giapponese Attrezzi/Dizionario Bilingue Illustrato per Bambini. Carlson Jr, Richard. 2019. (ITA.). 26p. (J). pap. 10.99 *(978-1-7944-0405-2(8))* Independently Published.

—Italiano-Giapponese Guaio/トラブル Libro Illustrato Bilingue per Bambini. Carlson, Richard. 2019. (ITA.). 24p. (J). pap. 10.99 *(978-1-0992-9663-5(3))* Independently Published.

Carlson, Suzanne. Italiano-Giapponese Mi Sento Ferito/ぼくは傷ついた Libro Illustrato Bilingue per Bambini. Carlson, Richard. 2019. (ITA.). 24p. (J). pap. 10.99 ***(978-1-6952-9794-4(6))*** Independently Published.

Carlson, Suzanne. Italiano-Giapponese Veicoli Dizionario Bilingue Illustrato per Bambini. Carlson Jr, Richard. 2018. (ITA.). 24p. (J). pap. 10.99 *(978-1-7200-2152-0(X))* Independently Published.

—Italiano-Greco Attrezzi/ Dizionario Bilingue Illustrato per Bambini. Carlson Jr, Richard. 2019. (ITA.). 26p. (J). pap. 10.99 *(978-1-7943-3433-5(5))* Independently Published.

—Italiano-Greco Guaio/Πρόβλημα Libro Illustrato Bilingue per Bambini. Carlson, Richard. 2019. (ITA.). 24p. (J). pap. 10.99 *(978-1-0992-6378-1(6))* Independently Published.

Carlson, Suzanne. Italiano-Greco Mi Sento Ferito/Πληγώθηκαν Τα Συναισθήματά Μου Libro Illustrato Bilingue per Bambini. Carlson, Richard. 2019. (ITA.). 24p. (J). pap. 10.99 ***(978-1-6950-5598-8(5))*** Independently Published.

Carlson, Suzanne. Italiano-Greco Veicoli Dizionario Bilingue Illustrato per Bambini. Carlson Jr, Richard. 2018. (ITA.). 24p. (J). pap. 10.99 *(978-1-7198-9371-8(3))* Independently Published.

—Italiano-Gujarati Attrezzi/ Dizionario Bilingue Illustrato per Bambini. Carlson Jr, Richard. 2019. (ITA.). 26p. (J). pap. 10.99 *(978-1-7943-3514-1(5))* Independently Published.

—Italiano-Gujarati Guaio/તકલીફ Libro Illustrato Bilingue per Bambini. Carlson, Richard. 2019. (ITA.). 24p. (J). pap. 10.99 *(978-1-0992-7789-4(2))* Independently Published.

Carlson, Suzanne. Italiano-Gujarati Mi Sento Ferito Libro Illustrato Bilingue per Bambini. Carlson, Richard. 2019. (ITA.). 24p. (J). pap. 10.99 ***(978-1-6950-5787-6(2))*** Independently Published.

Carlson, Suzanne. Italiano-Gujarati Veicoli Dizionario Bilingue Illustrato per Bambini. Carlson Jr, Richard. 2018. (ITA.). 24p. (J). pap. 10.99 *(978-1-7198-9377-0(2))* Independently Published.

—Italiano-Hausa Attrezzi/Kayan Aiki Dizionario Bilingue Illustrato per Bambini. Carlson Jr, Richard. 2019. (ITA.). 26p. (J). pap. 10.99 *(978-1-7943-3745-9(8))* Independently Published.

—Italiano-Hausa Guaio/Matsala Libro Illustrato Bilingue per Bambini. Carlson, Richard. 2019. (ITA.). 24p. (J). pap. 10.99 *(978-1-0992-8006-1(0))* Independently Published.

Carlson, Suzanne. Italiano-Hausa Mi Sento Ferito/Na Ji Jikkata Libro Illustrato Bilingue per Bambini. Carlson, Richard. 2019. (ITA.). 24p. (J). pap. 10.99 ***(978-1-6952-7239-2(0))*** Independently Published.

Carlson, Suzanne. Italiano-Hausa Veicoli-Abin Hawa/Mota Dizionario Bilingue Illustrato per Bambini. Carlson Jr, Richard. 2018. (ITA.). 24p. (J). pap. 10.99 *(978-1-7199-0712-5(9))* Independently Published.

—Italiano-Hindi Attrezzi/ Dizionario Bilingue Illustrato per Bambini. Carlson Jr, Richard. 2019. (ITA.). 26p. (J). pap. 10.99 *(978-1-7944-0173-0(3))* Independently Published.

—Italiano-Hindi Guaio/शरारत Libro Illustrato Bilingue per Bambini. Carlson, Richard. 2019. (ITA.). 24p. (J). pap. 10.99 *(978-1-0992-8103-7(2))* Independently Published.

Carlson, Suzanne. Italiano-Hindi Mi Sento Ferito/मेरी भावनाओं को ठेस पहुँची है Libro Illustrato Bilingue per Bambini. Carlson, Richard. 2019. (ITA.). 24p. (J). pap. 10.99 ***(978-1-6952-7479-2(2))*** Independently Published.

Carlson, Suzanne. Italiano-Indonesiano Attrezzi/Perkakas Dizionario Bilingue Illustrato per Bambini. Carlson Jr, Richard. 2019. (ITA.). 26p. (J). pap. 10.99 *(978-1-7944-0285-0(3))* Independently Published.

—Italiano-Indonesiano Guaio/Masalah Libro Illustrato Bilingue per Bambini. Carlson, Richard. 2019. (ITA.). 24p. (J). pap. 10.99 *(978-1-0992-8628-5(X))* Independently Published.

Carlson, Suzanne. Italiano-Indonesiano Mi Sento Ferito/Perasaanku Terluka Libro Illustrato Bilingue per Bambini. Carlson, Richard. 2019. (ITA.). 24p. (J). pap. 10.99 ***(978-1-6952-8220-9(5))*** Independently Published.

Carlson, Suzanne. Italiano-Indonesiano Veicoli/Kendaraan Dizionario Bilingue Illustrato per Bambini. Carlson Jr, Richard. 2018. (ITA.). 24p. (J). pap. 10.99 *(978-1-7200-2113-1(9))* Independently Published.

—Italiano-Inglese Veicoli/Vehicles Dizionario Bilingue Illustrato per Bambini. Carlson Jr, Richard. 2018. (ITA.). 24p. (J). pap. 10.99 *(978-1-7198-9194-3(X))* Independently Published.

—Italiano-Islandese Attrezzi/Verkfæri Dizionario Bilingue Illustrato per Bambini. Carlson Jr, Richard. 2019. (ITA.). 26p. (J). pap. 10.99 *(978-1-7944-0229-4(2))* Independently Published.

—Italiano-Islandese Guaio/Vandræði Libro Illustrato Bilingue per Bambini. Carlson, Richard. 2019. (ITA.). 24p. (J). pap. 10.99 *(978-1-0992-8526-4(7))* Independently Published.

Carlson, Suzanne. Italiano-Islandese Mi Sento Ferito/�g Er S�r�ur Libro Illustrato Bilingue per Bambini. Carlson, Richard. 2019. (ITA.). 24p. (J). pap. 10.99 ***(978-1-6952-7955-1(7))*** Independently Published.

Carlson, Suzanne. Italiano-Islandese Veicoli/Farartæki Dizionario Bilingue Illustrato per Bambini. Carlson Jr, Richard. 2018. (ITA.). 24p. (J). pap. 10.99 *(978-1-7200-2012-7(4))* Independently Published.

—Italiano-Kannada Attrezzi/Dizionario IO Bilingue Illustrato per Bambini. Carlson Jr, Richard. 2019. (ITA.). 26p. (J). pap. 10.99 *(978-1-7944-4162-0(X))* Independently Published.

—Italiano-Kannada Guaio/ತೊಂದರೆ Libro Illustrato Bilingue per Bambini. Carlson, Richard. 2019. (ITA.). 24p. (J). pap. 10.99 *(978-1-0992-9774-8(5))* Independently Published.

Carlson, Suzanne. Italiano-Kannada Mi Sento Ferito Libro Illustrato Bilingue per Bambini. Carlson, Richard. 2019. (ITA.). 24p. (J). pap. 10.99 ***(978-1-6955-0828-6(9))*** Independently Published.

Carlson, Suzanne. Italiano-Kannada Veicoli Dizionario Bilingue Illustrato per Bambini. Carlson Jr, Richard. 2018. (ITA.). 24p. (J). pap. 10.99 *(978-1-7200-2371-5(9))* Independently Published.

—Italiano-Kazako Guaio/Бәлеге ; қалу Libro Illustrato Bilingue per Bambini. Carlson, Richard. 2019. (ITA.). 24p. (J). pap. 10.99 *(978-1-0992-9834-9(2))* Independently Published.

Carlson, Suzanne. Italiano-Kazako Mi Sento Ferito/Сезімт ал бала туралы оқиға Libro Illustrato Bilingue per Bambini. Carlson, Richard. 2019. (ITA.). 24p. (J). pap. 10.99 ***(978-1-6955-1091-3(7))*** Independently Published.

Carlson, Suzanne. Italiano-Kazako Veicoli Dizionario Bilingue Illustrato per Bambini. Carlson Jr, Richard. 2018. (ITA.). 24p. (J). pap. 10.99 *(978-1-7200-2382-1(4))* Independently Published.

—Italiano-Khmer (Cambogiano) Attrezzi Dizionario Bilingue Illustrato per Bambini. Carlson Jr, Richard. 2019. (ITA.). 26p. (J). pap. 10.99 *(978-1-7944-4939-8(6))* Independently Published.

—Italiano-Khmer (Cambogiano) Guaio/បញ្ហ Libro Illustrato Bilingue per Bambini. Carlson, Richard. 2019. (ITA.). 24p. (J). pap. 10.99 *(978-1-0992-9951-3(9))* Independently Published.

Carlson, Suzanne. Italiano-Khmer (Cambogiano) Mi Sento Ferito Libro Illustrato Bilingue per Bambini. Carlson, Richard. 2019. (ITA.). 24p. (J). pap. 10.99 ***(978-1-6955-1366-2(5))*** Independently Published.

Carlson, Suzanne. Italiano-Khmer (Cambogiano) Veicoli Dizionario Bilingue Illustrato per Bambini. Carlson Jr, Richard. 2018. (ITA.). 24p. (J). pap. 10.99 *(978-1-7200-2411-8(1))* Independently Published.

—Italiano-Lao (Laotiano) Guaio Libro Illustrato Bilingue per Bambini. Carlson, Richard. 2019. (ITA.). 24p. (J). pap. 10.99 *(978-1-0993-9926-8(2))* Independently Published.

Carlson, Suzanne. Italiano-Lao (Laotiano) Mi Sento Ferito Libro Illustrato Bilingue per Bambini. Carlson, Richard. 2019. (ITA.). 24p. (J). pap. 10.99 ***(978-1-6955-1749-3(0))*** Independently Published.

Carlson, Suzanne. Italiano-Lao (Laotiano) Veicoli Dizionario Bilingue Illustrato per Bambini. Carlson Jr, Richard. 2018. (ITA.). 24p. (J). pap. 10.99 *(978-1-7200-4119-1(9))* Independently Published.

—Italiano-Lettone Guaio/Nelāgs Notikums Libro Illustrato Bilingue per Bambini. Carlson, Richard. 2019. (ITA.). 24p. (J). pap. 10.99 *(978-1-0994-0425-2(8))* Independently Published.

Carlson, Suzanne. Italiano-Lettone Mi Sento Ferito/Es Esmu Sāpināts Libro Illustrato Bilingue per Bambini. Carlson, Richard. 2019. (ITA.). 24p. (J). pap. 10.99 ***(978-1-6955-2038-7(6))*** Independently Published.

Carlson, Suzanne. Italiano-Lettone Veicoli Dizionario Bilingue Illustrato per Bambini. Carlson Jr, Richard. 2018. (ITA.). 24p. (J). pap. 10.99 *(978-1-7200-4141-2(5))* Independently Published.

—Italiano-Lituano Guaio/Beda Libro Illustrato Bilingue per Bambini. Carlson, Richard. 2019. (ITA.). 24p. (J). pap. 10.99 *(978-1-0994-0540-2(8))* Independently Published.

Carlson, Suzanne. Italiano-Lituano Mi Sento Ferito/Mane įskaudino Libro Illustrato Bilingue per Bambini. Carlson, Richard. 2019. (ITA.). 24p. (J). pap. 10.99 ***(978-1-6955-2317-3(2))*** Independently Published.

Carlson, Suzanne. Italiano-Lituano Veicoli Dizionario Bilingue Illustrato per Bambini. Carlson Jr, Richard. 2018. (ITA.). 24p. (J). pap. 10.99 *(978-1-7200-4194-8(6))* Independently Published.

—Italiano-Macedone Guaio/Беља Libro Illustrato Bilingue per Bambini. Carlson, Richard. 2019. (ITA.). 24p. (J). pap. 10.99 *(978-1-0994-0607-2(2))* Independently Published.

Carlson, Suzanne. Italiano-Macedone Mi Sento Ferito/Моите чувства се повредени Libro Illustrato Bilingue per Bambini. Carlson, Richard. 2019. (ITA.). 24p. (J). pap. 10.99 ***(978-1-6955-8627-7(1))*** Independently Published.

Carlson, Suzanne. Italiano-Macedone Veicoli Dizionario Bilingue Illustrato per Bambini. Carlson Jr, Richard. 2018. (ITA.). 24p. (J). pap. 10.99 *(978-1-7200-4262-4(4))* Independently Published.

—Italiano-Malayalam Guaio/ബുദ്ധിമുട്ടിക്കുക Libro Illustrato Bilingue per Bambini. Carlson, Richard. 2019. (ITA.). 24p. (J). pap. 10.99 *(978-1-0994-0977-6(2))* Independently Published.

Carlson, Suzanne. Italiano-Malayalam Mi Sento Ferito Libro Illustrato Bilingue per Bambini. Carlson, Richard. 2019. (ITA.). 24p. (J). pap. 10.99 ***(978-1-6959-3413-9(X))*** Independently Published.

Carlson, Suzanne. Italiano-Malayalam Veicoli Dizionario Bilingue Illustrato per Bambini. Carlson Jr, Richard. 2018. (ITA.). 24p. (J). pap. 10.99 *(978-1-7200-4385-0(X))* Independently Published.

—Italiano-Malese Guaio/Masalah Libro Illustrato Bilingue per Bambini. Carlson, Richard. 2019. (ITA.). 24p. (J). pap. 10.99 *(978-1-0994-0701-7(X))* Independently Published.

Carlson, Suzanne. Italiano-Malese Mi Sento Ferito/Perasaan Saya Disakiti Libro Illustrato Bilingue per Bambini. Carlson, Richard. 2019. (ITA.). 24p. (J). pap. 10.99 ***(978-1-6959-3217-3(X))*** Independently Published.

Carlson, Suzanne. Italiano-Malese Veicoli/Kenderaan Dizionario Bilingue Illustrato per Bambini. Carlson Jr, Richard. 2018. (ITA.). 24p. (J). pap. 10.99 *(978-1-7200-4274-7(8))* Independently Published.

—Italiano-Maltese Guaio/Inkwiet Libro Illustrato Bilingue per Bambini. Carlson, Richard. 2019. (ITA.). 24p. (J). pap. 10.99 *(978-1-0994-1235-6(8))* Independently Published.

Carlson, Suzanne. Italiano-Maltese Mi Sento Ferito/Weġġgħuni Libro Illustrato Bilingue per Bambini. Carlson, Richard. 2019. (ITA.). 24p. (J). pap. 10.99 ***(978-1-6959-3595-2(0))*** Independently Published.

Carlson, Suzanne. Italiano-Maltese Veicoli/Vetturi Dizionario Bilingue Illustrato per Bambini. Carlson Jr, Richard. 2018. (ITA.). 24p. (J). pap. 10.99 *(978-1-7200-4413-0(9))* Independently Published.

—Italiano-Marathi Guaio/त्रास Libro Illustrato Bilingue per Bambini. Carlson, Richard. 2019. (ITA.). 24p. (J). pap. 10.99 *(978-1-0995-1754-9(0))* Independently Published.

Carlson, Suzanne. Italiano-Marathi Mi Sento Ferito/माझ्या भावना दुखावल्या गेल्या आहेत Libro Il. Carlson, Richard. 2019. (ITA.). 24p. (J). pap. 10.99 ***(978-1-6959-3734-5(1))*** Independently Published.

Carlson, Suzanne. Italiano-Marathi Veicoli Dizionario Bilingue Illustrato per Bambini. Carlson Jr, Richard. 2018. (ITA.). 24p. (J). pap. 10.99 *(978-1-7200-4426-0(0))* Independently Published.

—Italiano-Mongolo Guaio/Хэрэгт орсон нь Libro Illustrato Bilingue per Bambini. Carlson, Richard. 2019. (ITA.). 24p. (J). pap. 10.99 *(978-1-0995-1907-9(1))* Independently Published.

Carlson, Suzanne. Italiano-Mongolo Mi Sento Ferito/Би гомдож байна Libro Illustrato Bilingue per Bambini. Carlson, Richard. 2019. (ITA.). 24p. (J). pap. 10.99 ***(978-1-6959-3847-2(X))*** Independently Published.

Carlson, Suzanne. Italiano-Mongolo Veicoli Dizionario Bilingue Illustrato per Bambini. Carlson Jr, Richard. 2018. (ITA.). 24p. (J). pap. 10.99 *(978-1-7200-4441-3(4))* Independently Published.

—Italiano-Montenegrino Guaio/Nevolja Libro Illustrato Bilingue per Bambini. Carlson, Richard. 2019. (ITA.). 24p. (J). pap. 10.99 *(978-1-0995-2170-6(X))* Independently Published.

Carlson, Suzanne. Italiano-Montenegrino Mi Sento Ferito/Moja Osjecanja Su Povrijeđena Libro Illustrato Bilingue per Bambini. Carlson, Richard. 2019. (ITA.). 24p. (J). pap. 10.99 ***(978-1-6959-4004-8(0))*** Independently Published.

Carlson, Suzanne. Italiano-Montenegrino Veicoli/Vozila Dizionario Bilingue Illustrato per Bambini. Carlson Jr, Richard. 2018. (ITA.). 24p. (J). pap. 10.99 *(978-1-7200-5483-2(5))* Independently Published.

—Italiano-Nepalese Guaio/समस्या ; Libro Illustrato Bilingue per Bambini. Carlson, Richard. 2019. (ITA.). 24p. (J). pap. 10.99 *(978-1-0995-2334-2(6))* Independently Published.

Carlson, Suzanne. Italiano-Nepalese Mi Sento Ferito/मेरो भावनामा चोट पुगेको छ Libro Illustrato Bilingue per Bambini. Carlson, Richard. 2019. (ITA.). 24p. (J). pap. 10.99 ***(978-1-6963-0570-9(5))*** Independently Published.

Carlson, Suzanne. Italiano-Nepalese Veicoli Dizionario Bilingue Illustrato per Bambini. Carlson Jr, Richard. 2018. (ITA.). 24p. (J). pap. 10.99 *(978-1-7200-5517-4(3))* Independently Published.

—Italiano-Norvegese Guaio/Trøbbel Libro Illustrato Bilingue per Bambini. Carlson, Richard. 2019. (ITA.). 24p. (J). pap. 10.99 *(978-1-0995-2999-3(9))* Independently Published.

Carlson, Suzanne. Italiano-Norvegese Mi Sento Ferito/ F�lelsene Mine Er S�ret Libro Illustrato Bilingue per Bambini. Carlson, Richard. 2019. (ITA.). 24p. (J). pap. 10.99 ***(978-1-6961-5094-1(9))*** Independently Published.

Carlson, Suzanne. Italiano-Norvegese Veicoli/Kjøretøyer Dizionario Bilingue Illustrato per Bambini. Carlson Jr, Richard. 2018. (ITA.). 24p. (J). pap. 10.99 *(978-1-7200-5559-4(9))* Independently Published.

—Italiano-Olandese Attrezzi/Gereedschappen Dizionario Bilingue Illustrato per Bambini. Carlson Jr, Richard. 2019. (ITA.). 26p. (J). pap. 10.99 *(978-1-7942-0693-9(0))* Independently Published.

—Italiano-Olandese Guaio/Problemen Libro Illustrato Bilingue per Bambini. Carlson, Richard. 2019. (ITA.). 24p. (J). pap. 10.99 *(978-1-0991-9200-5(5))* Independently Published.

Carlson, Suzanne. Italiano-Olandese Mi Sento Ferito/Mijn Gevoelens Zijn Gekwetst Libro Illustrato Bilingue per Bambini. Carlson, Richard. 2019. (ITA.). 24p. (J). pap. 10.99 ***(978-1-6950-4300-8(6))*** Independently Published.

Carlson, Suzanne. Italiano-Olandese Veicoli/Voertuigen Dizionario Bilingue Illustrato per Bambini. Carlson Jr, Richard. 2018. (ITA.). 24p. (J). pap. 10.99 *(978-1-7198-9161-5(3))* Independently Published.

—Italiano-Pangiabi Guaio Libro Illustrato Bilingue per Bambini. Carlson, Richard. 2019. (ITA.). 24p. (J). pap. 10.99 *(978-1-0996-8327-5(0))* Independently Published.

Carlson, Suzanne. Italiano-Pangiabi Mi Sento Ferito Libro Illustrato Bilingue per Bambini. Carlson, Richard. 2019. (ITA.). 24p. (J). pap. 10.99 ***(978-1-6961-6161-9(4))*** Independently Published.

Carlson, Suzanne. Italiano-Pangiabi Veicoli Dizionario Bilingue Illustrato per Bambini. Carlson Jr, Richard. 2018. (ITA.). 24p. (J). pap. 10.99 *(978-1-7200-7906-4(4))* Independently Published.

—Italiano-Pashtu Guaio/مصیبت Libro Illustrato Bilingue per Bambini. Carlson, Richard. 2019. (ITA.). 24p. (J). pap. 10.99 *(978-1-0995-3164-4(0))* Independently Published.

Carlson, Suzanne. Italiano-Pashtu Mi Sento Ferito Libro Illustrato Bilingue per Bambini. Carlson, Richard. 2019. (ITA.). 24p. (J). pap. 10.99 ***(978-1-6963-1576-0(X))*** Independently Published.

Carlson, Suzanne. Italiano-Pashtu Veicoli Dizionario Bilingue Illustrato per Bambini. Carlson Jr, Richard. 2018. (ITA.). 24p. (J). pap. 10.99 *(978-1-7200-6695-8(7))* Independently Published.

—Italiano-Persiano (Farsi) Guaio/دردسر Libro Illustrato Bilingue per Bambini. Carlson, Richard. 2019. (ITA.). 24p. (J). pap. 10.99 *(978-1-0995-3904-6(8))* Independently Published.

Carlson, Suzanne. Italiano-Persiano (Farsi) Mi Sento Ferito Libro Illustrato Bilingue per Bambini. Carlson, Richard. 2019. (ITA.). 24p. (J). pap. 10.99 ***(978-1-6964-6046-0(8))*** Independently Published.

Carlson, Suzanne. Italiano-Persiano (Farsi) Veicoli Dizionario Bilingue Illustrato per Bambini. Carlson Jr, Richard. 2018. (ITA.). 24p. (J). pap. 10.99 *(978-1-7200-7614-8(6))* Independently Published.

—Italiano-Polacco Guaio/Klopoty Libro Illustrato Bilingue per Bambini. Carlson, Richard. 2019. (ITA.). 24p. (J). pap. 10.99 *(978-1-0995-4320-3(7))* Independently Published.

Carlson, Suzanne. Italiano-Polacco Mi Sento Ferito/Zranione Uczucia Libro Illustrato Bilingue per Bambini. Carlson, Richard. 2019. (ITA.). 24p. (J). pap. 10.99 ***(978-1-6961-5283-9(6))*** Independently Published.

Carlson, Suzanne. Italiano-Polacco Veicoli/Pojazdy Dizionario Bilingue Illustrato per Bambini. Carlson Jr, Richard. 2018. (ITA.). 24p. (J). pap. 10.99 *(978-1-7200-7674-2(X))* Independently Published.

—Italiano-Portoghese (Brasiliano) Guaio/Encrenca Libro Illustrato Bilingue per Bambini. Carlson, Richard. 2019. (ITA.). 24p. (J). pap. 10.99 *(978-1-0995-5217-5(6))* Independently Published.

Carlson, Suzanne. Italiano-Portoghese (Brasiliano) Mi Sento Ferito/Meus Sentimentos Est�o Feridos Libro Illustrato Bilingue per Bambini. Carlson, Richard. 2019. (ITA.). 24p. (J). pap. 10.99 ***(978-1-6961-5489-5(8))*** Independently Published.

Carlson, Suzanne. Italiano-Portoghese (Brasiliano) Veicoli/Veículos Dizionario Bilingue Illustrato per Bambini. Carlson Jr, Richard. 2018. (ITA.). 24p. (J). pap. 10.99 *(978-1-7200-7824-1(6))* Independently Published.

—Italiano-Portoghese (Portogallo) Guaio/Sarilhos Libro Illustrato Bilingue per Bambini. Carlson, Richard. 2019. (ITA.). 24p. (J). pap. 10.99 *(978-1-0995-5280-9(X))* Independently Published.

Carlson, Suzanne. Italiano-Portoghese (Portogallo) Mi Sento Ferito/Os Meus Sentimentos Est�o Feridos Libro Illustrato Bilingue per Bambini. Carlson, Richard. 2019. (ITA.). 24p. (J). pap. 10.99 ***(978-1-6961-5744-5(7))*** Independently Published.

Carlson, Suzanne. Italiano-Portoghese (Portogallo) Veicoli/Veículos Dizionario Bilingue Illustrato per Bambini. Carlson Jr, Richard. 2018. (ITA.). 24p. (J). pap. 10.99 *(978-1-7200-7850-0(5))* Independently Published.

—Italiano-Rumeno Guaio/În încurcătură Libro Illustrato Bilingue per Bambini. Carlson, Richard. 2019. (ITA.). 24p. (J). pap. 10.99 *(978-1-0996-8457-9(9))* Independently Published.

Carlson, Suzanne. Italiano-Rumeno Mi Sento Ferito/Sunt Jignit Libro Illustrato Bilingue per Bambini. Carlson, Richard. 2019. (ITA.). 24p. (J). pap. 10.99 ***(978-1-6961-6763-5(9))*** Independently Published.

Carlson, Suzanne. Italiano-Rumeno Veicoli/Vehicule Dizionario Bilingue Illustrato per Bambini. Carlson Jr, Richard. 2018. (ITA.). 24p. (J). pap. 10.99 *(978-1-7200-8837-0(3))* Independently Published.

—Italiano-Russo Guaio/Проблема Libro Illustrato Bilingue per Bambini. Carlson, Richard. 2019. (ITA.). 24p. (J). pap. 10.99 *(978-1-0996-8609-2(1))* Independently Published.

Carlson, Suzanne. Italiano-Russo Mi Sento Ferito/Оскорбленные чувства Libro Illustrato Bilingue per Bambini. Carlson, Richard. 2019. (ITA.). 24p. (J). pap. 10.99 ***(978-1-6962-8649-7(2))*** Independently Published.

Carlson, Suzanne. Italiano-Serbo (Cirillico) Attrezzi/Dizionario Bilingue Illustrato per Bambini. Carlson Jr, Richard. 2019. (ITA.). 26p. (J). pap. 10.99 *(978-1-7944-4979-4(5))* Independently Published.

—Italiano-Serbo (Cirillico) Guaio/Невоља Libro Illustrato Bilingue per Bambini. Carlson, Richard. 2019. (ITA.). 24p. (J). pap. 10.99 *(978-1-0996-8968-0(6))* Independently Published.

Carlson, Suzanne. Italiano-Serbo (Cirillico) Mi Sento Ferito/Моја осећања су повређена Libro Illustrato Bilingue per Bambini. Carlson, Richard. 2019. (ITA.). 24p. (J). pap. 10.99 ***(978-1-6962-9170-5(4))*** Independently Published.

Carlson, Suzanne. Italiano-Serbo (Cirillico) Veicoli Dizionario Bilingue Illustrato per Bambini. Carlson Jr, Richard. 2018. (ITA.). 24p. (J). pap. 10.99 *(978-1-7200-8985-8(X))* Independently Published.

—Italiano-Serbo (Latino) Attrezzi/Alati Dizionario Bilingue Illustrato per Bambini. Carlson Jr, Richard. 2019. (ITA.). 26p. (J). pap. 10.99 *(978-1-7944-5002-8(5))* Independently Published.

—Italiano-Serbo (Latino) Guaio/Nevolja Libro Illustrato Bilingue per Bambini. Carlson, Richard. 2019. (ITA.). 24p. (J). pap. 10.99 *(978-1-0996-9129-4(X))* Independently Published.

Carlson, Suzanne. Italiano-Serbo (Latino) Mi Sento Ferito/Osecanja Su Mi Povređena Libro Illustrato Bilingue per Bambini. Carlson, Richard. 2019. (ITA.). 24p. (J). pap. 10.99 ***(978-1-6962-9254-2(9))*** Independently Published.

Carlson, Suzanne. Italiano-Serbo (Latino) Veicoli/Vozila Dizionario Bilingue Illustrato per Bambini. Carlson Jr, Richard. 2018. (ITA.). 24p. (J). pap. 10.99 *(978-1-7201-3906-5(7))* Independently Published.

—Italiano-Shangaiano Guaio/烦恼 Libro Illustrato Bilingue per Bambini. Carlson, Richard. 2019. (ITA.). 24p. (J). pap. 10.99 *(978-1-0998-2229-2(7))* Independently Published.

Carlson, Suzanne. Italiano-Shangaiano Mi Sento Ferito/我的感情受到了伤害 Libro Illustrato Bilingue per Bambini. Carlson, Richard. 2019. (ITA.). 24p. (J). pap. 10.99 ***(978-1-6963-0757-4(0))*** Independently Published.

Carlson, Suzanne. Italiano-Shangaiano Veicoli Dizionario Bilingue Illustrato per Bambini. Carlson Jr, Richard. 2018. (ITA.). 24p. (J). pap. 10.99 *(978-1-7201-3991-1(1))* Independently Published.

—Italiano-Singalese Attrezzi/Dizionario Bilingue Illustrato per Bambini. Carlson Jr, Richard. 2019. (ITA.). 26p. (J). pap. 10.99 *(978-1-7944-5030-1(0))* Independently Published.

—Italiano-Singalese Guaio/හිරිහැරය Libro Illustrato Bilingue per Bambini. Carlson, Richard. 2019. (ITA.). 24p. (J). pap. 10.99 *(978-1-0998-2353-4(6))* Independently Published.

Carlson, Suzanne. Italiano-Singalese Mi Sento Ferito Libro Illustrato Bilingue per Bambini. Carlson, Richard. 2019. (ITA.). 24p. (J). pap. 10.99 ***(978-1-6963-1718-4(5))*** Independently Published.

Carlson, Suzanne. Italiano-Singalese Veicoli Dizionario Bilingue Illustrato per Bambini. Carlson Jr, Richard. 2018. (ITA.). 24p. (J). pap. 10.99 *(978-1-7201-4042-9(1))* Independently Published.

—Italiano-Slovacco Attrezzi/Nástroje Dizionario Bilingue Illustrato per Bambini. Carlson Jr, Richard. 2019. (ITA.). 26p. (J). pap. 10.99 *(978-1-7944-5057-8(2))* Independently Published.

—Italiano-Slovacco Guaio/Problémy Libro Illustrato Bilingue per Bambini. Carlson Jr, Richard. 2019. (ITA.). 24p. (J). pap. 10.99 *(978-1-0998-2461-6(3))* Independently Published.

Carlson, Suzanne. Italiano-Slovacco Mi Sento Ferito/Ranili Moje City Libro Illustrato Bilingue per Bambini. Carlson, Richard. 2019. (ITA.). 24p. (J). pap. 10.99 ***(978-1-6963-1788-7(6))*** Independently Published.

Carlson, Suzanne. Italiano-Slovacco Veicoli/Vozidlá Dizionario Bilingue Illustrato per Bambini. Carlson Jr, Richard. 2018. (ITA.). 24p. (J). pap. 10.99 *(978-1-7201-4934-7(8))* Independently Published.

—Italiano-Sloveno (Slovenia) Attrezzi/Orodja Dizionario Bilingue Illustrato per Bambini. Carlson Jr, Richard. 2019. (ITA.). 26p. (J). pap. 10.99 *(978-1-7944-5558-0(2))* Independently Published.

—Italiano-Sloveno (Slovenia) Guaio/Tezava Libro Illustrato Bilingue per Bambini. Carlson, Richard. 2019. (ITA.). 24p. (J). pap. 10.99 *(978-1-0998-2588-0(1))* Independently Published.

Carlson, Suzanne. Italiano-Sloveno (Slovenia) Mi Sento Ferito/Moja Prizadeta čustva Libro Illustrato Bilingue per Bambini. Carlson, Richard. 2019. (ITA.). 24p. (J). pap. 10.99 ***(978-1-6963-1863-1(7))*** Independently Published.

Carlson, Suzanne. Italiano-Sloveno (Slovenia) Veicoli/Vozila Dizionario Bilingue Illustrato per Bambini. Carlson Jr, Richard. 2018. (ITA.). 24p. (J). pap. 10.99 *(978-1-7201-6127-1(5))* Independently Published.

—Italiano-Somalo Attrezzi/Qalab Dizionario Bilingue Illustrato per Bambini. Carlson Jr, Richard. 2019. (ITA.). 26p. (J). pap. 10.99 *(978-1-7944-5765-2(8))* Independently Published.

—Italiano-Somalo Guaio/Dhibaato Libro Illustrato Bilingue per Bambini. Carlson, Richard. 2019. (ITA.). 24p. (J). pap. 10.99 *(978-1-0998-2732-7(9))* Independently Published.

Carlson, Suzanne. Italiano-Somalo Mi Sento Ferito/Dareenadayda Ayaa Dhaawacmay Libro Illustrato Bilingue per Bambini. Carlson, Richard. 2019. (ITA.). 24p. (J). pap. 10.99 ***(978-1-6963-1964-5(1))*** Independently Published.

Carlson, Suzanne. Italiano-Somalo Veicoli/Gaadiid Dizionario Bilingue Illustrato per Bambini. Carlson Jr, Richard. 2018. (ITA.). 24p. (J). pap. 10.99 *(978-1-7201-6138-7(0))* Independently Published.

—Italiano-Spagnolo America Latina Attrezzi/Herramientas Dizionario Bilingue Illustrato per Bambini. Carlson Jr, Richard. 2019. (ITA.). 26p. (J). pap. 10.99 *(978-1-7944-5818-5(2))* Independently Published.

—Italiano-Spagnolo America Latina Guaio/Problema Libro Illustrato Bilingue per Bambini. Carlson, Richard. 2019. (ITA.). 24p. (J). pap. 10.99 *(978-1-0998-3071-6(0))* Independently Published.

Carlson, Suzanne. Italiano-Spagnolo America Latina Mi Sento Ferito/Han Herido Mis Sentimientos Libro Illustrato Bilingue per Bambini. Carlson, Richard. 2019. (ITA.). 24p. (J). pap. 10.99 ***(978-1-6963-2093-1(3))*** Independently Published.

Carlson, Suzanne. Italiano-Spagnolo America Latina Veicoli/Vehículos Dizionario Bilingue Illustrato per Bambini. Carlson Jr, Richard. 2018. (ITA.). 24p. (J). pap. 10.99 *(978-1-7201-7813-2(5))* Independently Published.

—Italiano-Spagnolo Castigliano Attrezzi/Herramientas Dizionario Bilingue Illustrato per Bambini. Carlson Jr, Richard. 2019. (ITA.). 26p. (J). pap. 10.99 *(978-1-7944-5837-6(9))* Independently Published.

—Italiano-Spagnolo Castigliano Guaio/Problema Libro Illustrato Bilingue per Bambini. Carlson, Richard. 2019. (ITA.). 24p. (J). pap. 10.99 *(978-1-0998-2972-7(0))* Independently Published.

Carlson, Suzanne. Italiano-Spagnolo Castigliano Mi Sento Ferito/Han Herido Mis Sentimientos Libro Illustrato Bilingue per Bambini. Carlson, Richard. 2019. (ITA.). 24p. (J). pap. 10.99 ***(978-1-6963-2018-4(6))*** Independently Published.

Carlson, Suzanne. Italiano-Spagnolo Castigliano Veicoli/Vehículos Dizionario Bilingue Illustrato per Bambini. Carlson Jr, Richard. 2018. (ITA.). 24p. (J). pap. 10.99 *(978-1-7201-6181-3(X))* Independently Published.

—Italiano-Svedese Attrezzi/Verktyg Dizionario Bilingue Illustrato per Bambini. Carlson Jr, Richard. 2019. (ITA.). 26p. (J). pap. 10.99 *(978-1-7945-0743-2(4))* Independently Published.

—Italiano-Svedese Guaio/Trubbel Libro Illustrato Bilingue per Bambini. Carlson, Richard. 2019. (ITA.). 24p. (J). pap. 10.99 *(978-1-0999-7398-7(8))* Independently Published.

Carlson, Suzanne. Italiano-Svedese Mi Sento Ferito/Mina K�nslor �r S�rade Libro Illustrato Bilingue per Bambini. Carlson, Richard. 2019. (ITA.). 24p. (J). pap. 10.99 ***(978-1-6963-2254-6(5))*** Independently Published.

Carlson, Suzanne. Italiano-Svedese Veicoli/Fordon Dizionario Bilingue Illustrato per Bambini. Carlson Jr, Richard. 2018. (ITA.). 24p. (J). pap. 10.99 *(978-1-7201-7892-7(5))* Independently Published.

—Italiano-Swahili Attrezzi/Zana Dizionario Bilingue Illustrato per Bambini. Carlson Jr, Richard. 2019. (ITA.). 26p. (J). pap. 10.99 *(978-1-7945-0702-9(7))* Independently Published.

—Italiano-Swahili Guaio/Shida Libro Illustrato Bilingue per Bambini. Carlson, Richard. 2019. (ITA.). 24p. (J). pap. 10.99 *(978-1-0999-7305-5(8))* Independently Published.

Carlson, Suzanne. Italiano-Swahili Mi Sento Ferito/Hisia Zangu Zinaumia Libro Illustrato Bilingue per Bambini. Carlson, Richard. 2019. (ITA.). 24p. (J). pap. 10.99 ***(978-1-6963-2184-6(0))*** Independently Published.

Carlson, Suzanne. Italiano-Tagalog Attrezzi/MGA Gamit Dizionario Bilingue Illustrato per Bambini. Carlson Jr, Richard. 2019. (ITA.). 26p. (J). pap. 10.99 *(978-1-7945-0799-9(X))* Independently Published.

—Italiano-Tagalog Guaio/Gulo Libro Illustrato Bilingue per Bambini. Carlson, Richard. 2019. (ITA.). 24p. (J). pap. 10.99 *(978-1-0999-7612-4(X))* Independently Published.

Carlson, Suzanne. Italiano-Tagalog Mi Sento Ferito/Nasaktan Ang Aking Damdamin Libro Illustrato Bilingue per Bambini. Carlson, Richard. 2019. (ITA.). 24p. (J). pap. 10.99 ***(978-1-6963-2326-0(6))*** Independently Published.

Carlson, Suzanne. Italiano-Tagalog Veicoli/MGA Sasakyan Dizionario Bilingue Illustrato per Bambini. Carlson Jr, Richard. 2018. (ITA.). 24p. (J). pap. 10.99 *(978-1-7201-7907-8(7))* Independently Published.

Carlson, Suzanne. Italiano-Tagico Mi Sento Ferito/эҳсосотм ҷриҳа дор шуда Libro Illustrato Bilingue per Bambini. Carlson, Richard. 2019. (ITA.). 24p. (J). pap. 10.99 ***(978-1-6963-2470-0(X))*** Independently Published.

Carlson, Suzanne. Italiano-Tamil Attrezzi Dizionario Bilingue Illustrato per Bambini. Carlson Jr, Richard. 2019. (ITA.). 26p. (J). pap. 10.99 *(978-1-7945-0814-9(7))* Independently Published.

—Italiano-Tamil Guaio Libro Illustrato Bilingue per Bambini. Carlson, Richard. 2019. (ITA.). 24p. (J). pap. 10.99 *(978-1-0999-7813-5(0))* Independently Published.

Carlson, Suzanne. Italiano-Tamil Mi Sento Ferito/எனது உணர்வுகள் காயமாகின Libro Illustrato Bilingue per Bambini. Carlson, Richard. 2019. (ITA.). 24p. (J). pap. 10.99 ***(978-1-6963-2636-0(2))*** Independently Published.

Carlson, Suzanne. Italiano-Tamil Veicoli Dizionario Bilingue Illustrato per Bambini. Carlson Jr, Richard. 2018. (ITA.). 24p. (J). pap. 10.99 *(978-1-7201-7925-2(5))* Independently Published.

—Italiano-Tedesco Attrezzi/Werkzeuge Dizionario Bilingue Illustrato per Bambini. Carlson Jr, Richard. 2019. (ITA.). 26p. (J). pap. 10.99 *(978-1-7943-3381-9(9))* Independently Published.

—Italiano-Tedesco Guaio/Ärger Libro Illustrato Bilingue per Bambini. Carlson, Richard. 2019. (ITA.). 24p. (J). pap. 10.99 *(978-1-0992-6137-4(6))* Independently Published.

Carlson, Suzanne. Italiano-Tedesco Mi Sento Ferito/Ich Wurde in Meinen Gef�hlen Verletzt Libro Illustrato Bilingue per Bambini. Carlson, Richard. 2019. (ITA.). 24p. (J). pap. 10.99 ***(978-1-6950-5455-4(5))*** Independently Published.

Carlson, Suzanne. Italiano-Tedesco Veicoli/Fahrzeuge Dizionario Bilingue Illustrato per Bambini. Carlson Jr, Richard. 2018. (ITA.). 24p. (J). pap. 10.99 *(978-1-7198-9361-9(6))* Independently Published.

—Italiano-Telugu Attrezzi/ Dizionario Bilingue Illustrato per Bambini. Carlson Jr, Richard. 2019. (ITA.). 26p. (J). pap. 10.99 *(978-1-7945-0873-6(2))* Independently Published.

—Italiano-Telugu Guaio Libro Illustrato Bilingue per Bambini. Carlson, Richard. 2019. (ITA.). 24p. (J). pap. 10.99 *(978-1-0999-7966-8(8))* Independently Published.

Carlson, Suzanne. Italiano-Telugu Mi Sento Ferito Libro Illustrato Bilingue per Bambini. Carlson, Richard. 2019. (ITA.). 24p. (J). pap. 10.99 ***(978-1-6963-2768-8(7))*** Independently Published.

Carlson, Suzanne. Italiano-Telugu Veicoli Dizionario Bilingue Illustrato per Bambini. Carlson Jr, Richard. 2018. (ITA.). 24p. (J). pap. 10.99 *(978-1-7201-7947-4(6))* Independently Published.

—Italiano-Thailandese Attrezzi/Dizionario Bilingue Illustrato per Bambini. Carlson Jr, Richard. 2019. (ITA.). 26p. (J). pap. 10.99 *(978-1-7945-0912-2(7))* Independently Published.

—Italiano-Thailandese Guaio/ยุ่งแล้วเชียว Libro Illustrato Bilingue per Bambini. Carlson, Richard. 2019. (ITA.). 24p. (J). pap. 10.99 *(978-1-0999-8108-1(5))* Independently Published.

Carlson, Suzanne. Italiano-Thailandese Mi Sento Ferito/ความรู้สึกของผมคือเสียใจ Libro Illustrato Bilingue per Bambini. Carlson, Richard. 2019. (ITA.). 24p. (J). pap. 10.99 ***(978-1-6963-2847-0(0))*** Independently Published.

Carlson, Suzanne. Italiano-Thailandese Veicoli Dizionario Bilingue Illustrato per Bambini. Carlson Jr, Richard. 2018. (ITA.). 24p. (J). pap. 10.99 *(978-1-7201-7966-5(2))* Independently Published.

—Italiano-Tigrino Attrezzi/ Dizionario Bilingue Illustrato per Bambini. Carlson Jr, Richard. 2019. (ITA.). 26p. (J). pap. 10.99 *(978-1-7945-1221-4(7))* Independently Published.

—Italiano-Tigrino Guaio/ፀገም Libro Illustrato Bilingue per Bambini. Carlson, Richard. 2019. (ITA.). 24p. (J). pap. 10.99 *(978-1-0999-8244-6(8))* Independently Published.

Carlson, Suzanne. Italiano-Tigrino Mi Sento Ferito/ስምዒተይ ተጎዲኡ እዩ Libro Illustrato Bilingue per Bambini. Carlson, Richard. 2019. (ITA.). 24p. (J). pap. 10.99 ***(978-1-6963-2937-8(X))*** Independently Published.

Carlson, Suzanne. Italiano-Turco Attrezzi/Aletler Dizionario Bilingue Illustrato per Bambini. Carlson Jr, Richard. 2019. (ITA.). 26p. (J). pap. 10.99 *(978-1-7945-1283-2(7))* Independently Published.

—Italiano-Turco Guaio/Üzüntü Libro Illustrato Bilingue per Bambini. Carlson, Richard. 2019. (ITA.). 24p. (J). pap. 10.99 *(978-1-0701-4538-9(6))* Independently Published.

Carlson, Suzanne. Italiano-Turco Mi Sento Ferito/Duygularım İncindi Libro Illustrato Bilingue per Bambini. Carlson, Richard. 2019. (ITA.). 24p. (J). pap. 10.99 ***(978-1-6963-3076-3(9))*** Independently Published.

Carlson, Suzanne. Italiano-Turco Veicoli/Araçlar Dizionario Bilingue Illustrato per Bambini. Carlson Jr, Richard. 2018. (ITA.). 24p. (J). pap. 10.99 *(978-1-7201-7996-2(4))* Independently Published.

—Italiano-Ucraino Attrezzi/Dizionario Bilingue Illustrato per Bambini. Carlson Jr, Richard. 2019. (ITA.). 26p. (J). pap. 10.99 *(978-1-7945-1358-7(2))* Independently Published.

—Italiano-Ucraino Guaio/Проблема Libro Illustrato Bilingue per Bambini. Carlson, Richard. 2019. (ITA.). 24p. (J). pap. 10.99 *(978-1-0701-4745-1(1))* Independently Published.

Carlson, Suzanne. Italiano-Ucraino Mi Sento Ferito/Мене зачепили за живе Libro Illustrato Bilingue per Bambini. Carlson, Richard. 2019. (ITA.). 24p. (J). pap. 10.99 ***(978-1-6963-3217-0(6))*** Independently Published.

Carlson, Suzanne. Italiano-Ucraino Veicoli Dizionario Bilingue Illustrato per Bambini. Carlson Jr, Richard. 2018. (ITA.). 24p. (J). pap. 10.99 *(978-1-7201-8019-7(9))* Independently Published.

—Italiano-Ungherese Attrezzi/Szerszámok Dizionario Bilingue Illustrato per Bambini. Carlson Jr, Richard. 2019. (ITA.). 26p. (J). pap. 10.99 *(978-1-7944-0196-9(2))* Independently Published.

—Italiano-Ungherese Guaio/Baj Libro Illustrato Bilingue per Bambini. Carlson, Richard. 2019. (ITA.). 24p. (J). pap. 10.99 *(978-1-0992-8439-7(2))* Independently Published.

Carlson, Suzanne. Italiano-Ungherese Mi Sento Ferito/Megb�nt�dtam Libro Illustrato Bilingue per Bambini. Carlson, Richard. 2019. (ITA.). 24p. (J). pap. 10.99 ***(978-1-6952-7733-5(3))*** Independently Published.

Carlson, Suzanne. Italiano-Ungherese Veicoli Dizionario Bilingue Illustrato per Bambini. Carlson Jr, Richard. 2018. (ITA.). 24p. (J). pap. 10.99 *(978-1-7200-1987-9(8))* Independently Published.

—Italiano-Urdu Attrezzi/Dizionario Bilingue Illustrato per Bambini. Carlson Jr, Richard. 2019. (ITA.). 26p. (J). pap. 10.99 *(978-1-7945-1439-3(2))* Independently Published.

—Italiano-Urdu Guaio/پریشانی Libro Illustrato Bilingue per Bambini. Carlson, Richard. 2019. (ITA.). 24p. (J). pap. 10.99 *(978-1-0701-9537-7(5))* Independently Published.

Carlson, Suzanne. Italiano-Urdu Mi Sento Ferito Libro Illustrato Bilingue per Bambini. Carlson, Richard. 2019. (ITA.). 24p. (J). pap. 10.99 ***(978-1-6964-6101-6(4))*** Independently Published.

Carlson, Suzanne. Italiano-Urdu Veicoli Dizionario Bilingue Illustrato per Bambini. Carlson Jr, Richard. 2018. (ITA.). 24p. (J). pap. 10.99 *(978-1-7201-8026-5(1))* Independently Published.

—Italiano-Uzbeco Attrezzi/Asboblar Dizionario Bilingue Illustrato per Bambini. Carlson Jr, Richard. 2019. (ITA.). 26p. (J). pap. 10.99 *(978-1-7945-1533-8(X))* Independently Published.

—Italiano-Uzbeco Guaio/Muammo Libro Illustrato Bilingue per Bambini. Carlson, Richard. 2019. (ITA.). 24p. (J). pap. 10.99 *(978-1-0702-1189-3(3))* Independently Published.

Carlson, Suzanne. Italiano-Uzbeco Mi Sento Ferito/His-Tuyg'ularim Yaralandi Libro Illustrato Bilingue per Bambini. Carlson, Richard. 2019. (ITA.). 24p. (J). pap. 10.99 ***(978-1-6963-3759-5(3))*** Independently Published.

Carlson, Suzanne. Italiano-Uzbeco Veicoli/Transport Vositalari Dizionario Bilingue Illustrato per Bambini. Carlson Jr, Richard. 2018. (ITA.). 24p. (J). pap. 10.99 *(978-1-7201-9244-2(8))* Independently Published.

—Italiano-Vietnamita Attrezzi/dng C; Dizionario Bilingue Illustrato per Bambini. Carlson Jr, Richard. 2019. (ITA.). 26p. (J). pap. 10.99 *(978-1-7945-1713-4(8))* Independently Published.

—Italiano-Vietnamita Guaio/Rắc Rối Libro Illustrato Bilingue per Bambini. Carlson, Richard. 2019. (ITA.). 24p. (J). pap. 10.99 *(978-1-0702-1275-3(X))* Independently Published.

Carlson, Suzanne. Italiano-Vietnamita Mi Sento Ferito/Cảm X�c Của M�nh Bị Tổn Thương Libro Illustrato Bilingue per Bambini. Carlson, Richard. 2019. (ITA.). 24p. (J). pap. 10.99 ***(978-1-6963-3939-1(1))*** Independently Published.

Carlson, Suzanne. Italiano-Vietnamita Veicoli Dizionario Bilingue Illustrato per Bambini. Carlson Jr, Richard. 2018. (ITA.). 24p. (J). pap. 10.99 *(978-1-7201-9273-2(1))* Independently Published.

—Italiano-Xhosa Attrezzi/Izixhobo Dizionario Bilingue Illustrato per Bambini. Carlson Jr, Richard. 2019. (ITA.). 26p. (J). pap. 10.99 *(978-1-7945-8026-8(3))* Independently Published.

—Italiano-Xhosa Guaio/Ingxaki Libro Illustrato Bilingue per Bambini. Carlson, Richard. 2019. (ITA.). 24p. (J). pap. 10.99 *(978-1-0702-1345-3(4))* Independently Published.

—Italiano-Xhosa Veicoli/Izithuthi Dizionario Bilingue Illustrato per Bambini. Carlson Jr, Richard. 2018. (ITA.). 24p. (J). pap. 10.99 *(978-1-7201-9305-0(3))* Independently Published.

Carlson, Suzanne. Italiano-Yiddish Mi Sento Ferito Libro Illustrato Bilingue per Bambini. Carlson, Richard. 2019. (ITA.). 24p. (J). pap. 10.99 ***(978-1-6964-6187-0(1))*** Independently Published.

Carlson, Suzanne. Italiano-Yoruba Attrezzi/Awan Irin Ie Dizionario Bilingue Illustrato per Bambini. Carlson Jr, Richard. 2019. (ITA.). 26p. (J). pap. 10.99 *(978-1-7946-4324-6(9))* Independently Published.

—Italiano-Yoruba Guaio Libro Illustrato Bilingue per Bambini. Carlson, Richard. 2019. (ITA.). 24p. (J). pap. 10.99 *(978-1-0702-1426-9(4))* Independently Published.

Carlson, Suzanne. Italiano-Yoruba Mi Sento Ferito/&#65533; d&#65533;n M&#65533; Iọ́k&#65533;n Mi Libro Illustrato Bilingue per Bambini. Carlson, Richard. 2019. (ITA.). 24p. (J). pap. 10.99 ***(978-1-6963-4680-1(0))*** Independently Published.

Carlson, Suzanne. Italiano-Yoruba Veicoli Dizionario Bilingue Illustrato per Bambini. Carlson Jr, Richard. 2018. (ITA.). 24p. (J). pap. 10.99 *(978-1-7201-9322-7(3))* Independently Published.

—Italiano-Zulu Attrezzi/Amathuluzi Dizionario Bilingue Illustrato per Bambini. Carlson Jr, Richard. 2019. (ITA.). 26p. (J). pap. 10.99 *(978-1-7950-1264-5(1))* Independently Published.

—Italiano-Zulu Gualo/Inkinga Libro Illustrato Bilingue per Bambini. Carlson, Richard. 2019. (ITA.). 24p. (J). pap. 10.99 *(978-1-0702-1556-3(2))* Independently Published.

Carlson, Suzanne. Italiano-Zulu Mi Sento Ferito/Ngiphatheke Kabuhlungu Libro Illustrato Bilingue per Bambini. Carlson, Richard. 2019. (ITA.). 24p. (J). pap. 10.99 ***(978-1-6963-4784-6(X))*** Independently Published.

Carlson, Suzanne. Italiano-Zulu Veicoli/Izimoto Dizionario Bilingue Illustrato per Bambini. Carlson Jr, Richard. 2018. (ITA.). 24p. (J). pap. 10.99 *(978-1-7201-9354-8(1))* Independently Published.

Carlson, Suzanne. Svenska-Afrikaans Fordon/Voertuie Barns Tv&#65533;spr&#65533;kiga Bildordbok. Carlson, Richard. 2019. (SWE.). 24p. (J). pap. 11.99 ***(978-1-6884-7470-3(6))*** Independently Published.

—Svenska-Afrikaans Mina K&#65533;nslor &#65533;r S&#65533;rade/My Gevoelens Is Gekwets Tv&#65533;spr&#65533;kig Bilderbok F&#65533;r Barn. Carlson, Richard. 2019. (SWE.). 24p. (J). pap. 11.99 ***(978-1-6964-6773-5(X))*** Independently Published.

—Svenska-Afrikaans Skolan/Skool Barns Tv&#65533;spr&#65533;kiga Bildordbok. Carlson, Richard. 2019. (SWE.). 24p. (J). pap. 11.99 ***(978-1-7024-5689-0(7))*** Independently Published.

—Svenska-Afrikaans Tid/Tyd Tv&#65533;spr&#65533;kig Bilderbok F&#65533;r Barn. Carlson, Richard. 2019. (SWE.). 28p. (J). pap. 11.99 ***(978-1-6984-0800-2(5))*** Independently Published.

Carlson, Suzanne. Svenska-Afrikaans Trubbel/Moeilikheid Tvåspråkig Bilderbok För Barn. Carlson, Richard. 2019. (SWE.). 24p. (J). pap. 11.99 *(978-1-0728-5316-9(7))* Independently Published.

Carlson, Suzanne. Svenska-Afrikaans Verktyg/Gereedskap Barns Tv&#65533;spr&#65533;kiga Bildordbok. Carlson, Richard. 2019. (SWE.). 26p. (J). pap. 11.99 ***(978-1-6906-5984-6(X))*** Independently Published.

—Svenska-Albanska Fordon/Automjetet Barns Tv&#65533;spr&#65533;kiga Bildordbok. Carlson, Richard. 2019. (SWE.). 24p. (J). pap. 11.99 ***(978-1-6886-1693-6(4))*** Independently Published.

—Svenska-Albanska Mina K&#65533;nslor &#65533;r S&#65533;rade/Ndjenjat e Mia Jan&#65533; T&#65533; l&#65533;nduara Tv&#65533;spr&#65533;kig Bilderbok F&#65533;r Barn. Carlson, Richard. 2019. (SWE.). 24p. (J). pap. 11.99 ***(978-1-6967-7879-4(4))*** Independently Published.

—Svenska-Albanska Skolan/Shkoll&#65533; Barns Tv&#65533;spr&#65533;kiga Bildordbok. Carlson, Richard. 2019. (SWE.). 24p. (J). pap. 11.99 ***(978-1-7024-6258-7(7))*** Independently Published.

—Svenska-Albanska Tid/Koha Tv&#65533;spr&#65533;kig Bilderbok F&#65533;r Barn. Carlson, Richard. 2019. (SWE.). 28p. (J). pap. 11.99 ***(978-1-6986-1684-1(8))*** Independently Published.

Carlson, Suzanne. Svenska-Albanska Trubbel/Shqetësim Tvåspråkig Bilderbok För Barn. Carlson, Richard. 2019. (SWE.). 24p. (J). pap. 11.99 *(978-1-0728-6250-5(6))* Independently Published.

Carlson, Suzanne. Svenska-Albanska Verktyg/Veglat Barns Tv&#65533;spr&#65533;kiga Bildordbok. Carlson, Richard. 2019. (SWE.). 26p. (J). pap. 11.99 ***(978-1-6906-6820-6(2))*** Independently Published.

—Svenska-Amhariska Fordon/ተሽከርካሪዎች Barns Tv&#65533;spr&#65533;kiga Bildordbok. Carlson, Richard. 2019. (SWE.). 24p. (J). pap. 11.99 ***(978-1-6886-1897-8(X))*** Independently Published.

—Svenska-Amhariska Mina K&#65533;nslor &#65533;r S&#65533;rade/ስሜቴተጎድቷል Tv&#65533;spr&#65533;kig Bilderbok F&#65533;r Barn. Carlson, Richard. 2019. (SWE.). 24p. (J). pap. 11.99 ***(978-1-6967-7965-4(0))*** Independently Published.

—Svenska-Amhariska Nummer/ቁጥሮች Bildordbok F&#65533;r Tv&#65533;spr&#65533;kiga Barn. Carlson, Richard. 2019. (SWE.). 26p. (J). pap. 11.99 ***(978-1-7092-2962-6(4))*** Independently Published.

—Svenska-Amhariska Skolan/ትምህርትቤት Barns Tv&#65533;spr&#65533;kiga Bildordbok. Carlson, Richard. 2019. (SWE.). 24p. (J). pap. 11.99 ***(978-1-7024-6847-3(X))*** Independently Published.

—Svenska-Amhariska Tid/ጊዜ Tv&#65533;spr&#65533;kig Bilderbok F&#65533;r Barn. Carlson, Richard. 2019. (SWE.). 28p. (J). pap. 11.99 ***(978-1-6986-1724-4(0))*** Independently Published.

Carlson, Suzanne. Svenska-Amhariska Trubbel/ችግር Tvåspråkig Bilderbok För Barn. Carlson, Richard. 2019. (SWE.). 24p. (J). pap. 11.99 *(978-1-0728-6309-0(X))* Independently Published.

Carlson, Suzanne. Svenska-Amhariska Verktyg/መሳሪያዎች Barns Tv&#65533;spr&#65533;kiga Bildordbok. Carlson, Richard. 2019. (SWE.). 26p. (J). pap. 11.99 ***(978-1-6906-9292-8(8))*** Independently Published.

—Svenska-Arabiska Fordon Barns Tv&#65533;spr&#65533;kiga Bildordbok. Carlson, Richard. 2019. (SWE.). 24p. (J). pap. 11.99 ***(978-1-6886-2701-7(4))*** Independently Published.

—Svenska-Arabiska Mina K&#65533;nslor &#65533;r S&#65533;rade Tv&#65533;spr&#65533;kig Bilderbok F&#65533;r Barn. Carlson, Richard. 2019. (SWE.). 24p. (J). pap. 11.99 ***(978-1-6967-8071-1(3))*** Independently Published.

—Svenska-Arabiska Nummer/الأرقام Bildordbok F&#65533;r Tv&#65533;spr&#65533;kiga Barn. Carlson, Richard. 2019. (SWE.). 26p. (J). pap. 11.99 ***(978-1-7095-2136-2(8))*** Independently Published.

—Svenska-Arabiska Skolan Barns Tv&#65533;spr&#65533;kiga Bildordbok. Carlson, Richard. 2019. (SWE.). 24p. (J). pap. 11.99 ***(978-1-7026-5850-8(3))*** Independently Published.

—Svenska-Arabiska Tid Tv&#65533;spr&#65533;kig Bilderbok F&#65533;r Barn. Carlson, Richard. 2019. (SWE.). 28p. (J). pap. 11.99 ***(978-1-6999-5185-9(3))*** Independently Published.

Carlson, Suzanne. Svenska-Arabiska Trubbel Tvåspråkig Bilderbok För Barn. Carlson, Richard. 2019. (SWE.). 24p. (J). pap. 11.99 *(978-1-0728-7629-8(9))* Independently Published.

Carlson, Suzanne. Svenska-Arabiska Verktyg Barns Tv&#65533;spr&#65533;kiga Bildordbok. Carlson, Richard. 2019. (SWE.). 26p. (J). pap. 11.99 ***(978-1-6906-9987-3(6))*** Independently Published.

—Svenska-Armeniska Fordon/Տրանսպորտայինմիջոցներ Barns Tv&#65533;spr&#65533;kiga Bildordbok. Carlson, Richard. 2019. (SWE.). 24p. (J). pap. 11.99 ***(978-1-6886-4129-7(7))*** Independently Published.

—Svenska-Armeniska Mina K&#65533;nslor &#65533;r S&#65533;rade/Եսվիրավորված եմ Tv&#65533;spr&#65533;kig Bilderbok F&#65533;r Barn. Carlson, Richard. 2019. (SWE.). 24p. (J). pap. 11.99 ***(978-1-6967-8198-5(1))*** Independently Published.

—Svenska-Armeniska Nummer/Թվեր Bildordbok F&#65533;r Tv&#65533;spr&#65533;kiga Barn. Carlson, Richard. 2019. (SWE.). 26p. (J). pap. 11.99 ***(978-1-7101-2473-6(3))*** Independently Published.

—Svenska-Armeniska Skolan/Դպրոց Barns Tv&#65533;spr&#65533;kiga Bildordbok. Carlson, Richard. 2019. (SWE.). 24p. (J). pap. 11.99 ***(978-1-7026-6961-0(0))*** Independently Published.

—Svenska-Armeniska Tid/Ժամանակ Tv&#65533;spr&#65533;kig Bilderbok F&#65533;r Barn. Carlson, Richard. 2019. (SWE.). 28p. (J). pap. 11.99 ***(978-1-6986-1887-6(5))*** Independently Published.

Carlson, Suzanne. Svenska-Armeniska Trubbel/Անախորժություն Tvåspråkig Bilderbok För Barn. Carlson, Richard. 2019. (SWE.). 24p. (J). pap. 11.99 *(978-1-0728-6676-3(5))* Independently Published.

Carlson, Suzanne. Svenska-Armeniska Verktyg/Գործիքներ Barns Tv&#65533;spr&#65533;kiga Bildordbok. Carlson, Richard. 2019. (SWE.). 26p. (J). pap. 11.99 ***(978-1-6907-0507-9(8))*** Independently Published.

—Svenska-Azerbajdzjanska Fordon/Nəqliyyat Vasitələri Barns Tv&#65533;spr&#65533;kiga Bildordbok. Carlson, Richard. 2019. (SWE.). 24p. (J). pap. 11.99 ***(978-1-6886-4291-1(9))*** Independently Published.

—Svenska-Azerbajdzjanska Mina K&#65533;nslor &#65533;r S&#65533;rade/Hisslərim Yaralandı Tv&#65533;spr&#65533;kig Bilderbok F&#65533;r Barn. Carlson, Richard. 2019. (SWE.). 24p. (J). pap. 11.99 ***(978-1-6967-8410-8(7))*** Independently Published.

—Svenska-Azerbajdzjanska Nummer/Say Bildordbok F&#65533;r Tv&#65533;spr&#65533;kiga Barn. Carlson, Richard. 2019. (SWE.). 26p. (J). pap. 11.99 ***(978-1-7101-3032-4(6))*** Independently Published.

—Svenska-Azerbajdzjanska Skolan/Məktəb Barns Tv&#65533;spr&#65533;kiga Bildordbok. Carlson, Richard. 2019. (SWE.). 24p. (J). pap. 11.99 ***(978-1-7028-1682-3(6))*** Independently Published.

—Svenska-Azerbajdzjanska Tid/Zaman Tv&#65533;spr&#65533;kig Bilderbok F&#65533;r Barn. Carlson, Richard. 2019. (SWE.). 28p. (J). pap. 11.99 ***(978-1-6986-2042-8(X))*** Independently Published.

Carlson, Suzanne. Svenska-Azerbajdzjanska Trubbel/Yaramazlıq Tvåspråkig Bilderbok För Barn. Carlson, Richard. 2019. (SWE.). 24p. (J). pap. 11.99 *(978-1-0728-6875-0(X))* Independently Published.

Carlson, Suzanne. Svenska-Azerbajdzjanska Verktyg/Alətlər Barns Tv&#65533;spr&#65533;kiga Bildordbok. Carlson, Richard. 2019. (SWE.). 26p. (J). pap. 11.99 ***(978-1-6908-3027-6(1))*** Independently Published.

—Svenska-Baskiska Fordon/Ibilgailuak Barns Tv&#65533;spr&#65533;kiga Bildordbok. Carlson, Richard. 2019. (SWE.). 24p. (J). pap. 11.99 ***(978-1-6886-4413-7(X))*** Independently Published.

—Svenska-Baskiska Mina K&#65533;nslor &#65533;r S&#65533;rade/Nire Sentimenduak Minduta Tv&#65533;spr&#65533;kig Bilderbok F&#65533;r Barn. Carlson, Richard. 2019. (SWE.). 24p. (J). pap. 11.99 ***(978-1-6967-8826-7(9))*** Independently Published.

—Svenska-Baskiska Nummer/Zenbakiak Bildordbok F&#65533;r Tv&#65533;spr&#65533;kiga Barn. Carlson, Richard. 2019. (SWE.). 26p. (J). pap. 11.99 ***(978-1-7104-1409-7(X))*** Independently Published.

—Svenska-Baskiska Skolan/Eskola Barns Tv&#65533;spr&#65533;kiga Bildordbok. Carlson, Richard. 2019. (SWE.). 24p. (J). pap. 11.99 ***(978-1-7028-5177-0(X))*** Independently Published.

—Svenska-Baskiska Tid/Denbora Tv&#65533;spr&#65533;kig Bilderbok F&#65533;r Barn. Carlson, Richard. 2019. (SWE.). 28p. (J). pap. 11.99 ***(978-1-6986-2356-6(9))*** Independently Published.

Carlson, Suzanne. Svenska-Baskiska Trubbel/Arazoa Tvåspråkig Bilderbok För Barn. Carlson, Richard. 2019. (SWE.). 24p. (J). pap. 11.99 *(978-1-0728-7789-9(9))* Independently Published.

Carlson, Suzanne. Svenska-Baskiska Verktyg/Tresnak Barns Tv&#65533;spr&#65533;kiga Bildordbok. Carlson, Richard. 2019. (SWE.). 26p. (J). pap. 11.99 ***(978-1-6908-4066-4(8))*** Independently Published.

—Svenska-Bengali Fordon/যানবাহন Barns Tv&#65533;spr&#65533;kiga Bildordbok. Carlson, Richard. 2019. (SWE.). 24p. (J). pap. 11.99 ***(978-1-6886-4830-2(5))*** Independently Published.

—Svenska-Bengali Mina K&#65533;nslor &#65533;r S&#65533;rade Tv&#65533;spr&#65533;kig Bilderbok F&#65533;r Barn. Carlson, Richard. 2019. (SWE.). 24p. (J). pap. 11.99 ***(978-1-6967-9292-9(4))*** Independently Published.

—Svenska-Bengali Nummer/সংখ্যা Bildordbok F&#65533;r Tv&#65533;spr&#65533;kiga Barn. Carlson, Richard. 2019. (SWE.). 26p. (J). pap. 11.99 ***(978-1-7104-3002-8(8))*** Independently Published.

—Svenska-Bengali Skolan/স্কুল Barns Tv&#65533;spr&#65533;kiga Bildordbok. Carlson, Richard. 2019. (SWE.). 24p. (J). pap. 11.99 ***(978-1-7028-5864-9(2))*** Independently Published.

—Svenska-Bengali Tid/সময় Tv&#65533;spr&#65533;kig Bilderbok F&#65533;r Barn. Carlson, Richard. 2019. (SWE.). 28p. (J). pap. 11.99 ***(978-1-6986-3223-0(1))*** Independently Published.

Carlson, Suzanne. Svenska-Bengali Trubbel/বিপদ Tvåspråkig Bilderbok För Barn. Carlson, Richard. 2019. (SWE.). 24p. (J). pap. 11.99 *(978-1-0729-9884-6(X))* Independently Published.

Carlson, Suzanne. Svenska-Bengali Verktyg Barns Tv&#65533;spr&#65533;kiga Bildordbok. Carlson, Richard. 2019. (SWE.). 26p. (J). pap. 11.99 ***(978-1-6908-5085-4(X))*** Independently Published.

—Svenska-Bosniska Fordon/Vozila Barns Tv&#65533;spr&#65533;kiga Bildordbok. Carlson, Richard. 2019. (SWE.). 24p. (J). pap. 11.99 ***(978-1-6886-5033-6(4))*** Independently Published.

—Svenska-Bosniska Mina K&#65533;nslor &#65533;r S&#65533;rade/Moja Osjecanja Su Povrijeđena Tv&#65533;spr&#65533;kig Bilderbok F&#65533;r Barn. Carlson, Richard. 2019. (SWE.). 24p. (J). pap. 11.99 ***(978-1-6967-9476-3(5))*** Independently Published.

—Svenska-Bosniska Nummer/Brojevi Bildordbok F&#65533;r Tv&#65533;spr&#65533;kiga Barn. Carlson, Richard. 2019. (SWE.). 26p. (J). pap. 11.99 ***(978-1-7110-1726-6(4))*** Independently Published.

—Svenska-Bosniska Skolan/Skola Barns Tv&#65533;spr&#65533;kiga Bildordbok. Carlson, Richard. 2019. (SWE.). 24p. (J). pap. 11.99 ***(978-1-7028-6117-5(1))*** Independently Published.

—Svenska-Bosniska Tid/Vrijeme Tv&#65533;spr&#65533;kig Bilderbok F&#65533;r Barn. Carlson, Richard. 2019. (SWE.). 28p. (J). pap. 11.99 ***(978-1-6988-9098-2(2))*** Independently Published.

Carlson, Suzanne. Svenska-Bosniska Trubbel/Problem Tvåspråkig Bilderbok För Barn. Carlson, Richard. 2019. (SWE.). 24p. (J). pap. 11.99 *(978-1-0730-0019-7(2))* Independently Published.

Carlson, Suzanne. Svenska-Bosniska Verktyg/Alati Barns Tv&#65533;spr&#65533;kiga Bildordbok. Carlson, Richard. 2019. (SWE.). 26p. (J). pap. 11.99 ***(978-1-6908-5766-2(8))*** Independently Published.

—Svenska-Bulgariska Fordon/Превознисредства Barns Tv&#65533;spr&#65533;kiga Bildordbok. Carlson, Richard. 2019. (SWE.). 24p. (J). pap. 11.99 ***(978-1-6886-5738-0(X))*** Independently Published.

—Svenska-Bulgariska Mina K&#65533;nslor &#65533;r S&#65533;rade/Чувствата мисанаранени Tv&#65533;spr&#65533;kig Bilderbok F&#65533;r Barn. Carlson, Richard. 2019. (SWE.). 24p. (J). pap. 11.99 ***(978-1-6967-9664-4(4))*** Independently Published.

—Svenska-Bulgariska Nummer/Числа; Bildordbok F&#65533;r Tv&#65533;spr&#65533;kiga Barn. Carlson, Richard. 2019. (SWE.). 26p. (J). pap. 11.99 ***(978-1-7110-2279-6(9))*** Independently Published.

—Svenska-Bulgariska Skolan/Училище Barns Tv&#65533;spr&#65533;kiga Bildordbok. Carlson, Richard. 2019. (SWE.). 24p. (J). pap. 11.99 ***(978-1-7028-6606-4(8))*** Independently Published.

—Svenska-Bulgariska Tid/Време Tv&#65533;spr&#65533;kig Bilderbok F&#65533;r Barn. Carlson, Richard. 2019. (SWE.). 28p. (J). pap. 11.99 ***(978-1-6988-9331-0(0))*** Independently Published.

Carlson, Suzanne. Svenska-Bulgariska Trubbel/Неприятност; Tvåspråkig Bilderbok För Barn. Carlson, Richard. 2019. (SWE.). 24p. (J). pap. 11.99 *(978-1-0730-0101-9(6))* Independently Published.

Carlson, Suzanne. Svenska-Bulgariska Verktyg/Инструменти Barns Tv&#65533;spr&#65533;kiga Bildordbok. Carlson, Richard. 2019. (SWE.). 26p. (J). pap. 11.99 ***(978-1-6908-6003-7(0))*** Independently Published.

—Svenska-Burmesiska Fordon Barns Tv&#65533;spr&#65533;kiga Bildordbok. Carlson, Richard. 2019. (SWE.). 24p. (J). pap. 11.99 ***(978-1-6888-3817-8(1))*** Independently Published.

—Svenska-Burmesiska Mina K&#65533;nslor &#65533;r S&#65533;rade Tv&#65533;spr&#65533;kig Bilderbok F&#65533;r Barn. Carlson, Richard. 2019. (SWE.). 24p. (J). pap. 11.99 ***(978-1-6968-0136-2(2))*** Independently Published.

—Svenska-Burmesiska Skolan Barns Tv&#65533;spr&#65533;kiga Bildordbok. Carlson, Richard. 2019. (SWE.). 24p. (J). pap. 11.99 ***(978-1-7028-7002-3(2))*** Independently Published.

—Svenska-Burmesiska Tid Tv&#65533;spr&#65533;kig Bilderbok F&#65533;r Barn. Carlson, Richard. 2019. (SWE.). 28p. (J). pap. 11.99 ***(978-1-6988-9571-0(2))*** Independently Published.

Carlson, Suzanne. Svenska-Burmesiska Trubbel Tvåspråkig Bilderbok För Barn. Carlson, Richard. 2019. (SWE.). 24p. (J). pap. 11.99 *(978-1-0730-0212-2(8))* Independently Published.

Carlson, Suzanne. Svenska-Burmesiska Verktyg Barns Tv&#65533;spr&#65533;kiga Bildordbok. Carlson, Richard. 2019. (SWE.). 26p. (J). pap. 11.99 ***(978-1-6908-6725-8(6))*** Independently Published.

—Svenska-Danska Fordon/K&#65533;ret&#65533;jer Barns Tv&#65533;spr&#65533;kiga Bildordbok. Carlson, Richard. 2019. (SWE.). 24p. (J). pap. 11.99 ***(978-1-6892-7202-5(3))*** Independently Published.

—Svenska-Danska Mina K&#65533;nslor &#65533;r S&#65533;rade/Mine F&#65533;lelser Blev S&#65533;ret Tv&#65533;spr&#65533;kig Bilderbok F&#65533;r Barn. Carlson, Richard. 2019. (SWE.). 24p. (J). pap. 11.99 ***(978-1-6968-1811-7(7))*** Independently Published.

—Svenska-Danska Nummer/Tal Bildordbok F&#65533;r Tv&#65533;spr&#65533;kiga Barn. Carlson, Richard. 2019. (SWE.). 26p. (J). pap. 11.99 ***(978-1-7113-2516-3(3))*** Independently Published.

—Svenska-Danska Skolan/Skole Barns Tv&#65533;spr&#65533;kiga Bildordbok. Carlson, Richard. 2019. (SWE.). 24p. (J). pap. 11.99 ***(978-1-7032-1950-0(3))*** Independently Published.

—Svenska-Danska Tid/Tid Tv&#65533;spr&#65533;kig Bilderbok F&#65533;r Barn. Carlson, Richard. 2019. (SWE.). 28p. (J). pap. 11.99 ***(978-1-6995-2216-5(2))*** Independently Published.

Carlson, Suzanne. Svenska-Danska Trubbel/Ballade Tvåspråkig Bilderbok För Barn. Carlson, Richard. 2019. (SWE.). 24p. (J). pap. 11.99 *(978-1-0731-4403-7(8))* Independently Published.

Carlson, Suzanne. Svenska-Danska Verktyg/V&#65533;rkt&#65533;j Barns Tv&#65533;spr&#65533;kiga Bildordbok. Carlson, Richard. 2019. (SWE.). 26p. (J). pap. 11.99 ***(978-1-6909-0738-1(X))*** Independently Published.

—Svenska-Dari Fordon Barns Tv&#65533;spr&#65533;kiga Bildordbok. Carlson, Richard. 2019. (SWE.). 24p. (J). pap. 11.99 ***(978-1-6892-7499-9(9))*** Independently Published.

—Svenska-Dari Mina K&#65533;nslor &#65533;r S&#65533;rade Tv&#65533;spr&#65533;kig Bilderbok F&#65533;r Barn. Carlson, Richard. 2019. (SWE.). 24p. (J). pap. 11.99 ***(978-1-6968-2012-7(X))*** Independently Published.

—Svenska-Dari Nummer/شمارهها Bildordbok F&#65533;r Tv&#65533;spr&#65533;kiga Barn. Carlson, Richard. 2019. (SWE.). 26p. (J). pap. 11.99 ***(978-1-7113-2829-4(4))*** Independently Published.

—Svenska-Dari Skolan/مکتب Barns Tv&#65533;spr&#65533;kiga Bildordbok. Carlson, Richard. 2019. (SWE.). 24p. (J). pap. 11.99 ***(978-1-7032-2012-4(9))*** Independently Published.

—Svenska-Dari Tid Tv&#65533;spr&#65533;kig Bilderbok F&#65533;r Barn. Carlson, Richard. 2019. (SWE.). 28p. (J). pap. 11.99 ***(978-1-7001-7954-8(3))*** Independently Published.

Carlson, Suzanne. Svenska-Dari Trubbel/مشکل Tvåspråkig Bilderbok För Barn. Carlson, Richard. 2019. (SWE.). 24p. (J). pap. 11.99 *(978-1-0731-4772-4(X))* Independently Published.

Carlson, Suzanne. Svenska-Dari Verktyg Barns Tv&#65533;spr&#65533;kiga Bildordbok. Carlson, Richard. 2019. (SWE.). 26p. (J). pap. 11.99 ***(978-1-6909-1536-2(6))*** Independently Published.

—Svenska-Egyptisk Arabiska Nummer/الأعداد Bildordbok F&#65533;r Tv&#65533;spr&#65533;kiga Barn. Carlson, Richard. 2019. (SWE.). 26p. (J). pap. 11.99 ***(978-1-7092-3537-5(3))*** Independently Published.

—Svenska-Egyptisk Arabiska Skolan Barns Tv&#65533;spr&#65533;kiga Bildordbok. Carlson, Richard. 2019. (SWE.). 24p. (J). pap. 11.99 ***(978-1-7026-5713-6(2))*** Independently Published.

—Svenska-Engelska Fordon/Vehicles Barns Tv&#65533;spr&#65533;kiga Bildordbok. Carlson, Richard. 2019. (SWE.). 24p. (J). pap. 11.99 ***(978-1-6892-8067-9(0))*** Independently Published.

—Svenska-Engelska Mina K&#65533;nslor &#65533;r S&#65533;rade/My Feelings Are Hurt Tv&#65533;spr&#65533;kig Bilderbok F&#65533;r Barn. Carlson, Richard. 2019. (SWE.). 24p. (J). pap. 11.99 ***(978-1-6968-2704-1(3))*** Independently Published.

—Svenska-Engelska Skolan/School Barns Tv&#65533;spr&#65533;kiga Bildordbok. Carlson,

Richard. 2019. (SWE.). 24p. (J). pap. 11.99 ***(978-1-7019-6249-1(7))*** Independently Published.

—Svenska-Engelska Tid/Time Tv&#65533;spr&#65533;kig Bilderbok F&#65533;r Barn. Carlson, Richard. 2019. (SWE.). 28p. (J). pap. 11.99 ***(978-1-6995-2867-9(5))*** Independently Published.

Carlson, Suzanne. Svenska-Engelska Trubbel/Trouble Tvåspråkig Bilderbok För Barn. Carlson, Richard. 2019. (SWE.). 24p. (J). pap. 11.99 *(978-1-0731-5219-3(7))* Independently Published.

Carlson, Suzanne. Svenska-Engelska Verktyg/Tools Barns Tv&#65533;spr&#65533;kiga Bildordbok. Carlson, Richard. 2019. (SWE.). 26p. (J). pap. 11.99 ***(978-1-6911-1821-2(4))*** Independently Published.

—Svenska-Estniska Fordon/S&#65533;idukid Barns Tv&#65533;spr&#65533;kiga Bildordbok. Carlson, Richard. 2019. (SWE.). 24p. (J). pap. 11.99 ***(978-1-6892-8241-3(X))*** Independently Published.

—Svenska-Estniska Mina K&#65533;nslor &#65533;r S&#65533;rade/Mu Tunded Said Haavata Tv&#65533;spr&#65533;kig Bilderbok F&#65533;r Barn. Carlson, Richard. 2019. (SWE.). 24p. (J). pap. 11.99 ***(978-1-6968-2844-4(9))*** Independently Published.

—Svenska-Estniska Nummer/Numbrid Bildordbok F&#65533;r Tv&#65533;spr&#65533;kiga Barn. Carlson, Richard. 2019. (SWE.). 26p. (J). pap. 11.99 ***(978-1-7113-3432-5(4))*** Independently Published.

—Svenska-Estniska Skolan/Kool Barns Tv&#65533;spr&#65533;kiga Bildordbok. Carlson, Richard. 2019. (SWE.). 24p. (J). pap. 11.99 ***(978-1-7032-2189-3(3))*** Independently Published.

—Svenska-Estniska Tid/Aeg Tv&#65533;spr&#65533;kig Bilderbok F&#65533;r Barn. Carlson, Richard. 2019. (SWE.). 28p. (J). pap. 11.99 ***(978-1-6997-3400-1(3))*** Independently Published.

Carlson, Suzanne. Svenska-Estniska Trubbel/Pahandus Tvåspråkig Bilderbok För Barn. Carlson, Richard. 2019. (SWE.). 24p. (J). pap. 11.99 *(978-1-0731-5360-2(6))* Independently Published.

Carlson, Suzanne. Svenska-Estniska Verktyg/T&#65533;&#65533;riistad Barns Tv&#65533;spr&#65533;kiga Bildordbok. Carlson, Richard. 2019. (SWE.). 26p. (J). pap. 11.99 ***(978-1-6911-1986-8(5))*** Independently Published.

—Svenska-F&#65533;renklad Kinesiska, Mandarin Mina K&#65533;nslor &#65533;r S&#65533;rade/我的感情受到了伤害 Tv&#65533;spr&#65533;kig Bilderbok F&#65533;r Barn. Carlson, Richard. 2019. (SWE.). 24p. (J). pap. 11.99 ***(978-1-6968-0745-6(X))*** Independently Published.

—Svenska-F&#65533;renklad Kinesiska, Mandarin Nummer/数字 Bildordbok F&#65533;r Tv&#65533;spr&#65533;kiga Barn. Carlson, Richard. 2019. (SWE.). 26p. (J). pap. 11.99 ***(978-1-7110-4335-7(4))*** Independently Published.

—Svenska-F&#65533;renklad Kinesiska, Mandarin Skolan/学校 Barns Tv&#65533;spr&#65533;kiga Bildordbok. Carlson, Richard. 2019. (SWE.). 24p. (J). pap. 11.99 ***(978-1-7031-7256-0(6))*** Independently Published.

—Svenska-F&#65533;renklad Kinesiska, Mandarin Tid/时间 Tv&#65533;spr&#65533;kig Bilderbok F&#65533;r Barn. Carlson, Richard. 2019. (SWE.). 28p. (J). pap. 11.99 ***(978-1-6990-9232-3(X))*** Independently Published.

—Svenska-F&#65533;renklad Kinesiska, Mandarin Verktyg/工具 Barns Tv&#65533;spr&#65533;kiga Bildordbok. Carlson, Richard. 2019. (SWE.). 26p. (J). pap. 11.99 ***(978-1-6908-9381-3(8))*** Independently Published.

—Svenska-Finska Fordon/Kulkuneuvot Barns Tv&#65533;spr&#65533;kiga Bildordbok. Carlson, Richard. 2019. (SWE.). 24p. (J). pap. 11.99 ***(978-1-6892-8455-4(2))*** Independently Published.

—Svenska-Finska Mina K&#65533;nslor &#65533;r S&#65533;rade/Tunteitani on Loukattu Tv&#65533;spr&#65533;kig Bilderbok F&#65533;r Barn. Carlson, Richard. 2019. (SWE.). 24p. (J). pap. 11.99 ***(978-1-6968-3042-3(7))*** Independently Published.

—Svenska-Finska Nummer/Numerot Bildordbok F&#65533;r Tv&#65533;spr&#65533;kiga Barn. Carlson, Richard. 2019. (SWE.). 26p. (J). pap. 11.99 ***(978-1-7113-5005-9(2))*** Independently Published.

—Svenska-Finska Skolan/Koulu Barns Tv&#65533;spr&#65533;kiga Bildordbok. Carlson, Richard. 2019. (SWE.). 24p. (J). pap. 11.99 ***(978-1-7032-2339-2(X))*** Independently Published.

—Svenska-Finska Tid/Aika Tv&#65533;spr&#65533;kig Bilderbok F&#65533;r Barn. Carlson, Richard. 2019. (SWE.). 28p. (J). pap. 11.99 ***(978-1-6997-3486-5(0))*** Independently Published.

Carlson, Suzanne. Svenska-Finska Trubbel/Kiusaaminen Tvåspråkig Bilderbok För Barn. Carlson, Richard. 2019. (SWE.). 24p. (J). pap. 11.99 *(978-1-0731-5634-4(6))* Independently Published.

Carlson, Suzanne. Svenska-Finska Verktyg/Ty&#65533;kalut Barns Tv&#65533;spr&#65533;kiga Bildordbok. Carlson, Richard. 2019. (SWE.). 26p. (J). pap. 11.99 ***(978-1-6911-2260-8(2))*** Independently Published.

—Svenska-Flaml&#65533;ndska (belgiska) Fordon/Voertuigen Barns Tv&#65533;spr&#65533;kiga Bildordbok. Carlson, Richard. 2019. (SWE.). 24p. (J). pap. 11.99 ***(978-1-6892-8836-1(1))*** Independently Published.

—Svenska-Flaml&#65533;ndska (belgiska) Mina K&#65533;nslor &#65533;r S&#65533;rade/Mijn Gevoelens Zijn Gekwetst Tv&#65533;spr&#65533;kig Bilderbok F&#65533;r Barn. Carlson, Richard. 2019. (SWE.). 24p. (J). pap. 11.99 ***(978-1-6968-3162-8(8))*** Independently Published.

—Svenska-Flaml&#65533;ndska (belgiska) Nummer/Cijfers Bildordbok F&#65533;r Tv&#65533;spr&#65533;kiga Barn. Carlson, Richard. 2019. (SWE.). 26p. (J). pap. 11.99 ***(978-1-7113-5225-1(X))*** Independently Published.

—Svenska-Flaml&#65533;ndska (belgiska) Tid/de Tijd Tv&#65533;spr&#65533;kig Bilderbok F&#65533;r Barn. Carlson, Richard. 2019. (SWE.). 28p. (J). pap. 11.99 ***(978-1-6997-3762-0(2))*** Independently Published.

—Svenska-Flaml&#65533;ndska (belgiska) Verktyg/Werktuigen Barns Tv&#65533;spr&#65533;kiga Bildordbok. Carlson, Richard. 2019. (SWE.). 26p. (J). pap. 11.99 ***(978-1-6911-2516-6(4))*** Independently Published.

Carlson, Suzanne. Svenska-Flamländska (belgiska) Trubbel/Problemen Tvåspråkig Bilderbok För Barn. Carlson, Richard. 2019. (SWE.). 24p. (J). pap. 11.99 *(978-1-0731-5884-3(5))* Independently Published.

—Svenska-Förenklad Kinesiska, Mandarin Trubbel/麻烦 Tvåspråkig Bilderbok För Barn. Carlson, Richard. 2019. (SWE.). 24p. (J). pap. 11.99 *(978-1-0731-2588-3(2))* Independently Published.

Carlson, Suzanne. Svenska-Franska Fordon/V&#65533;hicules Barns Tv&#65533;spr&#65533;kiga Bildordbok. Carlson, Richard. 2019. (SWE.). 24p. (J). pap. 11.99 ***(978-1-6894-8170-0(6))*** Independently Published.

—Svenska-Franska Mina K&#65533;nslor &#65533;r S&#65533;rade/on a Bless&#65533; Mes Sentiments Tv&#65533;spr&#65533;kig Bilderbok F&#65533;r Barn. Carlson, Richard. 2019. (SWE.). 24p. (J). pap. 11.99 ***(978-1-6968-3354-7(X))*** Independently Published.

—Svenska-Franska Nummer/Chiffres Bildordbok F&#65533;r Tv&#65533;spr&#65533;kiga Barn. Carlson, Richard. 2019. (SWE.). 26p. (J). pap. 11.99 ***(978-1-7113-7684-4(1))*** Independently Published.

—Svenska-Franska Skolan/&#65533;cole Barns Tv&#65533;spr&#65533;kiga Bildordbok. Carlson, Richard. 2019. (SWE.). 24p. (J). pap. 11.99 ***(978-1-7032-3322-3(0))*** Independently Published.

—Svenska-Franska Tid/le Temps Tv&#65533;spr&#65533;kig Bilderbok F&#65533;r Barn. Carlson, Richard. 2019. (SWE.). 28p. (J). pap. 11.99 ***(978-1-6997-3963-1(3))*** Independently Published.

Carlson, Suzanne. Svenska-Franska Trubbel/Problème Tvåspråkig Bilderbok För Barn. Carlson, Richard. 2019. (SWE.). 24p. (J). pap. 11.99 *(978-1-0731-6016-7(5))* Independently Published.

Carlson, Suzanne. Svenska-Franska Verktyg/Outils Barns Tv&#65533;spr&#65533;kiga Bildordbok. Carlson, Richard. 2019. (SWE.). 26p. (J). pap. 11.99 ***(978-1-6911-2760-3(4))*** Independently Published.

—Svenska-Galiciska Mina K&#65533;nslor &#65533;r S&#65533;rade/Os Meus Sentimentos Est&#65533;n Feridos Tv&#65533;spr&#65533;kig Bilderbok F&#65533;r Barn. Carlson, Richard. 2019. (SWE.). 24p. (J). pap. 11.99 ***(978-1-6969-6841-6(0))*** Independently Published.

—Svenska-Georgiska Fordon/სატრანსპორტოსაშუალებები Barns Tv&#65533;spr&#65533;kiga Bildordbok. Carlson, Richard. 2019. (SWE.). 24p. (J). pap. 11.99 ***(978-1-6894-8415-2(2))*** Independently Published.

—Svenska-Georgiska Mina K&#65533;nslor &#65533;r S&#65533;rade/ჩემი გრძნობები შეურაცხყოფილია Tv&#65533;spr&#65533;kig Bilderbok F&#65533;; Carlson, Richard. 2019. (SWE.). 24p. (J). pap. 11.99 ***(978-1-6969-7661-9(8))*** Independently Published.

—Svenska-Georgiska Nummer/რიცხვები Bildordbok F&#65533;r Tv&#65533;spr&#65533;kiga Barn. Carlson, Richard. 2019. (SWE.). 26p. (J). pap. 11.99 ***(978-1-7113-8082-7(2))*** Independently Published.

—Svenska-Georgiska Skolan/სკოლა Barns Tv&#65533;spr&#65533;kiga Bildordbok. Carlson, Richard. 2019. (SWE.). 24p. (J). pap. 11.99 ***(978-1-7035-0002-8(4))*** Independently Published.

—Svenska-Georgiska Tid/დრო Tv&#65533;spr&#65533;kig Bilderbok F&#65533;r Barn. Carlson, Richard. 2019. (SWE.). 28p. (J). pap. 11.99 ***(978-1-6997-4175-7(1))*** Independently Published.

Carlson, Suzanne. Svenska-Georgiska Trubbel/უსიამოვნება Tvåspråkig Bilderbok För Barn. Carlson, Richard. 2019. (SWE.). 24p. (J). pap. 11.99 *(978-1-0731-6408-0(X))* Independently Published.

Carlson, Suzanne. Svenska-Georgiska Verktyg/სამუშაო იარაღები Barns Tv&#65533;spr&#65533;kiga Bildordbok. Carlson, Richard. 2019. (SWE.). 26p. (J). pap. 11.99 ***(978-1-6911-3036-8(2))*** Independently Published.

—Svenska-Golfarabiska Fordon Barns Tv&#65533;spr&#65533;kiga Bildordbok. Carlson, Richard. 2019. (SWE.). 24p. (J). pap. 11.99 ***(978-1-6886-3436-7(3))*** Independently Published.

—Svenska-Golfarabiska Nummer/الأعداد Bildordbok F&#65533;r Tv&#65533;spr&#65533;kiga Barn. Carlson, Richard. 2019. (SWE.). 26p. (J). pap. 11.99 ***(978-1-7095-2430-1(8))*** Independently Published.

—Svenska-Golfarabiska Skolan Barns Tv&#65533;spr&#65533;kiga Bildordbok. Carlson, Richard. 2019. (SWE.). 24p. (J). pap. 11.99 ***(978-1-7026-6209-3(8))*** Independently Published.

—Svenska-Grekiska Fordon/Οχήματα Barns Tv&#65533;spr&#65533;kiga Bildordbok. Carlson, Richard. 2019. (SWE.). 24p. (J). pap. 11.99 ***(978-1-6894-9444-1(1))*** Independently Published.

—Svenska-Grekiska Mina K&#65533;nslor &#65533;r S&#65533;rade/Πληγώθηκαν Τα Συναισθήματά Μου Tv&#65533;spr&#65533;kig Bilderbok F&#65533;r Barn. Carlson, Richard. 2019. (SWE.). 24p. (J). pap. 11.99 ***(978-1-6969-8959-6(0))*** Independently Published.

—Svenska-Grekiska Nummer/Αριθμοί Bildordbok F&#65533;r Tv&#65533;spr&#65533;kiga Barn. Carlson, Richard. 2019. (SWE.). 26p. (J). pap. 11.99 ***(978-1-7119-1419-0(3))*** Independently Published.

—Svenska-Grekiska Skolan/Σχολείο; Barns Tv&#65533;spr&#65533;kiga Bildordbok. Carlson, Richard. 2019. (SWE.). 24p. (J). pap. 11.99 ***(978-1-7035-1043-0(7))*** Independently Published.

—Svenska-Grekiska Tid/Χρόνος Tv&#65533;spr&#65533;kig Bilderbok F&#65533;r Barn. Carlson, Richard. 2019. (SWE.). 28p. (J). pap. 11.99 ***(978-1-6999-0383-4(2))*** Independently Published.

Carlson, Suzanne. Svenska-Grekiska Trubbel/Πρόβλημα Tvåspråkig Bilderbok För Barn. Carlson, Richard. 2019. (SWE.). 24p. (J). pap. 11.99 *(978-1-0733-4937-1(3))* Independently Published.

Carlson, Suzanne. Svenska-Grekiska Verktyg/Εργαλεία Barns Tv&#65533;spr&#65533;kiga Bildordbok. Carlson, Richard. 2019. (SWE.). 26p. (J). pap. 11.99 ***(978-1-6913-0418-9(2))*** Independently Published.

—Svenska-Gujarati Fordon/વાહનો Barns Tv&#65533;spr&#65533;kiga Bildordbok. Carlson, Richard. 2019. (SWE.). 24p. (J). pap. 11.99 ***(978-1-6896-9082-9(8))*** Independently Published.

—Svenska-Gujarati Mina K&#65533;nslor &#65533;r S&#65533;rade Tv&#65533;spr&#65533;kig Bilderbok F&#65533;r Barn. Carlson, Richard. 2019. (SWE.). 24p. (J). pap. 11.99 ***(978-1-6970-1452-5(6))*** Independently Published.

—Svenska-Gujarati Nummer/આંકડા Bildordbok F&#65533;r Tv&#65533;spr&#65533;kiga Barn. Carlson, Richard. 2019. (SWE.). 26p. (J). pap. 11.99 ***(978-1-7119-1736-8(2))*** Independently Published.

—Svenska-Gujarati Skolan/શાળા (નિશાળ) Barns Tv&#65533;spr&#65533;kiga Bildordbok. Carlson, Richard. 2019. (SWE.). 24p. (J). pap. 11.99 ***(978-1-7035-1858-0(6))*** Independently Published.

—Svenska-Gujarati Tid/નવરાશ Tv&#65533;spr&#65533;kig Bilderbok F&#65533;r Barn. Carlson, Richard. 2019. (SWE.). 28p. (J). pap. 11.99 ***(978-1-6999-0555-5(X))*** Independently Published.

Carlson, Suzanne. Svenska-Gujarati Trubbel/તકલીફ Tvåspråkig Bilderbok För Barn. Carlson, Richard. 2019. (SWE.). 24p. (J). pap. 11.99 *(978-1-0733-5479-5(2))* Independently Published.

Carlson, Suzanne. Svenska-Gujarati Verktyg/સાધનો Barns Tv&#65533;spr&#65533;kiga Bildordbok. Carlson, Richard. 2019. (SWE.). 26p. (J). pap. 11.99 ***(978-1-6913-3836-8(2))*** Independently Published.

—Svenska-Haitisk Kreolska Fordon/Machin Yo Barns Tv&#65533;spr&#65533;kiga Bildordbok. Carlson, Richard. 2019. (SWE.). 24p. (J). pap. 11.99 ***(978-1-6896-9198-7(0))*** Independently Published.

—Svenska-Haitisk Kreolska Mina K&#65533;nslor &#65533;r S&#65533;rade/Santiman M Blese Tv&#65533;spr&#65533;kig Bilderbok F&#65533;r Barn. Carlson, Richard. 2019. (SWE.). 24p. (J). pap. 11.99 ***(978-1-6970-1875-2(0))*** Independently Published.

—Svenska-Haitisk Kreolska Nummer/Nimewo Yo Bildordbok F&#65533;r Tv&#65533;spr&#65533;kiga Barn. Carlson, Richard. 2019. (SWE.). 26p. (J). pap. 11.99 ***(978-1-7119-2952-1(2))*** Independently Published.

—Svenska-Haitisk Kreolska Skolan/Lek&#65533;l Barns Tv&#65533;spr&#65533;kiga Bildordbok. Carlson, Richard. 2019. (SWE.). 24p. (J). pap. 11.99 ***(978-1-7035-2995-1(2))*** Independently Published.

—Svenska-Haitisk Kreolska Tid/Tan Tv&#65533;spr&#65533;kig Bilderbok F&#65533;r Barn. Carlson, Richard. 2019. (SWE.). 28p. (J). pap. 11.99 ***(978-1-6999-0905-8(9))*** Independently Published.

Carlson, Suzanne. Svenska-Haitisk Kreolska Trubbel/Dezòd Tvåspråkig Bilderbok För Barn. Carlson, Richard. 2019. (SWE.). 24p. (J). pap. 11.99 *(978-1-0733-7095-5(X))* Independently Published.

Carlson, Suzanne. Svenska-Haitisk Kreolska Verktyg/Zouti Yo Barns Tv&#65533;spr&#65533;kiga Bildordbok. Carlson, Richard. 2019. (SWE.). 26p. (J). pap. 11.99 ***(978-1-6913-4055-2(3))*** Independently Published.

—Svenska-Hausa Fordon-Abin Hawa/Mota Barns Tv&#65533;spr&#65533;kiga Bildordbok. Carlson, Richard. 2019. (SWE.). 24p. (J). pap. 11.99 ***(978-1-6896-9334-9(7))*** Independently Published.

—Svenska-Hausa Mina K&#65533;nslor &#65533;r S&#65533;rade/Na Ji Jikkata Tv&#65533;spr&#65533;kig Bilderbok F&#65533;r Barn. Carlson, Richard. 2019. (SWE.). 24p. (J). pap. 10.99 ***(978-1-6970-2010-6(0))*** Independently Published.

—Svenska-Hausa Nummer/Lambobi Bildordbok F&#65533;r Tv&#65533;spr&#65533;kiga Barn. Carlson, Richard. 2019. (SWE.). 26p. (J). pap. 11.99 ***(978-1-7119-3380-1(5))*** Independently Published.

—Svenska-Hausa Skolan/Makaranta Barns Tv&#65533;spr&#65533;kiga Bildordbok. Carlson, Richard. 2019. (SWE.). 24p. (J). pap. 11.99 ***(978-1-7035-3615-7(0))*** Independently Published.

—Svenska-Hausa Tid/Lokaci Tv&#65533;spr&#65533;kig Bilderbok F&#65533;r Barn. Carlson, Richard. 2019. (SWE.). 28p. (J). pap. 11.99 ***(978-1-6999-1072-6(3))*** Independently Published.

Carlson, Suzanne. Svenska-Hausa Trubbel/Matsala Tvåspråkig Bilderbok För Barn. Carlson, Richard. 2019. (SWE.). 24p. (J). pap. 11.99 *(978-1-0734-4000-9(1))* Independently Published.

Carlson, Suzanne. Svenska-Hausa Verktyg/Kayan Aiki Barns Tv&#65533;spr&#65533;kiga Bildordbok. Carlson, Richard. 2019. (SWE.). 26p. (J). pap. 11.99 ***(978-1-6913-4272-3(6))*** Independently Published.

—Svenska-Hebreiska Fordon Barns Tv&#65533;spr&#65533;kiga Bildordbok. Carlson, Richard. 2019. (SWE.). 24p. (J). pap. 11.99 ***(978-1-6896-9520-6(X))*** Independently Published.

—Svenska-Hebreiska Mina K&#65533;nslor &#65533;r S&#65533;rade Tv&#65533;spr&#65533;kig Bilderbok F&#65533;r Barn. Carlson, Richard. 2019. (SWE.). 24p. (J). pap. 11.99 ***(978-1-6970-2174-5(3))*** Independently Published.

—Svenska-Hebreiska Nummer/מספרים Bildordbok F&#65533;r Tv&#65533;spr&#65533;kiga Barn. Carlson, Richard. 2019. (SWE.). 26p. (J). pap. 11.99 ***(978-1-7119-4031-1(3))*** Independently Published.

—Svenska-Hebreiska Skolan Barns Tv&#65533;spr&#65533;kiga Bildordbok. Carlson, Richard. 2019. (SWE.). 24p. (J). pap. 11.99 ***(978-1-7028-4333-1(5))*** Independently Published.

—Svenska-Hebreiska Tid Tv&#65533;spr&#65533;kig Bilderbok F&#65533;r Barn. Carlson, Richard. 2019. (SWE.). 28p. (J). pap. 11.99 ***(978-1-7001-8062-9(2))*** Independently Published.

Carlson, Suzanne. Svenska-Hebreiska Trubbel Tvåspråkig Bilderbok För Barn. Carlson, Richard. 2019. (SWE.). 24p. (J). pap. 11.99 *(978-1-0734-4096-2(6))* Independently Published.

Carlson, Suzanne. Svenska-Hebreiska Verktyg Barns Tv&#65533;spr&#65533;kiga Bildordbok. Carlson, Richard. 2019. (SWE.). 26p. (J). pap. 11.99 ***(978-1-6913-4699-8(3))*** Independently Published.

—Svenska-Hindi Fordon/वाहन Barns Tv&#65533;spr&#65533;kiga Bildordbok. Carlson, Richard. 2019. (SWE.). 24p. (J). pap. 11.99 ***(978-1-6896-9845-0(4))*** Independently Published.

—Svenska-Hindi Mina K&#65533;nslor &#65533;r S&#65533;rade/मेरी भावनाओं को ठेस पहुँची है Tv&#65533;spr&#65533;kig Bilderbok F&#65533;r Barn. Carlson, Richard. 2019. (SWE.). 24p. (J). pap. 11.99 ***(978-1-6970-2434-0(3))*** Independently Published.

—Svenska-Hindi Nummer/संख्याहरू Bildordbok F&#65533;r Tv&#65533;spr&#65533;kiga Barn. Carlson, Richard. 2019. (SWE.). 26p. (J). pap. 11.99 ***(978-1-7123-1860-7(8))*** Independently Published.

—Svenska-Hindi Skolan Barns Tv&#65533;spr&#65533;kiga Bildordbok. Carlson, Richard. 2019. (SWE.). 24p. (J). pap. 11.99 ***(978-1-7038-3329-4(5))*** Independently Published.

—Svenska-Hindi Tid/समय Tv&#65533;spr&#65533;kig Bilderbok F&#65533;r Barn. Carlson, Richard. 2019. (SWE.). 28p. (J). pap. 11.99 ***(978-1-6999-1816-6(3))*** Independently Published.

Carlson, Suzanne. Svenska-Hindi Trubbel/शरारत Tvåspråkig Bilderbok För Barn. Carlson, Richard. 2019. (SWE.). 24p. (J). pap. 11.99 *(978-1-0734-4218-8(7))* Independently Published.

Carlson, Suzanne. Svenska-Hindi Verktyg/औजार Barns Tv&#65533;spr&#65533;kiga Bildordbok. Carlson, Richard. 2019. (SWE.). 26p. (J). pap. 11.99 ***(978-1-6913-5007-0(9))*** Independently Published.

—Svenska-Holl&#65533;ndska Fordon/Voertuigen Barns Tv&#65533;spr&#65533;kiga Bildordbok. Carlson, Richard. 2019. (SWE.). 24p. (J). pap. 11.99 ***(978-1-6892-7709-9(2))*** Independently Published.

—Svenska-Holl&#65533;ndska Mina K&#65533;nslor &#65533;r S&#65533;rade/Mijn Gevoelens Zijn Gekwetst Tv&#65533;spr&#65533;kig Bilderbok F&#65533;r Barn. Carlson, Richard. 2019. (SWE.). 24p. (J). pap. 11.99 ***(978-1-6968-2142-1(8))*** Independently Published.

—Svenska-Holl&#65533;ndska Nummer/CIJFERS Bildordbok F&#65533;r Tv&#65533;spr&#65533;kiga Barn. Carlson, Richard. 2019. (SWE.). 26p. (J). pap. 11.99 ***(978-1-7113-3217-8(8))*** Independently Published.

—Svenska-Holl&#65533;ndska Skolan/School Barns Tv&#65533;spr&#65533;kiga Bildordbok. Carlson, Richard. 2019. (SWE.). 24p. (J). pap. 11.99 ***(978-1-7032-2132-9(X))*** Independently Published.

—Svenska-Holl&#65533;ndska Tid/Tijd Tv&#65533;spr&#65533;kig Bilderbok F&#65533;r Barn. Carlson, Richard. 2019. (SWE.). 28p. (J). pap. 11.99 ***(978-1-6995-2470-1(X))*** Independently Published.

—Svenska-Holl&#65533;ndska Verktyg/Gereedschappen Barns Tv&#65533;spr&#65533;kiga Bildordbok. Carlson, Richard. 2019. (SWE.). 26p. (J). pap. 11.99 ***(978-1-6909-1849-3(7))*** Independently Published.

Carlson, Suzanne. Svenska-Holländska Trubbel/Problemen Tvåspråkig Bilderbok För Barn. Carlson, Richard. 2019. (SWE.). 24p. (J). pap. 11.99 *(978-1-0731-4898-1(X))* Independently Published.

Carlson, Suzanne. Svenska-Indonesiska Fordon/Kendaraan Barns Tv&#65533;spr&#65533;kiga Bildordbok. Carlson, Richard. 2019. (SWE.). 24p. (J). pap. 11.99 ***(978-1-6898-2667-9(3))*** Independently Published.

C

—Svenska-Indonesiska Mina K&#65533;nslor &#65533;r S&#65533;rade/Perasaanku Terluka Tv&#65533;spr&#65533;kig Bilderbok F&#65533;r Barn. Carlson, Richard. 2019. (SWE.). 24p. (J). pap. 11.99 ***(978-1-6970-3075-4(0))*** Independently Published.

—Svenska-Indonesiska Nummer/Angka Bildordbok F&#65533;r Tv&#65533;spr&#65533;kiga Barn. Carlson, Richard. 2019. (SWE.). 26p. (J). pap. 11.99 ***(978-1-7123-3063-0(2))*** Independently Published.

—Svenska-Indonesiska Skolan/Sekolah Barns Tv&#65533;spr&#65533;kiga Bildordbok. Carlson, Richard. 2019. (SWE.). 24p. (J). pap. 11.99 ***(978-1-7038-4579-2(X))*** Independently Published.

—Svenska-Indonesiska Tid/Waktu Tv&#65533;spr&#65533;kig Bilderbok F&#65533;r Barn. Carlson, Richard. 2019. (SWE.). 28p. (J). pap. 11.99 ***(978-1-6999-5338-9(4))*** Independently Published.

Carlson, Suzanne. Svenska-Indonesiska Trubbel/Masalah Tvåspråkig Bilderbok För Barn. Carlson, Richard. 2019. (SWE.). 24p. (J). pap. 11.99 *(978-1-0734-4544-8(5))* Independently Published.

Carlson, Suzanne. Svenska-Indonesiska Verktyg/Perkakas Barns Tv&#65533;spr&#65533;kiga Bildordbok. Carlson, Richard. 2019. (SWE.). 26p. (J). pap. 11.99 ***(978-1-6917-1372-1(4))*** Independently Published.

—Svenska-Irl&#65533;ndsk Gaeliska Fordon/Feithicl&#65533; Barns Tv&#65533;spr&#65533;kiga Bildordbok. Carlson, Richard. 2019. (SWE.). 24p. (J). pap. 11.99 ***(978-1-6898-3519-0(2))*** Independently Published.

—Svenska-Irl&#65533;ndsk Gaeliska Mina K&#65533;nslor &#65533;r S&#65533;rade/T&#65533; M&#65533; Gortaithe Tv&#65533;spr&#65533;kig Bilderbok F&#65533;r Barn. Carlson, Richard. 2019. (SWE.). 24p. (J). pap. 11.99 ***(978-1-6970-3327-4(X))*** Independently Published.

—Svenska-Irl&#65533;ndsk Gaeliska Skolan/Scoil Barns Tv&#65533;spr&#65533;kiga Bildordbok. Carlson, Richard. 2019. (SWE.). 24p. (J). pap. 11.99 ***(978-1-7038-5294-3(X))*** Independently Published.

—Svenska-Irl&#65533;ndsk Gaeliska Tid/Am Tv&#65533;spr&#65533;kig Bilderbok F&#65533;r Barn. Carlson, Richard. 2019. (SWE.). 28p. (J). pap. 11.99 ***(978-1-6999-5855-1(6))*** Independently Published.

—Svenska-Irl&#65533;ndsk Gaeliska Verktyg/Uirlis&#65533; Barns Tv&#65533;spr&#65533;kiga Bildordbok. Carlson, Richard. 2019. (SWE.). 26p. (J). pap. 11.99 ***(978-1-6917-2138-2(7))*** Independently Published.

Carlson, Suzanne. Svenska-Irländsk Gaeliska Trubbel/Trioblóid Tvåspråkig Bilderbok För Barn. Carlson, Richard. 2019. (SWE.). 24p. (J). pap. 11.99 *(978-1-0734-4667-4(0))* Independently Published.

Carlson, Suzanne. Svenska-Isl&#65533;ndska Fordon/Farart&#65533;ki Barns Tv&#65533;spr&#65533;kiga Bildordbok. Carlson, Richard. 2019. (SWE.). 24p. (J). pap. 11.99 ***(978-1-6898-2479-8(4))*** Independently Published.

—Svenska-Isl&#65533;ndska Mina K&#65533;nslor &#65533;r S&#65533;rade/&#65533;g Er S&#65533;r&#65533;ur Tv&#65533;spr&#65533;kig Bilderbok F&#65533;r Barn. Carlson, Richard. 2019. (SWE.). 24p. (J). pap. 11.99 ***(978-1-6970-2779-2(2))*** Independently Published.

—Svenska-Isl&#65533;ndska Nummer/T&#65533;lur Bildordbok F&#65533;r Tv&#65533;spr&#65533;kiga Barn. Carlson, Richard. 2019. (SWE.). 26p. (J). pap. 11.99 ***(978-1-7123-2767-8(4))*** Independently Published.

—Svenska-Isl&#65533;ndska Skolan/Sk&#65533;li Barns Tv&#65533;spr&#65533;kiga Bildordbok. Carlson, Richard. 2019. (SWE.). 24p. (J). pap. 11.99 ***(978-1-7038-4160-2(3))*** Independently Published.

—Svenska-Isl&#65533;ndska Tid/T&#65533;mi Tv&#65533;spr&#65533;kig Bilderbok F&#65533;r Barn. Carlson, Richard. 2019. (SWE.). 28p. (J). pap. 11.99 ***(978-1-6999-3584-2(X))*** Independently Published.

—Svenska-Isl&#65533;ndska Verktyg/Verkf&#65533;ri Barns Tv&#65533;spr&#65533;kiga Bildordbok. Carlson, Richard. 2019. (SWE.). 26p. (J). pap. 11.99 ***(978-1-6917-0750-8(3))*** Independently Published.

Carlson, Suzanne. Svenska-Isländska Trubbel/Vandræði Tvåspråkig Bilderbok För Barn. Carlson, Richard. 2019. (SWE.). 24p. (J). pap. 11.99 *(978-1-0734-4443-4(0))* Independently Published.

Carlson, Suzanne. Svenska-Italienska Fordon/Veicoli Barns Tv&#65533;spr&#65533;kiga Bildordbok. Carlson, Richard. 2019. (SWE.). 24p. (J). pap. 11.99 ***(978-1-6898-3852-8(3))*** Independently Published.

—Svenska-Italienska Mina K&#65533;nslor &#65533;r S&#65533;rade/Mi Sento Ferito Tv&#65533;spr&#65533;kig Bilderbok F&#65533;r Barn. Carlson, Richard. 2019. (SWE.). 24p. (J). pap. 11.99 ***(978-1-6970-3496-7(9))*** Independently Published.

—Svenska-Italienska Nummer/Numeri Bildordbok F&#65533;r Tv&#65533;spr&#65533;kiga Barn. Carlson, Richard. 2019. (SWE.). 26p. (J). pap. 11.99 ***(978-1-7123-3482-9(4))*** Independently Published.

—Svenska-Italienska Skolan/Scuola Barns Tv&#65533;spr&#65533;kiga Bildordbok. Carlson, Richard. 2019. (SWE.). 24p. (J). pap. 11.99 ***(978-1-7038-4970-7(1))*** Independently Published.

—Svenska-Italienska Tid/Tempo Tv&#65533;spr&#65533;kig Bilderbok F&#65533;r Barn. Carlson, Richard. 2019. (SWE.). 28p. (J). pap. 11.99 ***(978-1-6999-6783-6(0))*** Independently Published.

Carlson, Suzanne. Svenska-Italienska Trubbel/Guaio Tvåspråkig Bilderbok För Barn. Carlson, Richard. 2019. (SWE.). 24p. (J). pap. 11.99 *(978-1-0734-5807-3(5))* Independently Published.

Carlson, Suzanne. Svenska-Italienska Verktyg/Attrezzi Barns Tv&#65533;spr&#65533;kiga Bildordbok. Carlson, Richard. 2019. (SWE.). 26p. (J). pap. 11.99 ***(978-1-6917-2515-1(3))*** Independently Published.

—Svenska-Japanska Fordon/のりもの Barns Tv&#65533;spr&#65533;kiga Bildordbok. Carlson, Richard. 2019. (SWE.). 24p. (J). pap. 11.99 ***(978-1-6898-4072-9(2))*** Independently Published.

—Svenska-Japanska Mina K&#65533;nslor &#65533;r S&#65533;rade/ぼくは傷ついた Tv&#65533;spr&#65533;kig Bilderbok F&#65533;r Barn. Carlson, Richard. 2019. (SWE.). 24p. (J). pap. 11.99 ***(978-1-6970-3696-1(1))*** Independently Published.

—Svenska-Japanska Nummer/数字 Bildordbok F&#65533;r Tv&#65533;spr&#65533;kiga Barn. Carlson, Richard. 2019. (SWE.). 26p. (J). pap. 11.99 ***(978-1-7123-4027-1(1))*** Independently Published.

—Svenska-Japanska Skolan/学校 Barns Tv&#65533;spr&#65533;kiga Bildordbok. Carlson, Richard. 2019. (SWE.). 24p. (J). pap. 11.99 ***(978-1-7038-6021-4(7))*** Independently Published.

—Svenska-Japanska Tid/じかん Tv&#65533;spr&#65533;kig Bilderbok F&#65533;r Barn. Carlson, Richard. 2019. (SWE.). 28p. (J). pap. 11.99 ***(978-1-7001-7421-5(5))*** Independently Published.

Carlson, Suzanne. Svenska-Japanska Trubbel/トラブル Tvåspråkig Bilderbok För Barn. Carlson, Richard. 2019. (SWE.). 24p. (J). pap. 11.99 *(978-1-0736-0932-1(4))* Independently Published.

Carlson, Suzanne. Svenska-Japanska Verktyg/工具 Barns Tv&#65533;spr&#65533;kiga Bildordbok. Carlson, Richard. 2019. (SWE.). 26p. (J). pap. 11.99 ***(978-1-6917-2880-0(2))*** Independently Published.

—Svenska-Jiddisch Mina K&#65533;nslor &#65533;r S&#65533;rade Tv&#65533;spr&#65533;kig Bilderbok F&#65533;r Barn. Carlson, Richard. 2019. (SWE.). 24p. (J). pap. 11.99 ***(978-1-6981-9635-0(0))*** Independently Published.

—Svenska-Kanaresiska Fordon Barns Tv&#65533;spr&#65533;kiga Bildordbok. Carlson, Richard. 2019. (SWE.). 24p. (J). pap. 11.99 ***(978-1-6898-4340-9(3))*** Independently Published.

—Svenska-Kanaresiska Mina K&#65533;nslor &#65533;r S&#65533;rade Tv&#65533;spr&#65533;kig Bilderbok F&#65533;r Barn. Carlson, Richard. 2019. (SWE.). 24p. (J). pap. 11.99 ***(978-1-6970-3931-3(6))*** Independently Published.

—Svenska-Kanaresiska Nummer/ಸಂಖ್ಯೆಗಳು Bildordbok F&#65533;r Tv&#65533;spr&#65533;kiga Barn. Carlson, Richard. 2019. (SWE.). 26p. (J). pap. 11.99 ***(978-1-7126-4761-5(X))*** Independently Published.

—Svenska-Kanaresiska Skolan Barns Tv&#65533;spr&#65533;kiga Bildordbok. Carlson, Richard. 2019. (SWE.). 24p. (J). pap. 11.99 ***(978-1-7041-6743-5(4))*** Independently Published.

—Svenska-Kanaresiska Tid Tv&#65533;spr&#65533;kig Bilderbok F&#65533;r Barn. Carlson, Richard. 2019. (SWE.). 28p. (J). pap. 11.99 ***(978-1-7006-2021-7(5))*** Independently Published.

Carlson, Suzanne. Svenska-Kanaresiska Trubbel/ತೊಂದರೆ Tvåspråkig Bilderbok För Barn. Carlson, Richard. 2019. (SWE.). 24p. (J). pap. 11.99 *(978-1-0736-1076-1(4))* Independently Published.

Carlson, Suzanne. Svenska-Kanaresiska Verktyg Barns Tv&#65533;spr&#65533;kiga Bildordbok. Carlson, Richard. 2019. (SWE.). 26p. (J). pap. 11.99 ***(978-1-6917-5920-0(1))*** Independently Published.

—Svenska-Kastiliansk Spanska Fordon/Veh&#65533;culos Barns Tv&#65533;spr&#65533;kiga Bildordbok. Carlson, Richard. 2019. (SWE.). 24p. (J). pap. 11.99 ***(978-1-6900-6056-7(5))*** Independently Published.

—Svenska-Kastiliansk Spanska Mina K&#65533;nslor &#65533;r S&#65533;rade/Han Herido Mis Sentimientos Tv&#65533;spr&#65533;kig Bilderbok F&#65533;r Barn. Carlson, Richard. 2019. (SWE.). 24p. (J). pap. 11.99 ***(978-1-6981-6605-6(2))*** Independently Published.

—Svenska-Kastiliansk Spanska Nummer/N&#65533;meros Bildordbok F&#65533;r Tv&#65533;spr&#65533;kiga Barn. Carlson, Richard. 2019. (SWE.). 26p. (J). pap. 11.99 ***(978-1-6701-7869-5(2))*** Independently Published.

—Svenska-Kastiliansk Spanska Skolan/Escuela Barns Tv&#65533;spr&#65533;kiga Bildordbok. Carlson, Richard. 2019. (SWE.). 24p. (J). pap. 11.99 ***(978-1-7053-8924-9(4))*** Independently Published.

—Svenska-Kastiliansk Spanska Tid/Tiempo Tv&#65533;spr&#65533;kig Bilderbok F&#65533;r Barn. Carlson, Richard. 2019. (SWE.). 28p. (J). pap. 11.99 ***(978-1-7019-1633-3(9))*** Independently Published.

Carlson, Suzanne. Svenska-Kastiliansk Spanska Trubbel/Problema Tvåspråkig Bilderbok För Barn. Carlson, Richard. 2019. (SWE.). 24p. (J). pap. 11.99 *(978-1-0742-6356-0(1))* Independently Published.

Carlson, Suzanne. Svenska-Kastiliansk Spanska Verktyg/Herramientas Barns Tv&#65533;spr&#65533;kiga Bildordbok. Carlson, Richard. 2019. (SWE.). 26p. (J). pap. 11.99 ***(978-1-6930-9832-1(6))*** Independently Published.

—Svenska-Katalanska Mina K&#65533;nslor &#65533;r S&#65533;rade/M'han Ferit Els Meus Sentiments Tv&#65533;spr&#65533;kig Bilderbok F&#65533;r Barn. Carlson, Richard. 2019. (SWE.). 24p. (J). pap. 11.99 ***(978-1-6968-0474-5(4))*** Independently Published.

—Svenska-Katalanska Nummer/Els Nombres Bildordbok F&#65533;r Tv&#65533;spr&#65533;kiga Barn. Carlson, Richard. 2019. (SWE.). 26p. (J). pap. 11.99 ***(978-1-7110-2503-2(8))*** Independently Published.

—Svenska-Katalanska Skolan/Escola Barns Tv&#65533;spr&#65533;kiga Bildordbok. Carlson, Richard. 2019. (SWE.). 24p. (J). pap. 11.99 ***(978-1-7028-7372-7(2))*** Independently Published.

—Svenska-Katalanska Tid/el Temps Tv&#65533;spr&#65533;kig Bilderbok F&#65533;r Barn. Carlson, Richard. 2019. (SWE.). 28p. (J). pap. 11.99 ***(978-1-6988-9826-1(6))*** Independently Published.

Carlson, Suzanne. Svenska-Katalanska Trubbel/Problemes Tvåspråkig Bilderbok För Barn. Carlson, Richard. 2019. (SWE.). 24p. (J). pap. 11.99 *(978-1-0730-0859-9(2))* Independently Published.

Carlson, Suzanne. Svenska-Katalanska Verktyg/Eines Barns Tv&#65533;spr&#65533;kiga Bildordbok. Carlson, Richard. 2019. (SWE.). 26p. (J). pap. 11.99 ***(978-1-6908-7059-3(1))*** Independently Published.

—Svenska-Kazakiska Mina K&#65533;nslor &#65533;r S&#65533;rade/Сезімталбалатуралыоқиға Tv&#65533;spr&#65533;kig Bilderbok F&#65533;r Barn. Carlson, Richard. 2019. (SWE.). 24p. (J). pap. 11.99 ***(978-1-6971-3566-4(8))*** Independently Published.

—Svenska-Kazakiska Skolan/Мектеп; Barns Tv&#65533;spr&#65533;kiga Bildordbok. Carlson, Richard. 2019. (SWE.). 24p. (J). pap. 11.99 ***(978-1-7044-1236-8(6))*** Independently Published.

—Svenska-Kazakiska Tid/Уақыт Tv&#65533;spr&#65533;kig Bilderbok F&#65533;r Barn. Carlson, Richard. 2019. (SWE.). 28p. (J). pap. 11.99 ***(978-1-7009-9519-3(7))*** Independently Published.

Carlson, Suzanne. Svenska-Kazakiska Trubbel/Бәлеге қалу Tvåspråkig Bilderbok För Barn. Carlson, Richard. 2019. (SWE.). 24p. (J). pap. 11.99 *(978-1-0736-1277-2(5))* Independently Published.

Carlson, Suzanne. Svenska-Kazakiska Verktyg/Құрал-саймандар Barns Tv&#65533;spr&#65533;kiga Bildordbok. Carlson, Richard. 2019. (SWE.). 26p. (J). pap. 11.99 ***(978-1-6917-6489-1(2))*** Independently Published.

—Svenska-Khmer (kambodjanska) Fordon Barns Tv&#65533;spr&#65533;kiga Bildordbok. Carlson, Richard. 2019. (SWE.). 24p. (J). pap. 11.99 ***(978-1-6898-4753-7(0))*** Independently Published.

—Svenska-Khmer (kambodjanska) Mina K&#65533;nslor &#65533;r S&#65533;rade/ខ្ញុំមានអារម្មណ៍ឈឺចាប់ Tv&#65533;spr&#65533;kig Bilderbok F&#65533;r Barn. Carlson, Richard. 2019. (SWE.). 24p. (J). pap. 11.99 ***(978-1-6971-3891-7(8))*** Independently Published.

—Svenska-Khmer (kambodjanska) Nummer/ចំនួនលេខ Bildordbok F&#65533;r Tv&#65533;spr&#65533;kiga Barn. Carlson, Richard. 2019. (SWE.). 26p. (J). pap. 11.99 ***(978-1-7127-2207-7(7))*** Independently Published.

—Svenska-Khmer (kambodjanska) Skolan Barns Tv&#65533;spr&#65533;kiga Bildordbok. Carlson, Richard. 2019. (SWE.). 24p. (J). pap. 11.99 ***(978-1-7044-1440-9(7))*** Independently Published.

—Svenska-Khmer (kambodjanska) Tid Tv&#65533;spr&#65533;kig Bilderbok F&#65533;r Barn. Carlson, Richard. 2019. (SWE.). 28p. (J). pap. 11.99 ***(978-1-7011-4138-4(8))*** Independently Published.

Carlson, Suzanne. Svenska-Khmer (kambodjanska) Trubbel/បញ្ហ Tvåspråkig Bilderbok För Barn. Carlson, Richard. 2019. (SWE.). 24p. (J). pap. 11.99 *(978-1-0736-1566-7(9))* Independently Published.

Carlson, Suzanne. Svenska-Khmer (kambodjanska) Verktyg Barns Tv&#65533;spr&#65533;kiga Bildordbok. Carlson, Richard. 2019. (SWE.). 26p. (J). pap. 11.99 ***(978-1-6917-7386-2(7))*** Independently Published.

—Svenska-Koreanska Fordon/운송수단 Barns Tv&#65533;spr&#65533;kiga Bildordbok. Carlson, Richard. 2019. (SWE.). 24p. (J). pap. 11.99 ***(978-1-6898-4908-1(8))*** Independently Published.

—Svenska-Koreanska Mina K&#65533;nslor &#65533;r S&#65533;rade/마음이 아팠어요 Tv&#65533;spr&#65533;kig Bilderbok F&#65533;r Barn. Carlson, Richard. 2019. (SWE.). 24p. (J). pap. 11.99 ***(978-1-6971-5461-0(1))*** Independently Published.

—Svenska-Koreanska Nummer/숫자 Bildordbok F&#65533;r Tv&#65533;spr&#65533;kiga Barn. Carlson, Richard. 2019. (SWE.). 26p. (J). pap. 11.99 ***(978-1-7127-2588-7(2))*** Independently Published.

—Svenska-Koreanska Skolan/학교 Barns Tv&#65533;spr&#65533;kiga Bildordbok. Carlson, Richard. 2019. (SWE.). 24p. (J). pap. 11.99 ***(978-1-7044-1641-0(8))*** Independently Published.

—Svenska-Koreanska Tid/시간 Tv&#65533;spr&#65533;kig Bilderbok F&#65533;r Barn. Carlson, Richard. 2019. (SWE.). 28p. (J). pap. 11.99 ***(978-1-7011-9089-4(3))*** Independently Published.

Carlson, Suzanne. Svenska-Koreanska Trubbel/장난 Tvåspråkig Bilderbok För Barn. Carlson, Richard. 2019. (SWE.). 24p. (J). pap. 11.99 *(978-1-0736-1769-2(6))* Independently Published.

Carlson, Suzanne. Svenska-Koreanska Verktyg/공구들 Barns Tv&#65533;spr&#65533;kiga Bildordbok. Carlson, Richard. 2019. (SWE.). 26p. (J). pap. 11.99 ***(978-1-6919-1169-1(0))*** Independently Published.

—Svenska-Kroatiska Fordon/Vozila Barns Tv&#65533;spr&#65533;kiga Bildordbok. Carlson, Richard. 2019. (SWE.). 24p. (J). pap. 11.99 ***(978-1-6890-8267-9(4))*** Independently Published.

—Svenska-Kroatiska Mina K&#65533;nslor &#65533;r S&#65533;rade/Moji Osjecaji Su Povrijeđeni Tv&#65533;spr&#65533;kig Bilderbok F&#65533;r Barn. Carlson, Richard. 2019. (SWE.). 24p. (J). pap. 11.99 ***(978-1-6968-1577-2(0))*** Independently Published.

—Svenska-Kroatiska Nummer/Brojevi Bildordbok F&#65533;r Tv&#65533;spr&#65533;kiga Barn. Carlson, Richard. 2019. (SWE.). 26p. (J). pap. 11.99 ***(978-1-7110-5482-7(8))*** Independently Published.

—Svenska-Kroatiska Skolan/Skola Barns Tv&#65533;spr&#65533;kiga Bildordbok. Carlson, Richard. 2019. (SWE.). 24p. (J). pap. 11.99 ***(978-1-7031-8126-5(3))*** Independently Published.

—Svenska-Kroatiska Tid/Vrijeme Tv&#65533;spr&#65533;kig Bilderbok F&#65533;r Barn. Carlson, Richard. 2019. (SWE.). 28p. (J). pap. 11.99 ***(978-1-6995-1525-9(5))*** Independently Published.

Carlson, Suzanne. Svenska-Kroatiska Trubbel/Nevolja Tvåspråkig Bilderbok För Barn. Carlson, Richard. 2019. (SWE.). 24p. (J). pap. 11.99 *(978-1-0731-3565-3(9))* Independently Published.

Carlson, Suzanne. Svenska-Kroatiska Verktyg/Alati Barns Tv&#65533;spr&#65533;kiga Bildordbok. Carlson, Richard. 2019. (SWE.). 26p. (J). pap. 11.99 ***(978-1-6908-9918-1(2))*** Independently Published.

—Svenska-Kurdiska Fordon Barns Tv&#65533;spr&#65533;kiga Bildordbok. Carlson, Richard. 2019. (SWE.). 24p. (J). pap. 11.99 ***(978-1-6898-5066-7(3))*** Independently Published.

—Svenska-Kurdiska Nummer/ژمارەکان Bildordbok F&#65533;r Tv&#65533;spr&#65533;kiga Barn. Carlson, Richard. 2019. (SWE.). 26p. (J). pap. 11.99 ***(978-1-7127-3134-5(3))*** Independently Published.

—Svenska-Kurdiska Skolan/قوتابخانە Barns Tv&#65533;spr&#65533;kiga Bildordbok. Carlson, Richard. 2019. (SWE.). 24p. (J). pap. 11.99 ***(978-1-7044-1810-0(0))*** Independently Published.

—Svenska-Kurdiska Tid/کات Tv&#65533;spr&#65533;kig Bilderbok F&#65533;r Barn. Carlson, Richard. 2019. (SWE.). 28p. (J). pap. 11.99 ***(978-1-7013-8374-6(8))*** Independently Published.

Carlson, Suzanne. Svenska-Kurdiska Trubbel/کێشە Tvåspråkig Bilderbok För Barn. Carlson, Richard. 2019. (SWE.). 24p. (J). pap. 11.99 *(978-1-0736-2042-5(5))* Independently Published.

Carlson, Suzanne. Svenska-Kurdiska Verktyg Barns Tv&#65533;spr&#65533;kiga Bildordbok. Carlson, Richard. 2019. (SWE.). 26p. (J). pap. 11.99 ***(978-1-6919-1589-7(0))*** Independently Published.

—Svenska-Lao (Laos) Fordon Barns Tv&#65533;spr&#65533;kiga Bildordbok. Carlson, Richard. 2019. (SWE.). 24p. (J). pap. 11.99 ***(978-1-6898-5327-9(1))*** Independently Published.

—Svenska-Lao (Laos) Mina K&#65533;nslor &#65533;r S&#65533;rade Tv&#65533;spr&#65533;kig Bilderbok F&#65533;r Barn. Carlson, Richard. 2019. (SWE.). 24p. (J). pap. 11.99 ***(978-1-6971-5928-8(1))*** Independently Published.

—Svenska-Lao (Laos) Nummer/ເລກຈໍານວນ Bildordbok F&#65533;r Tv&#65533;spr&#65533;kiga Barn. Carlson, Richard. 2019. (SWE.). 26p. (J). pap. 11.99 ***(978-1-7127-5133-6(6))*** Independently Published.

—Svenska-Lao (Laos) Skolan/ໂຮງຮຽນ Barns Tv&#65533;spr&#65533;kiga Bildordbok. Carlson, Richard. 2019. (SWE.). 24p. (J). pap. 11.99 ***(978-1-7044-2051-6(2))*** Independently Published.

—Svenska-Lao (Laos) Tid Tv&#65533;spr&#65533;kig Bilderbok F&#65533;r Barn. Carlson, Richard. 2019. (SWE.). 28p. (J). pap. 11.99 ***(978-1-7013-8731-7(X))*** Independently Published.

Carlson, Suzanne. Svenska-Lao (Laos) Trubbel Tvåspråkig Bilderbok För Barn. Carlson, Richard. 2019. (SWE.). 24p. (J). pap. 11.99 *(978-1-0737-5465-6(0))* Independently Published.

Carlson, Suzanne. Svenska-Lao (Laos) Verktyg Barns Tv&#65533;spr&#65533;kiga Bildordbok. Carlson, Richard. 2019. (SWE.). 26p. (J). pap. 11.99 ***(978-1-6919-2010-5(X))*** Independently Published.

—Svenska-Latinamerikansk Spanska Fordon/Veh&#65533;culos Barns Tv&#65533;spr&#65533;kiga Bildordbok. Carlson, Richard. 2019. (SWE.). 24p. (J). pap. 11.99 ***(978-1-6900-6212-7(6))*** Independently Published.

—Svenska-Latinamerikansk Spanska Mina K&#65533;nslor &#65533;r S&#65533;rade/Han Herido Mis Sentimientos Tv&#65533;spr&#65533;kig Bilderbok F&#65533;r Barn. Carlson, Richard. 2019. (SWE.). 24p. (J). pap. 11.99 ***(978-1-6981-7054-1(8))*** Independently Published.

—Svenska-Latinamerikansk Spanska Nummer/N&#65533;meros Bildordbok F&#65533;r Tv&#65533;spr&#65533;kiga Barn. Carlson, Richard. 2019. (SWE.). 26p. (J). pap. 11.99 ***(978-1-6701-8216-6(9))*** Independently Published.

—Svenska-Latinamerikansk Spanska Skolan/Escuela Barns Tv&#65533;spr&#65533;kiga Bildordbok. Carlson, Richard. 2019. (SWE.). 24p. (J). pap. 11.99 ***(978-1-7053-9046-7(3))*** Independently Published.

—Svenska-Latinamerikansk Spanska Tid/Tiempo Tv&#65533;spr&#65533;kig Bilderbok F&#65533;r Barn. Carlson, Richard. 2019. (SWE.). 28p. (J). pap. 11.99 ***(978-1-7019-1723-1(8))*** Independently Published.

Carlson, Suzanne. Svenska-Latinamerikansk Spanska Trubbel/Problema Tvåspråkig Bilderbok För Barn. Carlson, Richard. 2019. (SWE.). 24p. (J). pap. 11.99 *(978-1-0742-6498-7(3))* Independently Published.

Carlson, Suzanne. Svenska-Latinamerikansk Spanska Verktyg/Herramientas Barns Tv&#65533;spr&#65533;kiga Bildordbok. Carlson, Richard. 2019. (SWE.). 26p. (J). pap. 11.99 ***(978-1-6931-0154-0(8))*** Independently Published.

—Svenska-Lettiska Fordon/Transporta līdzekļi Barns Tv�spr�kiga Bildordbok. Carlson, Richard. 2019. (SWE.). 24p. (J). pap. 11.99 ***(978-1-6898-6311-7(0))*** Independently Published.

—Svenska-Lettiska Mina K�nslor �r S�rade/Es Esmu Sāpināts Tv�spr�kig Bilderbok F�r Barn. Carlson, Richard. 2019. (SWE.). 24p. (J). pap. 11.99 ***(978-1-6971-6434-3(X))*** Independently Published.

—Svenska-Lettiska Nummer/Skaitļi Bildordbok F�r Tv�spr�kiga Barn. Carlson, Richard. 2019. (SWE.). 26p. (J). pap. 11.99 ***(978-1-7127-5494-8(7))*** Independently Published.

—Svenska-Lettiska Skolan/Skola Barns Tv�spr�kiga Bildordbok. Carlson, Richard. 2019. (SWE.). 24p. (J). pap. 11.99 ***(978-1-7044-2346-3(5))*** Independently Published.

—Svenska-Lettiska Tid/Laiks Tv�spr�kig Bilderbok F�r Barn. Carlson, Richard. 2019. (SWE.). 28p. (J). pap. 11.99 ***(978-1-7014-0378-9(1))*** Independently Published.

Carlson, Suzanne. Svenska-Lettiska Trubbel/Nelāgs Notikums Tvåspråkig Bilderbok För Barn. Carlson, Richard. 2019. (SWE.). 24p. (J). pap. 11.99 *(978-1-0737-8522-3(X))* Independently Published.

Carlson, Suzanne. Svenska-Lettiska Verktyg/Darbarīki Barns Tv�spr�kiga Bildordbok. Carlson, Richard. 2019. (SWE.). 26p. (J). pap. 11.99 ***(978-1-6919-2725-8(2))*** Independently Published.

—Svenska-Levantinsk Arabiska Fordon Barns Tv�spr�kiga Bildordbok. Carlson, Richard. 2019. (SWE.). 24p. (J). pap. 11.99 ***(978-1-6886-3599-9(8))*** Independently Published.

—Svenska-Levantinsk Arabiska Nummer/الأعداد Bildordbok F�r Tv�spr�kiga Barn. Carlson, Richard. 2019. (SWE.). 26p. (J). pap. 11.99 ***(978-1-7098-2258-2(9))*** Independently Published.

—Svenska-Levantinsk Arabiska Skolan Barns Tv�spr�kiga Bildordbok. Carlson, Richard. 2019. (SWE.). 24p. (J). pap. 11.99 ***(978-1-7026-6409-7(0))*** Independently Published.

—Svenska-Litauiska Fordon/Transporto Priemones Barns Tv�spr�kiga Bildordbok. Carlson, Richard. 2019. (SWE.). 24p. (J). pap. 11.99 ***(978-1-6898-7026-9(5))*** Independently Published.

—Svenska-Litauiska Mina K�nslor �r S�rade/Mane įskaudino Tv�spr�kig Bilderbok F�r Barn. Carlson, Richard. 2019. (SWE.). 24p. (J). pap. 11.99 ***(978-1-6972-5641-3(4))*** Independently Published.

—Svenska-Litauiska Skolan/Mokykla Barns Tv�spr�kiga Bildordbok. Carlson, Richard. 2019. (SWE.). 24p. (J). pap. 11.99 ***(978-1-7044-2573-3(5))*** Independently Published.

—Svenska-Litauiska Tid/Laikas Tv�spr�kig Bilderbok F�r Barn. Carlson, Richard. 2019. (SWE.). 28p. (J). pap. 11.99 ***(978-1-7014-0547-9(4))*** Independently Published.

Carlson, Suzanne. Svenska-Litauiska Trubbel/Beda Tvåspråkig Bilderbok För Barn. Carlson, Richard. 2019. (SWE.). 24p. (J). pap. 11.99 *(978-1-0737-8765-4(6))* Independently Published.

Carlson, Suzanne. Svenska-Maghrebarabiska Fordon Barns Tv�spr�kiga Bildordbok. Carlson, Richard. 2019. (SWE.). 24p. (J). pap. 11.99 ***(978-1-6886-3801-3(6))*** Independently Published.

—Svenska-Maghrebarabiska Nummer/الأعداد Bildordbok F�r Tv�spr�kiga Barn. Carlson, Richard. 2019. (SWE.). 26p. (J). pap. 11.99 ***(978-1-7101-2041-7(X))*** Independently Published.

—Svenska-Maghrebarabiska Skolan Barns Tv�spr�kiga Bildordbok. Carlson, Richard. 2019. (SWE.). 24p. (J). pap. 11.99 ***(978-1-7026-6706-7(5))*** Independently Published.

—Svenska-Makedonska Fordon/Возила Barns Tv�spr�kiga Bildordbok. Carlson, Richard. 2019. (SWE.). 24p. (J). pap. 11.99 ***(978-1-6898-7185-3(7))*** Independently Published.

—Svenska-Makedonska Mina K�nslor �r S�rade/Моите
чувства се
повредени Tv�spr�kig Bilderbok F�r Barn. Carlson, Richard. 2019. (SWE.). 24p. (J). pap. 11.99 ***(978-1-6972-6065-6(9))*** Independently Published.

—Svenska-Makedonska Nummer/Броеви Bildordbok F�r Tv�spr�kiga Barn. Carlson, Richard. 2019. (SWE.). 26p. (J). pap. 11.99 ***(978-1-7130-1730-1(X))*** Independently Published.

—Svenska-Makedonska Skolan/Училиште Barns Tv�spr�kiga Bildordbok. Carlson, Richard. 2019. (SWE.). 24p. (J). pap. 11.99 ***(978-1-7044-2941-0(2))*** Independently Published.

—Svenska-Makedonska Tid/Време Tv�spr�kig Bilderbok F�r Barn. Carlson, Richard. 2019. (SWE.). 28p. (J). pap. 11.99 ***(978-1-7014-1853-0(3))*** Independently Published.

Carlson, Suzanne. Svenska-Makedonska Trubbel/Беља Tvåspråkig Bilderbok För Barn. Carlson, Richard. 2019. (SWE.). 24p. (J). pap. 11.99 *(978-1-0737-8948-1(9))* Independently Published.

Carlson, Suzanne. Svenska-Makedonska Verktyg/Алати Barns Tv�spr�kiga Bildordbok. Carlson, Richard. 2019. (SWE.). 26p. (J). pap. 11.99 ***(978-1-6919-5195-6(1))*** Independently Published.

—Svenska-Malay Fordon/Kenderaan Barns Tv�spr�kiga Bildordbok. Carlson, Richard. 2019. (SWE.). 24p. (J). pap. 11.99 ***(978-1-6898-7364-2(7))*** Independently Published.

—Svenska-Malay Mina K�nslor �r S�rade/Perasaan Saya Disakiti Tv�spr�kig Bilderbok F�r Barn. Carlson, Richard. 2019. (SWE.). 24p. (J). pap. 11.99 ***(978-1-6972-6318-3(6))*** Independently Published.

—Svenska-Malay Nummer/Nombor Bildordbok F�r Tv�spr�kiga Barn. Carlson, Richard. 2019. (SWE.). 26p. (J). pap. 11.99 ***(978-1-7130-8251-4(9))*** Independently Published.

—Svenska-Malay Skolan/Sekolah Barns Tv�spr�kiga Bildordbok. Carlson, Richard. 2019. (SWE.). 24p. (J). pap. 11.99 ***(978-1-7046-4933-7(1))*** Independently Published.

—Svenska-Malay Tid/Masa Tv�spr�kig Bilderbok F�r Barn. Carlson, Richard. 2019. (SWE.). 28p. (J). pap. 11.99 ***(978-1-7014-2022-9(8))*** Independently Published.

Carlson, Suzanne. Svenska-Malay Trubbel/Masalah Tvåspråkig Bilderbok För Barn. Carlson, Richard. 2019. (SWE.). 24p. (J). pap. 11.99 *(978-1-0737-9201-6(3))* Independently Published.

Carlson, Suzanne. Svenska-Malay Verktyg/Alat Barns Tv�spr�kiga Bildordbok. Carlson, Richard. 2019. (SWE.). 26p. (J). pap. 11.99 ***(978-1-6919-5360-8(1))*** Independently Published.

—Svenska-Malayalam Fordon Barns Tv�spr�kiga Bildordbok. Carlson, Richard. 2019. (SWE.). 24p. (J). pap. 11.99 ***(978-1-6898-7521-9(6))*** Independently Published.

—Svenska-Malayalam Mina K�nslor �r S�rade Tv�spr�kig Bilderbok F�r Barn. Carlson, Richard. 2019. (SWE.). 24p. (J). pap. 11.99 ***(978-1-6972-6730-3(0))*** Independently Published.

—Svenska-Malayalam Nummer/സംഖ്യകൾ Bildordbok F�r Tv�spr�kiga Barn. Carlson, Richard. 2019. (SWE.). 26p. (J). pap. 11.99 ***(978-1-7130-8772-4(3))*** Independently Published.

—Svenska-Malayalam Skolan Barns Tv�spr�kiga Bildordbok. Carlson, Richard. 2019. (SWE.). 24p. (J). pap. 11.99 ***(978-1-7046-5311-2(8))*** Independently Published.

—Svenska-Malayalam Tid Tv�spr�kig Bilderbok F�r Barn. Carlson, Richard. 2019. (SWE.). 28p. (J). pap. 11.99 ***(978-1-7004-1242-3(6))*** Independently Published.

Carlson, Suzanne. Svenska-Malayalam Trubbel/ബുദ്ധിമുട്ടിക്കുക Tvåspråkig Bilderbok För Barn. Carlson, Richard. 2019. (SWE.). 24p. (J). pap. 11.99 *(978-1-0737-9481-2(4))* Independently Published.

Carlson, Suzanne. Svenska-Malayalam Verktyg Barns Tv�spr�kiga Bildordbok. Carlson, Richard. 2019. (SWE.). 26p. (J). pap. 11.99 ***(978-1-6919-5461-2(6))*** Independently Published.

—Svenska-Maltesiska Fordon/Vetturi Barns Tv�spr�kiga Bildordbok. Carlson, Richard. 2019. (SWE.). 24p. (J). pap. 11.99 ***(978-1-6898-7772-5(3))*** Independently Published.

—Svenska-Maltesiska Mina K�nslor �r S�rade/Weġġgħuni Tv�spr�kig Bilderbok F�r Barn. Carlson, Richard. 2019. (SWE.). 24p. (J). pap. 11.99 ***(978-1-6972-7393-9(9))*** Independently Published.

—Svenska-Maltesiska Nummer/Numri Bildordbok F�r Tv�spr�kiga Barn. Carlson, Richard. 2019. (SWE.). 26p. (J). pap. 11.99 ***(978-1-7130-9887-4(3))*** Independently Published.

—Svenska-Maltesiska Skolan/Skola Barns Tv�spr�kiga Bildordbok. Carlson, Richard. 2019. (SWE.). 24p. (J). pap. 11.99 ***(978-1-7046-5431-7(9))*** Independently Published.

—Svenska-Maltesiska Tid/Il-Ħin Tv�spr�kig Bilderbok F�r Barn. Carlson, Richard. 2019. (SWE.). 28p. (J). pap. 11.99 ***(978-1-7014-2174-5(7))*** Independently Published.

Carlson, Suzanne. Svenska-Maltesiska Trubbel/Inkwiet Tvåspråkig Bilderbok För Barn. Carlson, Richard. 2019. (SWE.). 24p. (J). pap. 11.99 *(978-1-0740-4506-7(8))* Independently Published.

Carlson, Suzanne. Svenska-Maltesiska Verktyg/Għodda Barns Tv�spr�kiga Bildordbok. Carlson, Richard. 2019. (SWE.). 26p. (J). pap. 11.99 ***(978-1-6919-5550-3(7))*** Independently Published.

—Svenska-Marathi Fordon Barns Tv�spr�kiga Bildordbok. Carlson, Richard. 2019. (SWE.). 24p. (J). pap. 11.99 ***(978-1-6898-8522-5(X))*** Independently Published.

—Svenska-Marathi Mina K�nslor �r S�rade/माझ्या भावना दुखावल्या गेल्या आहेत Tv. Carlson, Richard. 2019. (SWE.). 24p. (J). pap. 11.99 ***(978-1-6972-7954-2(6))*** Independently Published.

—Svenska-Marathi Nummer/अंक Bildordbok F�r Tv�spr�kiga Barn. Carlson, Richard. 2019. (SWE.). 26p. (J). pap. 11.99 ***(978-1-7131-0188-8(2))*** Independently Published.

—Svenska-Marathi Skolan/शाळा Barns Tv�spr�kiga Bildordbok. Carlson, Richard. 2019. (SWE.). 24p. (J). pap. 11.99 ***(978-1-7046-5535-2(8))*** Independently Published.

—Svenska-Marathi Tid/वेळ Tv�spr�kig Bilderbok F�r Barn. Carlson, Richard. 2019. (SWE.). 28p. (J). pap. 11.99 ***(978-1-7014-2360-2(X))*** Independently Published.

Carlson, Suzanne. Svenska-Marathi Trubbel/त्रास Tvåspråkig Bilderbok För Barn. Carlson, Richard. 2019. (SWE.). 24p. (J). pap. 11.99 *(978-1-0740-6962-9(5))* Independently Published.

Carlson, Suzanne. Svenska-Mongoliska Fordon/Тээврийн хэрэгсэл Barns Tv�spr�kiga Bildordbok. Carlson, Richard. 2019. (SWE.). 24p. (J). pap. 11.99 ***(978-1-6898-8653-6(6))*** Independently Published.

—Svenska-Mongoliska Mina K�nslor �r S�rade/Би гомдож байна Tv�spr�kig Bilderbok F�r Barn. Carlson, Richard. 2019. (SWE.). 24p. (J). pap. 11.99 ***(978-1-6974-9813-4(2))*** Independently Published.

—Svenska-Mongoliska Nummer/Тоо Bildordbok F�r Tv�spr�kiga Barn. Carlson, Richard. 2019. (SWE.). 26p. (J). pap. 11.99 ***(978-1-6701-0840-1(6))*** Independently Published.

—Svenska-Mongoliska Skolan/Сургууль Barns Tv�spr�kiga Bildordbok. Carlson, Richard. 2019. (SWE.). 24p. (J). pap. 11.99 ***(978-1-7048-0643-3(7))*** Independently Published.

—Svenska-Mongoliska Tid/Цаг хугацаа Tv�spr�kig Bilderbok F�r Barn. Carlson, Richard. 2019. (SWE.). 28p. (J). pap. 11.99 ***(978-1-7014-2544-6(0))*** Independently Published.

Carlson, Suzanne. Svenska-Mongoliska Trubbel/Хэрэгт орсон нь Tvåspråkig Bilderbok För Barn. Carlson, Richard. 2019. (SWE.). 24p. (J). pap. 11.99 *(978-1-0740-7114-1(X))* Independently Published.

Carlson, Suzanne. Svenska-Mongoliska Verktyg/Багаж Barns Tv�spr�kiga Bildordbok. Carlson, Richard. 2019. (SWE.). 26p. (J). pap. 11.99 ***(978-1-6919-6098-9(5))*** Independently Published.

—Svenska-Montenegrinska Fordon/Vozila Barns Tv�spr�kiga Bildordbok. Carlson, Richard. 2019. (SWE.). 24p. (J). pap. 11.99 ***(978-1-6898-8852-3(0))*** Independently Published.

—Svenska-Montenegrinska Mina K�nslor �r S�rade/Moja Osjecanja Su Povrijeđena Tv�spr�kig Bilderbok F�r Barn. Carlson, Richard. 2019. (SWE.). 24p. (J). pap. 11.99 ***(978-1-6974-9927-8(9))*** Independently Published.

—Svenska-Montenegrinska Nummer/Бројеви Bildordbok F�r Tv�spr�kiga Barn. Carlson, Richard. 2019. (SWE.). 26p. (J). pap. 11.99 ***(978-1-6701-1071-8(0))*** Independently Published.

—Svenska-Montenegrinska Skolan/Skola Barns Tv�spr�kiga Bildordbok. Carlson, Richard. 2019. (SWE.). 24p. (J). pap. 11.99 ***(978-1-7048-0900-7(2))*** Independently Published.

—Svenska-Montenegrinska Tid/Vrijeme Tv�spr�kig Bilderbok F�r Barn. Carlson, Richard. 2019. (SWE.). 28p. (J). pap. 11.99 ***(978-1-7014-4539-0(5))*** Independently Published.

Carlson, Suzanne. Svenska-Montenegrinska Trubbel/Nevolja Tvåspråkig Bilderbok För Barn. Carlson, Richard. 2019. (SWE.). 24p. (J). pap. 11.99 *(978-1-0740-7358-9(4))* Independently Published.

Carlson, Suzanne. Svenska-Montenegrinska Verktyg/Алати Barns Tv�spr�kiga Bildordbok. Carlson, Richard. 2019. (SWE.). 26p. (J). pap. 11.99 ***(978-1-6921-8162-8(9))*** Independently Published.

—Svenska-Nepalesiska Fordon Barns Tv�spr�kiga Bildordbok. Carlson, Richard. 2019. (SWE.). 24p. (J). pap. 11.99 ***(978-1-6898-9081-6(9))*** Independently Published.

—Svenska-Nepalesiska Mina K�nslor �r S�rade/मेरो भावनामा चोट पुगेको छ Tv�spr�kig Bilderbok F�r Barn. Carlson, Richard. 2019. (SWE.). 24p. (J). pap. 11.99 ***(978-1-6975-0122-3(2))*** Independently Published.

—Svenska-Nepalesiska Nummer/संख्याहरू Bildordbok F�r Tv�spr�kiga Barn. Carlson, Richard. 2019. (SWE.). 26p. (J). pap. 11.99 ***(978-1-6701-1441-9(4))*** Independently Published.

—Svenska-Nepalesiska Skolan Barns Tv�spr�kiga Bildordbok. Carlson, Richard. 2019. (SWE.). 24p. (J). pap. 11.99 ***(978-1-7048-1692-0(0))*** Independently Published.

—Svenska-Nepalesiska Tid/समय Tv�spr�kig Bilderbok F�r Barn. Carlson, Richard. 2019. (SWE.). 28p. (J). pap. 11.99 ***(978-1-7016-3580-7(1))*** Independently Published.

Carlson, Suzanne. Svenska-Nepalesiska Trubbel/समस्या Tvåspråkig Bilderbok För Barn. Carlson, Richard. 2019. (SWE.). 24p. (J). pap. 11.99 *(978-1-0740-7594-1(3))* Independently Published.

Carlson, Suzanne. Svenska-Nepalesiska Verktyg Barns Tv�spr�kiga Bildordbok. Carlson, Richard. 2019. (SWE.). 26p. (J). pap. 11.99 ***(978-1-6921-8399-8(0))*** Independently Published.

—Svenska-Norska Fordon/Kj�ret�yer Barns Tv�spr�kiga Bildordbok. Carlson, Richard. 2019. (SWE.). 24p. (J). pap. 11.99 ***(978-1-6898-9336-7(2))*** Independently Published.

—Svenska-Norska Mina K�nslor �r S�rade/F�lelsene Mine Er S�ret Tv�spr�kig Bilderbok F�r Barn. Carlson, Richard. 2019. (SWE.). 24p. (J). pap. 11.99 ***(978-1-6975-0245-9(8))*** Independently Published.

—Svenska-Norska Nummer/Tall Bildordbok F�r Tv�spr�kiga Barn. Carlson, Richard. 2019. (SWE.). 26p. (J). pap. 11.99 ***(978-1-6701-1683-3(2))*** Independently Published.

—Svenska-Norska Skolan/Skole Barns Tv�spr�kiga Bildordbok. Carlson, Richard. 2019. (SWE.). 24p. (J). pap. 11.99 ***(978-1-7048-2661-5(6))*** Independently Published.

—Svenska-Norska Tid/Tid Tv�spr�kig Bilderbok F�r Barn. Carlson, Richard. 2019. (SWE.). 28p. (J). pap. 11.99 ***(978-1-7016-3968-3(8))*** Independently Published.

Carlson, Suzanne. Svenska-Norska Trubbel/Trøbbel Tvåspråkig Bilderbok För Barn. Carlson, Richard. 2019. (SWE.). 24p. (J). pap. 11.99 *(978-1-0740-7756-3(3))* Independently Published.

Carlson, Suzanne. Svenska-Norska Verktyg/Verkt�y Barns Tv�spr�kiga Bildordbok. Carlson, Richard. 2019. (SWE.). 26p. (J). pap. 11.99 ***(978-1-6921-8558-9(6))*** Independently Published.

—Svenska-Pashto Fordon Barns Tv�spr�kiga Bildordbok. Carlson, Richard. 2019. (SWE.). 24p. (J). pap. 11.99 ***(978-1-6900-2690-7(1))*** Independently Published.

—Svenska-Pashto Mina K�nslor �r S�rade Tv�spr�kig Bilderbok F�r Barn. Carlson, Richard. 2019. (SWE.). 24p. (J). pap. 11.99 ***(978-1-6975-0532-0(5))*** Independently Published.

—Svenska-Pashto Nummer/شم رېې Bildordbok F�r Tv�spr�kiga Barn. Carlson, Richard. 2019. (SWE.). 26p. (J). pap. 11.99 ***(978-1-6701-1879-0(7))*** Independently Published.

—Svenska-Pashto Skolan Barns Tv�spr�kiga Bildordbok. Carlson, Richard. 2019. (SWE.). 24p. (J). pap. 11.99 ***(978-1-7048-3934-9(3))*** Independently Published.

—Svenska-Pashto Tid Tv�spr�kig Bilderbok F�r Barn. Carlson, Richard. 2019. (SWE.). 28p. (J). pap. 11.99 ***(978-1-7016-4463-2(0))*** Independently Published.

Carlson, Suzanne. Svenska-Pashto Trubbel/مصیبت Tvåspråkig Bilderbok För Barn. Carlson, Richard. 2019. (SWE.). 24p. (J). pap. 11.99 *(978-1-0740-7924-6(8))* Independently Published.

Carlson, Suzanne. Svenska-Pashto Verktyg Barns Tv�spr�kiga Bildordbok. Carlson, Richard. 2019. (SWE.). 26p. (J). pap. 11.99 ***(978-1-6921-8934-1(4))*** Independently Published.

—Svenska-Persiska (farsi) Fordon Barns Tv�spr�kiga Bildordbok. Carlson, Richard. 2019. (SWE.). 24p. (J). pap. 11.99 ***(978-1-6900-2826-0(2))*** Independently Published.

—Svenska-Persiska (farsi) Mina K�nslor �r S�rade Tv�spr�kig Bilderbok F�r Barn. Carlson, Richard. 2019. (SWE.). 24p. (J). pap. 11.99 ***(978-1-6975-1040-9(X))*** Independently Published.

—Svenska-Persiska (farsi) Nummer/اعداد Bildordbok F�r Tv�spr�kiga Barn. Carlson, Richard. 2019. (SWE.). 26p. (J). pap. 11.99 ***(978-1-6701-2178-3(X))*** Independently Published.

—Svenska-Persiska (farsi) Skolan Barns Tv�spr�kiga Bildordbok. Carlson, Richard. 2019. (SWE.). 24p. (J). pap. 11.99 ***(978-1-7048-4157-1(7))*** Independently Published.

—Svenska-Persiska (farsi) Tid Tv�spr�kig Bilderbok F�r Barn. Carlson, Richard. 2019. (SWE.). 28p. (J). pap. 11.99 ***(978-1-7016-8424-9(1))*** Independently Published.

Carlson, Suzanne. Svenska-Persiska (farsi) Trubbel/دردسر Tvåspråkig Bilderbok För Barn. Carlson, Richard. 2019. (SWE.). 24p. (J). pap. 11.99 *(978-1-0742-1755-6(1))* Independently Published.

Carlson, Suzanne. Svenska-Persiska (farsi) Verktyg Barns Tv�spr�kiga Bildordbok. Carlson, Richard. 2019. (SWE.). 26p. (J). pap. 11.99 ***(978-1-6924-1807-6(6))*** Independently Published.

—Svenska-Polska Fordon/Pojazdy Barns Tv�spr�kiga Bildordbok. Carlson, Richard. 2019. (SWE.). 24p. (J). pap. 11.99 ***(978-1-6900-3434-6(3))*** Independently Published.

—Svenska-Polska Mina K�nslor �r S�rade/Zranione Uczucia Tv�spr�kig Bilderbok F�r Barn. Carlson, Richard. 2019. (SWE.). 24p. (J). pap. 11.99 ***(978-1-6975-1343-1(3))*** Independently Published.

—Svenska-Polska Nummer/Liczby Bildordbok F�r Tv�spr�kiga Barn. Carlson, Richard. 2019. (SWE.). 26p. (J). pap. 11.99 ***(978-1-6701-2337-4(5))*** Independently Published.

—Svenska-Polska Skolan/Szkola Barns Tv�spr�kiga Bildordbok. Carlson,

C

Richard. 2019. (SWE.). 24p. (J). pap. 11.99 ***(978-1-7048-4340-7(5))*** Independently Published.

—Svenska-Polska Tid/Czas Tv&#65533;spr&#65533;kig Bilderbok F&#65533;r Barn. Carlson, Richard. 2019. (SWE.). 28p. (J). pap. 11.99 ***(978-1-7016-8581-9(7))*** Independently Published.

Carlson, Suzanne. Svenska-Polska Trubbel/Klopoty Tvåspråkig Bilderbok För Barn. Carlson, Richard. 2019. (SWE.). 24p. (J). pap. 11.99 *(978-1-0742-1969-7(4))* Independently Published.

Carlson, Suzanne. Svenska-Polska Verktyg/Narzędzia Barns Tv&#65533;spr&#65533;kiga Bildordbok. Carlson, Richard. 2019. (SWE.). 26p. (J). pap. 11.99 ***(978-1-6924-2116-8(6))*** Independently Published.

—Svenska-Portugisiska (Brasilien) Fordon/Ve&#65533;culos Barns Tv&#65533;spr&#65533;kiga Bildordbok. Carlson, Richard. 2019. (SWE.). 24p. (J). pap. 11.99 ***(978-1-6900-3639-5(7))*** Independently Published.

—Svenska-Portugisiska (Brasilien) Mina K&#65533;nslor &#65533;r S&#65533;rade/Meus Sentimentos Est&#65533;o Feridos Tv&#65533;spr&#65533;kig Bilderbok F&#65533;r Barn. Carlson, Richard. 2019. (SWE.). 24p. (J). pap. 11.99 ***(978-1-6979-2037-6(3))*** Independently Published.

—Svenska-Portugisiska (Brasilien) Nummer/N&#65533;meros Bildordbok F&#65533;r Tv&#65533;spr&#65533;kiga Barn. Carlson, Richard. 2019. (SWE.). 26p. (J). pap. 11.99 ***(978-1-6701-2488-3(6))*** Independently Published.

—Svenska-Portugisiska (Brasilien) Skolan/Escola Barns Tv&#65533;spr&#65533;kiga Bildordbok. Carlson, Richard. 2019. (SWE.). 24p. (J). pap. 11.99 ***(978-1-7048-5166-2(1))*** Independently Published.

—Svenska-Portugisiska (Brasilien) Tid/Tempo Tv&#65533;spr&#65533;kig Bilderbok F&#65533;r Barn. Carlson, Richard. 2019. (SWE.). 28p. (J). pap. 11.99 ***(978-1-7016-8791-2(7))*** Independently Published.

Carlson, Suzanne. Svenska-Portugisiska (Brasilien) Trubbel/Encrenca Tvåspråkig Bilderbok För Barn. Carlson, Richard. 2019. (SWE.). 24p. (J). pap. 11.99 *(978-1-0742-2673-2(9))* Independently Published.

Carlson, Suzanne. Svenska-Portugisiska (Brasilien) Verktyg/Ferramentas Barns Tv&#65533;spr&#65533;kiga Bildordbok. Carlson, Richard. 2019. (SWE.). 26p. (J). pap. 11.99 ***(978-1-6924-2446-6(7))*** Independently Published.

—Svenska-Portugisiska (Portugal) Fordon/Ve&#65533;culos Barns Tv&#65533;spr&#65533;kiga Bildordbok. Carlson, Richard. 2019. (SWE.). 24p. (J). pap. 11.99 ***(978-1-6900-3748-4(2))*** Independently Published.

—Svenska-Portugisiska (Portugal) Mina K&#65533;nslor &#65533;r S&#65533;rade/Os Meus Sentimentos Est&#65533;o Feridos Tv&#65533;spr&#65533;kig Bilderbok F&#65533;r Barn. Carlson, Richard. 2019. (SWE.). 24p. (J). pap. 11.99 ***(978-1-6979-2091-8(8))*** Independently Published.

—Svenska-Portugisiska (Portugal) Nummer/N&#65533;meros Bildordbok F&#65533;r Tv&#65533;spr&#65533;kiga Barn. Carlson, Richard. 2019. (SWE.). 26p. (J). pap. 11.99 ***(978-1-6701-2633-7(1))*** Independently Published.

—Svenska-Portugisiska (Portugal) Skolan/Escola Barns Tv&#65533;spr&#65533;kiga Bildordbok. Carlson, Richard. 2019. (SWE.). 24p. (J). pap. 11.99 ***(978-1-7048-5269-0(2))*** Independently Published.

—Svenska-Portugisiska (Portugal) Tid/Tempo Tv&#65533;spr&#65533;kig Bilderbok F&#65533;r Barn. Carlson, Richard. 2019. (SWE.). 28p. (J). pap. 11.99 ***(978-1-7016-8938-1(3))*** Independently Published.

Carlson, Suzanne. Svenska-Portugisiska (Portugal) Trubbel/Sarilhos Tvåspråkig Bilderbok För Barn. Carlson, Richard. 2019. (SWE.). 24p. (J). pap. 11.99 *(978-1-0742-4165-0(7))* Independently Published.

Carlson, Suzanne. Svenska-Portugisiska (Portugal) Verktyg/Ferramentas Barns Tv&#65533;spr&#65533;kiga Bildordbok. Carlson, Richard. 2019. (SWE.). 26p. (J). pap. 11.99 ***(978-1-6924-2615-6(X))*** Independently Published.

—Svenska-Punjabi Fordon Barns Tv&#65533;spr&#65533;kiga Bildordbok. Carlson, Richard. 2019. (SWE.). 24p. (J). pap. 11.99 ***(978-1-6900-4227-3(3))*** Independently Published.

—Svenska-Punjabi Mina K&#65533;nslor &#65533;r S&#65533;rade Tv&#65533;spr&#65533;kig Bilderbok F&#65533;r Barn. Carlson, Richard. 2019. (SWE.). 24p. (J). pap. 11.99 ***(978-1-6979-3810-4(8))*** Independently Published.

—Svenska-Punjabi Nummer/ਗਿਣਤੀ Bildordbok F&#65533;r Tv&#65533;spr&#65533;kiga Barn. Carlson, Richard. 2019. (SWE.). 26p. (J). pap. 11.99 ***(978-1-6701-2805-8(9))*** Independently Published.

—Svenska-Punjabi Skolan/ਸਕੂਲ Barns Tv&#65533;spr&#65533;kiga Bildordbok. Carlson, Richard. 2019. (SWE.). 24p. (J). pap. 11.99 ***(978-1-7048-5402-1(4))*** Independently Published.

—Svenska-Punjabi Tid Tv&#65533;spr&#65533;kig Bilderbok F&#65533;r Barn. Carlson, Richard. 2019. (SWE.). 28p. (J). pap. 11.99 ***(978-1-7016-9280-0(5))*** Independently Published.

Carlson, Suzanne. Svenska-Punjabi Trubbel Tvåspråkig Bilderbok För Barn. Carlson, Richard. 2019. (SWE.). 24p. (J). pap. 11.99 *(978-1-0742-4736-2(1))* Independently Published.

Carlson, Suzanne. Svenska-Punjabi Verktyg Barns Tv&#65533;spr&#65533;kiga Bildordbok. Carlson, Richard. 2019. (SWE.). 26p. (J). pap. 11.99 ***(978-1-6925-4539-0(6))*** Independently Published.

—Svenska-Rum&#65533;nska Fordon/Vehicule Barns Tv&#65533;spr&#65533;kiga Bildordbok. Carlson, Richard. 2019. (SWE.). 24p. (J). pap. 11.99 ***(978-1-6900-4735-3(6))*** Independently Published.

—Svenska-Rum&#65533;nska Mina K&#65533;nslor &#65533;r S&#65533;rade/Sunt Jignit Tv&#65533;spr&#65533;kig Bilderbok F&#65533;r Barn. Carlson, Richard. 2019. (SWE.). 24p. (J). pap. 11.99 ***(978-1-6979-3933-0(3))*** Independently Published.

—Svenska-Rum&#65533;nska Nummer/Numere Bildordbok F&#65533;r Tv&#65533;spr&#65533;kiga Barn. Carlson, Richard. 2019. (SWE.). 26p. (J). pap. 11.99 ***(978-1-6701-3021-1(5))*** Independently Published.

—Svenska-Rum&#65533;nska Skolan/Școală Barns Tv&#65533;spr&#65533;kiga Bildordbok. Carlson, Richard. 2019. (SWE.). 24p. (J). pap. 11.99 ***(978-1-7048-5508-0(X))*** Independently Published.

—Svenska-Rum&#65533;nska Tid/Timpul Tv&#65533;spr&#65533;kig Bilderbok F&#65533;r Barn. Carlson, Richard. 2019. (SWE.). 28p. (J). pap. 11.99 ***(978-1-7016-9499-6(9))*** Independently Published.

—Svenska-Rum&#65533;nska Verktyg/Unelte Barns Tv&#65533;spr&#65533;kiga Bildordbok. Carlson, Richard. 2019. (SWE.). 26p. (J). pap. 11.99 ***(978-1-6925-5118-6(3))*** Independently Published.

Carlson, Suzanne. Svenska-Rumänska Trubbel/În încurcătură Tvåspråkig Bilderbok För Barn. Carlson, Richard. 2019. (SWE.). 24p. (J). pap. 11.99 *(978-1-0742-4826-0(0))* Independently Published.

Carlson, Suzanne. Svenska-Ryska Mina K&#65533;nslor &#65533;r S&#65533;rade/Оскорбленные чувства; Tv&#65533;spr&#65533;kig Bilderbok F&#65533;r Barn. Carlson, Richard. 2019. (SWE.). 24p. (J). pap. 11.99 ***(978-1-6979-4077-0(3))*** Independently Published.

—Svenska-Ryska Nummer/Числа; Bildordbok F&#65533;r Tv&#65533;spr&#65533;kiga Barn. Carlson, Richard. 2019. (SWE.). 26p. (J). pap. 11.99 ***(978-1-6701-3301-4(X))*** Independently Published.

—Svenska-Ryska Skolan/Школа; Barns Tv&#65533;spr&#65533;kiga Bildordbok. Carlson, Richard. 2019. (SWE.). 24p. (J). pap. 11.99 ***(978-1-7048-5612-4(4))*** Independently Published.

—Svenska-Ryska Tid/Время; Tv&#65533;spr&#65533;kig Bilderbok F&#65533;r Barn. Carlson, Richard. 2019. (SWE.). 28p. (J). pap. 11.99 ***(978-1-7017-0019-2(0))*** Independently Published.

Carlson, Suzanne. Svenska-Ryska Trubbel/Проблема; Tvåspråkig Bilderbok För Barn. Carlson, Richard. 2019. (SWE.). 24p. (J). pap. 11.99 *(978-1-0742-4956-4(9))* Independently Published.

Carlson, Suzanne. Svenska-Ryska Verktyg/Инструменты; Barns Tv&#65533;spr&#65533;kiga Bildordbok. Carlson, Richard. 2019. (SWE.). 26p. (J). pap. 11.99 ***(978-1-6925-5398-2(4))*** Independently Published.

—Svenska-Serbiska (kyrilliska) Fordon/Возила; Barns Tv&#65533;spr&#65533;kiga Bildordbok. Carlson, Richard. 2019. (SWE.). 24p. (J). pap. 11.99 ***(978-1-6900-4978-4(2))*** Independently Published.

—Svenska-Serbiska (kyrilliska) Mina K&#65533;nslor &#65533;r S&#65533;rade/Моја; осећања; су; повређена; Tv&#65533;spr&#65533;kig Bilderbok F&#65533;r Barn. Carlson, Richard. 2019. (SWE.). 24p. (J). pap. 11.99 ***(978-1-6979-5285-8(2))*** Independently Published.

—Svenska-Serbiska (kyrilliska) Nummer/Бројеви; Bildordbok F&#65533;r Tv&#65533;spr&#65533;kiga Barn. Carlson, Richard. 2019. (SWE.). 26p. (J). pap. 11.99 ***(978-1-6701-3905-4(0))*** Independently Published.

—Svenska-Serbiska (kyrilliska) Skolan/Школа; Barns Tv&#65533;spr&#65533;kiga Bildordbok. Carlson, Richard. 2019. (SWE.). 24p. (J). pap. 11.99 ***(978-1-7048-5852-4(6))*** Independently Published.

—Svenska-Serbiska (kyrilliska) Tid/Време; Tv&#65533;spr&#65533;kig Bilderbok F&#65533;r Barn. Carlson, Richard. 2019. (SWE.). 28p. (J). pap. 11.99 ***(978-1-7017-0753-5(5))*** Independently Published.

Carlson, Suzanne. Svenska-Serbiska (kyrilliska) Trubbel/Невоља; Tvåspråkig Bilderbok För Barn. Carlson, Richard. 2019. (SWE.). 24p. (J). pap. 11.99 *(978-1-0742-5152-9(0))* Independently Published.

Carlson, Suzanne. Svenska-Serbiska (kyrilliska) Verktyg/Алати; Barns Tv&#65533;spr&#65533;kiga Bildordbok. Carlson, Richard. 2019. (SWE.). 26p. (J). pap. 11.99 ***(978-1-6926-7227-0(4))*** Independently Published.

—Svenska-Serbiska (latinsk) Fordon/Vozila Barns Tv&#65533;spr&#65533;kiga Bildordbok. Carlson, Richard. 2019. (SWE.). 24p. (J). pap. 11.99 ***(978-1-6900-5187-9(6))*** Independently Published.

—Svenska-Serbiska (latinsk) Mina K&#65533;nslor &#65533;r S&#65533;rade/Osecanja Su Mi Povređena Tv&#65533;spr&#65533;kig Bilderbok F&#65533;r Barn. Carlson, Richard. 2019. (SWE.). 24p. (J). pap. 11.99 ***(978-1-6979-5408-1(1))*** Independently Published.

—Svenska-Serbiska (latinsk) Nummer/Brojevi Bildordbok F&#65533;r Tv&#65533;spr&#65533;kiga Barn. Carlson, Richard. 2019. (SWE.). 26p. (J). pap. 11.99 ***(978-1-6701-4149-1(7))*** Independently Published.

—Svenska-Serbiska (latinsk) Skolan/Skola Barns Tv&#65533;spr&#65533;kiga Bildordbok. Carlson, Richard. 2019. (SWE.). 24p. (J). pap. 11.99 ***(978-1-7048-5968-2(9))*** Independently Published.

—Svenska-Serbiska (latinsk) Tid/Vreme Tv&#65533;spr&#65533;kig Bilderbok F&#65533;r Barn. Carlson, Richard. 2019. (SWE.). 28p. (J). pap. 11.99 ***(978-1-7017-0996-6(1))*** Independently Published.

Carlson, Suzanne. Svenska-Serbiska (latinsk) Trubbel/Nevolja Tvåspråkig Bilderbok För Barn. Carlson, Richard. 2019. (SWE.). 24p. (J). pap. 11.99 *(978-1-0742-5274-8(8))* Independently Published.

Carlson, Suzanne. Svenska-Serbiska (latinsk) Verktyg/Alati Barns Tv&#65533;spr&#65533;kiga Bildordbok. Carlson, Richard. 2019. (SWE.). 26p. (J). pap. 11.99 ***(978-1-6926-7548-6(6))*** Independently Published.

—Svenska-Shanghainesiska Fordon/车辆 Barns Tv&#65533;spr&#65533;kiga Bildordbok. Carlson, Richard. 2019. (SWE.). 24p. (J). pap. 11.99 ***(978-1-6900-5263-0(5))*** Independently Published.

—Svenska-Shanghainesiska Mina K&#65533;nslor &#65533;r S&#65533;rade/我的感情受到了伤害 Tv&#65533;spr&#65533;kig Bilderbok F&#65533;r Barn. Carlson, Richard. 2019. (SWE.). 24p. (J). pap. 11.99 ***(978-1-6979-5533-0(9))*** Independently Published.

—Svenska-Shanghainesiska Nummer/数字 Bildordbok F&#65533;r Tv&#65533;spr&#65533;kiga Barn. Carlson, Richard. 2019. (SWE.). 26p. (J). pap. 11.99 ***(978-1-6701-4382-2(1))*** Independently Published.

—Svenska-Shanghainesiska Skolan/学校 Barns Tv&#65533;spr&#65533;kiga Bildordbok. Carlson, Richard. 2019. (SWE.). 24p. (J). pap. 11.99 ***(978-1-7048-6739-7(8))*** Independently Published.

—Svenska-Shanghainesiska Tid/时间; Tv&#65533;spr&#65533;kig Bilderbok F&#65533;r Barn. Carlson, Richard. 2019. (SWE.). 28p. (J). pap. 11.99 ***(978-1-7017-1458-8(2))*** Independently Published.

Carlson, Suzanne. Svenska-Shanghainesiska Trubbel/烦恼 Tvåspråkig Bilderbok För Barn. Carlson, Richard. 2019. (SWE.). 24p. (J). pap. 11.99 *(978-1-0742-5382-0(5))* Independently Published.

Carlson, Suzanne. Svenska-Singalesiska Fordon Barns Tv&#65533;spr&#65533;kiga Bildordbok. Carlson, Richard. 2019. (SWE.). 24p. (J). pap. 11.99 ***(978-1-6900-5499-3(9))*** Independently Published.

—Svenska-Singalesiska Mina K&#65533;nslor &#65533;r S&#65533;rade/මගේ හැඟීම් වලට රිදිලා Tv&#65533;spr&#65533;kig Bilderbok F&#65533;r Barn. Carlson, Richard. 2019. (SWE.). 24p. (J). pap. 11.99 ***(978-1-6979-7185-9(7))*** Independently Published.

—Svenska-Singalesiska Nummer/ඉලක්කම් Bildordbok F&#65533;r Tv&#65533;spr&#65533;kiga Barn. Carlson, Richard. 2019. (SWE.). 26p. (J). pap. 11.99 ***(978-1-6701-4645-8(6))*** Independently Published.

—Svenska-Singalesiska Skolan/පාසැල Barns Tv&#65533;spr&#65533;kiga Bildordbok. Carlson, Richard. 2019. (SWE.). 24p. (J). pap. 11.99 ***(978-1-7048-7110-3(7))*** Independently Published.

—Svenska-Singalesiska Tid/කාලය; Tv&#65533;spr&#65533;kig Bilderbok F&#65533;r Barn. Carlson, Richard. 2019. (SWE.). 28p. (J). pap. 11.99 ***(978-1-7017-1843-2(X))*** Independently Published.

Carlson, Suzanne. Svenska-Singalesiska Trubbel/හිරිහැරය; Tvåspråkig Bilderbok För Barn. Carlson, Richard. 2019. (SWE.). 24p. (J). pap. 11.99 *(978-1-0742-5555-8(0))* Independently Published.

Carlson, Suzanne. Svenska-Singalesiska Verktyg Barns Tv&#65533;spr&#65533;kiga Bildordbok. Carlson, Richard. 2019. (SWE.). 26p. (J). pap. 11.99 ***(978-1-6928-9258-6(4))*** Independently Published.

—Svenska-Slovakiska Fordon/Vozidl&#65533; Barns Tv&#65533;spr&#65533;kiga Bildordbok. Carlson, Richard. 2019. (SWE.). 24p. (J). pap. 11.99 ***(978-1-6900-5534-1(0))*** Independently Published.

—Svenska-Slovakiska Skolan/Skola Barns Tv&#65533;spr&#65533;kiga Bildordbok. Carlson, Richard. 2019. (SWE.). 24p. (J). pap. 11.99 ***(978-1-7048-7428-9(9))*** Independently Published.

—Svenska-Slovakiska Tid/Čas Tv&#65533;spr&#65533;kig Bilderbok F&#65533;r Barn. Carlson, Richard. 2019. (SWE.). 28p. (J). pap. 11.99 ***(978-1-7018-6603-4(X))*** Independently Published.

Carlson, Suzanne. Svenska-Slovakiska Trubbel/Problémy Tvåspråkig Bilderbok För Barn. Carlson, Richard. 2019. (SWE.). 24p. (J). pap. 11.99 *(978-1-0742-5725-5(1))* Independently Published.

Carlson, Suzanne. Svenska-Slovakiska Verktyg/N&#65533;stroje Barns Tv&#65533;spr&#65533;kiga Bildordbok. Carlson, Richard. 2019. (SWE.). 26p. (J). pap. 11.99 ***(978-1-6928-9984-4(8))*** Independently Published.

—Svenska-Slovenska Fordon/Vozila Barns Tv&#65533;spr&#65533;kiga Bildordbok. Carlson, Richard. 2019. (SWE.). 24p. (J). pap. 11.99 ***(978-1-6900-5801-4(3))*** Independently Published.

—Svenska-Slovenska Mina K&#65533;nslor &#65533;r S&#65533;rade/Moja Prizadeta čustva Tv&#65533;spr&#65533;kig Bilderbok F&#65533;r Barn. Carlson, Richard. 2019. (SWE.). 24p. (J). pap. 11.99 ***(978-1-6979-7568-0(2))*** Independently Published.

—Svenska-Slovenska Nummer/Stevila Bildordbok F&#65533;r Tv&#65533;spr&#65533;kiga Barn. Carlson, Richard. 2019. (SWE.). 26p. (J). pap. 11.99 ***(978-1-6701-6073-7(4))*** Independently Published.

—Svenska-Slovenska Skolan/Sola Barns Tv&#65533;spr&#65533;kiga Bildordbok. Carlson, Richard. 2019. (SWE.). 24p. (J). pap. 11.99 ***(978-1-7053-6229-7(X))*** Independently Published.

—Svenska-Slovenska Tid/Čas Tv&#65533;spr&#65533;kig Bilderbok F&#65533;r Barn. Carlson, Richard. 2019. (SWE.). 28p. (J). pap. 11.99 ***(978-1-7019-0386-9(5))*** Independently Published.

Carlson, Suzanne. Svenska-Slovenska Trubbel/Tezava Tvåspråkig Bilderbok För Barn. Carlson, Richard. 2019. (SWE.). 24p. (J). pap. 11.99 *(978-1-0742-5842-9(8))* Independently Published.

Carlson, Suzanne. Svenska-Slovenska Verktyg/Orodja Barns Tv&#65533;spr&#65533;kiga Bildordbok. Carlson, Richard. 2019. (SWE.). 26p. (J). pap. 11.99 ***(978-1-6929-0187-5(7))*** Independently Published.

—Svenska-Somaliska Fordon/Gaadiid Barns Tv&#65533;spr&#65533;kiga Bildordbok. Carlson, Richard. 2019. (SWE.). 24p. (J). pap. 11.99 ***(978-1-6900-5924-0(9))*** Independently Published.

—Svenska-Somaliska Mina K&#65533;nslor &#65533;r S&#65533;rade/Dareenadayda Ayaa Dhaawacmay Tv&#65533;spr&#65533;kig Bilderbok F&#65533;r Barn. Carlson, Richard. 2019. (SWE.). 24p. (J). pap. 11.99 ***(978-1-6979-7701-1(4))*** Independently Published.

—Svenska-Somaliska Nummer/Lambaro Bildordbok F&#65533;r Tv&#65533;spr&#65533;kiga Barn. Carlson, Richard. 2019. (SWE.). 26p. (J). pap. 11.99 ***(978-1-6701-6507-7(8))*** Independently Published.

—Svenska-Somaliska Skolan/Dugsi Barns Tv&#65533;spr&#65533;kiga Bildordbok. Carlson, Richard. 2019. (SWE.). 24p. (J). pap. 11.99 ***(978-1-7053-7774-1(2))*** Independently Published.

—Svenska-Somaliska Tid/Waqti Tv&#65533;spr&#65533;kig Bilderbok F&#65533;r Barn. Carlson, Richard. 2019. (SWE.). 28p. (J). pap. 11.99 ***(978-1-7019-1309-7(7))*** Independently Published.

Carlson, Suzanne. Svenska-Somaliska Trubbel/Dhibaato Tvåspråkig Bilderbok För Barn. Carlson, Richard. 2019. (SWE.). 24p. (J). pap. 11.99 *(978-1-0742-6167-2(4))* Independently Published.

Carlson, Suzanne. Svenska-Somaliska Verktyg/Qalab Barns Tv&#65533;spr&#65533;kiga Bildordbok. Carlson, Richard. 2019. (SWE.). 26p. (J). pap. 11.99 ***(978-1-6929-1637-4(8))*** Independently Published.

—Svenska-Swahili Fordon/Magari Barns Tv&#65533;spr&#65533;kiga Bildordbok. Carlson, Richard. 2019. (SWE.). 24p. (J). pap. 11.99 ***(978-1-6900-6362-9(9))*** Independently Published.

—Svenska-Swahili Mina K&#65533;nslor &#65533;r S&#65533;rade/Hisia Zangu Zinaumia Tv&#65533;spr&#65533;kig Bilderbok F&#65533;r Barn. Carlson, Richard. 2019. (SWE.). 24p. (J). pap. 11.99 ***(978-1-6981-7476-1(4))*** Independently Published.

—Svenska-Swahili Nummer/Namba Bildordbok F&#65533;r Tv&#65533;spr&#65533;kiga Barn. Carlson, Richard. 2019. (SWE.). 26p. (J). pap. 11.99 ***(978-1-6701-9098-7(6))*** Independently Published.

—Svenska-Swahili Skolan/Shule Barns Tv&#65533;spr&#65533;kiga Bildordbok. Carlson, Richard. 2019. (SWE.). 24p. (J). pap. 11.99 ***(978-1-7053-9889-0(8))*** Independently Published.

—Svenska-Swahili Tid/Muda Tv&#65533;spr&#65533;kig Bilderbok F&#65533;r Barn. Carlson, Richard. 2019. (SWE.). 28p. (J). pap. 11.99 ***(978-1-7019-6649-9(2))*** Independently Published.

Carlson, Suzanne. Svenska-Swahili Trubbel/Shida Tvåspråkig Bilderbok För Barn. Carlson, Richard. 2019. (SWE.). 24p. (J). pap. 11.99 *(978-1-0742-6884-8(9))* Independently Published.

Carlson, Suzanne. Svenska-Swahili Verktyg/Zana Barns Tv&#65533;spr&#65533;kiga Bildordbok. Carlson, Richard. 2019. (SWE.). 26p. (J). pap. 11.99 ***(978-1-6931-0903-4(4))*** Independently Published.

—Svenska-Tadzjikiska Mina K&#65533;nslor &#65533;r S&#65533;rade/эҳсосотм; ҷриҳа; дор; шуда; Tv&#65533;spr&#65533;kig Bilderbok F&#65533;r Barn. Carlson, Richard. 2019. (SWE.). 24p. (J). pap. 11.99 ***(978-1-6981-8326-8(7))*** Independently Published.

—Svenska-Tagalog Fordon/Mga Sasakyan Barns Tv&#65533;spr&#65533;kiga Bildordbok. Carlson, Richard. 2019. (SWE.). 24p. (J). pap. 11.99 ***(978-1-6900-6458-9(7))*** Independently Published.

—Svenska-Tagalog Mina K&#65533;nslor &#65533;r S&#65533;rade/Nasaktan Ang Aking Damdamin Tv&#65533;spr&#65533;kig Bilderbok F&#65533;r Barn. Carlson, Richard. 2019. (SWE.). 24p. (J). pap. 11.99 ***(978-1-6981-7580-5(9))*** Independently Published.

—Svenska-Tagalog Nummer/Mga Bilang Bildordbok F&#65533;r Tv&#65533;spr&#65533;kiga Barn. Carlson, Richard. 2019. (SWE.). 26p. (J). pap. 11.99 ***(978-1-6701-9298-1(9))*** Independently Published.

—Svenska-Tagalog Skolan/Paaralan Barns Tv&#65533;spr&#65533;kiga Bildordbok. Carlson, Richard. 2019. (SWE.). 24p. (J). pap. 11.99 ***(978-1-7054-0196-5(1))*** Independently Published.

—Svenska-Tagalog Tid/Oras Tv&#65533;spr&#65533;kig Bilderbok F&#65533;r Barn. Carlson, Richard. 2019. (SWE.). 28p. (J). pap. 11.99 ***(978-1-7019-7172-1(0))*** Independently Published.

Carlson, Suzanne. Svenska-Tagalog Trubbel/Gulo Tvåspråkig Bilderbok För Barn. Carlson, Richard. 2019. (SWE.). 24p. (J). pap. 11.99 *(978-1-0742-7037-7(1))* Independently Published.

Carlson, Suzanne. Svenska-Tagalog Verktyg/Mga Gamit Barns Tv&#65533;spr&#65533;kiga Bildordbok. Carlson, Richard. 2019. (SWE.). 26p. (J). pap. 11.99 ***(978-1-6931-1154-9(3))*** Independently Published.

—Svenska-Tamilska Fordon Barns Tv&#65533;spr&#65533;kiga Bildordbok. Carlson, Richard. 2019. (SWE.). 24p. (J). pap. 11.99 ***(978-1-6900-6650-7(4))*** Independently Published.

—Svenska-Tamilska Mina K&#65533;nslor &#65533;r S&#65533;rade/எனது உணர்வுகள் காயமாகின Tv&#65533;spr&#65533;kig Bilderbok F&#65533;r Barn. Carlson, Richard. 2019. (SWE.). 24p.

(J). pap. 11.99 ***(978-1-6981-8685-6(1))*** Independently Published.

—Svenska-Tamilska Nummer/எண்கள் Bildordbok F&#65533;r Tv&#65533;spr&#65533;kiga Barn. Carlson, Richard. 2019. (SWE.). 26p. (J). pap. 11.99 ***(978-1-6701-9542-5(2))*** Independently Published.

—Svenska-Tamilska Skolan Barns Tv&#65533;spr&#65533;kiga Bildordbok. Carlson, Richard. 2019. (SWE.). 24p. (J). pap. 11.99 ***(978-1-7054-0818-6(4))*** Independently Published.

—Svenska-Tamilska Tid Tv&#65533;spr&#65533;kig Bilderbok F&#65533;r Barn. Carlson, Richard. 2019. (SWE.). 28p. (J). pap. 11.99 ***(978-1-7019-8082-2(7))*** Independently Published.

Carlson, Suzanne. Svenska-Tamilska Trubbel Tvåspråkig Bilderbok För Barn. Carlson, Richard. 2019. (SWE.). 24p. (J). pap. 11.99 *(978-1-0744-1028-5(9))* Independently Published.

Carlson, Suzanne. Svenska-Tamilska Verktyg Barns Tv&#65533;spr&#65533;kiga Bildordbok. Carlson, Richard. 2019. (SWE.). 26p. (J). pap. 11.99 ***(978-1-6932-7360-5(8))*** Independently Published.

—Svenska-Telugu Fordon Barns Tv&#65533;spr&#65533;kiga Bildordbok. Carlson, Richard. 2019. (SWE.). 24p. (J). pap. 11.99 ***(978-1-6900-6861-7(2))*** Independently Published.

—Svenska-Telugu Mina K&#65533;nslor &#65533;r S&#65533;rade Tv&#65533;spr&#65533;kig Bilderbok F&#65533;r Barn. Carlson, Richard. 2019. (SWE.). 24p. (J). pap. 11.99 ***(978-1-6981-8801-0(3))*** Independently Published.

—Svenska-Telugu Nummer/నెంబర్లు Bildordbok F&#65533;r Tv&#65533;spr&#65533;kiga Barn. Carlson, Richard. 2019. (SWE.). 26p. (J). pap. 11.99 ***(978-1-6701-9736-8(0))*** Independently Published.

—Svenska-Telugu Skolan/పాఠశాల Barns Tv&#65533;spr&#65533;kiga Bildordbok. Carlson, Richard. 2019. (SWE.). 24p. (J). pap. 11.99 ***(978-1-7055-3375-8(2))*** Independently Published.

—Svenska-Telugu Tid/సమయం Tv&#65533;spr&#65533;kig Bilderbok F&#65533;r Barn. Carlson, Richard. 2019. (SWE.). 28p. (J). pap. 11.99 ***(978-1-7022-0274-9(7))*** Independently Published.

Carlson, Suzanne. Svenska-Telugu Trubbel Tvåspråkig Bilderbok För Barn. Carlson, Richard. 2019. (SWE.). 24p. (J). pap. 11.99 *(978-1-0744-1116-9(1))* Independently Published.

Carlson, Suzanne. Svenska-Telugu Verktyg Barns Tv&#65533;spr&#65533;kiga Bildordbok. Carlson, Richard. 2019. (SWE.). 26p. (J). pap. 11.99 ***(978-1-6932-7457-2(4))*** Independently Published.

—Svenska-Thail&#65533;ndska Fordon/ยานพาหนะ Barns Tv&#65533;spr&#65533;kiga Bildordbok. Carlson, Richard. 2019. (SWE.). 24p. (J). pap. 11.99 ***(978-1-6900-7028-3(5))*** Independently Published.

—Svenska-Thail&#65533;ndska Mina K&#65533;nslor &#65533;r S&#65533;rade/ความรู้สึกของผมคือเสียใจ Tv&#65533;spr&#65533;kig Bilderbok F&#65533;r Barn. Carlson, Richard. 2019. (SWE.). 24p. (J). pap. 11.99 ***(978-1-6981-8897-3(8))*** Independently Published.

—Svenska-Thail&#65533;ndska Nummer/จำนวน Bildordbok F&#65533;r Tv&#65533;spr&#65533;kiga Barn. Carlson, Richard. 2019. (SWE.). 26p. (J). pap. 11.99 ***(978-1-6701-9945-4(2))*** Independently Published.

—Svenska-Thail&#65533;ndska Skolan/โรงเรียน Barns Tv&#65533;spr&#65533;kiga Bildordbok. Carlson, Richard. 2019. (SWE.). 24p. (J). pap. 11.99 ***(978-1-7055-3717-6(0))*** Independently Published.

—Svenska-Thail&#65533;ndska Tid/เวลา Tv&#65533;spr&#65533;kig Bilderbok F&#65533;r Barn. Carlson, Richard. 2019. (SWE.). 28p. (J). pap. 11.99 ***(978-1-7022-0576-4(2))*** Independently Published.

—Svenska-Thail&#65533;ndska Verktyg Barns Tv&#65533;spr&#65533;kiga Bildordbok. Carlson, Richard. 2019. (SWE.). 26p. (J). pap. 11.99 ***(978-1-6932-7982-9(7))*** Independently Published.

Carlson, Suzanne. Svenska-Thailändska Trubbel/ยุ่งแล้วเชียว Tvåspråkig Bilderbok För Barn. Carlson, Richard. 2019. (SWE.). 24p. (J). pap. 11.99 *(978-1-0744-1274-6(5))* Independently Published.

Carlson, Suzanne. Svenska-Tigrinska Fordon/መጓዓዝያ Barns Tv&#65533;spr&#65533;kiga Bildordbok. Carlson, Richard. 2019. (SWE.). 24p. (J). pap. 11.99 ***(978-1-6900-7266-9(0))*** Independently Published.

—Svenska-Tigrinska Mina K&#65533;nslor &#65533;r S&#65533;rade/ስምዒተይ ተጎዲኡ እዩ Tv&#65533;spr&#65533;kig Bilderbok F&#65533;r Barn. Carlson, Richard. 2019. (SWE.). 24p. (J). pap. 11.99 ***(978-1-6981-9055-6(7))*** Independently Published.

—Svenska-Tigrinska Nummer/ቁፅሪ Bildordbok F&#65533;r Tv&#65533;spr&#65533;kiga Barn. Carlson, Richard. 2019. (SWE.). 26p. (J). pap. 11.99 ***(978-1-6702-0242-0(9))*** Independently Published.

—Svenska-Tigrinska Skolan/ቤት ትምህርቲ Barns Tv&#65533;spr&#65533;kiga Bildordbok. Carlson, Richard. 2019. (SWE.). 24p. (J). pap. 11.99 ***(978-1-7055-3979-8(3))*** Independently Published.

—Svenska-Tigrinska Tid/ግዘ Tv&#65533;spr&#65533;kig Bilderbok F&#65533;r Barn. Carlson, Richard. 2019. (SWE.). 28p. (J). pap. 11.99 ***(978-1-7022-0953-3(9))*** Independently Published.

Carlson, Suzanne. Svenska-Tigrinska Trubbel/ፀገም Tvåspråkig Bilderbok För Barn. Carlson, Richard. 2019. (SWE.). 24p. (J). pap. 11.99 *(978-1-0744-1359-0(8))* Independently Published.

Carlson, Suzanne. Svenska-Tigrinska Verktyg/መሳርሒ Barns Tv&#65533;spr&#65533;kiga Bildordbok. Carlson, Richard. 2019. (SWE.). 26p. (J). pap. 11.99 ***(978-1-6934-2131-0(3))*** Independently Published.

—Svenska-Tjeckiska Fordon/Dopravn&#65533; Prostředky Barns Tv&#65533;spr&#65533;kiga Bildordbok. Carlson, Richard. 2019. (SWE.). 24p. (J). pap. 11.99 ***(978-1-6892-7055-7(1))*** Independently Published.

—Svenska-Tjeckiska Mina K&#65533;nslor &#65533;r S&#65533;rade/M&#65533; City Jsou Zraněny Tv&#65533;spr&#65533;kig Bilderbok F&#65533;r Barn. Carlson, Richard. 2019. (SWE.). 24p. (J). pap. 10.99 ***(978-1-6968-1669-4(6))*** Independently Published.

—Svenska-Tjeckiska Nummer/Č&#65533;sla Bildordbok F&#65533;r Tv&#65533;spr&#65533;kiga Barn. Carlson, Richard. 2019. (SWE.). 26p. (J). pap. 11.99 ***(978-1-7110-5671-5(5))*** Independently Published.

—Svenska-Tjeckiska Skolan/Skola Barns Tv&#65533;spr&#65533;kiga Bildordbok. Carlson, Richard. 2019. (SWE.). 24p. (J). pap. 11.99 ***(978-1-7031-8364-1(9))*** Independently Published.

—Svenska-Tjeckiska Tid/Čas Tv&#65533;spr&#65533;kig Bilderbok F&#65533;r Barn. Carlson, Richard. 2019. (SWE.). 28p. (J). pap. 11.99 ***(978-1-6995-1919-6(6))*** Independently Published.

Carlson, Suzanne. Svenska-Tjeckiska Trubbel/Potíz Tvåspråkig Bilderbok För Barn. Carlson, Richard. 2019. (SWE.). 24p. (J). pap. 11.99 *(978-1-0731-4333-7(3))* Independently Published.

Carlson, Suzanne. Svenska-Tjeckiska Verktyg/N&#65533;stroje Barns Tv&#65533;spr&#65533;kiga Bildordbok. Carlson, Richard. 2019. (SWE.). 26p. (J). pap. 11.99 ***(978-1-6909-0395-6(3))*** Independently Published.

—Svenska-Traditionell Kinesisk Kantonesiska Fordon/交通工具 Barns Tv&#65533;spr&#65533;kiga Bildordbok. Carlson, Richard. 2019. (SWE.). 24p. (J). pap. 11.99 ***(978-1-6890-6312-8(2))*** Independently Published.

—Svenska-Traditionell Kinesisk Kantonesiska Mina K&#65533;nslor &#65533;r S&#65533;rade/我的情感受到了傷害 Tv&#65533;spr&#65533;kig Bilderbok F&#65533;r Barn. Carlson, Richard. 2019. (SWE.). 24p. (J). pap. 11.99 ***(978-1-6968-1396-9(4))*** Independently Published.

—Svenska-Traditionell Kinesisk Kantonesiska Nummer/數字 Bildordbok F&#65533;r Tv&#65533;spr&#65533;kiga Barn. Carlson, Richard. 2019. (SWE.). 26p. (J). pap. 11.99 ***(978-1-7110-4988-5(3))*** Independently Published.

—Svenska-Traditionell Kinesisk Kantonesiska Skolan/學校 Barns Tv&#65533;spr&#65533;kiga Bildordbok. Carlson, Richard. 2019. (SWE.). 24p. (J). pap. 11.99 ***(978-1-7031-7548-6(4))*** Independently Published.

—Svenska-Traditionell Kinesisk Kantonesiska Tid/時間 Tv&#65533;spr&#65533;kig Bilderbok F&#65533;r Barn. Carlson, Richard. 2019. (SWE.). 28p. (J). pap. 11.99 ***(978-1-6994-8897-3(5))*** Independently Published.

Carlson, Suzanne. Svenska-Traditionell Kinesisk Kantonesiska Trubbel/麻煩 Tvåspråkig Bilderbok För Barn. Carlson, Richard. 2019. (SWE.). 24p. (J). pap. 11.99 *(978-1-0731-2727-6(3))* Independently Published.

Carlson, Suzanne. Svenska-Traditionell Kinesisk Mandarin (Taiwan) Fordon/載具 Barns Tv&#65533;spr&#65533;kiga Bildordbok. Carlson, Richard. 2019. (SWE.). 24p. (J). pap. 11.99 ***(978-1-6890-7120-8(6))*** Independently Published.

—Svenska-Traditionell Kinesisk Mandarin (Taiwan) Mina K&#65533;nslor &#65533;r S&#65533;rade/我的感覺受傷了 Tv&#65533;spr&#65533;kig Bilderbok F&#65533;r Barn. Carlson, Richard. 2019. (SWE.). 24p. (J). pap. 11.99 ***(978-1-6968-1451-5(0))*** Independently Published.

—Svenska-Traditionell Kinesisk Mandarin (Taiwan) Nummer/數字 Bildordbok F&#65533;r Tv&#65533;spr&#65533;kiga Barn. Carlson, Richard. 2019. (SWE.). 26p. (J). pap. 11.99 ***(978-1-7110-5137-6(3))*** Independently Published.

—Svenska-Traditionell Kinesisk Mandarin (Taiwan) Skolan/學校 Barns Tv&#65533;spr&#65533;kiga Bildordbok. Carlson, Richard. 2019. (SWE.). 24p. (J). pap. 11.99 ***(978-1-7031-7837-1(8))*** Independently Published.

—Svenska-Traditionell Kinesisk Mandarin (Taiwan) Tid/時間 Tv&#65533;spr&#65533;kig Bilderbok F&#65533;r Barn. Carlson, Richard. 2019. (SWE.). 28p. (J). pap. 11.99 ***(978-1-6994-9447-9(9))*** Independently Published.

Carlson, Suzanne. Svenska-Traditionell Kinesisk Mandarin (Taiwan) Trubbel/麻煩 Tvåspråkig Bilderbok För Barn. Carlson, Richard. 2019. (SWE.). 24p. (J). pap. 11.99 *(978-1-0731-3424-3(5))* Independently Published.

Carlson, Suzanne. Svenska-Traditionell Kinesiska, Mandarin Fordon/載具 Barns Tv&#65533;spr&#65533;kiga Bildordbok. Carlson, Richard. 2019. (SWE.). 24p. (J). pap. 11.99 ***(978-1-6890-5432-4(8))*** Independently Published.

—Svenska-Traditionell Kinesiska, Mandarin Mina K&#65533;nslor &#65533;r S&#65533;rade/我的情感受到了傷害 Tv&#65533;spr&#65533;kig Bilderbok F&#65533;r Barn. Carlson, Richard. 2019. (SWE.). 24p. (J). pap. 11.99 ***(978-1-6968-0575-9(9))*** Independently Published.

—Svenska-Traditionell Kinesiska, Mandarin Nummer/數字 Bildordbok F&#65533;r Tv&#65533;spr&#65533;kiga Barn. Carlson, Richard. 2019. (SWE.). 26p. (J). pap. 11.99 ***(978-1-7110-4172-8(6))*** Independently Published.

—Svenska-Traditionell Kinesiska, Mandarin Skolan/學校 Barns Tv&#65533;spr&#65533;kiga Bildordbok. Carlson, Richard. 2019. (SWE.). 24p. (J). pap. 11.99 ***(978-1-7031-6943-0(3))*** Independently Published.

—Svenska-Traditionell Kinesiska, Mandarin Tid/時間 Tv&#65533;spr&#65533;kig Bilderbok F&#65533;r Barn. Carlson, Richard. 2019. (SWE.). 28p. (J). pap. 11.99 ***(978-1-6989-0051-3(1))*** Independently Published.

Carlson, Suzanne. Svenska-Traditionell Kinesiska, Mandarin Trubbel/麻煩 Tvåspråkig Bilderbok För Barn. Carlson, Richard. 2019. (SWE.). 24p. (J). pap. 11.99 *(978-1-0730-1063-9(5))* Independently Published.

Carlson, Suzanne. Svenska-Traditionell Kinesiska, Mandarin Verktyg/工具 Barns Tv&#65533;spr&#65533;kiga Bildordbok. Carlson, Richard. 2019. (SWE.). 26p. (J). pap. 11.99 ***(978-1-6908-9260-1(9))*** Independently Published.

—Svenska-Turkiska Mina K&#65533;nslor &#65533;r S&#65533;rade/Duygularım İncindi Tv&#65533;spr&#65533;kig Bilderbok F&#65533;r Barn. Carlson, Richard. 2019. (SWE.). 24p. (J). pap. 11.99 ***(978-1-6981-9197-3(9))*** Independently Published.

—Svenska-Turkiska Nummer/Sayılar Bildordbok F&#65533;r Tv&#65533;spr&#65533;kiga Barn. Carlson, Richard. 2019. (SWE.). 26p. (J). pap. 11.99 ***(978-1-6702-0384-7(0))*** Independently Published.

—Svenska-Turkiska Skolan/Okul Barns Tv&#65533;spr&#65533;kiga Bildordbok. Carlson, Richard. 2019. (SWE.). 24p. (J). pap. 11.99 ***(978-1-7056-1969-8(X))*** Independently Published.

—Svenska-Turkiska Tid/Zaman Tv&#65533;spr&#65533;kig Bilderbok F&#65533;r Barn. Carlson, Richard. 2019. (SWE.). 28p. (J). pap. 11.99 ***(978-1-7022-1226-7(2))*** Independently Published.

Carlson, Suzanne. Svenska-Turkiska Trubbel/Üzüntü Tvåspråkig Bilderbok För Barn. Carlson, Richard. 2019. (SWE.). 24p. (J). pap. 11.99 *(978-1-0744-1975-2(8))* Independently Published.

Carlson, Suzanne. Svenska-Turkiska Verktyg/Aletler Barns Tv&#65533;spr&#65533;kiga Bildordbok. Carlson, Richard. 2019. (SWE.). 26p. (J). pap. 11.99 ***(978-1-6934-2311-6(1))*** Independently Published.

—Svenska-Tyska Fordon/Fahrzeuge Barns Tv&#65533;spr&#65533;kiga Bildordbok. Carlson, Richard. 2019. (SWE.). 24p. (J). pap. 11.99 ***(978-1-6894-8641-5(4))*** Independently Published.

—Svenska-Tyska Mina K&#65533;nslor &#65533;r S&#65533;rade/Ich Wurde in Meinen Gef&#65533;hlen Verletzt Tv&#65533;spr&#65533;kig Bilderbok F&#65533;r Barn. Carlson, Richard. 2019. (SWE.). 24p. (J). pap. 11.99 ***(978-1-6969-8564-2(1))*** Independently Published.

—Svenska-Tyska Nummer/Zahlen Bildordbok F&#65533;r Tv&#65533;spr&#65533;kiga Barn. Carlson, Richard. 2019. (SWE.). 26p. (J). pap. 11.99 ***(978-1-7119-1051-2(1))*** Independently Published.

—Svenska-Tyska Skolan/Schule Barns Tv&#65533;spr&#65533;kiga Bildordbok. Carlson, Richard. 2019. (SWE.). 24p. (J). pap. 11.99 ***(978-1-7035-0242-8(6))*** Independently Published.

—Svenska-Tyska Tid/Zeit Tv&#65533;spr&#65533;kig Bilderbok F&#65533;r Barn. Carlson, Richard. 2019. (SWE.). 28p. (J). pap. 11.99 ***(978-1-6997-4445-1(9))*** Independently Published.

Carlson, Suzanne. Svenska-Tyska Trubbel/Ärger Tvåspråkig Bilderbok För Barn. Carlson, Richard. 2019. (SWE.). 24p. (J). pap. 11.99 *(978-1-0731-6687-9(2))* Independently Published.

Carlson, Suzanne. Svenska-Tyska Verktyg/Werkzeuge Barns Tv&#65533;spr&#65533;kiga Bildordbok. Carlson, Richard. 2019. (SWE.). 26p. (J). pap. 11.99 ***(978-1-6911-3229-4(2))*** Independently Published.

—Svenska-Ukainska Fordon/Транспортні засоби Barns Tv&#65533;spr&#65533;kiga Bildordbok. Carlson, Richard. 2019. (SWE.). 24p. (J). pap. 11.99 ***(978-1-6900-7677-3(1))*** Independently Published.

—Svenska-Ukainska Mina K&#65533;nslor &#65533;r S&#65533;rade/Мене зачепили за живе Tv&#65533;spr&#65533;kig Bilderbok F&#65533;r Barn. Carlson, Richard. 2019. (SWE.). 24p. (J). pap. 11.99 ***(978-1-6981-9259-8(2))*** Independently Published.

—Svenska-Ukainska Nummer/Цифри Bildordbok F&#65533;r Tv&#65533;spr&#65533;kiga Barn. Carlson, Richard. 2019. (SWE.). 26p. (J). pap. 11.99 ***(978-1-6702-0541-4(X))*** Independently Published.

—Svenska-Ukainska Skolan/Школа Barns Tv&#65533;spr&#65533;kiga Bildordbok. Carlson, Richard. 2019. (SWE.). 24p. (J). pap. 11.99 ***(978-1-7056-6410-0(5))*** Independently Published.

—Svenska-Ukainska Tid/Час Tv&#65533;spr&#65533;kig Bilderbok F&#65533;r Barn. Carlson, Richard. 2019. (SWE.). 28p. (J). pap. 11.99 ***(978-1-7022-1402-5(8))*** Independently Published.

Carlson, Suzanne. Svenska-Ukainska Trubbel/Проблема Tvåspråkig Bilderbok För Barn. Carlson, Richard. 2019. (SWE.). 24p. (J). pap. 11.99 *(978-1-0744-2123-6(X))* Independently Published.

Carlson, Suzanne. Svenska-Ukainska Verktyg/Інструменти Barns Tv&#65533;spr&#65533;kiga Bildordbok. Carlson, Richard. 2019. (SWE.). 26p. (J). pap. 11.99 ***(978-1-6934-2473-1(8))*** Independently Published.

—Svenska-Ungerska Fordon/J&#65533;rművek Barns Tv&#65533;spr&#65533;kiga Bildordbok. Carlson, Richard. 2019. (SWE.). 24p. (J). pap. 11.99 ***(978-1-6898-2240-4(6))*** Independently Published.

—Svenska-Ungerska Mina K&#65533;nslor &#65533;r S&#65533;rade/Megb&#65533;nt&#65533;dtam Tv&#65533;spr&#65533;kig Bilderbok F&#65533;r Barn. Carlson, Richard. 2019. (SWE.). 24p. (J). pap. 11.99 ***(978-1-6970-2620-7(6))*** Independently Published.

—Svenska-Ungerska Nummer/Sz&#65533;mok Bildordbok F&#65533;r Tv&#65533;spr&#65533;kiga Barn. Carlson, Richard. 2019. (SWE.). 26p. (J). pap. 11.99 ***(978-1-7123-2183-6(8))*** Independently Published.

—Svenska-Ungerska Skolan/Iskola Barns Tv&#65533;spr&#65533;kiga Bildordbok. Carlson, Richard. 2019. (SWE.). 24p. (J). pap. 11.99 ***(978-1-7038-3467-3(4))*** Independently Published.

—Svenska-Ungerska Tid/Idő Tv&#65533;spr&#65533;kig Bilderbok F&#65533;r Barn. Carlson, Richard. 2019. (SWE.). 28p. (J). pap. 11.99 ***(978-1-6999-3137-0(2))*** Independently Published.

Carlson, Suzanne. Svenska-Ungerska Trubbel/Baj Tvåspråkig Bilderbok För Barn. Carlson, Richard. 2019. (SWE.). 24p. (J). pap. 11.99 *(978-1-0734-4333-8(7))* Independently Published.

Carlson, Suzanne. Svenska-Ungerska Verktyg/Szersz&#65533;mok Barns Tv&#65533;spr&#65533;kiga Bildordbok. Carlson, Richard. 2019. (SWE.). 26p. (J). pap. 11.99 ***(978-1-6915-7964-8(5))*** Independently Published.

—Svenska-Urdu Mina K&#65533;nslor &#65533;r S&#65533;rade Tv&#65533;spr&#65533;kig Bilderbok F&#65533;r Barn. Carlson, Richard. 2019. (SWE.). 24p. (J). pap. 11.99 ***(978-1-6981-9331-1(9))*** Independently Published.

—Svenska-Urdu Nummer/گن تی Bildordbok F&#65533;r Tv&#65533;spr&#65533;kiga Barn. Carlson, Richard. 2019. (SWE.). 26p. (J). pap. 11.99 ***(978-1-6702-0704-3(8))*** Independently Published.

—Svenska-Urdu Skolan/سکول Barns Tv&#65533;spr&#65533;kiga Bildordbok. Carlson, Richard. 2019. (SWE.). 24p. (J). pap. 11.99 ***(978-1-7056-6586-2(1))*** Independently Published.

—Svenska-Urdu Tid Tv&#65533;spr&#65533;kig Bilderbok F&#65533;r Barn. Carlson, Richard. 2019. (SWE.). 28p. (J). pap. 11.99 ***(978-1-7022-1983-9(6))*** Independently Published.

Carlson, Suzanne. Svenska-Urdu Trubbel/پریشانی Tvåspråkig Bilderbok För Barn. Carlson, Richard. 2019. (SWE.). 24p. (J). pap. 11.99 *(978-1-0744-2196-0(5))* Independently Published.

Carlson, Suzanne. Svenska-Urdu Verktyg Barns Tv&#65533;spr&#65533;kiga Bildordbok. Carlson, Richard. 2019. (SWE.). 26p. (J). pap. 11.99 ***(978-1-6934-3027-5(4))*** Independently Published.

—Svenska-Uzbekiska Fordon/Transport Vositalari Barns Tv&#65533;spr&#65533;kiga Bildordbok. Carlson, Richard. 2019. (SWE.). 24p. (J). pap. 11.99 ***(978-1-6900-8379-5(4))*** Independently Published.

—Svenska-Uzbekiska Nummer/Sonlar Bildordbok F&#65533;r Tv&#65533;spr&#65533;kiga Barn. Carlson, Richard. 2019. (SWE.). 26p. (J). pap. 11.99 ***(978-1-6702-1137-8(1))*** Independently Published.

—Svenska-Uzbekiska Skolan/Maktab Barns Tv&#65533;spr&#65533;kiga Bildordbok. Carlson, Richard. 2019. (SWE.). 24p. (J). pap. 11.99 ***(978-1-7056-7165-8(9))*** Independently Published.

—Svenska-Uzbekiska Tid/Vaqt Tv&#65533;spr&#65533;kig Bilderbok F&#65533;r Barn. Carlson, Richard. 2019. (SWE.). 28p. (J). pap. 11.99 ***(978-1-7022-2144-3(X))*** Independently Published.

Carlson, Suzanne. Svenska-Uzbekiska Trubbel/Muammo Tvåspråkig Bilderbok För Barn. Carlson, Richard. 2019. (SWE.). 24p. (J). pap. 11.99 *(978-1-0744-2438-1(7))* Independently Published.

Carlson, Suzanne. Svenska-Uzbekiska Verktyg/Asboblar Barns Tv&#65533;spr&#65533;kiga Bildordbok. Carlson, Richard. 2019. (SWE.). 26p. (J). pap. 11.99 ***(978-1-6934-3125-8(4))*** Independently Published.

—Svenska-Vietnamesiska Fordon/Phương Tiện Barns Tv&#65533;spr&#65533;kiga Bildordbok. Carlson, Richard. 2019. (SWE.). 24p. (J). pap. 11.99 ***(978-1-6900-8502-7(9))*** Independently Published.

—Svenska-Vietnamesiska Mina K&#65533;nslor &#65533;r S&#65533;rade/Cảm X&#65533;c Của M&#65533;nh Bị Tổn Thương Tv&#65533;spr&#65533;kig Bilderbok F&#65533;r Barn. Carlson, Richard. 2019. (SWE.). 24p. (J). pap. 11.99 ***(978-1-6981-9467-7(6))*** Independently Published.

—Svenska-Vietnamesiska Nummer/Số Học Bildordbok F&#65533;r Tv&#65533;spr&#65533;kiga Barn. Carlson, Richard. 2019. (SWE.). 26p. (J). pap. 11.99 ***(978-1-6702-1358-7(7))*** Independently Published.

—Svenska-Vietnamesiska Tid/Thời Gian Tv&#65533;spr&#65533;kig Bilderbok F&#65533;r Barn. Carlson, Richard. 2019. (SWE.). 28p. (J). pap. 11.99 ***(978-1-7022-2384-3(1))*** Independently Published.

Carlson, Suzanne. Svenska-Vietnamesiska Trubbel/Rắc Rối Tvåspråkig Bilderbok För Barn. Carlson, Richard. 2019. (SWE.). 24p. (J). pap. 11.99 *(978-1-0744-2550-0(2))* Independently Published.

Carlson, Suzanne. Svenska-Vietnamesiska Verktyg/dụng Cụ Barns Tv&#65533;spr&#65533;kiga Bildordbok. Carlson, Richard. 2019. (SWE.). 26p. (J). pap. 11.99 ***(978-1-6934-3319-1(2))*** Independently Published.

—Svenska-Vitryska Fordon/Транспартныя сродкі Barns Tv&#65533;spr&#65533;kiga Bildordbok. Carlson, Richard. 2019. (SWE.). 24p. (J). pap. 11.99 ***(978-1-6886-4601-8(9))*** Independently Published.

—Svenska-Vitryska Mina K&#65533;nslor &#65533;r S&#65533;rade/Абражаныя пачуцці Tv&#65533;spr&#65533;kig Bilderbok F&#65533;r Barn. Carlson, Richard. 2019. (SWE.). 24p. (J). pap. 11.99 ***(978-1-6967-9201-1(0))*** Independently Published.

—Svenska-Vitryska Nummer/Лічбы Bildordbok F&#65533;r Tv&#65533;spr&#65533;kiga Barn. Carlson, Richard. 2019. (SWE.). 26p. (J). pap. 11.99 ***(978-1-7104-2272-6(6))*** Independently Published.

—Svenska-Vitryska Skolan/Школа Barns Tv&#65533;spr&#65533;kiga Bildordbok. Carlson, Richard. 2019. (SWE.). 24p. (J). pap. 11.99 ***(978-1-7028-5367-5(5))*** Independently Published.

—Svenska-Vitryska Tid/Час Tv&#65533;spr&#65533;kig Bilderbok F&#65533;r Barn. Carlson, Richard. 2019. (SWE.). 28p. (J). pap. 11.99 ***(978-1-6986-3120-2(0))*** Independently Published.

Carlson, Suzanne. Svenska-Vitryska Trubbel/Непрыемнасці; Tvåspråkig Bilderbok För Barn. Carlson, Richard. 2019. (SWE.). 24p. (J). pap. 11.99 *(978-1-0729-9804-4(1))* Independently Published.

Carlson, Suzanne. Svenska-Vitryska Verktyg/Інструменты Barns Tv&#65533;spr&#65533;kiga Bildordbok. Carlson, Richard. 2019. (SWE.). 26p. (J). pap. 11.99 ***(978-1-6908-4348-1(9))*** Independently Published.

—Svenska-Welsh Mina K&#65533;nslor &#65533;r S&#65533;rade/Fy Nheimladau Yn Brifo Tv&#65533;spr&#65533;kig Bilderbok F&#65533;r Barn. Carlson, Richard. 2019. (SWE.). 24p. (J). pap. 11.99 ***(978-1-6981-9550-6(8))*** Independently Published.

—Svenska-Welsh Verktyg/Offer Barns Tv&#65533;spr&#65533;kiga Bildordbok. Carlson, Richard. 2019. (SWE.). 26p. (J). pap. 11.99 ***(978-1-6934-3601-7(9))*** Independently Published.

—Svenska-Xhosa Fordon/Izithuthi Barns Tv&#65533;spr&#65533;kiga Bildordbok. Carlson, Richard. 2019. (SWE.). 24p. (J). pap. 11.99 ***(978-1-6900-8640-6(8))*** Independently Published.

—Svenska-Xhosa Nummer/Amanani Bildordbok F&#65533;r Tv&#65533;spr&#65533;kiga Barn. Carlson, Richard. 2019. (SWE.). 26p. (J). pap. 11.99 ***(978-1-6702-1693-9(4))*** Independently Published.

—Svenska-Xhosa Skolan/Isikolo Barns Tv&#65533;spr&#65533;kiga Bildordbok. Carlson, Richard. 2019. (SWE.). 24p. (J). pap. 11.99 ***(978-1-7056-7878-7(5))*** Independently Published.

—Svenska-Xhosa Tid/Ixesha Tv&#65533;spr&#65533;kig Bilderbok F&#65533;r Barn. Carlson, Richard. 2019. (SWE.). 28p. (J). pap. 11.99 ***(978-1-7022-2529-8(1))*** Independently Published.

Carlson, Suzanne. Svenska-Xhosa Trubbel/Ingxaki Tvåspråkig Bilderbok För Barn. Carlson, Richard. 2019. (SWE.). 24p. (J). pap. 11.99 *(978-1-0744-2677-4(0))* Independently Published.

Carlson, Suzanne. Svenska-Xhosa Verktyg/Izixhobo Barns Tv&#65533;spr&#65533;kiga Bildordbok. Carlson, Richard. 2019. (SWE.). 26p. (J). pap. 11.99 ***(978-1-6934-4083-0(0))*** Independently Published.

—Svenska-Yiddisch Verktyg Barns Tv&#65533;spr&#65533;kiga Bildordbok. Carlson, Richard. 2019. (SWE.). 26p. (J). pap. 11.99 ***(978-1-6934-4798-3(3))*** Independently Published.

—Svenska-Yoruba Fordon Barns Tv&#65533;spr&#65533;kiga Bildordbok. Carlson, Richard. 2019. (SWE.). 24p. (J). pap. 11.99 ***(978-1-6900-8810-3(9))*** Independently Published.

—Svenska-Yoruba Mina K&#65533;nslor &#65533;r S&#65533;rade/&#65533; d&#65533;n M&#65533; lọ́k&#65533;n Mi Tv&#65533;spr&#65533;kig Bilderbok F&#65533;r Barn. Carlson, Richard. 2019. (SWE.). 24p. (J). pap. 11.99 ***(978-1-6981-9750-0(0))*** Independently Published.

—Svenska-Yoruba Nummer Bildordbok F&#65533;r Tv&#65533;spr&#65533;kiga Barn. Carlson, Richard. 2019. (SWE.). 26p. (J). pap. 11.99 ***(978-1-6702-1888-9(0))*** Independently Published.

—Svenska-Yoruba Skolan Barns Tv&#65533;spr&#65533;kiga Bildordbok. Carlson, Richard. 2019. (SWE.). 24p. (J). pap. 11.99 ***(978-1-7056-8110-7(7))*** Independently Published.

—Svenska-Yoruba Tid/&#65533;k&#65533;k&#65533; Tv&#65533;spr&#65533;kig Bilderbok F&#65533;r Barn. Carlson, Richard. 2019. (SWE.). 28p. (J). pap. 11.99 ***(978-1-7022-2759-9(6))*** Independently Published.

Carlson, Suzanne. Svenska-Yoruba Trubbel Tvåspråkig Bilderbok För Barn. Carlson, Richard. 2019. (SWE.). 24p. (J). pap. 11.99 *(978-1-0744-3226-3(6))* Independently Published.

Carlson, Suzanne. Svenska-Yoruba Verktyg/Awọn Irin Iṣe Barns Tv&#65533;spr&#65533;kiga Bildordbok. Carlson, Richard. 2019. (SWE.). 26p. (J). pap. 11.99 ***(978-1-6934-5371-7(1))*** Independently Published.

—Svenska-Zulu Fordon/Izimoto Barns Tv&#65533;spr&#65533;kiga Bildordbok. Carlson, Richard. 2019. (SWE.). 24p. (J). pap. 11.99 ***(978-1-6906-3124-8(4))*** Independently Published.

—Svenska-Zulu Mina K&#65533;nslor &#65533;r S&#65533;rade/ Ngiphatheke Kabuhlungu Tv&#65533;spr&#65533;kig Bilderbok F&#65533;r Barn. Carlson, Richard. 2019. (SWE.). 24p. (J). pap. 11.99 ***(978-1-6981-9848-4(5))*** Independently Published.

—Svenska-Zulu Nummer/Izinombolo Bildordbok F&#65533;r Tv&#65533;spr&#65533;kiga Barn. Carlson, Richard. 2019. (SWE.). 26p. (J). pap. 11.99 ***(978-1-6702-2045-5(1))*** Independently Published.

—Svenska-Zulu Skolan/Isikole Barns Tv&#65533;spr&#65533;kiga Bildordbok. Carlson, Richard. 2019. (SWE.). 24p. (J). pap. 11.99 ***(978-1-7056-8364-4(9))*** Independently Published.

—Svenska-Zulu Tid/Isikhathi Tv&#65533;spr&#65533;kig Bilderbok F&#65533;r Barn. Carlson, Richard. 2019. (SWE.). 28p. (J). pap. 11.99 ***(978-1-7022-2922-7(X))*** Independently Published.

Carlson, Suzanne. Svenska-Zulu Trubbel/Inkinga Tvåspråkig Bilderbok För Barn. Carlson, Richard. 2019. (SWE.). 24p. (J). pap. 11.99 *(978-1-0744-3336-9(X))* Independently Published.

Carlson, Suzanne. Svenska-Zulu Verktyg/Amathuluzi Barns Tv&#65533;spr&#65533;kiga Bildordbok. Carlson, Richard. 2019. (SWE.). 26p. (J). pap. 11.99 ***(978-1-6934-5664-0(8))*** Independently Published.

Carlson, Suzanne. Italiano-Basco Guaio/Arazoa Libro Illustrato Bilingue per Bambini. Carlson, Suzanne. 2019. (ITA.). 24p. (J). pap. 10.99 *(978-1-0989-5550-2(1))* Independently Published.

Carlton Publishing Group. Fabulous Animals. 2016. (Cool & Calm Coloring for Kids Bks.). (ENG.). 48p. (J). (gr. 2-6). pap. 6.99 *(978-1-4380-0926-1(7)*, B.E.S. Publishing) Peterson's.

Carluccio, Maria. Dress Me Up! A Mix-And-Match Play Book. 2018. (ENG.). 16p. (J). (gr. -1 — 1). bds. 12.99 *(978-1-4521-6039-9(2))* Chronicle Bks. LLC.

—Jump into January. Blackstone, Stella. 2004. 32p. (J). 15.99 *(978-1-84148-629-1(9))* Barefoot Bks., Inc.

—On y Danse les Saisons. Blackstone, Stella. 2016. (FRE.). (J). pap. *(978-1-78285-298-8(0))* Barefoot Bks., Inc.

—Skip Through the Seasons. Blackstone, Stella. (J). 2010. 17p. bds. 14.99 *(978-1-84686-398-1(8))*; 2009. 32p. 16.99 *(978-1-84686-293-9(0))* Barefoot Bks., Inc.

—The Sounds Around Town. 2011. 24p. (J). (gr. -1-3). pap. 7.99 *(978-1-84686-430-8(5))* Barefoot Bks., Inc.

Carluccio, Maria. Un Recorrido Por Las Estaciones. Carluccio, Maria. Blackstone, Stella. 2009. 32p. (J). (gr. -1-2). pap. 7.99 *(978-1-84686-291-5(4))* Barefoot Bks., Inc.

—Skip Through the Seasons. Carluccio, Maria. Blackstone, Stella. 2006. (Seek-and-Find Bks.). 32p. (J). (gr. -1-k). pap. 7.99 *(978-1-905236-71-8(9))* Barefoot Bks., Inc.

—The Sounds Around Town. Carluccio, Maria. (ENG.). (J). 2016. 32p. (gr. -1-k). bds. 14.99 *(978-1-78285-281-0(6))*; 2010. 13p. 14.99 *(978-1-84686-362-2(7))* Barefoot Bks., Inc.

Carman, Debby. Cha Cha, the Dancing Dog. Carman, Debby. 2007. 28p. (J). (gr. -1-1). 14.99 *(978-0-9777340-5-4(6))* Faux Paw Media Group.

—Chewdalootie, Doing My Duty. Carman, Debby. 2007. 28p. (J). (gr. -1-1). 14.99 *(978-0-9777340-3-0(X))* Faux Paw Media Group.

—I'm Gronk & I'm Green. Carman, Debby. 2007. 28p. (J). (gr. -1-1). 14.99 *(978-0-9777340-0-9(5))* Faux Paw Media Group.

—Kittywimpuss Got Game. Carman, Debby. 2007. 28p. (J). (gr. -1-1). 14.99 *(978-0-9777340-4-7(8))* Faux Paw Media Group.

—The Nutcracker Cats of the Kremlin. Carman, Debby. 2007. 80p. (J). (gr. 1-7). 28.99 *(978-0-9777340-7-8(2))* Faux Paw Media Group.

—Purrlonia's Lullaby. Carman, Debby. 2008. 28p. (J). (gr. -1-1). 14.99 *(978-0-9777340-1-6(3))* Faux Paw Media Group.

Carman, William. The Little Secret. Saunders, Kate. 2012. (ENG.). 240p. (J). (gr. 3-6). pap. 11.99 *(978-0-312-67427-4(9)*, 900072842) Square Fish.

Carmb, Sara Lynn & Tadgell, Nicole. Real Sisters Pretend, 1 vol. Lambert, Megan Dowd & Daniels, Peter. 2016. (ENG.). 32p. (J). (gr. k-5). 16.95 *(978-0-88448-441-7(6)*, 884441) Tilbury Hse. Pubs.

Carmi, Giora. A Circle of Friends, 1 vol. 2006. (ENG.). 32p. (J). (gr. k-9). pap. 5.95 *(978-1-59572-060-3(X))* Star Bright Bks., Inc.

—A Journey to Paradise: And Other Jewish Tales. Schwartz, Howard. 2005. (Jewish Storyteller Ser.). 48p. (J). (gr. -1-3). 16.95 *(978-0-943706-21-4(1))*; pap. 9.95 *(978-0-943706-16-0(5))* Simcha Media Group. (Devora Publishing).

—The Magical Reindeer. Ocasio, David. 2004. (ENG.). 32p. per. 14.99 *(978-1-4134-2896-4(7))* Xlibris Corp.

—Night Lights: A Sukkot Story. Goldin, Barbara Diamond. 2004. (gr. k-3). 13.95 *(978-0-8074-0803-2(4)*, 142687) URJ Pr.

—The Rooster Prince. 2005. 48p. (J). (gr. 1-4). pap. 9.95 *(978-0-943706-49-8(1))*; (gr. 2-5). 16.95 *(978-0-943706-45-0(9))* Simcha Media Group. (Devora Publishing).

Carmi, Giora. Torah Commentary for Our Times: Volume 1: Genesis. Fields, Harvey J. 2020. (ENG.). 144p. (YA). pap. 26.95 ***(978-0-88123-252-3(1))*** Central Conference of American Rabbis/CCAR Pr.

Carmi, Giora. A Circle of Friends, 1 vol. Carmi, Giora. 2003. (ENG.). 32p. (J). 15.95 *(978-1-932065-00-8(8))* Star Bright Bks., Inc.

Carmichael, Peyton. The Donkey's Easter Tale, 1 vol. Colvin, Adele Bibb. 2008. (Donkey Tales Ser.). (ENG.). 32p. (J). (gr. k-3). 16.99 *(978-1-58980-593-4(3)*, Pelican Publishing) Arcadia Publishing.

Carnavas, Peter. Blue Whale Blues. Carnavas, Peter. 2016. (ENG.). 32p. (J). 11.99 *(978-1-61067-458-4(8))* Kane Miller.

Carnavas, Peter. A Quiet Girl. Carnavas, Peter. 2020. (ENG.). 32p. (J). (gr. k-2). 18.95 ***(978-1-77278-122-9(3))*** Pajama Pr. CAN. Dist: Ingram Publisher Services.

Carnehl, Jeff. Christmas Around the World. Trunkhill, Brenda. 2009. 32p. (J). (gr. k). 6.99 *(978-0-7586-1757-6(7))* Concordia Publishing Hse.

Carnell, Bobbie. Polly's Lost. Carnell, Bobbie. 2020. (Polly the Possum Ser.: Vol. 2). (ENG.). 30p. (J). pap. 6.95 ***(978-1-63051-836-3(0))*** Chiron Pubns.

Carnero, Carmen, jt. illus. see Martello, Annapaola.

Carney, Deborah. Walking along with My Dog. Taeckens, Geri. 2005. (J). 16.99 *(978-0-9774546-0-0(6))* Accessibilities.

Carney, Patrick. Homes: From Start to Finish. Carney, Patrick, photos by. Kreger, Claire. 2003. 32p. (J). 24.95 *(978-1-4103-0169-7(9)*, Blackbirch Pr., Inc.) Cengage Gale.

Carnovsky. Illuminature: Discover 180 Animals with Your Magic Three Color Lens. Williams, Rachel. 2016. (See 3 Images In 1 Ser.). (ENG.). 64p. (J). (gr. 3-6). 30.00 *(978-1-84780-887-5(5)*, Wide Eyed Editions) Quarto Publishing Group UK GBR. Dist: Hachette Bk. Group.

Carnovsky. Illuminightmare: Explore the Supernatural with Your Magic Three-Color Lens. Brownridge, Lucy. 2019. (See 3 Images In 1 Ser.). (ENG.). 64p. (J). (gr. 2-6). ***(978-1-78603-547-9(2)***, Wide Eyed Editions) Quarto Publishing Group UK.

—Illumisaurus: Explore the World of Dinosaurs with Your Magic Three Colour Lens. Brownridge, Lucy. 2020. (See 3 Images In 1 Ser.). (ENG.). 64p. (J). (gr. k-3). 30.00 ***(978-0-7112-5250-9(5)***, Wide Eyed Editions) Quarto Publishing Group UK GBR. Dist: Hachette Bk. Group.

Carol, Light. Chickensing Story Book Board. Carol, Light. 2003. 60p. (J). *(978-0-9745803-0-2(9))* Little Big Tomes.

Carol, Racklin-Siegel. Let My People Go! Goldstein, Jessica & Inker, Inna, eds. 2011. (ENG & HEB.). 32p. (J). pap. 10.95 *(978-0-939144-67-9(0))* EKS Publishing Co.

Carola, Dominic. Aladdin Live Action: a Friend Like Him. Francis, Suzanne. 2019. (ENG.). 40p. (J). (gr. -1-k). 16.99 *(978-1-368-03707-5(0))* Disney Pr.

Carola, Dominic & Feltman, Ryan. Dumbo Live Action Picture Book. Glass, Calliope. 2019. (ENG.). 40p. (J). (gr. -1-k). 16.99 *(978-1-368-02764-9(4))* Disney Pr.

Carolan, Christine. The Ballad of Booster Bogg. Jackson, Ellen B. 2011. (J). *(978-1-934860-07-6(7))* Shenanigan Bks.

—Flowers for Pudding Street. Mannone, Christine. 2009. (ENG.). 32p. (J). 15.95 *(978-1-934860-02-1(6))* Shenanigan Bks.

—Too Much of a Good Thing. Wasserman, Mira. 2003. 32p. (J). (gr. -1-3). pap. 6.95 *(978-1-58013-066-0(6))*; Vol. (ENG.). 15.95 *(978-1-58013-082-0(8))* Lerner Publishing Group. (Kar-Ben Publishing).

Carolan, Joanna. This Is My Piko. 2009. 58p. 17.95 incl. audio compact disk *(978-0-9715333-0-1(X))* Banana Patch Pr.

Carolan, Joanna F. Where Are My Slippers? A Book of Colors. Carolan, Dr. 32p. 2007. 17.95 *(978-0-9715333-7-0(7))*; 2005. (J). pap. 16.95 *(978-0-9715333-6-3(9))* Banana Patch Pr.

Carolan, Joanna F. Old Makana Had a Taro Farm. Carolan, Joanna F. 2008. 48p. 17.95 *(978-0-9715333-9-4(3))* Banana Patch Pr.

Carolan, Sean & Denson, Abby. Power Party, Vol. 1. Mccraken, Craig et al. 2013. (Powerpuff Girls Ser.). (ENG.). 148p. pap. 19.99 *(978-1-61377-733-6(7)*, 9781613777336) Idea & Design Works, LLC.

Carole, Isaacs. Toothbugs!, Alexander, Geoff. l.t. ed. 2005. 12p. (J). bds. 12.95 *(978-0-9760944-0-1(1))* Alexander-Marcus Publishing.

Caron, Melissa. Tales of the Bruhaven Bears: Book 1. West, Jeanie. Burian, Richard, ed. 2017. (ENG.). 98p. (J). pap. *(978-0-6480111-0-1(0))* Jeanie West.

—Tales of the Bruhaven Bears: Book 2: Izzy & Oskie. West, Jeanie. Burian, Richard, ed. 2018. (ENG.). 74p. (J). pap. *(978-0-6480111-1-8(9))* Jeanie West.

Caron, Mona. The Boy Without a Name. Shah, Idries. 2007. (ENG.). 32p. (J). pap. 9.99 *(978-1-883536-94-7(4)*, Hoopoe Bks.) I S H K.

—The Boy Without a Name: English-Dari Edition. Shah, Idries. 2017. (Hoopoe Teaching-Stories Ser.). (ENG.). (J). (gr. k-6). pap. 9.99 *(978-1-946270-09-2(1)*, Hoopoe Bks.) I S H K.

—The Boy Without a Name: English-Pashto Edition. Shah, Idries. 2017. (Hoopoe Teaching-Stories Ser.). (ENG & PUS.). (J). (gr. k-6). pap. 9.99 *(978-1-944493-54-7(9)*, Hoopoe Bks.) I S H K.

—The Boy Without a Name: English-Urdu Bilingual Edition. Shah, Idries. 2016. (URD & ENG.). (J). (gr. k-6). pap. 9.99 *(978-1-942698-73-9(9)*, Hoopoe Bks.) I S H K.

—The Boy Without a Name / el Nino Sin Nombre. Shah, Idries. Wirkala, Rita, tr. 2007. 32p. (J). 18.00 *(978-1-883536-92-3(8))*; pap. 7.99 *(978-1-883536-93-0(6))* I S H K. (Hoopoe Bks.).

—Many Worlds: Native Life along the Anza Trail. 2012. (ENG.). 24p. (J). pap. 7.95 *(978-1-59714-167-3(4))* Heyday.

Caron, Mona. Le Petit Gar&#65533;on Qui N'avait Pas de Nom: French-Arabic Edition. Shah, Idries. 2018. (Hoopoe Teaching-Stories Ser.). (FRE.). 40p. (J). (gr. 3-6). pap. 9.99 ***(978-1-949358-42-1(9)***, Hoopoe Bks.) I S H K.

Caron, Romi. Enquete Tres Speciale. Ducharme, Huguette. 2004. (Collection des 6 Ans: Vol. 32). (FRE.). 68p. (YA). 7.95 *(978-2-922565-94-2(7))* Editions de la Paix CAN. Dist: World of Reading, Ltd.

—Uumajut: Learn about Arctic Wildlife, 1 vol. Awa, Simon et al. ed. 2010. (ENG.). 32p. (J). (gr. 2-2). pap. 9.95 *(978-1-926569-08-6(3))* Inhabit Media Inc. CAN. Dist: Consortium Bk. Sales & Distribution.

—Uumajut - Learn about Arctic Wildlife!, 1 vol., Vol. 2. Awa, Simon et al. Otak, Leah, tr. ed. 2011. (ENG.). 48p. (J). (gr. 1-3). pap. 10.95 *(978-1-926569-22-2(9))* Inhabit Media Inc. CAN. Dist: Consortium Bk. Sales & Distribution.

Carpenter, Anthony. Big Bad Bible Giants, 1 vol. Strauss, Ed. 2005. (2:52 Ser.). (ENG.). 112p. (J). pap. 7.99 *(978-0-310-70869-8(9))* Zonderkidz.

—Creepy Creatures & Bizarre Beasts from the Bible, 1 vol. Osborne, Rick et al. 2004. (2:52 Ser.). (ENG.). 128p. (J). pap. 7.99 *(978-0-310-70654-0(8))* Zonderkidz.

—Iktomi y Muskrat. Jenkins, Amanda. 2016. (Jump into Genre Ser.). (SPA.). (J). (gr. 2). 5.25 *(978-1-4788-3613-1(X))* Newmark Learning LLC.

Carpenter, Anthony. Weird & Gross Bible Stuff, 1 vol. Carpenter, Anthony. Osborne, Rick et al. 2003. (2:52 Ser.). (ENG.). 112p. (J). pap. 7.99 *(978-0-310-70484-3(7))* Zonderkidz.

Carpenter, Christopher. Lilly's Heart: The Veterinary Clinic Cases Series. 2006. 32p. (J). per. 9.95 *(978-0-9766641-0-9(0))* Ichabod Ink.

Carpenter, Debra. Pete & Patricia Prairie Dog & their Pack of Prairie Pups. Lastoka, Mariann. 2003. 40p. 6.50 *(978-1-892860-05-7(8)*, 5) M R L, Inc.

Carpenter, Kathy L. Things We Wish to Say. Bauereis, Anna. 2020. (ENG.). 38p. (J). 16.95 ***(978-0-578-54222-5(6))*** Mascot Bks., Inc.

Carpenter, Mark And Anna. The Big Bible Storybook: 188 Bible Stories to Enjoy Together, 1 vol. Barfield, Maggie. 2009. 256p. (J). 18.99 *(978-0-8254-7424-8(8)*, Candle Bks.) Lion Hudson PLC GBR. Dist: Kregel Pubns.

Carpenter, Mike. Rhino Trouble. Olsen, Grant Orrin. 2015. (J). 14.99 *(978-1-4621-1665-2(5))* Cedar Fort, Inc./CFI Distribution.

Carpenter, Nancy. Abe Lincoln: Abe Lincoln. Winters, Kay. 2003. (ENG.). 40p. (J). (gr. k-3). 17.99 *(978-0-689-82554-5(4)*, Simon & Schuster Bks. For Young Readers) Simon & Schuster Bks. For Young Readers.

—Abe Lincoln: The Boy Who Loved Books. Winters, Kay. 2004. 38p. (J). (gr. -1-3). reprint ed. 17.00 *(978-0-7567-7969-6(3))* DIANE Publishing Co.

—Abe Lincoln: The Boy Who Loved Books. Winters, Kay. 2006. (ENG.). 40p. (J). (gr. k-3). reprint ed. 8.99 *(978-1-4169-1268-2(1)*, Aladdin) Simon & Schuster Children's Publishing.

—Apples to Oregon: Being the (Slightly) True Narrative of How a Brave Pioneer Father Brought Apples, Peaches, Pears, Plums, Grapes, & Cherries (and Children) Across the Plains. Hopkinson, Deborah. 2008. (ENG.). 40p. (J). (gr. -1-3). 7.99 *(978-1-4169-6746-0(X)*, Aladdin) Simon & Schuster Children's Publishing.

—Apples to Oregon: Being the (Slightly) True Narrative of How a Brave Pioneer Father Brought Apples, Peaches, Pears, Plums, Grapes, & Cherries (and Children) Across the Plains. Hopkinson, Deborah. 2004. (ENG.). 40p. (J). (gr. -1-3). 19.99 *(978-0-689-84769-1(6))* Simon & Schuster, Inc.

—Baby Radar. Nye, Naomi Shihab. 2003. 32p. (J). lib. bdg. 16.89 *(978-0-688-15949-8(4))* HarperCollins Pubs.

—Balderdash! John Newbery & the Boisterous Birth of Children's Books (Nonfiction Books for Kids, Early Elementary History Books) Markel, Michelle. 2017. (ENG.). 44p. (J). 17.99 *(978-0-8118-7922-4(4))* Chronicle Bks. LLC.

—Dear Mr. Washington. Cullen, Lynn. 2015. 32p. (J). (gr. k-3). 16.99 *(978-0-8037-3038-0(1)*, Dial Bks) Penguin Young Readers Group.

—Emma Dilemma: Big Sister Poems. George, Kristine O'Connell. 2011. (ENG.). 48p. (J). (gr. 1-4). 17.99 *(978-0-618-42842-7(9)*, 100346) Houghton Mifflin Harcourt Publishing Co.

—Fannie in the Kitchen: The Whole Story from Soup to Nuts of How Fannie Farmer Invented Recipes with Precise Measurements. Hopkinson, Deborah. 2004. (ENG.). 40p. (J). (gr. -1-4). reprint ed. 7.99 *(978-0-689-86997-6(5)*, Simon & Schuster/Paula Wiseman Bks.) Simon & Schuster/Paula Wiseman Bks.

—Good Guys, Bad Guys. Rocklin, Joanne. 2020. (ENG.). 32p. (J). (gr. -1-3). 16.99 *(978-1-4197-3417-5(2)*, 1138401, Abrams Bks. for Young Readers) Abrams, Inc.

—Have You Heard about Lady Bird? Poems about Our First Ladies. Singer, Marilyn. 2018. 56p. (J). (gr. -1-3). 17.99 *(978-1-4847-2660-0(X))* Disney Pr.

—I Could Do That! Esther Morris Gets Women the Vote. White, Linda Arms. 2005. (ENG.). 40p. (J). (gr. 2-4). 18.99 *(978-0-374-33527-4(3)*, 900022004, Farrar, Straus & Giroux (BYR)) Farrar, Straus & Giroux.

—Imogene's Last Stand. Fleming, Candace. 2014. (ENG.). 40p. (J). (gr. -1-3). lib. bdg. 18.80 *(978-1-62765-377-0(5))* Perfection Learning Corp.

—Imogene's Last Stand. Fleming, Candace. 2014. 40p. (J). (gr. -1-3). 7.99 *(978-0-385-38654-8(0)*, Dragonfly Bks.) Random Hse. Children's Bks.

—A Letter to My Teacher. Hopkinson, Deborah. 2017. (ENG.). 40p. (J). (gr. -1-3). 17.99 *(978-0-375-86845-0(3)*, Schwartz & Wade Bks.) Random Hse. Children's Bks.

—Lucky Ducklings. Moore, Eva. 2013. (ENG.). 32p. (J). (gr. k-2). 16.99 *(978-0-439-44861-1(1)*, Orchard Bks.) Scholastic, Inc.

—Mother Jones & Her Army of Mill Children. Winter, Jonah. 2020. (ENG.). 40p. (J). (gr. -1-3). 20.99 *(978-0-449-81292-1(8)*, Schwartz & Wade Bks.) Random Hse. Children's Bks.

—Only a Star. Facklam, Margery. 2004. 32p. (J). (gr. -1-3). pap. 8.00 *(978-0-8028-5174-1(6))* Eerdmans, William B. Publishing Co.

—A Picnic in October. Bunting, Eve. 2004. (ENG.). 32p. (J). (gr. -1-3). reprint ed. pap. 7.99 *(978-0-15-205065-8(5)*, 1195297) Houghton Mifflin Harcourt Publishing Co.

—Queen Victoria's Bathing Machine. 2014. (ENG.). 40p. (J). (gr. k-3). 18.99 *(978-1-4169-2753-2(0)*, Simon & Schuster/Paula Wiseman Bks.) Simon & Schuster/Paula Wiseman Bks.

—Thomas Jefferson & the Mammoth Hunt: The True Story of the Quest for America's Biggest Bones. Clickard, Carrie. 2019. (ENG.). 40p. (J). (gr. -1-3). 17.99 *(978-1-4814-4268-8(6)*, Beach Lane Bks.) Beach Lane Bks.

—Twister. Beard, Darleen Bailey & Beard, Darleen B. 2003. (ENG.). 32p. (J). (gr. -1-3). pap. 9.99 *(978-0-374-48014-1(1)*, 900020242) Square Fish.

—11 Experiments That Failed. Offill, Jenny. 2011. (ENG.). 40p. (J). (gr. -1-3). 17.99 *(978-0-375-84762-2(6),* Schwartz & Wade Bks.) Random Hse. Children's Bks.
—17 Things I'm Not Allowed to Do Anymore. Offill, Jenny. 2011. (ENG.). 32p. (J). (gr. -1-3). pap. 7.99 *(978-0-375-86601-2(9),* Dragonfly Bks.) Random Hse. Children's Bks.
Carpenter, Stephen. A Bad Case of the Giggles: Poems That Will Make You Laugh Out Loud. Lansky, Bruce. 2013. (Giggle Poetry Ser.). (ENG.). 128p. (J). (gr. 1-7). per. 9.99 *(978-1-4169-5197-1(0),* Running Pr.) Running Pr.
—I Hope I Don't Strike Out! & Other Funny Sports Poems. Lansky, Bruce. 2008. 30p. *(978-0-88166-535-2(5))* Meadowbrook Pr.
—If Kids Ruled the School: Kids' Favorite Funny School Poems. 2004. (Giggle Poetry Ser.). (ENG.). 80p. (J). (gr. k-7). pap. 8.99 *(978-0-689-03273-8(0),* Running Pr.) Running Pr.
—If Kids Ruled the School: More Kids' Favorite Funny School Poems. 2004. 73p. (J). 8.95 *(978-0-88166-468-3(5))* Meadowbrook Pr.
—I've Been Burping in the Classroom: And Other Silly Sing-along Songs. Lansky, Bruce, ed. 2007. 32p. (J). *(978-0-88166-521-5(5))* Meadowbrook Pr.
—I've Been Burping in the Classroom: And Other Silly Sing-Along Songs. 2007. (Giggle Poetry Ser.). (ENG.). 32p. (J). (gr. 1-7). 9.95 *(978-1-4169-2946-8(0),* Running Pr.) Running Pr.
—Mary Had a Little Jam: And Other Silly Rhymes. Lansky, Bruce. ed. 2017. (Giggle Poetry Ser.). (ENG.). 80p. (J). (gr. -1-2). pap. 8.99 *(978-1-4814-9278-2(0),* Running Pr.) Running Pr.
—Mary Had a Little Jam, & Other Silly Rhymes. 2004. 32p. (J). *(978-0-88166-470-6(7))* Meadowbrook Pr.
—Mary Had a Little Jam & Other Silly Rhymes: Expanded with Twice As Many Rhymes. 2016. 80p. (J). *(978-0-88166-597-0(5))* Meadowbrook Pr.
—Miles of Smiles: A Collection of Laugh-Out-Loud Poems. Lansky, Bruce, ed. 2013. (Giggle Poetry Ser.). (ENG.). 132p. (J). (gr. 1-7). pap. 9.99 *(978-0-689-03461-9(X),* Running Pr.) Running Pr.
—My Teacher's in Detention: Kids' Favorite Funny School Poems. Lansky, Bruce. 2006. (Giggle Poetry Ser.). (ENG.). 80p. (J). (gr. 1-7). per. 8.99 *(978-0-689-05245-3(6),* Running Pr.) Running Pr.
—Rolling in the Aisles: A Collection of Laugh-Out-Loud Poems. Lanksy, Bruce. 2004. 116p. (J). *(978-0-88166-473-7(1))* Meadowbrook Pr.
—What I Did on My Summer Vacation: Kids' Favorite Funny Poems about Summer Vacation. Lansky, Bruce. 2009. *(978-0-88166-539-0(8))* Meadowbrook Pr.
—What I Did on My Summer Vacation: Kids' Favorite Funny Summer Vacation Poems. 2009. (Giggle Poetry Ser.). (ENG.). 80p. (J). (gr. 1-9). pap. 8.99 *(978-1-4169-7047-7(9),* Running Pr.) Running Pr.
Carpenter, Suzanne. Happy Christmas Sglod. Morgan, Ruth. 2003. (ENG.). 32p. pap. 12.95 *(978-1-84323-261-2(8))* Beekman Bks., Inc.
—Rapping on the Window. Stephens, Chris S. 2004. (ENG.). 48p. pap. 12.95 *(978-1-84323-360-2(6))* Beekman Bks., Inc.
—So Hungry. Morden, Daniel. 2004. (ENG.). 32p. pap. 29.95 *(978-1-84323-455-5(6))* Beekman Bks., Inc.
Carpenter, Tad. Bitty Bot. McCanna, Tim. 2016. (Bitty Bot Ser.). (ENG.). 32p. (J). (gr. -1-3). 16.99 *(978-1-4814-4929-8(X),* Simon & Schuster Bks. For Young Readers) Simon & Schuster Bks. For Young Readers.
—Bitty Bot's Big Beach Getaway. McCanna, Tim. 2018. (Bitty Bot Ser.). (ENG.). 32p. (J). (gr. -1-3). 17.99 *(978-1-4814-4931-1(1),* Simon & Schuster/Paula Wiseman Bks.) Simon & Schuster/Paula Wiseman Bks.
—Monster's New Undies. Berger, Samantha. 2017. 40p. (J). (gr. -1-k). 16.99 *(978-0-545-87973-6(6),* Orchard Bks.) Scholastic, Inc.
—Ninja, Ninja, Never Stop! Tuell, Todd. (ENG.). (J). (gr. -1-k). 2020. 24p. bds. 7.99 *(978-1-4197-4307-8(4));* 2014. 32p. 14.95 *(978-1-4197-1027-8(3))* Abrams, Inc. (Abrams Appleseed).
—NRDC Simple Steps for Kids Activity Book. Smith, Molly & NRDC. 2010. (ENG.). 80p. (J). (gr. 3-17). pap., act. bk. ed. 12.99 *(978-0-8118-7141-9(X))* Chronicle Bks. LLC.
—Pantone: Color Puzzles: 6 Color-Matching Puzzles. Pantone. 2013. (ENG.). 12p. (J). (gr. -1 — 1). bds. 17.99 *(978-1-4197-0939-5(9),* Abrams Appleseed) Abrams, Inc.
—Science Experiments You Can Eat. Cobb, Vicki. 2016. (ENG.). 256p. (J). (gr. 3-7). pap. 9.99 *(978-0-06-237729-6(9))* HarperCollins Pubs.
—The Summer of May. Galante, Cecilia. 2012. (ENG.). 256p. (J). (gr. 4-6). 21.19 *(978-1-4169-8023-0(7),* Aladdin) Simon & Schuster Children's Publishing.
—Trick-Or-Treat: A Happy Haunter's Halloween. Leppanen, Debbie. 2013. (ENG.). 40p. (J). (gr. k-3). 16.99 *(978-1-4424-3398-4(1))* Simon & Schuster Children's Publishing.
—Tugboat Bill & the River Rescue. Brill, Calista. 2017. (ENG.). 40p. (J). (gr. -1-3). 17.99 *(978-0-06-236618-4(1),* HarperCollins) HarperCollins Pubs. Ltd. GBR. Dist: HarperCollins Pubs.
—Zoom! Zoom! Sounds of Things That Go in the City. Burleigh, Robert. 2014. (ENG.). 32p. (J). (gr. -1-3). 18.99 *(978-1-4424-8315-6(6),* Simon & Schuster Bks. For Young Readers) Simon & Schuster Bks. For Young Readers.
Carpentier, Margaux. Darwin's Tree of Life. Bright, Michael. 2019. (ENG.). 48p. (J). 18.95 *(978-1-62371-919-7(4),* Crocodile Bks.) Interlink Publishing Group, Inc.
Carr, A. E. K. Alice Eats Wonderland. Imholtz, August & Tannenbaum, Alison. 2009. (ENG.). 120p. pap. 14.95 *(978-1-4290-9106-0(1))* Applewood Bks.
Carr, Bethany. Dream BIG! Parker, Cassie. 2020. (Find Your Spark(le) Ser.). (ENG.). 128p. (J). (gr. 4-7). pap. 9.99 ***(978-1-78958-639-8(9))*** Top That! Publishing PLC GBR. Dist: Independent Pubs. Group.
—Follow Your Rainbow! Parker, Cassie. 2020. (Find Your Spark(le) Ser.). (ENG.). 128p. (J). (gr. 4-7). pap. 9.99 ***(978-1-78958-640-4(2))*** Top That! Publishing PLC GBR. Dist: Independent Pubs. Group.
—Sparkle-Go-seek Farm. Button, Katie. 2020. (Sparkle-Go-Seek Lift-The-Flap Bks.). (ENG.). 10p. (J). (— 1). bds. 8.99 ***(978-1-78958-571-1(6))*** Top That! Publishing PLC GBR. Dist: Independent Pubs. Group.
—Sparkle-Go-seek Ocean. Button, Katie. 2020. (Sparkle-Go-Seek Lift-The-Flap Bks.). (ENG.). 10p. (J). (— 1). bds. 8.99 ***(978-1-78958-572-8(4))*** Top That! Publishing PLC GBR. Dist: Independent Pubs. Group.
—Sparkle-Go-seek Rescue. Button, Katie. 2020. (Sparkle-Go-Seek Lift-The-Flap Bks.). (ENG.). 10p. (J). (— 1). bds. 8.99 ***(978-1-78958-574-2(0))*** Top That! Publishing PLC GBR. Dist: Independent Pubs. Group.
Carr, Greg. The Jiggleworm. Carr, Heather. ed. 2005. 18p. (J). 21.95 incl. audio compact disk *(978-0-9768450-0-3(8),* Giggletins) Le Bk. Moderne, LLC.
Carr, Holly. What is Pink? 2003. 24p. (J). (gr. -1-1). *(978-0-921156-92-5(8))* Rubicon Publishing, Inc.
—What is Pink? Rossetti, Christina. 2003. 24p. pap. *(978-1-894915-13-7(5))* Rubicon Publishing, Inc.
Carr, Karen. A Busy Day for Stegosaurus. Bentley, Dawn. (ENG.). 36p. (J). (gr. -1-2). 2005. 9.95 *(978-1-59249-156-8(1),* PS2451); 2004. 8.95 *(978-1-59249-210-7(X),* SD2401); 2004. 14.95 *(978-1-59249-153-7(7),* H2401); 2004. pap. 6.95 *(978-1-59249-154-4(5),* S2401) Soundprints.
—Dino Dung: The Scoop on Fossil Feces. Chin, Karen & Holmes, Thom. 2005. (Step into Reading Ser.). 48p. (J). (gr. 2-5). 11.65 *(978-0-7569-5163-4(1))* Perfection Learning Corp.
—The Hungry T-Rex. Galvin, Laura Gates & Studiomouse Staff. 2011. (Read, Play & Go Ser.). (ENG.). 20p. (gr. -1-k). 9.99 *(978-1-60727-288-5(1))* Studio Mouse LLC.
—It's Tyrannosaurus Rex! Bentley, Dawn. (Smithsonian's Prehistoric Pals Ser.). (ENG.). 36p. (J). (gr. -1-2). 2004. 8.95 *(978-1-59249-212-1(6),* SD2400); 2003. 9.95 *(978-1-59249-160-5(X),* PS2450) Soundprints.
—Lead the Way, Velociraptor! Bentley, Dawn. 2004. (Read & Discover (Soundprints) Ser.). (ENG.). 32p. (J). (gr. -1-3). pap. 3.95 *(978-1-59249-304-3(1),* S2031) Soundprints.
—Mosasaurus: Mighty Ruler of the Sea. Wagner, Karen. 2008. (ENG.). 36p. (J). (gr. k-2). 8.95 *(978-1-59249-782-9(9));* 2.95 *(978-1-59249-783-6(7));* 9.95 *(978-1-59249-784-3(5));* 14.95 *(978-1-59249-780-5(2))* Soundprints.
—Pterandon. Bailey, Gerry. 2011. (Smithsonian Prehistoric Zone Ser.). (ENG.). 32p. (J). (gr. k-3). *(978-0-7787-1800-0(X),* 1325446); pap. *(978-0-7787-1813-0(1),* 1325446) Crabtree Publishing Co.
—Pteranodon Soars. Bentley, Dawn. 2005. (Smithsonian's Prehistoric Pals Ser.). (ENG.). 36p. (J). (gr. -1-2). 8.95 *(978-1-59249-371-5(8),* SD2405); 9.95 *(978-1-59249-373-9(4),* PS2455); 14.95 *(978-1-59249-369-2(6),* H2405); 2.95 *(978-1-59249-372-2(6),* S2455); pap. 6.95 *(978-1-59249-370-8(X),* S2405) Soundprints.
—Snack Time, Tyrannosaurus Rex! Bentley, Dawn. 2004. (ENG.). 32p. (J). (gr. -1-3). pap. 3.95 *(978-1-59249-302-9(5),* S2033) Soundprints.
—Stegosaurus. Bailey, Gerry. 2011. (Smithsonian Prehistoric Zone Ser.). (ENG.). 32p. (J). (gr. k-3). *(978-0-7787-1803-1(4))* Crabtree Publishing Co.
—Surprise, Stegosaurus! Bentley, Dawn. 2004. (ENG.). 32p. (J). (gr. -1-3). pap. 3.95 *(978-1-59249-305-0(X),* S2032) Soundprints.
—Triceratops. Bentley, Dawn & Studio Mouse Staff. 2008. (ENG.). 24p. (J). (gr. 3-7). 4.99 *(978-1-59069-622-4(0))* Studio Mouse LLC.
—Triceratops. Bailey, Gerry. 2011. (Smithsonian Prehistoric Zone Ser.). (ENG.). 32p. (J). (gr. k-3). lib. bdg. *(978-0-7787-1804-8(2),* 1325450); pap. *(978-0-7787-1817-8(4),* 1325450) Crabtree Publishing Co.
—Triceratops Gets Lost. Bentley, Dawn. (Smithsonian's Prehistoric Pals Ser.). (J). 2009. 21.95 incl. audio compact disk *(978-1-59249-544-3(3));* 2005. (ENG.). 36p. (gr. -1-2). 8.95 *(978-1-59249-216-9(9),* SD2403); 2004. (ENG.). 36p. (gr. -1-2). pap. 6.95 *(978-1-59249-166-7(9),* S2403) Soundprints.
—Tylosaurus. Bailey, Gerry. 2011. (Smithsonian Prehistoric Zone Ser.). (ENG.). 32p. (J). (gr. k-3). *(978-0-7787-1805-5(0),* 1325451); pap. *(978-0-7787-1818-5(2),* 1325451) Crabtree Publishing Co.
—Tyrannosaurus Rex. Bentley, Dawn & Studio Mouse Staff. 2008. (ENG.). 24p. (J). (gr. 3-7). 4.99 *(978-1-59069-621-7(2))* Studio Mouse LLC.
—Tyrannosaurus Rex. Bailey, Gerry. 2011. (Smithsonian Prehistoric Zone Ser.). (ENG.). 32p. (J). (gr. k-3). *(978-0-7787-1806-2(9),* 1325452); pap. *(978-0-7787-1819-2(0),* 1325452) Crabtree Publishing Co.
—Velociraptor. Bentley, Dawn. 2005. (Smithsonian's Prehistoric Pals Ser.). (ENG.). 36p. (J). (gr. -1-2). 9.95 *(978-1-59249-168-1(5),* PS2453) Soundprints.
—Velociraptor. Bailey, Gerry. 2011. (Smithsonian Prehistoric Zone Ser.). (ENG.). 32p. (J). (gr. k-3). *(978-0-7787-1807-9(7));* pap. *(978-0-7787-1820-8(4))* Crabtree Publishing Co.
—Velociraptor: Small & Speedy. Bentley, Dawn. (ENG.). 36p. (J). (gr. -1-2). 2005. 9.95 *(978-1-59249-164-3(2),* PS2452); 2004. pap. 6.95 *(978-1-59249-162-9(6),* S2402) Soundprints.
—Velociraptor - Small & Speedy. Bentley, Dawn. 2004. (Smithsonian's Prehistoric Pals Ser.). (ENG.). 36p. (J). (gr. -1-2). 8.95 *(978-1-59249-214-5(2),* SD2402) Soundprints.
—Watch Out, Triceratops! Bentley, Dawn. 2004. (Read & Discover (Soundprints) Ser.). (ENG.). 32p. (J). (gr. -1-3). pap. 3.95 *(978-1-59249-303-6(3),* S2030) Soundprints.
—Woolly Mammoth. Bailey, Gerry. 2011. (Smithsonian Prehistoric Zone Ser.). (ENG.). 32p. (J). (gr. k-3). *(978-0-7787-1808-6(5),* 1325454); pap. *(978-0-7787-1821-5(2),* 1325454) Crabtree Publishing Co.
—Woolly Mammoth in Trouble. Bentley, Dawn. (Smithsonian's Prehistoric Pals Ser.). (ENG.). 36p. (J). (gr. -1-2). 2005. 14.95 *(978-1-59249-364-7(5),* H2404); 2005. 2.95 *(978-1-59249-367-8(X),* S2454); 2005. pap. 6.95 *(978-1-59249-365-4(3),* S2404); 2004. 8.95 *(978-1-59249-366-1(1),* SD2404); 2004. 9.95 *(978-1-59249-368-5(8),* PS2454) Soundprints.
Carr, Karen. Jurassic Shark. Carr, Karen. Diffily, Deborah. 2nd ed. 2004. (ENG.). 32p. (J). (gr. 4-6). pap. 27.95 *(978-1-59687-538-8(0),* ipicturebooks) ibooks, Inc.
Carr, Karen. A Busy Day for Stegosaurus. Carr, Karen, tr. Bentley, Dawn. 2005. (Smithsonian's Prehistoric Pals Ser.). (ENG.). 36p. (J). (gr. -1-2). 2.95 *(978-1-59249-155-1(3),* S2451) Soundprints.
—It's Tyrannosaurus Rex! Carr, Karen, tr. Bentley, Dawn. 2005. (Smithsonian's Prehistoric Pals Ser.). (ENG.). 36p. (J). (gr. -1-2). 14.95 *(978-1-59249-157-5(X),* H2400); pap. 6.95 *(978-1-59249-158-2(8),* S2400) Soundprints.
—Triceratops Gets Lost. Carr, Karen, tr. Bentley, Dawn. 2005. (Smithsonian's Prehistoric Pals Ser.). (ENG.). 36p. (J). (gr. -1-2). 14.95 *(978-1-59249-165-0(0),* H2403); 2.95 *(978-1-59249-167-4(7),* S2453) Soundprints.
—Velociraptor: Small & Speedy. Carr, Karen, tr. Bentley, Dawn. 2005. (Smithsonian's Prehistoric Pals Ser.). (ENG.). 36p. (J). (gr. -1-2). 14.95 *(978-1-59249-161-2(8),* H2402); 2.95 *(978-1-59249-163-6(4),* S2452) Soundprints.
Carr, Karent. Dinosaurs & More! Bentley, Dawn & Studio Mouse Staff. rev. ed. 2006. (ENG.). 60p. (J). 12.95 *(978-1-59069-487-9(2))* Soundprints.
Carr, Kathryn. Lizbeth Lou Got a Rock in Her Shoe. Howell, Troy. 2016. (ENG.). 36p. (J). (gr. k-7). 17.99 *(978-0-9913866-5-9(5))* Ripple Grove Pr.
Carr, Lindsey. Mice of the Round Table #1: a Tail of Camelot. Leung, Julie. (Mice of the Round Table Ser.: 1). (ENG.). (J). (gr. 3-7). 2017. 320p. pap. 6.99 *(978-0-06-240400-8(8));* 2016. 304p. 16.99 *(978-0-06-240399-5(0))* HarperCollins Pubs.
—Mice of the Round Table #2: Voyage to Avalon. Leung, Julie. (Mice of the Round Table Ser.: 2). (ENG.). (J). (gr. 3-7). 2018. 352p. pap. 6.99 *(978-0-06-240403-9(2));* 2017. 336p. 16.99 *(978-0-06-240402-2(4))* HarperCollins Pubs.
—Mice of the Round Table #3: Merlin's Last Quest. Leung, Julie. 2018. (Mice of the Round Table Ser.: 3). (ENG.). 368p. (J). (gr. 3-7). 16.99 *(978-0-06-240405-3(9))* HarperCollins Pubs.
Carr, Matt. Not So Different: What You Really Want to Ask about Having a Disability. Burcaw, Shane. 2017. (ENG.). 40p. (J). 17.99 *(978-1-62672-771-7(6),* 900172893) Roaring Brook Pr.
Carr, Matt. Superbat. Carr, Matt. 2017. (ENG.). 32p. (J). (gr. -1-k). 16.99 *(978-1-338-16052-9(4),* Scholastic Pr.) Scholastic, Inc.
Carr, Michael Douglas. The Boy Who Couldn't. Coverdale, Rachel. Let's Get Booked, Amanda, ed. 2019. (ENG.). 162p. (J). (gr. 3-6). pap. 8.87 ***(978-1-9161080-1-1(6))*** Willow Breeze Publishing.
Carr Roberts, Donna S. The Adventures of Mr. Fuzzy Ears: Searching for a Furry Friend. Carr Roberts, Donna S. 2018. (Adventures of Mr. Fuzzy Ears Ser.: Vol. 1). (ENG.). 36p. (J). 16.95 *(978-0-692-18421-9(X));* pap. 11.95 *(978-0-692-14309-4(2))* Mr. Fuzzy Ears LLC.
Carr, Stephen. The Curry Comb Caper. Carr, Debra. 2006. 48p. per. 8.95 *(978-1-933912-59-2(6))* Westview Publishing Co., Inc.
—The Feed Trough Thriller. Carr, Debra. 2007. 56p. per. 8.95 *(978-1-933912-66-0(9))* Westview Publishing Co., Inc.
—Misty Is Missing. Carr, Debra. 2008. 52p. pap. 8.95 *(978-0-9816172-7-5(1))* Westview Publishing Co., Inc.
Carr, Tabatha. A Lesson from a Tree. Mervyn, Catherine Antolino. 2008. 32p. pap. 12.95 *(978-0-9821153-2-9(6))* Living Waters Publishing Co.
Carrasco, José Manuel. El viaje de las semillas. 2008. 48p. *(978-84-95225-83-2(2))* Saure, Jean-Francois Editor.
Carrasco, Rick. A Dog Called Family. Davidson, Denise H. 2020. (ENG.). 26p. (J). pap. 10.00 ***(978-1-6591-7918-7(1))*** Independently Published.
Carratello, Veronica. Greta's Story: The Schoolgirl Who Went on Strike to Save the Planet. Camerini, Valentina. Giovannoni, Moreno, tr. 2019. (ENG.). 144p. (J). (gr. 3-7). 17.99 *(978-1-5344-6877-1(3),* Aladdin) Simon & Schuster Children's Publishing.
Carrel, Douglas. Monsterology: The Complete Book of Monstrous Creatures. Drake, Ernest. Steer, Dugald A., ed. 2008. (Ologies Ser.). (ENG.). 32p. (J). (gr. 3-7). 27.99 *(978-0-7636-3940-2(0))* Candlewick Pr.
Carrell, Douglas. Alienology. Grey, Allan. Steer, Dugald A., ed. 2010. (Ologies Ser.: 10). (ENG.). 32p. (J). (gr. 3-7). 21.99 *(978-0-7636-4565-6(6))* Candlewick Pr.
Carreres, Albert. Cars: Radiator Springs. Porter, Alan J. 2010. (World of Cars Ser.). (ENG.). 112p. (J). pap. 9.99 *(978-1-60886-502-4(9))* Boom! Studios.
—Cars: The Rookie. Porter, Alan J. 2009. (World of Cars Ser.). (ENG.). 112p. (J). 24.99 *(978-1-60886-522-2(3))* Boom! Studios.
—Cars Vol. 2: Radiator Springs. Porter, Alan J. 2010. (World of Cars Ser.). (ENG.). 112p. (J). 24.99 *(978-1-60886-528-4(2))* Boom! Studios.
—Cars: the Rookie. Porter, Alan J. 2011. (Kaboom! Graphic Novels Ser.). (ENG.). 112p. (J). (gr. 4-7). 26.19 *(978-1-934506-84-4(2))* Boom! Studios.
Carrescia, Reid. Magic on the Wall, 1 vol. Saccheri, Josephine. 2009. 11p. pap. 24.95 *(978-1-61546-374-9(7))* America Star Bks.
Carretero, Mónica. The Big Booger Battle. Acosta, Alicia. 2019. (ENG.). 40p. (J). 15.95 *(978-84-17123-91-8(1))* NubeOcho Ediciones ESP. Dist: Consortium Bk. Sales & Distribution.
—Clucky & the Magic Kettle. Pavon, Mar. Brokenbrow, Jon, tr. 2013. (Clucky Ser.). (ENG.). 30p. (J). (gr. -1-k). 15.95 *(978-84-15619-44-4(8))* Cuento de Luz SL ESP. Dist: Publishers Group West (PGW).
—Clucky in the Garden of Mirrors. Pavon, Mar. Brokenbrow, Jon, tr. 2011. (Clucky Ser.). (ENG.). 44p. (J). (gr. k-2). 14.95 *(978-84-15241-04-1(6))* Cuento de Luz SL ESP. Dist: Publishers Group West (PGW).
—Clucky the Hen. Pavon, Mar. Brokenbrow, Jon, tr. 2011. (Clucky Ser.). (ENG.). 32p. (J). (gr. -1-k). 14.95 *(978-84-15241-08-9(9))* Cuento de Luz SL ESP. Dist: Publishers Group West (PGW).
—Cuerpo de Nube. Eulate, Ana. 2011. (Luz Ser.). (SPA.). 26p. (J). (gr. 1-4). 14.95 *(978-84-937814-0-8(1))* Cuento de Luz SL ESP. Dist: Publishers Group West (PGW).
—El Emocionómetro Del Inspector Drilo. Isern, Susanna. 2018. (SPA.). 100p. (J). 22.95 *(978-84-17123-16-1(4))* NubeOcho Ediciones ESP. Dist: Consortium Bk. Sales & Distribution.
—La Gallina Cocorina. Pavon, Mar. 2011. (Cocorina Ser.). 32p. (J). (gr. k-2). 14.95 *(978-84-937814-6-0(0))* Cuento de Luz SL ESP. Dist: Publishers Group West (PGW).
—Inspector Croc's Emotion-O-Meter. Isern, Susanna. 2018. (ENG.). 100p. (J). 22.95 *(978-84-17123-07-9(5))* NubeOcho Ediciones ESP. Dist: Consortium Bk. Sales & Distribution.
—La Isla de Los Mocos. Acosta, Alicia. 2019. (ENG.). 40p. (J). 15.95 *(978-84-17123-90-1(3))* NubeOcho Ediciones ESP. Dist: Consortium Bk. Sales & Distribution.
—Little Cloud Lamb. Eulate, Ana. Brokenbrow, Jon, tr. 2011. (Light (Cuento de Luz) Ser.). (ENG.). 28p. (J). (gr. 1-4). 14.95 *(978-84-938240-2-0(X))* Cuento de Luz SL ESP. Dist: Publishers Group West (PGW).
—Mom Goes to War. Martin, Irene. Brokenbrow, Jon, tr. 2013. 24p. (J). (gr. 2-4). 15.95 *(978-84-15503-20-0(2))* Cuento de Luz SL ESP. Dist: Publishers Group West (PGW).
—Yago's Heartbeat. Miranda, Conchita. Brokenbrow, Jon, tr. 2011. (Light (Cuento de Luz) Ser.). (ENG.). 42p. (J). (gr. 1-4). 15.95 *(978-84-938240-3-7(8))* Cuento de Luz SL ESP. Dist: Publishers Group West (PGW).
Carretero, Mónica. Circo de Pulgas. Carretero, Mónica. 2011. (Artistas Mini-Animalistas Ser.). (SPA.). 34p. (J). (gr. k-2). 14.95 *(978-84-937814-5-3(2))* Cuento de Luz SL ESP. Dist: Publishers Group West (PGW).
—Fairy Handbook. Carretero, Mónica. Brokenbrow, Jon, tr. 2011. (Handbooks Ser.). (ENG.). 32p. (J). (gr. k-2). 14.95 *(978-84-937814-9-1(5))* Cuento de Luz SL ESP. Dist: Publishers Group West (PGW).
—La Familia Bola. Carretero, Mónica. 2011. (Artistas Mini-Animalistas Ser.). (SPA.). 32p. (J). (gr. k-2). 14.95 *(978-84-938240-4-4(6))* Cuento de Luz SL ESP. Dist: Publishers Group West (PGW).
—FLEA CIRCUS. Carretero, Mónica. Brokenbrow, Jon, tr. 2011. (Mini-Animalist Ser.). (ENG.). 32p. (J). (gr. k-2). 14.95 *(978-84-938240-0-6(3))* Cuento de Luz SL ESP. Dist: Publishers Group West (PGW).
—HAUNTED HOUSES HANDBOOK. Carretero, Mónica. Brokenbrow, Jon, tr. 2013. (Handbooks Ser.). (ENG.). 32p. (J). (gr. k-2). 15.95 *(978-84-15241-05-8(4))* Cuento de Luz SL ESP. Dist: Publishers Group West (PGW).
—Manual de Piratas. Carretero, Mónica. 2011. (Manuales Ser.). (SPA.). 34p. (J). (gr. k-2). 14.95 *(978-84-937814-3-9(6))* Cuento de Luz SL ESP. Dist: Publishers Group West (PGW).
—Pirate Handbook. Carretero, Mónica. Brokenbrow, Jon, tr. 2011. (Handbooks Ser.). 32p. (J). (gr. k-2). 14.95 *(978-84-937814-8-4(7))* Cuento de Luz SL ESP. Dist: Publishers Group West (PGW).
—ROLY-POLIES. Carretero, Mónica. Brokenbrow, Jon, tr. 2011. (Mini-Animalist Ser.). (ENG.). 32p. (J). (gr. k-2). 14.95 *(978-84-938240-1-3(1))* Cuento de Luz SL ESP. Dist: Publishers Group West (PGW).
—Witches Handbook. Carretero, Mónica. Brokenbrow, Jon, tr. 2012. (ENG.). 32p. (J). (gr. k-2). 14.95 *(978-84-15241-06-5(2))* Cuento de Luz SL ESP. Dist: Publishers Group West (PGW).
Carretero, M3/4nica. Los Latidos de Yago. Miranda, Conchita. 2011. (Luz Ser.). (SPA.). 40p. (J). (gr. 2-4). 15.95 *(978-84-937814-6-4(4))* Cuento de Luz SL ESP. Dist: Publishers Group West (PGW).
Carretero-Suarez, Mónica. Hansel, Gretel, & the Pudding Plot. Thomas, Isabel. (Fairy Tales Today Ser.). (ENG.). 24p. (J). (gr. -1-2). 2016. 9.95 *(978-1-4795-8748-3(6));* 2015. 23.99 *(978-1-4795-8614-1(5))* Capstone. (Picture Window Bks.).
Carrick, Donald. Journey to Topaz. Uchida, Yoshiko. 2015. (ENG.). 168p. pap. 10.00 *(978-1-890771-91-1(0))* Heyday.
—Patrick's Dinosaurs. Carrick, Carol. 2006. (ENG.). 32p. (J). (gr. -1-3). 10.99 *(978-0-618-73275-3(6),* 100517) Houghton Mifflin Harcourt Publishing Co.
Carrick, Paul. Mothers Are Like That. Carrick, Carol. 2007. (ENG.). 32p. (J). (gr. k — 1). 7.99 *(978-0-618-75241-6(2),* 100523) Houghton Mifflin Harcourt Publishing Co.
—Wired. Suen, Anastasia. 2007. 32p. (J). (gr. 1-4). pap. 7.95 *(978-1-57091-494-2(X));* (gr. k-3). 22.44 *(978-1-57091-599-4(7))* Charlesbridge Publishing, Inc.
Carrick, Paul. Watch Out for Wolfgang. Carrick, Paul. 2009. 32p. (J). (gr. -1-3). 16.95 *(978-1-57091-689-2(6))* Charlesbridge Publishing, Inc.
Carrick, Paul & Shillinglaw, Bruce. Dinosaur Parents, Dinosaur Young: Uncovering the Mystery of Dinosaur Families. Zoehfeld, Kathleen Weidner. 2006. 58p. (J). (gr. 3-6). tchr. ed. 22.44 *(978-0-395-91338-3(1))* Houghton Mifflin Harcourt Publishing Co.
Carrier, Jamie. The Story Tree: Year 1. Bergquist, S. a. 2020. (ENG.). 102p. (J). (gr. 2-6). 14.99 ***(978-1-7333079-1-8(5))*** Get It Factory, The.
Carrier, Jason. How Do Alligators Praise the Lord? Franklin, Kirk. 2005. 24p. (J). (gr. 4-7). 11.99 incl. audio compact disk *(978-1-59185-209-4(9),* Charisma Kids) Charisma Media.
Carrier, R. H. The Littlest Boat in the Big Sea. Carrier, R. H. 2019. (ENG.). 40p. (J). pap. 9.99 ***(978-1-0884-0315-0(8))*** Independently Published.

C

Carrier, Tracey Dahle. Come Worship with Me: A Journey Through the Church Year. Boling, Ruth L. 2010. (ENG.). (J). pap. 14.00 (978-0-664-23717-2(7)) Westminster John Knox Pr.

Carrigg, Susan. Sally Jo Survives Sixth Grade: A Journal. Keltz, Karen. 2013. 180p. pap. 9.99 (978-0-9857281-1-3(6)) HAPPY HOUSE PR.

Carrilho, Andre. Porch Lies: Tales of Slicksters, Tricksters, & Other Wily Characters. McKissack, Patricia. 2006. (ENG.). 160p. (J). (gr. 3-7). 19.99 (978-0-375-83619-0(5), Schwartz & Wade Bks.) Random Hse. Children's Bks.

—You Never Heard of Sandy Koufax?! Winter, Jonah. 2016. 40p. (J). (gr. -1-3). 7.99 (978-0-553-49842-4(8), Dragonfly Bks.) Random Hse. Children's Bks.

Carrillo, Azalea & Morrissey, Kay, photos by. IV Antología Nuevo Milenio: Narració y Poesia. Kassandra, ed. I.t. ed. 2003. (SPA.). 100p. (YA). pap. 12.00 (978-1-931481-48-9(2)) LiArt-Literature & Art.

Carrillo, Charles M. Shoes for the Santo Niño. Church, Peggy Pond. 2013. 64p. 25.95 (978-1-936744-23-7(6), Rio Grande Bks.) LPD Pr.

—Shoes for the Santo Niño: Zapitillos para el Santo Niño: A Bilingual Tale. Church, Peggy Pond. 2009. (SPA & ENG.). 61p. (J). pap. (978-1-890689-64-3(5), Rio Grande Bks.) LPD Pr.

Carrillo, J. Raul. Use Your Noodle! The Adventures of a Hollywood Poodle Named Doodle. Messick, Maxine. Hodsdon-Carr, Sandra, ed. Urrwin-Camara, Nancy, tr. 2004. (SPA.). 90p. 15.00 (978-0-9753508-0-5(3)) Aurora Bks.

Carrillo, Jorge. Flying High (Vuela Alto) Felix, Mph Sausan El Burai. 2016. (ENG.). (J). pap. 14.99 (978-0-9979788-2-7(1)) Mindstir Media.

Carrington, Janine. Mermaid Warrior Squad. Adams, Karin. 2018. (Lorimer Illustrated Humor Ser.). (ENG.). 152p. (J). (gr. 4-7). pap. 8.99 (978-1-4594-1146-3(3), 000a45c0-c367-4cec-a430-0c48e79b5fb2); lib. bdg. 27.99 (978-1-4594-1261-3(3), d82ac15c-5016-4d61-905a-760737715256) James Lorimer & Co. Ltd., Pubs. CAN. Dist: Lerner Publishing Group.

Carrington, Lorena. Vasilisa the Wise & Tales of Other Brave Young Women. 2017. (ENG.). (YA). pap. (978-0-6481030-6-6(4)) Serenity Press.

—Wiser Than Evening: Quotations from Poetry, Fairytales & Literature. 2018. (ENG.). 42p. (YA). (978-0-6483317-6-6(8)) Serenity Press.

Carrington, Marsha Gray. Coriander the Contrary Hen. Chaconas, Dori. 2007. (Carolrhoda Picture Bks.). (ENG.). 32p. (J). (gr. k-3). lib. bdg. 16.95 (978-1-57505-749-1(2), Carolrhoda Bks.) Lerner Publishing Group.

—Saving the Liberty Bell. Mcdonald, Megan. 2005. (ENG.). 32p. (J). (gr. k-3). 19.99 (978-0-689-85167-4(7), Atheneum/Richard Jackson Bks.) Simon & Schuster Children's Publishing.

Carrington, Matt. Dr. Mollie Cule Reboots the Robot: Awesome Science Activities You Can Do at Home. Muntz, Kendra & Kenis, Daniel. 2014. 160p. (J). (978-0-7166-0633-8(X)) World Bk., Inc.

—The Secret Files of Professor L. Otto Funn: Or, Stop Being a Slug, Open This Book, & Make Your Brain Happy. Gors, Steven E. 2013. 159p. (J). pap. (978-0-7166-1324-4(7)) World Bk., Inc.

Carrol, Patrick, jt. illus. see Brouhard, Crary.

Carroll, Chellie. The Book of Me: My Life, My Style, My Dreams. Bailey, Ellen & Williams, Imogen. 2018. (ENG.). 128p. (J). (gr. 4-6). pap. 12.95 (978-1-4549-2906-2(5)) Sterling Publishing Co., Inc.

Carroll, Emily. Baba Yaga's Assistant. McCoola, Marika. 136p. (J). (gr. 5-9). 2020. pap. 8.99 (978-1-5362-1310-2(1)); 2015. 16.99 (978-0-7636-6961-4(X)) Candlewick Pr.

—Speak: the Graphic Novel. Anderson, Laurie Halse. 2nd ed. 2018. (ENG.). 384p. (YA). 19.99 (978-0-374-30028-9(3), 900129381, Farrar, Straus & Giroux (BYR)) Farrar, Straus & Giroux.

Carroll, Hannah E. Carter's Star City Trolley Ride. Archual, Valerie. 2019. (ENG.). 28p. (J). pap. 9.99 (978-1-7244-7241-0(0)) CreateSpace Independent Publishing Platform.

Carroll, Jackie, jt. illus. see Huang, Linda.

Carroll, James Christopher. The Boy & the Moon. Carroll, James Christopher. 2010. (ENG.). 32p. (J). (gr. 1-4). 19.99 (978-1-58536-521-0(1), 202209) Sleeping Bear Pr.

—Papa's Backpack. Carroll, James Christopher. 2015. (ENG.). 32p. (J). (gr. 1-3). 15.99 (978-1-58536-613-2(7), 203942) Sleeping Bear Pr.

—A Song. Carroll, James Christopher. 2019. (ENG.). 32p. (J). (gr. 1-3). 19.99 (978-1-56846-331-5(6), Creative Editions) Creative Co., The.

Carroll, James Christopher & William, Lorna. Nathan Hale: Revolutionary War Hero. Klepeis, Alicia Z. 2018. (American Legends & Folktales Ser.). 32p. (gr. 3-3). 28.50 (978-1-5026-3689-8(1)) Cavendish Square Publishing LLC.

Carroll, Jim & William, Lorna. Buffalo Bill: Wild West Showman. Klepeis, Alicia Z. 2018. (American Legends & Folktales Ser.). 32p. (gr. 3-3). 28.50 (978-1-5026-3678-2(6)) Cavendish Square Publishing LLC.

—Uncle Sam: An American Icon. McMeans, Julia. 2018. (American Legends & Folktales Ser.). 32p. (gr. 3-3). 28.50 (978-1-5026-3697-3(2)) Cavendish Square Publishing LLC.

Carroll, Jr. Otis Best. Mansur, Motesem. 2011. 50p. pap. 24.95 (978-1-4560-4910-2(0)) America Star Bks.

Carroll, Katie. Brewster's New School. Carroll, Michael Shane. 2012. 24p. pap. 5.00 (978-1-937260-13-2(5)) Sleepytown Pr.

—Bye-Bye Brewster. Carroll, Michael Shane. 2012. 20p. pap. 5.00 (978-1-937260-14-9(3)) Sleepytown Pr.

Carroll, M. S. Diane Joan. Monty-Moo the Rabbit Says Get off My Tail. Carroll, M. S. Diane Joan. 2018. (ENG.). 26p. (J). pap. (978-1-78926-234-6(8)) Independent Publishing Network.

—Pandora's Frocks: - a Very Glam Meerkat Wedding. Carroll, M. S. Diane Joan. 2018. (ENG.). 26p. (J). pap. (978-1-78926-236-0(4)) Independent Publishing Network.

Carroll, Martha. The Angels & the Harp. Rea, Sylvia. 2017. (ENG.). (J). pap. 9.95 (978-1-944393-59-5(5)) RIVERRUN BOOKSTORE INC.

Carroll, Michael. Big Bang! The Tongue-Tickling Tale of a Speck That Became Spectacular. DeCristofano, Carolyn Cinami. 2005. 32p. (J). (gr. k-3). pap. 7.95 (978-1-57091-619-9(5)) Charlesbridge Publishing, Inc.

—A Black Hole Is Not a Hole. DeCristofano, Carolyn Cinami. 2017. 80p. (J). (gr. 4-7). pap. 9.99 (978-1-57091-784-4(1)) Charlesbridge Publishing, Inc.

—Max Goes to Jupiter (Second Edition) A Science Adventure with Max the Dog. Bennett, Jeffrey et al. 2nd ed. 2018. (Science Adventures with Max the Dog Ser.). (ENG.). 32p. (J). (gr. k-8). 15.00 (978-1-937548-82-7(1)) Big Kid Science.

—Max Goes to the Space Station: A Science Adventure with Max the Dog. Bennett, Jeffrey. 2013. (Science Adventures with Max the Dog Ser.). (ENG.). 32p. (J). (gr. 2-4). 15.00 (978-1-937548-28-5(7)) Big Kid Science.

—Max Viaja a Júpiter: Una Aventura de Ciencias con el Perro Max. Bennett, Jeffrey et al. 2018. (Science Adventures with Max the Dog Ser.). (SPA.). 32p. (J). (gr. 2-4). 15.00 (978-0-9721819-6-9(2)) Big Kid Science.

Carroll, Pam. Golden Numbers: A California Number Book. Domeniconi, David. 2008. (Count Your Way Across the U. S. A. Ser.). (ENG.). 40p. (J). 17.95 (978-1-58536-173-1(9)) Sleeping Bear Pr.

—M Is for Majestic: A National Parks Alphabet. Domeniconi, David. (ENG.). (J). (gr. k-6). 2007. 48p. per. 7.95 (978-1-58536-333-9(2)); 2003. 40p. 17.95 (978-1-58536-138-0(0)) Sleeping Bear Pr.

—One Nation: America by the Numbers. Scillian, Devin. 2004. (ENG.). 40p. (J). (gr. k-6). pap. 7.95 (978-1-58536-249-3(2)) Sleeping Bear Pr.

—S Is for Star: A Christmas Alphabet. Furlong, Reynolds Cynthia. 2004. (ENG.). 40p. (J). (gr. k-6). pap. 6.95 (978-1-58536-247-9(6)) Sleeping Bear Pr.

Carroll, Raymond. Abcs of Language & Literacy. Pinestein Press. 2007. 180p. per. 19.99 (978-0-9795364-4-1(8)) Chowder Bay Bks.

—Pre-K Prep! Pinestein Press. 2007. 180p. per. 19.99 (978-0-9795364-3-4(X)) Chowder Bay Bks.

Carroll, Rosemary. The Golden Rules of Etiquette at the Plaza. Bloch, Lyudmila & Civitano, Tom. 2004. 48p. (J). lib. bdg. 16.95 (978-0-9755390-0-2(0)) Fifth Ave Pr.

Carroll, Sissy DeWitt. Spike. Medicus, Christine. 2020. (Wingman Chronicles Ser.: Vol. 1). (ENG.). 46p. (J). pap. 9.95 **(978-1-950768-15-8(5))** ProsePress.

Carruthers, Adam. Little Ned. Wagner, Michael. 2020. (ENG.). 24p. (J). (gr. -1-k). 18.99 **(978-1-76012-927-9(5))** Little Hare Bks. AUS. Dist: Independent Pubs. Group.

Carruthers, Sandy. Peril at Summerland Park. Storrie, Paul D. 2012. (Twisted Journeys Ser.: 20). (ENG.). 112p. (J). (gr. 4-7). pap. 45.32 (978-0-7613-9290-3(4));No. 20. lib. bdg. 27.99 (978-0-7613-4935-8(9), 9780761349358) Lerner Publishing Group. (Graphic Universe™).

—Sunjata: Warrior King of Mali: A West African Legend. Fontes, Ron. 2008. (Graphic Myths & Legends Ser.). 48p. (J). (gr. 3-7). lib. bdg. 26.60 (978-0-8225-6758-5(X), Graphic Universe™) Lerner Publishing Group.

—Sunjata: Warrior King of Mali [a West African Legend]. Fontes, Justine & Fontes, Ron. 2009. (Graphic Myths & Legends Ser.). (ENG.). 48p. (J). (gr. 4-8). pap. 9.99 (978-1-58013-891-8(8), Graphic Universe™) Lerner Publishing Group.

—Terror in Ghost Mansion. Storrie, Paul D. 2007. (Twisted Journeys ® Ser.: 3). (ENG.). (J). (gr. 4-7). pap. 45.32 (978-0-8225-9467-3(6)) Lerner Publishing Group.

—Yu the Great: Conquering the Flood. Storrie, Paul D. 2007. (Graphic Myths & Legends Ser.). (ENG.). 48p. (gr. 4-8). lib. bdg. 27.93 (978-0-8225-3088-6(0)) Lerner Publishing Group.

—Yu the Great: Conquering the Flood [a Chinese Legend]. Storrie, Paul D. 2008. (Graphic Myths & Legends Ser.). (ENG.). 48p. (J). (gr. 4-8). per. 9.99 (978-0-8225-6562-8(5), Graphic Universe™) Lerner Publishing Group.

Carruthers, Stuart. Fiddly Fingers: The Misadventures of the Little Boy Who Touched Too Much. Carruthers, Stuart. 2019. (ENG.). 30p. (J). (gr. 4-6). 19.99 (978-1-63102-199-2(0)) Independent Pub.

Carse, A. Duncan. Hans Andersen's Fairy Tales - Illustrated by A. Duncan Carse. Andersen, Hans. 2016. (ENG.). (J). (978-1-4733-3524-0(8)) Read Bks.

Carselle, Cristobal. It's My Turn in the Front Seat: A Children's Rhyming Poetry & Coloring Book. Jaqua, Tiffani. 2020. (ENG.). 110p. (J). pap. 9.75 **(978-1-0764-4926-9(3))** Independently Published.

Carsey, Alice. Heidi. Spyri, Johanna. 2019. (ENG.). 204p. (J). (gr. 4-7). pap. 7.99 (978-1-4209-6135-5(7)) Digireads.com Publishing.

—Pinocchio. 2003. (Library of Tale Ser.).Tr. of Avventure di Pinocchio. (SPA.). 12p. (J). (gr. -1-7). pap. (978-958-30-0986-0(5)) Panamericana Editorial.

—Pinocchio. 2005.Tr. of Avventure di Pinocchio. (ENG.). 136p. (J). (gr. 2-5). 19.95 (978-1-933327-00-6(6)) Purple Bear Bks., Inc.

Carsey, Alice. Pinocchio: The Tale of a Puppet. Collodi, Carlo. 2019. (ENG.). 200p. (J). (gr. 2-4). pap. 9.99 **(978-1-7086-8620-8(7))** Independently Published.

Carsey, Alice. Pinocchio: the Tale of a Puppet. Collodi, C. 2007. (ENG.). 196p. per. (978-1-4065-1462-9(4)) Dodo Pr.

—Pinocchio, the Tale of a Puppet. 2011. 140p. pap. 12.99 (978-1-61203-095-1(5)) Bottom of the Hill Publishing.

Carson, Chuck. Every Cake Has a Baker. Tomo, Shane. 2020. (ENG.). 30p. (J). pap. 9.95 **(978-1-7326661-7-7(2))** Kaio Pubns., Inc.

Carson, Patty, et al. The Girl Who Saw a Flying Dinosaur: Patty Carson & Other Children, & Teenagers & Adults, Have Seen a Living Pterosaur, Sometimes Called a Pterodactyl. 2018. (ENG.). 58p. (J). pap. 7.80 (978-1-7277-7884-7(7)) CreateSpace Independent Publishing Platform.

Carson, Shawn. Keep-It-Cheap: Financially Surviving the Honey-Do List. Tompkins, Bill. 2007. (ENG.). 117p. (YA). spiral bd. (978-0-9741647-3-1(9)) NRG Pubns.

—Miss Molly's Adventure on the Farm: Another great adventure brought to you by Miss Molly & her dog Reyburn. Tompkins, Robyn Lee. 2006. (J). per. (978-0-9741647-7-9(1)) NRG Pubns.

Carson, Shawn K. Miss Molly's Adventure in the Park: Another Great Adventure Brought to You by Miss Molly & Her Dog Reyburn, 10 vols. Tompkins, Robyn Lee. I.t. ed. 2005. (ENG.). 60p. (J). per. (978-0-9741647-6-2(3)) NRG Pubns.

Carstiuc, Sorinel. Chasing Sunsets. Andrus, Kendra. 2017. (ENG.). 36p. (J). pap. 11.95 (978-0-9995444-0-2(3)) Wild Willow Pr.

—God Made Night. Andrus, Kendra. 2017. (ENG.). 36p. (J). pap. 11.95 (978-0-9995444-1-9(1)) Wild Willow Pr.

Cart, Jen. Pea Soup Fog. Smith, Constance. 2004. (ENG.). 32p. (J). (gr. -1-17). 15.95 (978-0-89272-643-1(1)) Down East Bks.

Carter, Abby. Andy Shane & the Barn Sale Mystery. Jacobson, Jennifer Richard. (Andy Shane Ser.: 5). 64p. (J). (gr. k-3). 2010. 4.99 (978-0-7636-4827-5(2)); 2009. 14.99 (978-0-7636-3599-2(5)) Candlewick Pr.

—Andy Shane & the Know-It-All: 4 Books In 1! Jacobson, Jennifer Richard. 2018. (Andy Shane Ser.). 256p. (J). (gr. k-3). 7.99 (978-1-5362-0046-1(8)) Candlewick Pr.

—Andy Shane & the Pumpkin Trick. Jacobson, Jennifer Richard. 2007. (Andy Shane Ser.: 2). (ENG.). 64p. (J). (gr. k-3). per. 4.99 (978-0-7636-3306-6(2)) Candlewick Pr.

—Andy Shane & the Pumpkin Trick. Jacobson, Jennifer Richard. 2008. (Andy Shane Ser.). (J). (gr. -1-3). 25.95 incl. audio (978-1-4301-0313-4(2)); pap. 16.95 incl. audio (978-1-4301-0312-7(4)) Live Oak Media.

—Andy Shane & the Queen of Egypt. Jacobson, Jennifer Richard. 2009. (Andy Shane Ser.: 3). 64p. (J). (gr. k-3). 4.99 (978-0-7636-4404-8(8)) Candlewick Pr.

—Andy Shane & the Very Bossy Dolores Starbuckle. Jacobson, Jennifer Richard. 2006. (Andy Shane Ser.: 1). 64p. (J). (gr. k-3). 4.99 (978-0-7636-3044-7(6)) Candlewick Pr.

—Andy Shane & the Very Bossy Dolores Starbuckle. Jacobson, Jennifer Richard. 2008. (Andy Shane Ser.). (J). (gr. -1-3). 25.95 incl. audio (978-1-4301-0321-9(3)); pap. 16.95 incl. audio (978-1-4301-0320-2(5)) Live Oak Media.

—Andy Shane, Hero at Last. Jacobson, Jennifer Richard. 2011. (Andy Shane Ser.: 6). 64p. (J). (gr. k-3). pap. 4.99 (978-0-7636-5293-7(8)) Candlewick Pr.

—Andy Shane Is Not in Love. Jacobson, Jennifer Richard. 2008. (Andy Shane Ser.: 4). 64p. (J). (gr. k-3). 17.44 (978-0-7636-3212-0(0)) Candlewick Pr.

—Andy Shane Is Not in Love. Jacobson, Jennifer Richard. 2009. (Andy Shane Ser.: 4). 64p. (J). (gr. k-3). 4.99 (978-0-7636-4403-1(X)) Candlewick Pr.

—The Best Chef in Second Grade. Kenah, Katharine. 2007. (I Can Read Bks.). 48p. (J). (gr. -1-3). lib. bdg. 16.89 (978-0-06-053562-9(8)) HarperCollins Pubs.

—The Best Chef in Second Grade. Kenah, Katharine. 2008. (I Can Read Level 2 Ser.). (ENG.). 48p. (J). (gr. k-3). pap. 4.99 (978-0-06-053563-6(6), HarperCollins) HarperCollins Pubs. Ltd. GBR. Dist: HarperCollins Pubs.

—The Best Seat in First Grade. Kenah, Katharine. 2020. (I Can Read Level 1 Ser.). 32p. (J). (gr. -1-3). pap. 4.99 (978-0-06-268644-2(5), HarperCollins) HarperCollins Pubs. Ltd. GBR. Dist: HarperCollins Pubs.

—The Best Seat in Kindergarten. Kenah, Katharine. 2019. (My First I Can Read Ser.). (ENG.). 32p. (J). (gr. -1-3). 16.99 (978-0-06-268641-1(0)) HarperCollins Pubs.

—The Best Seat in Kindergarten. Kenah, Katharine. 2019. (My First I Can Read Ser.). (ENG.). 32p. (J). (gr. -1-3). pap. 4.99 (978-0-06-268640-4(2), HarperCollins) HarperCollins Pubs. Ltd. GBR. Dist: HarperCollins Pubs.

—The Best Seat in Second Grade. Kenah, Katharine. 2006. (I Can Read Level 2 Ser.). (ENG.). 48p. (J). (gr. k-3). pap. 4.99 (978-0-06-000736-2(2)) HarperCollins Pubs.

—The Best Seat in Second Grade. Kenah, Katharine. 2006. (I Can Read Bks.). 48p. (J). (gr. -1-3). 11.65 (978-0-7569-6979-0(4)) Perfection Learning Corp.

—The Best Teacher in Second Grade. Kenah, Katharine. (I Can Read Level 2 Ser.). 48p. (J). 2007. (ENG.). (gr. k-3). pap. 4.99 (978-0-06-053566-7(0)); 2006. (gr. -1-3). lib. bdg. 17.89 (978-0-06-053565-0(2)) HarperCollins Pubs.

—The Best Teacher in Second Grade. Kenah, Katharine. 2007. (I Can Read Bks.). 48p. (gr. -1-3). 14.00 (978-0-7569-8105-1(0)) Perfection Learning Corp.

—The Curious Guide to Things That Aren't: Things You Can't Always Touch, See, or Hear. Can You Guess What They Are? Fixx, John & Fixx, James F. 2016. (ENG.). 112p. (J). (gr. 2-7). 12.95 (978-1-63322-176-5(8), Walter Foster Jr) Quarto Publishing Group USA.

—Daddies Do It Different. Sitomer, Alan Lawrence. 2012. (ENG.). 40p. (J). (gr. -1 — 1). 16.99 (978-1-4231-3315-5(3)) Hyperion Pr.

—Daddy's Zigzagging Bedtime Story. Sitomer, Alan Lawrence. 2014. (ENG.). 20p. (J). (gr. -1-k). 16.99 (978-1-4231-8420-1(3)) Hyperion Bks. for Children.

—Emma Dilemma & the Camping Nanny. Hermes, Patricia. 2019. (Emma Dilemma Ser.: 4). (ENG.). 146p. (J). (gr. 3-6). pap. 9.99 (978-1-4778-1079-8(X), 9781477810798, Two Lions) Amazon Publishing.

—Emma Dilemma & the New Nanny, 0 vols. Hermes, Patricia. 2010. (Emma Dilemma Ser.: 1). (ENG.). 114p. (J). (gr. 3-6). pap. 6.99 (978-0-7614-5619-3(8), 9780761456193, Two Lions) Amazon Publishing.

—Emma Dilemma & the Two Nannies, 0 vols. Hermes, Patricia. 2011. (Emma Dilemma Ser.: 2). (ENG.). 126p. (J). (gr. 3-6). pap. 9.99 (978-0-7614-5835-7(2), 9780761458357, Two Lions) Amazon Publishing.

—Emma Dilemma, the Nanny, & the Best Horse Ever, 0 vols. Hermes, Patricia. 2013. (Emma Dilemma Ser.: 6). (ENG.). 144p. (J). (gr. 3-6). pap. 9.99 (978-1-4778-1633-2(X), 9781477816332, Two Lions) Amazon Publishing.

—Emma Dilemma, the Nanny, & the Secret Ferret, 0 vols. Hermes, Patricia. 2010. (Emma Dilemma Ser.: 5). (ENG.). 112p. (J). (gr. 3-6). 15.99 (978-0-7614-5650-6(3), 9780761456506, Two Lions) Amazon Publishing.

—Full House: An Invitation to Fractions. Dodds, Dayle Ann. 2012. 32p. (J). (gr. 1-4). pap. 24.99 (978-0-7636-6090-1(6)) Candlewick Pr.

—Full House: An Invitation to Fractions. Dodds, Dayle Ann. 2009. 32p. (J). (gr. 1-4). pap. 7.99 (978-0-7636-4130-6(8)) Candlewick Pr.

—Hero at Last. Jacobson, Jennifer Richard. 2010. (Andy Shane Ser.: 6). 64p. (J). (gr. k-3). 14.99 (978-0-7636-3600-5(2)) Candlewick Pr.

—Human or Alien? Williams, Suzanne. 2004. (Marvelous Mind of Matthew Mcghee Age 8 Ser.). 57p. (J). (gr. 1-4). 11.65 (978-0-7569-5529-8(7)) Perfection Learning Corp.

—The Lucky Penny? Williams, Suzanne. 2004. 56p. (J). lib. bdg. 15.00 (978-1-4242-0909-5(9)) Fitzgerald Bks.

—Maggie's Monkeys. Sanders-Wells, Linda. 2009. (ENG.). 32p. (J). (gr. -1-2). 16.99 (978-0-7636-3326-4(7)) Candlewick Pr.

—Master of Minds? Williams, Suzanne. 2004. 58p. (J). lib. bdg. 15.00 (978-1-4242-0911-8(0)) Fitzgerald Bks.

—Master of Minds? Williams, Suzanne. 2004. (Marvelous Mind of Matthew Mcghee Age 8 Ser.). 58p. (J). 11.65 (978-0-7569-5530-4(0)) Perfection Learning Corp.

—Ollie's School Day: A Yes-And-No Story. Calmenson, Stephanie. 2019. 24p. (J). (-k). pap. 8.99 (978-0-8234-4521-9(6)) Holiday Hse., Inc.

—Slithery Jake. Provencher, Rose-Marie. 2004. (ENG.). 32p. (J). 15.99 (978-0-06-623820-3(X)) HarperCollins Pubs.

—Too Much Noise in the Library. Chapman, Susan Margaret. 2010. 32p. (J). (gr. 1-4). 17.95 (978-1-60213-026-5(4), Upstart Bks.) Highsmith Inc.

Carter, Alice. My Puppy Patch. Heras, Theo. 2019. (ENG.). 24p. (J). (gr. -1-1). 16.95 (978-1-77278-080-2(4)) Pajama Pr. CAN. Dist: Ingram Publisher Services.

—Our New Kittens. Heras, Theo. 2018. (ENG.). 24p. (J). (gr. -1-1). 15.95 (978-1-77278-060-4(X)) Pajama Pr. CAN. Dist: Ingram Publisher Services.

—Pierre & Paul: Avalanche! Adderson, Caroline. ed. 2020. (Pierre & Paul Ser.: 1). (ENG.). 32p. (J). (gr. -1-3). 16.95 (978-1-77147-327-9(4)) Owlkids Bks. Inc. CAN. Dist: Publishers Group West (PGW).

Carter, Alice. Teaching Mrs. Muddle. Nelson, Colleen. 2020. (ENG.). 32p. (J). (gr. -1-1). 17.95 **(978-1-77278-131-1(2))** Pajama Pr. CAN. Dist: Ingram Publisher Services.

Carter, Amy. The Little Baby Snoogle- Fleejer. Carter, Jimmy. 2014. (ENG.). 24p. (J). 19.95 (978-1-55728-671-0(X)) Univ. of Arkansas Pr.

Carter, Anne. Unitarian Universalism Is a Really Long Name. Dant, Jennifer. 2008. (ENG.). 30p. (J). (gr. 3-7). 12.00 (978-1-55896-508-9(4), Skinner Hse. Bks.) Unitarian Universalist Assn.

Carter, Barbara. Up & down with Lena Larocha. Power, Molly. 2013. 169p. pap. 15.00 (978-1-60571-176-8(4), Shires Press) Northshire Pr.

Carter, Dana. The Starrigans of Little Brook Bottom, 1 vol. Davis, Harold. 2007. (ENG.). 150p. (J). (gr. 3-7). per. (978-1-894294-85-0(8)) Breakwater Bks., Ltd.

Carter, David A. If You're a Robot & You Know It. Musical Robot. 2015. (ENG.). 14p. (J). (gr. -1-k). 16.99 (978-0-545-81980-0(6), Cartwheel Bks.) Scholastic, Inc.

—Who's under That Hat? A Lift-the-Flap Pop-up Adventure. Weeks, Sarah. 2006. 14p. (J). (gr. -1-2). 14.00 (978-1-4223-5440-7(7)) DIANE Publishing Co.

Carter, David A. Alpha Bugs: A Pop-Up Alphabet. Carter, David A. ed. 2006. (David Carter's Bugs Ser.). (ENG.). 28p. (J). (gr. -1-2). 13.99 (978-1-4169-0973-6(7), Little Simon) Little Simon.

—B Is for Box — the Happy Little Yellow Box: A Pop-Up Book. Carter, David A. 2014. (ENG.). 18p. (J). (gr. -1). 12.99 (978-1-4814-0295-8(1), Little Simon) Little Simon.

—Beach Bugs: A Sunny Pop-Up Book by David A. Carter. Carter, David A. 2008. (David Carter's Bugs Ser.). (ENG.). 16p. (J). (gr. -1-2). 12.99 (978-1-4169-5055-4(9), Little Simon) Little Simon.

—Bedtime Bugs: A Pop-Up Good Night Book by David A. Carter. Carter, David A. 2010. (David Carter's Bugs Ser.). (ENG.). 18p. (J). (gr. -1-2). 12.99 (978-1-4169-9960-7(4), Little Simon) Little Simon.

—The Big Bug Book: A Pop-Up Celebration by David A. Carter. Carter, David A. 2008. (David Carter's Bugs Ser.). (ENG.). 16p. (J). (gr. -1-2). 24.99 (978-1-4169-4095-1(2), Little Simon) Little Simon.

—Bitsy Bee Goes to School. Carter, David A. 2014. (David Carter's Bugs Ser.). (ENG.). 24p. (J). (gr. -1-1). pap. 3.99 (978-1-4424-9503-6(0), Simon Spotlight) Simon Spotlight.

—Blue 2 Vol. 2: A Pop-Up Book for Children of All Ages. Carter, David A. 2006. (ENG.). 18p. (J). (gr. 2-5). 29.99 (978-1-4169-1781-6(0), Little Simon) Little Simon.

—A Box of Bugs: 4 Pop-Up Concept Books. Carter, David A. ed. 2011. (David Carter's Bugs Ser.). (ENG.). 64p. (J). (gr. -1-3). 19.99 (978-1-4424-2989-5(5), Little Simon) Little Simon.

—Bugs at the Beach. Carter, David A. 2016. (David Carter's Bugs Ser.). (ENG.). 24p. (J). (gr. -1-1). pap. 4.99 (978-1-4814-4050-9(0), Simon Spotlight) Simon Spotlight.

—Bugs That Go! A Bustling Pop-Up Book. Carter, David A. 2011. (David Carter's Bugs Ser.). (ENG.). 18p. (J). (gr. -1-1). 12.99 (978-1-4169-4097-5(9), Little Simon) Little Simon.

—Builder Bugs: A Busy Pop-Up Book. Carter, David A. 2012. (David Carter's Bugs Ser.). (ENG.). 16p. (J). (gr. -1-2). 12.99 (978-1-4424-2648-1(9), Little Simon) Little Simon.

—Busy Bug Builds a Fort. Carter, David A. 2016. (David Carter's Bugs Ser.). (ENG.). 24p. (J). (gr. -1-1). pap. 3.99 (978-1-4814-4047-9(0), Simon Spotlight) Simon Spotlight.

—Colors: A Bugs Pop-Up Concept Book. Carter, David A. 2010. (David Carter's Bugs Ser.). (ENG.). 16p. (J). (gr.

-1-1). 9.99 *(978-1-4424-0830-2(8),* Little Simon) Little Simon.
—Counting: A Bugs Pop-Up Concept Book. Carter, David A. 2010. (David Carter's Bugs Ser.). (ENG.). 16p. (J). (gr. -1-1). 7.99 *(978-1-4424-0828-9(6),* Little Simon) Little Simon.
—Feely Bugs (Mini Edition) To Touch & Feel. Carter, David A. ed. 2005. (David Carter's Bugs Ser.). (ENG.). 14p. (J). (gr. -1-2). 12.99 *(978-1-4169-0326-0(7),* Little Simon) Little Simon.
—Five Cars Stuck & One Big Truck: A Pop-Up Road Trip. Carter, David A. 2017. (ENG.). 18p. (J). (gr. -1 — 1). bds. 15.99 *(978-1-4814-7119-0(8),* Little Simon) Little Simon.
—Halloween Bugs: Halloween Bugs, Vol. 16. Carter, David A. 2003. (David Carter's Bugs Ser.). (ENG.). 14p. (J). (gr. -1-3). 12.99 *(978-0-689-85916-8(3),* Little Simon) Little Simon.
—The Happy Little Yellow Box: A Pop-Up Book of Opposites. Carter, David A. 2012. (ENG.). 18p. (J). (gr. -1). 14.99 *(978-1-4169-4096-8(0),* Little Simon) Little Simon.
—How Many Bugs in a Box? A Pop-Up Counting Book. Carter, David A. ed. 2006. (David Carter's Bugs Ser.). (ENG.). 20p. (J). (gr. -1-1). 12.99 *(978-1-4169-0804-3(8),* Little Simon) Little Simon.
—Love Bugs: A Pop up Book. Carter, David A. ed. 2003. (ENG.). 12p. (J). (gr. 2-5). 7.99 *(978-0-689-85815-4(9),* Little Simon) Little Simon.
—Merry Christmas, Bugs! Carter, David A. 2014. (David Carter's Bugs Ser.). (ENG.). 24p. (J). (gr. -1-1). pap. 4.99 *(978-1-4424-9506-7(5),* Simon Spotlight) Simon Spotlight.
—Princess Bugs: A Touch-And-Feel Fairy Tale. Carter, David A. 2013. (David Carter's Bugs Ser.). (ENG.). 16p. (J). (gr. -1-2). 12.99 *(978-1-4424-5055-4(X),* Little Simon) Little Simon.
—School Bugs: An Elementary Pop-Up Book by David A. Carter. Carter, David A. 2009. (David Carter's Bugs Ser.). (ENG.). 20p. (J). (gr. -1-2). 12.99 *(978-1-4169-5056-1(7),* Little Simon) Little Simon.
—Snow Bugs: A Wintery Pop-Up Book. Carter, David A. 2009. (David Carter's Bugs Ser.). (ENG.). 20p. (J). (gr. -1-3). 12.99 *(978-1-4169-5054-7(0),* Little Simon) Little Simon.
—A Snowy Day in Bugland! Carter, David A. 2012. (David Carter's Bugs Ser.). (ENG.). 24p. (J). (gr. -1-1). 15.99 *(978-1-4424-3895-8(9));* pap. 3.99 *(978-1-4424-3894-1(0))* Simon Spotlight. (Simon Spotlight).
—Springtime in Bugland! Carter, David A. 2012. (David Carter's Bugs Ser.). (ENG.). 24p. (J). (gr. -1-1). 15.99 *(978-1-4424-3892-7(4));* pap. 3.99 *(978-1-4424-3890-3(8))* Simon Spotlight. (Simon Spotlight).
—Up & Down: A Bugs Pop-Up Concept Book. Carter, David A. 2010. (David Carter's Bugs Ser.). (ENG.). 16p. (J). (gr. -1-1). 9.99 *(978-1-4424-0831-9(6),* Little Simon) Little Simon.
—Welcome to Bugland! A Fun Foldout World from David A. Carter. Carter, David A. 2011. (David Carter's Bugs Ser.). (ENG.). 24p. (J). (gr. -1-3). 12.99 *(978-1-4424-1962-9(8),* Little Simon) Little Simon.
—White Noise: A Pop-Up Book for Children of All Ages. Carter, David A. 2009. (ENG.). 20p. (J). (gr. -1-3). 39.99 *(978-1-4169-4094-4(4),* Little Simon) Little Simon.
—Yellow Square: A Pop-Up Book for Children of All Ages. Carter, David A. 2008. (ENG.). 20p. (J). (gr. -1-3). 34.99 *(978-1-4169-4093-7(6),* Little Simon) Little Simon.
—The 12 Bugs of Christmas: A Pop-Up Christmas Counting Book. Carter, David A. 2011. (David Carter's Bugs Ser.). (ENG.). 24p. (J). (gr. -1-1). 12.99 *(978-1-4424-2649-8(7),* Little Simon) Little Simon.
—600 Black Spots: A Pop-Up Book for Children of All Ages. Carter, David A. 2007. (ENG.). 20p. (J). (gr. -1-2). 29.99 *(978-1-4169-4092-0(8),* Little Simon) Little Simon.
Carter, David A. & Carter, Noelle. Little Mouse & Daddy. Carter, David A. & Carter, Noelle. 2005. (Little Mouse Ser.). 12p. (J). 7.95 *(978-1-58117-223-2(0),* Intervisual/Piggy Toes) Bendon, Inc.
—Little Mouse & Mommy. Carter, David A. & Carter, Noelle. 2005. (Little Mouse Ser.). 12p. (J). 7.95 *(978-1-58117-224-9(9),* Intervisual/Piggy Toes) Bendon, Inc.
—Little Mouse Plays Peek-a-Boo. Carter, David A. & Carter, Noelle. 2005. (Little Mouse Ser.). 12p. (J). 7.95 *(978-1-58117-225-6(7),* Intervisual/Piggy Toes) Bendon, Inc.
—Little Mouse's Christmas. Carter, David A. & Carter, Noelle. 2005. 12p. (J). 7.95 *(978-1-58117-226-3(5),* Intervisual/Piggy Toes) Bendon, Inc.
Carter, Dunstan. The Haiku Zoo: The Haiku Zoo Book 2: Tiger. Watson, Mark. 2019. (Haiku Zoo Ser.: Vol. 2). (ENG.). 38p. (J). pap. *(978-1-9993686-1-6(4))* Watson, Mark Bks.
Carter, Fred, et al. The NEW Children of Color Holy Bible Hardcover Edition. Soles, Henry, ed. 2014. 880p. (gr. 2-18). 24.99 *(978-0-9638127-0-4(X))* Urban Spirit!.
Carter, Graham. The Gravedigger's Son. Moody, Patrick. 2017. 304p. (J). (gr. 2-7). 16.99 *(978-1-5107-1073-3(6),* Sky Pony Pr.) Skyhorse Publishing Co., Inc.
Carter, Graham. Alphamals: A-Z. Carter, Graham. 2017. (ENG.). 56p. (J). (-k). 17.99 *(978-0-7636-9557-6(2),* Big Picture Press) Candlewick Pr.
—Otto Blotter, Bird Spotter. Carter, Graham. 2019. (ENG.). 40p. (J). (gr. -1-3). 17.99 *(978-1-5415-7762-6(0))* Lerner Publishing Group.
Carter, Greg & Bascle, Brian. The Adventures of Marco Polo, 1 vol. Smalley, Roger. 2005. (Graphic History Ser.). (ENG.). 32p. (J). (gr. 3-9). 31.32 *(978-0-7368-3830-6(9),* Capstone Pr.) Capstone.
Carter, Jill. The Great Chicken Caper. Maxwell, Andre L. & Maxwell, Amanda L. 2012. 34p. (-18). 18.00 *(978-0-9881811-1-3(8))* Maxwell, Andre.
Carter, Kelly. Roxy & Chopper Visit the Animal Shelter. Garcia, Alaycia. 2011. 44p. pap. 24.95 *(978-1-4560-7336-7(2))* America Star Bks.
—Where Dreams Are Born. Wiggins, D. L. 2012. 26p. (J). 16.95 *(978-1-60131-128-3(1),* Castlebridge Bks.) Big Tent Bks.
Carter, Kris. Egypt. Gill, Heidi. 2012. (2 Kurious Kids Ser.: Vol. 5). (ENG.). 24p. (J). (gr. -1-5). 14.95 *(978-1-936319-93-0(4))* Mascot Bks., Inc.
—2 Kurious Kids: China. Gill, Heidi. 2012. 38p. (J). 14.95 *(978-1-936319-89-3(6))* Mascot Bks., Inc.
—2 Kurious Kids: France. Gill, Heidi. 2012. 38p. (J). 14.95 *(978-1-936319-90-9(X))* Mascot Bks., Inc.
—2 Kurious Kids: India. Gill, Heidi. 2012. 38p. (J). 14.95 *(978-1-936319-92-3(6))* Mascot Bks., Inc.
Carter, Leigh Anne. Look, See the Bird! Wilson, Bill & Fallon, Katie. 2017. (ENG.). 32p. (J). (gr. -1-2). 12.50 *(978-1-57826-687-6(4),* Hatherleigh Pr.) Hatherleigh Co., Ltd., The.
—Look, See the Farm! Wilson, Bill & Fallon, Katie. 2018. (ENG.). 1p. (J). (gr. -1-2). 12.50 *(978-1-57826-742-2(0),* Hatherleigh Pr.) Hatherleigh Co., Ltd., The.
Carter, Lydia, jt. illus. see Black, Joanna.
Carter, Maureen. The Tale of Jemima Puddle-Duck: A Story about Trust. 2006. (J). 6.99 *(978-1-59939-000-0(0))* Cornerstone Pr.
Carter, Mike. The Biting Cheese Bows Challenge. Thaler, Kathleen. 2018. (Navy Dad Series - Book 1 Ser.). (ENG.). 72p. (J). *(978-1-4602-8127-7(6));* pap. *(978-1-4602-8128-4(4))* FriesenPress.
Carter, Nancy, jt. illus. see Julien, Terry.
Carter, Noelle, jt. illus. see Carter, David A.
Carter, Paula Becker. Collect-n-Make Crafts for Kids. Lingo, Susan L. Stoker, Bruce, ed. 2006. 112p. (YA). (gr. 1-7). 15.99 *(978-0-7847-1198-9(4),* 02432) Standard Publishing.
—Collect-n-Play Games for Kids. Lingo, Susan L. Stoker, Bruce, ed. 2006. 112p. (YA). (gr. 1-7). 15.99 *(978-0-7847-1199-6(2),* 02433) Standard Publishing.
Carter, Robin. Are Mountains Getting Taller? Questions & Answers about the Changing Earth. Berger, Melvin & Berger, Gilda. 2003. (Question & Answer Ser.). (ENG.). 48p. (J). pap. 5.95 *(978-0-439-26673-4(4),* Scholastic Reference) Scholastic, Inc.
Carter, Sandy Lewis. Pookus & Buckie: A Children's Book Based on a True Story. Reed, Tom. l.t. ed. 2005. 36p. (J). per. 11.95 *(978-0-9749725-4-1(1),* 10000, Lonestar Abilene Publishing) LoneStar Abilene Publishing, LLC.
Carter, Sharon. Let's Learn the Hawaiian Alphabet. Murray, Patricia Lei. 2005. 24p. (J). 14.95 *(978-1-59700-102-1(3))* Island Heritage Publishing.
Carter, Stephanie. If Peace Is... Baskwill, Jane. 2003. (J). 23p. pap. 7.95 *(978-1-59034-449-1(9));* 24p. (gr. 11-18). 15.95 *(978-1-59034-448-4(0))* Mondo Publishing.
Carter, Steve. How Daddy Mouse Lost His Tail. Carter, Deborah. 2019. (ENG.). 24p. (J). pap. 7.49 *(978-0-473-47224-5(4))* Carter, Deborah.
Carter, Steve. Mops Goes to Pre-School. Carter, Deborah. 2019. (ENG.). 24p. (J). pap. 7.49 ***(978-0-473-48993-9(7))*** Carter, Deborah.
Cartobaleno. Castle Caper (Wallykazam!) Depken, Kristen L. 2015. (Pictureback(R) Ser.). (ENG.). 24p. (J). (gr. -1-2). 5.99 *(978-0-553-52313-3(9),* Random Hse. Bks. for Young Readers) Random Hse. Children's Bks.
—Catch a Wishing Star (Shimmer & Shine) Huntley, Tex. 2017. (Little Golden Book Ser.). (ENG.). 24p. (J). (-k). 4.99 *(978-1-5247-1667-7(7),* Golden Bks.) Random Hse. Children's Bks.
—A Dazzling Birthday! (Butterbean's Cafe) Carbone, Courtney. 2020. (Little Golden Book Ser.). (ENG.). 24p. (J). (-k). 4.99 *(978-1-9848-4774-4(0),* Golden Bks.) Random Hse. Children's Bks.
—Dragon Pox! (Shimmer & Shine) Carbone, Courtney. 2018. (Little Golden Book Ser.). (ENG.). 24p. (J). (-k). 4.99 *(978-1-5247-6798-3(0),* Golden Bks.) Random Hse. Children's Bks.
—Pet Talent Show! (Shimmer & Shine) Matheis, Mickie. 2017. (Little Golden Book Ser.). (ENG.). 24p. (J). (gr. -1-2). 4.99 *(978-1-5247-2060-5(7),* Golden Bks.) Random Hse. Children's Bks.
—The Sweetest Cupcake (Shimmer & Shine) Tillworth, Mary. 2016. (Pictureback(R) Ser.). (ENG.). 16p. (J). (gr. -1-2). 4.99 *(978-0-553-52201-3(9),* Random Hse. Bks. for Young Readers) Random Hse. Children's Bks.
—Treasure Twins! (Shimmer & Shine) Tillworth, Mary. 2017. (Little Golden Book Ser.). (ENG.). 24p. (J). (-k). 4.99 *(978-0-399-55792-7(X),* Golden Bks.) Random Hse. Children's Bks.
Cartobaleno Staff, jt. illus. see Golden Books.
Cartobaleno Staff, jt. illus. see Random House.
Carton, Holly. The Dancing Dogs: Literacy on the Move: Book 3. Cohen, Arlene N. 2020. (Literacy on the Move Ser.: Vol. 3). (ENG.). 44p. (J). pap. 10.00 ***(978-1-7344380-2-4(9))*** Moving Stories.
—The Dancing Reptiles: Literacy on the Move: Book 2. Cohen, Arlene N. 2020. (Literacy on the Move Ser.: Vol. 2). (ENG.). 60p. (J). 20.00 ***(978-0-578-68836-7(0))*** Moving Stories.
Carton, Rick. Frost Bites. Ogden, Charles. 2008. (Edgar & Ellen Nodyssey Ser.: 2). (ENG.). 192p. (J). (gr. 3-7). 23.99 *(978-1-4169-5464-4(3),* Simon & Schuster/Paula Wiseman Bks.) Simon & Schuster/Paula Wiseman Bks.
—High Wire. Ogden, Charles. 2006. (Edgar & Ellen Ser.: 5). (ENG.). 208p. (J). (gr. 3-7). 24.99 *(978-1-4169-1500-3(1),* Simon & Schuster/Paula Wiseman Bks.) Simon & Schuster/Paula Wiseman Bks.
—Hot Air. Ogden, Charles. 2008. (Edgar & Ellen Nodyssey Ser.: 1). (ENG.). 192p. (J). (gr. 3-7). 9.99 *(978-1-4169-5465-1(1),* Aladdin) Simon & Schuster Children's Publishing.
—Nod's Limbs. Ogden, Charles. 2007. (Edgar & Ellen Ser.: 6). (ENG.). 224p. (J). (gr. 3-7). 24.99 *(978-1-4169-1501-0(X),* Simon & Schuster/Paula Wiseman Bks.) Simon & Schuster/Paula Wiseman Bks.
—Pet's Revenge. Ogden, Charles. 2006. (Edgar & Ellen Ser.: 4). (ENG.). 192p. (J). (gr. 3-7). 23.99 *(978-1-4169-1408-2(0),* Simon & Schuster/Paula Wiseman Bks.) Simon & Schuster/Paula Wiseman Bks.
—Rare Beasts. Ogden, Charles. ed. 2006. (Edgar & Ellen Ser.: 1). (ENG.). 144p. (J). (gr. 3-7). 22.99 *(978-1-4169-1409-9(9),* Aladdin) Simon & Schuster Children's Publishing.
—Tourist Trap. Ogden, Charles. ed. 2006. (Edgar & Ellen Ser.: 2). (ENG.). 176p. (J). (gr. 3-7). 23.99 *(978-1-4169-1411-2(0),* Simon & Schuster/Paula Wiseman Bks.) Simon & Schuster/Paula Wiseman Bks.
—Under Town. Ogden, Charles. ed. 2006. (Edgar & Ellen Ser.: 3). (ENG.). 160p. (J). (gr. 3-7). 22.99 *(978-1-4169-1412-9(9),* Simon & Schuster/Paula Wiseman Bks.) Simon & Schuster/Paula Wiseman Bks.
Cartoon Saloon, Ltd. Scream Street: Fang of the Vampire. Donbavand, Tommy. 2009. (Scream Street Ser.: 1). (ENG.). 160p. (J). (gr. 3-7). pap. 5.99 *(978-0-7636-4608-0(3))* Candlewick Pr.
Cartoon Saloon, Ltd. Staff. Flesh of the Zombie, Bk. 4. Donbavand, Tommy. 2010. (Scream Street Ser.: 4). (ENG.). 128p. (J). (gr. 3-7). pap. 5.99 *(978-0-7636-4637-0(7))* Candlewick Pr.
—Heart of the Mummy, Bk. 3. Donbavand, Tommy. 2010. (Scream Street Ser.: 3). (ENG.). 128p. (J). (gr. 3-7). pap. 5.99 *(978-0-7636-4636-3(9))* Candlewick Pr.
—Skull of the Skeleton, 5. Donbavand, Tommy. 2010. (Scream Street Ser.: 5). (ENG.). 128p. (J). (gr. 2-4). 18.69 *(978-0-7636-4635-6(0))* Candlewick Pr.
Cartoon Saloon Staff. Blood of the Witch. Donbavand, Tommy. 2012. (Scream Street Ser.). (ENG.). 128p. (J). (gr. 3-7). 27.07 *(978-1-59961-993-4(8),* 13251, Chapter Bks.) Spotlight.
—Claw of the Werewolf, Bk. 6. Donbavand, Tommy. 2010. (Scream Street Ser.: 6). (ENG.). 128p. (J). (gr. 3-7). pap. 5.99 *(978-0-7636-4638-7(5))* Candlewick Pr.
—Claw of the Werewolf. Donbavand, Tommy. 2012. (Scream Street Ser.). (ENG.). 128p. (J). (gr. 3-7). 27.07 *(978-1-59961-997-2(0),* 13255, Chapter Bks.) Spotlight.
—Fang of the Vampire. Donbavand, Tommy. 2012. (Scream Street Ser.: Bk. 1). (ENG.). 160p. (J). (gr. 3-7). 27.07 *(978-1-59961-992-7(X),* 13250, Chapter Bks.) Spotlight.
—Flesh of the Zombie. Donbavand, Tommy. 2012. (Scream Street Ser.: Bk. 4). (ENG.). 128p. (J). (gr. 3-7). 27.07 *(978-1-59961-995-8(4),* 13253, Chapter Bks.) Spotlight.
—Heart of the Mummy. Donbavand, Tommy. 2012. (Scream Street Ser.: Bk. 3). (ENG.). 128p. (J). (gr. 3-7). 27.07 *(978-1-59961-994-1(6),* 13252, Chapter Bks.) Spotlight.
—Skull of the Skeleton. Donbavand, Tommy. 2012. (Scream Street Ser.: Bk. 5). (ENG.). 128p. (J). (gr. 3-7). 27.07 *(978-1-59961-996-5(2),* 13254, Chapter Bks.) Spotlight.
Cartwright, Amy. Dan Can! Powell, Marie. 2016. (Word Families Ser.). (ENG.). 16p. (J). (gr. k-3). 17.95 *(978-1-60753-924-7(1))* Amicus Publishing.
—Go to Bed, Ted! Powell, Marie. 2016. (Word Families Ser.). (ENG.). 16p. (gr. k-3). 17.95 *(978-1-60753-927-8(6))* Amicus Publishing.
—Jack & the Beanstalk. 2011. (J). pap. *(978-0-545-27434-0(6),* Cartwheel Bks.) Scholastic, Inc.
—The Map Trap. Powell, Marie. 2016. (Word Families Ser.). (ENG.). 16p. (J). (gr. k-3). 17.95 *(978-1-60753-928-5(4))* Amicus Publishing.
—My Very Busy Day. Prasadam-Halls, Smriti. Parragon Books, ed. 2019. (Start Little, Learn Big Children's First Words Board Book Ser.). (ENG.). 12p. (J). (gr. -1-k). bds. 9.99 *(978-1-68052-592-2(1),* 2002340, Parragon Books) Cottage Door Pr.
—Pirate Potty. Berger, Samantha. 2010. (ENG.). 24p. (J). (gr. -1 — 1). pap. 6.99 *(978-0-545-17295-0(0),* Cartwheel Bks.) Scholastic, Inc.
—Princess Potty. Berger, Samantha. 2010. (ENG.). 24p. (J). (gr. -1 — 1). pap. 5.99 *(978-0-545-17296-7(9),* Cartwheel Bks.) Scholastic, Inc.
—Stop, Pop! Powell, Marie. 2016. (Word Families Ser.). (ENG.). 16p. (gr. k-3). 17.95 *(978-1-60753-925-4(X))* Amicus Publishing.
—Things That Go. Prasadam-Halls, Smriti. Parragon Books, ed. 2019. (Start Little, Learn Big Children's First Words Board Book Ser.). (ENG.). 12p. (J). (gr. -1-k). bds. 9.99 *(978-1-68052-591-5(3),* 2002330, Parragon Books) Cottage Door Pr.
—When, Jen? Powell, Marie. 2016. (Word Families Ser.). (ENG.). 16p. (J). (gr. k-3). 17.95 *(978-1-60753-926-1(8))* Amicus Publishing.
—Win, Min! By Marie Powell: Illustrated by Amy Cartwright. Powell, Marie. 2016. (Word Families Ser.). (ENG.). 16p. (J). (gr. k-3). 17.95 *(978-1-60753-929-2(2))* Amicus Publishing.
—100 Words on the Farm: Discover & Learn. Byrd, Redd. Cottage Door Press, ed. 2018. (Discover & Learn Ser.). (ENG.). 12p. (J). (gr. -1-1). bds. 12.99 *(978-1-68052-369-0(4),* 1003340) Cottage Door Pr.
Cartwright, Christina. Grumpy Mom. Levitin, Sarah. 2019. (ENG.). 34p. (J). (gr. 4-5). pap. 7.99 *(978-0-578-43972-3(7))* levitin, sarah.
—Sonja's Wish. McPherson, Heather L. A. 2012. 26p. (J). pap. 11.95 *(978-1-61863-394-1(5))* Bookstand Publishing.
Cartwright, Mary. Glug, Glug, Glug. Baggott, Stella. 2007. (Bath Bks). 5p. (J). (gr. -1-k). 14.99 *(978-0-7945-1784-7(6),* Usborne) EDC Publishing.
Cartwright, Reg. The Three Golden Oranges. Flor, Alma Ada. 2012. (ENG.). 32p. (J). (gr. -1-3). 16.99 *(978-1-4424-7496-3(3),* Atheneum Bks. for Young Readers) Simon & Schuster Children's Publishing.
Cartwright, Shannon. Alaska ABC. 40th anniv. ed. 2018. (Paws IV Ser.). 32p. (J). (gr. -1-2). pap. 10.99 *(978-1-63217-166-5(X),* Little Bigfoot) Sasquatch Bks.
—Alaska's 12 Days of Summer. Chamberlin-Calamar, Pat. 2003. (Paws IV Ser.). 32p. (J). (gr. -1-2). pap. 10.99 *(978-1-57061-341-8(9),* Little Bigfoot) Sasquatch Bks.
—Alaska's Animals, You & I. 2016. (J). *(978-0-9896321-8-8(0))* Taku Graphics.
—Kiana's Iditarod. Gill, Shelley. 2008. (Paws IV Ser.). 32p. (J). (gr. -1-3). pap. 10.99 *(978-1-57061-589-4(6),* Little Bigfoot) Sasquatch Bks.
—Sitka Rose. Gill, Shelley. 2005. 32p. (J). (gr. -1-3). per. 7.95 *(978-1-57091-364-8(1))* Charlesbridge Publishing, Inc.
—Up on Denali: Alaska's Wild Mountain. Gill, Shelley. 2006. (Paws IV Ser.). 32p. (J). (gr. -1-2). pap. 10.99 *(978-1-57061-365-4(6),* Little Bigfoot) Sasquatch Bks.
Cartwright, Shannon & Love, Judy. Prickly Rose. Gill, Shelley. 2014. 32p. (J). (gr. -1-3). pap. 7.99 *(978-1-57091-357-0(9));* lib. bdg. 17.95 *(978-1-57091-356-3(0))* Charlesbridge Publishing, Inc.
Cartwright, Stephen. Big Pig on a Dig. Tyler, Jenny. 2004. (Easy Words to Read Ser.). (ENG.). 1p. (J). (gr. 1-18). pap. 6.99 *(978-0-7460-3021-9(5))* EDC Publishing.
—Big Pig on a Dig. Cox, Phil Roxbee. Tyler, Jenny, ed. rev. ed. 2006. (Phonics Readers Ser.). 16p. (J). (gr. -1-3). pap. 6.99 *(978-0-7945-1501-0(0),* Usborne) EDC Publishing.
—Big Red Tractor. Brooks, Felicity. 2006. (Usborne Farmyard Tales Jigsaw Bks.). 10p. (J). (gr. -1-k). bds. 7.99 *(978-0-7945-1130-2(9),* Usborne) EDC Publishing.
—Camping Out. Amery, Heather. 2005. (Usborne Farmyard Tales Ser.). 16p. (J). (gr. -1-17). pap., pap. 5.95 *(978-0-7945-0750-3(6),* Usborne) EDC Publishing.
—Céad Focal Sticker Book: The First Hundred Words. Amery, Heather. 2nd rev. ed. 2003. (GLE.). 38p. (J). pap. 15.95 *(978-0-7171-3651-3(5))* M.H. Gill & Co. U. C. IRL. Dist: Dufour Editions, Inc.
—Children's Songbook - Internet Referenced. 2004. (Songbooks Ser.). 32p. (J). pap. 6.95 *(978-0-7945-0710-7(7),* Usborne) EDC Publishing.
—Christmas Activities. Milbourne, Anna. 2004. (Activity Books). 32p. (J). pap. 6.95 *(978-0-7945-0564-6(3),* Usborne) EDC Publishing.
—Christmas Stencil Book. 2005. (Usborne Farmyard Tales Ser.). 10p. (J). (gr. -1-3). bds. 9.95 *(978-0-7945-1142-5(2),* Usborne) EDC Publishing.
—Cinderella. 2006. (First Stories Sticker Bks.). 16p. (J). (gr. -1-3). pap. 6.99 *(978-0-7945-1311-5(5),* Usborne) EDC Publishing.
—Cinderella Kid Kit with Pop Out Coach. Amery, Heather. 2006. (Usborne First Stories Ser.). 16p. (J). (gr. -1-3). pap. 8.99 *(978-1-58086-877-8(0),* Usborne) EDC Publishing.
—The Complete Book of First Experiences. Civardi, Anne. 2005. (Usborne First Experiences Ser.). 144p. (J). (gr. -1-3). 19.95 *(978-0-7945-1012-1(4),* Usborne) EDC Publishing.
—The Counting Train. Brooks, Felicity et al. 2006. (J). *(978-0-439-89922-2(2))* Scholastic, Inc.
—Curly the Pig Board Book. Amery, Heather. 2004. (Young Farmyard Tales Board Books Ser.). 10p. (J). bds. 3.95 *(978-0-7945-0468-7(X),* Usborne) EDC Publishing.
—Curly's Friends. Cox, Phil Roxbee. rev. ed. 2005. (Usborne Farmyard Tales Touchy-Feely Ser.). 10p. (J). (gr. -1-k). bds. 7.95 *(978-0-7945-1180-7(5),* Usborne) EDC Publishing.
—Dolly & the Train Sticker Book. Amery, Heather. 2005. 18p. (J). pap. 6.95 *(978-0-7945-1064-0(7),* Usborne) EDC Publishing.
—Donkey Cards. Amery, Heather. 2004. (Farmyard Tales Card Games Ser.). 52p. (J). 8.95 *(978-0-7945-0326-0(8),* Usborne) EDC Publishing.
—Dragons, Stories Of. Rawson, Christopher. 2004. (Young Reading Series One Ser.). 48p. (J). (gr. 2-18). pap. 5.95 *(978-0-7945-0446-5(9),* Usborne) EDC Publishing.
—Duck's Bathtime. Tyler, Jenny. 2005. 4p. (J). (gr. -1-3). 7.95 *(978-0-7945-0570-7(8),* Usborne) EDC Publishing.
—Fairytale Jigsaw Book. 2004. (Jigsaw Books Ser.). 20p. (J). 14.95 *(978-0-7945-0771-8(9),* Usborne) EDC Publishing.
—Fairytale Snap. 2005. (Snap Card Games Ser.). 52p. (J). 8.95 *(978-0-7945-0905-7(3),* Usborne) EDC Publishing.
—The Farm. Amery, Heather. 2008. (Usborne Talkabout Bks.). 12p. (J). (gr. -1-3). bds. 8.99 *(978-0-7945-1795-3(1),* Usborne) EDC Publishing.
—Farm Magnet Book. Civardi, Anna. 2009. (Magnet Bks). 10p. (J). bds. 19.99 *(978-0-7945-2231-5(9),* Usborne) EDC Publishing.
—Farmyard Tales Treasury - Internet Referenced. Amery, Heather. 2007. 96p. (J). 19.99 *(978-0-7945-1440-2(5),* Usborne) EDC Publishing.
—Fat Cat on a Mat. Cox, Phil Roxbee. Tyler, Jenny, ed. rev. ed. 2006. (Phonics Readers Ser.). 16p. (J). (gr. -1-3). pap. 6.99 *(978-0-7945-1502-7(9),* Usborne) EDC Publishing.
—Find the Bird. Roxbee-Cox, Phil. 2004. (Treasury of Farmyard Tales Ser.). (ENG.). 1p. (J). stu. ed., bds. 3.95 *(978-0-7460-3820-8(8))* EDC Publishing.
—Find the Duck. 2007. (Find-its Board Bks). 12p. (J). (gr. -1-k). bds. 6.99 *(978-0-7945-1804-2(4),* Usborne) EDC Publishing.
—Find the Duck. Cox, Phil Roxbee, ed. 2004. (Find It Board Bks.). (ENG.). 1p. (J). (gr. -1-18). bds. 3.95 *(978-0-7460-3821-5(6))* EDC Publishing.
—Find the Kitten. 2007. (Find-its Board Bks). 12p. (J). (gr. -1-k). bds. 6.99 *(978-0-7945-1803-5(6),* Usborne) EDC Publishing.
—Find the Kitten. Roxbee-Cox, Phil. rev. ed. 2004. (Treasury of Farmyard Tales Ser.). (ENG.). 1p. (J). bds. 3.99 *(978-0-7460-3822-2(4))* EDC Publishing.
—Find the Puppy. 2007. (Find-its Board Bks). 12p. (J). (gr. -1-k). bds. 6.99 *(978-0-7945-1802-8(8),* Usborne) EDC Publishing.
—Find the Puppy. Roxbee-Cox, Phil. rev. ed. 2004. (Treasury of Farmyard Tales Ser.). (ENG.). 1p. (J). bds. 3.99 *(978-0-7460-3824-6(0))* EDC Publishing.
—Find the Teddy. Roxbee-Cox, Phil. 2004. (Rhyming Board Bks.). (ENG.). 1p. (J). (gr. -1-18). bds. 3.95 *(978-0-7460-3825-3(9))* EDC Publishing.
—First Hundred Words. Amery, Heather. Tyler, Jenny, ed. 2006. (Usborne First Hundred Words Ser.). 32p. (J). (gr. -1). lib. bdg. 14.95 *(978-1-58086-505-0(4))* EDC Publishing.
—First Thousand Words: With Internet-Linked Pronunciation Guide. Amery, Heather. MacKinnon, Mairi, ed. 2007. (Usborne Internet-Linked First Thousand Words Ser.). 63p. (J). (gr. -1). 20.99 *(978-1-58086-987-4(4),* Usborne) EDC Publishing.
—First Thousand Words in Arabic. Amery, Heather. 2004. (First Thousand Words Ser.). (ENG.). 64p. (J). 12.99 *(978-0-7945-0030-6(7),* Usborne) EDC Publishing.

C

—First Thousand Words in Chinese: With Internet-Linked Pronunciation Guide. Amery, Heather. MacKinnon, Mairi, ed. Asian Absolute, tr. 2007. (Usborne Internet-Linked First Thousand Words Ser.). 63p. (J). 12.99 *(978-0-7945-1550-8(9),* Usborne) EDC Publishing.

—First Thousand Words in English. Amery, Heather. Irving, Nicole, ed. 2003. (First Thousand Words Ser.). 63p. (J). (gr. -1). lib. bdg. 20.95 *(978-1-58086-474-9(0))* EDC Publishing.

—First Thousand Words in Italian. Amery, Heather. rev. ed. 2004. (First Thousand Words Ser.). (ITA & ENG.). 64p. (J). (gr. -1-6). 12.99 *(978-0-7945-0286-7(5));* lib. bdg. 20.99 *(978-1-58086-560-9(7))* EDC Publishing. (Usborne).

—First Thousand Words in Japanese. Amery, Heather. rev. ed. 2004. (First Thousand Words Ser.). (JPN & ENG.). 64p. (J). (gr. -1-6). 12.95 *(978-0-7945-0480-9(9));* lib. bdg. 20.95 *(978-1-58086-552-4(6))* EDC Publishing. (Usborne).

—Frog on a Log. Cox, Phil Roxbee. Tyler, Jenny, ed. rev. ed. 2006. (Phonics Readers Ser.). 16p. (J). (gr. -1). pap. 6.99 *(978-0-7945-1504-1(5),* Usborne) EDC Publishing.

—Gnomes & Goblins. Rawson, Christopher. 2004. (Young Reading Series One Ser.). 48p. (J). (gr. 2-18). pap. 5.95 *(978-0-7945-0407-6(8),* Usborne) EDC Publishing.

—Going on a Plane. Civardi, Anne. Bates, Michelle, ed. rev. ed. 2005. (Usborne First Experiences Ser.). 16p. (J). pap. 4.99 *(978-0-7945-1005-3(1),* Usborne) EDC Publishing.

—Going to a Party. Civardi, Anne. Watt, Fiona, ed. 2007. (Usborne First Experiences Ser.). 16p. (J). (gr. -1-3). pap. 4.99 *(978-0-7945-1011-4(6),* Usborne) EDC Publishing.

—Going to School. Civardi, Anne. 2005. 16p. (J). pap. 4.95 *(978-0-7945-1008-4(6),* Usborne) EDC Publishing.

—Going to the Dentist. Civardi, Anne. Bates, Michelle, ed. rev. ed. 2005. (First Experiences Ser.). 16p. (J). (gr. -1). per. 4.95 *(978-0-7945-1007-7(8),* Usborne) EDC Publishing.

—Going to the Hospital. Civardi, Anne. Bates, Michelle, ed. rev. ed. 2005. (Usborne First Experiences Ser.). 16p. (J). (gr. -1-3). per. 4.99 *(978-0-7945-1006-0(X),* Usborne) EDC Publishing.

—Grumpy Goat. Amery, Heather. 2004. 16p. (J). pap. 5.95 *(978-0-7945-0788-6(3),* Usborne) EDC Publishing.

—Hen's Pens. Cox, Phil Roxbee. Tyler, Jenny, ed. rev. ed. 2006. (Phonics Readers Ser.). 16p. (J). (gr. -1-3). pap. 6.99 *(978-0-7945-1506-5(1),* Usborne) EDC Publishing.

—Hercules. 2004. (Young Reading Series Two Ser.). 64p. (J). (gr. 2-18). pap. 5.95 *(978-0-7945-0453-3(1),* Usborne) EDC Publishing.

—Hungry Donkey. Amery, Heather. Tyler, Jenny, ed. rev. ed. 2004. (Farmyard Tales Readers Ser.). 16p. (J). pap. 5.95 *(978-0-7945-0752-7(2),* Usborne) EDC Publishing.

—Jason & the Golden Fleece. 2004. (Young Reading Series Two Ser.). 64p. (J). (gr. 2-18). pap. 5.95 *(978-0-7945-0451-9(5),* Usborne) EDC Publishing.

—Latin Words Sticker Book. Sheikh-Miller, Jonathan. 2006. (Latin Words Sticker Book Ser.). 16p. (J). (gr. 1). pap. 8.99 *(978-0-7945-1145-6(7),* Usborne) EDC Publishing.

—Little Red Riding Hood. Amery, Heather. Tyler, Jenny, ed. 2004. (First Stories Ser.). 16p. (J). (gr. -1). lib. bdg. 12.95 *(978-1-58086-620-0(4),* Usborne) EDC Publishing.

—Ludo. 2004. (Farmyard Tales Card Games Ser.). (J). 12.95 *(978-0-7945-0310-9(1),* Usborne) EDC Publishing.

—Market Day. Amery, Heather. 2004. 16p. (J). pap. 5.95 *(978-0-7945-0783-1(2),* Usborne) EDC Publishing.

—Mermaids. Watt, Fiona. 2004. 10p. (J). 15.95 *(978-0-7945-0727-5(1),* Usborne) EDC Publishing.

—Mouse Moves House. Cox, Phil Roxbee. Tyler, Jenny, ed. rev. ed. 2006. (Phonic Readers Ser.). 16p. (J). (gr. -1-3). pap. 6.99 *(978-0-7945-1507-2(X),* Usborne) EDC Publishing.

—Moving House. Civardi, Anne. Bates, Michelle, ed. rev. ed. 2005. 16p. (J). (gr. -1-17). pap. 4.95 *(978-0-7945-1009-1(4),* Usborne) EDC Publishing.

—Naughty Woolly. Brooks, Felicity. 2006. (Usborne Farmyard Tales Jigsaw Bks.). 10p. (J). bds. 7.99 *(978-0-7945-1128-9(7),* Usborne) EDC Publishing.

—The New Baby. Civardi, Anne. Bates, Michelle, ed. rev. ed. 2005. 16p. (J). (gr. -1-17). pap. 4.99 *(978-0-7945-1003-9(5),* Usborne) EDC Publishing.

—New Pony. Amery, Heather. rev. ed. 2004. (Farmyard Tales Readers Ser.). 16p. (J). pap. 5.95 *(978-0-7945-0787-9(5),* Usborne) EDC Publishing.

—The Old Steam Train. Amery, Heather. rev. ed. 2007. (Farmyard Tales Readers Ser.). 16p. (J). (gr. -1-3). pap. 5.99 *(978-0-7945-0804-3(9),* Usborne) EDC Publishing.

—The Old Steam Train Kid Kit. Amery, Heather. rev. ed. 2007. (Kid Kits Ser.). (J). 16p. 13.99 *(978-1-60130-038-6(7));* 14p. pap. 13.99 *(978-1-60130-003-4(4))* EDC Publishing. (Usborne).

—Old steam train sticker Book. Amery, Heather. 2005. 18p. (J). pap. 6.95 *(978-0-7945-1066-4(3),* Usborne) EDC Publishing.

—La Oveja Rizos. Amery, Heather. 2004. (Titles in Spanish Ser.). (SPA.). 10p. (J). bds. 3.99 *(978-0-7460-6104-6(8),* Usborne) EDC Publishing.

—Red Tractor Board Book. Amery, Heather. 2004. (Young Farmyard Tales Board Books Ser.). 10p. (J). bds. 3.95 *(978-0-7945-0469-4(8),* Usborne) EDC Publishing.

—Runaway Tractor. Amery, Heather. 2004. 16p. (J). pap. 5.95 *(978-0-7945-0748-0(4),* Usborne) EDC Publishing.

—Rusty's Friends. Brooks, Felicity. 2006. (Usborne Farmyard Tales Jigsaw Bks.). 10p. (J). bds. 7.99 *(978-0-7945-1127-2(9),* Usborne) EDC Publishing.

—Rusty's Train Ride. Amery, Heather. rev. ed. 2007. (Farmyard Tales Readers Ser.). 16p. (J). (gr. -1-3). pap. 5.99 *(978-0-7945-0802-9(2),* Usborne) EDC Publishing.

—Sam Sheep Can't Sleep. Cox, Phil Roxbee. Tyler, Jenny, ed. rev. ed. 2006. (Usborne Phonics Bks.). 16p. (J). (gr. -1-k). 6.99 *(978-0-7945-1508-9(8),* Usborne) EDC Publishing.

—Scarecrow's Secret. Amery, Heather. Tyler, Jenny, ed. rev. ed. 2004. (Farmyard Tales Readers Ser.). 16p. (J). pap. 5.95 *(978-0-7945-0751-0(4),* Usborne) EDC Publishing.

—The Seaside. Amery, Heather. 2008. (Usborne Talkabout Bks.). 12p. (J). bds. 8.99 *(978-0-7945-1794-6(3),* Usborne) EDC Publishing.

—Shark in the Park. Cox, Phil Roxbee. Tyler, Jenny, ed. rev. ed. 2006. (Phonics Readers Ser.). 16p. (J). (gr. -1-k). pap. 6.99 *(978-0-7945-1509-6(6),* Usborne) EDC Publishing.

—Sleeping Beauty. 2006. (First Stories Sticker Bks.). 16p. (J). (gr. -1-3). pap. 6.99 *(978-0-7945-1313-9(1),* Usborne) EDC Publishing.

—Snowy Christmas Jigsaw Book. Amery, Heather. 2004. (Jigsaw Books Ser.). 14p. (J). 8.95 *(978-0-7945-0768-8(9),* Usborne) EDC Publishing.

—Stories of Giants. Rawson, Christopher. 2004. (Young Reading Ser.: Vol. 1). 48p. (J). (gr. 2-18). lib. bdg. 13.95 *(978-1-58086-614-9(X),* Usborne) EDC Publishing.

—Stories of Witches. Rawson, Christopher. 2004. (Young Reading Ser.: Vol. 1). 48p. (J). (gr. 2-18). lib. bdg. 13.95 *(978-1-58086-630-9(1),* Usborne) EDC Publishing.

—The Story of Flying. Sims, Lesley. 2004. (Young Reading Series Two Ser.). 64p. (J). (gr. 2-18). pap. 5.95 *(978-0-7945-0705-3(0),* Usborne) EDC Publishing.

—Surprise Visitors. Amery, Heather. 2004. 16p. (J). pap. 5.95 *(978-0-7945-0784-8(0),* Usborne) EDC Publishing.

—Ted in a Red Bed. Cox, Phil Roxbee. Tyler, Jenny, ed. rev. ed. 2006. (Phonics Reader, A: Easy Words to Read Ser.). 16p. (J). (gr. -1-3). 6.99 *(978-0-7945-1510-2(X),* Usborne) EDC Publishing.

—Ted's Shed. Cox, Phil Roxbee. Tyler, Jenny, ed. rev. ed. 2006. (Phonics Readers Ser.). 16p. (J). (gr. -1-3). pap. 6.99 *(978-0-7945-1511-9(8),* Usborne) EDC Publishing.

—Telling the Time. Amery, Heather. Tyler, Jenny & Lacey, Minna, eds. 2007. (Usborne Farmyard Tales Ser.). 24p. (J). (gr. -1-2). bds. 12.99 *(978-0-7945-1519-5(3),* Usborne) EDC Publishing.

—Three Little Pigs. 2006. (First Stories Sticker Bks.). 16p. (J). (gr. -1-3). pap. 6.99 *(978-0-7945-1386-3(7),* Usborne) EDC Publishing.

—Toad Makes a Road. Cox, Phil Roxbee. Tyler, Jenny, ed. rev. ed. 2006. (Phonics Readers Ser.). 16p. (J). (gr. -1-k). pap. 6.99 *(978-0-7945-1512-6(6),* Usborne) EDC Publishing.

—Ulysses. 2004. (Young Reading Series Two Ser.). 64p. (J). (gr. 2-18). pap. 5.95 *(978-0-7945-0452-6(3),* Usborne) EDC Publishing.

—The Usborne 1,2,3 Jigsaw Book. Brooks, Felicity & Tyler, Jenny. 2006. (Usborne Jigsaw Bks.). 12p. (J). (gr. -1-k). bds. 15.95 *(978-0-7945-1168-5(6),* Usborne) EDC Publishing.

—The Usborne Farmyard Tales Songbook. Marks, Anthony. Tyler, Jenny, ed. 2005. 31p. (J). (gr. -1-7). per. 6.95 *(978-0-7945-0918-7(5),* Usborne) EDC Publishing.

—Usborne Stories for Bedtime. Hawthorn, Phillip. Tyler, Jenny, ed. 2007. (Stories for Bedtime Ser.). 190p. (J). (gr. -1-3). 19.99 *(978-0-7945-1970-4(9),* Usborne) EDC Publishing.

—What's Happening at the Seaside? Amery, Heather. rev. ed. 2006. (What's Happening Ser.). 16p. (J). (gr. -1-3). 5.99 *(978-0-7945-1290-3(9),* Usborne) EDC Publishing.

—What's Happening on the Farm? Amery, Heather. rev. ed. 2006. (What's Happening? Ser.). 32p. (J). (gr. -1-3). 5.99 *(978-0-7945-1288-0(7),* Usborne) EDC Publishing.

—Where's Curly? Amery, H. 2004. (Treasury of Farmyard Tales Ser.). 16p. (J). (gr. 1-18). pap. 7.95 *(978-0-7945-0514-1(7));* lib. bdg. 15.95 *(978-1-58086-563-0(1))* EDC Publishing.

—Where's Woolly? Amery, Heather. Tyler, Jenny, ed. 2006. (Treasury of Farmyard Tales Ser.). 16p. (J). (gr. -1-18). 15.95 *(978-1-58086-531-9(3))* EDC Publishing.

—Who's Making That Mess? Hawthorn, Philip & Tyler, Jenny. 2008. (Luxury Flap Bks). (gr. -1-k). 9.99 *(978-0-7945-1694-9(7))* EDC Publishing.

—Who's Making That Noise? Hawthorne, Philip & Tyler, Jenny. 2005. (Flap Books Ser.). 16p. (J). (gr. 1-18). pap. 7.95 *(978-0-7945-0432-8(9),* Usborne) EDC Publishing.

—Who's Making That Smell? Tyler, Jenny & Hawthorn, Phillip. 2007. (Luxury Flap Bks). 16p. (J). (gr. -1-3). 9.99 *(978-0-7945-1696-3(3),* Usborne) EDC Publishing.

—Woolly Stops the Train. Amery, Heather. 2005. 18p. (J). pap. 6.95 *(978-0-7945-1063-3(9),* Usborne) EDC Publishing.

—Woolly the Sheep. Amery, Heather. 2004. (Young Farmyard Tales Board Books Ser.). 10p. (J). bds. 3.95 *(978-0-7945-0467-0(1),* Usborne) EDC Publishing.

—Ya Se Hacer Lazos. Watt, Fiona. 2005. (SPA.). 10p. (J). 7.95 *(978-0-7460-6626-3(0),* Usborne) EDC Publishing.

—Zoo Talkabout Board Book. Amery, Heather. 2008. (Talkabout Board Bks). 12p. (J). bds. 8.99 *(978-0-7945-1793-9(5),* Usborne) EDC Publishing.

Cartwright, Stephen. Abc Floor. Cartwright, Stephen. 2006. 16p. (J). bds. 15.99 *(978-0-7945-1367-2(0),* Usborne) EDC Publishing.

—Noisy Animals Board Bk. Cartwright, Stephen. 2007. 12p. (J). bds. 18.99 *(978-0-7945-1551-5(7),* Usborne) EDC Publishing.

—Usborne Phonics Flashcards: Dog. Cartwright, Stephen. 2007. (Usborne Flashcards Ser.). 48p. (J). (gr. -1-k). 9.99 *(978-0-7945-1516-4(9),* Usborne) EDC Publishing.

Cartwright, Stephen & Bird, Glen. Fairies. Watt, Fiona. 2004. 10p. (J). (gr. -1 — 1). per. 15.95 *(978-0-7945-0811-1(1),* Usborne) EDC Publishing.

—Fairies Jigsaw Book. Watt, Fiona. 2005. (Osborne Sparkly Jigsaws Ser.). 10p. (J). bds. 14.99 *(978-0-7945-1131-9(7),* Usborne) EDC Publishing.

—Mermaids Jigsaw Book. Watt, Fiona. 2006. (Osborne Sparkly Jigsaws Ser.). 10p. (J). bds. 14.99 *(978-0-7945-1189-0(9),* Usborne) EDC Publishing.

Cartwright, Stephen & Blundell, Kim. Snakes & Ladders. 2004. (Farmyard Tales Card Games Ser.). (J). 12.95 *(978-0-7945-0312-3(8),* Usborne) EDC Publishing.

Cartwright, Steven. Farmyard Tales Sticker Coloring Book. ed. 2011. (Coloring Bks). 20p. (J). pap. 5.99 *(978-0-7945-2959-8(3),* Usborne) EDC Publishing.

Cartwrigth, Aidan. Kindness Is... Tielesh, Simone. 2017. (ENG.). (J). pap. *(978-0-9939391-8-1(X))* Green Bamboo Publishing.

Carufel, Rick. Roly Poly's Adventures Calendar Book 2020. Mowbray, Elizabeth D. 2019. (ENG.). 32p. (J). pap. 9.99 ***(978-1-6534-2639-3(X))*** Independently Published.

Caruncho, Isabel. Un Topo en un Mar de Hierba. Prats, Joan de Déu. (SPA.). 31p. *(978-84-236-5040-8(5))* Edebé ESP. Dist: Lectorum Pubns., Inc.

Caruso, Frank. Heart Transplant. Vachss, Andrew. 2010. (ENG.). 117p. pap. 24.99 *(978-1-59582-575-9(4),* Dark Horse Books) Dark Horse Comics.

Caruso, Maria Victoria. The Mystery of Leo: El misterio de Leo. Gonzalez, Aurora Adriana. Ballester Kriska, Lorena Ivonne, ed. 2008.Tr. of misterio de Leo. (ENG & SPA.). 34p. (J). per. 15.95 *(978-0-9816973-0-7(5))* Spanish-Live.

Caruth, Jeannette. The Mountain Boy. Pages, Christina. 2007. (Nature Children Ser.). 39p. (J). (gr. -1-3). 12.95 *(978-0-9794863-9-5(4))* Summerland Publishing.

Carvajal, Cisco. Chuck Taylor & the Hormiguita. Carvajal, Cheryl. 2016. 32p. (J). pap. 10.00 *(978-1-939696-16-8(X))* Blue Dragon Publishing.

Carvalho, Bernado P. Plasticus Maritimus: An Invasive Species. Pego, Ana & Minhós Martins, Isabel. 2020. 176p. (J). (gr. 6). 19.95 ***(978-1-77164-643-7(8))*** Greystone Books Ltd. CAN. Dist: Publishers Group West (PGW).

Carvalho, Bernardo. Coming & Going. Martins, Isabel Minhós & Martins, Isabel Minhós. 2014. (ENG.). 48p. (J). (gr. -1-3). 16.95 *(978-1-84976-161-1(2))* Tate Publishing, Ltd. GBR. Dist: Hachette Bk. Group.

—Don't Cross the Line! Martins, Isabel Minhós. 2016. (ENG.). 40p. (J). (gr. k-3). 16.99 *(978-1-77657-074-4(X))* Gecko Pr. NZL. Dist: Lerner Publishing Group.

—The World in a Second. Martins, Isabel Minhós. 2015. (ENG.). 56p. (J). (gr. -1-3). 18.95 *(978-1-59270-157-5(4))* Enchanted Lion Bks., LLC.

Carvalho, Bernado P. Outside: A Guide to Discovering Nature. Peixe Dias, Maria Ana & Teixeira do Rosario, Ines. 2016. (ENG.). 368p. (J). (gr. 3-6). 27.99 *(978-1-84780-769-4(0),* Frances Lincoln Children's Bks.) Quarto Publishing Group UK GBR. Dist: Hachette Bk. Group.

—Outside: Discovering Animals. Dias, Maria Ana Peixe & Teixeira do Rosario, Ines. 2018. (ENG.). 208p. (J). (gr. 1-4). pap. 16.99 *(978-1-78603-160-0(4),* 303676, Frances Lincoln Children's Bks.) Quarto Publishing Group UK GBR. Dist: Hachette UK Distribution.

—Outside: Exploring Nature. Dias, Maria Ana Peixe & Teixeira do Rosario, Ines. ed. 2018. (ENG.). 176p. (J). (gr. 1-4). pap. 16.99 *(978-1-78603-161-7(2),* 303675, Frances Lincoln Children's Bks.) Quarto Publishing Group UK GBR. Dist: Hachette UK Distribution.

Carver, Allison. Charlotte's Bones: The Beluga Whale in a Farmer's Field, 1 vol. Rounds, Erin. 2018. (Tilbury House Nature Book Ser.: 0). (ENG.). 36p. (J). (gr. 1-5). 17.95 *(978-0-88448-485-1(8),* 884485) Tilbury Hse. Pubs.

Carver, Erin. Leafy Leafs Where Is Lester?, 1 vol. Carver, David. 34p. 2010. 24.95 *(978-1-4512-1069-9(8));* 2009. pap. 19.95 *(978-1-4489-2203-1(8))* PublishAmerica, Inc.

—Lester Returns Home with His New Friend La'doo, 1 vol. Carver, David. 2010. 28p. 24.95 *(978-1-4489-6340-9(0))* PublishAmerica, Inc.

Cary. Annie Oakley: The Shooting Star. Graves, Charles P. 2011. 80p. (gr. 4-7). 37.95 *(978-1-258-01390-5(8))* Literary Licensing, LLC.

—From Barter to Gold: The Story of Money. Russell, Solveig Paulson. 2011. 66p. 36.95 *(978-1-258-01865-8(9))* Literary Licensing, LLC.

—Treasure of the Revolution. Fox, Mary Virginia. 2011. 192p. 42.95 *(978-1-258-09675-5(7))* Literary Licensing, LLC.

Cary, Debbi. The Lost Monster Tales. Helm, Julie G. 2010. 212p. pap. 14.49 *(978-1-4490-3823-6(9))* AuthorHouse.

Cary, Debbi G., photos by. Merlin for Sherman. Helm, Julie G. 2010. 84p. pap. 26.49 *(978-1-4520-5183-3(6))* AuthorHouse.

Carzon, Walter. Five-Minute Bedtime Bible Stories. Parker, Amy. 2015. (American Bible Society Ser.). (ENG.). 192p. (J). (gr. -1-3). 12.99 *(978-0-545-79960-7(0),* Little Shepherd) Scholastic, Inc.

—Lee y Aprende. American Bible Society, American Bible & Parker, Amy. 2017. (American Bible Society Ser.). (SPA.). 38p. (J). (gr. -1 — 1). bds. 9.99 *(978-1-338-23345-2(9),* Scholastic en Espanol) Scholastic, Inc.

—My First Read & Learn Love & Kindness Bible Stories. American Bible Society, American Bible & Parker, Amy. 2017. (American Bible Society Ser.). (ENG.). 38p. (J). (— 1). bds. 9.99 *(978-1-338-18529-4(2),* Little Shepherd) Scholastic, Inc.

—Wonder Woman 1984: Destined for Greatness. West, Alexandra. 2020. (I Can Read Level 3 Ser.). (ENG.). 32p. (J). (gr. -1-3). pap. 4.99 *(978-0-06-296336-9(8),* HarperCollins) HarperCollins Pubs. Ltd. GBR. Dist: HarperCollins Pubs.

Carzon, Walter, jt. illus. see Artful Doodlers Limited Staff.

Casada, Giuseppina. The Magic Booger. Casada, Giuseppina. Carbini, Mariana, tr. 2019. (ENG.). 30p. (J). pap. 9.90 *(978-1-0960-1435-5(1))* Independently Published.

Casagrande, Donata Dal Molin. El Globo de Pablito. Brignole, Giancarla, tr. (Fabulas De Familia Ser.). (SPA.). 32p. *(978-970-20-0269-7(9))* Castillo, Ediciones, S. A. de C. V.

—Joseph & Chico: The Life of Pope Benedict XVI as Told by a Cat. Perego, Jeanne. Matt, Andrew, tr. from ITA. 2008. 36p. (J). (gr. k-7). 17.95 *(978-1-58617-252-7(2))* Ignatius Pr.

—Max & Benedict: A Bird's Eye View of the Pope's Daily Life. Perego, Jeanne et al. 2009. (ENG.). 52p. (J). (gr. 1-7). 17.95 *(978-1-58617-407-1(X))* Ignatius Pr.

Casal, Isabel. Poof 123: Touch & Learn Numbers - Ages 2-4 for Toddlers, Preschool & Kindergarten Kids. Berg, Arielle. 2018. (ENG.). 32p. (J). pap. *(978-0-9950441-3-5(9))* Heartlab Pr.

—Poof 123: Touch & Learn Numbers: Ages 2-4 for Toddlers, Preschool & Kindergarten Kids. Berg, Arielle. 2018. (ENG.). 30p. (J). pap. *(978-1-9993996-6-5(8))* Heartlab Pr.

—Poof ABC: Touch & Learn Alphabet - Ages 2-4 for Toddlers, Preschool & Kindergarten Kids. Berg, Arielle. 2018. (ENG.). 62p. (J). pap. *(978-0-9950441-1-1(2))* Heartlab Pr.

Casale, Paul. Danger: Dynamite!, 1 vol. Capeci, Anne. 2003. (Cascade Mountain Railroad Mysteries Ser.: 1). (ENG.). 144p. (J). (gr. 2-5). 12.95 *(978-1-56145-288-0(2))* Peachtree Publishing Co. Inc.

—Daredevils, 1 vol. Capeci, Anne. 2004. (Cascade Mountain Railroad Mysteries Ser.: 2). (ENG.). 144p. (J). (gr. 2-5). 12.95 *(978-1-56145-307-8(2))* Peachtree Publishing Co. Inc.

—Ghost Train, 1 vol., Vol. 3. Capeci, Anne. 2004. (Cascade Mountain Railroad Mysteries Ser.: 3). (ENG.). 144p. (J). (gr. 2-5). 12.95 *(978-1-56145-324-5(2))* Peachtree Publishing Co. Inc.

—Missing!, 1 vol. Capeci, Anne. 2005. (Cascade Mountain Railroad Mysteries Ser.: 4). (ENG.). 144p. (J). (gr. 2-5). 12.95 *(978-1-56145-334-4(X))* Peachtree Publishing Co. Inc.

—The Snowman Surprise. Keene, Carolyn. 63rd ed. 2004. (Nancy Drew Notebooks Ser.: 63). (ENG.). 80p. (J). (gr. 1-4). pap. 4.99 *(978-0-689-87411-6(1))* Simon & Schuster, Inc.

—Sonshine Girls: Operation Salvation. Morris, Rene. 2009. (ENG.). 164p. (J). pap. 6.99 *(978-0-9801861-5-4(3),* Summertime Bks.) Summerhill Pr.

—Sonshine Girls: Summer Secret. Morris, Rene. 2008. (ENG.). 164p. (J). pap. 6.99 *(978-0-9801861-2-3(9),* Summertime Bks.) Summerhill Pr.

—Wild Horse Country. Diaz, Katacha. 2005. (Wild Reading Adventures! Ser.). (ENG.). (J). (gr. -1-2). 32p. 8.95 *(978-1-59249-220-6(7),* SC7105); 36p. 15.95 *(978-1-59249-137-7(5),* B7105) Soundprints.

—Wild Horse Country. Diaz, Katacha & Bosson, Jo-Ellen. 2005. (Wild Reading Adventures! Ser.). (ENG.). 36p. (J). (gr. -1-2). 9.95 *(978-1-59249-140-7(5),* PS7155) Soundprints.

—Wild Horse Country. Diaz, Katacha. (Wild Reading Adventures! Ser.). (ENG.). (J). 2005. 36p. (gr. -1-2). pap. 6.95 *(978-1-59249-138-4(3),* S7105); 2005. 32p. (gr. -1-3). 19.95 *(978-1-59249-219-0(3),* BC7105); 2003. 36p. (gr. 2-2). pap. 2.95 *(978-1-59249-139-1(1),* S7155) Soundprints.

Casale, Paul. I Have Not Yet Begun to Fight: A Story about John Paul Jones. Casale, Paul, tr. Alphin, Elaine Marie & Alphin, Arthur B. 2004. (Creative Minds Biography Ser.). 64p. (J). 22.60 *(978-1-57505-601-2(1),* Carolrhoda Bks.); (ENG.). (gr. 4-8). pap. 9.99 *(978-1-57505-635-7(6))* Lerner Publishing Group.

Casale, Roberto. Little Binky Bear. 2009. (ENM & ENG.). 18p. (J). 7.99 *(978-0-9825700-0-5(7))* Show N' Tell Publishing.

—El Osito Binky. 2017.Tr. of Little Binky Bear. (J). 7.99 *(978-0-9986498-0-1(5))* Show N' Tell Publishing.

Casanova Ealo, Eduardo René. Las Hadas Calzan Botas: Poes�a Infantil Editorial Primigenios. Casanova Ealo, Eduardo René, ed. 2019. (SPA.). 62p. (J). pap. 15.99 ***(978-1-7026-4104-3(X))*** Independently Published.

Casas, Fritz. Blood Brotherhood, 1 vol. Sherman, M. Zachary. 2011. (Bloodlines Ser.). (ENG.). 88p. (J). (gr. 4-8). pap. 6.95 *(978-1-4342-3098-0(8));* 26.65 *(978-1-4342-2559-7(3))* Capstone. (Stone Arch Bks.).

—Control under Fire, 1 vol. Sherman, M. Zachary. 2011. (Bloodlines Ser.). (ENG.). 88p. (J). (gr. 4-8). pap. 6.95 *(978-1-4342-3100-0(3));* lib. bdg. 26.65 *(978-1-4342-2561-0(5))* Capstone. (Stone Arch Bks.).

—Fighting Phantoms, 1 vol. Sherman, M. Zachary. 2011. (Bloodlines Ser.). (ENG.). 88p. (J). (gr. 4-8). lib. bdg. 26.65 *(978-1-4342-2560-3(7),* Stone Arch Bks.) Capstone.

—A Time for War, 1 vol. Sherman, M. Zachary. 2011. (Bloodlines Ser.). (ENG.). 88p. (J). (gr. 4-8). 26.65 *(978-1-4342-2558-0(5),* Stone Arch Bks.) Capstone.

Casasanta, Illary. The Dinosaur Detectives, 4 Bks., Set. Baudet, Stephanie. 2016. (Dinosaur Detectives Ser.). (ENG.). (J). *(978-1-78226-275-6(X))* Sweet Cherry Publishing.

—The Dinosaur Detectives in the Amazon Rainforest. Baudet, Stephanie. 2016. (Dinosaur Detectives Ser.). (ENG.). 84p. (J). *(978-1-78226-265-7(2))* Sweet Cherry Publishing.

—The Dinosaur Detectives in the Frozen Desert. Baudet, Stephanie. 2016. (Dinosaur Detectives Ser.). (ENG.). 83p. (J). *(978-1-78226-267-1(9))* Sweet Cherry Publishing.

—The Dinosaur Detectives in the Rainbow Serpent. Baudet, Stephanie. 2016. (Dinosaur Detectives Ser.). (ENG.). 76p. (J). *(978-1-78226-268-8(7))* Sweet Cherry Publishing.

—The Dinosaur Detectives in the Scuttlebutt. Baudet, Stephanie. 2016. (Dinosaur Detectives Ser.). (ENG.). 76p. (J). *(978-1-78226-266-4(0))* Sweet Cherry Publishing.

Casciano, Christie & Moziak, Rose Mary Casciano. Haunted Hockey in Lake Placid. 2012. 72p. (J). pap. *(978-1-59531-040-8(1))* North Country Bks., Inc.

—The Puck Hog. 2011. 44p. (J). pap. 9.95 *(978-1-59531-037-8(1))* North Country Bks., Inc.

Cascio, Maria Cristina Lo & McNicholas, Shelagh. Little Ballerina Dancing Book. Watt, Fiona. 2007. (Little Ballerina Dancing Book Ser.). 12p. (J). bds. 15.99 incl. audio compact disk *(978-0-7945-1520-1(7),* Usborne) EDC Publishing.

Cascio, Maria Cristina Lo, jt. illus. see McNicholas, Shelagh.

Casco, Maria Cristina Lo. Saints Tell Their Stories. Mitchell, Patricia. 2009. 62p. (J). (gr. k-5). 12.95 *(978-1-59325-161-1(0))* Word Among Us Pr.

Case, Chris. Jacob's New Dress. Hoffman, Sarah & Hoffman, Ian. 2020. (ENG.). 32p. (J). (gr. -1-3). pap. 7.99 ***(978-0-8075-6375-5(7),*** 807563757) Whitman, Albert & Co.

Case, Chris. Jacob's Room to Choose. Hoffman, Ian & Hoffman, Sarah. 2019. 32p. (J). *(978-1-4338-3073-0(6),* Magination Pr.) American Psychological Assn.

Case, Doug & Case, Kaye. Valerie Valentine Visits Vincent Vampire. Case, Ph D. Kaye M. 2016. (ENG.). (YA). *(978-1-4602-8611-1(1));* pap. *(978-1-4602-8612-8(X))* FriesenPress.

Case, Jonathan. Before Tomorrowland. Case, Jonathan. Jensen, Jeff et al. 2015. (ENG.). 336p. (YA). (gr. 7-12). 16.99 *(978-1-4847-0421-9(5))* Disney Pr.

Case, Kaye, jt. illus. see Case, Doug.

Case, Richard, et al. Darkhold: Pages from the Book of Sins - the Complete Collection. 2018. (Darkhold: Pages from the Book of Sins - the Complete Collection: 1). 464p. (J). (gr. 4-17). pap. 39.99 *(978-1-302-91395-3(6))* Marvel Worldwide, Inc.

—Doctor Strange Epic Collection: Triumph & Torment. 2019. (ENG.). 488p. (YA). (gr. 8-17). pap. 39.99 *(978-1-302-92056-2(1))* Marvel Worldwide, Inc.

—Doctor Strange, Sorcerer Supreme Omnibus Vol. 1. 2017. (ENG.). 1064p. (J). (gr. 4-17). 125.00 *(978-1-302-90707-5(7))* Marvel Worldwide, Inc.

Caselli, Stefano. Avengers by Jason Aaron Vol. 4: War of the Realms. 2019. (Avengers by Jason Aaron Ser.: 4). (ENG.). 112p. (YA). (gr. 8-17). pap. 15.99 *(978-1-302-91462-2(6))* Marvel Worldwide, Inc.

—Avengers by Jason Aaron Vol. 5: Challenge of the Ghost Riders. 2020. 112p. (YA). (gr. 8-17). pap. 15.99 *(978-1-302-92093-7(6))* Marvel Worldwide, Inc.

Caselli, Stefano, et al. Fantastic Four by Dan Slott Vol. 3. 2019. (Fantastic Four by Dan Slott Ser.: 3). (ENG.). 120p. (YA). (gr. 4-17). pap. 17.99 *(978-1-302-91442-4(1))* Marvel Worldwide, Inc.

Caselli, Stefano. Invincible Iron Man: Ironheart Vol. 1: Riri Williams. 2018. (ENG.). 136p. (YA). (gr. 8-17). pap. 19.99 *(978-1-302-90672-6(0))* Marvel Worldwide, Inc.

—Invincible Iron Man Vol. 2: Choices. 2018. (ENG.). 136p. (YA). (gr. 8-17). 24.99 *(978-1-302-90673-3(9))* Marvel Worldwide, Inc.

—Ironheart: Riri Williams. 2019. 280p. (J). (gr. 4-7). pap. 12.99 *(978-1-302-91979-5(2))* Marvel Worldwide, Inc.

—West Coast Avengers Vol. 1: Best Coast. 2019. (West Coast Avengers - 2018 Ser.: 1). (ENG.). 144p. (YA). (gr. 8-17). pap. 17.99 *(978-1-302-91345-8(X))* Marvel Worldwide, Inc.

Casey, James, jt. illus. see Eldridge, Les.

Casey, Lukatz. Coconut Photo Journal. American Girl Editorial Staff, ed. 2005. (American Girl Today Ser.). (ENG.). 24p. (J). 9.95 *(978-1-58485-973-4(3),* American Girl) American Girl Publishing, Inc.

Casey, Quinn. My Dad Cancelled Christmas! Casey, Sean. 2008. 25p. (J). 15.95 *(978-0-9797297-0-6(X))* Cool Kids Create.

Casey, Robert, photos by. Every Kid Needs Things That Fly, 1 vol. Kinmont, Ritchie. 2005. (ENG., 136p. (J). pap. 14.95 *(978-1-58685-509-3(3),* 1241179) Gibbs Smith, Publisher.

Cash, Emory. Santa Almost Got Caught: Stories for Thanksgiving, Christmas, & the New Year. Neely, Kirk H. 2011. 152p. pap. 14.99 *(978-1-4575-0477-8(4))* Dog Ear Publishing, LLC.

Cash, Eric. Buster Tells It All: Stories from Pony Creek Ranch. Berry, Carolyn. 2011. 24p. (J). 16.95 *(978-1-61254-011-5(2))* Brown Books Publishing Group.

—Once upon a Time in Liverpool. Kristen, Judith. 2012. 40p. pap. 15.95 *(978-0-9849505-2-2(4))* Aquinas & Krone Publishing, LLC.

Cash, Paul. What's Wrong with Pauly? House, B. J. 2013. 36p. 11.99 *(978-0-9835843-6-0(2),* Lonely Swan Bks.) Cosmic Gargoyle Creative Solutions.

Cash-Walsh, Tina. Oscar the Oak. Wall, Kathy. 2018. (ENG.). 30p. (J). 20.00 *(978-0-9971001-0-5(9))* Kathy Wall.

Cashmore-Hingley, Michael. Do Not Disturb. Gabolinscy, Jack. 2013. 27p. (gr. 3-4). pap. *(978-1-77654-019-8(0),* Red Rocket Readers) Flying Start Bks.

—Funny Races. Holden, Pam. 2015. 16p. (-2). pap. *(978-1-77654-131-7(6),* Red Rocket Readers) Flying Start Bks.

Cashmore-Hingley, Michaela. Adventure Ride. Hughes, Susan. 2018. 21p. (J). pap. *(978-1-77654-243-7(6),* Red Rocket Readers) Flying Start Bks.

Casilla, Robert. Dolores Huerta: A Hero to Migrant Workers, 0 vols. Warren, Sarah E. 2012. (ENG.). 32p. (J). (gr. 1-3). 17.99 *(978-0-7614-6107-4(8),* 9780761461074, Two Lions) Amazon Publishing.

—First Day in Grapes, 1 vol. Perez, L. King. 2004. (ENG.). 32p. (J). pap. 9.95 *(978-1-55041-340-3(6),* a920fac5-51e0-4465-9963-9c60eb81b190) Fitzhenry & Whiteside, Ltd. CAN. Dist: Firefly Bks., Ltd.

—First Day in Grapes. Perez, L. King. 2014. (ENG.). (J). (gr. 1-4). lib. bdg. 20.05 *(978-1-62765-447-0(X))* Perfection Learning Corp.

—Jackie Robinson - He Led the Way. Prince, April Jones. 2007. (Penguin Young Readers, Level 3 Ser.). (ENG.). 48p. (J). (gr. 1-3). 4.99 *(978-0-448-44721-6(5),* Penguin Young Readers) Penguin Young Readers Group.

—Let's Salsa. Ruiz-Flores, Lupe & Rosales-Yeomans, Natalia. Rosales-Yeomans, Natalia, tr. 2013.Tr. of Bailemos Salsa. (SPA & ENG.). 32p. (J). 17.95 *(978-1-55885-762-9(1),* Piñata Books) Arte Publico Pr.

—The Little Painter of Sabana Grande. Markun, Patricia M. 2014. (ENG.). 32p. (J). (gr. -1-3). 13.99 *(978-1-4814-4458-3(1),* Simon & Schuster Bks. For Young Readers) Simon & Schuster Bks. For Young Readers.

Casilla, Robert. The Lunch Thief. Bromley, Anne C. 2020. (ENG.). 32p. (J). (gr. 3-7). pap. 9.95 ***(978-0-88448-837-8(3),*** 884837) Tilbury Hse. Pubs.

Casilla, Robert. A Picture Book of Jesse Owens. Adler, David A. 2019. (Picture Book Biography Ser.). 32p. (J). (gr. -1-3). pap. 7.99 *(978-0-8234-4270-6(5))* Holiday Hse., Inc.

—A Picture Book of John F. Kennedy. Adler, David A. 2018. (Picture Book Biography Ser.). (ENG.). 32p. (J). (gr. -1-3). 7.99 *(978-0-8234-4048-1(6))* Holiday Hse., Inc.

—A Picture Book of Martin Luther King, Jr. Adler, David A. 2004. (Picture Book Biography Ser.). (J). (gr. -1-3). pap. 18.95 incl. audio compact disk *(978-1-59112-773-4(4))* Live Oak Media.

—A Picture Book of Rosa Parks. Adler, David A. 2015. 32p. pap. 8.00 *(978-1-61003-405-0(8))* Center for the Collaborative Classroom.

—A Picture Book of Rosa Parks. Adler, David A. 2004. (J). (gr. -1-2). 28.95 incl. audio compact disk *(978-1-59112-762-8(9))* Live Oak Media.

—Primer dia en las Uvas. Perez, L. King. 2004. Orig. Title: First Day in Grapes. (SPA.). 32p. (J). (gr. 2-5). pap. 11.95 *(978-1-58430-240-7(2))* Lee & Low Bks., Inc.

—The Remembering Day / el Día de los Muertos. Mora, Pat & Ventura, Gabriela Baeza. 2015. (SPA & ENG.). 32p. (J). (gr. k-3). 17.95 *(978-1-55885-805-3(9),* Piñata Books) Arte Publico Pr.

Casipit, Mel. Jesus in Town. Pagratis, Magdalene. 2018. (ENG.). 32p. (J). pap. *(978-1-77335-085-1(4)); (978-1-77335-084-4(6))* Magdalene Pr.

—What Would Jesus Do? Book 2 of the Jesus Series. Pagratis, Magdalene. 2018. (ENG.). 32p. (J). pap. *(978-1-77335-093-6(5)); (978-1-77335-091-2(9));* pap. *(978-1-77335-092-9(7))* Magdalene Pr.

Caso, George R. The Mission. Caso, George R. 2003. 16p. (J). (gr. -1-6). pap. 4.95 *(978-0-9719290-1-2(7))* Caso, George R.

Cass, Bill. The Survivorship Net: A Parable for the Family, Friends, & Caregivers of People with Cancer. Owens, Jim. 2010. (ENG.). 48p. (J). (gr. 2). 14.95 *(978-0-60443-018-9(4))* American Cancer Society, Inc.

Cassaday, John. Astonishing X-Men - Volume 1: Gifted, Vol. 1. gif. ed. 2006. (ENG.). 152p. (YA). (gr. 8-17). pap. 14.99 *(978-0-7851-1531-1(5))* Marvel Worldwide, Inc.

—Astonishing X-Men - Volume 2: Dangerous, Vol. 2. 2007. (ENG.). 152p. (YA). (gr. 8-17). 14.99 *(978-0-7851-1677-6(X))* Marvel Worldwide, Inc.

—Astonishing X-Men by Joss Whedon & John Cassaday Omnibus. 2020. (ENG.). 672p. (YA). (gr. 8-17). 100.00 *(978-1-302-92268-9(8))* Marvel Worldwide, Inc.

Cassaday, John, et al. I Am Gandhi. Meltzer, Brad. 2018. (Ordinary People Change the World Ser.). 64p. (J). (gr. 5-9). pap. 8.99 *(978-0-525-55269-7(3),* Dial Bks) Penguin Young Readers Group.

Cassaday, John. Marvel Knights Captain America by Rieber & Cassaday: the New Deal. 2018. (Marvel Knights Ser.: 1). (ENG.). 160p. (YA). (gr. 8-17). pap. 17.99 *(978-1-302-91402-8(2))* Marvel Worldwide, Inc.

—The Planetary Omnibus. Ellis, Warren. 2014. (ENG.). 864p. 75.00 *(978-1-4012-4238-1(3))* DC Comics.

Cassaday, John & Martin, Laura. Skywalker Strikes. Aaron, Jason. 2016. (Star Wars: Skywalker Strikes Ser.). (ENG.). (J). (gr. 6-12). 24p. lib. bdg. 27.07 *(978-1-61479-530-8(4),* 21430); 24p. lib. bdg. 27.07 *(978-1-61479-532-2(0),* 21432); Vol. 1. 32p. lib. bdg. 27.07 *(978-1-61479-527-8(4),* 21427); Vol. 2. 24p. lib. bdg. 27.07 *(978-1-61479-528-5(2),* 21428); Vol. 3. 24p. lib. bdg. 27.07 *(978-1-61479-529-2(0),* 21429); Vol. 5. 24p. lib. bdg. 27.07 *(978-1-61479-531-5(2),* 21431) Spotlight. (Graphic Novels).

Cassara, J. & Jacinto, K. I. M. Secret Empire: United We Stand. 2017. (ENG.). 112p. (YA). (gr. 8-17). pap. 24.99 *(978-1-302-90855-3(3))* Marvel Worldwide, Inc.

Cassara, Josh. Falcon: Take Flight, Vol. 1. 2018. 112p. (YA). (gr. -1-17). pap. 19.99 *(978-1-302-91045-7(0))* Marvel Worldwide, Inc.

Cassara, Joshua, et al. Dawn of X Vol. 6. 2020. 176p. (gr. 10-17). pap. 17.99 ***(978-1-302-92161-3(4))*** Marvel Worldwide, Inc.

Cassatt, Mary. L' Amour de Cassatt / Cassatt's Love: Learn Family Relationships in French & English. Oui Love Books. 2019. (First Impressions Ser.: Vol. 3). (ENG.). 34p. (J). pap. 14.99 *(978-1-947961-69-2(1),* Oui Love Bks.) Odeon Livre.

—Mary Cassatt: Impressionist Painter, 1 vol. Harris, Lois V. 2007. (ENG.). 32p. (J). (gr. k-3). 16.99 *(978-1-58980-452-4(X),* Pelican Publishing) Arcadia Publishing.

Cassel, Lili. Jewish Heroes, 2 bks. Weilerstein, Sadie Rose. 208p. (J). (gr. 2-3). Bk. 1. 4.25 *(978-0-8381-0180-3(1));* Bk. 2. 4.25 *(978-0-8381-0177-3(1))* United Synagogue of America Bk. Service.

Cassels, Allison, jt. illus. see Muir, Toobz.

Cassels, Jean. Baby Animals. Rappoport, Bernice. 2004. (Treasure Tree Ser.). 32p. (J). *(978-0-7166-1615-3(7))* World Bk., Inc.

—The Cajun Nutcracker, 1 vol. Mock, Chara. 2011. (ENG.). 32p. (J). (gr. k-3). 16.99 *(978-1-58980-978-9(5),* Pelican Publishing) Arcadia Publishing.

—Two Bobbies. Larson, Kirby & Nethery, Mary. 2015. 36p. pap. 8.00 *(978-1-61003-411-1(2))* Center for the Collaborative Classroom.

—Two Bobbies: A True Story of Hurricane Katrina, Friendship, & Survival. Larson, Kirby & Nethery, Mary. 2008. (ENG.). 32p. (J). (gr. k-3). 17.99 *(978-0-8027-9754-4(7),* 900050366, Bloomsbury USA Childrens) Bloomsbury Publishing USA.

—Who Is My Mom? Nicholas, Melissa. l.t. ed. 2005. (Sadlier Phonics Reading Program). 8p. (gr. -1-1). 23.00 net. *(978-0-8215-7341-9(1))* Sadlier, William H. Inc.

Cassetta, Andrea. Mr Bothers. Frost, Lesley. 2007. 52p. per. 12.95 *(978-1-934246-59-7(X))* Peppertree Pr., The.

—The Truth about Dragons & Dinosaurs. Miranda, Edward. 2007. 32p. per. 10.95 *(978-1-934246-22-1(0))* Peppertree Pr., The.

Cassidy, Al. One Misty Morning. Dean, Lani. 2004. 36p. (J). 14.95 *(978-0-9645844-9-5(2))* Manor Hse. Publishing Co., Inc.

Cassidy, Albert, Jr. The Amazing Adventures of Dr. Snappy & Sam: Dr. Snappy vs. Subluxor. Cassidy, Albert, Jr. Bennedetti, Eric. Romanchick, Jennifer, ed. 2005. 16p. (J). 9.99 *(978-0-9770527-0-7(2))* All Health Chiropractic Ctrs. Inc.

Cassidy, Amber. One Windy Day. Goodhart, Pippa. 2016. (Reading Ladder Ser.). (ENG.). 48p. (J). (gr. k-2). 7.99 *(978-1-4052-8233-8(9))* Egmont Bks., Ltd. GBR. Dist: Independent Pubs. Group.

Cassidy, Dillon. I Remember. Cassidy, Dillon. 2018. (ENG.). 46p. (J). 24.99 *(978-0-692-04346-2(2));* pap. 16.99 *(978-0-692-19773-8(7))* Mother Bear Pr.

Cassidy, Nancy White. The Doll of Lilac Valley. Cheney, Cora. 2003. 128p. 11.95 *(978-0-9714612-5-3(2))* Green Mansion Pr. LLC.

Cassidy, Sean. Hanna Bear's Christmas, 1 vol. Devine, Monica. 2007. (ENG.). 32p. (J). (gr. -1-1). 9.95 *(978-1-55041-585-8(9),* ed32b98a-7cb8-481a-acf2-5432c5fa5f94) Fitzhenry & Whiteside, Ltd. CAN. Dist: Firefly Bks., Ltd.

—Wake up, Henry Rooster!, 1 vol. Ruurs, Margriet. 2006. (ENG.). 32p. (J). (gr. k-3). 19.95 *(978-1-55041-952-8(8),* 45ff6ba8-0ba0-4855-be4a-55990bed8e73) Trifolium Bks., Inc. CAN. Dist: Firefly Bks., Ltd.

Cassidy, Sean. A Woodpecker's Tale, 1 vol. Cassidy, Sean. 2020. (Tell Me More Storybook Ser.). (ENG.). 32p. (J). (gr. 1-4). pap. 12.95 ***(978-1-55455-481-2(0),*** 0c9b140f-a806-49a0-bccb-da06d5cc8f2b) Fitzhenry & Whiteside, Ltd. CAN. Dist: Firefly Bks., Ltd.

Cassie, Aidan. Little Juniper Makes It BIG. Cassie, Aidan. 2019. (ENG.). 40p. (J). 17.99 *(978-0-374-31045-5(9),* 900192886, Farrar, Straus & Giroux (BYR)) Farrar, Straus & Giroux.

—Sterling, Best Dog Ever. Cassie, Aidan. 2018. (ENG.). 40p. (J). 17.99 *(978-0-374-30614-4(1),* 900174300, Farrar, Straus & Giroux (BYR)) Farrar, Straus & Giroux.

—The Word for Friend. Cassie, Aidan. 2020. (ENG.). 40p. (J). 18.99 *(978-0-374-31046-2(7),* 900192888, Farrar, Straus & Giroux (BYR)) Farrar, Straus & Giroux.

Cassino, Mark, photos by. The Story of Snow: The Science of Winter's Wonder. Nelson, Jon. 2017. (ENG., 36p. (J). (gr. k-3). 7.99 *(978-1-4521-6436-6(3))* Chronicle Bks. LLC.

Cassity, Don. The Great Monkey Show! Holsey, Ron. 2018. 24p. (J). *(978-1-5490-4051-1(0))* Random Hse., Inc.

Cassity, Donald. Magnet Power! Huntley, Tex. 2017. (Step into Reading Ser.). (ENG.). 24p. (J). (gr. -1-1). lib. bdg. 12.99 *(978-1-5247-2069-8(0),* Random Hse. Bks. for Young Readers) Random Hse. Children's Bks.

—Meet Rusty Rivets! (Rusty Rivets) Random House. 2017. (Step into Reading Ser.). (ENG.). 24p. (J). (gr. -1-1). pap. 4.99 *(978-1-5247-1686-8(3));* lib. bdg. 12.99 *(978-1-5247-1687-5(1))* Random Hse. Children's Bks. (Random Hse. Bks. for Young Readers).

—The Missing Medal (Rusty Rivets) Huntley, Tex. 2017. (Step into Reading Ser.). (ENG.). 24p. (J). (gr. -1-1). pap. 4.99 *(978-1-5247-2068-1(2),* Random Hse. Bks. for Young Readers) Random Hse. Children's Bks.

—Tigerbot Saves the Day! (Rusty Rivets) Depken, Kristen L. 2019. (Step into Reading Ser.). (ENG.). 24p. (J). (gr. -1-1). 5.99 *(978-0-525-64829-1(1));* 12.99 *(978-0-525-64830-7(5))* Random Hse. Children's Bks. (Random Hse. Bks. for Young Readers).

Casson, Sophia. Toby's Very Important Question. Lemieux, Jean. 2004. 61p. (J). lib. bdg. 12.00 *(978-1-4242-1246-0(4))* Fitzgerald Bks.

Casson, Sophie. The Artist & Me. Peacock, Shane. 2016. (ENG.). 40p. (J). (gr. k-4). 16.95 *(978-1-77147-138-1(7),* Owlkids) Owlkids Bks. Inc. CAN. Dist: Publishers Group West (PGW).

—Le Fil de la Vie. Lemieux, Jean. 2004. (Premier Roman Ser.). (FRE.). 64p. (J). (gr. 1-4). pap. *(978-2-89021-644-0(6))* Diffusion du livre Mirabel (DLM).

—Helen's Birds, 1 vol. Cassidy, Sara. 2019. (ENG.). 44p. (J). (gr. 1-4). 18.95 *(978-1-77306-038-5(4))* Groundwood Bks. CAN. Dist: Publishers Group West (PGW).

—Pop Goes the Weasel: Classic Folk Sing-Along Songs. 2018. (Classic Sing-Along Folk Songs Ser.). (ENG.). 36p. (J). (gr. -1-k). pap. 7.95 *(978-2-924774-25-0(X))* La Montagne Secrete CAN. Dist: Independent Pubs. Group.

—She'll Be Coming 'Round the Mountain: Classic Folk Sing-Along Songs. 2018. (Classic Sing-Along Folk Songs Ser.). (ENG.). 36p. (J). (gr. -1-k). pap. 7.95 *(978-2-924774-23-6(3))* La Montagne Secrete CAN. Dist: Independent Pubs. Group.

—Toby & the Mysterious Creature. Lemieux, Jean. Cummins, Sarah, tr. 2008. (Formac First Novels Ser.). (ENG.). 64p. (J). (gr. 2-5). 14.95 *(978-0-88780-761-9(5),* 761) Formac Publishing Co., Ltd. CAN. Dist: Formac Lorimer Bks. Ltd.

—Toby Laughs Last, 1 vol. Lemieux, Jean. Cummins, Sarah, tr. 2006. (Formac First Novels Ser.: 59). (ENG.). 64p. (J). (gr. 2-5). 4.95 *(978-0-88780-716-9(X),* 716) Formac Publishing Co., Ltd. CAN. Dist: Formac Lorimer Bks. Ltd.

—Toby Shoots for Infinity. Lemieux, Jean. 2005. 61p. (J). lib. bdg. 12.00 *(978-1-4242-1201-9(4))* Fitzgerald Bks.

—Toby Shoots for Infinity. Lemieux, Jean. Cummins, Sarah, tr. 2005. (Formac First Novels Ser.: 55). (ENG.). 64p. (J). (gr. 2-5). 14.95 *(978-0-88780-685-8(6),* 685) Formac Publishing Co., Ltd. CAN. Dist: Formac Lorimer Bks. Ltd.

—Toby Shoots for Infinity, 1 vol. Lemieux, Jean. Cummins, Sarah, tr. 2005. (Formac First Novels Ser.: 55). (ENG.). 64p. (J). (gr. 2-5). 4.95 *(978-0-88780-684-1(8),* 684) Formac Publishing Co., Ltd. CAN. Dist: Formac Lorimer Bks. Ltd.

—Toby's Best Friend. Lemieux, Jean. Cummins, Sarah, tr. 2003. (Formac First Novels Ser.). (ENG.). 64p. (J). (gr. 2-5). 14.95 *(978-0-88780-611-7(2),* 611); (gr. 1-5). 4.95 *(978-0-88780-610-0(4),* 610) Formac Publishing Co., Ltd. CAN. Dist: Formac Lorimer Bks. Ltd.

—Toby's Very Important Question. Lemieux, Jean. Cummins, Sarah, tr. 2004. (Formac First Novels Ser.: 51). (ENG.). 64p. (J). (gr. 1-5). 14.95 *(978-0-88780-637-7(6),* 637) Formac Publishing Co., Ltd. CAN. Dist: Formac Lorimer Bks. Ltd.

—Twinkle, Twinkle, Little Star: Classic Folk Sing-Along Songs. 2018. (Classic Sing-Along Folk Songs Ser.). (ENG.). 36p. (J). (gr. -1-k). pap. 7.95 *(978-2-924774-24-3(1))* La Montagne Secrete CAN. Dist: Independent Pubs. Group.

Casson, Sophie. Toby & the Mysterious Creature, 1 vol. Casson, Sophie. Lemieux, Jean. Cummins, Sarah, tr. 2008. (Formac First Novels Ser.). (ENG.). 64p. (J). (gr. 2-5). 5.95 *(978-0-88780-759-6(3),* 759) Formac Publishing Co., Ltd. CAN. Dist: Formac Lorimer Bks. Ltd.

Casson, Sophie & Brochard, Philippe. Toby's Very Important Question, 1 vol. Lemieux, Jean. Cummins, Sarah, tr. 2004. (Formac First Novels Ser.: 51). (ENG.). 64p. (J). (gr. 1-5). 4.95 *(978-0-88780-636-0(8),* 636) Formac Publishing Co., Ltd. CAN. Dist: Formac Lorimer Bks. Ltd.

Castaldi, Elicia. Eighth Grade Is Making Me Sick: Ginny Davis's Year in Stuff. Holm, Jennifer L. 2012. (Ginny Davis's Year in Stuff Ser.: 1). 128p. (J). (gr. 3-7). 15.99 *(978-0-375-86851-1(8),* Random Hse. Bks. for Young Readers) Random Hse. Children's Bks.

—Middle School Is Worse Than Meatloaf: A Year Told Through Stuff. Holm, Jennifer L. (ENG.). 128p. (J). (gr. 3-7). 2011. pap. 9.99 *(978-1-4424-3663-3(8));* 2007. 14.99 *(978-0-689-85281-7(9))* Simon & Schuster Children's Publishing. (Atheneum Bks. for Young Readers).

Castaño, Julia. Miss Mary: The Irish Woman Who Saved the Lives of Hundreds of Children During World War II. Wilson, Bernard S. 2020. (ENG.). 144p. (J). pap. 9.95 ***(978-0-7171-8655-6(5))*** Gill Bks. IRL. Dist: Casemate Pubs. & Bk. Distributors, LLC.

Casteel, Erin. The ABCs of LSU. Taylor, Linda Colquitt. 2020. (ENG.). 32p. (J). 19.95 ***(978-0-8071-7387-9(8),*** 8180) Louisiana State Univ. Pr.

Casteel, Erin El. The Bread House. Windham, Rachel. 2019. (ENG.). 60p. (J). pap. 10.00 ***(978-1-0934-1502-5(9))*** Independently Published.

Casteel, Kay. The Legacy of Bletchley Park. Smith, Annie Laura. Hamilton, Dianne, ed. 2004. 130p. (J). pap. 6.99 *(978-0-9700752-5-3(1),* 0-9700752-5-1) Onstage Publishing, LLC.

—The Masterpiece: An Abbie Girl Spy Mystery. Butler, Darren J. 2004. (Abbie, Girl Spy Ser.: 4). (ENG.). 278p. (J). mass mkt. 8.50 *(978-0-9753367-3-1(8))* Onstage Publishing, LLC.

—Spies: A Gander's Cove Mystery. Taylor, Mary Ann. 2006. (J). mass mkt. 5.99 *(978-0-9753367-7-9(0))* Onstage Publishing, LLC.

—Traitors: A Gander's Cove Mystery. Taylor, Mary Ann. 2006. (J). mass mkt. 5.99 *(978-0-9753367-9-3(7))* Onstage Publishing, LLC.

—Will Paris Burn? Smith, Annie Laura. 2004. (ENG.). (YA). mass mkt. 6.99 *(978-0-9753367-4-8(6))* Onstage Publishing, LLC.

Casteel, Tom. The American Revolution: Experience the Battle for Independence. Dodge Cummings, Judy. 2015. (Build It Yourself Ser.). 128p. (J). (gr. 3-7). 22.95 *(978-1-61930-255-6(1),* 82a533b5-21de-4e07-be76-4ebeb6def6cf); pap. 17.95 *(978-1-61930-246-4(2),* 883232aa-eba5-440c-9010-885e8e9166a9) Nomad Pr.

—Ancient Civilizations: Aztecs, Maya, Incas! With 25 Social Studies Projects for Kids. Yasuda, Anita. 2019. (Explore Your World Ser.). (ENG.). 96p. (J). (gr. 3-4). 19.95 *(978-1-61930-831-2(2),* d9706ad8-1bd0-4424-a0fc-4592e8cdb1f8); pap. 14.95 *(978-1-61930-834-3(7),* b8aa0f32-9c14-480c-9252-7cb3a1625d9a) Nomad Pr.

—Ancient Civilizations: Egyptians! With 25 Social Studies Projects for Kids. Van Vleet, Carmella. 2019. (Explore Your World Ser.). (ENG.). 96p. (J). (gr. 3-4). 19.95 *(978-1-61930-835-0(5),* 02270c1d-91cd-4575-b081-a92c6e9cd01a); pap. 14.95 *(978-1-61930-838-1(X),* 499e8fb1-63e8-4dd5-98c8-f9d21ab8eae8) Nomad Pr.

—Ancient Civilizations: Greeks! With 25 Social Studies Projects for Kids. Van Vleet, Carmella. 2019. (Explore Your World Ser.). (ENG.). 96p. (J). (gr. 3-4). 19.95 *(978-1-61930-839-8(8),* 0ef5bd2e-2ad9-4269-b917-103d6b998a95); pap. 14.95 *(978-1-61930-842-8(8),* 1276f6f0-c4f9-42b0-b73e-797981b0d6a5) Nomad Pr.

—Ancient Civilizations: Romans! With 25 Social Studies Projects for Kids. Van Vleet, Carmella. 2019. (Explore Your World Ser.). (ENG.). 96p. (J). (gr. 3-4). 19.95 *(978-1-61930-843-5(6),* f3ce23e9-95ae-4344-b785-981e4177f932); pap. 14.95 *(978-1-61930-846-6(0),* 31b3923e-5178-41fb-8fab-d83634331f12) Nomad Pr.

—Biodiversity: Explore the Diversity of Life on Earth with Environmental Science Activities for Kids. Perdew, Laura. 2019. (Build It Yourself Ser.). (ENG.). 128p. (J). (gr. 4-6). 22.95 *(978-1-61930-748-3(0),* 39ed9edd-c8b2-4891-be68-469577a9bcaa); pap. 17.95 *(978-1-61930-751-3(0),* 61f4e274-f2d8-4f2d-a879-6807f31af2e7) Nomad Pr.

—Biomes: Discover the Earth's Ecosystems with Environmental Science Activities for Kids. Latham, Donna. 2019. (Build It Yourself Ser.). 128p. (J). (gr. 4-6). (ENG.). 22.95 *(978-1-61930-736-0(7),* 7f6f8980-a17e-42e7-912c-8805e2823273); pap. 17.95 *(978-1-61930-739-1(1),* 339e56f8-415d-4737-ade5-e8ca05d398ec) Nomad Pr.

—The Brain: Journey Through the Universe Inside Your Head. Mooney, Carla. 2015. (Inquire & Investigate Ser.). 128p. (J). (gr. 6-10). 22.95 *(978-1-61930-274-7(8),* 30972759-735d-4c97-b338-dfc1f813e69d) Nomad Pr.

—Cities: Discover How They Work. Reilly, Kathleen M. 2014. (Build It Yourself Ser.). 128p. (J). (gr. 3-7). 21.95 *(978-1-61930-213-6(6),* 0c513e90-f6e6-4737-a742-32ee7e7d897b) Nomad Pr.

—Explore Ancient Chinese Myths! With 25 Great Projects. Yasuda, Anita. 2017. (Explore Your World Ser.). 96p. (J). (gr. 3-4). 19.95 *(978-1-61930-607-3(7),* 3074ab73-5397-4feb-9d87-760e891e1bcc); pap. 14.95 *(978-1-61930-611-0(5),* 0af01a3b-d11c-4b42-9d11-b1f6b83061e5) Nomad Pr.

—Explorers of the New World: Discover the Golden Age of Exploration with 22 Projects. Mooney, Carla. 2011. (Build It Yourself Ser.). 128p. (J). (gr. 3-7). 21.95 *(978-1-936313-44-0(8),* 2771b643-d002-4dbb-9d06-494b38862cd2); pap. 15.95 *(978-1-936313-43-3(X),* 2ad1e208-8e2e-42a2-86e2-0af67fee6852) Nomad Pr.

—Extinction: What Happened to the Dinosaurs, Mastodons, & Dodo Birds? with 25 Projects. Perdew, Laura. 2017. (Build It Yourself Ser.). 128p. (J). (gr. 4-6). 22.95 *(978-1-61930-557-1(7),* ebd6ffcd-5dce-43fb-9754-7a1c9fb3e86a); pap. 17.95

(978-1-61930-561-8(5), f48fbd82-8d6e-45fb-af56-d498cdf2c826) Nomad Pr.

—Garbage: Follow the Path of Your Trash with Environmental Science Activities for Kids. Latham, Donna. 2019. (Build It Yourself Ser.). (ENG.). 128p. (J). (gr. 4-6). 22.95 *(978-1-61930-744-5(8),* 430a6646-9ec2-4fab-87f8-7783b212f78f); pap. 17.95 *(978-1-61930-747-6(2),* 6facb49a-ab5b-4df9-bc64-b753002236e6) Nomad Pr.

—The Great Depression: Experience the 1930s from the Dust Bowl to the New Deal. Amidon Lusted, Marcia. 2016. (Inquire & Investigate Ser.). 128p. (J). (gr. 6-10). 22.95 *(978-1-61930-336-2(1),* 097dbca2-51c9-41cd-bf76-d834fe46bb1a) Nomad Pr.

—The Great Depression: Experience the 1930's from the Dust Bowl to the New Deal. Amidon Lusted, Marcia. 2016. (Inquire & Investigate Ser.). 128p. (J). (gr. 6-10). pap. 17.95 *(978-1-61930-340-9(X),* a6de91f8-7bee-482a-b480-0eedf058b38b) Nomad Pr.

—The Holocaust: Racism & Genocide in World War II. Mooney, Carla. 2017. (Inquire & Investigate Ser.). 128p. (YA). (gr. 6-10). 22.95 *(978-1-61930-506-9(2),* 9c489ee6-029f-4e08-8d61-5e08cf3a2e3e) Nomad Pr.

—The Human Genome: Mapping the Blueprint of Human Life. Mooney, Carla. 2020. (Inquire & Investigate Ser.). 128p. (YA). (gr. 7-9). (ENG.). 22.95 *(978-1-61930-904-3(1),* 1c86258a-40fb-498b-ad33-890349818f56); pap. 17.95 *(978-1-61930-907-4(6),* 97a0ba84-a531-4079-8c73-459976141c71) Nomad Pr.

—Human Migration: Investigate the Global Journey of Humankind. Dodge Cummings, Judy. 2016. (Inquire & Investigate Ser.). 128p. (J). (gr. 6-10). 22.95 *(978-1-61930-371-3(X),* f53d81c8-8299-4b61-a012-d37e14b7a33e) Nomad Pr.

—Industrial Design: Why Smartphones Aren't Round & Other Mysteries with Science Activities for Kids. Mooney, Carla. 2018. (Build It Yourself Ser.). (ENG.). 128p. (J). (gr. 4-10). 22.95 *(978-1-61930-670-7(0),* 51a0770e-f5eb-48e7-a181-beedac3ed162) Nomad Pr.

—Innovators: The Stories Behind the People Who Shaped the World. Lusted, Marcia Amidon. 2017. (Build It Yourself Ser.). 128p. (J). (gr. 3-7). 22.95 *(978-1-61930-516-8(X),* a4027120-558b-415e-b4dd-837efcc2fe60) Nomad Pr.

—Inside the Human Body. Mooney, Carla. 2020. (Inquire & Investigate Ser.). 128p. (YA). (gr. 7-9). (ENG.). 22.95 *(978-1-61930-900-5(9),* ca30ff9d-db9f-4c40-8219-544505d4904c); pap. 17.95 *(978-1-61930-903-6(3),* 44dd6f55-9457-4707-adec-1d4cfcd12580) Nomad Pr.

—Lakes & Ponds! With 25 Science Projects for Kids. Haney, Johannah. 2018. (Explore Your World Ser.). 96p. (J). (gr. 3-4). 19.95 *(978-1-61930-699-8(9),* 5df51ec4-411b-48b5-8477-9f8aa0b1ccc7) Nomad Pr.

—Marshes & Swamps! With 25 Science Projects for Kids. O'Sullivan, J. K. 2018. (Explore Your World Ser.). 96p. (J). (gr. 3-4). 19.95 *(978-1-61930-705-6(7),* 4ad64041-072d-4df5-b995-48eda26ee03c) Nomad Pr.

—Maya: Amazing Inventions You Can Build Yourself. Bell-Rehwoldt, Sheri. 2nd ed. 2011. (Build It Yourself Ser.). 128p. (J). (gr. 3-7). 21.95 *(978-1-936749-61-4(0),* 1ee0a730-c3c2-4a61-8901-23dbc6777bd8); pap. 15.95 *(978-1-936749-60-7(2),* 1335c9a3-3490-43e2-b4c2-e747dc1304f0) Nomad Pr.

—Microbes: Discover an Unseen World. Burillo-Kirch, Christine. 2015. (Build It Yourself Ser.). 128p. (J). (gr. 3-7). 22.95 *(978-1-61930-306-5(X),* 9a464a28-0cce-4f0f-99cc-5074fedc2f7b) Nomad Pr.

—Natural Disasters: Investigate Earth's Most Destructive Forces with 25 Projects. Reilly, Kathleen M. 2012. (Build It Yourself Ser.). 128p. (J). (gr. 3-7). pap. 15.95 *(978-1-61930-146-7(6),* c658fb79-1d4f-46fc-b3b7-84de1159593b); 21.95 *(978-1-61930-147-4(4),* c83059d9-f723-404a-a061-f1a0ce0455bb) Nomad Pr.

—Natural Disasters! With 25 Science Projects for Kids. Haney, Johannah. 2020. (Explore Your World Ser.). (ENG.). 96p. (J). (gr. 3-4). 19.95 *(978-1-61930-859-6(2),* c9be4efd-d792-4e4b-9fdb-c05ee6adc4b9); pap. 14.95 *(978-1-61930-862-6(2),* 0f95604c-b424-4554-b36f-767d1f7fc3fc) Nomad Pr.

—Oceans & Seas! With 25 Science Projects for Kids. Yasuda, Anita. 2018. (Explore Your World Ser.). 96p. (J). (gr. 3-4). 19.95 *(978-1-61930-696-7(4),* 095fa984-a8ce-4576-8e47-ba0ad00123bf) Nomad Pr.

—The Oregon Trail: The Journey Across the Country from Lewis & Clark to the Transcontinental Railroad with 25 Projects. Gibson, Karen Bush. 2017. (Build It Yourself Ser.). 128p. (J). (gr. 4-6). pap. 17.95 *(978-1-61930-576-2(3),* 813842af-4fb2-4013-8a71-41ade2e56a24) Nomad Pr.

—The Oregon Trail: The Journey Across the Country from Lewis & Clark to the Transcontinental Railroad with 25 Projects. Bush Gibson, Karen. 2017. (Build It Yourself Ser.). 128p. (J). (gr. 4-6). 22.95 *(978-1-61930-572-4(0),* b108944d-1e3e-42d2-95b9-24c1cc4b8f9a) Nomad Pr.

—Planet Earth: Finding Balance on the Blue Marble with Environmental Science Activities for Kids. Reilly, Kathleen M. 2019. (Build It Yourself Ser.). (ENG.). 128p. (J). (gr. 4-6). 22.95 *(978-1-61930-740-7(5),* 4447afd6-d611-4e40-8a69-9f6e6a999259); pap. 17.95 *(978-1-61930-743-8(X),* 6c86a8d9-5a7d-4aa8-9562-7ddf5b250e36) Nomad Pr.

—Rivers & Streams! With 25 Science Projects for Kids. Siegel, Rebecca. 2018. (Explore Your World Ser.). 96p. (J). (gr. 3-4). 19.95 *(978-1-61930-702-5(2),* 0c304b8a-b31c-479c-a1b3-bcc05b4295fc) Nomad Pr.

—Robotics! With 25 Science Projects for Kids. Van Vleet, Carmella. 2019. (Explore Your World Ser.). 96p. (J). (gr. 3-4). 19.95 *(978-1-61930-810-7(X),* 4dfa8304-de34-4f8e-8ee9-2b5f72654f76); pap. 14.95 *(978-1-61930-813-8(4),* 4a12c1d2-1220-41da-b327-889abc45a849) Nomad Pr.

—Rocks & Minerals! With 25 Science Projects for Kids. Light Brown, Cynthia. 2020. (Explore Your World Ser.). (ENG.). 96p. (J). (gr. 3-4). 19.95 *(978-1-61930-871-8(1),* be7f2e21-90ef-48af-abaf-db4d5a698c05); pap. 14.95 *(978-1-61930-874-9(6),* 5dd0f304-f23b-4b8e-af50-73314fab5929) Nomad Pr.

—Science of Science Fiction. Wood, Mathew Brenden. 2017. (Inquire & Investigate Ser.). 128p. (J). (gr. 6-10). 22.95 *(978-1-61930-466-6(X),* ea6fc6d3-269e-45e4-a3b8-254784984b25) Nomad Pr.

—Science of Science Fiction. Wood, Mathew Brenden. 2017. (Inquire & Investigate Ser.). 128p. (J). (gr. 6-10). pap. 17.95 *(978-1-61930-470-3(8),* 0c213386-7e2b-4096-a73c-84949841369d) Nomad Pr.

—Skulls & Skeletons! With 25 Science Activities for Kids. Blobaum, Cindy. 2019. (Explore Your World Ser.). (ENG.). 96p. (J). (gr. 3-4). 19.95 *(978-1-61930-806-0(1),* 35165be9-cc48-406e-8857-947ffe75798d); pap. 14.95 *(978-1-61930-809-1(6),* 5b097690-9537-4bd9-ba49-35ce99f3b6e6) Nomad Pr.

—Terrorism: Violence, Intimidation, & Solutions for Peace. Mooney, Carla. 2017. (Inquire & Investigate Ser.). 128p. (YA). (gr. 7-9). 22.95 *(978-1-61930-592-2(5),* 06d5005e-5fa5-4189-ae4b-c318b40d9687) Nomad Pr.

—Terrorism: Violence, Intimidation, Terrorization, & Solutions for Peace. Mooney, Carla. 2017. (Inquire & Investigate Ser.). 128p. (YA). (gr. 7-9). pap. 17.95 *(978-1-61930-596-0(8),* b42d027e-9d9b-4347-883d-1ce0cd1ea5d2) Nomad Pr.

—U. S. Constitution: Discover How Democracy Works. Mooney, Carla. 2016. (Build It Yourself Ser.). 128p. (J). (gr. 3-7). pap. 17.95 *(978-1-61930-445-1(7),* d7c1ed64-7234-46b3-9c63-a92263154a9e) Nomad Pr.

—The U. S. Constitution: Discover How Democracy Works. Mooney, Carla. 2016. (Build It Yourself Ser.). 128p. (J). (gr. 3-7). 22.95 *(978-1-61930-441-3(4),* 3c3a5228-6955-4df0-b277-89799c67ef86) Nomad Pr.

—The Underground Railroad: Navigate the Journey from Slavery to Freedom. Dodge Cummings, Judy. 2017. (Build It Yourself Ser.). (ENG.). 128p. (J). (gr. 4-7). 22.95 *(978-1-61930-486-4(4),* 8f3d4dec-8da1-479e-ad8a-e0066dbafb46); pap. 17.95 *(978-1-61930-490-1(2),* 3b520754-9256-4b52-bc56-09f3812196b9) Nomad Pr.

—The Water Cycle! With 25 Science Projects for Kids. Yasuda, Anita. 2020. (Explore Your World Ser.). 96p. (J). (gr. 3-4). 19.95 *(978-1-61930-867-1(3),* 691ffcf4-78cb-4c96-911b-77d4f228dd69); pap. 14.95 *(978-1-61930-870-1(3),* 4c413add-55c0-455b-8376-4189154416bc) Nomad Pr.

—Weather & Climate! With 25 Science Projects for Kids. M. Reilly, Kathleen. 2020. (Explore Your World Ser.). (ENG.). 96p. (J). (gr. 3-4). 19.95 *(978-1-61930-863-3(0),* 475f6359-0b19-4e93-bfd7-4051032c5211); pap. 14.95 *(978-1-61930-866-4(5),* a3ddf223-ce9b-4a41-ae1d-ccc2f117f824) Nomad Pr.

Castel-Branco, Ines. La Gota de Agua: Según Raimon Panikkar. Panikkar, Raimon. 2019. (SPA.). 40p. (J). (gr. 2-4). pap. 17.95 *(978-84-17440-04-6(6))* Akiara Bks. ESP. Dist: Independent Pubs. Group.

Castelao, Patricia. ABANDONED! a Lion Called Kiki. Orr, Wendy. 2012. (Rainbow Street Shelter Ser.: 4). (ENG.). 128p. (J). (gr. 2-5). 15.99 *(978-0-8050-9501-2(2),* 900080591, Holt, Henry & Co. Bks. For Young Readers) Holt, Henry & Co.

—Anne of Green Gables, 1 vol. Montgomery, L. M. 2011. (Calico Illustrated Classics Ser.: No. 4). (ENG.). 112p. (J). (gr. 2-5). 29.93 *(978-1-61641-612-6(2),* 4039, Calico Chapter Bks.) ABDO Publishing Co.

—DISCOVERED! a Beagle Called Bella, 6. Orr, Wendy. 2013. (Rainbow Street Shelter Ser.: 6). (ENG.). 128p. (J). (gr. 2-5). 15.99 *(978-0-8050-9505-0(5),* 900080597, Holt, Henry & Co. Bks. For Young Readers) Holt, Henry & Co.

—Great Expectations, 1 vol. Dickens, Charles. 2010. (Calico Illustrated Classics Ser.: No. 1). (ENG.). 112p. (J). (gr. 2-5). 29.93 *(978-1-60270-706-1(5),* 3965, Calico Chapter Bks.) ABDO Publishing Co.

Castelao, Patricia. The One & Only Bob. Applegate, Katherine. 2020. (ENG.). 352p. (J). (gr. 3-7). 18.99 ***(978-0-06-299131-7(0),*** HarperCollins) HarperCollins Pubs. Ltd. GBR. Dist: HarperCollins Pubs.

Castelao, Patricia. The One & Only Ivan. Applegate, Katherine. (ENG.). (J). (gr. 3-7). 2015. 336p. pap. 8.99 *(978-0-06-199227-8(5),* HarperCollins); 2012. 320p. 18.99 ***(978-0-06-199225-4(9),*** Harper Torch) HarperCollins Pubs.

—The One & Only Ivan. Applegate, Katherine. 2015. (ENG.). (J). (gr. 3-7). lib. bdg. 18.60 *(978-1-62765-963-5(3))* Perfection Learning Corp.

—The One & Only Ivan. Applegate, Katherine. ed. 2015. (J). lib. bdg. 18.40 *(978-0-606-35481-3(6))* Turtleback.

—The One & Only Ivan: a Harper Classic. Applegate, Katherine. 2017. (Harper Classic Ser.). (ENG.). 336p. (J). (gr. 3-7). 16.99 *(978-0-06-264194-6(8),* HarperCollins) HarperCollins Pubs. Ltd. GBR. Dist: HarperCollins Pubs.

—The One & Only Ivan Full-Color Collector's Edition. Applegate, Katherine. 2015. (ENG.). 352p. (J). (gr. 3-7). 24.99 *(978-0-06-242524-9(2),* HarperCollins) HarperCollins Pubs.

Castelao, Patricia. The One & Only Ivan Movie Tie-In Edition: My Story. Applegate, Katherine. 2020. (ENG.). 336p. (J). (gr. 3-7). 18.99 ***(978-0-06-301413-8(0))***; 12.99 ***(978-0-06-301938-6(8))***; pap. 8.99 ***(978-0-06-301414-5(9))*** HarperCollins Pubs. Ltd. GBR. (HarperCollins). Dist: HarperCollins Pubs.

Castelao, Patricia. STOLEN! a Pony Called Pebbles. Orr, Wendy. 2012. (Rainbow Street Shelter Ser.: 5). (ENG.). 128p. (J). (gr. 2-5). pap. 5.99 *(978-0-8050-9504-3(7),* 900080596, Holt, Henry & Co. Bks. For Young Readers) Holt, Henry & Co.

—Wanted! - A Guinea Pig Called Henry. Orr, Wendy. 2012. (Rainbow Street Shelter Ser.: 3). (ENG.). 128p. (J). (gr. 2-5). 15.99 *(978-0-8050-8933-2(0),* 9780805089332, Holt, Henry & Co. Bks. For Young Readers) Holt, Henry & Co.

—Women Who Changed the World: 50 Amazing Americans. Calkhoven, Laurie. 2016. 96p. (J). *(978-1-5182-0923-9(8))* Scholastic, Inc.

Castellan, Andrea & De Vita, Massimo. Mickey Mouse: the Magnificent Doublejoke. Gray, Jonathan H. et al. 2018. (Mickey Mouse Ser.). 124p. (J). (gr. 4-7). pap. 12.99 *(978-1-68405-094-9(4))* Idea & Design Works, LLC.

Castellan, Andrea "Casty" & Mazzon, Michelle. Mickey Mouse & the World to Come. Castellan, Andrea "Casty". 2010. (ENG.). 112p. (J). (gr. 3-6). pap. 9.99 *(978-1-60886-562-8(2))* Boom! Studios.

Castellani, Andrea. Wild Imagination. Gretarsson, Huginn Thor. 2011. (ENG.). 34p. (J). pap. 9.99 *(978-1-0931-6151-9(5))* Independently Published.

Castellani, Leonel. Batman & the Ultimate Riddle. Steele, Michael Anthony. 2020. (DC Super Hero Adventures Ser.). (ENG.). 72p. (J). (gr. 3-5). pap. 6.95 *(978-1-4965-9199-9(2),* 142227); lib. bdg. 26.65 *(978-1-4965-8721-3(9),* 141591) Capstone. (Stone Arch Bks.).

—Hulked-Out Squaddies! Dezago, Todd. 2011. (Super Hero Squad Ser.). (ENG.). 24p. (J). (gr. 2-5). lib. bdg. 27.07 *(978-1-59961-859-3(1),* 13891, Marvel Age) Spotlight.

—Justice League & the False Destiny. Steele, Michael Anthony. 2020. (DC Super Hero Adventures Ser.). (ENG.). 72p. (J). (gr. 3-5). pap. 6.95 *(978-1-4965-9200-2(X),* 142228); lib. bdg. 26.65 *(978-1-4965-8722-0(7),* 141590) Capstone. (Stone Arch Bks.).

Castellani, Leonel. Superman & the Toxic Troublemaker. Sutton, Laurie S. 2020. (DC Super Hero Adventures Ser.). (ENG.). 72p. (J). (gr. 3-5). pap. 6.95 ***(978-1-4965-9963-6(2),*** 201655); lib. bdg. 26.65 ***(978-1-4965-9789-2(3),*** 200583) Capstone. (Stone Arch Bks.).

—Wonder Woman & the Cheetah Challenge. Sutton, Laurie S. 2020. (DC Super Hero Adventures Ser.). (ENG.). 72p. (J). (gr. 3-5). pap. 6.95 ***(978-1-4965-9964-3(0),*** 201656); lib. bdg. 26.65 ***(978-1-4965-9790-8(7),*** 200584) Capstone. (Stone Arch Bks.).

Castellani, Leonel & Dichiara, Marcelo. Baby on Board! Dezago, Todd. 2011. (Super Hero Squad Ser.). (ENG.). 24p. (J). (gr. 2-5). lib. bdg. 27.07 *(978-1-59961-858-6(3),* 13890, Marvel Age) Spotlight.

—Love Is in the Air! Dezago, Todd. 2011. (Super Hero Squad Ser.). (ENG.). 24p. (J). (gr. 2-5). lib. bdg. 27.07 *(978-1-59961-860-9(5),* 13892, Marvel Age) Spotlight.

—Super Hero Safari! Dezago, Todd. 2011. (Super Hero Squad Ser.). (ENG.). 24p. (J). (gr. 2-5). lib. bdg. 27.07 *(978-1-59961-861-6(3),* 13893, Marvel Age) Spotlight.

—When Slurks the Slime! Dezago, Todd. 2011. (Super Hero Squad Ser.). (ENG.). 24p. (J). (gr. 2-5). lib. bdg. 27.07 *(978-1-59961-863-0(X),* 13895, Marvel Age) Spotlight.

Castellani, Leonel & Schigiel, Gregg. DC Super Hero Adventures. Cohen, Ivan & Steele, Michael Anthony. 2020. (DC Super Hero Adventures Ser.). (ENG.). (J). (gr. 3-5). 213.20 ***(978-1-4965-9831-8(8),*** 200760); pap., pap., pap. 55.60 ***(978-1-5158-7351-8(X),*** 201808); 106.60 *(978-1-4965-8729-9(4),* 29813) Capstone. (Stone Arch Bks.).

Castellani, Terry. The Dog Who Cried Woof. McWood, Allison. 2019. (ENG.). 28p. (J). pap. ***(978-1-9992475-2-2(3))*** Annelid Pr.

Castellani, Terry. The Embarrassing Life of King Ficklefred. McWood, Allison. 2019. (ENG.). 28p. (J). pap. *(978-1-9994377-6-3(4))* Annelid Pr.

—Jasper Fabulous. McWood, Allison. 2019. (ENG.). 28p. (J). pap. *(978-1-9994377-3-2(X))* Annelid Pr.

Castellani, Terry. Margo the Nut Lady. McWood, Allison. 2019. (ENG.). 26p. (J). pap. ***(978-1-9994377-7-0(2))*** Annelid Pr.

Castellani, Terry. Spaghetti Gulch. McWood, Allison. 2018. (ENG.). 28p. (J). pap. *(978-0-9782729-7-5(8))* Annelid Pr.

Castellani, Terry. Stafford Girafford. McWood, Allison. 2019. (ENG.). 28p. (J). pap. ***(978-1-9992475-4-6(X))*** Annelid Pr.

Castellano, Giuseppe. C Is for City: An Alphabet Book. Zuravicky, Orli. 2011. (Mister Doodle Ser.). (ENG.). 40p. (J). (gr. -1-k). bds. 7.99 *(978-1-4424-2049-6(9),* Little Simon) Little Simon.

—A Color for Sketch: A Book about Colors. Zuravicky, Orli. 2011. (Mister Doodle Ser.). (ENG.). 34p. (J). (gr. -1-k). bds. 7.99 *(978-1-4424-3154-6(7),* Little Simon) Little Simon.

Castellanos, Guillo. Ulises y Los Diez Mil Bigotes. Estrada, Jorge. 2015. (SPA.). 128p. (J). (gr. 2-4). pap. 7.95 *(978-607-8237-87-6(X))* Nostra Ediciones MEX. Dist: Independent Pubs. Group.

Castelli, Francesco, jt. illus. see Pellizzari, Barbara.

Castelló, Laura. Queen: The Unauthorized Biography. Romero, Soledad. 2020. (Band Bios Ser.). 64p. (J). (-3). 14.99 *(978-1-7282-1091-9(7))* Sourcebooks, Inc.

Castillo, Cesar & Burruss, Melissa. Crybaby: Extinction. LaRocque, Greg. 2005. (YA). per. 9.99 *(978-1-933570-86-0(5))* Aardvark Global Publishing.

Castillo, Guillermo Graco. Komok, Nokek y los Flamencos. Gomez, Mercedes. rev. ed. 2006. (Castillo de la Lectura Naranja Ser.). (SPA & ENG.). 92p. (J). (gr. 4-7). pap. 7.95 *(978-968-5920-39-1(7))* Castillo, Ediciones, S. A. de C. V. MEX. Dist: Macmillan.

—Querido Tigre Quezada. Malpica, Antonio. rev. ed. 2006. (Castillo de la Lectura Roja Ser.). (SPA & ENG.). 232p. (YA). (gr. 7). pap. 8.95 *(978-968-5920-85-8(0))* Castillo, Ediciones, S. A. de C. V. MEX. Dist: Macmillan.

Castillo, Jesus. El Encargo de Fernanda. Riveros, Gabriela. rev. ed. 2006. (Castillo de la Lectura Blanca Ser.). (SPA & ENG.). 64p. (J). (gr. k-2). pap. 6.95 *(978-970-20-0126-3(9))* Castillo, Ediciones, S. A. de C. V. MEX. Dist: Macmillan.

—Mi Hermano Paco. Riveros, Gabriela. rev. ed. 2006. (Castillo de la Lectura Blanca Ser.). (SPA & ENG.). 72p. (J). (gr. k-2). pap. 6.95 *(978-970-20-0173-7(0))* Castillo, Ediciones, S. A. de C. V. MEX. Dist: Macmillan.

Castillo, Lauren. Christmas Is Here. King James Bible, Adapted From The. 2010. (ENG.). 32p. (J). (gr. -1-2). 12.99 *(978-1-4424-0822-7(7),* Simon & Schuster Bks. For Young Readers) Simon & Schuster Bks. For Young Readers.

—City Cat. Banks, Kate. 2013. (ENG.). 48p. (J). (gr. -1-2). 17.99 *(978-0-374-31321-0(0),* 900066290, Farrar, Straus & Giroux (BYR)) Farrar, Straus & Giroux.

—El Futbol Me Hace Feliz (Happy Like Soccer) Boelts, Maribeth. ed. 2016. (ENG & SPA.). 32p. (J). (gr. k-4). 17.20 *(978-0-606-39111-5(8))* Turtleback.

—Happy Like Soccer. Boelts, Maribeth. 2014. (ENG.). 32p. (J). (gr. k-4). pap. 6.99 *(978-0-7636-7049-8(9))* Candlewick Pr.

—Happy Like Soccer. Boelts, Maribeth. 2014. (ENG.). (J). (gr. k-4). lib. bdg. 17.60 *(978-1-62765-426-5(7))* Perfection Learning Corp.

—Imagina. Herrera, Juan Felipe. 2020. (SPA.). 32p. (J). (gr. k-4). 16.99 *(978-1-5362-1170-2(2))* Candlewick Pr.

—Imagine. Herrera, Juan Felipe. 2018. 32p. (J). (gr. k-4). 16.99 *(978-0-7636-9052-6(X))* Candlewick Pr.

—It Is Not Time for Sleeping. Graff, Lisa. 2016. (ENG.). 40p. (J). (gr. -1-3). 16.99 *(978-0-544-31930-1(3),* 1582434, Clarion Bks.) Houghton Mifflin Harcourt Trade & Reference Pubs.

—The Pig & Miss Prudence, 1 vol. Stanek, Linda. 2008. (ENG.). 32p. (J). (gr. -1-3). 15.95 *(978-1-59572-125-9(8))* Star Bright Bks., Inc.

—The Reader, 0 vols. Hest, Amy. 2012. (ENG.). 32p. (J). (gr. -1-1). 16.99 *(978-0-7614-6184-5(1),* 9780761461845, Two Lions) Amazon Publishing.

—Twenty Yawns, 0 vols. Smiley, Jane. 2016. (ENG.). 32p. (J). (gr. -1-2). 17.99 *(978-1-4778-2635-5(1),* 9781477826355, Two Lions) Amazon Publishing.

—Yard Sale. Bunting, Eve. 32p. (J). (gr. -1-2). 2017. 6.99 *(978-0-7636-9305-3(7))*; 2015. 16.99 *(978-0-7636-6542-5(8))* Candlewick Pr.

Castillo, Marcos. Hope Is Here! Kessler, Cristina. 2013. 27p. (J). *(978-1-934370-43-8(6))* Editorial Campana.

Castillo, Victoria. The Little Doctor / el Doctorcito. Guerra, Juan J. 2017. (ENG & SPA.). 32p. (J). (gr. k-3). 17.95 *(978-1-55885-846-6(6),* Piñata Books) Arte Publico Pr.

Castillon, Carly. I Need a Kazoot! Rovetch, L. Bob. 2006. (J). *(978-1-58987-055-0(7))* Kindermusik International.

—A Little Whale Tale. McKendry, Sam. 2005. (Stories to Share Ser.). 18p. (J). (gr. -1-k). 9.95 *(978-1-58117-146-4(3),* Intervisual/Piggy Toes) Bendon, Inc.

Castle, Astrid. Ricky of the River Pride. Sherratt, Linsay. 2018. (ENG.). pap. 5.00 *(978-1-4323-0703-5(7))* Penguin Random House South Africa ZAF. Dist: Casemate Pubs. & Bk. Distributors, LLC.

Castle, Caroline. Snip Snap Croc. Castle, Caroline. 2017. (Story Corner Ser.). (ENG.). 24p. (J). (gr. -1-k). lib. bdg. 19.99 *(978-1-68297-185-7(6))* QEB Publishing Inc.

Castle, Frances. Around the World in 50 Ways, 1 vol. Smith, Dan & Lonely Planet Kids. 2018. (Around the World Ser.). (ENG.). 164p. (J). (gr. 4-7). pap. 15.99 *(978-1-78657-756-6(9),* 5553) Lonely Planet Global Ltd. IRL. Dist: Hachette Bk. Group.

—Between Worlds: Folktales of Britain & Ireland. Crossley-Holland, Kevin, ed. 2019. (ENG.). 352p. (J). (gr. 5). 18.99 *(978-1-5362-0941-9(4))* Candlewick Pr.

Castle, Frances. Spot the Mistake: Journeys of Discovery. Wood, A. J. & Jolley, Mike. 2018. (Spot the Mistake Ser.). (ENG.). 48p. (J). (gr. 2-5). 19.99 ***(978-1-78603-130-3(2),*** Wide Eyed Editions) Quarto Publishing Group UK GBR. Dist: Hachette Bk. Group.

Castle, Frances. Spot the Mistake: Lands of Long Ago. Wood, A. J. & Jolley, Mike. 2017. (Spot the Mistake Ser.). (ENG.). 48p. (J). (gr. 2-5). 19.99 *(978-1-84780-964-3(2),* Wide Eyed Editions) Quarto Publishing Group UK GBR. Dist: Hachette Bk. Group.

Castle, Lynn. A Quetzalcóatl Tale of Corn, Vol. Haberstroh, Marilyn & Panik, Sharon. 2014. (Quetzalcóatl Tales Ser.). (ENG.). 48p. (J). (gr. k-5). pap. 9.95 *(978-1-60732-345-7(1))* Univ. Pr. of Colorado.

—Tale of Chocolate, Vol. Haberstroh, Marilyn & Panik, Sharon. 2014. (Quetzalcóatl Tales Ser.). (ENG.). 48p. (gr. k-5). pap., tchr. ed. 10.95 *(978-1-60732-322-8(2))* Univ. Pr. of Colorado.

Castleden, James. The Cockney Alphabet. 2014. (ENG.). 56p. pap. 14.00 *(978-1-909470-50-7(3))* Triarchy Press GBR. Dist: Independent Pubs. Group.

Castles, Heather. Little Land Adventures - Little Bird. James, Shilah & James, Michael. 2010. 24p. pap. *(978-1-926635-33-0(7))* Adlibbed, Ltd.

—Little Land Adventures - Little Iguan. James, Shilah & James, Michael. 2010. 24p. pap. *(978-1-926635-34-7(5))* Adlibbed, Ltd.

—Little Land Adventures - Little Pig. James, Shilah & James, Michael. 2010. 24p. pap. *(978-1-926635-35-4(3))* Adlibbed, Ltd.

—Little Land Adventures - Little Racoon. James, Shilah & James, Michael. 2010. 24p. pap. *(978-1-926635-36-1(1))* Adlibbed, Ltd.

Casto, Christina. Four Farm Boys: Turkey Times. Scholl, Jenny. 2010. 36p. (J). pap. 13.95 *(978-1-4327-5886-8(1))* Outskirts Pr., Inc.

Castor, C. Jared. Ursa Major: The Bear on a Quest for Honey. Gyas, Ulysses Arctos. 2019. (ENG.). 36p. (J). pap. 6.00 *(978-1-7938-1021-2(4))* Independently Published.

—Ursa Major: The Bear on a Zoological Expedition. Gyas, Ulysses Arctos. 2019. (ENG.). 36p. (J). pap. 6.00 *(978-1-0996-2351-6(0))* Independently Published.

—Ursa Major: The Bear Who Probed a Picky Palate. Gyas, Ulysses Arctos. 2019. (ENG.). 36p. (J). pap. 6.00 *(978-1-0902-1771-4(4))* Independently Published.

Castrillón, Melissa. Animazes: Extraordinary Animal Migrations. Haworth, Katie. 2019. (ENG.). 40p. (J). (gr. 1-4). 17.99 *(978-1-5362-0853-5(1),* Big Picture Press) Candlewick Pr.

Castrillon, Melissa. If I Had a Little Dream. Laden, Nina. 2017. (ENG.). 32p. (J). (gr. -1-3). 17.99 *(978-1-4814-3924-4(3),* Simon & Schuster/Paula Wiseman Bks.) Simon & Schuster/Paula Wiseman Bks.

—Mary Anning's Curiosity, 1 vol. Kulling, Monica. 2017. (ENG.). 120p. (J). (gr. 2-7). 14.95 *(978-1-55498-898-3(5))* Groundwood Bks. CAN. Dist: Publishers Group West (PGW).

—Yellow Kayak. Laden, Nina. 2018. (ENG.). 32p. (J). (gr. -1-3). 17.99 *(978-1-5344-0194-5(6)*, Simon & Schuster/Paula Wiseman Bks.) Simon & Schuster/Paula Wiseman Bks.

Castrillon, Melissa. The Balcony. Castrillon, Melissa. 2019. (ENG.). 48p. (J). (gr. -1-3). 18.99 *(978-1-5344-0588-2(7)*, Simon & Schuster/Paula Wiseman Bks.) Simon & Schuster/Paula Wiseman Bks.

Castrillón, Melissa & Castrillón, Melissa. Cartwheeling in Thunderstorms. Rundell, Katherine. 2014. (ENG.). 256p. (J). (gr. 3-7). 18.99 *(978-1-4424-9061-1(6)*, Simon & Schuster Bks. For Young Readers) Simon & Schuster Bks. For Young Readers.

Castrillón, Melissa, jt. illus. see Castrillón, Melissa.

Castro, Ali. Monster: Survival Guide. Dakota, Heather et al. 2015. 128p. (J). *(978-0-545-85166-4(1)*, Tangerine Pr.) Scholastic, Inc.

Castro, Beatriz. The Boy Who Thought Outside the Box: The Story of Video Game Inventor Ralph Baer. Wessels, Marcie. 2020. (People Who Shaped Our World Ser.). 48p. (J). (gr. k). 16.95 *(978-1-4549-3259-8(7))* Sterling Publishing Co., Inc.

—Collins Big Cat Phonics for Letters & Sounds - Pop Pop Pop!: Band 01B/Pink B, Bd. 1B. Baker, Catherine. 2018. (Collins Big Cat Phonics Ser.). (ENG.). 16p. (J). (gr. -1-k). pap. 6.99 *(978-0-00-825137-6(1))* HarperCollins Pubs. Ltd. GBR. Dist: Independent Pubs. Group.

—Duerme Cariño: (Slumber My Darling) Foster, Stephen. 2017. (Xist Kids Spanish Bks.). (SPA.). 32p. (J). (gr. -1-3). pap. 9.99 *(978-1-5324-0395-8(X))* Xist Publishing.

Castro, Beatriz. Earning Money. Hubbard, Ben. 2020. 32p. (J). ***(978-0-7787-7371-9(X))*** Crabtree Publishing Co.

—Saving Money. Hubbard, Ben. 2020. 32p. (J). ***(978-0-7787-7372-6(8))*** Crabtree Publishing Co.

Castro, Beatriz. Slumber My Darling / Duerme Carino. Foster, Stephen. Sandoval, Lenny, tr. 2017. (Xist Kids Bilingual Spanish English Ser.). (ENG & SPA.). 32p. (J). (gr. -1-3). pap. 9.99 *(978-1-5324-0351-4(8))* Xist Publishing.

Castro, Beatriz. Spending Money. Hubbard, Ben. 2020. 32p. (J). ***(978-0-7787-7373-3(6))*** Crabtree Publishing Co.

—What Is Money? Hubbard, Ben. 2020. 32p. (J). ***(978-0-7787-7381-8(7))*** Crabtree Publishing Co.

Castro, Christopher. The Pelican Family Counting Book. Castro, Shirley. 2006. (ENG.). (J). 15.00 *(978-0-9790307-0-3(6))* Castro, Shirley.

—The Pelican Family Series— Stelly & the Sticky, Gooey Taffy. Castro, Shirley. 2011. 36p. (J). 15.00 *(978-0-9790307-3-4(0))* Castro, Shirley.

—The Pelican Family Series— Telly's Story. Castro, Shirley. 2008. 36p. (J). 15.00 *(978-0-9790307-1-0(4))* Castro, Shirley.

Castro, Giovanni, et al. Work of Art, 5. 2014. (Hello Kitty Graphic Novels Ser.). (ENG.). 62p. (J). (gr. 3-5). 22.44 *(978-1-4844-4236-4(9))* Viz Media.

Castro, Jean Claudine. Rory Cooks: Rainbow Noodles!: a Story for Parents & Children about Healthy Eating. Castro, Jeanelle. 2019. (ENG.). 26p. (J). pap. 9.97 *(978-1-7956-5704-4(9))* Independently Published.

Castro L., Antonio. The Coyote under the Table (El Coyote Debajo de la Mesa) Hayes, Joe. 2011. (ENG.). 144p. (J). (gr. 1-7). 19.95 *(978-1-935955-21-4(7))* Cinco Puntos Pr.

—The Coyote under the Table (El Coyote Debajo de la Mesa) Hayes, Joe. 2011. (ENG.). 144p. (J). (gr. 1-7). pap. 12.95 *(978-1-935955-06-1(3))* Cinco Puntos Pr.

—El Día que Nevaron Tortillas. Hayes, Joe. 2003.Tr. of Day It Snowed Tortillas. (SPA.). 160p. (J). (gr. 4-6). pap. 12.95 *(978-0-938317-76-0(8))* Cinco Puntos Pr.

—Grandpa's Ha-La-loo-ya Hambone! Hayes, Joe. 2016. (ENG.). 32p. (J). (gr. -1-2). 16.95 *(978-1-941026-54-0(0))*; pap. 7.95 *(978-1-941026-55-7(9))* Cinco Puntos Pr.

—The Gum-Chewing Rattler. Hayes, Joe. 2008. (ENG.). 32p. (J). (gr. k-6). pap. 7.95 *(978-1-933693-19-4(3))* Cinco Puntos Pr.

—The Lovesick Skunk. Hayes, Joe. (ENG.). 32p. (J). 2016. 7.95 *(978-1-941026-04-5(4))*; 2010. 16.95 *(978-1-933693-81-1(9))* Cinco Puntos Pr.

—My Tata's Remedies - Los Remedios de Mi Tata. Rivera-Ashford, Roni Capin. 2015. (ENG.). 40p. (J). (gr. 1-6). pap. 8.95 *(978-1-935955-89-4(6))* Cinco Puntos Pr.

—Pajaro Verde. Hayes, Joe. 2005. (SPA.). 40p. (J). (gr. 4-6). pap. 8.95 *(978-0-938317-90-6(3))* Cinco Puntos Pr.

—Treasure on Gold Street/El Tesoro de la Calle D'Oro: A Neighborhood Story in Spanish & English. Byrd, Lee Merrill. 2003. (SPA.). 40p. (J). (gr. 4-6). 16.95 *(978-0-938317-75-3(X))* Cinco Puntos Pr.

—El Ttesoro en la Calle Oro: A Neighborhood Story in English & Spanish. Lee Merrill Byrd, Lee Merrill. 2007.Tr. of Treasure on Gold Street. (SPA.). 40p. (J). (gr. 4-6). pap. 8.95 *(978-1-933693-11-8(8))* Cinco Puntos Pr.

Castro, Luis F. A House with No Mouse. Tinsley, P. S. Deans, Nora L., ed. 2003. 28p. 14.95 *(978-0-9723213-1-0(4)*, Mousetime Bks.) Mousetime Media LLC.

Castro, Maria Elena, et al. Family Stories (Cuentos Familiares) Guerrero, Ernesto, tr. from ENG. 2006. (ENG & SPA.). 27p. 15.95 *(978-0-9716580-7-3(2))* Lectura Bks.

Castro, Mima. Celebrate Chinese New Year with the Fong Family. Flor Ada, Alma. 2006. (Cuentos para Celebrar / Stories to Celebrate Ser.). 30p. (gr. k-6). per. 11.95 *(978-1-59820-126-0(3))* Santillana USA Publishing Co., Inc.

—Una Fiesta Saludable. White, Amy. Kratky, Lada J., tr. 2009. (Colección Fácil de Leer Ser.). (SPA.). 16p. (gr. k-2). pap. 5.99 *(978-1-60396-417-3(7))* Ediciones Alfaguara ESP. Dist: Santillana USA Publishing Co., Inc.

—La Gallinita en la Ciudad: The Little Hen in the City. Argueta, Jorge. 2006. (Bilingual Bks). 32p. (gr. 3-5). 15.95 *(978-1-59820-093-5(3)*, Alfaguara) Santillana USA Publishing Co., Inc.

Castro, Mima. The Healthy Food Party. White, Amy. 2008. (Fácil de Leer / Easy to Read Ser.). (ENG.). 16p. (J). pap. 5.99 ***(978-1-59820-569-5(2)***, Santillana Texto) Santillana USA Publishing Co., Inc.

Castro, Patricia & Avila, Jorge. El Principe y el Mendigo. Twain, Mark. 2003. (Literatura Juvenil (Panamericana Editorial) Ser.).Tr. of Prince & the Pauper. (SPA.). 314p. (YA). (gr. 4-7). pap. *(978-958-30-0146-8(5))* Panamericana Editorial.

Castro, Silvia. Vicky y el Valle Encantado. Castro, Silvia. 2018. (SPA.). 32p. (J). pap. 9.15 *(978-1-7270-5246-6(3))* CreateSpace Independent Publishing Platform.

Castronovo, Katy. Where Do I Live? Duehl, Kristine. 2013. (Budding Biologist Ser.). (ENG.). 32p. (J). (gr. k-2). 9.99 *(978-0-9855481-1-7(8))* Budding Biologist.

Castulo Aten, Vicky Talaro & Ikaia Aten, Dayle Marc. A Mother's Prayer: A Life Changing Prayer for Children. French, Peter, photos by. Talaro, Theresa. 2007. 44p. (J). 23.99 *(978-1-59879-335-2(7)*, Lifevest) Lifevest Publishing, Inc.

Caswell, Kelly. Hickory Dickory Dock. (Classic Books with Holes Big Book Ser.). (J). 2014. 16p. spiral bd. *(978-1-84643-667-3(2))*; 2012. 14p. spiral bd. *(978-1-84643-510-2(2))*; 2012. 16p. pap. *(978-1-84643-499-0(8))* Child's Play International Ltd.

Caszatt-Allen, Wendy. The Disappearance of Dinosaur SUE®. PaleoJoe. 2006. (PaleoJoe's Dinosaur Detective Club Ser.: 1). 144p. (J). (gr. 2-5). pap. 8.95 *(978-1-934133-03-3(5)*, Mackinac Island Press, Inc.) Charlesbridge Publishing, Inc.

Catagan, Tino. La Reina de las Nieves. Andersen, Hans. Bravo-Villasante, Carmen, tr.Tr. of Snow Queen. (SPA.). (J). (gr. 2-4). 6.50 *(978-84-355-0695-3(9))* Minon, S.A. ESP. Dist: Lectorum Pubns., Inc.

Catalán, Laura. Make Your Own Time Travel Games. Pierce, Nick. 2017. (ENG.). 48p. (J). (gr. 2). pap. 8.95 *(978-1-911242-91-8(1)*, Scribo) Book Hse. GBR. Dist: Sterling Publishing Co., Inc.

Catalani, Ilaria & Sherron, Kate. Rugrats: Building Blocks. Andelfinger, Nicole & Kibblesmith, Daniel. 2019. (Rugrats Ser.). (ENG.). 112p. (J). pap. 14.99 *(978-1-68415-460-9(X))* Boom! Studios.

Catalano, Dominic. The Bremen Town Musicians: A Tale about Working Together. Grimm, Jacob & Grimm, Wilhelm K. 2006. (Famous Fables Ser.). (J). *(978-1-59939-039-0(6)*, Reader's Digest Young Families, Inc.) Studio Fun International.

—Clink, Clank, Clunk. Aroner, Miriam. 2006. (ENG.). 32p. (J). (gr. -1 — 1). 16.95 *(978-1-59078-270-5(4))* Boyds Mills Pr.

—My Sprig of Lilac: Remembering Abraham Lincoln. Coleman, Wim & Perrin, Pat. 2014. (Setting the Stage for Fluency Ser.). (ENG.). 40p. (J). (gr. 3-5). lib. bdg. 27.99 *(978-1-939656-54-4(0))* Red Chair Pr.

—The Shepherd's Christmas Story. Mackall, Dandi Daley. 2005. 32p. (J). (gr. 1-5). 12.99 *(978-0-7586-0904-5(3))* Concordia Publishing Hse.

—What's So Bad about the Big Bad Wolf?, 24 vols. Williams, Rozanne Lanczak. 2005. (Reading for Fluency Ser.). 8p. (J). pap. 2.49 *(978-1-59198-143-5(3)*, 4243) Creative Teaching Pr., Inc.

Catalanotto, Peter. Good-Bye, Sheepie, 0 vols. Burleigh, Robert. 2010. (ENG.). 32p. (J). (gr. -1-k). 16.99 *(978-0-7614-5598-1(1)*, 9780761455981, Two Lions) Amazon Publishing.

—My Mother's Voice. Ryder, Joanne. 2006. 32p. (J). (gr. -1-3). 16.99 *(978-0-06-029509-7(0))* HarperCollins Pubs.

—Sleepsong. Lyon, George Ella. 2008. (ENG.). 40p. (J). (gr. -1-k). 16.99 *(978-0-689-86973-0(8)*, Atheneum/Richard Jackson Bks.) Simon & Schuster Children's Publishing.

Catalanotto, Peter. Daisy 1, 2, 3. Catalanotto, Peter. 2003. (ENG.). 32p. (J). (gr. -1-1). 19.99 *(978-0-689-85457-6(9)*, Atheneum/Richard Jackson Bks.) Simon & Schuster Children's Publishing.

—Dylan's Day Out. Catalanotto, Peter. 2006. pap. 7.99 *(978-0-9777720-0-1(4))* Southpaw Books LLC.

—Emily's Art. Catalanotto, Peter. 2006. (ENG.). 32p. (J). (gr. k-3). 7.99 *(978-1-4169-2688-7(7)*, Atheneum Bks. for Young Readers) Simon & Schuster Children's Publishing.

—Ivan the Terrier. Catalanotto, Peter. 2007. (ENG.). 32p. (J). (gr. -1-3). 19.99 *(978-1-4169-1247-7(9)*, Atheneum/Richard Jackson Bks.) Simon & Schuster Children's Publishing.

—Kitten Red, Yellow, Blue. Catalanotto, Peter. 2005. (ENG.). 32p. (J). (gr. -1-k). 18.99 *(978-0-689-86562-6(7)*, Atheneum/Richard Jackson Bks.) Simon & Schuster Children's Publishing.

—Matthew A. B. C. Catalanotto, Peter. 2005. (ENG.). 32p. (J). (gr. -1-3). reprint ed. 7.99 *(978-1-4169-0330-7(5)*, Atheneum Bks. for Young Readers) Simon & Schuster Children's Publishing.

—Monkey & Robot. Catalanotto, Peter. 2014. (ENG.). 64p. (J). (gr. 1-4). pap. 7.99 *(978-1-4424-2979-6(8)*, Atheneum Bks. for Young Readers) Simon & Schuster Children's Publishing.

—Monkey & Robot: Friends & Neighbors. Catalanotto, Peter. 2019. (ENG.). 64p. (J). (gr. 1-4). 17.99 *(978-1-939547-59-0(8))* Creston Bks.

—More of Monkey & Robot. Catalanotto, Peter. 2014. (ENG.). 64p. (J). (gr. 1-4). 15.99 *(978-1-4424-5251-0(X)*, Atheneum/Richard Jackson Bks.) Simon & Schuster Children's Publishing.

—The Newbies. Catalanotto, Peter. 2015. (ENG.). 40p. (J). (gr. -1-3). 17.99 *(978-1-4814-1892-8(0))* Simon & Schuster Children's Publishing.

—Question Boy Meets Little Miss Know-It-All. Catalanotto, Peter. 2012. (ENG.). 40p. (J). (gr. -1-3). 17.99 *(978-1-4424-0670-4(4)*, Atheneum/Richard Jackson Bks.) Simon & Schuster Children's Publishing.

—The Veterans Day Visitor. Catalanotto, Peter. Schembri, Pamela. 2008. (Second Grade Friends Ser.). (ENG.). 64p. (J). (gr. 2-5). 17.99 *(978-0-8050-7840-4(1)*, 900030187, Holt, Henry & Co. Bks. For Young Readers) Holt, Henry & Co.

Cataldo, Melanie. Home by Another Way: A Christmas Story. Taylor, Barbara Brown. 2018. (ENG.). 40p. (J). (gr. 2-4). 18.00 *(978-1-947888-00-5(5)*, Flyaway Bks.) Westminster John Knox Pr.

—The Stranded Whale. Yolen, Jane. 2015. 32p. (J). (gr. k-4). 15.99 *(978-0-7636-6953-9(9))* Candlewick Pr.

Catanese, Donna. Dirty Larry. Hamsa, Bobbie. rev. ed. 2003. (Rookie Reader Ser.). (ENG.). 24p. (J). (gr. k-2). pap. 4.95 *(978-0-516-27493-5(7)*, Children's Pr.) Scholastic Library Publishing.

Catchpole, Diana. St Patrick & the Shamrock. Mortimer, Sheila. 2004. 8p. (J). 10.95 *(978-0-7171-3755-8(4))* M.H. Gill & Co. U. C. IRL. Dist: Dufour Editions, Inc.

—Trapped in the Witch's Lair: Peek Inside the Pop-Up Windows! Taylor, Dereen. 2014. (ENG.). 12p. (J). (gr. 2-7). 16.99 *(978-1-86147-320-2(6)*, Armadillo) Anness Publishing GBR. Dist: National Bk. Network.

Cate, Annette LeBlanc. Look Up! Bird-Watching in Your Own Backyard. Cate, Annette LeBlanc. 2019. 80p. (J). (gr. 3-7). 8.99 *(978-0-7636-9300-8(6))* Candlewick Pr.

—The Magic Rabbit. Cate, Annette LeBlanc. 2013. (ENG.). 32p. (J). (gr. -1-1). 21.19 *(978-0-7636-2672-3(4))*; 6.99 *(978-0-7636-6685-9(8))* Candlewick Pr.

Cate, Marijke Ten. Where Is My Sock? Cate, Marijke Ten. 2010. (ENG.). 24p. (J). (gr. -1-k). 16.95 *(978-1-59078-808-0(7))* Lemniscaat USA.

Cater, Angela. The Adventures of Sailor Sam. Cater, Angela. 2007. (ENG.). 32p. (J). pap. *(978-0-9555725-0-0(9))* Tabby Cat Pr.

—A Perfect Nest for Mrs Mallard. Cater, Angela. 2009. 32p. pap. *(978-0-9555725-2-4(5))* Tabby Cat Pr.

Cater, Rosina. Five Little Birds. Williams-Lemi, Siu. 2019. (ENG & MAO.). 26p. (J). pap. ***(978-0-473-49035-5(8))*** Kingfisher Publishing.

—The Happy Song. Williams-Lemi, Siu. 2020. (ENG.). 24p. (J). (gr. k-1). pap. ***(978-0-473-50996-5(2))*** Kingfisher Publishing.

—Ngati Fruit Salad. Williams-Lemi, Siu. 2020. (Loopy Tunes Rainbow Collection: Vol. 3). (ENG.). 28p. (J). pap. ***(978-0-473-52218-6(7))*** Kingfisher Publishing.

Caterini, Antonella. La Signora Delle Fiabe e Altre Fiabe. Plumeri Caterini, Mariella. 2015. (ITA.). 82p. (J). pap. *(978-88-940362-1-3(9))* Maria, Plumeri.

Caterisano, Sarah. Florida Santa: Is He Real? How Do We Know It? Clark, Ruth E. 2008. (ENG.). 32p. (J). (gr. -1-3). 16.95 *(978-0-9792963-0-7(7))* Hibiscus Publishing.

Cathcart, Sharyn. The Gull That Lost the Sea. Smith, Claude Clayton. 2008. (ENG.). 34p. pap. 5.95 *(978-0-9667359-7-0(8)*, BeanPole Bks.) Harren Communications, LLC.

Cathcart, Yvonne. Robyn Makes the News, 1 vol. Hutchins, Hazel J. & Hutchins, Hazel. 2003. (Formac First Novels Ser.: 27). (ENG.). 64p. (J). (gr. 1-5). 4.95 *(978-0-88780-593-6(0)*, 593) Formac Publishing Co., Ltd. CAN. Dist: Formac Lorimer Bks. Ltd.

—Robyn's Monster Play, 1 vol. Hutchins, Hazel. 2008. (Formac First Novels Ser.). (ENG.). 64p. (J). (gr. 2-5). 5.95 *(978-0-88780-748-0(8)*, 748) Formac Publishing Co., Ltd. CAN. Dist: Formac Lorimer Bks. Ltd.

—Robyn's Monster Play. Hutchins, Hazel. 2008. (Formac First Novels Ser.). (ENG.). 64p. (J). (gr. 2-5). 14.95 *(978-0-88780-750-3(X)*, 750) Formac Publishing Co., Ltd. CAN. Dist: Formac Lorimer Bks. Ltd.

—Robyn's Party-in-the-Park. Hutchins, Hazel. 2005. 59p. (J). lib. bdg. 12.00 *(978-1-4242-1203-3(0))* Fitzgerald Bks.

—Robyn's Party-in-the-Park. Hutchins, Hazel. 2005. (Formac First Novels Ser.: 31). (ENG.). 64p. (J). (gr. 2-5). 14.95 *(978-0-88780-663-6(5)*, 663) Formac Publishing Co., Ltd. CAN. Dist: Formac Lorimer Bks. Ltd.

—Robyn's Party in the Park, 1 vol. Hutchins, Hazel. 2005. (Formac First Novels Ser.: 31). (ENG.). 64p. (J). (gr. 2-5). 4.95 *(978-0-88780-662-9(7)*, 662) Formac Publishing Co., Ltd. CAN. Dist: Formac Lorimer Bks. Ltd.

—Skate, Robyn, Skate. Hutchins, Hazel J. & Hutchins, Hazel. 2004. (Formac First Novels Ser.: 30). (ENG.). 64p. (J). (gr. 1-5). 14.95 *(978-0-88780-627-8(9)*, 627) Formac Publishing Co., Ltd. CAN. Dist: Formac Lorimer Bks. Ltd.

—Skate, Robyn, Skate. Hutchins, Hazel. 2004. 57p. (J). lib. bdg. 12.00 *(978-1-4242-1244-6(8))* Fitzgerald Bks.

—Skate, Robyn, Skate, 1 vol. Hutchins, Hazel. 2004. (Formac First Novels Ser.: 30). (ENG.). 64p. (J). (gr. 1-5). 4.95 *(978-0-88780-626-1(0)*, 626) Formac Publishing Co., Ltd. CAN. Dist: Formac Lorimer Bks. Ltd.

—Tilt Your Head Rosie the Red, 1 vol. McCarney, Rosemary. 2015. (Rosie the Red Ser.). (ENG.). 24p. (J). (gr. 1-3). 15.95 *(978-1-927583-59-3(4))* Second Story Pr. CAN. Dist: Orca Bk. Pubs. USA.

Cathers Donohue, Christine. Wish for Winellda the Witch. Clark, Esther. 2019. (ENG.). 34p. (J). (gr. -1-3). pap. 11.99 ***(978-1-61254-389-5(8))*** Brown Books Publishing Group.

Catinot, Siobhan. Santa, Wipe Your Feet. Goldsbury, Sophie. 2019. (ENG.). 36p. (J). pap. 11.99 ***(978-1-7010-3599-7(5))*** Independently Published.

Catling, Andy. Brain Invaders. Dahl, Michael. 2016. (Igor's Lab of Fear Ser.). (ENG.). 40p. (J). (gr. 4-8). lib. bdg. 23.99 *(978-1-4965-3526-9(X)*, Stone Arch Bks.) Capstone.

—Electric Claw. Dahl, Michael. 2016. (Igor's Lab of Fear Ser.). (ENG.). 40p. (J). (gr. 4-8). lib. bdg. 23.99 *(978-1-4965-3527-6(8)*, Stone Arch Bks.) Capstone.

—Igor's Lab of Fear, 8 vols. Dahl, Michael. 2016. (Igor's Lab of Fear Ser.). (ENG.). 40p. (J). (gr. 4-8). lib. bdg., lib. bdg., lib. bdg. 191.92 *(978-1-4965-3542-9(1)*, Stone Arch Bks.) Capstone.

—Illustrated Treasury of Bedtime Stories. Kelly, Richard, ed. 2017. 384p. (J). 39.95 *(978-1-78209-987-1(5))* Miles Kelly Publishing, Ltd. GBR. Dist: Parkwest Pubns., Inc.

—Joseph & the Fearful Family. Smith, Fiona Veitch. 2018. (ENG.). 32p. pap. 10.00 *(978-0-281-07473-0(9))* InterVarsity Pr.

—Joseph & the Hidden Cup. Smith, Fiona Veitch. 2018. (ENG.). 32p. pap. 10.00 *(978-0-281-07474-7(7))* InterVarsity Pr.

—Joseph & the Jealous Brothers. Smith, Fiona Veitch. 2016. (ENG.). 32p. pap. 10.00 *(978-0-281-07469-3(0))* SPCK Publishing GBR. Dist: InterVarsity Pr.

—Joseph & the Lying Lady. Smith, Fiona Veitch. 2016. (ENG.). 32p. pap. 10.00 *(978-0-281-07470-9(4))* SPCK Publishing GBR. Dist: InterVarsity Pr.

—Joseph & the Rainbow Robe. Smith, Fiona Veitch. 2016. (ENG.). 32p. pap. 10.00 *(978-0-281-07468-6(2))* SPCK Publishing GBR. Dist: InterVarsity Pr.

—Lost Skeleton. Dahl, Michael. 2016. (Igor's Lab of Fear Ser.). (ENG.). 40p. (J). (gr. 4-8). lib. bdg. 23.99 *(978-1-4965-3529-0(4)*, Stone Arch Bks.) Capstone.

—The Lost Treasure of the Sunken City. Taylor, Martin. 2012. (J). *(978-1-4351-4330-2(2))* Barnes & Noble, Inc.

—Maze Monster. Dahl, Michael. 2016. (Igor's Lab of Fear Ser.). (ENG.). 40p. (J). (gr. 4-8). lib. bdg. 23.99 *(978-1-4965-3528-3(6)*, Stone Arch Bks.) Capstone.

—A Pirate Christmas Activity Book. Senior, Suzy. ed. 2019. (ENG.). 32p. (J). (gr. -1-k). pap. 6.99 *(978-0-7459-7728-7(6)*, Lion Children's) Lion Hudson PLC GBR. Dist: Independent Pubs. Group.

—The Sad Princess. Benton, Lynne. 2009. (Tadpoles Ser.). (ENG.). 24p. (J). (gr. k-2). pap. *(978-0-7787-3903-6(1))* Crabtree Publishing Co.

—The Sad Princess. Benton, Lynne. 2009. (Tadpoles Ser.). (ENG.). (J). (gr. k-k). lib. bdg. 17.55 *(978-1-61383-941-6(3))* Perfection Learning Corp.

Catling, Andy. What Would You Do? Moore-Mallinos, Jennifer. 2020. (ENG.). 96p. (J). (gr. -1-2). pap. 12.95 ***(978-0-8294-5013-2(0))*** Loyola Pr.

Catlow, Nikalas. Mind Your Own Business! A File of Super Secret Stuff. 2007. (ENG.). 224p. (J). 8.00 *(978-1-84046-763-5(0)*, Wizard Books) Icon Bks., Ltd. GBR. Dist: Publishers Group Canada.

Catlow, Nikalas. Pirates v. Ancient Egyptians in a Haunted Museum. Catlow, Nikalas. Wesson, Tim. 2012. (Mega Mash-Up Ser.: 4). (ENG.). 96p. (J). (gr. 2-5). pap. 6.99 *(978-0-7636-5901-1(0)*, Nosy Crow) Candlewick Pr.

Catlow, Nikalas & Wesson, Tim. Robots vs. Gorillas in the Desert. Catlow, Nikalas & Wesson, Tim. 2011. (Mega Mash-Up Ser.: 2). (ENG.). 96p. (J). (gr. 2-5). pap. 6.99 *(978-0-7636-5873-1(1)*, Nosy Crow) Candlewick Pr.

—Romans vs. Dinosaurs on Mars. Catlow, Nikalas & Wesson, Tim. 2011. (Mega Mash-Up Ser.: 3). (ENG.). 96p. (J). (gr. 2-5). pap. 6.99 *(978-0-7636-5872-4(3)*, Nosy Crow) Candlewick Pr.

Catnip. Little Cloud, Mrs. Pea, You Pointing at Me. Colouring Storybook. Jobi, M. S. Juhli. 2018. (ENG.). 56p. (J). pap. *(978-1-7751710-0-3(0))* Jobi, Juhli.

Catnip Design, Pamela Fattorelli. Bloodyrose. Adamas, Evalith. 2019. (ITA.). 268p. (J). pap. 13.50 *(978-1-7289-0166-4(9))* Independently Published.

Cato, Andrea. Rosie's Pink House, 1 vol. Blair, Candice. 2010. 18p. 24.95 *(978-1-4489-4619-8(0))* America Star Bks.

Caton, Margret. Blobfish Throws a Party. Paul, Miranda. 2017. (ENG.). 32p. (J). (gr. -1-3). 16.99 *(978-1-4998-0422-5(9))* Little Bee Books Inc.

Caton, Tim. The Book of Call & Response. Feierabend, John M. 2003. (First Steps in Music Ser.). (ENG.). 88p. (J). (gr. -1-2). pap. 14.95 *(978-1-57999-215-6(3))* G I A Pubns., Inc.

—The Book of Children's Song Tales. Feierabend, John M. 2003. (First Steps in Music Ser.). (ENG.). 104p. (J). (gr. -1-2). pap. 14.95 *(978-1-57999-213-2(7))* G I A Pubns., Inc.

—The Book of Echo Songs. Feierabend, John M. 2003. (First Steps in Music Ser.). (ENG.). 88p. (J). (gr. -1-2). pap. 14.95 *(978-1-57999-214-9(5))* G I A Pubns., Inc.

Catrinella, Laura. Chin Up. Firestone, Naomi. 2019. (ENG.). 32p. (J). ***(978-1-5255-3593-2(5))***; pap. ***(978-1-5255-3594-9(3))*** FriesenPress.

—Snowflake, Snowflake. Barone, Jennifer. 2019. (ENG.). 20p. (J). ***(978-1-5255-5090-4(X))***; pap. ***(978-1-5255-5091-1(8))*** FriesenPress.

—Something Lost Something Found. Paruzel-Gibson, Natalia. Ozunal, Bema, ed. 2020. (ENG.). 40p. (J). ***(978-1-5255-4381-4(4))***; pap. ***(978-1-5255-4382-1(2))*** FriesenPress.

Catrow, David. Are You Quite Polite? Silly Dilly Manners Songs. Katz, Alan. 2006. (ENG.). 32p. (J). (gr. -1-3). 17.99 *(978-0-689-86970-9(3)*, McElderry, Margaret K. Bks.) McElderry, Margaret K. Bks.

—The Boy Who Wouldn't Share. Reiss, Mike & Reiss, Mike. 2008. (ENG.). 32p. (J). (gr. 1-3). 16.99 *(978-0-06-059132-8(3))* HarperCollins Pubs.

—Cinderella Skeleton. San Souci, Robert D. 2004. (ENG.). 32p. (J). (gr. -1-3). reprint ed. pap. 7.99 *(978-0-15-205069-6(8)*, 1195310) Houghton Mifflin Harcourt Publishing Co.

—Don't Say That Word! Katz, Alan. 2007. (ENG.). 32p. (J). (gr. -1-3). 19.99 *(978-0-689-86971-6(1)*, McElderry, Margaret K. Bks.) McElderry, Margaret K. Bks.

—Dozens of Cousins. Crum, Shutta. 2013. (ENG.). 32p. (J). (gr. -1-3). 17.99 *(978-0-618-15874-4(X)*, 1013203) Houghton Mifflin Harcourt Publishing Co.

—Going, Going, Gone! And Other Silly Dilly Sports Songs. Katz, Alan. 2009. (ENG.). 32p. (J). (gr. -1-3). 16.99 *(978-1-4169-0696-4(7)*, McElderry, Margaret K. Bks.) McElderry, Margaret K. Bks.

—Have Fun, Molly Lou Melon. Lovell, Patty. 2012. (ENG.). 32p. (J). (gr. k-3). 17.99 *(978-0-399-25406-2(4)*, G.P. Putnam's Sons Books for Young Readers) Penguin Young Readers Group.

—How Murray Saved Christmas. Reiss, Mike. 2004. (Holiday Books: Christmas Ser.). 32p. (J). (gr. k-3). 21.19 *(978-0-14-250145-0(X)*, Puffin) Penguin Publishing Group.

—I Ain't Gonna Paint No More! Beaumont, Karen. (ENG.). (J). (gr. -1 — 1). 2012. 30p. bds. 11.99 *(978-0-547-87035-9(3)*, 1504857); 2005. 32p. 17.99 *(978-0-15-202488-8(3)*, 1192948) Houghton Mifflin Harcourt Publishing Co.

—I Ain't Gonna Paint No More! (board Book) Beaumont, Karen. 2019. (ENG.). 30p. (J). (— 1). bds. 7.99 *(978-0-358-00415-8(2)*, 1736741, HMH Books For Young Readers) Houghton Mifflin Harcourt Publishing Co.

—I Like Myself! Beaumont, Karen. (ENG.). 32p. (J). (gr. -1 — 1). 2010. bds. 11.99 *(978-0-547-40163-8(9)*, 1427978); 2004. 17.99 *(978-0-15-202013-2(6)*, 1191551) Houghton Mifflin Harcourt Publishing Co.

C

—I Like Myself! (board Book) Beaumont, Karen. 2016. (ENG.). 32p. (J). (— 1). bds. 7.99 *(978-0-544-64101-3(9)*, 1620821, HMH Books For Young Readers) Houghton Mifflin Harcourt Publishing Co.

—I Wanna Go Home. Kaufman Orloff, Karen. 2014. 32p. (J). (gr. k-3). 17.99 *(978-0-399-25407-9(2)*, G.P. Putnam's Sons Books for Young Readers) Penguin Young Readers Group.

—I Wanna Iguana. Kaufman Orloff, Karen. 2004. 32p. (J). (gr. -1-3). 17.99 *(978-0-399-23717-1(8)*, G.P. Putnam's Sons Books for Young Readers) Penguin Young Readers Group.

—I'm Still Here in the Bathtub: Brand New Silly Dilly Songs. Katz, Alan. 2003. (ENG.). 32p. (J). (gr. -1-3). 19.99 *(978-0-689-84551-2(0)*, McElderry, Margaret K. Bks.) McElderry, Margaret K. Bks.

—¡Me Gusta Cómo Soy! / I Like Myself! Beaumont, Karen. 2018. (ENG.). 30p. (J). (— 1). bds. 5.99 *(978-1-328-80904-9(8)*, 1688493, HMH Books For Young Readers) Houghton Mifflin Harcourt Publishing Co.

—Merry Un-Christmas. Reiss, Mike. 2006. 32p. (J). (gr. -1-2). lib. bdg. 16.89 *(978-0-06-059127-4(7))* HarperCollins Pubs.

—Mosquitoes Are Ruining My Summer! And Other Silly Dilly Camp Songs. Katz, Alan. 2011. (ENG.). 32p. (J). (gr. -1-3). 16.99 *(978-1-4169-5568-9(2)*, McElderry, Margaret K. Bks.) McElderry, Margaret K. Bks.

—My School's a Zoo! Smith, Stuart. 2004. 40p. (J). (gr. k-3). lib. bdg. 16.89 *(978-0-06-028511-1(7))* HarperCollins Pubs.

—On Top of the Potty: On Top of the Potty. Katz, Alan. 2008. (ENG.). 32p. (J). (gr. -1-3). 19.99 *(978-0-689-86215-1(6)*, McElderry, Margaret K. Bks.) McElderry, Margaret K. Bks.

—Our Tree Named Steve. Zweibel, Alan. 2007. 32p. (J). (gr. -1-k). pap. 7.99 *(978-0-14-240743-1(7)*, Puffin Books) Penguin Young Readers Group.

—Plantzilla. Nolen, Jerdine & Keliher, Brian. 2005. (ENG.). 32p. (J). (gr. -1-3). reprint ed. pap. 7.99 *(978-0-15-205392-5(1)*, 1196232) Houghton Mifflin Harcourt Publishing Co.

—Plantzilla Goes to Camp. Nolen, Jerdine. 2006. (ENG.). 32p. (J). (gr. k-3). 17.99 *(978-0-689-86803-0(0)*, Simon & Schuster/Paula Wiseman Bks.) Simon & Schuster/Paula Wiseman Bks.

—Smelly Locker: Silly Dilly School Songs. Katz, Alan. 2010. (ENG.). 32p. (J). (gr. -1-3). 7.99 *(978-1-4424-0251-5(2)*, McElderry, Margaret K. Bks.) McElderry, Margaret K. Bks.

—Smelly Locker: Silly Dilly School Songs. Katz, Alan. 2008. (ENG.). 32p. (J). (gr. -1-3). 16.99 *(978-1-4169-0695-7(9))* Simon & Schuster, Inc.

—Too Much Kissing! And Other Silly Dilly Songs about Parents. Katz, Alan. 2009. (ENG.). 32p. (J). (gr. -1-2). 16.99 *(978-1-4169-4199-6(1)*, McElderry, Margaret K. Bks.) McElderry, Margaret K. Bks.

—Westward Ho, Carlotta! Fleming, Candace. 2009. (ENG.). 36p. (J). (gr. -1-2). 10.99 *(978-1-4424-0218-8(0)*, Atheneum Bks. for Young Readers) Simon & Schuster Children's Publishing.

—Wet Dog! Broach, Elise. 2007. (ENG.). 32p. (J). (gr. k-3). pap. 6.99 *(978-0-14-240855-1(7)*, Puffin Books) Penguin Young Readers Group.

—When God Made Light. Turner, Matthew Paul. 2018. (ENG.). 48p. (J). (gr. -1-2). 11.99 *(978-1-60142-920-9(7)*, Convergent Bks.) Crown Publishing Group, The.

—When God Made You. Turner, Matthew Paul. 2017. (ENG.). 48p. (J). (gr. -1-2). 11.99 *(978-1-60142-918-6(5)*, Convergent Bks.) Crown Publishing Group, The.

—Where Did They Hide My Presents? Silly Dilly Christmas Songs. Katz, Alan. 2008. (ENG.). 32p. (J). (gr. -1-3). 6.99 *(978-1-4169-6830-6(X)*, McElderry, Margaret K. Bks.) McElderry, Margaret K. Bks.

Catrow, David. The Fly Flew In. Catrow, David. 2012. (I Like to Read Ser.). (ENG.). 24p. (J). (gr. -1-3). 14.95 *(978-0-8234-2418-4(9))* Holiday Hse., Inc.

—Fun in the Sun. Catrow, David. 2016. (ENG.). 32p. (J). (-k). 6.99 *(978-0-8234-3569-2(5))* Holiday Hse., Inc.

—We the Kids: The Preamble of the Constitution of the United States. Catrow, David. 2004. (J). (gr. k-5). 27.90 incl. audio *(978-0-8045-6914-9(2))* Spoken Arts, Inc.

—We the Kids: The Preamble to the Constitution of the United States. Catrow, David. 2005. (ENG.). 32p. (J). (gr. k-3). pap. 7.99 *(978-0-14-240276-4(1)*, Puffin Books) Penguin Young Readers Group.

Catrow, David, III & Catrow, David. I Wanna New Room. Kaufman Orloff, Karen. 2010. (ENG.). 32p. (J). (gr. k-3). 17.99 *(978-0-399-25405-5(6)*, G.P. Putnam's Sons Books for Young Readers) Penguin Young Readers Group.

Catrow, David, jt. illus. see Catrow, David, III.

Catterson, Stuart Mole. Ruby, Alfie & the Mother's Day Card. Gibb, Hil. 2019. (Ruby & Alfie Ser.: Vol. 1). (ENG.). 42p. (J). (gr. k-6). pap. *(978-0-9571911-2-9(X))* Haruki Publishing.

—A Tale of Two Sydneys. Gibb, Hil. 2018. (ENG.). 84p. (YA). (gr. 7-12). pap. *(978-0-9571911-0-5(3))* Haruki Publishing.

Cattish, Anna. Band Camp Rules. Cobb, Amy. 2016. (Band Geeks Set 2 Ser.). (ENG.). 112p. (J). (gr. 2-5). lib. bdg. 29.93 *(978-1-62402-172-5(7)*, 24523, Calico Chapter Bks.) ABDO Publishing Co.

—Band Geeks Set 2 (Set), 4 vols. Cobb, Amy. 2016. (Band Geeks Set 2 Ser.). 112p. (J). (gr. 2-5). lib. bdg. 114.00 *(978-1-62402-171-8(9)*, 24521, Calico Chapter Bks.) ABDO Publishing Co.

—Descendants: Fright at the Museum. Dawson, Delilah S. 2020. (ENG.). 72p. (J). (gr. 2-5). pap. 9.99 *(978-1-68405-415-2(X))* Idea & Design Works, LLC.

—Dude, Where's My Saxophone?, 1 vol. Cobb, Amy. 2015. (Band Geeks Ser.). (ENG.). 112p. (J). (gr. 2-5). 29.93 *(978-1-62402-073-5(9)*, 16721, Calico Chapter Bks.) ABDO Publishing Co.

—First Chair, 1 vol. Cobb, Amy. 2015. (Band Geeks Ser.). (ENG.). 112p. (J). (gr. 2-5). 29.93 *(978-1-62402-074-2(7)*, 16723, Calico Chapter Bks.) ABDO Publishing Co.

—Mr. Byrd Flies the Nest. Cobb, Amy. 2016. (Band Geeks Set 2 Ser.). (ENG.). 112p. (J). (gr. 2-5). lib. bdg. 29.93 *(978-1-62402-173-2(5)*, 24525, Calico Chapter Bks.) ABDO Publishing Co.

—Notes from a Pro, 1 vol. Cobb, Amy. 2015. (Band Geeks Ser.). (ENG.). 112p. (J). (gr. 2-5). 29.93 *(978-1-62402-075-9(5)*, 16725, Calico Chapter Bks.) ABDO Publishing Co.

—Nothing but Treble. Cobb, Amy. 2016. (Band Geeks Set 2 Ser.). (ENG.). 112p. (J). (gr. 2-5). lib. bdg. 29.93 *(978-1-62402-174-9(3)*, 24527, Calico Chapter Bks.) ABDO Publishing Co.

—Settling the Score. Cobb, Amy. 2016. (Band Geeks Set 2 Ser.). (ENG.). 112p. (J). (gr. 2-5). lib. bdg. 29.93 *(978-1-62402-175-6(1)*, 24529, Calico Chapter Bks.) ABDO Publishing Co.

—Shredding with the Geeks, 1 vol. Cobb, Amy. 2015. (Band Geeks Ser.). (ENG.). 112p. (J). (gr. 2-5). 29.93 *(978-1-62402-076-6(3)*, 16727, Calico Chapter Bks.) ABDO Publishing Co.

—Snaring the Trumpet, 1 vol. Cobb, Amy. 2015. (Band Geeks Ser.). (ENG.). 112p. (J). (gr. 2-5). 29.93 *(978-1-62402-077-3(1)*, 16729, Calico Chapter Bks.) ABDO Publishing Co.

—Swing Vote for Solo, 1 vol. Cobb, Amy. 2015. (Band Geeks Ser.). (ENG.). 112p. (J). (gr. 2-5). 29.93 *(978-1-62402-078-0(X)*, 16731, Calico Chapter Bks.) ABDO Publishing Co.

Cattish, Anna & Bartolini, Egle. Descendants: Twisted Field Trip. Vaughn, Jen et al. 2019. 80p. (J). (gr. 2-5). pap. 9.99 *(978-1-68405-298-1(X))* Idea & Design Works, LLC.

Caturano, Silvia. Anna: A Tender Story in a Silent Book. Caturano, Silvia. 2018. (ENG.). 44p. (J). pap. 12.00 ***(978-1-9864-0013-8(1))*** CreateSpace Independent Publishing Platform.

Catusanu, Mircea. How to Eat an Airplane. Pearson, Peter. 2016. (Bad Idea Book Club Ser.). (ENG.). 40p. (J). (gr. -1-3). 17.99 *(978-0-06-232062-9(9))* HarperCollins Pubs.

—How to Walk a Dump Truck. Pearson, Peter. 2019. (ENG.). 40p. (J). (gr. -1-3). 17.99 *(978-0-06-232063-6(7))* HarperCollins Pubs.

—Noah Webster's Fighting Words. Maurer, Tracy Nelson. 2017. (ENG.). 40p. (J). (gr. 2-5). 19.99 *(978-1-4677-9410-7(4)*, 9781467794107); E-Book 30.65 *(978-1-5124-2839-1(6))* Lerner Publishing Group. (Millbrook Pr.).

—Noah's Ark. Hazen, Barbara Shook. 2003. (Little Golden Book Ser.). 32p. (J). (gr. -1-2). 4.99 *(978-0-307-10440-3(0)*, Golden Bks.) Random Hse. Children's Bks.

—Wheels on the Move: Driving with Andy. Hissom, Jennie. 2006. (J). *(978-1-58987-141-0(3))* Kindermusik International.

Catusanu, Mircea & Wilkin, Eloise. Christmas Favorites. Golden Books Staff et al. 2009. 80p. (J). (gr. -1-2). 7.99 *(978-0-375-85778-2(8)*, Golden Bks.) Random Hse. Children's Bks.

Cauble, Christopher, photos by. What I Saw in Yellowstone: A Kid's Guide to Wonderland. Johanek, Durrae. 2012. (ENG., 40p. (J). (gr. 3-7). pap. 12.95 *(978-1-60639-035-1(X))* Riverbend Publishing.

Caulson, Kathleen. Power Reading: Games. Caulson, Kathleen. 2005. (J). 76p. (gr. 2-4). 29.95 *(978-1-883186-98-2(6)*, PPMXG2-3); 88p. (gr. 4-5). 79.95 *(978-1-883186-99-9(4)*, PPMXG45) National Reading Styles Institute, Inc.

Cauthen, Tommy. The Teacher's Gift. DeBray, Sherry. 2004. 30p. *(978-1-59421-007-5(1))* Seacoast Publishing, Inc.

Cauuet, Paul, jt. illus. see Itoïz, Mayana.

Cavaciuti, Susan. Someone Hurt Me. Cavaciuti, Susan. 2004. 222p. pap. 8.95 *(978-1-890995-20-1(7)*, Vital Health Publishing) Square One Pubs.

Cavada, Dario, jt. illus. see Baldassarra, Tomaso.

Cavagnaro, Larry. Sweet Sallie's Squirrel Scarf Factory. Cavagnaro, Teresa Dunham. 2012. 36p. 24.95 *(978-1-4626-6126-8(2))* America Star Bks.

Cavaliera, Lia. A Trilha. Madelinn, Mariana. 2018. (Recome�os Ser.: Vol. 1). (POR.). 196p. (J). pap. 9.00 ***(978-1-0864-0273-5(1))*** Independently Published.

Cavallaro, Mike. Curses! Foiled Again. Yolen, Jane. 2013. (Foiled Ser.: 2). (ENG.). 176p. (J). (gr. 6-9). pap. 16.99 *(978-1-59643-619-0(0)*, 900066527, First Second Bks.) Roaring Brook Pr.

—Foiled. Yolen, Jane. 2010. (Foiled Ser.: 1). (ENG.). 160p. (J). (gr. 6-9). pap. 18.99 *(978-1-59643-279-6(9)*, 900044183, First Second Bks.) Roaring Brook Pr.

—The Joker Virus. Peterson, Scott. 2012. (Dark Knight Ser.). (ENG.). 88p. (J). (gr. 3-7). lib. bdg. 26.65 *(978-1-4342-4096-5(7)*, Stone Arch Bks.) Capstone.

—The Moon Bandits. Sonneborn, Scott. 2013. (Man of Steel Ser.). (ENG.). 88p. (J). (gr. 3-7). pap. 5.95 *(978-1-4342-4223-5(4)*, Stone Arch Bks.) Capstone.

—Parasite's Feeding Frenzy. Peterson, Scott. 2012. (Man of Steel Ser.). (ENG.). 88p. (J). (gr. 3-7). pap. 5.95 *(978-1-4342-4221-1(8)*, Stone Arch Bks.) Capstone.

Cavallaro, Mike & DC Comics Staff. Moon Bandits. Sonneborn, Scott. 2013. (Man of Steel Ser.). (ENG.). 88p. (J). (gr. 3-7). 26.65 *(978-1-4342-4093-4(2)*, Stone Arch Bks.) Capstone.

Cavallaro, Mike & Levins, Tim. The Man of Gold. Weissburg, Paul. 2012. (Man of Steel Ser.). (ENG.). 88p. (J). (gr. 3-7). pap. 5.95 *(978-1-4342-4222-8(6)*, Stone Arch Bks.) Capstone.

Cavallini, Linda. Eek! That's Creepy! Look & Find. Lobo, Julia. 2010. 24p. (J). 7.98 *(978-1-60553-898-3(1))* Publications International, Ltd.

Cavallini, Valentina. Going to Mecca. Robert, Na'ima B. 2014. (ENG.). 32p. (J). (gr. k-6). pap. 8.99 *(978-1-84780-490-7(X)*, Frances Lincoln Children's Bks.) Quarto Publishing Group UK GBR. Dist: Hachette Bk. Group.

Cavanaugh, Stacy. The Next Steve Erwin, 1 vol. Dalton, Matthew. 2009. 16p. pap. 24.95 *(978-1-60836-635-4(9))* America Star Bks.

Cavanaugh, Wendy & LeVesque, Sherry, photos by. Pumpkin in the Sky: Let's bake a pie together, you & I, with Auntie Wendy. Cavanaugh, Wendy. 2011. 32p. (J). spiral bd. 20.00 *(978-0-9743121-1-8(8))* Eastlight Pr.

Cavazzano, Giorgio. Angry Birds Comics: Game Play, Vol. 1. Tobin, Paul et al. 2017. (Angry Birds Ser.). 80p. (J). (gr. 4-7). 12.99 *(978-1-63140-973-8(5))* Idea & Design Works, LLC.

Cavazzano, Giorgio, et al. Treasure above the Clouds. Barks, Carl & Fontana, Giorgio. 2019. (Uncle Scrooge Ser.). (ENG.). 96p. (J). (gr. 4-7). pap. 12.99 *(978-1-68405-424-4(9))* Idea & Design Works, LLC.

—Uncle Scrooge: the Tourist at the End of the Universe. Gray, Jonathan H. 2018. (Uncle Scrooge Ser.). 112p. (J). (gr. 2-5). pap. 12.99 *(978-1-68405-317-9(X))* Idea & Design Works, LLC.

Cavazzano, Giorgio & Fecchi, Massimo. Uncle Scrooge: Whom the Gods Would Destroy. Erickson, Byron et al. 2018. (Uncle Scrooge Ser.). 112p. (J). (gr. 2-5). pap. 12.99 *(978-1-68405-395-7(1))* Idea & Design Works, LLC.

Cavazzano, Giorgio, jt. illus. see Mastantuono, Corrado.

Cave, Joanne. Countdown to Christmas. Acampora, Courtney. 2018. (Christmas Gift Tags Ser.). (ENG.). 12p. (J). (— 1). bds. 14.99 *(978-1-68412-383-4(6)*, Silver Dolphin Bks.) Printers Row Publishing Group.

Cave, Yvonne, photos by. The Gardener's Encyclopaedia of New Zealand Native Plants. Paddison, Valda. 2003. 320p. (J). (gr. -1-3). *(978-1-86962-043-1(7)*, Godwit) Random Hse. New Zealand.

Caviezel, Giovanni. Little Bee. 2014. (Mini-Creatures Bks.). (ENG.). 8p. (J). (gr. -1 — 1). bds. 4.99 *(978-0-7641-6713-3(8)*, B.E.S. Publishing) Peterson's.

—Little Crab. 2014. (Mini-Creatures Bks.). (ENG.). 8p. (J). (gr. -1 — 1). bds. 4.99 *(978-0-7641-6714-0(6)*, B.E.S. Publishing) Peterson's.

—Little Snail. 2014. (Mini-Creatures Bks.). (ENG.). 8p. (J). (gr. -1 — 1). bds. 4.99 *(978-0-7641-6715-7(4)*, B.E.S. Publishing) Peterson's.

Caviezel, Giovanni, jt. illus. see Rigo, L.

Cayless, Sophie. Belle's Wild Ride: The Artful Adventure of a Butterfly & a Cabbie. Corlett, Mary Lee. 2015. (ENG.). 32p. (J). (gr. 3-7). 17.95 *(978-1-907804-51-9(X))* Giles, D. Ltd. GBR. Dist: Consortium Bk. Sales & Distribution.

—Sophie's Stuff. Sasscer, Abby. 2012. 36p. pap. 9.95 *(978-0-9854729-1-7(X))* Sasscer, Abby.

Cazac, Yoran. Little Man, Little Man: A Story of Childhood. Baldwin, James. Brody, Jennifer DeVere & Boggs, Nicholas, eds. 2018. (ENG.). 120p. (J). (gr. 3-6). 22.95 *(978-1-4780-0004-4(X))* Duke Univ. Pr.

Cazenove, Christophe. The Sisters Vol. 4: Selfie Awareness, Vol. 4. Murray, William. 2017. (Sisters Ser.: 4). (ENG.). 96p. (J). pap. 9.99 *(978-1-62991-799-3(0)*, 900180992) Papercutz.

—The Sisters Vol. 4: Selfie Awareness, Vol. 2. Murray, William. 2017. (Sisters Ser.: 4). (ENG.). 96p. (J). 14.99 *(978-1-62991-798-6(2)*, 9781629917986) Papercutz.

Cazet, Denys. Bob & Tom. Cazet, Denys. 2017. (ENG.). 40p. (J). (gr. -1-3). 17.99 *(978-1-4814-6140-5(0)*, Atheneum/Richard Jackson Bks.) Simon & Schuster Children's Publishing.

—Elvis the Rooster & the Magic Words. Cazet, Denys. 2004. (I Can Read Bks.). (ENG.). 48p. (J). (gr. k-3). 15.99 *(978-0-06-000509-2(2))* HarperCollins Pubs.

—Grandpa Spanielson's Chicken Pox Stories No. 1: The Octopus. Cazet, Denys. 2005. (I Can Read Bks.). 48p. (J). (gr. -1-3). lib. bdg. 16.89 *(978-0-06-051089-3(7))* HarperCollins Pubs.

—Minnie & Moo: The Attack of the Easter Bunnies. Cazet, Denys. 2004. (I Can Read Bks.). 48p. (J). (gr. k-3). (ENG.). 15.99 *(978-0-06-000506-1(8))*; lib. bdg. 17.89 *(978-0-06-000507-8(6))* HarperCollins Pubs.

—Minnie & Moo: The Case of the Missing Jelly Donut. Cazet, Denys. 2007. (Minnie & Moo Ser.). 45p. (J). (gr. -1-3). pap. 29.95 incl. audio *(978-1-4301-0088-1(5))* Live Oak Media.

—Minnie & Moo: The Night Before Christmas. Cazet, Denys. 2004. (Readalongs for Beginning Readers Ser.). 25.95 incl. audio *(978-1-59112-884-7(6))*; (J). pap. 31.95 incl. audio compact disk *(978-1-59112-889-2(7))*; (J). pap. 29.95 incl. audio *(978-1-59112-885-4(4))* Live Oak Media.

—Minnie & Moo: The Night of the Living Bed. Cazet, Denys. 2003. (I Can Read Bks.). 48p. (J). (gr. k-3). lib. bdg. 16.89 *(978-0-06-000504-7(1))* HarperCollins Pubs.

—Minnie & Moo Adventure Series. Cazet, Denys. 2004. pap. 45.95 incl. audio *(978-1-59112-849-6(8))*; pap. 51.95 incl. audio compact disk *(978-1-59112-850-2(1))* Live Oak Media.

—Minnie & Moo & the Haunted Sweater. Cazet, Denys. 2007. (I Can Read Level 3 Ser.). (ENG.). 48p. (J). (gr. k-3). 16.99 *(978-0-06-073016-1(1))* HarperCollins Pubs.

—Minnie & Moo & the Seven Wonders of the World. Cazet, Denys. 2003. (ENG.). 144p. (J). (gr. 2-5). 19.99 *(978-0-689-85330-2(0)*, Atheneum/Richard Jackson Bks.) Simon & Schuster Children's Publishing.

—Minnie & Moo Holiday Series. Cazet, Denys. 2004. pap. 45.95 incl. audio *(978-1-59112-851-9(X))*; pap. 51.95 incl. audio compact disk *(978-1-59112-852-6(8))* Live Oak Media.

—Minnie & Moo Meet Frankenswine. Cazet, Denys. 2004. (Readalongs for Beginning Readers Ser.). 28.95 incl. audio compact disk *(978-1-59112-876-2(5))*; (J). 25.95 incl. audio *(978-1-59112-262-3(7))*; (J). pap. 29.95 incl. audio *(978-1-59112-263-0(5))* Live Oak Media.

—Minnie & Moo: the Case of the Missing Jelly Donut. Cazet, Denys. 2006. (I Can Read Level 3 Ser.). (ENG.). 48p. (J). (gr. k-3). pap. 4.99 *(978-0-06-073009-3(9))* HarperCollins Pubs.

—Minnie & Moo: the Night of the Living Bed. Cazet, Denys. 2004. (I Can Read Level 3 Ser.). (ENG.). 48p. (J). (gr. k-3). pap. 4.99 *(978-0-06-000505-4(X))* HarperCollins Pubs.

—Minnie & Moo: Wanted Dead or Alive. Cazet, Denys. 2007. (I Can Read Level 3 Ser.). (ENG.). 48p. (J). (gr. k-3). pap. 4.99 *(978-0-06-073012-3(9))* HarperCollins Pubs.

—The Night of the Living Bed. Cazet, Denys. unabr. ed. 2005. (Minnie & Moo Ser.). (J). (gr. k-4). 25.95 incl. audio *(978-1-59519-389-6(8))*;Set. pap. 29.95 incl. audio *(978-1-59519-390-2(1))*;Set. pap. 31.95 incl. audio compact disk *(978-1-59519-394-0(4))* Live Oak Media.

—The Octopus. Cazet, Denys. 2008. (Grandpa Spanielson's Chicken Pox Stories Ser.). (J). (gr. -1-3). pap. 16.95 incl. audio *(978-1-4301-0455-1(4))*;Set. pap. 29.95 incl. audio *(978-1-4301-0457-5(0))*;Set. pap. 31.95 incl. audio compact disk *(978-1-4301-0460-5(0))* Live Oak Media.

—The Perfect Pumpkin Pie. Cazet, Denys. 2005. (ENG.). 32p. (J). (gr. -1-1). 17.99 *(978-0-689-86467-4(1)*, Atheneum/Richard Jackson Bks.) Simon & Schuster Children's Publishing.

—Snail & Slug. Cazet, Denys. 2016. (ENG.). 32p. (J). (gr. -1-3). 17.99 *(978-1-4814-4506-1(5)*, Atheneum/Richard Jackson Bks.) Simon & Schuster Children's Publishing.

—A Snout for Chocolate. Cazet, Denys. 2008. (Grandpa Spanielson's Chicken Pox Stories Ser.). (J). (gr. -1-3). pap. 16.95 incl. audio *(978-1-4301-0463-6(5))*;Set. pap. 29.95 incl. audio *(978-1-4301-0465-0(1))*;Set. pap. 31.95 incl. audio compact disk *(978-1-4301-0468-1(6))* Live Oak Media.

—Wanted Dead or Alive. Cazet, Denys. 2006. (I Can Read Bks.). 48p. (J). (gr. -1-3). (ENG.). 15.99 *(978-0-06-073010-9(2))*; lib. bdg. 16.89 *(978-0-06-073011-6(0))* HarperCollins Pubs.

—Wanted Dead or Alive. Cazet, Denys. 2008. (Minnie & Moo Ser.). (J). (gr. -1-3). pap. 16.95 incl. audio *(978-1-4301-0471-1(6))* Live Oak Media.

—Will You Read to Me? Cazet, Denys. 2007. (ENG.). 32p. (J). (gr. -1-1). 16.99 *(978-1-4169-0935-4(4)*, Atheneum/Richard Jackson Bks.) Simon & Schuster Children's Publishing.

C.B. Canga, C. B. Celebrating North Carolina: 50 States to Celebrate. Bauer, Marion Dane. 2014. (Green Light Readers Level 3 Ser.). (ENG.). 40p. (J). (gr. 1-4). pap. 4.99 *(978-0-544-28827-0(0)*, 1572121, HMH Books For Young Readers) Houghton Mifflin Harcourt Publishing Co.

—Celebrating Washington State: 50 States to Celebrate. Bauer, Marion Dane. 2014. (Green Light Readers Level 3 Ser.). (ENG.). 40p. (J). (gr. 1-4). pap. 4.99 *(978-0-544-28948-2(X)*, 1572173, HMH Books For Young Readers) Houghton Mifflin Harcourt Publishing Co.

Cboins, John. The Fox & the Grapes. Aesop, Aesop. 2010. (Short Tales Fables Ser.). (ENG.). 32p. (J). (gr. 1-4). lib. bdg. 27.07 *(978-1-60270-553-1(4)*, 13407, Short Tales) Magic Wagon.

—Jack & the Beanstalk. 2008. (Short Tales Fairy Tales Ser.). (ENG.). 32p. (J). (gr. 2-5). 27.07 *(978-1-60270-128-1(8)*, 594, Short Tales) Magic Wagon.

—Swiss Family Robinson: Shipwrecked. Wyss, Johann David. 2008. (Short Tales Classics Ser.). (ENG.). 32p. (J). (gr. 2-6). 24.21 *(978-1-60270-122-9(9)*, 13395, Short Tales) Magic Wagon.

CC, Myss. Arbogast & Qum: Les Mirages du Désert. David, L. L. L. 2018. (Arbogast & Qum Ser.: Vol. 2). (FRE.). 118p. (J). pap. *(978-2-490113-04-0(6))* Mademoiselle a trois ailes éditions.

—Arbogast et Qum: Les Abysses du Lac de Téméris. David, L. L. L. 2018. (Arbogast et Qum Ser.: Vol. 1). (FRE.). 100p. (J). pap. *(978-2-490113-02-6(X))* Mademoiselle a trois ailes éditions.

Ceasar, Fady. Nolia Fasolia: Read-Along Book: Arabic & English. Alexan, Julie. El-Ahraf, Amer, ed. 2011. (ARA & ENG.). 48p. pap. 5.99 *(978-0-9844310-1-4(2))* BigKids Bilingual Bks.

Cebu LL B, Vladimir. Healthy Heath & His Magic Fruits & Vegetables: A Book about Kids Nutrition, Kindness, & Celebrating Individuality. Poe, Kristen. 2018. (ENG.). 52p. (J). pap. 11.95 ***(978-0-692-19206-1(9))*** POE Holistic Health.

Cebu LIb, Vladimir. Color with Polly Pear. Shayne, Reesa. 2019. (Polly Pear Ser.: Vol. 3). (ENG.). 28p. (J). pap. 6.99 ***(978-1-6890-1611-7(6))*** Independently Published.

Cebu LIb, Vladimir. Workin' It. Young, Leah Marie. 2018. (ENG.). 30p. (J). pap. 10.99 *(978-1-7906-1363-2(9))* Independently Published.

Cebu, Vladimir. I Dream Cheer. Leigh, Summer. George, Nancy, ed. 2018. (ENG.). 26p. (J). pap. 12.99 *(978-1-7200-3184-0(3))* Independently Published.

Ceccarelli, Simona. Beasties Love Booties. Brooke, Susan Rich. 2020. (ENG.). 40p. (J). ***(978-1-5037-5249-8(6)*,** f9358540-3946-4614-82b7-fe274b527b65, p i kids) Phoenix International Publications, Inc.

Ceccarelli, Simona. If You Had Your Birthday Party on the Moon. Lapin, Joyce. 2019. 40p. (J). (gr. 2). 16.95 *(978-1-4549-2970-3(7))* Sterling Publishing Co., Inc.

Ceccarelli, Simona M. MSOP & DPAK: One Hot Day. Dunnihoo, Jeffrey C. 2018. (Soic & Friends Ser.: Vol. 3). (ENG.). 34p. (J). 19.45 ***(978-1-7322836-6-4(4))*** Pragma Design, Inc.

—SOIC y SOT: Los Microchips. Dunnihoo, Jeffrey C. 2019. (Soic y Amigos Ser.: Vol. 1). (SPA.). 28p. (J). 19.45 ***(978-1-7322836-7-1(2))*** Pragma Design, Inc.

Cecchi, Lorenzo, et al. The Vikings. McRae, Anne & Agosta, Loredana. 2008. (Back to Basics Ser.). 32p. (J). (gr. 2-5). lib. bdg. *(978-88-6098-051-9(8))* McRae Bks. Srl.

Ceccoli, Nicoletta. The Barefoot Book of Fairy Tales. Doyle, Malacy. 2005. 160p. (J). (gr. k-5). 19.99 *(978-1-84148-798-4(8))* Barefoot Bks., Inc.

—The Boo! Book. Lachenmeyer, Nathaniel. 2012. (ENG.). 46p. (J). (gr. -1-3). 17.99 *(978-1-4169-3513-1(4)*, Atheneum Bks. for Young Readers) Simon & Schuster Children's Publishing.

—Cinderella, 0 vols. Thomson, Sarah L. 2012. (ENG.). 32p. (J). (gr. k-3). 17.99 *(978-0-7614-6170-8(1)*, 9780761461708, Two Lions) Amazon Publishing.

—The Faerie's Gift. Batt, Tanya Robyn. 32p. (J). (gr. -1-3). 2008. (ENG.). 17.99 *(978-1-84686-230-4(2))*; 2003. 16.99 *(978-1-84148-998-8(0))* Barefoot Bks., Inc.

Ceccoli Nicoletta. Faeries Gift. Batt Tanya Robyn. 2006. 0032p. pap. 6.99 *(978-1-905236-73-2(5))* Barefoot Bks., Inc.

Ceccoli, Nicoletta. Faery's Gift. Batt, Tanya Robyn & Barefoot Books. 2015. 32p. (J). (gr. -1-2). 10.99 *(978-1-78285-145-5(3))* Barefoot Bks., Inc.
—Horns & Wrinkles. Helgerson, Joseph. 2008. (ENG.). 240p. (J). (gr. 5-7). pap. 7.99 *(978-0-618-98178-6(0),* 1025446) Houghton Mifflin Harcourt Publishing Co.
—Una Isla Bajo el Sol. Blackstone, Stella. 2003. (SPA.). 24p. (J). pap. 6.99 *(978-1-84148-144-9(0))* Barefoot Bks., Inc.
—An Island in the Sun. Blackstone, Stella & Barefoot Books Staff. 2005. (ENG.). 24p. (J). pap. 6.99 *(978-1-84148-079-4(7))* Barefoot Bks., Inc.
—Little Red Riding Hood. 2004. 32p. (J). 16.99 *(978-1-84148-621-5(3))* Barefoot Bks., Inc.
—The Princess & the White Bear King. Batt, Tanya Robyn. 2004. 40p. (J). 16.99 *(978-1-84148-339-9(7))* Barefoot Bks., Inc.
—The Princess & White Bear. Batt, Tanya Robyn. 2008. 40p. (J). (gr. -1-3). 17.99 *(978-1-84686-228-1(0))* Barefoot Bks., Inc.
—The Tear Thief. Duffy, Carol Ann & Stevenson, Juliet. 2011. 32p. (J). (gr. k-4). 9.99 *(978-1-84686-622-7(7))* Barefoot Bks., Inc.
—The Tear Thief. Duffy, Carol Ann. 2007. (ENG.). 32p. (J). (gr. -1-3). 16.99 *(978-1-84686-045-4(8))* Barefoot Bks., Inc.
—Tear Thief. Carol, Ann Duffy. 2018. (ENG.). 32p. (J). (gr. k-3). pap. 8.99 *(978-1-84686-394-3(5))* Barefoot Bks., Inc.
Ceccolini, Danielle. What Will It Be, Penelope? Corn, Tori. 2013. 32p. (J). (gr. -1-k). 16.95 *(978-1-62087-542-1(X),* 620542, Sky Pony Pr.) Skyhorse Publishing Co., Inc.
Ceceri, Kathy. The Silk Road: Explore the World's Most Famous Trade Route with 20 Projects. Ceceri, Kathy. 2011. (Build It Yourself Ser.). 128p. (J). (gr. 3-7). pap. 15.95 *(978-1-934670-62-0(6),* 55a7f34b-2501-42f0-a6b8-32d6fb613056) Nomad Pr.
Cecil, Jennifer, jt. illus. see Kelson, Ellen.
Cecil, Randy. And Here's to You! Elliott, David. 2009. 32p. (J). (gr. -1-2). pap. 6.99 *(978-0-7636-4126-9(X))* Candlewick Pr.
—Brontorina. Howe, James. 2013. 32p. (J). (gr. -1-3). 7.99 *(978-0-7636-5323-1(3))* Candlewick Pr.
—Dusty Locks & the Three Bears. Lowell, Susan. rev. ed. 2004. (ENG.). 32p. (J). (gr. -1-3). pap. 8.99 *(978-0-8050-7534-2(8),* 900021842) Square Fish.
—Evermore Dragon. Joosse, Barbara M. 2015. (Girl & Dragon Bks.). (ENG.). 32p. (J). (gr. -1-2). 15.99 *(978-0-7636-6882-2(6))* Candlewick Pr.
—How Do You Wokka-Wokka? Bluemle, Elizabeth. 2012. 32p. (J). (gr. -1-2). pap. 6.99 *(978-0-7636-6085-7(X))* Candlewick Pr.
—Looking for a Moose. Root, Phyllis. 2008. 40p. (J). (gr. -1-2). pap. 6.99 *(978-0-7636-3885-6(4))* Candlewick Pr.
—Lovabye Dragon. Joosse, Barbara M. 2012. (Girl & Dragon Bks.). (ENG.). 32p. (J). (gr. -1-2). 15.99 *(978-0-7636-5408-5(6))* Candlewick Pr.
—My Father the Dog. Bluemle, Elizabeth. (ENG.). 32p. (J). (gr. -1-3). 2008. pap. 6.99 *(978-0-7636-3077-5(2));* 2006. 15.99 *(978-0-7636-2222-0(2))* Candlewick Pr.
—One Is a Snail, Ten Is a Crab: A Counting by Feet Book. Sayre, April Pulley & Sayre, Jeff. 2006. (ENG.). 40p. (J). (gr. k-3). 6.99 *(978-0-7636-2631-0(7))* Candlewick Pr.
—One Is a Snail, Ten Is a Crab Big Book: A Counting by Feet Book. Sayre, Jeff & Sayre, April Pulley. 2010. 40p. (J). (gr. k-3). pap. 24.99 *(978-0-7636-4790-2(X))* Candlewick Pr.
—Sail Away Dragon. Joosse, Barbara M. 2017. (Girl & Dragon Bks.). 32p. (J). (gr. -1-2). 15.99 *(978-0-7636-7313-0(7))* Candlewick Pr.
Cecil, Randy. Douglas. Cecil, Randy. 2019. (ENG.). 120p. (J). (gr. k-3). 19.99 *(978-0-7636-3397-4(6))* Candlewick Pr.
—Duck. Cecil, Randy. 2008. (ENG.). 40p. (J). (gr. -1-2). 15.99 *(978-0-7636-3072-0(1))* Candlewick Pr.
—Lucy. Cecil, Randy. 2016. 144p. (J). (gr. k-3). 19.99 *(978-0-7636-6808-2(7))* Candlewick Pr.
Cedar, Emily. Miracles from Maddie. Fitzmaurice, John. 2010. 52p. pap. 21.25 *(978-1-4490-5332-1(7))* AuthorHouse.
Cee, Jess. Jessica Naturally. Gee, Shelley. 2019. (Jessica Ser.: Vol. 2). (ENG.). 108p. (J). pap. 8.99 ***(978-1-7121-5759-6(0))*** Independently Published.
Celej, Zuzanna. Dentro de Mi Imaginación (Inside My Imagination) Arteaga, Marta. 2020. (SPA.). 24p. (J). 9.95 ***(978-84-16733-96-5(1))*** Cuento de Luz SL ESP. Dist: Publishers Group West (PGW).
Celej, Zuzanna. Emmanuel Kelly: Dream Big! Sanchez, Mamen. Brokenbrow, Jon, tr. 2019. (What Really Matters Ser.). (ENG.). 24p. (J). 16.95 *(978-84-16733-40-8(6))* Cuento de Luz SL ESP. Dist: Publishers Group West (PGW).
—Emmanuel Kelly: ¡Sueña a lo grande! Sanchez, Mamen. 2019. (Lo Que de Verdad Importa Ser.). (SPA.). 24p. (J). 16.95 *(978-84-16733-39-2(2))* Cuento de Luz SL ESP. Dist: Publishers Group West (PGW).
—Inside My Imagination. Arteaga, Marta. Brokenbrow, Jon, tr. 2013. (ENG.). 24p. (J). (gr. k-2). 15.95 *(978-84-15503-59-0(8))* Cuento de Luz SL ESP. Dist: Publishers Group West (PGW).
—Mi Abuelo Pirata. Massons, Laia. Llasat, Isabel, tr. 2020. (SPA.). 32p. (J). (gr. k-2). pap. 17.95 *(978-84-17440-29-9(1))* Akiara Bks. ESP. Dist: Independent Pubs. Group.
—Where Are You, Agnes?, 1 vol. McWatt, Tessa. 2020. (ENG.). 44p. (J). (gr. k-3). 18.95 *(978-1-77306-140-5(2))* Groundwood Bks. CAN. Dist: Publishers Group West (PGW).
Celeskey, Matt. Children of Time: Evolution & the Human Story. Weaver, Anne H. 2012. (ENG.). 192p. (J). 19.95 *(978-0-8263-4442-7(9))* Univ. of New Mexico Pr.
Celestine, Karin. Bertram Likes to Sew. Celestine, Karin. 2018. (Celestine & the Hare Ser.). (ENG.). 48p. (J). (gr. k-2). 9.99 *(978-1-912213-61-0(3))* Graffeg Limited GBR. Dist: Independent Pubs. Group.
Celestino, Cleofas Ramirez. Axolotl: El Ajolote. Farfan, Flores & Antonio, Jose. 2003. (SPA.). 40p. (J). *(978-968-411-569-9(5))* Ediciones Era.
Celija, Maja. The Story of the Nose. Camilleri, Andrea. Sartarelli, Stephen, tr. 2016. (Save the Story Ser.: 6). (ENG.). 104p. (J). (gr. 3-7). 19.95 *(978-1-78269-017-7(4),* Pushkin Children's Bks.) Steerforth Pr.
Cella, Kristen, et al. He Loves Me, He Loves Me Not, No. 7. Mayhall, Robin. 2013. (My Boyfriend Is a Monster Ser.: 7). (ENG.). 128p. (YA). (gr. 7-12). lib. bdg. 29.32 *(978-0-7613-6005-6(0),* 9780761360056, Graphic Universe™) Lerner Publishing Group.
Celoni, Fabio. Disney Dracula, Starring Mickey Mouse (Graphic Novel) Enna, Bruno. 2019. (ENG.). 80p. (J). (gr. 3-7). pap. 10.99 *(978-1-5067-1217-8(7))* Dark Horse Comics.
Celoni, Fabio & Merli, Luca. Disney Frankenstein, Starring Donald Duck (Graphic Novel) Enna, Bruno. 2019. (ENG.). 80p. (J). (gr. 3-7). pap. 10.99 *(978-1-5067-1218-5(5))* Dark Horse Comics.
Cenizal, I. Our Dolls' Enchanted Wedding. Williams-Walker, Carol. 2019. (ENG.). 28p. (J). pap. ***(978-0-2288-1317-0(4))*** Tellwell Talent.
Cenizal, I. Where Are You, Moon? Lee, Charlotte A. 2018. (ENG.). 24p. (J). pap. 9.95 *(978-0-9905353-9-3(8))* B.A.D Mouse Publishing.
Cenkl, Jakub. I'm Not Afraid of the Dark. Harastová, Helena. 2017. (ENG.). 14p. (J). (gr. -1-3). 14.95 *(978-1-4549-2170-7(6))* Sterling Publishing Co., Inc.
Cenko, Doug. Zzzookeeper. Hutton, John. 2018. (ENG.). 32p. (J). (gr. -1-2). 17.99 *(978-1-936669-69-1(2))* Blue Manatee Press.
Cenko, Doug. My Papa Is a Princess. Cenko, Doug. 2018. (ENG.). 32p. (J). (gr. -1-2). 17.99 *(978-1-936669-70-7(6))* Blue Manatee Press.
Centineo, Ornella. A Day Out with Mom: A Day Out with Mom. Simmons, Roshonda & Simmons, Laura. 2018. (ENG.). 28p. (J). pap. 10.00 *(978-0-692-16869-1(9))* Simmons, Laura.
Ceolin, Andre. Droughts. Stewart, Melissa. 2017. (Let's-Read-And-Find-Out Science 2 Ser.). (ENG.). 40p. (J). (gr. -1-3). 17.99 *(978-0-06-238666-3(2));* pap. 6.99 *(978-0-06-238665-6(4))* HarperCollins Pubs.
Ceolin, André. Hanukah Hamster. Markel, Michelle. 2018. (ENG.). 32p. (J). (gr. k-2). 16.99 *(978-1-58536-399-5(5),* 204583) Sleeping Bear Pr.
—My Journey to the Stars. Kelly, Scott. (ENG.). 48p. (J). (gr. k-3). 2020. pap. 7.99 *(978-0-593-12465-9(0),* Dragonfly Bks.); 2017. 17.99 *(978-1-5247-6377-0(2),* Crown Books For Young Readers); 2017. lib. bdg. 20.99 *(978-1-5247-7031-0(0),* Crown Books For Young Readers) Random Hse. Children's Bks.
—My Journey to the Stars (Step into Reading) Kelly, Scott. 2019. (ENG.). 48p. (J). (gr. k-3). 12.99 *(978-0-525-64861-1(5),* Crown Books For Young Readers); pap. 4.99 *(978-1-5247-6380-0(2),* Random Hse. Bks. for Young Readers); lib. bdg. 15.99 *(978-1-5247-6378-7(0),* Random Hse. Bks. for Young Readers) Random Hse. Children's Bks.
—Yom Kippur Shortstop. Adler, David A. 2017. (J). *(978-1-68115-521-0(4))* Behrman Hse., Inc.
Cepeda, Joe. A Crazy Mixed-Up Spanglish Day. Montes, Marisa. 2004. (Get Ready for Gabi Ser.). 120p. (gr. 2-5). 14.00 *(978-0-7569-3403-3(6))* Perfection Learning Corp.
—A Crazy Mixed-Up Spanglish Day. Montes, Marisa. 2003. (Get Ready for Gabi Ser.). 128p. (J). 12.95 *(978-0-439-51710-2(9),* Scholastic Paperbacks) Scholastic, Inc.
—Cub's Big World. Thomson, Sarah L. 2013. (ENG.). 32p. (J). (gr. -1-3). 16.99 *(978-0-544-05739-5(2),* 1533708) Houghton Mifflin Harcourt Publishing Co.
—Freddy in Peril: Book Two in the Golden Hamster Saga. Reiche, Dietlof & Brownjohn, John. 2004. 202p. (J). pap. *(978-0-439-64984-1(6))* Scholastic, Inc.
—From North to South, 1 vol. Laínez, René Colato. 2014.Tr. of Del Norte Al Sur. (ENG & SPA.). 32p. (J). (gr. k-3). pap. 10.95 *(978-0-89239-304-6(1),* 2b1d4be8-c57b-4c3a-8e4e-f0f9d83af39e, Children's Book Press) Lee & Low Bks., Inc.
—From North to South/Del Norte Al Sur. Laínez, René Colato. 2010.Tr. of Del norte al Sur. (ENG & SPA.). 32p. (J). (gr. k-3). 17.95 *(978-0-89239-231-5(2))* Lee & Low Bks., Inc.
—Get Ready for Gabi No. 5: All in the Familia. Montes, Marisa. 2004. (ENG.). 112p. (J). (gr. 2-5). pap. *(978-0-439-66156-0(0),* Scholastic Paperbacks) Scholastic, Inc.
—Hey, Hey, Hay! Mihaly, Christy. 2018. 32p. (J). (gr. -1-3). 17.99 *(978-0-8234-3666-8(7))* Holiday Hse., Inc.
—The Journey of Oliver K. Woodman. Pattison, Darcy. 2009. (ENG.). 52p. (J). (gr. -1-3). pap. 7.99 *(978-0-15-206118-0(5),* 1099013) Houghton Mifflin Harcourt Publishing Co.
—Juan Bobo Busca Trabajo: Juan Bobo Goes to Work (Spanish Edition), 1 vol. Montes, Marisa. 2006. (SPA.). 32p. (J). (gr. -1-3). pap. 6.99 *(978-0-06-113681-8(6),* HarperCollins Español) HarperCollins Christian Publishing.
—Koi & the Kola Nuts: A Tale from Liberia. Aardema, Verna. rev. ed. 2003. (ENG.). 32p. (J). (gr. k-3). 16.99 *(978-0-689-85677-8(6),* Simon & Schuster/Paula Wiseman Bks.) Simon & Schuster/Paula Wiseman Bks.
—Mice & Beans. Ryan, Pam Muñoz. 2005. (gr. -1-3). lib. bdg. 17.00 *(978-0-7569-5089-7(9))* Perfection Learning Corp.
—Mice & Beans. Ryan, Pam Muñoz. 2005. (Scholastic Bookshelf Ser.). (ENG.). 32p. (J). (gr. -1-3). pap. 6.99 *(978-0-439-70136-5(8),* Scholastic Paperbacks) Scholastic, Inc.
—Peeny Butter Fudge. Morrison, Toni & Morrison, Slade. 2009. (ENG.). 32p. (J). (gr. -1-3). 19.99 *(978-1-4169-8332-3(5),* Simon & Schuster/Paula Wiseman Bks.) Simon & Schuster/Paula Wiseman Bks.
—Rip's Secret Spot. Butler, Kristi T. 2003. (Green Light Readers Level 1 Ser.). (ENG.). 24p. (J). (gr. -1-3). pap. 3.95 *(978-0-15-204849-5(9),* 1194642) Houghton Mifflin Harcourt Publishing Co.
—Side by Side/Lado a Lado: The Story of Dolores Huerta & Cesar Chavez/la Historia de Dolores Huerta y Cesar Chavez (Bilingual Spanish-English Children's Book) Brown, Monica. 2010.Tr. of Side by Side - The Story of Dolores Huerta & Cesar Chavez. (ENG.). 32p. (J). (gr. -1-3). 16.99 *(978-0-06-122781-3(1),* HarperCollins Español) HarperCollins Christian Publishing.
—Swing Sisters: The Story of the International Sweethearts of Rhythm. Deans, Karen. 2015. (ENG.). 32p. (J). (gr. -1-3). 16.95 *(978-0-8234-1970-8(3))* Holiday Hse., Inc.
—The Tapping Tale. Giglio, Judy. 2003. (Green Light Readers Level 1 Ser.). (ENG.). 24p. (J). (gr. -1-3). pap. 4.99 *(978-0-15-204852-5(9),* 1194651) Houghton Mifflin Harcourt Publishing Co.
—The Tortoise or the Hare. Morrison, Toni & Morrison, Slade. (ENG.). 32p. (J). (gr. -1-3). 2014. 8.99 *(978-1-4169-8335-4(X));* 2010. 17.99 *(978-1-4169-8334-7(1))* Simon & Schuster/Paula Wiseman Bks. (Simon & Schuster/Paula Wiseman Bks.).
—Try Your Best. McKissack, Robert L. 2004. (Green Light Readers Level 2 Ser.). (ENG.). 24p. (J). (gr. -1-3). pap. 3.95 *(978-0-15-205090-0(6),* 1195368) Houghton Mifflin Harcourt Publishing Co.
—Try Your Best. McKissack, Robert L. 2005. (Green Light Readers Level 2 Ser.). (gr. k-2). 13.95 *(978-0-7569-5630-1(7))* Perfection Learning Corp.
Cepeda, Joseph C., photos by. Emerald's Journal: A summer with Hatchlings. Allison, Pamela S. 2007. 24p. (J). lib. bdg. 16.95 *(978-0-9793474-1-2(6))* Sand Sage Pr.
Cerato, Mattia. ¡a Trabajar Duro! Garnett, Jaye. Cottage Door Press, ed. 2020. (Peek-A-Flap Board Bks.). (SPA.). 12p. (J). (gr. -1-1). bds. 8.99 ***(978-1-64638-060-2(6),*** 1002770-SLA) Cottage Door Pr.
Cerato, Mattia. Amusement Park Adventure. Kalz, Jill. 2010. (A-MAZE-Ing Adventures Ser.). (ENG.). 32p. (J). (gr. -1-2). lib. bdg. 27.32 *(978-1-4048-6023-0(1),* Picture Window Bks.) Capstone.
—Animal Friends: A Step-By-step Drawing & Story Book. Chagollan, Samantha. 2019. (Watch Me Read & Draw Ser.). (ENG.). 32p. (J). (gr. -1-2). lib. bdg. 26.65 *(978-1-60058-798-6(4),* Walter Foster Jr) Quarto Publishing Group USA.
—Dig! Chunky Peek a Flap Board Book. Garnett, Jaye. Cottage Door Press, ed. 2018. (Peek a Flap Ser.). (ENG.). 12p. (J). (gr. -1-1). bds. 8.99 *(978-1-68052-299-0(X),* 1002770) Cottage Door Pr.
—Farm Adventure. Kalz, Jill. 2010. (A-MAZE-Ing Adventures Ser.). (ENG.). 32p. (J). (gr. -1-2). lib. bdg. 27.32 *(978-1-4048-6038-4(X),* Picture Window Bks.) Capstone.
Cerato, Mattia. Hidden Picture Books for Kids Gift Set: Seek & Find Books in Chicago, Boston, New York City, & San Francisco. Guendelsberger, Erin. 2020. (ENG.). (J). (-5). 59.96 ***(978-1-7282-4063-3(8))*** Sourcebooks, Inc.
Cerato, Mattia. Hide & Seek Boston. Guendelsberger, Erin. 2019. (ENG.). 32p. (J). (-5). 14.99 *(978-1-4926-8422-0(8),* Sourcebooks Jabberwocky) Sourcebooks, Inc.
—Hide & Seek Chicago. Guendelsberger, Erin. 2019. (ENG.). 32p. (J). (-5). 14.99 *(978-1-4926-8420-6(1),* Sourcebooks Jabberwocky) Sourcebooks, Inc.
—Hide & Seek San Francisco. Guendelsberger, Erin. 2019. (ENG.). 32p. (J). (-5). 14.99 *(978-1-4926-8421-3(X),* Sourcebooks Jabberwocky) Sourcebooks, Inc.
—Just Imagine & Play! on the Site: Sticker & Press-Out Activity Book. Walter Foster Jr. Creative Team. 2017. (Just Imagine & Play! Ser.). (ENG.). 48p. (J). (gr. -1-1). pap. 9.95 *(978-1-63322-245-8(4),* 223677, Walter Foster Jr) Quarto Publishing Group USA.
—Rescue! Crowe, Carmen. Cottage Door Press, ed. 2019. (Early Bird Sound Books 5 Button Ser.). (ENG.). 12p. (J). (gr. -1-2). bds. 14.99 *(978-1-68052-637-0(5),* 1004300) Cottage Door Pr.
—School Adventure. Kalz, Jill. 2010. (A-MAZE-Ing Adventures Ser.). (ENG.). 32p. (J). (gr. -1-2). lib. bdg. 27.32 *(978-1-4048-6039-1(8),* Picture Window Bks.) Capstone.
—Watch Me Read & Draw: Animal Friends: A Step-By-step Drawing & Story Book. Chagollan, Samantha. 2018. (Watch Me Read & Draw Ser.). (ENG.). 36p. (J). (gr. -1-3). pap. 8.95 *(978-1-63322-659-3(X),* Walter Foster Jr) Quarto Publishing Group USA.
—Watch Me Read & Draw: the Nativity: A Step-By-step Drawing & Story Book. Walter Foster Jr. Creative Team. 2019. (Watch Me Read & Draw Ser.). (ENG.). 36p. (J). (gr. -1-3). pap. 8.95 *(978-1-63322-766-8(9),* 325976, Walter Foster Jr) Quarto Publishing Group USA.
—Watch Me Read & Draw: the Zoo: A Step-By-step Drawing & Story Book. Chagollan, Samantha. 2018. (Watch Me Read & Draw Ser.). (ENG.). 36p. (J). (gr. -1-3). pap. 8.95 *(978-1-63322-537-4(2),* Walter Foster Jr) Quarto Publishing Group USA.
—The Zoo: A Step-By-step Drawing & Story Book. Chagollan, Samantha. 2019. (Watch Me Read & Draw Ser.). (ENG.). 32p. (J). (gr. -1-2). lib. bdg. 26.65 *(978-1-60058-797-9(6),* Walter Foster Jr) Quarto Publishing Group USA.
Cerato, Mattia. Drew the Screw. Cerato, Mattia. 2016. (I Like to Read Ser.). (ENG.). 24p. (J). (gr. -1-3). 14.95 *(978-0-8234-3540-1(7))* Holiday Hse., Inc.
—Mom's New Friend. Cerato, Mattia. 2014. (Family Snaps Ser.). (ENG.). 32p. (J). (gr. k-2). pap. 6.99 *(978-1-939656-61-2(3))* Red Chair Pr.
—Sheep in the Closet. Cerato, Mattia. 2014. (Family Snaps Ser.). (ENG.). 32p. (J). (gr. k-2). pap. 6.99 *(978-1-939656-62-9(1))* Red Chair Pr.
—You Can Draw Construction Vehicles, 1 vol. Cerato, Mattia. 2011. (You Can Draw Ser.). (ENG.). 24p. (J). (gr. k-3). lib. bdg. 27.32 *(978-1-4048-6807-6(0),* Picture Window Bks.) Capstone.
—You Can Draw Dinosaurs, 1 vol. Cerato, Mattia. Bruning, Matt. 2010. (You Can Draw Ser.). (ENG.). 24p. (J). (gr. k-3). lib. bdg. 27.32 *(978-1-4048-6280-7(3),* Picture Window Bks.) Capstone.
Cerato, Mattia & Fisher, Diana. Watch Me Read & Draw: Dinosaurs. Chagollan, Samantha. 2019. (J). *(978-1-942875-82-6(7))* Quarto Publishing Group USA.
Cerato, Mattia & Sexton, Brenda. Easy-to-Draw Mythical Creatures. Cerato, Mattia & Sexton, Brenda. 2011. (You Can Draw Ser.). (ENG.). 48p. (J). (gr. k-3). pap. 5.19 *(978-1-4048-7059-8(8),* Picture Window Bks.) Capstone.
—Easy-to-Draw Vehicles. Cerato, Mattia & Sexton, Brenda. 2011. (You Can Draw Ser.). (ENG.). 48p. (J). (gr. k-3). pap. 5.19 *(978-1-4048-7058-1(X),* Picture Window Bks.) Capstone.
—Easy-To-Draw Vehicles: A Step-By-Step Drawing Book. Cerato, Mattia & Sexton, Brenda. 2014. (You Can Draw Ser.). (ENG.). 64p. (J). (gr. k-3). pap. 6.95 *(978-1-4795-5513-0(4),* Picture Window Bks.) Capstone.
Cerda, Edward. Me & My Flea Steed, Clyde, at Home on Ralph. Merrick, Sylvia Bach. 2011. 24p. pap. 24.95 *(978-1-60813-938-5(7))* America Star Bks.
Ceretti. Carnet Blanc Folies-Bergere. Ceretti. 2016. (Bnf Affiches Ser.). (FRE.). (J). pap. *(978-2-01-116959-4(3))* Hachette Groupe Livre.
—Carnet Ligne Folies-Bergere. Ceretti. 2016. (Bnf Affiches Ser.). (FRE.). (J). pap. *(978-2-01-116936-5(4))* Hachette Groupe Livre.
Cerisier, Emmanuel. Arab Science & Invention in the Golden Age. Blanchard, Anne. 2009. (ENG.). 80p. (J). (gr. 3). 19.95 *(978-1-59270-080-6(2))* Enchanted Lion Bks., LLC.
—Dick Whittington. Gifford, Clare. 2013. 64p. (YA). (gr. 2-4). 21.00 *(978-1-4081-8761-6(2),* 900122581, A&C Black Childrens & Educational) Bloomsbury Publishing Plc GBR. Dist: Macmillan.
—Gladiators. Lacey, Minna & Davidson, Susanna. 2006. (Usborne Young Reading Ser.). 64p. (J). (gr. 3-7). 8.99 *(978-0-7945-1268-2(2),* Usborne) EDC Publishing.
—Pompeii. Ball, Karen. 2006. (Usborne Young Reading Ser.). 64p. (J). (gr. 3-7). 8.99 *(978-0-7945-1270-5(4),* Usborne) EDC Publishing.
—River Rescue 1 Pathfinders. Millett, Peter. 2017. (Cambridge Reading Adventures Ser.). (ENG.). 24p. pap. 7.87 *(978-1-108-40071-8(X))* Cambridge Univ. Pr.
—The Silk Road White Band. Bradman, Tony. 2016. (Cambridge Reading Adventures Ser.). (ENG.). 15p. pap. 8.78 *(978-1-107-56232-5(5))* Cambridge Univ. Pr.
Cerisier, Emmanuel & Smith, Dave. A Time-Travel Guide to the Land of Jesus: Explore the World of the New Testament, 1 vol. Martin, Peter. ed. 2017. (ENG.). 64p. (J). (gr. 2-6). 16.99 *(978-0-7459-6589-5(X))* Lion Hudson PLC GBR. Dist: Independent Pubs. Group.
Cerizo, Lia. Will Puberty Last My Whole Life? REAL Answers to REAL Questions from Preteens about Body Changes, Sex, & Other Growing-Up Stuff. Metzger, Julie & Lehman, Robert. 2018. 224p. (J). (gr. 4-7). pap. 18.99 *(978-1-63217-179-5(1),* Little Bigfoot) Sasquatch Bks.
Cerney, Samantha May. The Three Little Green Pigs, Llc: A Recycling Pig Tale. Oldenburg, Richard. 2013. 28p. pap. 12.50 *(978-1-62516-649-4(4),* Strategic Bk. Publishing) Strategic Book Publishing & Rights Agency (SBPRA).

C

Cerniga, Kira. Vince, Boy Prince: And the Secrets of How Anyone Can Become a True Prince (or Princess), 1 vol. D'Amico, Carol. 2010. 18p. pap. 24.95 *(978-1-4489-7373-6(2))* PublishAmerica, Inc.
Cerocchi, Beatrice. Barefoot Books Amazing Places. Colombo, Miralda. 2020. (ENG.). 64p. (J). ***(978-1-64686-067-8(5))*** Barefoot Bks., Inc.
Cerone, Sal, jt. illus. see DeRosier, Cher.
Cerri, Mara. The Beach at Night. Ferrante, Elena. Goldstein, Ann, tr. 2016. (ENG.). 38p. 13.00 *(978-1-60945-370-1(0))* Europa Editions, Inc.
Cervadiku, Ylber. The Selfish Elf. Paskalenko, Olga. 2018. (ENG.). 44p. (J). pap. *(978-1-9999345-0-7(4))* Motley Topics Pr.
—Story of a New Israeli: Sippura Shel Olah Chadashah. MacLeod, Jennifer Tzivia. 2019. (ENG.). 36p. (J). (gr. k-2). *(978-1-988976-08-2(1));* pap. *(978-1-988976-07-5(3))* Safer Editions.
Cervantes, Christopher. The Fox Family Adventures: A Day at the Beach. Gorges, Chris & Gorges, Johnni. 2020. (Fox Family Adventures Ser.: Vol. 1). (ENG.). 28p. (J). pap. 10.99 ***(978-1-6592-6923-9(7))*** Independently Published.
Cervantes, Valeria. The Cucuy Stole My Cascarones / el Coco Me Robó Los Cascarones. Rivas, Spelile. Baeza Ventura, Gabriela, tr. 2013. (SPA & ENG.). 32p. (J). 17.95 *(978-1-55885-771-1(0),* Piñata Books) Arte Publico Pr.
—No Time for Monsters/No Hay Tiempo para Monstruos. Rivas, Spelile & Plascencia, Amira. 2010. (SPA & ENG.). 32p. (J). (gr. -1-3). 16.95 *(978-1-55885-445-1(2))* Arte Publico Pr.
Cesana, Laura. O Crescimento DOS G. Barroso, Maria do Sameiro, ed. Barroso, Maria do Sameiro, tr. 2018. (POR.). 64p. (J). pap. 6.50 *(978-1-7901-0326-3(6))* Independently Published.
Cesena, Denise. Respect - Companion Book. Smith, Anya. l.t. ed. 2003. 12p. (J). 2.00 *(978-0-9740418-5-8(8))* Night Light Pubns., LLC.
Cesena, Denise & Perez, Maureen T. Orderliness. Cesena, Denise. l.t. ed. 2003. 28p. (J). 10.00 *(978-0-9740418-2-7(3))* Night Light Pubns., LLC.
—Orderliness - Companion Book. Cesena, Denise. l.t. ed. 2003. 12p. (J). 2.00 *(978-0-9740418-3-4(1))* Night Light Pubns., LLC.
—Respect. Cesena, Denise. l.t. ed. 2003. 28p. (J). *(978-0-9740418-4-1(X))* Night Light Pubns., LLC.
Cesena, Denise, jt. illus. see Perez, Maureen T.
Cespedes-Alicea, Marcela. Best Friends Forever! (Nella the Princess Knight) Golden Books. 2017. (ENG.). 48p. (J). (gr. -1-2). pap. 4.99 *(978-1-5247-1677-6(4),* Golden Bks.) Random Hse. Children's Bks.
—Disney Vampirina: Guess Who! Hide & Shriek. 2018. (Deluxe Guess Who? Ser.). (ENG.). 12p. (J). (gr. -1-k). bds. 10.99 *(978-0-7944-4152-4(1),* Reader's Digest Children's Bks.) Studio Fun International.
Cespedes-Alicea, Marcela. A Halloween Surprise! (Butterbean's Cafe) Random House. 2020. (ENG.). 22p. (J). (— 1). bds. 6.99 ***(978-0-593-12201-3(1),*** Random Hse. Bks. for Young Readers) Random Hse. Children's Bks.
Cespedes-Alicea, Marcela. Purpleberry Surprise! (Nella the Princess Knight) Golden Books. 2017. (ENG.). 128p. (J). (gr. -1-2). pap. 7.99 *(978-1-5247-1673-8(1),* Golden Bks.) Random Hse. Children's Bks.
—A Toy for Trinket. Depken, Kristen L. 2019. (Step into Reading Ser.). (ENG.). 24p. (J). (gr. -1-1). 5.99

(978-1-9848-4807-9(0), Random Hse. Bks. for Young Readers) Random Hse. Children's Bks.
—1, 2, 3, Tea! (Shimmer & Shine) Random House. 2017. (ENG.). 24p. (J). (— 1). bds. 6.99 (978-1-5247-1719-3(3), Random Hse. Bks. for Young Readers) Random Hse. Children's Bks.
Cespedes-Alicea, Marcela & Devaney, Adam. Disney Vampirina: Treasure Haunters: Sliding Tab. 2018. (Sliding Tab Ser.). (ENG.). 12p. (J). (gr. -1-k). bds. 10.99 (978-0-7944-4200-2(5), Studio Fun International) Printers Row Publishing Group.
Cespedes-Alicea, Marcela, jt. illus. see Golden Books.
Cespedes, Marcela. Nickelodeon Butterbean's Cafe. PI Kids. 2020. (Look & Find Ser.). (ENG.). 18p. (J). bds. **(978-1-5037-5291-7(7),** 23e01035-5752-4580-a9ab-36f61cb47f64, p i kids) Phoenix International Publications, Inc.
Cestaro, Gregg, photos by. Wildly Austin: Austin's Landmark Art. Loving, Vikki. 2004. lib. bdg. 24.95 (978-0-9753990-0-2(4)) Wildly Austin.
Ceulemans, Églantine. Best Day Ever. Armstrong, Michael J. 2020. 32p. (J). (gr. -1). 16.95 **(978-1-4549-3097-6(7))** Sterling Publishing Co., Inc.
Ceulemans, Églantine. Captain Pug. James, Laura. 2017. (Adventures of Pug Ser.). (ENG.). 128p. (J). 16.99 (978-1-68119-380-9(9), 900172000, Bloomsbury USA Childrens) Bloomsbury Publishing USA.
—Cowboy Pug. James, Laura. 2017. (Adventures of Pug Ser.). (ENG.). 128p. (J). 16.99 (978-1-68119-824-8(X), 900188263); pap. 6.99 (978-1-68119-823-1(1), 900188267) Bloomsbury Publishing USA. (Bloomsbury USA Childrens).
Ceulemans, Eglantine. Marge in Charge. Fisher, Isla. (Marge in Charge Ser.: 1). (ENG.). (J). (gr. 3-7). 2018. 192p. pap. 6.99 (978-0-06-266219-4(8)); 2017. 176p. 15.99 (978-0-06-266218-7(X)) HarperCollins Pubs.
—Marge in Charge & the Missing Orangutan. Fisher, Isla. 2019. (Marge in Charge Ser.: 3). (ENG.). (J). (gr. 3-7). 160p. pap. 6.99 (978-0-06-266225-5(2)); 144p. 15.99 (978-0-06-266224-8(4)) HarperCollins Pubs.
—Marge in Charge & the Stolen Treasure. Fisher, Isla. (Marge in Charge Ser.: 2). (ENG.). (J). (gr. 3-7). 2019. 192p. pap. 6.99 (978-0-06-266222-4(8)); 2018. 176p. 15.99 (978-0-06-266221-7(X)) HarperCollins Pubs.
Ceulemans, Églantine. No Frogs in School. LaFaye, A. 2018. 32p. (J). (gr. -1-2). 16.95 (978-1-4549-2698-6(8)) Sterling Publishing Co., Inc.
—One-Third Nerd. Choldenko, Gennifer. (ENG.). 224p. (J). (gr. 3-7). 2020. pap. 6.99 (978-1-5247-1891-6(2), Yearling); 2019. 16.99 (978-1-5247-1888-6(2), Lamb, Wendy Bks.); 2019. lib. bdg. 19.99 (978-1-5247-1889-3(0), Lamb, Wendy Bks.) Random Hse. Children's Bks.
—Safari Pug. James, Laura. 2018. (Adventures of Pug Ser.). (ENG.). 112p. (J). 16.99 (978-1-68119-884-2(3), 900191401); pap. 6.99 (978-1-68119-883-5(5), 900191400) Bloomsbury Publishing USA. (Bloomsbury Children's Bks.).
—The Stepmonster. Nadin, Joanna. 2nd ed. 2016. (Reading Ladder Ser.). (ENG.). 48p. (J). (gr. k-2). pap. 7.99 (978-1-4052-8221-5(5)) Egmont Bks., Ltd. GBR. Dist: Independent Pubs. Group.
—The Stepmonster: Blue Banana. Nadin, Joanna. 2015. (Blue Banana Ser.). (ENG.). 48p. (J). (gr. k-2). pap. 8.99 (978-1-4052-7541-5(3)) Egmont Bks., Ltd. GBR. Dist: Independent Pubs. Group.
Cha, Hanna. Tiny Feet Between the Mountains. Cha, Hanna. 2019. (ENG.). 40p. (J). (gr. -1-3). 17.99 (978-1-5344-2992-5(1), Simon & Schuster Bks. For Young Readers) Simon & Schuster Bks. For Young Readers.
Cha, Jae Won. Mi Investigación / My Research Project. Bo-Hyun, Seo. 2019. (SPA.). 40p. (J). (gr. 3-7). pap. 16.99 (978-1-949061-45-1(0), Altea) Penguin Random House Grupo Editorial ESP. Dist: Penguin Random Hse. LLC.
Chabarb, jt. illus. see Niko.
Chabluk, Stefan. Floods! Dwyer, Helen. 2011. (Eyewitness Disaster Ser.). 32p. (gr. 3-3). 29.50 (978-1-60870-002-8(X)) Cavendish Square Publishing LLC.
—Volcanoes! Dwyer, Helen. 2011. (Eyewitness Disaster Ser.). 32p. (gr. 3-3). 29.50 (978-1-60870-006-6(2)) Cavendish Square Publishing LLC.
Chabot, Jacob. Boom Boom Mushroom #1. Tobin, Paul. 2017. (Plants vs. Zombies Ser.). (ENG.). 24p. (J). (gr. 3-7). lib. bdg. 27.07 (978-1-5321-4124-9(6), 26997, Graphic Novels) Spotlight.
—Boom Boom Mushroom #2. Tobin, Paul. 2017. (Plants vs. Zombies Ser.). (ENG.). 24p. (J). (gr. 3-7). lib. bdg. 27.07 (978-1-5321-4125-6(4), 26998, Graphic Novels) Spotlight.
—Boom Boom Mushroom #3. Tobin, Paul. 2017. (Plants vs. Zombies Ser.). (ENG.). 24p. (J). (gr. 3-7). lib. bdg. 27.07 (978-1-5321-4126-3(2), 26999, Graphic Novels) Spotlight.
—Cosmic Chaos! (Teenage Mutant Ninja Turtles) Golden Books. 2016. (Color Plus Crayons & Sticker Ser.). (ENG.). 48p. (J). (gr. -1-2). pap. 4.99 (978-0-553-53908-0(6), Golden Bks.) Random Hse. Children's Bks.
Chabot, Jacob, et al. Delicious!, 2. 2014. (Hello Kitty Graphic Novels Ser.). (ENG.). 64p. (J). (gr. 3-5). 22.44 (978-1-4844-2405-6(0)) Viz Media.
Chabot, Jacob. Garden Warfare #1. Tobin, Paul. 2017. (Plants vs. Zombies Ser.). (ENG.). 28p. (J). (gr. 3-7). lib. bdg. 27.07 (978-1-5321-4127-0(0), 27000, Graphic Novels) Spotlight.
—Garden Warfare #2. Tobin, Paul. 2017. (Plants vs. Zombies Ser.). (ENG.). 28p. (J). (gr. 3-7). lib. bdg. 27.07 (978-1-5321-4128-7(9), 27001, Graphic Novels) Spotlight.
—Garden Warfare #3. Tobin, Paul. 2017. (Plants vs. Zombies Ser.). (ENG.). 28p. (J). (gr. 3-7). lib. bdg. 27.07 (978-1-5321-4129-4(7), 27002, Graphic Novels) Spotlight.
Chabot, Jacob, et al. Gravity Falls: Lost Legends: 4 All-New Adventures! Hirsch, Alex. 2018. (ENG.). 144p. (J). (gr. 3-7). 19.99 (978-1-368-02142-5(5)) Disney Pr.
—Hello Kitty: Fashion Music Wonderland. 2015. 48p. (J). pap. 6.99 (978-1-4215-5903-2(X)) Viz Media.
Chabot, Jacob. Plants vs. Zombies Volume 6: Boom Boom Mushroom. Tobin, Paul. 2017. (Plants vs. Zombies Ser.: 6). (ENG.). 80p. (J). (gr. 3-7). 10.99 (978-1-5067-0037-3(3), Dark Horse Books) Dark Horse Comics.
—Science Comics: Robots & Drones: Past, Present, & Future. Scott, Mairghread. 2018. (Science Comics Ser.). (ENG.). 128p. (J). pap. 12.99 (978-1-62672-792-2(9), 900173910, First Second Bks.) Roaring Brook Pr.
Chabot, Jacob & Rainwater, Matt J. Plants vs. Zombies Volume 9: the Greatest Show Unearthed. Tobin, Paul. 2018. (ENG.). 80p. (J). (gr. 3-7). 9.99 (978-1-5067-0298-8(8), Dark Horse Books) Dark Horse Comics.
Chabot, Jean-Philippe. Sculpture. Pinet, Hélène. 2nd ed. 2018. (My First Discoveries Ser.). (ENG.). 36p. (J). (gr. k-2). spiral bd. 13.99 (978-1-85103-465-9(X), 185103465X) Moonlight Publishing, Ltd. GBR. Dist: Independent Pubs. Group.
Chad, Jon. Science Comics: Solar System: Our Place in Space. Mosco, Rosemary. 2018. (Science Comics Ser.). (ENG.). 128p. (J). 19.99 (978-1-62672-142-5(4), 900140352); pap. 12.99 (978-1-62672-141-8(6), 900140351) Roaring Brook Pr. (First Second Bks.).
Chad, Jon. Leo Geo & the Cosmic Crisis. Chad, Jon. 2013. (ENG.). 40p. (J). (gr. 2-6). 16.99 (978-1-59643-822-4(3), 900087335) Roaring Brook Pr.
—Science Comics: Volcanoes: Fire & Life. Chad, Jon. 2016. (Science Comics Ser.). (ENG.). 128p. (J). pap. 12.99 (978-1-62672-360-3(5), 900154792, First Second Bks.) Roaring Brook Pr.
Chadwell, Andrew C. When I Grow Up. Chadwell, Andrew C. 2019. (ENG.). 36p. (J). (gr. k-2). 15.95 (978-0-578-21799-4(6)) Drew Squared Publishing.
Chadwick, Cindy. Kaseybelle: The Tiniest Fairy in the Kingdom, 1 bk. Chastain, Sandra. 2004. 32p. (J). 14.95 (978-0-9673035-6-7(7), 24) BelleBks., Inc.
Chadwick-Holmes, Sara. Nine Ways to Empower Tweens #LifeSkills. Boucher, Kathleen. 2019. (ENG.). 132p. (J). **(978-0-2288-1881-6(8))**; pap. **(978-0-2288-1882-3(6))** Tellwell Talent.
Chadwick, Kat. Be Brave. Rochester, Karen. 2012. (ENG.). 40p. pap. 17.85 (978-0-9808710-1-2(8)) JoJo Publishing AUS. Dist: Baker & Taylor Publisher Services (BTPS).
Chadwick, Paul. Fragile Creature. Chadwick, Paul. 2006. (ENG.). 208p. pap. 12.95 (978-1-59307-464-7(6)) Dark Horse Comics.
Chaffey, Samantha. Birthday Surprise. Misra, Michelle. 2016. (Angel Wings Ser.: 2). (ENG.). 128p. (J). (gr. 1-4). pap. 5.99 (978-1-4814-5800-9(0), Aladdin) Simon & Schuster Children's Publishing.
—Jewels for a Princess. Baxter, Nicola. 2012. 12p. (J). (gr. 1-6). 16.99 (978-1-84322-926-1(9)) Anness Publishing GBR. Dist: National Bk. Network.
—My Ballet Theatre: Peek Inside the 3-D Windows. Baxter, Nicola. 2014. (ENG.). 24p. (J). (gr. -1-12). 16.99 (978-1-84322-949-0(8), Armadillo) Anness Publishing GBR. Dist: National Bk. Network.
—My Perfect Doll's House: Peek Inside the 3D Windows. Baxter, Nicola. 2013. (ENG.). 12p. (J). (gr. k-4). 16.99 (978-1-84322-924-7(2), Armadillo) Anness Publishing GBR. Dist: National Bk. Network.
—New Friends. Misra, Michelle. 2016. (Angel Wings Ser.: 1). (ENG.). 128p. (J). (gr. 1-4). pap. 5.99 (978-1-4814-5797-2(7), Aladdin) Simon & Schuster Children's Publishing.
—Party at the Fairy Palace: Peek Inside the 3D Windows. Baxter, Nicola. 2013. 12p. 16.99 (978-1-84322-725-0(8)) Anness Publishing GBR. Dist: National Bk. Network.
—Princess & the Jewels. Baxter, Nicola. 2018. 12p. (J). (gr. -1-12). 7.99 (978-1-84322-626-0(X), Armadillo) Anness Publishing GBR. Dist: National Bk. Network.
—Rainbows & Halos. Misra, Michelle. 2017. (Angel Wings Ser.: 4). (ENG.). 112p. (J). (gr. 1-4). pap. 5.99 (978-1-4814-5806-1(X), Simon & Schuster/Paula Wiseman Bks.) Simon & Schuster/Paula Wiseman Bks.
—Secrets & Sapphires. Misra, Michelle. 2016. (Angel Wings Ser.: 3). (ENG.). 128p. (J). (gr. 1-4). pap. 6.99 (978-1-4814-5803-0(5), Aladdin) Simon & Schuster Children's Publishing.
—Secrets & Sapphires. Misra, Michelle. 2016. (Angel Wings Ser.: 3). (ENG.). 128p. (J). (gr. 1-4). 16.99 (978-1-4814-5804-7(3), Simon & Schuster/Paula Wiseman Bks.) Simon & Schuster/Paula Wiseman Bks.
Chaffin, Daniel. City Doodles - Chicago, 1 vol. Lewis, Anna. 2013. (ENG.). 240p. (J). pap. 9.99 (978-1-4236-3479-9(9)) Gibbs Smith, Publisher.
Chagall, Marc. Self-Portrait with Seven Fingers. Lewis, J. Patrick. 2011. (ENG.). 40p. (J). (gr. 4-7). 18.99 (978-1-56846-211-0(5), Creative Editions) Creative Co., The.
Chaghatzbanian, Sonia. The Secret of Ferrell Savage. Gill, J. Duddy. (ENG.). 176p. (J). (gr. 3-7). 2015. pap. 7.99 (978-1-4424-6018-8(0)); 2014. 15.99 (978-1-4424-6017-1(2)) Simon & Schuster Children's Publishing. (Atheneum Bks. for Young Readers).
—Somewhere Among. Donwerth-Chikamatsu, Annie. 2016. (ENG.). 448p. (J). (gr. 4-7). 18.99 (978-1-4814-3786-8(0), Atheneum/Caitlyn Dlouhy Books) Simon & Schuster Children's Publishing.
Chagnaud, Y., jt. illus. see Ruffieux, Jean-Marie.
Chaira, Francesca di. Sleepytime Stories. Taplin, Sam. ed. 2011. (Baby Board Books Ser.). 12p. (J). ring bd. 12.99 (978-0-7945-3006-8(0), Usborne) EDC Publishing.
Chaisty, Chris & Lyle, Kevin. The Usborne Book of Face Painting. Moller, Ray, photos by. Caudron, Chris & Childs, Caro. Knighton, Kate, ed. 2007. (Activity Bks). 47p. (J). (gr. -1-3). 12.99 (978-0-7945-1783-0(8), Usborne) EDC Publishing.
Chakraborty, Pradip. Hilda Ma Tilda - Where's Finn? A Beautiful Illustrated Story Book for Children. Rockoff, Lisa & Weiner, Arlene. 2017. (ENG.). 1p. (J). pap. 9.95 (978-0-9986339-2-3(5)) Scribe Tribe, Inc.
Chalabi, Sawsan. H Is for Haiku: A Treasury of Haiku from a to Z. Rosenberg, Sydell. 2018. 40p. (J). 16.95 (978-0-9987999-7-1(1)) Penny Candy Bks., LLC.
Chaley, Dimitry. Marty the Martian Learns ABC. 2005. 24p. (J). bds. 6.99 (978-0-9747387-1-0(9)) EKADOO Publishing Group.
Chalk, Chris. Balancing Act: Band 18/Pearl (Collins Big Cat) Sparkes, Ali. 2014. (Collins Big Cat Ser.). (ENG.). 80p. (J). (gr. 5-5). pap. 12.95 (978-0-00-753010-6(2)) HarperCollins Pubs. Ltd. GBR. Dist: Independent Pubs. Group.
—From Wagon to Train. O'Dell, Kathryn L. 2017. (Text Connections Guided Close Reading Ser.). (J). (gr. 2). (978-1-4900-1854-6(9)) Benchmark Education Co.
—Journeys: Tales of Travel & Trailblazers. Litton, Jonathan. 2018. (ENG.). 96p. (J). (gr. 1-4). 24.99 (978-1-944530-13-6(4), 360 Degrees) Tiger Tales.
Chalk, Gary. Big Questions: Incredible Adventures in Thinking. Morrison, Matthew. 2007. (ENG.). 204p. (J). (gr. 4-8). pap. 7.95 (978-1-84046-670-6(7)) Icon Bks., Ltd. GBR. Dist: Publishers Group Canada.
—The Boy Who Cried Wolf! Schecter, Ellen. 2014. (ENG.). 34p. (J). 16.95 (978-1-59687-461-9(9), ipicturebooks) ibooks, Inc.
—Mariel of Redwall: A Tale from Redwall. Jacques, Brian. 2003. (Redwall Ser.: 4). (ENG.). 400p. (J). (gr. 5-5). pap. 9.99 (978-0-14-230239-2(2), Firebird) Penguin Young Readers Group.
—Mattimeo: A Tale from Redwall. Jacques, Brian. 2003. (Redwall Ser.: 3). (ENG.). 448p. (J). (gr. 5-7). pap. 9.99 (978-0-14-230240-8(6), Firebird) Penguin Young Readers Group.
—Redwall. Jacques, Brian. 20th anniv. ed. 2007. (Redwall Ser.: 1). (ENG.). 352p. (J). (gr. 5-18). 23.99 (978-0-399-24794-1(7), Philomel Bks.) Penguin Young Readers Group.
—Salamandastron: A Tale from Redwall. Jacques, Brian. 2003. (Redwall Ser.: 5). (ENG.). 400p. (J). (gr. 5-3). pap. 9.99 (978-0-14-250152-8(2), Firebird) Penguin Young Readers Group.
—The Six Crowns: Fair Wind to Widdershins. Jones, Allan. 2011. (Six Crowns Ser.: 2). (ENG.). 176p. (J). (gr. 2-5). 15.99 (978-0-06-200626-4(6), Greenwillow Bks.) HarperCollins Pubs.
—The Six Crowns: Fire over Swallowhaven. Jones, Allan. 2012. (Six Crowns Ser.: 3). (ENG.). 160p. (J). (gr. 2-5). 15.99 (978-0-06-200629-5(0), Greenwillow Bks.) HarperCollins Pubs.
—The Six Crowns: Full Circle. Jones, Allan. 2013. (Six Crowns Ser.: 6). (ENG.). 176p. (J). (gr. 3-7). 16.99 (978-0-06-200639-4(8), Greenwillow Bks.) HarperCollins Pubs.
—The Six Crowns: Sargasso Skies. Jones, Allan. 2013. (Six Crowns Ser.: 5). (ENG.). 176p. (J). (gr. 3-7). 16.99 (978-0-06-200636-3(3), Greenwillow Bks.) HarperCollins Pubs.
—The Six Crowns: Trundle's Quest. Jones, Allan. 2011. (Six Crowns Ser.: 1). (ENG.). 176p. (J). (gr. 2-5). pap. 5.99 (978-0-06-200625-7(8), Greenwillow Bks.) HarperCollins Pubs.
—The Six Crowns: Trundle's Quest. Jones, Allan. 2011. (Six Crowns Ser.: 1). (ENG.). 160p. (J). (gr. 2-5). 15.99 (978-0-06-200623-3(1), Greenwillow Bks.) HarperCollins Pubs.
—Taggerung: A Tale from Redwall. Jacques, Brian. 2003. (Redwall Ser.: 14). (ENG.). 448p. (J). (gr. 5-18). pap. 8.99 (978-0-14-250154-2(9), Firebird) Penguin Young Readers Group.
Challenger, Robert James. Eagle's Reflection: And Other Northwest Coast Stories, 1 vol. Challenger, Robert James. 2009. (ENG.). 48p. (J). (gr. 1-3). pap. 9.95 (978-1-895811-07-0(4)) Heritage Hse. CAN. Dist: Orca Bk. Pubs. USA.
—Grizzly's Home: And Other Northwest Coast Children's Stories, 1 vol. Challenger, Robert James. 2005. (ENG.). 48p. (J). (gr. 1-3). pap. 9.95 (978-1-894384-94-0(6)) Heritage Hse. CAN. Dist: Orca Bk. Pubs. USA.
—Nature's Circle: And Other Northwest Coast Children's Stories, 1 vol. Challenger, Robert James. 2009. (ENG.). 48p. (J). (gr. 1-3). pap. 9.95 (978-1-894384-77-3(6)) Heritage Hse. CAN. Dist: Orca Bk. Pubs. USA.
Challoner, Audrey. Summer at the Cabin. Roberts, Johanna Lonsdorf. Shaggy Dog Press, ed. 2007. 32p. (J). per. (978-0-9722007-2-1(X)) Shaggy Dog Pr.
Chalmers, Kirsty. Heartwood. Darling, Pollyanna. 2013. 66p. (J). pap. (978-0-9871164-4-4(4)) Imaginaria.
Chalmers, Mary. The Crystal Tree. Lindquist, Jennie D. 2008. (J). (gr. 2-6). 25.00 (978-0-8446-6287-9(9)) Smith, Peter Pub., Inc.
Chamberlain, Jon. The Five-Minute Brain Workout for Kids: 365 Amazing, Fabulous, & Fun Word Puzzles. Chamberlain, Kim. 2015. (ENG.). 416p. (J). (gr. 1-1). pap. 14.99 (978-1-63450-159-0(4), Sky Pony Pr.) Skyhorse Publishing Co., Inc.
Chamberlain, Margaret. The ABCs of Thanks & Please. Ohanesian, Diane. 2011. (J). (978-0-545-37962-5(8)) Scholastic, Inc.
—I'm Me! Sheridan, Sara. 2011. (ENG.). 32p. (J). (gr. -1-k). 17.99 (978-0-545-28222-2(5), Chicken Hse., The) Scholastic, Inc.
—Made by Raffi. Pomranz, Craig. 2016. (ENG.). 40p. (J). (gr. 1-4). pap. 9.99 (978-1-84780-596-6(5), Frances Lincoln Children's Bks.) Quarto Publishing Group UK GBR. Dist: Hachette Bk. Group.
—My Two Grandads. Benjamin, Floella. 2019. (ENG.). 32p. (J). (gr. k-3). pap. 9.99 (978-0-7112-4091-9(4), 324891, Frances Lincoln Children's Bks.) Quarto Publishing Group UK GBR. Dist: Hachette UK Distribution.
—My Two Grannies. Benjamin, Floella. 2009. (ENG.). 32p. (J). (gr. k-3). pap. 7.95 (978-1-84780-034-3(3), Frances Lincoln Children's Bks.) Quarto Publishing Group UK GBR. Dist: Hachette Bk. Group.
—Pink! Rickards, Lynne. 2009. (J). Non-ISBN Publisher.
—The Tale of Georgie Grub. Willis, Jeanne. 2012. (ENG.). 32p. (J). (gr. -1-k). pap. 12.99 (978-1-84939-065-1(7)) Andersen Pr. GBR. Dist: Independent Pubs. Group.
—Tattercoats. Greaves, Margaret. (ENG.). 32p. (J). (gr. -1-2). pap. (978-0-7112-0649-6(X)) ReiseArt Buchhandlung GmbH.
—The Very Wicked Headmistress. Mahy, Margaret. 2006. 94p. (J). (gr. 2-4). pap. 6.95 (978-1-903015-46-9(4)) Barn Owl Bks, London GBR. Dist: Independent Pubs. Group.
Chamberlain-Pecorino, Sarah. Ugly As a Toad. Fox, Julie. 2008. 24p. pap. 12.99 (978-1-4389-0002-5(3)) AuthorHouse.
Chamberlin, Emily Hall. The Wonderful Bed. Knevels, Gertrude. 2007. 124p. per. (978-1-4065-2920-3(6)) Dodo Pr.
Chamberlin, Maggie. The Adventures of Penny & Tubs: The City on the Sea. May, Marcie & Zerhusen, Margaret. 2012. (ENG.). 32p. (J). 16.95 (978-0-938467-61-8(1)) Headline Bks., Inc.
Chambers, Breanna. Take in the Good: Skills for Staying Positive & Living Your Best Life. Biegel, Gina. 2020. (ENG.). 208p. (YA). (gr. 8-12). pap. 17.95 (978-1-61180-771-4(9)) Shambhala Pubns., Inc.
Chambers, Brent. A Bird Is a Bird. Eggleton, Jill. 2003. (Rigby Sails Early Ser.). (ENG.). 16p. (gr. 1-2). pap. 6.95 (978-0-7578-8662-1(0)) Houghton Mifflin Harcourt Publishing Co.
Chambers-Goldberg, Micah. Daniel Boone, 1 vol. Blair, Eric. 2011. (My First Classic Story Ser.). (ENG.). 32p. (J). (gr. k-3). lib. bdg. 22.65 (978-1-4048-6578-5(0), Picture Window Bks.) Capstone.
—Even Superheroes Get Diabetes. Ganz-Schmitt, Sue. 36p. 2011. (gr. -1-3). 22.95 (978-1-59858-303-8(4)); 2007. (J). per. 15.95 (978-1-59858-302-1(6)) Dog Ear Publishing, LLC.
—Paul Bunyan, 1 vol. Blair, Eric. Robledo, Sol, tr. 2006. (Read-It! Readers en Español: Cuentos Exagerados Ser.).Tr. of Paul Bunyan. (SPA.). 32p. (J). (gr. k-3). 21.32 (978-1-4048-1657-2(7), Picture Window Bks.) Capstone.
—Pecos Bill, 1 vol. Blair, Eric. 2013. (My First Classic Story Ser.).Tr. of Pecos Bill. (ENG.). 32p. (J). (gr. k-3). pap. 7.10 (978-1-4795-1860-9(3), Picture Window Bks.) Capstone.
Chambers, Hannah. Auntie Uncle: Drag Queen Hero. Royce, Ellie. 2020. (ENG.). 32p. (J). (gr. -1-2). 17.99 (978-1-57687-935-1(6), powerHouse Bks.) powerHse. Bks.
Chambers, James Mathieu. I Want to Be in the Show, 1 vol. Chartrand, Jane & Nolan, Dionne. 2015. (ENG.). 32p. (J). (gr. 2-3). mass mkt. 10.95 (978-1-894717-52-6(X), 0d44bc98-86c4-4ffd-b172-9da31140eef8) Pemmican Pubns., Inc. CAN. Dist: Firefly Bks., Ltd.
Chambers, Mark. The Adventures of an Aluminum Can: A Story about Recycling. Inches, Alison. 2009. (Little Green Bks.). (ENG.). 24p. (J). (gr. -1-1). pap. 4.99 (978-1-4169-7221-1(8), Little Simon) Little Simon.
—Don't Close Your Eyes: A Silly Bedtime Story, 1 vol. Hostetler, Bob. 2019. 20p. (J). bds. 9.99 (978-1-4002-0951-4(X)) Nelson, Thomas Inc.
—Five Little Monkeys; and, Five Little Penguins. 2013. (ENG.). 24p. (J). (978-0-7787-1133-9(1)) Crabtree Publishing Co.
—Five Little Monkeys; Five Little Penguins. 2013. (ENG.). 24p. (J). pap. (978-0-7787-1151-3(X)) Crabtree Publishing Co.
—Jake Bakes a Monster Cake. Rowland, Lucy. 2017. (ENG.). 32p. (J). (gr. -1-1). 17.99 (978-1-4472-8668-4(5)); pap. 10.99 (978-1-4472-8670-7(7)) Pan Macmillan GBR. Dist: Independent Pubs. Group.
—Karate Kid. Kurstedt, Rosanne L. 2019. 40p. (J). (gr. -1-3). 14.99 (978-0-7624-9343-2(7), Running Pr. Kids) Running Pr.
—Kindergarten, Here I Come! Steinberg, D. J. 2012. (Here I Come! Ser.). (ENG.). 32p. (J). (gr. -1-k). pap. 5.99 (978-0-448-45624-9(9), Grosset & Dunlap) Penguin Young Readers Group.
Chambers, Mark, et al. My Favorite Fairy Tale Collection. 2014. (J). (978-1-4351-5723-1(0)) Little Tiger Pr.
Chambers, Mark. My Hamster Is a Genius. Lowe, Dave. 2018. (Stinky & Jinks Ser.). (ENG.). 112p. (J). (gr. 1-4). pap. 9.99 (978-1-84812-655-8(7)) Bonnier Publishing GBR. Dist: Independent Pubs. Group.
—My Hamster Is a Spy. Lowe, Dave. 2018. (Stinky & Jinks Ser.: 3). (ENG.). 112p. (J). (gr. k-3). pap. 9.99 (978-1-84812-657-2(3)) Bonnier Publishing GBR. Dist: Independent Pubs. Group.
—Noisy Pirates. Taplin, Sam. 2014. (ENG.). (J). 19.99 (978-0-7945-2814-0(7), Usborne) EDC Publishing.
—Pirate Pete & His Smelly Feet. Rowland, Lucy. 2017. (ENG.). 32p. (J). (gr. -1-1). 17.99 (978-1-5098-1776-4(X), Macmillan Children's Bks.) Pan Macmillan GBR. Dist: Independent Pubs. Group.
—Run! The Elephant Weighs a Ton! Frost, Adam. 2012. 128p. (J). (gr. -1-k). pap. 8.99 (978-1-4088-2707-9(7), 900086972, Bloomsbury Children's Bks.) Bloomsbury Publishing USA.
—Yoga Frog. Carpenter, Nora Shalaway. 2018. 40p. (J). (gr. -1-3). 14.99 (978-0-7624-6467-8(4), Running Pr. Kids) Running Pr.
—Zach & Lucy & the Museum of Natural Wonders. Pifferson Sisters, the. 2016. (Zach & Lucy Ser.). (ENG.). 40p. (J). (gr. 1-3). pap. 3.99 (978-1-4814-3935-0(9), Simon Spotlight) Simon Spotlight.
—Zach & Lucy & the Yoga Zoo. 2016. (Zach & Lucy Ser.). (ENG.). 40p. (J). (gr. 1-3). pap. 4.99 (978-1-4814-3938-1(3), Simon Spotlight) Simon Spotlight.
Chambers, Mary. Finding Anna Bee. Snider, Cindy Gay. 2007. 163p. (J). (gr. 3-7). per. 9.99 (978-0-8361-9392-3(X)) Herald Pr.
Chambers, Nick. Mr. Dan Has a Plan - We Can Fix It! - a Big Job: BuildUp Unit 1 Lap Book. Green, Lila et al. 2015. (Build up Core Phonics Ser.). (J). (gr. 1). (978-1-4900-2600-8(2)) Benchmark Education Co.

Chambers, Nick & Battuz, Christine. Shade Lake - Cole & Rose - Grace & Ace: BuildUp Unit 5 Lap Book. Lane, Tracy et al. 2015. (Build up Core Phonics Ser.). (J). (gr. 1). *(978-1-4900-2604-6(5))* Benchmark Education Co.

Chambers, Noah. All about the 12 Disciples. Snyder, Dave. 2020. (All About Ser.: Vol. 1). (ENG.). 100p. (J). pap. 6.99 ***(978-1-7908-0807-6(3))*** Independently Published.

Chambers, Sally. Big Cat. Shulman, Mark. 2004. 8p. (J). bds. 6.95 *(978-1-58925-737-5(5))* Tiger Tales.

—Foxy Fox. Shulman, Mark. 2004. 8p. (J). bds. 6.95 *(978-1-58925-738-2(3))* Tiger Tales.

Chambers, Z. Harvey's Adventures. Santini, Philip. 2011. 44p. pap. 24.95 *(978-1-4626-2078-4(7))* America Star Bks.

Chambliss, Matthew, et al, photos by. The Eastern Bluebird: A Guide for Young Birdwatchers. Houle, Donna Lee. 2011. 60p. (J). pap. 7.95 *(978-0-9846397-1-7(3)*, PitziGil Pr.) PitziGil Pubns.

Chambliss, Maxie. Dog & Cat. Fahiner, Paul & Fehlner, Paul. 2004. (My First Reader Ser.). (ENG.). 32p. (J). (gr. k-1). pap. 3.95 *(978-0-516-24626-0(7)*, Children's Pr.) Scholastic Library Publishing.

—Monsters! Namm, Diane. 2003. (My First Reader Ser.). (ENG.). 32p. (J). 18.50 *(978-0-516-22933-1(8)*, Children's Pr.) Scholastic Library Publishing.

—My Big Boy Potty. Cole, Joanna. 2004. (ENG.). 32p. (J). (gr. -1-3). 6.99 *(978-0-688-17042-4(0)*, HarperCollins) HarperCollins Pubs. Ltd. GBR. Dist: HarperCollins Pubs.

—My Big Girl Potty. Cole, Joanna. 2004. (ENG.). 32p. (J). (gr. -1 — 1). 7.99 *(978-0-688-17041-7(2)*, HarperCollins) HarperCollins Pubs. Ltd. GBR. Dist: HarperCollins Pubs.

—My Friend the Doctor. Cole, Joanna. 2005. (ENG.). 32p. (J). (gr. -1 — 1). 7.99 *(978-0-06-050500-4(1)*, HarperFestival) HarperCollins Pubs.

—Six Cheers for Ladybug. Fleming, Maria. 2005. (ENG.). 16p. (J). (gr. -1-1). pap. 2.99 *(978-0-439-69016-4(1))* Scholastic, Inc.

Chamorro, Marco. Angel de Mi Guarda (Libro + CD) Williams, Ricardo. 2015. (Serie Verde / Album Ilustrado Ser.). (SPA.). 24p. (J). pap. 14.95 *(978-9942-19-322-3(7))* Santillana USA Publishing Co., Inc.

—Torbellino. Iturralde, Edna. 2015. (Serie Verde / Album Ilustrado Ser.). (SPA.). 24p. (J). pap. 12.95 *(978-9942-19-340-7(5))* Santillana USA Publishing Co., Inc.

Champagne, Heather. The Adventures of Hip Hop: Hip Hop & the Blueberry Pancakes. Marshall, Denise. 2012. 36p. pap. 14.75 *(978-1-62212-331-5(X)*, Strategic Bk. Publishing) Strategic Book Publishing & Rights Agency (SBPRA).

Champagne, Heather, jt. illus. see Schley, Cheri.

Champagne, Melanie. My Aunt Came Back. 2008. (First Steps in Music Ser.). (ENG.). 32p. (J). (gr. -1-k). 17.95 *(978-1-57999-680-2(9))* G I A Pubns., Inc.

Champagne, Tony & Leonhard, Herb. Cinderella Battistella, 1 vol. Bruce, Bob & Cuthbert, David. 2017. (ENG.). 32p. (gr. k). 16.99 *(978-1-4556-2175-0(7)*, Pelican Publishing) Arcadia Publishing.

Champion, Daryl, jt. illus. see Champion, Dionne N.

Champion, Dionne N. & Champion, Daryl. The Spirit of the Baobab Tree. Champion, Dionne N. et al. 2008. 37p. (J). 31.99 *(978-1-4363-7842-0(7))* Xlibris Corp.

Champion, Tyler. Devils' Pass, 4 vols. Ireland, Justina. 2017. (Devils' Pass Ser.). (ENG.). 128p. (J). (gr. 4-8). 101.28 *(978-1-4965-5002-6(1)*, 26794, Stone Arch Bks.) Capstone.

—Devils' Pass, 6 vols. Ireland, Justina. 2018. (Devils' Pass Ser.). (ENG.). 128p. (J). (gr. 4-8). 155.94 *(978-1-4965-6528-0(2)*, 28445, Stone Arch Bks.) Capstone.

—Evie Allen vs. the Quiz Bowl Zombies. Ireland, Justina. 2017. (Devils' Pass Ser.). (ENG.). 128p. (J). (gr. 4-8). lib. bdg. 25.99 *(978-1-4965-4988-4(0)*, 135880, Stone Arch Bks.) Capstone.

—Jeff Allen vs. the Time Suck Vampire. Ireland, Justina. 2017. (Devils' Pass Ser.). (ENG.). 128p. (J). (gr. 4-8). lib. bdg. 25.99 *(978-1-4965-4986-0(4)*, 135878, Stone Arch Bks.) Capstone.

—Tiffany Donovan vs. the Cookie Elves of Destruction. Ireland, Justina. 2017. (Devils' Pass Ser.). (ENG.). 128p. (J). (gr. 4-8). lib. bdg. 25.99 *(978-1-4965-4987-7(2)*, 135879, Stone Arch Bks.) Capstone.

—Tiffany Donovan vs. the Poison Werewolves. Ireland, Justina. 2018. (Devils' Pass Ser.). (ENG.). 128p. (J). (gr. 4-8). lib. bdg. 25.99 *(978-1-4965-6525-9(8)*, 138528, Stone Arch Bks.) Capstone.

—Zach Lopez vs. the Shadow Cats. Ireland, Justina. 2018. (Devils' Pass Ser.). (ENG.). 128p. (J). (gr. 4-8). lib. bdg. 25.99 *(978-1-4965-6524-2(X)*, 138524, Stone Arch Bks.) Capstone.

—Zach Lopez vs. the Unicorns of Doom. Ireland, Justina. 2017. (Devils' Pass Ser.). (ENG.). 128p. (J). (gr. 4-8). lib. bdg. 25.99 *(978-1-4965-4989-1(9)*, 135881, Stone Arch Bks.) Capstone.

Champion, Vanessa. The Trepets Book Three Rabbit Race Day. Chance, C. 2007. 112p. per. *(978-0-9551289-2-9(7)*, Bumble Bks.) Dragonfly Bks. & Arts.

Champlin, DeeAnn. Eddie E & the Eggs. Champlin, DeeAnn. Date not set. (Little Lyrics Short Vowel Collection: Vol. 2). (J). (gr. k-2). pap. 12.00 *(978-1-893429-26-0(1))* Little Lyrics Pubns.

Chan, Charles. The Magic of Friendship in the Magical Kingdom. Louisa, Charlotte. 2017. (ENG.). 36p. (J). pap. *(978-0-9957419-5-9(6))* Magical Kingdom Publishing.

Chan, Florence. The Wandering God. Pantalleresco, Joshua. 2017. (Watcher Ser.: Vol. 3). (ENG.). (YA). (gr. 7-12). pap. *(978-1-987976-33-5(9))* Mirror World Publishing.

Chan, Harvey. Dead Man's Gold & Other Stories, 1 vol. Yee, Paul. 2004. (ENG.). 104p. (YA). pap. 9.95 *(978-0-88899-587-2(3))* Groundwood Bks. CAN. Dist: Publishers Group West (PGW).

—Ghost Train. Yee, Paul. 2004. 29p. (J). (gr. k-4). reprint ed. 16.00 *(978-0-7567-9083-7(2))* DIANE Publishing Co.

—Ghost Train, 1 vol. Yee, Paul. 2013. (ENG.). 32p. (J). (gr. k-5). 14.95 *(978-1-55498-389-6(4))* Groundwood Bks. CAN. Dist: Publishers Group West (PGW).

—No Return Land: You Are the Hero of This Book! Storm, Jeff. 2015. (Determine Your Destiny Ser.: Vol. 2). (ENG.). 176p. (J). (gr. 4-7). pap. *(978-1-77143-247-4(0))* CCB Publishing.

—Petrified World, Determine Your Destiny No. 1: You Are the Hero of This Book! Storm, Jeff. 2nd ed. 2014. 160p. pap. *(978-1-77143-159-0(8)*, CCB Publishing) CCB Publishing.

—Roses Sing on New Snow: A Delicious Tale. Yee, Paul. 32p. (J). 16.95 *(978-0-88899-144-7(4))* Groundwood Bks. CAN. Dist: Publishers Group West (PGW).

—The Young Masters of Time, Determine Your Destiny No. 3: You Are the Hero of This Book! Storm, Jeff. 2016. (Determine Your Destiny Ser.: Vol. 3). (ENG.). (J). pap. *(978-1-77143-287-0(X))* CCB Publishing.

Chan, Irene. ¡Al Bebé le Encanta Codificar! / Baby Loves Coding! Spiro, Ruth. 2019. (Baby Loves Science Ser.). (ENG.). 20p. (J). (— 1). bds. 8.99 *(978-1-62354-114-9(X))* Charlesbridge Publishing, Inc.

—¡Al Bebé le Encanta la Gravedad! / Baby Loves Gravity! Spiro, Ruth. 2019. (Baby Loves Science Ser.). (ENG.). 20p. (J). (— 1). bds. 8.99 *(978-1-62354-115-6(8))* Charlesbridge Publishing, Inc.

—¡Al Bebé le Encanta la Ingeniería Aeroespacial! / Baby Loves Aerospace Engineering! Spiro, Ruth. 2019. (Baby Loves Science Ser.). (ENG.). 22p. (J). (— 1). bds. 8.99 *(978-1-58089-983-3(8))* Charlesbridge Publishing, Inc.

—¡Al Bebé le Encantan Los Quarks! / Baby Loves Quarks! Spiro, Ruth. 2019. (Baby Loves Science Ser.). 22p. (J). (— 1). bds. 8.99 *(978-1-58089-984-0(6))* Charlesbridge Publishing, Inc.

—America ABC Board Book. Wilson, Samuel Troy. 2019. (ENG.). 32p. (J). (gr. -1 — 1). bds. 10.99 *(978-0-06-279527-4(9))* HarperCollins Pubs.

—Baby Loves Coding! Spiro, Ruth. 2018. (Baby Loves Science Ser.: 6). 20p. (J). (— 1). bds. 8.99 *(978-1-58089-884-3(X))* Charlesbridge Publishing, Inc.

—Baby Loves Gravity! Spiro, Ruth. 2018. (Baby Loves Science Ser.: 5). 22p. (J). (— 1). bds. 8.99 *(978-1-58089-836-2(X))* Charlesbridge Publishing, Inc.

—Baby Loves Green Energy! Spiro, Ruth. 2018. (Baby Loves Science Ser.: 7). 20p. (J). (— 1). bds. 8.99 *(978-1-58089-926-0(9))* Charlesbridge Publishing, Inc.

—Baby Loves Science Board Boxed Set. Spiro, Ruth. 2018. (Baby Loves Science Ser.). 88p. (J). (— 1). bds. 35.96 *(978-1-63289-035-1(6))* Charlesbridge Publishing, Inc.

—Baby Loves Scientists. Spiro, Ruth. 2019. (Baby Loves Science Ser.). 24p. (J). (— 1). 12.99 *(978-1-62354-149-1(2))* Charlesbridge Publishing, Inc.

—Baby Loves Structural Engineering! Spiro, Ruth. 2018. (Baby Loves Science Ser.: 8). 20p. (J). (— 1). bds. 8.99 *(978-1-58089-927-7(7))* Charlesbridge Publishing, Inc.

Chan, Irene. Baby Loves the Five Senses Boxed Set. Spiro, Ruth. 2020. (Baby Loves Science Ser.). (ENG.). 110p. (J). (— 1). bds. 44.95 ***(978-1-63289-058-0(5))*** Charlesbridge Publishing, Inc.

Chan, Irene. Baby Loves the Five Senses: Hearing! Spiro, Ruth. 2019. (Baby Loves Science Ser.). (ENG.). 20p. (J). (— 1). bds. 8.99 *(978-1-62354-102-6(6))* Charlesbridge Publishing, Inc.

—Baby Loves the Five Senses: Sight! Spiro, Ruth. 2019. (Baby Loves Science Ser.). (ENG.). 20p. (J). (— 1). bds. 8.99 *(978-1-62354-103-3(4))* Charlesbridge Publishing, Inc.

—Baby Loves the Five Senses: Smell! Spiro, Ruth. 2020. (Baby Loves Science Ser.). 20p. (J). (— 1). bds. 8.99 *(978-1-62354-153-8(0))* Charlesbridge Publishing, Inc.

Chan, Irene. Baby Loves the Five Senses: Taste! Spiro, Ruth. 2020. (Baby Loves Science Ser.). 20p. (J). (— 1). bds. 8.99 ***(978-1-62354-154-5(9))*** Charlesbridge Publishing, Inc.

Chan, Irene. Finding Kindness. Underwood, Deborah. 2019. (ENG.). 32p. (J). 17.99 *(978-1-250-23789-7(0)*, 900210834, Holt, Henry & Co. Bks. For Young Readers) Holt, Henry & Co.

Chan, Jenny. Consent: Deal with It Because It's Your Body, Your Choice. Evans, Keisha & Gonsalvez, N. B. 2020. (Lorimer Deal with It Ser.). (ENG.). 32p. (J). (gr. 4-9). 22.65 ***(978-1-4594-1506-5(X)***, dd50f39e-0d92-44f8-8c76-52f5fa5d1adf) James Lorimer & Co. Ltd., Pubs. CAN. Dist: Lerner Publishing Group.

Chan, Lidia. The Iron King. Kagawa, Julie. 2017. (Iron King Ser.). (SPA.). (YA). (gr. 7-12). pap. 19.99 *(978-1-948216-67-8(1))* TidalWave.

Chan, Melanie Linden. Moth & Wasp, Soil & Ocean: Remembering Chinese Scientist Pu Zhelong's Work for Sustainable Farming. Schmalzer, Sigrid. 2020. (ENG.). 40p. (J). (gr. 3-7). pap. 9.95 ***(978-0-88448-635-0(4)***, 884635) Tilbury Hse. Pubs.

Chan, Ron. Husbands. Espenson, Jane & Bell, Brad. Hahn, Sierra, ed. 2013. (ENG.). 80p. 14.99 *(978-1-61655-130-8(5))* Dark Horse Comics.

—Lawn of Doom #1. Tobin, Paul. 2019. (Plants vs. Zombies Ser.). (ENG.). 28p. (J). (gr. 3-7). lib. bdg. 27.07 *(978-1-5321-4383-0(4)*, 32886, Graphic Novels) Spotlight.

—Lawn of Doom #2. Tobin, Paul. 2019. (Plants vs. Zombies Ser.). (ENG.). 28p. (J). (gr. 3-7). lib. bdg. 27.07 *(978-1-5321-4384-7(2)*, 32887, Graphic Novels) Spotlight.

—Lawn of Doom #3. Tobin, Paul. 2019. (Plants vs. Zombies Ser.). (ENG.). 28p. (J). (gr. 3-7). lib. bdg. 27.07 *(978-1-5321-4385-4(0)*, 32888, Graphic Novels) Spotlight.

—Petal to the Metal #1. Tobin, Paul. 2017. (Plants vs. Zombies Ser.). (ENG.). 28p. (J). (gr. 3-7). lib. bdg. 27.07 *(978-1-5321-4130-0(0)*, 27003, Graphic Novels) Spotlight.

—Petal to the Metal #2. Tobin, Paul. 2017. (Plants vs. Zombies Ser.). (ENG.). 28p. (J). (gr. 3-7). lib. bdg. 27.07 *(978-1-5321-4131-7(9)*, 27004, Graphic Novels) Spotlight.

—Petal to the Metal #3. Tobin, Paul. 2017. (Plants vs. Zombies Ser.). (ENG.). 28p. (J). (gr. 3-7). lib. bdg. 27.07 *(978-1-5321-4132-4(7)*, 27005, Graphic Novels) Spotlight.

Chan, Ron, et al. Plants vs. Zombies Boxed Set 5. Tobin, Paul. 2019. (ENG.). 264p. (J). (gr. 3-7). 29.97 *(978-1-5067-1432-5(3)*, Dark Horse Books) Dark Horse Comics.

Chan, Ron. Plants vs. Zombies Volume 10: Rumble at Lake Gumbo. Tobin, Paul. 2018. (ENG.). 80p. (J). (gr. 3-7). 10.99 *(978-1-5067-0497-5(2)*, Dark Horse Books) Dark Horse Comics.

—Plants vs. Zombies Volume 12: Dino-Might. Tobin, Paul. 2019. (ENG.). 88p. (J). (gr. 3-7). 9.99 *(978-1-5067-0838-6(2)*, Dark Horse Books) Dark Horse Comics.

—Plants vs. Zombies Volume 8: Lawn of Doom. Tobin, Paul. 2017. (ENG.). 80p. (J). (gr. 2-5). 10.99 *(978-1-5067-0204-9(X)*, Dark Horse Books) Dark Horse Comics.

Chan, Ron & Rainwater, Matthew J. Lawnmageddon #1. Tobin, Paul. 2016. (Plants vs. Zombies Ser.). (ENG.). 28p. (J). (gr. 3-7). lib. bdg. 27.07 *(978-1-61479-540-7(1)*, 21447, Graphic Novels) Spotlight.

—Lawnmageddon #2. Tobin, Paul. 2016. (Plants vs. Zombies Ser.). (ENG.). 28p. (J). (gr. 3-7). lib. bdg. 27.07 *(978-1-61479-541-4(X)*, 21448, Graphic Novels) Spotlight.

—Lawnmageddon #3. Tobin, Paul. 2016. (Plants vs. Zombies Ser.). (ENG.). 28p. (J). (gr. 3-7). lib. bdg. 27.07 *(978-1-61479-542-1(8)*, 21449, Graphic Novels) Spotlight.

Chan, Ron & Soler, Sara. Plants vs. Zombies Volume 14: a Little Problem. Tobin, Paul. 2019. (ENG.). 88p. (J). (gr. 3-7). 10.99 *(978-1-5067-0840-9(4)*, Dark Horse Books) Dark Horse Comics.

Chan, Ruth. Amy the Red Panda Is Writing the Best Story in the World. Venable, Colleen Af. 2017. (ENG.). 40p. (J). (gr. -1-3). 17.99 *(978-0-06-233848-8(X)*, Greenwillow Bks.) HarperCollins Pubs.

Chan, Ruth. The Great Indoors. Falatko, Julie. 2019. (ENG.). 40p. (J). (gr. -1-k). 17.99 ***(978-1-368-00083-3(5))*** Little, Brown Bks. for Young Readers.

Chan, Ruth. Mervin the Sloth Is about to Do the Best Thing in the World. Venable, Colleen Af. 2016. (ENG.). 40p. (J). (gr. -1-3). 17.99 *(978-0-06-233847-1(1)*, Greenwillow Bks.) HarperCollins Pubs.

Chan, San Wei. Spear & Shield. *(978-0-9744905-0-2(4))* Santoon Bks.

Chan, Suwin. Buenas Noches, Estados Unidos. Gamble, Adam. 2012. (Buenas Noches Ser.). (SPA & ENG.). 28p. (J). (gr. k — 1). bds. 9.95 *(978-1-60219-069-6(0))* Good Night Bks.

—Good Night Alberta. Gamble, Adam & Jasper, Mark. 2017. (Good Night Our World Ser.). 20p. (J). (— 1). bds. 9.95 *(978-1-60219-442-7(4))* Good Night Bks.

—Good Night America. Gamble, Adam. 2006. (Good Night Our World Ser.). (ENG.). 28p. (J). (gr. k — 1). bds. 9.95 *(978-0-9777979-0-5(2))* Good Night Bks.

—Good Night Baby Animals. Gamble, Adam & Jasper, Mark. 2016. (Good Night Our World Ser.). (ENG.). 20p. (J). (— 1). bds. 9.95 *(978-1-60219-499-1(8))* Good Night Bks.

—Good Night Baby Dragons. Gamble, Adam & Jasper, Mark. 2018. (Good Night Our World Ser.). 20p. (J). (— 1). bds. 9.95 *(978-1-60219-511-0(0))* Good Night Bks.

—Good Night Bath Time. Gamble, Adam & Jasper, Mark. 2019. (Good Night Our World Ser.). 8p. (J). (— 1). 7.95 *(978-1-60219-797-8(0))* Good Night Bks.

—Good Night Books. Gamble, Adam & Jasper, Mark. 2017. (Good Night Our World Ser.). 20p. (J). (— 1). bds. 9.95 *(978-1-60219-470-0(X))* Good Night Bks.

—Good Night Maine. Gamble, Adam. 2007. (Good Night Our World Ser.). (ENG.). 18p. (J). (gr. k — 1). bds. 9.95 *(978-1-60219-010-8(0))* Good Night Bks.

—Good Night Mermaids. Gamble, Adam & Jasper, Mark. 2015. (Good Night Our World Ser.). (ENG.). 20p. (J). (— 1). bds. 9.95 *(978-1-60219-226-3(X))* Good Night Bks.

—Good Night Unicorns. Gamble, Adam & Jasper, Mark. 2019. (Good Night Our World Ser.). 20p. (J). (— 1). bds. 9.95 *(978-1-60219-791-6(1))* Good Night Bks.

—Good Night Yosemite. Gamble, Adam & Jasper, Mark. 2016. (Good Night Our World Ser.). (ENG.). 20p. (J). (— 1). bds. 9.95 *(978-1-60219-389-5(4))* Good Night Bks.

Chan, Suwin & Blackmore, Katherine. Good Night Yoga. Gamble, Adam et al. 2016. (Good Night Our World Ser.). (ENG.). 20p. (J). (— 1). bds. 9.95 *(978-1-60219-414-4(9))* Good Night Bks.

Chan, Yee Von. A Father's Love. Holt, Hannah. 2019. 32p. (J). (gr. -1-2). 17.99 *(978-0-525-51420-6(1)*, Philomel Bks.) Penguin Young Readers Group.

—Finding Christmas. Evans, Lezlie. 2017. (ENG.). 32p. (J). (gr. -1-3). 16.99 *(978-0-8075-2433-6(6)*, 807524336) Whitman, Albert & Co.

Chanani, Nidhi. Binny's Diwali. Umrigar, Thrity. 2020. (ENG.). 40p. (J). (gr. -1-3). 17.99 ***(978-1-338-36448-4(0)***, Scholastic Pr.) Scholastic, Inc.

Chanani, Nidhi. I Will Be Fierce. Birdsong, Bea. 2019. (ENG.). 40p. (J). 17.99 *(978-1-250-29508-8(4)*, 900195158) Roaring Brook Pr.

Chance, Robyn. C Is for Chin. Chance, Robyn. 2012. 38p. 18.95 *(978-1-936850-31-0(1))* Rhemalda Publishing.

Chandhok, Lena. Archaeology: Cool Women Who Dig. Yasuda, Anita. 2017. (Girls in Science Ser.). 112p. (J). (gr. 4-6). 19.95 *(978-1-61930-496-3(1)*, 6cc07de7-2b1d-4f45-97cc-7e6ee113164e) Nomad Pr.

—Architecture: Cool Women Who Design Structures. Schmermund, Elizabeth. 2017. (Girls in Science Ser.). 112p. (J). (gr. 4-6). 19.95 *(978-1-61930-542-7(9)*, d7b88266-7b15-42dd-9047-b3a22084ae40); pap. 9.95 *(978-1-61930-546-5(1)*, 09660b23-4677-4d08-a33e-53b9eea4d9a4) Nomad Pr.

—Aviation: Cool Women Who Fly. Van Vleet, Carmella. 2016. (Girls in Science Ser.). 112p. (J). (gr. 3-7). 19.95 *(978-1-61930-436-9(8)*, cabee642-94e2-4b4f-b1b0-5712458d4a82) Nomad Pr.

—Bots! Robotics Engineering: With Makerspace Activities for Kids. Ceceri, Kathy. 2019. (Build It Yourself Ser.). 128p. (J). (gr. 4-6). 22.95 *(978-1-61930-827-5(4)*, fc107804-ede1-4f0c-a7ff-d266633dfad2); pap. 17.95 *(978-1-61930-830-5(4)*, 8471778d-0d87-463f-b9f9-3d2090fd2fde) Nomad Pr.

—Civic Unrest: Investigate the Struggle for Social Change. Amidon Lusted, Marcia. 2015. (Inquire & Investigate Ser.). 128p. (J). (gr. 6-10). 22.95 *(978-1-61930-241-9(1)*, a1b71351-b0ed-41f7-b544-1a1cc176160f) Nomad Pr.

—Game Logic: Level up & Create Your Own Games with Science Activities for Kids. Smibert, Angie. 2019. (Build It Yourself Ser.). (ENG.). 128p. (J). (gr. 4-6). 22.95 *(978-1-61930-802-2(9)*, 56259ae0-f934-44ca-800e-a149997a4f9f); pap. 17.95 *(978-1-61930-805-3(3)*, b225c241-dc0f-462e-8dc7-1a6b84301e87) Nomad Pr.

—Marine Biology: Cool Women Who Dive. Bush Gibson, Karen. 2016. (Girls in Science Ser.). 112p. (J). (gr. 3-7). 19.95 *(978-1-61930-431-4(7)*, 32c15cc5-9841-424d-aeb2-af32155b90f6) Nomad Pr.

—Meteorology: Cool Women Who Weather Storms. Gibson, Karen Bush. 2017. (Girls in Science Ser.). 112p. (J). (gr. 4-6). pap. 9.95 *(978-1-61930-541-0(0)*, 95f7a2d3-eab4-4db3-9333-379377294132) Nomad Pr.

—Meteorology: Cool Women Who Weather Storms. Gibson, Bush Karen. 2017. (Girls in Science Ser.). 112p. (J). (gr. 4-6). 19.95 *(978-1-61930-537-3(2)*, 00f61013-80d2-47aa-b981-795bb8e082b9) Nomad Pr.

—Zoology: Cool Women Who Work with Animals. Swanson, Jennifer. 2017. (Girls in Science Ser.). 112p. (J). (gr. 3-7). 19.95 *(978-1-61930-501-4(1)*, 2def7fa1-0b20-4c62-b3f8-adca30e090b3) Nomad Pr.

Chandler, Alton, jt. illus. see Hayden, Seito.

Chandler, Emma. Thorn, 1 vol. Clauson, Heather & Grebe, John. 2018. (ENG.). 52p. (J). 22.99 *(978-1-59555-929-6(9))*; pap. 12.99 *(978-1-59555-931-9(0))* Elm Hill.

Chandler, Jeff. Bowling Alley Adjectives, 6 vols. Fisher, Doris & Gibbs, D. L. 2008. (Grammar All-Stars: the Parts of Speech Ser.). 32p. (gr. 2-5). pap. 10.50 *(978-0-8368-8908-6(8)*, Gareth Stevens Learning Library) Stevens, Gareth Publishing LLLP.

—Hole-in-One Adverbs. Fisher, Doris & Gibbs, D. L. 2008. (Grammar All-Stars Ser.). 32p. (J). (gr. 2-5). lib. bdg. 27.00 *(978-0-8368-8902-4(9)*, Gareth Stevens Learning Library) Stevens, Gareth Publishing LLLP.

Chandler, Jeff, photos by. Slam Dunk Pronouns. Fisher, Doris & Gibbs, D. L. 2008. (Grammar All-Stars Ser.). 32p. (J). (gr. 2-5). lib. bdg. 27.00 *(978-0-8368-8904-8(5)*, Gareth Stevens Learning Library) Stevens, Gareth Publishing LLLP.

Chandler, Jeff, jt. illus. see Angle, Scott.

Chandler, Joy. A Time to Fly: The Story of Annie the Butterfly. Cartie, Nancy. 2019. (ENG.). 38p. (J). pap. 11.99 ***(978-1-6939-0770-8(4))*** Independently Published.

Chandler, Shannon. New York City. Hannigan, Paula. 2012. (ENG.). 12p. (J). bds. 12.99 *(978-1-4494-1876-2(7))* Andrews McMeel Publishing.

—Safari: A Build & Play Story. Riegelman, Rianna & Accord Publishing Staff. 2012. (ENG.). 10p. (J). (gr. -1-1). bds. 15.99 *(978-1-4494-2191-5(1))* Andrews McMeel Publishing.

Chandler, Terrence. Conflict Resolution in American History, Gr. 8: Lessons from the Past, Lessons for Today. Friedman-Brunt, Elyse. 2003. 48p. (YA). pap., wbk. ed. 19.95 *(978-1-878227-89-8(0))* Peace Education Foundation.

—Conflict Resolution in American History, Grade 8: Lessons from the Past, Lessons for Today. Friedman-Brunt, Elyse. 2003. 200p. pap., instr.'s training gde. ed. 29.95 *(978-1-878227-88-1(2))* Peace Education Foundation.

Chandu & Manu. Draupadi: The Fire-Born Princess. Nagpal, Saraswati. 2013. (Campfire Graphic Novels Ser.: 9). (ENG.). 116p. (YA). (gr. 5-12). pap. 12.99 *(978-93-80741-09-3(X)*, Campfire) Steerforth Pr.

Chaney, Denise & Phillips, Deette. Unraveling: A Coloring Book. 2018. (ENG.). 74p. (YA). (gr. 7-12). pap. 12.00 *(978-0-692-19846-9(6))* Chaney, Denise Ann.

Chang, Angel. Most of the Better Natural Things in the World: (Juvenile Fiction, Nature Book for Kids, Wordless Picture Book) Eggers, Dave. 2019. (ENG.). 52p. (J). (gr. k-3). 17.99 *(978-1-4521-6282-9(4))* Chronicle Bks. LLC.

—When a Kid Like Me Fights Cancer. Stier, Catherine. 2019. 32p. (J). (gr. -1-3). 16.99 *(978-0-8075-6391-5(9)*, 807563919) Whitman, Albert & Co.

Chang, Bernard. Seven Wheels of Power. Barnes, Dawn. 2005. (Black Belt Club Ser.: No. 1). (ENG.). 173p. (J). (gr. 3-6). 17.44 *(978-0-439-63936-1(0))* Scholastic, Inc.

Chang, Chih-Wei. Baby Born, 1 vol. Suen, Anastasia. 2019. Orig. Title: Recien Nacido. (ENG.). 1p. (J). (gr. -1-1). pap. 9.95 ***(978-1-64379-094-7(3)***, 86659254-d0d5-46df-8da2-208c656ef747) Lee & Low Bks., Inc.

—Recién Nacido, 1 vol. Suen, Anastasia. 2019. (SPA.). 24p. (J). (gr. -1-1). pap. 9.95 ***(978-1-64379-099-2(4)***, 2654b436-b070-4b52-b4a2-b5eb486169cc) Lee & Low Bks., Inc.

Chang, Chong. Jin Jin & Rain Wizard. Chang, Grace. 2009. (ENG.). 48p. (J). (gr. -1-3). 16.95 *(978-1-59270-086-8(1))* Enchanted Lion Bks., LLC.

—Jin Jin the Dragon. Chang, Grace. 2008. (ENG.). 48p. (J). (gr. -1-3). 16.95 *(978-1-59270-102-5(7))* Enchanted Lion Bks., LLC.

Chang, Elsa. Despicable Me Little Golden Book. Kaplan, Arie. 2019. (Little Golden Book Ser.). (ENG.). 24p. (J). (gr. -1-2). 4.99 *(978-1-5247-7163-8(5)*, Golden Bks.) Random Hse. Children's Bks.

—Max on the Farm! (the Secret Life of Pets 2) Lewman, David. 2019. (Little Golden Book Ser.). (ENG.). 24p. (J). (-k). 4.99 *(978-1-9848-4994-6(8)*, Golden Bks.) Random Hse. Children's Bks.

—On the Case. 2018. (Sherlock Gnomes Ser.). (ENG.). 16p. (J). (gr. -1-2). pap. 5.99 *(978-1-5344-1430-3(4)*, Simon Spotlight) Simon Spotlight.

Chang, Flora. Sleepyhead. Silver Dolphin Staff. 2017. (ENG.). 10p. (J). (gr. -1 — 1). bds. 7.99 *(978-1-62686-874-8(3)*, Silver Dolphin Bks.) Printers Row Publishing Group.

C

Chang, Michelle. Goldfish & Chrysanthemums. Cheng, Andrea. 2003. (ENG.). 32p. (J). 16.95 *(978-1-58430-057-1(4))*; (gr. 1-3). pap. 10.95 *(978-1-60060-889-6(2)*, 4ce8cb40-bfa1-4bde-b4e5-1bee49f43596) Lee & Low Bks., Inc.

Chang, Pei-Yu. Snow for Everyone! Schneider, Antonie. 2019. (ENG.). 32p. (J). (gr. -1-2). 17.95 *(978-0-7358-4320-2(1))* North-South Bks., Inc.

Chang, Roy. Wuz Da Nite Befo: A Pidgin Christmas Story in Hawaii. Steele, Margaret. 2005. 24p. 10.95 *(978-1-56647-750-5(6))* Mutual Publishing LLC.

Chang, Tara Larsen & Gershman, Jo. Horse Magic - Or Not? Miller, Sibley. 2011. (Wind Dancers Ser.: 12). (ENG.). 80p. (J). (gr. 1-4). pap. 16.99 *(978-0-312-60545-2(5)*, 9780312605452) Feiwel & Friends.

—The Horse Must Go On. Miller, Sibley & Lenhard, Elizabeth. 2008. (Wind Dancers Ser.: 3). (ENG.). 80p. (J). (gr. 1-4). pap. 12.99 *(978-0-312-38282-7(0)*, 9780312382827) Feiwel & Friends.

—A Horse, of Course! Miller, Sibley. 2009. (Wind Dancers Ser.: 7). (ENG.). 80p. (J). (gr. 1-4). pap. 16.99 *(978-0-312-56402-5(3)*, 9780312564025) Feiwel & Friends.

—Horses Her Way. Miller, Sibley. 2009. (Wind Dancers Ser.: 6). (ENG.). 80p. (J). (gr. 1-4). pap. 16.99 *(978-0-312-56279-3(9)*, 9780312562793) Feiwel & Friends.

—Horses' Night Out. Miller, Sibley & Lenhard, Elizabeth. 2008. (Wind Dancers Ser.: 4). (ENG.). 80p. (J). (gr. 1-4). pap. 16.99 *(978-0-312-38283-4(9)*, 9780312382834) Feiwel & Friends.

—Horsey Trails. Miller, Sibley. 2011. (Wind Dancers Ser.: 11). (ENG.). 80p. (J). (gr. 1-4). pap. 16.99 *(978-0-312-60544-5(7)*, 9780312605445) Feiwel & Friends.

—If Wishes Were Horses. Miller, Sibley & Lenhard, Elizabeth. 2008. (Wind Dancers Ser.: 1). (ENG.). 80p. (J). (gr. 1-4). pap. 7.99 *(978-0-312-38280-3(4)*, 9780312382803) Feiwel & Friends.

Chang, Ting. The Helper. Zhu, Caitlyn. Knox-Collins, Ailynn, ed. 2019. (ENG.). 276p. (J). pap. 16.99 ***(978-0-9981849-7-5(7))*** Society of Young Inklings.

Chang, Warren. Encyclopedia Brown & the Case of the Slippery Salamander. Sobol, Donald J. 2003. (Encyclopedia Brown Ser.). 87p. (gr. 3-7). 16.00 *(978-0-7569-1619-0(4))* Perfection Learning Corp.

Changezi, Aisha. The Boy & the Owl: A Story about the Attributes of God Based on the Poem the Creed of Salvation. Mowjood, Siraj. 2015. (ENG.). 24p. (J). (gr. k-3). 17.95 *(978-1-941610-14-5(5))* Fons Vitae of Kentucky, Inc.

Channa, Abdul Malik. The Jinni on the Roof: A Ramadan Story. Rafi, Natasha. 2013. 40p. pap. 10.99 *(978-0-9888649-0-0(8))* Pamir LLC.

Chano, Teresa Ramos, et al. Hansel & Gretel Stories Around the World: 4 Beloved Tales. Meister, Cari. 2016. (Multicultural Fairy Tales Ser.). (ENG.). 32p. (J). (gr. k-2). lib. bdg. 27.99 *(978-1-4795-9706-2(6)*, Picture Window Bks.) Capstone.

—Hansel y Gretel: 4 Cuentos Predilectos de Alrededor Del Mundo. Meister, Cari. 2020. (Cuentos Multiculturales Ser.).Tr. of Hansel & Gretel Stories Around the World. (SPA.). 32p. (J). (gr. k-2). pap. 6.95 *(978-1-5158-6073-0(6)*, 142294); lib. bdg. 27.99 *(978-1-5158-5715-0(8)*, 142076) Capstone. (Picture Window Bks.).

Chano, Teresa Ramos & Madden, Colleen. Multicultural Fairy Tales. Meister, Cari. 2016. (Multicultural Fairy Tales Ser.). (ENG.). 32p. (J). (gr. k-2). lib. bdg., lib. bdg., lib. bdg. 167.94 *(978-1-4795-9707-9(4)*, Picture Window Bks.) Capstone.

Chanoa, Bernat. Fabulous Beekman Boys Present: Polka Spot: My Life in Pictures. 2017. (ENG.). (J). (gr. 3-6). pap. 19.99 *(978-1-948216-56-2(6))* TidalWave.

Chantland, Loren. Daniel Boone. Streissguth, Thomas. 2003. (On My Own Biographies Ser.). 48p. (J). (gr. 1-3). pap. 5.95 *(978-1-57505-532-9(5))* Lerner Publishing Group.

Chao, Alan. Papa's Garage. Hendrix, C. a. 2019. (ENG.). 40p. (J). (gr. k-4). 21.95 *(978-1-63263-778-9(2))* Booklocker.com, Inc.

Chao, Linus. Ali'i Kai. Matsuura, Richard & Matsuura, Ruth. (J). 7.95 *(978-1-887916-05-9(9))* Orchid Isle Publishing Co.

—Angels Masquerading on Earth. Matsuura, Richard & Matsuura, Ruth. (J). 7.95 *(978-1-887916-07-3(5))* Orchid Isle Publishing Co.

—Birthday Wish. Matsuura, Richard & Matsuura, Ruth. (J). 8.95 *(978-1-887916-04-2(0))* Orchid Isle Publishing Co.

—Gift from Santa. Matsuura, Richard & Matsuura, Ruth. (J). 7.95 *(978-1-887916-06-6(7))* Orchid Isle Publishing Co.

—Hawaiian Christmas Story. Matsuura, Richard & Matsuura, Ruth. (J). 8.95 *(978-1-887916-01-1(6))* Orchid Isle Publishing Co.

—Kalani & Primo. Matsuura, Richard & Matsuura, Ruth. (J). 8.95 *(978-1-887916-03-5(2))* Orchid Isle Publishing Co.

Chao, Mimi. In My World. Ma, Jillian. 2017. (ENG.). 36p. (J). (gr. -1-5). pap. 9.95 *(978-1-941765-43-2(2))* Future Horizons, Inc.

Chaperon, Carolyn. Sorial Promise: Book 1 of the Mindforce Saga. Vaughan, Christopher. 2016. (ENG.). (J). pap. 7.99 *(978-0-9863101-4-0(X))* Vaughan, Christopher.

Chaperon, Lison. El Amor Es Bondadoso, 1 vol. Sassi, Laura. 2019. (SPA.). 32p. (J). 15.99 *(978-0-8297-4227-5(1))* Vida Pubs.

—Love Is Kind, 1 vol. Sassi, Laura. 2019. (ENG.). 28p. (J). bds. 9.99 *(978-0-310-75484-8(4))* Zonderkidz.

Chapin, Jimmy, jt. illus. see Craig, Branden Chapin.

Chapin, Patrick. David Goes Fishing. White, James C. 2003. 32p. (J). 6.95 *(978-0-9747752-0-3(7))* White, James C.

Chapin, Patrick O. The Seven Presidents. Giunta, Brian. l.t. ed. 2003. 24p. (J). 8.95 *(978-1-58597-172-5(3))* Leathers Publishing.

Chapman, Cannaday. Feed Your Mind: A Story of August Wilson. Bryant, Jen. 2019. (ENG.). 48p. (J). (gr. 1-4). 17.99 *(978-1-4197-3653-7(1))* Abrams, Inc.

Chapman, Cat. The Best Mum in the World. Chapman, Pat. 2017. 32p. (J). (gr. -1-k). 14.99 *(978-1-927262-80-1(1))* Upstart Pr. NZL. Dist: Independent Pubs. Group.

—The Frog Who Lost His Underpants. MacIver, Juliette. 2014. (ENG.). 32p. (J). (gr. -1-1). 14.99 *(978-0-7636-6782-5(X))* Candlewick Pr.

—Yak & Gnu. MacIver, Juliette. 2015. (ENG.). 32p. (J). (gr. -1-2). 14.99 *(978-0-7636-7561-5(X))* Candlewick Pr.

Chapman, Chris, et al. How to Draw Horses. Smith, Lucy. 2006. (Young Artist Ser.). 32p. (J). (gr. 4-7). pap. 5.99 *(978-0-7945-1368-9(9)*, Usborne); pap. 13.99 *(978-1-58086-969-0(6))* EDC Publishing.

Chapman, David. Dick & Dom's Whoopee Book of Practical Jokes. Wood, Dominic & McCourt, Richard. 2015. (ENG.). 240p. (J). (gr. 4-6). pap. 10.99 *(978-1-4472-8495-6(X))* Pan Macmillan GBR. Dist: Independent Pubs. Group.

Chapman, Debbie. Mommy What Is a Ceo? Harris, Angela L. 2013. 32p. pap. 10.00 *(978-0-615-62527-0(4))* ALHsiccesslines.

Chapman, Frederick T. Big John's Secret. Jewett, Eleanore M. 2nd ed. 2004. (ENG.). 230p. (J). (gr. 7-9). pap. 12.95 *(978-1-883937-89-8(2))* Ignatius Pr.

—Door to the North: A Saga of 14th Century America. Coatsworth, Elizabeth. 2013. (Living History Library). (ENG.). 256p. (J). (gr. 7-9). pap. 15.95 *(978-1-932350-39-5(X))* Ignatius Pr.

—Famous Horses of the Civil War. Downey, Fairfax. 2011. 128p. 40.95 *(978-1-258-00351-7(1))* Literary Licensing, LLC.

—True & Untrue & Other Norse Tales. Undset, Sigrid, ed. 2013. (ENG.). 264p. pap. 16.95 *(978-0-8166-7828-0(6))* Univ. of Minnesota Pr.

—The White Winter: A Story of Scarlet Hill. Meigs, Elizabeth Bleecker. 2011. 208p. 44.95 *(978-1-258-08230-7(6))* Literary Licensing, LLC.

Chapman, Gaye. Incredibilia. Hawthorn, Libby. 2017. (ENG.). 40p. (J). (gr. -1-k). 19.99 *(978-1-76012-525-7(3))* Little Hare Bks. AUS. Dist: Independent Pubs. Group.

—My Sister Olive. Russell, Paula. 2012. (ENG.). 24p. (J). (gr. -1-k). 16.99 *(978-1-921272-88-2(0))* Little Hare Bks. AUS. Dist: Independent Pubs. Group.

Chapman, Gillian. Christmas. Henning, Heather. Bull, Nicola, ed. 2007. (Touch & Feel Ser.). 14p. (J). (gr. -1-3). bds. 10.49 *(978-0-7586-1383-7(0))* Concordia Publishing Hse.

—Creation. Henning, Heather. Bull, Nicola, ed. 2007. (Touch & Feel Ser.). 14p. (J). (gr. -1-3). bds. 10.49 *(978-0-7586-1384-4(9))* Concordia Publishing Hse.

—The Kids Bible. Lane, Leena. 2003. 64p. (J). 10.49 *(978-0-7586-0561-0(7))* Concordia Publishing Hse.

—My First Bible. Lane, Leena. 2005. 252p. (J). (gr. -1). 13.49 *(978-0-7586-0910-6(8))* Concordia Publishing Hse.

Chapman, Jane. Baa! Moo! What Will We Do? Benjamin, A. H. 2020. (Favorite Stories Ser.). (ENG.). 32p. (J). (gr. -1-2). 23.99 *(978-1-68010-195-9(1))* Tiger Tales.

—Bear Can't Sleep. Wilson, Karma. 2018. (Bear Bks.). (ENG.). 40p. (J). (gr. -1-3). 17.99 *(978-1-4814-5973-0(2)*, McElderry, Margaret K. Bks.) McElderry, Margaret K. Bks.

—Bear Counts. Wilson, Karma. 2015. (Bear Bks.). (ENG.). 32p. (J). (gr. -1-2). 17.99 *(978-1-4424-8092-6(0)*, McElderry, Margaret K. Bks.) McElderry, Margaret K. Bks.

—Bear Feels Scared. Wilson, Karma. 2011. (Bear Bks.). (ENG.). 34p. (J). (gr. -1 — 1). bds. 7.99 *(978-1-4424-2755-6(8)*, Little Simon) Little Simon.

—Bear Feels Scared. Wilson, Karma. 2008. (Bear Bks.). (ENG.). 40p. (J). (gr. -1-3). 17.99 *(978-0-689-85986-1(4)*, McElderry, Margaret K. Bks.) McElderry, Margaret K. Bks.

—Bear Feels Sick. Wilson, Karma. 2012. (Bear Bks.). (ENG.). 34p. (J). (gr. -1-2). bds. 7.99 *(978-1-4424-4093-7(7)*, Little Simon) Little Simon.

—Bear Feels Sick. Wilson, Karma. 2007. (Bear Bks.). (ENG.). 40p. (J). (gr. -1-3). 18.99 *(978-0-689-85985-4(6)*, McElderry, Margaret K. Bks.) McElderry, Margaret K. Bks.

Chapman, Jane. Bear Says Thanks. Wilson, Karma. 2020. (Classic Board Bks.). (ENG.). 34p. (J). (gr. -1-k). bds. 7.99 ***(978-1-5344-7418-5(8)***, Little Simon) Little Simon.

Chapman, Jane. Bear Says Thanks. Wilson, Karma. 2012. (Bear Bks.). (ENG.). 40p. (J). (gr. -1-3). 17.99 *(978-1-4169-5856-7(8)*, McElderry, Margaret K. Bks.) McElderry, Margaret K. Bks.

—Bear Sees Colors. Wilson, Karma. 2014. (Bear Bks.). (ENG.). 32p. (J). (gr. -1-3). 17.99 *(978-1-4424-6536-7(0)*, McElderry, Margaret K. Bks.) McElderry, Margaret K. Bks.

—Bear Snores On. Wilson, Karma. 2005. (Bear Bks.). (ENG.). 34p. (J). (gr. -1-k). bds. 7.99 *(978-1-4169-0272-0(4)*, Little Simon) Little Simon.

—Bear Stays up for Christmas. Wilson, Karma. 2011. (Bear Bks.). (ENG.). 34p. (J). (gr. -1 — 1). bds. 7.99 *(978-1-4424-2790-7(6)*, Little Simon) Little Simon.

—Bear Stays up for Christmas. Wilson, Karma. (Bear Bks.). (ENG.). 40p. (J). (gr. -1-3). 2008. 9.99 *(978-1-4169-5896-3(7))*; 2004. 17.99 *(978-0-689-85278-7(9))* McElderry, Margaret K. Bks. (McElderry, Margaret K. Bks.).

—Bear Wants More. Wilson, Karma. 2008. (Bear Bks.). (ENG.). 34p. (J). (gr. -1-2). bds. 7.99 *(978-1-4169-4922-0(4)*, Little Simon) Little Simon.

—Bear Wants More. Wilson, Karma. 2003. (Bear Bks.). (ENG.). 40p. (J). (gr. -1-3). 18.99 *(978-0-689-84509-3(X)*, McElderry, Margaret K. Bks.) McElderry, Margaret K. Bks.

—The Bears in the Bed & the Great Big Storm. Bright, Paul. 2020. (Favorite Stories Ser.). (ENG.). 32p. (J). (gr. -1-2). 23.99 *(978-1-68010-198-0(6))* Tiger Tales.

—Bear's Loose Tooth. Wilson, Karma. 2014. (Bear Bks.). (ENG.). 34p. (J). (gr. -1-k). bds. 7.99 *(978-1-4424-8936-3(7)*, Little Simon) Little Simon.

—Bear's Loose Tooth. Wilson, Karma. 2011. (Bear Bks.). (ENG.). 40p. (J). (gr. -1-3). 17.99 *(978-1-4169-5855-0(X)*, McElderry, Margaret K. Bks.) McElderry, Margaret K. Bks.

—Bear's New Friend. Wilson, Karma. 2009. (Bear Bks.). (ENG.). 34p. (J). (gr. -1-2). bds. 7.99 *(978-1-4169-5438-5(4)*, Little Simon) Little Simon.

—Bear's New Friend. Wilson, Karma. 2006. (Bear Bks.). (ENG.). 40p. (J). (gr. -1-3). 17.99 *(978-0-689-85984-7(8)*, McElderry, Margaret K. Bks.) McElderry, Margaret K. Bks.

—Big Bear Little Bear. Bedford, David. 2005. (Storytime Board Bks.). 18p. (J). (gr. -1-k). bds. 6.95 *(978-1-58925-770-2(7))* Tiger Tales.

—Big Bear, Small Mouse. Wilson, Karma. 2016. (Bear Bks.). (ENG.). 32p. (J). (gr. -1-3). 17.99 *(978-1-4814-5971-6(6)*, McElderry, Margaret K. Bks.) McElderry, Margaret K. Bks.

—Daddy Hug. Warnes, Tim. 2008. (ENG.). 32p. (J). (gr. -1-k). 17.99 *(978-0-06-058950-9(7))* HarperCollins Pubs.

—Don't Be Afraid, Little Pip. Wilson, Karma. 2009. (ENG.). 40p. (J). (gr. -1-2). 19.99 *(978-0-689-85987-8(2)*, McElderry, Margaret K. Bks.) McElderry, Margaret K. Bks.

—Dora's Chicks. Sykes, Julie. 2004. 32p. (J). pap. 6.95 *(978-1-58925-386-5(8))*; (gr. -1-2). 14.95 *(978-1-58925-015-4(X))* Tiger Tales.

—Dora's Eggs. Sykes, Julie. 2007. (Storytime Board Bks.). (J). (gr. -1-3). bds. 6.95 *(978-1-58925-801-3(0))* Tiger Tales.

—Duna y Dan. Jennings, Linda. (SPA.). 28p. (J). (gr. k-1). *(978-84-8418-027-2(1)*, ZZ4481) Zendrera Zariquiey, Editorial ESP. Dist: Lectorum Pubns., Inc.

—The Emperor's Egg Big Book: Read & Wonder Big Book. Jenkins, Martin. 2003. (Read & Wonder Ser.). (ENG.). 32p. (J). (gr. k-12). pap. 27.99 *(978-0-7636-2233-6(8))* Candlewick Pr.

—Goodnight, Ark, 1 vol. Sassi, Laura. (ENG.). (J). 2015. 24p. bds. 8.99 *(978-0-310-74938-7(7))*; 2014. 32p. 16.99 *(978-0-310-73784-1(2))* Zonderkidz.

—Goodnight, Manger, 1 vol. Sassi, Laura. 2015. (ENG.). 32p. (J). 17.99 *(978-0-310-74556-3(X))* Zonderkidz.

—A Long Way from Home. Baguley, Elizabeth. 2008. 32p. (J). (gr. 4-7). 15.95 *(978-1-58925-074-1(5))* Tiger Tales.

—The Magical Snow Garden. Corderoy, Tracey. 2014. (ENG.). 32p. (J). (gr. -1-2). 16.99 *(978-1-58925-162-5(8))* Tiger Tales.

—Mortimer's Christmas Manger. Wilson, Karma. 2007. (ENG.). 40p. (J). (gr. -1-3). 9.99 *(978-1-4169-5049-3(4)*, McElderry, Margaret K. Bks.) McElderry, Margaret K. Bks.

—One Duck Stuck: A Mucky Ducky Counting Book. Root, Phyllis. 2003. 40p. (J). (gr. k-k). pap. 6.99 *(978-0-7636-1566-6(8))* Candlewick Pr.

—One Duck Stuck: A Mucky Ducky Counting Book. Root, Phyllis. 2008. (ENG.). 40p. (J). (gr. k-k). pap. 24.99 *(978-0-7636-3817-7(X))* Candlewick Pr.

—One Tiny Turtle: Read & Wonder. Davies, Nicola. 2005. (Read & Wonder Ser.). (ENG.). 32p. (J). (gr. -1-3). reprint ed. pap. 7.99 *(978-0-7636-2311-1(3))* Candlewick Pr.

—Que Noche Mas Ruidosa! Hendry, Diana. 2003. (SPA.). 28p. (J). (gr. k-2). 16.95 *(978-84-488-0865-5(7)*, BS3550) Beascoa, Ediciones S.A. ESP. Dist: Lectorum Pubns., Inc.

—Silly Dilly Duckling. Freedman, Claire. 2014. (ENG.). 22p. (J). (gr. -1-k). bds. 8.99 *(978-1-58925-578-4(X))* Tiger Tales.

—The Snow Angel. Leeson, Christine. 2016. (ENG.). 32p. (J). (gr. -1-k). mass mkt. 3.99 *(978-1-58925-494-7(5))* Tiger Tales.

—Squish Squash Squeeze! Corderoy, Tracey. 2016. (ENG.). 32p. (J). (gr. -1-2). 16.99 *(978-1-68010-011-2(4))* Tiger Tales.

—Tigress. Dowson, Nick. 2008. (Read, Listen, & Wonder Ser.). (ENG.). 32p. (J). (gr. -1-3). pap. 8.99 *(978-0-7636-3872-6(2))* Candlewick Pr.

—Tigress. Dowson, Nick. 2007. (Read & Wonder Ser.). (ENG.). (J). (gr. -1-3). lib. bdg. 17.60 *(978-1-68065-159-1(5))* Perfection Learning Corp.

—Tigress, Pack. Dowson, Nick. 2008. (Read, Listen, & Wonder Ser.). (ENG.). 32p. (J). (gr. -1-3). pap. 9.99 *(978-0-7636-4189-4(8))* Candlewick Pr.

—Tigress: Read & Wonder. Dowson, Nick. 2007. (Read & Wonder Ser.). (ENG.). 32p. (J). (gr. -1-3). pap. 7.99 *(978-0-7636-3314-1(3))* Candlewick Pr.

—Time to Say Goodnight. Lloyd-Jones, Sally. 2006. (ENG.). 32p. (J). (gr. -1-2). 15.99 *(978-0-06-054328-0(0))* HarperCollins Pubs.

Chapman, Jane. The Very Noisy Night. Hendry, Diana. 2020. (ENG.). 22p. (J). (-k). bds. 9.99 ***(978-1-68010-646-6(5))*** Tiger Tales.

Chapman, Jane. The Very Snowy Christmas. Hendry, Diana. (J). 2013. (ENG.). 16p. (gr. -1-k). bds. 8.95 *(978-1-58925-617-0(4))*; 2007. 32p. pap. 6.95 *(978-1-58925-406-0(6))*; 2005. 32p. (gr. -1-2). 15.95 *(978-1-58925-051-2(6))* Tiger Tales.

—What's in the Egg, Little Pip? Wilson, Karma. 2010. (ENG.). 40p. (J). (gr. -1-3). 18.99 *(978-1-4169-4204-7(1)*, McElderry, Margaret K. Bks.) McElderry, Margaret K. Bks.

—Where Is Home, Little Pip? Wilson, Karma. 2008. (ENG.). 40p. (J). (gr. -1-3). 17.99 *(978-0-689-85983-0(X)*, McElderry, Margaret K. Bks.) McElderry, Margaret K. Bks.

Chapman, Jane. I Love You with All My Heart. Chapman, Jane. 2020. (ENG.). 32p. (J). (gr. -1-2). 17.99 *(978-1-68010-189-8(7))* Tiger Tales.

—Is It Christmas Yet? Chapman, Jane. (ENG.). (J). (gr. -1-k). 2015. 22p. bds. 8.99 *(978-1-58925-553-1(4))*; 2013. 32p. 14.99 *(978-1-58925-149-6(0))* Tiger Tales.

—Me Too, Grandma! Chapman, Jane. 2017. (ENG.). 32p. (J). (gr. -1-2). 16.99 *(978-1-68010-042-6(4))* Tiger Tales.

—No More Cuddles! Chapman, Jane. 2015. (ENG.). 32p. (J). (gr. -1-2). 16.99 *(978-1-58925-195-3(4))* Tiger Tales.

Chapman, Jane. The Snowiest Christmas Ever! Chapman, Jane. (ENG.). (J). 2020. 22p. (-k). bds. 9.99 ***(978-1-68010-635-0(X))***; 2019. 32p. (gr. -1-2). 17.99 *(978-1-68010-157-7(9))* Tiger Tales.

Chapman, Jane. With Your Paw in Mine. Chapman, Jane. 2018. (ENG.). 32p. (J). (gr. -1-2). 16.99 *(978-1-68010-084-6(X))* Tiger Tales.

Chapman, Jane. Baa! Moo! What Will We Do? Chapman, Jane, tr. Benjamin, A. H. 2003. 32p. (J). pap. 6.95 *(978-1-58925-381-0(7))* Tiger Tales.

—I Love My Mama. Chapman, Jane, tr. Kavanagh, Peter. 2003. 32p. (J). 12.95 *(978-1-85430-806-1(8)*, Simon & Schuster Bks. For Young Readers) Simon & Schuster Bks. For Young Readers.

Chapman, Jared. Be Glad Your Dad... (Is Not an Octopus!) Logelin, Matthew & Jensen, Sara. 2016. 48p. (J). (gr. -1-3). 16.99 *(978-0-316-25438-0(X))* Little Brown & Co.

—Codzilla. Zeltser, David. 2019. (ENG.). 40p. (J). (gr. -1-3). 17.99 *(978-0-06-257067-3(6))* HarperCollins Pubs.

—Didi Dodo, Future Spy: Double-O Dodo (Didi Dodo, Future Spy #3) Angleberger, Tom. 2020. (Flytrap Files Ser.). (ENG.). 112p. (J). (gr. 1-4). 12.99 *(978-1-4197-4097-8(0)*, 1259601, Amulet Bks.) Abrams, Inc.

—Didi Dodo, Future Spy: Recipe for Disaster (Didi Dodo, Future Spy #1) Angleberger, Tom. 2019. (Flytrap Files Ser.). (ENG.). (J). (gr. 1-4). 128p. pap. 5.99 *(978-1-4197-3706-0(6)*, 1259503); 112p. 12.99 *(978-1-4197-3370-3(2)*, 1259501) Abrams, Inc. (Amulet Bks.).

—Didi Dodo, Future Spy: Robo-Dodo Rumble (Didi Dodo, Future Spy #2) Angleberger, Tom. (Flytrap Files Ser.). (ENG.). (J). (gr. 1-4). 2020. 128p. pap. 5.99 *(978-1-4197-4117-3(9)*, 1259403); 2019. 112p. 12.99 *(978-1-4197-3688-9(4)*, 1259401) Abrams, Inc. (Amulet Bks.).

—Monster & Mouse Go Camping. Underwood, Deborah. 2018. (ENG.). 32p. (J). (gr. -1-3). 17.99 *(978-0-544-64832-6(3)*, 1621605, HMH Books For Young Readers) Houghton Mifflin Harcourt Publishing Co.

—T. Rex Time Machine. (ENG.). 44p. (J). (gr. -1-k). 2019. 16.99 *(978-1-4521-6155-6(0))*; 2018. 16.99 *(978-1-4521-6154-9(2))* Chronicle Bks. LLC.

—Wordplay. Lehrhaupt, Adam. 2017. 40p. (J). (gr. -1-3). 17.99 *(978-0-545-93428-2(1))* Scholastic, Inc.

Chapman, Jason. Battersea Dogs & Cats Home: I Want a Cat. Hubbard, Ben. ed. 2018. (Battersea Dogs & Cats Home Ser.). 32p. (J). (gr. k-2). pap. 9.99 *(978-1-4451-5070-3(0))*; 16.99 *(978-1-4451-5068-0(9))* Hachette Children's Group GBR. (Franklin Watts). Dist: Hachette Bk. Group.

—Battersea Dogs & Cats Home: I Want a Dog. Hubbard, Ben. ed. 2018. (Battersea Dogs & Cats Home Ser.). 32p. (J). (gr. k-2). pap. 9.99 *(978-1-4451-5067-3(0)*, Franklin Watts) Hachette Children's Group GBR. Dist: Hachette Bk. Group.

Chapman, Jason. Who's That Singing? A Pull-the-Tab Book. Chapman, Jason. 2010. (ENG.). 12p. (J). (gr. -1-1). bds. 9.99 *(978-1-4169-8736-9(3)*, Little Simon) Little Simon.

—Who's That Snoring? A Pull-the-Tab Bedtime Book. Chapman, Jason. 2010. (ENG.). 12p. (J). (gr. -1-1). bds. 9.99 *(978-1-4169-8937-0(4)*, Little Simon) Little Simon.

Chapman, Jenny. The Adventures of Rowdy Squirrel. Chapman, Rebecca. 2017. (ENG.). (J). 23.95 *(978-1-64079-259-3(7))*; pap. 13.95 *(978-1-64079-257-9(0))* Christian Faith Publishing.

Chapman, Jenny. The Magical Midwinter Star. Chapman, Jenny. 2016. (ENG.). 119p. (J). *(978-1-910637-06-7(8))*; (Tales from the Adventures of Algy Ser.: Vol. 3). pap. *(978-1-910637-07-4(6))* An Sithean Pr.

—The Tree with a Golden Heart. Chapman, Jenny. (Tales from the Adventures of Algy Ser.: Vol. 2). (ENG.). (J). (gr. 3-6). 2018. 174p. *(978-1-910637-09-8(2))*; 2017. pap. *(978-1-910637-08-1(4))* An Sithean Pr.

Chapman, Jesse. Skating on Thick Ice. Tobin, Richard K. LeBlanc, Rebecca, ed. 2013. 122p. (J). pap. 12.00 *(978-1-929882-96-0(3))* Biographical Publishing Co.

Chapman, Katriona. Illustrated Treasury of Bible Stories. Blake, Carly & Tig, Thomas. Kelly, Richard, ed. 2017. 384p. (J). 39.95 *(978-1-78617-052-1(3))* Miles Kelly Publishing, Ltd. GBR. Dist: Parkwest Pubns., Inc.

—Jo & Jess Go to the Dentist, 1 vol. Dale, Jay. 2012. (Wonder Words Ser.). (ENG.). 32p. (gr. k-2). pap. 5.99 *(978-1-4296-8912-0(9)*, Capstone Pr.) Capstone.

—The Miracle in Bethlehem: A Storyteller's Tale, 50 vols. Burton, Sarah. (ENG.). 64p. pap. 11.95 *(978-0-86315-663-2(0))* Floris Bks. GBR. Dist: SteinerBooks, Inc.

Chapman, Laura-Kate. The Kite Princess. Bell, Juliet Clare. 2012. 32p. (J). 9.99 *(978-1-84686-830-6(0))* Barefoot Bks., Inc.

Chapman, Lee. Tripper's Travels: An International Scrapbook, 1 vol. Chapman, Nancy Kapp & Chapman, Nancy. 2005. (ENG.). 32p. (J). (gr. 1-5). 16.95 *(978-0-7614-5240-9(0))* Marshall Cavendish Corp.

—Who's Knocking at the Door?, 1 vol. Stevens, Carla & Stevens, Chapman. 2004. (ENG.). 32p. (J). 16.95 *(978-0-7614-5168-6(4))* Marshall Cavendish Corp.

Chapman, Lynne. Bendro Bach. Rix, Jamie. Williams, Dylan, tr. from ENG. 2005. (WEL.). 36p. *(978-1-902416-84-7(8))* Cymdeithas Lyfrau Ceredigion.

—Class One Farmyard Fun. Jarman, Julia. 2018. (Class One, Two & Three Ser.). 32p. (J). (gr. -1-k). pap. 9.99 *(978-1-4449-2716-0(7))* Hachette Children's Group GBR. Dist: Hachette Bk. Group.

—Class Three at Sea. Jarman, Julia. 2008. (ENG.). 32p. (J). (gr. k-3). 16.95 *(978-0-8225-7617-4(1)*, Carolrhoda Bks.) Lerner Publishing Group.

—Class Two at the Zoo. Jarman, Julia. 2007. (Carolrhoda Picture Bks.). (ENG.). 32p. (J). (gr. k-2). 16.95 *(978-0-8225-7132-2(3)*, Carolrhoda Bks.) Lerner Publishing Group.

—Dos Pies Suben, Dos Pies Bajan. Love, Pamela. 2005. (Rookie Reader Español Ser.). (SPA & ESP.). 31p. (J). (gr. k-2). per. 4.95 *(978-0-516-25532-3(0)*, Children's Pr.) Scholastic Library Publishing.

—Dos pies suben, dos pies Bajan: Two Feet up, Two Feet Down. Love, Pamela. 2005. (Rookie Reader Español Ser.). 32p. (gr. k-2). 19.50 *(978-0-516-25252-0(6)*, Children's Pr.) Scholastic Library Publishing.

—Mr Strongmouse & the Baby. Oram, Hiawyn. 2006. (ENG.). 32p. (J). pap. *(978-1-84362-588-9(1)*, Orchard Bks.) Scholastic, Inc.

—The Odds Get Even. Hall, Pam. 2005. 16p. (J). 12.95 *(978-1-58117-216-4(8)*, Intervisual/Piggy Toes) Bendon, Inc.

—Two Feet up, Two Feet Down. Love, Pamela. 2005. (Rookie Reader Español Ser.). (ENG.). 32p. (J). (gr. k-2). pap. 4.95 *(978-0-516-24646-8(1)*, Children's Pr.) Scholastic Library Publishing.

Chapman, Michelle. A Monster in the Attic. Crosby, June. 2011. 16p. pap. 24.95 *(978-1-4560-6959-9(4))* America Star Bks.

Chapman, Neil. The Boy with the Pudding Touch. North, Laura. 2014. (Race Ahead with Reading Ser.). (ENG.). 32p. (J). pap. *(978-0-7787-1364-7(4))* Crabtree Publishing Co.

—Pirate Pete. Benton, Lynne. 2008. (Tadpoles Ser.). (ENG.). 24p. (J). (gr. -1-3). pap. *(978-0-7787-3892-3(2))* Crabtree Publishing Co.

—Toad's Getting Married. Metcalf, Ken. 2016. (ENG.). 66p. (J). pap. *(978-1-86151-463-9(8),* Mereo Bks.) Mereo Bks.

—Treasure Island. Stevenson, Robert Louis. 2004. 320p. (J). *(978-1-4054-3773-8(1))* Parragon, Inc.

Chapman, Pat. The Best Dad in the World. Chapman, Patricia. 2016. 24p. (J). (-k). 14.99 *(978-1-927262-74-0(7))* Upstart Pr. NZL. Dist: Independent Pubs. Group.

Chapman, Richard. Immigration Nation: The American Identity in the Twenty-First Century. Cummings, Judy Dodge. 2019. (Inquire & Investigate Ser.). (ENG.). 128p. (YA). (gr. 7-9). 22.95 *(978-1-61930-760-5(X),* dc4e41a5-23af-47c9-9fc6-aae8bb731877); pap. 17.95 *(978-1-61930-763-6(4),* 5206ed12-5df5-4a32-a323-c039a99f5476) Nomad Pr.

Chapman, Richard, jt. illus. see Dasgupta, Sudipta.

Chapman, Robert. A Gift for Abuelita/Un Regalo para Abuelita: Celebrating the Day of the Dead/En Celebration del Dia de los Muertos. Luenn, Nancy. 2004.Tr. of Un Regalo para Abuelita: En Celebration del Dia de los Muertos. (ENG, SPA & MUL.). 32p. (J). (gr. k-3). 15.95 *(978-0-87358-688-7(3))* Cooper Square Publishing Llc.

Chapman, Robert E. The Boy Who Could See. Carmona, Adela. 2008. 32p. pap. 24.95 *(978-1-60672-697-6(8))* PublishAmerica, Inc.

Chapman, Simon. In the Himalayas. Chapman, Simon. 2005. 103p. (J). lib. bdg. 20.00 *(978-1-4242-0626-1(X))* Fitzgerald Bks.

—In the Jungle. Chapman, Simon. 2005. 116p. (J). lib. bdg. 20.00 *(978-1-4242-0630-8(8))* Fitzgerald Bks.

—On Safari. Chapman, Simon. 2005. 111p. (J). lib. bdg. 20.00 *(978-1-4242-0633-9(2))* Fitzgerald Bks.

—Under the Sea. Chapman, Simon. 2005. 112p. (J). lib. bdg. 20.00 *(978-1-4242-0631-5(6))* Fitzgerald Bks.

Chapman, Susan. Monkey Business. Hood, Sue. 2005. (J). bds. *(978-1-890647-17-9(9))* TOMY International, Inc.

—Why I Praise You, God. Adams, Michelle Medlock. 2006. 20p. (J). (gr. -1). bds. 5.49 *(978-0-7586-0912-0(4))* Concordia Publishing Hse.

Chapman, Susanna. Elizabeth Warren's Big, Bold Plans. Thompson, Laurie Ann. 2020. (ENG.). 40p. (J). (gr. -1-3). 17.99 ***(978-1-5344-7580-9(X),*** Atheneum Bks. for Young Readers) Simon & Schuster Children's Publishing.

Chapman, Susanna. The Girl Who Ran: Bobbi Gibb, the First Woman to Run the Boston Marathon. Poletti, Frances & Yee, Kristina. 2017. (J). *(978-1-943200-47-4(5))* Compendium, Inc., Publishing & Communications.

Chapmanworks Staff. Camping Fun. Parent, Nancy. 2004. (Barbie Glittery Window Bks.). 12p. (J). (gr. -1-1). bds. 4.99 *(978-1-57584-331-5(5),* Reader's Digest Children's Bks.) Studio Fun International.

Chappell, Warren. The Dark Frigate. Hawes, Charles Boardman. 2018. (ENG.). 240p. (gr. 3-7). pap. 7.99 *(978-0-486-82392-8(X))* Dover Pubns., Inc.

—The Extraordinary Education of Johnny Longfoot in His Search for the Magic Hat. Besterman, Catherine. 2011. 160p. 41.95 *(978-1-258-08544-5(5))* Literary Licensing, LLC.

—The Light in the Forest. Richter, Conrad. 2005. (Everyman's Library Children's Classics Ser.). (ENG.). 176p. (J). (gr. 5-7). 15.95 *(978-1-4000-4426-9(X),* Everyman's Library) Knopf Doubleday Publishing Group.

—Wolf Story. McCleery, William. 2012. (ENG.). 88p. (J). (gr. k-4). 15.95 *(978-1-59017-589-7(1),* NYR Children's Collection) New York Review of Bks., Inc., The.

Character Building Studio. Kermit the Brave (Disney Muppet Babies) Shaw, Eric. 2019. (ENG.). 22p. (J). (— 1). bds. 6.99 *(978-0-7364-3980-0(3),* RH/Disney) Random Hse. Children's Bks.

—Super Fabulous! (Disney Muppet Babies) Brown, Robyn. 2019. (ENG.). 22p. (J). (— 1). bds. 6.99 *(978-0-7364-3993-0(5),* RH/Disney) Random Hse. Children's Bks.

Charbonnel, Olivier & Mostyn, David. Santa's Factory. Hooper, Ruth. 2004. 6p. (J). (gr. k-4). reprint ed. 16.00 *(978-0-7567-7585-8(X))* DIANE Publishing Co.

Charest, Travis. X-Men Red Vol. 2: Waging Peace, Vol. 2. 2019. (ENG.). 136p. (YA). (gr. 8-17). pap. 17.99 *(978-1-302-91168-3(6))* Marvel Worldwide, Inc.

Charette, Geraldine. Cyberbullying: And Ctrl Alt Delete It, 1 vol. MacEachern, Robyn. (Lorimer Deal with It Ser.). (ENG.). 32p. (gr. 4-9). 2016. (J). 24.95 *(978-1-55277-496-0(1),* 496); 2008. (YA). pap. 12.95 *(978-1-55277-037-5(0),* 037) James Lorimer & Co. Ltd., Pubs. CAN. Dist: Lerner Publishing Group, Formac Lorimer Bks. Ltd.

Charette, Geraldine, et al. Deal with It Series Bullying & Conflict Resource Guide, 1 vol. Carmichael, Tricia & MacDonald, Allison, eds. 2011. (Lorimer Deal with It Ser.). (ENG.). 104p. (J). (gr. 4-6). 24.95 *(978-1-55277-693-3(X),* 693) James Lorimer & Co. Ltd., Pubs. CAN. Dist: Formac Lorimer Bks. Ltd.

Charko, Kasia. Bats in Trouble, 1 vol. McDowell, Pamela. 2017. (Orca Echoes Ser.). (ENG.). 96p. (J). (gr. 1-3). pap. 6.95 *(978-1-4598-1403-5(7))* Orca Bk. Pubs. USA.

—Cougar Frenzy, 1 vol. McDowell, Pamela. 2019. (Orca Echoes Ser.). (ENG.). 96p. (J). (gr. 1-3). pap. 7.95 *(978-1-4598-2064-7(9))* Orca Bk. Pubs. USA.

—Marsh Island, 1 vol. Bates, Sonya Spreen. 2009. (Orca Echoes Ser.). (ENG.). 64p. (J). (gr. 1-3). pap. 6.95 *(978-1-55469-117-3(6))* Orca Bk. Pubs. USA.

—Ospreys in Danger, 1 vol. McDowell, Pamela. 2014. (Orca Echoes Ser.). (ENG.). 64p. (J). (gr. 1-3). pap. 6.95 *(978-1-4598-0283-4(7))* Orca Bk. Pubs. USA.

—Salamander Rescue, 1 vol. McDowell, Pamela. 2016. (Orca Echoes Ser.). (ENG.). 80p. (J). (gr. 1-3). pap. 7.95 *(978-1-4598-1123-2(2))* Orca Bk. Pubs. USA.

—Sharing Snowy, 1 vol. Helmer, Marilyn. 2008. (Orca Echoes Ser.). (ENG.). 64p. (J). (gr. 1-3). pap. 6.95 *(978-1-55469-021-3(8))* Orca Bk. Pubs. USA.

—Smuggler's Cave, 1 vol. Bates, Sonya. 2010. (Orca Echoes Ser.). (ENG.). 64p. (J). (gr. 1-3). pap. 6.95 *(978-1-55469-308-5(X))* Orca Bk. Pubs. USA.

—Thunder Creek Ranch, 1 vol. Bates, Sonya. 2013. (Orca Echoes Ser.). (ENG.). 64p. (J). (gr. 1-3). pap. 6.95 *(978-1-4598-0112-7(1))* Orca Bk. Pubs. USA.

—Wildcat Run, 1 vol. Bates, Sonya. 2011. (Orca Echoes Ser.). (ENG.). 64p. (J). (gr. 1-3). pap. 6.95 *(978-1-55469-830-1(8))* Orca Bk. Pubs. USA.

Charles, Akins. Zig the Pig Goes to School. Heiney, Sue P. I.t. ed. 2004. 32p. (J). 7.00 *(978-0-9761700-0-6(0))* Zig the Pig.

Charles-Blumenthal, Nelly. Petit Malabar Raconte la Lune, la Terre et le Soleil. Duprat, Jean. 2010. (A. M. Docus Ser.). (FRE.). 72p. (J). *(978-2-226-20927-6(1))* Albin-Michel, Editions.

Charles, Joan. Lost in Lexicon: An Adventure in Words & Numbers. Noyce, Pendred. 2011. (ENG.). 368p. (J). (gr. 3). pap. 12.95 *(978-0-9830219-2-6(9))* Mighty Media Pr.

Charles M. Schulz Creative Associates & Scott, Vicki. Peanuts: Merry Christmas, Charlie Brown: Look & Find. 2018. (Look & Find Ser.). (ENG.). 24p. (J). ***(978-1-5037-3705-1(5),*** adf231df-567d-4eec-ba76-cbb2ce2170d2, p i kids) Phoenix International Publications, Inc.

Charles Robinson. The Happy Prince & Other Tales. Wilde, Oscar. 2012. 84p. pap. 3.47 *(978-1-60386-460-2(1),* Watchmaker Publishing) Wexford College Pr.

Charles Santore. The Velveteen Rabbit (Kohl's Edition) Charles Santore. 2012. (ENG.). 48p. (J). 5.00 *(978-1-60464-032-8(4),* Applesauce Pr.) Cider Mill Pr. Bk. Pubs., LLC.

Charles, Simpson. P'nut Butter & Rubber. Sonnebeyatta, Kemba. 2012. (ENG.). (J). *(978-0-9770904-6-4(9))* Africana Homestead Legacy Pubs., Inc.

Charles, Thoth. Mandela Mindset: Coloring Book 1. Thoth Octave Books. 2019. (Mandela Mindset Ser.: Vol. 1). (ENG.). 44p. (J). pap. 8.59 ***(978-1-6985-5617-8(9))*** Independently Published.

—Mandela Mindset: Coloring Book 2. Thoth Octave Books. 2019. (Mandela Mindset Ser.: Vol. 2). (ENG.). 46p. (J). pap. 8.59 ***(978-1-6985-5735-9(3))*** Independently Published.

—Mandela Mindset: Coloring Book 3. Thoth Octave Books. 2019. (Mandela Mindset Ser.: Vol. 3). (ENG.). 46p. (J). pap. 8.59 ***(978-1-6985-5794-6(9))*** Independently Published.

—Mandela Mindset: Coloring Book 4. Thoth Octave Books. 2019. (Mandela Mindset Ser.: Vol. 4). (ENG.). 46p. (J). pap. 8.59 ***(978-1-6985-5876-9(7))*** Independently Published.

—Mandela Mindset: Coloring Book 5. Thoth Octave Books. 2019. (Mandela Mindset Ser.: Vol. 5). (ENG.). 46p. (J). pap. 6.10 ***(978-1-6986-5472-0(3))*** Independently Published.

Charlip, Remy. Fortunately. Charlip, Remy. 2017. (Classic Board Bks.). (ENG.). 44p. (J). (gr. -1-k). bds. 8.99 *(978-1-5344-0087-0(7),* Little Simon) Little Simon.

Charlip, Remy & Rettenmund, Tamara. Little Old Big Beard & Big Young Little Beard: A Short & Tall Tale, 1 vol. Charlip, Remy. (ENG.). (J). 2006. 300p. (gr. -1-3). pap. 5.95 *(978-0-7614-5288-1(5));* 2003. 32p. 16.95 *(978-0-7614-5142-6(0))* Marshall Cavendish Corp.

Charlotte Hansen. Those are MY Private Parts. Hansen, Diane. 2004. (J). per. *(978-0-9761988-0-2(0))* Hansen, Diane.

Charlotte, J. M. The Little Mermaid Retold. Andersen, Hans. 2013. 48p. 18.00 *(978-0-9895422-0-3(3))* MHC Ministries.

Charlton, Kirk. I Want to Be a Jazz Musician. Charlton, Kirk. 2018. (I Wannabe Ser.: Vol. 2). (ENG.). 52p. (J). pap. 12.95 *(978-1-940734-65-1(7))* May December Pubns. LLC.

—I Want to Be a Marine Biologist. Charlton, Kirk. 2018. (I Wannabe Ser.: Vol. 1). (ENG.). 52p. (J). pap. 12.95 *(978-1-940734-64-4(9))* May December Pubns. LLC.

Charlton, Krik. I Want to Be an Artist. Charlton, Kirk. 2019. (I Wannabe Ser.: Vol. 4). (ENG.). 52p. (J). pap. 12.95 *(978-1-940734-68-2(1))* May December Pubns. LLC.

Charm, Derek, et al. Powerpuff Girls: Power up My Mojo. Mancini, Haley & Goldman, Jake. 2017. (Powerpuff Girls Ser.: 2). (ENG.). 76p. (J). (gr. 4-7). 12.99 *(978-1-63140-871-7(2))* Idea & Design Works, LLC.

Charm, Derek. Star Trek Starfleet Academy. Johnson, Mike & Parrott, Ryan. 2016. (Star Trek Ser.). 120p. pap. 19.99 *(978-1-63140-663-8(9),* 9781631406638) Idea & Design Works, LLC.

Charm, Derek, et al. Star Wars Adventures #1: Better the Devil You Know, Part 1. Scott, Cavan. 2018. (Star Wars Adventures Ser.). (ENG.). 24p. (J). (gr. 4-9). lib. bdg. 27.07 *(978-1-5321-4285-7(4),* 31111, Graphic Novels) Spotlight.

—Star Wars Adventures #6: Rose Knows. Dawson, Delilah S. & Manning, Shaun. 2018. (Star Wars Adventures Ser.). (ENG.). 24p. (J). (gr. 4-9). lib. bdg. 27.07 *(978-1-5321-4290-1(0),* 31116, Graphic Novels) Spotlight.

—Star Wars Adventures Omnibus, Vol. 1. Walker, Landry Q. & Scott, Cavan. 2020. (Star Wars Adventures Omnibus Ser.: 1). (ENG.). 304p. (J). (gr. 4-7). pap. 29.99 *(978-1-68405-328-5(5))* Idea & Design Works, LLC.

—Star Wars Adventures: Tales from Vader's Castle. Scott, Cavan. 2019. (Star Wars Adventures Ser.). (ENG.). 120p. (J). (gr. 2-5). pap. 12.99 *(978-1-68405-407-7(9))* Idea & Design Works, LLC.

—Star Wars Adventures Vol. 1: Heroes of the Galaxy, Vol. 1. Scott, Cavan & Walker, Landry Q. 2017. (Star Wars Adventures Ser.: 1). (ENG.). 80p. (J). (gr. 2-5). pap. 9.99 *(978-1-68405-205-9(X))* Idea & Design Works, LLC.

Charm, Derek. Star Wars Adventures Vol. 2: Unexpected Detour, Vol. 2. Walker, Landry Q. 2018. (Star Wars Adventures Ser.: 2). (ENG.). 80p. (J). (gr. 2-5). pap. 9.99 *(978-1-68405-169-4(X))* Idea & Design Works, LLC.

Charm, Derek, et al. Star Wars Adventures Vol. 3: Endangered. Dawson, Delilah S. & Fisch, Sholly. 2018. (Star Wars Adventures Ser.: 3). (ENG.). 80p. (J). (gr. 2-5). pap. 9.99 *(978-1-68405-249-3(1))* Idea & Design Works, LLC.

Charm, Derek. Star Wars Adventures Vol. 4: Smuggler's Blues. Scott, Cavan et al. 2018. (Star Wars Adventures Ser.: 4). (ENG.). 80p. (J). (gr. 2-5). pap. 9.99 *(978-1-68405-344-5(7))* Idea & Design Works, LLC.

Charm, Derek, et al. Star Wars Adventures Vol. 9: Fight the Empire! Scott, Cavan & Flynn, Ian. 2020. (Star Wars Adventures Ser.: 9). (ENG.). 88p. (J). (gr. 4-7). pap. 9.99 *(978-1-68405-674-3(8))* Idea & Design Works, LLC.

—The Unbeatable Squirrel Girl Vol. 11: Call Your Squirrelfriends. 2019. (Unbeatable Squirrel Girl - 2015 Ser.: 11). 120p. (YA). (gr. 4-17). pap. 15.99 *(978-1-302-91448-6(0))* Marvel Worldwide, Inc.

Charm, Derek. The Unbeatable Squirrel Girl Vol. 12: To All the Squirrels I've Loved Before. 2020. 112p. (YA). (gr. 4-17). pap. 15.99 *(978-1-302-91724-1(2))* Marvel Worldwide, Inc.

Charm, Derek & Mauricet. Star Wars Adventures Vol. 8: Defend the Republic! Dawson, Delilah S. et al. 2020. (Star Wars Adventures Ser.: 8). (ENG.). 72p. (J). (gr. 4-7). pap. 9.99 *(978-1-68405-619-4(5))* Idea & Design Works, LLC.

Charm, Derek & Sommariva, Jon. Star Wars Adventures: Destroyer Down. Beatty, Scott. 2019. (Star Wars Adventures Ser.). (ENG.). 72p. (J). (gr. 4-7). pap. 9.99 *(978-1-68405-509-8(1))* Idea & Design Works, LLC.

Charnick, Tim. God's Zoo. Christian, Focus & Tnt Ministries Staff. 2005. (On the Way Ser.). (ENG.). 96p. (J). per. 17.99 *(978-1-84550-069-6(5),* 6e315646-4128-44fc-9523-c53096e238d8) Christian Focus Pubns. GBR. Dist: Baker & Taylor Publisher Services (BTPS).

Charnley, Dan. 72 Minutes in the Woods. Soar, A. E. 2019. (ENG.). 302p. (J). pap. 11.99 ***(978-1-6920-6210-1(7))*** Independently Published.

Charnoff, Amichai. Prince Long Leggs: Growing Tall. Charnoff, Sam. 2016. (Prince Long Leggs Ser.: Vol. 1). (ENG.). (J). (gr. k-2). 15.00 *(978-0-692-81729-2(8))* Amichai Charnoff.

Charretier, Elsa. Journey to Star Wars: the Rise of Skywalker a Finn & Poe Adventure. Scott, Cavan. 2019. (Choose Your Destiny Chapter Book Ser.). (ENG.). 144p. (J). (gr. 1-3). pap. 5.99 *(978-1-368-04338-0(0),* Disney Lucasfilm Press) Disney Publishing Worldwide.

—Star Wars: A Luke & Leia Adventure. Scott, Cavan. 2018. 137p. (J). *(978-1-5444-1928-2(7),* Disney Lucasfilm Press) Disney Publishing Worldwide.

—Star Wars a Luke & Leia Adventure: A Choose Your Destiny Chapter Book. Scott, Cavan. 2018. (Choose Your Destiny Chapter Book Ser.). (ENG.). 144p. (J). (gr. 1-3). pap. 5.99 *(978-1-368-02424-2(6),* Disney Lucasfilm Press) Disney Publishing Worldwide.

Charretier, Elsa, et al. Star Wars Adventures #2: Better the Devil You Know, Part 2. Scott, Cavan & Charretier, Elsa. Colinet, Pierrick. 2018. (Star Wars Adventures Ser.). (ENG.). 24p. (J). (gr. 4-9). lib. bdg. 27.07 *(978-1-5321-4286-4(2),* 31112, Graphic Novels) Spotlight.

Charretier, Elsa. Star Wars an Obi-Wan & Anakin Adventure: A Choose Your Destiny Chapter Book. Scott, Cavan. 2019. (Choose Your Destiny Chapter Book Ser.). (ENG.). 144p. (J). (gr. 1-3). pap. 5.99 *(978-1-368-04337-3(2),* Disney Lucasfilm Press) Disney Publishing Worldwide.

—Star Wars: Choose Your Destiny (Book 1) a Han & Chewie Adventure. Scott, Cavan. 2018. (Choose Your Destiny Chapter Book Ser.). (ENG.). 144p. (J). (gr. 1-3). pap. 5.99 *(978-1-368-01624-7(3),* Disney Lucasfilm Press) Disney Publishing Worldwide.

—The Unstoppable Wasp: G. I. R. L. Power. 2019. (ENG.). 184p. (J). (gr. 4-7). pap. 12.99 *(978-1-302-91656-5(4))* Marvel Worldwide, Inc.

—The Unstoppable Wasp Vol. 1: Unstoppable! 2017. (ENG.). 136p. (YA). (gr. 8-17). pap. 12.99 *(978-1-302-90646-7(1))* Marvel Worldwide, Inc.

Charretier, Elsa, et al. The Unstoppable Wasp Vol. 2: Agents of G. I. R. L. 2018. (ENG.). 120p. (YA). (gr. 8-17). pap. 15.99 *(978-1-302-90647-4(X))* Marvel Worldwide, Inc.

Charretier, Elsa. Windhaven (Graphic Novel) Martin, George R. R. & Tuttle, Lisa. 2018. (ENG.). 240p. 27.00 *(978-0-553-39366-8(9),* Bantam) Random House Publishing Group.

Charretier, Elsa & Wilson, Megan. Unstoppable! #1. Whitley, Jeremy. 2019. (Unstoppable Wasp Ser.). (ENG.). 24p. (J). (gr. 6-12). lib. bdg. 27.07 *(978-1-5321-4365-6(6),* 31885, Marvel Age) Spotlight.

—Unstoppable! #2. Whitley, Jeremy. 2019. (Unstoppable Wasp Ser.). (ENG.). 24p. (J). (gr. 6-12). lib. bdg. 27.07 *(978-1-5321-4366-3(4),* 31886, Marvel Age) Spotlight.

—Unstoppable! #3. Whitley, Jeremy. 2019. (Unstoppable Wasp Ser.). (ENG.). 24p. (J). (gr. 6-12). lib. bdg. 27.07 *(978-1-5321-4367-0(2),* 31887, Marvel Age) Spotlight.

—Unstoppable! #4. Whitley, Jeremy. 2019. (Unstoppable Wasp Ser.). (ENG.). 24p. (J). (gr. 6-12). lib. bdg. 27.07 *(978-1-5321-4368-7(0),* 31888, Marvel Age) Spotlight.

—The Unstoppable Wasp (Set), 4 vols. Whitley, Jeremy. 2019. (Unstoppable Wasp Ser.). (ENG.). 24p. (J). (gr. 6-12). lib. bdg. 108.28 *(978-1-5321-4364-9(8),* 31884, Marvel Age) Spotlight.

Chartier, Normand. Maine Marmalade. Pochocki, Ethel. 2004. (ENG.). 32p. (J). (gr. k-17). 15.95 *(978-0-89272-558-8(3))* Down East Bks.

—'Til the Cows Come Home. Icenoggle, Jodi. 2010. (ENG.). 32p. (J). (gr. k-2). pap. 9.95 *(978-1-59078-800-4(1))* Boyds Mills Pr.

Chartkoff, Eli. Aschenputtel Coloring Book. Grimm, Wilhelm & Grimm, Jakob. 2019. (ENG.). 54p. (J). pap. 9.99 ***(978-1-7031-2044-8(2))*** Independently Published.

Chartrand, G. Flour Sack Flora, 1 vol. Delaronde, D. L. 2015. (ENG.). 32p. (J). (gr. 2-3). pap. 10.95 *(978-1-894717-05-2(8),* ae2821a7-cb2a-45e0-9457-fa52193d9d81) Pemmican Pubns., Inc. CAN. Dist: Firefly Bks., Ltd.

—Flour Sack Friends, 1 vol. Delaronde, D. L. 2015. (ENG.). 32p. (J). (gr. 2-3). pap. 10.95 *(978-1-894717-18-2(X),* e78f3345-35f8-4a04-a11c-2b02ff5e114d) Pemmican Pubns., Inc. CAN. Dist: Firefly Bks., Ltd.

Chase, Andra. Aloha Potter! - hardcover Book. Talley, Linda. 2004. 30p. (J). *(978-1-55942-200-0(9))* Witcher Productions.

—Ludmila's Way. Talley, Linda. 2003. (J). 17.95 *(978-1-55942-190-4(8))* Witcher Productions.

Chase, Andra. Stanley's "This Is the Life!" Chase, Andra. Rebein, Alyssa Chase. 2008. (J). *(978-1-55942-570-4(9))* Witcher Productions.

Chase, Anita, et al. Tundra Adventures. Chase, Anita et al. 2006. (Adventure Story Collection Ser.). 28p. (J). (gr. 2-6). pap. 10.00 *(978-1-58084-254-9(2))* Lower Kuskokwim Schl. District.

Chase, Janet. The Lady & the Knight. Chase, Janet, . 2019. (ENG.). (J). pap. 9.99 ***(978-1-7340950-2-9(4))*** Harris Publishing, Inc.

Chase, Kit. Little Sweet Pea, God Loves You, 1 vol. 2019. (ENG.). 32p. (J). 15.99 *(978-0-310-76699-5(0))* Zonderkidz.

—You're My Little Sweet Pea, 1 vol. 2019. (ENG.). 16p. (J). bds. 9.99 *(978-0-310-76656-8(7))* Zonderkidz.

Chase, Kit. Oliver's Tree. Chase, Kit. 2014. 32p. (J). (gr. -1-k). 16.99 *(978-0-399-25700-1(4),* G.P. Putnam's Sons Books for Young Readers) Penguin Young Readers Group.

Chase, Linda. Creature or Critter? Griner, Jack. 2005. 107p. (J). per. 12.95 *(978-1-59879-064-1(1))* Lifevest Publishing, Inc.

Chase, Michelle B. & Chase, Tanor R. Las Aventuras de Max, el Camión Volteador: El Mejor Día de Nieve! = the Adventures of Max the Dump Truck: The Greatest Snow Day Ever! Shea, Christine. 2007. (ENG & SPA.). (J). *(978-1-933002-01-9(8))* PublishingWorks.

Chase, Rhoda. The Christmas Reindeer. Burgess, Thornton W. 2013. (Dover Children's Classics Ser.). (ENG.). 152p. (J). (gr. k-3). pap. 5.99 *(978-0-486-49153-0(6))* Dover Pubns., Inc.

Chase, Rhoda C. The Sandman's Hour - Stories for Bedtime. Walker, Abbie Phillips. Pogue, Kaye, ed. 2018. (ENG.). 124p. (J). pap. 6.20 *(978-1-7287-3885-7(7))* Independently Published.

Chase, Tanor R., jt. illus. see Chase, Michelle B.

Chast, Roz. No Fair! No Fair! And Other Jolly Poems of Childhood. Trillin, Calvin. 2016. (ENG.). 40p. (J). (gr. -1-3). 17.99 *(978-0-545-82578-8(4),* Orchard Bks.) Scholastic, Inc.

Chast, Roz. Around the Clock. Chast, Roz. 2015. (ENG.). 32p. (J). (gr. -1-3). 18.99 *(978-1-4169-8476-4(3),* Atheneum Bks. for Young Readers) Simon & Schuster Children's Publishing.

—Marco Goes to School. Chast, Roz. 2012. (ENG.). 32p. (J). (gr. -1-3). 16.99 *(978-1-4169-8475-7(5),* Atheneum Bks. for Young Readers) Simon & Schuster Children's Publishing.

—Too Busy Marco. Chast, Roz. 2010. (ENG.). 32p. (J). (gr. -1-3). 16.99 *(978-1-4169-8474-0(7),* Atheneum Bks. for Young Readers) Simon & Schuster Children's Publishing.

Chast, Roz & Feiffer, Jules. Nursery Rhyme Comics: 50 Timeless Rhymes from 50 Celebrated Cartoonists. Various Authors Staff. Davis, Vanessa, ed. 2011. (ENG.). 128p. (J). (gr. -1-3). 21.99 *(978-1-59643-600-8(X),* 900065610, First Second Bks.) Roaring Brook Pr.

Chastain, Madye Lee. The Cow-Tail Switch: And Other West African Stories. Courlander, Harold & Herzog, George. 2008. (ENG.). 160p. (J). (gr. 3-7). pap. 10.99 *(978-0-312-38006-9(2),* 900050529) Square Fish.

Chatel, Kim, photos by. A Talent for Quiet. Chatel, Kim. 2009. 32p. pap. 10.95 *(978-1-935137-56-6(5))* Guardian Angel Publishing, Inc.

Chatelain, Éva. A Squirmy, Wormy Surprise. Meyerhoff, Jenny. 2017. (Friendship Garden Ser.: 6). (ENG.). 128p. (J). (gr. 2-5). 16.99 *(978-1-4814-7055-1(8));* pap. 5.99 *(978-1-4814-7054-4(X))* Simon & Schuster Children's Publishing. (Aladdin).

—Sweet Peas & Honeybees. Meyerhoff, Jenny. 2016. (Friendship Garden Ser.: 4). (ENG.). 128p. (J). (gr. 2-5). pap. 5.99 *(978-1-4814-3917-6(0),* Aladdin) Simon & Schuster Children's Publishing.

Chatelain, Éva & Chatelain, Éva. Green Thumbs-Up! Meyerhoff, Jenny. 2015. (Friendship Garden Ser.: 1). (ENG.). 176p. (J). (gr. 2-5). pap. 6.99 *(978-1-4814-3904-6(9),* Aladdin) Simon & Schuster Children's Publishing.

—Project Peep. Meyerhoff, Jenny. 2016. (Friendship Garden Ser.: 3). (ENG.). 144p. (J). (gr. 2-5). pap. 5.99 *(978-1-4814-3913-8(8),* Aladdin) Simon & Schuster Children's Publishing.

—Pumpkin Spice. Meyerhoff, Jenny. 2015. (Friendship Garden Ser.: 2). (ENG.). 144p. (J). (gr. 2-5). pap. 5.99 *(978-1-4814-3909-1(X),* Aladdin) Simon & Schuster Children's Publishing.

Chatelain, Éva, jt. illus. see Chatelain, Éva.

Chater, Mack. Buried in Rubble: True Stories of Surviving Earthquakes. Collins, Terry. 2015. (True Stories of Survival Ser.). (ENG.). 32p. (J). (gr. 3-9). lib. bdg. 31.32 *(978-1-4914-6570-7(0),* Capstone Pr.) Capstone.

Chater, Mack, et al. True Stories of Survival. Yomtov, Nel. 2015. (True Stories of Survival Ser.). (ENG.). 32p. (J). (gr. 3-9). 125.28 *(978-1-4914-6915-6(3),* 22969, Capstone Pr.) Capstone.

Chatham, Dennis J. Professor Rock Ltd. Hatch Jr., B. J. Butch. 2003. 32p. (J). 14.95 *(978-1-56167-808-2(2))* American Literary Pr.

Chatmon, Tayliyah. Tidy Tessa. Goldson, Cpo. 2018. (ENG.). 28p. (J). pap. 10.99 *(978-0-692-18566-7(6))* Restore Order Professional Organizing.

C

Chatterjee, Madly. The Children of Slowville Activity Book: Activity & Colouring Book Bilingual English/French. Chatterjee, Madly. 2019. (Children of Slowville Ser.). (ENG.). 44p. (J). (gr. 1-3). pap. 9.95 ***(978-1-9160491-2-3(5))*** Peacock Tree Publishing.

—The Children of Slowville Book 2: Les Enfants de Slowville Tome 2. Chatterjee, Madly. 2019. (Book Ser.: Vol. 2). (ENG.). 46p. (J). (gr. 1-3). pap. 10.95 ***(978-1-7257-7657-9(X))*** Peacock Tree Publishing.

Chatterjee, Pratyush, jt. illus. see Chatterjee, Rituparna.

Chatterjee, Rituparna & Chatterjee, Pratyush. Anabelle y Las Migajas: A-Doo-Run-Run. Wachs, Greg. 2019. (SPA.). 42p. (J). pap. 9.95 ***(978-1-0767-8581-7(6))*** Independently Published.

Chatterjee, Somnath. Dev & Ollie: Camel Caper. Aggarwal, Shweta. 2017. (ENG.). 34p. (J). pap. ***(978-0-9932328-2-4(5))*** Curious Minds Pr. Ltd.

Chatterjee, Susnata. The Children's Garden. Talwar, Ankoor & Talwar, Abhinav. 2009. 32p. pap. 16.49 *(978-1-4389-9309-6(9))* AuthorHouse.

Chatterji, Somnath. I Am Tan! Denise, Carolyn. 2012. (ENG.). 18p. (J). (gr. -1-3). pap. 19.95 *(978-0-9835651-3-0(9))* Levi Bass Publishing.

—I Can Do It Myself! Denise, Carolyn. 2012. (ENG.). 16p. (J). (gr. -1-3). pap. 19.95 *(978-0-9835651-4-7(7))* Levi Bass Publishing.

Chatterley, Cedric N., photos by. Sokita Celebrates the New Year: A Cambodian American Holiday. Lau, Barbara & Nesbitt, Kris. 2004. 32p. (J). per. 9.95 *(978-0-9747456-0-2(X))* Greensboro Historical Museum, Inc.

Chatterley, Patricia. Callon: Educational. Donohoe, Honor. 2017. (Circular Wood Ser.: Vol. 1). (ENG.). 66p. (J). (gr. 2-4). pap. *(978-1-912521-00-5(8))* Cahar Pubns.

Chatterton, Ann, jt. illus. see Chatterton, Martin.

Chatterton, Chris. All the Fun Winter Things #4. Perl, Erica S. 2019. (Arnold & Louise Ser.). (ENG.). 64p. (J). (gr. 1-3). 6.99 *(978-1-5247-9048-6(6),* Penguin Workshop) Penguin Young Readers Group.

—CRASH! BOOM! a Math Tale. Harris, Robie H. 2018. (ENG.). 32p. (J). (-k). 15.99 *(978-0-7636-7827-2(9))* Candlewick Pr.

—The Digger Disaster. Impey, Rose. 2017. 24p. (J). pap. 9.99 *(978-1-4088-7244-4(7),* 9781408872444, Bloomsbury Children's Bks.) Bloomsbury Publishing USA.

—Fruit on a Stick. Schmauss, Judy Kentor. 2015. (Early Rising Readers Ser.). (J). (gr. -1-k). 5.83 *(978-1-4788-1589-1(2))* Newmark Learning LLC.

—Frutas en un Pincho. Schmauss, Judy Kentor. 2016. (Early Rising Readers Ser.). (SPA.). (J). (gr. -1). 6.67 *(978-1-4788-3674-2(1))* Newmark Learning LLC.

—The Great Louweezie #1. Perl, Erica S. 2019. (Arnold & Louise Ser.: 1). (ENG.). 64p. (J). (gr. 1-3). 6.99 *(978-1-5247-9039-4(7));* lib. bdg. 15.99 *(978-1-5247-9040-0(0))* Penguin Young Readers Group. (Penguin Workshop).

—Happy Fell #3. Perl, Erica S. 2019. (Arnold & Louise Ser.: 3). (ENG.). 64p. (J). (gr. 1-3). 6.99 *(978-1-5247-9045-5(1),* Penguin Workshop) Penguin Young Readers Group.

—Lost & Found #2. Perl, Erica S. 2019. (Arnold & Louise Ser.: 2). (ENG.). 64p. (J). (gr. 1-3). 6.99 *(978-1-5247-9042-4(7));* lib. bdg. 15.99 *(978-1-5247-9043-1(5))* Penguin Young Readers Group. (Penguin Workshop).

—Now I Am 3! Brown, Ruby. 2016. (ENG.). 24p. (J). (gr. -1 — 1). 19.99 *(978-1-76012-332-1(3))* Hardie Grant Egmont Pty, Ltd. AUS. Dist: Independent Pubs. Group.

—Now What? a Math Tale. Harris, Robie H. 2019. 32p. (J). (-k). 15.99 *(978-0-7636-7828-9(7))* Candlewick Pr.

Chatterton, Chris. The Princess Rules (the Princess Rules) Gregory, Philippa. 2020. (Princess Rules Ser.). (ENG.). 256p. (J). 6.99 ***(978-0-00-838831-7(8),*** HarperCollins Children's Bks.) HarperCollins Pubs. Ltd. GBR. Dist: HarperCollins Pubs.

Chatterton, Chris. There's a Bison Bouncing on the Bed! Bright, Paul. 2016. (ENG.). 32p. (J). (gr. -1-2). 16.99 *(978-1-68010-006-8(8))* Tiger Tales.

Chatterton, Chris, jt. illus. see Guillain, Charlotte.

Chatterton, Martin. Danny Dreadnought Saves the World. Emmett, Jonathan. 2016. (Reading Ladder Ser.). (ENG.). 48p. (J). (gr. k-2). pap. 7.99 *(978-1-4052-8219-2(3))* Egmont Bks., Ltd. GBR. Dist: Independent Pubs. Group.

—The Emperor's New Clones. Emmett, Jonathan. 2nd ed. 2016. (Reading Ladder Ser.). (ENG.). 48p. (J). (gr. k-2). pap. 7.99 *(978-1-4052-8252-9(5))* Egmont Bks., Ltd. GBR. Dist: Independent Pubs. Group.

—The Mummy Family Find Fame. Bradman, Tony. 2nd ed. 2016. (Reading Ladder Ser.). (ENG.). 48p. (J). (gr. k-2). pap. 7.99 *(978-1-4052-8241-3(X))* Egmont Bks., Ltd. GBR. Dist: Independent Pubs. Group.

—My First Thesaurus. Beal, George. 2019. (Kingfisher First Reference Ser.). (ENG.). 144p. (J). pap. 10.99 *(978-0-7534-7480-8(8),* 900196731, Kingfisher) Roaring Brook Pr.

—Prince Albert's Birthday. Clarke, Jane. 2005. 24p. (J). lib. bdg. 23.65 *(978-1-59646-748-4(7))* Dingles & Co.

—Technoslime Terror! Griffiths, Mark. 2013. (ENG.). 288p. (J). pap. 6.99 *(978-0-85707-537-6(3),* Simon & Schuster Children's) Simon & Schuster, Ltd. GBR. Dist: Simon & Schuster, Inc.

—Weava the Wilful Witch. Mandrake, Tiffany. 2011. (Little Horrors Ser.: 6). (ENG.). 112p. (J). (gr. 2-4). pap. 7.99 *(978-1-921714-02-3(6))* Little Hare Bks. AUS. Dist: Independent Pubs. Group.

Chatterton, Martin. The Surprise Party. Chatterton, Martin. Bradman, Tony. 2005. (Red Bananas Ser.). (ENG.). 48p. (J). lib. bdg. *(978-0-7787-1068-4(8))* Crabtree Publishing Co.

Chatterton, Martin & Chatterton, Ann. Stranger from Somewhere in Time. McBratney, Sam. 2004. (Yellow Bananas Ser.). (ENG.). (J). (gr. 3-4). lib. bdg. 16.05 *(978-0-7569-1510-0(4))* Perfection Learning Corp.

Chatterton, Martin, jt. illus. see Trimmer, Tony.

Chatzikonstantinou, Danny. Humpty Dumpty Flip-Side Rhymes. Harbo, Christopher L. 2015. (Flip-Side Nursery Rhymes Ser.). (ENG.). 24p. (J). (gr. -1-2). lib. bdg. 27.99 *(978-1-4795-5986-2(5),* Picture Window Bks.) Capstone.

—Little Bo Peep Flip-Side Rhymes. Harbo, Christopher L. 2015. (Flip-Side Nursery Rhymes Ser.). (ENG.). 24p. (J). (gr. -1-2). lib. bdg. 27.99 *(978-1-4795-5989-3(X),* Picture Window Bks.) Capstone.

—My Grandma's a Ninja. Tarpley, Todd. 2015. 40p. (J). 17.95 *(978-0-7358-4199-4(3))* North-South Bks., Inc.

—Officer Katz & Houndini: A Tale of Two Tails. Gianferrari, Maria. 2016. (ENG.). 32p. (J). (gr. -1-2). 17.99 *(978-1-4814-2265-9(0),* Aladdin) Simon & Schuster Children's Publishing.

Chatzikonstantinou, Danny & Jack, Colin. Flip-Side Nursery Rhymes. Harbo, Christopher. 2015. (Flip-Side Nursery Rhymes Ser.). (ENG.). (J). (gr. -1-2). 103.80 *(978-1-4795-6023-3(5),* Picture Window Bks.) Capstone.

Chatzikonstantinou, Danny, jt. illus. see Jack, Colin.

Chau, Alina. Lunar New Year. Eliot, Hannah. 2018. (Celebrate the World Ser.). (ENG.). 24p. (J). (gr. -1 — 1). bds. 8.99 *(978-1-5344-3303-8(1),* Little Simon) Little Simon.

—The Nian Monster. Wang, Andrea. 2016. (ENG.). 32p. (J). (gr. -1-3). 16.99 *(978-0-8075-5642-9(4),* 807556424) Whitman, Albert & Co.

—The Treehouse Heroes: The Forgotten Beast. Amara, Phil. 2012. (ENG.). 36p. (J). (gr. -1-3). 15.95 *(978-1-59702-034-3(6))* Immedium.

Chau, Alina, et al. The World Is Yours (Disney Princess) Roth, Megan. 2020. (ENG.). 32p. (J). (gr. -1-2). 10.99 ***(978-0-7364-4080-6(1),*** RH/Disney) Random Hse. Children's Bks.

Chau, Alina. The Year of the Sheep. Chin, Oliver. 2014. (Tales from the Chinese Zodiac Ser.: 10). (ENG.). 36p. (J). (gr. -1-3). 15.95 *(978-1-59702-104-3(0))* Immedium.

Chau, Annie. Lawnteel at Home. Maccaull, Angus. 2016. (ENG.). (J). pap. *(978-0-9949240-4-9(6))* Outside the Lines Pr.

Chau, Annie. Lawnteel at School. Maccaull, Angus. 2019. (ENG.). 40p. (J). pap. ***(978-0-9958692-9-5(4))*** Outside the Lines Pr.

Chau, Annie. Lawnteel at the Store. Maccaull, Angus. 2015. (ENG.). (J). pap. *(978-0-9949240-2-5(X))* Outside the Lines Pr.

Chau, Ming, photos by. Walking on Solid Ground. Cheung, Shu Pui et al. Wei, Deborah & Kodish, Debora, eds. 2004. (ENG & CHI., 64p. (J). pap. 12.95 *(978-0-9644937-4-2(8),* 09644937-4-8) Philadelphia Folklore Project.

Chaud, Benjamin. La Fée Coquillette et le Concours de Fées. Levy, Didier. 2010. (A. M. Alb. Ill. C. Ser.). (FRE.). 34p. (J). *(978-2-226-20709-8(0))* Albin-Michel, Editions.

—La Fée Coquillette Mène L'Enquête. Levy, Didier. 2010. (A. M. Alb. Ill. C. Ser.). (FRE.). 32p. (J). *(978-2-226-20953-5(0))* Albin-Michel, Editions.

—Pomelo Begins to Grow. Badescu, Ramona. 2011. (Pomelo the Garden Elephant Ser.). (ENG.). 48p. (J). (gr. -1-2). 16.95 *(978-1-59270-111-7(6))* Enchanted Lion Bks., LLC.

—Pomelo Est Amoureux. Badescu, Ramona. 2003. (A. M. Alb. Ill. C. Ser.). (FRE.). 88p. (J). *(978-2-226-14070-8(0))* Albin-Michel, Editions.

—Pomelo Explores Color. Badescu, Ramona. 2012. (Pomelo the Garden Elephant Ser.). (ENG.). 120p. (J). (gr. -1). 15.95 *(978-1-59270-126-1(4))* Enchanted Lion Bks., LLC.

—Pomelo Grandit. Badescu, Ramona. 2010. (A. M. Alb. Ill. C. Ser.). (FRE.). 42p. (J). *(978-2-226-19566-1(1))* Albin-Michel, Editions.

—Pomelo Se Demande. Badescu, Ramona. 2006. (A. M. Alb. Ill. C. Ser.). (FRE.). 88p. (J). *(978-2-226-14942-8(2))* Albin-Michel, Editions.

—Pomelo's Big Adventure. Badescu, Ramona. 2014. (Pomelo the Garden Elephant Ser.). 40p. (J). (gr. -1-3). 17.95 *(978-1-59270-158-2(2))* Enchanted Lion Bks., LLC.

—Pomelo's Opposites. Badescu, Ramona. 2013. (Pomelo the Garden Elephant Ser.). (ENG.). 120p. (J). 15.95 *(978-1-59270-132-2(9))* Enchanted Lion Bks., LLC.

Chaudhary, Aman. Mo Smells Sweet Dreams: A Scentsational Journey. Hyde, Margaret E. 2012. (Mo's Nose Ser.). (ENG.). 24p. (J). (-k). 17.95 *(978-0-9816255-8-4(4))* Mo's Nose, LLC.

—Mo Smells the Ballpark. Hyde, Margaret. 2014. 24p. (J). (gr. -1-k). 14.95 *(978-1-62873-668-7(2),* Sky Pony Pr.) Skyhorse Publishing Co., Inc.

Chaudhary, Somak. When I'm Older. Flory, Neil. 2018. (ENG.). 32p. (J). (gr. -1-1). 17.99 *(978-1-76029-632-2(5))* Allen & Unwin AUS. Dist: Independent Pubs. Group.

Chauffrey, Celia. Little Red Riding Hood. Don, Lari. 2019. (ENG.). 32p. (J). (gr. -1-2). pap. *(978-1-78285-413-5(4))* Barefoot Bks., Ltd.

Chauffrey, Célia. The Nutcracker. Maccarone, Grace. 2016. (ENG.). 40p. (J). (gr. -1-3). 17.99 *(978-1-4998-0281-8(1))* Little Bee Books Inc.

Chauffrey, Celia. Peter & the Moon, 1 vol. Briere-Haquet, Alice. 2012. (Big Picture Book Ser.). (ENG.). 48p. (J). (gr. k). 16.95 *(978-2-7338-1940-1(2))* Auzou, Philippe Editions FRA. Dist: Consortium Bk. Sales & Distribution.

Chauffrey, Celia. Little Red Riding Hood. Chauffrey, Celia. Don, Lari & Staunton, Imelda. 2012. 32p. (J). (gr. -1-3). 9.99 *(978-1-84686-768-2(1));* 16.99 *(978-1-84686-766-8(5))* Barefoot Bks., Inc.

Chauvin, D. & Uderzo, M. The Falklands War. Rideau, J. & Asso, B. 2011. (Cinebook Recounts Ser.). (ENG.). 48p. pap. 11.95 *(978-1-84918-056-6(3))* CineBook GBR. Dist: National Bk. Network.

Chauvin, Daniel & Uderzo, Marcel. Biggles Recounts the Falklands War: Volume 1. Asso, Bernard & Rideau, Joel. 2007. (ENG.). 48p. per. 9.99 *(978-1-905460-22-9(8))* CineBook GBR. Dist: National Bk. Network.

Chavarri, Elisa. Fairly Fairy Tales. Codell, Esmé Raji. 2011. (ENG.). 32p. (J). (gr. -1-3). 18.99 *(978-1-4169-9086-4(0),* Aladdin) Simon & Schuster Children's Publishing.

—Fly Blanky Fly. Lewis, Anne Margaret. 2012. (ENG.). 40p. (J). (gr. -1-2). 16.99 *(978-0-06-199996-3(2))* HarperCollins Pubs.

—Maybe Mother Goose. Codell, Esmé Raji. 2016. (ENG.). 32p. (J). (gr. -1-3). 17.99 *(978-1-4814-4036-3(5),* Aladdin) Simon & Schuster Children's Publishing.

—Rainbow Weaver/Tejedora del Arcoíris. Marshall, Linda Elovitz. ed. 2016. (ENG & SPA.). 40p. (J). (gr. 1-4). 19.95 *(978-0-89239-374-9(2))* Lee & Low Bks., Inc.

Chaveevah, Banks Ferguson. Good Morning Lovey! Hickey, Joshalyn M. 2005. (ENG.). 28p. (J). 12.00 *(978-0-9718939-3-1(4))* BaHar Publishing, L.C.

Chaves, Guido. La Cucarachita Martina. Gonzalez, Ana Carlota. 2015. 24p. (J). (gr. -1-2). pap. 12.95 *(978-9942-05-769-3(2),* Alfaguara Infantil) Santillana Ecuador ECU. Dist: Santillana USA Publishing Co., Inc.

—La Cucarachita Martina. Carlota Gonzalez, Ana. 2015. (Serie Verde / Album Ilustrado Ser.). (SPA.). 24p. (J). pap. 12.95 *(978-9942-19-330-8(8))* Santillana USA Publishing Co., Inc.

—Martina, Las Estrellas y un Cachito de Luna. Iturralde, Edna. 2015. 24p. (J). (gr. -1-2). pap. 12.95 *(978-9942-05-068-7(X),* Alfaguara Infantil) Santillana Ecuador ECU. Dist: Santillana USA Publishing Co., Inc.

Chavez, Diego. Sometimes We Do. Moses, Omowale. 2019. (MathTalk Ser.). (ENG.). 32p. (J). (gr. -1-k). 16.95 *(978-1-943431-47-2(7))* Tumblehome Learning.

Chavez, Karina. El Monstruo Que No Pod�a Asustar. Silva, J. M. 2019. (SPA.). 38p. (J). pap. 9.98 ***(978-1-6908-7946-6(7))*** Independently Published.

Chavez, Karina. Pily y Su Miedo a la Oscuridad. Silva, J. M. 2019. (SPA.). 30p. (J). pap. 9.98 *(978-1-0975-0573-9(1))* Independently Published.

Chawla, Neena. Bear Claws. Scheunemann, Pam. 2006. (Fact & Fiction Ser.). 24p. (J). pap. 48.42 *(978-1-59679-926-4(9));* (ENG.). lib. bdg. 27.07 *(978-1-59679-925-7(0),* 2721, SandCastle) ABDO Publishing Co.

—Cat Tails. Scheunemann, Pam. 2006. (Fact & Fiction Ser.). 24p. (J). pap. 48.42 *(978-1-59679-928-8(5));* (ENG.). lib. bdg. 27.07 *(978-1-59679-927-1(7),* 2723, SandCastle) ABDO Publishing Co.

—Crocodile Tears, 1 vol. Scheunemann, Pam. 2006. (Critter Chronicles Ser.). (ENG.). 24p. (J). (gr. k-3). lib. bdg. 27.07 *(978-1-59928-436-1(7),* 4968, SandCastle) ABDO Publishing Co.

—Goldfish Bowl, 1 vol. Salzmann, Mary Elizabeth. 2006. (Animal Tales Ser.). (ENG.). 24p. (J). (gr. k-3). lib. bdg. 27.07 *(978-1-59679-939-4(0),* 2735, SandCastle) ABDO Publishing Co.

—Goldfish Bowl (6-pack) Salzmann, Mary Elizabeth. 2006. (Fact & Fiction Ser.). 24p. (J). pap. 59.57 *(978-1-59679-940-0(4))* ABDO Publishing Co.

—Homing Pigeon, 1 vol. Doudna, Kelly. 2006. (Critter Chronicles Ser.). (ENG.). 24p. (J). (gr. k-3). lib. bdg. 27.07 *(978-1-59928-440-8(5),* 4972, SandCastle) ABDO Publishing Co.

—Jellyfish Role, 1 vol. Doudna, Kelly. 2006. (Critter Chronicles Ser.). (ENG.). 24p. (J). (gr. k-3). lib. bdg. 27.07 *(978-1-59928-446-0(4),* 4978, SandCastle) ABDO Publishing Co.

—Lamb Chops. Doudna, Kelly. 2006. (Fact & Fiction Ser.). 24p. (J). pap. 48.42 *(978-1-59679-948-6(X));* (ENG.). lib. bdg. 27.07 *(978-1-59679-947-9(1),* 2743, SandCastle) ABDO Publishing Co.

—La Lana de la Oveja. Doudna, Kelly. 2006. (Cuentos de Animales Ser.).Tr. of Lamb Chops. (SPA.). 24p. (J). (gr. k-3). lib. bdg. 27.07 *(978-1-59928-661-7(0),* 5012, SandCastle) ABDO Publishing Co.

—Leaping Lizards, 1 vol. Salzmann, Mary Elizabeth. 2006. (Critter Chronicles Ser.). (ENG.). 24p. (J). (gr. k-3). lib. bdg. 27.07 *(978-1-59928-450-7(2),* 4982, SandCastle) ABDO Publishing Co.

—Monarch Butterfly, 1 vol. Kompelien, Tracy. 2006. (Critter Chronicles Ser.). (ENG.). 24p. (J). (gr. k-3). lib. bdg. 27.07 *(978-1-59928-454-5(5),* 4986, SandCastle) ABDO Publishing Co.

—Monkey Business. Hanson, Anders. 2006. (Fact & Fiction Ser.). 24p. (J). pap. 48.42 *(978-1-59679-952-3(8));* (ENG.). lib. bdg. 27.07 *(978-1-59679-951-6(X),* 2747, SandCastle) ABDO Publishing Co.

—Pack Rat. Doudna, Kelly. 2006. (Fact & Fiction Ser.). 24p. (J). pap. 48.42 *(978-1-59679-956-1(0));* (ENG.). lib. bdg. 27.07 *(978-1-59679-955-4(2),* 2751, SandCastle) ABDO Publishing Co.

—Peacock Fan, 1 vol. Scheunemann, Pam. 2006. (Critter Chronicles Ser.). (ENG.). 24p. (J). (gr. k-3). lib. bdg. 27.07 *(978-1-59928-460-6(X),* 4992, SandCastle) ABDO Publishing Co.

—Penguin Suit. Doudna, Kelly. 2006. (Fact & Fiction Ser.). 24p. (J). pap. 48.42 *(978-1-59679-958-5(7));* (ENG.). lib. bdg. 27.07 *(978-1-59679-957-8(9),* 2753, SandCastle) ABDO Publishing Co.

—Squirrel Hollow. Doudna, Kelly. 2006. (Fact & Fiction Ser.). 24p. (J). pap. 48.42 *(978-1-59679-968-4(4));* (ENG.). lib. bdg. 27.07 *(978-1-59679-967-7(6),* 2763, SandCastle) ABDO Publishing Co.

Chayamachi, Suguro. Devil May Cry, No. 3. Chayamachi, Suguro. 2005. 168p. pap. 9.99 *(978-1-59816-031-4(1))* TOKYOPOP, Inc.

Chayka, Doug. Four Feet, Two Sandals. Williams, Karen Lynn & Mohammad, Khadra. rev. ed. 2016. 32p. (gr. 2-5). 18.70 *(978-0-8028-5296-0(3))* Kendall Hunt Publishing Co.

—The Secret Shofar of Barcelona. Greene, Jacqueline Dembar. 2009. (High Holidays Ser.). (ENG.). 32p. (J). (gr. k-3). 17.95 *(978-0-8225-9915-9(5),* Kar-Ben Publishing) Lerner Publishing Group.

—The Secret Shofar of Barcelona, Vol. Dembar Greene, Jacqueline. 2009. (ENG.). 32p. (J). (gr. k-3). pap. 7.95 *(978-0-8225-9944-9(9),* Kar-Ben Publishing) Lerner Publishing Group.

—Yasmin's Hammer. Malaspina, Ann. 2010. (ENG.). 40p. (J). (gr. k-6). 18.95 *(978-1-60060-359-4(9))* Lee & Low Bks., Inc.

Chaykin, Howard. Magneto. Chaykin, Howard. 2011. (X-Men: First Class Ser.: No. 2). (ENG.). 24p. (J). (gr. 2-6). 27.07 *(978-1-59961-949-1(0),* 15636, Marvel Age) Spotlight.

Chaykin, Howard & Williamson, Alan. Star Wars: the Original Trilogy - the Movie Adaptations. 2020. (ENG.). 384p. (YA). (gr. 4-17). pap. 34.99 *(978-1-302-92379-2(X))* Marvel Worldwide, Inc.

Chebret, Sébastien. Daisy the Digger. Bently, Peter. 2020. (Whizzy Wheels Academy Ser.). (ENG.). 24p. (J). (gr. -1-1). lib. bdg. 26.65 *(978-0-7112-4331-6(X))* QEB Publishing Inc.

—Dylan the Dump Truck. Bently, Peter. 2020. (Whizzy Wheels Academy Ser.). (ENG.). 24p. (J). (gr. -1-1). lib. bdg. 26.65 *(978-0-7112-4348-4(4))* QEB Publishing Inc.

—Fergus the Fire Engine. Bently, Peter. 2020. (Whizzy Wheels Academy Ser.). (ENG.). 24p. (J). (gr. -1-1). lib. bdg. 26.65 *(978-0-7112-4790-1(0))* QEB Publishing Inc.

—Little Worlds. Collet, Géraldine. 2018. 32p. (J). *(978-1-4338-2819-5(7),* Magination Pr.) American Psychological Assn.

—Tess the Tractor. Bently, Peter. 2020. (Whizzy Wheels Academy Ser.). (ENG.). 24p. (J). (gr. -1-1). lib. bdg. 26.65 *(978-0-7112-4791-8(9))* QEB Publishing Inc.

Chebret, Sébastien. Whizzy Wheels Academy: Dylan the Dump Truck. Bently, Peter. 2019. (Whizzy Wheels Academy Ser.). (ENG.). 20p. (J). (gr. -1-k). bds. 9.95 ***(978-0-7112-4347-7(6))*** QEB Publishing Inc.

Checcetto, Marco. Daredevil by Chip Zdarsky Vol. 3: Through Hell. 2020. 112p. (YA). (gr. 8-17). pap. 15.99 *(978-1-302-92018-0(9))* Marvel Worldwide, Inc.

—Gamora: Memento Mori. 2017. (ENG.). 112p. (YA). (gr. 8-17). pap. 15.99 *(978-0-7851-9782-9(6))* Marvel Worldwide, Inc.

—Old Man Hawkeye Vol. 2: The Whole World Blind. 2019. (Old Man Hawkeye Ser.: 2). (ENG.). 136p. (gr. 10-17). pap. 17.99 *(978-1-302-91125-6(2))* Marvel Worldwide, Inc.

Chedru, Delphine. Animals at Night: A Glow-In-the-Dark Book. Jankeliowitch, Anne. Bodeux, Eve, tr. 2017. (ENG.). 40p. (J). (gr. 3-7). 19.99 *(978-1-4926-5319-6(5))* Sourcebooks, Inc.

Chee. Second Wave. Nelson, Michael Alan. 2008. (ENG.). 128p. per. 14.99 *(978-1-934506-06-6(0))* Boom! Studios.

Chee, jt. illus. see Azaceta, Paul.

Chee, (IL. Star Trek Motion Picture Trilogy. Schmidt, Andy & Barr, Mike W. 2010. (Star Trek Ser.). 216p. pap. 24.99 *(978-1-60010-660-6(9),* 9781600106606) Idea & Design Works, LLC.

Chee, Cheng-Khee. Noel. Johnston, Tony. 2005. (ENG.). 32p. (J). (gr. k-3). lib. bdg. 16.95 *(978-1-57505-752-1(2),* Carolrhoda Bks.) Lerner Publishing Group.

Cheetham, Stephen. Off to the Park! 2014. (Tactile Bks.). 12p. (J). spiral bd. *(978-1-84643-502-7(1))* Child's Play International Ltd.

Chelich, Michael. The Dog & the Jet Ski. Dworkin, James B. 2016. (ENG.). 38p. (J). pap. 9.99 ***(978-1-0807-6105-0(5))*** Independently Published.

Chelsea, David. Snow Angel. Chelsea, David. 2016. (ENG.). 112p. (J). (gr. 3-7). pap. 9.99 *(978-1-61655-940-3(3))* Dark Horse Comics.

Chelsey, Emily. Got Milk? How? Donlon, Bridget. 2012. (-18). 26p. 29.95 *(978-1-62709-613-3(2));* 28p. pap. 24.95 *(978-1-4626-8033-7(X))* America Star Bks.

Chen, Belinda. Bath Buddies - on the Farm. 2018. (Bath Buddies Ser.). (ENG.). 8p. (J). (gr. -1 — 1). 9.95 ***(978-1-78603-306-2(2))*** QEB Publishing Inc.

Chen, Belinda. Bath Buddies: Things That Go. QED Publishing. 2018. (Bath Buddies Ser.). (ENG.). 8p. (J). (gr. -1 — 1). 9.95 *(978-1-78603-308-6(9))* QEB Publishing Inc.

Chen, Benjamin. Peanut Butter & the Jellyfish. Chen, Stephen Benjamin. 2018. (ENG.). 22p. (J). (gr. 1-4). 18.00 *(978-0-692-14249-3(5))* Chen, Stephen.

Chen, Dream. Butterflies on the First Day of School. Silvestro, Annie. 2019. (ENG.). 32p. (J). (gr. -1). 16.95 *(978-1-4549-2119-6(6))* Sterling Publishing Co., Inc.

Chen, Elaine. My Day with Gong Gong. Yee, Sennah. 2020. (ENG.). 36p. (J). (-2). 18.95 ***(978-1-77321-429-0(2))*** Annick Pr., Ltd. CAN. Dist: Publishers Group West (PGW).

Chen, Eszter. What I Can Learn from the Incredible & Fantastic Life of Oprah Winfrey. Medina, Melissa & Colting, Fredrik. 2017. 32p. (J). 14.95 *(978-0-9977145-8-6(1))* Moppet Bks.

Chen, Helen, jt. illus. see Golden Books.

Chen, Ju-Hong. Eliza's Cherry Trees: Japan's Gift to America, 1 vol. Zimmerman, Andrea. 2011. (ENG.). 32p. (J). (gr. k-3). 16.99 *(978-1-58980-954-3(8),* Pelican Publishing) Arcadia Publishing.

—The Jade Stone: A Chinese Folktale, 1 vol. 2019. (ENG.). 34p. (J). (gr. k-3). 11.95 *(978-1-4556-2467-6(5),* Pelican Publishing) Arcadia Publishing.

—The Jade Stone: A Chinese Folktale, 1 vol. 2005. (ENG.). 32p. (J). (gr. k-3). 16.99 *(978-1-58980-359-6(0),* Pelican Publishing) Arcadia Publishing.

Chen, Kerry. The Odd Anteater Named Snifflebell Chen, Kerry. 2020. (ENG.). 24p. (J). pap. 16.46 ***(978-1-6552-4575-6(9))*** Independently Published.

Chen, Kuo Kan, et al. Forensic Science. Frith, Alex. 2007. (Forensic Science Ser.). 96p. (J). (gr. 4-7). pap. 10.99 *(978-0-7945-1689-5(0),* Usborne) EDC Publishing.

Chen, Kuo Kang. How to Draw Robots & Aliens. Cook, Janet. Tatchell, Judy, ed. 2006. (Young Artist Ser.). 32p. (J). (gr. 4-7). pap. 5.99 *(978-0-7945-1370-2(0),* Usborne) EDC Publishing.

—Weather. Level 7. Clarke, Catriona. 2006. (Usborne Beginners Ser.). 32p. (J). (gr. 4-7). lib. bdg. 12.99 *(978-1-58086-892-1(4),* Usborne) EDC Publishing.

Chen, Kuo Kang, et al. The World of the Microscope. Oxlade, Chris & Stockley, Corinne. 2008. (Usborne Science & Experiments Ser.). 48p. (J). (gr. 5-11). pap. 8.99 *(978-0-7945-1524-9(X),* Usborne) EDC Publishing.

Chen, Kuo Kang & Mayer, Uwe. Sun, Moon & Stars. Turnbull, Stephanie. 2006. (Beginners Nature: Level 2 Ser.). 32p. (J). (gr. 1-3). 4.99 *(978-0-7945-1399-3(9),* Usborne) EDC Publishing.

Chen, Kuo Kang & Smith, Guy. Illustrated Dictionary of Biology. Stockley, Corinne. Rogers, Kirsteen, ed. 2007. (Illustrated Dictionaries Ser.). 128p. (J). (gr. 4-7). pap. 12.99 *(978-0-7945-1559-1(2),* Usborne) EDC Publishing.
—The Usborne Illustrated Dictionary of Science. Stockley, Corinne et al. Rogers, Kirsteen, ed. rev. ed. 2007. (Illustrated Dictionaries Ser.). 382p. (J). (gr. 4-7). pap. 29.99 *(978-0-7945-1847-9(8),* Usborne) EDC Publishing.
Chen, Kuo Kang, jt. illus. see Slane, Andrea.
Chen, Kuo Kang, jt. illus. see Spenceley, Annabel.
Chen, Lidan. Ben 10 Original Graphic Novel: the Truth Is Out There. Lee, C. B. 2019. (ENG.). 80p. (J). pap. 7.99 *(978-1-68415-319-0(0))* Boom! Studios.
—Ben 10: the Manchester Mystery. Lee, C. B. 2020. (Ben 10 Ser.). (ENG.). 80p. (J). pap. 7.99 *(978-1-68415-496-8(0))* Boom! Studios.
Chen, M. M. Lady Mechanika Volume 3: The Lost Boys of West Abbey, vol. 3. Chen, M. M. Benitez, Joe. 2017. (ENG.). 64p. (YA). pap. 7.99 *(978-0-9966030-4-1(2),* 41b7929e-1a9f-42f6-a15e-8cb89a0f1150) Benitez Productions.
Chen, Sean, et al. Iron Man: Heroes Return - the Complete Collection Vol. 1. 2019. (ENG.). 504p. (J). (gr. 4-17). pap. 39.99 *(978-1-302-91606-0(8))* Marvel Worldwide, Inc.
Chen, Vincent. Hot Pot Night! Chen, Vincent. 2020. 40p. (J). (gr. -1-2). 16.99 ***(978-1-62354-120-0(4))*** Charlesbridge Publishing, Inc.
Chen, Yuyi. Amy Is Famous. Bottner, Barbara. 2019. (ENG.). 40p. (J). 17.99 *(978-1-250-13490-5(0),* 900178001) Imprint IND. Dist: Macmillan.
Chen, Yuyi. Artemis & the Awesome Animals: Little Goddess Girls 4. Holub, Joan & Williams, Suzanne. 2020. (Quix Ser.). (ENG.). 96p. (J). (gr. k-3). 17.99 ***(978-1-5344-3115-7(2))***; pap. 5.99 ***(978-1-5344-3114-0(4))*** Simon & Schuster Children's Publishing. (Aladdin).
—Athena & the Island Enchantress: Little Goddess Girls 5. Holub, Joan & Williams, Suzanne. 2020. (Quix Ser.). (ENG.). 96p. (J). (gr. k-3). 17.99 ***(978-1-5344-7959-3(7))***; pap. 5.99 ***(978-1-5344-7958-6(9))*** Simon & Schuster Children's Publishing. (Aladdin).
Chen, Yuyi. Athena & the Magic Land: Little Goddess Girls 1. Holub, Joan & Williams, Suzanne. 2019. (Quix Ser.). (ENG.). 96p. (J). (gr. k-3). pap. 5.99 *(978-1-5344-3105-8(5),* Simon & Schuster/Paula Wiseman Bks.) Simon & Schuster/Paula Wiseman Bks.
—Going to Grandma's House: Shaped Board Book. Wing, Scarlett. 2016. (I Can Do It Ser.). (ENG.). 10p. (J). (gr. -1-k). bds. 8.99 *(978-1-68052-114-6(4),* 1001070) Cottage Door Pr.
—Ho Ho Ho: Peek-A-Flap Board Book. Berry Byrd, Holly. Cottage Door Press, ed. 2018. (ENG.). 12p. (J). (gr. -1-k). bds. 8.99 *(978-1-68052-344-7(9),* 1003160) Cottage Door Pr.
—Persephone & the Giant Flowers: Little Goddess Girls 2. Holub, Joan & Williams, Suzanne. 2019. (Quix Ser.: Bk. 2). (ENG.). 96p. (J). (gr. k-3). 16.99 *(978-1-5344-3109-6(8))*; pap. 5.99 *(978-1-5344-3108-9(X))* Simon & Schuster Children's Publishing. (Aladdin).
Chen, Zhiyuan. Mimi Goes Potty. Chou, Yih-fen. 2011. (J). *(978-0-9845523-9-9(1))* Heryin Publishing Corp.
—Mimi Tidies Up. Chou, Yih-fen. 2011. (J). *(978-0-9845523-6-8(7))* Heryin Publishing Corp.
—The Potty Story. Chou, Yih-fen. 2011. (J). *(978-0-9845523-8-2(3))* Heryin Publishing Corp.
Chen, Ziyue. Enough! 20 Protesters Who Changed America. Easton, Emily. 2018. (ENG.). 48p. (J). (gr. k-3). 17.99 *(978-1-9848-3197-2(6))*; lib. bdg. 20.99 *(978-1-9848-3199-6(2))* Random Hse. Children's Bks. (Crown Books For Young Readers).
—How Women Won the Vote: Alice Paul, Lucy Burns, & Their Big Idea. Bartoletti, Susan Campbell. 2020. (ENG.). 80p. (J). (gr. 3-7). 18.99 *(978-0-06-284130-8(0),* HarperCollins) HarperCollins Pubs. Ltd. GBR. Dist: HarperCollins Pubs.
—Just Right Family: An Adoption Story. Lopez, Silvia. 2018. (ENG.). 32p. (J). (gr. -1-k). 16.99 *(978-0-8075-4082-4(X),* 080754082X) Whitman, Albert & Co.
—Mela & the Elephant. Phumiruk, Dow. 2018. (ENG.). 32p. (J). (gr. k-3). 16.99 *(978-1-58536-998-0(5),* 204407) Sleeping Bear Pr.
—Rocket-Bye Baby: a Spaceflight Lullaby. Smith, Danna. 2019. (Little Golden Book Ser.). (ENG.). 24p. (J). (-k). 4.99 *(978-1-5247-6894-2(4),* Golden Bks.) Random Hse. Children's Bks.
—Some Days. Orloff, Karen Kaufman. 2019. 40p. (J). (gr. -1). 16.95 *(978-1-4549-2620-7(1))* Sterling Publishing Co., Inc.
Cheney, Tracy. Totem Poles: An Ancient Art. Batdorf, Carol. 2005. (Act Ser.). (ENG.). 24p. (Orig.). (gr. 1-6). pap. 4.95 *(978-0-88839-248-0(6))* Hancock Hse. Pubs.
Cheng, Andrea. Etched in Clay: The Life of Dave, Enslaved Potter & Poet, 1 vol. 2018. (ENG.). 160p. (J). (gr. 4-12). pap. 12.95 *(978-1-62014-807-5(2),* 761f0cf5-a4cc-451d-8ef8-6da9df473fff) Lee & Low Bks., Inc.
Cheng, Andrea. Etched in Clay: The Life of Dave, Enslaved Potter & Poet. Cheng, Andrea. 2013. (ENG.). 146p. (J). 17.95 *(978-1-60060-451-5(X))* Lee & Low Bks., Inc.
Cheng, Kyan. School Spells. Kuenzler, Lou. 2019. (Bella Broomstick Ser.: 2). (ENG.). 224p. (J). (gr. 3-7). pap. 7.99 *(978-1-5247-6783-9(2),* Random Hse. Bks. for Young Readers) Random Hse. Children's Bks.
Cheng-Liang, Zhu. A New Year's Reunion. Yu, Li Qiong. 2013. (ENG.). (J). (gr. -1-2). lib. bdg. 16.60 *(978-1-62765-381-7(3))* Perfection Learning Corp.
—A New Year's Reunion: A Chinese Story. Li-Qiong, Yu. 2013. (ENG.). 40p. (J). (gr. -1-2). 6.99 *(978-0-7636-6748-1(X))* Candlewick Pr.
—What I Like Most. Murphy, Mary. 2020. (ENG.). 32p. (J). (gr. -1-2). 16.99 *(978-1-5362-0940-2(6))* Candlewick Pr.
Cheng, Puay Koon. I Trapped a Dolphin but It Really Wasn't My Fault. Humphreys, Neil. 2013. (Abbie Rose & the Magic Suitcase Ser.). (ENG.). 24p. (J). (gr. -1-3). pap. 9.90 *(978-981-4408-51-6(4))* Marshall Cavendish International (Asia) Private Ltd. SGP. Dist: National Bk. Network.
—Picking up a Penguin's Egg Really Got Me into Trouble. Humphreys, Neil. 2014. (Abbie Rose & the Magic Suitcase Ser.). (ENG.). 24p. (J). (gr. -1-3). pap. 9.90 *(978-981-4484-18-3(0))* Marshall Cavendish International (Asia) Private Ltd. SGP. Dist: National Bk. Network.
Cherif, Jennifer. Abbey & Friends M Is for Manners. Jesse, Mary. 2003. 48p. (J). 15.95 *(978-0-9729958-0-1(3))* Hexagon Blue.
Chermayeff, Ivan. Sun Moon Star. Vonnegut, Kurt. 2016. 64p. (J). (gr. k-4). 22.95 *(978-1-60980-724-5(3),* Triangle Square) Seven Stories Pr.
Cherna. Patch's Country Quilt. Cherna. 2013. 54p. 25.95 *(978-1-60571-188-1(8))*; 50p. pap. 17.95 *(978-1-60571-187-4(X))* Northshire Pr.
Chernett, Dan. Clean up! Our Earth Day Project - 6 Pack: Set of 6 with Teacher Materials Common Core Edition. Adams, Alison. 2017. (Text Connections Guided Close Reading Ser.). (J). (gr. k-1). 40.00 *(978-1-5021-5484-2(6))* Benchmark Education Co.
Chernichaw, Ian. Blue's Bad Dream. Albee, Sarah & Hood, Susan. 2006. (Blue's Clues Ser.: 21). (ENG.). 24p. (J). (gr. -1-2). pap. 3.99 *(978-1-4169-1553-9(2),* Simon Spotlight/Nickelodeon) Simon Spotlight/Nickelodeon.
—Blue's Big Parade! Spelvin, Justin. 2005. (Blue's Clues Ser.). (ENG.). 24p. (J). pap. 3.99 *(978-0-689-87673-8(4),* Simon Spotlight/Nickelodeon) Simon Spotlight/Nickelodeon.
—Blue's Checkup. Albee, Sarah. 2003. (Blue's Clues Ser.). (ENG.). 24p. (J). pap. 3.99 *(978-0-689-85449-1(8),* Simon Spotlight/Nickelodeon) Simon Spotlight/Nickelodeon.
Chernyak, Inna. Happy Holidays, Pirates: Lift-The-flap Book. Clever Publishing & Koval, Tatiana. 2018. (Clever Flaps Ser.). (ENG.). 14p. (J). (gr. -1-1). bds. 12.99 *(978-1-948418-45-4(2))* Clever Media Group.
Chernyshova, Anna. The Abandoned Hamster. Nolan, Tina. 2018. (Animal Rescue Center Ser.). (ENG.). 128p. (J). (gr. 1-4). 19.99 *(978-1-68010-088-4(2))* Tiger Tales.
—Catch That Egg! Rowland, Lucy. 2019. (ENG.). 24p. (J). (-k). bds. 8.99 *(978-1-5247-9306-7(X),* Grosset & Dunlap) Penguin Young Readers Group.
—The Home-Alone Kitten. Nolan, Tina. 2016. (Animal Rescue Center Ser.). (ENG.). 112p. (J). (gr. 1-4). pap. 4.99 *(978-1-58925-493-0(7))* Tiger Tales.
—The Homeless Foal. Nolan, Tina. 2017. (Animal Rescue Center Ser.). (ENG.). 112p. (J). (gr. 1-4). pap. 4.99 *(978-1-58925-498-5(8))* Tiger Tales.
—The Injured Fox Kit. Nolan, Tina. 2017. (Animal Rescue Center Ser.). (ENG.). 112p. (J). (gr. 1-4). pap. 4.99 *(978-1-58925-499-2(6))* Tiger Tales.
Chernyshova, Anna. Laugh-Out-Loud Christmas Jokes: Lift-The-flap. Elliott, Rob. 2020. (Laugh-Out-Loud Jokes for Kids Ser.). 28p. (J). (gr. -1-3). 6.99 ***(978-0-06-294390-3(1),*** HarperFestival) HarperCollins Pubs.
Chernyshova, Anna. Laugh-Out-Loud Halloween Jokes: Lift-The-Flap. Elliott, Rob. 2019. (Laugh-Out-Loud Jokes for Kids Ser.). (ENG.). 28p. (J). (gr. -1-3). pap. 6.99 *(978-0-06-284535-1(7))* HarperCollins Pubs.
—The Lost Duckling. Nolan, Tina. 2017. (Animal Rescue Center Ser.). (ENG.). 128p. (J). (gr. 1-4). 19.99 *(978-1-68010-057-0(2))* Tiger Tales.
—Penguin & Moose. Hall, Hannah C. 2019. (Penguin & Moose Ser.). 32p. (J). (gr. -1-3). 16.99 *(978-1-5460-1433-1(0),* Worthy Kids/Ideals) Worthy Publishing.
—The Runaway Rabbit. Nolan, Tina. 2017. (Animal Rescue Center Ser.). (ENG.). 128p. (J). (gr. 1-4). 19.99 *(978-1-68010-058-7(0))* Tiger Tales.
—Santa Selfie. Bently, Peter. 2018. (ENG.). 32p. (J). (gr. -1-1). pap. 10.99 *(978-1-5098-3114-2(2))* Pan Macmillan GBR. Dist: Independent Pubs. Group.
—Sounds All Around. Pfeffer, Wendy. 2016. (Let's-Read-And-Find-Out Science 1 Ser.). (ENG.). 40p. (J). (gr. -1-3). pap. 6.99 *(978-0-06-238669-4(7))* HarperCollins Pubs.
—The Unwanted Puppy. Nolan, Tina. 2016. (Animal Rescue Center Ser.). (ENG.). 112p. (J). (gr. 1-4). pap. 4.99 *(978-1-58925-492-3(9))* Tiger Tales.
Cherrington, Gary. The Spy Who Played Baseball. Jones, Carrie. 2018. (ENG.). 32p. (J). (gr. k-4). 17.99 *(978-1-5124-0313-8(X),* 9781512403138, Kar-Ben Publishing) Lerner Publishing Group.
Cherry, Gale. The Best Book in the Library. Sue, Grandma. 2010. 20p. 12.49 *(978-1-4490-9704-2(9))* AuthorHouse.
Cherry, Lynne. Where Butterflies Grow. Ryder, Joanne. 2014. 32p. pap. 7.00 *(978-1-61003-313-8(2))* Center for the Collaborative Classroom.
Cheryl H. Hahn. Dog Gone: Boomer's Story. Greene, Brenda. 2005. 127p. (YA). per. 8.99 *(978-0-9770279-0-3(2))* Three Willows Pr.
Cheshenko, Valentina. Fillmore the Dragon. Zapple, Elias. 2018. (Jellybean the Dragon Stories American-English Ser.: Vol. 3). (ENG.). 128p. (J). (gr. 4-6). pap. *(978-1-912704-18-7(8))*; pap. *(978-1-912704-19-4(6))* Heads or Tales Pr.
Chess, Victoria. Beautiful Buehla & the Zany Zoo Makeover. Hogg, Gary. 2006. 32p. (J). (gr. -1-2). 15.99 *(978-0-06-009420-1(6),* Tegen, Katherine Bks) HarperCollins Pubs.
—The Beautiful Butterfly: A Folktale from Spain. Sierra, Judy. 2005. 32p. (J). (gr. k-4). reprint ed. 19.00 *(978-0-7567-9593-1(1))* DIANE Publishing Co.
—The Scaredy Cats. Bottner, Barbara. 2013. (ENG.). 32p. (J). (gr. -1-3). 16.99 *(978-1-4814-2166-9(2),* Simon & Schuster Bks. For Young Readers) Simon & Schuster Bks. For Young Readers.
—Teeny Tiny Tingly Tales. Van Laan, Nancy. 2008. (ENG.). 32p. (J). (gr. -1-2). 8.99 *(978-1-4169-7572-4(1),* Simon & Schuster/Paula Wiseman Bks.) Simon & Schuster/Paula Wiseman Bks.
—Ten Sly Piranhas. Wise, William. 2004. 32p. (J). (gr. -1-k). pap. 6.99 *(978-0-14-240074-6(2),* Puffin Books) Penguin Young Readers Group.
Chess, Victoria. Fletcher & Zenobia. Chess, Victoria. Gorey, Edward. 2016. 72p. (J). (gr. k-2). 14.95 *(978-1-59017-963-5(3),* NYR Children's Collection) New York Review of Bks., Inc., The.
Chessa, Francesca. Library Lily. Shields, Gillian. 2011. (ENG.). 26p. (YA). 16.00 *(978-0-8028-5401-8(X))* Eerdmans, William B. Publishing Co.
—Love-a-Duck. Brown, Alan James. 2010. (ENG.). 32p. (J). (gr. -1-1). pap. 16.95 *(978-0-8234-2263-0(1))* Holiday Hse., Inc.
—Who Has Wiggle-Waggle Toes? Shiefman, Vicky. 2019. 40p. (J). (-k). 17.99 *(978-0-8234-3864-8(3))* Holiday Hse., Inc.
Chessa, Francesca. A Button Muddle. Chessa, Francesca. 2003. 32p. (YA). pap. *(978-1-85602-461-7(X),* Pavilion Children's Books) Pavilion Bks.
Chessare, Michele. A Lion to Guard Us. Bulla, Clyde Robert. 2018. (Trophy Bk.). (ENG.). 128p. (J). (gr. 3-7). pap. 6.99 *(978-0-06-440333-7(5),* HarperCollins) HarperCollins Pubs. Ltd. GBR. Dist: HarperCollins Pubs.
Chesterman, Adrian. Ankylosaurus. Bailey, Gerry. 2011. (Smithsonian Prehistoric Zone Ser.). (ENG.). 32p. (J). (gr. k-3). *(978-0-7787-1797-3(6),* 1325443); pap. *(978-0-7787-1810-9(7),* 1325443) Crabtree Publishing Co.
—Ankylosaurus Fights Back. Galvin, Laura Gates. 2007. (Smithsonian's Prehistoric Pals Ser.). (ENG.). 36p. (J). 8.95 *(978-1-59249-681-5(4))*; (J). 14.95 *(978-1-59249-679-2(2))*; (J). pap. 6.95 *(978-1-59249-680-8(6))*; (J). (gr. -1-3). 2.95 *(978-1-59249-682-2(2))*; 9.95 *(978-1-59249-683-9(0))* Soundprints.
—Polar Bear Horizon. Halfmann, Janet. (Smithsonian Oceanic Collection). (J). 2009. 24.95 incl. audio compact disk *(978-1-59249-665-5(2))*; 2006. (ENG.). 32p. 8.95 *(978-1-59249-569-6(9))*; 2006. (ENG.). 32p. 4.95 *(978-1-59249-567-2(2))*; 2006. (ENG.). 32p. (gr. -1-3). 15.95 *(978-1-59249-565-8(6))*; 2006. (ENG.). 32p. (gr. -1-3). mass mkt. 6.95 *(978-1-59249-566-5(4))* Soundprints.
—Polar Bear Horizon. Halfman, Janet. 2006. (Smithsonian Oceanic Collection). (ENG.). 32p. (J). 19.95 *(978-1-59249-568-9(0))*; (gr. -1-3). 9.95 *(978-1-59249-570-2(2))* Soundprints.
Chesterman, Al. Little Book of Dinosaurs. Winner, Cherie. 2005. (Little Bks.). (ENG.). 24p. (J). (gr. -1-2). pap. 5.95 *(978-1-58728-516-5(9))* Cooper Square Publishing Llc.
Chesworth, Michael. America the Musical 1776-1899: A Nation's History Through Music. Gershenson, Harold P. 2005. 21p. (J). *(978-1-58987-116-8(2))* Kindermusik International.
—America the Musical 1900-2000: A Nation's History Through Music. Gershenson, Harold P. 2006. (J). *(978-1-58987-201-1(0))* Kindermusik International.
—Fluffy: Scourge of the Sea. Bateman, Teresa. 2006. 32p. (J). (gr. -1-2). pap. 7.95 *(978-1-58089-152-3(7))* Charlesbridge Publishing, Inc.
—Frieda B. & the Zillabeast. Bowers, Renata. 2013. 32p. (J). lib. bdg. 15.00 *(978-0-9843862-0-8(3))* Frieda B.
—Mom for Mayor. Edwards, Nancy. 2006. (ENG.). 96p. (J). (gr. 1-5). 16.95 *(978-0-8126-2743-5(1))* Cricket Bks.
Chesworth, Michael & Pearce, Carl. Many Ways to Learn: A Kid's Guide to LD. Stern, Judith M. & Ben-Ami, Uzi. 2nd rev. ed. 2010. 112p. (J). (gr. 3-8). 14.95 *(978-1-4338-0739-8(4))*; pap. 9.95 *(978-1-4338-0740-4(8))* American Psychological Assn. (Magination Pr.).
Chesworth, Michael D. Truman's Loose Tooth, Wurm, Kristine. 2005. (ENG.). 32p. (J). (gr. -1-3). 16.95 *(978-0-9768513-0-1(X))* Spirited Publishing, LLC.
Chetaud, Helene. Where is Santa's Beard? Leroy, Jean;Chetaud. 2017. (ENG.). 12p. (J). 16.00 *(978-1-4711-6126-1(9),* Simon & Schuster Children's) Simon & Schuster, Ltd. GBR. Dist: Simon & Schuster, Inc.
Chettle, Julie. Happy Misunderstanding: How Folly Gets his Name. Buller, Ginny. 2012. (ENG.). 29p. (J). pap. 16.95 *(978-1-4327-8234-4(7))* Outskirts Pr., Inc.
Cheung, Aggie. Mommy, You're the Best! 2018. (Special Delivery Bks.). (ENG.). 8p. (J). (— 1). bds. 6.49 *(978-1-68412-274-5(0),* Silver Dolphin Bks.) Printers Row Publishing Group.
Cheung, Aries. The Bonsai Bear. Libster, Bernard. 2006. 31p. (J). (gr. k-4). reprint ed. 16.00 *(978-1-4223-5857-3(7))* DIANE Publishing Co.
Cheung, Charly. Macbeth. Shakespeare, William. 2013. (William Shakespeare Ser.). (ENG.). 64p. pap. 6.95 *(978-1-906230-47-0(1))* Real Reads Ltd. GBR. Dist: Casemate Pubs. & Bk. Distributors, LLC.
—A Midsummer Night's Dream. Shakespeare, William. 2013. (William Shakespeare Ser.). (ENG.). 64p. pap. 6.95 *(978-1-906230-44-9(7))* Real Reads Ltd. GBR. Dist: Casemate Pubs. & Bk. Distributors, LLC.
—Romeo & Juliet. Shakespeare, William. 2013. (William Shakespeare Ser.). (ENG.). 64p. pap. 6.95 *(978-1-906230-45-6(5))* Real Reads Ltd. GBR. Dist: Casemate Pubs. & Bk. Distributors, LLC.
—The Tempest. Shakespeare, William. 2014. (William Shakespeare Ser.). (ENG.). 64p. pap. 6.95 *(978-1-906230-46-3(3))* Real Reads Ltd. GBR. Dist: Casemate Pubs. & Bk. Distributors, LLC.
Cheung, Jim, et al. Blood for Blood, Vol. 2. Marz, Ron. 2003. (Scion Traveler Ser.: Vol. 2). 208p. (YA). (gr. 7-18). pap. 9.95 *(978-1-931484-75-6(9))* CrossGeneration Comics, Inc.
—Conflict of Conscience. Marz, Ron. 2003. (Scion Traveler Ser.: Vol. 1). 192p. (YA). (gr. 7-18). pap. 9.95 *(978-1-931484-58-9(9))* CrossGeneration Comics, Inc.
—Divided Loyalties, Vol. 3. Marz, Ron. 2003. (Scion Traveler Ser.: Vol. 3). 176p. (YA). (gr. 7-18). pap. 9.95 *(978-1-931484-94-7(5))* CrossGeneration Comics, Inc.
—The Far Kingdom, Vol. 5. Marz, Ron. 2003. (Scion Ser.: Vol. 5). 160p. (YA). (gr. 7-18). pap. 15.95 *(978-1-931484-81-7(3))* CrossGeneration Comics, Inc.
—Sanctuary, Vol. 4. Marz, Ron. (Scion Traveler Ser.: Vol. 4). 160p. (YA). 2004. pap. 9.95 *(978-1-59314-044-1(4))*; 2003. (gr. 7-18). pap. 15.95 *(978-1-931484-50-3(3))* CrossGeneration Comics, Inc.
—Scion Vol. 6: The Royal Wedding. Marz, Ron. 2004. (Scion Ser.). 160p. (YA). pap. 15.95 *(978-1-59314-034-2(7))* CrossGeneration Comics, Inc.
—X-Men vs. Apocalypse: the Twelve Omnibus. 2020. (ENG.). 1272p. (YA). (gr. 4-17). 125.00 *(978-1-302-92287-0(4))* Marvel Worldwide, Inc.
Cheung, Lori A., photos by. My Amazing Day: A Celebration of Wonder & Gratitude. Fisher-Golton, Karin. 2013. (ENG., 26p. (J). bds. 8.99 *(978-0-9896145-1-1(4))* Pacific Dogwood Pr.
Cheung, Silvia. Little Avocado's Big Adventure. Puffinton, Brick. Cottage Door Press, ed. 2019. (Finger Puppet Board Book Ser.). (ENG.). 12p. (J). (gr. -1 — 1). bds. 6.99 *(978-1-68052-734-6(7),* 1004550) Cottage Door Pr.
Chevalier, Carole. The Contest. Cyril, Melita. 2018. (ENG.). 38p. (J). pap. *(978-1-7751608-4-7(X))* Q for Quinn.
Chewning, Randy. Ben & Bailey Build a Book Report. Lynette, Rachel. 2012. (Writing Builders Ser.). 32p. (J). (gr. 2-4). lib. bdg. 25.27 *(978-1-59953-506-7(8))* Norwood Hse. Pr.
—Parade Day. Schmauss, Judy Kentor. 2006. (Reader's Clubhouse Level 2 Reader Ser.). 24p. (J). (gr. k-1). pap. 3.99 *(978-0-7641-3293-3(8),* B.E.S. Publishing) Peterson's.
—Signing at Home: Sign Language for Kids, 1 vol. Clay, Kathryn & Vonne, Mira. 2013. (Time to Sign Ser.). (ENG.). 32p. (J). (gr. -1-2). 27.99 *(978-1-62065-051-6(7))* Capstone.
Chewning, Randy, et al. Time to Sign: Sign Language for Kids, 1 vol. Clay, Kathryn & Vonne, Mira. 2013. (Time to Sign Ser.). (ENG.). 112p. (J). (gr. -1-2). pap. 8.95 *(978-1-62065-687-7(6),* Capstone Pr.) Capstone.
Chewning, Randy. Where Does the Garbage Go? Showers, Paul. 2015. (Let's-Read-And-Find-Out Science 2 Ser.). (ENG.). 32p. (J). (gr. -1-3). pap. 6.99 *(978-0-06-238200-9(4))* HarperCollins Pubs.
—Where Does the Garbage Go? Showers, Paul. 2015. (Let's-Read-And-Find-Out Science 2 Ser.). (ENG.). (J). (gr. -1-3). lib. bdg. 17.60 *(978-1-68065-160-7(9))* Perfection Learning Corp.
Chiacchiera, Moreno & Todd, Michelle. Ancient Homes. Taylor, Saranne. 2014. (Young Architect Ser.). (ENG.). 32p. (J). (gr. 3-3). *(978-0-7787-1437-8(3))* Crabtree Publishing Co.
—Animal Homes. Taylor, Saranne. 2014. (Young Architect Ser.). (ENG.). 32p. (J). (gr. 3-3). *(978-0-7787-1438-5(1))* Crabtree Publishing Co.
—Futuristic Homes. Taylor, Saranne. 2014. (Young Architect Ser.). (ENG.). 32p. (J). (gr. 3-3). *(978-0-7787-1439-2(X))* Crabtree Publishing Co.
—Green Homes. Taylor, Saranne. 2014. (Young Architect Ser.). (ENG.). 32p. (J). (gr. 3-3). *(978-0-7787-1452-1(7))* Crabtree Publishing Co.
Chiang, Andy. Harold Takes a Trip: Harold & the Purple Crayon. Marsoli, Lisa Ann. 2005. 10p. (J). 7.95 *(978-1-58117-262-1(1),* Intervisual/Piggy Toes) Bendon, Inc.
Chiang, Maggie, et al. In Focus: Space. Jenner, Elizabeth. 2020. (ENG.). 28p. (J). (gr. 2). 24.99 *(978-1-944530-29-7(0),* 360 Degrees) Tiger Tales.
Chiang, Shirley. Dream of the Red Chamber. Xueqin, Cao. 2013. (Chinese Classics Ser.). (ENG.). 64p. pap. 6.95 *(978-1-906230-36-4(6))* Real Reads Ltd. GBR. Dist: Casemate Pubs. & Bk. Distributors, LLC.
—The Girl Who Blamed the World. MacKey, Cindy. 2013. 50p. pap. 16.50 *(978-0-9892699-0-2(6))* Cyrano Bks.
—Impressionists Sticker Book. Courtauld, Sarah & Davies, Kate. ed. 2011. (Art Ser.). 32p. (J). pap. 9.99 *(978-0-7945-2961-1(5),* Usborne) EDC Publishing.
—Journey to the West. Cheng'en, Wu. 2013. (Chinese Classics Ser.). (ENG.). 64p. pap. 6.95 *(978-1-906230-34-0(X))* Real Reads Ltd. GBR. Dist: Casemate Pubs. & Bk. Distributors, LLC.
—The Three Kingdoms. Guanzhong, Luo. 2013. (Chinese Classics Ser.). (ENG.). 64p. pap. 6.95 *(978-1-906230-35-7(8))* Real Reads Ltd. GBR. Dist: Casemate Pubs. & Bk. Distributors, LLC.
—The Water Margin. Naian, Shi. 2013. (Chinese Classics Ser.). (ENG.). 64p. pap. 6.95 *(978-1-906230-37-1(4))* Real Reads Ltd. GBR. Dist: Casemate Pubs. & Bk. Distributors, LLC.
Chiara, Francesca De. Little Stories for Bedtime. Taplin, Sam. 2010. (Bedtime Stories Ser.). 12p. (J). bds. 12.99 *(978-0-7945-2673-3(X),* Usborne) EDC Publishing.
—Polar Bears. Watt, Fiona. 2010. (Luxury Touchy-Feely Board Bks). 10p. (J). bds. 15.99 *(978-0-7945-2544-6(X),* Usborne) EDC Publishing.
Chibuzo, Chris. Why I Didnt Cry: I Kept Pushing. Uchendu, Gideon Julius. 2019. (My Motivation Ser.: Vol. 25). (ENG.). 52p. (J). pap. 8.99 *(978-1-0904-9547-1(1))* Independently Published.
Chicado, Emilian. Drive Me to the Moon. Cisco the Original. 2016. (ENG.). (J). (gr. k-6). pap. 11.95 *(978-1-68181-601-2(6))* Strategic Book Publishing & Rights Agency (SBPRA).
Chicaiza, Cesar. El Jarabe Del Cielo. Coronado Parra, Sergio & Coronado Martin, Jesus Angel, eds. 2019. (Cuentos de ni�os para Ni�os Ser.: Vol. 2). (SPA.). 38p. (J). pap. 9.99 ***(978-1-7023-3751-9(0))*** Independently Published.
—La Leyenda Del Mago de Hielo. Coronado Parra, Sergio. Coronado Martin, Jesus Angel, ed. 2019. (Cuentos de ni�os para Ni�os Ser.: Vol. 1). (SPA.). 44p. (J). pap. 9.99 ***(978-1-6998-3892-1(5))*** Independently Published.
—El Planeta BOB. Coronado Parra, Sergio. Coronado Martin, Jesus Angel, ed. 2019. (Cuentos de ni�os para

C

Ni�os Ser.: Vol. 3). (SPA.). 38p. (J). pap. 9.99 ***(978-1-7033-2254-5(1))*** Independently Published.

Chichester Clark, Emma. Cunning Cat Tales. Cecil, Laura. 2006. 71p. (J). (gr. k-4). reprint ed. pap. 17.00 *(978-1-4223-5013-3(4))* DIANE Publishing Co.

—Enchantment: Fairy Tales, Ghost Stories & Tales of Wonder. Crossley-Holland, Kevin. 2003. 128p. (YA). reprint ed. 22.00 *(978-0-7567-6961-1(2))* DIANE Publishing Co.

—Hans Christian Andersen's Fairy Tales. Waddell, Martin & Andersen, Hans. 2014. 127p. (J). *(978-1-4351-5626-5(9))* Barnes & Noble, Inc.

—The McElderry Book of Grimms' Fairy Tales. 2006. (ENG.). 128p. (J). (gr. 1-5). 24.99 *(978-1-4169-1798-4(5)*, McElderry, Margaret K. Bks.) McElderry, Margaret K. Bks.

—Miss Wire's Christmas Surprise. Whybrow, Ian. 2007. 45p. (J). (gr. -1-3). pap. 3.95 *(978-0-7534-6136-5(6)*, Kingfisher) Roaring Brook Pr.

—Mrs. Vole the Vet. Ahlberg, Allan. (ENG.). 24p. (J). pap. 6.95 *(978-0-14-037880-1(4))* Penguin Bks., Ltd. GBR. Dist: Trafalgar Square Publishing.

—No More Kissing! 2015. (J). *(978-1-4351-5751-4(6))* Barnes & Noble, Inc.

—The Pied Piper of Hamelin. Morpurgo, Michael. 2011. (ENG.). 64p. (J). (gr. k-4). 16.99 *(978-0-7636-4824-4(8))* Candlewick Pr.

—Pinocchio: in His Own Words. Morpurgo, Michael. 2018. (ENG.). 272p. (J). 17.99 *(978-0-00-825769-9(8)*, HarperCollins Children's Bks.) HarperCollins Pubs. Ltd. GBR. Dist: HarperCollins Pubs.

—Thumbelina. Andersen, Hans & Falloon, Jane. 2006.Tr. of Tommelise. 38p. (J). (gr. k-4). reprint ed. 16.00 *(978-1-4223-5373-8(7))* DIANE Publishing Co.

—Toto: the Dog-Gone Amazing Story of the Wizard of Oz. Morpurgo, Michael. 2017. (ENG.). 284p. (J). 17.99 *(978-0-00-825256-4(4)*, HarperCollins Children's Bks.) HarperCollins Pubs. Ltd. GBR. Dist: HarperCollins Pubs.

—A Treasury of Shakespeare's Verse. Shakespeare, William. Pollinger, Gina, ed. 2006. 96p. (J). (gr. 4-8). reprint ed. pap. 12.00 *(978-1-4223-5444-5(X))* DIANE Publishing Co.

Chichester Clark, Emma. Bears Don't Read! Chichester Clark, Emma. 2016. 32p. (J). 12.99 *(978-1-61067-366-2(2))* Kane Miller.

—Come to School Too, Blue Kangaroo! Chichester Clark, Emma. 2013. (ENG.). 32p. (J). pap. 9.99 *(978-0-00-725868-0(2)*, HarperCollins Children's Bks.) HarperCollins Pubs. Ltd. GBR. Dist: HarperCollins Pubs.

—Happy Birthday, Blue Kangaroo! Chichester Clark, Emma. 2020. (ENG.). 32p. (J). pap. 6.99 *(978-0-00-826630-1(1)*, HarperCollins Children's Bks.) HarperCollins Pubs. Ltd. GBR. Dist: HarperCollins Pubs.

—I'll Show You, Blue Kangaroo! Chichester Clark, Emma. 2019. (ENG.). 32p. (J). pap. 6.99 *(978-0-00-826627-1(1)*, HarperCollins Children's Bks.) HarperCollins Pubs. Ltd. GBR. Dist: HarperCollins Pubs.

—It Was You, Blue Kangaroo. Chichester Clark, Emma. 2018. (ENG.). 32p. (J). pap. 6.99 *(978-0-00-826626-4(3)*, HarperCollins Children's Bks.) HarperCollins Pubs. Ltd. GBR. Dist: HarperCollins Pubs.

—Love Is My Favorite Thing. Chichester Clark, Emma. 2015. (ENG.). 32p. (J). (gr. -1-k). 16.99 *(978-0-399-17503-9(2)*, Nancy Paulsen Books) Penguin Young Readers Group.

—Lulu & the Treasure Hunt (Wagtail Town) Chichester Clark, Emma. 2013. (Wagtail Town Ser.). (ENG.). 32p. (J). pap. 9.99 *(978-0-00-742517-4(1)*, HarperCollins Children's Bks.) HarperCollins Pubs. Ltd. GBR. Dist: HarperCollins Pubs.

—Merry Christmas, Blue Kangaroo! Chichester Clark, Emma. 2017. (ENG.). 32p. (J). 17.99 *(978-0-00-824219-0(4)*, HarperCollins Children's Bks.) HarperCollins Pubs. Ltd. GBR. Dist: HarperCollins Pubs.

—Mimi's Book of Counting. Chichester Clark, Emma. 2004. 24p. (J). 9.95 *(978-1-57091-573-4(3))* Charlesbridge Publishing, Inc.

—Mimi's Book of Opposites. Chichester Clark, Emma. 2004. 24p. (J). 9.95 *(978-1-57091-574-1(1))* Charlesbridge Publishing, Inc.

—Piper. Chichester Clark, Emma. 2007. 32p. (J). (gr. k-3). 17.00 *(978-0-8028-5314-1(5)*, Eerdmans Bks For Young Readers) Eerdmans, William B. Publishing Co.

—Plenty of Love to Go Around. Chichester Clark, Emma. 2016. (ENG.). 32p. (J). (-k). 17.99 *(978-0-399-54666-2(9)*, Nancy Paulsen Books) Penguin Young Readers Group.

—Plum & Rabbit & Me (Humber & Plum, Book 3), Bk. 3. Chichester Clark, Emma. 2010. (Humber & Plum Ser.: 3). (ENG.). 32p. (J). (gr. -1-k). pap. 9.99 *(978-0-00-727325-6(8)*, HarperCollins Children's Bks.) HarperCollins Pubs. Ltd. GBR. Dist: HarperCollins Pubs.

—We Are Not Fond of Rat: Band 02B/Red B (Collins Big Cat Phonics) Chichester Clark, Emma. 2006. (Collins Big Cat Phonics Ser.). (ENG.). 16p. (J). (gr. -1-1). pap. 6.99 *(978-0-00-723590-2(9))* HarperCollins Pubs. Ltd. GBR. Dist: Independent Pubs. Group.

—What Shall We Do, Blue Kangaroo? Chichester Clark, Emma. 2019. (ENG.). 32p. (J). pap. 6.99 *(978-0-00-826629-5(8)*, HarperCollins Children's Bks.) HarperCollins Pubs. Ltd. GBR. Dist: HarperCollins Pubs.

—When I First Met You, Blue Kangaroo! Chichester Clark, Emma. 2018. (ENG.). 32p. (J). pap. 6.99 *(978-0-00-825430-8(3)*, HarperCollins Children's Bks.) HarperCollins Pubs. Ltd. GBR. Dist: HarperCollins Pubs.

—Where Are You, Blue Kangaroo? Chichester Clark, Emma. 2019. (ENG.). 32p. (J). pap. 6.99 *(978-0-00-826628-8(X)*, HarperCollins Children's Bks.) HarperCollins Pubs. Ltd. GBR. Dist: HarperCollins Pubs.

Chichester Clark, Emma. Will & Squill. Chichester Clark, Emma, tr. 2006. 32p. (J). (gr. -1-k). 15.95 *(978-1-57505-936-5(3)*, Carolrhoda Bks.) Lerner Publishing Group.

Chicote, Marta. La Música Del Mar (the Music of the Sea) Isern, Susanna. 2020. (SPA.). 24p. (J). 9.95 ***(978-84-16733-97-2(X))*** Cuento de Luz SL ESP. Dist: Publishers Group West (PGW).

Chien, Cátia. A Boy & a Jaguar. Rabinowitz, Alan. 2014. (ENG.). 32p. (J). (gr. -1-3). 17.99 *(978-0-547-87507-1(X)*, 1505753, HMH Books For Young Readers) Houghton Mifflin Harcourt Publishing Co.

Chien, Catia. My Blue Is Happy. Young, Jessica. 2013. (ENG.). 32p. (J). (gr. -1-3). 16.99 *(978-0-7636-5125-1(7))* Candlewick Pr.

—Things to Do. Magliaro, Elaine. 2017. (ENG.). 40p. (J). (gr. -1-k). 16.99 *(978-1-4521-1124-7(3))* Chronicle Bks. LLC.

Chien, Cátia. The Town of Turtle. Cuevas, Michelle. 2018. (ENG.). 40p. (J). (gr. -1-3). 17.99 *(978-0-544-74982-5(0)*, 1633373, HMH Books For Young Readers) Houghton Mifflin Harcourt Publishing Co.

Chikoyak, Andrew J. The Common Snipe. Joe, Anna Rose. Afcan, Paschal, ed. Afcan, Paschal, tr. 2004. (J). pap. 7.50 *(978-1-58084-224-2(0))* Lower Kuskokwim Schl. District.

—Tukutukuaraller. Joe, Anna Rose. Afcan, Paschal, ed. Afcan, Paschal, tr. 2004. (J). pap. 7.50 *(978-1-58084-225-9(9))* Lower Kuskokwim Schl. District.

Child, Jeremy. Found You, Magic Fish! Butterfield, Moira. 2010. (Magic Bath Bks.). (ENG.). 8p. (J). (gr. -1 — 1). 5.99 *(978-0-7641-9791-8(6)*, B.E.S. Publishing) Peterson's.

—Wake up, Magic Duck! Butterfield, Moira. 2010. (Magic Bath Bks.). (ENG.). 8p. (J). (gr. -1 — 1). 5.99 *(978-0-7641-9792-5(4)*, B.E.S. Publishing) Peterson's.

Child, Lauren. I'd Like a Little Word, Leonie! Oldfield, Jenny. (ENG.). 99p. (J). pap. 8.99 *(978-0-340-78501-0(2))* Macmillan Pubs., Ltd. GBR. Dist: Trafalgar Square Publishing.

—Not Now, Nathan! Oldfield, Jenny. (ENG.). 107p. (J). pap. 7.99 *(978-0-340-78502-7(0))* Macmillan Pubs., Ltd. GBR. Dist: Trafalgar Square Publishing.

—What's the Matter, Maya? Oldfield, Jenny. (ENG.). 106p. (J). pap. *(978-0-340-78503-4(9))* Hodder & Stoughton.

Child, Lauren. Absolutely One Thing: Featuring Charlie & Lola. Child, Lauren. (Charlie & Lola Ser.). (ENG.). 32p. (J). (gr. -1-3). 2018. 8.99 *(978-1-5362-0038-6(7))*; 2016. 17.99 *(978-0-7636-8728-1(6))* Candlewick Pr.

—But Excuse Me That Is My Book. Child, Lauren. 2006. (Charlie & Lola Ser.). (ENG.). 32p. (J). (gr. -1-3). 17.99 *(978-0-8037-3096-0(9)*, Dial Bks) Penguin Young Readers Group.

—Catch Your Death. Child, Lauren. 2015. (Ruby Redfort Ser.: 3). (ENG.). 432p. (J). (gr. 5-9). 17.99 *(978-0-7636-5469-6(8))* Candlewick Pr.

—Clarice Bean: The Utterly Complete Collection. Child, Lauren. 2008. (Clarice Bean Ser.). (ENG.). 656p. (J). (gr. 3-7). pap. 16.99 *(978-0-7636-4115-3(4))* Candlewick Pr.

—Clarice Bean, Don't Look Now. Child, Lauren. 2008. (Clarice Bean Ser.: 3). (ENG.). 256p. (J). (gr. 3-7). pap. 7.99 *(978-0-7636-3935-8(4))* Candlewick Pr.

—Clarice Bean Spells Trouble. Child, Lauren. 2006. (Clarice Bean Ser.: 2). (ENG.). 192p. (J). (gr. 3-7). pap. 7.99 *(978-0-7636-2903-8(0))* Candlewick Pr.

—Clarice Bean Spells Trouble. Child, Lauren. 2006. (Clarice Bean Ser.). 189p. (J). (gr. 3-6). 13.65 *(978-0-7569-7919-5(6))* Perfection Learning Corp.

—Clarice Bean, That's Me. Child, Lauren. 2010. (Clarice Bean Ser.). (ENG.). 32p. (J). (gr. 1-4). pap. 8.99 *(978-0-7636-4795-7(0))* Candlewick Pr.

—A Dog with Nice Ears: Featuring Charlie & Lola. Child, Lauren. 2018. (Charlie & Lola Ser.). (ENG.). 32p. (J). (gr. -1-2). 17.99 *(978-1-5362-0036-2(0))* Candlewick Pr.

—Guess Who's Babysitting? Child, Lauren. 2010. (Clarice Bean Ser.). (ENG.). 32p. (J). (gr. 1-4). pap. 8.99 *(978-0-7636-4797-1(7))* Candlewick Pr.

—I Absolutely Must Do Coloring Now or Painting or Drawing. Child, Lauren. 2006. (Charlie & Lola Ser.). (ENG.). 24p. (J). (gr. -1-k). 4.99 *(978-0-448-44415-4(1)*, Grosset & Dunlap) Penguin Young Readers Group.

—I Am Not Sleepy & I Will Not Go to Bed. Child, Lauren. (Charlie & Lola Ser.). (ENG.). (J). (gr. -1-2). 2008. 16p. 19.99 *(978-0-7636-4098-9(0))*; 2005. 32p. reprint ed. pap. 8.99 *(978-0-7636-2970-0(7))* Candlewick Pr.

—I Am Too Absolutely Small for School. Child, Lauren. (Charlie & Lola Ser.). (ENG.). 32p. (J). (gr. -1-2). 2004. 16.99 *(978-0-7636-2403-3(9))*; 2005. reprint ed. per. 8.99 *(978-0-7636-2887-1(5))* Candlewick Pr.

—I Am Too Absolutely Small for School. Child, Lauren. 2005. (ENG.). (J). (gr. -1-1). lib. bdg. 14.65 *(978-0-7569-6495-5(4))* Perfection Learning Corp.

—I Will Never Not Ever Eat a Tomato. Child, Lauren. 2003. (Charlie & Lola Ser.). (ENG.). 32p. (J). (gr. -1-3). reprint ed. 8.99 *(978-0-7636-2180-3(3))* Candlewick Pr.

—My Wobbly Tooth Must Not Ever Never Fall Out. Child, Lauren. 2006. (Charlie & Lola Ser.). (ENG.). 32p. (J). (gr. -1-2). mass mkt. 6.99 *(978-0-448-44255-6(8))*, Grosset & Dunlap) Penguin Young Readers Group.

—The New Small Person. Child, Lauren. 2018. (ENG.). 32p. (J). (gr. -1-3). 7.99 *(978-0-7636-9974-1(8))* Candlewick Pr.

—Ruby Redfort Blink & You Die. Child, Lauren. (Ruby Redfort Ser.). (ENG.). 544p. (J). (gr. 5-9). 2019. pap. 8.99 *(978-1-5362-0863-4(9))*; 2018. 18.99 *(978-0-7636-5472-6(8))* Candlewick Pr.

—Ruby Redfort Catch Your Death. Child, Lauren. 2018. (Ruby Redfort Ser.: 3). (ENG.). 528p. (J). (gr. 5-9). pap. 7.99 *(978-0-7636-8846-2(0))* Candlewick Pr.

—Ruby Redfort Feel the Fear. Child, Lauren. (Ruby Redfort Ser.: 4). (ENG.). 528p. (J). (gr. 5-9). 2018. pap. 7.99 *(978-0-7636-9452-4(5))*; 2016. 16.99 *(978-0-7636-5470-2(1))* Candlewick Pr.

—Ruby Redfort Look into My Eyes. Child, Lauren. (Ruby Redfort Ser.: 1). (ENG.). 400p. (J). (gr. 5-9). 2018. pap. 7.99 *(978-1-5362-0047-8(6))*; 2013. pap. 7.99 *(978-0-7636-6257-8(7))* Candlewick Pr.

—Ruby Redfort Pick Your Poison. Child, Lauren. (Ruby Redfort Ser.: 5). (ENG.). 528p. (J). (gr. 5-9). 2018. pap. 7.99 *(978-1-5362-0049-2(2))*; 2017. 16.99 *(978-0-7636-5471-9(X))* Candlewick Pr.

—Ruby Redfort Take Your Last Breath. Child, Lauren. (Ruby Redfort Ser.: 2). (ENG.). 432p. (J). (gr. 5-9). 2018. pap. 7.99 *(978-1-5362-0048-5(4))*; 2013. 16.99 *(978-0-7636-5468-9(X))* Candlewick Pr.

—Slightly Invisible. Child, Lauren. (Charlie & Lola Ser.). (ENG.). 40p. (J). (gr. -1-3). 2016. 8.99 *(978-0-7636-9014-4(7))*; 2011. 16.99 *(978-0-7636-5347-7(0))* Candlewick Pr.

—Slightly Invisible. Child, Lauren. ed. 2016. (Charlie & Lola Ser.). (ENG.). 40p. (J). (gr. -1-3). 19.65 *(978-0-606-39107-8(X))* Turtleback.

—Take Your Last Breath. Child, Lauren. 2014. (Ruby Redfort Ser.: 2). (ENG.). 432p. (J). (gr. 5-9). pap. 7.99 *(978-0-7636-6932-4(6))* Candlewick Pr.

—Utterly Me, Clarice Bean. Child, Lauren. 2005. (Clarice Bean Ser.). (ENG.). (J). 190p. (gr. 4-6). 18.69 *(978-0-7636-2186-5(2))*; 208p. (gr. 3-7). reprint ed. pap. 7.99 *(978-0-7636-2788-1(7))* Candlewick Pr.

—Utterly Me, Clarice Bean. Child, Lauren. 2006. (Clarice Bean Ser.). 16.00 *(978-0-7569-6567-9(5))* Perfection Learning Corp.

Child, Ruthie. Dave's Timely Adventures: The Thieves of Time. Kuttner, Benjamin. 2019. (Dave's Timely Adventures Ser.: Vol. 2). (ENG.). 208p. (J). pap. 8.99 ***(978-1-6511-5744-2(8))*** Independently Published.

Childers, Basil, photos by. Tuning Up: A Visit with Eric Kimmel. Kimmel, Eric A. 2005. (Meet the Author Ser.). (ENG., 32p. (J). 14.95 *(978-1-57274-822-4(2)*, 732, Meet the Author) Owen, Richard C. Pubs., Inc.

Childers, Whitney. Macaroni the Great & the Sea Beast. Childers, Whitney. 2018. (ENG.). 26p. (J). (gr. -1-3). pap. 9.99 *(978-1-5324-0768-0(8))* Xist Publishing.

Children of Appalachia. Teddy Bear Helps on the Farm. Children of Appalachia. 2007. 64p. (J). per. 14.95 *(978-0-929915-73-9(9))* Headline Bks., Inc.

Children-Oln. Jeremiah & the Man, 6 vols., Vol. 1. Terbay, Susan Handle. Mariants, tr. 2007. 43p. (J). (gr. 1-6). pap. *(978-0-9628309-8-3(4))* Marianist Pr.

Children's Art-Friends of Kateri, jt. illus. see McCauley, Marlene.

Childrens Books Staff & Lambe, Steve. Smell You Later! Childrens Books Staff. 2012. (Fanboy & Chum Chum Ser.). (ENG.). 96p. (J). (gr. 2-4). 21.19 *(978-1-4424-2834-8(1)*, Simon Spotlight) Simon & Schuster Children's Publishing.

Childs, Sam. Boobela & the Belching Giant. Friedman, Joe. ed. 2010. (ENG.). 128p. 12.99 *(978-1-4440-0046-7(2))* Orion Publishing Group, Ltd. GBR. Dist: Hachette Bk. Group.

—Boobela, Worm & Potion Power. Friedman, Joe. ed. 2010. (ENG.). 128p. 12.99 *(978-1-4440-0045-0(4))* Orion Publishing Group, Ltd. GBR. Dist: Hachette Bk. Group.

Chilton, Noel. The Tale of the Pronghorned Cantaloupe. Steinsiek, Sabra Brown. 2009. (SPA & ENG.). 48p. (J). (gr. -1-3). pap. 17.95 *(978-1-890689-85-8(8)*, Rio Grande Bks.) LPD Pr.

Chilton, Noël. Tía's Tamales. Baca, Ana. 2012. (ENG & SPA.). 32p. (J). pap. 16.95 *(978-0-8263-5027-5(5))* Univ. of New Mexico Pr.

Chilton, Noel Dora. The Tale of the Pronghorned Cantaloupe. Steinsiek, Sabra Brown. 2013. 48p. 24.95 *(978-1-936744-11-4(2)*, Rio Grande Bks.) LPD Pr.

Chilvers, Nigel. Giants & Trolls. Peebles, Alice. 2015. (Mythical Beasts Ser.). (ENG.). 32p. (J). (gr. 3-6). 27.99 *(978-1-4677-6340-0(3)*, 9781467763400, Hungry Tomato ®) Lerner Publishing Group.

—Mighty Mutants. Peebles, Alice. 2015. (Mythical Beasts Ser.). (ENG.). 32p. (J). (gr. 3-6). lib. bdg. 27.99 *(978-1-4677-6343-1(8)*, 9781467763431, Hungry Tomato ®) Lerner Publishing Group.

—Monsters of the Gods. Peebles, Alice. 2015. (Mythical Beasts Ser.). (ENG.). 32p. (J). (gr. 3-6). 27.99 *(978-1-4677-6342-4(X)*, 9781467763424, Hungry Tomato ®) Lerner Publishing Group.

—My First Thomas: All Aboard Animals! Fischer, Maggie. 2019. (ENG.). 12p. (J). (— 1). bds. 10.99 *(978-0-7944-4265-1(X)*, Studio Fun International) Printers Row Publishing Group.

Chilvers, Nigel. My First Thomas: Let's Go, Thomas! Fischer, Maggie. 2020. (Storytime Sliders Ser.). (ENG.). 10p. (J). (— 1). bds. 9.99 ***(978-0-7944-4535-5(7)***, Studio Fun International) Printers Row Publishing Group.

Chilvers, Nigel. Thomas & Friends: All Aboard! Winslow, Claire. 2019. (Look & Find Ser.). (ENG.). 18p. (J). *(978-1-5037-4796-8(4)*, 805b9e26-c59a-4b33-8a87-c5334c2ba10c, p i kids) Phoenix International Publications, Inc.

—Thomas & Friends: Full Steam Ahead. Fischer, Maggie. 2018. (ENG.). 10p. (J). (gr. -1-k). bds. 9.99 *(978-0-7944-4166-1(1)*, Reader's Digest Children's Bks.) Studio Fun International.

—Thomas & Friends: Sleepytime Thomas. Fischer, Maggie. 2018. (Carry along Play Book Ser.). (ENG.). 14p. (J). (gr. -1-k). 14.99 *(978-0-7944-4210-1(2)*, Studio Fun International) Printers Row Publishing Group.

—Thomas & Friends: Teamwork Makes the Steam Work. Fischer, Maggie. 2020. (Deluxe Guess Who? Ser.). (ENG.). 12p. (J). (— 1). bds. 10.99 *(978-0-7944-4488-4(1)*, Studio Fun International) Printers Row Publishing Group.

—Thomas & Friends: the Great Train Mystery. Fischer, Maggie. 2018. (ENG.). 10p. (J). (gr. -1-k). bds. 9.99 *(978-0-7944-4112-8(2)*, Reader's Digest Children's Bks.) Studio Fun International.

Chilvers, Nigel & Disney Storybook Art Team. Disney Junior Vampirina: Look & Find. Harmening, Derek. 2018. (Look & Find Ser.). (ENG.). 24p. (J). ***(978-1-5037-3757-0(8)***, b7586903-d934-4884-b26f-1abf30735958, p i kids) Phoenix International Publications, Inc.

Chin, Foo Swee. Zeet. Chin, Foo Swee. 2003. 32p. (Orig.). pap. 2.95 *(978-0-943151-75-5(9))* Slave Labor Bks.

Chin, Jason. Chinese New Year. Jango-Cohen, Judith. 2005. (On My Own Holidays Ser.). 48p. (J). (gr. 1-3). lib. bdg. 25.26 *(978-1-57505-653-1(4))*; (ENG.). (gr. 2-4). pap. 7.99 *(978-1-57505-763-7(8)*, First Avenue Editions) Lerner Publishing Group.

—The Day the World Exploded: The Earthshaking Catastrophe at Krakatoa. Winchester, Simon. 2008. 96p. (J). (gr. 5-9). lib. bdg. 23.89 *(978-0-06-123983-0(6))* HarperCollins Pubs.

—My Big Fat Secret: How Jenna Takes Control of Her Emotions & Eating. Schechter, Lynn R. 2009. 64p. (J). (gr. 3-7). 14.95 *(978-1-4338-0540-0(5))*; pap. 9.95 *(978-1-4338-0541-7(3))* American Psychological Assn. (Magination Pr.).

—Nine Months: Before a Baby Is Born. Paul, Miranda. 2019. (ENG.). 32p. (J). (gr. -1-3). 18.99 *(978-0-8234-4161-7(X)*, Neal Porter Bks) Holiday Hse., Inc.

—Water Is Water: A Book about the Water Cycle. Paul, Miranda. 2015. (ENG.). 40p. (J). (gr. 1-5). 18.99 *(978-1-59643-984-9(X)*, 900128158) Roaring Brook Pr.

—Where Do Polar Bears Live? Thomson, Sarah L. 2009. (Let's-Read-And-Find-Out Science 2 Ser.). (ENG.). 40p. (J). (gr. k-4). 16.99 *(978-0-06-157518-1(6))*; pap. 5.99 *(978-0-06-157517-4(8))* HarperCollins Pubs. (Collins).

Chin, Jason. Coral Reefs: A Journey Through an Aquatic World Full of Wonder. Chin, Jason. 2011. (ENG.). 40p. (J). (gr. k-4). 18.99 *(978-1-59643-563-6(1)*, 900062702) Roaring Brook Pr.

—Gravity. Chin, Jason. 2014. (ENG.). 32p. (J). (gr. k-3). 18.99 *(978-1-59643-717-3(0)*, 900075228) Roaring Brook Pr.

—Island: A Story of the Galápagos. Chin, Jason. 2012. (ENG.). 40p. (J). (gr. k-3). 18.99 *(978-1-59643-716-6(2)*, 900075227) Roaring Brook Pr.

—Redwoods. Chin, Jason. 2009. (ENG.). 40p. (J). (gr. -1-3). 18.99 *(978-1-59643-430-1(9)*, 900054268) Roaring Brook Pr.

Chin, Lili. Don't Judge a Book by Its Cover. Fleck, Denise. 2013. 24p. pap. 14.99 *(978-1-4575-1758-7(2))* Dog Ear Publishing, LLC.

Chin, Louie. Don't Ask a Dinosaur. Esenwine, Matt Forrest & Bruss, Deborah. 2018. (ENG.). 32p. (J). (gr. -1-2). 17.99 *(978-1-57687-841-5(4)*, powerHouse Bks.) powerHse. Bks.

Chin Mueller, Olivia. Babies in the Forest: Chunky Lift a Flap Board Book. Swift, Ginger. Cottage Door Press, ed. 2017. (Chunky Lift-A-Flap Board Book Ser.). (ENG.). 12p. (J). (gr. -1-k). bds. 7.99 *(978-1-68052-188-7(8)*, 1001860) Cottage Door Pr.

Chin Mueller, Olivia. Chocolate Challenge: Royal Sweets 5. Perelman, Helen. 2020. (Quix Ser.). (ENG.). 80p. (J). (gr. k-3). 17.99 ***(978-1-5344-5506-1(X))***; pap. 5.99 ***(978-1-5344-5505-4(1))*** Simon & Schuster Children's Publishing. (Aladdin).

Chin Mueller, Olivia. The Marshmallow Ghost: Royal Sweets 4. Perelman, Helen. 2019. (Quix Ser.). (ENG.). 80p. (J). (gr. k-3). 16.99 *(978-1-4814-9487-8(2))*; pap. 5.99 *(978-1-4814-9486-1(4))* Simon & Schuster Children's Publishing. (Aladdin).

—A Royal Rescue: Royal Sweets 1. Perelman, Helen. 2018. (Quix Ser.). (ENG.). 80p. (J). (gr. k-3). 16.99 *(978-1-4814-9478-6(3))*; pap. 5.99 *(978-1-4814-9477-9(5))* Simon & Schuster Children's Publishing. (Aladdin).

—Stolen Jewels: Royal Sweets 3. Perelman, Helen. 2019. (Quix Ser.). (ENG.). 80p. (J). (gr. k-3). 16.99 *(978-1-4814-9484-7(8))*; pap. 5.99 *(978-1-4814-9483-0(X))* Simon & Schuster Children's Publishing. (Aladdin).

—Sugar Secrets: Royal Sweets 2. Perelman, Helen. 2018. (Quix Ser.). (ENG.). 80p. (J). (gr. k-3). 16.99 *(978-1-4814-9481-6(3))*; pap. 5.99 *(978-1-4814-9480-9(5))* Simon & Schuster Children's Publishing. (Aladdin).

Chin Mueller, Olivia, jt. illus. see Rowe, Helen.

Chin, Todd. Bernice's Bad Hair Days. Cardin, Jodi. 2009. 56p. (J). pap. *(978-1-60800-004-3(4))* LifeReloaded Specialty Publishing LLC.

China, Aisha. Lisa with Her Baby Brother. China, Aisha. 2018. (MUL.). 20p. (J). pap. 12.95 *(978-1-64096-161-6(5))* Newman Springs Publishing, Inc.

Chinchinian, Harry. The Princess & the Beggar II: Continuing Adventures. Chinchinian, Harry. 2005. 176p. (J). lib. bdg. 18.95 *(978-1-892476-11-1(8))* Plum Tree Pr.

Ching, Jerry Yu. The Greatest King. Ching, Jerry Yu. Onghai, Mike. 2nd I.t. ed. 2003. 52p. *(978-0-9743215-0-9(8))* WebCartoons, LLC.

Ching, Kai Yun & Li, Wai-Yant. From the Stars in the Sky to the Fish in the Sea. 2017. 40p. (J). (gr. -1-3). 17.95 *(978-1-55152-709-3(X))* Arsenal Pulp Pr. CAN. Dist: Consortium Bk. Sales & Distribution.

Chiodi, Maira. Monster Knows Excuse Me, 1 vol. Miller, Connie Colwell. 2014. (Monster Knows Manners Ser.). (ENG.). 24p. (J). (gr. -1-2). pap. 6.95 *(978-1-4795-2953-7(2))*; lib. bdg. 25.32 *(978-1-4795-2202-6(3))* Capstone. (Picture Window Bks.).

—Monster Knows Manners, 1 vol. Miller, Connie Colwell. 2014. (Monster Knows Manners Ser.). (ENG.). 24p. (J). (gr. -1-2). lib. bdg., lib. bdg., lib. bdg. 101.28 *(978-1-4795-3346-6(7)*, Picture Window Bks.) Capstone.

Chiodi, Maira Kistemann. Adverbs Say Finally! Dahl, Michael. 2019. (Word Adventures: Parts of Speech Ser.). (ENG.). 32p. (J). (gr. k-3). pap. 7.95 *(978-1-5158-4061-9(1)*, 140055); lib. bdg. 27.99 *(978-1-5158-3872-2(2)*, 139591) Capstone. (Picture Window Bks.).

—Conjunctions Say Join Us! Dahl, Michael. 2019. (Word Adventures: Parts of Speech Ser.). (ENG.). 32p. (J). (gr. k-3). pap. 7.95 *(978-1-5158-4107-4(1)*, 140145); lib. bdg. 27.99 *(978-1-5158-4099-2(9)*, 140139) Capstone. (Picture Window Bks.).

—Prepositions Say under Where? Dahl, Michael. 2019. (Word Adventures: Parts of Speech Ser.). (ENG.). 32p. (J). (gr. k-3). pap. 7.95 *(978-1-5158-4106-7(5)*, 140144); lib. bdg. 27.99 *(978-1-5158-4098-5(0)*, 140137) Capstone. (Picture Window Bks.).

—Verbs Say Go! Dahl, Michael. 2019. (Word Adventures: Parts of Speech Ser.). (ENG.). 32p. (J). (gr. k-3). pap. 7.95 *(978-1-5158-4059-6(X)*, 140053); lib. bdg. 27.99 *(978-1-5158-3870-8(6)*, 139589) Capstone. (Picture Window Bks.).

Chiodi, Maira Kistemann & Lowen, Lauren. Word Adventures: Parts of Speech. Dahl, Michael. 2019. (Word Adventures: Parts of Speech Ser.). (ENG.). (J). (gr. k-3). 223.92 *(978-1-5158-3873-9(0)*, 28865); pap., pap., pap. 63.60 *(978-1-5158-4078-7(6)*, 29163) Capstone. (Picture Window Bks.).

Chiodo, Charles. Chiodo Bros. ' Allen Xmas. Chiodo, Stephen & Strain, Jim. 2015. (ENG.). 100p. (J). (gr. -1). pap. 17.95 *(978-0-9729388-4-6(2))* Baby Tattoo Bks.

Chiodo, Joe. The Adventures of Wonderbaby: From A to Z. Chin, Oliver. 2005. (ENG.). 32p. (J). bds. 8.95 *(978-1-59702-001-5(X))* Immedium.

Chipka, Sandy. Ok, Said Carrie Katherine, 1 vol. Flaggert, Candy. 2008. (ENG.). 25p. 24.95 *(978-1-60563-502-6(2))* America Star Bks.

Chirco, Antonella. BibleRhymes' Christmas Story, bk. 3. McCardell, Ken. ed. 2008. (BibleRhymes Ser.: 3). 28p. (J). 17.95 *(978-0-9790605-2-6(4)*, BibleRhymes) BibleRhymes Publishing, L.L.C.

—BibleRhymes' Creation. McCardell, Ken. 2007. (BibleRhymes Ser.). 32p. (J). 17.95 *(978-0-9790605-0-2(8)*, BibleRhymes) BibleRhymes Publishing, L.L.C.

—BibleRhymes' Noah & the Ark, bk. 2. McCardell, Ken. 2007. (BibleRhymes Ser.: 2). 28p. (J). 17.95 *(978-0-9790605-1-9(6)*, BibleRhymes) BibleRhymes Publishing, L.L.C.

Chironna, Ronald. Galloping Gertrude: By Motorcar In 1908. Loeper, John J. 2011. 80p. (J). lib. bdg. 19.95 *(978-0-9727940-1-5(8))* Hieropub LLC.

Chisholm, Lael. A Country Yarn. Haylock, Heather. 2019. (Granny Mcflitter Ser.). 32p. (J). (gr. k-2). 16.99 *(978-0-14-377323-8(2))* Penguin Group New Zealand, Ltd. NZL. Dist: Independent Pubs. Group.

—Granny Mcflitter, the Champion Knitter. Haylock, Heather. 2018. (Granny Mcflitter Ser.). 32p. (J). (gr. k-2). 16.99 *(978-0-14-377054-1(3))* Penguin Group New Zealand, Ltd. NZL. Dist: Independent Pubs. Group.

Chism, Wesley. Laquita the Mosquito. Chism, Wesley. 2018. (ENG.). 32p. (J). pap. 10.00 *(978-1-7239-4623-3(0))* Independently Published.

—That Pesty Fly. Chism, Wesley. 2018. (ENG.). 24p. (J). pap. 10.00 *(978-1-7904-2933-2(1))* Independently Published.

Chitombo, Patience. From Adam to Noah in Coloring Pages: Genesis 1 To 9. Zinjiba-Nyakutya, Peshie. 2012. 64p. pap. 12.50 *(978-1-61897-769-4(5)*, Strategic Bk. Publishing) Strategic Book Publishing & Rights Agency (SBPRA).

Chitouras, Barbara. Little Women. Lindskoog, Kathryn, ed. 2003. (Classics for Young Readers Ser.). 432p. (J). per. 12.99 *(978-0-87552-734-5(5))* P & R Publishing.

Chitrakar, Manu. I See the Promised Land: A Life of Martin Luther King, Jr., 1 vol. Flowers, Arthur. rev. ed. 2013. (ENG.). 156p. (J). (gr. 6). 16.95 *(978-1-55498-328-5(2))* Groundwood Bks. CAN. Dist: Publishers Group West (PGW).

Chitrakar, Moyna. Sita's Ramayana, 1 vol. Arni, Samhita & Valmiki. 2011. (ENG.). 152p. (J). (gr. 4). 24.95 *(978-1-55498-145-8(X))* Groundwood Bks. CAN. Dist: Publishers Group West (PGW).

Chitwood, Suzanne, jt. illus. see Chitwood, Suzanne Tanner.

Chitwood, Suzanne Tanner & Chitwood, Suzanne. Boom Chicka Rock. Archambault, John. 2004. 32p. (J). (gr. -1-k). 16.99 *(978-0-399-23587-0(6)*, Philomel Bks.) Penguin Young Readers Group.

Chiu, Alex. In the Garden. Reid, Hunter. 2018. (Fluorescent Pop! Ser.). (ENG.). 14p. (J). (gr. -1-k). bds. 5.99 *(978-1-4998-0594-9(2))* Little Bee Books Inc.

—In the Rainforest. Reid, Hunter. 2017. (Fluorescent Pop! Ser.). (ENG.). 14p. (J). (gr. -1-k). bds. 5.99 *(978-1-4998-0420-1(2))* Little Bee Books Inc.

—Mighty Dinos. Reid, Hunter. 2017. (Fluorescent Pop! Ser.). (ENG.). 14p. (J). (gr. -1-k). bds. 5.99 *(978-1-4998-0524-6(1))* Little Bee Books Inc.

—Noisy Robots. Reid, Hunter. 2017. (Fluorescent Pop! Ser.). (ENG.). 14p. (J). (gr. -1-k). bds. 5.99 *(978-1-4998-0523-9(3))* Little Bee Books Inc.

—Vroom! Zoom! Reid, Hunter. 2018. (Fluorescent Pop! Ser.). (ENG.). 14p. (J). (gr. -1-k). bds. 5.99 *(978-1-4998-0595-6(0))* Little Bee Books Inc.

Chiu, Andrew. The Apollo 11 Moon Landing: July 20 1969, 1 vol. Yomtov, Nel. 2014. (24-Hour History Ser.). (ENG.). 48p. (J). (gr. 3-9). pap. 8.95 *(978-1-4329-9298-9(8))*; lib. bdg. 33.99 *(978-1-4329-9292-7(9))* Capstone. (Heinemann).

—Earthquakes, Tsunamis, & Volcanoes: Bridges Edition, Set Of 10. Piddock, Charles. 2013. (Prime Plus Ser.). (J). (gr. 6-8). 99.00 net. *(978-1-4509-9931-1(X))* Benchmark Education Co.

—Earthquakes, Tsunamis, & Volcanoes: Prime Bridges Edition. Piddock, Charles. 2013. (Prime Ser.). (YA). (gr. 6-8). pap. *(978-1-4509-9682-2(5))* Benchmark Education Co.

—Earthquakes, Tsunamis, & Volcanoes: Set Of 10. Piddock, Charles. 2013. (Prime Plus Ser.). (J). (gr. 6-8). 99.00 net. *(978-1-4509-9907-6(7))* Benchmark Education Co.

—Earth's Lithosphere: Bridges Edition, Set Of 10. Hirschmann, Kris. 2013. (Prime Plus Ser.). (J). (gr. 6-8). 99.00 net. *(978-1-4509-9930-4(1))* Benchmark Education Co.

—Earth's Lithosphere: Prime Bridges Edition. Hirschmann, Kris. 2013. (Prime Ser.). (YA). (gr. 6-8). pap. *(978-1-4509-9681-5(7))* Benchmark Education Co.

—Earth's Lithosphere: Set Of 10. Hirschmann, Kris. 2013. (Prime Plus Ser.). (J). (gr. 6-8). 99.00 net. *(978-1-4509-9906-9(9))* Benchmark Education Co.

—The Human Footprint: Bridges Edition, Set Of 10. Worth, Richard. 2013. (Prime Plus Ser.). (J). (gr. 6-8). 99.00 net. *(978-1-4509-9933-5(6))* Benchmark Education Co.

—The Human Footprint: Prime Bridges Edition. Worth, Richard. 2013. (Prime Ser.). (YA). (gr. 6-8). pap. *(978-1-4509-9684-6(1))* Benchmark Education Co.

—The Human Footprint: Set Of 10. Worth, Richard. 2013. (Prime Plus Ser.). (J). (gr. 6-8). 99.00 net. *(978-1-4509-9909-0(3))* Benchmark Education Co.

—Weathering & Erosion: Bridges Edition, Set Of 10. Hirschmann, Kris. 2013. (Prime Plus Ser.). (J). (gr. 6-8). 99.00 net. *(978-1-4509-9932-8(8))* Benchmark Education Co.

—Weathering & Erosion: Prime Bridges Edition. Hirschmann, Kris. 2013. (Prime Ser.). (YA). (gr. 6-8). pap. *(978-1-4509-9683-9(3))* Benchmark Education Co.

—Weathering & Erosion: Set Of 10. Hirschmann, Kris. 2013. (Prime Plus Ser.). (J). (gr. 6-8). 99.00 net. *(978-1-4509-9908-3(5))* Benchmark Education Co.

Chiu, Bessie. Ariana Leaves San Francisco. Martha, Morales. 2011. 28p. pap. 8.50 *(978-1-61170-017-6(5))* Robertson Publishing.

Chloloula, jt. illus. see Germain-Therrien, Chloé.

Cho, Eun-Yeong. No Soy Floja: Los �rganos Del Cuerpo. Hyeon, So. 2018. (Click Click: Ciencia B�sica / Basic Science Ser.). (SPA.). 32p. (J). pap. 17.99 ***(978-1-64101-216-4(1))*** Santillana USA Publishing Co., Inc.

Cho, Frank. Marvel Monograph: the Art of Frank Cho. 2020. (ENG.). 112p. (gr. 10-17). pap. 19.99 *(978-1-302-92416-4(8))* Marvel Worldwide, Inc.

Cho, Michael. Max Finder Mystery Collected Casebook Volume 1, Vol. 1. O'Donnell, Liam. 2006. (Max Finder Mystery Collected Casebook Ser.: 1). (ENG.). 96p. (J). (gr. 3-6). pap. 9.95 *(978-2-89579-116-4(3)*, Owlkids) Owlkids Bks. Inc. CAN. Dist: Publishers Group West (PGW).

—Max Finder Mystery Collected Casebook Volume 2, Vol. 2. O'Donnell, Liam. 2007. (Max Finder Mystery Collected Casebook Ser.: 2). (ENG.). 96p. (J). (gr. 3-6). 9.95 *(978-2-89579-121-8(X))* Owlkids Bks. Inc. CAN. Dist: Publishers Group West (PGW).

—Max Finder Mystery Collected Casebook Volume 3 Vol. 3, Vol. 3. O'Donnell, Liam. 2007. (Max Finder Mystery Collected Casebook Ser.: 3). (ENG.). 96p. (J). (gr. 3-6). pap. 9.95 *(978-2-89579-149-2(X)*, Owlkids) Owlkids Bks. Inc. CAN. Dist: Publishers Group West (PGW).

—Media Madness: An Insider's Guide to Media. Ali, Dominic. 2005. 64p. (J). (gr. 5-9). 9.95 *(978-1-55337-175-5(5))* Kids Can Pr., Ltd. CAN. Dist: Hachette Bk. Group.

Cho, Mu Young, jt. illus. see Random House Editors.

Cho, Seung-Yup. Phantom, Vol. 4. Lee, Ki-Hoon. 2008. (Phantom (Tokyopop) Ser.). 192p. (gr. 8). pap. 9.99 *(978-1-59816-773-3(1))* TOKYOPOP, Inc.

Cho, Sumin. Desastre en el Musical. Gunderson, Jessica. 2020. (Drama en la Secundaria Ser.).Tr. of School Musical Meltdown. (SPA.). 64p. (J). (gr. 3-6). pap. 6.95 *(978-1-4965-9318-4(9)*, 142348); lib. bdg. 25.99 *(978-1-4965-9163-0(1)*, 142080) Capstone. (Stone Arch Bks.).

—El Dilema de la Primera Cita. Mason, Jane B. 2020. (Drama en la Secundaria Ser.).Tr. of First-Date Dilemma. (SPA.). 64p. (J). (gr. 3-6). pap. 6.95 *(978-1-4965-9316-0(2)*, 142346); lib. bdg. 25.99 *(978-1-4965-9161-6(5)*, 142078) Capstone. (Stone Arch Bks.).

—Drama en la Secundaria. Mason, Jane B. 2020. (Drama en la Secundaria Ser.).Tr. of Junior High Drama. (SPA.). (J). (gr. 3-6). pap., pap., pap. 27.80 *(978-1-4965-9337-5(5)*, 30086, Stone Arch Bks.) Capstone.

—Drama en la Secundaria. Simonson, Louise. 2020. (Drama en la Secundaria Ser.).Tr. of Junior High Drama. (SPA.). (J). (gr. 3-6). 103.96 *(978-1-4965-9185-2(2)*, 29929, Stone Arch Bks.) Capstone.

—The First-Date Dilemma. Mason, Jane B. 2018. (Junior High Drama Ser.). (ENG.). 64p. (J). (gr. 3-6). 25.99 *(978-1-4965-4709-5(8)*, 135223, Stone Arch Bks.) Capstone.

—El Gran Chisme. Simonson, Louise. 2020. (Drama en la Secundaria Ser.).Tr. of Runaraound Rumor. (SPA.). 64p. (J). (gr. 3-6). pap. 6.95 *(978-1-4965-9315-3(4)*, 142345); lib. bdg. 25.99 *(978-1-4965-9160-9(7)*, 142077) Capstone. (Stone Arch Bks.).

—Junior High Drama, 4 vols. Simonson, Louise & Mason, Jane B. 2018. (Junior High Drama Ser.). (ENG.). 64p. (J). (gr. 3-6). 103.96 *(978-1-4965-4754-5(3)*, 26528); pap., pap., pap. 27.80 *(978-1-4965-7419-0(2)*, 28679) Capstone. (Stone Arch Bks.).

—Las Malvadas de la Escuela Secundaria. Simonson, Louise. 2020. (Drama en la Secundaria Ser.).Tr. of Middle School Mean Queens. (SPA.). 64p. (J). (gr. 3-6). pap. 6.95 *(978-1-4965-9317-7(0)*, 142347); lib. bdg. 25.99 *(978-1-4965-9162-3(3)*, 142079) Capstone. (Stone Arch Bks.).

—The Runaround Rumor. Simonson, Louise. 2018. (Junior High Drama Ser.). (ENG.). 64p. (J). (gr. 3-6). 25.99 *(978-1-4965-4708-8(X)*, 135222, Stone Arch Bks.) Capstone.

—The School Musical Meltdown. Gunderson, Jessica. 2018. (Junior High Drama Ser.). (ENG.). 64p. (J). (gr. 3-6). 25.99 *(978-1-4965-4711-8(X)*, 135225, Stone Arch Bks.) Capstone.

Cho, Ye-Jeong. �qui�n Manda en Los Bosques? Interacciones en un Ecosistema. Lee, Yu-Jeong. 2018. (Click Click: Ciencia B�sica / Basic Science Ser.). (SPA.). 32p. (J). pap. 18.99 ***(978-1-64101-212-6(9))*** Santillana USA Publishing Co., Inc.

Chocheli, Niko. The Legend of the Cross. Hart, Chrissi. 2014. (ENG.). 32p. (J). (gr. -1-3). pap. 19.99 *(978-1-62395-570-0(X))* Xist Publishing.

Chodagiri, Shanthi. The Pursuit of Pizan, 1 vol. Heap, Bridgette. 2009. 35p. pap. 24.95 *(978-1-61546-994-9(X))* America Star Bks.

Chodos-Irvine, Margaret. Apple Pie Fourth of July. Wong, Janet S. 2006. (ENG.). 40p. (J). (gr. -1-3). pap. 7.99 *(978-0-15-205708-4(0)*, 1197158) Houghton Mifflin Harcourt Publishing Co.

—Where Lily Isn't. Paschkis, Julie. 2020. (ENG.). 336p. (J). 17.99 *(978-1-250-18425-2(8)*, 900191038, Holt, Henry & Co. Bks. For Young Readers) Holt, Henry & Co.

Choi, Allan. Barbie & the Three Musketeers: A Junior Novelization. Dumas, Alexandre. 2009. 93p. (J). *(978-0-545-09413-9(5))* Scholastic, Inc.

Choi, Allan, jt. illus. see Ulkutay Design Group.

Choi, Allan Jai-Ho. Chimmy '5 in 1' Language Alphabet Book. Paigerac, Patricia. 2007. 56p. (J). 23.00 *(978-0-9801137-0-9(9))* Paigerac, Patricia M.

Choi, Cheol-Min. How Does It Protect Itself? Camouflage. Oh, Hyeon-Gyeong. 2017. (Science Storybooks Ser.). (ENG.). 32p. (J). (gr. k-4). lib. bdg. 27.99 *(978-1-925235-16-6(5)*, Big and SMALL) ChoiceMaker Pty. Ltd., The AUS. Dist: Lerner Publishing Group.

Choi, Connie. Anyone's Game. Chiang, Sylv. 2018. (Cross Ups Ser.). 200p. (J). pap. 9.95 *(978-1-77321-046-9(7))* Annick Pr., Ltd. CAN. Dist: Publishers Group West (PGW).

—Rising Star (Cross Ups, Book 3) Chiang, Sylv. 2019. (Cross Ups Ser.: 3). 208p. (J). (gr. 4). (ENG.). 18.95 *(978-1-77321-312-5(1))*; pap. 9.95 *(978-1-77321-311-8(3))* Annick Pr., Ltd. CAN. Dist: Publishers Group West (PGW).

—Tournament Trouble (Cross Ups, Book 1) Chiang, Sylv. 2018. (Cross Ups Ser.: 1). 200p. (J). (gr. 3-6). (ENG.). 18.95 *(978-1-77321-009-4(2))*; pap. 9.95 *(978-1-77321-008-7(4))* Annick Pr., Ltd. CAN. Dist: Publishers Group West (PGW).

Choi, Eun-yeong. The Farting Princess: Digestion. Jang, Ki-Seon. 2017. (Science Storybooks Ser.). (ENG.). 32p. (J). (gr. k-4). lib. bdg. 27.99 *(978-1-925235-38-8(6)*, Big and SMALL) ChoiceMaker Pty. Ltd., The AUS. Dist: Lerner Publishing Group.

—What a Beautiful World! The Earth's Layers. Shin, Seon-Woong. 2017. (Science Storybooks Ser.). (ENG.). 32p. (J). (gr. k-4). lib. bdg. 27.99 *(978-1-925235-39-5(4)*, Big and SMALL) ChoiceMaker Pty. Ltd., The AUS. Dist: Lerner Publishing Group.

Choi, Hayelin. Alice Waters & the Trip to Delicious. Martin, Jacqueline Briggs. 2014. (Food Heroes Ser.). (ENG.). 32p. (J). (gr. k). 18.95 *(978-0-9836615-6-6(1))* READERS to EATERS.

Choi, Il-Ho. Chrono Code, 2 vols. Shin, Eui-Cheol. 2nd rev. ed. 2005. (Chrono Code Ser.: Vol. 2). 208p. per. 9.99 *(978-1-59532-551-8(4))* TOKYOPOP, Inc.

—Chrono Code, 2 vols., Vol. I. Kim, Sarah, tr. from KOR. 2005. 192p. pap. 9.99 *(978-1-59532-550-1(6))* TOKYOPOP, Inc.

Choi, Link. The Dragon Hunters. Russell, James. 2017. (Dragon Brothers Ser.: 1). (ENG.). 32p. (J). (-4). 16.99 *(978-1-4926-4861-1(2)*, 9781492648611, Sourcebooks Jabberwocky) Sourcebooks, Inc.

—The Dragon Riders. Russell, James. 2017. (J). (-4). (Dragon Brothers Ser.: 3). 32p. 16.99 *(978-1-4926-4867-3(1)*, Sourcebooks Jabberwocky); 40p. pap. ***(978-1-4926-4989-2(9))*** Sourcebooks, Inc.

Choi, Mike, et al. Cable: the Last Hope Vol. 2. 2018. (Cable: the Last Hope Ser.: 2). (ENG.). 496p. (YA). (gr. 8-17). pap. 39.99 *(978-1-302-91394-6(8))* Marvel Worldwide, Inc.

—X-Men Milestones: Messiah War. 2020. 248p. (YA). (gr. 8-17). pap. 24.99 *(978-1-302-92284-9(X))* Marvel Worldwide, Inc.

Choi, Min-ho. Little Red Riding Hood. Brothers Grimm. 2015. (World Classics Ser.). (ENG.). 32p. (J). (gr. k-4). pap. 5.00 *(978-1-925186-62-8(8)*, Big and SMALL) ChoiceMaker Pty. Ltd., The AUS. Dist: Lerner Publishing Group.

—Little Red Riding Hood. Brothers Grimm. Cowley, Joy, ed. 2015. (World Classics Ser.). (ENG.). 32p. (gr. k-4). (J). 10.00 *(978-1-925186-68-0(7))*; 26.65 *(978-1-925246-16-2(7))*; 7.99 *(978-1-925246-68-1(X))*; 26.65 *(978-1-925246-42-1(6))* ChoiceMaker Pty. Ltd., The AUS. (Big and SMALL). Dist: Lerner Publishing Group.

Choi, Stef. Ruby Lu, Star of the Show. Look, Lenore. (ENG.). 144p. (J). (gr. 1-5). 2012. pap. 6.99 *(978-1-4169-1776-2(4))*; 2011. 15.99 *(978-1-4169-1775-5(6))* Simon & Schuster Children's Publishing. (Atheneum Bks. for Young Readers).

Choi Sung Hwan, Aragon Noel. Best Friends for Life. Miller, Jennifer. 2006. (Trollz Ser.). (ENG.). 120p. (J). pap. 4.99 *(978-0-439-80311-3(X))* Scholastic, Inc.

—Ready to Glow. Ruditis, Paul. 2005. (Trollz Ser.). (ENG.). 80p. (J). pap. 5.99 *(978-0-439-80313-7(6))* Scholastic, Inc.

Choi, Woo Bin, et al. The Advent of Ultron #1. Zub, Jim. 2017. (Avengers K Set 2 Ser.). (ENG.). 28p. (J). (gr. 2-8). lib. bdg. 27.07 *(978-1-5321-4001-3(0)*, 25468, Marvel Age) Spotlight.

—The Advent of Ultron #2. Zub, Jim. 2017. (Avengers K Set 2 Ser.). (ENG.). 28p. (J). (gr. 2-8). lib. bdg. 27.07 *(978-1-5321-4002-0(9)*, 25469, Marvel Age) Spotlight.

—The Advent of Ultron #3. Zub, Jim. 2017. (Avengers K Set 2 Ser.). (ENG.). 28p. (J). (gr. 2-8). lib. bdg. 27.07 *(978-1-5321-4003-7(7)*, 25470, Marvel Age) Spotlight.

—The Advent of Ultron #4. Zub, Jim. 2017. (Avengers K Set 2 Ser.). (ENG.). 28p. (J). (gr. 2-8). lib. bdg. 27.07 *(978-1-5321-4004-4(5)*, 25471, Marvel Age) Spotlight.

—The Advent of Ultron #5. Zub, Jim. 2017. (Avengers K Set 2 Ser.). (ENG.). 32p. (J). (gr. 2-8). lib. bdg. 27.07 *(978-1-5321-4005-1(3)*, 25472, Marvel Age) Spotlight.

—The Advent of Ultron #6. Zub, Jim. 2017. (Avengers K Set 2 Ser.). (ENG.). 28p. (J). (gr. 2-8). lib. bdg. 27.07 *(978-1-5321-4006-8(1)*, 25473, Marvel Age) Spotlight.

—Avengers K, 6 vols., Set. Zub, Jim. 2016. (Avengers K Ser.). (ENG.). 28p. (J). (gr. 2-8). lib. bdg. 162.42 *(978-1-61479-567-4(3)*, 24348, Marvel Age) Spotlight.

—Avengers K Book 5: Assembling the Avengers. 2017. (ENG.). 168p. (YA). (gr. 8-17). pap. 24.99 *(978-1-302-90413-5(2))* Marvel Worldwide, Inc.

—Avengers vs. Ultron #1. Zub, Jim. 2016. (Avengers K Ser.). (ENG.). 28p. (J). (gr. 2-8). lib. bdg. 27.07 *(978-1-61479-568-1(1)*, 24349, Marvel Age) Spotlight.

—Avengers vs. Ultron #2. Zub, Jim. 2016. (Avengers K Ser.). (ENG.). 28p. (J). (gr. 2-8). lib. bdg. 27.07 *(978-1-61479-569-8(X)*, 24350, Marvel Age) Spotlight.

—Avengers vs. Ultron #3. Zub, Jim. 2016. (Avengers K Ser.). (ENG.). 28p. (J). (gr. 2-8). lib. bdg. 27.07 *(978-1-61479-570-4(3)*, 24351, Marvel Age) Spotlight.

—Avengers vs. Ultron #4. Zub, Jim. 2016. (Avengers K Ser.). (ENG.). 28p. (J). (gr. 2-8). lib. bdg. 27.07 *(978-1-61479-571-1(1)*, 24352, Marvel Age) Spotlight.

—Avengers vs. Ultron #5. Zub, Jim. 2016. (Avengers K Ser.). (ENG.). 28p. (J). (gr. 2-8). lib. bdg. 27.07 *(978-1-61479-572-8(X)*, 24353, Marvel Age) Spotlight.

—Avengers vs. Ultron #6. Zub, Jim. 2016. (Avengers K Ser.). (ENG.). 28p. (J). (gr. 2-8). lib. bdg. 27.07 *(978-1-61479-573-5(8)*, 24354, Marvel Age) Spotlight.

Choi, Yang-sook. Liang's Treasure: China. Yun, Yeo-rim. 2015. (Global Kids Storybooks Ser.). (ENG.). 32p. (J). (gr. 1-4). pap. 8.99 *(978-1-925233-48-3(0)*, Big and SMALL) ChoiceMaker Pty. Ltd., The AUS. Dist: Lerner Publishing Group.

—Liang's Treasure: China. Yun, Yeo-rim. Cowley, Joy, ed. 2015. (Global Kids Storybooks Ser.). (ENG.). 32p. (gr. 1-4). 26.65 *(978-1-925246-05-6(1))*; 26.65 *(978-1-925246-31-5(0))*; 7.99 *(978-1-925246-57-5(4))* ChoiceMaker Pty. Ltd., The AUS. (Big and SMALL). Dist: Lerner Publishing Group.

Choi, Yangsook. Basket Weaver & Catches Many Mice. Gill, Janet. 2005. 30p. (J). (gr. k-4). reprint ed. 19.00 *(978-0-7567-9420-0(X))* DIANE Publishing Co.

—Landed. Lee, Milly. 2006. (ENG.). 40p. (J). (gr. 2-6). 18.99 *(978-0-374-34314-9(4)*, 900029288, Farrar, Straus & Giroux (BYR)) Farrar, Straus & Giroux.

Choi, Yangsook. The Name Jar. Choi, Yangsook. 2003. 40p. (J). (gr. -1-2). pap. 7.99 *(978-0-440-41799-6(6)*, Dragonfly Bks.) Random Hse. Children's Bks.

Choksi, Nishant. Really, Really Big Questions about Space & Time. Brake, Mark. 2012. (Really, Really Big Questions Ser.). (ENG.). 64p. (J). (gr. 4-7). pap. 24.94 *(978-0-7534-6747-3(X)*, 900085123) Kingfisher Publications, plc GBR. Dist: Children's Plus, Inc.

Chollat, Emilie. Lettuce In! And Other Knock-Knock Jokes. Gallo, Tina. 2011. (Little Simon Sillies Ser.). (ENG.). 20p. (J). (gr. -1-1). 5.99 *(978-1-4424-1404-4(9)*, Little Simon) Little Simon.

—The Please & Thank You Book. Hazen, Barbara Shook. 2009. (Little Golden Book Ser.). 24p. (J). (gr. -1-2). 4.99 *(978-0-375-84758-5(8)*, Golden Bks.) Random Hse. Children's Bks.

Choltus, Rebekah L. Joe's Room. Choltus, Rebekah L. 32p. (J). pap. 14.95 *(978-1-932560-40-4(8))* Llumina Pr.) Aeon Publishing Inc.

Chomiak, Joseph, jt. illus. see Tremlin, Nathan.

Chomichuk, G. M. B., et al. This Place: 150 Years Retold, 1 vol. Vowel, Chelsea et al. 2019. (ENG.). 296p. (YA). (gr. 9-12). pap. *(978-1-55379-758-6(2)*, HighWater Pr.) Portage & Main Pr.

Chomichuk, G. M. B. Will I See, 1 vol. Robertson, David A. 2017. (ENG.). 54p. (YA). (gr. 8-12). pap. 18.95 *(978-1-55379-674-9(8)*, HighWater Pr.) Portage & Main Pr. CAN. Dist: Orca Bk. Pubs. USA.

Chomyn, Rebecca Nase. Who Paints the World. Nase, Lesley P. 2018. (ENG.). 40p. (J). (gr. k-6). pap. 12.95 *(978-0-9849992-0-0(5))* Moonspinners Enterprise.

Chong, Luther, photos by. Counting Petals: Using Flowers of Hawaii. Whitman, Nancy C. 2009. 31p. (J). *(978-1-4363-8562-6(8))* Xlibris Corp.

Choo, Brian. The Big Picture Book. Long, John. 2005. (ENG.). 48p. (J). (gr. 4-7). 24.99 *(978-1-74114-328-7(4))* Allen & Unwin AUS. Dist: Independent Pubs. Group.

Choosing The Best Publishing. Choosing the Best Path 6th Edition Leader Kit. Choosing The Best Publishing. 3rd ed. 2004. *(978-0-9724890-2-7(9))* Choosing The Best Publishing.

Choquette, Gabriel. Max & Voltaire Getting to Know You. Bail, Mina Mauerstein. 2015. 66p. (J). pap. 16.95 *(978-1-59095-151-4(4))* TotalRecall Pubns.

—Max et Voltaire Faisons Connaissance. Bail, Mina Mauerstein. Demmer, A. M., tr. 2016. (FRE.). (J). (gr. k-6). pap. 14.95 *(978-1-59095-538-3(2)*, ExamWise) Total Recall Learning, Inc.

Chorao, Kay. Time for Bed, Baby Ted. Sartell, Debra. 2010. (ENG.). 32p. (J). (gr. -1). 16.95 *(978-0-8234-1968-5(1))* Holiday Hse., Inc.

Chorao, Kay. Baby's Lap Book. Chorao, Kay. ed. 2004. 64p. (J). (gr. -1 — 1). 18.99 *(978-0-525-47330-5(0)*, Dutton Books for Young Readers) Penguin Young Readers Group.

—D Is for Drums: A Colonial Williamsburg ABC. Chorao, Kay. 2006. 30p. (J). (gr. k-4). reprint ed. 17.00 *(978-1-4223-5240-3(4))* DIANE Publishing Co.

—Ed & Kip. Chorao, Kay. 2015. (I Like to Read Ser.). (ENG.). 24p. (J). (gr. -1-3). 6.99 *(978-0-8234-3398-8(6))* Holiday Hse., Inc.

Chorkung. Dinosaurs. 2017. (First Explorers Ser.). (ENG.). 10p. (J). (— 1). bds. 8.95 *(978-1-4549-2655-9(4))* Sterling Publishing Co., Inc.

—Sea Creatures. 2017. (First Explorers Ser.). (ENG.). 10p. (J). (— 1). bds. 8.95 *(978-1-4549-2658-0(9))* Sterling Publishing Co., Inc.

Chotiner, Barbara. The Beautiful Garden of Eden. Bower, Gary. 2017. (Faith That God Built Book Ser.). (ENG.). 32p. (J). 14.99 *(978-1-4964-1743-5(7)*, 20_28618, Tyndale Kids) Tyndale Hse. Pubs.

—The Frightening Philippi Jail. Bower, Gary. 2017. (Faith That God Built Book Ser.). (ENG.). 32p. (J). 14.99 *(978-1-4964-1750-3(X)*, 20_28652) Tyndale Hse. Pubs.

—The Hurry-Up Exit from Egypt. Bower, Gary. 2017. (Faith That God Built Book Ser.). (ENG.). 32p. (J). 14.99 *(978-1-4964-1745-9(3)*, 20_28620) Tyndale Hse. Pubs.

—A Patch on the Peak of Ararat. Bower, Gary. 2017. (Faith That God Built Book Ser.). (ENG.). 32p. (J). 14.99 *(978-1-4964-1744-2(5)*, 20_28619, Tyndale Kids) Tyndale Hse. Pubs.

Chou, Joey. B. Bear & Lolly: Catch That Cookie! Livingston, A. A. 2015. (ENG.). 32p. (J). (gr. -1-3). 15.99 *(978-0-06-219791-7(6))* HarperCollins Pubs.

—B. Bear & Lolly: off to School. Livingston, A. A. 2014. (ENG.). 32p. (J). (gr. -1-3). 15.99 *(978-0-06-219788-7(6))* HarperCollins Pubs.

C

—Betsy B's Big Blue Bouncing Bubble. Williams, Dawn. 2007. 56p. (J). (gr. -1-3). 15.00 *(978-0-9770783-3-2(7))* SunriseHouse Pubs.

—Cyril T. Centipede Looks for New Shoes, 1. Williams, Dawn. 2006. 48p. (J). (gr. -1-3). 15.00 *(978-0-9770783-0-1(2))* SunriseHouse Pubs.

—Drac Is Back! 2015. (Hotel Transylvania 2 Ser.). (ENG.). 24p. (J). (gr. -1-2). pap. 3.99 *(978-1-4814-4811-6(0),* Simon Spotlight) Simon Spotlight.

—Giraffe Rescue Company. Sagerman, Evan. 2016. (J). *(978-1-4424-1366-5(2))* Simon & Schuster Children's Publishing.

—How Hooper the Hyaena Lost His Laugh. Williams, Dawn. 2008. 56p. (J). (gr. -1-3). 15.00 *(978-0-9770783-4-9(5))* SunriseHouse Pubs.

—I'm a Ballerina! Fliess, Sue. 2015. (Little Golden Book Ser.). 24p. (J). (-k). 4.99 *(978-0-553-49758-8(8),* Golden Bks.) Random Hse. Children's Bks.

—I'm a Dragon. Loehr, Mallory. 2019. (Little Golden Book Ser.). 24p. (J). (-k). 4.99 *(978-1-9848-4944-1(1),* Golden Bks.) Random Hse. Children's Bks.

—I'm a Narwhal. Loehr, Mallory. 2019. (Little Golden Book Ser.). 24p. (J). (-k). 4.99 *(978-0-525-64576-4(4),* Golden Bks.) Random Hse. Children's Bks.

Chou, Joey. I'm a Reindeer. Loehr, Mallory. 2020. (Little Golden Book Ser.). 24p. (J). (-k). 4.99 ***(978-0-593-12561-8(4),*** Golden Bks.) Random Hse. Children's Bks.

Chou, Joey. I'm a Unicorn. Loehr, Mallory. 2018. (Little Golden Book Ser.). (ENG.). 24p. (J). (-k). 4.99 *(978-1-5247-1512-0(3),* Golden Bks.) Random Hse. Children's Bks.

—Make & Play: Christmas. Nosy Crow Staff. 2017. (ENG.). 26p. (J). (gr. -1-2). 11.99 *(978-0-7636-9616-0(1),* Nosy Crow) Candlewick Pr.

—Make & Play: Easter. Nosy Crow. 2018. (ENG.). 26p. (J). (gr. -1-2). 11.99 *(978-0-7636-9693-1(5),* Nosy Crow) Candlewick Pr.

—Make & Play: Nativity. Nosy Crow Staff. 2017. (ENG.). 26p. (J). (gr. -1-2). 11.99 *(978-0-7636-9617-7(X),* Nosy Crow) Candlewick Pr.

—Monster & Son. LaRochelle, David. 2016. (ENG.). 32p. (J). (gr. -1 — 1). 16.99 *(978-1-4521-2937-2(1))* Chronicle Bks. LLC.

—Olaf's Frozen Adventure. 2017. (J). *(978-1-5379-5893-4(3),* Golden Bks.) Random Hse. Children's Bks.

—Olaf's Frozen Adventure (Disney Frozen) Posner-Sanchez, Andrea. 2018. (ENG.). 22p. (J). (— 1). bds. 6.99 *(978-0-7364-3856-8(4),* RH/Disney) Random Hse. Children's Bks.

—Olaf's Frozen Adventure Little Golden Book (Disney Frozen) Posner-Sanchez, Andrea. 2017. (Little Golden Book Ser.). (ENG.). 24p. (J). (-k). 4.99 *(978-0-7364-3835-3(1),* Golden/Disney) Random Hse. Children's Bks.

—Ruby's Chinese New Year. Lee, Vickie. 2017. (ENG.). 40p. (J). 17.99 *(978-1-250-13338-0(6),* 900177279, Holt, Henry & Co. Bks. For Young Readers) Holt, Henry & Co.

—Say What? Diterlizzi, Angela. 2011. (ENG.). 32p. (J). (gr. -1-k). 15.99 *(978-1-4169-8694-2(4),* Beach Lane Bks.) Beach Lane Bks.

—Thanksgiving Activity Book. Jones, Karl & Price, Stern. 2015. 16p. (J). (gr. 3-7). bds. 9.99 *(978-0-8431-8296-5(2),* Price Stern Sloan) Penguin Young Readers Group.

—Very Little Venus & the Very Friendly Fly. Williams, Dawn. 2007. 48p. (J). 15.00 *(978-0-9770783-2-5(9))* SunriseHouse Pubs.

—When the Snow Is Deeper Than My Boots Are Tall. Reidy, Jean. 2019. (ENG.). 32p. (J). 16.99 *(978-1-250-12712-9(2),* 900175379, Holt, Henry & Co. Bks. For Young Readers) Holt, Henry & Co.

—Winston J. Worm Hunts for a New Name. Williams, Dawn. 2010. 52p. (J). 15.00 *(978-0-9770783-5-6(3))* SunriseHouse Pubs.

—12 Lucky Animals: a Bilingual Baby Book. Lee, Vickie. 2018. (ENG.). 24p. (J). bds. 7.99 *(978-1-250-18424-5(X),* 900191035, Holt, Henry & Co. Bks. For Young Readers) Holt, Henry & Co.

Chou, Joey. Crazy by the Letters. Chou, Joey. 2006. 15.99 *(978-0-9788670-0-3(9))* Choo Choo Clan.

Choudhary, Sandeep. Fun & Games with Lad & Slim: [none]. Murray, Bruce A. & Murray, Geralyn (Geri). 2019. (Geniebooks Ser.: Vol. 2). (ENG.). 218p. (J). (gr. k-2). pap. 19.95 ***(978-0-578-50399-8(9))*** GenieBks.

Chougule, Shailja Jain. My Experiments with Truth. Gandhi, Mahatma. 2016. (ENG.). 64p. pap. 6.95 *(978-1-906230-88-3(9))* Real Reads Ltd. GBR. Dist: Casemate Pubs. & Bk. Distributors, LLC.

Chouinard, Barbara Jean. Anthony's Adventures in Growing Up: (Series #1) I'm a Big Boy Now. C-Harrington, Debra M. 2020. (ENG.). 30p. (J). 23.00 ***(978-1-64426-191-0(X))*** Dorrance Publishing Co., Inc.

Choux, Nathalie. A Beary Merry Christmas. Meunier, Henri. 2017. (Super-Duper Duo Ser.). (ENG.). 32p. (J). (gr. -1-3). 8.99 *(978-1-328-76678-6(0),* 1680915, HMH Books For Young Readers) Houghton Mifflin Harcourt Publishing Co.

—Easter Eggscapade. Meunier, Henri. 2018. (Super-Duper Duo Ser.). (ENG.). 32p. (J). (gr. -1-3). 8.99 *(978-1-328-76679-3(9),* 1680917, HMH Books For Young Readers) Houghton Mifflin Harcourt Publishing Co.

—Make Us Laugh! A Laugh-Out-Loud Sound Book. Babin, Stéphanie. 2020. (ENG.). 18p. (J). (gr. -1 — 1). 15.99 *(978-2-408-01613-5(4))* Editions Tourbillon FRA. Dist: Hachette Bk. Group.

Chow, Candice, jt. illus. see Lee, Jenn Manley.

Chow, Candice, jt. illus. see Lee, Jennifer A.

Chow, Derrick. Come Play with Me. Hillert, Margaret. 2016. (BeginningtoRead Ser.). (ENG.). 32p. (J). (-2). 22.60 *(978-1-59953-814-3(8));* (gr. -1-2). pap. 11.94 *(978-1-60357-976-6(1))* Norwood Hse. Pr.

Chown, Lori. A Magical World Becomes the Night. Chown, Lori. Goeman, Jan, ed. 2017. (ENG.). 34p. (J). pap. 15.00 *(978-0-9997161-0-6(7))* Utopian Dreams Gifts.

Choy, Julien. Manga Classics: Hamlet. Shakespeare, William. 2020. (ENG.). 476p. (YA). (gr. 9-12). 24.99 *(978-1-947808-11-9(7),* afd8afdd-8e5c-4a92-b206-259fc6fadf30); pap. 17.99 *(978-1-947808-12-6(5),* 2dc3712e-d7fc-4f57-a65f-b81491002c46) Manga Classics Inc.

Chris, Healey. Jackie's Got Game! A Story about Diabetes. Steinberg, Howard. 2005. (J). 9.99 *(978-0-9777463-0-9(5))* dLife - For Your Diabetes Life.

Chris, Wright. The Legend of Skylar Swift, the Fastest Boy on Earth. Patterson, Eric. 2010. 122p. pap. 6.95 *(978-1-935105-49-7(3))* Avid Readers Publishing Group.

Chrisagis, Shawn. Who & What Am I? Good News Gang. Chrisagis, Brian. 2006. 24p. (J). 9.99 *(978-1-59958-014-2(4))* Journey Stone Creations, LLC.

ChrisCross. KINO Vol. 2: The End of All Lies. Casey, Joe. 2018. (ENG.). 144p. (YA). pap. 14.99 *(978-1-941302-83-5(1),* 9d306e25-8522-4745-9e26-fdfb3ff5a768, Lion Forge) Oni Pr., Inc.

Christe, Moreno. The Wild Cats of Piran. Young, Scott Alexander. 2014. (ENG.). 136p. (J). (gr. 5). pap. 10.99 *(978-0-9900043-0-1(9),* Young Europe Bks.) New Europe Bks.

Christelow, Eileen. The Flimflam Man. Beard, Darleen Bailey. 2003. (ENG.). 96p. (J). (gr. 2-5). per. 11.99 *(978-0-374-42345-2(8),* 900021220, Farrar, Straus & Giroux (BYR)) Farrar, Straus & Giroux.

Christelow, Eileen. Vote! Christelow, Eileen. 2004. 48p. (J). (gr. 1-5). 47.60 *(978-0-618-51723-7(5),* Clarion Bks.) Houghton Mifflin Harcourt Trade & Reference Pubs.

Christensen, Andrew. Canals & Dams: Investigate Feats of Engineering with 25 Projects. Latham, Donna. 2013. (Build It Yourself Ser.). 128p. (J). (gr. 3-7). 21.95 *(978-1-61930-169-6(5),* 2672547e-8821-478c-9473-09f9d38863b0); pap. 16.95 *(978-1-61930-165-8(2),* 3fda4ef0-be4d-47d4-847c-e2127ecdae00) Nomad Pr.

—Skyscrapers: Investigate Feats of Engineering with 25 Projects. Latham, Donna. 2013. (Build It Yourself Ser.). 128p. (J). (gr. 3-7). pap. 16.95 *(978-1-61930-193-1(8),* 930e30b8-2461-4448-b985-08287f8aca34) Nomad Pr.

—3-D Engineering: Design & Build Your Own Prototypes. May, Vicki V. 2015. (Build It Yourself Ser.). 128p. (J). (gr. 3-7). 22.95 *(978-1-61930-311-9(6),* 28f43073-dbc9-4302-8b35-e2af23419a5d) Nomad Pr.

Christensen, Bodil Sebrina. Lille Pearls Spejlbillede: N. Kinnear, Sarah Ann. Holland, Mette Sk, tr. 2018. (DAN.). 40p. (J). pap. 9.99 *(978-1-7293-7304-0(6))* Independently Published.

Christensen, Bodil Sebrina. Little Pearl's Reflection: The Song of the Unicorns. Kinnear, Sarah Ann. 2019. (Little Pearl's Reflection Ser.: Vol. 6). (ENG.). 40p. (J). pap. 9.99 ***(978-1-9843-7489-9(3))*** CreateSpace Independent Publishing Platform.

Christensen, Bodil Sebrina. Little Pearl's Reflection: Where Is Asterix? Kinnear, Sarah Ann. 2019. (Little Pearl's Reflection Ser.: Vol. 5). (ENG.). 40p. (J). pap. 9.99 *(978-1-9843-7488-2(5))* CreateSpace Independent Publishing Platform.

Christensen, Bonnie. Breaking into Print: Before & after the Invention of the Printing Press. Krensky, Stephen. 2003. 30p. (J). (gr. 3-8). reprint ed. 18.00 *(978-0-7567-6843-0(8))* DIANE Publishing Co.

—Ida B. Wells: Let the Truth Be Told. Myers, Walter Dean. (ENG.). 40p. (J). (gr. -1-3). 2015. pap. 7.99 *(978-0-06-054468-3(6));* 2008. 16.99 *(978-0-06-027705-5(X))* HarperCollins Pubs. (Amistad).

—Moon over Tennessee: A Boy's Civil War Journal. Crist-Evans, Craig. 2003. (ENG.). 64p. (J). (gr. 5-7). pap. 8.95 *(978-0-618-31107-1(6),* 460020) Houghton Mifflin Harcourt Publishing Co.

—Pompeii: Lost & Found. Osborne, Mary Pope. 2006. (ENG.). 40p. (J). (gr. -1-2). 16.95 *(978-0-375-82889-8(3),* Knopf Bks. for Young Readers) Random Hse. Children's Bks.

Christensen, Bonnie. Django: World's Greatest Jazz Guitarist. Christensen, Bonnie. 2011. (ENG.). 32p. (J). (gr. k-4). pap. 9.99 *(978-1-59643-696-1(4),* 900073117) Roaring Brook Pr.

—Elvis: The Story of the Rock & Roll King. Christensen, Bonnie. 2015. (ENG.). 32p. (J). (gr. 1-4). 18.99 *(978-0-8050-9447-3(4),* 900077612, Holt, Henry & Co. Bks. For Young Readers) Holt, Henry & Co.

—Woody Guthrie: Poet of the People. Christensen, Bonnie. 2009. (ENG.). 32p. (J). (gr. -1-2). pap. 7.99 *(978-0-553-11203-0(1),* Dragonfly Bks.) Random Hse. Children's Bks.

Christensen, David. All about Real Bears. Williams, Rozanne Lanczak. 2006. (Learn to Write Ser.). 8p. (J). (gr. k-2). pap. 3.49 *(978-1-59198-288-3(X),* 6182) Creative Teaching Pr., Inc.

—All about Real Bears. Williams, Rozanne Lanczak. Maio, Barbara & Faulkner, Stacey, eds. 2006. (J). per. 6.99 *(978-1-59198-339-2(8))* Creative Teaching Pr., Inc.

Christensen, David & Leary, Catherine. Fairy Tale Rock. Williams, Rozanne Lanczak. 2005. (Reading for Fluency Ser.). 16p. (J). pap. 3.49 *(978-1-59198-153-4(0),* 4252) Creative Teaching Pr., Inc.

Christensen, Donald. The Macaroon Moon: A Book of Poems & Rhymes for Children. Haan, Wanda. 2004. 32p. (J). 17.95 *(978-0-913337-51-6(X))* Southfarm Pr.

Christensen, Donna. Mommy, May I Hug the Fish?, 1 vol. Bowman, Crystal. 2007. (I Can Read! Ser.).Tr. of Mamá, Puedo Abrazar Al Pez?. (ENG.). 32p. (J). (gr. -1-1). pap. 4.99 *(978-0-310-71468-2(0))* Zonderkidz.

Christensen, Tomas. The Thing about Swings. 2018. (ENG.). 56p. (J). 14.95 *(978-1-61961-835-0(4))* Mascot Bks., Inc.

Christenson, Anna, et al. Animal Tracks Activity Book, 1 vol. Ortler, Brett. 2015. (Color & Learn Ser.). (ENG.). 64p. (J). (gr. 3-7). pap. 6.95 *(978-1-59193-538-4(5),* Adventure Pubns.) AdventureKEEN.

Christenson, Anna, jt. illus. see Nitzsche, Shane.

Christenson, Emme Jo, jt. illus. see Christenson, Lisa.

Christenson, Lisa. Harley Hippo & the Crane Game. Christenson, Lisa. 2005. (J). per. *(978-0-9725311-0-8(6),* Pickled Eggs Press (TM)) Bk. Entree(TM).

Christenson, Lisa & Christenson, Emme Jo. Seasons on the Sofa. Christenson, Lisa & Christenson, Emme Jo. 2006. per. *(978-0-9725311-3-9(0),* Pickled Eggs Press (TM)) Bk. Entree(TM).

—Who Ate the Moon? Christenson, Lisa & Christenson, Emme Jo. 2006. (J). per. *(978-0-9725311-2-2(2),* Pickled Eggs Press (TM)) Bk. Entree(TM).

Christenson, Maren. Jingle Jangle Jungle Jeepers. Dutson, Shelly. 2009. 24p. pap. 12.50 *(978-1-4490-1061-4(X))* AuthorHouse.

Christian, Heather. Bible Awareness Series, 6 vols. Widmer, Becky. Date not set. (J). (gr. -1-18). 9.95 *(978-1-888537-00-0(0))* Publisher Plus.

Christiana, David. Fairy Haven & the Quest for the Wand. Levine, Gail Carson. 2007. 191p. (J). *(978-1-4287-6391-3(0))* Disney Pr.

—Gold & Silver, Silver & Gold: Tales of Hidden Treasure. Schwartz, Alvin. 2009. (ENG.). 144p. (J). (gr. 4-8). pap. 16.99 *(978-0-374-42582-1(5),* 900063090, Farrar, Straus & Giroux (BYR)) Farrar, Straus & Giroux.

—El Pais de Nunca Jamas y el Secreto de la Hadas. Levine, Gail Carson. Pombo, Juan Manuel, tr. 2005. (SPA.). 239p. (J). *(978-958-04-8969-6(6))* Norma S.A.

Christiane. White Gloves & Party Manners. Young, Mariabelle & Buchwald, Ann. 2012. (ENG.). 65p. (J). (gr. 4-7). pap. 14.95 *(978-0-88331-000-7(7))* Luce, Robert B. Pubs.

Christiansen, Lee. Eagle Boy: A Pacific Northwest Native Tale. Vaughan, Richard Lee. 2008. 32p. (J). (gr. -1-3). pap. 10.99 *(978-1-57061-592-4(6),* Little Bigfoot) Sasquatch Bks.

—On This Spot: An Expedition Back Through Time. Goodman, Susan. 2004. (ENG.). 32p. (J). (gr. k-5). 17.99 *(978-0-688-16913-8(9),* Greenwillow Bks.) HarperCollins Pubs.

Christie, Gregory R. The Palm of My Heart: Poetry by African American Children. Adedjouma, Davida. 2013. (ENG.). 32p. (J). (gr. -1-18). pap. 10.95 *(978-1-880000-76-2(8))* Lee & Low Bks., Inc.

—Richard Wright y el Carne de Biblioteca. Miller, William. 2003. (SPA.). (J). 32p. 16.95 *(978-1-58430-180-6(5));* pap. 6.95 *(978-1-58430-181-3(3))* Lee & Low Bks., Inc.

Christie, R. Love to Langston, 1 vol. Medina, Tony. 2005. (ENG.). 40p. (J). (gr. 1-7). pap. 11.95 *(978-1-58430-283-4(6))* Lee & Low Bks., Inc.

Christie, R. Gregory. Almost Zero: A Dyamonde Daniel Book. Grimes, Nikki. 2010. (Dyamonde Daniel Book Ser.: 3). (ENG.). 128p. (J). (gr. 2-4). 12.99 *(978-0-399-25177-1(4),* G.P. Putnam's Sons Books for Young Readers) Penguin Young Readers Group.

—Answering the Cry for Freedom: Stories of African Americans & the American Revolution. Woelfle, Gretchen. 2016. (ENG.). 240p. (J). (gr. 4-7). 19.99 *(978-1-62979-306-1(X),* Calkins Creek) Boyds Mills Pr.

—Bad News for Outlaws: The Remarkable Life of Bass Reeves, Deputy U. S. Marshal. Nelson, Vaunda Micheaux. 2009. (ENG.). 40p. (J). (gr. 3-6). lib. bdg. 19.99 *(978-0-8225-6764-6(4),* Carolrhoda Bks.) Lerner Publishing Group.

—The Book Itch: Freedom, Truth & Harlem's Greatest Bookstore. Nelson, Vaunda Micheaux. 2015. (ENG.). 32p. (J). (gr. 2-4). lib. bdg. 17.99 *(978-0-7613-3943-4(4),* 9780761339434); E-Book 27.99 *(978-1-4677-4618-2(5))* Lerner Publishing Group. (Carolrhoda Bks.).

—Brothers in Hope: The Story of the Lost Boys of Sudan, 1 vol. Williams, Mary. 2013. (ENG.). 40p. (J). 18.95 *(978-1-58430-232-2(1))* Lee & Low Bks., Inc.

—The Champ. Bolden, Tonya. 2007. (gr. k-3). 17.00 *(978-0-7569-7940-9(4))* Perfection Learning Corp.

—The Champ: the Story of Muhammad Ali. Bolden, Tonya. 2007. (ENG.). 40p. (J). (gr. 1-4). pap. 7.99 *(978-0-440-41782-8(1),* Dragonfly Bks.) Random Hse. Children's Bks.

—Freedom in Congo Square. Boston Weatherford, Carole. 2016. (ENG.). 40p. (J). (gr. -1-3). 17.99 *(978-1-4998-0103-3(3))* Little Bee Books Inc.

—Halfway to Perfect: A Dyamonde Daniel Book. Grimes, Nikki. (Dyamonde Daniel Book Ser.: 4). (ENG.). 128p. (J). (gr. 2-4). 2018. 6.99 *(978-0-425-29175-7(8),* Puffin Books); 2012. 12.99 *(978-0-399-25178-8(2),* G.P. Putnam's Sons Books for Young Readers) Penguin Young Readers Group.

—Jazz Baby. Wheeler, Lisa. 2007. (ENG.). 40p. (J). (gr. -1-3). 17.99 *(978-0-15-202522-9(7),* 1193042) Houghton Mifflin Harcourt Publishing Co.

—Keep Climbing, Girls. Richards, Beah E. 2006. (ENG.). 32p. (J). (gr. -1-3). 19.99 *(978-1-4169-0264-5(3),* Simon & Schuster Bks. For Young Readers) Simon & Schuster Bks. For Young Readers.

—Lift As You Climb: The Story of Ella Baker. Powell, Patricia Hruby. 2020. (ENG.). 48p. (J). (gr. -1-3). 17.99 *(978-1-5344-0623-0(9),* McElderry, Margaret K. Bks.) McElderry, Margaret K. Bks.

—Love to Langston. Medina, Tony. 2006. (J). (gr. 1-7). 17.10 *(978-0-7569-7016-1(4))* Perfection Learning Corp.

—Make Way for Dyamonde Daniel. Grimes, Nikki. (Dyamonde Daniel Book Ser.: 1). (ENG.). (J). (gr. 2-4). 2010. 112p. pap. 6.99 *(978-0-14-241555-9(3),* Puffin Books); 2009. 96p. 12.99 *(978-0-399-25175-7(8),* G.P. Putnam's Sons Books for Young Readers) Penguin Young Readers Group.

—Memphis, Martin, & the Mountaintop: The Sanitation Strike Of 1968. Duncan, Alice Faye. 2018. (ENG.). 40p. (J). (gr. 2-5). 17.99 *(978-1-62979-718-2(9),* Calkins Creek) Boyds Mills Pr.

—No Crystal Stair: A Documentary Novel of the Life & Work of Lewis Michaux, Harlem Bookseller. Nelson, Vaunda Micheaux. 2018. (ENG.). 192p. (YA). (gr. 7-12). pap. 9.99 *(978-1-5415-1491-1(2),* 9781541514911, Carolrhoda Lab™) Lerner Publishing Group.

—Rich: a Dyamonde Daniel Book. Grimes, Nikki. 2009. (Dyamonde Daniel Book Ser.: 2). (ENG.). 112p. (J). (gr. 2-4). 12.99 *(978-0-399-25176-4(6),* G.P. Putnam's Sons Books for Young Readers) Penguin Young Readers Group.

—Roots & Blues: A Celebration. Adoff, Arnold. 2011. (ENG.). 96p. (J). (gr. 5-7). 17.99 *(978-0-547-23554-7(2),* 1083184) Houghton Mifflin Harcourt Publishing Co.

—Sugar Hill: Harlem's Historic Neighborhood. Weatherford, Carole Boston. 2014. (ENG.). 32p. (J). (gr. k-3). 16.99 *(978-0-8075-7650-2(6),* 807576506) Whitman, Albert & Co.

—A Time to Act: John F. Kennedy's Big Speech. Corey, Shana. 2017. (ENG.). 56p. (J). (gr. 3). 18.95 *(978-0-7358-4275-5(2))* North-South Bks., Inc.

—The United States V. Jackie Robinson. Bardhan-Quallen, Sudipta. 2018. (ENG.). 40p. (J). (gr. -1-3). 17.99 *(978-0-06-228784-7(2),* Balzer & Bray) HarperCollins Pubs.

—Yesterday I Had the Blues. Ashford Frame, Jeron. 2nd rev. ed. 2008. 32p. (J). (gr. -1-2). pap. 7.99 *(978-1-58246-260-8(7),* Tricycle Pr.) Random Hse. Children's Bks.

Christie, R. Gregory & Steptoe, Javaka. Thirteen Ways of Looking at a Black Boy. Medina, Tony. 2018. (ENG.). 40p. (J). 16.95 *(978-0-9987999-4-0(7))* Penny Candy Bks., LLC.

Christine Battuz, Christine. Goodnight, Sleepy Animals: A Nightlight Book. 2016. (Nightlight Book Ser.). 14p. (J). (gr. -1-k). bds. 12.99 *(978-2-89718-338-7(1),* CrackBoom! Bks.) Chouette Publishing CAN. Dist: Publishers Group West (PGW).

Christine, Grove. My Mom Has a Job. Snead, Kathi. 2004. (J). *(978-0-9747385-1-2(4))* City of Manassas Department of Social Services.

Christlike, Daniel. Hearing the Voice of God for Children. Carini, Lori Hosanna. 2018. (ENG.). 74p. (J). pap. 12.99 *(978-1-7288-2886-2(4))* Independently Published.

Christman, Therese. Cecil Centipede's Career. Ramsay, Betsy. 2005. 25p. (J). per. 19.99 *(978-1-4208-7870-7(0))* AuthorHouse.

Christmas, Dozay. Loon Rock. Trottier, Maxine. Sylliboy, Helen, tr. ed. (ENG.). 22p. (J). (gr. k-2). pap. *(978-0-920336-84-7(1))* Cape Breton Univ. Pr.

Christmas, Dozay (Arlene). Les Savoirs Perdus / Panuijkatasikl Kina'masuti'l, 1 vol. Isaac, Michael James. 2017. (FRE.). 48p. 17.00 ***(978-1-55266-968-6(8),*** 23644) Community Bks. CAN. Dist: Columbia Univ. Pr.

Christmas Gifts, Fortnite. Fortnite Christmas (Part 2) Fortnite Coloring Books for Kids Fortnite Christmas Gifts (Unofficial Book) Turner, Page. 2018. (ENG.). 90p. (J). pap. 12.99 *(978-1-7257-1633-9(X))* CreateSpace Independent Publishing Platform.

Christmas, Lawrence. Totally Turtles! (Teenage Mutant Ninja Turtles) Gilbert, Matthew J. 2020. (Little Golden Book Ser.). (ENG.). 24p. (J). (-k). 4.99 ***(978-0-593-17937-6(4),*** Golden Bks.) Random Hse. Children's Bks.

Christodoulou, Jean. The Night Before Christmas in Africa, 1 vol. Foster, Jesse et al. 2010. (Night Before Christmas Ser.). (ENG.). 32p. (J). (gr. k-3). 16.99 *(978-1-58980-847-8(9),* Pelican Publishing) Arcadia Publishing.

Christoph, James. Pingpong Perry Experiences How a Book Is Made, 1 vol. Donovan, Sandy. 2010. (In the Library). (ENG.). 24p. (J). (gr. k-4). lib. bdg. 27.32 *(978-1-4048-5759-9(1),* Picture Window Bks.) Capstone.

Christoph, Jamey. Bones in the White House: Thomas Jefferson's Mammoth. Ransom, Candice. 2020. 40p. (J). (gr. -1-2). 17.99 *(978-0-525-64607-5(8))* Knopf Doubleday Publishing Group.

—Clackety Track: Poems about Trains. Brown, Skila. 2019. 32p. (J). (gr. k-3). 16.99 *(978-0-7636-9047-2(3))* Candlewick Pr.

—Cursive Writing: Around the World in 26 Letters. Flash Kids Editors, ed. 2012. 112p. (J). (gr. 2-4). pap. 5.95 *(978-1-4114-6345-5(5),* Spark Publishing Group) Sterling Publishing Co., Inc.

—Diggin' Dirt: Science Adventures with Kitanai the Origami Dog, 1 vol. Troupe, Thomas Kingsley. 2013. (Origami Science Adventures Ser.). (ENG.). 24p. (J). (gr. -1-3). pap. 6.95 *(978-1-4048-8066-5(6));* lib. bdg. 27.99 *(978-1-4048-7969-0(2))* Capstone. (Picture Window Bks.).

—Glowing with Electricity: Science Adventures with Glenda the Origami Firefly, 1 vol. Troupe, Thomas Kingsley. 2014. (Origami Science Adventures Ser.). (ENG.). 24p. (J). (gr. -1-3). lib. bdg. 27.99 *(978-1-4795-2189-0(2),* Picture Window Bks.) Capstone.

—Gordon Parks: How the Photographer Captured Black & White America. Weatherford, Carole Boston. 2015. (ENG.). 32p. (J). (gr. -1-3). 16.99 *(978-0-8075-3017-7(4),* 807530174) Whitman, Albert & Co.

—Kitanai & Cavity Croc Brush Their Teeth. Troupe, Thomas Kingsley. 2015. (Kitanai's Healthy Habits Ser.). (ENG.). 24p. (J). (gr. -1-2). lib. bdg. 27.32 *(978-1-4795-6080-6(4),* Picture Window Bks.) Capstone.

—Kitanai & Filthy Flamingo Wash Up. Troupe, Thomas Kingsley. 2015. (Kitanai's Healthy Habits Ser.). (ENG.). 24p. (J). (gr. -1-2). lib. bdg. 27.32 *(978-1-4795-6081-3(2),* Picture Window Bks.) Capstone.

—Kitanai & Hungry Hare Eat Healthfully. Troupe, Thomas Kingsley. 2015. (Kitanai's Healthy Habits Ser.). (ENG.). 24p. (J). (gr. -1-2). pap. 8.95 *(978-1-4795-6114-8(2),* Picture Window Bks.) Capstone.

—Kitanai & Lazy Lizard Get Fit. Troupe, Thomas Kingsley. 2015. (Kitanai's Healthy Habits Ser.). (ENG.). 24p. (J). (gr. -1-2). lib. bdg. 27.32 *(978-1-4795-6083-7(9),* Picture Window Bks.) Capstone.

—Kitanai's Healthy Habits. Troupe, Thomas Kingsley. 2015. (Kitanai's Healthy Habits Ser.). (ENG.). 24p. (J). (gr. -1-2). lib. bdg., lib. bdg., lib. bdg. 109.28 *(978-1-4795-6255-8(6),* Picture Window Bks.) Capstone.

—Let's Rock! Science Adventures with Rudie the Origami Dinosaur, 1 vol. Braun, Eric. 2013. (Origami Science Adventures Ser.). (ENG.). 24p. (J). (gr. -1-3). pap. 6.95 *(978-1-4048-8068-9(2));* lib. bdg. 27.99 *(978-1-4048-7971-3(4))* Capstone. (Picture Window Bks.).

—Lookin' for Light: Science Adventures with Manny the Origami Moth, 1 vol. Braun, Eric. 2014. (Origami Science Adventures Ser.). (ENG.). 24p. (J). (gr. -1-3). lib. bdg. 27.99 (978-1-4795-2186-9(8), Picture Window Bks.) Capstone.

—Magnet Power! Science Adventures with MAG-3000 the Origami Robot, 1 vol. Troupe, Thomas Kingsley. 2013. (Origami Science Adventures Ser.). (ENG.). 24p. (J). (gr. -1-3). pap. 6.95 (978-1-4048-8070-2(4)); lib. bdg. 27.99 (978-1-4048-7972-0(2)) Capstone. (Picture Window Bks.).

—Outside My Window. Ashman, Linda. 2018. (ENG.). 40p. (J). 17.00 (978-0-8028-5465-0(6), Eerdmans Bks For Young Readers) Eerdmans, William B. Publishing Co.

—Plant Parts Smarts: Science Adventures with Charlie the Origami Bee, 1 vol. Braun, Eric. 2013. (Origami Science Adventures Ser.). (ENG.). 24p. (J). (gr. -1-3). pap. 6.95 (978-1-4048-8072-6(0)); lib. bdg. 27.99 (978-1-4048-7970-6(6)) Capstone. (Picture Window Bks.).

—Simply Sound: Science Adventures with Jasper the Origami Bat, 1 vol. Braun, Eric. 2014. (Origami Science Adventures Ser.). (ENG.). 24p. (J). (gr. -1-3). lib. bdg. 27.99 (978-1-4795-2187-6(6), Picture Window Bks.) Capstone.

—Stonewall: a Building. an Uprising. a Revolution. Sanders, Rob. 2019. (ENG.). 40p. (J). (gr. k-3). 17.99 (978-1-5247-1952-4(8), Random Hse. Bks. for Young Readers) Random Hse. Children's Bks.

—Wild Weather: Science Adventures with Sonny the Origami Bird, 1 vol. Troupe, Thomas Kingsley. 2014. (Origami Science Adventures Ser.). (ENG.). 24p. (J). (gr. -1-3). lib. bdg. 27.99 (978-1-4795-2188-3(4), Picture Window Bks.) Capstone.

Christophe, Jamey. Up in the Leaves: The True Story of the Central Park Treehouses. Boss, Shira. 2018. (ENG.). 40p. (J). (gr. k-3). 16.95 (978-1-4549-2071-7(8)) Sterling Publishing Co., Inc.

Christopher, Danny. A Children's Guide to Arctic Birds, 1 vol. Pelletier, Mia. 2014. (ENG.). 32p. (J). (gr. k-2). 16.95 (978-1-927095-67-6(0)) Inhabit Media Inc. CAN. Dist: Consortium Bk. Sales & Distribution.

—A Children's Guide to Arctic Butterflies, 1 vol. Pelletier, Mia. 2019. (ENG.). 40p. (J). (gr. k-2). 16.95 (978-1-77227-177-5(2)) Inhabit Media Inc. CAN. Dist: Consortium Bk. Sales & Distribution.

—The Legend of the Fog, 1 vol. Mikkigak, Qaunaq & Schwartz, Joanne. 2017. (ENG.). 40p. (J). (gr. k-2). pap. 10.95 (978-1-77227-136-2(5)) Inhabit Media Inc. CAN. Dist: Consortium Bk. Sales & Distribution.

—Polar Bear, 1 vol. Flaherty, William. 2016. (Animals Illustrated Ser.). (ENG.). 24p. (J). (gr. -1-k). 12.95 (978-1-77227-079-2(2)) Inhabit Media Inc. CAN. Dist: Consortium Bk. Sales & Distribution.

Christopher, Danny & Sandland, Amanda. Una Huna: What Is This? Aglukark, Susan. 2019. (ENG.). 36p. (J). 16.95 (978-1-77227-226-0(4)) Inhabit Media Inc. CAN. Dist: Consortium Bk. Sales & Distribution.

Christopher, Jennifer, jt. illus. see Christopher, Marie.

Christopher, John Tyler, jt. illus. see Andrade, Filipe.

Christopher, Lawrence. The Tickle Fingers: Where Is Pinky? Christopher, Lawrence. 2006. (ENG.). 24p. (J). (gr. -1-18). 9.95 (978-0-9712278-3-5(7)) MF Unlimited.

Christopher, Marie & Christopher, Jennifer. What If a Fork Was a Spoon. Christopher, Jennifer R. 2006. (ENG.). 29p. (J). (gr. -1-3). per. 19.99 (978-1-4257-0847-4(1)) Xlibris Corp.

Christopher, Nathan. Humpty Dumpty Lived near a Wall. Hughes, Derek. 2020. 48p. (J). (gr. 5). 14.99 (978-1-5247-9302-9(7), Penguin Workshop) Penguin Young Readers Group.

Christopher, Wright. Something Lurking in the Bell Tower. Patterson, Eric. 2007. 99p. (J). pap. 6.95 (978-0-9797106-1-2(8)) Avid Readers Publishing Group.

Christophersen, Christine. Kakadu Calling: Stories for Kids. Christophersen, Jane Garlil. 2007. 64p. (J). (gr. 2-7). pap. 9.95 (978-1-921248-00-9(9)) Magabala Bks. AUS. Dist: Independent Pubs. Group.

Christou, Bethany. Slow Samson. Christou, Bethany. 2020. (ENG.). 40p. (J). (gr. -1-2). 16.99 (978-1-5362-1547-2(3), Templar) Candlewick Pr.

Christy, Jana. And Then Comes Christmas. Brenner, Tom. 2014. (And Then Comes Ser.). (ENG.). 32p. (J). (gr. -1-3). 15.99 (978-0-7636-5342-2(X)) Candlewick Pr.

—Around the Neighborhood: A Counting Lullaby, 0 vols. Thomson, Sarah L. 2012. (ENG.). 32p. (J). (gr. -1-3). 16.99 (978-0-7614-6164-7(7), 9780761461647, Two Lions) Amazon Publishing.

—A Dandelion Wish. Thorpe, Kiki. ed. 2013. (Never Girls Ser.: 3). lib. bdg. 16.00 (978-0-606-32199-0(3)) Turtleback.

—A Dandelion Wish/from the Mist (Disney: the Never Girls) Thorpe, Kiki. 2015. (Never Girls Ser.). (ENG.). 256p. (J). (gr. 1-4). 9.99 (978-0-7364-3460-7(7), RH/Disney) Random Hse. Children's Bks.

—A Fairy's Gift (Disney: the Never Girls) Thorpe, Kiki. 2017. (Never Girls Ser.). (ENG.). 224p. (J). (gr. 1-4). 7.99 (978-0-7364-3773-8(8), RH/Disney) Random Hse. Children's Bks.

—Finding Tinker Bell #1: Beyond Never Land (Disney: the Never Girls) Thorpe, Kiki. 2018. (Never Girls Ser.: 1). (ENG.). 128p. (J). (gr. 1-4). 6.99 (978-0-7364-3599-4(9), RH/Disney) Random Hse. Children's Bks.

—Finding Tinker Bell #2 (Disney: the Never Girls) Thorpe, Kiki. 2018. (Never Girls Ser.: 2). (ENG.). 128p. (J). (gr. 1-4). lib. bdg. 12.99 (978-0-7364-8183-0(4), RH/Disney) Random Hse. Children's Bks.

—Finding Tinker Bell #2: Through the Dark Forest (Disney: the Never Girls) Thorpe, Kiki. 2018. (Never Girls Ser.: 2). (ENG.). 128p. (J). (gr. 1-4). 6.99 (978-0-7364-3651-9(0), RH/Disney) Random Hse. Children's Bks.

—Finding Tinker Bell #3: on the Lost Coast (Disney: the Never Girls) Thorpe, Kiki. 2018. (Never Girls Ser.: 3). (ENG.). 128p. (J). (gr. 1-4). 6.99 (978-0-7364-3760-8(6)); lib. bdg. 12.99 (978-0-7364-9020-7(5)) Random Hse. Children's Bks. (RH/Disney).

—Finding Tinker Bell #5: to the Forgotten Castle (Disney: the Never Girls) Thorpe, Kiki. 2019. (Never Girls Ser.). (ENG.). 128p. (J). (gr. 1-4). 6.99 (978-0-7364-3955-8(2)); 12.99 (978-0-7364-8270-7(9)) Random Hse. Children's Bks. (RH/Disney).

Christy, Jana. Finding Tinker Bell: Books #1-6 (Disney: the Never Girls), 6 vols. Thorpe, Kiki. 2020. (Never Girls Ser.). (ENG.). 768p. (J). (gr. 1-4). 41.94 (978-0-7364-4127-8(1), RH/Disney) Random Hse. Children's Bks.

Christy, Jana. Frankie Liked to Sing. Seven, John. 2015. (ENG.). 32p. (J). (gr. -1-3). 16.95 (978-1-4197-1644-7(1), Abrams Bks. for Young Readers) Abrams, Inc.

—Gorilla Gardener: How to Help Nature Take over the World. Seven, John. 2017. (Wee Rebel Ser.). (ENG.). 44p. (J). (gr. -1). 16.95 (978-1-945665-00-4(9)) Manic D Pr.

—Happy Birthday, Tree! A Tu B'Shevat Story. Rosenberg, Madelyn. 2014. (AV2 Fiction Readalong Ser.: Vol. 106). (ENG.). (J). (gr. -1-2). lib. bdg. 32.71 (978-1-4896-2404-8(X), AV2 by Weigl) Weigl Pubs., Inc.

—Happy, Sad, Silly, Mad. Seven, John. 2012. (ENG.). 26p. (J). (-k). bds. 6.99 (978-1-4494-2229-5(2)) Andrews McMeel Publishing.

—I'm the Big One Now! Poems about Growing Up. Singer, Marilyn. 2019. (ENG.). 32p. (J). (gr. -1-3). 16.95 (978-1-62979-169-2(5), Wordsong) Boyds Mills Pr.

—In a Blink. Thorpe, Kiki. ed. 2013. (Never Girls Ser.: 1). lib. bdg. 16.00 (978-0-606-26977-3(0)) Turtleback.

—My Never Land Journal (Disney: the Never Girls) RH Disney Staff & Depken, Kristen L. 2014. (Never Girls Ser.). (ENG.). 128p. (J). (gr. 1-4). 12.99 (978-0-553-49685-7(9), RH/Disney) Random Hse. Children's Bks.

—Never Girls #1: in a Blink (Disney: the Never Girls) Thorpe, Kiki. 2013. (Never Girls Ser.: 1). (ENG.). 128p. (J). (gr. 1-4). 5.99 (978-0-7364-2794-4(5), RH/Disney) Random Hse. Children's Bks.

—Never Girls #10: on the Trail (Disney: the Never Girls) Thorpe, Kiki. 2015. (Never Girls Ser.: 10). (ENG.). 128p. (J). (gr. 1-4). 5.99 (978-0-7364-3306-8(6), RH/Disney) Random Hse. Children's Bks.

—Never Girls #11: into the Waves (Disney: the Never Girls) Thorpe, Kiki. 2016. (Never Girls Ser.: 11). (ENG.). 128p. (J). (gr. 1-4). 5.99 (978-0-7364-3525-3(5), RH/Disney) Random Hse. Children's Bks.

—Never Girls #12: in the Game (Disney: the Never Girls) Thorpe, Kiki. 2016. (Never Girls Ser.: 12). (ENG.). 128p. (J). (gr. 1-4). 5.99 (978-0-7364-3527-7(1), RH/Disney) Random Hse. Children's Bks.

—Never Girls #2: the Space Between (Disney: the Never Girls) Thorpe, Kiki. 2013. (Never Girls Ser.: 2). (ENG.). 128p. (J). (gr. 1-4). 5.99 (978-0-7364-2795-1(3), RH/Disney) Random Hse. Children's Bks.

—Never Girls #3: a Dandelion Wish (Disney: the Never Girls) Thorpe, Kiki. 2013. (Never Girls Ser.: 3). (ENG.). 128p. (J). (gr. 1-4). 5.99 (978-0-7364-2796-8(1), RH/Disney) Random Hse. Children's Bks.

—Never Girls #4: from the Mist (Disney: the Never Girls) Thorpe, Kiki. 2013. (Never Girls Ser.: 4). (ENG.). 128p. (J). (gr. 1-4). 5.99 (978-0-7364-2797-5(X), RH/Disney) Random Hse. Children's Bks.

—Never Girls #5: Wedding Wings (Disney: the Never Girls) Thorpe, Kiki. 2014. (Never Girls Ser.: 5). (ENG.). 128p. (J). (gr. 1-4). 5.99 (978-0-7364-3077-7(6), RH/Disney) Random Hse. Children's Bks.

—Never Girls #6: the Woods Beyond (Disney: the Never Girls) Thorpe, Kiki. 2014. (Never Girls Ser.: 6). (ENG.). 128p. (J). (gr. 1-4). 5.99 (978-0-7364-3096-8(2), RH/Disney) Random Hse. Children's Bks.

—Never Girls #7: a Pinch of Magic (Disney: the Never Girls) Thorpe, Kiki. 2014. (Never Girls Ser.: 7). (ENG.). 128p. (J). (gr. 1-4). 5.99 (978-0-7364-3097-5(0), RH/Disney) Random Hse. Children's Bks.

—Never Girls #8: Far from Shore (Disney: the Never Girls) Thorpe, Kiki. 2015. (Never Girls Ser.: 8). (ENG.). 128p. (J). (gr. 1-4). lib. bdg. 12.99 (978-0-7364-8166-3(4), RH/Disney) Random Hse. Children's Bks.

—Never Girls #9: Before the Bell (Disney: the Never Girls) Thorpe, Kiki. 2015. (Never Girls Ser.: 9). (ENG.). 128p. (J). (gr. 1-4). 5.99 (978-0-7364-3304-4(X), RH/Disney) Random Hse. Children's Bks.

—Never Girls: Books 4-6 (Disney: the Never Girls) Thorpe, Kiki. 2016. (Never Girls Ser.). (ENG.). 384p. (J). (gr. 1-4). 15.99 (978-0-7364-3581-9(6), RH/Disney) Random Hse. Children's Bks.

—The Never Girls Collection #2 (Disney: the Never Girls) Books 5-8, 4 vols. Thorpe, Kiki. 2015. (Never Girls Ser.). (ENG.). 512p. (J). (gr. 1-4). 23.96 (978-0-7364-3462-1(3), RH/Disney) Random Hse. Children's Bks.

—The Never Girls Collection #3 (Disney: the Never Girls) Books 9-12, 4 vols. Thorpe, Kiki. 2016. (Never Girls Ser.). (ENG.). 512p. (J). (gr. 1-4). 23.96 (978-0-7364-3521-5(2), RH/Disney) Random Hse. Children's Bks.

—The Never Girls Volume 1: Books 1-3 (Disney: the Never Girls) Thorpe, Kiki. 2016. (Never Girls Ser.). (ENG.). 384p. (J). (gr. 1-4). 15.99 (978-0-7364-3580-2(8), RH/Disney) Random Hse. Children's Bks.

—The Never Girls Volume 3: Books 7-9 (Disney: the Never Girls) Thorpe, Kiki. 2017. (Never Girls Ser.). (ENG.). 384p. (J). (gr. 1-4). 15.99 (978-0-7364-3819-3(X), RH/Disney) Random Hse. Children's Bks.

—The Ocean Story, 1 vol. Seven, John. 2011. (Fiction Picture Bks.). (ENG.). 32p. (J). (gr. k-2). lib. bdg. 23.99 (978-1-4048-6785-7(6), Picture Window Bks.) Capstone.

—Penelope Popper, Book Doctor. Buzzeo, Toni. 2011. 32p. (J). 17.95 (978-1-60213-054-8(X), Upstart Bks.) Highsmith Inc.

—Pixie Puzzles, Games, & More! Posner-Sanchez, Andrea. 2014. (Never Girls Ser.). (ENG.). 256p. (J). (gr. 1-4). 6.99 (978-0-7364-3152-1(7), Golden/Disney) Random Hse. Children's Bks.

—The Princess & the Pea. Golden Books Staff & Andersen, Hans. 2013. (Little Golden Book Ser.). Orig. Title: Prindsessen paa aerten. 24p. (J). (-k). 4.99 (978-0-307-97951-3(2), Golden Bks.) Random Hse. Children's Bks.

—The Smile That Went Around the World. Karst, Patrice. rev. ed. 2014. (ENG.). 22p. (J). 15.95 (978-0-87516-875-3(2), Devorss Pubns.) DeVorss & Co.

—The Space Between. Thorpe, Kiki. ed. 2013. (Never Girls Ser.: 2). lib. bdg. 16.00 (978-0-606-26974-2(6)) Turtleback.

—Under the Lagoon. Thorpe, Kiki. 2016. (Never Girls Ser.). 128p. (J). (gr. 1-4). 5.99 (978-0-7364-3529-1(8), RH/Disney) Random Hse. Children's Bks.

—Up the Misty Peak. Thorpe, Kiki. 2019. (Never Girls Ser.: 4). (ENG.). 128p. (J). (gr. 1-4). 6.99 (978-0-7364-3873-5(4)); lib. bdg. 12.99 (978-0-7364-3874-2(2)) Random Hse. Children's Bks. (RH/Disney).

—We're Getting a Pet! Fliess, Sue. 2015. (Little Golden Book Ser.). 24p. (J). (-k). 4.99 (978-0-385-37554-2(9), Golden Bks.) Random Hse. Children's Bks.

—What NOT to Give Your Mom on Mother's Day, 0 vols. Self Simpson, Martha. 2013. (ENG.). 24p. (J). (gr. -1-2). 12.99 (978-1-4778-1647-9(X), 9781477816479, Two Lions) Amazon Publishing.

—When the Snow Falls. Sweeney, Linda Booth. 2017. 32p. (J). (-k). 16.99 (978-0-399-54720-1(7), G.P. Putnam's Sons Books for Young Readers) Penguin Young Readers Group.

—The Woods Beyond. Thorpe, Kiki. 2014. (Never Girls Ser.: 6). (ENG.). 128p. (J). (gr. 1-4). lib. bdg. 12.99 (978-0-7364-8148-9(6), RH/Disney) Random Hse. Children's Bks.

—The Woods Beyond. Thorpe, Kiki. ed. 2014. (Never Girls Ser.: 6). lib. bdg. 16.00 (978-0-606-35545-2(6)) Turtleback.

Christy, Jana & Mitchell, Jana Christy. How to Hug, 0 vols. MacDonald, Maryann. 2011. (ENG.). 32p. (J). (gr. -1-3). 16.99 (978-0-7614-5804-3(2), 9780761458043, Two Lions) Amazon Publishing.

Christy, Jana & Zhang, Nancy. On Pins & Needles. Taylor, Chloe. 2013. (Sew Zoey Ser.: 2). (ENG.). 160p. (J). (gr. 3-7). 15.99 (978-1-4424-7937-1(X), Simon Spotlight) Simon Spotlight.

Christy, Jana, jt. illus. see RH Disney Staff.

Chromik, Vanessa. Boys Can Be Strong & Emotional: Growth Mindset. Cordova, Esther Pia. 2019. (Growth Mindset Ser.: Vol. 3). (ENG.). 32p. (J). (gr. k-2). (978-3-948298-00-5(9)) Cordova, Esther Pia Power Of Yet.

—Boys Can Be Strong & Emotional: Growth Mindset. Cordova, Esther Pia. 2019. (Growth Mindset Ser.: Vol. 3). (ENG.). 32p. (J). pap. (978-3-948298-01-2(7)) Cordova, Esther Pia Power Of Yet.

Chromik, Vanessa. Little Bears Can Do Big Things: Growth Mindset. Cordova, Esther Pia. 2019. (ENG.). 34p. (J). pap. (978-3-948298-07-4(6)) Cordova, Esther Pia Power Of Yet.

Chronister, Amanda. Claim to Fame, 1 vol. Wallace, Nancy K. 2013. (Abby & the Book Bunch Ser.). (ENG.). 80p. (J). (gr. 2-5). 29.93 (978-1-61641-912-7(1), 2, Calico Chapter Bks.) ABDO Publishing Co.

—The Haunted Sleepover, 1 vol. Wallace, Nancy K. 2013. (Abby & the Book Bunch Ser.). (ENG.). 80p. (J). (gr. 2-5). 29.93 (978-1-61641-913-4(X), 3, Calico Chapter Bks.) ABDO Publishing Co.

—Movie Mishaps, 1 vol. Wallace, Nancy K. 2013. (Abby & the Book Bunch Ser.). (ENG.). 80p. (J). (gr. 2-5). 29.93 (978-1-61641-914-1(8), 4, Calico Chapter Bks.) ABDO Publishing Co.

—The Mystery of the Golden Key, 1 vol. Wallace, Nancy K. 2013. (Abby & the Book Bunch Ser.). (ENG.). 80p. (J). (gr. 2-5). 29.93 (978-1-61641-915-8(6), 5, Calico Chapter Bks.) ABDO Publishing Co.

—Out to Lunch, 1 vol. Wallace, Nancy K. 2013. (Abby & the Book Bunch Ser.). (ENG.). 80p. (J). (gr. 2-5). 29.93 (978-1-61641-916-5(4), 6, Calico Chapter Bks.) ABDO Publishing Co.

—Presumed Missing, 1 vol. Wallace, Nancy K. 2013. (Abby & the Book Bunch Ser.). (ENG.). 80p. (J). (gr. 2-5). 29.93 (978-1-61641-917-2(2), 7, Calico Chapter Bks.) ABDO Publishing Co.

Chronister, Michele E. My First Book of Catholic Pictures Seek & Find. Chronister, Michele E. 2019. (ENG.). 28p. (J). pap. 9.99 (978-1-7906-2769-1(9)) Independently Published.

Chronopoulos, Maria. La Marathonienne. Desautels, Denise. 2004. (Poetry Ser.). (FRE.). 36p. (J). (gr. 7). pap. (978-2-89021-673-0(X)) Diffusion du livre Mirabel (DLM).

Chrustowski, Rick. Higgledy-Piggledy Chicks. Joosse, Barbara M. 2010. 40p. (J). (gr. -1-k). (ENG.). 16.99 (978-0-06-075042-8(1)); lib. bdg. 17.89 (978-0-06-075043-5(X)) HarperCollins Pubs. (Greenwillow Bks.).

Chrustowski, Rick. Bee Dance. Chrustowski, Rick. 2015. (ENG.). 32p. (J). (gr. -1-3). 18.99 (978-0-8050-9919-5(0), 900125638, Holt, Henry & Co. Bks. For Young Readers) Holt, Henry & Co.

—My Little Fox. Chrustowski, Rick. 2017. (ENG.). 40p. (J). (gr. -1-k). 17.99 (978-1-4814-6961-6(4), Beach Lane Bks.) Beach Lane Bks.

Chrystall, Claire. ABC: A Busy Fingers Book. Harris, Sue. 2003. 10p. (J). bds. 10.95 (978-1-57145-936-7(7), Silver Dolphin Bks.) Readerlink Distribution Services, LLC.

—Shapes. Hunt, Janie. 2003. (Busy Finger Ser.). 10p. (J). bds. 10.95 (978-1-57145-938-1(3), Silver Dolphin Bks.) Readerlink Distribution Services, LLC.

Chrzanowski, Rose-Ann. Welcome to Our Family. Kuczenski, Tyler. 2020. (ENG.). 36p. (J). 29.99 (978-1-6655-0198-9(7)); pap. 16.99 (978-1-6655-0199-6(5)) AuthorHouse.

Chu, April. Ada Byron Lovelace & the Thinking Machine. Wallmark, Laurie. 2015. (ENG.). 40p. (J). (gr. -1-6). 17.99 (978-1-939547-20-0(2)) Creston Bks.

—Down by the River: A Family Fly Fishing Story. Weiner, Andrew. 2018. (ENG.). 40p. (J). (gr. k-2). 17.99 (978-1-4197-2293-6(X), Abrams Bks. for Young Readers) Abrams, Inc.

—In a Village by the Sea. Van, Muon. 2015. (ENG.). 32p. (J). (gr. k-3). 16.95 (978-1-939547-15-6(6)) Creston Bks.

—Summoning the Phoenix: Poems & Prose about Chinese Musical Instruments, 1 vol. Jiang, Emily. 2014. (ENG.). 32p. (J). 18.95 (978-1-885008-50-3(3)) Lee & Low Bks., Inc.

Chu, Carol. My Misadventures As a Teenage Rock Star. Raskin, Joyce. 2011. (ENG.). 112p. (YA). (gr. 7-18). pap. 8.99 (978-0-547-39311-7(3), 1426898) Houghton Mifflin Harcourt Publishing Co.

Chu, Kate & Long, May. Charlotte's Garden. Partin, Charlotte Corry. Bine-Stock, Eve Heidi, ed. 2005. 29p. per. 18.95 (978-0-9748933-3-4(1)) E & E Publishing.

Chua, Charlene. Amy Wu & the Perfect Bao. Zhang, Kat. 2019. (Amy Wu Ser.). (ENG.). 40p. (J). (gr. -1-3). 17.99 (978-1-5344-1133-3(X), Simon & Schuster/Paula Wiseman Bks.) Simon & Schuster/Paula Wiseman Bks.

—The Belt of Fire. Chin, Oliver. 2013. (Julie Black Belt Ser.). (ENG.). 40p. (J). (gr. -1-3). 15.95 (978-1-59702-079-4(6)) Immedium.

Chua, Charlene. Elisapee & Her Baby Seagull, 1 vol. Mike, Nancy. 2020. (ENG.). 44p. (J). 11.95 (978-1-77227-293-2(0)) Inhabit Media Inc. CAN. Dist: Consortium Bk. Sales & Distribution.

Chua, Charlene. Fishing with Grandma, 1 vol. Avingaq, Susan & Vsetula, Maren. 2016. (ENG.). 32p. (J). (gr. k-2). pap. 10.95 (978-1-77227-084-6(9)) Inhabit Media Inc. CAN. Dist: Consortium Bk. Sales & Distribution.

Chua, Charlene. Genius Jolene. Cassidy, Sara. 2020. (Orca Echoes Ser.). (ENG.). 112p. (J). (gr. 1-3). pap. 7.95 (978-1-4598-2529-1(2)) Orca Bk. Pubs. USA.

Chua, Charlene. Going Up! Lee, Sherry J. 2020. (ENG.). 40p. (J). (gr. -1-2). 17.99 (978-1-5253-0113-1(6)) Kids Can Pr., Ltd. CAN. Dist: Hachette Bk. Group.

—The Great Googlini, 1 vol. Cassidy, Sara. 2018. (Orca Echoes Ser.). (ENG.). 112p. (J). (gr. 1-3). pap. 6.95 (978-1-4598-1703-6(6)) Orca Bk. Pubs. USA.

—Julie Black Belt: The Kung Fu Chronicles. Chin, Oliver. 2008. (Julie Black Belt Ser.). (ENG.). 36p. (J). (gr. k-1). 15.95 (978-1-59702-009-1(5)) Immedium.

—The Pencil, 1 vol. Avingaq, Susan & Vsetula, Maren. 2019. (ENG.). 36p. (J). 16.95 (978-1-77227-216-1(7)) Inhabit Media Inc. CAN. Dist: Consortium Bk. Sales & Distribution.

—Shubh Diwali! Soundar, Chitra. 2019. (ENG.). 32p. (J). (gr. -1-3). 16.99 (978-0-8075-7355-6(8), 807573558) Whitman, Albert & Co.

Chua, Charlene. What I Wear (English), 1 vol. 2018. (Nunavummi Ser.). (ENG.). 12p. (gr. k-k). 7.95 (978-0-2287-0151-4(1)) Inhabit Education CAN. Dist: Consortium Bk. Sales & Distribution.

Chua, Charlene. The Wind Plays Tricks. Howard, Virginia. 2019. (ENG.). 32p. (J). (gr. -1-3). 16.99 (978-0-8075-8735-5(4), 807587354) Whitman, Albert & Co.

Chua, Charlene. Hug? Chua, Charlene. 2020. (ENG.). 32p. (J). (gr. -1-2). 16.99 (978-1-5253-0206-0(X)) Kids Can Pr., Ltd. CAN. Dist: Hachette Bk. Group.

Chullabrahm, T. M. The Kid Who Ate Dog Food. Penner, Evelyn. 2008. 32p. (J). 15.99 (978-0-9796500-0-0(3)) Peppernut Publishing.

Chun, Anthony. Little Red Rocket: Kids Picture Book 4-8 Girls. Chun, Anthony. 2017. (ENG.). (J). pap. 10.97 (978-0-9994539-0-2(4)) Chun, Anthony.

Chun, Eugene. Invisibles. Chun, Eleanor. 2019. (ENG.). 36p. (J). pap. (978-1-5255-4818-5(2)) FriesenPress.

Chung, Arree. The Danger Gang & the Isle of Feral Beasts! Bramucci, Stephen. 2018. (ENG.). 352p. (J). 16.99 (978-1-61963-694-1(8), 900145711, Bloomsbury Children's Bks.) Bloomsbury Publishing USA.

—The Danger Gang & the Pirates of Borneo! Bramucci, Stephen. 2018. 304p. (J). pap. 7.99 (978-1-68119-434-9(1), 900172649, Bloomsbury Children's Bks.) Bloomsbury Publishing USA.

—The Fix-It Man. Hood, Susan. 2016. (ENG.). 40p. (J). (gr. -1-3). 17.99 (978-0-06-237085-3(5)) HarperCollins Pubs.

—How to Pee: Potty Training for Girls. Spector, Todd. 2016. (ENG.). 40p. (J). 12.99 (978-1-62779-297-4(X), 9781627792974, Holt, Henry & Co. Bks. For Young Readers) Holt, Henry & Co.

—How to Pee: Potty Training for Boys: Potty Training for Boys. Spector, Todd. 2015. (ENG.). 40p. (J). (— 1). 12.99 (978-0-8050-9773-3(2), 900118954, Holt, Henry & Co. Bks. For Young Readers) Holt, Henry & Co.

Chung, Arree. Mixed: a Colorful Story. Chung, Arree. 2018. (ENG.). 40p. (J). 18.99 (978-1-250-14273-3(3), 900180378, Holt, Henry & Co. Bks. For Young Readers) Holt, Henry & Co.

—Ninja! Chung, Arree. 2014. (Ninja! Ser.: 1). (ENG.). 40p. (J). (gr. -1-2). 18.99 (978-0-8050-9911-9(5), 900125303, Holt, Henry & Co. Bks. For Young Readers) Holt, Henry & Co.

Chung, Chi. Emily Dickinson. Bolin, Frances Schoonmaker, ed. 2008. (Poetry for Young People Ser.: 2). 48p. (J). (gr. 3). pap. 6.95 (978-1-4027-5473-9(6)) Sterling Publishing Co., Inc.

—God's Oak Tree. Nolan, Allia Zobel. 2007. 16p. (J). (gr. -1). 12.99 (978-0-8254-5536-0(7)) Kregel Pubns.

—God's Rainbow. Nolan, Allia Zobel. 2007. 16p. (J). 12.99 (978-0-8254-5537-7(5)) Kregel Pubns.

—A House for Little Red. Hillert, Margaret. 2016. (BeginningtoRead Ser.). (ENG.). 32p. (J). (gr. -1-2). 22.60 (978-1-59953-798-6(2)); pap. 11.94 (978-1-60357-939-1(7)) Norwood Hse. Pr.

—Poetry for Young People: Emily Dickinson. Bolin, Frances Schoonmaker, ed. 2014. (Poetry for Young People Ser.: 2). (ENG.). 48p. (J). (gr. 3). 14.95 (978-1-4549-1346-7(0)) Sterling Publishing Co., Inc.

—Rick & Rachel Build a Research Report. Gallion, Sue Lowell. 2014. (Writing Builders Ser.). (ENG.). 32p. (J). (gr. 2-4). pap. 11.94 (978-1-60357-557-7(X)); lib. bdg. 25.27 (978-1-59953-583-8(1)) Norwood Hse. Pr.

—When God Tucks in the Day. Nolan, Allia Zobel. 2005. 16p. (J). 12.99 (978-0-8254-5524-7(3)) Kregel Pubns.

C

Chung, Nahyun. Dreaming of Newport: Counting down Around the Town. Everin, Gretchen. 2019. (Dreaming Of... Ser.). (ENG.). 16p. (J). bds. 9.95 *(978-1-64194-130-3(8)*, Commonwealth Editions) Applewood Bks.
Chung, Ruth. 4,962,571. Eissler, Trevor. 2011. (ENG.). 32p. (J). 20.00 *(978-0-9835558-0-3(X))* June Bks., LLC.
Chung, Veronica. The Hidden Link: An Awesome Beginning. McAvoy, Coleen. 2018. (ENG.). 60p. (J). *(978-1-5255-3338-9(X))*; pap. *(978-1-5255-3339-6(8))* FriesenPress.
Chung-Wipff, Caroline. Kevin the Complainer. Chung-Wipff, Caroline. 2019. (ENG.). 46p. (J). pap. 6.00 *(978-1-0909-7574-4(0))* Independently Published.
Chuong, édéric Pham. Scare City. Jenkins, Paul. 2019. (ENG.). 120p. (gr. 5-12). 14.95 *(978-1-64337-575-5(X)*, BU908) Humanoids, Inc.
Churbuck, Esther V. Tommy Sweet-Tooth & Little girl Blue. Gates, Josephine Scribner. 2007. 64p. (J). lib. bdg. 59.00 *(978-1-60304-014-3(5))* Dollworks.
Church, Anna & Taylor, Nicole. Hug-A-Bug Travels to Peru. Church, Anna. 2013. 44p. pap. 12.00 *(978-0-9831449-4-6(X))* Mighty Lion Ventures.
Church, Caroline Jayne. Dear Bunny: A Bunny Love Story. Morgan, Michaela. 2006. (Scholastic Bookshelf Ser.). (ENG.). 32p. (J). (gr. k-2). 18.69 *(978-0-439-74834-6(8))* Scholastic, Inc.
—La Gallina Hambrienta. Waring, Richard & Jayne, Waring -. 2003. (SPA.). 28p. (J). (gr. k-2). 17.99 *(978-84-261-3339-7(8))* Juventud, Editorial ESP. Dist: Lectorum Pubns., Inc.
—How Do I Love You? Bauer, Marion Dane. 2009. (ENG.). 26p. (J). (gr. -1-k). bds. 8.99 *(978-0-545-07270-0(0)*, Cartwheel Bks.) Scholastic, Inc.
—How Do I Love You? / ¿Cómo Te Quiero? Bauer, Marion Dane. 2014. (ENG & SPA.). 24p. (J). (gr. -1-k). bds. 8.99 *(978-0-545-66525-4(6)*, Scholastic en Espanol) Scholastic, Inc.
—I Love You Through & Through. Rossetti-Shustak, Bernadette. 2005. (ENG.). 24p. (J). (gr. k — 1). bds. 8.95 *(978-0-439-67363-1(1)*, Cartwheel Bks.) Scholastic, Inc.
—I Love You Through & Through: Board Book & Plush. Rossetti-Shustak, Bernadette. 2014. (Caroline Jayne Church Ser.). (ENG.). 24p. (J). (gr. -1 — 1). 14.99 *(978-0-545-64792-2(4)*, Cartwheel Bks.) Scholastic, Inc.
—I Love You Through & Through at Christmas, Too! Rossetti-Shustak, Bernadette. 2018. (Caroline Jayne Church Ser.). (ENG.). 26p. (J). (gr. -1 — 1). bds. 8.99 *(978-1-338-23010-9(7)*, Cartwheel Bks.) Scholastic, Inc.
—I Love You Through & Through at Christmas, Too! / ¡En Navidad También Te Quiero! Rossetti-Shustak, Bernadette. 2018. (Caroline Jayne Church Ser.). (ENG & SPA.). 26p. (J). (gr. -1 — 1). bds. 8.99 *(978-1-338-29949-6(2)*, Scholastic en Espanol) Scholastic, Inc.
—I Love You Through & Through (Te Quiero, Yo Te Quiero) Rossetti-Shustak, Bernadette. ed. 2013. (Caroline Jayne Church Ser.). (ENG & SPA.). 24p. (J). (gr. -1 — 1). bds. 8.95 *(978-0-545-58416-6(7))* Scholastic, Inc.
—Peek-A-Boo Farm. Editors of Studio Fun International. 2018. (ENG.). 10p. (J). (gr. -1-k). 8.99 *(978-0-7944-4067-1(3)*, Reader's Digest Children's Bks.) Studio Fun International.
—Snuggle up, Little Penguin! Randall, Ronne. 2003. (Little Friends Ser.). 14p. (J). 12.95 *(978-1-57145-919-0(7)*, Silver Dolphin Bks.) Readerlink Distribution Services, LLC.
—You Are My Sunshine. Davis, Jimmie. 2011. (ENG.). 12p. (J). (gr. k — 1). bds. 6.99 *(978-0-545-07552-7(1)*, Cartwheel Bks.) Scholastic, Inc.
Church, Caroline Jayne. Giggle! Church, Caroline Jayne. 2013. (ENG.). 10p. (J). (— 1). bds. 7.99 *(978-0-545-35082-2(4)*, Cartwheel Bks.) Scholastic, Inc.
—Goodnight, I Love You. Church, Caroline Jayne. 2012. (ENG.). 20p. (J). (gr. -1-k). bds. 8.99 *(978-0-545-39215-0(2)*, Cartwheel Bks.) Scholastic, Inc.
—Here Comes Christmas! Church, Caroline Jayne. 2010. (ENG.). 14p. (J). (gr. k — 1). bds. 7.99 *(978-0-545-11817-0(4)*, Cartwheel Bks.) Scholastic, Inc.
—Here Comes Halloween! Church, Caroline Jayne. 2009. (ENG.). 8p. (J). (gr. k — 1). bds. 7.99 *(978-0-545-11815-6(8)*, Cartwheel Bks.) Scholastic, Inc.
—I Am a Big Brother! Church, Caroline Jayne. 2015. 32p. (J). (gr. -1 — 1). bds. 6.99 *(978-0-545-68886-4(8)*, Cartwheel Bks.) Scholastic, Inc.
—I Am a Big Brother! (¡Soy un Hermano Mayor!) Church, Caroline Jayne. 2015. (Caroline Jayne Church Ser.). (ENG & SPA.). 24p. (J). (gr. -1 — 1). 6.99 *(978-0-545-84717-9(6)*, Scholastic en Espanol) Scholastic, Inc.
—I Am a Big Sister! Church, Caroline Jayne. 2015. 32p. (J). (gr. -1 — 1). bds. 6.99 *(978-0-545-68898-7(1)*, Cartwheel Bks.) Scholastic, Inc.
—I Am a Big Sister! (¡Soy una Hermana Mayor!) Church, Caroline Jayne. 2015. (ENG & SPA.). 24p. (J). (gr. -1 — 1). 6.99 *(978-0-545-84718-6(4)*, Scholastic en Espanol) Scholastic, Inc.
—I Love My Puppy. Church, Caroline Jayne. 2015. (Love Meez Ser.). 10p. (J). (gr. -1 — 1). bds. 7.99 *(978-0-545-83594-7(1)*, Cartwheel Bks.) Scholastic, Inc.
—I Love You! Church, Caroline Jayne. 2012. (ENG.). 6p. (J). (— 1). 12.99 *(978-0-545-46140-5(5)*, Cartwheel Bks.) Scholastic, Inc.
—Let's Get Dressed! Church, Caroline Jayne. 2012. (ENG.). 10p. (J). (gr. -1 — 1). bds. 7.99 *(978-0-545-43637-3(0))* Scholastic, Inc.
—Little Apple Goat. Church, Caroline Jayne. 2007. (ENG.). 28p. (J). (gr. k-3). 16.00 *(978-0-8028-5320-2(X)*, Eerdmans Bks For Young Readers) Eerdmans, William B. Publishing Co.
—Potty Time! Church, Caroline Jayne. 2012. (ENG.). 10p. (J). (gr. -1-k). bds. 7.99 *(978-0-545-35080-8(8)*, Cartwheel Bks.) Scholastic, Inc.
—Rain, Rain, Go Away. Church, Caroline Jayne. 2013. (ENG.). 12p. (J). (— 1). bds. 6.99 *(978-0-545-48542-5(8)*, Cartwheel Bks.) Scholastic, Inc.
—Sweet Child of Mine: A Caroline Jayne Church Treasury. Church, Caroline Jayne. 2014. 24p. (J). (— 1). bds. 8.99 *(978-0-545-64771-7(1)*, Cartwheel Bks.) Scholastic, Inc.
—Ten Tiny Toes. Church, Caroline Jayne. 2014. (ENG.). 22p. (J). (— 1). bds. 8.99 *(978-0-545-53601-1(4)*, Cartwheel Bks.) Scholastic, Inc.
—Thank You Prayer. Church, Caroline Jayne. Page, Josephine. 2005. (Caroline Jayne Church Ser.). (ENG.). 24p. (J). (gr. -1-k). 8.99 *(978-0-439-68099-8(9)*, Cartwheel Bks.) Scholastic, Inc.
—Twinkle, Twinkle, Little Star. Church, Caroline Jayne. 2014. 12p. (J). (— 1). bds. 6.99 *(978-0-545-51806-2(7)*, Cartwheel Bks.) Scholastic, Inc.
Church, Elizabeth Comfort. The Pancake Stories: Cuentos Del Panqueque. Church, Peggy Pond. Chilton, Noël, tr. 2013. (ENG & SPA.). 96p. (J). 12.95 *(978-0-8263-5387-0(8))* Univ. of New Mexico Pr.
Church, Malik. The Monk & the Prince. Morselli, Jean-Paul. 2020. (Path of the Prince Ser.: Vol. 1). (ENG.). 34p. (J). pap. 19.99 ***(978-1-6568-7788-8(0))*** Independently Published.
Church, Peter. The Purim Surprise, Vol. Simpson, Lesley. 2004. (Purim Ser.). (ENG.). 32p. (J). (gr. -1-3). pap. 6.95 *(978-1-58013-090-5(9)*, Kar-Ben Publishing) Lerner Publishing Group.
Churchill, Ian, et al. X-Men/Avengers: Onslaught Vol. 1. 2020. 440p. (YA). (gr. 8-17). pap. 39.99 *(978-1-302-92281-8(5))* Marvel Worldwide, Inc.
Churchill, Ian, jt. illus. see Dodson, Terry.
Churchill, Jessica, photos by. Shalamazoo. Shaboo, Joseph R. Date not set. 56p. (J). (gr. 2-5). *(978-0-9700380-0-5(3))* Purple Pig Publishing.
Churchill, Ryan. Kate & Abby's Favorite Things. Nana. 2017. (ENG.). (J). 22.95 *(978-1-64028-743-3(4))*; pap. 12.95 *(978-1-64028-741-9(8))* Christian Faith Publishing.
Churilla, Brian. Achilles. Long, Christopher E. 2008. (Short Tales Greek Myths Ser.). (ENG.). 32p. (J). (gr. 3-6). 27.07 *(978-1-60270-133-5(4)*, 13431, Short Tales) Magic Wagon.
Chuzzlewit, Abraham R. My Sister Is a Preemie: A Children's Guide to the NICU Experience. Vitterito, Joseph A., 2nd. 2012. 30p. (J). (-18). pap. 15.99 *(978-0-9882940-9-7(5))* Bryson Taylor Publishing.
Chwast, Seymour. My Daddy & Me. Spinelli, Jerry. 2006. (ENG.). 40p. (J). (gr. -1-2). pap. 7.99 *(978-0-553-11303-7(8)*, Dragonfly Bks.) Random Hse. Children's Bks.
—Out of the Bag: The Paper Bag Players Book of Plays. Martin, Judith. 2005. 48p. (J). (gr. k-4). reprint ed. pap. 14.00 *(978-0-7567-8530-7(8))* DIANE Publishing Co.
Chwast, Seymour. Arno & the MiniMachine. Chwast, Seymour. 2019. 32p. (J). (gr. -1-3). 17.95 *(978-1-60980-879-2(7)*, Triangle Square) Seven Stories Pr.
—Bobo's Smile. Chwast, Seymour. 2012. (ENG.). 32p. (J). (gr. 1-3). 14.99 *(978-1-56846-221-9(2)*, Creative Editions) Creative Co., The.
—Dr. Dolittle. Chwast, Seymour. 2015. (ENG.). 40p. (J). (gr. 4-7). 18.99 *(978-1-56846-258-5(1)*, Creative Editions) Creative Co., The.
—Tall City, Wide Country. Chwast, Seymour. 2013. (ENG.). 32p. (J). (gr. -1-k). 15.99 *(978-1-56846-228-8(X)*, Creative Editions) Creative Co., The.
Chylak, Jolie Catherine. The Legend of the Angel Wing Shell. Steele, Kathleen Marie. 2009. 20p. pap. 24.95 *(978-1-60749-134-7(6))* America Star Bks.
Ciaffaglione, Sebastian. The Crystal Code, Bk. 4. Newsome, Richard. ed. 2013. (ENG.). 378p. (gr. 2-7). pap. 8.99 *(978-1-922079-03-9(0))* Text Publishing Co. AUS. Dist: Consortium Bk. Sales & Distribution.
Ciarnau, Viorel. The Adventures of Cardigan. Ciarnau, Elaine Bosvik. 2019. (ENG.). 64p. (J). *(978-1-5255-5099-7(3))*; pap. *(978-1-5255-5100-0(0))* FriesenPress.
Cibis, Inge. My Name Is Schnuckiputz: Just Call Me Schnucki. Dinklage, Rosemarie. 2019. (Four Legged Friends Ser.: Vol. 1). (ENG.). 122p. (J). pap. 23.30 ***(978-1-6763-3125-4(5))*** Independently Published.
Ciccarelli, Gary, jt. illus. see Hillam, Corbin.
Ciccarelli, Gary, jt. illus. see Otoshi, Kathryn.
Ciccotello, Mike. Twins: A Picture Book. Ciccotello, Mike. 2019. (ENG.). 32p. (J). 17.99 *(978-0-374-31212-1(5)*, 900199035, Farrar, Straus & Giroux (BYR)) Farrar, Straus & Giroux.
Cicero, Julian. Al Reves Esta Bien. Luna, Arcadio. 2006. (Castillo de la Lectura Blanca Ser.). (ENG.). 14p. (J). (gr. -1-k). pap. 7.95 *(978-970-20-0841-5(7))* Castillo, Ediciones, S. A. de C. V. MEX. Dist: Macmillan.
Cicero, Julián. El Príncipe Feliz y Otros Cuentos. Wilde, Oscar. 2017. (Serie Naranja Ser.). (SPA.). 104p. (J). (gr. 3-8). pap. 7.99 *(978-970-58-0208-9(4))* Santillana USA Publishing Co., Inc.
Cicero, Julian. La Risa de los Cocodrilos. Baranda, Maria. 2009. (SPA.). 70p. (J). (gr. 3-6). pap. *(978-968-5389-67-9(5))* El Naranjo, Ediciones.
—Unas Vacaciones Horribles. Jinks, Catherine. rev. ed. 2007. (Castillo de la Lectura Verde Ser.). 88p. (J). (gr. 2-4). pap. 7.95 *(978-970-20-0852-1(2))* Castillo, Ediciones, S. A. de C. V. MEX. Dist: Macmillan.
—Zarabulli: Cantares de Alla y de Aqui. Masera, Mariana. rev. ed. 2006. (Otra Escalera Ser.). (SPA & ENG.). 48p. (J). (gr. k). pap. 10.95 *(978-968-5920-70-4(2))* Castillo, Ediciones, S. A. de C. V. MEX. Dist: Macmillan.
Cichos, Tomek. Bee in the Barn. Wildfong, Tonya. 2012. 22p. (J). 12.95 *(978-0-9860056-0-2(6))* TBSM Publishing.
Cicierega, Emmy. Gravity Falls: Dipper & Mabel & the Curse of the Time Pirates' Treasure! A Select Your Own Choose-Venture! Rowe, Jeffrey. 2016. (ENG.). 288p. (J). (gr. 3-7). 12.99 *(978-1-4847-4668-4(6))* Disney Pr.
Cide, Jane. Secret Message Origami: Pass Secret Notes That Only Your Friends Can Read! (with 120 Origami Sheets) Odd Dot. 2020. (ENG.). 288p. (J). pap. 9.99 *(978-1-250-23596-1(0)*, 900210413, Odd Dot) St. Martin's Pr.
Ciencin, Scott, et al. Trial by Fire. Salvatore, R. A. 2003. 160p. (YA). (gr. 7-18). pap. 15.95 *(978-1-931484-62-6(7))* CrossGeneration Comics, Inc.
Ciesemier, Kali. I Am Princess X. Priest, Cherie. 2015. 304p. (YA). (gr. 7). 18.99 *(978-0-545-62085-7(6)*, Levine, Arthur A. Bks.) Scholastic, Inc.
Ciesinka, Izabela. The Adventures of Northern the Moose & a Dragon Named Zeus. Chapman, Karean. 2010. 38p. pap. 12.95 *(978-1-935268-44-4(9))* Halo Publishing International.
Ciesinki, Izabela. Marllow. Johnson, Cheryl. 2007. 27p. (J). 14.95 *(978-0-9785728-4-6(X))* Digi-Tall Media.
Ciesinska, Izabela. Dmitri: The Kind Storyteller Book One of Five. Karandeev, Oleg. 2006. 76p. (YA). per. 15.95 *(978-0-9785728-9-1(0))* Digi-Tall Media.
—Dmitri II: The Kind Storyteller Book Two of Five. Karandeev, Oleg. 2007. 76p. (YA). per. 15.95 *(978-0-9793944-3-0(0))* Digi-Tall Media.
—Doctor Dave's Dragon Tales. Fast, David R. 2007. 160p. (J). per. 13.95 *(978-0-9793944-8-5(1))* Digi-Tall Media.
—Kate & the Family Tree. Bernard, Margaret Mitchell. Duncan, Shirley, ed. 2009. 24p. pap. 14.99 *(978-1-4251-7408-8(6))* Trafford Publishing.
—Look at Me, a Muscian I Want to Be. Chapman, Karean. 2011. 32p. pap. 12.95 *(978-1-935268-75-8(9))* Halo Publishing International.
—Look at Me, a Veterinarian I Want to Be. Chapman, Karean. 2011. 32p. pap. 12.95 *(978-1-935268-76-5(7))* Halo Publishing International.
—Starr Light & the Christmas Story. Warren, G. A. 2009. 32p. (J). 14.95 *(978-1-935268-09-3(0))* Halo Publishing International.
—What We Believe. Haskan, Kim. 2016. (ENG.). (J). *(978-0-9950709-0-5(3))* Kelebek Publishing.
Cillyart, (cindy M. Bowles). Twin Tails: Journey to Oceanus: TWIN TAILS Book Three. Cillyart, (cindy M. Bowles). 2019. (Twin Tails Book Ser.: Vol. 3). (ENG.). 228p. (J). (gr. 2-6). pap. 15.00 ***(978-0-9985955-6-6(X))*** CILLYart4U.
Cimatoribus, Alessandra. Mighty Mountains, Swirling Seas. Bloom, Valerie. 2015. (Collins Big Cat Ser.). (ENG.). 32p. (J). (gr. 2-2). pap. 7.95 *(978-0-00-759126-8(8))* HarperCollins Pubs. Ltd. GBR. Dist: Independent Pubs. Group.
—Monkey's Magic Pipe. Thomson, Pat. 2014. (Traditional Tales Ser.). (ENG.). 24p. (J). (gr. 1-2). pap. 6.95 *(978-1-62521-586-4(X)*, Capstone Classroom) Capstone.
—One Night in a Stable. Visconti, Guido. 2004. 32p. (J). 16.00 *(978-0-8028-5279-3(3))* Eerdmans, William B. Publishing Co.
Ciminelli, Matthew Joseph. Where's My Father? Ciminelli, Marilyn Johnson. 2006. (ENG.). 24p. per. 12.99 *(978-1-59926-657-2(1))* Xlibris Corp.
CINAR Animation Staff. Caillou, Spends the Day with Daddy. Pleau-Murissi, Marilyn. 2004. (Clubhouse Usa Ser.). 24p. (J). (gr. -1-18). 3.95 *(978-2-89450-523-6(X))* Ellipsis Pr.
CINAR Corporation Staff. Caillou, What's That Noise. Johnson, Marion. 2004. (Clubhouse Usa Ser.). (ENG.). 24p. (J). pap. 3.95 *(978-2-89450-489-5(6))* Ellipsis Pr.
Cinar, Lisa. Bear's Winter Party, 1 vol. Hodge, Deborah. 2016. (ENG.). 32p. (J). (gr. -1-2). 16.95 *(978-1-55498-853-2(5))* Groundwood Bks. CAN. Dist: Publishers Group West (PGW).
Cinar, Lisa. Clara Humble & the Kitten Caboodle. Humphrey, Anna. 2020. (Clara Humble Ser.: 3). (ENG.). 232p. (J). (gr. 2-6). pap. 11.95 ***(978-1-77147-423-8(8))*** Owlkids Bks. Inc. CAN. Dist: Publishers Group West (PGW).
Cinar, Lisa. Clara Humble: Quiz Whiz. Humphrey, Anna. 2020. (Clara Humble Ser.: 2). (ENG.). 240p. (J). (gr. 1-5). pap. 10.95 *(978-1-77147-401-6(7))* Owlkids Bks. Inc. CAN. Dist: Publishers Group West (PGW).
—You & Me Both. Narsimhan, Mahtab. 2020. (ENG.). 24p. (J). (gr. -1-5). 16.95 *(978-1-77147-366-8(5))* Owlkids Bks. Inc. CAN. Dist: Publishers Group West (PGW).
Cinar, Yildiray. Friendly Neighborhood Spider-Man Vol. 2: Hostile Takeovers. 2020. (Friendly Neighborhood Spider-Man - 2018 Ser.: 2). (ENG.). 112p. (YA). (gr. 4-17). pap. 17.99 *(978-1-302-91691-6(2))* Marvel Worldwide, Inc.
—Weapon X Vol. 5: Weapon X-Force. 2019. (Weapon X (2017) Ser.: 5). (ENG.). 112p. (YA). (gr. 8-17). pap. 17.99 *(978-1-302-91224-6(0))* Marvel Worldwide, Inc.
Cincinnati Zoo and Botanical Garden Staff, photos by. Fiona's Feelings. Hutton, John. 2018. (ENG., 14p. (J). (— 1). bds. 7.99 *(978-1-936669-65-3(X))* Blue Manatee Press.
—Fiona's Friends. Hutton, John. 2018. (ENG., 14p. (J). (— 1). bds. 7.99 *(978-1-936669-68-4(4))* Blue Manatee Press.
Cindrich, Mary. Let's Chat about Democracy: Exploring Forms of Government in a Treehouse. Balconi, Michelle a & Laffer, Arthur B. 2018. (ENG.). 48p. (J). (gr. 1-5). 18.99 *(978-0-9906846-5-7(2))* Gichigami Pr.
—Let's Chat about Democracy: Exploring Forms of Government in a Treehouse. Balconi, Michelle a & Laffer, Arthur B. 2018. (ENG.). 48p. (J). (gr. 1-5). pap. 14.99 *(978-0-9906846-4-0(4))* Gichigami Pr.
Cinelli, Lisa. Josefina, the Christmas Cow: A Tale of Hope & Faith. Benson, P. Bryn. 2005. 35p. (J). (gr. -1-3). per. 9.95 *(978-0-929636-47-4(3))* Syren Bk. Co.
—Peter Fished the Springs of Galilee. Bahamon, Claire. Sampson, Anne, ed. 2015. (ENG.). 32p. (J). pap. 7.99 *(978-0-9961139-0-8(8))* Donkey's Quest Pr.
Cinq-Mars, Mathilde. Clarence's Big Secret. MacGregor, Roy & MacGregor Cation, Christine. 2020. (ENG.). 32p. (J). (gr. k-5). 17.95 *(978-1-77147-331-6(2))* Owlkids Bks. Inc. CAN. Dist: Publishers Group West (PGW).
—Grand Tintamarre! Chansons et Comptines Acadiennes. 2018. (ENG & FRE.). 36p. (J). (gr. k-2). 16.95 *(978-2-924217-76-4(8))* La Montagne Secrete CAN. Dist: Independent Pubs. Group.
—Mr. Mergler, Beethoven, & Me, 1 vol. Gutnick, David. 2018. (ENG.). 32p. (J). (gr. 1-3). 18.95 *(978-1-77260-059-9(8))* Second Story Pr. CAN. Dist: Orca Bk. Pubs. USA.
—My Mommy, My Mama, My Brother, & Me, 1 vol. Meisner, Natalie. 2019. (ENG.). 32p. (J). 22.95 *(978-1-77108-741-4(2)*, 093493e2-4fb0-4a6e-af04-cd5015e6ef47) Nimbus Publishing, Ltd. CAN. Dist: Baker & Taylor Publisher Services (BTPS).
Cioffi, Ben. The Gospel for Children. Piantedosi, John J. 2011. (J). pap. *(978-1-56548-370-5(7))* New City Community Pr.
Cioffi, Dom. Digby & the Lake Monster. l.t. ed. 2006. 36p. (J). per. *(978-0-9745931-0-4(9))* Vermont Bookworks.
Ciraolo, Simona. Can't Catch Me! Knapman, Timothy. 2017. (ENG.). 32p. (J). (-k). 15.99 *(978-0-7636-9496-8(7))* Candlewick Pr.
—Lights! Camera! Alice! The Thrilling True Adventures of the First Woman Filmmaker. Rockliff, Mara. 2018. (ENG.). 60p. (J). (gr. k-3). 17.99 *(978-1-4521-4134-3(7))* Chronicle Bks. LLC.
—Whatever Happened to My Sister? 2015. 40p. (J). (gr. k-3). 17.95 *(978-1-909263-52-9(4))* Flying Eye Bks. GBR. Dist: Penguin Random Hse. LLC.
Ciresi-Abremski, M. Kathleen. Buzzy the Vegetarian Vulture. Johnson, Calvin. 2012. 28p. pap. 12.95 *(978-1-61493-109-6(7))* Peppertree Pr., The.
Cis, Valeria. Bubbe's Belated Bat Mitzvah, Vol. Pinson, Isabel. 2014. (ENG.). 32p. (J). (gr. -1-3). 7.95 *(978-1-4677-1950-6(1)*, 9781467719506, Kar-Ben Publishing) Lerner Publishing Group.
—A Heart Just Like My Mother's, Vol. Nargi, Lela. 2018. (ENG.). 32p. (J). (gr. -1-2). pap. 7.99 *(978-1-5124-2099-9(9)*, 9781512420999, Kar-Ben Publishing) Lerner Publishing Group.
—Millie's Chickens. Williams, Brenda. 40p. (J). (gr. k-4). 2015. pap. 8.99 *(978-1-78285-083-0(X))*; 2014. 16.99 *(978-1-78285-082-3(1))* Barefoot Bks., Inc.
—A Tale of Two Seders. Portnoy, Mindy Avra. 2010. (ENG.). 32p. (J). (gr. k-4). lib. bdg. 17.95 *(978-0-8225-9907-4(4))*; Vol. pap. 7.95 *(978-0-8225-9931-9(7)*, 9780822599319) Lerner Publishing Group. (Kar-Ben Publishing).
Cis, Valeria. The Beeman. Cis, Valeria. Krebs, Laurie. 2008. 40p. (J). (gr. -1-3). 16.99 *(978-1-84686-146-8(2))* Barefoot Bks., Inc.
Cisco II, Wendell. Rainbows, Elephants, a Sun . . . oh My! Mann, Kamryn. 2018. (ENG.). 20p. (J). pap. 11.95 *(978-1-937449-36-0(X))* YAV.
Cisner, Naftali. Count with Mendel. Cisner, Naftali. 2003. 10p. (J). bds. 5.95 *(978-1-880582-84-8(8)*, CWMH) Judaica Pr., Inc., The.
—Get Ready for Shabbos with Mendel. Cisner, Naftali. 2003. 10p. (J). bds. 5.95 *(978-1-880582-03-9(1))* Judaica Pr., Inc., The.
Cisneros, Kevin. Shoelaces: The Secret Art of Fresco Painting. Cisneros, Kevin. Cadney, Mary, ed. collector's l.t. ed. 2004. 120p. (YA). 119.00 *(978-0-9658481-7-6(5))* Belisarian Bks.
Cissna, Kent. Clouds for Breakfast. Eisen, Laura. 2013. 60p. pap. 14.95 *(978-0-9882113-4-6(3))*; pap. 14.95 *(978-0-9882113-7-7(8))* StarryBks.
—Clouds for Breakfast (Korean/English Edition) Eisen, Laura. 2013. (KOR.). (J). pap. 14.95 *(978-0-9882113-3-9(5))* StarryBks.
—Nubes para Desayunar. Eisen, Laura. 2013. 60p. pap. 14.95 *(978-0-9882113-2-2(7))* StarryBks.
Cittadino, Kristen, jt. illus. see Cittadino, Kyle.
Cittadino, Kyle & Cittadino, Kristen. The Sleigh. Russo, Frank M. 2012. 24p. 24.95 *(978-1-4626-6916-5(6))*; pap. 24.95 *(978-1-4626-7662-0(6))* America Star Bks.
Civati, Chiara. Waking Beauty: Is She for Real? Fraser, Hugh. 2016. (ENG.). (J). (gr. 4-6). pap. *(978-0-9955429-0-7(2))* Storynory.
Civiello, Emmanuel. A Bit of Madness. Civiello, Emmanuel. Mosdi, Thomas. 2005. (ENG.). 200p. pap. 24.95 *(978-0-9753808-9-5(3))* Devil's Due Digital, Inc. - A Checker Digital Co.
Clack, Barbra. Good Night Cowboy. Dromgoole, Glenn. 2006. (ENG.). 24p. (J). (gr. -1-k). 15.95 *(978-1-931721-51-6(3)*, 8881eb28-4741-4243-b214-11aad6390010) Night Heron Media.
—Good Night Little Texan. Dromgoole, Glenn. 2012. (ENG.). 24p. (J). (gr. k-2). 15.95 *(978-1-936474-10-3(7)*, fd802ca2-d96b-4396-bae7-2e758a7aeba8) Night Heron Media.
Clack, Barbra. Good Night Cowgirl. Clack, Barbra. Dromgoole, Glenn. 2006. (ENG.). 24p. (J). (gr. -1-k). 15.95 *(978-1-931721-80-6(7)*, 190e123d-8fa7-4a39-aeb7-0540e8381d2d) Night Heron Media.
Claerhout, Paul. Willy Nilly Volume 1. Brehm, David L. 2013. 94p. (J). pap. 19.95 *(978-0-9860669-0-0(7))* Blue Logic Publishing.
Claeys, Bobby. My Name Is Benjamin! Claeys, Bobby. 2019. (ENG.). 26p. (J). pap. 9.99 *(978-1-0745-8779-6(0))* Independently Published.
Clamp Staff. Rg Veda, Vol. 2. Furukawa, Haruko, tr. from JPN. rev. ed. 2005. 192p. pap. 14.99 *(978-1-59532-485-6(2)*, Tokyopop Adult) TOKYOPOP, Inc.
—Tokyo Babylon, Vol. 6. Yoshimoto, Ray, tr. from JPN. rev. ed. 2005. 176p. pap. 9.99 *(978-1-59532-050-6(4))* TOKYOPOP, Inc.
Clamp Staff. Angelic Layer, 2 vols., Vol. 2. Clamp Staff. Horn, Carl Gustav, ed. 2013. (Angelic Layer Ser.). (ENG.). 472p. pap. 19.99 *(978-1-61655-128-5(3))* Dark Horse Comics.
—Cardcaptor Sakura, 4 vols., Vol. 3. Clamp Staff. 2012. (Cardcaptor Sakura Ser.: 3). (ENG.). 600p. pap. 19.99 *(978-1-59582-808-8(7))* Dark Horse Comics.
—Cardcaptor Sakura, 6 vols., Vol. 2. Clamp Staff. Onishi, Mika, tr. rev. ed. 2004. 192p. (J). pap. 9.99 *(978-1-59182-879-2(1)*, Tokyopop Kids) TOKYOPOP, Inc.
—Cardcaptor Sakura, Vol. 4. Clamp Staff. rev. ed. 2005. 200p. (J). pap. 9.99 *(978-1-59182-881-5(3)*, Tokyopop Kids) TOKYOPOP, Inc.
—RG Veda, Vol. 3. Clamp Staff. 3rd rev. ed. 2005. (RG Veda Ser.). 184p. per. 14.99 *(978-1-59532-486-3(0)*, Tokyopop Adult) TOKYOPOP, Inc.
Clamp Staff. Rg Veda. Clamp Staff, creator. 2005. pap. 14.99 *(978-1-59532-484-9(4)*, Tokyopop Adult) TOKYOPOP, Inc.

—Tokyo Babylon, Vol. 7. Clamp Staff, creator. rev. ed. 2005. 160p. pap. 9.99 *(978-1-59532-051-3(2))* TOKYOPOP, Inc.

Clancy, Catherine. Phoebe Sees the Light. Maurer, Eileen Reno. 2018. (ENG.). 32p. (J). (gr. 4-6). 20.00 *(978-0-578-42376-0(6))* Eileen Reno Maurer.

Clanton, Ben. Jasper John Dooley: NOT in Love. Adderson, Caroline. 2015. (Jasper John Dooley Ser.). (ENG.). 132p. (J). (gr. 2-5). pap. 7.95 *(978-1-77138-343-1(7))* Kids Can Pr., Ltd. CAN. Dist: Hachette Bk. Group.

—Jasper John Dooley: Star of the Week. Adderson, Caroline. 2014. (Jasper John Dooley Ser.). (ENG.). 128p. (J). (gr. 2-5). pap. 7.95 *(978-1-77138-119-2(1))* Kids Can Pr., Ltd. CAN. Dist: Hachette Bk. Group.

—Max Finds an Egg. Blevins, Wiley. 2015. (Penguin Young Readers, Level 1 Ser.). (ENG.). 32p. (J). (gr. k-1). pap. 4.99 *(978-0-448-47993-4(1))*, Penguin Young Readers) Penguin Young Readers Group.

—Max Finds an Egg. Blevins, Wiley. 2015. (Penguin Young Readers: Level 1 Ser.). (ENG.). (J). (gr. k-1). lib. bdg. 14.60 *(978-1-62765-742-6(8))* Perfection Learning Corp.

—Max Has a Fish. Blevins, Wiley. 2012. (Penguin Young Readers, Level 1 Ser.). (ENG.). 32p. (J). (gr. k-1). pap. 4.99 *(978-0-448-46158-8(7))*, Penguin Young Readers) Penguin Young Readers Group.

—Monster Boogie. Berkner, Laurie. 2018. (ENG.). 40p. (J). (gr. -1-3). 17.99 *(978-1-4814-6465-9(5))*, Simon & Schuster Bks. For Young Readers) Simon & Schuster Bks. For Young Readers.

—We Are the Dinosaurs. Berkner, Laurie. 2017. (ENG.). 40p. (J). (gr. -1-3). 18.99 *(978-1-4814-6463-5(9))*, Simon & Schuster Bks. For Young Readers) Simon & Schuster Bks. For Young Readers.

Clanton, Ben. Boo Who? Clanton, Ben. 32p. (J). 2018. (-k). bds. 7.99 *(978-0-7636-9967-3(5))*; 2017. (ENG.). (gr. -1-2). 15.99 *(978-0-7636-8824-0(X))* Candlewick Pr.

—It Came in the Mail. Clanton, Ben. (ENG.). 40p. (J). (gr. -1-3). 2019. 7.99 *(978-1-5344-5321-0(0))*; 2016. 17.99 *(978-1-4814-0360-3(5))* Simon & Schuster Bks. For Young Readers. (Simon & Schuster Bks. For Young Readers).

—Rex Wrecks It! Clanton, Ben. (J). 2017. 32p. (-k). bds. 7.99 *(978-0-7636-9308-4(1))*; 2014. 40p. (gr. -1-2). 15.99 *(978-0-7636-6501-2(0))* Candlewick Pr.

—Rot, the Cutest in the World! Clanton, Ben. 2017. (ENG.). 40p. (J). (gr. -1-3). 17.99 *(978-1-4814-6762-9(X))*, Atheneum Bks. for Young Readers) Simon & Schuster Children's Publishing.

—Something Extraordinary. Clanton, Ben. 2015. (ENG.). 40p. (J). (gr. -1-3). 18.99 *(978-1-4814-0358-0(3))*, Simon & Schuster Bks. For Young Readers) Simon & Schuster Bks. For Young Readers.

Clanton, Connie. The Boy Who Cried Wolf: The Boy Who Cried Wolf. 2012. (SGN, ARA, BOS, CHI & ENG.). 32p. (J). pap. 19.95 incl. DVD *(978-0-9818139-1-2(7))* ASL Tales.

Clar, David Austin. The First Easter, 1 vol. DeBoer, Jesslyn. 2005. (Easter Board Bks.). (ENG.). 12p. (J). bds. 3.99 *(978-0-310-70842-1(7))* Zonderkidz.

—¡Listos... Ya! Donovan, Gail. 2003. (Rainbow Fish & Friends Ser.). 24p. (J). mass mkt. 3.99 *(978-1-59014-123-6(7))* Night Sky Bks.

—My Day with Jesus, 1 vol. Davidson, Alice Joyce. 2005. (Easter Board Bks.). (ENG.). 16p. (J). bds. 3.99 *(978-0-310-70843-8(5))* Zonderkidz.

—100th Day Fun. Donovan, Gail. 2003. (Rainbow Fish & Friends Ser.). 24p. (J). lib. bdg. 9.95 *(978-1-59014-141-0(5))* Night Sky Bks.

Clar, David Austin & Hantel, Johanna. Good Food. Jensen, Patricia & Demar, Regier. 2006. (My First Reader Ser.). (ENG.). 32p. (J). (gr. k-1). per. 3.95 *(978-0-516-24969-8(X))*, Children's Pr.) Scholastic Library Publishing.

Clar, David Austin, jt. illus. see Goodell, Jon.

Clara, Miss. The Princess & the Pea. Gresham, Xanthe. 2013. 40p. (J). 17.99 *(978-1-84686-905-1(6))* Barefoot Bks., Inc.

—Princess & the Pea. Gresham, Xanthe & Knight, Gresham. 2017. (ENG.). 40p. (J). (gr. -1-3). pap. 12.99 *(978-1-78285-355-8(3))* Barefoot Bks., Inc.

—The Snow Queen. Lowes, Sarah. 64p. (J). 2013. 17.99 *(978-1-84686-964-8(1))*; 2011. (gr. 1-5). pap. 9.99 *(978-1-84686-662-3(6))* Barefoot Bks., Inc.

—The Twelve Dancing Princesses. Hoffman, Mary. (J). 2013. 40p. (gr. 1-5). 17.99 *(978-1-84686-966-2(8))*; 2012. 64p. (gr. 2-6). pap. 9.99 *(978-1-84686-838-2(6))* Barefoot Bks., Inc.

Claremont, Heather. Thank You, Jesus. Lundy, Charlotte. Waldrep, Evelyn L., ed. 2003. 32p. (gr. k-3). 15.95 *(978-0-9670280-1-9(9))* Bay Light Publishing.

Clarey, Patricio. Arena of Monsters. Dahl, Michael. 2020. (Escape from Planet Alcatraz Ser.). (ENG.). 40p. (J). (gr. 3-6). pap. 5.95 *(978-1-4965-9301-6(4))*, 142313); lib. bdg. 23.99 *(978-1-4965-8671-1(9))*, 141423) Capstone. (Stone Arch Bks.).

—Attack of the Drones. Dahl, Michael. 2019. (Escape from Planet Alcatraz Ser.). (ENG.). 40p. (J). (gr. 3-6). lib. bdg. 23.99 *(978-1-4965-8315-4(9))*, 140490, Stone Arch Bks.) Capstone.

—Beyond the Farthest Star. Dahl, Michael. 2020. (Escape from Planet Alcatraz Ser.). (ENG.). 40p. (J). (gr. 3-6). pap. 5.95 *(978-1-4965-9302-3(2))*, 142314); lib. bdg. 23.99 *(978-1-4965-8673-5(5))*, 141424) Capstone. (Stone Arch Bks.).

—Bug Team Alpha, 6 vols. Sutton, Laurie S. 2018. (Bug Team Alpha Ser.). (ENG.). 112p. (J). (gr. 3-6). 155.94 *(978-1-4965-5972-2(X))*, 27621, Stone Arch Bks.) Capstone.

—The Canyon of Giants. Dahl, Michael. 2020. (Escape from Planet Alcatraz Ser.). (ENG.). 40p. (J). (gr. 3-6). pap. 5.95 *(978-1-4965-9304-7(9))*, 142316); lib. bdg. 23.99 *(978-1-4965-8677-3(8))*, 141426) Capstone. (Stone Arch Bks.).

Clarey, Patricio. Dead Letters. Dahl, Michael. 2020. (Secrets of the Library of Doom Ser.). (ENG.). 40p. (J). (gr. 3-5). pap. 5.95 ***(978-1-4965-9897-4(0)***, 201274); lib. bdg. 23.99 ***(978-1-4965-9723-6(0)***, 199357) Capstone. (Stone Arch Bks.).

Clarey, Patricio. Diamonds of Doom. Dahl, Michael. 2020. (Escape from Planet Alcatraz Ser.). (ENG.). 40p. (J). (gr. 3-6). pap. 5.95 *(978-1-4965-9303-0(0))*, 142315); lib. bdg. 23.99 *(978-1-4965-8675-9(1))*, 141425) Capstone. (Stone Arch Bks.).

Clarey, Patricio. Don't Read This! Dahl, Michael. 2020. (Secrets of the Library of Doom Ser.). (ENG.). 40p. (J). (gr. 3-5). pap. 5.95 ***(978-1-4965-9898-1(9)***, 201275); lib. bdg. 23.99 ***(978-1-4965-9721-2(4)***, 199355) Capstone. (Stone Arch Bks.).

—The Eraser Strikes Back. Dahl, Michael. 2020. (Secrets of the Library of Doom Ser.). (ENG.). 40p. (J). (gr. 3-5). pap. 5.95 ***(978-1-4965-9901-8(2)***, 201278); lib. bdg. 23.99 ***(978-1-4965-9722-9(2)***, 199356) Capstone. (Stone Arch Bks.).

—The Index Insects. Dahl, Michael. 2020. (Secrets of the Library of Doom Ser.). (ENG.). 40p. (J). (gr. 3-5). pap. 5.95 ***(978-1-4965-9902-5(0)***, 201279); lib. bdg. 23.99 ***(978-1-4965-9724-3(9)***, 199358) Capstone. (Stone Arch Bks.).

—Invisible Ink. Dahl, Michael. 2020. (Secrets of the Library of Doom Ser.). (ENG.). 40p. (J). (gr. 3-5). pap. 5.95 ***(978-1-4965-9899-8(7)***, 201276); lib. bdg. 23.99 ***(978-1-4965-9720-5(6)***, 199354) Capstone. (Stone Arch Bks.).

Clarey, Patricio. Juggernaut. Sutton, Laurie S. 2018. (Bug Team Alpha Ser.). (ENG.). 112p. (J). (gr. 3-6). lib. bdg. 25.99 *(978-1-4965-5958-6(4))*, 137178, Stone Arch Bks.) Capstone.

—The Pit of No Return. Dahl, Michael. 2019. (Escape from Planet Alcatraz Ser.). (ENG.). 40p. (J). (gr. 3-6). lib. bdg. 23.99 *(978-1-4965-8311-6(6))*, 140486, Stone Arch Bks.) Capstone.

Clarey, Patricio. Raiders of the Lost Archives. Dahl, Michael. 2020. (Secrets of the Library of Doom Ser.). (ENG.). 40p. (J). (gr. 3-5). pap. 5.95 ***(978-1-4965-9900-1(4)***, 201277); lib. bdg. 23.99 ***(978-1-4965-9719-9(2)***, 199352) Capstone. (Stone Arch Bks.).

Clarey, Patricio. Seven Doors to Death. Dahl, Michael. 2020. (Escape from Planet Alcatraz Ser.). (ENG.). 40p. (J). (gr. 3-6). pap. 5.95 *(978-1-4965-9305-4(7))*, 142317); lib. bdg. 23.99 *(978-1-4965-8679-7(4))*, 141427) Capstone. (Stone Arch Bks.).

—Terror Wood. Dahl, Michael. 2020. (Escape from Planet Alcatraz Ser.). (ENG.). 40p. (J). (gr. 3-6). pap. 5.95 *(978-1-4965-9306-1(5))*, 142318); lib. bdg. 23.99 *(978-1-4965-8681-0(6))*, 141428) Capstone. (Stone Arch Bks.).

—The Time Vortex. Sutton, Laurie S. 2018. (Bug Team Alpha Ser.). (ENG.). 112p. (J). (gr. 3-6). lib. bdg. 25.99 *(978-1-4965-5957-9(6))*, 137177, Stone Arch Bks.) Capstone.

—Voyage to the Metal Moon. Dahl, Michael. 2019. (Escape from Planet Alcatraz Ser.). (ENG.). 40p. (J). (gr. 3-6). lib. bdg. 23.99 *(978-1-4965-8314-7(0))*, 140489, Stone Arch Bks.) Capstone.

Clarey, Patricio & Fei, Shen. Escape from Planet Alcatraz. Dahl, Michael. 2019. (Escape from Planet Alcatraz Ser.). (ENG.). (J). (gr. 3-6). 143.94 *(978-1-4965-8317-8(5))*, 29314, Stone Arch Bks.) Capstone.

Clark, Alan M. & Koszowski, Allen. The House of the Temple. Lumley, Brian. collector's ed. 2004. 115p. (YA). 45.00 *(978-0-9728656-3-0(2))* Endeavor Pr.

Clark, Andi. Brooklyn & Bailey: Tails of a Girl & Her Dog. Hicks, Courtney E. 2019. (ENG.). 22p. (J). (gr. k-2). 18.99 *(978-0-578-46095-6(5))* CEH Creative.

Clark, Andy, jt. illus. see Bond, Clint.

Clark, Anna & Clark, Daniel. Babies Love Numbers: Life-A-Flap Book. Wing, Scarlett. Cottage Door Press, ed. 2019. (Chunky Lift a Flap Board Book Ser.). (ENG.). 12p. (J). (gr. -1-k). bds. 7.99 *(978-1-68052-780-3(0))*, 1005031) Cottage Door Pr.

Clark, Anna & Daniel. Numeros: Lif-A-Flap Book. Wing, Scarlett. Cottage Door Press, ed. 2020. (SPA.). 12p. (J). (gr. -1-k). bds. 7.99 *(978-1-68052-842-8(4))*, 1005030-SLA) Cottage Door Pr.

Clark, Barbara Hoserman. The Tale of Rebekah Rabbit. Meade, Jean McCurdy. 2009. 28p. pap. 12.95 *(978-1-59858-970-2(9))* Dog Ear Publishing, LLC.

Clark, Bartholomew & Clark, Bill. God, I Need to Talk to You about Lying. Carr, Dan. 16p. (J). 1.19 *(978-0-7586-0512-2(9))* Concordia Publishing Hse.

—God, I Need to Talk to You about Sharing. Carr, Dan. 16p. (J). 1.19 *(978-0-7586-0511-5(0))* Concordia Publishing Hse.

—God, I Need to Talk to You about Stealing. Carr, Dan. 16p. (J). 1.19 *(978-0-7586-0509-2(9))* Concordia Publishing Hse.

—God, I Need to Talk to You about Vandalism. Carr, Dan. 16p. (J). 1.19 *(978-0-7586-0510-8(2))* Concordia Publishing Hse.

Clark, Bill. God, I Need to Talk to You about Bad Words. Leigh, Susan K. 2005. 16p. (J). pap. 1.19 *(978-0-7586-0793-5(8))* Concordia Publishing Hse.

—God, I Need to Talk to You about Bullying. Leigh, Susan K. 2005. 16p. (J). pap. 1.19 *(978-0-7586-0796-6(2))* Concordia Publishing Hse.

—God, I Need to Talk to You about Greed. Leigh, Susan K. 2005. 16p. (J). pap. 1.19 *(978-0-7586-0795-9(4))* Concordia Publishing Hse.

—God, I Need to Talk to You about Whining. Leigh, Susan K. 2005. pap. 1.19 *(978-0-7586-0794-2(6))* Concordia Publishing Hse.

—Jesus & the Woman at the Well. Busch, Melinda Kay. 2005. (Arch Bks.). (ENG.). 16p. (J). 1.99 *(978-0-7586-0675-4(3))* Concordia Publishing Hse.

—Tiny Baby Moses. Dietrich, Julie. 2003. (Arch Bks.). (ENG.). 16p. (J). (gr. k-4). 1.99 *(978-0-570-07581-3(5))* Concordia Publishing Hse.

Clark, Bill, jt. illus. see Clark, Bartholomew.

Clark, Bradley. The Little Cowboy & the Big Cowboy. Hillert, Margaret. 2016. (BeginningtoRead Ser.). (ENG.). 32p. (J). (gr. -1-2). pap. 11.94 *(978-1-60357-940-7(0))*; (gr. 1-2). 22.60 *(978-1-59953-799-3(0))* Norwood Hse. Pr.

Clark, Bradley. El Vaquero Pequeño y el Vaquero Grande. Hillert, Margaret. 2020. (Beginning-To-Read: Spanish Easy Stories Ser.). (SPA.). 32p. (J). (-2). 22.60 ***(978-1-68450-878-5(9))***; pap. 11.94 ***(978-1-68404-536-5(3))*** Norwood Hse. Pr.

Clark, Brenda. Bravo Benjamin! Bourgeois, Paulette. ed. 2004.Tr. of Good Job Franklin!. (FRE.). (J). (gr. -1-2). spiral bd. *(978-0-616-11142-0(8))* Canadian National Institute for the Blind/Institut National Canadien pour les Aveugles.

—Finders Keepers for Franklin. Bourgeois, Paulette. 2013. (Franklin Ser.). (ENG.). 32p. (J). (gr. -1-3). pap. 6.99 *(978-1-77138-003-4(9))* Kids Can Pr., Ltd. CAN. Dist: Hachette Bk. Group.

—Franklin & Harriet. Bourgeois, Paulette. 2nd ed. 2011. (Franklin Ser.). (ENG.). 32p. (J). (gr. -1-3). pap. 6.99 *(978-1-55453-727-3(4))* Kids Can Pr., Ltd. CAN. Dist: Hachette Bk. Group.

—Franklin & the Computer. Bourgeois, Paulette. 2003. (Franklin Ser.: Bk. 16). 32p. (J). pap. 4.50 *(978-0-439-43121-7(2))* Scholastic, Inc.

—Franklin & the Thunderstorm. Bourgeois, Paulette. 2nd ed. 2011. (Franklin Ser.). (ENG.). 32p. (J). (gr. -1-3). pap. 6.99 *(978-1-55453-729-7(0))* Kids Can Pr., Ltd. CAN. Dist: Hachette Bk. Group.

—Franklin & the Tooth Fairy. Bourgeois, Paulette. 2nd ed. 2011. (Franklin Ser.). (ENG.). 32p. (J). (gr. -1-3). pap. 6.99 *(978-1-55453-734-1(7))* Kids Can Pr., Ltd. CAN. Dist: Hachette Bk. Group.

—Franklin Es un Mandon. Bourgeois, Paulette. Varela, Alejandra López, tr.Tr. of Franklin Is Bossy. (SPA.). 10.95 *(978-1-930332-16-4(5))*, LC6564) Lectorum Pubns., Inc.

—Franklin Fibs. Bourgeois, Paulette. 2nd ed. 2011. (Franklin Ser.). (ENG.). 32p. (J). (gr. -1-3). pap. 6.99 *(978-1-55453-774-7(6))* Kids Can Pr., Ltd. CAN. Dist: Hachette Bk. Group.

—Franklin Goes to School. Bourgeois, Paulette. 2013. (Franklin Ser.). (ENG.). 32p. (J). (gr. -1-3). pap. 6.99 *(978-1-77138-010-2(1))* Kids Can Pr., Ltd. CAN. Dist: Hachette Bk. Group.

—Franklin Goes to the Hospital. Bourgeois, Paulette. 2nd ed. 2011. (Franklin Ser.). (ENG.). 32p. (J). (gr. -1-3). 6.99 *(978-1-55453-725-9(8))* Kids Can Pr., Ltd. CAN. Dist: Hachette Bk. Group.

—Franklin Has a Sleepover. Bourgeois, Paulette. 2nd ed. 2011. (Franklin Ser.). (ENG.). 32p. (J). (gr. -1-3). pap. 6.99 *(978-1-55453-736-5(3))* Kids Can Pr., Ltd. CAN. Dist: Hachette Bk. Group.

—Franklin in the Dark. Bourgeois, Paulette. 2013. (Franklin Ser.). (ENG.). 32p. (J). (gr. -1-3). pap. 6.99 *(978-1-77138-007-2(1))* Kids Can Pr., Ltd. CAN. Dist: Hachette Bk. Group.

—Franklin in the Dark: 25th Anniversary Edition. Bourgeois, Paulette. 2nd ed. 2011. (Franklin Ser.). (ENG.). 48p. (J). (gr. -1-3). 18.95 *(978-1-55453-616-0(2))* Kids Can Pr., Ltd. CAN. Dist: Hachette Bk. Group.

—Franklin Is Bossy. Bourgeois, Paulette. 2nd ed. 2011. (Franklin Ser.). (ENG.). 32p. (J). (gr. -1-3). 6.99 *(978-1-55453-785-3(1))* Kids Can Pr., Ltd. CAN. Dist: Hachette Bk. Group.

—Franklin Is Lost. Bourgeois, Paulette. 2nd ed. 2011. (Franklin Ser.). (ENG.). 32p. (J). (gr. -1-3). pap. 6.99 *(978-1-55453-735-8(5))* Kids Can Pr., Ltd. CAN. Dist: Hachette Bk. Group.

—Franklin Is Messy. Bourgeois, Paulette. 2013. (Franklin Ser.). (ENG.). 32p. (J). (gr. -1-3). pap. 6.99 *(978-1-77138-000-3(4))* Kids Can Pr., Ltd. CAN. Dist: Hachette Bk. Group.

—Franklin Rides a Bike. Bourgeois, Paulette. 2nd ed. 2011. (Franklin Ser.). (ENG.). 32p. (J). (gr. -1-3). pap. 6.99 *(978-1-55453-731-0(2))* Kids Can Pr., Ltd. CAN. Dist: Hachette Bk. Group.

—Franklin Says I Love You. Bourgeois, Paulette. 2nd ed. 2011. (Franklin Ser.). (ENG.). 32p. (J). (gr. -1-3). pap. 6.99 *(978-1-55453-728-0(2))* Kids Can Pr., Ltd. CAN. Dist: Hachette Bk. Group.

—Franklin Wants a Pet. Bourgeois, Paulette. 2013. (Franklin Ser.). (ENG.). 32p. (J). (gr. -1-3). pap. 6.99 *(978-1-77138-004-1(7))* Kids Can Pr., Ltd. CAN. Dist: Hachette Bk. Group.

—Franklin y el Dia de Accion de Gracias. Bourgeois, Paulette. Varela, Alejandra López, tr.Tr. of Franklin's Thanksgiving. (SPA.). (J). (gr. k-2). 10.95 *(978-1-930332-07-2(6))*, LC30184) Lectorum Pubns., Inc.

—Franklin's Baby Sister. Bourgeois, Paulette. (Franklin Ser.). (ENG.). 32p. (J). (gr. -1-3). *(978-1-55074-858-1(0))* Kids Can Pr., Ltd.

—Franklin's Baby Sister. Bourgeois, Paulette. 2013. (Franklin Ser.). (ENG.). 32p. (J). (gr. -1-3). pap. 6.99 *(978-1-77138-002-7(0))* Kids Can Pr., Ltd. CAN. Dist: Hachette Bk. Group.

—Franklin's Bad Day. Bourgeois, Paulette. 2nd ed. 2011. (Franklin Ser.). (ENG.). 32p. (J). (gr. -1-3). pap. 6.99 *(978-1-55453-732-7(0))* Kids Can Pr., Ltd. CAN. Dist: Hachette Bk. Group.

—Franklin's Blanket. Bourgeois, Paulette. 2nd ed. 2011. (Franklin Ser.). (ENG.). 32p. (J). (gr. -1-3). pap. 6.99 *(978-1-55453-733-4(9))* Kids Can Pr., Ltd. CAN. Dist: Hachette Bk. Group.

—Franklin's Christmas: A Sticker Activity Book. Bourgeois, Paulette. 2003. 16p. (J). (ENG.). 6.95 *(978-1-55337-561-6(0))*; 6.95 *(978-1-55337-506-7(8))* Kids Can Pr., Ltd. CAN. Dist: Hachette Bk. Group.

—Franklin's Christmas Gift. Bourgeois, Paulette. 2013. (Franklin Ser.). (ENG.). 32p. (J). (gr. -1-3). pap. 6.99 *(978-1-77138-001-0(2))* Kids Can Pr., Ltd. CAN. Dist: Hachette Bk. Group.

—Franklin's Class Trip. Bourgeois, Paulette. 2012. (Franklin Ser.). (ENG.). 32p. (J). (gr. -1-3). pap. 6.99 *(978-1-55453-936-9(6))* Kids Can Pr., Ltd. CAN. Dist: Hachette Bk. Group.

—Franklin's Family Treasury. Bourgeois, Paulette. 2003. (Franklin Ser.). (ENG.). 128p. (J). (gr. -1-3). 15.95 *(978-1-55337-479-4(7))* Kids Can Pr., Ltd. CAN. Dist: Hachette Bk. Group.

—Franklin's Halloween. Bourgeois, Paulette. 2nd ed. 2011. (Franklin Ser.). (ENG.). 32p. (J). (gr. -1-3). pap. 6.99 *(978-1-55453-786-0(X))* Kids Can Pr., Ltd. CAN. Dist: Hachette Bk. Group.

—Franklin's New Friend. Bourgeois, Paulette. (Franklin Ser.). (ENG.). 32p. (J). (gr. -1-3). *(978-1-55074-363-0(5))* Kids Can Pr., Ltd.

—Franklin's New Friend. Bourgeois, Paulette. 2nd ed. 2011. (Franklin Ser.). (ENG.). 32p. (J). (gr. -1-3). pap. 6.99 *(978-1-55453-773-0(8))* Kids Can Pr., Ltd. CAN. Dist: Hachette Bk. Group.

—Franklin's School Play. Bourgeois, Paulette. 2012. (Franklin Ser.). (ENG.). 32p. (J). (gr. -1-3). pap. 5.95 *(978-1-55453-935-2(8))* Kids Can Pr., Ltd. CAN. Dist: Hachette Bk. Group.

—Franklin's Secret Club. Bourgeois, Paulette. 2012. (Franklin Ser.). (ENG.). 32p. (J). (gr. -1-3). pap. 6.99 *(978-1-55453-934-5(X))* Kids Can Pr., Ltd. CAN. Dist: Hachette Bk. Group.

—Franklin's Thanksgiving. Bourgeois, Paulette. 2013. (Franklin Ser.). (ENG.). 32p. (J). (gr. -1-3). pap. 6.99 *(978-1-77138-005-8(5))* Kids Can Pr., Ltd. CAN. Dist: Hachette Bk. Group.

—Franklin's Valentines. Bourgeois, Paulette. 2013. (Franklin Ser.). (ENG.). 32p. (J). (gr. -1-3). pap. 6.99 *(978-1-77138-006-5(3))* Kids Can Pr., Ltd. CAN. Dist: Hachette Bk. Group.

—Fun with Franklin: A Learning to Read Book. Bourgeois, Paulette. (Franklin Ser.). (J). (gr. -1-3). pap. *(978-1-55074-646-4(4))* Kids Can Pr., Ltd.

—Hurry up Franklin. Bourgeois, Paulette. 2012. (Franklin Ser.). (ENG.). 32p. (J). (gr. -1-3). pap. 6.99 *(978-1-55453-819-5(X))* Kids Can Pr., Ltd. CAN. Dist: Hachette Bk. Group.

—La Manta de Franklin. Bourgeois, Paulette. Varela, Alejandra López, tr.Tr. of Franklin's Blanket. (SPA.). (J). (gr. k-2). pap. 5.95 *(978-1-880507-98-8(6))*, LC30178); ring bd. 10.95 *(978-1-880507-99-5(4))*, LC30179) Lectorum Pubns., Inc.

Clark Brown, Jane. Marvin One Too Many. Paterson, Katherine. 2003. 25.95 incl. audio *(978-1-59112-254-8(6))*; 28.95 incl. audio compact disk *(978-1-59112-635-5(5))*; pap. 31.95 incl. audio compact disk *(978-1-59112-636-2(3))*; (J). pap. 29.95 incl. audio *(978-1-59112-255-5(4))* Live Oak Media.

Clark, Callan. Bubbles & the Berry Bush. Mokry, Shannon L. 2017. (Bubbles the Bubble Blowing Dragon Ser.: Vol. 1). (ENG.). (J). 17.99 *(978-0-9987112-0-1(9))* Sillygeese Publishing, LLC.

—Bubbles & the Shark Attack. Mokry, Shannon L. 2018. (Bubbles the Bubble Blowing Dragon Ser.: Vol. 2). (ENG.). 34p. (J). 18.99 *(978-0-9987112-6-3(8))*; pap. 11.99 *(978-0-9987112-7-0(6))* Sillygeese Publishing, LLC.

Clark, Casey. Noah's Boat. Swinson, Joyce Ann. 2007. 32p. per. 24.95 *(978-1-4241-9012-6(6))* America Star Bks.

Clark College Continuing Eduction. I See You: In English & Tigrinya. Ready Set Go Books. Dessalegn, Aklilu, tr. 2019. (ENG.). 38p. (J). pap. 9.99 *(978-1-0958-3496-1(7))* Independently Published.

Clark College Economic and Community Dev & Baughman, Lee. We Are Full of Life: In English & Amharic. Ready Set Go Books. 2019. (ENG.). 36p. (J). pap. 9.99 ***(978-1-6972-4595-0(1))*** Independently Published.

Clark, Daniel, jt. illus. see Clark, Anna.

Clark, David. Ants. Heos, Bridget. 2017. (Just Like Us! Ser.). (ENG.). 32p. (J). (gr. -1-3). 14.99 *(978-0-544-57043-6(X))*, 1612569, HMH Books For Young Readers) Houghton Mifflin Harcourt Publishing Co.

—Birds. Heos, Bridget. 2017. (Just Like Us! Ser.). (ENG.). 32p. (J). (gr. -1-3). 14.99 *(978-0-544-57044-3(8))*, 1612570, HMH Books For Young Readers) Houghton Mifflin Harcourt Publishing Co.

—Curious Creatures: Animal Poems. Polisar, Barry Louis. 2010. (Rainbow Morning Music Picture Bks.). (ENG.). 32p. (J). (gr. 2-4). 14.95 *(978-0-938663-52-2(6))* Rainbow Morning Music Alternatives.

—Fakers: An Insider's Guide to Cons, Hoaxes, & Scams. Poole, Hilary W. & Wood, H. P. 2018. 176p. (J). (gr. 5). lib. bdg. 18.99 *(978-1-58089-743-3(6))* Charlesbridge Publishing, Inc.

—Fractions in Disguise: A Math Adventure. Einhorn, Edward. 2014. (Charlesbridge Math Adventures Ser.). (J). (gr. 2-5). (ENG.). 32p. pap. 7.95 *(978-1-57091-774-5(4))*; 240p. lib. bdg. 16.95 *(978-1-57091-773-8(6))* Charlesbridge Publishing, Inc.

—Gakky Two-Feet. Dolenz, Micky. 2006. (J). *(978-1-4156-8089-6(2))*, Putnam Juvenile) Penguin Publishing Group.

—Just Like Us! Ants. Heos, Bridget. 2019. (Just Like Us! Ser.). (ENG.). 32p. (J). (gr. -1-3). pap. 7.99 *(978-0-358-00385-4(7))*, 1736314, HMH Books For Young Readers) Houghton Mifflin Harcourt Publishing Co.

—Just Like Us! Birds. Heos, Bridget. 2019. (Just Like Us! Ser.). (ENG.). 32p. (J). (gr. -1-3). pap. 7.99 *(978-0-358-00386-1(5))*, 1736316, HMH Books For Young Readers) Houghton Mifflin Harcourt Publishing Co.

—Just Like Us!, Cats. Heos, Bridget. 2019. (Just Like Us! Ser.). (ENG.). 32p. (J). (gr. -1-3). 14.99 *(978-1-328-79184-9(X))*, 1685035, HMH Books For Young Readers) Houghton Mifflin Harcourt Publishing Co.

—Just Like Us! Cats. Heos, Bridget. 2019. (Just Like Us! Ser.). (ENG.). 32p. (J). (gr. -1-3). pap. 7.99 *(978-0-358-00389-2(X))*, 1736322, HMH Books For Young Readers) Houghton Mifflin Harcourt Publishing Co.

—Just Like Us! Crocs. Heos, Bridget. 2019. (Just Like Us! Ser.). (ENG.). 32p. (J). (gr. -1-3). 14.99 *(978-1-328-79192-4(0))*, 1685046); pap. 7.99 *(978-0-358-00390-8(3))*, 1736324) Houghton Mifflin Harcourt Publishing Co. (HMH Books For Young Readers).

C

—Just Like Us!, Fish. Heos, Bridget. 2018. (Just Like Us! Ser.). (ENG.). 32p. (J). (gr. -1-3). 14.99 (978-0-544-57095-5(2), 1612572, HMH Books For Young Readers) Houghton Mifflin Harcourt Publishing Co.

—Just Like Us! Fish. Heos, Bridget. 2019. (Just Like Us! Ser.). (ENG.). 32p. (J). (gr. -1-3). pap. 7.99 (978-0-358-00387-8(3), 1736318, HMH Books For Young Readers) Houghton Mifflin Harcourt Publishing Co.

—Just Like Us!, Plants. Heos, Bridget. 2018. (Just Like Us! Ser.). (ENG.). 32p. (J). (gr. -1-3). 14.99 (978-0-544-57094-8(4), 1612571, HMH Books For Young Readers) Houghton Mifflin Harcourt Publishing Co.

—Just Like Us! Plants. Heos, Bridget. 2019. (Just Like Us! Ser.). (ENG.). 32p. (J). (gr. -1-3). pap. 7.99 (978-0-358-00388-5(1), 1736320, HMH Books For Young Readers) Houghton Mifflin Harcourt Publishing Co.

—Never Insult a Killer Zucchini. Azose, Elana & Amancio, Brandon. 2016. 32p. (J). (gr. 2-5). lib. bdg. 16.95 (978-1-58089-618-4(9)) Charlesbridge Publishing, Inc.

—Pirate Bob. Lasky, Kathryn. alt. ed. 2008. 32p. (J). (gr. k-3). per. 8.95 (978-1-57091-647-2(0)) Charlesbridge Publishing, Inc.

—Something Fishy. Polisar, Barry Louis. 2013. (Rainbow Morning Music Picture Bks.). 32p. (J). (gr. 2-4). 14.95 (978-0-938663-53-9(4)) Rainbow Morning Music Alternatives.

—What's for Dinner? Quirky, Squirmy Poems from the Animal World. Hauth, Katherine B. 2011. (ENG.). 48p. (J). (gr. 2-5). pap. 8.95 (978-1-57091-472-0(9)) Charlesbridge Publishing, Inc.

Clark, David, jt. illus. see Hohn, David.

Clark, Debbie. Alphabet of Music. Schwaeber, Barbie Heit. 2009. (ENG.). 40p. 9.95 (978-1-59249-995-3(3)) Soundprints.

Clark, Debbie, jt. illus. see Santillan, Jorge.

Clark, Desiree. The Divine in Me. Leigh, Maya. 2019. (ENG.). 30p. (J). pap. 9.99 **(978-1-0721-0823-8(2))** Independently Published.

Clark, Don. All Is Merry & Bright. Burton, Jeffrey. 2018. (Shine Bright Book Ser.). (ENG.). 26p. (J). (gr. -1 — 1). 24.99 (978-1-5344-2912-3(3), Little Simon) Little Simon.

—The Biggest Story: How the Snake Crusher Brings Us Back to the Garden. DeYoung, Kevin. 2015. (ENG.). 132p. 17.99 (978-1-4335-4244-2(7)) Crossway.

—The Biggest Story ABC. DeYoung, Kevin. 2017. (ENG.). 32p. (J). bds. 12.99 (978-1-4335-5818-4(1)) Crossway.

—The Incredibles (Disney/Pixar the Incredibles) Sazaklis, John. 2018. (Little Golden Book Ser.). (ENG.). 24p. (J). (-k). 4.99 (978-0-7364-3863-6(7), Golden/Disney) Random Hse. Children's Bks.

—The World Shines for You. Burton, Jeffrey. 2017. (Shine Bright Book Ser.). (ENG.). 26p. (J). (gr. -1 — 1). 24.99 (978-1-4814-9632-2(8), Little Simon) Little Simon.

Clark, Donna Osborn. What about Johnson? Johnson, Harvell. Howard, Vanetta, ed. 2013. 132p. pap. 11.95 (978-0-9885056-0-5(6)) Word on Da Street Publishing.

Clark, Elijah Brady. Who Pooped in the Park? Robson, Gary D. 2006. 48p. (J). pap. 11.95 (978-1-56037-388-9(1)) Farcountry Pr.

—Who Pooped in the Park? Grand Canyon National Park. Robson, Gary D. 2005. 80p. (J). pap. 11.95 (978-1-56037-319-3(9)) Farcountry Pr.

—Who Pooped in the Park? Rocky Mountain National Park: Scats & Tracks for Kids. Robson, Gary D. 2005. 48p. (J). (gr. -1-5). per. 11.95 (978-1-56037-320-9(2)) Farcountry Pr.

—Who Pooped in the Park? Yosemite National Park. Robson, Gary D. 2005. 80p. (J). pap. 11.95 (978-1-56037-318-6(0)) Farcountry Pr.

Clark, Elizabeth Palmer. Lysis Goes to the Play. Snedeker, Caroline Dale. 2003. 62p. (J). per. 8.95 (978-0-9667067-4-1(9)) American Home-School Publishing, LLC.

Clark, Emma Chichester. The Mcelderry Book of Aesop's Fables. Morpurgo, Michael. 2005. (ENG.). 96p. (J). (gr. 1-5). 24.99 (978-1-4169-0290-4(2), McElderry, Margaret K. Bks.) McElderry, Margaret K. Bks.

—Three Little Monkeys. Blake, Quentin. 2017. (ENG.). 40p. (J). (gr. -1-3). 18.99 (978-0-06-267067-0(0), HarperCollins) HarperCollins Pubs. Ltd. GBR. Dist: HarperCollins Pubs.

Clark, Graeme Andrew. Haggis Macdougall & His Very Long Tail. McMillan, Katie Lorna. 2017. (ENG.). 34p. (J). (gr. k-3). pap. (978-1-9997427-9-6(6)) Laughing Monkey Publishing.

—Haggis Macdougall & the Pirate King. McMillan, Katie Lorna. 2017. (ENG.). 36p. (J). (gr. k-2). pap. (978-1-9997427-7-5(X)) Laughing Monkey Publishing.

—Haggis Macdougall Saves Santa. McMillan, Katie Lorna. 2018. (Haggis Macdougall Ser.). (ENG.). 34p. (J). (gr. k-2). pap. (978-1-9997427-6-8(1)) Laughing Monkey Publishing.

—Haggis Macdougall Saves the Day. McMillan, Katie Lorna. 2017. (ENG.). 32p. (J). (gr. k-2). pap. (978-1-9997427-8-2(8)) Laughing Monkey Publishing.

Clark, Irene. Basic Kit - Kindergarten. Bradshaw, Georgine & Wrighton, Charlene. 2005. Orig. Title: Basic Kit II. (J). 249.95 (978-1-886441-31-6(6)) Zoo-phonics, Inc.

—Basic Kit - Preschool. Wrighton, Charlene & Bradshaw, Georgine. 2005. Orig. Title: Basis Kit I. (J). 249.95 (978-1-886441-30-9(8)) Zoo-phonics, Inc.

—Kindergarten Zoo-per Kit. Bradshaw, Georgine & Wrighton, Charlene. 2005. (J). 499.95 (978-1-886441-34-7(0), ZOP4219) Zoo-phonics, Inc.

—Preschool Zoo-per Kit. Bradshaw, Georgine & Wrighton, Charlene. 2005. (J). 449.95 (978-1-886441-32-3(4), ZOP4218) Zoo-phonics, Inc.

—Set of Color Mini-Books (29 Titles) Bradshaw, Georgine & Wrighton, Charlene. 2005. (J). 39.95 (978-1-886441-42-2(1), CMB4356) Zoo-phonics, Inc.

Clark, Jeff. The Amazing Spider-Man. Thomas, Rich. 2012. (Marvel Origins Ser.). (ENG.). 48p. (J). (gr. k-5). lib. bdg. 27.07 (978-1-61479-007-5(8), 11335, Marvel Age) Spotlight.

—The Mighty Thor. Thomas, Rich. 2012. (Marvel Origins Ser.). (ENG.). 48p. (J). (gr. k-5). lib. bdg. 27.07 (978-1-61479-011-2(6), 11339, Marvel Age) Spotlight.

Clark, Justin. The Legend of the Great Alow II: The Three Forbidden Scrolls. Clark, Justin. 2019. (Legend of the Great Alow Ser.: Vol. 2). (ENG.). 78p. (J). pap. 6.99 **(978-1-0899-9660-6(8))** Independently Published.

Clark, K. C. Dancing Waters. Tulley, Tara. 2004. (J). (978-0-9759468-1-7(1)) Balanced Families.

Clark, Karen & White, Ian. Flash, Bang, Wheee! Bing, Bang, Boum! 2004. 24p. (J). (978-1-85269-354-1(1)) Mantra Lingua.

—Flash, Bang, Wheee! Shkreptime, Gjemim Dhe Vershellime! 2004. 24p. (J). (978-1-85269-349-7(5)) Mantra Lingua.

Clark, Laura. Puppies & Planets & a Cucumber. Areyan. 2017. (ENG.). 96p. (J). pap. (978-0-9876264-1-7(8)) Moptops Publishing.

Clark, Leslie Ann. Peepsqueak! Clark, Leslie Ann. 2012. (ENG.). 32p. (J). (gr. -1-k). 12.99 (978-0-06-207801-8(1)) HarperCollins Pubs.

—Peepsqueak Wants a Friend! Clark, Leslie Ann. 2013. (ENG.). 32p. (J). (gr. -1-3). 15.99 (978-0-06-207804-9(6)) HarperCollins Pubs.

Clark, Linda. Dear Mum, I Miss You! Ross, Stewart. 54p. (J). (978-0-237-52318-3(3)) Evans Brothers, Ltd.

Clark, Linda McConeghy. Cow & the Magic Shoes. Spradlin, Amber L. 2019. (ENG.). 100p. (J). (gr. -1-1). pap. 34.99 **(978-0-9964421-8-3(9))** Hocks Out Press.

Clark Mancuso, Jackie. Hudson in Provence: A Paris-Chien Adventure. Clark Mancuso, Jackie. l.t. ed. 2015. (Paris-Chien Adventure Ser.). (ENG.). 32p. (J). (gr. k-2). 17.95 (978-0-9886058-4-8(8)) La Librairie Parisienne.

Clark, Mary. The Life & Adventures of Santa Claus. Baum, L. Frank. 2007. 156p. (gr. 4-7). 23.95 (978-1-60206-778-3(3)); per. 9.95 (978-1-60206-777-6(5)) Cosimo, Inc.

Clark, Mary Cowles. The Life & Adventures of Santa Claus. Baum, L. Frank. 2011. 200p. (978-1-84902-560-7(6)) Benediction Classics.

—The Life & Adventures of Santa Claus. Baum, L. Frank. 2015. (Penguin Christmas Classics Ser.: 6). (ENG.). 160p. (gr. 12). 16.00 (978-0-14-312853-3(1), Penguin Classics) Penguin Publishing Group.

Clark, Mary Cowles. The LIFE & ADVENTURES of SANTA CLAUS (Illustrated) / a KIDNAPPED SANTA CLAUS. Baum, L. Frank. Barry, ed. 2019. (ENG.). 124p. (J). pap. 39.85 **(978-1-6788-4771-5(2))** Independently Published.

Clark, Matthew. Inhumans: Lunar, Vol. 1. McKeever, Sean. 2004. (Marvel Heroes Ser.). 144p. (YA). (gr. 7-18). pap. 14.99 (978-0-7851-1303-4(7)) Marvel Worldwide, Inc.

Clark, Matthew Levi. The Substitute Teacher Named Mr King. King, Seth David. 2005. 24p. (gr. 2-6). 12.00 (978-0-9640837-6-9(0)) Ascension Education.

Clark, Mez. A Cheesy Little Joke Book. Puffinton, Brick. Cottage Door Press, ed. 2019. (Finger Puppet Board Book Ser.). (ENG.). 12p. (J). (gr. -1 — 1). bds. 6.99 (978-1-68052-736-0(3), 1004570) Cottage Door Pr.

Clark, Nathan. Ann Drew Jackson. Clark, Joan. 2007. 122p. per. 17.95 (978-1-931282-45-1(5)) Autism Asperger Publishing Co.

Clark, Neil. Let's Draw Aliens & Spaceships with Crayola ®! Allen, Kathy. 2019. (Let's Draw with Crayola ®! Ser.). (ENG.). 32p. (J). (gr. -1-3). pap. 6.99 (978-1-5415-4606-6(7), Lerner Pubns.) Lerner Publishing Group.

—Let's Draw Aliens & Spaceships with Crayola®! Allen, Kathy. 2019. (Let's Draw with Crayola ®! Ser.). (ENG.). 32p. (J). (gr. -1-3). 27.99 (978-1-5415-1103-3(4), Lerner Pubns.) Lerner Publishing Group.

Clark, Neil. The Book of Cars & Trucks. Clark, Neil. 2019. (Clever Cogz Ser.). (ENG.). 24p. (J). (gr. k-2). 14.95 **(978-1-78603-630-8(4))** QEB Publishing Inc.

—The Book of Space Rockets. Clark, Neil. 2019. (Clever Cogz Ser.). (ENG.). 24p. (J). (gr. k-2). 14.95 **(978-1-78603-633-9(9))** QEB Publishing Inc.

—Rusty the Squeaky Robot. Clark, Neil. 2018. (ENG.). 32p. (J). (gr. -1-1). 17.95 **(978-1-910277-52-2(5)**, Words & Pictures) Quarto Publishing Group UK GBR. Dist: Hachette Bk. Group.

Clark, Nicole K. Pigment the Rainbow Pig. Clark, Nicole K. Date not set. (J). (gr. -1-2). (978-1-892176-18-9(1)) PremaNations Publishing.

Clark, Sharon. Dream. Clark, Sharon. 2018. (ENG.). 40p. (J). (gr. k-3). (978-0-6484268-0-6(7)) Dream Blossom Pr.

Clark, Steve. All about Eels: Read Well Level K Unit 2 Storybook. Sprick, Marilyn et al. 2003. (Read Well Level K Ser.). 20p. (J). (978-1-57035-674-2(2)) Cambium Education, Inc.

—All about Eels: Read Well Level K Unit 2 Teacher Storybook. Sprick, Marilyn et al. 2003. (Read Well Level K Ser.). 20p. (J). (978-1-57035-697-1(1)) Cambium Education, Inc.

—Hey Diddle Diddle: Read Well Level K Unit 16 Storybook. Sprick, Marilyn & Sprick, Jessica. 2003. (Read Well Level K Ser.). 20p. (J). (978-1-57035-687-2(4), 55562) Cambium Education, Inc.

Clark, Tim, photos by. Davy Asks His Dad. Clark, Harriet. 2012. 32p. pap. (978-1-77097-977-2(8)) FriesenPress.

Clark, Warren. Lowdown on Earthworms, 1 vol. Dixon, Norma. 2005. (Up Close with Animals Ser.). (ENG.). 32p. (J). (gr. 5-8). pap. 9.95 (978-1-55005-119-3(9), 1ed99c01-db2d-4167-b4b6-988e567b0f4d) Trifolium Bks., Inc. CAN. Dist: Firefly Bks., Ltd.

Clark, Wendy. My Brother's A Pirate, 1 vol. Nannini, Randi. 2010. 14p. pap. 24.95 (978-1-4489-8576-0(5)) America Star Bks.

Clark, Wook-Jin. The Not-So Secret Society: Tale of the Gummy. Daley, Matthew et al. 2017. (ENG.). 128p. (J). (gr. 3). pap. 9.99 (978-1-60886-997-8(0)) Boom! Studios.

Clark, Yvonne, jt. illus. see Pettikas-Barnes, Judy.

Clarke & Clarke. Melusine - Hocus Pocus. Gilson. 2007. (Melusine Ser.: 1). (ENG.). 48p. (J). (gr. -1-12). per. 9.99 (978-1-905460-20-5(1)) CineBook GBR. Dist: National Bk. Network.

Clarke, jt. illus. see Clarke.

Clarke, Alan. The Big Brother. Dagg, Stephanie. 2003. (Pandas Ser.: 24). (ENG.). 64p. (J). pap. 11.00 (978-0-86278-779-0(3)) O'Brien Pr., Ltd., The IRL. Dist: Casemate Pubs. & Bk. Distributors, LLC.

—Eddie Lenihan's Irish Tales of Mystery. Lenihan, Eddie. 2006. (ENG.). 224p. (J). 33.95 (978-1-85635-519-3(5)) Mercier Pr., Ltd., The IRL. Dist: Dufour Editions, Inc.

—Fionn Mac Cumhail's Amazing Stories, Bk. 3. Lenihan, Eddie. 2015. (Irish Mystery & Magic Collection: 3). (ENG.). 64p. (J). 5.50 (978-1-78117-359-6(1)) Mercier Pr., Ltd., The IRL. Dist: Casemate Pubs. & Bk. Distributors, LLC.

—Fionn Mac Cumhail's Tales from Ireland, Bk. 1. Lenihan, Eddie. 2015. (Mystery & Magic Collection: 1). (ENG.). 64p. (J). 5.50 (978-1-78117-357-2(5)) Mercier Pr., Ltd., The IRL. Dist: Casemate Pubs. & Bk. Distributors, LLC.

—Fionn MacCumhail's Epic Adventures, Bk. 2. Lenihan, Edmund. 2015. (Irish Mystery & Magic Collection: 2). (ENG.). 64p. (J). 5.50 (978-1-78117-358-9(3)) Mercier Pr., Ltd., The IRL. Dist: Casemate Pubs. & Bk. Distributors, LLC.

Clarke, Alan, jt. illus. see Askin, Corrina.

Clarke, Asiya. Allah Gave Me Two Ears to Hear. Arif, Amrana. 2015. (ENG.). 32p. (J). 8.95 (978-0-86037-353-7(3)) Kube Publishing Ltd. GBR. Dist: Consortium Bk. Sales & Distribution.

—Allah Gave Me Two Hands & Feet. 2015. (ENG.). 32p. (J). 8.95 (978-0-86037-348-3(7)) Kube Publishing Ltd. GBR. Dist: Consortium Bk. Sales & Distribution.

Clarke, Benjamin S. The House Who Found Its Home. Vincolisi, Marnie. 2013. 32p. pap. 10.95 (978-0-9823732-3-1(6)) Light Internal Publishing.

Clarke, Caroline. The Mystery of the Portuguese Waltzes, 1 vol. Simas, Richard. 2019. (ENG.). 44p. (J). (gr. 4-7). pap. 9.95 **(978-1-927917-25-1(5))** Running the Goat, Bks. & Broadsides CAN. Dist: Orca Bk. Pubs. USA.

Clarke, Catherine. Believe-In Your Special Gift. Davies, S. V. Smith, Katharine, ed. 2018. (Believe-In Ser.: Vol. 3). (ENG.). 34p. (J). pap. (978-1-9995963-7-8(4)) Spiffing covers.

Clarke, Daniel. Freeing Freddie the Dream Weaver: A Guide to Realizing Your Dreams - a Workbook. Feinberg, Brent & Normand, Kim. 2017. (ENG.). 72p. (J). pap. 19.95 (978-0-7570-0460-5(1)) Square One Pubs.

—Freeing Freddie the Dream Weaver: Reader. Feinberg, Brent. 2017. (ENG.). 48p. (J). 16.95 (978-0-7570-0458-2(X)) Square One Pubs.

—Freeing Freddie the Dream Weaver: Ultimate Activity Book. Feinberg, Brent & Normand, Kim. 2017. (ENG.). 56p. (J). pap. 16.95 (978-0-7570-5459-4(5)) Square One Pubs.

—Freeing Freddie the Dream Weaver: Workbook. Feinberg, Brent & Normand, Kim. 2017. (ENG.). 72p. (J). pap. 19.95 (978-0-7570-5460-0(9)) Square One Pubs.

Clarke, Gail. Dormouse Snoremouse. Clarke, Gail. 2019. (ENG.). 30p. (J). (gr. k-2). **(978-1-912406-35-7(7))**; pap. **(978-1-912406-34-0(9))** Gupole Pubns.

Clarke, Gail & O'Reilly, Zoe. Mischief at the Waterhole. Clarke, Gail. 2017. (ENG.). (J). (gr. k-3). (978-1-912406-24-1(1)); 25p. pap. (978-1-912406-17-3(9)) Gupole Pubns.

Clarke, Greg. The Blood-Hungry Spleen & Other Poems about Our Parts. Wolf, Allan. 2008. 56p. (J). (gr. 3-7). per. 9.99 (978-0-7636-3806-1(4)) Candlewick Pr.

Clarke, Harry. Fairy Tales of Charles Perrault: [Complete & Illustrated]. Perrault, Charles. Mansion, J. E., tr. 2019. (ENG.). 154p. (J). (gr. k-4). **(978-625-7959-46-9(2))** Uhrayoglu, Murat E Kitap Projesi.

Clarke, Harry & Perrault, Charles. Classic Fairy Tales of Charles Perrault. 2013. (ENG.). 224p. (J). 34.00 (978-0-7171-5408-1(4)) M.H. Gill & Co. U. C. IRL. Dist: Dufour Editions, Inc.

Clarke, Herbert, photos by. An Introduction to Southern California Birds. Clarke, Herbert. rev. ed. 192p. (J). (gr. 4). pap. 14.00 (978-0-87842-233-3(1), 413) Mountain Pr. Publishing Co., Inc.

Clarke, Jimmy, photos by. Play-by-Play Snowboarding. Lurie, Jon. 2003. (Play-by-Play Ser.). 80p. (J). (gr. 5-18). pap. 7.95 (978-0-8225-9881-7(7)) Lerner Publishing Group.

Clarke, Judith, et al. Rosetta's Daring Day. Papademetriou, Lisa. 2009. (Disney Fairies Chapters Ser.). (ENG.). 117p. (J). (gr. 1-4). 18.69 (978-0-7364-2509-4(8)) Random House Publishing Group.

Clarke, Judith Holmes. La Aventura de Rosetta. Papademetriou, Lisa. Pombo, Mauricio, tr. 2008.Tr. of Rosetta's Daring Day. (SPA.). 107p. (J). pap. (978-958-45-0849-2(0)) Norma S.A.

Clarke, Judith Holmes & Disney Storybook Artists Staff. Lily's Pesky Plant. Larsen, Kirsten. 2006. (Disney Fairies Chapters Ser.). (ENG.). 110p. (J). (gr. 1-4). 18.69 (978-0-7364-2374-8(5)) Random Hse. Bks. for Young Readers.

Clarke, Lyndia A. Tidy up Tommy. Clarke, Lyndia A. 2005. (J). 1700.00 (978-0-9762898-6-9(5)) LightHouse Pr.

Clarke, Roger. Do Mice Eat Rice? Clarke, Roger. Wight, Al. 2005. (ENG.). 32p. (J). (gr. -1-3). 12.95 (978-0-8048-3643-2(4)) Tuttle Publishing.

Clarke, Simonne-Anais. A Guide to Things We Wear. Lauren, Olivia & John, Melissa-Sue. 2018. (Olivia Lauren Ser.: Vol. 5). (ENG.). 34p. (J). 19.99 **(978-1-948071-30-7(4))** Lauren Simone Publishing Hse.

Clarke, Simonne-Anais & Clarke, Zachary-Michael. Gratitude Journal for Kids. Morgan, Priscilla. 2019. (ENG.). 34p. (J). pap. 11.99 **(978-1-948071-39-0(8))** Lauren Simone Publishing Hse.

Clarke, Simonne-Anais & Clarke, Zachary-Michael. Olivia Lauren's Occupations a to Z: A Children's Guide to Jobs & Careers. John Ph D, Melissa-Sue. 2017. (ENG.). (J). pap. 9.99 (978-0-9979520-2-5(4)) Lauren Simone Publishing Hse.

Clarke, Zachary-Michael, jt. illus. see Clarke, Simonne-Anais.

Clarkson, Bryony. Owl Always Love You. Hegarty, Patricia. 2020. (ENG.). 14p. (J). (-k). bds. 8.99 **(978-1-68010-640-4(6))** Tiger Tales.

Clarkson, Giselle. Hazel & the Snails. Blanchard, Nan. 2019. 108p. (J). (gr. 4-7). pap. 15.00 (978-0-9951135-8-9(0)) Massey University Press NZL. Dist: Independent Pubs. Group.

—Secret World of Butterflies. Meredith, Courtney Sina. 2018. (ENG.). 32p. (J). (gr. -1-2). pap. 9.99 (978-1-76063-360-8(7)) Allen & Unwin AUS. Dist: Independent Pubs. Group.

Clarkson, Jackie. Birthday Bus. Ackland, Nick & Clever Publishing. 2019. (Wonder Wheels Ser.). (ENG.). 10p. (J). (gr. -1 — 1). bds. 8.99 (978-1-948418-81-2(9)) Clever Media Group.

—Camper Fun. Ackland, Nick & Clever Publishing. 2019. (Wonder Wheels Ser.). (ENG.). 10p. (J). (gr. -1 — 1). bds. 8.99 (978-1-948418-82-9(7)) Clever Media Group.

—Safari Park. Ackland, Nick & Clever Publishing. 2019. (Wonder Wheels Ser.). (ENG.). 10p. (J). (gr. -1 — 1). bds. 8.99 (978-1-948418-83-6(5)) Clever Media Group.

—Train Trip. Ackland, Nick & Clever Publishing. 2019. (Wonder Wheels Ser.). (ENG.). 10p. (J). (gr. -1 — 1). bds. 8.99 (978-1-948418-84-3(3)) Clever Media Group.

Clarkson, Janet M. Petoskey Stone Soup. Mothershead, Martha Fulford. 2006. 32p. (J). 18.95 (978-0-9785465-0-2(4)) Leelanau Pr.

Clarkson, Karen. Saltypie: A Choctaw Journey from Darkness into Light. Tingle, Tim. 2010. (ENG.). 40p. (J). (gr. 2-6). 17.95 (978-1-933693-67-5(3)) Cinco Puntos Pr.

Clary, Holly. Fables from the North. McDonald, Rhonda. 2019. (ENG.). 70p. (J). pap. 16.00 (978-1-7293-8796-2(9)) SDC Publishing, LLC.

Class, Virginia Tyree. Auntie Silly & the Crazy Cousins Day Parade, 1 vol. Fields, Melissa. 2010. 20p. pap. 24.95 (978-1-4489-8140-3(9)) PublishAmerica, Inc.

Classified. Journey to Star Wars: the Rise of Skywalker - Allegiance. 2019. (ENG.). 112p. (YA). (gr. 4-17). pap. 15.99 (978-1-302-91924-5(5)) Marvel Worldwide, Inc.

Claude, Jean. Animals. Channing, Margot. 2017. (First Words & Pictures Ser.). (ENG.). 14p. (J). (gr. -1 — 1). bds. 9.99 (978-1-68152-200-5(4)) Amicus.

—Around Town. Channing, Margot. 2018. (First Words & Pictures Ser.). (ENG.). 14p. (J). (gr. -1 — 1). bds. 9.99 (978-1-68152-410-8(4)) Amicus.

—At Home. Channing, Margot. 2018. (First Words & Pictures Ser.). (ENG.). 14p. (J). (gr. -1 — 1). bds. 9.99 (978-1-68152-411-5(2)) Amicus.

—Be Brave, Little Tiger! Brown, Margaret Wise. 2019. (Margaret Wise Brown Classics Ser.). (ENG.). 32p. (J). (gr. -1-k). 12.99 (978-1-68412-744-3(0), Silver Dolphin Bks.) Printers Row Publishing Group.

—Bears Make the Best Math Buddies. Oliver, Carmen. 2019. (ENG.). 32p. (J). (gr. k-2). lib. bdg. 17.95 (978-1-68446-079-3(4), 140866, Capstone Editions) Capstone.

—Bears Make the Best Reading Buddies. Oliver, Carmen. 2016. (Fiction Picture Bks.). (ENG.). 32p. (J). (gr. -1-1). lib. bdg. 21.27 (978-1-4795-9181-7(5), Picture Window Bks.) Capstone.

Claude, Jean. Bears Make the Best Science Buddies. Oliver, Carmen. 2020. (ENG.). 32p. (J). (gr. k-2). 17.99 **(978-1-68446-083-0(2)**, 140868, Capstone Editions) Capstone.

Claude, Jean. Bears Make the Best Writing Buddies. Oliver, Carmen. 2020. (ENG.). 32p. (J). (gr. k-2). 17.95 (978-1-68446-081-6(6), 140867, Capstone Editions) Capstone.

—Collins Big Cat Phonics for Letters & Sounds - Tusks: Band 04/Blue, Bd. 4. Clarke, Jane. 2018. (Collins Big Cat Phonics Ser.). (ENG.). 16p. (J). (gr. k-1). pap. 6.99 (978-0-00-825162-8(2)) HarperCollins Pubs. Ltd. GBR. Dist: Independent Pubs. Group.

—Cuentos Ilustrados de Ficción. Oliver, Carmen. (Cuentos Ilustrados de Ficción Ser.). (SPA.). (J). (gr. -1-1). 2020. pap., pap. 15.90 (978-1-5158-6114-0(7), 30111); 2019. 63.91 (978-1-5158-4691-8(1), 29726) Capstone. (Picture Window Bks.).

—Henry Hyena, Why Won't You Laugh? Jantzen, Doug. 2015. (ENG.). 32p. (J). (gr. -1-2). 17.99 (978-1-4814-2822-4(5), Aladdin) Simon & Schuster Children's Publishing.

—Make a Mobile: Solar System. 2020. (ENG.). 8p. (J). 9.99 (978-1-83857-657-8(6), 929507ca-62bc-4425-a50b-facd346b8b18) Arcturus Publishing GBR. Dist: Baker & Taylor Publisher Services (BTPS).

—My First Book of Jungle Animals. Peebles, Alice. 2019. (Arcturus My First Ser.). (ENG.). 48p. (J). 9.99 (978-1-78950-029-5(X), c64cb56e-893e-44a0-87b5-9ec25a9c4087) Arcturus Publishing GBR. Dist: Baker & Taylor Publisher Services (BTPS).

—No Hay Nada Más Chistoso Que Leer con un Oso. Oliver, Carmen. (Cuentos Ilustrados de Ficción Ser.).Tr. of Bears Make the Best Reading Buddies. (SPA.). 32p. (J). (gr. -1-1). 2020. pap. 7.95 (978-1-5158-6081-5(7), 142360); 2019. lib. bdg. 21.27 (978-1-5158-4665-9(2), 141302) Capstone. (Picture Window Bks.).

—On the Go. Channing, Margot. 2017. (First Words & Pictures Ser.). (ENG.). 14p. (J). (gr. -1 — 1). bds. 9.99 (978-1-68152-201-2(2)) Amicus.

—Rainforest. Crowe, Carmen. Cottage Door Press, ed. 2019. (Early Bird Sound Books 5 Button Ser.). (ENG.). 12p. (J). (gr. -1-2). bds. 14.99 (978-1-68052-700-1(2), 1004330) Cottage Door Pr.

—Rainforest Sticker Book. Channing, Margot. ed. 2018. (Scribblers Fun Activity Ser.). 32p. (J). (gr. k-2). pap. 5.95 (978-1-912233-17-5(7), Scribblers) Book Hse. GBR. Dist: Sterling Publishing Co., Inc.

—Safari. Channing, Margot. ed. 2019. 16p. (J). (gr. -1). bds. 6.95 (978-1-912537-91-4(5), Scribblers) Book Hse. GBR. Dist: Sterling Publishing Co., Inc.

—See, Search, Find: on the Go. Channing, Margot. 2019. (ENG.). 16p. (J). (gr. -1). bds. 6.95 (978-1-912904-69-3(1), Scribblers) Book Hse. GBR. Dist: Sterling Publishing Co., Inc.

Claudio, Eloy. Gavin's Wonderful World of Sprinkles: Childrens Book. Gomez, Crystal M. 2015. (ENG.). (J). pap. 9.95 *(978-1-60730-499-9(6))* Michaelson Entertainment.

Claudio-Vinci, Jean. Disney PIXAR the Incredibles 2: Secret Identities. Disney Pixar & Gage, Christos. 2019. (ENG.). 72p. (J). (gr. 3-7). pap. 10.99 *(978-1-5067-1392-2(0),* Dark Horse Books) Dark Horse Comics.

Clauzel, Dorothee. Petits Minous, Gros Toutous. Cottereau, Roger-Pol. Livio Editions, ed. 2018. (FRE.). 94p. (J). pap. ***(978-2-35455-001-1(4))*** Livio Informatique.

Claverie, Jean. We Are Brothers. Nadon, Yves. 2018. (ENG.). 32p. (J). (gr. -1-1). 18.99 *(978-1-56846-292-9(1),* Creative Editions) Creative Co., The.

Clay, Adam & Whelon, Chuck. Pocket Fun: Super Funny Jokes. 2020. (Pocket Fun Ser.: 7). (ENG.). 96p. (J). pap. 6.99 *(978-1-83857-633-2(9),* 34dac50f-8e9b-406b-98ec-5e6dfc30e780) Arcturus Publishing GBR. Dist: Baker & Taylor Publisher Services (BTPS).

Clay, Cliff. Blacks in Ohio II, Vol. 1. Moore, Mary. Caesor, Ebraska, ed. (YA). (gr. 6-18). pap. 12.95 *(978-0-913678-31-2(7))* New Day Pr.

Clay, Dorian. Freddie Loses His Game. Clay, Dorian. 2012. 64p. pap. 12.99 *(978-1-938056-03-1(5))* ARIVA Publishing.

Clay, Doris. Prince Cody Meets A Monster. Robison, Peggy. 2004. 40p. pap. 9.95 *(978-0-9708395-7-2(X))* Legacy Publishing Services, Inc.

—Prince Cody Runs Ahead of the Hurricane. Robison, Peggy. 2005. 64p. per. 9.95 *(978-0-9764982-7-8(8))* Legacy Publishing Services, Inc.

Clay, Joshua. Lucy Swan's Circle. Furman, Necah Stewart & Huff, Bailey. 2005. (Friends of Fairlane Woods Ser.). (ENG.). 40p. (J). (gr. -1-3). per. 16.99 *(978-1-4134-8666-7(5))* Xlibris Corp.

Clay, Julia. The Lord Is My Shepherd, 1 vol. ed. 2014. (ENG.). 32p. (J). 9.99 *(978-1-78128-143-7(2),* Candle Bks.) Lion Hudson PLC GBR. Dist: Kregel Pubns.

—Our Father, 1 vol. ed. 2014. (ENG.). 32p. (J). 9.99 *(978-1-78128-144-4(0),* Candle Bks.) Lion Hudson PLC GBR. Dist: Kregel Pubns.

Clay, Julie. Sleep Tight, Sleepy Bears. Brown, Margaret Wise. 2019. (Margaret Wise Brown Classics Ser.). (ENG.). 32p. (J). (gr. -1-k). 12.99 *(978-1-68412-760-3(2),* Silver Dolphin Bks.) Printers Row Publishing Group.

Clay, Wil. Auntee Edna. Smothers, Ethel Footman. 2004. 32p. (J). pap. 8.00 *(978-0-8028-5246-5(7));* 16.00 *(978-0-8028-5154-3(1))* Eerdmans, William B. Publishing Co.

Claycomb, Norma L. Tail Talks. Hesselbein, Deborah A. 2008. 48p. per. 15.95 *(978-1-59858-560-5(6))* Dog Ear Publishing, LLC.

Clayman, Fillys, et al. Spanish Emergent Reader 1: Mira como Juego; ¡Curitas!; Los Animales del Zoológico; Construyendo una Casa; la Alberca; ¡Agua y Jabón!; Me Visto; Mi Gato, 8 bks. Libritos Mios staff et al. Ellas, Annette, tr. 2003.Tr. of Emergent Reader 1. (SPA.). 8p. (J). 120.00 *(978-1-893986-24-4(1))* Keep Bks.

Clayton, Christian. Crazy Loco. Rice, David & Rice, David Talbot. 2003. 144p. (YA). (gr. 7-11). 7.99 *(978-0-14-250056-9(9),* Speak) Penguin Young Readers Group.

Clayton, Dallas. Make Magic! Do Good! Clayton, Dallas. 2012. 112p. (J). (gr. 2-5). 17.99 *(978-0-7636-5746-8(8))* Candlewick Pr.

Clayton, Elaine. Gee Whiz. Smiley, Jane. 2013. (Horses of Oak Valley Ranch Ser.: Bk. 5). (ENG.). 272p. (J). (gr. 5). 16.99 *(978-0-375-86969-3(7),* Knopf Bks. for Young Readers) Random Hse. Children's Bks.

—Georges & the Jewels. Smiley, Jane. 2010. (Horses of Oak Valley Ranch Ser.). (ENG.). (J). (gr. 5-9). lib. bdg. 17.60 *(978-1-61383-023-9(8))* Perfection Learning Corp.

Clayton Junior. Free the Lines. Clayton Junior. 2017. (ENG.). 32p. (J). (gr. -1-2). 17.95 *(978-1-910277-29-4(0),* Words & Pictures) Quarto Publishing Group UK GBR. Dist: Hachette Bk. Group.

Clayton, Kim. Footprints on the Ceiling: Your Child's Footprint Completes the Story. Hetzer, Michael. 2nd ed. 2005. 32p. (J). 18.95 *(978-0-9728222-2-0(4))* Webster Henrietta Publishing.

—Footprints on the Ceiling (Collector's Edition) Your Child's Footprint Completes the Story. Hetzer, Michael. 2004. 32p. (J). 18.95 *(978-0-9728222-1-3(6))* Webster Henrietta Publishing.

—The Get Well Picture. Hetzer, Michael. 2005. (J). 2nd collector's ed. 32p. 18.95 *(978-0-9728222-5-1(9));* 3rd ed. 18.95 *(978-0-9728222-6-8(7))* Webster Henrietta Publishing.

—A Hug for Percy Porcupine. Hetzer, Michael. 2005. 32p. (J). (gr. k-2). 2nd collector's ed. 18.95 *(978-0-9728222-4-4(0));* 3rd ed. 18.95 *(978-0-9728222-3-7(2))* Webster Henrietta Publishing.

—No More Handprints: Your Child's Handprint Completes the Story. Hetzer, Michael. 2nd ed. 2005. 32p. (J). 18.95 *(978-0-9728222-0-6(8))* Webster Henrietta Publishing.

Clayton, Lew. Felina's New Home: A Florida Panther Story, 1 vol. Wlodarski, Loran. 2010. (ENG.). 32p. (J). (gr. -1-3). 16.95 *(978-1-60718-068-5(5))* Arbordale Publishing.

Clayton, Peirce. Piggyback Backpack: I'm Not Ready for School. Clayton, Peirce a. 2018. (ENG.). 38p. (J). (gr. k-6). pap. 14.00 *(978-1-7326245-4-2(2))* Cridge Mumbly Publishing.

Clayton, Peirce a. Cridge Mumbly: Johnny Appleseeds Cousin. Clayton, Peirce a. 2018. (ENG.). 36p. (J). (gr. k-6). pap. 14.00 *(978-1-7326245-0-4(X))* Cridge Mumbly Publishing.

—The First Grandpa: Grandpas Nonsense Tales. Clayton, Peirce a. 2018. (ENG.). 38p. (J). (gr. k-6). pap. 14.00 *(978-1-7326245-1-1(8))* Cridge Mumbly Publishing.

—Grandma Shhh ... The Quietest Place. Clayton, Peirce a. 2018. (ENG.). 34p. (J). (gr. k-6). pap. 14.00 *(978-1-7326245-5-9(0))* Cridge Mumbly Publishing.

—The Thief Prince: Stealing Is Bad for You. Clayton, Peirce a. 2018. (ENG.). 42p. (J). (gr. k-6). pap. 14.00 *(978-1-7326245-3-5(4))* Cridge Mumbly Publishing.

—Train Town: The Town That Sees the World. Clayton, Peirce a. 2018. (ENG.). 34p. (J). (gr. k-6). pap. 14.00 *(978-1-7326245-2-8(6))* Cridge Mumbly Publishing.

Clayton, Sean & Spears, Ashley. Melvin the Mailman. Clayton, Lisa. 2005. 8p. (J). 3.49 *(978-0-9773723-0-0(8))* Trent's Prints.

Clearwater, Linda. Duckling Is Patient. Simon, Mary Manz. 2006. (First Virtues for Toddlers Ser.). 20p. (J). 5.99 *(978-0-7847-1410-2(X),* 04038) Standard Publishing.

—Kitty Shows Kindness. Simon, Mary Manz. 2006. (First Virtues for Toddlers Ser.). 20p. (J). 5.99 *(978-0-7847-1408-9(8),* 04036) Standard Publishing.

Clearwater, Linda & Couri, Kathy. Bear Obeys. Simon, Mary Manz. 2006. (First Virtues for Toddlers Ser.). 20p. (J). 5.99 *(978-0-7847-1416-4(9),* 04068) Standard Publishing.

—Tiger Forgives. Simon, Mary Manz. 2006. (First Virtues for Toddlers Ser.). 20p. (J). 5.99 *(978-0-7847-1413-3(4),* 04065) Standard Publishing.

Clearwater, Linda, jt. illus. see Couri, Kathy.

Clearwater, Linda, jt. illus. see Harris, Phyllis.

Cleary, Christine Desmond. Angels for Little People. O'Reilly, Orla Marie. 2006. (ENG.). 36p. pap. 16.95 *(978-1-85390-908-5(4))* Veritas Pubns. IRL. Dist: Casemate Pubs. & Bk. Distributors, LLC.

Cleary, Janice. Come to Jesus: A Kids' Book for Eucharistic Adoration. Flanagan, Anne. 2006. (J). 4.50 *(978-0-8198-1577-4(2))* Pauline Bks. & Media.

Clecak, Greg. OMG Where Are You? Arellano, Samantha X. 2019. (ENG.). 36p. (J). (gr. k-4). 19.99 ***(978-0-578-54366-6(4))*** Samantha Xiong Arellano.

Clegg, Dave. Bear's Bad Day: Bullies Can Change. Blevins, Wiley. 2015. (Funny Bone Readers (tm) — Dealing with Bullies Ser.). (ENG.). 24p. (J). (gr. k-2). lib. bdg. 19.99 *(978-1-63440-012-1(7))* Red Chair Pr.

—Carnival on Neptune (Book 5) Dinardo, Jeff. 2019. (Funny Bone Books (tm) First Chapters — the Jupiter Twins Ser.). (ENG.). 32p. (J). (gr. k-2). 19.99 *(978-1-63440-750-2(4));* pap. 4.99 *(978-1-63440-754-0(7))* Red Chair Pr.

—Field Trip to Mars (Book 1) Dinardo, Jeff. 2018. (Funny Bone Books (tm) First Chapters — the Jupiter Twins Ser.). (ENG.). 32p. (J). (gr. k-2). pap. 4.99 *(978-1-63440-253-8(7));* lib. bdg. 19.99 *(978-1-63440-249-1(9))* Red Chair Pr.

—Lost on Earth. Dinardo, Jeff. 2018. (Funny Bone Books (tm) First Chapters — the Jupiter Twins Ser.: Vol. 2). (ENG.). 32p. (J). (gr. k-2). lib. bdg. 19.99 *(978-1-63440-250-7(2))* Red Chair Pr.

—Lost on Earth (Book 2) Dinardo, Jeff. 2018. (Funny Bone Books (tm) First Chapters — the Jupiter Twins Ser.). (ENG.). 32p. (J). (gr. k-2). pap. 4.99 *(978-1-63440-254-5(5))* Red Chair Pr.

—Music on Mercury (Book 7) Dinardo, Jeff. 2019. (Funny Bone Books (tm) First Chapters — the Jupiter Twins Ser.). (ENG.). 32p. (J). (gr. k-2). 19.99 *(978-1-63440-752-6(0));* pap. 4.99 *(978-1-63440-756-4(3))* Red Chair Pr.

—New Kid on Jupiter (Book 8) Dinardo, Jeff. 2019. (Funny Bone Books (tm) First Chapters — the Jupiter Twins Ser.). (ENG.). 32p. (J). (gr. k-2). 19.99 *(978-1-63440-753-3(9))* Red Chair Pr.

—The New Kid on Jupiter (Book 8) Dinardo, Jeff. 2019. (Funny Bone Books (tm) First Chapters — the Jupiter Twins Ser.). (ENG.). 32p. (J). (gr. k-2). pap. 4.99 *(978-1-63440-757-1(1))* Red Chair Pr.

—Party on Pluto (Book 4) Dinardo, Jeff. 2018. (Funny Bone Books (tm) First Chapters — the Jupiter Twins Ser.). (ENG.). 32p. (J). (gr. k-2). pap. 4.99 *(978-1-63440-256-9(1));* lib. bdg. 19.99 *(978-1-63440-252-1(9))* Red Chair Pr.

—Scout Trip to Saturn. Dinardo, Jeff. 2018. (Funny Bone Books (tm) First Chapters — the Jupiter Twins Ser.: Vol. 3). (ENG.). 32p. (J). (gr. k-2). lib. bdg. 19.99 *(978-1-63440-251-4(0))* Red Chair Pr.

—Scout Trip to Saturn (Book 3) Dinardo, Jeff. 2018. (Funny Bone Books (tm) First Chapters — the Jupiter Twins Ser.). (ENG.). 32p. (J). (gr. k-2). pap. 4.99 *(978-1-63440-255-2(3))* Red Chair Pr.

—Seed Power: Discovering How Plants Grow. Prokos, Anna. 2017. (Imagine That! Ser.). (ENG.). 32p. (J). (gr. 2-4). lib. bdg. 26.65 *(978-1-63440-151-7(4));* E-Book 39.99 *(978-1-63440-163-0(8))* Red Chair Pr.

—Star Light, Star Bright: Exploring Our Solar System. Prokos, Anna. 2017. (Imagine That! Ser.). (ENG.). 32p. (J). (gr. 2-4). lib. bdg. 26.65 *(978-1-63440-152-4(2));* E-Book 39.99 *(978-1-63440-164-7(6))* Red Chair Pr.

—Vacation on Venus (Book 6) Dinardo, Jeff. 2019. (Funny Bone Books (tm) First Chapters — the Jupiter Twins Ser.). (ENG.). 32p. (J). (gr. k-2). 19.99 *(978-1-63440-751-9(2));* pap. 4.99 *(978-1-63440-755-7(5))* Red Chair Pr.

Cleland, Josh. Go, New York, Go! duopress labs. 2018. (ENG.). 22p. (J). (gr. -1-k). bds. 9.95 *(978-1-946064-97-4(1),* 806497) Duo Pr. LLC.

—I Want a Real Bike in Oregon. Kimmel, Eric A. 2018. (ENG.). 32p. (J). (gr. 1-3). 17.99 *(978-1-5132-6127-0(4),* West Winds Pr.) West Margin Pr.

—Portland Baby. Kerley, Barbara. 2017. (Local Baby Bks.). (ENG.). 22p. (J). (gr. -1-k). bds. 8.95 *(978-1-946064-05-9(X),* 806405) Duo Pr. LLC.

Cleland, Josh. Trick or Treat Songs. VonFeder, Rosa. Cottage Door Press, ed. 2020. (Halloween Interactive Children's Take along Song Book with 5 Sing-Along Tunes Ser.). (ENG.). 10p. (J). (gr. -1-2). bds. 14.99 ***(978-1-68052-939-5(0),*** 1005820) Cottage Door Pr.

Cleland, Josh. Zoom! Beep! Vroom! Busy Cities. duopress labs. 2018. (ENG.). 22p. (J). (gr. -1 — 1). bds. 9.95 *(978-1-947458-27-7(2),* 805827, Duo Pr. Llc (US)) Duo Pr. LLC.

Clelland, Ron. Guess Who's Coming? Green, Carol. 2018. (ENG.). 26p. (J). pap. 15.00 *(978-1-7904-3733-7(4))* Independently Published.

Clem, Margaret H. Elbert ein Swine, Genius Pig. Clem, Margaret H. 2003. (ENG.). 32p. (J). (gr. k-4). pap. 6.95 *(978-1-878044-12-9(5))* Mayhaven Publishing, Inc.

—Elbert ein Swine Learns Line Dancing No. 2. Clem, Margaret H. 2003. (ENG.). 32p. (J). (gr. k-4). pap. 9.95 *(978-1-878044-28-0(1))* Mayhaven Publishing, Inc.

Clemenston, John. More Little Mouse Deer Tales. Hughes, Mónica. 2005. 24p. (J). lib. bdg. 23.65 *(978-1-59646-730-9(4))* Dingles & Co.

Clement, Devyn, jt. illus. see Steele, Andrew.

Clement, Edgar. El Hombre Qve Se Convirtio en Toro: Y Otras Historias de la Inquisicion. Cortes Hernandez, Santiago & Cortes, Santiago. 2006. (Otra Escalera Ser.). (ENG.). 60p. (J). (gr. -1-k). pap. 12.95 *(978-970-20-0831-6(X))* Castillo, Ediciones, S. A. de C. V. MEX. Dist: Macmillan.

—Sonrie! McGaughrean, Geraldine et al. rev. ed. 2006. (Castillo de la Lectura Naranja Ser.). (ENG.). 120p. (J). (gr. 4-6). pap. 7.95 *(978-970-20-0853-8(0))* Castillo, Ediciones, S. A. de C. V. MEX. Dist: Macmillan.

Clement, Gary. A Coyote Solstice Tale, 1 vol. King, Thomas. 2009. (ENG.). 64p. (gr. -1). 14.95 *(978-0-88899-929-0(1))* Groundwood Bks. CAN. Dist: Publishers Group West (PGW).

—Get Growing! Savage, Candace. (J). pap. 6.95 *(978-1-55054-203-5(6),* Da Capo Pr. Inc.) Hachette Bks.

Clement, Gary, et al. Mother Goose, 1 vol. Lottridge, Celia. 2009. (ENG.). 64p. (J). (gr. k — 1). bds. 9.95 *(978-0-88899-933-7(X))* Groundwood Bks. CAN. Dist: Publishers Group West (PGW).

Clement, Gary. My Winter City, 1 vol. Gladstone, James. 2019. (ENG.). 32p. (J). (gr. k-2). 19.95 *(978-1-77306-010-1(4))* Groundwood Bks. CAN. Dist: Publishers Group West (PGW).

—One-Eye! Two-Eyes! Three-Eyes! A Very Grimm Fairy Tale. Shepard, Aaron. 2006. (ENG.). 32p. (J). (gr. k-2). 18.99 *(978-0-689-86740-8(9),* Atheneum Bks. for Young Readers) Simon & Schuster Children's Publishing.

—Oy, Feh, So?, 1 vol. Fagan, Cary. 2013. (ENG.). 40p. (J). (gr. -1-3). 17.95 *(978-1-55498-148-9(4))* Groundwood Bks. CAN. Dist: Publishers Group West (PGW).

—Stories from Adam & Eve to Ezekiel, 1 vol. Lottridge, Celia Barker. 2004. (ENG.). 144p. (J). 24.95 *(978-0-88899-490-5(7))* Groundwood Bks. CAN. Dist: Publishers Group West (PGW).

—Swimming, Swimming, 1 vol. 2015. (ENG.). 48p. (J). (gr. -1-2). 18.95 *(978-1-55498-449-7(1))* Groundwood Bks. CAN. Dist: Publishers Group West (PGW).

—Ten Old Men & a Mouse. Fagan, Cary. 2007. 32p. (J). (gr. -1-1). 18.95 *(978-0-88776-716-6(8),* Tundra Bks.) Tundra Bks. CAN. Dist: Penguin Random Hse. LLC.

Clement, Marilyn. Edgar, the Near-Sighted Eagle. Bettenberg, Barbie. 2008. 27p. (J). *(978-0-9822534-0-3(0))* Cricket XPress of Minnesota.

Clement, Michelle. Qui Aimerais-Je Devenir? Billan, Rumeet. 2018. (FRE.). 40p. (J). (gr. k-3). pap. *(978-1-989025-46-8(3))* Page Two Bks., Inc.

—¿quién Quiero Llegar a Ser? Billan, Rumeet. 2018. (SPA.). 40p. (J). (gr. k-3). pap. *(978-1-989025-45-1(5))* Page Two Bks., Inc.

Clement, Morgan. A Card for My Father. Thornhill, Samantha. 2018. (ENG.). 40p. (J). 16.95 *(978-0-9987999-6-4(3))* Penny Candy Bks., LLC.

Clement, Rod. Grandpa's Teeth. Clement, Rod. 2005. (Trophy Picture Bks.). (ENG.). 32p. (J). (gr. -1-3). 7.99 *(978-0-06-443557-4(1))* Perfection Learning Corp.

—Olga the Brolga. Clement, Rod. 2004. 32p. *(978-0-207-19701-7(6))* HarperCollins Pubs. Australia.

Clement, Sarah. Half for You & Half for Me: Favorite Nursery Rhymes & the Stories Behind Them, 1 vol. Govier, Katherine. 2014. (ENG.). 176p. (J). (gr. -1-3). 22.95 *(978-1-77050-212-3(2),* 31686dd3-b7e4-4921-ba5e-94ce6299b0bb) Whitecap Bks., Ltd. CAN. Dist: Firefly Bks., Ltd.

Clement, Stacy. God's Special Creation. Davis, Rebecca. de Papenbrock, Dervy Romero, tr. unabr. ed. 2003. (ENG & SPA.). 30p. (J). (gr. k-3). spiral bd. 8.00 *(978-0-9720881-3-8(X),* B004) His Hands, Inc.

Clement, Theresa. I See You Little Andrew. Boggs-Johnson, Stefanie. 2018. (ENG.). 24p. (J). (gr. k-6). pap. 12.99 *(978-1-63132-059-0(9))* Advanced Publishing LLC.

Clemente, Luca. Il Viaggio Di Vlad Nel Mondo-Di-La. Popescu, Sinziana. Salone, Sara, tr. 2015. (ITA.). 252p. (J). *(978-606-93279-8-2(5))* Mediamorphosis.

Clements, Ashley, jt. illus. see Smith, Ian.

Clements, Frida. The Wandering Goose: A Modern Fable of How Love Goes. Earnhardt, Heather L. 2013. 64p. 15.95 *(978-1-57061-881-9(X))* Sasquatch Bks.

Clements, Ruth Sypherd. Beasley's Christmas Party. Tarkington, Booth. 2004. reprint ed. pap. 15.95 *(978-1-4179-0186-9(1))* Kessinger Publishing, LLC.

Clemesha, Andrea Zimmerman,David. Fire Engine Man. Clemesha, Andrea Zimmerman,David. 2016. (Digger Man Ser.: 2). (ENG.). 15p. (J). bds. 7.99 *(978-1-62779-503-6(0),* 900152955, Holt, Henry & Co. Bks. For Young Readers) Holt, Henry & Co.

Clemesha, David & Zimmerman, Andrea. Fire Engine Man. Clemesha, David & Zimmerman, Andrea. 2007. (Digger Man Ser.: 2). (ENG.). 32p. (J). (gr. -1-k). 18.99 *(978-0-8050-7905-0(X),* 900031314, Holt, Henry & Co. Bks. For Young Readers) Holt, Henry & Co.

Clemesha, David, jt. illus. see Zimmerman, Andrea.

Cleminson, Katie. Loved to Bits. Heapy, Teresa. 2018. (ENG.). 32p. (J). 17.99 *(978-1-250-18694-2(3),* 900191735) Roaring Brook Pr.

Clemmons, Najah. Always My Twin. Samuels, Valerie R. 2006. (ENG.). 30p. pap. 15.22 *(978-1-4120-6036-3(2))* Trafford Publishing.

—When Life Gives Me Lemons I Make Lemonade. James, Queen Elizabeth. 2019. (ENG.). 42p. (J). pap. 13.00 *(978-1-9818-4395-4(7))* CreateSpace Independent Publishing Platform.

Cleofas, Jasmine. Grumpy the Stump. Feizo, Alicia & Cavanagh, Larry. 2019. (ENG.). 22p. (J). (gr. k-2). pap. 11.99 *(978-5-532-37877-3(0),* ExamWise) Total Recall Learning, Inc.

Clerici, Lorenzo. The Dog Book: A Minibombo Book. Clerici, Lorenzo. 2017. (Minibombo Ser.). (ENG.). 32p. (J). (-k). 9.99 *(978-0-7636-9487-6(8))* Candlewick Pr.

Clester, Shane. Birthday Surprise! (Top Wing) Berrios, Frank. 2019. (Little Golden Book Ser.). (ENG.). 24p. (J). (-k). 4.99 *(978-0-525-64752-2(X),* Golden Bks.) Random Hse. Children's Bks.

Clester, Shane. Blue Bay Mystery (the Boxcar Children: Time to Read, Level 2) 2020. (Time to Read Ser.). (ENG.). 48p. (J). (gr. k-2). pap. 3.99 ***(978-0-8075-0800-8(4),*** 0807508004); 12.99 ***(978-0-8075-0795-7(4),*** 807507954) Whitman, Albert & Co.

—The Boxcar Children Early Reader Set #1 (the Boxcar Children: Time to Read, Level 2) Warner, Gertrude Chandler. 2019. (Time to Read Ser.). (ENG.). 208p. (J). (gr. k-2). pap. 14.99 ***(978-0-8075-0832-9(2),*** 807508322) Whitman, Albert & Co.

Clester, Shane. The Boxcar Children (the Boxcar Children: Time to Read, Level 2) Warner, Gertrude Chandler. (Time to Read Ser.). (ENG.). 48p. (J). (gr. k-2). 2019. pap. 3.99 *(978-0-8075-0835-0(7),* 807508357); 2018. 12.99 *(978-0-8075-0839-8(X),* 080750839X) Whitman, Albert & Co.

—Collins Big Cat Phonics for Letters & Sounds - Map Man: Band 01A/Pink A, Bd. 1A. Clarke, Zoë. 2018. (Collins Big Cat Phonics Ser.). (ENG.). 16p. (J). (gr. -1-k). pap. 6.99 *(978-0-00-825131-4(2))* HarperCollins Pubs. Ltd. GBR. Dist: Independent Pubs. Group.

—The Falcon (Marvel Avengers) Berrios, Frank. 2020. (Little Golden Book Ser.). (ENG.). 24p. (J). (-k). 4.99 *(978-0-593-17323-7(6),* Golden Bks.) Random Hse. Children's Bks.

—The Holiday Heroes Save Christmas. Wallace, Adam & Wallace, Adam. 2018. 32p. (J). (-3). 10.99 *(978-1-4926-6970-8(9),* Sourcebooks Jabberwocky) Sourcebooks, Inc.

Clester, Shane. I Am a Padawan (Star Wars) Eckstein, Ashley. 2020. (Little Golden Book Ser.). (ENG.). 24p. (J). (-k). 4.99 ***(978-0-7364-4046-2(1),*** Golden Bks.) Random Hse. Children's Bks.

Clester, Shane. I Am She-Ra! (She-Ra) Sazaklis, John. 2019. (Little Golden Book Ser.). (ENG.). 24p. (J). (-k). 4.99 *(978-1-9848-5035-5(0),* Golden Bks.) Random Hse. Children's Bks.

Clester, Shane. I Am Skeletor! (He-Man) Berrios, Frank. 2020. (Little Golden Book Ser.). 24p. (J). (-k). 4.99 ***(978-0-593-12185-6(6),*** Golden Bks.) Random Hse. Children's Bks.

—The Lighthouse Mystery (the Boxcar Children: Time to Read, Level 2) 2020. (Time to Read Ser.). (ENG.). 48p. (J). (gr. k-2). 12.99 ***(978-0-8075-4548-5(1),*** 0807545481) Whitman, Albert & Co.

—Mike's Mystery (the Boxcar Children: Time to Read, Level 2) 2020. (Time to Read Ser.). (ENG.). 48p. (J). (gr. k-2). pap. 3.99 ***(978-0-8075-5139-4(2),*** 807551392) Whitman, Albert & Co.

Clester, Shane. Mike's Mystery (the Boxcar Children: Time to Read, Level 2) Warner, Gertrude Chandler. 2019. (Time to Read Ser.). (ENG.). 48p. (J). (gr. k-2). 12.99 *(978-0-8075-5142-4(2),* 807551422) Whitman, Albert & Co.

Clester, Shane. Miles Morales (Marvel Spider-Man) Berrios, Frank. 2020. (Little Golden Book Ser.). (ENG.). 24p. (J). (-k). 5.99 ***(978-0-593-17324-4(4),*** Golden Bks.) Random Hse. Children's Bks.

Clester, Shane. Mystery Ranch (the Boxcar Children: Time to Read, Level 2) Warner, Gertrude Chandler. 2019. (Time to Read Ser.). (ENG.). 48p. (J). (gr. k-2). pap. 3.99 *(978-0-8075-5435-7(9),* 807554359); 12.99 *(978-0-8075-5402-9(2),* 807554022) Whitman, Albert & Co.

—The Picky Eater. Parkinson, Betsy. 2018. (Little Boost Ser.). (ENG.). 32p. (J). (gr. -1-2). 14.95 *(978-1-5158-2943-0(X),* 138476); lib. bdg. 23.99 *(978-1-5158-2942-3(1),* 138475) Capstone. (Picture Window Bks.).

—Spider-Man, Spider-Man! Includes CD with Song! Disney Storybook Art Team. 2018. (ENG.). 32p. (J). (gr. -1-k). 12.99 *(978-1-368-02769-4(5),* Marvel Pr.) Disney Publishing Worldwide.

—Surprise Island (the Boxcar Children: Time to Read, Level 2) Warner, Gertrude Chandler. (Time to Read Ser.). (ENG.). 64p. (J). (gr. k-2). 2019. pap. 3.99 *(978-0-8075-7679-3(4),* 807576794); 2018. 12.99 *(978-0-8075-7675-5(1),* 807576751) Whitman, Albert & Co.

—Team Top Wing! (Top Wing) Matheis, Mickie. 2019. (Little Golden Book Ser.). (ENG.). 24p. (J). (-k). 4.99 *(978-0-525-70792-9(1),* Golden Bks.) Random Hse. Children's Bks.

—The Threat of Thanos. Kaplan, Arie. 2018. (J). *(978-1-5444-0930-6(3),* Golden Bks.) Random Hse. Children's Bks.

—The Threat of Thanos (Marvel Avengers) Kaplan, Arie. 2018. (Little Golden Book Ser.). (ENG.). 24p. (J). (-k). 4.99 *(978-1-5247-6856-0(1),* Golden Bks.) Random Hse. Children's Bks.

Clester, Shane. The Woodshed Mystery (the Boxcar Children: Time to Read, Level 2) 2020. (Time to Read Ser.). (ENG.). 48p. (J). (gr. k-2). pap. 3.99 ***(978-0-8075-9216-8(1),*** 0807592161); 12.99 ***(978-0-8075-9210-6(2),*** 807592102) Whitman, Albert & Co.

Clester, Shane. The Yellow House Mystery (the Boxcar Children: Time to Read, Level 2) Warner, Gertrude Chandler. 2019. (Time to Read Ser.). (ENG.). 48p. (J). (gr. k-2). pap. 3.99 *(978-0-8075-9370-7(2),* 807593702); 12.99 *(978-0-8075-9367-7(2),* 807593672) Whitman, Albert & Co.

Clester, Shane. 13th Street #1: Battle of the Bad-Breath Bats. Bowles, David. 2020. (HarperChapters Ser.). (ENG.). 96p. (J). (gr. 1-5). 15.99 ***(978-0-06-294780-2(X));*** pap. 5.99 ***(978-0-06-294779-6(6))*** HarperCollins Pubs. Ltd. GBR. (HarperCollins). Dist: HarperCollins Pubs.

—13th Street #2: the Fire-Breathing Ferret Fiasco. Bowles, David. 2020. (HarperChapters Ser.). 96p. (J). (gr. 1-5). 15.99 ***(978-0-06-294783-3(4));*** pap. 5.99 ***(978-0-06-294782-6(6))*** HarperCollins Pubs. Ltd. GBR. (HarperCollins). Dist: HarperCollins Pubs.

C

—13th Street #3: Clash of the Cackling Cougars. Bowles, David. 2020. (HarperChapters Ser.). 96p. (J). (gr. 1-5). 15.99 ***(978-0-06-294786-4(9))***; pap. 5.99 ***(978-0-06-294785-7(0))*** HarperCollins Pubs. Ltd. GBR. (HarperCollins). Dist: HarperCollins Pubs.

Clester, Shane, jt. illus. see Harrison, J. J.

Cleveland, Fred. The Navajo Brothers & the Stolen Herd. Grammer, Maurine. 2004. 120p. (gr. 4-7). pap. 9.95 *(978-1-878610-23-2(6))* Red Crane Bks., Inc.

Cleyet-Merle, Laurence. Animal Stencil Book. 2006. (Stencil Bks.). 14p. (J). (gr. -1-3). bds. 12.99 *(978-0-7945-1140-1(6)*, Usborne) EDC Publishing.

—The Rhyme Bible Storybook, 1 vol. Sattgast, L. J. 2012. 344p. (J). 17.99 *(978-0-310-72602-9(6))* Zonderkidz.

—The Rhyme Bible Storybook for Little Ones, 1 vol. Sattgast, L. J. rev. ed. 2015. (ENG.). 40p. (J). bds. 9.99 *(978-0-310-75363-6(5))* Zonderkidz.

Clibbon, Lucy. Fabulous Fairies. Clibbon, Meg. 2010. (My World Of... Ser.). (ENG.). 32p. (J). (gr. k-2). 21.19 *(978-1-84089-551-3(9))* Evans Brothers, Ltd. GBR. Dist: Children's Plus, Inc.

—The Fairyland Olympics. Clibbon, Meg et al. 2008. (ENG.). 32p. (J). (gr. k-2). *(978-1-84089-504-9(7))* Zero to Ten, Ltd.

—Imagine You're a Ballerina. Clibbon, Meg. 2006. 32p. (J). (gr. -1-4). 19.95 *(978-1-55451-020-7(1)*, 9781554510207) Annick Pr., Ltd. CAN. Dist: Publishers Group West (PGW).

—Imagine You're a Princess! Princess Megerella & Princess Lulubelle. Clibbon, Meg. 2005. (ENG.). 32p. (J). (gr. -1-4). pap. 7.95 *(978-1-55037-920-4(8)*, 9781550379204) Annick Pr., Ltd. CAN. Dist: Publishers Group West (PGW).

—Magical Christmas. Clibbon, Meg & Meg, Merry. 2008. (ENG.). 32p. (J). (gr. k-2). *(978-1-84089-377-9(X))* Zero to Ten, Ltd.

—My Pretty Pink Fairy Journal. Clibbon, Meg et al. 2008. (Meg & Lucy Journals). (ENG.). 112p. (J). (gr. k-2). *(978-1-84089-467-7(9))* Zero to Ten, Ltd.

—My Wicked Pirate Journal. Clibbon, Meg et al. 2008. (Meg & Lucy Journals). (ENG.). 112p. (J). (gr. k-2). *(978-1-84089-466-0(0))* Zero to Ten, Ltd.

—Shimmering Mermaids. Clibbon, Meg. 2011. (My World Of Ser.). (ENG.). 32p. (J). (gr. k-2). pap. 9.99 *(978-1-84089-594-0(2))* Meg and Lucy Bks. GBR. Dist: Independent Pubs. Group.

—Sparkly Princesses. Clibbon, Meg. 2010. (My World Of... Ser.). (ENG.). 32p. (J). (gr. k-2). 21.19 *(978-1-84089-542-1(X))* Evans Brothers, Ltd. GBR. Dist: Children's Plus, Inc.

—Wicked Pirates. Clibbon, Meg. 2010. (My World Of... Ser.). (ENG.). 32p. (J). (gr. k-2). 21.19 *(978-1-84089-552-0(7))* Evans Brothers, Ltd. GBR. Dist: Children's Plus, Inc.

Clibbon, Lucy, jt. illus. see Loveheart, Lucy.

Cliette, Emanuel & Zieroth, Emily. Mom's First Days of School. Joseph, Terrica. 2018. (ENG.). 32p. (J). pap. 9.99 *(978-1-970016-25-3(6))* Fruit Springs, LLC.

Cliff, Tony. Let's Get Sleepy! Cliff, Tony. 2020. (ENG.). 32p. (J). 17.99 *(978-1-250-30784-2(8)*, 900198143) Imprint IND. Dist: Macmillan.

Clifford, Caroline. The Gospel on Five Fingers: The Story of Mother Theresa, 1 bk. Coming, Soon. Gosselin, Katie & Bono, Ignacio, trs. 2005. (J). 5.00 *(978-0-9765180-1-3(5))* Catholic World Mission.

—Jesus, I Trust in You! The Story of Saint Faustina, Missionary of Divine Mercy. Luetkemeyer, Jenny. Kiszkurno, Irene & Chacon, Cesar, trs. 2004. (SPA & POL.). 32p. (J). (gr. k-5). 5.00 *(978-0-9747571-2-4(8))* Catholic World Mission.

Clift, Eva. Gulliver's Travels: And A Discussion of Tolerance. Swift, Jonathan. 2003. (Values in Action Illustrated Classics Ser.). 191p. (J). *(978-1-59203-029-3(7))* Learning Challenge, Inc.

—Heidi: With a Discussion of Optimism. Spyri, Johanna. 2003. (Values in Action Illustrated Classics Ser.). 190p. (J). *(978-1-59203-030-9(0))* Learning Challenge, Inc.

—The Red Badge of Courage: With a Discussion of Self-Esteem. Crane, Stephen. 2003. (Values in Action Illustrated Classics Ser.). 190p. (J). *(978-1-59203-034-7(3))* Learning Challenge, Inc.

Clift, Eva. The Call of the Wild. Clift, Eva, tr. London, Jack. 2003. (Values in Action Illustrated Classics Ser.). (J). *(978-1-59203-047-7(5))* Learning Challenge, Inc.

—Frankenstein: With a Discussion of Tolerance. Clift, Eva, tr. Shelley, Mary. 2003. (Values in Action Illustrated Classics Ser.). (J). *(978-1-59203-048-4(3))* Learning Challenge, Inc.

—The Merry Adventures of Robin Hood: With a Discussion of Fellowship. Clift, Eva, tr. Pyle, Howard. 2003. (Values in Action Illustrated Classics Ser.). (J). *(978-1-59203-044-6(0))* Learning Challenge, Inc.

—The Strange Case of Dr. Jekyll & Mr. Hyde: With a Discussion of Moderation. Clift, Eva, tr. Stevenson, Robert Louis. 2003. (Values in Action Illustrated Classics Ser.). (J). *(978-1-59203-053-8(X))* Learning Challenge, Inc.

Clifton-Brown, Holly. Alphabreaths: The ABCs of Mindful Breathing. Willard, Christopher & Rechtschaffen, Daniel. 2019. (ENG.). 32p. (J). 17.95 *(978-1-68364-197-1(3)*, 900220906) Sounds True, Inc.

—Big Birthday. Hosford, Kate. 2012. (Carolrhoda Picture Bks.). (ENG.). 32p. (J). (gr. k-2). lib. bdg. 16.95 *(978-0-7613-5410-9(7))* Lerner Publishing Group.

Clifton-Brown, Holly. Does Your Dog Speak Hebrew? A Book of Animal Sounds. Bari, Ellen. 2020. (Very First Board Bks.). (ENG.). 14p. (J). (gr. -1 — 1). bds. 7.99 ***(978-1-5415-6089-5(2)***, Kar-Ben Publishing) Lerner Publishing Group.

Clifton-Brown, Holly. The Flower Girl Wore Celery. Gordon, Meryl G. 2016. (ENG.). 32p. (J). (gr. -1-5). 9.99 *(978-1-4677-7844-2(3)*, 9781467778442, Kar-Ben Publishing) Lerner Publishing Group.

—Lion's Lullaby. Kelly, Mij. 2016. (ENG.). 32p. (J). (gr. -1 — 1). 16.99 *(978-1-4847-2526-9(3))* Disney Pr.

—Lion's Lullaby. Kelly, Mij. 2017. (ENG.). 32p. (J). (gr. -1 — 1). bds. 8.99 *(978-1-4847-2549-8(2))* Hyperion Bks. for Children.

—Move Your Mood! A Guide for Kids about Mind-Body Connection. Miles, Brenda & Patterson, Colleen A. 2016. 32p. (J). *(978-1-4338-2112-7(5)*, Magination Pr.) American Psychological Assn.

—So Many Smarts! Genhart, Michael. 2017. 32p. (J). *(978-1-4338-2722-8(0)*, Magination Pr.) American Psychological Assn.

—Stella Brings the Family. Schiffer, Miriam B. 2015. (ENG.). 36p. (J). (gr. k-3). 16.99 *(978-1-4521-1190-2(1))* Chronicle Bks. LLC.

—The Story of Gilbert Baker & the Rainbow Flag. Pitman, Gayle E. 2018. 32p. (J). *(978-1-4338-2902-4(9)*, Magination Pr.) American Psychological Assn.

Clifton Brown, Holly. Tell Me a Story, Rory. Willis, Jeanne. 2019. 32p. (J). (gr. -1 — 1). pap. 9.99 *(978-1-4449-1768-0(4))* Hachette Children's Group GBR. Dist: Hachette Bk. Group.

Clifton-Brown, Holly. Where Are You, Blue? Fry, Sonali. 2015. (Dot Town Ser.). (ENG.). 32p. (J). (gr. -1 — 1). bds. 8.99 *(978-1-4814-3589-5(2)*, Little Simon) Little Simon.

Clifton Johnson. Walking. Thoreau, Henry. 2010. 100p. pap. 3.49 *(978-1-60386-305-6(2)*, Watchmaker Publishing) Wexford College Pr.

Clifton, Tom. Under One Flag: A Year at Rohwer. Parkhurst, Liz S. 2006. (ENG.). 32p. (J). (gr. 3-7). 16.95 *(978-0-87483-759-9(6)*, 1241971) August Hse. Pubs., Inc.

Climo, Liz. Can Somebody Please Scratch My Back? John, Jory. 2018. (ENG.). 40p. (J). (gr. -1-3). 16.99 *(978-0-7352-2854-2(X)*, Dial Bks) Penguin Young Readers Group.

Climo, Liz. First Day Critter Jitters. John, Jory. 2020. 40p. (J). (gr. -1-3). 17.99 ***(978-0-7352-2855-9(8)***, Dial Bks) Penguin Young Readers Group.

Climo, Liz. You Don't Want a Unicorn! Dyckman, Ame. 2017. (ENG.). 40p. (J). (gr. -1-3). 17.99 *(978-0-316-34347-3(1))* Little Brown & Co.

—You Don't Want a Unicorn! Dyckman, Ame. 2019. 24p. (J). (gr. -1 — 1). bds. 7.99 *(978-0-316-48886-0(0))* Little, Brown Bks. for Young Readers.

Climpson, Sue. Incredible Quests: Epic Journeys in Myth & Legend. Steele, Philip. 2006. 48p. (J). (gr. 3-7). pap. 11.99 *(978-1-84476-247-7(5))* Anness Publishing GBR. Dist: National Bk. Network.

—Legendary Quests: Mythological Journeys & Heroic Adventures, from the Voyages of Odysseus to the Hunt for the Holy Grail. 2020. 80p. (J). (gr. -1-12). 15.00 *(978-1-86147-865-8(8)*, Armadillo) Anness Publishing GBR. Dist: National Bk. Network.

Cline, Ian, photos by. Brownie the Monkey Visits the Zoo. Ramoutar, Tagore. 2012. 38p. pap. *(978-1-907837-48-7(5))* Longshot Ventures, Ltd.

Cline, Mike. Franky Fox's Fun with English Activity Book, Level A1. Cline, Mike. Yi-Cline, Nancy. Yi-Cline, Nancy, ed. 2007. 62p. pap. 7.99 *(978-0-9777419-1-5(5)*, SIAB) Lingo Pr. LLC.

—Franky Fox's Fun with English Level A1. Cline, Mike. Yi-Cline, Nancy. Yi-Cline, Nancy, ed. 2007. 65p. 14.99 *(978-0-9777419-0-8(7)*, SITB) Lingo Pr. LLC.

Cline, Mike, jt. illus. see Maher, Adele.

Clinedinst, B. West, jt. illus. see Varian, George.

Clipp, Joan. Phoebe's Family: A Story about Egg Donation. Stamm, Linda J. 2015. (J). pap. *(978-0-9755810-7-0(4))* Graphite Pr.

—Scarlett's Story: A Tale about Embryo Donation. Stamm, Linda J. 2017. (J). pap. *(978-1-938313-17-2(8))* Graphite Pr.

Cliquet, Ronan. The Creeping Doom. Van Lente, Fred. 2008. (Iron Man Ser.: No. 1). (ENG.). 24p. (J). (gr. 2-6). 27.07 *(978-1-59961-551-6(7)*, 10025, Marvel Age) Spotlight.

—Hand in Hand. David, Peter. 2013. (Wolverine: First Class Ser.). (ENG.). 24p. (J). (gr. 2-6). Pt. 1. lib. bdg. 27.07 *(978-1-61479-176-8(7)*, 15324); Pt. 2. lib. bdg. 27.07 *(978-1-61479-177-5(5)*, 15325) Spotlight. (Marvel Age).

Cliquet, Ronan. Marvel Vault of Heroes: Thor. Simonson, Louise et al. 2020. 208p. (J). (gr. 4-7). pap. 19.99 ***(978-1-68405-666-8(7))*** Idea & Design Works, LLC.

Cliquet, Ronan, jt. illus. see Rousseau, Craig.

Clish, Lori. Fish Don't Swim in a Tree. Clish, Marian L. (J). (gr. k-3). pap. 7.95 *(978-1-928632-12-2(2))* Writers Marketplace:Consulting, Critiquing & Publishing.

—The Owl Who Couldn't Say Whoo. Staheli, Bee, ed. l.t. ed. (J). (gr. k-5). pap. 7.95 *(978-1-928632-50-4(5))* Writers Marketplace:Consulting, Critiquing & Publishing.

Clo, Kathy. Mommy, Did I Grow in Your Tummy? Where Some Babies Come From. Gordon, Elaine R. Date not set. 28p. (Orig.). (J). (gr. -1-4). pap. 9.95 *(978-0-9634561-0-6(5))* EM Greenberg Pr., Inc.

Clohosy Cole, Tom. Destination: Space. Englert, Christoph. 2016. (ENG.). 64p. (J). (gr. 3-7). 19.99 *(978-1-84780-840-0(9)*, Wide Eyed Editions) Quarto Publishing Group UK GBR. Dist: Hachette Bk. Group.

Cloke, Rene. The Adventures of Tom Thumb. 2012. (ENG.). 24p. (J). pap. 6.50 *(978-1-84135-545-0(3))* Award Pubns. Ltd. GBR. Dist: Parkwest Pubns., Inc.

—Aladdin & His Magical Lamp. 2012. (ENG.). 24p. pap. 6.50 *(978-1-84135-534-4(8))* Award Pubns. Ltd. GBR. Dist: Parkwest Pubns., Inc.

—Bible Stories for Children. Wilkin, Wendy. 2012. (ENG.). 32p. (J). 9.95 *(978-0-86163-797-3(6))* Award Pubns. Ltd. GBR. Dist: Parkwest Pubns., Inc.

—By the River Bank, 4 vols. Bishop, Michael. 2012. (ENG.). 30p. (J). 4.95 *(978-1-84135-784-3(7))* Award Pubns. Ltd. GBR. Dist: Parkwest Pubns., Inc.

—Cinderella. 2012. (ENG.). 24p. pap. 6.50 *(978-1-84135-535-1(6))* Award Pubns. Ltd. GBR. Dist: Parkwest Pubns., Inc.

—In the Wild Wood, 4 vols. Bishop, Michael. 2012. (ENG.). 64p. (J). 4.95 *(978-1-84135-785-0(5))* Award Pubns. Ltd. GBR. Dist: Parkwest Pubns., Inc.

—Little Red Riding Hood. 2012. (ENG.). 24p. pap. 6.50 *(978-1-84135-540-5(2))* Award Pubns. Ltd. GBR. Dist: Parkwest Pubns., Inc.

—The Little Tin Soldier. 2012. (ENG.). 24p. (J). pap. 6.50 *(978-1-84135-542-9(9))* Award Pubns. Ltd. GBR. Dist: Parkwest Pubns., Inc.

—More Bible Stories for Children. Carruth, Jane. 2012. (ENG.). 32p. (J). 9.95 *(978-0-86163-770-6(4))* Award Pubns. Ltd. GBR. Dist: Parkwest Pubns., Inc.

—Mr Toad Comes Home, 4 vols. Bishop, Michael. 2012. (ENG.). 30p. (J). 4.95 *(978-1-84135-787-4(1))* Award Pubns. Ltd. GBR. Dist: Parkwest Pubns., Inc.

—Mr Toad in Trouble, 4 vols. Bishop, Michael. 2012. (ENG.). 30p. (J). 4.95 *(978-1-84135-786-7(3))* Award Pubns. Ltd. GBR. Dist: Parkwest Pubns., Inc.

—My First Picture Book of Nursery Rhymes. 2012. (ENG.). 24p. 9.95 *(978-1-84135-581-8(X))* Award Pubns. Ltd. GBR. Dist: Parkwest Pubns., Inc.

—Pinocchio. 2012. (ENG.). 24p. pap. 6.50 *(978-1-84135-538-2(0))* Award Pubns. Ltd. GBR. Dist: Parkwest Pubns., Inc.

—Puss in Boots. 2012. (ENG.). 24p. (J). pap. 6.50 *(978-1-84135-539-9(9))* Award Pubns. Ltd. GBR. Dist: Parkwest Pubns., Inc.

—Snow White & the Seven Dwarfs. 2012. (ENG.). 24p. pap. 6.50 *(978-1-84135-541-2(0))* Award Pubns. Ltd. GBR. Dist: Parkwest Pubns., Inc.

—Storytime Classics. 2012. (ENG.). 144p. (J). 12.50 *(978-1-84135-521-4(6))* Award Pubns. Ltd. GBR. Dist: Parkwest Pubns., Inc.

—The Three Little Pigs. 2012. (ENG.). 24p. pap. 6.50 *(978-1-84135-544-3(5))* Award Pubns. Ltd. GBR. Dist: Parkwest Pubns., Inc.

—The Ugly Duckling. 2012. (ENG.). 24p. (J). pap. 6.50 *(978-1-84135-543-6(7))* Award Pubns. Ltd. GBR. Dist: Parkwest Pubns., Inc.

Cloke, Rene. Favourite Bible Stories: Best-Loved Tales from the New Testament. Cloke, Rene. 2014. (ENG.). 32p. 10.50 *(978-1-84135-982-3(3))* Award Pubns. Ltd. GBR. Dist: Parkwest Pubns., Inc.

Clonts, E. M. M. Childrens Adoration Prayer Book. Hartley, Bob. 2012. 114p. pap. 24.95 *(978-0-615-58840-7(9))* Deeper Waters.

Close, Colleen & Close, Rex. My Closest Friend. Close, Colleen. 2006. (ENG.). 24p. pap. 8.00 *(978-1-4120-6375-3(2))* Trafford Publishing.

Close, Laura Ferraro. 5 Steps to Drawing Magical Creatures. StJohn, Amanda. 2018. (5 Steps to Drawing Ser.). (ENG.). 32p. (J). (gr. k-3). 29.93 *(978-1-5038-2480-5(2)*, 212242) Child's World, Inc., The.

—5 Steps to Drawing Sea Creatures. StJohn, Amanda. 2018. (5 Steps to Drawing Ser.). (ENG.). 32p. (J). (gr. k-3). 29.93 *(978-1-5038-2485-0(3)*, 212245) Child's World, Inc., The.

Close, Rex, jt. illus. see Close, Colleen.

Clouette, Katie. Benjamin the Bear. Shakespeare, Nancy. 2013. (Benjamin the Bear Ser.). (ENG.). (J). (gr. -1-3). 14.95 *(978-1-62086-312-1(X))* Mascot Bks., Inc.

—Benjamin the Bear Gets a Sister. Shakespeare, Nancy. 2013. (Benjamin the Bear Ser.). (ENG.). (J). (gr. -1-3). 14.95 *(978-1-62086-316-9(2))* Mascot Bks., Inc.

—Benjamin the Bear Goes on a Picnic. Shakespeare, Nancy. 2013. (Benjamin the Bear Ser.). (ENG.). (J). (gr. -1-3). 14.95 *(978-1-62086-314-5(6))* Mascot Bks., Inc.

—Benjamin the Bear Goes to Kindergarten. Shakespeare, Nancy. 2013. (Benjamin the Bear Ser.). (ENG.). (J). (gr. -1-k). 14.95 *(978-1-62086-320-6(0))* Mascot Bks., Inc.

—Benjamin the Bear Rides on an Airplane. Shakespeare, Nancy. 2013. (Benjamin the Bear Ser.). (ENG.). (J). (gr. -1-3). 14.95 *(978-1-62086-318-3(9))* Mascot Bks., Inc.

Clough, Zeke. It's a PanDA Thing - a Visit to the World of PDA: A Visit to the World of Pathological Demand Avoidance. Jackson, Rachel. 2019. (Thing Ser.: Vol. 3). (ENG.). 38p. (J). pap. *(978-1-9996769-4-0(7))* Changing Things Publishing.

Clover, Gordon. Sammy Squirrel & Rodney Raccoon: A Stanley Park Tale. Lawrence, Duane. 2007. (ENG.). 106p. (J). pap. *(978-1-894694-54-4(6))* Granville Island Publishing.

Clow, Alexine. Jenny's Dreams. Clow, Alexine. 2010. 20p. pap. 10.95 *(978-1-936051-89-2(3))* Peppertree Pr., The.

Clowes, Rachel. Christmas Love Letters from God: Bible Stories, 1 vol. Nellist, Glenys. 2016. (Love Letters from God Ser.). (ENG.). 32p. (J). 17.99 *(978-0-310-74824-3(0))* Zonderkidz.

—Girls' Love Letters from God: Bible Stories for a Girl's Heart, 1 vol. Nellist, Glenys. 2017. (Love Letters from God Ser.). (ENG.). 32p. (J). 16.99 *(978-0-310-75328-5(7))* Zonderkidz.

Cloyne, Rachel. The Fairy Tale Colouring Book. Cloyne, Rachel. 2014. (ENG.). 32p. (J). (gr. 1-4). pap. 8.99 *(978-1-78055-252-1(1))* O'Mara, Michael Bks., Ltd. GBR. Dist: Independent Pubs. Group.

Clucas, Jack & Jackson, Max. 123, Anteater Stuck up a Tree. Clucas, Jack & Jackson, Max. 2019. (ENG.). 32p. (J). (— 1). 16.99 *(978-1-78055-531-7(8))* O'Mara, Michael Bks., Ltd. GBR. Dist: Independent Pubs. Group.

Clulow, Hanako. The River. Hegarty, Patricia. 2016. (J). 12.99 *(978-1-61067-468-3(5))* Kane Miller.

—10 Reasons to Love... a Bear. Barr, Catherine & Natural History Museum. 2018. (10 Reasons to Love A... Ser.). (ENG.). 24p. (J). (gr. -1-1). 14.99 *(978-1-78603-016-0(0)*, Frances Lincoln Children's Bks.) Quarto Publishing Group UK GBR. Dist: Hachette Bk. Group.

—10 Reasons to Love A... Turtle. Barr, Catherine. 2017. (10 Reasons to Love A... Ser.). (ENG.). 24p. (J). (gr. -1-1). 14.99 *(978-1-84780-941-4(3)*, Frances Lincoln Children's Bks.) Quarto Publishing Group UK GBR. Dist: Hachette Bk. Group.

Clulow, Hanako. 50 Reasons to Love Animals. Barr, Catherine. 2020. (ENG.). 40p. (J). (gr. -1-1). ***(978-0-7112-5246-2(7))*** Frances Lincoln Childrens Bks.

Cneut, Carll. City Lullaby. Singer, Marilyn. 2007. (ENG.). 32p. (J). (gr. -1-3). 16.99 *(978-0-618-60703-7(X)*, 100441) Houghton Mifflin Harcourt Publishing Co.

—Willy. Kockere, Geert De. 2011. (ENG.). 32p. (YA). (gr. -1-3). 14.00 *(978-0-8028-5395-0(1)*, Eerdmans Bks For Young Readers) Eerdmans, William B. Publishing Co.

Co, Aileen & Dayton, Melissa. Friends of God: Catholic Bible Study for Children. Manhardt, Laurie Watson. 2006. (Come & See Kids Ser.). 124p. (J). (gr. -1-2). per. 9.95 *(978-1-931018-41-8(3))* Emmaus Road Publishing.

Coady, Chris. The Pebble in My Pocket: A History of Our Earth. Hooper, Meredith. rev. ed. 2015. (ENG.). 40p. (J). (gr. 2-5). pap. 9.99 *(978-1-84780-768-7(2)*, Frances Lincoln Children's Bks.) Quarto Publishing Group UK GBR. Dist: Hachette Bk. Group.

Coalson, Glo. En Las Piernas de Mamá. Scott, Ann Herbert. 2007.Tr. of On Mother's Lap. (ENG.). 14p. (J). (gr. k — 1). bds. 5.95 *(978-0-618-75247-8(1)*, 100529) Houghton Mifflin Harcourt Publishing Co.

Coat, Janik. Aleph. Coat, Janik. 2019. (ENG.). 128p. (J). (gr. -1-k). 19.99 *(978-1-77657-205-2(X))* Gecko Pr. NZL. Dist: Lerner Publishing Group.

Coates, Jennifer. This Is Farmer Greg. Howard-Parham, Pam. l.t. ed. 2005. (HRL Board Book Ser.). (gr. -1-k). pap. 10.95 *(978-1-57332-305-5(5)*, HighReach Learning, Incorporated) Carson-Dellosa Publishing, LLC.

Coates, Kathy. Batty about Texas, 1 vol. Smith, J. 2008. (ENG.). 32p. (J). (gr. k-3). 16.99 *(978-1-58980-582-8(8)*, Pelican Publishing) Arcadia Publishing.

—The Buzz on Honeybees, 1 vol. Kaemmerlen, Cathy. 2012. (ENG.). 32p. (J). (gr. k-3). 16.99 *(978-1-4556-1457-8(2)*, Pelican Publishing) Arcadia Publishing.

Coates, Kathy, jt. illus. see Knowlton, Charlotte.

Coates, Sean. Kayla's Magic Eyes. Hinton, Cheryl. Ellis, Althia Melody, ed. 2013. 26p. 13.00 *(978-0-578-11929-8(3))* Mosaic Paradigm Group, LLC.

Cobalt Illustrations Studio Staff, jt. illus. see Low, William.

Cobb, Josh, jt. illus. see Cobb, Vicki.

Cobb, Rebecca. The Day War Came. Davies, Nicola. 2018. (ENG.). 32p. (J). (gr. 1-4). 16.99 *(978-1-5362-0173-4(1))* Candlewick Pr.

Cobb, Vicki & Cobb, Josh. Light Action! Amazing Experiments with Optics. 2005. (Press Monographs: PM150). 208p. (J). 17.00 *(978-0-8194-5851-3(1))* SPIE.

Cobleigh, Carolynn. Edgar Allan Poe. Bagert, Brod, ed. 2008. (Poetry for Young People Ser.: 3). 48p. (J). (gr. 3-7). pap. 6.95 *(978-1-4027-5472-2(8))* Sterling Publishing Co., Inc.

—Poetry for Young People: Edgar Allan Poe. Bagert, Brod, ed. 2014. (Poetry for Young People Ser.: 3). 48p. (J). (gr. 3). 14.95 *(978-1-4549-1348-1(7))* Sterling Publishing Co., Inc.

Coburn, Alisa. Billie's Animal Hospital Adventure. Rippin, Sally. 2017. (ENG.). 24p. (J). 10.99 *(978-1-61067-607-6(6))* Kane Miller.

—Billie's Outer Space Adventure. Rippin, Sally. 2017. (ENG.). 24p. (J). 10.99 *(978-1-61067-608-3(4))* Kane Miller.

—Billie's Wild Jungle Adventure. Rippin, Sally. 2017. (ENG.). 24p. (J). 10.99 *(978-1-61067-553-6(3))* Kane Miller.

—Billie's Yummy Bakery Adventure. Rippin, Sally. 2017. (ENG.). 24p. (J). 10.99 *(978-1-61067-554-3(1))* Kane Miller.

—Hello, Door. Heim, Alastair. 2018. (ENG.). 32p. (J). (gr. -1-3). 16.99 *(978-1-4998-0536-9(5))* Little Bee Books Inc.

—I Want to Be ... a Lion Tamer. Brown, Ruby. 2016. (ENG.). 22p. (J). bds. 8.99 *(978-1-61067-405-8(7))* Kane Miller.

—I Want to Be ... an Astronaut. Brown, Ruby. 2016. (ENG.). 22p. (J). bds. 8.99 *(978-1-61067-406-5(5))* Kane Miller.

—Love You Too. Heim, Alastair. (ENG.). (J). (gr. -1-k). 2019. 26p. bds. 7.99 *(978-1-4998-0990-9(5))*; 2016. 32p. 16.99 *(978-1-4998-0174-3(2))* Little Bee Books Inc.

Coburn, Dylan. Adam & the Golden Horseshoe. Page, Adam. 2020. (Elite Team Ser.). (ENG.). 40p. (J). (gr. k-2). 16.95 ***(978-0-9993886-2-4(2))*** Mrs. Weisz Bks.

Coburn, Dylan. You Can Have a Party Anywhere!, 6 vols. Eggleton, Jill. 2005. (ENG.). (J). (gr. 1-2). pap. 50.00 *(978-1-4189-1008-2(2))* Rigby Education.

Coburn, Maggie. Patrick & the Fire: A Legend about Saint Patrick. Bilinsky, Cornelia Mary. 2017. 25p. (J). pap. *(978-0-8198-6037-8(9))* Pauline Bks. & Media.

Cocca-Leffler, Maryann. Carl the Complainer. Petitions. Knudsen, Michelle. 2006. (Social Studies Connects® Ser.). (ENG.). 32p. (J). (gr. 1-3). pap. 5.95 *(978-1-57565-157-6(2))* Astra Publishing Hse.

—Thanksgiving at the Tappletons' Spinelli, Eileen. 2015. (ENG.). 32p. (J). (gr. -1-3). pap. 7.99 *(978-0-06-236397-8(2))* HarperCollins Pubs.

Cocca-Leffler, Maryann. Dog Wash Day. Cocca-Leffler, Maryann. 2004. (All Aboard Picture Reader Ser.). 32p. (J). (gr. -1-k). mass mkt. 4.99 *(978-0-448-43370-7(2)*, Grosset & Dunlap) Penguin Young Readers Group.

—Easter Bunny in Training. Cocca-Leffler, Maryann. 2009. (Sneak a Peek Ser.). 16p. (J). (gr. -1-3). pap. 6.99 *(978-0-06-125673-8(0))* HarperCollins Pubs.

—A Homemade Together Christmas. Cocca-Leffler, Maryann. 2015. (ENG.). 32p. (J). (gr. -1-3). 16.99 *(978-0-8075-3366-6(1)*, 807533661) Whitman, Albert & Co.

—It's Halloween Night. Cocca-Leffler, Maryann. 2009. (Sneak a Peek Ser.). (ENG.). 16p. (J). (gr. -1-3). 6.99 *(978-0-06-125674-5(9)*, HarperFestival) HarperCollins Pubs.

—Jack's Talent. Cocca-Leffler, Maryann. 2007. (ENG.). 32p. (J). (gr. -1-3). 17.99 *(978-0-374-33681-3(4)*, 900038443, Farrar, Straus & Giroux (BYR)) Farrar, Straus & Giroux.

Cocca-Leffler, Maryann. Janine. Cocca-Leffler, Maryann. (ENG.). 32p. (J). (gr. -1-3). 2020. pap. 7.99 ***(978-0-8075-3759-6(4)***, 807537594); 2015. 16.99 *(978-0-8075-3754-1(3)*, 807537543) Whitman, Albert & Co.

Cocca-Leffler, Maryann. Janine & the Field Day Finish. Cocca-Leffler, Maryann. 2016. (ENG.). 32p. (J). (gr. -1-3). 16.99 *(978-0-8075-3756-5(X)*, 080753756X) Whitman, Albert & Co.

—Let It Rain. Cocca-Leffler, Maryann. 2013. (ENG.). 24p. (J). (gr. k-3). pap. 16.19 *(978-0-545-45343-1(7))* Scholastic, Inc.

—Let It Snow. Cocca-Leffler, Maryann. 2010. (ENG.). 24p. (J). (gr. -1-k). pap. 3.99 *(978-0-545-20880-2(7))* Scholastic, Inc.

—Mr. Tanen's Ties. Cocca-Leffler, Maryann. 2004. (ENG.). 32p. (J). (gr. k-2). pap. 6.95 *(978-0-8075-5302-2(6))* Whitman, Albert & Co.
—Princess K. I. M. & the Lie That Grew. Cocca-Leffler, Maryann. 2013. (AV2 Fiction Readalong Ser.). (ENG.). (J). (gr. k-3). 34.28 *(978-1-62127-889-4(1)*, AV2 by Weigl) Weigl Pubs., Inc.
—Rain Brings Frogs: A Little Book of Hope. Cocca-Leffler, Maryann. 2011. (ENG.). 32p. (J). (gr. -1-2). 9.99 *(978-0-06-196106-9(X))* HarperCollins Pubs.
—Same Way Ben. Cocca-Leffler, Maryann. 2019. (ENG.). 32p. (J). (gr. -1-3). 16.99 *(978-0-8075-7222-1(5)*, 807572225) Whitman, Albert & Co.
—Spotlight on Stacey: Colonial History. Cocca-Leffler, Maryann. 2007. (Social Studies Connects ® Ser.). (ENG.). 32p. (J). (gr. 1-3). pap. 5.95 *(978-1-57565-236-8(6))* Astra Publishing Hse.
—Theo's Mood: A Book of Feelings. Cocca-Leffler, Maryann. 2013. (ENG.). 24p. (J). (gr. -1-3). 15.99 *(978-0-8075-7778-3(2)*, 807577782) Whitman, Albert & Co.
Cocciolone, Kathy Roberts. You Can't Get into More Trouble Than Gator Pervis!! Hammock, Sarah Owens. 2007. 32p. (J). 12.95 *(978-1-934246-27-6(1))* Peppertree Pr., The.
Cochard, David. The Legend of Honey Hollow. 2008. 46p. (J). 16.99 *(978-0-9799444-0-6(6))* Joey Publishing.
—Miracle in Sumatra: The Story of Gutsy Gus. McNaney, Jeanne. 2009. (ENG.). 32p. (J). (gr. -1-3). 16.95 *(978-0-9814534-6-0(5))* Ovation Bks.
Cochran, Christina. The Mini Message Man & the Great Candy Caper. Cochran, Cheryl. 2011. 40p. pap. 24.95 *(978-1-4560-7565-1(9))* America Star Bks.
Cochran, Josh. The Real Monsters. Bardhan-Quallen, Sudipta. 2008. (Mysteries Unwrapped Ser.). (ENG.). 88p. (J). (gr. 5-8). 18.69 *(978-1-4027-3776-3(9))* Sterling Publishing Co., Inc.
Cochran, Josh. Inside & Out: New York. Cochran, Josh. 2014. (ENG.). 16p. (J). (gr. 2-5). 17.99 *(978-0-7636-7520-2(2)*, Big Picture Press) Candlewick Pr.
Cochran, Shaun. Hole in the Wall. Hansen, Tevin. 2017. 300p. (J). 14.99 *(978-1-941429-54-9(8))* Handersen Publishing.
—Hole in the Wall: (humorous Action & Adventure - Ages 8+) Hansen, Tevin. l.t. ed. 2014. (ENG.). 300p. (J). (gr. 2-7). pap. 11.99 *(978-1-941429-00-6(9))* Handersen Publishing.
Cockburn, Gerrie L. Why Turtles Have Shells. Cockburn, Gerrie L. Cockburn, Ian, ed. (Friendship Ser.). 31p. (Orig.). (J). (gr. k-4). pap. 5.95 *(978-1-887461-00-9(0))* Cockburn Publishing.
Cockcroft, Jason. Amazing Animal Homes. Packham, Chris. 2018. (ENG.). 32p. (J). (gr. -1). 14.95 *(978-1-4549-3007-5(1))* Sterling Publishing Co., Inc.
—Bad Mermaids Make Waves. Pounder, Sibéal. 2018. (Bad Mermaids Ser.). (ENG.). 256p. (J). 13.99 *(978-1-68119-792-0(8)*, 900187211, Bloomsbury Children's Bks.) Bloomsbury Publishing USA.
—Jason & the Golden Fleece. Riordan, James. 2004. 64p. (YA). *(978-1-84507-271-1(5))* ReiseArt Buchhandlung GmbH.
—The Oxford Book of Bible Stories. Doherty, Berlie. 2014. (ENG.). 272p. pap. 18.95 *(978-0-19-278210-6(X))* Oxford Univ. Pr., Inc.
—Pilgrim's Progress. McCaughrean, Geraldine. (ENG.). 112p. (J). pap. 16.99 *(978-0-340-72754-6(3))* Hodder & Stoughton GBR. Dist: Trafalgar Square Publishing.
—Room for a Little One: A Christmas Tale. Waddell, Martin. 2008. (ENG.). 26p. (J). (gr. -1-2). bds. 7.99 *(978-1-4169-6177-2(1)*, Little Simon) Little Simon.
—Room for a Little One: A Christmas Tale. Waddell, Martin. (ENG.). 32p. (J). (gr. -1-3). 2006. 11.99 *(978-1-4169-2518-7(X))*; 2004. 19.99 *(978-0-689-86841-2(3))* McElderry, Margaret K. Bks. (McElderry, Margaret K. Bks.).
—Saint Paul, 1 vol. Self, David. 2009. 48p. (J). (gr. 2-7). 14.95 *(978-0-8254-7906-9(1)*, Lion Children's) Lion Hudson PLC GBR. Dist: Kregel Pubns.
COCKCROFT, JASON. The Spirit of Christmas. Benson, Nicky. 2014. (ENG.). 32p. (J). (gr. -1-2). 16.99 *(978-1-58925-188-5(1))* Tiger Tales.
Cockcroft, Jason. The Spirit of Christmas: A Giving Tradition. Benson, Nicky. 2014. (ENG.). 32p. (J). (gr. -1-3). 24.99 *(978-1-58925-530-2(5))* Tiger Tales.
COCKCROFT, JASON. How to Take Care of Your Dinosaur. COCKCROFT, JASON. 2019. (ENG.). 32p. (J). (-k). 15.99 *(978-1-5362-0568-8(0)*, Nosy Crow) Candlewick Pr.
Cockcroft, Jason. Jason & the Golden Fleece. Cockcroft, Jason, tr. Riordan, James. 2003. (ENG.). 64p. (J). *(978-0-7112-2081-2(6))* ReiseArt Buchhandlung GmbH.
Cockeram, Tom. Stegalegs & the Stormflower: A Jilly Jonah Book. Angel, Katharine Ann. 2019. (Jilly Jonah Ser.: Vol. 2). (ENG.). 106p. (J). (gr. 3-6). pap. ***(978-1-913071-25-7(1))*** 2QT, Ltd. (Publishing).
Cocklico, Marion. My First Fairy Tales: Goldilocks & the Three Bears. 2019. (My First Fairy Tales Ser.). (ENG.). 10p. (J). bds. 10.99 *(978-2-7338-6149-3(2))* Auzou, Philippe Editions FRA. Dist: Consortium Bk. Sales & Distribution.
—No More Diapers. 2018. (Big Steps Ser.). (ENG.). 12p. (J). (— 1). bds. 8.95 *(978-1-4549-2951-2(0))* Sterling Publishing Co., Inc.
Cockrille, Eva Vagreti. Bitty Fish: Short Vowel I. deRubertis, Barbara. 2006. (Let's Read Together ® Ser.). (ENG.). 32p. (J). (gr. -1-2). pap. 5.95 *(978-1-57565-002-9(9))* Astra Publishing Hse.
—Bouncy Mouse: Vowel Combinations Oi, Ou. deRubertis, Barbara. 2006. (Let's Read Together ® Ser.). (ENG.). 32p. (J). (gr. -1-3). pap. 5.95 *(978-1-57565-043-2(6))* Astra Publishing Hse.
—Foxy Fox: Short Vowel O. deRubertis, Barbara. 2006. (Let's Read Together ® Ser.). (ENG.). 32p. (J). (gr. -1-2). pap. 5.95 *(978-1-57565-003-6(7))* Astra Publishing Hse.
—Janey Crane: Long Vowel A. deRubertis, Barbara. 2006. (Let's Read Together ® Ser.). (ENG.). 32p. (J). (gr. -1-2). pap. 5.95 *(978-1-57565-022-7(3))* Astra Publishing Hse.
—Lucky Duck: Short Vowel U. deRubertis, Barbara. 2006. (Let's Read Together ® Ser.). (ENG.). 32p. (J). (gr. -1-2). pap. 5.95 *(978-1-57565-004-3(5))* Astra Publishing Hse.
—Marty Aardvark: Vowel Combination Ar. deRubertis, Barbara. 2006. (Let's Read Together ® Ser.). (ENG.). 32p. (J). (gr. -1-3). pap. 5.95 *(978-1-57565-042-5(8))* Astra Publishing Hse.
—Penny Hen: Short Vowel E. deRubertis, Barbara. 2006. (Let's Read Together ® Ser.). (ENG.). 32p. (J). (gr. -1-2). pap. 5.95 *(978-1-57565-001-2(0))* Astra Publishing Hse.
—Perky Otter: Vowel Combination Er. deRubertis, Barbara. 2006. (Let's Read Together ® Ser.). (ENG.). 32p. (J). (gr. -1-3). pap. 5.95 *(978-1-57565-045-6(2))* Astra Publishing Hse.
—Rooney 'Roo: Vowel Combination Oo. deRubertis, Barbara. 2006. (Let's Read Together ® Ser.). (ENG.). 32p. (J). (gr. -1-3). pap. 5.95 *(978-1-57565-044-9(4))* Astra Publishing Hse.
—Suzy Mule: Long Vowel U. deRubertis, Barbara. 2006. (Let's Read Together ® Ser.). (ENG.). 32p. (J). (gr. -1-2). pap. 5.95 *(978-1-57565-026-5(6))* Astra Publishing Hse.
—Tiny Tiger: Long Vowel I. deRubertis, Barbara. 2006. (Let's Read Together ® Ser.). (ENG.). 32p. (J). (gr. -1-2). pap. 5.95 *(978-1-57565-024-1(X))* Astra Publishing Hse.
—Wally Walrus: Vowel Combinations Al, Au, Aw. deRubertis, Barbara. 2006. (Let's Read Together ® Ser.). (ENG.). 32p. (J). (gr. -1-3). pap. 5.95 *(978-1-57565-046-3(0))* Astra Publishing Hse.
—Zeely Zebra: Long Vowel E. deRubertis, Barbara. 2006. (Let's Read Together ® Ser.). (ENG.). 32p. (J). (gr. -1-2). pap. 5.95 *(978-1-57565-023-4(1))* Astra Publishing Hse.
Cockrum, Dave, et al. The Uncanny X-Men Omnibus Vol. 1. 2020. 848p. (J). (gr. 4-17). 100.00 ***(978-1-302-92480-5(X))*** Marvel Worldwide, Inc.
Cockrum, Dave, et al. X-Men Classic Omnibus. 2017. 1040p. (J). (gr. 4-17). 125.00 *(978-1-302-90811-9(1))* Marvel Worldwide, Inc.
—X-Men: Starjammers by Dave Cockrum. 2019. (ENG.). 456p. (YA). (gr. 4-17). pap. 39.99 *(978-1-302-92046-3(4))* Marvel Worldwide, Inc.
Coco, Cha. Zaira y los Delfines. Pavon, Mar. 2012. (SPA.). 32p. (J). (gr. k-2). 14.95 *(978-84-15241-02-7(X))* Cuento de Luz SL ESP. Dist: Publishers Group West (PGW).
Cocoretto. Beach. 2019. (Making Tracks Ser.: 4). 12p. (J). bds. *(978-1-78628-295-8(X))* Child's Play International Ltd.
—City. Child's Play. 2017. (Wheels at Work (US Edition) Ser.: 4). (ENG.). 12p. (J). bds. *(978-1-78628-081-7(7))* Child's Play International Ltd.
—Construction. Child's Play. 2017. (Wheels at Work (US Edition) Ser.: 4). (ENG.). 12p. (J). bds. *(978-1-78628-083-1(3))* Child's Play International Ltd.
—Emergency. Child's Play. 2017. (Wheels at Work (US Edition) Ser.: 4). (ENG.). 12p. (J). bds. *(978-1-78628-080-0(9))* Child's Play International Ltd.
—Farm. 2019. (Making Tracks Ser.: 4). 12p. (J). bds. *(978-1-78628-296-5(8))* Child's Play International Ltd.
—Farm. Child's Play. 2017. (Wheels at Work (US Edition) Ser.: 4). (ENG.). 12p. (J). bds. *(978-1-78628-082-4(5))* Child's Play International Ltd.
—Getting Ready. Child's Play. 2016. (Tactile Bks.). 12p. (J). spiral bd. *(978-1-84643-886-8(1))* Child's Play International Ltd.
—Off to the Beach! Child's Play. 2016. (Tactile Bks.). 12p. (J). spiral bd. *(978-1-84643-923-0(X))* Child's Play International Ltd.
—Park. 2019. (Making Tracks Ser.: 4). 12p. (J). bds. *(978-1-78628-293-4(3))* Child's Play International Ltd.
—Peekaboo! in the Jungle! 2016. (Peekaboo! Ser.: 4). 12p. (J). spiral bd. *(978-1-84643-866-0(7))* Child's Play International Ltd.
—Peekaboo! in the Ocean! 2016. (Peekaboo! Ser.: 4). 12p. (J). spiral bd. *(978-1-84643-867-7(5))* Child's Play International Ltd.
—Peekaboo! in the Snow! 2016. (Peekaboo! Ser.: 4). 12p. (J). spiral bd. *(978-1-84643-865-3(9))* Child's Play International Ltd.
—Peekaboo! on the Farm! 2016. (Peekaboo! Ser.: 4). 12p. (J). spiral bd. *(978-1-84643-864-6(0))* Child's Play International Ltd.
—Snow. 2019. (Making Tracks Ser.: 4). 12p. (J). bds. *(978-1-78628-294-1(1))* Child's Play International Ltd.
—What's That Noise? CHOO! CHOO! Guess the Vehicle! Child's Play. 2015. (What's That Noise? Ser.: 4). 12p. (J). spiral bd. *(978-1-84643-746-5(6))* Child's Play International Ltd.
—What's That Noise? SNAP! SNAP! Guess the Animal! Child's Play. 2015. (What's That Noise? Ser.: 4). 12p. (J). spiral bd. *(978-1-84643-748-9(2))* Child's Play International Ltd.
—What's That Noise? TAP! TAP! Guess the Toy! Child's Play. 2015. (What's That Noise? Ser.: 4). 12p. (J). spiral bd. *(978-1-84643-747-2(4))* Child's Play International Ltd.
—What's That Noise? TOOT! TOOT! Guess the Instrument! Child's Play. 2015. (What's That Noise? Ser.: 4). 12p. (J). spiral bd. *(978-1-84643-749-6(0))* Child's Play International Ltd.
—What's up Crocodile? Sport. Child's Play. 2018. (What's Up? Ser.: 4). 12p. (J). spiral bd. *(978-1-78628-051-0(5))* Child's Play International Ltd.
—What's up Fox? Dressing Up. Child's Play. 2018. (What's Up? Ser.: 4). 12p. (J). bds. *(978-1-78628-156-2(2))* Child's Play International Ltd.
—What's up Penguin? Art. Child's Play. 2018. (What's Up? Ser.: 4). 12p. (J). bds. *(978-1-78628-154-8(6))* Child's Play International Ltd.
—What's up Tiger? Food. Child's Play. 2018. (What's Up? Ser.: 4). 12p. (J). bds. *(978-1-78628-157-9(0))* Child's Play International Ltd.
Coddington, D. There's a Monster in My House: A Book about Children's Human Rights. E-Collen, D. 2019. (ENG.). 20p. (J). *(978-1-5255-3767-7(9))* FriesenPress.
Codor, Richard. Too Many Latkes! Codor, Richard. 2011. (ENG.). 44p. (J). (gr. -1-3). pap. 9.95 *(978-0-87441-882-8(8))* Behrman Hse., Inc.
Coe, Anne. Here Is the Southwestern Desert. Dunphy, Madeleine. 2006. (Web of Life Ser.). (ENG.). 32p. (J). (gr. -1-3). 16.95 *(978-0-9773795-7-6(4))*; pap. 9.95 *(978-0-9773795-6-9(6))* Web of Life Children's Bks.
Coe, Kimberly. My Dad Is A Marine. Coe, Kimberly. 2007. 46p. (J). per. 12.00 *(978-0-9787113-1-3(9)*, Ithaca Pr.) Authors & Artists Publishers of New York, Inc.
Coelho, Jorge & Beaulieu, Jean-François. Disney Kingdoms: the Haunted Mansion #1. Williamson, Joshua. 2016. (Disney Kingdoms: the Haunted Mansion Ser.). (ENG.). 24p. (J). (gr. 1-5). lib. bdg. 27.07 *(978-1-61479-587-2(8)*, 24368, Graphic Novels) Spotlight.
—Disney Kingdoms: the Haunted Mansion #2. Williamson, Joshua. 2016. (Disney Kingdoms: the Haunted Mansion Ser.). (ENG.). 24p. (J). (gr. 1-5). lib. bdg. 27.07 *(978-1-61479-588-9(6)*, 24369, Graphic Novels) Spotlight.
—Disney Kingdoms: the Haunted Mansion #3. Williamson, Joshua. 2016. (Disney Kingdoms: the Haunted Mansion Ser.). (ENG.). 24p. (J). (gr. 1-5). lib. bdg. 27.07 *(978-1-61479-589-6(4)*, 24370, Graphic Novels) Spotlight.
—Disney Kingdoms: the Haunted Mansion #4. Williamson, Joshua. 2016. (Disney Kingdoms: the Haunted Mansion Ser.). (ENG.). 24p. (J). (gr. 1-5). lib. bdg. 27.07 *(978-1-61479-590-2(8)*, 24371, Graphic Novels) Spotlight.
—Disney Kingdoms: the Haunted Mansion #5. Williamson, Joshua. 2016. (Disney Kingdoms: the Haunted Mansion Ser.). (ENG.). 24p. (J). (gr. 1-5). lib. bdg. 27.07 *(978-1-61479-591-9(6)*, 24372, Graphic Novels) Spotlight.
—Disney Kingdoms: the Haunted Mansion (Set), 5 vols. Williamson, Joshua. 2016. (Disney Kingdoms: the Haunted Mansion Ser.). (ENG.). 24p. (J). (gr. 1-5). lib. bdg. 135.35 *(978-1-61479-586-5(X)*, 24367, Graphic Novels) Spotlight.
Coelho, Rogério. Books Do Not Have Wings. Barnes, Brynne. 2016. (ENG.). 32p. (J). (gr. k-3). 16.99 *(978-1-58536-964-5(0)*, 204112) Sleeping Bear Pr.
—One Earth. Spinelli, Eileen. 2020. 32p. (J). (gr. -1-3). 17.99 *(978-1-5460-1539-0(6)*, Worthy Kids/Ideals) Worthy Publishing.
—Roof Octopus. Branam, Lucy. 2018. (ENG.). 32p. (J). (gr. k-3). 16.99 *(978-1-58536-997-3(7)*, 204327) Sleeping Bear Pr.
Coelho, Sunaina. Tickle Me, Don't Tickle Me: And Other Poems for Magnificent, Turbo-Loaded, Triple-Charged Children. Pinto, Jerry. 2019. (ENG.). 98p. (J). pap. ***(978-93-89231-57-1(4))*** Speaking Tiger Publishing.
Coelho, Sunaina. When I Was a Boy: Scenes & Stories from My Childhood. Ruskin Bond. 2018. (ENG.). 202p. (J). (gr. 3-6). pap. *(978-93-88326-61-2(X))* Speaking Tiger Publishing.
Coello, Iban. Venom by Donny Cates Vol. 3: Absolute Carnage. 2020. (ENG.). 112p. (YA). (gr. 8-17). pap. 15.99 *(978-1-302-91997-9(0))* Marvel Worldwide, Inc.
Coello, Iban & Beyruth, Danilo. Venom: War of the Realms. 2019. (Venom by Donny Cates Ser.: 3). (ENG.). 128p. (YA). (gr. 8-17). pap. 15.99 *(978-1-302-91696-1(3))* Marvel Worldwide, Inc.
Coello, Iban & Stegman, Ryan. Venom by Donny Cates Vol. 1. 2019. (ENG.). 280p. (YA). (gr. 8-17). 34.99 *(978-1-302-91967-2(9))* Marvel Worldwide, Inc.
Coello, Iban, jt. illus. see Ottley, Ryan.
Coerr, Eleanor. Circus Day in Japan: Bilingual English & Japanese Text. Coerr, Eleanor. Matsunari, Yumi, tr. ed. 2016. (ENG.). 48p. (J). (gr. -1-3). 9.95 *(978-0-8048-4743-8(6))* Tuttle Publishing.
Coevoet, Sylvie. Rouge. Averous, Helene. 2013. 38p. pap. *(978-967-10358-2-5(5))* MHC Asia Group.
Coffey, Durwood. Running for Home. McDiarmid, Gail S. & McGee, Marilyn S. 2013. 76p. pap. 15.95 *(978-0-9854677-0-8(3))* SunDog Enterprises.
Coffey, Kevin. Bad Dog? Blom, Tracy. 2018. (ENG.). 24p. (J). pap. 9.99 *(978-0-9906871-6-0(3))* Blom Pubns.
—Bear-Ly There with Compass. French, Mary B. 2012. 122p. pap. 6.00 *(978-0-9852821-0-3(X))* Mary B./French.
—The Candy Roses of Cape Care. Canale, Suzie Hearl. 2012. 38p. (J). 14.95 *(978-1-937406-67-7(9))* Mascot Bks., Inc.
—A Loop of String: String Stories & String Stunts: Traditional & Original String Figures & Stories. Stotter, Ruth. 2009. 110p. (J). pap. 22.95 *(978-1-58790-170-6(6))* Regent Pr.
—New England a to Z. Baker, Alison. 2012. 38p. (J). 14.95 *(978-1-62086-065-6(1))* Mascot Bks., Inc.
—So Big yet So Small. Weiland, Peter. 2012. (J). 14.95 *(978-1-937406-16-5(4))* Mascot Bks., Inc.
Coffin, Douglas. One Maine Christmas Eve, 1 vol. Coffin, Douglas. 2015. (ENG.). 32p. (J). (gr. -1-12). 16.95 *(978-0-88448-469-1(6)*, 884469) Tilbury Hse. Pubs.
Coffin, Marilyn. The Ducks' New Friends. Stephenson, Nancy Ann. l.t. ed. 2006. 34p. (J). per. 9.99 *(978-1-59879-164-8(8))* Lifevest Publishing, Inc.
Cofrancesco, Fay. Where's Green? Heiss, Renee & Stewart, Gary a. 2013. (Enteletrons(r) Ser.: Vol. 1). (ENG.). 24p. (J). (gr. k-2). pap. 14.95 *(978-0-9887813-0-6(1))* Entelechy Education, LLC.
Cogan, John. Belle's Star. Gotsch, Connie. 2009. (Belle Ser.: 1). (ENG.). 136p. (J). (-1). pap. 8.99 *(978-1-932926-01-9(1))* Artemesia Publishing, LLC.
—Belle's Trial. Gotsch, Connie. 2010. (Belle Ser.: 2). (ENG.). 152p. (J). (gr. 5-1). pap. 8.99 *(978-1-932926-12-5(7)*, Kinkajou Pr.) Artemesia Publishing, LLC.
Cogan, Kim. Cooper's Lesson. Shin, Sun Yung. ed. 2015. (ENG & KOR.). 32p. (J). (gr. k-3). pap. 9.95 *(978-0-89239-361-9(0)*, Children's Book Press) Lee & Low Bks., Inc.
Cogan, Kim. Cooper's Lesson. Cogan, Kim, tr. Shin, Sun Yung. Paek, Min, tr. from ENG. 2004. (ENG & KOR.). 32p. (J). 16.95 *(978-0-89239-193-6(6))* Lee & Low Bks., Inc.
Cogancherry, Helen. Floating House. Sanders, Scott Russell. 2011. 40p. (J). lib. bdg. 18.00 *(978-1-59098-425-3(0))* Wooster Bk. Co., The.
—Warm as Wool. Sanders, Scott Russell. 2007. (J). lib. bdg. 18.00 *(978-1-59098-421-5(8))* Wooster Bk. Co., The.
Cogdill, Jill K. Cracker the Crab & the Sideways Afternoon. 2003. 40p. (J). lib. bdg. 19.95 *(978-0-9725560-0-2(1))* Cracker the Crab LLC.
Coglitore, Diego Horacio. Ciencias Monstruosas. Biskup, Agnieszka Józefina. 2019. (Ciencias Monstruosas Ser.). (SPA.). (J). (gr. 3-9). 156.60 *(978-1-5435-8290-1(7)*, 29729) Capstone.
—Vampiros y Células. Biskup, Agnieszka Józefina. 2019. (Ciencias Monstruosas Ser.). (SPA.). 32p. (J). (gr. 3-9). lib. bdg. 31.32 *(978-1-5435-8266-6(4)*, 141276) Capstone.
Cogswell, Matthew. Thor's Wedding Day: By Thialfi, the Goat Boy. Coville, Bruce. 2008. (ENG.). 144p. (J). (gr. 3-7). pap. 7.99 *(978-0-15-205872-2(9)*, 1197633) Houghton Mifflin Harcourt Publishing Co.
Coh, Smiljana. Cinderella. Castor, Harriet. 2016. (ENG.). 24p. (J). (gr. -1-k). 19.99 *(978-1-4052-7175-2(2))* Egmont Bks., Ltd. GBR. Dist: Independent Pubs. Group.
Coh, Smiljana. Heal the Earth. Lennon, Julian & Davis, Bart. (Julian Lennon White Feather Flier Advent Ser.: 2). (J). (gr. -1-1). 2020. (ENG.). 38p. bds. 9.99 *(978-1-5107-5188-0(2))*; 2018. 40p. 17.99 *(978-1-5107-2853-0(8))* Skyhorse Publishing Co., Inc. (Sky Pony Pr.).
—Heal the Earth (author Signed Copies) Lennon, Julian & Davis, Bart. 2018. (ENG.). 40p. (J). 17.99 *(978-1-5107-3994-9(7)*, Sky Pony Pr.) Skyhorse Publishing Co., Inc.
—Julian Lennon White Feather Flier 3-Book Box Set. Lennon, Julian & Davis, Bart. 2019. (Julian Lennon's Children's Adventures Ser.). (ENG.). 120p. (J). (gr. -1-1). 35.00 *(978-1-5107-4673-2(0)*, Sky Pony Pr.) Skyhorse Publishing Co., Inc.
—Touch the Earth. Lennon, Julian & Davis, Bart. (ENG.). 40p. (J). 2020. (Julian Lennon White Feather Flier Advent Ser.: 1). (gr. -1-1). bds. 9.99 *(978-1-5107-5187-3(4))*; 2017. 17.99 *(978-1-5107-3121-9(0))*; 2017. (Julian Lennon White Feather Flier Advent Ser.: 1). (gr. -1-k). 17.99 *(978-1-5107-2083-1(9))* Skyhorse Publishing Co., Inc. (Sky Pony Pr.).
Coh, Smiljana. I Have a Brother. Coh, Smiljana. 2012. (ENG.). 24p. (J). (gr. -1-2). 9.95 *(978-1-58925-124-3(5))* Tiger Tales.
—I Have a Sister. Coh, Smiljana. 2012. (ENG.). 24p. (J). (gr. -1-2). 9.95 *(978-1-58925-125-0(3))* Tiger Tales.
Cohee, Ron. Go, Go, Go! Lagonegro, Melissa. 2011. (Step into Reading Ser.). (ENG.). 32p. (J). (gr. k-3). pap. 4.99 *(978-0-7364-2765-4(1))*; lib. bdg. 12.99 *(978-0-7364-8091-8(9))* Random Hse. Children's Bks. (RH/Disney).
—I Am a Jedi (Star Wars) Golden Books. 2016. (Little Golden Book Ser.). (ENG.). 24p. (J). (-k). 4.99 *(978-0-7364-3487-4(9)*, Golden Bks.) Random Hse. Children's Bks.
—Return of the Jedi. 2015. (J). *(978-1-4806-9362-3(6)*, Golden Bks.) Random Hse. Children's Bks.
—Star Wars: Return of the Jedi (Star Wars) Smith, Geof. 2015. (Little Golden Book Ser.). (ENG.). 24p. (J). (-k). 4.99 *(978-0-7364-3548-2(4)*, Golden Bks.) Random Hse. Children's Bks.
—Tales of the Force (Star Wars) Golden Books. 2017. (Big Golden Book Ser.). (ENG.). 48p. (J). (gr. -1-2). 10.99 *(978-1-5247-7090-7(6)*, Golden Bks.) Random Hse. Children's Bks.
Cohee, Ron & Posner-Sanchez, Andrea. Peeps in Pajamas (Peeps) 2017. (Little Golden Book Ser.). 24p. (J). (-k). 4.99 *(978-1-5247-1907-4(2)*, Golden Bks.) Random Hse. Children's Bks.
Cohee, Ron, jt. illus. see Webber, John.
Cohen, A. R. Chadwick & Friends: A Lift-The-Flap Board Book, 1 vol. Cummings, Priscilla. 2018. (ENG.). 22p. (J). bds. 12.99 *(978-0-7643-5579-0(1)*, 16206) Schiffer Publishing, Ltd.
—The Chadwick Coloring Book, 1 vol. Cummings, Priscilla. 2009. (ENG.). 32p. (J). (gr. -1-3). pap. 3.95 *(978-0-87033-389-7(5)*, 3617, Cornell Maritime Pr./Tidewater Pubs.) Schiffer Publishing, Ltd.
—A Chadwick Treasury: The Four Classic Stories of an Adventurous Blue Crab & His Chesapeake Bay Friends, 1 vol. Cummings, Priscilla. 2019. (ENG.). 128p. 26.99 *(978-0-7643-5704-6(2)*, 16398) Schiffer Publishing, Ltd.
Cohen, Allen R. Chadwick & the Garplegrungen, 1 vol. Cummings, Priscilla. 2009. (ENG.). 30p. (J). (gr. -1-3). 8.95 *(978-0-87033-377-4(1)*, 9780870333774, Cornell Maritime Pr./Tidewater Pubs.) Schiffer Publishing, Ltd.
Cohen, Brie, photos by. Dandy Desserts. Cornell, Kari. 2013. (You're the Chef Ser.). (ENG., 32p. (gr. 3-5). lib. bdg. 26.60 *(978-0-7613-6644-7(X)*, Millbrook Pr.) Lerner Publishing Group.
—Delicious Vegetarian Main Dishes. Larson, Jennifer S. 2013. (You're the Chef Ser.). (ENG., 32p. (gr. 3-5). lib. bdg. 26.60 *(978-0-7613-6635-5(0)*, Millbrook Pr.) Lerner Publishing Group.
—Marvelous Muffins, Breads, & Pancakes. Cornell, Kari. 2013. (You're the Chef Ser.). (ENG., 32p. (gr. 3-5). lib. bdg. 26.60 *(978-0-7613-6636-2(9)*, Millbrook Pr.) Lerner Publishing Group.
—Perfect Pizza Recipes. Larson, Jennifer S. 2013. (You're the Chef Ser.). (ENG., 32p. (J). (gr. 3-5). lib. bdg. 26.60 *(978-0-7613-6637-9(7)*, Millbrook Pr.) Lerner Publishing Group.
—Super Pasta & Rice Dishes. Larson, Jennifer S. 2013. (You're the Chef Ser.). (ENG., 32p. (gr. 3-5). lib. bdg. 26.60 *(978-0-7613-6641-6(5)*, Millbrook Pr.) Lerner Publishing Group.
—Sweet Cookies & Bars. Cornell, Kari. 2013. (You're the Chef Ser.). (ENG., 32p. (J). (gr. 3-5). lib. bdg. 26.65 *(978-0-7613-6638-6(5)*, Millbrook Pr.) Lerner Publishing Group.
—Tasty Sandwiches. Larson, Jennifer S. 2013. (You're the Chef Ser.). (ENG., 32p. (J). (gr. 3-5). lib. bdg. 26.65 *(978-0-7613-6643-0(1)*, Millbrook Pr.) Lerner Publishing Group.
—Terrific Veggies on the Side. Cornell, Kari. 2013. (You're the Chef Ser.). (ENG., 32p. (gr. 3-5). lib. bdg. 26.60 *(978-0-7613-6640-9(7)*, Millbrook Pr.) Lerner Publishing Group.
—Yummy Soup & Salad Recipes. Larson, Jennifer S. 2013. (You're the Chef Ser.). (ENG., 32p. (gr. 3-5). lib. bdg.

26.60 (978-0-7613-6633-1(4), Millbrook Pr.) Lerner Publishing Group.

Cohen, Deene. Yesterday's Child. Benjamin, Ruth. (YA). 16.95 (978-1-56062-176-8(1), CFR122H); pap. 13.95 (978-1-56062-177-5(X), CFR122S) C I S Communications, Inc.

Cohen, Dov Ber. The Magnificent Nine. Zubarev, Misha. 2018. (ENG.). 40p. (J). 19.95 (978-0-9861106-2-7(0)) Ariella Publishing.

Cohen, Elly. Peg Bearskin. Dinn, Philip & Jones, Andy. 2003. (ENG.). 32p. (J). pap. (978-0-9688712-7-0(5)) Running the Goat, Bks. & Broadsides.

Cohen, Greg A. The Littlest Maccabee: An Original Story. Rouss, Sylvia A. 2006. (J). (978-1-932687-76-7(9), Pitspopany Pr.) Simcha Media Group.

Cohen, Izhar. The Wolf's Story: What Really Happened to Little Red Riding Hood. Forward, Toby. 2005. (ENG.). 32p. (J). (gr. -1-3). 17.99 (978-0-7636-2785-0(2)) Candlewick Pr.

Cohen, Jan Barger. Lighting a Lamp: A Diwali Story. Zucker, Jonny. 2004. (Festival Time Ser.). (ENG.). 24p. (J). (gr. -1-1). pap. 8.99 (978-0-7641-2670-3(9), B.E.S. Publishing) Peterson's.

Cohen, Jesse, photos by. Elephant & Mommy. Galvin, Laura. 2003. (Let's Go to the Zoo Ser.). (ENG., 16p. (J). (gr. -1-k). 5.95 (978-1-56899-911-1(9), B9007) Soundprints.

Cohen, Jessie. Tamarin's Mealtime. Galvin, Laura Gates. 2005. (Let's Go to the Zoo! Ser.). (ENG.). 16p. (J). (gr. -1-k). 5.95 (978-1-56899-858-9(9)) Soundprints.

—Tiger Cub See-and-Do. Galvin, Laura Gates. 2005. (Let's Go to the Zoo! Ser.). (ENG.). 16p. (J). (gr. -1-k). 5.95 (978-1-56899-856-5(2), B9006) Soundprints.

Cohen, Jessie, photos by. Flamingo Grows Up. 2005. (Let's Go to the Zoo! Ser.). (ENG., 16p. (J). (gr. -1-k). 5.95 (978-1-56899-974-6(7), B9009) Soundprints.

—New Baby Giraffe. Galvin, Laura. 2003. (Let's Go to the Zoo! Ser.). (ENG., 16p. (J). (gr. -1-k). 5.95 (978-1-56899-798-8(1), B9003) Soundprints.

—Sea Lion Swims. Lamm, Drew. 2005. (Let's Go to the Zoo! Ser.). (ENG., 16p. (J). (gr. -1-k). 5.95 (978-1-56899-976-0(3), B9010) Soundprints.

Cohen, Lynda. Beach Feet. Jackson, Marjorie. 2005. (ENG.). 8p. (J). pap. 5.75 (978-1-57274-750-0(1), 2123, Bks. for Young Learners) Owen, Richard C. Pubs., Inc.

Cohen, Miriam. Two Little Mittens, 1 vol. Cohen, Miriam. 2006. (ENG.). 32p. (J). (gr. -1). pap. 6.95 (978-1-59572-044-3(8)) Star Bright Bks., Inc.

Cohen, Santiago. Good Night San Francisco. Gamble, Adam. 2006. (Good Night Our World Ser.). (ENG.). 22p. (J). (gr. k — 1). bds. 9.95 (978-0-9777979-5-0(3)) Good Night Bks.

—The Yiddish Fish. 2014. (ENG.). 32p. (J). (gr. -1-k). 16.95 (978-1-62914-633-1(1), Sky Pony Pr.) Skyhorse Publishing Co., Inc.

Cohen, Sheldon. The Flying Canoe. Fischman, Sheila, tr. from FRE. 2004. (ENG.). 24p. (J). (gr. 3-7). 15.95 (978-0-88776-636-7(6), Tundra Bks.) Tundra Bks. CAN. Dist: Penguin Random Hse. LLC.

Cohen, Sheldon. The Hockey Sweater. Carrier, Roch. Fischman, Sheila, tr. from FRE. 2020. Orig. Title: Le Chandail de Hockey. (ENG.). 24p. (J). (— 1). bds. 8.99 (978-0-7352-6868-5(1), Tundra Bks.) Tundra Bks. CAN. Dist: Penguin Random Hse. LLC.

Cohen, Sheldon. Kishka for Koppel, 1 vol. Davis, Aubrey. 2011. (ENG.). 32p. (J). (gr. -1-k). 19.95 (978-1-55469-299-6(7)) Orca Bk. Pubs. USA.

Cohen, Tod. It's Seder Time!, Vol. Cohen, Tod, photos by. Kropf, Latifa Berry. 2004. (ENG.). 24p. (J). (gr. -1-1). 12.95 (978-1-58013-092-9(5), Kar-Ben Publishing) Lerner Publishing Group.

—It's Sukkah Time, Vol. Cohen, Tod, photos by. Kropf, Latifa Berry. 2003. (Sukkot & Simchat Torah Ser.). (ENG.). 24p. (J). (gr. -1-1). 12.95 (978-1-58013-084-4(4), Kar-Ben Publishing) Lerner Publishing Group.

Cohen, Tod, photos by. It's Hanukkah Time!, Vol. Kropf, Latifa Berry. (ENG., 24p. (J). (gr. -1-1). 2011. pap. 8.95 (978-0-7613-8306-2(9)); 2004. 12.95 (978-1-58013-120-9(4)) Lerner Publishing Group. (Kar-Ben Publishing).

—It's Israel's Birthday!, Vol. Dietrick, Ellen. 2008. (ENG., 24p. (J). (gr. -1-1). pap. 12.95 (978-0-8225-7668-6(6), Kar-Ben Publishing) Lerner Publishing Group.

—It's Purim Time!, Vol. Kropf, Latifa Berry. (ENG., 24p. (J). 2012. (gr. -1-1). pap. 8.95 (978-0-7613-8493-9(6)); 2005. (gr. 2-6). lib. bdg. 12.95 (978-1-58013-153-7(0)) Lerner Publishing Group. (Kar-Ben Publishing).

—It's Shofar Time!, Vol. Kropf, Latifa Berry. 2006. (ENG., 24p. (J). (gr. -1-1). lib. bdg. 12.95 (978-1-58013-158-2(1), Kar-Ben Publishing) Lerner Publishing Group.

—It's Sukkah Time!, Vol. Kropf, Latifa Berry. 2012. (ENG., 24p. (J). (gr. -1-1). 9.95 (978-1-4677-0741-1(4), Kar-Ben Publishing) Lerner Publishing Group.

—It's Time Set. Kropf, Latifa Berry. 24p. (J). (gr. -1-1). 58.28 (978-1-58013-192-6(1), Kar-Ben Publishing) Lerner Publishing Group.

—It's Tot Shabbat! Danis, Naomi. 2011. (ENG., 24p. (J). (gr. -1-1). lib. bdg. 14.95 (978-0-7613-4515-2(9), 9780761345152, Kar-Ben Publishing) Lerner Publishing Group.

—Ten Good Rules: A Counting Book. Topek, Susan Remick. 2007. (ENG., 24p. (J). (gr. -1-1). lib. bdg. 15.95 (978-0-8225-7293-0(1), Kar-Ben Publishing) Lerner Publishing Group.

Cohn, Riley. Martin in the Narthex. 2011. (ENG.). 40p. (J). 14.95 (978-0-940672-82-6(0)) Shearer Publishing.

Cohn, Scott. I Am Bane. Rosen, Lucy. 2012. (Dark Knight Rises Ser.). (ENG.). 24p. (J). (gr. -1-2). pap. 3.99 (978-0-06-213222-2(9), HarperFestival) HarperCollins Pubs.

Coillen, Lisa P. Time for Bed. Jarrell, Pamela R. l.t. ed. 2005. (HRL Board Book Ser.). (J). (gr. -1-k). pap. 10.95 (978-1-57332-325-3(X), HighReach Learning, Incorporated) Carson-Dellosa Publishing, LLC.

Cointe, François & Cointe, François. The Book of When. Jaffé, Laura & Jaffé, Laura. 2008. (ENG.). 96p. (J). (gr. 3-7). 17.95 (978-0-8109-7240-7(9), Abrams Bks. for Young Readers) Abrams, Inc.

Cointe, François, jt. illus. see Cointe, François.

Coipel, Olivier. House of M. 2006. 224p. (YA). (gr. 8-17). pap. 24.99 (978-0-7851-1721-6(0)) Marvel Worldwide, Inc.

Coirault, Christine. How Do I Say That? (¿Cómo se Dice?) Wise, Sue. 2006. (How Do I Say That?/ Cómo se dice? Ser.). (ENG & SPA.). 32p. (gr. k-4). pap. 10.50 (978-0-8368-6583-7(9), Gareth Stevens Learning Library) Stevens, Gareth Publishing LLLP.

—My First Book of Learning. 2009. (J). (978-1-74089-930-7(X)) Fog City Pr.

Cojocaru, Diane. Catalina & the King's Wall. Costello, Patricia. 2018. (ENG.). 34p. (J). (gr. k-5). pap. 9.99 (978-1-63233-101-4(2)) Elfrig Publishing.

Coke, Sherrie. Tommy's New Shell, 2nd in series. Evangelista, Susan. 2005. 24p. (J). bds. 19.95 (978-0-9769602-0-1(6)) Evangelista, Susan.

Coker, Carla. God's World & Me from A to Z. Langley, Judy. 2004. 32p. (gr. -1). 8.99 (978-1-56309-367-8(7), New Hope Pubs.) Iron Stream Media.

Coker, Paul, Jr. Henrietta: The Homely Duckling. Hahn, Phil. 2004. (Weewisdom Bks.). 47p. (J). 16.95 (978-0-87159-293-4(2), 168, Unity Hse.) Unity Schl. of Christianity.

Coker, Tomm, et al. Tales Through the Marvel Universe. 2020. (ENG.). 136p. (YA). (gr. 8-17). pap. 24.99 (978-1-302-91746-3(3)) Marvel Worldwide, Inc.

Colabucci, Rin. You Sparkle Inside. Kann, Rachel. 2018. (ENG.). 44p. (J). pap. 19.99 (978-1-885021-11-3(9)) Orange Ocean Pr.

Colan, Gene, et al. Captain Marvel: the Many Lives of Carol Danvers. 2020. (ENG.). 288p. (YA). (gr. 8-17). pap. 29.99 **(978-1-302-92506-2(7))** Marvel Worldwide, Inc.

Colan, Gene, et al. Daredevil Epic Collection: a Woman Called Widow. 2019. (ENG.). 512p. (YA). (gr. 4-17). pap. 39.99 (978-1-302-92034-0(0)) Marvel Worldwide, Inc.

—Guardians of the Galaxy: Tomorrow's Heroes Omnibus. 2019. (Guardians of the Galaxy: Tomorrow's Heroes Omnibus Ser.: 1). (ENG.). 752p. (J). (gr. 4-17). 100.00 (978-1-302-91554-4(1)) Marvel Worldwide, Inc.

Colan, Gene & Romita, John. Captain America Epic Collection: Bucky Reborn. 2017. 400p. (J). (gr. 4-17). pap. 39.99 (978-1-302-90419-7(1)) Marvel Worldwide, Inc.

Colangelo, Dina. Rocky: The Rockefeller Christmas Tree. Nicassio, Jennie E. 2016. (ENG.). (J). (gr. k-3). pap. 13.97 (978-0-692-77187-7(5)) NIEJE Production LLC.

Colangione-B, Christie. The Biggest Splash. Badavino, Jimmy. 2019. (ENG.). 34p. (J). pap. 12.50 **(978-1-7005-5816-9(1))** Independently Published.

Colavecchio, Alan. Seymour & the Big Red Rhino. Powers, John. 2005. 32p. (J). (gr. -1-3). 14.95 (978-1-929039-21-0(2)) Ambassador Bks., Inc.

Colbath, Shirl. Ruby & Nolan's Great Adventures in Space: The Merpeople. Colbath, Brenda. 2019. (Book: 6 Ser.: Vol. 6). (ENG.). 90p. (J). pap. 5.99 **(978-1-6990-4765-1(0))** Independently Published.

—Sleep Travelers Book: 2: the Amusement Park. Colbath, Brenda. 2019. (Amusement Park Ser.: Vol. 2). (ENG.). 68p. (J). pap. 5.99 **(978-1-6981-6687-2(7))** Independently Published.

Colbert, la Vivian. Asha's Journey to Her Incredible Self: Love, Faith, Hope & Dreams. Hutsell, Jacqueline S. 2020. (ENG.). 23p. (J). pap. 14.95 **(978-1-9772-2667-9(1))** Outskirts Pr., Inc.

Colbert, Megan Benham. The Enchanted Paradise of Sugar Creek. Paneck, Becky. 2016. (Sugar Creek Ser.: Vol. 1). (ENG.). (J). (gr. k-4). pap. 12.00 (978-1-942168-62-1(4), Compass Flower Pr.) AKA:yoLa.

Colby, Devon English, jt. illus. see Nielsen, Gwyn English.

Colby, Garry. Bizarre Bible Stories: Flying Pigs, Walking Bones, & 24 Other Things That Really Happened. Cooley, Dan. 2011. 160p. (gr. k). pap. 14.99 (978-0-8010-4520-2(7)) Heritage Builders, LLC.

—Jack B. Nimble Jumps. Fuerst, Jeffrey B. 2009. (Reader's Theater Nursery Rhymes & Songs Set B Ser.). 48p. (J). pap. (978-1-60859-154-1(9)) Benchmark Education Co.

—Jack Be Nimble. Fuerst, Jeffrey B. 2010. (Rising Readers Ser.). (J). 3.49 (978-1-60719-698-3(0)) Newmark Learning LLC.

—Picture That! Bible Storybook over 65 Stories, 1 vol. Harrast, Tracy. 2011. (ENG.). 160p. (J). (gr. -1-2). pap. 9.99 (978-0-310-72590-9(9)) Zonderkidz.

Colby, J. Z., et al. Trilogy One. Colby, J. Z. ed. 2010. (Nebador Ser.: Books One, Two, and Three). (ENG.). 641p. (YA). pupil's gde. ed. 49.95 (978-1-936253-17-3(8)) Nebador Archives.

Colby, J. Z. & Powers, Mireille Xioulan. Flight Training, Kibi & the Search for Happiness. Colby, J. Z. & Persons, Katelynn. 2011. (Nebador Ser.: Book Four). 178p. (YA). pap. 10.95 (978-1-936253-27-2(5)) Nebador Archives.

Cole, Al. Room for One More. Harris, Jane Ellen. 2007. 24p. (J). (gr. -1-3). pap. 11.98 (978-0-9800733-0-0(8), LSP) LSP Digital, LLC.

Cole, Allison. Emily Sparkes & the Competition Calamity: Book 2. Fitzgerald, Ruth. 2017. (Emily Sparkes Ser.). 288p. (J). (gr. 4-6). pap. 8.99 (978-0-349-00184-5(7)) Little, Brown Bks. for Young Readers.

Cole, Amy & Roberts, Joshua. Bobby the Blue-Footed Booby Gets Bullied. Bowles, Sharon. 2016. (ENG.). (J). (gr. k-3). 17.99 (978-0-692-67659-2(7)) Bowles, Sharon.

Cole, Amy, jt. illus. see Hayes, Steve.

Cole, Babette. How to Put Your Parents to Bed. Larsen, Mylisa. 2016. (ENG.). 32p. (J). (gr. -1-3). 17.99 (978-0-06-232064-3(5)) HarperCollins Pubs.

Cole, Babette. Princess Smartypants. Cole, Babette. 2005. (ENG.). 32p. (J). (gr. -1-3). 17.99 (978-0-399-24398-1(4), G.P. Putnam's Sons Books for Young Readers) Penguin Young Readers Group.

Cole, Brock. George Washington's Teeth. Chandra, Deborah & Comora, Madeleine. 2007. (ENG.). 40p. (J). (gr. -1-3). pap. 8.99 (978-0-312-37604-8(9), 900048324) Square Fish.

Cole, Brock. The Goats. Cole, Brock. 2010. (ENG.). 192p. (YA). (gr. 7-10). pap. 9.99 (978-0-312-61191-0(9), 900065536) Square Fish.

Cole, Dick. The Falling Flowers. Reed, Jennifer. 2005. (Falling Flowers Ser.). 32p. (J). (gr. -1-3). 16.95 (978-1-885008-28-2(7), Shen's Bks.) Lee & Low Bks., Inc.

Cole, Gina. Adapt. 2005. 40p. (J). 17.00 (978-0-9659538-3-2(1)) Soul Vision Works Publishing.

Cole, Henry. Adventures of Katy Duck. Capucilli, Alyssa Satin. 2016. (J). (978-1-4814-8110-6(X), Simon Spotlight) Simon Spotlight.

—And Tango Makes Three. Richardson, Justin & Parnell, Peter. 2005. (ENG.). 32p. (J). (gr. -1-3). 17.99 (978-0-689-87845-9(1), Simon & Schuster Bks. For Young Readers) Simon & Schuster Bks. For Young Readers.

—Bad Boys. Palatini, Margie. 40p. (J). (gr. -1-2). 2003. lib. bdg. 16.89 (978-0-06-000103-2(8)); 2003. (ENG.). 15.99 (978-0-06-000102-5(X), Tegen, Katherine Bks); 2006. (ENG.). reprint ed. 7.99 (978-0-06-000104-9(6), Tegen, Katherine Bks) HarperCollins Pubs.

—Bad Boys Get Cookie! Palatini, Margie. 2006. 32p. (J). (gr. -1-3). 18.89 (978-0-06-074437-3(5)); (ENG.). 17.99 (978-0-06-074436-6(7), Tegen, Katherine Bks) HarperCollins Pubs.

—Bad Boys Get Henpecked! Palatini, Margie. 2009. (ENG.). 32p. (J). (gr. -1-2). 17.99 (978-0-06-074433-5(2), Tegen, Katherine Bks) HarperCollins Pubs.

—Big Chickens. Helakoski, Leslie. 2008. (ENG.). 32p. (J). (gr. -1-k). pap. 7.99 (978-0-14-241057-8(8), Puffin Books) Penguin Young Readers Group.

—Big Chickens. Helakoski, Leslie. 2008. (J). (gr. -1-3). lib. bdg. 14.65 (978-0-7569-8913-2(2)) Perfection Learning Corp.

—Big Chickens Fly the Coop. Helakoski, Leslie. 2010. 32p. (J). (gr. -1-k). pap. 7.99 (978-0-14-241464-4(6), Puffin Books) Penguin Young Readers Group.

—Chaucer's First Winter. Krensky, Stephen. (ENG.). 32p. (J). (gr. -1-1). 2010. 9.99 (978-1-4424-1658-1(0)); 2009. 17.99 (978-1-4169-9026-0(7)) Simon & Schuster Bks. For Young Readers. (Simon & Schuster Bks. For Young Readers).

—Chicken Butt. Perl, Erica S. 2009. (ENG.). 32p. (J). (gr. -1-1). 13.95 (978-0-8109-8325-0(7), Abrams Bks. for Young Readers) Abrams, Inc.

—Chicken Butt's Back! Perl, Erica S. 2011. (ENG.). 32p. (J). (gr. -1-17). 13.95 (978-0-8109-9729-5(0), Abrams Bks. for Young Readers) Abrams, Inc.

—City Chicken. Dorros, Arthur. 2003. 40p. (J). (gr. -1-3). 16.89 (978-0-06-028483-1(8)) HarperCollins Pubs.

—Clara Caterpillar. Edwards, Pamela Duncan. 2004. (ENG.). 40p. (J). (gr. -1-1). reprint ed. pap. 7.99 (978-0-06-443691-5(8)) HarperCollins Pubs.

—Emmett & the Bright Blue Cape. Capucilli, Alyssa Satin. 2017. (Ready-To-Reads Ser.). (ENG.). 24p. (J). (gr. -1-1). 16.99 (978-1-4814-5873-3(6)); pap. 4.99 (978-1-4814-5869-6(8)) Simon Spotlight. (Simon Spotlight).

—Ferocious Fluffity: A Mighty Bite-Y Class Pet. Perl, Erica S. 2016. (ENG.). 32p. (J). (gr. k-2). 16.95 (978-1-4197-2182-3(8), Abrams Bks. for Young Readers) Abrams, Inc.

—La Gallinita de la Pradera, 1 vol. Hopkins, Jackie Mims. 2015. (SPA.). 32p. (J). (gr. 1-3). 17.95 (978-1-56145-841-7(4)) Peachtree Publishing Co. Inc.

—Honk! Duncan Edwards, Pamela. 2014. 32p. pap. 8.00 (978-1-61003-226-1(8)) Center for the Collaborative Classroom.

—Katy Duck. Capucilli, Alyssa Satin. 2007. (Katy Duck Ser.). (ENG.). 16p. (J). (gr. -1-k). bds. 7.99 (978-1-4169-1901-8(5), Little Simon) Little Simon.

—Katy Duck & the Tip-Top Tap Shoes. Capucilli, Alyssa Satin. 2013. (Ready-To-Read Level 1 Ser.). (ENG.). 24p. (J). (gr. -1-1). 17.44 (978-1-4424-5246-6(3), Simon Spotlight) Simon & Schuster Children's Publishing.

—Katy Duck & the Tip-Top Tap Shoes. Capucilli, Alyssa Satin. 2013. (Katy Duck Ser.). (ENG.). 24p. (J). (gr. -1-1). pap. 3.99 (978-1-4424-5245-9(5), Simon Spotlight) Simon Spotlight.

—Katy Duck, Big Sister. Capucilli, Alyssa Satin. 2007. (ENG.). 14p. (J). (gr. -1-k). bds. 7.99 (978-1-4169-4209-2(2), Little Simon) Little Simon.

—Katy Duck, Center Stage. Capucilli, Alyssa Satin. 2008. (Katy Duck Ser.). (ENG.). 16p. (J). (gr. -1-k). bds. 7.99 (978-1-4169-3338-0(7), Little Simon) Little Simon.

—Katy Duck, Dance Star. Capucilli, Alyssa Satin. 2008. (Katy Duck Ser.). (ENG.). 16p. (J). (gr. -1-k). bds. 7.99 (978-1-4169-3337-3(9), Little Simon) Little Simon.

—Katy Duck, Dance Star / Katy Duck, Center Stage. Capucilli, Alyssa Satin. 2009. (Katy Duck Ser.). (ENG.). 24p. (J). (gr. -1-k). pap. 3.99 (978-1-4169-8279-1(5), Little Simon) Little Simon.

—Katy Duck, Flower Girl. Capucilli, Alyssa Satin. 2013. (Katy Duck Ser.). (ENG.). 24p. (J). (gr. -1-1). 16.99 (978-1-4424-7279-2(0)); pap. 3.99 (978-1-4424-7278-5(2)) Simon Spotlight. (Simon Spotlight).

—Katy Duck Goes to Work. Capucilli, Alyssa Satin. 2014. (Katy Duck Ser.). (ENG.). 24p. (J). (gr. -1-1). pap. 3.99 (978-1-4424-7281-5(2), Simon Spotlight) Simon Spotlight.

—Katy Duck Makes a Friend. Capucilli, Alyssa Satin. 2012. (Katy Duck Ser.). (ENG.). 24p. (J). (gr. -1-1). 16.99 (978-1-4424-1977-3(6)); pap. 4.99 (978-1-4424-1976-6(8)) Simon Spotlight. (Simon Spotlight).

—Katy Duck Meets the Babysitter. Capucilli, Alyssa Satin. 2012. (Katy Duck Ser.). (ENG.). 24p. (J). (gr. -1-1). 15.99 (978-1-4424-5242-8(0)); pap. 3.99 (978-1-4424-5241-1(2)) Simon Spotlight. (Simon Spotlight).

—Katy Duck Ready-To-Read Value Pack: Starring Katy Duck; Katy Duck Makes a Friend; Katy Duck Meets the Babysitter; Katy Duck & the Tip-Tip Tap Shoes; Katy Duck, Flower Girl; Katy Duck Goes to Work. Capucilli, Alyssa Satin. 2014. (Katy Duck Ser.). (ENG.). 144p. (J). (gr. -1-1). pap. 15.96 (978-1-4814-2600-8(1), Simon Spotlight) Simon Spotlight.

—Katy Duck's Happy Halloween. Capucilli, Alyssa Satin. 2014. (Katy Duck Ser.). (ENG.). 24p. (J). (gr. -1-1). pap. 3.99 (978-1-4424-9806-8(4), Simon Spotlight) Simon Spotlight.

—The Leprechaun's Gold. Edwards, Pamela Duncan. 2006. (ENG.). 40p. (J). (gr. -1-2). reprint ed. 7.99 (978-0-06-443878-0(3), Tegen, Katherine Bks) HarperCollins Pubs.

—Little Bo in Italy: The Continued Adventures of Bonnie Boadicea. Edwards, Julie Andrews. 2010. (ENG.). 112p. (J). (gr. 1-4). 19.99 (978-0-06-008908-5(3)) HarperCollins Pubs.

—Maxi the Little Taxi. Upton, Elizabeth. 2016. (ENG.). 32p. (J). (gr. -1-k). 17.99 (978-0-545-79860-0(4), Scholastic Pr.) Scholastic, Inc.

—Mouse Was Mad. Urban, Linda. (ENG.). 40p. (J). (gr. -1-3). 2012. pap. 7.99 (978-0-547-72750-9(X), 1483175, HMH Books For Young Readers); 2009. 17.99 (978-0-15-205337-6(9), 1098982) Houghton Mifflin Harcourt Publishing Co.

—Naughty Little Monkeys. Aylesworth, Jim. 2006. (ENG.). 32p. (J). (gr. -1-2). reprint ed. 6.99 (978-0-14-240562-8(0), Puffin Books) Penguin Young Readers Group.

—Nelly May Has Her Say. DeFelice, Cynthia C. 2013. (ENG.). 32p. (J). (gr. -1-3). 16.99 (978-0-374-39899-6(2), 900060600, Farrar, Straus & Giroux (BYR)) Farrar, Straus & Giroux.

—Oink? Palatini, Margie. 2006. (ENG.). 40p. (J). (gr. -1-3). 19.99 (978-0-689-86258-8(X), Simon & Schuster Bks. For Young Readers) Simon & Schuster Bks. For Young Readers.

—The Old House. Edwards, Pamela Duncan. 2007. (ENG.). 32p. (J). (gr. k-2). 21.19 (978-0-525-47796-9(9)) Penguin Young Readers Group.

—One Pup's Up. Chall, Marsha Wilson. 2010. (ENG.). 32p. (J). (gr. -1 — 1). 16.99 (978-1-4169-7960-9(3), McElderry, Margaret K. Bks.) McElderry, Margaret K. Bks.

—Prairie Chicken Little, 1 vol. Hopkins, Jackie Mims. (ENG.). 32p. (J). 2015. (gr. 1-3). pap. 7.95 (978-1-56145-834-9(1)); 2013. (gr. -1-3). 15.95 (978-1-56145-694-9(2)) Peachtree Publishing Co. Inc.

—Ralph & the Rocket Ship. Capucilli, Alyssa Satin. 2016. (Ready-To-Reads Ser.). (ENG.). 24p. (J). (gr. -1-1). pap. 3.99 (978-1-4814-5866-5(3), Simon Spotlight) Simon Spotlight.

—Roar! A Noisy Counting Book. Edwards, Pamela Duncan. Date not set. 32p. (J). (gr. -1-2). pap. 5.99 (978-0-06-443572-7(5)) HarperCollins Pubs.

—Santa's Stuck. Greene, Rhonda Gowler. 2006. (ENG.). 32p. (J). (gr. -1-3). pap. 6.99 (978-0-14-240686-1(4), Puffin Books) Penguin Young Readers Group.

—Shiver Me Letters: A Pirate ABC. Sobel, June. (ENG.). 32p. (J). (gr. -1-3). 2009. pap. 7.99 (978-0-15-206679-6(9), 1199768); 2006. 17.99 (978-0-15-216732-5(3), 1201748) Houghton Mifflin Harcourt Publishing Co.

—The Sissy Duckling. Fierstein, Harvey. 2014. (ENG.). 40p. (J). (gr. -1-3). pap. 9.99 (978-1-4424-9817-4(X), Little Simon) Little Simon.

—The Sissy Duckling. Fierstein, Harvey. 2005. (ENG.). 40p. (J). (gr. k-3). reprint ed. 9.99 (978-1-4169-0313-0(5), Simon & Schuster Bks. For Young Readers) Simon & Schuster Bks. For Young Readers.

—Starring Katy Duck. Capucilli, Alyssa Satin. 2011. (Ready-To-Read Level 1 Ser.). (ENG.). 24p. (J). (gr. -1-1). lib. bdg. 17.44 (978-1-4424-1975-9(X), Simon Spotlight) Simon & Schuster Children's Publishing.

—Starring Katy Duck. Capucilli, Alyssa Satin. 2011. (Katy Duck Ser.). (ENG.). 24p. (J). (gr. -1-1). pap. 4.99 (978-1-4424-1974-2(1), Simon Spotlight) Simon Spotlight.

—Surfer Chick. Dempsey, Kristy. 2018. (ENG.). 32p. (J). (gr. -1-k). pap. 4.99 (978-1-4197-2931-7(4), Abrams Bks. for Young Readers) Abrams, Inc.

—A Teeny Tiny Halloween, 1 vol. Wohl, Lauren L. 2017. (ENG.). 32p. (J). (gr. -1-2). 7.95 (978-1-943978-20-5(4), 9781943978205) WunderMill, Inc.

—Three Hens & a Peacock, 1 vol. Laminack, Lester L. 2011. (ENG.). 32p. (J). (gr. -1-3). 16.99 (978-1-56145-564-5(4)) Peachtree Publishing Co. Inc.

—Three Hens & a Peacock, 1 vol. Laminack, Lester L. 2014. (ENG.). 32p. (J). (gr. -1-3). pap. 7.95 (978-1-56145-726-7(4)) Peachtree Publishing Co. Inc.

—Tubby the Tuba. Tripp, Paul. 2006. 32p. (J). (gr. -1-3). 17.99 (978-0-525-47717-4(9), Dutton Books for Young Readers) Penguin Young Readers Group.

—The Twelve Days of Christmas in Virginia. Corbett, Sue. (Twelve Days of Christmas in America Ser.). (J). (-k). 2018. 22p. bds. 7.95 (978-1-4549-2929-1(4)); 2009. 40p. 12.95 (978-1-4027-6344-1(1)) Sterling Publishing Co., Inc.

—Why Do Kittens Purr? Bauer, Marion Dane. 2007. (ENG.). 32p. (J). (gr. -1-2). 9.99 (978-1-4169-6850-4(4), Aladdin) Simon & Schuster Children's Publishing.

—With a Little Help from My Friends. Lennon, John & McCartney, Paul. 2019. (ENG.). 40p. (J). (gr. -1-3). 17.99 (978-1-5344-2983-3(2), Little Simon) Little Simon.

—The Worrywarts. Edwards, Pamela Duncan. 2003. (ENG.). 32p. (J). (gr. -1-1). 7.99 (978-0-06-443516-1(4)) HarperCollins Canada, Ltd. CAN. Dist: HarperCollins Pubs.

—Z Is for Zookeeper: A Zoo Alphabet. Smith, Roland & Smith, Marie. (ENG.). 40p. (J). (gr. k-6). 2005. 16.95 (978-1-58536-158-8(5)); 2007. pap. 7.95 (978-1-58536-329-2(4)) Sleeping Bear Pr.

Cole, Henry. Another Quest for Celeste. Cole, Henry. (Nest for Celeste Ser.: 2). (ENG.). (J). (gr. 3-7). 2020. 288p. pap. 7.99 (978-0-06-265813-5(1)); 2018. 272p. 16.99 (978-0-06-265812-8(3)) HarperCollins Pubs. (Tegen, Katherine Bks).

—Big Bug. Cole, Henry. 2018. (Classic Board Bks.). (ENG.). 28p. (J). (gr. -1 — 1). bds. 7.99 (978-1-5344-1690-1(0), Little Simon) Little Simon.

—Big Bug. Cole, Henry. 2014. (ENG.). 32p. (J). (gr. -1-2). 15.99 (978-1-4424-9897-6(8), Little Simon) Little Simon.

—Brambleheart: A Story about Finding Treasure & the Unexpected Magic of Friendship. Cole, Henry. 2017. (Brambleheart Ser.: 1). (ENG.). 288p. (J). (gr. 3-7). pap. 6.99 *(978-0-06-224544-1(9),* Tegen, Katherine Bks) HarperCollins Pubs.

—Brambleheart: A Story about Finding Treasure & the Unexpected Magic of Friendship. Cole, Henry. 2016. (Brambleheart Ser.: 1). (ENG.). 272p. (J). (gr. 3-7). 16.99 *(978-0-06-224546-5(5),* Tegen, Katherine Bks) HarperCollins Pubs.

—Brambleheart #2: Bayberry Island: An Adventure about Friendship & the Journey Home. Cole, Henry. (Brambleheart Ser.: 2). (ENG.). (J). (gr. 3-7). 2018. 192p. pap. 6.99 *(978-0-06-224562-5(7));* 2017. 176p. 16.99 *(978-0-06-224551-9(1))* HarperCollins Pubs. (Tegen, Katherine Bks).

—The Littlest Evergreen. Cole, Henry. 2011. (ENG.). 32p. (J). (gr. -1-2). 16.99 *(978-0-06-114619-0(6),* Tegen, Katherine Bks) HarperCollins Pubs.

—A Nest for Celeste: A Story about Art, Inspiration, & the Meaning of Home. Cole, Henry. (Nest for Celeste Ser.: 1). (ENG.). 352p. (J). (gr. 3-7). 2012. pap. 6.99 *(978-0-06-170412-3(1));* 2010. 16.99 *(978-0-06-170410-9(5))* HarperCollins Pubs. (Tegen, Katherine Bks).

—Nesting. Cole, Henry. 2020. (ENG.). 40p. (J). (gr. -1-3). 17.99 *(978-0-06-288592-0(8),* Tegen, Katherine Bks) HarperCollins Pubs.

—On Meadowview Street. Cole, Henry. 2007. (ENG.). 32p. (J). (gr. -1-3). 17.99 *(978-0-06-056481-0(4),* Greenwillow Bks.) HarperCollins Pubs.

—On the Way to the Beach. Cole, Henry. 2003. (ENG.). 32p. (J). (gr. -1-3). 16.99 *(978-0-688-17515-3(5),* Greenwillow Bks.) HarperCollins Pubs.

—The Somewhat True Adventures of Sammy Shine, 1 vol. Cole, Henry. 2016. (ENG.). 272p. (J). (gr. 3-6). 16.95 *(978-1-56145-866-0(X))* Peachtree Publishing Co. Inc.

—The Somewhat True Adventures of Sammy Shine, 1 vol. Cole, Henry. 2018. (ENG.). 272p. (J). (gr. 3-7). pap. 7.95 *(978-1-56145-778-6(7))* Peachtree Publishing Co. Inc.

—Spot & Dot. Cole, Henry. 2019. (ENG.). 32p. (J). (gr. -1-3). 17.99 *(978-1-5344-2555-2(1),* Little Simon) Little Simon.

—Spot, the Cat. Cole, Henry. 2016. (ENG.). 32p. (J). (gr. -1-3). 18.99 *(978-1-4814-4225-1(2),* Little Simon) Little Simon.

—Trudy. Cole, Henry. 2009. (ENG.). 32p. (J). (gr. -1-3). 17.99 *(978-0-06-154267-1(9),* Greenwillow Bks.) HarperCollins Pubs.

—Try a Little Kindness: A Guide to Being Better. Cole, Henry. 2018. (ENG.). 32p. (J). (gr. -1-k). 17.99 *(978-1-338-25641-3(6),* Scholastic Pr.) Scholastic, Inc.

—Unspoken: A Story from the Underground Railroad. Cole, Henry. 2012. (ENG.). 40p. (J). (gr. k-2). 19.99 *(978-0-545-39997-5(1),* Scholastic Pr.) Scholastic, Inc.

Cole, Henry. Gigi & Lulu's Gigantic Fight. Cole, Henry, tr. Edwards, Pamela Duncan. 2004. 40p. (J). (gr. -1-2). lib. bdg. 15.89 *(978-0-06-050753-4(5))* HarperCollins Pubs.

Cole, Henry & Bond, Felicia. Jack & Jill's Treehouse. Edwards, Pamela Duncan. 2008. 24p. (J). (gr. -1-2). lib. bdg. 17.89 *(978-0-06-009078-4(2),* Tegen, Katherine Bks) HarperCollins Pubs.

Cole, Herbert. A Child's Book of Warriors. Canton, William. 2012. 290p. (J). pap. 12.75 *(978-1-936639-21-2(1))* St. Augustine Academy Pr.

Cole, Jeff. Numbers: A Silly Slider Book. Accord Publishing Staff & Andrews McMeel Publishing, LLC Staff. 2011. (ENG.). 12p. (J). (gr. -1-k). bds. 10.99 *(978-1-4494-0174-0(0))* Andrews McMeel Publishing.

Cole, Jeff. Eyeball Animation Drawing Book: Underwater Safari Edition. Cole, Jeff. Andrews McMeel Publishing, LLC Staff. 2009. (ENG.). 84p. (J). (gr. -1). pap. 14.99 *(978-0-7407-8106-3(5))* Andrews McMeel Publishing.

Cole, Joanna, jt. illus. see Cuddy, Robbin.

Cole, Joanne. Bod in the Park. Cole, Michael. 2017. (Bod Ser.). (ENG.). 32p. (J). (gr. -1-1). 9.99 *(978-1-4052-8059-4(X))* Egmont Bks., Ltd. GBR. Dist: Independent Pubs. Group.

—Bod on the Beach. Cole, Michael. 2017. (Bod Ser.). (ENG.). 32p. (J). (gr. -1-1). 9.99 *(978-1-4052-8060-0(3))* Egmont Bks., Ltd. GBR. Dist: Independent Pubs. Group.

—Bod's Present. Cole, Michael. 2016. (Bod Ser.). (ENG.). 48p. (J). (gr. -1-1). 9.99 *(978-1-4052-7754-9(8))* Egmont Bks., Ltd. GBR. Dist: Independent Pubs. Group.

Cole, Lisa. Chessie of the Chesapeake Bay. Cole, Lisa. 2011. 110p. pap. 9.95 *(978-1-936343-94-2(0))* Peppertree Pr., The.

Cole, Lo. A Whisper from Grey. Greig, Louise. 2019. (ENG.). 32p. (J). (gr. -1-k). pap. 10.99 *(978-1-4052-9083-8(8))* Egmont Bks., Ltd. GBR. Dist: Independent Pubs. Group.

Cole, Mernie. You Let the Cat Out of the Bag! (and Other Crazy Animal Sayings) Klingel, Cynthia Fitterer & Klingel, Cynthia. 2007. (Sayings & Phrases Ser.). (ENG.). 24p. (J). (gr. 2-5). 14.21 *(978-1-59296-903-6(8),* 200791) Child's World, Inc., The.

Cole, Mernie & Gallagher-Cole, Mernie. Hold Your Horses! (And Other Peculiar Sayings) Amoroso, Cynthia. 2011. (Sayings & Phrases Ser.). (ENG.). 24p. (J). (gr. 2-5). lib. bdg. 14.21 *(978-1-60253-681-4(3),* 200780) Child's World, Inc., The.

—You're Clean as a Whistle! (And Other Silly Sayings) Klingel, Cynthia Fitterer & Klingel, Cynthia. 2007. (Sayings & Phrases Ser.). (ENG.). 24p. (J). (gr. 2-5). 14.21 *(978-1-59296-905-0(4),* 200792) Child's World, Inc., The.

Cole, Mernie Gallagher. My Superhero Mind. Thatch, Jaina Marie. 2019. (ENG.). 34p. (J). (gr. k-2). 24.95 ***(978-0-578-59280-0(0))*** Thatch, Jaina.

Cole, Nichole. Cajun Babies: Journey to Safety. Ketterer, Cynthia Griffin. 2018. (ENG.). 24p. (J). pap. 9.99 *(978-1-7901-2354-4(2))* Independently Published.

Cole, Raymond A. A Slip in Time: The Book of Eventide. Cole, T. M. 2006. (YA). per. 10.75 *(978-0-9777677-0-0(1))* Silver Cloak Pubns.

Cole, Sarah. Big Fun Christmas Crafts & Activities: Over 200 Quick & Easy Activities for Holiday Fun! Press, Judy. 2006. (ENG.). 128p. (J). (gr. -1-3). 16.95 *(978-0-8249-6787-1(9),* Ideal Pubns.) Worthy Publishing.

Cole, Tom Clohosy. The Red Prince. Roscoe, Charlie. 2016. (ENG.). 32p. (J). (-k). 16.99 *(978-0-7636-8912-4(2),* Templar) Candlewick Pr.

Cole, Tom Clohosy. Wall. Cole, Tom Clohosy. 2014. (ENG.). 32p. (J). (gr. -1-3). 16.99 *(978-0-7636-7560-8(1),* Templar) Candlewick Pr.

Coleman, Brandon. I Love Socks! Murff, Tonette. 2019. (ENG.). 34p. (J). pap. 14.42 ***(978-1-0711-0619-8(8))*** Independently Published.

Coleman, Joan. The Jungle Gym. Cobb, Anton. 2018. (ENG.). 26p. (J). (gr. k-2). pap. 11.99 *(978-0-578-42236-7(0))* JUNGLE Gym, The.

Coleman, Joan. My Sister Would Make a Good President. Simplyharmony. 2019. (ENG.). 26p. (J). pap. 14.44 ***(978-0-578-56435-7(1))*** Hom, Jonathan.

Coleman, Joan. Time Traveling in Bandon: Activity & Coloring Book. Coleman, Andrew & Proehl, Jim, eds. 2019. (ENG.). 28p. (J). pap. 8.95 *(978-1-0752-0527-9(1))* Independently Published.

Coleman Lester, Gwen. Toby & the Secret Code. Townsend, Una Belle. 2016. (ENG.). 36p. (J). (gr. k-3). 18.99 *(978-0-9966205-9-8(1))* Doodle and Peck Publishing.

Coleman, Sadie. The Biggest Heart Ever. Coleman, Sadie. 2013. 24p. 14.99 *(978-0-9881969-0-2(5))* Vorpal Words, LLC.

Coleman, Sandra Js. Doofy Goes to School: The Bossy Goat. Sorrell, Elizabeth Lee. 2018. (Doofy Goes to School Ser.: Vol. 1). (ENG.). 34p. (J). (gr. k-5). 19.99 *(978-0-9995800-5-9(1))* Yarbrough Hse. Publishing.

—Nutcracker Versus Nutcracker. Sorrell, Elizabeth Lee. 2017. (ENG.). (J). (gr. k-5). 19.99 *(978-0-9995800-0-4(0))* Yarbrough Hse. Publishing.

Coleman, Sandra Js. Porter's Magic Paintbrush. Sorrell, Elizabeth Lee. 2019. (Faceless Nutcracker Ser.: Vol. 3). (ENG.). 32p. (J). (gr. k-6). 19.99 ***(978-1-7330965-2-2(3))*** Yarbrough Hse. Publishing.

Coleman, Sarah J. Out to Get You: 13 Tales of Weirdness & Woe. Allen, Josh. 2019. 176p. (J). (gr. 4-7). 16.99 *(978-0-8234-4366-6(3))* Holiday Hse., Inc.

Coleman, Stephanie Fizer. Bird Count, 1 vol. Richmond, Susan Edwards. 2019. (ENG.). 32p. (J). (gr. -1-3). 17.95 *(978-1-56145-954-4(2))* Peachtree Publishing Co. Inc.

—Fact-Packed Animal Activity Book. Potter, William. 2018. (ENG.). 96p. (J). pap. 12.99 *(978-1-78828-498-1(4),* d0efd84e-a0e8-473c-8cb2-c1ebb0323029) Arcturus Publishing GBR. Dist: Baker & Taylor Publisher Services (BTPS).

—Fact-Packed Dinosaur Activity Book. Potter, William. 2018. (ENG.). 96p. (J). pap. 12.99 *(978-1-78828-499-8(2),* b205c136-9df1-4fb7-9319-a5a49550f318) Arcturus Publishing GBR. Dist: Baker & Taylor Publisher Services (BTPS).

—From Cocoa Beans to Chocolate. Heos, Bridget. 2018. (Who Made My Lunch? Ser.). (ENG.). 24p. (J). (gr. k-3). pap. 9.99 *(978-1-68152-145-9(8))* Amicus.

—From Cocoa Beans to Chocolate. Heos, Bridget. 2017. (Who Made My Lunch? Ser.). (ENG.). 24p. (gr. 1-4). 20.95 *(978-1-68151-120-7(7))* Amicus Publishing.

—From Grapes to Jelly. Heos, Bridget. 2018. (Who Made My Lunch? Ser.). (ENG.). 24p. (J). (gr. k-3). pap. 9.99 *(978-1-68152-147-3(4))* Amicus.

—From Grapes to Jelly. Heos, Bridget. 2017. (Who Made My Lunch? Ser.). (ENG.). 24p. (gr. 1-4). 20.95 *(978-1-68151-122-1(3))* Amicus Publishing.

—From Milk to Cheese. Heos, Bridget. 2018. (Who Made My Lunch? Ser.). (ENG.). 24p. (J). (gr. k-3). pap. 9.99 *(978-1-68152-144-2(X))* Amicus.

—From Milk to Cheese. Heos, Bridget. 2017. (Who Made My Lunch? Ser.). (ENG.). 24p. (gr. 1-4). 20.95 *(978-1-68151-119-1(3))* Amicus Publishing.

—From Milk to Ice Cream. Heos, Bridget. 2017. (Who Made My Lunch? Ser.). (ENG.). 24p. (gr. 1-4). 20.95 *(978-1-68151-121-4(5))* Amicus Publishing.

—From Peanuts to Peanut Butter: By Bridget Heos: Illustrated by Stephanie Fizer Coleman. Heos, Bridget. 2017. (Who Made My Lunch? Ser.). (ENG.). 24p. (gr. 1-4). 20.95 *(978-1-68151-123-8(1))* Amicus Publishing.

—From Wheat to Bread. Heos, Bridget. 2017. (Who Made My Lunch? Ser.). (ENG.). 24p. (gr. 1-4). 20.95 *(978-1-68151-118-4(5))* Amicus Publishing.

—Hidden World: Forest. Walden, Libby. 2018. (ENG.). 18p. (J). (gr. -1-2). 14.99 *(978-1-944530-14-3(2),* 360 Degrees) Tiger Tales.

—Hidden World: Ocean. Walden, Libby. 2018. (ENG.). 18p. (J). (gr. -1-2). 14.99 *(978-1-944530-15-0(0),* 360 Degrees) Tiger Tales.

—Lali's Feather. Zia, Farhana. 2020. (ENG.). 32p. (J). (gr. -1-3). 17.99 *(978-1-68263-129-4(X))* Peachtree Publishing Co. Inc.

—Meet My Family! Animal Babies & Their Families. Salas, Laura Purdie. 2018. (ENG.). 32p. (J). (gr. k-3). 19.99 *(978-1-5124-2532-1(X),* Millbrook Pr.) Lerner Publishing Group.

—Ninita's Big World: The True Story of a Deaf Pygmy Marmoset. Marsh, Sarah Glenn. 2019. (ENG.). 32p. (J). (gr. -1-3). 17.99 *(978-1-328-77001-1(X),* 1680998, Clarion Bks.) Houghton Mifflin Harcourt Trade & Reference Pubs.

—Runaway Pumpkins. Bateman, Teresa. 2020. 32p. (J). (gr. -1-2). lib. bdg. 16.99 *(978-1-58089-681-8(2))* Charlesbridge Publishing, Inc.

Coleman, Stephanie Fizer. Sounds of the Wild. Butterfield, Moira. 2020. (ENG.). 24p. (J). (gr. k-3). 19.99 ***(978-1-944530-28-0(2),*** 360 Degrees) Tiger Tales.

Coleman, Stephanie Fizer. Super Marsupials: Kangaroos, Koalas, Wombats, & More. Kenah, Katharine. 2019. (Let's-Read-And-Find-Out Science 1 Ser.). (ENG.). 40p. (J). (gr. -1-3). pap. 6.99 *(978-0-06-249529-7(1))* HarperCollins Pubs.

Coleman, Winfield. The Thunder Egg, Vol. Myers, Tim J. 2015. 28p. (J). (gr. k-4). 15.95 *(978-1-937786-39-7(0),* Wisdom Tales) World Wisdom, Inc.

Coles, James. The Many Adventures of Pengey Penguin. Burns, John. 2005. 207p. (J). per. 17.95 *(978-0-9774227-0-8(4))* San Francisco Story Works.

Coles, Mary. Brontosaurus Brunch: A Smorgasbord of Dinosaur Delights. Peers, Judi. 3rd ed. 2011. *(978-0-9810964-2-1(5))* Praise Publishing.

Coleson, Julie. How Six Little Ipu Got Their Names. Coleson, Julie. Brimmer, Debi. 2005. 30p. (J). 9.95 incl. audio compact disk *(978-1-57306-186-5(7))* Bess Pr., Inc.

Coll, Ivar Da. El Barbero y el Coronel. MacHado, Ana Maria.Tr. of Barber & the Colonel. (SPA.). (J). (gr. 2-3). 7.95 *(978-958-04-5035-1(8),* NR1718) Norma S.A. COL. Dist: Distribuidora Norma, Inc., Lectorum Pubns., Inc.

—Una Cama para Tres. Reyes, Yolanda. 2004. (SPA.). 36p. (J). (gr. k-3). 14.95 *(978-958-704-055-5(4))* Santillana USA Publishing Co., Inc.

Coll, Ivar Da. Carlos. Coll, Ivar Da. 2003. (SPA.). 52p. (J). (gr. k-3). pap. 9.95 *(978-958-8061-64-1(4))* Santillana USA Publishing Co., Inc.

Colla, Juan Carlos. The Maybe Magnificent Day. Berryhill-Castaneda, Rhonda. 2019. (ENG.). 28p. (J). pap. 12.99 *(978-1-61225-425-8(X))* Mirror Publishing.

Collado, John. Great Cape o' Colors: Career Costumes for Kids. Beckstrand, Karl. 2018. (Careers for Kids Ser.: Vol. 4). (ENG.). 30p. (J). 26.55 *(978-1-7320696-3-3(8))* Premio Publishing & Gozo Bks., LLC.

Collar, Orpheus. The Kane Chronicles - Book One Red Pyramid: the Graphic Novel, Bk. 1. Collar, Orpheus. Riordan, Rick. 2012. (Kane Chronicles Ser.: 1). (ENG.). 192p. (J). (gr. 5-9). 21.99 *(978-1-4231-5068-8(6))* Hyperion Pr.

—The Kane Chronicles, Book Three the Serpent's Shadow: the Graphic Novel. Collar, Orpheus. Riordan, Rick. 2017. (Kane Chronicles Ser.). (ENG.). 160p. (J). (gr. 5-9). 21.99 *(978-1-4847-8132-6(5));* pap. 12.99 *(978-1-4847-8234-7(8))* Hyperion Bks. for Children.

—Kane Chronicles, the, Book One the Red Pyramid: the Graphic Novel (Kane Chronicles, the, Book One), Bk. 1. Collar, Orpheus. Riordan, Rick. 2012. (Kane Chronicles Ser.: 1). (ENG.). 192p. (J). (gr. 5-9). pap. 12.99 *(978-1-4231-5069-5(4))* Hyperion Pr.

Collar, Orpheus & Dodé, Antoine. Percy Jackson & the Olympians the Battle of the Labyrinth: the Graphic Novel (Percy Jackson & the Olympians) Riordan, Rick & Venditti, Robert. 2018. (Percy Jackson & the Olympians Ser.: 4). (ENG.). 128p. (J). (gr. 5-9). 21.99 *(978-1-4847-8235-4(6));* pap. 12.99 *(978-1-4847-8639-0(4))* Hyperion Bks. for Children.

—Percy Jackson & the Olympians the Last Olympian: the Graphic Novel. Riordan, Rick & Venditti, Robert. 2019. (Percy Jackson & the Olympians Ser.). (ENG.). 128p. (J). (gr. 5-9). 21.99 *(978-1-4847-8233-0(X));* pap. 12.99 *(978-1-4847-8638-3(6))* Hyperion Bks. for Children.

Collar, Orpheus, jt. illus. see Dodé, Antoine.

Collectif. Fables Jean de la Fontaines. 2008. (A. M. Alb. Ill. C. Ser.). (FRE.). (J). *(978-2-226-18945-5(9))* Albin-Michel, Editions.

—45 Games - On the Plane. Auzou Publishing Staff. 2019. 52p. (J). spiral bd. 6.99 *(978-2-7338-6737-2(7))* Auzou, Philippe Editions FRA. Dist: Consortium Bk. Sales & Distribution.

—45 Games: in the Summer. 2019. (ENG.). 50p. (J). 6.99 *(978-2-7338-6736-5(9))* Auzou, Philippe Editions FRA. Dist: Consortium Bk. Sales & Distribution.

Collection/Jupiterimages Unlimited. Farm Animal Friends: A Mega Sticker Book. Ciminera, Siobhan. 2009. (ENG.). 48p. (J). (gr. -1-2). 12.99 *(978-1-4169-6786-6(9),* Simon Scribbles) Simon Scribbles.

—Stuck on Christmas! A Mega Sticker Book. Ciminera, Siobhan. 2008. (ENG.). 48p. (J). (gr. -1-2). 12.99 *(978-1-4169-6784-2(2),* Simon Scribbles) Simon Scribbles.

Collective Work Staff. The Arabian Nights, 7 vols. Melodie. 2012. 32p. (J). (gr. 1). 19.95 *(978-2-7338-2150-3(4))* Auzou, Philippe Editions FRA. Dist: Consortium Bk. Sales & Distribution.

Collenberger, Chris. The Day the Sun Called Out Sick!!! Belle, Deborah A. 2013. 30p. pap. 12.99 *(978-0-9853406-0-5(6))* Scribez, Scarebz & Vibez.

Coller, Casey W., et al. My Little Pony: Friendship Is Magic Volume 19. Rice, Christina & Whitley, Jeremy. 2020. (My Little Pony Ser.: 19). 120p. (J). (gr. 4-7). pap. 17.99 ***(978-1-68405-685-9(3))*** Idea & Design Works, LLC.

Coller, H. Seven Sisters at Queen Anne's. Smith, Evelyn. 2013. 162p. pap. *(978-1-909423-07-7(6))* Bks. to Treasure.

Collet-Derby, Pierre. Goodnight Selfie. Menchin, Scott. 2015. 32p. (J). (gr. -1-3). 16.99 *(978-0-7636-3182-6(5))* Candlewick Pr.

Collet-Derby, Pierre. Barnaby Never Forgets. Collet-Derby, Pierre. 2017. 32p. (J). (gr. k-3). 16.99 *(978-0-7636-8853-0(3))* Candlewick Pr.

Collet, Maëva. Wondrous Women Who Changed the World. Jacoby, Jenny. 2019. (Role Models Ser.). (ENG.). 64p. (J). 19.99 *(978-1-68412-951-5(6),* Thunder Bay Pr.) Printers Row Publishing Group.

Collett, Farrell R. Jerry Lindsey: Explorer to the San Juan. Luce, Willard. 2011. 88p. 38.95 *(978-1-258-07330-5(7))* Literary Licensing, LLC.

Collett, Susan. The Christmas Dragon. Collett, Susan, . 2007. 64p. (J). pap. 5.95 *(978-0-9678115-1-2(1))* Dragonseed Pr.

Colletti, Marco, jt. illus. see Cortes, Mario.

Colletti, Marco, jt. illus. see Laguna, Fabio.

Collicott, Sharleen. The Chicken Sisters. Numeroff, Laura Joffe. abr. ed. 2003. (J). (gr. -1-2). 28.95 incl. audio compact disk *(978-1-59112-533-4(2))* Live Oak Media.

Collicott, Sharleen. Mildred & Sam. Collicott, Sharleen. (I Can Read Bks.). (J). 2008. 64p. (gr. -1-2). lib. bdg. 17.89 *(978-0-06-058115-2(8),* Geringer, Laura Book); 2004. (ENG.). 48p. (gr. k-3). pap. 4.99 *(978-0-06-000200-8(X));* 2003. 48p. (gr. -1-18). 15.99 *(978-0-06-026681-3(3))* HarperCollins Pubs.

—Mildred & Sam & Their Babies. Collicott, Sharleen. 2005. (I Can Read Bks.). 48p. (J). (gr. -1-2). 15.99 *(978-0-06-058111-4(5),* Geringer, Laura Book) HarperCollins Pubs.

Collicutt, Paul. World's Weirdest Reptiles. Jackson, Tom. 2018. (Extreme Reptiles Ser.). (ENG.). 32p. (J). (gr. 3-6). lib. bdg. 27.99 *(978-1-5415-0089-1(X),* Hungry Tomato ®) Lerner Publishing Group.

Collicutt, Paul. Murder on the Robot City Express. Collicutt, Paul. 2010. (Robot City Ser.: 4). (ENG.). 48p. (J). (gr. 3-7). pap. 8.99 *(978-0-7636-5015-5(3),* Templar) Candlewick Pr.

—Rust Attack! Collicutt, Paul. 2009. (Robot City Ser.: 2). (ENG.). 48p. (J). (gr. 3-7). pap. 8.99 *(978-0-7636-4594-6(X),* Templar) Candlewick Pr.

Collier, photos by. ABCs of South African Animals. Collier, . 2015. 32p. (gr. -1-1). pap. 12.99 *(978-0-692-59277-9(6))* Educational Consulting by Design, LLC.

Collier, Bryan. Barack Obama: Son of Promise, Child of Hope. Grimes, Nikki. (ENG.). 48p. (J). (gr. k-3). 2012. 9.99 *(978-1-4424-4092-0(9));* 2008. pap. 18.99 *(978-1-4169-7144-3(0))* Simon & Schuster Bks. For Young Readers. (Simon & Schuster Bks. For Young Readers).

—Barack Obama: Son of Promise, Child of Hope (Book & CD) Grimes, Nikki. 2012. (ENG.). 48p. (J). (gr. k-3). pap. 9.99 *(978-1-4424-5077-6(0),* Little Simon) Little Simon.

—Between the Lines: How Ernie Barnes Went from the Football Field to the Art Gallery. Wallace, Sandra Neil. 2018. (ENG.). 48p. (J). (gr. -1-3). 17.99 *(978-1-4814-4387-6(9),* Simon & Schuster Bks. For Young Readers) Simon & Schuster Bks. For Young Readers.

—By & By: Charles Albert Tindley, the Father of Gospel Music. Weatherford, Carole Boston. 2020. (ENG.). 48p. (J). (gr. -1-3). 17.99 *(978-1-5344-2636-8(1))* Simon & Schuster Children's Publishing.

—City Shapes. Murray, Diana. 2016. 40p. (J). (gr. -1-3). 18.99 *(978-0-316-37092-9(4))* Little Brown & Co.

—Dave the Potter: Artist, Poet, Slave. Hill, Laban Carrick. 2010. (ENG.). 40p. (J). (gr. -1-3). 19.99 *(978-0-316-10731-0(X))* Little, Brown Bks. for Young Readers.

—Dave the Potter: Artist, Poet, Slave. Hill, Laban Carrick. 2011. 40p. (J). (gr. -1-2). 37.75 *(978-1-4618-1710-9(2))* Recorded Bks., Inc.

—Doo-Wop Pop. Schotter, Roni. 2008. 40p. (J). (gr. -1-3). lib. bdg. 17.89 *(978-0-06-057974-6(9),* Amistad) HarperCollins Pubs.

—Hey Black Child. Perkins, Useni Eugene. (J). (gr. -1 — 1). 2019. 22p. 7.99 *(978-0-316-36029-6(5));* 2017. 40p. 18.99 *(978-0-316-36030-2(9))* Little, Brown Bks. for Young Readers.

—I, Too, Am America. Hughes, Langston. 2012. (ENG.). 40p. (J). (gr. -1-3). 19.99 *(978-1-4424-2008-3(1),* Simon & Schuster Bks. For Young Readers) Simon & Schuster Bks. For Young Readers.

—John's Secret Dreams: The Life of John Lennon. Rappaport, Doreen. 2016. (Big Words Book Ser.: 6). (ENG.). 48p. (J). (gr. -1-3). pap. 8.99 *(978-1-4847-4962-3(6))* Hyperion Bks. for Children.

—The Jump at the Sun Treasury: An African American Picture Book Collection. Price, Hope Lynne. 2004. 205p. (J). (gr. 4-8). reprint ed. 17.00 *(978-0-7567-7328-1(8))* DIANE Publishing Co.

—Lift Your Light a Little Higher: The Story of Stephen Bishop: Slave-Explorer. Henson, Heather. 2016. (ENG.). 32p. (J). (gr. -1-3). 17.99 *(978-1-4814-2095-2(X),* Atheneum/Caitlyn Dlouhy Books) Simon & Schuster Children's Publishing.

—Lincoln & Douglass: An American Friendship. Giovanni, Nikki. 2013. (ENG.). 40p. (J). (gr. 2-6). 9.99 *(978-1-250-01869-4(2),* 900087706) Square Fish.

—Lincoln & Douglass: An American Friendship. Giovanni, Nikki. 2011. (J). (gr. -1-3). 29.95 *(978-0-545-13457-6(9))* Weston Woods Studios, Inc.

—Martin's Big Words: The Life of Dr. Martin Luther King, Jr. Rappaport, Doreen. rev. ed. 2007. (Big Words Book Ser.: 1). (ENG.). 40p. (J). (gr. 1-3). pap. 7.99 *(978-1-4231-0635-7(0),* Jump at the Sun) Hyperion Bks. for Children.

—My Country, 'Tis of Thee: How One Song Reveals the History of Civil Rights. Murphy, Claire Rudolf. 2014. (ENG.). 48p. (J). (gr. k-4). 17.99 *(978-0-8050-8226-5(3),* 900041119, Holt, Henry & Co. Bks. For Young Readers) Holt, Henry & Co.

—Rosa. Giovanni, Nikki. rev. ed. 2005. (ENG.). 40p. (J). (gr. -1-3). 18.99 *(978-0-8050-7106-1(7),* 900029805, Holt, Henry & Co. Bks. For Young Readers) Holt, Henry & Co.

—Rosa. Giovanni, Nikki. 2007. (ENG.). 40p. (J). (gr. -1-3). per. 8.99 *(978-0-312-37602-4(2),* 900048322) Square Fish.

—Rosa. Giovanni, Nikki. 2011. (J). (gr. 2-5). 29.95 *(978-0-545-04261-1(5))* Weston Woods Studios, Inc.

—Rosa Storytime Set, 1 vol. Giovanni, Nikki. unabr. ed. 2014. (Macmillan Young Listeners Story Time Sets Ser.). (ENG.). 40p. (J). (gr. -1-3). 12.99 *(978-1-4272-4397-3(2),* 9781427243973) Macmillan Audio.

—Thurgood. Winter, Jonah. 2019. 40p. (J). (gr. k-4). 17.99 *(978-1-5247-6533-0(3));* (ENG.). 20.99 *(978-1-5247-6534-7(1))* Random Hse. Children's Bks. (Schwartz & Wade Bks.).

—Trombone Shorty. Andrews, Troy. 2015. (ENG.). 40p. (J). (gr. -1-3). 17.95 *(978-1-4197-1465-8(1),* Abrams Bks. for Young Readers) Abrams, Inc.

—Twelve Rounds to Glory: The Story of Muhammad Ali. Smith, Charles R., Jr. 2007. (ENG.). 80p. (J). (gr. 5). 19.99 *(978-0-7636-1692-2(3))* Candlewick Pr.

—Twelve Rounds to Glory (12 Rounds to Glory) The Story of Muhammad Ali. Smith Jr., Charles R. 2010. (ENG.). 80p. (J). (gr. 5). pap. 12.99 *(978-0-7636-5002-5(1))* Candlewick Pr.

—Visiting Langston. Perdomo, Willie. 2006. (gr. -1-3). 19.00 *(978-0-7569-6802-1(X))* Perfection Learning Corp.

—Visiting Langston. Perdomo, Willie. 2005. (ENG.). 32p. (J). (gr. -1-3). reprint ed. pap. 9.99 *(978-0-8050-7881-7(9),* 900030908) Square Fish.

—Your Moon, My Moon: A Grandmother's Words to a Faraway Child. Maclachlan, Patricia. 2011. (ENG.). 32p. (J). (gr. -1-3). 16.99 *(978-1-4169-7950-0(6),* Simon &

C

Schuster Bks. For Young Readers) Simon & Schuster Bks. For Young Readers.

—The 5 o'Clock Band. Andrews, Troy. 2018. (ENG.). 40p. (J). (gr. -1-3). 17.99 *(978-1-4197-2836-5(9),* Abrams Bks. for Young Readers) Abrams, Inc.

Collier, Bryan. Uptown, 4 bks., Set. Collier, Bryan. 2007. (J). (gr. k-3). pap. 39.95 incl. audio compact disk *(978-1-4301-0055-3(9))* Live Oak Media.

—Uptown. Collier, Bryan. rev. ed. 2004. (ENG.). 32p. (J). (gr. -1-3). pap. 8.99 *(978-0-8050-7399-7(X),* 900020161) Square Fish.

Collier, Bryan, jt. illus. see Willems, Mo.

Collier, John & Morin, Paul. At Break of Day. Grimes, Nikki. 2004. 32p. (J). (gr. -1-3). 17.00 *(978-0-8028-5104-8(5))* Eerdmans, William B. Publishing Co.

Collier, Kelly. A Horse Named Steve. Collier, Kelly. 2017. (ENG.). 32p. (J). (gr. -1-3). 16.95 *(978-1-77138-736-1(X))* Kids Can Pr., Ltd. CAN. Dist: Hachette Bk. Group.

—Team Steve. Collier, Kelly. 2018. (Steve the Horse Ser.). (ENG.). 40p. (J). (gr. -1-3). 16.99 *(978-1-77138-932-7(X))* Kids Can Pr., Ltd. CAN. Dist: Hachette Bk. Group.

Collier, Kevin. Campfire Bedtime Stories. Kennett Rudkin, Lisa. 2018. (ENG.). 58p. (J). pap. *(978-1-7750736-5-9(3))* Publishing Hse. Publishing.

—Campfire Bedtime Stories. Rudkin, Lisa Kennet. 2018. (ENG.). 58p. (J). (gr. 2-4). *(978-1-7750736-6-6(1))* PageMaster Publication Services, Inc.

—J P S Halloween Parade. Houdek, Andi. 2012. 20p. pap. 9.95 *(978-1-61633-263-1(8))* Guardian Angel Publishing, Inc.

—Magical Mea. Cole, Penelope Anne. 2013. 24p. 19.95 *(978-1-61633-394-2(4));* pap. 10.95 *(978-1-61633-395-9(2))* Guardian Angel Publishing, Inc.

—Magico Mateo. Cole, Penelope Anne. 2013. 24p. pap. 10.95 *(978-1-61633-421-5(5))* Guardian Angel Publishing, Inc.

—Michael & the Magic Dinosaur. Bloomberg, Sandi. 2012. 30p. pap. 13.95 *(978-1-61244-066-8(5))* Halo Publishing International.

—One Nutty Family. Byers, James. 2012. 16p. pap. 9.95 *(978-1-61633-200-6(X))* Guardian Angel Publishing, Inc.

—Start with Your Heart. Skordy, Anne Marie. 2011. 32p. (J). pap. 12.95 *(978-1-60131-089-7(7))* Big Tent Bks.

—Stop That Pudding! Houdek, Andi. 2010. 16p. pap. 9.95 *(978-1-61633-079-8(1))* Guardian Angel Publishing, Inc.

—What in the World Should I Be. Jones, Debra M. 2010. 16p. pap. 9.95 *(978-1-61633-037-8(6))* Guardian Angel Publishing, Inc.

Collier, Kevin Scott. The Adventures of Brutus & Baby: A Haunted Halloween. Rogers, Michelle Elizabeth. 2010. 50p. pap. 16.50 *(978-1-60860-592-7(2),* Eloquent Bks.) Strategic Book Publishing & Rights Agency (SBPRA).

—The Best Christmas Gift. Appel, Cindy. 2005. (J). E-Book 6.00 incl. cd-rom *(978-1-933090-19-1(7))* Guardian Angel Publishing, Inc.

—A Blessed Bethlehem Birth: As told by Abraham & Anna Mousenstern. McElligott, Walter Lee. 2006. 28p. (J). E-Book 5.00 incl. cd-rom *(978-1-933090-21-4(9))* Guardian Angel Publishing, Inc.

—Bobby Cottontail's Gift. James, Catherine. 2008. 28p. pap. 10.95 *(978-1-935137-07-8(7));* 2006. 32p. (J). E-Book 9.95 incl. cd-rom *(978-1-933090-24-5(3))* Guardian Angel Publishing, Inc.

—Chizzy's Topsy Tale. Shepherd, Donna J. 2008. 20p. pap. 10.95 *(978-1-935137-10-8(7))* Guardian Angel Publishing, Inc.

—Dotty's Topsy Tale. Shepherd, Donna J. 2009. 16p. pap. 9.95 *(978-1-935137-55-9(7))* Guardian Angel Publishing, Inc.

—Magical Matthew. Cole, Penelope Anne. 2012. 24p. 19.95 *(978-1-61633-325-6(1))* Guardian Angel Publishing, Inc.

—Magical Matthew. Cole, Penelope Ann. 2012. 24p. pap. 10.95 *(978-1-61633-326-3(X))* Guardian Angel Publishing, Inc.

—Mateo Magico. Cole, Penelope Anne. 2018. (SPA.). 40p. (J). pap. 9.50 *(978-1-943196-12-8(5))* Magical Bk. Works.

—MIA Magica. Cole, Penelope Anne. 2018. (SPA.). 42p. (J). pap. 9.50 *(978-1-943196-13-5(3))* Magical Bk. Works.

—Mice in My Tummy. Houdek, Andrea. 2012. 16p. pap. 9.95 *(978-1-61633-219-8(0))* Guardian Angel Publishing, Inc.

—The Misadventures of Rooter & Snuffle. Lyle-Soffe, Shari. 2008. 20p. pap. 9.95 *(978-1-933090-88-7(X));* 2006. 28p. (J). E-Book 5.00 incl. cd-rom *(978-1-933090-43-6(X))* Guardian Angel Publishing, Inc.

—Nothing Stops Noah. Lyle-Soffe, Shari. 2008. 24p. pap. 10.95 *(978-1-935137-19-1(0))* Guardian Angel Publishing, Inc.

—On the Go with Rooter & Snuffle. Lyle-Soffe, Shari. 2008. 20p. pap. 9.95 *(978-1-933090-96-2(0))* Guardian Angel Publishing, Inc.

—OUCH! Sunburn. Shepherd, Donna J. 2007. 27p. (J). E-Book 9.95 incl. cd-rom *(978-1-933090-60-3(X))* Guardian Angel Publishing, Inc.

—Peaches & Cream, 1 vol. Squires, R. L. 2009. 31p. pap. 24.95 *(978-1-60749-164-4(8))* America Star Bks.

—Piccolo. Lake, Mary. 2007. (J). (gr. -1-3). 25p. 14.99 *(978-1-59879-358-1(6));* per. 10.99 *(978-1-59879-253-9(9))* Lifevest Publishing, Inc.

—The Sad Little House. James, Catherine. 2008. 24p. pap. 10.95 *(978-1-935137-06-1(9));* 2006. 28p. (J). E-Book 9.95 incl. cd-rom *(978-1-933090-18-4(9))* Guardian Angel Publishing, Inc.

—Sam Feels Better Now! An Interactive Story for Children. Osborne, Jill. 2008. 44p. (J). pap. 15.95 *(978-1-932690-60-6(3))* Loving Healing Pr., Inc.

—Sully's Topsy Tale. Shepherd, Donna J. 2010. 20p. pap. 10.95 *(978-1-61633-047-7(3))* Guardian Angel Publishing, Inc.

—Trouble Finds Rooter & Snuffle. Lyle-Soffe, Shari. 2008. 20p. pap. 9.95 *(978-1-933090-72-6(3))* Guardian Angel Publishing, Inc.

—We're Brothers & Sisters. Cahill, Bear. 2008. 20p. pap. 9.95 *(978-1-933090-70-2(7))* Guardian Angel Publishing, Inc.

Collier, Kevin Scott. Hope, the Angelfish. Collier, Kevin Scott. 2008. 24p. pap. 10.95 *(978-1-933090-17-7(0))* Guardian Angel Publishing, Inc.

—Journeys of Hope, Pearl of Wisdom. Collier, Kevin Scott. 2006. 28p. (J). E-Book 9.95 incl. cd-rom *(978-1-933090-31-3(6))* Guardian Angel Publishing, Inc.

—Professor Horace, Cryptozoologist. Collier, Kevin Scott. 2008. 20p. pap. 9.95 *(978-1-935137-14-6(X))* Guardian Angel Publishing, Inc.

Collier, Kevin Scott & LeBlanc, Giselle. The New Puppy. Hall, Raelene. 2013. 16p. pap. 9.95 *(978-1-61633-415-4(0))* Guardian Angel Publishing, Inc.

Collier, Mary. The Caterpillar. Schmauss, Judy Kentor. 2006. (Reader's Clubhouse Level 1 Reader Ser.). (ENG.). 24p. (J). (gr. k-1). pap. 4.99 *(978-0-7641-3286-5(5),* B.E.S. Publishing) Peterson's.

—My Clothes/Mi Ropa. Rosa-Mendoza, Gladys. Abello, Patricia & Weber, Amy, eds. 2005. (#1 Bilingual Board Book Ser.). (SPA & ENG.). 20p. (J). (gr. -1). bds. 6.95 *(978-1-931398-15-2(1))* Me+Mi Publishing.

Collier-Morales, Roberta. August, 1 vol. Kesselring, Mari. 2009. (Months of the Year Ser.). (ENG.). 24p. (J). (gr. k-2). 27.07 *(978-1-60270-635-4(2),* 11577, Looking Glass Library) Magic Wagon.

—Cuatro Buenos Amigos. Hillert, Margaret. 2018. (BeginningtoRead Ser.).Tr. of Four Good Friends. (SPA.). 32p. (J). (gr. -1-2). pap. 11.94 *(978-1-68404-234-0(8))* Norwood Hse. Pr.

—Four Good Friends. Hillert, Margaret. 2016. (BeginningtoRead Ser.). (ENG.). 32p. (J). (-2). lib. bdg. 22.60 *(978-1-59953-780-1(X));* (gr. -1-2). pap. 11.94 *(978-1-60357-906-3(0))* Norwood Hse. Pr.

—Inside Out. Halley, Wendy Stofan. 2003. 32p. 15.95 *(978-0-9701907-5-8(1))* Illumination Arts Publishing Co., Inc.

—July, 1 vol. Kesselring, Mari. 2009. (Months of the Year Ser.). (ENG.). 24p. (J). (gr. k-2). 27.07 *(978-1-60270-634-7(4),* 11575, Looking Glass Library) Magic Wagon.

—June, 1 vol. Kesselring, Mari. 2009. (Months of the Year Ser.). (ENG.). 24p. (J). (gr. k-2). 27.07 *(978-1-60270-633-0(6),* 11573, Looking Glass Library) Magic Wagon.

—The Lost Coin. Dreyer, Nicole E. 2006. (ENG.). 16p. (J). pap. 1.99 *(978-0-7586-0873-4(X))* Concordia Publishing Hse.

—El Mago Que Salvo el Mundo. Bennett, Jeffrey. 2011. (SPA.). 32p. (J). (gr. 2-4). 15.00 *(978-0-9721819-5-2(4))* Big Kid Science.

—The Thankful Leper: The Story of the Ten Lepers: Luke 17:11-19 & 2 Kings 5:1-15 for Children. Hinkle, Cynthia A. 2006. (Arch Bks.). (J). 2.49 *(978-0-7586-1284-7(2))* Concordia Publishing Hse.

—The Wizard Who Saved the World. Bennett, Jeffrey. 2011. (ENG.). 32p. (J). (gr. 2-4). 15.00 *(978-0-9721819-4-5(6))* Big Kid Science.

Collier-Morales, Roberta. Cuatro Buenos Amigos. Collier-Morales, Roberta. Hillert, Margaret & Del Risco, Eida. 2018. (BeginningtoRead Ser.).Tr. of Four Good Friends. (SPA.). 32p. (J). (gr. -1-2). lib. bdg. 22.60 *(978-1-59953-950-8(0))* Norwood Hse. Pr.

Collier-Morales, Roberta, jt. illus. see Jack Pullan.

Collier, Roberta. Frohliche Weihnachten: Learning Songs & Traditions in German. Rauenhorst, Linda. 2007. (Teach Me Ser.). (GER & ENG.). 32p. (J). (gr. -1-3). 19.95 *(978-1-59972-063-0(9))* Teach Me Tapes, Inc.

Collignon, Veronica. Happiness Hacks: How to Find Energy & Inspiration. Andrus, Aubre & Bluth, Karen. 2017. (Stress-Busting Survival Guides). (ENG.). 48p. (J). (gr. 4-8). lib. bdg. 31.99 *(978-1-5157-6820-3(1),* 135349, Capstone Pr.) Capstone.

—Me Time: How to Manage a Busy Life. Andrus, Aubre & Bluth, Karen. 2017. (Stress-Busting Survival Guides). (ENG.). 48p. (J). (gr. 4-8). lib. bdg. 31.99 *(978-1-5157-6821-0(X),* 135350, Capstone Pr.) Capstone.

—Project You: More Than 50 Ways to Calm down, de-Stress, & Feel Great. Andrus, Aubre & Bluth, Karen. 2017. (ENG.). 160p. (YA). (gr. 4-8). pap. 14.95 *(978-1-63079-091-2(5),* 135352, Switch Pr.) Capstone.

—Stress Less: How to Achieve Inner Calm & Relaxation. Andrus, Aubre & Bluth, Karen. 2017. (Stress-Busting Survival Guides). (ENG.). 48p. (J). (gr. 4-8). lib. bdg. 31.99 *(978-1-5157-6822-7(8),* 135351, Capstone Pr.) Capstone.

Collin, Renaud. Minions 3: Viva le Boss! HC. Lapuss, Stephane. 2018. 48p. (J). (gr. 1-4). 14.99 *(978-1-78773-016-8(6))* Titan Bks. Ltd. GBR. Dist: Penguin Random Hse. LLC.

—Minions Paella! Lapuss', Stephane. 2020. (J). (gr. 4-7). pap. 6.99 *(978-1-78773-024-3(7))* Titan Bks. Ltd. GBR. Dist: Penguin Random Hse. LLC.

—Minions Volume 3: Viva le Boss! Lapuss, Stephane. 2019. 48p. (J). (gr. 1-4). pap. 6.99 *(978-1-78773-017-5(4))* Titan Bks. Ltd. GBR. Dist: Penguin Random Hse. LLC.

Collina, Sumiti. Katarina Ballerina. Peck, Tiler & Harris, Kyle. 2020. (Katarina Ballerina Ser.: 1). (ENG.). 192p. (J). (gr. 3-7). 16.99 ***(978-1-5344-5276-3(1),*** Aladdin) Simon & Schuster Children's Publishing.

Collinet, Rob. Kids' Kookiest Riddles. Charney, Steve. 2010. (Jokes & Riddles Ser.). (ENG.). 96p. (J). (gr. k-3). 17.44 *(978-1-4027-7850-6(3))* Sterling Publishing Co., Inc.

Collingridge, Catharine. The Fairy Bell Sisters #5: Sylva & the Lost Treasure. McNamara, Margaret. 2014. (Fairy Bell Sisters Ser.: 5). (ENG.). 144p. (J). (gr. 1-5). pap. 4.99 *(978-0-06-226720-7(5))* HarperCollins Pubs.

—The Fairy Bell Sisters #5: Sylva & the Lost Treasure Vol. 5. McNamara, Margaret. 2014. (Fairy Bell Sisters Ser.: 5). (ENG.). 144p. (J). (gr. 1-5). 15.99 *(978-0-06-226721-4(3))* HarperCollins Pubs.

—The Fairy Bell Sisters #6: Christmas Fairy Magic. McNamara, Margaret. 2014. (Fairy Bell Sisters Ser.: 6). (ENG.). 144p. (J). (gr. 1-5). pap. 4.99 *(978-0-06-226723-8(X),* Balzer & Bray) HarperCollins Pubs.

Collingridge, Richard. Blackberry Blue & Other Fairy Tales. Gavin, Jamila. 2015. 240p. (J). (gr. 4-6). 12.99 *(978-1-84853-107-9(9))* Transworld Publishers Ltd. GBR. Dist: Independent Pubs. Group.

Collingridge, Richard. Lionheart. Collingridge, Richard. 2016. (ENG.). 32p. (J). (gr. -1-k). 17.99 *(978-0-545-83321-9(3))* Scholastic, Inc.

—Tiny Little Rocket. Collingridge, Richard. 2018. (ENG.). 32p. (J). (gr. -1-k). 17.99 *(978-1-338-18949-0(2))* Scholastic, Inc.

Collins, Andrew Dawe. Zombies Are Cool. Giangregorio, Anthony. 2013. 38p. pap. 9.99 *(978-1-61199-073-7(4))* Living Dead Pr.

Collins, Chuck. When Love Walked the Earth: An African Myth Retold By. Chiphe, Eva Harley. 2018. (ENG.). 38p. (J). pap. 12.99 *(978-0-692-10905-2(6))* EvaHarleyChiphe.

Collins, Chuckie. Las Ni. Green, Jakayla M. Pouncil, Nory, ed. 2018. (SPA.). 36p. (J). pap. 12.99 *(978-1-7287-7967-6(7))* Independently Published.

Collins, Courtney. I Love to Exercise. Brown, Phoenix. 2008. 28p. pap. 24.95 *(978-1-60563-727-3(0))* America Star Bks.

Collins, Daryl. The Fume in the Tomb. O'neal, Katherine Pebley. 2004. 68p. (J). lib. bdg. 15.00 *(978-1-4242-0901-9(3))* Fitzgerald Bks.

Collins, Daryll. The Itsy Bity Spider. Fuerst, Jeffrey B. 2010. (Rising Readers Ser.). (J). 3.49 *(978-1-60719-689-1(1))* Newmark Learning LLC.

Collins, Daryll, et al. Laff-O-Tronic Animal Jokes!, 1 vol. Dahl, Michael. 2013. (Laff-O-Tronic Joke Books! Ser.). (ENG.). 96p. (J). (gr. 1-3). 25.32 *(978-1-4342-6020-8(8),* Stone Arch Bks.) Capstone.

—Laff-O-Tronic Monster Jokes!, 1 vol. Dahl, Michael. 2013. (Laff-O-Tronic Joke Books! Ser.). (ENG.). 96p. (J). (gr. 1-3). 25.32 *(978-1-4342-6021-5(6),* Stone Arch Bks.) Capstone.

—Laff-O-Tronic School Jokes!, 1 vol. Dahl, Michael. 2013. (Laff-O-Tronic Joke Books! Ser.). (ENG.). 96p. (J). (gr. 1-3). 25.32 *(978-1-4342-6022-2(4),* Stone Arch Bks.) Capstone.

—Laff-O-Tronic Sports Jokes!, 1 vol. Dahl, Michael. 2013. (Laff-O-Tronic Joke Books! Ser.). (ENG.). 96p. (J). (gr. 1-3). 25.32 *(978-1-4342-6023-9(2),* Stone Arch Bks.) Capstone.

Collins, Daryll. Phonics Comics: Super Sam - Level 3: Issue 1. Marks, Melanie. 2006. (ENG.). 24p. (J). (gr. 1-17). per. 3.99 *(978-1-58476-420-5(1),* IKIDS) Innovative Kids.

—Sport Illustrated Kids Baseball Jokes! Hoena, Blake. 2017. (Sports Illustrated Kids All-Star Jokes! Ser.). (ENG.). 64p. (J). (gr. 2-6). lib. bdg. 22.65 *(978-1-4965-5092-7(7),* 136060, Stone Arch Bks.) Capstone.

—Sport Illustrated Kids Football Jokes. Hoena, Blake. 2017. (Sports Illustrated Kids All-Star Jokes! Ser.). (ENG.). 64p. (J). (gr. 2-6). lib. bdg. 22.65 *(978-1-4965-5093-4(5),* 136061, Stone Arch Bks.) Capstone.

Collins, Daryll & Holgate, Douglas. Laff-O-Tronic Joke Books. Dahl, Michael. 2013. (Laff-O-Tronic Joke Books! Ser.). (ENG.). 96p. (J). (gr. 1-3). pap., pap., pap. 14.85 *(978-1-4342-6224-0(3),* Stone Arch Bks.) Capstone.

—Laff-O-Tronic Monster Jokes! Dahl, Michael. 2013. (Laff-O-Tronic Joke Books! Ser.). (ENG.). 96p. (J). (gr. k-3). pap. 29.70 *(978-1-4342-6239-4(1),* Stone Arch Bks.) Capstone.

Collins, Daryll, jt. illus. see Holgate, Douglas.

Collins, Dawn. The Way of the Bear: A Story the Whole Family Colors. Roberts, Kathy. 2016. (Family Coloring Storybooks Ser.: Vol. 1). (ENG.). (J). (gr. k-3). pap. *(978-1-988245-21-8(4))* Mindful Word, The.

—We All Have Wings: A Story the Whole Family Colors. Roberts, Kathy. 2016. (Family Coloring Storybooks Ser.: Vol. 2). (ENG.). (J). (gr. k-3). pap. *(978-1-988245-65-2(6))* Mindful Word, The.

Collins, Don. Head Case Lacrosse Goalie: Sports Fiction with a Winning Edge. Chambers, Sam T. et al. 2009. (ENG.). 95p. (gr. 4-7). pap. 9.95 *(978-1-933979-40-3(2),* 968d1f06-ae22-438f-ae78-3706af59df92) Night Heron Media.

Collins, Erica. Aloha Activity Book. Collins, Erica. 2009. 24p. pap. 4.98 *(978-1-933735-59-7(7))* Pacifica Island Art, Inc.

Collins, Heather. The Bare Naked Book. Stinson, Kathy. 20th anniv. ed. 2006. (ENG.). 32p. (J). (gr. -1-1). pap. 6.95 *(978-1-55451-049-8(X),* 9781554510498) Annick Pr., Ltd. CAN. Dist: Publishers Group West (PGW).

—Get Outside: The Kids Guide to Fun in the Great Outdoors. Drake, Jane & Love, Ann. 2012. (ENG.). 176p. (J). (gr. 1-5). 16.95 *(978-1-55453-802-7(5))* Kids Can Pr., Ltd. CAN. Dist: Hachette Bk. Group.

—Hey Diddle Diddle. 2003. (Traditional Nursery Rhymes Ser.). (ENG.). 12p. (J). (gr. -1 — 1). bds. 3.95 *(978-1-55337-078-9(3))* Kids Can Pr., Ltd. CAN. Dist: Hachette Bk. Group.

—Jack & Jill. 2003. (Traditional Nursery Rhymes Ser.). (ENG.). 12p. (J). (gr. -1 — 1). bds. 3.95 *(978-1-55337-075-8(9))* Kids Can Pr., Ltd. CAN. Dist: Hachette Bk. Group.

—The Kids Book of the Night Sky. Love, Ann & Drake, Jane. 2004. (Family Fun Ser.). (ENG.). 144p. (J). (gr. 3-7). pap. 16.95 *(978-1-55337-128-1(3))* Kids Can Pr., Ltd. CAN. Dist: Hachette Bk. Group.

—Little Miss Muffet. 2003. (Traditional Nursery Rhymes Ser.). (ENG.). 12p. (J). (gr. -1 — 1). bds. 3.95 *(978-1-55337-076-5(7))* Kids Can Pr., Ltd. CAN. Dist: Hachette Bk. Group.

—Pat-A-Cake. 2003. (Traditional Nursery Rhymes Ser.). (ENG.). 12p. (J). (gr. -1 — 1). bds. 3.95 *(978-1-55337-077-2(5))* Kids Can Pr., Ltd. CAN. Dist: Hachette Bk. Group.

—Rain Tonight: A Story of Hurricane Hazel. Pitt, Steve. 2004. (ENG.). 48p. (J). (gr. 3-7). pap. 6.95 *(978-0-88776-641-1(2),* Tundra Bks.) Tundra Bks. CAN. Dist: Penguin Random Hse. LLC.

—She Dared: True Stories of Heroines, Scoundrels, & Renegades. Butts, Ed. 2005. 128p. (J). (gr. 5-9). pap. 8.95 *(978-0-88776-718-0(4),* Tundra Bks.) Tundra Bks. CAN. Dist: Penguin Random Hse. LLC.

Collins, Jacob. The Christmas Candle. Evans, Richard. (ENG.). 32p. (J). (gr. -1-3). 2007. 11.99 *(978-1-4169-5047-9(8));* 2006. 9.99 *(978-1-4169-2682-5(8))* Simon & Schuster Bks. For Young Readers. (Simon & Schuster Bks. For Young Readers).

Collins, Julia B. Ohio Men, Vol. 2. Georgiady, Nicholas P. et al. 2nd rev. ed. Date not set. 44p. (J). (gr. 4-8). pap. 4.50 *(978-0-917961-04-5(8))* Argee Pubs.

Collins, Kelsey. Annie Mouse's Route 66 Adventure: A Photo Journal, vols. 6, vol. 5. Slanina, Anne Maro. 2011. (ENG.). 48p. (J). pap. 14.99 *(978-0-9793379-6-3(8))* Annie Mouse Bks.

—Annie Mouse's Route 66 Family Vacation. Slanina, Anne. 2014. (Adventures of Annie Mouse Ser.). (ENG.). 150p. (J). pap. 9.99 *(978-0-9914094-1-9(8))* Annie Mouse Bks.

Collins, Linda. Boppy & Me. Mazur, Gabrielle. 2013. 38p. pap. 12.95 *(978-1-4507-3906-1(7))* Bush Publishing Inc.

Collins III, John W. Abba!! Abba!! Collins, Lynda A. 2006. (ENG.). 30p. pap. 12.99 *(978-1-4120-9937-0(4))* Trafford Publishing.

Collins, Lois. Crumbdog. Collins, Lois. 2018. (ENG.). 46p. (J). *(978-1-912576-04-3(X))* Boughton, George Publishing.

Collins, Mark C. Grandma Stinks! Collins, Mark C. 2017. (ENG.). (J). (gr. k-4). 17.95 *(978-0-692-83463-3(X))* BRIGHT IDEAS GRAPHICS.

Collins, Matt. Basketball Belles: How Two Teams & One Scrappy Player Put Women's Hoops on the Map. Macy, Sue. 2019. 40p. (J). (gr. 1-4). pap. 7.99 *(978-0-8234-4175-4(X))* Holiday Hse., Inc.

—Out in Left Field. Lemna, Don. 2013. (ENG.). 224p. (J). (gr. 4-6). 22.44 *(978-0-8234-2313-2(1))* Holiday Hse., Inc.

—A Picture Book of Alexander Hamilton. Adler, David A. 2019. (Picture Book Biography Ser.). (ENG.). 32p. (J). (gr. -1-3). 17.99 *(978-0-8234-3961-4(5))* Holiday Hse., Inc.

—A Picture Book of Daniel Boone. Adler, David A. & Adler, Michael S. 2013. (Picture Book Biography Ser.). (ENG.). 32p. (J). (gr. -1-3). 17.95 *(978-0-8234-2748-2(X))* Holiday Hse., Inc.

—A Picture Book of Harry Houdini. Adler, David A. & Adler, Michael S. 2010. (Picture Book Biography Ser.). (ENG.). 32p. (J). (gr. k-3). pap. 7.99 *(978-0-8234-2302-6(6))* Holiday Hse., Inc.

—Roller Derby Rivals. Macy, Sue. (J). 2019. 40p. (gr. 1-4). pap. 7.99 *(978-0-8234-4185-3(7));* 2014. (ENG.). 32p. (gr. -1-3). 16.95 *(978-0-8234-2923-3(7))* Holiday Hse., Inc.

—Trudy's Big Swim: How Gertrude Ederle Swam the English Channel & Took the World by Storm. Macy, Sue. 40p. (J). (gr. 1-4). 2019. pap. 8.99 *(978-0-8234-4189-1(X));* 2017. (ENG.). 16.95 *(978-0-8234-3665-1(9))* Holiday Hse., Inc.

Collins, Mike. A Christmas Carol. Dickens, Charles. 2012. (ENG.). 160p. (Orig.). (gr. 6). lib. bdg. 24.95 *(978-1-907127-40-3(2))* Classical Comics GBR. Dist: Publishers Group West (PGW).

Collins, Mike, et al. A Christmas Carol the Graphic Novel - Original Text: British Edition. Dickens, Charles. ed. 2008. 160p. (Orig.). pap. *(978-1-906332-17-4(7))* Classical Comics.

Collins, Mike. The Chronicles of Arthur: Sword of Fire & Ice. Matthews, John. 2009. (ENG.). 128p. (J). (gr. 3-7). pap. 14.99 *(978-1-4169-5908-3(4),* Aladdin) Simon & Schuster Children's Publishing.

—The Chronicles of Arthur: Sword of Fire & Ice. Matthews, John. 2009. (ENG.). 128p. (J). (gr. 3-7). 21.99 *(978-1-4169-8683-6(9),* Simon & Schuster/Paula Wiseman Bks.) Simon & Schuster/Paula Wiseman Bks.

Collins, Nathan. Anthology of Amazing Women: Trailblazers Who Dared to Be Different. Lawrence, Sandra. 2018. (ENG.). 128p. (J). (gr. 3-7). 17.99 *(978-1-4998-0690-8(6))* Little Bee Books Inc.

Collins, P. The Time Travellers' Aussie Mystery. Collins, S. & Collins, E. 2016. (ENG.). (J). pap. *(978-0-9943344-5-9(1))* South Seas Publishing.

—The Time Travellers' Date with Disaster. Collins, S. & Collins, E. 2018. (ENG.). 110p. (J). (gr. k-6). pap. *(978-0-9943344-6-6(X))* South Seas Publishing.

Collins, P. The Time Travellers' World Cup Conspiracy. Collins, S. & Collins, E. 2019. (ENG.). 142p. (J). pap. ***(978-0-9943344-9-7(4))*** South Seas Publishing.

Collins, Peggy. Eat This! Kid's Field Guide to Fast Food Advertising, 1 vol. Curtis, Andrea. 2018. (ENG.). 40p. (J). (gr. 5-12). pap. 16.95 *(978-0-88995-532-5(8),* 19479690-5878-4db4-b1cc-60245e73e16d) Trifolium Bks., Inc. CAN. Dist: Firefly Bks., Ltd.

—Hungry for Math: Poems to Munch On, 1 vol. Winters, Kari-Lynn & Sherritt-Fleming, Lori. 2014. (ENG.). 32p. (J). (gr. 1-4). 18.95 *(978-1-55455-307-5(5),* aac6e31d-b110-4a20-92b4-40aa93d7223b) Fitzhenry & Whiteside, Ltd. CAN. Dist: Firefly Bks., Ltd.

—Hungry for Science, 1 vol. Winters, Kari-Lynn & Sherritt-Fleming, Lori. 2018. (ENG.). 32p. (J). (gr. k-3). 18.95 *(978-1-55455-396-9(2),* 50a381d4-f6e4-47a0-ad42-a243e4fd7137) Fitzhenry & Whiteside, Ltd. CAN. Dist: Firefly Bks., Ltd.

—Tallula's Atishoo! A Marvellously Mucky Adventure. a Special Limited Edition - Griffiths, Nei. 2015. (ENG.). (J). *(978-1-908702-13-5(3))* Corner To Learn Ltd.

—Tooter's Stinky Wish, 1 vol. Cretney, Brian. 2011. (Tell Me More Storybook Ser.). (ENG.). 32p. (J). (gr. k-2). 18.95 *(978-1-55455-165-1(X),* fd62d527-5e0e-47e6-a80f-450bf77d5068) Trifolium Bks., Inc. CAN. Dist: Firefly Bks., Ltd.

Collins, Peggy. In the Garden. Collins, Peggy. 2009. (ENG.). 40p. (J). 14.95 *(978-1-60433-026-7(0),* Applesauce Pr.) Cider Mill Pr. Bk. Pubs., LLC.

Collins Powell, Judy. You Have Been Invited! Howell, Brian. 2012. (ENG.). 48p. 18.99 *(978-0-9882892-0-8(2))* Wheat State Media LLC.

Collins, Ross. Alligator Action, No. 14. Sparkes, Ali. 2014. (S. W. I. T. C. H. Ser.: 14). (ENG.). 112p. (J). (gr. 2-5). lib. bdg. 27.99 *(978-1-4677-2117-2(4),* 9781467721172, Darby Creek) Lerner Publishing Group.

—The Bag of Bones: The Second Tale from the Five Kingdoms. French, Vivian. 2009. (Tales from the Five

Kingdoms Ser.: 2). (ENG.). 256p. (J). (gr. 3-7). 14.99 *(978-0-7636-4255-6(X))* Candlewick Pr.
—Billy Monster's Daymare. Durant, Alan. 2008. 32p. (J). (gr. -1-2). pap. 6.95 *(978-1-58925-412-1(0))* Tiger Tales.
—Chameleon Chaos, No. 10. Sparkes, Ali. 2014. (S. W. I. T. C. H. Ser.: 10). (ENG.). 112p. (J). (gr. 2-5). lib. bdg. 27.99 *(978-1-4677-2113-4(1)*, 9781467721134, Darby Creek) Lerner Publishing Group.
—The Flight of Dragons: The Fourth Tale from the Five Kingdoms. French, Vivian. 2011. (Tales from the Five Kingdoms Ser.: 4). (ENG.). 208p. (J). (gr. 3-7). 15.99 *(978-0-7636-5083-4(8))* Candlewick Pr.
—The Flight of Dragons: The Fourth Tale from the Five Kingdoms. French, Vivian. 2012. (Tales from the Five Kingdoms Ser.: 4). (ENG.). 256p. (J). (gr. 3-7). pap. 5.99 *(978-0-7636-5133-6(8))* Candlewick Pr.
—Fly Frenzy, No. 2. Sparkes, Ali. 2013. (S. W. I. T. C. H. Ser.: 2). (ENG.). 104p. (J). (gr. 2-5). pap. 7.95 *(978-1-4677-0711-4(2)*, 9781467707114, Darby Creek) Lerner Publishing Group.
—Gecko Gladiator, No. 12. Sparkes, Ali. 2014. (S. W. I. T. C. H. Ser.: 12). (ENG.). 104p. (J). (gr. 2-5). lib. bdg. 27.99 *(978-1-4677-2115-8(8)*, 9781467721158, Darby Creek) Lerner Publishing Group.
—The Heart of Glass: The Third Tale from the Five Kingdoms. French, Vivian. 2010. (Tales from the Five Kingdoms Ser.: 3). (ENG.). 256p. (J). (gr. 3-7). 14.99 *(978-0-7636-4814-5(0))* Candlewick Pr.
—Hugh's Blue Day. Hodgson, Karen J. 2010. 32p. (J). (gr. -1-k). pap. 9.99 *(978-1-907432-00-2(0))* Hogs Back Bks. GBR. Dist: Independent Pubs. Group.
—I Am a Tiger. Newson, Karl. 2019. (ENG.). 32p. (J). (gr. -1-k). 17.99 *(978-1-338-34989-4(9)*, Scholastic Pr.) Scholastic, Inc.
—Littlenose Collection: the Explorer. Grant, John. 2014. (ENG.). 336p. (J). pap. 8.99 *(978-1-4711-2135-7(6)*, Simon & Schuster Children's) Simon & Schuster, Ltd. GBR. Dist: Simon & Schuster, Inc.
—Littlenose Collection: the Magician. Grant, John. 2014. (ENG.). 352p. (J). pap. 8.99 *(978-1-4711-2137-1(2)*, Simon & Schuster Children's) Simon & Schuster, Ltd. GBR. Dist: Simon & Schuster, Inc.
—Littlenose the Magician. Grant, John. 2009. (ENG.). 112p. (J). (gr. k-12). pap. 5.99 *(978-1-84738-201-6(0)*, Simon & Schuster Children's) Simon & Schuster, Ltd. GBR. Dist: Simon & Schuster, Inc.
—Lizard Loopy, Bk. 9. Sparkes, Ali. 2014. (S. W. I. T. C. H. Ser.: 9). (ENG.). 104p. (J). (gr. 2-5). lib. bdg. 27.99 *(978-1-4677-2112-7(3)*, 9781467721127, Darby Creek) Lerner Publishing Group.
—The Music of Zombies. French, Vivian. 2013. (Tales from the Five Kingdoms Ser.: 5). (ENG.). 304p. (J). (gr. 3-7). 15.99 *(978-0-7636-5930-1(4))* Candlewick Pr.
—Newt Nemesis, No. 8. Sparkes, Ali. 2014. (S. W. I. T. C. H. Ser.: 8). (ENG.). 88p. (J). (gr. 2-5). lib. bdg. 27.99 *(978-1-4677-3233-8(8)*, 9781467732338, Darby Creek) Lerner Publishing Group.
—Oh, George! Graves, Sue. 2005. (Reading Corner Ser.). 24p. (J). (gr. k-3). lib. bdg. 22.80 *(978-1-59771-000-8(8))* Sea-To-Sea Pubns.
—The Robe of Skulls: The First Tale from the Five Kingdoms. French, Vivian. 2009. (Tales from the Five Kingdoms Ser.: 1). (ENG.). 208p. (J). (gr. 3-7). pap. 7.99 *(978-0-7636-4364-5(5))* Candlewick Pr.
—The Robe of Skulls: The First Tale from the Five Kingdoms. French, Vivian. 2008. (Tales from the Five Kingdoms Ser.: 1). (ENG.). 208p. (J). (gr. 4-6). 18.69 *(978-0-7636-3531-2(6))* Candlewick Pr.
—When I Woke up I Was a Hippopotamus. MacRae, Tom. 2011. (Andersen Press Picture Books Ser.). (J). 16.95 *(978-0-7613-8099-3(X))* Andersen Pr. GBR. Dist: Lerner Publishing Group.
Collins, Ross. The Elephantom. Collins, Ross. 2015. (ENG.). 40p. (J). (gr. -1-2). 16.99 *(978-0-7636-7591-2(1)*, Templar) Candlewick Pr.
—There's a Bear on My Chair. Collins, Ross. 2018. (ENG.). 24p. (J). (-k). bds. 7.99 *(978-1-5362-0014-0(X)*, Nosy Crow) Candlewick Pr.
—This Is a Dog. Collins, Ross. 2020. (ENG.). 32p. (J). (-k). 16.99 *(978-1-5362-1200-6(8)*, Nosy Crow) Candlewick Pr.
—This Zoo Is Not for You. Collins, Ross. 2018. (ENG.). 32p. (J). (gr. -1-2). 16.99 *(978-1-5362-0015-7(8)*, Nosy Crow) Candlewick Pr.
—What Does an Anteater Eat? Collins, Ross. 2019. (ENG.). 32p. (J). (-k). 16.99 *(978-1-5362-0591-6(5)*, Nosy Crow) Candlewick Pr.
Collins, Ross. Attila, Loolagax & the Eagle. Collins, Ross, tr. McAuliffe, Nichola. 2003. 128p. (J). pap. 10.99 *(978-0-7475-6499-7(X))* Bloomsbury Publishing Plc GBR. Dist: Independent Pubs. Group.
Collins, Sally J. Hamish Mchaggis & the Edinburgh Adventure. Strachan, Linda. 2005. (Hamish Mchaggis Ser.). 26p. (J). per. 9.00 *(978-0-9546701-7-7(5))* GW Publishing GBR. Dist: Gatewood Pr.
—Hamish Mchaggis & the Ghost of Glamis. Strachan, Linda. 2005. (Hamish Mchaggis Ser.). 26p. (J). per. 9.00 *(978-0-9546701-9-1(1))* GW Publishing GBR. Dist: Gatewood Pr.
—Hamish Mchaggis & the Search for the Loch Ness Monster. Strachan, Linda. 2005. 32p. (J). pap. 9.00 *(978-0-9546701-5-3(9))* GW Publishing GBR. Dist: Gatewood Pr.
—Hamish Mchaggis & the Skye Surprise. Strachan, Linda. 2005. (Hamish Mchaggis Ser.). 26p. (J). pap. 9.00 *(978-0-9546701-8-4(3))* GW Publishing GBR. Dist: Gatewood Pr.
Collins, Sarah. The Boy Who Wandered Too Far into the Forest. Collins, Linda Stenberg. 2019. (ENG.). 24p. (J). pap. 13.95 *(978-1-64471-717-2(4))* Covenant Bks.
Collins, Sarah Jean. God Made the Ocean. Collins, Sarah Jean. 2019. (God Made Ser.). (ENG.). 22p. (J). bds. 7.99 *(978-1-4964-3633-7(4)*, 20_32104, Tyndale Kids) Tyndale Hse. Pubs.
—God Made the Rain Forest. Collins, Sarah Jean. 2020. (God Made Ser.). (ENG.). 20p. (J). bds. 7.99 *(978-1-4964-3632-0(6)*, 20_32354, Tyndale Kids) Tyndale Hse. Pubs.
Collins, Simon. The Enchanted Bus: Lily & the Lost Soldiers. Stamp, Anne. 2017. (ENG.). 68p. (J). pap. *(978-1-909985-22-3(8))* Green, Callisto.
—Space Bugs & Selfies: A Story about Being Yourself, Space Bugs & Farting. Genn, Lex. 2018. (ENG.). 30p. (J). (gr. k-6). pap. *(978-1-911589-48-8(2)*, Choir Pr., The) Action Publishing Technology Ltd.
Collins Staff. American Flag Q & A. Thomson, Sarah L. 2008. 48p. (J). (gr. k-4). 16.99 *(978-0-06-089959-2(X)*, Collins) HarperCollins Pubs.
Collins, Stephen. Baby's First Bank Heist. Whalley, Jim. 2019. (ENG.). 32p. (J). 17.99 *(978-1-5476-0062-5(4)*, 900196647, Bloomsbury Children's Bks.) Bloomsbury Publishing USA.
Collinson, Lorraine. The Early Days & Misadventures of Ravensthorpe Tinker: A Cocker Spaniel Tale. Collinson, Lorraine. 2018. (Ravensthorpe Tinker Ser.: Vol. 1). (ENG.). 42p. (J). (gr. 2-4). pap. *(978-1-911589-68-6(7)*, Choir Pr., The) Action Publishing Technology Ltd.
Colllins, Linda. Boppy & Me. Mazur, Gabrielle. 2013. 38p. 14.97 *(978-1-4507-3897-2(4))* Bush Publishing Inc.
Colman, Audrey. Walter Canis Inflatus: Walter the Farting Dog, Latin-Language Edition. Kotzwinkle, William & Murray, Glenn. Dobbin, Rob, tr. from ENG. 2004. (Walter the Farting Dog Ser.).Tr. of Walter the Farting Dog. (LAT.). 32p. (J). (gr. k-4). 15.95 *(978-1-58394-110-2(X)*, Frog Children's Bks.) North Atlantic Bks.
—Walter el Perro Pedorrero. Kotzwinkle, William & Murray, Glenn. Bohorquez, Eduardo, tr. from ENG. 2004. (Walter the Farting Dog Ser.).Tr. of Walter the Farting Dog. (SPA.). 32p. (J). (gr. k-4). 15.95 *(978-1-58394-103-4(7)*, Frog Children's Bks.) North Atlantic Bks.
—Walter the Farting Dog: Banned from the Beach. Kotzwinkle, William et al. 2009. (ENG.). 32p. (J). (gr. k-3). pap. 7.99 *(978-0-14-241394-4(1)*, Puffin Books) Penguin Young Readers Group.
—Walter the Farting Dog Goes on a Cruise. Kotzwinkle, William et al. (ENG.). 32p. (J). (gr. k-3). 2008. pap. 7.99 *(978-0-14-241142-1(6)*, Puffin Books); 2006. 16.99 *(978-0-525-47714-3(4)*, Dutton Books for Young Readers) Penguin Young Readers Group.
—Walter the Farting Dog Goes on a Cruise. Katzwinkle, William et al. 2008. (J). 13.99 *(978-1-59319-939-5(2))* LeapFrog Enterprises, Inc.
—Walter the Farting Dog: Trouble at the Yard Sale. Kotzwinkle, William & Murray, Glenn. 2006. (ENG.). 32p. (J). (gr. k-3). reprint ed. pap. 7.99 *(978-0-14-240626-7(0)*, Puffin Books) Penguin Young Readers Group.
Cologne, Starla. Miss Flavia & the Cookie Cottage. Schmidt, Kristina Edelkamp. 2009. 28p. pap. 7.99 *(978-1-935125-61-7(3))* Robertson Publishing.
Coloji, Livia. Everything Tells Us about God. Hyde, Katherine Bolger. l.t. ed. 2018. (ENG.). 32p. (J). 19.95 *(978-1-944967-29-1(X))* Ancient Faith Publishing.
—The Fable of the Bully Dragon: Facing Your Fears. Dinardo, Jeff. 2015. (Funny Bone Readers (tm) — Dealing with Bullies Ser.). (ENG.). 24p. (J). (gr. k-2). lib. bdg. 19.99 *(978-1-63440-000-8(3))* Red Chair Pr.
Coloji, Livia. Five Minute Bedtime Stories. Cottage Door Press, ed. 2020. (ENG.). 192p. (J). (gr. -1-2). 9.99 ***(978-1-68052-860-2(2)***, 2003150) Cottage Door Pr.
Coloji, Livia. Look Inside Nativity, 1 vol. Rock, Lois. ed. 2016. (ENG.). 12p. (J). (gr. -1 — 1). 12.99 *(978-0-7459-7611-2(5)*, Lion Books) Lion Hudson PLC GBR. Dist: Independent Pubs. Group.
—Look Inside Noah's Ark. Rock, Lois. ed. 2016. (ENG.). 12p. (J). (gr. k-2). 12.99 *(978-0-7459-7612-9(3))* Lion Hudson PLC GBR. Dist: Independent Pubs. Group.
Coloma, Lester. Tea Leaves. Coloma, Lester, tr. Lipp, Frederick J. 2003. (J). 32p. (gr. 1-6). 15.95 *(978-1-59034-998-4(9))*; 33p. pap. *(978-1-59034-999-1(7))* Mondo Publishing.
Colombet, Julie. Hair! Animal Fur, Wool, & More. Singer, Marilyn. 2019. (ENG.). 40p. (J). (gr. 2-5). 26.65 *(978-1-5124-4915-0(6)*, Millbrook Pr.) Lerner Publishing Group.
Colombet, Julie. The Society of Distinguished Lemmings, 1 vol. Colombet, Julie. 2020. (ENG.). 40p. (J). (gr. 1-5). 17.99 *(978-1-68263-156-0(7))* Peachtree Publishing Co. Inc.
Colombo, Alexandra. It's Raining, It's Pouring: Set Of 6. Strom, Laura Layton. 2014. (Shared Reading Foundations Ser.). (J). (gr. 1). 36.00 net. *(978-1-4900-0044-2(5))* Benchmark Education Co.
—It's Raining, It's Pouring Book Set. Strom, Laura Layton. 2014. (Shared Reading Foundations Ser.). (J). (gr. 1). 72.00 net. *(978-1-4900-0014-5(3))* Benchmark Education Co.
—The Lemonade Stand. Lindeen, Mary. 2015. (Early Rising Readers Ser.). (J). (gr. -1-k). 5.83 *(978-1-4788-1577-8(9))* Newmark Learning LLC.
—Michael Recycle. Bethel, Ellie. 2008. (Michael Recycle Ser.). 28p. (J). (gr. 1-3). 15.99 *(978-1-60010-224-0(7)*, 9781600102240) Idea & Design Works, LLC.
—Michael Recycle & Bootleg Peg. Patterson, Ellie. 2014. (Michael Recycle Ser.). 28p. (J). (gr. 1-3). 17.99 *(978-1-61377-708-4(6)*, 9781613777084) Idea & Design Works, LLC.
—Michael Recycle & the Tree Top Cops. Patterson, Ellie. 2012. (Michael Recycle Ser.). (ENG.). 24p. (J). (gr. 1-3). 15.99 *(978-1-61377-161-7(4)*, 9781613771617) Idea & Design Works, LLC.
—Michael Recycle Meets Borat the Space Cat. Patterson, Ellie. 2020. (Michael Recycle Ser.). 24p. (J). (gr. 1-3). 15.99 *(978-1-68405-653-8(5))* Idea & Design Works, LLC.
—Michael Recycle Meets Litterbug Doug. Bethel, Ellie. 2009. (Michael Recycle Ser.). 24p. (J). (gr. 1-3). 15.99 *(978-1-60010-392-6(8)*, 9781600103926) Idea & Design Works, LLC.
—Michael Recycle Saves Christmas. Bethel, Ellie. 2010. (Michael Recycle Ser.). 32p. (J). (gr. 1-3). 15.99 *(978-1-60010-843-3(1)*, 9781600108433) Idea & Design Works, LLC.
—One Snowy Day. Parkes, Brenda. 2015. (Shared Reading Contemporary Tales Ser.). (J). (gr. k-1). *(978-1-4900-2120-1(5))* Benchmark Education Co.
—One Snowy Day: Big Book Edition. Parkes, Brenda. 2015. (Shared Reading Contemporary Tales Ser.). (J). (gr. k-1). 16.99 *(978-1-4900-2115-7(9))* Benchmark Education Co.
—El Puesto de Limonada. Lindeen, Mary. 2016. (Early Rising Readers Ser.). (SPA.). (J). (gr. -1). 6.67 *(978-1-4788-3701-5(2))* Newmark Learning LLC.
Colombo, Alexandra. Young Fionn: Small Kid, Big Legend. Moore, Ronan. 2020. (ENG.). 224p. (J). pap. 10.95 ***(978-0-7171-8586-3(9))*** Gill Bks. IRL. Dist: Casemate Pubs. & Bk. Distributors, LLC.
Colombo, Alexandra & Zahler, Thom. Michael Recycle's Environmental Adventures. Wharton, Ellie. 2017. (Michael Recycle Ser.). 88p. (J). (gr. 1-3). 14.99 *(978-1-63140-985-1(9))* Idea & Design Works, LLC.
Colombo, Angelo. Alex & Penny's Italy Jigsaw Book. Francia, Giada. 2007. (ENG.). 14p. (gr. 1-3). pap. 14.95 *(978-88-544-0242-3(7)*, White Star) Rizzoli International Pubns., Inc.
—Alex & Penny's Wild West Jigsaw Book. Francia, Giada. 2007. (ENG.). 14p. (gr. 1-3). pap. 14.95 *(978-88-544-0285-0(0)*, White Star) Rizzoli International Pubns., Inc.
—Ballooning over Italy: An Extraordinary Voyage Packed with Games & Fantastic Adventures; Special Agents. Francia, Giada, ed. Ezrin, Amy, tr. 2007. (Alex & Penny Ser.). (ENG.). 80p. (J). (gr. 2-5). 14.95 *(978-88-544-0160-0(9)*, White Star) Rizzoli International Pubns., Inc.
Colombo, David. Silly Soup. Helms, Tina, photos by. Korty, Carol. Landes, William-Alan, ed. 2003. (Plays & Play Collections). 128p. (Orig.). (J). (gr. k-6). pap. 17.00 *(978-0-88734-679-8(0))* Players Pr., Inc.
Colombo, Sophia. Bullet Journal: Cute Dot Grid Narwhals Notebook (Composition Book, Journal) (5 X 8") Colombo, Sophia. 2019. (ENG.). 134p. (J). pap. 6.99 ***(978-1-7083-4220-3(6))*** Independently Published.
Colon, Daniel. Where Is the Empire State Building? Pascal, Janet B. & Who HQ. 2015. (Where Is? Ser.). (ENG.). 112p. (J). (gr. 3-7). 5.99 *(978-0-448-48426-6(9)*, Penguin Workshop) Penguin Young Readers Group.
—Where Is the Grand Canyon? Who HQ & O'Connor, Jim. 2015. (Where Is? Ser.). (ENG.). 112p. (J). (gr. 3-7). 5.99 *(978-0-448-48357-3(2)*, Penguin Workshop) Penguin Young Readers Group.
Colon, Ernie. Everything You Need for Simple Science Fair Projects: Grades 3-5. Friedhoffer, Bob. 2006. (Scientific American Science Fair Projects Ser.). 48p. (gr. 3-5). lib. bdg. 27.00 *(978-0-7910-9054-1(X))* Facts On File, Inc.
—Everything You Need for Winning Science Fair Projects: Grades 5-7. Friedhoffer, Bob. 2006. (Scientific American Science Fair Projects Ser.). 48p. (gr. 4-6). lib. bdg. 27.00 *(978-0-7910-9056-5(6))* Facts On File, Inc.
Colon, Ernie, jt. illus. see Drozd, Jerzy.
Colon Pena, Eduardo. El Tesoro Del Pirata. Colon Pena, Eduardo. Ortiz Bello, Frank Joseph, ed. 2018. (SPA.). 34p. (J). pap. 12.00 *(978-1-881741-81-7(8))* Ediciones Eleos.
Colon, Raul. Abuelo. Dorros, Arthur. 2014. (ENG.). 32p. (J). (gr. -1-3). 17.99 *(978-0-06-168627-6(1))* HarperCollins Pubs.
Colón, Raúl. Annie & Helen. Hopkinson, Deborah. 2012. 48p. (J). (gr. -1-3). 17.99 *(978-0-375-85706-5(0)*, Schwartz & Wade Bks.) Random Hse. Children's Bks.
—Good-Bye, Havana! Hola, New York! Colon, Edie. 2011. (ENG.). 32p. (J). (gr. -1-3). 19.99 *(978-1-4424-0674-2(7)*, Simon & Schuster/Paula Wiseman Bks.) Simon & Schuster/Paula Wiseman Bks.
—How to Bake an American Pie. Wilson, Karma. 2007. (ENG.). 40p. (J). (gr. -1-3). 19.99 *(978-0-689-86506-0(6)*, McElderry, Margaret K. Bks.) McElderry, Margaret K. Bks.
—My Name Is Gabito: The Life of Gabriel Garcia Marquez. Brown, Monica. 2007. (ENG.). 32p. (J). (gr. -1-3). 15.95 *(978-0-87358-934-5(3))* Cooper Square Publishing Llc.
—My Name Is Gabito/Me Llamo Gabito: The Life of Gabriel Garcia Marquez/la Vida de Gabriel Garcia Marquez. Brown, Monica. 2007. (ENG, SPA & MUL.). 32p. (J). (gr. -1-3). 15.95 *(978-0-87358-908-6(4))* Cooper Square Publishing Llc.
Colon, Raul. Once upon a Time/Habia una Vez: Traditional Latin American Tales/Cuentos Tradicionales Latinoamericanos (Bilingual Spanish-English Children's Book) Martinez, Rueben. 2010. (ENG.). 96p. (J). (gr. -1-3). 19.99 *(978-0-06-146895-7(9)*, HarperCollins Español) HarperCollins Christian Publishing.
Colón, Raúl. Play Ball! Posada, Jorge. 2006. (ENG.). 32p. (J). (gr. 2-4). 21.19 *(978-1-4169-0687-2(8))* Simon & Schuster, Inc.
—Roberto Clemente: Pride of the Pittsburgh Pirates. Winter, Jonah. 2008. (ENG.). 40p. (J). (gr. -1-3). 8.99 *(978-1-4169-5082-0(6)*, Atheneum Bks. for Young Readers) Simon & Schuster Children's Publishing.
—Roberto Clemente: Pride of the Pittsburgh Pirates. Winter, Jonah. 2005. (ENG.). 40p. (J). (gr. k-3). 22.44 *(978-0-689-85643-3(1))* Simon & Schuster, Inc.
—Sí, Puedes. Posada, Jorge. 2010.Tr. of Play Ball!. (SPA.). 32p. (J). (gr. 1-5). 8.99 *(978-1-4169-9826-6(8)*, Simon & Schuster/Paula Wiseman Bks.) Simon & Schuster/Paula Wiseman Bks.
—Tomas & the Library Lady. Mora, Pat. 2007. (gr. k-3). 18.00 *(978-0-7569-7935-5(8))* Perfection Learning Corp.
Colón, Raúl. Imagine! Colón, Raúl. 2018. (ENG.). 48p. (J). (gr. -1-3). 17.99 *(978-1-4814-6273-0(3)*, Simon & Schuster/Paula Wiseman Bks.) Simon & Schuster/Paula Wiseman Bks.
Colonna, Morgan. Muir Magic! Selvaraj, Sasha Emma. 2018. (ENG.). 22p. (J). (gr. 1-3). pap. 9.99 *(978-1-7335173-0-0(8))* Emma, Sasha.
Colorcocktail. EZ & the Intangibles. Katz, Bob. 2018. (ENG.). 150p. (J). (gr. 4-7). 20.95 *(978-1-947548-45-9(X)*, Fitzroy Bks.) Regal Hse. Publishing, LLC.
Coloring Books, Kitanie. Doodle Dots. Riley, Jessie. 2016. (ENG.). (J). (gr. k-6). pap. 12.95 *(978-1-935734-87-1(3))* Kitanie Bks.
—One Big Gigantic Herd of Invisible Cosmic Zebras Coloring Book. Riley, Jessie. 2016. (ENG.). (YA). (gr. 7-12). pap. 10.95 *(978-1-935734-88-8(1))* Kitanie Bks.
Colpoys, Allison. All the Ways to Be Smart. Bell, Davina. 2019. (ENG.). 32p. (J). (gr. -1-1). 16.99 *(978-1-947534-96-4(3))* Scribe Pubns. AUS. Dist: Consortium Bk. Sales & Distribution.
—Captain Starfish. Bell, Davina. 2018. (ENG.). 40p. (J). (gr. -1-3). 16.99 *(978-1-4197-2837-2(7)*, Abrams Bks. for Young Readers) Abrams, Inc.
—Grandpa's Stories. Coelho, Joseph. 2019. (ENG.). 32p. (J). (gr. -1-3). 16.99 *(978-1-4197-3498-4(9)*, Abrams Bks. for Young Readers) Abrams, Inc.
Colquhoun, Christine. Pick-a-WooWoo - the Little Sparkle in Me: My Sparkle Is A Gift to Feel Hear & See, 16 vols., Vol. 15. Colquhoun, Christine. 2010. 32p. pap. *(978-0-9806520-8-6(1))* Pick-a-Woo Woo Pubs.
Colson, A. W. & Renda, Joseph. Manassas, Please Slow Down. Glenn, Judith. 2010. 60p. pap. 21.99 *(978-1-4490-6682-6(8))* AuthorHouse.
Colton, Ellie. Bible Blessings. Elkins, Stephen. 2003. (Lulla-Bible Series for Little Ones). 32p. (J). 9.99 incl. audio compact disk *(978-0-8054-2761-5(9))* B&H Publishing Group.
—The Bible Prayer Collection: 30 Life Changing Prayers from the Bible for Children. Elkins, Stephen. 2003. 64p. (J). (gr. k-3). 9.99 incl. audio compact disk *(978-0-8054-2758-5(9))* B&H Publishing Group.
—Bible Prayers. Elkins, Stephen. 2003. (Lulla-Bible Series for Little Ones). 32p. (J). 9.99 incl. audio compact disk *(978-0-8054-2755-4(4))* B&H Publishing Group.
—Bible Promises. Elkins, Stephen. 2003. (Lulla-Bible Series for Little Ones). 32p. (J). 9.99 incl. audio compact disk *(978-0-8054-2756-1(2))* B&H Publishing Group.
—Bible Verses. Elkins, Stephen. 2003. (Lulla-Bible Series for Little Ones). 32p. (J). 9.99 incl. audio compact disk *(978-0-8054-2757-8(0))* B&H Publishing Group.
—First Steps in Faith: Beginning Lessons of God's Love. Elkins, Stephen. 2006. (First Steps in Faith Ser.). 25p. (J). (gr. -1-k). bds. 9.99 incl. audio compact disk *(978-0-8054-2662-5(0))* B&H Publishing Group.
—First Steps in Prayer. Elkins, Stephen. 2006. (First Steps Ser.). 32p. (J). 9.99 *(978-0-8054-2663-2(9))* B&H Publishing Group.
—First Steps to God: Beginning Lessons of God's Love. Elkins, Stephen. 2006. (First Steps Ser.). 25p. (J). (gr. -1-k). 9.99 incl. audio compact disk *(978-0-8054-2661-8(2))* B&H Publishing Group.
—The LullaBible: A Musical Treasury for Mother & Baby. Elkins, Stephen. 2004. (J). (gr. -1). 223p. 14.99 *(978-0-8054-2388-4(5))*; 224p. 19.99 incl. audio *(978-0-8054-2389-1(3))* B&H Publishing Group.
—My LullaBible A to Z Promise Book. Elkins, Stephen. 2007. 36p. (J). (gr. -1). bds. 14.99 incl. audio compact disk *(978-0-8054-2657-1(4))* B&H Publishing Group.
Colton, Nicola. The Cool Cat Club. Colton, Nicola. 2020. (Jasper & Scruff Ser.: 1). (ENG.). 96p. (J). (gr. 1-4). 18.99 *(978-1-68010-202-4(8))*; pap. 6.99 *(978-1-68010-460-8(8))* Tiger Tales.
—The Treasure Hunt. Colton, Nicola. 2020. (Jasper & Scruff Ser.: 2). (ENG.). 96p. (J). (gr. 1-4). 18.99 *(978-1-68010-203-1(6))*; pap. 6.99 *(978-1-68010-461-5(6))* Tiger Tales.
Columbin, Corey. Silly Rhymes for Fun Times. Wigden, Susan. 2011. 20p. pap. 11.95 *(978-1-60888-107-9(5))* Nimble Bks. LLC.
Columbo, Silvia. Child's Bible. Mediana, Rose. 2019. (ENG.). (J). pap. 16.95 *(978-0-8091-6791-3(3))* Paulist Pr.
Colwell, Emerson/Mylon, Jr. The Fisher Cat. Colwell, Emerson/Mylon, Jr. 2009. (ENG.). 36p. (J). pap. 14.95 *(978-0-9840916-1-4(0))* TINK INK Publishing.
Comahig, Aljon. Deekin Duck & the Road to Find Purpose. Wolfe, Kathryn. 2016. (ENG.). (J). 22.95 *(978-1-63525-809-7(X))* Christian Faith Publishing.
Combes, M. On the Go. 2019. (My First Interactive Board Book Ser.). (ENG.). 12p. (J). bds. 9.99 *(978-2-7338-6734-1(2))* Auzou, Philippe Editions FRA. Dist: Consortium Bk. Sales & Distribution.
Combs, Bradley. Lexi's Tea Party. Tuttle, Mark. 2011. 32p. pap. 24.95 *(978-1-4560-9919-0(1))* America Star Bks.
Combs, Covers by. Dragon Rising: A Mulan Inspired Fantasy. Craven, Melissa A. & Haines, Caitlin, eds. 2020. (Hidden Warrior Ser.: Vol. 1). (ENG.). 312p. (J). pap. 14.99 ***(978-1-6617-9608-2(7))*** Independently Published.
Combs, Covers by. Glass Princess. Lynn, M. Craven, Melissa A., ed. 2019. (Fantasy & Fairytales Ser.: Vol. 5). (ENG.). 292p. (J). pap. 14.99 *(978-1-7974-7470-0(7))* Independently Published.
Combs, Paul. The Floating Zoo. Scarff, Ruth. 2003. 21p. (J). pap. *(978-0-87398-289-4(4))* Sword of the Lord Pubs.
Comella, Angels. Let's Talk about God/Hablemos de Dios. Comella, Angels. Twomey, Lisa A., tr. from SPA. 2005. (SPA & ENG.). 28p. (J). (gr. -1-3). 9.95 *(978-0-8146-2361-9(1))* Liturgical Pr.
Comer, Bella. Barry Blue & the Blueberry Trall. Comer, Bella. 2019. (ENG.). 26p. (J). 18.00 *(978-0-9990090-6-2(0))* Hilliard Pr.
Comfort, Louise. Find & Speak English Words: Look, Find, Say. Millar, Louise. 2018. (Find & Speak Ser.). (ENG.). 64p. (J). (gr. -1-k). pap. 9.99 *(978-1-911509-40-0(3))* B Small Publishing GBR. Dist: Independent Pubs. Group.
—Find & Speak Spanish Words: Look, Find, Say. Millar, Louise. 2018. (Find & Speak Ser.). (ENG.). 64p. (J). (gr. -1-k). pap. 9.99 *(978-1-911509-42-4(X))* B Small Publishing GBR. Dist: Independent Pubs. Group.
—Hide & Speak French. Bruzzone, Catherine & Martinneau, Susan. 2003. (Hide & Speak Ser.). (ENG.). 32p. (J). (gr. 2-6). pap. 8.99 *(978-0-7641-2588-1(5)*, B.E.S. Publishing) Peterson's.
—Hide & Speak Spanish. Bruzzone, Catherine & Martineau, Susan. 2003. (Hide & Speak Ser.). (ENG.). 32p. (J). (gr. 2-6). pap. 9.99 *(978-0-7641-2589-8(3)*, B.E.S. Publishing) Peterson's.
—My French Sticker Dictionary: Everyday Words & Popular Themes in Colorful Sticker Scenes. Bruzzone, Catherine

C

& Millar, Louise. 2013. (Sticker Dictionaries Ser.). (ENG.). 24p. (J). (gr. -1-1). pap. 6.99 *(978-1-4380-0253-8(X)*, B.E.S. Publishing) Peterson's.

—El Palacio de Las Hadas. Bateson, Maggie. Sánchez Abulí, Enrique, tr. 2007. (SPA & ENG.). 14p. (J). (gr. 2-4). pap. 34.95 *(978-84-666-1678-2(0))* Ediciones B ESP. Dist: Independent Pubs. Group.

Comfort, Louise & Dix, Steph. French-English Picture Dictionary. Bruzzone, Catherine et al. ed. 2011. (First Bilingual Picture Dictionaries Ser.). (ENG.). 48p. (J). (gr. 2-4). pap. 7.99 *(978-0-7641-4660-2(2)*, B.E.S. Publishing) Peterson's.

Comfort, Mike & Baisley, Stephen. Discovering Oregon. Matchette, Dennis, photos by. Matchette, Katharine E. (YA). (gr. 5-9). spiral bd. 13.00 *(978-0-9645045-4-7(5))* Deka Pr.

Comics, Marvel. Marvel's Black Widow Prelude. 2020. (ENG.). 136p. (YA). (gr. 8-17). pap. 14.99 *(978-1-302-92108-8(8))* Marvel Worldwide, Inc.

Comicup Design Sudio SL Staff. Doo Good Together, Scooby-Doo! Jones, Christianne. 2019. (Scooby-Doo! Ser.). (ENG.). 32p. (J). (gr. -1-1). lib. bdg. 17.95 *(978-1-68446-108-0(1)*, 141347, Capstone Editions) Capstone.

Comins, Andy. The Frog Scientist. Turner, Pamela S. 2011. (Scientists in the Field Ser.). (ENG.). 64p. (J). (gr. 5-7). pap. 9.99 *(978-0-547-57698-5(6)*, 1458452) Houghton Mifflin Harcourt Publishing Co.

—Stronger Than Steel: Spider Silk DNA & the Quest for Better Bulletproof Vests, Sutures, & Parachute Rope. Heos, Bridget. (Scientists in the Field Ser.). (ENG.). 80p. (J). (gr. 5-7). 2017. pap. 9.99 *(978-0-544-93247-0(1)*, 1657957, HMH Books For Young Readers); 2013. 18.99 *(978-0-547-68126-9(7)*, 1475667) Houghton Mifflin Harcourt Publishing Co.

Comins, Andy, photos by. Crow Smarts: Inside the Brain of the World's Brightest Bird. Turner, Pamela S. 2016. (Scientists in the Field Ser.). (ENG., 80p. (J). (gr. 5-7). 18.99 *(978-0-544-41619-2(8)*, 1597282, HMH Books For Young Readers) Houghton Mifflin Harcourt Publishing Co.

—The Orca Scientists. Valice, Kimberly Lynn Perez. 2018. (Scientists in the Field Ser.). (ENG., 80p. (J). (gr. 5-7). 18.99 *(978-0-544-89826-4(5)*, 1653794, HMH Books For Young Readers) Houghton Mifflin Harcourt Publishing Co.

Communication Design (Firm) Staff, jt. illus. see Meganck, Robert.

Comoglio, Eduardo. The Kangaroo That Couldn't Jump. Phethean, Lee. 2019. (ENG.). 26p. (J). pap. 9.95 ***(978-1-6983-9512-8(4))*** Independently Published.

Compere, Janet. Louis Braille. Davidson, Margaret. (FRE.). 80p. (J). pap. 5.99 *(978-0-590-71110-4(5))* Scholastic, Inc.

Compiet, Iris. Court of Shadows. Roux, Madeleine. (House of Furies Ser.: 2). (ENG.). (YA). (gr. 9). 2019. 448p. pap. 9.99 *(978-0-06-249871-7(1))*; 2018. 432p. 17.99 *(978-0-06-249870-0(3))* HarperCollins Pubs. (HarperTeen).

—House of Furies. Roux, Madeleine. 2018. (House of Furies Ser.: 1). (ENG.). 432p. (YA). (gr. 9). pap. 9.99 *(978-0-06-249859-5(2)*, HarperTeen) HarperCollins Pubs.

—Tomb of Ancients. Roux, Madeleine. 2019. (House of Furies Ser.: 3). (ENG.). 384p. (J). (gr. 9). 17.99 *(978-0-06-249873-1(8)*, HarperTeen) HarperCollins Pubs.

Comport, Sally Wern. Ada's Violin: The Story of the Recycled Orchestra of Paraguay. Hood, Susan. 2016. (ENG.). 40p. (J). (gr. -1-3). 18.99 *(978-1-4814-3095-1(5)*, Simon & Schuster Bks. For Young Readers) Simon & Schuster Bks. For Young Readers.

—Bearwalker. Bruchac, Joseph. 2010. (ENG.). 240p. (J). (gr. 5). pap. 7.99 *(978-0-06-112315-3(3)*, HarperCollins) HarperCollins Pubs. Ltd. GBR. Dist: HarperCollins Pubs.

—The Dark Pond. Bruchac, Joseph. 2005. (ENG.). 160p. (J). (gr. 5-18). pap. 7.99 *(978-0-06-052998-7(9))* HarperCollins Pubs.

—The Dark Pond. Bruchac, Joseph. 2005. 142p. (gr. 5-9). 17.00 *(978-0-7569-5436-9(3))* Perfection Learning Corp.

—Dream March: Dr. Martin Luther King, Jr., & the March on Washington. Nelson, Vaunda Micheaux. 2017. (Step into Reading Ser.). (ENG.). 48p. (J). (gr. k-3). lib. bdg. 12.99 *(978-1-101-93670-2(3)*, Random Hse. Bks. for Young Readers) Random Hse. Children's Bks.

—Dream March: Dr. Martin Luther King, Jr. , & the March on Washington. Nelson, Vaunda Micheaux. 2017. (Step into Reading Ser.). (ENG.). 48p. (J). (gr. k-3). 4.99 *(978-1-101-93669-6(X)*, Random Hse. Bks. for Young Readers) Random Hse. Children's Bks.

—First Kids. Davis, Gibbs. 2009. (Step into Reading: Step 4 Ser.). (ENG.). 48p. (J). (gr. 1-3). lib. bdg. 16.19 *(978-0-375-92218-3(0))* Random House Publishing Group.

—First Kids. Davis, Gibbs. 2004. (Step into Reading Ser.). (ENG.). 48p. (J). (gr. 2-4). pap. 4.99 *(978-0-375-82218-6(6)*, Random Hse. Bks. for Young Readers) Random Hse. Children's Bks.

—For Your Paws Only. Frederick, Heather Vogel. 2006. (Spy Mice Ser.: 2). (ENG.). 272p. (J). (gr. 3-6). pap. 5.99 *(978-1-4169-4025-8(1)*, Simon & Schuster Bks. For Young Readers) Simon & Schuster Bks. For Young Readers.

—For Your Paws Only. Frederick, Heather Vogel. 2005. (Spy Mice Ser.). (ENG.). 272p. (J). (gr. 4-6). 9.95 *(978-1-4169-0573-8(1))* Simon & Schuster Children's Publishing.

—How to Disappear Completely & Never Be Found. Nickerson, Sara. 2003. (ENG.). 288p. (J). (gr. 5-18). pap. 5.99 *(978-0-06-441027-4(7))* HarperCollins Pubs.

—Louisiana Purchase. Roop, Peter & Roop, Connie. 2004. 84p. (J). lib. bdg. 15.00 *(978-1-4242-0908-8(0))* Fitzgerald Bks.

—Louisiana Purchase. Roop, Peter & Roop, Connie. 2004. (Ready-For-Chapters Ser.). (ENG.). 80p. (J). (gr. 2-5). pap. 6.99 *(978-0-689-86443-8(4)*, Simon & Schuster/Paula Wiseman Bks.) Simon & Schuster/Paula Wiseman Bks.

—Love Will See You Through: Martin Luther King Jr. 's Six Guiding Beliefs (as Told by His Niece) Watkins, Angela Farris. 2014. (ENG.). 32p. (J). (gr. 1-6). 18.99 *(978-1-4169-8693-5(6)*, Simon & Schuster Bks. For Young Readers) Simon & Schuster Bks. For Young Readers.

—Night Wings. Bruchac, Joseph. 2018. (ENG.). 224p. (J). (gr. 3-7). pap. 6.99 *(978-0-06-112321-4(8))* HarperCollins Pubs.

—On Point. Khan, Hena. 2018. (Zayd Saleem, Chasing the Dream Ser.: 2). (ENG.). 144p. (J). (gr. 2-5). 16.99 *(978-1-5344-1202-6(6))*; pap. 6.99 *(978-1-5344-1201-9(8))* Simon & Schuster Bks. For Young Readers. (Salaam Reads).

—Pirate's Revenge. Malcolm, Jahnna N. 2003. 77p. (J). *(978-1-931020-09-1(4))* HOP, LLC.

—Power Forward. Khan, Hena. 2018. (Zayd Saleem, Chasing the Dream Ser.: 1). (ENG.). 144p. (J). (gr. 2-5). 16.99 *(978-1-5344-1198-2(4))*; pap. 6.99 *(978-1-5344-1199-9(2))* Simon & Schuster Bks. For Young Readers. (Salaam Reads).

—The Return of Skeleton Man. Bruchac, Joseph. 144p. (J). 2006. (gr. 5-9). lib. bdg. 16.89 *(978-0-06-058091-9(7))*; 2. 2008. (Skeleton Man Ser.: 2). (ENG.). (gr. 3-8). pap. 7.99 *(978-0-06-058092-6(5))* HarperCollins Pubs.

—Skeleton Man. Bruchac, Joseph. 2003. 114p. (J). (gr. 5). 12.65 *(978-0-7569-3399-9(4))* Perfection Learning Corp.

—The Story of Thanksgiving. Bartlett, Robert Merrill. rev. ed. 2004. 30p. (J). (gr. k-4). reprint ed. *(978-0-7567-7757-9(7))* DIANE Publishing Co.

—The Story of Thanksgiving. Bartlett, Robert Merrill. Date not set. 40p. (J). (gr. 2-5). 5.99 *(978-0-06-446238-9(2))* HarperCollins Pubs.

—Treasure Island: The Treasure Map. Stevenson, Robert Louis. 2007. (Easy Reader Classics Ser.). (ENG.). 32p. (J). (gr. k-3). lib. bdg. 27.07 *(978-1-59961-342-0(5)*, 6219) Spotlight.

—Vampire State Building. Levy, Elizabeth. 2003. (ENG.). 112p. (J). pap. 4.99 *(978-0-06-000052-3(X))* HarperCollins Pubs.

—El Violín de Ada (Ada's Violin) La Historia de la Orquesta de Instrumentos Reciclados Del Paraguay. Hood, Susan. McConnell, Shelley, tr. 2016. (SPA.). 40p. (J). (gr. -1-3). 18.99 *(978-1-4814-6657-8(7)*, Simon & Schuster Bks. For Young Readers) Simon & Schuster Bks. For Young Readers.

—Whisper in the Dark. Bruchac, Joseph. 2009. (ENG.). 192p. (J). (gr. 5). pap. 7.99 *(978-0-06-058089-6(5))* HarperCollins Pubs.

Comport, Sally Wern. Zayd Saleem, Chasing the Dream: Power Forward; on Point; Bounce Back. Khan, Hena. 2020. (Zayd Saleem, Chasing the Dream Ser.). (ENG.). 416p. (J). (gr. 2-7). 19.99 ***(978-1-5344-6947-1(8)***, Salaam Reads); pap. 8.99 ***(978-1-5344-6946-4(X)***, Simon & Schuster Bks. For Young Readers) Simon & Schuster Bks. For Young Readers.

Compton, Annette. God's Paintbrush. Sasso, Sandy Eisenberg. 2nd anniv. annot. ed. 2004. (ENG.). 32p. (J). (gr. -1-2). 18.99 *(978-1-58023-195-4(0)*, a3804693-b3d2-4881-b712-82b40c7f6cb2, Jewish Lights Publishing) LongHill Partners, Inc.

—I Am God's Paintbrush. Sasso, Sandy Eisenberg. 2009. (ENG.). 24p. (J). 22.99 *(978-1-68336-795-6(2))*; pap. 12.99 *(978-1-68336-794-9(4))* LongHill Partners, Inc. (Skylight Paths Publishing).

Compton, Donna. Wood, Hay, & Pigs. Koenig, Albert. 2005. (J). 8.99 *(978-1-4183-0078-4(0))* Christ Inspired, Inc.

Computers, Dream. The Ninth Inning. Bader, Jerry (Zaza). 2017. (ENG.). (J). *(978-1-988647-24-1(X))*; pap. *(978-1-988647-23-4(1))* MRPwebmedia.

—Two Dragons Named Shoe. Bader, Jerry (Zaza). 2016. (ENG.). (J). *(978-0-9953426-6-8(0))*; pap. *(978-0-9953426-5-1(2))* MRPwebmedia.

Comstock, Chris. The Hat Peddler. Susedik, Tina. 2014. 41p. (J). pap. 14.00 *(978-0-9667527-7-9(5))* Maple Lane Writing & Desktop Publishing.

Comstock, Eric. The Great Dictionary Caper. Sierra, Judy. 2018. (ENG.). 40p. (J). (gr. -1-3). 17.99 *(978-1-4814-8004-8(9)*, Simon & Schuster/Paula Wiseman Bks.) Simon & Schuster/Paula Wiseman Bks.

Comstock, Eric. I Heard a Sound. Ward, David J. 2020. (ENG.). 40p. (J). (gr. 1-4). 18.99 ***(978-0-8234-3704-7(3))*** Holiday Hse., Inc.

Comstock, Eric. Tangled: A Story about Shapes. Miranda, Anne. 2019. (ENG.). 40p. (J). (gr. -1-3). 17.99 *(978-1-4814-9721-3(9)*, Simon & Schuster/Paula Wiseman Bks.) Simon & Schuster/Paula Wiseman Bks.

Comstock, Eric. Charlie Piechart & the Case of the Missing Dog. Comstock, Eric. Sadler, Marilyn. 2018. (Charlie Piechart Ser.). (ENG.). 40p. (J). (gr. -1-3). 17.99 *(978-0-06-237058-7(8))* HarperCollins Pubs.

—Charlie Piechart & the Case of the Missing Hat. Comstock, Eric. Sadler, Marilyn. 2016. (Charlie Piechart Ser.). (ENG.). 40p. (J). (gr. -1-3). 17.99 *(978-0-06-237056-3(1)*, Tegen, Katherine Bks) HarperCollins Pubs.

—Charlie Piechart & the Case of the Missing Pizza Slice. Comstock, Eric. Sadler, Marilyn. 2015. (Charlie Piechart Ser.). (ENG.). 40p. (J). (gr. -1-3). 17.99 *(978-0-06-237054-9(5)*, Tegen, Katherine Bks) HarperCollins Pubs.

Comstock, Tiger. T-Tek, the Unbearable T-rex. Comstock, Keirah. 2019. (ENG.). 42p. (J). pap. 12.99 *(978-1-0986-2282-4(0))* Independently Published.

COMTA. An Archdemon's Dilemma: How to Love Your Elf Bride: Volume 1. Teshima, Fuminori. Hikoki, tr. 2019. (Archdemon's Dilemma: How to Love Your Elf Bride (light Novel) Ser.: 1). (ENG.). 250p. pap. 14.99 *(978-1-7183-5700-6(1))* J-Novel Club.

—An Archdemon's Dilemma: How to Love Your Elf Bride: Volume 2. Teshima, Fuminori. Hikoki, tr. 2019. (Archdemon's Dilemma: How to Love Your Elf Bride (light Novel) Ser.: 2). 250p. pap. 14.99 *(978-1-7183-5701-3(X))* J-Novel Club.

Conahan, Carolyn. Stubby the Fearless Squid. Davis-Pyles, Barbara. 2019. 32p. (J). (gr. k-4). 17.99 *(978-1-63217-199-3(6)*, Little Bigfoot) Sasquatch Bks.

Conahan, Carolyn Digby. Bubble Homes & Fish Farts. Bayrock, Fiona. 2009. 48p. (J). (gr. 1-4). pap. 7.95 *(978-1-57091-670-0(5))* Charlesbridge Publishing, Inc.

—The Discontented Gopher: A Prairie Tale. Baum, L. Frank. 2006. (Prairie Tales Ser.). 40p. (J). (gr. 3-7). 14.95 *(978-0-9749195-9-1(4)*, South Dakota State Historical Society Pr.) South Dakota Historical Society Pr.

—The Twelve Days of Christmas in Oregon. Blackaby, Susan. (Twelve Days of Christmas in America Ser.). (J). (-k). 2018. 22p. bds. 7.95 *(978-1-4549-2997-0(9))*; 2014. 40p. 12.95 *(978-1-4549-0891-3(2))* Sterling Publishing Co., Inc.

Conard, Vincent. Charis: A Journey to Pandora's Jar. Walters, Nicole Y. 2013. 214p. 32.95 *(978-1-62015-318-5(1)*, Booktrope Editions) Booktrope.

Conaway, Jim. The Ultimate Travel Time Bible. Elkins, Stephen. 2007. 170p. (J). (gr. -1-3). 14.99 incl. audio compact disk *(978-0-8054-2647-2(7))* B&H Publishing Group.

Concannon, Sue. The Breezes of Inspire. Ruth, Nick. 2005. (Remin Chronicles: 2). (ENG.). 264p. (J). (gr. 3-7). 16.95 *(978-0-9745603-3-5(2))* Imaginator Pr.

—The Dark Dreamweaver. Ruth, Nick. 2007. (Remin Chronicles: 1). (ENG.). 256p. (J). (gr. 4-7). per. 11.95 *(978-0-9745603-5-9(9))* Imaginator Pr.

Condé, J. M. The Hollow Tree & Deep Woods Book, Being a New Edition in One Volume of the Hollow Tree & in the Deep Woods with Several New Stories & Pictu. Paine, Albert Bigelow. 2012. 174p. *(978-1-78139-176-1(9))* Benediction Classics.

Conde, Manuel. Lost & Found. Madonna, Lenae. 2012. 38p. (J). 16.95 *(978-1-60131-115-3(X)*, Castlebridge Bks.) Big Tent Bks.

Conder, Jonathan Paul. The Wishing Elf. Tallant, Wesley. 2017. (ENG.). 36p. (J). (gr. 2-6). pap. 7.99 *(978-1-68160-289-9(X))* Crimson Cloak Publishing.

Cone, Carl. There's a Season for All. Shu, Sammy. 2006. 54p. (J). (gr. -1-3). 16.95 *(978-0-9778211-0-5(2)*, Raynestorm Bks.) Silver Rose Publishing.

Cone, Carl. There's a Season for All. Cone, Carl. 2008. (ENG.). pap. 14.95 *(978-0-9801555-6-3(8))* Argus Enterprises International, Inc.

Cone, William. The Night Before Christmas. Moore, Clement C. 2005. (Rabbit Ears-A Classic Tale Ser.). (ENG.). 32p. (J). (gr. 2-6). 28.50 *(978-1-59197-751-3(7)*, 12953, Picture Bk.) Spotlight.

Conforti, John W. Lucy the Elephant & Sami the Mouse: The Birthday Party. Evelyn. 2004. (J). *(978-0-9740115-1-6(7))* WeBeANS Corp.

Conforti, John W. Lucy the Elephant & Sami the Mouse: A Bedtime Story. Conforti, John W., tr. Evelyn. 2003. (J). *(978-0-9740115-0-9(9))* WeBeANS Corp.

Congdon, Lisa. Imogen: The Mother of Modernism & Three Boys. Novesky, Amy. 2012. (ENG.). 32p. (J). (gr. -1-3). 16.95 *(978-1-937359-32-4(8)*, Cameron Books) Cameron + Co.

Conger, Holli. All the Colors That I See. B&H Kids Editorial Staff. 2018. (Little Words Matter(tm) Ser.). (ENG.). 22p. (J). (gr. -1 — 1). bds. 7.99 *(978-1-4627-9475-1(0)*, 005801980, B&H Kids) B&H Publishing Group.

—Backyard Pirates. Feldman, Thea. 2007. (Magnix Imagination Activity Bks.). 6p. bds. 5.99 *(978-1-932915-40-2(0))* Sandvik Innovations, LLC.

—Chinese New Year, 1 vol. Marsico, Katie. 2009. (Cultural Holidays Ser.). (ENG.). 32p. (J). (gr. k-4). 28.50 *(978-1-60270-600-2(X)*, 5038, Looking Glass Library) Magic Wagon.

—Choose Good Food! My Eating Tips. Bellisario, Gina. 2014. (Cloverleaf Books (tm) — My Healthy Habits Ser.). (ENG.). 24p. (J). (gr. k-2). lib. bdg. 25.32 *(978-1-4677-1350-4(3)*, 9781467713504, Millbrook Pr.) Lerner Publishing Group.

—Christmas, 1 vol. Owens, L. L. 2009. (Cultural Holidays Ser.). (ENG.). 32p. (J). (gr. k-4). 28.50 *(978-1-60270-601-9(8)*, 5040, Looking Glass Library) Magic Wagon.

—Christmas (board Book) B&H Kids Editorial Staff. 2016. (Little Words Matter(tm) Ser.). (ENG.). 24p. (J). (gr. -1 — 1). bds. 8.99 *(978-1-4336-4454-2(1)*, 005787712, B&H Kids) B&H Publishing Group.

—Cinco de Mayo, 1 vol. Owens, L. L. 2009. (Cultural Holidays Ser.). (ENG.). 32p. (J). (gr. k-4). 28.50 *(978-1-60270-602-6(6)*, 5042, Looking Glass Library) Magic Wagon.

—Daniela's Day of the Dead. Bullard, Lisa. 2012. (Cloverleaf Books (tm) — Fall & Winter Holidays Ser.). (ENG.). 24p. (J). (gr. k-2). lib. bdg. 25.32 *(978-0-7613-5084-2(5)*, 9780761350842, Millbrook Pr.) Lerner Publishing Group.

—David. B&H Kids Editorial Staff. 2016. (Little Words Matter(tm) Ser.). (ENG.). 24p. (J). (gr. -1 — 1). bds. 8.99 *(978-1-4336-8651-1(1)*, 005728397, B&H Kids) B&H Publishing Group.

—Does the Sun Sleep? Noticing Sun, Moon, & Star Patterns. Rustad, Martha E. H. 2015. (Cloverleaf Books (tm) — Nature's Patterns Ser.). (ENG.). 24p. (J). (gr. k-2). 25.32 *(978-1-4677-8560-0(1)*, 9781467785600, Millbrook Pr.) Lerner Publishing Group.

—Easter (board Book) B&H Kids Editorial Staff. 2017. (Little Words Matter(tm) Ser.). (ENG.). 24p. (J). (gr. -1 — 1). bds. 8.99 *(978-1-4336-4453-5(3)*, 005787711, B&H Kids) B&H Publishing Group.

—Hailey's Halloween. Bullard, Lisa. 2012. (Cloverleaf Books (tm) — Fall & Winter Holidays Ser.). (ENG.). 24p. (J). (gr. k-2). 7.99 *(978-0-7613-8586-8(X)*, 9780761385868); lib. bdg. 25.32 *(978-0-7613-5083-5(7)*, 9780761350835) Lerner Publishing Group. (Millbrook Pr.).

—Hanukkah, 1 vol. Owens, L. L. 2009. (Cultural Holidays Ser.). (ENG.). 32p. (J). (gr. k-4). 28.50 *(978-1-60270-603-3(4)*, 5044, Looking Glass Library) Magic Wagon.

—How Big Is It? A Book about Adjectives. Meister, Cari. 2016. (Say What?: Parts of Speech Ser.). (ENG.). 16p. (J). (gr. k-3). 17.95 *(978-1-60753-930-8(6))* Amicus Publishing.

—How Fast Is It? A Book about Adverbs. Meister, Cari. 2016. (Say What?: Parts of Speech Ser.). (ENG.). 16p. (J). (gr. k-3). 17.95 *(978-1-60753-931-5(4))* Amicus Publishing.

Conger, Holli. Hunter's Pyjamas. Telfer, Tori & Telfer, Rhonda. 2020. (ENG.). 32p. (J). pap. ***(978-1-922331-46-5(5))*** Library For All Limited.

Conger, Holli. If You're Happy & You Know It, Sound Book. B&H Kids Editorial Staff. 2016. (Little Words Matter(tm) Ser.). (ENG.). 12p. (J). (gr. -1 — 1). bds. 12.99 *(978-1-4336-8678-8(3)*, 005733103, B&H Kids) B&H Publishing Group.

—Is a Bald Eagle Really Bald? Rustad, Martha E. H. 2014. (Cloverleaf Books (tm) — Our American Symbols Ser.). (ENG.). 24p. (J). (gr. k-2). pap. 8.99 *(978-1-4677-4466-9(2)*, 9781467744669, Millbrook Pr.) Lerner Publishing Group.

—Jesus. B&H Kids Editorial Staff. 2015. (Little Words Matter(tm) Ser.). (ENG.). 24p. (J). (— 1). bds. 8.99 *(978-1-4336-8648-1(1)*, 005728394, B&H Kids) B&H Publishing Group.

—Jesus Loves Me, Sound Book. B&H Kids Editorial Staff. 2015. (Little Words Matter(tm) Ser.). (ENG.). 12p. (J). (— 1). bds. 12.99 *(978-1-4336-8675-7(9)*, 005733100, B&H Kids) B&H Publishing Group.

—Little Words Matter Bible Storybook (padded Board Book) B&H Kids Editorial Staff, ed. 2015. (Little Words Matter(tm) Ser.). (ENG.). 38p. (J). (gr. -1 — 1). bds. 9.99 *(978-1-4336-8643-6(0)*, 005727302, B&H Kids) B&H Publishing Group.

—Marco's Cinco de Mayo. Bullard, Lisa. 2012. (Cloverleaf Books (tm) — Holidays & Special Days Ser.). (ENG.). 24p. (J). (gr. k-2). pap. 8.99 *(978-0-7613-8580-6(0)*, 9780761385806, Millbrook Pr.) Lerner Publishing Group.

—Mitzi's Mitzvah, Vol. Koster, Gloria. 2013. (Very First Board Bks.). (ENG.). 12p. (J). (gr. -1 — 1). bds. 5.95 *(978-1-4677-0695-7(7)*, 9781467706957, Kar-Ben Publishing) Lerner Publishing Group.

—Moses. B&H Kids Editorial Staff. 2016. (Little Words Matter(tm) Ser.). (ENG.). 24p. (J). (gr. -1 — 1). bds. 8.99 *(978-1-4336-8650-4(3)*, 005728396, B&H Kids) B&H Publishing Group.

—My Family Celebrates Day of the Dead. Bullard, Lisa. 2018. (Holiday Time (Early Bird Stories (tm)) Ser.). (ENG.). 24p. (J). (gr. k-2). pap. 7.99 *(978-1-5415-2739-3(9))*; lib. bdg. 27.99 *(978-1-5415-2008-0(4)*, Lerner Pubns.) Lerner Publishing Group.

—My Family Celebrates Halloween. Bullard, Lisa. 2018. (Holiday Time (Early Bird Stories (tm)) Ser.). (ENG.). 24p. (J). (gr. k-2). 27.99 *(978-1-5415-2010-3(6)*, Lerner Pubns.) Lerner Publishing Group.

—My Little Words Devotional (Padded) 2017. (Little Words Matter(tm) Ser.). (ENG.). 38p. (J). bds. 9.99 *(978-1-4627-5933-0(5)*, 005795785, B&H Kids) B&H Publishing Group.

—My Religion, Your Religion. Bullard, Lisa. 2015. (Cloverleaf Books (tm) — Alike & Different Ser.). (ENG.). 24p. (J). (gr. k-2). pap. 8.99 *(978-1-4677-6033-1(1)*, 9781467760331); lib. bdg. 25.32 *(978-1-4677-4905-3(2)*, 9781467749053) Lerner Publishing Group. (Millbrook Pr.).

—No School Today: A Book about Nouns. Meister, Cari. 2016. (Say What?: Parts of Speech Ser.). (ENG.). 16p. (J). (gr. k-3). 17.95 *(978-1-60753-934-6(9))* Amicus Publishing.

—Noah's Ark. B&H Kids Editorial Staff. 2015. (Little Words Matter(tm) Ser.). (ENG.). 24p. (J). (— 1). bds. 8.99 *(978-1-4336-8649-8(X)*, 005728395, B&H Kids) B&H Publishing Group.

—Now I Lay Me down to Sleep, Sound Book. B&H Kids Editorial Staff. 2016. (Little Words Matter(tm) Ser.). (ENG.). 12p. (J). (gr. -1 — 1). bds. 12.99 *(978-1-4336-8677-1(5)*, 005733102, B&H Kids) B&H Publishing Group.

—Ouch! It Bit Me! A Book about Interjections. Meister, Cari. 2016. (Say What?: Parts of Speech Ser.). (ENG.). 16p. (J). (gr. k-3). 17.95 *(978-1-60753-932-2(2))* Amicus Publishing.

—Pepperoni or Sausage? A Book about Conjunctions. Meister, Cari. 2016. (Say What?: Parts of Speech Ser.). (ENG.). 16p. (J). (gr. k-3). 17.95 *(978-1-60753-935-3(7))* Amicus Publishing.

—Poison Alert! My Tips to Avoid Danger Zones at Home. Bellisario, Gina. 2014. (Cloverleaf Books (tm) — My Healthy Habits Ser.). (ENG.). 24p. (J). (gr. k-2). lib. bdg. 25.32 *(978-1-4677-1353-5(8)*, 9781467713535, Millbrook Pr.) Lerner Publishing Group.

—Prayers for Bedtime (padded Board Book) B&H Kids Editorial Staff. 2016. (Little Words Matter(tm) Ser.). (ENG.). 38p. (J). (gr. -1 — 1). 9.99 *(978-1-4336-8645-0(7)*, 005727304, B&H Kids) B&H Publishing Group.

—A Raindrop's Journey, 1 vol. Slade, Suzanne. (Follow It! Ser.). (ENG.). 24p. (J). (gr. 1-3). 2011. pap. 7.49 *(978-1-4048-6712-3(0))*; 2010. lib. bdg. 27.32 *(978-1-4048-6266-1(8))* Capstone. (Picture Window Bks.).

—Ramadan, 1 vol. Anderson, Sheila. 2009. (Cultural Holidays Ser.). (ENG.). 32p. (J). (gr. k-4). 28.50 *(978-1-60270-605-7(0)*, 5048, Looking Glass Library) Magic Wagon.

—Rashad's Ramadan & Eid Al-Fitr. Bullard, Lisa. 2012. (Cloverleaf Books (tm) — Holidays & Special Days Ser.). (ENG.). 24p. (J). (gr. k-2). pap. 8.99 *(978-0-7613-8583-7(5)*, 9780761385837); lib. bdg. 25.32 *(978-0-7613-5079-8(9)*, 9780761350798) Lerner Publishing Group. (Millbrook Pr.).

—Shai's Shabbat Walk. Vol. Gellman, Ellie B. 2014. (ENG.). 12p. (J). (gr. -1 — 1). bds. 5.95 *(978-1-4677-4949-7(4)*, Kar-Ben Publishing) Lerner Publishing Group.

—Take a Bath! My Tips for Keeping Clean. Bellisario, Gina. 2014. (Cloverleaf Books (tm) — My Healthy Habits Ser.). (ENG.). 24p. (J). (gr. k-2). lib. bdg. 25.32 *(978-1-4677-1352-8(X)*, 9781467713528, Millbrook Pr.) Lerner Publishing Group.

—Thank You, God, from a to Z. B&H Kids Editorial Staff. 2018. (Little Words Matter(tm) Ser.). (ENG.). 22p. (J). (— 1).

bds. 7.99 *(978-1-5359-1705-6(9)*, 005806050, B&H Kids) B&H Publishing Group.

—This Is My Neighborhood. Bullard, Lisa. 2016. (Cloverleaf Books (tm) — Where I Live Ser.). (ENG.). 24p. (J). (gr. k-2). 25.32 *(978-1-4677-9521-0(6)*, 9781467795210, Millbrook Pr.) Lerner Publishing Group.

—This Is My State. Bullard, Lisa. 2016. (Cloverleaf Books (tm) — Where I Live Ser.). (ENG.). 24p. (J). (gr. k-2). 25.32 *(978-1-4677-9523-4(2)*, 9781467795234, Millbrook Pr.) Lerner Publishing Group.

—What Is It Doing? A Book about Verbs. Meister, Cari. 2016. (Say What?: Parts of Speech Ser.). (ENG.). 16p. (J). (gr. k-3). 17.95 *(978-1-60753-933-9(0))* Amicus Publishing.

—When Will It Rain? Noticing Weather Patterns. Rustad, Martha E. H. 2015. (Cloverleaf Books (tm) — Nature's Patterns Ser.). (ENG.). 24p. (J). (gr. k-2). 25.32 *(978-1-4677-8557-0(1)*, 9781467785570, Millbrook Pr.) Lerner Publishing Group.

—Which Shape Should I Be? 2019. (Little Words Matter(tm) Ser.). (ENG.). 22p. (J). (— 1). bds. 7.99 *(978-1-5359-5942-1(8)*, 005815678, B&H Kids) B&H Publishing Group.

—Who Ate It? A Book about Pronouns. Meister, Cari. 2016. (Say What?: Parts of Speech Ser.). (ENG.). 16p. (J). (gr. k-3). 17.95 *(978-1-60753-937-7(3))* Amicus Publishing.

—Who Is up There? A Book about Prepositions. Meister, Cari. 2016. (Say What?: Parts of Speech Ser.). (ENG.). 16p. (J). (gr. k-3). 17.95 *(978-1-60753-936-0(5))* Amicus Publishing.

—The Whole World in His Hands, Sound Book. B&H Kids Editorial Staff. 2015. (Little Words Matter(tm) Ser.). (ENG.). 12p. (J). (— 1). bds. 12.99 *(978-1-4336-8676-4(7)*, 005733101, B&H Kids) B&H Publishing Group.

—Why Is the Statue of Liberty Green? Rustad, Martha E. H. 2014. (Cloverleaf Books (tm) — Our American Symbols Ser.). (ENG.). 24p. (J). (gr. k-2). pap. 8.99 *(978-1-4677-4470-6(0)*, 9781467744706); lib. bdg. 25.32 *(978-1-4677-2139-4(5)*, 9781467721394) Lerner Publishing Group. (Millbrook Pr.).

—1, 2, 3 God Made Me. B&H Kids Editorial Staff. 2018. (Little Words Matter(tm) Ser.). (ENG.). 22p. (J). (— 1). bds. 7.99 *(978-1-4627-7407-4(5)*, 005797599, B&H Kids) B&H Publishing Group.

Conger, Hollil. Marco's Cinco de Mayo. Bullard, Lisa. 2012. (Holidays & Special Days Ser.). 24p. (J). (gr. k-2). pap. 39.62 *(978-0-7613-9249-1(1)*, Millbrook Pr.) Lerner Publishing Group.

—Rashad's Ramadan & Eid Al-Fitr. Bullard, Lisa. 2012. (Holidays & Special Days Ser.). 24p. (J). (gr. k-2). pap. 39.62 *(978-0-7613-9250-7(5)*, Millbrook Pr.) Lerner Publishing Group.

Conklin, Paul, photos by. Gavriel & Jemal: Two Boys of Jerusalem. Ashabranner, Brent. 2005. 94p. (J). (gr. 4-10). reprint ed. 12.00 *(978-0-7567-9758-4(6))* DIANE Publishing Co.

Conley, Chelsea. Daddy's Submarine: The Life of Submarine Children. Patterson, Bethany. 2019. (ENG.). 26p. (J). pap. 12.00 *(978-1-7928-2594-1(3))* Independently Published.

Conley, Laurie A. Peter Polo & the Snow Beast of Hunza. Bradley, Craig. 2020. (ENG.). 108p. (J). (gr. 4-6). 21.95 ***(978-1-947860-96-4(8))***; pap. 12.95 ***(978-1-947860-97-1(6))*** Brandylane Pubs., Inc. (Belle Isle Bks.).

Conley, Laurie A. What Is the Women's Rights Movement? Hopkinson, Deborah & Who HQ. 2018. (What Was? Ser.). 112p. (J). (gr. 3-7). 5.99 *(978-1-5247-8629-8(2))*; lib. bdg. 15.99 *(978-1-5247-8631-1(4))* Penguin Young Readers Group. (Penguin Workshop).

—Where Is the Vatican? Stine, Megan & Who HQ. 2019. (Where Is? Ser.). 112p. (J). (gr. 3-7). 5.99 *(978-1-5247-9259-6(4))*; 15.99 *(978-1-5247-9260-2(8))* Penguin Young Readers Group. (Penguin Workshop).

Conley, Stephanie. My Extra Special Brother: How to Love, Understand, & Celebrate Your Sibling with Special Needs. Heyman, Carly. l.t. ed. 2003. 112p. pap. 12.95 *(978-0-9727865-0-8(3)*, 1003894) Fragile X Assn. of Georgia.

Conn, Alexandra. Turtlebird's Double Dip Shuffle. Fass, Tara. 2013. 18p. pap. 10.00 *(978-0-9838120-4-3(7))* Huqua Pr.

Connally, Erin, jt. illus. see Dobbins, Erin.

Connally, Perry L., Sr. Hard Heads Make Soft Bottoms. Switzer, Vern. 2007. 34p. (J). 15.95 *(978-0-9753542-2-3(1))* Rural Farm Productions.

—Lucy the Cantaloupe. Switzer, Vern. 2005. 32p. (J). 15.95 *(978-0-9753542-1-6(3))* Rural Farm Productions.

Connally, Perry L., Sr., jt. illus. see Listokin, David.

Connell, Chris. The Muddy Cuddle. Dwyer, Hjm. 2019. (ENG.). 22p. (J). *(978-1-78623-519-0(6))*; pap. *(978-1-78623-495-7(5))* Grosvenor Hse. Publishing Ltd.

Connell, Jacqueline. Is There Magic in the Mountains, Mamma? Cook, Maureen McNamee. 2008. 23p. pap. 24.95 *(978-1-60672-673-0(0))* America Star Bks.

Connell, Lauren. Designed to Shine! Read Aloud Rhymes for Any Size Heart. Resor, Joy. 2018. (ENG.). 66p. (J). (gr. k-6). 22.00 *(978-0-9840353-4-2(6))* Joy on Your Shoulders TM.

Connell, Tom. Code It! 4 Creative STEM Projects for Budding Engineers — Programming Edition. Alliston, Caroline. 2019. (Build It! Ser.). (ENG.). 32p. (J). (gr. 2-5). lib. bdg. 27.99 *(978-0-7112-4223-4(2))* QEB Publishing Inc.

—Race It! 5 Creative STEM Projects for Budding Engineers — Speed Edition. Alliston, Caroline. 2019. (Build It! Ser.). (ENG.). 32p. (J). (gr. 2-5). lib. bdg. 27.99 *(978-0-7112-4221-0(6))* QEB Publishing Inc.

—Wire It! 6 Creative STEM Projects for Budding Engineers — Electric Circuit Edition. Alliston, Caroline. 2019. (Build It! Ser.). (ENG.). 32p. (J). (gr. 2-5). lib. bdg. 27.99 *(978-0-7112-4222-7(4))* QEB Publishing Inc.

Connelly, Devin. The Day the Books Cried. Marsh Longmeyer, Carole. 2016. (Bluffton Bks.). (ENG.). (J). (gr. -1-3). lib. bdg. 24.99 *(978-0-635-12533-0(1))*; 7.99 *(978-0-635-12532-3(3))* Bluffton Bks.

Connelly, Gwen. Dayenu! A Passover Haggadah for Families & Children. Leon, Carol Boyd. 2008. 32p. (J). (gr. 1-3). 16.95 incl. audio compact disk *(978-1-60280-041-0(3))*; pap. 8.95 incl. audio compact disk *(978-1-60280-039-7(1))*; spiral bd. 16.95 incl. audio compact disk *(978-1-60280-040-3(5))*; bds. 24.95 incl. audio compact disk *(978-1-60280-042-7(1))* Ktav Publishing Hse., Inc.

—Let's Celebrate St. Patrick's Day. Roop, Peter & Roop, Connie. 2003. 32p. (J). (gr. 3-6). pap. 6.95 *(978-0-7613-1782-1(1))*; lib. bdg. 22.90 *(978-0-7613-2505-5(0))* Lerner Publishing Group. (Millbrook Pr.).

—No Bigger Than My Teddy Bear. Pankow, Valerie. 2nd ed. 2004. 32p. (J). 6.95 *(978-0-9728460-0-4(X))* Family Bks.

—The Story of Ruth. Vol. Schur, Maxine Rose. 2005. (ENG.). 32p. (J). (gr. 2-4). lib. bdg. 16.95 *(978-1-58013-114-8(X)*, Kar-Ben Publishing) Lerner Publishing Group.

Connelly, Gwen & Holmberg, Ansgar. Days of Faith: Student Planner & Assignment Book 2004-2005. Fischer, Carl. 2004. 108p. (J). spiral bd. 3.25 *(978-0-89837-199-4(6)*, 9805) Pflaum Publishing Group.

Connelly, Gwen, jt. illus. see Holmberg, Ansgar.

Connelly, Sheila. The Young People's Book of Saints: Sixty-Three Saints of the Western Church from the First to the Twentieth Century. Ross Williamson, Hugh. 2009. (J). 15.95 *(978-1-933184-62-3(0))* Sophia Institute Pr.

Conner, Eulala. 5 Steps to Drawing People. Hall, Pamela. 2018. (5 Steps to Drawing Ser.). (ENG.). 32p. (J). (gr. k-3). 29.93 *(978-1-5038-2484-3(5)*, 212244) Child's World, Inc., The.

Conner, Paula. Girls Who Looked under Rocks: The Lives of Six Pioneering Naturalists, 1 vol. Atkins, Jeannine. 2011. (ENG.). 64p. (J). (gr. 5-10). pap. 11.95 *(978-1-58469-011-5(9)*, Dawn Pubns.) Sourcebooks, Inc.

Conner, Sarah. Adam & Eve, 1 vol. Williamson, Karen. ed. 2017. (Candle Little Lambs Ser.). (ENG.). 24p. (J). pap. 2.99 *(978-1-78128-324-0(9)*, Candle Bks.) Lion Hudson PLC GBR. Dist: Kregel Pubns.

—Baby Jesus, 1 vol. Williaon, Karen. ed. 2015. (Candle Little Lambs Ser.). (ENG.). 24p. (J). (gr. -1-k). pap. 2.99 *(978-1-78128-188-8(2)*, Candle Bks.) Lion Hudson PLC GBR. Dist: Kregel Pubns.

—Daniel & the Lions, 1 vol. Williaon, Karen. ed. 2015. (Candle Little Lambs Ser.). (ENG.). 24p. (J). (gr. -1-k). pap. 2.99 *(978-1-78128-162-8(9)*, Candle Bks.) Lion Hudson PLC GBR. Dist: Kregel Pubns.

—David & Goliath, 1 vol. Williaon, Karen. ed. 2015. (Candle Little Lambs Ser.). (ENG.). 24p. (J). (gr. -1-k). pap. 2.99 *(978-1-78128-160-4(2)*, Candle Bks.) Lion Hudson PLC GBR. Dist: Kregel Pubns.

—The First Easter, 1 vol. Williamson, Karen. ed. 2016. (Candle Little Lambs Ser.). (ENG.). 24p. (J). pap. 2.99 *(978-1-78128-243-4(9)*, Candle Bks.) Lion Hudson PLC GBR. Dist: Kregel Pubns.

—Genius Communication Inventions: From Morse Code to the Internet. Turner, Matt. 2017. (Incredible Inventions Ser.). (ENG.). 32p. (J). (gr. 3-6). 27.99 *(978-1-5124-3210-7(5)*, 9781512432107, Hungry Tomato ®) Lerner Publishing Group.

—Genius Engineering Inventions: From the Plow to 3D Printing. Turner, Matt. 2017. (Incredible Inventions Ser.). (ENG.). 32p. (J). (gr. 3-6). 27.99 *(978-1-5124-3211-4(3)*, 9781512432114, Hungry Tomato ®) Lerner Publishing Group.

—Genius Optical Inventions: From the X-Ray to the Telescope. Turner, Matt. 2017. (Incredible Inventions Ser.). (ENG.). 32p. (J). (gr. 3-6). 27.99 *(978-1-5124-3208-4(3)*, 9781512432084, Hungry Tomato ®) Lerner Publishing Group.

—Genius Transportation Inventions: From the Wheel to Spacecraft. Turner, Matt. 2017. (Incredible Inventions Ser.). (ENG.). 32p. (J). (gr. 3-6). 27.99 *(978-1-5124-3209-1(1)*, 9781512432091, Hungry Tomato ®) Lerner Publishing Group.

—Joseph, 1 vol. Williamson, Karen. ed. 2016. (Candle Little Lambs Ser.). (ENG.). 24p. (J). pap. 2.99 *(978-1-78128-278-6(1)*, Candle Bks.) Lion Hudson PLC GBR. Dist: Kregel Pubns.

—Mary & Martha, 1 vol. Williamson, Karen. ed. 2016. (Candle Little Lambs Ser.). (ENG.). 24p. (J). pap. 2.99 *(978-1-78128-279-3(X)*, Candle Bks.) Lion Hudson PLC GBR. Dist: Kregel Pubns.

—Paul, 1 vol. Williamson, Karen. ed. 2016. (Candle Little Lambs Ser.). (ENG.). 24p. (J). pap. 2.99 *(978-1-78128-276-2(5)*, Candle Bks.) Lion Hudson PLC GBR. Dist: Kregel Pubns.

—The Prodigal Son, 1 vol. Williamson, Karen. ed. 2017. (Candle Little Lambs Ser.). (ENG.). 24p. (J). pap. 2.99 *(978-1-78128-325-7(7)*, Candle Bks.) Lion Hudson PLC GBR. Dist: Kregel Pubns.

—Samuel, 1 vol. Williamson, Karen. ed. 2017. (Candle Little Lambs Ser.). (ENG.). 24p. (J). pap. 2.99 *(978-1-78128-326-4(5)*, Candle Bks.) Lion Hudson PLC GBR. Dist: Kregel Pubns.

—Zacchaeus, 1 vol. Williamson, Karen. ed. 2016. (Candle Little Lambs Ser.). (ENG.). 24p. (J). pap. 2.99 *(978-1-78128-277-9(3)*, Candle Bks.) Lion Hudson PLC GBR. Dist: Kregel Pubns.

Conner, Sarah & Allsopp, Sophie. The Good Samaritan, 1 vol. Williamson, Karen & Rock, Lois. ed. 2017. (Candle Little Lambs Ser.). (ENG.). 24p. (J). pap. 2.99 *(978-1-78128-323-3(0)*, Candle Bks.) Lion Hudson PLC GBR. Dist: Kregel Pubns.

Connolly, Danie. The Third Turtledove. Connolly, Danie. 2018. (ENG.). 54p. (J). pap. 14.95 *(978-0-9970546-2-0(X))* Absolutely Perfect!.

Connor, Chris. Charlotte Sometimes. Farmer, Penelope. 2007. (ENG.). 208p. (J). (gr. 7-9). 17.95 *(978-1-59017-221-6(3)*, NYR Children's Collection) New York Review of Bks., Inc., The.

Connor, Michael. An Buachaill Bo. Perdue, Gillian. 2006. (Sraith Sos Ser.: 13). (GLE.). 64p. (J). pap. 11.00 *(978-1-84717-006-4(4))* O'Brien Pr., Ltd., The IRL. Dist: Casemate Pubs. & Bk. Distributors, LLC.

—Conor's Canvas. Perdue, Gillian. 2007. (Pandas Ser.: 35). (ENG.). 64p. (J). pap. 9.95 *(978-1-84717-043-9(9))* O'Brien Pr., Ltd., The IRL. Dist: Casemate Pubs. & Bk. Distributors, LLC.

—Conor's Concert. Perdue, Gillian. 2003. (Pandas Ser.: 26). (ENG.). 64p. (J). pap. 11.00 *(978-0-86278-847-6(1))* O'Brien Pr., Ltd., The IRL. Dist: Casemate Pubs. & Bk. Distributors, LLC.

—Danny Brown & His Daft Dog. Dawson, Brianóg Brady. 2nd rev. ed. 2018. (Danny Brown Ser.). (ENG.). 64p. (J). 12.00 *(978-1-78849-011-5(8))* O'Brien Pr., Ltd., The IRL. Dist: Casemate Pubs. & Bk. Distributors, LLC.

—Danny Brown & the Big Surprise. Dawson, Brianog Brady. 2018. (Danny Brown Ser.). (ENG.). 64p. (J). 12.00 *(978-1-78849-010-8(X))* O'Brien Pr., Ltd., The IRL. Dist: Casemate Pubs. & Bk. Distributors, LLC.

—Danny Brown & the Monster Toothbrush. Dawson, Brianog Brady & Nolan, Alan. 2017. (Danny Brown Ser.). (ENG.). 64p. (J). 11.00 *(978-1-84717-880-0(4))* O'Brien Pr., Ltd., The IRL. Dist: Casemate Pubs. & Bk. Distributors, LLC.

—Danny Brown & the Talking Teeth. Dawson, Brianog Brady. 2017. (Danny Brown Ser.). (ENG.). 64p. (J). 12.00 *(978-1-84717-879-4(0))* O'Brien Pr., Ltd., The IRL. Dist: Casemate Pubs. & Bk. Distributors, LLC.

—Pageboy Danny. Dawson, Brianóg Brady. 2006. (Pandas Ser.: 34). (ENG.). 64p. (J). pap. 11.00 *(978-0-86278-950-3(8))* O'Brien Pr., Ltd., The IRL. Dist: Dufour Editions, Inc.

Connor, Michael. Danny's Pesky Pet. Connor, Michael, tr. Dawson, Brianog Brady. 2003. (Pandas Ser.: 25). (ENG.). 64p. (J). pap. 11.00 *(978-0-86278-803-2(X))* O'Brien Pr., Ltd., The IRL. Dist: Dufour Editions, Inc.

Connor, Robin. Power Reading: Classics/Jungle Book. Cole, Bob. 2004. 94p. (J). (gr. 4-18). vinyl bd. 39.95 *(978-1-883186-61-6(7)*, PPCL2) National Reading Styles Institute, Inc.

—Power Reading: Comic Book/Jungle Book. Cole, Bob. 2005. 62p. (J). (gr. 3-18). vinyl bd. 39.95 *(978-1-883186-74-6(9)*, PPCLC2) National Reading Styles Institute, Inc.

Connor, Sarah. Incredible Inventions: From the Wheel to Spacecraft, the First Written Word to the Internet. Turner, Matt. 2019. (ENG.). 96p. (J). (gr. 2-6). 19.99 *(978-1-913077-15-0(2)*, bd667eae-1a3d-4087-b95a-c12154505433, Beetle Bks.) Hungry Tomato Ltd. GBR. Dist: Baker & Taylor Publisher Services (BTPS).

Connors, Jerrold. Now, Louie! Connors, Jerrold. 2006. 40p. (J). 12.99 *(978-0-9721416-1-1(8))* Alligator Boogaloo.

Connors, Mary. Mandy Miller & the Brownie Troop. Gatewood, June S. 2009. 48p. pap. 17.49 *(978-1-4389-1727-6(9))* AuthorHouse.

—Patric the Pony Finds a Friend. Edmonds, Lin. 2009. 32p. pap. 12.99 *(978-1-4389-5167-6(1))* AuthorHouse.

—Proto: Que faire quand un dinosaure nait dans votre Jardin? Heywood, Grand-Mere Geny. 2010. 56p. pap. 23.99 *(978-1-4490-5786-2(1))* AuthorHouse.

Conrad, Cindy. How Do You Butterfly? Welch, Donnie. 2018. (ENG.). 36p. (J). pap. 12.00 *(978-1-7908-0279-1(2))* Independently Published.

Conrad, Jessica J. Ducks Can't Ballerina. Hawthorne, Jaime. 2018. (ENG.). 32p. (J). pap. 14.99 *(978-1-7309-2194-0(9))* Independently Published.

Conrad, Liz. The Baby Hustle: An Interactive Book with Wiggles & Giggles! Schoenberg, Jane. 2010. (ENG.). 12p. (J). (gr. -1 — 1). bds. 7.99 *(978-1-4169-8050-6(4)*, Little Simon) Little Simon.

—Little Bunny. 2009. (My Sparkling Springtime Friends Ser.). (ENG.). 10p. (J). bds. 3.95 *(978-1-58117-865-4(4)*, Intervisual/Piggy Toes) Bendon, Inc.

—Little Chick. 2009. (My Sparkling Springtime Friends Ser.). (ENG.). 10p. (J). bds. 3.95 *(978-1-58117-866-1(2)*, Intervisual/Piggy Toes) Bendon, Inc.

—Little Duck. 2009. (My Sparkling Springtime Friends Ser.). (ENG.). 10p. (J). bds. 3.95 *(978-1-58117-867-8(0)*, Intervisual/Piggy Toes) Bendon, Inc.

—Little Lamb. 2009. (My Sparkling Springtime Friends Ser.). (ENG.). 10p. (J). bds. 3.95 *(978-1-58117-868-5(9)*, Intervisual/Piggy Toes) Bendon, Inc.

—Skeleton Shake. 2008. (ENG.). 12p. (J). 6.95 *(978-1-58117-798-5(4)*, Intervisual/Piggy Toes) Bendon, Inc.

Consentino, Ralph. Peanut Bear: What's in the Forest? 2018. (ENG.). 24p. (J). bds. 7.99 *(978-1-68383-235-5(3))* Insight Editions.

Considine, Declan. The Adventures of Feefeen & Friends. Noughton, Barbara. *(978-0-9575814-1-8(6))* Universal Humourous Pubs.

Consolazio, Pamela A. Rule of Three. Archer, Nick & Mcdonald, Megan. 2009. (Sisters Club Ser.: 2). 240p. (J). (gr. 3-7). 15.99 *(978-0-7636-4153-5(7))* Candlewick Pr.

Constable, Tim. The Adventures of Billy Bog Brush: The Fire Brigade. Campbell, Ian. 2018. (ENG.). 26p. (J). pap. *(978-1-912562-80-0(4))* Clink Street Publishing.

—The Adventures of Billy Bog Brush: The Lost Boy. Campbell, Ian. 2019. (ENG.). 40p. (J). pap. *(978-1-912562-82-4(0))* Clink Street Publishing.

Constance, Catherine. The Adventures of Bumble the Bus: A Day Out in London. Allister, Lizzie. 2016. (ENG.). 14p. (J). pap. *(978-1-78623-798-9(9))* Grosvenor Hse. Publishing Ltd.

Constantin, Pascale. Al lado de una Hormiga: Next to an Ant. Rockliff, Mara. 2005. (Rookie Reader Español Ser.). (ENG & SPA.). 24p. (J). (gr. k-2). 19.50 *(978-0-516-25251-3(8)*, Children's Pr.) Scholastic Library Publishing.

—Bible Stories for Growing Kids. Rivers, Francine & Coibion, Shannon Rivers. 2007. (ENG.). 216p. (J). (gr. 1-5). 15.99 *(978-1-4143-0569-1(9)*, 4600123) Tyndale Hse. Pubs.

—The Facttracker. Eaton, Jason Carter. 2008. 272p. (J). (gr. 3-7). 16.99 *(978-0-06-056434-6(2))* HarperCollins Pubs.

—Historias Bíblicas para Niños Bilingüe. Rivers, Francine & Coibion, Shannon Rivers. ed. 2008.Tr. of Bible Stories for Kids Bilingual. 216p. (J). 14.99 *(978-1-4143-1981-0(9)*, 4600971, Tyndale Espanol) Tyndale Hse. Pubs.

—Never Kick a Ghost & Other Silly Chillers. Sierra, Judy. 2011. (I Can Read Level 2 Ser.). (ENG.). 32p. (J). (gr. k-3). pap. 4.99 *(978-0-06-143521-8(X))* HarperCollins Pubs.

—Next to an Ant. Rockliff, Mara. 2011. (ENG.). 32p. (J). (gr. -1-1). lib. bdg. 23.00 *(978-0-531-26447-8(5)*, Children's Pr.) Scholastic Library Publishing.

—Raising a Little Stink. Sydor, Colleen. 2006. 32p. (J). (gr. -1-2). 16.95 *(978-1-55337-896-9(2))* Kids Can Pr., Ltd. CAN. Dist: Hachette Bk. Group.

Constantine, Adam. The Usborne Illustrated Dictionary of Math. Large, Tori. 2007. 128p. (J). (gr. 4-7). pap. 12.99 *(978-0-7945-1629-1(7)*, Usborne) EDC Publishing.

—The Usborne Illustrated Dictonary of Math. Large, Tori. Rogers, Kirsteen, ed. 2007. (Usborne Illustrated Dictionaries Ser.). 128p. (YA). (gr. 7). lib. bdg. 20.99 *(978-1-60130-013-3(1)*, Usborne) EDC Publishing.

Consuegra, Carlos Manuel Diaz. The Czar & the Shirt. Tolstoy, Leo. Leal, Mireya Fonseca, ed. 2003. (Library of Tale Ser.). (SPA.). 12p. (J). (gr. -1-7). pap. *(978-958-30-0984-6(9))* Panamericana Editorial.

Conte, Angie Moon & Conte, Laurelle Moon. Cousin Camp Conversations: A Children's Story about Religion. Rogers, William A. 2019. (Cousin Camp Conversations Ser.: Vol. 1). (ENG.). 50p. (J). pap. 12.95 *(978-0-578-45901-1(9))* RBHC LLC.

Conte, Laurelle Moon, jt. illus. see Conte, Angie Moon.

Conteh Morgan, Jane. Meet Jesus: The Life & Lessons of a Beloved Teacher. Gunny, Lynn Tuttle. 2008. (ENG.). 36p. (J). (gr. 3-7). pap. 12.00 *(978-1-55896-524-9(6)*, Skinner Hse. Bks.) Unitarian Universalist Assn.

Conteh-Morgan, Jane. Oink-Oink: And Other Animal Sounds. Group, Cricket Magazine. 2007. (ENG.). 20p. (J). (gr. k-k). bds. 7.95 *(978-0-8126-7934-2(2))* Cricket Bks.

Contento, Dindo. The Dancing Christmas Tree. 2019. (ENG.). 26p. (J). pap. 10.00 ***(978-1-7043-9849-5(5))*** Independently Published.

Context Productions. Remembering Heroes. Context Productions. 2019. (Discovering Heroes® Ser.: 2). (ENG.). 46p. (J). (gr. 3-6). 24.99 *(978-1-7329913-0-9(8))*; pap. 12.99 *(978-1-7329913-1-6(6))* Context Productions.

Conti, Angela M. Miss Swirly Pepper: The Case of the Bread & Wine. Conti, Angela M. 2018. (Miss Swirly Pepper Ser.: Vol. 3). (ENG.). 52p. (J). (gr. k-6). 16.99 *(978-1-943574-14-8(6))* Big Eyes Publishing.

—Miss Swirly Pepper: The Case of the Spicy Pretzel. Conti, Angela M. 2018. (Miss Swirly Pepper Ser.: Vol. 1). (ENG.). 44p. (J). (gr. k-6). 14.99 *(978-1-943574-16-2(2))* Big Eyes Publishing.

Conti, Gia. The Sentimental Hippo & His Friends. Abate, Melinda & Jarquin, Paula. 2019. (ENG.). 28p. (J). pap. 10.00 *(978-1-0817-4998-9(9))* Independently Published.

Contreras-Freeland, Gina, jt. illus. see Freeland, Devon.

Convert, Helene. Magnetology: Vehicles. Baumann, Anne-Sophie. 2020. (Magnetology Ser.). (ENG.). 12p. (J). (gr. k-3). bds. 21.99 Éditions Tourbillon FRA. Dist: Hachette Bk. Group.

Convert, Hélène. The Ultimate Book of Horses. Laboucarie, Sandra. 2020. (Ultimate Book Ser.: 7). (ENG.). 22p. (J). (gr. k-3). 21.99 Éditions Tourbillon FRA. Dist: Hachette Bk. Group.

Convington, Adrian. Heaven: How to Get There. Maynor, Lynnette. 2016. (ENG.). (J). pap. 11.99 *(978-1-4984-9034-4(4))* Salem Author Services.

Conway, Aaron. Alex the Sea Turtle. 2007. 26p. (J). *(978-0-9777923-0-6(7))* Shiloh Children's Bks.

—Pamela la Impaciente y los Microbios. Overland, Sarah. Arroyo Seppa, Carmen, tr. 2006. (SPA & ENG.). 32p. (J). (gr. k-2). per. 7.95 *(978-1-930650-39-8(6))* mTrellis Publishing, Inc.

Conway, Jeanne. Kindertransport: A Child's Journey. Sosa, Kena. 2019. (ENG.). 52p. (J). (gr. 3-5). 20.99 *(978-1-940310-90-9(3))* 4RV Pub.

Conway, Jeanne. Louie Finds a Friend: A Louie the Duck Story. Zabel, Vivian. 2019. (Louie the Duck Story Ser.: Vol. 2). (ENG.). 48p. (J). (gr. k-5). 21.99 ***(978-1-950074-04-4(8))***; pap. 16.99 ***(978-1-950074-03-7(X))*** 4RV Pub.

Conway, Jeanne. Storm Sentinel. Lopresti, Tony. 2019. (ENG.). 48p. (J). (gr. k-3). 21.99 *(978-1-950074-00-6(5))* 4RV Pub.

—Storm Sentinel. Lo Presti, Tony. 2019. (ENG.). 48p. (J). (gr. k-3). pap. 18.99 *(978-1-950074-01-3(3))* 4RV Pub.

—This Isn't My Bed. McNair, Mike. 2019. (ENG.). 36p. (J). (gr. k-2). 21.99 *(978-1-940310-74-9(1))*; pap. 18.99 *(978-1-940310-73-2(3))* 4RV Pub.

—Wave Excitement: A Louie the Duck Story. Zabel, Vivian. 2018. (Louie the Duck Stories Ser.: Vol. 1). (ENG.). 56p. (J). (gr. k-4). 21.99 *(978-1-940310-76-3(8))*; pap. 15.99 *(978-1-940310-75-6(X))* 4RV Pub.

—Wild, Wild Wind. Hurst, Jodi Heaton. 2019. (ENG.). 48p. (J). (gr. k-3). 22.99 *(978-1-940310-94-7(6))*; pap. 17.99 *(978-1-940310-93-0(8))* 4RV Pub.

Conway, Tricia. Parabola O Jednom Mostu. Farah, Barbara. 2006. 44p. (gr. 4-7). per. 14.99 *(978-1-59919-011-2(7))* Elim Publishing.

Conyers, Courtney. Adventures on the Farm. Jacobs, Jerry L. 2012. 38p. pap. 10.99 *(978-0-9855202-6-7(4))* Kids At Heart Publishing, LLC.

Coogan, Carol. Gaia Girls: Way of Water. Welles, Lee. 2007. (Gaia Girls Ser.). (ENG.). 336p. (J). (gr. 4-7). 18.95 *(978-1-933609-02-7(8))* Chelsea Green Publishing.

—Way of Water. Welles, Lee. 2007. (Gaia Girls Ser.: 2). (ENG.). 336p. (YA). (gr. 4-7). pap. 24.95 *(978-1-933609-03-4(6))* Chelsea Green Publishing.

Cook, Ande. Bible Heroes. Ditchfield, Christin. 2004. (Little Golden Book Ser.). 32p. (J). (gr. -1-2). 4.99 *(978-0-375-82816-4(8)*, Golden Bks.) Random Hse. Children's Bks.

Cook, Danielle. Letters from Pyggles, 1. 2003. 24p. 9.00 *(978-0-9729914-0-7(9))* Oden, Rachel.

C

Cook, Euan. Crush Hour: A 4D Book. Dahl, Michael. 2018. (School Bus of Horrors Ser.). (ENG.). 40p. (J). (gr. 4-8). pap. 4.95 *(978-1-4965-6275-3(5)*, 138006); lib. bdg. 23.99 *(978-1-4965-6269-2(0)*, 137996) Capstone. (Stone Arch Bks.).

—Dead End: A 4D Book. Dahl, Michael. 2018. (School Bus of Horrors Ser.). (ENG.). 40p. (J). (gr. 4-8). pap. 4.95 *(978-1-4965-6274-6(7)*, 138005); lib. bdg. 23.99 *(978-1-4965-6268-5(2)*, 137995) Capstone. (Stone Arch Bks.).

—Destruction Zone: A 4D Book. Dahl, Michael. 2018. (School Bus of Horrors Ser.). (ENG.). 40p. (J). (gr. 4-8). pap. 4.95 *(978-1-4965-6273-9(9)*, 138004); lib. bdg. 23.99 *(978-1-4965-6267-8(4)*, 137994) Capstone. (Stone Arch Bks.).

—The Digger 2 Wayfarers. Eldridge, Jim. 2017. (Cambridge Reading Adventures Ser.). (ENG.). 32p. pap. 6.74 *(978-1-108-40093-0(0))* Cambridge Univ. Pr.

—Friday Night Headlights: A 4D Book. Dahl, Michael. 2018. (School Bus of Horrors Ser.). (ENG.). 40p. (J). (gr. 4-8). pap. 4.95 *(978-1-4965-6277-7(1)*, 138008); lib. bdg. 23.99 *(978-1-4965-6271-5(2)*, 137999) Capstone. (Stone Arch Bks.).

—The Squeals on the Bus: A 4D Book. Dahl, Michael. 2018. (School Bus of Horrors Ser.). (ENG.). 40p. (J). (gr. 4-8). pap. 4.95 *(978-1-4965-6278-4(X)*, 138009); lib. bdg. 23.99 *(978-1-4965-6272-2(0)*, 138000) Capstone. (Stone Arch Bks.).

—Under the Hood: A 4D Book. Dahl, Michael. 2018. (School Bus of Horrors Ser.). (ENG.). 40p. (J). (gr. 4-8). pap. 4.95 *(978-1-4965-6276-0(3)*, 138007); lib. bdg. 23.99 *(978-1-4965-6270-8(4)*, 137997) Capstone. (Stone Arch Bks.).

Cook, Geoff. D Is for down Under: An Australia Alphabet. Scillian, Devin. 2010. (Discover the World Ser.). (ENG.). 40p. (J). (gr. 1-3). 17.95 *(978-1-58536-445-9(2)*, 202170) Sleeping Bear Pr.

Cook, Jeffrey. Sundays with Daddy. Kelly, Kelley R. 2010. 32p. pap. 13.99 *(978-1-4490-6082-4(X))* AuthorHouse.

Cook, Katie. Star Wars: a Very Vader Valentine's Day. King, Trey. 2013. (ENG.). 16p. (J). (gr. 3-7). pap. 6.99 *(978-0-545-51560-3(2))* Scholastic, Inc.

—Star Wars ABC-3PO: Alphabet Book. Glass, Calliope & Kennedy, Caitlin. 2016. (ENG.). 48p. (J). (gr. -1-k). 12.99 *(978-1-4847-4142-9(0)*, Disney Lucasfilm Press) Disney Publishing Worldwide.

—Star Wars Creatures Big & Small. Glass, Calliope & Kennedy, Caitlin. 2019. (ENG.). 48p. (J). (gr. 1-3). 10.99 *(978-1-368-05082-1(4)*, Disney Lucasfilm Press) Disney Publishing Worldwide.

—Star Wars OBI-123: A Book of Numbers. Glass, Calliope & Kennedy, Caitlin. 2017. (ENG.). 48p. (J). (gr. 1-3). 12.99 *(978-1-4847-6812-9(4)*, Disney Lucasfilm Press) Disney Publishing Worldwide.

—Star Wars: Search Your Feelings. Glass, Calliope & Kennedy, Caitlin. 2018. (ENG.). 48p. (J). (gr. 1-3). 10.99 *(978-1-368-02736-6(9)*, Disney Lucasfilm Press) Disney Publishing Worldwide.

Cook, Katie & Ashworth, Nichol. Fraggle Rock: Tails & Tales. Randolph, Grace et al. Beedle, Tim, ed. 2011. (Fraggle Rock Ser.: 2). (ENG.). 136p. (J). (gr. 4). 19.95 *(978-1-936393-13-8(1))* Boom Entertainment, Inc.

Cook, Katie & Disney Book Group. Art of Coloring Journey to Star Wars: the Last Jedi: Keepsake Coloring Book. Disney Book Group. 2017. (ENG.). 128p. (YA). (gr. 9-17). pap. 15.99 *(978-1-368-01754-1(1)*, Disney Lucasfilm Press) Disney Publishing Worldwide.

Cook, Laurie. Amelia Asks May I Have A Pet. Mathews, Madge. 2008. 24p. (J). 3.99 *(978-0-9796536-1-2(4)*, EPI Kid Bks.) EPI Bks.

—Brandon's Really Bad, Really Good Day. Mathews, Madge. 2007. (J). 3.99 *(978-0-9726075-1-3(X))* EPI Bks.

—Brandon's Really Big Birthday Surprise. Mathews, Madge. 2008. 24p. (J). 3.99 *(978-0-9796536-0-5(6)*, EPI Kid Bks.) EPI Bks.

Cook, Lynette R. Faraway Worlds: Planets Beyond Our Solar System. Halpern, Paul. 2004. 32p. (J). (gr. 2-5). pap. 7.99 *(978-1-57091-617-5(9))* Charlesbridge Publishing, Inc.

Cook, Monique. Beulah the Lunchroom Bully. Marie, K. 2011. 20p. pap. 24.95 *(978-1-4560-5224-9(1))* America Star Bks.

Cook, Peter. Canada Doodles, 1 vol. Radford, Megan. ed. 2014. (ENG.). 240p. (J). pap. 9.99 *(978-1-4236-3621-2(X))* Gibbs Smith, Publisher.

Cook, Selene. Flight of the Pegasus: Buttercup Gets Her Wings. Coker, Suzanne & Coker, Brennlen, eds. 2019. (ENG.). 96p. (J). pap. 5.99 *(978-1-7984-8904-8(X))* Independently Published.

Cook, Soledad. Ocean of Emotions: A Fun & Interactive Path to Mindfulness. Leitch, Patricia a. 2019. (Kindfulkids Adventure Ser.: Vol. 2). (ENG.). 64p. (J). pap. 13.99 *(978-0-9980349-1-1(6))* Hom, Jonathan.

Cook, Terry. A Moose at the Bus Stop. Cook, Terry. 2013. 24p. pap. 10.95 *(978-1-61633-378-2(2))* Guardian Angel Publishing, Inc.

Cooke, Bev. Timmy the Tadpole, 1 vol. Wrucke, Mary. 2009. 25p. pap. 24.95 *(978-1-60813-776-3(7))* America Star Bks.

Cooke, Charlotte. A Bedtime Journey. Smith, Suzanne. 2017. (Littlest Dreamer Ser.). (ENG.). 32p. (J). (gr. -1-k). pap. 10.99 *(978-1-4052-7689-4(4))* Egmont Bks., Ltd. GBR. Dist: Independent Pubs. Group.

—Lucille Gets Jealous, 1 vol. Gassman, Julie A. 2012. (Little Boost Ser.). (ENG.). 32p. (J). (gr. -1-1). lib. bdg. 23.99 *(978-1-4048-6797-0(X)*, Picture Window Bks.) Capstone.

—A Song for All Seasons. Brown, Margaret Wise. 2019. (Margaret Wise Brown Classics Ser.). (ENG.). 32p. (J). (gr. -1-k). 12.99 *(978-1-68412-765-8(3)*, Silver Dolphin Bks.) Printers Row Publishing Group.

—Wish upon a Dream. Brown, Margaret Wise. 2019. (Margaret Wise Brown Classics Ser.). (ENG.). 32p. (J). (gr. -1-k). 12.99 *(978-1-68412-745-0(9)*, Silver Dolphin Bks.) Printers Row Publishing Group.

Cooke, Grace. An Egyptian Adventure. Durkin, Frances. 2019. (Histronauts Ser.). (ENG.). (J). 88p. pap. 10.99 *(978-1-63163-240-2(X)*, 163163240X); 81p. lib. bdg. 29.99 *(978-1-63163-239-6(6)*, 1631632396) North Star Editions. (Jolly Fish Pr.).

—A Roman Adventure. Durkin, Frances. 2019. (Histronauts Ser.). (ENG.). (J). 88p. pap. 10.99 *(978-1-63163-244-0(2)*, 1631632442); 81p. lib. bdg. 29.99 *(978-1-63163-243-3(4)*, 1631632434) North Star Editions. (Jolly Fish Pr.).

—A Viking Adventure. Durkin, Frances. 2019. (Histronauts Ser.). (ENG.). 88p. (J). pap. 10.99 *(978-1-63163-364-5(3)*, 1631633643); lib. bdg. 29.99 *(978-1-63163-363-8(5)*, 1631633635) North Star Editions. (Jolly Fish Pr.).

Cooke, Lucy, photos by. A Little Book of Sloth. Cooke, Lucy. 2013. (ENG., 64p. (J). (gr. k). 18.99 *(978-1-4424-4557-4(2)*, McElderry, Margaret K. Bks.) McElderry, Margaret K. Bks.

Cooke, Stephanie. Adora the Albino Alligator. Edwards, Rhonda. 2019. (ENG.). 32p. (J). pap. 9.98 *(978-0-7443-2415-0(7))* CamCat Publishing.

Cooke, Tom & Brannon, Tom. Twinkle, Twinkle, Little Bug. Ross, Katharine. 2014. (Step into Reading Ser.). (ENG.). 32p. (J). (gr. -1-1). pap. 3.99 *(978-0-679-87666-3(9)*, Random Hse. Bks. for Young Readers) Random Hse. Children's Bks.

Cooley, Rhonda. Old Witch Hazel. Cooley, Zach. 2019. (ENG.). 26p. (J). pap. 13.00 *(978-1-7950-5495-9(6))* Independently Published.

Coombs, Jonathan. Do You Know the Cucuy? Conoces Al Cucuy? Galindo, Claudia & Pluecker, John. 2008. (SPA & ENG.). 32p. (J). (gr. -1-2). 16.95 *(978-1-55885-492-5(4)*, Piñata Books) Arte Publico Pr.

—It's Bedtime, Cucuy!/A la Cama, Cucuy. Galindo, Claudia. Pluecker, John, tr. from ENG. 2008. (SPA & ENG.). 32p. (J). (gr. -1-2). 16.95 *(978-1-55885-491-8(6)*, Piñata Books) Arte Publico Pr.

Coombs, Patricia. Laugh with the Moon. Coombs, Patricia. Burg, Shana. 2013. 256p. (J). (gr. 5-6). pap. 7.99 *(978-0-440-42210-5(8)*, Yearling) Random Hse. Children's Bks.

Coon, Cyndi. Art That Pops! How to Make Wacky 3-D Creations That Jump, Spin, & Spring! 2006. 48p. (J). pap. *(978-0-439-81337-2(9))* Scholastic, Inc.

Coonan, Felicity, jt. illus. see Ober, Jules.

Cooney, Barbara. El Nino Espiritu: Una Historia de la Navidad. Bierhorst, John. Aramburu, Francisco Gonzalez, tr. 2003.Tr. of Spirit Child: A Story of the Nativity. (SPA.). 26p. (J). (gr. 3-7). reprint ed. 20.00 *(978-0-7567-6882-9(9))* DIANE Publishing Co.

—Roxaboxen. McLerran, Alice. 2004. (ENG.). 32p. (J). (gr. -1-3). pap. 7.99 *(978-0-06-052633-7(5))* HarperCollins Pubs.

—The Story of Holly & Ivy. Godden, Rumer. 2006. (ENG.). 32p. (J). (gr. k-3). 17.99 *(978-0-670-06219-5(7)*, Viking Books for Young Readers) Penguin Young Readers Group.

—When the Sky Is Like Lace, 1 vol. Horwitz, Elinor Lander. 2015. (ENG.). 32p. (J). 17.95 *(978-1-939017-47-5(5)*, 50bff2c0-f742-4934-b12b-ee45b2b2dd27) Islandport Pr., Inc.

Cooney, Barbara. Island Boy: 30th Anniversary Edition. Cooney, Barbara. 30th ed. 2018. 44p. (J). (-k). 17.99 *(978-0-451-48092-7(9)*, Viking Books for Young Readers) Penguin Young Readers Group.

—Miss Rumphius. Cooney, Barbara. 2004. 28p. (J). (gr. k-2). reprint ed. pap. 6.00 *(978-0-7567-7107-2(2))* DIANE Publishing Co.

Coons, Dean. The Lion of Oz & the Badge of Courage. Baum, Roger S. 2nd ed. 2003. 247p. (J). 24.95 *(978-1-57072-255-4(2))* Overmountain Pr.

Coope, Katy. How to Make Manga Characters: Band 17/Diamond (Collins Big Cat) Coope, Katy. 2008. (Collins Big Cat Ser.). (ENG.). 56p. (J). (gr. 5-6). pap. 12.99 *(978-0-00-723102-7(4))* HarperCollins Pubs. Ltd. GBR. Dist: Independent Pubs. Group.

Cooper, Adrian, photos by. Beijing. Pellegrini, Nancy. 2007. (Global Cities Ser.). 61p. (gr. 5-8). lib. bdg. 30.00 *(978-0-7910-8848-7(0)*, Chelsea Hse.) Facts On File, Inc.

—Los Angeles. Barber, Nicola. 2007. (Global Cities Ser.). 64p. (gr. 5-8). lib. bdg. 30.00 *(978-0-7910-8847-0(2)*, Chelsea Hse.) Facts On File, Inc.

Cooper, Adrian, jt. photos by see Bowden, Rob.

Cooper, Barbara & Cooper, Jayson E. Charlie's Game. Cooper, Jayson E. 2019. (ENG.). 26p. (J). pap. 9.99 *(978-1-0777-4452-3(8))* Independently Published.

Cooper, Blair. Hello Blue Devil! Aryal, Aimee. 2004. 22p. (J). 19.95 *(978-1-932888-26-3(8))* Mascot Bks., Inc.

—Hello, Demon Deacon! Aryal, Aimee. 2004. 24p. (J). 19.95 *(978-1-932888-14-0(4))* Mascot Bks., Inc.

—Hello Mr. Wuf! Aryal, Aimee. 2004. 24p. (J). 19.95 *(978-1-932888-06-5(3))* Mascot Bks., Inc.

—Hello Rameses! Aryal, Aimee. 2004. 24p. (J). 19.95 *(978-1-932888-17-1(9))* Mascot Bks., Inc.

—Hello Wildcat! Aryal, Aimee. 2004. 24p. (J). 19.95 *(978-1-932888-33-1(0))* Mascot Bks., Inc.

Cooper-Davies, Amber. The Wedding Week: Around the World in Seven Weddings. Allan, Chimaechi. 2015. 40p. (YA). pap. *(978-0-9931349-4-4(7))* Kio Global Ltd.

Cooper, Dawn. The Animal Book, 1 vol. Martin, Ruth & Lonely Planet Kids. 2017. (ENG.). 164p. (J). (gr. 4-7). 19.99 *(978-1-78657-434-3(9)*, 5372) Lonely Planet Global Ltd. IRL. Dist: Hachette Bk. Group.

—Ocean Emporium. Brooks, Susie. 2019. (ENG.). 64p. (J). (gr. k-4). lib. bdg. 18.99 *(978-1-58089-828-7(9))* Charlesbridge Publishing, Inc.

Cooper, Debbie. Ancient Maya: Cultures of the Caribbean & Central America, 2 bks. l.t. ed. 2005. 32p. (J). per. 9.99 *(978-0-9760406-1-3(1)*, A Kidz World) ABUAA, Inc.

—The Garifuna: Cultures of the Caribbean & Central America, l.t. ed. 2005. 32p. (J). 9.99 *(978-0-9760406-0-6(3)*, 6-0-3, A Kidz World) ABUAA, Inc.

Cooper, Deborah. Searching for Grizzlies. Mangelsen, Thomas, photos by. Hirschi, Ron. 2005. (ENG.). 32p. (J). (gr. 2-k). 16.95 *(978-1-59078-014-5(0))* Boyds Mills Pr.

Cooper, Deborah, jt. illus. see Mangelsen, Thomas D.

Cooper, Elisha. Beach. Cooper, Elisha. 2006. (ENG.). 40p. (J). (gr. -1-k). 18.99 *(978-0-439-68785-0(3)*, Orchard Bks.) Scholastic, Inc.

—Bear Dreams. Cooper, Elisha. 2006. 40p. (J). (gr. -1-2). 16.99 *(978-0-06-087428-5(7)*, Greenwillow Bks.) HarperCollins Pubs.

—Homer. Cooper, Elisha. 2012. (ENG.). 32p. (J). (gr. -1-3). 16.99 *(978-0-06-201248-7(7)*, Greenwillow Bks.) HarperCollins Pubs.

Cooper, Emmanuel. A Saturday Surprise. Battle, Cleaton D. 2006. 68p. (J). pap. 11.95 *(978-1-59663-504-3(5)*, Castle Keep Pr.) Rock, James A. & Co. Pubs.

Cooper, Floyd. Back of the Bus. Reynolds, Aaron. 32p. (J). (gr. 1-3). 2013. 8.99 *(978-0-14-751058-7(9)*, Puffin Books); 2010. 16.99 *(978-0-399-25091-0(3)*, Philomel Bks.) Penguin Young Readers Group.

—Back of the Bus. Reynolds, Aaron. 2013. (ENG.). (J). (gr. 1-3). lib. bdg. 19.60 *(978-1-62765-943-7(9))* Perfection Learning Corp.

—A Beach Tail. Williams, Karen Lynn. 2010. (ENG.). 32p. (J). (gr. -1-2). 17.95 *(978-1-59078-712-0(9))* Boyds Mills Pr.

—Becoming Billie Holiday. Weatherford, Carole Boston. 2008. (ENG.). 120p. (YA). (gr. 4-7). 19.95 *(978-1-59078-507-2(X)*, Wordsong) Boyds Mills Pr.

—Ben & the Emancipation Proclamation. Sherman, Patrice. 2009. (ENG.). 32p. (J). (gr. 3-7). 17.00 *(978-0-8028-5319-6(6)*, Eerdmans Bks For Young Readers) Eerdmans, William B. Publishing Co.

—The Blacker the Berry. Thomas, Joyce Carol. 2008. (ENG.). 32p. (J). (gr. -1-3). 16.99 *(978-0-06-025375-2(4)*, Amistad) HarperCollins Pubs.

—Brick by Brick. Smith, Charles R., Jr. 2012. (ENG.). 32p. (J). (gr. -1-3). 17.99 *(978-0-06-192082-0(7)*, Amistad) HarperCollins Pubs.

—Brick by Brick. Smith, Charles R., Jr. 2015. (ENG.). 32p. (J). (gr. -1-3). pap. 7.99 *(978-0-06-192084-4(3)*, Amistad) HarperCollins Pubs.

—A Dance Like Starlight: One Ballerina's Dream. Dempsey, Kristy. 2014. 32p. (J). (gr. k-3). 17.99 *(978-0-399-25284-6(3)*, Philomel Bks.) Penguin Young Readers Group.

—Frederick Douglass: the Lion Who Wrote History. Myers, Walter Dean. 2017. (ENG.). 40p. (J). (gr. -1-3). 17.99 *(978-0-06-027709-3(2))* HarperCollins Pubs.

—In the Land of Milk & Honey. Thomas, Joyce Carol. 2012. (ENG.). 32p. (J). (gr. -1-3). 16.99 *(978-0-06-025383-7(5)*, Amistad) HarperCollins Pubs.

—The Last Stop Before Heaven. De Baun, Hillary Hall. 2012. (ENG.). 236p. (J). pap. 9.00 *(978-0-8028-5398-1(6)*, Eerdmans Bks For Young Readers) Eerdmans, William B. Publishing Co.

—Miss Crandall's School for Young Ladies & Little Misses of Color. Alexander, Elizabeth & Nelson, Marilyn. 2007. (ENG.). 48p. (J). (gr. 1-4). 17.95 *(978-1-59078-456-3(1)*, Wordsong) Boyds Mills Pr.

—Mississippi Morning. Vander Zee, Ruth. 2004. 32p. (J). 16.00 *(978-0-8028-5211-3(4))* Eerdmans, William B. Publishing Co.

—Queen of the Track: Alice Coachman, Olympic High-Jump Champion. Lang, Heather. 2012. (ENG.). 40p. (J). (gr. k-4). 16.95 *(978-1-59078-850-9(8))* Boyds Mills Pr.

—Ride to Remember: A Civil Rights Story. Langley, Sharon & Nathan, Amy. 2020. (ENG.). 40p. (J). (gr. 1-4). 18.99 *(978-1-4197-3685-8(X)*, 1149701, Abrams Bks. for Young Readers) Abrams, Inc.

—Sisters & Champions: the True Story of Venus & Serena Williams. Bryant, Howard. 2018. 32p. (J). (gr. -1-3). 17.99 *(978-0-399-16906-9(7)*, Philomel Bks.) Penguin Young Readers Group.

—A Spy Called James: The True Story of James Lafayette, Revolutionary War Double Agent. Rockwell, Anne. 2016. (ENG.). 32p. (J). (gr. 2-5). lib. bdg. 18.99 *(978-1-4677-4933-6(8)*, 9781467749336); E-Book 29.32 *(978-1-4677-6178-9(8))* Lerner Publishing Group. (Carolrhoda Bks.).

—Taneesha Never Disparaging. Perry, M. LaVora. 2008. (ENG.). 216p. (J). (gr. 2-7). pap. 8.95 *(978-0-86171-550-3(0))* Wisdom Pubns.

—These Hands. Mason, Margaret H. (ENG.). 32p. (J). (gr. -1-3). 2015. 7.99 *(978-0-544-55546-4(5)*, 1610453, HMH Books For Young Readers); 2011. 16.99 *(978-0-547-21566-2(5)*, 1060722) Houghton Mifflin Harcourt Publishing Co.

—Where's Rodney? Bogan, Carmen. 2017. (ENG.). 32p. (J). (gr. -1-1). 16.99 *(978-1-930238-73-2(8))* Yosemite Conservancy.

Cooper, Floyd. Jump! From the Life of Michael Jordan. Cooper, Floyd. 2004. (ENG.). 40p. (J). (gr. 1-4). 17.99 *(978-0-399-24230-4(9)*, Philomel Bks.) Penguin Young Readers Group.

—Juneteenth for Mazie. Cooper, Floyd. 2015. (Fiction Picture Bks.). (ENG.). 40p. (J). (gr. 1-4). lib. bdg. 25.32 *(978-1-4795-5819-3(2)*, Picture Window Bks.) Capstone.

—Max & the Tag-Along Moon. Cooper, Floyd. (ENG.). 32p. (J). (gr. -1-2). 2015. pap. 8.99 *(978-0-14-751546-9(7)*, Puffin Books); 2013. 17.99 *(978-0-399-23342-5(3)*, Philomel Bks.) Penguin Young Readers Group.

—Max & the Tag-Along Moon. Cooper, Floyd. 2015. (ENG.). (J). (gr. -1-2). lib. bdg. 19.60 *(978-1-62765-741-9(X))* Perfection Learning Corp.

—The Ring Bearer. Cooper, Floyd. 2017. (ENG.). 32p. (J). (gr. -1-2). 16.99 *(978-0-399-16740-9(4)*, Philomel Bks.) Penguin Young Readers Group.

Cooper, France. Oh, Do You Know? A Read-and-Sing Book. Gifford, Myrna. 2003. 12p. (J). 9.95 *(978-0-9720763-5-7(2))* Action Factor, Inc.

Cooper, Frances. Meet the Lit Kids: A Read-and-Sing Book. Gifford, Myrna. 2003. 12p. (J). 9.95 *(978-0-9720763-7-1(9))* Action Factor, Inc.

—Name Those Vowels: A Read-and-Sing Book. Gifford, Myrna. 2003. 12p. (J). 9.95 *(978-0-9720763-4-0(4))* Action Factor, Inc.

—Outlaws: A Read-and-Sing Book. Gifford, Myrna Ross. 2005. 12p. (J). 9.95 *(978-0-9754618-1-5(8))* Action Factor, Inc.

—Silent E: A Read-and-Sing Book. Gifford, Myrna Ross. 2005. 12p. (J). 9.95 *(978-0-9754618-0-8(X))* Action Factor, Inc.

—Spelling Families: A Read-and-Sing Book. Gifford, Myrna. 2003. 12p. (J). 9.95 *(978-0-9720763-6-4(0))* Action Factor, Inc.

—Talking & Walking: A Read-and-Sing Book. Gifford, Myrna. 2005. 12p. (J). 9.95 *(978-0-9720763-9-5(5))* Action Factor, Inc.

—Two Little Letters: A Read-and-Sing Book. Gifford, Myrna. 2005. 12p. (J). 9.95 *(978-0-9720763-8-8(7))* Action Factor, Inc.

—What's That Sound? A Read-and-Sing Book. Gifford, Myrna. 2003. 12p. (J). 9.95 *(978-0-9720763-3-3(6))* Action Factor, Inc.

Cooper, Gene. Who, Who... Who Is Reading My Book? Cooper, Gene. 2014. (J). 11.95 *(978-0-615-85312-3(9))* Cooper, Gene.

Cooper, Helen. The Hippo at the End of the Hall. Cooper, Helen. 2019. (ENG.). 352p. (J). (gr. 2-4). 17.99 *(978-1-5362-0448-3(X))* Candlewick Pr.

—Pumpkin Soup: A Picture Book. Cooper, Helen. 2005. (ENG.). 32p. (J). (gr. -1-3). per. 8.99 *(978-0-374-46031-0(0)*, 900030431) Square Fish.

Cooper, Helen S. Tatty-Ratty. Cooper, Helen S. 2004. 28p. (J). (gr. k-3). reprint ed. 19.00 *(978-0-7567-7214-7(1))* DIANE Publishing Co.

Cooper, Jay. Adventures of the Super Zeroes. Bolts, Russ. 2020. (Bots Ser.: 7). (ENG.). 128p. (J). (gr. k-4). 16.99 *(978-1-5344-6093-5(4))*; pap. 5.99 *(978-1-5344-6092-8(6))* Little Simon. (Little Simon).

—The Bots Collection: The Most Annoying Robots in the Universe; the Good, the Bad, & the Cowbots; 20,000 Robots under the Sea; the Dragon Bots. Bolts, Russ. ed. 2019. (Bots Ser.). (ENG.). 512p. (J). (gr. k-4). pap. 23.99 *(978-1-5344-4642-7(7)*, Little Simon) Little Simon.

—Delivery Trucks! Burton, Jeffrey. 2017. (ENG.). 12p. (J). bds. 7.99 *(978-1-4814-9219-5(5)*, Little Simon) Little Simon.

—The Dragon Bots. Bolts, Russ. 2019. (Bots Ser.: 4). (ENG.). 128p. (J). (gr. k-4). 16.99 *(978-1-5344-4420-1(3))*; pap. 5.99 *(978-1-5344-4419-5(X))* Little Simon. (Little Simon).

—Food Trucks! A Lift-The-Flap Meal on Wheels! Burton, Jeffrey. 2016. (ENG.). 12p. (J). (gr. -1). bds. 7.99 *(978-1-4814-6521-2(X)*, Little Simon) Little Simon.

—The Good, the Bad, & the Cowbots. Bolts, Russ. 2019. (Bots Ser.: 2). (ENG.). 128p. (J). (gr. k-4). 16.99 *(978-1-5344-3692-3(8))*; pap. 5.99 *(978-1-5344-3691-6(X))* Little Simon. (Little Simon).

Cooper, Jay. The Lost Camera. Bolts, Russ. 2020. (Bots Ser.: 8). (ENG.). 128p. (J). (gr. k-9). 17.99 ***(978-1-5344-6096-6(9))***; pap. 5.99 ***(978-1-5344-6095-9(0))*** Little Simon. (Little Simon).

Cooper, Jay. The Most Annoying Robots in the Universe. Bolts, Russ. 2019. (Bots Ser.: 1). (ENG.). 128p. (J). (gr. k-4). 16.99 *(978-1-5344-3689-3(8))*; pap. 5.99 *(978-1-5344-3688-6(X))* Little Simon. (Little Simon).

—The Secret Space Station. Bolts, Russ. 2020. (Bots Ser.: 6). (ENG.). 128p. (J). (gr. k-4). 16.99 *(978-1-5344-4504-8(8))*; pap. 5.99 *(978-1-5344-4503-1(X))* Little Simon. (Little Simon).

—A Tale of Two Classrooms. Bolts, Russ. 2019. (Bots Ser.: 5). (ENG.). 128p. (J). (gr. k-4). 16.99 *(978-1-5344-4501-7(3))*; pap. 5.99 *(978-1-5344-4500-0(5))* Little Simon. (Little Simon).

—20,000 Robots under the Sea. Bolts, Russ. 2019. (Bots Ser.: 3). (ENG.). 128p. (J). (gr. k-4). 16.99 *(978-1-5344-4417-1(3))*; pap. 5.99 *(978-1-5344-4416-4(5))* Little Simon. (Little Simon).

Cooper, Jayson E., jt. illus. see Cooper, Barbara.

Cooper, Jenny. Birds to Color. Cullis, Megan. ed. 2012. (Coloring Bks). 32p. (J). pap. 5.99 *(978-0-7945-3285-7(3)*, Usborne) EDC Publishing.

—Butterflies Coloring Book. Cullis, Megan. ed. 2012. (Coloring Bks). 32p. (J). pap. 5.99 *(978-0-7945-3113-3(X)*, Usborne) EDC Publishing.

—Do Your Ears Hang Low? 2017. (ENG.). 40p. (J). (gr. -1). 14.95 *(978-1-4549-1614-7(1))* Sterling Publishing Co., Inc.

—Flowers to Color. Meredith, Susan. ed. 2013. (Nature Coloring Bks). 32p. (J). pap. 5.99 *(978-0-7945-3058-7(3)*, Usborne) EDC Publishing.

—Forest Life to Color. ed. 2013. (Nature Coloring Bks). 32p. (J). pap. 5.99 *(978-0-7945-3305-2(1)*, Usborne) EDC Publishing.

—Fruit for You, 6 pack. Holden, Pam. 2009. (Red Rocket Readers Ser.). 16p. (gr. -1-1). pap. *(978-1-877363-01-6(4)*, Red Rocket Readers) Flying Start Bks.

Cooper, Jenny. Grandma's Lost Her Corgis. Davidson, Joy H. ed. 2020. (ENG.). 32p. (J). (gr. -1-1). 16.95 ***(978-1-913337-36-0(7)***, Scribblers) Book Hse. GBR. Dist: Sterling Publishing Co., Inc.

Cooper, Jenny. Nature to Color. Meredith, Susan & Cullis, Megan. 2013. (ENG.). 96p. (J). 9.99 *(978-0-7945-1913-1(X)*, Usborne) EDC Publishing.

—Oh No! Look What the Cat Dragged In. Davidson, Joy H. ed. 2019. (ENG.). 40p. (J). (gr. -1-1). 16.95 *(978-1-912904-60-0(8)*, Scribblers) Book Hse. GBR. Dist: Sterling Publishing Co., Inc.

—Oh, So Many Kisses (padded Board Book) Finn, Maura. 2019. (ENG.). 24p. (J). (— 1). bds. 8.99 *(978-0-358-07427-4(4)*, 1745372, HMH Books For Young Readers) Houghton Mifflin Harcourt Publishing Co.

—Rainforest to Color. ed. 2013. (Nature Coloring Bks). 32p. (J). pap. 5.99 *(978-0-7945-3306-9(X)*, Usborne) EDC Publishing.

—Show Me a Shape, 6 pack. Holden, Pam. 2009. (Red Rocket Readers Ser.). 16p. (gr. -1-1). pap. *(978-1-877363-27-6(8)*, Red Rocket Readers) Flying Start Bks.

—Show Me a Shape - BIG BOOK. Holden, Pam. 2016. 16p. (-1). pap. *(978-1-77654-160-7(X)*, Red Rocket Readers) Flying Start Bks.

—Sina & the Eel: A Tale from Samoa. Watson, Leilani. 2016. 24p. (J). pap. 9.95 *(978-1-927244-56-2(0))* Flying Start Bks. NZL. Dist: Flying Start Bks.

—Sina & the Eel (Big Book Edition) A Tale from Samoa. Watson, Leilani. 2016. 24p. (J). pap. *(978-1-927244-66-1(8))* Flying Start Bks.

—A Treasury of NZ Poems for Children. Green, Paula. 2017. (ENG.). 288p. (J). (gr. k-2). 39.95 *(978-0-14-377219-4(8))* Penguin Group New Zealand, Ltd. NZL. Dist: Independent Pubs. Group.

—Undersea Life to Color. Meredith, Susan. 2014. (ENG.). (J). pap. 5.99 *(978-0-7945-2854-6(6)*, Usborne) EDC Publishing.

Cooper, Jenny & King, Sue. Monkeys. Bowman, Lucy. ed. 2011. (Beginner's Nature Ser.). 32p. (J). ring bd. 4.99 *(978-0-7945-2978-9(X)*, Usborne) EDC Publishing.

Cooper, Jenny & Watson, Richard. Owls. Bone, Emily. 2013. (Usborne Beginners Ser.). (ENG.). 32p. (J). 9.99 *(978-0-7945-3401-1(5)*, Usborne) EDC Publishing.

Cooper, Jon. Joe's Jungle Hair. Aldridge, Paul. 2020. (ENG.). 36p. (J). pap. 13.99 ***(978-1-910903-16-2(7))*** AudioGO.

Cooper, Joseph. A Bridge to Our Tradition. Moskowitz, Nachama Skolnik. Lewy, Faye Tillis, ed. 2004. (gr. 4-6). pap., tchr. ed., tchr.'s training gde. ed. 22.95 *(978-0-8074-0761-5(5)*, 208060) URJ Pr.

—A Bridge to Our Tradition: Pirkei Avot. Moskowitz, Nachama Skolnik. Lewy, Faye Tillis, ed. 2004. (gr. 4-6). pap. 13.95 *(978-0-8074-0760-8(7)*, 160504) URJ Pr.

Cooper, Kelly. Good Night Diggers. Gamble, Adam & Jasper, Mark. 2018. (Good Night Our World Ser.). 32p. (J). (— 1). bds. 9.95 *(978-1-60219-678-0(8))* Good Night Bks.

Cooper, Martha, photos by. The Jump Rope Book. Laredo, Elizabeth. 2004. 284p. (J). (gr. k-4). reprint ed. pap. 10.00 *(978-0-7567-7775-3(5))* DIANE Publishing Co.

—The Marble Book. Chevat, Richie. 2004. 186p. (J). (gr. k-4). reprint ed. pap. 10.00 *(978-0-7567-7776-0(3))* DIANE Publishing Co.

Cooper, Nicole. The Adventures of Ryan Lincoln. Standish, Joyce, ed. 2012. 46p. (J). pap. 10.00 *(978-0-9716244-5-0(3))* TLS Publishing.

Cooper, Paul. Seafarers: Chronicles of the Suspense & Romance of the Sea. Niedworok, Claudio O. Knight, Tori, ed. Date not set. 80p. (Orig.). (YA). pap. 11.95 *(978-1-882133-05-5(6))* Barefoot Pr.

Cooper, Sharon, jt. illus. see Kirkby, Joanne.

Cooper, Simon. Flight of the Pummeled Parakeet. Hay, Sam. 2015. (Undead Pets Ser.: 6). (ENG.). 112p. (J). (gr. 1-3). 5.99 *(978-0-448-47800-5(5)*, Grosset & Dunlap) Penguin Young Readers Group.

—Gasp of the Ghoulish Guinea Pig. Hay, Sam. 2016. (Undead Pets Ser.: 7). (ENG.). 112p. (J). (gr. 1-3). 5.99 *(978-0-448-49003-8(X)*, Grosset & Dunlap) Penguin Young Readers Group.

—Goldfish from Beyond the Grave. Hay, Sam. 2015. (Undead Pets Ser.: 4). (ENG.). 112p. (J). (gr. 1-3). 5.99 *(978-0-448-47798-5(X)*, Grosset & Dunlap) Penguin Young Readers Group.

—Hour of the Doomed Dog. Hay, Sam. 2016. (Undead Pets Ser.: 8). (ENG.). 112p. (J). (gr. 1-3). 5.99 *(978-0-448-49004-5(8)*, Grosset & Dunlap) Penguin Young Readers Group.

—Return of the Hungry Hamster. Hay, Sam. 2014. (Undead Pets Ser.: 1). (ENG.). 112p. (J). (gr. 1-3). 5.99 *(978-0-448-47795-4(5)*, Grosset & Dunlap) Penguin Young Readers Group.

—Rise of the Zombie Rabbit. Hay, Sam. 2015. (Undead Pets Ser.: 5). (ENG.). 112p. (J). (gr. 1-3). 5.99 *(978-0-448-47799-2(8)*, Grosset & Dunlap) Penguin Young Readers Group.

Cooper, Stephanie. Cat in the Tree. Archambault, John. 2007. (J). *(978-1-58669-230-8(5))* Childcraft Education Corp.

Cooper, Wade. Farm Animals. Cooper, Wade. 2009. (Scholastic Reader Level 2 Ser.). (ENG.). 32p. (J). (gr. -1-3). pap. 3.99 *(978-0-545-09993-6(5)*, Cartwheel Bks.) Scholastic, Inc.

Coote, Maree. Andy Web Artist: Artist. Coote, Maree. 2018. (ENG.). 24p. (J). (gr. k-2). 22.99 *(978-0-9924917-5-8(4))* Melbournestyle Bks. AUS. Dist: Independent Pubs. Group.

—The Black Pot Belly. Coote, Maree. 2005. (ENG.). 20p. (J). (gr. -1-3). 22.99 *(978-0-9757047-1-4(0))* Melbournestyle Bks. AUS. Dist: Independent Pubs. Group.

—Letters from New York: Making Pictures with the A-B-C. Coote, Maree. 2018. (ENG.). 24p. (J). (gr. k-2). 17.99 *(978-0-9924917-6-5(2))* Melbournestyle Bks. AUS. Dist: Independent Pubs. Group.

—The Seacret of Driftus & Sprout. Coote, Maree. 2005. (ENG.). 24p. (J). (gr. -1-3). 22.99 *(978-0-9757047-0-7(2))* Melbournestyle Bks. AUS. Dist: Independent Pubs. Group.

Coote, Mark. Pushing & Pulling: Band 01A/Pink a (Collins Big Cat) Hughes, Mónica. 2005. (Collins Big Cat Ser.). (ENG.). 16p. (J). (gr. -1-k). pap. 5.99 *(978-0-00-718541-2(3))* HarperCollins Pubs. Ltd. GBR. Dist: Independent Pubs. Group.

Coover, Colleen. Bandette Volume 1: Presto! Tobin, Paul. 2020. (ENG.). 144p. (YA). (gr. 7-9). pap. 14.99 ***(978-1-5067-1923-8(6)**, Dark Horse Books)* Dark Horse Comics.

Coovert, J. P. Charlie Joe Jackson's Guide to Extra Credit. Greenwald, Tommy. 2013. (Charlie Joe Jackson Ser.: 2). (ENG.). 288p. (J). (gr. 4-7). pap. 7.99 *(978-1-250-01670-6(3)*, 900087084) Square Fish.

—Charlie Joe Jackson's Guide to Not Growing Up. Greenwald, Tommy. 2016. (Charlie Joe Jackson Ser.: 6). (ENG.). 192p. (J). 13.99 *(978-1-62672-169-2(6)*, 9781626721692) Roaring Brook Pr.

—Charlie Joe Jackson's Guide to Not Growing Up. Greenwald, Tommy. 2018. (Charlie Joe Jackson Ser.: 6). (ENG.). 208p. (J). pap. 7.99 *(978-1-250-15835-2(4)*, 900185487) Square Fish.

—Charlie Joe Jackson's Guide to Not Reading. Greenwald, Tommy. 2012. (Charlie Joe Jackson Ser.). (ENG.). (J). (gr. 4-7). lib. bdg. 17.60 *(978-1-68065-309-0(1))* Perfection Learning Corp.

—The Last Invisible Boy. Kuhlman, Evan. (ENG.). 240p. (J). (gr. 5-9). 2010. pap. 7.99 *(978-1-4169-6089-8(9))*; 2008. 16.99 *(978-1-4169-5797-3(9))* Simon & Schuster Children's Publishing. (Atheneum Bks. for Young Readers).

—Why Fish Fart: Gross but True Things You'll Wish You Didn't Know. Gould, Francesca. 2014. (ENG.). 144p. (J). (gr. 3-7). pap. 8.99 *(978-0-399-16598-6(3)*, G.P. Putnam's Sons Books for Young Readers) Penguin Young Readers Group.

Cope, Jane. Dad's Cake. Nash, Margaret. 2009. (Tadpoles Ser.). (ENG.). (J). (gr. k-k). lib. bdg. 17.55 *(978-1-61383-942-3(1))* Perfection Learning Corp.

—Little Bad Riding Hood. Jarman, Julia. 2014. (Tadpoles: Fairytale Twists Ser.). (ENG.). 32p. (J). (gr. 1-2). *(978-0-7787-0442-3(4))*; pap. *(978-0-7787-0450-8(5))* Crabtree Publishing Co.

Cope-Robinson, Lyn. Cat Tails. Cope-Robinson, Lyn. l.t. ed. 2003. 32p. (J). lib. bdg. *(978-1-887774-14-7(9)*, Wynden) Canmore Pr.

Copeland, Eric. The Adventures of Brer Rabbit & Friends. Dorling Kindersley Publishing Staff. 2006. (ENG.). 64p. (J). (gr. 5-12). per. 6.99 *(978-0-7566-1813-1(4)*, DK Children) Dorling Kindersley Publishing, Inc.

—Lewis Carroll. Mendelson, Edward, ed. 2008. (Poetry for Young People Ser.: 11). 48p. (J). (gr. 3). pap. 6.95 *(978-1-4027-5474-6(4))* Sterling Publishing Co., Inc.

Copeland, Greg. The Frederick Douglass You Never Knew. 2004. (You Never Knew Ser.). (ENG.). 80p. (J). (gr. 4-6). pap. 6.95 *(978-0-516-25837-9(0)*, Children's Pr.) Scholastic Library Publishing.

—The George Washington You Never Knew. Collier, James Lincoln. 2004. (You Never Knew Ser.). (ENG.). 80p. (J). (gr. 4-6). pap. 6.95 *(978-0-516-25833-1(8)*, Children's Pr.) Scholastic Library Publishing.

—The Tecumseh You Never Knew. Collier, James Lincoln. 2004. (You Never Knew Ser.). (ENG.). 80p. (J). 25.50 *(978-0-516-24426-6(4)*, Children's Pr.) Scholastic Library Publishing.

Copeland, Gregory. What Is Rock & Roll? O'Connor, Jim. 2017. 105p. (J). *(978-1-5379-2401-4(X)*, Penguin Workshop) Penguin Young Readers Group.

—What Is Rock & Roll? Who HQ & O'Connor, Jim. 2017. (What Was? Ser.). 112p. (J). (gr. 3-7). 5.99 *(978-0-451-53381-4(X))*; lib. bdg. 15.99 *(978-0-451-53383-8(6))* Penguin Young Readers Group. (Penguin Workshop).

—What Is the Stanley Cup? Herman, Gail & Who HQ. 2019. (What Was? Ser.). 112p. (J). (gr. 3-7). 5.99 *(978-1-5247-8647-2(0))*; lib. bdg. 15.99 *(978-1-5247-8648-9(9))* Penguin Young Readers Group. (Penguin Workshop).

—What Is the Story of Doctor Who? Cooper, Gabriel P. & Who HQ. 2019. (What Is the Story Of? Ser.). 112p. (J). (gr. 3-7). (ENG.). 6.99 *(978-1-5247-9106-3(7))*; 15.99 *(978-1-5247-9107-0(5))* Penguin Young Readers Group. (Penguin Workshop).

—What Was the Age of the Dinosaurs? Stine, Megan. 2017. 108p. (J). *(978-1-5182-2584-0(5)*, Grosset & Dunlap) Penguin Publishing Group.

—What Was the Age of the Dinosaurs? Stine, Megan & Who HQ. 2017. (What Was? Ser.). 112p. (J). (gr. 3-7). 5.99 *(978-0-451-53264-0(3))*; lib. bdg. 15.99 *(978-0-451-53266-4(X))* Penguin Young Readers Group. (Penguin Workshop).

—What Was the Titanic? Sabol, Stephanie & Who HQ. 2018. (What Was? Ser.). 112p. (J). (gr. 3-7). 5.99 *(978-0-515-15726-0(0))*; lib. bdg. 15.99 *(978-0-515-15728-4(7))* Penguin Young Readers Group. (Penguin Workshop).

—What Was Woodstock? Holub, Joan. 2016. (What Was-? Chapter Ser.). (ENG.). 112p. (J). (gr. 3-6). 18.69 *(978-1-4844-6936-1(4))* Penguin Publishing Group.

—What Was Woodstock? Holub, Joan & Who HQ. 2016. (What Was? Ser.). 112p. (J). (gr. 3-7). 5.99 *(978-0-448-48696-3(2)*, Penguin Workshop) Penguin Young Readers Group.

—Where Is Walt Disney World? Holub, Joan & Who HQ. 2018. (Where Is? Ser.). (ENG.). 112p. (J). (gr. 3-7). 5.99 *(978-0-515-15843-4(7))*; lib. bdg. 15.99 *(978-0-515-15845-8(3))* Penguin Young Readers Group. (Penguin Workshop).

—Who Is Bruce Springsteen? Sabol, Stephanie & Who HQ. 2016. (Who Was? Ser.). 112p. (J). (gr. 3-7). 5.99 *(978-0-448-48703-8(9)*, Penguin Workshop) Penguin Young Readers Group.

—Who Is Jackie Chan? Jensen Shaffer, Jody & Who HQ. 2020. (Who Was? Ser.). 112p. (J). (gr. 3-7). 5.99 *(978-1-5247-9162-9(8))*; 15.99 *(978-1-5247-9163-6(6))* Penguin Young Readers Group. (Penguin Workshop).

—Who Was Andy Warhol? Anderson, Kirsten & Who HQ. 2014. (Who Was? Ser.). 112p. (J). (gr. 3-7). 5.99 *(978-0-448-48242-2(8)*, Penguin Workshop) Penguin Young Readers Group.

—Who Was Aretha Franklin? Medina, Nico & Who HQ. 2018. (Who Was? Ser.). 112p. (J). (gr. 3-7). 5.99 *(978-0-451-53239-8(2))*; lib. bdg. 15.99 *(978-0-451-53241-1(4))* Penguin Young Readers Group. (Penguin Workshop).

—Who Was Bob Marley? Ellison, Katie & Who HQ. 2017. (Who Was? Ser.). 112p. (J). (gr. 3-7). 5.99 *(978-0-448-48919-3(8)*, Penguin Workshop) Penguin Young Readers Group.

—Who Was Coretta Scott King? Herman, Gail & Who HQ. 2017. (Who Was? Ser.). 112p. (J). (gr. 3-7). 5.99 *(978-0-451-53261-9(9))*; lib. bdg. 15.99 *(978-0-451-53263-3(5))* Penguin Young Readers Group. (Penguin Workshop).

—Who Was Frank Lloyd Wright? Labrecque, Ellen & Who HQ. 2015. (Who Was? Ser.). 112p. (J). (gr. 3-7). 5.99 *(978-0-448-48313-9(0)*, Penguin Workshop) Penguin Young Readers Group.

—Who Was Harriet Beecher Stowe? Rau, Dana Meachen. 2015. (Who Was-? Chapters Ser.). (ENG.). 112p. (J). (gr. 4-6). 18.69 *(978-1-4844-5253-0(4))* Penguin Young Readers Group.

—Who Was Harriet Beecher Stowe? Rau, Dana Meachen & Who HQ. 2015. (Who Was? Ser.). 112p. (J). (gr. 3-7). 5.99 *(978-0-448-48301-6(7)*, Penguin Workshop) Penguin Young Readers Group.

—Who Was Harvey Milk? Grinapol, Corinne A. & Who HQ. 2020. (Who Was? Ser.). 112p. (J). (gr. 3-7). 5.99 *(978-1-5247-9278-7(0))*; 15.99 *(978-1-5247-9279-4(9))* Penguin Young Readers Group. (Penguin Workshop).

—Who Was Jesse Owens? Buckley, James, Jr. et al. 2015. (Who Was? Ser.). (ENG.). 112p. (J). (gr. 3-7). 5.99 *(978-0-448-48307-8(6)*, Penguin Workshop) Penguin Young Readers Group.

—Who Was Jesse Owens? Buckley, James. 2015. 106p. (J). *(978-1-4806-9215-2(8)*, Grosset & Dunlap) Penguin Publishing Group.

—Who Was Jules Verne? Buckley, James & Who HQ. 2016. (Who Was? Ser.). (ENG.). 112p. (J). (gr. 3-7). 5.99 *(978-0-448-48850-9(7)*, Penguin Workshop) Penguin Young Readers Group.

Copeland, Gregory. Who Was Kobe Bryant? Labrecque, Ellen & Who HQ. 2020. (Who HQ NOW Ser.). 56p. (J). (gr. 3-7). 4.99 ***(978-0-593-22570-7(8))***; 12.99 ***(978-0-593-22571-4(6))*** Penguin Young Readers Group. (Penguin Workshop).

Copeland, Gregory. Who Was Lucille Ball? Pollack, Pam & Belviso, Meg. 2017. 107p. (J). *(978-1-4806-9203-9(4)*, Grosset & Dunlap) Penguin Publishing Group.

—Who Was Lucille Ball? Belviso, Meg et al. 2017. (Who Was? Ser.). 112p. (J). (gr. 3-7). 5.99 *(978-0-448-48303-0(3)*, Penguin Workshop) Penguin Young Readers Group.

—Who Was Napoleon? Gigliotti, Jim & Who HQ. 2018. (Who Was? Ser.). 112p. (J). (gr. 3-7). (ENG.). 5.99 *(978-0-448-48860-8(4))*; lib. bdg. 15.99 *(978-1-5247-8853-7(8))* Penguin Young Readers Group. (Penguin Workshop).

—Who Was Norman Rockwell? Fabiny, Sarah & Who HQ. 2019. (Who Was? Ser.). 112p. (J). (gr. 3-7). 5.99 *(978-0-448-48864-6(7))*; lib. bdg. 15.99 *(978-1-5247-9096-7(6))* Penguin Young Readers Group. (Penguin Workshop).

—Who Was Seabiscuit? Buckley, James. 2015. (Who Was-? Chapters Ser.). (ENG.). 112p. (J). (gr. 4-6). 18.69 *(978-1-4844-6962-0(3))* Penguin Publishing Group.

—Who Was Seabiscuit? Buckley, James & Who HQ. 2015. (Who Was? Ser.). (ENG.). 112p. (J). (gr. 3-7). 5.99 *(978-0-448-48309-2(2)*, Penguin Workshop) Penguin Young Readers Group.

—Who Was Stephen Hawking? Who HQ & Gigliotti, Jim. 2019. (Who Was? Ser.). (ENG.). 112p. (J). (gr. 3-7). 5.99 *(978-0-451-53248-0(1))*; 15.99 *(978-0-451-53250-3(3))* Penguin Young Readers Group. (Penguin Workshop).

Copelman, Evelyn. Once There Was a King: A Tournament of Stories. Alden, Raymond MacDonald. 2011. 194p. 42.95 *(978-1-258-08031-0(1))* Literary Licensing, LLC.

Copiel, Olivier. Red Zone, 2 vols., Vol. 2. Johns, Geoff. 2004. (Avengers Ser.). 160p. (YA). pap. 14.99 *(978-0-7851-1099-6(2))* Marvel Worldwide, Inc.

Copple, Lauren. Tonight: A Book of God's Bedtime Promises. Assell, Emily. 2019. (Generation Claimed Ser.). (ENG.). 20p. (J). bds. 7.99 *(978-1-4964-3624-5(5)*, 20_32346, Tyndale Kids) Tyndale Hse. Pubs.

Copplestone, Jim. Noah's Bed. Jones, Liz. 2004. 32p. (J). *(978-1-84507-002-1(X))* ReiseArt Buchhandlung GmbH.

Coppo, Marianna. Good Boy. 2020. (ENG.). 48p. (J). (gr. k-3). 17.99 *(978-1-4521-7774-8(0))* Chronicle Bks. LLC.

Copter, Steve. Medikidz Explain Living with ADHD, Vol. Chilman-Blair, Kim et al. 2014. (ENG.). 16p. (J). pap. *(978-1-906935-84-9(X))* Medikidz Ltd.

Corace, Jen. Baby Wren & the Great Gift, 1 vol. Lloyd-Jones, Sally. 2016. (ENG.). 32p. (J). 16.99 *(978-0-310-73389-8(8))* Zonderkidz.

—The Entomological Tales of Augustus T. Percival. Low, Dene. 2009. 208p. (J). (gr. 6-8). 18.69 *(978-0-547-15250-9(7))* Houghton Mifflin Harcourt Publishing Co.

—A Little Books Boxed Set Featuring Little Pea Little Hoot Little Oink: (Baby Board Books, Nursery Rhymes, Children's Book Sets, Nursery Books), 3 vols., Set. Rosenthal, Amy Krouse. 2009. (ENG.). 80p. (J). (gr. -1 — 1). bds. 19.99 *(978-0-8118-7054-2(5))* Chronicle Bks. LLC.

—Little Hoot. Rosenthal, Amy Krouse. 2016. (ENG.). 28p. (J). (gr. -1-k). bds. 7.99 *(978-1-4521-5207-3(1))* Chronicle Bks. LLC.

—Little Oink. Rosenthal, Amy Krouse. (ENG.). (J). 2017. 24p. bds. 7.99 *(978-1-4521-5319-3(1))*; 2009. 36p. (gr. -1-17). 14.99 *(978-0-8118-6655-2(6))*; 2009. 14.99 *(978-0-8118-8331-3(0))* Chronicle Bks. LLC.

—Little Pea. Rosenthal, Amy Krouse. 2015. (ENG.). 32p. (J). (gr. -1-k). bds. 7.99 *(978-1-4521-4289-0(0))* Chronicle Bks. LLC.

—Little Pea: (Children's Book, Books for Baby, Books about Picky Eaters, Board Books for Kids) Rosenthal, Amy Krouse. 2005. (ENG.). 36p. (J). (gr. -1-17). 15.99 *(978-0-8118-4658-5(X))* Chronicle Bks. LLC.

Corace, Jen. Night Wishes. Hopkins, Lee Bennett, ed. 2020. 40p. (J). ***(978-0-8028-5496-4(6)**,* Eerdmans Bks For Young Readers) Eerdmans, William B. Publishing Co.

Corace, Jen. Sweet Dreams. Lewis, Rose. 2012. (ENG.). 32p. (J). (gr. -1-2). 16.95 *(978-1-4197-0189-4(4)*, Abrams Bks. for Young Readers) Abrams, Inc.

—Telephone. Barnett, Mac. 2014. (ENG.). 40p. (J). (gr. -1-3). 16.99 *(978-1-4521-1023-3(9))* Chronicle Bks. LLC.

—This Plus That: Life's Little Equations. Rosenthal, Amy Krouse. 2011. (ENG.). 40p. (J). (gr. -1-3). 15.99 *(978-0-06-172655-2(9))* HarperCollins Pubs.

Corace, Jennifer. Brave Jane Austen: The Story of Jane Austen: Reader, Writer, Author, Rebel. Pliscou, Lisa. 2018. (ENG.). 48p. (J). 17.99 *(978-1-62779-643-9(6)*, 900157358, Holt, Henry & Co. Bks. For Young Readers) Holt, Henry & Co.

Coray, Stacy A. Cailloo Goes to the Fair. Hensley, Sarah M. l.t. ed. 2005. (HRL Board Book Ser.). (J). (gr. k-18). pap. 10.95 *(978-1-57332-328-4(4)*, HighReach Learning, Incorporated) Carson-Dellosa Publishing, LLC.

—Katie's Snacks. Hensley, Sarah M. l.t. ed. (HRL Big Book Ser.). (J). (gr. k-18). 2005. pap. 10.95 *(978-1-57332-337-6(3))*; 2004. pap. 10.95 *(978-1-57332-338-3(1))* Carson-Dellosa Publishing, LLC. (HighReach Learning, Incorporated).

Corazones Valientes, Corazones. Tortillas & Lullabies/Tortillas y Cancioncitas: Bilingual Spanish-English Children's Book. Reiser, Lynn. 2008. (Rise & Shine Ser.).Tr. of Tortillas y Cancioncitas. (ENG.). 48p. (J). (gr. -1-3). pap. 6.99 *(978-0-06-089185-5(8)*, Greenwillow Bks.) HarperCollins Pubs.

Corazza, Joe. The Frog Prince: A Story about Keeping Your Word. 2006. (J). 6.99 *(978-1-59939-008-6(6))* Cornerstone Pr.

Corbalán, Begoña. The Eagle Nest. Dell, Pamela. 2016. (Spring Forward Ser.). (J). (gr. 1). *(978-1-4900-9382-6(6))* Benchmark Education Co.

Corbalan, Begona. En Las Estaciones. Craddock, Petra. 2016. (Early Rising Readers Ser.). (SPA.). 16p. (J). (gr. 1-1). 6.67 *(978-1-4788-3732-9(2))* Newmark Learning LLC.

—Goyo en la Libreria. Canetti, Yanitzia. 2017. (Rising Readers Ser.). (SPA.). (J). (gr. 2). 5.83 *(978-1-4788-2719-1(X))* Newmark Learning LLC.

—In the Seasons. Craddock, Petra. 2015. (Early Rising Readers Ser.). (J). (gr. -1-k). 5.83 *(978-1-4788-1697-3(X))* Newmark Learning LLC.

Corbalán, Begoña. Mary's Lamb Goes to School: Lap Book Edition. Smith, Carrie. 2016. (My First Reader's Theater Tales Ser.). (J). (gr. k). *(978-1-5021-5506-1(0))* Benchmark Education Co.

—Mary's Lamb Goes to School: Small Book Edition. Smith, Carrie. 2016. (My First Reader's Theater Tales Ser.). (J). (gr. k). *(978-1-5021-5511-5(7))* Benchmark Education Co.

Corbett, Barry. Gormon: The Sentinel Awakes. Corbett, Barry. 2005. per. 3.95 *(978-0-9762294-1-4(2)*, Griffin Comics) Corbett Features.

Corbett, Liza. Rabbit Tricks. Posner, Tina. 2006. 8p. (J). pap. *(978-0-439-73513-1(0))* Scholastic, Inc.

Corbin, Hillam, jt. illus. see Valko, Diane.

Corbin, Marissa. The Seasons of Life. Murray, Barbara. 2013. 36p. 19.95 *(978-0-9885370-8-8(7))* RIVERRUN BOOKSTORE INC.

Corbineau, Antoine. City Mazes Around the World. Babin, Stephanie. 2020. (ENG.). 36p. (J). (gr. k-3). 18.99 ***(978-2-408-01967-9(2))*** Editions Tourbillon FRA. Dist: Hachette Bk. Group.

Corbineau, Antoine. Diggers. Brown, Margaret Wise. 2019. (Margaret Wise Brown Classics Ser.). (ENG.). 32p. (J). (gr. -1-k). 12.99 *(978-1-68412-742-9(4)*, Silver Dolphin Bks.) Printers Row Publishing Group.

—On Your Mark, Get Set, Gold! An Irreverent Guide to the Sports of the Summer Games. Allen, Scott. 2020. (ENG.). 96p. (J). (gr. 5). 19.99 *(978-1-5362-1398-0(5)*, Nosy Crow) Candlewick Pr.

Corcoran, Graham. Dare to Dream: Irish People Who Took on the World (and Won)! Webb, Sarah. 2019. (ENG.). 64p. 24.99 *(978-1-78849-127-3(0))* O'Brien Pr., Ltd., The IRL. Dist: Casemate Pubs. & Bk. Distributors, LLC.

Corcoran, Mark. The Three Sisters. Higgins, Kitty. ed. 2004. (Reader's Theater Ser.). (J). pap. *(978-1-4108-2312-0(1)*, A23121) Benchmark Education Co.

Cordeiro, James. Destructive Reentry. Van Lente, Fred. 2009. (Iron Man Ser.: No. 2). (ENG.). 24p. (J). (gr. 2-6). lib. bdg. 27.07 *(978-1-59961-589-9(4)*, 10030, Marvel Age) Spotlight.

—Enter the Dragon. Van Lente, Fred. 2008. (Iron Man Ser.: No. 1). (ENG.). 24p. (J). (gr. 2-6). 27.07 *(978-1-59961-552-3(5)*, 10026, Marvel Age) Spotlight.

—Heart of Steel. Van Lente, Fred. 2008. (Iron Man Ser.: No. 1). (ENG.). 24p. (J). (gr. 2-6). 27.07 *(978-1-59961-553-0(3)*, 10027, Marvel Age) Spotlight.

—Hostile Takeover. Van Lente, Fred. 2008. (Iron Man Ser.: No. 1). (ENG.). 24p. (J). (gr. 2-6). 27.07 *(978-1-59961-554-7(1)*, 10028, Marvel Age) Spotlight.

Cordeiro, James, jt. illus. see Nolan, Graham.

Cordell, Matthew. Baby Clown. LaReau, Kara. 2020. (ENG.). 32p. (J). (gr. -1-2). 16.99 *(978-0-7636-9743-3(5))* Candlewick Pr.

—First Grade Dropout. Vernick, Audrey. 2019. (ENG.). 32p. (J). (gr. -1-3). pap. 7.99 *(978-1-328-59631-4(1)*, 1731314, HMH Books For Young Readers) Houghton Mifflin Harcourt Publishing Co.

—First Grade Dropout. Vernick, Audrey. 2015. (ENG.). 32p. (J). (gr. -1-3). 17.99 *(978-0-544-12985-6(7)*, 1544741, Clarion Bks.) Houghton Mifflin Harcourt Trade & Reference Pubs.

—Forgive Me, I Meant to Do It: False Apology Poems. Levine, Gail Carson. 2012. (ENG.). 80p. (J). (gr. 3-7). lib. bdg. 16.89 *(978-0-06-178726-3(4))* HarperCollins Pubs.

—Gone Camping: A Novel in Verse. Wissinger, Tamera Will. (ENG.). 112p. (J). (gr. 1-4). 2019. pap. 7.99 *(978-1-328-59634-5(6)*, 1731320); 2017. 15.99 *(978-0-544-63873-0(5)*, 1620560) Houghton Mifflin Harcourt Publishing Co. (HMH Books For Young Readers).

—Gone Fishing. Wissinger, Tamera Will. 2015. (ENG.). (J). (gr. 5-7). lib. bdg. 17.60 *(978-1-62765-721-1(5))* Perfection Learning Corp.

—If the S in Moose Comes Loose. Hermann, Peter. 2018. (ENG.). 48p. (J). (gr. -1-3). 17.99 *(978-0-06-229510-1(1))* HarperCollins Pubs.

—If You Were a Chocolate Mustache. Lewis, J. Patrick. 2020. (ENG.). 160p. (J). (gr. 3-6). pap. 9.99 *(978-1-68437-705-3(6)*, Wordsong) Boyds Mills Pr.

—Itsy-Bitsy Baby Mouse. Meadows, Michelle. 2012. (ENG.). 40p. (J). (gr. -1-2). 15.99 *(978-1-4169-3786-9(2)*, Simon & Schuster Bks. For Young Readers) Simon & Schuster Bks. For Young Readers.

—Justin Case: School, Drool, & Other Daily Disasters. Vail, Rachel. 2011. (Justin Case Ser.: 1). (ENG.). 272p. (J). (gr.

C

2-4). pap. 7.99 *(978-0-312-56357-8(4)*, 900074758) Square Fish.

—Justin Case: Shells, Smells, & the Horrible Flip-Flops of Doom, 2. Vail, Rachel. 2013. (Justin Case Ser.: 2). (ENG.). 208p. (J). (gr. 2-4). pap. 7.99 *(978-1-250-02723-8(3)*, 900098294) Square Fish.

—The Knowing Book. Dotlich, Rebecca Kai. 2016. (ENG.). 32p. (J). (gr. 2). 16.95 *(978-1-59078-926-1(1))* Boyds Mills Pr.

—Leap Back Home to Me. Thompson, Lauren. 2011. (ENG.). 32p. (J). (gr. -1-3). 19.99 *(978-1-4169-0664-3(9)*, McElderry, Margaret K. Bks.) McElderry, Margaret K. Bks.

—Like Bug Juice on a Burger. Sternberg, Julie. 2013. (ENG.). 176p. (J). (gr. 2-5). 15.95 *(978-1-4197-0190-0(8)*, Amulet Bks.) Abrams, Inc.

—Like Carrot Juice on a Cupcake. Sternberg, Julie. 2014. (ENG.). 192p. (J). (gr. 2-5). 15.95 *(978-1-4197-1033-9(8)*, Amulet Bks.) Abrams, Inc.

—Like Pickle Juice on a Cookie. Sternberg, Julie. (ENG.). (J). (gr. 3-7). 2016. 144p. pap. 6.95 *(978-1-4197-2050-5(3))*; 2011. 128p. 15.95 *(978-0-8109-8424-0(5))* Abrams, Inc. (Amulet Bks.).

—Lost. Found: A Picture Book. Arnold, Marsha Diane. 2015. (ENG.). 32p. (J). (gr. -1-3). 16.99 *(978-1-62672-017-6(7)*, 900131521) Roaring Brook Pr.

—Rock 'n' Roll Soul. Verde, Susan. 2018. (ENG.). 32p. (J). (gr. k-2). 16.99 *(978-1-4197-2849-5(0)*, Abrams Bks. for Young Readers) Abrams, Inc.

—Rooting for You. Hood, Susan. 2014. (ENG.). 32p. (J). (gr. -1-k). 16.99 *(978-1-4231-5230-9(1))* Disney Pr.

—Second Grade Holdout. Vernick, Audrey. 2017. (ENG.). 32p. (J). (gr. -1-3). 18.99 *(978-0-544-87681-1(4)*, 1649576, Clarion Bks.) Houghton Mifflin Harcourt Trade & Reference Pubs.

—Shells, Smells, & the Horrible Flip-Flops of Doom. Vail, Rachel. 2012. (Justin Case Ser.: 2). (ENG.). 192p. (J). (gr. 2-4). 16.99 *(978-1-250-00081-1(5)*, 900078833) Feiwel & Friends.

—Special Delivery. Stead, Philip C. 2015. (ENG.). 40p. (J). (gr. -1-2). 17.99 *(978-1-59643-931-3(9)*, 9781596439313) Roaring Brook Pr.

—Toot Toot Zoom! Root, Phyllis. 2009. (ENG.). 40p. (J). (gr. -1-2). 15.99 *(978-0-7636-3452-0(2))* Candlewick Pr.

—What Floats in a Moat? Berry, Lynne. 2013. (ENG.). 48p. (J). (gr. k-4). 18.99 *(978-1-4169-9763-4(6)*, Simon & Schuster Bks. For Young Readers) Simon & Schuster Bks. For Young Readers.

Cordell, Matthew. Another Brother. Cordell, Matthew. 2018. (ENG.). 40p. (J). pap. 8.99 *(978-1-250-20762-3(2)*, 900201653) Square Fish.

—Hello! Hello! Cordell, Matthew. 2012. 56p. (J). (gr. -1-4). 16.99 *(978-1-4231-5906-3(3))* Hyperion Pr.

—Trouble Gum. Cordell, Matthew. 2018. (ENG.). 48p. (J). pap. 8.99 *(978-1-250-20767-8(3)*, 900201656) Square Fish.

Cordell, Matthew. Wish. Cordell, Matthew. 2018. (Wish Ser.: 1). 36p. (J). bds. 8.99 ***(978-1-4847-8846-2(X))*** Little, Brown Bks. for Young Readers.

Cordell, Matthew & Brown, Richard. Gone Fishing: A Novel. Wissinger, Tamera Will & Long, Earlene R. 2015. (ENG.). 128p. (J). (gr. 1-4). pap. 6.99 *(978-0-544-43931-3(7)*, 1596830, HMH Books For Young Readers) Houghton Mifflin Harcourt Publishing Co.

Cordero, Ana E. KJ's Adventures: KJ Takes a Trip to the Wild Life Preserve. Lewis, Kevin. Webb, Kim, ed. 2019. (ENG.). 28p. (J). pap. 12.00 ***(978-1-7031-4435-2(X))*** Independently Published.

Cordero Vidal, Andria. When Jesus Comes Back. Hayes, Daisy. 2016. (ENG.). 30p. (J). pap. 7.95 *(978-1-4787-7782-3(6))* Outskirts Pr., Inc.

Cordes, Jennifer. Seasons at Grandma & Grandpa´s Lake. Pollard, Vicki. 2017. (ENG.). 38p. (J). pap. 12.99 *(978-1-9811-3862-3(5))* CreateSpace Independent Publishing Platform.

Cordes, Miriam. Farewell, Grandpa Elephant: What Happens When a Loved One Dies? Abedí, Isabel. 2012. 28p. (J). (gr. -1-k). 16.95 *(978-1-61608-655-8(6)*, 608655, Sky Pony Pr.) Skyhorse Publishing Co., Inc.

Cordier, Severine. Gandhi: His Life, His Struggles, His Words. de Lambilly, Elisabeth. 2010. (Great Spiritual Figures of Modern Times Ser.). (ENG.). 72p. (J). (gr. 3-6). 16.95 *(978-1-59270-094-3(2))* Enchanted Lion Bks., LLC.

Cordish, Janet Luckey. Dolly Dolphin. Cordish, Janet Luckey. 2004. 32p. (J). (gr. k-3). 19.95 *(978-0-9661315-6-7(8))* FreeStar Pr.

—First Ice Cream Cone. Cordish, Janet Luckey. 2004. 32p. (J). (gr. -1-3). 19.95 *(978-0-9661315-5-0(X))* FreeStar Pr.

Cordner, Theo & Bolder, Joe. Minecraft Combat Handbook. Milton, Stephanie & Soares, Paul. 2015. 95p. (J). *(978-0-545-82319-7(6))* Scholastic, Inc.

Cordner, Theo, jt. illus. see Burlinson, James.

Córdova, Amy. Amadito & the Hero Children: Amadito y Los Niños Héroes. Lamadrid, Enrique R. 2011. (J). (SPA & ENG.). *(978-0-8263-4978-1(1))*; (gr. 6). 60p. E-Book *(978-0-8263-4980-4(3))* Univ. of New Mexico Pr.

Cordova, Amy. Namaste!, 1 vol. Cohn, Diana. 2012. (ENG.). 32p. (J). pap. 9.95 *(978-1-62148-005-1(4))* SteinerBooks, Inc.

Córdova, Amy. Roses for Isabella, 34 vols. Cohn, Diana. 2011. (ENG.). 32p. (J). 17.95 *(978-0-88010-731-0(6))* SteinerBooks, Inc.

Cordova, Amy. What Can You Do with a Rebozo? / ¿Qué Puedes Hacer con un Rebozo? Tafolla, Carmen. 2009. (J). (gr. -1-2). 30p. 14.99 *(978-1-58246-270-7(4))*; 32p. pap. 7.99 *(978-1-58246-271-4(2))* Random Hse. Children's Bks. (Tricycle Pr.).

Cordova, Amy. Abuelita's Heart. Cordova, Amy. 2008. (ENG.). 32p. (J). (gr. -1-3). 13.99 *(978-1-4169-7576-2(4)*, Simon & Schuster/Paula Wiseman Bks.) Simon & Schuster/Paula Wiseman Bks.

—Talking Eagle & the Lady of Roses: The Story of Juan Diego & Our Lady of Guadalupe, 1 vol. Cordova, Amy. Gollogly, Gene. 2010. (ENG.). 40p. (J). (gr. k-7). 17.95 *(978-0-88010-719-8(7))* SteinerBooks, Inc.

Córdova, Amy & Córdova, Amy. The First Tortilla: A Bilingual Story. Anaya, Rudolfo. Lamadrid, Enrique R., tr. 2012. (ENG & SPA.). 32p. (J). pap. 16.95 *(978-0-8263-4215-7(9))* Univ. of New Mexico Pr.

—La Llorona: The Crying Woman. Anaya, Rudolfo. Lamadrid, Enrique R., tr. 2011. (ENG & SPA.). 40p. (J). 19.95 *(978-0-8263-4460-1(7))* Univ. of New Mexico Pr.

—The Santero's Miracle: A Bilingual Story. Anaya, Rudolfo. Lamadrid, Enrique R., tr. 2004. (ENG.). 32p. (J). 19.95 *(978-0-8263-2847-2(4))* Univ. of New Mexico Pr.

Córdova, Amy, jt. illus. see Córdova, Amy.

Cordoves, Barbara, pseud & Cordoves, Gladys M. The Legend of Zias. Cordoves, Barbara & Cordoves, Gladys M. (Zias' Adventures Ser.). 44p. (J). pap. 7.99 *(978-0-9637252-0-2(3))* Cordoves, Barbara & Gladys M.

Cordoves, Gladys M., jt. illus. see Cordoves, Barbara, pseud.

Coreana, Aliyah. All New Superstar Kids: Rhyming Moral Fun. Rhodes, Gavin. 2017. (ENG.). 58p. (J). (gr. k-6). pap. *(978-1-78719-630-8(5))* Authors OnLine, Ltd.

—Superstar Kids: Rhyming Moral Fun. Rhodes, Gavin. 2016. (ENG.). (J). (gr. k-6). pap. *(978-1-78719-186-0(9))* Authors OnLine, Ltd.

Corey, Rj. Coral the Curious Octopus: Coral Meets Crunch. Corey, Rj. 2019. (Coral the Curious Octopus Ser.: Vol. 2). (ENG.). 36p. (J). pap. 9.99 ***(978-1-7087-6899-7(8))*** Independently Published.

Corey, Victoria. Larry the Lawnmower. Archambault, Jeanne. 2004. 32p. (J). 14.95 *(978-0-9763031-0-7(8))*; per. 10.00 *(978-0-9763031-1-4(6))* Jitterbug Bks.

Corfee, Stephanie. Doodle with Attitude. Corfee, Stephanie. 2016. (Doodle with Attitude Ser.). (ENG.). 32p. (J). (gr. 4-8). lib. bdg., lib. bdg., lib. bdg. 85.95 *(978-1-4914-7949-0(3))* Capstone.

—Free Spirit Doodles. Corfee, Stephanie. 2016. (Doodle with Attitude Ser.). (ENG.). 32p. (J). (gr. 4-8). lib. bdg. 28.65 *(978-1-4914-7945-2(0))* Capstone.

—Girl Plus Pen: Doodle, Draw, Color, & Express Your Individual Style. Corfee, Stephanie. 2016. (Craft It Yourself Ser.). (ENG.). 144p. (J). (gr. 3-9). pap. 12.95 *(978-1-62370-596-1(7)*, Capstone Young Readers) Capstone.

—Quirky, Cute Doodles. Corfee, Stephanie. 2016. (Doodle with Attitude Ser.). (ENG.). 32p. (J). (gr. 4-8). lib. bdg. 28.65 *(978-1-4914-7944-5(2))* Capstone.

—Twirly Girly Doodles. Corfee, Stephanie. 2016. (Doodle with Attitude Ser.). (ENG.). 32p. (J). (gr. 4-8). lib. bdg. 28.65 *(978-1-4914-7943-8(4))* Capstone.

Corfield, Robin Bell. Fire & Stone, Wind & Tide: Poems About the Elements. Waters, Fiona. 2006. 43p. (gr. 4-8). reprint ed. 24.00 *(978-1-4223-5595-4(0))* DIANE Publishing Co.

Corichi, Yadhira. Elisa Escuchaba el Canto de Las Ballenas. Hernandez, Ruben. rev. ed. 2003. (Castillo de la Lectura Blanca Ser.). (SPA & ENG.). 48p. (J). (gr. 1-3). pap. 6.95 *(978-970-20-0141-6(2))* Castillo, Ediciones, S. A. de C. V. MEX. Dist: Macmillan.

Corke, Estelle. Beach Socks, 1 vol. Daley, Michael J. 2013. (ENG.). 10p. (J). bds. 6.99 *(978-1-59572-637-7(3))* Star Bright Bks., Inc.

—The Christmas Star, 1 vol. Box, Su. 2009. 18p. (J). bds. 9.95 *(978-0-8254-7891-6(X)*, Lion Children's) Lion Hudson PLC GBR. Dist: Kregel Pubns.

—Collins Big Cat Phonics for Letters & Sounds - Pip!: Band 01A/Pink A. Ditchburn, Suzannah. 2020. (Collins Big Cat Phonics for Letters & Sounds Ser.). (ENG.). 16p. (J). (gr. -1-k). pap. 6.99 *(978-0-00-835758-0(7))* HarperCollins Pubs. Ltd. GBR. Dist: Independent Pubs. Group.

—Collins Big Cat Phonics for Letters & Sounds - up on Deck: Band 01B/Pink B, Bd. 1B. Baker, Catherine. 2018. (Collins Big Cat Phonics Ser.). (ENG.). 16p. (J). (gr. -1-k). pap. 6.99 *(978-0-00-825138-3(X))* HarperCollins Pubs. Ltd. GBR. Dist: Independent Pubs. Group.

—Daddy's Girl. James, Helen Foster. 2017. 32p. (J). (gr. -1-2). 15.99 *(978-0-8249-5681-3(8))* Worthy Publishing.

—Daniel & the Lions, 1 vol. Piper, Sophie. 2009. (Bible Story Time Ser.). 32p. (J). 5.95 *(978-0-8254-7837-6(5)*, Lion Children's) Lion Hudson PLC GBR. Dist: Kregel Pubns.

—David & Goliath, 1 vol. Piper, Sophie. 2009. (Bible Story Time Ser.). 32p. (J). 5.95 *(978-0-8254-7835-2(9)*, Lion Children's) Lion Hudson PLC GBR. Dist: Kregel Pubns.

—The First Easter, 1 vol. Piper, Sophie. (Bible Story Time Ser.). 32p. (J). 2009. 5.95 *(978-0-8254-7832-1(4))*; Pack, 2019. (ENG.). (gr. -1). pap. 23.99 ***(978-0-7459-7834-5(7))*** Lion Hudson PLC GBR. (Lion Children's). Dist: Kregel Pubns., Independent Pubs. Group.

—The Gingerbread Man. 2007. (Flip-Up Fairy Tales Ser.). 24p. (J). *(978-1-84643-144-9(1))*; (gr. -1-2). *(978-1-84643-078-7(X))* Child's Play International Ltd.

—God Made Daddy Special, 1 vol. Nellist, Glenys. 2018. (ENG.). 20p. (J). bds. 9.99 *(978-0-310-76243-0(X))* Zonderkidz.

—God Made Mommy Special, 1 vol. Nellist, Glenys. 2018. (ENG.). 20p. (J). bds. 9.99 *(978-0-310-76233-1(2))* Zonderkidz.

—God Made You Nose to Toes, 1 vol. Parrott, Leslie. 2017. (ENG.). 18p. (J). bds. 9.99 *(978-0-310-75740-5(1))* Zonderkidz.

—Goldilocks & the Three Bears. (Flip-Up Fairy Tales Ser.). 24p. (J). 2007. (gr. -1-2). *(978-1-84643-085-5(2))*; 2005. (ENG.). (gr. 1-2). pap. *(978-1-904550-19-8(3))* Child's Play International Ltd.

—Jesus & the Fishermen, 1 vol. Piper, Sophie. 2009. (Bible Story Time Ser.). 32p. (J). 5.95 *(978-0-8254-7833-8(2)*, Lion Children's) Lion Hudson PLC GBR. Dist: Kregel Pubns.

—Jonah & the Whale, 1 vol. Piper, Sophie. 2009. (Bible Story Time Ser.). 32p. (J). 5.95 *(978-0-8254-7836-9(7)*, Lion Children's) Lion Hudson PLC GBR. Dist: Kregel Pubns.

—The Lion Bible Story Box. Piper, Sophie. ed. 2016. (ENG.). 32p. (J). pap. 16.99 *(978-0-7459-7687-7(5))* Lion Hudson PLC GBR. Dist: Independent Pubs. Group.

—Oh Holy Night. Harrast, Tracy. 2006. 10p. (J). (gr. -1-k). bds. 10.49 *(978-0-7586-1129-1(3))* Concordia Publishing Hse.

—The Story of the Nativity, 1 vol. Harrast, Tracy. 2010. 24p. (J). (gr. -1-1). bds. 14.99 *(978-0-8254-5549-0(9))* Kregel Pubns.

—The Strongest Mouse: A Tale from East Africa. Wilton, Briar. 2016. 24p. (J). pap. 9.95 *(978-1-927244-59-3(5))* Flying Start Bks. NZL. Dist: Flying Start Bks.

—The Strongest Mouse (Big Book Edition) A Tale from East Africa. Wilton, Briar. 2016. 24p. (J). pap. *(978-1-927244-69-2(2))* Flying Start Bks.

Corley, Rob & Bancroft, Tom. My First Message: A Devotional Bible for Kids. Peterson, Eugene H., tr. 2007. (ENG.). 384p. (J). 24.99 *(978-1-57683-448-0(4)*, 4610275) Tyndale Hse. Pubs.

Corley, Rob, jt. illus. see Bancroft, Tom.

Cormack, Allan & Cormack, Deborah Drew Brook. Volcanoes Inside & Out. Souza, Dorothy M. 2005. (On My Own Science Ser.). 48p. (J). (gr. 3-7). lib. bdg. 25.26 *(978-1-57505-761-3(1))* Lerner Publishing Group.

Cormack, Allan & Drew-Brook, Deborah. Ghost Wolf. Bradford, Karleen. 2005. 59p. (J). lib. bdg. 20.00 *(978-1-4242-1254-5(5))* Fitzgerald Bks.

—Ghost Wolf, 1 vol. Bradford, Karleen. 2005. (Orca Echoes Ser.). (ENG.). 64p. (J). (gr. 1-3). per. 6.95 *(978-1-55143-341-7(9))* Orca Bk. Pubs. USA.

Cormack, Allan, jt. illus. see Drew-Brook, Deborah.

Cormack, Deborah Drew Brook, jt. illus. see Cormack, Allan.

Cormier, France. The Nut That Fell from the Tree. Bhadra, Sangeeta. 2020. (ENG.). 32p. (J). (gr. -1-2). 17.99 ***(978-1-5253-0119-3(5))*** Kids Can Pr., Ltd. CAN. Dist: Hachette Bk. Group.

Cormier, France. Through the Elephant's Door, 1 vol. De Blois, Hélène. 2019. (ENG.). 48p. (J). (gr. 1-3). 19.95 *(978-1-4598-2193-4(9))* Orca Bk. Pubs. USA.

Corn, Atlantis. Beauford the Patriotic Donkey. Bouk, T. A. & Thomas, Jewel. 2018. (ENG.). 64p. (J). pap. 19.99 *(978-1-7294-5643-9(X))* Independently Published.

Cornejo, Andrés. Mary's Magic Word: Story & Activity Book. Gittle, Aviva & Megson, Mark. 2017. (ENG.). (J). pap. 12.95 *(978-1-942736-09-7(6))* Aviva Gittle Publishing.

Cornejo, Eulalia. Mi libro. Cordova, Soledad. 2015. 24p. (J). (gr. -1-2). pap. 12.95 *(978-9978-07-525-8(9)*, Alfaguara Infantil) Santillana Ecuador ECU. Dist: Santillana USA Publishing Co., Inc.

—Verde Fue Mi Selva. Iturralde, Edna. Arroba, Doris et al, eds. 2008. (Alfaguara Infantil Ser.).Tr. of My Forest Was Green. 152p. (J). (gr. 5-8). pap. *(978-9978-07-097-0(4))* Ediciones Alfaguara.

—Verde Manzana. Williams, Ricardo. 2015. 24p. (J). (gr. -1-2). pap. 12.95 *(978-9942-05-938-3(5)*, Alfaguara Infantil) Santillana Ecuador ECU. Dist: Santillana USA Publishing Co., Inc.

—Verde Manzana (Libro + CD) Williams, Ricardo. 2015. (Serie Verde / Album Ilustrado Ser.). (SPA.). 24p. (J). pap. 12.95 *(978-9942-19-342-1(1))* Santillana USA Publishing Co., Inc.

Cornejo, Eulalia. Porque Existes Tú. Cornejo, Eulalia. 2015. (Serie Verde / Álbum Ilustrado Ser.). (SPA.). 24p. (J). (gr. -1-2). pap. 12.95 *(978-9942-19-338-4(3))* Santillana Ecuador ECU. Dist: Santillana USA Publishing Co., Inc.

Cornejo, Oscar Kein. Aventura en la Puerta Del Diablo. Panama, Ernesto. 2019. (Las Aventuras de Pepito, Pelota y Pelotilla Ser.: Vol. 1). (SPA.). 50p. (J). pap. 11.00 *(978-1-0936-3057-2(4))* Independently Published.

Cornelison, Reuel. Cat Got Your Tongue? A Book of Idioms. White, Russ. l.t. ed. 2004. 44p. (J). per. *(978-0-9742885-0-5(0)*, 00) White, Russ.

Cornelison, Sue. Don't Put Yourself down in Circus Town: A Story about Self-Confidence. Sileo, Frank J. 2014. 32p. (J). pap. *(978-1-4338-1914-8(7)*, Magination Pr.) American Psychological Assn.

—Hooray for Babies! Meyers, Susan. 2019. (ENG.). 32p. (J). (— 1). 14.99 *(978-1-328-52847-6(2)*, 1722054, HMH Books For Young Readers) Houghton Mifflin Harcourt Publishing Co.

—Inch & Miles: The Journey to Success. Wooden, John et al. 2003. 39p. (J). pap. *(978-0-7891-6073-7(0))* Perfection Learning Corp.

—Lost & Found Cat: The True Story of Kunkush's Incredible Journey. Kuntz, Doug & Shrodes, Amy. (J). (gr. -1-3). 2019. (ENG.). 48p. pap. 7.99 *(978-1-5247-1550-2(6)*, Dragonfly Bks.); 2017. 40p. 17.99 *(978-1-5247-1547-2(6)*, Crown Books For Young Readers) Random Hse. Children's Bks.

—Mango Moon. de Anda, Diane. 2019. (ENG.). 32p. (J). (gr. -1-3). 16.99 *(978-0-8075-4957-5(6)*, 807549576) Whitman, Albert & Co.

—My Little Golden Book about Martin Luther King Jr. Bader, Bonnie. 2018. (Little Golden Book Ser.). (ENG.). 24p. (J). (-k). 4.99 *(978-0-525-57870-3(6)*, Golden Bks.) Random Hse. Children's Bks.

—Sofia's Dream. Wilson, Land. O'Malley, Judy, ed. 2016. (ENG.). 40p. (J). (gr. -1-2). 18.95 *(978-0-9829938-1-1(1)*, Little Pickle Pr.) Sourcebooks, Inc.

—Sofia's Dream. Wilson, Land. 2nd rev. ed. 2020. 40p. (J). (-2). 17.99 *(978-1-4926-9873-9(3)*, Little Pickle Pr.) Sourcebooks, Inc.

Cornelison, Sue F. Inch & Miles: The Journey to Success. Wooden, John et al. 2003. (Inch & Miles Ser.). 40p. (J). (gr. k-3). 15.95 *(978-0-7569-1410-3(8)*, 3957506) Perfection Learning Corp.

—The Twelve Days of Christmas in Iowa. 2010. (Twelve Days of Christmas in America Ser.). 40p. (J). (gr. k). 12.95 *(978-1-4027-6710-4(2))* Sterling Publishing Co., Inc.

Cornelison, Susan F. Fiesta. Wooden, John. 2007. (Coach John Wooden for Kids Ser.). 63p. (J). (gr. k-3). lib. bdg. 11.65 *(978-0-7569-7791-7(6))*; pap., per. 4.99 *(978-0-7891-7187-0(2))* Perfection Learning Corp.

—Howard B. Wigglebottom Learns about Sportsmanship: Winning Isn't Everything. Binkow, Howard & Ana, Reverend. 2012. (Howard B. Wigglebottom Ser.). (ENG.). 32p. (J). (gr. -1-3). 15.00 *(978-0-9826165-6-7(2)*, We Do Listen) We Do Listen Foundation.

—Howard B. Wigglebottom Learns to Listen. Binkow, Howard & Ana, Reverend. 2008. (Howard B. Wigglebottom Ser.). (ENG.). 32p. (J). (gr. -1-3). 15.00 *(978-0-9715390-1-3(4)*, We Do Listen) We Do Listen Foundation.

—Howard B. Wigglebottom Listens to His Heart. Binkow, Howard & Ana, Reverend. 2nd ed. 2008. (Howard B. Wigglebottom Ser.). (ENG.). 32p. (J). (gr. -1-3). 15.00 *(978-0-9715390-2-0(2)*, We Do Listen) We Do Listen Foundation.

Cornelius, Brad. We're Having a Tuesday. Simoneau, D. K. 2006. (ENG.). 32p. (J). 16.95 *(978-1-933302-13-3(5))* AC Pubns. Group LLC.

Cornell, Alexis. Big Data: Information in the Digital World with Science Activities for Kids. Mooney, Carla. 2018. (Build It Yourself Ser.). (ENG.). 128p. (J). (gr. 4-10). 22.95 *(978-1-61930-679-0(4)*, 8e99fbfc-de3f-4f18-ad80-c12a741c6285) Nomad Pr.

—Bioengineering: Discover How Nature Inspires Human Designs. Burillo-Kirch, Christine. 2016. (Build It Yourself Ser.). 128p. (J). (gr. 3-7). 22.95 *(978-1-61930-366-9(3)*, 373d3757-bd9c-4e43-aac9-6b012df9aaba) Nomad Pr.

—Climate Change: The Science Behind Melting Glaciers & Warming Oceans with Hands-On Science Activities. Sneideman, Josh & Twamley, Erin. 2020. (Build It Yourself Ser.). 128p. (J). (gr. 4-7). (ENG.). 22.95 *(978-1-61930-896-1(7)*, 6abbb19f-e40d-42c2-9fda-0a2f20fcddfe); pap. 17.95 *(978-1-61930-899-2(1)*, 271451c4-9a39-4ec4-9c9c-6d804ccbdc07) Nomad Pr.

—Evolution: How Life Adapts to a Changing Environment with 25 Projects. Mooney, Carla. 2017. (Build It Yourself Ser.). 128p. (J). (gr. 4-6). 22.95 *(978-1-61930-597-7(6)*, f5c4ecd8-1bc1-41fb-9e48-2e208c0318fd); pap. 17.95 *(978-1-61930-601-1(8)*, 983cace2-3f4c-4f99-bf61-014f99d2167a) Nomad Pr.

—Feminism: The March Toward Equal Rights for Women. Dearman, Jill. 2019. (Inquire & Investigate Ser.). 128p. (YA). (gr. 7-9). 22.95 *(978-1-61930-752-0(9)*, df66a727-f7d7-46de-ac2a-49ea2b9ee0d2); pap. 17.95 *(978-1-61930-755-1(3)*, 25ad39a3-16f8-4315-833a-e51ec4f3fcf6) Nomad Pr.

—Gender Identity: Beyond Pronouns & Bathrooms. Cook, Maria. 2019. (Inquire & Investigate Ser.). 128p. (YA). (gr. 7-9). 22.95 *(978-1-61930-756-8(1)*, 4f5afc16-3c14-4b5b-a2ac-4ae97d5b0fa1); pap. 17.95 *(978-1-61930-759-9(6)*, 3414c4ea-ab8c-4725-8bb8-9fcd7f03bedd) Nomad Pr.

—The Human Body: Get under the Skin with Science Activities for Kids. Reilly, Kathleen M. 2019. (Build It Yourself Ser.). 128p. (J). (gr. 4-6). 22.95 *(978-1-61930-798-8(7)*, cff2e9d9-aa0e-476f-a620-9a4741a053ce); pap. 17.95 *(978-1-61930-801-5(0)*, 2197c1e3-631d-4951-bd1e-e3e7c938f2fa) Nomad Pr.

Cornell du Houx, Emily, jt. illus. see du Houx, Ramona.

Cornell du Houx, Emily M. D. Martin Mcmillan & the Lost Inca City. Russell, Elaine. 2005. 128p. (gr. 5-18). pap. 10.00 *(978-1-882190-86-7(6))* Polar Bear & Co.

Cornell, Kevin. Chapter Two Is Missing. Lieb, Josh. 2019. 48p. (J). (gr. -1-1). 17.99 *(978-1-9848-3548-2(3)*, Razorbill) Penguin Young Readers Group.

—The Chicken Squad. Cronin, Doreen. 2014. 92p. (J). *(978-0-605-90609-9(2))* Simon & Schuster Children's Publishing.

—The Chicken Squad: The First Misadventure. Cronin, Doreen. (Chicken Squad Ser.: 1). (ENG.). 112p. (J). (gr. 2-5). 2015. pap. 7.99 *(978-1-4424-9677-4(0))*; 2014. 12.99 *(978-1-4424-9676-7(2))* Simon & Schuster Children's Publishing. (Atheneum Bks. for Young Readers).

—The Legend of Diamond Lil: A J. J. Tully Mystery. Cronin, Doreen. (ENG.). 144p. (J). (gr. 1-5). 2013. pap. 5.99 *(978-0-06-177997-8(0))*; 2012. lib. bdg. 15.89 *(978-0-06-198578-2(3))* HarperCollins Pubs.

—Lulu Is Getting a Sister: (Who WANTS Her? Who NEEDS Her?) Viorst, Judith. (Lulu Ser.). (ENG.). 192p. (J). (gr. 1-5). 2019. pap. 7.99 *(978-1-4814-7191-6(0))*; 2018. 16.99 *(978-1-4814-7190-9(2))* Simon & Schuster.

—Shark Kiss, Octopus Hug. Reed, Lynn Rowe. 2014. (ENG.). 32p. (J). (gr. -1-3). 14.99 *(978-0-06-220320-5(7))* HarperCollins Pubs.

—The Terrible Two. Barnett, Mac & John, Jory. 2016. (Terrible Two Ser.). (ENG.). 224p. (J). (gr. 3-7). pap. 7.95 *(978-1-4197-1925-7(4))* Abrams, Inc.

—The Terrible Two Get Worse. Barnett, Mac & John, Jory. 2016. (Terrible Two Ser.). (ENG.). 224p. (J). (gr. 3-7). 13.95 *(978-1-4197-1680-5(8)*, 1093701, Amulet Bks.) Abrams, Inc.

—The Terrible Two Go Wild. Barnett, Mac & John, Jory. 2018. (ENG.). 240p. (J). (gr. 3-7). pap. 7.99 *(978-1-4197-3205-8(6)*, 1093803, Amulet Bks.) Abrams, Inc.

—Terrible Two Go Wild. John, Jory & Barnett, Mac. 2018. (Terrible Two Ser.). (ENG.). 224p. (J). (gr. 3-7). 13.99 *(978-1-4197-2185-4(2)*, 1093801, Amulet Bks.) Abrams, Inc.

—The Terrible Two Wild. Barnett, Mac & John, Jory. 2018. (Terrible Two Ser.). (ENG.). 224p. (J). (gr. 3-7). pap. 7.99 *(978-1-4197-2341-4(3))* Abrams, Inc.

—The Terrible Two's Last Laugh. Barnett, Mac & John, Jory. 2019. (ENG.). 224p. (J). (gr. 3-7). pap. 7.99 *(978-1-4197-3621-6(3)*, 1093903, Amulet Bks.) Abrams, Inc.

—The Trouble with Chickens. Cronin, Doreen. 2012. (J. J. Tully Mysteries Ser.). (ENG.). (J). (gr. 1-5). lib. bdg. 16.60 *(978-1-61383-650-7(3))* Perfection Learning Corp.

—The Trouble with Chickens: A J. J. Tully Mystery. Cronin, Doreen. (ENG.). (J). (gr. 1-5). 2012. 144p. pap. 7.99 *(978-0-06-121534-6(1))*; 2011. 128p. 14.99 *(978-0-06-121532-2(5))* HarperCollins Pubs.

Cornell, Kevin. Go to Sleep, Monster! Cornell, Kevin. 2016. (ENG.). 32p. (J). (gr. -1-3). 17.99 *(978-0-06-234915-6(5)*, Balzer & Bray) HarperCollins Pubs.

—Lucy Fell down the Mountain. Cornell, Kevin. 2018. (ENG.). 40p. (J). 17.99 *(978-0-374-30608-3(7)*, 900174207, Farrar, Straus & Giroux (BYR)) Farrar, Straus & Giroux.

Cornell, Kevin & Gilpin, Stephen. The Complete Chicken Squad Misadventures: The Chicken Squad; the Case of the Weird Blue Chicken; into the Wild; Dark Shadows; Gimme Shelter; Bear Country. Cronin, Doreen. ed. 2019. (Chicken Squad Ser.). (ENG.). 704p. (J). (gr. 2-5). 77.99 *(978-1-5344-6391-2(7)*, Atheneum/Caitlyn Dlouhy Books) Simon & Schuster Children's Publishing.

Cornell, Kevin, jt. illus. see Smith, Lane.

Cornell, Laura. Annie Bananie. Komaiko, Leah. 2003. (ENG.). 32p. (J). (gr. -1-3). pap. 7.99 *(978-0-06-051912-4(6))* HarperCollins Pubs.

—The Best Christmas Pageant Ever (picture Book Edition) Robinson, Barbara. 2011. (ENG.). 40p. (J). (gr. -1-3). 16.99 *(978-0-06-089074-2(6))* HarperCollins Pubs.

—Big Words for Little People. Curtis, Jamie Lee. 2008. (ENG.). 40p. (J). (gr. -1-3). 16.99 *(978-0-06-112759-5(0))* HarperCollins Pubs.

—Boy/Girl Book. Curtis, Jamie Lee. Date not set. 32p. (J). (gr. -1-3). 5.99 *(978-0-06-443639-7(X))* HarperCollins Pubs.

—Heather Has Two Mommies. Newman, Lesléa. (ENG.). 32p. (J). (gr. -1-2). 2016. 6.99 *(978-0-7636-9042-7(2))*; 2015. 18.99 *(978-0-7636-6631-6(9))* Candlewick Pr.

—I'm Gonna Like Me: Letting off a Little Self-Esteem. Curtis, Jamie Lee. 2007. (ENG.). 32p. (J). (gr. -1-3). 17.99 *(978-0-06-028761-0(6)*, HarperCollins) HarperCollins Pubs. Ltd. GBR. Dist: HarperCollins Pubs.

—Is There Really a Human Race? Curtis, Jamie Lee. 2006. (ENG.). 40p. (J). (gr. -1-3). 16.99 *(978-0-06-075346-7(3))* HarperCollins Pubs.

—It's Hard to Be Five: Learning How to Work My Control Panel. Curtis, Jamie Lee. 2004. 40p. (J). (gr. -1-3). lib. bdg. 17.89 *(978-0-06-008096-9(5)*, Cotler, Joanna Books) HarperCollins Pubs.

—It's Hard to Be Five: Learning How to Work My Control Panel. Curtis, Jamie Lee. 2007. (ENG.). 40p. (J). (gr. -1-3). 17.99 *(978-0-06-008095-2(7)*, HarperCollins) HarperCollins Pubs. Ltd. GBR. Dist: HarperCollins Pubs.

—Jamie Lee Curtis's Books to Grow by Treasury. Curtis, Jamie Lee. 2009. (ENG.). 208p. (J). (gr. -1-3). 24.99 *(978-0-06-180364-2(2))* HarperCollins Pubs.

—M. O. M. (Mom Operating Manual) Cronin, Doreen. 2011. (ENG.). 56p. (J). (gr. -1-3). 16.99 *(978-1-4169-6150-5(X)*, Atheneum Bks. for Young Readers) Simon & Schuster Children's Publishing.

—Me, Myselfie & I: a Cautionary Tale. Curtis, Jamie Lee. 2018. (ENG.). 40p. (J). 17.99 *(978-1-250-13827-9(2)*, 900179059) Feiwel & Friends.

—My Brave Year of Firsts: Tries, Sighs, & High Fives. Curtis, Jamie Lee. 2012. (ENG.). 40p. (J). (gr. -1-3). 16.99 *(978-0-06-144155-4(4))* HarperCollins Pubs.

—My Mommy Hung the Moon: A Love Story. Curtis, Jamie Lee. 2010. (ENG.). 40p. (J). (gr. -1-3). 17.99 *(978-0-06-029016-0(1))* HarperCollins Pubs.

—Today I Feel Silly & Other Moods That Make My Day. Curtis, Jamie Lee. 2007. (ENG.). 40p. (J). (gr. -1-3). 17.99 *(978-0-06-024560-3(3)*, HarperCollins) HarperCollins Pubs. Ltd. GBR. Dist: HarperCollins Pubs.

Corner, Chris. Little Bear: a Folktale from Greenland: Band 10 White/Band 14 Ruby (Collins Big Cat Progress) Casey, Dawn. 2014. (Collins Big Cat Progress Ser.). (ENG.). 32p. (J). (gr. 3-4). pap. 10.99 *(978-0-00-751925-5(7))* HarperCollins Pubs. Ltd. GBR. Dist: Independent Pubs. Group.

Cornia, Christian. Brina the Cat #1: The Gang of the Feline Sun. Salati, Giorgio. 2020. (Brina Ser.: 1). (ENG.). 88p. (J). 14.99 *(978-1-5458-0425-4(7)*, 900211578); pap. 9.99 *(978-1-5458-0426-1(5)*, 900211579) Papercutz.

—Finding Yorgy. Harper, Benjamin. 2020. (Michael Dahl Presents: Side-Splitting Stories Ser.). (ENG.). 72p. (J). (gr. 3-6). pap. 5.95 *(978-1-4965-9208-8(5)*, 142236); lib. bdg. 25.32 *(978-1-4965-8704-6(9)*, 141438) Capstone. (Stone Arch Bks.).

—Fred Flintstone's Adventures with Levers: Lift That Load! Weakland, Mark. 2016. (Flintstones Explain Simple Machines Ser.). (ENG.). 24p. (J). (gr. k-2). lib. bdg. 27.99 *(978-1-4914-8473-9(X))* Capstone.

—The Middle Ages: New Conquests & Dynasties. Farndon, John. 2018. (Human History Timeline Ser.). (ENG.). 32p. (J). (gr. 3-6). 27.99 *(978-1-5124-5972-2(0)*, Hungry Tomato ®) Lerner Publishing Group.

—The Middle Colonies: Bridges Edition. Burgan, Michael. 2015. (Prime Plus Ser.). (YA). (gr. 6-8). pap. *(978-1-4900-1940-6(5))* Benchmark Education Co.

—The Middle Colonies: Bridges Edition Set of 6 with Common Core Indicators. Burgan, Michael. 2015. (Prime Plus Ser.). (YA). (gr. 6-8). 69.00 net. *(978-1-4900-2036-5(5))* Benchmark Education Co.

—The Modern World: The Last Hundred Years. Farndon, John. 2018. (Human History Timeline Ser.). (ENG.). 32p. (J). (gr. 3-6). lib. bdg. 27.99 *(978-1-5124-5974-6(7)*, Hungry Tomato ®) Lerner Publishing Group.

—The New England Colonies: Bridges Edition. Burgan, Michael. 2015. (Prime Plus Ser.). (YA). (gr. 6-8). pap. *(978-1-4900-1939-0(1))* Benchmark Education Co.

—The New England Colonies: Bridges Edition Set of 6 with Common Core Indicators. Burgan, Michael. 2015. (Prime Plus Ser.). (YA). (gr. 6-8). 69.00 net. *(978-1-4900-2035-8(7))* Benchmark Education Co.

—The Rise of Western Society: Sailing Ships & Revolutions. Farndon, John. 2018. (Human History Timeline Ser.). (ENG.). 32p. (J). (gr. 3-6). lib. bdg. 27.99 *(978-1-5124-5973-9(9)*, Hungry Tomato ®) Lerner Publishing Group.

—Scooby-Doo! a Science of Electricity Mystery: The Mutant Crocodile. Peterson, Megan Cooley. 2017. (Scooby-Doo Solves It with S. T. E. M. Ser.). (ENG.). 32p. (J). (gr. 3-6). pap. 7.95 *(978-1-5157-3702-5(0))*; lib. bdg. 28.65 *(978-1-5157-3698-1(9))* Capstone. (Capstone Pr.).

—Scooby-Doo! a Science of Magnetism Mystery: The Magnetic Monster. Peterson, Megan Cooley. 2017. (Scooby-Doo Solves It with S. T. E. M. Ser.). (ENG.). 32p. (J). (gr. 3-6). pap. 7.95 *(978-1-5157-3703-2(9))*; lib. bdg. 28.65 *(978-1-5157-3699-8(7))* Capstone. (Capstone Pr.).

—Scooby-Doo! a States of Matter Mystery: Revenge from a Watery Grave. Peterson, Megan Cooley. 2016. (Scooby-Doo Solves It with S. T. E. M. Ser.). (ENG.). 32p. (J). (gr. 3-6). 28.65 *(978-1-5157-2592-3(8)*, Capstone Pr.) Capstone.

—Scooby-Doo! & the Buried City of Pompeii: The Ghastly Guide. Weakland, Mark. 2018. (Unearthing Ancient Civilizations with Scooby-Doo! Ser.). (ENG.). 32p. (J). (gr. 3-6). lib. bdg. 27.99 *(978-1-5157-7512-6(7)*, 135892, Capstone Pr.) Capstone.

—Scooby-Doo! & the Cliff Dwellings of Mesa Verde: The Ghostly Gaze. Weakland, Mark. 2018. (Unearthing Ancient Civilizations with Scooby-Doo! Ser.). (ENG.). 32p. (J). (gr. 3-6). lib. bdg. 27.99 *(978-1-5157-7511-9(9)*, 135891, Capstone Pr.) Capstone.

Cornia, Christian, et al. Scooby-Doo! Unmasks Monsters: The Truth Behind Zombies, Werewolves, & Other Spooky Creatures. Weakland, Mark & Collins, Terry. 2015. (ENG.). 144p. (J). (gr. k-2). pap. 9.95 *(978-1-62370-216-8(X))* Capstone.

Cornia, Christian. Smash! Wile E. Coyote Experiments with Simple Machines, 1 vol. Weakland, Mark. 2014. (Wile E. Coyote, Physical Science Genius Ser.). (ENG.). 32p. (J). (gr. 3-6). 31.32 *(978-1-4765-4222-5(8)*, Capstone Pr.) Capstone.

—The Southern Colonies: Bridges Edition. Burgan, Michael. 2015. (Prime Plus Ser.). (YA). (gr. 6-8). pap. *(978-1-4900-1941-3(3))* Benchmark Education Co.

—The Southern Colonies: Bridges Edition Set of 6 with Common Core Indicators. Burgan, Michael. 2015. (Prime Plus Ser.). (YA). (gr. 6-8). 69.00 net. *(978-1-4900-2037-2(3))* Benchmark Education Co.

—Splat! Wile E. Coyote Experiments with States of Matter, 1 vol. Slade, Suzanne. 2014. (Wile E. Coyote, Physical Science Genius Ser.). (ENG.). 32p. (J). (gr. 3-6). 31.32 *(978-1-4765-4224-9(4)*, Capstone Pr.) Capstone.

—Super Scavengers. Harper, Benjamin. 2020. (Michael Dahl Presents: Side-Splitting Stories Ser.). (ENG.). 72p. (J). (gr. 3-6). pap. 5.95 *(978-1-4965-9210-1(7)*, 142238); lib. bdg. 25.32 *(978-1-4965-8706-0(5)*, 141440) Capstone. (Stone Arch Bks.).

—Thud! Wile E. Coyote Experiments with Forces & Motion, 1 vol. Weakland, Mark. 2014. (Wile E. Coyote, Physical Science Genius Ser.). (ENG.). 32p. (J). (gr. 3-6). 31.32 *(978-1-4765-4221-8(X)*, Capstone Pr.) Capstone.

Cornia, Christian, et al. Unmasking Monsters with Scooby-Doo! Collins, Terry & Weakland, Mark. 2015. (Unmasking Monsters with Scooby-Doo! Ser.). (ENG.). 24p. (J). (gr. k-2). lib. bdg., lib. bdg., lib. bdg. 159.90 *(978-1-4914-1797-3(8))* Capstone.

Cornia, Christian. When Unicorns Poop. Castle, Lexie. 2019. 32p. (J). (gr. -1-3). 16.99 *(978-0-7624-6712-9(6)*, Running Pr. Kids) Running Pr.

—Yogi Bear's Guide to Animal Tracks. Weakland, Mark. 2015. (Yogi Bear's Guide to the Great Outdoors Ser.). (ENG.). 32p. (J). (gr. k-2). lib. bdg. 28.65 *(978-1-4914-6545-5(X))* Capstone.

—Yogi Bear's Guide to Plants. Weakland, Mark. 2015. (Yogi Bear's Guide to the Great Outdoors Ser.). (ENG.). 32p. (J). (gr. k-2). lib. bdg. 28.65 *(978-1-4914-6547-9(6))* Capstone.

Cornia, Christian & Brizuela, Dario. Unearthing Ancient Civilizations with Scooby-Doo! Weakland, Mark. 2018. (Unearthing Ancient Civilizations with Scooby-Doo! Ser.). (ENG.). 32p. (J). (gr. 3-6). 111.96 *(978-1-5157-7532-4(1)*, 26799, Capstone Pr.) Capstone.

Cornia, Christian, jt. illus. see Beach, Bryan.

Cornia, Christian, jt. illus. see Beavers, Ethen.

Corniaux, Christian. The Rise of Civilization: First Cities & Empires. Farndon, John. 2018. (Human History Timeline Ser.). (ENG.). 32p. (J). (gr. 3-6). 27.99 *(978-1-5124-5971-5(2)*, Hungry Tomato ®) Lerner Publishing Group.

Cornish, D. M. Foundling. Cornish, D. M. 2007. (Monster Blood Tattoo Ser.). 434p. (gr. 7-12). 20.00 *(978-0-7569-7957-7(9))* Perfection Learning Corp.

Cornish, David. Emu's Halloween. Mangan, Anne. 2017. 32p. 9.99 *(978-0-7322-9890-6(3))* HarperCollins Pubs. Australia AUS. Dist: HarperCollins Pubs.

—Here Comes a Kiss. Mccleary, Stacey. 2015. (ENG.). 24p. (J). (gr. -1-k). pap. 9.99 *(978-1-76012-122-8(3))* Little Hare Bks. AUS. Dist: Independent Pubs. Group.

Cornue, Don. The Firflake: A Christmas Story. Cardno, Anthony R. 2008. 56p. pap. 8.95 *(978-0-595-52468-6(0))* iUniverse, Inc.

Cornwall, Gaia. The Unicorn Came to Dinner. DeStefano, Lauren. 2020. (ENG.). 10p. (J). bds. 18.99 *(978-1-250-31040-8(7)*, 900198666) Roaring Brook Pr.

Cornwall, Gaia. Jabari Jumps. Cornwall, Gaia. (ENG.). 32p. (J). (gr. -1-3). 2020. 7.99 *(978-1-5362-0290-8(8))*; 2017. 16.99 *(978-0-7636-7838-8(4))* Candlewick Pr.

—Jabari Saltа. Cornwall, Gaia. 2020. 32p. (J). (gr. -1-3). 7.99 *(978-1-5362-1254-9(7))* Candlewick Pr.

Cornwall, Gaia. Jabari Tries. Cornwall, Gaia. 2020. (ENG.). 32p. (J). (gr. -1-3). 16.99 ***(978-1-5362-0716-3(0))*** Candlewick Pr.

Cornwell, Brendan W. Aesop in Goudy. 2007. 48p. (J). 20.00 *(978-0-9711321-1-5(9))* Blue Tree LLC.

Coroa, Carolina. Trailblazer: Lily Parr, the Unstoppable Star of Women's Soccer. Dale, Elizabeth. 2020. (ENG.). 32p. (J). (gr. -1-3). 17.99 ***(978-1-84886-645-4(3))*** Maverick Arts Publishing GBR. Dist: Lerner Publishing Group.

Corona, Jorge. But Games Can Never Hurt Me & Sleep Over. Fisch, Sholly & Hagan, Merrill. 2019. (DC Teen Titans Go! Ser.). (ENG.). 32p. (J). (gr. 2-6). lib. bdg. 21.93 *(978-1-4965-7998-0(4)*, 139829, Stone Arch Bks.) Capstone.

Corona, Jorge. Stare Master and Royal Pains. Fisch, Sholly & Hagan, Merrill. 2020. (DC Teen Titans Go! Ser.). (ENG.). 32p. (J). (gr. 2-6). lib. bdg. 21.93 ***(978-1-4965-9941-4(1)***, 201382, Stone Arch Bks.) Capstone.

—Starstruck and No Jacket Required. Hagan, Merrill. 2020. (DC Teen Titans Go! Ser.). (ENG.). 32p. (J). (gr. 2-6). lib. bdg. 21.93 ***(978-1-4965-9939-1(X)***, 201380, Stone Arch Bks.) Capstone.

Corona, Jorge & Bates, Ben. Party, Party & Silicon Valley Cyborg. Wolfram, Amy & Sanchez, Ricardo. 2019. (DC Teen Titans Go! Ser.). (ENG.). 32p. (J). (gr. 2-6). lib. bdg. 21.93 *(978-1-4965-7995-9(X)*, 139826, Stone Arch Bks.) Capstone.

Corona, Jorge & Gugliotti, Chris. Robin the First & Teen Titans Go ... Fish! Wolfram, Amy & Fisch, Sholly. 2019. (DC Teen Titans Go! Ser.). (ENG.). 32p. (J). (gr. 2-6). lib. bdg. 21.93 *(978-1-4965-7996-6(8)*, 139827, Stone Arch Bks.) Capstone.

Corona, Jorge & Hernandez, Lea. One Potato, Two Potato, Couch Potato and the Rocky Road to Love. Fisch, Sholly & Wolfram, Amy. 2020. (DC Teen Titans Go! Ser.). (ENG.). 32p. (J). (gr. 2-6). lib. bdg. 21.93 ***(978-1-4965-9940-7(3)***, 201381, Stone Arch Bks.) Capstone.

Corona, Jorge & Hernandez, Lea. Prank'd! & Don't Look. Fisch, Sholly & Wolfram, Amy. 2019. (DC Teen Titans Go! Ser.). (ENG.). 32p. (J). (gr. 2-6). lib. bdg. 21.93 *(978-1-4965-7997-3(6)*, 139828, Stone Arch Bks.) Capstone.

Corona, Jorge & Sandoval, Tony. Adventure Time Comics Vol. 3. Kennedy Johnson, Phillip. 2017. (Adventure Time Comics Ser.: 3). (ENG.). 112p. (J). (gr. 4-7). pap. 14.99 *(978-1-68415-041-0(8))* Boom! Studios.

Corona, Jorge, jt. illus. see Bates, Ben.

Corona, Jorge, jt. illus. see Brizuela, Dario.

Corona, Jorge, jt. illus. see Hernandez, Lea.

Coronado, Jinky. Avalon High: Coronation #2: Homecoming, 2. Cabot, Meg. 2008. (Avalon High Coronation Ser.: Bk. 2). (ENG.). 192p. (YA). (gr. 8-12). pap. 9.99 *(978-0-06-117709-5(1))* HarperCollins Pubs.

—Avalon High: Coronation #3: Hunter's Moon. Cabot, Meg. 2009. (Avalon High Coronation Ser.: Bk. 3). (ENG.). 160p. (YA). (gr. 8-18). pap. 9.99 *(978-0-06-117710-1(5))* HarperCollins Pubs.

—The Merlin Prophecy. Cabot, Meg. 2007. (Avalon High Coronation Ser.: Bk. 1). 128p. pap. 7.99 *(978-1-4278-0106-7(1))* TOKYOPOP, Inc.

Corpi, Lucha & Fields, Lisa. The Triple Banana Split Boy/El Nino Goloso. Corpi, Lucha & Fields, Lisa. 2009. (SPA & ENG.). 32p. (J). (gr. -1-4). 16.95 *(978-1-55885-504-5(1))* Arte Publico Pr.

Corpus, Mary. Reading Beauty, 1 vol. Cockroft, Kimberly. 2018. (ENG.). 32p. (J). (gr. -1-3). 16.99 *(978-1-4556-2359-4(8)*, Pelican Publishing) Arcadia Publishing.

Corpus, Mary Grace. Broccoli for Breakfast. James, Matilda. 2018. (ENG.). 32p. (J). (gr. -1-3). pap. 9.99 *(978-1-5324-0764-2(5))* Xist Publishing.

—Sergeant Bill & His Horse Bob. Dans, Peter E. 2015.Tr. of 28. (ENG.). (J). 17.95 *(978-1-933822-97-6(X))* Camino Bks., Inc.

Corr, Christopher. All Aboard for the Bobo Road. Davies, Stephen. 2016. (ENG.). 32p. (J). (gr. -1-3). 17.99 *(978-1-5124-1598-8(7)*, 9781512415988) Lerner Publishing Group.

—Around the World: A Colorful Atlas for Kids. Ganeri, Anita. 2015. (ENG.). 64p. (J). (gr. k-2). 17.99 *(978-0-8075-0443-7(2)*, 807504432) Whitman, Albert & Co.

—Ebby Meets Felicity. Hickey, Matt. 2004. 32p. (J). 14.95 *(978-1-84458-141-2(1))* Avalon Publishing.

—Heaven in a Poem: An Anthology of Poems. 48p. 19.99 *(978-0-7459-4259-9(8)*, Lion Books) Lion Hudson PLC GBR. Dist: Trafalgar Square Publishing.

—Indian Tales. Nanji, Shenaaz. 2017. (ENG.). 96p. (J). (gr. 1-4). pap. 16.99 *(978-1-78285-357-2(X))* Barefoot Bks., Inc.

—My Granny Went to Market: A Round-the-World Counting Rhyme. Blackstone, Stella. 24p. (J). 2006. (gr. -1-2). pap. 6.99 *(978-1-905236-62-6(X))*; 2005. 16.99 *(978-1-84148-792-2(9))* Barefoot Bks., Inc.

—My Travel Journal. Mudpuppy Press Staff. 2005. (J). 9.99 *(978-0-7353-0882-4(9))* Galison.

—Nos Vamos a Mexico! Una Aventura Bajo el Sol. Krebs, Laurie & Blackstone, Stella. Canetti, Yanitzia James, tr. 2006. 32p. (J). (gr. k-5). pap. 8.99 *(978-1-84686-014-0(8))* Barefoot Bks., Inc.

—Off We Go to Mexico. Krebs, Laurie. 2006. (ENG.). 32p. (J). 16.99 *(978-1-905236-40-4(9))* Barefoot Bks., Inc.

—Off We Go to Mexico! An Adventure in the Sun. Krebs, Laurie. 2008. 32p. (J). (gr. k-5). pap. 8.99 *(978-1-84686-159-8(4))* Barefoot Bks., Inc.

—Where's Everybody Going? Samuel, Quentin. 2003. 24p. (J). *(978-1-84089-218-5(8))* Zero to Ten, Ltd.

—Whole World: PB with CD. 2010. (ENG.). 32p. (J). (gr. -1-2). 9.99 *(978-1-84686-085-0(7))* Barefoot Bks., Inc.

—Why Is Everybody So Excited. Samuel, Quentin. 2003. 24p. (J). *(978-1-84089-219-2(6))* Zero to Ten, Ltd.

—A Year Full of Stories: 52 Classic Stories from All Around the World. McAllister, Angela. 2016. (ENG.). 128p. (J). (gr. 1-4). 22.99 *(978-1-84780-868-4(9)*, Frances Lincoln Children's Bks.) Quarto Publishing Group UK GBR. Dist: Hachette Bk. Group.

Corr, Christopher. Indian Tales: A Barefoot Collection. Corr, Christopher. Nanji, Shenaaz. 2007. (ENG.). 96p. (J). (gr. 2-18). 19.99 *(978-1-84686-083-6(0))* Barefoot Bks., Inc.

—Whole World. Corr, Christopher. Penner, Fred. 2007. (ENG.). 32p. (J). (gr. -1-4). 16.99 *(978-1-84686-043-0(1))* Barefoot Bks., Inc.

Corr Scott, Briana. The Mermaid Handbook: A Guide to the Mermaid Way of Life, Including Recipes, Folklore, & More, 1 vol. Widrig, Taylor. 2020. (ENG.). 88p. (J). pap. 14.95 ***(978-1-77108-865-7(6)***, e3feb951-627b-44aa-96de-c7a29dd88c61) Nimbus Publishing, Ltd. CAN. Dist: Baker & Taylor Publisher Services (BTPS).

Corradengo, Giorgia. Rise & Shine, Mr. Porcupine! Blaeser, Keatyn. 2018. (ENG.). 32p. (J). pap. 10.99 *(978-1-5329-5649-2(5))* CreateSpace Independent Publishing Platform.

Corradetti, Chiara. K Is for King Arthur. Bahney, Kelly. 2020. (ENG.). 32p. (J). pap. 10.99 ***(978-1-6777-3480-1(9))*** Independently Published.

Corradino, Davide. Ela's World: A Playful Story about Heritage & World Cultures. Caputo-Wickham, Laura. l.t. ed. 2019. (ENG.). 28p. (J). (gr. k-1). pap. 6.99 ***(978-1-938712-21-0(8))*** Long Bridge Publishing.

Corrado, Lynda. Norman: The Great Escape. Corrado, Lynda. 2020. (Norman Ser.: Vol. 1). (ENG.). 106p. (J). (gr. 3-5). pap. 6.99 ***(978-0-9835647-7-5(9))*** White Horse Flying Pubns.

Corral, Roy, photos by. Children of the First People: Fresh Voices of Alaska's Native Kids. 2019. (ENG., 48p. (J). (gr. 1-5). 24.99 *(978-1-5132-6198-0(3))*; (gr. 3-5). pap. 13.99 *(978-1-5132-6197-3(5))* West Margin Pr. (Alaska Northwest Bks.).

Correll, Gemma. Annie's Life in Lists. Mahoney, Kristin Mary. 2018. 272p. (J). (gr. 3-7). 16.99 *(978-1-5247-6509-5(0)*, Knopf Bks. for Young Readers) Random Hse. Children's Bks.

—Being a Girl. Long, Hayley. 2016. (ENG.). 224p. (J). pap. 12.99 *(978-1-4494-7797-4(6))* Andrews McMeel Publishing.

—Mind Your Head. Dawson, James & Hewitt, Olivia. 2016. (ENG.). 208p. (YA). (gr. 7). pap. 12.99 *(978-1-4714-0531-0(1))* Bonnier Publishing GBR. Dist: Independent Pubs. Group.

—Pig & Pug. Berry, Lynne. 2015. (ENG.). 40p. (J). (gr. -1-3). 16.99 *(978-1-4814-2131-7(X)*, Simon & Schuster Bks. For Young Readers) Simon & Schuster Bks. For Young Readers.

—Uncle Shawn & Bill & the Almost Entirely Unplanned Adventure. Kennedy, A. L. 2018. (ENG.). 192p. (J). pap. 5.99 *(978-1-61067-740-0(4))* Kane Miller.

—Uncle Shawn & Bill & the Pajimminy Crimminy Unusual Adventure. Kennedy, A. L. 2019. (ENG.). 272p. (J). pap. 5.99 *(978-1-61067-741-7(2))* Kane Miller.

Corrette, Keith F., photos by. Sally Sue & the Hospice of Saint John. Mesplay, Gail G. 2003. 44p. (J). (gr. -1-6). pap. 15.00 *(978-0-9742849-0-3(4))* Hospice of Saint John, The.

Corrigan, Caroline. Women Artists a to Z. LaBarge, Melanie. 2020. (ENG.). 64p. (J). (gr. -1-2). 19.99 *(978-0-593-10872-7(8)*, Dial Bks) Penguin Young Readers Group.

Corrigan, Patrick. Billy & the Balloons. Dale, Elizabeth. ed. 2020. 32p. (J). (gr. -1-1). 16.95 ***(978-1-913337-16-2(2)***, Scribblers) Book Hse. GBR. Dist: Sterling Publishing Co., Inc.

Corrigan, Patrick. If I Were a Park Ranger. Stier, Catherine. 2019. (ENG.). 32p. (J). (gr. -1-3). 16.99 *(978-0-8075-3545-5(1)*, 807535451) Whitman, Albert & Co.

—The Little Squeegy Bug, 0 vols. Martin, Bill, Jr. & Sampson, Michael. 2005. (ENG.). 32p. (J). (gr. -1-2). reprint ed. pap. 9.99 *(978-0-7614-5243-0(5)*, 9780761452430, Two Lions) Amazon Publishing.

Corrigan, Patrick. Mister T. V. The Story of John Logie Baird. Fulton, Julie. 2020. (ENG.). 32p. (J). (gr. -1-3). 17.99 ***(978-1-84886-646-1(1))*** Maverick Arts Publishing GBR. Dist: Lerner Publishing Group.

Corrigan, Patrick. OopsyDaisy! Dale, Elizabeth. 2019. (Picture Bks.). (ENG.). 32p. (J). pap. 16.99 *(978-1-78700-981-3(5))* Willow Tree Bks. GBR. Dist: Independent Pubs. Group.

Corrigan, Patrick. The Story of the Mayflower. Pingry, Patricia A. 2020. (ENG.). 24p. (J). (gr. -1 — 1). 7.99 ***(978-1-5460-3378-3(5)***, Worthy Kids/Ideals) Worthy Publishing.

Corrigan, Patrick. Tow Truck Joe. Sobel, June. 2019. (Tow Truck Joe Ser.). (ENG.). 32p. (J). (gr. -1-3). 17.99 *(978-0-358-05312-5(9)*, 1742722, HMH Books For Young Readers) Houghton Mifflin Harcourt Publishing Co.

—Trick-Or-Treat with Tow Truck Joe. Sobel, June. 2020. (Tow Truck Joe Ser.). (ENG.). 12p. (J). (gr. -1-2). 8.99 *(978-0-358-06367-4(1)*, 1743695, HMH Books For Young Readers) Houghton Mifflin Harcourt Publishing Co.

Corrigan, Sophie. The Heart of a Mouse. Pang, Mandy. 2016. (ENG.). (J). (gr. 1-3). pap. *(978-0-9935872-1-4(6))* Pang, Mandy.

Corrigan, Sophie. Pugtato Finds a Thing, 1 vol. Zondervan. 2020. 32p. (J). 17.99 ***(978-0-310-76781-7(4))*** Zonderkidz.

Corrin, Ashleigh. Layla's Happiness. Tallie, Mariahadessa Ekere. 2019. (ENG.). 48p. 17.95 *(978-1-59270-288-6(0))* Enchanted Lion Bks., LLC.

Corry, Lydia. Eight Princesses & a Magic Mirror. Farrant, Natasha. 2020. (ENG.). 224p. (J). 19.95 *(978-1-324-01556-7(X)*, 341556, Norton Young Readers) Norton, W. W. & Co., Inc.

Corso, Bertina, jt. illus. see Corso, Erika.

Corso, Erika & Corso, Bertina. The Day You Came. Corso, Erika. 2006. (ENG.). 20p. (J). per. 12.95 *(978-1-59800-242-3(2))* Outskirts Pr., Inc.

Cort, Ben. Aliens in Underpants Save the World. Freedman, Claire. 2012. (Underpants Bks.). (ENG.). 32p. (J). (gr. -1-2). 18.99 *(978-1-4424-2768-6(X)*, Simon & Schuster/Paula Wiseman Bks.) Simon & Schuster/Paula Wiseman Bks.

—Aliens Love Dinopants. Freedman, Claire. 2016. (Underpants Bks.). (ENG.). 32p. (J). (gr. -1-2). 17.99 *(978-1-4814-6736-0(0)*, Aladdin) Simon & Schuster Children's Publishing.

—Aliens Love Panta Claus. Freedman, Claire. 2011. (Underpants Bks.). (ENG.). 32p. (J). (gr. -1-2). 18.99 *(978-1-4424-2830-0(9)*, Simon & Schuster/Paula Wiseman Bks.) Simon & Schuster/Paula Wiseman Bks.

—Dinosaurs Love Underpants. Freedman, Claire. 2009. (Underpants Bks.). (ENG.). 32p. (J). (gr. -1-2). 17.99 *(978-1-4169-8938-7(2)*, Aladdin) Simon & Schuster Children's Publishing.

—Monstersaurus. Freedman, Claire. 2013. (J). *(978-1-4351-4952-6(1))* Barnes & Noble, Inc.

—Monstersaurus. Freedman, Claire. 2011. (ENG.). 32p. *(978-1-84738-904-6(X))* Simon & Schuster, Ltd.

—Nora: The Girl Who Ate & Ate & Ate ... Weale, Andrew. 2012. 32p. (J). (gr. -1-k). pap. 13.99 *(978-1-84939-382-9(6))* Andersen Pr. GBR. Dist: Independent Pubs. Group.

—Octopus's Garden. Starr, Ringo. 2014. (ENG.). 32p. (J). (gr. -1-3). 19.99 (978-1-4814-0362-7(1), Aladdin) Simon & Schuster Children's Publishing.

—Pirate Blunderbeard: Worst. Mission. Ever. (Pirate Blunderbeard, Book 3) Sparkes, Amy. 2019. (Pirate Blunderbeard Ser.: 3). (ENG.). 160p. (J). 4.99 (978-0-00-830827-8(6), HarperCollins Children's Bks.) HarperCollins Pubs. Ltd. GBR. Dist: HarperCollins Pubs.

—Pirate Blunderbeard: Worst. Movie. Ever. (Pirate Blunderbeard, Book 4) Sparkes, Amy. 2019. (Pirate Blunderbeard Ser.: 4). (ENG.). 144p. (J). 4.99 (978-0-00-830828-5(4), HarperCollins Children's Bks.) HarperCollins Pubs. Ltd. GBR. Dist: HarperCollins Pubs.

—Pirate Blunderbeard: Worst. Pirate. Ever. (Pirate Blunderbeard, Book 1) Sparkes, Amy. 2019. (Pirate Blunderbeard Ser.: 1). (ENG.). 160p. (J). 4.99 (978-0-00-830825-4(X), HarperCollins Children's Bks.) HarperCollins Pubs. Ltd. GBR. Dist: HarperCollins Pubs.

—Pirate Blunderbeard: Worst. Vacation. Ever. (Pirate Blunderbeard, Book 2) Sparkes, Amy. 2019. (Pirate Blunderbeard Ser.: 2). (ENG.). 160p. (J). 4.99 (978-0-00-830826-1(8), HarperCollins Children's Bks.) HarperCollins Pubs. Ltd. GBR. Dist: HarperCollins Pubs.

—Pirates Love Underpants. Freedman, Claire. 2013. (Underpants Bks.). (ENG.). 32p. (J). (gr. -1-2). 17.99 (978-1-4424-8512-9(4), Simon & Schuster/Paula Wiseman Bks.) Simon & Schuster/Paula Wiseman Bks.

—Watch Out for Muddy Puddles! Faulks, Ben. 2018. (ENG.). 32p. (J). 16.99 (978-1-68119-627-5(1), 900179490, Bloomsbury USA Childrens) Bloomsbury Publishing USA.

Cortazar, Alicia Canas. Cuando Llega la Noche. Martín Anguita, Carmen & Carmen, Martín Anguita. 2008. (SPA.). 32p. (J). 10.99 (978-84-241-5400-4(2)) Everest Editora ESP. Dist: Lectorum Pubns., Inc.

—Cuéntame un Cuento, Que Voy a Comer. Martín Anguita, Carmen & Carmen, Martín Anguita. 2008. (SPA.). 32p. (J). 10.99 (978-84-241-5752-4(4)) Everest Editora ESP. Dist: Lectorum Pubns., Inc.

—El Cumpleaños de Laika. Martín Anguita, Carmen & Carmen, Martín Anguita. 2008. (SPA.). 32p. (J). 10.99 (978-84-241-5803-3(2)) Everest Editora ESP. Dist: Lectorum Pubns., Inc.

—Marta y Mamá Juegan a Recordar. Martín Anguita, Carmen & Carmen, Martín Anguita. 2008. (SPA.). 32p. (J). 10.99 (978-84-241-5390-8(1)) Everest Editora ESP. Dist: Lectorum Pubns., Inc.

—Marta y Su Dragón (Martha & Her Dragon) Martín Anguita, Carmen & Carmen, Martín Anguita. 2008. (SPA.). 32p. (J). 10.99 (978-84-241-5444-8(4)) Everest Editora ESP. Dist: Lectorum Pubns., Inc.

—El Primer Día de Colegio de David. Martín Anguita, Carmen & Carmen, Martín Anguita. 2008. (SPA.). 32p. (J). 10.99 (978-84-241-5790-6(7)) Everest Editora ESP. Dist: Lectorum Pubns., Inc.

—Una Tarde en el Circo. Martín Anguita, Carmen & Carmen, Martín Anguita. 2008. (SPA.). 32p. (J). 10.99 (978-84-241-5459-2(2)) Everest Editora ESP. Dist: Lectorum Pubns., Inc.

Corteggiani, Francois. Third Nile. Gray, Jonathan H. et al. 2017. (Uncle Scrooge Ser.). (ENG.). 124p. (J). (gr. 4-7). pap. 12.99 (978-1-68405-087-1(1)) Idea & Design Works, LLC.

Corteletti Agua Viva, Mauricio. Nana Speaks Nanese. Brennan, Laura. 2019. (ENG.). 54p. (J). pap. 12.99 (978-1-7323846-0-6(6)) Brennan, Laura.

Cortes, Darvin. Mommy Can't Feed the Baby? Colwill, Simone. 2020. (ENG.). 40p. (J). (gr. k-6). pap. (978-0-473-49878-8(2)) Bks. for Caring Kids.

Cortes, Laura Gutierrez & Gutierrez, Lucia Doblas. The Eagle Learns about Christmas - el Águila Aprende Sobre la Navidad. Puerto, Ledezna. 2018. (MUL.). 52p. (J). pap. 13.95 (978-1-64471-035-7(8)) Covenant Bks.

—Valentine Is a Shape: Valentin Es una Figura. Puerto, Ledezna. 2018. (MUL.). 56p. (J). pap. 14.95 (978-1-64300-116-6(7)) Covenant Bks.

Cortes, Mario, et al. Ariel Is My Babysitter (Disney Princess) Posner-Sanchez, Andrea. 2016. (Little Golden Book Ser.). (ENG.). 24p. (J). (gr. -1-k). 4.99 (978-0-7364-3446-1(1), Golden/Disney) Random Hse. Children's Bks.

Cortes, Mario. The Aristocats. Bornec, Didier Le. 2020. (Disney Classics Ser.). (ENG.). 48p. (J). (gr. 2-6). lib. bdg. 28.50 (978-1-5321-4532-2(2), 35181, Graphic Novels) Spotlight.

—Bambi. Maine, Régis. 2020. (Disney Classics Ser.). (ENG.). 48p. (J). (gr. 2-6). lib. bdg. 28.50 (978-1-5321-4535-3(7), 35182, Graphic Novels) Spotlight.

Cortés, Mario. Cinderella. Maine, Régis. 2020. (Disney Princesses Ser.). (ENG.). 48p. (J). (gr. 2-6). lib. bdg. 28.50 (978-1-5321-4560-5(8), 35207, Graphic Novels) Spotlight.

Cortes, Mario. Disney Before the Story: Elsa's Icy Rescue. Egan, Kate. 2020. (Disney Before the Story Ser.). (ENG.). 128p. (J). (gr. k-3). pap. 6.99 (978-1-368-05605-2(9)) Disney Pr.

Cortes, Mario. Disney Cinderella: the Story of the Movie in Comics. Maine, Régis. 2020. (ENG.). 48p. (J). (gr. 3-7). 10.99 (978-1-5067-1737-1(3), Dark Horse Books) Dark Horse Comics.

—Lady & the Tramp. Corteggiani, François. 2020. (Disney Classics Ser.). (ENG.). 48p. (J). (gr. 2-6). lib. bdg. 28.50 (978-1-5321-4538-4(1), 35185, Graphic Novels) Spotlight.

—Mulan. Ehrbar, Bob Foster. 2020. (Disney Princesses Ser.). (ENG.). 48p. (J). (gr. 2-6). lib. bdg. 28.50 (978-1-5321-4564-3(0), 35211, Graphic Novels) Spotlight.

—Peter Pan. Bornec, Didier Le. 2020. (Disney Classics Ser.). (ENG.). 48p. (J). (gr. 2-6). lib. bdg. 28.50 (978-1-5321-4542-1(X), 35188, Graphic Novels) Spotlight.

—Sleeping Beauty. Maine, Régis. 2020. (Disney Princesses Ser.). (ENG.). 48p. (J). (gr. 2-6). lib. bdg. 28.50 (978-1-5321-4567-4(5), 35214, Graphic Novels) Spotlight.

Cortes, Mario, et al. Smash Trash! Driscoll, Laura & Random House Disney Staff. 2008. (Step into Reading Ser.). (ENG.). 32p. (J). (gr. k-3). pap. 3.99 (978-0-7364-2515-5(2), RH/Disney) Random Hse. Children's Bks.

Cortes, Mario & Colletti, Marco. Follow That Hippo! (Disney Junior: the Lion Guard) Posner-Sanchez, Andrea. 2016. (Big Golden Book Ser.). (ENG.). 32p. (J). (-k). 9.99 (978-0-7364-3391-4(0), Golden/Disney) Random Hse. Children's Bks.

Cortes, Osvaldo. Descubre la historia de los Ninos. Lara, Jose Luis Trueba. (Serie Descubre Ser.). (SPA.). 96p. (J). (gr. 3-5). pap. 18.95 (978-970-29-1057-2(9)) Santillana USA Publishing Co., Inc.

—Descubre... La Tierra y el Cosmos. Trueba, Jose Luis. 2004. (Ser. Descubre). (SPA.). 96p. (J). (gr. 3-5). pap. 18.95 (978-970-29-0509-7(5)) Santillana USA Publishing Co., Inc.

—Descubre... Las Raices de Mexico. Trueba, Jose Luis. 2004. (Ser. Descubre). (SPA.). 96p. (J). (gr. 3-5). pap. 18.95 (978-970-29-0508-0(7)) Santillana USA Publishing Co., Inc.

—Descubre... Los Animales. Trueba, Jose Luis. 2004. (Ser. Descubre). 96p. (J). (gr. 3-5). pap. 18.95 (978-970-29-0510-3(9)) Santillana USA Publishing Co., Inc.

Cortes, Paulina. Comrade, Bliss Ain't Playing: Un Cuento de la Republica Dominicana. Baez, Josefina. 2008. (Marisol Ser.: Vol. 1). (ENG.). 100p. (Orig.). (gr. k-3). pap. 12.95 (978-1-882161-01-0(7)) I.Om.Be Pr.

Cortes, Ricardo. Boundary. Terrell, Heather. 2015. (Books of Eva Ser.). (ENG.). 276p. (YA). (gr. 9). pap. 10.99 (978-1-61695-620-2(8), Soho Teen) Soho Pr., Inc.

—Party: A Mystery. Kincaid, Jamaica. 2019. (ENG.). 32p. (J). 17.95 (978-1-61775-716-7(0)) Akashic Bks.

—Relic (the Books of Eva I) Terrell, Heather. 2014. (Books of Eva Ser.: 1). (ENG.). 288p. (YA). (gr. 9). pap. 9.99 (978-1-61695-406-2(X), Soho Teen) Soho Pr., Inc.

—Seriously, Just Go to Sleep. Mansbach, Adam. 2012. (ENG.). 32p. (gr. k-5). 15.95 (978-1-61775-078-6(6)) Akashic Bks.

Cortez, Jess S. My Trip to the Harbor. Cortez, Jess S., photos by. ed. 2005. 16p. (J). (978-0-9776291-0-7(4)) Jesus Estanislado.

Cortina, Eliel & Cortina, Elio. If You Teach a Giraffe to Fly. Morgan, Zach. 2020. (ENG.). 24p. (J). pap. 16.99 (978-1-7283-6027-0(7)) AuthorHouse.

Cortina, Elio, jt. illus. see Cortina, Eliel.

Cortright, Robert S., photos by. Bridging the World. Cortright, Robert S. 2003. 208p. 35.00 (978-0-9641963-3-9(6)) Bridge Ink.

Corts, Enrique. Back to the Ice Age. Nickel, Scott. 2008. (Graphic Sparks Ser.). (ENG.). 40p. (J). (gr. 2-5). pap. 5.95 (978-1-4342-0500-1(2), Stone Arch Bks.) Capstone.

—T. Rex vs Robo-Dog 3000. Nickel, Scott. 2008. (Graphic Sparks Ser.). (ENG.). 40p. (J). (gr. 2-5). pap. 5.95 (978-1-4342-0857-6(5), Stone Arch Bks.) Capstone.

Corum, Jaime. D Is for Derby: A Kentucy Derby Alphabet. Wilbur, Helen L. 2014. (ENG.). 38p. (J). (gr. 3-6). 16.95 (978-1-58536-813-6(X), 203008) Sleeping Bear Pr.

Corvaisier, Laurent. Songs in the Shade of the Flamboyant Tree: French Creole Lullabies & Nursery Rhymes, 1 vol. 2012. (ENG.). 52p. (J). (gr. -1-k). 16.95 (978-2-923163-82-6(6)) La Montagne Secrete CAN. Dist: Independent Pubs. Group.

Corvino, Lucy. The Adventures of Robin Hood: Retold from the Howard Pyle Original. Pyle, Howard. 2005. (Classic Starts® Ser.). 160p. (J). (gr. 2-4). 6.95 (978-1-4027-1257-9(X)) Sterling Publishing Co., Inc.

—The Adventures of Sherlock Holmes: Retold from the Sir Arthur Conan Doyle Original. Doyle, A. Conan. 2005. (Classic Starts® Ser.). 160p. (J). (gr. 2-4). 6.95 (978-1-4027-1217-3(0)) Sterling Publishing Co., Inc.

—The Adventures of Tom Sawyer: Retold from the Mark Twain Original. Twain, Mark. 2005. (Classic Starts® Ser.). 160p. (J). (gr. 2-4). 6.95 (978-1-4027-1216-6(2)) Sterling Publishing Co., Inc.

—Anne of Green Gables. Montgomery, L. M. 2005. (Classic Starts® Ser.). 160p. (J). (gr. 2-4). 6.95 (978-1-4027-1130-5(1)) Sterling Publishing Co., Inc.

—Arabian Nights. 2008. (Classic Starts® Ser.). 160p. (J). (gr. 2-4). 6.95 (978-1-4027-4573-7(7)) Sterling Publishing Co., Inc.

—Black Beauty. Sewell, Anna. 2005. (Classic Starts® Ser.). 160p. (J). (gr. 2-4). 6.95 (978-1-4027-1144-2(1)) Sterling Publishing Co., Inc.

—The Call of the Wild. London, Jack. 2005. (Classic Starts® Ser.). 160p. (J). (gr. 2-4). 6.95 (978-1-4027-1274-6(X)) Sterling Publishing Co., Inc.

Corvino, Lucy. Classic Starts®: Anne of Green Gables. Montgomery, Lucy Maud. 2020. (Classic Starts® Ser.). (ENG.). 160p. (J). (gr. 2-4). pap. 6.95 (978-1-4549-3794-4(7)) Sterling Publishing Co., Inc.

—Classic Starts®: Black Beauty. Sewell, Anna. 2020. (Classic Starts® Ser.). (ENG.). 160p. (J). (gr. 2-4). pap. 6.95 (978-1-4549-3795-1(5)) Sterling Publishing Co., Inc.

—Classic Starts®: Little Women. Alcott, Louisa May. 2020. (Classic Starts® Ser.). (ENG.). 160p. (J). (gr. 2-4). pap. 6.95 (978-1-4549-3797-5(1)) Sterling Publishing Co., Inc.

—Classic Starts®: the Adventures of Robin Hood. Pyle, Howard. 2020. (Classic Starts® Ser.). (ENG.). 160p. (J). (gr. 2-4). pap. 6.95 (978-1-4549-3800-2(5)) Sterling Publishing Co., Inc.

—Classic Starts®: the Adventures of Sherlock Holmes. Doyle, A. Conan. 2020. (Classic Starts® Ser.). (ENG.). 160p. (J). (gr. 2-4). pap. 6.95 (978-1-4549-3801-9(3)) Sterling Publishing Co., Inc.

—Classic Starts®: the Adventures of Tom Sawyer. Twain, Mark. 2020. (Classic Starts® Ser.). (ENG.). 160p. (J). (gr. 2-4). pap. 6.95 (978-1-4549-3802-6(1)) Sterling Publishing Co., Inc.

—Classic Starts®: the Call of the Wild. London, Jack. 2020. (Classic Starts® Ser.). (ENG.). 160p. (J). (gr. 2-4). pap. 6.95 (978-1-4549-3803-3(X)) Sterling Publishing Co., Inc.

—Classic Starts®: the Secret Garden. Burnett, Frances Hodgson. 2020. (Classic Starts® Ser.). (ENG.). 160p. (J). (gr. 2-4). pap. 6.95 (978-1-4549-3804-0(8)) Sterling Publishing Co., Inc.

—Classic Starts®: Treasure Island. Stevenson, Robert Louis. 2020. (Classic Starts® Ser.). (ENG.). 160p. (J). (gr. 2-4). pap. 6.95 (978-1-4549-3808-8(0)) Sterling Publishing Co., Inc.

Corvino, Lucy. The Hunchback of Notre-Dame. Hugo, Victor. 2008. (Classic Starts® Ser.). 160p. (J). (gr. 2-4). 6.95 (978-1-4027-4575-1(3)) Sterling Publishing Co., Inc.

—The Jungle Book. Kipling, Rudyard. 2008. (Classic Starts® Ser.). 160p. (J). (gr. 2-4). 6.95 (978-1-4027-4576-8(1)) Sterling Publishing Co., Inc.

—A Little Princess. Zamorsky, Tania & Burnett, Frances Hodgson. 2005. (Classic Starts® Ser.). 160p. (J). (gr. 2-4). 6.95 (978-1-4027-1275-3(8)) Sterling Publishing Co., Inc.

—Little Women. Alcott, Louisa May. 2005. (Classic Starts® Ser.). 160p. (J). (gr. 2-4). 6.95 (978-1-4027-1236-4(7)) Sterling Publishing Co., Inc.

—Robert Louis Stevenson. Schoonmaker, Frances, ed. 2008. (Poetry for Young People Ser.: 9). 48p. (J). (gr. 3-7). pap. 6.95 (978-1-4027-5476-0(0)) Sterling Publishing Co., Inc.

—The Secret Garden. Burnett, Frances Hodgson. 2005. (Classic Starts® Ser.). 160p. (J). (gr. 2-4). 6.95 (978-1-4027-1319-4(3)) Sterling Publishing Co., Inc.

—Treasure Island. Stevenson, Robert Louis. 2005. (Classic Starts® Ser.). 160p. (J). (gr. 2-4). 6.95 (978-1-4027-1318-7(5)) Sterling Publishing Co., Inc.

—The Voyages of Doctor Dolittle. Lofting, Hugh. 2008. (Classic Starts® Ser.). 160p. (J). (gr. 2-4). 6.95 (978-1-4027-4574-4(5)) Sterling Publishing Co., Inc.

Corvino, Lucy. The Christmas Garland. Corvino, Lucy, tr. Flinn, Lisa & Younger, Barbara. 2003. 32p. (J). 14.95 (978-0-8249-5460-4(2), Ideal Pubns.) Worthy Publishing.

Corwin, Judith Hoffman. Native American Crafts of the Northeast & Southeast. Corwin, Judith Hoffman. 2003. (Native American Crafts Ser.). (ENG.). 48p. (J). (gr. 3-6). pap. 7.95 (978-0-531-15593-6(5), Watts, Franklin) Scholastic Library Publishing.

—Native American Crafts of the Plains & Plateau. Corwin, Judith Hoffman. 2003. (Native American Crafts Ser.). (ENG.). 48p. (J). (gr. 3-6). pap. 7.95 (978-0-531-15595-0(1), Watts, Franklin) Scholastic Library Publishing.

Corwin, Stuart. The Cryptic Cat. Corwin, Susan Simon. 2006. 99p. (YA). (978-0-9790632-0-6(5)) Lucky Duck Designs.

Cory, Fanny Y. Sunshine Annie. Gates, Josephine Scribner. 2007. 148p. (J). lib. bdg. 59.00 (978-1-60304-011-2(0)) Dollworks.

Cos, Manrique & Parra, Lola. La Gruta de la Serpiente. Parra, Mónica. 2016. (SPA.). (J). pap. (978-84-946255-1-0(9)) Editorial Proyecto Educa.

Cosanti, Francesca. Hansel & Gretel. 2017. (ENG.). 40p. (J). (gr. 1). 16.95 (978-88-544-1186-9(8)) White Star ITA. Dist: Sterling Publishing Co., Inc.

—Little Red Riding Hood. 2017. (ENG.). 40p. (J). (gr. 1). 16.95 (978-88-544-1185-2(X)) White Star ITA. Dist: Sterling Publishing Co., Inc.

Cosco, Rafaella. Little Hands Life of Jesus. Mackenzie, Carine. 2008. (ENG.). 144p. (J). 10.99 (978-1-84550-339-0(2), a1e94d2a-fe5b-4990-a8df-1277db0a1e72) Christian Focus Pubns. GBR. Dist: Baker & Taylor Publisher Services (BTPS).

Cosco, Raffaella. Little Hands Story Bible. MacKenzie, Carine. rev. ed. 2009. (ENG.). 144p. (J). (gr. -1-3). 10.99 (978-1-84550-435-9(6), 25532b9a-56ca-420e-a783-aa0a1ef20ce8) Christian Focus Pubns. GBR. Dist: Baker & Taylor Publisher Services (BTPS).

Cosford, Nina. Coco Chanel. Alkayat, Zena. 2016. (Library of Luminaries Ser.). (ENG.). 128p. 16.95 (978-1-4521-5024-6(9)) Chronicle Bks. LLC.

—Dublin. 2012. (Panorama Pops Ser.). (ENG.). 30p. (J). (gr. k-4). 8.99 (978-0-7636-6153-3(8)) Candlewick Pr.

Cosgrove, Kate. And the Bullfrogs Sing: A Life Cycle Begins. Harrison, David L. 2019. 32p. (J). (gr. -1-3). 17.99 (978-0-8234-3834-1(1)) Holiday Hse., Inc.

—The Purple Pussycat. Hillert, Margaret. 2016. (BeginningtoRead Ser.). (ENG.). 32p. (J). (gr. -1-2). pap. 11.94 (978-1-60357-944-5(3)); 21st ed. (gr. k-2). 22.60 (978-1-59953-803-7(2)) Norwood Hse. Pr.

Cosgrove, Lee. Finn Maccool & the Giant's Causeway. Dougherty, John. 2014. (Traditional Tales Ser.). (ENG.). 32p. (J). (gr. 1-2). pap. 7.95 (978-1-62521-556-7(8), Capstone Classroom) Capstone.

—Narwhals & Pirates. Finch, Rusty. Cottage Door Press, ed. 2020. (Very Busy Board Book to Look, Match Search & Laugh! Ser.). (ENG.). 12p. (J). (gr. -1-1). bds. 14.99 (978-1-68052-823-7(8), 1005360) Cottage Door Pr.

Cosgrove, Lee. Night of the Living Ted. Hutchison, Barry. 2020. (Living Ted Ser.: 1). (ENG.). 192p. (J). (gr. 3-7). 9.99 (978-0-593-17428-9(3), Delacorte Bks. for Young Readers) Random Hse. Children's Bks.

—Sharks Can't Smile! And Other Amazing Facts. Dennis, Elizabeth. 2020. (Super Facts for Super Kids Ser.). (ENG.). 32p. (J). (gr. k-2). 17.99 (978-1-5344-6772-9(6)); pap. 4.99 (978-1-5344-6771-2(8)) Simon Spotlight. (Simon Spotlight).

Cosgrove, Lee. Shhh! It's a Surprise Party! 22 Button Sound Book. Fowler, Cherry. 2017. (Early Bird Sound Bks.). (ENG.). 16p. (J). (gr. -1-k). bds. 16.99 (978-1-68052-241-9(8), 1002270) Cottage Door Pr.

Cosgrove, Lee. Tigers Can't Purr! And Other Amazing Facts. Feldman, Thea. 2020. (Super Facts for Super Kids Ser.). (ENG.). 32p. (J). (gr. k-2). 17.99 (978-1-5344-6775-0(0)); pap. 4.99 (978-1-5344-6774-3(2)) Simon Spotlight. (Simon Spotlight).

Cosgrove, Matt. Macca the Alpaca. Cosgrove, Matt. 2020. (Macca the Alpaca Ser.). (ENG.). 24p. (J). (gr. -1-k). 14.99 (978-1-338-60282-1(9), Scholastic Pr.) Scholastic, Inc.

Cosley, Jamie, jt. illus. see Richardson, Markayla.

Cosmo, A. J. & Hinojosa, Felix. Nuts 3: Happy Birthday, Chestnut! Pearson, Angela, ed. 2018. (Nuts Ser.: Vol. 3). (ENG.). 46p. (J). pap. 11.99 (978-1-7240-8115-5(2)) Independently Published.

Cosneau, Géraldine. Hello, New York! Franceschelli, Christopher. 2018. (ENG.). 46p. (J). (gr. -1 — 1). bds. 12.99 (978-1-4197-2829-7(6), Abrams Appleseed) Abrams, Inc.

—Hello, Paris! Franceschelli, Christopher. 2018. (ENG.). 46p. (J). (gr. -1 — 1). bds. 12.99 (978-1-4197-2830-3(X), Abrams Appleseed) Abrams, Inc.

Cosneau, Olivia. Six Little Birds. Little Gestalten, Little, ed. 2019. (ENG.). 16p. 19.95 (978-3-89955-828-9(6)) Die Gestalten Verlag DEU. Dist: Ingram Publisher Services.

Cosner, Jeff. Smoke Hole Adventure. Lough, Whitney. 2013. 36p. (J). 12.00 (978-0-87012-833-2(7)) McClain Printing Co.

Cossette, Julie. Maine Monsters: A Search & Find Book. 2018. (ENG.). 22p. (J). (gr. -1). bds. 9.99 (978-2-924734-14-8(2)) City Monsters Bks. CAN. Dist: Publishers Group West (PGW).

—Play & Learn Activity Cards: Activity Card Set. Byrd, Redd. Cottage Door Press, ed. 2018. (Activity Card Set Ser.). (ENG.). 16p. (J). (gr. -1-k). bds. 12.99 (978-1-68052-323-2(6), 1002990) Cottage Door Pr.

—Where Do I Live? Animals & Their Homes. Downy, Rufus. Cottage Door Press, ed. 2019. (Colorforms Activity Bks.). (ENG.). 12p. (J). (gr. -1-2). bds. 12.99 (978-1-68052-742-1(8), 1004630) Cottage Door Pr.

Cossey, Jean Ann. The Best Treasure. Jones, Cathy Anderson. 2016. (ENG.). (J). 19.95 (978-1-4787-8465-4(2)); pap. 14.95 (978-1-4787-8456-2(3)) Outskirts Pr., Inc.

Cost, Steve. An Omelet Fit for a King. Stewart, Maria. 2013. 24p. pap. 14.99 (978-1-936453-23-8(1)) Bezalel Bks.

Costa, Alessandro, jt. illus. see Facciotto, Giuseppe.

Costa, Jana. Sleeping Beauty. 2007. (Usborne Young Reading: Series One Ser.). 48p. (J). 8.99 (978-0-7945-1458-7(8), Usborne) EDC Publishing.

—Stories of Magic Ponies. Davidson, Susanna. 2007. (Young Reading Series 1 Gift Bks). 48p. (J). 8.99 (978-0-7945-1790-8(0), Usborne) EDC Publishing.

Costa, Maria. El Patito Bello. Canetti, Yanitzia & Yanitzia, Canetti. 2009. (SPA.). 32p. (J). (gr. 1-4). 12.99 (978-84-241-7071-4(7)) Everest Editora ESP. Dist: Lectorum Pubns., Inc.

Costa, Marta. Busy Colors: Spin the Wheel for a Learning Adventure! Clever Publishing. 2019. (Clever Wheels Ser.). (ENG.). 8p. (J). (gr. -1 — 1). bds. 8.99 (978-1-948418-73-7(8), 332284) Clever Media Group.

—Busy Numbers: Spin the Wheel to Learn Numbers! Clever Publishing. 2020. (Clever Wheels Ser.). (ENG.). 8p. (J). (gr. -1 — 1). bds. 8.99 (978-1-948418-72-0(X), 331767) Clever Media Group.

—Busy Shapes: Spin the Wheel to Learn Shapes! Clever Publishing. 2020. (Clever Wheels Ser.). (ENG.). 8p. (J). (gr. -1 — 1). bds. 8.99 (978-1-948418-74-4(6)) Clever Media Group.

—David & the Lost Lamb. Bauers, W. C. 2018. (Tiny Bible Tales Ser.). 14p. (J). (-k). bds. 7.99 (978-1-5247-8590-1(3), Grosset & Dunlap) Penguin Young Readers Group.

—Jonah & the Whale. Bauers, W. C. 2018. (Tiny Bible Tales Ser.). 14p. (J). (-k). bds. 7.99 (978-1-5247-8592-5(X), Grosset & Dunlap) Penguin Young Readers Group.

—Noah's Ark. Reed, Avery & Bader, Bonnie. 2016. (Penguin Young Readers, Level 2 Ser.). 32p. (J). (gr. 1-2). 3.99 (978-0-448-48967-4(8), Penguin Young Readers) Penguin Young Readers Group.

—Preposterous Rhinoceros. Gunaratnam, Tracy. 2019. (Early Bird Readers — Purple (Early Bird Stories (tm)) Ser.). (ENG.). 32p. (J). (gr. k-3). 27.99 (978-1-5415-4226-6(6), 9781541542266); pap. 7.99 (978-1-5415-7425-0(7), 9781541574250) Lerner Publishing Group. (Lerner Pubns.).

Costa, Rosaria. The Bat Cave. Walker, Jonathan. Zahn, Lisa, ed. 2019. (ENG.). 38p. (J). (gr. 2-4). (978-1-9997606-4-9(6)); pap. (978-1-9997606-5-6(4)) Chirpy Stories.

—Bill & the Little Red Plane. Walker, Jonathan. Zahn, Lisa, ed. 2017. (ENG.). (J). (gr. 1-2). (978-1-9997606-0-1(3)); pap. (978-1-9997606-1-8(1)) Chirpy Stories.

Costa, Violaine. Francis of Assisi: Wolf Tamer of the Middle Ages. Pasteau, Delphine. 2019. (ENG.). 32p. (J). (gr. -1). pap. 9.99 (978-1-64060-207-6(0), 02076) Paraclete Pr., Inc.

Costa, Violaine. Friends Again. Amiot, Karine-Marie. 2020. (ENG.). 34p. (J). (gr. k-2). 13.99 (978-1-62164-338-8(7)) Ignatius Pr.

Costamagna, Beatrice. ABC & 123 Learning Songs: Deluxe Sound Book Wood Module. Wing, Scarlett. Cottage Door Press, ed. 2017. (Early Bird Song Ser.). (ENG.). 10p. (J). (gr. -1-2). bds. 18.99 (978-1-68052-147-4(0), 1001510) Cottage Door Pr.

—Crocodile Snap! 2016. (Crunchy Board Bks.). (ENG.). 12p. (J). (gr. -1-1). bds. 6.99 (978-1-4998-0201-6(3)) Little Bee Books Inc.

—Lift-The-Flap Baby Animals. Prasadam-Halls, Smriti. 2019. (Start Little, Learn Big Ser.). (ENG.). 12p. (J). (gr. -1-k). bds. 8.99 (978-1-68052-594-6(8), 2002360, Parragon Books) Cottage Door Pr.

—Under the Sea Dot-To-Dots. Tafuni, Gabriele. 2019. (Children's Dot-To-Dot Titles Ser.). (ENG.). 96p. (J). pap. 9.99 (978-1-78888-306-1(3), b83400ea-af7e-4e6f-961a-515184608351) Arcturus Publishing GBR. Dist: Baker & Taylor Publisher Services (BTPS).

—Vampire Bite! Little Bee Books. 2018. (Crunchy Board Bks.). (ENG.). 12p. (J). (gr. -1-1). bds. 6.99 (978-1-4998-0701-1(5)) Little Bee Books Inc.

—Wolf Crunch! 2016. (Crunchy Board Bks.). (ENG.). 12p. (J). (gr. -1-1). bds. 6.99 (978-1-4998-0200-9(5)) Little Bee Books Inc.

Costanza, Salvatore, et al. Champions: Blame It on the Train. Marz, Ron & Rodriguez, David A. 2018. (Skylanders Ser.). (ENG.). 24p. (J). (gr. 1-5). lib. bdg. 27.07 *(978-1-5321-4243-7(9)*, 28571, Graphic Novels) Spotlight.

Costanza, Stephen. The Christmas Spider's Miracle. Noble, Trinka Hakes. 2011. (ENG.). 32p. (YA). (gr. k-3). 16.95 *(978-1-58536-602-6(1))* Sleeping Bear Pr.

—Smudge & the Book of Mistakes: A Christmas Story. 2012. (ENG.). 48p. (J). (gr. 1-5). 17.95 *(978-1-58536-483-1(5))* Sleeping Bear Pr.

Costello, Brooke. BE KIND, Silly: A Child's Quest for a Kinder World. Allison, Lily & Allison, Makayla. 2019. (ENG.). 42p. (J). pap. 12.11 ***(978-1-0976-0811-9(5))*** Independently Published.

Costello, David & Costello, David Hyde. A Crow of His Own. Lambert, Megan Dowd. 32p. (J). (gr. -1-1). 2019. pap. 7.99 *(978-1-58089-448-7(8))*; 2015. lib. bdg. 16.95 *(978-1-58089-447-0(X))* Charlesbridge Publishing, Inc.

Costello, David Hyde. I Can Help: A Picture Book. Costello, David Hyde. 2010. (ENG.). 32p. (J). (gr. -1-1). 15.99 *(978-0-374-33526-7(5)*, 900029630, Farrar, Straus & Giroux (BYR)) Farrar, Straus & Giroux.

—Little Pig Joins the Band. Costello, David Hyde. 2014. 32p. (J). (gr. -1-3). pap. 7.95 *(978-1-58089-265-0(5))* Charlesbridge Publishing, Inc.

—Little Pig Joins the Band. Costello, David Hyde. 2012. 29.95 incl. audio compact disk *(978-1-4301-1139-9(9))* Live Oak Media.

—Little Pig Saves the Ship. Costello, David Hyde. 2017. 32p. (J). (gr. -1-2). 14.99 *(978-1-58089-715-0(0))* Charlesbridge Publishing, Inc.

—Little Pig Saves the Ship (1 Hardcover/1 CD) Costello, David Hyde. 2018. (ENG.). (J). (gr. -1-2). 29.95 *(978-1-4301-3112-0(8))* Live Oak Media.

Costello, David Hyde, jt. illus. see Costello, David.

Costello, Dolores. The Sad Sad Monster. Costello, Dolores. 2017. (ENG.). 32p. (J). (gr. -1-2). pap. 9.99 *(978-1-5324-0192-3(2))* Xist Publishing.

—The Sad, Sad Monster / el Triste Triste Monstruo. Costello, Dolores. 2018. (Xist Kids Bilingual Spanish English Ser.). (ENG & SPA.). 32p. (J). (gr. -1-3). pap. 9.99 *(978-1-5324-0685-0(1))* Xist Publishing.

—El Triste Triste Monstruo. Costello, Dolores. 2018. (Xist Kids Spanish Bks.). (SPA.). 32p. (J). (gr. -1-3). pap. 9.99 *(978-1-5324-0707-9(6))* Xist Publishing.

Costello, Jim. Nana's Quilt: Stitched in St. John'S, Newfoundland & Labrador, 1 vol. Lane, Lori & Winsor, Kathy. 2007. (ENG.). 32p. (J). (gr. -1-4). per. *(978-1-894294-82-9(3))* Breakwater Bks., Ltd.

Costello, Jim, photos by. Poppy & Allie: Hooked on St. John's, Newfoundland, 1 vol. Lane, Lori & Winsor, Kathy. 2009. (ENG., 32p. (J). (gr. 1-8). pap. *(978-1-897174-22-7(5))* Breakwater Bks., Ltd.

Costello, Shawn. Estas Manos: Manitas de Mi Familia. Caraballo, Samuel. 2014.Tr. of These Hands: My Family's Hands. (ENG & SPA.). (J). 17.95 *(978-1-55885-795-7(8)*, Piñata Books) Arte Publico Pr.

—Luke's Mule. Schmauss, Judy Kentor. 2006. (Reader's Clubhouse Level 2 Reader Ser.). (ENG.). 24p. (J). (gr. k-1). pap. 3.99 *(978-0-7641-3297-1(0)*, B.E.S. Publishing) Peterson's.

—Private Joel & the Sewell Mountain Seder. Fireside, Bryna J. 2008. (Passover Ser.). 47p. (J). (gr. 3-6). lib. bdg. 16.95 *(978-0-8225-7240-4(0)*, Kar-Ben Publishing) Lerner Publishing Group.

Costelloe, Lynn. Daisy, the Dutiful Donkey's Daughter. Bird, Rosita. 2020. (Animal Alphabet Ser.: Vol. 4). (ENG.). 30p. (J). pap. 10.99 ***(978-1-68160-714-6(X))*** Crimson Cloak Publishing.

Costelloe, Lynn. Emma Tate Learns to Skate. Bird, Rosita. 2017. (Emma Tate Ser.: Vol. 3). (ENG.). 30p. (J). (gr. 1-5). pap. 9.99 *(978-1-68160-514-2(7))* Crimson Cloak Publishing.

—Night Noises. Beere, Lisa. 2016. (ENG.). (J). pap. 9.59 *(978-1-68160-200-4(8))* Crimson Cloak Publishing.

Costmagna, Beatrice. Polar Bear Romp! 2016. (Crunchy Board Bks.). (ENG.). 12p. (J). (gr. -1-1). bds. 6.99 *(978-1-4998-0345-7(1))* Little Bee Books Inc.

Costner, Howard. Sixth Grade Was a Nightmare, & Seventh Is Worse: A 12-Year Old Speaks Out. Cheng, Haw. Thurman, Joann M., ed. Date not set. 128p. (J). (gr. 3-9). 11.95 *(978-0-89896-335-9(4))* Larksdale.

—The Tenth Rifle. Marvin, Isabel R. Date not set. 128p. (Orig.). (J). (gr. 3-8). pap. 9.95 *(978-0-89896-109-6(2))* Larksdale.

Cota, Cecilia. Punto y Rayo: Los Puntos Cardinales y Los Mapas. Doddoli, Consuelo. rev. ed. 2006. (Otra Escalera Ser.). (SPA & ENG.). 24p. (J). (gr. 2-4). pap. 9.95 *(978-968-5920-68-1(0))* Castillo, Ediciones, S. A. de C. V. MEX. Dist: Macmillan.

Côté, Geneviève. Ella May & the Wishing Stone. Fagan, Cary. (ENG.). 32p. (J). (gr. -1-1). 2014. pap. 8.99 *(978-1-77049-410-7(3))*; 2011. 17.95 *(978-1-77049-225-7(9))* Tundra Bks. CAN. (Tundra Bks.). Dist: Penguin Random Hse. LLC.

Cote, Genevieve. Flare. George, Kallie. 2014. (ENG.). 34p. (J). (gr. -1-3). 12.95 *(978-1-927018-50-7(1))* Simply Read Bks. CAN. Dist: Ingram Publisher Services.

—Hey Little Baby! Leigh, Heather. 2012. (ENG.). 32p. (J). (gr. -1-1). 14.99 *(978-1-4169-8979-0(X)*, Beach Lane Bks.) Beach Lane Bks.

—The Magic Beads. Nielsen-Fernlund, Susin. 2007. (ENG.). 32p. (J). (gr. -1-3). 16.95 *(978-1-894965-47-7(7))* Simply Read Bks. CAN. Dist: Ingram Publisher Services.

—Minn & Jake. Wong, Janet S. & Wong, Janet G. 2008. (ENG.). 160p. (J). (gr. 4-6). pap. 21.19 *(978-0-374-40021-7(0)*, 9780374400217, Farrar, Straus & Giroux) Farrar, Straus & Giroux.

Côté, Geneviève. Minn & Jake's Almost Terrible Summer. Wong, Janet S. 2008. (ENG.). 112p. (J). (gr. 2-5). 16.99 *(978-0-374-34977-6(0)*, 9780374349776, Farrar, Straus & Giroux (BYR)) Farrar, Straus & Giroux.

—Missuk's Snow Geese. Renaud, Anne. 2008. 36p. (J). (gr. -1-3). 16.95 *(978-1-894965-82-8(5))* Simply Read Bks. CAN. Dist: Ingram Publisher Services.

—Noni Is Nervous. Hartt-Sussman, Heather. 2013. (ENG.). 24p. (J). (gr. -1-2). 17.95 *(978-1-77049-323-0(9)*, Tundra Bks.) Tundra Bks. CAN. Dist: Penguin Random Hse. LLC.

—Noni Says No. Hartt-Sussman, Heather. 2011. (ENG.). 24p. (J). (gr. -1-2). 17.95 *(978-1-77049-233-2(X)*, Tundra Bks.) Tundra Bks. CAN. Dist: Penguin Random Hse. LLC.

—Shooting Star Rider. Jin, Nayoung. 2017. 36p. (J). (gr. -1-3). 16.95 *(978-1-77229-020-2(3))* Simply Read Bks. CAN. Dist: Ingram Publisher Services.

—Spark. George, Kallie. 2013. 34p. (J). (gr. -1-3). 12.95 *(978-1-927018-24-8(2))* Simply Read Bks. CAN. Dist: Ingram Publisher Services.

Cote, Genevieve. Splash. George, Kallie. 2016. (Tiny Tails Ser.: 3). 44p. (J). (gr. -1-3). 12.95 *(978-1-927018-77-4(3))* Simply Read Bks. CAN. Dist: Ingram Publisher Services.

Côté, Geneviève. W Is for Wapiti! An Alphabet Songbook. Duchesne, Christiane. 2012. (ENG.). 48p. (J). (gr. -1-k). 16.95 *(978-2-923163-83-3(4))* La Montagne Secrete CAN. Dist: Independent Pubs. Group.

Côté, Geneviève. Me & You. Côté, Geneviève. 2009. (Piggy & Bunny Ser.). (ENG.). 32p. (J). (gr. -1-k). 16.95 *(978-1-55453-446-3(1))* Kids Can Pr., Ltd. CAN. Dist: Hachette Bk. Group.

Côté, Geneviève & Côté, Geneviève. The Lady of Shalott. Tennyson, Alfred Lord. 2009. (Visions in Poetry Ser.). (ENG.). 48p. (J). (gr. 5-9). 9.95 *(978-1-55453-457-9(7))* Kids Can Pr., Ltd. CAN. Dist: Hachette Bk. Group.

—Little Word Catcher, 1 vol. Simard, Danielle. 2008. (ENG.). 32p. (J). (gr. 1-3). 14.95 *(978-1-897187-44-9(0))* Second Story Pr. CAN. Dist: Orca Bk. Pubs. USA.

—Mr. King's Castle. Côté, Geneviève & Côté, Geneviève. 2013. (Mr. King Ser.). (ENG.). 32p. (J). (gr. -1-2). 16.95 *(978-1-55453-972-7(2))* Kids Can Pr., Ltd. CAN. Dist: Hachette Bk. Group.

—Mr. King's Things. Côté, Geneviève & Côté, Geneviève. 2012. (Mr. King Ser.). (ENG.). 32p. (J). (gr. -1-2). 16.95 *(978-1-55453-700-6(2))* Kids Can Pr., Ltd. CAN. Dist: Hachette Bk. Group.

—Starring Me & You, 0 vols. Côté, Geneviève & Côté, Geneviève. 2014. (Piggy & Bunny Ser.). (ENG.). 32p. (J). (gr. -1-k). 16.95 *(978-1-894786-39-3(4))* Kids Can Pr., Ltd. CAN. Dist: Hachette Bk. Group.

Côté, Geneviève, jt. illus. see Côté, Geneviève.

Côté, Geneviève. Mr. King's Machine. Côté, Geneviève. 2016. (Mr. King Ser.). (ENG.). 32p. (J). (gr. -1-2). 16.95 *(978-1-77138-021-8(7))* Kids Can Pr., Ltd. CAN. Dist: Hachette Bk. Group.

Côté, Genvièvе. Violette, la Reine Muette. Pelletier, Marthe. 2004. (Mon Roman Ser.). (FRE.). 96p. (J). (gr. 2). pap. *(978-2-89021-708-9(6))* Diffusion du livre Mirabel (DLM).

Cote, Nancy. Big Mama's Baby. Borgo, Lacy Finn. 2007. (ENG.). 32p. (J). (gr. k-2). 15.95 *(978-1-59078-187-6(2))* Boyds Mills Pr.

—Dixie Wants an Allergy. Corn, Tori. 2014. 32p. (J). (gr. -1-k). 16.95 *(978-1-62087-991-7(3)*, Sky Pony Pr.) Skyhorse Publishing Co., Inc.

—The Leprechaun Who Lost His Rainbow, 1 vol. Callahan, Sean. 2010. (ENG.). 32p. (J). (gr. 1-3). pap. 6.99 *(978-0-8075-4455-6(8)*, 807544558) Whitman, Albert & Co.

—Makayla Cares about Others. Kroll, Virginia. 2007. (Way I Act Bks.). (ENG.). 24p. (J). (gr. k-3). lib. bdg. 15.99 *(978-0-8075-4945-2(2)*, 807549452) Whitman, Albert & Co.

—Puddle Jumpers. Lewis, Anne Margaret. 2016. 32p. (J). (gr. -1-k). 16.99 *(978-1-63450-185-9(3)*, Sky Pony Pr.) Skyhorse Publishing Co., Inc.

—Round the Turkey: A Grateful Thanksgiving. Kimmelman, Leslie. 2012. (J). 34.28 *(978-1-61913-130-9(7))* Weigl Pubs., Inc.

—Watch the Birdie! 2016. (ENG.). 32p. (J). (gr. -1-k). 16.99 *(978-1-63450-202-3(7)*, Sky Pony Pr.) Skyhorse Publishing Co., Inc.

—Watch the Cookie! 2014. (ENG.). 32p. (J). (gr. -1-k). 16.95 *(978-1-62914-630-0(7)*, Sky Pony Pr.) Skyhorse Publishing Co., Inc.

—When I Feel Angry. Spelman, Cornelia. 2012. (J). reprint ed. lib. bdg. 32.71 *(978-1-61913-139-2(0))* Weigl Pubs., Inc.

Cotes Stanley, Marsha. Gypsy the Goat. Miller, Vern. 2013. 36p. pap. 11.95 *(978-1-61153-082-7(2))* Light Messages Publishing.

Cotroneo, Marilisa. Attack of the Cute. Jaycox, Jaclyn. 2019. (Boo Bks.). (ENG.). 32p. (J). (gr. k-2). lib. bdg. 21.32 *(978-1-5158-4483-9(8)*, 140579, Picture Window Bks.) Capstone.

—Blood & Cookies. Varlow, Scarlet. 2019. (Creature Feature Ser.). (ENG.). 112p. (J). (gr. 2-5). lib. bdg. 29.93 *(978-1-5321-3496-8(7)*, 31911, Calico Chapter Bks.) ABDO Publishing Co.

—Creature Feature (Set), 4 vols. Varlow, Scarlet. 2019. (Creature Feature Ser.). 112p. (J). (gr. 2-5). lib. bdg. 114.00 *(978-1-5321-3495-1(9)*, 31909, Calico Chapter Bks.) ABDO Publishing Co.

—The Creature in the Fireplace. Varlow, Scarlet. 2019. (Creature Feature Ser.). (ENG.). 112p. (J). (gr. 2-5). lib. bdg. 29.93 *(978-1-5321-3497-5(5)*, 31913, Calico Chapter Bks.) ABDO Publishing Co.

—Sticks & Stones. Varlow, Scarlet. 2019. (Creature Feature Ser.). (ENG.). 112p. (J). (gr. 2-5). lib. bdg. 29.93 *(978-1-5321-3498-2(3)*, 31915, Calico Chapter Bks.) ABDO Publishing Co.

—Zombie Mode. Varlow, Scarlet. 2019. (Creature Feature Ser.). (ENG.). 48p. (J). (gr. 2-5). lib. bdg. 29.93 *(978-1-5321-3499-9(1)*, 31917, Calico Chapter Bks.) ABDO Publishing Co.

Cotroneo, Marilisa & Fabicka, Patrycja. Boo Books. Bird, Benjamin et al. 2019. (Boo Bks.). (ENG.). (J). (gr. k-2). 127.92 *(978-1-5158-4494-5(3)*, 29334, Picture Window Bks.) Capstone.

—Scare Ball. Bird, Benjamin. 2019. (Boo Bks.). (ENG.). 32p. (J). (gr. k-2). lib. bdg. 21.32 *(978-1-5158-4487-7(0)*, 140583, Picture Window Bks.) Capstone.

Cotta-Flood, Stephanie. Harold Angel. Dahl, Steven. 2012. 40p. (J). *(978-0-9883420-0-2(6))* Thotsup LLC.

Cotteleer, Kaly. Timo & the Soft White Light. Meijer, Margreet. Meyer, Liesbeth, tr. 2019. (ENG.). 32p. (J). *(978-94-92593-29-0(7))* Graviant Educatieve Uitgaven.

Cotteleer, Kaly. Timo et la Douce Lumi�re Blanche. Meijer, Margreet. Taggak Amatsiaq, Daniel, tr. 2019. (FRE.). 32p. (J). ***(978-94-92593-37-5(8))*** Graviant Educatieve Uitgaven.

Cottell, James. Cangrejo y Ballena: Mindfulness para niños: la Introducción Más Fácil, Sencilla y Bella a la Atención Plena para Niños. Kerr, Christiane. Orrego, Marcela, tr. 2019. (SPA.). 32p. (J). pap. ***(978-1-9999378-1-2(3))*** Mindful Storytime.

Cottell, James. Crabe et Baleine: La Pleine Conscience Pour les Petits - une Introduction Douce et Efficace. Kerr, Christiane & Pallis, Mark. 2019. (ENG.). 32p. (J). pap. *(978-1-9999378-3-6(X))* Mindful Storytime.

—Krabbe und Wal: Achtsamkeit Für Kinder, Entspannung Kindergerechtes Buch Zum Vorlesen Mit Lustiger Geschichte und Achtsamkeitsübungen Kinder, Atmen und Konzentration. Yoga-Freunde Werden Es Lieben. Kerr, Christiane & Pallis, Mark. 2019. (GER.). 32p. (J). pap. *(978-1-9999378-2-9(1))* Mindful Storytime.

Cotterill, Charlotte. Hack & Whack. Simon, Francesca. 2017. (ENG.). 32p. (J). (gr. -1-k). 16.95 *(978-0-571-32871-0(7)*, Faber & Faber Children's Bks.) Faber & Faber, Inc.

Cotterill, Samantha. Charlotte & the Rock. Martin, Stephen W. 2017. (ENG.). 32p. (J). (-k). 17.99 *(978-1-101-99389-7(8)*, Dial Bks) Penguin Young Readers Group.

—The Forever Garden. Snyder, Laurel. 2017. 40p. (J). (gr. -1-3). 17.99 *(978-0-553-51273-1(0))*; (ENG.). lib. bdg. 20.99 *(978-0-553-51274-8(9))* Random Hse. Children's Bks. (Schwartz & Wade Bks.).

—Jinx & the Doom Fight Crime! Mantchev, Lisa. 2018. (ENG.). 32p. (J). (gr. -1-3). 16.99 *(978-1-4814-6701-8(8)*, Simon & Schuster/Paula Wiseman Bks.) Simon & Schuster/Paula Wiseman Bks.

—Just Add Glitter. DiTerlizzi, Angela. 2018. (ENG.). 32p. (J). (gr. -1-3). 18.99 *(978-1-4814-0967-4(0)*, Beach Lane Bks.) Beach Lane Bks.

—Once upon a Slime. Maxwell, Andy. 2018. 40p. (J). (gr. -1-3). 17.99 *(978-0-316-39326-3(6))* Little Brown & Co.

Cotterill, Samantha. Can I Play Too? Cotterill, Samantha. 2020. (Little Senses Ser.). 32p. (J). (gr. -1-2). 16.99 *(978-0-525-55346-5(0)*, Dial Bks) Penguin Young Readers Group.

—No More Bows. Cotterill, Samantha. 2017. (ENG.). 40p. (J). (gr. -1-3). 17.99 *(978-0-06-240870-9(4))* HarperCollins Pubs.

—Nope. Never. Not for Me! Cotterill, Samantha. 2019. (Little Senses Ser.). (ENG.). 32p. (J). (gr. -1-2). 16.99 *(978-0-525-55344-1(4)*, Dial Bks) Penguin Young Readers Group.

—This Beach Is Loud! Cotterill, Samantha. 2019. (Little Senses Ser.). 32p. (J). (gr. -1-2). 16.99 *(978-0-525-55345-8(2)*, Dial Bks) Penguin Young Readers Group.

Cottin, Menena. It's Our Nature. Orozco, Rebeca. 2012. (ENG.). 24p. (J). (gr. k-3). 12.95 *(978-1-77049-283-7(6)*, Tundra Bks.) Tundra Bks. CAN. Dist: Penguin Random Hse. LLC.

Cottingham, Tracy. Choose Your Own Journey. Brooks, Susie. 2017. (J). 11.99 *(978-1-61067-537-6(1))* Kane Miller.

—Yellow. Doering, Amanda. 2018. (Sing Your Colors! Ser.). (ENG.). 24p. (J). (gr. -1-2). 33.99 *(978-1-68410-312-6(6)*, 140705); lib. bdg. 33.99 incl. audio compact disk *(978-1-68410-131-3(X)*, 31853) Cantata Learning.

Cotton, Catherine. The Tadpole Family. Peters, Michelle Lee. 2018. (ENG.). 22p. (J). pap. 9.99 *(978-0-692-14933-1(3))* Peters, Michelle Lee.

Cotton, Sarah. Jackson Sundown: Native American Bronco Buster, 1 vol. Fisher, Doris. 2018. (ENG.). 32p. (gr. -1-3). 16.99 *(978-1-4556-2361-7(X)*, Pelican Publishing) Arcadia Publishing.

Cotton, Sue. Iza & Her Magic Seashell. Adrian, Mikel. 2018. (ENG.). 28p. (J). (gr. k-2). pap. 15.95 *(978-1-61493-631-2(5))* Peppertree Pr., The.

—Iza & the Magic Suitcase. Adrian, Mikel. 2018. (ENG.). 24p. (J). (gr. k-3). pap. 14.95 *(978-1-61493-632-9(3))* Peppertree Pr., The.

Cotton, Sue Lynn. The Adventures of Granville, Coming to America. MacKenzie-Krysko, Claudia & Krysko, Kenneth L. 2013. 24p. pap. 12.95 *(978-1-61493-227-7(1))* Peppertree Pr., The.

—The Adventures of the Nutters, the Tree Highway. Ringley, Patrick & Brown, Anne Corbett. 2013. 48p. pap. 19.95 *(978-1-61493-207-9(7))* Peppertree Pr., The.

—Dinky Duck's Adventure. Hattaway, Carol. 2012. 16p. pap. 12.95 *(978-1-61493-128-7(3))* Peppertree Pr., The.

—Elric's Florida Holiday. Colhoun, Sheelah. 2012. 20p. pap. 13.95 *(978-1-61493-110-2(0))* Peppertree Pr., The.

—It's Fun to Feed the Little Lambs. Colhoun, Sheelah. 2013. 32p. pap. 14.95 *(978-1-61493-185-0(2))* Peppertree Pr., The.

—Iza & Her Magic Seashell. Adrian, Mikel. 2012. 28p. 24.95 *(978-1-61493-077-8(5))* Peppertree Pr., The.

—The Mouse Who Came to Lunch. Snyder, Susan E. 2018. (ENG.). 20p. (J). (gr. k-4). 21.95 *(978-1-61493-617-6(X))* Peppertree Pr., The.

—Rounding Rescue, a Rounding Numbers Story. Lostorto, Eric. 2013. 16p. pap. 11.95 *(978-1-61493-217-8(4))* Peppertree Pr., The.

—Spaced Out Gerbil. Lang, Kathy. 2013. 20p. pap. 12.95 *(978-1-61493-190-4(9))* Peppertree Pr., The.

—The Tooth Be Told. Howell, Julie Ann. 2011. 24p. 18.95 *(978-1-61493-061-7(9))* Peppertree Pr., The.

—Waiting for Wings, Angel's Journey from Shelter Dog to Therapy Dog. Musick, Stacy. 2012. 32p. 21.95 *(978-1-61493-055-6(4))*; pap. 12.95 *(978-1-61493-054-9(6))* Peppertree Pr., The.

Cotton, Valerie. The Adventures of Cowboy Jake. White, Alice. 2018. (ENG.). 20p. (J). (gr. k-4). 22.95 *(978-1-61493-625-1(0))*; pap. 14.95 *(978-1-61493-622-0(6))* Peppertree Pr., The.

Cottone-Kolthoff, Carol. Chocolate, a Glacier Grizzly. Christian, Peggy. (Humane Society of the United States Animal Tales Ser.). 32p. (J). (gr. 1-5). 34.95 incl. audio *(978-1-882728-64-0(5))*; pap. 9.95 incl. audio *(978-1-882728-67-1(X))*; pap. 19.95 incl. audio *(978-1-882728-69-5(6))* Benefactory, Inc., The.

Cottrell, Amanda Marie. It Is Okay to Feel. Cottrell, Amanda Marie. 2017. (ENG.). 50p. (J). pap. *(978-1-7751434-0-6(6))* Art Mindfulness & Creativity.

Cottrill, Peter. Mrs. McGee's Coconut. Zobel-Nolan, Allia. 2009. 32p. (J). (gr. -1-2). 15.95 *(978-1-58925-079-6(6))*; pap. 6.95 *(978-1-58925-414-5(7))* Tiger Tales.

Couch, Crista. Cooper's Big Bear Hug. Woo, Melissa. 2012. 32p. (J). 9.95 *(978-1-59530-352-3(9))* Hallmark Card, Inc.

Couch, Greg. Aladdin & the Magic Lamp, 1 vol. Kunstler, James Howard. 2005. (Rabbit Ears-A Classic Tale Ser.). (ENG.). 36p. (J). (gr. 2-6). 28.50 *(978-1-59679-221-0(3)*, 12930, Picture Bk.) Spotlight.

—The Boy Who Invented TV. Krull, Kathleen. 2014. (ENG.). (J). (gr. 1-4). lib. bdg. 18.60 *(978-1-62765-575-0(1))* Perfection Learning Corp.

—The Boy Who Invented TV: The Story of Philo Farnsworth. Krull, Kathleen. 40p. (J). (gr. 1-4). 2014. 7.99 *(978-0-385-75557-3(0)*, Dragonfly Bks.); 2009. 16.99 *(978-0-375-84561-1(5)*, Knopf Bks. for Young Readers) Random Hse. Children's Bks.

—Nothing but Trouble: The Story of Althea Gibson. Stauffacher, Sue. 2011. 40p. (J). (gr. -1-2). pap. 7.99 *(978-0-375-86544-2(6)*, Dragonfly Bks.) Random Hse. Children's Bks.

—Pretty Little Lilly & the Magical Light. Hornsby, Ashley. 2007. 32p. (J). 15.95 *(978-0-9777241-0-9(7))* Cepia LLC.

—Wild Child. Plourde, Lynn. 2003. (ENG.). 32p. (J). (gr. -1-3). 7.99 *(978-0-689-86349-3(7)*, Aladdin) Simon & Schuster Children's Publishing.

Coudray, Philippe. A Goofy Guide to Penguins, Level 1. Coudray, Jean-Luc. 2016. (ENG.). 40p. (J). (gr. k). 12.95 *(978-1-935179-96-2(9))* TOON Books / RAW Junior, LLC.

Coulson, David. Laugh It Up! 501 Super-Silly Jokes, Riddles, & Cartoons from Highlights. Highlights for Children Editorial Staff. 2013. (Laugh Attack! Ser.). (ENG.). 256p. (J). (gr. 3-6). 18.69 *(978-1-62091-071-9(3))* Boyds Mills Pr.

Coulter, Dare. My N. C. from A-Z. Lanier, Michelle. 2020. (ENG.). 32p. (J). 14.95 *(978-0-86526-499-1(6)*, 01OSPS) North Carolina Office of Archives & History.

Coulton, Mia, photos by. All about Danny. Coulton, Mia. 2003. (ENG., pap. 5.35 *(978-0-9720295-3-7(2))* Maryruth Bks., Inc.

—At Grandma Ruth's House. Coulton, Mia. 2008. (ENG., pap. 5.35 *(978-1-933624-32-7(9))* Maryruth Bks., Inc.

—Circus Fish. Coulton, Mia. 2008. (ENG., pap. 5.35 *(978-1-933624-29-7(9))* Maryruth Bks., Inc.

—Danny & Abby Play Tag. Coulton, Mia. 2004. (ENG., pap. 5.35 *(978-0-9746475-3-1(5))* Maryruth Bks., Inc.

—Danny & Bee's Book of Opposites. Coulton, Mia. 2006. (ENG., pap. 5.35 *(978-1-933624-02-0(7))* Maryruth Bks., Inc.

—Danny & Dad Go Shopping. Coulton, Mia. 2003. (ENG., pap. 5.35 *(978-0-9720295-4-4(0))* Maryruth Bks., Inc.

—Danny & Heather Share. Coulton, Mia. 2003. (ENG., 16p. pap. 5.35 *(978-0-9720295-8-2(3))* Maryruth Bks., Inc.

—Danny & the Little Worm. Coulton, Mia. 2004. (ENG., pap. 5.35 *(978-0-9746475-6-2(X))* Maryruth Bks., Inc.

—Danny Can Sort. Coulton, Mia. 2003. (ENG., pap. 5.35 *(978-0-9720295-6-8(7))* Maryruth Bks., Inc.

—Danny Likes Red. Coulton, Mia. 2003. (ENG., pap. 5.35 *(978-0-9720295-2-0(4))* Maryruth Bks., Inc.

—Danny Likes to Help. Coulton, Mia. 2005. (ENG., pap. 5.35 *(978-0-9746475-9-3(4))* Maryruth Bks., Inc.

—Danny Paints a Picture. Coulton, Mia. 2004. (ENG., pap. 5.35 *(978-0-9746475-5-5(1))* Maryruth Bks., Inc.

—Danny's Big Adventure. Coulton, Mia. 2004. (ENG., per. 9.95 *(978-0-9746475-0-0(0))* Maryruth Bks., Inc.

—Danny's Castle. Coulton, Mia. 2005. (ENG., 16p. pap. 5.35 *(978-1-933624-00-6(0))* Maryruth Bks., Inc.

—Danny's Favorite Shapes. Coulton, Mia. 2004. (ENG., pap. *(978-0-9746475-4-8(3))* Maryruth Bks., Inc.

—Danny's Party. Coulton, Mia. 2004. (ENG., (J). pap. 5.35 *(978-0-9746475-1-7(9))* Maryruth Bks., Inc.

—Danny's Rocket. Coulton, Mia. 2009. (ENG., pap. 5.35 *(978-1-933624-40-2(X))* Maryruth Bks., Inc.

—Danny's Special Tree. Coulton, Mia. 2008. (ENG., pap. 6.95 *(978-1-933624-25-9(6))* Maryruth Bks., Inc.

—Danny's Timeline. Coulton, Mia. 2004. (ENG., pap. 5.35 *(978-0-9746475-2-4(7))* Maryruth Bks., Inc.

—Danny's Window. Coulton, Mia. 2005. (ENG., pap. 5.35 *(978-0-9746475-8-6(6))* Maryruth Bks., Inc.

—Five Danny Dogs. Coulton, Mia. 2005. (ENG., pap. 5.35 *(978-1-933624-01-3(9))* Maryruth Bks., Inc.

—Get down Danny. Coulton, Mia. 2003. (ENG., pap. 5.35 *(978-0-9720295-1-9(9))* Maryruth Bks., Inc.

—I Am Danny. Coulton, Mia. 2003. (ENG., pap. 5.35 *(978-0-9720295-7-5(5))* Maryruth Bks., Inc.

—A New Home for Fish. Coulton, Mia. 2007. (ENG., pap. 5.35 *(978-1-933624-14-3(0))* Maryruth Bks., Inc.

—Pirate Fish. Coulton, Mia. 2007. (ENG., pap. 5.35 *(978-1-933624-15-0(9))* Maryruth Bks., Inc.

—Spy Danny. Coulton, Mia. 2006. (ENG., pap. 5.35 *(978-1-933624-03-7(5))* Maryruth Bks., Inc.

—Super Danny. Coulton, Mia. 2012. (ENG., 13p. bds. 6.99 *(978-1-933197-90-6(0))* Orange Frazer Pr.

Counseller, Jane. It's All About Sam or Is It? All about Grace. Housenick, Nicole. 2019. (ENG.). 38p. (J). pap. 15.95 ***(978-1-9822-3492-8(X)***, Balboa Pr.) Author Solutions, Inc.

Counts, Monika. Alabama Countdown to Touchdown. 2010. (Countdown to Touchdown Ser.). 20p. (J). 14.95 *(978-1-61524-080-7(2)*, Intervisual/Piggy Toes) Bendon, Inc.

C

—Florida Countdown to Touchdown. 2010. (Countdown to Touchdown Ser.). 20p. 14.95 *(978-1-61524-082-1(9),* Intervisual/Piggy Toes) Bendon, Inc.

—LSU Countdown to Touchdown. 2010. (Countdown to Touchdown Ser.). 20p. 14.95 *(978-1-61524-081-4(0),* Intervisual/Piggy Toes) Bendon, Inc.

Countz, Tracey Hudson. Amelia's Dash. Countz, Tracey Hudson. 2019. (ENG.). 66p. (J). pap. 15.99 ***(978-1-7232-9680-2(5))*** CreateSpace Independent Publishing Platform.

Courageous $oul. The Lonely Flower. !Myster?Ous M! & Courageous $Oul. 2011. 20p. pap. 24.95 *(978-1-4560-6950-6(0))* America Star Bks.

Couri, Kathryn A. Goodnight Bear: A Book & Night Light. Bentley, Dawn. 2005. (Stories to Share Ser.). 12p. (J). 12.95 *(978-1-58117-034-4(3),* Intervisual/Piggy Toes) Bendon, Inc.

Couri, Kathy. The Night Before Easter: Special Edition. Wing, Natasha. 2019. (Night Before Ser.). 32p. (J). (gr. -1-3). 8.99 *(978-1-5247-9285-5(3),* Grosset & Dunlap) Penguin Young Readers Group.

Couri, Kathy & Clearwater, Linda. Puppy Makes Friends. Simon, Mary Manz. 2006. (First Virtues for Toddlers Ser.). 20p. (J). 5.99 *(978-0-7847-1414-0(2),* 04066) Standard Publishing.

—Squirrel Says Thank You. Simon, Mary Manz. 2006. (First Virtues for Toddlers Ser.). 20p. (J). 5.99 *(978-0-7847-1415-7(0),* 04067) Standard Publishing.

Couri, Kathy, jt. illus. see Clearwater, Linda.

Court, Moira. Colour Me. Kwaymullina, Ezekiel. 2018. 40p. (J). (gr. -1-k). pap. 12.95 *(978-1-925164-66-4(7))* Fremantle Pr. AUS. Dist: Independent Pubs. Group.

Courtin, Thierry. Twin to Twin. O'Hair, Margaret. 2003. (ENG.). 32p. (J). (gr. -1-3). 17.99 *(978-0-689-84494-2(8),* McElderry, Margaret K. Bks.) McElderry, Margaret K. Bks.

Courtney-Clarke, Margaret. My Painted House, My Friendly Chicken, & Me. Angelou, Maya. 2003. (ENG.). 48p. (gr. -1-2). 7.99 *(978-0-375-82567-5(3))* Perfection Learning Corp.

Courtney, Richard. Animals Everywhere! (Thomas & Friends) Awdry, W. 2011. (Step into Reading Ser.). (ENG.). 32p. (J). (gr. -1-1). pap. 4.99 *(978-0-375-86812-2(7),* Random Hse. Bks. for Young Readers) Random Hse. Children's Bks.

—Christmas in Wellsworth. Awdry, W. 2010. (Thomas in Town Ser.). (ENG.). 32p. (J). (gr. -1-2). 5.99 *(978-0-375-86356-1(7),* Random Hse. Bks. for Young Readers) Random Hse. Children's Bks.

—Easter Engines. Awdry, Wilbert V. 2012. (Step into Reading Ser.). (ENG.). 32p. (J). (gr. -1-1). pap. 3.99 *(978-0-307-92996-9(5),* Random Hse. Bks. for Young Readers) Random Hse. Children's Bks.

—Five Tank Engine Tales (Thomas & Friends) Random House. 2015. (Step into Reading Ser.). (ENG.). 160p. (J). (gr. -1-1). pap. 8.99 *(978-0-385-38496-4(3),* Random Hse. Bks. for Young Readers) Random Hse. Children's Bks.

—Flynn Saves the Day (Thomas & Friends) Awdry, Wilbert V. 2011. (Step into Reading Ser.). (ENG.). 32p. (J). (gr. -1-1). pap. 3.99 *(978-0-375-86935-8(2),* Random Hse. Bks. for Young Readers) Random Hse. Children's Bks.

—The Good Sport. Awdry, W. 2016. 24p. (J). *(978-1-5182-1481-3(9))* Random Hse., Inc.

—Halloween in Anopha. Awdry, Wilbert V. 2008. (Thomas in Town Ser.). (ENG.). 32p. (J). (gr. -1-2). 5.99 *(978-0-375-84413-3(9),* Random Hse. Bks. for Young Readers) Random Hse. Children's Bks.

—Let's Find Out: Dinosaurs. Behrens, Janice. Date not set. (ENG.). 24p. (J). 8.99 *(978-0-439-87321-5(5))* Scholastic, Inc.

—The Lost Ship. Awdry, W. 2015. (Step into Reading Ser.). (ENG.). 32p. (J). (gr. -1-1). lib. bdg. 12.99 *(978-0-553-52172-6(1),* Random Hse. Bks. for Young Readers) Random Hse. Children's Bks.

—The Lost Ship (Thomas & Friends) Awdry, W. 2015. (Step into Reading Ser.). (ENG.). 32p. (J). (gr. -1-1). 5.99 *(978-0-553-52171-9(3),* Random Hse. Bks. for Young Readers) Random Hse. Children's Bks.

—Not So Fast, Bash & Dash! Awdry, Wilbert V. 2013. (Step into Reading Ser.). (ENG.). 24p. (J). (gr. -1-1). 3.99 *(978-0-449-81539-7(0),* Random Hse. Bks. for Young Readers) Random Hse. Children's Bks.

—Railway Rhymes. Awdry, Wilbert V. & Hooke, R. Schuyler. 2005. (ENG.). 36p. (J). (gr. k — 1). bds. 11.99 *(978-0-375-83175-1(4),* Random Hse. Bks. for Young Readers) Random Hse. Children's Bks.

—Reds Against Blues! 2016. 22p. (J). *(978-1-4806-9772-0(9))* Random Hse., Inc.

—Reds Against Blues! (Thomas & Friends) Random House. 2016. (Step into Reading Ser.). (ENG.). 24p. (J). (gr. -1-1). 4.99 *(978-1-101-93284-1(8),* Random Hse. Bks. for Young Readers) Random Hse. Children's Bks.

—Stuck in the Mud. Corey, Shana & Awdry, Wilbert V. 2009. (Step into Reading Ser.). (ENG.). 32p. (J). (gr. -1-1). pap. 4.99 *(978-0-375-86177-2(7),* Random Hse. Bks. for Young Readers) Random Hse. Children's Bks.

—Thomas' 123 Book. Awdry, W. 2013. (Pictureback(R) Ser.). (ENG.). 24p. (J). (gr. -1-2). pap. 3.99 *(978-0-307-98203-2(3),* Random Hse. Bks. for Young Readers) Random Hse. Children's Bks.

—Thomas & Friends: down at the Docks (Thomas & Friends) Awdry, W. 2003. (Pictureback(R) Ser.). (ENG.). 24p. (J). (gr. -1-2). pap. 3.99 *(978-0-375-82592-7(4),* Random Hse. Bks. for Young Readers) Random Hse. Children's Bks.

—Thomas & Friends Summer 2016 Movie Step into Reading (Thomas & Friends) Webster, Christy & Awdry, W. 2016. (Step into Reading Ser.). (ENG.). 24p. (J). (gr. -1-1). 4.99 *(978-1-101-94031-0(X),* Random Hse. Bks. for Young Readers) Random Hse. Children's Bks.

—Thomas & Percy & the Dragon. Awdry, W. 2003. (Step into Reading Ser.). (ENG.). 32p. (J). (gr. -1-1). pap. 4.99 *(978-0-375-82230-8(5),* Random Hse. Bks. for Young Readers) Random Hse. Children's Bks.

—Thomas & the Runaway Pumpkins (Thomas & Friends) Random House & Kleinberg, Naomi. 2018. (Little Golden Book Ser.). (ENG.). 24p. (J). (gr. -1-2). 4.99 *(978-0-385-37391-3(0),* Golden Bks.) Random Hse. Children's Bks.

—Thomas & the Shark. Awdry, Wilbert V. 2013. (Step into Reading Ser.). (ENG.). 32p. (J). (gr. -1-1). pap. 3.99 *(978-0-307-98200-1(9),* Random Hse. Bks. for Young Readers) Random Hse. Children's Bks.

—Thomas' Color Book (Thomas & Friends) Random House. 2017. (Pictureback(R) Ser.). (ENG.). 24p. (J). (gr. -1-2). 4.99 *(978-1-101-93723-5(8),* Random Hse. Bks. for Young Readers) Random Hse. Children's Bks.

—Thomas Comes to Breakfast. Awdry, W. 2004. (Step into Reading Ser.). (ENG.). 32p. (J). (gr. -1-1). pap. 4.99 *(978-0-375-82892-8(3),* Random Hse. Bks. for Young Readers) Random Hse. Children's Bks.

—Thomas Gets a Snowplow. 2004. (Pictureback(R) Ser.). (ENG.). 24p. (J). (gr. -1-2). 3.99 *(978-0-375-82783-9(8),* Random Hse. Bks. for Young Readers) Random Hse. Children's Bks.

—Thomas Goes Fishing. Awdry, W. 2005. (Step into Reading Ser.). (ENG.). 32p. (J). (gr. -1-1). pap. 4.99 *(978-0-375-83118-8(5),* Random Hse. Bks. for Young Readers) Random Hse. Children's Bks.

—Thomas' Night Before Christmas. Hooke, R. Schuyler. 2013. (Little Golden Book Ser.). (ENG.). 24p. (J). (gr. -1-k). 4.99 *(978-0-449-81663-9(X),* Golden Bks.) Random Hse. Children's Bks.

—Thomas' Opposites Book (Thomas & Friends) Webster, Christy. 2017. (Pictureback(R) Ser.). (ENG.). 24p. (J). (gr. -1-2). pap. 4.99 *(978-1-5247-1604-2(9),* Random Hse. Bks. for Young Readers) Random Hse. Children's Bks.

—A Valentine for Percy. Awdry, W. 2015. 24p. (J). *(978-1-4806-9757-7(5))* Random Hse., Inc.

—A Valentine for Percy (Thomas & Friends) Random House. 2015. (Step into Reading Ser.). (ENG.). 24p. (J). (gr. -1-1). 4.99 *(978-1-101-93287-2(2),* Random Hse. Bks. for Young Readers) Random Hse. Children's Bks.

Courtney, Richard & Stubbs, Tommy. Story Time Collection. Awdry, W. 2014. (ENG.). 320p. (J). (gr. -1-2). 15.99 *(978-0-553-49678-9(6),* Random Hse. Bks. for Young Readers) Random Hse. Children's Bks.

Courtney, Richard H. The Close Shave. Awdry, Wilbert V. 2008. (Step into Reading Ser.). (ENG.). 32p. (J). (gr. -1-1). pap. 3.99 *(978-0-375-85180-3(1),* Random Hse. Bks. for Young Readers) Random Hse. Children's Bks.

Courtney-Tickle, Jessica. Animal Journeys. Hegarty, Patricia. 2017. (ENG.). 76p. (J). (gr. 2-12). 12.99 *(978-1-944530-04-4(5),* 360 Degrees) Tiger Tales.

—The Perfectly Perfect Wish. Mantchev, Lisa. 2020. (ENG.). 32p. (J). (gr. -1-3). 17.99 *(978-1-5344-0619-3(0),* Simon & Schuster/Paula Wiseman Bks.) Simon & Schuster/Paula Wiseman Bks.

—The Story Orchestra: Four Seasons in One Day: Press the Note to Hear Vivaldi's Music. 2016. (Story Orchestra Ser.). (ENG.). 24p. (J). (gr. 1-4). 25.99 *(978-1-84780-877-6(8),* 314669, Frances Lincoln Children's Bks.) Quarto Publishing Group UK GBR. Dist: Hachette Bk. Group.

Courtney-Tickle, Jessica. Little Christmas Tree. Courtney-Tickle, Jessica. 2018. (ENG.). 12p. (J). (-k). bds. 15.99 *(978-1-5362-0311-0(4),* Big Picture Press) Candlewick Pr.

Courtright, Molly M. My Beagle Ali Baba Who Had 40 Fleas: A Counting Book for Young Children. Pyle, Jacqueline. 2017. (ENG.). (J). (gr. k-1). pap. 10.99 *(978-1-942922-35-3(3))* Wee Creek Pr. LLC.

Cousin, Matthieu. Afraid of Everything. Tierney, Adam. 2020. 96p. (J). (gr. 5-9). 19.99 *(978-1-68405-627-9(6))* Idea & Design Works, LLC.

Cousineau, Anik. Anna at the Aquarium. George, Tracilyn. 2019. (ENG.). 24p. (J). pap. 9.99 *(978-1-0926-0574-8(6))* Independently Published.

Cousineau, Normand. Atalante: La Coureuse la Plus Rapide au Monde. Galloway, Priscilla. 2006. (FRE.). 75p. (J). (gr. k-4). reprint ed. pap. 15.00 *(978-1-4223-5394-3(X))* DIANE Publishing Co.

Cousins, Lucy. Nursery Rhymes. ed. 2015. (First Nursery Rhymes Ser.). (ENG.). 16p. (J). (-k). bds. 9.99 *(978-1-4472-6105-6(4))* Pan Macmillan GBR. Dist: Independent Pubs. Group.

Cousins, Lucy. Bathtime with Ducky Duckling. Cousins, Lucy. 2020. (ENG.). 8p. (J). (— 1). 7.99 *(978-1-5362-0965-5(1))* Candlewick Pr.

—Beep, Beep, Maisy! Cousins, Lucy. 2017. (Maisy Ser.). (ENG.). 16p. (J). (-k). bds. 12.99 *(978-0-7636-9407-4(X))* Candlewick Pr.

—Colors with Little Fish. Cousins, Lucy. 2019. (Little Fish Ser.). (ENG.). 24p. (J). (— 1). bds. 7.99 *(978-1-5362-0611-1(3))* Candlewick Pr.

—Count with Little Fish. Cousins, Lucy. 2018. (Little Fish Ser.). (ENG.). 22p. (J). (— 1). bds. 7.99 *(978-1-5362-0024-9(7))* Candlewick Pr.

—Count with Maisy, Cheep, Cheep, Cheep! Cousins, Lucy. 2015. (Maisy Ser.). (ENG.). 32p. (J). (-k). 15.99 *(978-0-7636-7643-8(8))* Candlewick Pr.

—Create with Maisy: A Maisy First Arts-and-Crafts Book. Cousins, Lucy. 2012. (Maisy Ser.). (ENG.). 48p. (J). (gr. -1-3). 16.99 *(978-0-7636-6122-9(8))* Candlewick Pr.

—Doctor Maisy. Cousins, Lucy. 2006. (Maisy Ser.). 24p. (gr. k-k). pap. 3.99 *(978-0-7636-1613-7(3))* Candlewick Pr.

—Hooray for Birds! Cousins, Lucy. 2018. (ENG.). 34p. (J). (— 1). bds. 8.99 *(978-1-5362-0156-7(1))* Candlewick Pr.

—Hooray for Fish! Cousins, Lucy. (ENG.). (J). (— 1). 2017. 34p. bds. 8.99 *(978-0-7636-9352-7(9));* 2005. 40p. 17.99 *(978-0-7636-2741-6(0))* Candlewick Pr.

—¡Hurra, Pecesito! Cousins, Lucy. 2019. (Little Fish Ser.). (SPA.). 34p. (J). (— 1). bds. 8.99 *(978-1-5362-0904-4(X))* Candlewick Pr.

—I Am Little Fish! a Finger Puppet Book. Cousins, Lucy. 2018. (Little Fish Ser.). (ENG.). 16p. (J). (— 1). bds. 12.99 *(978-1-5362-0023-2(9))* Candlewick Pr.

—I'm the Best. Cousins, Lucy. 2013. (ENG.). 32p. (J). (-k). 6.99 *(978-0-7636-6348-3(4))* Candlewick Pr.

—Jazzy in the Jungle. Cousins, Lucy. 2013. (ENG.). 32p. (J). (-k). 15.99 *(978-0-7636-6806-8(0))* Candlewick Pr.

Cousins, Lucy. Let's Play Monsters! Cousins, Lucy. 2020. (ENG.). 40p. (J). (-k). 16.99 ***(978-1-5362-1060-6(9))*** Candlewick Pr.

Cousins, Lucy. Letters from Maisy. Cousins, Lucy. 2020. (Maisy Ser.). (ENG.). 32p. (J). (-k). 14.99 *(978-1-5362-1293-8(8))* Candlewick Pr.

Cousins, Lucy. Little Fish & Friends: a Touch-And-Feel Book. Cousins, Lucy. 2020. (ENG.). 14p. (J). (— 1). 11.99 ***(978-1-5362-1512-0(0))*** Candlewick Pr.

Cousins, Lucy. Little Fish & Mommy. Cousins, Lucy. 2019. (Little Fish Ser.). (ENG.). 22p. (J). (— 1). bds. 8.99 *(978-1-5362-0612-8(1))* Candlewick Pr.

—Maisy at Home: a First Words Book. Cousins, Lucy. 2019. (Maisy Ser.). (ENG.). 22p. (J). (— 1). bds. 8.99 *(978-1-5362-0385-1(8))* Candlewick Pr.

—Maisy, Charley, & the Wobbly Tooth. Cousins, Lucy. 2009. (Maisy Ser.). (ENG.). 32p. (J). (gr. k-k). pap. 6.99 *(978-0-7636-4369-0(6))* Candlewick Pr.

—Maisy Drives the Bus. Cousins, Lucy. 2006. (Maisy Ser.). (ENG.). 24p. (gr. k-k). 3.99 *(978-0-7636-1085-2(2))* Candlewick Pr.

—Maisy Explores: a First Words Book. Cousins, Lucy. 2020. (Maisy Ser.). (ENG.). 20p. (J). (— 1). bds. 8.99 *(978-1-5362-1291-4(1))* Candlewick Pr.

—Maisy Gets a Pet. Cousins, Lucy. 2020. (Maisy Ser.). (ENG.). 32p. (J). (-k). 12.99 *(978-1-5362-1159-7(1))* Candlewick Pr.

—Maisy Goes Camping. Cousins, Lucy. 2009. (Maisy Ser.). (ENG.). 32p. (J). (gr. k-k). pap. 6.99 *(978-0-7636-4368-3(8))* Candlewick Pr.

—Maisy Goes on a Plane. Cousins, Lucy. 2015. (Maisy Ser.). (ENG.). 32p. (J). (-k). 12.99 *(978-0-7636-7825-8(2))* Candlewick Pr.

—Maisy Goes on a Plane: A Maisy First Experiences Book. Cousins, Lucy. 2017. (Maisy Ser.). (ENG.). 32p. (J). (-k). 6.99 *(978-0-7636-9791-4(5))* Candlewick Pr.

—Maisy Goes on a Sleepover. Cousins, Lucy. 2016. (Maisy Ser.). (ENG.). 32p. (J). (gr. -1-2). 6.99 *(978-0-7636-8947-6(5))* Candlewick Pr.

—Maisy Goes on a Sleepover. Cousins, Lucy. ed. 2016. (Maisy First Experiences Ser.). (ENG.). 32p. (gr. -1-2). 17.20 *(978-0-606-39089-7(8))* Turtleback.

—Maisy Goes on Vacation. Cousins, Lucy. 2012. (Maisy Ser.). (ENG.). 32p. (J). (gr. -1-2). pap. 6.99 *(978-0-7636-6039-0(6))* Candlewick Pr.

—Maisy Goes Shopping: Complete with Durable Play Scene: A Fold-Out & Play Book. Cousins, Lucy. 2019. (Maisy Ser.). (ENG.). 16p. (J). (-k). bds. 8.99 *(978-1-5362-0862-7(0))* Candlewick Pr.

—Maisy Goes Swimming. Cousins, Lucy. 2017. (Maisy Ser.). (ENG.). 16p. (J). (-k). 14.99 *(978-0-7636-9461-6(4))* Candlewick Pr.

—Maisy Goes to a Show. Cousins, Lucy. (Maisy Ser.). (ENG.). 32p. (J). (-k). 2020. 6.99 *(978-1-5362-1295-2(4));* 2019. 12.99 *(978-1-5362-0463-6(3))* Candlewick Pr.

—Maisy Goes to a Wedding. Cousins, Lucy. (Maisy Ser.). (ENG.). 32p. (J). (-k). 2019. 6.99 *(978-1-5362-0614-2(8));* 2018. 12.99 *(978-1-5362-0011-9(5))* Candlewick Pr.

—Maisy Goes to Bed. Cousins, Lucy. 2016. (Maisy Ser.). (ENG.). 16p. (J). (gr. -1-2). 14.99 *(978-0-7636-9249-0(2))* Candlewick Pr.

—Maisy Goes to London. Cousins, Lucy. 2016. (Maisy Ser.). (ENG.). 32p. (J). (-k). 15.99 *(978-0-7636-8399-3(X))* Candlewick Pr.

—Maisy Goes to Preschool: A Maisy First Experiences Book. Cousins, Lucy. (Maisy Ser.). (ENG.). 32p. (J). 2010. (gr. k-k). pap. 6.99 *(978-0-7636-5086-5(2));* 2009. (gr. -1-k). 12.99 *(978-0-7636-4254-9(1))* Candlewick Pr.

—Maisy Goes to the City. Cousins, Lucy. 2014. (Maisy Ser.). (ENG.). 32p. (J). (gr. -1-2). 6.99 *(978-0-7636-6834-1(6))* Candlewick Pr.

—Maisy Goes to the Hospital. Cousins, Lucy. 2009. (Maisy Ser.). (ENG.). 32p. (J). (gr. k-k). pap. 6.99 *(978-0-7636-4372-0(6))* Candlewick Pr.

—Maisy Goes to the Library: A Maisy First Experience Book. Cousins, Lucy. 2009. (Maisy Ser.). (ENG.). 32p. (J). (gr. k-k). pap. 6.99 *(978-0-7636-4371-3(8))* Candlewick Pr.

—Maisy Goes to the Local Bookstore. Cousins, Lucy. 2018. (Maisy Ser.). (ENG.). 32p. (J). (-k). 6.99 *(978-1-5362-0085-0(9))* Candlewick Pr.

—Maisy Goes to the Local Bookstore: A Maisy First Experiences Book. Cousins, Lucy. 2017. (Maisy Ser.). (ENG.). 32p. (J). (-k). 12.99 *(978-0-7636-9255-1(7))* Candlewick Pr.

—Maisy Goes to the Movies: A Maisy First Experiences Book. Cousins, Lucy. 2014. (Maisy Ser.). (ENG.). 32p. (J). (gr. -1-2). 6.99 *(978-0-7636-7237-9(8))* Candlewick Pr.

—Maisy Goes to the Museum. Cousins, Lucy. 2009. (Maisy Ser.). (ENG.). 32p. (J). (gr. k-k). pap. 6.99 *(978-0-7636-4370-6(X))* Candlewick Pr.

—Maisy Learns to Swim: A Maisy First Experience Book. Cousins, Lucy. 2015. (Maisy Ser.). (ENG.). 32p. (J). (-k). 6.99 *(978-0-7636-7749-7(3))* Candlewick Pr.

—Maisy Plays Soccer. Cousins, Lucy. 2014. (Maisy Ser.). 32p. (J). (gr. -1-2). pap. 6.99 *(978-0-7636-7238-6(6))* Candlewick Pr.

—Maisy's Amazing Big Book of Words. Cousins, Lucy. 2007. (Maisy Ser.). (ENG.). 64p. (J). (gr. k-k). 15.99 *(978-0-7636-0794-4(0))* Candlewick Pr.

—Maisy's Animals: a First Words Book. Cousins, Lucy. 2020. (Maisy Ser.). (ENG.). 20p. (J). (— 1). bds. 8.99 *(978-1-5362-1292-1(X))* Candlewick Pr.

—Maisy's Animals Los Animales de Maisy: A Maisy Dual Language Book. Cousins, Lucy. 2009. (Maisy Ser.). 16p. (J). (gr. -1-2). bds. 5.99 *(978-0-7636-4517-5(6))* Candlewick Pr.

—Maisy's Birthday Party Sticker Book. Cousins, Lucy. 2015. (Maisy Ser.). (ENG.). 16p. (J). (gr. -1-2). pap. 7.99 *(978-0-7636-7735-0(3))* Candlewick Pr.

—Maisy's Bus. Cousins, Lucy. 2017. (Maisy Ser.). (ENG.). 18p. (J). (— 1). bds. 5.99 *(978-0-7636-9406-7(1))* Candlewick Pr.

—Maisy's Christmas Party: With 6 Festive Letters & Secret Surprises! Cousins, Lucy. 2019. (Maisy Ser.). (ENG.). 32p. (J). (-k). 14.99 *(978-1-5362-0861-0(2))* Candlewick Pr.

—Maisy's Christmas Presents. Cousins, Lucy. 2016. (Maisy Ser.). (ENG.). 16p. (J). (-k). 14.99 *(978-0-7636-9248-3(4))* Candlewick Pr.

—Maisy's Christmas Tree. Cousins, Lucy. 2014. (Maisy Ser.). (ENG.). 16p. (J). (-k). bds. 6.99 *(978-0-7636-7457-1(5))* Candlewick Pr.

—Maisy's Clothes la Ropa de Maisy: A Maisy Dual Language Book. Cousins, Lucy. 2009. (Maisy Ser.). 16p. (J). (gr. -1-2). bds. 6.99 *(978-0-7636-4518-2(4))* Candlewick Pr.

Cousins, Lucy. Maisy's Construction Site: Push, Slide, & Play! Cousins, Lucy. 2020. (Maisy Ser.). (ENG.). 8p. (J). (— 1). bds. 9.99 ***(978-1-5362-1294-5(6))*** Candlewick Pr.

Cousins, Lucy. Maisy's Day Out: A First Words Book. Cousins, Lucy. 2019. (Maisy Ser.). (ENG.). 22p. (J). (— 1). bds. 8.99 *(978-1-5362-0386-8(6))* Candlewick Pr.

—Maisy's Digger: A Go with Maisy Board Book. Cousins, Lucy. 2015. (Maisy Ser.). (ENG.). 18p. (J). (— 1). bds. 5.99 *(978-0-7636-8010-7(9))* Candlewick Pr.

—Maisy's Farm: Complete with Durable Play Scene. Cousins, Lucy. 2019. (Maisy Ser.). (ENG.). 16p. (J). (-k). bds. 8.99 *(978-1-5362-0613-5(X))* Candlewick Pr.

—Maisy's Field Day. Cousins, Lucy. 2016. (Maisy Ser.). (ENG.). 32p. (J). (-k). 12.99 *(978-0-7636-8441-9(4))* Candlewick Pr.

—Maisy's Fire Engine: A Maisy Shaped Board Book. Cousins, Lucy. 2009. (Maisy Ser.). (ENG.). 16p. (J). (gr. k-k). bds. 5.99 *(978-0-7636-4252-5(5))* Candlewick Pr.

—Maisy's First Clock. Cousins, Lucy. 2011. (Maisy Ser.). (ENG.). 16p. (J). (gr. k-k). bds. 14.99 *(978-0-7636-5095-7(1))* Candlewick Pr.

—Maisy's First Colors: A Maisy Concept Book. Cousins, Lucy. 2013. (Maisy Ser.). (ENG.). 14p. (J). (-k). bds. 6.99 *(978-0-7636-6804-4(4))* Candlewick Pr.

—Maisy's Food Los Alimentos de Maisy: A Maisy Dual Language Book. Cousins, Lucy. 2009. (Maisy Ser.). 16p. (J). (gr. -1-2). bds. 5.99 *(978-0-7636-4519-9(2))* Candlewick Pr.

—Maisy's House. Cousins, Lucy. 2018. (Maisy Ser.). (ENG.). 16p. (J). (-k). bds. 8.99 *(978-1-5362-0378-3(5))* Candlewick Pr.

—Maisy's Morning on the Farm. Cousins, Lucy. 2006. (Maisy Ser.). (ENG.). 24p. (gr. k-k). 3.99 *(978-0-7636-1611-3(7))* Candlewick Pr.

—Maisy's Placemat Doodle Book. Cousins, Lucy. 2014. (Maisy Ser.). (ENG.). 104p. (J). (-k). pap. 11.99 *(978-0-7636-7108-2(8))* Candlewick Pr.

—Maisy's Plane. Cousins, Lucy. 2015. (Maisy Ser.). (ENG.). 18p. (J). (— 1). bds. 5.99 *(978-0-7636-7304-8(8))* Candlewick Pr.

—Maisy's Preschool: Complete with Durable Play Scene. Cousins, Lucy. 2019. (Maisy Ser.). 16p. (J). (-k). bds. 8.99 *(978-1-5362-0678-4(4))* Candlewick Pr.

—Maisy's Race Car: A Go with Maisy Board Book. Cousins, Lucy. 2015. (Maisy Ser.). (ENG.). 18p. (J). (— 1). bds. 5.99 *(978-0-7636-8011-4(7))* Candlewick Pr.

—Maisy's Sailboat. Cousins, Lucy. 2017. (Maisy Ser.). (ENG.). 18p. (J). (— 1). bds. 6.99 *(978-0-7636-9405-0(3))* Candlewick Pr.

—Maisy's Toys Los Juguetes de Maisy: A Maisy Dual Language Book. Cousins, Lucy. 2009. (Maisy Ser.). 16p. (J). (gr. -1-2). bds. 5.99 *(978-0-7636-4520-5(6))* Candlewick Pr.

—Maisy's Tractor. Cousins, Lucy. 2015. (Maisy Ser.). (ENG.). 18p. (J). (— 1). bds. 6.99 *(978-0-7636-7305-5(6))* Candlewick Pr.

—Maisy's Train: A Maisy Shaped Board Book. Cousins, Lucy. 2009. (Maisy Ser.). (ENG.). 16p. (J). (gr. k-k). bds. 5.99 *(978-0-7636-4251-8(7))* Candlewick Pr.

—Maisy's Valentine Sticker Book. Cousins, Lucy. 2005. (Maisy Ser.). (ENG.). 16p. (J). (gr. k-k). pap. 4.99 *(978-0-7636-2713-3(5))* Candlewick Pr.

—Maisy's Wonderful Weather Book. Cousins, Lucy. 2006. (Maisy Ser.). (ENG.). 14p. (J). (gr. -1). 11.99 *(978-0-7636-2987-8(1))* Candlewick Pr.

—Noah's Ark. Cousins, Lucy. 2004. 22p. (J). (gr. k-k). bds. 6.99 *(978-0-7636-2446-0(2))* Candlewick Pr.

—Peck, Peck, Peck. Cousins, Lucy. 2013. (ENG.). 32p. (J). (-k). 15.99 *(978-0-7636-6621-7(1))* Candlewick Pr.

—Peck Peck Peck. Cousins, Lucy. 2016. (ENG.). 32p. (J). (— 1). bds. 8.99 *(978-0-7636-8946-9(7))* Candlewick Pr.

—Shapes with Little Fish. Cousins, Lucy. 2020. (Little Fish Ser.). (ENG.). 18p. (J). (— 1). bds. 8.99 *(978-1-5362-1296-9(2))* Candlewick Pr.

—Splish, Splash, Ducky! Cousins, Lucy. 2018. (ENG.). 40p. (J). (-k). 16.99 *(978-0-7636-9844-7(X))* Candlewick Pr.

—Sweet Dreams, Maisy. Cousins, Lucy. 2009. (Maisy Ser.). (ENG.). 32p. (J). (gr. -1-2). bds. 6.99 *(978-0-7636-4532-8(X))* Candlewick Pr.

—Swim with Little Fish! a Bath Book. Cousins, Lucy. 2019. (Little Fish Ser.). (ENG.). 8p. (J). (— 1). 7.99 *(978-1-5362-0729-3(2))* Candlewick Pr.

—Where Are Maisy's Friends? A Maisy Lift-The-Flap Book. Cousins, Lucy. 2010. (Maisy Ser.). (ENG.). 12p. (J). (-k). bds. 5.99 *(978-0-7636-4669-1(5))* Candlewick Pr.

—Where Does Maisy Live? A Maisy Lift-The-Flap Book. Cousins, Lucy. 2010. (Maisy Ser.). (ENG.). 12p. (J). (-k). bds. 6.99 *(978-0-7636-4668-4(7))* Candlewick Pr.

—Where Is Little Fish? Cousins, Lucy. 2018. (Little Fish Ser.). (ENG.). 16p. (J). (— 1). bds. 7.99 *(978-0-7636-9486-9(X))* Candlewick Pr.

—Where Is Maisy? Cousins, Lucy. 2010. (Maisy Ser.). (ENG.). 14p. (J). (gr. k-k). bds. 5.99 *(978-0-7636-4673-8(3))* Candlewick Pr.

—Yummy: Eight Favorite Fairy Tales. Cousins, Lucy. 2009. (ENG.). 128p. (J). (gr. -1-2). 19.99 *(978-0-7636-4474-1(9))* Candlewick Pr.

Couteaud, Cheryl. A Monster for Halloween. Couteaud, Cheryl. 2009. 24p. pap. 10.96 *(978-1-4251-8563-3(0))* Trafford Publishing.

Coutinho, Ivan. Mary Our Mother Col Bk (5pk) Ramalho, Rosa. 2017. (ENG.). 40p. (J). pap. 3.95 *(978-0-8198-4964-9(2))* Pauline Bks. & Media.

Coutts, Lisa. The Elf Flute. Branford, Anna. 2015. 44p. (J). *(978-1-61067-628-1(9))* Kane Miller.
—The Elf Flute: Lily the Elf. Branford, Anna. 2017. 44p. (J). pap. 4.99 *(978-1-61067-532-1(0))* Kane Miller.
—Hello God. Simons, Moya. 2019. 160p. (Orig.). pap. 4.99 *(978-0-7322-8534-0(8))* HarperCollins Pubs. Australia AUS. Dist: HarperCollins Pubs.
—The Midnight Owl. Branford, Anna. 2016. 47p. (J). *(978-1-61067-625-0(4))* Kane Miller.
—The Midnight Owl: Lily the Elf. Branford, Anna. 2017. 47p. (J). pap. 4.99 *(978-1-61067-529-1(0))* Kane Miller.
—The Precious Ring. Branford, Anna. 2015. 44p. (J). *(978-1-61067-626-7(2))* Kane Miller.
—The Precious Ring: Lily the Elf. Branford, Anna. 2017. 44p. (J). pap. 4.99 *(978-1-61067-530-7(4))* Kane Miller.
—The Wishing Seed: Lily the Elf. Branford, Anna. 2017. 47p. (J). pap. 4.99 *(978-1-61067-531-4(2))* Kane Miller.
Couvillian, Shelley & Steuerwald, Joy. Checking In. Arrow, Emily. 2019. (My Feelings, My Choices Ser.). (ENG.). 24p. (J). (gr. -1-2). 33.99 *(978-1-68410-404-8(1)*, 141214) Cantata Learning.
Coverly, Dave. How to Care for Your T-Rex. Baker, Ken. 2019. (ENG.). 36p. (J). 17.99 *(978-1-250-13751-7(9)*, 900178842, Holt, Henry & Co. Bks. For Young Readers) Holt, Henry & Co.
—The Very Inappropriate Word. Tobin, Jim. 2013. (ENG.). 36p. (J). (gr. k-3). 16.99 *(978-0-8050-9474-9(1)*, 900079391, Holt, Henry & Co. Bks. For Young Readers) Holt, Henry & Co.
Coverly, Dave. Night of the Living Worms: A Speed Bump & Slingshot Misadventure. Coverly, Dave. 2015. (Speed Bump & Slingshot Misadventure Ser.). (ENG.). 128p. (J). (gr. 2-5). 13.99 *(978-0-8050-8886-1(5)*, 9780805088861, Holt, Henry & Co. Bks. For Young Readers) Holt, Henry & Co.
—Night of the Living Worms: A Speed Bump & Slingshot Misadventure. Coverly, Dave. ed. 2016. (Speed Bump & Slingshot Misadventure Ser.: 1). (ENG.). 121p. (J). (gr. 2-5). 16.00 *(978-0-606-39299-0(8))* Turtleback.
—Night of the Living Zombie Bugs. Coverly, Dave. 2017. (Speed Bump & Slingshot Misadventure Ser.: 3). (ENG.). 144p. (J). 13.99 *(978-1-250-11400-6(4)*, 900171359, Holt, Henry & Co. Bks. For Young Readers) Holt, Henry & Co.
—Night of the Living Zombie Bugs. Coverly, Dave. 2018. (Speed Bump & Slingshot Misadventure Ser.: 3). (ENG.). 144p. (J). pap. 6.99 *(978-1-250-17721-6(9)*, 900171360) Square Fish.
Covey, Rosemary Feit. Beauty & the Serpent: Thirteen Tales of Unnatural Animals. Porte, Barbara Ann. 2008. (ENG.). 128p. (YA). (gr. 7). pap. 7.99 *(978-1-4169-7579-3(9)*, Simon & Schuster/Paula Wiseman Bks.) Simon & Schuster/Paula Wiseman Bks.
Covi, jt. illus. see Antonio.
Coville, Katherine. Aliens Ate My Homework. Coville, Bruce. 2008. (Rod Allbright & the Galactic Patrol Ser.). 179p. (gr. 3-7). 17.00 *(978-0-7569-8466-3(1))* Perfection Learning Corp.
—Aliens Ate My Homework. Coville, Bruce. 2007. (Rod Allbright & the Galactic Patrol Ser.). (ENG.). 192p. (J). (gr. 3-7). pap. 7.99 *(978-1-4169-3883-5(4)*, Aladdin) Simon & Schuster Children's Publishing.
—Aliens Ate My Homework Collection: Aliens Ate My Homework; I Left My Sneakers in Dimension X; the Search for Snout; Aliens Stole My Body. Coville, Bruce. ed. 2018. (Rod Allbright & the Galactic Patrol Ser.). (ENG.). 848p. (J). (gr. 3-7). pap. 27.99 *(978-1-5344-1514-0(9)*, Aladdin) Simon & Schuster Children's Publishing.
—Aliens Stole My Body. Coville, Bruce. 2008. (Rod Allbright & the Galactic Patrol Ser.). (ENG.). 240p. (J). (gr. 3-7). pap. 7.99 *(978-1-4169-5359-3(0)*, Simon & Schuster/Paula Wiseman Bks.) Simon & Schuster/Paula Wiseman Bks.
—The Dragon of Doom. Coville, Bruce. 2005. (Moongobble & Me Ser.: Bk. 1). (ENG.). 80p. (J). (gr. 1-5). pap. 6.99 *(978-0-689-85757-7(8)*, Aladdin) Simon & Schuster Children's Publishing.
—The Evil Elves. Coville, Bruce. 2006. (Moongobble & Me Ser.: Bk. 3). (ENG.). 80p. (J). (gr. 1-5). pap. 6.99 *(978-0-689-85759-1(4)*, Simon & Schuster/Paula Wiseman Bks.) Simon & Schuster/Paula Wiseman Bks.
—Goblins in the Castle. Coville, Bruce. 2015. (ENG.). 208p. (J). (gr. 3-7). 17.99 *(978-1-4814-3900-8(6)*, Aladdin) Simon & Schuster Children's Publishing.
—I Left My Sneakers in Dimension X. Coville, Bruce. 2007. (Rod Allbright & the Galactic Patrol Ser.). (ENG.). 192p. (J). (gr. 3-7). pap. 7.99 *(978-1-4169-3882-8(6)*, Simon & Schuster/Paula Wiseman Bks.) Simon & Schuster/Paula Wiseman Bks.
—The Mischief Monster. Coville, Bruce. 2008. (Moongobble & Me Ser.: Bk. 4). (ENG.). 80p. (J). (gr. 1-5). pap. 6.99 *(978-1-4169-0808-1(0)*, Aladdin) Simon & Schuster Children's Publishing.
—The Mischief Monster. Coville, Bruce. 2007. (Moongobble & Me Ser.: Bk. 4). (ENG.). 80p. (J). (gr. 3-6). 16.19 *(978-1-4169-0807-4(2))* Simon & Schuster, Inc.
—The Monster's Ring. Coville, Bruce. 2008. (Magic Shop Book Ser.: 1). (ENG.). 128p. (J). (gr. 5-7). pap. 7.99 *(978-0-15-206442-6(7)*, 1199254) Houghton Mifflin Harcourt Publishing Co.
Coville, Katherine. Moongobble & Me Magical Collection: The Dragon of Doom; the Weeping Werewolf; the Evil Elves; the Mischief Monster; the Naughty Nork. Coville, Bruce. ed. 2020. (Moongobble & Me Ser.). (ENG.). 448p. (J). (gr. 1-5). pap. 32.99 ***(978-1-5344-5784-3(4)***, Aladdin) Simon & Schuster Children's Publishing.
Coville, Katherine. More Short & Shivery: Thirty Terrifying Tales. San Souci, Robert D. 2015. (ENG.). 224p. (J). (gr. 3-7). 6.99 *(978-0-440-41857-3(7)*, Yearling) Random Hse. Children's Bks.
—The Naughty Nork. Coville, Bruce. (Moongobble & Me Ser.). (ENG.). (J). 2009. 128p. (gr. 1-5). pap. 6.99 *(978-1-4169-0810-4(2))*; 2008. 80p. (gr. 2-4). 17.44 *(978-1-4169-0809-8(9))* Simon & Schuster Children's Publishing. (Aladdin).
—The Search for Snout. Coville, Bruce. 2007. (Rod Allbright & the Galactic Patrol Ser.). (ENG.). 224p. (J). (gr. 3-7). pap. 7.99 *(978-1-4169-4980-0(1)*, Simon & Schuster/Paula Wiseman Bks.) Simon & Schuster/Paula Wiseman Bks.
—The Weeping Werewolf. Coville, Bruce. 2006. (Moongobble & Me Ser.). 68p. (gr. 1-5). 16.00 *(978-0-7569-6582-2(9))* Perfection Learning Corp.
—The Weeping Werewolf. Coville, Bruce. 2005. (Moongobble & Me Ser.: Bk. 2). (ENG.). 80p. (J). (gr. 1-5). pap. 6.99 *(978-0-689-85758-4(6)*, Aladdin) Simon & Schuster Children's Publishing.
Coville, Katherine, jt. illus. see Gerstein, Mordicai.
Covo, Pedro. The Elephant Keeper: Caring for Orphaned Elephants in Zambia. Ruurs, Margriet. 2017. (CitizenKid Ser.). (ENG.). 48p. (J). (gr. 3-7). 18.99 *(978-1-77138-561-9(8))* Kids Can Pr., Ltd. CAN. Dist: Hachette Bk. Group.
Covolo, David. Ned & the General: A Lesson about Deployment. Madison, Ron. 2004. (J). 24p. 8.95 *(978-1-887206-24-2(8))*; 26p. (gr. -1-3). *(978-1-887206-25-9(6))* Ned's Head Productions.
—Ned & the World's Religions: As Seen Through the Eyes of Children. Madison, Ron. 2008. 36p. (J). 14.95 *(978-1-887206-26-6(4))* Ned's Head Productions.
—Ned Learns to Say No: A Lesson about Drugs. Madison, Ron. l.t. ed. 2003. (Health & Safety Ser.). 24p. pap. 4.95 *(978-1-887206-23-5(X))* Ned's Head Productions.
Cowan, Denys, et al. Power Man & Iron Fist Epic Collection: Doombringer. 2019. (ENG.). 440p. (YA). (gr. 4-17). pap. 39.99 *(978-1-302-92071-5(5))* Marvel Worldwide, Inc.
Cowan, Madison. Beyond the Pond & Back. Chambers, G. S. 2020. (It Takes a Pond Ser.: Vol. 2). (ENG.). 152p. (J). pap. 8.99 ***(978-1-7339710-4-1(1))*** Theophany Pr.
—Tadpoles on the Loose. Chambers, G. S. 2019. (It Takes a Pond Ser.: Vol. 1). (ENG.). 150p. (J). pap. 8.99 ***(978-1-7339710-3-4(3))*** Theophany Pr.
Cowcher, Robin. Digger. Dumbleton, Mike. 2018. (ENG.). 32p. (J). (gr. k-3). 19.99 *(978-1-76029-673-5(2))* Allen & Unwin AUS. Dist: Independent Pubs. Group.
Cowden, Steve. Cheese Louise!, 1 vol. Slater, David Michael. 2005. (ENG.). 32p. (J). (gr. 2-4). pap. 8.95 *(978-1-55285-721-2(2)*, 06900264-88aa-418a-82dc-f0cf9f18dd41) Whitecap Bks., Ltd. CAN. Dist: Firefly Bks., Ltd.
Cowdery, Nichola. This Little Piggy Wore a T-Shirt. Make Believe Ideas Ltd. 2020. (ENG.). 12p. (J). bds. ***(978-1-78947-362-9(4))*** Make Believe Ideas.
Cowdrey, Richard. Animals on the Go. Brett, Jessica. 2003. (Green Light Readers Level 2 Ser.). (ENG.). 24p. (J). (gr. -1-3). pap. 3.95 *(978-0-15-204827-3(8)*, 1194577) Houghton Mifflin Harcourt Publishing Co.
—Bad Dog, Marley! Grogan, John. (ENG.). 40p. (J). (gr. -1-3). 2011. pap. 7.99 *(978-0-06-117116-1(6))*; 2007. 17.99 *(978-0-06-117114-7(X))* HarperCollins Pubs.
—Bad Dog, Marley! Beloved Book & Plush Puppy. Grogan, John. 2007. 40p. (J). (gr. -1-3). 24.99 *(978-0-06-143496-9(5))* HarperCollins Pubs.
—Bambi: A Life in the Woods. Salten, Felix. 2013. (Bambi's Classic Animal Tales Ser.). (ENG.). 272p. (J). (gr. 3-7). pap. 8.99 *(978-1-4424-6745-3(2)*, Aladdin) Simon & Schuster Children's Publishing.
—Bambi's Children: The Story of a Forest Family. Salten, Felix. Tilley, R. Sudgen, ed. Fles, Barthold, tr. 2014. (Bambi's Classic Animal Tales Ser.). (ENG.). 368p. (J). (gr. 3-7). pap. 7.99 *(978-1-4424-8745-1(3)*, Aladdin) Simon & Schuster Children's Publishing.
—The Christmas Baby. Bauer, Marion Dane. 2009. (ENG.). 32p. (J). (gr. -1-k). 15.99 *(978-1-4169-7885-5(2)*, Simon & Schuster Bks. For Young Readers) Simon & Schuster Bks. For Young Readers.
—Fiona: La Bebé Hipo, 1 vol. 2019. (SPA.). 32p. (J). 16.99 *(978-1-4002-1247-7(2))* Vida Pubs.
—Fiona the Hippo, 1 vol. 2018. (Fiona the Hippo Book Ser.). (ENG.). (J). 32p. 17.99 *(978-0-310-76639-1(7))*; 30p. bds. 8.99 *(978-0-310-76636-0(2))* Zonderkidz.
—The Legend of St. Nicholas: A Story of Christmas Giving, 1 vol. Mackall, Dandi Daley. 2014. (ENG.). 32p. (J). 16.99 *(978-0-310-73115-3(1))* Zonderkidz.
—The Legend of the Candy Cane, 1 vol. Zondervan Staff & Walburg, Lori. 2014. (ENG.). 30p. (J). bds. 9.99 *(978-0-310-74672-0(8))* Zonderkidz.
—The Legend of the Christmas Cookie, 1 vol. Mackall, Dandi Daley. 2015. (ENG.). 32p. (J). 16.99 *(978-0-310-74767-3(8))* Zonderkidz.
—The Legend of the Easter Robin: An Easter Story of Compassion & Faith, 1 vol. Mackall, Dandi Daley. 2016. (ENG.). 30p. (J). 16.99 *(978-0-310-74964-6(6))* Zonderkidz.
—The Legend of the Sand Dollar, Newly Illustrated Edition: An Inspirational Story of Hope for Easter, 1 vol. Auer, Chris. 2017. (ENG.). 32p. (J). 17.99 *(978-0-310-74980-6(8))* Zonderkidz.
—The Legends of Christmas Treasury: Inspirational Stories of Faith & Giving, 1 vol. Mackall, Dandi Daley & Walburg, Lori. 2017. (ENG.). 96p. (J). 19.99 *(978-0-310-75743-6(6))* Zonderkidz.
—The Legends of Easter Treasury: Inspirational Stories of Faith & Hope, 1 vol. Mackall, Dandi Daley et al. 2018. (ENG.). 96p. (J). 19.99 *(978-0-310-75759-7(2))* Zonderkidz.
—Marley & the Kittens. Grogan, John. 2010. (Marley Ser.). (ENG.). 40p. (J). (gr. -1-3). 17.99 *(978-0-06-171486-3(0))*; lib. bdg. 18.89 *(978-0-06-171487-0(9))* HarperCollins Pubs.
—Marley: Farm Dog. Grogan, John. 2011. (I Can Read Level 2 Ser.). (ENG.). 32p. (J). (gr. k-3). pap. 4.99 *(978-0-06-198937-7(1))* HarperCollins Pubs.
—Marley Goes to School. Grogan, John. (Marley Ser.). 40p. (J). (gr. -1-3). 2012. (ENG.). 9.99 *(978-0-06-211366-5(6))*; 2009. lib. bdg. 18.89 *(978-0-06-156152-8(5))* HarperCollins Pubs.
—Marley: Marley & the Runaway Pumpkin. Grogan, John. 2010. (I Can Read Level 2 Ser.). (ENG.). 32p. (J). (gr. k-3). pap. 4.99 *(978-0-06-185389-0(5))* HarperCollins Pubs.
—Marley: Marley Learns a Lesson. Grogan, John. 2013. (I Can Read Level 2 Ser.). (ENG.). 32p. (J). (gr. -1-3). 16.99 *(978-0-06-207487-4(3))* HarperCollins Pubs.
—Marley: Marley Looks for Love. Grogan, John. 2010. (Marley Ser.). (ENG.). 16p. (J). (gr. -1-1). 6.99 *(978-0-06-185590-0(1)*, HarperFestival) HarperCollins Pubs.
—Marley: Marley Steals the Show. Grogan, John. 2010. (Marley Ser.). (ENG.). 24p. (J). (gr. -1-2). pap. 3.99 *(978-0-06-185377-7(1)*, HarperFestival) HarperCollins Pubs.
—Marley: Marley's Big Adventure. Grogan, John. 2009. (I Can Read Level 2 Ser.). (ENG.). 32p. (J). (gr. k-3). pap. 4.99 *(978-0-06-185383-8(6))* HarperCollins Pubs.
—Marley: Marley's World Reusable Sticker Book. Grogan, John. 2010. (Marley Ser.). (ENG.). 12p. (J). (gr. -1-3). pap. 6.99 *(978-0-06-185397-5(6)*, HarperFestival) HarperCollins Pubs.
—Marley: Messy Dog. Grogan, John. 2011. (I Can Read Level 2 Ser.). (ENG.). 32p. (J). (gr. k-3). 16.99 *(978-0-06-198940-7(1))*; pap. 4.99 *(978-0-06-198939-1(8))* HarperCollins Pubs.
—Marley: Sit, Marley, Sit! Grogan, John. 2010. (Marley Ser.). (ENG.). 24p. (J). (gr. -1-2). pap. 3.99 *(978-0-06-185380-7(1)*, HarperFestival) HarperCollins Pubs.
—Marley: Snow Dog Marley. Grogan, John. 2010. (I Can Read Level 2 Ser.). (ENG.). 32p. (J). (gr. k-3). pap. 4.99 *(978-0-06-185392-0(5))* HarperCollins Pubs.
—Marley: Strike Three, Marley! Grogan, John. 2010. (I Can Read Level 2 Ser.). (ENG.). 32p. (J). (gr. k-3). pap. 4.99 *(978-0-06-185386-9(0))* HarperCollins Pubs.
—Marley: Thanks, Mom & Dad! Grogan, John. 2011. (Marley Ser.). (ENG.). 24p. (J). (gr. -1-2). pap. 3.99 *(978-0-06-185381-4(X)*, HarperFestival) HarperCollins Pubs.
—Marley: the Dog Who Cried Woof. Grogan, John. 2011. (I Can Read Level 2 Ser.). (ENG.). 32p. (J). (gr. k-3). pap. 4.99 *(978-0-06-198943-8(6))* HarperCollins Pubs.
—Marley's Christmas Pageant. Grogan, John. 2013. (Marley Ser.). (ENG.). 16p. (J). (gr. -1-3). 6.99 *(978-0-06-185382-1(8)*, HarperFestival) HarperCollins Pubs.
—Marley's Storybook Treasury: Marley's Big Adventure; Strike Three, Marley!, Marley & the Runaway Pumpkin; Snow Dog Marley; Thanks, Mom & Dad!; Marley: Messy Dog. Grogan, John. 2012. (I Can Read Level 2 Ser.). (ENG.). 192p. (J). (gr. k-3). 11.99 *(978-0-06-212331-2(9))* HarperCollins Pubs.
—The Puppy That No One Wanted. DeStefano, Anthony. 2015. (ENG.). 32p. (gr. -1-k). 18.99 *(978-1-61636-928-6(0)*, T36928, Servant Bks.) Franciscan Media.
—Snow Dog Marley. Grogan, John. 2010. (I Can Read Book: Level 2 Ser.). (ENG.). 32p. (J). (gr. k-2). 16.19 *(978-0-06-185393-7(3))* HarperCollins Pubs.
—The Tarantula in My Purse & 172 Other Wild Pets: True-Life Stories to Read Aloud. George, Jean Craighead. 2019. (Trophy Bk.). (ENG.). 144p. (J). (gr. 3-7). reprint ed. pap. 6.99 *(978-0-06-446201-3(3)*, HarperCollins) HarperCollins Pubs. Ltd. GBR. Dist: HarperCollins Pubs.
—Trick or Treat, Marley! Grogan, John. (Marley Ser.). (ENG.). 40p. (J). (gr. -1-3). 2013. 9.99 *(978-0-06-211368-9(2))*; 2011. 17.99 *(978-0-06-185755-3(6))* HarperCollins Pubs. (HarperFestival).
—A Very Marley Christmas. Grogan, John. (Marley Ser.). (ENG.). 40p. (J). (gr. -1-3). 2014. 9.99 *(978-0-06-211367-2(4))*; 2008. 17.99 *(978-0-06-137292-6(7))* HarperCollins Pubs.
—A Very Marley Christmas. Grogan, John. (ENG.). 32p. pap. *(978-0-00-728723-9(2)*, HarperCollins Children's Bks.) HarperCollins Pubs. Ltd.
Cowdrey, Richard & Halverson, Lydia. Marley: Firehouse Dog. Grogan, John. 2012. (I Can Read Level 2 Ser.). (ENG.). 32p. (J). (gr. -1-3). 16.99 *(978-0-06-207484-3(9))*; pap. 4.99 *(978-0-06-207483-6(0))* HarperCollins Pubs.
—Marley's Big Adventure. Grogan, John & Hill, Susan. 2009. (I Can Read Book 2 Ser.). 32p. (J). (gr. -1-3). 16.99 *(978-0-06-185384-5(4))* HarperCollins Pubs.
Cowdrey, Richard & Whipple, Rick. Marley: a Thanksgiving to Remember. Grogan, John. 2011. (Marley Ser.). (ENG.). 16p. (J). (gr. -1-1). pap. 6.99 *(978-0-06-185591-7(X)*, HarperFestival) HarperCollins Pubs.
—Marley: Not a Peep! Grogan, John. 2012. (I Can Read Level 2 Ser.). (ENG.). 32p. (J). (gr. k-3). pap. 4.99 *(978-0-06-207477-5(6))* HarperCollins Pubs.
—Marley: the Dog Who Ate My Homework. Grogan, John. 2012. (I Can Read Level 2 Ser.). (ENG.). 32p. (J). (gr. k-3). pap. 4.99 *(978-0-06-207480-5(6))* HarperCollins Pubs.
Cowdrey, Richard, jt. illus. see Bernardin, James.
Cowen-Fletcher, Jane. Baby Be Kind. Cowen-Fletcher, Jane. 2012. 18p. (J). (gr. k — 1). bds. 6.99 *(978-0-7636-5647-8(X))* Candlewick Pr.
—Hello, Puppy! Cowen-Fletcher, Jane. 2010. 32p. (J). (gr. -1-k). 12.99 *(978-0-7636-4303-4(3))* Candlewick Pr.
Cowen, Linda. Mason's This-And-That Day. Kotchman, Sue. 2016. (ENG.). (J). (gr. k-6). 17.00 *(978-1-941251-84-3(6))* Thewordverve.
—Namaste, Great Gray. Davis, Beverly. 2017. (Namaste, Great Gray Ser.: Vol. 3). (ENG.). (J). (gr. 1-6). 18.00 *(978-1-941251-92-8(7))*; pap. 12.00 *(978-1-941251-91-1(9))* Thewordverve.
Cowgur, Eldon. Made for Each Other, 2 vols., No. 2. Storrie, Paul D. 2011. (My Boyfriend Is a Monster Ser.: 2). (ENG.). 128p. (YA). (gr. 7-12). 29.32 *(978-0-7613-5601-1(0)*, 9780761356011, Graphic Universe™) Lerner Publishing Group.
—#02 Made for Each Other. Storrie, Paul D. 2011. (My Boyfriend Is a Monster Ser.). 128p. (YA). pap. 56.72 *(978-0-7613-7604-0(6)*, Graphic Universe™) Lerner Publishing Group.
Cowherd, Kevin. Cal Ripken Jr. 's All-Stars Super-Sized Slugger. Ripken Jr., Cal. 2013. (Cal Ripken Jr. 's All Stars Ser.: 2). 208p. (J). (gr. 3-7). pap. 6.99 *(978-1-4231-4004-7(4))* Hyperion Pr.
Cowhey, Dennis E. Murder & Betrayal. Guzaldo, Jessica. DeFalco, Julie & Cowhey, Dennis R., eds. 2003. 72p. (YA). (gr. 7-8). pap. 9.95 *(978-0-9642823-2-1(1))* Key Answer Products, Inc.
Cowles Clark, Mary. The Life & Adventures of Santa Claus. Baum, L. Frank. 2017. (ENG.). 162p. 12.99 *(978-1-5098-4174-5(1)*, 900183885, Collector's Library, The) Pan Macmillan GBR. Dist: Macmillan.
Cowles, Rose. Achoo! The Most Interesting Book You'll Ever Read about Germs. Romanek, Trudee. 2003. (Mysterious You Ser.). (ENG.). 40p. (J). (gr. 4-9). pap. 8.95 *(978-1-55337-451-0(7))* Kids Can Pr., Ltd. CAN. Dist: Hachette Bk. Group.
—The Queen, the Bear & the Bumblebee. Petty, Dini. 32p. (J). 19.95 *(978-1-55285-151-7(6))* Whitecap Bks., Ltd. CAN. Dist: Graphic Arts Ctr. Publishing Co.
—Science Detectives: How Scientists Solved Six Real-Life Mysteries. Editors of YES Mag. 2006. (ENG.). 48p. (J). (gr. 3-7). pap. 8.95 *(978-1-55337-995-9(0))* Kids Can Pr., Ltd. CAN. Dist: Hachette Bk. Group.
—Squirt! The Most Interesting Book You'll Ever Read about Blood. Romanek, Trudee. 2006. (Mysterious You Ser.). 40p. (J). (gr. 4-9). 7.95 *(978-1-55337-777-1(X))* Kids Can Pr., Ltd. CAN. Dist: Hachette Bk. Group.
Cowles, The Misses. Social Life in Old Virginia Before the War (Illustrated Edition) Page, Thomas Nelson. 2017. (ENG.). 48p. (J). pap. *(978-1-4068-8696-2(3))* Echo Library.
Cowley, Katz. The Dinky Donkey. Smith, Craig. 2019. (ENG.). 24p. (J). (gr. -1-k). pap. 7.99 *(978-1-338-60083-4(4))* Scholastic, Inc.
—Wilbee the Bumblebee. Smith, Craig & Thomson, Maureen. 2019. (ENG.). 32p. (J). (gr. -1-k). pap. 7.99 *(978-1-338-57521-7(X)*, Scholastic Paperbacks) Scholastic, Inc.
—The Wonky Donkey. Smith, Craig. 2010. (ENG.). 24p. (J). (gr. -1-k). pap. 7.99 *(978-0-545-26124-1(4)*, Scholastic Paperbacks) Scholastic, Inc.
Cowley, Ray B. First Day at Bouddi School. Bourke, Debra. 2012. 32p. pap. 18.00 *(978-1-4349-8469-2(9)*, RoseDog Bks.) Dorrance Publishing Co., Inc.
Cowman, Joseph. All in One Day. Huber, Mike. 2014. (ENG.). 32p. (gr. -1-k). 15.95 *(978-1-60554-207-2(5))* Redleaf Pr.
—The Amazing Erik. Huber, Mike. 2014. (ENG.). 32p. (gr. -1). 15.95 *(978-1-60554-209-6(1))* Redleaf Pr.
—Bree Finds a Friend. Huber, Mike. 2014. (ENG.). 32p. (gr. -1). 15.95 *(978-1-60554-211-9(3))* Redleaf Pr.
—Evette's Invitation. Huber, Mike. 2014. (ENG.). 32p. (gr. -1). 15.95 *(978-1-60554-212-6(1))* Redleaf Pr.
Cowman, Joseph. Gus' Fortunate Misfortune. Pepka, Susan. 2018. (ENG.). 62p. (J). 15.00 ***(978-0-9966422-3-1(4))*** Full Cycle Pubns.
—Habbi: The Hard Working Camel. Daggenhurst, T. S. 2017. (ENG.). 37p. (J). 12.00 ***(978-0-9905819-0-1(X))*** Full Cycle Pubns.
Cowman, Joseph. Jesus & His Friends. Pingry, Patricia A. 2017. (ENG.). 24p. (J). (gr. -1-k). bds. 9.99 *(978-1-945470-24-0(0))* Worthy Publishing.
—K Is for Kindergarten. Dealey, Erin. 2017. (ENG.). 32p. (J). (gr. -1-1). 16.99 *(978-1-58536-995-9(0)*, 204326) Sleeping Bear Pr.
—Mama's Gloves. Huber, Mike. 2014. (ENG.). 32p. (gr. -1). 15.95 *(978-1-60554-210-2(5))* Redleaf Pr.
—Noah & His Friends. Pingry, Patricia A. 2017. (ENG.). 24p. (J). (gr. -1-k). bds. 9.99 *(978-1-945470-25-7(9))* Worthy Publishing.
—Noah Chases the Wind. Worthington, Michelle. 2015. (ENG.). 32p. (J). (gr. -1-3). 16.95 *(978-1-60554-356-7(X))* Redleaf Pr.
—Nothing: Nothing Can Separate You from God's Love! Creech, Natalee. 2019. 32p. (J). (gr. -1-3). 16.99 *(978-0-8249-5703-2(2)*, Worthy Kids/Ideals) Worthy Publishing.
—The Nutcracker's Night Before Christmas. Brockett, Keith. 2015. (ENG.). 32p. (J). (gr. 1-3). 15.99 *(978-1-58536-889-1(X)*, 203954) Sleeping Bear Pr.
—Rita & the Firefighters. Huber, Mike. 2014. (ENG.). 32p. (gr. -1-k). 15.95 *(978-1-60554-208-9(3))* Redleaf Pr.
Cowne, Joanne, jt. illus. see Levy, Ruth.
Cowper-Thomas, Wendy. Colby's New Home. Sinex, Roxana Faith. 2004. (J). pap. *(978-0-87743-705-5(X))* Baha'i Publishing Trust, U.S.
—The First Gift. Cobb, Judith A. 2008. (J). pap. *(978-0-87743-708-6(4))* Baha'i Publishing Trust, U.S.
—Something Important. 2010. (J). *(978-0-87743-711-6(4))* Baha'i Publishing Trust, U.S.
Cox, Birck. The Encyclopedia of Skin & Skin Disorders. Turkington, Carol & Dover, Jeffrey S. 3rd rev. ed. 2006. (Facts on File Library of Health & Living). 480p. (C). (gr. 9). 75.00 *(978-0-8160-6403-8(2))* Facts On File, Inc.
Cox, Brian T. Lions, Lions Everywhere: The Story of Daniel as told by God's Animals. Loesch, Joe. Hutchinson, Cheryl, ed. 2004. (Bible Stories for Kids Ser.). 56p. (J). bds. 16.95 incl. audio compact disk *(978-1-932332-24-7(3))* Toy Box Productions.
Cox, Brian T. Florence Nightingale: Called to Serve with Buffalo Biff & Farley's Raiders. Wood, Jill G. 2006. (Time Traveler's Adventure Ser.). 56p. (J). 13.50 incl. audio compact disk *(978-1-932332-29-2(4))* Toy Box Productions.
—Joshua - Victory Through God: As Told by God's Animals. Loesch, Joe. 2006. 56p. (J). 13.50 incl. audio compact disk *(978-1-932332-62-9(6))* Toy Box Productions.
—Rosa Parks: Not Giving In with Buffalo Bill & Farley's Raiders. Collins, James. 2006. (Time Traveler's Adventure Ser.). 56p. (J). 13.50 incl. audio compact disk *(978-1-932332-17-9(0))* Toy Box Productions.
—Theodore Roosevelt: With Buffalo Bill & Farley's Raiders. Collins, James. 2006. (Time Traveler's Adventure Ser.).

C

56p. (J). 13.50 incl. audio compact disk *(978-1-932332-60-5(X))* Toy Box Productions.

Cox, Carolyn. Lion Children's Bible. Alexander, Pat. 2nd ed. 2004. (ENG.). 256p. (J). (gr. 2-6). pap. 8.99 *(978-0-7459-4912-3(6))* Lion Hudson PLC GBR. Dist: Independent Pubs. Group.

Cox, Chad, jt. illus. see Hillmann, Joe.

Cox, Daniel J. Borealis: A Polar Bear Cub's First Year, 1 vol. Grambo, Rebecca L. 2003. (Wild Beginnings Ser.: 1). (ENG.). 48p. (J). (gr. -1-3). pap. 9.95 *(978-1-55285-465-5(5),* 6e2459b4-75ef-4307-982d-9eb5b8f6b8d6) Whitecap Bks., Ltd. CAN. Dist: Firefly Bks., Ltd.

Cox, Danielle Murrell. My Hair. Cox, Danielle Murrell. 2020. 24p. (J). (gr. -1 — 1). bds. 7.99 *(978-0-06-289765-7(9),* HarperFestival) HarperCollins Pubs.

Cox, David. Bike Daredevils. Arena, Felice & Kettle, Phil. 2004. (J). pap. *(978-1-59336-371-0(0))* Mondo Publishing.

—Bull Riding. Arena, Felice & Kettle, Phil. 2004. (J). pap. *(978-1-59336-370-3(2))* Mondo Publishing.

—I Hate Books! Walker, Kate. 2007. 88p. (J). (gr. 1-4). 16.95 *(978-0-8126-2745-9(8))* Cricket Bks.

—Olympics. Arena, Felice & Kettle, Phil. 2004. (J). pap. *(978-1-59336-374-1(5))* Mondo Publishing.

—Race Car Dreamers. Arena, Felice & Kettle, Phil. 2004. (J). pap. *(978-1-59336-375-8(3))* Mondo Publishing.

Cox, Glendyne Dewhurst. Haley Honeybee: Finds the Magic Rose. Burton M.Sc., Kathryn Mac. Diarmid. 2013. 50p. pap. *(978-0-9917941-0-2(9))* Burton, K. Publishing.

Cox, Janis. The Kingdom of Thrim. Cox, Janis. 2017. (ENG.). (J). pap. 9.99 *(978-0-9952290-2-0(3))* Creativity Pr.

Cox, Jennifer. Parchburg Tears. James, Sy. 2019. (ENG.). 52p. (J). (gr. 2-6). pap. 16.95 ***(978-1-64388-203-1(1))*** Luminare Pr., LLC.

Cox, Jon. Crazy Man & the Plums. 2005. (Wind River Stories Ser.). (ENG & ARP.). 32p. (J). 14.95 *(978-0-9759806-1-3(0))* Painted Pony, Inc.

—Yuse: The Bully & the Bear. Washakie, John. 2nd ed. 2004. 47p. (J). 14.95 *(978-0-9759806-0-6(2))* Painted Pony, Inc.

Cox, Kim. Chester's Presents. McNease, Mitzy. ed. 2006. 28p. (J). 10.95 *(978-0-9779488-0-2(3))* Blancmange Publishing LLC.

Cox, Kristine. The Human/Symbiote War. Cox, Kristine, ed. Cox, Enoch Ashton. 2018. (Symbiote Creator Ser.: Vol. 2). (ENG.). 116p. (J). pap. 10.30 *(978-1-7310-6151-5(X))* Independently Published.

Cox, Nancy. Elise the Elephant. Campbell, Jennifer. 2012. 32p. pap. 16.99 *(978-1-4567-9920-5(7))* AuthorHouse.

Cox, Palmer. Busy Brownies (Illustrated Edition) 2017. (ENG.). (J). pap. *(978-1-4068-8505-7(3))* Echo Library.

Cox, Palmer. The Brownies: Their Book. Cox, Palmer. ed. 2011. (Dover Children's Classics Ser.). (ENG.). 144p. (Orig.). (J). (gr. 1-6). pap. 7.95 *(978-0-486-21265-4(3))* Dover Pubns., Inc.

Cox, Paul. The Elevator Man. Trachtenberg, Stanley. 2009. 34p. (J). (gr. -1-3). 18.00 *(978-0-8028-5315-8(3))* Eerdmans, William B. Publishing Co.

Cox, Rhonda, photos by. Best Friends. Cox, Rhonda. 2003. (ENG., 16p. (J). pap. 15.00 *(978-1-57274-699-2(8),* BB2126, Bks. for Young Learners) Owen, Richard C. Pubs., Inc.

—Pigs Peek. Cox, Rhonda. 2003. (ENG., 12p. (J). pap. 15.00 *(978-1-57274-698-5(X),* BB2180, Bks. for Young Learners) Owen, Richard C. Pubs., Inc.

Cox, Russ. The Boy Whose Face Froze Like That. Plourde, Lynn. 2020. 32p. (J). (gr. -1-3). 17.99 *(978-0-7624-9347-0(X),* Running Pr. Kids) Running Pr.

—Lost at Sea. Soderberg, Erin. 2019. (Puppy Pirates Ser.: 7). 96p. (J). (gr. 1-4). 5.99 *(978-0-525-57923-6(0),* Random Hse. Bks. for Young Readers) Random Hse. Children's Bks.

Cox, Russ. Sleeping Beauty. Gunderson, Jessica. 2020. (Fairy Tales Ser.). (ENG.). 32p. (J). (gr. k-2). pap. 6.95 ***(978-1-5158-7276-4(9),*** 201237); lib. bdg. 21.32 ***(978-1-5158-7119-4(3),*** 199340) Capstone. (Picture Window Bks.).

Cox, Russ. This Cowgirl Ain't Kiddin' about the Potty. Fortson, Sarah Glenn. 2019. (J). *(978-1-4413-3165-6(4))* Peter Pauper Pr. Inc.

—The Tortoise & the Hare, Narrated by the Silly but Truthful Tortoise. Loewen, Nancy. 2018. (Other Side of the Fable Ser.). (ENG.). 24p. (J). (gr. -1-3). lib. bdg. 27.99 *(978-1-5158-2867-9(0),* 138405, Picture Window Bks.) Capstone.

—Whatever Says Mark: Knowing & Using Punctuation, 1 vol. Collins, Terry. 2013. (Language on the Loose Ser.). (ENG.). 24p. (J). (gr. 2-4). 28.65 *(978-1-4048-8318-5(5),* Picture Window Bks.) Capstone.

Cox, Russ, jt. illus. see Guerlais, Gérald.

Cox, Steve. Amazing Life of Jesus. Zobel-Nolan, Allia. 2005. 10p. (J). 10.99 *(978-0-8254-5522-3(7))* Kregel Pubns.

—Ants in My Pants. Vantrease, Norma. 2004. (Rookie Readers Ser.). 31p. (J). 12.60 *(978-0-7569-4280-9(2))* Perfection Learning Corp.

—Ants in My Pants. Vantrease, Norma. 2004. (Rookie Reader Skill Set Ser.). (ENG.). 32p. (J). (gr. k-2). pap. 4.95 *(978-0-516-25839-3(7),* Children's Pr.) Scholastic Library Publishing.

—Bible Adventures. Ellis, Gwen. 2006. 20p. (J). (gr. -1-k). bds. 9.49 *(978-0-7586-1130-7(7))* Concordia Publishing Hse.

—Boris the Boastful Frog. Hodgson, Karen J. 2015. 32p. (J). (gr. -1-1). pap. 9.99 *(978-1-907432-10-1(8))* Hogs Back Bks. GBR. Dist: Independent Pubs. Group.

—The Bremen Town Ghosts. Blevins, Wiley. 2017. (Scary Tales Retold Ser.). (ENG.). 24p. (J). (gr. k-3). pap. 6.99 *(978-1-63440-169-2(7),* 9781634401692) Red Chair Pr.

—The Bremen Town Ghosts. Blevins, Wiley. 2017. (Scary Tales Retold Ser.). (ENG.). 24p. (J). (gr. k-3). lib. bdg. 23.99 *(978-1-63440-165-4(4))* Red Chair Pr.

—The Cat, the Mouse, & the Runaway Train. Bently, Peter. 2013. (J). *(978-1-4351-4968-7(8))* Barnes & Noble, Inc.

—Cinderella & the Vampire Prince. Blevins, Wiley. 2016. (Scary Tales Retold Ser.). (ENG.). 24p. (J). (gr. k-3). lib. bdg. 23.99 *(978-1-63440-090-9(9))* Red Chair Pr.

—Goldilocks & the Three Ghosts. Blevins, Wiley. 2016. (Scary Tales Retold Ser.). (ENG.). 24p. (J). (gr. k-3). lib. bdg. 23.99 *(978-1-63440-093-0(3))* Red Chair Pr.

—Hansel & Gretel & the Haunted Hut. Blevins, Wiley. 2016. (Scary Tales Retold Ser.). (ENG.). 24p. (J). (gr. k-3). pap. 6.99 *(978-1-63440-097-8(6))* Red Chair Pr.

—Hansel & Gretel & the Haunted Hut. Blevins, Wiley. 2016. (Scary Tales Retold Ser.). (ENG.). 24p. (J). (gr. k-3). lib. bdg. 23.99 *(978-1-63440-096-1(8))* Red Chair Pr.

—Is That You, Monster? Check Inside the Secret Pockets If You Dare! 2013. (Not a Bedtime Story! Ser.). (ENG.). 22p. (J). (gr. -1-1). 12.99 *(978-0-7641-6608-2(5),* B.E.S. Publishing) Peterson's.

—Jack & the Bloody Beanstalk. Blevins, Wiley. 2016. (Scary Tales Retold Ser.). (ENG.). 24p. (J). (gr. k-3). lib. bdg. 23.99 *(978-1-63440-099-2(2))* Red Chair Pr.

—Leah & Leshawn Build a Letter. Lynette, Rachel. 2012. (Writing Builders Ser.). 32p. (J). (gr. 2-4). pap. 11.94 *(978-1-60357-390-0(9));* lib. bdg. 25.27 *(978-1-59953-510-4(6))* Norwood Hse. Pr.

—Little Dead Riding Hood. Blevins, Wiley. 2016. (Scary Tales Retold Ser.). (ENG.). 24p. (J). (gr. k-3). lib. bdg. 23.99 *(978-1-63440-102-9(6))* Red Chair Pr.

—The Marvelous Toy. Paxton, Tom. 2014. 22p. (J). (gr. -1-2). bds. 7.95 *(978-1-62354-043-2(7))* Charlesbridge Publishing, Inc.

—Moses' Big Adventure. Nolan, Allia Zobel. 2004. 12p. (J). bds. 10.99 *(978-0-8254-5521-6(9))* Kregel Pubns.

—Mother Goose Rhyme Time Animals. Faurot, Kimberly. 2006. 68p. (gr. -1-1). pap. 16.95 *(978-1-932146-66-0(0),* Upstart Bks.) Highsmith Inc.

—Mother Goose Rhyme Time Night. Faurot, Kimberly. 2006. 72p. (gr. -1-1). pap. 16.95 *(978-1-932146-65-3(2),* Upstart Bks.) Highsmith Inc.

—Mother Goose Rhyme Time People. Faurot, Kimberly. 2006. 66p. (gr. -1-1). pap. 16.95 *(978-1-932146-67-7(9),* Upstart Bks.) Highsmith Inc.

—Mrs. Paddington & the Silver Mousetraps: A Hair-Raising History of Women's Hairstyles in 18th-Century London. Skroback Hennessey, Gail. 2020. (ENG.). 40p. (J). (gr. 3-6). 18.99 *(978-1-63440-900-1(0))* Red Chair Pr.

—Peek & Find Bible Stories. Zobel-Nolan, Allia. 2003. 14p. (J). (gr. -1-k). bds. 7.49 *(978-0-7586-0413-2(0))* Concordia Publishing Hse.

—Peek & Find Christmas Story. Zobel-Nolan, Allia. 2004. 14p. (J). bds. 7.49 *(978-0-7586-0718-8(0))* Concordia Publishing Hse.

—The Princess & the Poison Pea. Blevins, Wiley. 2017. (Scary Tales Retold Ser.). (ENG.). 24p. (J). (gr. k-3). pap. 6.99 *(978-1-63440-170-8(0))* Red Chair Pr.

—The Princess & the Poison Pea. Blevins, Wiley. 2017. (Scary Tales Retold Ser.). (ENG.). 24p. (J). (gr. k-3). lib. bdg. 23.99 *(978-1-63440-166-1(2),* 9781634401661) Red Chair Pr.

—Rapunzel & the Werewolf. Blevins, Wiley. 2017. (Scary Tales Retold Ser.). (ENG.). 24p. (J). (gr. k-3). pap. 6.99 *(978-1-63440-171-5(9))* Red Chair Pr.

—Rapunzel & the Werewolf. Blevins, Wiley. 2017. (Scary Tales Retold Ser.). (ENG.). 24p. (J). (gr. k-3). lib. bdg. 23.99 *(978-1-63440-167-8(0),* 9781634401678) Red Chair Pr.

—Snow White & the Seven Trolls. Blevins, Wiley. 2016. (Scary Tales Retold Ser.). (ENG.). 24p. (J). (gr. k-3). lib. bdg. 23.99 *(978-1-63440-105-0(0))* Red Chair Pr.

—Stuff! Reduce, Reuse, Recycle, 0 vols. Kroll, Steven. 2012. (ENG.). 32p. (J). (gr. -1-3). pap. 7.99 *(978-0-7614-6237-8(6),* 9780761462378, Two Lions) Amazon Publishing.

—Ten Missing Princesses. Blevins, Wiley. 2017. (Scary Tales Retold Ser.). (ENG.). 24p. (J). (gr. k-3). pap. 6.99 *(978-1-63440-172-2(7),* 9781634401722) Red Chair Pr.

—Ten Missing Princesses. Blevins, Wiley. 2017. (Scary Tales Retold Ser.). (ENG.). 24p. (J). (gr. k-3). lib. bdg. 23.99 *(978-1-63440-168-5(9))* Red Chair Pr.

Cox, Tom. Things My Father Taught Me Through Sports. . . Playing the Game of Football. Maiocco, Chris & Maiocco, Kimberly. 2003. 24p. (J). 12.99 *(978-0-9720417-1-3(0))* His Kids Publishing, Inc.

—Things My Father Taught Me Through Sports... Playing the Game of Baseball: Playing the Game of Baseball. Maiocco, Chris & Maiocco, Kimberly. 2003. 20p. (J). 12.99 *(978-0-9720417-0-6(2),* 0-9720417-0-2) His Kids Publishing, Inc.

Cox, Val. Freaksville. Keswick, Kitty. 2010. 328p. (YA). (gr. 8-12). pap. 16.99 *(978-1-61603-001-8(1))* Leap Bks.

—Under My Skin. Graves, Judith. 2010. 328p. (YA). (gr. 8-18). pap. 16.99 *(978-1-61603-000-1(3))* Leap Bks.

Coxe, Molly. Blues for Unicorn: Long Vowel U. Coxe, Molly. 2019. (Bright Owl Bks.). (ENG.). 40p. (J). (gr. -1-1). 27.99 *(978-1-63592-109-0(0));* pap. 5.99 *(978-1-63592-110-6(4))* Astra Publishing Hse.

—Cubs in a Tub: Short Vowel U. Coxe, Molly. 2018. (Bright Owl Bks.). (ENG.). 40p. (J). (gr. -1-1). pap. 5.99 *(978-1-57565-985-5(9));* lib. bdg. 27.99 *(978-1-57565-984-8(0))* Astra Publishing Hse.

—Go Home, Goat. Coxe, Molly. 2019. (Bright Owl Bks.). (ENG.). 40p. (J). (gr. -1-1). 27.99 *(978-1-63592-100-7(7))* Astra Publishing Hse.

—Greedy Beetle. Coxe, Molly. 2019. (Bright Owl Bks.). (ENG.). 40p. (J). (gr. -1-1). 27.99 *(978-1-63592-103-8(1))* Astra Publishing Hse.

—Hop Frog: Short Vowel O. Coxe, Molly. 2018. (Bright Owl Bks.). (ENG.). 40p. (J). (gr. -1-1). pap. 5.99 *(978-1-57565-982-4(4));* lib. bdg. 27.99 *(978-1-57565-981-7(6))* Astra Publishing Hse.

—Lion Spies a Tiger: Long Vowel I. Coxe, Molly. 2019. (Bright Owl Bks.). (ENG.). 40p. (J). (gr. -1-1). 27.99 *(978-1-63592-106-9(6))* Astra Publishing Hse.

—Princess Pig: Short Vowel I. Coxe, Molly. 2018. (Bright Owl Bks.). (ENG.). 40p. (J). (gr. -1-1). pap. 5.99 *(978-1-57565-979-4(4));* lib. bdg. 27.99 *(978-1-57565-978-7(6))* Astra Publishing Hse.

—Rat Attack: Short Vowel A. Coxe, Molly. 2018. (Bright Owl Bks.). (ENG.). 40p. (J). (gr. -1-1). pap. 5.99 *(978-1-57565-973-2(5));* lib. bdg. 27.99 *(978-1-57565-972-5(7))* Astra Publishing Hse.

—Wet Hen: Short Vowel E. Coxe, Molly. 2018. (Bright Owl Bks.). (ENG.). 40p. (J). (gr. -1-1). pap. 5.99 *(978-1-57565-976-3(X));* lib. bdg. 27.99 *(978-1-57565-975-6(1))* Astra Publishing Hse.

Coxon, Michele. Oh No, Woolly Bear!, 1 vol. McFadden, Patricia. 2008. (ENG.). 32p. (J). (gr. -1-3). 6.50 *(978-1-59572-149-5(5))* Star Bright Bks., Inc.

Coxon, Michele. Have You Fed the Cat?, 1 vol. Coxon, Michele. 2004. (ENG.). 32p. (J). 15.95 *(978-1-932065-90-9(3))* Star Bright Bks., Inc.

—Have You Fed the Cat? (Spanish/English) Coxon, Michele. 2004. (SPA & ENG.). 32p. (J). 15.95 *(978-1-59572-001-6(4));* pap. 5.95 *(978-1-59572-002-3(2))* Star Bright Bks., Inc.

—Kitten's Adventure (Spanish/English), 1 vol. Coxon, Michele. 2006. (SPA.). 32p. (J). (gr. -1-k). pap. 5.95 *(978-1-59572-048-1(0))* Star Bright Bks., Inc.

—Termites on a Stick: A Chimp Learns to Use a Tool, 1 vol. Coxon, Michele. 2008. (ENG.). 32p. (J). (gr. -1-3). 17.95 *(978-1-59572-121-1(5))* Star Bright Bks., Inc.

—Termites on a Stick: A Chimpanzee Learns to Use a Tool, 1 vol. Coxon, Michele. 2008. (ENG.). 32p. (J). pap. 7.95 *(978-1-59572-183-9(5))* Star Bright Bks., Inc.

Coy, Eve. Daddy-Sitting. 2019. (ENG.). 32p. (J). (gr. -1-3). 17.99 *(978-1-328-48989-0(2),* 1716810, Clarion Bks.) Houghton Mifflin Harcourt Trade & Reference Pubs.

Coy, Eve. The Huffalots. Coy, Eve. 2020. (ENG.). 32p. (J). (gr. -1-3). 17.99 ***(978-1-7284-1579-6(9))*** Lerner Publishing Group.

Crabapple, Molly. The Raindrop Keeper. DePalma, Johnny. 2006. (J). per. 8.50 *(978-0-9791127-1-3(0))* Umbrelly Bks.

—The Raindrop Keeper: (Limited Edition Hardcover) DePalma, Johnny. 2006. 50p. (J). 16.50 *(978-0-9791127-8-2(8))* Umbrelly Bks.

—What Flowers Say: And Other Stories. Sand, George. Erskine Hirko, Holly, tr. 2014. (ENG.). 208p. (J). (gr. 2-7). pap. 15.95 *(978-1-55861-857-2(0))* Feminist Pr. at The City Univ. of New York.

Crabtree, Andy. Many Moods of Maddie: Bossy Boots. Hastings, Suanne. 2006. (Baby Sitter Ser.). 24p. (J). (gr. -1-3). *(978-0-9769348-0-6(9))* Tastica, Suanne Creations Inc.

Crabtree, Marc. Gerbils. Crabtree, Marc, photos by. Sjonger, Rebecca & Kalman, Bobbie. 2003. (Pet Care Ser.). (ENG.). 32p. (J). lib. bdg. *(978-0-7787-1752-2(6))* Crabtree Publishing Co.

—Guinea Pigs. Crabtree, Marc, photos by. Kalman, Bobbie & MacAulay, Kelley. 2003. (Pet Care Ser.). (ENG.). 32p. (J). lib. bdg. *(978-0-7787-1755-3(0))* Crabtree Publishing Co.

—Hamsters. Crabtree, Marc, photos by. Sjonger, Rebecca & Kalman, Bobbie. 2003. (Pet Care Ser.). (ENG.). 32p. (J). lib. bdg. *(978-0-7787-1753-9(4))* Crabtree Publishing Co.

—Mice. Crabtree, Marc, photos by. Sjonger, Rebecca & Kalman, Bobbie. 2003. (Pet Care Ser.). (ENG.). 32p. (J). pap. *(978-0-7787-1786-7(0));* lib. bdg. *(978-0-7787-1754-6(2))* Crabtree Publishing Co.

—Ponies. Crabtree, Marc, photos by. MacAulay, Kelley & Kalman, Bobbie. 2004. (Pet Care Ser.). (ENG.). 32p. (J). pap. *(978-0-7787-1790-4(9))* Crabtree Publishing Co.

—Rabbits. Crabtree, Marc, photos by. MacAulay, Kelley & Kalman, Bobbie. 2004. (Pet Care Ser.). (ENG.). 32p. (J). pap. *(978-0-7787-1788-1(7))* Crabtree Publishing Co.

Crabtree, Marc, photos by. Los Cachorros. Sjonger, Rebecca & Kalman, Bobbie. 2006. (Cuidado de las Mascotas Ser.). 32p. (J). (gr. 3-7). (SPA., pap. *(978-0-7787-8477-7(0));* (ENG & SPA., lib. bdg. *(978-0-7787-8455-5(X))* Crabtree Publishing Co.

—Los Caniches o Poodles. MacAulay, Kelley & Kalman, Bobbie. rev. ed. 2007. (Cuidado de las Mascotas Ser.). (SPA & ENG., 32p. (J). (gr. -1-4). pap. *(978-0-7787-8483-8(5))* Crabtree Publishing Co.

—Los Cobayos. Kalman, Bobbie & MacAulay, Kelley. 2006. (Cuidado de las Mascotas Ser.). (SPA., 32p. (J). (gr. 3-7). pap. *(978-0-7787-8479-1(7));* lib. bdg. *(978-0-7787-8457-9(6))* Crabtree Publishing Co.

—Los Cocker Spaniel. MacAulay, Kelley & Kalman, Bobbie. rev. ed. 2007. (Cuidado de las Mascotas Ser.). (SPA., 32p. (J). (gr. 1-5). pap. *(978-0-7787-8480-7(0))* Crabtree Publishing Co.

—Cocker Spaniels. MacAulay, Kelley & Kalman, Bobbie. 2006. (Pet Care Ser.). (ENG., 32p. (J). (gr. -1-3). pap. *(978-0-7787-1792-8(5),* 1259503); lib. bdg. *(978-0-7787-1760-7(7),* 1259503) Crabtree Publishing Co.

—Los Dálmatas. MacAulay, Kelley & Kalman, Bobbie. rev. ed. 2007. (Cuidado de las Mascotas Ser.). (SPA., 32p. (J). (gr. 1-5). pap. *(978-0-7787-8481-4(9))* Crabtree Publishing Co.

—Dalmatians. MacAulay, Kelley & Kalman, Bobbie. 2006. (Pet Care Ser.). (ENG., 32p. (J). (gr. -1-3). pap. *(978-0-7787-1793-5(3),* 1259504); lib. bdg. *(978-0-7787-1761-4(5),* 1259504) Crabtree Publishing Co.

—Los Gatitos. Walker, Niki & Kalman, Bobbie. 2006. (Cuidado de las Mascotas Ser.). (SPA., 32p. (J). (gr. 3-7). pap. *(978-0-7787-8476-0(2));* lib. bdg. *(978-0-7787-8454-8(1))* Crabtree Publishing Co.

—Los Hamsters. Sjonger, Rebecca & Kalman, Bobbie. 2006. (Cuidado de las Mascotas Ser.). (ENG & SPA., 32p. (J). (gr. 3-7). lib. bdg. *(978-0-7787-8456-2(8))* Crabtree Publishing Co.

—Judo in Action. Crossingham, John & Kalman, Bobbie. 2005. (Sports in Action Ser.). (ENG., 32p. (J). (gr. 2-3). pap. *(978-0-7787-0362-4(2))* Crabtree Publishing Co.

—Labrador Retrievers. MacAulay, Kelley & Kalman, Bobbie. 2006. (Pet Care Ser.). (ENG., 32p. (J). (gr. -1-4). lib. bdg. *(978-0-7787-1762-1(3))* Crabtree Publishing Co.

—Los Hámsters. Sjonger, Rebecca & Kalman, Bobbie. 2006. (Cuidado de las Mascotas Ser.). (SPA & ENG., 32p. (J). (gr. 3-7). pap. *(978-0-7787-8478-4(9))* Crabtree Publishing Co.

—Los Perros Labrador. MacAulay, Kelley & Kalman, Bobbie. rev. ed. 2007. (Cuidado de las Mascotas Ser.). (SPA & ENG., 32p. (J). (gr. -1-4). pap. *(978-0-7787-8482-1(7))* Crabtree Publishing Co.

—Poodles. MacAulay, Kelley & Kalman, Bobbie. 2006. (Pet Care Ser.). (ENG., 32p. (J). (gr. -1-4). lib. bdg. *(978-0-7787-1763-8(1),* 1259506) Crabtree Publishing Co.

—Taekwondo in Action. MacAulay, Kelley & Kalman, Bobbie. 2004. (Sports in Action Ser.). (ENG., 32p. (J). pap. *(978-0-7787-0358-7(4))* Crabtree Publishing Co.

—Yoga in Action. MacAulay, Kelley & Kalman, Bobbie. 2005. (Sports in Action Ser.). (ENG., 32p. (J). (gr. 2-3). pap. *(978-0-7787-0364-8(9))* Crabtree Publishing Co.

Crabtree, Marc & Rouse, Bonna. Field Events in Action. Crabtree, Marc, photos by. Kalman, Bobbie. 2004. (Sports in Action Ser.). (ENG.). 32p. (J). lib. bdg. *(978-0-7787-0340-2(1))* Crabtree Publishing Co.

Crabtree, Marc, jt. illus. see Reiach, Margaret Amy.

Crabtree Staff. Mustang. 2010. (Superstar Cars Ser.). (ENG.). 64p. (J). pap. *(978-0-7787-2152-9(3))* Crabtree Publishing Co.

Crackboom Staff. Peep Through ... My Animals. 2018. 22p. (J). (gr. -1). bds. 7.99 *(978-2-924786-27-7(4),* CrackBoom! Bks.) Chouette Publishing CAN. Dist: Publishers Group West (PGW).

—Peep Through ... My Colors. 2018. 22p. (J). (gr. -1). bds. 7.99 *(978-2-924786-29-1(0),* CrackBoom! Bks.) Chouette Publishing CAN. Dist: Publishers Group West (PGW).

—Peep Through ... My Numbers. 2018. 22p. (J). (gr. -1). bds. 7.99 *(978-2-924786-25-3(8),* CrackBoom! Bks.) Chouette Publishing CAN. Dist: Publishers Group West (PGW).

—Peep Through ... My Vehicles. 2018. 22p. (J). (gr. -1). bds. 7.99 *(978-2-924786-31-4(2),* CrackBoom! Bks.) Chouette Publishing CAN. Dist: Publishers Group West (PGW).

Craddock, Erik. BC Mambo. Craddock, Erik. 2009. (Stone Rabbit Ser.: 1). (ENG.). 96p. (J). (gr. 3-7). pap. 6.99 *(978-0-375-84360-0(4),* Random Hse. Bks. for Young Readers) Random Hse. Children's Bks.

—Deep-Space Disco. Craddock, Erik. 2009. (Stone Rabbit Ser.: 3). 96p. (J). (gr. 3-7). pap. 6.99 *(978-0-375-85876-5(8),* Random Hse. Bks. for Young Readers) Random Hse. Children's Bks.

—Night of the Living Dust Bunnies. Craddock, Erik. 2011. (Stone Rabbit Ser.: 6). 96p. (J). (gr. 3-7). pap. 6.99 *(978-0-375-86724-8(4),* Random Hse. Bks. for Young Readers) Random Hse. Children's Bks.

—Ninja Slice. Craddock, Erik. 2010. (Stone Rabbit Ser.: 5). 96p. (J). (gr. 3-7). pap. 6.99 *(978-0-375-86723-1(6),* Random Hse. Bks. for Young Readers) Random Hse. Children's Bks.

—Robot Frenzy. Craddock, Erik. 2013. (Stone Rabbit Ser.: 8). 96p. (J). (gr. 2-5). pap. 6.99 *(978-0-375-86913-6(1),* Random Hse. Bks. for Young Readers) Random Hse. Children's Bks.

—Stone Rabbit #8: Robot Frenzy. Craddock, Erik. 2013. (Stone Rabbit Ser.: 8). (ENG.). 96p. (J). (gr. 2-5). lib. bdg. 12.99 *(978-0-375-96913-3(6),* Random Hse. Bks. for Young Readers) Random Hse. Children's Bks.

—Superhero Stampede: Stone Rabbit #4. Craddock, Erik. 2010. (Stone Rabbit Ser.: 4). 96p. (J). (gr. 3-7). pap. 6.99 *(978-0-375-85877-2(6),* Random Hse. Bks. for Young Readers) Random Hse. Children's Bks.

Craft, Danna. Sereena's Secret. Harris, Rae Ann & Weintraub, David. 2005. (ENG & YID.). 40p. (J). 16.95 *(978-1-932687-41-5(6));* pap. 9.95 *(978-1-932687-42-2(4))* Simcha Media Group. (Devora Publishing).

Craft, Donna. Benjamin's Big Lesson. Laven, Zp. 2011. 20p. pap. 12.95 *(978-1-61493-009-9(0))* Peppertree Pr., The.

—Happy for a Honk & a Wave. McGregor, Janet C. 2010. 20p. pap. 12.95 *(978-1-936343-04-1(5))* Peppertree Pr., The.

Craft, James. Five Little Honeybees. 2009. (ENG.). 12p. 5.95 *(978-1-58117-907-1(3),* Intervisual/Piggy Toes) Bendon, Inc.

Craft, Jerry. Looking to the Clouds for Daddy. Candelario, Margo. 2009. (J). *(978-0-9820221-7-7(4))* Hunter, Karen Media.

—The Zero Degree Zombie Zone. Bass, Patrik Henry. 2014. (ENG.). 144p. (J). (gr. 3-7). 16.99 *(978-0-545-13210-7(X),* Scholastic Pr.) Scholastic, Inc.

Craft, Jerry. New Kid. Craft, Jerry. 2019. (ENG.). 256p. (J). (gr. 3-7). 21.99 *(978-0-06-269120-0(1));* pap. 12.99 *(978-0-06-269119-4(8))* HarperCollins Pubs.

Craft, K. Y. Christmas Moon. Craft, Mahlon. 2003. 32p. (J). 15.95 *(978-1-58717-056-0(6));* lib. bdg. *(978-1-58717-057-7(4))* Chronicle Bks. LLC. (SeaStar Bks.).

Craft, Kinuko Y. The Adventures of Tom Thumb. Mayer, Marianna. 2005. 28p. (J). (gr. k-4). reprint ed. 16.00 *(978-0-7567-9642-6(3))* DIANE Publishing Co.

—Beauty & the Beast. Craft, Mahlon F. 2016. (ENG.). 32p. (J). (gr. -1-3). 17.99 *(978-0-06-053919-1(4),* HarperCollins) HarperCollins Pubs. Ltd. GBR. Dist: HarperCollins Pubs.

—King Midas & the Golden Touch. Craft, Charlotte. 2003. (ENG.). 32p. (J). (gr. -1-3). pap. 7.99 *(978-0-06-054063-0(X))* HarperCollins Pubs.

Craft, Liz. What Color Will It Be? Abud Jr, Gary. 2019. (Science with Scarlett Ser.: Vol. 1). (ENG.). 36p. (J). (gr. -1-3). 25.00 *(978-1-64300-999-5(0));* pap. 14.95 *(978-1-64300-998-8(2))* Covenant Bks.

Cragg, Marcelyn Martin. Amanda & the Angel. Hutchings, Harriet Anne. 2010. 24p. pap. 9.95 *(978-1-936051-81-6(8))* Peppertree Pr., The.

Craig & Karl. Sticker Art Jungle. 2017. (Sticker Art Ser.). (ENG.). 24p. (J). (gr. -1-k). pap. 7.99 *(978-1-78603-004-7(7),* Frances Lincoln Children's Bks.) Quarto Publishing Group UK GBR. Dist: Hachette Bk. Group.

—Sticker Art Savanna. 2017. (Sticker Art Ser.). (ENG.). 24p. (J). (gr. -1-k). pap. 7.99 *(978-1-78603-006-1(3),* Frances Lincoln Children's Bks.) Quarto Publishing Group UK GBR. Dist: Hachette Bk. Group.

—Sticker Art Woodland. 2017. (Sticker Art Ser.). (ENG.). 24p. (J). (gr. -1-k). pap. 7.99 *(978-1-78603-007-8(1),* Frances

Lincoln Children's Bks.) Quarto Publishing Group UK GBR. Dist: Hachette Bk. Group.

Craig, Branden Chapin & Chapin, Jimmy. Thunder Is Not Scary. Rehberg, Emily. 2013. 26p. pap. 12.00 *(978-0-9800108-3-1(7))* Bilbo Bks.

Craig, Charles. Saint John Paul II: Be Not Afraid. Wallace, Susan Helen. 2011. (Encounter the Saints Ser.). 128p. (J). (gr. 3-7). pap. 8.95 *(978-0-8198-1178-3(5))* Pauline Bks. & Media.

Craig, Charlie. Joseph from Germany: The Life of Pope Benedict XVI for Children. Mohan, Claire Jordan. 2007. 38p. (J). 8.95 *(978-0-8198-3988-6(4))* Pauline Bks. & Media.

Craig, Chris. Indigo Boy & Crystalline Girl. McCracken, Connie. 2009. 24p. pap. 10.95 *(978-1-4269-0423-3(1))* Trafford Publishing.

Craig, Dan. Mom Has Left & Gone to Vegas. Dasilva, D. 2008. 32p. pap. 19.95 *(978-1-59858-603-9(3))* Dog Ear Publishing, LLC.

Craig, Daniel. The Light of Christmas. Evans, Richard Paul. 2016. (ENG.). 32p. (J). (gr. -1-3). 9.99 *(978-1-4814-6612-7(7)*, Aladdin) Simon & Schuster Children's Publishing.

Craig, David. A Day That Changed America - The Alamo: Surrounded & Outnumbered,They Chose to Make a Defiant Last Stand. Tanaka, Shelley. 2003. (ENG.). 48p. (gr. 3-17). 16.99 *(978-0-7868-1923-2(5))* Hyperion Pr.

—Earthquake! A Day That Changed America. Tanaka, Shelley. 2006. 48p. (J). (gr. 4-8). reprint ed. 17.00 *(978-1-4223-5635-7(3))* DIANE Publishing Co.

—Gettysburg: The Legendary Battle & the Address That Inspired a Nation. Tanaka, Shelley. 2003. (Day That Changed America Ser.). (ENG.). 48p. 16.99 *(978-0-7868-1922-5(7))* Hyperion Pr.

—Hudson. Weaver, Janice. 2010. 48p. (J). (gr. 3-7). 22.95 *(978-0-88776-814-9(8)*, Tundra Bks.) Tundra Bks. CAN. Dist: Penguin Random Hse. LLC.

—A Is for Airplane: An Aviation Alphabet. Riehle, Mary Ann McCabe. 2009. (Science Alphabet Ser.). (ENG.). 40p. (J). (gr. 1-4). 19.99 *(978-1-58536-358-2(8)*, 202143) Sleeping Bear Pr.

—The Long White Scarf, 1 vol. Trottier, Maxine. 2005. (ENG.). 32p. (J). *(978-1-55005-147-6(4))* Fitzhenry & Whiteside, Ltd.

Craig, Gary. I Can Be Anything Creative Activity Book. Craig, Gary. 2006. 41p. (J). pap. 5.99 *(978-0-9786813-2-6(0))* Elora Pr.

Craig, Helen. Amy's Three Best Things. Pearce, Philippa. 2013. (ENG.). 40p. (J). (gr. -1-3). 15.99 *(978-0-7636-6314-8(X))* Candlewick Pr.

Craig, Helen. Angelina & the Princess. Holabird, Katharine. 2020. (Angelina Ballerina Ser.). (ENG.). 32p. (J). (gr. -1-3). 17.99 ***(978-1-5344-6961-7(3)***, Little Simon) Little Simon.

Craig, Helen. Angelina Ballerina. Holabird, Katharine. 2019. (Angelina Ballerina Ser.). (ENG.). 32p. (J). (gr. -1-3). 17.99 *(978-1-5344-5151-3(X)*, Little Simon) Little Simon.

—Angelina Ballerina & the Tea Party. Holabird, Katharine. 2019. (Angelina Ballerina Ser.). (ENG.). 32p. (J). (gr. -1-1). 17.99 *(978-1-5344-5427-9(6))*; pap. 4.99 *(978-1-5344-5426-2(8))* Simon Spotlight. (Simon Spotlight).

Craig, Helen. Angelina Ballerina Dresses Up. Holabird, Katharine. 2020. (Angelina Ballerina Ser.). (ENG.). 32p. (J). (gr. -1-1). pap. 7.99 ***(978-1-5344-6951-8(6)***, Simon Spotlight) Simon Spotlight.

—Angelina Ballerina Loves Ice-Skating! Holabird, Katharine. 2020. (Angelina Ballerina Ser.). (ENG.). 22p. (J). (gr. -1-k). bds. 7.99 ***(978-1-5344-6959-4(1)***, Simon Spotlight) Simon Spotlight.

—Angelina Ballerina Tries Again. Holabird, Katharine. 2020. (Angelina Ballerina Ser.). (ENG.). 32p. (J). (gr. -1-1). 17.99 ***(978-1-5344-6446-9(8))***; pap. 4.99 ***(978-1-5344-6445-2(X))*** Simon Spotlight. (Simon Spotlight).

Craig, Helen. Angelina Ice Skates. Holabird, Katharine. 2006. (Angelina Ballerina (8x8) Ser.). (ENG.). (J). (gr. -1-2). lib. bdg. 17.60 *(978-0-7569-7320-9(1))* Perfection Learning Corp.

—Angelina Loves. Holabird, Katharine. 2019. (Angelina Ballerina Ser.). (ENG.). 22p. (J). (gr. -1-k). bds. 6.99 *(978-1-5344-5686-0(4)*, Simon Spotlight) Simon Spotlight.

—Angelina's Perfect Party. Holabird, Katharine. 2011. (Angelina Ballerina Ser.). (ENG.). 24p. (J). (gr. -1-1). 17.44 *(978-0-448-45617-1(6))* Penguin Young Readers Group.

—The Bunny Who Found Easter Gift Edition. Zolotow, Charlotte. 2018. (ENG.). 40p. (J). (gr. -1-3). 8.99 *(978-1-328-69467-6(4)*, 1671423, HMH Books For Young Readers) Houghton Mifflin Harcourt Publishing Co.

—Center Stage. Holabird, Katharine. 2019. (Angelina Ballerina Ser.). (ENG.). 16p. (J). (gr. -1-3). 6.99 *(978-1-5344-5482-8(9)*, Simon Spotlight) Simon Spotlight.

—A Dance of Friendship. Holabird, Katharine. 2006. (Angelina Ballerina Ser.). (ENG.). 23p. (J). (gr. -1-1). 16.19 *(978-0-448-44115-3(2))* Penguin Young Readers Group.

Craig, Helen. Dancing Day. Holabird, Katharine. 2020. (Angelina Ballerina Ser.). (ENG.). 14p. (J). (gr. -1-k). bds. 6.99 ***(978-1-5344-6304-2(6)***, Simon Spotlight) Simon Spotlight.

Craig, Helen. A Day at Miss Lilly's. Holabird, Katharine. 2007. (Angelina Ballerina Ser.). (ENG.). 24p. (J). (gr. -1-1). pap. 4.99 *(978-0-448-44548-9(4)*, Grosset & Dunlap) Penguin Publishing Group.

—A Finder's Magic. Pearce, Philippa. 2009. (ENG.). 128p. (J). (gr. 2-4). 15.99 *(978-0-7636-4072-9(7))* Candlewick Pr.

Craig, Helen. Meet Angelina Ballerina. Holabird, Katharine. 2020. (Angelina Ballerina Ser.). (ENG.). 24p. (J). (gr. -1-2). pap. 5.99 ***(978-1-5344-4250-4(2)***, Simon Spotlight) Simon Spotlight.

—Sleepover Party! Holabird, Katharine. 2020. (Angelina Ballerina Ser.). (ENG.). 32p. (J). (gr. -1-1). 17.99 ***(978-1-5344-6954-9(0))***; pap. 4.99 ***(978-1-5344-6953-2(2))*** Simon Spotlight. (Simon Spotlight).

Craig, Helen. Snowy Sunday. Root, Phyllis. 2015. (ENG.). 24p. (J). (-k). 14.99 *(978-0-7636-3627-2(4))* Candlewick Pr.

—The Yellow House. Morrison, Blake. 2011. (ENG.). 32p. (J). (gr. -1-2). 15.99 *(978-0-7636-4959-3(7))* Candlewick Pr.

Craig, Johnny. The Vault of Horror, Vol. 3. Gaines, Bill et al. Chabon, Daniel, ed. 2014. (ENG.). 200p. 49.99 *(978-1-61655-292-3(1))* Dark Horse Comics.

Craig, Johnny, jt. illus. see Tuska, George.

Craig, Karen. One for Me, One for You: A Book about Sharing. Albee, Sarah. 2006. (Blue's Clues Ser.: 20). (ENG.). 24p. (J). (gr. -1-3). pap. 3.99 *(978-1-4169-1300-9(9)*, Simon Spotlight/Nickelodeon) Simon Spotlight/Nickelodeon.

—A Visit to the Firehouse. Tuchman, Lauryn & Silverhardt, Lauryn. 2009. (Blue's Clues Ser.). (ENG.). 24p. (J). (gr. -1-2). pap. 3.99 *(978-1-4169-7193-1(9)*, Simon Spotlight/Nickelodeon) Simon Spotlight/Nickelodeon.

Craig, Megan. Hello Big Red! Aryal, Aimee. 2004. 24p. (J). 19.95 *(978-1-932888-24-9(1))* Mascot Bks., Inc.

—Hello, Hook 'Em! Aryal, Aimee. 2004. 24p. (J). (gr. -1-3). lib. bdg. 19.95 *(978-1-932888-10-2(1))* Mascot Bks., Inc.

—Hello, Pistol Pete! Aryal, Aimee. 2007. 24p. (J). lib. bdg. 14.95 *(978-1-932888-38-6(1))* Mascot Bks., Inc.

—Howdy Reveille! Aryal, Aimee. 2004. 24p. (J). 19.95 *(978-1-932888-18-8(7))* Mascot Bks., Inc.

Craigan, Charles J. Mayuk the Grizzly Bear: A Legend of the Sechelt People. braille ed. 2004. (J). (gr. k-3). spiral bd. *(978-0-616-07562-3(6))* Canadian National Institute for the Blind/Institut National Canadien pour les Aveugles.

Craighead, Hailey. Grayson's Goggles. McBride, Roxie. 2019. (Alphabet Vocabulary Ser.: Vol. 3). (ENG.). 42p. (J). (gr. k-4). pap. 9.99 ***(978-1-0878-1831-3(1))*** Children's Author.

Craighead, Hailey. The Little Book Monster That Ate My Puppy Book. Callaway, Janice W. 2019. (ENG.). 34p. (J). (gr. k-2). pap. 10.00 *(978-0-578-46569-2(8))* Callaway, Janice.

—Spectacular Shenanigans. McBride, Roxie. 2018. (ENG.). 84p. (J). (gr. k-6). pap. 12.99 *(978-0-692-13151-0(5))* Children's Author.

Crain, Clayton. Cable Vol. 2: The Newer Mutants. 2018. (ENG.). 112p. (YA). (gr. 8-17). pap. 15.99 *(978-1-302-90483-8(3))* Marvel Worldwide, Inc.

—Carnage, U. S. A. Wells, Zeb. 2017. (ENG.). 112p. (YA). (gr. 8-17). pap. 19.99 *(978-1-302-90741-9(7))* Marvel Worldwide, Inc.

—Spider-Geddon. 2019. (ENG.). 200p. (J). (gr. 4-17). pap. 24.99 *(978-1-302-91475-2(8))* Marvel Worldwide, Inc.

—Venom vs. Carnage. 2007. 96p. (YA). (gr. 8-17). pap. 9.99 *(978-0-7851-1524-3(2))* Marvel Worldwide, Inc.

Crain, Clayton, et al. X-Men Milestones: Necrosha. 2020. (ENG.). 448p. (YA). (gr. 8-17). pap. 39.99 ***(978-1-302-92395-2(1))*** Marvel Worldwide, Inc.

Craine, Nick. I Can Read Fearless Girls #1: Roberta Bondar: I Can Read Level 1. Howden, Sarah. 2019. (ENG.). 32p. (J). (gr. -1-2). pap. 4.99 *(978-1-4434-5981-5(X)*, Collins) HarperCollins Pubs.

—I Can Read Fearless Girls #2: Misty Copeland: I Can Read Level 1. Howden, Sarah. 2019. (ENG.). 32p. (J). (gr. -1-2). pap. 4.99 *(978-1-4434-5982-2(8)*, Collins) HarperCollins Pubs.

—I Can Read Fearless Girls #3: Viola Desmond: I Can Read Level 1. Howden, Sarah. 2019. (ENG.). 32p. (J). (gr. -1-2). pap. 4.99 *(978-1-4434-5983-9(6)*, Collins) HarperCollins Pubs.

—I Can Read Fearless Girls #4: Lucy Maud Montgomery: I Can Read Level 1. Howden, Sarah. 2019. (ENG.). 32p. (J). (gr. -1-2). pap. 4.99 *(978-1-4434-5984-6(4)*, Collins) HarperCollins Pubs.

—I Can Read Fearless Girls #5: Michelle Obama: I Can Read Level 1. Howden, Sarah. 2019. (ENG.). 32p. (J). (gr. -1-2). pap. 4.99 *(978-1-4434-5985-3(2)*, Collins) HarperCollins Pubs.

—I Can Read Fearless Girls #6: Ruth Graves Wakefield: I Can Read Level 1. Howden, Sarah. 2019. (ENG.). 32p. (J). (gr. -1-2). pap. 4.99 *(978-1-4434-5986-0(0)*, Collins) HarperCollins Pubs.

—I Can Read Hockey Stories: Hayley's Journey. Howden, Sarah. 2018. (I Can Read Hockey Stories Ser.). (ENG.). 32p. (J). (gr. -1-3). pap. 4.99 *(978-1-4434-5733-0(7)*, Collins) HarperCollins Pubs.

—I Can Read Hockey Stories: Hockey at Home. Braithwaite, Meg. 2018. (I Can Read Hockey Stories Ser.). (ENG.). 32p. (J). (gr. -1-3). pap. 4.99 *(978-1-4434-5734-7(5)*, Collins) HarperCollins Pubs.

—I Can Read Hockey Stories: the Best First Game. Braithwaite, Meg. 2018. (I Can Read Hockey Stories Ser.). (ENG.). 32p. (J). (gr. -1-3). pap. 4.99 *(978-1-4434-5730-9(2)*, Collins) HarperCollins Pubs.

—I Can Read Hockey Stories: the Golden Goal. Braithwaite, Meg. 2018. (I Can Read Hockey Stories Ser.). (ENG.). 32p. (J). (gr. -1-3). pap. 4.99 *(978-1-4434-5732-3(9)*, Collins) HarperCollins Pubs.

—I Can Read Hockey Stories: the Masked Man. Braithwaite, Meg. 2018. (I Can Read Hockey Stories Ser.). (ENG.). 32p. (J). (gr. -1-3). pap. 4.99 *(978-1-4434-5729-3(9)*, Collins) HarperCollins Pubs.

—I Can Read Hockey Stories: What's in a Number. Braithwaite, Meg. 2018. (I Can Read Hockey Stories Ser.). (ENG.). 32p. (J). (gr. -1-3). pap. 4.99 *(978-1-4434-5731-6(0)*, Collins) HarperCollins Pubs.

—Lucy Maud Montgomery: Creator of Anne of Green Gables: I Can Read Level 1. Howden, Sarah. 2020. (ENG.). 32p. (J). pap. 4.99 *(978-1-4434-6026-2(5)*, Collins) HarperCollins Pubs.

—Michelle Obama: First Lady & Superhero: I Can Read Level 1. Howden, Sarah. 2020. (ENG.). 32p. (J). pap. 4.99 *(978-1-4434-6027-9(3)*, Collins) HarperCollins Pubs.

—Misty Copeland: Ballet Star: I Can Read Level 1. Howden, Sarah. 2020. (ENG.). 32p. (J). pap. 4.99 *(978-1-4434-6024-8(9)*, Collins) HarperCollins Pubs.

—Roberta Bondar: Space Explorer: I Can Read Level 1. Howden, Sarah. 2020. (ENG.). 32p. (J). pap. 4.99 *(978-1-4434-6023-1(0)*, Collins) HarperCollins Pubs.

—Ruth Graves Wakefield: One Smart Cookie: I Can Read Level 1. Howden, Sarah. 2020. (ENG.). 32p. (J). pap. 4.99 *(978-1-4434-6028-6(1)*, Collins) HarperCollins Pubs.

—Viola Desmond: a Hero for Us All: I Can Read Level 1. Howden, Sarah. 2020. (ENG.). 32p. (J). pap. 4.99 *(978-1-4434-6025-5(7)*, Collins) HarperCollins Pubs.

—5-Minute Basketball Stories. Howden, Sarah. 2018. (J). (gr. k-2). 172p. 16.99 *(978-1-4434-5716-3(7))*; 176p. 15.99 *(978-1-4434-5672-2(1))* HarperCollins Pubs. (Collins).

—5-Minute Hockey Stories. Braithwaite, Meg. 2017. (ENG.). 192p. (J). (gr. -1-2). 14.50 *(978-1-4434-5398-1(6))* HarperCollins Pubs.

—5-Minute Stories for Fearless Girls. Howden, Sarah. 2018. 176p. (J). 16.99 *(978-1-4434-5542-8(3)*, Collins) HarperCollins Pubs.

Craker, James a. The Cloud That Fell to Earth. Craker, James a. Lane, Jennifer, ed. 2016. (ENG.). (J). pap. *(978-0-9956795-0-4(9))* Kixel Publishing.

Cramer. A Year Without Dad. Brunson, Jodi. 2003. (J). per. 10.00 *(978-0-9740683-1-2(4))* Authors & Artists Publishers of New York, Inc.

Cramer, Rie. Grimm's Fairy Tales. Racehorse for Young Readers & The Brothers Grimm. 2018. (Children's Classic Collections). 176p. (J). (gr. -1-3). 12.99 *(978-1-63158-252-3(6)*, Racehorse Publishing) Skyhorse Publishing Co., Inc.

Crampton, Shane. Scarlett's Spectacles: A Cheerful Choice for a Happy Heart. Surette, Janet. 2019. (ENG.). 24p. (J). (gr. -1-2). bds. 12.99 *(978-1-5359-5905-6(3)*, 005815433, B&H Kids) B&H Publishing Group.

Crampton, Shane. Stay Wild My Child. Archer, Mandy. 2020. (ENG.). 40p. (J). (gr. -1-3). 16.99 ***(978-1-77402-121-7(8))*** Kidsbooks, LLC.

—Surgery on Sunday. Harrison, Kat. 2020. (ENG.). 28p. (J). (gr. k-4). 17.95 ***(978-1-7347075-0-2(X))***; pap. 9.95 ***(978-1-7347075-1-9(8))*** Warren Publishing, Inc.

Crampton, Shane. Yoga Baby. Flinn, Amanda. 2020. (ENG.). 24p. (J). (gr. -1 — 1). bds. 7.99 *(978-1-5064-5699-7(5)*, Beaming Books) Augsburg Fortress, Pubs.

Crane, Ben. Tall Tales of the Wild West: A Humorous Collection of Cowboy Poems & Songs. Ode, Eric. 2007. 32p. *(978-0-88166-524-6(X))* Meadowbrook Pr.

Crane, Devin. Yoda: The Story of a Cat & His Kittens. Stern, Beth. 2014. 32p. (J). (gr. -1-3). 18.99 *(978-1-4814-4407-1(7)*, Aladdin) Simon & Schuster Children's Publishing.

—Yoda Gets a Buddy. Stern, Beth. 2015. (ENG.). 32p. (J). (gr. -1-3). 17.99 *(978-1-4814-6969-2(X)*, Aladdin) Simon & Schuster Children's Publishing.

Crane, Eddie. Little Gregory. Bradex, Melissa A. 2009. 32p. pap. 14.99 *(978-1-4490-3549-5(3))* AuthorHouse.

Crane, Jordan & Burkert, Nancy Ekholm. James & the Giant Peach: (Penguin Classics Deluxe Edition) Dahl, Roald. 2011. (Penguin Classics Deluxe Edition Ser.). 160p. (gr. 3-7). 16.00 *(978-0-14-310634-0(1)*, Penguin Classics) Penguin Publishing Group.

Crane, Noelle L. The Clever Pug. Crane, Noelle L. 2013. 66p. pap. 9.99 *(978-0-9846119-8-0(3))* Pluriverse Publishing.

Crane, Robert, photos by. Counting Colors in Texas, 1 vol. Kralovansky, Susan. 2018. (SPA & ENG., 10p. bds. 9.95 *(978-1-4556-2383-9(0)*, Pelican Publishing) Arcadia Publishing.

Crane, Walter. Beauty & the Beast. Beaumont, Jeanne Marie Le Prince De. 2013. 28p. pap. *(978-1-909115-62-0(2))* Planet, The.

—Bedtime Stories: Little Red Riding Hood & Puss In Boots. Perrault, Charles. 2019. (ENG.). 36p. (J). *(978-1-910880-74-6(4))* Robin Bks. Ltd.

—The Children's Plutarch: Tales of the Romans. Gould, F. J. 2012. 260p. *(978-1-78139-160-0(2))* Benediction Classics.

—A Christmas Posy (Illustrated Edition) Molesworth. 2018. (ENG.). 108p. (J). pap. *(978-1-4068-8750-1(1))* Echo Library.

—Goldilocks & the Three Bears. Old Mother Hubbard. Jacobs, Joseph. 2018. (ENG.). 32p. (J). *(978-1-910880-58-6(2))* Robin Bks. Ltd.

Crane, Walter. Grimms' Fairy Tales (Illustrated by Walter Crane) Grimm, Jacob & Grimm, Wilhelm. 2016. (ENG.). 194p. (J). ***(978-1-78139-729-9(5))*** Benediction Classics.

Crane, Walter. Grimm's Household Stories. Grimm, Wilhelm. Crane, Lucy, tr. 2010. (Vintage Books Restored Ser.: Vol. 8). (ENG.). 316p. (J). pap. *(978-606-92253-7-0(6))* Mediamorphosis.

—Jack & the Beanstalk. Jacobs, Joseph. 2013. 20p. pap. *(978-1-909115-63-7(0))* Planet, The.

Crane, Walter, et al. Mother Goose's Nursery Rhymes: A Collection of Alphabets, Rhymes, Tales, & Jingles. 2010. (ENG.). 324p. (gr. -1-k). pap. 19.95 *(978-1-4290-9005-6(7))* Applewood Bks.

Crane, Walter. Mr Michael Mouse Unfolds His Tale. 2011. 36p. pap. 35.95 *(978-1-258-07891-1(0))* Literary Licensing, LLC.

—Toy Book. l.t. ed. 2012. (Vintage Books Restored Ser.: Vol. 9). (ENG.). 86p. (J). pap. *(978-606-92253-6-3(8))* Mediamorphosis.

Crane, Walter. The Baby's Opera - a Book of Old Rhymes with New Dresses - Illustrated by Walter Crane. Crane, Walter. 2016. (ENG.). (J). *(978-1-4733-3494-6(2))* Read Bks.

—Baby's Own Aesop - Being the Fables Condensed in Rhyme with Portable Morals - Illustrated by Walter Crane. Crane, Walter. 2016. (ENG.). (J). *(978-1-4733-3488-5(8))* Read Bks.

—The Song of Sixpence Picture Book - Containing Sing a Song of Sixpence, Princess Belle Etoile, an Alphabet of Old Friends - Illustrated by Walter Crane. Crane, Walter. 2016. (ENG.). (J). *(978-1-4733-3493-9(4))* Read Bks.

Crane, Walter & Hood, Jacomb. The Happy Prince & Other Tales. Wilde, Oscar. 2019. (ENG.). 56p. (J). pap. 5.50 *(978-1-0986-7488-5(X))* Independently Published.

Crane, Walter & Hood, Jacomb. The Happy Prince & Other Tales (1888) Collection of Stories for Children. Wilde, Oscar. 2019. (ENG.). 96p. (J). pap. 7.60 ***(978-1-6984-6866-2(0))*** Independently Published.

Craner, Ben. I Can Be a Missionary, Too. Craner, Ben, tr. 2003. (J). *(978-1-57008-965-7(5))* Deseret Bk. Co.

Cranford, Darren. Aerial: A Spider's Tale. ReWalt, Nancy E. 2009. 32p. (J). 16.95 *(978-0-9821110-0-0(2))* Ronan Enterprises, Inc.

—Aerial: A Trip to Remember. ReWalt, Nancy E. 2010. 32p. (J). 16.95 *(978-0-9821110-1-7(0))* Ronan Enterprises, Inc.

—Aerial Meets Farmer Fedamore. Rewalt, Nancy E. 2012. 64p. (J). 17.95 *(978-0-9821110-3-1(7))* Ronan Enterprises, Inc.

—Jeep: The Coyote Who Flew in World War II. Moller, Sharon Chickering. 2014. 59p. (J). pap. 9.95 *(978-0-9860799-0-0(1))* Chickering-Moller Project.

—Lost & Found: Goldilocks & the Three Bears Revisited. Rewalt, Nancy E. 2012. 64p. (J). pap. 6.95 *(978-0-9821110-2-4(9))* Ronan Enterprises, Inc.

—PawPrints on Your Heart. White, Becky. 2013. 64p. (J). 18.95 *(978-0-9860169-0-5(X))* Vision Chapters Publishing Co.

—The Sugar Goblin: The Return of Tricks for Treats. Boyle, Crystal & Boyle, Michael. 2015. 32p. (J). 16.99 *(978-0-9860859-0-1(1))* Sugar Goblin LLC, The.

Crangle, Claudine. Priscilla the Pack Rat: Making Room for Friendship. 2017. 32p. (J). 15.95 *(978-1-4338-2335-0(7)*, Magination Pr.) American Psychological Assn.

—Woolfred Does Not Eat Dandelions. 2014. 32p. (J). *(978-1-4338-1672-7(5))*; pap. *(978-1-4338-1673-4(3))* American Psychological Assn. (Magination Pr.).

Crank, Donny. Cluck, Cluck, Cluck Splash! Kruse, Donald W. 2012. 48p. pap. 12.95 *(978-1-59663-856-3(7)*, Castle Keep Pr.) Rock, James A. & Co. Pubs.

—Fleas, Please. Kruse, Donald W. 2012. 48p. pap. 12.95 *(978-1-59663-858-7(3)*, Castle Keep Pr.) Rock, James A. & Co. Pubs.

—The Ghost of Wolverine Forest, Part 3: Azazel's Revenge! Kruse, Donald W. 2nd ed. 2019. (Ghost of Wolverine Forest Ser.: Vol. 3). (ENG.). 84p. (YA). (gr. 7-12). pap. 8.99 *(978-0-9994571-7-7(9))* Zaccheus Entertainment Co.

—Gorilla Soup! Kruse, Donald W. 2017. (ENG.). (J). (gr. k-5). pap. 14.95 *(978-0-9981972-2-7(X))* Zaccheus Entertainment Co.

—Hey, Charlie! Kruse, Donald W. 2017. (ENG.). (J). (gr. k-6). pap. 14.95 *(978-0-9981972-1-0(1))* Zaccheus Entertainment Co.

—Jasper Has Left the Building! Kruse, Donald W. 2013. 50p. pap. 12.95 *(978-1-59663-863-1(X)*, Castle Keep Pr.) Rock, James A. & Co. Pubs.

—Jasper Has Returned! Kruse, Donald W. 2016. (ENG.). (J). (gr. k-5). pap. 14.95 *(978-0-9969964-8-8(6))* Zaccheus Entertainment Co.

—Monster at o'Malley's Mansion. Kruse, Donald W. 2016. (ENG.). (J). (gr. k-5). pap. 14.95 *(978-0-9969964-9-5(4))* Zaccheus Entertainment Co.

—Take a Bath — -Please! Kruse, Donald W. 2017. (ENG.). (J). (gr. k-5). pap. 14.95 *(978-0-9969964-0-2(0))* Zaccheus Entertainment Co.

—There's a Goof on My Roof. Kruse, Donald W. 2012. 48p. pap. 12.95 *(978-1-59663-855-6(9)*, Castle Keep Pr.) Rock, James A. & Co. Pubs.

—There's a Goof on My Roof! Kruse, Donald W. 2017. (ENG.). (J). (gr. k-5). pap. 14.95 *(978-0-9981972-3-4(8))* Zaccheus Entertainment Co.

—Waldo, Blue, & Glad Max Too! Kruse, Donald W. 2017. (ENG.). (J). (gr. k-6). pap. 14.95 *(978-0-9981972-0-3(3))* Zaccheus Entertainment Co.

Cratty, Aaron. The Stuff in the Back of the Desk. Brink, LeeAnn. 2006. 24p. (J). per. 10.95 *(978-1-934246-05-4(0))* Peppertree Pr., The.

Cravath, Lynne. Big Max & the Mystery of the Missing Giraffe. Platt, Kin. 2006. (I Can Read Level 2 Ser.). (ENG.). 64p. (J). (gr. k-3). pap. 4.99 *(978-0-06-009920-6(8))* HarperCollins Pubs.

Cravath, Lynne Avril. Amazing You! Getting Smart about Your Private Parts. Saltz, Gail. 2008. (ENG.). 32p. (J). (gr. -1-2). pap. 7.99 *(978-0-14-241058-5(6)*, Puffin Books) Penguin Young Readers Group.

—Amazing You: Getting Smart about Your Private Parts: A First Guide to Body Awareness for Pre-Schoolers. Saltz, Gail. 2005. 32p. (J). (gr. -1-2). 17.99 *(978-0-525-47389-3(0)*, Dutton Books for Young Readers) Penguin Young Readers Group.

—Big Max & the Mystery of the Missing Giraffe. Platt, Kin. 2005. (I Can Read Bks.). 64p. (J). (gr. -1). 15.99 *(978-0-06-009918-3(6))*; lib. bdg. 17.89 *(978-0-06-009919-0(4))* HarperCollins Pubs.

—Changing You! A Guide to Body Changes & Sexuality. Saltz, Gail. 2009. 32p. (J). (gr. 1-3). pap. 6.99 *(978-0-14-241479-8(4)*, Puffin Books) Penguin Young Readers Group.

—The Twelve Days of Christmas in Louisiana. Cassels, Jean. 2007. (Twelve Days of Christmas in America Ser.). 40p. (J). (gr. k-3). 12.95 *(978-1-4027-3814-2(5))* Sterling Publishing Co., Inc.

Cravath, Lynne Avril & Avril, Lynne. The Show-and-Tell Lion. Abercrombie, Barbara. 2006. (ENG.). 32p. (J). (gr. -1-2). 19.99 *(978-0-689-86408-7(6)*, McElderry, Margaret K. Bks.) McElderry, Margaret K. Bks.

Craven, Josh. Hayrides. Craven, Josh. 2011. 16p. pap. 24.95 *(978-1-4626-1123-2(0))* America Star Bks.

Crawford, Alice. Splish, Splat!, 1 vol. Domney, Alexis. 2011. (ENG.). 24p. (J). (gr. 1-3). 15.95 *(978-1-897187-88-3(2))* Second Story Pr. CAN. Dist: Orca Bk. Pubs. USA.

Crawford, Andy, photos by. Bread & Pizza. Blake, Susannah. 2009. (Make & Eat Ser.). 24p. (J). (gr. 3-5). 27.25 *(978-1-4358-2858-2(5)*, PowerKids Pr.) Rosen Publishing Group, Inc., The.

—Cookies & Cakes. Blake, Susannah. 2009. (Make & Eat Ser.). 24p. (J). (gr. 3-5). 27.25 *(978-1-4358-2859-9(3)*, PowerKids Pr.) Rosen Publishing Group, Inc., The.

—Sandwiches & Snacks. Blake, Susannah. 2009. (Make & Eat Ser.). 24p. (J). (gr. 5). 27.25 *(978-1-4358-2857-5(7)*, PowerKids Pr.) Rosen Publishing Group, Inc., The.

—This Is My Dump Truck. Oxlade, Chris. 2008. (Mega Machine Drivers Ser.). 30p. (J). (gr. k). lib. bdg. 28.50 *(978-1-59771-105-0(5))* Sea-To-Sea Pubns.

—Vegetarian Food. Blake, Susannah. 2009. (Make & Eat Ser.). 24p. (J). (gr. 3-5). 27.25 *(978-1-4358-2860-5(7),* PowerKids Pr.) Rosen Publishing Group, Inc., The.

Crawford, Andy, photos by. Fun with Opposites. Crawford, Andy. (J). pap. 9.99 *(978-0-590-24640-8(2))* Scholastic, Inc.

Crawford, Dale. Tales of Tails from the Blue Heron Ranch, Grandbear the Storyteller. 2nd l.t. ed. 2003. 128p. (J). per. 12.00 *(978-0-9729759-0-2(X))* Guru Graphics.

Crawford, Elizabeth. Cave: An Evocation of the Beginnings of Art. Hirose, George, photos by. Lewis, Richard. 2003. (ENG.). 56p. pap. 14.00 *(978-1-929299-03-4(6))* Touchstone Ctr. Pubns.

Crawford, Greg. The Flying Mouse. Otten, Charlotte. 2014. (ENG.). 32p. (J). (gr. -1-3). 17.95 *(978-1-59373-152-6(3))* Bunker Hill Publishing, Inc.

Crawford, Gregory. I Can Show You I Care: Compassionate Touch for Children. Cotta, Susan. 2003. 32p. (J). (gr. k-4). 18.95 *(978-1-55643-433-4(2))* North Atlantic Bks.

Crawford, Gregory. Harriet's Hairballs. Crawford, Gregory, tr. Chin, Oliver Clyde. 2003. 32p. (J). 15.95 *(978-1-58394-078-5(2),* Frog Ltd.) North Atlantic Bks.

Crawford, K. Trouble in Troublesome Creek. Allen, Nancy. 2011. (ENG.). 32p. (gr. -1-3). pap. 11.95 *(978-1-933176-36-9(9))* Red Rock Pr., Inc.

Crawford, K. Michael. The Munched-up Flower Garden. 2006. (Troublesome Creek Kids Story Ser.). (ENG.). 32p. (J). (gr. -1-3). 16.95 *(978-1-933176-04-8(0));* pap. 10.95 *(978-1-933176-06-2(7))* Red Rock Pr., Inc.

—Trouble in Troublesome Creek: A Troublesome Creek Kids Story. Allen, Nancy Kelly. 2010. (ENG.). 32p. (J). (gr. -1-3). 16.95 *(978-1-933176-32-1(6))* Red Rock Pr., Inc.

Crawford, K. Michael. The Mystery of Journeys Crowne-an Adventure Drawing Game. Crawford, K. Michael. 2008. 52p. pap. 14.95 *(978-0-9817940-0-6(9))* Virtualbookworm.com Publishing, Inc.

Crawford, L. H. Tales of Mr. Snuggywhiskers: The Spring Tales. Crawford, C. F. 2016. (ENG.). (J). (gr. 2-5). pap. 11.00 *(978-0-9976422-1-6(1))* Lauco Pr.

—Tales of Mr. Snuggywhiskers: The Summer Tales. Crawford, C. F. 2018. (ENG.). 188p. (J). (gr. 1-5). pap. 11.00 *(978-0-9976422-3-0(8))* Lauco Pr.

Crawford, Mel. Dale Evans & the Lost Gold Mine. Hill, Monica. 2011. 32p. pap. 35.95 *(978-1-258-01715-6(6))* Literary Licensing, LLC.

—Gene Autry. Fletcher, Steffi. 2011. 32p. pap. 35.95 *(978-1-258-02076-7(9))* Literary Licensing, LLC.

—Gerald Mcboing Boing. Seuss, Dr. 2017. (Classic Seuss Ser.). (ENG.). 40p. (J). (gr. k-4). 16.99 *(978-1-5247-1635-6(9));* lib. bdg. 19.99 *(978-1-5247-1757-5(6))* Random Hse. Children's Bks. (Random Hse. Bks. for Young Readers).

—Rin Tin Tin & the Outlaw. Verral, Charles Spain. 2011. 28p. pap. 35.95 *(978-1-258-04034-5(4))* Literary Licensing, LLC.

—Roy Rogers & Cowboy Toby. Beecher, Elizabeth. 2011. 30p. 35.95 *(978-1-258-03514-3(6))* Literary Licensing, LLC.

Crawford, Mel, jt. illus. see Helweg, Hans.

Crawford, Robert. The Legend of the Old Man of the Mountain. Ortakales, Denise. 2004. (Legends Ser.). (ENG.). 40p. (J). 17.95 *(978-1-58536-236-3(0))* Sleeping Bear Pr.

—Poetry for Kids: Carl Sandburg. Sandburg, Carl. Benzel, Kathryn, ed. 2017. (ENG.). 48p. (J). (gr. 3-8). 16.95 *(978-1-63322-151-2(2),* 224355, Moondance) Quarto Publishing Group USA.

—T Is for Taj Mahal: An India Alphabet. Bajaj, Varsha. 2011. (Discover the World Ser.). (ENG.). 40p. (J). (gr. k-6). 17.95 *(978-1-58536-504-3(1))* Sleeping Bear Pr.

Crawford-White, Helen. Dream on, Amber. Shevah, Emma. (ENG.). (J). (gr. 3-7). 2016. 288p. pap. 11.99 *(978-1-4926-3592-5(8),* 9781492635925); 2015. 272p. 12.99 *(978-1-4926-2250-5(8),* 9781492622505) Sourcebooks, Inc. (Sourcebooks Jabberwocky).

—Dream on, Amber. Shevah, Emma. ed. 2016. (ENG.). 272p. (J). (gr. 3-7). 18.40 *(978-0-606-39305-8(6))* Turtleback.

—The Little Mermaid. Andersen, Hans Christian. Hoekstra, Misha, tr. 2020. (ENG.). 64p. (J). (gr. 2-5). pap. 9.99 *(978-1-78269-249-2(5),* Pushkin Children's Bks.) Steerforth Pr.

Crawley, Annie. Plastic, Ahoy! Investigating the Great Pacific Garbage Patch. Newman, Patricia. 2014. (ENG.). 48p. (J). (gr. 3-6). lib. bdg. 30.65 *(978-1-4677-1283-5(3),* 9781467712835, Millbrook Pr.) Lerner Publishing Group.

Crawley, Annie, photos by. Zoo Scientists to the Rescue. Newman, Patricia. 2017. (ENG.). 64p. (J). (gr. 4-8). lib. bdg. 33.32 *(978-1-5124-1571-1(5),* 9781512415711, Millbrook Pr.) Lerner Publishing Group.

Crawley, Ceron. Mike at the Aquarium. Oliver, Sw. 2019. (Mike Ser.: Vol. 1). (ENG.). 26p. (J). pap. 9.99 *(978-1-393-79226-0(X))* Draft2Digital.

Creagh, Lachlan. Ambush at Cisco Swamp. Irwin, Robert & Wells, Jack. 2014. (Robert Irwin Dinosaur Hunter Ser.: 2). 96p. (J). (gr. 2-4). 7.99 *(978-1-86471-846-1(3))* Random Hse. Australia AUS. Dist: Independent Pubs. Group.

—Armoured Defence. Irwin, Robert & Wells, Jack. 2014. (Robert Irwin Dinosaur Hunter Ser.: 3). 96p. (J). (gr. 2-4). 7.99 *(978-1-74275-091-0(5))* Random Hse. Australia AUS. Dist: Independent Pubs. Group.

—The Dinosaur Feather. Irwin, Robert & Wells, Jack. 2014. (Robert Irwin Dinosaur Hunter Ser.: 4). 96p. (J). (gr. 2-4). 7.99 *(978-1-74275-092-7(3))* Random Hse. Australia AUS. Dist: Independent Pubs. Group.

Creamer, Joan Klatil. The Magic Sceptre - the Legend of Blue Santa Claus. Creamer, Joan Klatil. ed. 2006. 32p. (J). 16.95 *(978-0-9778476-3-1(2))* Silver Snowflake Publishing.

Creamer, Kathy. Splash! Cowley, Joy. 2004. (ENG.). 8p. (gr. 1-1). pap. 3.97 net. *(978-1-56270-764-4(7),* Dominie Elementary) Savvas Learning Co.

Create, INKmagine and. Blanklines: Black. Halverson, Care. 2019. (Blanklines Journal Ser.: Vol. 2). (ENG.). 116p. (J). pap. 5.99 *(978-1-7979-6919-0(6))* Independently Published.

—BlankLines: Brush & Quill Grey. Halverson, Care. 2019. (Blanklines Journal Ser.: Vol. 6). (ENG.). 116p. (J). pap. 5.99 *(978-1-0987-6199-8(5))* Independently Published.

—Blanklines: Purple Wolf. Halverson, Care. 2019. (Blanklines Journal Ser.: Vol. 3). (ENG.). 116p. (J). pap. 5.99 *(978-1-7986-6811-5(4))* Independently Published.

Creations, Adriatica & Studios, Milktee. Beware the Violet. Miller, Sara, ed. 2019. (Eulogimenoi Ser.: Vol. 1). (ENG.). 378p. (J). pap. 13.99 ***(978-1-6958-5359-1(8))*** Independently Published.

Creations, Muje. The Holiday Boys & the Tall Man: A Creation of Teachable Lessons for Children. Daniel, Onicka J. 2017. (ENG.). (J). pap. 12.99 *(978-0-692-95713-4(8))* Daniel, Onicka J.

Creative, Howell Edwards. Movies Are Magic: A Kid's History of the Moving Image from the Dawn of Time to About 1939. Churchill, Jennifer Anne. 2018. (Movies Are Magic Ser.: Vol. 1). (ENG.). 34p. (J). pap. 16.95 *(978-1-7243-6430-2(8))* CreateSpace Independent Publishing Platform.

Creative Illustrations Studio & Good Times At Home LLC. The Night Before Christmas. Moore, Clement C. & Curto Family, The. 2012. (J). pap. 9.99 *(978-0-9840338-5-0(8))* Good Times at Home LLC.

Creative, Roundhouse. I Can Throw a Tantrum Too! Carriera, Angelina. 2016. (ENG.). (J). pap. *(978-0-9944325-2-0(6))* Ralston, Angelina.

—MR & Mrs Bloodsucker's Travel Adventure. Carriera, Angelina. 2016. (ENG.). (J). pap. *(978-0-9944325-5-1(0))* Ralston, Angelina.

—The Only Planet. Carriera, Angelina. 2016. (ENG.). (J). pap. *(978-0-9944591-3-8(0))* Ralston, Angelina.

—The Sugar Hunting Party Poo-Pers. Carriera, Angelina. 2016. (ENG.). (J). pap. *(978-0-9944325-0-6(X))* Ralston, Angelina.

—The Sugar Hunting Party Poo-Pers: The Play. Carriera, Angelina. 2016. (ENG.). (J). pap. *(978-0-9944325-1-3(8))* Ralston, Angelina.

—Who Will Be in Heaven? The Boys' Version. Carriera, Angelina. 2016. (ENG.). (J). pap. *(978-0-9944325-4-4(2))* Ralston, Angelina.

—Who Will Be in Heaven? The Girls' Version. Carriera, Angelina. 2016. (ENG.). (J). pap. *(978-0-9944325-3-7(4))* Ralston, Angelina.

Crecelius, Tim. The Story Travelers Bible. Madder, Tracey. 2017. (ENG.). 368p. (J). 16.99 *(978-1-4964-0915-7(9),* 20_11548, Tyndale Kids) Tyndale Hse. Pubs.

Creeden, Mitchell. When Pigmen Fly: Redstone Junior High #6. Stevens, Cara J. 2019. (Redstone Junior High Ser.: 6). (ENG.). 192p. (J). (gr. 3-7). pap. 11.99 *(978-1-5107-4110-2(0),* Sky Pony Pr.) Skyhorse Publishing Co., Inc.

Creek, Chris. Who Is This Jesus? A Hidden Picture Book. Creek, Lorie. 2012. (J). 18.99 *(978-1-60908-909-2(X))* Deseret Bk. Co.

Creeper Art, Crafty. Diary of Jack the Kid - a Minecraft LitRPG - FULL Season ONE (1) Unofficial Minecraft Books for Kids, Teens, & Nerds - LitRPG Adventure Fan Fiction Diary Series. Steve, Skeleton. Steve Minecrafty, Wimpy Noob, ed. 2019. (ENG.). 652p. (J). pap. 24.95 ***(978-1-6865-7943-1(8))*** Independently Published.

Creeper Art, Crafty. Diary of Jack the Kid - a Minecraft LitRPG - Season 1 Episode 5 (Book 5) Unofficial Minecraft Books for Kids, Teens, & Nerds - LitRPG Adventure Fan Fiction Diary Series. Steve, Skeleton. Steve Minecrafty, Wimpy Noob, ed. 2019. (Skeleton Steve & the Noob Mobs Minecraft Diaries Collection: Vol. 5). (ENG.). 372p. (J). pap. 14.95 *(978-1-0966-4341-8(3))* Independently Published.

Creeper Art, Crafty. Diary of Jack the Kid - a Minecraft LitRPG - Season 1 Episode 6 (Book 6) Unofficial Minecraft Books for Kids, Teens, & Nerds - LitRPG Adventure Fan Fiction Diary Series. Steve, Skeleton. Steve Minecrafty, Wimpy Noob, ed. 2019. (Skeleton Steve & the Noob Mobs Minecraft Diaries Collection: Vol. 6). (ENG.). 388p. (J). pap. 14.95 ***(978-1-0868-2549-7(7))*** Independently Published.

Creeper Art, Crafty. Diary of Jack the Kid Litrpg - Season 1 Episode 4: An Unofficial Minecraft Book. Steve, Skeleton. Steve Minecrafty, Wimpy Noob, ed. 2019. (Skeleton Steve & the Noob Mobs Minecraft Diaries Collection: Vol. 4). (ENG.). 404p. (J). pap. 14.95 *(978-1-7950-4260-4(5))* Independently Published.

—Diary of Minecraft Skeleton Steve the Noob Years - Season 5 Episode 1 (Book 25) Unofficial Minecraft Books for Kids, Teens, & Nerds - Adventure Fan Fiction Diary Series. Steve, Skeleton. Steve Minecrafty, Wimpy Noob, ed. 2019. (Skeleton Steve & the Noob Mobs Minecraft Diaries Collection: Vol. 25). (ENG.). 378p. (J). pap. 13.95 *(978-1-7930-9819-1(0))* Independently Published.

Creeper Art, Crafty. Diary of Minecraft Skeleton Steve the Noob Years - Season 5 Episode 4 (Book 28) Unofficial Minecraft Books for Kids, Teens, & Nerds - Adventure Fan Fiction Diary Series. Steve, Skeleton. Steve Minecrafty, Wimpy Noob, ed. 2019. (Skeleton Steve & the Noob Mobs Minecraft Diaries Collection: Vol. 28). (ENG.). 320p. (J). pap. 13.95 ***(978-1-6990-8253-9(7))*** Independently Published.

—Diary of Minecraft Skeleton Steve the Noob Years - Season 5 Episode 5 (Book 29) Unofficial Minecraft Books for Kids, Teens, & Nerds - Adventure Fan Fiction Diary Series. Steve, Skeleton. Steve Minecrafty, Wimpy Noob, ed. 2019. (Skeleton Steve & the Noob Mobs Minecraft Diaries Collection: Vol. 29). (ENG.). 312p. (J). pap. 13.95 ***(978-1-6778-4032-8(3))*** Independently Published.

Creeper Art, Crafty. Minecraft Diary of Skeleton Steve the Noob Years - Full Season Four (4) Unofficial Minecraft Books for Kids, Teens, & Nerds - Adventure Fan Fiction Diary Series. Steve, Skeleton. Steve Minecrafty, Wimpy Noob, ed. 2019. (Minecraft Book Collections - Skeleton Steve & the Noob Mobs Ser.: Vol. 16). (ENG.). 706p. (J). pap. 24.95 *(978-1-7938-5684-5(2))* Independently Published.

Crehore, Amy. Machu Picchu: The Story of the Amazing Inkas & Their City in the Clouds. Mann, Elizabeth. 2006. (Wonders of the World Book Ser.). (ENG.). 48p. (J). (gr. 4-8). pap. 12.95 *(978-1-931414-10-4(6),* 6a82696d-260f-49c3-b432-7c04b1cdea4d) Mikaya Pr.

Creighton-Pester, David. Arf! Buzz! Cluck! A Rather Noisy Alphabet. Seltzer, Eric. 2018. (ENG.). 24p. (J). (gr. -1 — 1). bds. 7.99 *(978-1-5344-1297-2(2),* Little Simon) Little Simon.

—Fast Fox & Slow Snail. Treleaven, Lou. 2019. (Early Bird Readers — Blue (Early Bird Stories (tm)) Ser.). (ENG.). 32p. (J). (gr. -1-2). pap. 7.99 *(978-1-5415-4616-5(4))* Lerner Publishing Group.

—God's Protection Covers Me, Vol. Houts, Amy. 2019. (ENG.). 32p. (J). (gr. -1-k). 15.99 *(978-1-5064-4856-5(9),* Beaming Books) Augsburg Fortress, Pubs.

—Max & Bear. Quinn, Susan. 2018. (Story Corner Ser.). (ENG.). 24p. (J). (gr. -1-k). lib. bdg. 19.99 *(978-1-68297-317-2(4))* QEB Publishing Inc.

—Who's Afraid of the Dark? When You're Only Little, the Night Can Be Big & Scary. Joyce, Melanie. 2017. (ENG.). 24p. (J). 9.99 *(978-1-78670-649-2(0))* Igloo Bks. GBR. Dist: Simon & Schuster, Inc.

Crelencia, Archangelo. Running with Reed: Be a Better Somebody Coloring Book. Keen, Tammi Croteau & Kotalik, Reed. 2019. (ENG.). 26p. (J). pap. 5.95 *(978-1-7931-2809-6(X))* Independently Published.

Crème, Aurora C. Two Tipsy Tots, 1 vol. Arnold, Ginger Fudge. 2009. 32p. pap. 24.95 *(978-1-4489-1891-1(X))* America Star Bks.

Cremeans, Robert. La Colonia de Arco Iris. Tiller, Steve. Date not set. (SPA.). (J). 15.95 *(978-1-932317-02-2(3))* Right Stuff Kids Bks.

—Connectada al Corazon. Tiller, Steve. Date not set. (SPA.). (J). 15.95 *(978-1-932317-01-5(5))* Right Stuff Kids Bks.

Crenshaw, Derek. The Dinosaurs Went Marching On. Acopiado, Ginger. 2007. 24p. (J). pap. 4.95 *(978-0-9729093-1-0(1))* Tike Time, Inc.

Crenshaw, Ellen T. Kiss Number 8. Venable, Colleen Af. 2019. (ENG.). 320p. (YA). 24.99 *(978-1-250-19693-4(0),* 900194272); pap. 17.99 *(978-1-59643-709-8(X),* 900074316) Roaring Brook Pr. (First Second Bks.).

Crenshaw, Madison. ABC March. Crenshaw, Dawn. 2020. (ENG.). 30p. (J). pap. 15.00 ***(978-1-7224-4854-7(7))*** CreateSpace Independent Publishing Platform.

Crespo, George. T-Boy of the Bayou. McGaw, Wayne T. 2003. 32p. (J). (gr. -1-3). 15.95 *(978-0-87614-648-4(5),* Carolrhoda Bks.) Lerner Publishing Group.

Cress, Michelle H. Families. Cook, Barbara L. l.t. ed. 2004. (HRL Board Book Ser.). 8p. (J). (gr. -1-1). pap. 10.95 *(978-1-57332-280-5(6),* HighReach Learning, Incorporated) Carson-Dellosa Publishing, LLC.

—Jonah Starts School. Mullican, Judy. l.t. ed. 2003. (HRL Big Book Ser.). 8p. (J). (gr. -1-1). pap. 10.95 *(978-1-57332-268-3(7));* pap. 10.95 *(978-1-57332-269-0(5))* Carson-Dellosa Publishing, LLC. (HighReach Learning, Incorporated).

Cressey, Roger. Owliviah. Winbolt-Lewis, Martin. 2013. 56p. (J). pap. *(978-1-78222-075-6(5))* Paragon Publishing, Rothersthorpe.

Cressey, Roger. The Talking Giraffe. Cressey, Roger. 2013. 118p. pap. *(978-1-78222-143-2(3))* Paragon Publishing, Rothersthorpe.

Cressy, Mike. The Legend of Atlantis, 1 vol. Troupe, Thomas Kingsley. 2012. (Legend Has It Ser.). (ENG.). 32p. (J). (gr. 2-4). lib. bdg. 27.99 *(978-1-4048-6656-0(6),* Picture Window Bks.) Capstone.

Crestan, David. Welcome to School: Helping Friends with Autism. James, Colin & Newton, Jennifer, photos by. Barrette, Melanie. James, Colin, ed. 2005. 16p. (J). (gr. k-6). pap. 12.00 *(978-1-928598-11-4(0))* Pyramid Educational Products, Inc.

Crewe, Robert. My Mommy Prays. Bright, Yvanna D. Crewe, Jan, ed. 2016. (ENG.). (J). pap. 14.99 *(978-0-9981891-0-9(3))* Bright Hse. Publishing, LLC.

Crews, Donald. Fire! 2016. (J). *(978-0-06-237349-6(8),* Greenwillow Bks.) HarperCollins Pubs.

—How Many Blue Birds Flew Away? A Counting Book with a Difference. Giganti, Paul. 2005. 32p. (J). lib. bdg. 16.89 *(978-0-06-000763-8(X))* HarperCollins Pubs.

Crews, Donald. Diez Puntos Negros: Ten Black Dots (Spanish Edition), 1 vol. Crews, Donald. 2009. (SPA.). 32p. (J). (gr. -1-3). 16.99 *(978-0-06-177138-5(4),* HarperCollins Español) HarperCollins Christian Publishing.

—Freight Train. Crews, Donald. 2003. 24p. (J). (SPA & ENG.). lib. bdg., bds. 16.89 *(978-0-06-056203-8(X));* (ENG.). (gr. -1-3). 16.99 *(978-0-688-80165-6(X),* Greenwillow Bks.); (ENG.). (gr. -1-3). pap. 7.99 *(978-0-688-11701-6(5),* Greenwillow Bks.) HarperCollins Pubs.

—Freight Train/Tren de Carga: Bilingual Spanish-English Children's Book. Crews, Donald. 24p. (J). (gr. -1-3). 2008. (ENG.). pap. 7.99 *(978-0-06-056204-5(8));* 2003. (SPA.). 16.99 *(978-0-06-056202-1(1))* HarperCollins Pubs. (Greenwillow Bks.).

—Freight Train/Tren de Carga Board Book: Bilingual Spanish-English Children's Book. Crews, Donald. 2016. (ENG.). 32p. (J). (gr. -1 — 1). bds. 7.99 *(978-0-06-245708-0(X),* Greenwillow Bks.) HarperCollins Pubs.

—Ten Black Dots Board Book. Crews, Donald. 2010. (ENG.). 32p. (J). (gr. -1-3). bds. 7.99 *(978-0-06-185779-9(3),* Greenwillow Bks.) HarperCollins Pubs.

Crews, Nina. The Neighborhood Mother Goose. Crews, Nina. 2003. (ENG.). 64p. (J). (gr. -1-3). 17.99 *(978-0-06-051573-7(2),* Greenwillow Bks.) HarperCollins Pubs.

—The Neighborhood Sing-Along. Crews, Nina. 2011. (ENG.). 64p. (J). (gr. -1-3). 17.99 *(978-0-06-185063-9(2),* Greenwillow Bks.) HarperCollins Pubs.

—Seeing into Tomorrow: Haiku by Richard Wright. Crews, Nina. Wright, Richard. 2018. (ENG.). 32p. (J). (gr. k-4). 19.99 *(978-1-5124-1865-1(X),* Millbrook Pr.) Lerner Publishing Group.

Creyts, Patrick. Easter Extras: Faith-Filled Ideas for Easter Week. Schultz, Joani et al. 2007. 24p. pap. 6.99 *(978-0-7644-3694-9(5))* Group Publishing, Inc.

Crichlow, Ernest. Forever Free: The Story of the Emancipation Proclamation. Sterling, Dorothy. 2012. 216p. 44.95 *(978-1-258-25034-8(9));* pap. 29.95 *(978-1-258-25547-3(2))* Literary Licensing, LLC.

Crilley, Mark. Miki Falls: Autumn. Crilley, Mark. 2007. (Miki Falls Ser.: 3). (ENG.). 176p. (YA). (gr. 8-12). pap. 9.99 *(978-0-06-084618-3(6),* HarperCollins) HarperCollins Pubs. Ltd. GBR. Dist: HarperCollins Pubs.

—Miki Falls: Spring. Crilley, Mark. 2007. (Miki Falls Ser.: 1). (ENG.). 176p. (YA). (gr. 8-12). pap. 8.99 *(978-0-06-084616-9(X))* HarperCollins Pubs.

—Miki Falls: Summer. Crilley, Mark. 2007. (Miki Falls Ser.: 2). (ENG.). 176p. (YA). (gr. 8-12). pap. 8.99 *(978-0-06-084617-6(8))* HarperCollins Pubs.

—Miki Falls: Winter. Crilley, Mark. 2008. (Miki Falls Ser.: 4). (ENG.). 176p. (YA). (gr. 8-12). pap. 9.99 *(978-0-06-084619-0(4))* HarperCollins Pubs.

Crimmins, Carol. The Sun Played Hide-And-Seek: A Personification Story. Cleary, Brian. 2017. (ENG.). 32p. (J). (gr. 2-5). lib. bdg. 26.65 *(978-1-4677-2648-1(6),* 9781467726481, Millbrook Pr.) Lerner Publishing Group.

Crip. Dance Class 3-In-1 #1. Beka. 2019. (Dance Class Graphic Novels Ser.: 1). (ENG.). 160p. (J). pap. 14.99 *(978-1-5458-0533-6(4),* 900197414) Papercutz.

—Dance Class 3-In-1 #2. Beka. 2020. (Dance Class Graphic Novels Ser.: 2). (ENG.). 160p. (J). pap. 14.99 *(978-1-5458-0482-7(6),* 900219635) Papercutz.

Crisenbery, Casey. Ringo the Helpful Raccoon. Kelley, Khris. 2012. 38p. (J). 14.95 *(978-1-937406-70-7(9))* Mascot Bks., Inc.

Crisp, Dan. Animals. Isaacs, Connie. 2018. (Sticker Play Ser.). (ENG.). 60p. (J). (gr. k). pap. 5.99 *(978-1-78700-613-3(1))* Top That! Publishing PLC GBR. Dist: Independent Pubs. Group.

—The Ants Go Marching. (Classic Books with Holes 8x8 with CD Ser.). (J). 2013. (ENG.). 16p. (gr. -1). pap. incl. audio compact disk *(978-1-84643-622-2(2));* 2013. (ENG.). 16p. (gr. -1). pap. *(978-1-84643-618-5(4));* 2009. 16p. (gr. -1-1). spiral bd. *(978-1-84643-207-1(3));* 2009. (ENG.). 16p. pap. incl. audio compact disk *(978-1-84643-256-9(1));* 2007. 14p. spiral bd. *(978-1-84643-109-8(3));* 2007. 16p. (gr. 1-2). pap. *(978-1-84643-105-0(0))* Child's Play International Ltd.

—At the Beach: Look up, Look Around, Look Down: 3-In-1 Board Book. Wing, Scarlett. Cottage Door Press, ed. 2018. (Baby Einstein Ser.). (ENG.). 30p. (J). (gr. -1-1). bds. 9.99 *(978-1-68052-350-8(3),* 1003220) Cottage Door Pr.

—Backyard All Year: Touch & Feel Multi Board Book. Wing, Scarlett. Cottage Door Press, ed. 2017. (Baby Einstein Ser.). (ENG.). 10p. (J). (gr. -1-k). bds. 9.99 *(978-1-68052-224-2(8),* 1002110) Cottage Door Pr.

—Big & Little: Chunky Lift a Flap Board Book. Wing, Scarlett. 2017. (Baby Einstein Ser.). (ENG.). 12p. (J). (gr. -1-k). bds. 7.99 *(978-1-68052-222-8(1),* 1002090) Cottage Door Pr.

—A Bright New Star: With Color-Changing Star Light. Ranson, Erin. 2007. (Story Book Ser.). 16p. (J). (gr. -1-3). bds. *(978-1-84666-161-7(7),* Tide Mill Pr.) Top That! Publishing PLC.

—Busy Bus. Brooks, Felicity & Durber, Matt. 2007. (Play Bks). 10p. (J). bds. 10.99 *(978-0-7945-1701-4(3),* Usborne) EDC Publishing.

—Busy Truck. Allen, Francesca & Brooks, Felicity. 2007. (Usborne Play Bks.). 10p. (J). (gr. -1-k). bds. 10.99 *(978-0-7945-1453-2(7),* Usborne) EDC Publishing.

—Circles & Squares: Chunky Lift a Flap Board Book. Wing, Scarlett. Cottage Door Press, ed. 2017. (Baby Einstein Ser.). (ENG.). 12p. (J). (gr. -1-k). bds. 7.99 *(978-1-68052-280-8(9),* 1002650) Cottage Door Pr.

—CityBLOCKS Stacking Blocks. Smartink Books Staff. 2011. (ENG.). 10p. (J). (gr. -1-17). 21.99 *(978-1-4521-0275-7(9))* Chronicle Bks. LLC.

—Colors Everywhere: Shake & Play. Wing, Scarlett. Cottage Door Press, ed. 2019. (Baby Einstein Ser.). (ENG.). 10p. (J). (gr. -1-k). bds. 8.99 *(978-1-68052-601-1(4),* 1004160) Cottage Door Pr.

—Dinosaurs. Isaacs, Connie. 2018. (Sticker Play Ser.). (ENG.). 60p. (J). (gr. k). pap. 5.99 *(978-1-78700-614-0(X))* Top That! Publishing PLC GBR. Dist: Independent Pubs. Group.

—Discover 100 First Words: Case Bound Big Book. Wing, Scarlett. 2018. (Baby Einstein Ser.). (ENG.). 22p. (J). (gr. -1-k). bds. 9.99 *(978-1-68052-351-5(1),* 1003230) Cottage Door Pr.

—Farmer Jill, 1 vol. Dale, Jay. 2012. (Wonder Words Ser.). (ENG.). 32p. (gr. k-2). pap. 5.99 *(978-1-4296-8926-7(9),* Capstone Pr.) Capstone.

—Favorite First Words: Lift-A-Tab Book. Wing, Scarlett. Cottage Door Press, ed. 2017. (Baby Einstein Ser.). (ENG.). 8p. (J). (gr. -1-k). bds. 8.99 *(978-1-68052-244-0(2),* 1002300) Cottage Door Pr.

—Five Little Men in a Flying Saucer. (Classic Books with Holes Big Book Ser.). (J). 2006. 16p. spiral bd. *(978-1-84643-007-7(0));* 2005. 14p. spiral bd. *(978-1-904550-58-7(4));* 2005. 16p. pap. *(978-1-904550-30-3(4))* Child's Play International Ltd.

—London: A Colourful City. 2012. (ENG.). 18p. (J). (gr. -1 — 1). bds. 9.99 *(978-1-4052-6468-6(3))* Egmont Bks., Ltd. GBR. Dist: Independent Pubs. Group.

—Look & Learn Rainbow. Garnett, Jaye. Cottage Door Press, ed. 2020. (Finger Puppet Board Book Baby Einstein Ser.). (ENG.). 12p. (J). (gr. -1 — 1). bds. 6.99 *(978-1-68052-848-0(3),* 1005600) Cottage Door Pr.

—Old MacDonald Had a Farm. Linn, Susie. 2019. (Counting to Ten Bks.). (ENG.). 22p. (J). 9.99 *(978-1-78700-978-3(5))* Top That! Publishing PLC GBR. Dist: Independent Pubs. Group.
—Play & Learn Activity Cards: Activity Card Set. Wing, Scarlett. 2018. (Baby Einstein Ser.). (ENG.). 16p. (J). (gr. -1-k). bds. 14.99 *(978-1-68052-307-2(4),* 1002820) Cottage Door Pr.
—Play & Learn Together: Flip a Flap Board Book. Wing, Scarlett. 2017. (Baby Einstein Ser.). (ENG.). 10p. (J). (gr. -1-k). bds. 9.99 *(978-1-68052-221-1(3),* 1002080) Cottage Door Pr.
—Under the Stars: Turn & Learn Wood Disc Board Book. Wing, Scarlett. Cottage Door Press, ed. 2017. (Baby Einstein Ser.). (ENG.). 8p. (J). (gr. -1-k). bds. 12.99 *(978-1-68052-223-5(X),* 1002100) Cottage Door Pr.
—Who Am I? Mirror & Me. Wing, Scarlett. Cottage Door Press, ed. 2019. (Baby Einstein Mirror & Me Children's Interactive Mirrored Board Book Ser.). (ENG.). 10p. (J). (gr. -1-k). bds. 8.99 *(978-1-68052-494-9(1),* 1003690) Cottage Door Pr.
—World of Exploration: Chunky Peek a Flap Board Book. Garnett, Jaye. 2018. (Baby Einstein Ser.). (ENG.). 12p. (J). (-k). bds. 8.99 *(978-1-68052-317-1(1),* 1002930) Cottage Door Pr.
Crisp, Dan & Betowers. Write & Erase ABC And 123. Downy, Rufus. Cottage Door Press, ed. 2019. (Early Bird Learning Ser.). (ENG.). 16p. (J). (gr. -1-1). bds. 9.99 *(978-1-68052-311-9(2),* 1002860) Cottage Door Pr.
Crisp, Dan, jt. illus. see Tugeau, Jeremy.
Crispin, Gerald W. God Speaks Through Dreams: But Who's Listening?, No. 1. Crispin, Gerald W., photos by. Crispin, Vera G., ed. unabr. ed. 2003. 160p. (gr. 10-18). reprint ed. pap. 19.95 *(978-0-9744015-1-5(X))* Benchmark Book Craft.
Crissey, Noah. The Loneliest Christmas Tree. Crissey, Brian. 2004. 32p. (J). bds. 25.00 *(978-1-893183-35-3(1),* 598) Granite Publishing, LLC.
—The Loneliest Christmas Tree. Crissey, Brian L. 2004. (J). *(978-1-930724-12-9(8)); (978-1-930724-13-6(6))* Granite Publishing, LLC.
Cristina, Mavrodin. Messy Jessie! Trott, Jack. 2020. (ENG.). 40p. (J). pap. 12.90 ***(978-1-7283-5357-9(2))*** AuthorHouse.
Crittenden, Nina Victor. Cedric & the Dragon. Raum, Elizabeth. 2010. (ENG.). 32p. (J). 16.95 *(978-1-934617-05-2(9),* Alma Little) Elva Resa Publishing, LLC.
Croatto, Barbara. The Three Visitors: The Story of Knock. Gormally, Elenor. 2014. (ENG.). 32p. (J). pap. 11.00 *(978-1-84730-554-1(7))* Veritas Pubns. IRL. Dist: Casemate Pubs. & Bk. Distributors, LLC.
Crockett-Blassingame, Linda. See the Ocean. 2006. 32p. (J). 14.95 *(978-0-9778143-0-5(0))* Inclusive Books LLC.
Crockett, Linda. Of Corn Silk & Black Braids. Johnson, Vincent L. 2005. 32p. (J). (gr. k-3). 17.95 *(978-0-9657033-2-1(0))* Marzetta Bks.
Croft, Eddie. The Little Plane That Could. Delaurentis, Robert & Gilbert, Susan. 2020. (ENG.). 48p. (J). pap. 10.99 ***(978-1-7324937-1-1(5))*** Flying Thru Life Pubns.
Croft, James. Surprising Sharks: Read & Wonder. Davies, Nicola. 2005. (Read & Wonder Ser.). (ENG.). 32p. (J). (gr. -1-3). reprint ed. pap. 7.99 *(978-0-7636-2742-3(9))* Candlewick Pr.
Croft, James Lee. Meet Gator: A Picture Clues Touch & Feel Book. DePrisco, Dorothea. 2005. (Learn to Read Ser.). 10p. (J). (gr. -1-18). 10.95 *(978-1-58117-123-5(4),* Intervisual/Piggy Toes) Bendon, Inc.
Croghan, Ron. The Adventures of Joey, the Dog Who Barks at Puddles. Holmgren, Patti. 2017. (ENG.). (J). 21.95 *(978-1-63525-207-1(5));* pap. 12.95 *(978-1-63575-482-7(8))* Christian Faith Publishing.
Croissant-Madden, Gayle. My Wild, Wild Hair! Croissant-Madden, Gayle. 2006. (J). 10.00 *(978-0-9786478-0-3(7))* airjam.com.
Croll, Carolyn. Cheerios Count to 100. Fontes, Justine. 2005. (J). *(978-0-439-70341-3(7))* Scholastic, Inc.
—The Story of Christmas Story Book Set & Advent Calendar: Story Book Set & Advent Calendar. ed. 2008. (ENG.). 96p. (J). (gr. -1-12). 17.99 *(978-0-7611-5250-7(4),* 15250) Workman Publishing Co., Inc.
—What Will the Weather Be? DeWitt, Lynda. 2015. (Let's-Read-And-Find-Out Science 2 Ser.). (ENG.). 32p. (J). (gr. -1-3). pap. 6.99 *(978-0-06-238198-9(9))* HarperCollins Pubs.
Cromwell, Danielle. My Ten Cents. Young, T. M. Victoria Washington and Carla Watts, ed. 2013. 24p. pap. 24.95 *(978-1-4626-5790-2(7))* America Star Bks.
—Playing Church. Young, T. M. Washington, Victoria, ed. 2012. 32p. pap. 24.95 *(978-1-4626-7883-9(1))* America Star Bks.
—What's Love Got to Do with It. Young, T. M. Vickie Washington and Carla Watts, ed. 2013. 32p. pap. 24.95 *(978-1-4626-0889-8(2))* America Star Bks.
Cronan, Paul. The Last Synapsid. Mason, Timothy. 2011. (ENG.). 320p. (J). (gr. 4-6). lib. bdg. 22.44 *(978-0-385-90567-1(X),* Yearling) Random Hse. Children's Bks.
Cronin, Janet. The Dog Machine. Andreae, Giles. 2013. (World of Happy Ser.). (ENG.). 32p. (J). (gr. -1-k). 5.99 *(978-1-4052-5841-8(1))* Egmont Bks., Ltd. GBR. Dist: Independent Pubs. Group.
—The Ministry of Niceness. Andreae, Giles. 2013. (World of Happy Ser.). (ENG.). 32p. (J). (gr. -1-k). 5.99 *(978-1-4052-5843-2(8))* Egmont Bks., Ltd. GBR. Dist: Independent Pubs. Group.
—My Little World of Happy, 9 vols. Andreae, Giles. 2013. (World of Happy Ser.). (ENG.). 90p. (J). (— 1). bds. 15.99 *(978-1-4052-6082-4(3))* Egmont Bks., Ltd. GBR. Dist: Independent Pubs. Group.
—Planet of the Bears. Andreae, Giles & World of Happy Staff. 2013. (World of Happy Ser.). (ENG.). 32p. (J). (gr. -1-k). 5.99 *(978-1-4052-5845-6(4))* Egmont Bks., Ltd. GBR. Dist: Independent Pubs. Group.
Cronin, Laurie. Oliver's Surprise: A Boy, a Schooner, & the Great Hurricane Of 1938. Cronin, Carol Newman. rev. ed. 2009. (ENG.). 150p. (J). (gr. 4-7). pap. 9.95 *(978-1-934848-62-3(X))* GemmaMedia.
Cronin, Laurie Ann. Cape Cod Surprise: Oliver Matches Wits with Hurricane Carol. Cronin, Carol Newman. 2010. (ENG.). 150p. (J). pap. 9.95 *(978-1-934848-47-0(6))* GemmaMedia.
Cronin, Tricia Lynn. Don't Use Granny's Toothbrush. Bianchi, Ann. 2019. (ENG.). 48p. (J). 24.95 ***(978-0-578-61225-6(9))*** Bianchi, Ann.
Croom, Terry. Grandma's Here. 2013. 20p. (J). pap. 9.99 *(978-0-9888650-2-0(5))* Soar Publishing, LLC.
Crosby, Amy. Mud Boy: A Story about Bullying. Siggs, Sarah. ed. 2019. (ENG.). 48p. 17.95 ***(978-1-78592-870-3(8),*** 697073) Kingsley, Jessica Pubs. GBR. Dist: Hachette UK Distribution.
Crosby-Fairall, Marjorie. The Boy in the Big Blue Glasses. Gervay, Susanne. (ENG.). 32p. (J). (gr. -1-3). 2019. 17.99 *(978-1-925335-99-6(2),* 331746); 2nd ed. 2020. pap. 15.99 ***(978-1-925820-56-0(4),*** 337887) Exisle Publishing Pty Ltd. AUS. (EK Bks.). Dist: Hachette Bk. Group.
Crosby, Jeff. Brave Cloelia: Retold from the Account in the History of Early Rome by the Roman Historian Titus Livius. Curry, Jane Louise & Livy. 2004. (ENG.). 34p. 17.95 *(978-0-89236-763-4(6))* Oxford Univ. Pr., Inc.
—Otis Steele & the Taileebone: A Southern Tall Tale, 1 vol. McDermott, Tom. 2013. (ENG.). 32p. (J). (gr. k-2). 16.99 *(978-1-4556-1736-4(9),* Pelican Publishing) Arcadia Publishing.
Crosby, Jeff & Jackson, Shelley Ann. Little Lions, Bull Baiters & Hunting Hounds: A History of Dog Breeds. Crosby, Jeff & Jackson, Shelley Ann. 2008. (ENG.). 72p. (J). (gr. k-12). 19.95 *(978-0-88776-815-6(6),* Tundra Bks.) Tundra Bks. CAN. Dist: Penguin Random Hse. LLC.
Crosby, Jeff, jt. illus. see Jackson, Shelley.
Crosier, Mike. Entrepreneurship: Create Your Own Business. Kahan, Alex. 2014. (Build It Yourself Ser.). 128p. (J). (gr. 3-7). pap. 17.95 *(978-1-61930-265-5(9),* 9ddab2eb-932a-4367-b518-7fa44b1e64d7) Nomad Pr.
—Explore Canals & Dams! With 25 Great Projects. Yasuda, Anita. 2018. (Explore Your World Ser.). 96p. (J). (gr. 3-5). 19.95 *(978-1-61930-645-5(X),* bab1c11c-a1a3-4c57-9ab3-d90711fb4e76) Nomad Pr.
—Explore Skyscrapers! With 25 Great Projects. Schmermund, Elizabeth. 2018. (Explore Your World Ser.). 96p. (J). (gr. 3-5). 19.95 *(978-1-61930-651-6(4),* 16f2e428-9481-4626-be78-e32a9b8b7759) Nomad Pr.
—Explore Tunnels! With 25 Great Projects. Moore, Jeanette. 2018. (Explore Your World Ser.). 96p. (J). (gr. 3-5). 19.95 *(978-1-61930-648-6(4),* e23173e7-53a0-4e88-97e3-d574a0951812) Nomad Pr.
—Video Games: Design & Code Your Own Adventure. Ceceri, Kathy. 2015. (Build It Yourself Ser.). 128p. (J). (gr. 3-7). 22.95 *(978-1-61930-291-4(8),* a540a01d-35ec-417a-bc43-2c2f55cdfb83) Nomad Pr.
Crosland, Dave, et al. Invader ZIM Vol. 5, Vol. 5. Trueheart, Eric & Crosland, Dave. 2018. (Invader ZIM Ser.: 5). (ENG.). 128p. (J). pap. 19.99 *(978-1-62010-478-1(4),* 9781620104781, Lion Forge) Oni Pr., Inc.
Cross, Chris. Nothing to Lose. David, Peter. 2003. (Captain Marvel Ser.). 144p. (YA). pap. 12.99 *(978-0-7851-1104-7(2))* Marvel Worldwide, Inc.
Cross, James. Dancing Fruit Put on a Show! Wilkes, Ruth. 2013. (ENG.). (J). pap. 7.99 *(978-1-62154-282-7(3))* Aquarius Pr.
—Dancing Fruit Put on a Show! Wilkes, Ruth. 2013. 48p. 18.99 *(978-1-62314-797-6(2))* Willow Publishing.
Cross, Jo Ellen. Remembering to Breathe. Chisolm, Melinda. 2009. 31p. pap. 24.95 *(978-1-60703-914-3(1))* America Star Bks.
Cross, Kevin. A Little Dachshund's Tale. Jean, April. 2012. 36p. pap. 9.95 *(978-1-61897-367-2(3),* Strategic Bk. Publishing) Strategic Book Publishing & Rights Agency (SBPRA).
Cross, Neal. G Is for Georgia. Sullivan, E. J. 2006. 24p. (J). *(978-1-58173-524-6(3))* Sweetwater Pr.
—T Is for Tennessee. Sullivan, E. J. 2007. (State Alphabet Bks.). 24p. (J). (gr. -1-3). *(978-1-58173-527-7(8))* Sweetwater Pr.
Cross, Rachael. Lucy: The Wintertime Bunny. Livingood, James. 2019. (Lucy Ser.: Vol. 4). (ENG.). 26p. (J). pap. 9.25 ***(978-1-7102-4691-9(X))*** Independently Published.
Crossett, Laura. Happy Harry's World Turns Upside Down. Ferris, Nicola. 2020. (ENG.). 32p. (J). pap. ***(978-1-9998842-7-7(2))*** Bear Pr.
Crossett, Warren. The Sound of the Sea. Harvey, Jacqueline. 2005. 32p. (J). *(978-0-7344-0742-9(4),* Lothian Children's Bks.) Hachette Australia.
Crossland, Caroline. Cinderella. Umansky, Kaye. 2012. 48p. *(978-0-88734-072-7(5))* Players Pr., Inc.
—The Emperor's New Clothes. Umansky, Kaye. 2012. *(978-0-88734-074-1(1))* Players Pr., Inc.
—Sleeping Beauty. Umansky, Kaye. 2003. (Plays & Play Collections). 48p. (J). pap. 15.00 *(978-0-7136-5371-7(X),* A&C Black) Bloomsbury Publishing Plc GBR. Dist: Players Pr., Inc.
—Sleeping Beauty. Umansky, Kaye. 2012. *(978-0-88734-070-3(9))* Players Pr., Inc.
Crossley, David. ABC. 2004. (Baby's First Learning Ser.). 12p. (J). bds. 4.99 *(978-1-85854-890-6(X))* Brimax Books Ltd. GBR. Dist: Byeway Bks.
—Baby's First Learning Book: 123. 2004. 10p. (J). bds. 2.99 *(978-0-681-03556-0(0))* Autumn Publishing Group, LLC.
—First Words. 2004. (Baby's First Learning Ser.). 10p. (J). bds. 4.99 *(978-1-85854-892-0(6))* Brimax Books Ltd. GBR. Dist: Byeway Bks.
—On the Farm. 2004. (Baby's First Learning Ser.). 12p. (J). bds. 4.99 *(978-1-85854-893-7(4))* Brimax Books Ltd. GBR. Dist: Byeway Bks.
—123. 2004. (Baby's First Learning Ser.). 12p. (J). bds. 4.99 *(978-1-85854-891-3(8))* Brimax Books Ltd. GBR. Dist: Byeway Bks.
Crossley, Kezzia. N Is for Nutrition: Rhymes by the Alphabet. Skene, Todd & Aulakh, Amneet. 2018. (ENG.). 42p. (J). (gr. k-3). *(978-1-7751147-0-3(8))* Heart Happy Kids Media.
Crosson, Cierra. Rain, Rain, Come Today. Magee, Kanika. 2004. (J). *(978-0-9748834-2-7(5))* Ebenezer A.M.E. Church.
Crouch, Frances. Alexander the Moose. Dixon, Karen S. 2004. 23p. pap. 24.95 *(978-1-4137-3626-7(2))* PublishAmerica, Inc.
Crouch, Julian. Maggot Moon. Gardner, Sally. (ENG.). 288p. (YA). (gr. 7). 2014. pap. 9.99 *(978-0-7636-7169-3(X));* 2013. 16.99 *(978-0-7636-6553-1(3))* Candlewick Pr.
Crouch, Karen Hillard. One Enchanted Evening. Moulton, Mark Kimball. 2003. 32p. (J). 14.95 *(978-0-8249-5480-2(7),* Ideal Pubns.) Worthy Publishing.
Croucher, Barry. Frogs & Toads. Whittley, Sarah & Showler, Dave. rev. ed. 2004. (Golden Guide from St. Martin's Press Ser.). (ENG.). 160p. pap. 6.95 *(978-0-312-32241-0(0),* 9780312322410, Golden Guides from Saint Martin's Pr.) St. Martin's Pr.
Crough, Noelle. �Por Qu� No Puedo Leer? Torres, Alexander Jose. Hernandez, Roberto, ed. 2019. (Spanish Version Ser.: Vol. 1). (SPA.). 24p. (J). pap. 11.00 ***(978-1-7089-4828-3(7))*** Independently Published.
Crouth, Julia. Wibble Wobble. Mills, David. 2004. (ENG & POL.). 32p. (J). pap. *(978-1-85269-996-3(5));* pap. *(978-1-85269-991-8(4));* pap. *(978-1-85269-986-4(8));* pap. *(978-1-85269-981-9(7));* pap. *(978-1-85269-976-5(0));* pap. *(978-1-85269-971-0(X));* pap. *(978-1-85269-966-6(3));* pap. *(978-1-85269-961-1(2));* pap. *(978-1-85269-951-2(5));* pap. *(978-1-85269-946-8(9));* pap. *(978-1-85269-937-6(X));* pap. *(978-1-85269-932-1(9));* pap. *(978-1-85269-927-7(2));* pap. *(978-1-85269-922-2(1));* pap. *(978-1-85269-917-8(5));* pap. *(978-1-85269-912-3(4));* pap. *(978-1-85269-907-9(8));* pap. *(978-1-85269-902-4(7));* pap. *(978-1-85269-926-0(4))* Mantra Lingua.
—Wibbly Wobbly Tooth. Mills, David. 2004. (ENG & ARA.). 32p. (J). pap. *(978-1-85269-931-4(0));* pap. *(978-1-85269-936-9(1));* pap. *(978-1-85269-941-3(8));* pap. *(978-1-85269-956-7(6))* Mantra Lingua.
Crouthamel, Cheryl. Miracle. Pinter, Jason. 2018. (ENG.). 30p. (J). (gr. -1-3). 13.99 *(978-1-947993-39-6(9));* 18.99 *(978-1-947993-40-2(2))* Polis Bks. (Armina Pr.).
Crovara, Francesca. El Pescadito de Oro. Mantegazza, Giovanna. 2019. (SPA.). 12p. (J). (gr. -1-1). 5.95 *(978-84-414-1256-9(1))* Editorial Edaf, S.L. ESP. Dist: Spanish Pubs., LLC.
Crow, Heather. Mosey's Field, 1 vol. Lockhart, Barbara. 2013. (ENG.). 32p. 16.99 *(978-0-7643-4388-9(2),* 4802) Schiffer Publishing, Ltd.
—Wind & Oyster Jack, 1 vol. Moore, Marcia. 2017. (ENG.). 32p. (J). 14.99 *(978-0-7643-5422-9(1),* 7745) Schiffer Publishing, Ltd.
Crow, Isaias. You Are the Vision. Corrado, Meagan. 2019. (ENG.). 42p. (J). pap. 10.00 *(978-1-7325813-2-6(0))* Storiez: Meagan Corrado.
Crow, Katie. The Ranch Race. Carkhuff Jr., Sam. 2012. 36p. 16.99 *(978-1-939054-03-6(6));* pap. 11.99 *(978-1-939054-02-9(8))* Rowe Publishing.
Crow, Virginia. Rosie Jane & the Swodgerump: The First Rosie Jane Poem. Crow, Susan. 2019. (ENG.). 20p. (J). pap. *(978-0-9957860-8-0(9))* Crowvus.
Crowe, Carolyn Walker. Hairy, Scary, but Mostly Merry Fairies! Curing Nature Deficiency Through Folklore, Imagination, & Creative Activities. Raney, Renee Simmons. 2017. (ENG.). 128p. pap. 15.95 *(978-1-58838-328-0(8),* NewSouth Bks.) NewSouth, Inc.
Crowe, Jeanine. Little Lessons from St. Therese of Lisieux: An Introduction to Her Words & Wisdom. Martin, Therese. 2019. (ENG.). 44p. (J). pap. 11.95 *(978-1-68192-522-6(2))* Our Sunday Visitor, Publishing Div.
Crowe, Louise. Fergus Finds a Friend, 38 vols. Steven, Kenneth. 2010. (ENG.). 32p. (J). (gr. -1-1). 11.95 *(978-0-86315-778-3(5))* Floris Bks. GBR. Dist: Consortium Bk. Sales & Distribution.
—Tama the Extraordinary Cat: The True Story of the Cat Who Saved a Railway Company & Became a Goddess. a Story for Children & People Who Love Cats. Rutherford, Jill. 2018. (ENG.). 58p. (J). pap. *(978-1-9996133-0-3(9))* Little Wren Pr.
Crowe, Michelle. The Hardrock Rooster of Rose-Nose Mound. Anderson, Donald. 2017. (ENG.). (YA). (gr. 7-12). pap. 11.95 *(978-0-9881993-2-3(7))* CK Books Publishing.
Crowell, Helen. The Little Red Present. Pierce, Brian. 2007. 32p. (J). per. 8.00 *(978-0-9793269-1-2(5))* Straub, Rick.
Crowell, Knox. Andy & Jerome. Williams, Heather L. l.t. ed. 2004. (HRL Big Book Ser.). 8p. (J). (gr. -1-1). pap. 10.95 *(978-1-57332-276-8(8));* pap. 10.95 *(978-1-57332-277-5(6))* Carson-Dellosa Publishing, LLC. (HighReach Learning, Incorporated).
—At the Park. Hensley, Sarah M. l.t. ed. 2006. 10p. (J). (gr. -1-k). pap. 10.95 *(978-1-57332-354-3(3),* HighReach Learning, Incorporated) Carson-Dellosa Publishing, LLC.
—Caillou Waits for Dinner. Howard-Parham, Pam. l.t. ed. 2004. (HRL Board Book Ser.). (J). (gr. -1-1). pap. 10.95 *(978-1-57332-289-8(X),* HighReach Learning, Incorporated) Carson-Dellosa Publishing, LLC.
—A Cold Winter Day. Muench-Williams, Heather. l.t. ed. 2006. (HRL Board Book Ser.). (J). (gr. -1-k). pap. 10.95 *(978-1-57332-326-0(8),* HighReach Learning, Incorporated) Carson-Dellosa Publishing, LLC.
—Helping Farmer Joe. Hensley, Sarah M. l.t. ed. 2004. (HRL Little Book Ser.). (J). (gr. -1). pap. 10.95 *(978-1-57332-296-6(2));* pap. 10.95 *(978-1-57332-295-9(4))* Carson-Dellosa Publishing, LLC. (HighReach Learning, Incorporated).
—Let's Build a Snowman: Cuddle Book. Black, Jessica L. & Mullican, Judy. 6p. (J). (gr. -1-1). bds. 10.95 *(978-1-57332-222-5(9),* HighReach Learning, Incorporated) Carson-Dellosa Publishing, LLC.
—Playing on the Playground. Howard-Parham, Pam. l.t. ed. 2005. (HRL Little Book Ser.). (J). (gr. k-18). pap. 10.95 *(978-1-57332-336-9(5));* pap. 10.95 *(978-1-57332-335-2(7))* Carson-Dellosa Publishing, LLC. (HighReach Learning, Incorporated).
—Water Fun. Hensley, Sarah M. l.t. ed. 2005. (J). (gr. -1-k). pap. 10.95 *(978-1-57332-342-0(X));* pap. 10.95 *(978-1-57332-343-7(8))* Carson-Dellosa Publishing, LLC. (HighReach Learning, Incorporated).
—Who Is in the Backyard? Jarrell, Pamela R. l.t. ed. 2004. (HRL Board Book Ser.). 8p. (J). (gr. -1). pap. 10.95 *(978-1-57332-281-2(4),* HighReach Learning, Incorporated) Carson-Dellosa Publishing, LLC.
Crowell, Pers. The Whistling Stallion. Holt, Stephen. 2011. 224p. 44.95 *(978-1-258-10199-2(8))* Literary Licensing, LLC.
Crowley, Adam A., photos by. Gus Learns to Fly: Self-Defense Is Self-Discovery. Richardson, Kimberly Stanton. 2012. (ENG., 44p. (J). (gr. k). pap. 18.00 *(978-0-939165-64-3(3))* NewSage Pr., LLC.
Crowley, Ashley. The Boy & the Blue Moon. O'Leary, Sara. 2018. (ENG.). 40p. (J). 17.99 *(978-1-62779-774-0(2),* 9781627797740, Holt, Henry & Co. Bks. For Young Readers) Holt, Henry & Co.
—One Wave at a Time: A Story about Grief & Healing. Thompson, Holly. 2018. (ENG.). 32p. (J). (gr. -1-3). 16.99 *(978-0-8075-6112-6(6),* 807561126) Whitman, Albert & Co.
—Pup 681: A Sea Otter Rescue Story. Reidy, Jean. 2019. (ENG.). 40p. (J). 17.99 *(978-1-250-11450-1(0),* 900171459, Holt, Henry & Co. Bks. For Young Readers) Holt, Henry & Co.
Crowley, Ashley. Officer Panda: Fingerprint Detective. Crowley, Ashley. 2015. (Officer Panda Ser.: 1). (ENG.). 32p. (J). (gr. -1-3). 17.99 *(978-0-06-236626-9(2))* HarperCollins Pubs.
—Officer Panda: Sky Detective. Crowley, Ashley. 2016. (Officer Panda Ser.: 2). (ENG.). 32p. (J). (gr. -1-3). 17.99 *(978-0-06-236627-6(0))* HarperCollins Pubs.
Crowley, Cheryl. The Adventures of Webb Ellis, a Tale from the Heart of Africa: The Return of the Protectors. Rieback, Milton. 2006. (J). lib. bdg. 19.95 *(978-0-9777440-0-8(0))* Inyati Press.
Crown Peak Publishing. Just Be You. Crown Peak Publishing. 2008. (ENG.). 40p. (J). 19.95 *(978-0-9645663-5-4(4))* Crown Peak Publishing.
Crowson, Andrew. Flip Flap Christmas. Crowson, Andrew. 2003. 12p. (J). bds. *(978-1-85602-476-1(8),* Pavilion Children's Books) Pavilion Bks.
—Flip Flap Prehistoric. Crowson, Andrew. 2003. 12p. (J). pap. *(978-1-85602-474-7(1),* Pavilion Children's Books) Pavilion Bks.
—Flip Flap Safari. Crowson, Andrew. 2003. 12p. (J). bds. *(978-1-85602-473-0(3),* Pavilion Children's Books) Pavilion Bks.
—Flip Flap Spooky. Crowson, Andrew. 2003. 12p. (J). bds. *(978-1-85602-475-4(X),* Pavilion Children's Books) Pavilion Bks.
Crowther, Calvin. Flash & Bones & the Empty Tomb of Herobrine. Crowther, Calvin. Smith, Jared, ed. 2014. (ENG.). (J). pap. 12.99 *(978-1-945906-00-8(6))* Interactive Stories.
Crowther, Jeff. Attack of the Cling-Ons, 1 vol. Ciencin, Scott. 2011. (Graphic Sparks Ser.). (ENG.). 40p. (J). (gr. 2-4). pap. 5.95 *(978-1-4342-3067-6(8));* lib. bdg. 23.99 *(978-1-4342-2637-2(9))* Capstone. (Stone Arch Bks.).
Crowther, Jeff. Baking Apples. Gates, Margo. 2020. (Plant Life Cycles (Pull Ahead Readers — Fiction) Ser.). (ENG.). 16p. (J). (gr. -1-1). 22.65 ***(978-1-5415-9026-7(0),*** Lerner Pubns.) Lerner Publishing Group.
Crowther, Jeff. The Evil Echo, 1 vol. Nickel, Scott & Dahl, Michael. 2010. (Princess Candy Ser.). (ENG.). 40p. (J). (gr. 2-5). 23.99 *(978-1-4342-1977-0(1));* pap. 5.95 *(978-1-4342-2804-8(5))* Capstone. (Stone Arch Bks.).
—The Green Queen of Mean. Dahl, Michael & Nickel, Scott. 2010. (Princess Candy Ser.). (ENG.). 40p. (J). (gr. 2-5). pap. 5.95 *(978-1-4342-2803-1(7),* Stone Arch Bks.) Capstone.
—Hungry Little Bear. Gates, Margo. 2019. (Science All Around Me (Pull Ahead Readers — Fiction) Ser.). (ENG.). 16p. (J). (gr. -1-1). 22.65 *(978-1-5415-5852-6(9),* 9781541558526, Lerner Pubns.) Lerner Publishing Group.
—Into the Clouds. Gates, Margo. 2019. (Let's Look at Weather (Pull Ahead Readers — Fiction) Ser.). (ENG.). 16p. (J). (gr. -1-1). 22.65 *(978-1-5415-5840-3(5),* 9781541558403, Lerner Pubns.) Lerner Publishing Group.
—The Marshmallow Mermaid. Dahl, Michael. 2010. (Princess Candy Ser.). (ENG.). 40p. (J). (gr. 2-5). pap. 5.95 *(978-1-4342-2802-4(9),* Stone Arch Bks.) Capstone.
—No Bugs Here. Gates, Margo. 2019. (Let's Look at Animal Habitats (Pull Ahead Readers — Fiction) Ser.). (ENG.). 16p. (J). (gr. -1-1). pap. 6.99 *(978-1-5415-7307-9(2),* ee4999c2-5960-4ac6-8b2f-470fe28201d0, Lerner Pubns.) Lerner Publishing Group.
—Princess Candy: The Complete Comics Collection. Dahl, Michael & Nickel, Scott. ed. 2020. (Stone Arch Graphic Novels Ser.). (ENG.). 144p. (J). (gr. 3-6). pap. 8.95 *(978-1-4965-9320-7(0),* 142350); lib. bdg. 27.99 *(978-1-4965-8731-2(6),* 141609) Capstone. (Stone Arch Bks.).
Crowther, Jeff, et al. Stone Arch Graphic Novels. Dahl, Michael et al. 2020. (Stone Arch Graphic Novels Ser.). (ENG.). (J). (gr. 3-6). 111.96 *(978-1-4965-8738-1(3),* 29817); pap., pap., pap. 35.80 *(978-1-4965-9344-3(8),* 30109) Capstone. (Stone Arch Bks.).
Crowther, Jeff. Sugar Hero. Dahl, Michael. (Princess Candy Ser.). (ENG.). 40p. (J). (gr. 2-5). 2010. pap. 5.95 *(978-1-4342-2801-7(0));* 2009. lib. bdg. 23.99 *(978-1-4342-1587-1(3))* Capstone. (Stone Arch Bks.).
Crowther, Kitty. The Runaways. Stark, Ulf. 2019. (ENG.). 144p. (J). (gr. k-5). 17.99 *(978-1-77657-233-5(5))* Gecko Pr. NZL. Dist: Lerner Publishing Group.
Crowther, Kitty. Stories of the Night. Crowther, Kitty. 2018. (ENG.). 64p. (J). (gr. -1-k). 17.99 *(978-1-77657-197-0(5))* Gecko Pr. NZL. Dist: Lerner Publishing Group.

C

Crowther, Robert. Deep down under Ground: A Pop-up Book of Amazing Facts & Feats. Crowther, Robert. 2004. 18p. (J). (gr. 3-8). reprint ed. pap. 22.00 *(978-0-7567-7179-9(X))* DIANE Publishing Co.

—Robert Crowther's Pop-Up Dinosaur ABC. Crowther, Robert. 2015. (ENG.). 10p. (J). (gr. -1-3). 19.99 *(978-0-7636-7296-6(3))* Candlewick Pr.

—Soccer: Facts & Stats & the World Cup & Superstars: A Pop-up Book. Crowther, Robert. 2004. 14p. (J). (gr. 2-8). reprint ed. 18.00 *(978-0-7567-7368-7(7))* DIANE Publishing Co.

Crowton, Melissa. Baby Code! Horning, Sandra. 2018. (Girls Who Code Ser.). 14p. (J). (— 1). bds. 7.99 *(978-0-399-54257-2(4),* Penguin Workshop) Penguin Young Readers Group.

—The Kids on the Bus: A Spin-The-Wheel Book of Emotions (School Bus Book, Interactive Board Book for Toddlers, Wheels on the Bus) Hall, Kirsten. 2020. (ENG.). 16p. (J). (gr. -1 — 1). bds. 9.99 *(978-1-4521-6825-8(3))* Chronicle Bks. LLC.

—Mousie, I Will Read to You. Cole, Rachael. 2018. 40p. (J). (gr. -1-2). 17.99 *(978-1-5247-1536-6(0),* Schwartz & Wade Bks.) Random Hse. Children's Bks.

Crozat, Francois. Los Gatos de Maria Tatin. Chausse, Sylvie. 2003. (SPA.). 32p. (J). (gr. k-2). *(978-84-8418-067-8(0),* ZZ30446) Zendrera Zariquiey, Editorial ESP. Dist: Lectorum Pubns., Inc.

Cruickshank, Jessica. When the Stars Wrote Back: Poems. Mateer, Trista. 2020. (ENG.). 208p. (YA). (gr. 9). 14.99 ***(978-0-593-17267-4(1))***; lib. bdg. 17.99 ***(978-0-593-17268-1(X))*** Random Hse. Children's Bks. (Random Hse. Bks. for Young Readers).

Cruikshank, George. Philosophy in Sport Made Science in Earnest: Being an Attempt to Illustrate the First Principles of Natural Philosophy by the Aid of the Popular Toys & Sports. Paris, John Ayrton. 2013. (Cambridge Library Collection - Education Ser.). (ENG.). Volume 1. 340p. pap. 40.99 *(978-1-108-05739-4(X))*; Volume 2. 328p. pap. 40.99 *(978-1-108-05740-0(3))*; Volume 3. 220p. pap. 30.99 *(978-1-108-05741-7(1))* Cambridge Univ. Pr.

—Punch & Judy. Landes, William-Alan, ed. 2003. (Classic Plays Ser.). 24p. (YA). (gr. 4-12). pap. 7.50 *(978-0-88734-290-5(6))* Players Pr., Inc.

Crum, A. M. The Lucky Farm Boy, 1 vol. Mertz, Alyssa. 2009. 28p. pap. 24.95 *(978-1-60813-892-0(5))* PublishAmerica, Inc.

Crum, Anna-Maria. The Christmas Tree Cried: The Story of the White House Christmas Tree. McAdam, Claudia Cangilla. 2004. 32p. (J). 16.95 *(978-0-9748995-5-8(0),* 1236093) Two Sons Pr., Inc.

—Kangaroos: Read Well Level K Unit 15 Storybook. Sprick, Jessica. 2003. (Read Well Level K Ser.). 20p. (J). *(978-1-57035-686-5(6),* 55554) Cambium Education, Inc.

—Maria's Mysterious Mission. Cangilla-McAdam, Claudia. 2007. 32p. (J). (gr. 3-7). 12.95 *(978-1-56579-588-4(1))* Fielder, John Publishing.

—Tallie's Christmas Lights Surprise!, 1 vol. Pease, Elaine. 2012. (ENG.). 32p. (J). (gr. k-3). 16.99 *(978-1-4556-1586-5(2),* Pelican Publishing) Arcadia Publishing.

Crum, Anna-Maria, jt. illus. see Shupe, Bobbi.

Crum, Jeanette. Tales from the Chicken Yard & Other Fowl Stories: Chicken Tales. Moreno, Elizabeth. 2019. (Tales from the Chicken Yard & Other Fowl Stories Ser.: Vol. 1). (ENG.). 142p. (J). (gr. 2-6). pap. 12.75 *(978-1-970079-26-5(6))* Dettling Moreno, Elizabeth.

—Tales from the Chicken Yard & Other Fowl Stories: Chicken Tales Coloring Book. Moreno, Elizabeth. 2019. (Tales from the Chicken Yard & Other Fowl Stories Ser.). (ENG.). 54p. (J). (gr. k-4). pap. 8.75 *(978-1-970079-29-6(0))* Dettling Moreno, Elizabeth.

Crumbo, Elizabeth. Cheese Crackers. Macklin, Eckley. 2018. (ENG.). 34p. (J). pap. 12.00 *(978-1-7310-1491-7(0))* Independently Published.

Crumley, Tiffani. A Calftales Christmas. Crumley, Karen B. 2017. (ENG.). 28p. (J). pap. 9.95 *(978-0-9836690-5-0(8))* Purple Sage Publishing.

—A Calftales Easter. Crumley, Karen D. 2018. (ENG.). 32p. (J). pap. 10.00 *(978-0-9836690-6-7(6))* Purple Sage Publishing.

—A Calftales Halloween. Crumley, Karen B. 2017. (ENG.). (J). pap. 9.95 *(978-0-9836690-4-3(X))* Purple Sage Publishing.

Crump, Christopher. The Valley of Secrets. Hussey, Charmian. 2006. (ENG.). 400p. (J). (gr. 7-12). per. 17.99 *(978-1-4169-0015-3(2),* Simon Pulse) Simon Pulse.

Crump, Fred, Jr. Three Kings & a Star. Crump, Fred, Jr. 2010. 40p. (J). (gr. -1-3). 12.95 *(978-1-932715-52-1(5))* UMI (Urban Ministries, Inc.).

Crump, Fred, Jr. The Little Mermaid. Crump, Fred, Jr., retold by. 2007. 32p. (J). 12.95 *(978-1-934056-72-1(3))*; pap. 9.95 *(978-1-60352-063-8(5))* UMI (Urban Ministries, Inc.).

Crump, Leslie. Right Guard Grant. Barbour, Ralph Henry. 2011. 304p. 48.95 *(978-1-258-10515-0(2))* Literary Licensing, LLC.

Crump, Lil. Anna at the Art Museum. Hutchins, Hazel & Herbert, Gail. 2018. 36p. (J). (gr. k-2). 18.95 *(978-1-77321-043-8(2))* Annick Pr., Ltd. CAN. Dist: Publishers Group West (PGW).

—DNA Detective. Lloyd Kyi, Tanya. 2015. (ENG.). 120p. (YA). (gr. 5-8). 24.95 *(978-1-55451-774-9(5),* 9781554517749) Annick Pr., Ltd. CAN. Dist: Publishers Group West (PGW).

—The Great Number Rumble: A Story of Math in Surprising Places. Lee, Cora & O'Reilly, Gillian. 2nd ed. 2016. (ENG.). 104p. (J). (gr. 3-7). pap. 12.95 *(978-1-55451-849-4(0))* Annick Pr., Ltd. CAN. Dist: Publishers Group West (PGW).

Cruse, Howard. The Swimmer with a Rope in His Teeth: A Shadow Fable, Vol. Shaffer, Jeanne E. 2004. (ENG.). 1p. pap. 15.98 *(978-1-59102-181-0(2),* Pyr Bks.) Start Publishing LLC.

Crutchfield, Jim, jt. illus. see Laughbaum, Steve.

Cruz, Abigail Dela. Archer: Book 4. Lynn, Jenna. 2018. (Robyn Hood Ser.). (ENG.). 48p. (J). (gr. 3-7). lib. bdg. 29.93 *(978-1-5321-3379-4(0),* 31181, Spellbound) Magic Wagon.

—Hoodnapped: Book 3. Lynn, Jenna. 2018. (Robyn Hood Ser.). (ENG.). 48p. (J). (gr. 3-7). lib. bdg. 29.93 *(978-1-5321-3378-7(2),* 31179, Spellbound) Magic Wagon.

—Metropolis Orphanage: Book 1. Lynn, Jenna. 2018. (Robyn Hood Ser.). (ENG.). 48p. (J). (gr. 3-7). lib. bdg. 29.93 *(978-1-5321-3376-3(6),* 31175, Spellbound) Magic Wagon.

—Rivals: Book 2. Lynn, Jenna. 2018. (Robyn Hood Ser.). (ENG.). 48p. (J). (gr. 3-7). lib. bdg. 29.93 *(978-1-5321-3377-0(4),* 31177, Spellbound) Magic Wagon.

—Robyn Hood (Set), 4 vols. Lynn, Jenna. 2018. (Robyn Hood Ser.). 48p. (J). (gr. 3-7). lib. bdg. 114.00 *(978-1-5321-3375-6(8),* 31173, Spellbound) Magic Wagon.

Cruz, Bruno. The Cat with the Hemingway Paw. Wisma, Mare. 2019. (ENG.). 30p. (J). (gr. k-3). 16.50 ***(978-1-7324576-3-8(8))*** Abdullah, Mary.

—The Trials & Tribulations of Mischief the Extraordinary Cat. Wisma, Mare. 2020. (ENG.). 38p. (J). (gr. k-6). pap. 14.99 ***(978-1-7324576-6-9(2))*** Abdullah, Mary.

Cruz, Bruno D. The Trials & Tribulations of Mischief the Extraordinary Cat. Wisma, Mare. 2019. (ENG.). 38p. (J). (gr. k-6). 19.50 ***(978-1-7324576-1-4(1))*** Abdullah, Mary.

Cruz, Cheryl. Goodbye, Santa. Hineman, Jonathan. 2013. 26p. (J). 16.95 *(978-1-60131-172-6(9))* Big Tent Bks.

—The Million Year Meal. Lucas, Ian & Medoza, Chris. 2012. 32p. (J). 19.95 *(978-1-60131-099-6(4))* Big Tent Bks.

Cruz, D. Nina. Mis abuelos y yo / My Grandparents & I. Caraballo, Samuel. Brammer, Ethriam Cash, tr. (ENG & SPA.). 32p. 16.95 *(978-1-55885-407-9(X),* Piñata Books) Arte Publico Pr.

—The Rowdy, Rowdy Ranch / Alla en el Rancho Grande. Brammer, Ethriam Cash. 2003. (ENG & SPA.). 32p. (J). 16.95 *(978-1-55885-409-3(6),* Piñata Books) Arte Publico Pr.

Cruz, David Garcia. Mini but Mighty. Marz, Ron & Rodriguez, David A. 2015. (Skylanders Set 1 Ser.). (ENG.). 24p. (J). (gr. 1-5). lib. bdg. 27.07 *(978-1-61479-386-1(7),* 18217, Graphic Novels) Spotlight.

Cruz, David Garcia, jt. illus. see Ossio, Fico.

Cruz, Ernesto R. Two Years Before the Mast: Student Activity Book. Sohl, Marcia & Dackerman, Gerald. (Now Age Illustrated Ser.). (J). (gr. 4-12). stu. ed. 1.25 *(978-0-88301-294-9(4))* Pendulum Pr., Inc.

Cruz, Olga. La Tetera M�gica de Paulita. Fernandez, Margarita. La Fabrica de Suenos, ed. 2019. (SPA.). 40p. (J). pap. ***(978-84-120660-4-3(9))*** La Fabrica De Suenos S.C.

Cruz, Ray. Alexander & the Terrible, Horrible, No Good, Very Bad Day. Viorst, Judith. 2014. (Classic Board Bks.). (ENG.). 34p. (J). (gr. -1 — 1). bds. 7.99 *(978-1-4424-9816-7(1),* Little Simon) Little Simon.

—Alexander & the Terrible, Horrible, No Good, Very Bad Day. Viorst, Judith. 2009. (ENG.). 32p. (J). (gr. -1-2). 17.99 *(978-1-4169-8595-2(6),* Atheneum Bks. for Young Readers) Simon & Schuster Children's Publishing.

—Alexander & the Terrible, Horrible, No Good, Very Bad Day: Lap Edition. Viorst, Judith. 2014. (ENG.). 34p. (J). (gr. -1 — 1). bds. 12.99 *(978-1-4814-1412-8(7),* Little Simon) Little Simon.

—Sing, Little Sack! I Canta, Saquito!: a Folktale from Puerto Rico. Jaffe, Nina. 2006. 48p. (J). (gr. 2-3). reprint ed. 19.00 *(978-1-4223-5573-2(X))* DIANE Publishing Co.

Cruz, Roger. The Bird, the Beast & the Lizard. Parker, Jeff. Paniccia, Mark, ed. 2007. (X-Men: First Class Ser.: No. 1). (ENG.). 24p. (J). (gr. 2-6). lib. bdg. 27.07 *(978-1-59961-398-7(0),* 15629, Marvel Age) Spotlight.

—A Life of the Mind. Parker, Jeff. Paniccia, Mark, ed. 2007. (X-Men: First Class Ser.: No. 1). (ENG.). 24p. (J). (gr. 2-6). lib. bdg. 27.07 *(978-1-59961-399-4(9),* 15630, Marvel Age) Spotlight.

—Seeing Red. Parker, Jeff. Paniccia, Mark, ed. 2007. (X-Men: First Class Ser.: No. 1). (ENG.). 24p. (J). (gr. 2-6). 27.07 *(978-1-59961-400-7(6),* 15631, Marvel Age) Spotlight.

—X-Men 101. Parker, Jeff. Paniccia, Mark, ed. 2007. (X-Men: First Class Ser.: No. 1). (ENG.). 24p. (J). (gr. 2-6). lib. bdg. 27.07 *(978-1-59961-401-4(4),* 15632, Marvel Age) Spotlight.

Cruz, Roger & Wieringo, Mike. Spider-Man: Friendly Neighborhood Spider-Man by Peter David - the Complete Collection. 2017. (ENG.). 480p. (J). (gr. 4-17). pap. 39.99 *(978-1-302-90436-4(1))* Marvel Worldwide, Inc.

Cruz, Stefane Christine. Guerra Entre Deuses: Comeco Do Caos. Alves, Vitor Souza. 2016. (POR.). (J). pap. *(978-85-920831-5-1(X))* WM.

Cruzan, Patricia & Solly, Gloria. Molly's Mischievous Dog. l.t. ed. 2004. 121p. (J). per. *(978-0-9653543-3-2(4))* Clear Creek Pubs.

Crysler, Ian, photos by. Seed to Sunflower: A First Look Board Book. Reid, Barbara. 2004. 12p. (J). (gr. k-2). reprint ed. 10.00 *(978-0-7567-7853-8(0))* DIANE Publishing Co.

Crystian, Carol Payne. Jas & Poetic Lucy. Crystian, Carol Payne. l.t. ed. 2006. 21p. (J). (gr. -1-3). per. 10.99 *(978-1-59879-154-9(0))* Lifevest Publishing, Inc.

Csavas, Sally. Tiny Story, Vol. 1. Price, Diane J. 2008. 28p. (J). 9.00 *(978-0-9789637-0-5(9))* Price, Diane Joan.

Csicsko, David Lee. The Skin You Live In. Tyler, Michael. 2005. (ENG.). 32p. (J). (gr. k-2). 15.95 *(978-0-9759580-0-1(3))* Chicago Children's Museum.

Csortos, Kyle. Bullyfish. Ulch, Virginia. 2019. (Educator Edition Ser.: Vol. 4). (ENG.). 28p. (J). pap. 12.95 *(978-1-7938-2174-4(7))* Independently Published.

—Happy to Bee Me. Ulch, Virginia. 2019. (Educator Edition Ser.: Vol. 5). (ENG.). 34p. (J). pap. 12.95 *(978-1-7938-0153-1(3))* Independently Published.

—I Love You Anyway: A Tail of Understanding ADHD. Ulch, Virginia. 2019. (Educator Edition Ser.: Vol. 2). (ENG.). 34p. (J). pap. 12.95 *(978-1-7934-9895-3(4))* Independently Published.

—Love You, Teddy Educator Edition: A Tail of Loss & Hope. Ulch, Virginia. 2019. (Educator Edition Ser.: Vol. 3). (ENG.). 30p. (J). pap. 12.95 *(978-1-7934-9466-5(5))* Independently Published.

Csotonyi, Julius. Discovering Bugs. 2017. (Discovering Ser.). (ENG.). 96p. (J). 19.95 *(978-1-60433-689-4(7),* Applesauce Pr.) Cider Mill Pr. Bk. Pubs., LLC.

—Discovering Whales, Dolphins & Porpoises. Gauthier, Kelly. 2020. (Discovering Ser.). (ENG.). 112p. (J). 19.95 *(978-1-60433-961-1(6),* Applesauce Pr.) Cider Mill Pr. Bk. Pubs., LLC.

—Pinocchio Rex & Other Tyrannosaurs. Stewart, Melissa & Brusatte, Steve. 2017. (Let's-Read-And-Find-Out Science 2 Ser.). (ENG.). 40p. (J). (gr. -1-3). 17.99 *(978-0-06-249093-3(1))*; pap. 6.99 *(978-0-06-249091-9(5))* HarperCollins Pubs.

—Prehistoric Predators. Switek, Brian. 2015. (ENG.). 96p. (J). 19.95 *(978-1-60433-552-1(1),* Applesauce Pr.) Cider Mill Pr. Bk. Pubs., LLC.

—The T Rex Handbook. Switek, Brian. 2016. (Discovering Ser.). (ENG.). 64p. (J). 12.95 *(978-1-60433-603-0(X),* Applesauce Pr.) Cider Mill Pr. Bk. Pubs., LLC.

—Why Does T. Rex Have Such Short Arms? And Other Questions about... Dinosaurs. Stewart, Melissa. 2014. (Good Question! Ser.). (ENG.). 32p. (J). (gr. 1). pap. 6.95 *(978-1-4549-0679-7(0))* Sterling Publishing Co., Inc.

Csotonyi, Julius T. Dinosaurs of the Alberta Badlands. Persons, W. Scott. 2018. (ENG.). 144p. (J). pap. *(978-1-55017-821-0(0))* Harbour Publishing Co., Ltd.

—Discovering Sharks. Parham, Donna Potter. 2016. (Discovering Ser.). (ENG.). 96p. (J). 19.95 *(978-1-60433-604-7(8),* Applesauce Pr.) Cider Mill Pr. Bk. Pubs., LLC.

Cubillas, Roberto. Juanita y el Conejo Perdido. Huidobro, Norma. 2019. (Torre Roja Ser.). (SPA.). 86p. (J). pap. ***(978-987-545-475-0(3))*** Norma Ediciones, S.A.

Cubillas, Roberto. Mimosaurio! Pez, Alberto. (SPA.). (J). 8.95 *(978-958-04-6035-0(3))* Norma S.A. COL. Dist: Distribuidora Norma, Inc.

Cubillas, Roberto. Mitos Griegos. Blanco, Cecilia. 2020. (SPA.). 64p. (J). (gr. 2-5). 12.95 ***(978-987-3994-29-6(7))*** El Gato de Hojalata ARG. Dist: Penguin Random Hse. LLC.

—Mitos Vikingos / Viking Myths. Blanco, Cecilia. 2020. (SPA.). 64p. (J). (gr. 2-5). 12.95 ***(978-987-3994-30-2(0))*** El Gato de Hojalata ARG. Dist: Penguin Random Hse. LLC.

Cucca, Vincenzo, et al. The Mystery of Sheristan, Vol. 7. Kesel, Barbara. 2004. (Meridian Ser.: Vol. 7). 160p. (YA). pap. 15.95 *(978-1-59314-056-4(8))* CrossGeneration Comics, Inc.

Cucca, Vincenzo & Hao, Katrina Mae. Frosty's First Christmas (Frosty the Snowman) Random House. 2016. (ENG.). 12p. (J). (-k). bds. 6.99 *(978-0-399-55012-6(7),* RH/Disney) Random Hse. Children's Bks.

Cuccia, David. The Five Frogs on Biscuit Bay. Piolata, Tommy. 2018. (ENG.). 36p. (J). 19.99 *(978-1-63337-246-7(4))*; pap. 12.99 *(978-1-63337-245-0(6))* Roland Golf Services.

Cuccia, David. There's a Crazy Dog under the Palace! Cuccia, David. 2019. (ENG.). 44p. (J). (gr. 1-6). pap. 14.99 ***(978-1-63337-321-1(5))*** Roland Golf Services.

—Who Ate the Gelato?! Cuccia, David. 2019. (ENG.). 88p. (J). (gr. 1-6). pap. 19.99 ***(978-1-63337-322-8(3))*** Roland Golf Services.

Cucco, Giuliano. Red Spider Hero. Miller, John. 2015. (ENG.). 40p. (J). (gr. -1-3). 16.95 *(978-1-59270-176-6(0))* Enchanted Lion Bks., LLC.

—Winston & George. Miller, John. 2014. (ENG.). 56p. (J). (gr. k-3). 17.95 *(978-1-59270-145-2(0))* Enchanted Lion Bks., LLC.

Cuchelo, Marta. Marina: No Quiero Perderte. Bonet, Wilmeliz. 2018. (Herederos Del Mar Ser.: Vol. 1). (SPA.). 340p. (J). pap. 14.99 *(978-1-7238-2078-6(4))* Independently Published.

Cudby, Simon, photos by. Motocross Exposure. Cudby, Simon. 2004. 24.95 *(978-0-9766918-0-8(9))* MX No Fear.

Cudd, Savannah. The True Story of the Big Red Onion. Fitzgerald, D. M. 2013. 36p. 18.99 *(978-0-9890288-7-5(9))*; pap. 10.99 *(978-0-9890288-5-1(2))* Mindstir Media.

Cuddehe, Judy Link. The Heron Chronicles. Cuddehe, Judy Link. 2013. 54p. pap. 13.00 *(978-0-9836659-6-0(6))* Found Link.

Cuddy, Robbin. Clifford Helps Santa. Sander, Sonia & Bridwell, Norman. 2006. (Clifford the Big Red Dog Ser.). (J). pap. *(978-0-439-90456-8(0))* Scholastic, Inc.

—Learn to Draw Birds & Butterflies: Step-By-Step Instructions for More Than 25 Winged Creatures. Walter Foster Jr. Creative Team. 2016. (Learn to Draw: Expanded Edition Ser.). (ENG.). 64p. (J). (gr. 3-5). 33.32 *(978-1-939581-96-9(6),* Walter Foster Jr) Quarto Publishing Group USA.

—Learn to Draw Cats & Kittens: Step-By-Step Instructions for More Than 25 Favorite Feline Friends. Walter Foster Jr. Creative Team. 2015. (Learn to Draw: Expanded Edition Ser.). (ENG.). 64p. (J). (gr. 3-5). 33.32 *(978-1-939581-66-2(4),* Walter Foster Jr) Quarto Publishing Group USA.

—Learn to Draw Exotic Animals: Step-By-Step Instructions for More Than 25 Unusual Animals. Walter Foster Jr. Creative Team. 2016. (Learn to Draw: Expanded Edition Ser.). (ENG.). 64p. (J). (gr. 3-5). 33.32 *(978-1-939581-97-6(4),* Walter Foster Jr) Quarto Publishing Group USA.

—Learn to Draw Forest Animals: Step-By-Step Instructions for More Than 25 Woodland Creatures. Walter Foster Jr. Creative Team. 2015. (Learn to Draw: Expanded Edition Ser.). (ENG.). 64p. (J). (gr. 3-5). 33.32 *(978-1-939581-68-6(0),* Walter Foster Jr) Quarto Publishing Group USA.

—Learn to Draw Horses & Ponies: Step-By-Step Instructions for More Than 25 Different Breeds. Walter Foster Jr. Creative Team. 2015. (Learn to Draw: Expanded Edition Ser.). (ENG.). 64p. (J). (gr. 3-5). 33.32 *(978-1-939581-65-5(6),* Walter Foster Jr) Quarto Publishing Group USA.

—Learn to Draw Pets: Step-By-Step Instructions for More Than 25 Cute & Cuddly Animals. Walter Foster Jr. Creative Team. 2015. (Learn to Draw: Expanded Edition Ser.). (ENG.). 64p. (J). (gr. 3-5). 33.32 *(978-1-939581-53-2(2),* Walter Foster Jr) Quarto Publishing Group USA.

—Learn to Draw Polar Animals: Draw More Than 25 Favorite Arctic & Antarctic Wildlife Critters. Walter Foster Jr. Creative Team. 2015. (Learn to Draw: Expanded Edition Ser.). (ENG.). 64p. (J). (gr. 3-5). 33.32 *(978-1-939581-51-8(6),* Walter Foster Jr) Quarto Publishing Group USA.

—Learn to Draw Rainforest & Jungle Animals: Learn to Draw & Color 21 Different Exotic Creatures, Step by Easy Step, Shape by Simple Shape! Phan, Sandy. 2014. 40p. (J). *(978-1-939581-25-9(7))* Quarto Publishing Group USA.

—Learn to Draw Safari Animals: Step-By-Step Instructions for More Than 25 Exotic Animals. Walter Foster Jr. Creative Team. 2015. (Learn to Draw: Expanded Edition Ser.). (ENG.). 64p. (J). (gr. 3-5). 33.32 *(978-1-939581-67-9(2),* Walter Foster Jr) Quarto Publishing Group USA.

—Learn to Draw Sea Creatures. Walter Foster Jr. Creative Team. 2015. (Learn to Draw: Expanded Edition Ser.). (ENG.). 64p. (J). (gr. 3-5). 33.32 *(978-1-939581-54-9(0),* Walter Foster Jr) Quarto Publishing Group USA.

—Learn to Draw Zoo Animals: Step-By-Step Instructions for More Than 25 Popular Animals. Walter Foster Jr. Creative Team. 2016. (Learn to Draw: Expanded Edition Ser.). (ENG.). 64p. (J). (gr. 3-5). lib. bdg. 33.32 *(978-1-939581-99-0(0),* Walter Foster Jr) Quarto Publishing Group USA.

Cuddy, Robbin & Cole, Joanna. The Magic School Bus in the Bat Cave. Lane, Jeanette & Cole, Joanna. 2006. (J). pap. *(978-0-439-89934-5(6))* Scholastic, Inc.

Cuddy, Robbin & Walter Foster Jr. Creative Team. Learn to Draw Dinosaurs: Step-By-Step Instructions for More Than 25 Prehistoric Creatures. Walter Foster Jr. Creative Team. 2015. (Learn to Draw: Expanded Edition Ser.). (ENG.). 64p. (J). (gr. 3-5). 33.32 *(978-1-939581-70-9(2),* Walter Foster Jr) Quarto Publishing Group USA.

Cuddy, Robin. Baby Meerkats. Clarke, Ginjer L. 2010. (Penguin Young Readers, Level 3 Ser.). (ENG.). 48p. (J). (gr. 1-3). 4.99 *(978-0-448-45106-0(9),* Penguin Young Readers) Penguin Young Readers Group.

—Baby Otter. Clarke, Ginjer L. 2009. (Penguin Young Readers, Level 3 Ser.). (ENG.). 48p. (J). (gr. 1-3). mass mkt. 4.99 *(978-0-448-45105-3(0),* Penguin Young Readers) Penguin Young Readers Group.

—Simba's Moon. Weiss, Ellen. Date not set. (ENG.). 32p. (J). (gr. -1-2). 12.99 *(978-0-7868-3267-5(3))* Disney Pr.

Cuddy, Robin & Wummer, Amy. Baby Elephant. Clarke, Ginjer L. 2009. (Penguin Young Readers, Level 3 Ser.). (ENG.). 48p. (J). (gr. 1-3). mass mkt. 4.99 *(978-0-448-44825-1(4),* Penguin Young Readers) Penguin Young Readers Group.

Cudignotto, Elettra. Sean Goes to Barcelona: A Children's Book about Soccer & Goals. Preminger, Tanya. 2019. (Sean Wants to Be Messi Ser.: Vol. 2). (ENG.). 76p. (J). (gr. k-4). 22.99 *(978-0-578-48039-8(5))* Preminger, Tanya.

—The Zoo on the Sea: Noah & the Ark. West, Claudia S. 2019. (Grammy Giggle' Bible Stories Ser.: Vol. 1). (ENG.). 42p. (J). (gr. k-2). 17.95 *(978-1-7338784-0-1(8))* Heyer Publishing.

Cudignotto, Elettra F. Fish Tummy Soup: (the Inside Scoop on Jonah) West, Claudia S. 2019. (Grammy Giggle' Bible Stories Ser.: Vol. 2). (ENG.). 42p. (J). (gr. k-3). 17.95 ***(978-1-7338784-1-8(6))*** Heyer Publishing.

Cue, Harold. Yankee Doodle: The Story of A Pioneer Boy & His Dog. Bartlett, Arthur C. 2011. 322p. 50.95 *(978-1-258-06634-5(3))* Literary Licensing, LLC.

Cuellar, Olga. Arco Iris de Poesia: Poemmas de las Americas y Espana. Andricain, Sergio. 2008. (SPA.). 40p. (J). (gr. -1-3). 15.99 *(978-1-930332-59-1(9))* Lectorum Pubns., Inc.

—El Jardin de la Emperatriz Casia. Wang, Gabrielle. Holguin, Magdalena, tr. 2004. (SPA.). 108p. (YA). 8.95 *(978-958-04-7346-6(3))* Norma S.A. COL. Dist: Distribuidora Norma, Inc.

—Que Extranos Son Los Terricolas/Earthlings, How Weird They Are! Rodriguez, Antonio Orlando. 2006. (Bilingual Collection). (SPA.). 51p. (J). (gr. k-2). *(978-958-30-1737-7(X))* Panamericana Editorial.

—Los Siete Mejores Cuentos Chinos. Hoyos, Hector. 2004. (SPA.). (J). (gr. 3-5). *(978-958-04-7210-0(6))* Norma S.A.

—Los Siete Mejores Cuentos Indios. Hoyos, Hector. 2004. (SPA.). 55p. (J). (gr. 3-5). *(978-958-04-7213-1(0))* Norma S.A.

Cuentas, Joel. Do You See the Sea Horse? Book of Homophones. Talbot, Virginia. 2019. (ENG.). 24p. (J). 23.95 ***(978-1-64096-868-4(7))***; pap. 13.95 ***(978-1-64096-538-6(6))*** Newman Springs Publishing, Inc.

Cuevas, Andres Mario Ramirez. Circuito Interior: Los Deportistas Por Dentro. Santillan, Maria Luisa. rev. ed. 2006. (Otra Escalera Ser.). (SPA & ENG.). 24p. (J). (gr. 2-4). pap. 9.95 *(978-968-5920-72-8(9))* Castillo, Ediciones, S. A. de C. V. MEX. Dist: Macmillan.

Cuevas, Ernesto & Cuevas, Ernesto, Jr. Featherless: Desplumado. Herrera, Juan Felipe. 2004. (ENG & SPA.). 32p. (J). (gr. 1-4). 16.95 *(978-0-89239-195-0(2))* Lee & Low Bks., Inc.

Cuevas, Ernesto, Jr., jt. illus. see Cuevas, Ernesto.

Cuevas, Ernesto, jt. illus. see Herrera, Juan Felipe.

Cuevas, Jezreel. Richie Doodles: An Adventure of a Young Richard Feynman. Mouton, M. J. 2018. (Tiny Thinkers Ser.). 24p. (J). (gr. k-3). 16.95 *(978-0-9983147-1-6(4),* Secular Media Group) Rare Bird Bks.

Cuevas, Jezreel S. Carl Went to the Library: An Adventure of a Young Carl Sagan. Mouton, M. J. 2018. (Tiny Thinkers Ser.). 24p. (J). (gr. k-4). 16.95 *(978-0-9983147-9-2(X))* Rare Bird Bks.

Culbertson, James Forrest. Louisiana: The Land & Its People, 1 vol. Eakin, Sue et al. 5th ed. 2006. (ENG.). 560p. 35.00 (978-1-58980-303-9(5), Pelican Publishing) Arcadia Publishing.

Culkin-Lawrence, Teresa. Lara Saves the Concert, 7 vols. Smith, Annette. 2006. (ENG.). (J). (gr. 1-2). pap. 65.33 (978-1-4189-1606-0(4)) Houghton Mifflin Harcourt Supplemental Pubs.

Cullen, Jennifer. Animal Earthquake. Cullen, Jennifer. 2019. (ENG.). 24p. (J). pap. 9.99 (978-1-0705-4367-3(5)) Independently Published.

—Faces Undercover. Cullen, Jennifer. 2019. (ENG.). 26p. (J). pap. 9.99 (978-1-0991-1678-0(3)) Independently Published.

Cullen, Lisa Anne. Three Wild Pigs: A Carolina Folktale. Cullen, Lisa Anne. 2018. (Young Palmetto Bks.). (ENG.). 32p. (J). 18.99 (978-1-61117-944-6(0)) Univ. of South Carolina Pr.

Cullen, Philip. The Friendship Fairies. Kennedy, Lucy. 2020. (ENG.). 160p. (J). pap. 9.95 **(978-0-7171-8949-6(X))** Gill Bks. IRL. Dist: Casemate Pubs. & Bk. Distributors, LLC.

Cully, Sheilagh. Oopsie Daisy: The Deaf & Partially Blind Ray of Aussie Sunshine. Marsh, Deborah. Cully, Meghan, ed. 2020. (ENG.). 40p. (J). pap. 12.99 **(978-1-0951-2296-9(7))** Independently Published.

Culotta, Kent. D Is for Dump Truck: A Construction Alphabet. Shoulders, Michael. 2016. (ENG.). 32p. (J). (gr. k-3). 16.99 (978-1-58536-975-1(6), 204115) Sleeping Bear Pr.

—Too Many Tomatoes. Ode, Eric. 2016. (ENG.). 32p. (J). 11.99 (978-1-61067-400-3(6)) Kane Miller.

—The Twelve Days of Christmas in Kentucky. Christensen, Evelyn B. (Twelve Days of Christmas in America Ser.). (J). (-k). 2018. 22p. bds. 7.95 (978-1-4549-3033-4(0)); 2016. 32p. 12.95 (978-1-4549-1959-9(0)) Sterling Publishing Co., Inc.

Culpepper, Gina G. Felix & Culpepper, Victoria Lynn Felix. Brownie the Lonely Dragon. Culpepper, Peter Ryan & Culpepper, Gina G. Felix. Make-a-Wish Foundation Staff, ed. l.t. ed. 2003. 32p. 17.95 (978-0-9740435-0-0(8), 1) Culpepper, Felix International, Inc.

Culpepper, Victoria Lynn Felix, jt. illus. see Culpepper, Gina G. Felix.

Culver, Dennis. Chicken Boy: The Amazing Adventures of a Super Hero with Autism. Allen, Gregory G. 2012. 32p. pap. 9.99 (978-0-9853441-0-8(5)) ASD Publishing.

Cumbers, Jenna. Attack My Anxiety! Sachdev, Amomrat. 2016. (ENG.). (J). (gr. k-6). pap. (978-1-928034-15-5(2)) ED-ucation Publishing.

Cumming, Hannah. The Cloud. Cumming, Hannah. 2010. (Child's Play Library). (ENG.). 32p. (J). (gr. 1-2). pap. (978-1-84643-343-6(6)) Child's Play International Ltd.

—The Lost Stars. Cumming, Hannah. 2011. (Child's Play Library). 32p. (J). (978-1-84643-416-7(5)) Child's Play International Ltd.

—The Red Boat. Cumming, Hannah. 2012. (Child's Play Library). 32p. (J). (ENG.). (978-1-84643-493-8(9)); (978-1-84643-481-5(5)) Child's Play International Ltd.

Cumming, Hannah & Noakes, Polly. Focusing on Feelings Book Set Of 4. Cumming, Hannah et al. 2020. (Social & Emotional Learning Sets Ser.). (ENG.). 144p. (J). pap., pap., pap. **(978-1-78628-536-2(3))** Child's Play International Ltd.

Cummings, Art, jt. illus. see Lopshire, Robert.

Cummings, Erika. Blueberry's Gift. Mudge, Tenney. 2019. (ENG.). 34p. (J). (gr. k-4). pap. 16.95 **(978-1-7339720-2-4(1)**, Harbour Bks.) Mariner Publishing.

Cummings, Erika. Ruby at the Gate. Moses, Robert. 2nd ed. 2018. (ENG.). 20p. (J). pap. 9.95 (978-0-9992885-3-5(9)) Mariner Publishing.

Cummings, Maris. Seeking Serenity. Stella, Pilar. 2008. (ENG.). (J). (gr. -1-3). pap. 17.95 (978-1-60037-451-7(4)) Morgan James Publishing.

Cummings, Matt & Yan, Edison. Summer Brain Quest: Between Grades 2 And 3. Walker, Persephone et al. 2017. (Summer Brain Quest Ser.). (ENG.). 160p. (J). (gr. 2-3). pap. 12.95 (978-0-7611-8918-3(1), 18918) Workman Publishing Co., Inc.

Cummings, Pat. Beauty & the Beast. Lee, H. Chuku. 2014. (ENG.). 32p. (J). (gr. -1-3). 17.99 (978-0-688-14819-5(0), Amistad) HarperCollins Pubs.

—Pickin' Peas. MacDonald, Margaret Read. 2014. (ENG.). 32p. pap. 8.95 (978-1-939160-83-6(9)) August Hse. Pubs., Inc.

—Storm in the Night. Stolz, Mary. 2020. (Trophy Picture Bks.). (ENG.). 32p. (J). (gr. -1-3). pap. 7.99 (978-0-06-443256-6(4), HarperCollins) HarperCollins Pubs. Ltd. GBR. Dist: HarperCollins Pubs.

—The World's Wide Open. Stroud, Bettye. 2016. (J). (978-0-689-84026-5(8)) Simon & Schuster Bks. For Young Readers.

Cummings, Pat. Harvey Moon, Museum Boy. Cummings, Pat. 2008. 32p. (J). (gr. -1-3). lib. bdg. 18.89 (978-0-06-057861-9(0)) HarperCollins Pubs.

Cummings, Steven. Champions by Jim Zub Vol. 1: Beat the Devil, Vol. 1. 2019. (ENG.). 112p. (YA). (gr. 8-17). pap. 17.99 (978-1-302-91671-8(8)) Marvel Worldwide, Inc.

—Champions by Jim Zub Vol. 2: Give & Take. 2019. (Champions by Jim Zub Ser.: 2). (ENG.). 112p. (YA). (gr. 8-17). pap. 15.99 (978-1-302-91672-5(6)) Marvel Worldwide, Inc.

—Uglies: Cutters (Graphic Novel) Westerfeld, Scott & Grayson, Devin. 2012. (Uglies Graphic Novels Ser.: 2). 176p. (YA). (gr. 8-12). pap. 12.99 (978-0-345-52723-3(2), Del Rey) Random House Publishing Group.

Cummings, Troy. Captain Kidd's Crew Experiments with Sinking & Floating, 1 vol. Weakland, Mark. 2012. (In the Science Lab Ser.). (ENG.). 24p. (J). (gr. k-3). pap. 9.95 (978-1-4048-7236-3(1)); lib. bdg. 27.32 (978-1-4048-7144-1(6)) Capstone. (Picture Window Bks.).

—Caring for Your Lion. Sauer, Tammi. 2017. (ENG.). 32p. (J). (gr. -1). 16.95 (978-1-4549-1609-3(5)) Sterling Publishing Co., Inc.

—Cars & Trucks. 2018. (ENG.). 5p. (J). (gr. -1 — 1). 15.99 (978-1-4521-6546-2(7)) Chronicle Bks. LLC.

—Mighty Truck. Barton, Chris. 2016. (ENG.). 32p. (J). (gr. -1-3). 17.99 (978-0-06-234478-6(1)) HarperCollins Pubs.

—Mighty Truck: Surf's Up! Barton, Chris. 2019. (I Can Read Level 1 Ser.). (ENG.). 32p. (J). (gr. -1-3). 16.99 (978-0-06-234476-2(5)); pap. 4.99 (978-0-06-234475-5(7)) HarperCollins Pubs.

—Mighty Truck: Muddymania! Barton, Chris. 2017. (ENG.). 32p. (J). (gr. -1-3). 17.99 (978-0-06-234479-3(X)) HarperCollins Pubs.

—Mighty Truck on the Farm. Barton, Chris. 2018. (I Can Read Level 1 Ser.). (ENG.). 32p. (J). (gr. -1-3). 16.99 (978-0-06-234467-0(6)); pap. 4.99 (978-0-06-234466-3(8)) HarperCollins Pubs.

—Mighty Truck: the Traffic Tie-Up. Barton, Chris. 2018. (I Can Read Level 1 Ser.). (ENG.). 32p. (J). (gr. -1-3). 16.99 (978-0-06-234470-0(6)); pap. 4.99 (978-0-06-234469-4(2)) HarperCollins Pubs.

—Mighty Truck: Zip & Beep. Barton, Chris. 2018. (I Can Read Level 1 Ser.). (ENG.). 32p. (J). (gr. -1-3). 16.99 (978-0-06-234473-1(0)); pap. 4.99 (978-0-06-234472-4(2)) HarperCollins Pubs.

—Monster Notebook. 2017. (J). (978-1-5364-2396-9(3)) Scholastic, Inc.

Cummings, Troy. More Bears! Nesbitt, Kenn. (J). (-3). 2020. 32p. 8.99 **(978-1-7282-2304-9(0))**; 2017. (ENG.). 28p. bds. 7.99 (978-1-4926-5467-4(1)); 2010. (ENG.). 32p. 14.99 (978-1-4022-3835-2(5)) Sourcebooks, Inc. (Sourcebooks Jabberwocky).

Cummings, Troy. The Twelve Days of Christmas in Indiana. Griffin, Donna. (Twelve Days of Christmas in America Ser.). (J). (-k). 2017. 22p. bds. 7.95 (978-1-4549-2793-8(3)); 2014. 40p. 12.95 (978-1-4549-0888-3(2)) Sterling Publishing Co., Inc.

Cummings, Troy. Attack of the Shadow Smashers. Cummings, Troy. 2013. (Notebook of Doom Ser.: 3). (ENG.). 96p. (J). (gr. 1-3). pap. 4.99 (978-0-545-55297-4(4)) Scholastic, Inc.

—Attack of the Shadow Smashers: #3. Cummings, Troy. 2018. (Notebook of Doom Ser.). (ENG.). 96p. (J). (gr. 2-5). lib. bdg. 27.07 (978-1-5321-4274-1(9), 31091, Chapter Bks.) Spotlight.

—Battle of the Boss-Monster. Cummings, Troy. 2017. (Notebook of Doom Ser.: 13). (ENG.). 96p. (J). (gr. 1-3). lib. bdg. 15.99 (978-1-338-03457-8(X)); pap. 4.99 (978-1-338-03456-1(1)) Scholastic, Inc.

—Brute-Cake. Cummings, Troy. 2019. (Binder of Doom Ser.: 1). (ENG.). 96p. (J). (gr. 1-3). pap. 4.99 (978-1-338-31466-3(1)) Scholastic, Inc.

—Charge of the Lightning Bugs. Cummings, Troy. 2015. (Notebook of Doom Ser.: 8). (ENG.). 96p. (J). (gr. 1-3). 15.99 (978-0-545-79554-8(0)); pap. 4.99 (978-0-545-79555-5(9)) Scholastic, Inc.

—Charge of the Lightning Bugs: #8. Cummings, Troy. 2018. (Notebook of Doom Ser.). (ENG.). 96p. (J). (gr. 2-5). lib. bdg. 27.07 (978-1-5321-4279-6(X), 31096, Chapter Bks.) Spotlight.

—Chomp of the Meat-Eating Vegetables. Cummings, Troy. 2014. (Notebook of Doom Ser.: 4). (ENG.). 96p. (J). (gr. 1-3). pap. 4.99 (978-0-545-55299-8(0)) Scholastic, Inc.

—Chomp of the Meat-Eating Vegetables: #4. Cummings, Troy. 2018. (Notebook of Doom Ser.). (ENG.). 96p. (J). (gr. 2-5). lib. bdg. 27.07 (978-1-5321-4275-8(7), 31092, Chapter Bks.) Spotlight.

—Day of the Night Crawlers. Cummings, Troy. 2013. (Notebook of Doom Ser.: 2). 96p. (J). (gr. 1-3). pap. 4.99 (978-0-545-49325-3(0)) Scholastic, Inc.

—Day of the Night Crawlers: #2. Cummings, Troy. 2018. (Notebook of Doom Ser.). (ENG.). 96p. (J). (gr. 2-5). lib. bdg. 27.07 (978-1-5321-4273-4(0), 31090, Chapter Bks.) Spotlight.

—The Eensy Weensy Spider Freaks Out! (Big-Time!) Cummings, Troy. 2015. 40p. (J). (gr. -1-2). 7.99 (978-0-553-49672-7(7), Dragonfly Bks.) Random Hse. Children's Bks.

—Flurry of the Snombies. Cummings, Troy. 2015. (Notebook of Doom Ser.: 7). (ENG.). 96p. (J). (gr. 1-3). pap. 4.99 (978-0-545-79550-0(8)) Scholastic, Inc.

—Flurry of the Snombies: #7. Cummings, Troy. 2018. (Notebook of Doom Ser.). (ENG.). 96p. (J). (gr. 2-5). lib. bdg. 27.07 (978-1-5321-4278-9(1), 31095, Chapter Bks.) Spotlight.

—March of the Vanderpants - A Branches Book. Cummings, Troy. 2017. (Notebook of Doom Ser.: 12). (ENG.). 96p. (J). (gr. 1-3). pap. 4.99 (978-1-338-03452-3(9)) Scholastic, Inc.

—March of the Vanderpants: #12. Cummings, Troy. 2018. (Notebook of Doom Ser.). (ENG.). 96p. (J). (gr. 2-5). lib. bdg. 27.07 (978-1-5321-4283-3(8), 31100, Chapter Bks.) Spotlight.

—Monster Notebook. Cummings, Troy. 2017. (Notebook of Doom Ser.). (ENG.). 144p. (J). (gr. 1-3). pap. 6.99 (978-1-338-15742-0(6)) Scholastic, Inc.

—The Notebook of Doom Collection, Bks. 1-3. Cummings, Troy. 2016. (Notebook of Doom Ser.). (ENG.). 288p. (J). (gr. 1-3). pap. 9.99 (978-1-338-10199-7(4)) Scholastic, Inc.

—Pop of the Bumpy Mummy. Cummings, Troy. 2014. (Notebook of Doom Ser.: 6). (ENG.). 96p. (J). (gr. 1-3). pap. 4.99 (978-0-545-69898-6(7)) Scholastic, Inc.

—Pop of the Bumpy Mummy: #6. Cummings, Troy. 2018. (Notebook of Doom Ser.). (ENG.). 96p. (J). (gr. 2-5). lib. bdg. 27.07 (978-1-5321-4277-2(3), 31094, Chapter Bks.) Spotlight.

—Rise of the Balloon Goons. Cummings, Troy. 2013. (Notebook of Doom Ser.: 1). (ENG.). 96p. (J). (gr. 1-3). pap. 4.99 (978-0-545-49323-9(4)) Scholastic, Inc.

—Rise of the Balloon Goons: #1. Cummings, Troy. 2018. (Notebook of Doom Ser.). (ENG.). 96p. (J). (gr. 2-5). lib. bdg. 27.07 (978-1-5321-4272-7(2), 31089, Chapter Bks.) Spotlight.

—Rumble of the Coaster Ghost. Cummings, Troy. 2016. (Notebook of Doom Ser.: 9). (ENG.). 96p. (J). (gr. 1-3). pap. 4.99 (978-0-545-86497-8(6)) Scholastic, Inc.

—Rumble of the Coaster Ghost: #9. Cummings, Troy. 2018. (Notebook of Doom Ser.). (ENG.). 96p. (J). (gr. 2-5). lib. bdg. 27.07 (978-1-5321-4280-2(3), 31097, Chapter Bks.) Spotlight.

—Snap of the Super-Goop: A Branches Book. Cummings, Troy. 2016. (Notebook of Doom Ser.: 10). (ENG.). 96p. (J). (gr. 1-3). 24.99 (978-0-545-86500-5(X)) Scholastic, Inc.

—Snap of the Super-Goop - A Branches Book. Cummings, Troy. 2016. (Notebook of Doom Ser.: 1). (ENG.). 96p. (J). (gr. 1-3). pap. 4.99 (978-0-545-86499-2(2)) Scholastic, Inc.

—Snap of the Super-Goop: #10. Cummings, Troy. 2018. (Notebook of Doom Ser.). (ENG.). 96p. (J). (gr. 2-5). lib. bdg. 27.07 (978-1-5321-4281-9(1), 31098, Chapter Bks.) Spotlight.

—Sneeze of the Octo-Schnozz: #11. Cummings, Troy. 2018. (Notebook of Doom Ser.). (ENG.). 96p. (J). (gr. 2-5). lib. bdg. 27.07 (978-1-5321-4282-6(X), 31099, Chapter Bks.) Spotlight.

—Sneeze of the Octo-Schnozz: a Branches Book (the Notebook of Doom #11) Cummings, Troy. 2016. (Notebook of Doom Ser.: 11). (ENG.). 96p. (J). (gr. 1-3). pap. 4.99 (978-1-338-03448-6(0)) Scholastic, Inc.

—Whack of the P-Rex: #5. Cummings, Troy. 2018. (Notebook of Doom Ser.). (ENG.). 96p. (J). (gr. 2-5). lib. bdg. 27.07 (978-1-5321-4276-5(5), 31093, Chapter Bks.) Spotlight.

Cummins, Ian. Yellow Banana: The Banana Split. McCreadie, Avlon. 2017. (ENG.). 26p. (J). (gr. k-6). pap. 11.99 (978-1-946540-60-7(9)) Strategic Book Publishing & Rights Agency (SBPRA).

Cummins, Lucy Ruth. From Ed's to Ned's. Sterer, Gideon. 2020. (ENG.). 48p. (J). (gr. -1-2). 20.99 (978-0-525-64807-9(0)); 17.99 **(978-0-525-64806-2(2))** Random Hse. Children's Bks. (Knopf Bks. for Young Readers).

—The Love Letter. Denise, Anika Aldamuy. 2019. (ENG.). 40p. (J). (gr. -1-3). 17.99 (978-0-06-274157-8(8), HarperCollins) HarperCollins Pubs. Ltd. GBR. Dist: HarperCollins Pubs.

—The Taking Tree: A Selfish Parody. Travesty, Shrill. 2010. (ENG.). 48p. (J). (gr. -1-2). 19.99 (978-1-4424-0763-3(8), Simon & Schuster Bks. For Young Readers) Simon & Schuster Bks. For Young Readers.

—This Is Not a Valentine. Higgins, Carter. 2017. (ENG.). 48p. (J). (gr. k-3). 14.99 (978-1-4521-5374-2(4)) Chronicle Bks. LLC.

—Truman. Reidy, Jean. 2019. (ENG.). 48p. (J). (gr. -1-3). 17.99 (978-1-5344-1664-2(1)) Simon & Schuster Children's Publishing.

Cummins, Lucy Ruth. A Hungry Lion, or a Dwindling Assortment of Animals. Cummins, Lucy Ruth. 2016. (ENG.). 40p. (J). (gr. -1-3). 17.99 (978-1-4814-4889-5(7)) Simon & Schuster Children's Publishing.

—Stumpkin. Cummins, Lucy Ruth. 2018. (ENG.). 56p. (J). (gr. -1-3). 17.99 (978-1-5344-1362-7(6), Atheneum Bks. for Young Readers) Simon & Schuster Children's Publishing.

Cummins, Lucy Ruth & Buisán, David. The Cold #5. Huddleston, Tom. 2019. (Star Wars: Adventures in Wild Space Ser.). (ENG.). 144p. (J). (gr. 3-7). lib. bdg. 27.07 (978-1-5321-4322-9(2), 31852, Chapter Bks.) Spotlight.

—The Darkness #4. Huddleston, Tom. 2019. (Star Wars: Adventures in Wild Space Ser.). (ENG.). 144p. (J). (gr. 3-7). lib. bdg. 27.07 (978-1-5321-4321-2(4), 31851, Chapter Bks.) Spotlight.

—The Escape: Prelude. Scott, Cavan. 2019. (Star Wars: Adventures in Wild Space Ser.). (ENG.). 88p. (J). (gr. 3-7). lib. bdg. 27.07 (978-1-5321-4317-5(6), 31847, Chapter Bks.) Spotlight.

—The Heist #3. Scott, Cavan. 2019. (Star Wars: Adventures in Wild Space Ser.). (ENG.). 144p. (J). (gr. 3-7). lib. bdg. 27.07 (978-1-5321-4320-5(6), 31850, Chapter Bks.) Spotlight.

—The Nest #2. Huddleston, Tom. 2019. (Star Wars: Adventures in Wild Space Ser.). (ENG.). 144p. (J). (gr. 3-7). lib. bdg. 27.07 (978-1-5321-4319-9(2), 31849, Chapter Bks.) Spotlight.

—The Rescue #6. Huddleston, Tom. 2019. (Star Wars: Adventures in Wild Space Ser.). (ENG.). 176p. (J). (gr. 3-7). lib. bdg. 27.07 (978-1-5321-4323-6(0), 31853, Chapter Bks.) Spotlight.

—The Snare #1. Scott, Cavan. 2019. (Star Wars: Adventures in Wild Space Ser.). (ENG.). 144p. (J). (gr. 3-7). lib. bdg. 27.07 (978-1-5321-4318-2(4), 31848, Chapter Bks.) Spotlight.

—Star Wars: Adventures in Wild Space (Set), 7 vols. 2019. (Star Wars: Adventures in Wild Space Ser.). (ENG.). 104p. (J). (gr. 3-7). lib. bdg. 189.49 (978-1-5321-4316-8(8), 31846, Chapter Bks.) Spotlight.

Cummins, Pat. Squashed in the Middle. Winthrop, Elizabeth. 2008. (J). (gr. k-4). 25.95 incl. audio (978-1-4301-0440-7(6)); 28.95 incl. audio compact disk (978-1-4301-0443-8(0)) Live Oak Media.

Cummins, Scott. The Gate of No Return. Morris, Rooster. 2004. (ENG.). (J). per. 7.95 (978-0-9755895-1-9(2), 0-9755895-1-2) Axle Publishing Co., Inc.

Cuneo, Nina. Sheep Won't Sleep. Cox, Judy. 2019. 32p. (J). (gr. -1-3). pap. 8.99 (978-0-8234-4369-7(8)) Holiday Hse., Inc.

—Sheep Won't Sleep: Counting by 2s, 5s, And 10s. Cox, Judy. 2017. (ENG.). 32p. (J). (gr. -1-3). 17.99 (978-0-8234-3701-6(9)) Holiday Hse., Inc.

Cunha, Anna. A Story about Afiya. Berry, James. 2020. 32p. (J). (gr. k-2). 17.99 (978-1-911373-33-9(1)) Lantana Publishing GBR. Dist: Lerner Publishing Group.

Cuniff, Joe. The Littlest Peanut: A Baby Book for the Teeny Tiny Ones. Wilson, Shannan. 2011. 32p. 16.95 (978-1-61254-023-8(6)) Brown Books Publishing Group.

Cunliffe, Ian. Cock-A-doodle-moo! Litton, Jonathan. 2016. (My First Ser.). (ENG.). 12p. (J). (gr. -1-k). bds. 12.99 (978-1-58925-232-5(2)) Tiger Tales.

—Farm. Ross, Isabel. 2018. (My First Ser.). (ENG.). 12p. (J). (gr. -1-k). bds. 9.99 (978-1-68010-539-1(6)) Tiger Tales.

—Friends That Go Stroller Cards. 2019. (ENG.). 20p. (J). (— 1). 9.99 (978-1-68412-515-9(4), Silver Dolphin Bks.) Printers Row Publishing Group.

—Megaboy. 2016. (ENG.). 24p. (J). 9.95 (978-1-78557-908-0(8)) Igloo Bks. GBR. Dist: Simon & Schuster, Inc.

—Ten Tiny Dinosaurs. Brooks, Susie. 2018. (ENG.). 22p. (J). (gr. -1-k). bds. 12.99 (978-1-68412-298-1(8), Silver Dolphin Bks.) Printers Row Publishing Group.

Cunliffe, Ian. I Want to Be a Witch. Cunliffe, Ian. (ENG.). 32p. (J). (gr. -1-k). 2016. mass mkt. 3.99 (978-1-58925-495-4(3)); 2014. 16.99 (978-1-58925-159-5(8)) Tiger Tales.

Cunliffe, Ian & Artful Doodlers, Artful. Farm Sticker Activities. Rusling, Annette. 2014. (My First Ser.). (ENG.). 96p. (J). (gr. -1-2). pap. 9.99 (978-1-58925-303-2(5)) Tiger Tales.

Cunningham, Ann Elizabeth. Sadie Can Count: A Multi-sensory Book, Cunningham, Ann Elizabeth. l.t. ed. 2006. 16p. (J). bds. 29.95 (978-0-9770054-8-2(8)) Sensational Bks.

Cunningham, Bob. Ivan the Invacar & the Cave. Boles, Jim. 2013. 52p. pap. 19.95 (978-0-9858052-2-7(6)) People Ink Pr.

—Ivan the Invacar Helps Big Dog. Boles, Jim. 2012. 56p. pap. 19.95 (978-0-9845983-5-9(9)) People Ink Pr.

—Ivan the Invacar Saves the Wobbly Hubcap. Boles, S. 2014. (J). pap. 7.95 (978-0-9893267-3-5(X)) People Ink Pr.

Cunningham, Charles E. The Puzzle. Beal, Tracy Lynn. 2008. 17p. pap. 24.95 (978-1-60610-078-3(5)) America Star Bks.

Cunningham, David. Snowbound Mystery. Warner, Gertrude Chandler. 2020. (Boxcar Children Ser.). (ENG.). 128p. (J). (gr. 2-6). lib. bdg. 27.07 **(978-1-5321-4479-0(2)**, 35169, Chapter Bks.) Spotlight.

—Tree House Mystery. Warner, Gertrude Chandler. 2020. (Boxcar Children Ser.). (ENG.). 128p. (J). (gr. 2-6). lib. bdg. 27.07 **(978-1-5321-4481-3(4)**, 35171, Chapter Bks.) Spotlight.

Cunningham, Imogen, et al, photos by. In Real Life: Six Women Photographers. Sills, Leslie. 2005. (ENG., 80p. (J). pap. 9.95 (978-0-8234-1752-0(2)) Holiday Hse., Inc.

Cunningham, Kelley. Poison Plate, 1 vol. Sobel, M. et al. 2006. (Vortex Bks.). (ENG.). 112p. (J). (gr. 5-9). per. 7.19 (978-1-59889-280-2(0), Stone Arch Bks.) Capstone.

—The Ultimate How-To-Draw Real Stuff Book. 2006. 48p. (J). (978-0-439-81336-5(0)) Scholastic, Inc.

Cunningham, Paul. Braving the Storm, 6 vols., Vol. 2. Dateno, Maria Grace. 2013. 70p. (J). pap. 5.95 (978-0-8198-1204-9(8)) Pauline Bks. & Media.

—Courageous Quest. Dateno, Maria Grace. 2014. 81p. (J). pap. 5.95 (978-0-8198-1628-3(0)) Pauline Bks. & Media.

—Danger at Sea. Dateno, Maria Grace. 2013. 80p. (J). pap. 5.95 (978-0-8198-1891-1(7)) Pauline Bks. & Media.

—Discovery at Dawn. Dateno, Maria Grace. 2014. (ENG.). 79p. (J). pap. 5.95 (978-0-8198-1895-9(X)) Pauline Bks. & Media.

—Mystery of the Missing Jars. Dateno, Maria Grace. 2014. 77p. (J). 5.95 (978-0-8198-4922-9(7)) Pauline Bks. & Media.

—Shepherds to the Rescue, 6 vols., Vol. 1. Dateno, Maria Grace. 2013. 71p. (J). pap. 5.95 (978-0-8198-7251-7(2)) Pauline Bks. & Media.

Cunningham, R. We Are All People: A Children's Book about Tolerance. Catton, Lucas A. 2019. (ENG.). 36p. (J). pap. 14.99 **(978-0-578-55240-8(X))** Catton Communications.

Cunningham, Rob. My Uncle Rob. Sandler, Steve. 2008. 32p. (J). pap. 12.95 (978-0-9715721-5-7(1)) Washington Pubs.

Cunningham, S. C. Ginormous Jo's Missing a Loved One. Cunningham, S. C. 2019. (Ginormous Ser.: Vol. 11). (ENG.). 54p. (J). pap. 11.99 **(978-1-6889-3699-7(8))** Independently Published.

Cunningham, S. C. Ginormous Jo's One Good Thing. Cunningham, S. C. 2019. (Ginormous Ser.: Vol. 9). (ENG.). 52p. (J). pap. 11.10 (978-1-0815-5595-5(5)) Independently Published.

—Ginormous Jo's Silly Bullies. Cunningham, S. C. 2019. (Ginormous Ser.: Vol. 4). (ENG.). 44p. (J). pap. 10.99 (978-1-0976-1932-0(X)) Independently Published.

—Ginormous Jo's Welcoming Arms. Cunningham, S. C. 2019. (Ginormous Ser.: Vol. 5). (ENG.). 46p. (J). pap. 10.99 (978-1-0986-9884-3(3)) Independently Published.

Cunningham, S. C. Ginormous Jo's Worry Detective. Cunningham, S. C. 2019. (Ginormous Ser.: Vol. 10). (ENG.). 54p. (J). pap. 11.50 **(978-1-0865-9885-8(7))** Independently Published.

Cunningham, S. C. Ginormous Jo's You Are Special. Cunningham, S. C. 2019. (Ginormous Ser.: Vol. 6). (ENG.). 44p. (J). pap. 10.99 (978-1-0991-3091-5(3)) Independently Published.

Cunningham, S. C. & Raven, Scarlett. Ginormous Joe's Broken Bark. Cunningham, S. C. 2019. (Ginormous Ser.: Vol. 1). (ENG.). 44p. (J). pap. 10.99 **(978-1-7058-2179-4(0))** Independently Published.

Cunningham, Sam. Vlad & the First World War: A Flea in History. Cunningham, Kate. 2017. (Flea in History Ser.: Vol. 2). (ENG.). (J). (gr. 3-5). pap. (978-0-9955205-2-3(6)) Reading Riddle.

Cunningham, Sam. Vlad & the Florence Nightingale Adventure. Cunningham, Kate. 2020. (Flea in History Ser.). (ENG.). 34p. (J). pap. **(978-0-9955205-6-1(9))** Reading Riddle.

Cunningham, Sam. Vlad & the Great Fire of London. Cunningham, Kate. 2016. (ENG.). (J). (gr. 1-3). pap. (978-0-9955205-0-9(X)) Reading Riddle.

Cunningham, Sam. Vlad & the Great Fire of London Activity Book. Cunningham, Kate. 2017. (ENG.). 28p. (J). (gr. 2-4). pap. **(978-0-9955205-3-0(4))** Reading Riddle.

—Vlad & the Space Race. Cunningham, Kate. 2019. (ENG.). 34p. (J). (gr. k-2). pap. **(978-1-913338-00-8(2))** Reading Riddle.

Cunyat, Pol. The Not-So-Deadly Dragon. Tulien, Sean. 2016. (Thud & Blunder Ser.). (ENG.). 56p. (J). (gr. 1-3). lib. bdg. 23.99 (978-1-4965-3220-6(1), Stone Arch Bks.) Capstone.

—The Not-So-Evil Wizard. Tulien, Sean. 2016. (Thud & Blunder Ser.). (ENG.). 56p. (J). (gr. 1-3). pap. 4.95

C

(978-1-4965-3225-1(2)); lib. bdg. 23.99 *(978-1-4965-3221-3(X))* Capstone. (Stone Arch Bks.).

—The Not-So-Helpless Princess. Tulien, Sean & Hoena, Blake. 2016. (Thud & Blunder Ser.). (ENG.). 56p. (J). (gr. 1-3). lib. bdg. 23.99 *(978-1-4965-3218-3(X)*, Stone Arch Bks.) Capstone.

—The Not-So-Heroic Knight. Tulien, Sean & Hoena, Blake. 2016. (Thud & Blunder Ser.). (ENG.). 56p. (J). (gr. 1-3). lib. bdg. 23.99 *(978-1-4965-3219-0(8)*, Stone Arch Bks.) Capstone.

Cupolo, Eileen. My Super Stupendous Day at the Beach. Webb, Jane K. 2012. 24p. pap. 12.95 *(978-1-61493-044-0(9))* Peppertree Pr., The.

Cupples, Pat. The Disappearing Magician. Dickson, Louise. 2007. (Kids Can Read Ser.). 32p. (J). (gr. 1-2). 3.95 *(978-1-55453-034-2(2))* Kids Can Pr., Ltd. CAN. Dist: Hachette Bk. Group.

—The Drop of Doom. Mason, Adrienne. 2007. (Kids Can Read Ser.). 32p. (J). (gr. 1-2). 3.95 *(978-1-55453-036-6(9))*; 14.95 *(978-1-55453-035-9(0))* Kids Can Pr., Ltd. CAN. Dist: Hachette Bk. Group.

—Lost & Found. Mason, Adrienne. 2008. (Kids Can Read Ser.). 32p. (J). (gr. 1-2). 14.95 *(978-1-55453-251-3(5))*; pap. 3.95 *(978-1-55453-252-0(3))* Kids Can Pr., Ltd. CAN. Dist: Hachette Bk. Group.

Cupples, Pat, jt. illus. see Cupples, Patricia.

Cupples, Patricia & Cupples, Pat. Secret Spies. Mason, Adrienne. 2008. (Kids Can Read Ser.). 32p. (J). (gr. 1-2). 14.95 *(978-1-55453-276-6(0))* Kids Can Pr., Ltd. CAN. Dist: Hachette Bk. Group.

Curato, Mike. What If... Berger, Samantha. 2018. 40p. (J). (gr. -1-3). 17.99 *(978-0-316-39096-5(8))* Little, Brown Bks. for Young Readers.

—Worm Loves Worm. Austrian, J. J. 2016. (ENG.). 32p. (J). (gr. -1-3). 17.99 *(978-0-06-238633-5(6))* HarperCollins Pubs.

Curato, Mike. Flamer. Curato, Mike. 2020. (ENG.). 368p. (YA). 25.99 ***(978-1-62779-641-5(X)***, 900157313); pap. 17.99 ***(978-1-250-75614-5(6)***, 900226014) Holt, Henry & Co. (Holt, Henry & Co. Bks. For Young Readers).

Curato, Mike. Little Elliot, Big City. Curato, Mike. (Little Elliot Ser.: 1). (ENG.). (J). 2016. 34p. bds. 7.99 *(978-1-62779-698-9(3)*, 900158360); 2014. 40p. (gr. -1-3). 17.99 *(978-0-8050-9825-9(9)*, 900121237) Holt, Henry & Co. (Holt, Henry & Co. Bks. For Young Readers).

—Little Elliot, Big Family. Curato, Mike. 2015. (Little Elliot Ser.: 2). (ENG.). 40p. (J). (gr. -1-3). 17.99 *(978-0-8050-9826-6(7)*, 900121238, Holt, Henry & Co. Bks. For Young Readers) Holt, Henry & Co.

—Little Elliot, Big Fun. Curato, Mike. 2016. (Little Elliot Ser.: 3). (ENG.). 40p. (J). 17.99 *(978-0-8050-9827-3(5)*, 900121239, Holt, Henry & Co. Bks. For Young Readers) Holt, Henry & Co.

—Little Elliot, Fall Friends. Curato, Mike. 2017. (Little Elliot Ser.: 4). (ENG.). 40p. (J). 17.99 *(978-1-62779-640-8(1)*, 900157312, Holt, Henry & Co. Bks. For Young Readers) Holt, Henry & Co.

—Merry Christmas, Little Elliot. Curato, Mike. (Little Elliot Ser.: 5). (ENG.). (J). 2019. 30p. bds. 7.99 *(978-1-250-20984-9(6)*, 900203329); 2018. 40p. 17.99 *(978-1-250-18589-1(0)*, 900191442) Holt, Henry & Co. (Holt, Henry & Co. Bks. For Young Readers).

Curiel, A. M. & Arroyo, Daniel. The Magic Butterfly & the Flower of Life: (books for Kids - Picture Book - Bedtime Stories for Kids - Children's Books) Curiel, A. M. 2018. (ENG.). 60p. (J). pap. 12.99 *(978-1-7237-5910-9(4))* Independently Published.

Curlee, Lynn. Ballpark: The Story of America's Baseball Fields. Curlee, Lynn. 2008. (ENG.). 48p. (J). (gr. -1-3). 9.99 *(978-1-4169-5360-9(4)*, Atheneum Bks. for Young Readers) Simon & Schuster Children's Publishing.

—Ballpark: The Story of America's Baseball Fields. Curlee, Lynn. 2008. (ENG.). 48p. (J). (gr. 1-5). 22.44 *(978-0-689-86742-2(5))* Simon & Schuster, Inc.

—Capital. Curlee, Lynn. 2006. (ENG.). 48p. (J). (gr. 4-7). 22.99 *(978-1-4169-1801-1(9)*, Atheneum Bks. for Young Readers) Simon & Schuster Children's Publishing.

—The Great Nijinsky: God of Dance. Curlee, Lynn. 2019. 120p. (YA). (gr. 7). lib. bdg. 19.99 *(978-1-58089-800-3(9)*, Charlesbridge Teen) Charlesbridge Publishing, Inc.

—Liberty. Curlee, Lynn. 2003. (ENG.). 48p. (J). (gr. 2-7). 9.99 *(978-0-689-85683-9(0)*, Atheneum Bks. for Young Readers) Simon & Schuster Children's Publishing.

—Mythological Creatures: A Classical Bestiary. Curlee, Lynn. 2008. (ENG.). 40p. (J). (gr. 3-7). 19.99 *(978-1-4169-1453-2(6)*, Atheneum Bks. for Young Readers) Simon & Schuster Children's Publishing.

—Parthenon. Curlee, Lynn. 2011. (ENG.). 40p. (J). (gr. 3-7). 19.99 *(978-1-4424-3094-5(X)*, Atheneum Bks. for Young Readers) Simon & Schuster Children's Publishing.

—Skyscraper. Curlee, Lynn. 2007. (ENG.). 48p. (J). (gr. 3-7). 19.99 *(978-0-689-84489-8(1)*, Atheneum Bks. for Young Readers) Simon & Schuster Children's Publishing.

—Trains. Curlee, Lynn. 2009. (ENG.). 48p. (J). (gr. 4-6). 19.99 *(978-1-4169-4848-3(1)*, Atheneum Bks. for Young Readers) Simon & Schuster Children's Publishing.

Curless, Allan. The Long Patrol: A Tale from Redwall. Jacques, Brian. 2004. (Redwall Ser.: 10). (ENG.). 368p. (J). (gr. 5-3). 8.99 *(978-0-14-240245-0(1)*, Firebird) Penguin Young Readers Group.

—Triss: A Tale from Redwall. Jacques, Brian. 2004. (Redwall Ser.: 15). (ENG.). 400p. (J). (gr. 5-7). pap. 8.99 *(978-0-14-240248-1(6)*, Firebird) Penguin Young Readers Group.

Curley, Carol. The What If Book. Sammarco, Teresa "T". 2013. (J). lib. bdg. 16.95 *(978-1-59598-236-0(1))* HenschelHAUS Publishing, Inc.

Curley, Gabriel. Zion & Zara Stories: The Big Bike Race. Li, Nalah-. 2019. (Zion & Zara Stories Ser.: Vol. 1). (ENG.). 22p. (J). (gr. k-6). 16.00 ***(978-0-578-53690-3(0))*** Color In The Lines LLC.

Curmi, Serena. Smile, Principessa! Enderle, Judith Ross & Gordon, Stephanie Jacob. 2012. (ENG.). 40p. (J). (gr. -1-1). 16.99 *(978-1-4424-3096-9(6)*, McElderry, Margaret K. Bks.) McElderry, Margaret K. Bks.

Curnick, Pippa. Different? Same! Tekavec, Heather. 2017. (ENG.). 32p. (J). (gr. -1-1). 16.99 *(978-1-77138-565-7(0))* Kids Can Pr., Ltd. CAN. Dist: Hachette Bk. Group.

—The First Egg Hunt. Guillain, Charlotte & Guillain, Adam. 2019. (ENG.). 32p. (J). (gr. -1-k). pap. 9.99 *(978-1-4052-8628-2(8))* Egmont Bks., Ltd. GBR. Dist: Independent Pubs. Group.

—Let's Explore... Jungle, 1 vol. Feroze, Jen & Lonely Planet Kids. 2016. (Let's Explore Ser.). (ENG.). 48p. (J). (gr. 1-3). pap. 9.99 *(978-1-76034-038-4(3)*, 5144) Lonely Planet Global Ltd. IRL. Dist: Hachette Bk. Group.

—Let's Explore... Ocean, 1 vol. Feroze, Jen & Lonely Planet Kids. 2016. (Let's Explore Ser.). (ENG.). 48p. (J). (gr. 1-3). pap. 9.99 *(978-1-76034-040-7(5)*, 5146) Lonely Planet Global Ltd. IRL. Dist: Hachette Bk. Group.

—Let's Explore... Safari, 1 vol. Webb, Christina & Lonely Planet Kids. 2016. (Let's Explore Ser.). (ENG.). 48p. (J). (gr. 1-3). pap. 9.99 *(978-1-76034-039-1(1)*, 5145) Lonely Planet Global Ltd. IRL. Dist: Hachette Bk. Group.

Curnow, Bobby. Pony Tales, Vol. 1. Zahler, Thomas F. et al. 2013. (MLP Pony Tales Ser.: 1). 152p. pap. 19.99 *(978-1-61377-740-4(X)*, 9781613777404) Idea & Design Works, LLC.

Currant, Gary. Code Blue Calling All Capitals!, 1 vol. Hall, Pamela. 2009. (Grammar's Slammin' Ser.). (ENG.). 32p. (J). (gr. k-4). 28.50 *(978-1-60270-614-9(X)*, 8976, Looking Glass Library) Magic Wagon.

—Find Your Function at Conjunction Junction, 1 vol. Hall, Pamela. 2009. (Grammar's Slammin' Ser.). (ENG.). 32p. (J). (gr. k-4). 28.50 *(978-1-60270-615-6(8)*, 8978, Looking Glass Library) Magic Wagon.

—The Muscle-Bound Compounds, 1 vol. Hall, Pamela. 2009. (Grammar's Slammin' Ser.). (ENG.). 32p. (J). (gr. k-4). 28.50 *(978-1-60270-616-3(6)*, 8980, Looking Glass Library) Magic Wagon.

—The Old Gray Mare. Fuerst, Jeffrey B. 2010. (Rising Readers Ser.). (J). 3.49 *(978-1-60719-692-1(1))* Newmark Learning LLC.

—The Old Gray Mare IS What She Used to Be. Fuerst, Jeffrey B. 2009. (Reader's Theater Nursery Rhymes & Songs Set B Ser.). 48p. (J). pap. *(978-1-60859-162-6(X))* Benchmark Education Co.

—Punk-Tuation Celebration, 1 vol. Hall, Pamela. 2009. (Grammar's Slammin' Ser.). (ENG.). 32p. (J). (gr. k-4). 28.50 *(978-1-60270-617-0(4)*, 8982, Looking Glass Library) Magic Wagon.

—Stand-in Pronouns Save the Scene!, 1 vol. Hall, Pamela. 2009. (Grammar's Slammin' Ser.). (ENG.). 32p. (J). (gr. k-4). 28.50 *(978-1-60270-618-7(2)*, 8984, Looking Glass Library) Magic Wagon.

—Wheel of Subject-Verb Agreement, 1 vol. Hall, Pamela. 2009. (Grammar's Slammin' Ser.). (ENG.). 32p. (J). (gr. k-4). 28.50 *(978-1-60270-619-4(0)*, 8986, Looking Glass Library) Magic Wagon.

Currant, Gary, jt. illus. see Sharp, Chris.

Currel, Augusta. My First Communion Bible. Moss, Mary Martha. 2018. (ENG.). 128p. (J). pap. 19.95 *(978-0-8198-4965-6(0))* Pauline Bks. & Media.

Curreli, Augusta. My Bible: The Story of God's Love. Wright, Melissa & Curelli, Augusta. 2004. 236p. (J). 24.95 *(978-0-8198-4834-5(4)*, 332-223) Pauline Bks. & Media.

Curreli, Augusta & Lombardo, Irina. Holy Friends: Thirty Saints & Blesseds of the Americas. Amadeo, Diana M. 2005. 134p. (J). (gr. 3-7). 19.95 *(978-0-8198-3384-6(3))* Pauline Bks. & Media.

Curren, Cindy. The Leaf That Was Left. Bryan-Brown, Kim. l.t. ed. 2006. 32p. (J). 16.95 *(978-0-9772564-0-2(5))* Them Potatoes.

Currey, Andrew K. The Littlest Ladybug. Marranzino, Sami. 2012. 32p. pap. 24.95 *(978-1-4626-7781-8(9))* America Star Bks.

Currey, Anna. Hush-a-Bye, Baby: And Other Nursery Rhymes. 2003. (ENG.). 14p. (J). bds. 8.99 *(978-0-333-78086-2(8))* Macmillan Pubs., Ltd. GBR. Dist: Trafalgar Square Publishing.

—One Ted Falls Out of Bed. Donaldson, Julia. (ENG.). (J). 2014. 26p. (gr. -1 — 1). bds. 13.95 *(978-1-4472-0995-9(8))*; 2015. 32p. (— 1). pap. 7.99 *(978-1-4472-6614-3(5))* Pan Macmillan GBR. Dist: Independent Pubs. Group.

—Pat-a-Cake: And Other Nursery Rhymes. 2003. (ENG.). 14p. (J). bds. 6.95 *(978-0-333-78083-1(3))* Macmillan Pubs., Ltd. GBR. Dist: Trafalgar Square Publishing.

—Ring-a-Ring O' Roses: And Other Nursery Rhymes. 2003. (ENG.). 14p. (J). bds. 6.95 *(978-0-333-78084-8(1))* Macmillan Pubs., Ltd. GBR. Dist: Trafalgar Square Publishing.

—Rosie's Hat. Donaldson, Julia. ed. 2015. (ENG.). 32p. (J). (-k). pap. 11.99 *(978-1-4472-6612-9(9))* Pan Macmillan GBR. Dist: Independent Pubs. Group.

—Sophie in Charge. Umansky, Kaye. 2005. 30p. (J). 9.95 *(978-1-56148-478-2(4)*, Good Bks.) Skyhorse Publishing Co., Inc.

—When the World Is Full of Friends. Shields, Gillian. (ENG.). (J). 2019. 26p. bds. 7.99 *(978-1-5476-0067-0(5)*, 900196734, Bloomsbury Children's Bks.); 2018. 32p. 16.99 *(978-1-68119-626-8(3)*, 900179835, Bloomsbury USA Childrens) Bloomsbury Publishing USA.

—When the World Is Ready for Bed (padded Board) Shields, Gillian. 2010. (ENG.). 26p. (J). (gr. -1 — 1). bds. 7.99 *(978-1-59990-533-4(7)*, 900068691, Bloomsbury USA Childrens) Bloomsbury Publishing USA.

—When the World Was Waiting for You. Shields, Gillian. (ENG.). 26p. (J). 2018. bds. 9.99 *(978-1-5476-0033-5(0)*, 900196018, Bloomsbury Children's Bks.); 2012. (gr. -1 — 1). bds. 7.99 *(978-1-59990-849-6(2)*, 900081566, Bloomsbury USA Childrens) Bloomsbury Publishing USA.

—Who Goes There? Wilson, Karma. 2013. (ENG.). 40p. (J). (gr. -1-3). 16.99 *(978-1-4169-8002-5(4)*, McElderry, Margaret K. Bks.) McElderry, Margaret K. Bks.

—The Wishing Club: A Story about Fractions. Napoli, Donna Jo. rev. ed. 2007. (ENG.). 32p. (J). (gr. 1-4). 18.99 *(978-0-8050-7665-3(4)*, 900042104, Holt, Henry & Co. Bks. For Young Readers) Holt, Henry & Co.

Currey, Anna. Truffle Goes to Town. Currey, Anna. 2003. 32p. (YA). *(978-1-85602-429-7(6)*, Pavilion Children's Books) Pavilion Bks.

Currey, Erica Leigh. Finding Nemo: Reef Rescue. Croall, Marie. 2009. (ENG.). 112p. (J). 24.99 *(978-1-60886-524-6(X))* Boom! Studios.

—Finding Nemo: Reef Rescue. Croall, Marie. 2011. (Kaboom! Graphic Novels Ser.). (ENG.). 112p. (J). (gr. 4-7). 26.19 *(978-1-934506-88-2(5))* Boom! Studios.

Currie, Justin. Quackers Wants to Fly. Wolff, Susan. 2013. 32p. pap. 8.95 *(978-1-60653-074-0(7))* High Hill Pr.

Curriel, Hector. Umpire in a Skirt: The Amanda Clement Story. Kratz, Marilyn. 2011. 52p. (J). pap. 9.95 *(978-0-9845041-2-1(5)*, South Dakota State Historical Society Pr.) South Dakota Historical Society Pr.

Curry, Garrett A. Sugarfootn' in the South with Brer' Rabbit: How Handclapping Got Started in the Church Sugarfootstrade; Tattle-Tales Series. El Wilson, Barbara. 2010. 24p. 12.99 *(978-1-4520-3145-3(2))* AuthorHouse.

Curry, Tiana. Autumn Princess Purry: My Life. Curry, Grisel. 2019. (ENG.). 38p. (J). pap. 9.13 ***(978-1-6946-4874-7(5))*** Independently Published.

Curry, Tom. A Fine St. Patrick's Day. Wojciechowski, Susan. 2008. (ENG.). 40p. (J). (gr. -1-2). pap. 7.99 *(978-0-385-73640-4(1)*, Dragonfly Bks.) Random Hse. Children's Bks.

—Galileo's Universe. Lewis, J. Patrick. 2005. (Creative Editions Ser.). 18p. (YA). (gr. 4-7). 24.95 *(978-1-56846-183-0(6))* Creative Co., The.

Curtis, Bruce, photos by. Kids' Container Gardening: Year-Round Projects for Inside & Out. Krezel, Cindy. 2nd ed. 2010. (ENG., 88p. (J). (gr. 1-6). pap. 14.95 *(978-1-883052-75-1(0))* Ball Publishing.

Curtis, E. Ends of Rainbow. Varsell, Linda. 2003. 260p. (J). per. 8.00 *(978-0-9725479-5-6(9))* Rainbow Communications.

—The Humane Touch. Varsell, Linda. 2003. 316p. per. 10.00 *(978-0-9728737-0-3(8))* Rainbow Communications.

—A Journey for Rainbows. Varsell, Linda. 2003. 166p. (YA). per. 6.00 *(978-0-9725479-1-8(6))* Rainbow Communications.

—The Rainbow Breakers. Varsell, Linda. 2003. 232p. per. 7.00 *(978-0-9725479-3-2(2))* Rainbow Communications.

—The Rainbow Circle. Varsell, Linda. 2003. 428p. (J). per. 10.00 *(978-0-9725479-9-4(1))* Rainbow Communications.

—The Rainbow Dreamers. Varsell, Linda. 2003. 262p. per. 8.00 *(978-0-9725479-4-9(0))* Rainbow Communications.

—The Rainbow Makers. Varsell, Linda. 2003. 148p. per. 6.00 *(978-0-9725479-2-5(4))* Rainbow Communications.

—The Rainbow Planet. Varsell, Linda. 2003. 162p. (J). per. 6.00 *(978-0-9725479-7-0(5))* Rainbow Communications.

—The Rainbow Remnants. Varsell, Linda. 2003. 204p. (J). per. 7.00 *(978-0-9725479-8-7(3))* Rainbow Communications.

—The Rainbow Rescue. Varsell, Linda. 2003. 200p. (J). per. 7.00 *(978-0-9725479-6-3(7))* Rainbow Communications.

—With a Human Touch. Varsell, Linda. 2003. 178p. per. 6.00 *(978-0-9725479-0-1(8))* Rainbow Communications.

Curtis, Jane S. When Is Spring? Curtis, Jane S. 2019. (ENG.). 32p. (J). pap. 9.13 ***(978-1-6877-3328-3(7))*** Independently Published.

Curtis, Neil. Cat & Fish. Grant, Joan. 2005. (ENG.). 32p. (J). (gr. k-3). 16.95 *(978-1-894965-14-9(0))* Simply Read Bks. CAN. Dist: Ingram Publisher Services.

—Cat & Fish Go to See. Grant, Joan. 2006. (ENG.). 32p. (J). (gr. -1-3). 16.95 *(978-1-894965-39-2(6))* Simply Read Bks. CAN. Dist: Ingram Publisher Services.

Curtis, Stacy. The Dragon Stone, 0 vols. Regan, Dian. 2013. (Rocky Cave Kids Ser.). (ENG.). 96p. (J). (gr. 2-4). pap. 9.99 *(978-1-4778-1632-5(1)*, 9781477816325, Two Lions) Amazon Publishing.

—Goob & His Grandpa: Habit 7. Covey, Sean. (7 Habits of Happy Kids Ser.: 7). (ENG.). 32p. (J). (gr. -1-1). 2018. 6.99 *(978-1-5344-1584-3(X))*; 2013. 7.99 *(978-1-4424-7653-0(2))* Simon & Schuster Bks. For Young Readers. (Simon & Schuster Bks. For Young Readers).

—Just the Way I Am: Habit 1. Covey, Sean. (7 Habits of Happy Kids Ser.: 1). (ENG.). 32p. (J). (gr. -1-1). 2018. 6.99 *(978-1-5344-1577-5(7))*; 2009. 7.99 *(978-1-4169-9423-7(8))* Simon & Schuster Bks. For Young Readers. (Simon & Schuster Bks. For Young Readers).

—Just the Way I Am: Habit 1. Covey, Sean. 2019. (7 Habits of Happy Kids Ser.: 1). (ENG.). 32p. (J). (gr. k-2). 17.99 *(978-1-5344-4445-4(9))*; pap. 4.99 *(978-1-5344-4444-7(0))* Simon Spotlight. (Simon Spotlight).

—Lily & the Yucky Cookies: Habit 5. Covey, Sean. (7 Habits of Happy Kids Ser.: 5). (ENG.). 32p. (J). (gr. -1-1). 2018. 6.99 *(978-1-5344-1582-9(3))*; 2013. 7.99 *(978-1-4424-7649-3(4))* Simon & Schuster Bks. For Young Readers. (Simon & Schuster Bks. For Young Readers).

Curtis, Stacy. Lily & the Yucky Cookies: Habit 5. Covey, Sean. 2020. (7 Habits of Happy Kids Ser.: 5). (ENG.). 32p. (J). (gr. k-2). 17.99 ***(978-1-5344-4457-7(2))***; pap. 4.99 ***(978-1-5344-4456-0(4))*** Simon Spotlight. (Simon Spotlight).

Curtis, Stacy. A Place for Everything: Habit 3. Covey, Sean. (7 Habits of Happy Kids Ser.: 3). (ENG.). 32p. (J). (gr. -1-1). 2018. 6.99 *(978-1-5344-1580-5(7))*; 2010. 7.99 *(978-1-4169-9425-1(4))* Simon & Schuster Bks. For Young Readers. (Simon & Schuster Bks. For Young Readers).

—A Place for Everything: Habit 3. Covey, Sean. 2019. (7 Habits of Happy Kids Ser.: 3). (ENG.). 32p. (J). (gr. k-2). 17.99 *(978-1-5344-4451-5(3))*; pap. 4.99 *(978-1-5344-4450-8(5))* Simon Spotlight. (Simon Spotlight).

—Raymond & Graham: Bases Loaded. Knudson, Mike & Wilkinson, Steve. 2011. (Raymond & Graham Ser.: 3). 160p. (J). (gr. 3-7). 6.99 *(978-0-14-241751-5(3)*, Puffin Books) Penguin Young Readers Group.

—Ricky Vargas: The Funniest Kid in the World. Katz, Alan. 2011. (J). pap. *(978-0-545-24583-8(4)*, Cartwheel Bks.) Scholastic, Inc.

—Sammy & the Pecan Pie: Habit 4. Covey, Sean. (7 Habits of Happy Kids Ser.: 4). (ENG.). 32p. (J). (gr. -1-1). 2018. 6.99 *(978-1-5344-1581-2(5))*; 2013. 7.99 *(978-1-4424-7647-9(8))* Simon & Schuster Bks. For Young Readers. (Simon & Schuster Bks. For Young Readers).

—Sammy & the Pecan Pie: Habit 4. Covey, Sean. 2019. (7 Habits of Happy Kids Ser.: 4). (ENG.). 32p. (J). (gr. k-2). 17.99 *(978-1-5344-4454-6(8))*; pap. 4.99 *(978-1-5344-4453-9(X))* Simon Spotlight. (Simon Spotlight).

—Snack Attack. Krensky, Stephen. 2008. (Ready-To-Reads Ser.). (ENG.). 32p. (J). (gr. -1-1). pap. 4.99 *(978-1-4169-0238-6(4)*, Simon Spotlight) Simon Spotlight.

—Sophie & the Perfect Poem: Habit 6. Covey, Sean. (7 Habits of Happy Kids Ser.: 6). (ENG.). 32p. (J). (gr. -1-1). 2018. 6.99 *(978-1-5344-1583-6(1))*; 2013. 7.99 *(978-1-4424-7651-6(6))* Simon & Schuster Bks. For Young Readers. (Simon & Schuster Bks. For Young Readers).

Curtis, Stacy. Sophie & the Perfect Poem: Habit 6. Covey, Sean. 2020. (7 Habits of Happy Kids Ser.: 6). (ENG.). 32p. (J). (gr. k-2). 17.99 ***(978-1-5344-4460-7(2))***; pap. 4.99 ***(978-1-5344-4459-1(9))*** Simon Spotlight. (Simon Spotlight).

Curtis, Stacy. To Be a Cat. Haig, Matt. (ENG.). 304p. (J). (gr. 3-7). 2014. pap. 8.99 *(978-1-4424-5406-4(7))*; 2013. 16.99 *(978-1-4424-5405-7(9))* Simon & Schuster Children's Publishing.

—When I Grow Up: Habit 2. Covey, Sean. (7 Habits of Happy Kids Ser.: 2). (ENG.). 32p. (J). (gr. -1-1). 2018. 6.99 *(978-1-5344-1579-9(3))*; 2009. 7.99 *(978-1-4169-9424-4(6))* Simon & Schuster Bks. For Young Readers. (Simon & Schuster Bks. For Young Readers).

—When I Grow Up: Habit 2. Covey, Sean. 2019. (7 Habits of Happy Kids Ser.: 2). (ENG.). 32p. (J). (gr. k-2). 17.99 *(978-1-5344-4448-5(3))*; pap. 4.99 *(978-1-5344-4447-8(5))* Simon Spotlight. (Simon Spotlight).

—The 7 Habits of Happy Kids. Covey, Sean. 2008. (ENG.). 96p. (J). (gr. -1-3). 19.99 *(978-1-4169-5776-8(6)*, Simon & Schuster Bks. For Young Readers) Simon & Schuster Bks. For Young Readers.

—The 7 Habits of Happy Kids Collection: Just the Way I Am; When I Grow up; a Place for Everything; Sammy & the Pecan Pie; Lily & the Yucky Cookies; Sophie & the Perfect Poem; Goob & His Grandpa. Covey, Sean. ed. 2013. (7 Habits of Happy Kids Ser.). (ENG.). 224p. (J). (gr. -1-1). 55.99 *(978-1-4424-9617-0(7)*, Simon & Schuster Bks. For Young Readers) Simon & Schuster Bks. For Young Readers.

—The 7 Habits of Happy Kids Paperback Collection: Just the Way I Am; When I Grow up; a Place for Everything; Sammy & the Pecan Pie; Lily & the Yucky Cookies; Sophie & the Perfect Poem; Goob & His Grandpa. Covey, Sean. ed. 2018. (7 Habits of Happy Kids Ser.). (ENG.). 224p. (J). (gr. -1-1). pap. 48.99 *(978-1-5344-1585-0(8)*, Simon & Schuster Bks. For Young Readers) Simon & Schuster Bks. For Young Readers.

Curtiss, Melody. Naming: Book One of the Magic of Io Series. Robinson, Kelley. 2013. 138p. pap. 8.95 *(978-0-9745865-1-9(X)*, SarahRose Children's Bks.) SarahRose Publishing.

Curtiss, Natalie. Speed of the Dark / German Edition: Babl Children's Books in German & English. Swidler, Patrick. l.t. ed. 2016. (ENG.). (J). 14.99 *(978-1-68304-200-6(X))* Babl Books, Incorporated.

Curto, Rosa M. The Virtue of Effort. Montaner, Vinyet & Cabrera, Alex. 2020. (Virtues Ser.). (ENG.). 32p. (J). (gr. -1-2). pap. 9.95 ***(978-0-8294-5036-1(X))*** Loyola Pr.

—The Virtue of Listening. Cabrera, Alex & Montaner, Vinyet. 2020. (Virtues Ser.). (ENG.). 32p. (J). (gr. -1-2). pap. 9.95 ***(978-0-8294-5037-8(8))*** Loyola Pr.

—The Virtue of Patience. Cabrera, Alex & Montaner, Vinyet. 2020. (Virtues Ser.). (ENG.). 32p. (J). (gr. -1-2). pap. 9.95 ***(978-0-8294-5038-5(6))*** Loyola Pr.

—The Virtue of Prudence. Cabrera, Alex & Montaner, Vinyet. 2020. (Virtues Ser.). (ENG.). 32p. (J). (gr. -1-2). pap. 9.95 ***(978-0-8294-5035-4(1))*** Loyola Pr.

Curto, Rosa M. & Curto, Rosa Maria. I Have Asthma. Moore-Malinos, Jennifer & Moore-Mallinos, Jennifer. 2007. (What Do You Know about? Bks.). 36p. (J). (gr. k-2). pap. 7.99 *(978-0-7641-3785-3(9)*, B.E.S. Publishing) Peterson's.

Curto, Rosa Maria. La Ratita Presumida. Bailer, Darice & Dominguez, Madelca. 2007. (SPA & ENG.). 28p. (J). *(978-0-545-03031-1(5))* Scholastic, Inc.

—The Three R's: Reuse, Reduce, Recycle. Roca, Nuria. 2007. (What Do You Know about? Bks.). 36p. (J). (gr. -1-1). pap. 7.99 *(978-0-7641-3581-1(3)*, B.E.S. Publishing) Peterson's.

Curto, Rosa Maria, jt. illus. see Curto, Rosa M.

Curvey, Mary A., et al. Alton ABC. Johnson, Reneé B. 2019. (ENG.). (gr. k). *(978-0-578-46891-4(3))* Johnson, Renee B.

Curwen, James E. The Dragon's Castle. Potter, Beverly. 2019. (ENG.). 40p. (J). pap. 9.99 ***(978-1-7079-2112-6(1))*** Independently Published.

Curzon, Brett. Hungry for Worms. Rosen, Robert. 2017. (Seasons Around Me Ser.). (ENG.). 24p. (gr. -1-2). pap. 8.95 *(978-1-68342-776-6(9)*, 9781683427766) Rourke Educational Media.

—My Routine. Nino, Carl. 2017. (All about Me Ser.). (ENG.). 24p. (gr. -1-2). 29.93 *(978-1-68342-705-6(X)*, 9781683427056) Rourke Educational Media.

—Our Snowy Day. Rosen, Robert. 2017. (Seasons Around Me Ser.). (ENG.). 24p. (gr. -1-2). pap. 8.95 *(978-1-68342-797-1(1)*, 9781683427971) Rourke Educational Media.

—We Can Reuse It! Marks, Craig. 2017. (I Help My Friends Ser.). (ENG.). 24p. (gr. -1-2). pap. 8.95

(978-1-68342-783-4(1), 9781683427834) Rourke Educational Media.
—What I Want to Be. Abbott, Victoria. 2017. (All about Me Ser.). (ENG.). 24p. (gr. -1-2). 29.93 *(978-1-68342-741-4(6)*, 9781683427414); pap. 8.95 *(978-1-68342-793-3(9)*, 9781683427933) Rourke Educational Media.
Cusack, Elizabeth. Cartwheeling. Whitaker, Joan. 2013. 24p. 22.95 *(978-1-61493-189-8(5))*; pap. 12.95 *(978-1-61493-188-1(7))* Peppertree Pr., The.
Cushley, Aaron. How Many Mice Make an Elephant? And Other Big Questions about Size & Distance. Turner, Tracey. 2020. (How Many Ser.). (ENG.). 48p. (J). 16.99 *(978-0-7534-7565-2(0)*, 900219366, Kingfisher) Roaring Brook Pr.
—Valentine's Day. Berne, Emma Carlson. 2018. (Holidays in Rhythm & Rhyme Ser.). (ENG.). 24p. (gr. k-2). lib. bdg. 33.99 *(978-1-68410-398-0(3)*, 140368); lib. bdg. 33.99 incl. audio compact disk *(978-1-68410-124-5(7)*, 31840) Cantata Learning.
Cushman, Doug. The Amazing Trail of Seymour Snail. Hazen, Lynn E. 2009. (ENG.). 64p. (J). (gr. 1-4). 17.99 *(978-0-8050-8698-0(6)*, 9780805086980, Holt, Henry & Co. Bks. For Young Readers) Holt, Henry & Co.
—Birthday at the Panda Palace. Calmenson, Stephanie. 2007. 32p. (J). (gr. -1-3). 15.99 *(978-0-06-052663-4(7))* HarperCollins Pubs.
—Double Play: Monkeying Around with Addition. Franco, Betsy. 2011. 32p. (J). (gr. -1-2). 15.99 *(978-1-58246-384-1(0)*, Tricycle Pr.) Random Hse. Children's Bks.
—Dracula & Frankenstein Are Friends. Tegen, Katherine. 2003. 32p. (J). (gr. -1-3). 15.99 *(978-0-06-000115-5(1))* HarperCollins Pubs.
—Feliz Dia de Gracias, Gus!, 1 vol. Williams, Jacklyn. Abello, Patricia, tr. from ENG. 2006. (Read-It! Readers en Español: Gus el Erizo Ser.). (SPA.). 32p. (gr. k-3). lib. bdg. 19.99 *(978-1-4048-2690-8(4)*, Picture Window Bks.) Capstone.
—Here Comes the Choo Choo! Roth, Carol. 2007. (J). *(978-0-15-205582-0(7))* Harcourt Trade Pubs.
—The Invisible Man. Yorinks, Arthur. 2011. (ENG.). 32p. (J). (gr. -1-3). 16.99 *(978-0-06-156148-1(7))* HarperCollins Pubs.
—Let's Try It Out in the Air. Simon, Seymour & Fauteux, Nicole. 2003. (Let's Try It Out Ser.). 28p. (J). (gr. -1-3). lib. bdg. 14.65 *(978-0-7569-1477-6(9))* Perfection Learning Corp.
—Let's Try It Out in the Water: Hands-on Early-Learning Science Activities. Simon, Seymour & Fauteux, Nicole. 2003. (Let's Try It Out Ser.). (J). (gr. -1-3). 14.65 *(978-0-7569-1478-3(7))* Perfection Learning Corp.
—Nighttime: Too Dark to See. Strasser, Todd. 2008. 79p. (J). *(978-0-439-80068-6(4))* Scholastic, Inc.
—The Snow Blew Inn. Regan, Dian. 2011. (ENG.). 32p. (J). 16.95 *(978-0-8234-2351-4(4))* Holiday Hse., Inc.
—Thanksgiving Mice! Roberts, Bethany. 2005. 32p. (J). (gr. -1 — 1). 5.95 *(978-0-618-60486-9(3))* Houghton Mifflin Harcourt Publishing Co.
—Valentine Mice! Roberts, Bethany. 2016. (Green Light Readers Level 1 Ser.). (ENG.). 32p. (J). (gr. -1-3). 12.99 *(978-0-544-80897-3(5)*, 1641296, HMH Books For Young Readers) Houghton Mifflin Harcourt Publishing Co.
—Valentine Mice! Board Book. Roberts, Bethany. 2011. (Green Light Readers Level 1 Ser.). (ENG.). 28p. (J). (gr. k — 1). bds. 5.99 *(978-0-547-37144-3(6)*, 1423785) Houghton Mifflin Harcourt Publishing Co.
—What a Day It Was at School! Prelutsky, Jack. 40p. (J). (gr. k-5). 2009. (ENG.). pap. 6.99 *(978-0-06-082337-5(2)*, Greenwillow Bks.); 2006. 16.99 *(978-0-06-082335-1(6))* HarperCollins Pubs.
—What Grandmas Can't Do. Wood, Douglas. (ENG.). 32p. (J). (gr. -1-3). 2008. 7.99 *(978-1-4169-5483-5(X))*; 2005. 19.99 *(978-0-689-84647-2(9))* Simon & Schuster Bks. For Young Readers. (Simon & Schuster Bks. For Young Readers).
—What Santa Can't Do. Wood, Douglas. 2008. (ENG.). 32p. (J). (gr. -1-3). 16.99 *(978-1-4169-6747-7(8)*, Simon & Schuster Bks. For Young Readers) Simon & Schuster Bks. For Young Readers.
—What Time Is It, Mr. Crocodile? Sierra, Judy. 2007. (ENG.). 32p. (J). (gr. -1-3). pap. 7.99 *(978-0-15-205850-0(8)*, 1197570) Houghton Mifflin Harcourt Publishing Co.
Cushman, Doug. Dirk Bones & the Mystery of the Haunted House. Cushman, Doug. 2009. (I Can Read Level 1 Ser.). (ENG.). 32p. (J). (gr. k-3). pap. 4.99 *(978-0-06-073767-2(0))* HarperCollins Pubs.
—Dirk Bones & the Mystery of the Missing Books. Cushman, Doug. 2009. (I Can Read Level 1 Ser.). (ENG.). 32p. (J). (gr. -1-3). 16.99 *(978-0-06-073768-9(9))* HarperCollins Pubs.
—Inspector Hopper's Mystery Year, No. 2. Cushman, Doug. 2003. (I Can Read Bks.). 64p. (J). (gr. k-3). 15.99 *(978-0-06-008962-7(8))*; 16.89 *(978-0-06-008963-4(6))* HarperCollins Pubs.
—Pigmares: Porcine Poems of the Silver Screen. Cushman, Doug. 2012. 44p. (J). (gr. 2-5). 12.95 *(978-1-58089-401-2(1))* Charlesbridge Publishing, Inc.
—Space Cat. Cushman, Doug. 2006. (I Can Read Level 1 Ser.). (ENG.). 32p. (J). (gr. -1-3). pap. 4.99 *(978-0-06-008967-2(9))* HarperCollins Pubs.
—Space Cat. Cushman, Doug. 2006. (I Can Read Bks.). 32p. (gr. -1-3). 14.00 *(978-0-7569-6977-6(8))* Perfection Learning Corp.
Cushner, Susie, photos by. The Bride & Groom First & Forever Cookbook. Barber, Mary Corpening et al. 2003. (ENG., 272p. (gr. 8-17). 35.00 *(978-0-8118-3493-3(X))* Chronicle Bks. LLC.
—Denyse Schmidt Quilts: 30 Colorful Quilt & Patchwork Projects. Schmidt, Denyse. 2005. (ENG., 176p. (gr. 8-17). pap. 24.95 *(978-0-8118-4442-0(0))* Chronicle Bks. LLC.
—5 Spices, 50 Dishes: Simple Indian Recipes Using Five Common Spices. Kahate, Ruta. 2007. (ENG., 132p. (gr. 8-17). pap. 19.95 *(978-0-8118-5342-2(X))* Chronicle Bks. LLC.
Custard, P. T. & Pearson, David. Kid Canine - Superhero! Custard, P. T. 2008. 32p. (J). 13.95 *(978-0-9785317-1-3(X))* Black Plum Bks.
Cutbill, Andy. Albie & the Big Race. 2004. (ENG.). 32p. (J). pap. 9.99 *(978-0-00-712212-7(8))* HarperCollins Pubs. Ltd. GBR. Dist: Trafalgar Square Publishing.
Cutchin, Marcia. Feathers: A Jewish Tale from Eastern Europe. 2005. (ENG.). 36p. (J). (gr. k-3). 16.95 *(978-0-87483-755-1(3)*, 1249133) August Hse. Pubs., Inc.
Cuthbert, R M & Vincent, Allison. Reindeer. Cuthbert, R M. 2006. 30p. (J). 12.95 *(978-1-56167-908-9(9))* American Literary Pr.
Cuthbertson, Ollie. Stranger in the Snow. Benton, Lynne. 2010. (Let's Read! Spanish-English Ser.).Tr. of Extrano en la Nieve. (ENG.). 32p. (J). (gr. k-3). 17.44 *(978-0-7641-4473-8(1)*, B.E.S. Publishing) Peterson's.
—Stranger in the Snow/L'etranger dans la Neige: French/English Edition. Barron's Educational Series & Benton, Lynne. 2010. (Let's Read! French-English Ser.). (ENG.). 32p. (J). (gr. k-3). 17.44 *(978-0-7641-4475-2(8)*, B.E.S. Publishing) Peterson's.
Cutler, Dave. When I Wished I Was Alone. Cutler, Dave. 2003. 36p. (J). 16.95 *(978-0-9671851-0-1(6))* GreyCore Pr.
Cutler, Erin. Grandma's Table. Pontefract, Michelle. 2020. (ENG.). 34p. (J). pap. ***(978-1-989506-16-5(X))*** Pandamonium Publishing Hse.
Cutler, Marcus. Lark & the Dessert Disaster, 1 vol. Deen, Natasha. 2019. (Orca Echoes Ser.). (ENG.). 104p. (J). (gr. 1-3). pap. 6.95 *(978-1-4598-2067-8(3))* Orca Bk. Pubs. USA.
—Lark & the Diamond Caper, 1 vol. Deen, Natasha. 2017. (Orca Echoes Ser.). (ENG.). 96p. (J). (gr. 1-3). pap. 7.95 *(978-1-4598-1400-4(2))* Orca Bk. Pubs. USA.
—Lark Takes a Bow, 1 vol. Deen, Natasha. 2018. (Orca Echoes Ser.). (ENG.). 96p. (J). (gr. 1-3). pap. 7.95 *(978-1-4598-1715-9(X))* Orca Bk. Pubs. USA.
—The Owl & the Two Rabbits. Sammurtok, Nadia. 2019. (ENG.). 32p. (J). 16.95 *(978-1-77227-236-9(1))* Inhabit Media Inc. CAN. Dist: Consortium Bk. Sales & Distribution.
—The Walrus & the Caribou. Harper, Maika. 2020. 32p. (J). 16.95 *(978-1-77227-256-7(6))* Inhabit Media Inc. CAN. Dist: Consortium Bk. Sales & Distribution.
Cutler, Warren. The Seal Pup. Thach, James Otis. 2010. 128p. (J). (gr. k-7). 24.95 *(978-0-9825663-0-5(1))* Bowrider Pr.
Cutting, David. Betty Boop Paper Dolls. 2016. (ENG.). 32p. (J). (gr. 3-6). 11.99 *(978-0-486-80171-1(3))* Dover Pubns., Inc.
—Danny & the Dinosaur: Too Tall. Hale, Bruce. 2015. 29p. (J). *(978-1-4806-8575-8(5))* Harper & Row Ltd.
—GIANTmicrobes — Cells Coloring Book. GIANTmicrobes®. 2014. (ENG.). 32p. (J). (gr. k-5). pap. 3.99 *(978-0-486-78017-7(1))* Dover Pubns., Inc.
—GIANTmicrobes — Germs & Microbes Coloring Book. GIANTmicrobes®. 2014. (ENG.). 32p. (J). (gr. k-5). pap. 3.99 *(978-0-486-78018-4(X))* Dover Pubns., Inc.
—Syd Hoff's Danny & the Dinosaur & the Big Storm. Hale, Bruce. 2017. (J). *(978-1-5182-4495-7(5))* HarperCollins Pubs. Ltd.
—Syd Hoff's Danny & the Dinosaur & the New Puppy. Hale, Bruce & Hoff, Syd. 2015. 32p. (J). *(978-1-4806-8576-5(3))* Harper & Row Ltd.
Cutting, David, jt. illus. see Hoff, Syd.
Cutting, David A. I Love to Sing. Matheson, Anne. 2014. (ENG.). 32p. (J). (gr. 1-5). 7.99 *(978-1-4867-0001-1(2))* Flowerpot Children's Pr. Inc. CAN. Dist: Cardinal Pubs. Group.
—'Twas the Night Before Christmas. Moore, Clement C. 2019. (Flowerpot Holiday Ser.). (ENG.). 20p. (J). (gr. k-2). bds. 7.99 *(978-1-4867-1774-3(8)*, cbf3bb14-baf9-4bb3-b2cc-b6b74208d821) Flowerpot Pr.
Cuuet, Paul, jt. illus. see Itoïz, Mayana.
Cuxart, Bernardette. Cuentame un Cuento, No. 4. (SPA.). 96p. (J). (gr. k-3). *(978-84-480-1602-9(5)*, TM8095) Timun Mas, Editorial S.A. ESP. Dist: Lectorum Pubns., Inc.
Cuzik, David. Captain Cook. Levene, Rebecca. 2005. (Usborne Famous Lives Gift Bks.). 61p. (J). (gr. -1-3). 8.95 *(978-0-7945-1051-0(5)*, Usborne) EDC Publishing.
—Nelson. Lacey, Minna. 2006. (Usborne Famous Lives Gift Bks.). 64p. (J). 8.95 *(978-0-7945-1121-0(X)*, Usborne) EDC Publishing.
—The Usborne Story of Music. O'Brien, Eileen. Danes, Emma & Hooper, Caroline, eds. 2006. (Story of Music Ser.). 32p. (J). (gr. 4). lib. bdg. 15.99 *(978-1-58086-935-5(1)*, Usborne) EDC Publishing.
—The Usborne Story of Music. O'Brien, Eileen. Danes, Emma, ed. 2006. 32p. (J). (gr. 4-7). per. 7.99 *(978-0-7945-1403-7(0)*, Usborne) EDC Publishing.
Cyber Group Studios, Cyber Group. Gigantosaurus: Don't Cave In. Cyber Group Studios, Cyber Group. 2019. (Gigantosaurus Ser.). (ENG.). (J). (gr. -1-2). 32p. 12.99 *(978-1-5362-1207-5(5))*; 34p. 5.99 *(978-1-5362-0988-4(0))* Candlewick Pr. (Candlewick Entertainment).
—Gigantosaurus: Dream Big, Bill. Cyber Group Studios, Cyber Group. 2020. (Gigantosaurus Ser.). (ENG.). 32p. (J). (gr. -1-2). pap. 5.99 *(978-1-5362-1406-2(X)*, Candlewick Entertainment) Candlewick Pr.
—Gigantosaurus: Rock Out, Rocky. Cyber Group Studios, Cyber Group. 2020. (Gigantosaurus Ser.). (ENG.). 32p. (J). (gr. -1-2). pap. 5.99 *(978-1-5362-1408-6(6)*, Candlewick Entertainment) Candlewick Pr.
—Gigantosaurus: Smart Move, Mazu. Cyber Group Studios, Cyber Group. 2020. (Gigantosaurus Ser.). (ENG.). 32p. (J). (gr. -1-2). pap. 5.99 *(978-1-5362-1407-9(8)*, Candlewick Entertainment) Candlewick Pr.
Cyber Group Studios, Cyber Group. Gigantosaurus: the Groundwobbler. Cyber Group Studios, Cyber Group. 2020. (Gigantosaurus Ser.). (ENG.). 32p. (J). (gr. -1-2). 12.99 ***(978-1-5362-1556-4(2))***; pap. 5.99 ***(978-1-5362-1665-3(8))*** Candlewick Pr. (Candlewick Entertainment).
—Gigantosaurus: the Holiday Party. Cyber Group Studios, Cyber Group. 2020. (Gigantosaurus Ser.). (ENG.). 32p. (J). (gr. -1-2). pap. 5.99 ***(978-1-5362-1340-9(3)*****,** Candlewick Entertainment) Candlewick Pr.
Cyber Group Studios, Cyber Group. Gigantosaurus: the Last Dragonfly. Cyber Group Studios, Cyber Group. 2020. (Gigantosaurus Ser.). (ENG.). (J). (gr. -1-2). 32p. 12.99 *(978-1-5362-1400-0(0))*; 36p. 5.99 *(978-1-5362-1401-7(9))* Candlewick Pr. (Candlewick Entertainment).
—Gigantosaurus: Try Again, Tiny. Cyber Group Studios, Cyber Group. 2020. (Gigantosaurus Ser.). (ENG.). 32p. (J). (gr. -1-2). pap. 5.99 *(978-1-5362-1409-3(4)*, Candlewick Entertainment) Candlewick Pr.
Cyr, Cathy. Jay the Jet Seed: Book 2 of the Earth Whispers Series. Cyr, Cathy. 2018. (ENG.). 46p. (J). pap. *(978-1-987982-30-5(4))* Artistic Warrior Publishing.
—Leila's Journey. Cyr, Cathy. 2018. (ENG.). 42p. (J). pap. *(978-1-987982-28-2(2))* Artistic Warrior Publishing.
Cyr, Cathy. Tumble Anna to the Rescue. Cyr, Cathy. 2019. (ENG.). 46p. (J). pap. ***(978-1-987982-40-4(1))*** Artistic Warrior Publishing.
Cyr, Christopher. Who Will Bell the Cat? McKissack, Patricia C. 2018. (ENG.). 32p. (J). (gr. -1-3). 17.95 *(978-0-8234-3700-9(0))* Holiday Hse., Inc.
Cyr, Christopher & Cyr, James. Pete-O Burrito & the Lucky Stripes. Cyr, Liz. 2012. 28p. 24.95 *(978-1-4626-5566-3(1))* America Star Bks.
Cyr, James, jt. illus. see Cyr, Christopher.
Cyrus, Kurt. Agent Q, or the Smell of Danger! Anderson, M. T. (Pals in Peril Tale Ser.). (ENG.). (J). (gr. 5-9). 2011. 320p. pap. 8.99 *(978-1-4424-2640-5(3))*; 2010. 304p. 16.99 *(978-1-4169-8640-9(5))* Beach Lane Bks. (Beach Lane Bks.).
—The Bones of Fred McFee. Bunting, Eve. 2005. (ENG.). 32p. (J). (gr. -1-3). pap. 7.99 *(978-0-15-205423-6(5)*, 1196323) Houghton Mifflin Harcourt Publishing Co.
—The Clue of the Linoleum Lederhosen. Anderson, M. T. 2010. (Pals in Peril Tale Ser.). (ENG.). (J). (gr. 5-9). 272p. pap. 6.99 *(978-1-4424-0702-2(6))*; 2. 256p. 17.99 *(978-1-4424-0697-1(6))* Beach Lane Bks. (Beach Lane Bks.).
—He Laughed with His Other Mouths. Anderson, M. T. 2014. (Pals in Peril Tale Ser.). (ENG.). 304p. (J). (gr. 5-9). 17.99 *(978-1-4424-5110-0(6)*, Beach Lane Bks.) Beach Lane Bks.
—Hibernation Station. Meadows, Michelle. 2010. (ENG.). 40p. (J). (gr. -1-3). 18.99 *(978-1-4169-3788-3(9)*, Simon & Schuster Bks. For Young Readers) Simon & Schuster Bks. For Young Readers.
—Jasper Dash & the Flame-Pits of Delaware. Anderson, M. T. (Pals in Peril Tale Ser.). (ENG.). (J). (gr. 5-9). 2010. 448p. pap. 8.99 *(978-1-4424-0838-8(3))*; 3. 2009. 432p. 16.99 *(978-1-4169-8639-3(1))* Beach Lane Bks. (Beach Lane Bks.).
—Pest Fest. Durango, Julia. 2012. (ENG.). 40p. (J). (gr. -1-2). 19.99 *(978-1-4424-3095-2(8)*, Simon & Schuster Bks. For Young Readers) Simon & Schuster Bks. For Young Readers.
—Sixteen Cows. Wheeler, Lisa. 2006. (ENG.). 32p. (J). (gr. -1-3). reprint ed. pap. 7.99 *(978-0-15-205592-9(4)*, 1196819) Houghton Mifflin Harcourt Publishing Co.
—Twenty Big Trucks in the Middle of the Street. Lee, Mark. (J). 2015. 30p. (-k). bds. 7.99 *(978-0-7636-7650-6(0))*; 2013. 32p. (gr. -1-2). 17.99 *(978-0-7636-5809-0(X))* Candlewick Pr.
—Veinte Camiones Grandes en Medio de la Calle. Lee, Mark. 2015. 30p. (J). (-k). bds. 7.99 *(978-0-7636-7651-3(9))* Candlewick Pr.
—Whales on Stilts! Anderson, M. T. 2010. (Pals in Peril Tale Ser.). (ENG.). (J). (gr. 5-9). 224p. pap. 8.99 *(978-1-4424-0701-5(8))*; 1. 208p. 17.99 *(978-1-4424-0695-7(X))* Beach Lane Bks. (Beach Lane Bks.).
—Whales on Stilts! Anderson, M. T. 2006. (M. T. Anderson's Thrilling Tales Ser.). 188p. (gr. 5-9). 15.95 *(978-0-7569-7213-4(2))* Perfection Learning Corp.
—What in the World? Sets in Nature. Day, Nancy Raines. 2015. (ENG.). 32p. (J). (gr. -1-3). 17.99 *(978-1-4814-0060-2(6)*, Beach Lane Bks.) Beach Lane Bks.
—Word Builder. Paul, Ann Whitford. 2009. (ENG.). 32p. (J). (gr. k-2). 18.99 *(978-1-4169-3981-8(4)*, Simon & Schuster Bks. For Young Readers) Simon & Schuster Bks. For Young Readers.
—Zombie Mommy. Anderson, M. T. (Pals in Peril Tale Ser.). (ENG.). 224p. (J). (gr. 5-9). 2012. pap. 6.99 *(978-1-4424-5440-8(7))*; 2011. 16.99 *(978-1-4169-8641-6(3))* Beach Lane Bks. (Beach Lane Bks.).
—Zombie Mommy. Anderson, M. T. 2011. (M. T. Anderson's Thrilling Tales Ser.). 240p. 16.99 *(978-1-4424-3068-6(0))* Simon & Schuster Children's Publishing.
Cyrus, Kurt. Be a Good Dragon. Cyrus, Kurt. 2018. (ENG.). 32p. (J). (gr. k-3). 16.99 *(978-1-58536-383-4(9)*, 204395) Sleeping Bear Pr.
—Billions of Bricks: A Counting Book about Building. Cyrus, Kurt. 2016. (ENG.). 32p. (J). 18.99 *(978-1-62779-273-8(2)*, 900144946, Holt, Henry & Co. Bks. For Young Readers) Holt, Henry & Co.
—Shake a Leg, Egg! Cyrus, Kurt. 2017. (ENG.). 32p. (J). (gr. -1-3). 17.99 *(978-1-4814-5848-1(5)*, Beach Lane Bks.) Beach Lane Bks.
Czekaj, Jef. The Circulatory Story. Corcoran, Mary. 2010. (ENG.). 44p. (J). (gr. 3-7). pap. 7.95 *(978-1-58089-209-4(4))* Charlesbridge Publishing, Inc.
—The Quest to Digest. Corcoran, Mary K. 2006. 32p. (J). (gr. 3-7). pap. 7.95 *(978-1-57091-665-6(9))* Charlesbridge Publishing, Inc.
Czekaj, Jef. Austin, Lost in America: A Geography Adventure. Czekaj, Jef. 2015. (ENG.). 40p. (J). (gr. -1-3). 17.99 *(978-0-06-228017-6(1))* HarperCollins Pubs.
—A Call for a New Alphabet. Czekaj, Jef. 2011. 48p. (J). (gr. 1-4). pap. 5.95 *(978-1-58089-229-2(9))* Charlesbridge Publishing, Inc.
—Cat Secrets. Czekaj, Jef. 2011. (ENG.). 32p. (J). (gr. -1-3). 16.99 *(978-0-06-192088-2(6)*, Balzer & Bray) HarperCollins Pubs.
—Dog Rules. Czekaj, Jef. 2016. (ENG.). 32p. (J). (gr. -1-3). 17.99 *(978-0-06-228018-3(X))* HarperCollins Pubs.
—Oink-A-Doodle-Moo. Czekaj, Jef. 2012. (ENG.). 32p. (J). (gr. -1-1). 16.99 *(978-0-06-206011-2(2))* HarperCollins Pubs.
Czernecki, Stefan. Aziz the Story Teller. Hughes, V. I. 2006. 29p. (J). (gr. k-4). reprint ed. 17.00 *(978-1-4223-5298-4(6))* DIANE Publishing Co.
—For Sure! for Sure! Andersen, Hans & White, Mus. 2005. (ENG.). 32p. (J). (gr. k-3). 16.95 *(978-0-87483-742-1(1))* August Hse. Pubs., Inc.
—For Sure! for Sure! Andersen, Hans. White, Mus, tr. from DAN. 2006. 29p. (J). (gr. k-4). reprint ed. 17.00 *(978-1-4223-5208-3(0))* DIANE Publishing Co.
—Holy Mole! A Folktale from Mexico. McAlister, Caroline. 2006. (ENG.). 32p. (J). (gr. k-3). 16.95 *(978-0-87483-775-9(8))* August Hse. Pubs., Inc.
—Mama God, Papa God: A Caribbean Tale, 1 vol. Keens-Douglas, Richardo & Tradewind Books Staff. 2016. (ENG.). 20p. (J). (gr. -1-k). 16.95 *(978-1-896580-16-6(5))* Tradewind Bks. CAN. Dist: Orca Bk. Pubs. USA.
—Viva Zapata!, 1 vol. Smith, Emilie & Tejada, Marguerita. 2009. (ENG.). 32p. (J). (gr. -1-k). 14.95 *(978-1-896580-55-5(6))* Tradewind Bks. CAN. Dist: Orca Bk. Pubs. USA.
—Zigzag. San Souci, Robert D. 2005. (ENG.). 32p. (J). (gr. -1-2). 16.95 *(978-0-87483-764-3(2))* August Hse. Pubs., Inc.
Czernichowska. A Contar Gatos. Schmauss, Judy Kentor. 2016. (Early Rising Readers Ser.). (SPA.). (J). (gr. -1). 6.67 *(978-1-4788-3669-8(5))* Newmark Learning LLC.
Czernichowska, Joanna. Arriba. Nunez, Jaclyn. 2016. (Early Rising Readers Ser.). (SPA.). (J). (gr. -1). 6.67 *(978-1-4788-3656-8(3))* Newmark Learning LLC.
—Groundhog & the Sun. Dalton, Kippy. 2016. (Spring Forward Ser.). (J). (gr. 1). *(978-1-4900-9369-7(9))* Benchmark Education Co.
—Hansel & Gretel - 6 Pack: Set of 6 with Common Core Teacher Materials. 2015. (Classic Tales Ser.). (J). (gr. k-1). 39.00 *(978-1-5125-8343-4(X))* Benchmark Education Co.
—La Marea Está Llegando. Lee, Calee M. 2018. (Xist Kids Spanish Bks.). (SPA.). 32p. (J). (gr. -1-3). pap. 9.99 *(978-1-5324-0717-8(3))* Xist Publishing.
—Mi Monito. Lindeen, Mary. 2016. (Early Rising Readers Ser.). (SPA.). 16p. (J). (gr. 1-1). 6.67 *(978-1-4788-4178-4(8))* Newmark Learning LLC.
—Mi Trineo. Koons, Linda. 2016. (Early Rising Readers Ser.). (SPA.). (J). (gr. -1). 6.67 *(978-1-4788-3687-2(3))* Newmark Learning LLC.
—Mr. Max - Gabe, Kate, & Dave - a Home for Moles: StartUp Unit 9 Lap Book. Robinson, Lisa et al. 2015. (Start up Core Phonics Ser.). (J). (gr. k). *(978-1-4900-2598-8(7))* Benchmark Education Co.
—My Monkey. Lindeen, Mary. 2015. (Early Rising Readers Ser.). (J). (gr. -1-k). 5.83 *(978-1-4788-2142-7(6))* Newmark Learning LLC.
—My Sled. Koons, Linda. 2015. (Early Rising Readers Ser.). (J). (gr. -1-k). 5.83 *(978-1-4788-1698-0(8))* Newmark Learning LLC.
—On Top. Nunez, Jaclyn. 2015. (Early Rising Readers Ser.). (J). (gr. -1-k). 5.83 *(978-1-4788-1596-9(5))* Newmark Learning LLC.
—Opinions about Two Fairy Tales: Baba Yaga & Hansel & Gretel. Strom, Laura Layton et al. 2014. (Text Connections Ser.). (J). (gr. 3). *(978-1-4509-9649-5(3))* Benchmark Education Co.
—El Perro y el Lobo. Swain, Cynthia. 2016. (Jump into Genre Ser.). (SPA.). (J). (gr. 3). 5.25 *(978-1-4788-3620-9(2))* Newmark Learning LLC.
—¿Quién le Pone el Cascabel Al Gato? Blane, Antonio. 2016. (Jump into Genre Ser.). (SPA.). (J). (gr. 3). 5.25 *(978-1-4788-3619-3(9))* Newmark Learning LLC.
—The Tide Is Coming in / la Marea Está Llegando. Lee, Calee M. 2018. (Xist Kids Bilingual Spanish English Ser.). (ENG & SPA.). 32p. (J). (gr. -1-3). pap. 9.99 *(978-1-5324-0687-4(8))* Xist Publishing.
—The Wind & the Sun. Parkes, Brenda. 2015. (Shared Reading Classics Ser.). (J). (gr. k-1). *(978-1-4900-2109-6(4))* Benchmark Education Co.
—The Wind & the Sun: Big Book Edition. Parkes, Brenda. 2015. (Shared Reading Classics Ser.). (J). (gr. k-1). *(978-1-4900-2105-8(1))* Benchmark Education Co.
Czernichowska, Joanna & Leonidou, Niki. Opinions about Two Fairy Tales - Baba Yaga & Hansel & Gretel: Set Of 6. Strom, Laura Layton. 2014. (Text Connections Ser.). (J). (gr. 3). 49.00 net. *(978-1-4900-0125-8(5))* Benchmark Education Co.
Czub, Martyna. The Little Philosophers & the Tree of Knowledge. Maerz, Juel. 2019. (Little Philosophers Ser.). (ENG.). 32p. (J). (gr. -1-3). *(978-1-5255-3476-8(9))*; pap. *(978-1-5255-3477-5(7))* FriesenPress.
Czubinski, Amber. The Many Adventures of Pig Batter: A Day at the Park, 1 vol. Czubinski, Robert. 2009. 20p. pap. 24.95 *(978-1-61546-495-1(6))* America Star Bks.

D

D' Angelo, Toni R. My Papa Saw the Easter Bunny in a Cornfield in Missouri. Ethier, Robert M. 2019. (ENG.). 30p. (J). pap. 20.99 *(978-1-7283-2085-4(2))* AuthorHouse.
D, Baby & M, Baby. Mmm! INSECTALICIOUS! G, Paula. 2019. (ENG.). 32p. (J). ***(978-1-5255-6036-1(0))***; pap. ***(978-1-5255-6037-8(9))*** FriesenPress.
D, Osborne. A Countess at School. Channon, E. M. 2016. (ENG.). 154p. (J). (gr. 4-6). pap. *(978-1-909423-68-8(8))* Bks. to Treasure.

D

D�vila, Claudia. Viminy Crowe's Comic Book. Jocelyn, Marthe & Scrimger, Richard. (ENG.). (J). (gr. 4-7). 2017. 336p. pap. 9.99 *(978-1-101-91893-7(4))*; 2014. 330p. 17.99 *(978-1-77049-479-4(0))* Tundra Bks. CAN. (Tundra Bks.). Dist: Penguin Random Hse. LLC.

Da Coll, Ivar. Azucar! Da Coll, Ivar. 2005. (SPA.). (J). 14.99 *(978-1-930332-65-2(3))* Lectorum Pubns., Inc.

—Hamamelis, Miosotis y el Senor Sorpresa. Da Coll, Ivar. 2005. (SPA.). 24p. (J). *(978-958-704-218-4(2))* Ediciones Alfaguara.

—Hamamelis y el Secreto. Da Coll, Ivar. 2005. (SPA.). 24p. (J). pap. *(978-958-704-219-1(0))* Ediciones Alfaguara.

—Jose Tomillo, Maria Juana. Da Coll, Ivar. 2004. (SPA.). 53p. pap. *(978-958-04-7662-7(4))* Norma S.A.

—No, No Fui Yo! Da Coll, Ivar. 2005. (SPA.). 40p. (J). pap. *(978-958-704-220-7(4))* Ediciones Alfaguara.

Da Fonte, Jos� Rodrigues. El Ferrocarril de Foz-Tua a Braganza. Cu�llar, Domingo, tr. 2019. (SPA.). 154p. (J). pap. 30.00 ***(978-1-0863-6936-6(X))*** Independently Published.

Da S Barbosa, Rute Julia. Amber. N S de Moura, Terry. 2019. (ENG.). 204p. (J). pap. 8.49 ***(978-1-0713-1282-7(0))*** Independently Published.

Da Sacco, Francesca. Because I Cleaned My Room. Cowan, Matthew. 2019. (ENG.). 34p. (J). pap. ***(978-0-473-50759-6(5))*** HookMedia Co. Ltd.

Da-Young Im, Linda, jt. illus. see Ju-Young Im, Joy.

d'Abadie, Joelle. Ishmael: The Shepherd Boy of Bethlehem. Haumonte, Odile. 2014. (ENG.). 32p. (J). (gr. 1-7). 14.99 *(978-1-58617-987-8(X))* Ignatius Pr.

—A Missal for Little Ones. 2015. (ENG.). 64p. (J). (gr. -1-2). 12.99 *(978-1-62164-037-0(X))* Ignatius Pr.

Dabbs, Douglas. The Legend's Granddaughter: Not Quite Super, Book 1. Carr, Patrick W. 2007. 281p. (J). pap. *(978-0-9793168-0-7(4))* NQSBks.

Dabi, Hila. Marvelee. Geva, Aviv. Sasson, Ziona, tr. 2019. (ENG.). 26p. (J). pap. 19.99 ***(978-1-0965-0072-8(8))*** Independently Published.

Dabija, Violeta. East of the Sun, West of the Moon. Powling, Chris. 2014. (Traditional Tales Ser.). (ENG.). 32p. (J). (gr. 2-3). pap. 7.95 *(978-1-62521-552-9(5)*, Capstone Classroom) Capstone.

—A Leaf Can Be ... Salas, Laura Purdie. 2012. (Can Be ... Bks.). (ENG.). 32p. (J). (gr. k-2). lib. bdg. 17.99 *(978-0-7613-6203-6(7)*, 9780761362036, Millbrook Pr.) Lerner Publishing Group.

—A Rock Can Be ... Salas, Laura Purdie. 2015. (Can Be ... Bks.). (ENG.). 32p. (J). (gr. k-2). lib. bdg. 17.99 *(978-1-4677-2110-3(7)*, 9781467721103, Millbrook Pr.) Lerner Publishing Group.

—The Twelve Days of Christmas. 2013. (ENG.). 24p. (J). 18.99 *(978-0-7945-3330-4(2)*, Usborne) EDC Publishing.

—Water Can Be ... Salas, Laura Purdie. 2014. (Can Be ... Bks.). (ENG.). 32p. (J). (gr. k-2). 17.99 *(978-1-4677-0591-2(8)*, 9781467705912, Millbrook Pr.) Lerner Publishing Group.

Dabney, Undra & Goettling, Nickalas. My Daddy Does GOOD Things, Too! Gaffney, Linda. 2006. 55p. per. 10.99 *(978-0-9787501-0-7(1))* Gaffney, Linda.

Daboin, Edwin. I Wish You Success: Thriving from the Inside Out. Jones, Eevi. 2020. (Braving the World Ser.: Vol. 4). (ENG.). 40p. (J). (gr. 1-6). 16.00 ***(978-1-952517-95-2(8))***; 16.00 ***(978-1-952517-90-7(7))*** LHC Publishing.

—My Daddy Is a Podcast Host: A Podcast Book for Kids. Jones, Eevi. 2020. (Changemakers Ser.: Vol. 1). (ENG.). 42p. (J). 16.00 ***(978-1-7323733-9-6(6))*** LHC Publishing.

D'Abreo, Marie. Beautiful: Un Viaje a Trav�s Del Espejo. Lingopro Solutions & Mulitz, Libby, trs. 2019. (Beautiful Ser.: Vol. 1). (SPA.). 134p. (J). (gr. 3-7). pap. 10.99 ***(978-1-7333589-0-3(0))*** Far Out Pr.

D'Abreo, Marie. Beautiful: Un Voyage à Travers le Miroir. Lingopro Solutions & Goyer, Isabelle, trs. 2019. (Beautiful Ser.: Vol. 1). (FRE.). 134p. (J). (gr. 3-7). pap. 10.99 *(978-0-9915285-3-0(0))* Far Out Pr.

D'Abreo, Marie. Beautiful: A Girl's Trip Through the Looking Glass. D'Abreo, Marie. 2018. (ENG.). 134p. (J). (gr. 3-7). 18.99 *(978-0-9915285-1-6(4))* Far Out Pr.

D'Abreo, Marie. Beautiful: Game of Crones. D'Abreo, Marie. 2019. (Beautiful Ser.: Vol. 3). (ENG.). 156p. (J). (gr. 3-6). 18.99 ***(978-1-7333589-1-0(9))***; pap. 10.99 *(978-0-9915285-9-2(X))* Far Out Pr.

D'Abreo, Marie. Beautiful: Living with the Frenemy. D'Abreo, Marie. 2018. (ENG.). 150p. (J). (gr. 3-7). 18.99 *(978-0-9915285-8-5(1))* Far Out Pr.

Dacey, Bob. Hermit Crab's Home: Safe in a Shell. Halfmann, Janet. 2007. (ENG.). 32p. 19.95 *(978-1-59249-735-5(7))*; 8.95 *(978-1-59249-736-2(5))*; (J). pap. 6.95 *(978-1-59249-733-1(0))* Soundprints.

Dacey, Bob & Bandelin, Debra. Abigail Adams: First Lady of the American Revolution. Lakin, Patricia. 2006. (Ready-To-read SOFA Ser.). (ENG.). 48p. (J). (gr. 1-3). pap. 4.99 *(978-0-689-87032-3(9)*, Simon Spotlight) Simon Spotlight.

—Davy Crockett A Life on the Frontier. Krensky, Stephen. ed. 2005. (Ready-to-Read Ser.). 48p. (J). lib. bdg. 15.00 *(978-1-59054-959-9(7))* Fitzgerald Bks.

—Hermit Crab's Home: Safe in a Shell. Halfmann, Janet. (Smithsonian Oceanic Collection Ser.). (ENG.). 32p. (J). (gr. -1-3). 2011. 19.95 *(978-1-60727-650-0(X))*; 2007. 4.95 *(978-1-59249-734-8(9))*; 2007. 16.95 *(978-1-59249-732-4(2))*; 2007. 9.95 *(978-1-59249-737-9(3))* Soundprints.

—Pelican's Catch. Halfmann, Janet. (Smithsonian Oceanic Collection Ser.). (ENG.). 32p. (J). 2011. (gr. -1-3). 8.95 *(978-1-60727-657-9(7))*; 2011. (gr. -1-3). 19.95 *(978-1-60727-656-2(9))*; 2005. (gr. -1-2). 4.95 *(978-1-59249-286-2(X)*, B4076); 2005. (gr. -1-2). 19.95 *(978-1-59249-310-4(6)*, BC4026); 2005. (gr. -1-2). 9.95 *(978-1-59249-311-1(4)*, PB4076); 2005. (gr. -1-2). 15.95 *(978-1-59249-287-9(8)*, B4026); 2004. (gr. 2-7). 8.95 *(978-1-59249-309-8(2)*, SC4026); 2004. (gr. -1-3). 6.95 *(978-1-59249-285-5(1)*, S4026) Soundprints.

—The Star-Spangled Banner. Winstead, Amy. 2003. (ENG.). 32p. (J). 18.65 *(978-0-8249-5462-8(9)*, Ideal Pubns.) Worthy Publishing.

—Teddy Roosevelt: The People's President. Gayle, Sharon Shavers & Gayle, Sharon. Dacey, Bob & Bandelin, Debra, trs. 2004. (Ready-To-read SOFA Ser.). (ENG.). 32p. (J). (gr. 1-3). pap. 4.99 *(978-0-689-85825-3(6)*, Simon Spotlight) Simon Spotlight.

Dacey, Bob, jt. illus. see Bandelin, Debra.

Dachamont Earth, Kaewket, jt. illus. see Hedison, Debby.

Dacus, Bobbie. Saving Emma. Willoughby, Bebe. 2005. (J). pap. 12.95 *(978-0-9763945-0-1(2))* King St Bks./Stabler-Leadbeater Apothecary Museum.

D'Adamo, Anthony. Pierre, the Young Watchmaker. Berg, Jean Horton. 2011. 190p. 42.95 *(978-1-258-08171-3(7))* Literary Licensing, LLC.

Dade, Raheem. Mommy, Why Can't I Be Rich? Ms. G. 2005. 20p. (J). 7.00 *(978-0-9724621-1-2(2))* Unlimited Possibilities Publishing, LLC.

Daeuble, Marta. The Big Book of Everything Underground. Sekaninová, Štěpánka. ed. 2017. (ENG.). 24p. (J). (gr. 2). 14.95 *(978-1-912006-82-3(0))* Book Hse. GBR. Dist: Sterling Publishing Co., Inc.

Daff, Russ. Power Cut Turquoise Band. Millett, Peter. 2016. (Cambridge Reading Adventures Ser.). (ENG.). 24p. pap. 8.08 *(978-1-316-60586-8(8))* Cambridge Univ. Pr.

—Take Zayan with You! Green Band. Millett, Peter. 2016. (Cambridge Reading Adventures Ser.). (ENG.). 16p. pap. 7.37 *(978-1-107-57587-5(7))* Cambridge Univ. Pr.

—What Has a Pointed Head & Eats Lizards? Kanner, Robert. 2008. (J). *(978-1-59646-832-0(7))* Dingles & Co.

—What Has Armor & a Tail Club? Kanner, Robert. 2008. (J). *(978-1-59646-828-3(9))* Dingles & Co.

—What Has Three Horns & a Sharp Beak? Zocchi, Judith Mazzeo. 2008. (J). *(978-1-59646-820-7(3))* Dingles & Co.

—What Weighs 70,000 Pounds & Swallows Stones? Kanner, Robert. 2008. (J). *(978-1-59646-840-5(8))* Dingles & Co.

Dafflon, Adele. Let's Play, Funny Flamingo! Deutsch, Georgiana. 2020. (ENG.). 10p. (J). (-k). bds. 9.99 *(978-1-68010-611-4(2))* Tiger Tales.

—Let's Play, Happy Giraffe! Deutsch, Georgiana. 2020. (ENG.). 10p. (J). (-k). bds. 9.99 *(978-1-68010-610-7(4))* Tiger Tales.

Dafflon, Adele. Let's Play, Noisy Dinosaur! Deutsch, Georgiana. 2020. (ENG.). 10p. (J). (-k). bds. 9.99 ***(978-1-68010-631-2(7))*** Tiger Tales.

Dages, Juliette Garesche. Learning about Virtues: A Guide to Making Good Choices. Dages, Juliette Garesche. 2009. (J). pap. 7.95 *(978-0-87029-420-4(2))* Abbey Pr.

Daggett, Irma, jt. illus. see Pighin, Marcel.

Dahanayaka, Aishu. Peyton's Special Day. Johnson, Cynthia. 2019. (ENG.). 42p. (J). pap. 11.99 ***(978-1-6959-8929-0(5))*** Independently Published.

Dahl, Michael & Jensen, Brian. Rápido, Más Rápido, Muy Rápido: Animales Que se Muevan a Grandes Velocidades. Dahl, Michael & Jensen, Brian. Translations.com Staff, tr. 2012. (Los Extremos y Los Animales/Animal Extremes Ser.).Tr. of Fast, Faster, Fastest-Animals That Move at Great Speeds. (ENG.). 24p. (J). (gr. k-2). lib. bdg. 27.32 *(978-1-4048-7317-9(1)*, Picture Window Bks.) Capstone.

Dahl, Roald. Beastly Ballons. Top That Publishing Editors, ed. 2005. 24p. (J). pap. *(978-1-905359-55-4(1))* Top That! Publishing PLC.

—Fiendish Faces. Top That Publishing Editors, ed. 2005. 24p. (J). pap. *(978-1-905359-53-0(5))* Top That! Publishing PLC.

—Ghastly Grub. Top That Publishing Editors, ed. 2005. 24p. (J). pap. *(978-1-905359-54-7(3))* Top That! Publishing PLC.

—Magical Mischief. Top That Publishing Editors, ed. 2005. 24p. (J). pap. *(978-1-905359-51-6(9))* Top That! Publishing PLC.

—Silly Scribbles. Top That Publishing Editors, ed. 2005. 24p. (J). pap. *(978-1-905359-52-3(7))* Top That! Publishing PLC.

—Stupendous Stampers. Top That Publishing Editors, ed. 2005. 24p. (J). pap. *(978-1-905359-50-9(0))* Top That! Publishing PLC.

Dahl, Sarah. Hollywood Style: Fun Fashions You Can Sketch, 1 vol. Bolte, Mari. 2013. (Drawing Fun Fashions Ser.). (ENG.). 32p. (J). (gr. 3-9). lib. bdg. 28.65 *(978-1-62065-037-0(1))* Capstone.

—Rock Star Style: Fun Fashions You Can Sketch, 1 vol. Bolte, Mari. 2013. (Drawing Fun Fashions Ser.). (ENG.). 32p. (J). (gr. 3-9). lib. bdg. 28.65 *(978-1-62065-036-3(3))* Capstone.

Dahle, Stefanie. There's No One I Love Like You. Langreuter, Jutta. 2018. (ENG.). 28p. (J). (— 1). bds. 9.95 *(978-0-7358-4321-9(X))* North-South Bks., Inc.

Dahle, Stephanie. So Happy Together! Langreuter, Jutta. 2017. (ENG.). 32p. (J). (gr. -1-3). 17.95 *(978-0-7358-4279-3(5))* North-South Bks., Inc.

Dahm, Andrea. Gus Finds God. Foley, Michael P. 2018. (ENG.). 44p. (J). (gr. -1-3). 22.95 *(978-1-947792-60-9(1))*; pap. 11.95 *(978-1-947792-61-6(X))* Emmaus Road Publishing.

Dahn Tran, Art. I Make. Blom, Tracy & DiResta, Jimmy. 2019. (ENG.). 32p. (J). 15.99 ***(978-1-7336349-3-9(2))*** Blom Pubns.

Daigle, Brian. Texas Farm Girl. Crownover, Rebecca. 2013. (ENG.). (J). (gr. -1-3). 14.95 *(978-1-62086-265-0(4))* Mascot Bks., Inc.

Daigle, Casie. The Fish That Went Roar. Daigle, Damien. 2011. 28p. pap. 24.95 *(978-1-4560-5080-1(X))* America Star Bks.

Daigle, Stephan, jt. illus. see Galouchko, Annouchka Gravel.

Daigle, Sylvie. Tu N'es Plus Seul, Nazaire. Dube, Jasmine. 2003. (Premier Roman Ser.). (FRE.). 64p. (J). (gr. 2-5). pap. *(978-2-89021-286-2(6))* Diffusion du livre Mirabel (DLM).

Daigneault, Sylvie. C Is for Canada. Ulmer, Michael. 2017. (ENG.). 32p. (J). (gr. 1-3). 16.99 *(978-1-58536-973-7(X)*, 204218) Sleeping Bear Pr.

—Egg Hunts! Fireworks! Pumpkins! Reindeer! Edwards, Pamela Duncan. 2018. (ENG.). 32p. (J). (gr. k-2). 16.99 *(978-1-58536-403-9(7)*, 204584) Sleeping Bear Pr.

—The Good Garden: How One Family Went from Hunger to Having Enough. Milway, Katie Smith. (CitizenKid Ser.). (ENG.). 32p. (J). (gr. 3-7). 2020. pap. 10.99 *(978-1-5253-0406-4(2))*; 2010. 18.99 *(978-1-55453-488-3(7))* Kids Can Pr., Ltd. CAN. Dist: Hachette Bk. Group.

—Piece by Piece. Shaw, Stephanie. 2017. (ENG.). 32p. (J). (gr. 1-4). 16.99 *(978-1-58536-999-7(3)*, 204318) Sleeping Bear Pr.

Dailey, Allison, jt. illus. see Dailey, Dan.

Dailey, Dan & Dailey, Allison. Glassigator. 2007. 33p. (J). *(978-0-935172-29-4(7))* Hudson Hills Pr. LLC.

Dailey, Nathaniel. A Day with Grand-Pere. Green, Gary. 2017. (ENG.). (J). 19.95 *(978-0-9972312-4-3(6))* Stewart, H. K. Creative Services, Inc.

Daily, Don. The Classic Tales of Brer Rabbit. Harris, Joel Chandler. 2008. 56p. (J). (gr. -1-3). 9.95 *(978-0-7624-3219-6(5)*, Running Pr. Kids) Running Pr.

—The Classic Treasury of Aesop's Fables. Aesop. 2007. 56p. (J). (gr. -1-3). 9.95 *(978-0-7624-2876-2(7)*, Running Pr. Kids) Running Pr.

—Grimms' Fairy Tales. 2014. (Classic Edition Ser.). (ENG.). 64p. (J). 18.95 *(978-1-60433-498-2(3)*, Applesauce Pr.) Cider Mill Pr. Bk. Pubs., LLC.

—The Jungle Book: The Classic Edition. Kipling, Rudyard. 2014. (ENG.). 64p. (J). (gr. -1). 18.95 *(978-1-60433-475-3(4))* Cider Mill Pr. Bk. Pubs., LLC.

—The Nutcracker. Hoffmann, E. T. A. 2019. 26p. (J). (gr. -1 — 1). bds. 12.99 *(978-0-7624-9571-9(5)*, Running Pr. Kids) Running Pr.

—The Nutcracker: A Young Reader's Edition of the Holiday Classic. Hoffmann, E. T. A. 2003. (ENG.). 56p. (J). (gr. -1-3). 12.95 *(978-0-7624-1633-2(5)*, 53656638, Running Pr. Kids) Running Pr.

—The Wind in the Willows: The Classic Edition. Grahame, Kenneth. 2014. (Classic Edition Ser.). (ENG.). 72p. (J). (gr. -1). 18.95 *(978-1-60433-478-4(9)*, Applesauce Pr.) Cider Mill Pr. Bk. Pubs., LLC.

Daily, Don. The Twelve Days of Christmas Cats (Hardcover) The Classic Edition. Daily, Don. 2014. (Classic Edition Ser.). (ENG.). 48p. (J). 18.95 *(978-1-60433-495-1(9)*, Applesauce Pr.) Cider Mill Pr. Bk. Pubs., LLC.

Daily, Rick. The Ghost House. Thomas, Jesse Lee. 2011. 30p. pap. 16.00 *(978-1-4349-8472-2(9)*, RoseDog Bks.) Dorrance Publishing Co., Inc.

Daines, Cameron. The Cats of Storm Mountain. Daines, McKay. 2003. 294p. (YA). 28.95 *(978-0-9749467-1-9(0))*; pap. 17.99 *(978-0-9749467-0-2(2))* Shine Publishing Hse.

Dair, Catherine. Wind Me up, One More Time: When Holidays Attack. Trenten, K. S. E, Jaymi, ed. 2019. (ENG.). 242p. (J). pap. 13.99 ***(978-1-7089-7611-8(6))*** Independently Published.

Daisy, April. The Lonely Dragon. Daisy, April. 2005. (J). per. 7.95 *(978-1-59466-074-0(3)*, Little Ones) Port Town Publishing.

—The Monster's in My Room. Daisy, April. 2005. (J). per. 7.95 *(978-1-59466-048-1(4)*, Little Ones) Port Town Publishing.

Daisy, Jeanie. Donna's New Dress. Cox, Amy. 2019. (ENG.). 46p. (J). 14.99 ***(978-1-945464-94-2(1))*** Cox & Castelluccio.

Dakins, Todd. Abigail Is a Big Girl. Hoffman, Don. 2nd ed. 2016. (Billy & Abby Ser.). (ENG.). 28p. (J). (gr. -1-k). pap. 3.99 *(978-1-943154-03-6(1))* Peek-A-Boo Publishing.

—Billy Is a Big Boy. Hoffman, Don. 2nd ed. 2016. (Billy & Abby Ser.). (ENG.). 28p. (J). (gr. -1-k). pap. 3.99 *(978-1-943154-02-9(3))* Peek-A-Boo Publishing.

—Bobcat Bootcamp in Orange City. Pritchard, Jean. 2007. (J). *(978-0-9652491-6-4(6))* Cook, Ken Co.

—A Counting Book with Billy & Abigail. Hoffman, Don. 2nd ed. 2016. (Billy & Abby Ser.). (ENG.). 24p. (J). (gr. -1-k). pap. 3.99 *(978-1-943154-08-1(2))* Peek-A-Boo Publishing.

—Find Your Music. Hoffman, Don & Palmer, Priscilla. 2016. (ENG.). 32p. (J). (gr. -1-k). pap. 3.99 *(978-1-943154-06-7(6))* Peek-A-Boo Publishing.

—Good Morning, Good Night Billy & Abigail. Hoffman, Don. 2nd ed. 2016. (Billy & Abby Ser.). (ENG.). 24p. (J). (gr. -1-k). pap. 3.99 *(978-1-943154-09-8(0))* Peek-A-Boo Publishing.

—A Very Special Snowflake. Hoffman, Don. 2nd ed. 2016. (ENG.). 28p. (J). (gr. -1-k). pap. 3.99 *(978-1-943154-01-2(5))* Peek-A-Boo Publishing.

—Yoga Poga Shmoga! Jones, Sonia. 2016. (ENG.). 36p. (J). (gr. k-2). pap. 3.99 *(978-1-943154-32-6(5)*, See-Saw Publishing) Peek-A-Boo Publishing.

—Yoga Poga Shmoga! Jones, Sonia. 2016. (ENG.). 36p. (J). (gr. k-2). 7.95 *(978-1-943154-33-3(3)*, See-Saw Publishing) Peek-A-Boo Publishing.

Dal Chele, Egido Victor. Zoonauts: The Secret of Animalville. Mueller, Richard. Gosline, Sheldon, ed. 2003. 210p. (J). 14.95 *(978-0-9719496-6-9(2))* Shangri-La Pubns.

Dal Lago, Alberto, jt. illus. see Parks, Phil.

Dalby, C. Reginald. James & the Express (Thomas & Friends) Awdry, W. 2016. (ENG.). 24p. (J). (— 1). bds. 6.99 *(978-1-101-93758-7(0)*, Random Hse. Bks. for Young Readers) Random Hse. Children's Bks.

—Percy's Promise (Thomas & Friends) Awdry, W. 2017. (ENG.). 24p. (J). (— 1). bds. 6.99 *(978-0-399-55774-3(1)*, Random Hse. Bks. for Young Readers) Random Hse. Children's Bks.

—Thomas & Gordon (Thomas & Friends) Random House. 2016. (ENG.). 24p. (J). (— 1). bds. 6.99 *(978-1-101-93139-4(6)*, Random Hse. Bks. for Young Readers) Random Hse. Children's Bks.

Dalby, Danny Brooks. Lara Ladybug. Florie, Christine. 2011. (Rookie Ready to Learn: Animals Ser.). (ENG.). 32p. (J). (gr. -1-1). lib. bdg. 25.00 *(978-0-531-26417-1(3)*, Children's Pr.) Scholastic Library Publishing.

Dalby, Danny Brooks. La Mariquita Lara. Dalby, Danny Brooks. Florie, Christine. 2011. (Rookie Ready to Learn Español Ser.). (SPA.). 32p. (J). pap. 5.95 *(978-0-531-26783-7(0))*; lib. bdg. 23.00 *(978-0-531-26115-6(8))* Scholastic Library Publishing. (Children's Pr.).

Dale, Andrew N. Pipsy & Friends. Ivens, Marian. 2020. (ENG.). 32p. (J). pap. 12.90 ***(978-1-7283-5359-3(9))*** AuthorHouse.

Dale, Hannah. Mr. Hare's Big Secret. 2016. (ENG.). 32p. (J). (gr. -1-2). 16.99 *(978-0-553-53856-4(X)*, Doubleday Bks. for Young Readers) Random Hse. Children's Bks.

Dale, Ian. The Advent Storybook: 25 Bible Stories Showing Why Jesus Came. Richie, Laura. 2018. (ENG.). 64p. (J). 13.99 *(978-0-8307-7608-5(7)*, 145331) Cook, David C.

—The Easter Storybook: 40 Bible Stories Showing Who Jesus Is. Richie, Laura. 2020. (ENG.). 96p. (J). 18.99 *(978-0-8307-7860-7(8)*, 149072) Cook, David C.

Dale, Penny. Jamie & Angus Together. Fine, Anne. 2007. (Jame & Angus Ser.). (ENG.). 112p. (J). (gr. -1-1). 15.99 *(978-0-7636-3374-5(7))* Candlewick Pr.

Dale, Penny. Dinosaur Christmas! Dale, Penny. 2020. (ENG.). 32p. (J). (-k). 16.99 ***(978-1-5362-1449-9(3)***, Nosy Crow) Candlewick Pr.

Dale, Penny. Dinosaur Dig! Dale, Penny. 2012. (Dinosaurs on the Go Ser.). (ENG.). 14p. (J). (gr. k-k). bds. 6.99 *(978-0-7636-6270-7(4)*, Nosy Crow) Candlewick Pr.

—Dinosaur Farm! Dale, Penny. 2019. (Dinosaurs on the Go Ser.). (ENG.). 32p. (J). (-k). 15.99 *(978-0-7636-9936-9(5)*, Nosy Crow) Candlewick Pr.

—Dinosaur Pirates! Dale, Penny. 2017. (Dinosaurs on the Go Ser.). (ENG.). 32p. (J). (-k). 15.99 *(978-0-7636-9330-5(8)*, Nosy Crow) Candlewick Pr.

—Dinosaur Rescue! Dale, Penny. 2016. (Dinosaurs on the Go Ser.). (ENG.). 24p. (J). (-k). bds. 6.99 *(978-0-7636-8000-8(1)*, Nosy Crow) Candlewick Pr.

—Dinosaur Rocket! Dale, Penny. 2015. (Dinosaurs on the Go Ser.). (ENG.). 32p. (J). (-k). 16.99 *(978-0-7636-7999-6(2)*, Nosy Crow) Candlewick Pr.

—Dinosaur Zoom! Dale, Penny. (Dinosaurs on the Go Ser.). (ENG.). (J). (-k). 2014. 24p. bds. 6.99 *(978-0-7636-7394-9(3))*; 2013. 32p. 15.99 *(978-0-7636-6448-0(0))* Candlewick Pr. (Nosy Crow).

—Dinosaurs on the Go! Dale, Penny. 2016. (Dinosaurs on the Go Ser.). (ENG.). (J). (-k). bds. 19.99 *(978-0-7636-8936-0(X)*, Nosy Crow) Candlewick Pr.

—Ten in the Bed. Dale, Penny. 2007. (ENG.). 24p. (J). (— 1). bds. 6.99 *(978-0-7636-3514-5(6))* Candlewick Pr.

Dale, Rae. Kids for Hire. Costain, Meredith. 2004. iv, 36p. (J). pap. *(978-0-7608-6748-8(8))* Sundance/Newbridge Educational Publishing.

—The Legend of Big Red. Roy, James. 2005. (UQP Children's Fiction Ser.). 96p. (J). pap. *(978-0-7022-3528-3(8))* Univ. of Queensland Pr.

Dale-Scott, Lindsay. First 100 Engineering Words. Ferrie, Chris. 2020. (My First STEAM Words Ser.). 24p. (J). bds. 6.99 *(978-1-7282-1126-8(3))* Sourcebooks, Inc.

—First 100 Mathematics Words: First STEAM Words. Ferrie, Chris. 2020. (My First STEAM Words Ser.). 24p. (J). bds. 6.99 *(978-1-7282-1128-2(X))* Sourcebooks, Inc.

—First 100 Science Words: First STEAM Words. Ferrie, Chris. 2020. (My First STEAM Words Ser.). 24p. (J). bds. 6.99 *(978-1-7282-1124-4(7))* Sourcebooks, Inc.

—First 100 Technology Words: First STEAM Words. Ferrie, Chris. 2020. (My First STEAM Words Ser.). 24p. (J). bds. 6.99 *(978-1-7282-1125-1(5))* Sourcebooks, Inc.

—A Gingerbread Christmas. Acampora, Courtney. 2018. (Christmas Gift Tags Ser.). (ENG.). 12p. (J). (— 1). bds. 4.99 *(978-1-68412-382-7(8)*, Silver Dolphin Bks.) Printers Row Publishing Group.

—Little Vampire's Big Smile: Small Padded Board Book. VonFeder, Rosa. 2016. (Little Bird Stories Ser.). (ENG.). 12p. (J). (gr. -1-k). bds. 6.99 *(978-1-68052-109-2(8)*, 1001020) Cottage Door Pr.

—My First 100 Art Words. Ferrie, Chris. 2020. (My First STEAM Words Ser.). 24p. (J). bds. 6.99 *(978-1-7282-1127-5(1))* Sourcebooks, Inc.

—The Night Before Christmas: A Light-Up Book. Moore, Clement Clarke. 2018. 24p. (J). (gr. -1 — 1). 11.99 *(978-0-7624-9332-6(1)*, Running Pr. Kids) Running Pr.

—Trick or Treat: 3 Button Handle Book. VonFeder, Rosa. Cottage Door Press, ed. 2017. (Halloween Interactive Take-Along Early Bird Children's Sound Book Ser.). (ENG.). 12p. (J). (gr. -1-k). bds. 9.99 *(978-1-68052-197-9(7)*, 1001950) Cottage Door Pr.

—Wild Bios: Frida Catlo. Acampora, Courtney & Fischer, Maggie. 2019. (Wild Bios Ser.). (ENG.). 16p. (J). (— 1). bds. 7.99 *(978-1-68412-558-6(8)*, Silver Dolphin Bks.) Printers Row Publishing Group.

Dale-Scott, Lindsay, jt. illus. see RH Disney Staff.

Dale-Scott, Lindsay, jt. illus. see RH Disney.

Dale-Scott, Lindsey. Belly Breathe. Kimmelman, Leslie. 2018. (ENG.). 22p. (J). (gr. -1 — 1). bds. 7.99 *(978-0-8075-2167-0(1)*, 807521671) Whitman, Albert & Co.

Dale, Shelley. Juan Quezada. Quezada, Juan. 2003. (SPA.). 40p. (J). pap. 9.95 *(978-0-9708617-1-9(0))*; (gr. -1-8). 16.95 *(978-0-9708617-0-2(2))* Norman Bks.

—Juan Quezada. Quezada, Juan. Mlawer, Teresa, tr. 2003. 40p. (J). (gr. k-6). 16.95 *(978-0-9708617-4-0(5))*; pap. 9.95 *(978-0-9708617-5-7(3))* Norman Bks.

Dale, Unity-Joy. Seeds of Hope Bereavement & Loss Activity Book: Helping Children & Young People Cope with Change Through Nature. Jay, Caroline. 2014. (ENG.). 88p. (J). pap. 22.95 *(978-1-84905-546-8(7)*, 694642) Kingsley, Jessica Pubs. GBR. Dist: Hachette UK Distribution.

—What Does Dead Mean? A Book for Young Children to Help Explain Death & Dying. Jay, Caroline & Thomas, Jenni. 2012. (ENG.). 32p. (J). 15.95 *(978-1-84905-355-6(3)*, 694370) Kingsley, Jessica Pubs. GBR. Dist: Hachette UK Distribution.

Dalena, Antonello. Angry Birds Comics: Furious Fowl. Tobin, Paul et al. 2018. (Angry Birds Ser.). 80p. (J). (gr. 2-5). 12.99 *(978-1-68405-153-3(3))* Idea & Design Works, LLC.

Dalena, Antonello. Cars. Sisti, Alessandro. 2020. (Disney & Pixar Movies Ser.). (ENG.). 52p. (J). (gr. 2-6). lib. bdg. 28.50 ***(978-1-5321-4546-9(2)***, 35193, Graphic Novels) Spotlight.

D'Alesi, Hugo. Carnet Blanc, Bateaux a Helices. 2016. (Bnf Monuments Ser.). (FRE.). (J). pap. *(978-2-01-116968-6(2))* Hachette Groupe Livre.

Daley Daley, Ken. Auntie Luce's Talking Paintings, 1 vol. Latour, Francie. 2018. (ENG.). 36p. (J). (gr. k-3). 18.95 *(978-1-77306-041-5(4))* Groundwood Bks. CAN. Dist: Publishers Group West (PGW).

Daley, Ken. Joseph's Big Ride. Farish, Terry. 2017. (ENG.). 32p. (J). (gr. -1-2). pap. 9.95 *(978-1-55451-805-0(9))* Annick Pr., Ltd. CAN. Dist: Publishers Group West (PGW).

Daley-Prado, M. J. Gordon & the Magic Fishbowl, 1 vol. Nestell, Mark. 2010. 26p. pap. 24.95 *(978-1-4489-8495-4(5))* America Star Bks.

—Peanut Bunny & the Christmas Lights. Adams-Cantrell;, Renee. 2009. 48p. pap. 24.95 *(978-1-60610-432-3(2))* America Star Bks.

Dalhaimer Bartkowski, Anna. Maggie Visits Grandpa: A Coloring Adventure. Dalhaimer Bartkowski, Anna. 2007. 32p. pap. 8.99 *(978-0-9790720-1-7(8))* Infinite Adventure.

Dalien, Linnae. Annual Race at Beaver Town. Dalien, Luke. 2019. (ENG.). 28p. (J). pap. 9.99 *(978-1-7929-2257-2(4))* Independently Published.

—Clovers & Gold a Magical Tale. Dalien, Luke. 2019. (Adventures of the Silly Little Beaver Ser.: Vol. 15). (ENG.). 34p. (J). pap. 9.99 *(978-1-7982-8994-5(6))* Independently Published.

—The Diagnosis: Epic Battle with Muscular Dystrophy. Dalien, Luke. 2018. (Mark the Mighty Muskrat Ser.: Vol. 1). (ENG.). 30p. (J). pap. 9.99 *(978-1-7904-8946-6(6))* Independently Published.

—The Explanation: Epic Battle with Muscular Dystrophy. Dalien, Luke. 2019. (Mark the Mighty Muskrat Ser.: Vol. 2). (ENG.). 30p. (J). pap. 9.99 *(978-1-0914-7413-0(3))* Independently Published.

—Friendship Is Golden. Dalien, Luke. 2018. (ENG.). 28p. (J). pap. 9.99 *(978-1-7908-0514-3(7))* Independently Published.

—Lesson from the Pimple. Dalien, Luke. 2018. (Adventures of the Silly Little Beaver Ser.: Vol. 11). (ENG.). 28p. (J). pap. 9.99 *(978-1-7918-0963-8(4))* Independently Published.

—Lost Friend. Dalien, Luke. 2018. (Adventures of the Silly Little Beaver Ser.: Vol. 3). (ENG.). 26p. (J). pap. 9.99 *(978-1-7926-2028-7(4))* Independently Published.

—Loud Bang in the Night. Dalien, Luke. 2018. (Adventures of the Silly Little Beaver Ser.: Vol. 9). (ENG.). 30p. (J). pap. 9.99 *(978-1-7920-0665-4(9))* Independently Published.

—The Mysterious Box. Dalien, Luke. 2018. (Adventures of the Silly Little Beaver Ser.: Vol. 8). (ENG.). 30p. (J). pap. 9.99 *(978-1-7926-1993-9(6))* Independently Published.

—Pushing for Success. Dalien, Luke. 2019. (ENG.). 28p. (J). pap. 9.99 *(978-1-7932-0608-4(2))* Independently Published.

—A True Beaver Family Christmas Miracle. Dalien, Luke. 2018. (Adventures of the Silly Little Beaver Ser.: Vol. 12). (ENG.). 32p. (J). pap. 9.99 *(978-1-7913-7902-5(8))* Independently Published.

—The Unsigned Valentine. Dalien, Luke. 2019. (Adventures of the Silly Little Beaver Ser.: Vol. 14). (ENG.). 30p. (J). pap. 9.99 *(978-1-7945-0362-5(5))* Independently Published.

—Winter Preparation. Dalien, Luke. 2018. (ENG.). 30p. (J). pap. 9.99 *(978-1-7908-0151-0(6))* Independently Published.

Dall, Christopher M. Tell Me a Story. Grant, Susan. 2013. 56p. pap. *(978-1-4602-1356-8(4))* FriesenPress.

Dall, John. The Christmas Santa Had No Beard. H M Bricker & Bricker, Howard Michael. ed. 2011.Tr. of Navidad Que Santa Claus No Tovo Barba. (ENG & SPA.). 34p. (J). 15.45 *(978-0-615-42163-6(6))* H M Bricker.

Dallocchio, Federico, et al. Knight Errant: Aflame, Vol. 1. Miller, John Jackson. 2012. (Star Wars: Knight Errant Ser.). (ENG.). 24p. (J). (gr. 6-12). 27.07 *(978-1-59961-986-6(5),* 13824, Graphic Novels) Spotlight.

—Star Wars - Knight Errant: Aflame, Vol. 2. Miller, John Jackson. 2012. (Star Wars: Knight Errant Ser.). (ENG.). 24p. (J). (gr. 6-12). 27.07 *(978-1-59961-987-3(3),* 13825, Graphic Novels) Spotlight.

Dallocchio, Federico & Rosado, Will. Summit Vol. 2: Price of Power. Chu, Amy. 2018. (ENG.). 144p. (YA). pap. 14.99 *(978-1-5493-0285-5(X),* e29c3ea1-fd36-4f1e-b6da-4ea258b1f5ae, Lion Forge) Oni Pr., Inc.

Dalrymple, Farel. The Wrenchies. Dalrymple, Farel. 2014. (ENG.). 304p. (YA). (gr. 9). pap. 19.99 *(978-1-59643-421-9(X),* 9781596434219, First Second Bks.) Roaring Brook Pr.

Dalton, Alex & Gallant, S. L. DreamWorks Classics Volume 4. Bark, Jasper et al. 2016. (DreamWorks Classics Ser.). 64p. (J). (gr. 1-4). 6.99 *(978-1-78276-249-2(3))* Titan Bks. Ltd. GBR. Dist: Penguin Random Hse. LLC.

Dalton, Alex & Laguna, Fabio. Monsters vs. Aliens: the M Files. Titan Books Staff et al. 2009. (ENG.). 48p. pap. 4.95 *(978-1-84856-281-3(0),* Titan Bks.) Titan Bks. Ltd. GBR. Dist: Penguin Random Hse. LLC.

Dalton, Alex, jt. illus. see Hebb, Matt.

Dalton, Max. The Lonely Phone Booth. Ackerman, Peter. 2010. (ENG.). 32p. (J). (gr. k-2). 16.95 *(978-1-56792-414-5(X))* Godine, David R. Pub.

—The Screaming Chef: A Picture Book. Ackerman, Peter. 2017. (ENG.). 32p. (J). 17.95 *(978-1-56792-598-2(7))* Godine, David R. Pub.

Dalton, Pamela. Brother Sun, Sister Moon. Paterson, Katherine. 2011. (ENG.). 36p. (J). (gr. -1-1). 17.99 *(978-0-8118-7734-3(5))* Chronicle Bks. LLC.

—The Story of Christmas. 2011. (ENG.). 32p. (J). (gr. -1-17). 17.99 *(978-1-4521-0470-6(0))* Chronicle Bks. LLC.

—The Sun with Loving Light, 1 vol. Bloomquist, Stephen, ed. 2014. Orig. Title: Der Sonne Licht. (ENG.). 110p. (J). *(978-1-936367-63-4(7))* Waldorf Publications.

—Under the Silver Moon: Lullabies, Night Songs, & Poems. 2017. (ENG.). 48p. (J). 17.99 *(978-1-4521-1673-0(3))* Chronicle Bks. LLC.

Dalvand, Reza. The Day of Your Arrival. Brown, Dolores. 2019. (ENG.). 36p. (J). 15.95 *(978-84-17673-02-4(4))* NubeOcho Ediciones ESP. Dist: Consortium Bk. Sales & Distribution.

—El día en Que Llegaste. Brown, Dolores. 2019. (ENG.). 36p. (J). 15.95 *(978-84-17673-01-7(6))* NubeOcho Ediciones ESP. Dist: Consortium Bk. Sales & Distribution.

Dalvand, Reza. What Could That Be? Dalvand, Reza. 2020. (ENG.). 32p. (J). (gr. -1-3). 18.99 *(978-1-338-53019-3(4),* Orchard Bks.) Scholastic, Inc.

Dalvy, Jon B. The Ballad of Titha Mae: A Fantasy in Twelve Parts. Dalvy, Jon B. 2018. (Titha Mae Ser.: Vol. 1). (ENG.). (J). (gr. 4-6). 304p. 28.99 *(978-0-692-06188-6(6));* 2nd ed. 346p. pap. 16.99 *(978-0-692-06506-8(7))* Nechalec Pr.

Daly, Elle. I Will Get You. Lane, Alex. 2014. (Traditional Tales Ser.). (ENG.). 16p. (J). (gr. -1-k). pap. 6.95 *(978-1-62521-570-3(3),* Capstone Classroom) Capstone.

Daly, Jude. The Gift of the Sun. Stewart, Dianne. 2019. (ENG.). 32p. (J). pap. 8.95 *(978-1-4314-2857-1(4))* Jacana Media ZAF. Dist: Independent Pubs. Group.

—Inside the Books: Readers & Libraries Around the World. Buzzeo, Toni. 2012. 32p. (J). 17.95 *(978-1-60213-058-6(2),* Upstart Bks.) Highsmith Inc.

—Lila & the Secret of Rain. Conway, David. 2011. (ENG.). 32p. (J). (gr. k-3). 12.99 *(978-1-84780-035-0(1),* Frances Lincoln Children's Bks.) Quarto Publishing Group UK GBR. Dist: Hachette Bk. Group.

Daly, Jude. To Everything There Is a Season. Daly, Jude. 2006. 32p. (Orig.). (J). (gr. -1-3). 16.00 *(978-0-8028-5286-1(6),* Eerdmans Bks For Young Readers) Eerdmans, William B. Publishing Co.

Daly, Karen Anne. A Dinosaur under My Bed. Mitchell, Colleen. 2013. 24p. (J). pap. 7.49 *(978-0-9853600-2-3(X))* Thistlewood Publishing.

—Mrs Mouse's Garden Party in Giggleswick Village. Westover, Gail. 2012. 26p. pap. 9.95 *(978-0-9821507-9-5(2))* Thistlewood Publishing.

Daly, Lisa. Christmas O'Clock: A Collection. Deluca, Alison. 2013. 198p. pap. 9.99 *(978-1-939296-98-6(6))* Myrddin Publishing Group.

Daly, Meghan. Little Harper Grace & the Hummingbird. Preza, Jessie. 2008. (ENG.). 36p. (J). pap. 9.95 *(978-0-615-24059-6(3))* Poppy Blossom Pr.

Daly, Niki. Daddy Island. Wells, Philip. 2015. 24p. (J). (gr. -1-k). pap. 7.99 *(978-1-84148-198-2(X))* Barefoot Bks., Inc.

—Fly, Eagle, Fly: An African Tale. Gregorowski, Christopher. 2008. (ENG.). 36p. (J). (gr. -1-3). 12.99 *(978-1-4169-7599-1(3),* Aladdin) Simon & Schuster Children's Publishing.

Daly, Niki. The Greatest Skating Race: A World War II Story from the Netherlands. Daly, Niki. Borden, Louise. 2004. (ENG.). 48p. (J). (gr. 4-7). 19.99 *(978-0-689-84502-4(2),* McElderry, Margaret K. Bks.) McElderry, Margaret K. Bks.

—Little Artists. Daly, Niki. 2016. (ENG.). 5p. (J). bds. 10.99 *(978-1-61067-436-2(7))* Kane Miller.

—Pretty Salma: A Little Red Riding Hood Story from Africa. Daly, Niki. 2007. (ENG.). 32p. (J). (gr. -1-3). 17.99 *(978-0-618-72345-4(5),* 100514, Clarion Bks.) Houghton Mifflin Harcourt Trade & Reference Pubs.

Daly, Sue V. Everybody Loves Mookie. Kristen, Judith. 2008. (ENG.). 44p. (J). pap. 15.95 *(978-0-9800448-4-3(7))* Aquinas & Krone Publishing, LLC.

Dalzell, Lucy. A Journey Through Art: A Global Art Adventure. Rosen, Aaron. 2018. (ENG.). 144p. (J). (gr. 4-8). 22.95 *(978-0-500-65101-8(9),* 565101) Thames & Hudson.

Dalziel, Linda. The Adventures of Turbo-Color along Book: Color along Book. Pearson, Alexis. 2018. (Adventures of Turbo Ser.: Vol. 2). (ENG.). 60p. (J). pap. 9.99 *(978-1-7903-6264-6(4))* Independently Published.

Damaggio, Rodolfo. Episode I Vol. 1: The Phantom Menace. Gilroy, Henry. 2009. (Star Wars Ser.: No. 1). (ENG.). 32p. (J). (gr. 6-12). 27.07 *(978-1-59961-608-7(4),* 13764, Graphic Novels) Spotlight.

—Episode I Vol. 2: The Phantom Menace. Gilroy, Henry. 2009. (Star Wars Ser.: No. 1). (ENG.). 32p. (J). (gr. 6-12). 27.07 *(978-1-59961-609-4(2),* 13765, Graphic Novels) Spotlight.

—Episode I Vol. 3: The Phantom menace. Gilroy, Henry. 2009. (Star Wars Ser.: No. 1). (ENG.). 32p. (J). (gr. 6-12). 27.07 *(978-1-59961-610-0(6),* 13766, Graphic Novels) Spotlight.

—Episode I Vol. 4: The Phantom Menace. Gilroy, Henry. 2009. (Star Wars Ser.: No. 1). (ENG.). 32p. (J). (gr. 6-12). 27.07 *(978-1-59961-611-7(4),* 13767, Graphic Novels) Spotlight.

Damant, Aurore. The Five o'Clock Ghost #4, No. 4. Butler, Dori Hillestad. 2015. (Haunted Library: 4). (ENG.). 144p. (J). (gr. 1-3). 5.99 *(978-0-448-46248-6(6),* Grosset & Dunlap) Penguin Young Readers Group.

—The Ghost at the Fire Station #6, No. 6. Butler, Dori Hillestad. 2015. (Haunted Library: 6). 128p. (J). (gr. 1-3). bds. 6.99 *(978-0-448-48334-4(3),* Grosset & Dunlap) Penguin Young Readers Group.

—The Ghost Backstage. Butler, Dori Hillestad. 2014. (Haunted Library: 3). 128p. (J). (gr. 1-3). 5.99 *(978-0-448-46246-2(X),* Grosset & Dunlap) Penguin Young Readers Group.

—The Ghost in the Attic, No. 2. Butler, Dori Hillestad. 2014. (Haunted Library: 2). 128p. (J). (gr. 1-3). 5.99 *(978-0-448-46244-8(3),* Grosset & Dunlap) Penguin Young Readers Group.

—The Ghost in the Tree House #7. Butler, Dori Hillestad. 2016. (Haunted Library: 7). (ENG.). 128p. (J). (gr. 1-3). 5.99 *(978-0-448-48940-7(6),* Grosset & Dunlap) Penguin Young Readers Group.

—The Ghosts at the Movie Theater. Butler, Dori Hillestad. 2017. (Haunted Library: 9). 128p. (J). (gr. 1-3). 5.99 *(978-0-451-53435-4(2),* Grosset & Dunlap) Penguin Young Readers Group.

—The Ghosts at the Movie Theater #9. Butler, Dori Hillestad. 2017. (Haunted Library: 9). (ENG.). 128p. (J). (gr. 1-3). 14.99 *(978-0-451-53436-1(0),* Grosset & Dunlap) Penguin Young Readers Group.

—The Haunted Library #1. Butler, Dori Hillestad. 2014. (Haunted Library: 1). 128p. (J). (gr. 1-3). 5.99 *(978-0-448-46242-4(7),* Grosset & Dunlap) Penguin Young Readers Group.

—The King of Too Many Things. Snyder, Laurel. 2017. (ENG.). 32p. (J). (gr. -1-3). 17.99 *(978-1-62336-874-6(X),* 9781623368746, Rodale Kids) Random Hse. Children's Bks.

—The Secret Room. Butler, Dori Hillestad & dePaola, Tomie. 2015. (Haunted Library: 5). 128p. (J). (gr. 1-3). bds. 5.99 *(978-0-448-48332-0(7),* Grosset & Dunlap) Penguin Young Readers Group.

—The Underground Ghosts #10: A Super Special. Butler, Dori Hillestad. 2017. (Haunted Library: 10). (ENG.). 192p. (J). (gr. 1-3). 7.99 *(978-0-515-15711-6(2),* Grosset & Dunlap) Penguin Young Readers Group.

Damato, Tamara. All That Jazz. Damato, Tamara. 2019. (ENG.). 28p. (J). pap. 10.00 ***(978-1-6994-2967-9(7))*** Independently Published.

Dameron, Ned. Charlie the Choo-Choo. Evans, Beryl. 2016. (ENG.). 24p. (J). (gr. -1). 14.99 *(978-1-5344-0123-5(7),* Simon & Schuster Bks. For Young Readers) Simon & Schuster Bks. For Young Readers.

Damerum, Kanako, et al. Abracadabra Strings - Abracadabra Double Bass Book 1. Lillywhite, Rosalind & Marshall, Andrew. Moss, Carla & Sebba, Jane, eds. 2005. (Abracadabra Ser.). (ENG.). 64p. (J). pap. 24.95 incl. audio compact disk *(978-0-7136-7097-4(5))* HarperCollins Pubs. Ltd. GBR. Dist: Independent Pubs. Group.

Damerum, Kanako & Parks, Paul. Abracadabra Violin, Bk. 1. Davey, Peter. Hussey, Christopher & Sebba, Jane, eds. 2nd ed. 2004. (Abracadabra Strings Ser.). (ENG.). 64p. (J). pap. 10.95 *(978-0-7136-6308-2(1),* A&C Black) Bloomsbury Publishing Plc GBR. Dist: Consortium Bk. Sales & Distribution.

Damian, Margo Gabrielle. The Elephant's Euphonium: A Little Tusker's Adventures in Africa. Fladung, Bonnie J. 2018. (Little Global Adventurers Ser.). (ENG.). 46p. (J). (gr. 2-5). 19.99 *(978-1-7327242-1-1(0))* Feather Star Pr.

Damian, Margo Gabrielle. The Elephant's Euphonium: A Little Tusker's Adventures in Africa. Currie, James Alexander & Fladung, Bonnie J. 2018. (Little Global Adventurers Ser.: Vol. 1). (ENG.). 46p. (J). pap. 9.99 ***(978-1-7327242-0-4(2))*** Feather Star Pr.

Damiao, Thais. Beauty & the Beast. Gunderson, Jessica. 2020. (Fairy Tales Ser.). (ENG.). 32p. (J). (gr. k-2). pap. 6.95 ***(978-1-5158-7271-9(8),*** 201229); lib. bdg. 21.32 ***(978-1-5158-7117-0(7),*** 199338) Capstone. (Picture Window Bks.).

Damião, Thais. Rumble! Vroom! Zoom! Let's Listen to Things That Go! Cottage Door Press & Parragon Books, eds. 2019. (ENG.). 10p. (J). (gr. -1-2). bds. 12.99 *(978-1-68052-681-3(2),* 2002830, Parragon Books) Cottage Door Pr.

D'Amico, Carmela & D'Amico, Steven. Ella: The Elegant Elephant. D'Amico, Carmela & D'Amico, Steven. unabr. ed. 2006. (ENG.). 56p. (J). (gr. -1-3). pap. 10.99 incl. DVD *(978-0-439-87589-9(7))* Scholastic, Inc.

D'Amico, Steven. Ella Sets the Stage. D'Amico, Carmela. 2006. 41p. (J). pap. 16.99 *(978-0-439-83153-6(9),* Levine, Arthur A. Bks.) Scholastic, Inc.

—The Hanukkah Hop! Silverman, Erica. 2011. (ENG.). 32p. (J). (gr. -1-3). 12.99 *(978-1-4424-0604-9(6),* Simon & Schuster Bks. For Young Readers) Simon & Schuster Bks. For Young Readers.

D'Amico, Steven, jt. illus. see D'Amico, Carmela.

Damm, Antje. The Visitor. Damm, Antje. 2018. (ENG.). 32p. (J). (gr. -1-k). 17.99 *(978-1-77657-188-8(6))* Gecko Pr. NZL. Dist: Lerner Publishing Group.

—Waiting for Goliath. Damm, Antje. 2017. (ENG.). 32p. (J). (gr. -1-3). 16.99 *(978-1-77657-141-3(X))* Gecko Pr. NZL. Dist: Lerner Publishing Group.

—The Wolf & the Fly. Damm, Antje. 2020. (ENG.). 22p. (J). (gr. -1-k). bds. 9.99 *(978-1-77657-280-9(7))* Gecko Pr. NZL. Dist: Lerner Publishing Group.

Damm, Heidi Kahrs. Krabben Klara Og Konkylien: Kampen Mot Plast I Havet. Bjelland, Hildegunn. Sanne, Thea Marie, ed. 2019. (NOR.). 136p. (J). pap. *(978-82-8391-060-5(4))* Tegn Forlag.

Damm, Heidi Kahrs. Ninjana: Det Store Skredet. Sanne, Thea Marie, ed. Bjelland, Hildegunn, tr. 2019. (Ninjana Ser.: Vol. 1). (NNO.). 102p. (J). pap. ***(978-82-8391-054-4(X))*** Tegn Forlag.

Dammann, Anke. Chester Crumbleberry. Dammann, Anke. 2005. 32p. 15.95 *(978-1-893815-11-7(0))* Pie in the Sky Publishing, LLC.

Dammer, Mike. Little Puff. Hillert, Margaret. 2016. (BeginningtoRead Ser.). (ENG.). 32p. (J). (gr. -1-2). pap. 11.94 *(978-1-60357-941-4(9));* (gr. k-2). 22.60 *(978-1-59953-800-6(8))* Norwood Hse. Pr.

Dammer, Mike. Pequeño Soplador. Hillert, Margaret. 2020. (Beginning-To-Read: Spanish Easy Stories Ser.). (SPA.). 32p. (J). (-2). 22.60 ***(978-1-68450-870-9(3));*** pap. 11.94 ***(978-1-68404-544-0(4))*** Norwood Hse. Pr.

Dammer, Mike. Phonics Comics: Cave Dave - Level 1. McAdams Moore, Carol. 2007. (ENG.). 24p. (J). (gr. 1-17). per. 3.99 *(978-1-58476-552-3(6))* Innovative Kids.

—Say It Again! 501 Wacky Word Puzzles from Highlights. Highlights for Children Staff. 2013. (Highlights(TM) Laugh Attack! Joke Bks.). (ENG.). 256p. (J). (gr. 1-4). pap. 5.95 *(978-1-62091-072-6(1),* Highlights) Boyds Mills Pr.

Damon Danielson. The Sleepover. Garnett, Tarreka. 2013. 32p. pap. 14.97 *(978-1-62212-249-3(6),* Strategic Bk. Publishing) Strategic Book Publishing & Rights Agency (SBPRA).

Damon, Emma. All Kinds of People. Safran, Sheri. 2012. (ENG.). 12p. (J). (gr. -1). 12.99 *(978-1-60887-160-5(6))* Insight Editions.

Damone, G. L., 3rd. Interrupted Journey's: Wyoming's Haunted Historic Trails. Del Bene, Terry A. et al. 2005. (YA). per. 15.95 *(978-0-9722217-5-7(1))* Horse Creek Pubns.

Dan, Houser. Creepy Kitchen. Lee, Newman. Elizabeth, Neering, ed. 2012. 40p. (J). pap. 10.00 *(978-1-62314-873-7(1))* Fisticuff Publishing.

Dana, Steve. Bookworm: Discovering Idioms, Sayings & Expressions. Emigh, Karen. 2013. (ENG.). 32p. (J). pap. 9.95 *(978-1-935274-88-9(0),* 9781935274889) Future Horizons, Inc.

—Who Took My Shoe? Emigh, Karen. 2003. (ENG.). 19p. (J). (gr. 1-6). pap. 9.95 *(978-1-885477-95-8(3))* Future Horizons, Inc.

Danalis, John. The Girl in the Cave. Eaton, Anthony. 2004. 128p. (J). pap. *(978-0-7022-3437-8(0))* Univ. of Queensland Pr.

—Licking Lizards. Risson, Toni. 2005. 128p. (Orig.). (J). pap. *(978-0-7022-3524-5(5))* Univ. of Queensland Pr.

Danalis, John. Dog 37. Danalis, John. 2004. 96p. (Orig.). (J). pap. *(978-0-7022-3431-6(1))* Univ. of Queensland Pr.

Danby, Aaron, jt. illus. see Martin, M. J.

Dancy, Karla. Bazo: A Coloring Book about Love & Letting Go. Jacobson M D, Walter E. 2018. (ENG.). 60p. (J). pap. 12.63 *(978-1-5025-5040-8(7))* CreateSpace Independent Publishing Platform.

D'Anda, Carlos. In the Shadow of Yavin, 6 vols. ABDO Publishing Company Staff & Wood, Brian. 2014. (Star Wars: in the Shadow of Yavin Ser.: 6). (ENG.). 24p. (J). (gr. 6-12). lib. bdg. 162.42 *(978-1-61479-285-7(2),* 1656, Graphic Novels) Spotlight.

—Star Wars. Wood, Brian. 2014. (Star Wars: in the Shadow of Yavin Ser.: Vol. 1). (ENG.). 24p. (J). (gr. 6-12). 27.07 *(978-1-61479-286-4(0),* 1657, Graphic Novels) Spotlight.

Dandan-Albano, Corazon. All about the Philippines: Stories, Songs & Crafts for Kids. Jimenez, Gidget Roceles. 2015. (ENG.). 64p. (J). (gr. 3-6). 16.95 *(978-0-8048-4072-9(5))* Tuttle Publishing.

—All about the Philippines: Stories, Songs, Crafts & Games for Kids. Jimenez, Gidget Roceles. 2017. 64p. (J). (gr. 3-6). 14.95 *(978-0-8048-4848-0(3))* Tuttle Publishing.

—Filipino Celebrations: A Treasury of Feasts & Festivals. Romulo, Liana. ed. 2012. 48p. (J). (gr. k-4). 16.95 *(978-0-8048-3821-4(6))* Tuttle Publishing.

—Filipino Friends. Romulo, Liana. 2006. 32p. (J). (gr. 1-3). pap. 15.95 *(978-0-8048-3822-1(4))* Tuttle Publishing.

D'Andrade, Hugh. The Grimm Conclusion. Gidwitz, Adam. 2013. (ENG.). 368p. (J). (gr. 5). 17.99 *(978-0-525-42615-8(9),* Dutton Books for Young Readers) Penguin Young Readers Group.

—In a Glass Grimmly. Gidwitz, Adam. 2012. (ENG.). 336p. (J). (gr. 5). 17.99 *(978-0-525-42581-6(0),* Dutton Books for Young Readers) Penguin Young Readers Group.

—A Tale Dark & Grimm. Gidwitz, Adam et al. 2010. (ENG.). 272p. (J). (gr. 5-18). 17.99 *(978-0-525-42334-8(6),* Dutton Books for Young Readers) Penguin Young Readers Group.

D'Andrea, Lisa. A Most Remarkable Mouse. Zoboli, Giovanna. 2016. 40p. (J). (gr. -1-4). 17.95 *(978-1-59270-213-8(9))* Enchanted Lion Bks., LLC.

Dane, Donna. Circle Time Book: For Holiday & Seasons. Wilmes, Liz et al. 2004. 128p. (J). pap. 12.95 *(978-0-943452-00-5(7),* 20002) Building Blocks, LLC.

—Felt Board Fun: For Everyday & Holidays. Wilmes, Liz & Wilmes, Dick. 2004. 244p. (J). pap. 16.95 *(978-0-943452-02-9(3))* Building Blocks, LLC.

Danelli, Maureen. Mouse & the Big Show. Danelli, Jimmy. 2016. (ENG.). (J). pap. 12.99 *(978-0-692-78740-3(2))* Straight From The Heart Publishing.

Danger, Chris. Stella: The Dog with the Big Heart. Feldman, Thea. 2015. (Hero Dog Ser.). (ENG.). 32p. (J). (gr. k-2). pap. 3.99 *(978-1-4814-2243-7(X))* Simon & Schuster Children's Publishing.

D

Daniel, Alan. Bunnicula: 40th Anniversary Edition. Howe, James & Howe, Deborah. ed. 2019. (Bunnicula & Friends Ser.). (ENG.). 144p. (J). (gr. 3-7). pap. 10.99 *(978-1-5344-3593-3(X),* Atheneum Bks. for Young Readers) Simon & Schuster Children's Publishing.

—Bunnicula: A Rabbit-Tale of Mystery. Howe, Deborah & Howe, James. 2006. (Bunnicula & Friends Ser.). (ENG.). 128p. (J). (gr. 3-7). pap. 7.99 *(978-1-4169-2817-1(0),* Atheneum Bks. for Young Readers) Simon & Schuster Children's Publishing.

—Bunnicula Strikes Again! Howe, James. 2007. (Bunnicula & Friends Ser.). (ENG.). 144p. (J). (gr. 3-7). pap. 7.99 *(978-1-4169-3968-9(7),* Atheneum Bks. for Young Readers) Simon & Schuster Children's Publishing.

—Eh? To Zed: A Canadian Abecedarium, 1 vol. Major, Kevin. 2003. (ENG.). 32p. (J). (gr. -1-1). pap. 9.95 *(978-0-88995-272-0(8),* c54baa76-4444-4b16-8e16-1fc3bde3ef31) Trifolium Bks., Inc. CAN. Dist: Firefly Bks., Ltd.

—Fireside Al's Treasury of Christmas Stories, 1 vol. Maitland, Alan. 2007. (ENG.). 64p. (J). (gr. 4-7). 19.95 *(978-0-88995-382-6(1),* ae947c11-2f0c-4f7f-8cfa-d698567e388b) Red Deer Pr. CAN. Dist: Firefly Bks., Ltd.

—The Grand Escape. Naylor, Phyllis Reynolds. 2005. (ENG.). 160p. (J). (gr. 3-7). pap. 7.99 *(978-0-689-87407-9(3),* Atheneum Bks. for Young Readers) Simon & Schuster Children's Publishing.

—The Healing of Texas Jake. Naylor, Phyllis Reynolds. 2005. (ENG.). 128p. (J). (gr. 3-7). pap. 7.99 *(978-0-689-87406-2(5),* Atheneum Bks. for Young Readers) Simon & Schuster Children's Publishing.

Daniel, Alan, et al. Much More Munsch! A Robert Munsch Collection. Munsch, Robert. 2019. (ENG.). 184p. (J). 24.99 *(978-0-439-93571-5(7))* Scholastic Canada, Ltd. CAN. Dist: Publishers Group West (PGW).

Daniel, Alan. Polo's Mother. Naylor, Phyllis Reynolds. 2006. (ENG.). 176p. (J). (gr. 3-7). pap. 7.99 *(978-0-689-87404-8(9),* Atheneum Bks. for Young Readers) Simon & Schuster Children's Publishing.

—Return to Howliday Inn. Howe, James. 2007. (Bunnicula & Friends Ser.). (ENG.). 192p. (J). (gr. 3-7). pap. 7.99 *(978-1-4169-3967-2(9),* Atheneum Bks. for Young Readers) Simon & Schuster Children's Publishing.

—Return to Howliday Inn. Howe, James. ed. 2007. (Bunnicula Ser.: 5). (gr. 4-7). lib. bdg. 17.20 *(978-1-4177-9044-9(X))* Turtleback.

Daniel, Alan & Daniel, Lea. Aaron's Hair. Munsch, Robert et al. 2020. (ENG.). 32p. (J). pap. 7.99 (978-0-439-98716-5(4)) Scholastic Canada, Ltd. CAN. Dist: Publishers Group West (PGW).

—Albert Einstein: Genius of the Twentieth Century. Lakin, Patricia. 2005. (Ready-To-read SOFA Ser.). (ENG.). 48p. (J). (gr. 1-3). pap. 4.99 (978-0-689-87034-7(5), Simon Spotlight) Simon Spotlight.

—Amelia Earhart: Amelia Earhart: More Than A Flier. Lakin, Patricia. ed. 2005. 48p. (J). lib. bdg. 15.00 (978-1-59054-957-5(0)) Fitzgerald Bks.

—Amelia Earhart: More Than a Flier. Lakin, Patricia & Daniel, Alan. Daniel, Lea. 2003. (Ready-To-read SOFA Ser.). (ENG.). 48p. (J). (gr. 1-3). pap. 4.99 (978-0-689-85575-7(3), Simon Spotlight) Simon Spotlight.

—My Home Bay, 1 vol. Carter, Anne Laurel. 2003. (ENG.). 32p. (J). (gr. k-1). 6.95 (978-0-88995-284-3(1), 14a4dae9-f7ec-465b-b10e-3a3eb64cba6c) Red Deer Pr. CAN. Dist: Firefly Bks., Ltd.

—Roundup at the Palace, 1 vol. Waldron, Kathleen Cook. 2006. (ENG.). 32p. (J). (gr. -1). 17.95 (978-0-88995-319-2(8)) Red Deer Pr. CAN. Dist: Ingram Publisher Services.

—Under a Prairie Sky, 1 vol. Carter, Anne Laurel. 2004. (ENG.). 32p. (J). (gr. -1-k). pap. 13.95 (978-1-55143-282-3(X)) Orca Bk. Pubs. USA.

Daniel, Alan, jt. illus. see Shapiro, Deborah.

Daniel, Beverly. The Adventures of Madilyn Millicent Middleton-Mew. Daniel, Beverly. Daniel, Cindy, ed. 2013. 64p. pap. 8.95 (978-0-9789429-6-0(5)) Batelier Publishing.

Daniel, Carol. Fun to Learn Opposites: Kaleidoscope Book. Jackaman, Philippa. 16p. (J). (978-1-84322-125-8(X)) Bookmart Ltd.

Daniel, Danielle. You Hold Me Up, 1 vol. Gray Smith, Monique. 2017. (ENG.). 32p. (J). (gr. -1-k). 19.95 (978-1-4598-1447-9(9)) Orca Bk. Pubs. USA.

—You Hold Me up /Ki Kîhcêyimin Mâna, 1 vol. Gray Smith, Monique. Collins, Mary Cardinal, tr. ed. 2018. (ENG & CRE.). 32p. (J). (gr. -1-k). 19.95 (978-1-4598-2175-0(0)) Orca Bk. Pubs. USA.

Daniel, Ellen. The Twilight Ride of the Pink Fairy. Demeritt, Mary Anne. 2006. 36p. (J). pap. 17.95 (978-1-58597-410-8(2)) Leathers Publishing.

Daniel, Lea, jt. illus. see Daniel, Alan.

Daniel, R. F. "I Can Tell You Stories, If You Gather Near"... The Big Bear of Arkansas. Sandage, Charley. 2004. 46p. (J). (gr. k-2). pap. 14.95 (978-0-9638956-7-7(2)) Archeological Assessments, Inc.

Daniel, Rick. Math Rapmatics: Mathematical Rhymes Right on Time. Van Horn, Stephanie. 2011. 24p. (J). 18.00 (978-0-9814945-9-3(5)) AK Classics, LLC.

Daniel Tiger Style Guide. Let's Look with Daniel & Friends! A Very Busy Board Book! Cottage Door Press, ed. 2020. (Very Busy Board Book to Look, Match Search & Laugh! Daniel Tiger's Neighborhood Ser.). (ENG.). 12p. (J). (gr. -1-1). bds. 14.99 (978-1-68052-825-1(4), 1005380) Cottage Door Pr.

Daniele, Guido. Handimals: Animals in Art & Nature. Lopez, Silvia. 2019. (ENG.). 40p. (J). 18.99 (978-1-62779-891-4(9), 900161981, Holt, Henry & Co. Bks. For Young Readers) Holt, Henry & Co.

Daniels, Erin. One Small Piece. Daniels, Cash. 2019. (ENG.). 32p. (J). pap. 9.99 (978-1-7946-1352-2(8)) Independently Published.

Daniels, Gail. Pretty Princess: Words. Daniels, Gail. 2004. 12p. (J). bds. 3.99 (978-1-85997-812-2(6)); bds. 5.99 (978-1-85997-868-9(1)) Byeway Bks.

—Pretty Princess: Words. Daniels, Gail. 2003. (J). per. (978-1-884907-45-6(8)) Paradise Pr., Inc.

Daniels, Greg. I Want off This Stinkin' Plane, 1 vol. McInnes, Dawn Daniels. 2010. 18p. pap. 24.95 (978-1-4489-7809-0(2)) PublishAmerica, Inc.

Daniels, Landon. Rowan, My Boat: A Child's Fantasy Story with Music. Ackley, Ginger. 2019. (ENG.). 30p. (J). pap. 17.95 (978-1-0884-5306-3(6)) Independently Published.

Daniels, Regina. Three Days & Four Knights. Auxier, Bryan. 2004. 66p. (J). pap. 3.95 (978-0-9719144-2-1(7)) Where? Pr., Inc.

—Where Have All the Unicorns Gone? Auxier, Bryan. l.t. ed. 2003. 16p. (J). 7.95 (978-0-9719144-1-4(9)) Where? Pr., Inc.

Daniels, Shaelyn. Malia the Merfairy & the Lucky Rainbow Cake (Bilingual Spanish English Version) Triplin, Jamie a. 2019. (ENG.). 48p. (J). pap. 10.95 (978-1-0793-5997-8(4)) Independently Published.

Daniels, Sterling N., 2nd. Yas. Daniels, Sterling N., 2nd. 36p. (J). (gr. k-3). pap. 4.95 (978-0-9628081-2-8(1)) D. A. W. Enterprise.

Danielson, Damon. Bully's Game Day Rules. Smith, Sherri Graves. 2013. (ENG.). (J). 14.95 (978-1-62086-334-3(0)) Mascot Bks., Inc.

—Cimarron's Game Day Rules. Smith, Sherri Graves. 2013. (ENG.). (J). 14.95 (978-1-62086-230-8(1)) Mascot Bks., Inc.

—Cocky's Game Day Rules. Smith, Sherri Graves. 2013. (ENG.). (J). 14.95 (978-1-62086-085-4(6)) Mascot Bks., Inc.

—Nittany Lion's Game Day Rules. Smith, Sherri Graves. 2013. (ENG.). (J). 14.95 (978-1-62086-233-9(6)) Mascot Bks., Inc.

—Reveille's Game Day Rules. Smith, Sherri Graves. 2013. (ENG.). (J). (gr. -1-3). 14.95 (978-1-62086-350-3(2)) Mascot Bks., Inc.

—Tiger's Game Day Rules. Smith, Sherri Graves. 2013. (ENG.). (J). (gr. -1-3). 14.95 (978-1-62086-086-1(4)) Mascot Bks., Inc.

Danilewicz, Jamie. Make the World Pink, I Think. Petersen, Pat. 2012. 26p. 24.95 (978-1-4626-3028-8(6)) America Star Bks.

Danilova, Daria. Silly Limbic: A Tail of Bravery. Harvey, Miss Naomi. 2018. (ENG.). 36p. (J). pap. (978-1-9997664-0-5(7)) Harvey, Naomi.

Danilova, Lida. Rainy Day Drawing: More Than 100 Pages for Drawing, Coloring, & Creating. Clever Publishing. 2019. (Clever Activity Pad Ser.). (ENG.). 104p. (J). (gr. -1-1). pap. 4.99 (978-1-948418-03-4(7)) Clever Media Group.

Danilova, Valeriya. I Know Things That Go: Lift-The-flap Book. Clever Publishing. 2018. (Clever Questions Ser.). (ENG.). 16p. (J). (gr. -1-1). bds. 9.99 (978-1-948418-36-2(3)) Clever Media Group.

Danioth, David. A Mother's Promise. Humphrey, Lisa. 2004. 32p. (J). per. 15.95 (978-0-9701907-9-6(4)) Illumination Arts Publishing Co., Inc.

Danis Drouot, Lucile. Boston Monsters: A Search-And-Find Book. 2017. (ENG.). 22p. (J). (gr. -1). bds. 9.99 (978-2-924734-05-6(3)) City Monsters Bks. CAN. Dist: Publishers Group West (PGW).

—New York Monsters: A Search-And-Find Book. Paradis, Anne. 2017. (ENG.). 22p. (J). bds. 9.99 (978-2-924734-02-5(9)) City Monsters Bks. CAN. Dist: Publishers Group West (PGW).

—Washington D. C. Monsters: A Search-And-Find Book. 2017. (ENG.). 22p. (J). (gr. -1). bds. 9.99 (978-2-924734-06-3(1)) City Monsters Bks. CAN. Dist: Publishers Group West (PGW).

Dann, Geoff & Gorton, Steve. Espías. Platt, Richard. 2003. (SPA.). 64p. (J). 14.95 (978-84-372-2319-3(9)) Altea, Ediciones, S.A. - Grupo Santillana ESP. Dist: Santillana USA Publishing Co., Inc.

Dann, Penny. Christmas at Last! Hearn, Sam. 2015. (ENG.). 16p. (J). (gr. -1-k). bds. 10.99 (978-0-545-79455-8(2), Cartwheel Bks.) Scholastic, Inc.

—Missing! Mellor, Jodie. 2010. (Mystery Pups Ser.). (ENG.). 112p. (J). (gr. k-2). pap. 6.99 (978-1-84738-226-9(6)) Simon & Schuster, Ltd. GBR. Dist: Independent Pubs. Group.

—Too Many Tickles! Taylor, Thomas. ed. 2014. (ENG.). 24p. (J). (gr. -1-k). 17.99 (978-0-230-75265-8(9)) Pan Macmillan GBR. Dist: Independent Pubs. Group.

—What Are Friends For? Grindley, Sally. 2020. (ENG.). 32p. (J). 17.99 (978-0-7534-7619-2(3), 900226434, Kingfisher) Roaring Brook Pr.

—What Will I Do Without You? Grindley, Sally. 2020. (ENG.). 32p. (J). 17.99 (978-0-7534-7620-8(7), 900226436, Kingfisher) Roaring Brook Pr.

—Will You Forgive Me? Grindley, Sally. 2020. (ENG.). 32p. (J). 17.99 (978-0-7534-7621-5(5), 900226435, Kingfisher) Roaring Brook Pr.

Danna Sr., Gerald. Miss Poppy & Red Jeans: Adventure to Willie Willie's Garden. Danna, Minnie. 2012. 66p. pap. 12.95 (978-0-9852608-0-4(7)) Flower Publishing.

Dannenmann, Alexandra. El Reino M�gico: Un Libro de Colorear para Adultos para So�ar y Relajarse. Dannenmann, Alexandra. Del Val Nunez, Mabel, tr. 2019. (SPA.). 58p. (J). pap. 6.99 (978-1-7026-9602-9(2)) Independently Published.

Danner, Maggie. How Teddy Bears Find Their Homes. Waldman, David K. 2nd ed. 2015. (ENG.). 154p. (gr. k-2). pap. 38.40 (978-0-945522-02-7(9)) BookBaby.

Danny Snell. Aussie Kids: Meet Mia by the Jetty. Brian, Janeen. 2020. (Aussie Kids Ser.). 64p. (J). (gr. k-2). 12.99 (978-1-76089-366-8(8), Puffin) Penguin Random Hse. AUS. Dist: Independent Pubs. Group.

Danowski, Sonja. The Forever Flowers. Rosen, Michael J. 2014. (ENG.). 32p. (J). (gr. 1-3). 18.99 (978-1-56846-273-8(5), Creative Editions) Creative Co., The.

—Grandma Lives in a Perfume Village. Suzhen, Fang. 2015. 48p. (J). (gr. -1-2). 19.95 (978-0-7358-4216-8(7)) North-South Bks., Inc.

Danse, Catline. Lola et la Tartine de Chocolat. Danse, Catline. 2019. (FRE.). 38p. (J). pap. 10.00 (978-1-0889-4018-1(8)) Independently Published.

Dansereau, Steve. Goodbye Little Dude: A Remarkable Story of Kindness, Hope, & Love. Trotsky, Rebecca & Smyth, Marie. 2018. (ENG.). 32p. (J). (gr. 1-3). pap. 12.99 (978-1-970002-01-0(8)) Curran Pr. and Editorial Consulting, LLC.

—A Mouse in the House: A True Story about the Mice Who Came into Our Home after Hurricane Sandy. Tarpinian, Steve. 2018. (ENG.). 34p. (J). (gr. 4-6). pap. 12.99 (978-0-692-06685-0(3)) mellano, jean.

Danso, Al. Maddie the Mathematician: The Discovery of Polygons. Joseph, Nnenia. 2018. (Maddie the Mathematician Ser.: Vol. 3). (ENG.). 26p. (J). (gr. k-5). 19.99 (978-1-64316-557-8(7)) Primedia eLaunch LLC.

Danson, Lesley. Cairo the Camel: A Tale of Responsibility. Law, Felicia. 2010. (Animal Fair Values Ser.). (ENG.). 32p. (J). (gr. -1-3). pap. 10.55 (978-1-60754-911-6(5)) Windmill Bks.

—Darwin the Dolphin: A Tale of Bravery & Courage. Law, Felicia. 2010. (Animal Fair Values Ser.). 32p. (J). (gr. -1-3). pap. 10.55 (978-1-60754-810-2(0)); lib. bdg. 25.60 (978-1-60754-806-5(2)) Windmill Bks.

—Dragon Magic. Goodhart, Pippa. 2nd ed. 2016. (Reading Ladder Ser.). (ENG.). 48p. (J). (gr. k-2). 7.99 (978-1-4052-8244-4(4)) Egmont Bks., Ltd. GBR. Dist: Independent Pubs. Group.

—Hide-and-Seek Bunnies. Watt, Fiona. 2007. (Touchy-Feely Flap Bks). 10p. (J). (gr. -1-k). bds. 16.99 (978-0-7945-1566-9(5), Usborne) EDC Publishing.

—Hudson the Hippo: A Tale of Self-Control. Law, Felicia. 2010. (Animal Fair Values Ser.). (ENG.). 32p. (J). (gr. -1-3). pap. 10.55 (978-1-60754-913-0(1)) Windmill Bks.

—Kimberly the Koala: A Tale of Independence. Law, Felicia. 2010. (Animal Fair Values Ser.). (ENG.). 32p. (J). (gr. -1-3). pap. 10.55 (978-1-60754-909-3(3)); lib. bdg. 25.60 (978-1-60754-902-4(6)) Windmill Bks.

—Pearl Fairweather Pirate Captain: Teaching Children Gender Equality, Respect, Empowerment, Diversity, Leadership, Recognising Bullying. Sanders, Jayneen. 2017. (ENG.). 40p. (J). (gr. k-5). (978-1-925089-15-8(0), Educate2Empower Publishing) UpLoad Publishing Pty, Ltd.

—Snow White. (Flip-Up Fairy Tales Ser.). 24p. (J). 2007. (gr. -1-2). (978-1-84643-096-1(8)); 2006. (gr. 1-2). (978-1-84643-023-7(2)) Child's Play International Ltd.

Dantat, Dan & Santat, Dan. Fire! ¡Fuego! Brave Bomberos. Elya, Susan Middleton. ed. 2012. 40p. (J). (gr. -1-1). pap. 17.99 (978-1-59990-461-0(6), 900064754, Bloomsbury USA Childrens) Bloomsbury Publishing USA.

D'Antoni, Colleen. Cajun 'Ti Beau & the Cocodries, 1 vol. Gibson, Cay. 2014. (ENG.). 32p. (J). (gr. k-3). 16.99 (978-1-4556-1947-4(7), Pelican Publishing) Arcadia Publishing.

D'Antonio, Sandra. Do Whales Have Wings? A Book about Animal Bodies. Dahl, Michael. 2003. (Animals All Around Ser.). (ENG.). 24p. (J). (gr. -1-2). per. 8.95 (978-1-4048-0373-2(4), Picture Window Bks.) Capstone.

Dao, Linh. Amazing Animal Friendships: Odd Couples in Nature. Hanááčková, Pavla. ed. 2017. (ENG.). 36p. (J). (gr. k-4). 14.95 (978-1-912006-48-9(0)) Book Hse. GBR. Dist: Sterling Publishing Co., Inc.

Dapo, Bleps. Where's My Teddy (Tetun Edition) - Ha'u-Nia Teddy Iha Ne'ebé? Mirio, Bridgette. 2020. (TET.). 18p. (J). pap. (978-1-922331-52-6(X)) Library For All Limited.

D'Aquino, Andrea. Classics Reimagined, Alice's Adventures in Wonderland. Carroll, Lewis. unabr. ed. 2015. (Classics Reimagined Ser.). (ENG.). 312p. 30.00 (978-1-63159-075-7(8), Rockport Publishers) Quarto Publishing Group USA.

Daranga, Ana-Maria. Mango & His Friends Have a Party. Ionescu, Julian. 2012. (ENG.). 32p. (J). (gr. k-2). pap. 13.95 (978-0-86527-510-2(6)) Fertig, Howard Publisher.

—Tomato & Her Friends Have a Party. Ionescu, Julian. 2012. (Tomato & Her Friends Have a Party). (ENG.). (J). (gr. k-2). pap. 13.95 (978-0-86527-509-6(2)) Fertig, Howard Publisher.

Darby, Hope. Terra Porkorum: The Planet of the Pigs. Salvati, Urbano. 2018. (ENG.). 36p. (J). (gr. k-6). pap. 13.95 (978-1-946540-69-0(2)) Strategic Book Publishing & Rights Agency (SBPRA).

Darby, Stephania Pierce, jt. illus. see Jones, C. Denise West.

Darby, Stephania Pierce, jt. illus. see Jones, Denise West.

Darchicourt, David. Sir Pigglesworth's Adventures in San Juan, PR. Wagner, JoAnn. 2017. (Sir Pigglesworth Adventure Ser.: Vol. 7). (ENG.). (J). (gr. 1-4). 16.95 (978-1-68055-082-5(9)); pap. 8.95 (978-1-68055-081-8(0)) Sir Pigglesworth Publishing, Inc.

Darcy, Liam. Emily's Pumpkin. Gates, Margo. 2019. (Science All Around Me (Pull Ahead Readers — Fiction) Ser.). (ENG.). 16p. (J). (gr. -1-1). pap. 6.99 (978-1-5415-7338-3(2), 9781541573383, Lerner Pubns.) Lerner Publishing Group.

—The Fish. Gates, Margo. 2019. (Let's Look at Animal Habitats (Pull Ahead Readers — Fiction) Ser.). (ENG.). 16p. (J). (gr. -1-1). 22.65 (978-1-5415-5863-2(4), 9781541558632, Lerner Pubns.) Lerner Publishing Group.

—Hiding from Lightning. Gates, Margo. 2019. (Let's Look at Weather (Pull Ahead Readers — Fiction) Ser.). (ENG.). 16p. (J). (gr. -1-1). pap. 6.99 (978-1-5415-7321-5(8), 9781541573215, Lerner Pubns.) Lerner Publishing Group.

Dardik, Helen. Bagel in Love. Wing, Natasha. 2018. 32p. (J). (gr. -1). 16.95 (978-1-4549-2239-1(7)) Sterling Publishing Co., Inc.

—Lite'N Up! Laugh Yourself Skinny. Klein, Samara Q. 2009. (ENG.). 156p. pap. 14.95 (978-0-9777383-5-9(3)) Plain White Pr., LLC.

Dardik, Helen, et al. The Magical Unicorn Society Official Handbook. Phipps, Selwyn E. 2018. (Magical Unicorn Society Ser.: 1). (ENG.). 128p. (J). 12.99 (978-1-250-20619-0(7), 900201438) Feiwel & Friends.

Dardik, Helen. Oh! Christmas Tree! Small Padded Board Book. Berry Byrd, Holly. Cottage Door Press, ed. 2016. (Little Bird Stories Ser.). (ENG.). 12p. (J). (gr. -1-k). bds. 6.99 (978-1-68052-110-8(1), 1001030) Cottage Door Pr.

—The Story of Christmas. 2017. 24p. (J). (gr. -1 — 1). 9.95 (978-0-7624-6242-1(6), Running Pr. Kids) Running Pr.

—The Story of David & Goliath. Running Press. 2018. 24p. (J). (gr. -1 — 1). bds. 9.95 (978-0-7624-6332-9(5), Running Pr. Kids) Running Pr.

—The Story of Easter. 2019. 384p. (J). (gr. -1 — 1). bds. 9.95 (978-0-7624-9269-5(4), Running Pr. Kids) Running Pr.

D'Argo, Laura. The Adventures of Puss-A-Too-Too & Skunk-a-Pedius. Bakus, Bob, ed. 2013. (ENG.). (J). 21.99 (978-1-4849-6456-9(X)) CreateSpace Independent Publishing Platform.

—Suzy Season Loves Fall. Posner, Renee & Quinton, Sasha. 2003. (Be Mine Bears Ser.). (J). bds. 4.99 (978-1-58209-352-9(0)) Bks. Are Fun, Ltd.

—Suzy Season Loves Spring. Posner, Renee & Quinton, Sasha. (Be Mine Bears Ser.). (J). bds. 4.99 (978-1-58209-350-5(4)) Bks. Are Fun, Ltd.

—Suzy Season Loves Summer. Posner, Renee & Quinton, Sasha. (Be Mine Bears Ser.). (J). bds. 4.99 (978-1-58209-351-2(2)) Bks. Are Fun, Ltd.

—Suzy Season Loves Winter. Posner, Renee & Quinton, Sasha. 2003. (Be Mine Bears Ser.). (J). bds. 4.99 (978-1-58209-353-6(9)) Bks. Are Fun, Ltd.

—The Wright Brothers for Kid: How They Invented the Airplane, 21 Activities Exploring the Science & History of Flight. Carson, Mary Kay. 2003. (For Kids Ser.). (ENG.). 160p. (J). (gr. 4). pap. 18.95 (978-1-55652-477-6(3)) Chicago Review Pr., Inc.

D'Ariggo, Jay, jt. illus. see Michelle, Jean.

Darley, F. O. C. A Visit from Saint Nicholas. Moore, Clement. 2019. (ENG.). 22p. (J). (gr. k-3). pap. (978-625-7959-14-8(4)) Uhrayoglu, Murat E Kitap Projesi.

Darley, Heidi. Meet Zade! Bringing Home a New Puppy. Copeland, Milada & Eliason, Donna. 2020. (Meet Zade! Ser.). (ENG.). 40p. (J). (978-1-5255-7296-8(2)); pap. (978-1-5255-7297-5(0)) FriesenPress.

Darling, Geneviève. What Makes Girls Sick & Tired, 1 vol. de Pesloüan, Lucile. 2019. (ENG.). 48p. (YA). (gr. 8-12). pap. 13.95 (978-1-77260-096-4(2)) Second Story Pr. CAN. Dist: Orca Bk. Pubs. USA.

Darling, Louis. Beezus & Ramona. Cleary, Beverly. (gr. 3-5). pap. (978-0-545-24980-5(5)) Scholastic, Inc.

—Henry & Beezus. Cleary, Beverly. 2017. (Henry Huggins Ser.: 2). (ENG.). 176p. (J). (gr. 3-7). 16.99 (978-0-06-265236-2(2)) HarperCollins Pubs.

—Henry & Ribsy. Cleary, Beverly. 2017. (Henry Huggins Ser.: 3). (ENG.). 176p. (J). (gr. 3-7). 16.99 (978-0-06-265237-9(0)) HarperCollins Pubs.

—Henry & the Clubhouse. Cleary, Beverly. 2017. (Henry Huggins Ser.: 5). (ENG.). 176p. (J). (gr. 3-7). 16.99 (978-0-06-265239-3(7)) HarperCollins Pubs.

—Henry & the Paper Route. Cleary, Beverly. 2017. (Henry Huggins Ser.: 4). (ENG.). 176p. (J). (gr. 3-7). 16.99 (978-0-06-265238-6(9)) HarperCollins Pubs.

—Henry Huggins. Cleary, Beverly. 2017. (Henry Huggins Ser.: 1). (ENG.). 160p. (J). (gr. 3-7). 16.99 (978-0-06-265235-5(4)) HarperCollins Pubs.

—Henry Huggins: Henry Huggins (Spanish Edition), 1 vol. Cleary, Beverly. 2004. (Henry Huggins Ser.: 1). (SPA.). 160p. (J). (gr. 3-7). pap. 7.99 (978-0-06-073600-2(3), HarperCollins Español) HarperCollins Christian Publishing.

—Ramona la Chinche. Cleary, Beverly. Palacios, Argentina, tr. ed. 2006. (Ramona Quimby Spanish Ser.: 2).Tr. of Ramona the Pest. (SPA.). 181p. (J). (gr. 4-7). lib. bdg. 16.00 (978-0-613-00464-0(7)) Turtleback.

—El Ratoncito de la Moto: The Mouse & the Motorcycle (Spanish Edition), 1 vol. Cleary, Beverly. 2006. (Ralph Mouse Ser.: 1).Tr. of Mouse & the Motorcycle. (SPA.). 160p. (J). (gr. 3-7). pap. 7.99 (978-0-06-000057-8(0)) HarperCollins Español.

—Ribsy. Cleary, Beverly. 2017. (Henry Huggins Ser.: 6). (ENG.). 192p. (J). (gr. 3-7). 16.99 (978-0-06-265240-9(0)) HarperCollins Pubs.

Darling, Rachel. Jack. Farrell, Bianca. 2019. (ENG.). (J). 22p. (978-1-925952-01-8(0)); 20p. pap. (978-1-925952-02-5(9)) Vivid Publishing.

Darling, Wendy Anne. The Curse of Time Book 1 Bloodstone. Mallon, M. J. Chesebro, Colleen, ed. 2018. (ENG.). 242p. (J). pap. (978-1-9998224-3-9(9)) Kyrosmagica Publishing.

Darlington, Stacey. Athena's Curse: A Novel Twist on the Medusa Myth. Darlington-Davis, S. 2019. (ENG.). 222p. (J). pap. 12.00 (978-1-7964-0194-3(3)) Independently Published.

D'Armata, Frank, jt. illus. see Epting, Steve.

Darmawan, Iwan. Little Bo. Porter, Inman L. 2016. (Little Bo Ser.: Vol. 1). (ENG.). (J). (gr. k-3). pap. 14.99 (978-0-9979766-1-8(6)) Porter, Inman.

Darnell, K. L. The American Reader. Wargin, Kathy-jo. 2006. (Readers Ser.). (ENG.). 96p. (J). (gr. 1-5). 12.95 (978-1-58536-095-6(3)) Sleeping Bear Pr.

—The New Jersey Reader. Noble, Trinka Hakes. 2009. (Readers Ser.). (ENG.). 96p. 12.95 (978-1-58536-438-1(X)) Sleeping Bear Pr.

—The New York Reader. Burg, Ann E. 2008. (Readers Ser.). (ENG.). 96p. (J). pap. 5.95 (978-1-58536-349-0(9)) Sleeping Bear Pr.

—The Ohio Reader. Schonberg, Marcia. rev. ed. 2007. (State Readers Ser.). (ENG.). 96p. (J). (gr. 1-5). 12.95 (978-1-58536-321-6(9)) Sleeping Bear Pr.

—Pennsylvania Reader. Noble, Trinka Hakes. rev. ed. 2007. (State Readers Ser.). (ENG.). 96p. (J). (gr. 1-5). 12.95 (978-1-58536-320-9(0)) Sleeping Bear Pr.

Darnell, Kate. The Missouri Reader. Young, Judy Dockrey. 2010. (Readers Ser.). (ENG.). 96p. (J). 12.95 (978-1-58536-437-4(1)) Sleeping Bear Pr.

D'Arnoux, Charles Albert. Nutcracker: And Mouse King. Hoffmann, E. T. A. Hope, Ascott Robert, tr. 2019. (ENG.). 152p. (J). (gr. k-6). pap. (978-625-7959-22-3(5)) Uhrayoglu, Murat E Kitap Projesi.

Darrenkamp, Julia Mary. My First Book about Mary. Orfeo, Christine Virginia. 2007. 63p. (Orig.). (J). (gr. 3-7). per. 7.95 (978-0-8198-4861-1(1)) Pauline Bks. & Media.

—My Scriptural Rosary. Roddy, Lauren S. rev. ed. 2006. (J). 4.95 (978-0-8198-4845-1(X)) Pauline Bks. & Media.

Darroch, Jane & Riley, Scott. The Story of Monet & Renoir. Frey, Lisa A. Frey, Lisa A. & Darroch, Jane, eds. 2004. (Color & Learn Book Ser.). 32p. (gr. k-4). pap. 12.99 (978-0-9707110-1-4(8)) Starshell Pr., Ltd.

Dart, Christopher. Gwensie's Bedtime Dreams with Grandma. Bowles, Mark & Zamarripa-Lopez, Elizabeth. 2018. (ENG.). 34p. (J). pap. 15.00 (978-1-7262-6126-5(3)) CreateSpace Independent Publishing Platform.

Dart, Christopher. How to Stop Armadillo Tears. Gandara, Juanita Quinones & Bowles, Mark. 2020. (ENG.). 36p. (J). pap. 19.99 (978-1-6502-3281-2(0)) Independently Published.

Dart, Eleanor. God's Hour in the Nursery: Activity Book. Bolton, Mother Margaret. 2019. (ENG.). 56p. (J). (gr. k-1). pap. 12.95 (978-1-64051-080-7(X)) St. Augustine Academy Pr.

Dartes, Staci. Prince de'Mario's Adventure, 1 vol. Smith, Nerissia. 2009. 29p. pap. 24.95 (978-1-61582-972-9(5)) America Star Bks.

Dartez, Cecilia & Green, Andy. Jenny Giraffe's Mardi Gras Ride, 1 vol. Dartez, Cecilia. 2018. (Jenny Giraffe Ser.). (ENG.). 32p. (gr. -1-3). 8.99 (978-1-4556-2387-7(3), Pelican Publishing) Arcadia Publishing.

Darwin, Erwin L. Sparky Ames of the Ferry Command. Snell, Roy Judson. 2012. 246p. 46.95 (978-1-258-25306-6(2)); pap. 31.95 (978-1-258-25572-5(3)) Literary Licensing, LLC.

Darwin, Jami. The Gift of Paper. Andres, Isaac. 2018. (ENG.). 36p. (J). pap. 14.95 (978-0-9843922-7-8(0)) Little Balloon Pr.

Das, Abira. Amazing Adventures with Grammy & Me. Smith, Mari K. 2019. (ENG.). 38p. (J). pap. 9.99 (978-1-6892-5081-8(X)) Independently Published.

—A Bobby-Dazzler of a Pouch. Halfmann, Janet. 2020. (ENG.). 38p. (J). 20.99 (978-1-951263-11-9(1)) Pen It! Pubns., LLC.

—A Bobby-Dazzler of a Pouch! Halfmann, Janet. 2020. (ENG.). 38p. (J). pap. 13.99 **(978-1-951263-12-6(X))** Pen It! Pubns., LLC.

Das, Abira. Cai Apprend à être Courageux. Touchais, Samantha. 2019. (FRE.). 32p. (J). pap. 10.99 *(978-1-7989-1515-8(4))* Independently Published.

—Don't Go to Monster Town. Sabio, Gary. 2017. (ENG.). 28p. (J). (gr. k-1). pap. *(978-1-9998430-0-7(2))* Sabio, Gary.

Das, Abira. Fearless Felicia. Hanimyan, Angela. 2020. (ENG.). 24p. (J). **(978-1-5255-6580-9(X))**; pap. **(978-1-5255-6581-6(8))** FriesenPress.

Das, Abira. Girls Breaking the Mold. Joseph, Angela Banner. 2017. (ENG.). (J). pap. 14.99 *(978-1-943945-05-4(5))* Joseph, Dr. Angela Banner.

—Onyx Mcfly Saves the Day! Judkins, Crystal. 2016. (ENG.). (J). pap. 10.00 *(978-0-9978304-0-8(9))* Two Pens and a Grind Pubns.

—Roll with It! Marguerite, Sue. 2019. (ENG.). 28p. (J). pap. 12.98 *(978-1-7956-6117-1(8))* Independently Published.

Das Grup, Das. Friends, Fashion, & Fun! (Barbie) Man-Kong, Mary. 2012. (ENG.). 224p. (J). (gr. -1-2). pap. 5.99 *(978-0-375-87358-4(9)*, Golden Bks.) Random Hse. Children's Bks.

—I Can Be... a Baby Doctor (Barbie) Depken, Kristen L. 2013. (Step into Reading Ser.). (ENG.). 32p. (J). (gr. -1-1). pap. 4.99 *(978-0-307-98112-7(6)*, Random Hse. Bks. for Young Readers) Random Hse. Children's Bks.

Dasen, Shannon L. The Story of Honk, the Goose. LaBadie, Sally J. 2019. (ENG.). 28p. (J). *(978-1-5255-4567-2(1))*; pap. *(978-1-5255-4568-9(X))* FriesenPress.

Dasgupta, Ishaan & Sadr, Ayeshe. What Would It Be Like? Krishna, McArthur. 2016. (ENG.). 34p. (J). (gr. 2-4). 17.99 *(978-0-692-58721-8(7)*, Little Adventures) Amberjack Publishing Co.

Dasgupta, Sanghamitra. The Adventures of Princess Jellibean. Goodeaux, Cindi Handley. 2018. (ENG.). 52p. (J). (gr. 1-5). pap. 10.99 *(978-1-68160-697-2(6))* Crimson Cloak Publishing.

—Don't Call Me a Dinosaur. MacGregor, Cynthia. 2018. (ENG.). 32p. (J). (gr. k-4). pap. 8.99 *(978-1-68160-639-2(9))* Crimson Cloak Publishing.

—Gimli the Goblin. Beere, Lisa. 2019. (ENG.). 56p. (J). (gr. k-7). pap. 11.99 *(978-1-68160-644-6(5))* Crimson Cloak Publishing.

—Grandpa Moon. Goodeaux, Cindi Handley. 2019. (ENG.). 34p. (J). pap. 11.99 *(978-1-68160-319-3(5))* Crimson Cloak Publishing.

—I Wish I Could Trade Parents. MacGregor, Cynthia. 2018. (ENG.). 42p. (J). (gr. k-6). pap. 12.99 *(978-1-68160-653-8(4))* Crimson Cloak Publishing.

Dasgupta, Sanghamitra. Little Wave. Lawati, A. 2017. (ENG.). 26p. (J). (gr. k-6). pap. 8.99 **(978-1-68160-407-7(8))** Crimson Cloak Publishing.

Dasgupta, Sanghamitra. Mama's Map. Goodeaux, Cindi Handley. 2019. (Jellibean Adventures Ser.: Vol. 2). (ENG.). 48p. (J). (gr. 1-4). pap. 10.99 *(978-1-68160-661-3(5))* Crimson Cloak Publishing.

—Princess Kayleigh Magic Unicorn Kisses. Auna, Kayleigh. 2018. (Princess Kayleigh Ser.: Vol. 2). (ENG.). 30p. (J). pap. 9.50 *(978-1-7901-6380-9(3))* Independently Published.

Dasgupta, Sanghamitra. The Tale of Gabe's Tail. Hoover, Elizabeth. 2020. (ENG.). 24p. (J). pap. 12.99 **(978-1-952011-09-2(4))** Pen It! Pubns., LLC.

—When Cats Fly. Goodeaux, Cindi Handley. 2020. (Jellibean Adventures Ser.: Vol. 3). (ENG.). 42p. (J). pap. 10.99 **(978-1-68160-710-8(7))** Crimson Cloak Publishing.

—The Year Mrs. Claus Drove the Sleigh. MacGregor, Cynthia. 2019. (ENG.). 34p. (J). pap. 9.99 **(978-1-68160-702-3(6))** Crimson Cloak Publishing.

—You're an Aries. North, Lynne. 2020. (Zodiac Ser.: Vol. 1). (ENG.). 34p. (J). pap. 9.99 **(978-1-68160-713-9(1))** Crimson Cloak Publishing.

Dasgupta, Sanghamitra. The 2000th Warrior: A Journey of Faith. Marriott, Russell S. & Marriott, Kelly. 2018. (2000th Warrior Ser.: Vol. 1). (ENG.). 66p. (J). (gr. k-3). pap. 9.99 *(978-0-692-13367-5(4))* Bury Your Inner Weapons Publishing Co.

DasGupta, Sayantani. The Chaos Curse (Kiranmala & the Kingdom Beyond #3) DasGupta, Sayantani. 2020. (Kiranmala & the Kingdom Beyond Ser.: 3). (ENG.). 400p. (J). (gr. 3-7). 17.99 *(978-1-338-35589-5(9)*, Scholastic Pr.) Scholastic, Inc.

Dasgupta, Sudipta. A Basketful of Kittens: The Bff Gang's Kitten Rescue Adventure. Szabo, Erika M. Carey, Lorraine, ed. 2018. (ENG.). 38p. (J). pap. 9.95 *(978-1-7179-7173-9(3))* Independently Published.

—Jungle Dreams. Blom, Tracy. 2018. (ENG.). 36p. (J). pap. 10.00 *(978-0-9906871-9-1(8))* Blom Pubns.

Dasgupta, Sudipta & Chapman, Richard. Race Relations: The Struggle for Equality in America. Diggs, Barbara. 2019. (Inquire & Investigate Ser.). (ENG.). 128p. (YA). (gr. 7-9). 22.95 *(978-1-61930-552-6(6)*, a31038f0-a895-4286-b046-019191dd321a); pap. 17.95 *(978-1-61930-555-7(0)*, 8fe802ee-0862-4647-8c74-3e4c71b715b9) Nomad Pr.

Dasgupta, Sudipta Steve. Peanut Visits Mounds State Park. Gerstorff, Katherine Chaffin. 2018. (Peanut Adventure Ser.: Vol. 1). (ENG.). 50p. (J). (gr. k-6). 34.99 *(978-0-692-16431-0(6))* Gerstorff, Katherine.

Dash, Manas. Roary the Lion: Rides the Train. McFarran, Travis. 2018. (Roary the Lion Ser.: Vol. 1). (ENG.). 20p. (J). (gr. k-3). 6.99 *(978-0-578-42659-4(5))* True Measure.

Dash, Victor. Fat Cat & the Time Shift. Fly, Annie. 2019. (ENG.). 30p. (J). pap. 5.39 **(978-1-0897-1627-3(3))** Independently Published.

Dashiell, Margaret. Haworth Idyll: A Fantasy. Trigg, Roberta. 2012. 88p. 38.95 *(978-1-258-23556-7(0))*; pap. 23.95 *(978-1-258-24510-8(8))* Literary Licensing, LLC.

Daste, Larry. Looney Limericks. Jacobs, Frank, ed. 2011. (Dover Children's Activity Bks.). (ENG.). 64p. (gr. 3). pap. 3.00 *(978-0-486-40615-2(6))* Dover Pubns., Inc.

Dattola, Chiara. One Little Bean: Observation - Life Cycle. Kim, Cecil. Cowley, Joy, ed. 2015. (Step up - Creative Thinking Ser.). (ENG.). 32p. (gr. -1-2). 26.65 *(978-1-925246-12-4(4))*; 7.99 *(978-1-925246-64-3(7))*; 26.65 *(978-1-925246-38-4(8))*; (J). 10.00 *(978-1-925186-40-6(7))* ChoiceMaker Pty. Ltd., The AUS. (Big and SMALL). Dist: Lerner Publishing Group.

Datz, Jim. The Spiritglass Charade: A Stoker & Holmes Novel. Gleason, Colleen. 2015. (Stoker & Holmes Ser.: 2). (ENG.). 368p. (YA). (gr. 7-12). pap. 9.99 *(978-1-4521-2885-6(5))* Chronicle Bks. LLC.

—Whose Tools? Buzzeo, Toni. 2015. (ENG.). 16p. (J). (gr. -1 — 1). bds. 9.95 *(978-1-4197-1431-3(7))* Abrams, Inc.

—Whose Truck? Buzzeo, Toni. 2015. (ENG.). 24p. (J). (gr. -1 — 1). bds. 10.99 *(978-1-4197-1612-6(3))* Abrams, Inc.

Datz, Margot. Nighttide on a Vineyard Farm. Schaal, Patty. 2010. (J). *(978-0-9827146-1-4(0))* Vineyard Stories.

Daubney, Kate. The Airport. Goldsmith, Mike. 2015. (! Explore Ser.). (ENG.). 12p. (J). (gr. -1-k). bds. 6.95 *(978-1-4549-1495-2(5))* Sterling Publishing Co., Inc.

—Hocus Pocus Diplodocus. Howson, Steve. 2019. (Early Bird Readers — Purple (Early Bird Stories (tm)) Ser.). (ENG.). 32p. (J). (gr. k-3). 27.99 *(978-1-5415-4225-9(8)*, 9781541542259); pap. 7.99 *(978-1-5415-7424-3(9)*, 9781541574243) Lerner Publishing Group. (Lerner Pubns.).

—Jumping Monkeys: Lap Book Edition. Smith, Carrie. 2016. (My First Reader's Theater Tales Ser.). (J). (gr. k). *(978-1-5021-5507-8(9))* Benchmark Education Co.

—Jumping Monkeys: Small Book Edition. Smith, Carrie. 2016. (My First Reader's Theater Tales Ser.). (J). (gr. k). *(978-1-5021-5512-2(5))* Benchmark Education Co.

Daugherty, James. Abe Lincoln Grows Up. Sandburg, Carl. 2009. (ENG.). 224p. (YA). (gr. 7-18). reprint ed. pap. 7.99 *(978-0-15-602615-4(5)*, 1063351) Houghton Mifflin Harcourt Publishing Co.

—A Child's First Book of American History. Miers, Earl Schenck. 2013. 320p. (J). *(978-1-893103-41-2(2))* Beautiful Feet Bks.

D'Aulaire, Edgar Parin, jt. illus. see D'Aulaire, Ingri.

D'Aulaire, Ingri & D'Aulaire, Edgar Parin. Abraham Lincoln. 75th ed. 2015. (J). *(978-1-893103-60-3(9))* Beautiful Feet Bks.

—D'Aulaires' Book of Norwegian Folktales. 2016. (ENG.). 192p. 24.95 *(978-0-8166-9932-2(1))* Univ. of Minnesota Pr.

Dauterman, Russell. The Art of War of the Realms. 2019. (ENG.). 224p. (YA). (gr. -1-17). pap. 34.99 *(978-1-302-91764-7(1))* Marvel Worldwide, Inc.

Dauterman, Russell, et al. Mighty Thor Vol. 3: The Asgard/Shi'ar War. 2018. 160p. (YA). (gr. 8-17). pap. 19.99 *(978-1-302-90309-1(8))* Marvel Worldwide, Inc.

—Mighty Thor Vol. 4: The War Thor. 2018. (Cable (2017) Ser.: 4). (ENG.). 136p. (YA). (gr. 8-17). pap. 19.99 *(978-1-302-90659-7(3))* Marvel Worldwide, Inc.

Dauterman, Russell. Mighty Thor Vol. 4: The War Thor. 2018. (ENG.). 136p. (YA). (gr. 8-17). 24.99 *(978-1-302-90658-0(5))* Marvel Worldwide, Inc.

Dauterman, Russell, et al. The Mighty Thor Vol. 5: The Death of the Mighty Thor. 2018. (ENG.). 136p. (YA). (gr. 8-17). 34.99 *(978-1-302-90660-3(7))* Marvel Worldwide, Inc.

—Mighty Thor Vol. 5: The Death of the Mighty Thor. 2018. (Mighty Thor (2015) Ser.: 5). (ENG.). 168p. (YA). (gr. 8-17). pap. 24.99 *(978-1-302-90661-0(5))* Marvel Worldwide, Inc.

—Thor by Jason Aaron & Russell Dauterman Vol. 3, Vol. 3. 2019. (ENG.). 528p. (YA). (gr. -1-17). 44.99 *(978-1-302-91738-8(2))* Marvel Worldwide, Inc.

Dauterman, Russell & Ribic, Esad. Thor by Jason Aaron: the Complete Collection Vol. 2. 2020. 448p. (YA). (gr. 8-17). pap. 39.99 *(978-1-302-92386-0(2))* Marvel Worldwide, Inc.

Dauterman, Russell, jt. illus. see Garres, Rafa.

Dautremer, Rébecca. L' Amoureux. 2003. (Albums Gautier-Languereau Ser.: Vol. 3909884). (FRE.). (J). pap. *(978-2-01-390988-4(8))* Gautier-Languereau.

—Cahier Petit Format Princesses N 2. 2007. (Papeterie Ser.: Vol. 3913795). (FRE.). (J). *(978-2-01-391379-9(6))* Gautier-Languereau.

—Le Carton a Dessins Petit Poucet. Lechermeier, Philippe. 2010. (Papeterie Ser.: Vol. 3933033). (FRE.). (J). *(978-2-01-393303-2(7))* Gautier-Languereau.

—Mini-Pochette Princesses N 2. 2009. (Papeterie Ser.: Vol. 3930963). (FRE.). (J). *(978-2-01-393096-3(8))* Gautier-Languereau.

Dautremer, Rebecca. Nasreddine. Weulersse, Odile & Merz, Kathleen. 2013. (ENG.). 34p. (J). 17.00 *(978-0-8028-5416-2(8)*, Eerdmans Bks For Young Readers) Eerdmans, William B. Publishing Co.

Dautremer, Rébecca. Les Petits Papiers de Rebecca Dautremer. 2009. (Papeterie Ser.: Vol. 3931706). (FRE.). (J). *(978-2-01-393170-0(0))* Gautier-Languereau.

—Pg 7 - une Lettre Pour Lily la Licorne. Ponchon, Christian. 2007. (Petits Gautier Ser.: Vol. 3913324). (FRE.). (J). pap. *(978-2-01-391332-4(X))* Gautier-Languereau.

Davalos, Felipe. Al fin en Casa, 1 vol. Elya, Susan Middleton. 2011.Tr. of Home at Last. (SPA.). 32p. (J). (gr. 1-5). pap. 10.95 *(978-1-60060-654-0(7)*, d2e50112-f071-4617-bb42-a5082b42e907) Lee & Low Bks., Inc.

Dávalos, Felipe. All the Way to Morning. Harshman, Marc. 2006. (J). per. 7.95 *(978-1-891852-49-7(3))* Quarrier Pr.

Davalos, Felipe. Eyes of the Jaguar. Flor Ada, Alma. 2004. (Puertas Al Sol / Gateways to the Sun Ser.). 48p. (gr. k-6). pap. 17.95 *(978-1-58105-970-0(1))* Santillana USA Publishing Co., Inc.

—Gone Forever: An Alphabet of Extinct Animals. Markle, Sandra & Markle, William. 2007. (ENG.). 40p. (J). (gr. 4-6). 14.99 *(978-1-4169-6138-3(0)*, Simon & Schuster/Paula Wiseman Bks.) Simon & Schuster/Paula Wiseman Bks.

Dávalos, Felipe. Home at Last. Elya, Susan Middleton. 2013. (ENG.). 32p. (J). 16.95 *(978-1-58430-020-5(5))* Lee & Low Bks., Inc.

Davalos, Felipe, et al. On the Wings of the Condor. Flor Ada, Alma & Campoy, F. Isabel. (Gateways to the Sun). 48p. (J). (gr. k-6). pap. 13.95 *(978-1-58105-964-9(7))* Santillana USA Publishing Co., Inc.

Davalos, Felipe, 1st. Our Lady of Guadalupe, 1 vol. Serrano, Francisco. 2nd ed. 2011. (ENG.). 12p. (gr. -1). 22.95 *(978-1-55498-074-1(7))* Groundwood Bks. CAN. Dist: Publishers Group West (PGW).

Dávalos, Felipe. The Secret Stars, 1 vol. Slate, Joseph. 2005. (ENG.). 32p. (J). pap. 5.95 *(978-0-7614-5152-5(8))* Marshall Cavendish Corp.

—Una Semilla de Luz. Flor Ada, Alma & Campoy, F. Isabel. 2003. (Coleccion Derechos Del Nino Ser.). (SPA.). 32p. (J). (gr. 3-5). pap. 7.95 *(978-84-204-5818-2(X))* Santillana USA Publishing Co., Inc.

Davalos, Felipe, et al. Tales Our Abuelitas Told: A Hispanic Folktale Collection. Flor Ada, Alma & Campoy, F. Isabel. 2006. (ENG.). 128p. (J). (gr. k-5). 19.99 *(978-0-689-82583-5(8)*, Atheneum Bks. for Young Readers) Simon & Schuster Children's Publishing.

Dávalos, Felipe. La Virgen de Guadalupe. Serrano, Francisco.Tr. of Virgin of Guadalupe. (SPA.). (J). (gr. 2-4). 18.00 *(978-968-494-070-3(X))* Centro de Informacion y Desarrollo de la Comunicacion y la Literatura MEX. Dist: Lectorum Pubns., Inc.

Davauer, Nathaniel. Goodnight Loon. Sauer, Abe. 2014. (ENG.). 28p. (J). 9.95 *(978-0-8166-9703-8(5))* Univ. of Minnesota Pr.

Dave, Davis. Northfighters - the View from the Christallis. Colm, Dowd. 2018. (Northfighters Ser.: Vol. 1). (ENG.). 356p. (YA). (gr. 7-12). pap. **(978-1-9994666-1-9(6))** Northfighters.

Dave, Kelsey. If the World Needed a Hug. Robbins, Lisa. 2018. (ENG.). 28p. (J). pap. 11.99 *(978-1-945620-42-3(0))* Hear My Heart Publishing.

Dave, Pooja. Bus Ride Impossible! Chandnani, Armaan. 2019. (ENG.). 44p. (J). pap. 9.99 *(978-1-7240-2897-6(9))* Independently Published.

Dave Stephens. Billy the Friendly Blue Bird. Jay Fowler. 2018. (ENG.). 28p. (J). (gr. -1-2). pap. 9.99 *(978-1-4808-6735-2(7))* Archway Publishing.

Dave, Vijay, jt. photos by see Bhargava, Neirah.

Davenier, Christine. The Cat with Seven Names. Johnston, Tony. 2013. 40p. (J). (gr. k-3). 16.95 *(978-1-58089-381-7(3))* Charlesbridge Publishing, Inc.

—Dear Santa, Love, Rachel Rosenstein. Peet, Amanda & Troyer, Andrea. 2015. 40p. (J). (gr. -1-2). 17.99 *(978-0-553-51061-4(4)*, Doubleday Bks. for Young Readers) Random Hse. Children's Bks.

—Dessert First. Durand, Hallie. 2010. (ENG.). 176p. (J). (gr. 2-5). pap. 5.99 *(978-1-4169-6386-8(3)*, Atheneum Bks. for Young Readers) Simon & Schuster Children's Publishing.

—Dessert First, 1. Durand, Hallie. 2009. (Dessert Ser.). (ENG.). 160p. (J). (gr. 4-6). 18.69 *(978-1-4169-6385-1(5))* Simon & Schuster, Inc.

—Emily Writes: Emily Dickinson & Her Poetic Beginnings. Yolen, Jane. 2020. (ENG.). 40p. (J). 18.99 *(978-1-250-12808-9(0)*, 900175642, Holt, Henry & Co. Bks. For Young Readers) Holt, Henry & Co.

—Iris & Walter. Guest, Elissa Haden. alt. ed. 2012. (Iris & Walter Ser.). (ENG.). 44p. (J). (gr. 1-4). pap. 4.99 *(978-0-547-74555-8(9)*, 1486268) Houghton Mifflin Harcourt Publishing Co.

—Iris & Walter. Guest, Elissa Haden. 2006. (Iris & Walter Ser.). 43p. (gr. 1-4). 15.95 *(978-0-7569-7008-6(3))* Perfection Learning Corp.

—Iris & Walter: Lost & Found. Guest, Elissa Haden. 2014. (Iris & Walter Ser.). (ENG.). 44p. (J). (gr. 1-4). pap. 4.99 *(978-0-544-22789-7(1)*, 1563719, HMH Books For Young Readers) Houghton Mifflin Harcourt Publishing Co.

—Iris & Walter: Lost & Found. Guest, Elissa Haden. 2014. (Green Light Readers Level 3 Ser.). (ENG.). (J). (gr. 1-4). lib. bdg. 14.60 *(978-1-62765-682-5(0))* Perfection Learning Corp.

—Iris & Walter - The School Play. Guest, Elissa Haden. 2006. (Iris & Walter Ser.). 44p. (gr. 1-4). 15.95 *(978-0-7569-6679-9(5))* Perfection Learning Corp.

—Iris & Walter & Baby Rose. Guest, Elissa Haden. 2012. (Iris & Walter Ser.). (ENG.). 44p. (J). (gr. 1-4). pap. 4.99 *(978-0-547-85064-1(6)*, 1501049) Houghton Mifflin Harcourt Publishing Co.

—Iris & Walter & Baby Rose. Guest, Elissa Haden. ed. 2012. (Iris & Walter — Green Light Reader Ser.). lib. bdg. 13.55 *(978-0-606-26612-3(7))* Turtleback.

—Iris & Walter & Cousin Howie. Guest, Elissa Haden. (Iris & Walter Ser.). (ENG.). 44p. (J). 2003. (gr. k-3). 18.69 *(978-0-15-216695-3(5))*; 2012. (gr. 1-4). pap. 4.99 *(978-0-547-85068-9(9)*, 1501050) Houghton Mifflin Harcourt Publishing Co.

—Iris & Walter & the Birthday Party. Guest, Elissa Haden. 2013. (Green Light Readers Level 3 Ser.). (ENG.). 44p. (J). (gr. 1-4). pap. 4.99 *(978-0-544-10498-3(6)*, 1540803) Houghton Mifflin Harcourt Publishing Co.

—Iris & Walter & the Field Trip. Guest, Elissa Haden. 2013. (Green Light Readers Level 3 Ser.). (ENG.). 44p. (J). (gr. 1-4). pap. 4.99 *(978-0-544-10665-9(2)*, 1540873) Houghton Mifflin Harcourt Publishing Co.

—Iris & Walter & the Field Trip. Guest, Elissa Haden. (Green Light Readers Level 3 Ser.). (J). (gr. 1-4). 2013. (ENG.). lib. bdg. 14.60 *(978-1-62765-349-7(X))*; 2007. 44p. 13.60 *(978-0-7569-8041-2(0))* Perfection Learning Corp.

—Iris & Walter & the Substitute Teacher. Guest, Elissa Haden. 2006. (Iris & Walter Ser.). 44p. (gr. 1-4). 15.95 *(978-0-7569-7122-9(5))* Perfection Learning Corp.

—Iris & Walter: Substitute Teacher. Guest, Elissa Haden. 2014. (Iris & Walter Ser.). (ENG.). 44p. (J). (gr. 1-4). pap. 4.99 *(978-0-544-22788-0(3)*, 1563718, HMH Books For Young Readers) Houghton Mifflin Harcourt Publishing Co.

—Iris & Walter: the School Play. Guest, Elissa Haden. 2015. (Iris & Walter Ser.). (ENG.). 44p. (J). (gr. 1-4). pap. 4.99 *(978-0-544-45602-0(5)*, 1599387, HMH Books For Young Readers) Houghton Mifflin Harcourt Publishing Co.

—Iris & Walter, the Sleepover. Guest, Elissa Haden. 2006. (Iris & Walter Ser.). 44p. (gr. 1-4). 15.95 *(978-0-7569-6681-2(7))* Perfection Learning Corp.

—Iris & Walter: the Sleepover. Guest, Elissa Haden. alt. ed. 2012. (Iris & Walter Ser.). (ENG.). 44p. (J). (gr. 1-4). pap. 4.99 *(978-0-547-74556-5(7)*, 1486269) Houghton Mifflin Harcourt Publishing Co.

—Iris & Walter: True Friends. Guest, Elissa Haden. 2015. (Iris & Walter Ser.). (ENG.). 44p. (J). (gr. 1-4). pap. 4.99 *(978-0-544-45603-7(3)*, 1599388, HMH Books For Young Readers) Houghton Mifflin Harcourt Publishing Co.

—Just Desserts. Durand, Hallie. (ENG.). (J). (gr. 2-5). 2011. 224p. pap. 5.99 *(978-1-4169-6388-2(X))*; 2010. 208p. 15.99 *(978-1-4169-6387-5(1))* Simon & Schuster Children's Publishing. (Atheneum Bks. for Young Readers).

—Me I Am! Prelutsky, Jack. 2007. (ENG.). 32p. (J). (gr. -1-1). 18.99 *(978-0-374-34902-8(9)*, 900021998, Farrar, Straus & Giroux (BYR)) Farrar, Straus & Giroux.

—Miss Lina's Ballerinas. Maccarone, Grace. 2010. (Miss Lina's Ballerinas Ser.). (ENG.). 40p. (J). (gr. -1-1). 18.99 *(978-0-312-38243-8(X)*, 900051152) Feiwel & Friends.

—Miss Lina's Ballerinas & the Wicked Wish. Maccarone, Grace. 2012. (Miss Lina's Ballerinas Ser.). (ENG.). 40p. (J). (gr. k-1). 16.99 *(978-1-250-00580-9(9)*, 900081278) Feiwel & Friends.

—Nadia: The Girl Who Couldn't Sit Still. Gray, Karlin. 2016. (ENG.). 40p. (J). (gr. 1-4). 17.99 *(978-0-544-31960-8(5)*, 1582245, HMH Books For Young Readers) Houghton Mifflin Harcourt Publishing Co.

—No Room for Dessert. Durand, Hallie. 2012. (ENG.). 192p. (J). (gr. 2-5). pap. 6.99 *(978-1-4424-0361-1(6)*, Atheneum Bks. for Young Readers) Simon & Schuster Children's Publishing.

—The Other Dog. L'Engle, Madeleine. ed. 2018. (ENG.). 48p. (J). (gr. -1-k). 17.99 *(978-1-4521-7189-0(0))* Chronicle Bks. LLC.

—The Other Dog. L'Engle, Madeleine. 2003. 37p. (J). (gr. 2-5). reprint ed. 16.00 *(978-0-7567-6970-3(1))* DIANE Publishing Co.

—Piper Reed, Campfire Girl. Holt, Kimberly Willis. 2011. (Piper Reed Ser.: 4). (ENG.). 176p. (J). (gr. 3-6). pap. 7.99 *(978-0-312-67482-3(1)*, 900072895) Square Fish.

—Piper Reed, Clubhouse Queen. Holt, Kimberly Willis. 2011. (Piper Reed Ser.: 2). (ENG.). 160p. (J). (gr. 3-6). 15.99 *(978-0-8050-9431-2(8)*, 9780805094312, Holt, Henry & Co. Bks. For Young Readers) Holt, Henry & Co.

—Piper Reed, Clubhouse Queen. Holt, Kimberly Willis. 2011. (Piper Reed Ser.: 2). (ENG.). 176p. (J). (gr. 3-6). pap. 7.99 *(978-0-312-61676-2(7)*, 900076846) Square Fish.

—Piper Reed, Forever Friend, 6. Holt, Kimberly Willis. 2012. (Piper Reed Ser.: 6). (ENG.). 160p. (J). (gr. 3-6). 18.69 *(978-0-8050-9008-6(8)*, 900058970, Holt, Henry & Co.) Holt, Henry & Co.

—Piper Reed, Forever Friend. Holt, Kimberly Willis. 2013. (Piper Reed Ser.: 6). (ENG.). 176p. (J). (gr. 3-6). pap. 7.99 *(978-1-250-02725-2(X)*, 900098296) Square Fish.

—Piper Reed, Navy Brat. Holt, Kimberly Willis. 2011. (Piper Reed Ser.: 1). (ENG.). 176p. (J). (gr. 3-6). pap. 7.99 *(978-0-312-62548-1(0)*, 900077153) Square Fish.

—Piper Reed, Party Planner. Holt, Kimberly Willis. 2011. (Piper Reed Ser.: 3). (ENG.). 176p. (J). (gr. 3-6). pap. 7.99 *(978-0-312-61677-9(5)*, 900076848) Square Fish.

—Piper Reed, Rodeo Star. Holt, Kimberly Willis. 2012. (Piper Reed Ser.: 5). (ENG.). 176p. (J). (gr. 3-6). pap. 7.99 *(978-1-250-00409-3(8)*, 900080156) Square Fish.

—Piper Reed, Rodeo Star. (Piper Reed No. 5) Holt, Kimberly Willis. 2011. (Piper Reed Ser.: 5). (ENG.). 160p. (J). (gr. 3-6). 15.99 *(978-0-8050-9007-9(X)*, 900058968, Holt, Henry & Co. Bks. For Young Readers) Holt, Henry & Co.

—Poetry for Kids: Emily Dickinson. Dickinson, Emily. Snively, Susan, ed. 2016. (Poetry for Kids Ser.). (ENG.). 48p. (J). (gr. 3-7). 16.95 *(978-1-63322-117-8(2)*, Moondance) Quarto Publishing Group USA.

—Sally Jean, the Bicycle Queen. Best, Cari. 2006. (ENG.). 32p. (J). (gr. -1-3). 17.99 *(978-0-374-36386-4(2)*, 9780374363864, Farrar, Straus & Giroux (BYR)) Farrar, Straus & Giroux.

—Samantha on a Roll. Ashman, Linda. 2011. (ENG.). 40p. (J). (gr. -1-4). 17.99 *(978-0-374-36399-4(4)*, 9780374363994, Farrar, Straus & Giroux (BYR)) Farrar, Straus & Giroux.

Davenier, Christine. Simon at the Art Museum. Soontornvat, Christina. 2020. (ENG.). 40p. (J). (gr. -1-3). 17.99 **(978-1-5344-3752-4(5)**, Atheneum Bks. for Young Readers) Simon & Schuster Children's Publishing.

Davenier, Christine. Snowy Race. Prince, April Jones. 2019. 40p. (J). (gr. -1-2). 18.99 *(978-0-8234-4141-9(5)*, Margaret Ferguson Books) Holiday Hse., Inc.

—The Stars Just up the Street. Soltis, Sue. 2020. (ENG.). 40p. (J). (gr. -1-3). 16.99 *(978-0-7636-9834-8(2))* Candlewick Pr.

—The Very Fairy Princess. Andrews, Julie & Hamilton, Emma Walton. 2010. (Very Fairy Princess Ser.). 32p. (J). (gr. -1-3). 18.00 *(978-0-316-04050-1(9))* Little, Brown Bks. for Young Readers.

—The Very Fairy Princess: a Fairy Merry Christmas. Andrews, Julie & Hamilton, Emma Walton. 2012. (Passport to Reading Ser.). (ENG.). 32p. (J). (gr. -1-3). pap. 4.99 *(978-0-316-21962-4(2))* Little, Brown Bks. for Young Readers.

—The Very Fairy Princess: a Spooky, Sparkly Halloween. Andrews, Julie & Hamilton, Emma Walton. 2015. (ENG.). 32p. (J). (gr. -1-3). 18.00 *(978-0-316-28304-5(5))* Little, Brown Bks. for Young Readers.

—The Very Fairy Princess: a Winter Wonderland Surprise. Andrews, Julie & Hamilton, Emma Walton. 2015. (Very Fairy Princess Ser.). 32p. (J). (gr. -1-3). pap. 5.99 *(978-0-316-28306-9(1))* Little, Brown Bks. for Young Readers.

—The Very Fairy Princess Follows Her Heart. Andrews, Julie & Hamilton, Emma Walton. 2013. (Very Fairy Princess Ser.). 32p. (J). (gr. -1-3). 16.99 *(978-0-316-18559-2(0))* Little Brown & Co.

—The Very Fairy Princess: Graduation Girl! Andrews, Julie & Hamilton, Emma Walton. 2014. (Very Fairy Princess Ser.).

D

32p. (J). (gr. -1-3). 18.99 *(978-0-316-21960-0(6))* Little, Brown Bks. for Young Readers.

—The Very Fairy Princess Sparkles in the Snow. Andrews, Julie & Hamilton, Emma Walton. 2013. (Very Fairy Princess Ser.). (ENG.). 32p. (J). (gr. -1-3). 18.00 *(978-0-316-21963-1(0))* Little Brown & Co.

—The Very Fairy Princess: Teacher's Pet. Andrews, Julie & Hamilton, Emma Walton. 2013. (Passport to Reading Ser.). 32p. (J). (gr. -1-3). 4.99 *(978-0-316-21959-4(2))* Little Brown & Co.

—The Very Fairy Princess: Valentines from the Heart. Andrews, Julie & Hamilton, Emma Walton. 2015. (Very Fairy Princess Ser.). 32p. (J). (gr. -1-3). pap. 5.99 *(978-0-316-28324-3(X))* Little, Brown Bks. for Young Readers.

Davenier, Christine & Gilbert, Rob. It's Raining, It's Pouring. Peter, Paul & Eagle, Kim. 2012. 32p. (J). (-k). 17.95 *(978-1-936140-77-0(2))* Charlesbridge Publishing, Inc.

Davenport, Andy. The ABC's of Handling Money God's Way. Dayton, Howard & Dayton, Beverly. 2003. (ENG.). 96p. (J). pap., tchr. ed. 11.99 *(978-0-8024-3151-6(8))* Moody Pubs.

—The Secret of Handling Money God's Way. Dayton, Howard & Dayton, Beverly. 2003. (ENG.). 96p. (J). pap., tchr. ed. 10.99 *(978-0-8024-3153-0(4))* Moody Pubs.

Davenport, Chris. Confronting a Bully, 1 vol. Finley, Danielle. 2009. 12p. pap. 24.95 *(978-1-61546-146-2(9))* America Star Bks.

Davenport, Martha. Liefy's Journey Home. Davenport, Martha. 2019. (ENG.). 32p. (J). pap. 9.99 ***(978-1-6925-5289-3(9))*** Independently Published.

Davenport, Maxine & Roberts, Cindy. On the Farm: First Frieze. 2015. (ENG.). 10p. (J). 7.00 *(978-1-61067-422-5(7))* Kane Miller.

—What Can You Spot? 2018. (J). *(978-1-4998-0737-0(6))* Little Bee Books Inc.

—1 2 3 Counting: First Frieze. 2015. (ENG.). 10p. (J). 7.00 *(978-1-61067-421-8(9))* Kane Miller.

Davenport, Miles. Kissing the Biker's Boo-Boo. Davenport, Jack & Davenport, Piper. 2019. (Dogs of Fire Wolf Pup Story Ser.: Vol. 1). (ENG.). 38p. (J). pap. 14.99 *(978-1-0729-5861-1(9))* Independently Published.

Davenport, Philip. The Race to Hornswaggle Rock. Quayle, Ruth. 2019. 224p. (J). (gr. 3). pap. 14.99 ***(978-1-78344-828-9(8))*** Andersen Pr. GBR. Dist: Independent Pubs. Group.

Davey, Martin. The Prehistoric Games, 1 vol. Lawler, Janet. 2016. (ENG.). 32p. (J). (gr. 3-8). 16.99 *(978-1-4556-2138-5(2),* Pelican Publishing) Arcadia Publishing.

Davey, Owen. Curiositree: Natural World: A Visual Compendium of Wonders from Nature - Jacket Unfolds into a Huge Wall Poster! Jolley, Mike & Wood, A. J. 2016. (Curiositree Ser.). (ENG.). 112p. (J). (gr. 3-6). 27.99 *(978-1-84780-782-3(8),* Wide Eyed Editions) Quarto Publishing Group UK GBR. Dist: Hachette Bk. Group.

—Fanatical about Frogs. 2019. (About Animals Ser.). (ENG.). 40p. (J). (gr. k-4). 19.95 *(978-1-912497-98-0(0))* Flying Eye Bks. GBR. Dist: Penguin Random Hse. LLC.

—Foxly's Feast. 2014. (ENG.). 32p. (J). (-k). 14.95 *(978-1-62914-608-9(0),* Sky Pony Pr.) Skyhorse Publishing Co., Inc.

—Pinball Science: Everything That Matters about Matter. Graham, Ian. 2017. (ENG.). 32p. (J). (gr. 2-5). 24.95 *(978-1-68297-199-4(6))* QEB Publishing Inc.

Davey, Owen. Laika: Astronaut Dog. Davey, Owen. 2013. (ENG.). 32p. (J). (gr. k-3). 15.99 *(978-0-7636-6822-8(2),* Templar) Candlewick Pr.

—My First Pop-Up Dinosaurs: 15 Incredible Pop-Ups. Davey, Owen. 2019. (ENG.). 20p. (J). (gr. -1-2). 16.99 *(978-1-5362-0566-4(4))* Candlewick Pr.

—Night Knight. Davey, Owen. 2012. (ENG.). 32p. (J). (gr. k-k). 15.99 *(978-0-7636-5838-0(3),* Templar) Candlewick Pr.

Davey, Paul. Sauerkraut. Jones, Kelly. 2019. (ENG.). 288p. (J). (gr. 3-7). lib. bdg. 19.99 *(978-1-5247-6596-5(1),* Knopf Bks. for Young Readers) Random Hse. Children's Bks.

Davey, Sharon. Phoenix Goes to School: A Story to Support Transgender & Gender Diverse Children. Finch, Michelle & Finch, Phoenix. 2018. (ENG.). 40p. (C). 15.95 *(978-1-78592-821-5(X),* 696833) Kingsley, Jessica Pubs. GBR. Dist: Hachette UK Distribution.

—The Rabbi Slurps Spaghetti. Kimmelman, Leslie. 2019. (J). *(978-1-68115-543-2(5),* Apples & Honey Pr.) Behrman Hse., Inc.

Davick, Linda. Kindergarten Countdown. Hays, Anna Jane. 2013. 24p. (J). (gr. -1-2). 6.99 *(978-0-385-75371-5(3),* Dragonfly Bks.) Random Hse. Children's Bks.

—We Love Our School! Sierra, Judy. 2016. 24p. (J). (gr. -1-2). 6.99 *(978-1-101-94025-9(5),* Dragonfly Bks.) Random Hse. Children's Bks.

—We Love Our School! A Read-Together Rebus Story. Sierra, Judy. 2011. 24p. (J). (gr. -1-2). 7.99 *(978-0-375-86728-6(7),* Knopf Bks. for Young Readers) Random Hse. Children's Bks.

—We Love You, Rosie! Rylant, Cynthia. 2017. (ENG.). 48p. (J). (gr. -1-2). 17.99 *(978-1-4424-6511-4(5),* Beach Lane Bks.) Beach Lane Bks.

—What Riley Wore. Arnold, Elana K. 2019. (ENG.). 40p. (J). (gr. -1-3). 17.99 *(978-1-4814-7260-9(7),* Beach Lane Bks.) Beach Lane Bks.

—10 Easter Egg Hunters: A Holiday Counting Book. Schulman, Janet. (J). 2015. 32p. (— 1). 4.99 *(978-0-553-50784-3(2),* Dragonfly Bks.); 2012. 26p. (gr. -1 — 1). bds. 6.99 *(978-0-375-86637-1(X),* Knopf Bks. for Young Readers); 2011. 32p. (gr. -1 — 1). 8.99 *(978-0-375-86787-3(2),* Knopf Bks. for Young Readers) Random Hse. Children's Bks.

—10 Trick-Or-Treaters. Schulman, Janet. 2008. (ENG.). 32p. (J). (gr. -1-2). pap. 7.99 *(978-0-385-73614-5(2),* Dragonfly Bks.) Random Hse. Children's Bks.

—10 Trick-or-Treaters: A Halloween Counting Book. Schulman, Janet. 2009. 26p. (J). (gr. -1-2). bds. 6.99 *(978-0-375-85347-0(2),* Knopf Bks. for Young Readers) Random Hse. Children's Bks.

—10 Trim-the-Tree'ers. Schulman, Janet. 2011. 32p. (J). (gr. -1 — 1). bds. 6.99 *(978-0-375-87302-7(3),* Knopf Bks. for Young Readers) Random Hse. Children's Bks.

—10 Valentine Friends. Schulman, Janet. 2012. 26p. (J). (gr. -1 — 1). bds. 6.99 *(978-0-375-87130-6(6),* Knopf Bks. for Young Readers) Random Hse. Children's Bks.

Davick, Linda. I Love You, Nose! I Love You, Toes! Davick, Linda. 2013. (ENG.). 32p. (J). (gr. -1-1). 17.99 *(978-1-4424-6037-9(7),* Beach Lane Bks.) Beach Lane Bks.

—It's Not Easy Being Mimi. Davick, Linda. (Mimi's World Ser.: 1). (ENG.). (J). (gr. 1-4). 2019. 192p. pap. 6.99 *(978-1-4424-5890-1(9));* 2018. 176p. 13.99 *(978-1-4424-5889-5(5))* Beach Lane Bks. (Beach Lane Bks.).

—Mimi's Treasure Trouble. Davick, Linda. 2019. (Mimi's World Ser.: 2). (ENG.). 240p. (J). (gr. 1-4). 13.99 *(978-1-4424-5892-5(5),* Beach Lane Bks.) Beach Lane Bks.

—Say Hello! Davick, Linda. 2015. (ENG.). 40p. (J). (gr. -1-3). 17.99 *(978-1-4814-2867-5(5),* Beach Lane Bks.) Beach Lane Bks.

David, Amanda. Bedwin, 1 vol. Michael. 2009. (ENG.). 46p. 24.95 *(978-1-60813-258-4(7))* America Star Bks.

David, Amor. How Does God See Me? Rashad, Girmen. 2008. (Little Christian Ser.). 24p. 9.99 *(978-0-9819100-0-0(9))* Elkarez Publishing Co.

David Antram. The Story of Lewis & Clark. Morley, Jacqueline. 2017. (Explorers Ser.). 32p. (gr. 3-6). 31.35 *(978-1-910706-89-3(2))* Book Hse. GBR. Dist: Black Rabbit Bks.

David, Brittany. Where Is the Dog, Where Is the Cat? A Biscuit & Gravy Adventure. Bunyap, K. W. 2019. (ENG.). 36p. (J). pap. 15.00 *(978-1-9837-9130-7(X))* CreateSpace Independent Publishing Platform.

David Hardy. Aussie Kids: Meet Zoe & Zac at the Zoo. Murrell, Belinda. 2020. (Aussie Kids Ser.). 64p. (J). (gr. 1-3). 12.99 ***(978-1-76089-365-1(X),*** Puffin) Penguin Random Hse. AUS. Dist: Independent Pubs. Group.

David, Jamie. Johann Sebastian Humpbach. David, Jamie. 2009. 167p. pap. 14.95 *(978-0-615-31840-0(1))* Chai Yo Maui Pr.

David, Jason. Red Is Beautiful: Chiih Nizhoni. John, Roberta. Ruffenach, Jessie, ed. Thomas, Peter, tr. from NAV. 2003. (ENG & NAV.). 32p. (J). (gr. 4-7). 17.95 *(978-1-893354-37-1(7))* Salina Bookshelf Inc.

David, Mark. The Case of the Graveyard Ghost & Other Mysteries. Ball, Duncan. 2005. 192p. (Orig.). *(978-0-207-20044-1(0))* HarperCollins Pubs. Australia.

David, Matt. The Missing Playbook. Dixon, Franklin W. 2016. (Hardy Boys Clue Book Ser.: 2). (ENG.). 96p. (J). (gr. 1-4). 16.99 *(978-1-4814-5178-9(2));* pap. 5.99 *(978-1-4814-5177-2(4))* Simon & Schuster Children's Publishing. (Aladdin).

—Scavenger Hunt Heist. Dixon, Franklin W. 2017. (Hardy Boys Clue Book Ser.: 5). (ENG.). 96p. (J). (gr. 1-4). pap. 5.99 *(978-1-4814-8516-6(4),* Simon & Schuster/Paula Wiseman Bks.) Simon & Schuster/Paula Wiseman Bks.

—A Skateboard Cat-Astrophe. Dixon, Franklin W. 2017. (Hardy Boys Clue Book Ser.: 6). (ENG.). 96p. (J). (gr. 1-4). 16.99 *(978-1-4814-8870-9(8));* pap. 5.99 *(978-1-4814-8869-3(4))* Simon & Schuster Children's Publishing. (Aladdin).

—Talent Show Tricks. Dixon, Franklin W. 2016. (Hardy Boys Clue Book Ser.: 4). (ENG.). 96p. (J). (gr. 1-4). pap. 5.99 *(978-1-4814-5180-2(4),* Aladdin) Simon & Schuster Children's Publishing.

—Talent Show Tricks. Dixon, Franklin W. 2016. (Hardy Boys Clue Book Ser.: 4). (ENG.). 96p. (J). (gr. 1-4). 16.99 *(978-1-4814-5181-9(2),* Simon & Schuster/Paula Wiseman Bks.) Simon & Schuster/Paula Wiseman Bks.

—The Video Game Bandit. Dixon, Franklin W. 2016. (Hardy Boys Clue Book Ser.: 1). (ENG.). 96p. (J). (gr. 1-4). 16.99 *(978-1-4814-5053-9(0));* pap. 5.99 *(978-1-4814-5052-2(2))* Simon & Schuster Children's Publishing. (Aladdin).

—Water-Ski Wipeout. Dixon, Franklin W. 2016. (Hardy Boys Clue Book Ser.: 3). (ENG.). 96p. (J). (gr. 1-4). pap. 5.99 *(978-1-4814-5055-3(7),* Aladdin) Simon & Schuster Children's Publishing.

—Water-Ski Wipeout. Dixon, Franklin W. 2016. (Hardy Boys Clue Book Ser.: 3). (ENG.). 96p. (J). (gr. 1-4). 16.99 *(978-1-4814-5056-0(5),* Simon & Schuster/Paula Wiseman Bks.) Simon & Schuster/Paula Wiseman Bks.

David, R. Joseph & His Brothers. 2010. 12p. *(978-965-91286-0-0(6))* Sifrei Bet Shearim Ltd.

David, Racheli. Doda Golda Comes for Pesach. Paretzky, Leah. 2012. 24p. 10.95 *(978-1-60091-195-8(1))* Israel Bookshop Pubns.

—Hot! Hot! Hot! Rosenberg, Faigy & Weiss, Esti. 2013. 32p. 10.95 *(978-1-60091-268-9(0))* Israel Bookshop Pubns.

—Let's Use Them Right: Social Skills for My Hands, Feet, & Mouth. Schwartz, Sara Leah. 2013. 39p. 16.95 *(978-1-60091-276-4(1))* Israel Bookshop Pubns.

—Look What My Parents Give Me. Ginsburg, Sara. 2014. 29p. (J). *(978-1-4226-1489-1(1))* Mesorah Pubns., Ltd.

—Moshe Goes to Yeshiva. Levy, Rochel. 2012. 24p. 11.95 *(978-1-60091-212-2(5))* Israel Bookshop Pubns.

Daviddi, Evelyn. Here & There. Smith, Tamara Ellis. 2019. (ENG.). 32p. (J). (gr. -1-4). pap. *(978-1-78285-742-6(7))* Barefoot Bks., Ltd.

Davide, Dennis. Alissa & Her Clever Dog, Cyber: Book 1: War Driving. Conger, Mathew. 2019. (ENG.). 28p. (J). pap. 21.99 *(978-1-7960-1950-6(X))* Xlibris Corp.

Davidge, Jesse. Mathemagick: The Point & the Invisible Hand. Davidge, James. 2014. (ENG.). 64p. (YA). pap. 9.95 *(978-1-897411-80-3(4))* Bayeux Arts, Inc. CAN. Dist: Chicago Distribution Ctr.

Davidow, Shelley. Early Phonetic Readers: 6 Book Collection. Davidow, Shelley. 2020. (ENG.). 116p. (J). (gr. 1-3). pap. 17.95 ***(978-1-931061-00-1(9))*** Jalmar Pr.

Davids, Paul, photos by. The Fountain of Youth. Davids, Paul. 56p. (Orig.). (YA). (gr. 5-9). pap. 9.95 *(978-0-939031-01-6(9))* Pictorial Legends.

Davidson, Andrew. Tales of the Peculiar. Riggs, Ransom. (ENG.). (gr. 7). 2017. 208p. (J). pap. 14.99 *(978-0-399-53854-4(2),* Penguin Books); 2016. 192p. (YA). 24.99 *(978-0-399-53853-7(4),* Dutton Books for Young Readers) Penguin Young Readers Group.

Davidson, Annie. Unfolding Journeys Rocky Mountain Explorer, 1 vol. Ross, Stewart & Lonely Planet Kids. 2016. (Unfolding Journeys Ser.). (ENG.). 16p. (J). (gr. 4-7). 17.99 *(978-1-78657-107-6(2),* 5243) Lonely Planet Global Ltd. IRL. Dist: Hachette Bk. Group.

Davidson, Blanche. Pancho Finds A Home. Cogan, Karen. 2007. 32p. (J). 19.95 *(978-1-929115-16-7(4))* Azro Pr., Inc.

Davidson, Breanne. Brutus Plays on Thin Ice. Briggs, Jeannette. 2019. (ENG.). 28p. (J). *(978-0-2288-1288-3(7));* pap. *(978-0-2288-1287-6(9))* Tellwell Talent.

Davidson, Carli, photos by. Heads & Tails. 2017. (ENG., 20p. (J). bds. 8.99 *(978-1-4521-5137-3(7))* Chronicle Bks. LLC.

—Shake, Wiggle & Roll. 2017. (ENG., 20p. (J). bds. 8.99 *(978-1-4521-5136-6(9))* Chronicle Bks. LLC.

Davidson, Chris. Family Gatherings, 1 vol. Owens, L. L. 2010. (Let's Be Social Ser.). (ENG.). 32p. (J). (gr. k-4). 28.50 *(978-1-60270-798-6(7),* 11039, Looking Glass Library) Magic Wagon.

—Go Worship, 1 vol. Owens, L. L. 2010. (Let's Be Social Ser.). (ENG.). 32p. (J). (gr. k-4). 28.50 *(978-1-60270-800-6(2),* 11043, Looking Glass Library) Magic Wagon.

—Hide & Seek Moon: The Moon Phases, 1 vol. Koontz, Robin Michal. 2010. (First Graphics: Nature Cycles Ser.). (ENG.). 24p. (J). (gr. 1-3). 24.65 *(978-1-4296-5365-7(5))* Capstone.

—Hide & Seek Moon: The Moon Phases, 1 vol. Koontz, Robin. 2011. (First Graphics: Nature Cycles Ser.). (ENG.). 24p. (gr. 1-3). (J). pap. 6.29 *(978-1-4296-6229-1(8));* pap. 35.70 *(978-1-4296-6398-4(7))* Capstone.

—Join a Team, 1 vol. Owens, L. L. 2010. (Let's Be Social Ser.). (ENG.). 32p. (J). (gr. k-4). 28.50 *(978-1-60270-801-3(0),* 11045, Looking Glass Library) Magic Wagon.

—Water Goes Round: The Water Cycle, 1 vol. Koontz, Robin Michal. 2010. (First Graphics: Nature Cycles Ser.). (ENG.). 24p. (J). (gr. 1-3). lib. bdg. 24.65 *(978-1-4296-5364-0(7))* Capstone.

—Water Goes Round: The Water Cycle, 1 vol. Koontz, Robin. 2011. (First Graphics: Nature Cycles Ser.). (ENG.). 24p. (gr. 1-3). (J). pap. 6.29 *(978-1-4296-6231-4(X));* pap. 35.70 *(978-1-4296-6400-4(2))* Capstone.

Davidson, Dawn. The Pirate's Tale of Papa's Gold Tooth. Marino, Richard M. 2019. (ENG.). 26p. (J). (gr. k-3). pap. 10.99 ***(978-1-61254-375-8(8))*** Brown Books Publishing Group.

Davidson, Dawn Doughty. Glowstone Peak. Dye, David & Hurt, Karin. 2018. (ENG.). 50p. (J). (gr. 1-3). 24.97 *(978-1-7322647-0-0(8))* Let's Grow Leaders.

Davidson, Diana. Cole, the Little White Horse. Giesbrecht, Brian. 2019. (ENG.). 32p. (J). ***(978-1-5255-5749-1(1));*** pap. ***(978-1-5255-5750-7(5))*** FriesenPress.

Davidson, Jamie. On the Wings of Angels: Inspirational Verses for Everyday Living. Woodsmall, Marilyne. 2004. (YA). per. 22.00 *(978-1-892876-10-2(8))* Next Step Pr.

Davidson, Kevin. Catholic Bible Stories for Children. Ball, Ann & Will, Julianne M. 2006. 208p. (J). (gr. -1-3). 19.95 *(978-1-59276-243-9(3))* Our Sunday Visitor, Publishing Div.

—Catholic Bible Stories for Children: 1st Communion Edition. Ball, Ann & Will, Julianne M. 2006. 208p. (J). (gr. -1-3). 19.95 *(978-1-59276-221-7(2))* Our Sunday Visitor, Publishing Div.

—Making Things Right: The Sacrament of Reconciliation. Leichner, Jeannine Timko. 2005. 70p. pap. 6.95 *(978-1-59276-157-9(7))* Our Sunday Visitor, Publishing Div.

Davidson, Mary. Fiddle Me a Riddle & Bring Me the Moon. Plunkett, Windyann. 2011. 24p. pap. 24.95 *(978-1-4626-3920-5(8))* America Star Bks.

Davidson, Michael. Ready, Teddy, Go! Davidson, Michael. 2013. (ENG.). 32p. (J). (gr. -1-k). 18.99 ***(978-1-4083-2023-5(1),*** Orchard Bks.) Hachette Children's Group GBR. Dist: Hachette Bk. Group.

Davidson, Mike, et al. Draw What? A Doodling, Drawing, & Coloring Book. 2014. (ENG.). (J). (gr. -1-3). *(978-1-74352-285-1(1))* Hinkler Bks. Pty, Ltd.

Davidson, Pat, jt. illus. see Gully, Mario.

Davidson, Paul. Can You Survive an Asteroid Strike? An Interactive Doomsday Adventure. Doeden, Matt. 2016. (You Choose: Doomsday Ser.). (ENG.). 112p. (J). (gr. 3-7). lib. bdg. 32.65 *(978-1-4914-8109-7(9),* Capstone Pr.) Capstone.

—EDGE: I HERO: Monster Hunter: Vampire. Skidmore, Steve & Barlow, Steve. 2019. (EDGE: I HERO: Monster Hunter Ser.). 64p. (J). (gr. 1-5). 9.99 *(978-1-4451-5936-2(8),* Franklin Watts) Hachette Children's Group GBR. Dist: Hachette Bk. Group.

—Shuri Vol. 2: 24/7 Vibranium. 2019. (ENG.). 112p. (YA). (gr. 4-17). pap. 15.99 *(978-1-302-91854-5(0))* Marvel Worldwide, Inc.

Davidsson, Ashton, jt. illus. see Amber, Holly.

Davie, Helen K. Dolphin Talk: Whistles, Clicks, & Clapping Jaws. Pfeffer, Wendy. 2003. (Let's-Read-and-Find-Out Science Ser.). 40p. (J). (gr. k-4). (ENG.). 15.99 *(978-0-06-028801-3(9));* (ENG.). pap. 5.99 *(978-0-06-445210-6(7));* lib. bdg. 16.89 *(978-0-06-028802-0(7))* HarperCollins Pubs.

—What Lives in a Shell? Zoehfeld, Kathleen Weidner. 2015. (Let's-Read-And-Find-Out Science 1 Ser.). (ENG.). 32p. (J). (gr. -1-3). pap. 6.99 *(978-0-06-238196-5(2))* HarperCollins Pubs.

Davies, Andy Robert. Clothesline Clues to Jobs People Do. Heling, Kathryn & Hembrook, Deborah. (J). (gr. -1-2). 2014. 240p. pap. 7.95 *(978-1-58089-252-0(3));* 2012. (ENG.). 40p. 14.95 *(978-1-58089-251-3(5))* Charlesbridge Publishing, Inc.

—Clothesline Clues to Sports People Play. Heling, Kathryn & Hembrook, Deborah. 2015. 40p. (J). (gr. -1-2). lib. bdg. 14.95 *(978-1-58089-602-3(2))* Charlesbridge Publishing, Inc.

—Clothesline Clues to the First Day of School. Heling, Kathryn & Hembrook, Deborah. 2019. 40p. (J). (gr. -1-2). pap. 7.99 *(978-1-58089-579-8(4))* Charlesbridge Publishing, Inc.

—Truck Stuck. Wolf, Sallie. (J). (— 1). 2017. 28p. bds. 7.99 *(978-1-58089-781-5(9));* 2009. 32p. pap. 7.95 *(978-1-58089-257-5(4))* Charlesbridge Publishing, Inc.

Davies, Benji. All Right Already! A Snowy Story. John, Jory. 2018. (ENG.). 32p. (J). (gr. -1-3). 17.99 *(978-0-06-237099-0(5))* HarperCollins Pubs.

Davies, Benji. Also an Octopus. Tokuda-Hall, Maggie. (ENG.). 32p. (J). (gr. -1-2). 2020. 7.99 ***(978-1-5362-1591-5(0));*** 2016. 16.99 *(978-0-7636-7084-9(7))* Candlewick Pr.

Davies, Benji. Big Friends. Sarah, Linda. 2016. (ENG.). 32p. (J). 18.99 *(978-1-62779-330-8(5),* 900146698, Holt, Henry & Co. Bks. For Young Readers) Holt, Henry & Co.

—Bizzy Bear: Ambulance Rescue. Nosy Crow. 2018. (Bizzy Bear Ser.). (ENG.). 8p. (J). (— 1). bds. 7.99 *(978-1-5362-0256-4(8),* Nosy Crow) Candlewick Pr.

—Bizzy Bear: Christmas Helper. Nosy Crow. 2016. (Bizzy Bear Ser.). (ENG.). 8p. (J). (— 1). bds. 7.99 *(978-0-7636-8004-6(4),* Nosy Crow) Candlewick Pr.

—Bizzy Bear: Deep-Sea Diver. Nosy Crow Staff. 2016. (Bizzy Bear Ser.). (ENG.). 8p. (J). (— 1). bds. 7.99 *(978-0-7636-8647-5(6),* Nosy Crow) Candlewick Pr.

—Bizzy Bear: Dinosaur Safari. Nosy Crow Staff. 2015. (Bizzy Bear Ser.). (ENG.). 8p. (J). (— 1). bds. 7.99 *(978-0-7636-8170-8(9),* Nosy Crow) Candlewick Pr.

—Bizzy Bear: Do-It-Yourself Day. Nosy Crow Staff. 2017. (Bizzy Bear Ser.). (ENG.). 8p. (J). (— 1). bds. 7.99 *(978-0-7636-9328-2(6),* Nosy Crow) Candlewick Pr.

—Bizzy Bear: Fun on the Farm. Nosy Crow Staff. 2011. (Bizzy Bear Ser.). (ENG.). 8p. (J). (gr. k — 1). bds. 7.99 *(978-0-7636-5879-3(0),* Nosy Crow) Candlewick Pr.

—Bizzy Bear: Knights' Castle. Nosy Crow Staff. 2015. (Bizzy Bear Ser.). (ENG.). 8p. (J). (— 1). bds. 7.99 *(978-0-7636-7602-5(0),* Nosy Crow) Candlewick Pr.

—Bizzy Bear: Let's Get to Work! Nosy Crow Staff. 2012. (Bizzy Bear Ser.). (ENG.). 8p. (J). (gr. k — 1). bds. 7.99 *(978-0-7636-5899-1(5),* Nosy Crow) Candlewick Pr.

—Bizzy Bear: Let's Go & Play. Nosy Crow Staff. 2011. (Bizzy Bear Ser.). (ENG.). 8p. (J). (gr. k — 1). bds. 7.99 *(978-0-7636-5880-9(4),* Nosy Crow) Candlewick Pr.

—Bizzy Bear: off We Go! Nosy Crow Staff. 2012. (Bizzy Bear Ser.). (ENG.). 8p. (J). (gr. k — 1). bds. 7.99 *(978-0-7636-5900-4(2),* Nosy Crow) Candlewick Pr.

—Bizzy Bear: Race Car Driver. Nosy Crow. 2019. (Bizzy Bear Ser.). (ENG.). 8p. (J). (— 1). bds. 7.99 *(978-1-5362-0559-6(1),* Nosy Crow) Candlewick Pr.

—Bizzy Bear: Space Rocket. Nosy Crow Staff. 2015. (Bizzy Bear Ser.). (ENG.). 8p. (J). (— 1). bds. 7.99 *(978-0-7636-8003-9(6),* Nosy Crow) Candlewick Pr.

—Bizzy Bear: Spooky House. Nosy Crow. 2017. (Bizzy Bear Ser.). (ENG.). 8p. (J). (— 1). bds. 7.99 *(978-0-7636-9327-5(8),* Nosy Crow) Candlewick Pr.

—Bizzy Bear: Train Engineer. Nosy Crow. 2019. (Bizzy Bear Ser.). (ENG.). 8p. (J). (— 1). bds. 7.99 *(978-1-5362-0985-3(6),* Nosy Crow) Candlewick Pr.

—Bizzy Bear: Zookeeper. Nosy Crow Staff. 2015. (Bizzy Bear Ser.). (ENG.). 8p. (J). (— 1). bds. 7.99 *(978-0-7636-7603-2(9),* Nosy Crow) Candlewick Pr.

—Come Home Already! John, Jory. 2017. (ENG.). 32p. (J). (gr. -1-3). 17.99 *(978-0-06-237097-6(9),* 118990985) HarperCollins Pubs.

—The Dragon & the Nibblesome Knight. Woollard, Elli. 2018. (ENG.). 32p. (J). 17.99 *(978-1-250-15020-2(5),* 900182510, Holt, Henry & Co. Bks. For Young Readers) Holt, Henry & Co.

—Fire Rescue! Nosy Crow Staff. 2013. (Bizzy Bear Ser.). (ENG.). 8p. (J). (— 1). bds. 7.99 *(978-0-7636-6518-0(5),* Nosy Crow) Candlewick Pr.

—Goodnight Already! John, Jory. 2014. (ENG.). 32p. (J). (gr. -1-3). 17.99 *(978-0-06-228620-8(X))* HarperCollins Pubs.

—I Love You Already! John, Jory. 2015. (ENG.). 32p. (J). (gr. -1-3). 17.99 *(978-0-06-237095-2(2))* HarperCollins Pubs.

—In the Castle. Milbourne, Anna. 2006. (English Heritage Ser.). 24p. (J). (gr. -1-3). 9.99 *(978-0-7945-1243-9(7),* Usborne) EDC Publishing.

—On a Pirate Ship. Courtauld, Sarah. 2007. (Picture Bks). 24p. (J). (gr. -1-3). 9.99 *(978-0-7945-1712-0(9),* Usborne) EDC Publishing.

—Pirate Adventure. Nosy Crow Staff. 2013. (Bizzy Bear Ser.). (ENG.). 8p. (J). (— 1). bds. 7.99 *(978-0-7636-6519-7(3),* Nosy Crow) Candlewick Pr.

Davies, Benji. Grandad's Island. Davies, Benji. 2016. (ENG.). 32p. (J). (gr. -1-3). 16.99 *(978-0-7636-9005-2(8))* Candlewick Pr.

—The Storm Whale. Davies, Benji. 2014. (ENG.). 32p. (J). (gr. -1-3). 17.99 *(978-0-8050-9967-6(0),* 900128170, Holt, Henry & Co. Bks. For Young Readers) Holt, Henry & Co.

—Tad. Davies, Benji. 2020. (ENG.). 32p. (J). (gr. -1-3). 17.99 *(978-0-06-256359-0(9),* HarperCollins) HarperCollins Pubs. Ltd. GBR. Dist: HarperCollins Pubs.

Davies, Bronwen. Scholastic Reader Level 1: Get the Giggles: A First Joke Book. 2014. (Scholastic Reader Level 1 Ser.). (ENG.). 32p. (J). (gr. -1-2). pap. 3.99 *(978-0-545-54087-2(9))* Scholastic, Inc.

Davies, Caroline. Duck. 2013. (Shake & Play Bath Bks.). (ENG.). 8p. (J). (gr. -1 — 1). 5.99 *(978-1-4380-7339-2(9),* B.E.S. Publishing) Peterson's.

—Fish. 2013. (Shake & Play Bath Bks.). (ENG.). 8p. (J). (gr. -1 — 1). 5.99 *(978-1-4380-7340-8(2),* B.E.S. Publishing) Peterson's.

—Frog. 2017. (Shake & Play Bath Bks.). (ENG.). 8p. (J). (gr. -1 — 1). 5.99 *(978-1-4380-7841-0(2),* B.E.S. Publishing) Peterson's.

—Seahorse. 2017. (Shake & Play Bath Bks.). (ENG.). 8p. (J). (gr. -1 — 1). 5.99 *(978-1-4380-7842-7(0),* B.E.S. Publishing) Peterson's.

—Turtle. 2013. (Shake & Play Bath Bks.). (ENG.). 8p. (J). (gr. -1 — 1). 5.99 *(978-1-4380-7341-5(0)*, B.E.S. Publishing) Peterson's.
—Whale. 2013. (Shake & Play Bath Bks.). (ENG.). 8p. (J). (gr. -1 — 1). 5.99 *(978-1-4380-7342-2(9)*, B.E.S. Publishing) Peterson's.
Davies, Caroline. Hey, Diddle Diddle. Davies, Caroline, tr. 2004. (Baby's First Nursery Rhymes Ser.). 12p. (J). bds. 3.99 *(978-1-85854-622-3(2))* Brimax Books Ltd. GBR. Dist: Byeway Bks.
—Humpty Dumpty. Davies, Caroline, tr. 2004. (Baby's First Nursery Rhymes Ser.). 12p. (J). bds. 3.99 *(978-1-85854-610-0(9))* Brimax Books Ltd. GBR. Dist: Byeway Bks.
—Little Miss Muffet. Davies, Caroline, tr. 2004. (Baby's First Nursery Rhymes Ser.). 12p. (J). bds. 3.99 *(978-1-85854-623-0(0))* Brimax Books Ltd. GBR. Dist: Byeway Bks.
—Pat-A-Cake. Davies, Caroline, tr. 2004. (Baby's First Nursery Rhymes Ser.). 12p. (J). bds. 3.99 *(978-1-85854-611-7(7))* Brimax Books Ltd. GBR. Dist: Byeway Bks.
Davies, Dorian Spencer. Welsh Castles Colouring Book. Davies, Dorian Spencer. ed. 2020. (ENG.). 24p. pap. 7.99 ***(978-1-78461-677-9(X))*** Y Lolfa GBR. Dist: Casemate Pubs. & Bk. Distributors, LLC.
Davies, Hannah & Gunnell, Beth. Pretty Patterns: Beautiful Patterns to Color! 2013. (ENG.). 96p. (J). (gr. -1-2). 7.99 *(978-1-4424-5181-0(5)*, Little Simon) Little Simon.
Davies, Hannah & Ryan, Nellie. Pretty Costumes: Beautiful Costumes to Color! 2013. (ENG.). 96p. (J). (gr. -1-2). 7.99 *(978-1-4424-5180-3(7)*, Little Simon) Little Simon.
Davies, James. Polly & the Pirates. Bradman, Tony & Banana, Red. 2014. (Red Bananas Ser.). (ENG.). 48p. (J). (gr. k-2). pap. 5.99 *(978-1-4052-6412-9(8))* Egmont Bks., Ltd. GBR. Dist: Independent Pubs. Group.
—Polly & the Pirates. Bradman, Tony. 2nd ed. 2016. (Reading Ladder Ser.). (ENG.). 48p. (J). (gr. k-2). 7.99 *(978-1-4052-8249-9(5))* Egmont Bks., Ltd. GBR. Dist: Independent Pubs. Group.
—Space Penguins. Courtenay, Lucy. 2015. (Space Penguins Ser.). (ENG.). 112p. (J). (gr. 2-3). lib. bdg., lib. bdg., lib. bdg. 90.60 *(978-1-4965-0255-1(8)*, Stone Arch Bks.) Capstone.
—Space Penguins Cosmic Crash! Courtenay, L. A. 2015. (Space Penguins Ser.). (ENG.). 112p. (J). (gr. 2-3). lib. bdg. 22.65 *(978-1-4342-9785-3(3)*, Stone Arch Bks.) Capstone.
—Space Penguins Galaxy Race! Courtenay, L. A. 2015. (Space Penguins Ser.). (ENG.). 112p. (J). (gr. 2-3). lib. bdg. 22.65 *(978-1-4342-9783-9(7)*, Stone Arch Bks.) Capstone.
—Space Penguins Meteor Madness! Courtenay, L. A. 2015. (Space Penguins Ser.). (ENG.). 112p. (J). (gr. 2-3). lib. bdg. 22.65 *(978-1-4342-9782-2(9)*, Stone Arch Bks.) Capstone.
—Space Penguins Star Attack! Courtenay, L. A. 2015. (Space Penguins Ser.). (ENG.). 112p. (J). (gr. 2-3). lib. bdg. 22.65 *(978-1-4342-9784-6(5)*, Stone Arch Bks.) Capstone.
Davies, Joe. Meet MR Love & Mrs You & Their Wonderful Planet. Small, Martin. 2018. (ENG.). 42p. (J). pap. *(978-1-78623-423-0(8))* Grosvenor Hse. Publishing Ltd.
Davies, Kate. The Children's Book of Green Habits. Giles, Sophie. 2014. (ENG.). 32p. (J). pap. 10.00 *(978-1-84135-908-3(4))* Award Pubns. Ltd. GBR. Dist: Parkwest Pubns., Inc.
—The Children's Book of Healthy Habits. Giles, Sophie. 2014. (ENG.). 40p. (J). pap. 10.00 *(978-1-84135-972-4(6))* Award Pubns. Ltd. GBR. Dist: Parkwest Pubns., Inc.
—Little Squeak School. 2014. (J). *(978-1-4351-5582-4(3))* Barnes & Noble, Inc.
—Princess Tales. Award, Anna. 2017. (ENG.). 96p. (J). 15.00 *(978-1-84135-523-8(2))* Award Pubns. Ltd. GBR. Dist: Parkwest Pubns., Inc.
—Science in the Kitchen. Heddle, Rebecca. Edom, Helen, ed. rev. ed. 2007. (Usborne Science Activities Ser.). 24p. (J). (gr. 3-7). pap. 5.99 *(978-0-7945-1405-1(7)*, Usborne) EDC Publishing.
—Tick Tock! Tell the Time: Follow Liam Through His Busy Day. 2017. (ENG.). 10p. (J). (gr. -1-2). bds. 8.99 *(978-0-7641-6874-1(6)*, B.E.S. Publishing) Peterson's.
—Welcome to the Mouse House. 2014. (J). *(978-1-4351-5583-1(1))* Barnes & Noble, Inc.
Davies, Kelly. Can I Tell You about Auditory Processing Disorder? A Guide for Friends, Family & Professionals. Mountjoy, Alyson. 2018. (Can I Tell You About...? Ser.). (ENG.). 56p. pap. 14.95 *(978-1-78592-494-1(X)*, 696840) Kingsley, Jessica Pubs. GBR. Dist: Hachette UK Distribution.
Davies, Lauretta. God's Amazing Book. Ruckman, Kathleen. 2007. (ENG.). 28p. (J). (gr. -1-2). 10.99 *(978-1-59317-201-5(X))* Warner Pr., Inc.
Davies, Matt. Nerdy Birdy. Reynolds, Aaron. 2015. (Nerdy Birdy Ser.). (ENG.). 40p. (J). (gr. k-3). 17.99 *(978-1-62672-127-2(0)*, 900138461) Roaring Brook Pr.
Davies, Michelle. Debbie's Letter to God. Griffin, Marcia. 2005. (J). pap. 8.00 *(978-0-8059-6409-7(6))* Dorrance Publishing Co., Inc.
Davies, Nic, jt. illus. see Martin, Caroline.
Davies, Taffy. Be a Church Detective: A Young Person's Guide to Old Churches. Fewins, Clive & Open Churches Trust Staff. ed. 2005. (ENG.). 48p. (J). pap. 12.99 *(978-1-85311-628-5(9)*, Canterbury Pr. Norwich) Hymns Ancient & Modern Ltd GBR. Dist: Norwich Bks. & Music.
—The Curious History of God. Stannard, Russell. 2003. (ENG.). 96p. (J). (gr. -1-3). pap. 7.95 *(978-1-932031-27-0(8))* Templeton Pr.
Davies, Vanessa, photos by. Cooking with Kids. Collister, Linda. 128p. 2007. per. *(978-1-84597-488-6(3))*; 2003. (ENG., (gr. 6-11). tchr. ed. *(978-1-84172-498-0(X))* Ryland Peters & Small.
—Crafting with Kids: Creative Fun for Children Aged 3-10. Woram, Catherine. 2006. (ENG., 128p. (J). (gr. 3-7). pap. *(978-1-84597-252-3(X))* Ryland Peters & Small.
Dávila, Claudia. Bus to the Badlands. Ruurs, Margriet. 2018. 80p. (J). *(978-1-5490-7424-0(5))* Orca Bk. Pubs.
—Bus to the Badlands, 1 vol. Ruurs, Margriet. 2018. (Orca Echoes Ser.). (ENG.). 88p. (J). (gr. 1-3). pap. 6.95 *(978-1-4598-1670-1(6))* Orca Bk. Pubs. USA.
—Change It! Solids, Liquids, Gases & You. Mason, Adrienne. 2006. (Primary Physical Science Ser.). (ENG.). 32p. (J). (gr. -1-2). 7.95 *(978-1-55337-838-9(5))* Kids Can Pr., Ltd. CAN. Dist: Hachette Bk. Group.
—Child Soldier: When Boys & Girls Are Used in War. Humphreys, Jessica Dee. 2020. (CitizenKid Ser.). (ENG.). 48p. (J). (gr. 5-9). pap. 10.99 *(978-1-5253-0405-7(4))* Kids Can Pr., Ltd. CAN. Dist: Hachette Bk. Group.
—Child Soldier: When Boys & Girls Are Used in War. Humphreys, Jessica Dee & Chikwanine, Michel. 2015. (CitizenKid Ser.). (ENG.). 48p. (J). (gr. 5-9). 17.95 *(978-1-77138-126-0(4))* Kids Can Pr., Ltd. CAN. Dist: Hachette Bk. Group.
—Christmas: 20 Dreamy Ways to Relax & Feel Great. Wallace, Mary & Wallace, Jessica. Smith, Scott McBride, ed. 2009. (ENG.). 20p. (gr. 4-8). pap. 6.25 *(978-1-897379-47-9(1)*, 00220309) Novus Via Music Group Inc. CAN. Dist: Leonard, Hal Corp.
—Ghost of the Mill House, 1 vol. Ruurs, Margriet. 2019. (Orca Echoes Ser.). (ENG.). 104p. (J). (gr. 1-3). pap. 7.95 *(978-1-4598-2035-7(5))* Orca Bk. Pubs. USA.
—It's Your Room: A Decorating Guide for Real Kids. Weaver, Janice & Wishinsky, Frieda. 2006. (ENG.). 64p. (J). (gr. 4-7). per. 14.95 *(978-0-88776-711-1(7)*, Tundra Bks.) Tundra Bks. CAN. Dist: Penguin Random Hse. LLC.
—Move It! Motion, Forces & You. Mason, Adrienne. 2005. (Primary Physical Science Ser.). (ENG.). 32p. (J). (gr. -1-2). pap. 7.95 *(978-1-55337-759-7(1))* Kids Can Pr., Ltd. CAN. Dist: Hachette Bk. Group.
—Ruby's Birds, 1 vol. Thompson, Mya. 2019. (ENG.). 36p. (J). 16.95 *(978-1-943645-33-6(7)*, 900bcd9d-3ef8-4193-83bf-c69bbc73ef5c, Cornell Lab Publishing Group, The) WunderMill, Inc.
Davila, Claudia. Ruby's Birds, 1 vol. Thompson, Mya. 2020. (ENG.). 36p. (J). (gr. -1-3). 8.95 *(978-1-943645-62-6(0)*, d7479f64-3091-48e5-a7c1-1ca528ff45e6, Cornell Lab Publishing Group, The) WunderMill, Inc.
Dávila, Claudia. Sweet! The Delicious Story of Candy. Love, Ann & Drake, Jane. 2009. (ENG.). 64p. (J). (gr. 4-7). pap. 12.95 *(978-0-88776-962-7(4)*, Tundra Bks.) Tundra Bks. CAN. Dist: Penguin Random Hse. LLC.
—Touch It! Materials, Matter & You. Mason, Adrienne. 2005. (Primary Physical Science Ser.). (ENG.). 32p. (J). (gr. -1-2). 7.95 *(978-1-55337-761-0(3))* Kids Can Pr., Ltd. CAN. Dist: Hachette Bk. Group.
Dávila, Claudia. Super Red Riding Hood. Dávila, Claudia. 2014. (ENG.). 32p. (J). (gr. -1-2). 16.95 *(978-1-77138-020-1(9))* Kids Can Pr., Ltd. CAN. Dist: Hachette Bk. Group.
Davis, Aaron. I Know God Is Real. Hardy, C. Cherie. 2017. (ENG.). (J). pap. 10.95 *(978-1-946753-23-6(8))* Avant-garde Bks.
Davis, Alan, et al. Fantastic Four: Heroes Return - the Complete Collection Vol. 1. 2019. (ENG.). 504p. (J). (gr. 4-17). pap. 39.99 *(978-1-302-91623-7(8))* Marvel Worldwide, Inc.
Davis, Alan. Guardians of the Galaxy: Mother Entropy. 2017. (ENG.). 136p. (J). (gr. 4-17). pap. 15.99 *(978-1-302-90488-3(4))* Marvel Worldwide, Inc.
—Righteous Ray-Ray Has a Bad Day Beginning Readers Edition. Smith, Raymond R. 2012. 26p. pap. 9.99 *(978-0-9883634-1-0(0))* Righteous Bks.
—Thanos: the Infinity Ending. 2019. (ENG.). 112p. (YA). (gr. 8-17). 24.99 *(978-1-302-90816-4(2))* Marvel Worldwide, Inc.
Davis, Alan, et al. X-Men: Reload by Chris Claremont Vol. 2: House of M. 2019. (ENG.). 400p. (YA). (gr. 8-17). pap. 34.99 *(978-1-302-92053-1(7))* Marvel Worldwide, Inc.
—Young Avengers by Allan Heinberg & Jim Cheung: the Children's Crusade. 2017. 248p. (YA). (gr. 8-17). pap. 34.99 *(978-1-302-90875-1(8))* Marvel Worldwide, Inc.
Davis, Alan. Killraven. Davis, Alan. 2003. (Spider-Man Ser.). 144p. (YA). pap. 16.99 *(978-0-7851-1083-5(6))* Marvel Worldwide, Inc.
Davis, Allen. Chipmunk at Hollow Tree Lane. Sherrow, Victoria. 2011. (Smithsonian's Backyard Ser.). (ENG.). 32p. (J). (gr. -1-3). 8.95 *(978-1-60727-635-7(6))*; 19.95 *(978-1-60727-634-0(8))* Soundprints.
—Cottontail at Clover Crescent. Lamm, Drew C. 2005. (Smithsonian's Backyard Ser.). (ENG.). 32p. (J). (gr. -1-2). pap. 6.95 *(978-1-59249-112-4(X)*, S5005) Soundprints.
—Why the Snake Crawls on Its Belly. Kimmel, Eric A. 2005. 32p. (J). (gr. 1-4). 14.95 *(978-1-930143-20-3(6)*, Devora Publishing) Simcha Media Group.
—Woodchuck at Blackberry Road. Lamm, C. Drew. 2011. (Smithsonian's Backyard Ser.). (ENG.). 32p. (J). (gr. -1-3). 19.95 *(978-1-60727-644-9(5))* Soundprints.
Davis, Amy. Princesses Can Be Pirates Too! Zellerhoff, Christi. 2012. 38p. 17.99 *(978-1-935961-68-0(3))*; pap. 8.99 *(978-1-935961-95-6(0))* Booktrope. (Booktrope Editions).
Davis, Angela, jt. illus. see Davis, Charles.
Davis, Anne. Bud & Gabby. Davis, Anne. 2006. 32p. (J). (gr. -1-2). lib. bdg. 16.89 *(978-0-06-075351-1(X))* HarperCollins Pubs.
—No Dogs Allowed!, No. 1. Davis, Anne. 2011. (ENG.). 32p. (J). (gr. -1-3). 16.99 *(978-0-06-075353-5(6))* HarperCollins Pubs.
Davis, Ashley. Lorenzo the Lizard. Williams, Iris M. 2016. (ENG.). (J). pap. 10.95 *(978-1-942022-81-7(6))* Butterfly Typeface, The.
Davis, Ashley. Emery, It's Time for Bed: The Magnificent Rainbow! Davis, Ashley. Williams, Iris M., ed. 2016. (ENG.). (J). pap. 10.95 *(978-1-942022-79-4(4))* Butterfly Typeface, The.
—Fishtopia. Davis, Ashley. 2018. (ENG.). 42p. (J). pap. 13.95 *(978-1-947656-67-3(8))* Butterfly Typeface, The.
—A Frog in the Tree. Davis, Ashley. Williams, Iris M., ed. 2016. (ENG.). (J). pap. 10.95 *(978-1-942022-77-0(8))* Butterfly Typeface, The.
Davis, Autum. The Window That Showed God's Glory. Davis, Rosemarie. 2018. (ENG.). 24p. (J). 21.95 *(978-1-64300-337-5(2))*; pap. 12.95 *(978-1-64300-336-8(4))* Covenant Bks.
Davis, Autum Marie Zane. The Truck That Could Not Move. Davis, Rosemarie Swadley. 2018. (ENG.). 26p. (J). pap. 12.95 *(978-1-64003-405-1(6))* Covenant Bks.
Davis, Benjamin. Echoes from the Farm. Jefferson, Jonathan T. 2016. (ENG.). (J). *(978-1-4602-9673-8(7))*; pap. *(978-1-4602-9674-5(5))* FriesenPress.
Davis, Betsy, jt. illus. see Davis, Shelley.
Davis, Bob. Tommy Turtle Learns about Contentment/LB's Sweetest Song: Two Books in One. Wilson, Beth & Brown, D'Anna. 2016. (ENG.). (J). pap. 11.99 *(978-1-945620-04-1(8))* Hear My Heart Publishing.
Davis, Carol Marie. The Adventures of Moon Spirit, a Girl from Florida's Past. Davis, Carol Marie. 2008. 60p. pap. 8.95 *(978-0-9821654-2-3(0))* Peppertree Pr., The.
Davis, Carolina A. Puppy's Tail. Powell, Richard. 2003. (Animal Tails Ser.). 12p. (J). 3.95 *(978-1-58925-674-3(3))* Tiger Tales.
Davis, Caroline. Kitty's Tail. Powell, Richard. 2003. (Animal Tails Ser.). 10p. (J). 3.95 *(978-1-58925-673-6(5))* Tiger Tales.
—My Babies. Emma Treehouse Ltd. 2007. (Easy Flaps Ser.). 10p. (J). (gr. -1). bds. 6.95 *(978-1-58925-822-8(3))* Tiger Tales.
—My Friends. Emma Treehouse Ltd. 2007. (Easy Flaps Ser.). 10p. (J). (gr. -1). bds. 6.95 *(978-1-58925-823-5(1))* Tiger Tales.
—My Pets. Emma Treehouse Ltd. 2007. (Easy Flaps Ser.). 10p. (J). (gr. -1). bds. 6.95 *(978-1-58925-824-2(X))* Tiger Tales.
—My Toys. Emma Treehouse Ltd. 2007. (Easy Flaps Ser.). 10p. (J). (gr. -1). bds. 6.95 *(978-1-58925-825-9(8))* Tiger Tales.
—Old MacDonald's: Barnyard Tales. Baxter, Nicola. 256p. (J). *(978-0-7525-8771-4(4))* Parragon Bk. Service Ltd.
Davis, Caroline. Babies. Davis, Caroline. 2010. (ENG.). 20p. (J). bds. *(978-1-4083-0786-1(3)*, Orchard Bks.) Hachette Children's Group GBR. Dist: Hachette Bk. Group.
—Bugs. Davis, Caroline. 2010. (ENG.). 20p. (J). bds. *(978-1-4083-0784-7(7)*, Orchard Bks.) Hachette Children's Group GBR. Dist: Hachette Bk. Group.
—Diggers. Davis, Caroline. 2010. (ENG.). 20p. (J). bds. *(978-1-4083-0785-4(5)*, Orchard Bks.) Hachette Children's Group GBR. Dist: Hachette Bk. Group.
—Sparkly Farm. Davis, Caroline. 2008. (Tiger Tales Ser.). 8p. (J). (gr. -1). bds. 6.95 *(978-1-58925-831-0(2))* Tiger Tales.
—Sparkly Garden. Davis, Caroline. 2008. (Tiger Tales Ser.). 8p. (J). (gr. -1). bds. 6.95 *(978-1-58925-830-3(4))* Tiger Tales.
—Sparkly Ocean. Davis, Caroline. 2008. (Tiger Tales Ser.). 8p. (J). (gr. -1). bds. 6.95 *(978-1-58925-832-7(0))* Tiger Tales.
—Yum Yum! Davis, Caroline. 2010. (ENG.). 20p. (J). bds. *(978-1-4083-0787-8(1)*, Orchard Bks.) Hachette Children's Group GBR. Dist: Hachette Bk. Group.
Davis, Catherine Baptista. One Is Fun. DeRosa Bodie, Leona. 2007. 30p. (J). (gr. -1). bds. 12.95 *(978-1-4243-2961-8(2))* Independent Publisher Services.
Davis, Chad L. Little Peter & Sela. Toledo, Leila J. l.t. ed. 2004. 17p. (J). pap. 8.95 *(978-0-9753118-0-6(8))* Bimini Bks.
Davis, Charles & Davis, Angela. Mashed Banana Pie. Jakeman, Melissa. 2018. (ENG.). 32p. (J). pap. *(978-0-646-98961-7(8))* Jakeman, Melissa.
Davis, Christine. The Shelter Dog. Davis, Christine. 2008. 32p. (J). (gr. -1-3). 11.95 *(978-0-9659225-4-8(5))* Lighthearted Pr., Inc.
Davis, Christopher. Funky Little Monkey. Buttar, Debbie. 2015. (ENG.). 20p. (J). 14.99 *(978-0-9794302-5-1(9))* GMEC Publishing.
Davis, Christopher Owen, jt. illus. see Speer, Julie.
Davis, Dan. Dan the Bucket Truck. Cox, Katie. 2019. (ENG.). 38p. (J). pap. 12.99 *(978-1-0746-2988-5(4))* Independently Published.
—Scooby-Doo & the Creepy Chef, 1 vol. McCann, Jesse Leon. 2010. (Scooby-Doo! Ser.: No. 1). (ENG.). 24p. (J). (gr. k-4). lib. bdg. 27.07 *(978-1-59961-676-6(9)*, 13236, Picture Bk.) Spotlight.
Davis, Dan & Suriano, Andy. Charge of the Army Eternal, 1 vol. Torres, J. 2013. (Batman: the Brave & the Bold Ser.). (ENG.). 32p. (J). (gr. 2-5). 22.60 *(978-1-4342-4706-3(6)*, Stone Arch Bks.) Capstone.
Davis, Dan W., jt. illus. see Suriano, Andy.
Davis, Daniel M. After Halloween. McClellan, Sara, ed. 2007. 64p. (J). per. 20.00 *(978-0-9774173-4-6(4))* Steam Crow Pr.
Davis, Dennis. What God Has Always Wanted: The Bible's Big Idea from Genesis Through Revelation. Boyd, Charles F. 2006. 22p. (J). (gr. -1-3). *(978-1-57229-725-8(5))* FamilyLife.
Davis, Dick. From Here to There. Keckler, Ben. 2005. (Express Yourself Ser.). 42p. (J). (gr. 3-7). lib. bdg. 16.95 *(978-0-9769093-0-9(8))* Eagle Creek Pubns., LLC.
—Incredibly Lonely, That's Me. Keckler, Ben. 2007. (Express Yourself Ser.). 42p. (J). (gr. 3-7). 17.95 *(978-0-9769093-2-3(4))* Eagle Creek Pubns., LLC.
Davis, Eleanor. The Secret Science Alliance & the Copycat Crook. Davis, Eleanor. 2009. (ENG.). 160p. (YA). (gr. 3-6). pap. 17.99 *(978-1-59990-396-5(2)*, 900062420, Bloomsbury USA Childrens) Bloomsbury Publishing USA.
Davis, Guy & Sikoryak, Bob. Fantastic Four: Unstable Molecules. Sturm, James. 2003. (Fantastic Four Legends Ser.: Vol. 1). 128p. (YA). pap. 13.99 *(978-0-7851-1112-2(3))* Marvel Worldwide, Inc.
Davis, Hilary. The Teacup Café. Farrin, Patty. 2018. (J). 19.95 *(978-1-63381-142-3(5))*; pap. 15.95 *(978-1-63381-143-0(3))* Custom Museum Publishing LLC.
Davis, Jack. Crazy Campsongs. Petersen, George & Jenkins, J. J. 2003. 64p. (J). bds. 9.99 *(978-0-9726794-9-7(9))* Jenpet Publishing.
Davis, Jack & Williamson, Al. The Adventures of the Fly. Simon, Joe. 2004. (Red Circle Ser.). (ENG.). 96p. pap. 12.95 *(978-1-879794-18-4(7)*, Archie Comics) Archie Comic Pubns., Inc.
Davis, Jack E. Bunion Burt. Hayles, Marsha. 2009. (ENG.). 32p. (J). (gr. -1-3). 16.99 *(978-1-4169-4132-3(0)*, McElderry, Margaret K. Bks.) McElderry, Margaret K. Bks.
—Dirty Joe, the Pirate: A True Story. Harley, Bill. 2008. (ENG.). 32p. (J). (gr. k-3). 17.99 *(978-0-06-623780-0(7))* HarperCollins Pubs.
—Don't Count on Dracula. Greenburg, Dan. 2004. (Zack Files Ser.). 58p. lib. bdg. 15.00 *(978-0-7569-2236-8(4))* Perfection Learning Corp.
—Goldie & the Three Hares. Palatini, Margie. 2011. (ENG.). 32p. (J). (gr. -1-2). 17.99 *(978-0-06-125314-0(6)*, Tegen, Katherine Bks) HarperCollins Pubs.
—Halfway Hank. Fallon, Joe & Scarborough, Ken. 2005. 40p. (J). 15.99 *(978-0-06-623636-0(3))* HarperCollins Pubs.
—Here Comes T. Rex Cottontail. Grambling, Lois G. 2010. (ENG.). 32p. (J). (gr. -1-1). pap. 7.99 *(978-0-06-053134-8(7)*, Tegen, Katherine Bks) HarperCollins Pubs.
—How I Went from Bad to Verse. Greenburg, Dan. 2004. (Zack Files Ser.). 59p. lib. bdg. 15.00 *(978-0-7569-2235-1(6))* Perfection Learning Corp.
—I Am the Dog. Pinkwater, Daniel M. 2010. (ENG.). 32p. (J). (gr. -1-3). 16.99 *(978-0-06-055505-4(X))* HarperCollins Pubs.
—It's Itchcraft!, 30 vols. Greenburg, Dan. 2003. (Zack Files Ser.: 30). (ENG.). 128p. (J). (gr. 2-5). pap. 4.99 *(978-0-448-42888-8(1)*, Grosset & Dunlap) Penguin Young Readers Group.
—It's Itchcraft! Greenburg, Dan. 2004. (Zack Files Ser.). 118p. lib. bdg. 15.00 *(978-0-7569-2238-2(0))* Perfection Learning Corp.
—Just Add Water... & Scream! Greenburg, Dan. 2004. (Zack Files Ser.). 56p. lib. bdg. 15.00 *(978-0-7569-2239-9(9))* Perfection Learning Corp.
—Marsupial Sue Presents the Runaway Pancake. Lithgow, John. 2008. (ENG.). 40p. (J). (gr. -1-3). 7.99 *(978-0-689-87848-0(6)*, Simon & Schuster Bks. For Young Readers) Simon & Schuster Bks. For Young Readers.
—Moose Tracks! Wilson, Karma. 2006. (ENG.). 32p. (J). (gr. -1-2). 17.99 *(978-0-689-83437-0(3)*, McElderry, Margaret K. Bks.) McElderry, Margaret K. Bks.
—T. Rex & the Mother's Day Hug. Grambling, Lois G. 2011. (ENG.). 32p. (J). (gr. -1-1). pap. 7.99 *(978-0-06-053128-7(2)*, Tegen, Katherine Bks) HarperCollins Pubs.
—T. Rex Trick-or-Treats. Grambling, Lois G. 2005. 32p. (J). 12.99 *(978-0-06-050252-2(5)*, Tegen, Katherine Bks) HarperCollins Pubs.
—T. Rex Trick-Or-Treats. Grambling, Lois G. 2008. (ENG.). 32p. (J). (gr. -1-3). pap. 7.99 *(978-0-06-050254-6(1)*, Tegen, Katherine Bks) HarperCollins Pubs.
—Yo-Yo Man. Pinkwater, Daniel M. 2007. (ENG.). 32p. (J). (gr. -1-3). 16.99 *(978-0-06-055502-3(5))* HarperCollins Pubs.
Davis, Jack E. Sweet Tooth. Davis, Jack E. Palatini, Margie. 2004. (ENG.). 40p. (J). (gr. -1-3). 19.99 *(978-0-689-85159-9(6)*, Simon & Schuster Bks. For Young Readers) Simon & Schuster Bks. For Young Readers.
Davis, Jacqui. Sleeping Beauty: An Islamic Tale. Gilani, Fawzia. 2018. (Islamic Fairy Tales Ser.). (ENG.). 40p. (J). (gr. k-4). 14.00 *(978-0-86037-597-5(8))* Kube Publishing Ltd. GBR. Dist: Consortium Bk. Sales & Distribution.
Davis, Jacqui, jt. illus. see Finlayson, Luke.
Davis, Jason. Hurricane Hound. Lee, Gia. 2011. 40p. pap. 24.95 *(978-1-4560-9743-1(1))* America Star Bks.
Davis, Jeff. The Hand That Scared Jenny. Rosas, Beverly. 2008. 47p. pap. 24.95 *(978-1-4241-9138-3(6))* PublishAmerica, Inc.
Davis, Jeffrey. Martin the Mouse Meets the Great Owl. Stemmler, Jennifer. 2019. (ENG.). 26p. (J). pap. 9.99 ***(978-1-7016-5235-4(8))*** Independently Published.
Davis, John Watson. The King of the Golden City: An Allegory for Children. Loyola, Mother Mary. 2nd ed. 2005. 128p. (J). per. *(978-0-9764691-0-0(3))* Little Way Pr.
Davis, Jon. Baby! Zeavin, Carol & Silverbush, Rhona. 2020. (J). ***(978-1-4338-3250-5(X)*** , Magination Pr.) American Psychological Assn.
Davis, Jon. Boo-Boo! Zeavin, Carol. 2018. 16p. (J). *(978-1-4338-2875-1(8)*, Magination Pr.) American Psychological Assn.
—Bye-Bye! Zeavin, Carol & Silverbush, Rhona. 2018. 16p. (J). *(978-1-4338-2876-8(6)*, Magination Pr.) American Psychological Assn.
—The Clever Friend. Kane, Kim. 2018. (Ginger Green, Playdate Queen Ser.). (ENG.). 64p. (J). (gr. 1-3). pap. 5.95 *(978-1-5158-2013-0(0)*, 136660, Picture Window Bks.) Capstone.
—The Coziest Place. Michalak, Jamie. 2013. (ENG.). 32p. (J). (gr. -1-k). 14.99 *(978-1-58925-121-2(0))* Tiger Tales.
—The Crazy Friend. Kane, Kim. 2017. (Ginger Green, Playdate Queen Ser.). (ENG.). 64p. (J). (gr. 1-3). lib. bdg. 23.32 *(978-1-5158-1947-9(7)*, 136630, Picture Window Bks.) Capstone.
—The Fancy Friend. Kane, Kim. 2017. (Ginger Green, Playdate Queen Ser.). (ENG.). 64p. (J). (gr. 1-3). lib. bdg. 23.32 *(978-1-5158-1948-6(5)*, 136631, Picture Window Bks.) Capstone.
—Ginger Green + Cousins = Total Chaos!, Volume 4. Kane, Kim. 2020. (Ginger Green Ser.: 4). (ENG.). 144p. (J). (gr. k-2). pap. 8.99 *(978-1-76050-206-5(5))* Hardie Grant Egmont Pty, Ltd. AUS. Dist: Independent Pubs. Group.
—Is Absolutely Mad for Birthdays! (Mostly), Volume 1. Kane, Kim. 2019. (Ginger Green Ser.: 1). (ENG.). 144p. (J). (gr. k-2). pap. 8.99 *(978-1-76050-105-1(0))* Hardie Grant Egmont Pty, Ltd. AUS. Dist: Independent Pubs. Group.
—The Knish War on Rivington Street. Oppenheim, Joanne. 2017. (ENG.). 32p. (J). (gr. -1-3). 16.99 *(978-0-8075-4182-1(6)*, 807541826) Whitman, Albert & Co.

D

—The New Friend. Kane, Kim. 2017. (Ginger Green, Playdate Queen Ser.). (ENG.). 64p. (J). (gr. 1-3). lib. bdg. 23.32 (978-1-5158-1946-2(9), 136629, Picture Window Bks.) Capstone.

—The Next Door Friend. Kane, Kim. 2017. (Ginger Green, Playdate Queen Ser.). (ENG.). 64p. (J). (gr. 1-3). lib. bdg. 23.32 (978-1-5158-1949-3(3), 136632, Picture Window Bks.) Capstone.

—The NOT-MUCH Sleepover Starring Ginger Green, Volume 2. Kane, Kim. 2019. (Ginger Green Ser.: 2). (ENG.). 144p. (J). (gr. k-2). pap. 8.99 (978-1-76050-106-8(9)) Hardie Grant Egmont Pty, Ltd. AUS. Dist: Independent Pubs. Group.

—The Only Friend. Kane, Kim. 2018. (Ginger Green, Playdate Queen Ser.). (ENG.). 64p. (J). (gr. 1-3). pap. 5.95 (978-1-5158-2012-3(2), 136659, Picture Window Bks.) Capstone.

Davis, Jon. Potty! Zeavin, Carol & Silverbush, Rhona. 2020. (J). **(978-1-4338-3251-2(8)**, Magination Pr.) American Psychological Assn.

Davis, Jon. The Truth (and Myths) about American Heroes. Peacock, L. A. 2016. 96p. (J). (978-0-545-83027-0(3)) Scholastic, Inc.

—The Truth (and Myths) about Disasters. Peacock, L. A. 2014. 96p. (J). pap. (978-0-545-70565-3(7)) Scholastic, Inc.

—Why Do My Teeth Fall Out? And Other Questions Kids Have about the Human Body, 1 vol. Montgomery, Heather L. 2011. (Kids' Questions Ser.). (ENG.). 24p. (J). (gr. k-2). pap. 7.49 (978-1-4048-6534-1(9), Picture Window Bks.) Capstone.

Davis, Kaley. Beau Bandit's Tale. Richardville, Carol. 2004. (J). per. 16.99 (978-1-932503-23-4(4)) Insight Publishing Group.

Davis, Katheryn & Van Slyke, Rebecca. Storybook Art: Hands-On Art for Children in the Styles of 100 Great Picture Book Illustrators. Kohl, MaryAnn F. & Potter, Jean. 2003. (Bright Ideas for Learning Ser.: 7). 144p. (J). (gr. -1-6). pap. 18.95 (978-0-935607-03-1(X)) Chicago Review Pr., Inc.

Davis, Kathryn Lynn. Christmas Shapes. Gerver, Jane E. 2010. (ENG.). 14p. (J). (gr. -1 — 1). bds. 6.99 (978-1-4169-9759-7(8), Little Simon) Little Simon.

Davis, Kathryn Lynn. The First Thanksgiving: A Lift-The-Flap Book. Davis, Kathryn Lynn. 2010. (ENG.). 14p. (J). (gr. -1 — 1). bds. 5.99 (978-1-4424-0807-4(3), Little Simon) Little Simon.

Davis, Kathryn Lynn, jt. illus. see Davis, Nancy.

Davis, Katie. Little Chicken's Big Day. Davis, Katie. Davis, Jerry. 2011. (ENG.). 40p. (J). (gr. -1 — 1). 14.99 (978-1-4424-1401-3(4), McElderry, Margaret K. Bks.) McElderry, Margaret K. Bks.

Davis, Lambert. Seaside Dream. Bates, Janet Costa. 2013. (ENG.). 32p. (J). (gr. k-5). 17.95 (978-1-60060-347-1(5)) Lee & Low Bks., Inc.

—Seaside Dream, 1 vol. Bates, Janet. 2016. (ENG.). 32p. (J). pap. 9.95 (978-1-62014-256-1(2)) Lee & Low Bks., Inc.

—Snow Bear. Stafford, Liliana. 32p. (J). pap. (978-0-88899-441-7(9)) Groundwood Bks.

Davis, Leann. The Little Wooden Cup. Usrey, Jody. 2020. (ENG.). 36p. (J). pap. 9.95 **(978-1-7041-2530-5(8))** Independently Published.

Davis, Lynn. Meet Harry & Herman: Colorbook. Watson, Kathy. 2018. (ENG.). 22p. (J). (gr. 2-6). pap. (978-94-93105-02-7(4)) MinistryHouse Pr.

Davis, Lynne. Little Dongs for Little Souls: Sharing God's Love. Elkins, Stephen. 2005. 32p. (J). 9.99 incl. audio compact disk (978-0-8054-2673-1(6)) B&H Publishing Group.

—Little Songs for Little Souls: God Cares for Me. Elkins, Stephen. 2005. 32p. (J). 9.99 incl. audio compact disk (978-0-8054-2675-5(2)) B&H Publishing Group.

—Little Songs for Little Souls: I Can Be Happy in Jesus. Elkins, Stephen. 2005. 32p. (J). 9.99 incl. audio compact disk (978-0-8054-2676-2(0)) B&H Publishing Group.

—Little Songs for Little Souls: I Can Praise the Lord. Elkins, Stephen. 2005. 32p. (J). 9.99 incl. audio compact disk (978-0-8054-2677-9(9)) B&H Publishing Group.

Davis, Marcus. Joey & the Ancient Horn: A Mystery Revealed. Watkins, T. a. 2007. 333p. (J). (gr. -1). per. 12.95 (978-0-9762788-0-1(4)) Great I-AM Publishing Co., The.

Davis, Mika. Little Ola Goes to Church. Lycett, Sonia Lawson. 2017. (ENG.). 24p. (J). pap. 14.99 (978-1-5434-6373-6(8)) Xlibris Corp.

Davis Molloy, Christa-Ann. Dance Quadrille & Play Quelbe. Adisa, Opal Palmer. 2019. (ENG.). 36p. (J). 17.99 (978-1-7338299-4-6(6)) CaribbeanReads.

Davis, Nancy. Flicker Flash. Graham, Joan Bransfield et al. 2003. (ENG.). 32p. (J). (gr. -1-3). pap. 7.99 (978-0-618-31102-6(5), 486711) Houghton Mifflin Harcourt Publishing Co.

—Older Than the Stars. Fox, Karen C. 2011. (ENG.). 32p. (J). (gr. 2-5). pap. 7.95 (978-1-57091-788-2(4)) Charlesbridge Publishing, Inc.

Davis, Nancy. Halloween Faces. Davis, Nancy. 2010. (ENG.). 18p. (J). (gr. k — 1). bds. 6.99 (978-0-545-16586-0(5), Cartwheel Bks.) Scholastic, Inc.

Davis, Nancy & Davis, Kathryn Lynn. Wake Up! Wake Up! Davis, Nancy & Davis, Kathryn Lynn. 2011. (ENG.). 14p. (J). (gr. -1 — 1). bds. 5.99 (978-1-4424-1217-0(8), Little Simon) Little Simon.

—Who's at Home? Gerver, Jane E. 2010. (ENG.). 14p. (J). (gr. -1 — 1). bds. 6.99 (978-1-4169-9758-0(X), Little Simon) Little Simon.

Davis, Nelle. Eight Little Legs. Gravelle, Karen. 2004. (ENG.). 20p. (gr. k-2). pap. 8.95 (978-1-57874-042-0(8), Kaeden Bks.) Kaeden Corp.

Davis, Oslo. Henry Lawson Treasury. Lawson, Henry. 2015. 160p. (J). (gr. 6). pap. 17.99 (978-0-85798-513-2(2)) Random Hse. Australia AUS. Dist: Independent Pubs. Group.

Davis, Pharis. Eugene the Mouse at the Big Farmhouse: The Contentment of a Creative Mouse. Skinner, Lynn. 2018. (ENG.). 34p. (J). (gr. k-2). pap. 11.99 (978-0-9991679-6-0(0)) Skinner, Lynn C.

Davis, Renée. Bartholomew's Wish. Coffey, Nathan. 2018. (ENG.). 32p. (J). pap. (978-1-5255-2143-0(8)); (978-1-5255-2142-3(X)) FriesenPress.

Davis, Rich. Happy Easter, Tiny! Meister, Cari. 2018. (Tiny Ser.). 32p. (J). (gr. k-1). pap. 3.99 (978-1-5247-8385-3(4), Penguin Young Readers) Penguin Young Readers Group.

—Happy Thanksgiving, Tiny! Meister, Cari. 2018. (Tiny Ser.). 32p. (J). (gr. k-1). pap. 3.99 (978-1-5247-8388-4(9), Penguin Young Readers) Penguin Young Readers Group.

—Hi-Ho, Tiny. Meister, Cari. 2015. (Tiny Ser.). (ENG.). 32p. (J). (gr. k-1). pap. 4.99 (978-0-448-48291-0(6), Penguin Young Readers) Penguin Young Readers Group.

—Tiny Goes Back to School. Meister, Cari. 2014. (Tiny Ser.). 32p. (J). (gr. k-1). pap. 4.99 (978-0-448-48134-0(0), Penguin Young Readers) Penguin Young Readers Group.

—Tiny Goes Camping. Meister, Cari. 2007. (Tiny Ser.). 32p. (J). (gr. k-1). mass mkt. 4.99 (978-0-14-056741-0(0), Penguin Young Readers) Penguin Young Readers Group.

—Tiny Goes to the Movies. Meister, Cari. 2016. (Tiny Ser.). 32p. (J). (gr. k-1). pap. 4.99 (978-0-448-48295-8(9), Penguin Young Readers) Penguin Young Readers Group.

—Tiny Saves the Day. Meister, Cari. 2016. (Tiny Ser.). 32p. (J). (gr. k-1). 4.99 (978-0-448-48293-4(2), Penguin Young Readers) Penguin Young Readers Group.

—Tiny the Birthday Dog. Meister, Cari. 2013. (Tiny Ser.). 32p. (J). (gr. k-1). pap. 4.99 (978-0-448-46478-7(0), Penguin Young Readers) Penguin Young Readers Group.

Davis, Rob. Sólo para Chicos: ¿Qué Me Está Pasando? Mi Pubertad. Crossick, Matt. Parragon Books, ed. 2019. (SPA.). 96p. (YA). (gr. 4-9). 7.99 (978-1-68052-579-3(4), 2002210-SLA, Parragon Books) Cottage Door Pr.

Davis, Robert. My Nativity 1-2-3s. Sumner, Esther Yu. 2018. (ENG.). 32p. (J). 14.99 (978-1-4621-2246-2(9)) Cedar Fort, Inc./CFI Distribution.

Davis, Robyn L. Good Times with Gregory: Airplanes: A Visit to A 747. Davis, Helen J. 2008. (Good Times with Gregory Ser.). 37p. (J). (gr. -1-4). 12.95 (978-1-935122-11-1(8)) K&B Products.

—Good Times with Gregory: Birds: Rescuing a Baby Bird. Davis, Helen J. 2008. (Good Times with Gregory Ser.). 54p. (J). (gr. -1-4). 12.95 (978-1-935122-10-4(X)) K&B Products.

Davis, Sandy. Fun Facts about Animals - from a to Z. Davis, Nina. 2016. (ENG.). (J). pap. (978-0-9939038-5-4(1)) LMonD Pubns.

Davis, Sarah. Cruise Control: The Anti-Princess Club 5. Turnbull, Samantha. 2017. (Anti-Princess Club Ser.: 5). (ENG.). 192p. (J). (gr. 2-4). pap. 9.99 (978-1-76029-188-4(9)) Allen & Unwin AUS. Dist: Independent Pubs. Group.

—Fearless. Thompson, Colin. 2015. 32p. 17.99 (978-0-7333-2025-5(2)) ABC Bks. AUS. Dist: HarperCollins Pubs.

—Saige Paints the Sky. Haas, Jessie. ed. 2012. (American Girl Today Ser.: Bk. 2). lib. bdg. 17.15 (978-0-606-31569-2(1)) Turtleback.

—That's Not a Hippopotamus! MacIver, Juliette. 2016. (ENG.). 32p. (J). (gr. -1-1). 16.99 (978-1-927271-96-4(7), 9781927271964) Gecko Pr. NZL. Dist: Lerner Publishing Group.

Davis, Shane. Fantastic Four: The Menace of Monster Isle! Dezago, Todd. 2006. (Spider-Man Team Up Ser.). (ENG.). 24p. (J). (gr. 2-6). lib. bdg. 27.07 (978-1-59961-006-1(X), 13646, Marvel Age) Spotlight.

Davis, Shelley & Davis, Betsy. Billy's Big Tomato. White, Gene. 2013. 24p. pap. 11.00 (978-0-9886360-9-5(3)) Kids At Heart Publishing, LLC.

Davis, Shelley L. A. The Boinking Bubble MacHine. Reece, Eva. 2013. 24p. pap. 12.99 (978-0-9886360-2-6(6)) Kids At Heart Publishing, LLC.

Davis, Shelley La. Brownie Calf & the Barnyard Babies. Reece, Eva. 2012. 24p. pap. 12.99 (978-0-9836641-8-5(8)) Kids At Heart Publishing, LLC.

Davis, Stephen. The Awakening: An Icelandic Classic. Chopin, Kate. 2014. (American Classics Ser.). (ENG.). 64p. pap. 6.95 (978-1-906230-78-4(1)) Real Reads Ltd. GBR. Dist: Casemate Pubs. & Bk. Distributors, LLC.

Davis, Tim. The Case of the Purple Diamonds. 2011. 88p. pap. 9.95 (978-1-934606-07-0(3)) TAG Publishing, LLC.

—Charlie the Chopper & the Greatest Toymaker. Yuen, Dan. 2010. 26p. (J). (978-0-88144-480-3(4)) Yorkshire Publishing Group.

—Funny Money. Temko, Florence. 2005. 48p. (J). (gr. -1-3). per. 4.99 (978-1-58196-037-2(9), Darby Creek) Lerner Publishing Group.

—Lunchroom Laughs Joke Book. Pellowski, Michael J. 2005. (ENG.). 128p. (gr. 2-6). per. 3.99 (978-1-58196-032-7(8), Darby Creek) Lerner Publishing Group.

Davis, Will. Clemency Pogue: Fairy Killer. Petty, J. T. 2011. (ENG.). 128p. (J). (gr. 3-7). pap. 7.99 (978-1-4424-3097-6(4), Simon & Schuster Bks. For Young Readers) Simon & Schuster Bks. For Young Readers.

Davis, Yvonne. Tuck-Me-In Tales: Bedtime Stories from Around the World. MacDonald, Margaret Read. 2005. (ENG.). 64p. (J). (gr. -1-2). 19.95 (978-0-87483-461-1(9)) August Hse. Pubs., Inc.

Davis, Yvonne LeBrun. The Girl Who Wore Too Much: A Folktale from Thailand. 2015. (ENG.). 32p. (J). (gr. k-3). pap. 8.95 (978-1-939160-93-5(6)) August Hse. Pubs., Inc.

—The Round Book: Rounds Kids Love to Sing. MacDonald, Margaret Read & Jaeger, Winifred. 2006. (ENG.). 136p. (J). (gr. -1-3). per. 18.95 (978-0-87483-786-5(3)) August Hse. Pubs., Inc.

Daviscourt, Anna. T. Rex. Garnett, Jaye. Cottage Door Press, ed. 2020. (Finger Puppet Board Book Smithsonian Kids Ser.). (ENG.). 12p. (J). (gr. -1 — 1). bds. 6.99 (978-1-68052-811-4(4), 1005240) Cottage Door Pr.

Davison, Jennifer. Daniel & the Very Hungry Lions. Thornborough, Tim. 2019. (Very Best Bible Stories Ser.). (ENG.). 24p. (J). (978-1-78498-332-1(2)) Good Bk. Co., The.

—David & the Very Big Giant. Thornborough, Tim. 2019. (Very Best Bible Stories Ser.). (ENG.). 24p. (J). (978-1-78498-381-9(0)) Good Bk. Co., The.

—Jonah & the Very Big Fish. Thornborough, Tim. 2019. (Very Best Bible Stories Ser.). (ENG.). 24p. (J). (978-1-78498-379-6(9)) Good Bk. Co., The.

—Noah & the Very Big Boat. Thornborough, Tim. 2019. (Very Best Bible Stories Ser.). (ENG.). 24p. (J). (978-1-78498-380-2(2)) Good Bk. Co., The.

Davison, Jennifer. The Very Last Leaf. Wade, Stef. 2020. (ENG.). 32p. (J). (gr. k-2). 17.99 **(978-1-68446-104-2(9)**, 141337, Capstone Editions) Capstone.

Davison, Jennifer. A Very Noisy Christmas. Thornborough, Tim. 2018. (ENG.). 24p. (J). pap. (978-1-78498-290-4(3)) Good Bk. Co., The.

Davisson, Vanessa. Adventures of Baroness of the Arizona Desert. Garr, Rebecca. 2010. 60p. pap. 18.95 (978-1-60911-958-4(4), Eloquent Bks.) Strategic Book Publishing & Rights Agency (SBPRA).

Daviz, Paul. Amazing Earth: Dinosaurs. 2020. (Amazing Earth Ser.). (ENG.). 24p. (J). (gr. 3-7). 16.99 **(978-1-64517-042-6(X)**, Silver Dolphin Bks.) Printers Row Publishing Group.

—Amazing Earth: Jungles. 2020. (Amazing Earth Ser.). (ENG.). 24p. (J). (gr. 3-7). 16.99 **(978-1-64517-041-9(1)**, Silver Dolphin Bks.) Printers Row Publishing Group.

—Amazing Earth: Oceans. 2020. (Amazing Earth Ser.). (ENG.). 24p. (J). (gr. 3-7). 16.99 **(978-1-64517-040-2(3)**, Silver Dolphin Bks.) Printers Row Publishing Group.

—Who's Playing in the Jungle? Watson, Lydia. 2020. (ENG.). 10p. (J). (gr. -1-k). bds. 15.99 **(978-1-64517-125-6(6)**, Silver Dolphin Bks.) Printers Row Publishing Group.

—Who's Swimming in the Ocean? Watson, Lydia. 2020. (ENG.). 10p. (J). (gr. -1-k). bds. 15.99 **(978-1-64517-124-9(8)**, Silver Dolphin Bks.) Printers Row Publishing Group.

Dawes, Will, jt. illus. see Haw, Brenda.

Dawid. Supers (Book One) A Little Star Past Cassiopeia. Maupomé, édéric. 2019. (ENG.). 112p. (J). (gr. 2-5). pap. 14.99 (978-1-60309-439-9(3)) Top Shelf Productions.

Dawley, Sarah. You Are Special Little Bee. Doty, Sara. 2009. 16p. pap. 10.99 (978-1-4389-7040-0(4)) AuthorHouse.

Dawn, Baumer. The Detective Company. Baldwin, Rich & Jones, Sandie. 2004. 183p. (YA). pap. 9.95 (978-0-9742920-0-7(1), 2001) Buttonwood Pr.

Dawn Phillips. Glasses for Me? Oh No! By Kaleena Ma. 2009. 40p. pap. 18.49 (978-1-4389-5418-9(2)) AuthorHouse.

Dawson, Clare. Heavenward Bound. Branscombe, E. T. W. 2019. (ENG.). 96p. (J). (gr. 2-6). pap. 10.95 **(978-1-64051-105-7(9))** St. Augustine Academy Pr.

Dawson, Courtney. ABC of Body Safety & Consent: Teach Children about Body Safety, Consent, Safe/unsafe Touch, Private Parts, Body Boundaries & Respect. Sanders, Jayneen. 2020. (ENG.). 42p. (J). (gr. k-5). **(978-1-925089-59-2(2))**; pap. **(978-1-925089-58-5(4))** UpLoad Publishing Pty, Ltd.

Dawson, Courtney. Help Wanted, Must Love Books. Sumner Johnson, Janet. 2020. (ENG.). 32p. (J). (gr. -1-2). 17.95 (978-1-68446-075-5(1), 140527, Capstone Editions) Capstone.

Dawson, Courtney. A Vote Is a Powerful Thing. Stier, Catherine. 2020. (ENG.). 32p. (J). (gr. -1-3). 16.99 **(978-0-8075-8498-9(3)**, 0807584983) Whitman, Albert & Co.

Dawson, Isabel. Stories of Mystery, Adventure & Fun from Calling All Girls. Gipson, Morrell, ed. 2011. 252p. 46.95 (978-1-258-10497-9(0)) Literary Licensing, LLC.

Dawson, Janine. The Awful Pawful. Odgers, Darrel & Odgers, Sally. 2007. (Jack Russell: Dog Detective Ser.: 5). 96p. (J). (gr. 1-6). pap. 4.99 (978-1-933605-53-1(7)) Kane Miller.

—The Blue Stealer. Odgers, Darrel & Odgers, Sally. 2009. (Jack Russell: Dog Detective Ser.: 9). 96p. (J). (gr. 2-6). pap. 4.99 (978-1-935279-09-9(2)) Kane Miller.

—The Buried Biscuits. Odgers, Sally & Odgers, Darrel. 2008. (Jack Russell: Dog Detective Ser.: 7). 96p. (J). (gr. 1-6). pap. 4.99 (978-1-933605-77-7(4)) Kane Miller.

—Bush Rescue. Odgers, Darrel & Odgers, Sally. 2016. 89p. (J). (978-1-61067-563-5(0)) Kane Miller.

—Bush Rescue: Pup Patrol. Odgers, Sally & Darrel. 2017. 96p. (J). pap. 4.99 (978-1-61067-519-2(3)) Kane Miller.

—Cranky Paws. Odgers, Darrel & Odgers, Sally. 2009. (Pet Vet Ser.: 1). 96p. (J). (gr. 2-6). pap. 4.99 (978-1-935279-01-3(7)) Kane Miller.

—Dog Den Mystery. Odgers, Sally & Odgers, Darrel. 2006. (Jack Russell: Dog Detective Ser.: 1). 96p. (J). (gr. 1-5). pap. 4.99 (978-1-933605-18-0(9)) Kane Miller.

—Farm Rescue. Odgers, Darrel & Odgers, Sally. 2016. 92p. (J). (978-1-61067-562-8(2)) Kane Miller.

—Farm Rescue: Pup Patrol. Odgers, Sally & Darrel. 2017. 96p. (J). pap. 4.99 (978-1-61067-518-5(5)) Kane Miller.

—The Ham Heist. Odgers, Darrel & Odgers, Sally. 2010. (Jack Russell: Dog Detective Ser.: 11). 96p. (J). (gr. 2-6). pap. 4.99 (978-1-935279-75-4(0)) Kane Miller.

—Inspector Jacques. Odgers, Darrel & Odgers, Sally. 2010. (Jack Russell: Dog Detective Ser.: 10). 96p. (J). (gr. 2-4). pap. 4.99 (978-1-935279-17-4(3)) Kane Miller.

—The Kitnapped Creature. Odgers, Darrel & Odgers, Sally. 2008. (Jack Russell: Dog Detective Ser.: 8). 96p. (J). (gr. 2-6). pap. 4.99 (978-1-933605-82-1(0)) Kane Miller.

—The Kitten's Tale. Odgers, Darrel & Odgers, Sally. 2010. (Pet Vet Ser.: 5). 96p. (J). (gr. 2-6). pap. 4.99 (978-1-935279-76-1(9)) Kane Miller.

—Lily Quench 6 Hand of Manuelo, Vol. 6. Prior, Natalie Jane. 2004. (ENG.). 176p. (J). (gr. 3-7). 6.99 (978-0-14-240222-1(2), Puffin Books) Penguin Young Readers Group.

—Lily Quench 7 the Search for King Dragon. Prior, Natalie Jane. 2005. (ENG.). 192p. (J). (gr. 3-7). 6.99 (978-0-14-240267-2(2), Puffin Books) Penguin Young Readers Group.

—Lily Quench & the Dragon of Ashby, 1. Prior, Natalie. 2004. (Lily Quench Ser.). (ENG.). 160p. (J). (gr. 3-6). 17.44 (978-0-14-240020-3(3), Puffin) Penguin Publishing Group.

—Lily Quench & the Hand of Manuelo. Prior, Natalie Jane. 2004. x, 166p. (Orig.). (J). pap. (978-0-7336-1654-9(2), Hodder Children's Books) Hachette Children's Group.

—The Lying Postman. Odgers, Sally & Odgers, Darrel. 2007. (Jack Russell: Dog Detective Ser.: 4). 96p. (J). pap. 4.99 (978-1-933605-31-9(6), 05319) Kane Miller.

—The Mare's Tale. Odgers, Darrel & Odgers, Sally. 2009. (Pet Vet Ser.: 2). 96p. (J). (gr. 2-6). pap. 4.99 (978-1-935279-02-0(5)) Kane Miller.

—The Mugged Pug. Odgers, Darrel & Odgers, Sally. 2007. 76p. (J). (978-0-439-88018-3(1)) Scholastic, Inc.

—The Mugged Pug. Odgers, Sally & Odgers, Darrel. 2007. (Jack Russell: Dog Detective Ser.: 3). 96p. (J). pap. 4.99 (978-1-933605-32-6(4), 05326) Kane Miller.

—The Phantom Mudder. Odgers, Sally & Odgers, Darrel. 2006. (Jack Russell: Dog Detective Ser.: 2). 96p. (J). (gr. 1-5). pap. 4.99 (978-1-933605-19-7(7)) Kane Miller.

—Pudding & Chips, 28 vols. Matthews, Penny. 2005. (ENG.). 40p. (J). (gr. k-3). (978-0-86315-496-6(4)) Floris Bks.

—The Pup's Tale: Pet Vet Book 6. Odgers, Darrel & Sally. 2015. 96p. (J). pap. 4.99 (978-1-61067-351-8(4)) Kane Miller.

—The Python Problem. Odgers, Darrel & Odgers, Sally. 2010. (Pet Vet Ser.: 4). 96p. (J). (gr. 2-4). pap. 4.99 (978-1-935279-16-7(5)) Kane Miller.

—The Sausage Situation. Odgers, Darrel & Odgers, Sally. 2007. (Jack Russell: Dog Detective Ser.: 6). 96p. (J). (gr. 1-6). pap. 4.99 (978-1-933605-54-8(5)) Kane Miller.

—Storm Rescue: Pup Patrol. Odgers, Sally & Darrel. 2018. 89p. (J). pap. 4.99 (978-1-61067-657-1(2)) Kane Miller.

Dawson, Jessica Paige. Walla on the Hiking Trail. Dawson, Jessica Paige. 2018. (ENG.). 62p. (J). (gr. 4-6). 19.99 (978-0-578-43348-6(6)); pap. 12.99 (978-0-578-42853-6(9)) Walla Bks.

Dawson, Lillian. Things Evie Eats. W, Suzie. 2016. (ENG.). 31p. (J). pap. (978-0-9574662-5-8(0)) Beresford Publishing Hse.

Dawson, Michelle. Fluke. Gibbes, Lesley. 2019. 32p. pap. 6.99 (978-1-921504-96-9(X), Working Title Pr.) HarperCollins Pubs. Australia AUS. Dist: HarperCollins Pubs.

Dawson, Sandy & McGee, E. Alan, photos by. The Springer Ghost Book: A Theatre Haunting in the Deep South. Pierce, Paul. 2003. 92p. 19.99 (978-0-9741819-0-5(0)) Pierce, Paul.

Dawson, Scott. The Attacks of September 11th, 2001. Tarshis, Lauren. 2012. (I Survived Ser.: 6). (ENG.). 112p. (J). (gr. 3-7). pap. 5.99 (978-0-545-20700-3(2), Scholastic Paperbacks) Scholastic, Inc.

—El Naufragio del Titanic, 1912. Tarshis, Lauren. 2019. (Sobreviví Ser.: 1). (SPA.). 112p. (J). (gr. 2-5). pap. 5.99 (978-1-338-35915-2(0), Scholastic en Espanol) Scholastic, Inc.

—I Survived Hurricane Katrina 2005. Tarshis, Lauren. 2011. (I Survived Ser.: 3). (ENG.). 112p. (J). (gr. 2-5). pap. 5.99 (978-0-545-20696-9(0), Scholastic Paperbacks) Scholastic, Inc.

—I Survived the Bombing of Pearl Harbor 1941. Tarshis, Lauren. 2011. (I Survived Ser.: 4). (ENG.). 112p. (J). (gr. 2-5). pap. 5.99 (978-0-545-20698-3(7), Scholastic Paperbacks) Scholastic, Inc.

—I Survived the Destruction of Pompeii, AD 79. Tarshis, Lauren. 2014. 95p. (J). (978-0-545-77568-7(X), Scholastic Pr.) Scholastic, Inc.

—I Survived the Japanese Tsunami 2011. Tarshis, Lauren. 2013. (I Survived Ser.: No. 8). 83p. (J). (978-0-545-62981-2(0)) Scholastic, Inc.

—I Survived the Joplin Tornado 2011. Tarshis, Lauren. 2015. (I Survived Ser.: 12). (ENG.). 112p. (J). (gr. 2-5). pap. 5.99 (978-0-545-65848-5(9), Scholastic Paperbacks) Scholastic, Inc.

—I Survived the San Francisco Earthquake 1906. Tarshis, Lauren. 2012. (I Survived Ser.: 5). (ENG.). 112p. (J). (gr. 2-5). pap. 5.99 (978-0-545-20699-0(5), Scholastic Paperbacks) Scholastic, Inc.

—I Survived the Shark Attacks of 1916. Tarshis, Lauren. 2010. (I Survived Ser.: 2). (ENG.). 112p. (J). (gr. 2-5). pap. 5.99 (978-0-545-20695-2(2), Scholastic Paperbacks) Scholastic, Inc.

—I Survived the Sinking of the Titanic 1912. Tarshis, Lauren. 2010. (I Survived Ser.: 1). (ENG.). 112p. (J). (gr. 2-5). 4.99 (978-0-545-20694-5(4), Scholastic Paperbacks) Scholastic, Inc.

—Sobreviví el Terremoto de San Francisco 1906. Tarshis, Lauren. 2019. (Sobreviví Ser.).Tr. of I Survived #5: I Survived the San Francisco Earthquake 1906. (SPA.). 112p. (J). (gr. 2-5). pap. 5.99 (978-1-338-60121-3(0), Scholastic en Espanol) Scholastic, Inc.

Dawson, Scott. Sobreviví - Los Ataques de Tiburones de 1916. Dawson, Scott. Tarshis, Lauren. 2018. (Sobreviví Ser.: 2). (SPA.). 112p. (J). (gr. 2-5). pap. 5.99 (978-1-338-33123-3(X), Scholastic en Espanol) Scholastic, Inc.

Dawson, Sheldon. Do unto Otters: And Other Bedtime Thymes, 1 vol. Anderson, G. 2015. (ENG.). 48p. (J). (gr. k-2). pap. 10.95 (978-1-894717-34-2(1), c6772e11-d22e-43f7-8441-84c7816d89d0) Pemmican Pubns., Inc. CAN. Dist: Firefly Bks., Ltd.

—Duck's Bay. Delaronde, Deborah L. 2004. 48p. (J). pap. (978-1-894717-24-3(4), Spotlight Poets) Pemmican Pubns., Inc.

—If I Was the Mayor. Howell, Lauren. 2005. 32p. (J). per. (978-0-9735798-1-9(1)) Three Bears Publishing.

—Thomas & the Métis Cart: Tummas Ek Ekwa Li Michif Sharey, 1 vol. Murray, Bonnie. Flamand, Rita, tr. 2015. (ENG.). 32p. (J). pap. 10.95 (978-1-894717-47-2(3), feda32f8-9f48-43bb-8642-7f4307f3c2a9) Pemmican Pubns., Inc. CAN. Dist: Firefly Bks., Ltd.

Dawson, Willow. Avis Dolphin, 1 vol. Wishinsky, Frieda. 2015. (ENG.). 128p. (J). (gr. 3-7). 16.95 *(978-1-55498-489-3(0))* Groundwood Bks. CAN. Dist: Publishers Group West (PGW).
—The Big Green Book of the Big Blue Sea. Becker, Helaine. 2012. (ENG.). 80p. (J). (gr. 3-7). 15.95 *(978-1-55453-746-4(0))*; pap. 9.95 *(978-1-55453-747-1(9))* Kids Can Pr., Ltd. CAN. Dist: Hachette Bk. Group.
—No Girls Allowed: Tales of Daring Women Dressed as Men for Love, Freedom & Adventure. Hughes, Susan. 2008. 80p. (J). (gr. 4-7). 16.95 *(978-1-55453-177-6(2))* Kids Can Pr., Ltd. CAN. Dist: Hachette Bk. Group.
—No Girls Allowed: Tales of Daring Women Dressed As Men for Love, Freedom & Adventure. Hughes, Susan. 2008. (ENG.). 80p. (J). (gr. 4-7). pap. 12.99 *(978-1-55453-178-3(0))* Kids Can Pr., Ltd. CAN. Dist: Hachette Bk. Group.
Dawson, Willow. Lila & Ecco's Do-It-Yourself Comics Club. Dawson, Willow. 2010. 112p. (J). (gr. 3-7). 16.95 *(978-1-55453-438-8(0))* Kids Can Pr., Ltd. CAN. Dist: Hachette Bk. Group.
Daxiong Staff. Star Wars Adventures: Boba Fett & the Ship of Fear. Barlow, Jeremy. 2013. (Star Wars Digests Ser.). (ENG.). 80p. (J). (gr. 3-8). lib. bdg. 29.93 *(978-1-61479-056-3(6))*, 13759, Graphic Novels) Spotlight.
Day, Alexandra. Edens Picture Book, No. 3. Edens, Cooper. Date not set. (J). 14.99 *(978-0-06-205153-0(9))* HarperCollins Pubs.
—The Teddy Bears' Picnic. Kennedy, Jimmy. 2015. (Classic Board Bks.). (ENG.). 34p. (J). (gr. -1-k). bds. 8.99 *(978-1-4814-2274-1(X))*, Little Simon) Little Simon.
Day, Alexandra. Carl & the Puppies. Day, Alexandra. 2011. (My Readers Ser.). (ENG.). 32p. (J). (gr. -1-1). pap. 4.99 *(978-0-312-62483-5(2))*, 900066471) Square Fish.
—Carl at the Dog Show, 1 vol. Day, Alexandra. 2012. (Carl Ser.). (ENG.). 40p. (J). (gr. -1-1). 16.99 *(978-0-374-31083-7(1))*, 900064340, Farrar, Straus & Giroux (BYR)) Farrar, Straus & Giroux.
—Carl's Halloween. Day, Alexandra. 2015. (Carl Ser.). (ENG.). 32p. (J). (gr. -1-2). 14.99 *(978-0-374-31082-0(3))*, 900064341, Farrar, Straus & Giroux (BYR)) Farrar, Straus & Giroux.
—Carl's Snowy Afternoon. Day, Alexandra. 2009. (Carl Ser.). (ENG.). 32p. (J). (gr. -1-1). 13.99 *(978-0-374-31086-8(6))*, 900042212, Farrar, Straus & Giroux (BYR)) Farrar, Straus & Giroux.
—Carl's Summer Vacation. Day, Alexandra. 2008. (Carl Ser.). (ENG.). 32p. (J). (gr. -1-1). 16.99 *(978-0-374-31085-1(8))*, 900042214, Farrar, Straus & Giroux (BYR)) Farrar, Straus & Giroux.
Day, Betsy. Animal Habitats! Learning about North American Animals & Plants Through Art, Science & Creative Play. Press, Judy. (ENG.). 128p. (J). (gr. 3-7). 2008. per. 12.95 *(978-0-8249-6756-7(9))*; 2005. 14.95 *(978-0-8249-6778-9(X))* Worthy Publishing. (Ideal Pubns.).
—My Happy Heart Books: A Touch-And-Feel Book Boxed Set, Vol. Osteen, Victoria. ed. 2009. (ENG.). 66p. (J). (gr. -1-k). 19.99 *(978-1-4169-5549-8(6))*, Little Simon Inspirations) Little Simon Inspirations.
Day, Bruce. Rodney Robbins & the Rainy-Day Pond. Stegall, Kim. 2010. 29p. (J). *(978-1-60682-058-2(3))* BJU Pr.
Day, Caroline, jt. illus. see Thompson, Josephine.
Day, Francis. The Luck of the Dudley Grahams (Illustrated Edition) Haines, Alice Calhoun. 2018. (ENG.). 108p. (J). pap. *(978-1-4068-1651-8(5))* Echo Library.
Day, J. David, photos by. Canyonlands National Park Favorite Jeep Roads & Hiking Trails. Day, J. David. 2004. (ENG., 296p. pap. 14.95 *(978-0-9660858-2-2(5))* Rincon Publishing Co.
Day, Jeff. What Is Funny? Boritzer, Etan. 2004. 40p. 14.95 *(978-0-9637597-8-8(7))*; 32p. pap. 6.95 *(978-0-9637597-9-5(5))* Lane, Veronica Bks.
Day, Kathleen. Ruby & the Magic Key. Thomson, Lu. Patrick, J. J., ed. 2017. (ENG.). (J). pap. *(978-1-9997854-5-1(2))* Cynefin Road.
Day, Larry. Beware! Raczka, Bob. 2019. 32p. (J). (gr. -1-2). lib. bdg. 15.99 *(978-1-58089-683-2(9))* Charlesbridge Publishing, Inc.
—Bim, Bam, Bop...and Oona. Martin, Jacqueline Briggs. 2019. (ENG.). 32p. (J). 16.95 *(978-1-5179-0395-4(5))* Univ. of Minnesota Pr.
—Civil War Battleship: The Monitor. Thompson, Gare. 2003. (Penguin Young Readers, Level 4 Ser.). 48p. (J). (gr. 3-4). mass mkt. 4.99 *(978-0-448-43245-8(5))*, Penguin Young Readers) Penguin Young Readers Group.
—Colonial Voices: Hear Them Speak: The Outbreak of the Boston Tea Party Told from Multiple Points-Of-View! Winters, Kay. 2015. 48p. (J). (gr. 4-7). 8.99 *(978-0-14-751162-1(3))*, Puffin Books) Penguin Young Readers Group.
—Found. Newman, Jeff. 2018. (ENG.). 48p. (J). (gr. -1-3). 18.99 *(978-1-5344-1006-0(6))*, Simon & Schuster Bks. For Young Readers) Simon & Schuster Bks. For Young Readers.
—George Did It. Jurmain, Suzanne Tripp. 2007. (ENG.). 40p. (J). (gr. k-4). pap. 6.99 *(978-0-14-240895-7(6))*, Puffin Books) Penguin Young Readers Group.
—George Did It. Jurmain, Suzanne Tripp. 2007. (gr. -1-3). 17.00 *(978-0-7569-8161-7(1))* Perfection Learning Corp.
—Let It Begin Here! Lexington & Concord: First Battles of the American Revolution. Fradin, Dennis Brindell. 2009. (ENG.). 40p. (J). (gr. 2-4). pap. 8.99 *(978-0-8027-9711-7(3))*, 900049550, Bloomsbury USA Childrens) Bloomsbury Publishing USA.
—Lion, Lion. Busch, Miriam. 2014. (ENG.). 32p. (J). (gr. -1-3). 17.99 *(978-0-06-227104-4(0))* HarperCollins Pubs.
—The Monitor: The Iron Warship That Changed the World. Thompson, Gare. 2003. (All Aboard Reading: Station Stop 3 Ser.). (ENG.). 48p. (J). (gr. 2-4). 16.19 *(978-0-448-43283-0(8))* Penguin Young Readers Group.
—My Fourth of July. Spinelli, Jerry. 2019. 40p. (J). (gr. -1-3). 18.99 *(978-0-8234-4288-1(8))*, Neal Porter Bks) Holiday Hse., Inc.
—Raisin, the Littlest Cow. Busch, Miriam. 2017. (ENG.). 40p. (J). (gr. -1-3). 17.99 *(978-0-06-242763-2(6))* HarperCollins Pubs.
—Voices from the Underground Railroad. Winters, Kay. 2018. 48p. (J). (gr. 2-4). 18.99 *(978-0-8037-4092-1(1))*, Dial Bks) Penguin Young Readers Group.
—Who Was Annie Oakley? Spinner, Stephanie. 2003. (Who Was...? Ser.). 109p. (gr. 4-7). 15.00 *(978-0-7569-1588-9(0))* Perfection Learning Corp.
—Worst of Friends: Thomas Jefferson, John Adams & the True Story of an American Feud. Jurmain, Suzanne Tripp. 2011. (ENG.). 32p. (J). (gr. 1-3). 17.99 *(978-0-525-47903-1(1))*, Dutton Books for Young Readers) Penguin Young Readers Group.
—Yankee Doodle & the Redcoats: Soldiering in the Revolutionary War. Beller, Susan Provost. 2003. (Single Titles Ser.). (ENG.). 96p. (gr. 5-8). lib. bdg. 26.60 *(978-0-7613-2612-0(X))*, Twenty-First Century Bks.) Lerner Publishing Group.
Day, Linda S. Milestones. Darby, Joel et al. Grant, Lisa, ed. l.t. ed. 2004. 32p. (J). 12.95 *(978-0-9759579-0-5(2))* Denver Broncos.
—The Pocket Fairies of Middleburg. Zern, Linda L. 2004. (J). per. 9.95 *(978-0-9753098-0-3(3))* LinWood Hse. Publishing.
Day, Linda S. Frogazoom! Day, Linda S. Butterworth, MyLinda. l.t. ed. 2003. 32p. (J). (gr. k-3). pap. 16.95 *(978-1-890905-03-3(8))*, Day to Day Bks.) Day to Day Enterprises.
—There's a Frog on a Log in the Bog. Day, Linda S. Day, Robert O. 2003. (J). (gr. 3-6). 212p. pap. 8.95 *(978-1-890905-50-7(X))*, Day to Day Bks.); (Just So Wild Ser.: Vol. 1). 14.95 *(978-1-890905-51-4(8))*, Eco Fiction Bks.) Day to Day Enterprises.
Day, Margery. The Canada Goose & You. Burrows, Jennifer S. 2009. 32p. (J). pap. 15.95 *(978-0-9791606-9-1(3))* E & E Publishing.
Day, Maurice. The Animal Etiquette Book of Rhymes. LeCron, Helen Cowles. 2014. (ENG.). 64p. (J). (gr. 1-5). pap. 4.99 *(978-0-486-78234-8(4))* Dover Pubns., Inc.
—Little Jack Rabbit's Favorite Bunny Tales. Cory, David. 2014. (ENG.). 320p. (J). (gr. 1-5). pap. 12.99 *(978-0-486-78556-1(4))* Dover Pubns., Inc.
Day, Michael. The Palm Tree & the Storm. Smith, Suzette. 2018. (ENG.). 32p. (J). *(978-1-5255-2643-5(X))*; pap. *(978-1-5255-2644-2(8))* FriesenPress.
Day, Pooh. Jetta Dog Goes to the Beach. Forbes, Kristi. 2018. (ENG.). 24p. (J). 22.95 *(978-1-4808-5038-5(1))*; pap. 12.45 *(978-1-4808-5037-8(3))* Archway Publishing.
Day, Rob. Voices in Poetry: Walt Whitman. Loewen, Nancy. 2015. (Voices in Poetry Ser.). (ENG.). 48p. (J). (gr. 5-8). pap. 12.00 *(978-1-62832-057-2(5))*, Creative Paperbacks) Creative Co., The.
—Walt Whitman. Loewen, Nancy. 2014. 47p. 35.65 *(978-1-60818-329-6(7))*, Creative Education) Creative Co., The.
Day, Sonny & Maroney, Biddy. Hello to You, Moon. Morgan, Sally. (ENG.). 24p. (J). (— 1). 2019. pap. 11.99 *(978-1-76050-307-9(X))*; 2018. 18.99 *(978-1-76012-546-2(6))* Little Hare Bks. AUS. Dist: Independent Pubs. Group.
Daykin, Louise. Goldilocks & the Three Bears. 2004. 32p. (J). *(978-1-84444-054-2(0))*; (SER & ENG.). *(978-1-84444-053-5(2))*; (ITA & ENG.). *(978-1-84444-050-4(8))*; (CZE & ENG.). *(978-1-84444-049-8(4))*; (TUR & ENG.). *(978-1-84444-047-4(8))*; (ENG & SPA.). *(978-1-84444-046-7(X))*; (SOM & ENG.). *(978-1-84444-045-0(1))*; *(978-1-84444-042-9(7))*; (GER & ENG.). *(978-1-84444-041-2(9))*; *(978-1-84444-039-9(7))*; (ALB & ENG.). *(978-1-84444-035-1(4))* Mantra Lingua.
—Goldilocks & the Three Bears. Clynes, Kate. 32p. (J). 2004. (ENG & PAN.). pap. *(978-1-84444-043-6(5))*; 2004. (ENG & POR.). pap. *(978-1-84444-044-3(3))*; 2004. (FRE & ENG.). pap. *(978-1-84444-040-5(0))*; 2004. (ENG & URD.). pap. *(978-1-84444-048-1(6))*; 2004. (ENG & POL.). pap. *(978-1-84444-051-1(6))*; 2004. (ENG & ARA.). pap. *(978-1-84444-036-8(2))*; 2004. (ENG & HIN.). pap. *(978-1-84444-059-7(1))*; 2003. (CHI & ENG.). pap. *(978-1-84444-038-2(9))*; 2003. (BEN & ENG.). pap. *(978-1-84444-037-5(0))*; 2003. (RUS & ENG.). pap. *(978-1-84444-052-8(4))* Mantra Lingua.
—Not Again, Red Riding Hood! Clynes, Kate. 2004. 32p. (J). (HIN & ENG.). *(978-1-85269-998-7(1))*; (ENG & GUJ.). pap. *(978-1-85269-993-2(0))*; (GER & ENG.). pap. *(978-1-85269-988-8(4))*; (FRE & ENG.). pap. *(978-1-85269-983-3(3))*; (ENG & PER.). pap. *(978-1-85269-978-9(7))*; (ENG & CZE.). pap. *(978-1-85269-973-4(6))*; (ENG & CHI.). pap. *(978-1-85269-968-0(X))*; (ENG & VIE.). pap. *(978-1-85269-959-8(0))*; (ENG & ARA.). pap. *(978-1-85269-958-1(2))*; (ENG & URD.). pap. *(978-1-85269-954-3(X))*; (ENG & ALB.). pap. *(978-1-85269-953-6(1))*; (ENG & TUR.). pap. *(978-1-85269-949-9(3))*; (ENG & TAM.). pap. *(978-1-85269-944-4(2))*; (ENG & SPA.). pap. *(978-1-85269-939-0(6))*; (ENG & SOM.). pap. *(978-1-85269-934-5(5))*; (ENG & SER.). pap. *(978-1-85269-929-1(9))*; (ENG & RUS.). pap. *(978-1-85269-924-6(8))*; (POR & ENG.). pap. *(978-1-85269-919-2(1))*; (ENG & POL.). pap. *(978-1-85269-914-7(0))*; (ENG & PAN.). pap. *(978-1-85269-909-3(4))*; (ENG & ITA.). pap. *(978-1-85269-904-8(3))* Mantra Lingua.
Daykin, Louise. Goldilocks & the Three Bears. Daykin, Louise, tr. 2004. 31p. (J). *(978-1-84444-057-3(5))* Mantra Lingua.
—Goldilocks & the Three Bears. Daykin, Louise, tr. Clynes, Kate. 2003. (VIE & ENG.). 32p. (J). pap. 12.95 *(978-1-84444-055-9(9))* Mantra Lingua GBR. Dist: Chinasprout, Inc.
Dayn, Penelope. Fat Rat, Fat Cat — -Because Cats & Rats Are Also People. Dyan, Penelope. 2008. 40p. pap. 11.95 *(978-1-935118-11-4(0))* Bellissima Publishing, LLC.
Dayton, Charles, photos by. Secrets of the Loon. Salas, Laura Purdie. 2020. (ENG., 32p. (J). 16.95 *(978-1-68134-158-3(1))* Minnesota Historical Society Pr.
Dayton, Melissa, jt. illus. see Aileen Co.
Dayton, Melissa, jt. illus. see Co, Aileen.
Day6. SCOOB! a Dog's Best Friend (Scooby-Doo) Huntley, Tex. 2020. (Step into Reading Ser.). (ENG.). 24p. (J). (gr. -1-2). pap. 5.99 *(978-0-593-17872-0(6))*; lib. bdg. 12.99 *(978-0-593-17873-7(4))* Random Hse. Children's Bks. (Random Hse. Bks. for Young Readers).
Daze, Stephanie. Mom Works. Beere, Lisa. 2019. (ENG.). 28p. (J). pap. 9.99 ***(978-1-68160-694-1(1))*** Crimson Cloak Publishing.
Dazo, Bong, et al. Star Wars Legends Epic Collection: the Old Republic Vol. 3. 2019. 432p. (J). (gr. 4-17). pap. 39.99 *(978-1-302-91646-6(7))* Marvel Worldwide, Inc.
dB, Silvio. Cleansing the World: Flood Myths Around the World. Hoena, Blake. 2017. (Universal Myths Ser.). (ENG.). 48p. (J). (gr. 3-9). lib. bdg. 31.32 *(978-1-5157-6627-8(6))*, 135198, Capstone Pr.) Capstone.
—Ninjas: Japan's Stealthy Secret Agents. Chandler, Matthew Allan. 2019. (Graphic History: Warriors Ser.). (ENG.). 32p. (J). (gr. 3-9). pap. 7.95 *(978-1-5435-5929-3(8))*, 139907); lib. bdg. 31.32 *(978-1-5435-5503-5(9))*, 139375) Capstone.
—Vikings: Scandinavia's Ferocious Sea Raiders. Yomtov, Nel. 2019. (Graphic History: Warriors Ser.). (ENG.). 32p. (J). (gr. 3-9). pap. 7.95 *(978-1-5435-5931-6(X))*, 139909); lib. bdg. 31.32 *(978-1-5435-5506-6(3))*, 139378) Capstone.
DBG. The Story of Spider-Man (Level 2) DBG. 2012. (World of Reading Ser.). (ENG.). 32p. (J). (gr. 1-3). pap. 3.99 *(978-1-4231-5409-9(6))* Marvel Worldwide, Inc.
—These Are the Avengers Level 1 Reader. DBG. 2012. (World of Reading Ser.). (ENG.). 32p. (J). (gr. -1-k). pap. 3.99 *(978-1-4231-5398-6(7))*, Marvel Pr.) Disney Publishing Worldwide.
—This Is Spider-Man Level 1 Reader. DBG. 2012. (World of Reading Ser.). (ENG.). 32p. (J). (gr. -1-k). pap. 3.99 *(978-1-4231-5408-2(8))*, Marvel Pr.) Disney Publishing Worldwide.
—World of Reading Avengers Boxed Set: Level 1. DBG. 2015. (World of Reading Ser.: 2). (ENG.). 192p. (J). (gr. 1-3). pap. 12.99 *(978-1-4847-0438-7(X))*, Marvel Pr.) Disney Publishing Worldwide.
—World of Reading This Is Captain America: Level 1. DBG. 2014. (World of Reading Ser.). (ENG.). 32p. (J). (gr. -1-k). pap. 3.99 *(978-1-4847-1267-2(6))*, Marvel Pr.) Disney Publishing Worldwide.
DC Comics. Super Friends: Flying High (DC Super Friends) Eliopulos, Nick. 2008. (Step into Reading Ser.). (ENG.). 32p. (J). (gr. -1-1). pap. 4.99 *(978-0-375-85208-4(5))*, Random Hse. Bks. for Young Readers) Random Hse. Children's Bks.
DC Comics Staff. Emperor of the Airwaves, 1 vol. Lemke, Donald B. et al. 2013. (Batman Ser.). (ENG.). 56p. (J). (gr. 3-6). pap. 4.95 *(978-1-4342-1364-8(1))*, Stone Arch Bks.) Capstone.
DC Comics Staff, jt. illus. see Cavallaro, Mike.
DC Comics Staff, jt. illus. see Levins, Tim.
DC Comics Staff, jt. illus. see Vecchio, Luciano.
de Almeida, Melissa, jt. illus. see Onque, Suliman.
De Amicis, Giulia. The Human Body at a Glance. 2019. (ENG.). 72p. (J). (gr. 3). 16.95 *(978-88-544-1528-7(6))* White Star ITA. Dist: Sterling Publishing Co., Inc.
—Ocean: Secrets of the Deep. Weiss, Sabrina. 2019. (ENG.). 72p. (J). (gr. 2-6). 19.99 *(978-1-9999680-7-6(7))* What on Earth Bks GBR. Dist: Ingram Publisher Services.
De Angel, M. Hello, Wilbur! Olson, Lute. 2007. 24p. (J). lib. bdg. 14.95 *(978-1-932888-40-9(3))* Mascot Bks., Inc.
De Angel, Miguel. Cort Spells It Out. Aryal, Aimee. 2006. (Cort the Sport Adventures Ser.). 24p. (J). (gr. -1-3). per. 5.95 *(978-1-932888-62-1(4))*, 91-101-01) Mascot Bks., Inc.
—Go, Pack, Go! Aryal, Aimee. 2007. 24p. (J). (gr. -1-3). 14.95 *(978-1-932888-94-2(2))* Mascot Bks., Inc.
—Hello, Cosmo! Edwards, Pat & Edwards, LaVell. 2006. 24p. (J). lib. bdg. 17.95 *(978-1-932888-45-4(4))* Mascot Bks., Inc.
—How 'Bout Them Cowboys! Aryal, Aimee. 2007. 24p. (J). 17.95 *(978-1-932888-90-4(X))* Mascot Bks., Inc.
—How 'Bout Them Dawgs! Dooley, Vince. 2006. 24p. (J). lib. bdg. 17.95 *(978-1-932888-46-1(2))* Mascot Bks., Inc.
—Let's Go, Chiefs! Aryal, Aimee. 2007. 24p. (J). lib. bdg. 14.95 *(978-1-932888-93-5(4))* Mascot Bks., Inc.
—Let's Go, Giants! Aryal, Aimee. 2007. 24p. (J). lib. bdg. 14.95 *(978-1-932888-92-8(6))* Mascot Bks., Inc.
—Let's Go, Panthers! Aryal, Aimee. 2007. 24p. (J). (gr. -1-3). 14.95 *(978-1-932888-97-3(7))* Mascot Bks., Inc.
—Let's Go, Patriots! 2007. 24p. (J). (gr. -1-3). 14.95 *(978-1-932888-98-0(5))* Mascot Bks., Inc.
—Let's Go, Seahawks! Aryal, Aimee. 2007. 24p. (J). lib. bdg. 14.95 *(978-1-932888-95-9(0))* Mascot Bks., Inc.
—Let's Go, Vikings! Aryal, Aimee. 2007. 24p. (J). 14.95 *(978-1-932888-99-7(3))* Mascot Bks., Inc.
—Roll Tide! Stabler, Ken. 2006. 24p. (J). lib. bdg. 17.95 *(978-1-932888-48-5(9))* Mascot Bks., Inc.
—War Eagle! Dye, Pat. 2006. 24p. (J). lib. bdg. 17.95 *(978-1-932888-47-8(0))* Mascot Bks., Inc.
—Yea, It's Hokie Game Day! Beamer, Cheryl & Beamer, Frank. 2006. 24p. (J). lib. bdg. 17.95 *(978-1-932888-44-7(6))* Mascot Bks., Inc.
De Angel, Miguel & Moore, D. Hello, Brutus! Aryal, Aimee. 2006. 24p. (J). lib. bdg. 14.95 *(978-1-932888-51-5(9))* Mascot Bks., Inc.
—Let's Go, White Sox! Aryal, Aimee. 2007. 24p. (J). lib. bdg. 14.95 *(978-1-932888-87-4(X))* Mascot Bks., Inc.
de Beer, Hans. Little Polar Bear. de Beer, Hans. 2011. (Little Polar Bear Ser.). 32p. (J). (gr. -1-3). pap. 7.95 *(978-0-7358-4052-2(0))* North-South Bks., Inc.
De Beer, Hans, pseud. El Pequeno Coco. Romanelli, Serena. Lamas, Blanca Rosa, tr. from GER. 2004.Tr. of Kleiner Dodo was Spielst du?. (SPA.). 24p. (J). (gr. k-4). reprint ed. 16.00 *(978-0-7567-7707-4(0))* DIANE Publishing Co.
De Bezenac, Agnes. Abraham - Bible People: The Short Story of Abraham. De Bezenac, Agnes. De Bezenac, Salem. 2018. (Bible People Ser.: Vol. 3). (ENG.). 26p. (J). (gr. k-2). 11.50 *(978-1-63474-231-3(1))*; pap. 7.50 *(978-1-63474-242-9(7))* iCharacter.org.
—Abraham Coloring Book: A Story Coloring Book. De Bezenac, Agnes. De Bezenac, Salem. 2017. (Story Coloring Bks.: Vol. 3). (ENG.). (J). (gr. k-1). pap. 4.95 *(978-1-63474-079-1(3))* iCharacter.org.
—Apple Shnapple: Encouraging Kids to Eat Healthy Snacks. De Bezenac, Agnes. De Bezenac, Salem. 2017. (Eat Right Ser.: Vol. 1). (ENG.). (J). (gr. k-2). 11.49 *(978-1-63474-057-9(2))*, Kidible) iCharacter.org.
—La Armadura de Dios: Efesios 6:10-18. De Bezenac, Agnes. De Bezenac, Salem. 2014. (Capitulos de la Biblia para Ninos Ser.: Vol. 8). (SPA.). (J). (gr. k-2). 11.49 *(978-1-62387-657-9(5))* iCharacter.org.
—The Armor of God: Ephesians 6:10-18. De Bezenac, Agnes. De Bezenac, Salem. 2014. (Bible Chapters for Kids Ser.: Vol. 8). (ENG.). (J). (gr. k-2). 11.49 *(978-1-62387-656-2(7))* iCharacter.org.
De Bezenac, Agnes. Be Happy: Baby Book. De Bezenac, Agnes. 2020. (ENG.). 34p. (J). pap. 7.00 ***(978-1-63474-348-8(2))*** iCharacter.org.
De Bezenac, Agnes. Beans Bummer: Have You Tried Beans This Way? De Bezenac, Agnes. De Bezenac, Salem. 2017. (Eat Right Ser.: Vol. 5). (ENG.). (J). (gr. k-2). 11.49 *(978-1-63474-053-1(X))*, Kidible) iCharacter.org.
—The Bear Family Diorama: Paper Toys Mini World. De Bezenac, Agnes. 2017. (Tiny Thoughts Paper Toys Ser.: Vol. 1). (ENG.). (J). (gr. k-2). pap. 7.95 *(978-1-62387-732-3(6))* iCharacter.org.
De Bezenac, Agnes. Beauty Tips: Coloring Journal. De Bezenac, Agnes. De Bezenac, Salem. 2019. (ENG.). 198p. (J). (gr. 5-6). pap. 9.00 ***(978-1-63474-297-9(4))***; (Pretty Joys Ser.: Vol. 8). 16.00 ***(978-1-63474-298-6(2))*** iCharacter.org. (Kidible).
—The Bible & My Crayons: Coloring & Activity Book. De Bezenac, Agnes. 2015. (Big Bible, Little Me Ser.). (ENG.). 250p. (J). (gr. k-2). pap. 12.00 ***(978-1-63474-329-7(6))*** iCharacter.org.
—The Bible & My Crayons: Coloring & Activity Book. De Bezenac, Agnes. De Bezenac, Salem. 2015. (Big Bible, Little Me Ser.). (ENG.). 250p. (J). (gr. k-2). 15.00 ***(978-1-63474-322-8(9))*** iCharacter.org.
De Bezenac, Agnes. Bible Thoughts on Christmas Presents: Why Do We Give Presents? De Bezenac, Agnes. De Bezenac, Salem. 2013. (Bible Thoughts Ser.). (ENG.). (J). (gr. k-1). 11.49 *(978-1-62387-663-0(X))* iCharacter.org.
—A Birthday of Meaningful Fun: Games & Activities. De Bezenac, Agnes. 2017. (ENG.). (J). (gr. k-3). pap. 9.95 *(978-1-63474-075-3(0))*, Kidible) iCharacter.org.
—Cheerfulness - Games & Activities: Games & Activities to Help Build Moral Character. De Bezenac, Agnes. De Bezenac, Salem. 2017. (Cut Out & Play Ser.: Vol. 9). (ENG.). (J). (gr. k-2). pap. 6.45 *(978-1-62387-627-2(3))*, Kidible) iCharacter.org.
De Bezenac, Agnes. Children of the Bible: Learning Values of Character from Kids in Bible Times. De Bezenac, Agnes. De Bezenac, Salem. (ENG.). (J). (gr. k-2). 2019. 62p. 15.00 ***(978-1-63474-323-5(7))***; 2014. 12.00 *(978-1-62387-670-8(2))* iCharacter.org.
De Bezenac, Agnes. Courage - Games & Activities: Games & Activities to Help Build Moral Character. De Bezenac, Agnes. De Bezenac, Salem. 2017. (Cut Out & Play Ser.: Vol. 14). (ENG.). (J). (gr. k-2). pap. 6.45 *(978-1-62387-631-9(1))*, Kidible) iCharacter.org.
—Daniel Coloring Book: A Story Coloring Book. De Bezenac, Agnes. De Bezenac, Salem. 2017. (Story Coloring Bks.: Vol. 4). (ENG.). (J). (gr. k-2). pap. 4.95 *(978-1-63474-080-7(7))* iCharacter.org.
De Bezenac, Agnes. David - Bible People: The Story of David. De Bezenac, Agnes. De Bezenac, Salem. 2019. (Bible People Ser.: Vol. 5). (ENG.). 26p. (J). (gr. k-2). 12.00 ***(978-1-63474-305-1(9))***; pap. 7.00 ***(978-1-63474-304-4(0))*** iCharacter.org.
—Dieu Est Bon: Le Psaume 34. De Bezenac, Agnes. De Bezenac, Salem. 2019. (Chapitres de la Bible Pour Enfants Ser.: Vol. 5). (FRE.). 34p. (J). (gr. k-1). pap. 6.00 ***(978-1-63474-334-1(2))*** iCharacter.org.
De Bezenac, Agnes. Eat Right: Take a Bite. De Bezenac, Agnes. De Bezenac, Salem. 2017. (Eat Right Ser.). (ENG.). (J). (gr. k-2). 18.95 *(978-1-63474-073-9(4))*; pap. 11.95 *(978-1-63474-074-6(2))* iCharacter.org. (Kidible).
—Les Enfants de la Bible: Les Enfants de l'Époque Biblique Parlent Aux Enfants D'Aujourd'hui. De Bezenac, Agnes. De Bezenac, Salem. 2nd ed. 2015. (FRE.). 62p. (J). (gr. k-2). pap. 8.80 *(978-1-63474-279-5(6))* iCharacter.org.
—Esther - Bible People: The Story of Esther. De Bezenac, Agnes. De Bezenac, Salem. 2018. (Bible People Ser.: Vol. 6). (ENG.). 26p. (J). (gr. k-2). 11.50 *(978-1-63474-229-0(X))*; pap. 6.00 *(978-1-63474-239-9(7))* iCharacter.org.
—Family Fun Activity Ideas: Activity Ideas with Meaning. De Bezenac, Agnes. De Bezenac, Salem. 2018. (ENG.). 100p. (J). (gr. 2-6). pap. 5.00 *(978-1-62387-731-6(8))*; pap. 8.00 *(978-1-63474-234-4(6))* iCharacter.org. (Kidible).
—Find Solutions - Games & Activities: Games & Activities to Help Build Moral Character. De Bezenac, Agnes. De Bezenac, Salem. 2017. (Cut Out & Play Ser.: Vol. 10). (ENG.). (J). (gr. k-2). pap. 6.45 *(978-1-62387-628-9(1))*, Kidible) iCharacter.org.
—Fun Bible Lessons on Diligence: Values That Stick. De Bezenac, Agnes. De Bezenac, Salem. 2017. (Biblegum Ser.: Vol. 1). (ENG.). (J). (gr. k-2). pap. 4.50 *(978-1-62387-592-3(7))* iCharacter.org.
—Fun Bible Lessons on Gratitude: Values That Stick. De Bezenac, Agnes. De Bezenac, Salem. 2017. (Biblegum Ser.: Vol. 2). (ENG.). (J). (gr. k-2). pap. 4.50 *(978-1-62387-593-0(5))* iCharacter.org.
—Fun Bible Lessons on Self-Control: Values That Stick. De Bezenac, Agnes. De Bezenac, Salem. 2017. (Biblegum Ser.: Vol. 3). (ENG.). (J). (gr. k-2). pap. 4.50 *(978-1-62387-594-7(3))* iCharacter.org.

D

—God Talks with Me about Friendship. De Bezenac, Agnes. De Bezenac, Salem. 2017. (God Talks with Me Ser.: Vol. 3). (ENG.). (J). (gr. k-1). 11.49 *(978-1-63474-012-8(2))* iCharacter.org.

—God Talks with Me about Overcoming Fears. De Bezenac, Agnes. De Bezenac, Salem. 2017. (God Talks with Me Ser.). (ENG.). (J). (gr. k-2). pap. 6.45 *(978-1-63474-032-6(7))*; 11.49 *(978-1-63474-009-8(2))* iCharacter.org.

—God Talks with Me about Thankfulness. De Bezenac, Agnes. De Bezenac, Salem. 2017. (God Talks with Me Ser.: Vol. 4). (ENG.). (J). (gr. k-1). 11.49 *(978-1-63474-013-5(0))* iCharacter.org.

—Hanging Out with Jesus: Life Lessons with Jesus & His Childhood Friends. De Bezenac, Agnes. De Bezenac, Salem. 2017. (ENG.). (J). (gr. k-1). 15.45 *(978-1-63474-059-3(9))*; pap. 10.95 *(978-1-63474-070-8(X))* iCharacter.org.

De Bezenac, Agnes. Happy Birthday to You. De Bezenac, Agnes. l.t. ed. 2020. (ENG.). 42p. (J). pap. 6.95 ***(978-1-63474-357-0(1))*** iCharacter.org.

—Heroes of Value - Activity Book. De Bezenac, Agnes. De Bezenac, Salem. 2019. (ENG.). 90p. (J). (gr. 1-4). 13.00 ***(978-1-63474-303-7(2))***; pap. 8.00 ***(978-1-63474-302-0(4))*** iCharacter.org.

—High Fives Coloring Craze: Journaling Collection. De Bezenac, Agnes. 2018. (Pretty Joys Ser.: Vol. 6). (ENG.). 138p. (J). (gr. 4-6). 13.00 ***(978-1-63474-324-2(5))*** iCharacter.org.

De Bezenac, Agnes. Honesty - Games & Activities: Games & Activities to Help Build Moral Character. De Bezenac, Agnes. De Bezenac, Salem. 2017. (Cut Out & Play Ser.: Vol. 13). (ENG.). (J). (gr. k-2). pap. 6.45 *(978-1-62387-630-2(3)*, Kidible) iCharacter.org.

—I Am Honest: Cut & Glue Activity Book. De Bezenac, Agnes. De Bezenac, Salem. 2018. (Tiny Thoughts Cut & Glue Ser.: Vol. 13). (ENG.). 32p. (J). (gr. k-2). pap. 4.90 *(978-1-63474-116-3(1)*, Kidible) iCharacter.org.

—I Have Courage: Cut & Glue Activity Book. De Bezenac, Agnes. De Bezenac, Salem. 2018. (Tiny Thoughts Cut & Glue Ser.: Vol. 14). (ENG.). 32p. (J). (gr. k-2). pap. 4.50 *(978-1-63474-115-6(3)*, Kidible) iCharacter.org.

—I Show Respect: Cut & Glue Activity Book. De Bezenac, Agnes. De Bezenac, Salem. 2018. (Tiny Thoughts Cut & Glue Ser.: Vol. 5). (ENG.). 32p. (J). (gr. k-2). pap. 4.50 *(978-1-63474-117-0(X)*, Kidible) iCharacter.org.

—Irish Blessings for Girls: Coloring Book. De Bezenac, Agnes. De Bezenac, Salem. 2018. (ENG.). 50p. (J). (gr. 4-6). pap. 5.00 *(978-1-63474-237-5(0)*, Kidible) iCharacter.org.

—It Grows: But Can You Grow a Pizza? De Bezenac, Agnes. De Bezenac, Salem. 2017. (Eat Right Ser.: Vol. 2). (ENG.). (J). (gr. k-2). 11.49 *(978-1-63474-056-2(4)*, Kidible) iCharacter.org.

De Bezenac, Agnes. The Journal of Me: A Safekeep of Growth & Values. De Bezenac, Agnes. De Bezenac, Salem. 2019. (ENG.). 98p. (J). 28.50 ***(978-1-63474-300-6(8))***; (gr. 1-4). pap. 17.00 ***(978-1-63474-290-0(7))*** iCharacter.org. (Kidible).

—JOY Prayer Journal - Coloring Craze: Journaling Collection. De Bezenac, Agnes. 2018. (Pretty Joys Ser.: Vol. 5). (ENG.). 110p. (J). (gr. 4-6). 12.00 ***(978-1-63474-326-6(1))*** iCharacter.org.

De Bezenac, Agnes. Kindness - Games & Activities: Games & Activities to Help Build Moral Character. De Bezenac, Agnes. De Bezenac, Salem. 2017. (Cut Out & Play Ser.: Vol. 12). (ENG.). (J). (gr. k-2). pap. 7.99 *(978-1-63474-076-0(9)*, Kidible) iCharacter.org.

De Bezenac, Agnes. Let's Color Values: Ages 3-4. De Bezenac, Agnes. 2019. (Fun with Values Ser.: Vol. 1). (ENG.). 82p. (J). (gr. k-1). 12.00 ***(978-1-63474-314-3(8)***, Kidible) iCharacter.org.

—Let's Color Values: Ages 4-5. De Bezenac, Agnes. 2019. (Fun with Values Ser.: Vol. 2). (ENG.). 82p. (J). (gr. k-1). 12.00 ***(978-1-63474-315-0(6)***, Kidible) iCharacter.org.

—Let's Color Values: Ages 5-6. De Bezenac, Agnes. 2019. (Fun with Values Ser.: Vol. 3). (ENG.). 82p. (J). (gr. k-2). 12.00 ***(978-1-63474-316-7(4)***, Kidible) iCharacter.org.

De Bezenac, Agnes. Mary Coloring Book: A Story Coloring Book. De Bezenac, Agnes. 2017. (ENG.). (J). (gr. k-1). pap. 5.45 *(978-1-62387-589-3(7))* iCharacter.org.

—Mini Steps to Greatness: Growing up & Making Smart Choices. De Bezenac, Agnes. De Bezenac, Salem. (ENG.). (J). (gr. k-1). 2017. pap. 8.25 *(978-1-63474-019-7(X))*; 2016. 14.45 *(978-1-63474-033-3(5))* iCharacter.org. (Kidible).

—Mini Steps to Happiness: Growing up with the Fruit of the Spirit. De Bezenac, Agnes. De Bezenac, Salem. (ENG.). (J). (gr. k-1). 2017. pap. 8.45 *(978-1-63474-023-4(8))*; 2016. pap. 15.95 *(978-1-63474-034-0(3))* iCharacter.org.

De Bezenac, Agnes. Mon Journal à Moi. De Bezenac, Agnes. De Bezenac, Salem. 2020. (FRE.). 98p. (J). 18.00 ***(978-1-63474-374-7(1))*** iCharacter.org.

—Mon Workbook des Valeurs Avec la Bible. De Bezenac, Agnes. 2020. (FRE.). 82p. (J). pap. 7.50 ***(978-1-63474-351-8(2))*** iCharacter.org.

—My Bible Values Coloring Book. De Bezenac, Agnes. 2019. (ENG.). 58p. (J). (gr. 1-2). 12.00 ***(978-1-63474-308-2(3))***; pap. 7.00 ***(978-1-63474-307-5(5))*** iCharacter.org.

De Bezenac, Agnes. My Friends Journal Coloring Craze: Journaling Collection. De Bezenac, Agnes. De Bezenac, Salem. 2018. (Pretty Joys Ser.: Vol. 7). (ENG.). 54p. (J). (gr. 4-6). pap. 7.00 *(978-1-63474-235-1(4))* iCharacter.org.

—My Great Day: A Day That Rhymes. De Bezenac, Agnes. De Bezenac, Salem. 2017. (ENG.). (J). (gr. k). 14.45 *(978-1-63474-068-5(8))*; pap. 7.99 *(978-1-62387-613-5(3))* iCharacter.org. (Kidible).

—My Great Day with God: Rhymes That Teach. De Bezenac, Agnes. De Bezenac, Salem. (ENG.). (J). (gr. k-1). 2017. pap. 7.45 *(978-1-62387-616-6(8))*; 2016. 11.45 *(978-1-62387-660-9(5))* iCharacter.org.

—My Little Prayers for All Occasions: Please & Thank You, God! De Bezenac, Agnes. De Bezenac, Salem. 2017. (ENG.). (J). (gr. k-1). 16.95 *(978-1-63474-060-9(2))*; pap. 8.99 *(978-1-63474-069-2(6))* iCharacter.org.

De Bezenac, Agnes. My Story Journal: A Personal Time Capsule with Stories & Bible Verses. De Bezenac, Agnes. De Bezenac, Salem. 2019. (ENG.). 98p. (J). pap. 18.00 ***(978-1-63474-291-7(5))***; (gr. 1-4). 19.00 ***(978-1-63474-301-3(6))*** iCharacter.org.

—My Word Time Journal - Coloring Craze: Journaling Collection. De Bezenac, Agnes. 2018. (Pretty Joys Ser.: Vol. 3). (ENG.). 220p. (J). (gr. 4-6). 14.00 ***(978-1-63474-325-9(3))*** iCharacter.org.

De Bezenac, Agnes. New Testament Coloring & Activity Book: Big Bible, Little Me. De Bezenac, Agnes. De Bezenac, Salem. 2015. (Big Bible, Little Me Ser.). (ENG.). (J). (gr. k-2). pap. 6.60 *(978-1-62387-728-6(8))* iCharacter.org.

—No to Anger - Games & Activities: Games & Activities to Help Build Moral Character. De Bezenac, Agnes. De Bezenac, Salem. 2017. (Cut Out & Play Ser.: Vol. 2). (ENG.). (J). (gr. k-2). pap. 6.45 *(978-1-62387-620-3(6)*, Kidible) iCharacter.org.

—Noah - Bible People: The Story of Noah. De Bezenac, Agnes. De Bezenac, Salem. 2018. (Bible People Ser.: Vol. 1). (ENG.). 26p. (J). (gr. k-2). 11.50 *(978-1-63474-186-6(2))*; pap. 5.00 *(978-1-63474-226-9(5))* iCharacter.org.

—Noah Coloring Book: A Story Coloring Book. De Bezenac, Agnes. De Bezenac, Salem. 2017. (ENG.). (J). (gr. k-1). pap. 5.25 *(978-1-62387-588-6(9))* iCharacter.org.

—Nuevo Testamento - Cuaderno para Colorear y de Actividades (Bilingue) New Testament Coloring & Activity Book (Bilingual) De Bezenac, Agnes. De Bezenac, Salem. 2015. (SPA.). (J). (gr. k-2). pap. 6.95 *(978-1-62387-591-6(9))* iCharacter.org.

—Obedience - Games & Activities: Games & Activities to Help Build Moral Character. De Bezenac, Agnes. De Bezenac, Salem. 2017. (Cut Out & Play Ser.: Vol. 1). (ENG.). (J). (gr. k-2). pap. 6.45 *(978-1-62387-619-7(2)*, Kidible) iCharacter.org.

—Patience - Games & Activities: Games & Activities to Help Build Moral Character. De Bezenac, Agnes. De Bezenac, Salem. 2017. (Cut Out & Play Ser.: Vol. 11). (ENG.). (J). (gr. k-2). pap. 6.45 *(978-1-62387-629-6(X)*, Kidible) iCharacter.org.

—Perseverance - Games & Activities: Games & Activities to Help Build Moral Character. De Bezenac, Agnes. De Bezenac, Salem. 2017. (Cut Out & Play Ser.: Vol. 3). (ENG.). (J). (gr. k-2). pap. 6.45 *(978-1-62387-621-0(4)*, Kidible) iCharacter.org.

—Princess Joline: Life Lessons & Fun with Princes Joline. De Bezenac, Agnes. De Bezenac, Salem. (ENG.). (J). (gr. k-2). 2017. pap. 6.95 *(978-1-62387-704-0(0))*; 2016. 14.95 *(978-1-62387-659-3(1))* iCharacter.org.

—Respect - Games & Activities: Games & Activities to Help Build Moral Character. De Bezenac, Agnes. De Bezenac, Salem. 2017. (Cut Out & Play Ser.: Vol. 5). (ENG.). (J). (gr. k-2). pap. 6.45 *(978-1-62387-623-4(0)*, Kidible) iCharacter.org.

—Responsibility - Games & Activities: Games & Activities to Help Build Moral Character. De Bezenac, Agnes. De Bezenac, Salem. 2017. (Cut Out & Play Ser.: Vol. 6). (ENG.). (J). (gr. k-2). pap. 6.45 *(978-1-62387-624-1(9)*, Kidible) iCharacter.org.

—Safe with God: Psalm 91. De Bezenac, Agnes. De Bezenac, Salem. 2017. (Bible Chapters for Kids Ser.: Vol. 7). (ENG.). (J). (gr. k-1). 11.49 *(978-1-62387-057-7(7))* iCharacter.org.

—Sharing - Games & Activities: Games & Activities to Help Build Moral Character. De Bezenac, Agnes. De Bezenac, Salem. 2017. (Cut Out & Play Ser.: Vol. 16). (ENG.). (J). (gr. k-2). pap. 6.99 *(978-1-62387-633-3(8)*, Kidible) iCharacter.org.

—Shyness - Games & Activities: Games & Activities to Help Build Moral Character. De Bezenac, Agnes. De Bezenac, Salem. 2017. (Cut Out & Play Ser.: Vol. 7). (ENG.). (J). (gr. k-2). pap. 6.45 *(978-1-62387-625-8(7))* iCharacter.org.

—Smile for Soup: Veggies Hidden Away. De Bezenac, Agnes. De Bezenac, Salem. 2017. (Eat Right Ser.: Vol. 4). (ENG.). (J). (gr. k-2). 11.49 *(978-1-63474-054-8(8)*, Kidible) iCharacter.org.

—Teamwork - Games & Activities: Games & Activities to Help Build Moral Character. De Bezenac, Agnes. De Bezenac, Salem. 2017. (Cut Out & Play Ser.: Vol. 15). (ENG.). (J). (gr. k-2). pap. 6.99 *(978-1-62387-632-6(X)*, Kidible) iCharacter.org.

—Thankfulness - Games & Activities: Games & Activities to Help Build Moral Character. De Bezenac, Agnes. De Bezenac, Salem. 2017. (Cut Out & Play Ser.: Vol. 8). (ENG.). (J). (gr. k-2). pap. 6.45 *(978-1-62387-626-5(5)*, Kidible) iCharacter.org.

—Tiny Thoughts on Anger: How to Handle Anger. De Bezenac, Agnes. De Bezenac, Salem. 2013. (Tiny Thoughts Ser.: Vol. 2). (ENG.). (J). (gr. k-1). 11.49 *(978-1-63474-037-1(8)*, Kidible) iCharacter.org.

—Tiny Thoughts on Cheerfulness: It's Better with a Smile! De Bezenac, Agnes. De Bezenac, Salem. 2014. (Tiny Thoughts Ser.: Vol. 9). (ENG.). (J). (gr. k-1). 11.49 *(978-1-63474-044-9(0)*, Kidible) iCharacter.org.

—Tiny Thoughts on Courage: Try Something New! De Bezenac, Agnes. De Bezenac, Salem. 2014. (Tiny Thoughts Ser.: Vol. 14). (ENG.). (J). (gr. k-1). 11.49 *(978-1-63474-050-0(5)*, Kidible) iCharacter.org.

—Tiny Thoughts on Finding Solutions: We Can Work This Out! De Bezenac, Agnes. De Bezenac, Salem. 2014. (Tiny Thoughts Ser.: Vol. 10). (ENG.). (J). (gr. k-1). 11.49 *(978-1-63474-045-6(9)*, Kidible) iCharacter.org.

—Tiny Thoughts on Honesty: How I Feel When I Steal. De Bezenac, Agnes. De Bezenac, Salem. (Tiny Thoughts Ser.: Vol. 13). (ENG.). (J). (gr. k-1). 2017. pap. 6.45 *(978-1-63474-071-5(8))*; 2014. 11.49 *(978-1-63474-049-4(1))* iCharacter.org. (Kidible).

—Tiny Thoughts on Kindness: Thinking of Others. De Bezenac, Agnes. De Bezenac, Salem. 2015. (Tiny Thoughts Ser.: Vol. 12). (ENG.). (J). (gr. k-1). 11.49 *(978-1-63474-048-7(3)*, Kidible) iCharacter.org.

—Tiny Thoughts on Patience: It's Wise to Wait! De Bezenac, Agnes. De Bezenac, Salem. 2015. (Tiny Thoughts Ser.: Vol. 11). (ENG.). (J). (gr. k-1). 11.49 *(978-1-63474-046-3(7)*, Kidible) iCharacter.org.

—Tiny Thoughts on Perseverance: Don't Give Up! De Bezenac, Agnes. De Bezenac, Salem. 2013. (Tiny Thoughts Ser.: Vol. 3). (ENG.). (J). (gr. k-1). 11.49 *(978-1-63474-038-8(6)*, Kidible) iCharacter.org.

—Tiny Thoughts on Responsibility: Helping Out at Home. De Bezenac, Agnes. De Bezenac, Salem. 2014. (Tiny Thoughts Ser.: Vol. 6). (ENG.). (J). (gr. k-1). 11.49 *(978-1-63474-041-8(6)*, Kidible) iCharacter.org.

—Tiny Thoughts on Sharing: The Joys of Being Unselfishness. De Bezenac, Agnes. De Bezenac, Salem. 2017. (Tiny Thoughts Ser.). (ENG.). (J). (gr. k-1). 11.49 *(978-1-63474-062-3(9))*; pap. 6.45 *(978-1-63474-072-2(6))* iCharacter.org. (Kidible).

—Tiny Thoughts on Shyness: Greeting Others Cheerfully. De Bezenac, Agnes. De Bezenac, Salem. 2014. (Tiny Thoughts Ser.: Vol. 7). (ENG.). (J). (gr. k-1). 11.49 *(978-1-63474-042-5(4)*, Kidible) iCharacter.org.

—Tiny Thoughts on Teamwork: As a Team It Works Better! De Bezenac, Agnes. De Bezenac, Salem. 2014. (Tiny Thoughts Ser.: Vol. 15). (ENG.). (J). (gr. k-1). 11.49 *(978-1-63474-051-7(3)*, Kidible) iCharacter.org.

—Tiny Thoughts on Thankfulness: Let's Be Content! De Bezenac, Agnes. De Bezenac, Salem. 2014. (Tiny Thoughts Ser.: Vol. 8). (ENG.). (J). (gr. k-1). 11.49 *(978-1-63474-043-2(2)*, Kidible) iCharacter.org.

—Tiny Thoughts on Unselfishness: The Joys of Sharing. De Bezenac, Agnes. De Bezenac, Salem. 2014. (Tiny Thoughts Ser.: Vol. 16). (ENG.). (J). (gr. k-1). 11.49 *(978-1-63474-052-4(1)*, Kidible) iCharacter.org.

De Bezenac, Agnes. What in My Head Is Going On? Stages of Grief & Loss, for Children. De Bezenac, Agnes. 2020. (ENG.). 28p. (J). pap. 6.00 ***(978-1-63474-362-4(8)***, Kidible) iCharacter.org.

De Bezenac, Agnes. Where Is Grandpa? My Visit to the Cemetery. De Bezenac, Agnes. De Bezenac, Salem. (ENG.). (J). (gr. k-2). 2017. pap. 6.45 *(978-1-63474-018-0(1))*; 2015. 11.75 *(978-1-62387-669-2(9))* iCharacter.org.

De Bezenac, Agnes. Wisdom for Little Brains: With a Healthy Dose of Coloring. De Bezenac, Agnes. 2019. (ENG.). 104p. (J). (gr. k-2). pap. 6.00 ***(978-1-63474-309-9(1))*** iCharacter.org.

De Bezenac, Agnes. Wise Words: Taken from the Book of Proverbs in the Bible. De Bezenac, Agnes. De Bezenac, Salem. 2014. (Bible Chapters for Today Ser.: Vol. 9). (ENG.). (J). pap. 9.95 *(978-1-62387-685-2(0))* iCharacter.org.

De Bezenac, Agnes. You Are Beautiful: A Coloring Gift Book. De Bezenac, Agnes. De Bezenac, Salem. 2019. (Pretty Joys Ser.: Vol. 9). (ENG.). 214p. (J). (gr. 4-6). 14.00 ***(978-1-63474-327-3(X))***; pap. 9.00 ***(978-1-63474-328-0(8))*** iCharacter.org. (Kidible).

De Bezenac, Agnes. 14 Adventures with Chris: 2 Minute Stories. De Bezenac, Agnes. De Bezenac, Salem. 2018. (ENG.). 34p. (J). (gr. k-2). 18.50 *(978-1-63474-244-3(3))*; pap. 8.90 *(978-1-63474-233-7(8))* iCharacter.org.

—14 Jesus Tales: Fictional Stories of Jesus As a Little Boy. De Bezenac, Agnes. De Bezenac, Salem. 2017. (ENG.). (J). (gr. k-2). 11.49 *(978-1-63474-058-6(0))*; pap. 6.45 *(978-1-62387-729-3(6))* iCharacter.org.

De Board, Suzanne C. Clarence Catches a Cold. De Board, Suzanne C. 2019. (ENG.). 32p. (J). pap. 10.99 ***(978-0-9989905-4-5(X))*** Pen Pearls.

de Boer, Ester. Raymund & the Fear Monster. Higginson, Megan. 2019. (Raymund & the Fear Ser.). (ENG.). 52p. (J). (gr. k-6). pap. ***(978-0-6483381-1-6(8))*** Blue Brumby Bks.

De Boer, Michel. Bobby Boast a Lot. Howat, Irene. 2005. (Little Lots Ser.). (ENG.). 16p. (J). pap. 4.99 *(978-1-85792-978-2(0)*, 5c7a4f2f-d048-416d-8721-6f8787e402c2) Christian Focus Pubns. GBR. Dist: Baker & Taylor Publisher Services (BTPS).

—Granny Grump a Lot. Howat, Irene. 2005. (Little Lots Ser.). (ENG.). 16p. (J). pap. 4.99 *(978-1-85792-980-5(2)*, 5919b601-88fa-4172-9b42-454325030327) Christian Focus Pubns. GBR. Dist: Baker & Taylor Publisher Services (BTPS).

—Harry Help a Lot. Howat, Irene. 2005. (Little Lots Ser.). (ENG.). 16p. (J). pap. 4.99 *(978-1-85792-976-8(4)*, fcec1821-67e7-4b7c-9fd1-fcc4d9f22276) Christian Focus Pubns. GBR. Dist: Baker & Taylor Publisher Services (BTPS).

—Lorna Look a Lot. Howat, Irene. 2005. (Little Lots Ser.). (ENG.). 16p. (J). pap. 4.99 *(978-1-85792-979-9(9)*, 37c2f301-25b2-4f4a-8002-0055c03e6c6b) Christian Focus Pubns. GBR. Dist: Baker & Taylor Publisher Services (BTPS).

—Lucy Lie a Lot. Howat, Irene. 2005. (Little Lots Ser.). (ENG.). 16p. (J). pap. 4.99 *(978-1-85792-975-1(6)*, eb22f140-5286-4d7c-80c4-f280d475680f) Christian Focus Pubns. GBR. Dist: Baker & Taylor Publisher Services (BTPS).

—William Work a Lot. Howat, Irene. 2005. (Little Lots Ser.). (ENG.). 16p. (J). pap. 4.99 *(978-1-85792-977-5(2)*, 8f1f0fd9-c9ad-4f16-b958-c85726936a5c) Christian Focus Pubns. GBR. Dist: Baker & Taylor Publisher Services (BTPS).

de Brun, Brendan Joseph. The Talking Llama: la Llama Que Habla. de Brun, Kieran Christopher. 2005. (J). pap. 16.00 *(978-0-8059-6910-8(1))* Dorrance Publishing Co., Inc.

De Brunhoff, Jean. Babar & Zephir. De Brunhoff, Jean. 2005. 38p. (J). (gr. k-4). reprint ed. 16.00 *(978-0-7567-8935-0(4))* DIANE Publishing Co.

de Bruyn, Sassafras. I Give You My Heart. van Hest, Pimm. 2017. (ENG.). 56p. (J). (gr. 1-1). 32.95 *(978-1-60537-356-0(7))* Clavis Publishing.

De Castro, Ines E. The Teddy Bear Faeries. De Castro, Ines E. 2011. 24p. (J). (gr. -1-3). 16.95 *(978-1-935359-72-2(X))* Bk. Pubs. Network.

De Conno, Gianni. Poemas a la Luna/ Poems to the Moon. 2009. (SPA.). 28p. (YA). (gr. 5-18). *(978-84-263-7338-0(0))* Vives, Luis Editorial (Edelvives).

de Dios, Olga. The Hips on the Drag Queen Go Swish, Swish, Swish. Hot Mess, Lil Miss. 2020. 40p. (J). (gr. -1-3). 17.99 *(978-0-7624-6765-5(7)*, Running Pr. Kids) Running Pr.

de Domenico, Helouise. Maxon Carter e Os Artefatos de Merlin. Moraes, Elton. 2019. (Série Maxon Carter Ser.: Vol. 1). (POR.). 278p. (J). pap. 10.41 *(978-1-0948-7203-2(2))* Independently Published.

De Gante, Guillermo. El Espejo en el Agua. Estrada, E. Gabriela Aguileta. rev. ed. 2006. (Castillo de la Lectura Naranja Ser.). (SPA & ENG.). 124p. (J). (gr. 4-7). pap. 7.95 *(978-970-20-0131-7(5))* Castillo, Ediciones, S. A. de C. V. MEX. Dist: Macmillan.

de Georgi, Sergio. Robot to the Rescue: Robots. Lawrence, Kay. 2018. (Makers Make It Work Ser.). (ENG.). 32p. (J). (gr. k-3). 25.32 *(978-1-63592-011-6(6))*; pap. 5.99 *(978-1-57565-987-9(5))* Astra Publishing Hse.

de Giorgi, Sergio. Building God's Kingdom: Diggit Saves the Day, 1 vol. Holmes, Andy. 2014. (ENG.). 22p. (J). bds. 9.99 *(978-0-529-11100-5(4))* Nelson, Thomas Inc.

De Giorgi, Sergio. Eight Great Planets! A Song about the Planets, 1 vol. Salas, Laura Purdie. 2010. (Science Songs Ser.). (ENG.). 24p. (J). (gr. 1-3). lib. bdg. 27.32 *(978-1-4048-5765-0(6)*, Picture Window Bks.) Capstone.

de Giorgi, Sergio. Tipper Tells a Lie, 1 vol. Holmes, Andy. 2014. (ENG.). 22p. (J). bds. 9.99 *(978-0-529-11213-2(2))* Nelson, Thomas Inc.

de Groat, Diane. Anastasia on Her Own. Lois, Lowry. 2016. (Anastasia Krupnik Story Ser.). (ENG.). 176p. (J). (gr. 5-7). pap. 7.99 *(978-0-544-54027-9(1)*, 1608838, HMH Books For Young Readers) Houghton Mifflin Harcourt Publishing Co.

De Horna, Luis. El Dragon y la Mariposa. Ende, Michael. 2003.Tr. of Der Lindwurm und der Schmetterling. (SPA.). 48p. (J). (gr. k-3). pap. 8.95 *(978-84-204-3710-1(7))* Santillana USA Publishing Co., Inc.

de Horna, Luis. El Dragon y la Mariposa. 2014. (ENG & SPA.). (J). pap. 8.95 *(978-607-01-1869-2(3)*, Alfaguara) Santillana USA Publishing Co., Inc.

De Hugo, Pierre. Fish Underwater. Delafosse, Claude. Stanley-Baker, Penelope, tr. 2012. (ENG.). 38p. (J). (gr. -1-k). spiral bd. 14.99 *(978-1-85103-409-3(9))* Moonlight Publishing, Ltd. GBR. Dist: Independent Pubs. Group.

de Hugo, Pierre & Bour, Laura. Polar Bears. de Hugo, Pierre & Bour, Laura. Stanley-Baker, Penelope, tr. 2013. (ENG.). 36p. (J). (gr. -1-k). spiral bd. 13.99 *(978-1-85103-418-5(8))* Moonlight Publishing, Ltd. GBR. Dist: Independent Pubs. Group.

de Iulis, Mattia. Invisible Woman: Partners in Crime. 2020. (ENG.). 112p. (YA). (gr. 4-17). pap. 15.99 *(978-1-302-91697-8(1))* Marvel Worldwide, Inc.

de Jesus Alvarez, Maria. Estoy Orgullosa de Mi Pasado. White, Amy. Kratky, Lada J., tr. 2009. (Colección Fácil de Leer Ser.). (SPA.). 16p. (gr. k-2). pap. 5.99 *(978-1-60396-421-0(5))* Ediciones Alfaguara ESP. Dist: Santillana USA Publishing Co., Inc.

de Klerk, Roger. Foxy Learns Colors, 1 vol. 2009. (Foxy Learns Ser.). (ENG.). 16p. (J). pap. 4.95 *(978-1-59496-181-6(6))* Teora USA LLC.

—Foxy Learns Shapes, 1 vol. 2009. (Foxy Learns Ser.). (ENG.). 16p. (J). pap. 4.95 *(978-1-59496-179-3(4))* Teora USA LLC.

—Foxy Learns to Add, 1 vol. 2009. (Foxy Learns Ser.). (ENG.). 16p. (J). pap. 4.95 *(978-1-59496-178-6(6))* Teora USA LLC.

—Foxy Learns to Tell Time, 1 vol. 2009. (Foxy Learns Ser.). (ENG.). 16p. (J). pap. 4.95 *(978-1-59496-180-9(8))* Teora USA LLC.

—Moses in the Bulrushes. Andrews, Jackie. 2012. (ENG.). 24p. (J). 8.50 *(978-1-84135-807-9(X))* Award Pubns. Ltd. GBR. Dist: Parkwest Pubns., Inc.

De Kleuver, Lorraine. When the Uneverythingable Happened. De Kleuver, Lorraine. 2018. (ENG.). 30p. (J). (gr. k-6). pap. *(978-0-6480017-9-9(2))* Aly's Bks.

de La Cour, Gary, et al. Mother Goose Lullabies. Studio Mouse Staff. rev. ed. 2007. (ENG.). 24p. (J). 4.99 *(978-1-59069-559-3(3))* Studio Mouse LLC.

—Twinkle Twinkle: And Other Sleepy-Time Rhymes. 2005. (Mother Goose Ser.). (ENG.). 36p. (J). (gr. -1-k). 12.95 *(978-1-59249-464-4(1)*, 1D016) Soundprints.

—Wheels on the Bus. rev. ed. 2007. (ENG.). 24p. (J). (gr. -1-3). 4.99 *(978-1-59069-562-3(3))* Studio Mouse LLC.

De La Cour, Gary. Counting in the Snow. De La Cour, Gary, creator. gif. ed. 2005. 10p. (J). bds. 9.99 *(978-1-57791-186-9(5))* Brighter Minds Children's Publishing.

De La Cruz, Erin Harris. Frank Is a Chihuahua. Morrison, Kevin. 2007. 32p. (J). (gr. 1-4). *(978-1-929039-43-2(3))* Ambassador Bks., Inc.

de la Cruz López, Casimiro, jt. illus. see de la Cruz, María Hernández.

de la Cruz, María Hernández & de la Cruz López, Casimiro. The Journey of Tunuri & the Blue Deer: A Huichol Indian Story. Endredy, James. 2003. (ENG.). 32p. (J). (gr. -1-6). 15.95 *(978-1-59143-016-2(X))* Bear & Co.

de la Fuente, Francisco & Wheatley, Doug. How to Train Your Dragon: Dragonvine. DeBlois, Dean et al. 2018. (ENG.). 80p. (J). (gr. 4-7). 10.99 *(978-1-61655-953-3(5)*, Dark Horse Books) Dark Horse Comics.

De La Fuente, Mary, jt. illus. see Horowitz, Alena Netia.

de la Fuente, Pilar. A Halloween Story: A frightfully delightful tale by a 5-year-old, for other little monsters Everywhere. Fernandez, Alberto. 2007.Tr. of Historia de Halloween. 48p. (J). *(978-0-9796465-0-8(2))* Maroma Bks.

—A Halloween Story: A frightfully-delightful tale, by a 5-year-old, for other little monsters, Everywhere. Fernandez, Alberto. 2007. (J). pap. 9.95 *(978-0-9796465-2-2(9))* Maroma Bks.

de la Lastra, Virginia. Young George & the Dragon. Ortega, Emily Grace. 2018. (ENG.). 170p. (J). pap. 9.00 *(978-1-7239-2087-5(8))* Independently Published.

de la Pena, Marisa. How to Deal: Tarot for Everyday Life. Main, Sami. 2018. (ENG.). 240p. (YA). (gr. 8). pap. 15.99 *(978-0-06-266217-0(1))* HarperCollins Pubns.

de la Prada, Sandra. Seek & Find Cities, 1 vol. Lonely Planet Kids & Baker, Kate. 2019. (ENG.). 48p. (J). (gr. 1-3). pap. 9.99 *(978-1-78868-618-1(7))* Lonely Planet Global Ltd. IRL. Dist: Hachette Bk. Group.

de la Prada, Sandra. Way Past Worried. Adelman, Hallee. 2020. (Great Big Feelings Ser.). (ENG.). 32p. (J). (gr. -1-4). 16.99 ***(978-0-8075-8686-0(2)***, 0807586862) Whitman, Albert & Co.

de la Rue, James. Darkmouth #1: the Legends Begin. Hegarty, Shane. 2016. (Darkmouth Ser.: 1). (ENG.). 432p. (J). (gr. 3-7). pap. 7.99 *(978-0-06-231130-6(1))* HarperCollins Pubs.

—Darkmouth #2: Worlds Explode. Hegarty, Shane. 2016. (Darkmouth Ser.: 2). (ENG.). 464p. (J). (gr. 3-7). 17.99 *(978-0-06-231132-0(8))* HarperCollins Pubs.

De La Torre, Eric, jt. illus. see Fernandez, Elizabeth.

De La Torre, Roberto, et al. Captain Marvel: Carol Danvers - the Ms. Marvel Years Vol. 1. 2018. (ENG.). 432p. (YA). (gr. 8-17). pap. 34.99 *(978-1-302-91014-3(0))* Marvel Worldwide, Inc.

de la Vega, Jimena. You Can't Invite a Fish to a Dance Party. Williams, Jessica. 2019. (ENG.). 34p. (J). (gr. k-2). ***(978-1-9995397-3-3(7))***; pap. ***(978-1-9995397-2-6(9))*** All Write Here Publishing.

de Landro, Valentin, jt. illus. see Miyazawa, Takeshi.

De Lauretis, Gregorio. Made for Me. Bush, Zack. (ENG.). (J). (gr. k-3). 2019. 20p. bds. 12.99 *(978-1-64170-200-3(1)*, 550200); 2018. 32p. 16.99 *(978-1-945547-69-0(3)*, 554769) Familius LLC.

De Leon, Joanne. Filipino Children's Favorite Stories: Fables, Myths & Fairy Tales. Romulo, Liana. 2020. 64p. (J). (gr. k-5). 14.99 *(978-0-8048-5021-6(6))* Tuttle Publishing.

De Leon, Schenker. Teachers Are the Best: Book 1 Question Learns about Humans. Green, Joan. 2017. (ENG.). 30p. pap. 21.99 *(978-1-5434-2308-2(6))* Xlibris Corp.

—Teachers Are the Best: Book 2 Taz Teaches Tiz. Green, Joan. 2017. (ENG.). 28p. pap. 21.99 *(978-1-5434-2310-5(8))* Xlibris Corp.

—Teachers Are the Best: Book 3 Tiz & Blue Bear. Green, Joan. 2017. (ENG.). 28p. pap. 21.99 *(978-1-5434-2382-2(5))* Xlibris Corp.

—Teachers Are the Best: Book 4 Mr. Owl. Green, Joan. 2017. (ENG.). 28p. pap. 21.99 *(978-1-5434-2400-3(7))* Xlibris Corp.

De Lima, Ana. An Atlas of Imaginary Places. Cassany, Mia. 2018. (ENG.). 40p. (J). (gr. -1-3). 19.95 *(978-3-7913-7347-8(1))* Prestel Verlag GmbH & Co KG. DEU. Dist: Penguin Random Hse. LLC.

De Lorenzi, Paolo. Disney Hamlet, Starring Donald Duck (Graphic Novel) Salati, Giorgio. 2019. (ENG.). 72p. (J). (gr. 3-7). pap. 10.99 *(978-1-5067-1219-2(3))* Dark Horse Comics.

De Lorenzi, Paolo, et al. Uncle Scrooge: the World of Ideas. Panaro, Carlo & Stabile, Vito. 2019. (Uncle Scrooge Ser.). (ENG.). 96p. (J). (gr. 4-7). pap. 12.99 *(978-1-68405-572-2(5))* Idea & Design Works, LLC.

De Lorenzi, Paolo, jt. illus. see Freccero, Andrea.

de los reyes Cruz, Cheryl. DemiChat & the Lost Mummy. Brisland, Toni. 2013. 142p. (J). pap. 14.95 *(978-1-60131-173-3(7))* Big Tent Bks.

De Luca, Daniela. The Animal Atlas. McRae, Anne. 2008. (ENG.). 29p. (J). (gr. -1-3). 16.95 *(978-88-88166-38-4(6))* McRae Bks. Srl ITA. Dist: Independent Pubs. Group.

—The Atlas of Ancient Civilizations. Morris, Neil. 2008. (ENG.). 28p. (J). (gr. -1-3). 17.95 *(978-88-900466-0-5(0))* McRae Bks. Srl ITA. Dist: Independent Pubs. Group.

—Buster the Kangaroo. McRae, Anne & Morris, Neil. 2017. 31p. (J). *(978-0-7166-3523-9(2))* World Bk., Inc.

—Celia the Tiger. McRae, Anne & Morris, Neil. 2017. 31p. (J). *(978-0-7166-3524-6(0))* World Bk., Inc.

—The Children's Pictorial Atlas of the World. Cooper, Alison & McRae, Anne. 2008. (ENG.). 45p. (J). (gr. -1-3). 17.95 *(978-88-88166-05-6(X))* McRae Bks. Srl ITA. Dist: Independent Pubs. Group.

—Josh the Anteater. McRae, Anne & Morris, Neil. 2017. 31p. (J). *(978-0-7166-3525-3(9))* World Bk., Inc.

—Mattie the Polar Bear. McRae, Anne & Morris, Neil. 2017. 31p. (J). *(978-0-7166-3526-0(7))* World Bk., Inc.

—Meyers Bunter Weltatlas fuer Kinder. (GER.). 50p. *(978-3-411-07781-6(6))* Bibliographisches Institut & F. A. Brockhaus AG DEU. Dist: i. b. d., Ltd.

De Luca, Francesca. Nana's Garden. Juliano, Larissa & Clever Publishing. 2020. (Clever Family Stories Ser.). (ENG.). 20p. (J). (gr. -1-17). bds. 8.99 *(978-1-949998-98-6(3))* Clever Media Group.

De Lucio-Brock, Anita. Grandma & Me at the Flea: Los Meros Meros Remateros. Herrera, Juan Felipe. 2013. (ENG & SPA.). 32p. (J). pap. 10.95 *(978-0-89239-279-7(7)*, Children's Book Press) Lee & Low Bks., Inc.

de Marcken, Gail. Born to Pull: The Glory of Sled Dogs. Cary, Bob. 2009. (ENG.). 96p. (J). pap. 12.95 *(978-0-8166-6773-4(X))* Univ. of Minnesota Pr.

—Princess Tales: Once upon a Time in Rhyme with Seek-and-Find Pictures. Maccarone, Grace. 2013. (ENG.). 32p. (J). (gr. -1-1). 16.99 *(978-0-312-67958-3(0)*, 900073561) Feiwel & Friends.

De Marco, Arielle. Penny Sue the Pure Hearted. Degarmo, Serena. 2013. 30p. pap. 7.99 *(978-1-936341-55-9(7))* DeWard Publishing Co., Ltd.

De Mario, Camy. The Brave Teddy Bear. Garrett, Charlie. 2019. (ENG.). 32p. (J). pap. 9.13 ***(978-1-6882-2558-9(7))*** Independently Published.

De Montignie, Leon. Mudpoo & the Fungus Mystery. Klein, Peter. 2013. (ENG.). 72p. (J). 23.49 *(978-0-9874104-9-8(0))* JoJo Publishing AUS. Dist: Baker & Taylor Publisher Services (BTPS).

—Mudpoo & the Magic Tree Stump. Klein, Peter. 2012. (ENG.). 234p. (J). 23.49 *(978-0-9871448-5-0(5))* JoJo Publishing AUS. Dist: Baker & Taylor Publisher Services (BTPS).

de Moraes, Thiago. The Zoomers' Handbook. de Moraes, Ana. 2016. (ENG.). 32p. (J). (gr. -1-3). 17.99 *(978-1-5124-0424-1(1)*, 9781512404241) Lerner Publishing Group.

De Muth, Roger. Messy Bessie: Where's My Homework? Ziefert, Harriet. 2007. (J). *(978-1-4287-4707-4(9))* Handprint Bks.

De Negri, Andrea. The Cheese Experiment. Stilton, Geronimo & Tramontozzi, Lidia Morson. 2016. 103p. (J). *(978-1-5182-1588-9(2))* Scholastic, Inc.

de Polonia - Nill, Nina. This Is My School. Weakland, Mark. 2019. (School Rules Ser.). (ENG.). 24p. (J). (gr. k-2). pap. 8.95 *(978-1-5158-4066-4(2)*, 140060, Picture Window Bks.) Capstone.

—Who's Who at School. Weakland, Mark. 2019. (School Rules Ser.). (ENG.). 24p. (J). (gr. k-2). lib. bdg. 28.65 *(978-1-5158-3852-4(8)*, 139575, Picture Window Bks.) Capstone.

de Polonia, Nina. Ants Everywhere! Rosen, Robert. 2017. (Seasons Around Me Ser.). (ENG.). 24p. (gr. -1-2). 29.93 *(978-1-68342-740-7(8)*, 9781683427407); pap. 8.95 *(978-1-68342-792-6(0)*, 9781683427926) Rourke Educational Media.

—Building a Snowman. James, Lauren & Kisloski, Carolyn. 2017. (Play Time Ser.). (ENG.). 24p. (gr. -1-2). pap. 8.95 *(978-1-68342-784-1(X)*, 9781683427841) Rourke Educational Media.

—Chill of the Ice Dragon. West, Tracey. 2018. (Dragon Masters Ser.: 9). (ENG.). 96p. (J). (gr. 1-3). pap. 4.99 *(978-1-338-16986-7(6))* Scholastic, Inc.

De Polonia, Nina. The Family Photo. Rosen, Robert. 2017. (Family Time Ser.). (ENG.). 24p. (gr. -1-2). 29.93 *(978-1-68342-712-4(2)*, 9781683427124) Rourke Educational Media.

de Polonia, Nina. The Family Photo. Rosen, Robert. 2017. (Family Time Ser.). (ENG.). 24p. (gr. -1-2). pap. 8.95 *(978-1-68342-764-3(5)*, 9781683427643) Rourke Educational Media.

—Growing Up. Walters, Abby. 2017. (School Days Ser.). (ENG.). 24p. (gr. -1-2). pap. 8.95 *(978-1-68342-799-5(8)*, 9781683427995) Rourke Educational Media.

—Jonny's Neighborhood. Ko, Hannah. 2017. (All about Me Ser.). (ENG.). 24p. (gr. -1-2). 29.93 *(978-1-68342-726-1(2)*, 9781683427261) Rourke Educational Media.

De Polonia, Nina. My Favorite Sport. Rosen, Robert. 2017. (Play Time Ser.). (ENG.). 24p. (gr. -1-2). 29.93 *(978-1-68342-716-2(5)*, 9781683427162) Rourke Educational Media.

de Polonia, Nina. My Favorite Sport. Rosen, Robert. 2017. (Play Time Ser.). (ENG.). 24p. (gr. -1-2). pap. 8.95 *(978-1-68342-768-1(8)*, 9781683427681) Rourke Educational Media.

—My Great Body. Shah, Summer & Kisloski, Carolyn. 2017. (All about Me Ser.). (ENG.). 24p. (gr. -1-2). pap. 8.95 *(978-1-68342-752-0(1)*, 9781683427520) Rourke Educational Media.

—Shine of the Silver Dragon. West, Tracey. 2018. (Dragon Masters Ser.: 11). (ENG.). 96p. (J). (gr. 1-3). pap. 4.99 *(978-1-338-26365-7(X))* Scholastic, Inc.

De Polonia, Nina. Shine of the Silver Dragon. West, Tracey. 2018. (Dragon Masters Ser.: 11). (ENG.). 96p. (J). (gr. 1-3). 15.99 *(978-1-338-26366-4(8))* Scholastic, Inc.

de Pretto, Lorenzo. The Discovery of America. Crippa, Luca et al. Cooper-McGuinness, Nanette, tr. 2009. (Geronimo Stilton Graphic Novels Ser.: 1). (ENG.). (J). (gr. 2-6). 9.99 *(978-1-59707-158-1(7)*, 900063006) Papercutz.

De Quay, John Paul. Break the Siege: Make Your Own Catapults. Ives, Rob. 2016. (Tabletop Wars Ser.). (ENG.). 32p. (J). (gr. 3-6). 27.99 *(978-1-5124-0638-2(4)*, 9781512406382, Hungry Tomato ®) Lerner Publishing Group.

—Castle Attack: Make Your Own Medieval Battlefield. Ives, Rob. 2016. (Tabletop Wars Ser.). (ENG.). 32p. (J). (gr. 3-6). 27.99 *(978-1-5124-0639-9(2)*, 9781512406399, Hungry Tomato ®) Lerner Publishing Group.

De Quay, John Paul, jt. illus. see Dean, Venitia.

de Regil, Tania. A New Home. de Regil, Tania. 2019. 32p. (J). (gr. -1-3). 16.99 *(978-1-5362-0193-2(6))* Candlewick Pr.

—Un Nuevo Hogar. de Regil, Tania. 2019. 32p. (J). (gr. -1-3). 16.99 *(978-1-5362-0675-3(X))* Candlewick Pr.

De Rond, Roxana. Milo & Monty. 2020. (Child's Play Library). (ENG.). 32p. (J). (gr. -1-2). *(978-1-78628-352-8(2))* Child's Play International Ltd.

de Ruiter, Jo. Dump Truck Duck. Bryant, Megan E. 2016. (ENG.). 32p. (J). (gr. -1-3). 16.99 *(978-0-8075-1736-9(4)*, 807517364) Whitman, Albert & Co.

—Sleeping Handsome & the Princess Engineer. Woodward, Kay. 2015. (Fairy Tales Today Ser.). (ENG.). 24p. (J). (gr. -1-2). 23.99 *(978-1-4795-8615-8(3)*, Picture Window Bks.) Capstone.

de Ruiter, Jo. Will You Be Friends with Me? Bostrom, Kathleen Long. 2020. (ENG.). 24p. (J). (gr. -1 — 1). 7.99 ***(978-1-5460-3380-6(7)***, Worthy Kids/Ideals) Worthy Publishing.

De Saulles, Tony. Huesos, Sangre y Otros Pedazos del Cuerpo. Arnold, Nick. 2003. (Coleccion Esa Horrible Cienca). (SPA.). 156p. (YA). (gr. 5-8). *(978-84-272-2051-5(0)*, ML8311) Molino, Editorial ESP. Dist: Lectorum Pubns., Inc.

De Saulles, Tony. The Poo That Animals Do. Mason, Paul. 2018. 32p. (J). (gr. 1-6). 13.99 ***(978-1-5263-0394-3(9)***, Wayland) Hachette Children's Group GBR. Dist: Hachette Bk. Group.

De Saulles, Tony. Esa Caotica Quimica. De Saulles, Tony. Arnold, Nick. 2003. (Coleccion Esa Horrible Cienca). (SPA.). 158p. (YA). *(978-84-272-2052-2(9)*, ML8312) Molino, Editorial ESP. Dist: Lectorum Pubns., Inc.

—Esa Deslumbrante Luz. De Saulles, Tony. Arnold, Nick. (SPA.). 158p. (YA). (gr. 5-8). *(978-84-272-2063-8(4))* Molino, Editorial ESP. Dist: Lectorum Pubns., Inc.

—Esa Electrizante Electricidad. De Saulles, Tony. Arnold, Nick. (SPA.). 160p. (YA). (gr. 5-8). *(978-84-272-2066-9(9))* Molino, Editorial ESP. Dist: Lectorum Pubns., Inc.

—Esas Perversas Plantas. De Saulles, Tony. Arnold, Nick. (SPA.). 160p. (YA). (gr. 5-8). *(978-84-272-2062-1(6))* Molino, Editorial ESP. Dist: Lectorum Pubns., Inc.

—Ese Voluminoso Cerebro. De Saulles, Tony. Arnold, Nick. 2003. (Coleccion Esa Horrible Cienca). (SPA.). 158p. (YA). *(978-84-272-2065-2(0)*, ML31376) Molino, Editorial ESP. Dist: Lectorum Pubns., Inc.

—Esos Microscopicos Monstruos. De Saulles, Tony. Arnold, Nick. (SPA.). 144p. (YA). (gr. 5-8). *(978-84-272-2092-8(8))* Molino, Editorial ESP. Dist: Lectorum Pubns., Inc.

de Sève, Peter & O'Hara, Catherine. Finn McCoul. Gleeson, Brian. 2005. (Rabbit Ears-A Classic Tale Ser.). (ENG.). 36p. (J). (gr. 2-6). 28.50 *(978-1-59679-223-4(X)*, 12932, Picture Bk.) Spotlight.

de Silva, Manoshi. Ronan's Dinosaur. Aloysius, Nadishka. 2018. (ENG.). 106p. (J). pap. *(978-955-51847-5-5(5))* Aloysius, Nadishka.

De Soto, Ben. The Adventures of Dynamic Doolittle: The Problem with Paulie Python. Chachas, George & Wojtak, James. 2011. 31p. (J). pap. 9.95 *(978-0-9793144-1-4(0))* Doolittle Edutainment Corp.

—Doolittle's Very, Very Bad Day. Chachas, George & Wojtak, James. 2011. 26p. (J). pap. 9.95 *(978-0-9793144-2-1(9))* Doolittle Edutainment Corp.

—The Story of Doolittle: An Exceptional Young Gorilla. Chachas, George & Wojtak, James. 2011. 32p. (J). pap. 9.95 *(978-0-9793144-0-7(2))* Doolittle Edutainment Corp.

de Sousa, Isis. ¡mamá, Hay una Nube en la Cocina! Ortiz Bello, Frank Joseph. 2018. (SPA.). 38p. (J). pap. 15.00 *(978-1-881741-83-1(4))* Ediciones Eleos.

—La Mancha Pegajosa. Terron Tamez, Irma Ilia. Ortiz Bello, Frank Joseph, ed. 2019. (SPA.). 34p. (J). pap. 15.00 *(978-1-881741-86-2(9))* Ediciones Eleos.

De Spiegeleer, Chantal, jt. illus. see Sterne, René.

de Tagyos, Paul Rátz. Barnyard Fun, 0 vols. Wright, Maureen. 2013. (ENG.). 24p. (J). (gr. -1-3). 16.99 *(978-1-4778-1643-1(7)*, 9781477816431, Two Lions) Amazon Publishing.

De Tagyos, Paul Rátz. Ferret Fun, 0 vols. Rostoker-Gruber, Karen. 2011. (ENG.). 32p. (J). (gr. k-3). 17.99 *(978-0-7614-5817-3(4)*, 9780761458173, Two Lions) Amazon Publishing.

De Villiers, Patricia. An Adoption Story: Little Stork's New Home. Robertson, Carolyn. 2017. (ENG.). (J). pap. *(978-0-9931153-4-9(9))* Sparklypoo Pubns.

de Vita, Flor. Just One Itsy Bitsy Little Bite / Sólo un Mordadita Chiquitita. Garza, Xavier. 2018. (ENG & SPA.). 32p. (J). (gr. -1-3). 17.95 *(978-1-55885-872-5(5)*, Piñata Books) Arte Publico Pr.

De Vita, Flor. When Julia Danced Bomba / Cuando Julia Bailaba Bomba. Ortiz, Raquel M. & Ventura, Gabriela Baeza. 2019. (ENG & SPA.). 32p. (J). (gr. 1-3). 17.95 *(978-1-55885-886-2(5))* Arte Publico Pr.

De Vita, Massimo, jt. illus. see Castellan, Andrea.

De Vries, Bruce. What Do You See, Mrs Night Heron? Hasselbring, Janet. 2010. 32p. pap. 12.95 *(978-1-936343-03-4(7))* Peppertree Pr., The.

de Vries, Marloes. That 17th Hat. Eissler, Trevor. 2012. 32p. (J). 20.00 *(978-0-9835558-1-0(8))* June Bks., LLC.

De Weerd, Kelsey. I Can't Believe You Said That! Cook, Julia. 2014. (ENG.). 32p. (J). pap. 10.95 *(978-1-934490-67-9(9))* Boys Town Pr.

—I Just Don't Like the Sound of No! My Story about Accepting No for an Answer & Disagreeing the Right Way. Cook, Julia. 2011. (ENG.). 32p. (J). *(978-1-934490-26-6(1))* Boys Town Pr.

—I Just Don't Like the Sound of No! My Story about Accepting 'No' for an Answer & Disagreeing the Right Way!: My Story about Accepting 'No' for an Answer & Disagreeing... the Right Way! Cook, Julia. 2011. (ENG.). 32p. (J). 10.95 *(978-1-934490-25-9(3))* Boys Town Pr.

—I Just Want to Do It My Way! Cook, Julia. 2013. (ENG.). 32p. (J). 16.95 *(978-1-934490-44-0(X))* Boys Town Pr.

—I Just Want to Do It My Way! My Story about Staying on Task & Asking for Help! Cook, Julia. 2013. (ENG.). 32p. (J). 10.95 *(978-1-934490-43-3(1))* Boys Town Pr.

—Priscilla & the Perfect Storm. McCumbee, Stephie. 2014. (ENG.). 32p. (J). pap. 10.95 *(978-1-934490-60-0(1))* Boys Town Pr.

—Sorry, I Forgot to Ask! My Story about Asking Permission & Making an Apology! Cook, Julia. 2012. (ENG.). 32p. 16.95 *(978-1-934490-29-7(6))*; pap. 10.95 *(978-1-934490-28-0(8))* Boys Town Pr.

—Teamwork Isn't My Thing, & I Don't Like to Share! Cook, Julia. 2012. (ENG.). 32p. (J). pap. 10.95 *(978-1-934490-35-8(0))* Boys Town Pr.

—The Worst Day of My Life Ever! Cook, Julia. 2011. (ENG.). 32p. (J). 16.95 *(978-1-934490-21-1(0))*; pap. 10.95 *(978-1-934490-20-4(2))* Boys Town Pr.

De Witt, Elfrieda. Santa Mouse. Brown, Michael. 2019. (Santa Mouse Book Ser.). (ENG.). 32p. (J). (gr. -1-1). 17.99 *(978-1-5344-3793-7(2)*, Little Simon) Little Simon.

De Witt, Elfrieda. Santa Mouse Christmas Surprise: A Lift-The-Flap Book. Brown, Michael. 2020. (Santa Mouse Book Ser.). (ENG.). 12p. (J). (gr. -1-k). bds. 7.99 ***(978-1-5344-3801-9(7)***, Little Simon) Little Simon.

de Wolf, Alex. Reuben & Barney's Day on the Farm, 54 vols. Kuiper, Nannie. 2012. Orig. Title: Buiten Op de Boerderij. (ENG.). 28p. (J). 17.95 *(978-0-86315-858-2(7))* Floris Bks. GBR. Dist: Consortium Bk. Sales & Distribution.

Deacon, Alexis. Jim's Lion. Hoban, Russell. 2014. (ENG.). 64p. (J). (gr. 1-4). 15.99 *(978-0-7636-6517-3(7))* Candlewick Pr.

—Soonchild. Hoban, Russell. 2012. (ENG.). 144p. (YA). (gr. 9). 15.99 *(978-0-7636-5920-2(7))* Candlewick Pr.

Deacon, Alexis & Deacon, Alexis. Voyages in the Underworld of Orpheus Black. Sedgwick, Julian & Sedgwick, Marcus. 2019. (ENG.). 320p. (J). (gr. 7). 17.99 *(978-1-5362-0437-7(4))* Candlewick Pr.

Deacon, Alexis, jt. illus. see Deacon, Alexis.

Deadner, Courtney R. The Mystery of Jupiter. Hunter, Katharine King. 2016. (ENG.). (J). pap. 12.95 *(978-1-942022-76-3(X))* Butterfly Typeface, The.

Deal, David, photos by. Best Behavior: A Celebration of Good Manners for Our African-American Children. Henry, Debra. 2004. (J). per. 15.00 *(978-0-9758611-0-3(7))* Black Society Pages, Inc.

Deal, L. Kate. The Boxcar Children. Warner, Gertrude Chandler. 2020. (Boxcar Children Ser.). (ENG.). 160p. (J). (gr. 2-6). lib. bdg. 27.07 ***(978-1-5321-4473-8(3)***, 35163, Chapter Bks.) Spotlight.

Deal, L. Kate. The Boxcar Children. collector's ed. 2009. (Boxcar Children Mysteries Ser.). (ENG.). 168p. (J). (gr. 1-5). 18.99 *(978-0-8075-0850-3(0)*, 807508500) Whitman, Albert & Co.

—The Boxcar Children Journal. 2017. (Boxcar Children Mysteries Ser.). (ENG.). 160p. (J). (gr. 1-5). 15.99 *(978-0-8075-0725-4(3)*, 807507253) Whitman, Albert & Co.

Dean, David. The Barefoot Book of Children. Strickland, Tessa & DePalma, Kate. 2016. (ENG.). 64p. (J). (gr. k-5). 19.99 *(978-1-78285-296-4(4))* Barefoot Bks., Inc.

—Barefoot Books Children of the World. Strickland, Tessa & DePalma, Kate. 2019. (ENG.). 64p. (J). (gr. -1-3). pap. *(978-1-78285-332-9(4))* Barefoot Bks., Ltd.

—Barefoot Books World Atlas. Crane, Nick. 2011. 52p. (J). (gr. 3-6). 19.99 *(978-1-84686-333-2(3))* Barefoot Bks., Inc.

—The Reluctant Rajput. Moverley, Richard. 2005. (Yellow Go Bananas Ser.). (ENG.). 48p. (J). (gr. 3-4). *(978-0-7787-2745-3(9))*; lib. bdg. *(978-0-7787-2723-1(8))* Crabtree Publishing Co.

—Saying Grace: Blessings for the Family Table. McElwain, Sarah, ed. 2003. (ENG.). 120p. (gr. 8-17). 14.95 *(978-0-8118-4025-5(5))* Chronicle Bks. LLC.

Dean, Gwendolyne (Wendy). The Adventures of Mr. Wilson: Beyond the Gate. Horine, Dolores & Horine, Dennis. 2019. (Series 1 Ser.: Vol. 1). (ENG.). 38p. (J). pap. 12.99 *(978-0-578-44699-8(5))* Treecat Publishing.

Dean, J. B. Your Unlucky, Rotten, Dreadful Day: Journey Jumper Books. Dean, J. B. 2019. (Journey Jumper Bks.: Vol. 3). (ENG.). 108p. (J). pap. 6.99 ***(978-1-0801-9205-2(0))*** Independently Published.

Dean, James. I Love My White Shoes. 2010. (Pete the Cat Ser.). (J). lib. bdg. *(978-0-06-107623-7(6))* HarperCollins Pubs.

—Mighty Dads. Holub, Joan. 2014. (ENG.). 40p. (J). (gr. -1-k). 16.99 *(978-0-545-60968-5(2)*, Scholastic Pr.) Scholastic, Inc.

—Pete the Cat: Scuba-Cat. 2016. (I Can Read Book: My First Ser.). (ENG.). 32p. (J). (gr. -1-1). 17.44 *(978-1-4844-7052-7(4))* HarperCollins Pubs.

—Pete the Cat: Snow Daze. 2016. (I Can Read Book: My First Ser.). (ENG.). 32p. (J). (gr. -1-1). 17.44 *(978-1-4844-9513-1(6))* HarperCollins Pubs.

—Pete the Cat & His Four Groovy Buttons. Litwin, Eric & Dean, Kimberly. 2012. (Pete the Cat Ser.). (ENG.). 40p. (J). (gr. -1-2). lib. bdg. 17.89 *(978-0-06-211059-6(4))* HarperCollins Pubs.

—Pete the Cat & His Four Groovy Buttons. Litwin, Eric & Dean, Kimberly. 2012. (Pete the Cat Ser.). (ENG.). 40p. (J). (gr. -1-2). 17.99 *(978-0-06-211058-9(6)*, HarperCollins) HarperCollins Pubs. Ltd. GBR. Dist: HarperCollins Pubs.

—Pete the Cat & the Lost Tooth. 2017. 32p. (J). *(978-1-5182-4986-0(8)*, 118857967) Harper & Row Ltd.

—Pete the Cat & the Surprise Teacher. 2017. 32p. (J). *(978-1-5182-3399-9(6))* Harper & Row Ltd.

—Pete the Cat & the Treasure Map. 2017. (J). *(978-1-5182-3828-4(9))* HarperCollins Pubs. Ltd.

—Pete the Cat: I Love My White Shoes. Litwin, Eric & Dean, Kimberly. 2010. (Pete the Cat Ser.). (ENG.). 40p. (J). (gr. -1-3). 17.99 *(978-0-06-190622-0(0))*; lib. bdg. 17.89 *(978-0-06-190623-7(9))* HarperCollins Pubs.

—Pete the Cat: Rocking in My School Shoes. Litwin, Eric & Dean, Kimberly. 2011. (Pete the Cat Ser.). (ENG.). 40p. (J). (gr. -1-3). 17.99 *(978-0-06-191024-1(4))*; lib. bdg. 17.89 *(978-0-06-191025-8(2))* HarperCollins Pubs.

—Pete the Cat Saves Christmas. Litwin, Eric & Dean, Kimberly. (Pete the Cat Ser.). (ENG.). 40p. (J). (gr. -1-3). 2019. 9.99 *(978-0-06-294516-7(5))*; 2012. lib. bdg. 18.89 *(978-0-06-211063-3(2))* HarperCollins Pubs.

—Pete the Cat Saves Christmas: Includes Sticker Sheet! Litwin, Eric & Dean, Kimberly. 2014. (Pete the Cat Ser.). (ENG.). 40p. (J). (gr. -1-3). 17.99 *(978-0-06-211062-6(4)*, HarperCollins) HarperCollins Pubs. Ltd. GBR. Dist: HarperCollins Pubs.

—Sir Pete the Brave. 2016. 32p. (J). *(978-1-5182-0881-2(9))* Harper & Row Ltd.

—Tool School. Holub, Joan. 2017. (ENG.). 32p. (J). (gr. -1-k). 16.99 *(978-0-545-68520-7(6)*, Scholastic Pr.) Scholastic, Inc.

Dean, James. Pete the Cat 12-Book Phonics Fun! Includes 12 Mini-Books Featuring Short & Long Vowel Sounds. Dean, James. Dean, Kimberly. 2017. (My First I Can Read Ser.). (ENG.). 144p. (J). (gr. -1-3). pap. 12.99 *(978-0-06-240452-7(0))* HarperCollins Pubs.

—Pete the Cat: 5-Minute Bedtime Stories: Includes 12 Cozy Stories! Dean, James. Dean, Kimberly. 2020. (Pete the Cat Ser.). (ENG.). 192p. (J). (gr. -1-3). 12.99 *(978-0-06-295334-6(6)*, HarperCollins) HarperCollins Pubs. Ltd. GBR. Dist: HarperCollins Pubs.

—Pete the Cat: 5-Minute Pete the Cat Stories: Includes 12 Groovy Stories! Dean, James. Dean, Kimberly. 2017. (Pete the Cat Ser.). (ENG.). 192p. (J). (gr. -1-3). 12.99 *(978-0-06-247019-5(1)*, HarperFestival) HarperCollins Pubs.

—Pete the Cat: a Pet for Pete. Dean, James. Dean, Kimberly. 2014. (My First I Can Read Ser.). (ENG.). 32p. (J). (gr. -1-3). pap. 4.99 *(978-0-06-230379-0(1))* HarperCollins Pubs.

—Pete the Cat & His Magic Sunglasses. Dean, James. Dean, Kimberly. 2013. (Pete the Cat Ser.). (ENG.). 40p. (J). (gr. -1-3). 17.99 *(978-0-06-227556-1(9))*; lib. bdg. 18.89 *(978-0-06-227557-8(7))* HarperCollins Pubs.

—Pete the Cat & the Bad Banana. Dean, James. Dean, Kimberly. 2014. (My First I Can Read Ser.). (ENG.). 32p. (J). (gr. -1-3). pap. 4.99 *(978-0-06-230382-0(1))* HarperCollins Pubs.

—Pete the Cat & the Bedtime Blues. Dean, James. Dean, Kimberly. 2015. (Pete the Cat Ser.). (ENG.). 40p. (J). (gr. -1-3). 17.99 *(978-0-06-230430-8(5))*; lib. bdg. 18.89 *(978-0-06-230431-5(3))* HarperCollins Pubs.

—Pete the Cat & the Cool Cat Boogie. Dean, James. Dean, Kimberly. 2017. (Pete the Cat Ser.). (ENG.). 40p. (J). (gr. -1-3). 17.99 *(978-0-06-240434-3(2))*; lib. bdg. 18.89 *(978-0-06-240909-6(3))* HarperCollins Pubs.

D

—Pete the Cat & the Cool Caterpillar. Dean, James. Dean, Kimberly. 2018. (I Can Read Level 1 Ser.). (ENG.). 32p. (J). (gr. -1-3). 16.99 *(978-0-06-267522-4(2))* HarperCollins Pubs.

—Pete the Cat & the Cool Caterpillar. Dean, James. Dean, Kimberly. 2018. (I Can Read Level 1 Ser.). (ENG.). 32p. (J). (gr. -1-3). pap. 4.99 *(978-0-06-267521-7(4),* HarperCollins) HarperCollins Pubs. Ltd. GBR. Dist: HarperCollins Pubs.

—Pete the Cat & the Itsy Bitsy Spider. Dean, James. Dean, Kimberly. 2019. (Pete the Cat Ser.). (ENG.). 32p. (J). (gr. -1-3). 9.99 *(978-0-06-267544-6(3),* HarperFestival) HarperCollins Pubs.

—Pete the Cat & the Lost Tooth. Dean, James. Dean, Kimberly. 2017. (My First I Can Read Ser.). (ENG.). 32p. (J). (gr. -1-3). 16.99 *(978-0-06-267519-4(2),* 118857967); pap. 4.99 *(978-0-06-267518-7(4),* 118857967) HarperCollins Pubs.

—Pete the Cat & the Missing Cupcakes. Dean, James. Dean, Kimberly. 2016. (Pete the Cat Ser.). (ENG.). 40p. (J). (gr. -1-3). 17.99 *(978-0-06-230434-6(8))* HarperCollins Pubs.

—Pete the Cat & the Missing Cupcakes. Dean, James. Dean, Kimberly. 2016. (Pete the Cat Ser.). (ENG.). 40p. (J). (gr. -1-3). lib. bdg. 18.89 *(978-0-06-230435-3(6),* HarperCollins) HarperCollins Pubs. Ltd. GBR. Dist: HarperCollins Pubs.

—Pete the Cat & the New Guy. Dean, James. Dean, Kimberly. 2014. (Pete the Cat Ser.). (ENG.). 40p. (J). (gr. -1-3). 17.99 *(978-0-06-227560-8(7),* HarperCollins); lib. bdg. 18.89 *(978-0-06-227561-5(5))* HarperCollins Pubs.

—Pete the Cat & the Perfect Pizza Party. Dean, James. Dean, Kimberly. 2019. (Pete the Cat Ser.). (ENG.). 40p. (J). (gr. -1-3). 17.99 *(978-0-06-240437-4(7));* lib. bdg. 18.89 *(978-0-06-240910-2(7))* HarperCollins Pubs.

—Pete the Cat & the Supercool Science Fair. Dean, James. Dean, Kimberly. 2019. (Pete the Cat Ser.). (ENG.). 24p. (J). (gr. -1-3). 4.99 *(978-0-06-286835-0(7),* HarperFestival) HarperCollins Pubs.

—Pete the Cat & the Surprise Teacher. Dean, James. Dean, Kimberly. 2017. (My First I Can Read Ser.). (ENG.). 32p. (J). (gr. -1-3). 4.99 *(978-0-06-240428-2(8),* HarperCollins) HarperCollins Pubs. Ltd. GBR. Dist: HarperCollins Pubs.

—Pete the Cat & the Tip-Top Tree House. Dean, James. Dean, Kimberly. 2017. (My First I Can Read Ser.). (ENG.). 32p. (J). (gr. -1-3). pap. 4.99 *(978-0-06-240431-2(8))* HarperCollins Pubs.

—Pete the Cat & the Tip-Top Tree House (backpack Special Edition) Dean, James. 2017. (My First I Can Read Ser.). 32p. (J). (gr. -1-3). 4.50 *(978-0-06-274847-8(5))* HarperCollins Pubs.

—Pete the Cat & the Treasure Map. Dean, James. Dean, Kimberly. 2017. (Pete the Cat Ser.). (ENG.). 24p. (J). (gr. -1-3). pap. 4.99 *(978-0-06-240441-1(5),* HarperFestival) HarperCollins Pubs.

—Pete the Cat: Big Easter Adventure. Dean, James. Dean, Kimberly. 2014. (Pete the Cat Ser.). (ENG.). 24p. (J). (gr. -1-3). 10.99 *(978-0-06-219867-9(X))* HarperCollins Pubs.

—Pete the Cat: Big Reading Adventures: 5 Far-Out Books in 1 Box! Dean, James. Dean, Kimberly. 2018. (My First I Can Read Ser.). (ENG.). 160p. (J). (gr. -1-3). pap. 19.99 *(978-0-06-287259-3(1))* HarperCollins Pubs.

—Pete the Cat: Cavecat Pete. Dean, James. Dean, Kimberly. 2015. (Pete the Cat Ser.). (ENG.). 24p. (J). (gr. -1-3). pap. 4.99 *(978-0-06-219863-1(7),* HarperFestival) HarperCollins Pubs.

—Pete the Cat Checks Out the Library. Dean, James. Dean, Kimberly. 2018. (Pete the Cat Ser.). (ENG.). 24p. (J). (gr. -1-3). pap. 4.99 *(978-0-06-267532-3(X),* HarperFestival) HarperCollins Pubs.

—Pete the Cat: Construction Destruction: Includes over 30 Stickers! Dean, James. Dean, Kimberly. 2015. (Pete the Cat Ser.). (ENG.). 24p. (J). (gr. -1-3). pap. 4.99 *(978-0-06-219861-7(0),* HarperFestival) HarperCollins Pubs.

Dean, James. Pete the Cat: Crayons Rock! Dean, James. Dean, Kimberly. 2020. (Pete the Cat Ser.). (ENG.). 40p. (J). (gr. -1-3). 18.99 ***(978-0-06-286855-8(1));*** lib. bdg. 19.89 ***(978-0-06-287207-4(9))*** HarperCollins Pubs. Ltd. GBR. (HarperCollins). Dist: HarperCollins Pubs.

—Pete the Cat Falling for Autumn. Dean, James. Dean, Kimberly. 2020. (Pete the Cat Ser.). (ENG.). 24p. (J). (gr. -1-3). 10.99 ***(978-0-06-286848-0(9),*** HarperCollins) HarperCollins Pubs. Ltd. GBR. Dist: HarperCollins Pubs.

Dean, James. Pete the Cat: Firefighter Pete: Includes over 30 Stickers! Dean, James. Dean, Kimberly. 2018. (Pete the Cat Ser.). (ENG.). 24p. (J). (gr. -1-3). pap. 4.99 *(978-0-06-240445-9(8),* HarperFestival) HarperCollins Pubs.

—Pete the Cat: Five Little Bunnies. Dean, James. Dean, Kimberly. 2020. (Pete the Cat Ser.). (ENG.). 24p. (J). (gr. -1-3). 9.99 *(978-0-06-286829-9(2))* HarperCollins Pubs.

—Pete the Cat: Five Little Ducks. Dean, James. Dean, Kimberly. 2017. (Pete the Cat Ser.). (ENG.). 32p. (J). (gr. -1-3). 9.99 *(978-0-06-240448-0(2))* HarperCollins Pubs.

—Pete the Cat: Five Little Pumpkins. Dean, James. Dean, Kimberly. 2015. (Pete the Cat Ser.). (ENG.). 32p. (J). (gr. -1-3). 9.99 *(978-0-06-230418-6(6),* HarperFestival) HarperCollins Pubs.

—Pete the Cat Giant Sticker Book. Dean, James. Dean, Kimberly. 2016. (Pete the Cat Ser.). (ENG.). 100p. (J). (gr. -1-3). pap. 12.99 *(978-0-06-230423-0(2),* HarperFestival) HarperCollins Pubs.

—Pete the Cat: Go, Pete, Go! Dean, James. Dean, Kimberly. 2016. (Pete the Cat Ser.). (ENG.). 24p. (J). (gr. -1-3). pap. 4.99 *(978-0-06-240439-8(3),* HarperFestival) HarperCollins Pubs.

—Pete the Cat Goes Camping. Dean, James. Dean, Kimberly. 2018. (I Can Read Level 1 Ser.). (ENG.). 32p. (J). (gr. -1-3). 16.99 *(978-0-06-267530-9(3));* pap. 4.99 *(978-0-06-267529-3(X))* HarperCollins Pubs.

—Pete the Cat: Meet Pete. Dean, James. Dean, Kimberly. 2017. (Pete the Cat Ser.). (ENG.). 18p. (J). (gr. -1 — 1). bds. 8.99 *(978-0-06-267517-0(6),* HarperFestival) HarperCollins Pubs.

—Pete the Cat: My First I Can Draw. Dean, James. Dean, Kimberly. 2016. (Pete the Cat Ser.). (ENG.). 160p. (J). (gr. -1-3). pap. 9.99 *(978-0-06-230443-8(7),* HarperFestival) HarperCollins Pubs.

—Pete the Cat: Old MacDonald Had a Farm. Dean, James. Dean, Kimberly. 2014. (Pete the Cat Ser.). (ENG.). 32p. (J). (gr. -1-3). 9.99 *(978-0-06-219873-0(4))* HarperCollins Pubs.

—Pete the Cat: Old MacDonald Had a Farm Board Book. Dean, James. Dean, Kimberly. 2016. (Pete the Cat Ser.). (ENG.). 32p. (J). (gr. -1 — 1). bds. 7.99 *(978-0-06-238160-6(1),* HarperFestival) HarperCollins Pubs.

Dean, James. Pete the Cat: Old MacDonald Had a Farm Sound Book. Dean, James. Dean, Kimberly. 2020. (Pete the Cat Ser.). (ENG.). 34p. (J). (gr. -1 — 1). bds. 12.99 ***(978-0-06-298225-4(7),*** HarperFestival) HarperCollins Pubs.

Dean, James. Pete the Cat: Out of This World. Dean, James. Dean, Kimberly. 2017. (Pete the Cat Ser.). (ENG.). 24p. (J). (gr. -1-3). pap. 4.99 *(978-0-06-240443-5(1),* HarperFestival) HarperCollins Pubs.

—Pete the Cat: Pete at the Beach. Dean, James. Dean, Kimberly. 2013. (My First I Can Read Ser.). (ENG.). 32p. (J). (gr. -1-3). 16.99 *(978-0-06-211073-2(X));* pap. 4.99 *(978-0-06-211072-5(1))* HarperCollins Pubs.

—Pete the Cat: Pete's Big Lunch. Dean, James. Dean, Kimberly. 2013. (My First I Can Read Ser.). (ENG.). 32p. (J). (gr. -1-3). 16.99 *(978-0-06-211070-1(5))* HarperCollins Pubs.

—Pete the Cat: Play Ball! Dean, James. Dean, Kimberly. 2013. (My First I Can Read Ser.). (ENG.). 32p. (J). (gr. -1-3). 16.99 *(978-0-06-211067-1(5))* HarperCollins Pubs.

—Pete the Cat: Robo-Pete. Dean, James. Dean, Kimberly. 2015. (Pete the Cat Ser.). (ENG.). 24p. (J). (gr. -1-3). pap. 4.99 *(978-0-06-230427-8(5),* HarperFestival) HarperCollins Pubs.

—Pete the Cat: Rock on, Mom & Dad! Dean, James. Dean, Kimberly. 2015. (Pete the Cat Ser.). (ENG.). 24p. (J). (gr. -1-3). pap. 6.99 *(978-0-06-230408-7(9),* HarperFestival) HarperCollins Pubs.

—Pete the Cat: Scuba-Cat. Dean, James. Dean, Kimberly. 2016. (My First I Can Read Ser.). (ENG.). 32p. (J). (gr. -1-3). pap. 4.99 *(978-0-06-230388-2(0))* HarperCollins Pubs.

—Pete the Cat: Secret Agent. Dean, James. Dean, Kimberly. 2020. (Pete the Cat Ser.). (ENG.). 24p. (J). (gr. -1-3). 4.99 *(978-0-06-286842-8(X),* HarperCollins) HarperCollins Pubs. Ltd. GBR. Dist: HarperCollins Pubs.

—Pete the Cat: Sir Pete the Brave. Dean, James. Dean, Kimberly. 2016. (My First I Can Read Ser.). (ENG.). 32p. (J). (gr. -1-3). pap. 4.99 *(978-0-06-240421-3(0),* HarperCollins) HarperCollins Pubs. Ltd. GBR. Dist: HarperCollins Pubs.

—Pete the Cat: Snow Daze. Dean, James. Dean, Kimberly. 2016. (My First I Can Read Ser.). (ENG.). 32p. (J). (gr. -1-3). 16.99 *(978-0-06-240425-1(3))* HarperCollins Pubs.

—Pete the Cat Storybook Collection: 7 Groovy Stories! Dean, James. Dean, Kimberly. 2016. (Pete the Cat Ser.). (ENG.). 192p. (J). (gr. -1-3). 11.99 *(978-0-06-230425-4(9))* HarperCollins Pubs.

—Pete the Cat Storybook Favorites: Includes 7 Stories Plus Stickers! Dean, James. Dean, Kimberly. 2019. (Pete the Cat Ser.). (ENG.). 192p. (J). (gr. -1-3). 13.99 *(978-0-06-289484-7(6))* HarperCollins Pubs.

Dean, James. Pete the Cat: Super Pete. Dean, James. Dean, Kimberly. 2020. (I Can Read Level 1 Ser.). (ENG.). 32p. (J). (gr. -1-3). 16.99 ***(978-0-06-286853-4(5));*** pap. 4.99 ***(978-0-06-286850-3(0))*** HarperCollins Pubs. Ltd. GBR. (HarperCollins). Dist: HarperCollins Pubs.

Dean, James. Pete the Cat Take-Along Storybook Set: 5-Book 8x8 Set. Dean, James. Dean, Kimberly. 2017. (Pete the Cat Ser.). (ENG.). 120p. (J). (gr. -1-3). pap. 11.99 *(978-0-06-240447-3(4),* HarperFestival) HarperCollins Pubs.

—Pete the Cat: the First Thanksgiving. Dean, James. Dean, Kimberly. 2013. (Pete the Cat Ser.). (ENG.). 16p. (J). (gr. -1-3). 6.99 *(978-0-06-219869-3(6),* HarperFestival) HarperCollins Pubs.

—Pete the Cat: the Great Leprechaun Chase: Includes 12 St. Patrick's Day Cards, Fold-Out Poster, & Stickers! Dean, James. Dean, Kimberly. 2019. (Pete the Cat Ser.). (ENG.). 24p. (J). (gr. -1-3). 10.99 *(978-0-06-240450-3(4))* HarperCollins Pubs.

—Pete the Cat: the Petes Go Marching. Dean, James. Dean, Kimberly. 2018. (Pete the Cat Ser.). (ENG.). 24p. (J). (gr. -1-3). 9.99 *(978-0-06-230412-4(7))* HarperCollins Pubs.

—Pete the Cat: the Wheels on the Bus. Dean, James. Dean, Kimberly. 2013. (Pete the Cat Ser.). (ENG.). 32p. (J). (gr. -1-3). 9.99 *(978-0-06-219871-6(8))* HarperCollins Pubs.

—Pete the Cat: Too Cool for School. Dean, James. Dean, Kimberly. 2014. (My First I Can Read Ser.). (ENG.). 32p. (J). (gr. -1-3). 16.99 *(978-0-06-211076-3(4));* pap. 4.99 *(978-0-06-211075-6(6))* HarperCollins Pubs.

—Pete the Cat Treasury: Five Groovy Stories. Dean, James. Dean, Kimberly. 2017. (Pete the Cat Ser.). (ENG.). 160p. (J). (gr. -1-3). 21.99 *(978-0-06-274036-6(9))* HarperCollins Pubs.

—Pete the Cat: Trick or Pete. Dean, James. Dean, Kimberly. 2017. (Pete the Cat Ser.). (ENG.). 16p. (J). (gr. -1-3). pap. 6.99 *(978-0-06-219870-9(X),* HarperFestival) HarperCollins Pubs.

—Pete the Cat: Twinkle, Twinkle, Little Star. Dean, James. Dean, Kimberly. 2014. (Pete the Cat Ser.). (ENG.). 32p. (J). (gr. -1-3). 9.99 *(978-0-06-230416-2(X),* HarperFestival) HarperCollins Pubs.

—Pete the Cat: Twinkle, Twinkle, Little Star Board Book. Dean, James. Dean, Kimberly. 2016. (Pete the Cat Ser.). (ENG.). 32p. (J). (gr. -1 — 1). bds. 7.99 *(978-0-06-238161-3(X),* HarperFestival) HarperCollins Pubs.

—Pete the Cat: Valentine's Day Is Cool. Dean, James. Dean, Kimberly. 2013. (Pete the Cat Ser.). (ENG.). 24p. (J). (gr. -1-3). 10.99 *(978-0-06-219865-5(3),* HarperFestival) HarperCollins Pubs.

—Pete the Cat's 12 Groovy Days of Christmas. Dean, James. Dean, Kimberly. 2018. (Pete the Cat Ser.). (ENG.). 48p. (J). (gr. -1-3). 12.99 *(978-0-06-267527-9(3))* HarperCollins Pubs.

—Pete the Cat's Big Doodle & Draw Book. Dean, James. Dean, Kimberly. 2015. (Pete the Cat Ser.). (ENG.). 128p. (J). (gr. -1-3). pap. 12.99 *(978-0-06-230442-1(9),* HarperFestival) HarperCollins Pubs.

—Pete the Cat's Family Road Trip. Dean, James. Dean, Kimberly. 2020. (I Can Read Level 1 Ser.). (ENG.). 32p. (J). (gr. -1-3). 16.99 *(978-0-06-286839-8(X));* pap. 4.99 *(978-0-06-286838-1(1))* HarperCollins Pubs. Ltd. GBR. (HarperCollins). Dist: HarperCollins Pubs.

—Pete the Cat's Giant Groovy Book: 9 Books in One. Dean, James. Dean, Kimberly. 2019. (My First I Can Read Ser.). (ENG.). 288p. (J). (gr. -1-3). 16.99 *(978-0-06-286830-5(6))* HarperCollins Pubs.

—Pete the Cat's Got Class. Dean, James. Dean, Kimberly. 2016. (Pete the Cat Ser.). (ENG.). 24p. (J). (gr. -1-3). 9.99 *(978-0-06-230410-0(0))* HarperCollins Pubs.

—Pete the Cat's Groovy Bake Sale. Dean, James. Dean, Kimberly. 2018. (My First I Can Read Ser.). (ENG.). 32p. (J). (gr. -1-3). 16.99 *(978-0-06-267525-5(7));* pap. 4.99 *(978-0-06-267524-8(9))* HarperCollins Pubs.

—Pete the Cat's Groovy Guide to Kindness. Dean, James. Dean, Kimberly. 2020. (Pete the Cat Ser.). (ENG.). 48p. (J). (gr. -1-3). 12.99 *(978-0-06-297402-0(5),* HarperCollins) HarperCollins Pubs. Ltd. GBR. Dist: HarperCollins Pubs.

—Pete the Cat's Groovy Guide to Life. Dean, James. Dean, Kimberly. 2015. (Pete the Cat Ser.). (ENG.). 48p. (J). (gr. -1-3). 12.99 *(978-0-06-235135-7(4))* HarperCollins Pubs.

—Pete the Cat's Groovy Guide to Love. Dean, James. Dean, Kimberly. 2015. (Pete the Cat Ser.). (ENG.). 48p. (J). (gr. -1-3). 12.99 *(978-0-06-243061-8(0))* HarperCollins Pubs.

Dean, James. Pete the Cat's Happy Halloween. Dean, James. Dean, Kimberly. 2020. (Pete the Cat Ser.). (ENG.). 18p. (J). (gr. -1 — 1). bds. 8.99 ***(978-0-06-286844-2(6),*** HarperFestival) HarperCollins Pubs.

Dean, James. Pete the Cat's Sing-Along Story Collection: 3 Great Books from One Cool Cat. Dean, James. Dean, Kimberly. 2014. (Pete the Cat Ser.). (ENG.). 96p. (J). (gr. -1-3). 19.99 *(978-0-06-230420-9(8))* HarperCollins Pubs.

—Pete the Cat's Super Cool Reading Collection. Dean, James. Dean, Kimberly. 2014. (My First I Can Read Ser.). (ENG.). 160p. (J). (gr. -1-3). pap. 19.99 *(978-0-06-230424-7(0))* HarperCollins Pubs.

—Pete the Cat's Train Trip. Dean, James. Dean, Kimberly. 2015. (My First I Can Read Ser.). (ENG.). 32p. (J). (gr. -1-3). pap. 4.99 *(978-0-06-230385-1(6))* HarperCollins Pubs.

—Pete the Cat's Trip to the Supermarket. Dean, James. Dean, Kimberly. 2019. (I Can Read Level 1 Ser.). (ENG.). 32p. (J). (gr. -1-3). 16.99 *(978-0-06-267538-5(9))* HarperCollins Pubs.

—Pete the Cat's Trip to the Supermarket. Dean, James. Dean, Kimberly. 2019. (I Can Read Level 1 Ser.). (ENG.). 32p. (J). (gr. -1-3). pap. 4.99 *(978-0-06-267537-8(0),* HarperCollins) HarperCollins Pubs. Ltd. GBR. Dist: HarperCollins Pubs.

—Pete the Cat's World Tour: Includes over 30 Stickers! Dean, James. Dean, Kimberly. 2018. (Pete the Cat Ser.). (ENG.). 24p. (J). (gr. -1-3). pap. 4.99 *(978-0-06-267535-4(4),* HarperFestival) HarperCollins Pubs.

—Pete the Kitty & Baby Animals. Dean, James. Dean, Kimberly. 2018. (Pete the Cat Ser.). (ENG.). 18p. (J). (gr. -1 — 1). bds. 8.99 *(978-0-06-267534-7(6),* HarperFestival) HarperCollins Pubs.

—Pete the Kitty & the Case of the Hiccups. Dean, James. Dean, Kimberly. 2018. (My First I Can Read Ser.). (ENG.). 32p. (J). (gr. -1-3). 16.99 *(978-0-06-286827-5(6))* HarperCollins Pubs.

—Pete the Kitty & the Case of the Hiccups. Dean, James. Dean, Kimberly. 2018. (My First I Can Read Ser.). (ENG.). 32p. (J). (gr. -1-3). pap. 4.99 *(978-0-06-286826-8(8),* HarperCollins) HarperCollins Pubs. Ltd. GBR. Dist: HarperCollins Pubs.

—Pete the Kitty & the Groovy Playdate. Dean, James. Dean, Kimberly. 2018. (Pete the Cat Ser.). (ENG.). 40p. (J). (gr. -1-3). 17.99 *(978-0-06-267540-8(0));* lib. bdg. 18.89 *(978-0-06-267541-5(9))* HarperCollins Pubs.

Dean, James. Pete the Kitty & the Unicorn's Missing Colors. Dean, James. Dean, Kimberly. 2020. (My First I Can Read Ser.). (ENG.). 32p. (J). (gr. -1-3). 16.99 ***(978-0-06-286846-6(2));*** pap. 4.99 ***(978-0-06-286845-9(4))*** HarperCollins Pubs. Ltd. GBR. (HarperCollins). Dist: HarperCollins Pubs.

Dean, James. Pete the Kitty Goes to the Doctor. Dean, James. Dean, Kimberly. 2019. (My First I Can Read Ser.). (ENG.). 32p. (J). (gr. -1-3). 16.99 *(978-0-06-286833-6(0))* HarperCollins Pubs.

—Pete the Kitty Goes to the Doctor. Dean, James. Dean, Kimberly. 2019. (My First I Can Read Ser.). (ENG.). 32p. (J). (gr. -1-3). pap. 4.99 *(978-0-06-286832-9(2),* HarperCollins) HarperCollins Pubs. Ltd. GBR. Dist: HarperCollins Pubs.

—Pete the Kitty: I Love Pete the Kitty. Dean, James. Dean, Kimberly. 2017. (Pete the Cat Ser.). (ENG.). 24p. (J). (gr. -1 — 1). bds. 7.99 *(978-0-06-243581-1(7),* HarperFestival) HarperCollins Pubs.

Dean, James. Pete the Kitty's Cozy Christmas Touch & Feel Board Book. Dean, James. Dean, Kimberly. 2020. (Pete the Cat Ser.). (ENG.). 12p. (J). (gr. -1 — 1). bds. 8.99 ***(978-0-06-286831-2(4),*** HarperFestival) HarperCollins Pubs.

Dean, James. Pete the Kitty's First Day of Preschool. Dean, James. Dean, Kimberly. 2019. (Pete the Cat Ser.). (ENG.). 24p. (J). (gr. -1 — 1). bds. 7.99 *(978-0-06-243582-8(5),* HarperFestival) HarperCollins Pubs.

—Rock on, Mom & Dad! Dean, James. ed. 2015. (Pete the Cat (HarperCollins) Ser.). (J). lib. bdg. 17.20 *(978-0-606-36490-4(0))* Turtleback.

—Snow Daze. Dean, James. ed. 2016. (Pete the Cat I Can Read Ser.). (ENG.). 32p. (J). (gr. -1-3). lib. bdg. 13.55 *(978-0-606-39264-8(5))* Turtleback.

—Time for Bed, Pete the Kitty: A Touch & Feel Book. Dean, James. Dean, Kimberly. 2018. (Pete the Cat Ser.). (ENG.). 12p. (J). (gr. -1-3). bds. 8.99 *(978-0-06-286825-1(X),* HarperFestival) HarperCollins Pubs.

Dean, James, jt. illus. see Dean, Kim.

Dean, Jarrett. Adventure Dog Koopa & His Best Day Ever: Getting Adopted. Moritz, Laurie. 2019. (Imagining Better Feelings Ser.: Vol. 1). (ENG.). 56p. (J). pap. 12.99 ***(978-1-6773-1035-7(9))*** Independently Published.

Dean, Joyce. Singing Lessons. Ballou, Jill. 2019. (ENG.). 30p. (J). pap. 9.95 ***(978-0-9981468-5-0(4))*** Bicycle Bell Bks.

Dean, Karen. Kitty Kate's Tea Party. Dean, Karen. 2009. (ENG.). 48p. (J). *(978-1-934363-30-0(8))* Zoe Life Publishing.

Dean, Kim & Dean, James. Pete the Cat & the Missing Cupcakes. 2016. (J). *(978-0-605-95181-5(0))* Harper & Row Ltd.

Dean Kleven Studios & Finley, Shawn. Tonka Rescue Trucks! Joyce, Bridget & Furman, Eric. 2007. (Fold & Go Vehicles Ser.). 15.98 *(978-1-4127-2981-9(5))* Publications International, Ltd.

Dean, Michael. Percy the Penguin's Adventure. Brown, Babs. 2016. (ENG.). 50p. (J). (gr. 1-3). pap. *(978-1-910077-96-2(8))* 2QT, Ltd. (Publishing).

Dean, Rachael. B Is for Ballet: a Dance Alphabet (American Ballet Theatre) Allman, John Robert. 2020. (American Ballet Theatre Ser.). (ENG.). 48p. (J). (gr. -1-2). 18.99 ***(978-0-593-18094-5(1));*** lib. bdg. 21.99 ***(978-0-593-18095-2(X))*** Random Hse. Children's Bks. (Doubleday Bks. for Young Readers).

Dean, Venetia. Stickmen's Guide to Your Body: A Stickman Bonanza on Your Brilliant Brain, Gurgling Guts, Beating Heart & Muscles & Bones All Work. Farndon, John. 2nd ed. 2020. (Stickmen's Guides: 2). (ENG.). 96p. (J). (gr. 2-6). 19.99 *(978-1-913077-17-4(9),* aa8fd9d4-3440-4443-bc66-83537cea39db, Beetle Bks.) Hungry Tomato Ltd. GBR. Dist: Baker & Taylor Publisher Services (BTPS).

Dean, Venetia, jt. illus. see Scott, Kimberly.

Dean, Venitia. Earthquakes White Band. Harper, Kathryn. 2016. (Cambridge Reading Adventures Ser.). (ENG.). 24p. pap. 8.08 *(978-1-316-50342-3(9))* Cambridge Univ. Pr.

—Forces & Motion Through Infographics. Rowell, Rebecca. 2013. (Super Science Infographics Ser.). (ENG.). 32p. (J). (gr. 3-5). pap. 8.99 *(978-1-4677-1591-1(3));* lib. bdg. 26.65 *(978-1-4677-1291-0(4),* Lerner Pubns.) Lerner Publishing Group.

—Plague! Epidemics & Scourges Through the Ages. Farndon, John. 2017. (Sickening History of Medicine Ser.). (ENG.). 32p. (J). (gr. 3-6). 27.99 *(978-1-5124-1557-5(X),* 9781512415575); E-Book 42.65 *(978-1-5124-3632-7(1),* 9781512436327); E-Book 42.65 *(978-1-5124-2709-7(8));* E-Book 4.99 *(978-1-5124-3634-1(8),* 9781512436341) Lerner Publishing Group. (Hungry Tomato ®).

—Quacks & con Artists: The Dubious History of Doctors. Farndon, John. 2017. (Sickening History of Medicine Ser.). (ENG.). 32p. (J). (gr. 3-6). 27.99 *(978-1-5124-1560-5(X),* 9781512415605); E-Book 42.65 *(978-1-5124-2712-7(8));* E-Book 42.65 *(978-1-5124-3635-8(6),* 9781512436358); E-Book 4.99 *(978-1-5124-3636-5(4),* 9781512436365) Lerner Publishing Group. (Hungry Tomato ®).

—Stickmen's Guide to Your Beating Heart. Farndon, John. 2017. (Stickmen's Guides to Your Awesome Body Ser.). (ENG.). 32p. (J). (gr. 3-6). 27.99 *(978-1-5124-3215-2(6),* 9781512432152, Hungry Tomato ®) Lerner Publishing Group.

—Stickmen's Guide to Your Brilliant Brain. Farndon, John. 2017. (Stickmen's Guides to Your Awesome Body Ser.). (ENG.). 32p. (J). (gr. 3-6). 27.99 *(978-1-5124-3213-8(X),* 9781512432138, Hungry Tomato ®) Lerner Publishing Group.

—Stickmen's Guide to Your Gurgling Guts. Farndon, John. 2017. (Stickmen's Guides to Your Awesome Body Ser.). (ENG.). 32p. (J). (gr. 3-6). 27.99 *(978-1-5124-3212-1(1),* 9781512432121, Hungry Tomato ®) Lerner Publishing Group.

—Stickmen's Guide to Your Mighty Muscles & Bones. Farndon, John. 2017. (Stickmen's Guides to Your Awesome Body Ser.). (ENG.). 32p. (J). (gr. 3-6). 27.99 *(978-1-5124-3214-5(8),* 9781512432145, Hungry Tomato ®) Lerner Publishing Group.

—Strange Medicine. Farndon, John. 2017. (Sickening History of Medicine Ser.). (ENG.). 32p. (J). (gr. 3-6). 27.99 *(978-1-5124-1559-9(6),* 9781512415599, Hungry Tomato ®) Lerner Publishing Group.

—Strange Medicine: A History of Medical Remedies. Farndon, John. ed. 2017. (Sickening History of Medicine Ser.). (ENG.). 32p. (J). (gr. 3-6). E-Book 4.99 *(978-1-5124-3640-2(2),* 9781512436402); E-Book 42.65 *(978-1-5124-2711-0(X));* E-Book 42.65 *(978-1-5124-3638-9(0),* 9781512436389) Lerner Publishing Group. (Hungry Tomato ®).

—Tiny Killers: When Bacteria & Viruses Attack. Farndon, John. 2017. (Sickening History of Medicine Ser.). (ENG.). 32p. (J). (gr. 3-6). 27.99 *(978-1-5124-1558-2(8),* 9781512415582); E-Book 42.65 *(978-1-5124-3641-9(0),* 9781512436419); E-Book 42.65 *(978-1-5124-2710-3(1));* E-Book 4.99 *(978-1-5124-3642-6(9),* 9781512436426) Lerner Publishing Group. (Hungry Tomato ®).

—Weather & Climate Through Infographics. Rowell, Rebecca. 2013. (Super Science Infographics Ser.). (ENG.). 32p. (J). (gr. 3-5). pap. 8.99 *(978-1-4677-1595-9(6));* lib. bdg. 26.65 *(978-1-4677-1292-7(2),* Lerner Pubns.) Lerner Publishing Group.

Dean, Venitia & De Quay, John Paul. Stickmen's Guide to Cities in Layers. Chambers, Catherine. 2016. (Stickmen's Guides to This Incredible Earth Ser.). (ENG.). 32p. (J). (gr. 3-6). 27.99 *(978-1-5124-0620-7(1),* 9781512406207, Hungry Tomato ®) Lerner Publishing Group.

—Stickmen's Guide to Earth's Atmosphere in Layers. Chambers, Catherine. 2016. (Stickmen's Guides to This Incredible Earth Ser.). (ENG.). 32p. (J). (gr. 3-6). 27.99 *(978-1-5124-0617-7(1)*, 9781512406177, Hungry Tomato ®) Lerner Publishing Group.
—Stickmen's Guide to Mountains & Valleys in Layers. Chambers, Catherine. 2016. (Stickmen's Guides to This Incredible Earth Ser.). (ENG.). 32p. (J). (gr. 3-6). 27.99 *(978-1-5124-0618-4(X)*, 9781512406184, Hungry Tomato ®) Lerner Publishing Group.
—Stickmen's Guide to Oceans in Layers. Chambers, Catherine. 2016. (Stickmen's Guides to This Incredible Earth Ser.). (ENG.). 32p. (J). (gr. 3-6). 27.99 *(978-1-5124-0619-1(8)*, 9781512406191, Hungry Tomato ®) Lerner Publishing Group.
Deanes, Brittany. Princess Elise & the Missing Royal Treats. Turner, Bianca. 2019. (ENG.). 32p. (J). 25.00 ***(978-1-951300-81-4(5))*** Liberation's Publishing.
Deangeli, Marguerite. The Lances of Lynwood. Yonge, Charlotte. 2018. (ENG.). 222p. (J). (gr. 6). pap. 14.95 *(978-0-9991706-5-6(1))* Hillside Education.
DeAnguelo Hout, Sarah. Leap & Twirl. Anderson, Steven. 2012. 34p. (J). pap. 10.99 *(978-0-692-01667-1(8))* BalletMet Dance Centre.
Dearinger, Jenifer Peters. A Stone's Crow. Dearinger, Jenifer Peters. 2018. (ENG.). 28p. (J). pap. 10.00 *(978-1-9877-8380-3(8))* CreateSpace Independent Publishing Platform.
Dearolf, Jeremy. Magic Stones. Jaccodine, Kristen R. 2018. (ENG.). 52p. (J). pap. 13.99 *(978-0-9978108-1-3(5))* K Jacks Publishing.
Dearsley, Ross. Secrets of Bearhaven. Rocha, K. E. 2016. (Bearhaven Ser.: 1). (ENG.). 256p. (J). (gr. 3-7). 14.99 *(978-0-545-81303-7(4)*, Scholastic Pr.) Scholastic, Inc.
Deas, Michael. Huddle up! Cuddle Up! Hegedus, Bethany. 2020. 40p. (J). (gr. -1-2). 17.99 ***(978-0-593-11562-6(7)***, Viking Books for Young Readers) Penguin Young Readers Group.
Deas, Mike. Adventures at Camp Lots-O-Fun, 1 vol. Helmer, Marilyn. 2010. (Orca Echoes Ser.). (ENG.). 64p. (J). (gr. 1-3). pap. 6.95 *(978-1-55469-347-4(0))* Orca Bk. Pubs. USA.
—Aliens among Us: Invasive Animals & Plants in British Columbia, 1 vol. Van Tol, Alex. 2015. (ENG.). 144p. (J). pap. 14.95 *(978-0-7726-6853-0(1)*, 3c93c366-fe45-4839-b5e9-f4cf4cc8a30e) Royal British Columbia Museum CAN. Dist: Independent Pubs. Group.
—Dalen & Gole: Scandal in Port Angus, 1 vol. 2011. (ENG.). 128p. (J). (gr. 4-7). pap. 9.95 *(978-1-55469-800-4(6))* Orca Bk. Pubs. USA.
—Field Day Fun. Griffin, Molly Beth. 2019. (School Sidekicks Ser.). (ENG.). 32p. (J). (gr. -1-2). lib. bdg. 21.32 *(978-1-5158-4418-1(8)*, 140513, Picture Window Bks.) Capstone.
—Field Trip Trouble. Griffin, Molly Beth. 2019. (School Sidekicks Ser.). (ENG.). 32p. (J). (gr. -1-2). lib. bdg. 21.32 *(978-1-5158-4416-7(1)*, 140510, Picture Window Bks.) Capstone.
—Food Fight, 1 vol. O'Donnell, Liam. 2010. (Graphic Guides: 5). (ENG.). 64p. (J). (gr. 4-7). pap. 9.95 *(978-1-55469-067-1(6))* Orca Bk. Pubs. USA.
—The Great Garage Sale, 1 vol. Helmer, Marilyn. 2013. (Orca Echoes Ser.). (ENG.). 64p. (J). (gr. 1-3). pap. 6.95 *(978-1-4598-0060-1(5))* Orca Bk. Pubs. USA.
—Hard Hat Heroes. Griffin, Molly Beth. 2019. (School Sidekicks Ser.). (ENG.). 32p. (J). (gr. -1-2). lib. bdg. 21.32 *(978-1-5158-4417-4(X)*, 140511, Picture Window Bks.) Capstone.
—I, Witness, 1 vol. McClintock, Norah. 2012. (ENG.). 144p. (YA). (gr. 8-12). pap. 16.95 *(978-1-55469-789-2(1))* Orca Bk. Pubs. USA.
—Media Meltdown: A Graphic Guide Adventure, 1 vol. O'Donnell, Liam. 2009. (Graphic Guides: 4). (ENG.). 64p. (J). (gr. 4-7). pap. 9.95 *(978-1-55469-065-7(X))* Orca Bk. Pubs. USA.
—Power Play, 1 vol. O'Donnell, Liam. 2011. (Graphic Guides: 6). (ENG.). 64p. (J). (gr. 4-7). pap. 9.95 *(978-1-55469-069-5(2))* Orca Bk. Pubs. USA.
—Ramp Rats: A Graphic Guide Adventure, 1 vol. O'Donnell, Liam. 2008. (Graphic Guides: 2). (ENG.). 64p. (J). (gr. 4-7). pap. 9.95 *(978-1-55143-880-1(1))* Orca Bk. Pubs. USA.
Deas, Mike. Scallywag on the Salish Sea, 1 vol. Cassidy, Sara. 2019. (ENG.). 80p. (J). (gr. 1-3). pap. 9.95 ***(978-1-77203-278-9(6))*** Heritage Hse. CAN. Dist: Orca Bk. Pubs. USA.
Deas, Mike. School Sidekicks. Griffin, Molly Beth. 2019. (School Sidekicks Ser.). (ENG.). (J). (gr. -1-2). 170.56 *(978-1-5158-4424-2(2)*, 29320, Picture Window Bks.) Capstone.
—Shadow Island, 1 vol. Deas, Nancy. 2019. (Sueño Bay Adventures Ser.: 1). (ENG.). 192p. (J). (gr. 1-3). pap. 14.95 *(978-1-4598-1961-0(6))* Orca Bk. Pubs. USA.
—Soccer Sabotage: A Graphic Guide Adventure, 1 vol. O'Donnell, Liam. 2009. (Graphic Guides: 3). (ENG.). 64p. (J). (gr. 4-7). pap. 9.95 *(978-1-55143-884-9(4))* Orca Bk. Pubs. USA.
—Tank & Fizz: The Case of Firebane's Folly, 1 vol. O'Donnell, Liam. 2018. (Tank & Fizz Ser.: 4). (ENG.). 256p. (J). (gr. 4-7). pap. 9.95 *(978-1-4598-1261-1(1))* Orca Bk. Pubs. USA.
—Tank & Fizz: the Case of the Battling Bots, 1 vol. O'Donnell, Liam. 2016. (Tank & Fizz Ser.: 2). (ENG.). 176p. (J). (gr. 4-7). pap. 9.95 *(978-1-4598-0813-3(4))* Orca Bk. Pubs. USA.
—Tank & Fizz: the Case of the Missing Mage, 1 vol. O'Donnell, Liam. 2017. (Tank & Fizz Ser.: 3). (ENG.). 208p. (J). (gr. 4-7). pap. 9.95 *(978-1-4598-1258-1(1))* Orca Bk. Pubs. USA.
—Tank & Fizz: the Case of the Slime Stampede, 1 vol. O'Donnell, Liam. 2015. (Tank & Fizz Ser.: 1). (ENG.). 152p. (J). (gr. 4-7). pap. 9.95 *(978-1-4598-0810-2(X))* Orca Bk. Pubs. USA.
—Tank & Fizz: the Case of the Tentacle Terror, 1 vol. O'Donnell, Liam. 2019. (Tank & Fizz Ser.: 5). (ENG.). 208p. (J). (gr. 4-7). pap. 9.95 *(978-1-4598-1952-8(7))* Orca Bk. Pubs. USA.
—Test Trouble. Griffin, Molly Beth. 2019. (School Sidekicks Ser.). (ENG.). 32p. (J). (gr. -1-2). lib. bdg. 21.32 *(978-1-5158-4419-8(6)*, 140512, Picture Window Bks.) Capstone.
—Wild Ride: A Graphic Guide Adventure, 1 vol. O'Donnell, Liam. 2007. (Graphic Guides: 1). (ENG.). 64p. (J). (gr. 4-7). pap. 9.95 *(978-1-55143-756-9(2))* Orca Bk. Pubs. USA.
Deas, Rich. 10 Fat Turkeys. Johnston, Tony. (ENG.). (J). (gr. -1-k). 2009. 28p. bds. 6.99 *(978-0-545-16469-6(9))*; 2004. 32p. pap. 3.99 *(978-0-439-45948-8(6))* Scholastic, Inc. (Cartwheel Bks.).
Deas, Robert. Manga Shakespeare: Macbeth. Shakespeare, William. 2008. (ENG.). 208p. (YA). (gr. 7-11). pap. 14.99 *(978-0-8109-7073-1(2)*, Amulet Bks.) Abrams, Inc.
Deasey, Kevin, jt. illus. see Rice, Kaleb.
Debbie, Nana. Elisabeth: The Baby Blue Whale. Debbie, Nana. 2020. (ENG.). 54p. (J). pap. 14.00 ***(978-0-9998833-5-8(6))*** MAKE BELIEVE PUBLISHING.
Deberdeev, Timur. Granny Can't Remember Me: A Children's Book about Alzheimer's. McCormick, Susan. 2018. (ENG.). 34p. (J). (gr. k-2). pap. 7.99 *(978-0-9986187-0-8(5))* Carroll Pr.
Debi Rogers. Kaylea Grows Up: Mommy & Me Days. Summer Rogers Martin. 2009. 20p. pap. 10.99 *(978-1-4389-5908-5(7))* AuthorHouse.
Debon, Nicolas. Florence Nightingale. Zemlicka, Shannon. (On My Own Biographies Ser.). 48p. (gr. 2-5). 2005. 23.93 *(978-0-87614-917-1(4))*; 2003. (ENG.). (J). pap. 7.99 *(978-0-87614-102-1(5)*, First Avenue Editions) Lerner Publishing Group.
—Liberty or Death: A Story about Patrick Henry. McPherson, Stephanie Sammartino. 2003. (Creative Minds Biographies Ser.). (ENG.). 64p. (gr. 4-8). 22.60 *(978-1-57505-178-9(8)*, Carolrhoda Bks.) Lerner Publishing Group.
—The Red Sash, 1 vol. Pendziwol, Jean E. 2005. (ENG.). 40p. (J). (gr. k-3). 18.95 *(978-0-88899-589-6(X))* Groundwood Bks. CAN. Dist: Publishers Group West (PGW).
—Thing-Thing. Fagan, Cary. 2008. 32p. (J). (gr. -1-1). 18.95 *(978-0-88776-839-2(3)*, Tundra Bks.) Tundra Bks. CAN. Dist: Penguin Random Hse. LLC.
—Timmerman Was Here. Sydor, Colleen. 2009. 32p. (J). (gr. -1-1). 19.95 *(978-0-88776-890-3(3)*, Tundra Bks.) Tundra Bks. CAN. Dist: Penguin Random Hse. LLC.
—The Warlord's Alarm, 1 vol. Pilegard, Virginia Walton. 2006. (Warlord's Ser.). (ENG.). 32p. (J). (gr. k-3). 16.99 *(978-1-58980-378-7(7)*, Pelican Publishing) Arcadia Publishing.
—The Warlord's Kites, 1 vol. Pilegard, Virginia Walton. 2004. (Warlord's Ser.). (ENG.). 32p. (J). (gr. k-3). 16.99 *(978-1-58980-180-6(6)*, Pelican Publishing) Arcadia Publishing.
—The Warlord's Messengers, 1 vol. Pilegard, Virginia Walton. 2005. (Warlord's Ser.). (ENG.). 32p. (J). (gr. k-3). 16.99 *(978-1-58980-271-1(3)*, Pelican Publishing) Arcadia Publishing.
—The Warlord's Puppeteers, 1 vol. Pilegard, Virginia Walton. 2003. (Warlord's Ser.: 4). (ENG.). 32p. (J). (gr. k-3). 16.99 *(978-1-58980-077-9(X)*, Pelican Publishing) Arcadia Publishing.
Deborah, Allwright. The Best Pet Ever. Victoria, Roberts. 2010. (ENG.). 32p. (J). (gr. -1-2). 15.95 *(978-1-58925-089-5(3))* Tiger Tales.
Deborah, Brown Armes. Grandpa Still Remembers: Life Changing Stories for Kids of All Ages from a Missionary Kid in Africa. Brown, Paul Henry. 2013. 162p. pap. 14.95 *(978-1-61153-027-8(X))* Light Messages Publishing.
Deborah Niland. There's a Hippopotamus on Our Roof Eating Cake 40th Anniversary Edition. Edwards, Hazel. 40th ed. 2020. (ENG.). 32p. (J). (-k). 19.99 ***(978-1-76089-627-0(6)***, Puffin) Penguin Random Hse. AUS. Dist: Independent Pubs. Group.
DeBord, Kim Jackson. Smell My Elephant. DeBord, Tina Ballon. 2017. (ENG.). 32p. (J). (gr. k-3). 16.99 *(978-1-58536-992-8(6)*, 204235) Sleeping Bear Pr.
Debra, Hoskins. Nosy the Passover Lamb. Pettingell, Karen. 2017. (ENG.). (J). pap. 13.99 *(978-0-9987731-0-0(7))* Frankie Dove Publishing.
Debriffe, Blandine. Bonne Nuit, Lucie ! Curtiss, Dominique. 2019. (FRE.). 24p. (J). (gr. k-3). ***(978-2-89687-821-5(1))*** chouetteditions.com.
DeBroech, Sarah. Beach Ball's Return. Van Tassel, Mary A. 2011. 28p. pap. 24.95 *(978-1-4512-2124-4(X))* America Star Bks.
—In Your Heart. Reyes, Cameron. 2011. 28p. pap. 24.95 *(978-1-4560-1009-6(3))* America Star Bks.
DeBroeck, Sarah. Abc People of the Bible. Collins, Chris. 2011. 44p. pap. 24.95 *(978-1-4560-2820-6(0))* America Star Bks.
—Jacob's Journey. Bailey, Leslie J. 2011. 28p. pap. 24.95 *(978-1-4560-9951-0(5))* America Star Bks.
—Moses P Rose Has Broken His Nose. Saupé, Rick. 2012. 28p. pap. 24.95 *(978-1-4626-0547-7(8))* America Star Bks.
—Small & Sassy. Atwater, Jillene. 2011. 36p. pap. 24.95 *(978-1-4489-8374-2(6))* America Star Bks.
—Thomas & the Toad King. Cardoso, Kelly. 2011. 28p. pap. 24.95 *(978-1-4560-0956-4(7))* America Star Bks.
—Working As a Team: Down to the End of the Road & Back. Lynch, Lauren Boehm. 2011. 28p. pap. 24.95 *(978-1-4560-0986-1(9))* America Star Bks.
—The Yellow Butterfly. Lynch, Lauren Boehm. 2011. 28p. pap. 24.95 *(978-1-4560-0982-3(6))* America Star Bks.
Debusschere, Jeanette. Anchors & Sails: A Reading Program for Beginners. Jaremko, Bev. 2004. (ENG.). 332p. pap. 35.55 *(978-1-4120-2128-9(6))* Trafford Publishing.
Decaire, Camela. Paper Doll Fashion Fun: Make paper doll clothes with the supplies Inside! Anton, Carrie, ed. 2007. 54p. (J). (gr. 4-7). pap. 17.95 *(978-1-59369-284-1(6))* American Girl Publishing, Inc.
DeCarlo, Mike, et al. Here Come the Heroes! (DC Super Friends) Wrecks, Billy. 2013. (ENG.). 224p. (J). (gr. -1-2). pap. 5.99 *(978-0-449-81610-3(9)*, Golden Bks.) Random Hse. Children's Bks.
—T. Rex Trouble! (DC Super Friends) Shealy, Dennis R. 2011. (Step into Reading Ser.). (ENG.). 32p. (J). (gr. -1-1). pap. 4.99 *(978-0-375-86777-4(5)*, Random Hse. Bks. for Young Readers) Random Hse. Children's Bks.
Decedue, Julie. Frankie Goes to Fenway: The Tale of the Faithful, Red Sox-Loving Mouse. Clark, Seneca & Giardi, Sandy. 2008. 56p. (J). 18.95 *(978-0-9767276-3-7(3))* Three Bean Pr.
—Lily & the Imaginary Zoo, 1. Clark, Seneca & Giardi, Sandy. 2005. (ENG.). 30p. (J). 15.95 *(978-0-9767276-1-3(7))* Three Bean Pr.
—The Yellowest Yellow Lab. Clark, Seneca & Giardi, Sandy. 2005. 30p. (J). 11.95 *(978-0-9767276-2-0(5))* Three Bean Pr.
Decenciere, Isabelle. The Wrinkled-at-the Knees Elephant & Other Tuneful Tales. Binder, Betsy. 2008. 28p. (J). pap. 19.95 incl. audio compact disk *(978-0-615-26652-7(5))* Velvet Pony Stories.
—The Wrinkled-At-the-Knees Elephant & Other Tuneful Tales: The Wrinkled-At-the-Knees Elephant & Other Tuneful Tales. Binder, Betsy. 2016. (ENG.). (J). pap. 18.95 *(978-0-692-80080-5(8))* Velvet Pony Stories.
Decis, Anne. Blanca Nieve y los Siete Gigantones. Canetti, Yanitzia & Yanitzia, Canetti. 2009. (SPA.). 32p. (J). (gr. k-2). 12.99 *(978-84-241-7061-5(X))* Everest Editora ESP. Dist: Lectorum Pubns., Inc.
—Colores que se Aman. Abril, Paco & Francisco, Abril Berán. 2004.Tr. of Colors that Love Each Other. (SPA.). 32p. (J). (gr. 2-3). 14.99 *(978-84-241-7989-2(7))* Everest Editora ESP. Dist: Lectorum Pubns., Inc.
—Cuentame un Cuento, Vol. 5. Comelles, Salvador. 2003. (SPA.). 96p. *(978-84-480-1674-6(2)*, TM30559) Timun Mas, Editorial S.A. ESP. Dist: Lectorum Pubns., Inc.
—Me Duele la Lengua. Mainé, Margarita. 3rd ed. (SPA.). 32p. (J). (gr. 1-3). *(978-84-236-4016-4(7))* Edebé ESP. Dist: Lectorum Pubns., Inc.
Decker, C. B. Alley Oops. Levy, Janice. 2005. (ENG.). 32p. (J). (gr. k-3). 17.95 *(978-0-9729225-4-8(7))* Flashlight Pr.
—Avi the Ambulance & the Snowy Day. Carlson, Claudia & Koffsky, Ann D. 2017. (J). *(978-1-68115-528-9(1))* Behrman Hse., Inc.
—Dr. Ruth Talks with the Animals. Westheimer, Ruth K. et al. 2019. (J). *(978-1-68115-551-7(6)*, Apples & Honey Pr.) Behrman Hse., Inc.
—Farmer Kobi's Hanukkah Match. Rostoker-Gruber, Karen & Isaacs, Ronald H. 2015. (J). pap. *(978-0-87441-924-5(7))*; Vol. (ENG.). *(978-1-68115-501-2(X))* Behrman Hse., Inc.
Decker, Cynthia. Stories of Dinosaurs. Punter, Russell. 2006. (Usborne Young Reading: Series One Ser.). 48p. (J). (gr. 2). lib. bdg. 13.99 *(978-1-58086-940-9(8))*; per. 5.99 *(978-0-7945-1363-4(8))* EDC Publishing. (Usborne).
Decker, Jacqueline. A Kittery Kayaker. Bull, Webster. 2007. (Little Limericks Ser.). (ENG.). 24p. (J). (gr. k-3). 12.95 *(978-1-933212-36-4(5)*, Commonwealth Editions) Applewood Bks.
Decker, Tim. The Punk Ethic. Decker, Tim. 2012. (ENG.). 188p. (YA). 18.95 *(978-1-60898-120-5(7))*; pap. 9.95 *(978-1-60898-121-2(5))* namelos llc.
DeCristoforo, Jennifer. Lucky Bamboo Book of Crafts: Over 100 Projects & Ideas Celebrating Chinese Culture, vols. 2, vol. 101. DeCristoforo, Jennifer. 2013. (ENG & CHI.). 136p. 26.99 *(978-0-9884648-0-3(2))* Lucky Bamboo Crafts.
Decuir, Jessica. Escape from the Clutches of Earth. Elrod, Jonathan C. 2018. (New Pilgrim Age, a Future's Look at the Past Ser.: Vol. 1). (ENG.). 146p. (J). pap. 8.99 *(978-1-7217-3579-2(8))* CreateSpace Independent Publishing Platform.
Dedering, Victoria. Snuckle-Bee & Snuckle-Bun: The Bee-Attitudes. Written By Susan J. Perry; Illustrated B. 2011. 32p. pap. 24.95 *(978-1-4560-8787-6(8))* America Star Bks.
Dedieu, Emilie. Le Petit Cireur de Chaussures. Curtiss, Dominique. 2017. (FRE.). 50p. (J). pap. *(978-2-89687-633-4(2))* chouetteditions.com.
Dedieu, Thierry. Snowmen Live Forever. 2019. (ENG.). 40p. (J). *(978-0-8028-5526-8(1)*, Eerdmans Bks For Young Readers) Eerdmans, William B. Publishing Co.
Dee, Kati. My Secret Best Friend. Rogers-Busboom, Kimberly. 2009. 24p. lib. bdg. 16.99 *(978-0-9823145-2-4(3))* Dirks Publishing, LLC.
Deedman, Heidi. Too Many Toys! Deedman, Heidi. 2015. (ENG.). 32p. (J). (gr. -1-1). 15.99 *(978-0-7636-7861-6(9))* Candlewick Pr.
Deen, David. Monsters: The Hunt & the Capture. Weiss, Bobbi & Weiss, David. 2008. (ENG.). 24p. (J). (gr. 2-17). 19.99 *(978-1-58476-727-5(8))* Innovative Kids.
Deeptown, Danny. Captain Green & the Plastic Scene. Bookless, Evelyn. 2019. (ENG.). 32p. (J). (gr. -1-1). 10.00 *(978-981-4794-77-0(5))* Marshall Cavendish International (Asia) Private Ltd. SGP. Dist: National Bk. Network.
—Counting Sheep. Chorley, Pippa. 2020. (ENG.). 32p. (J). (gr. -1-12). 10.00 *(978-981-4841-19-1(6))* Marshall Cavendish International (Asia) Private Ltd. SGP. Dist: National Bk. Network.
Dees, Leighanne. Flying Feet: A Story of Irish Dance. Burgard, Anna Marlis. 2006. 31p. (J). (gr. 4-8). 16.00 *(978-1-4223-5255-7(2))* DIANE Publishing Co.
DeFazio, Deborah. Peek-a-Boo Moon. Crick, Stephanie. 2004. 16p. (J). per. 9.95 *(978-0-9746397-3-4(7))* Pinefield Publishing.
DeFelice, Bonnie. The Adventures of Zsa-Zsa & Gabby-Lou: Dangers at the Seashore. DeFelice, Jennie & Landry, Jennifer. 2005. (J). lib. bdg. 19.95 *(978-0-9767072-0-2(9))* Two Dogz.
Defelice, Bonnie. The Adventures of Zsa Zsa & Gabby Lou in New Orleans. Defelice, Jennie & Landry, Jennifer. 2006. (J). lib. bdg. 21.95 *(978-0-9767072-1-9(7))* Two Dogz.
Defenbaugh, David. Alexander, It's Time for Bed! Lluch, Alex A. 2006. 30p. (J). (gr. -1-3). 14.95 *(978-1-887169-59-2(8))* WS Publishing.
—Alphabet: I Like to Learn the ABCs! Lluch, Alex A. 2014. (ENG.). 30p. (J). bds. 8.95 *(978-1-61351-077-3(2))* WS Publishing.
—Animal Alphabet: Slide & Seek the ABCs. Lluch, Alex A. 2013. 13p. (J). (-k). bds. 12.99 *(978-1-61351-041-4(1))* WS Publishing.
—Big Bugs, Small Bugs: If You Could Be a Bug, Which Bug Would You Be? Lluch, Alex. 2005. 28p. (J). (gr. -1-k). bds. 7.95 *(978-1-887169-62-2(8))* WS Publishing.
—Do I Look Good in Color? Lluch, Alex. 2006. (J). (gr. -1-k). 32p. 14.95 *(978-1-887169-63-9(6))*; (ENG.). 30p. bds. 7.95 *(978-1-887169-57-8(1))* WS Publishing.
—Numbers - I Like to Count from 1 to 10! Lluch, Alex A. 2014. (ENG.). 30p. (J). bds. 8.95 *(978-1-61351-078-0(0))* WS Publishing.
—Trace & Learn the ABCs: And Have Fun Playing Peek-A-Boo Who? Lluch, Alex A. 2014. (ENG.). 26p. (J). bds. 8.95 *(978-1-61351-082-7(9))* WS Publishing.
Deffenbaugh, Dena. Alice's ABC's: Version 2. Reid, Demetra. 2010. 66p. pap. 14.00 *(978-0-9802275-8-1(5))* Candalyse Publishing.
Defigueiredo, Antonieta. Comment Grandirent les Jumeaux: Recueil de Brèves Histoires Pour Petits et Jeunes Enfants. Barroso, Maria do Sameiro, ed. de Thracy, Athanase Vantchev, tr. 2019. (FRE.). 68p. (J). pap. 5.99 *(978-1-0782-6554-6(2))* Independently Published.
Degen, Bruce. At the Waterworks. Cole, Joanna. 2004. (Magic School Bus Ser.). (ENG.). 40p. (J). (gr. -1-3). pap. 7.99 *(978-0-590-40360-3(5))* Scholastic, Inc.
—Climb the Family Tree, Jesse Bear! Carlstrom, Nancy White. 2004. (Jesse Bear Ser.). (ENG.). 32p. (J). (gr. -1-1). 18.99 *(978-0-689-80701-5(5)*, Simon & Schuster Bks. For Young Readers) Simon & Schuster Bks. For Young Readers.
—Guess Who's Coming, Jesse Bear. Carlstrom, Nancy White. 2012. (ENG.). 32p. (J). (gr. -1-1). 16.99 *(978-0-689-84820-9(X)*, Aladdin) Simon & Schuster Children's Publishing.
—If You Were a Writer. Nixon, Joan Lowery. 2014. 32p. pap. 7.00 *(978-1-61003-353-4(1))* Center for the Collaborative Classroom.
—Inside the Human Body. Cole, Joanna. 2011. (Magic School Bus Ser.). (ENG.). (J). (gr. 2-5). pap. 18.99 incl. audio compact disk *(978-0-545-24086-4(7))*; audio compact disk 10.99 *(978-0-545-24083-3(2))* Scholastic, Inc.
—Jazzmatazz! Calmenson, Stephanie. 2008. 32p. (J). (gr. -1). lib. bdg. 17.89 *(978-0-06-077290-1(5))* HarperCollins Pubs.
—The Josefina Story Quilt. Coerr, Eleanor. 2003. (I Can Read Level 3 Ser.). (ENG.). 64p. (J). (gr. k-3). pap. 4.99 *(978-0-06-444129-2(6)*, HarperCollins) HarperCollins Pubs. Ltd. GBR. Dist: HarperCollins Pubs.
—The Josefina Story Quilt. Coerr, Eleanor. ed. 2003. (I Can Read! Level 3 Ser.). 64p. (J). (gr. 2-4). lib. bdg. 13.55 *(978-0-8335-2723-3(1))* Turtleback.
—Lost in the Solar System. Cole, Joanna. 2010. (Magic School Bus Ser.). (ENG.). (J). (gr. 2-5). audio compact disk 18.99 *(978-0-545-22337-9(7))* Scholastic, Inc.
—The Magic School Bus & the Climate Challenge. Cole, Joanna. (ENG.). (J). (gr. 2-5). 2014. 40p. 6.99 *(978-0-545-65599-6(4))*; 2010. 48p. 16.99 *(978-0-590-10826-3(3)*, Scholastic Pr.) Scholastic, Inc.
—The Magic School Bus Gets Baked in a Cake: A Book about Kitchen Chemistry. Beech, Linda Ward. Duchesne, Lucie, tr. from ENG. (Magic School Bus Ser.). (FRE.). 32p. (J). (gr. 1-4). pap. 5.99 *(978-0-590-24660-6(7))* Scholastic, Inc.
—The Magic School Bus on the Ocean Floor. Cole, Joanna. 2010. (Magic School Bus Ser.). (ENG.). (J). (gr. 2-5). audio compact disk 10.99 *(978-0-545-22751-3(8))* Scholastic, Inc.
—The Time of the Dinosaurs. (Magic School Bus Ser.). (FRE.). (J). (gr. 1-4). pap. 6.99 *(978-0-590-24641-5(0))* Scholastic, Inc.
—What a Scare, Jesse Bear. Carlstrom, Nancy White. 2012. (ENG.). 32p. (J). (gr. -1-1). 16.99 *(978-0-689-85190-2(1)*, Simon & Schuster/Paula Wiseman Bks.) Simon & Schuster/Paula Wiseman Bks.
—Where Is Christmas, Jesse Bear? Carlstrom, Nancy White. 2003. (ENG.). 32p. (J). (gr. -1-1). 13.99 *(978-0-689-86233-5(4)*, Aladdin) Simon & Schuster Children's Publishing.
Degen, Bruce. I Gotta Draw. Degen, Bruce. 2012. (ENG.). 40p. (J). (gr. k-4). 16.99 *(978-0-06-028417-6(X))* HarperCollins Pubs.
—I Said, Bed! Degen, Bruce. 2015. (I Like to Read Ser.). (ENG.). 24p. (J). (gr. -1-3). 6.99 *(978-0-8234-3311-7(0))* Holiday Hse., Inc.
—Jamberry. Degen, Bruce. 25th enl. anniv. ed. 2008. (I Can Read Bks.). (ENG.). 32p. (J). (gr. -1-3). pap. 7.99 *(978-0-06-443068-5(5)*, HarperCollins) HarperCollins Pubs. Ltd. GBR. Dist: HarperCollins Pubs.
—Jamberry Padded Board Book. Degen, Bruce. 2017. (ENG.). 34p. (J). (gr. -1 — 1). bds. 9.99 *(978-0-06-264379-7(7)*, HarperFestival) HarperCollins Pubs.
—Nate Likes to Skate. Degen, Bruce. 2016. (I Like to Read Ser.). (ENG.). 24p. (J). (gr. -1-3). 7.99 *(978-0-8234-3543-2(1))*; 14.95 *(978-0-8234-3456-5(7))* Holiday Hse., Inc.
—Snow Joke. Degen, Bruce. 2014. (I Like to Read Ser.). (ENG.). 24p. (J). (gr. -1-3). 14.95 *(978-0-8234-3065-9(0))* Holiday Hse., Inc.
Degen, Bruce & Bracken, Carolyn. The Human Body. Cole, Joanna et al. 2014. (Magic School Bus Presents Ser.). (ENG.). 32p. (J). (gr. 1-3). pap. 6.99 *(978-0-545-68364-7(5))* Scholastic, Inc.
—Insects: A Nonfiction Companion to the Original Magic School Bus Series. Cole, Joanna & Jackson, Tom. 2014. (Magic School Bus Presents Ser.). (ENG.). 32p. (J). (gr. 1-3). pap. 6.99 *(978-0-545-68587-0(7)*, Scholastic Paperbacks) Scholastic, Inc.
deGennaro, Sue. Clarrie's Pig Day Out. Storer, Jen. 2019. 32p. pap. 6.99 *(978-0-7333-3445-0(8))* ABC Bks. AUS. Dist: HarperCollins Pubs.

D

—Millie Loves Ants. French, Jackie. 2019. 32p. pap. 6.99 *(978-1-4607-5179-4(5))* HarperCollins Pubs.

—The Princess & the Packet of Frozen Peas, 1 vol. Wilson, Tony. 2012. (ENG.). 32p. (J). 16.95 *(978-1-56145-635-2(7))* Peachtree Publishing Co. Inc.

—The Princess & the Packet of Frozen Peas, 1 vol. Wilson, Tony. 2018. (ENG.). 32p. (J). (gr. -1-3). pap. 7.95 *(978-1-68263-051-8(X))* Peachtree Publishing Co. Inc.

deGennaro, Sue. The Pros & Cons of Being a Frog. deGennaro, Sue. 2016. (ENG.). 40p. (J). (gr. -1-3). 17.99 *(978-1-4814-7130-5(9)*, Simon & Schuster/Paula Wiseman Bks.) Simon & Schuster/Paula Wiseman Bks.

Deghand, Tim, jt. illus. see Feyh, Alexa.

Degnan, Mai Ly. Martin Luther King Jr. ed. 2020. (Little People, BIG DREAMS Ser.: 33). (ENG.). 32p. (J). (gr. -1-1). 14.99 ***(978-0-7112-4566-2(5)***, 328307, Frances Lincoln Children's Bks.) Quarto Publishing Group UK GBR. Dist: Hachette UK Distribution.

Degphilip. Cocoa for Santa: Adam. Schachtner, Brian W. 2019. (ENG.). 28p. (J). pap. 9.95 ***(978-1-7288-0777-5(8))*** Independently Published.

Degphilip. Cocoa for Santa: Addison. Schachtner, Brian W. 2018. (ENG.). 28p. (J). pap. 12.99 *(978-1-7238-9932-4(1))* Independently Published.

Degphilip. Cocoa for Santa: Adrian. Schachtner, Brian W. 2019. (ENG.). 28p. (J). pap. 9.95 ***(978-1-7288-0783-6(2))*** Independently Published.

—Cocoa for Santa: Aedon. Schachtner, Brian W. 2019. (ENG.). 28p. (J). pap. 9.95 ***(978-1-7288-0793-5(X))*** Independently Published.

—Cocoa for Santa: Aiden. Schachtner, Brian W. 2019. (ENG.). 28p. (J). pap. 9.95 ***(978-1-7288-0802-4(2))*** Independently Published.

—Cocoa for Santa: Alex. Schachtner, Brian W. 2019. (ENG.). 28p. (J). pap. 9.95 ***(978-1-7288-0811-6(1))*** Independently Published.

—Cocoa for Santa: Alexander. Schachtner, Brian W. 2019. (ENG.). 28p. (J). pap. 9.95 ***(978-1-7288-0818-5(9))*** Independently Published.

—Cocoa for Santa: Andrew. Schachtner, Brian W. 2019. (ENG.). 28p. (J). pap. 9.95 ***(978-1-7288-0825-3(1))*** Independently Published.

—Cocoa for Santa: Andy. Schachtner, Brian W. 2019. (ENG.). 28p. (J). pap. 9.95 ***(978-1-7288-0835-2(9))*** Independently Published.

Degphilip. Cocoa for Santa: Audrey. Schachtner, Brian W. 2018. (ENG.). 28p. (J). pap. 12.99 *(978-1-7240-0464-2(6))* Independently Published.

Degphilip. Cocoa for Santa: Ayden. Schachtner, Brian W. 2018. (ENG.). 28p. (J). pap. 9.95 ***(978-1-7288-0882-6(0))*** Independently Published.

—Cocoa for Santa: Ben. Schachtner, Brian W. 2018. (ENG.). 28p. (J). pap. 9.95 ***(978-1-7288-0889-5(8))*** Independently Published.

—Cocoa for Santa: Benjamin. Schachtner, Brian W. 2018. (ENG.). 28p. (J). pap. 9.95 ***(978-1-7288-0896-3(0))*** Independently Published.

—Cocoa for Santa: Brayden. Schachtner, Brian W. 2018. (ENG.). 28p. (J). pap. 9.95 ***(978-1-7288-0904-5(5))*** Independently Published.

—Cocoa for Santa: Bryson. Schachtner, Brian W. 2018. (ENG.). 28p. (J). pap. 9.95 ***(978-1-7288-0910-6(X))*** Independently Published.

—Cocoa for Santa: Caleb. Schachtner, Brian W. 2018. (ENG.). 28p. (J). pap. 9.95 ***(978-1-7288-0924-3(X))*** Independently Published.

—Cocoa for Santa: Cameron. Schachtner, Brian W. 2018. (ENG.). 28p. (J). pap. 9.95 ***(978-1-7288-0928-1(2))*** Independently Published.

—Cocoa for Santa: Carson. Schachtner, Brian W. 2018. (ENG.). 28p. (J). pap. 9.95 ***(978-1-7288-0935-9(5))*** Independently Published.

—Cocoa for Santa: Carter. Schachtner, Brian W. 2018. (ENG.). 28p. (J). pap. 9.95 ***(978-1-7288-0946-5(0))*** Independently Published.

—Cocoa for Santa: Charles. Schachtner, Brian W. 2018. (ENG.). 28p. (J). pap. 9.95 ***(978-1-7288-4572-2(6))*** Independently Published.

—Cocoa for Santa: Chase. Schachtner, Brian W. 2018. (ENG.). 28p. (J). pap. 9.95 ***(978-1-7288-4593-7(9))*** Independently Published.

—Cocoa for Santa: Chris. Schachtner, Brian W. 2018. (ENG.). 28p. (J). pap. 9.95 ***(978-1-7288-4610-1(2))*** Independently Published.

—Cocoa for Santa: Christian. Schachtner, Brian W. 2018. (ENG.). 28p. (J). pap. 9.95 ***(978-1-7288-4627-9(7))*** Independently Published.

—Cocoa for Santa: Conner. Schachtner, Brian W. 2018. (ENG.). 28p. (J). pap. 9.95 ***(978-1-7288-4701-6(X))*** Independently Published.

—Cocoa for Santa: Connor. Schachtner, Brian W. 2018. (ENG.). 28p. (J). pap. 9.95 ***(978-1-7288-4711-5(7))*** Independently Published.

—Cocoa for Santa: Copper. Schachtner, Brian W. 2018. (ENG.). 28p. (J). pap. 9.95 ***(978-1-7288-4731-3(1))*** Independently Published.

Degphilip. Cocoa for Santa: Cora. Schachtner, Brian W. 2018. (ENG.). 28p. (J). pap. 12.99 *(978-1-7240-0881-7(1))* Independently Published.

—Cocoa for Santa: Daisy. Schachtner, Brian W. 2018. (ENG.). 28p. (J). pap. 12.99 *(978-1-7240-0947-0(8))* Independently Published.

Degphilip. Cocoa for Santa: Daniel. Schachtner, Brian W. 2018. (ENG.). 28p. (J). pap. 9.95 ***(978-1-7288-4739-9(7))*** Independently Published.

—Cocoa for Santa: Dominic. Schachtner, Brian W. 2018. (ENG.). 28p. (J). pap. 9.95 ***(978-1-7288-4783-2(4))*** Independently Published.

—Cocoa for Santa: Dylan. Schachtner, Brian W. 2018. (ENG.). 28p. (J). pap. 9.95 ***(978-1-7288-4792-4(3))*** Independently Published.

—Cocoa for Santa: Eli. Schachtner, Brian W. 2018. (ENG.). 28p. (J). pap. 9.95 ***(978-1-7288-4807-5(5))*** Independently Published.

—Cocoa for Santa: Elias. Schachtner, Brian W. 2018. (ENG.). 28p. (J). pap. 9.95 ***(978-1-7288-4818-1(0))*** Independently Published.

—Cocoa for Santa: Elijah. Schachtner, Brian W. 2018. (ENG.). 28p. (J). pap. 9.95 ***(978-1-7288-4867-9(9))*** Independently Published.

Degphilip. Cocoa for Santa: Emilia. Schachtner, Brian W. 2018. (ENG.). 28p. (J). pap. 12.99 *(978-1-7240-4484-6(2))* Independently Published.

—Cocoa for Santa: Emily. Schachtner, Brian W. 2018. (ENG.). 28p. (J). pap. 12.99 *(978-1-7240-4501-0(6))* Independently Published.

Degphilip. Cocoa for Santa: Emma. Schachtner, Brian W. 2018. (ENG.). 28p. (J). pap. 9.95 ***(978-1-7240-4548-5(2))*** Independently Published.

—Cocoa for Santa: Erin. Schachtner, Brian W. 2018. (ENG.). 28p. (J). pap. 9.95 ***(978-1-7240-4579-9(2))*** Independently Published.

—Cocoa for Santa: Ethan. Schachtner, Brian W. 2018. (ENG.). 28p. (J). pap. 9.95 ***(978-1-7288-4884-6(9))*** Independently Published.

—Cocoa for Santa: Ezekiel. Schachtner, Brian W. 2018. (ENG.). 28p. (J). pap. 9.95 ***(978-1-7288-4934-8(9))*** Independently Published.

—Cocoa for Santa: Ezra. Schachtner, Brian W. 2018. (ENG.). 28p. (J). pap. 9.95 ***(978-1-7288-4945-4(4))*** Independently Published.

Degphilip. Cocoa for Santa: Faith. Schachtner, Brian W. 2018. (ENG.). 28p. (J). pap. 12.99 *(978-1-7240-4630-7(6))* Independently Published.

Degphilip. Cocoa for Santa: Francis. Schachtner, Brian W. 2018. (ENG.). 28p. (J). pap. 9.95 ***(978-1-7288-4967-6(5))*** Independently Published.

—Cocoa for Santa: Frank. Schachtner, Brian W. 2018. (ENG.). 28p. (J). pap. 9.95 ***(978-1-7288-4985-0(3))*** Independently Published.

—Cocoa for Santa: Grayson. Schachtner, Brian W. 2018. (ENG.). 28p. (J). pap. 9.95 ***(978-1-7288-5041-2(X))*** Independently Published.

—Cocoa for Santa: Greyson. Schachtner, Brian W. 2018. (ENG.). 28p. (J). pap. 9.95 ***(978-1-7288-5062-7(2))*** Independently Published.

Degphilip. Cocoa for Santa: Hannah. Schachtner, Brian W. 2018. (ENG.). 28p. (J). pap. 12.99 *(978-1-7240-4719-9(1))* Independently Published.

Degphilip. Cocoa for Santa: Henry. Schachtner, Brian W. 2018. (ENG.). 28p. (J). pap. 9.95 ***(978-1-7288-5073-3(8))*** Independently Published.

—Cocoa for Santa: Hudson. Schachtner, Brian W. 2018. (ENG.). 28p. (J). pap. 9.95 ***(978-1-7288-5081-8(9))*** Independently Published.

—Cocoa for Santa: Ian. Schachtner, Brian W. 2018. (ENG.). 28p. (J). pap. 9.95 ***(978-1-7288-5105-1(X))*** Independently Published.

—Cocoa for Santa: Isaac. Schachtner, Brian W. 2018. (ENG.). 28p. (J). pap. 9.95 ***(978-1-7288-5112-9(2))*** Independently Published.

—Cocoa for Santa: Isabella. Schachtner, Brian W. 2018. (ENG.). 28p. (J). pap. 9.95 ***(978-1-7240-4825-7(2))*** Independently Published.

—Cocoa for Santa: Isaiah. Schachtner, Brian W. 2018. (ENG.). 28p. (J). pap. 9.95 ***(978-1-7288-5123-5(8))*** Independently Published.

—Cocoa for Santa: Jace. Schachtner, Brian W. 2018. (ENG.). 28p. (J). pap. 9.95 ***(978-1-7288-5140-2(8))*** Independently Published.

—Cocoa for Santa: Jack. Schachtner, Brian W. 2018. (ENG.). 28p. (J). pap. 9.95 ***(978-1-7288-5147-1(5))*** Independently Published.

—Cocoa for Santa: Jameson. Schachtner, Brian W. 2018. (ENG.). 28p. (J). pap. 9.95 ***(978-1-7288-5190-7(4))*** Independently Published.

—Cocoa for Santa: Jason. Schachtner, Brian W. 2018. (ENG.). 28p. (J). pap. 9.95 ***(978-1-7288-5195-2(5))*** Independently Published.

Degphilip. Cocoa for Santa: Jaxon. Schachtner, Brian W. 2018. (ENG.). 28p. (J). pap. 12.99 *(978-1-7288-8180-5(3))* Independently Published.

Degphilip. Cocoa for Santa: Jaxson. Schachtner, Brian W. 2018. (ENG.). 28p. (J). pap. 9.95 ***(978-1-7288-9353-2(4))*** Independently Published.

—Cocoa for Santa: Jayden. Schachtner, Brian W. 2018. (ENG.). 28p. (J). pap. 9.95 ***(978-1-7288-9363-1(1))*** Independently Published.

—Cocoa for Santa: John. Schachtner, Brian W. 2018. (ENG.). 28p. (J). pap. 9.95 ***(978-1-7288-9387-7(9))*** Independently Published.

—Cocoa for Santa: Jonathan. Schachtner, Brian W. 2018. (ENG.). 28p. (J). pap. 9.95 ***(978-1-7288-9395-2(X))*** Independently Published.

—Cocoa for Santa: Jordan. Schachtner, Brian W. 2018. (ENG.). 28p. (J). pap. 9.95 ***(978-1-7288-9409-6(3))*** Independently Published.

—Cocoa for Santa: Jose. Schachtner, Brian W. 2018. (ENG.). 28p. (J). pap. 9.95 ***(978-1-7288-9446-1(8))*** Independently Published.

—Cocoa for Santa: Joseph. Schachtner, Brian W. 2018. (ENG.). 28p. (J). pap. 9.95 ***(978-1-7288-9455-3(7))*** Independently Published.

—Cocoa for Santa: Josh. Schachtner, Brian W. 2018. (ENG.). 28p. (J). pap. 9.95 ***(978-1-7288-9476-8(X))*** Independently Published.

—Cocoa for Santa: Josiah. Schachtner, Brian W. 2018. (ENG.). 28p. (J). pap. 9.95 ***(978-1-7288-9520-8(0))*** Independently Published.

—Cocoa for Santa: Kayden. Schachtner, Brian W. 2018. (ENG.). 28p. (J). pap. 9.95 ***(978-1-7288-9542-0(1))*** Independently Published.

Degphilip. Cocoa for Santa: Kennedy. Schachtner, Brian W. 2018. (ENG.). 28p. (J). pap. 12.99 *(978-1-7240-8396-8(1))* Independently Published.

Degphilip. Cocoa for Santa: Kevin. Schachtner, Brian W. 2018. (ENG.). 28p. (J). pap. 9.95 ***(978-1-7288-9554-3(5))*** Independently Published.

—Cocoa for Santa: Leo. Schachtner, Brian W. 2018. (ENG.). 28p. (J). pap. 9.95 ***(978-1-7288-9601-4(0))*** Independently Published.

—Cocoa for Santa: Levi. Schachtner, Brian W. 2018. (ENG.). 28p. (J). pap. 9.95 ***(978-1-7288-9631-1(2))*** Independently Published.

—Cocoa for Santa: Lincoln. Schachtner, Brian W. 2018. (ENG.). 28p. (J). pap. 9.95 ***(978-1-7288-9665-6(7))*** Independently Published.

—Cocoa for Santa: Logan. Schachtner, Brian W. 2018. (ENG.). 28p. (J). pap. 9.95 ***(978-1-7288-9675-5(4))*** Independently Published.

Degphilip. Cocoa for Santa: Lucy. Schachtner, Brian W. 2018. (ENG.). 28p. (J). pap. 12.99 *(978-1-7241-1996-4(6))* Independently Published.

—Cocoa for Santa: Madison. Schachtner, Brian W. 2018. (ENG.). 28p. (J). pap. 12.99 *(978-1-7241-5490-3(7))* Independently Published.

Degphilip. Cocoa for Santa: Mateo. Schachtner, Brian W. 2018. (ENG.). 28p. (J). pap. 9.95 ***(978-1-7288-9736-3(X))*** Independently Published.

—Cocoa for Santa: Maya. Schachtner, Brian W. 2018. (ENG.). 28p. (J). pap. 9.95 ***(978-1-7241-5524-5(5))*** Independently Published.

Degphilip. Cocoa for Santa: Melanie. Schachtner, Brian W. 2018. (ENG.). 28p. (J). pap. 12.99 *(978-1-7241-5529-0(6))* Independently Published.

—Cocoa for Santa: Mia. Schachtner, Brian W. 2018. (ENG.). 28p. (J). pap. 12.99 *(978-1-7241-5534-4(2))* Independently Published.

Degphilip. Cocoa for Santa: Mya. Schachtner, Brian W. 2018. (ENG.). 28p. (J). pap. 9.95 ***(978-1-7286-7797-2(1))*** Independently Published.

—Cocoa for Santa: Roman. Schachtner, Brian W. 2018. (ENG.). 28p. (J). pap. 9.95 ***(978-1-7289-3792-2(2))*** Independently Published.

—Cocoa for Santa: Savannah. Schachtner, Brian W. 2019. (ENG.). 28p. (J). pap. 9.95 ***(978-1-7288-0561-0(9))*** Independently Published.

—Cocoa for Santa: Serafina. Schachtner, Brian W. 2019. (ENG.). 28p. (J). pap. 9.95 ***(978-1-7288-0585-6(6))*** Independently Published.

—Cocoa for Santa: Serenity. Schachtner, Brian W. 2019. (ENG.). 28p. (J). pap. 9.95 ***(978-1-7288-0594-8(5))*** Independently Published.

—Cocoa for Santa: Skylar. Schachtner, Brian W. 2019. (ENG.). 28p. (J). pap. 9.95 ***(978-1-7288-0606-8(2))*** Independently Published.

—Cocoa for Santa: Sofia. Schachtner, Brian W. 2019. (ENG.). 28p. (J). pap. 9.95 ***(978-1-7288-0616-7(X))*** Independently Published.

—Cocoa for Santa: Sophia. Schachtner, Brian W. 2019. (ENG.). 28p. (J). pap. 9.95 ***(978-1-7288-0622-8(4))*** Independently Published.

—Cocoa for Santa: Stella. Schachtner, Brian W. 2019. (ENG.). 28p. (J). pap. 9.95 ***(978-1-7288-0629-7(1))*** Independently Published.

—Cocoa for Santa: Susan. Schachtner, Brian W. 2019. (ENG.). 28p. (J). pap. 9.95 ***(978-1-7288-0636-5(4))*** Independently Published.

Degphilip. Cocoa for Santa: Theodore. Schachtner, Brian W. 2018. (ENG.). 28p. (J). pap. 12.99 *(978-1-7289-3846-2(5))* Independently Published.

Degphilip. Cocoa for Santa: Valentina. Schachtner, Brian W. 2019. (ENG.). 28p. (J). pap. 9.95 ***(978-1-7288-0668-6(2))*** Independently Published.

—Cocoa for Santa: Victoria. Schachtner, Brian W. 2019. (ENG.). 28p. (J). pap. 9.95 ***(978-1-7288-0676-1(3))*** Independently Published.

—Cocoa for Santa: Violet. Schachtner, Brian W. 2019. (ENG.). 28p. (J). pap. 9.95 ***(978-1-7288-0687-7(9))*** Independently Published.

Degphilip. Cocoa for Santa: William. Schachtner, Brian W. 2018. (ENG.). 28p. (J). pap. 12.99 *(978-1-7289-3866-0(X))* Independently Published.

Degphilip. Cocoa for Santa: Wyatt. Schachtner, Brian W. 2018. (ENG.). 28p. (J). pap. 9.95 ***(978-1-7289-3875-2(9))*** Independently Published.

—Cocoa for Santa: Xavier. Schachtner, Brian W. 2018. (ENG.). 28p. (J). pap. 9.95 ***(978-1-7289-3890-5(2))*** Independently Published.

—Cocoa for Santa: Zoey. Schachtner, Brian W. 2019. (ENG.). 28p. (J). pap. 9.95 ***(978-1-7287-4861-0(5))*** Independently Published.

Degphilip. H. O. M. e Is Where L. O. V. E. Brightly Speaks. Lim, Adele M. 2018. (ENG.). 32p. (J). pap. *(978-1-912145-16-4(2))* Acorn Independent Pr.

—Many Lands, One Bridge. Lim, Adele M. 2018. (ENG.). 44p. (J). pap. *(978-1-912145-66-9(9))* Acorn Independent Pr.

Degphillip. Cocoa for Santa: Taylor. Schachtner, Brian W. 2019. (ENG.). 28p. (J). pap. 9.95 ***(978-1-7288-0651-8(8))*** Independently Published.

DeGraaf, Rebecca L., jt. photos by see DeGraaf, Rob L.

DeGraaf, Rob L. & DeGraaf, Rebecca L., photos by. Fat Tire Favorites: South Florida off-Road Bicycling. DeGraaf, Rob L. DeGraaf, Rebecca L., ed. 2003. Orig. Title: Guide to South Florida off-Road Bicycling. 111p. per. 12.95 *(978-0-9678385-2-6(5))* DeGraaf Publishing.

DeGrand, David. Twisted Tongues: Jokes, Comics, Facts, & Tongue Twisters — All 100% Gross! Lively, Kit & Lewman, David. 2020. (ENG.). 208p. (J). (gr. 2-7). pap. 8.95 ***(978-1-5235-1016-0(1)***, 101016) Workman Publishing Co., Inc.

DeGrand, David. What Makes a Monster? Discovering the World's Scariest Creatures. Keating, Jess. 2017. (World of Weird Animals Ser.). 40p. (J). (gr. 1-4). 17.99 *(978-0-553-51230-4(7)*, Knopf Bks. for Young Readers) Random Hse. Children's Bks.

—The Zombie Chasers #5: Nothing Left to Ooze. Kloepfer, John. 2014. (Zombie Chasers Ser.: 5). (ENG.). (J). (gr. 3-7). 240p. pap. 6.99 *(978-0-06-223099-7(9))*; 224p. 16.99 *(978-0-06-223098-0(0))* HarperCollins Pubs.

—The Zombie Chasers #6: Zombies of the Caribbean. Kloepfer, John. (Zombie Chasers Ser.: 6). (ENG.). (J). (gr. 3-7). 2015. 240p. pap. 6.99 *(978-0-06-229025-0(8))*; 2014. 224p. 16.99 *(978-0-06-229024-3(X))* HarperCollins Pubs.

—The Zombie Chasers #7: World Zombination. Kloepfer, John. 2015. (Zombie Chasers Ser.: 7). (ENG.). 240p. (J). (gr. 3-7). 16.99 *(978-0-06-229027-4(4))* HarperCollins Pubs.

deGroat, Diane. Bug in a Rug. Gilson, Jamie. 2003. (ENG.). 80p. (J). pap. 7.95 *(978-0-618-31670-0(1)*, 150103) Houghton Mifflin Harcourt Publishing Co.

—Charlie & the Christmas Kitty. Drummond, Ree. 2012. (Charlie the Ranch Dog Ser.). (ENG.). 40p. (J). (gr. -1-3). 17.99 *(978-0-06-199657-3(2))* HarperCollins Pubs.

—Charlie & the New Baby. Drummond, Ree. 2014. (Charlie the Ranch Dog Ser.). (ENG.). 40p. (J). (gr. -1-3). 17.99 *(978-0-06-229750-1(3))* HarperCollins Pubs.

—Charlie Goes to School. Drummond, Ree. 2013. (Charlie the Ranch Dog Ser.). (ENG.). 40p. (J). (gr. -1-3). 17.99 *(978-0-06-221920-6(0))* HarperCollins Pubs.

—Charlie Plays Ball. Drummond, Ree. 2015. (Charlie the Ranch Dog Ser.). (ENG.). 40p. (J). (gr. -1-3). 17.99 *(978-0-06-229752-5(X))* HarperCollins Pubs.

—Charlie the Ranch Dog. Drummond, Ree. 2011. (Charlie the Ranch Dog Ser.). (ENG.). 40p. (J). (gr. -1-3). 17.99 *(978-0-06-199655-9(6))* HarperCollins Pubs.

—Charlie the Ranch Dog: Charlie Goes to the Doctor. Drummond, Ree. 2014. (I Can Read Level 1 Ser.). (ENG.). 32p. (J). (gr. -1-3). pap. 4.99 *(978-0-06-221917-6(0))* HarperCollins Pubs.

—Charlie the Ranch Dog: Charlie's New Friend. Drummond, Ree. 2014. (I Can Read Level 1 Ser.). (ENG.). 32p. (J). (gr. -1-3). 16.99 *(978-0-06-221915-2(4))*; pap. 4.99 *(978-0-06-221914-5(6))* HarperCollins Pubs.

—Charlie the Ranch Dog: Charlie's Snow Day. Drummond, Ree. 2013. (I Can Read Level 1 Ser.). (ENG.). 32p. (J). (gr. -1-3). 16.99 *(978-0-06-221912-1(X))*; pap. 4.99 *(978-0-06-221911-4(1))* HarperCollins Pubs.

—Charlie the Ranch Dog: Rock Star. Drummond, Ree. 2015. (I Can Read Level 1 Ser.). (ENG.). 32p. (J). (gr. -1-3). pap. 4.99 *(978-0-06-234777-0(2))* HarperCollins Pubs.

—Charlie the Ranch Dog: Where's the Bacon? Drummond, Ree. 2013. (I Can Read Level 1 Ser.). (ENG.). 32p. (J). (gr. -1-3). 16.99 *(978-0-06-221909-1(X))*; pap. 4.99 *(978-0-06-221908-4(1))* HarperCollins Pubs.

deGroat, Diane. Ants in Your Pants, Worms in Your Plants! (Gilbert Goes Green) deGroat, Diane. 2011. (Gilbert Ser.). (ENG.). 32p. (J). (gr. -1-3). 16.99 *(978-0-06-176511-7(2))* HarperCollins Pubs.

—April Fool! Watch Out at School! deGroat, Diane. 2009. (Gilbert Ser.). 32p. (J). (gr. -1-3). (ENG.). 17.99 *(978-0-06-143042-8(0))*; lib. bdg. 18.89 *(978-0-06-143043-5(9))* HarperCollins Pubs.

—Brand-New Pencils, Brand-New Books. deGroat, Diane. 2005. (ENG.). 32p. (J). (gr. -1-3). 15.99 *(978-0-06-072613-3(X))* HarperCollins Pubs.

—Brand-New Pencils, Brand-New Books. deGroat, Diane. 2007. (Gilbert & Friends Ser.). (J). (gr. -1-3). 14.65 *(978-0-7569-8087-0(9))* Perfection Learning Corp.

—Brand-New Pencils, Brand-new Books. deGroat, Diane. 2007. (ENG.). 32p. (J). (gr. -1-3). pap. 7.99 *(978-0-06-072616-4(4))* HarperCollins Pubs.

—Gilbert & the Lost Tooth. deGroat, Diane. 2012. (I Can Read Level 2 Ser.). (ENG.). 32p. (J). (gr. k-3). 16.99 *(978-0-06-125214-3(X))*; pap. 4.99 *(978-0-06-125216-7(6))* HarperCollins Pubs.

—Gilbert, the Surfer Dude. deGroat, Diane. 2010. (I Can Read Level 2 Ser.). (ENG.). 32p. (J). (gr. k-3). pap. 4.99 *(978-0-06-125213-6(1))* HarperCollins Pubs.

—Good Night, Sleep Tight, Don't Let the Bedbugs Bite! deGroat, Diane. 2008. (ENG.). 32p. (J). (gr. -1-3). pap. 6.99 *(978-0-06-134061-1(8))* HarperCollins Pubs.

—Happy Birthday to You, You Belong in a Zoo. deGroat, Diane. 2007. (Gilbert & Friends Ser.). (ENG.). 32p. (J). (gr. -1-3). pap. 7.99 *(978-0-06-001029-4(0))* HarperCollins Pubs.

—Happy Birthday to You, You Belong in a Zoo. deGroat, Diane. 2007. (Gilbert & Friends Ser.). (gr. -1-3). 17.00 *(978-0-7569-8108-2(5))* Perfection Learning Corp.

—Jingle Bells, Homework Smells, Vol. deGroat, Diane. 2003. (ENG.). 32p. (J). (gr. -1-3). pap. 7.99 *(978-0-688-17545-0(7))* HarperCollins Pubs.

—Jingle Bells, Homework Smells. deGroat, Diane. 2008. (J). (gr. -1-3). pap. 16.95 incl. audio *(978-1-4301-0419-3(8))* Live Oak Media.

—Last One in Is a Rotten Egg! deGroat, Diane. 2011. (Gilbert Ser.). (ENG.). 32p. (J). (gr. -1-3). pap. 7.99 *(978-0-06-089296-8(X))* HarperCollins Pubs.

—No More Pencils, No More Books, No More Teacher's Dirty Looks! deGroat, Diane. (Gilbert Ser.). 32p. (J). (gr. -1-3). 2009. (ENG.). pap. 7.99 *(978-0-06-079116-2(0))*; 2006. 15.99 *(978-0-06-079114-8(4))*; 2006. (ENG.). lib. bdg. 18.89 *(978-0-06-079115-5(2))* HarperCollins Pubs.

—Trick or Treat, Smell My Feet. deGroat, Diane. 2008. (J). (gr. -1-7). pap. 16.95 incl. audio *(978-1-4301-0425-4(2))* Live Oak Media.

deGroat, Diane & Whipple, Rick. Charlie the Ranch Dog: Stuck in the Mud. Drummond, Ree. 2015. (I Can Read Level 1 Ser.). (ENG.). 32p. (J). (gr. -1-3). 16.99 *(978-0-06-234775-6(6))*; pap. 4.99 *(978-0-06-234774-9(8))* HarperCollins Pubs.

Deguchi, Ryusei. Abenobashi: Magical Shopping Arcade, 2 vols. Akahori, Satoru. 2004. Vol. 1. pap. 14.99 *(978-1-59182-790-0(6))*; Vol. 2. 192p. pap. 14.99 *(978-1-59182-791-7(4))* TOKYOPOP, Inc. (Tokyopop Adult).

Dehennin, Stephanie. Curious Pearl Explains States of Matter: 4D an Augmented Reality Science Experience. Braun, Eric. 2017. (Curious Pearl, Science Girl 4D Ser.). (ENG.). 24p. (J). (gr. k-2). lib. bdg. 23.99 *(978-1-5158-1342-2(8)*, 135144, Picture Window Bks.) Capstone.

—Curious Pearl Identifies the Reason for Seasons: 4D an Augmented Reality Science Experience. Braun, Eric. 2017. (Curious Pearl, Science Girl 4D Ser.). (ENG.). 24p. (J). (gr. k-2). lib. bdg. 23.99 *(978-1-5158-1343-9(6)*, 135145, Picture Window Bks.) Capstone.

—Curious Pearl Investigates Light: 4D an Augmented Reality Science Experience. Braun, Eric. 2017. (Curious Pearl, Science Girl 4D Ser.). (ENG.). 24p. (J). (gr. k-2). lib. bdg. 23.99 *(978-1-5158-1345-3(2)*, 135147, Picture Window Bks.) Capstone.
—Curious Pearl Observes Migration: 4D an Augmented Reality Science Experience. Braun, Eric. 2017. (Curious Pearl, Science Girl 4D Ser.). (ENG.). 24p. (J). (gr. k-2). lib. bdg. 23.99 *(978-1-5158-1344-6(4)*, 135146, Picture Window Bks.) Capstone.
—Curious Pearl, Science Girl 4D. Braun, Eric. 2017. (Curious Pearl, Science Girl 4D Ser.). (ENG.). 24p. (J). (gr. k-2). 95.96 *(978-1-5158-1362-0(2)*, 26484, Picture Window Bks.) Capstone.
—Dream Big. Kronenberg, Kat. 2017. (ENG.). 48p. (gr. -1-5). 15.95 *(978-1-62634-347-4(0))* Greenleaf Book Group.
Dehennin, Stephanie & Lewis, Anthony. Curious Pearl - Kicks off Forces & Motion: 4D an Augmented Reading Science Experience. Braun, Eric. 2018. (Curious Pearl, Science Girl 4D Ser.). (ENG.). 24p. (J). (gr. k-2). lib. bdg. 23.99 *(978-1-5158-2970-6(7)*, 138573, Picture Window Bks.) Capstone.
—Curious Pearl Tinkers with Simple Machines: 4D an Augmented Reading Science Experience. Braun, Eric. 2018. (Curious Pearl, Science Girl 4D Ser.). (ENG.). 24p. (J). (gr. k-2). lib. bdg. 23.99 *(978-1-5158-2973-7(1)*, 138575, Picture Window Bks.) Capstone.
Dehghanpisheh, Corine. Buddy's Dream. Dehghanpisheh, Corine. 2013. 34p. pap. 12.95 *(978-0-9851930-4-1(2))* Dehghanpisheh, Corine.
—Can We Play Again? Dehghanpisheh, Corine. 2012. 32p. pap. 12.95 *(978-0-9851930-1-0(8))* Dehghanpisheh, Corine.
Deines, Brian. Adrift at Sea: A Vietnamese Boy's Story of Survival. Skrypuch, Marsha Forchuk. 2016. (ENG.). 40p. (J). (gr. 1-4). 19.95 *(978-1-77278-005-5(7))* Pajama Pr. CAN. Dist: Ingram Publisher Services.
—A Bear in War. Endrulat, Harry & Innes, Stephanie. 2009. (ENG.). 40p. (J). (gr. k-3). *(978-1-55470-097-4(3))* Me to We.
—A Bear in War. Innes, Stephanie & Endrulat, Harry. 2019. 40p. (J). (gr. k-4). pap. 14.95 *(978-1-77278-086-4(3))* Pajama Pr. CAN. Dist: Ingram Publisher Services.
—Bear on the Homefront, 1 vol. Innes, Stephanie & Endrulat, Harry. 2014. (ENG.). 32p. (J). (gr. k-3). 17.95 *(978-1-927485-13-2(4))* Pajama Pr. CAN. Dist: Ingram Publisher Services.
—Elephant Journey: The True Story of Three Zoo Elephants & Their Rescue from Captivity. Laidlaw, Rob. 2016. (ENG.). 40p. (J). (gr. 1-4). 19.95 *(978-1-927485-77-4(0))* Pajama Pr. CAN. Dist: Ingram Publisher Services.
—En la Granja del Tío Juan. Fitz-Gibbon, Sally. 2005. (SPA.). 32p. (J). (gr. -1-1). 16.95 *(978-1-55041-878-1(5)*, 826cc839-309d-4326-a8ed-21b99f53e362); pap. 8.95 *(978-1-55041-883-5(1)*, cdc3c008-cbb1-4458-b03b-171ea8b42a6a) Fitzhenry & Whiteside, Ltd. CAN. Dist: Firefly Bks., Ltd.
—Forever: The Annual Hockey Classic, 1 vol. MacGregor, Roy. 2005. (ENG.). 64p. (J). (gr. 4-7). 19.95 *(978-0-88995-306-2(6)*, 775f4c3d-501e-491c-a20b-8f74a86420fc) Red Deer Pr. CAN. Dist: Firefly Bks., Ltd.
—Fox on the Ice, 1 vol. Highway, Tomson. 2010. (Songs of the North Wind Ser.). (ENG.). 32p. (J). (gr. -1-2). pap. 12.95 *(978-1-897252-66-6(8)*, 79cefaad-cb14-4988-b27e-bd002c957d59) Fifth Hse. Pubs. CAN. Dist: Firefly Bks., Ltd.
—Lullaby Berceuse: A Warm Prairie Night. Kaldor, Connie & Campagne, Carmen. 2006. (ENG & FRE.). 40p. (J). (gr. -1-2). 16.95 *(978-2-923163-22-2(2))* La Montagne Secrete CAN. Dist: Independent Pubs. Group.
—Number 21, 1 vol. Hundal, Nancy. 2004. (ENG.). 32p. (J). (gr. -1-k). pap. 9.95 *(978-1-55041-905-4(6)*, 6682640b-2679-4cbe-b01c-d427bceb8ef1) Trifolium Bks., Inc. CAN. Dist: Firefly Bks., Ltd.
—On Uncle John's Farm, 1 vol. Fitz-Gibbon, Sally. 2006. (ENG.). 32p. (J). (gr. -1-1). 6.95 *(978-1-55041-886-6(6)*, 400c3a90-22a7-4e12-9964-b0f0b18d0bb0) Trifolium Bks., Inc. CAN. Dist: Firefly Bks., Ltd.
—Prairie Summer, 1 vol. Hundal, Nancy. 2003. (ENG.). 40p. (J). (gr. k-3). pap. 9.95 *(978-1-55041-710-4(X)*, cc34fcd7-f944-4ce6-a294-21d8f9fa12d5) éditeur, Annika Parance CAN. Dist: Firefly Bks., Ltd.
—SkySisters. Bourdeau Waboose, Jan. 2007. (ENG.). 32p. (gr. k-3). 8.95 *(978-1-55074-699-0(5))* Kids Can Pr., Ltd. CAN. Dist: Perfection Learning Corp.
Deines, Brian, et al. A World of Kindness. Del Rizzo, Suzanne. Featherstone, Ann, ed. 2020. (ENG.). 32p. (J). (gr. -1-1). 12.95 *(978-1-77278-109-0(6))* Pajama Pr. CAN. Dist: Ingram Publisher Services.
Deisadze, Zaur. Andy's Cherry Tree. Haxhia, Miranda. 2007. (POL & ENG.). 32p. (J). pap. 12.95 *(978-1-60195-094-9(2))* International Step by Step Assn.
—To Have a Dog. Brezinova, Ivona. 2007. (POL & ENG.). 32p. (J). pap. 12.95 *(978-1-60195-106-9(X))* International Step by Step Assn.
Deisboeck, Thomas. The Case of the Plastic Rings: The Adventures of Planetman. Cioffi, Karen. 2020. (Adventures of Planetman Ser.: Vol. 1). (ENG.). 48p. (J). 21.99 ***(978-1-950074-18-1(8))***; pap. 17.99 ***(978-1-950074-17-4(X))*** 4RV Pub.
Deisher, Kathleen E. Beyond the Gloesmur: Book 1 in the Gloesmur Scrolls. Deisher, Kathleen E. 2003. (Gloesmur Scrolls Ser.). 270p. (J). pap. 13.95 *(978-1-892135-00-1(0))* Lamp Post Publishing, Inc.
Deiss, Veronique. Je Veux des Lunettes ! Moundlic, Charlotte. 2010. (A. M. Zephyr Ser.). (FRE.). 40p. (J). *(978-2-226-20727-2(9))* Albin-Michel, Editions.
DeJesus, Melissa. Fan Art. Tregay, Sarah. 2014. (ENG.). 368p. (YA). (gr. 8). 17.99 *(978-0-06-224315-7(2)*, Tegen, Katherine Bks) HarperCollins Pubs.
—Sokora Refugees. Segamu. 2006. (Sokora Refugees Ser.: Vol. 2). 192p. pap. 9.99 *(978-1-59816-551-7(8))* TOKYOPOP, Inc.
—Sokora Refugees, Vol. 1. 2005. 192p. pap. 14.99 *(978-1-59532-736-9(3)*, Tokyopop Adult) TOKYOPOP, Inc.
DeJesus, Robert. Another Nastybook: The Curse of the Tweeties. Yourgrau, Barry. 2006. 171p. (J). (gr. 5-9). lib. bdg. 13.89 *(978-0-06-057982-1(X)*, Cotler, Joanna Books) HarperCollins Pubs.
DeJong Artman, Catherine & Artman, Townsend. The Further Adventures of a Lucky Dog: Owney, U. S. Rail Mail Mascot. Wales, Dirk. 2009. 32p. (J). (gr. -1-7). 17.95 *(978-0-9632459-6-0(1))* Great Plains Pr.
Dek, Maria. Good Morning Neighbor: (Picture Book on Sharing, Kindness, & Working As a Team, Ages 4-8) Cali, Davide. 2018. (ENG.). 48p. (J). (gr. -1-2). 17.95 *(978-1-61689-699-7(X))* Princeton Architectural Pr.
—Look, It's Raining: (rainy Day Inspiration for Kids, Ages 3-6, Encourages Exploration & Independence) Pierloot, Mathieu. 2019. (ENG.). (J). (gr. -1-1). 17.95 *(978-1-61689-828-1(3))* Princeton Architectural Pr.
DeKnight, Cathy. A Family of His Own. Brown, Stacia Bradley. 2004. (J). 14.95 *(978-1-58597-283-8(5))* Leathers Publishing.
Del Ángel, Jorge. Cuentos para una Noche de Insomnio. Estrada, Jorge. 2014. (SPA.). 88p. (J). (gr. k-2). pap. 7.95 *(978-607-8237-37-1(3))* Nostra Ediciones MEX. Dist: Independent Pubs. Group.
del Conte, Mia. Andy's Discovery. Benjamin, Matthew C. 2003. 78p. (J). per. 8.95 *(978-0-9744672-0-7(0))* Adventure & Discovery Pr.
—Ricky's Adventure. Benjamin, Matthew C. 2003. 94p. (J). per. 8.95 *(978-0-9744672-1-4(9))* Adventure & Discovery Pr.
Del Duca, Leila. Wonder Woman: Tempest Tossed. Anderson, Laurie Halse. 2020. 208p. (J). (gr. 9). pap. 16.99 ***(978-1-4012-8645-3(3))*** DC Comics.
Del Mundo, Mike, et al. Thor by Jason Aaron Vol. 4. 2020. (ENG.). 272p. (YA). (gr. 8-17). 34.99 ***(978-1-302-92385-3(4))*** Marvel Worldwide, Inc.
Del Mundo, Mike. Thor Vol. 3: War's End. 2019. (Thor - 2018 Ser.: 3). 120p. (YA). (gr. 8-17). pap. 15.99 *(978-1-302-91445-5(6))* Marvel Worldwide, Inc.
Del Mundo, Mike, jt. illus. see Moore, Tony.
Del Mundo, Mike, jt. illus. see Noto, Phil.
del Pennino, Mario. Marvel Super Hero Adventures: Captain Marvel. 2019. (ENG.). 112p. (J). (gr. 1-3). pap. 9.99 *(978-1-302-91569-8(X))* Marvel Worldwide, Inc.
Del Rizzo, Suzanne. Gerbil, Uncurled, 1 vol. Hughes, Alison. 2015. (ENG.). 32p. (J). (gr. -1-2). 18.95 *(978-1-55455-332-7(6)*, da681f37-da55-467a-a08f-56a959582ce0) Fitzhenry & Whiteside, Ltd. CAN. Dist: Firefly Bks., Ltd.
—Sun Dog. Kerbel, Deborah. 2018. (ENG.). 32p. (J). (gr. k-2). 17.95 *(978-1-77278-038-3(3))* Pajama Pr. CAN. Dist: Ingram Publisher Services.
Del Rizzo, Suzanne. My Beautiful Birds. Del Rizzo, Suzanne. 2017. (ENG.). 32p. (J). (gr. 1-3). 18.95 *(978-1-77278-010-9(3))* Pajama Pr. CAN. Dist: Ingram Publisher Services.
Del Russo, John William, Sr. & Del Russo, John William. How Scooter Gets His Tail Back. Godsey, J. P. "Gus". 2014. (ENG.). 46p. (gr. 2-6). pap. 9.95 *(978-1-63047-003-6(1))* Morgan James Publishing.
Del Russo, John William, jt. illus. see Del Russo, John William, Sr.
Del Toro, Mark. Somewhere in Texas. Fitzgibbon, Diana. Gonzales, Diana, ed. 2004. 32p. (J). *(978-0-9747587-0-1(1))* Mike-Auri Bks.
del Valle, Clara J., photos by. Gisselle's Adventures in Color. Ames, Heidi L. 2010. 36p. pap. 14.95 *(978-1-60844-436-6(8))* Dog Ear Publishing, LLC.
Dela Cruz, Abigail. Babies in the Ocean. Swift, Ginger. Cottage Door Press, ed. 2020. (Babies Love Ser.). (ENG.). 12p. (J). (gr. -1 — 1). bds. 7.99 ***(978-1-68052-979-1(X)***, 1006070) Cottage Door Pr.
Dela Cruz, Abigail. Lights & Music Christmas Songs: Lights & Music Board Book. Berry Byrd, Holly. Cottage Door Press, ed. 2018. (ENG.). 12p. (J). (gr. -1-k). bds. 16.99 *(978-1-68052-347-8(3)*, 1003190) Cottage Door Pr.
dela Noche Milne, April. The Imperfect Garden, 1 vol. Assaly, Melissa. 2019. (ENG.). 36p. (J). (gr. -1-3). 19.95 *(978-1-55455-408-9(X)*, c0b88459-11cb-4208-8378-1f3f29717580) Fitzhenry & Whiteside, Ltd. CAN. Dist: Firefly Bks., Ltd.
Delaborde, Gilles, photos by. Face-to-Face with the Horse: Faster Than the Wind. Tracqui, Valérie. 2004. (Face to Face Ser.). 28p. (J). (gr. -1-2). 9.95 *(978-1-57091-450-8(8))* Charlesbridge Publishing, Inc.
Delacre, Lulu. El Flamboyan Amarillo. Leon, Georgina Lazaro & León, Georgina Lázaro. 2nd ed. 2016.Tr. of Yellow Flame Tree. (SPA.). 32p. (J). 14.99 *(978-1-930332-55-3(6))* Lectorum Pubns., Inc.
—Pasando Páginas: La Historia de Mi Vida. Sotomayor, Sonia. 2018. (SPA.). 40p. (J). (gr. -1-3). 17.99 *(978-0-525-51549-4(6)*, Philomel Bks.) Penguin Young Readers Group.
—Shake It, Morena! And Other Folklore from Puerto Rico. Bernier-Grand, Carmen T. 2007. 48p. (J). (gr. -1-3). per. 6.95 *(978-0-8225-7026-4(2)*, First Avenue Editions) Lerner Publishing Group.
—The Storyteller's Candle: La Velita de Los Cuentos, 1 vol. González, Lucía. 2013. (ENG & SPA.). 32p. (J). (gr. 1-6). pap. 10.95 *(978-0-89239-237-7(1)*, 4189b703-66e4-4060-90bf-83a19b9d69a9, Children's Book Press) Lee & Low Bks., Inc.
—Turning Pages: My Life Story. Sotomayor, Sonia. 2018. 40p. (J). (gr. -1-3). 17.99 *(978-0-525-51408-4(2)*, Philomel Bks.) Penguin Young Readers Group.
—Los Zapaticos de Rosa. Martí, José & José, Martí. 2003. (SPA.). 84p. *(978-84-241-3352-8(8)*, LC4069) Everest Editora ESP. Dist: Lectorum Pubns., Inc.
Delacre, Lulu. How Far Do You Love Me? Delacre, Lulu. (ENG.). (J). 2014. pap. 8.95 *(978-1-62014-208-0(2))*; 2013. 32p. 11.95 *(978-1-60060-882-7(5))* Lee & Low Bks., Inc.
—Jay & Ben. Delacre, Lulu. Swanson, Katharine. 2013. (ENG.). 18p. (J). bds. 20.00 *(978-1-60060-460-7(9))* Lee & Low Bks., Inc.
Delacre, Lulu. Luci Soars. Delacre, Lulu. 2020. 32p. (J). (gr. -1-3). 17.99 ***(978-1-9848-1288-9(2)***, Philomel Bks.) Penguin Young Readers Group.
Delacre, Lulu. ¡Olinguito, de la A a la Z!: Descubriendo el Bosque Nublado: Olinguito, from A to Z!: Unveiling the Cloud Forest, 1 vol. Delacre, Lulu. ed. 2016. (ENG & SPA.). 40p. (J). (gr. k-6). 19.95 *(978-0-89239-327-5(0)*, 2eec40ce-f5f4-4c0d-b218-7596bbd920f2) Lee & Low Bks., Inc.
—Rafi & Rosi. Delacre, Lulu. 2005. (I Can Read Bks.). 64p. (J). (gr. k-3). pap. 3.99 *(978-0-06-009897-1(X)*, Rayo) HarperCollins Pubs.
—Rafi & Rosi. Delacre, Lulu. 2016. (Rafi & Rosi Ser.). (ENG.). 63p. (J). (gr. k-3). pap. 10.95 *(978-0-89239-377-0(7))* Lee & Low Bks., Inc.
—Rafi & Rosi: Music!, 1 vol. Delacre, Lulu. 2019. (Rafi & Rosi Ser.). (ENG.). 64p. (J). (gr. 1-3). pap. 10.95 *(978-0-89239-431-9(5)*, b24cace3-0cfe-4b8d-93f2-01a717f2c8c2, Children's Book Press) Lee & Low Bks., Inc.
—Rafi y Rosi. Delacre, Lulu. 2016. (Rafi & Rosi Ser.).Tr. of Rafi & Rosi. (SPA.). (J). pap. 10.95 *(978-0-89239-378-7(5))* Lee & Low Bks., Inc.
—Rafi y Rosi ¡Música!, 1 vol. Delacre, Lulu. 2019. (Rafi & Rosi Ser.). (SPA.). 64p. (J). (gr. k-3). pap. 9.95 *(978-0-89239-432-6(3)*, 31bc392c-8751-4831-bdd9-a9a7da26b9cd, Children's Book Press) Lee & Low Bks., Inc.
—Rafi y Rosi ¡Piratas! Delacre, Lulu. 2018. (Rafi & Rosi Ser.). (SPA.). 64p. (J). 16.95 *(978-0-89239-428-9(5))* Lee & Low Bks., Inc.
—Salsa Stories. Delacre, Lulu. 2012. (ENG.). 112p. (J). (gr. 2-5). pap. 6.99 *(978-0-545-43098-2(4)*, Scholastic Pr.) Scholastic, Inc.
—Us, in Progress: Short Stories about Young Latinos. Delacre, Lulu. (ENG.). 256p. (J). (gr. 3-7). 2019. pap. 7.99 *(978-0-06-239215-2(8))*; 2017. 16.99 *(978-0-06-239214-5(X))* HarperCollins Pubs.
Delacre, Lulu. Arrorro Mi Nino: Latino Lullabies & Gentle Games, 1 vol. Delacre, Lulu, compiled by. 2004. (ENG & SPA.). 32p. (J). 16.95 *(978-1-58430-159-2(7))* Lee & Low Bks., Inc.
Delacroix, Sibylle. Jesus Stories from the Bible. Grossetête, Charlotte et al. 2018. (ENG.). 48p. (J). (gr. -1-4). 15.99 *(978-1-62164-226-8(7))* Ignatius Pr.
DeLage, Charlene. Buds & Blossoms: A Book about Flowers, 1 vol. Blackaby, Susan. 2003. (Growing Things Ser.). (ENG.). 24p. (J). (gr. -1-2). per. 8.95 *(978-1-4048-0388-6(2)*, Picture Window Bks.) Capstone.
Delage, Charlene. Catching Sunlight: A Book about Leaves, 1 vol. Blackaby, Susan. 2003. (Growing Things Ser.). (ENG.). 24p. (J). (gr. -1-2). per. 8.95 *(978-1-4048-0387-9(4)*, Picture Window Bks.) Capstone.
DeLage, Charlene. Green & Growing: A Book about Plants. Blackaby, Susan. 2003. (Growing Things Ser.). (ENG.). 24p. (J). (gr. -1-2). 27.32 *(978-1-4048-0107-3(3)*, Picture Window Bks.) Capstone.
Delage, Charlene. El Patito Feo. Blackaby, Susan. Ruíz, Carlos, tr. 2006. (Read-It! Readers en Español: Cuentos de Hadas Ser.). (SPA.). 32p. (J). (gr. k-3). 21.32 *(978-1-4048-1644-2(5)*, Picture Window Bks.) Capstone.
—Plant Packages: A Book about Seeds, 1 vol. Blackaby, Susan. 2003. (Growing Things Ser.). (ENG.). 24p. (J). (gr. -1-2). per. 8.95 *(978-1-4048-0384-8(X)*, Picture Window Bks.) Capstone.
DeLage, Charlene. Plant Plumbing: A Book about Roots & Stems. Blackaby, Susan. 2003. (Growing Things Ser.). (ENG.). 24p. (J). (gr. -1-2). 27.32 *(978-1-4048-0109-7(X))*; per. 8.95 *(978-1-4048-0385-5(8))* Capstone. (Picture Window Bks.).
Delage, Kristi, jt. illus. see Hanson, Sandy.
Delahaye, Genine. Baby Peekaboo! Tiger Tales. 2019. (You're My Baby Ser.). (ENG.). 12p. (J). (gr. 2 — 1). bds. 9.99 *(978-1-68010-594-0(9))* Tiger Tales.
—Hickory, Dickory, Dock. Tiger Tales. 2017. (ENG.). 24p. (J). (gr. -1-k). bds. 9.99 *(978-1-68010-525-4(6))* Tiger Tales.
—It's Your Birthday! 2018. (Special Delivery Bks.). (ENG.). 8p. (J). (gr. -1 — 1). bds. 6.49 *(978-1-68412-266-0(X)*, Silver Dolphin Bks.) Printers Row Publishing Group.
—This Little Piggy. Tiger Tales. 2018. (ENG.). 24p. (J). (gr. -1-k). bds. 9.99 *(978-1-68010-536-0(1))* Tiger Tales.
—To Baby, with Love. 2018. (Special Delivery Bks.). (ENG.). 8p. (J). (— 1). bds. 6.49 *(978-1-68412-267-7(8)*, Silver Dolphin Bks.) Printers Row Publishing Group.
Delainey, James. The Savage River: Seventy-One Days with Simon Fraser, 1 vol. Campbell, Marjorie Wilkins. 2003. (ENG.). 149p. (YA). (gr. 10-12). pap. 8.95 *(978-1-894856-24-9(4)*, 210ee4b2-62b9-434c-916c-7e367941b473) Fifth Hse. Pubs. CAN. Dist: Firefly Bks., Ltd.
Delandro Hardison, Brian. The Journey of Odysseus, Vol. DeHoratius, Ed. 2009. (Follow Your Fates Ser.). (ENG.). 116p. (J). pap. 12.00 *(978-0-86516-710-0(9))* Bolchazy-Carducci Pubs.
Delaney, A. I Think That It Is Wonderful (Sesame Street) Korr, David. 2018. (Little Golden Book Ser.). 24p. (J). (-k). 4.99 *(978-1-5247-6826-3(X)*, Golden Bks.) Random Hse. Children's Bks.
Delaney, Deborah. Me, the Center of the Universe. Villafana, Yolanda. 2019. (ENG.). 28p. (J). pap. 9.99 ***(978-1-7016-7035-8(6))*** Independently Published.
DeLaney, Edgar Azell. The Magical Hammock. DeLaney, Edgar Azell. 2004. (ENG.). 83p. (J). 19.95 *(978-0-9759013-0-4(3))* Special Edition Studios, Inc.
Delaney, John. Scooby-Doo in Hear No Evil, 1 vol. Kress, Earl. 2010. (Scooby-Doo Graphic Novels Ser.: No. 1). (ENG.). 24p. (J). (gr. 2-6). 27.07 *(978-1-59961-694-0(7)*, 562, Graphic Novels) Spotlight.
Delaney, Molly. Mat Man Hats. Olsen, Jan Z. 2008. (ENG.). 36p. stu. ed. 13.75 *(978-1-891627-93-4(7))* Handwriting Without Tears.
—Mat Man on the Go. Olsen, Jan Z. 2010. (ENG.). stu. ed. 13.75 *(978-1-934825-39-6(5))* Handwriting Without Tears.
—Mat Man Opposites. Olsen, Jan Z. 2009. (ENG.). stu. ed. 13.75 *(978-1-891627-94-1(5))* Handwriting Without Tears.
—Mat Man Shapes. Olsen, Jan Z. 2007. (ENG.). 32p. stu. ed. 13.75 *(978-1-891627-92-7(9))* Handwriting Without Tears.
—No Peas, Please! Athey, Victoria. 2005. (ENG.). 20p. (gr. k-2). pap. 8.95 *(978-1-57874-087-1(8)*, Kaeden Bks.) Kaeden Corp.
—Which Way Did They Go? Williams, Rozanne Lanczak. Hamaguchi, Carla, ed. 2003. (Sight Word Readers Ser.). 16p. (J). (gr. k-2). pap. 2.99 *(978-1-57471-971-0(8)*, 3593) Creative Teaching Pr., Inc.
—Zero's Slider. Christopher, Matt. 2009. (New Peach Street Mudders Sports Library). 64p. (J). (gr. 2-4). lib. bdg. 23.93 *(978-1-59953-323-0(5))* Norwood Hse. Pr.
DeLange, Alex Pardo. The Empanadas That Abuela Made/Las Empandas Que Hacia la Abuela. Bertrand, Diane Gonzales. Ventura, Gabriela Baeza, tr. (ENG & SPA.). 32p. (J). 16.95 *(978-1-55885-388-1(X)*, Piñata Books) Arte Publico Pr.
Delange, Alex Pardo. Pepita on Pepper Street/Pepita en la Calle Pepper. Lachtman, Ofelia Dumas. Monsivais, Maria Estela, tr. from ENG. 2008. (SPA & ENG.). 32p. (J). (gr. -1-3). 16.95 *(978-1-55885-443-7(6)*, Piñata Books) Arte Publico Pr.
—Pepita Packs Up: Pepita Empaca. Lachtman, Ofelia Dumas. Ventura, Gabriela Baeza, tr. from ENG. 2005. 48p. (J). (gr. -1-k). lib. bdg. 16.95 *(978-1-55885-431-4(2)*, Piñata Books) Arte Publico Pr.
—Sip, Slurp, Soup, Soup/Caldo, Caldo, Caldo. Bertrand, Diane Gonzales. Castilla, Julia Mercedes, tr. 2008. (SPA & ENG.). 32p. (J). (gr. -1-2). pap. 7.95 *(978-1-55885-241-9(7)*, Piñata Books) Arte Publico Pr.
DeLange, Alex Pardo. Sip, Slurp, Soup Soup/Caldo Caldo Caldo: CD & Book Set. Bertrand, Diane Gonzales. 2008. 32p. (J). pap. 19.95 *(978-0-9815686-1-4(0))* Lorito Bks., Inc.
Delano, Aryn. The Sky Is the Limit: The Story of Ms. Margaret's Magic Hats. Delano, Aryn. 2019. (Sky Is the Limit Ser.: Vol. 1). (ENG.). 40p. (J). (gr. k-4). 17.00 *(978-0-578-46906-5(5))* Murray, Aryn D.
Delanssay, Cathy. Give Me Moon. Galliez, Roxane Marie. 2009. 44p. (J). (gr. -1-3). 14.99 *(978-0-8416-7138-6(9))* Hammond World Atlas Corp.
—The Secret Life of Princesses. Hanna, Virginie. 2009. 26p. (J). (gr. -1-3). 17.99 *(978-0-8437-1476-0(X))* Hammond World Atlas Corp.
Delanssay, Cathy, et al. 18 Historias de Princesas y de Hadas. Agin, Elodie et al. Oyaga, Irene, tr. from FRE. 2010. (SPA.). 118p. (J). (gr. 1-4). 24.95 *(978-84-96939-04-2(9))* Roca Editorial ESP. Dist: Spanish Pubs., LLC.
Delany, Shannon. Tangled Lines: Paradise in Peril. Doerr, Bonnie J. Hashway, Kelly, ed. 2016. (ENG.). (J). (gr. 3-6). pap. 15.99 *(978-1-61603-079-7(8))* Leap Bks.
Delapaz, Archie. Grommet & Shaka. Krasny, M. J. S. 2019. (ENG.). 48p. (J). pap. 14.99 ***(978-1-7342210-8-4(9))*** Mindstir Media.
Delaurent, Trisha, photos by. Isabella's Aviary. Zajac, Kristen. 2016. (ENG., (J). 19.95 *(978-1-61633-820-6(2))*; pap. 11.95 *(978-1-61633-821-3(0))* Guardian Angel Publishing, Inc.
Delclos, Jordi V. Vero y el Fantasma de Canterville. Puerto, Carlos. 2005. 121p. (J). (gr. 6-10). 14.40 *(978-84-263-5180-7(8))* Vives, Luis Editorial (Edelvives) ESP. Dist: Lectorum Pubns., Inc.

D

Delclòs, Jordi Vila. A Meeting in the Sky. Singh, Rina. 2019. (ENG.). 32p. (J). (gr. 3-5). 19.99 *(978-1-56846-310-0(3)*, Creative Editions) Creative Co., The.
Delcoglin, Nathan. Bella's Umbrella. Delcoglin, Gwen. 2007. 28p. (J). (gr. -1-3). per. 10.99 *(978-1-59879-315-4(2))* Lifevest Publishing, Inc.
Delderfield, Angela. The Adventures of Charlie. Moseley, Sophia. 2012. 106p. pap. *(978-1-78148-757-0(X))* Grosvenor Hse. Publishing Ltd.
Delehanty, Joan M. Manners I. Care. Bruce, David. 2006. 32p. (J). 16.95 *(978-0-9771143-2-0(5))* Child Life Bks., LLC.
—What Does the Wind Say? Silvano, Wendi. 2006. (ENG.). 32p. (J). (gr. -1-k). 15.95 *(978-1-55971-954-4(0))* Cooper Square Publishing Llc.
DeLeon, Roy. Margaret & the Pope Go to Assisi. Sweeney, Jon M. 2020. (Pope's Cat Ser.). (ENG.). 64p. (J). (gr. 1-4). pap. 10.99 *(978-1-64060-170-3(8)*, 01703) Paraclete Pr., Inc.
—Margaret's First Holy Week. Sweeney, Jon M. 2019. (Pope's Cat Ser.). (ENG.). 64p. (J). (gr. 1-4). pap. 9.99 *(978-1-61261-937-8(1))* Paraclete Pr., Inc.
—Margaret's Night in St. Peter's (a Christmas Story) Sweeney, Jon M. 2018. (Pope's Cat Ser.: 2). (ENG.). 64p. (J). (gr. 1-4). pap. 10.99 *(978-1-61261-936-1(3))* Paraclete Pr., Inc.
—The Pope's Cat. Sweeney, Jon M. 2018. (Pope's Cat Ser.: 1). (ENG.). 64p. (J). (gr. 1). pap. 9.99 *(978-1-61261-935-4(5))* Paraclete Pr., Inc.
Delessert, Etienne. The Happy Prince. Wilde, Oscar. 2008. (Creative Short Stories Ser.). 32p. (YA). (gr. 9-18). lib. bdg. 28.50 *(978-1-58341-582-5(3)*, Creative Education) Creative Co., The.
—I Hate to Read! Marshall, Rita. 2013. (ENG.). 32p. (J). (gr. k-17). 16.99 *(978-1-56846-232-5(8)*, Creative Editions) Creative Co., The.
—I Hate to Read! Marshall, Rita. 2008. (J). (gr. k-3). 27.95 incl. audio *(978-0-8045-6973-6(8))*; 29.95 incl. audio compact disk *(978-0-8045-4198-5(1))* Spoken Arts, Inc.
—I Still Hate to Read! Marshall, Rita. 2008. (ENG.). 32p. (J). (gr. 1-3). 19.95 *(978-1-56846-174-8(7)*, Creative Editions) Creative Co., The.
—I Still Hate to Read! Marshall, Rita. 2008. (J). (gr. k-3). 27.95 incl. audio *(978-0-8045-6974-3(6))*; 29.95 incl. audio compact disk *(978-0-8045-4199-2(X))* Spoken Arts, Inc.
—John Keats. Kirkpatrick, Patricia. 2005. (Voices in Poetry Ser.). 43p. (J). (gr. 5-9). 21.95 *(978-1-58341-345-6(6)*, Creative Education) Creative Co., The.

—The Lonely Pine. Frisch, Aaron. 2011. (ENG.). 32p. (J). (gr. 1-3). 17.99 (978-1-56846-214-1(X), Creative Editions) Creative Co., The.

—The Ransom of Red Chief. Henry, O. 2008. (Creative Short Stories Ser.). 32p. (YA). (gr. 9-18). lib. bdg. 28.50 (978-1-58341-585-6(8), Creative Education) Creative Co., The.

Delessert, Etienne. A Glass. Delessert, Etienne. 2013. (ENG.). 32p. (J). (gr. 4-7). 18.99 (978-1-56846-257-8(3), Creative Editions) Creative Co., The.

—A Was an Apple Pie. Delessert, Etienne. 2005. (Creative Editions Ser.). 28p. (J). (gr. -1-3). 18.95 (978-1-56846-196-0(8)) Creative Co., The.

Delezenne, Christine. The Courage of Elfina. Jacob, André. Ouriou, Susan, tr. 2019. (ENG.). 64p. (YA). (gr. 7-12). 24.95 (978-1-4594-1419-8(5), a798247b-2030-41ba-8013-c0ff357ccc3f) James Lorimer & Co. Ltd., Pubs. CAN. Dist: Lerner Publishing Group.

—Le Monde de Xéros. Plante, Raymond. 2004. (Roman Jeunesse Ser.). (FRE.). 96p. (J). (gr. 4-7). pap. (978-2-89021-615-0(2)) Diffusion du livre Mirabel (DLM).

Delf, Brian. Atlas Visual del Mundo. Kemp, Richard. (SPA.). 80p. (YA). (gr. 5-8). (978-84-216-1576-8(9), BU4606) Bruño, Editorial ESP. Dist: Lectorum Pubns., Inc.

Delgado Cabeza, Yaritza. La Comarca de la Abuela Chicha. Baratutes Benavides, Eldys. 2019. (SPA.). 76p. (J). pap. 22.50 (978-1-6988-1571-8(9)) Independently Published.

—El P�jaro de Fuego. Baratutes Benavides, Eldys. 2019. (SPA.). 36p. (J). pap. 18.50 (978-1-6985-1568-7(5)) Independently Published.

—Petrushka. Fraguela, José Raúl. 2019. (SPA.). 38p. (J). pap. 24.50 (978-1-6993-8555-5(6)) Independently Published.

Delgado, Chieko. Where Is Dahnya's Rosary: A Family Rosary Book. Bernardine, Isabela. 2017. (ENG.). 36p. (J). (gr. k-4). (978-0-692-19912-1(8)) Rosmini House.

Delgado, Edgar, jt. illus. see Larroca, Salvador.

Delgado, Francisco. Birdie's Beauty Parlor: El Salón de Belleza de Birdy. Byrd, Lee Merrill. 2018. (SPA & ENG.). (J). (978-1-947627-02-4(3)) Cinco Puntos Pr.

Delgado, Francisco. ¡Sí, Se Puede! Cohn, Diana.Tr. of Yes, We Can!. (SPA.). 32p. (J). 2009. (gr. k-2). pap. 8.95 (978-0-938317-89-0(X)); 2008. (gr. 1-5). 15.95 (978-0-938317-66-1(0)) Cinco Puntos Pr.

—Lover Boy / Juanito el Carinoso: A Bilingual Counting Book. Byrd, Lee Merrill. 2005. (ENG.). 32p. (J). (gr. -1-2). 15.95 (978-0-938317-38-8(5)) Cinco Puntos Pr.

Delgado, Juan. Angel Travieso y la Flor Encantada: Angelín Bravín y Maltecita Florecita. del Pino Batueca, Belkis, ed. 2018. (SPA.). 68p. (J). pap. 5.50 (978-1-7177-2203-4(2)) Independently Published.

Delgado, Luis Antoni, jt. illus. see Schoening, Dan.

Delgado, Luis Antonio, jt. illus. see Schoening, Dan.

Delicado, Federico. Finch. Sobrino, Javier. Brokenbrow, Jon, tr. 2019. (ENG.). 28p. (J). 16.95 (978-84-16733-52-1(X)) Cuento de Luz SL ESP. Dist: Publishers Group West (PGW).

—Pinzón. Sobrino, Javier. 2019. (SPA.). 28p. (J). 16.95 (978-84-16733-51-4(1)) Cuento de Luz SL ESP. Dist: Publishers Group West (PGW).

Delice, Shelly Meredith. A Monster Named Criney Who Makes Kids Whiney. Zuckerman, Heather. 2005. 32p. (J). (gr. -1-3). 15.95 (978-0-9744307-0-6(6)) Merry Lane Pr.

Delinois, Alix. Eight Days: A Story of Haiti. Danticat, Edwidge. 2010. (ENG.). 32p. (J). (gr. -1-1). 17.99 (978-0-545-27849-2(X), Orchard Bks.) Scholastic, Inc.

—Greetings, Leroy, 1 vol. Sadu, Itah. 2017. (ENG.). 32p. (J). (gr. -1-2). 18.95 (978-1-55498-760-3(1)) Groundwood Bks. CAN. Dist: Publishers Group West (PGW).

—Muhammad Ali: The People's Champion. Myers, Walter Dean. (ENG.). 40p. (J). (gr. -1-3). 2016. pap. 7.99 (978-0-06-443718-9(3), Amistad); 2009. 16.99 (978-0-06-029131-0(1), Collins) HarperCollins Pubs.

—Mumbet's Declaration of Independence. Woelfle, Gretchen. 2014. (ENG.). 32p. (J). (gr. 1-4). 17.95 (978-0-7613-6589-1(3), 9780761365891, Carolrhoda Bks.) Lerner Publishing Group.

Delioglu, Mustafa. Kangaroo Clues. Finke, Margot. 2013. 16p. pap. 9.95 (978-1-61633-368-3(5)) Guardian Angel Publishing, Inc.

Delios, Kim, photos by. Aussie Toddlers Can. Magabala Books Staff. l.t. ed. 2006. 10p. (J). bds. (978-1-875641-88-8(2)) Magabala Bks.

Delisa, Patricia. Little Red Riding Hood: The Classic Grimm's Fairy Tale, 1 vol. Flaxman, Andrew. 2006. (ENG.). 32p. (J). (gr. -1-3). 14.95 (978-0-88010-571-2(2), Bell Pond Bks.) SteinerBooks, Inc.

Delisle, Anne-Claire. Really & Truly. Rivard, Émilie & Rivard, Émilie. 2012. (ENG.). 24p. (J). (gr. -1-3). 15.95 (978-1-926973-40-1(2)) Owlkids Bks. Inc. CAN. Dist: Publishers Group West (PGW).

Delisle, Kathryn H. It's Christmas Again! Frrich, Lewandowski & Riccards, Michael. 2007. 32p. (J). 14.95 (978-1-929039-44-9(1)) Ambassador Bks., Inc.

Deliu, Andreea. Daddy Gave Me the Magic. Stoica, Dana Irina. 2019. (ENG.). 32p. (J). pap. 10.99 (978-1-0731-1838-0(X)) Independently Published.

Deliu, Andreea. Mommy Gave Me the Moon. Stoica, Dana Irina. 2018. (Generosity Book Collection). (ENG.). 30p. (J). 15.99 (978-0-692-16913-1(X)) Stoica, Dana.

Delk, Chrissy. The Girl Who Owned a City: Graphic Novel. Nelson, O. T. 2012. (Single Titles Ser.). (ENG.). 128p. (YA). (gr. 5-12). lib. bdg. 29.27 (978-0-7613-4903-7(0), Graphic Universe™) Lerner Publishing Group.

Dell, Jacob J., photos by. A Piece of Notre Dame: A pictorial guide to the University of Notre Dame, leading you on an insightful tour of the often unnoticed, yet beautifully crafted details of Campus. Dell, Jacob J. Dell, Rachel E. Wilson, Robin M., ed. 2005. 14.87 (978-0-9744544-0-5(0)) Dell, Jacob J.

Della-Rovere, Cynthia. Bush, Blair, & Iraq: Days of Decision, 1 vol. Langley, Andrew. 2013. (Days of Decision Ser.). (ENG.). 64p. (J). (gr. 6-11). pap. 10.95 (978-1-4329-7640-8(0), Heinemann) Capstone.

Dell'edera, Werther. Thicker Than Blackwater, Vol. 2. Azzarello, Brian & Zezelj, Danijel. rev. ed. 2007. (Loveless Ser.). (ENG.). 168p. pap. 14.99 (978-1-4012-1250-6(6), Vertigo) DC Comics.

Dellepiane, Rhonda Mullins. Ruthie Goes to Town: Stories of a Little Amish Girl. Garrett, Ruth Irene. 2005. (Little Ruthie Ser.). (ENG.). 48p. (J). (gr. -1-3). 14.95 (978-0-9773198-2-4(2), Joey Bks.) Acclaim Pr., Inc.

Dellow, Sarah, jt. illus. see Kubler, Annie.

Delmar, Natasha. Fatima la Fileuse et la Tente: French-Arabic Edition. Shah, Idries. 2018. (Hoopoe Teaching-Stories Ser.). (FRE.). 40p. (J). (gr. 3-6). pap. 9.99 (978-1-949358-44-5(5), Hoopoe Bks.) I S H K.

Delmar, Natasha. Fatima the Spinner & the Tent: English-Dari Edition. Shah, Idries. 2017. (Hoopoe Teaching-Stories Ser.). (ENG.). (J). (gr. k-6). pap. 9.99 (978-1-946270-11-5(3), Hoopoe Bks.) I S H K.

—Fatima the Spinner & the Tent: English-Pashto Edition. Shah, Idries. 2017. (Hoopoe Teaching-Stories Ser.). (ENG & PUS.). (J). (gr. 2-6). pap. 9.99 (978-1-944493-56-1(5), Hoopoe Bks.) I S H K.

—Fatima the Spinner & the Tent: English-Urdu Bilingual Edition. Shah, Idries. 2016. (URD & ENG.). (J). (gr. 1-6). pap. 9.99 (978-1-942698-75-3(5), Hoopoe Bks.) I S H K.

—The Old Woman & the Eagle. Shah, Idries. 32p. (J). 2005. (gr. -1-3). pap., pap. 6.99 (978-1-883536-28-2(6)); 2003. 18.00 (978-1-883536-27-5(8), OLWE1) I S H K. (Hoopoe Bks.).

—The Old Woman & the Eagle: English-Dari Edition. Shah, Idries. 2017. (Hoopoe Teaching-Stories Ser.). (ENG.). (J). (gr. k-6). pap. 9.99 (978-1-946270-16-0(4), Hoopoe Bks.) I S H K.

—The Old Woman & the Eagle: English-Pashto Edition. Shah, Idries. 2017. (Hoopoe Teaching-Stories Ser.). (ENG & PUS.). (J). (gr. 1-6). pap. 9.99 (978-1-944493-61-5(1), Hoopoe Bks.) I S H K.

—The Old Woman & the Eagle: English-Urdu Bilingual Edition. Shah, Idries. 2016. (URD & ENG.). (J). (gr. k-6). pap. 9.99 (978-1-942698-78-4(X), Hoopoe Bks.) I S H K.

—The Old Woman & the Eagle HB/CD English. Shah, Idries. 2005. (Sounds of Afghanistan Ser.). (J). (gr. -1-3). 28.95 incl. audio compact disk (978-1-883536-77-0(4), Hoopoe Bks.) I S H K.

Delmar, Natasha. La Vieille Dame et L'aigle: French-Arabic Edition. Shah, Idries. 2018. (Hoopoe Teaching-Stories Ser.). (FRE.). 40p. (J). (gr. k-4). pap. 9.99 (978-1-949358-50-6(X), Hoopoe Bks.) I S H K.

Delmar, Natasha. The Wisdom of Ahmad Shah: An Afghan Legend: English-Dari Edition. Bazger Salam, Palwasha. 2017. (Hoopoe Teaching-Stories Ser.). (ENG.). (J). (gr. k-6). pap. 9.99 (978-1-946270-19-1(9), Hoopoe Bks.) I S H K.

—The Wisdom of Ahmad Shah: English-Pashto Edition. Salam, Palwasha Bazger. 2017. (Hoopoe Teaching-Stories Ser.). (ENG & PUS.). (J). (gr. 2-6). pap. 9.99 (978-1-944493-64-6(6), Hoopoe Bks.) I S H K.

Deloache, Shawn. Medikidz Explain Haemophilia: What's up with Louis? Chilman-Blair, Kim & Hersov, Kate. 2011. 32p. (J). pap. (978-1-906935-29-0(7)) Medikidz Ltd.

—Medikidz Explain Inflammatory Bowel Disease: What's up with Adam?, Vol. Chilman-Blair, Kim & Hersov, Kate. 2011. (ENG.). 32p. (J). pap. (978-1-906935-65-8(3)) Medikidz Ltd.

DeLoatch, Diane. I Can Do It Just Like You. Cason Gilmore, Sabrina F. 2019. (ENG.). 26p. (J). pap. 9.99 (978-1-0748-0461-9(9)) Independently Published.

Delonas, Sean. Twas the Day after Christmas. Snell, Gordon. Date not set. 32p. (J). (gr. -1-3). 5.99 (978-0-06-443675-5(6)) HarperCollins Pubs.

Delort, Nicolas, photos by. Divergent. Roth, Veronica. (Divergent Ser.: 1). (ENG., (YA). (gr. 9). 2014. 576p. pap. 12.99 (978-0-06-238724-0(3)); 2011. 496p. 18.99 (978-0-06-202402-2(7)) HarperCollins Pubs. (Tegen, Katherine Bks).

—Divergent Collector's Edition. Roth, Veronica. collector's ed. 2014. (Divergent Ser.: 1). (ENG., 576p. (YA). (gr. 9). 19.99 (978-0-06-235217-0(2), Tegen, Katherine Bks) HarperCollins Pubs.

—Divergent Movie Tie-In Edition. Roth, Veronica. movie tie-in ed. 2014. (Divergent Ser.: 1). (ENG.). 496p. (YA). (gr. 9). 17.99 (978-0-06-228984-1(5), Tegen, Katherine Bks) HarperCollins Pubs.

Delosh, Diana Ting. Shoes! Brott, Wayne. 2013. (ENG.). (J). (gr. -1-3). 14.95 (978-1-62086-239-1(5)) Mascot Bks., Inc.

Deloudi, Sofia. Mia Träumt: Abenteuer in Einer Wundersamen Parallelwelt. Steurer, Walter. 2019. (GER.). 74p. (J). pap. 14.66 (978-1-9874-2979-4(6)) CreateSpace Independent Publishing Platform.

Delsi, Dawna. Great Tastes of Michigan. Glupker, Dianne. 2006. (J). per. 9.95 (978-0-9769846-1-0(X)) Harambee Pr.

Delsi, Dawna. Great Lights of Michigan. Delsi, Dawna. Glupker, Dianne. 2005. (J). per. 9.95 (978-0-9769846-0-3(1), 318924) Harambee Pr.

DeLuca, Francesca. Grandma's Kitchen: Padded Board Book. Lodi, Madison. Cottage Door Press, ed. 2017. (Love You Always Ser.). (ENG.). 20p. (J). (gr. -1-1). bds. 9.99 (978-1-68052-275-4(2), 1002600) Cottage Door Pr.

Demarest, Chris. Breakfast at Danny's Diner: A Book about Multiplication. Stamper, Judith Bauer. 2003. (All Aboard Math Reader Ser.). 48p. (J). (gr. 2-4). 11.65 (978-0-7569-1695-4(X)) Perfection Learning Corp.

—Ding-Dong, Trick or Treat! Ziefert, Harriet. 2004. 22p. (J). (gr. -1-3). reprint ed. pap. 12.00 (978-0-7567-8258-0(9)) DIANE Publishing Co.

Demarest, Chris. The Donkey's Tale: Level 2. Oppenheim, Joanne. 2020. (ENG.). 34p. (J). pap. 9.95 (978-1-876965-76-1(2)) ibooks, Inc.

Demarest, Chris. Go, Fractions! Stamper, Judith Bauer & Stamper, Judith. 2003. (All Aboard Math Readers Ser.). 48p. (J). (gr. k-3). 16.19 (978-0-448-43113-0(0)) Penguin Young Readers Group.

—Hush That Hullabaloo! Merritt, Donna Marie. 2017. (ENG.). 38p. (J). (gr. 1-6). 19.99 (978-1-64372-011-1(2)) MacLaren-Cochrane Publishing, Inc.

—Hush That Hullabaloo! Merritt, Donna. 2017. (ENG.). 38p. (J). (gr. 1-6). pap. 15.99 (978-1-64372-217-7(4)) Lulu Pr., Inc.

—Hush That Hullabaloo! Dyslexic Edition: Dyslexic Font. Merritt, Donna. 2017. (ENG.). 38p. (J). (gr. 1-6). 19.99 (978-1-64372-218-4(2)); pap. 15.99 (978-1-64372-219-1(0)) Lulu Pr., Inc.

—Red Sled. Thomas, Patricia. (ENG.). 32p. (J). (gr. -1-k). 2013. pap. 6.95 (978-1-62091-592-9(8)); 2008. 16.95 (978-1-59078-559-1(2)) Boyds Mills Pr.

Demarest, Chris. Alpha Bravo Charlie: The Military Alphabet. Demarest, Chris. 2005. (ENG.). 40p. (J). (gr. 1-5). 19.99 (978-0-689-86928-0(2), McElderry, Margaret K. Bks.) McElderry, Margaret K. Bks.

—Firefighters a to Z. Demarest, Chris. 2003. (ENG.). 32p. (J). (gr. -1-3). 7.99 (978-0-689-85999-1(6), McElderry, Margaret K. Bks.) McElderry, Margaret K. Bks.

—Firefighters a to Z. Demarest, Chris. 2003. (ENG.). (J). (gr. -1-3). lib. bdg. 18.60 (978-1-68065-340-3(7)) Perfection Learning Corp.

—Hurricane Hunters! Riders on the Storm. Demarest, Chris. 2006. (ENG.). 40p. (J). (gr. -1-5). 19.99 (978-0-689-86168-0(0), McElderry, Margaret K. Bks.) McElderry, Margaret K. Bks.

—Mayday! Mayday! A Coast Guard Rescue. Demarest, Chris. 2004. (ENG.). 40p. (J). (gr. -1-5). 17.99 (978-0-689-85161-2(8), McElderry, Margaret K. Bks.) McElderry, Margaret K. Bks.

Demarest, Chris L. Leaping Beauty: And Other Animal Fairy Tales. Maguire, Gregory. 2006. (ENG.). 224p. (J). (gr. 3-7). reprint ed. pap. 7.99 (978-0-06-056419-3(9)) HarperCollins Pubs.

Demarest, William. Not Now! Said the Cow. Oppenheim, Joanne. 2018. (Bank Street Ready-To-Read Ser.). (ENG.). 36p. (J). (gr. 1-3). pap. 11.95 (978-1-876965-56-3(8), ipicturebooks) ibooks, Inc.

Demaret, David. Dream Monsters: A 4D Book. Kammer, Gina. 2018. (Mind Drifter Ser.). (ENG.). 128p. (J). (gr. 3-8). lib. bdg. 26.65 (978-1-4965-5896-1(0), 137057, Stone Arch Bks.) Capstone.

—Enemy Mind: A 4D Book. Kammer, Gina. 2018. (Mind Drifter Ser.). (ENG.). 128p. (J). (gr. 3-8). lib. bdg. 26.65 (978-1-4965-5898-5(7), 137059, Stone Arch Bks.) Capstone.

—Mind Drifter. Kammer, Gina. 2018. (Mind Drifter Ser.). (ENG.). 128p. (J). (gr. 3-8). 106.60 (978-1-4965-5908-1(8), 27558, Stone Arch Bks.) Capstone.

—Reject Rebound: A 4D Book. Kammer, Gina. 2018. (Mind Drifter Ser.). (ENG.). 128p. (J). (gr. 3-8). lib. bdg. 26.65 (978-1-4965-5899-2(5), 137061, Stone Arch Bks.) Capstone.

—Wicked Stepsister: A 4D Book. Kammer, Gina. 2018. (Mind Drifter Ser.). (ENG.). 128p. (J). (gr. 3-8). lib. bdg. 26.65 (978-1-4965-5897-8(9), 137058, Stone Arch Bks.) Capstone.

Dematons, Charlotte. Holland & a Thousand Things about Holland. 2013. (ENG.). 176p. (J). (gr. 3). 29.95 (978-1-935954-33-0(4), 9781935954330) Lemniscaat USA.

—Raf. de Vries, Anke. 2009. (ENG.). 32p. (J). (gr. -1-3). 16.95 (978-1-59078-749-6(8)) Lemniscaat USA.

DeMatte, Darcey. God Did Make Little Green Apples. Assunto, Cecelia. 2012. 30p. (J). pap. 12.95 (978-1-61314-028-4(2)) Innovo Publishing, LLC.

Demers, David, photos by. My Grandpa Loves Trains: A Picture Storybook for Preschoolers. Demers, David. Demers, Lee Ann. l.t. ed. 2005. 76p. (J). 27.95 (978-0-922993-36-9(X)) Marquette Bks.

—My Grandpa Loves Trains: A Storybook for Preschoolers. Demers, David. Demers, Lee Ann. l.t. ed. 2005. 76p. (J). per. 19.95 (978-0-922993-23-9(8)) Marquette Bks.

Demetriou, Pedro. Joke-O-Rama. 2018. (ENG.). 64p. (J). (gr. 1-3). pap. 5.99 (978-1-68412-292-9(9), Silver Dolphin Bks.) Printers Row Publishing Group.

Demetris, Alex. Grandma's Box of Memories: Helping Grandma to Remember. Demetris, Jean. 2014. (ENG.). 32p. (J). 17.95 (978-1-84905-993-0(4), 694253) Kingsley, Jessica Pubs. GBR. Dist: Hachette UK Distribution.

Demi. The Conference of the Birds. 2012. 44p. (J). (gr. -1-3). 19.95 (978-1-937786-02-1(1)) World Wisdom, Inc.

—Grass Sandals: The Travels of Basho. Spivak, Dawnine. 2009. (ENG.). 40p. (J). (gr. 4-6). 13.99 (978-1-4424-0936-1(3), Atheneum Bks. for Young Readers) Simon & Schuster Children's Publishing.

—Mahavira: The Hero of Nonviolence, Vol. Jain, Manoj. 2014. (ENG.). 28p. (J). (gr. k-4). 17.95 (978-1-937786-21-2(8), Wisdom Tales) World Wisdom, Inc.

Demi. The Boy Who Painted Dragons. Demi. 2007. (ENG.). 52p. (J). (gr. 2-5). 21.99 (978-1-4169-2469-2(8), McElderry, Margaret K. Bks.) McElderry, Margaret K. Bks.

—Buddha. Demi. 2018. (ENG.). 48p. (J). pap. 9.99 (978-1-250-29407-4(X), 900195035) Square Fish.

—Buddha Stories. Demi. 2018. (ENG.). 32p. (J). pap. 9.99 (978-1-250-29408-1(8), 900195036) Square Fish.

—Columbus, 0 vols. Demi. 2012. (ENG.). 64p. (J). (gr. 4-7). 19.99 (978-0-7614-6167-8(1), 9780761461678, Two Lions) Amazon Publishing.

—The Dalai Lama: With a Foreword by His Holiness the Dalai Lama. Demi. 2018. (ENG.). 32p. (J). pap. 9.99 (978-1-250-29406-7(1), 900195034) Square Fish.

—The Empty Pot. Demi. 2007. (ENG.). 32p. (J). (gr. -1-3). pap. 25.99 (978-0-8050-8227-2(1), 9780805082272, Holt, Henry & Co. Bks. For Young Readers) Holt, Henry & Co.

—The Fantastic Adventures of Krishna, Vol. Demi. 2013. (ENG.). 44p. (J). (gr. -1-3). 19.95 (978-1-937786-05-2(6), Wisdom Tales) World Wisdom, Inc.

—The Girl Who Drew a Phoenix. Demi. 2008. (ENG.). 52p. (J). (gr. 2-5). 29.99 (978-1-4169-5347-0(7), McElderry, Margaret K. Bks.) McElderry, Margaret K. Bks.

—The Greatest Power. Demi. 2004. (ENG.). 40p. (J). (gr. -1-3). 24.99 (978-0-689-84503-1(0), McElderry, Margaret K. Bks.) McElderry, Margaret K. Bks.

—The Hungry Coat: A Tale from Turkey. Demi. 2004. (ENG.). 40p. (J). (gr. 1-5). 21.99 (978-0-689-84680-9(0), McElderry, Margaret K. Bks.) McElderry, Margaret K. Bks.

—Jesus. Demi. 2005. (ENG.). 48p. (J). (gr. 2-5). 24.99 (978-0-689-86905-1(3), McElderry, Margaret K. Bks.) McElderry, Margaret K. Bks.

—The Legend of Saint Nicholas. Demi. 2003. (ENG.). 40p. (J). (gr. k-5). 21.99 (978-0-689-84681-6(9), McElderry, Margaret K. Bks.) McElderry, Margaret K. Bks.

—The Magic Pillow. Demi. 2008. (ENG.). 40p. (J). (gr. 2-5). 24.99 (978-1-4169-2470-8(1), McElderry, Margaret K. Bks.) McElderry, Margaret K. Bks.

—Marie Curie. Demi. 2018. (ENG.). 40p. (J). 19.99 (978-1-62779-389-6(5), 900148733, Holt, Henry & Co. Bks. For Young Readers) Holt, Henry & Co.

—Mozart: Gift of God. Demi. 2019. (ENG.). 48p. (J). (gr. -1-3). 15.99 (978-1-62164-300-5(X)) Ignatius Pr.

—Muhammad. Demi. 2003. (ENG.). 48p. (J). (gr. 2-5). 19.95 (978-0-689-85264-0(9), McElderry, Margaret K. Bks.) McElderry, Margaret K. Bks.

—The Shady Tree. Demi. 2016. (ENG.). 32p. (J). 17.99 (978-1-62779-769-6(6), 900159550, Holt, Henry & Co. Bks. For Young Readers) Holt, Henry & Co.

DeMicco, Michelle. Easy-to-Make Bible Story Puppets. Bendt, Valerie. 2005. 184p. (J). per. 24.00 (978-1-885814-17-3(8)) Valerie Bendt.

Demidova, Olga. Bernard Pepperlin. Hoffman, Cara. 2019. (ENG.). 224p. (J). (gr. 3-7). 16.99 (978-0-06-286544-1(7)) HarperCollins Pubs.

—A Friendship Yarn. Moser, Lisa. 2019. (ENG.). 32p. (J). (gr. -1-3). 16.99 (978-0-8075-0762-9(8), 807507628) Whitman, Albert & Co.

—In the Forest: Look up, Look Around, Look Down. Garnett, Jaye. Cottage Door Press, ed. 2018. (3 in 1 Tall Padded Board Book Ser.). (ENG.). 30p. (J). (gr. -1-k). bds. 9.99 (978-1-68052-349-2(X), 1003210) Cottage Door Pr.

—Little Green Frog: Chunky Lift a Flap Board Book. Swift, Ginger. Cottage Door Press, ed. 2016. (Chunky Lift a Flap Board Book Ser.). (ENG.). 12p. (J). (gr. -1-k). bds. 7.99 (978-1-68052-082-8(2), 1000650) Cottage Door Pr.

Demidova, Olga, et al. Nature Friends: Slipcase 4-Pack Including Little Blue Boat, Little Green Frog, Little Yellow Bee, & Little Red Barn. Swift, Ginger. Cottage Door Press, ed. 2018. (ENG.). 48p. (J). (gr. -1-k). bds., bds., bds. 24.99 (978-1-68052-340-9(6), 9001200) Cottage Door Pr.

Demidova, Olga. La Ranita Verde. Swift, Ginger. Cottage Door Press, ed. 2020. (Chunky Lift a Flap Board Book Ser.). (SPA.). 12p. (J). (gr. -1 — 1). bds. 7.99 (978-1-64638-058-9(4), 1000650-SLA) Cottage Door Pr.

Demidova, Olga. Snow White. Tiger Tales. 2019. (Fairy Tale Classics Ser.). (ENG.). 32p. (J). (gr. -1-2). lib. bdg. 23.99 (978-1-68010-161-4(7)) Tiger Tales.

—To the Moon & Back: Deluxe Multi Activity Book. Garnett, Jaye. 2017. (Smithsonian Kids Ser.). (ENG.). 12p. (J). (gr. -1-1). bds. 12.99 (978-1-68052-235-8(3), 1002210) Cottage Door Pr.

Demidova, Olga & Longhi, Katya. Yellow Bee & Green Frog 2 Pack: Chunky Lift a Flap Board Book 2 Pack. Swift, Ginger. Cottage Door Press, ed. 2016. (Chunky Lift a Flap Ser.). (ENG.). 24p. (J). (gr. -1-k). bds. 15.98 (978-1-68052-164-1(0), 9000460) Cottage Door Pr.

Demidova, Tania & Williams, Sharon. Collins Musicals - the Twelve Days of Christmas: a Dastardly Dazzling Musical. Sebba, Jane & Bakhurst, Samantha. Sanderson, Ana, ed. 2005. (and C Black Musicals Ser.). (ENG.). 64p. (J). (gr. 2-6). pap. 32.95 incl. audio compact disk (978-0-7136-7256-5(0)) HarperCollins Pubs. Ltd. GBR. Dist: Independent Pubs. Group.

Demirel, Selcuk. Banjo of Destiny, 1 vol. Fagan, Cary. 2012. (ENG.). 128p. (J). (gr. 3). pap. 8.95 (978-1-55498-086-4(0)) Groundwood Bks. CAN. Dist: Publishers Group West (PGW).

Demmer, Melanie. Apple & Annie, the Hamster Duo. Florence, Debbi Michiko. 2019. (My Furry Foster Family Ser.). (ENG.). 72p. (J). (gr. k-2). pap. 7.95 (978-1-5158-4561-4(3), 141149); lib. bdg. 23.32 (978-1-5158-4473-0(0), 140574) Capstone. (Picture Window Bks.).

—Betty the Bearded Dragon. Florence, Debbi Michiko. 2019. (My Furry Foster Family Ser.). (ENG.). 72p. (J). (gr. k-2). pap. 7.95 (978-1-5158-4559-1(1), 141147); lib. bdg. 23.32 (978-1-5158-4476-1(5), 140576) Capstone. (Picture Window Bks.).

—Buttons the Kitten. Florence, Debbi Michiko. 2019. (My Furry Foster Family Ser.). (ENG.). 72p. (J). (gr. k-2). pap. 7.95 (978-1-5158-4562-1(1), 141150); lib. bdg. 23.32 (978-1-5158-4474-7(9), 140575) Capstone. (Picture Window Bks.).

—I Love You, Daddy! Evans, Edie. 2019. (Little Golden Book Ser.). 16p. (J). (-k). 4.99 (978-1-9848-9251-5(7), Golden Bks.) Random Hse. Children's Bks.

—I Love You, Mommy! Evans, Edie. 2019. (Little Golden Book Ser.). 16p. (J). (-k). 4.99 (978-1-9848-5257-1(4), Golden Bks.) Random Hse. Children's Bks.

Demmer, Melanie. Kingston the Great Dane. Florence, Debbi Michiko. 2020. (My Furry Foster Family Ser.). (ENG.). 72p. (J). (gr. k-2). pap. 7.95 (978-1-5158-7331-0(5), 201741); lib. bdg. 23.32 (978-1-5158-7092-0(8), 199187) Capstone. (Picture Window Bks.).

—Murray the Ferret. Florence, Debbi Michiko. 2020. (My Furry Foster Family Ser.). (ENG.). 72p. (J). (gr. k-2). pap. 7.95 (978-1-5158-7330-3(7), 201740); lib. bdg. 23.32 (978-1-5158-7091-3(X), 199184) Capstone. (Picture Window Bks.).

—My Furry Foster Family. Florence, Debbi Michiko. (My Furry Foster Family Ser.). (ENG.). (J). (gr. k-2). 2020. 186.56 (978-1-5158-7096-8(0), 199190); 2020. pap., pap., pap. 63.60 (978-1-5158-7341-9(2), 201798); 2019. 93.28 (978-1-5158-4481-5(1), 29333); 2019. pap., pap., pap. 31.80 (978-1-5158-4604-8(0), 29665) Capstone. (Picture Window Bks.).

Demmer, Melanie. On the Farm: Look up, Look down, Look Around: 3-In-1 Board Book. Garnett, Jaye. Cottage Door Press, ed. 2018. (3 in 1 Tall Padded Board Book Ser.). (ENG.). 30p. (J). (gr. -1-1). bds. 9.99 *(978-1-68052-348-5(1)*, 1003200) Cottage Door Pr.
—A Place for Pluto. Wade, Stef. (ENG.). (J). (gr. k-3). 2019. 30p. bds. 7.99 *(978-1-68446-093-9(X)*, 141308); 2018. 32p. 15.95 *(978-1-68446-004-5(2)*, 138587) Capstone. (Capstone Editions).
—Problem at the Playground (Undersea Mystery Club Book 1) Carbone, Courtney. 2019. (Undersea Mystery Club Ser.). (ENG.). 80p. (J). 12.99 *(978-1-5248-5547-5(2))*; pap. 6.99 *(978-1-5248-5524-6(3))* Andrews McMeel Publishing.
Demmer, Melanie. Roo the Rabbit. Florence, Debbi Michiko. 2020. (My Furry Foster Family Ser.). (ENG.). 72p. (J). (gr. k-2). pap. 7.95 ***(978-1-5158-7332-7(3)***, 201742); lib. bdg. 23.32 ***(978-1-5158-7093-7(6)***, 199188) Capstone. (Picture Window Bks.).
—Tiki the Cockatoo. Florence, Debbi Michiko. 2020. (My Furry Foster Family Ser.). (ENG.). 72p. (J). (gr. k-2). pap. 7.95 ***(978-1-5158-7329-7(3)***, 201739); lib. bdg. 23.32 ***(978-1-5158-7090-6(1)***, 199181) Capstone. (Picture Window Bks.).
Demmer, Melanie. Trouble with Treasure (Undersea Mystery Club Book 2) Carbone, Courtney. 2020. (Undersea Mystery Club Ser.). (ENG.). 112p. (J). 12.99 *(978-1-5248-5784-4(X))*; pap. 6.99 *(978-1-5248-5572-7(3))* Andrews McMeel Publishing.
—Truman the Dog. Florence, Debbi Michiko. 2019. (My Furry Foster Family Ser.). (ENG.). 72p. (J). (gr. k-2). pap. 7.95 *(978-1-5158-4560-7(5)*, 141148); lib. bdg. 23.32 *(978-1-5158-4475-4(7)*, 140577) Capstone. (Picture Window Bks.).
Demmers, Justina. Closet Creeps: A Bedtime Mystery. Mele, Leo. 2011. 20p. pap. 24.95 *(978-1-4560-9002-9(X))* America Star Bks.
Demming, Karen. Has a Donkey Ever Brought You Breakfast in Bed? Brannon, Pat. 2012. 38p. pap. 10.00 *(978-1-938634-90-1(X))* Freedom of Speech Publishing, Inc.
Demong, Todd. 100 Girls. Gallardo, Adam. 2008. (ENG.). 176p. (YA). (gr. 9-18). pap. 9.99 *(978-1-4169-6109-3(7)*, Simon Pulse) Simon Pulse.
—100 Girls Vol. 1: Vol 1: the First Girl, Vol. 1. Gallardo, Adam. 2008. (YA). 9.95 *(978-0-9763095-3-6(X))* Arcana Studio, Inc.
DeMonico, Rick. Teacher's Pet. Tobin, C. 2005. (Maya & Miguel Ser.). (ENG.). (J). (gr. -1-3). lib. bdg. 16.60 *(978-0-7569-6473-3(3))* Perfection Learning Corp.
deMontignie, Leon. The (True) Adventures of Mudpoo. Klein, Peter. 2012. (ENG.). 48p. (J). 23.49 *(978-0-9870734-9-5(4))* JoJo Publishing AUS. Dist: Baker & Taylor Publisher Services (BTPS).
Dempsey, Sheena. The Clamshell Show (Mermaid School #2) Courtenay, Lucy. 2020. (Mermaid School Ser.). (ENG.). 128p. (J). (gr. 1-4). 14.99 *(978-1-4197-4520-1(4)*, 1695001); pap. 6.99 *(978-1-4197-4521-8(2)*, 1695003) Abrams, Inc. (Amulet Bks.).
—Hungry Babies. Cotton, Fearne. 2020. 32p. (J). (-k). pap. 14.99 *(978-1-78344-758-9(3))* Andersen Pr. GBR. Dist: Independent Pubs. Group.
—Mermaid School. Courtenay, Lucy. 2020. (Mermaid School Ser.). (ENG.). 128p. (J). (gr. 1-4). 14.99 *(978-1-4197-4518-8(2)*, 1694901); pap. 6.99 *(978-1-4197-4519-5(0)*, 1694903) Abrams, Inc. (Amulet Bks.).
—Yoga Babies. Cotton, Fearne. 2018. (ENG.). 32p. (J). (gr. -1-k). 11.99 *(978-1-4380-5030-0(5)*, B.E.S. Publishing) Peterson's.
Dempsey, Sheena. Bruno & Titch. Dempsey, Sheena. 2014. (ENG.). 32p. (J). (gr. -1-2). 16.99 *(978-0-7636-7316-1(1))* Candlewick Pr.
Dempster, Al. Cinderella's Friends (Disney Classic) Werner, Jane. 2017. (Little Golden Book Ser.). (ENG.). 24p. (J). (-k). 4.99 *(978-0-7364-3713-4(4)*, Golden/Disney) Random Hse. Children's Bks.
—Walt Disney's Peter Pan (Disney Classic) RH Disney. 2007. (Little Golden Book Ser.). (ENG.). 24p. (J). (gr. -1-2). 4.99 *(978-0-7364-0238-5(1)*, Golden/Disney) Random Hse. Children's Bks.
—Walt Disney's Pinocchio Little Golden Board Book (Disney Classic) RH Disney. 2020. (Little Golden Book Ser.). (ENG.). 26p. (J). (gr. -1-2). bds. 7.99 *(978-0-7364-4095-0(X)*, Golden/Disney) Random Hse. Children's Bks.
Demski, James, Jr. Elect Me!, 1 vol. Manushkin, Fran. 2008. (Read-It! Readers: Social Studies). (ENG.). 32p. (J). (gr. k-2). 21.32 *(978-1-4048-4911-2(4)*, Picture Window Bks.) Capstone.
—Eric No Juega, 1 vol. Jones, Christianne C. Ruíz, Carlos, tr. 2006. (Read-It! Readers en Español: Story Collection).Tr. of Eric Won't Do It. (SPA.). 24p. (J). (gr. -1-3). 21.32 *(978-1-4048-1683-1(6)*, Picture Window Bks.) Capstone.
Den Ouden, Marijke. Fun with Asian Food: A Kids' Cookbook. Den Ouden, Marijke. Sanmugam, Devagi. 2005. (ENG.). 32p. (J). (gr. -1-3). 15.95 *(978-0-7946-0339-7(4)*, PeriplusEdition) Tuttle Publishing.
Denaro, Sal. Hello, I'm Sir Frettirick! Let's Say Hello to Our New Friends! Stratten, Lou. Bennett, Judy, ed. 2006. (J). (gr. -1-2). pap. 6.95 incl. audio compact disk *(978-0-9747173-1-9(2))* Stratten, Lou.
DeNault, Shirl. Mema Has Cancer, 1 vol. McBride, Linda Ray. 2008. (ENG.). 29p. 24.95 *(978-1-60610-833-8(6))* America Star Bks.
Denchfield, Nick & Sharp, Anne. Pop-up Minibeast Adventure. 2004. 16p. (J). (gr. k-4). reprint ed. 25.00 *(978-0-7567-8204-7(X))* DIANE Publishing Co.
Denef, Barbara. Timmy's Tornado. Vliestra, David. 2020. (ENG.). 32p. (J). (gr. -1). 17.95 ***(978-1-60537-585-4(3))*** Clavis Publishing.
Denetsosie, Hoke. Little Herder in Winter: Haigo Na'nilkaadi' Ya'zhi' Clark, Ann Nolan & Harrington, John P. 2011. 116p. 39.95 *(978-1-258-03041-4(1))* Literary Licensing, LLC.
Deneux, Xavier. Badaboom Badabump! Baou, Bartelemi. 2019. (ENG.). 10p. (J). (gr. -1 — 1). 19.99 Éditions Tourbillon FRA. Dist: Hachette Bk. Group.
—Dress up Jojo. 2017. (ENG.). 10p. (J). (gr. -1 — 1). bds. 14.99 Éditions Tourbillon FRA. Dist: Hachette Bk. Group.
—Hail Mary. Bus, Sabrina. 2nd ed. 2006. 12p. (J). (gr. -1). bds. 8.00 *(978-0-8028-5312-7(9)*, Eerdmans Bks For Young Readers) Eerdmans, William B. Publishing Co.
—Our Father. Bus, Sabrina. 2nd ed. 2006. (ENG.). 12p. (J). (gr. -1). bds. 8.00 *(978-0-8028-5313-4(7)*, Eerdmans Bks For Young Readers) Eerdmans, William B. Publishing Co.
Deng, Sally. Yusra Swims. Abery, Julie. 2020. 32p. (J). (gr. 1-3). 19.99 *(978-1-56846-329-2(4)*, Creative Editions) Creative Co., The.
Denham, Caitlin. Rocketry: Investigate the Science & Technology of Rockets & Ballistics. Mooney, Carla. 2014. (Build It Yourself Ser.). 128p. (J). (gr. 3-7). 22.95 *(978-1-61930-232-7(2)*, c2bdf537-0b24-4a4f-ac1d-3fd246e839b8) Nomad Pr.
Denham, Gemma. Daniel & the Lions' Den, 1 vol. David, Juliet. 2009. (Candle Playbook Ser.). 18p. (J). bds. 7.99 *(978-0-8254-7385-2(3)*, Candle Bks.) Lion Hudson PLC GBR. Dist: Kregel Pubns.
—Noah & His Boat, 1 vol. David, Juliet. 2008. (Candle Playbook Ser.). 18p. (J). bds. 7.99 *(978-0-8254-7378-4(0)*, Candle Bks.) Lion Hudson PLC GBR. Dist: Kregel Pubns.
Denich, E. A. The Long Con. Meconis, Dylan & Coleman, Ben. 2019. (Long Con Ser.: 1). (ENG.). 136p. (YA). pap. 19.99 *(978-1-62010-571-9(3)*, Lion Forge) Oni Pr., Inc.
Dening, Abby. The Pages Between Us. Leavitt, Lindsey & Mellom, Robin. 2016. (Pages Between Us Ser.: 1). (ENG.). 288p. (J). (gr. 3-7). 16.99 *(978-0-06-237771-5(X))* HarperCollins Pubs.
—The Pages Between Us: in the Spotlight. Leavitt, Lindsey & Mellom, Robin. 2017. (Pages Between Us Ser.: 2). (ENG.). 336p. (J). (gr. 3-7). 16.99 *(978-0-06-237774-6(4))* HarperCollins Pubs.
Denis, Florencia. The Best Gift. Ryan, Ann Marie. 2011. (My Phonics Readers: Level 1 Ser.). 24p. (J). (gr. -1-1). 24.25 *(978-1-84898-507-0(X))* Sea-To-Sea Pubns.
Denis, Stephane. George Most Wanted. Lee, Ingrid. 2005. 62p. (J). lib. bdg. 20.00 *(978-1-4242-1253-8(7))* Fitzgerald Bks.
—George Most Wanted, 1 vol. Lee, Ingrid. 2005. (Orca Echoes Ser.). (ENG.). 64p. (J). (gr. 1-3). per. 6.95 *(978-1-55143-472-8(5))* Orca Bk. Pubs. USA.
—George, the Best of All!, 1 vol. Lee, Ingrid. 2006. (Orca Echoes Ser.). (ENG.). 64p. (J). (gr. 1-3). pap. 4.99 *(978-1-55143-623-4(X))* Orca Bk. Pubs. USA.
—The True Story of George. Lee, Ingrid. 2004. 62p. (J). lib. bdg. 20.00 *(978-1-4242-1262-0(6))* Fitzgerald Bks.
—The True Story of George, 1 vol. Lee, Ingrid. 2004. (Orca Echoes Ser.). (ENG.). 64p. (J). (gr. 1-3). pap. 6.95 *(978-1-55143-293-9(5))* Orca Bk. Pubs. USA.
Denise & Fernando. Winter Is for Snowflakes. Knudsen, Michelle. 2003. (Please Read to Me Ser.). (ENG.). 24p. (J). (gr. -1-1). 16.19 *(978-0-375-82215-5(1))* Random House Publishing Group.
Denise, Christopher. Baking Day at Grandma's. Denise, Anika. 2014. 32p. (J). (gr. -1-k). 16.99 *(978-0-399-24244-1(9)*, Philomel Bks.) Penguin Young Readers Group.
—Bunny in the Middle. Denise, Anika A. 2019. (ENG.). 40p. (J). 17.99 *(978-1-250-12036-6(5)*, 900173006, Holt, Henry & Co. Bks. For Young Readers) Holt, Henry & Co.
—Conejo y Tortuga van a la Escuela. Floyd, Lucy. Flor Ada, Alma & Campoy, F. Isabel, trs. 2010. (Green Light Readers Level 1 Ser.).Tr. of Rabbit & Turtle Go to School. (ENG.). 28p. (J). (gr. -1-3). pap. 4.99 *(978-0-547-33898-9(8)*, 1418429) Houghton Mifflin Harcourt Publishing Co.
—Digger Pig & the Turnip. Cohen, Caron Lee. 2003. (Green Light Readers Level 2 Ser.). (ENG.). 24p. (J). (gr. -1-3). pap. 4.99 *(978-0-15-204829-7(4)*, 1194582) Houghton Mifflin Harcourt Publishing Co.
—Firefly Hollow. McGhee, Alison. (ENG.). 304p. (J). (gr. 3-7). 2016. pap. 9.99 *(978-1-4424-2337-4(4)*, Atheneum/Caitlyn Dlouhy Books); 2015. 16.99 *(978-1-4424-2336-7(6)*, Atheneum Bks. for Young Readers) Simon & Schuster Children's Publishing.
—Following Grandfather. Wells, Rosemary. 2012. (ENG.). 64p. (J). (gr. 1-4). 14.99 *(978-0-7636-5069-8(2))* Candlewick Pr.
—Groundhug Day. Pace, Anne Marie. 2017. (ENG.). 48p. (J). (gr. -1-3). 17.99 *(978-1-4847-5356-9(9))* Disney Pr.
—If I Could. Milord, Susan. 2009. (ENG.). 32p. (J). (gr. k-k). 15.99 *(978-0-7636-4342-3(4))* Candlewick Pr.
—Me with You. Dempsey, Kristy. 2013. 28p. (J). (gr. -1-k). bds. 7.99 *(978-0-399-16262-6(3)*, Philomel Bks.) Penguin Young Readers Group.
—Rabbit & Turtle Go to School. Floyd, Lucy. 2003. (Green Light Readers Level 1 Ser.). (ENG.). 24p. (J). (gr. -1-3). pap. 4.99 *(978-0-15-204851-8(0)*, 1194648) Houghton Mifflin Harcourt Publishing Co.
—The Redwall Cookbook. Jacques, Brian. 2005. (Redwall Ser.). (ENG.). 104p. (J). (gr. 5-5). pap. 24.99 *(978-0-399-23791-1(7)*, Philomel Bks.) Penguin Young Readers Group.
—That's What Friends Are For. Lewis, J. Patrick. 2012. (I Am A Reader! Ser.). (ENG.). 40p. (J). (gr. k-3). pap. 3.99 *(978-1-58536-687-3(0))* Sleeping Bear Pr.
—Tugg & Teeny. Lewis, J. Patrick. 2011. (I AM a READER!: Tugg & Teeny Ser.). (ENG.). 40p. (J). (gr. 2-3). pap. 3.99 *(978-1-58536-685-9(4)*, 202329);Bk. 1. lib. bdg. 9.95 *(978-1-58536-514-2(9)*, 202204) Sleeping Bear Pr.
—Tugg & Teeny: That's What Friends Are For. Lewis, J. Patrick. 2012. (I Am a Reader: Tugg & Teeny Ser.). (ENG.). 40p. (J). (gr. k-2). lib. bdg. 16.19 *(978-1-58536-516-6(5))* Sleeping Bear Pr.
—Tugg & Teeny - Jungle Suprises, Bk. 2. Lewis, J. Patrick. 2012. (I Am a Reader: Tugg & Teeny Ser.). (ENG.). 40p. (J). (gr. k-2). lib. bdg. 16.19 *(978-1-58536-515-9(7))* Sleeping Bear Pr.
—Tugg & Tweeny - Jungle Surprises, Bk. 2. Lewis, J. Patrick. 2011. (I am a Reader Ser.). (ENG.). 40p. (J). (gr. k-2). pap. 3.99 *(978-1-58536-686-6(2))* Sleeping Bear Pr.
Denison, Susan. Jake & Josh Go Camping. Quarles, Pamela. 2007. 40p. per. 14.00 *(978-1-59858-407-3(3))* Dog Ear Publishing, LLC.
Denlinger, Sam. Marathon Mouse. Dixon, Amy. 2012. (ENG.). 32p. (J). (gr. -1-k). 16.95 *(978-1-61608-966-5(0)*, 608966, Sky Pony Pr.) Skyhorse Publishing Co., Inc.
Denman, Michael, et al. Alphabet of African Animals. Galvin, Laura Gates. 2008. (ENG.). 40p. (J). (gr. -1-2). 17.95 *(978-1-59249-854-3(X))* Soundprints.
Denman, Michael. Bible Story Hidden Pictures: Coloring & Activity Book. Fogle, Robin. 2006. (J). (gr. 1-5). 1.79 *(978-1-59317-161-2(7))* Warner Pr., Inc.
—The Miller, His Son & Their Donkey. Sommer, Carl. 2014. (Sommer-Time Story Classics Ser.). (ENG.). 32p. (J). (gr. k-4). 16.95 *(978-1-57537-085-9(9))* Advance Publishing, Inc.
—Stone Soup. Sommer, Carl. 2014. (Sommer-Time Story Classics Ser.). (ENG.). 32p. (J). (gr. k-4). 16.95 *(978-1-57537-078-1(6))* Advance Publishing, Inc.
Denman, Michael & Huiett, William. Judy the Elephant. Galvin, Laura Gates. (African Wildlife Foundation Ser.). (ENG.). 36p. (J). (gr. -1-2). 2005. 2.95 *(978-1-59249-171-1(5)*, S6552); 2005. 9.95 *(978-1-59249-172-8(3)*, PS6552); 2004. 8.95 *(978-1-59249-198-8(7)*, SD6502) Soundprints.
—Kakuda the Giraffe. Galvin, Laura Gates. (ENG.). 36p. (J). (gr. -1-2). 2006. 2.95 *(978-1-59249-187-2(1)*, S6551); 2005. 8.95 *(978-1-59249-206-0(1)*, SD6501); 2003. 9.95 *(978-1-59249-188-9(X)*, PS6551) Soundprints.
—Leperit the Zebra. Grey, Chelsea Gillian. 2005. (Internet Interactive Ser.). (ENG.). 36p. (J). (gr. -1-3). 8.95 *(978-1-59249-440-8(4)*, SD6505); (gr. 2-2). 14.95 *(978-1-59249-438-5(2)*, H6505); (gr. 2-2). pap. 6.95 *(978-1-59249-439-2(0)*, S6505) Soundprints.
Denman, Michael & Huiett, William J. Land of the Wild Llama: A Story of the Patagonian Andes. Fraggalosch, Audrey. 2005. (Wild Habitats Ser.). (ENG.). (J). (gr. 1-4). 32p. 19.95 *(978-1-931465-83-0(5)*, BC7022); 36p. 15.95 *(978-1-931465-81-6(9)*, B7022) Soundprints.
—Land of the Wild Llama: A Story of the Patagonian Andes, Including 10" Toy. Fraggalosch, Audrey. 2005. (Wild Habitats Ser.). (ENG.). 36p. (J). (gr. 1-4). 17.95 *(978-1-931465-86-1(X)*, PS7022) Soundprints.
Denman, Michael L. The Town Musicians of Bremen. Sommer, Carl. 2016. (J). *(978-1-57537-947-0(3))* Advance Publishing, Inc.
Denman, Michael L. & Huiett, William J. Judy the Elephant. Galvin, Laura Gates. Denman, Michael L. & Huiett, William J., trs. 2005. (African Wildlife Foundation Ser.). (ENG.). 36p. (J). (gr. -1-2). 14.95 *(978-1-59249-169-8(3)*, H6502); 6.95 *(978-1-59249-170-4(7)*, S6502) Soundprints.
—Kakuda the Giraffe. Galvin, Laura Gates. Denman, Michael L. & Huiett, William J., trs. 2005. (Meet Africa's Animals Ser.). (ENG.). 36p. (J). (gr. -1-2). 14.95 *(978-1-59249-185-8(5)*, H6501); pap. 6.95 *(978-1-59249-186-5(3)*, S6501) Soundprints.
—Leperit the Zebra: African Wildlife Foundation. Grey, Chelsea Gillian. 2005. (Meet Africa's Animals Ser.). (ENG.). 36p. (J). (gr. -1-2). 2.95 *(978-1-59249-441-5(2)*, S6555) Soundprints.
Denmark, Thomas. Knights & Castles. Torpie, Kate. 2008. (ENG.). 24p. (J). (gr. 2-17). 19.99 *(978-1-58476-726-8(X))* Innovative Kids.
Denmon, Noa. A Place Inside of Me: A Poem to Heal the Heart. Elliott, Zetta. 2020. (ENG.). 32p. (J). 17.99 *(978-0-374-30741-7(5)*, 900179868, Farrar, Straus & Giroux (BYR)) Farrar, Straus & Giroux.
Denne, John, photos by. High Riders, Saints & Death Cars: A Life Saved by Art, 1 vol. Herrera, Nicholas. 2011. (ENG., 56p. (J). (gr. 4-18). 24.95 *(978-0-88899-854-5(6))* Groundwood Bks. CAN. Dist: Publishers Group West (PGW).
Dennen, Sue. The Moving Book: A Kids' Survival Guide. Davis, Gabriel. 2nd ed. 2008. 160p. (J). spiral bd. 22.95 *(978-0-912301-92-1(9))* First Bks.
Dennis, Cindy. Pick That Penny Up! All Proceeds Go to the Give a Child a Voice Foundation. Dennis, Cindy. 2019. (Give a Child a Voice Ser.: Vol. 8). (ENG.). 30p. (J). pap. 9.99 *(978-1-0971-0401-7(X))* Independently Published.
Dennis, Jane. Far from This Earth & Other Stories. Oliver, Chad. Olson, Priscilla, ed. 2003. (NESFA's Choice Ser.: 25). 480p. 24.00 *(978-1-886778-48-1(5)*, NESFA Pr.) New England Science Fiction Assn., Inc.
—A Star Above It & Other Stories. Oliver, Chad. Olson, Priscilla, ed. 2003. (NESFA's Choice Ser.: 24). 480p. 24.00 *(978-1-886778-45-0(0)*, NESFA Pr.) New England Science Fiction Assn., Inc.
Dennis, Jeannette. Kitty Kitty Rescues Mr. Gator. Queen, Kindness. 2017. (Virtuous Volumes Ser.: Vol. 2). (ENG.). (J). 17.99 *(978-0-9889060-2-0(3))* Kindness Queen's Empire, The.
Dennis, Kathryn. Too Many Questions. Dennis, Kathryn. 2016. (ENG.). 32p. (J). 10.99 *(978-1-61067-460-7(X))* Kane Miller.
Dennis, Nadine. Lincoln & the Lilac Lilies. Stafford, Mary. 2005. (Fantastic World of Lincoln Llama Ser.). 24p. 6.95 *(978-0-9735663-0-7(2))* Amethyst Hse Publishing, Inc. CAN. Dist: Hushion Hse. Publishing, Ltd.
—Lincoln's Day of Discovery, Vol. 2. Stafford, Mary. 2005. (Fantastic World of Lincoln Llama Ser.). 24p. 6.95 *(978-0-9735663-1-4(0))* Amethyst Hse Publishing, Inc. CAN. Dist: Hushion Hse. Publishing, Ltd.
—Lincoln's Journey of Journeys, Vol. 3. Stafford, Mary. 2005. (Fantastic World of Lincoln Llama Ser.). 24p. 6.95 *(978-0-9735663-2-1(9))* Amethyst Hse Publishing, Inc. CAN. Dist: Hushion Hse. Publishing, Ltd.
Dennis, Peter. The Adventures of King Arthur. 2003. (Young Reading Ser.). 64p. (J). (gr. k-7). pap. 5.99 *(978-0-7945-0447-2(7)*, Usborne) EDC Publishing.
—The Adventures of King Arthur. 2003. (Usborne Young Reading: Series Two Ser.). 64p. (J). (gr. k-7). 8.99 *(978-0-7945-1871-4(0)*, Usborne) EDC Publishing.
—Castle. 2006. (Leap Through Time Ser.). 31p. (J). *(978-0-7607-7523-3(0))* backpackbooks.
—Conquest! Can You Build a Roman City? Bruce, Julia. 2009. (Step into History Ser.). 32p. (gr. 3-3). lib. bdg. 24.94 *(978-0-7660-3478-5(X))* Enslow Publishing, LLC.
—Dinosaurs Through Time. Harris, Nicolas. 2009. (Fast Forward Ser.). 32p. (YA). (gr. 2-5). lib. bdg. 27.25 *(978-1-4358-2802-5(X))* Rosen Publishing Group, Inc., The.
—Family Bible. Costecalde, Claude-Bernard & Costecalde, Claude. 2016. (ENG.). 384p. (J). (gr. 5-12). 29.99 *(978-0-7894-1503-5(8)*, DK Children) Dorling Kindersley Publishing, Inc.
—The First Humans. Harris, Nicholas. 2006. 31p. (J). *(978-0-7607-7528-8(1))* backpackbooks.
—Pirates. DeGagne, Mandie. 2012. 31p. (J). *(978-1-58865-594-3(6))* Kidsbooks, LLC.
—Pyramid. Harris, Nicholas. 2006. 31p. (J). *(978-0-7607-7526-4(5))* backpackbooks.
—Sail! Can You Command a Sea Voyage? Bruce, Julia. 2009. (Step into History Ser.). 32p. (gr. 3-3). lib. bdg. 24.94 *(978-0-7660-3477-8(1))* Enslow Publishing, LLC.
Dennis, Peter & Draper, Richard. The Usborne Book of Explorers. Everett, Felicity & Reid, Struan. rev. ed. 2007. (Famous Lives Ser.). 47p. (J). (gr. 4-7). pap. 8.99 *(978-0-7945-1533-1(9)*, Usborne) EDC Publishing.
Dennis, Sarah. Animal Habitats: Search & Find Activity Book (for Young Naturalists Ages 6-9) Hutchinson, Sam. 2019. (ENG.). 32p. (J). (gr. 1-4). 16.95 *(978-1-61689-849-6(6))* Princeton Architectural Pr.
—Cinderella: A Cut-Paper Book. 2015. (ENG.). 52p. (J). (gr. -1-k). 19.99 *(978-1-85707-843-5(8))* Tango Bks. GBR. Dist: Independent Pubs. Group.
Dennis, Sarah. Endangered Animals: And How You Can Help. Hutchinson, Sam. 2020. (ENG.). 32p. (J). (gr. 1-4). 17.95 ***(978-1-61689-940-0(9))*** Princeton Architectural Pr.
Dennis, Sarah. Rip & Stick Insects & Flowers. Hutchinson, Sam. 2018. (Rip & Stick Ser.). (ENG.). 64p. (J). (gr. -1-k). 8.99 *(978-1-911509-07-3(1))* B Small Publishing GBR. Dist: Independent Pubs. Group.
—Rip & Stick Jungle Animals. Hutchinson, Sam. 2018. (Rip & Stick Ser.). (ENG.). 64p. (J). (gr. -1-k). 8.99 *(978-1-911509-06-6(3))* B Small Publishing GBR. Dist: Independent Pubs. Group.
Dennis, Tammy D. The Crumb Snatchers. Thompson, Debra. 2012. 24p. pap. 12.95 *(978-1-61493-037-2(6))* Peppertree Pr., The.
Dennis, Wesley. Album of Horses. Henry, Marguerite. 2015. (ENG.). 208p. (J). (gr. 3-7). 19.99 *(978-1-4814-4258-9(9)*, Aladdin) Simon & Schuster Children's Publishing.
—Benjamin West & His Cat Grimalkin. Henry, Marguerite. 2014. (ENG.). 160p. (J). (gr. 3-7). pap. 7.99 *(978-1-4814-0394-8(X)*, Aladdin) Simon & Schuster Children's Publishing.
—Black Gold. Henry, Marguerite. 2016. (ENG.). 208p. (J). (gr. 3-7). 19.99 *(978-1-4814-6212-9(1)*, Aladdin) Simon & Schuster Children's Publishing.
—Cinnabar, the One O'Clock Fox. Henry, Marguerite. 2015. (ENG.). 144p. (J). (gr. 3-7). 19.99 *(978-1-4814-0401-3(6)*, Aladdin) Simon & Schuster Children's Publishing.
—Cinnabar, the One o'Clock Fox. Henry, Marguerite. 2014. (ENG.). 144p. (J). (gr. 3-7). pap. 7.99 *(978-1-4814-0400-6(8)*, Aladdin) Simon & Schuster Children's Publishing.
—Justin Morgan Had a Horse. Henry, Marguerite. (ENG.). 176p. (J). (gr. 3-7). 2015. 19.99 *(978-1-4814-2562-9(5))*; 2006. pap. 7.99 *(978-1-4169-2785-3(9))* Simon & Schuster Children's Publishing. (Aladdin).
—King of the Wind: The Story of the Godolphin Arabian. Henry, Marguerite. 2006. (ENG.). 176p. (J). (gr. 3-7). pap. 7.99 *(978-1-4169-2786-0(7)*, Aladdin) Simon & Schuster Children's Publishing.
—Marguerite Henry Treasury of Horses (Boxed Set) Set: Misty of Chincoteague, Justin Morgan Had a Horse, King of the Wind. Henry, Marguerite. ed. 2007. (ENG.). 528p. (J). (gr. 3-7). pap. 23.99 *(978-1-4169-3954-2(7)*, Aladdin) Simon & Schuster Children's Publishing.
—Misty of Chincoteague. Henry, Marguerite. 2007. 173p. (gr. 3-7). 17.00 *(978-0-7569-8227-0(8))* Perfection Learning Corp.
—Misty of Chincoteague. Henry, Marguerite. 60th ed. 2006. (ENG.). 176p. (J). (gr. 3-7). pap. 7.99 *(978-1-4169-2783-9(2)*, Aladdin) Simon & Schuster Children's Publishing.
Dennis, Wesley. Misty of Chincoteague Essential Collection: Misty of Chincoteague; Stormy, Misty's Foal; Sea Star; Misty's Twilight. Henry, Marguerite. ed. 2020. (ENG.). 736p. (J). (gr. 3-7). pap. 31.99 ***(978-1-5344-5783-6(6)***, Aladdin) Simon & Schuster Children's Publishing.
Dennis, Wesley. Sea Star: Orphan of Chincoteague. Henry, Marguerite. 2007. (ENG.). 176p. (J). (gr. 3-7). pap. 7.99 *(978-1-4169-2784-6(0)*, Aladdin) Simon & Schuster Children's Publishing.
—Stormy, Misty's Foal. Henry, Marguerite. (ENG.). (J). (gr. 3-7). 2015. 256p. 21.99 *(978-1-4814-2561-2(7))*; 2007. 224p. pap. 7.99 *(978-1-4169-2788-4(3))* Simon & Schuster Children's Publishing. (Aladdin).
—Ticktock & Jim: Famous Horse Stories. Robertson, Keith. 2011. 250p. 46.95 *(978-1-258-10102-2(5))* Literary Licensing, LLC.
—White Stallion of Lipizza. Henry, Marguerite. 2014. (ENG.). 192p. (J). (gr. 3-7). pap. 7.99 *(978-1-4814-0391-7(5)*, Aladdin) Simon & Schuster Children's Publishing.
Denomm�-Warren, Madison & Brooke, jt. illus. see Maresky, David.
Denos, Julia. Camping Out. Denton, P. J. 2007. (Sleepover Squad Ser.: 2). (ENG.). 96p. (J). (gr. 1-4). pap. 5.99 *(978-1-4169-2791-4(3)*, Simon & Schuster/Paula Wiseman Bks.) Simon & Schuster/Paula Wiseman Bks.
—The Fairy Bell Sisters #1: Sylva & the Fairy Ball. McNamara, Margaret. 2013. (Fairy Bell Sisters Ser.: 1). (ENG.). 128p. (J). (gr. 1-5). 15.99 *(978-0-06-222802-4(1))*; pap. 4.99

D

(978-0-06-222801-7(3)) HarperCollins Pubs. (Balzer & Bray).

—The Fairy Bell Sisters #2: Rosy & the Secret Friend. McNamara, Margaret. 2013. (Fairy Bell Sisters Ser.: 2). (ENG.). 128p. (J). (gr. 1-5). 15.99 *(978-0-06-222805-5(6))*; pap. 4.99 *(978-0-06-222804-8(8))* HarperCollins Pubs. (Balzer & Bray).

—The Fairy Bell Sisters #3: Golden at the Fancy-Dress Party. McNamara, Margaret. 2013. (Fairy Bell Sisters Ser.: 3). (ENG.). 144p. (J). (gr. 1-5). 15.99 *(978-0-06-222808-6(0))*, Balzer & Bray) HarperCollins Pubs.

—The Fairy Bell Sisters #3: Golden at the Fancy-Dress Party No. 3. McNamara, Margaret. 2013. (Fairy Bell Sisters Ser.: 3). (ENG.). 144p. (J). (gr. 1-5). pap. 4.99 *(978-0-06-222807-9(2)*, Balzer & Bray) HarperCollins Pubs.

—The Fairy Bell Sisters #4: Clara & the Magical Charms. McNamara, Margaret. 2013. (Fairy Bell Sisters Ser.: 4). (ENG.). 128p. (J). (gr. 1-5). pap. 4.99 *(978-0-06-222810-9(2)*, Balzer & Bray) HarperCollins Pubs.

—Girls Against Boys. Denton, P. J. 2013. (Sleepover Squad Ser.: 7). (ENG.). 96p. (J). (gr. 1-4). pap. 4.99 *(978-1-4169-5933-5(5)*, Simon & Schuster/Paula Wiseman Bks.) Simon & Schuster/Paula Wiseman Bks.

—Grandma's Gloves. Castellucci, Cecil. 2010. (ENG.). 32p. (J). (gr. k-3). 15.99 *(978-0-7636-3168-0(X))* Candlewick Pr.

—I Had a Favorite Dress. Ashburn, Boni. 2011. (ENG.). 32p. (J). (gr. -1-1). 16.95 *(978-1-4197-0016-3(2)*, Abrams Bks. for Young Readers) Abrams, Inc.

—Just Being Audrey. Cardillo, Margaret. 2011. (ENG.). 32p. (J). (gr. -1-3). 16.99 *(978-0-06-185283-1(X))* HarperCollins Pubs.

—Just Being Jackie. Cardillo, Margaret. 2018. (ENG.). 32p. (J). (gr. -1-3). 17.99 *(978-0-06-248502-1(4)*, Balzer & Bray) HarperCollins Pubs.

—Keeping Secrets. Denton, P. J. 4th ed. 2008. (Sleepover Squad Ser.: 4). (ENG.). 96p. (J). (gr. 1-4). pap. 4.99 *(978-1-4169-2801-0(4)*, Aladdin) Simon & Schuster Children's Publishing.

—Letters to Leo. Hest, Amy. 2012. (ENG.). 160p. (J). (gr. 3-7). 14.99 *(978-0-7636-3695-1(9))* Candlewick Pr.

—Letters to Leo. Hest, Amy. 2014. 160p. (J). (gr. 3-7). pap. 6.99 *(978-0-7636-7165-5(7))* Candlewick Pr.

—Lexie. Couloumbis, Audrey. 2012. (ENG.). 208p. (J). (gr. 3-7). pap. 6.99 *(978-0-375-85633-4(1)*, Yearling) Random Hse. Children's Bks.

—The New Girl. Denton, P. J. 6th ed. 2008. (Sleepover Squad Ser.: 6). (ENG.). 80p. (J). (gr. 1-4). pap. 5.99 *(978-1-4169-5932-8(7)*, Simon & Schuster/Paula Wiseman Bks.) Simon & Schuster/Paula Wiseman Bks.

—Pony Party! Denton, P. J. 5th ed. 2008. (Sleepover Squad Ser.: 5). (ENG.). 96p. (J). (gr. 1-4). pap. 5.99 *(978-1-4169-5931-1(9)*, Aladdin) Simon & Schuster Children's Publishing.

—Sojourner Truth: Path to Glory. Merchant, Peter. 2007. (Ready-To-Read Level 3 Ser.). (ENG.). 47p. (J). (gr. 1-3). lib. bdg. 16.19 *(978-0-689-87208-2(9)*, Aladdin) Simon & Schuster Children's Publishing.

—Sojourner Truth: Path to Glory. Merchant, Peter. 2007. (Ready-To-read SOFA Ser.). (ENG.). 48p. (J). (gr. 1-3). pap. 4.99 *(978-0-689-87207-5(0)*, Simon Spotlight) Simon Spotlight.

—The Trouble with Brothers. Denton, P. J. 2007. (Sleepover Squad Ser.: 3). (ENG.). 96p. (J). (gr. 1-4). pap. 5.99 *(978-1-4169-2800-3(6)*, Simon & Schuster/Paula Wiseman Bks.) Simon & Schuster/Paula Wiseman Bks.

—Where Do Angels Sleep? Strong, Cynda. 2007. 24p. (J). (gr. -1-3). 14.99 *(978-0-7586-1298-4(2))* Concordia Publishing Hse.

Denos, Julia. Swatch: the Girl Who Loved Color. Denos, Julia. 2016. (ENG.). 40p. (J). (gr. -1-3). 17.99 *(978-0-06-236638-2(6))* HarperCollins Pubs.

Densham, Lauren. Reuben & Joseph. Vellacott, Natalie. 2019. (ENG.). 186p. (J). pap. 8.89 *(978-1-5481-3421-1(X))* CreateSpace Independent Publishing Platform.

—Reuben's Big Test. Vellacott, Natalie. 2019. (ENG.). 294p. (J). pap. 11.44 *(978-1-7921-9244-9(4))* Independently Published.

Denslow, W. W. La Mirinda Sorchisto de Oz. Baum, L. Frank. Broadribb, Donald, tr. 2012. 278p. pap. 24.00 *(978-1-59569-245-0(2))* Mondial.

—The Wizard of Oz. Baum, L. Frank. 2012. (Stepping Stone Book(TM) Ser.). 112p. (J). (gr. 1-4). 5.99 *(978-0-375-86994-5(8)*, Random Hse. Bks. for Young Readers) Random Hse. Children's Bks.

Denslow, W. w. The Wonderful Wizard of Oz. Baum, L. Frank. Wolstenholme, Susan, ed. 2008. (Oxford World's Classics Ser.). (ENG.). 336p. pap. 13.95 *(978-0-19-954064-8(0))* Oxford Univ. Pr., Inc.

Denslow, W. W. The Wonderful Wizard of Oz. Baum, L. Frank. 2015. (Dover Children's Classics Ser.). (ENG.). 308p. (J). (gr. 3-6). reprint ed. pap. 16.99 *(978-0-486-20691-2(2))* Dover Pubns., Inc.

Denslow, W. W. The Pearl & the Pumpkin: A Classic Halloween Tale. Denslow, W. W. West, Paul. 2009. (Dover Children's Classics Ser.). (ENG.). 264p. (J). (gr. 2-5). pap. 12.99 *(978-0-486-47031-3(8))* Dover Pubns., Inc.

Denslow, W. W. & Menten, Ted. The Wonderful Wizard of Oz. Baum, L. Frank. 2010. (Dover Read & Listen Ser.). (ENG.). 112p. (J). (gr. 1-5). pap. 14.99 *(978-0-486-47725-1(8))* Dover Pubns., Inc.

Denson, Abby, jt. illus. see Carolan, Sean.

Denton, Ivan. Blizzard No. 5: Don't Give Up. Denton, Ivan. Sargent, Dave. 2004. 36p. (J). pap. 10.95 *(978-1-59381-009-2(1))* Ozark Publishing.

—Misty's Miracle No. 4: Overcome Fear, 6 vols. Denton, Ivan. Sargent, Dave. 2004. 36p. (J). pap. 10.95 *(978-1-59381-005-4(9))* Ozark Publishing.

—My Grandpa Is a Cowboy: Learning Is Fun #1, 6 vols. Denton, Ivan. Sargent, Dave. 2004. 36p. (J). pap. 10.95 *(978-1-59381-001-6(6))* Ozark Publishing.

Denton, Kady MacDonald. A Bedtime for Bear. Becker, Bonny. 2010. (J). (Bear & Mouse Ser.: 3). (ENG.). 48p. (gr. -1-2). 16.99 *(978-0-7636-4101-6(4))*; *(978-0-7636-5364-4(0))* Candlewick Pr.

—Before I Go to Sleep: Bible Stories, Poems, & Prayers for Children. Pilling, Ann. 2019. (ENG.). 96p. (J). 12.99 *(978-0-7534-7583-6(9)*, 900219441, Kingfisher) Roaring Brook Pr.

—A Birthday for Bear. Becker, Bonny. (Candlewick Sparks Ser.). (J). 2013. 56p. (gr. k-4). pap. 4.99 *(978-0-7636-6861-7(3))*; 2012. (ENG.). 48p. (gr. -1-2). 17.99 *(978-0-7636-5823-6(5))* Candlewick Pr.

—A Child's Treasury of Nursery Rhymes. 2004. (J). (gr. k). audio compact disk 12.95 *(978-0-618-49306-7(9))* Houghton Mifflin Harcourt Trade & Reference Pubs.

—A Christmas for Bear. Becker, Bonny. 2017. (Bear & Mouse Ser.). (ENG.). 48p. (J). (gr. k-4). 16.99 *(978-0-7636-4923-4(6))* Candlewick Pr.

—A Library Book for Bear. Becker, Bonny. 2014. (Bear & Mouse Ser.). 32p. (J). (gr. -1-2). 17.99 *(978-0-7636-4924-1(4))* Candlewick Pr.

—The Queen of France. Wadham, Tim. 2011. (ENG.). 32p. (J). (gr. -1-3). 16.99 *(978-0-7636-4102-3(2))* Candlewick Pr.

—A Sea-Wishing Day. Heidbreder, Robert. 2007. 32p. (J). (gr. -1-3). 15.95 *(978-1-55337-707-8(9))* Kids Can Pr., Ltd. CAN. Dist: Hachette Bk. Group.

—A Second Is a Hiccup: A Child's Book of Time. Hutchins, Hazel J. 2004. (ENG.). 32p. (J). *(978-0-439-97400-4(3)*, North Winds Pr) Scholastic Canada, Ltd.

—A Second Is a Hiccup: A Child's Book of Time. Hutchins, Hazel. 2008. (J). 16.99 *(978-0-439-83110-9(5)*, Levine, Arthur A. Bks.) Scholastic, Inc.

—The Sniffles for Bear. Becker, Bonny. (Bear & Mouse Ser.). 32p. (J). (gr. -1-2). 2019. 6.99 *(978-0-7636-6539-5(8))*; 2011. (ENG.). 16.99 *(978-0-7636-4756-8(X))* Candlewick Pr.

—Two Homes. Masurel, Claire. 2003. (ENG.). 40p. (J). (gr. -1-2). 7.99 *(978-0-7636-1984-8(1))* Candlewick Pr.

—A Visitor for Bear. Becker, Bonny. (Bear & Mouse Ser.). (ENG.). 56p. (J). (gr. -1-2). 2012. pap. 7.99 *(978-0-7636-4611-0(3))*; 2008. 17.99 *(978-0-7636-2807-9(7))* Candlewick Pr.

—A Visitor for Bear. Becker, Bonny. ed. 2012. lib. bdg. 17.20 *(978-0-606-26930-8(4))* Turtleback.

—What Are You Doing, Benny? Fagan, Cary. 2019. (ENG.). 36p. (J). (gr. -1-2). 17.99 *(978-1-77049-857-0(5)*, Tundra Bks.) Tundra Bks. CAN. Dist: Penguin Random Hse. LLC.

Denton, Shannon E. The Mystery of the Roanoke Colony, 1 vol. Englar, Xavier & Niz, Xavier W. 2006. (Graphic History Ser.). (ENG.). 32p. (J). (gr. 3-9). per. 8.10 *(978-0-7368-9657-3(0))* Capstone.

Denton, Terry. Beastly Tales: Six Crazy Creature Capers. Tulloch, Richard. 2006. (ENG.). 144p. (J). (gr. k-2). pap. 13.99 *(978-1-74166-189-7(7))* Random Hse. Australia AUS. Dist: Independent Pubs. Group.

—Beastly Tales: Six Crazy Stories. Tulloch, Richard. 2014. 144p. (J). (gr. k-3). 12.99 *(978-0-85798-731-0(3))* Random Hse. Australia AUS. Dist: Independent Pubs. Group.

—The Big Fat Cow That Goes Kapow: 10 Easy-To-Read Stories. Griffiths, Andy. 2010. (ENG.). 144p. (J). (gr. -1-3). pap. 7.99 *(978-0-312-65301-9(8)*, 900069442) Square Fish.

—Boomerang & Bat: The Story of the Real First Eleven. Greenwood, Mark. 2016. (ENG.). 32p. (J). (gr. 2-7). 24.99 *(978-1-74331-924-6(X))* Allen & Unwin AUS. Dist: Independent Pubs. Group.

—The Cat on the Mat Is Flat. Griffiths, Andy. 2009. (ENG.). 192p. (J). (gr. -1-3). pap. 7.99 *(978-0-312-53584-1(8)*, 900054770) Square Fish.

—The Cat, the Rat, & the Baseball Bat. Griffiths, Andy. 2013. (My Readers Ser.). (ENG.). 32p. (J). (gr. -1-1). pap. 4.99 *(978-1-250-02774-0(8)*, 900104562) Square Fish.

—Ed & Ted & Ted's Dog Fred. Griffiths, Andy. 2014. (My Readers Ser.). (ENG.). 32p. (J). (gr. -1-1). 15.99 *(978-1-250-04447-1(2)*, 900128346) Square Fish.

—Killer Koalas from Outer Space & Lots of Other Very Bad Stuff That Will Make Your Brain Explode! Griffiths, Andy. 2012. (ENG.). 192p. (J). (gr. 3-7). pap. 7.99 *(978-1-250-01017-9(9)*, 900084754) Square Fish.

—The Looming Lamplight. Dubosarsky, Ursula. 2015. (Cryptic Casebook of Coco Carlomagno & Alberta Ser.: 2). (ENG.). 96p. (J). (gr. 1-3). 9.99 *(978-1-74331-259-9(8))* Allen & Unwin AUS. Dist: Independent Pubs. Group.

—The Treehouse Fun Book. Griffiths, Andy & Griffiths, Jill. 2016. (Treehouse Bks.). (ENG.). 192p. (J). 12.99 *(978-1-250-11775-5(5)*, 900172281) Feiwel & Friends.

—The Treehouse Fun Book. Griffiths, Andy & Griffiths, Jill. 2017. (Treehouse Bks.). (ENG.). 192p. (J). pap. 7.99 *(978-1-250-14325-9(X)*, 900180483) Square Fish.

—The Treehouse Joke Book. Griffiths, Andy. 2020. (Treehouse Bks.). (ENG.). 304p. (J). pap. 9.99 *(978-1-250-25950-9(9)*, 900221044) Feiwel & Friends.

—The Upside-Down History of Down-Under. Lloyd, Alison;Denton. 2019. 304p. (J). (gr. 4-6). 24.99 *(978-0-14-378866-9(3))* Random Hse. Australia AUS. Dist: Independent Pubs. Group.

—What Body Part Is That? A Wacky Guide to the Funniest, Weirdest, & Most Disgustingest Parts of Your Body. Griffiths, Andy. 2013. (ENG.). 208p. (J). (gr. 3-7). pap. 9.99 *(978-1-250-03406-9(X)*, 900120576) Square Fish.

—The Worm Who Knew Karate! Lever, Jill. 2019. 32p. (J). (gr. k-3). 15.99 *(978-0-14-350602-7(1)*, Puffin) Penguin Bks., Ltd. GBR. Dist: Independent Pubs. Group.

—The 13-Story Treehouse: Monkey Mayhem! Griffiths, Andy. 2013. (Treehouse Bks.: 1). (ENG.). 256p. (J). (gr. 1-5). 13.99 *(978-1-250-02690-3(3)*, 900098155) Feiwel & Friends.

—The 13-Story Treehouse: Monkey Mayhem! Griffiths, Andy. 2015. (Treehouse Bks.: 1). (ENG.). 272p. (J). (gr. 1-5). pap. 7.99 *(978-1-250-07065-4(1)*, 900148615) Square Fish.

—The 26-Story Treehouse: Pirate Problems! Griffiths, Andy. 2014. (Treehouse Bks.: 2). (ENG.). 352p. (J). (gr. 1-5). 13.99 *(978-1-250-02691-0(1)*, 900098156) Feiwel & Friends.

—The 39-Story Treehouse: Mean Machines & Mad Professors! Griffiths, Andy. 2015. (Treehouse Bks.: 3). (ENG.). 352p. (J). (gr. 1-5). 13.99 *(978-1-250-02692-7(X)*, 900098157) Feiwel & Friends.

—The 39-Story Treehouse: Mean Machines & Mad Professors! Griffiths, Andy. 2016. (Treehouse Bks.: 3). (ENG.). 368p. (J). pap. 7.99 *(978-1-250-07511-6(4)*, 900151529) Square Fish.

—The 52-Story Treehouse: Vegetable Villains! Griffiths, Andy. 2016. (Treehouse Bks.: 4). (ENG.). 336p. (J). (gr. 2-5). 13.99 *(978-1-250-02693-4(8)*, 900098158) Feiwel & Friends.

—The 52-Story Treehouse: Vegetable Villains! Griffiths, Andy. 2017. (Treehouse Bks.: 4). (ENG.). 352p. (J). pap. 7.99 *(978-1-250-10379-6(7)*, 900163638) Square Fish.

—The 65-Story Treehouse: Time Travel Trouble! Griffiths, Andy. 2018. (Treehouse Bks.: 5). (ENG.). 400p. (J). pap. 7.99 *(978-1-250-10247-8(2)*, 900163128) Square Fish.

—The 78-Story Treehouse. Griffiths, Andy. 2018. (Treehouse Bks.: 6). (ENG.). 384p. (J). 13.99 *(978-1-250-10485-4(8)*, 900164004) Feiwel & Friends.

—The 78-Story Treehouse: Moo-Vie Madness! Griffiths, Andy. 2019. (Treehouse Bks.: 6). (ENG.). 400p. (J). pap. 7.99 *(978-1-250-10483-0(1)*, 900164005) Square Fish.

—The 91-Story Treehouse. Griffiths, Andy. 2018. (Treehouse Bks.: 7). (ENG.). 384p. (J). 13.99 *(978-1-250-10488-5(2)*, 900164007) Feiwel & Friends.

—The 104-Story Treehouse: Dental Dramas & Jokes Galore! Griffiths, Andy. 2019. (Treehouse Bks.: 8). (ENG.). 368p. (J). 13.99 *(978-1-250-30149-9(1)*, 900196710) Feiwel & Friends.

—The 117-Story Treehouse: Dots, Plots & Daring Escapes! Griffiths, Andy. 2019. (Treehouse Bks.: 9). (ENG.). 384p. (J). 13.99 *(978-1-250-31720-9(7)*, 900199916) Feiwel & Friends.

Denton, Terry. Summer in the City. Denton, Terry. 2008. (ENG.). 132p. (J). (gr. 2-5). pap. 11.99 *(978-1-74175-130-7(6))* Allen & Unwin AUS. Dist: Independent Pubs. Group.

—The Ultimate Wave. Denton, Terry. 2003. (Storymaze Ser.: Vol. 1). (ENG.). 144p. (J). (gr. 3-7). pap. 11.99 *(978-1-86508-378-0(X))* Allen & Unwin AUS. Dist: Independent Pubs. Group.

—The Wooden Cow. Denton, Terry. 2003. (Storymaze Ser.: Vol. 3). (ENG.). 120p. (J). (gr. 3-6). pap. 11.99 *(978-1-86508-783-2(1))* Allen & Unwin AUS. Dist: Independent Pubs. Group.

DeNucci, Corinne. Ava Goes to Africa. DeNucci, Sharon. 2010. 32p. pap. 16.99 *(978-1-4520-4091-2(5))* AuthorHouse.

—Grammie & the Gecko. Denucci, Sharon. 2008. 40p. pap. 16.99 *(978-1-4389-1790-0(2))* AuthorHouse.

Denyer, Paul. Plug & Glug. Court, Terry. 2016. (ENG.). 26p. (J). pap. *(978-1-909874-95-4(7)*, Mereo Bks.) Mereo Bks.

Deo, Laura. I Love You, Little Moo. Temple, Tilly. 2019. (ENG.). 10p. (J). (-k). bds. 9.99 *(978-1-68010-624-4(4))* Tiger Tales.

—The Moon Explorer's Model Book: Includes 2 Fantastic Models. Potter, William. 2019. (ENG.). 8p. (J). bds. 9.99 *(978-1-78950-033-2(8)*, 78d90cea-9940-485c-b401-741c6e5f25a3) Arcturus Publishing GBR. Dist: Baker & Taylor Publisher Services (BTPS).

Deo, Laura. Let's Trace Numbers. Deo, Laura. 2018. (Ready to Write Ser.). (ENG.). 48p. (J). pap. 5.99 *(978-1-78828-510-0(7)*, b723b0c0-7a04-450d-9eb3-4cfa9d361668) Arcturus Publishing GBR. Dist: Baker & Taylor Publisher Services (BTPS).

—Ready to Write: Let's Learn Phonics. Deo, Laura. Casey, Catherine. 2019. (ENG.). 48p. (J). pap. 5.99 *(978-1-78950-042-4(7)*, ea603749-bcc5-4bec-bbe6-2e23e929b7d0) Arcturus Publishing GBR. Dist: Baker & Taylor Publisher Services (BTPS).

—Ready to Write!: Let's Trace Letters. Deo, Laura. 2018. (Ready to Write Ser.). (ENG.). 48p. (J). pap. 5.99 *(978-1-78828-509-4(3)*, ab5df5b0-e28d-4bfb-ba51-59e0fde9eef8) Arcturus Publishing GBR. Dist: Baker & Taylor Publisher Services (BTPS).

—Ready to Write: Let's Trace Shapes. Deo, Laura. Casey, Catherine. 2019. (ENG.). 48p. (J). pap. 5.99 *(978-1-78950-602-0(6)*, aea176b8-6aac-4cdb-b341-3e1e918bd3ab) Arcturus Publishing GBR. Dist: Baker & Taylor Publisher Services (BTPS).

Deodato, Mike. Infinity Wars. 2019. 272p. (YA). (gr. 8-17). pap. 34.99 *(978-1-302-91356-4(5))* Marvel Worldwide, Inc.

Deodato, Mike, et al. Infinity Wars by Gerry Duggan: the Complete Collection. 2019. (ENG.). 592p. (YA). (gr. 8-17). 50.00 *(978-1-302-91496-7(0))* Marvel Worldwide, Inc.

—New Avengers by Brian Michael Bendis: the Complete Collection Vol. 7. 2017. 440p. (YA). (gr. 8-17). pap. 39.99 *(978-1-302-90868-3(5))* Marvel Worldwide, Inc.

—Star Wars: Vader Down (Set), 6 vols. Aaron, Jason & Gillen, Kieron. 2016. (Star Wars: Vader Down Ser.). (ENG.). 24p. (J). (gr. 6-12). lib. bdg. 162.42 *(978-1-61479-560-5(6)*, 24394, Graphic Novels) Spotlight.

Deodato, Mike & Bagley, Mark. Invincible Iron Man Vol. 3: Civil War II. 2017. (ENG.). 136p. (YA). (gr. 8-17). pap. 15.99 *(978-1-302-90321-3(7))* Marvel Worldwide, Inc.

Deodato, Mike & Martin, Laura. Vader down: Volume 1. Aaron, Jason. 2016. (Star Wars: Vader Down Ser.). (ENG.). 36p. (J). (gr. 6-12). lib. bdg. 27.07 *(978-1-61479-561-2(4)*, 24395, Graphic Novels) Spotlight.

—Vader down: Volume 3. Aaron, Jason. 2016. (Star Wars: Vader Down Ser.). (ENG.). 24p. (J). (gr. 6-12). lib. bdg. 27.07 *(978-1-61479-563-6(0)*, 24397, Graphic Novels) Spotlight.

—Vader down: Volume 5. Aaron, Jason. 2016. (Star Wars: Vader Down Ser.). (ENG.). 24p. (J). (gr. 6-12). lib. bdg. 27.07 *(978-1-61479-565-0(7)*, 24399, Graphic Novels) Spotlight.

DePalma, Mary Newell. Bow-Wow Wiggle Waggle. 2012. (ENG.). 32p. (J). 14.00 *(978-0-8028-5408-7(7)*, Eerdmans Bks For Young Readers) Eerdmans, William B. Publishing Co.

—Now It Is Summer. Spinelli, Eileen. 2011. (ENG.). 36p. (YA). (gr. -1-3). 16.00 *(978-0-8028-5340-0(4)*, Eerdmans Bks For Young Readers) Eerdmans, William B. Publishing Co.

—Now It Is Winter. Spinelli, Eileen. 2004. 32p. (J). 16.00 *(978-0-8028-5244-1(0))* Eerdmans, William B. Publishing Co.

—The Squeaky Door. MacDonald, Margaret Read. 2006. (ENG.). 40p. (J). (gr. -1-1). 16.99 *(978-0-06-028373-5(4))* HarperCollins Pubs.

—Swimming Sal. Molski, Carol. 2009. 36p. (J). (gr. -1-3). 17.00 *(978-0-8028-5327-1(7)*, Eerdmans Bks For Young Readers) Eerdmans, William B. Publishing Co.

DePalma, Mary Newell. A Grand Old Tree. DePalma, Mary Newell. 2005. (ENG.). 32p. (J). (gr. -1-3). 17.99 *(978-0-439-62334-6(0)*, Levine, Arthur A. Bks.) Scholastic, Inc.

Depalma, Victoria. This Is My Body: A Safety for Little Girls. DePalma, Vanessa. 2003. 15p. (J). (gr. -1-4). *(978-0-9728135-0-1(0))* DePalma, Vanessa.

dePaola, Tomie. The Comic Adventures of Old Mother Hubbard & Her Dog. 2020. (ENG.). 32p. (J). (gr. -1-3). 17.99 ***(978-1-5344-6662-3(2)***, Simon & Schuster Bks. For Young Readers) Simon & Schuster Bks. For Young Readers.

dePaola, Tomie. Cookie's Week. Ward, Cindy. 2015. 32p. pap. 7.00 *(978-1-61003-528-6(3))* Center for the Collaborative Classroom.

—Erandi's Braids. Madrigal, Antonio Hernandez. 2015. 32p. pap. 7.00 *(978-1-61003-530-9(5))* Center for the Collaborative Classroom.

—Frida Kahlo: The Artist Who Painted Herself. Frith, Margaret. 2003. (Smart about Art Ser.). (ENG.). 32p. (J). (gr. k-4). 6.99 *(978-0-448-42677-8(3)*, Grosset & Dunlap) Penguin Young Readers Group.

—God Is Great, God Is Good. Baker, Sanna Anderson. 2020. (ENG.). 24p. (J). (gr. -1 — 1). bds. 8.99 *(978-1-4197-4094-7(6)*, Abrams Appleseed) Abrams, Inc.

—I Love You Sun / I Love You Moon: Te Amo Sol / Te Amo Luna. Pandell, Karen. 2003.Tr. of I Love You, Sun - I Love You, Moon. 12p. (J). (gr. -1 — 1). bds. 7.99 *(978-0-399-24165-9(5)*, G.P. Putnam's Sons Books for Young Readers) Penguin Young Readers Group.

—I Will Talk to You, Little One. Grann, Phyllis E. 2020. (ENG.). 16p. (J). (— 1). bds. 9.99 *(978-1-5344-0253-9(5)*, Little Simon) Little Simon.

—Little Poems for Tiny Ears. Oliver, Lin. 2014. 32p. (J). (gr. -1 — 1). 16.99 *(978-0-399-16605-1(X)*, Nancy Paulsen Bks.) Penguin Publishing Group.

—The Moon's Almost Here. MacLachlan, Patricia. 2016. (ENG.). 32p. (J). (gr. -1-3). 17.99 *(978-1-4814-2062-4(3)*, McElderry, Margaret K. Bks.) McElderry, Margaret K. Bks.

—My First Chanukah. 2008. (ENG.). 14p. (J). (gr. -1-k). bds. 6.99 *(978-0-448-44859-6(9)*, Grosset & Dunlap) Penguin Young Readers Group.

—The Night Before Christmas. Moore, Clement C. (J). 2019. 22p. (— 1). bds. 8.99 *(978-0-8234-4351-2(5))*; 2010. (ENG.). 24p. (gr. -1 — 1). bds. 8.95 *(978-0-8234-2284-5(4))* Holiday Hse., Inc.

—Strega Nona & the Twins. 2017. (J). *(978-1-5379-5057-0(6)*, Simon Spotlight) Simon Spotlight.

—Wings. Klein, Cheryl B. 2019. (ENG.). 40p. (J). (gr. -1-3). 17.99 *(978-1-5344-0510-3(0)*, Atheneum Bks. for Young Readers) Simon & Schuster Children's Publishing.

dePaola, Tomie. Adelita. dePaola, Tomie. 2004. (ENG.). 40p. (J). (gr. -1-3). pap. 7.99 *(978-0-14-240187-3(0)*, Puffin Books) Penguin Young Readers Group.

—Andy & Sandy & the Big Talent Show. dePaola, Tomie. Lewis, Jim. (Andy & Sandy Book Ser.). (ENG.). 32p. (J). (gr. -1-3). 2019. 5.99 *(978-1-5344-1375-7(8))*; 2017. 8.99 *(978-1-4814-7947-9(4))* Simon & Schuster Bks. For Young Readers. (Simon & Schuster Bks. For Young Readers).

—Andy & Sandy & the First Snow. dePaola, Tomie. (Andy & Sandy Book Ser.). (ENG.). 32p. (J). (gr. -1-3). 2018. 5.99 *(978-1-5344-1374-0(X))*; 2016. 8.99 *(978-1-4814-4159-9(0))* Simon & Schuster Bks. For Young Readers. (Simon & Schuster Bks. For Young Readers).

—The Andy & Sandy Collection: When Andy Met Sandy; Andy & Sandy's Anything Adventure; Andy & Sandy & the First Snow; Andy & Sandy & the Big Talent Show. dePaola, Tomie. ed. 2017. (Andy & Sandy Book Ser.). (ENG.). 128p. (J). (gr. -1-3). 35.99 *(978-1-5344-1369-6(3)*, Simon & Schuster Bks. For Young Readers) Simon & Schuster Bks. For Young Readers.

—The Andy & Sandy Paperback Collection: When Andy Met Sandy; Andy & Sandy's Anything Adventure; Andy & Sandy & the First Snow; Andy & Sandy & the Big Talent Show. dePaola, Tomie. ed. 2019. (Andy & Sandy Book Ser.). (ENG.). 128p. (J). (gr. -1-3). pap. 23.99 *(978-1-5344-1376-4(6)*, Simon & Schuster Bks. For Young Readers) Simon & Schuster Bks. For Young Readers.

—Andy & Sandy's Anything Adventure. dePaola, Tomie. 2018. (Andy & Sandy Book Ser.). (ENG.). 32p. (J). (gr. -1-3). 5.99 *(978-1-5344-1373-3(1)*, Simon & Schuster Bks. For Young Readers) Simon & Schuster Bks. For Young Readers.

—Andy & Sandy's Anything Adventure. dePaola, Tomie. 2016. (Andy & Sandy Book Ser.). (ENG.). 32p. (J). (gr. -1-3). 8.99 *(978-1-4814-4157-5(4)*, Simon & Schuster Bks. For Young Readers) Simon & Schuster Bks. For Young Readers.

—Andy, That's My Name. dePaola, Tomie. 2019. (ENG.). 32p. (J). (gr. -1-3). 7.99 *(978-1-5344-3014-3(8)*, Simon & Schuster Bks. For Young Readers) Simon & Schuster Bks. For Young Readers.

—The Birds of Bethlehem. dePaola, Tomie. 2012. 40p. (J). (gr. -1-k). 17.99 *(978-0-399-25780-3(2)*, Nancy Paulsen Books) Penguin Young Readers Group.
—The Clown of God. dePaola, Tomie. (ENG.). 48p. (J). (gr. -1-3). 2019. 7.99 *(978-1-5344-3012-9(1))*; 2018. 18.99 *(978-1-5344-1427-3(4))* Simon & Schuster Bks. For Young Readers. (Simon & Schuster Bks. For Young Readers).
—Days of the Blackbird: A Tale of Northern Italy. dePaola, Tomie. 2005. (J). 13.65 *(978-0-7569-5888-6(1))* Perfection Learning Corp.
—Four Friends at Christmas. dePaola, Tomie. 2009. (ENG.). 32p. (J). (gr. -1-1). 12.99 *(978-1-4169-9175-5(1)*, Aladdin) Simon & Schuster Children's Publishing.
—Four Friends in Autumn. dePaola, Tomie. 2004. (ENG.). 32p. (J). (gr. -1-3). 18.99 *(978-0-689-85980-9(5)*, Simon & Schuster Bks. For Young Readers) Simon & Schuster Bks. For Young Readers.
—Four Friends in Summer. dePaola, Tomie. 2003. (ENG.). 32p. (J). (gr. -1-3). reprint ed. 17.99 *(978-0-689-85693-8(8)*, Simon & Schuster Bks. For Young Readers) Simon & Schuster Bks. For Young Readers.
dePaola, Tomie. Guess Who's Coming to Santa's for Dinner? dePaola, Tomie. 2020. (ENG.). 48p. (J). (gr. -1-3). 18.99 ***(978-1-5344-6649-4(5)***, Simon & Schuster Bks. For Young Readers) Simon & Schuster Bks. For Young Readers.
dePaola, Tomie. Haircuts for Little Lambs. dePaola, Tomie. 2020. (ENG.). 26p. (J). (gr. -1-k). bds. 8.99 *(978-1-5344-6058-4(6)*, Little Simon) Little Simon.
dePaola, Tomie. Hurry, Santa! dePaola, Tomie. 2020. (ENG.). 14p. (J). (gr. -1-k). bds. 7.99 ***(978-1-5344-6405-6(0)***, Little Simon) Little Simon.
dePaola, Tomie. Jack. dePaola, Tomie. 2014. 40p. (J). (gr. -1-k). 17.99 *(978-0-399-16154-4(6)*, Nancy Paulsen Books) Penguin Young Readers Group.
—Joy to the World: Tomie's Christmas Stories. dePaola, Tomie. 2013. 112p. (J). (gr. -1-2). 12.99 *(978-0-14-750952-9(1)*, Puffin Books) Penguin Young Readers Group.
—The Legend of Old Befana: An Italian Christmas Story. dePaola, Tomie. (ENG.). 32p. (J). (gr. -1-3). 2019. 7.99 *(978-1-5344-3011-2(3))*; 2017. 17.99 *(978-1-4814-7763-5(3))* Simon & Schuster Bks. For Young Readers. (Simon & Schuster Bks. For Young Readers).
—Let the Whole Earth Sing Praise. dePaola, Tomie. 2011. 28p. (J). (gr. -1-k). 15.99 *(978-0-399-25478-9(1)*, G.P. Putnam's Sons Books for Young Readers) Penguin Young Readers Group.
—Little Grunt & the Big Egg: A Prehistoric Fairy Tale. dePaola, Tomie. 2008. 32p. (J). (gr. -1-3). pap. 7.99 *(978-0-14-241143-8(4)*, Puffin Books) Penguin Young Readers Group.
—The Magical World of Strega Nona: a Treasury. dePaola, Tomie. 2015. (ENG.). 224p. (J). (gr. k-3). 40.00 *(978-0-399-17345-5(5)*, Nancy Paulsen Books) Penguin Young Readers Group.
dePaola, Tomie. Marianna May & Nursey. dePaola, Tomie. 2020. (ENG.). 32p. (J). (gr. -1-3). 17.99 ***(978-1-5344-6646-3(0)***, Simon & Schuster Bks. For Young Readers) Simon & Schuster Bks. For Young Readers.
dePaola, Tomie. Meet the Barkers: Morgan & Moffat Go to School. dePaola, Tomie. 2003. (Barker Twins Ser.). 32p. (J). (gr. -1-3). 7.99 *(978-0-14-250083-5(6)*, Puffin Books) Penguin Young Readers Group.
—Michael Bird-Boy. dePaola, Tomie. (ENG.). 32p. (J). (gr. -1-3). 2019. 7.99 *(978-1-5344-3015-0(6))*; 2015. 16.99 *(978-1-4814-4333-3(X))* Simon & Schuster Bks. For Young Readers. (Simon & Schuster Bks. For Young Readers).
—More Mother Goose Favorites. dePaola, Tomie. 2007. (gr. -1-3). 14.00 *(978-0-7569-8138-9(7))* Perfection Learning Corp.
—My First Christmas. dePaola, Tomie. 2008. (ENG.). 14p. (J). (gr. -1-k). bds. 6.99 *(978-0-448-44860-2(2)*, Grosset & Dunlap) Penguin Young Readers Group.
—My First Easter. dePaola, Tomie. 2008. (ENG.). 14p. (J). (gr. -1-k). bds. 5.99 *(978-0-448-44790-2(8)*, Grosset & Dunlap) Penguin Young Readers Group.
—My First Passover, Vol. dePaola, Tomie. 2015. (ENG.). 14p. (J). (gr. -1-k). bds. 5.99 *(978-0-448-44791-9(6)*, Grosset & Dunlap) Penguin Young Readers Group.
—Now One Foot, Now the Other. dePaola, Tomie. 48p. (J). (gr. k-3). 2006. pap. 8.99 *(978-0-14-240104-0(8)*, Puffin Books); 2005. reprint ed. 17.99 *(978-0-399-24259-5(7)*, G.P. Putnam's Sons Books for Young Readers) Penguin Young Readers Group.
—Oliver Button Is a Sissy. dePaola, Tomie. (ENG.). 48p. (J). (gr. -1-3). 2019. 7.99 *(978-1-5344-3016-7(4))*; 2017. 17.99 *(978-1-4814-7757-4(9))* Simon & Schuster Bks. For Young Readers. (Simon & Schuster Bks. For Young Readers).
—Quiet. dePaola, Tomie. 2018. (ENG.). 32p. (J). (gr. -1-3). 17.99 *(978-1-4814-7754-3(4)*, Simon & Schuster Bks. For Young Readers) Simon & Schuster Bks. For Young Readers.
—Stagestruck. dePaola, Tomie. 2005. (ENG.). 32p. (J). (gr. -1-1). 21.19 *(978-0-399-24338-7(0))* Penguin Young Readers Group.
—Stagestruck. dePaola, Tomie. 2007. (gr. -1-3). 17.00 *(978-0-7569-8159-4(X))* Perfection Learning Corp.
dePaola, Tomie. The Story of the Three Wise Kings. dePaola, Tomie. 2020. (ENG.). 32p. (J). (gr. -1-3). 17.99 ***(978-1-5344-6652-4(5)***, Simon & Schuster Bks. For Young Readers) Simon & Schuster Bks. For Young Readers.
dePaola, Tomie. Strega Nona. dePaola, Tomie. 2017. (Strega Nona Book Ser.). (ENG.). 36p. (J). (gr. -1-k). bds. 8.99 *(978-1-4814-8724-5(8)*, Little Simon) Little Simon.
—Strega Nona: Book & CD. dePaola, Tomie. 2011. (Strega Nona Book Ser.). (ENG.). 40p. (J). (gr. -1-3). pap. 9.99 *(978-1-4424-3355-7(8)*, Little Simon) Little Simon.
—Strega Nona & Her Tomatoes. dePaola, Tomie. 2017. (Strega Nona Book Ser.). (ENG.). 32p. (J). (gr. -1-1). pap. 4.99 *(978-1-4814-8134-2(7)*, Simon Spotlight) Simon Spotlight.
—Strega Nona & the Twins. dePaola, Tomie. 2017. (Strega Nona Book Ser.). (ENG.). 32p. (J). (gr. -1-1). pap. 4.99 *(978-1-4814-8137-3(1)*, Simon Spotlight) Simon Spotlight.
—Strega Nona Takes a Vacation. dePaola, Tomie. 2003. 32p. (J). (gr. -1-3). pap. 7.99 *(978-0-14-250076-7(3)*, Puffin Books) Penguin Young Readers Group.
—Strega Nona Takes a Vacation. dePaola, Tomie. 2003. (J). (gr. -1-3). 13.65 *(978-0-7569-1469-1(8))* Perfection Learning Corp.
—Strega Nona's Gift. dePaola, Tomie. 2011. 32p. (J). (gr. -1-3). 17.99 *(978-0-399-25649-3(0)*, Nancy Paulsen Books) Penguin Young Readers Group.
—Strega Nona's Harvest. dePaola, Tomie. 32p. (J). (gr. -1-3). 2012. (ENG.). mass mkt. 7.99 *(978-0-14-242338-7(6)*, Puffin Books); 2009. 16.99 *(978-0-399-25291-4(6)*, G.P. Putnam's Sons Books for Young Readers) Penguin Young Readers Group.
—Strega Nona's Magic Lessons. dePaola, Tomie. (Strega Nona Book Ser.). (ENG.). 32p. (J). (gr. -1-3). 2019. 7.99 *(978-1-5344-3013-6(X))*; 2017. 17.99 *(978-1-4814-7759-8(5))* Simon & Schuster Bks. For Young Readers. (Simon & Schuster Bks. For Young Readers).
—Strega Nona's Magic Ring. dePaola, Tomie. (Strega Nona Book Ser.). (ENG.). 32p. (J). (gr. -1-3). 2019. 7.99 *(978-1-5344-3017-4(2))*; 2018. 17.99 *(978-1-4814-7761-1(7))* Simon & Schuster Bks. For Young Readers. (Simon & Schuster Bks. For Young Readers).
—Things Will Never Be the Same. dePaola, Tomie. 2004. (26 Fairmount Avenue Bks.). 69p. (J). (gr. 3-7). 13.65 *(978-0-7569-2951-0(2))* Perfection Learning Corp.
—Too Many Bunnies. dePaola, Tomie. 2020. (ENG.). 26p. (J). (gr. -1-k). bds. 8.99 *(978-1-5344-6056-0(X)*, Little Simon) Little Simon.
—What a Year. dePaola, Tomie. 2003. (26 Fairmount Avenue Bks.). 72p. (gr. 2-5). 16.00 *(978-0-7569-1546-9(5))* Perfection Learning Corp.
—When Andy Met Sandy. dePaola, Tomie. 2018. (Andy & Sandy Book Ser.). (ENG.). 32p. (J). (gr. -1-3). 5.99 *(978-1-5344-1372-6(3)*, Simon & Schuster Bks. For Young Readers) Simon & Schuster Bks. For Young Readers.
—When Andy Met Sandy. dePaola, Tomie. 2016. (Andy & Sandy Book Ser.). (ENG.). 32p. (J). (gr. -1-3). 8.99 *(978-1-4814-4155-1(8)*, Simon & Schuster Bks. For Young Readers) Simon & Schuster Bks. For Young Readers.
—26 Fairmount Avenue. dePaola, Tomie. 2005. 58p. (J). (gr. k-4). reprint ed. 14.00 *(978-0-7567-8722-6(X))* DIANE Publishing Co.
DePaola, Daniel. Dingo & Willy's Donuts. Allen, Katy C. 2012. 74p. pap. 6.99 *(978-0-9857160-3-5(7))*; pap. 6.99 *(978-0-9857160-1-1(0))* Baysmore Bks.
DePauw, Sandra A. The Don't-Give-Up Kid: And Learning Differences. Gehret, Jeanne. 2003. 40p. (J). (gr. 1-5). 2nd rev. ed. 13.95 *(978-0-9625136-3-3(6))*; 3rd rev. ed. pap. 9.95 *(978-1-884281-10-5(9))* Verbal Images Pr.
Depew, Robert, jt. illus. see Zapater Oliva, Carlos.
Depinet, Linda. God Just Needed Another Angel. Depinet, Linda. 2003. 32p. (J). pap. 12.95 *(978-1-59098-844-2(2))* Wooster Bk. Co., The.
DePorter, Vince. The Song That Never Ends. Banks, Steven. ed. 2005. 32p. (J). lib. bdg. 15.00 *(978-1-59054-984-1(8))* Fitzgerald Bks.
—The Song That Never Ends. Banks, Steven. 2004. (Spongebob Squarepants Ser.). 32p. (J). (gr. k-2). 11.65 *(978-0-7569-5374-4(X))* Perfection Learning Corp.
—Special Delivery! Banks, Steven. 2003. (SpongeBob SquarePants Ser.: Vol. 2). (ENG.). 32p. (J). pap. 3.99 *(978-0-689-85887-1(6)*, Simon Spotlight/Nickelodeon) Simon Spotlight/Nickelodeon.
—Special Delivery. Banks, Steven. 2005. (Ready-to-Read Ser.). 32p. (J). lib. bdg. 15.00 *(978-1-59054-986-5(4))* Fitzgerald Bks.
—Stop the Presses! Banks, Steven. 2005. 22p. (J). lib. bdg. 15.00 *(978-1-4242-0973-6(0))* Fitzgerald Bks.
Deporter, Vincent. Scooby-Doo & the Mystery Date, 1 vol. Strom, Frank. 2010. (Scooby-Doo Graphic Novels Ser.: No. 1). (ENG.). 24p. (J). (gr. 2-6). 27.07 *(978-1-59961-689-6(0)*, 557, Graphic Novels) Spotlight.
—Scooby-Doo in Don't Play Dummy with Me, 1 vol. Busch, Robbie. 2010. (Scooby-Doo Graphic Novels Ser.: No. 1). (ENG.). 24p. (J). (gr. 2-6). 27.07 *(978-1-59961-693-3(9)*, 561, Graphic Novels) Spotlight.
—Scooby-Doo in Fangs, but No Fangs!, 1 vol. Fisch, Sholly. 2013. (Scooby-Doo Graphic Novels Ser.). (ENG.). 24p. (J). (gr. 2-6). lib. bdg. 27.07 *(978-1-61479-051-8(5)*, 584, Graphic Novels) Spotlight.
Deppe, Iris. Noah's Ark. Allison, Catherine. Parragon Books & Cottage Door Press, eds. 2019. (ENG.). 32p. (J). (gr. -1-3). 9.99 *(978-1-68052-551-9(4)*, 2001300, Parragon Books) Cottage Door Pr.
Deppe, Iris. Tag Your Dreams: Poems of Play & Persistence. Jules, Jacqueline. 2020. (ENG.). 40p. (J). (gr. 1-5). 17.99 ***(978-0-8075-6726-5(4)***, 807567264) Whitman, Albert & Co.
Deppe, Iris. What Can You See? Animals in the Night: Use the Star Light to Find Hidden Animals! Austin, Ruth. 2018. (ENG.). 32p. (J). (gr. k-2). 21.99 *(978-0-7603-6316-4(1))* becker&mayer! books.
Depratto, Marcel, jt. illus. see Brignaud, Pierre.
Depriest, Mitchell a. My Dad's Hero. Depriest, Mitchell a. Depriest, M. a. 2019. (ENG.). 26p. (J). pap. 9.13 *(978-1-7312-4649-3(8))* Independently Published.
DePrince, Erik & Volinski, Jessica. Not Everyone Is Nice: Helping Children Learn Caution with Strangers. Alimonti, Frederick. 2003. (Let's Talk Ser.). 48p. (J). pap. 9.95 *(978-0-88282-233-4(0))* New Horizon Pr. Pubs., Inc.
Der Saim, Van. Invisible Magic Wand(r) Sequel to Hot Chocolate Underpants. Jacimin, Rafael. 2019. (Hot Chocolate Underpants Ser.: Vol. 2). (ENG.). 32p. (J). pap. 12.00 *(978-1-5203-4616-8(6))* Independently Published.
Derby, Cindy. Born, 1 vol. Sobol, John. 2020. (ENG.). 24p. (J). (gr. -1-2). 18.95 *(978-1-77306-169-6(0))* Groundwood Bks. CAN. Dist: Publishers Group West (PGW).
—Outside In. Underwood, Deborah. 2020. (ENG.). 40p. (J). (gr. -1-3). 17.99 *(978-1-328-86682-0(3)*, 1695831, HMH Books For Young Readers) Houghton Mifflin Harcourt Publishing Co.
Derby, Cindy. How to Walk an Ant. Derby, Cindy. 2019. (ENG.). 40p. (J). 17.99 *(978-1-250-16262-5(9)*, 900186339) Roaring Brook Pr.
Derby, Sarah. It's a Scamp's Life! Kezar, Wanda. 2013. 186p. pap. 14.99 *(978-1-62839-371-2(8))* Salem Author Services.
Derby, T. L. The Hanukkah Fable of Little Dreidel & Silver Menorah. Rouss, Sylvia. ed. 2019. (ENG.). 30p. (J). (gr. k-6). pap. 15.99 ***(978-1-64372-294-8(8)***, Huskies Pub) MacLaren-Cochrane Publishing, Inc.
Derenne, Juliette & Barroux, Sophie. Queen Margot - The Age of Innocence. Cadic, Olivier & Gheysens, Francois. 2007. (Queen Margot Ser.: 1). (ENG.). 48p. (J). (gr. 4-7). per. 13.95 *(978-1-905460-10-6(4))* CineBook GBR. Dist: National Bk. Network.
Dérib. The River of Forgetfulness. Job. 2013. (Yakari Ser.: 10). (ENG.). 48p. pap. 11.95 *(978-1-84918-140-2(3))* CineBook GBR. Dist: National Bk. Network.
Derib. Yakari & Nanabozo. Job. 2014. (Yakari Ser.: 11). (ENG.). 48p. pap. 11.95 *(978-1-84918-177-8(2))* CineBook GBR. Dist: National Bk. Network.
Dérib. Yakari & the Coyote. Job. 2012. (Yakari Ser.: 9). (ENG.). 48p. (J). (gr. 1-6). pap. 11.95 *(978-1-84918-101-3(2))* CineBook GBR. Dist: National Bk. Network.
—Yakari & the Grizzly. Job. 2007. (Yakari Ser.: 4). (ENG.). 46p. (J). (gr. 4-7). per. 9.99 *(978-1-905460-16-8(3))* CineBook GBR. Dist: National Bk. Network.
Derington, Nick, et al. Graphic Science 4D. Adamson, Thomas Kristian et al. 2019. (Graphic Science 4D Ser.). (ENG.). (J). (gr. 3-9). pap., pap., pap. 190.80 *(978-1-5435-8135-5(8)*, 29506); 831.60 *(978-1-5435-7255-1(3)*, 29336); pap., pap., pap. 159.00 *(978-1-5435-6064-0(4)*, 29203); 693.00 *(978-1-5435-5888-3(7)*, 28932) Capstone.
—Graphic Science 4D. Biskup, Agnieszka Józefina et al. 2019. (Graphic Science 4D Ser.). (ENG.). (J). (gr. 3-9). pap., pap., pap. 79.50 *(978-1-5435-6033-6(4)*, 29186) Capstone.
Derington, Nick. The Illuminating World of Light with Max Axiom, Super Scientist, 1 vol. Sohn, Emily. 2008. (Graphic Science Ser.). (ENG.). 32p. (J). (gr. 3-9). pap. 8.10 *(978-1-4296-1768-0(3))* Capstone.
—The Illuminating World of Light with Max Axiom, Super Scientist: 4D an Augmented Reading Science Experience. Sohn, Emily Beth. 2019. (Graphic Science 4D Ser.). (ENG.). 32p. (J). (gr. 3-9). pap. 7.95 *(978-1-5435-6001-5(6)*, 140062); lib. bdg. 34.65 *(978-1-5435-5868-5(2)*, 139789) Capstone.
—Understanding Viruses with Max Axiom, Super Scientist, 1 vol. Biskup, Agnieszka. 2010. (Graphic Science Ser.). (ENG.). 32p. (J). (gr. 3-9). pap. 8.10 *(978-1-4296-3453-3(7))* Capstone.
—Understanding Viruses with Max Axiom, Super Scientist: 4D an Augmented Reading Science Experience. Biskup, Agnieszka Józefina. 2019. (Graphic Science 4D Ser.). (ENG.). 32p. (J). (gr. 3-9). pap. 7.95 *(978-1-5435-6032-9(6)*, 140079); lib. bdg. 34.65 *(978-1-5435-5877-7(1)*, 139802) Capstone.
Dernavich, Drew. Elvin Link, Please Report to the Principal's Office! Dernavich, Drew. 2020. (ENG.). 224p. (J). 16.99 *(978-1-62779-209-7(0)*, 900141078, Holt, Henry & Co. Bks. For Young Readers) Holt, Henry & Co.
—It's Not Easy Being Number Three. Dernavich, Drew. 2016. (ENG.). 40p. (J). 16.99 *(978-1-62779-208-0(2)*, 900141077, Holt, Henry & Co. Bks. For Young Readers) Holt, Henry & Co.
Derome, Pierre-André. La Petite Lili Est un Genie. Gauthier, Gilles. 2004. (Premier Roman Ser.). (FRE.). 64p. (J). (gr. 1-4). pap. *(978-2-89021-686-0(1))* Diffusion du livre Mirabel (DLM).
DeRosa, Dee. I'm a Princess. Hall, Kirsten. 2004. (My First Reader Ser.). (ENG.). 32p. (J). (gr. k-1). pap. 3.95 *(978-0-516-24630-7(5)*, Children's Pr.) Scholastic Library Publishing.
DeRose, Adam. A Very Scary Halloween Tail. Tucking-Strickler, Devan. 2019. (Very Scary Tail Ser.: Vol. 3). (ENG.). 26p. (J). pap. 9.98 ***(978-1-7024-3193-4(2))*** Independently Published.
DeRose, Kim. Handstand Kids Mexican Cookbook. Garfield, Yvette & Azima, Cricket. 2008. 52p. (J). (gr. -1-3). 28.00 *(978-0-9792107-2-3(0))* Handstand Kids.
DeRosier, Cher & Cerone, Sal. The Pea & the Grape. DeRosier, Cher. 2005. (ENG.). (J). ring bd. incl. cd-rom *(978-1-891685-60-6(0))* Dearborn Publishing.
d'Errico, Camilla. Camilla d'Errico's Burn. d'Errico, Camilla. Sanders, Scott. 2009. (ENG.). 160p. (YA). (gr. 7-18). pap. 9.99 *(978-1-4169-7873-2(9)*, Simon Pulse) Simon Pulse.
Dershowitz, Yosef. Cartons in the Air & Other Stories. Weinbach, Shaindel. (J). 14.99 *(978-0-89906-992-0(4)*, CARH) Mesorah Pubns., Ltd.
—The Friendly Persuader & Other Stories. Weinbach, Shaindel. (J). 14.99 *(978-0-89906-970-8(3)*, FRIH) Mesorah Pubns., Ltd.
Derstine, Charlene. God Made Nuts. Martin, Mary. 2012. 53p. (J). *(978-0-7399-2501-0(6))* Rod & Staff Pubs., Inc.
Desai, Makarand. Bug Off. Clark, Shawnie. 2018. (ENG.). 36p. (J). (gr. k-6). 17.99 *(978-1-365-86169-7(4))*; pap. 13.99 *(978-1-365-86171-0(6))* Lulu Pr., Inc.
—Bug Off. Clark, Shawnie. ed. 2018. (ENG.). 32p. (J). (gr. k-6). 17.99 *(978-1-64372-192-7(5))*; pap. 13.99 *(978-1-64372-193-4(3))* MacLaren-Cochrane Publishing, Inc. (Huskies Pub).
—Bug off Dyslexic Edition: Dyslexic Font. Clark, Shawnie. ed. 2018. (ENG.). 34p. (J). (gr. k-6). 19.99 *(978-1-64372-063-0(5))*; pap. 15.99 *(978-1-64372-062-3(7))* MacLaren-Cochrane Publishing, Inc.
DeSaix, Deborah Durland. The Grand Mosque of Paris: A Story of How Muslims Rescued Jews During the Holocaust. Ruelle, Karen Gray. 2009. (ENG.). 40p. (J). (gr. 2-18). 18.95 *(978-0-8234-2159-6(7))* Holiday Hse., Inc.
—Hidden on the Mountain: Stories of Children Sheltered from the Nazis in le Chambon. Ruelle, Karen Gray. 2007. (ENG.). 272p. (J). (gr. 5-18). 24.95 *(978-0-8234-1928-9(2))* Holiday Hse., Inc.
DeSantis, Andrea. Space Kids: An Introduction for Young Explorers. 2018. (ENG.). 40p. (J). (gr. 2). 24.95 *(978-3-89955-795-4(6))* Die Gestalten Verlag DEU. Dist: Ingram Publisher Services.
DeSantis, Mary. A. J. & Grandpa's Cap. Dickerson, Martha Perry. 2019. (ENG.). 40p. (J). pap. 9.99 ***(978-1-6969-4260-7(8))*** Independently Published.
DeSantis, Mike. Aiden Pike: Step Right Up! Ryan, Mary C. 2017. (ENG.). 70p. (J). pap. 6.95 *(978-0-9678115-4-3(6))* Dragonseed Pr.
—Rock Away Blues. Mackall, Dandi Daley. 2017. 32p. (J). (gr. -1-k). 16.99 *(978-1-5107-0835-8(9)*, Sky Pony Pr.) Skyhorse Publishing Co., Inc.
DeSantis, Susan. Little Too-Tall: A Book about Friendship. Moncure, Jane Belk. 2013. (Magic Castle Readers Ser.). (ENG.). 32p. (J). (gr. -1-2). 14.21 *(978-1-62323-568-0(5)*, 206303) Child's World, Inc., The.
—Rabbits' Habits: A Book about Good Habits. Moncure, Jane Belk. 2013. (Magic Castle Readers Ser.). (ENG.). 32p. (J). (gr. -1-2). 14.21 *(978-1-62323-569-7(3)*, 206304) Child's World, Inc., The.
—'Smile,' Says Little Crocodile: A Book about Good Habits. Moncure, Jane Belk. 2013. (Magic Castle Readers Ser.). (ENG.). 32p. (J). (gr. -1-2). 14.21 *(978-1-62323-570-3(7)*, 206305) Child's World, Inc., The.
—Yes, No, Little Hippo: A Book about Safety. Moncure, Jane Belk. 2013. (Magic Castle Readers Ser.). (ENG.). 32p. (J). (gr. -1-2). 14.21 *(978-1-62323-571-0(5)*, 206306) Child's World, Inc., The.
—5 Steps to Drawing Machines at Work. Kesselring, Susan. 2018. (5 Steps to Drawing Ser.). (ENG.). 32p. (J). (gr. k-3). 29.93 *(978-1-5038-2482-9(9)*, 212241) Child's World, Inc., The.
—5 Steps to Drawing Zoo Animals. Kesselring, Susan. 2018. (5 Steps to Drawing Ser.). (ENG.). 32p. (J). (gr. k-3). 29.93 *(978-1-5038-2486-7(1)*, 212246) Child's World, Inc., The.
Desautels, Stacie. Blue Bear Finds a Rainbow. Betts, McKenzie Leigh. Abbott, Candy, ed. 2011. 24p. (J). 15.00 *(978-1-886068-51-3(8))* Fruitbearer Publishing, LLC.
—Pink Bear's Journey: I Love Me, Who Do You Love? Betts, McKenzie Leigh. 2013. (ENG.). 48p. (J). 15.00 *(978-1-886068-72-8(0))* Fruitbearer Publishing, LLC.
DesChamps, Eric. The Ark Plan. Martin, Laura. ed. 2017. (Edge of Extinction Ser.: 1). (ENG.). (J). (gr. 3-7). lib. bdg. 17.20 *(978-0-606-40046-6(X))* Turtleback.
Deschamps, Eric. Edge of Extinction #1: the Ark Plan. Martin, Laura. (Edge of Extinction Ser.: 1). (ENG.). (J). (gr. 3-7). 2017. 384p. pap. 6.99 *(978-0-06-241623-0(5))*; 2016. 368p. 16.99 *(978-0-06-241622-3(7))* HarperCollins Pubs.
—Edge of Extinction #2: Code Name Flood. Martin, Laura. 2018. (Edge of Extinction Ser.: 2). (ENG.). 368p. (J). (gr. 3-7). pap. 7.99 *(978-0-06-241626-1(X))* HarperCollins Pubs.
Desharnais, Margo. An Icon for Christmas: Sophia's Gift: an Icon Christmas Story to Color. Katris Gonis, Theofania. 2005. (ENG.). 24p. (J). (gr. k-3). pap. 5.95 *(978-1-880971-94-9(1))* Light & Life Publishing Co.
DeShazo, Sharon B., jt. illus. see Jackson, April Eley.
DeSica, Melissa. Wordsworth Dances the Waltz. Kakugawa, Frances. 2007. 32p. (J). 10.95 *(978-0-9790647-3-9(2))* Watermark Publishing, LLC.
Desierto, Derek. A Is for Awesome! 23 Iconic Women Who Changed the World. Chen, Eva. 2019. (ENG.). 32p. (J). bds. 9.99 *(978-1-250-21599-4(4)*, 900206602) Feiwel & Friends.
—Juno Valentine & the Fantastic Fashion Adventure. Chen, Eva. 2019. (Juno Valentine Ser.). (ENG.). 32p. (J). 18.99 *(978-1-250-29730-3(3)*, 900195909) Feiwel & Friends.
—Juno Valentine & the Magical Shoes. Chen, Eva. 2018. (Juno Valentine Ser.). (ENG.). 32p. (J). 18.99 *(978-1-250-29726-6(5)*, 900195905) Feiwel & Friends.
Desierto, Derek. 3 2 1 Awesome! 20 Fearless Women Who Dared to Be Different. Chen, Eva. 2020. (ENG.). 24p. (J). bds. 9.99 ***(978-1-250-62402-4(9)***, 900224110) Feiwel & Friends.
Design, Chelms & Mena, Jessica. The Adventures of Cleanis & Pristina: Bath Time. Allen, Terry. 2018. (ENG.). 28p. (J). pap. 11.95 *(978-1-9867-3880-4(9))* CreateSpace Independent Publishing Platform.
Design, Leslie. Shazam!: Freddy's Guide to Super Hero-Ing. Behling, Steve. 2019. (Shazam! Ser.). (ENG.). 144p. (J). (gr. 3-7). pap. 9.99 *(978-0-06-288418-3(2))* HarperCollins Pubs.
Design, Leslie, jt. illus. see Montgomery, Grant.
Design, Munyx. El Secreto de Tu Mirada (Bilog�a Secretos) Gomez, Raquelita. 2019. (Secretos Ser.: Vol. 2). (SPA.). 322p. (J). pap. 15.20 ***(978-1-0709-1910-2(1))*** Independently Published.
Design, Prettygrafik. Merry Christmas: Christmas Journal. Miracles, Miniature. 2018. (ENG.). 126p. (J). pap. 7.80 *(978-1-7309-0521-6(8))* Independently Published.
Design, Warren. Clouded Hearts: Short Story #2 Prequel to Chroma Chronicles Book Series. Roman, Elani. 2019. (ENG.). 124p. (J). pap. 6.99 ***(978-1-7072-9866-2(1))*** Independently Published.
Design, Wonder. Wally the Whale & Ocean Pollution: Naturebella's Kids Books Earth Series. Le Gendre, Kimaada. 2019. (Earth Ser.: Vol. 1). (ENG.). 48p. (J). pap. 12.95 *(978-1-7326320-7-3(3))* Le Gendre, Kimaada.
Designs, Dena. Sunshine Doodle Book. Publications International Ltd. Staff, ed. 2016. 80p. (J). spiral bd. *(978-1-68022-410-8(7)*, 1680224107, PIL Kids) Publications International, Ltd.

D

Designs, Marion, photos by. Ellen G Goes to the Haunted Planetarium. Crews, G. S. 2009. 50p. pap. 20.00 *(978-0-9795236-4-9(8))* Crews Pubns., LLC.

Desimini, Lisa. The Great Big Green. Gifford, Peggy. 2014. (ENG.). 32p. (J). (gr. -1-3). 15.95 *(978-1-62091-629-2(0))* Boyds Mills Pr.

—Iris Has a Virus. Alda, Arlene. 2008. 24p. (J). (gr. -1-1). 18.95 *(978-0-88776-844-6(X),* Tundra Bks.) Tundra Bks. CAN. Dist: Penguin Random Hse. LLC.

—Lulu's Piano Lesson. Alda, Arlene. 2010. 32p. (J). (gr. -1-1). 16.95 *(978-0-88776-930-6(6),* Tundra Bks.) Tundra Bks. CAN. Dist: Penguin Random Hse. LLC.

—The Snowflake Sisters. Lewis, J. Patrick. 2012. (ENG.). 32p. (J). (gr. -1-3). pap. 16.99 *(978-1-4424-6719-4(3),* Atheneum Bks. for Young Readers) Simon & Schuster Children's Publishing.

DeSimone, Corkey Hay. The Planet Hue. DeSimone, Corkey Hay. 2003. (J). 14.95 *(978-0-9747921-0-1(1))* Gentle Giraffe Pr.

DeSimone, Suzanne. My Princess Boy. Kilodavis, Cheryl. 2010. (ENG.). 36p. (J). (gr. -1-3). 17.99 *(978-1-4424-2988-8(7),* Aladdin) Simon & Schuster Children's Publishing.

Desira, Angela. A Trust of Treasures. Sinclair, Mehded Maryam. 2010. (ENG.). 29p. (J). (gr. k). 14.95 *(978-0-86037-462-6(9))* Kube Publishing Ltd. GBR. Dist: Consortium Bk. Sales & Distribution.

Desisto, Allie. Some Kids Just Can't Sit Still! Desisto, Allie. Goldstein, Sam. 2009. (ENG.). 32p. (J). (gr. 2-4). pap. 15.95 *(978-1-886941-73-1(4))* Specialty Pr., Inc.

Desjardins, Vincent. Mercy: The Incredible Story of Henry Bergh, Founder of the ASPCA & Friend to Animals. Furstinger, Nancy. 2016. (ENG.). 192p. (J). (gr. 5-7). 16.99 *(978-0-544-65031-2(X),* 1621873, HMH Books For Young Readers) Houghton Mifflin Harcourt Publishing Co.

Deskcube. The Volcano: The Adventures of Antboy & Mr Cricket. Stevens, A. P. Finn, N. K., ed. 2008. (ENG.). 29p. pap. 9.95 *(978-0-9798886-0-1(3))* Mugsy and Sugar Pressed.

Desmet, Sara. Scared Silly. Desmet, Sara. 2006. 32p. (J). (gr. -1-3). 15.95 *(978-1-60108-009-7(3))* Red Cygnet Pr.

Desmoinaux, Christel. Passover Is Here! Passover Is Here! Pearlman, Bobby. 2005. (ENG.). 16p. (J). (gr. k-2). pap. 6.99 *(978-0-689-86587-9(2),* Little Simon) Little Simon.

Desmoineaux, Christel. Rosy Posey Is Not Dirty! Hanna, Virginie. 2012. (My Little Picture Book Ser.). (ENG.). 32p. (J). pap. 6.95 *(978-2-7338-1947-0(X))* Auzou, Philippe Editions FRA. Dist: Consortium Bk. Sales & Distribution.

Desmond, Hillary. Jake & the Big Cake Mistake. Beall, Kirsten. 2011. 36p. pap. 24.95 *(978-1-4626-4524-4(0))* America Star Bks.

Desmond, Jenni. Blue Monster Wants It All! Willis, Jeanne. 2018. (ENG.). 32p. (J). (gr. -1-2). 16.99 *(978-1-68010-077-8(7))* Tiger Tales.

—I Have a Little Seedling. Meister, Cari. 2018. (New Books for Newborns Ser.). (ENG.). 16p. (J). (— 1). bds. 7.99 *(978-1-5344-1002-2(3),* Little Simon) Little Simon.

—Joy. Ismail, Yasmeen. 2020. (ENG.). 32p. (J). (gr. -1-2). 16.99 *(978-1-5362-0934-1(1))* Candlewick Pr.

—Migration: Incredible Animal Journeys. Unwin, Mike. 2019. (ENG.). 48p. (J). 18.99 *(978-1-5476-0097-7(7),* 900198454, Bloomsbury Children's Bks.) Bloomsbury Publishing USA.

—On the Night of the Shooting Star. Hest, Amy. 2017. (ENG.). 32p. (J). (-k). 16.99 *(978-0-7636-9154-7(2))* Candlewick Pr.

—¿Quieres Ser Mi Amigo? Hest, Amy. 2019. (SPA.). 40p. (J). 15.95 *(978-84-17673-10-9(5))* NubeOcho Ediciones ESP. Dist: Consortium Bk. Sales & Distribution.

Desmond, Jenni. Albert's Tree. Desmond, Jenni. 2018. (ENG.). 32p. (J). (gr. -1-2). 15.99 *(978-0-7636-9688-7(9))* Candlewick Pr.

Desnitskaya, Anna. The Apartment: a Century of Russian History. Litvina, Alexandra. Bouis, Antonina W., tr. 2019. (ENG.). 64p. (J). (gr. 3-7). 24.99 *(978-1-4197-3403-8(2),* Abrams Bks. for Young Readers) Abrams, Inc.

Després, Geneviève. Best Friend Trouble, 1 vol. Itani, Frances. 2014. (ENG.). 32p. (J). (gr. -1-k). 19.95 *(978-1-55469-891-2(X))* Orca Bk. Pubs. USA.

—The Highest Number in the World. MacGregor, Roy. 2014. (ENG.). 32p. (J). (gr. 1-4). 17.99 *(978-1-77049-575-3(4),* Tundra Bks.) Tundra Bks. CAN. Dist: Penguin Random Hse. LLC.

Desputeaux, Helene. Baby Science: How Babies Really Work! Douglas, Ann. 2004. 32p. (J). (gr. k-4). reprint ed. pap. 7.00 *(978-0-7567-8455-3(7))* DIANE Publishing Co.

Desputeaux, Hélène. Purple, Green & Yellow. Munsch, Robert. 2018. (Classic Munsch Ser.). 32p. (J). (gr. -1-2). pap. 6.95 *(978-1-77321-033-9(5))* Annick Pr., Ltd. CAN. Dist: Publishers Group West (PGW).

Desputeaux, Hélène & Desputeaux, Hélène. Purple, Green & Yellow. Munsch, Robert. 2018. (Classic Munsch Ser.). (ENG.). 36p. (J). (gr. -1-2). 19.95 *(978-1-77321-034-6(3))* Annick Pr., Ltd. CAN. Dist: Publishers Group West (PGW).

Desputeaux, Hélène, jt. illus. see Desputeaux, Hélène.

Desrocher, Jack. Eat Right! How You Can Make Good Food Choices. Doeden, Matt. 2008. (Health Zone Ser.). (ENG.). 64p. (gr. 4-7). lib. bdg. 30.60 *(978-0-8225-7552-8(3))* Lerner Publishing Group.

—Keep Your Cool! What You Should Know about Stress. Leder, Jane Mersky & Donovan, Sandy. 2008. (Health Zone Ser.). (ENG.). 64p. (gr. 4-7). lib. bdg. 30.60 *(978-0-8225-7555-9(8))* Lerner Publishing Group.

—Stay Clear! What You Should Know about Skin Care. Donovan, Sandy. 2008. (Health Zone Ser.). (ENG.). 64p. (gr. 4-7). lib. bdg. 30.60 *(978-0-8225-7550-4(7))* Lerner Publishing Group.

—Stay Fit! How You Can Get in Shape. Doeden, Matt. 2008. (Health Zone Ser.). 64p. (YA). (gr. 4-7). lib. bdg. 30.60 *(978-0-8225-7553-5(1))* Lerner Publishing Group.

—Stay Safe! How You Can Keep Out of Harm's Way. Nelson, Sara Kirsten. 2008. (Health Zone Ser.). (ENG.). 64p. (gr. 4-7). lib. bdg. 30.60 *(978-0-8225-7551-1(5))* Lerner Publishing Group.

—Take a Stand! What You Can Do about Bullying. Golus, Carrie. 2008. (Health Zone Ser.). 64p. (YA). (gr. 4-7). lib. bdg. 30.60 *(978-0-8225-7554-2(X))* Lerner Publishing Group.

Desrocher, Jack & Fairman, Jennifer. Amazing DNA. Johnson, Rebecca L. 2007. (Microquests Ser.). (ENG.). 48p. (gr. 3-5). lib. bdg. 29.27 *(978-0-8225-7139-1(0),* Millbrook Pr.) Lerner Publishing Group.

—Daring Cell Defenders. Johnson, Rebecca L. 2007. (Microquests Ser.). 48p. (J). (gr. 4-7). lib. bdg. 29.27 *(978-0-8225-7140-7(4),* Millbrook Pr.) Lerner Publishing Group.

—Mighty Animal Cells. Johnson, Rebecca L. 2007. (Microquests Ser.). (ENG.). 48p. (gr. 3-5). lib. bdg. 29.27 *(978-0-8225-7137-7(4),* Millbrook Pr.) Lerner Publishing Group.

—Powerful Plant Cells. Johnson, Rebecca L. 2007. (Microquests Ser.). (ENG.). 48p. (gr. 3-5). lib. bdg. 29.27 *(978-0-8225-7141-4(2),* Millbrook Pr.) Lerner Publishing Group.

—Ultra-Organized Cell Systems. Johnson, Rebecca L. 2007. (Microquests Ser.). (ENG.). 48p. (gr. 3-5). lib. bdg. 29.27 *(978-0-8225-7138-4(2),* Millbrook Pr.) Lerner Publishing Group.

Desrochers, Fache. Liliana Loretta Larue. McGreevy, Anne Kelly. 2017. (ENG.). 28p. (J). pap. 8.95 *(978-1-68350-069-8(5))* Morgan James Publishing.

DesRosiers, Trisha. Bella's Blessings. Stokes, Brenda. 2012. 50p. (J). (gr. -1-3). 17.95 *(978-1-897476-61-1(2))* Simply Read Bks. CAN. Dist: Ingram Publisher Services.

Destarisa, Rosalia. I Love My Grandpa (Bilingual Chinese with Pinyin & English - Simplified Chinese Version) A Dual Language Children's Book. Liu, Katrina. 2019. (ENG & CHI.). 34p. (J). (gr. k-1). 15.99 ***(978-1-7339671-0-5(9))*** Liu, Katrina.

—I Love My Grandpa (Bilingual Chinese with Pinyin & English - Traditional Chinese Version) A Dual Language Children's Book. Liu, Katrina. 2019. (ENG & CHI.). 34p. (J). (gr. k). 15.99 ***(978-1-7339671-4-3(1))*** Liu, Katrina.

—Mina's Scavenger Hunt (Bilingual Chinese with Pinyin & English - Simplified Chinese Version) A Dual Language Children's Book. Liu, Katrina. 2019. (ENG.). 36p. (J). (gr. k). 15.99 ***(978-1-7339671-6-7(8))*** Liu, Katrina.

—Mina's Scavenger Hunt (Bilingual Chinese with Pinyin & English - Traditional Chinese Version) A Dual Language Children's Book. Liu, Katrina. 2019. (CHI & ENG.). 36p. (J). (gr. k-1). 15.99 ***(978-1-7339671-7-4(6))*** Liu, Katrina.

Destiny Images Staff. Collecting Data: Pick a Pancake. Burstein, John. 2003. (Math Monsters Ser.). 24p. (J). (gr. k-4). lib. bdg. 21.00 *(978-0-8368-3805-3(X),* Weekly Reader Leveled Readers) Stevens, Gareth Publishing LLLP.

—Keeping Track of Time: Go Fly a Kite! Burstein, John. 2003. (Math Monsters Ser.). 24p. (J). (gr. k-4). lib. bdg. 21.00 *(978-0-8368-3810-7(6),* Weekly Reader Leveled Readers) Stevens, Gareth Publishing LLLP.

—Measuring: The Perfect Playhouse. Burstein, John. 2003. (Math Monsters Ser.). 24p. (J). (gr. k-4). lib. bdg. 22.00 *(978-0-8368-3813-8(0),* Weekly Reader Leveled Readers) Stevens, Gareth Publishing LLLP.

—Patterns: What's on the Wall? Burstein, John. 2003. (Math Monsters Ser.). 24p. (J). (gr. k-4). lib. bdg. 22.00 *(978-0-8368-3816-9(5),* Weekly Reader Leveled Readers) Stevens, Gareth Publishing LLLP.

—Using Computers: Machine with a Mouse. Burstein, John. 2003. (Math Monsters Ser.). 24p. (J). (gr. k-4). lib. bdg. 22.00 *(978-0-8368-3817-6(3),* Weekly Reader Leveled Readers) Stevens, Gareth Publishing LLLP.

Desvaux, Olivier. The Little Dancer: A Children's Book Inspired by Edgar Degas. Elschner, Géraldine. 2020. (Children's Books Inspired by Famous Artworks Ser.). (ENG.). 32p. (J). (gr. -1-3). 14.95 ***(978-3-7913-7449-9(4))*** Prestel Verlag GmbH & Co KG. DEU. Dist: Penguin Random Hse. LLC.

Deters, Kevin. Care Bears Sing & Play: Follow-the-Lights Piano Songbook. 2006. (Care Bears Ser.). 24p. (J). (gr. -1-3). bds. 13.99 *(978-1-57791-300-9(0))* Brighter Minds Children's Publishing.

Detmold, Edward J. & Detmold, Maurice. The Jungle Book. Kipling, Rudyard. 2010. (Calla Editions Ser.). (ENG.). 192p. 30.00 *(978-1-60660-009-2(5))* Dover Pubns., Inc.

Detmold, Maurice, jt. illus. see Detmold, Edward J.

Detwiler, Susan. After a While Crocodile: Alexa's Diary, 1 vol. Barr, Brady & Curtis, Jennifer Keats. 2016. (ENG & SPA.). 32p. (J). (gr. k-3). 17.95 *(978-1-62855-834-0(2))* Arbordale Publishing.

—Até Mais Tarde, Crocodilo- o Diário de Alexa: (after a While Crocodile: Alexa's Diary in Portuguese) Barr, Brady & Curtis, Jennifer Keats. Sacciotto, Adriana & Wiedemann, Tatiana, trs. 2019. (POR.). 32p. (J). 11.95 *(978-1-64351-401-7(6))* Arbordale Publishing.

—'Avanzando ... de Aquí para Allá: Migraciones Masivas, 1 vol. Cohn, Scotti. 2013. (SPA.). 32p. (J). (gr. -1-4). pap. 11.95 *(978-1-62855-350-5(2))* Arbordale Publishing.

—Avanzando ... de Aquí para Allá 1 vol. Migraciones Masivas. Cohn, Scotti. 2013. (SPA.). 32p. (J). (gr. -1-4). 17.95 *(978-1-60718-712-7(4),* 9781607187127) Arbordale Publishing.

—Bat Count: A Citizen Science Story, 1 vol. Forrester, Anna. 2017. (ENG.). 32p. (J). (gr. k-3). 17.95 *(978-1-62855-894-4(6))* Arbordale Publishing.

—Big Cat, Little Kitty, 1 vol. Cohn, Scotti. 2011. (ENG.). 32p. (J). (gr. -1-3). 16.95 *(978-1-60718-124-8(X));* pap. 8.95 *(978-1-60718-134-7(7))* Arbordale Publishing.

—Contando Los Murciélagos: Una Historia de Ciencias Cívicas. Forrester, Anna. 2017. (SPA.). 32p. (J). (gr. k-3). pap. 11.95 *(978-1-62855-896-8(2))* Arbordale Publishing.

—The First Teddy Bear. Kay, Helen. 2nd enl. ed. 2005. 38p. (J). (gr. -1-3). 18.95 *(978-0-88045-154-3(8));* per. 11.95 *(978-0-88045-153-6(X))* Stemmer Hse. Pubs.

—Gatão, Gatinho (Big Cat, Little Kitty in Portuguese) Cohn, Scotti. Sacciotto, Adriana & Wiedemann, Tatiana, trs. 2019. (POR.). 32p. (J). (gr. k-3). pap. 11.95 *(978-1-64351-409-3(1))* Arbordale Publishing.

Detwiler, Susan. Grand F�lin, Petit Chat: (big Cat, Little Kitty in French) Cohn, Scotti. Troff, Sophie, tr. 2019. (FRE.). 32p. (J). (gr. k-1). 11.95 ***(978-1-64351-727-8(9))*** Arbordale Publishing.

Detwiler, Susan. Hasta la Vista, Cocodrilo: El Diario de Alexa. Barr, Brady & Curtis, Jennifer Keats. 2016. (SPA.). 32p. (J). (gr. k-3). pap. 11.95 *(978-1-62855-836-4(9))* Arbordale Publishing.

—One Wolf Howls, 1 vol. Cohn, Scotti. 2009. (ENG.). 32p. (J). (gr. -1-3). 16.95 *(978-1-934359-92-1(0))* Arbordale Publishing.

—Pandas' Earthquake Escape, 1 vol. Perry, Phyllis J. 2010. (ENG.). 32p. (J). (gr. -1-3). 16.95 *(978-1-60718-071-5(5));* pap. 8.95 *(978-1-60718-082-1(0))* Arbordale Publishing.

Deuchars, Marion. Art Play. 2016. (ENG.). 224p. (J). (gr. 2-6). pap. 19.99 *(978-1-78067-877-1(0),* King, Laurence Publishing) Orion Publishing Group, Ltd. GBR. Dist: Hachette Bk. Group.

Devals, Nicole. Arthur in Venice. Ferrero Menut, Caroline. 2019. (ENG.). 48p. (J). pap. *(978-1-913162-09-2(5))* Grace Note Pubns.

Devaney, Adam. Bug Babies. Reasoner, Charles. 2009. (Baby Animal Board Bks.). 12p. (J). (gr. -1-k). bds. 7.99 *(978-1-934650-51-6(X))* Just For Kids Pr., LLC.

—Dinosaur Babies. Reasoner, Charles. 2009. (Baby Animal Board Bks.). 12p. (J). (gr. -1-k). bds. 7.99 *(978-1-934650-49-3(8))* Just For Kids Pr., LLC.

—Disney Puppy Dog Pals: Paws-Itively Alien! 2018. (ENG.). 10p. (J). (gr. -1-k). bds. 9.99 *(978-0-7944-4201-9(3),* Studio Fun International) Printers Row Publishing Group.

—Disney Puppy Dog Pals: Take Me Out to the Pug Game. 2018. (ENG.). 10p. (J). (gr. -1-k). bds. 11.99 *(978-0-7944-4159-3(9),* Reader's Digest Children's Bks.) Studio Fun International.

—Disney Puppy Dog Pals: Wags & Gags. Fischer, Maggie. 2019. (Deluxe Guess Who? Ser.). (ENG.). 12p. (J). (gr. -1-k). 10.99 *(978-0-7944-4304-7(4),* Studio Fun International) Printers Row Publishing Group.

—Disney Vampirina: Vamping Trip. 2019. (Hidden Stories Ser.). (ENG.). 10p. (J). (gr. -1-k). 12.99 *(978-0-7944-4247-7(1),* Studio Fun International) Printers Row Publishing Group.

—Drac's in Love! 2018. (Hotel Transylvania 3: Summer Vacation Ser.). (ENG.). 32p. (J). (gr. k-2). pap. 4.99 *(978-1-5344-1834-9(2),* Simon Spotlight) Simon Spotlight.

—DreamWorks Trolls: Poppy Lends a Hand. Layman, Barbara. 2018. (Hugs Book Ser.). (ENG.). 12p. (J). (gr. -1-k). bds. 10.99 *(978-0-7944-4077-0(0),* Reader's Digest Children's Bks.) Studio Fun International.

—DreamWorks Trolls: the Legend of Hug Time. 2018. (ENG.). 32p. (J). (gr. -1-k). bds. 12.99 *(978-0-7944-4078-7(9),* Reader's Digest Children's Bks.) Studio Fun International.

—Fan-Tab-U-Lus: Dinosaurs. Reasoner, Charles. 2011. (Fan-Tab-U-Lus Bks.). (ENG.). 12p. (J). (gr. -1). bds. 9.99 *(978-1-935498-58-2(4))* Just For Kids Pr., LLC.

—Fan-Tab-U-Lus: Jungle Animals. Reasoner, Charles. 2011. (Fan-Tab-U-Lus Bks.). (ENG.). 12p. (J). (gr. -1-3). bds. 9.99 *(978-1-935498-55-1(X))* Just For Kids Pr., LLC.

—Farm Babies. Reasoner, Charles. 2009. (Baby Animal Board Bks.). 12p. (J). (gr. -1-k). bds. 7.99 *(978-1-934650-52-3(8))* Just For Kids Pr., LLC.

—Jungle. Reasoner, Charles. 2009. (Learning Tab Board Bks.). 10p. (J). (gr. -1-k). bds. 9.99 *(978-1-934650-79-0(X))* Just For Kids Pr., LLC.

—Monster Cruise! 2018. (Hotel Transylvania 3: Summer Vacation Ser.). (ENG.). 24p. (J). (gr. -1-2). pap. 3.99 *(978-1-5344-1768-7(0),* Simon Spotlight) Simon Spotlight.

—Scooby-Doo & the High Tech House of the Future, 1 vol. 2015. (Scooby-Doo Comic Readers Ser.). (ENG.). 32p. (J). (gr. -1-3). lib. bdg. 27.07 *(978-1-61479-452-3(9),* 19431, Graphic Novels) Spotlight.

—12 Days of Dinosaurs: A Jurassic Classic Christmas Carol. Fischer, Maggie. 2019. (ENG.). 20p. (J). (gr. -1-k). bds. 9.99 *(978-1-68412-664-4(9),* Silver Dolphin Bks.) Printers Row Publishing Group.

Devaney, Adam & Doherty, Paula. Jungle Babies. Reasoner, Charles. 2009. (Baby Animal Board Bks.). 12p. (J). (gr. -1-k). bds. 7.99 *(978-1-934650-50-9(1))* Just For Kids Pr., LLC.

Devaney, Adam, jt. illus. see Cespedes-Alicea, Marcela.

Devard, Nancy. A Mom Like No Other. Scholastic, Inc. Staff & Taylor-Butler, Christine. 2004. (Just for You Ser.). (ENG.). 32p. pap. 3.99 *(978-0-439-56853-1(6),* Teaching Resources) Scholastic, Inc.

—The Mystery of the Missing Dog. Scholastic, Inc. Staff & Hooks, Gwendolyn. 2004. (Just for You Ser.). (ENG.). 32p. (gr. k-3). pap. 3.99 *(978-0-439-56864-7(1),* Teaching Resources) Scholastic, Inc.

—The Secret Olivia Told Me. Joy, N. 2007. 32p. (J). (gr. -1-3). 16.95 *(978-1-933491-08-0(6))* Just Us Bks., Inc.

Devaux, Clement. Attention Aux Ogres ! Ramadier, Cedric. 2010. (A. M. Alb. Ill. C. Ser.). (FRE.). (J). *(978-2-226-20956-6(5))* Albin-Michel, Editions.

Deverell, Richard. How They Lived in Bible Times. Jones, Graham. 2003. 48p. 6.49 *(978-1-85999-435-1(0))* Scripture Union GBR. Dist: Gabriel Resources.

Deverell, Richard & King, Chris. Pop-up Pets. Deverell, Christine. 2005. 12p. (J). (gr. k-4). reprint ed. 20.00 *(978-0-7567-8776-9(9))* DIANE Publishing Co.

—Sparkly Sea. 14p. (J). *(978-1-85081-374-3(4))* Frederick, Robert.

Devernay, Laëtitia. Shapes All Around. Riggs, Kate. 2018. (ENG.). 14p. (J). (gr. -1-k). bds. 8.99 *(978-1-56846-317-9(0),* Creative Editions) Creative Co., The.

Devia, Maria Teresa. Soldados en la Lluvia. Malpica, Tono. 2019. (Torre Amarilla Ser.). (SPA.). 166p. (J). pap. ***(978-958-45-4131-4(5))*** Norma Ediciones, S.A.

DeVince, James, jt. illus. see Porcheron, Tammy.

Devine, Quentin. It's Raining & I'm Okay: A Calming Story to Help Children Relax When They Go Out & About. Devine, Adele. 2017. (ENG.). 40p. (J). 14.95 *(978-1-78592-319-7(6),* 696556) Kingsley, Jessica Pubs. GBR. Dist: Hachette UK Distribution.

DeVito, Anthony T. The Story of Lilly & Lou: Based on a True Story. Lucia, Doriane. 2008. 56p. (J). pap. *(978-0-9809995-4-9(5),* CCB Publishing) CCB Publishing.

Devlin, Harry. Cranberry Halloween. Devlin, Wende. 2013. (Cranberryport Ser.). (ENG.). (J). (gr. -1-3). 18.95 *(978-1-930900-69-1(4))* Purple Hse. Pr.

—Cranberry Thanksgiving. Devlin, Wende. 2012. (ENG.). 32p. (J). (gr. -1-3). 18.95 *(978-1-930900-63-9(5))* Purple Hse. Pr.

—Old Black Witch! Devlin, Wende. 2012. (ENG.). 32p. (J). (gr. -1-3). 18.95 *(978-1-930900-62-2(7))* Purple Hse. Pr.

—Old Witch & the Polka Dot Ribbon. Devlin, Wende. 2014. (ENG.). (J). (gr. k-3). 18.95 *(978-1-930900-71-4(6))* Purple Hse. Pr.

Devries, Shane. The Christmasaurus. Fletcher, Tom. 2018. (ENG.). 384p. (J). (gr. 3-7). 13.99 *(978-1-5247-7330-4(1));* lib. bdg. 16.99 *(978-1-5247-7331-1(X))* Random Hse. Children's Bks. (Random Hse. Bks. for Young Readers).

—The Creakers. Fletcher, Tom. 2019. (ENG.). 368p. (J). (gr. 3-7). 19.99 *(978-1-5247-7335-9(2),* Random Hse. Bks. for Young Readers) Random Hse. Children's Bks.

Dewald, Anna. Follow Your Wings. Friend, Kayla. 2017. (ENG.). 34p. (J). pap. 12.95 *(978-1-64028-592-7(X))* Christian Faith Publishing.

Dewar, Bob. The Whisky Muse: Collected & Introduced by Robin Laing. Laing, Robin. 2nd ed. 2003. (ENG.). 224p. per. 19.95 *(978-1-84282-041-4(9))* Luath Pr. Ltd. GBR. Dist: Independent Pubs. Group.

Dewar, Ken. H Is for Hockey: A NHL Alumni Alphabet. Shea, Kevin. 2015. (Av2 Fiction Readalong 2016 Ser.). (ENG.). (J). (gr. k-2). lib. bdg. 34.28 *(978-1-4896-3741-3(9),* AV2 by Weigl) Weigl Pubs., Inc.

—H Is for Hockey: An NHL Alumni Alphabet. Shea, Kevin. 2012. (ENG.). 32p. (J). (gr. 1-5). 16.95 *(978-1-58536-794-8(X)); (978-1-58536-814-3(8))* Sleeping Bear Pr.

Dewdney, Anna. All-Star Fever. Christopher, Matt. 2009. (New Peach Street Mudders Sports Library). 64p. (J). (gr. 2-4). lib. bdg. 23.93 *(978-1-59953-315-5(4))* Norwood Hse. Pr.

—Christmas in the Barn. Brown, Margaret Wise. 2016. (ENG.). 40p. (J). (gr. -1-3). 17.99 *(978-0-06-237986-3(0))* HarperCollins Pubs.

—Shadow over Second. Christopher, Matt. 2009. (New Peach Street Mudders Sports Library). 64p. (J). (gr. 2-4). lib. bdg. 23.93 *(978-1-59953-320-9(0))* Norwood Hse. Pr.

Dewdney, Anna. Grumpy Gloria. Dewdney, Anna. 2006. 32p. (J). (gr. -1-k). 17.99 *(978-0-670-06123-5(9),* Viking Books for Young Readers) Penguin Young Readers Group.

—Llama Llama Birthday Party! Dewdney, Anna. 2013. (Llama Llama Ser.). 16p. (J). (gr. -1-k). 6.99 *(978-0-448-45880-9(2),* Grosset & Dunlap) Penguin Young Readers Group.

—Llama Llama Jingle Bells. Dewdney, Anna. 2014. (Llama Llama Ser.). (ENG.). 14p. (J). (— 1). bds. 6.99 *(978-0-451-46980-9(1),* Viking Books for Young Readers) Penguin Young Readers Group.

—Llama Llama Mad at Mama. Dewdney, Anna. 2007. (Llama Llama Ser.). (ENG.). 40p. (J). (gr. -1-k). 18.99 *(978-0-670-06240-9(5),* Viking Books for Young Readers) Penguin Young Readers Group.

—Llama Llama Red Pajama. Dewdney, Anna. (Llama Llama Ser.). (ENG.). (J). 2018. 34p. (-k). bds. 14.99 *(978-0-451-48063-7(5));* 2014. 40p. (gr. -1-k). 25.00 *(978-0-451-46990-8(9));* 2005. 40p. (gr. -1-k). 17.99 *(978-0-670-05983-6(8))* Penguin Young Readers Group. (Viking Books for Young Readers).

—Llama Llama Trick or Treat. Dewdney, Anna. 2014. (Llama Llama Ser.). (ENG.). 12p. (J). (— 1). bds. 5.99 *(978-0-451-46978-6(X),* Viking Books for Young Readers) Penguin Young Readers Group.

DeWeerd, Kelsey. El Peor Dia de TODA Mi Vida. Cook, Julia. 2012. (SPA.). 32p. (J). pap. 10.95 *(978-1-934490-34-1(2))* Boys Town Pr.

Deweese, Susan. The Acorn Nuts. Beck, Bev. 2011. 32p. pap. 24.95 *(978-1-4626-2233-7(X))* America Star Bks.

DeWeese, Susan. The Birthday Present. Beck, Bev. 2011. 40p. pap. 24.95 *(978-1-4560-8398-4(8))* America Star Bks.

—The Curwood Acorns. Breece, Beverly. 2012. 40p. pap. 24.95 *(978-1-4626-8202-7(2))* America Star Bks.

Dewey, Ariane & Aruego, Jose. The Big, Big Wall. Howard, Reginald. ed. 2003. (Green Light Readers Level 1 Ser.). (J). (gr. -1-3). 13.50 *(978-0-613-66350-2(0))* Turtleback.

—The Big, Big Wall/No Puedo Bajar. Howard, Reginald. Flor Ada, Alma & Campoy, F. Isabel, trs. 2009. (Green Light Readers Level 1 Ser.). (ENG.). 28p. (J). (gr. -1-3). pap. 4.99 *(978-0-547-25548-4(9),* 1388304) Houghton Mifflin Harcourt Publishing Co.

—Gregory, the Terrible Eater. Sharmat, Mitchell. 2009. (Scholastic Bookshelf Ser.). (ENG.). 32p. (J). (gr. -1-3). pap. 6.99 *(978-0-545-12931-2(1))* Scholastic, Inc.

Dewey, Ariane, jt. illus. see Aruego, Jose.

Dewey, Jennifer Owings. Alligators & Crocodiles. Dennard, Deborah. (Our Wild World Ser.). (ENG.). 48p. (J). (gr. 2-5). 2008. pap. 8.95 *(978-1-55971-859-2(5));* 2003. 10.95 *(978-1-55971-860-8(9))* Cooper Square Publishing Llc.

—Lizards. Dennard, Deborah. 2003. (Our Wild World Ser.). (ENG.). 48p. (J). (gr. 2-5). 10.95 *(978-1-55971-858-5(7));* pap. 8.95 *(978-1-55971-857-8(9))* Cooper Square Publishing Llc.

—Snakes. Dennard, Deborah. 2003. (Our Wild World Ser.). (ENG.). 48p. (J). (gr. 2-5). pap. 7.95 *(978-1-55971-855-4(2))* Cooper Square Publishing Llc.

—Turtles. Dennard, Deborah. 2003. (Our Wild World Ser.). (ENG.). 48p. (J). (gr. 2-5). pap. 7.95 *(978-1-55971-861-5(7))* Cooper Square Publishing Llc.

Dewey, Jennifer Owings. Reptiles: Explore the Fascinating Worlds of Alligators & Crocodiles, Lizards, Snakes, Turtles. Dewey, Jennifer Owings, tr. Dennard, Deborah. 2004. (Our Wild World Ser.). (ENG.). 192p. (J). (gr. 3-6). 16.95 *(978-1-55971-880-6(3))* Cooper Square Publishing Llc.

Dewey, Simon. I'm Trying to Be Like Jesus. Dobson, Cynthia Lund. 2010. (J). 19.99 *(978-1-60641-846-8(7))* Deseret Bk. Co.

—The Life of Our Lord: Illustrated 200th Anniversary Edition. Dickens, Charles. 2012. 17.99 *(978-1-60907-185-1(9)*, Shadow Mountain) Shadow Mountain Publishing.

DeWildt, Jim. What Am I? New Jersey. Lewis, Anne Margaret. 2007. 32p. (J). 9.95 *(978-1-934133-19-4(1)*, Mackinac Island Press, Inc.) Charlesbridge Publishing, Inc.

DeWitt, Aaron. Boom! Bellow! Bleat! Animal Poems for Two or More Voices. Heard, Georgia. 2019. 32p. (J). (gr. k-4). 17.95 *(978-1-62091-520-2(0)*, Wordsong) Boyds Mills Pr.

—Dreaming of You. Vanderwater, Amy Ludwig. 2018. (ENG.). 32p. (J). (gr. -1-k). 17.95 *(978-1-62979-212-5(8))* Boyds Mills Pr.

Dewitt-Grush, Patricia, et al. Brave with Beauty: A Story of Afghanistan. Schur, Maxine Rose. 2019. (ENG.). 46p. (J). (gr. 2-4). 19.99 *(978-1-949528-97-8(9)*, Yali Bks.) Yali Publishing LLC.

Dewitt Grush, Patricia, jt. illus. see DeWitt, Robin.

Dewitt Grush, Patricia, jt. illus. see Dewitt, Robin.

Dewitt, Kenny. Sneakers Hangs Out. Gosule, Bette & Longmire, Lynda. 2012. 26p. (J). 14.95 *(978-1-60131-129-0(X)*, Castlebridge Bks.) Big Tent Bks.

Dewitt, Levi. Co-Man & Poppa Meet Kanka. Wright, Mary. 2013. 24p. pap. 24.95 *(978-1-62709-328-6(1))* America Star Bks.

DeWitt, Robin. Rehan & the Mysterious Book. Warsi, Farozan. 2020. (ENG.). 32p. (J). ***(978-1-5255-4805-5(0))***; pap. ***(978-1-5255-4806-2(9))*** FriesenPress.

DeWitt, Robin & Dewitt Grush, Patricia. Brewster Rooster. Underwood, Barbara. 2006.Tr. of Carla's New Glasses. (ENG.). 32p. (gr. 1-2). pap. 9.95 *(978-1-57874-108-3(4)*, Kaeden Bks.) Kaeden Corp.

Dewitt, Robin & Dewitt Grush, Patricia. Ethel the Emu. Wiley, Pamela. 2007. (ENG.). 32p. (gr. 1-3). pap. 9.95 *(978-1-57874-335-3(4)*, Kaeden Bks.) Kaeden Corp.

DeWolf, Holly. What's Going on at the Time Tonight?, 1 vol. Mercer, Gerald. ed. 2013. (ENG.). 32p. (J). (gr. k-3). 19.95 *(978-1-77108-004-0(3)*, 088cdf2d-fb2f-45af-8a0d-d5937adb928d) Nimbus Publishing, Ltd. CAN. Dist: Baker & Taylor Publisher Services (BTPS).

Dewyea, Glenn. The Pumpkin Se. Dohr, Robert. 2012. 32p. pap. 13.50 *(978-1-61204-337-1(2)*, Strategic Bk. Publishing) Strategic Book Publishing & Rights Agency (SBPRA).

Dey, Lorraine. Maddy Patti & the Great Curiosity: Helping Children Understand Diabetes. Bilderback Abel, Mary & Borg, Stan W. 2015. (Let's Talk Ser.). (ENG.). 48p. (J). (gr. k-5). 9.95 *(978-0-88282-490-1(2))* New Horizon Pr. Pubs., Inc.

—A Sweater for Duncan. Malone, Margaret Gay. 2010. (ENG.). 32p. (J). (gr. -1-12). lib. bdg. 16.95 *(978-1-936299-06-5(2)*, Raven Tree Pr.,Csi) Continental Sales, Inc.

Dey, Romi. Crazy Pizza Day. Dobkin, Bonnie. 2010. (J). *(978-1-60617-150-9(X))* Teaching Strategies, LLC.

DeYoe, Katie & Aaron. The Mighty Quinn. Parnell, Robyn. 2013. (ENG.). 272p. (gr. 2-7). pap. 10.95 *(978-1-938063-10-7(4)*, Mighty Media Junior Readers) Mighty Media Pr.

Dezakin, Akin. Campo Abierto (Open Field) Hagen, Oddmund. Santos, Nuria G., tr. from NOR. 2003. (Rosa y Manzana Ser.). (SPA.). 32p. 16.95 *(978-84-89804-42-5(7))* Lóguez Ediciones ESP. Dist: Baker & Taylor Bks.

Dezsö, Andrea. Lies, Knives, & Girls in Red Dresses. Koertge, Ron. 2012. 96p. (YA). (gr. 9). 17.99 *(978-0-7636-4406-2(4))* Candlewick Pr.

Dezuniga, Tony, et al. Punisher: Back to the War Omnibus. 2017. (ENG.). 720p. (YA). (gr. 8-17). 100.00 *(978-1-302-90823-2(5))* Marvel Worldwide, Inc.

DGPH Stufio. Amazing Ancients!: Egypt. Vernon-Melzer, Gabby. 2019. (Amazing Ancients! Ser.). 32p. (J). (gr. 3-7). pap. 9.99 *(978-1-5247-9062-2(1)*, Penguin Workshop) Penguin Young Readers Group.

—Amazing Ancients! World of the Maya. Kule, Elaine A. 2020. (Amazing Ancients! Ser.). (ENG.). 32p. (J). (gr. 3-7). pap. 10.99 *(978-0-593-09306-1(2)*, Penguin Workshop) Penguin Young Readers Group.

DGPH Stufio Staff, jt. illus. see Vaisberg, Diego.

D'hamers, Heidi. Duck's Easter Egg Hunt. Richards, Dawn. 2014. (J). *(978-1-4351-5243-4(3))* Barnes & Noble, Inc.

D'heur, Valérie. Heart in the Pocket. Bourguignon, Laurence. 2008. 26p. (J). (gr. -1-3). 16.50 *(978-0-8028-5343-1(9))* Eerdmans, William B. Publishing Co.

Di Baldo, Fabrizio. Turtle Is a Hero Green Band. Pritchard, Gabby. 2016. (Cambridge Reading Adventures Ser.). (ENG.). 16p. pap. 7.37 *(978-1-107-55046-9(7))* Cambridge Univ. Pr.

Di Bartolo, Jim. The Dragon's Pearl. Jordan, Devin. 2010. (ENG.). 352p. (YA). (gr. 5-9). pap. 8.99 *(978-1-4169-6411-7(8)*, Simon & Schuster Bks. For Young Readers) Simon & Schuster Bks. For Young Readers.

—Lips Touch: Three Times. Taylor, Laini. 288p. (gr. 7-7). 2011. (YA). pap. 14.99 *(978-0-545-05586-4(5))*; 2009. (J). 17.99 *(978-0-545-05585-7(7))* Scholastic, Inc. (Levine, Arthur A. Bks.).

—Night of Cake & Puppets. Taylor, Laini. 2017. (Daughter of Smoke & Bone Ser.). (ENG.). 256p. (YA). (gr. 10-17). 16.99 *(978-0-316-43919-0(3))* Little, Brown Bks. for Young Readers.

Di Bartolo, Jim. In the Shadows. Di Bartolo, Jim. White, Kiersten. 2014. (ENG.). 384p. (YA). (gr. 7). 21.99 *(978-0-545-56144-0(2)*, Scholastic Pr.) Scholastic, Inc.

Di Benedetto, Angelo. How the Donkeys Came to Haiti & Other Folk Tales. 124p. (J). (gr. 4-9). 12.95 *(978-0-8159-5706-5(8))* Devin-Adair Pubs., Inc.

di Chiara, Francesca. The Sun & the Wind. 2007. (First Reading Level 1 Ser.). 32p. (J). (gr. -1-3). 8.99 *(978-0-7945-1811-0(7)*, Usborne) EDC Publishing.

Di Chiara, Marcelo. Batman: Overdrive. Fontana, Shea. 2020. 136p. (J). (gr. 2). pap. 9.99 *(978-1-4012-8356-8(X))* DC Comics.

di Gaudesi, Andrea Ricciardi. El Girasol: Por Dentro y Por Fuera. Hipp, Andrew. Brusca, Maria Cristina, tr. 2004. (Explora la Naturaleza (Getting into Nature) Ser.). (SPA.). 27p. (J). (gr. 3-7). lib. bdg. 27.25 *(978-1-4042-2868-9(3))* Rosen Publishing Group, Inc., The.

Di Gennaro, Andrea. Mark Twain. Carew-Miller, Anna. 2003. (Great Names Ser.). (J). 19.95 *(978-957-745-414-0(3))* Mason Crest.

di Gesu, Tara. The Life of the Buddha. Sanche, Heather. 2020. (ENG.). 44p. (J). (gr. -1-3). 17.95 *(978-1-61180-629-8(1)*, Bala Kids) Shambhala Pubns., Inc.

Di Giacomo, Kris. Brief Thief. Escoffier, Michaël. 2013. (ENG.). 32p. (J). (gr. -1-3). 16.95 *(978-1-59270-131-5(0))* Enchanted Lion Bks., LLC.

—The Day I Lost My Superpowers. Escoffier, MichaUl. 2014. 32p. (J). (gr. -1-3). 16.95 *(978-1-59270-144-5(2))* Enchanted Lion Bks., LLC.

—Enormous Smallness: The Story of e. e. Cummings. Burgess, Matthew. 2015. 64p. (J). (gr. -1-3). 17.95 *(978-1-59270-171-1(X))* Enchanted Lion Bks., LLC.

—Have You Seen My Trumpet? Escoffier, Michaël. 2016. 48p. (J). (gr. -1-3). 17.95 *(978-1-59270-201-5(5))* Enchanted Lion Bks., LLC.

—Me First! Escoffier, Michaël. 2013. (ENG.). 24p. (J). 14.00 *(978-1-59270-136-0(1))* Enchanted Lion Bks., LLC.

—My Dad at the Zoo. Saudo, Coralie. 2016. (ENG.). 32p. (J). (gr. -1-2). 17.95 *(978-1-59270-190-2(6))* Enchanted Lion Bks., LLC.

—My Dad Is Big & Strong, But... A Bedtime Story. Saudo, Coralie. 2012. (ENG.). 32p. (J). (gr. -1-2). 16.95 *(978-1-59270-122-3(1))* Enchanted Lion Bks., LLC.

—Rabbit & the Not-So-Big-Bad Wolf. Escoffier, Michaël. 2013. (ENG.). 32p. (J). (gr. -1-3). 16.95 *(978-0-8234-2813-7(3))* Holiday Hse., Inc.

—Take Away the A. Escoffier, Michaël. 2014. 56p. (J). (gr. -1-3). 17.95 *(978-1-59270-156-8(6))* Enchanted Lion Bks., LLC.

—Where's the Baboon? Escoffier, Michaël. 2015. 40p. (J). (gr. -1-3). 17.95 *(978-1-59270-189-6(2))* Enchanted Lion Bks., LLC.

Di Giandomenico, Carmine, et al. Spider-Man Noir: the Complete Collection. Hine, David et al. 2019. 264p. (YA). (gr. -1-17). pap. 24.99 *(978-1-302-91958-0(X))* Marvel Worldwide, Inc.

Di Gianvittorio, Rita. Getting along with Lola Bird. Di Gianvittorio, Rita. 2018. (ENG.). 36p. (J). (gr. k-2). pap. *(978-1-7752708-0-5(7))* Gianvittorio, Rita Di.

Di Giorgio, Mariachiara. Professional Crocodile. Zoboli, Giovanna. 2017. (ENG.). 32p. (J). (gr. k-3). 17.99 *(978-1-4521-6506-6(8))* Chronicle Bks. LLC.

Di Gravio, Maria Luisa. Diabetes Doesn't Stop Maddie! Marsh, Sarah Glenn. 2020. (ENG.). 32p. (J). (gr. -1-3). 16.99 ***(978-0-8075-4703-8(4)***, 807547034) Whitman, Albert & Co.

Di Gravio, Maria Luisa. Finding a Dove for Gramps. Amstutz, Lisa J. 2018. (ENG.). 32p. (J). 16.99 *(978-0-8075-1279-1(6)*, 807512796) Whitman, Albert & Co.

Di Lernia, Giuseppe. Jack & the Beanstalk. Dorling Kindersley Publishing Staff. 2019. (Storytime Lap Bks.). (ENG.). 30p. (J). (-k). bds. 12.99 *(978-1-4654-8279-2(2)*, DK Children) Dorling Kindersley Publishing, Inc.

—Jonah & the Whale. Dorling Kindersley Publishing Staff. 2018. (Storytime Lap Bks.). (ENG.). 30p. (J). (-k). bds. 12.99 *(978-1-4654-7000-3(X)*, DK Children) Dorling Kindersley Publishing, Inc.

—Noah's Ark. Dorling Kindersley Publishing Staff. 2018. (ENG.). 30p. (J). (-k). bds. 12.99 *(978-1-4654-6999-1(0)*, DK Children) Dorling Kindersley Publishing, Inc.

—Pinocchio. DK. 2019. (Storytime Lap Bks.). (ENG.). 30p. (J). (-k). bds. 12.99 *(978-1-4654-7849-8(3)*, DK Children) Dorling Kindersley Publishing, Inc.

—The Three Little Pigs. DK. 2019. (ENG.). 30p. (J). (-k). bds. 12.99 *(978-1-4654-7848-1(5)*, DK Children) Dorling Kindersley Publishing, Inc.

—The Ugly Duckling. Dorling Kindersley Publishing Staff. 2019. (Storytime Lap Bks.). (ENG.). 30p. (J). (-k). bds. 12.99 *(978-1-4654-8278-5(4)*, DK Children) Dorling Kindersley Publishing, Inc.

Di Mambro, Pompeo. The Child Far Away. Forbus, Jason Ray. (ENG.). (J). 2020. 50p. ***(978-88-3346-507-4(1))***; 2018. 46p. pap. *(978-88-3346-109-0(2))* Ali Ribelli Edizioni.

—L' Enfant Lointain. Forbus, Jason Ray. (FRE.). (J). 2020. 50p. ***(978-88-3346-509-8(8))***; 2018. 46p. pap. *(978-88-3346-110-6(6))* Ali Ribelli Edizioni.

—Il Fanciullo Lontano. Forbus, Jason Ray. 2020. (ITA.). 50p. (J). ***(978-88-3346-506-7(3))*** Ali Ribelli Edizioni.

—El ni�o Lejano. Forbus, Jason Ray. 2020. (SPA.). 50p. (J). ***(978-88-3346-508-1(X))*** Ali Ribelli Edizioni.

—O Menino Long�nquo. Forbus, Jason Ray. 2020. (POR.). 50p. (J). ***(978-88-3346-510-4(1))*** Ali Ribelli Edizioni.

Di Mambro, Pompeo. Pojken Från Fjärran. Forbus, Jason Ray. 2018. (SWE.). 46p. (J). pap. *(978-88-3346-113-7(0))* Ali Ribelli Edizioni.

Di Mambro, Pompeo. Pojken Fr�n Fj�rran. Forbus, Jason Ray. 2020. (SWE.). 50p. (J). ***(978-88-3346-514-2(4))*** Ali Ribelli Edizioni.

—A T�voli Gyermek. Forbus, Jason Ray. 2020. (HUN.). 50p. (J). ***(978-88-3346-512-8(8))*** Ali Ribelli Edizioni.

Di Mambro, Pompeo. A Távoli Gyermek. Forbus, Jason Ray. 2018. (HUN.). 46p. (J). pap. *(978-88-3346-118-2(1))* Ali Ribelli Edizioni.

Di Mambro, Pompeo. Tolių Vaikas. Forbus, Jason Ray. 2020. (LIT.). 50p. (J). ***(978-88-3346-511-1(X))*** Ali Ribelli Edizioni.

—Uzaktaki �ocuk. Forbus, Jason Ray. 2020. (TUR.). 50p. (J). ***(978-88-3346-513-5(6))*** Ali Ribelli Edizioni.

Di Marco, Audrey. Little Brave Bear. Kolar, Marsha. 2005. 17p. (J). per. *(978-0-9766804-0-6(8))* CottonWood Publishing Co.

Di Meo, Mattia. Ben 10 Original Graphic Novel: for Science! Lee, C. B. 2019. (Ben 10 Ser.). (ENG.). 80p. (J). pap. 7.99 *(978-1-68415-373-2(5))* Boom! Studios.

di Meo, Mattia. Regular Show Original Graphic Novel Vol. 6: Comic Conned. Andelfinger, Nicole. 2018. (Regular Show Ser.). (ENG.). 144p. (J). (gr. 4-7). pap. 14.99 *(978-1-68415-280-3(1))* Boom! Studios.

Di Meo, Mattia. Rocko's Modern Afterlife. Burch, Anthony. 2020. (Rocko's Modern Life Ser.). (ENG.). 112p. (J). pap. 14.99 *(978-1-68415-488-3(X))* Boom! Studios.

Di Meo, Simone, et al. This Is Doctor Strange. 2016. 30p. (J). *(978-1-5182-2636-6(1))* Disney Pr.

—This Is Doctor Strange. West, Alexandra. 2017. (World of Reading Level 1 Ser.). (ENG.). 32p. (J). (gr. -1-3). 27.07 *(978-1-5321-4057-0(6)*, 25423) Spotlight.

di Nicuolo, Daniele. West Coast Avengers Vol. 2: City of Evils, Vol. 2. 2019. (ENG.). 112p. (YA). pap. 17.99 *(978-1-302-91346-5(8))* Marvel Worldwide, Inc.

Di Prospero, Francisco & Lagarrigue, Carolina. The White House. Di Prospero, Francisco. 2019. (ENG.). 40p. (J). pap. 11.50 *(978-1-0911-0787-8(4))* Independently Published.

di Salvo, Roberto. Marvel Rising: Heroes of the Round Table. 2019. (ENG.). 112p. (YA). (gr. 4-17). pap. 12.99 *(978-1-302-91826-2(5))* Marvel Worldwide, Inc.

di Salvo, Roberto, jt. illus. see Marvel Press Artist.

Di Spirito, Emanuele. Noah: Fiabe con Versione in Inglese. Mollo, Maria. Di Spirito, Nicola Antonio, tr. 2019. (I Piccoli Ser.: Vol. 7). (ITA.). 62p. (J). pap. 16.67 ***(978-1-6777-5188-4(6))*** Independently Published.

Di Vito, Andrea. The Buddy System. Van Lente, Fred. 2009. (Wolverine: First Class Ser.). (ENG.). 24p. (J). (gr. 2-6). lib. bdg. 27.07 *(978-1-59961-669-8(6)*, 15317, Marvel Age) Spotlight.

Di Vito, Andrea, et al. Gladiator Triumphant, Vol. 2. Dixon, Chuck. 2004. (Brath Ser.: Vol. 2). 160p. (YA). pap. 9.95 *(978-1-59314-045-8(2))* CrossGeneration Comics, Inc.

Di Vito, Andrea. Marvel Super Heroes: Larger Than Life. 2017. (ENG.). 136p. (J). (gr. 4-17). pap. 15.99 *(978-1-302-90889-8(8))* Marvel Worldwide, Inc.

—Suprise!! Van Lente, Fred. 2009. (Wolverine: First Class Ser.). (ENG.). 24p. (J). (gr. 2-6). lib. bdg. 27.07 *(978-1-59961-674-2(2)*, 15322, Marvel Age) Spotlight.

Di Vito, Andrea & Buran, Jon. Avengers: Mighty Origins. 2018. (ENG.). 152p. (YA). (gr. 8-17). pap. 17.99 *(978-0-7851-8525-3(9))* Marvel Worldwide, Inc.

Di Vito, Andrea & Kolins, Scott. Thor: Ragnaroks. 2017. (ENG.). 448p. (YA). (gr. 8-17). pap. 34.99 *(978-1-302-90794-5(8))* Marvel Worldwide, Inc.

Di Vito, Andrea & Pantazis, Pete. This Is Black Widow. Wong, Clarissa. 2015. 32p. (J). *(978-1-4844-4992-9(4))* Disney Pr.

Di Vito, Andrea & Pantazis, Peter. This Is Black Widow. Wong, Clarissa. 2017. (World of Reading Level 1 Ser.). (ENG.). 32p. (J). (gr. -1-3). 27.07 *(978-1-5321-4050-1(9)*, 25421) Spotlight.

Di Vito, Andrea & Rosenberg, Rachelle. Avengers: The\New Team. Wyatt, Chris. 2017. (World of Reading Level 1 Ser.). (ENG.). 32p. (J). (gr. -1-3). lib. bdg. 27.07 *(978-1-5321-4049-5(5)*, 25420) Spotlight.

Di Vito, Andrea, jt. illus. see Nauck, Todd.

Diakite, Baba Wague. The Pot of Wisdom. Badoe, Adwoa. 2008. (ENG.). 64p. (J). (gr. 1-5). pap. 14.95 *(978-0-88899-869-9(4))* Groundwood Bks. CAN. Dist: Publishers Group West (PGW).

Diamond, Donna. Bridge to Terabithia. Paterson, Katherine. 2008. (ENG.). 208p. (J). (gr. 3-7). pap. 7.99 *(978-0-06-073401-5(9)*, HarperTeen) HarperCollins Pubs.

—Bridge to Terabithia. Paterson, Katherine. 2017. (ENG.). 192p. (J). (gr. 3-7). 16.99 *(978-0-690-01359-7(0)*, HarperCollins) HarperCollins Pubs. Ltd. GBR. Dist: HarperCollins Pubs.

—Bridge to Terabithia. Paterson, Katherine. l.t. ed. 2007. (Literacy Bridge Middle Reader Ser.). 187p. (J). (gr. 4-7). 23.95 *(978-0-7862-9620-0(8))* Thorndike Pr.

—Bridge to Terabithia 40th Anniversary Edition. Paterson, Katherine. 2017. (Trophy Bk.). (ENG.). 192p. (J). (gr. 3-7). reprint ed. pap. 7.99 *(978-0-06-440184-5(7)*, HarperCollins) HarperCollins Pubs. Ltd. GBR. Dist: HarperCollins Pubs.

—Bridge to Terabithia: a Harper Classic. Paterson, Katherine. 2017. (Harper Classic Ser.). (ENG.). 192p. (J). (gr. 3-7). 16.99 *(978-0-06-265874-6(3))* HarperCollins Pubs.

—Bridge to Terabithia Movie Tie-In Edition. Paterson, Katherine. movie tie-in ed. 2006. (ENG.). (J). (gr. 3-7). 176p. pap. 7.99 *(978-0-06-122728-8(5))*; 208p. pap. 6.99 *(978-0-06-125370-6(7))* HarperCollins Pubs. (HarperFestival).

—Molly & the Sword. Shlasko, Robert. 2004. 32p. (J). 15.95 *(978-0-9745077-4-3(1))* Jane & Street Pubs. Ltd.

—Walter: The Story of a Rat. Wersba, Barbara. 2012. (ENG.). 64p. (gr. 4-6). 24.94 *(978-1-932425-41-3(1))*; (J). pap. 8.95 *(978-1-59078-948-3(2))* Boyds Mills Pr.

Diamond, Donna. The Shadow. Diamond, Donna. 2010. 32p. (J). (gr. k-3). 15.99 *(978-0-7636-4878-7(7))* Candlewick Pr.

Diamond, Shendl. The True Story of Critter Angels by Yani. Diamond, Shendl, text. 2005. (J). 15.95 *(978-0-9764724-3-8(0))* LikeMinds Pr.

Diana. Tee Hee. Carmen, Indigo. 2008. 24p. pap. 24.95 *(978-1-4241-9959-4(X))* America Star Bks.

Diana, Andreea. The Neverland Rascals: To Neverland. Snyder, Ted. Espinosa, Sharon, ed. 2015. (Neverland Rascals Ser.). (ENG.). (J). pap. 19.99 *(978-0-9965019-1-0(6))* Snyder, Ted.

Diana Cox. Bebe's Big Adventure: A Bebe & Muckle Book. Laverty, Neil. 2013. 44p. pap. 17.97 *(978-1-62212-612-5(2)*, Strategic Bk. Publishing) Strategic Book Publishing & Rights Agency (SBPRA).

Diane, Brown. Forty Winks. Allen, Nancy. 2016. (ENG.). (J). (gr. k-3). 19.99 *(978-1-940310-46-6(6))* 4RV Pub.

Diaper, Barry. Bertie the Buffalo. Jones, Wendy H. 2019. (ENG.). 32p. (J). (gr. -1-2). pap. 12.99 *(978-1-910786-52-9(7)*, cfa3bbe8-2cd5-4236-bae2-fcd10296ec12, Sarah Grace Publishing) Malcolm Down Publishing Ltd. GBR. Dist: Baker & Taylor Publisher Services (BTPS).

Diaper, Barry. Bertie the Buffalo Colouring Book. Jones, Wendy H. 2020. (ENG.). 30p. (J). (gr. -1-1). pap. 7.99 ***(978-1-912863-33-4(2)***, b09565fe-f00e-4a0a-aa3d-346e74e50a4d, Sarah Grace Publishing) Malcolm Down Publishing Ltd. GBR. Dist: Baker & Taylor Publisher Services (BTPS).

Dias, Jodie E. & Weston, Wendy J. Alex & the Spirit of Christmas. Keen, Marian E. 2019. (Adventures of Alexander Catt Ser.: Vol. 1). (ENG.). 52p. (J). (gr. 2-4). pap. ***(978-1-988220-19-2(X))*** Keen Ideas Publishing.

Dias, Ron, et al. Beauty & the Beast. Slater, Teddy. 2004. (Little Golden Book Ser.). (ENG.). 24p. (J). (gr. -1-2). 4.99 *(978-0-7364-2197-3(1)*, Golden/Disney) Random Hse. Children's Bks.

Dias, Ron. Cinderella (Disney Princess) RH Disney. 2005. (Little Golden Book Ser.). (ENG.). 24p. (J). (gr. -1-k). lib. bdg. 4.99 *(978-0-7364-2362-5(1)*, Golden/Disney) Random Hse. Children's Bks.

Dias, Ron, jt. illus. see DiCicco, Sue.

Dias, Ron, jt. illus. see Langley, Bill.

Diaz, Bianca. La Casa de Algún Día. Durango, Julia. 2020. 32p. (J). (gr. -1-2). (SPA.). 16.99 *(978-1-62354-231-3(6))*; pap. 7.99 *(978-1-62354-135-4(2))* Charlesbridge Publishing, Inc.

—The One Day House. Durango, Julia. 32p. (J). (gr. -1-2). 2020. pap. 7.99 *(978-1-62354-134-7(4))*; 2017. (ENG.). lib. bdg. 16.99 *(978-1-58089-709-9(6))* Charlesbridge Publishing, Inc.

Díaz, Carlos Manuel. Amigo Se Escribe con H. Heredia, María Fernanda. 2019.Tr. of Friend Is Spelled with Ph. (SPA.). 126p. (J). (gr. 4-6). pap. 12.99 *(978-958-04-7160-8(6)*, Norma) Norma S.A. COL. Dist: Distribuidora Norma, Inc.

Diaz, David. Angel Face. Weeks, Sarah. 2014. (ENG.). 32p. (J). (gr. -1-2). 13.99 *(978-1-4814-5045-4(X)*, Atheneum Bks. for Young Readers) Simon & Schuster Children's Publishing.

—Before You Came. Charest, Emily MacLachlan & MacLachlan, Patricia. 2011. (ENG.). 32p. (J). (gr. -1-3). 16.99 *(978-0-06-051234-7(2))*; lib. bdg. 17.89 *(978-0-06-051235-4(0))* HarperCollins Pubs. (Tegen, Katherine Bks).

—The Castle Corona. Creech, Sharon. 2007. 336p. (J). (gr. 4-7). lib. bdg. 19.89 *(978-0-06-084622-0(4)*, Cotler, Joanna Books) HarperCollins Pubs.

—The Castle Corona. Creech, Sharon. 2013. (ENG.). 352p. (J). (gr. 3-7). pap. 7.99 *(978-0-06-206395-3(2)*, HarperCollins) HarperCollins Pubs. Ltd. GBR. Dist: HarperCollins Pubs.

—César: ¡Sí, Se Puede! Yes, We Can!, 0 vols. Bernier-Grand, Carmen T. 2011. (ENG.). 49p. (J). (gr. 3-7). pap. 7.99 *(978-0-7614-5833-3(6)*, 9780761458333, Two Lions) Amazon Publishing.

—La Cinturita de Anansi, Level 3. Cabral, Len. Flor Ada, Alma, tr. 3rd ed. 2003. (Dejame Leer Ser.). (SPA.). 16p. (J). (gr. -1-3). 6.50 *(978-0-673-36294-0(9)*, Good Year Bks.) Celebration Pr.

—Counting Ovejas. Weeks, Sarah. 2006. (ENG.). 40p. (J). (gr. -1-2). 19.99 *(978-0-689-86750-7(6)*, Atheneum Bks. for Young Readers) Simon & Schuster Children's Publishing.

—Diego: Bigger Than Life, 0 vols. Bernier-Grand, Carmen. 2009. (ENG.). 64p. (J). (gr. 8-13). 18.99 *(978-0-7614-5383-3(0)*, 9780761453833) Amazon Publishing.

—Feliz Navidad: Two Stories Celebrating Christmas. Feliciano, Jose. 2005. 23p. (J). reprint ed. 16.00 *(978-0-7567-8587-1(1))* DIANE Publishing Co.

—The Gospel Cinderella. Thomas, Joyce Carol. 2004. 40p. (J). (gr. k-5). lib. bdg. 16.89 *(978-0-06-025388-2(6)*, Cotler, Joanna Books) HarperCollins Pubs.

—The Little Scarecrow Boy. Brown, Margaret Wise. 2005. (ENG.). 40p. (J). (gr. -1-2). reprint ed. pap. 7.99 *(978-0-06-077891-0(1))* HarperCollins Pubs.

—Mama, Look! Murphy, Patricia. 2017. (ENG.). 40p. (J). (gr. -1-1). 17.99 *(978-1-4998-0080-7(0))* Little Bee Books Inc.

—Martin de Porres: The Rose in the Desert. Schmidt, Gary D. 2012. (ENG.). 32p. (J). (gr. 1-4). lib. bdg. 18.99 *(978-0-547-61218-8(4)*, 1464622) Houghton Mifflin Harcourt Publishing Co.

—Maya's Blanket, 1 vol. Brown, Monica & Domínguez, Adriana. ed. 2015. (SPA & ENG.). 32p. (J). (gr. k-4). 18.95 *(978-0-89239-292-6(4)*, 77f32a2a-93a1-4933-89d5-9f212904879e) Lee & Low Bks., Inc.

—Me, Frida. Novesky, Amy. (ENG.). 32p. (J). (gr. -1-3). 2015. pap. 9.95 *(978-1-4197-1516-7(X))*; 2010. 18.99 *(978-0-8109-8969-6(7))* Abrams, Inc. (Abrams Bks. for Young Readers).

—Neighborhood Odes. Soto, Gary. 2005. (ENG.). 80p. (J). (gr. 3-7). pap. 7.99 *(978-0-15-205364-2(6)*, 1196154) Houghton Mifflin Harcourt Publishing Co.

—Picasso: I the King, Yo el Rey, 0 vols. Bernier-Grand, Carmen T. 2012. (ENG.). 64p. (J). (gr. 5-10). 19.99 *(978-0-7614-6177-7(9)*, 9780761461777) Amazon Publishing.

—The Pot That Juan Built. Andrews-Goebel, Nancy. 2013. (ENG.). 32p. (J). (gr. 1-18). 17.95 *(978-1-58430-038-0(8))* Lee & Low Bks., Inc.

—Rin, Rin, Rin - Do, Re, Mi. Orozco, Jose-Luis. 2005. (ENG.). 32p. (J). (gr. -1-k). 3.99 *(978-0-439-75531-3(X)*, Orchard Bks.) Scholastic, Inc.

—Sharing the Seasons: A Book of Poems. 2010. (ENG.). 96p. (J). (gr. 3-7). 24.99 *(978-1-4169-0210-2(4)*, McElderry, Margaret K. Bks.) McElderry, Margaret K. Bks.

—La Vasija Que Juan Fabrico. Andrews-Goebel, Nancy. 2004. (SPA.). 32p. (J). (gr. 2-5). pap. 10.95 *(978-1-58430-230-8(5))* Lee & Low Bks., Inc.

D

—La Vasija Que Juan Fabrico. Andrews-Goebel, Nancy. Cortes, Eunice, tr. 2004. (SPA.). (J). 16.95 *(978-1-58430-229-2(1))* Lee & Low Bks., Inc.
—The Wanderer. Creech, Sharon. 2011. (ENG.). 304p. (J). (gr. 3-7). pap. 7.99 *(978-0-06-441032-8(3)*, HarperCollins) HarperCollins Pubs. Ltd. GBR. Dist: HarperCollins Pubs.
—Wilma Unlimited. Krull, Kathleen. 2015. 44p. pap. 7.00 *(978-1-61003-502-6(X))* Center for the Collaborative Classroom.
—Yes! We Are Latinos. Flor Ada, Alma & Campoy, F. Isabel. 2016. 96p. (J). (gr. 5). pap. 9.95 *(978-1-58089-549-1(2))* Charlesbridge Publishing, Inc.
—Yes! We Are Latinos. Ada, Alma Flor & Campoy, F. Isabel. 2013. 96p. (J). (gr. 5). 18.95 *(978-1-58089-383-1(X))* Charlesbridge Publishing, Inc.
Diaz, David, jt. illus. see Nelson, Annika.
Diaz, Francesca. Popigami: When Everyday Paper Pops! Diaz, James. 2007. (ENG.). 8p. (J). (gr. -1). 19.95 *(978-1-58117-641-4(4)*, Intervisual/Piggy Toes) Bendon, Inc.
Diaz, Gabriel. The Hoop Kid from Elmdale Park. Bernard, Teko & Wilson, Wayne L. 2013. 126p. pap. 7.99 *(978-0-9860593-0-8(7))* Elmdale Park Books.
Diaz, Irene & Xian Nu Studio Staff. Sanctuary, Vol. 1. Marr, Melissa. 2009. (Wicked Lovely: Desert Tales Ser.: 1). (ENG.). 176p. (YA). (gr. 8-18). pap. 9.99 *(978-0-06-149354-6(6))* HarperCollins Pubs.
Diaz, James & Gerth, Melanie. Numbers: Learning Fun for Little Ones! 2007. 10p. (J). reprint ed. *(978-1-4223-6683-7(9))* DIANE Publishing Co.
Diaz, Jo. The Dragon Who Farted Fire. Jooste, David. 2019. (ENG.). 48p. (J). pap. 11.99 *(978-1-7956-7783-7(X))* Independently Published.
—Hong Kong: Wildlife for Kids. Jooste, David. 2019. (Scruff the Dog Ser.: Vol. 12). (ENG.). 40p. (J). pap. 9.99 *(978-1-0756-5485-5(8))* Independently Published.
—Invisible Magic Dust: A Scruff the Dog Story. Jooste, David. 2019. (ENG.). 46p. (J). pap. 9.99 *(978-1-0974-0397-4(1))* Independently Published.
—The Puppy Has Fleas: A Scruff the Dog Story. Jooste, David. 2019. (ENG.). 52p. (J). pap. 10.99 *(978-1-0931-8167-8(2))* Independently Published.
—Shipwrecked: Tatty the Bird. Jooste, David. 2018. (Scruff the Dog Ser.: Vol. 6). (ENG.). 42p. (J). pap. 9.99 *(978-1-7310-8825-3(6))* Independently Published.
Diaz, Jonathan, photos by. True Heroes: A Treasury of Modern-Day Fairy Tales Written by Best-Selling Authors. Diaz, Jonathan, ed. Hale, Shannon et al. 2015. (ENG.). 208p. (J). (gr. 3-6). 19.99 *(978-1-62972-103-3(4)*, 5140400, Shadow Mountain) Shadow Mountain Publishing.
Diaz, Kimberly J. Bajos y Altos. Fernandez, Queta. 2016. (Early Rising Readers Ser.). (SPA.). (J). (gr. -1). 6.67 *(978-1-4788-3668-1(7))* Newmark Learning LLC.
Diaz, Maine. I Am Dam Tough, 1 vol. Morelli, Licia. 2020. (ENG.). 32p. (J). (gr. 2-6). 17.95 ***(978-0-88448-780-7(6)***, 884780) Tilbury Hse. Pubs.
Diaz, Maine. The Runaway Chicken: Woodworking. Thorpe, Kiki. 2018. (Makers Make It Work Ser.). (ENG.). 32p. (J). (gr. k-3). 25.32 *(978-1-63592-012-3(4))*; pap. 5.99 *(978-1-57565-991-6(3))* Astra Publishing Hse.
—Slime King. Daly, Catherine. 2019. (Makers Make It Work Ser.). (ENG.). 32p. (J). (gr. k-3). 25.32 *(978-1-63592-121-2(X))* Astra Publishing Hse.
—Spring into Action. Brigandi, Pat. 2018. (Dinosaur Pals Ser.). (ENG.). 24p. (J). (gr. -1-2). 14.95 *(978-1-63322-460-5(0)*, Seagrass) Quarto Publishing Group USA.
Diaz, Manuel. Fame: Adele. Troy, Michael. Davis, Darren G., ed. 2017. (Fame Ser.). (ENG.). (YA). (gr. 8-12). pap. 5.99 *(978-1-948216-30-2(2))* TidalWave.
—Tribute: Freddie Mercury. Lynch, Mike. Davis, Darren G., ed. 2017. (Tribute Ser.). (ENG.). (YA). pap. 5.99 *(978-1-948216-03-6(5))* TidalWave.
Diaz, Paco. Marvel's Avengers: Road to A-Day. 2020. (ENG.). 112p. (YA). (gr. 8-17). pap. 15.99 ***(978-0-7851-9465-1(7))*** Marvel Worldwide, Inc.
Díaz, Raquel. Sapito Azul. Sánchez Beras, César. 2004. (SPA.). 32p. (J). *(978-1-58018-056-6(6))* Cambridge BrickHouse, Inc.
Diaz Reguera, Raquel. El Animal Perfecto. 2017. (SPA.). 40p. (J). (gr. -1-3). 15.95 *(978-84-946333-8-6(4))* NubeOcho Ediciones ESP. Dist: Consortium Bk. Sales & Distribution.
—The Perfect Animal. 2017. (ENG.). 40p. (J). (gr. -1-3). 15.95 *(978-84-946333-9-3(2))* NubeOcho Ediciones ESP. Dist: Consortium Bk. Sales & Distribution.
Diaz, Sonia. My Friends. Castellanos, Graciela. 2019. (ENG.). 24p. (J). pap. 9.50 ***(978-1-6920-6847-9(4))*** Independently Published.
Diaz, Viviana. Spooky & Spookier: Four American Ghost Stories. Houran, Lori Haskins. 2015. (Step into Reading Ser.). (ENG.). 48p. (J). (gr. 2-4). 4.99 *(978-0-553-53396-5(7)*, Random Hse. Bks. for Young Readers) Random Hse. Children's Bks.
Dibble, Traci. Great White Sharks. Cline, Gina. 2009. (1B Animal Behaviors Ser.). (ENG.). 36p. (J). pap. 9.60 *(978-1-61406-045-1(2))* American Reading Co.
—The Lion Pride. Zorzi, Gina & Cline, Gina. 2010. (2G Predator Animals Ser.). (ENG.). 32p. (J). (gr. k-2). pap. 8.00 *(978-1-61541-500-7(9))* American Reading Co.
Dibble, Traci. Brown Bears. Dibble, Traci. 2012. (1-3Y Animals Ser.). (ENG.). 16p. (J). (gr. k-2). pap. 9.60 *(978-1-61541-375-1(8))* American Reading Co.
—Cobras. Dibble, Traci. 2011. (1-3Y Wild Animals Ser.). (ENG.). 16p. (J). (gr. k-2). pap. 9.60 *(978-1-61541-367-6(7))* American Reading Co.
—Hammerhead Sharks. Dibble, Traci. 2009. (1-3Y Marine Life Ser.). (ENG.). 16p. (J). pap. 8.00 *(978-1-61406-037-6(1))* American Reading Co.
—Robber Flies. Dibble, Traci. Washington, Joi. 2014. (1-3Y Bugs Ser.). (ENG.). 16p. (J). (gr. k-2). pap. 9.60 *(978-1-61541-294-5(8))* American Reading Co.
—Sea Turtles. Dibble, Traci. Johnson, Gee & Cline, Gina. 2010. (2G Marine Life Ser.). (ENG.). 32p. (J). (gr. k-2). pap. 9.60 *(978-1-61541-399-7(5))* American Reading Co.

DiBiase, Judy. More Award-Winning Science Fair Projects. Bochinski, Julianne Blair. 2003. (ENG.). 228p. (J). (gr. 6-12). pap. 22.00 *(978-0-471-27337-0(6)*, Wiley) Wiley, John & Sons, Inc.
Dibley, Glin. Joy in Mudville. Raczka, Robert. 2014. (ENG.). 32p. (J). (gr. -1-3). 17.95 *(978-0-7613-6015-5(8)*, 9780761360155, Carolrhoda Bks.) Lerner Publishing Group.
—Kid Tea, 0 vols. Ficocelli, Elizabeth. 2013. (ENG.). 36p. (J). (gr. -1-1). pap. 9.99 *(978-1-4778-4738-1(3)*, 9781477847381, Two Lions) Amazon Publishing.
—Kid Tea. Ficocelli, Elizabeth. 2009. 32p. (J). (gr. -1). bds. 7.99 *(978-0-7614-5533-2(7))* Marshall Cavendish Corp.
—The Stupendous Dodgeball Fiasco. Rosensweig, Jay B. & Repka, Janice. 2012. 181p. (J). (gr. 4-6). 21.19 *(978-0-525-47346-6(7))* Penguin Young Readers Group.
DiChiara, Marcelo. Teen Titans Go! to Camp. Fisch, Sholly. 2020. 152p. (J). (gr. 3-7). pap. 9.99 ***(978-1-77950-317-6(2))*** DC Comics.
Dichiara, Marcelo. Things That Go Bump in the Night! Dezago, Todd. 2011. (Super Hero Squad Ser.). (ENG.). 24p. (J). (gr. 2-5). lib. bdg. 27.07 *(978-1-59961-862-3(1)*, 13894, Marvel Age) Spotlight.
DiChiara, Marcelo & Garbowska, Agnes. Past Times at Super Hero High. Fontana, Shea. 2020. (DC Super Hero Girls Ser.). (ENG.). 128p. (J). (gr. 2-6). lib. bdg. 31.99 ***(978-1-5158-7435-5(4)***, 202140, Stone Arch Bks.) Capstone.
Dichiara, Marcelo, jt. illus. see Castellani, Leonel.
DiCianni, Ron. Tell Me about Heaven. Alcorn, Randy. 2007. (ENG.). 64p. (J). 19.99 *(978-1-58134-853-8(3)*, 1271662) Crossway.
—Tell Me the Promises. Eareckson Tada, Joni & Jensen, Steve. 2004. 48p. (gr. 5-7). 17.99 *(978-0-89107-904-0(1))* Crossway.
—Tell Me the Story: A Story for Eternity. Lucado, Max. ed. 2015. (ENG.). 48p. (J). 19.99 *(978-1-4335-4744-7(9))* Crossway.
Dicicco, Joe. Planet Baseball, Dominican Republic Edition, Volume 1: Making the Play, Vol. 1. Dicicco, Joe. Jimenez, Ruben D., tr. I.t. ed. 2009.Tr. of Beisbol de Planeta. (ENG & SPA.). 14p. (J). (gr. -1-3). 7.95 *(978-1-929528-01-1(9))* Punta Gorda Pr.
—Planet Baseball, Japanese Edition, Volume 1: Making the Play, Vol. 1. Dicicco, Joe. Jimenez, Ruben D., tr. I.t. ed. 2009. (JPN & ENG.). 14p. (J). (gr. -1-3). 7.95 *(978-1-929528-03-5(5))* Punta Gorda Pr.
—Planet Baseball, Puerto Rico: Volume 1, Making the Play, Vol. 1. Dicicco, Joe. Jimenez, Ruben D., tr. I.t. ed. 2009.Tr. of Beisbol de Planeta. (ENG & SPA.). 14p. (J). (gr. -1-3). 7.95 *(978-1-929528-02-8(7))* Punta Gorda Pr.
DiCicco Studios, et al. Disney Princess. 2016. (Look & Find Ser.). (ENG.). 24p. (J). *(978-1-5037-1214-0(1)*, 32e5e0d7-b912-4ac1-8043-5bd69f84df2b, p i kids) Phoenix International Publications, Inc.
DiCicco Studios, jt. illus. see Disney Storybook Art Team.
DiCicco, Sue. Bath Time with Ariel (Disney Princess) Posner-Sanchez, Andrea. 2015. (Board Book Ser.). (ENG.). 24p. (J). (— 1). bds. 6.99 *(978-0-7364-3310-5(4)*, RH/Disney) Random Hse. Children's Bks.
DiCicco, Sue, et al. Disney Junior Mickey Mouse Clubhouse: Let It Snow! Holiday Gift Set. PI Kids. 2020. (Look & Find Ser.). (ENG.). 16p. (J). bds., bds. ***(978-1-5037-5660-1(2)***, e6e53e29-2ebf-48de-9a4f-ad254348d268, p i kids) Phoenix International Publications, Inc.
DiCicco, Sue. Jack & Jill & T-Ball Bill. Pierce, Terry. 2018. (Step into Reading Ser.). (ENG.). 32p. (J). (gr. -1-1). pap. 4.99 *(978-1-5247-1413-0(5)*, Random Hse. Bks. for Young Readers) Random Hse. Children's Bks.
—The Little Mermaid (Disney Princess) Teitelbaum, Michael. 2003. (Little Golden Book Ser.). (ENG.). 24p. (J). (gr. -1-2). 4.99 *(978-0-7364-2177-5(7)*, Golden/Disney) Random Hse. Children's Bks.
—The Little Red Caboose. Depken, Kristen L. 2018. (Step into Reading Ser.). (ENG.). 32p. (J). (gr. -1-1). lib. bdg. 12.99 *(978-1-5247-1427-7(5)*, Random Hse. Bks. for Young Readers) Random Hse. Children's Bks.
—The Poky Little Puppy & the Pumpkin Patch. Muldrow, Diane. 2018. (Little Golden Book Ser.). (ENG.). 24p. (J). (-k). 4.99 *(978-0-399-55698-2(2)*, Golden Bks.) Random Hse. Children's Bks.
—The Poky Little Puppy's Playtime. Golden Books. 2017. 16p. (J). (— 1). 8.99 *(978-0-399-55289-2(8)*, Golden Bks.) Random Hse. Children's Bks.
—The Poky Little Puppy's Valentine. Muldrow, Diane. 2019. 12p. (J). (— 1). bds. 5.99 *(978-1-9848-5007-2(5)*, Golden Bks.) Random Hse. Children's Bks.
—The Poky Little Puppy's Wonderful Winter Day. Chandler, Jean. 2017. (Little Golden Book Ser.). (J). (-k). 24p. 4.99 *(978-0-399-55292-2(8))*; *(978-1-5379-5880-4(1))* Random Hse. Children's Bks. (Golden Bks.).
—Quiet Time with Belle (Disney Princess) Posner-Sanchez, Andrea. 2016. (ENG.). 24p. (J). (gr. -1 — 1). bds. 6.99 *(978-0-7364-3441-6(0)*, RH/Disney) Random Hse. Children's Bks.
—The Shy Little Kitten. Depken, Kristen L. & Schurr, Cathleen. 2015. (Step into Reading Ser.). (ENG.). 32p. (J). (gr. -1-1). 12.99 *(978-0-375-97377-2(X)*, Random Hse. Bks. for Young Readers) Random Hse. Children's Bks.
—The Shy Little Kitten's Christmas. Depken, Kristen L. 2018. (Step into Reading Ser.). 32p. (J). (gr. -1-1). pap. 4.99 *(978-1-5247-6809-6(X)*, Random Hse. Bks. for Young Readers) Random Hse. Children's Bks.
—The Shy Little Kitten's New Friends. Golden Books. 2019. (ENG.). 16p. (J). (— 1). bds. 8.99 *(978-0-399-55644-9(3)*, Golden Bks.) Random Hse. Children's Bks.
—Tawny Scrawny Lion. Depken, Kristen L. & Jackson, Kathryn. 2016. (Step into Reading Ser.). 32p. (J). (gr. -1-1). pap. 4.99 *(978-1-101-93424-1(7)*, Random Hse. Bks. for Young Readers) Random Hse. Children's Bks.
—Tootle. Redbank, Tennant & Crampton, Gertrude. 2017. (Step into Reading Ser.). 32p. (J). (gr. -1-1). pap. 4.99 *(978-0-399-55520-6(X)*, Random Hse. Bks. for Young Readers) Random Hse. Children's Bks.

DiCicco, Sue. Feelings. DiCicco, Sue. 2010. 10p. 9.95 *(978-1-60747-743-3(2)*, Pickwick Pr.) Phoenix Bks., Inc.
—Manners. DiCicco, Sue. 2010. 10p. 9.95 *(978-1-60747-749-5(1)*, Pickwick Pr.) Phoenix Bks., Inc.
—1, 2 at the Zoo. DiCicco, Sue. 2012. (ENG.). 10p. (J). (— 1). bds. 6.99 *(978-0-545-43239-9(1))* Scholastic, Inc.
DiCicco, Sue & Dias, Ron. Sleeping Beauty. Teitelbaum, Michael & Golden Books Staff. 2004. (Little Golden Book Ser.). (ENG.). 24p. (J). (gr. -1-k). 4.99 *(978-0-7364-2198-0(X)*, Golden/Disney) Random Hse. Children's Bks.
DiCicco, Sue & Hathi, Garva. The Saggy Baggy Elephant. Redbank, Tennant & Jackson, Kathryn. 2016. (Step into Reading Ser.). 32p. (J). (gr. -1-1). pap. 4.99 *(978-0-553-53588-4(9)*, Random Hse. Bks. for Young Readers) Random Hse. Children's Bks.
DiCicco, Sue & Mawhinney, Art. Diego y los Dinosaurios. 2008. (Go, Diego, Go! Ser.). Orig. Title: Diego's Great Dinosaur Rescue. (SPA & ENG.). 24p. (J). (gr. -1-2). pap. 3.99 *(978-1-4169-5871-0(1)*, Libros Para Ninos) Libros Para Ninos.
—Diego's Great Dinosaur Rescue. 2008. (Go, Diego, Go! Ser.). (ENG.). 24p. (J). (gr. -1-2). pap. 3.99 *(978-1-4169-5867-3(3)*, Simon Spotlight/Nickelodeon) Simon Spotlight/Nickelodeon.
DiCicco, Sue, jt. illus. see Disney Storybook Art Team.
DiCicco, Sue, jt. illus. see RH Disney Staff.
Dick, Judy. The Seder Activity Book. Dick, Judy. 2004. 39p. (gr. k-3). pap., act. bk. ed. 9.95 *(978-0-8074-0728-8(3)*, 101097) URJ Pr.
Dick, Peggy. Draw & Write Through History: Creation Through Jonah. Gressman, Carylee Anne. Wolf, Aaron D., ed. 2006. (J). per. 12.95 *(978-0-9778597-0-2(3))* CPR Pubng.
Dick, Regina Frances, jt. illus. see Richards, Virginia Helen.
Dickason, Chris. Brain Games for Clever Kids. Moore, Gareth. 2014. (ENG.). 192p. (J). (gr. 3-7). pap. 7.99 *(978-1-78055-249-1(1))* O'Mara, Michael Bks., Ltd. GBR. Dist: Independent Pubs. Group.
—Brain Gaming for Clever Kids. Moore, Gareth. 2018. (Clever Kids Ser.). (ENG.). 192p. (J). (gr. 2-6). pap. 6.99 *(978-1-4380-1237-7(3)*, B.E.S. Publishing) Peterson's.
—Hello Dinosaurs! Holub, Joan. 2019. (Hello Book Ser.). (ENG.). 26p. (J). (gr. -1 — 1). bds. 8.99 *(978-1-5344-1870-7(9)*, Little Simon) Little Simon.
—Hello Knights! Holub, Joan. 2018. (Hello Book Ser.). (ENG.). 26p. (J). (gr. -1 — 1). bds. 8.99 *(978-1-5344-1868-4(7)*, Little Simon) Little Simon.
—Hello Knights! Ninjas! Robots! & Dinosaurs! Hello Knights!; Hello Ninjas!; Hello Robots!; Hello Dinosaurs! Holub, Joan. ed. 2019. (Hello Book Ser.). (ENG.). 104p. (J). (— 1). bds. 35.99 *(978-1-5344-4320-4(7)*, Little Simon) Little Simon.
—Hello Ninjas! Holub, Joan. 2018. (Hello Book Ser.). (ENG.). 26p. (J). (gr. -1 — 1). bds. 8.99 *(978-1-5344-1869-1(5)*, Little Simon) Little Simon.
—Hello Robots! Holub, Joan. 2019. (Hello Book Ser.). (ENG.). 26p. (J). (gr. -1 — 1). bds. 8.99 *(978-1-5344-1871-4(7)*, Little Simon) Little Simon.
—Math Games for Clever Kids. Moore, Gareth. 2018. (Clever Kids Ser.). (ENG.). 192p. (J). (gr. 2-6). pap. 6.99 *(978-1-4380-1238-4(1)*, B.E.S. Publishing) Peterson's.
Dickason, Chris. The Clever Kids' Dickason, Chris. 2015. (ENG.). 32p. (J). (gr. 1). pap., act. bk. ed. 6.99 *(978-1-78055-319-1(6))* O'Mara, Michael Bks., Ltd. GBR. Dist: Independent Pubs. Group.
—The Diggers & Trucks Colouring Book. Dickason, Chris. 2017. (ENG.). 64p. (J). (gr. k-2). pap. 8.99 *(978-1-78055-250-7(5))* O'Mara, Michael Bks., Ltd. GBR. Dist: Independent Pubs. Group.
—The Planes, Trains & Cars Colouring Book. Dickason, Chris. Buster Books Staff. 2017. (ENG.). 64p. (J). (gr. k-2). pap. 6.99 *(978-1-78055-251-4(3))* O'Mara, Michael Bks., Ltd. GBR. Dist: Independent Pubs. Group.
—Quiz Book for Clever Kids. Dickason, Chris. Moore, Gareth & Farnsworth, Lauren. 2015. (ENG.). 192p. (J). (gr. 1-5). pap. 7.99 *(978-1-78055-314-6(5))* O'Mara, Michael Bks., Ltd. GBR. Dist: Independent Pubs. Group.
Dickason, Kailyn. Charlie & the Time-Traveling Flip-Phone. Sobel, Ron. 2019. (ENG.). 96p. (J). pap. 12.95 *(978-1-7927-1858-8(6))* Independently Published.
—Gwenivere the Great Travels the World: Activity & Coloring Book. Flanagan, Jessica a. 2018. (ENG.). 42p. (J). pap. 9.99 *(978-1-7175-2189-7(4))* CreateSpace Independent Publishing Platform.
Dickens, Christina. I Have a New Puppy! Now What? A Puppy Survival Guide for Kids. Hunt, James. 2007. (Fireman James & Flame Ser.). 40p. (J). (gr. 1-3). 14.99 *(978-0-9769401-0-4(8))* Hunt, J. L. Publishing.
Dickens, Earl. Real Fossils. Benanti, Carol. Frank, Michael, ed. (Real Collections). 32p. (Orig.). (J). (gr. 3-8). pap. 6.95 *(978-1-880592-06-9(1))* Pace Products, Inc.
Dickens, Frank. Albert Herbert Hawkins: The Naughtiest Boy in the World. Dickens, Frank. 32p. (J). (gr. -1-3). 12.95 *(978-0-87592-000-9(4))* Scroll Pr., Inc.
Dickerson, Patrick a. Samidi's Trunk. Smith, Laura E. 2019. (ENG.). 34p. (J). pap. 10.00 ***(978-1-948747-56-1(1))*** J2B Publishing LLC.
Dickert, Sheryl. The Night Before Christmas in New York, 1 vol. Phillips, Betty Lou & Herndon, Roblyn. 2013. 32p. 9.99 *(978-1-4236-3440-9(3))* Gibbs Smith, Publisher.
—The Night Before Christmas in Texas, 1 vol. Phillips, Betty Lou & Herndon, Roblyn. 2013. (ENG.). 32p. 9.99 *(978-1-4236-3509-3(4))* Gibbs Smith, Publisher.
Dickinson, John. The Draco Twins Make a Discovery. Basile, Carol. 2018. (Draco Twins Make a Discovery Ser.: Vol. 1). (ENG.). 34p. (J). (gr. k-5). 18.99 *(978-1-7324359-2-6(8))* Dragon Gate Media.
Dickinson, John Michael. The Draco Twins Make a Discovery. Basile, Carol Jean. 2018. (Draco Twins Ser.: Vol. 1). (ENG.). 34p. (J). (gr. k-5). pap. 9.99 *(978-1-7324359-1-9(X))* Dragon Gate Media.

Dickinson, Rebecca. Anybody Home?, 1 vol. Berkes, Marianne. 2013. (ENG.). 32p. (J). (gr. -1-3). 17.95 *(978-1-60718-618-2(7)*, 9781607186182); pap. 9.95 *(978-1-60718-630-4(6))* Arbordale Publishing.
—Hay Alguien en Casa?, 1 vol. Berkes, Marianne. 2013. (SPA.). 32p. (J). (gr. -1-3). 17.95 *(978-1-60718-714-1(0))* Arbordale Publishing.
Dickison, Forrest. Gray Flowers. Radford, Dave. 2018. (ENG.). 24p. (J). pap. 11.95 *(978-1-947644-46-5(7))* Canon Pr.
—Hello, Ninja. Wilson, N. D. 2019. (ENG.). 32p. (J). (gr. -1-3). 14.99 *(978-0-06-287195-4(1))* HarperCollins Pubs.
Dickison, Forrest. Hello, Ninja. Hello, Georgie. Wilson, N. D. 2020. (ENG.). 32p. (J). (gr. -1-3). 14.99 ***(978-0-06-287197-8(8)***, HarperCollins) HarperCollins Pubs. Ltd. GBR. Dist: HarperCollins Pubs.
Dickison, Forrest. The Riot & the Dance Teacher's Guide. Wilson, Gordon. 2015. (ENG.). 236p. (YA). pap. 20.00 *(978-1-59128-193-1(8))* Canon Pr.
—The Sword of Abram. 2013. (J). *(978-1-59128-046-0(X))* Canon Pr.
Dickman, Michael. The Cat & the Kids of Millbrae. Banerjee, Timir. 2011. 24p. pap. 24.95 *(978-1-4560-9721-9(0))* America Star Bks.
Dickson, Bill. Big Rig Daddy: A Ride in the Truck of All Trucks. Wildman, Dale. 2006. 24p. (J). per. 2.99 *(978-1-59958-007-4(1))* Journey Stone Creations, LLC.
—The Bremen Town Musicians: A Retelling of the Grimm's Fairy Tale, 1 vol. Blair, Eric. 2013. (My First Classic Story Ser.). (ENG.). 32p. (J). (gr. k-3). pap. 7.10 *(978-1-4795-1848-7(4)*, Picture Window Bks.) Capstone.
—Daniel & the Lions. Petach, Heidi. 2013. (Happy Day Ser.). (ENG.). 16p. (J). pap. 2.49 *(978-1-4143-9298-1(2)*, 4608288) Tyndale Hse. Pubs.
—David & Goliath. 2013. (Happy Day Ser.). (ENG.). 16p. (J). pap. 2.49 *(978-1-4143-9324-7(5)*, 4608314) Tyndale Hse. Pubs.
—The Shoemaker & His Elves: A Retelling of the Grimm's Fairy Tale, 1 vol. Blair, Eric. 2013. (My First Classic Story Ser.). (ENG.). 32p. (J). (gr. k-3). pap. 7.10 *(978-1-4795-1849-4(2)*, Picture Window Bks.) Capstone.
—What Kind of Cow Are You? Being Content with How God Made You. Dwire, Joyann. 2006. 24p. (J). per. 2.99 *(978-1-59958-006-7(3))* Journey Stone Creations, LLC.
Dickson, Daryl. Paddy O'Melon: The Irish Kangaroo. Cooper, Julia. 2017. (ENG.). 32p. (J). (gr. -1-3). 12.99 *(978-1-925335-63-7(1)*, EK Bks.) Exisle Publishing Pty Ltd. AUS. Dist: Hachette Bk. Group.
Dickson, Irene. Blocks. Dickson, Irene. (ENG.). (J). (— 1). 2018. 26p. bds. 8.99 *(978-1-5362-0272-4(X))*; 2016. 32p. 14.99 *(978-0-7636-8656-7(5))* Candlewick Pr. (Nosy Crow).
—Stick. Dickson, Irene. 2018. (ENG.). 32p. (J). (-k). 14.99 *(978-1-5362-0016-4(6)*, Nosy Crow) Candlewick Pr.
Dicmas, Courtney. Bathtime. Dicmas, Courtney. 2014. (Wild! Ser.: 4). 14p. (J). (gr. k-k). spiral bd. *(978-1-84643-686-4(9))* Child's Play International Ltd.
—Bedtime. Dicmas, Courtney. 2014. (Wild! Ser.: 4). 14p. (J). (gr. k-k). spiral bd. *(978-1-84643-687-1(7))* Child's Play International Ltd.
—Colors. Dicmas, Courtney. ed. 2017. (Wild! Concepts Ser.: 4). (ENG.). 14p. (J). bds. *(978-1-84643-996-4(5))* Child's Play International Ltd.
—Colors/Colores. Dicmas, Courtney. Mlawer, Teresa, tr. 2019. (Spanish/English Bilingual Editions Ser.). (ENG & SPA.). 14p. (J). bds. *(978-1-78628-393-1(X))* Child's Play International Ltd.
—Colours. Dicmas, Courtney. 2017. (Wild! Concepts Ser.: 4). 14p. (J). spiral bd. *(978-1-84643-995-7(7))* Child's Play International Ltd.
—The Great Googly Moogly. Dicmas, Courtney. 2014. (Child's Play Library). (ENG.). 32p. (J). *(978-1-84643-640-6(0))* Child's Play International Ltd.
—Harold Finds a Voice. Dicmas, Courtney. 2013. (Child's Play Library). 32p. (J). *(978-1-84643-550-8(1))* Child's Play International Ltd.
—Lemur Dreamer. Dicmas, Courtney. 2018. (J). 12.99 *(978-1-61067-767-7(6))* Kane Miller.
—Mealtime. Dicmas, Courtney. 2014. (Wild! Ser.: 4). 14p. (J). (gr. k-k). spiral bd. *(978-1-84643-684-0(2))* Child's Play International Ltd.
—A New School for Charlie. Dicmas, Courtney. 2020. (Child's Play Library). 32p. (J). (gr. -1-1). *(978-1-78628-342-9(5))* Child's Play International Ltd.
—Numbers. Dicmas, Courtney. 2017. (Wild! Concepts Ser.: 4). 14p. (J). spiral bd. *(978-1-84643-993-3(0))* Child's Play International Ltd.
—Numbers/Numeros. Dicmas, Courtney. Mlawer, Teresa, tr. 2019. (Spanish/English Bilingual Editions Ser.). (ENG & SPA.). 14p. (J). bds. *(978-1-78628-395-5(6))* Child's Play International Ltd.
—Opposites. Dicmas, Courtney. 2017. (Wild! Concepts Ser.: 4). 14p. (J). spiral bd. *(978-1-84643-997-1(3))* Child's Play International Ltd.
—Opposites/Opuestos. Dicmas, Courtney. Mlawer, Teresa, tr. 2019. (Spanish/English Bilingual Editions Ser.). (ENG & SPA.). 14p. (J). bds. *(978-1-78628-394-8(8))* Child's Play International Ltd.
—Playtime. Dicmas, Courtney. 2014. (Wild! Ser.: 4). 14p. (J). (gr. k-k). spiral bd. *(978-1-84643-685-7(0))* Child's Play International Ltd.
—Shapes. Dicmas, Courtney. 2017. (Wild! Concepts Ser.: 4). 14p. (J). spiral bd. *(978-1-84643-994-0(9))* Child's Play International Ltd.
—Shapes/Formas. Dicmas, Courtney. Mlawer, Teresa, tr. 2019. (Spanish/English Bilingual Editions Ser.). (ENG & SPA.). 14p. (J). bds. *(978-1-78628-396-2(4))* Child's Play International Ltd.
—WILD! Mealtime/¡QUÉ LOCURA! a la Hora de Comer. Dicmas, Courtney. ed. 2016. (Spanish/English Bilingual Editions Ser.: 4). (ENG & SPA.). 14p. (J). bds. *(978-1-84643-905-6(1))* Child's Play International Ltd.
—WILD! Playtime/¡QUÉ LOCURA! a la Hora de Jugar. Dicmas, Courtney. ed. 2016. (Spanish/English Bilingual

Editions Ser.: 4). (ENG & SPA.). 14p. (J). bds. *(978-1-84643-906-3(X))* Child's Play International Ltd.

Dicmas, Courtney, jt. illus. see Hibbs, Gillian.

Diddams, Huon. Run Spider, Run! Diddams, Tracey. 2018. (ENG.). 38p. (J). pap. *(978-0-6482855-0-2(2))* Trace Writing.

Didier, Samwise. Traveler. Scholastic, Inc. Staff & Weisman, Greg. 2016. (World of Warcraft: Traveler Ser.: 1). (ENG.). 384p. (J). (gr. 3-7). 14.99 *(978-0-545-90667-8(9))* Scholastic, Inc.

Diederen, Suzanne. Just the Right Size. Grubman, Bonnie. 2018. (ENG.). 32p. (J). 17.95 *(978-1-60537-365-2(6))*; 9.95 *(978-1-60537-428-4(8))* Clavis Publishing.

—A Kiss for Giraffe. Koppens, Judith. 2019. (ENG.). 40p. (J). 14.95 *(978-1-60537-407-9(5))* Clavis Publishing.

Diederen, Suzanne. A Kiss for Giraffe (Target) Koppens, Judith. 2019. (ENG.). 16p. (J). 9.99 ***(978-1-60537-539-7(X))*** Clavis Publishing.

Diederen, Suzanne. Larry & Lola. What Do We Buy? van der Linden, Elly. 2017. (Larry & Lola Ser.). (ENG.). 32p. (J). 14.95 *(978-1-60537-347-8(8))* Clavis ROM. Dist: Publishers Group West (PGW).

—Little Bear Wants to Grow. Koppens, Judith. 2019. (ENG.). 32p. (J). 14.95 *(978-1-60537-408-6(3))* Clavis Publishing.

Diederich, Ellen Jean. Where's Petunia? Diederich, Ellen Jean. Wert, Lynette, ed. gif. l.t. ed. 2003. (ENG.). 32p. (J). (gr. 1-4). per. 18.99 *(978-0-9728654-0-1(3))* Givinity Pr.

Diefendorf, Cathy. Diving for el Corazon. Damitz, Charlie. 2007. (ENG.). 101p. (J). pap. 10.95 *(978-0-9744446-3-5(4))* All About Kids Publishing.

—Ginger Leads the Way. O'Donnell, Liam. (Pet Tales Ser.). (ENG.). 32p. (J). (gr. -1-2). 2005. 4.95 *(978-1-59249-358-6(0),* 1B023); 2005. 2.95 *(978-1-59249-359-3(9),* 1B024); 2004. 9.95 *(978-1-59249-360-9(2),* 1B025) Soundprints.

—Pepper: A Snowy Search. O'Donnell, Liam. 2004. (Pet Tales Ser.). (ENG.). 32p. (J). (gr. -1-3). 4.95 *(978-1-59249-361-6(0),* 1B026) Soundprints.

—Pepper, a Snowy Search. O'Donnell, Liam. (Pet Tales Ser.). (ENG.). 32p. (J). (gr. -1-2). 2005. 2.95 *(978-1-59249-362-3(9),* 1B027); 2004. 9.95 *(978-1-59249-363-0(7),* 1B028) Soundprints.

Diego, Barbosa. Is It Ice Cream Yet? McLennan, Alison. 2019. (ENG.). 38p. (J). pap. *(978-1-925986-61-7(6))* Library For All Limited.

Diego, Rapi. Repugnante Pajarraco y Otros Regalos. Hinojosa, Francisco. 2014. (Serie Naranja Ser.). (SPA.). 104p. (J). pap. 9.95 *(978-1-64101-143-3(2))* Santillana USA Publishing Co., Inc.

—La Sapita Sabia y Otros Cuentos. Ferré, Rosario. (SPA.). 48p. (J). (gr. 3-5). pap. 8.95 *(978-968-19-0353-4(6))* Santillana USA Publishing Co., Inc.

Diego, Rapi & Flores, Martha. El Jardin del Nino: Una Historia de Esperanza. Foreman, Michael. 2009. (SPA.). 30p. (J). (gr. 1-3). 14.99 *(978-1-933032-56-6(1))* Lectorum Pubns., Inc.

—El Lorito Pelon. Foreman, Michael. 2008. (SPA.). 30p. (J). (gr. 1-3). 15.99 *(978-1-930332-56-0(4))* Lectorum Pubns., Inc.

Diehl, Chey. Billie the Octopus. Kay, Lotus. 2019. (ENG.). 28p. (J). (gr. k-5). 14.99 ***(978-1-63233-231-8(0))***; pap. 9.99 ***(978-1-63233-236-3(1))*** Eifrig Publishing.

—More Beautiful Than Heaven. Kay, Lotus. 2019. (ENG.). 30p. (J). (gr. k-5). 14.99 ***(978-1-63233-225-7(6))***; pap. 9.99 ***(978-1-63233-224-0(8))*** Eifrig Publishing.

Diehl, Laura. The Legend of Shi-Lin. Beatty, Sharon Lee. 2015. (ENG.). 112p. (J). pap. 7.99 *(978-0-692-36341-6(6))* Purple Unicorn Pr.

Diehl, Nichole. Old Testament Heroines of the Faith. Lo, Monica. 2007. 82p. per. 17.99 *(978-1-59879-224-9(5),* Lifevest) Lifevest Publishing, Inc.

Diemberger, Jana. Monacello: The Little Monk. McCaughrean, Geraldine. 2013. (Monacello Trilogy Ser.: 1). 64p. (J). (gr. 4-7). pap. 13.99 *(978-1-907912-03-0(7))* Phoenix Yard Bks. GBR. Dist: Independent Pubs. Group.

Diemert, Katherine. When Planet Earth Was New. Gladstone, James. 2017. (ENG.). 40p. (J). (gr. -1-5). 18.95 *(978-1-77147-203-6(0))* Owlkids Bks. Inc. CAN. Dist: Publishers Group West (PGW).

Dieterichs, Shelley. Ben Gives a Gift. Hoffmann, Sara E. 2013. (My Reading Neighborhood: Kindergarten Sight Word Stories Ser.). (ENG.). 16p. (J). (gr. -1-1). pap. 5.99 *(978-1-4677-1164-7(0),* 9781467711647) Lerner Publishing Group.

—Little Sister, Big Mess! Gerver, Jane E. 2007. (Rookie Reader Skill Set Ser.). (ENG.). 32p. (J). (gr. -1-3). 19.50 *(978-0-531-17545-3(6),* Children's Pr.) Scholastic Library Publishing.

—Sam Is Six. Hoffmann, Sara E. 2013. (My Reading Neighborhood: Kindergarten Sight Word Stories Ser.). (ENG.). 16p. (J). (gr. -1-1). pap. 5.99 *(978-1-4677-1163-0(2),* 9781467711630) Lerner Publishing Group.

—Sam Sees Snow. Hoffmann, Sara E. 2013. (My Reading Neighborhood: Kindergarten Sight Word Stories Ser.). (ENG.). 16p. (J). (gr. -1-1). pap. 5.99 *(978-1-4677-1167-8(5),* 9781467711678) Lerner Publishing Group.

Dieterlé, Nathalie. Jojo & the Food Fight! Lévy, Didier & Rosinsky, Lisa. 2018. (ENG.). 32p. (J). (gr. -1-2). 16.99 *(978-1-78285-409-8(6))* Barefoot Bks., Inc.

Dieterle, Nathalie. Jojo & the Food Fight. Lévy, Didier. 2018. (ENG.). 32p. (J). (gr. -1-2). pap. 8.99 *(978-1-78285-410-4(X))* Barefoot Bks., Inc.

Diethelm, David. David & the Bear. Diethelm, Jerry. 2020. (ENG.). 36p. (J). pap. ***(978-1-945432-33-0(0))*** Aurora Production AG.

Dietrich, Andrea. Hooligan Bear Home. Toynton, Ian. 2012. 32p. (J). 15.95 *(978-1-60131-108-5(7))* Big Tent Bks.

—Hooligan Bear New Friends. Toynton, Ian. 2012. 34p. (J). 15.95 *(978-1-60131-107-8(9))* Big Tent Bks.

Dietrich, Sean. Hansel & Gretel: The Graphic Novel, 1 vol. 2008. (Graphic Spin Ser.). (ENG.). 40p. (J). (gr. 3-6). 25.32 *(978-1-4342-0767-8(6),* Stone Arch Bks.) Capstone.

—Hansel & Gretel: The Graphic Novel, 1 vol. Stone Arch Books (Firm: Afton, Minn.) Staff. 2008. (Graphic Spin Ser.). (ENG.). 40p. (J). (gr. 3-6). pap. 5.95 *(978-1-4342-0863-7(X),* Stone Arch Bks.) Capstone.

—Hansel y Gretel: La Novela Grafica. Andersen, Hans & Stone Arch Books Staff. 2010. (Graphic Spin en Español Ser.). (SPA.). 40p. (J). (gr. 3-6). pap. 5.95 *(978-1-4342-2271-8(3),* Stone Arch Bks.) Capstone.

—Hansel y Gretel: La Novela Grafica. Andersen, Hans & Capstone Press Staff. 2010. (Graphic Spin en Español Ser.). (SPA.). 40p. (J). (gr. 3-6). lib. bdg. 25.32 *(978-1-4342-1901-5(1),* Stone Arch Bks.) Capstone.

—Sleeping Beauty. Capstone Press Staff. 2009. (Graphic Spin Ser.). (ENG.). 40p. (J). (gr. 3-6). pap. 5.95 *(978-1-4342-1393-8(5),* Stone Arch Bks.) Capstone.

Dietz, Mike. Funny Boy Meets the Dumbbell Dentist from Deimos (with Dangerous Dental Decay) Gutman, Dan. 2012. (Funny Boy Ser.). (ENG.). 120p. (J). (gr. 2-5). pap. 10.99 *(978-1-4532-7070-7(1))* Open Road Integrated Media, Inc.

—Funny Boy Takes on the Chit-Chatting Cheeses from Chattanooga. Gutman, Dan. 2012. (Funny Boy Ser.). (ENG.). 138p. (J). (gr. 2-5). pap. 10.99 *(978-1-4532-9530-4(5))* Open Road Integrated Media, Inc.

—Funny Boy Versus the Bubble-Brained Barbers from the Big Bang. Gutman, Dan. 2012. (Funny Boy Ser.). (ENG.). 144p. (J). (gr. 2-5). pap. 10.99 *(978-1-4532-9532-8(1))* Open Road Integrated Media, Inc.

Dieumegard, Mari. The Old Mainer & the Sea. Flahive, Jean. 2017. (ENG.). 32p. (J). 17.95 *(978-1-944762-27-8(2),* 2b2bca2a-ff00-4d1b-ba38-c94f01dcc653) Islandport Pr., Inc.

Diez, Dalia Alvarado. El Secreto del Sauce. Dreser, Elena. 2003. (SPA.). 44p. (J). (gr. 3-5). pap. 6.95 *(978-968-19-0617-7(9))* Santillana USA Publishing Co., Inc.

Diez-Luckie, Cathy. Kitty Goes Splash. Hill, Merle Roddy. 2005. (ENG.). 12p. (J). 5.75 *(978-1-57274-823-1(0),* 2171, Bks. for Young Learners) Owen, Richard C. Pubs., Inc.

—The Paper Bag. Ford, Carolyn. 2005. (ENG.). 8p. (J). 5.75 *(978-1-57274-756-2(0),* 2494, Bks. for Young Learners) Owen, Richard C. Pubs., Inc.

Diez, Miguel Angel. Grandpa Monty's Muddles. Zafrilla, Marta. Brokenbrow, Jon, tr. 2012. (ENG.). 32p. (J). (gr. 2-4). 15.95 *(978-84-15241-17-1(8))* Cuento de Luz SL ESP. Dist: Publishers Group West (PGW).

Difonzo, Nick Francis. Allen B & the Open Gate. Crosby, Matthew. 2017. (ENG.). 32p. (J). (gr. 1-5). pap. 9.99 *(978-1-5324-0175-6(2))* Xist Publishing.

Digby, Desmond. The Selected Adventures of Bottersnikes & Gumbles. Wakefield, S. A. 2017. 224p. 6.99 *(978-1-4607-5192-3(2))* HarperCollins Pubs. Australia AUS. Dist: HarperCollins Pubs.

Diggins, Julia E. & Bell, Corydon. String, Straightedge & Shadow: The Story of Geometry. Diggins, Julia E. 2003. (J). per. 16.95 *(978-1-892857-07-1(3))* Whole Spirit Pr.

Diggins, Matthew. Andrew & the Secret Gallery. Diggins, Matthew. (J). 2008. 32p. pap. 6.95 *(978-1-60108-026-4(3))*; 2007. 30p. (gr. 1-5). 15.95 *(978-1-60108-016-5(6))* Red Cygnet Pr.

Diggle, Daniel James. Barbara: A Sssslithering Adventure of Self Discovery. Diggle, David Mark. 2011. 24p. (J). pap. *(978-0-9871657-9-4(8))* Diggle de Doo Productions Pty, Ltd.

—Brian: Eats Himself Smarter. Diggle, David Mark. 2011. 24p. (J). pap. *(978-0-9871657-4-9(7))* Diggle de Doo Productions Pty, Ltd.

—Ewan: From Bullied to Superhero in One Afternoon. Diggle, David Mark. 2011. 24p. (J). pap. *(978-0-9871657-0-1(4))* Diggle de Doo Productions Pty, Ltd.

—Frederick: Thinking Makes Breathing Easy. Diggle, David Mark. 2011. 24p. (J). pap. *(978-0-9871657-8-7(X))* Diggle de Doo Productions Pty, Ltd.

—George & Toby: Won't Have A Baaa of Bed Wetting. Diggle, David Mark. 2011. 24p. (J). pap. *(978-0-9871657-5-6(5))* Diggle de Doo Productions Pty, Ltd.

—Melanie: Honestly Finds Herself Out of Her Depth. Diggle, David Mark. 2011. 24p. (J). pap. *(978-0-9871657-1-8(2))* Diggle de Doo Productions Pty, Ltd.

—Sammy: Leaves His Mark. Diggle, David Mark. 2011. 24p. (J). pap. *(978-0-9871657-3-2(9))* Diggle de Doo Productions Pty, Ltd.

Diggory, Nick. A Big Box of Bananas, 1 vol. Dale, Jay. 2012. (Engage Literacy Blue Ser.). (ENG.). 16p. (J). (gr. k-2). pap. 5.99 *(978-1-4296-8980-9(3),* Capstone Pr.) Capstone.

—Lazy Old Pirates, 1 vol. Dale, Jay. 2012. (Wonder Words Ser.). (ENG.). 32p. (gr. k-2). pap. 5.99 *(978-1-4296-8930-4(7),* Capstone Pr.) Capstone.

—Two Old Pirates, 1 vol. Dale, Jay. 2012. (Wonder Words Ser.). (ENG.). 32p. (gr. k-2). pap. 5.99 *(978-1-4296-8928-1(5),* Capstone Pr.) Capstone.

—What Is the Matter, Mrs. Long?, 1 vol. Dale, Jay. 2012. (Engage Literacy Green Ser.). (ENG.). 32p. (gr. k-2). pap. 5.99 *(978-1-4296-9030-0(5),* Capstone Pr.) Capstone.

Digital Island. Petting Farm Fun, Vol. 3. Hood, Karen Jean Matsko. Whispering Pine Press International, ed. 2014. (Hood Picture Book Ser.). (ENG.). 46p. (J). 24.95 *(978-1-59434-885-3(5))* Whispering Pine Pr. International, Inc.

—Petting Farm Fun: Hood Picture Book Series, Vol. 3. Hood, Karen Jean Matsko. Whispering Pine Press International, ed. 2014. (Hood Picture Book Ser.). (ENG.). 46p. (J). 84.99 *(978-1-59434-914-0(2))*; pap. 15.95 *(978-1-59434-618-7(6))* Whispering Pine Pr. International, Inc.

—Petting Farm Fun: Hood Picture Book Series - Book 3, Vol. 3. Hood, Karen Jean Matsko. Whispering Pine Press International Staff, ed. 2015. (Hood Picture Book Ser.). (ENG.). 46p. (J). pap. 15.95 *(978-1-59434-905-8(3))* Whispering Pine Pr. International, Inc.

Digital Light Studio. Sunny Bunnies: the Magic Wand: A Lift-The-Flap Book. 2019. (Sunny Bunnies Ser.). 10p. (J). (gr. -1). bds. 7.99 *(978-2-89802-073-5(7),* CrackBoom! Bks.) Chouette Publishing CAN. Dist: Publishers Group West (PGW).

Digman, Kristina. Our Apple Tree. Naslund, Gorel Kristina. 2006. (ENG.). 32p. (J). (gr. -1-3). pap. 8.99 *(978-1-59643-191-1(1),* 900039774) Square Fish.

Dienno, Trish. Toolbox. Ireland, Charles E. 2006. (J). *(978-1-892142-30-6(9))* Cedar Tree Bks.

Dikaya, Alexandra. Sweet Treats Activity Book: Tons of Fun Activities! Mazes, Drawing, Matching Games & More! Danilova, Lida & Clever Publishing. 2020. (Clever Activity Book Ser.). (ENG.). 48p. (J). (gr. -1-17). pap. 4.99 *(978-1-949998-87-0(8))* Clever Media Group.

Dillamore, Lucy. Nipper & the Lunchbox. Dillamore, Lucy. 2018. (Child's Play Library). 32p. (J). *(978-1-78628-180-7(5))* Child's Play International Ltd.

Dillard, Sarah. Five Wishing Stars: Disappearing Die Cut. Runnells, Treesha. 2005. (ENG.). 12p. (J). 14.95 *(978-1-58117-265-2(6),* Intervisual/Piggy Toes) Bendon, Inc.

—If You Were a Divided-By Sign, 1 vol. Shaskan, Trisha Speed. 2009. (Math Fun Ser.). (ENG.). 24p. (J). (gr. 2-4). pap. 7.95 *(978-1-4048-5196-2(8))*; lib. bdg. 28.65 *(978-1-4048-5195-5(X))* Capstone. (Picture Window Bks.).

—If You Were a Polygon, 1 vol. Aboff, Marcie. 2009. (Math Fun Ser.). (ENG.). 24p. (J). pap. 7.95 *(978-1-4048-5692-9(7),* Picture Window Bks.) Capstone.

—If You Were a Set, 1 vol. Aboff, Marcie. 2008. (Math Fun Ser.). (ENG.). 24p. (J). (gr. 2-4). 28.65 *(978-1-4048-4799-6(5))*; pap. 7.95 *(978-1-4048-4800-9(2))* Capstone. (Picture Window Bks.).

—If You Were a Set [LTD Commodities]. Aboff, Marcie. 2010. (Math Fun Ser.). 24p. pap. 3.50 *(978-1-4048-6258-6(7),* Picture Window Bks.) Capstone.

—If You Were a Times Sign, 1 vol. Shaskan, Trisha Speed. 2009. (Math Fun Ser.). (ENG.). 24p. (J). (gr. 2-4). pap. 7.95 *(978-1-4048-5211-2(5))*; lib. bdg. 28.65 *(978-1-4048-5210-5(7))* Capstone. (Picture Window Bks.).

—If You Were an Even Number, 1 vol. Aboff, Marcie. 2008. (Math Fun Ser.). (ENG.). 24p. (J). (gr. 2-4). 28.65 *(978-1-4048-4796-5(0))*; pap. 7.95 *(978-1-4048-4797-2(9))* Capstone. (Picture Window Bks.).

—If You Were an Even Number [LTD Commodities]. Aboff, Marcie. 2010. (Math Fun Ser.). 24p. pap. 3.50 *(978-1-4048-6259-3(5),* Picture Window Bks.) Capstone.

—If You Were an Even Number [Scholastic]. Aboff, Marcie. 2010. (Math Fun Ser.). 24p. pap. 0.47 *(978-1-4048-6547-1(0),* Picture Window Bks.) Capstone.

—If You Were an Inch or a Centimeter, 1 vol. Aboff, Marcie. 2009. (Math Fun Ser.). (ENG.). 24p. (J). (gr. 2-4). pap. 7.95 *(978-1-4048-5199-3(2),* Picture Window Bks.) Capstone.

—If You Were an Odd Number [LTD Commodities]. Aboff, Marcie. 2010. (Math Fun Ser.). 24p. pap. 3.50 *(978-1-4048-6260-9(9),* Picture Window Bks.) Capstone.

—If You Were an Odd Number [Scholastic]. Aboff, Marcie. 2010. (Math Fun Ser.). 24p. pap. 0.47 *(978-1-4048-6546-4(2),* Picture Window Bks.) Capstone.

—My Magnetic Opposites: Big & Little: Best Friends. Feldman, Thea. 2007. (Magnix Learning Fun Ser.). 10p. (gr. -1-k). bds. 9.95 *(978-1-932915-39-6(7))* Sandvik Innovations, LLC.

—Ten Wishing Stars: A Countdown to Bedtime Book. Runnells, Treesha. 2006. (ENG.). 22p. (J). 9.95 *(978-1-58117-187-7(0),* Intervisual/Piggy Toes) Bendon, Inc.

—Toca y Siente las Historias de la Biblia. Larson, Beverly. Pineda, Nancy, tr. 2003. (Touch & Feel Ser.). (SPA.). (J). (gr. -1-k). bds. 8.99 *(978-0-7899-1088-2(8))* Editorial Unilit.

—Traveling in Two's: The Journey to Noah's Ark. Auerbach, Annie. 2005. 8p. (J). 10.95 *(978-1-58117-236-2(2),* Intervisual/Piggy Toes) Bendon, Inc.

—What Do You Say? Please & Thank You. Wax, Wendy. 2005. (J). *(978-1-58987-108-3(1))* Kindermusik International.

Dillard, Sarah. Extraordinary Warren: A Super Chicken. Dillard, Sarah. 2014. (Pix Ser.). (ENG.). 64p. (J). (gr. 1-4). 12.99 *(978-1-4424-5340-1(0),* Aladdin) Simon & Schuster Children's Publishing.

Dillard, Sarah. Extraordinary Warren's World: Extraordinary Warren; Extraordinary Warren Saves the Day. Dillard, Sarah. 2020. (ENG.). 128p. (J). (gr. 1-4). 19.99 ***(978-1-5344-6347-9(X))***; pap. 7.99 ***(978-1-5344-6346-2(1))*** Simon & Schuster Children's Publishing. (Aladdin).

Dillard, Sarah. First Day at Zoo School. Dillard, Sarah. 2014. (ENG.). 40p. (J). (gr. k-2). 14.99 *(978-1-58536-890-7(3),* 203670) Sleeping Bear Pr.

—I Don't Like Rain! Dillard, Sarah. 2020. (ENG.). 40p. (J). (gr. -1-3). 17.99 *(978-1-5344-0678-0(6),* Aladdin) Simon & Schuster Children's Publishing.

—I Wish It Would Snow! Dillard, Sarah. 2018. (ENG.). 40p. (J). (gr. -1-3). 17.99 *(978-1-5344-0676-6(X),* Aladdin) Simon & Schuster Children's Publishing.

Dillard, Sarah, jt. illus. see Carabelli, Francesca.

Dilley, Kristi. Squiggy the Squirrel Meets Wallis the Woodpecker. Dilley, Kristi. 2013. 28p. pap. 9.99 *(978-1-937165-47-5(7))* Orange Hat Publishing.

Dillingham, Charlene. The Friendship Thief. Roach, Hesta. (J). (gr. k-5). pap. 9.99 *(978-0-9660583-3-8(X))* Sakura Pr.

Dillman, Jennifer. Tiffany at Tea Time: (A Tiffany T. Book) Gow, Kailin. 2004. (J). 14.95 *(978-1-59457-929-5(6))* Sparklesoup LLC.

—Tiffany at the Top of the World: (A Tiffany T. Book) Gow, Kailin. 2004. (J). 14.95 *(978-1-59457-928-8(8))* Sparklesoup LLC.

Dillon, Derry. Countess Markievicz: An Adventurous Life. Carroll, Ann. 2017. (ENG.). (J). pap. *(978-1-78199-870-0(1))* Poolbeg Pr.

—Freddy Buttons & the Apple Bandits. Dillon, Fiona. 2016. (Freddy Buttons Ser.: 5). (ENG.). 40p. (J). pap. 12.00 *(978-1-909895-87-4(3))* Orpen Pr. IRL. Dist: Dufour Editions, Inc.

—Niall of the Nine Hostages. Carroll, Ann. 2017. (ENG.). 50p. (J). pap. *(978-1-78199-901-1(5))* Poolbeg - In A Nutshell.

—Pádraig Pearse & the Easter Rising 1916. Smith, Rod. 2017. (ENG.). 50p. (J). pap. *(978-1-78199-888-5(4))* Poolbeg - In A Nutshell.

—The Story of Saint Patrick. Carroll, Ann. 2017. (ENG.). 50p. (J). pap. *(978-1-78199-268-5(1))* Poolbeg - In A Nutshell.

—Ten Women of the 1916 Rising. Carroll, Ann. 2017. (ENG.). (J). pap. *(978-1-78199-877-9(9))* Poolbeg Pr.

Dillon, Diane. I Can Be Anything! Don't Tell Me I Can't! Dillon, Diane. 2018. (ENG.). 32p. (J). (gr. -1-3). 17.99 *(978-1-338-16690-3(5),* Blue Sky Pr., The) Scholastic, Inc.

Dillon, Diane & Dillon, Leo. The Hundred Penny Box. Mathis, Sharon Bell. 2006. (ENG.). 48p. (J). (gr. 1-4). pap. 7.99 *(978-0-14-240702-8(X),* Puffin Books) Penguin Young Readers Group.

Dillon, Diane, jt. illus. see Dillon, Leo.

Dillon, James. Busy Book of Vehicles. Make Believe Ideas Ltd. 2019. (Busy Book of Vehicles Ser.). (ENG.). 14p. (J). (gr. -1-7). bds. *(978-1-78843-651-9(2))* Make Believe Ideas.

—Funderpants! Make Believe Ideas Ltd. 2019. (ENG.). 32p. (J). (gr. -1-1). pap. *(978-1-78947-016-1(1))*; *(978-1-78947-017-8(X))* Make Believe Ideas.

—Funderpants! Greening, Rosie. 2019. 12p. (J). bds. *(978-1-78843-996-1(1))* Make Believe Ideas.

Dillon, James. God Loves You Just the Way You Are. Make Believe Ideas Ltd. 2020. (ENG.). 32p. (J). (gr. -1-7). ***(978-1-78947-577-7(5))*** Make Believe Ideas.

Dillon, James. H Is for Happy-Saurus. Make Believe Ideas Ltd. 2019. (ENG.). 14p. (J). (gr. -1-7). bds. *(978-1-78843-979-4(1))* Make Believe Ideas.

—I Love You Just the Way You Are. Greening, Rosie. 2019. (Story Book Ser.). (ENG.). 32p. (J). (gr. -1-7). *(978-1-78843-663-2(6))* Make Believe Ideas.

Dillon, Jana. Lucky O'Leprechaun in School, 1 vol. Dillon, Jana. 2003. (Lucky O'Leprechaun Ser.). (ENG.). 32p. (J). (gr. k-3). 16.99 *(978-1-58980-035-9(4),* Pelican Publishing) Arcadia Publishing.

Dillon, Leo, et al. Dream: A Tale of Wonder, Wisdom & Wishes. Bosak, Susan V. 2004. 40p. (J). *(978-1-896232-04-1(3),* TCP Pr.) Communication Project, The.

Dillon, Leo & Dillon, Diane. Ashanti to Zulu: African Traditions. Musgrove, Margaret. 2004. 28p. (YA). (gr. 4-8). reprint ed. pap. 14.00 *(978-0-7567-7106-5(4))* DIANE Publishing Co.

—The Color Wizard. Brenner, Barbara. 2015. (ENG.). (J). 16.95 *(978-1-59687-479-4(1),* ipicturebooks) ibooks, Inc.

—The Goblin & the Empty Chair. Fox, Mem. 2009. (ENG.). 32p. (J). (gr. k-3). 17.99 *(978-1-4169-8585-3(9),* Beach Lane Bks.) Beach Lane Bks.

—Hakon of Rogen's Saga. Haugaard, Erik Christian. 2013. (ENG.). 144p. pap. 11.95 *(978-0-8166-8127-3(9))* Univ. of Minnesota Pr.

—The Hundred Penny Box. Mathis, Sharon Bell. 2006. 47p. (gr. 1-4). 18.00 *(978-0-7569-6786-4(4))* Perfection Learning Corp.

—If Kids Ran the World. Dillon, Leo & Dillon, Diane. 2014. (ENG.). 32p. (J). 18.99 *(978-0-545-44196-4(X),* Blue Sky Pr., The) Scholastic, Inc.

—The People Could Fly: American Black Folktales. Hamilton, Virginia. 2009. (ENG.). 192p. (J). (gr. k-12). 24.99 *(978-0-394-86925-4(7),* Knopf Bks. for Young Readers) Random Hse. Children's Bks.

—The People Could Fly: The Picture Book. Hamilton, Virginia. 32p. (J). (gr. k-12). 2015. 7.99 *(978-0-553-50780-5(X),* Dragonfly Bks.); 2004. 16.95 *(978-0-375-82405-0(7),* Knopf Bks. for Young Readers) Random Hse. Children's Bks.

—The Porcelain Cat. Hearn, Michael Patrick. 2004. (ENG.). 32p. (J). (gr. 4-7). 16.95 *(978-1-59687-175-5(X))* IBks., Inc.

—The Porcelain Cat. Hearn, Michael Patrick. 2004. 32p. (J). (gr. -1). 16.95 *(978-0-689-03592-0(6),* Milk & Cookies) ibooks, Inc.

—The Secret River. Rawlings, Marjorie Kinnan. 2011. (ENG.). 56p. (J). (gr. -1-3). 19.99 *(978-1-4169-1179-1(0),* Atheneum Bks. for Young Readers) Simon & Schuster Children's Publishing.

—Switch on the Night. Bradbury, Ray & ANZ014 Staff. 2004. 40p. (J). (gr. -1-2). reprint ed. pap. 7.99 *(978-0-553-11244-3(9),* Dragonfly Bks.) Random Hse. Children's Bks.

—The Tale of the Mandarin Ducks. Paterson, Katherine. 2004. 32p. (J). (gr. k-4). reprint ed. 15.00 *(978-0-7567-7698-5(8))* DIANE Publishing Co.

Dillon, Leo, jt. illus. see Dillon, Diane.

Dillon, Leo and Diane. Two Little Trains. Brown, Margaret Wise. 2003. (ENG.). 32p. (J). (gr. -1-k). pap. 7.99 *(978-0-06-443568-0(7))* HarperCollins Pubs.

—Where Have You Been? Brown, Margaret Wise. 2004. (ENG.). 32p. (J). (gr. -1-1). 16.99 *(978-0-06-028378-0(5))*; lib. bdg. 16.89 *(978-0-06-028379-7(3))* HarperCollins Pubs.

Dillon, Paul. Blunder or Brainstorm: Fact & Fiction of Famous Inventors & Inventions. Polette, Nancy. 2006. (YA). pap. 11.95 *(978-1-931334-91-4(9))* Pieces of Learning.

—N Is for Never Forget: POW-MIA a to Z. Polette, Nancy. 2017. (ENG.). 40p. (YA). (gr. 7). 16.95 *(978-1-934617-36-6(9))* Elva Resa Publishing, LLC.

Dillon, Stephanie. Here Comes Sandy Claus: The Launch of Christmas Eve. Leisner, Amy. 2019. (ENG.). 38p. (J). pap. 9.95 ***(978-1-7016-4702-2(8))*** Independently Published.

Dillon, Wade. The Alamo from A to Z, 1 vol. Chemerka, William R. 2011. (ABC Ser.). (ENG.). 32p. (J). (gr. k-3). 16.99 *(978-1-4556-1461-5(0),* Pelican Publishing) Arcadia Publishing.

—Davy Crockett from a to Z, 1 vol. Chemerka, William R. 2013. (ABC Ser.). (ENG.). 32p. (J). (gr. k-3). 16.99

D

(978-1-4556-1835-4(7), Pelican Publishing) Arcadia Publishing.

DiLorenzo, Barbara. Renato & the Lion. DiLorenzo, Barbara. 2017. 44p. (J). (gr. k-2). 17.99 *(978-0-451-47641-8(7)*, Viking Books for Young Readers) Penguin Young Readers Group.

Dima. Ice Cream Land. Lianou, Villy. 2016. (ENG.). (J). pap. *(978-618-5232-36-8(7))* Fylatos, Ekdoseis.

Dimaculangan, Pierre. Precy the Autumn Pumpkin: A Christian Story for Young Children. Dimaculangan, Pierre. Famin, Debbie. 2019. (ENG.). 26p. (J). pap. 12.00 *(978-1-0987-4221-8(4))* Independently Published.

DiMartino, Joseph Michael. Hacksaw Jim. DiMartino, Dawn Marie Paone. 2019. (ENG.). 34p. (J). pap. 5.99 *(978-1-9876-9439-0(2))* CreateSpace Independent Publishing Platform.

Dimatteo, Richard. Study Strategies for Early School Success: Seven Steps to Improve Your Learning. Sirotowitz, Sandi et al. 2003. (Seven Steps Family Guides). (ENG.). 146p. pap. 18.00 *(978-1-886941-55-7(6))* Specialty Pr., Inc.

DiMatteo, Richard A. Eukee the Jumpy Jumpy Elephant. Corman, Clifford L. & Trevino, Esther. 2009. (ENG.). 26p. (J). (gr. -1-1). pap. 10.95 *(978-1-886941-75-5(0))* Specialty Pr., Inc.

Dimaya, Emerson & Calero, Dennis. The Murders in the Rue Morgue, 1 vol. Bowen, Carl & Poe, Edgar Allen. 2013. (Edgar Allan Poe Graphic Novels Ser.). (ENG.). 72p. (J). (gr. 5-9). 27.99 *(978-1-4342-3033-1(3))*; pap. 6.10 *(978-1-4342-4259-4(5))* Capstone. (Stone Arch Bks.).

Dimbylow, Jube. Mr Squealy Goes to Town. Norton Kreider, Barbara. 2013. 24p. pap. *(978-1-921883-41-5(3)*, MBS Pr.) Pick-a-Woo Woo Pubs.

—Mr Squealy Makes a Friend. Norton Kreider, Barbara. 2013. 24p. pap. *(978-1-921883-52-1(9))* Pick-a-Woo Woo Pubs.

—Mr Squealy Meets Scarecrow. Norton Kreider, Barbara. 2013. 24p. pap. *(978-1-921883-53-8(7))* Pick-a-Woo Woo Pubs.

—The Surprise Party. Norton Kreider, Barbara. 2013. 30p. pap. *(978-1-921883-37-8(5)*, MBS Pr.) Pick-a-Woo Woo Pubs.

Dimitri, Simona. The Balloon Launch. Bird, Helen. 2005. 32p. (J). lib. bdg. 9.00 *(978-1-4242-0887-6(4))* Fitzgerald Bks.

—Big Yellow Balloon. Bird, Helen. 2009. (Get Set Readers Ser.). 32p. (J). (gr. -1-2). lib. bdg. 25.60 *(978-1-60754-268-1(4))* Windmill Bks.

—Peek Inside Animal Homes. Milbourne, Anna. 2014. (Peek Inside Board Bks.). (ENG.). 14p. (gr. -1). bds. 11.99 *(978-0-7945-2549-1(0)*, Usborne) EDC Publishing.

—This Is My Tractor. Brooks, Felicity. 2009. (Noisy Touchy-Feely Board Bks). 10p. (J). bds. 16.99 *(978-0-7945-2473-9(7)*, Usborne) EDC Publishing.

Dimitriadis, Nick. A Hungry Lion in My Tummy. Vollmer, Cheryl. 2009. 24p. pap. 9.99 *(978-0-9825255-9-3(1))* Epigraph Bks.

Dimitrova, Teodora. Leonard & Loulou. Buerki, Esther. 2019. (ENG.). 32p. (gr. k-5). pap. 12.95 *(978-1-64279-251-5(9))* Morgan James Publishing.

DiMotta, Michael J. Animals at Play: Rules of the Game. Bekoff, Marc. 2008. (Animals & Ethics Ser.). (ENG.). 32p. (J). (gr. 4-6). 19.95 *(978-1-59213-551-6(X))* Temple Univ. Pr.

Dina, Madalina. The Robot Who Couldn't Cry. Hodgson, Karen J. 2010. 32p. (J). (gr. -1-2). pap. 9.99 *(978-1-907432-01-9(9))* Hogs Back Bks. GBR. Dist: Independent Pubs. Group.

Dinallo, Alissa. I Love My Mum Because. James, Petra. 2019. (ENG.). 32p. (J). (gr. -1-k). 11.99 ***(978-1-76078-438-6(9))*** Pan Macmillan Australia Pty, Ltd. AUS. Dist: Independent Pubs. Group.

Dindar, Kubra. A Day on the Farm Playing Along, 1 vol. Ochs, Tom. 2009. 25p. pap. 24.95 *(978-1-60749-405-8(1))* America Star Bks.

Dineen, Tom. Taking Hearing Impairment to School. Schneider, Elaine Ernst. Schader, Karen, ed. 2004. (Special Kids in School Ser.: Fifteenth). (J). per. 11.95 *(978-1-891383-23-6(X)*, 70015) JayJo Bks., LLC.

—Taking Speech Disorders to School. Bryant, John E. Schader, Karen, ed. 2004. (Special Kids in School Ser.: Sixteenth). (J). per. 11.95 *(978-1-891383-24-3(8)*, 70016) JayJo Bks., LLC.

Dingeldein, Noelle. Walter's Wheels. Dingeldein, Noelle. 2015. (ENG.). 14p. (J). (gr. -1 — 1). bds. 7.99 *(978-1-936669-36-3(6)*, 1395558) Blue Manatee Press.

Dingess, Tracey. Pookie Wants Out! The Continuing Adventures of a Hamster's Tale. Hauth, Susan. 2019. (ENG.). 134p. (J). pap. 8.49 ***(978-1-7021-0104-2(5))*** Independently Published.

Diolosa, Tommaso. La Storia Di Doson - Doson's Story. Carini, Cristina. 2016. (Yellow Ser.). (ENG.). 36p. (J). (gr. k-6). pap. *(978-88-97551-28-7(9))* Edizioni Lalbero.

Dion, Nathalie. Artsy Babies Wear Paint. Colman, Michelle Sinclair. 2011. (Urban Babies Wear Black Book Ser.). 20p. (J). (gr. k — 1). bds. 6.99 *(978-1-58246-371-1(9)*, Tricycle Pr.) Random Hse. Children's Bks.

—Beach Babies Wear Shades. Colman, Michelle Sinclair. 2007. (Urban Babies Wear Black Book Ser.). 18p. (J). (gr. k — 1). bds. 6.99 *(978-1-58246-204-2(6)*, Tricycle Pr.) Random Hse. Children's Bks.

—The Big Night Out. Beker, Jeanne. 2005. 80p. (J). (gr. 4-7). pap. 15.95 *(978-0-88776-719-7(2)*, Tundra Bks.) Tundra Bks. CAN. Dist: Penguin Random Hse. LLC.

—Foodie Babies Wear Bibs. Colman, Michelle Sinclair. 2008. (Urban Babies Wear Black Book Ser.). 20p. (J). (— 1). bds. 6.99 *(978-1-58246-254-7(2)*, Tricycle Pr.) Random Hse. Children's Bks.

Dion, Nathalie. I Found Hope in a Cherry Tree, 1 vol. Pendziwol, Jean E. 2020. (ENG.). 32p. (J). (gr. -1-2). 18.95 ***(978-1-77306-220-4(4))*** Groundwood Bks. CAN. Dist: Publishers Group West (PGW).

Dion, Nathalie. Passion for Fashion: Careers in Style. Beker, Jeanne. 2008. 80p. (J). (gr. 5-9). pap. 18.95 *(978-0-88776-800-2(8)*, Tundra Bks.) Tundra Bks. CAN. Dist: Penguin Random Hse. LLC.

—Rocker Babies Wear Jeans. Colman, Michelle Sinclair. 2009. (Urban Babies Wear Black Book Ser.). 20p. (J). (gr. -1 — 1). bds. 6.99 *(978-1-58246-291-2(7)*, Tricycle Pr.) Random Hse. Children's Bks.

—Sporty Babies Wear Sweats. Colman, Michelle Sinclair. 2010. (Urban Babies Wear Black Book Ser.). (ENG.). 20p. (J). (gr. -1 — 1). bds. 6.99 *(978-1-58246-313-1(1)*, Tricycle Pr.) Random Hse. Children's Bks.

—Urban Babies Wear Black. Colman, Michelle Sinclair. 2005. (Urban Babies Wear Black Book Ser.). 20p. (J). (gr. k — 1). 6.99 *(978-1-58246-158-8(9)*, Tricycle Pr.) Random Hse. Children's Bks.

—What's in Your Purse? Samoun, Abigail. 2014. (ENG.). 12p. (J). (gr. -1-17). 17.99 *(978-1-4521-1701-0(2))* Chronicle Bks. LLC.

Dionne, Deanna. Sally Lumpkin's Party: A story of 6 true Friends. Blankenship, Julianna. 2008. 32p. pap. 15.56 *(978-1-4343-6860-7(2))* AuthorHouse.

Dionne, Nina. Samuel's Exeter Walkabout. Tomaszewski, Suzanne Lyon. 2003. 37p. (J). *(978-0-9744855-0-8(0))* Gold Charm Publishing, LLC.

DiOrio, Ariel. The Mystery of the Missing Menorahs: A Hanukkah Humdinger! 2007. 52p. (J). pap. 9.95 *(978-0-9659546-4-8(1))* Oak Leaf Systems.

DiPaolo, Katharine, jt. illus. see Marantz, Larissa.

Dippold, Jane. Farmers' Market Day. Trent, Shanda. 2013. (ENG.). 32p. (J). (gr. -1-1). 12.95 *(978-1-58925-115-1(6))* Tiger Tales.

—A Great Idea? An Up2U Character Education Adventure, 1 vol. Suen, Anastasia. 2015. (Up2U Adventures Ser.). (ENG.). 80p. (J). (gr. 2-5). 29.93 *(978-1-62402-093-3(3)*, 17355, Calico Chapter Bks.) ABDO Publishing Co.

—Jessica's Bear. Bennett, Donna I. 2003. (ENG.). 32p. (J). pap. 9.95 *(978-1-878044-57-0(5))* Mayhaven Publishing, Inc.

—New Girl: An Up2U Character Education Adventure, 1 vol. Suen, Anastasia. 2013. (Up2U Adventures Ser.). (ENG.). 80p. (J). (gr. 2-5). lib. bdg. 29.93 *(978-1-61641-968-4(7)*, 15219, Calico Chapter Bks.) ABDO Publishing Co.

—Papa Jethro, Vol. Cohen, Deborah Bodin. 2007. (Jewish Identity Ser.). (ENG.). 32p. (J). (gr. -1-1). per. 7.95 *(978-1-58013-252-7(9)*, Kar-Ben Publishing) Lerner Publishing Group.

—Traveling Babies. Galbraith, Kathryn Osebold. 2006. (Animal Babies Ser.). (ENG.). 32p. (J). (gr. -1-k). 16.95 *(978-1-55971-939-1(7))* Cooper Square Publishing Llc.

Dirk, Martin Scott. Lauryn Lost Her Sock. James, Leigh. 2019. (ENG.). 30p. (J). pap. 9.99 ***(978-1-6731-6240-0(1))*** Independently Published.

Dirksen, Lucy. Fetch! Clinedinst, Paula. 2018. (ENG.). 34p. (J). (gr. -1-3). 17.99 *(978-1-948225-19-9(0))* Thewordverve.

DiRocco, Carl. Dear Big, Mean, Ugly Monster. Berglin, Ruth. 2006. 40p. (J). (gr. -1-7). pap. 14.95 *(978-1-58760-072-2(2)*, Child & Family Pr.) Child Welfare League of America, Inc.

—Elliot Stone & the Mystery of the Summer Vacation Sea Monster. Chase, L. P. 2011. (ENG.). 165p. (J). pap. 8.99 *(978-0-9792918-7-6(9))* Blue Marlin Pubns.

—Madison & the Two-Wheeler, 1 vol. Braver, Vanita. 2007. (ENG.). 32p. (J). (gr. -1-3). 14.95 *(978-1-59572-109-9(6))* Star Bright Bks., Inc.

—Madison's Patriotic Project, 1 vol. Braver, Vanita. 2007. (ENG.). 32p. (J). 14.95 *(978-1-59572-110-5(X))* Star Bright Bks., Inc.

—Make Sense! Haddon, Jean. 2006. (Silly Millies Ser.). 32p. (J). (gr. 3-7). per. 5.95 *(978-0-8225-6472-0(6)*, First Avenue Editions); (ENG.). (gr. k-2). lib. bdg. 21.27 *(978-0-7613-3403-3(3)*, Millbrook Pr.) Lerner Publishing Group.

—Mystery of the Bear Cub, 1 vol. Wight, Tamra. 2017. (Cooper & Packrat Ser.: 4). (ENG.). 216p. (J). 16.95 *(978-1-944762-25-4(6)*, 9781944762254) Islandport Pr., Inc.

—Mystery on Pine Lake: A Cooper & Packrat Mystery, 1 vol. Wight, Tamra. 2015. (Cooper & Packrat Ser.: 1). (ENG.). 152p. (J). pap. 12.95 *(978-1-939017-02-4(5)*, 9781939017024) Islandport Pr., Inc.

—Our Principal Promised to Kiss a Pig. Dakos, Kalli & DesMarteau, Alicia. (ENG.). 32p. (J). 2017. (gr. -1-3). pap. 7.99 *(978-0-8075-6635-0(7)*, 807566357); 2004. (gr. 2-5). 16.99 *(978-0-8075-6629-9(2))* Whitman, Albert & Co.

Dirr, Karen. The Back Pain Book: A Self-Help Guide for the Daily Relief of Back & Neck Pain, 1 vol. Hage, Mike. 2nd rev. ed. 2005. (ENG.). 256p. pap. 16.95 *(978-1-56145-342-9(0))* Peachtree Publishing Co. Inc.

DiRubbio, Jennifer. Around One Log: Chipmunks, Spiders, & Creepy Insiders, 1 vol. Fredericks, Anthony D. 2011. (ENG.). 32p. (J). (gr. -1-5). 16.95 *(978-1-58469-137-2(9))* Dawn Pubns.

—Around One Log: Chipmunks, Spiders, & Creepy Insiders. Fredericks, Anthony D. 2004. (ENG.). 32p. (J). (gr. -1-4). pap. 8.95 *(978-1-58469-138-9(7)*, Dawn Pubns.) Sourcebooks, Inc.

—Going Home: The Mystery of Animal Migration. Berkes, Marianne. 2010. (ENG.). 32p. (J). (gr. -1-4). pap. 8.95 *(978-1-58469-127-3(1))*; (gr. k-4). 16.95 *(978-1-58469-126-6(3))* Sourcebooks, Inc. (Dawn Pubns.).

—In One Tidepool: Crabs, Snails, & Salty Tails. Fredericks, Anthony D. 2004. (Sharing Nature with Children Book Ser.). 32p. (J). (gr. -1-2). 16.95 *(978-1-58469-039-9(9))* Dawn Pubns.

—Nature Did It First: Engineering Through Biomimicry, 1 vol. Ansberry, karen. 2020. 32p. (J). (gr. k-5). 16.95 *(978-1-58469-657-5(5))*; pap. 8.95 *(978-1-58469-658-2(3))* Sourcebooks, Inc. (Dawn Pubns.).

—Near One Cattail: Turtles, Logs, & Leaping Frogs. Fredericks, Anthony D. 2005. (ENG.). 32p. (J). (-4). 16.95 *(978-1-58469-070-2(4))*; pap. 8.95 *(978-1-58469-071-9(2))* Sourcebooks, Inc. (Dawn Pubns.).

—On One Flower: Butterflies, Ticks & a Few More Icks, 1 vol. Fredericks, Anthony D. 2006. (ENG.). 32p. (J). (gr. -1-4). 8.95 *(978-1-58469-087-0(9))*; 16.95 *(978-1-58469-086-3(0))* Sourcebooks, Inc. (Dawn Pubns.).

—Under One Rock: Bugs, Slugs, & Other Ughs. Fredericks, Anthony D. 2004. (Sharing Nature with Children Book Ser.). 32p. (J). 16.95 *(978-1-58469-028-3(3))* Dawn Pubns.

DiRubbio, Jennifer. Around One Cactus: Owls, Bats, & Leaping Rats. DiRubbio, Jennifer, tr. Fredericks, Anthony D. (Sharing Nature with Children Book Ser.). 32p. (J). 2004. pap. 7.95 *(978-1-58469-052-8(6))*; 2003. (ENG.). 24.94 *(978-1-58469-051-1(8))* Dawn Pubns.

DiSalvo, Len. Lima Bear's Halloween. Weck, Peter. 2012. (Lima Bear Stories Ser.). 40p. (J). 15.95 *(978-1-933872-16-2(0))* Lima Bear Pr LLC, The.

DiSalvo-Ryan, DyAnne. City Green. DiSalvo-Ryan, DyAnne. 2019. (ENG.). 32p. (J). (gr. -1-3). pap. 7.99 *(978-0-06-290614-4(3))* HarperCollins Pubs.

Disbury, Tom. Junk: A Spectacular Tale of Trash. Day, Nicholas & Nicholas Best Staff. 2018. (ENG.). 32p. (J). (gr. k-3). 16.99 *(978-1-58536-400-8(2)*, 204586) Sleeping Bear Pr.

—Knight Owls: Ready-To-Read Pre-Level 1. Seltzer, Eric. 2019. (Ready-To-Reads Ser.). (ENG.). 32p. (J). (gr. -1-k). 17.99 *(978-1-5344-4881-0(0))*; pap. 4.99 *(978-1-5344-4880-3(2))* Simon Spotlight. (Simon Spotlight).

—Party Pigs! Seltzer, Eric. 2019. (Ready-To-Reads Ser.). (ENG.). 32p. (J). (gr. -1-k). 17.99 *(978-1-5344-2879-9(8))*; pap. 4.99 *(978-1-5344-2878-2(X))* Simon Spotlight. (Simon Spotlight).

—Sea Sheep. Seltzer, Eric. 2020. (Ready-To-Reads Ser.). (ENG.). 32p. (J). (gr. -1-k). 17.99 *(978-1-5344-6134-5(5))*; pap. 4.99 *(978-1-5344-6133-8(7))* Simon Spotlight. (Simon Spotlight).

—Space Cows. Seltzer, Eric. 2018. (Ready-To-Reads Ser.). (ENG.). 32p. (J). (gr. -1-k). 17.99 *(978-1-5344-2876-8(3))*; pap. 4.99 *(978-1-5344-2875-1(5))* Simon Spotlight. (Simon Spotlight).

Dishaw, Karen. Cereal for Breakfast Cereal for Lunch. Cooperman, Ben. 2013. 42p. pap. *(978-0-9919356-0-4(8))* Teacherben Publishing.

—Era Chimera. Perrine, Jared. 2018. (ENG.). 36p. (J). pap. 9.99 *(978-0-9985067-0-8(2))* Overhead Pr., LLC.

DiSilvio, Rich. Danny & the Dreamweaver. Poe, Mark. 2016. (ENG.). 98p. (YA). (gr. 7-12). pap. 6.75 *(978-0-9976807-3-7(3)*, DV Bks.) Digital Vista, Inc.

DiSilvio, Rich. Meet My Famous Friends. DiSilvio, Rich. 2016. (ENG.). (YA). (gr. 5-12). 28.99 *(978-0-9976807-5-1(X))*; 34p. pap. 14.99 *(978-0-9976807-6-8(8))* Digital Vista, Inc. (DV Bks.).

Disney. Disney Alice in Wonderland: the Story of the Movie in Comics. Disney. 2020. (ENG.). 48p. (J). (gr. 3-7). 10.99 ***(978-1-5067-1735-7(7)***, Dark Horse Books) Dark Horse Comics.

—Disney Lady & the Tramp: the Story of the Movie in Comics. Disney. 2020. (ENG.). 48p. (J). (gr. 3-7). 10.99 ***(978-1-5067-1734-0(9)***, Dark Horse Books) Dark Horse Comics.

Disney Book Group. Art of Coloring: Mickey & Minnie: 100 Images to Inspire Creativity. Disney Book Group. 2017. (Art of Coloring Ser.). 128p. pap. 15.99 *(978-1-4847-8973-5(3)*, Disney Editions) Disney Pr.

—Beauty & the Beast: The Enchantment. Disney Book Group. Geron, Eric. 2017. (ENG.). 24p. (J). (gr. -1-k). pap. 5.99 *(978-1-4847-8283-5(6))* Disney Pr.

—Beauty & the Beast, Level 2: Something More. Disney Book Group. Geron, Eric. 2017. (World of Reading Ser.). (ENG.). 32p. (J). (gr. -1-3). pap. 4.99 *(978-1-4847-8284-2(4))* Disney Pr.

—Disney Emoji: Questions & Quizzes to Disney-Fy Your World! Disney Book Group. 2017. (ENG.). 112p. (J). (gr. 7-9). pap. 9.99 *(978-1-368-01354-3(6))* Disney Pr.

Disney Book Group & Brown, Adrienne. Walt Disney: Drawn from Imagination. Scollon, Bill. 2018. (ENG.). 144p. (J). (gr. 3-7). pap. 7.99 *(978-1-368-02757-1(1))* Disney Pr.

Disney Book Group, jt. illus. see Cook, Katie.

Disney Books. Disney Bunnies an Eggcellent Day. Disney Books. 2017. (ENG.). 12p. (J). (gr. -1-k). bds. 7.99 *(978-1-4847-7369-7(1))* Disney Pr.

Disney Storybook Art Team. Aladdin Read-Along Storybook & CD. Disney Book Group. 2019. (Read-Along Storybook & CD Ser.). (ENG.). 32p. (J). (gr. -1-k). pap. 6.99 *(978-1-368-04155-3(8))* Disney Pr.

Disney Storybook Art Team. Ariel's Voice / la Voz de Ariel (English-Spanish) (Disney the Little Mermaid) (Level up! Readers) Collado Píriz, Laura, tr. 2020. (Disney Bilingual Ser.: 36). (ENG.). 32p. (J). (gr. k-3). pap. 3.99 ***(978-1-4998-0879-7(8))***; 16.99 ***(978-1-4998-0880-3(1))*** Little Bee Books Inc. (BuzzPop).

Disney Storybook Art Team. Artemis Fowl: Genius at Work: Codes, Activities, Puzzles, & More. Disney Books. 2020. (ENG.). 32p. (J). (gr. k-3). pap. 6.99 *(978-1-368-05238-2(X))* Disney Pr.

—The Beast Within: A Tale of Beauty's Prince. Valentino, Serena. 2014. (Villains Ser.). (ENG.). 224p. (YA). (gr. 7-17). 16.99 *(978-1-4231-5912-4(8))* Disney Pr.

—Beauty & the Beast Read-Along Storybook & CD. Disney Book Group. 2017. (Read-Along Storybook & CD Ser.). (ENG.). 32p. (J). (gr. 1-3). pap. 6.99 *(978-1-4847-7606-3(2))* Disney Pr.

—Beauty & the Beast: the Story of Belle. Disney Book Group. 2016. (ENG.). 112p. (J). (gr. -1-k). 12.99 *(978-1-4847-6720-7(9))* Disney Pr.

Disney Storybook Art Team. Bedtime Favorites. Disney Books. 2020. (Storybook Collection). (ENG.). 304p. (J). (gr. -1-k). 17.99 ***(978-1-368-04483-7(2))*** Disney Pr.

Disney Storybook Art Team. Bedtime Storybook Library. 2017. (ENG.). 144p. (J). (gr. 1-3). 12.99 *(978-1-368-01067-2(9))* Disney Pr.

—Belle's Winter Adventure (Disney Princess) Richards, Kitty. 2017. (ENG.). 22p. (J). (— 1). bds. 6.99 *(978-0-7364-3697-7(9)*, RH/Disney) Random Hse. Children's Bks.

—Boo to You, Winnie the Pooh. Disney Book Group. 2019. (ENG.). 18p. (J). (gr. -1-k). bds. 6.99 *(978-1-368-04358-8(5))* Disney Pr.

—Buddies Collection. Disney Book Group. 2018. (ENG.). 240p. (J). (gr. 1-3). 10.99 *(978-1-368-02711-3(3))* Disney Pr.

—C Is for Christmas. Disney Book Group. 2019. (ENG.). 26p. (J). (gr. -1-k). bds. 12.99 *(978-1-368-03891-1(3))* Disney Pr.

—Cars 3 Read-Along Storybook & CD. Disney Books. 2017. (Read-Along Storybook & CD Ser.). (ENG.). 32p. (J). (gr. 1-3). pap. 6.99 *(978-1-4847-8134-0(1))* Disney Pr.

—Catch That Fish! / ¡Atrapa Ese Pez! (English-Spanish) (Disney Junior: Mickey & the Roadster Racers) Collado Píriz, Laura, tr. 2018. (Disney Bilingual Ser.: 11). (ENG.). 24p. (J). (gr. -1-2). pap. 4.99 *(978-1-4998-0797-4(X)*, BuzzPop) Little Bee Books Inc.

—Cinderella Read-Along Storybook & CD. Disney Book Group. 2nd ed. 2012. (Read-Along Storybook & CD Ser.). (ENG.). 32p. (J). (gr. 1-3). pap. 6.99 *(978-1-4231-6321-3(4))* Disney Pr.

—Descendants 2 Evie's Fashion Book. Disney Book Group. 2017. (ENG.). 144p. (J). (gr. 3-7). 12.99 *(978-1-368-00251-6(X))* Disney Pr.

—Descendants 2: Mal's Spell Book 2: More Wicked Magic, Bk. 2. Disney Book Group. 2017. (ENG.). 192p. (J). (gr. 3-7). 12.99 *(978-1-368-00041-3(X))* Disney Pr.

—Descendants 2: Uma's Wicked Book: For Villain Kids. Disney Book Group. 2018. (ENG.). 192p. (J). (gr. 3-7). 12.99 *(978-1-368-02432-7(7))* Disney Pr.

—Descendants: Mal's Diary. Disney Book Group. 2015. (ENG.). 192p. (J). (gr. 3-7). 9.99 *(978-1-4847-2685-3(5))* Disney Pr.

—Descendants: Mal's Spell Book. Disney Book Group. 2015. (ENG.). 192p. (J). (gr. 3-7). 11.99 *(978-1-4847-2638-9(3))* Disney Pr.

—Disney. 2019. (ENG.). 96p. (J). pap., pap. *(978-1-5037-4910-8(X)*, dd478962-5144-4b84-96cb-ad832da89a3c, p i kids) Phoenix International Publications, Inc.

Disney Storybook Art Team. Disney. 2020. (ENG.). 64p. (J). pap., pap. ***(978-1-5037-5284-9(4)***, 3cb280aa-2521-4b89-83f1-449184126217, p i kids) Phoenix International Publications, Inc.

Disney Storybook Art Team. Disney: 8-Book Set. Broderick, Kathy & Beck, Riley. 2019. (ENG.). 192p. (J). *(978-1-5037-4988-7(6)*, d94bc8db-3b9c-4599-8d79-5693fc1c73ae, p i kids) Phoenix International Publications, Inc.

—Disney 5-Minute Christmas Stories. Disney Books. 2016. (5-Minute Stories Ser.). (ENG.). 192p. (J). (gr. 1-3). 12.99 *(978-1-4847-2741-6(X))* Disney Pr.

—Disney 5-Minute Fairy Tales. Disney Book Group. 2013. (5-Minute Stories Ser.). (ENG.). 192p. (J). (gr. -1 — 1). 12.99 *(978-1-4231-6766-2(X))* Disney Pr.

—Disney Aladdin: Movie Storybook / Libro Basado en la Película (English-Spanish) Collado Píriz, Laura, tr. 2019. (Disney Bilingual Ser.: 19). (ENG.). 24p. (J). (gr. -1-2). pap. 4.99 *(978-1-4998-0943-5(3)*, BuzzPop) Little Bee Books Inc.

—Disney Animals Dot-To-Dot: Connect Hundreds of Dots on Every Page! Disney Book Group. 2018. (Dot-To-Dot Book Ser.). (ENG.). 128p. (YA). (gr. 7-12). pap. 14.99 *(978-1-368-01924-8(2)*, Disney Editions) Disney Pr.

—Disney Animals Storybook Collection. Disney Books. 2019. (Storybook Collection). (ENG.). 304p. (J). (gr. 1-3). 16.99 *(978-1-368-04198-0(1))* Disney Pr.

—Disney Baby. Brooke, Susan Rich. 2019. (ENG.). 120p. (J). bds., bds. *(978-1-5037-4646-6(1)*, fccf855b-5fbf-4c29-b322-643df10cd7fa, p i kids) Phoenix International Publications, Inc.

—Disney Baby: Day & Night. Wage, Erin Rose. 2019. (Take-A-Look Ser.). (ENG.). 20p. (J). *(978-1-5037-4674-9(7)*, 9fd9b765-de4f-4719-af46-cdb9b3ece77d, p i kids) Phoenix International Publications, Inc.

—Disney Baby: First Look & Find Book & Giant Puzzle. Broderick, Kathy. 2019. (Look & Find Ser.). (ENG.). 16p. (J). *(978-1-5037-4633-6(X)*, 25aac9bf-4399-4044-9bda-f6e94bf9fd21, p i kids) Phoenix International Publications, Inc.

—Disney Baby: First Look & Find Book Giant Activity Card Set. Broderick, Kathy. 2018. (Look & Find Ser.). (ENG.). 18p. (J). *(978-1-5037-3503-3(6)*, 86375f2e-30b2-41ca-b901-a87019301347, p i kids) Phoenix International Publications, Inc.

—Disney Baby: Hide & Seek Animals. Skwish, Emily. 2019. (Look & Find Ser.). (ENG.). 16p. (J). *(978-1-5037-3704-4(7)*, d39016a7-c0da-4eb0-a11b-afb92b2bb3db, p i kids) Phoenix International Publications, Inc.

—Disney Baby: Jingle Bells Sing-Along. Skwish, Emily. 2019. (Play-A-Song Ser.). (ENG.). 14p. (J). bds. *(978-1-5037-3681-8(4)*, a4cc2de4-c20a-497e-b3c7-ab82078aa39f, p i kids) Phoenix International Publications, Inc.

—Disney Baby: Let's Learn Together. Winslow, Claire. 2020. (Play-A-Sound Ser.). (ENG.). 20p. (J). spiral bd. *(978-1-5037-4596-4(1)*, a28dce37-d071-4943-899a-c3ea64c6e6c0, p i kids) Phoenix International Publications, Inc.

—Disney Baby: Peek-A-Boo. Broderick, Kathy. 2020. (Look & Find Ser.). (ENG.). 14p. (J). *(978-1-5037-5265-8(8)*, 42238c2b-2aa2-4663-8711-ac0fd9aa2f43, p i kids) Phoenix International Publications, Inc.

—Disney Baby: Read & Play with My Disney Friends! p i kids. 2018. (ENG.). 104p. (J). *(978-1-5037-3977-2(5)*, a58831a1-5136-496f-87ac-b1701fc990c0, p i kids) Phoenix International Publications, Inc.

—Disney Baby 100 First Words Lift-The-Flap. Disney Book Group. 2018. (ENG.). 12p. (J). (gr. -1 — 1). bds. 10.99 *(978-1-4847-1801-8(1))* Disney Pr.

Disney Storybook Art Team. Disney Baby: ABCs: Little First Look & Find Book & Puzzle. PI Kids. 2020. (Look & Find Ser.). (ENG.). 16p. (J). bds., bds. ***(978-1-5037-5588-8(6),*** 2c6c056a-f2a1-4abd-ac1f-969d1267d28f, p i kids) Phoenix International Publications, Inc.

Disney Storybook Art Team. Disney Baby Baby Animals. Disney Book Group. 2019. (ENG.). 24p. (J). (gr. -1 — 1). bds. 7.99 *(978-1-368-04267-3(8))* Disney Pr.

—Disney Baby First Colors, Shapes, Numbers. Disney Book Group. 2018. (ENG.). 24p. (J). (gr. -1 — 1). bds. 7.99 *(978-1-368-03702-0(X))* Disney Pr.

—Disney Baby Good Night, Farm. Disney Books. 2020. (ENG.). 10p. (J). (gr. -1 — 1). bds. 8.99 *(978-1-368-05001-2(8))* Disney Pr.

—Disney Baby I Love You This Much! Disney Book Group. 2016. (ENG.). 24p. (J). (gr. -1 — 1). bds. 6.99 *(978-1-4847-7823-4(5))* Disney Pr.

—Disney Baby Look at Me! Disney Book Group. 2016. (ENG.). 12p. (J). (gr. -1 — 1). bds. 8.99 *(978-1-4847-1915-2(8))* Disney Pr.

—Disney Baby: My 123s. Disney Books. 2020. (ENG.). 14p. (J). (gr. -1 — 1). bds. 9.99 *(978-1-368-05268-9(1))* Disney Pr.

—Disney Baby My ABCs. Disney Books. 2018. (ENG.). 14p. (J). (gr. -1 — 1). bds. 9.99 *(978-1-368-01397-0(X))* Disney Pr.

—Disney Baby My First Christmas. Disney Book Group. 2017. (ENG.). 12p. (J). (gr. -1 — 1). bds. 8.99 *(978-1-368-00725-2(2))* Disney Pr.

—Disney Baby My First Colors. Disney Book Group. 2016. (ENG.). 10p. (J). (gr. -1 — 1). bds. 6.99 *(978-1-4847-2943-4(9))* Disney Pr.

—Disney Baby My First Easter. Disney Book Group. 2018. (ENG.). 12p. (J). (gr. -1 — 1). bds. 8.99 *(978-1-368-01116-7(0))* Disney Pr.

—Disney Baby My First Halloween. Disney Book Group. 2017. (ENG.). 12p. (J). (gr. -1 — 1). bds. 8.99 *(978-1-4847-9936-9(4))* Disney Pr.

—Disney Baby My First Valentine's Day. Disney Book Group. 2019. (ENG.). 12p. (J). (gr. -1 — 1). bds. 8.99 *(978-1-368-04216-1(3))* Disney Pr.

—Disney Baby My First Words. Disney Books. 2016. (ENG.). 24p. (J). (gr. -1 — 1). bds. 7.99 *(978-1-4847-5261-6(9))* Disney Pr.

—Disney Baby My First Year: Record & Share Baby's Firsts. Disney Books. 2016. (ENG.). 20p. (J). (gr. -1 — 1). 12.99 *(978-1-4847-4367-6(9))* Disney Pr.

—Disney Baby My Little Lullabies Read-Along Storybook & CD. Disney Book Group. 2019. (Read-Along Storybook & CD Ser.). (ENG.). 32p. (J). (gr. -1 — 1). bds. 10.99 *(978-1-368-02373-3(8))* Disney Pr.

—Disney Baby on the Farm. Disney Books. 2017. (ENG.). 12p. (J). (gr. -1-k). bds. 8.99 *(978-1-4847-8248-4(8))* Disney Pr.

—Disney Baby One, Two, Winnie the Pooh. Disney Book Group. 2018. (ENG.). 10p. (J). (gr. -1 — 1). bds. 8.99 *(978-1-368-02372-6(X))* Disney Pr.

—Disney Baby Peek-A-boo Winnie the Pooh. Disney Book Group. 2016. (ENG.). 10p. (J). (gr. -1 — 1). bds. 8.99 *(978-1-4847-7824-1(3))* Disney Pr.

Disney Storybook Art Team. Disney Baby Say Good Night. Disney Books. 2020. (Touch-And-feel Book Ser.). (ENG.). 10p. (J). (gr. -1 — 1). bds. 8.99 ***(978-1-368-05501-7(X))*** Disney Pr.

Disney Storybook Art Team. Disney Baby Shapes All Around. Disney Book Group. 2017. (ENG.). 18p. (J). (gr. -1 — 1). bds. 8.99 *(978-1-368-00079-6(7))* Disney Pr.

—Disney Baby Things That Go. Disney Book Group. 2019. (ENG.). 10p. (J). (gr. -1 — 1). bds. 8.99 *(978-1-368-03704-4(6))* Disney Pr.

—Disney Bunnies All Ears. Glass, Calliope. 2016. (ENG.). 12p. (J). (gr. -1 — 1). bds. 7.99 *(978-1-4847-2210-7(8))* Disney Pr.

—Disney Bunnies Goodnight, Thumper! Disney Books. 2020. (ENG.). 14p. (J). (gr. -1-k). bds. 6.99 *(978-1-368-02334-4(7))* Disney Pr.

—Disney Bunnies I Love You, My Bunnies Reissue with Stickers. Disney Books. 2017. (ENG.). 24p. (J). (gr. -1-k). pap. 4.99 *(978-1-4847-7370-3(5))* Disney Pr.

—Disney Bunnies Thumper & the Noisy Ducky. Driscoll, Laura. 2014. (ENG.). 12p. (J). (gr. -1 — 1). bds. 6.99 *(978-1-4231-8487-4(4))* Disney Pr.

—Disney Bunnies Thumper Finds a Friend. Disney Books. 2010. (ENG.). 32p. (J). (gr. -1-k). pap. 3.99 *(978-1-4231-2313-2(1))* Disney Pr.

—Disney Bunnies Thumper's Furry Friends. Disney Books. 2010. (Touch-And-feel Book Ser.). (ENG.). 12p. (J). (gr. -1-k). bds. 6.99 *(978-1-4231-1840-4(5))* Disney Pr.

—Disney Bunnies Thumper's Hoppy Home: A Lift-The-Flap Board Book. Disney Books. 2018. (ENG.). 10p. (J). (gr. -1-k). bds. 8.99 *(978-1-4847-7371-0(3))* Disney Pr.

—Disney Christmas Storybook Collection. Glass, Calliope & Risco, Elle D. 2014. (Storybook Collection). (ENG.). 304p. (J). (gr. -1-k). 16.99 *(978-1-4231-8450-8(5))* Disney Pr.

—Disney Classics Storybook Treasury. Disney Book Group. 2016. (Storybook Treasury Ser.). (ENG.). 256p. (J). (gr. 1-3). 30.00 *(978-1-4847-8960-5(1))* Disney Pr.

—Disney First Tales Disney Frozen Do You Want a Hug? Disney Book Group. 2016. (ENG.). 64p. (J). (gr. 1-3). 10.99 *(978-1-4847-8775-5(7))* Disney Pr.

Disney Storybook Art Team. Disney Frozen. 2020. (ENG.). 64p. (J). pap., pap. ***(978-1-5037-5283-2(6),*** befb929f-b0c0-44ed-b513-a7079fd1ad12, p i kids) Phoenix International Publications, Inc.

Disney Storybook Art Team. Disney Frozen: Sing-Along Songs. 2019. (Play-A-Song Ser.). (ENG.). 12p. (J). *(978-1-5037-4726-5(3),* 3c19904c-76e3-4804-a4a7-e0c7c17e95db, p i kids) Phoenix International Publications, Inc.

—Disney Frozen 2. 2019. (Play-A-Sound Ser.). (ENG.). 12p. (J). *(978-1-5037-4765-4(4),* b0c2558f-6276-46b2-8df6-db4d66dc1e71, p i kids) Phoenix International Publications, Inc.

—Disney Frozen 2. Skwish, Emily. 2019. (Play-A-Sound Ser.). (ENG.). 24p. (J). *(978-1-5037-4602-2(X),* 934ce587-859e-4eed-a9d5-7072b37d7c73, p i kids) Phoenix International Publications, Inc.

—Disney Frozen 2. 2019. (Play-A-Sound Ser.). (ENG.). 12p. (J). *(978-1-5037-4727-2(1),* 856a6a27-be5b-4e8a-8a51-bf2354bb470f, p i kids) Phoenix International Publications, Inc.

Disney Storybook Art Team. Disney Frozen 2: Olaf & Friends. PI Kids. 2020. (ENG.). 24p. (J). ***(978-1-5037-5471-3(5),*** 625d8f3a-c8a8-440f-8556-15e3227ae5ff, p i kids) Phoenix International Publications, Inc.

—Disney Frozen 2: Enchanted Journey. 2020. (Play-A-Sound Ser.). (ENG.). 12p. (J). bds. ***(978-1-5037-5721-9(8),*** 118afaaf-0c7b-4886-ade9-b0521465ab7b, p i kids) Phoenix International Publications, Inc.

Disney Storybook Art Team. Disney Frozen 2: Movie Storybook / Libro Basado en la Película (English-Spanish) Collado Píriz, Laura, tr. 2019. (Disney Bilingual Ser.: 30). (ENG.). 24p. (J). (gr. -1-2). pap. 4.99 *(978-1-4998-0953-4(0),* BuzzPop) Little Bee Books Inc.

—Disney Frozen: Movie Storybook / Libro Basado en la Película (English-Spanish) Ortiz, Elvira, tr. 2018. (Disney Bilingual Ser.: 6). (ENG.). 24p. (J). (gr. -1-2). pap. 4.99 *(978-1-4998-0786-8(4),* BuzzPop) Little Bee Books Inc.

—Disney Frozen Storybook Collection. Disney Book Group. 2019. (Storybook Collection). (ENG.). 304p. (J). (gr. k-3). 16.99 *(978-1-368-05177-4(4))* Disney Pr.

—Disney High School Musical 3 Making Memories, No. 1. Nathan, Sarah & Disney Book Group. 2009. (High School Musical 3: Senior Year Ser.). (ENG.). 24p. (J). (gr. 3-6). pap. 16.19 *(978-1-4231-1204-4(0))* Disney Pr.

—Disney It's a Small World Furry Friends. Disney Book Group. 2011. (Touch-And-feel Book Ser.). (ENG.). 16p. (J). (gr. -1-k). bds. 7.99 *(978-1-4231-4183-9(0))* Disney Pr.

—Disney It's a Small World Guess Who! Disney Book Group. 2012. (ENG.). 14p. (J). (gr. -1-k). bds. 6.99 *(978-1-4231-6008-3(8))* Disney Pr.

—Disney It's a Small World Hello, World! Disney Books. 2011. (ENG.). 14p. (J). (gr. -1-k). bds. 6.99 *(978-1-4231-4140-2(7))* Disney Pr.

—Disney Junior: Sing with Me. Keast, Jennifer H. & Brooke, Susan Rich. 2015. (Sing with Me Ser.). (ENG.). 192p. (J). *(978-1-5037-0003-1(8),* f126dc3f-d064-4b9d-9228-dc9a2b0960af, p i kids) Phoenix International Publications, Inc.

—Disney Junior Fancy Nancy. Winslow, Claire. 2019. (ENG.). 120p. (J). *(978-1-5037-4644-2(5),* 7b9d3020-2738-4996-994a-4f6171279a50, p i kids) Phoenix International Publications, Inc.

Disney Storybook Art Team. Disney Junior Mickey Christmas Tales. Disney Books. 2020. (ENG.). 72p. (J). (gr. -1-k). pap. 9.99 ***(978-1-368-06539-9(2))*** Disney Pr.

Disney Storybook Art Team. Disney Junior Mickey Top o' the Clubhouse. Disney Book Group. 2019. (ENG.). 24p. (J). (gr. -1-k). pap. 4.99 *(978-1-368-05764-6(0))* Disney Pr.

—Disney Junior Minnie. Brooke, Susan Rich & Skwish, Emily. 2020. (Me Reader Jr Ser.). (ENG.). 80p. (J). bds., bds. *(978-1-5037-5254-2(2),* a6611284-f8a8-4368-8daa-6b73f9a09840, p i kids) Phoenix International Publications, Inc.

—Disney Junior Minnie: Best Friends. Keast, Jennifer H. 2019. (Play-A-Sound Ser.). (ENG.). 10p. (J). bds., bds. *(978-1-5037-4872-9(3),* 9e526e10-511e-41c0-99ae-48f98e1d28f7, p i kids) Phoenix International Publications, Inc.

—Disney Junior Minnie: I'm Ready to Read: Minnie. Tawa, Renee. 2019. (Play-A-Sound Ser.). (ENG.). 24p. (J). *(978-1-5037-4698-5(4),* b6cdd26e-eabc-4efa-bdde-6cc94cfaa806, p i kids) Phoenix International Publications, Inc.

Disney Storybook Art Team. Disney Junior Puppy Dog Pals: Happy Howl-Oween! PI Kids. 2020. (Play-A-Sound Ser.). (ENG.). 12p. (J). bds. ***(978-1-5037-5289-4(5),*** 08682a1e-117f-4e96-a653-da2ea4e115c8, p i kids) Phoenix International Publications, Inc.

—Disney Junior Puppy Dog Pals: The Purr-Fect Toy. PI Kids. 2020. (Play-A-Sound Ser.). (ENG.). 12p. (J). bds. ***(978-1-5037-5214-6(3),*** e6074af5-8a69-4dc4-9cde-999e25412bdc, p i kids) Phoenix International Publications, Inc.

Disney Storybook Art Team. Disney Junior Storybook Collection. Disney Book Group. 2014. (Storybook Collection). (ENG.). 304p. (J). (gr. -1-k). 16.99 *(978-1-4231-7875-0(0))* Disney Pr.

—Disney Mickey & Friends: Let's Go. Harmening, Derek. 2019. (Play-A-Sound Ser.). (ENG.). 10p. (J). bds., bds. *(978-1-5037-4873-6(1),* 258510e9-bcb5-4796-b109-3997e179ff61, p i kids) Phoenix International Publications, Inc.

—Disney Mickey & Friends: Let's Go Camping. Harmening, Derek. 2018. (Play-A-Sound Ser.). (ENG.). 10p. (J). *(978-1-5037-4028-0(5),* 5c228b62-c979-4cdb-a0ee-3ab581ab1835, p i kids) Phoenix International Publications, Inc.

Disney Storybook Art Team, et al. Disney Mickey & Friends: Read & Play with Mickey & Minnie. p i kids. 2018. (ENG.). 104p. (J). *(978-1-5037-3985-7(6),* b6a2f7c3-5d53-4bbc-9a2f-a17527bfdb8f, p i kids) Phoenix International Publications, Inc.

Disney Storybook Art Team. Disney Mickey & Friends: Let's Go Camping! 2020. (Play-A-Sound Ser.). (ENG.). 12p. (J). bds. ***(978-1-5037-5720-2(X),*** bff64bbb-bcbf-44f4-8969-a0cf1941a546, p i kids) Phoenix International Publications, Inc.

Disney Storybook Art Team. Disney Mickey Mouse: the Scariest Halloween Story Ever! Read-Along Storybook & CD. Disney Book Group. 2018. (Read-Along Storybook & CD Ser.). (ENG.). 32p. (J). (gr. 1-3). pap. 6.99 *(978-1-368-02052-7(6))* Disney Pr.

—Disney Minnie: My Friend Minnie! Skwish, Emily. 2019. (ENG.). 120p. (J). *(978-1-5037-4362-5(4),* d1f8f7e4-ce5d-4d08-a6d4-10353e0a6622, p i kids) Phoenix International Publications, Inc.

—Disney Mulan: Movie Storybook / Diàn Yǐng Tóng Huà Gù Shi (English-Mandarin) Wang, Tom, tr. 2019. (Disney Bilingual Ser.: 31). (ENG.). 24p. (J). (gr. -1-2). pap. 4.99 *(978-1-4998-0951-0(4),* BuzzPop) Little Bee Books Inc.

—Disney Mulan: Movie Storybook / Libro Basado en la Película (English-Spanish) Collado Píriz, Laura, tr. 2019. (Disney Bilingual Ser.: 32). (ENG.). 24p. (J). (gr. -1-2). pap. 4.99 *(978-1-4998-0952-7(2),* BuzzPop) Little Bee Books Inc.

—Disney: My First Smart Pad Library: Interactive Activity Pad & 8-Book Set. Broderick, Kathy & Beck, Riley. 2019. (Play-A-Sound Ser.). (ENG.). 192p. (J). *(978-1-5037-4065-5(X),* d3b64a3d-d53d-4fd9-b12f-77e718aa4a1a, p i kids) Phoenix International Publications, Inc.

—Disney Nursery Rhymes Read-Along Storybook & CD. Disney Book Group. 2011. (Read-Along Storybook & CD Ser.). (ENG.). 32p. (J). (gr. -1-k). 10.99 *(978-1-4231-3743-6(4))* Disney Pr.

—Disney Pixar. Beck, Riley. 2019. (ENG.). 120p. (J). *(978-1-5037-4361-8(6),* 9485dba9-5fd2-4b08-ba9e-c7bec2c7117d, p i kids) Phoenix International Publications, Inc.

—Disney Princess: Princess Sing-Along. Keast, Jennifer H. 2014. (Play-A-Song Ser.). (ENG.). 12p. (J). bds. *(978-1-4508-7605-6(6),* 2c2589dc-a7f1-4e7a-b761-45ce8ab71efa, p i kids) Phoenix International Publications, Inc.

—Disney Princess: Princess Songs Around the World. Skwish, Emily. 2019. (Play-A-Song Ser.). (ENG.). 12p. (J). *(978-1-5037-4600-8(3),* c4f37c14-d197-4f5a-823c-8745072457c0, p i kids) Phoenix International Publications, Inc.

Disney Storybook Art Team. Disney Princess: Starlight Dreams. PI Kids. 2020. (Play-A-Song Ser.). (ENG.). 12p. (J). bds. ***(978-1-5037-5191-0(0),*** 3ae28a34-9cfc-485b-9cc3-0d927964525f, p i kids) Phoenix International Publications, Inc.

—Disney Princess: Talking Quiz Book. PI Kids. 2020. (Play-A-Sound Ser.). (ENG.). 96p. (J). ***(978-1-5037-5320-4(4),*** caf1f3e6-98ed-45f0-9103-da5913b8045f, p i kids) Phoenix International Publications, Inc.

Disney Storybook Art Team. Disney Princess 5-Minute Princess Stories. Disney Books. 2019. (5-Minute Stories Ser.). (ENG.). 192p. (J). (gr. 1-3). 12.99 *(978-1-4847-1641-0(8))* Disney Pr.

—The Disney Princess Cookbook. Disney Book Group. 2013. (ENG.). 144p. (J). (gr. 1-3). 15.99 *(978-1-4231-6324-4(9))* Disney Pr.

—Disney Princess Jasmine: the Jewel Orchard. Disney Book Group & O'Ryan, Ellie. 2013. (Disney Princess Chapters Ser.). (ENG.). 96p. (J). (gr. 2-4). pap. 17.44 *(978-1-4231-6978-9(6))* Disney Pr.

—Disney Princess Magical Tales Read-Along Storybook & CD Collection. Disney Books. 2019. (Read-Along Storybook & CD Ser.). (ENG.). 96p. (J). (gr. -1-k). pap. 9.99 *(978-1-368-02809-7(8))* Disney Pr.

—Disney Princess Me Reader Electronic Reader & 8-Book Library. Publications International Ltd. Staff, ed. 2013. (Me Reader Ser.). (ENG.). 192p. (J). (gr. k-4). *(978-1-4508-6873-0(8),* 88cfbb37-84fd-4e47-841b-46035288bb22) Phoenix International Publications, Inc.

—Disney Princess My First Bedtime Storybook. Disney Books. 2019. (My First Bedtime Storybook Ser.). (ENG.). 72p. (J). (gr. -1-k). 10.99 *(978-1-368-03915-4(4))* Disney Pr.

—Disney Princess P Is for Princess. Auerbach, Annie & Disney Books. 2013. (ENG.). 26p. (J). (gr. -1-k). bds. 12.99 *(978-1-4231-6471-5(7))* Disney Pr.

—Disney Princess Read-Along Storybook & CD Boxed Set. Disney Book Group. 2017. (Read-Along Storybook & CD Ser.). (ENG.). 128p. (J). (gr. 1-3). pap. 12.99 *(978-1-368-00262-2(5))* Disney Pr.

—Disney Princess Storybook Collection (4th Edition) Disney Book Group. 2015. (Storybook Collection). (ENG.). 304p. (J). (gr. -1-k). 16.99 *(978-1-4847-1283-2(8),* 1394934) Disney Pr.

—Disney Princess Storybook Treasury. Disney Book Group. 2016. (Storybook Treasury Ser.). (ENG.). 256p. (J). (gr. 1-3). 30.00 *(978-1-4847-8959-9(8))* Disney Pr.

—Disney Princess the Little Book of Big Ideas. Disney Book Group. 2019. (ENG.). 72p. (J). (gr. -1-k). bds. 14.99 *(978-1-368-04647-3(9))* Disney Pr.

—Disney Puppy Dog Pals. Scollon, Bill. 2020. (Me Reader Ser.). (ENG.). 192p. (J). *(978-1-5037-5213-9(5),* 549e29e0-8fde-42a6-92c2-0da5ec470cbe, p i kids) Phoenix International Publications, Inc.

—Disney Puppy Dog Pals: Fun on the Farm. Winslow, Claire. 2019. (Play-A-Sound Ser.). (ENG.). 10p. (J). *(978-1-5037-4601-5(1),* 145c8a4f-384f-4c78-b31c-a030848311dd, p i kids) Phoenix International Publications, Inc.

—Disney Storybook Collection (3rd Edition) Disney Book Group. 2015. (Storybook Collection). (ENG.). 304p. (J). (gr. -1-k). 16.99 *(978-1-4847-1348-8(6))* Disney Pr.

—Disney Tangled: Movie Storybook / Libro Basado en la Película (English-Spanish) Ortiz, Elvira, tr. 2018. (Disney Bilingual Ser.: 5). (ENG.). 24p. (J). (gr. -1-2). pap. 4.99 *(978-1-4998-0785-1(6),* BuzzPop) Little Bee Books Inc.

—Disney the Lion King: Movie Storybook / Libro Basado en la Película (English-Spanish) Collado Píriz, Laura, tr. 2019. (Disney Bilingual Ser.: 20). (ENG.). 24p. (J). (gr. -1-2). pap. 4.99 *(978-1-4998-0941-1(7),* BuzzPop) Little Bee Books Inc.

—Disney the Little Mermaid: Movie Storybook / Libro Basado en la Película (English-Spanish) Collado Píriz, Laura, tr. 2018. (Disney Bilingual Ser.: 13). (ENG.). 24p. (J). (gr. -1-2). pap. 4.99 *(978-1-4998-0796-7(1),* BuzzPop) Little Bee Books Inc.

—Disney Who's Who. Disney Book Group. 2017. (ENG.). 432p. (J). (gr. 1-3). pap. 11.99 *(978-1-368-00992-8(1))* Disney Pr.

—Disney Winnie the Pooh: Learning Mats. 2009. (ENG.). (J). *(978-1-4127-6598-5(6),* d32522f8-328a-4abe-9111-2165186c27d0, p i kids) Phoenix International Publications, Inc.

Disney Storybook Art Team. Disney*Pixar: Talking Quiz Book. PI Kids. 2020. (Play-A-Sound Ser.). (ENG.). 96p. (J). ***(978-1-5037-5196-5(1),*** 1fa8cac1-a11e-4041-852f-37bd4a3f26b6, p i kids) Phoenix International Publications, Inc.

Disney Storybook Art Team. Disney*Pixar Board Book & CD Treasury Box. Disney Book Group. 2017. (Board Book & CD Treasury Box Ser.). (ENG.). 18p. (J). (gr. -1-k). 12.99 *(978-1-368-00323-0(0))* Disney Pr.

—Disney*Pixar My First Bedtime Storybook. Disney Books. 2019. (My First Bedtime Storybook Ser.). (ENG.). 72p. (J). (gr. -1-k). 10.99 *(978-1-368-03913-0(8))* Disney Pr.

—Disney*Pixar Read-Along Storybook & CD Box Set. Disney Book Group. 2017. (Read-Along Storybook & CD Ser.). (ENG.). 128p. (J). (gr. 1-3). pap. 12.99 *(978-1-368-00264-6(1))* Disney Pr.

—Disney*Pixar Storybook Collection: Tales to Finish: Color Your Own Storybook Collection! Disney Book Group. 2017. (Disney*Pixar Storybook Collection: Tales to Finish Ser.). (ENG.). 128p. (J). (gr. 1-3). 10.99 *(978-1-4847-9942-0(9))* Disney Pr.

—Disney*Pixar Tales of Teamwork: A Lift-And-Seek Book. Roth, Megan. 2019. (Lift-And-Seek Ser.). (ENG.). 12p. (J). (gr. -1-k). bds. 10.99 *(978-1-368-03892-8(1))* Disney Pr.

—Disney*Pixar Toy Story 4: No Toy Left Behind. 2019. (Play-A-Sound Ser.). (ENG.). 14p. (J). bds. *(978-1-5037-4352-6(7),* 157c543a-9351-426e-9f9b-3f87b45348c1, p i kids) Phoenix International Publications, Inc.

—Disney/Pixar Toy Story 4: Movie Storybook / Libro Basado en la Película (English-Spanish) Collado Píriz, Laura, tr. 2019. (Disney Bilingual Ser.: 18). (ENG.). 24p. (J). (gr. -1-2). pap. 4.99 *(978-1-4998-0944-2(1),* BuzzPop) Little Bee Books Inc.

—Disney's Countdown to Christmas: A Story a Day. 2017. (ENG.). 64p. (J). (gr. 1-3). 10.99 *(978-1-4847-3052-2(6))* Disney Pr.

—Disney's Movie Night Read-Along Storybook & CD Collection: 3-In-1 Feature Animation Bind-up. Disney Book Group. 2018. (Read-Along Storybook & CD Ser.). (ENG.). 96p. (J). (gr. 1-3). pap. 9.99 *(978-1-368-02864-6(0))* Disney Pr.

—Do You Want to Play? / ¿Quieres Jugar? (English-Spanish) (Disney Frozen) Cregg, R. J. Ortiz, Elvira, tr. 2018. (Disney Bilingual Ser.: 8). (ENG.). 16p. (J). (gr. -1-k). bds. 6.99 *(978-1-4998-0790-5(2),* BuzzPop) Little Bee Books Inc.

—Doc Mcstuffins Jingle Bell Doc. Higginson, Sheila Sweeny & Disney Book Group. 2013. (ENG.). 12p. (J). (gr. -1-k). bds. 6.99 *(978-1-4231-8386-0(X))* Disney Pr.

—DuckTales: Woo-Oo! Read-along Storybook & CD. Disney Book Group. 2018. (Read-Along Storybook & CD Ser.). (ENG.). 32p. (J). (gr. 1-3). pap. 6.99 *(978-1-368-02049-7(6))* Disney Pr.

—E Is for Easter. Disney Book Group. 2019. (ENG.). 26p. (J). (gr. -1-k). bds. 12.99 *(978-1-368-03911-6(1))* Disney Pr.

—Elena of Avalor a Palace Fit for a Princess. Disney Book Group. 2016. (ENG.). 16p. (J). (gr. 1-3). 12.99 *(978-1-4847-5872-4(2))* Disney Pr.

—Elena of Avalor My Best Friend's Birthday. Disney Book Group & Olivas, Silvia. 2017. (ENG.). 24p. (J). (gr. 1-3). pap. 4.99 *(978-1-4847-7495-3(7))* Disney Pr.

—Elena of Avalor Song of the Sirenas. Ruderman, Rachel. 2018. (ENG.). 24p. (J). (gr. 1-3). pap. 4.99 *(978-1-368-02047-3(X))* Disney Pr.

—Fairest of All: A Tale of the Wicked Queen. Valentino, Serena & Disney Book Group. 2009. (Villains Ser.: 1). (ENG.). 256p. (YA). (gr. 7-12). 15.99 *(978-1-4231-0629-6(6))* Disney Pr.

—Farm Animals / Animales de Granja (English-Spanish) (Disney Baby) Cregg, R. J. Collado Píriz, Laura, tr. 2019. (Disney Bilingual Ser.: 17). (ENG.). 16p. (J). (gr. -1-k). bds. 6.99 *(978-1-4998-0908-4(5),* BuzzPop) Little Bee Books Inc.

—Finding Dory (Read-Along Storybook & CD) 2016. (Read-Along Storybook & CD Ser.). (ENG.). 32p. (J). (gr. 1-3). pap. 6.99 *(978-1-4847-2586-3(7))* Disney Pr.

—Finding Nemo Read-Along Storybook & CD. Disney Books. 2012. (Read-Along Storybook & CD Ser.). (ENG.). 32p. (J). (gr. -1 — 1). pap. 6.99 *(978-1-4231-6028-1(2))* Disney Pr.

Disney Storybook Art Team. Frozen 2 Read-Along Storybook & CD. Disney Book Group. 2019. (Read-Along Storybook & CD Ser.). (ENG.). 32p. (J). (gr. 1-3). pap. 6.99 ***(978-1-368-04280-2(5))*** Disney Pr.

Disney Storybook Art Team. Frozen Holiday Special Big Golden Book (Disney Frozen) RH Disney Staff. 2017. (Big Golden Book Ser.). (ENG.). 48p. (J). (gr. -1-2). 10.99 *(978-0-7364-3695-3(2),* Golden/Disney) Random Hse. Children's Bks.

—Frozen: Olaf & the Three Polar Bears. Glass, Calliope. 2018. (ENG.). 32p. (J). (gr. 1-3). 12.99 *(978-1-368-02140-1(9))* Disney Pr.

—Frozen Olaf's Night Before Christmas Book & CD. Disney Book Group. 2015. (ENG.). 32p. (J). (gr. 1-3). 12.99 *(978-1-4847-2468-2(2))* Disney Pr.

—Frozen Read-Along Storybook & CD. Disney Book Group. 2013. (Read-Along Storybook & CD Ser.). (ENG.). 32p. (J). (gr. -1-k). pap. 6.99 *(978-1-4231-7064-8(4))* Disney Pr.

—Frozen Reindeers Are Better Than People. Disney Book Group. 2015. (ENG.). 12p. (J). (gr. -1-k). bds. 6.99 *(978-1-4847-2469-9(0))* Disney Pr.

—Gabby Duran's Intergalactic Babysitter Orientation Guide. Disney Books & Davis, Carin. 2020. (ENG.). 176p. (J). (gr. 3-7). 12.99 *(978-1-368-05359-4(9))* Disney Pr.

—Going Batty / Vampireando (English-Spanish) (Disney Vampirina) Collado Píriz, Laura, tr. 2019. (Disney Bilingual Ser.: 23). (ENG.). 24p. (J). (gr. -1-2). pap. 4.99 *(978-1-4998-0942-8(5),* BuzzPop) Little Bee Books Inc.

—Good, Clean Fun / Diversión Buena y Limpia (English-Spanish) (Disney Puppy Dog Pals) Collado Píriz, Laura, tr. 2018. (Disney Bilingual Ser.: 10). (ENG.). 24p. (J). (gr. -1-2). pap. 4.99 *(978-1-4998-0787-5(2),* BuzzPop) Little Bee Books Inc.

—Guardians of the Galaxy Hallo-Scream Spook-tacular!!! Palacios. 2016. (ENG.). 24p. (J). (gr. 1-3). pap. 5.99 *(978-1-4847-3214-4(6),* Marvel Pr.) Disney Publishing Worldwide.

—H Is for Halloween. Disney Book Group. 2018. (ENG.). 26p. (J). (gr. -1-k). bds. 12.99 *(978-1-368-01999-6(4))* Disney Pr.

—Happy Birthday, Mickey! Read-Along Storybook & CD. Vitale, Brooke. 2018. (Read-Along Storybook & CD Ser.). (ENG.). 12p. (J). (gr. -1-k). bds. 8.99 *(978-1-368-02148-7(4))* Disney Pr.

—Haunted Clubhouse. Disney Book Group. 2010. (ENG.). 12p. (J). (gr. -1-k). bds. 6.99 *(978-1-4231-2832-8(X))* Disney Pr.

—Head to Toe! P. I. Kids Staff. 2017. (Play-A-Song Ser.). (ENG.). 20p. (J). *(978-1-5037-2567-6(7),* 07e8d9f3-f8d6-4a3e-8760-64873900ac9a, p i kids) Phoenix International Publications, Inc.

—Hello, My Friend / Bonjour, Mon Amie (English-French) (Disney Fancy Nancy) Stein, Carol. Roche, Camille, tr. 2019. (Disney Bilingual Ser.: 15). (ENG.). 16p. (J). (gr. -1-k). bds. 6.99 *(978-1-4998-0794-3(5),* BuzzPop) Little Bee Books Inc.

—How Is Mickey Feeling? / ¿Cómo Se Siente Mickey? (English-Spanish) (Disney Mickey Mouse) Cregg, R. J. Ortiz, Elvira, tr. 2018. (Disney Bilingual Ser.: 7). (ENG.). 16p. (J). (gr. -1-k). bds. 6.99 *(978-1-4998-0789-9(9))* Little Bee Books Inc.

—I Love My Family / Amo a Mi Familia (English-Spanish) (Disney Elena of Avalor) Stack, Stevie. Ortiz, Elvira, tr. 2018. (Disney Bilingual Ser.: 9). (ENG.). 16p. (J). (gr. -1-k). bds. 6.99 *(978-1-4998-0791-2(0),* BuzzPop) Little Bee Books Inc.

—Jasmine's Story (Disney Aladdin) Lagonegro, Melissa. 2019. (Pictureback(R) Ser.). (ENG.). 24p. (J). (gr. -1-2). 5.99 *(978-0-7364-3940-4(4),* RH/Disney) Random Hse. Children's Bks.

—Jingle Bell Pups. Disney Book Group. 2019. (ENG.). 12p. (J). (gr. -1-k). bds. 7.99 *(978-1-368-04839-2(0))* Disney Pr.

—Journey Together & Apart / un Viaje Juntos y Separados (English-Spanish) (Disney Frozen 2) (Level up! Readers) Cregg, R. J. Collado Píriz, Laura, tr. 2019. (Disney Bilingual Ser.: 28). (ENG.). 32p. (J). (gr. -1-2). pap. 3.99 *(978-1-4998-0877-3(1));* 16.99 *(978-1-4998-0878-0(X))* Little Bee Books Inc. (BuzzPop).

—Junior Encyclopedia of Animated Characters. Disney Book Group. 2014. (ENG.). 144p. (J). (gr. 1-3). 12.99 *(978-1-4231-8914-5(0))* Disney Pr.

—Kingdom Keepers: Disney after Dark. Pearson, Ridley. 2020. (Kingdom Keepers Ser.). 336p. (J). (gr. 5-9). 16.99 *(978-1-368-05632-8(6))* Hyperion Bks. for Children.

—Kingdom Keepers III: Disney in Shadow. Pearson, Ridley. 2020. (Kingdom Keepers Ser.). 576p. (J). (gr. 5-9). pap. 8.99 *(978-1-368-04627-5(4))* Hyperion Bks. for Children.

—The Legend of Sleepy Hollow Book & CD. Disney Book Group. 2019. (ENG.). 32p. (J). (gr. -1-k). pap. 6.99 *(978-1-368-02244-6(8))* Disney Pr.

—LEGO Disney Princess: a Dragon in the Castle? Chapter Book 2. Brody, Jessica. 2018. (ENG.). 96p. (J). (gr. 1-3). pap. 6.99 *(978-1-368-02415-0(7))* Disney Pr.

—LEGO Disney Princess: the Secret Room. Brody, Jessica. 2019. (ENG.). 96p. (J). (gr. 1-3). pap. 6.99 *(978-1-368-02666-6(4))* Disney Pr.

—LEGO Disney Princess: the Surprise Storm: Chapter Book 1. Brody, Jessica. 2018. (ENG.). 96p. (J). (gr. 1-3). pap. 6.99 *(978-1-368-02414-3(9))* Disney Pr.

—Let It Glow (Disney Frozen: Northern Lights) Francis, Suzanne. 2017. (Big Golden Book Ser.). (ENG.). 48p. (J). (gr. -1-2). 9.99 *(978-0-7364-3678-6(2),* Golden/Disney) Random Hse. Children's Bks.

—Let's Write the Alphabet: My Write-And-Erase Book. Harmening, Derek. 2017. (Play-A-Sound Ser.). (ENG.). 16p. (J). *(978-1-5037-1690-2(2),* 7ffbca28-388e-419f-bd64-cfd25413bb46, p i kids) Phoenix International Publications, Inc.

—The Lion Guard, Meet the New Guard. Disney Book Group. 2016. (ENG.). 10p. (J). (gr. -1-k). bds. 8.99 *(978-1-4847-1914-5(X))* Disney Pr.

—The Lion Guard Read-Along Storybook & CD the Power of the Roar. Disney Book Group. 2017. (Read-Along Storybook & CD Ser.). (ENG.). 32p. (J). (gr. -1-k). pap. 6.99 *(978-1-4847-2950-2(1))* Disney Pr.

—The Lion Guard Return of the Roar: Purchase Includes Disney EBook! Disney Book Group. 2015. (ENG.). 40p. (J). (gr. -1-k). 16.99 *(978-1-4847-1551-2(9))* Disney Pr.

—The Lion King Deluxe Step into Reading (Disney the Lion King) Carbone, Courtney. 2019. (Step into Reading Ser.). (ENG.). 24p. (J). (gr. -1-1). 5.99 *(978-0-7364-3985-5(4),* RH/Disney) Random Hse. Children's Bks.

—The Lion King Read-Along Storybook & CD. Disney Book Group. 2019. (Read-Along Storybook & CD Ser.). (ENG.). 32p. (J). (gr. -1-k). pap. 6.99 *(978-1-368-04156-0(6))* Disney Pr.

—The Little Mermaid Read-Along Storybook & CD. Disney Book Group. 2013. (Read-Along Storybook & CD Ser.). (ENG.). 32p. (J). (gr. -1-k). pap. 6.99 *(978-1-4231-6889-8(5))* Disney Pr.

—The Little Mermaid: the Story of Ariel. Disney Book Group. 2016. (ENG.). 112p. (J). (gr. -1-k). 12.99 *(978-1-4847-6728-3(4))* Disney Pr.

—M Is for Mickey. Disney Books. 2017. (ENG.). 26p. (J). (gr. -1-k). bds. 12.99 *(978-1-4847-8221-7(6))* Disney Pr.

—M Is for Minnie. Roth, Megan. 2019. (Touch & Trace Ser.). (ENG.). 26p. (J). (gr. -1-k). bds. 10.99 *(978-1-368-04202-4(3))* Disney Pr.

—Magical Moments: A Light-Up Board Book. Disney Book Group. 2018. (Light-Up Board Book Ser.). (ENG.). 10p. (J). (gr. -1-k). 12.99 *(978-1-368-01895-1(5))* Disney Pr.

—Making the Cut. Grace, N. B. & Disney Book Group. 2nd ed. 2010. (Sonny with a Chance Ser.). (ENG.). 128p. (J). (gr. 3-6). pap. 17.44 *(978-1-4231-2276-0(3))* Disney Pr.

—Meet Maui. Posner-Sanchez, Andrea. 2017. (Pictureback(R) Ser.). (ENG.). 24p. (J). (gr. -1-2). pap. 4.99 *(978-0-7364-3738-7(X),* RH/Disney) Random Hse. Children's Bks.

—Meet the Cars. Disney Books. 2017. (ENG.). 144p. (J). (gr. -1-k). 12.99 *(978-1-368-00783-2(X))* Disney Pr.

—A Merry Christmas Cookbook. Disney Book Group. 2014. (ENG.). 64p. (J). (gr. 1-3). 10.99 *(978-1-4231-6322-0(2))* Disney Pr.

—Mickey & Friends Best Friends Day. Vitale, Brooke. 2019. (Ears Bks.). (ENG.). 12p. (J). (gr. -1-k). bds. 7.99 *(978-1-368-02332-0(0))* Disney Pr.

—Mickey & Friends Mickey's Snowy Christmas. Disney Book Group. 2019. (ENG.). 12p. (J). (gr. -1-k). bds. 8.99 *(978-1-368-04376-2(3))* Disney Pr.

—Mickey & Friends Mickey's Spooky Night. Disney Book Group. 2017. (ENG.). 24p. (J). (gr. 1-3). bds. 10.99 *(978-1-368-01920-0(X))* Disney Pr.

—Mickey & Friends Mickey's Spooky Night: Purchase Includes Mobile App for IPhone & IPad! Read & Play. Disney Book Group. 2014. (ENG.). 24p. (J). (gr. 1-3). bds. 10.99 *(978-1-4847-0841-5(5))* Disney Pr.

—Mickey & Minnie's Storybook Collection. Disney Book Group. 2015. (Storybook Collection). (ENG.). 304p. (J). (gr. 1-3). 16.99 *(978-1-4231-3508-1(3,* 1394887) Disney Pr.

—Mickey Mouse Clubhouse Mickey's Halloween. Disney Book Group. 2015. (ENG.). 10p. (J). (gr. -1-k). bds. 8.99 *(978-1-4847-2096-7(2))* Disney Pr.

—Mickey Mouse Clubhouse Minnie's Rainbow. Higginson, Sheila Sweeny & Disney Book Group. rev. ed. 2008. (ENG.). 24p. (J). (gr. -1-k). pap. 3.99 *(978-1-4231-0743-9(8))* Disney Pr.

—Mickey Mouse Clubhouse Minnie's Valentine. Higginson, Sheila Sweeny & Disney Book Group. rev. ed. 2007. (ENG.). 24p. (J). (gr. -1-k). pap. 4.99 *(978-1-4231-0746-0(2))* Disney Pr.

—Mickey Mouse Clubhouse Road Trip. Disney Book Group. 2011. (ENG.). 10p. (J). (gr. -1-k). bds. 8.99 *(978-1-4231-4416-8(3))* Disney Pr.

—Mickey Mouse Clubhouse Whose Birthday Is It? Higginson, Sheila Sweeny & Disney Books. 2007. (ENG.). 16p. (J). (gr. -1-k). 4.99 *(978-1-4231-0652-4(0))* Disney Pr.

—Mickey Ready, Set, Fun! A Lift-And-Seek Book. Disney Book Group. 2019. (Lift-And-Seek Ser.). (ENG.). 12p. (J). (gr. -1-k). bds. 10.99 *(978-1-368-03893-5(X))* Disney Pr.

—Mickey Saves Santa. Disney Book Group. 2009. (ENG.). 24p. (J). (gr. -1-k). pap. 5.99 *(978-1-4231-1846-6(4))* Disney Pr.

—Mickey's Christmas Carol Read-Along Storybook & CD. Disney Book Group. 2017. (Read-Along Storybook & CD Ser.). (ENG.). 32p. (J). (gr. 1-3). pap. 6.99 *(978-1-368-01602-5(2))* Disney Pr.

—Mickey's Christmas Storybook Treasury. 2017. (Storybook Treasury Ser.). (ENG.). 256p. (J). (gr. 1-3). 30.00 *(978-1-368-00256-1(0))* Disney Pr.

—Mickey's Halloween Treat. Feldman, Thea & Disney Book Group. 2008. (ENG.). 16p. (J). (gr. -1-k). pap. 4.99 *(978-1-4231-0983-9(X))* Disney Pr.

—Miguel's Guitar / la Guitarra de Miguel (English-Spanish) (Disney/Pixar Coco) (Level up! Readers) López, Mariel, tr. 2019. (Disney Bilingual Ser.: 26). (ENG.). 32p. (J). (gr. k-3). pap. 3.99 *(978-1-4998-0881-0(X));* 16.99 *(978-1-4998-0882-7(8))* Little Bee Books Inc. (BuzzPop).

—Minnie Be My Sparkly Valentine. Scollon, Bill & Disney Book Group. 2014. (ENG.). 24p. (J). (gr. -1-k). pap. 5.99 *(978-1-4231-6414-2(8))* Disney Pr.

—Minnie Easter Bonnet Parade: Includes Stickers. Scollon, Bill & Disney Books. 2013. (ENG.). 24p. (J). (gr. -1-k). pap. 5.99 *(978-1-4231-6416-6(4))* Disney Pr.

—Minnie Knows Bows. Disney Book Group. 2019. (Ears Bks.). (ENG.). 12p. (J). (gr. -1-k). bds. 7.99 *(978-1-368-04501-8(4))* Disney Pr.

—Minnie Minnie's Costume Contest. Higginson, Sheila Sweeny & Disney Book Group. 2014. (ENG.). 12p. (J). (gr. -1-k). bds. 7.99 *(978-1-4231-9427-9(6))* Disney Pr.

Disney Storybook Art Team. Minnie Minnie's Rainbow. Disney Books. 2020. (ENG.). 24p. (J). (gr. -1-k). pap. 6.99 ***(978-1-368-04983-2(4))*** Disney Pr.

Disney Storybook Art Team. Minnie Saves Christmas Read-Along Storybook & CD. Disney Book Group. 2018. (Read-Along Storybook & CD Ser.). (ENG.). 14p. (J). (gr. -1-k). bds. 8.99 *(978-1-368-02234-7(0))* Disney Pr.

—Moana & Pua (Disney Moana) Lagonegro, Melissa. 2019. (Step into Reading Ser.). (ENG.). 24p. (J). (gr. -1-1). 5.99 *(978-0-7364-3957-2(9),* RH/Disney) Random Hse. Children's Bks.

—Moana Read-Along Storybook & CD. 2016. (Read-Along Storybook & CD Ser.). (ENG.). 32p. (J). (gr. 1-3). pap. 6.99 *(978-1-4847-4361-4(X))* Disney Pr.

—Mulan Read-Along Storybook & CD. Disney Books. 2020. (Read-Along Storybook & CD Ser.). (ENG.). 32p. (J). (gr. 1-3). pap. 6.99 *(978-1-368-01617-9(0))* Disney Pr.

—My 1St Libraries Disney Baby Animals. Publications International Ltd. Staff. 2011. (ENG.). 120p. (J). bds. 6.10 net. *(978-1-4508-1571-0(5),* c4f9fe85-eb40-41c9-8932-5b3a0f814696) Phoenix International Publications, Inc.

—My First 1000 Words / Mis Primeras 1000 Palabras (English-Spanish) (Disney) A Picture Word Book / un Libro de Palabras. Collado Píriz, Laura, tr. 2019. (Disney Bilingual Ser.: 22). (ENG.). 144p. (J). (gr. -1-k). 16.99 *(978-1-4998-0985-5(9),* BuzzPop) Little Bee Books Inc.

—My First Disney Classics Bedtime Storybook. Disney Book Group. 2018. (My First Bedtime Storybook Ser.). (ENG.). 72p. (J). (gr. -1-k). 10.99 *(978-1-368-02810-3(1))* Disney Pr.

—My First Mickey Mouse Bedtime Storybook. Disney Book Group. 2019. (My First Bedtime Storybook Ser.). (ENG.). 72p. (J). (gr. -1-k). 10.99 *(978-1-368-04484-4(0))* Disney Pr.

—Olaf's Frozen Adventure Olaf's Journey: A Light-Up Board Book. Disney Book Group. 2017. (Light-Up Board Book Ser.). (ENG.). 10p. (J). (gr. -1-k). bds. 12.99 *(978-1-368-00674-3(4))* Disney Pr.

—Olaf's Frozen Adventure Read-Along Storybook & CD. 2017. (Read-Along Storybook & CD Ser.). (ENG.). 32p. (J). (gr. 1-3). pap. 6.99 *(978-1-4847-8491-4(X))* Disney Pr.

—Onward: Ian & Barley's Magical Book of Jokes, Puns, & Gags. Disney Books. 2020. (ENG.). 48p. (J). (gr. k-3). pap. 4.99 *(978-1-368-06163-6(X))* Disney Pr.

Disney Storybook Art Team, et al. Onward: Quests of Yore. Renzetti, Rob. 2020. (ENG.). 192p. (J). (gr. 3-7). 16.99 *(978-1-368-05209-2(6))* Disney Pr.

Disney Storybook Art Team. Onward Read-Along Storybook & CD. Disney Books. 2020. (Read-Along Storybook & CD Ser.). (ENG.). 32p. (J). (gr. 1-3). pap. 6.99 *(978-1-368-04553-7(7))* Disney Pr.

—Onward: the Search for the Phoenix Gem: An In-Questigation. Behling, Steve. 2020. (ENG.). 256p. (J). (gr. 3-7). 10.99 *(978-1-368-05210-8(X))* Disney Pr.

—Pawcation! Depken, Kristen L. & Diaz, Ella. 2017. (Pictureback(R) Ser.). (ENG.). 16p. (J). (gr. -1-2). pap. 4.99 *(978-0-7364-3712-7(6),* RH/Disney) Random Hse. Children's Bks.

—Peter Pan Read-Along Storybook & CD. Disney Book Group. 2013. (Read-Along Storybook & CD Ser.). (ENG.). 32p. (J). (gr. -1-k). pap. 6.99 *(978-1-4231-8034-0(8))* Disney Pr.

—Phineas & Ferb Big-Top Bonanza. Grace, N. B. & Disney Book Group. 5th ed. 2011. (Phineas & Ferb Chapters Ser.: 5). (ENG.). 112p. (J). (gr. 3-7). pap. 17.44 *(978-1-4231-1800-8(6))* Disney Pr.

—Phineas & Ferb Comic Reader the Beak Strikes! Green, John & Disney Book Group. 2011. (Phineas & Ferb Comic Readers Ser.). (ENG.). 32p. (J). (gr. 1-3). pap. 17.44 *(978-1-4231-3740-5(X))* Disney Pr.

—Phineas & Ferb How to Conquer the Tri-State Area (by Heinz Doofenshmirtz) Disney Book Group & O'Ryan, Ellie. 2010. (Phineas & Ferb Chapters Ser.). (ENG.). 80p. (J). (gr. 3-7). pap. 17.44 *(978-1-4231-3465-7(6))* Disney Pr.

—Phineas & Ferb Runaway Hit, No. 2. Bergen, Lara & Disney Book Group. 2nd ed. 2011. (Phineas & Ferb Chapters Ser.: 2). (ENG.). 112p. (J). (gr. 3-7). pap. 17.44 *(978-1-4231-1797-1(2))* Disney Pr.

—Phineas & Ferb Speed Demons. Jones, Jasmine & Disney Book Group. 2011. (Phineas & Ferb Chapters Ser.: 1). (ENG.). 112p. (J). (gr. 3-7). pap. 17.44 *(978-1-4231-1628-8(3))* Disney Pr.

Disney Storybook Art Team. Phineas & Ferb's Guide to Life. Disney Books. 2020. (Guide to Life Ser.). (ENG.). 144p. (J). (gr. 3-7). 9.99 ***(978-1-368-06573-3(2))*** Disney Pr.

Disney Storybook Art Team. Pocahontas Read-Along Storybook & CD. Disney Books. 2020. (Read-Along Storybook & CD Ser.). (ENG.). 32p. (J). (gr. 1-3). pap. 6.99 *(978-1-368-04819-4(6))* Disney Pr.

—Pooh's Honey Adventure. Disney Book Group. 2011. (Disney Early Reader: Level Pre-1 Ser.). (ENG.). 32p. (J). (gr. -1-1). pap. 16.19 *(978-1-4231-3593-7(8))* Disney Pr.

—Poor Unfortunate Soul: A Tale of the Sea Witch. Valentino, Serena. 2016. (Villains Ser.: 3). (ENG.). 208p. (YA). (gr. 7-12). 17.99 *(978-1-4847-2405-7(4))* Disney Pr.

—Princess Bedtime Stories (2nd Edition) Disney Books. 2017. (Storybook Collection). (ENG.). 304p. (J). (gr. 1-3). 16.99 *(978-1-4847-4711-7(9))* Disney Pr.

—Puppy Dog Pals the Last Pup-Icorn. Disney Book Group. 2020. (ENG.). 24p. (J). (gr. -1-k). pap. 4.99 *(978-1-368-05290-0(8))* Disney Pr.

—Rain or Shine / Lluvia o Sol (English-Spanish) (Disney Baby) Stack, Stevie. Collado Píriz, Laura, tr. 2019. (Disney Bilingual Ser.: 16). (ENG.). 16p. (J). (gr. -1-k). bds. 6.99 *(978-1-4998-0793-6(7),* BuzzPop) Little Bee Books Inc.

—Rapunzel Loves Colors / a Rapunzel le Encantan Los Colores (English-Spanish) (Disney Tangled) (Level up! Readers) Cregg, R. J. Collado Píriz, Laura, tr. 2020. (Disney Bilingual Ser.: 34). (ENG.). 32p. (J). (gr. -1-1). 16.99 *(978-1-4998-0995-4(6));* pap. 3.99 *(978-1-4998-0994-7(8))* Little Bee Books Inc. (BuzzPop).

—Say Please! / ¡Di Por Favor! (English-Spanish) (Disney Puppy Dog Pals) Cregg, R. J. Collado Píriz, Laura, tr. 2019. (Disney Bilingual Ser.: 14). (ENG.). 16p. (J). (gr. -1-k). bds. 6.99 *(978-1-4998-0795-0(3),* BuzzPop) Little Bee Books Inc.

—Scary Storybook Collection. 3rd ed. 2017. (Storybook Collection). (ENG.). 304p. (J). (gr. 1-3). 16.99 *(978-1-4847-3239-7(1))* Disney Pr.

—School of Secrets: Ally's Mad Mystery (Disney Descendants), Bk. 3. Brody, Jessica. 2017. (School of Secrets Ser.: 3). (ENG.). 192p. (J). (gr. 3-7). bds. 9.99 *(978-1-4847-7866-1(9))* Disney Pr.

—School of Secrets: Carlos's Scavenger Hunt (Disney Descendants) Brody, Jessica. 2017. (School of Secrets Ser.: 5). (ENG.). 192p. (J). (gr. 3-7). 9.99 *(978-1-368-01398-7(8))* Disney Pr.

—School of Secrets: CJ's Treasure Chase (Disney Descendants) Brody, Jessica. 2016. (School of Secrets Ser.: 1). (ENG.). 192p. (J). (gr. 3-7). 9.99 *(978-1-4847-7864-7(2))* Disney Pr.

—School of Secrets: Freddie's Shadow Cards (Disney Descendants) Brody, Jessica. 2016. (School of Secrets Ser.: 2). (ENG.). 192p. (J). (gr. 3-7). 9.99 *(978-1-4847-7865-4(0))* Disney Pr.

—Serena Valentino's Villains Box Set: Books 1-3, Set. Valentino, Serena. 2017. (ENG.). 640p. (YA). (gr. 7-17). 44.99 *(978-1-368-00905-8(0))* Disney Pr.

—Shake It up Bring It!, 2. Disney Book Group. 2012. (Shake It Up Ser.: 2). (ENG.). 128p. (J). (gr. 2-4). pap. 17.44 *(978-1-4231-6336-7(2))* Disney Pr.

—Show-And-Tell / Mostrar y Contar (English-Spanish) (Disney Olaf's Frozen Adventure) Collado Píriz, Laura, tr. 2019. (Disney Bilingual Ser.: 21). (ENG.). 24p. (J). (gr. -1-2). pap. 4.99 *(978-1-4998-0798-1(8),* BuzzPop) Little Bee Books Inc.

—Sofia the First Me & Our Mom. Hapka, Catherine & Disney Book Group. 2015. (ENG.). 24p. (J). (gr. -1-k). pap. 4.99 *(978-1-4847-0688-6(9))* Disney Pr.

—Sofia the First S is for Sofia. Disney Book Group. 2015. (ENG.). 26p. (J). (gr. -1-k). bds. 12.99 *(978-1-4847-1804-9(6))* Disney Pr.

—The Sorcerer's Apprentice: A Classic Mickey Mouse Tale. Vitale, Brooke. 2018. (ENG.). 40p. (J). (gr. 1-3). 10.99 *(978-1-368-02331-3(2))* Disney Pr.

Disney Storybook Art Team. The Soundtrack Series Frozen: Let It Go. Disney Book Group. 2019. (Soundtrack Ser.). (ENG.). 32p. (J). (gr. -1-k). 12.99 ***(978-1-368-02139-5(5))*** Disney Pr.

Disney Storybook Art Team. The Soundtrack Series the Lion King: I Just Can't Wait to Be King. Disney Book Group. 2019. (Soundtrack Ser.). (ENG.). 32p. (J). (gr. -1-k). 12.99 *(978-1-368-04550-6(2))* Disney Pr.

—Star Darlings Astra's Mixed-Up Mission. Zappa, Shana Muldoon & Zappa, Ahmet. 2016. (Star Darlings Ser.: 8). (ENG.). 176p. (J). (gr. 3-7). pap. 6.99 *(978-1-4847-1427-0(X))* Disney Pr.

—Star Darlings Piper's Perfect Dream. Zappa, Shana Muldoon & Zappa, Ahmet. 2016. (Star Darlings Ser.: 7). (ENG.). 176p. (J). (gr. 3-7). pap. 6.99 *(978-1-4847-1426-3(1))* Disney Pr.

—T. O. T. S. You've Gotta Be Kitten Me (with Stickers!) Disney Book Group. 2019. (ENG.). 24p. (J). (gr. -1-k). pap. 4.99 *(978-1-368-04566-7(9))* Disney Pr.

—Tangled & Tangled Ever after Read-Along Storybook & CD Bindup. Disney Book Group. 2017. (Read-Along Storybook & CD Ser.). (ENG.). 64p. (J). (gr. 1-3). pap. 8.99 *(978-1-4847-8780-9(3))* Disney Pr.

—Tangled Read-Along Storybook & CD. Disney Book Group. 2010. (Read-Along Storybook & CD Ser.). (ENG.). 32p. (J). (gr. -1 — 1). pap. 6.99 *(978-1-4231-3742-9(6))* Disney Pr.

—Tea Party Trouble / Problème de Thé (English-French) (Disney Fancy Nancy) Roche, Camille, tr. 2018. (Disney Bilingual Ser.: 12). (ENG.). 24p. (J). (gr. -1-2). pap. 4.99 *(978-1-4998-0788-2(0))* Little Bee Books Inc.

—Thank You, Pooh. Disney Book Group. 2018. (Ears Bks.). (ENG.). 10p. (J). (gr. -1-k). bds. 7.99 *(978-1-368-02319-1(3))* Disney Pr.

—Thrill-O-rama! Richards, Kitty & Disney Book Group. 4th ed. 2011. (Phineas & Ferb Chapters Ser.: 4). (ENG.). 112p. (J). (gr. 3-7). pap. 17.44 *(978-1-4231-1799-5(9))* Disney Pr.

—Toy Story 4 - Made to Play! Random House & Bouchard, Natasha. 2019. (Step into Reading Ser.). (ENG.). 24p. (J). (gr. -1-1). 5.99 *(978-0-7364-3987-9(0),* RH/Disney) Random Hse. Children's Bks.

—Toy Story 4 Read-Along Storybook & CD. Disney Books. 2019. (Read-Along Storybook & CD Ser.). (ENG.). 32p. (J). (gr. 1-3). pap. 6.99 *(978-1-368-04281-9(3))* Disney Pr.

—Toy Story 4: the Junior Novelization (Disney/Pixar Toy Story 4) 2019. (ENG.). 144p. (J). (gr. 3-7). 6.99 *(978-0-7364-3998-5(6),* RH/Disney) Random Hse. Children's Bks.

—Toy Story Read-Along Storybook & CD. Disney Books. 2010. (Read-Along Storybook & CD Ser.). (ENG.). 32p. (J). (gr. -1 — 1). pap. 6.99 *(978-1-4231-3349-0(8))* Disney Pr.

—Toy Story Read-Along Storybook & CD Collection. Disney Books. 2019. (Read-Along Storybook & CD Ser.). (ENG.). 96p. (J). (gr. 1-3). pap. 9.99 *(978-1-368-04282-6(1))* Disney Pr.

—Toy Story Storybook Collection. Disney Books. 2019. (Storybook Collection). (ENG.). 304p. (J). (gr. -1-k). 16.99 *(978-1-4847-4719-3(4))* Disney Pr.

—Vampirina Vampire for President. Disney Books. 2020. (ENG.). 24p. (J). (gr. -1-k). 16.99 *(978-1-368-05271-9(1))* Disney Pr.

—Vampirina Vee's Tricks & Treats. Disney Book Group. 2019. (ENG.). 24p. (J). (gr. -1-k). pap. 5.99 *(978-1-368-02788-5(1))* Disney Pr.

—A Very Handy Holiday. Ring, Susan & Disney Book Group. 2008. (Handy Manny Ser.). (ENG.). 24p. (J). (gr. -1-1). pap. 16.19 *(978-1-4231-1028-6(5))* Disney Pr.

—Welcome to Auradon: a Descendants 3 Sticker & Activity Book. Disney Book Group. 2019. (ENG.). 88p. (J). (gr. 1-3). pap. 8.99 *(978-1-368-04955-9(9))* Disney Pr.

—What a Team! Glass, Calliope. 2017. (Pictureback(R) Ser.). (ENG.). 24p. (J). (gr. -1-2). pap. 4.99 *(978-0-7364-3688-5(X),* RH/Disney) Random Hse. Children's Bks.

—Whisker Haven Tales with the Palace Pets: Sticker Storybook. Green, Rico. 2015. (ENG.). 48p. (J). (gr. -1-k). 12.99 *(978-1-4847-2995-3(1))* Disney Pr.

—Whisker Haven Tales with the Palace Pets: Berry's Halloween Costume Trouble: Read-Along Storybook & CD. Green, Rico. 2016. (Read-Along Storybook & CD Ser.). (ENG.). 32p. (J). (gr. -1-k). pap. 6.99 *(978-1-4847-4707-0(0))* Disney Pr.

—Winnie the Pooh Pooh's Halloween Pumpkin. Hapka, Catherine & Disney Book Group. 2013. (ENG.). 10p. (J). (gr. -1-k). bds. 5.99 *(978-1-4231-6767-9(8))* Disney Pr.

—Winnie the Pooh Pooh's Secret Garden. Hapka, Catherine & Disney Book Group. 2012. (ENG.). 24p. (J). (gr. -1-k). pap. 4.99 *(978-1-4231-4845-6(2))* Disney Pr.

—Winnie the Pooh Storybook Treasury. Disney Book Group. 2019. (Storybook Treasury Ser.). (ENG.). 256p. (J). (gr. 1-3). 30.00 *(978-1-368-01861-6(0))* Disney Pr.

—Winnie the Pooh Sweet Dreams, Roo. Hapka, Catherine & Disney Books. 2012. (ENG.). 24p. (J). (gr. -1-k). bds. 6.99 *(978-1-4231-4843-2(6))* Disney Pr.

—World of Reading Disney Bunnies 3-In-1 Listen-along Reader (Level 1) 3 Fun Fuzzy Tales. Disney Books. 2019. (World of Reading Ser.). (ENG.). 96p. (J). (gr. -1-k). pap. 7.99 *(978-1-368-01921-7(8))* Disney Pr.

—World of Reading: Disney Bunnies Thumper & the Egg (Level 1 Reader) Disney Books. 2018. (World of Reading Ser.). (ENG.). 32p. (J). (gr. -1-k). pap. 4.99 *(978-1-4847-9965-9(8))* Disney Pr.

—World of Reading Disney Christmas Collection 3-In-1 Listen-along Reader (Level 1) 3 Festive Tales with CD! Disney Book Group. 2019. (World of Reading Ser.). (ENG.). 96p. (J). (gr. -1-k). pap. 7.99 *(978-1-368-04487-5(5))* Disney Pr.

—World of Reading Disney Classic Characters Level 1 Boxed Set, Set. Disney Book Group. 2017. (World of Reading

Ser.). (ENG.). 192p. (J). (gr. 1-3). pap. 12.99 *(978-1-4847-9921-5(6))* Disney Pr.

—World of Reading: Disney Junior Five Tales of Fun! (Level 1 Reader Bindup) Disney Books. 2018. (World of Reading Ser.). (ENG.). 160p. (J). (gr. -1-k). pap. 7.99 *(978-1-368-01909-5(9))* Disney Pr.

Disney Storybook Art Team. World of Reading Disney Junior Mickey: Friendship Tales. Disney Books. 2020. (World of Reading Ser.). (ENG.). 160p. (J). (gr. -1-k). pap. 7.99 ***(978-1-368-05542-0(7))*** Disney Pr.

Disney Storybook Art Team. World of Reading Disney Princess Level 1 Boxed Set. Disney Book Group. 2017. (World of Reading Ser.). (ENG.). 192p. (J). (gr. 1-3). pap. 12.99 *(978-1-4847-9940-6(2))* Disney Pr.

Disney Storybook Art Team. World of Reading Disney's Spooky Collection 3-In-1 Listen-along Reader (Level 1 Reader) 3 Scary Stories with CD! Disney Books. 2020. (World of Reading Ser.). (ENG.). 96p. (J). (gr. -1-k). pap. 7.99 ***(978-1-368-04488-2(3))*** Disney Pr.

Disney Storybook Art Team. World of Reading: Elena of Avalor Isabel's School Adventure. Disney Book Group. 2017. (World of Reading Ser.). (ENG.). 32p. (J). (gr. 1-3). pap. 4.99 *(978-1-4847-4798-8(4))* Disney Pr.

—World of Reading Hauntley Girls. Disney Books. 2020. (World of Reading Ser.). (ENG.). 32p. (J). (gr. -1-k). 16.99 *(978-1-368-05327-3(0))* Disney Pr.

—World of Reading LEGO Disney Princess: Lost & Found (Level 1) Disney Book Group. 2018. (World of Reading Ser.). (ENG.). 32p. (J). (gr. -1-k). pap. 4.99 *(978-1-368-02304-7(5))* Disney Pr.

—World of Reading LEGO Disney Princess: the Best Tree House Ever (Level 2) Disney Book Group. 2019. (World of Reading Ser.). (ENG.). 32p. (J). (gr. 1-3). pap. 4.99 *(978-1-368-02681-9(8))* Disney Pr.

—World of Reading LEGO Disney Princess: the Friendship Bridge (Level 2) Disney Book Group. 2018. (World of Reading Ser.). (ENG.). 32p. (J). (gr. 1-3). pap. 4.99 *(978-1-368-02305-4(3))* Disney Pr.

—World of Reading Mickey & the Roadster Racers Mickey's Perfecto Day (Level 1 Reader) With Stickers. Disney Book Group. 2017. (World of Reading Ser.). (ENG.). 32p. (J). (gr. -1-k). pap. 4.99 *(978-1-368-01028-3(8))* Disney Pr.

Disney Storybook Art Team. World of Reading: Mickey Mouse Mixed-Up Adventures Campy Camper Day (Level 1 Reader) Disney Books. 2020. (World of Reading Ser.). (ENG.). 32p. (J). (gr. -1-k). pap. 4.99 ***(978-1-368-04489-9(1))*** Disney Pr.

Disney Storybook Art Team. World of Reading: Miles from Tomorrowland How I Saved My Summer Vacation: Level 1. Disney Book Group. 2016. (World of Reading Ser.). (ENG.). 32p. (J). (gr. -1-k). pap. 3.99 *(978-1-4847-2962-5(5))* Disney Pr.

—World of Reading: Minnie Tales. Disney Book Group. 2020. (World of Reading Ser.). (ENG.). 160p. (J). (gr. -1-k). pap. 7.99 *(978-1-368-05288-7(6))* Disney Pr.

Disney Storybook Art Team. World of Reading Phineas & Ferb Another Grand Adventure. Disney Books. 2020. (World of Reading Ser.). (ENG.). 160p. (J). (gr. k-3). pap. 7.99 ***(978-1-368-06575-7(9))*** Disney Pr.

Disney Storybook Art Team. World of Reading: Puppy Dog Pals Lucky Pups (Level 1 Word Swap Reader) Vitale, Brooke. 2019. (World of Reading Ser.). (ENG.). 16p. (J). (gr. -1-k). pap. 4.99 *(978-1-368-02787-8(3))* Disney Pr.

Disney Storybook Art Team. World of Reading Puppy Dog Pals: One Small Ruff for Pup-Kind (Reader with Fun Facts) Disney Books. 2020. (World of Reading Ser.). (ENG.). 32p. (J). (gr. -1-k). pap. 4.99 ***(978-1-368-05593-2(1))*** Disney Pr.

Disney Storybook Art Team. World of Reading: T. O. T. S. Panda Excess (Level 1 Reader with Stickers) Disney Book Group. 2019. (World of Reading Ser.). (ENG.). 32p. (J). (gr. -1-k). pap. 4.99 *(978-1-368-04568-1(5))* Disney Pr.

Disney Storybook Art Team. World of Reading T. O. T. S. Whale, Hello There. Disney Books. 2020. (ENG.). 32p. (J). (gr. -1-k). pap. 4.99 ***(978-1-368-05784-4(5))*** Disney Pr.

Disney Storybook Art Team. World of Reading Villains 3-In-1 Listen-along Reader (World of Reading Level 1) 3 Terrible Tales with CD! 2018. (World of Reading Ser.). (ENG.). 96p. (J). (gr. -1-k). pap. 7.99 *(978-1-4847-9922-2(4))* Disney Pr.

—5-Minute Disney Classic Stories. Disney Book Group. 2018. (5-Minute Stories Ser.). (ENG.). 192p. (J). (gr. 1-3). 12.99 *(978-1-368-00676-7(0))* Disney Pr.

—5-Minute Disney*Pixar Stories. Disney Book Group. 2012. (5-Minute Stories Ser.). (ENG.). 192p. (J). (gr. -1-k). 12.99 *(978-1-4231-6520-0(9))* Disney Pr.

—5-Minute Disney*Pixar Stories. Disney Books. 2019. (5-Minute Stories Ser.). (ENG.). 192p. (J). (gr. 1-3). 12.99 *(978-1-368-00109-0(2))* Disney Pr.

—5-Minute Easter Stories. Disney Books. 2020. (5-Minute Stories Ser.). (ENG.). 192p. (J). (gr. 1-3). 12.99 *(978-1-368-04194-2(9))* Disney Pr.

Disney Storybook Art Team. 5-Minute Frozen. Disney Book Group. 2019. (5-Minute Stories Ser.). (ENG.). 192p. (J). (gr. 1-3). 12.99 ***(978-1-368-04195-9(7))*** Disney Pr.

Disney Storybook Art Team. 5-Minute Girl Power Stories. Disney Books. 2020. (5-Minute Stories Ser.). (ENG.). 192p. (J). (gr. 1-3). 12.99 *(978-1-368-04196-6(5))* Disney Pr.

—5-Minute Halloween Stories. 2018. (5-Minute Stories Ser.). (ENG.). 192p. (J). (gr. 1-3). 12.99 *(978-1-368-00257-8(9))* Disney Pr.

—5-Minute Mickey Mouse Stories. Disney Books. 2018. (5-Minute Stories Ser.). (ENG.). 192p. (J). (gr. 1-3). 12.99 *(978-1-368-02235-4(9))* Disney Pr.

—5-Minute Minnie Tales. Disney Book Group. 2014. (5-Minute Stories Ser.). (ENG.). 192p. (J). (gr. 1-3). 12.99 *(978-1-4847-0452-3(5))* Disney Pr.

—5-Minute Puppy Dog Pals Stories. Disney Books. 2019. (5-Minute Stories Ser.). (ENG.). 192p. (J). (gr. 1-3). 12.99 *(978-1-368-04700-5(9))* Disney Pr.

—5-Minute Racing Stories. Disney Books. 2017. (5-Minute Stories Ser.). (ENG.). 192p. (J). (gr. 1-3). 12.99 *(978-1-368-00075-8(4))* Disney Pr.

Disney Storybook Art Team. 5-Minute Sleepy Time Stories. Disney Books. 2020. (5-Minute Stories Ser.). (ENG.). 208p. (J). (gr. k-3). 14.99 ***(978-1-368-05538-3(9))*** Disney Pr.

Disney Storybook Art Team. 5-Minute Snuggle Stories. Disney Books. 2013. (5-Minute Stories Ser.). (ENG.). 192p. (J). (gr. -1 — 1). 12.99 *(978-1-4231-6765-5(1))* Disney Pr.

—5-Minute Spooky Stories. Disney Book Group. 2014. (5-Minute Stories Ser.). (ENG.). 192p. (J). (gr. -1-k). 12.99 *(978-1-4231-8915-2(9))* Disney Pr.

—5-Minute under the Sea Stories. Disney Books. 2020. (5-Minute Stories Ser.). (ENG.). 192p. (J). (gr. k-3). 12.99 *(978-1-368-05552-9(4))* Disney Pr.

—5-Minute Winnie the Pooh Stories. Disney Book Group. 2017. (5-Minute Stories Ser.). (ENG.). 192p. (J). (gr. 1-3). 12.99 *(978-1-368-01399-4(6))* Disney Pr.

—365 Bedtime Stories. Disney Book Group. 2017. (365 Stories Ser.). (ENG.). 368p. (J). (gr. 1-3). 15.99 *(978-1-368-01821-0(1))* Disney Pr.

Disney Storybook Art Team & Batson, Alan. The Kitchen Catastrophe. Redbank, Tennant. 2016. (ENG.). 64p. (J). (gr. 1-4). 5.99 *(978-0-7364-3643-4(X)*, RH/Disney) Random Hse. Children's Bks.

Disney Storybook Art Team & DiCicco Studios. Disney: Let's Play! First Look & Find. PI Kids. 2018. (Look & Find Ser.). (ENG.). 18p. (J). ***(978-1-5037-4331-1(4)***, 1d2d4d0d-d20a-4dff-96c2-fe4fb70321e3, p i kids) Phoenix International Publications, Inc.

Disney Storybook Art Team & DiCicco, Sue. Disney Junior Mickey Mouse Clubhouse: Little First Look & Find Book & Puzzle. PI Kids. 2020. (Look & Find Ser.). (ENG.). 16p. (J). bds., bds. ***(978-1-5037-5591-8(6)***, 023a143d-ffd7-4416-81da-4ce2f9e78b03, p i kids) Phoenix International Publications, Inc.

Disney Storybook Art Team & Houston, Lauren. Disney Baby My First Words. Disney Book Group. 2014. (ENG.). 24p. (J). (gr. -1 — 1). bds. 7.99 *(978-1-4847-0915-3(2))* Disney Pr.

Disney Storybook Art Team & Imaginism Studio. Disney Junior. 2020. (Me Reader Ser.). (ENG.). 192p. (J). *(978-1-5037-5111-8(2)*, 33a9f411-fca1-4f6f-bdbc-de5c0343e72b, p i kids) Phoenix International Publications, Inc.

—Disney Junior Fancy Nancy. Winslow, Claire. 2019. (ENG.). 60p. (J). bds., bds. *(978-1-5037-5251-1(8)*, 19e72e37-6fa7-4b1b-83e2-156226b9d0f4, p i kids) Phoenix International Publications, Inc.

—Disney Junior Fancy Nancy. Broderick, Kathy. 2019. (Look & Find Ser.). (ENG.). (J). 20p. *(978-1-5037-5071-5(X)*, a94083ec-c892-4831-bc25-9b195cd8cfe6); 18p. *(978-1-5037-4645-9(3)*, d040b972-8474-4a91-8ef4-8b6a7e308388) Phoenix International Publications, Inc. (p i kids).

—Disney Junior Fancy Nancy. Broderick, Kathy et al. 2019. (Me Reader Ser.). (ENG.). 192p. (J). *(978-1-5037-4604-6(6)*, 5c034f19-e91d-44ac-b250-2adfa8b1d30f, p i kids) Phoenix International Publications, Inc.

Disney Storybook Art Team & Imaginism Studios, Inc. Vampirina Home Scream Home: Read-Along Storybook & CD. Disney Book Group. 2018. (Read-Along Storybook & CD Ser.). (ENG.). 32p. (J). (gr. -1-k). pap. 6.99 *(978-1-368-02065-7(8))* Disney Pr.

—Vampirina Snowplace Like Home. Disney Book Group. 2018. (ENG.). 24p. (J). (gr. -1-k). pap. 5.99 *(978-1-368-01563-9(8))* Disney Pr.

—Vampirina Vee's Monster Bash: With Puffy Stickers! Disney Book Group. 2018. (ENG.). 24p. (J). (gr. -1-k). pap. 5.99 *(978-1-368-02060-2(7))* Disney Pr.

—World of Reading: Vampirina the Surprise Party (Pre-Level 1 Reader) With Stickers. Disney Book Group. 2017. (World of Reading Ser.). (ENG.). 32p. (J). (gr. -1-k). pap. 4.99 *(978-1-368-01027-6(X))* Disney Pr.

—World of Reading: Vampirina Vampirina in the Fall (Level 1) Disney Book Group. 2018. (World of Reading Ser.). (ENG.). 32p. (J). (gr. -1-k). pap. 4.99 *(978-1-368-01564-6(6))* Disney Pr.

Disney Storybook Art Team & Imaginism Studios Staff. Disney - Fancy Nancy: Ooh la La! - I Love Being Fancy! Broderick, Kathy. 2019. (Play-A-Sound Ser.). (ENG.). 12p. (J). *(978-1-5037-4594-0(5)*, 0e72296e-91ab-4cfc-85c8-8186135d9f94, p i kids) Phoenix International Publications, Inc.

Disney Storybook Art Team & Melaranci, Elisabetta. Disney Before the Story: Anna Finds a Friend. Egan, Kate. 2020. (Disney Before the Story Ser.). (ENG.). 128p. (J). (gr. k-3). pap. 6.99 *(978-1-368-05604-5(0))* Disney Pr.

Disney Storybook Art Team & No New Art Needed. Gravity Falls Pining Away. Disney Book Group. 2014. (Gravity Falls Chapter Book Ser.: 1). (ENG.). 112p. (J). (gr. 1-3). pap. 4.99 *(978-1-4847-1139-2(4))* Disney Pr.

Disney Storybook Art Team & Premise Entertainment. Happy Birthday, Puppy Pals! Disney Book Group. 2018. (ENG.). 24p. (J). (gr. -1-k). pap. 5.99 *(978-1-368-01086-3(5))* Disney Pr.

—Puppy Dog Pals Best Pug Pals. Disney Book Group. 2018. (ENG.). 12p. (J). (gr. -1-k). bds. 8.99 *(978-1-368-00420-6(2))* Disney Pr.

—Puppy Dog Pals Bingo & Rolly's Jokes & Riddles. Disney Book Group. 2017. (ENG.). 48p. (J). (gr. -1-k). pap. 4.99 *(978-1-368-00617-0(5))* Disney Pr.

—Puppy Dog Pals Design-A-Dog. Disney Book Group. 2017. (ENG.). 24p. (J). (gr. -1-k). pap. 4.99 *(978-1-368-00418-3(0))* Disney Pr.

—Puppy Dog Pals Haunted Howl-Oween: With Glow-In-the-Dark Stickers! Disney Book Group. 2018. (ENG.). 24p. (J). (gr. -1-k). pap. 5.99 *(978-1-368-01561-5(1))* Disney Pr.

—Puppy Dog Pals Puppy Dog Pals Mission: Fun: A Lift-The-Flap Book. Disney Book Group. 2018. (Lift-And-Seek Ser.). (ENG.). 12p. (J). (gr. -1-k). bds. 10.99 *(978-1-368-01029-0(6))* Disney Pr.

—Puppy Dog Pals Read-Along Storybook & CD Adventures in Puppy-Sitting. Disney Book Group. 2017. (Read-Along Storybook & CD Ser.). (ENG.). 32p. (J). (gr. -1-k). pap. 6.99 *(978-1-368-01030-6(X))* Disney Pr.

—Vampirina Read-Along Book & CD Vee's Slumber Party. Disney Book Group. 2017. (Read-Along Storybook & CD Ser.). (ENG.). 32p. (J). (gr. -1-k). pap. 6.99 *(978-1-368-00620-0(5))* Disney Pr.

—World of Reading: Puppy Dog Pals Ice, Ice, Puggy (Level 1 Reader) With Stickers. Disney Book Group. 2017. (World of Reading Ser.). (ENG.). 32p. (J). (gr. -1-k). pap. 4.99 *(978-1-368-01031-3(8))* Disney Pr.

—World of Reading: Puppy Dog Pals Pups on a Mission (Level 1 Reader Plus Fun Facts) Disney Books. 2018. (World of Reading Ser.). (ENG.). 32p. (J). (gr. -1-k). pap. 4.99 *(978-1-368-02044-2(5))* Disney Pr.

—World of Reading: Vampirina Scare B & B: Level 1 with Stickers. Disney Book Group. 2017. (World of Reading Ser.). (ENG.). 32p. (J). (gr. -1-k). pap. 4.99 *(978-1-368-00965-2(4))* Disney Pr.

Disney Storybook Art Team & Shimabukuro, Denise. Disney Before the Story: Mulan's Secret Plan. Roehl, Tessa. 2020. (Disney Before the Story Ser.). (ENG.). 128p. (J). (gr. k-3). pap. 6.99 *(978-1-368-05603-8(2))* Disney Pr.

Disney Storybook Art Team, jt. illus. see Chilvers, Nigel.

Disney Storybook Art Team, jt. illus. see Fang, Susan Chen.

Disney Storybook Art Team, jt. illus. see Loter, Inc.

Disney Storybook Art Team, jt. illus. see Mawhinney, Art.

Disney Storybook Art Team, jt. illus. see No New Art Needed.

Disney Storybook Art Team, jt. illus. see Random House Disney Staff.

Disney Storybook Art Team, jt. illus. see Random House Disney.

Disney Storybook Art Team, jt. illus. see RH Disney Staff.

Disney Storybook Art Team, Disney Storybook. All Around Arendelle (Disney Frozen) Stephens, Elle. 2020. (ENG.). 64p. (J). (gr. -1-2). 15.99 ***(978-0-7364-4084-4(4)***, RH/Disney) Random Hse. Children's Bks.

Disney Storybook Art Team, Disney Storybook. Anna, Elsa, & Friends (Disney Frozen 2) RH Disney. 2019. (ENG.). 18p. (J). (— 1). bds. 8.99 *(978-0-7364-4057-8(7)*, RH/Disney) Random Hse. Children's Bks.

—Aurora's Story (Disney Princess) RH Disney. 2019. (Pictureback(R) Ser.). (ENG.). 24p. (J). (gr. -1-2). 5.99 *(978-0-7364-4058-5(5)*, RH/Disney) Random Hse. Children's Bks.

—Behold! the Majestic Unicorn (and Other Not-So-Magical Beings) (Disney/Pixar Onward) RH Disney. 2020. (ENG.). 40p. (J). (gr. -1-2). 9.99 *(978-0-7364-4096-7(8)*, RH/Disney) Random Hse. Children's Bks.

—A Day with Dad (Disney/Pixar Onward) RH Disney. 2020. (Step into Reading Ser.). (ENG.). 32p. (J). (gr. k-2). 5.99 *(978-0-7364-4051-6(8)*, RH/Disney) Random Hse. Children's Bks.

—Disney Junior Fancy Nancy: 5-Minute Stories: Includes 12 Fancy Stories! 2019. (Disney Junior Fancy Nancy Ser.). (ENG.). 192p. (J). (gr. -1 — 1). 12.99 *(978-0-06-284397-5(4))* HarperCollins Pubs.

—Disney Junior Fancy Nancy: Camp Fancy: Includes over 50 Stickers! Tucker, Krista. 2019. (Disney Junior Fancy Nancy Ser.). (ENG.). 24p. (J). (gr. -1-3). pap. 4.99 *(978-0-06-284376-0(1)*, HarperFestival) HarperCollins Pubs.

—Disney Junior Fancy Nancy: Chez Nancy. Parent, Nancy. 2018. (I Can Read Level 1 Ser.). (ENG.). 32p. (J). (gr. -1-3). 16.99 *(978-0-06-288864-8(1))* HarperCollins Pubs.

—Disney Junior Fancy Nancy: Chez Nancy. Parent, Nancy. 2018. (I Can Read Level 1 Ser.). (ENG.). 32p. (J). (gr. -1-3). pap. 4.99 *(978-0-06-279825-1(1)*, HarperCollins) HarperCollins Pubs. Ltd. GBR. Dist: HarperCollins Pubs.

—Disney Junior Fancy Nancy: Easter Bonnet Bug-A-Boo: A Scratch & Sniff Story. Tucker, Krista. 2020. (Disney Junior Fancy Nancy Ser.). (ENG.). 24p. (J). (gr. -1-3). 10.99 *(978-0-06-284380-7(X)*, HarperFestival) HarperCollins Pubs.

—Disney Junior Fancy Nancy: Ice Skater Extraordinaire. Tucker, Krista. 2018. (Disney Junior Fancy Nancy Ser.). (ENG.). 24p. (J). (gr. -1-3). pap. 6.99 *(978-0-06-284395-1(8)*, HarperFestival) HarperCollins Pubs.

—Disney Junior Fancy Nancy: Mademoiselle Mom. Parent, Nancy. 2019. (I Can Read Level 1 Ser.). (ENG.). 32p. (J). (gr. -1-3). 16.99 *(978-0-06-288867-9(6))* HarperCollins Pubs.

—Disney Junior Fancy Nancy: Mademoiselle Mom. Parent, Nancy. 2019. (I Can Read Level 1 Ser.). (ENG.). 32p. (J). (gr. -1-3). pap. 4.99 *(978-0-06-284383-8(4)*, HarperCollins) HarperCollins Pubs. Ltd. GBR. Dist: HarperCollins Pubs.

—Disney Junior Fancy Nancy: Nancy & the Mermaid Ballet. Parent, Nancy. 2020. (Disney Junior Fancy Nancy Ser.). (ENG.). 24p. (J). (gr. -1-3). 4.99 *(978-0-06-298333-6(4)*, HarperCollins) HarperCollins Pubs. Ltd. GBR. Dist: HarperCollins Pubs.

—Disney Junior Fancy Nancy: Nancy & the Nice List. Tucker, Krista. 2019. (Disney Junior Fancy Nancy Ser.). (ENG.). 24p. (J). (gr. -1-3). pap. 9.99 *(978-0-06-284379-1(6)*, HarperFestival) HarperCollins Pubs.

—Disney Junior Fancy Nancy: Nancy Goes to Work. Tucker, Krista. 2019. (Disney Junior Fancy Nancy Ser.). (ENG.). 24p. (J). (gr. -1-3). pap. 6.99 *(978-0-06-284382-1(6)*, HarperFestival) HarperCollins Pubs.

—Disney Junior Fancy Nancy: Nancy Makes Her Mark. Parent, Nancy. 2018. (I Can Read Level 1 Ser.). (ENG.). 32p. (J). (gr. -1-3). 16.99 *(978-0-06-288865-5(X))* HarperCollins Pubs.

—Disney Junior Fancy Nancy: Nancy Makes Her Mark. Parent, Nancy. 2018. (I Can Read Level 1 Ser.). (ENG.). 32p. (J). (gr. -1-3). pap. 4.99 *(978-0-06-279828-2(6)*, HarperCollins) HarperCollins Pubs. Ltd. GBR. Dist: HarperCollins Pubs.

—Disney Junior Fancy Nancy: Nancy Takes the Case. Saxon, Victoria. 2020. (I Can Read Level 1 Ser.). (ENG.). 32p. (J). (gr. -1-3). 16.99 *(978-0-06-288872-3(2))*; pap. 4.99 *(978-0-06-284393-7(1))* HarperCollins Pubs.

—Disney Junior Fancy Nancy: Nancy's Fancy Heirloom. Evans-Sanden, Marisa. 2020. (I Can Read Level 1 Ser.). (ENG.). 32p. (J). (gr. -1-3). 16.99 *(978-0-06-298332-9(6))*; pap. 4.99 *(978-0-06-298335-0(0))* HarperCollins Pubs. Ltd. GBR. (HarperCollins). Dist: HarperCollins Pubs.

—Disney Junior Fancy Nancy: Nancy's Ghostly Halloween: Includes over 50 Stickers! Tucker, Krista. 2018. (Disney Junior Fancy Nancy Ser.). (ENG.). 24p. (J). (gr. -1-3). pap. 4.99 *(978-0-06-279827-5(8)*, HarperFestival) HarperCollins Pubs.

—Disney Junior Fancy Nancy: Operation Fix Marabelle. Parent, Nancy. 2020. (I Can Read Level 1 Ser.). (ENG.). 32p. (J). (gr. -1-3). 16.99 *(978-0-06-288871-6(4))*; pap. 4.99 *(978-0-06-284391-3(5))* HarperCollins Pubs. Ltd. GBR. (HarperCollins). Dist: HarperCollins Pubs.

—Disney Junior Fancy Nancy: School de Fancy. Parent, Nancy. 2018. (Disney Junior Fancy Nancy Ser.). (ENG.). 20p. (J). (gr. -1-3). bds. 9.99 *(978-0-06-284396-8(6))* HarperCollins Pubs.

—Disney Junior Fancy Nancy: the Case of the Disappearing Doll. Parent, Nancy. 2019. (I Can Read Level 1 Ser.). (ENG.). 32p. (J). (gr. -1-3). 16.99 *(978-0-06-288868-6(4))* HarperCollins Pubs.

—Disney Junior Fancy Nancy: the Case of the Disappearing Doll. Parent, Nancy. 2019. (I Can Read Level 1 Ser.). (ENG.). 32p. (J). (gr. -1-3). pap. 4.99 *(978-0-06-284385-2(0)*, HarperCollins) HarperCollins Pubs. Ltd. GBR. Dist: HarperCollins Pubs.

—Disney Junior Fancy Nancy: What's Your Fancy? Tucker, Krista. 2019. (Disney Junior Fancy Nancy Ser.). (ENG.). 40p. (J). (gr. -1-3). 15.99 *(978-0-06-284473-6(3))* HarperCollins Pubs.

—Ducky & Bunny Help Out! (Disney/Pixar Toy Story 4) RH Disney. 2020. (Step into Reading Ser.). (ENG.). 24p. (J). (gr. -1-1). 12.99 *(978-0-7364-8291-2(1))*; 5.99 *(978-0-7364-4055-4(0))* Random Hse. Children's Bks. (RH/Disney).

—Dumbo (Disney Classic) RH Disney. 2004. (Little Golden Book Ser.). (ENG.). 24p. (J). (gr. -1-2). 4.99 *(978-0-7364-2309-0(5)*, Golden/Disney) Random Hse. Children's Bks.

—Elsa's Epic Journey (Disney Frozen 2) Amerikaner, Susan. 2019. (Step into Reading Ser.). (ENG.). 32p. (J). (gr. -1-1). 5.99 *(978-0-7364-4026-4(7))*; 12.99 *(978-0-7364-8283-7(0))* Random Hse. Children's Bks. (RH/Disney).

—Frozen 2 Big Golden Book (Disney Frozen 2) 2019. (Big Golden Book Ser.). (ENG.). 48p. (J). (gr. -1-2). 10.99 *(978-0-7364-4034-9(8)*, Golden/Disney) Random Hse. Children's Bks.

—Frozen 2: the Deluxe Junior Novelization (Disney Frozen 2) Blaze, David. 2019. (ENG.). 208p. (J). (gr. 3-7). 14.99 *(978-0-7364-4030-1(5)*, RH/Disney) Random Hse. Children's Bks.

—Jack-Jack Attack (Disney/Pixar the Incredibles) Andrews, Mark & Swager, Krista. 2018. (Little Golden Book Ser.). (ENG.). 24p. (J). (gr. k-k). 4.99 *(978-0-7364-2377-9(X)*, Golden/Disney) Random Hse. Children's Bks.

—The Lion King Deluxe Step into Reading (Disney the Lion King) Carbone, Courtney. 2019. (Step into Reading Ser.). (ENG.). 24p. (J). (gr. -1-1). 12.99 *(978-0-7364-8276-9(8)*, RH/Disney) Random Hse. Children's Bks.

—Made to Play! (Disney/Pixar Toy Story 4) Bouchard, Natasha. 2019. (Step into Reading Ser.). (ENG.). 24p. (J). (gr. -1-1). 12.99 *(978-0-7364-8277-6(6)*, RH/Disney) Random Hse. Children's Bks.

Disney Storybook Art Team, Disney Storybook. Moana Little Golden Board Book (Disney Princess) RH Disney. 2020. (ENG.). 26p. (J). (gr. -1-2). bds. 7.99 ***(978-0-7364-4070-7(4)***, Golden/Disney) Random Hse. Children's Bks.

Disney Storybook Art Team, Disney Storybook. Moana's New Friend (Disney Moana) Liberts, Jennifer. 2019. (Step into Reading Ser.). (ENG.). 24p. (J). (gr. -1-1). 12.99 *(978-0-7364-8279-0(2)*, RH/Disney) Random Hse. Children's Bks.

—Mom & Me (Disney Princess) Hurley, Kalikolehua. 2020. (Pictureback(R) Ser.). (ENG.). 24p. (J). (gr. -1-2). 5.99 *(978-0-7364-4042-4(9)*, RH/Disney) Random Hse. Children's Bks.

—Mulan's Story (Disney Princess) Katschke, Judy. 2020. (Pictureback(R) Ser.). (ENG.). 24p. (J). (gr. -1-2). 5.99 *(978-0-7364-4043-1(7)*, RH/Disney) Random Hse. Children's Bks.

—Olaf's Little Library (Disney Frozen) 4 Board Books. RH Disney. 2020. (ENG.). 96p. (J). (— 1). bds. 15.99 *(978-0-7364-4097-4(6)*, RH/Disney) Random Hse. Children's Bks.

—Old Friends, New Friends (Disney/Pixar Toy Story 4) Bouchard, Natasha. 2019. (Step into Reading Ser.). (ENG.). 24p. (J). (gr. -1-1). 5.99 *(978-0-7364-4011-0(9)*, RH/Disney) Random Hse. Children's Bks.

Disney Storybook Art Team, Disney Storybook. The One & Only Ivan: New Friends. Hosten, Colin. 2020. (I Can Read Level 1 Ser.). (ENG.). 32p. (J). (gr. -1-3). pap. 4.99 ***(978-0-06-301709-2(1)***, HarperCollins) HarperCollins Pubs. Ltd. GBR. Dist: HarperCollins Pubs.

Disney Storybook Art Team, Disney Storybook. Onward Deluxe Step into Reading #1 (Disney/Pixar Onward) RH Disney. 2020. (Step into Reading Ser.). (ENG.). 32p. (J). (gr. k-2). 12.99 *(978-0-7364-8289-9(X)*, RH/Disney) Random Hse. Children's Bks.

—Onward: the Deluxe Junior Novelization (Disney/Pixar Onward) Francis, Suzanne. 2020. (ENG.). 144p. (J). (gr. 2-5). 9.99 *(978-0-7364-4050-9(X)*, RH/Disney) Random Hse. Children's Bks.

—A Puppy for Miguel (Disney/Pixar Coco) Lagonegro, Melissa. 2019. (Step into Reading Ser.). (ENG.). 24p. (J). (gr. -1-1). 12.99 *(978-0-7364-8275-2(X)*, RH/Disney) Random Hse. Children's Bks.

—Spirits of Nature (Disney Frozen 2) Bouchard, Natasha. 2019. (Step into Reading Ser.). (ENG.). 24p. (J). (gr. -1-1).

5.99 *(978-0-7364-4028-8(3)*, RH/Disney) Random Hse. Children's Bks.

Disney Storybook Art Team, Disney Storybook. Walt Disney's Alice in Wonderland Little Golden Board Book (Disney Classic) RH Disney. 2020. (ENG.). 26p. (J). (gr. -1-2). bds. 7.99 ***(978-0-7364-4071-4(2)***, Golden/Disney) Random Hse. Children's Bks.

Disney Storybook Art Team, Disney Storybook. Walt Disney's Cinderella Little Golden Board Book (Disney Classic) RH Disney. 2020. (Little Golden Book Ser.). (ENG.). 26p. (J). (gr. -1-2). bds. 7.99 *(978-0-7364-4094-3(1)*, Golden/Disney) Random Hse. Children's Bks.

—We'll Always Have Each Other (Disney Frozen 2) Edwards, John. 2019. (Pictureback(R) Ser.). (ENG.). 24p. (J). (gr. -1-2). 5.99 *(978-0-7364-4035-6(6)*, RH/Disney) Random Hse. Children's Bks.

—The Wizard in You! (Disney/Pixar Onward) Behling, Steve. 2020. (Pictureback(R) Ser.). (ENG.). 24p. (J). (gr. -1-2). 5.99 *(978-0-7364-3961-9(7)*, RH/Disney) Random Hse. Children's Bks.

Disney Storybook Art Team, Disney Storybook. You're Worth Melting for (Disney Frozen) Roth, Megan. 2020. (ENG.). 32p. (J). (gr. -1-2). 10.99 ***(978-0-7364-4081-3(X)***, RH/Disney) Random Hse. Children's Bks.

Disney Storybook Art Team, Disney Storybook, jt. illus. see Balian, Nick.

Disney Storybook Artists. Aurora Plays the Part. RH Disney Staff. 2018. (Stepping Stone Book(TM) Ser.). (ENG.). 128p. (J). (gr. 1-4). 6.99 *(978-0-7364-3795-0(9)*, RH/Disney) Random Hse. Children's Bks.

—Be Mindful, Donald! A Mickey & Friends Story. Saxon, Vickie. 2018. (Disney Learning Everyday Stories Ser.). (ENG.). 32p. (J). (gr. k-3). pap. 8.99 *(978-1-5415-3284-7(8)*, Lerner Pubns.) Lerner Publishing Group.

Disney Storybook Artists. Disney Junior Vampirina. PI Kids. 2020. (Play-A-Sound Ser.). (ENG.). 12p. (J). bds. ***(978-1-5037-5215-3(1)***, 70671f70-e3bb-4c79-b989-d5df2df2ffb6, p i kids) Phoenix International Publications, Inc.

—Disney Mickey Mouse Clubhouse. PI Kids. 2020. (ENG.). 120p. (J). bds., bds. ***(978-1-5037-5611-3(4)***, fce427ae-7b73-4e58-9405-d0c2931ff02d, p i kids) Phoenix International Publications, Inc.

Disney Storybook Artists. Disney Princess Beginnings: Aurora Plays the Part. RH Disney Staff. 2018. (Stepping Stone Book(TM) Ser.). (ENG.). 128p. (J). (gr. 1-4). lib. bdg. 12.99 *(978-0-7364-8260-8(1)*, RH/Disney) Random Hse. Children's Bks.

—Hatastrophe (Disney Muppet Babies) Random House. 2019. (Little Golden Book Ser.). (ENG.). 24p. (J). (gr. -1-2). 4.99 *(978-0-7364-3995-4(1)*, Golden/Disney) Random Hse. Children's Bks.

—Just Like Me? A Frozen Story. Saxon, Vickie. 2018. (Disney Learning Everyday Stories Ser.). (ENG.). 32p. (J). (gr. k-3). pap. 8.99 *(978-1-5415-3292-2(9)*, Lerner Pubns.) Lerner Publishing Group.

—The Lion King (Disney the Lion King) Liberts, Jennifer. 2019. (Big Golden Book Ser.). (ENG.). 48p. (J). (gr. -1-2). 10.99 *(978-0-7364-3977-0(3)*, Golden/Disney) Random Hse. Children's Bks.

—Merida: Legend of the Emeralds. O'Ryan, Ellie. 2017. (Disney Princess Ser.). (ENG.). 96p. (J). (gr. 2-6). lib. bdg. 27.07 *(978-1-5321-4121-8(1)*, 26994, Chapter Bks.) Spotlight.

—Moana & Pua (Disney Moana) Lagonegro, Melissa. 2019. (Step into Reading Ser.). (ENG.). 24p. (J). (gr. -1-1). 12.99 *(978-0-7364-8271-4(7)*, RH/Disney) Random Hse. Children's Bks.

—Moana's New Friend (Disney Moana) Liberts, Jennifer. 2019. (Step into Reading Ser.). (ENG.). 24p. (J). (gr. -1-1). 5.99 *(978-0-7364-3991-6(9)*, RH/Disney) Random Hse. Children's Bks.

—Nala & Simba (Disney the Lion King) Tillworth, Mary. 2019. (Step into Reading Ser.). (ENG.). 24p. (J). (gr. -1-1). 5.99 *(978-0-7364-4013-4(5)*, RH/Disney) Random Hse. Children's Bks.

—The Night Sky: A Frozen Discovery Book. Dichter, Paul. 2018. (Disney Learning Discovery Bks.). (ENG.). 48p. (J). (gr. 2-5). pap. 8.99 *(978-1-5415-3268-7(6)*, Lerner Pubns.) Lerner Publishing Group.

—The Ocean World: A Finding Dory Discovery Book. Dichter, Paul. 2018. (Disney Learning Discovery Bks.). (ENG.). 48p. (J). (gr. 2-5). pap. 8.99 *(978-1-5415-3272-4(4)*, Lerner Pubns.) Lerner Publishing Group.

—The Pacific Islands: A Moana Discovery Book. Dichter, Paul. 2018. (Disney Learning Discovery Bks.). (ENG.). 48p. (J). (gr. 2-5). pap. 8.99 *(978-1-5415-3276-2(7)*, Lerner Pubns.) Lerner Publishing Group.

—Phineas & Ferb Christmas Vacation. Disney Book Group. 2011. (Phineas & Ferb 8x8 Ser.). (ENG.). 24p. (J). (gr. k-3). pap. 18.69 *(978-1-4231-3732-0(9))* Disney Pr.

—A Puppy for Miguel (Disney/Pixar Coco) Lagonegro, Melissa. 2019. (Step into Reading Ser.). (ENG.). 24p. (J). (gr. -1-1). pap. 5.99 *(978-0-7364-3983-1(8)*, RH/Disney) Random Hse. Children's Bks.

—The Science of Cars: A Cars Discovery Book. Heiman, Larry. 2018. (Disney Learning Discovery Bks.). (ENG.). 48p. (J). (gr. 2-5). pap. 8.99 *(978-1-5415-3280-9(5)*, Lerner Pubns.) Lerner Publishing Group.

—Tiana: The Stolen Jewel. Glass, Calliope. 2017. (Disney Princess Ser.). (ENG.). 96p. (J). (gr. 2-6). lib. bdg. 27.07 *(978-1-5321-4122-5(X)*, 26995, Chapter Bks.) Spotlight.

—Tiana's Winter Treats. Homberg, Ruth. 2018. (Step into Reading Ser.). (ENG.). 24p. (J). (gr. -1-1). lib. bdg. 12.99 *(978-0-7364-3871-1(8)*, RH/Disney) Random Hse. Children's Bks.

—Tiana's Winter Treats (Disney Princess) Homberg, Ruth. 2018. (Step into Reading Ser.). (ENG.). 24p. (J). (gr. -1-1). pap. 4.99 *(978-0-7364-3870-4(X)*, RH/Disney) Random Hse. Children's Bks.

—Who Needs a Hug? A Finding Dory Story. Sycamore, Beth. 2018. (Disney Learning Everyday Stories Ser.). (ENG.). 32p. (J). (gr. k-3). pap. 8.99 *(978-1-5415-3296-0(1)*, Lerner Pubns.) Lerner Publishing Group.

—World of Reading World of Reading: Disney Jr. 's Best Day Ever! 3-In-1 Listen-along Reader (Level 1) Disney Books. 2020. (World of Reading Ser.). (ENG.). 96p. (J). (gr. -1-k). pap. 7.99 *(978-1-368-04497-4(2))* Disney Pr.

Disney Storybook Artists, jt. illus. see Lee, Grace.

Disney Storybook Artists, Disney Storybook. Be Mindful, Donald! A Mickey & Friends Story. Saxon, Vickie. 2018. (Disney Learning Everyday Stories Ser.). (ENG.). 32p. (J). (gr. k-3). lib. bdg. 31.99 *(978-1-5415-3255-7(4)*, Lerner Pubns.) Lerner Publishing Group.

—Coding with Anna & Elsa: A Frozen Guide to Blockly. Prottsman, Kiki. 2018. (ENG.). 48p. (J). (gr. 2-5). lib. bdg. 31.99 *(978-1-5415-3266-3(X)*, Lerner Pubns.) Lerner Publishing Group.

—Hotheads: An Inside Out Story. Higginson, Sheila. 2018. (Disney Learning Everyday Stories Ser.). (ENG.). 32p. (J). (gr. k-3). lib. bdg. 31.99 *(978-1-5415-3250-2(3)*, Lerner Pubns.) Lerner Publishing Group.

—Just Like Me? A Frozen Story. Saxon, Vickie. 2018. (Disney Learning Everyday Stories Ser.). (ENG.). 32p. (J). (gr. k-3). lib. bdg. 31.99 *(978-1-5415-3251-9(1)*, Lerner Pubns.) Lerner Publishing Group.

—The Night Sky: A Frozen Discovery Book. Dichter, Paul. 2018. (Disney Learning Discovery Bks.). (ENG.). 48p. (J). (gr. 2-5). lib. bdg. 31.99 *(978-1-5415-3260-1(0)*, Lerner Pubns.) Lerner Publishing Group.

—The Ocean World: A Finding Dory Discovery Book. Dichter, Paul. 2018. (Disney Learning Discovery Bks.). (ENG.). 48p. (J). (gr. 2-5). lib. bdg. 31.99 *(978-1-5415-3259-5(7)*, Lerner Pubns.) Lerner Publishing Group.

—The Pacific Islands: A Moana Discovery Book. Dichter, Paul. 2018. (Disney Learning Discovery Bks.). (ENG.). 48p. (J). (gr. 2-5). lib. bdg. 31.99 *(978-1-5415-3258-8(9)*, Lerner Pubns.) Lerner Publishing Group.

—The Science of Cars: A Cars Discovery Book. Heiman, Larry. 2018. (Disney Learning Discovery Bks.). (ENG.). 48p. (J). (gr. 2-5). lib. bdg. 31.99 *(978-1-5415-3261-8(9)*, Lerner Pubns.) Lerner Publishing Group.

—Who Needs a Hug? A Finding Dory Story. Sycamore, Beth. 2018. (Disney Learning Everyday Stories Ser.). (ENG.). 32p. (J). (gr. k-3). lib. bdg. 31.99 *(978-1-5415-3254-0(6)*, Lerner Pubns.) Lerner Publishing Group.

Disney Storybook Artists Staff. Alice in Wonderland (Disney Alice in Wonderland) Bobowicz, Pamela. 2013. (Step into Reading Ser.). (ENG.). 32p. (J). (gr. -1-1). pap. 3.99 *(978-0-7364-3027-2(X)*, RH/Disney) Random Hse. Children's Bks.

—Always a Princess (Disney Princess) Posner-Sanchez, Andrea. 2011. (ENG.). 48p. (J). (gr. k — 1). bds. 10.99 *(978-0-7364-2848-4(8)*, RH/Disney) Random Hse. Children's Bks.

Disney Storybook Artists Staff, et al. Disney's the Lion King. 2007. (Play-A-Sound Ser.). 16p. (J). (gr. -1-3). 16.98 *(978-1-4127-8776-5(9))* Publications International, Ltd.

Disney Storybook Artists Staff. Fabulous Fashions. Walter Foster Jr. Creative Team. 2014. (Learn to Draw Favorite Characters: Expanded Edition Ser.). (ENG.). 64p. (J). (gr. 3-5). 33.32 *(978-1-939581-32-7(X)*, Walter Foster Jr) Quarto Publishing Group USA.

—Finding Nemo. 2007. (Play-A-Sound Ser.). 15p. (J). (gr. -1-3). 15.98 *(978-1-4127-8754-3(8))* Publications International, Ltd.

—Furry, Fluffy & Fabulous! (Disney Princess: Palace Pets) RH Disney Staff. 2014. (Big Golden Book Ser.). (ENG.). 64p. (J). (gr. -1-2). 9.99 *(978-0-7364-3263-4(9)*, Golden/Disney) Random Hse. Children's Bks.

—A Horse to Love: An Enchanted Stables Story. Lagonegro, Melissa & RH Disney Staff. 2007. (Pictureback(R) Ser.). (ENG.). 16p. (J). (gr. -1-2). pap. 3.99 *(978-0-7364-2504-9(7)*, RH/Disney) Random Hse. Children's Bks.

—The Incredible Elastigirl. Bouchard, Natasha. 2018. (Step into Reading Ser.). (ENG.). 32p. (J). (gr. -1-1). pap. 5.99 *(978-0-7364-3857-5(2)*, RH/Disney) Random Hse. Children's Bks.

—Learn to Draw Mickey & His Friends. Walter Foster Jr. Creative Team. 2014. (Learn to Draw Favorite Characters: Expanded Edition Ser.). (ENG.). 64p. (J). (gr. 3-5). lib. bdg. 33.32 *(978-1-939581-15-0(X)*, Walter Foster Jr) Quarto Publishing Group USA.

—Learn to Draw Winnie the Pooh. Walter Foster Jr. Creative Team. 2014. (Learn to Draw Favorite Characters: Expanded Edition Ser.). (ENG.). 64p. (J). (gr. 3-5). lib. bdg. 33.32 *(978-1-939581-16-7(8)*, Walter Foster Jr) Quarto Publishing Group USA.

—Let's Cruise! RH Disney Staff. 2017. (ENG.). 12p. (J). (gr. k — 1). bds. 10.99 *(978-0-7364-2391-5(5)*, RH/Disney) Random Hse. Children's Bks.

—Minnie: Minnie's Valentine. Disney Book Group Staff & Higginson, Sheila Sweeny. 2013. 10p. 5.99 *(978-1-4231-8811-7(X))* Disney Pr.

—My Firstlibrary 12 Board Books Mickey Mouse. Publications International Ltd. Staff & p i kids. 2014. (ENG.). 120p. (J). bds. 6.10 net. *(978-1-4127-6851-1(9)*, e3102c8d-4b95-4dd0-94da-67af996c766f) Phoenix International Publications, Inc.

—Rani: Two Friendship Tales. Papademetriou, Lisa & Morris, Kimberly. 2010. (Disney Fairies Ser.). (ENG.). 240p. (J). (gr. 1-4). 24.94 *(978-0-7364-2730-2(9))* Random House Publishing Group.

—Run, Remy, Run! Richards, Kitty & RH Disney Staff. 2007. (Step into Reading Ser.). (ENG.). 32p. (J). (gr. k-3). pap. 3.99 *(978-0-7364-2476-9(8)*, RH/Disney) Random Hse. Children's Bks.

—Snow White & the Seven Dwarfs. Berrios, Frank & RH Disney Staff. 2006. (Read-Aloud Board Book Ser.). (ENG.). 24p. (J). (gr. k — 1). bds. 4.99 *(978-0-7364-2426-4(1)*, RH/Disney) Random Hse. Children's Bks.

—Toy Story. Walter Foster Jr. Creative Team. 2014. (Learn to Draw Favorite Characters: Expanded Edition Ser.). (ENG.). 64p. (J). (gr. 3-5). lib. bdg. 33.32 *(978-1-939581-12-9(5)*, Walter Foster Jr) Quarto Publishing Group USA.

—The Uncanny X-Men. Thomas, Rich. 2012. (Marvel Origins Ser.). (ENG.). 48p. (J). (gr. k-5). lib. bdg. 27.07 *(978-1-61479-012-9(4)*, 11340, Marvel Age) Spotlight.

—Wreck-It Ralph 2 Movie Storybook (Disney Wreck-It Ralph 2) Scollon, Bill. 2018. (ENG.). 96p. (J). (gr. -1-2). pap. 9.99 *(978-0-7364-3754-7(1)*, RH/Disney) Random Hse. Children's Bks.

Disney Storybook Artists Staff & Random House Disney Staff. Driving Buddies. Jordan, Apple. 2006. (Step into Reading Ser.). (ENG.). 32p. (J). (gr. k-3). pap. 4.99 *(978-0-7364-2339-7(7)*, RH/Disney) Random Hse. Children's Bks.

Disney Storybook Artists Staff & Studio Iboix Staff. Aurora & the Helpful Dragon/Tiana & Her Furry Friend. Random House Editors & RH Disney Staff. 2011. (Pictureback(R) Ser.). (ENG.). 32p. (J). (gr. -1-2). pap. 4.99 *(978-0-7364-2757-9(0)*, RH/Disney) Random Hse. Children's Bks.

Disney Storybook Artists Staff & Thammavongsa, Christine. The Little Mermaid. 2007. (Play-A-Sound Bks.). 18p. (J). (gr. -1-3). bds. 16.98 *(978-1-4127-8775-8(0))* Publications International, Ltd.

Disney Storybook Artists Staff & Walt Disney Studios Staff. Bambi. Golden Books Staff. Chambers, Whittaker, tr. 2004. (Little Golden Book Ser.). (ENG.). 24p. (J). (gr. -1-2). 4.99 *(978-0-7364-2308-3(7)*, Golden/Disney) Random Hse. Children's Bks.

Disney Storybook Artists Staff, jt. illus. see Batson, Alan.

Disney Storybook Artists Staff, jt. illus. see Clarke, Judith Holmes.

Disney Storybook Artists Staff, jt. illus. see Lee, Grace.

Disney Storybook Artists Staff, jt. illus. see Mawhinney, Art.

Disney Storybook Artists Staff, jt. illus. see Random House Editors.

Disney Storybook Artists Staff, jt. illus. see RH Disney Staff.

Disney Storybook Artists Staff, jt. illus. see Studio IBOIX.

Dissanayake, Thakshila. The True Story of the Spiritual Awakening of Lord Ganesha: Interactive Personal Development Book with Exercises for All. Janik, Kate. 2019. (Lord Ganesha True Stories Ser.: Vol. 1). (ENG.). 50p. (J). pap. 24.90 ***(978-1-7129-2415-0(X))*** Independently Published.

Dister, Jillian. Snowy Day. Soto, Anabel. 2019. (ENG.). 30p. (J). pap. 15.99 ***(978-1-9866-9528-2(X))*** CreateSpace Independent Publishing Platform.

Ditama, Bow. Mahoromatic, Vol. 5. rev. ed. 2005. 184p. pap. 14.99 *(978-1-59182-915-7(1)*, Tokyopop Adult) TOKYOPOP, Inc.

—Mahoromatic: Automatic Maiden, 4 vols., Vol. 1. Nakayama, Bunjuro. 2004. 192p. pap. 14.99 *(978-1-59182-729-0(9)*, Tokyopop Adult) TOKYOPOP, Inc.

—Mahoromatic: Automatic Maiden, 6 vols. Nakayama, Bunjuro. rev. ed. Vol. 3. 2004. 192p. pap. 14.99 *(978-1-59182-731-3(0))*; Vol. 6. 2005. 190p. pap. 14.99 *(978-1-59182-916-4(X))* TOKYOPOP, Inc. (Tokyopop Adult).

—Mahoromatic: Automatic Maiden: The Misato Residence's Maid, 6 vols., Vol. 4. Nakayama, Bunjuro. rev. ed. 2004. 192p. pap. 14.99 *(978-1-59182-732-0(9)*, Tokyopop Adult) TOKYOPOP, Inc.

DiTerlizzi, Tony. The Beloved Dearly. Cooney, Doug. 2003. (ENG.). 192p. (J). (gr. 3-7). pap. 7.99 *(978-0-689-86354-7(3)*, Simon & Schuster Bks. For Young Readers) Simon & Schuster Bks. For Young Readers.

—Dracula. Stoker, Bram. 2009. (Puffin Classics Ser.). 640p. (J). (gr. 5-7). 6.99 *(978-0-14-132566-8(6)*, Puffin Books) Penguin Young Readers Group.

—Hanging Out. Johnston, Tony. 2003. (Alien & Possum Ser.). 48p. (J). 11.65 *(978-0-7569-1544-5(9))* Perfection Learning Corp.

—The Spider & the Fly: 10th Anniversary Edition. Howitt, Mary. ed. 2012. (ENG.). 40p. (J). (gr. 1-4). 17.99 *(978-1-4424-5454-5(7)*, Simon & Schuster Bks. For Young Readers) Simon & Schuster Bks. For Young Readers.

—The Story of Diva & Flea. Willems, Mo. 2015. (ENG.). 80p. (J). (gr. 1-3). 14.99 *(978-1-4847-2284-8(1))* Disney Pr.

DiTerlizzi, Tony. Arthur Spiderwick's Field Guide to the Fantastical World Around You. DiTerlizzi, Tony. Black, Holly. 2005. (Spiderwick Chronicles Ser.). (ENG.). 142p. (J). (gr. 3). 24.99 *(978-0-689-85941-0(4)*, Simon & Schuster Bks. For Young Readers) Simon & Schuster Bks. For Young Readers.

—Arthur Spiderwick's Field Guide to the Fantastical World Around You: Movie Tie-In Edition. DiTerlizzi, Tony. Black, Holly. movie tie-in ed. 2008. (Spiderwick Chronicles Ser.). (ENG.). 142p. (J). (gr. 3-7). 24.99 *(978-1-4169-6095-9(3)*, Simon & Schuster Bks. For Young Readers) Simon & Schuster Bks. For Young Readers.

—The Battle for WondLa. DiTerlizzi, Tony. 2014. (Search for WondLa Ser.: 3). (ENG.). 496p. (J). (gr. 5). 17.99 *(978-1-4169-8314-9(7)*, Simon & Schuster Bks. For Young Readers) Simon & Schuster Bks. For Young Readers.

—Beyond the Spiderwick Chronicles (Boxed Set) Set: The Nixies Song; a Giant Problem; the Wyrm King, Set. DiTerlizzi, Tony. Black, Holly. ed. 2009. (Beyond the Spiderwick Chronicles Ser.: Nos. 1-3). (ENG.). 528p. (J). (gr. 2-5). 39.99 *(978-1-4169-9011-6(9)*, Simon & Schuster Bks. For Young Readers) Simon & Schuster Bks. For Young Readers.

—Big Fun! DiTerlizzi, Tony. DiTerlizzi, Angela. 2009. (Adventure of Meno Ser.: 1). (ENG.). 48p. (J). (gr. -1-k). 9.99 *(978-1-4169-7148-1(3)*, Simon & Schuster Bks. For Young Readers) Simon & Schuster Bks. For Young Readers.

—The Broken Ornament. DiTerlizzi, Tony. 2018. (ENG.). 48p. (J). (gr. -1-3). 17.99 *(978-1-4169-3976-4(8)*, Simon & Schuster Bks. For Young Readers) Simon & Schuster Bks. For Young Readers.

—Care & Feeding of Sprites. DiTerlizzi, Tony. Black, Holly. 2006. (Spiderwick Chronicles Ser.). (ENG.). 48p. (J). (gr. 2-7). 19.99 *(978-1-4169-2757-0(3)*, Simon & Schuster Bks. For Young Readers) Simon & Schuster Bks. For Young Readers.

—The Field Guide. DiTerlizzi, Tony. Black, Holly. 2003. (Spiderwick Chronicles Ser.: 1). (ENG.). 128p. (J). (gr. 1-5). 12.99 *(978-0-689-85936-6(8)*, 53409542, Simon & Schuster Bks. For Young Readers) Simon & Schuster Bks. For Young Readers.

—The Field Guide. DiTerlizzi, Tony. Black, Holly. ed. (Spiderwick Chronicles Ser.: 1). (ENG.). (J). 2013. 128p. (gr. 1-5). 17.99 *(978-1-4424-8693-5(7))*; 2013. 144p. (gr. 1-5). pap. 7.99 *(978-1-4424-8692-8(9))*; 2008. 128p. (gr. 2-5). 10.99 *(978-1-4169-5017-2(6))* Simon & Schuster Bks. For Young Readers. (Simon & Schuster Bks. For Young Readers).

—G Is for One Gzonk! An Alpha-Number-bet Book. DiTerlizzi, Tony. 2006. (ENG.). 80p. (J). (gr. -1-2). 29.99 *(978-0-689-85290-9(8)*, Simon & Schuster Bks. For Young Readers) Simon & Schuster Bks. For Young Readers.

—A Giant Problem. DiTerlizzi, Tony. Black, Holly. 2008. (Beyond the Spiderwick Chronicles Ser.: 2). (ENG.). 176p. (J). (gr. 2-5). 12.99 *(978-0-689-87132-0(5)*, Simon & Schuster Bks. For Young Readers) Simon & Schuster Bks. For Young Readers.

—A Hero for WondLa. DiTerlizzi, Tony. (Search for WondLa Ser.: 2). (ENG.). (J). (gr. 5). 2013. 480p. pap. 12.99 *(978-1-4169-8313-2(9))*; 2012. 464p. 17.99 *(978-1-4169-8312-5(0))* Simon & Schuster Bks. For Young Readers. (Simon & Schuster Bks. For Young Readers).

—The Ironwood Tree. DiTerlizzi, Tony. Black, Holly. ed. 2013. (Spiderwick Chronicles Ser.: 4). (ENG.). (J). (gr. 1-5). 128p. 15.99 *(978-1-4424-8702-4(X))*; 144p. pap. 7.99 *(978-1-4424-8701-7(1))* Simon & Schuster Bks. For Young Readers. (Simon & Schuster Bks. For Young Readers).

—The Ironwood Tree. DiTerlizzi, Tony. Black, Holly. 4th ed. 2004. (Spiderwick Chronicles Ser.: 4). (ENG.). 128p. (J). (gr. 2-6). 10.99 *(978-0-689-85939-7(2)*, Simon & Schuster Bks. For Young Readers) Simon & Schuster Bks. For Young Readers.

—Jimmy Zangwow's Out-Of-This-World Moon-Pie Adventure. DiTerlizzi, Tony. 2003. (ENG.). 40p. (J). (gr. k-3). 8.99 *(978-0-689-85563-4(X)*, Simon & Schuster Bks. For Young Readers) Simon & Schuster Bks. For Young Readers.

—Kenny & the Dragon. DiTerlizzi, Tony. 2012. (Kenny & the Dragon Ser.). (ENG.). 176p. (J). (gr. 3-7). pap. 8.99 *(978-1-4424-3651-0(4)*, Simon & Schuster Bks. For Young Readers) Simon & Schuster Bks. For Young Readers.

—Kenny & the Dragon. DiTerlizzi, Tony. 2008. 160p. (J). (gr. 3-7). 15.99 Simon & Schuster Children's Publishing.

—Kenny & the Dragon. DiTerlizzi, Tony. 2008. (Kenny & the Dragon Ser.). (ENG.). 160p. (J). (gr. 3-7). 17.99 *(978-1-4169-3977-1(6))* Simon & Schuster, Inc.

—Lucinda's Secret. DiTerlizzi, Tony. Black, Holly. ed. 2013. (Spiderwick Chronicles Ser.: 3). (ENG.). (J). (gr. 1-5). 128p. 17.99 *(978-1-4424-8700-0(3))*; 144p. pap. 7.99 *(978-1-4424-8697-3(X))* Simon & Schuster Bks. For Young Readers. (Simon & Schuster Bks. For Young Readers).

—Lucinda's Secret, BK. 3. DiTerlizzi, Tony. Black, Holly. 3rd ed. 2003. (Spiderwick Chronicles Ser.: 3). (ENG.). 128p. (J). (gr. 2-7). 12.99 *(978-0-689-85938-0(4)*, Simon & Schuster Bks. For Young Readers) Simon & Schuster Bks. For Young Readers.

—The Nixie's Song. DiTerlizzi, Tony. Black, Holly. 2007. (Beyond the Spiderwick Chronicles Ser.: 1). (ENG.). 192p. (J). (gr. 2-6). 12.99 *(978-0-689-87131-3(7)*, Simon & Schuster Bks. For Young Readers) Simon & Schuster Bks. For Young Readers.

—Notebook for Fantastical Observations. DiTerlizzi, Tony. Black, Holly. 2005. (Spiderwick Chronicles Ser.). (ENG.). 240p. (J). (gr. 2-6). 14.99 *(978-1-4169-0345-1(3)*, Simon & Schuster Bks. For Young Readers) Simon & Schuster Bks. For Young Readers.

—The Search for WondLa. DiTerlizzi, Tony. 2012. (Search for WondLa Ser.: 1). (ENG.). 512p. (J). (gr. 5). pap. 12.99 *(978-1-4169-8311-8(2)*, Simon & Schuster Bks. For Young Readers) Simon & Schuster Bks. For Young Readers.

—The Search for WondLa, 1. DiTerlizzi, Tony. 2010. (Search for WondLa Ser.: 1). (ENG.). 496p. (J). (gr. 5-8). 17.99 *(978-1-4169-8310-1(4))* Simon & Schuster, Inc.

—The Search for Wondla, Book 1. DiTerlizzi, Tony. 2012. (Search for Wondla Ser.: Vol. 1). (ENG.). (J). (gr. 5). lib. bdg. 20.60 *(978-1-68065-141-6(2))* Perfection Learning Corp.

—The Seeing Stone. DiTerlizzi, Tony. Black, Holly. (Spiderwick Chronicles Ser.: 2). (ENG.). (J). (gr. 1-5). ed. 2013. 128p. 17.99 *(978-1-4424-8695-9(3))*; ed. 2013. 144p. pap. 7.99 *(978-1-4424-8694-2(5))*; Bk. 2. 2nd ed. 2003. 128p. 12.99 *(978-0-689-85937-3(6)*, 53409541) Simon & Schuster Bks. For Young Readers. (Simon & Schuster Bks. For Young Readers).

—The Spiderwick Chronicles, the Complete Series Set: The Field Guide; the Seeing Stone; Lucinda's Secret; the Ironwood Tree; the Wrath of Mulgrath. DiTerlizzi, Tony. Black, Holly. ed. 2013. (Spiderwick Chronicles Ser.). (ENG.). (J). (gr. 1-5). 752p. pap. 39.99 *(978-1-4424-8798-7(4))*; 672p. 79.99 *(978-1-4424-8797-0(6))* Simon & Schuster Bks. For Young Readers. (Simon & Schuster Bks. For Young Readers).

—Ted. DiTerlizzi, Tony. 2004. (ENG.). 40p. (J). (gr. -1-3). reprint ed. 8.99 *(978-0-689-86374-5(8)*, Simon & Schuster Bks. For Young Readers) Simon & Schuster Bks. For Young Readers.

—Uh-Oh Sick! DiTerlizzi, Tony. DiTerlizzi, Angela. 2010. (Adventure of Meno Ser.: 4). (ENG.). 52p. (J). (gr. -1-k). 9.99 *(978-1-4169-7153-5(X)*, Simon & Schuster Bks. For

Young Readers) Simon & Schuster Bks. For Young Readers.
—Wet Friend! DiTerlizzi, Tony. DiTerlizzi, Angela. 2009. (Adventure of Meno Ser.: 2). (ENG.). 48p. (J). (gr. -1-k). 9.99 *(978-1-4169-7149-8(1)*, Simon & Schuster Bks. For Young Readers) Simon & Schuster Bks. For Young Readers.
—The Wrath of Mulgarath. DiTerlizzi, Tony. Black, Holly. (Spiderwick Chronicles Ser.: 5). (ENG.). (J). ed. 2013. 160p. (gr. 1-5). 15.99 *(978-1-4424-8704-8(6))*; ed. 2013. 176p. (gr. 1-5). pap. 7.99 *(978-1-4424-8703-1(8))*; 5th ed. 2004. 160p. (gr. 2-6). 10.99 *(978-0-689-85940-3(6))* Simon & Schuster Bks. For Young Readers. (Simon & Schuster Bks. For Young Readers).
—The Wyrm King. DiTerlizzi, Tony. Black, Holly. 2009. (Beyond the Spiderwick Chronicles Ser.: 3). (ENG.). 224p. (J). (gr. 2-7). 12.99 *(978-0-689-87133-7(3)*, Simon & Schuster Bks. For Young Readers) Simon & Schuster Bks. For Young Readers.
—Yummy Trip! DiTerlizzi, Tony. DiTerlizzi, Angela. 2010. (Adventure of Meno Ser.: 3). (ENG.). 48p. (J). (gr. -1-k). 9.99 *(978-1-4169-7150-4(5)*, Simon & Schuster Bks. For Young Readers) Simon & Schuster Bks. For Young Readers.
Ditewig, Diann. Eddie & Harry. Kretzmann, Jane. 2014. 48p. (J). *(978-0-9846739-3-3(8))* Cornerstone Pr. Chicago.
Ditko, Steve, et al. Doctor Strange: Lords of Fear. 2018. (ENG.). 264p. (J). (gr. 4-17). pap. 29.99 *(978-1-302-90786-0(7))* Marvel Worldwide, Inc.
Ditko, Steve. Marvel Masters of Suspense: Stan Lee & Steve Ditko Omnibus Vol. 1. 2019. (ENG.). 688p. (YA). (gr. -1-17). 100.00 *(978-1-302-91875-0(3))* Marvel Worldwide, Inc.
—Marvel Masters of Suspense: Stan Lee & Steve Ditko Omnibus Vol. 2. 2020. (ENG.). 696p. (YA). (gr. -1-17). 100.00 *(978-1-302-92209-2(2))* Marvel Worldwide, Inc.
Ditko, Steve, et al. Spider-Man: Spider-Verse - Fearsome Foes. 2018. (Into the Spider-Verse: Fearsome Foes Ser.: 1). (ENG.). 136p. (J). (gr. 5-9). pap. 9.99 *(978-1-302-91412-7(X))* Marvel Worldwide, Inc.
—Spider-Man vs. the Vulture. 2017. (ENG.). 320p. (J). (gr. 4-17). pap. 34.99 *(978-1-302-90706-8(9))* Marvel Worldwide, Inc.
—Spider-Man/Doctor Strange: the Way to Dusty Death. 2017. (ENG.). 336p. (YA). (gr. 8-17). pap. 34.99 *(978-1-302-90701-3(8))* Marvel Worldwide, Inc.
Ditko, Steve, jt. illus. see Tuska, George.
Ditner, Jillian. Creepy, Crawly Tattoo Bugs: 60 Temporary Tattoos That Teach. Roehrig, Artemis. 2019. (Tattoos That Teach Ser.). (ENG.). 14p. (J). pap. 7.95 *(978-1-63586-196-9(9)*, 626196) Storey Publishing, LLC.
Dittus, Jade Moon. Blinky the Magical Elf. Andrew-Kollmann, Marcia. 2012. 28p. pap. 24.95 *(978-1-4626-5345-4(6))* America Star Bks.
DIVINCENZO, Yoselem G. Paisaje de Risas. Robles Echeverria, Maria De Jesus & ALONSO CURIEL, Jorge David. 2013. 72p. pap. 14.99 *(978-1-61196-924-5(7))* Pintos, Yoselem G.
DiVito, Andrea, et al. Brath. Dixon, Chuck. 2003. (Brath Ser.: Vol. 1). 160p. (YA). (gr. 6-18). pap. 9.95 *(978-1-931484-87-9(2))* CrossGeneration Comics, Inc.
DiVito, Anna. Eleanor Roosevelt & the Scary Basement. Merchant, Peter. 2006. (Ready-To-read COFA Ser.). (ENG.). 32p. (J). (gr. k-2). pap. 3.99 *(978-0-689-87205-1(4)*, Simon & Schuster/Paula Wiseman Bks.) Simon & Schuster/Paula Wiseman Bks.
—A Kids' Guide to America's Bill of Rights: Revised Edition. Krull, Kathleen. 2015. (ENG.). 240p. (J). (gr. 3-7). pap. 6.99 *(978-0-06-235230-9(X))* HarperCollins Pubs.
—A Kids' Guide to America's First Ladies. Krull, Kathleen. 2017. (Kids' Guide to American History Ser.). (ENG.). 256p. (J). (gr. 4-6). 21.19 *(978-1-5364-0248-3(6))*; (gr. 3-7). pap. 6.99 *(978-0-06-238106-4(7))* HarperCollins Pubs.
—A Kids' Guide to the American Revolution. Krull, Kathleen. 2018. (Kids' Guide to American History Ser.: 2). (ENG.). 224p. (J). (gr. 3-7). 16.99 *(978-0-06-238110-1(5))*; pap. 6.99 *(978-0-06-238109-5(1))* HarperCollins Pubs.
—Thomas Edison to the Rescue! Goldsmith, Howard. 2003. (Ready-To-read COFA Ser.). (ENG.). 32p. (J). (gr. k-2). pap. 4.99 *(978-0-689-85331-9(9)*, Simon Spotlight) Simon Spotlight.
—Who Was Johnny Appleseed? Holub, Joan & Who HQ. 2005. (Who Was? Ser.). 112p. (J). (gr. 3-7). pap. 5.99 *(978-0-448-43968-6(9)*, Penguin Workshop) Penguin Young Readers Group.
—Why Do Birds Sing? Holub, Joan. 2004. (Penguin Young Readers, Level 3 Ser.). 48p. (J). (gr. 1-3). mass mkt. 3.99 *(978-0-14-240106-4(4)*, Penguin Young Readers) Penguin Young Readers Group.
—Why Do Birds Sing? Holub, Joan. 2004. (Easy-to-Read Ser.). 47p. 14.00 *(978-0-7569-3114-8(2))* Perfection Learning Corp.
—Why Do Horses Neigh? Holub, Joan. 2003. (Penguin Young Readers, Level 3 Ser.). 48p. (J). (gr. 1-3). pap. 4.99 *(978-0-14-230119-7(1)*, Penguin Young Readers) Penguin Young Readers Group.
—Why Do Snakes Hiss? And Other Questions about Snakes, Lizards, & Turtles. Holub, Joan. 2004. (Penguin Young Readers, Level 3 Ser.). 48p. (J). (gr. 1-3). mass mkt. 3.99 *(978-0-14-240105-7(6)*, Penguin Young Readers) Penguin Young Readers Group.
DiVito, Anna. Annie Oakley Saves the Day. DiVito, Anna. ed. 2005. 32p. (J). lib. bdg. 15.00 *(978-1-59054-939-1(2))* Fitzgerald Bks.
—Annie Oakley Saves the Day. DiVito, Anna. 2004. (Ready-To-read COFA Ser.). (ENG.). 32p. (J). (gr. k-2). pap. 4.99 *(978-0-689-86520-6(1)*, Simon Spotlight) Simon Spotlight.
Dix, Steph, jt. illus. see Comfort, Louise.
Dixey, Kay. Life in an Irish Castle: The Journal of a 17th Century Castles in Times of Peace & War. Crosbie, Duncan. 2007. (ENG.). 19p. (J). 37.95 *(978-0-7171-4273-6(6))* M.H. Gill & Co. U. C. IRL. Dist: Dufour Editions, Inc.
Dixit, Rama. Space Travelers Land at Buckingham Palace. Walker, Peter Lancaster. 2007. 275p. (J). 19.95 *(978-1-934138-12-0(6))* Bouncing Ball Bks., Inc.
Dixon, Carol. Friends with a Difference. Pope, Ellen Dittman. 2009. (J). *(978-0-929915-92-0(5))* Headline Bks., Inc.
—If I Had My Way — /By Rock S. Wilson; Illustrated by Carol Dixon. Wilson, Rock. 2010. 32p. (J). *(978-0-929915-44-9(5))* Headline Bks., Inc.
—Pros & Cons of an Outdoor John. Brooks, Karl. 2013. 36p. pap. 24.95 *(978-1-63000-813-0(3))* America Star Bks.
Dixon, Chuck, jt. illus. see Hama, Larry.
Dixon, Corey. Larry, Lisa & the Missing Kite, 1 vol. McLaurin, Corey F. 2009. 20p. pap. 24.95 *(978-1-61546-590-3(1))* America Star Bks.
Dixon, Darla. What Really Happened During the Middle Ages: A Collection of Historical Biographies, 4. 2007. (What Really Happened Ser.). 222p. per. 15.95 *(978-1-932786-22-4(8))* Knowledge Quest.
—What Really Happened in Ancient Times: A Collection of Historical Biographies, 4. 2007. (What Really Happened Ser.). 240p. per. 15.95 *(978-1-932786-21-7(X))*; 2nd ed. 2016. (What Really Happened... Ser.: Vol. 1). (ENG.). (J). pap. 15.95 *(978-1-932786-59-0(7))* Knowledge Quest.
—What Really Happened in Colonial Times: A Collection of Historical Biographies. Johnson, Terri. 2007. (What Really Happened Ser.). 224p. (J). (gr. 4-7). per. 15.95 *(978-1-932786-23-1(6))* Knowledge Quest.
—What Really Happened in Colonial Times: A Collection of Historical Biographies. 2nd ed. 2016. (What Really Happened Ser.: Vol. 3). (ENG.). (J). pap. 15.95 *(978-1-932786-60-6(0))* Knowledge Quest.
—What Really Happened in Medieval Times: A Collection of Historical Biographies. 2nd ed. 2016. (What Really Happened Ser.: Vol. 2). (ENG.). (J). pap. 15.95 *(978-1-932786-58-3(9))* Knowledge Quest.
Dixon, Debra Spina & Spina Dixon, Debra. Painting on a Canvas: Art Adventures for Kids, 1 vol. Wheeler, Annie. 2006. (ENG.). 64p. (J). (gr. 3-7). pap. 9.95 *(978-1-58685-839-1(4))* Gibbs Smith, Publisher.
Dixon, Gary. Blackjack's Hare Raising Adventure. Papaj, Dana. 2005. (J). *(978-1-932583-20-5(3))* Bates Jackson Engraving Co., Inc.
Dixon, Heather. Music Box. Kramer, Ron. 2016. (ENG.). (J). (gr. 3-6). 18.99 *(978-0-692-80099-7(9))* PANDA BKS. PR.
Dixon, Laura Emily. Talking to a Child with Bone Marrow Disease. 2004. 32p. (J). pap. *(978-0-9755572-0-4(3))* Aplastic Anemia + MDS International Foundation.
Dixon, Nehemiah F. Ryan Elias Finds: The Truth Behind Lying. Gross, Carmen. 2008. 27p. pap. 24.95 *(978-1-60474-945-8(8))* America Star Bks.
Dixon, Samantha. Running Wild: Awesome Animals in Motion. Watson, Galadriel. 2020. 68p. (J). (gr. 2-5). 18.95 *(978-1-77321-370-5(9))*; pap. 12.95 *(978-1-77321-369-9(5))* Annick Pr., Ltd. CAN. Dist: Publishers Group West (PGW).
Dixon, Sierra B. How Special Are You? Well You're One of a Kind! Pauling, Precious L. 2019. (ENG.). 46p. (J). pap. 14.97 ***(978-1-6866-5279-0(8))***; pap. 14.97 ***(978-1-0897-8566-8(6))*** Independently Published.
Dixon, Tennessee. Long Johns for a Small Chicken. Blanc, Esther Silverstein & Eagle, Godeane. 2003. (J). 16.95 *(978-1-884244-23-0(8))* volcano pr.
Dizin, Pascal, et al. Grace: Based on the Jeff Buckley Story. DeBartolo, Tiffanie. 2019. (ENG.). 160p. 26.99 *(978-1-250-19692-7(2)*, 900194270, First Second Bks.) Roaring Brook Pr.
Djasim, Urville. The Introverted Mosquito. Ward de Paz, Adrian & Ward, Janelle. 2020. (ENG.). 36p. (J). pap. 9.99 ***(978-1-6512-3937-7(1))*** Independently Published.
Djokic, Barbara. Charlie Is Bilingual. Mazloum, Jade. 2019. (ENG.). 26p. (J). pap. 9.90 *(978-1-0751-9956-1(5))* Independently Published.
d'Lacey, Chris. Icefire. d'Lacey, Chris. ed. 2007. (Last Dragon Chronicles Ser.: 2). lib. bdg. 19.65 *(978-1-4177-9138-5(1))* Turtleback.
Dlugos, Pamela J. Messages from Heaven: Be a Shining Star. Dlugos, Pamela J. Date not set. 64p. (J). (gr. 4-6). pap. 10.95 *(978-0-9661564-0-9(4))* Rejoyce Pubns.
Dmitriev, Sergei. Tales of Classical Ballet, Uralskaia, Valeria et al. Talmi, Mary, ed. Loutchinina, Ekaterina, tr. from RUS. 2004. 40p. (J). *(978-0-9743082-1-0(8)*, Moscow Ballet) Sports Marketing International, Inc.
Do, Gam, jt. illus. see Gamdo.
Do Gam, Rin Bo. Insects & Spiders. Cowley, Joy, ed. 2015. (Science Storybooks Ser.). (ENG.). 32p. (gr. k-3). 7.99 *(978-1-925246-75-9(2)*, Big and SMALL) ChoiceMaker Pty. Ltd., The AUS. Dist: Lerner Publishing Group.
Do, Khanh. The Sad Polar Bear. Do, Madison. 2019. (ENG.). 28p. (J). pap. 12.99 ***(978-1-7021-2103-3(8))*** Independently Published.
Do, Linh Dan Quy. Thần Thoại Của dân Việt. Ngo, Quy Linh Thi. 2019. (VIE.). 30p. (J). (gr. 3-4). pap. 25.00 *(978-0-9746135-3-6(3))* Y Linh.
Do Yeon, Kim. ¿Los Animales Se Comunican? / ¿Do They Talk? Hye Suk, Eom. 2018. (Click Click: Ciencia Básica / Basic Science Ser.). (SPA.). 40p. (J). (gr. 3-7). pap. 16.99 *(978-1-949061-46-8(9)*, Altea) Penguin Random House Grupo Editorial ESP. Dist: Penguin Random Hse. LLC.
Doak, Angela. My First Book of Canadian Birds, 1 vol. Miller, Andrea. 2018. (ENG.). 32p. (J). 22.95 *(978-1-77108-653-0(X)*, d65d85bf-c48b-4d24-9cac-27c63ea3f515) Nimbus Publishing, Ltd. CAN. Dist: Baker & Taylor Publisher Services (BTPS).
Doan, Nam. My First Mandarin Words with Gordon & Li Li: With Gordon & Li Li. McSween, Michele Wong. 2018. (ENG.). 24p. (J). (gr. -1 — 1). bds. 9.99 *(978-1-338-25372-6(7)*, Cartwheel Bks.) Scholastic, Inc.
Doane, Pelagie. The Phantom Friend, No. 30. Sutton, Margaret. 2008. (Judy Bolton Ser.). (ENG.). 188p. (J). (gr. 4-7). pap. 14.95 *(978-1-4290-9050-6(2))* Applewood Bks.
—Unfinished House #11, No. 11. Sutton, Margaret. 2008. (Judy Bolton Ser.). (ENG.). 196p. (J). (gr. 4-7). pap. 14.95 *(978-1-4290-9031-5(6))* Applewood Bks.
—The Yellow Phantom: A Judy Bolton Mystery. Sutton, Margaret. 2011. 222p. 44.95 *(978-1-258-10044-5(4))* Literary Licensing, LLC.
Dob, Bob. Blimpo: the Third Circle of Heck Vol. 3. Basye, Dale E. 2011. (Heck Ser.: 3). 464p. (J). (gr. 3-7). pap. 9.99 *(978-0-375-85677-8(3)*, Yearling) Random Hse. Children's Bks.
—Fibble: the Fourth Circle of Heck. Basye, Dale E. 2012. (Heck Ser.: 4). 384p. (J). (gr. 4-7). pap. 7.99 *(978-0-375-85679-2(X)*, Yearling) Random Hse. Children's Bks.
—Precocia: the Sixth Circle of Heck. Basye, Dale E. 2013. (Heck Ser.: 6). 432p. (J). (gr. 3-7). 7.99 *(978-0-375-86807-8(0)*, Yearling) Random Hse. Children's Bks.
—Rapacia: The Second Circle of Heck. Basye, Dale E. 2010. (Heck Ser.: 2). 384p. (J). (gr. 3-7). pap. 7.99 *(978-0-375-84078-4(8)*, Yearling) Random Hse. Children's Bks.
—The Seventh Circle of Heck: Wise Acres. Basye, Dale E. 2013. (Heck Ser.). 448p. (J). (gr. 4-7). 16.99 *(978-0-307-98185-1(1)*, Random Hse. Bks. for Young Readers) Random Hse. Children's Bks.
—Snivel, 5. Basye, Dale E. 2013. (Heck Ser.). (ENG.). 448p. (J). (gr. 6-8). lib. bdg. 22.44 *(978-0-375-96834-1(2))* Random Hse. Bks. for Young Readers.
—Snivel: Where the Whiny kids Go. Basye, Dale E. 2013. (Heck Ser.: 5). 448p. (J). (gr. 4-7). 8.99 *(978-0-375-86806-1(2)*, Yearling) Random Hse. Children's Bks.
—Where the Bad Kids Go. Basye, Dale E. 2009. (Heck Ser.: 1). 304p. (J). (gr. 3-7). 6.99 *(978-0-375-84076-0(1)*, Yearling) Random Hse. Children's Bks.
—Wise Acres. Basye, Dale E. 2014. (Heck Ser.: 7). 448p. (J). (gr. 4-7). 8.99 *(978-0-307-98188-2(6)*, Yearling) Random Hse. Children's Bks.
Dobbins, Erin & Connally, Erin. B Is for Baylor. Cook, Jane Hampton. 2010. (Big Bear Bks.). (ENG.). 64p. (gr. 17). 29.95 *(978-1-60258-270-5(X))* Baylor Univ. Pr.
Dobbyn, Nigel. Cesar Chavez: Friend to Farm Workers. Cipriano, Jeri. 2020. (Beginner Biography (LOOK! Books (tm)) Ser.). (ENG.). 24p. (J). (gr. k-2). pap. 6.99 ***(978-1-63440-970-4(1))***; lib. bdg. 25.32 ***(978-1-63440-969-8(8))*** Red Chair Pr.
Dobbyn, Nigel. Macbeth. Shakespeare, William. Sutliff Sanders, Joe, tr. 2008. (ENG.). 144p. (gr. 4-18). pap. 16.95 *(978-1-906332-46-4(0)*, Classical Comics, Ltd.); (gr. 5-18). pap. 16.95 *(978-1-906332-45-7(2))*; (gr. 7-18). pap. 16.95 *(978-1-906332-44-0(4)*, Classical Comics, Ltd.) Classical Comics GBR. Dist: Publishers Group West (PGW).
Dobbyn, Nigel. Maria Tallchief: Native America's Prima Ballerina. Walters, Jennifer Marino. 2020. (Beginner Biography (LOOK! Books (tm)) Ser.). (ENG.). 24p. (J). (gr. k-2). pap. 6.99 ***(978-1-63440-049-7(6))***; lib. bdg. 25.32 ***(978-1-63440-999-5(X))*** Red Chair Pr.
Dobenberga, Eliza. The Vegefolk Tales: The Big Clean Up. Nowland, Gillian. 2020. (Vegefolk Ser.: Vol. 1). (ENG.). 30p. (J). (gr. k-4). pap. ***(978-1-78963-079-4(7)***, Choir Pr., The) Action Publishing Technology Ltd.
Dobler, Shirley Jean. Permilia: A Western Children's Book. Pierce, Mary E. 2013. 62p. (J). 25.00 *(978-1-936617-15-9(3))* Lemon Pr. LLC.
d'Obrin, Felix. ZZ Dogs. Franks, T. S. 2003. (J). 15.99 *(978-0-9722304-0-7(8)*, 5000, ZZ Dogs Pr.) That's Life Publishing, Inc.
Dobrinska, Pat. Together, We Are Family. Condon, Kelly M. 2016. (ENG.). (J). 18.95 *(978-0-9968237-6-0(X))* BlueMoonGreenLake.
Dobson, Clive. Jessica's X-Ray. Zonta, Pat. 2006. 28p. (J). (gr. 1-3). pap. 9.95 *(978-1-55297-577-0(0)*, bbc1ffbd-c44d-419b-9a6b-ca613cb5eeb1) Firefly Bks., Ltd.
Dobson, Kathy. Sinterklaas. Dobson, Kathy. 2017. (ENG.). (J). (gr. -1-3). 20.00 *(978-0-9982820-3-9(0))* Dobson, Kathy.
Dobson, Len. Diamond Downhill. Dingles, Molly. 2005. (Community of Shapes Ser.). 32p. (J). pap. 10.95 *(978-1-59646-240-3(X))*; lib. bdg. 21.65 *(978-1-59646-043-0(1))*; per. 10.95 *(978-1-59646-241-0(8))* Dingles & Co.
—Diamond Downhill/Cuesta abajo en forma de Rombo. Dingles, Molly. 2005. (Community of Shapes Ser.).Tr. of Cuesta abajo en forma de Rombo. (ENG & SPA.). 32p. (J). pap. 10.95 *(978-1-59646-242-7(6))*; lib. bdg. 20.65 *(978-1-59646-044-7(X))*; per. 10.95 *(978-1-59646-243-4(4))* Dingles & Co.
—Rectangle Ranch. Dingles, Molly. 2005. (Community of Shapes Ser.). 32p. (J). pap. 10.95 *(978-1-59646-244-1(2))*; lib. bdg. 21.65 *(978-1-59646-035-5(0))*; per. 10.95 *(978-1-59646-245-8(0))* Dingles & Co.
—Rectangle Ranch/Rancho Rectangular. Dingles, Molly. 2005. (Community of Shapes Ser.).Tr. of Rancho Rectangular. (ENG & SPA.). 32p. (J). pap. 10.95 *(978-1-59646-246-5(9))*; lib. bdg. 20.65 *(978-1-59646-036-2(9))*; per. 10.95 *(978-1-59646-247-2(7))* Dingles & Co.
Dobson, Mark. The Recyclables: Skips First Day at Work. Ellis, Lee. 2019. (Recyclables Ser.: Vol. 1). (ENG.). 34p. (J). pap. 9.13 ***(978-1-7112-7883-4(1))*** Independently Published.
Dobson, S. Gaston. A Salute to Black Civil Rights Leaders. Green, Richard L. et al, eds. (Empak "Black History" Publication). (J). pap. 1.00 *(978-0-9616156-3-5(X))* Empak Publishing Co.
Docampo, Valeria. Always Daddy's Princess, 1 vol. Kingsbury, Karen. rev. ed. 2013. (ENG.). 32p. (J). 15.99 *(978-0-310-71647-1(0))* Zonderkidz.
—Cara & the Wizard, 2 vols. Flannigan, Liz. 2013. (Magic Stories Ser.). 48p. (J). (gr. 1-4). pap. 8.99 *(978-1-84686-780-4(0))* Barefoot Bks., Inc.
—Celebrate Kwanzaa with Boots & Her Kittens. Flor Ada, Alma. 2007. (Cuentos para Celebrar / Stories to Celebrate Ser.). 30p. (gr. k-6). per. 11.95 *(978-1-59820-135-2(2))* Santillana USA Publishing Co., Inc.
—Cinderstella: A Tale of Planets Not Princes. Miles, Brenda & Sweet, Susan D. 2016. 32p. (J). *(978-1-4338-2270-4(9)*, Magination Pr.) American Psychological Assn.
—Jacqueline & the Beanstalk: A Tale of Facing Giant Fears. Sweet, Susan D. & Miles, Brenda. 2017. 32p. (J). 15.95 *(978-1-4338-2682-5(8)*, Magination Pr.) American Psychological Assn.
—The Library Pages. Morton, Carlene. 2010. 32p. (J). (gr. k-4). 17.95 *(978-1-60213-045-6(0)*, Upstart Bks.) Highsmith Inc.
—Lunette, the True Story of the Tooth Fairy. Cruise, Robin. 2015. (J). *(978-1-938298-89-9(6))* Compendium, Inc., Publishing & Communications.
—Medio Pollito: A Spanish Tale, 0 vols. Kimmel, Eric A. 2010. (ENG.). 32p. (J). (gr. k-3). 17.99 *(978-0-7614-5705-3(4)*, 9780761457053, Two Lions) Amazon Publishing.
—The New York City Ballet Presents a Classic Picture Book Collection: The Nutcracker; the Sleeping Beauty; Swan Lake. New York City Ballet. ed. 2019. (ENG.). 120p. (J). (gr. -1-3). 53.99 *(978-1-5344-6242-7(2)*, Little Simon) Little Simon.
—The Nutcracker. New York City Ballet. (Classic Board Bks.). (ENG.). (J). (gr. -1-3). 2018. 38p. bds. 7.99 *(978-1-5344-2843-0(7))*; 2016. 40p. 17.99 *(978-1-4814-5829-0(9))* Little Simon. (Little Simon).
—Oni & the Eagle. Flanagan, Liz. 2014. (J). *(978-1-84686-876-4(9))* Barefoot Bks., Ltd.
—The Sleeping Beauty. New York City Ballet. 2017. (ENG.). 40p. (J). (gr. -1-3). 17.99 *(978-1-4814-5831-3(0)*, Little Simon) Little Simon.
—Starlight Grey. Flannigan, Liz. 2013. (Magic Stories Ser.). 48p. (J). (gr. 1-4). pap. 8.99 *(978-1-84686-778-1(9))* Barefoot Bks., Inc.
—Swan Lake. New York City Ballet. 2019. (ENG.). 40p. (J). (gr. -1-3). 17.99 *(978-1-4814-5833-7(7)*, Little Simon) Little Simon.
—The Three Little Tamales, 0 vols. Kimmel, Eric A. 2009. (ENG.). 40p. (J). (gr. -1-3). 17.99 *(978-0-7614-5519-6(1)*, 9780761455196, Two Lions) Amazon Publishing.
—Tip-Tap Pop, 0 vols. Lynn, Sarah. 2010. (ENG.). 32p. (J). (gr. -1-4). 17.99 *(978-0-7614-5712-1(7)*, 9780761457121, Two Lions) Amazon Publishing.
—Whatever You Grow up to Be, 1 vol. Kingsbury, Karen. rev. ed. 2014. (ENG.). 32p. (J). 17.99 *(978-0-310-71646-4(2))* Zonderkidz.
Docherty, Helen. The Snatchabook. Docherty, Helen. 2013. (ENG.). 32p. (J). (-2). 16.99 *(978-1-4022-9082-4(9)*, 9781402290824, Sourcebooks Jabberwocky) Sourcebooks, Inc.
Docherty, Thomas. Bombs & Blackberries. Donaldson, Julia. 2019. 48p. (J). (gr. 3-7). 16.99 *(978-1-4449-3879-1(7))* Hachette Children's Group GBR. Dist: Hachette Bk. Group.
—The Cat Who Ate Christmas. Chase, Lil. 2018. (ENG.). 96p. (J). (gr. 1-5). 13.99 *(978-0-7624-6475-3(5)*, Running Pr. Kids) Running Pr.
—The Lighthouse under the Clouds. Gutzschhahn, Uwe-Michael. 2008. (ENG.). 32p. (J). (gr. -1-k). 19.00 *(978-1-906367-03-9(5))* National Maritime Museum GBR. Dist: Independent Pubs. Group.
Docherty, Thomas. Pirate Nell's Tale to Tell: A Storybook Adventure. Docherty, Helen. 2020. 40p. (J). (-4). 17.99 ***(978-1-4926-9867-8(9)***, Sourcebooks Jabberwocky) Sourcebooks, Inc.
Docherty, Thomas. Polly & the Puffin: the New Friend: Book 3. Colgan, Jenny. 2018. (Polly & the Puffin Ser.). 96p. (J). (gr. 1-6). pap. 11.99 *(978-1-5102-0090-6(8))* Little, Brown Bks. for Young Readers.
—The Storybook Knight. Docherty, Helen. 2016. (ENG.). 32p. (J). (-4). 17.99 *(978-1-4926-3814-8(5)*, 9781492638148, Sourcebooks Jabberwocky) Sourcebooks, Inc.
Docherty, Thomas. Big Scary Monster. Docherty, Thomas. 2010. (ENG.). 40p. (J). (gr. -1-2). 15.99 *(978-0-7636-4787-2(X)*, Templar) Candlewick Pr.
—Little Boat. Docherty, Thomas. 2009. (ENG.). 40p. (J). (gr. -1-2). 15.99 *(978-0-7636-4428-4(5)*, Templar) Candlewick Pr.
—To the Beach. Docherty, Thomas. 2009. (ENG.). 40p. (J). (gr. -1-2). 15.99 *(978-0-7636-4429-1(3)*, Templar) Candlewick Pr.
Dockray, Tracy. Ellen Tebbits. Cleary, Beverly. 2008. (ENG.). 192p. (J). (gr. 3-7). 16.99 *(978-0-688-21264-3(6))*; pap. 7.99 *(978-0-380-70913-7(9))* HarperCollins Pubs. Ltd. GBR. (HarperCollins). Dist: HarperCollins Pubs.
—Emily's Runaway Imagination. Cleary, Beverly. 2008. (Cleary Reissue Ser.). (ENG.). 288p. (J). (gr. 3-7). pap. 7.99 *(978-0-380-70923-6(6)*, HarperCollins) HarperCollins Pubs. Ltd. GBR. Dist: HarperCollins Pubs.
—The Fix-It Friends: Eyes on the Prize. Kear, Nicole C. 2018. (Fix-It Friends Ser.: 5). (ENG.). 160p. (J). pap. 7.99 *(978-1-250-08672-3(8)*, 900157583) Imprint IND. Dist: Macmillan.
—The Fix-It Friends: Have No Fear! Kear, Nicole C. 2017. (Fix-It Friends Ser.: 1). (ENG.). 144p. (J). pap. 5.99 *(978-1-250-08584-9(5)*, 900157364) Imprint IND. Dist: Macmillan.
—The Fix-It Friends: Sticks & Stones. Kear, Nicole C. 2017. (Fix-It Friends Ser.: 2). (ENG.). 144p. (J). pap. 7.99 *(978-1-250-08586-3(1)*, 900157366) Imprint IND. Dist: Macmillan.
—The Fix-It Friends: the Show Must Go On. Kear, Nicole C. 2017. (Fix-It Friends Ser.: 3). (ENG.). 160p. (J). pap. 5.99 *(978-1-250-08668-6(X)*, 900157576) Imprint IND. Dist: Macmillan.
—The Fix-It Friends: Three's a Crowd. Kear, Nicole C. 2018. (Fix-It Friends Ser.: 6). (ENG.). 176p. (J). pap. 6.99 *(978-1-250-08674-7(4)*, 900157587) Imprint IND. Dist: Macmillan.
—The Fix-It Friends: Wish You Were Here. Kear, Nicole C. 2017. (Fix-It Friends Ser.: 4). (ENG.). 160p. (J). pap. 5.99 *(978-1-250-08670-9(1)*, 900157581) Imprint IND. Dist: Macmillan.

D

—Izzy & Oscar. Estes, Allison & Stark, Dan. 2015. (ENG.). 40p. (J). (-2). 16.99 *(978-1-4926-0150-0(0)*, 9781492601500, Sourcebooks Jabberwocky) Sourcebooks, Inc.

—Mitch & Amy. Cleary, Beverly. 2008. (Cleary Reissue Ser.). (ENG.). 288p. (J). (gr. 3-7). pap. 6.99 *(978-0-380-70925-0(2)*, HarperCollins) HarperCollins Pubs. Ltd. GBR. Dist: HarperCollins Pubs.

—Muggie Maggie. Cleary, Beverly. 2015. (Cleary Reissue Ser.). (ENG.). 96p. (J). (gr. 3-7). reprint ed. pap. 7.99 *(978-0-380-71087-4(0)*, HarperCollins) HarperCollins Pubs. Ltd. GBR. Dist: HarperCollins Pubs.

—Otis Spofford. Cleary, Beverly. 2008. (Cleary Reissue Ser.). (ENG.). 208p. (J). (gr. 3-7). reprint ed. pap. 7.99 *(978-0-380-70919-9(8)*, HarperCollins) HarperCollins Pubs. Ltd. GBR. Dist: HarperCollins Pubs.

—Socks. Cleary, Beverly. (Avon Camelot Bks.). (ENG.). 160p. (J). (gr. 3-7). 2015. pap. 7.99 *(978-0-380-70926-7(0))*; 2008. 16.99 *(978-0-688-20067-1(2))* HarperCollins Pubs. Ltd. GBR. (HarperCollins). Dist: HarperCollins Pubs.

—The Tushy Book. Manushkin, Fran. 2011. (ENG.). 22p. (J). (gr. -1-k). bds. 7.99 *(978-0-312-65913-4(X)*, 9780312659134) Feiwel & Friends.

Dockray, Tracy. Bright Dreams: The Brilliant Ideas of Nikola Tesla. Dockray, Tracy. 2020. (ENG.). 32p. (J). (gr. 3-5). lib. bdg. 18.99 ***(978-1-68446-141-7(3)***, 141992, Capstone Editions) Capstone.

Dockray, Tracy. My Life Story. Dockray, Tracy. 2003. 40p. (J). lib. bdg. 15.95 *(978-1-58717-218-2(6)*, SeaStar Bks.) Chronicle Bks. LLC.

Dockray, Tracy Arah, jt. illus. see Howard, Linda.

Dockrill, Katy. A Voice for the Spirit Bears: How One Boy Inspired Millions to Save a Rare Animal. Oliver, Carmen. 2019. (CitizenKid Ser.). (ENG.). 32p. (J). (gr. 1-4). 16.99 *(978-1-77138-979-2(6))* Kids Can Pr., Ltd. CAN. Dist: Hachette Bk. Group.

Docktor, Irv. We Were There in the Klondike Gold Rush. Appel, Benjamin & Clark, Henry W. 2011. 188p. 42.95 *(978-1-258-05908-8(8))* Literary Licensing, LLC.

Dodan, Mihaela. Charlie Makes a Donut. Letourneau, Dolly. 2018. (ENG.). 34p. (J). 15.99 *(978-0-692-07912-6(2))* Letourneau.

Dodd, Emma. Big Brothers Don't Take Naps. Borden, Louise. 2011. (ENG.). 32p. (J). (gr. -1-3). 17.99 *(978-1-4169-5503-0(8)*, McElderry, Margaret K. Bks.) McElderry, Margaret K. Bks.

—Dog & Friends: Birthday. 2017. 12p. (J). (gr. -1-12). bds. 9.99 *(978-1-86147-836-8(4)*, Armadillo) Anness Publishing GBR. Dist: National Bk. Network.

—Dog & Friends: Busy Day. 2017. 12p. (J). (gr. -1-12). bds. 9.99 *(978-1-86147-835-1(6)*, Armadillo) Anness Publishing GBR. Dist: National Bk. Network.

—Dog's 123: A Canine Counting Adventure! 2016. (ENG.). 14p. bds. 14.99 *(978-1-86147-698-2(1)*, Armadillo) Anness Publishing GBR. Dist: National Bk. Network.

—Dog's ABC: An Alphabet Adventure! 2016. 14p. bds. 14.99 *(978-1-86147-699-9(X)*, Armadillo) Anness Publishing GBR. Dist: National Bk. Network.

—Dog's Farmyard Friends: A Touch & Tickle Book - with Fun-To-Feel Flocking! 2016. (ENG.). 12p. (J). (gr. -1-1). bds. 14.99 *(978-1-86147-719-4(8)*, Armadillo) Anness Publishing GBR. Dist: National Bk. Network.

—I Love My Daddy [board Book]. Andreae, Giles. 2014. (ENG.). 26p. (J). (gr. -1 — 1). bds. 6.99 *(978-1-4231-9970-0(7))* Hyperion Bks. for Children.

—I Love My Dinosaur. Andreae, Giles. 2019. 32p. (J). (gr. -1-k). pap. 9.99 *(978-1-4083-4557-3(9)*, Orchard Bks.) Hachette Children's Group GBR. Dist: Hachette Bk. Group.

—I Love My Grandma. Andreae, Giles. 2016. (ENG.). 32p. (J). (gr. -1-3). 16.99 *(978-1-4847-3407-0(6))* Disney Pr.

—I Love My Grandma. Andreae, Giles. 2018. (ENG.). 24p. (J). (gr. -1 — 1). bds. 7.99 *(978-1-4847-3409-4(2))* Hyperion Bks. for Children.

—I Love My Mommy. Andreae, Giles. 2013. (ENG.). 26p. (J). (gr. -1 — 1). bds. 6.99 *(978-1-4231-6825-6(9))* Hyperion Pr.

—I Love You, Baby. Andreae, Giles. 2015. (ENG.). 32p. (J). (gr. -1-3). 15.99 *(978-1-4847-2230-5(2))* Disney Publishing Worldwide.

—I Love You, Baby. Andreae, Giles. 2016. (ENG.). 26p. (J). (gr. -1 — 1). bds. 6.99 *(978-1-4847-2261-9(2))* Hyperion Bks. for Children.

—I Saw Anaconda. Clarke, Jane. 2017. (ENG.). 24p. (J). (-k). 14.99 *(978-0-7636-9336-7(7)*, Nosy Crow) Candlewick Pr.

—Let's Make a Movie. Smith, Kath. 2003. (ENG.). 32p. (J). *(978-1-84089-190-4(4))* Zero to Ten, Ltd.

—My Mum's Best. Nilsen, Anna. 2011. 24p. bds. *(978-1-84089-679-4(5))* Zero to Ten, Ltd.

—Tick Tock Dog: A Tell the Time Book - with a Special Movable Clock! 2016. (ENG.). 12p. (J). (gr. -1-k). bds. 14.99 *(978-1-86147-718-7(X)*, Armadillo) Anness Publishing GBR. Dist: National Bk. Network.

Dodd, Emma. Always. Dodd, Emma. (Emma Dodd's Love You Bks.). (ENG.). (J). (— 1). 2018. 22p. bds. 9.99 *(978-1-5362-0057-7(3))*; 2014. 24p. 12.99 *(978-0-7636-7544-8(X))* Candlewick Pr. (Templar).

Dodd, Emma. Christmas Is Joy. Dodd, Emma. 2020. (Emma Dodd's Love You Bks.). (ENG.). 24p. (J). (-k). 14.99 ***(978-1-5362-1545-8(7)***, Templar) Candlewick Pr.

Dodd, Emma. Counting Our Blessings. Dodd, Emma. 2020. (ENG.). 24p. (J). (-k). 14.99 *(978-1-5362-1018-7(8)*, Templar) Candlewick Pr.

—Dog's Colorful Day: A Messy Story about Colors & Counting. Dodd, Emma. 2003. (ENG.). 32p. (J). (gr. k-k). 7.99 *(978-0-14-250019-4(4)*, Puffin Books) Penguin Young Readers Group.

—Everything. Dodd, Emma. 2015. (Emma Dodd's Love You Bks.). (ENG.). 24p. (J). (-k). 12.99 *(978-0-7636-7128-0(2)*, Templar) Candlewick Pr.

—Forever. Dodd, Emma. (Emma Dodd's Love You Bks.). (ENG.). (J). (— 1). 2019. 22p. bds. 9.99 *(978-1-5362-0812-2(4))*; 2013. 24p. 12.99 *(978-0-7636-7132-7(0))* Candlewick Pr. (Templar).

—Foxy. Dodd, Emma. 2012. (ENG.). 40p. (J). (gr. -1-2). 14.99 *(978-0-06-201419-1(6))* HarperCollins Pubs.

—Foxy in Love. Dodd, Emma. 2013. (ENG.). 40p. (J). (gr. -1-3). 17.99 *(978-0-06-201422-1(6))* HarperCollins Pubs.

—Happy. Dodd, Emma. (Emma Dodd's Love You Bks.). (ENG.). (J). (— 1). 2017. 22p. bds. 9.99 *(978-0-7636-9642-9(0))*; 2015. 24p. 12.99 *(978-0-7636-8008-4(7))* Candlewick Pr. (Nosy Crow).

—Love. Dodd, Emma. (Emma Dodd's Love You Bks.). (ENG.). (J). (— 1). 2018. 22p. bds. 9.99 *(978-0-7636-9941-3(1))*; 2016. 24p. 12.99 *(978-0-7636-8941-4(6))* Candlewick Pr. (Nosy Crow).

—Messy Fingers. Dodd, Emma. 2009. (ENG.). 14p. (J). (gr. -1). 15.95 *(978-0-230-71310-9(6))* Pan Macmillan GBR. Dist: Independent Pubs. Group.

—More & More. Dodd, Emma. 2014. (Emma Dodd's Love You Bks.). (ENG.). 24p. (J). (-k). 12.99 *(978-0-7636-7543-1(1)*, Templar) Candlewick Pr.

—Together. Dodd, Emma. (Emma Dodd's Love You Bks.). (ENG.). (J). (— 1). 2018. 22p. bds. 9.99 *(978-0-7636-9940-6(3))*; 2016. 24p. 12.99 *(978-0-7636-8940-7(8))* Candlewick Pr. (Nosy Crow).

—What Matters Most. Dodd, Emma. 2020. (ENG.). 24p. (J). (-k). 14.99 *(978-1-5362-1017-0(X)*, Templar) Candlewick Pr.

Dodd, Emma. When I Grow Up. Dodd, Emma. (Emma Dodd's Love You Bks.). (ENG.). (J). (— 1). 2020. 22p. bds. 9.99 ***(978-1-5362-1548-9(1))***; 2015. 24p. 12.99 *(978-0-7636-7985-9(2))* Candlewick Pr. (Templar).

—When You Were Born. Dodd, Emma. (Emma Dodd's Love You Bks.). (ENG.). (J). (— 1). 2020. 22p. bds. 9.99 ***(978-1-5362-1549-6(X))***; 2015. 24p. 14.99 *(978-0-7636-7405-2(2))* Candlewick Pr. (Templar).

Dodd, Emma. Wish. Dodd, Emma. (Emma Dodd's Love You Bks.). (ENG.). (J). (— 1). 2017. 22p. bds. 9.99 *(978-0-7636-9643-6(9))*; 2015. 24p. 12.99 *(978-0-7636-8009-1(5))* Candlewick Pr. (Nosy Crow).

Dodd, Joseph D. Kraken Ka The Komodo Dragon. Belknap, Jodi P. & Montgomery, Tamara. 2007. 32p. pap. 19.95 incl. audio compact disk *(978-0-9723420-7-0(9))* Belknap Publishing & Design.

Dodd, Lynley. Hairy Maclary's Caterwaul Caper. Dodd, Lynley. 2009. (Hairy Maclary & Friends Ser.). (ENG.). 32p. (J). (gr. -1-2). pap. 6.99 *(978-1-58246-307-0(7)*, Tricycle Pr.) Random Hse. Children's Bks.

—Zachary Quack Minimonster. Dodd, Lynley. 2006. (Gold Star First Readers Ser.). 32p. (gr. -1-3). lib. bdg. 23.00 *(978-0-8368-6187-7(6)*, Gareth Stevens Learning Library) Stevens, Gareth Publishing LLLP.

Dodd, Marion. Mystic by the A,B, Sea. Dodd, Marion. 2006. (J). 17.95 *(978-0-9773725-2-2(9))* Flat Hammock Pr.

Dodé, Antoine & Collar, Orpheus. The Heroes of Olympus, Book Two, the Son of Neptune: the Graphic Novel. Riordan, Rick & Venditti, Robert. 2017. (Heroes of Olympus Ser.). (ENG.). 192p. (J). (gr. 5-9). 21.99 *(978-1-4847-1621-2(3))* Disney Pr.

Dodé, Antoine, jt. illus. see Collar, Orpheus.

Dodge, Barbara A. Counting on the Bay. Siwak, Brenda S. 2006. (J). per. 14.95 *(978-0-9790906-0-8(1))* Pleasant Plains Pr.

Dodson, Bert. An Affectionate Farewell: the Story of Old Abe & Old Bob. Krisher, Trudy. 2015. (ENG.). 32p. (J). (gr. 6-2). 17.95 *(978-1-59373-155-7(8))* Bunker Hill Publishing, Inc.

—Cousin John: The Story of a Boy & a Small Smart Pig. Paine, Walter. 2006. (ENG.). 96p. (J). (gr. 3-9). 17.95 *(978-1-59373-057-4(8))* Bunker Hill Publishing, Inc.

—Favor Johnson: A Christmas Story. Lange, Willem. 2009. (ENG.). 32p. (J). (gr. 1-3). 16.95 *(978-1-59373-082-6(9))* Bunker Hill Publishing, Inc.

—Finch Discoveries: An Inspiring Tale of Adaptation to a Changing Environment. Wallis, Ginger. 2013. 34p. pap. 12.95 *(978-0-9847662-2-2(7))* Dancing Journey Pr.

—Grammie's Secret Cupboard. Reynolds, Cynthia Furlong. 2007. 32p. (J). (gr. -1-3). 17.95 *(978-1-58726-310-1(6)*, Mitten Pr.) Ann Arbor Editions LLC.

—Not I, Not I. Hillert, Margaret. 21st ed. 2016. (BeginningtoRead Ser.). (ENG.). 32p. (J). (-2). lib. bdg. 22.60 *(978-1-59953-785-6(0))* Norwood Hse. Pr.

—Paul Revere & the Bell Ringers. Winter, Jonah. ed. 2005. 32p. (J). lib. bdg. 15.00 *(978-1-59054-952-0(X))* Fitzgerald Bks.

—Paul Revere & the Bell Ringers. Winter, Jonah. 2003. (Ready-To-read COFA Ser.). (ENG.). 32p. (J). (gr. k-2). pap. 4.99 *(978-0-689-85635-8(0)*, Simon Spotlight) Simon Spotlight.

—Stranger in Right Field. Christopher, Matt. 2009. (New Peach Street Mudders Sports Library). 64p. (J). (gr. 2-4). lib. bdg. 23.93 *(978-1-59953-322-3(7))* Norwood Hse. Pr.

—Super Grandpa. Schwartz, David. 2005. (ENG.). 32p. (J). (gr. 2-4). pap. 6.95 *(978-1-889910-34-5(1))* Tortuga Pr.

—Super Grandpa. Schwartz, David. 2nd rev. ed. 2005. (ENG.). 32p. (J). (gr. 2-4). 18.95 *(978-1-889910-33-8(3))* Tortuga Pr.

—Superabuelo. Schwartz, David M. Ferrer, Martín Luis Guzmán, tr. 2005. (SPA.). 32p. (J). (gr. 2-4). 18.95 *(978-1-889910-37-6(6))*; pap. 6.95 *(978-1-889910-38-3(4))* Tortuga Pr.

—The White-Footed Mouse. Lange, Willem. 2012. (ENG.). 32p. (J). (gr. 1-3). 17.95 *(978-1-59373-109-0(4))* Bunker Hill Publishing, Inc.

—Yo No, Yo No. Hillert, Margaret. 2018. (BeginningtoRead Ser.).Tr. of Not I, Not I. (SPA.). 32p. (J). (gr. -1-2). pap. 11.94 *(978-1-68404-245-6(3))* Norwood Hse. Pr.

Dodson, Bert. Helping Santa: My First Christmas Adventure with Grandma. Dodson, Bert. 2011. (ENG.). 32p. (J). (gr. -1-1). 17.95 *(978-1-59373-093-2(4))* Bunker Hill Publishing, Inc.

—Yo No, Yo No. Dodson, Bert. Hillert, Margaret & Del Risco, Eida. 2018. (BeginningtoRead Ser.).Tr. of Not I, Not I. (SPA.). 32p. (J). (gr. -1-2). lib. bdg. 22.60 *(978-1-59953-901-4(6))* Norwood Hse. Pr.

Dodson, Bert, jt. illus. see Jack Pullan.

Dodson, Emma. Hattie the Dancing Hippo. Powell, Jillian. 2009. (Get Ready (Windmill Books) Ser.). 32p. (J). (gr. k-2). lib. bdg. 25.60 *(978-1-60754-264-3(1))* Windmill Bks.

—Hattie the Dancing Hippo. Powell, Jillian. 2011. 32p. pap. *(978-1-84089-709-8(0))* Zero to Ten, Ltd.

—Hooey Higgins & the Shark. Voake, Steve. 2012. (Hooey Higgins Ser.). (ENG.). 112p. (J). (gr. 2-5). 14.99 *(978-0-7636-5782-6(4))* Candlewick Pr.

—Hooey Higgins & the Tremendous Trousers. Voake, Steve. 2014. (Hooey Higgins Ser.). (ENG.). 144p. (J). (gr. 2-5). 14.99 *(978-0-7636-6923-2(7))* Candlewick Pr.

—Lots of Nuts. Munton, Gill. 2014. (Traditional Tales Ser.). (ENG.). 12p. (J). (gr. -1-k). pap. 5.95 *(978-1-62521-582-6(7)*, Capstone Classroom) Capstone.

Dodson, Emma. Speckle the Spider. Dodson, Emma. 2010. (ENG.). 32p. (J). (gr. -1-2). 14.99 *(978-0-7636-4778-0(0))* Candlewick Pr.

Dodson, Terry & Churchill, Ian. Cable & X-Force: Onslaught Rising. 2018. (ENG.). 360p. (J). (gr. 4-17). pap. 34.99 *(978-1-302-90949-9(5))* Marvel Worldwide, Inc.

Dodwell, Dayle. My Goat Gertrude. Dobson, Starr. ed. (ENG.). 32p. (J). (gr. 1-3). 2012. pap. 12.95 *(978-1-55109-920-0(9)*, 3a0ba8b5-15f7-487c-83f4-11e73de22b24); 2011. 18.95 *(978-1-55109-861-6(X)*, e8b874ed-0cbb-4d40-baee-eaf4e4d16295) Nimbus Publishing, Ltd. CAN. Dist: Baker & Taylor Publisher Services (BTPS).

Doe, Juan. Ice Man & Angel. Clevinger, Brian. 2011. (X-Men: First Class Ser.: No. 2). (ENG.). 24p. (J). (gr. 2-6). 27.07 *(978-1-59961-948-4(2)*, 15635, Marvel Age) Spotlight.

Doe, Juan, jt. illus. see Haspiel, Dean.

Doehring, Aurora. The Bible According to Grandpa. Bernstein, Jordan. 2011. 34p. pap. 6.50 *(978-0-9743414-3-9(6))* Adventure in Discovery.

Doehring, Phoebe. Chip's Sharing Day. Derkez, Linda. 2012. 16p. pap. 9.95 *(978-1-61633-245-7(X))* Guardian Angel Publishing, Inc.

Doell, Glenn. Creative Coloring Books: The What If. . . series. Doell, Glenn, concept. 2003. (What If. . . ser.). 41p. (J). spiral bd. 8.95 *(978-0-9742438-0-1(9))* Curtis Elliott Designs, Ltd.

Doering, Kimber. Two Beautiful Butterflies. Moody, Gloria. l.t. ed. 2005. 25p. (YA). per. 8.99 *(978-1-59879-002-3(1))* Lifevest Publishing, Inc.

Doerrfeld, Cori. Barnyard Baby. Broach, Elise. 2013. (Baby Seasons Ser.). 14p. (J). (gr. -1 — 1). bds. 7.99 *(978-0-316-21203-8(2))* Little, Brown Bks. for Young Readers.

—The Cold Winter Day, 1 vol. Emerson, Carl. 2008. (Read-It! Readers: Science Ser.). (ENG.). 32p. (J). (gr. k-2). lib. bdg. 21.32 *(978-1-4048-2627-4(0)*, Picture Window Bks.) Capstone.

—Fingers for Halloween. Lewis, Brandt. 2017. 12p. (J). (gr. -1 — 1). bds. 7.99 *(978-0-316-37800-0(3))* Little, Brown Bks. for Young Readers.

—Fingers for Lunch. Lewis, Brandt. 2016. 16p. (J). (gr. -1 — 1). bds. 7.99 *(978-0-316-37799-7(6))* Little, Brown Bks. for Young Readers.

—Goalkeeper Goof, 1 vol. Meister, Cari. 2009. (My First Graphic Novel Ser.). (ENG.). 32p. (J). (gr. k-2). pap. 6.25 *(978-1-4342-1409-6(5)*, Stone Arch Bks.) Capstone.

—Rah-Rah Ruby!, 1 vol. Jones, Christianne C. 2009. (My First Graphic Novel Ser.). (ENG.). 32p. (J). (gr. k-2). pap. 6.25 *(978-1-4342-1412-6(5)*, Stone Arch Bks.) Capstone.

—Sleepy Toes. McNeil, Kelli. 2017. 26p. (J). (gr. -1 — 1). bds. 8.99 *(978-1-338-03072-3(8)*, Cartwheel Bks.) Scholastic, Inc.

—Snuggle Bunny (a StoryPlay Book) Dopirak, Kate. 2016. (ENG.). 40p. (J). (gr. -1-k). 5.99 *(978-0-545-81536-9(3)*, Cartwheel Bks.) Scholastic, Inc.

—That's Life! Dyckman, Ame. 2020. 40p. (J). (gr. -1-3). 17.99 *(978-0-316-48548-7(9))* Little, Brown Bks. for Young Readers.

—The True Adventures of Esther the Wonder Pig. Jenkins, Steve et al. 2018. 40p. (J). (gr. -1-3). 17.99 *(978-0-316-55476-3(6))* Little, Brown Bks. for Young Readers.

—Welcome to Your World, Baby. Shields, Brooke. 2008. 32p. (J). (gr. -1-3). lib. bdg. 17.89 *(978-0-06-125312-6(X))* HarperCollins Pubs.

Doerrfeld, Cori. Good Dog. Doerrfeld, Cori. 2018. (ENG.). 40p. (J). (gr. -1-3). 17.99 *(978-0-06-266286-6(4))* HarperCollins Pubs.

—Maggie & Wendel: Imagine Everything! Doerrfeld, Cori. 2016. (ENG.). 48p. (J). (gr. -1-3). 17.99 *(978-1-4814-3974-9(X)*, Simon & Schuster Bks. For Young Readers) Simon & Schuster Bks. For Young Readers.

—The Rabbit Listened. Doerrfeld, Cori. 2018. (ENG.). 40p. (J). (-k). 17.99 *(978-0-7352-2935-8(X)*, Dial Bks) Penguin Young Readers Group.

—Wild Baby. Doerrfeld, Cori. 2019. (ENG.). 32p. (J). (gr. -1-3). 17.99 *(978-0-06-269894-0(X))* HarperCollins Pubs.

—Wild Baby Board Book. Doerrfeld, Cori. 2019. (ENG.). 36p. (J). (gr. -1 — 1). bds. 7.99 *(978-0-06-269893-3(1)*, HarperFestival) HarperCollins Pubs.

Doerrfeld, Cori & Lyles, Christopher. Make Me Giggle: Writing Your Own Silly Story, 1 vol. Loewen, Nancy. 2009. (Writer's Toolbox Ser.). (ENG.). 32p. (J). (gr. 2-4). pap. 8.95 *(978-1-4048-5704-9(4)*, Picture Window Bks.) Capstone.

Doerrfeld, Cori & Page, Tyler. Créele a Tus Ojos. Doerrfeld, Cori & Page, Tyler. 2020. (Cici: un Cuento de Hada (Cici: a Fairy's Tale) Ser.). 48p. (J). (gr. 2-5). 26.65 ***(978-1-5415-7935-4(6)***, Graphic Universe™) Lerner Publishing Group.

—Créele a Tus Ojos (Believe Your Eyes) Libro 1 (Book 1) Doerrfeld, Cori. 2020. (Cici: un Cuento de Hada (Cici: a Fairy's Tale) Ser.). (SPA.). 48p. (J). (gr. 2-5). pap. 7.99 ***(978-1-7284-1288-7(9)***, Graphic Universe™) Lerner Publishing Group.

Doerrfeld, Cori & Page, Tyler. A Perfect View, No. 3. Doerrfeld, Cori. 2017. (Cici: a Fairy's Tale Ser.: 3). 48p. (J). (gr. 2-5). 26.65 *(978-1-4677-6154-3(0)*, 9781467761543, Graphic Universe™) Lerner Publishing Group.

—A Perfect View: Book 3. Doerrfeld, Cori. ed. 2017. (Cici: a Fairy's Tale Ser.: 3). (ENG.). 48p. (J). (gr. 2-5). E-Book 39.99 *(978-1-5124-2700-4(4)*, 9781512427004);No. 3. pap. 7.99 *(978-1-5124-3068-4(4)*, 9781512430684) Lerner Publishing Group. (Graphic Universe™).

—Truth in Sight, No. 2. Doerrfeld, Cori. 2016. (Cici: a Fairy's Tale Ser.: 2). 48p. (J). (gr. 2-5). lib. bdg. 26.65 *(978-1-4677-6153-6(2)*, 9781467761536, Graphic Universe™) Lerner Publishing Group.

Doery, Marya. The Squid Kids. Robinson, Virginia. 2008. 44p. pap. 24.95 *(978-1-4241-9901-3(8))* America Star Bks.

Doescher, Erik. Batman's Birthday Surprise! (DC Super Friends) Berrios, Frank. 2016. (Pictureback(R) Ser.). (ENG.). 16p. (J). (gr. -1-2). 4.99 *(978-0-553-53983-7(3)*, Random Hse. Bks. for Young Readers) Random Hse. Children's Bks.

—The Big Splash! Fontana, Shea. 2018. (Pictureback Favorites Ser.). (ENG.). 24p. (J). (gr. -1-1). 18.69 *(978-1-5364-3056-1(0))* Random Hse. Bks. for Young Readers.

—Big Splash! (DC Super Hero Girls) Fontana, Shea. 2018. (Pictureback(R) Ser.). (ENG.). 24p. (J). (gr. -1-2). pap. 5.99 *(978-1-5247-6868-3(5)*, Random Hse. Bks. for Young Readers) Random Hse. Children's Bks.

—Bizarro Is Born!, 1 vol. Simonson, Louise. (Superman Ser.). (ENG.). 56p. (J). (gr. 3-6). 2013. pap. 4.95 *(978-1-4342-1725-7(6))*; 2009. 26.65 *(978-1-4342-1567-3(9))* Capstone. (Stone Arch Bks.).

—Brave Batgirl! (DC Super Friends) Webster, Christy. 2017. (Step into Reading Ser.). (ENG.). 24p. (J). (gr. -1-1). pap. 4.99 *(978-1-5247-1711-7(8)*, Random Hse. Bks. for Young Readers) Random Hse. Children's Bks.

—Captain Cold's Arctic Eruption, 1 vol. Mason, Jane B. 2011. (Flash Ser.). (ENG.). 56p. (J). (gr. 3-6). pap. 4.95 *(978-1-4342-3089-8(9))*; lib. bdg. 26.65 *(978-1-4342-2617-4(4))* Capstone. (Stone Arch Bks.).

—The Cold Caper! Carbone, Courtney. 2017. (J). *(978-1-5182-2647-2(7))* Random Hse., Inc.

—Colorful Cadets! (Top Wing) Golden Books. 2019. (ENG.). 48p. (J). (gr. -1-2). pap. 4.99 *(978-0-525-64771-3(6)*, Golden Bks.) Random Hse. Children's Bks.

—Cosmic Conquest. Sutton, Laurie S. 2018. (You Choose Stories: Justice League Ser.). (ENG.). 112p. (J). (gr. 2-6). pap. 6.95 *(978-1-4965-6559-4(2)*, 138572); lib. bdg. 32.65 *(978-1-4965-6555-6(X)*, 138568) Capstone. (Stone Arch Bks.).

—DC Super Friends Joke Book (DC Super Friends) Carmona, George. 2017. (ENG.). 64p. (J). (gr. -1-2). 5.99 *(978-1-5247-1975-3(7)*, Random Hse. Bks. for Young Readers) Random Hse. Children's Bks.

—Dream Team! (Top Wing) Lewman, David. 2019. (Pictureback(R) Ser.). (ENG.). 16p. (J). (gr. -1-2). 5.99 *(978-0-525-64826-0(7)*, Random Hse. Bks. for Young Readers) Random Hse. Children's Bks.

—Fast As the Flash! Webster, Christy. 2018. 24p. (J). *(978-1-5444-0227-7(9))* Random Hse., Inc.

—Fast As the Flash! (DC Super Friends) Webster, Christy. 2018. (Step into Reading Ser.). (ENG.). 24p. (J). (gr. -1-1). pap. 4.99 *(978-1-5247-6864-5(2))*; lib. bdg. 12.99 *(978-1-5247-6865-2(0))* Random Hse. Children's Bks. (Random Hse. Bks. for Young Readers).

—Gorilla Warfare, 1 vol. Sutton, Laurie S. et al. 2011. (Flash Ser.). (ENG.). 56p. (J). (gr. 3-6). pap. 4.95 *(978-1-4342-3087-4(2)*, Stone Arch Bks.) Capstone.

—The Green Team! (Corn & Peg) Clauss, Lauren. 2020. (Step into Reading Ser.). (ENG.). 24p. (J). (gr. -1-1). 5.99 *(978-0-593-12395-9(6)*, Random Hse. Bks. for Young Readers) Random Hse. Children's Bks.

—Halloween 1, 2, 3! (Top Wing) Random House. 2019. (ENG.). 22p. (J). (— 1). bds. 6.99 *(978-1-9848-4783-6(X)*, Random Hse. Bks. for Young Readers) Random Hse. Children's Bks.

Doescher, Erik, et al. Heroes United! - Attack of the Robot! Shealy, Dennis R. & Random House Staff. 2008. (Pictureback(R) Ser.). (ENG.). 32p. (J). (gr. -1-2). pap. 4.99 *(978-0-375-84409-6(0)*, Random Hse. Bks. for Young Readers) Random Hse. Children's Bks.

—Heroes vs. Villains/Space Chase! (DC Super Friends) Wrecks, Billy. 2013. (Pictureback(R) Ser.). (ENG.). 32p. (J). (gr. -1-2). pap. 4.99 *(978-0-307-97616-1(5)*, Random Hse. Bks. for Young Readers) Random Hse. Children's Bks.

Doescher, Erik. How to Draw Batman & His Friends & Foes. Sautter, Aaron. 2015. (Drawing DC Super Heroes Ser.). (ENG.). 32p. (J). (gr. 3-9). lib. bdg. 28.65 *(978-1-4914-2153-6(3)*, Stone Arch Bks.) Capstone.

—How to Draw Superman & His Friends & Foes. Sautter, Aaron. 2015. (Drawing DC Super Heroes Ser.). (ENG.). 32p. (J). (gr. 3-9). lib. bdg. 28.65 *(978-1-4914-2156-7(8)*, Stone Arch Bks.) Capstone.

—The League of Laughs. Manning, Matthew K. 2018. (You Choose Stories: Justice League Ser.). (ENG.). 112p. (J). (gr. 2-6). pap. 6.95 *(978-1-4965-6556-3(8)*, 138569); lib. bdg. 32.65 *(978-1-4965-6552-5(5)*, 138566) Capstone. (Stone Arch Bks.).

—The Portal of Doom. Sutton, Laurie S. 2018. (You Choose Stories: Justice League Ser.). (ENG.). 112p. (J). (gr. 2-6). pap. 6.95 *(978-1-4965-6558-7(4)*, 138571); lib. bdg. 32.65 *(978-1-4965-6554-9(1)*, 138567) Capstone. (Stone Arch Bks.).

—Reptile Rumble! (DC Super Friends) Wrecks, Billy. 2014. (Step into Reading Ser.). (ENG.). 32p. (J). (gr. -1-1). 4.99 *(978-0-385-37403-3(8)*, Random Hse. Bks. for Young Readers) Random Hse. Children's Bks.

—The Secret of Shazam! (DC Super Friends) Webster, Christy. 2019. (Step into Reading Ser.). (ENG.). 24p. (J). (gr. -1-1). 12.99 *(978-0-525-64852-9(6))*; pap. 4.99 *(978-0-525-64851-2(8))* Random Hse. Children's Bks. (Random Hse. Bks. for Young Readers).

—Shark Attack! Wrecks, Billy. 2017. 24p. (J). *(978-1-5182-2649-6(3))* Random Hse., Inc.

—Shark Attack! (DC Super Friends) Wrecks, Billy. 2017. (Step into Reading Ser.). (ENG.). 24p. (J). (gr. -1-1). pap. 4.99 *(978-0-399-55846-7(2)*, Random Hse. Bks. for Young Readers) Random Hse. Children's Bks.

—Shell Shocker, 1 vol. Sonneborn, Scott. 2011. (Flash Ser.). (ENG.). 56p. (J). (gr. 3-6). pap. 4.95 *(978-1-4342-3092-8(9)*, Stone Arch Bks.) Capstone.

—Shell Shocker, 1 vol. DeCarlo, Mike et al. 2011. (Flash Ser.). (ENG.). 56p. (J). (gr. 3-6). lib. bdg. 26.65 *(978-1-4342-2615-0(8)*, Stone Arch Bks.) Capstone.

—Super-Villain Showdown, 1 vol. Kupperberg, Paul. 2013. (Superman Ser.). (ENG.). 56p. (J). (gr. 3-6). pap. 4.95 *(978-1-4342-1736-3(1)*, Stone Arch Bks.) Capstone.

—Supergirl Takes off! (DC Super Friends) Carbone, Courtney. 2016. (Step into Reading Ser.). (ENG.). 24p. (J). (gr. -1-1). 4.99 *(978-0-399-55344-8(4)*, Random Hse. Bks. for Young Readers) Random Hse. Children's Bks.

—The Ultimate Weapon. Manning, Matthew K. 2018. (You Choose Stories: Justice League Ser.). (ENG.). 112p. (J). (gr. 2-6). pap. 6.95 *(978-1-4965-6557-0(6)*, 138570); lib. bdg. 32.65 *(978-1-4965-6553-2(3)*, 138565) Capstone. (Stone Arch Bks.).

—Wonder Woman: an Amazing Hero! (DC Super Friends) Tillworth, Mary. 2017. (Big Golden Book Ser.). (ENG.). 32p. (J). (gr. -1-2). 9.99 *(978-1-5247-1840-4(8)*, Golden Bks.) Random Hse. Children's Bks.

—Wonder Woman to the Rescue! Carbone, Courtney & Marston, William Moulton. 2016. 24p. (J). *(978-1-4806-9760-7(5))* Random Hse., Inc.

—Wonder Woman to the Rescue! (DC Super Friends) Carbone, Courtney. 2016. (Step into Reading Ser.). (ENG.). 24p. (J). (gr. -1-1). 4.99 *(978-1-101-93308-4(9)*, Random Hse. Bks. for Young Readers) Random Hse. Children's Bks.

—Wrath of the Weather Wizard, 1 vol. Lemke, Donald B. 2011. (Flash Ser.). (ENG.). 56p. (J). (gr. 3-6). lib. bdg. 26.65 *(978-1-4342-2613-6(1)*, Stone Arch Bks.) Capstone.

—Wrath of the Weather Wizard, 1 vol. Lemke, Donald B. et al. 2011. (Flash Ser.). (ENG.). 56p. (J). (gr. 3-6). pap. 4.95 *(978-1-4342-3090-4(2)*, Stone Arch Bks.) Capstone.

—You Choose Stories: Justice League. Sutton, Laurie S. & Manning, Matthew K. 2018. (You Choose Stories: Justice League Ser.). (ENG.). 112p. (J). (gr. 2-6). 130.60 *(978-1-4965-6568-6(1)*, 28474, Stone Arch Bks.) Capstone.

Doescher, Erik & Levins, Tim. Drawing DC Super Heroes. Sautter, Aaron. 2015. (Drawing DC Super Heroes Ser.). (ENG.). 32p. (J). (gr. 3-9). lib. bdg., lib. bdg., lib. bdg. 114.60 *(978-1-4914-2553-4(9)*, Stone Arch Bks.) Capstone.

—How to Draw Batman, Superman, & Other DC Super Heroes & Villains. Sautter, Aaron. 2015. (DC Super Heroes Ser.). (ENG.). 144p. (J). (gr. 3-9). pap. 14.95 *(978-1-62370-231-1(3)*, Stone Arch Bks.) Capstone.

Doescher, Erik & Spaziante, Patrick. Batman's Hero Files (DC Super Friends) Wrecks, Billy. 2015. (Step into Reading Ser.). (ENG.). 24p. (J). (gr. -1-1). 4.99 *(978-0-553-50808-6(3)*, Random Hse. Bks. for Young Readers) Random Hse. Children's Bks.

Doescher, Erik, jt. illus. see Random House.

Doescher, Erik, jt. illus. see RH Disney Staff.

Dog Artlist Collection Staff. The Dog from Arf! Arf! to Zzzzzz. Dog Artlist Collection Staff. 2004. 40p. (J). (ENG.). 14.99 *(978-0-06-059857-0(3))*; lib. bdg. 16.89 *(978-0-06-059858-7(1))* HarperCollins Pubs.

Doggett, Al. Clara's Imagination. Edwards, Helen L. 2005. 19.95 *(978-0-9765414-0-0(8))* Bad Publishing.

Doggett, Allen B. Hans Brinker or the Silver Skates A Story of Life in Holland. Dodge, Mary Mapes. 2004. reprint ed. pap. 34.95 *(978-1-4179-4127-8(8))* Kessinger Publishing, LLC.

Doggett, W. Kirk. Physiology of the Eye. Phillips, Carey R. & Johannen, Kevin C. 2nd ed. 2005. (C). cd-rom 95.00 *(978-0-9759464-1-1(2)*, Interactive Eye, L.L.C.) Interactive Knowledge, Inc.

Dogi, Fiammetta. On the Farm. Riggs, Kate. 2015. (ENG.). 14p. (J). (gr. -1 — 1). bds. 7.99 *(978-1-56846-272-1(7)*, Creative Editions) Creative Co., The.

—El Roble: Por Dentro y Por Fuera. Hipp, Andrew. Gonzalez, Tomas, tr. from ENG. 2004. (Explora la Naturaleza (Getting into Nature) Ser.). (SPA.). 27p. (J). (gr. 3-7). lib. bdg. 25.25 *(978-1-4042-2864-1(0))* Rosen Publishing Group, Inc., The.

—A Seed Needs Sun. Riggs, Kate. 2014. (ENG.). 14p. (J). (gr. -1-k). 7.99 *(978-1-56846-254-7(9)*, Creative Editions) Creative Co., The.

—Sounds of the Forest. Riggs, Kate. 2019. (ENG.). 14p. (J). (gr. -1-k). bds. 8.99 *(978-1-56846-318-6(9)*, Creative Editions) Creative Co., The.

—That's Creepy! Riggs, Kate. 2013. (ENG.). 14p. (J). (gr. -1-k). bds. 7.99 *(978-1-56846-236-3(0)*, Creative Editions) Creative Co., The.

—Wild Backyard. Riggs, Kate. 2016. (ENG.). 14p. (J). (gr. -1 — 1). bds. 7.99 *(978-1-56846-287-5(5)*, Creative Editions) Creative Co., The.

Dogi, Flammetta. Dinosaurs. Ganeri, Anita. 2007. (Back to Basics Ser.). 32p. (J). lib. bdg. *(978-88-6098-048-9(8))* McRae Bks. Srl.

—Mammals. McRae, Anne & Agosta, Loredana. 2007. (Back to Basics Ser.). 32p. (J). lib. bdg. *(978-88-6098-047-2(X))* McRae Bks. Srl.

—The Solar System. Williams, Brian & Egan, Vicky. 2007. (Back to Basics Ser.). 32p. (J). lib. bdg. *(978-88-6098-049-6(6))* McRae Bks. Srl.

Dogliani, Daniela. The Boy Who Cried Wolf. Parkes, Brenda. 2015. (Shared Reading Classics Ser.). (J). (gr. k-1). *(978-1-4900-2108-9(6))* Benchmark Education Co.

—The Boy Who Cried Wolf: Big Book Edition. Parkes, Brenda. 2015. (Shared Reading Classics Ser.). (J). (gr. k-1). *(978-1-4900-2104-1(3))* Benchmark Education Co.

—Hug Me. 2014. (ENG.). 26p. (J). bds. 8.99 *(978-1-78440-558-8(2))* Igloo Bks. GBR. Dist: Simon & Schuster, Inc.

—Tug! Tug! & Lots of Spots. Jinks, Jenny. 2020. (Early Bird Readers — Pink (Early Bird Stories (tm)) Ser.). (ENG.). 32p. (J). (gr. -1-2). pap. 7.99 *(978-1-5415-8728-1(6)*, Lerner Pubns.) Lerner Publishing Group.

Dohanish, Jason. Buddy's Bedtime. O'Shea, Pauleen. 2007. 32p. (J). 14.95 *(978-0-9778063-0-0(8))* Idlehour Entertainment.

Doherty, Ann. Prince Rama of the Solar Dynasty Pt. 1: Prince in Exile, the Journey Begins. Doherty, Vrinda & Valmiki. 2011. (ENG.). 212p. (J). 29.95 *(978-0-9817273-1-8(X)*, f9b1cb4a-e44d-457e-b008-81129b5e2805) Torchlight Publishing.

Doherty, Anna. Big Ideas for Curious Minds: An Introduction to Philosophy. The School of Life, The School. 2019. 160p. (J). (gr. 4). 24.99 *(978-1-9997471-4-5(3))* First Church lam, The Schl. of Life Ministry of Solehealism, The GBR. Dist: Consortium Bk. Sales & Distribution.

Doherty, Catherine. Breaking Free. Mulrine, Jennifer. 2008. 112p. (YA). (gr. 7-18). pap. *(978-1-897039-32-8(8))* High Interest Publishing (HIP).

—Dancing on the Edge. Jennings, Sharon. 2007. (HIP Edge Ser.). 112p. (YA). (gr. 7-18). pap. *(978-1-897039-27-4(1))* High Interest Publishing (HIP).

—The Edge Is Burning. Kropp, Paul. 2008. 112p. (YA). (gr. 7-18). pap. *(978-1-897039-33-5(6))* High Interest Publishing (HIP).

—Foul Shot. Kropp, Paul. 96p. pap. *(978-1-897039-25-0(5))* High Interest Publishing (HIP).

—I Didn't Do It! Kropp, Paul. 72p. pap. *(978-1-897039-23-6(9))* High Interest Publishing (HIP).

—Outrage. Varrato, Tony. 2007. (HIP Edge Ser.). 112p. (YA). (gr. 7-18). pap. *(978-1-897039-28-1(X))* High Interest Publishing (HIP).

—Stealing Home. Durkin, Shawn. 96p. pap. *(978-1-897039-24-3(7))* High Interest Publishing (HIP).

Doherty, Dave. There Once Was a Place Called P.O.P. 2008. 93p. (J). 61.99 *(978-1-4363-6190-3(7))* Xlibris Corp.

Doherty, Kathy. The Royal Search for Shenanigans: The Secrets of Zen Castle. Clark, Nita Marie. 2017. (Secrets of Zen Castle Ser.: 1). (ENG.). (J). (gr. 2-6). pap. 8.99 *(978-0-578-19321-2(3))* A Neat Read Publishing LLC.

Doherty, Meghan. How Not to Be a Dick: An Everyday Etiquette Guide. Doherty, Meghan. 2013. (ENG.). 192p. (YA). (gr. 8-12). 17.99 *(978-1-936976-02-7(1)*, Zest Bks.) Lerner Publishing Group.

Doherty, Paula. El Arca de Noé (Noah's Ark) 2015. (SPA.). 26p. (J). bds. 8.95 *(978-1-78557-209-8(1))* Igloo Bks. GBR. Dist: Simon & Schuster, Inc.

—Dinosaurs. Reasoner, Charles. 2009. (Little Big Flap Bks.). 10p. (J). (gr. -1-k). 9.99 *(978-1-934650-24-0(2))* Just For Kids Pr., LLC.

—Farm Animals. Reasoner, Charles. 2009. (Little Big Flap Bks.). 10p. (J). (gr. -1-k). 9.99 *(978-1-934650-23-3(4))* Just For Kids Pr., LLC.

—Insects. Reasoner, Charles. 2009. (Little Big Flap Bks.). 10p. (J). (gr. -1-k). bds. 9.99 *(978-1-934650-21-9(8))* Just For Kids Pr., LLC.

—Jungle Animals. Reasoner, Charles. 2009. (Little Big Flap Bks.). 10p. (J). (gr. -1-k). 9.99 *(978-1-934650-22-6(6))* Just For Kids Pr., LLC.

—My Giant Fold-Out Book: Christmas. Harrast, Tracy. 2008. 10p. (J). (gr. -1). bds. 13.49 *(978-0-7586-1425-4(X))* Concordia Publishing Hse.

Doherty, Paula. Mi Biblia para la Hora de Dormir. Doherty, Paula. Godfrey, Jan & Urízar de Ramírez, Mayra. 2015. (SPA.). 96p. (J). 14.99 *(978-1-4143-9874-7(3)*, 4608864) Tyndale Hse. Pubs.

Doherty, Paula, jt. illus. see Devaney, Adam.

Dohm, Ingrid. Alex Is Mr. Jolly. Skinner, Lynn C. 2020. (ENG.). 36p. (J). pap. 11.99 ***(978-1-7336531-4-5(7))*** Skinner, Lynn C.

Dohm, Ingrid. Anytime Is Party Time for Eugene the Mouse: The Wisdom of a Creative Mouse. Skinner, Lynn C. 2018. (ENG.). 34p. (J). (gr. k-6). pap. 11.99 *(978-0-9991679-8-4(7))* Skinner, Lynn C.

Dohm, Ingrid. Happy Birthday Dolly. Skinner, Lynn C. 2020. (ENG.). 32p. (J). pap. 11.99 ***(978-1-7336531-2-1(0))*** Skinner, Lynn C.

Dohm, Katrina G. Drop the Puck, It's Hockey Season. Jones Beehler, Jayne J. 2015. (Official Adventures Ser.). (ENG.). (J). (gr. 2-5). 17.95 *(978-1-59298-881-5(4))* Beaver's Pond Pr., Inc.

Dolan, Amy. A Boy Named Bucky, Vol. 1. Adams, Mark. 2006. 17p. (J). pap. 5.00 *(978-0-9670245-5-4(2))* Enthusi Adams, Inc.

—Bucky's Best Friend, Vol. 1. Adams, Mark. 2006. 15p. (J). pap. 5.00 *(978-0-9670245-4-7(4))* Enthusi Adams, Inc.

Dolan, Elys. The Mystery of the Haunted Farm. Dolan, Elys. 2016. (ENG.). (J). (gr. -1-3). 17.99 *(978-0-7636-8658-1(1)*, Nosy Crow) Candlewick Pr.

—Nuts in Space. Dolan, Elys. 2015. (ENG.). 32p. (J). (gr. k-3). 17.99 *(978-0-7636-7609-4(8)*, Nosy Crow) Candlewick Pr.

—Weasels. Dolan, Elys. 2014. (ENG.). 32p. (J). (gr. k-3). 17.99 *(978-0-7636-7100-6(2)*, Nosy Crow) Candlewick Pr.

Dolby, Jan. Be Happy to Be You. Hull, Diane. 2018. (ENG.). 32p. (J). (gr. k-6). pap. 13.99 *(978-1-387-59698-0(5))* Lulu Pr., Inc.

—Be Happy to Be You. Hull, Diane Margaret. 2018. (ENG.). 32p. (J). (gr. k-6). 17.99 *(978-1-387-59700-0(0))* Lulu Pr., Inc.

—Be Happy to Be You Dyslexic Font. Hull, Diane. 2018. (ENG.). 32p. (J). (gr. k-6). 17.99 *(978-1-387-59701-7(9))*; pap. 13.99 *(978-1-387-59699-7(3))* Lulu Pr., Inc.

—Gabby, 1 vol. Grant, Joyce. (ENG.). 32p. (J). 2019. (gr. k-2). 12.95 *(978-1-55455-471-3(3)*, 21316c2e-dc64-4899-b70e-6db47877dad2); 2012. (gr. -1-1). 18.95 *(978-1-55455-250-4(8)*, 66868761-cf42-44d0-b984-e2d49d08ec11) Fitzhenry & Whiteside, Ltd. CAN. Dist: Firefly Bks., Ltd.

—Gabby Drama Queen, 1 vol. Grant, Joyce. 2013. (ENG.). 32p. (J). (gr. -1-1). 18.95 *(978-1-55455-310-5(5)*, 4f68df11-6f30-42e4-98bd-0b52b8e1c948) Trifolium Bks., Inc. CAN. Dist: Firefly Bks., Ltd.

—Lucky Me, 1 vol. Rozler, Lora. 2017. (ENG.). 36p. (J). (gr. -1-3). 18.95 *(978-1-55455-410-2(1)*, 85a5f0f7-a2a7-4f52-b3a0-85a39c952feb) Fitzhenry & Whiteside, Ltd. CAN. Dist: Firefly Bks., Ltd.

—The Nifty Thrifty. Ferguson Fuller, Sandy. 2017. (ENG.). (J). (gr. k-6). 17.99 *(978-1-365-86165-9(1))*; pap. 13.99 *(978-1-365-86166-6(X))* Lulu Pr., Inc.

Dolby, Jan. The Nifty Thrifty. Ferguson Fuller, Sandy. ed. 2017. (ENG.). 32p. (J). (gr. k-6). 17.99 ***(978-1-64372-030-2(9))***; pap. 17.99 ***(978-1-64372-277-1(8))*** MacLaren-Cochrane Publishing, Inc. (Huskies Pub).

Dolby, Jan. The Nifty Thrifty Dyslexic Font. Ferguson Fuller, Sandy. 2017. (ENG.). 34p. (J). (gr. k-6). 21.99 *(978-1-365-86167-3(8))*; pap. 15.99 *(978-1-365-86168-0(6))* Lulu Pr., Inc.

Dolby, Jan. The Nifty Thrifty Dyslexic Font. Ferguson Fuller, Sandy. ed. 2017. (ENG.). 30p. (J). (gr. k-6). 19.99 ***(978-1-64372-279-5(4))***; pap. 15.99 ***(978-1-64372-278-8(6))*** MacLaren-Cochrane Publishing, Inc.

Dolce, Ellen. Children's Bible Stories. Kennedy, Dana & Wilson, Etta. 2009. 160p. (J). (gr. -1). 16.99 *(978-0-7586-1634-0(1))* Concordia Publishing Hse.

Doliveux, Maelle. Good Night, Wind: A Yiddish Folktale. Marshall, Linda Elovitz. 2019. 32p. (J). (gr. -1-3). 17.99 *(978-0-8234-3788-7(4))* Holiday Hse., Inc.

Dollak, Nicholas. Frannie & Pickles. McClear, Preston. 2003. 48p. (J). (gr. k-5). 16.95 *(978-1-929084-13-5(7))* Malibu Bks. for Children.

Dollar, Diane A., jt. illus. see Garretson, Jerri.

Dolotovskaia, Evgenia. The Adventures of Nature Nate & Chompy's Christmas Tree: Holistic Thinking Kids. Hoeschele, Micah & Hammill, Kristy. 2019. (Adventures of Nature Nate Ser.: Vol. 2). (ENG.). 34p. (J). pap. ***(978-1-7751638-9-3(X))*** Hammill, Kristy.

Dolotovskaia, Evgenia. Prince Jayden... the Curious One! My Brave Adventure. Riggins, Gabrielle A. M. 2019. (ENG.). 24p. (J). pap. 15.00 *(978-1-9860-3818-8(1))* CreateSpace Independent Publishing Platform.

—You're Perfect the Way You Are! Nelson, Richard. 2018. (ENG.). 24p. (J). (gr. k-1). *(978-1-7752839-2-8(5))* Nelson, Richard.

Dolotovskaia, Evgenia. The Adventures of Nature Nate & His Mud Kitchen: Holistic Thinking Kids. Hammill, Kristy. 2019. (Adventures of Nature Nate Ser.: Vol. 1). (ENG.). 32p. (J). pap. ***(978-1-7751638-8-6(1))*** Hammill, Kristy.

Dolphin, Ikue & Dolphin, Ivan. The Friendly Butterfly: A Heart-Warming Tale of Sharing, Understanding Differences, Keeping a Positive Attitude & Learning to Count Numbers. Dolphin, Miles, ed. 2019. (ENG.). 28p. (J). pap. 9.99 ***(978-1-7967-9040-5(0))*** Independently Published.

Dolphin, Ivan, jt. illus. see Dolphin, Ikue.

Domagala, Anne. Alice the Cabin Dog. Rasmussen, John. 2019. (ENG.). 24p. (J). pap. 9.50 *(978-1-0924-2287-1(0))* Independently Published.

Dombek, Jeff. Caveman Art Teacher. Dombek, Jeff. 2004. 28p. (J). pap. 4.95 *(978-0-9752597-0-2(9))* Corn Tassel Pr.

Dombrowski, Johnny. The Warrior Challenge: 8 Quests for Boys to Grow up with Kindness, Courage, & Grit. Beede, John. 2020. 272p. (J). (gr. 5-7). 16.99 ***(978-0-593-17529-3(8))***; (ENG.). lib. bdg. 19.99 ***(978-0-593-17530-9(1))*** Random Hse. Children's Bks. (Random Hse. Bks. for Young Readers).

Dombrowski, Theo. A Book of Tricksters: Tales from Many Lands, 1 vol. Stott, Jon C. 2010. (ENG.). 144p. (J). (gr. 4-7). pap. 12.95 *(978-1-926613-69-7(4))* Heritage Hse. CAN. Dist: Orca Bk. Pubs. USA.

Domeniconi, Paolo. Lola Shapes the Sky. Greenley, Wendy. 2019. (ENG.). 32p. (J). (gr. 1-3). 19.99 *(978-1-56846-319-3(7)*, Creative Editions) Creative Co., The.

—Oscar the Guardian Cat, 1 vol. Segre, Chiara Valentina. 2018. (ENG.). 32p. (J). (gr. k-6). 16.99 *(978-1-4236-4934-2(6))* Gibbs Smith, Publisher.

—Taste the Clouds. Marshall, Rita. 2016. (ENG.). 14p. (J). (gr. -1-k). bds. 8.99 *(978-1-56846-285-1(9)*, Creative Editions) Creative Co., The.

Domergue, Agnes. Oh My, Oh No! Charrier, Lisa. 2014. (ENG.). 32p. (J). (gr. -1-1). 15.95 *(978-0-7624-5409-9(1)*, Running Pr. Kids) Running Pr.

Domi. La Carrera del Sapo y el Venado, 1 vol. Mora, Pat. 2004. (SPA.). 32p. (J). pap. 9.95 *(978-0-88899-650-3(0))* Groundwood Bks. CAN. Dist: Publishers Group West (PGW).

—The Honey Jar, 1 vol. Liano, Dante & Menchu, Rigoberta. Unger, David, tr. 2006. (ENG.). 64p. (J). (gr. 3). 18.95 *(978-0-88899-670-1(5))* Groundwood Bks. CAN. Dist: Publishers Group West (PGW).

—Napí Va a la Montaña, 1 vol. Ramirez, Antonio. 2006. (SPA.). 48p. (J). (gr. k-3). 18.95 *(978-0-88899-715-9(9))* Groundwood Bks. CAN. Dist: Publishers Group West (PGW).

—La Noche Que Se Cayó la Luna. Mora, Pat. 2009. (SPA.). 32p. (J). (gr. k-k). pap. 6.95 *(978-0-88899-963-4(1))* Groundwood Bks. CAN. Dist: Publishers Group West (PGW).

—The Secret Legacy. Menchu, Rigoberta & Liano, Dante. Unger, David, tr. 2008. (ENG.). 64p. (J). (gr. k-3). 19.95 *(978-0-88899-896-5(1))* Groundwood Bks. CAN. Dist: Publishers Group West (PGW).

—Senora Reganona: A Mexican Bedtime Story. Sanroman, Susana. 2006. 20p. (J). (gr. k-4). reprint ed. 15.00 *(978-1-4223-5466-7(0))* DIANE Publishing Co.

Domi & Domi. Napí Goes to the Mountain, 1 vol. Ramirez, Antonio. Amado, Elisa, tr. 2006. (ENG.). 48p. (J). (gr. k-3). 18.95 *(978-0-88899-713-5(2))* Groundwood Bks. CAN. Dist: Publishers Group West (PGW).

Domi, jt. illus. see Domi.

Domi, Carlos. The Girl from Chimel, 1 vol. Menchu, Rigoberta & Liano, Dante. Unger, David, tr. 2005. (ENG.). 56p. (J). (gr. 4-7). 18.95 *(978-0-88899-666-4(7))* Groundwood Bks. CAN. Dist: Publishers Group West (PGW).

—The Night the Moon Fell: A Maya Myth, 1 vol. Mora, Pat. 2009. (ENG.). 32p. (J). (gr. k-k). pap. 6.95 *(978-0-88899-938-2(0))* Groundwood Bks. CAN. Dist: Publishers Group West (PGW).

Domineske, Alice. Summer Daze. Shaw, Mary E. 2019. (ENG.). 30p. (J). pap. 19.00 ***(978-1-64530-152-3(4))*** Dorrance Publishing Co., Inc.

Domingos, Daniel. Spike Coloring Book: Coloring Book. Domingos, Daniel. 2020. (ENG.). 52p. (J). pap. 5.99 ***(978-1-6574-8432-0(7))*** Independently Published.

Domingos, Rafael. Deep Sea Dance. Nesbitt, Kenn. 2019. (ENG.). 28p. (J). pap. 11.99 *(978-1-9874-9244-6(7))* CreateSpace Independent Publishing Platform.

Dominguez. The Story of Colors (La Historia de los Colores) A Bilingual Folktale from the Jungles of Chiapas. Marcos, Subcomandante. Bar Din, Anne, tr. 2003. (SPA.). 40p. (J). (gr. 4-6). pap. 8.95 *(978-0-938317-71-5(7))* Cinco Puntos Pr.

Domínguez, Ángel. Beauty & the Beast. Quiller-Couch, Arthur. 2017. (ENG.). 96p. (J). (gr. 2-7). 12.99 *(978-1-63158-115-1(5)*, Racehorse Publishing) Skyhorse Publishing Co., Inc.

Domínguez, Angel. A Christmas Carol. Dickens, Charles. 2019. (ENG.). 128p. (Orig.). (J). (gr. 1-6). 14.99 *(978-1-63158-453-4(7)*, Racehorse Publishing) Skyhorse Publishing Co., Inc.

Dominguez, Angela. Kaia & the Bees. Boelts, Maribeth. 2020. (ENG.). 40p. (J). (gr. -1-3). 16.99 *(978-1-5362-0105-5(7))* Candlewick Pr.

—Kaia y Las Abejas. Boelts, Maribeth. 2020. (SPA.). 40p. (J). (gr. -1-3). 16.99 *(978-1-5362-1413-0(2))* Candlewick Pr.

—Mango, Abuela, & Me. Medina, Meg. 32p. (J). (gr. k-3). 2017. (ENG.). 7.99 *(978-0-7636-9513-2(0))*; 2015. 16.99 *(978-0-7636-6900-3(8))* Candlewick Pr.

—Mango, Abuela y Yo. Medina, Meg. 2015. 32p. (J). (gr. k-3). 7.99 *(978-0-7636-8099-2(0))* Candlewick Pr.

—Marta! Big & Small. Arena, Jen. 2016. (ENG.). 32p. (J). 17.99 *(978-1-62672-243-9(9)*, 900146476) Roaring Brook Pr.

—La Noche Buena: A Christmas Story. Sacre, Antonio. 2010. (ENG.). 32p. (J). (gr. -1-3). 17.95 *(978-0-8109-8967-2(0)*, Abrams Bks. for Young Readers) Abrams, Inc.

—Quiero Ayudar! Flor Ada, Alma. 2010.Tr. of Let Me Help!. (ENG & SPA.). 32p. (J). (gr. -1-3). 16.95 *(978-0-89239-232-2(0))* Lee & Low Bks., Inc.

Dominguez, Angela. How Do You Say? / ¿Cómo Se Dice? Dominguez, Angela. ed. 2016. (ENG.). 32p. (J). 18.99 *(978-1-62779-496-1(4)*, 900152614, Holt, Henry & Co. Bks. For Young Readers) Holt, Henry & Co.

—Maria Had a Little Llama / María Tenía una Llamita. Dominguez, Angela. ed. 2013.Tr. of Maria Had a Little Llama. (SPA.). 32p. (J). (gr. -1-2). 17.99 *(978-0-8050-9333-9(8)*, 900070912, Holt, Henry & Co. Bks. For Young Readers) Holt, Henry & Co.

Dominguez, Angela N. Carmen Learns English. Cox, Judy. 2010. (ENG.). 32p. (J). (gr. -1-3). 16.95 *(978-0-8234-2174-9(0))* Holiday Hse., Inc.

Dominguez, Maria. Sofi & the Magic, Musical Mural. Ortiz, Raquel M. & Ventura, Gabriela Baeza. 2015. (SPA & ENG.). (J). 17.95 *(978-1-55885-803-9(2)*, Piñata Books) Arte Publico Pr.

Dominguez, Oliver. Electrical Wizard: How Nikola Tesla Lit up the World. Rusch, Elizabeth. (Candlewick Biographies Ser.). (J). 2015. (ENG.). 56p. (gr. 3-7). 14.99 *(978-0-7636-7978-1(X))*; 2013. 40p. (gr. 2-5). 17.99 *(978-0-7636-5855-7(3))* Candlewick Pr.

—Luis Paints the World. Farish, Terry. 2016. (ENG.). 32p. (J). (gr. k-4). 19.99 *(978-1-4677-5796-6(9)*, 9781467757966); E-Book 30.65 *(978-1-5124-0667-2(8)*, 9781512406672) Lerner Publishing Group. (Carolrhoda Bks.).

—Miracle Mud: Lena Blackburne & the Secret Mud That Changed Baseball. Kelly, David A. 2013. (ENG.). 32p. (J). (gr. 2-5). lib. bdg. 16.99 *(978-0-7613-8092-4(2)*, 9780761380924, Millbrook Pr.) Lerner Publishing Group.

—Papa Francisco: Creador de Puentes. Otheguy, Emma. 2018. (SPA.). 32p. (J). 17.99 *(978-1-5476-0013-7(6)*, 900194853, Bloomsbury Children's Bks.) Bloomsbury Publishing USA.

—Pope Francis: Builder of Bridges. Otheguy, Emma. 2018. (ENG.). 48p. (J). 17.99 *(978-1-68119-560-5(7)*, 900177833, Bloomsbury Children's Bks.) Bloomsbury Publishing USA.

Domínguez, Oscar. The Call of the Wild. London, Jack. 2019. 176p. (J). (gr. 6-6). 14.99 *(978-1-63158-393-3(X)*, Racehorse Publishing) Skyhorse Publishing Co., Inc.

—Frankenstein. Shelley, Mary. 2017. 208p. (J). 14.99 *(978-1-63158-184-7(8)*, Racehorse Publishing) Skyhorse Publishing Co., Inc.

Dominguez, Richard. Cómo Comprender la Fotosíntesis con Max Axiom, Supercientífico. O'Donnell, Liam & Barnett, Charles, III. 2013. (Ciencia Gráfica Ser.). (SPA.). 32p. (J). (gr. 3-9). pap. 8.10 *(978-1-62065-984-7(0))* Capstone.

—The Shocking World of Electricity with Max Axiom, Super Scientist, 1 vol. O'Donnell, Liam. 2007. (Graphic Science Ser.). (ENG.). 32p. (J). (gr. 3-9). pap. 8.10 *(978-0-7368-7888-3(2)*, 1264936, Capstone Pr.) Capstone.

—The Shocking World of Electricity with Max Axiom Super Scientist: 4D an Augmented Reading Science Experience. O'Donnell, Liam. 2018. (Graphic Science 4D Ser.). (ENG.). 32p. (J). (gr. 3-9). lib. bdg. 34.65 *(978-1-5435-2949-4(6)*, 138538, Capstone Pr.) Capstone.

—The Shocking World of Electricity with Max Axiom Super Scientist: An Augmented Reading Science Experience. O'Donnell, Liam. 2018. (Graphic Science 4D Ser.). (ENG.). 32p. (J). (gr. 3-9). pap. 7.95 *(978-1-5435-2960-9(7)*, 138560, Capstone Pr.) Capstone.

—Understanding Photosynthesis with Max Axiom Super Scientist: 4D an Augmented Reading Science Experience. O'Donnell, Liam. 2018. (Graphic Science 4D

D

Ser.). (ENG.). 32p. (J). (gr. 3-9). lib. bdg. 34.65 *(978-1-5435-2952-4(6)*, 138541, Capstone Pr.) Capstone.
—Understanding Photosynthesis with Max Axiom Super Scientist: An Augmented Reading Science Experience. O'Donnell, Liam. 2018. (Graphic Science 4D Ser.). (ENG.). 32p. (J). (gr. 3-9). pap. 7.95 *(978-1-5435-2963-0(1)*, 138563, Capstone Pr.) Capstone.
Dominguez, Richard & Barnett, Charles. Understanding Photosynthesis with Max Axiom, Super Scientist, 1 vol. O'Donnell, Liam & Barnett III, Charles. 2007. (Graphic Science Ser.). (ENG.). 32p. (J). (gr. 3-9). 31.32 *(978-0-7368-6841-9(0)*, 1264938, Capstone Pr.) Capstone.
Dominguez, Richard & Barnett, Charles, III. Understanding Photosynthesis with Max Axiom, Super Scientist, 1 vol. O'Donnell, Liam. 2007. (Graphic Science Ser.). (ENG.). 32p. (J). (gr. 3-9). per. 8.10 *(978-0-7368-7893-7(9)*, 1264938, Capstone Pr.) Capstone.
Dominguez, Richard, jt. illus. see Martin, Cynthia.
Dominguez, Stephanie. George Ferris' Grand Idea: The Ferris Wheel. Glatzer, Jenna. 2015. (Story Behind the Name Ser.). (ENG.). 32p. (J). (gr. 2-4). pap. 7.95 *(978-1-4795-7165-9(2))*; lib. bdg. 29.32 *(978-1-4795-7135-2(0))* Capstone. (Picture Window Bks.).
Dominik, Karen. The Perfect Gift. Dominik, Karen. 2020. (J). pap. 12.99 ***(978-0-578-70159-2(6))*** Dominik, Karen.
Dominquez, Richard, et al. Madam C. J. Walker & New Cosmetics, 1 vol. Krohn, Katherine E. 2006. (Inventions & Discovery Ser.). (ENG.). 32p. (J). (gr. 3-9). 8.10 *(978-0-7368-9647-4(3)*, Capstone Pr.) Capstone.
Domm, Jeff. The Hatchling's Journey: A Blanding's Turtle Story, 1 vol. Domm, Kristin. 2003. (ENG.). 40p. (J). (gr. -1-3). pap. 10.95 *(978-1-55109-438-0(X)*, 18339eaf-35d8-426a-b76e-f595995316eb) Nimbus Publishing, Ltd. CAN. Dist: Baker & Taylor Publisher Services (BTPS).
Domm, Jeffrey. Tangled in the Bay: The Story of a Baby Right Whale, 1 vol. Tobin, Deborah. 2003. (ENG.). 32p. (J). (gr. 4-7). pap. 10.95 *(978-1-55109-441-0(X)*, 4fa9eeec-8d39-4a2e-b3fa-0d41e33d2c0d) Nimbus Publishing, Ltd. CAN. Dist: Baker & Taylor Publisher Services (BTPS).
Domm, Jeffrey C. Atlantic Puffin: Little Brother of the North, 1 vol. Domm, Kristin Bieber. 2005. (ENG.). 32p. (J). (gr. -1-3). pap. 9.95 *(978-1-55109-518-9(1)*, 12cd67dc-a5b9-4f1f-b121-dd863d4dc15) Nimbus Publishing, Ltd. CAN. Dist: Baker & Taylor Publisher Services (BTPS).
—Eagle of the Sea, 1 vol. Domm, Kristin Bieber. ed. 2010. (ENG.). 32p. (J). (gr. 1-3). 9.95 *(978-1-55109-749-7(4)*, 0d703446-89b4-4375-8dd1-1191df878c0d) Nimbus Publishing, Ltd. CAN. Dist: Baker & Taylor Publisher Services (BTPS).
Domschke, Angelika. Stranded in Space: The Stellar Life of Jpeg the Robot Dog. Atticus, C. J. 2013. 119p. (J). pap. 6.95 *(978-0-9887780-2-3(5))* Atticus, C. J.
Donaera, Patrizia. Cats. Milbourne, Anna. 2006. (Beginners Nature: Level 1 Ser.). 32p. (J). (gr. k-2). 4.99 *(978-0-7945-1394-8(8)*, Usborne) EDC Publishing.
—El Pastorcito Mentiroso y Otras Fabulas de Esopo. Osei, Leah et al. rev. ed. 2019. (Literary Text Ser.). (SPA.). 32p. (gr. 3-4). pap. 9.99 *(978-1-4938-0061-2(2))* Teacher Created Materials, Inc.
—The Taming. Krum, Atticus. 2014. (ENG.). 227p. (J). pap. 12.99 *(978-0-9885349-1-9(6))* Huntly Hse.
Donaera, Patrizia & Fox, Christyan. Cats. Milbourne, Anna. 2006. (Usborne Beginners Ser.). 32p. (J). (gr. 1). lib. bdg. 12.99 *(978-1-58086-942-3(4)*, Usborne) EDC Publishing.
Donaera, Patrizia & Haggerty, Tim. Seashore. Beckett-Bowman, Lucy. 2008. (Beginners Nature Ser.). 32p. (J). (gr. -1-3). 4.99 *(978-0-7945-2061-8(8)*, Usborne) EDC Publishing.
Donaera, Patrizia & Larkum, Adam. Night Animals: Level 1. Meredith, Sue. 2007. (Beginners Ser.). 32p. (J). 4.99 *(978-0-7945-1656-7(4)*, Usborne) EDC Publishing.
Donaera, Patrizia & Mayer, Uwe. Dogs. Helbrough, Emma. 2006. (Beginners Nature: Level 1 Ser.). 32p. (J). (gr. k-2). 4.99 *(978-0-7945-1395-5(6))*; (gr. 1). lib. bdg. 12.99 *(978-1-58086-943-0(2))* EDC Publishing. (Usborne).
Donaera, Patrizia & Wray, Zoe. Tadpoles & Frogs. Milbourne, Anna. 2007. (Usborne Beginners Ser.). 32p. (J). 4.99 *(978-0-7945-1345-0(X)*, Usborne) EDC Publishing.
Donahoe, Tina. Mathematical Marie: And the Playground of Fractions. Donahoe, Charlotte. 2019. (Mathematical Marie Ser.: Vol. 2). (ENG.). 34p. (J). (gr. 1-4). pap. 10.99 *(978-1-970079-45-6(2))* Brown Books Publishing Group.
Donahue, Carol J. How Willy Got His Magic Hat. Donahue, Carol J. 2019. (Adventures of Cool Willy Green Ser.: Vol. 1). (ENG.). 40p. (J). pap. 15.99 *(978-1-7267-9871-6(2))* Independently Published.
Donahue, Jim. The Christmas Lantern. Bishop, Karen C. 2008. 32p. (J). *(978-0-615-20131-3(8))* Three River Rambler.
Donahue, Linda. A Gifted Book. Johnston, Camille. 2008. 19p. pap. 24.95 *(978-1-60563-329-9(1))* America Star Bks.
Donaldson, Jennifer. The Earth, the Alphabet, & Me. Pesout, Christine. 2011. (J). *(978-0-615-47220-1(6))* Pesout, Christine.
Donaldson, Julia. The Wrong Kind of Bark. Parsons, Garry. 2nd ed. 2016. (Reading Ladder Ser.). (ENG.). 48p. (J). (gr. k-2). pap. 7.99 *(978-1-4052-8237-6(1))* Egmont Bks., Ltd. GBR. Dist: Independent Pubs. Group.
Donaldson, Keavoughn. Meet Cire Brown: Meet Cire Brown. Debrow, April. 2019. (ENG.). 26p. (J). pap. 12.99 *(978-1-0740-5673-5(6))* Independently Published.
Donaldson, Leo. Toby & Friends Coloring & Activity Book: Toby Teaches Kids to Learn, & Improve Their Pen Control with This Educational Activity Book. Ideal for 3-5 Year Old's. Donaldson, Leo. 2019. (ENG.). 74p. (J). pap. 6.49 ***(978-1-7043-0035-1(5))*** Independently Published.
Donaldson, Stephen G., photos by. From Tree to House. Nelson, Robin. 2004. (Start to Finish Ser.). 24p. (J). (gr. -1-3). lib. bdg. 18.60 *(978-0-8225-1392-6(7)*, Lerner Pubns.) Lerner Publishing Group.
Donato, Janice. How Cold Was It? Barclay, Jane. ed. 2004. (J). (gr. k-3). spiral bd. *(978-0-616-11862-7(7))* Canadian National Institute for the Blind/Institut National Canadien pour les Aveugles.
—How Hot Was It? Barclay, Jane. Cole, Kathryn, ed. (ENG.). 24p. (J). 14.95 *(978-1-894222-70-9(9))* Lobster Pr. CAN. Dist: Univ. of Toronto Pr.
Donato, Michael A. Squanto & the First Thanksgiving: The Legendary American Tale. Metaxas, Eric. 2004. 36p. (J). (gr. 3-8). reprint ed. 19.00 *(978-0-7567-7123-2(4))* DIANE Publishing Co.
Donbavand, Tommy. Flame of the Dragon. Donbavand, Tommy. 2015. (Scream Street Ser.: 13). (ENG.). 192p. (J). (gr. 3-7). pap. 5.99 *(978-0-7636-5765-9(4))* Candlewick Pr.
—Hunger of the Yeti. Donbavand, Tommy. 2015. (Scream Street Ser.: 11). (ENG.). 128p. (J). (gr. 3-7). pap. 5.99 *(978-0-7636-5763-5(8))* Candlewick Pr.
—Secret of the Changeling. Donbavand, Tommy. 2015. (Scream Street Ser.: 12). (ENG.). 128p. (J). (gr. 3-7). pap. 5.99 *(978-0-7636-5764-2(6))* Candlewick Pr.
Donbo, Koge. Pita-Ten, Vol. 8. Donbo, Koge, creator. rev. ed. 2005. 208p. pap. 9.99 *(978-1-59532-017-9(2))* TOKYOPOP, Inc.
Donehey, Jennifer Caulfield. An Octopus Named Mom. Flaherty, Kathleen Marion. 2012. (ENG.). 32p. (J). 16.95 *(978-0-9767276-8-2(4))* Three Bean Pr.
Doner, Kim. The Buffalo in the Mall. Griffis, Molly. 32p. 8.95 *(978-1-57168-635-0(5))* Eakin Pr.
—Q Is for Quark: A Science Alphabet Book. Schwartz, David & Schwartz, David M. 2009. 64p. (J). (gr. 3-7). pap. 9.99 *(978-1-58246-303-2(4)*, Tricycle Pr.) Random Hse. Children's Bks.
Doner, Kim & Radzinski, Kandy. S Is for Sooner: An Oklahoma Alphabet. Scillian, Devin. 2003. (Discover America State by State Ser.). (ENG.). 40p. (J). 17.95 *(978-1-58536-062-8(7))* Sleeping Bear Pr.
Doneva, Steliyana. Adam's Animals. Schwartz, Barry L. 2017. (J). *(978-1-68115-530-2(3))* Behrman Hse., Inc.
—An Extraordinary Ordinary Moth. Gray, Karlin. 2018. (ENG.). 32p. (J). (gr. k-3). 16.99 *(978-1-58536-372-8(3)*, 204401) Sleeping Bear Pr.
—When Hillary Rodham Clinton Played Ice Hockey. Ruiz, Rachel. 2017. (Leaders Doing Headstands Ser.). (ENG.). 32p. (J). (gr. 1-4). lib. bdg. 28.65 *(978-1-5158-1573-0(0)*, 136243, Picture Window Bks.) Capstone.
Dong, Monique. Busy Noisy Safari: 10B Sound Book. Crowe, Carmen. 2018. (Interactive Early Bird Children's Song Book with 10 Sing-Along Tunes Ser.). (ENG.). 10p. (J). (gr. -1-1). bds. 18.99 *(978-1-68052-321-8(X)*, 1002970) Cottage Door Pr.
—Jesus Loves Me Songbook: Song Book Wood Module with Handle. Swift, Ginger. Cottage Door Press, ed. 2019. (Little Sunbeams Ser.). (ENG.). 12p. (J). (gr. -1-2). bds. 14.99 *(978-1-68052-371-3(6)*, 1003360) Cottage Door Pr.
—Kids Who Are Saving the Planet. Calkhoven, Laurie. 2020. (You Should Meet Ser.). (ENG.). 48p. (J). (gr. 1-3). 17.99 *(978-1-5344-5647-1(3))*; pap. 4.99 *(978-1-5344-5646-4(5))* Simon Spotlight. (Simon Spotlight).
—Mae Jemison. Calkhoven, Laurie. 2016. (You Should Meet Ser.). (ENG.). 48p. (J). (gr. 1-3). pap. 4.99 *(978-1-4814-7649-2(1)*, Simon Spotlight) Simon Spotlight.
—Misty Copeland. Calkhoven, Laurie. 2016. (You Should Meet Ser.). (ENG.). 48p. (J). (gr. 1-3). pap. 4.99 *(978-1-4814-7043-8(4)*, Simon Spotlight) Simon Spotlight.
—Precious Baby, Vol. Ferreri, Della Ross. 2019. (ENG.). 20p. (J). (gr. -1 — 1). 7.99 *(978-1-5064-4773-5(2)*, Beaming Books) Augsburg Fortress, Pubs.
—Roberta Gibb. Calkhoven, Laurie. 2018. (You Should Meet Ser.). (ENG.). 48p. (J). (gr. 1-3). 16.99 *(978-1-5344-0972-9(6))*; pap. 4.99 *(978-1-5344-0971-2(8))* Simon Spotlight. (Simon Spotlight).
Dong-sung, Kim. Suro: The First King of Gaya. Hye-sook, Lee. Park, Christian J., tr. 2011. (ENG.). 44p. 14.00 *(978-89-91913-48-6(2)*, 2040) Seoul Selection KOR. Dist: Univ. of Hawaii Pr.
Donivan, Marilee. Luna's Ladder. Matson, Faith. 2020. (ENG.). 32p. (J). pap. 9.95 ***(978-1-940728-14-8(2))*** Sunrise Mountain Bks.
Donnan, Matt. The Exploration Station: The Stormlands. Phelps, B. B. 2019. (Exploration Station Ser.: Vol. 2). (ENG.). 90p. (J). pap. 6.49 ***(978-1-6861-9354-5(8))*** Independently Published.
Donnelly, Jenifer. Daddy's Heroes: Gibby's Homer: the 1988 World Series. Garcia, Tom & Naga, Karun. 2007. (1988 World Ser.). 32p. (J). (gr. -1-3). pap. 9.95 *(978-0-9792111-0-2(7))* Daddy's Heroes, Inc.
Donnelly, John J. Edgar the Farting Dragon. Greenwood, Lisa K. 2018. (ENG.). 38p. (J). (gr. k-3). 19.95 *(978-0-692-08066-5(X))* Greenwood, Lisa K.
Donnelly, Karen. A Christmas Carol. Dickens, Charles. 2013. (Charles Dickens Ser.). (ENG.). 64p. (Orig.). pap. 6.95 *(978-1-906230-02-9(1))* Real Reads Ltd. GBR. Dist: Casemate Pubs. & Bk. Distributors, LLC.
—Daisy May. Ure, Jean. 2011. (ENG.). 96p. (J). pap. 5.99 *(978-0-00-713369-7(3)*, HarperCollins Children's Bks.) HarperCollins Pubs. Ltd. GBR. Dist: HarperCollins Pubs.
—David Copperfield. Tavner, Gill & Dickens, Charles. 2009. (Real Reads Ser.). 64p. (J). (gr. 4-8). pap. 13.55 *(978-1-60754-383-1(4))* Windmill Bks.
—Dazzling Danny. Ure, Jean. 2011. (ENG.). 96p. (J). pap. 5.99 *(978-0-00-713370-3(7)*, HarperCollins Children's Bks.) HarperCollins Pubs. Ltd. GBR. Dist: HarperCollins Pubs.
—Family Fan Club. Ure, Jean. 2011. (ENG.). 160p. (J). (gr. 4-7). pap. 7.99 *(978-0-00-717237-5(0)*, HarperCollins Children's Bks.) HarperCollins Pubs. Ltd. GBR. Dist: HarperCollins Pubs.
—Great Expectations. Dickens, Charles. 2013. (Charles Dickens Ser.). (ENG.). 64p. pap. 6.95 *(978-1-906230-01-2(3))* Real Reads Ltd. GBR. Dist: Casemate Pubs. & Bk. Distributors, LLC.
—Hard Times. Dickens, Charles. 2014. (Charles Dickens Ser.). (ENG.). 64p. pap. 6.95 *(978-1-906230-05-0(6))* Real Reads Ltd. GBR. Dist: Casemate Pubs. & Bk. Distributors, LLC.
—Hard Times. Tavner, Gill & Dickens, Charles. 2009. (Real Reads Ser.). 64p. (J). (gr. 4-8). pap. 13.55 *(978-1-60754-386-2(9))* Windmill Bks.
—Jesus of Nazareth. Moore, Alan & Tavner, Gill. 2014. (New Testament Ser.). (ENG.). 64p. pap. 6.95 *(978-1-906230-24-1(2))* Real Reads Ltd. GBR. Dist: Casemate Pubs. & Bk. Distributors, LLC.
—Judas Iscariot. Moore, Alan & Tavner, Gill. 2014. (New Testament Ser.). (ENG.). 64p. pap. 6.95 *(978-1-906230-28-9(5))* Real Reads Ltd. GBR. Dist: Casemate Pubs. & Bk. Distributors, LLC.
—Lucky Stars #2: Wish upon a Pet. Bright, Phoebe. 2012. (Lucky Stars Ser.). (ENG.). 96p. (J). (gr. 2-5). 5.99 *(978-0-545-41999-4(9)*, Scholastic Paperbacks) Scholastic, Inc.
—Lucky Stars #3: Wish upon a Song. Bright, Phoebe. 2012. (Lucky Stars Ser.: 3). (ENG.). 96p. (J). (gr. 2-5). pap. 5.99 *(978-0-545-42000-6(8)*, Scholastic Paperbacks) Scholastic, Inc.
—Mary Magdalene. Moore, Alan & Tavner, Gill. 2014. (New Testament Ser.). (ENG.). 64p. pap. 6.95 *(978-1-906230-27-2(7))* Real Reads Ltd. GBR. Dist: Casemate Pubs. & Bk. Distributors, LLC.
—Mary of Galilee. Moore, Alan & Tavner, Gill. 2014. (New Testament Ser.). (ENG.). 64p. pap. 6.95 *(978-1-906230-25-8(0))* Real Reads Ltd. GBR. Dist: Casemate Pubs. & Bk. Distributors, LLC.
—Oliver Twist. Dickens, Charles. 2013. (Charles Dickens Ser.). (ENG.). 64p. pap. 6.95 *(978-1-906230-00-5(5))* Real Reads Ltd. GBR. Dist: Casemate Pubs. & Bk. Distributors, LLC.
—Paul of Tarsus. Moore, Alan & Tavner, Gill. 2014. (New Testament Ser.). (ENG.). 64p. pap. 6.95 *(978-1-906230-29-6(3))* Real Reads Ltd. GBR. Dist: Casemate Pubs. & Bk. Distributors, LLC.
—Simon Peter. Moore, Alan & Tavner, Gill. 2014. (New Testament Ser.). (ENG.). 64p. pap. 6.95 *(978-1-906230-26-5(9))* Real Reads Ltd. GBR. Dist: Casemate Pubs. & Bk. Distributors, LLC.
Donnelly, Liza. The End of the Rainbow. Donnelly, Liza. 2015. (I Like to Read Ser.). (ENG.). 24p. (J). (gr. -1-3). 7.99 *(978-0-8234-3396-4(X))*; 14.95 *(978-0-8234-3291-2(2))* Holiday Hse., Inc.
Donner, Brad, photos by. A Complete Book about Death for Kids. Grollman, Earl A. & Johnson, Joy. 2006. (ENG., 46p. (J). pap. 7.95 *(978-1-56123-191-1(6))* Centering Corp.
Donny, Crank. Jasper Has Left the Building! Kruse, Donald W. 2016. (ENG.). (J). (gr. k-5). pap. 14.95 *(978-0-9969964-7-1(8))* Zaccheus Entertainment Co.
D'Onofrio, Eleonora. Yokai Stories. Davisson, Zack. 2018. 64p. (J). (gr. 2-7). 16.95 *(978-1-63405-914-5(X))* Chin Music Pr.
Donohue, Dorothy. All in One Hour, 0 vols. Crummel, Susan Stevens. 2009. (ENG.). 40p. (J). (gr. k-3). pap. 9.99 *(978-0-7614-5537-0(X)*, 9780761455370, Two Lions) Amazon Publishing.
—City Dog, Country Dog, 0 vols. Crummel, Susan Stevens. 2010. (ENG.). 42p. (J). (gr. k-4). pap. 9.99 *(978-0-7614-5538-7(8)*, 9780761455387, Two Lions) Amazon Publishing.
—Sherlock Bones & the Missing Cheese, 0 vols. Crummel, Susan Stevens. 2012. (ENG.). 40p. (J). (gr. k-3). 17.99 *(978-0-7614-6186-9(8)*, 9780761461869, Two Lions) Amazon Publishing.
—Ten-Gallon Bart, 0 vols. Crummel, Susan Stevens. 2010. (ENG.). 32p. (J). (gr. k-3). pap. 9.99 *(978-0-7614-5719-0(4)*, 9780761457190, Two Lions) Amazon Publishing.
—Ten-Gallon Bart Beats the Heat, 0 vols. Crummel, Susan Stevens. 2010. (ENG.). 40p. (J). (gr. k-3). 17.99 *(978-0-7614-5634-6(1)*, 9780761456346, Two Lions) Amazon Publishing.
Donohue, Dorothy. City Dog & Country Dog. Donohue, Dorothy. Crummel, Susan Stevens. unabr. ed. 2006. (J). (gr. k-3). 27.95 incl. audio *(978-0-8045-6942-2(8)*, SAC6942) Spoken Arts, Inc.
Donoso, Marcela. Pablo. Lazaro, Georgina. 2008. (Cuando los Grandes Eran Pequenos Ser.). (SPA.). 32p. (J). (gr. 3-5). 14.99 *(978-1-933032-09-2(X))* Lectorum Pubns., Inc.
Donovan, Derec. Forget-Me-Not. Bedard, Tony. 2005. (Rogue Ser.). 144p. (YA). (gr. 8-12). pap. 14.99 *(978-0-7851-1734-6(2))* Marvel Worldwide, Inc.
Donovan, Jane Monroe. Black Beauty's Early Days in the Meadow. Sewell, Anna. rev. ed. 2006. (ENG.). 32p. (J). (gr. k-6). 15.95 *(978-1-58536-296-7(4))* Sleeping Bear Pr.
—My Daddy Likes to Say. Brennan-Nelson, Denise. 2009. (ENG.). 32p. (J). (gr. k-6). 15.95 *(978-1-58536-432-9(0))* Sleeping Bear Pr.
—My Grandma Likes to Say. Brennan-Nelson, Denise. rev. ed. 2007. (ENG.). 32p. (J). (gr. k-6). 16.95 *(978-1-58536-284-4(0))* Sleeping Bear Pr.
—My Momma Likes to Say. Brennan-Nelson, Denise. 2003. (ENG.). 32p. (J). (gr. k-6). 15.95 *(978-1-58536-106-9(2))* Sleeping Bear Pr.
Donovan, Jane Monroe. Small, Medium & Large. Donovan, Jane Monroe. 2010. (ENG.). 32p. (J). (gr. 1-4). 15.95 *(978-1-58536-447-3(9)*, 202172) Sleeping Bear Pr.
Donovan, Jane Monroe, jt. illus. see Monroe Donovan, Jane.
Donovan, Natasha. The Eagle Mother. Huson, Brett D. 2020. (Mothers of Xsan Ser.: 3). (ENG.). 32p. (J). (gr. 3-7). *(978-1-55379-859-0(7)*, HighWater Pr.) Portage & Main Pr.
—The Grizzly Mother, 1 vol. Huson, Brett D. 2019. (Mothers of Xsan Ser.: 2). (ENG.). 32p. (J). (gr. 5-8). *(978-1-55379-776-0(0)*, HighWater Pr.) Portage & Main Pr.
—The Sockeye Mother, 1 vol. Huson, Brett D. 2017. (Mothers of Xsan Ser.: 1). (ENG.). 32p. (J). (gr. 3-7). *(978-1-55379-739-5(6)*, HighWater Pr.) Portage & Main Pr.
Donovan, Patte. Tobey Boland & the Blackstone Canal. Rooney, Thomas L. 2005. 30p. (J). *(978-1-929039-30-2(1))* Ambassador Bks., Inc.
Donoyan, Laurent. Le Château du Roi Bocana. Garrec, Sophie. 2019. (FRE.). 38p. (J). pap. *(978-2-9555174-4-4(5))* Bekalle-Akwe (Henri Junior).
Donploypetch, Jintanan, jt. illus. see Nugent, Suzanne.
Donze, Lisa. Squanto & the First Thanksgiving. Kessel, Joyce K. rev. ed. 2003. (On My Own Holidays Ser.). (ENG.). 48p. (gr. 2-4). lib. bdg. 25.26 *(978-0-87614-941-6(7))* Lerner Publishing Group.
—Squanto & the First Thanksgiving, 2nd Edition. Kessel, Joyce K. 2nd rev. ed. 2003. (On My Own Holidays Ser.). (ENG.). 48p. (J). (gr. 2-4). pap. 7.99 *(978-1-57505-585-5(6)*, First Avenue Editions) Lerner Publishing Group.
—Squanto y el Primer Dia de Accion de Gracias. Kessel, Joyce K. 2007. (Yo Solo - Festividades (on My Own - Holidays) Ser.). 48p. (J). (gr. 4-7). per. 6.95 *(978-0-8225-7795-9(X))* Lerner Publishing Group.
—Squanto y el Primer Día de Acción de Gracias. Kessel, Joyce K. Translations.com Staff, tr. from ENG. 2007. (Yo Solo - Festividades (on My Own - Holidays) Ser.). (SPA.). 48p. (gr. 2-4). lib. bdg. 25.26 *(978-0-8225-7792-8(5))* Lerner Publishing Group.
Doodler, Todd H. One Potato, Two Potato. Doodler, Todd H. 2013. (ENG.). 32p. (J). (gr. -1-k). 14.99 *(978-1-4424-8517-4(5)*, Little Simon) Little Simon.
—Rawr! Doodler, Todd H. 2013. 40p. (J). (gr. -1-k). 12.99 *(978-0-545-51118-6(6)*, Scholastic Pr.) Scholastic, Inc.
—Super Rawr! Doodler, Todd H. 2016. 40p. (J). (gr. -1-k). pap. 12.99 *(978-0-545-79969-0(4)*, Scholastic Pr.) Scholastic, Inc.
—Veggies with Wedgies. Doodler, Todd H. 2014. (ENG.). 32p. (J). (gr. -1-k). 16.99 *(978-1-4424-9340-7(2)*, Little Simon) Little Simon.
—Veggies with Wedgies Present Doin' the Wedgie. Doodler, Todd H. 2015. (ENG.). 26p. (J). (gr. -1-k). bds. 7.99 *(978-1-4424-9351-3(8)*, Little Simon) Little Simon.
Doody, Lori. The Puffin Problem, 1 vol. Doody, Lori. 2017. (ENG.). 44p. (J). (gr. -1-3). pap. 9.95 ***(978-1-927917-14-5(X))*** Running the Goat, Bks. & Broadsides CAN. Dist: Orca Bk. Pubs. USA.
Doody, Lori & Doody, Lori. Mallard, Mallard, Moose, 1 vol. 2018. (ENG.). 40p. (J). (gr. -1-3). pap. 9.95 ***(978-1-927917-16-9(6))*** Running the Goat, Bks. & Broadsides CAN. Dist: Orca Bk. Pubs. USA.
Doody, Lori, jt. illus. see Doody, Lori.
Dooling, Carly. The Magic of We. Anderson, Danielle. 2018. (ENG.). 40p. (J). 17.95 *(978-0-9964016-3-0(6))* Third Man Books.
—The Magic of We: Paperback. Anderson, Danielle. 2019. (ENG.). 40p. (J). pap. 14.95 *(978-0-9974578-6-5(4))* Third Man Books.
Dooling, Michael. The Amazing Life of Benjamin Franklin. Giblin, James Cross. 2006. 48p. (gr. -1-3). 18.00 *(978-0-7569-6551-8(9))* Perfection Learning Corp.
—The Amazing Life of Benjamin Franklin. Giblin, James Cross. 2006. (ENG.). 48p. (J). (gr. 3-6). per. 7.99 *(978-0-439-81065-4(5)*, Scholastic Paperbacks) Scholastic, Inc.
Dooling, Michael. The Great Horse-Less Carriage Race. Dooling, Michael. 2005. (ENG.). 32p. (J). (gr. k-3). tchr. ed. 16.95 *(978-0-8234-1640-0(2))* Holiday Hse., Inc.
—Young Thomas Edison. Dooling, Michael. 2005. (ENG.). 40p. (J). (gr. -1-3). 17.95 *(978-0-8234-1868-8(5))* Holiday Hse., Inc.
Dooling, Michael & Sayles, Elizabeth. Won't Papa Be Surprised! Cohlene, Terri. 2003. 32p. (J). 16.89 *(978-0-688-13094-7(1))* HarperCollins Pubs.
Doolittle, Bev. Reading the Wild. Maclay, Elise. 2005. 32p. (J). (gr. k-4). reprint ed. 17.00 *(978-0-7567-9649-5(0))* DIANE Publishing Co.
Doolittle, Michael. Motorcycles! Goodman, Susan E. 2007. (Step into Reading: Step 3 Ser.). (ENG.). 48p. (J). (gr. k-2). lib. bdg. 16.19 *(978-0-375-94116-0(9))* Random Hse. Bks. for Young Readers.
—Trains! Goodman, Susan E. 2012. (Step into Reading Ser.). 48p. (J). (gr. 1-4). pap. 4.99 *(978-0-375-86941-9(7)*, Random Hse. Bks. for Young Readers) Random Hse. Children's Bks.
Doolittle, Michael, photos by. Choppers! Goodman, Susan E. 2004. (Step into Reading Ser.: Vol. 4). 48p. (J). (gr. 2-4). pap. 4.99 *(978-0-375-82517-0(7)*, Random Hse. Bks. for Young Readers) Random Hse. Children's Bks.
Doolittle, Michael J. Monster Trucks! Goodman, Susan E. 2010. (Step into Reading Ser.). (ENG.). 48p. (J). (gr. k-3). pap. 4.99 *(978-0-375-86208-3(0)*, Random Hse. Bks. for Young Readers) Random Hse. Children's Bks.
—Motorcycles! Goodman, Susan E. 2007. (Step into Reading Ser.). 48p. (J). (gr. k-3). per. 4.99 *(978-0-375-84116-3(4)*, Random Hse. Bks. for Young Readers) Random Hse. Children's Bks.
—Ultimate Field Trip #5: Blasting off to Space Academy. Goodman, Susan E. 2011. (ENG.). 48p. (J). (gr. 3-7). pap. 19.99 *(978-1-4424-4345-7(6)*, Atheneum Bks. for Young Readers) Simon & Schuster Children's Publishing.
Doolittle, Michael J. Life on the Ice. Doolittle, Michael J., photos by. Goodman, Susan E. 2006. 32p. (J). 22.60 *(978-0-7613-2775-2(4)*, Millbrook Pr.) Lerner Publishing Group.
Dooney, Michael. Teenage Mutant Ninja Turtles: the Ultimate Collection Volume 1, Vol. 1. Eastman, Kevin & Laird, Peter. 2012. (TMNT Ultimate Collection: 1). (ENG.). 320p. 49.99 *(978-1-61377-007-8(3)*, 9781613770078) Idea & Design Works, LLC.
Dor, jt. illus. see Manet.
Dorado, Steve. The Empty Pot: A Chinese Folk Tale, 1 vol. Guillain, Charlotte. 2014. (Folk Tales from Around the World Ser.). (ENG.). 24p. (J). (gr. -1-3). pap. 6.95 *(978-1-4109-6697-1(6)*, Raintree) Capstone.
—Finn MacCool & the Giant's Causeway: An Irish Folk Tale, 1 vol. Guillain, Charlotte. 2014. (Folk Tales from Around the

World Ser.). (ENG.). 24p. (J). (gr. -1-3). pap. 6.95 *(978-1-4109-6699-5(2)*, Raintree) Capstone.
—Folk Tales from Around the World, 1 vol. Guillain, Charlotte. 2014. (Folk Tales from Around the World Ser.). (ENG.). 24p. (J). (gr. -1-3). pap., pap., pap. 41.70 *(978-1-4109-6702-2(6)*, Raintree) Capstone.
—The Foolish, Timid Rabbit: An Indian Folk Tale, 1 vol. Guillain, Charlotte. 2014. (Folk Tales from Around the World Ser.). (ENG.). 24p. (J). (gr. -1-3). pap. 6.95 *(978-1-4109-6700-8(X)*, Raintree) Capstone.
—The Tree of Life: An Amazonian Folk Tale, 1 vol. Guillain, Charlotte. 2014. (Folk Tales from Around the World Ser.). (ENG.). 24p. (J). (gr. -1-3). pap. 6.95 *(978-1-4109-6698-8(4)*, Raintree) Capstone.
—The Unhappy Stonecutter: A Japanese Folk Tale, 1 vol. Guillain, Charlotte. 2014. (Folk Tales from Around the World Ser.). (ENG.). 24p. (J). (gr. -1-3). pap. 6.95 *(978-1-4109-6696-4(8)*, Raintree) Capstone.
—Why the Spider Has Long Legs: An African Folk Tale, 1 vol. Guillain, Charlotte. 2014. (Folk Tales from Around the World Ser.). (ENG.). 24p. (J). (gr. -1-3). pap. 6.95 *(978-1-4109-6701-5(8)*, Raintree) Capstone.
Doran, Colleen. Beauty & the Beast. Weiss, Bobbi Jg. 2020. (Disney Princesses Ser.). (ENG.). 48p. (J). (gr. 2-6). lib. bdg. 28.50 ***(978-1-5321-4558-2(6)***, 35205, Graphic Novels) Spotlight.
Doran, David. Orchestra. Nuovo, Avalon. 2019. (ENG.). 80p. (J). (gr. 2-5). 19.95 *(978-1-912497-86-7(7))* Flying Eye Bks. GBR. Dist: Penguin Random Hse. LLC.
—Where Is God? Ferry, Therese. 2012. (ENG.). 26p. 12.95 *(978-1-85607-778-1(0))* Columba Pr. IRL. Dist: Dufour Editions, Inc.
Doran, Fran. The Boarding House. Melton, Marcia. 2012. 153p. (J). pap. 12.00 *(978-1-937849-03-0(1))* Raven Publishing Inc. of Montana.
Doran, Melissa. My Naturama Nature Journal: Open Your Eyes to the Wonders of Irish Nature. Fewer, Michael. 2017. (ENG.). 240p. (J). pap. 25.00 *(978-0-7171-7545-1(6))* Gill Bks. IRL. Dist: Casemate Pubs. & Bk. Distributors, LLC.
—Naturama. Fewer, Michael. 2017. (ENG.). 96p. (J). 42.00 *(978-0-7171-6980-1(4))* Gill Bks. IRL. Dist: Casemate Pubs. & Bk. Distributors, LLC.
Dorankamp, Michelle. Why Boys & Girls Are Different. Greene, Carol. 2008. (J). pap. 12.99 *(978-0-7586-1409-4(8))* Concordia Publishing Hse.
Dore, Gustave. Don Quixote. Part I (Illustrated) Barry, ed. Ormsby, John, tr. 2019. (Don Quixote. (Complete Illustrated Edition in Two Parts) Ser.: Vol. 1). (ENG.). 712p. (J). pap. 39.85 *(978-1-0819-7092-5(8))* Independently Published.
Dore, Gustave. L' Ing&#65533;nieux Hidalgo DON QUICHOTTE de la Manche. (Roman Illustr&#65533; Par Gustave Dor&#65533;) Barry, ed. Viardot, Louis, tr. 2019. (Don Quichotte (Version Compl&#65533;te Illustr&#65533;e en Deux Volumes) Ser.: Vol. 2). (FRE.). 646p. (J). pap. 29.80 ***(978-1-0859-1798-8(3))*** Independently Published.
Dore, Gustave. L' Ingénieux Hidalgo DON QUICHOTTE de la Manche. (Roman Illustré Par Gustave Doré) Barry, ed. Viardot, Louis, tr. 2019. (Don Quichotte (Version Complète Illustrée en Dex Volumes) Ser.: Vol. 1). (FRE.). 650p. (J). pap. 29.80 *(978-1-0841-5483-4(8))* Independently Published.
Doré, Gustave. River Legends of the Thames & Rhine. Brabourne, Edward Hugessen Knatchbull-Hugessen. 2005. (J). pap. *(978-0-486-44372-0(8))* Dover Pubns., Inc.
—The Surprising Adventures of Baron Munchausen. Raspe, Rudolf Erich. 2012. (Everyman's Library Children's Classics Ser.). (ENG.). 208p. 20.00 *(978-0-307-96147-1(8)*, Everyman's Library) Knopf Doubleday Publishing Group.
Dorémus, Gaëtan, jt. illus. see Rocco.
Doremus, Robert. Jeb Stuart: Boy in the Saddle. Winders, Gertrude Hecker. 2011. 202p. 44.95 *(978-1-258-08155-3(5))* Literary Licensing, LLC.
—Mystery in the Old Red Barn. Orton, Louise Fuller. 2016. (ENG.). (J). pap. 9.99 *(978-1-4794-2290-6(8))* Wildside Pr., LLC.
Dorenkamp, Michelle. The Christmas Message. Miller, Claire. 2006. (Arch Bks.). 16p. (J). 1.99 *(978-0-7586-0872-7(1))* Concordia Publishing Hse.
—The Easter Day Surprise. Fryar, Jane L. 2008. 32p. (Orig.). (J). (gr. k-4). 13.49 *(978-0-7586-1445-2(4))* Concordia Publishing Hse.
—From Adam to Easter. Bohnet, Eric. 2014. (Arch Bks.). (ENG.). 16p. (J). pap. 2.49 *(978-0-7586-4602-6(X))* Concordia Publishing Hse.
—Get up, Lazarus! Schkade, Jonathan. 2004. (Arch Bks.). (ENG.). 16p. (J). 1.99 *(978-0-7586-0480-4(7))* Concordia Publishing Hse.
—God Calls Abraham... God Calls You! Busch, Melinda Kay. 2003. (Arch Bks.). (ENG.). 16p. (J). (gr. k-4). 1.99 *(978-0-7586-0502-3(1))* Concordia Publishing Hse.
—Jesus Enters Jerusalem. Fryar, Jane L. 2004. (ENG.). 16p. (J). 1.99 *(978-0-7586-0641-9(9))* Concordia Publishing Hse.
—Los Tres Cerditos. Hillert, Margaret. 2018. (BeginningtoRead Ser.). (SPA.). 32p. (J). (gr. -1-2). pap. 11.94 *(978-1-68404-240-1(2))* Norwood Hse. Pr.
—Six Dogs & a Police Officer. Sonberg, Caryn. 2006. 31p. pap. 8.40 *(978-1-55501-776-7(2))* Ballard & Tighe Pubs.
—The Three Little Pigs. Hillert, Margaret. 2016. (BeginningtoRead Ser.). (ENG.). 32p. (J). (-2). lib. bdg. 22.60 *(978-1-59953-789-4(3))* Norwood Hse. Pr.
Dorenkamp, Michelle. Los Tres Cerditos. Dorenkamp, Michelle. Hillert, Margaret & Del Risco, Eida. 2018. (BeginningtoRead Ser.). (SPA.). 32p. (J). (gr. -1-2). lib. bdg. 22.60 *(978-1-59953-956-0(X))* Norwood Hse. Pr.
Dorenkamp, Michelle, jt. illus. see Jack Pullan.
Dorenkamp Repa, Michelle. Lydia Believes. Hovland, Stephenie. 2014. (Arch Bks.). (ENG.). 16p. (J). (gr. k-4). pap. 2.49 *(978-0-7586-4607-1(0))* Concordia Publishing Hse.
Dorfman, Elsa, photos by. No Hair Day. 2004. (Wgbh Specials Ser.). (gr. 7-18). 19.95 *(978-1-57807-730-4(3)*, WG1205) WGBH Boston Video.
Dorion, Leah. Moon Time Prayer. Gaudet, Cindy. 2nd ed. 2018. (ENG.). 80p. (J). pap. *(978-1-7752231-4-6(0))* MotherButterfly Bks.
Dorion, Sarah. Bestoj en Nia Domo. Metz, Zdravka. 2019. (Mas-Libro Ser.: Vol. 222). (EPO.). 66p. (J). pap. *(978-2-36960-174-6(4))* Unesko-Grupo Narbonia.
Dorland, Andrew. Harold Can't Stand to Be Alone. Cowie, Ken. 2006. 24p. per. *(978-0-9781338-3-2(8))* Soul Asylum Poetry.
Dormal, Alexis. Anna Banana & the Chocolate Explosion. Roques, Dominique. 2015. (Anna Banana Ser.). (ENG.). 28p. (J). (gr. k-2). 15.99 *(978-1-62672-020-6(7)*, 900131617, First Second Bks.) Roaring Brook Pr.
Dorman, Brandon. Axel la Camioneta: un Camino Rocoso: Axel the Truck: Rocky Road (Spanish Edition) Riley, J. D. Mendoza, Isabel, tr. 2020. (My First I Can Read Ser.). (SPA.). 32p. (J). (gr. -1-3). 16.99 ***(978-0-06-298041-0(6))***; pap. 4.99 ***(978-0-06-298040-3(8))*** HarperCollins Pubs. (Greenwillow Bks.).
—Axel la Camioneta: una Carrera en la Playa: Axel the Truck: Beach Race (Spanish Edition) Riley, J. D. Mendoza, Isabel, tr. 2020. (My First I Can Read Ser.). (SPA.). 32p. (J). (gr. -1-3). 16.99 ***(978-0-06-298029-8(7))***; pap. 4.99 ***(978-0-06-298028-1(9))*** HarperCollins Pubs. (Greenwillow Bks.).
Dorman, Brandon. Axel the Truck: Beach Race. Riley, J. D. 2013. (My First I Can Read Ser.). (ENG.). 32p. (J). (gr. -1-3). 16.99 *(978-0-06-222230-5(9))*; pap. 4.99 *(978-0-06-222229-9(5))* HarperCollins Pubs. (Greenwillow Bks.).
—Axel the Truck: Field Trip. Riley, J. D. 2019. (My First I Can Read Ser.). (ENG.). 24p. (J). (gr. -1-3). 16.99 *(978-0-06-269281-8(X))*; pap. 4.99 *(978-0-06-269280-1(1))* HarperCollins Pubs. (Greenwillow Bks.).
—Axel the Truck: Rocky Road. Riley, J. D. 2013. (My First I Can Read Ser.). (ENG.). 32p. (J). (gr. -1-3). 16.99 *(978-0-06-222232-9(5))*; pap. 4.99 *(978-0-06-222231-2(7))* HarperCollins Pubs. (Greenwillow Bks.).
—Axel the Truck: Speed Track. Riley, J. D. 2018. (My First I Can Read Ser.). (ENG.). 24p. (J). (gr. -1-3). 16.99 *(978-0-06-269279-5(8))*; pap. 4.99 *(978-0-06-269278-8(X))* HarperCollins Pubs. (Greenwillow Bks.).
—Be Glad Your Nose Is on Your Face: And Other Poems: Some of the Best of Jack Prelutsky. Prelutsky, Jack. 2008. (ENG.). 208p. (J). (gr. 1-5). 22.99 *(978-0-06-157653-9(0)*, Greenwillow Bks.) HarperCollins Pubs.
—Between the Light. Berkeley, Jon. 2008. (Julie Andrews Collection). (J). lib. bdg. 17.89 *(978-0-06-075514-0(8))* HarperCollins Pubs.
—The Blade of Shattered Hope. Dashner, James. 2011. (13th Reality Ser.: 3). (ENG.). 528p. (J). (gr. 3-7). pap. 8.99 *(978-1-4424-0871-5(5)*, Aladdin) Simon & Schuster Children's Publishing.
—Can You Fly High, Wright Brothers? Berger, Melvin & Berger, Gilda. 2007. (Scholastic Science Supergiants Ser.: Vol. 1). (ENG.). 48p. (J). (gr. 2-5). pap. 4.99 *(978-0-439-83378-3(7))* Scholastic, Inc.
—The Caretaker's Guide to Fablehaven. Mull, Brandon. 2015. (ENG.). 128p. (J). (gr. 4). 24.99 *(978-1-62972-091-3(7)*, 5139120, Shadow Mountain) Shadow Mountain Publishing.
—The Christmas Sweater: A Picture Book. Beck, Glenn et al. 2009. (ENG.). 40p. (J). (gr. -1-2). 17.99 *(978-1-4169-9543-2(9)*, Aladdin) Simon & Schuster Children's Publishing.
—Crashing the Party. Finn, Perdita. 2007. 109p. (J). *(978-0-439-74436-2(9))* Scholastic, Inc.
—The Curvy Tree: A Tale from the Land of Stories. Colfer, Chris. 2015. (Land of Stories Ser.). 32p. (J). (gr. -1-3). 17.00 *(978-0-316-40685-7(6))* Little Brown & Co.
—Did It Take Creativity to Find Relativity, Albert Einstein? Berger, Melvin & Berger, Gilda. 2007. (Scholastic Science Supergiants Ser.). (ENG.). 48p. (J). (gr. 2-5). pap. 4.99 *(978-0-439-83384-4(1)*, Scholastic Nonfiction) Scholastic, Inc.
—Dragonwatch: A Fablehaven Adventure. Mull, Brandon. 2018. (Dragonwatch Ser.: 1). (ENG.). 384p. (J). (gr. 3-8). pap. 9.99 *(978-1-4814-8502-9(4)*, Aladdin) Simon & Schuster Children's Publishing.
—Fablehaven. Mull, Brandon. 2007. (Fablehaven Ser.: 1). (ENG.). 384p. (J). (gr. 3-8). pap. 8.99 *(978-1-4169-4720-2(5)*, Aladdin) Simon & Schuster Children's Publishing.
—Fablehaven Complete Set (Boxed Set) Set: Fablehaven; Rise of the Evening Star; Grip of the Shadow Plague; Secrets of the Dragon Sanctuary; Keys to the Demon Prison. Mull, Brandon. ed. 2011. (Fablehaven Ser.). (ENG.). 2512p. (J). (gr. 3-8). pap. 49.99 *(978-1-4424-2977-2(1)*, Aladdin) Simon & Schuster Children's Publishing.
—Falcon Quinn & the Black Mirror. Boylan, Jennifer Finney. 2011. (Falcon Quinn Ser.: 1). (ENG.). 512p. (J). (gr. 5-9). pap. 7.99 *(978-0-06-172834-1(9)*, Tegen, Katherine Bks) HarperCollins Pubs.
—Giant Dance Party. Bird, Betsy. 2013. (ENG.). 32p. (J). (gr. k-3). 17.99 *(978-0-06-196083-3(7)*, Greenwillow Bks.) HarperCollins Pubs.
—Grasshopper Magic. Jonell, Lynne. (Magical Mix-Ups Ser.: 3). (ENG.). 112p. (J). (gr. 1-4). 2014. pap. 4.99 *(978-0-307-93123-8(4))*; 2013. 12.99 *(978-0-375-87084-2(9))* Random Hse. Children's Bks. (Random Hse. Bks. for Young Readers).
—Grip of the Shadow Plague. Mull, Brandon. 2008. (Fablehaven Ser.: 3). (ENG.). 480p. (J). (gr. 3-7). 19.99 *(978-1-59038-898-3(4)*, 5004776, Shadow Mountain) Shadow Mountain Publishing.
—Grip of the Shadow Plague. Mull, Brandon. 2009. (Fablehaven Ser.: 3). (ENG.). 512p. (J). (gr. 3-8). pap. 9.99 *(978-1-4169-8603-4(0)*, Aladdin) Simon & Schuster Children's Publishing.
—Halloween Night. Murray, Marjorie Dennis. (ENG.). 40p. (J). (gr. k-4). 2013. pap. 7.99 *(978-0-06-185773-7(4))*; 2010. 9.99 *(978-0-06-201293-7(2))* HarperCollins Pubs. (Greenwillow Bks.).
—Hamster Magic. Jonell, Lynne. 2012. (Magical Mix-Ups Ser.: 1). (ENG.). 112p. (J). (gr. 1-4). pap. 5.99 *(978-0-375-86616-6(7)*, Random Hse. Bks. for Young Readers) Random Hse. Children's Bks.
—I Know He Is There: A Lift-A-Flap Book about Faith. Thornley, Rebecca Gundersen. 2006. (J). *(978-1-59038-550-0(0))* Deseret Bk. Co.
—In the Garden. Buehner, Caralyn. 2007. (J). 18.95 *(978-1-59038-403-9(2))* Deseret Bk. Co.
—Keys to the Demon Prison. Mull, Brandon. 2011. (Fablehaven Ser.: 5). (ENG.). 640p. (J). (gr. 3-8). pap. 9.99 *(978-1-4169-9029-1(1)*, Aladdin) Simon & Schuster Children's Publishing.
—The Land of Stories: A Treasury of Classic Fairy Tales. Colfer, Chris. 2016. 323p. (J). *(978-0-316-55193-9(7))* Little Brown & Co.
Dorman, Brandon, et al. The Mother Goose Diaries. Colfer, Chris. 2015. 121p. (J). *(978-0-316-38332-5(5))* Little Brown & Co.
Dorman, Brandon. The Not Even Once Club: My Promise to Heavenly Father. Nelson, Wendy Watson. 2013. 18.99 *(978-1-60907-337-4(1))* Deseret Bk. Co.
—The Palace of Laughter. Berkeley, Jon. 2006. (Wednesday Tales Ser.: No. 1). 427p. (J). (gr. 3-7). 16.99 *(978-0-06-075507-2(5)*, Julie Andrews Collection) HarperCollins Pubs.
—The Palace of Laughter: The Wednesday Tales No. 1. Berkeley, Jon. 2007. (Wednesday Tales Ser.: No. 1). (ENG.). 464p. (J). (gr. 3-7). pap. 8.99 *(978-0-06-075509-6(1))* HarperCollins Pubs.
—Pingo & the Playground Bully. Mull, Brandon. 2012. (Pingo Ser.: 2). (ENG.). 32p. (J). (gr. k-3). 17.99 *(978-1-60907-178-3(6)*, 5082090, Shadow Mountain) Shadow Mountain Publishing.
—Queen Red Riding Hood's Guide to Royalty. Colfer, Chris. 2015. 118p. (J). *(978-0-316-38339-4(2))* Little Brown & Co.
—Rise of the Evening Star. Mull, Brandon. 2007. (Fablehaven Ser.: 2). (ENG.). 456p. (J). (gr. 3-7). 19.99 *(978-1-59038-742-9(2)*, 4981432, Shadow Mountain) Shadow Mountain Publishing.
—Rise of the Evening Star. Mull, Brandon. 2008. (Fablehaven Ser.: 2). (ENG.). 480p. (J). (gr. 3-8). pap. 8.99 *(978-1-4169-5770-6(7)*, Aladdin) Simon & Schuster Children's Publishing.
—Secrets of the Dragon Sanctuary. Mull, Brandon. 2010. (Fablehaven Ser.: 4). (ENG.). 560p. (J). (gr. 3-8). pap. 9.99 *(978-1-4169-9028-4(3)*, Aladdin) Simon & Schuster Children's Publishing.
—The Slippery Map. 2007. 288p. (J). (gr. 3-7). lib. bdg. 17.89 *(978-0-06-079109-4(8))* HarperCollins Pubs.
—The Snow Angel. Beck, Glenn & Schoebinger, Chris. 2011. (ENG.). 40p. (J). (gr. -1-2). 7.99 *(978-1-4424-4448-5(7)*, Simon & Schuster/Paula Wiseman Bks.) Simon & Schuster/Paula Wiseman Bks.
—Snowman Magic. Tegen, Katherine. 2012. (ENG.). 32p. (J). (gr. -1-3). 12.99 *(978-0-06-201445-0(5))* HarperCollins Pubs.
—The Story of the Jack O'Lantern. Tegen, Katherine. 2010. (ENG.). 32p. (J). (gr. -1-3). 12.99 *(978-0-06-143088-6(9))* HarperCollins Pubs.
—The Tiger's Egg. Berkeley, Jon. (Wednesday Tales Ser.: No. 2). (J). 2009. (ENG.). 432p. pap. 7.99 *(978-0-06-075512-6(1)*, Harper Trophy); 2007. 416p. (gr. 3-7). 16.99 *(978-0-06-075510-2(5)*, Julie Andrews Collection) HarperCollins Pubs.
—Trollbella Throws a Party: A Tale from the Land of Stories. Colfer, Chris. 2017. (Land of Stories Ser.). (ENG.). 32p. (J). (gr. -1-3). 17.99 *(978-0-316-38340-0(6))* Little Brown & Co.
—The Void of Mist & Thunder. Dashner, James. 2013. (13th Reality Ser.: 4). (ENG.). 496p. (J). (gr. 3-7). pap. 9.99 *(978-1-4424-0873-9(1)*, Aladdin) Simon & Schuster Children's Publishing.
—Wild Water Magic. Jonell, Lynne. 2014. (Magical Mix-Ups Ser.: 4). (ENG.). 112p. (J). (gr. 1-4). 12.99 *(978-0-375-87085-9(7)*, Random Hse. Bks. for Young Readers) Random Hse. Children's Bks.
—The Wishing Spell. Colfer, Chris. 2012. 438p. (J). pap. *(978-0-316-45393-6(5))* Little Brown & Co.
—Worlds Collide. Colfer, Chris. 2017. 434p. (J). *(978-0-316-43920-6(7))* Little Brown & Co.
Dorman, Brandon. Hoolie & the Hooligans, Book 1: The Alien That Ate My Socks. Dorman, Brandon. 2016. (Hoolie & the Hooligans Ser.: 1). (ENG.). 224p. (J). (gr. 2-7). 13.99 *(978-1-62972-222-1(7)*, Shadow Mountain) Shadow Mountain Publishing.
—Pirates of the Sea! Dorman, Brandon. 2011. (ENG.). 32p. (J). (gr. -1-3). 16.99 *(978-0-06-204068-8(5)*, Greenwillow Bks.) HarperCollins Pubs.
Dorman, Brandon & Call, Greg. Up & down the Scratchy Mountains. Snyder, Laurel. 2008. (ENG.). 256p. (J). (gr. 4-6). lib. bdg. 22.44 *(978-0-375-94719-3(1))* Random House Publishing Group.
—Up & down the Scratchy Mountains. Snyder, Laurel. 2010. 272p. (J). (gr. 3-7). 7.99 *(978-0-375-84720-2(0)*, Yearling) Random Hse. Children's Bks.
Dormer, Frank. Ebenezer Has a Word for Everything, 1 vol. Rowe, Chelsea H. 2018. (ENG.). 32p. (J). (gr. -1-3). 17.95 *(978-1-56145-848-6(1))* Peachtree Publishing Co. Inc.
Dormer, Frank W. Aggie & Ben: Three Stories. Ries, Lori. 2006. (Aggie & Ben Ser.). (ENG.). 48p. (J). (gr. -1-1). lib. bdg. 18.69 *(978-1-57091-594-9(6))* Charlesbridge Publishing, Inc.
—Aggie Gets Lost. Ries, Lori. 2020. (Aggie & Ben Ser.). 48p. (J). (gr. -1-3). pap. 5.99 *(978-1-57091-634-2(9))* Charlesbridge Publishing, Inc.
—Aggie the Brave. Ries, Lori. (Aggie & Ben Ser.). 48p. (J). (gr. -1-3). 2012. pap. 5.95 *(978-1-57091-636-6(5))*; 2010. 12.95 *(978-1-57091-635-9(7))* Charlesbridge Publishing, Inc.
—Dinos Are Forever. Trine, Greg. 2014. (Adventures of Jo Schmo Ser.: 1). (ENG.). 112p. (J). (gr. 1-4). pap. 6.99 *(978-0-544-00325-5(X)*, 1526367, HMH Books For Young Readers) Houghton Mifflin Harcourt Publishing Co.
—Good Dog, Aggie. Ries, Lori. (Aggie & Ben Ser.). 48p. (J). (gr. -1-3). 2012. pap. 5.95 *(978-1-57091-646-5(2))*; 2009. 12.95 *(978-1-57091-645-8(4))* Charlesbridge Publishing, Inc.
—Octopus Escapes! Lachenmeyer, Nathaniel. 2018. 32p. (J). (-k). lib. bdg. 16.99 *(978-1-58089-795-2(9))* Charlesbridge Publishing, Inc.
—Pinkbeard's Revenge. Trine, Greg. 2015. (Adventures of Jo Schmo Ser.: 4). (ENG.). 128p. (J). (gr. 1-4). pap. 7.99 *(978-0-544-45601-3(7)*, 1599386, HMH Books For Young Readers) Houghton Mifflin Harcourt Publishing Co.
—Shifty Business. Trine, Greg. (Adventures of Jo Schmo Ser.: 3). (ENG.). 112p. (J). (gr. 1-4). 2014. pap. 5.99 *(978-0-544-33911-8(8)*, 1584482, HMH Books For Young Readers); 2013. 12.99 *(978-0-547-80796-6(1)*, 1495240) Houghton Mifflin Harcourt Publishing Co.
—Three Stories. Ries, Lori. 2007. (Aggie & Ben Ser.). 48p. (J). (gr. -1-3). 5.95 *(978-1-57091-649-6(7))* Charlesbridge Publishing, Inc.
—Wyatt Burp Rides Again. Trine, Greg. (Adventures of Jo Schmo Ser.: 2). (ENG.). 112p. (J). (gr. 1-4). 2014. pap. 6.99 *(978-0-544-01899-0(0)*, 1528127, HMH Books For Young Readers); 2012. 12.99 *(978-0-547-80795-9(3)*, 1495239) Houghton Mifflin Harcourt Publishing Co.
Dormer, Frank W. Firefighter Duckies! Dormer, Frank W. 2017. (ENG.). 40p. (J). (gr. -1-3). 17.99 *(978-1-4814-6090-3(0)*, Atheneum Bks. for Young Readers) Simon & Schuster Children's Publishing.
—The Sword in the Stove. Dormer, Frank W. 2016. (ENG.). 40p. (J). (gr. -1-3). 17.99 *(978-1-4814-3167-5(6))* Simon & Schuster, Inc.
—Tita y Ben: Tres Cuentos. Dormer, Frank W. Ries, Lori & Canetti, Yanitzia. 2010. 48p. (J). (gr. -1-3). 13.95 *(978-1-57091-934-3(8))*; pap. 6.99 *(978-1-57091-935-0(6))* Charlesbridge Publishing, Inc.
Dormishev, Lilly. Seascape. Van Risseghem, Kristin D. Lister, Dionne, ed. 2018. (ENG.). 212p. (J). pap. 10.99 *(978-1-943207-41-1(0))* Kasian Publishing.
Dornadic, Alicia. Collaboration: Ways We Work Together. Moniz, Tomas. 2018. (ENG.). 38p. (J). 14.95 *(978-1-84935-312-0(3))* AK Pr. GBR. Dist: Consortium Bk. Sales & Distribution.
Dornemann, Volker. Taekwondo Kids: From White Belt to Yellow/Green Belt. Rumpf, Wolfgang. 2007. 136p. (J). pap. 14.95 *(978-1-84126-214-7(5))* Meyer & Meyer Sport, Ltd. GBR. Dist: Cardinal Pubs. Group.
Dorosheva, Sveta. Anne Frank. Sanchez Vegara, Maria Isabel. 2018. (Little People, Big Dreams Ser.: Vol. 15). (ENG.). 32p. (J). (gr. -1-2). ***(978-1-78603-229-4(5))*** Frances Lincoln Childrens Bks.
Dorros, Arthur. What Makes Day & Night. Branley, Franklyn M. 2015. (Let's-Read-And-Find-Out Science 2 Ser.). (ENG.). 32p. (J). (gr. -1-3). pap. 6.99 *(978-0-06-238197-2(0))* HarperCollins Pubs.
Doscher, Susan. Emmy Sue & the Blue Moo. Doscher, E. L. M. S. 2010. 20p. pap. 9.99 *(978-1-935125-92-1(3))* Robertson Publishing.
Doss, Andrea. Do Your Ears Hang Low? Everett, Melissa. 2017. (ENG.). 20p. (J). (gr. -1-2). bds. *(978-1-4867-1242-7(8))* Flowerpot Children's Pr. Inc.
—Do Your Ears Hang Low? Bell, Lucy & Everett, Melissa. 2014. (ENG.). 20p. (J). (gr. -1-2). bds. 8.99 *(978-1-4867-0358-6(5))* Flowerpot Children's Pr. Inc. CAN. Dist: Cardinal Pubs. Group.
—Good Night, Sleep Tight. Flowerpot Press, ed. 2019. (Bedtime Prayers Ser.). (ENG.). 20p. (J). (gr. k-1). bds. 7.99 *(978-1-4867-1578-7(8)*, 55003805-d0ba-4708-9201-e599a30230e1) Flowerpot Pr.
—Little Red Riding Hood. 2017. (5 Minute Storytime Ser.). (ENG.). 32p. (J). (gr. k-3). 6.99 *(978-1-4867-1275-5(4)*, 2d9d6b59-dd56-477e-81de-10f55d1100b1) Flowerpot Pr.
—Mary Had a Little Lamb. Bell, Lucy. 2017. (ENG.). 20p. (J). (gr. -1-2). bds. *(978-1-4867-1241-0(X))* Flowerpot Children's Pr. Inc.
Dostalova, Petronela. The Things. Dostalova, Petronela. 2019. (Child's Play Library). 32p. (J). *(978-1-78628-190-6(2))*; pap. *(978-1-78628-189-0(9))* Child's Play International Ltd.
Dotneboya, Katerina. Pokeweed: An Illustrated Novella. Tucker, Brian L. 2018. (ENG.). 118p. (YA). (gr. 7-12). pap. 14.95 *(978-1-68433-109-3(9))* Black Rose Writing.
Dotneboya, Katerina. The Scary, Gray Shark. Tucker, Brian L. 2020. (ENG.). 20p. (J). pap. 15.95 ***(978-1-68433-410-0(1))*** Black Rose Writing.
D'Ottavi, Francesca. Bee Life. Evans, Lynette. 2013. (ENG.). 32p. (J). (gr. -1). 12.99 *(978-1-60887-198-8(3))* Insight Editions.
—La Biblia Juvenil Ilustrada. Griswood, John, ed. Sanz Falcon, Maria Teresa, tr. from ENG. 2006. (SPA.). 320p. (J). (gr. -1-3). 24.95 *(978-1-58087-088-7(0)*, 0278) Stampley, C. D. Enterprises, Inc.
—The Illustrated Bible. Morris, Neil & Morris, Ting. McRae Books Staff, ed. 2008. (ENG.). 320p. (J). (gr. -1). 24.95 *(978-88-88166-34-6(3))* McRae Bks. Srl ITA. Dist: Independent Pubs. Group.
—Isis & Osiris, 1 vol. 2012. (Egyptian Myths Ser.). (ENG.). 32p. (J). (gr. 3-5). lib. bdg. 29.32 *(978-1-4048-7148-9(9)*, Picture Window Bks.) Capstone.
—Sarah Palin: Political Rebel, 1 vol. Yomtov, Nelson. 2011. (American Graphic Ser.). (ENG.). 32p. (J). (gr. 3-9). lib. bdg. 31.32 *(978-1-4296-6018-1(X)*, Capstone Pr.) Capstone.
—Sarah Palin: Political Rebel, 1 vol. Yomtov, Nel. 2011. (American Graphic Ser.). (ENG.). 32p. (gr. 3-9). pap. 8.10 *(978-1-4296-7341-9(9))*; pap. 47.70 *(978-1-4296-7342-6(7))* Capstone. (Capstone Pr.).
Dotty, Zens. The First Time I Heard the Gospel. Rolling, Greg. 2012. 24p. pap. 11.99 *(978-0-9827446-9-7(2))* Quoir.

D

Doty, Eldon. An Illustrated Timeline of Transportation, 1 vol. Spengler, Kremena T. 2011. (Visual Timelines in History Ser.). (ENG.). 32p. (J). (gr. 2-4). pap. 7.49 (978-1-4048-7019-2(9), Picture Window Bks.) Capstone.

—Mummies: Truth & Rumors. Montgomery, Heather L. 2010. (Truth & Rumors Ser.). (ENG.). 32p. (J). (gr. 3-9). lib. bdg. 28.65 (978-1-4296-3950-7(4), Capstone Pr.) Capstone.

—Pirates: Truth & Rumors, 1 vol. Price, Sean Stewart. 2010. (Truth & Rumors Ser.). (ENG.). 32p. (J). (gr. 3-9). lib. bdg. 28.65 (978-1-4296-4746-5(9), Capstone Pr.) Capstone.

—Sports. Price, Sean Stewart. 2010. (Truth & Rumors Ser.). (ENG.). 32p. (J). (gr. 3-9). lib. bdg. 28.65 (978-1-4296-4747-2(7), Capstone Pr.) Capstone.

—Titanic: Truth & Rumors. Burgan, Michael. 2010. (Truth & Rumors Ser.). (ENG.). 32p. (J). (gr. 3-9). lib. bdg. 28.65 (978-1-4296-3951-4(2), Capstone Pr.) Capstone.

—U. S. Presidents: Truth & Rumors. Price, Sean Stewart. 2010. (Truth & Rumors Ser.). (ENG.). 32p. (J). (gr. 3-9). lib. bdg. 28.65 (978-1-4296-3952-1(0), Capstone Pr.) Capstone.

Doty, Eldon C. Fast Dan. Pearson, Mary E. 2003. (Rookie Reader Skill Set Ser.). (ENG.). 32p. (J). (gr. k-2). pap. 4.95 (978-0-516-27494-2(5), Children's Pr.) Scholastic Library Publishing.

Doub, Alexander. The Prodigal Pig. Means, Grant. 2019. (Three Little Pigs Ser.: Vol. 1). (ENG.). 36p. (J). pap. 10.00 **(978-1-7121-5482-3(6))** Independently Published.

Doubleday, Dorothy. Little Bear & the Marco Polo. Minarik, Else Holmelund. 2010. (I Can Read Level 1 Ser.). (ENG.). 32p. (J). (gr. k-3). 16.99 (978-0-06-085485-0(5)); pap. 4.99 (978-0-06-085487-4(1)) HarperCollins Pubs.

Doucet, Bob. All for a Game, 1 vol. Abdo, Kenny. 2013. (Haven't Got a Clue! Ser.). (ENG.). 80p. (J). (gr. 3-6). lib. bdg. 29.93 (978-1-61641-950-9(4), 9425, Calico Chapter Bks.) ABDO Publishing Co.

—Amazing American Curls, 1 vol. Hengel, Katherine. 2011. (Cat Craze Ser.). (ENG.). 24p. (J). (gr. -1-4). 28.50 (978-1-61714-829-3(6), 4144, Super SandCastle) ABDO Publishing Co.

—The Apple State Treasure Hunt: A Story about Washington. Hengel, Katherine. 2011. (Fact & Fable: State Stories Ser.). (ENG.). 24p. (J). (gr. -1-4). 28.50 (978-1-61714-679-4(X), 7179, Super SandCastle) ABDO Publishing Co.

—Awesome Abyssinians, 1 vol. Hanson, Anders. 2009. (Cat Craze Ser.). (ENG.). 24p. (J). (gr. k-4). 28.50 (978-1-60453-721-5(3), 4130, Super SandCastle) ABDO Publishing Co.

—Bea on Broadway: A Story about New York. Kenney, Karen Latchana. 2008. (Fact & Fable: State Stories Ser.). (ENG.). 24p. (J). (gr. -1-4). 28.50 (978-1-60453-182-4(7), 7151, Super SandCastle) ABDO Publishing Co.

—Bold Boxers, 1 vol. Hanson, Anders. 2009. (Dog Daze Ser.). (ENG.). 24p. (J). (gr. -1-4). 28.50 (978-1-60453-615-7(2), 5201, Super SandCastle) ABDO Publishing Co.

—Brainy Brittanys, 1 vol. Hengel, Katherine. 2009. (Dog Daze Ser.). (ENG.). 24p. (J). (gr. -1-4). 28.50 (978-1-60453-616-4(0), 5203, Super SandCastle) ABDO Publishing Co.

—Burly Bulldogs, 1 vol. Hengel, Katherine. 2010. (Dog Daze Ser.). (ENG.). 24p. (J). (gr. -1-4). 28.50 (978-1-61613-376-4(7), 5215, Super SandCastle) ABDO Publishing Co.

—Buster's Trip to Cape Cod: A Story about Massachusetts. Gaarder-Juntti, Oona. 2010. (Fact & Fable: State Stories Ser.). 24p. (J). (gr. -1-4). 27.07 (978-1-60453-921-9(6), 7165, Super SandCastle) ABDO Publishing Co.

—Chipper Chihuahuas, 1 vol. Hengel, Katherine. 2010. (Dog Daze Ser.). (ENG.). 24p. (J). (gr. -1-4). 28.50 (978-1-61613-377-1(5), 5217, Super SandCastle) ABDO Publishing Co.

—Comic Relief, 1 vol. Abdo, Kenny. 2013. (Haven't Got a Clue! Ser.). (ENG.). 80p. (J). (gr. 3-6). lib. bdg. 29.93 (978-1-61641-951-6(2), 9427, Calico Chapter Bks.) ABDO Publishing Co.

—Daring Dalmatians, 1 vol. Scheunemann, Pam. 2010. (Dog Daze Ser.). (ENG.). 24p. (J). (gr. -1-4). 28.50 (978-1-61613-378-8(3), 5219, Super SandCastle) ABDO Publishing Co.

—Delightful Devon Rexes, 1 vol. Hengel, Katherine. 2011. (Cat Craze Ser.). (ENG.). 24p. (J). (gr. -1-4). 28.50 (978-1-61714-830-9(X), 4146, Super SandCastle) ABDO Publishing Co.

—Dixie's Big Heart: A Story about Alabama. Tuminelly, Nancy. 2011. (Fact & Fable: State Stories Ser.). (ENG.). 24p. (J). (gr. -1-4). lib. bdg. 28.50 (978-1-61714-680-0(3), 7181, Super SandCastle) ABDO Publishing Co.

—Duck, Dive, Rock & Roll, 1 vol. Abdo, Kenny. 2013. (Haven't Got a Clue! Ser.). (ENG.). 80p. (J). (gr. 3-6). lib. bdg. 29.93 (978-1-61641-952-3(0), 9429, Calico Chapter Bks.) ABDO Publishing Co.

—Frenchy's Float: A Story about Louisiana. Scheunemann, Pam. 2010. (Fact & Fable: State Stories Ser.). (ENG.). 24p. (J). (gr. -1-4). 28.50 (978-1-60453-922-6(4), 7167, Super SandCastle) ABDO Publishing Co.

—Give Me Liberty or Give Me Detention!, 1 vol. Abdo, Kenny. 2013. (Haven't Got a Clue! Ser.). (ENG.). 80p. (J). (gr. 3-6). lib. bdg. 29.93 (978-1-61641-953-0(9), 9431, Calico Chapter Bks.) ABDO Publishing Co.

—Griz Finds Gold: A Story about California. Lindeen, Mary. 2008. (Fact & Fable: State Stories Ser.). (ENG.). 24p. (J). (gr. -1-4). 28.50 (978-1-60453-183-1(5), 7153, Super SandCastle) ABDO Publishing Co.

—Hip Himalayans, 1 vol. Hengel, Katherine. 2009. (Cat Craze Ser.). (ENG.). 24p. (J). (gr. k-4). 28.50 (978-1-60453-722-2(1), 4132, Super SandCastle) ABDO Publishing Co.

—Jumping Jack Russell Terriers, 1 vol. Scheunemann, Pam. 2009. (Dog Daze Ser.). (ENG.). 24p. (J). (gr. -1-4). 28.50 (978-1-60453-617-1(9), 5205, Super SandCastle) ABDO Publishing Co.

—Leaping Lily: A Story about Georgia. Dolphin, Colleen. 2010. (Fact & Fable: State Stories Ser.). (ENG.). 24p. (J). (gr. -1-4). 28.50 (978-1-60453-924-0(0), 7171, Super SandCastle) ABDO Publishing Co.

—Lena & the Lady's Slippers: A Story about Minnesota. Scheunemann, Pam. 2011. (Fact & Fable: State Stories Ser.). (ENG.). 24p. (J). (gr. -1-4). 28.50 (978-1-61714-681-7(1), 7183, Super SandCastle) ABDO Publishing Co.

—The Lonesome Star: A Story about Texas. Kenney, Karen Latchana. 2008. (Fact & Fable: State Stories Ser.). (ENG.). 24p. (J). (gr. -1-4). 28.50 (978-1-60453-184-8(3), 7155, Super SandCastle) ABDO Publishing Co.

—Lovely Labrador Retrievers, 1 vol. Scheunemann, Pam. 2009. (Dog Daze Ser.). 24p. (J). (gr. -1-4). 27.07 (978-1-60453-618-8(7), 5207, Super SandCastle) ABDO Publishing Co.

—The Lucky Buckeye: A Story about Ohio. Leebrick, Kristal. 2008. (Fact & Fable: State Stories Ser.). (ENG.). 24p. (J). (gr. -1-4). 28.50 (978-1-60453-185-5(1), 7157, Super SandCastle) ABDO Publishing Co.

—Marvelous Maine Coons, 1 vol. Scheunemann, Pam. 2009. (Cat Craze Ser.). (ENG.). 24p. (J). (gr. k-4). 28.50 (978-1-60453-723-9(X), 4134, Super SandCastle) ABDO Publishing Co.

—Missy the Show-Me Mule: A Story about Missouri. Tuminelly, Nancy. 2011. (Fact & Fable: State Stories Ser.). (ENG.). 24p. (J). (gr. -1-4). 28.50 (978-1-61714-682-4(X), 7185, Super SandCastle) ABDO Publishing Co.

—Outgoing Oriental Shorthairs, 1 vol. Hengel, Katherine. 2011. (Cat Craze Ser.). (ENG.). 24p. (J). (gr. -1-4). 28.50 (978-1-61714-831-6(8), 4148, Super SandCastle) ABDO Publishing Co.

—Perky Poodles, 1 vol. Scheunemann, Pam. 2010. (Dog Daze Ser.). (ENG.). 24p. (J). (gr. -1-4). 28.50 (978-1-61613-379-5(1), 5221, Super SandCastle) ABDO Publishing Co.

—Pizza Pie in the Sky: A Story about Illinois. Kenney, Karen Latchana. 2008. (Fact & Fable: State Stories Ser.). 24p. (J). (gr. -1-4). 27.07 (978-1-60453-186-2(X), 7159, Super SandCastle) ABDO Publishing Co.

—Popular Persians, 1 vol. Scheunemann, Pam. 2009. (Cat Craze Ser.). (ENG.). 24p. (J). (gr. k-4). 28.50 (978-1-60453-724-6(8), 4136, Super SandCastle) ABDO Publishing Co.

—Proud Portuguese Water Dogs, 1 vol. Hengel, Katherine. 2010. (Dog Daze Ser.). (ENG.). 24p. (J). (gr. -1-4). 28.50 (978-1-61613-380-1(5), 5223, Super SandCastle) ABDO Publishing Co.

—Psych-Out!, 1 vol. Abdo, Kenny. 2013. (Haven't Got a Clue! Ser.). (ENG.). 80p. (J). (gr. 3-6). lib. bdg. 29.93 (978-1-61641-954-7(7), 9433, Calico Chapter Bks.) ABDO Publishing Co.

—Rachel's Home on Bear Mountain: A Story about Connecticut. Salzmann, Mary Elizabeth. 2011. (Fact & Fable: State Stories Ser.). (ENG.). 24p. (J). (gr. -1-4). lib. bdg. 28.50 (978-1-61714-683-1(8), 7187, Super SandCastle) ABDO Publishing Co.

—Rocky's Outdoor Adventure: A Story about Colorado. Dolphin, Colleen. 2011. (Fact & Fable: State Stories Ser.). (ENG.). 24p. (J). (gr. -1-4). lib. bdg. 28.50 (978-1-61714-684-8(6), 7189, Super SandCastle) ABDO Publishing Co.

—Rupert & the Liberty Bell: A Story about Pennsylvania. Hengel, Katherine. 2010. (Fact & Fable: State Stories Ser.). (ENG.). 24p. (J). (gr. -1-4). 28.50 (978-1-60453-926-4(7), 7175, Super SandCastle) ABDO Publishing Co.

—S Is for Spirit Bear: A British Columbia Alphabet. Roberts, G. Gregory. rev. ed. 2006. (Discover Canada Province by Province Ser.). (ENG.). 40p. (J). (gr. 3-7). 18.95 (978-1-58536-291-2(3)) Sleeping Bear Pr.

—Shaggy Shih Tzus, 1 vol. Hanson, Anders. 2009. (Dog Daze Ser.). (ENG.). 24p. (J). (gr. -1-4). 28.50 (978-1-60453-619-5(5), 5209, Super SandCastle) ABDO Publishing Co.

—Sleek Siamese, 1 vol. Hanson, Anders. 2009. (Cat Craze Ser.). (ENG.). 24p. (J). (gr. k-4). 28.50 (978-1-60453-725-3(6), 4138, Super SandCastle) ABDO Publishing Co.

—Smooth Sphynx, 1 vol. Hengel, Katherine. 2009. (Cat Craze Ser.). (ENG.). 24p. (J). (gr. k-4). 28.50 (978-1-60453-726-0(4), 4140, Super SandCastle) ABDO Publishing Co.

—Strong Siberian Huskies, 1 vol. Hengel, Katherine. 2009. (Dog Daze Ser.). (ENG.). 24p. (J). (gr. -1-4). 28.50 (978-1-60453-620-1(9), 5211, Super SandCastle) ABDO Publishing Co.

—The Sunshine Champs: A Story about Florida. Kenney, Karen Latchana. 2008. (Fact & Fable: State Stories Ser.). (ENG.). 24p. (J). (gr. -1-4). 28.50 (978-1-60453-187-9(8), 7161, Super SandCastle) ABDO Publishing Co.

—Super Saint Bernards, 1 vol. Salzmann, Mary Elizabeth. 2010. (Dog Daze Ser.). (ENG.). 24p. (J). (gr. -1-4). 28.50 (978-1-61613-381-8(3), 5225, Super SandCastle) ABDO Publishing Co.

—Sweet Scottish Folds, 1 vol. Hengel, Katherine. 2011. (Cat Craze Ser.). (ENG.). 24p. (J). (gr. k-4). 28.50 (978-1-61714-833-0(4), 4152, Super SandCastle) ABDO Publishing Co.

—Terrific Tabbies, 1 vol. Hengel, Katherine. 2011. (Cat Craze Ser.). (ENG.). 24p. (J). (gr. k-4). 28.50 (978-1-61714-834-7(2), 4154, Super SandCastle) ABDO Publishing Co.

—Triple Take, 1 vol. Abdo, Kenny. 2013. (Haven't Got a Clue! Ser.). (ENG.). 80p. (J). (gr. 3-6). lib. bdg. 29.93 (978-1-61641-955-4(5), 9435, Calico Chapter Bks.) ABDO Publishing Co.

Doucet, Rashad. Alabaster Shadows. Gardner, Matt. 2015. (ENG.). 184p. (J). pap. 12.99 (978-1-62010-264-0(1), 9781620102640, Lion Forge) Oni Pr., Inc.

Doucette, Constance. A Moose for Mackenzie. Ballard, Lisa. 2008. 32p. pap. 24.95 (978-1-60610-123-0(4)) America Star Bks.

Dougall, Dawn. Gracey at the Grange: Stories for Children 6-To-60. Chish-Graham, Betty. 2016. (ENG.). (J). (gr. k-6). pap. (978-1-77317-001-5(5)) Prism Pubs.

Dougherty, Charles L. Giant of the Western Trail: Father Peter de Smet. McHugh, Michael. 2011. 186p. 42.95 (978-1-258-05887-6(1)) Literary Licensing, LLC.

—Priest, Patriot & Leader: The Story of Archbishop Carroll. Betz, Eva K. 2011. 188p. 42.95 (978-1-258-03693-5(2)) Literary Licensing, LLC.

Dougherty, Dan. Band Nerds: Poetry from the 13th Chair Trombone Player. Corchin, D. J. 2020. (Band Nerds Ser.). 144p. (YA). (gr. 7-12). pap. 12.99 **(978-1-7282-1982-0(5))** Sourcebooks, Inc.

Dougherty, Dan. The Marching Band Nerds Handbook. Corchin, Dj. 2012. 136p. 22.95 (978-0-9834876-7-8(7)); pap. 12.95 (978-0-9819645-7-7(5)) phazelFOZ Co., LLC., The.

Dougherty, Dan. The Marching Band Nerds Handbook: Rules from the 13th Chair Trombone Player. Corchin, D. J. 2020. (Band Nerds Ser.). (ENG.). 128p. (YA). (gr. 7-12). pap. 12.99 **(978-1-7282-1976-9(0))** Sourcebooks, Inc.

Dougherty, Dan. A Thousand No's. Corchin, D. J. 2020. 48p. (J). (-3). 17.99 (978-1-7282-1919-6(1)) Sourcebooks, Inc.

Dougherty, Rachel. The Twelve Days of Christmas in Pennsylvania. Peaslee Levine, Martha. (Twelve Days of Christmas in America Ser.). (J). (-k). 2018. 22p. bds. 7.95 (978-1-4549-3052-5(7)); 2014. 40p. 12.95 (978-1-4549-0889-0(0)) Sterling Publishing Co., Inc.

—Your Life As a Pioneer on the Oregon Trail. Gunderson, Jessica. 2012. (Way It Was Ser.). (ENG.). 32p. (J). (gr. 2-5). pap. 8.95 (978-1-4048-7250-9(7), Picture Window Bks.) Capstone.

Dougherty, Rachel. Secret Engineer: How Emily Roebling Built the Brooklyn Bridge. Dougherty, Rachel. 2019. (ENG.). 40p. (J). 17.99 (978-1-250-15532-0(0), 900184621) Roaring Brook Pr.

Doughty, Clare, jt. illus. see Giraffe, Red.

Doughty, Rebecca. One of Those Days. Rosenthal, Amy Krouse. 2006. 32p. (J). (gr. -1-3). 16.99 (978-0-399-24365-3(8), G.P. Putnam's Sons Books for Young Readers) Penguin Young Readers Group.

—31 Usos para Mama. Ziefert, Harriet. Sarfatti, Esther, tr. 2006. (Montana Encantada Ser.). (SPA.). 32p. (J). (gr. -1-k). pap. 8.50 (978-84-241-8777-4(6)) Lectorum Pubns., Inc.

Douglas, Allen. Diary of a Runaway Griffin. Coville, Bruce. 2016. (Enchanted Files Ser.: 2). (ENG.). 272p. (J). (gr. 3-7). 16.99 (978-0-385-39255-6(9), Random Hse. Bks. for Young Readers) Random Hse. Children's Bks.

—Drone Academy, 4 vols. Manning, Matthew K. 2018. (Drone Academy Ser.). (ENG.). 112p. (J). (gr. 4-8). 106.60 (978-1-4965-6085-8(X), 27719, Stone Arch Bks.) Capstone.

—The Last Dogs: Dark Waters. Holt, Christopher. 2013. (Last Dogs Ser.: 2). (ENG.). 352p. (J). (gr. 3-7). pap. 8.99 (978-0-316-20009-7(3)) Little, Brown Bks. for Young Readers.

—The Last Dogs: Journey's End. Holt, Christopher. 2014. (Last Dogs Ser.: 4). (ENG.). 320p. (J). (gr. 3-7). 17.00 (978-0-316-20007-3(7)) Little, Brown Bks. for Young Readers.

—The Last Dogs: the Long Road. Holt, Christopher. 2014. (Last Dogs Ser.: 3). (ENG.). 352p. (J). (gr. 3-7). pap. 8.99 (978-0-316-20016-5(6)) Little, Brown Bks. for Young Readers.

—Operation Copycat. Manning, Matthew K. 2018. (Drone Academy Ser.). (ENG.). 112p. (J). (gr. 4-8). lib. bdg. 26.65 (978-1-4965-6075-9(2), 137497, Stone Arch Bks.) Capstone.

—Operation Foxhunt. Manning, Matthew K. 2018. (Drone Academy Ser.). (ENG.). 112p. (J). (gr. 4-8). lib. bdg. 26.65 (978-1-4965-6074-2(4), 137496, Stone Arch Bks.) Capstone.

—Operation Runaway. Manning, Matthew K. 2018. (Drone Academy Ser.). (ENG.). 112p. (J). (gr. 4-8). lib. bdg. 26.65 (978-1-4965-6073-5(6), 137495, Stone Arch Bks.) Capstone.

—Operation Stargazer. Manning, Matthew K. 2018. (Drone Academy Ser.). (ENG.). 112p. (J). (gr. 4-8). lib. bdg. 26.65 (978-1-4965-6076-6(0), 137498, Stone Arch Bks.) Capstone.

—Warriors: Dawn of the Clans #4: the Blazing Star. Hunter, Erin. 2014. (Warriors: Dawn of the Clans Ser.: 4). (ENG.). 320p. (J). (gr. 3-7). 16.99 (978-0-06-206358-8(8)) HarperCollins Pubs.

Douglas, Allen, jt. illus. see McLoughlin, Wayne.

Douglas, Allen, jt. illus. see Richardson, Owen.

Douglas, Bettye, et al. Portrait of a People: The Bettye Douglas Forum, Inc. Multicultural Resource Book. Douglas, Bettye. 222p. (YA). (gr. 5-13). 100.00 (978-0-9703183-1-2(6)) Douglas, Bettye Forum, Inc., The.

Douglas, Chloe. The Princess & the Cafe on the Moat. Markarian, Margie & Hoover, John. 2018. (ENG.). 32p. (J). (gr. k-3). 16.99 (978-1-58536-397-1(9), 204402) Sleeping Bear Pr.

Douglas, Garbrielle. Safari Oklahoma Presents: God Bless America Historical. Douglas, Bettye. 2003. 22p. (J). (gr. 2-7). wbk. ed. 19.95 (978-0-9703183-6-7(7)) Douglas, Bettye Forum, Inc., The.

Douglas, Janine. The Muselings. Wicke, Ed. 2012. 212p. pap. 9.99 (978-0-9840718-8-3(1)) Blacknblue Pr.

Douglas, Karlon. Addison: Personalized Ima Gonna Color My Happy Easter Coloring Book for Kids. Art, Black River. 2019. (ENG.). 52p. (J). pap. 6.99 (978-1-0918-0825-6(2)) Independently Published.

—Aiden: Personalized Ima Gonna Color My Happy Easter Coloring Book for Kids. Art, Black River. 2019. (ENG.). 52p. (J). pap. 6.99 (978-1-0919-1369-1(2)) Independently Published.

—Alex: Personalized Ima Gonna Color My Happy Easter Coloring Book for Kids. Art, Black River. 2019. (ENG.). 52p. (J). pap. 6.99 (978-1-0919-1371-4(4)) Independently Published.

—Amelia: Personalized Ima Gonna Color My Happy Easter Coloring Book for Kids. Art, Black River. 2019. (ENG.). 52p. (J). pap. 6.99 (978-1-0918-0826-3(0)) Independently Published.

—Anderson's Writing Tablet: Personalized Primary Writing Tablet for Kids, 65 Sheets of Blank Lined Practice Paper with 1 Ruling Designed for Children Learning How to Write in Preschool, Kindergarten or First Grade. Button, Big Red. 2019. (ENG.). 68p. (J). pap. 6.99 (978-1-0812-4544-3(1)) Independently Published.

—Andrew: Personalized Ima Gonna Color My Happy Easter Coloring Book for Kids. Art, Black River. 2019. (ENG.). 52p. (J). pap. 6.99 (978-1-0919-1372-1(2)) Independently Published.

—Andy's Writing Tablet: Personalized Book for Kids, Primary Writing Tablet with 65 Sheets of Blank Lined Practice Paper with 1 Ruling Designed for Children Learning How to Write in Pre-K, Kindergarten or First Grade. Button, Big Red. 2019. (ENG.). 68p. (J). pap. 6.99 (978-1-0814-0152-8(4)) Independently Published.

—Anthony: Personalized Ima Gonna Color My Happy Easter Coloring Book for Kids. Art, Black River. 2019. (ENG.). 52p. (J). pap. 6.99 (978-1-0919-1599-2(7)) Independently Published.

—Aubrey: Personalized Ima Gonna Color My Happy Easter Coloring Book for Kids. Art, Black River. 2019. (ENG.). 52p. (J). pap. 6.99 (978-1-0918-0829-4(5)) Independently Published.

—Ava: Personalized Ima Gonna Color My Happy Easter Coloring Book for Kids. Art, Black River. 2019. (ENG.). 52p. (J). pap. 6.99 (978-1-0918-0831-7(7)) Independently Published.

—Benjamin: Personalized Ima Gonna Color My Happy Easter Coloring Book for Kids. Art, Black River. 2019. (ENG.). 52p. (J). pap. 6.99 (978-1-0919-1600-5(4)) Independently Published.

—Boom Boom Unicorns: Cute Unicorn Farting Rainbows Themed Book with 105 Lined Pages to Write in That Can Be Used As a Journal or Notebook. Art, Black River. l.t. ed. 2018. (ENG.). 108p. (J). pap. 5.99 (978-1-7904-9589-4(X)) Independently Published.

—Chay's Gonna Trace Some Letters: Personalized Tracing Workbook for Kids Learning to Write the Letters of the Alphabet, Paper with 1 Ruling for Children in Preschool, Kindergarten & First Grade. Art, Black River. 2018. (ENG.). 108p. (J). pap. 8.99 (978-1-7191-3876-5(1)) CreateSpace Independent Publishing Platform.

—Chloe: Personalized Ima Gonna Color My Happy Easter Coloring Book for Kids. Art, Black River. 2019. (ENG.). 52p. (J). pap. 6.99 (978-1-0918-1195-9(4)) Independently Published.

—Dalton's Writing Tablet: Personalized Book for Kids, Primary Writing Tablet with 65 Sheets of Blank Lined Practice Paper with 1 Ruling Designed for Children Learning How to Write in Pre-K, Kindergarten or First Grade. Button, Big Red. 2019. (ENG.). 68p. (J). pap. 6.99 (978-1-0814-0155-9(9)) Independently Published.

—David: Personalized Ima Gonna Color My Happy Easter Coloring Book for Kids. Art, Black River. 2019. (ENG.). 52p. (J). pap. 6.99 (978-1-0919-1602-9(0)) Independently Published.

—Dori's Gonna Trace Some Letters: Personalized Tracing Workbook for Kids Learning to Write the Letters of the Alphabet, Paper with 1 Ruling for Children in Preschool, Kindergarten & First Grade. Art, Black River. 2018. (ENG.). 108p. (J). pap. 8.99 (978-1-7907-0720-1(X)) Independently Published.

—Elizabeth: Personalized Ima Gonna Color My Happy Easter Coloring Book for Kids. Art, Black River. 2019. (ENG.). 52p. (J). pap. 6.99 (978-1-0918-1196-6(2)) Independently Published.

—Ella: Personalized Ima Gonna Color My Happy Easter Coloring Book for Kids. Art, Black River. 2019. (ENG.). 52p. (J). pap. 6.99 (978-1-0918-1197-3(0)) Independently Published.

—Elliana's Writing Tablet: Personalized Primary Writing Tablet for Kids, 65 Sheets of Blank Lined Practice Paper with 1 Ruling Designed for Children Learning How to Write in Preschool, Kindergarten or First Grade. Button, Big Red. 2019. (ENG.). 68p. (J). pap. 6.99 (978-1-0813-7923-0(5)) Independently Published.

—Ethan: Personalized Ima Gonna Color My Happy Easter Coloring Book for Kids. Art, Black River. 2019. (ENG.). 52p. (J). pap. 6.99 (978-1-0919-8616-9(9)) Independently Published.

—Happy 10th Birthday: Better Than a Birthday Card! Cute Rainbow Farting Unicorn Themed Birthday Book with 105 Lined Pages to Write in That Can Be Used As a Journal or Notebook. Art, Black River. l.t. ed. 2018. (ENG.). 108p. (J). pap. 5.99 (978-1-7313-4760-2(X)) Independently Published.

—Happy 10th Birthday: Colorful Unicorn Sketch Book for Kids. Perfect for Doodling, Drawing & Sketching. Way Better Than a Birthday Card! Art, Black River. 2019. (ENG.). 102p. (J). pap. 5.99 (978-1-0976-1925-2(7)) Independently Published.

—Happy 10th Birthday: Poppin' Purple Sketch Book for Kids. Perfect for Doodling, Drawing & Sketching. Way Better Than a Birthday Card! Art, Black River. 2019. (ENG.). 102p. (J). pap. 5.99 (978-1-0977-7438-8(4)) Independently Published.

—Happy 10th Birthday: Pretty Pink Sketch Book for Kids. Perfect for Doodling, Drawing & Sketching. Way Better Than a Birthday Card! Art, Black River. 2019. (ENG.). 102p. (J). pap. 5.99 (978-1-0977-7446-3(5)) Independently Published.

—Happy 32nd Birthday: Better Than a Birthday Card! Neon Sign Themed Birthday Book with 105 Lined Pages to Write in That Can Be Used As a Journal or Notebook. Art, Black River. l.t. ed. 2018. (ENG.). 108p. (J). pap. 6.99 (978-1-7261-3617-4(5)) CreateSpace Independent Publishing Platform.

—Happy 3rd Birthday: Bright Green Primary Writing Tablet for 3 Year Old Kids Learning to Write, 65 Sheets of Blank Lined Practice Paper with 1 Ruling Designed for Preschoolers. Art, Black River. 2018. (ENG.). 68p. (J). pap. 5.99 (978-1-7258-6971-4(3)) CreateSpace Independent Publishing Platform.

—Happy 3rd Birthday: Poppin' Purple Primary Writing Tablet for 3 Year Old Kids Learning to Write, 65 Sheets of Blank Lined Practice Paper with 1 Ruling Designed for Preschoolers. Art, Black River. 2018. (ENG.). 68p. (J). pap. 5.99 *(978-1-7258-7012-3(6))* CreateSpace Independent Publishing Platform.

—Happy 45th Birthday: Better Than a Birthday Card! Neon Sign Themed Birthday Book with 105 Lined Pages to Write in That Can Be Used As a Journal or Notebook. Art, Black River. l.t. ed. 2018. (ENG.). 108p. (J). pap. 6.99 *(978-1-7261-3680-8(9))* CreateSpace Independent Publishing Platform.

—Happy 47th Birthday: Better Than a Birthday Card! Neon Sign Themed Birthday Book with 105 Lined Pages to Write in That Can Be Used As a Journal or Notebook. Art, Black River. l.t. ed. 2018. (ENG.). 108p. (J). pap. 6.99 *(978-1-7261-3808-6(9))* CreateSpace Independent Publishing Platform.

—Happy 48th Birthday: Better Than a Birthday Card! Neon Sign Themed Birthday Book with 105 Lined Pages to Write in That Can Be Used As a Journal or Notebook. Art, Black River. l.t. ed. 2018. (ENG.). 108p. (J). pap. 6.99 *(978-1-7261-3807-9(0))* CreateSpace Independent Publishing Platform.

—Happy 49th Birthday: Better Than a Birthday Card! Neon Sign Themed Birthday Book with 105 Lined Pages to Write in That Can Be Used As a Journal or Notebook. Art, Black River. l.t. ed. 2018. (ENG.). 108p. (J). pap. 6.99 *(978-1-7261-3806-2(2))* CreateSpace Independent Publishing Platform.

—Happy 4th Birthday: Bright Green Primary Writing Tablet for 4 Year Old Kids Learning How to Write, 65 Sheets of Blank Lined Practice Paper with 1 Ruling Designed for Preschoolers. Art, Black River. 2018. (ENG.). 68p. (J). pap. 5.99 *(978-1-7258-6979-0(9))* CreateSpace Independent Publishing Platform.

—Happy 4th Birthday: Poppin' Purple Primary Writing Tablet for 4 Year Old Kids Learning How to Write, 65 Sheets of Blank Lined Practice Paper with 1 Ruling Designed for Preschoolers. Art, Black River. 2018. (ENG.). 68p. (J). pap. 5.99 *(978-1-7258-7016-1(9))* CreateSpace Independent Publishing Platform.

—Happy 50th Birthday: Better Than a Birthday Card! Neon Sign Themed Birthday Book with 105 Lined Pages to Write in That Can Be Used As a Journal or Notebook. Art, Black River. l.t. ed. 2018. (ENG.). 108p. (J). pap. 6.99 *(978-1-7261-3805-5(4))* CreateSpace Independent Publishing Platform.

—Happy 7th Birthday: Colorful Unicorn Sketch Book for Kids. Perfect for Doodling, Drawing & Sketching. Way Better Than a Birthday Card! Art, Black River. 2019. (ENG.). 102p. (J). pap. 5.99 *(978-1-0976-1922-1(2))* Independently Published.

—Happy 7th Birthday: Poppin' Purple Sketch Book for Kids. Perfect for Doodling, Drawing & Sketching. Way Better Than a Birthday Card! Art, Black River. 2019. (ENG.). 102p. (J). pap. 5.99 *(978-1-0977-7434-0(1))* Independently Published.

—Happy 7th Birthday: Pretty Pink Sketch Book for Kids. Perfect for Doodling, Drawing & Sketching. Way Better Than a Birthday Card! Art, Black River. 2019. (ENG.). 102p. (J). pap. 5.99 *(978-1-0977-7442-5(2))* Independently Published.

—Happy 9th Birthday: Poppin' Purple Sketch Book for Kids. Perfect for Doodling, Drawing & Sketching. Way Better Than a Birthday Card! Art, Black River. 2019. (ENG.). 102p. (J). pap. 5.99 *(978-1-0977-7440-1(6))* Independently Published.

—Happy 9th Birthday: Pretty Pink Sketch Book for Kids. Perfect for Doodling, Drawing & Sketching. Way Better Than a Birthday Card! Art, Black River. 2019. (ENG.). 102p. (J). pap. 5.99 *(978-1-0977-7445-6(7))* Independently Published.

Douglas, Karlon. Jack's Gonna Trace Some Letters: Personalized Primary Letter Tracing Workbook for Kids Learning How to Write the Letters of the Alphabet, Practice Handwriting Paper with 1 Ruling Designed for Children in Preschool & Kindergarten. Art, Black River. 2019. (ENG.). 56p. (J). pap. 6.99 ***(978-1-6951-6585-4(3))*** Independently Published.

Douglas, Karlon. Jacob: Personalized Ima Gonna Color My Happy Easter Coloring Book for Kids. Art, Black River. 2019. (ENG.). 52p. (J). pap. 6.99 *(978-1-0919-8622-0(3))* Independently Published.

—Jayden: Personalized Ima Gonna Color My Happy Easter Coloring Book for Kids. Art, Black River. 2019. (ENG.). 52p. (J). pap. 6.99 *(978-1-0919-8624-4(X))* Independently Published.

—Jett's Writing Tablet: Personalized Book for Kids, Primary Writing Tablet with 65 Sheets of Blank Lined Practice Paper with 1 Ruling Designed for Children Learning How to Write in Pre-K, Kindergarten or First Grade. Button, Big Red. 2019. (ENG.). 68p. (J). pap. 6.99 *(978-1-0814-0166-5(4))* Independently Published.

—Joanna's Writing Tablet: Personalized Primary Writing Tablet for Kids, 65 Sheets of Blank Lined Practice Paper with 1 Ruling Designed for Children Learning How to Write in Preschool, Kindergarten or First Grade. Button, Big Red. 2019. (ENG.). 68p. (J). pap. 6.99 *(978-1-0813-7926-1(X))* Independently Published.

—Joseph: Personalized Ima Gonna Color My Happy Easter Coloring Book for Kids. Art, Black River. 2019. (ENG.). 52p. (J). pap. 6.99 *(978-1-0919-9312-9(2))* Independently Published.

—Joshua: Personalized Ima Gonna Color My Happy Easter Coloring Book for Kids. Art, Black River. 2019. (ENG.). 52p. (J). pap. 6.99 *(978-1-0919-9313-6(0))* Independently Published.

Douglas, Karlon. Karl's Writing Tablet: Personalized Book for Kids, Primary Writing Tablet with 65 Sheets of Blank Lined Practice Paper with 1 Ruling Designed for Children Learning How to Write in Pre-K, Kindergarten or First Grade. Button, Big Red. 2019. (ENG.). 68p. (J). pap. 6.99 ***(978-1-6920-7854-6(2))*** Independently Published.

Douglas, Karlon. Katie's Writing Tablet: Personalized Primary Writing Tablet for Kids, 65 Sheets of Blank Lined Practice Paper with 1 Ruling Designed for Children Learning How to Write in Preschool, Kindergarten or First Grade. Button, Big Red. 2019. (ENG.). 68p. (J). pap. 6.99 *(978-1-0813-7929-2(4))* Independently Published.

Douglas, Karlon. Keira's Writing Tablet: Personalized Book for Kids, Pink Primary Writing Tablet with 65 Sheets of Blank Lined Handwriting Practice Paper with 1 Ruling Designed for Children Learning How to Write in Pre-K, Kindergarten or First Grade. Button, Big Red. 2019. (ENG.). 68p. (J). pap. 6.99 ***(978-1-6969-7865-1(3))*** Independently Published.

Douglas, Karlon. Liam: Personalized Ima Gonna Color My Happy Easter Coloring Book for Kids. Art, Black River. 2019. (ENG.). 52p. (J). pap. 6.99 *(978-1-0919-9314-3(9))* Independently Published.

—Marco's Writing Tablet: Personalized Primary Writing Tablet for Kids, 65 Sheets of Blank Lined Practice Paper with 1 Ruling Designed for Children Learning How to Write in Preschool, Kindergarten or First Grade. Button, Big Red. 2019. (ENG.). 68p. (J). pap. 6.99 *(978-1-0813-6084-9(4))* Independently Published.

—Matthew: Personalized Ima Gonna Color My Happy Easter Coloring Book for Kids. Art, Black River. 2019. (ENG.). 52p. (J). (gr. 6-12). pap. 6.99 *(978-1-0921-0760-0(6))* Independently Published.

Douglas, Karlon. Mein Name Ist Johann: Spa� Mad Scientist Personalisierte Prim�r Name Tracking Arbeitsbuch F�r Kinder Lernen, Wie Man Ihren Vornamen PraxisPapier Mit 1 Linien F�r Kinder in Vorschule und Kindergarten Schreiben. Button, Big Red. 2019. (GER.). 54p. (J). pap. 6.99 ***(978-1-6999-0971-3(7))*** Independently Published.

Douglas, Karlon. Mein Name Ist Louis: Spaß Dino Monster Personalisierte Primäre Namensverfolgung Arbeitsbuch Für Kinder Lernen, Wie Man Ihren Vornamen Übungspapier Mit 1 Linien Für Kinder in Vorschule und Kindergarten Schreiben. Button, Big Red. 2019. (GER.). 54p. (J). pap. 6.99 *(978-1-0731-1526-6(7))* Independently Published.

—Mein Name Ist Luke: Spaß Dino Monster Personalisierte Primäre Namensverfolgung Arbeitsbuch Für Kinder Lernen, Wie Man Ihren Vornamen Übungspapier Mit 1 Linien Für Kinder in Vorschule und Kindergarten Schreiben. Button, Big Red. 2019. (GER.). 54p. (J). pap. 6.99 *(978-1-0731-1923-3(8))* Independently Published.

—Mein Name Ist Noa: Spaß Dino Monster Personalisierte Primäre Namensverfolgung Arbeitsbuch Für Kinder Lernen, Wie Man Ihren Vornamen Übungspapier Mit 1 Linien Für Kinder in Vorschule und Kindergarten Schreiben. Button, Big Red. 2019. (GER.). 54p. (J). pap. 6.99 *(978-1-0731-1926-4(2))* Independently Published.

Douglas, Karlon. Mi Nombre Es Alana: Libro de Trabajo de Seguimiento de Nombre y Letra. Button, Big Red. 2020. (SPA.). 110p. (J). pap. 5.99 ***(978-1-6583-1809-9(9))*** Independently Published.

—Mi Nombre Es Maria: Libro de Trabajo de Seguimiento de Nombre y Letra. Button, Big Red. 2019. (SPA.). 110p. (J). pap. 5.99 ***(978-1-6769-2490-6(6))*** Independently Published.

Douglas, Karlon. Michael: Personalized Ima Gonna Color My Happy Easter Coloring Book for Kids. Art, Black River. 2019. (ENG.). 52p. (J). (gr. 6-12). pap. 6.99 *(978-1-0921-0759-4(2))* Independently Published.

—My First Name Is Amila: Personalized Primary Name Tracing Workbook for Kids Learning How to Write Their First Name, Practice Paper with 1 Ruling Designed for Children in Preschool & Kindergarten. Button, Big Red. 2019. (ENG.). 54p. (J). pap. 6.99 *(978-1-7942-9725-8(1))* Independently Published.

—My First Name Is Aria: Personalized Primary Name Tracing Workbook for Kids Learning How to Write Their First Name, Practice Paper with 1 Ruling Designed for Children in Preschool & Kindergarten. Button, Big Red. 2019. (ENG.). 54p. (J). pap. 6.99 *(978-1-7932-0824-8(7))* Independently Published.

—My First Name Is Aubree: Personalized Primary Name Tracing Workbook for Kids Learning How to Write Their First Name, Practice Paper with 1 Ruling Designed for Children in Preschool & Kindergarten. Button, Big Red. 2019. (ENG.). 54p. (J). pap. 6.99 *(978-1-7946-1367-6(6))* Independently Published.

—My First Name Is Bella: Personalized Primary Name Tracing Workbook for Kids Learning How to Write Their First Name, Practice Paper with 1 Ruling Designed for Children in Preschool & Kindergarten. Button, Big Red. 2019. (ENG.). 54p. (J). pap. 6.99 *(978-1-7954-9744-2(0))* Independently Published.

—My First Name Is Brody: Personalized Primary Name Tracing Workbook for Kids Learning How to Write Their First Name, Practice Paper with 1 Ruling Designed for Children in Preschool & Kindergarten. Button, Big Red. 2019. (ENG.). 54p. (J). pap. 6.99 *(978-1-0924-1632-0(3))* Independently Published.

—My First Name Is Camila: Personalized Primary Name Tracing Workbook for Kids Learning How to Write Their First Name, Practice Paper with 1 Ruling Designed for Children in Preschool & Kindergarten. Button, Big Red. 2019. (ENG.). 54p. (J). pap. 6.99 *(978-1-7932-0847-7(6))* Independently Published.

—My First Name Is Connor: Personalized Primary Name Tracing Workbook for Kids Learning How to Write Their First Name, Practice Paper with 1 Ruling Designed for Children in Preschool & Kindergarten. Button, Big Red. 2019. (ENG.). 54p. (J). pap. 6.99 *(978-1-7955-0005-0(0))* Independently Published.

—My First Name Is Devon: Personalized Primary Name Tracing Workbook for Kids Learning How to Write Their First Name, Practice Paper with 1 Ruling Designed for Children in Preschool & Kindergarten. Button, Big Red. 2019. (ENG.). 54p. (J). pap. 6.99 *(978-1-0911-0875-2(7))* Independently Published.

—My First Name Is Gannon: Personalized Primary Name Tracing Workbook for Kids Learning How to Write Their First Name, Practice Paper with 1 Ruling Designed for Children in Preschool & Kindergarten. Button, Big Red. 2019. (ENG.). 54p. (J). pap. 6.99 *(978-1-7964-8162-4(9))* Independently Published.

—My First Name Is Genesis: Personalized Primary Name Tracing Workbook for Kids Learning How to Write Their First Name, Practice Paper with 1 Ruling Designed for Children in Preschool & Kindergarten. Button, Big Red. 2019. (ENG.). 54p. (J). pap. 6.99 *(978-1-7954-9746-6(7))* Independently Published.

—My First Name Is Jonathan: Personalized Primary Name Tracing Workbook for Kids Learning How to Write Their First Name, Practice Paper with 1 Ruling Designed for Children in Preschool & Kindergarten. Button, Big Red. 2019. (ENG.). 54p. (J). pap. 6.99 *(978-1-7931-9602-6(8))* Independently Published.

—My First Name Is Jordan: Personalized Primary Name Tracing Workbook for Kids Learning How to Write Their First Name, Practice Paper with 1 Ruling Designed for Children in Preschool & Kindergarten. Button, Big Red. 2019. (ENG.). 54p. (J). pap. 6.99 *(978-1-7946-1279-2(3))* Independently Published.

—My First Name Is Kaylee: Personalized Primary Name Tracing Workbook for Kids Learning How to Write Their First Name, Practice Paper with 1 Ruling Designed for Children in Preschool & Kindergarten. Button, Big Red. 2019. (ENG.). 54p. (J). pap. 6.99 *(978-1-7932-0949-8(9))* Independently Published.

Douglas, Karlon. My First Name Is Marcie: Fun Walrus Themed Personalized Primary Name Tracing Workbook for Kids Learning How to Write Their First Name, Practice Paper with 1 Ruling Designed for Children in Preschool & Kindergarten. Button, Big Red. 2019. (ENG.). 54p. (J). pap. 6.99 ***(978-1-6910-3331-7(6))*** Independently Published.

Douglas, Karlon. My First Name Is Mykayla: Personalized Primary Name Tracing Workbook for Kids Learning How to Write Their First Name, Practice Paper with 1 Ruling Designed for Children in Preschool & Kindergarten. Button, Big Red. 2019. (ENG.). 54p. (J). pap. 6.99 *(978-1-0917-1934-7(9))* Independently Published.

—My First Name Is Naliyah: Personalized Primary Name Tracing Workbook for Kids Learning How to Write Their First Name, Practice Paper with 1 Ruling Designed for Children in Preschool & Kindergarten. Button, Big Red. 2019. (ENG.). 54p. (J). pap. 6.99 *(978-1-0916-7036-5(6))* Independently Published.

—My First Name Is Nathan: Personalized Primary Name Tracing Workbook for Kids Learning How to Write Their First Name, Practice Paper with 1 Ruling Designed for Children in Preschool & Kindergarten. Button, Big Red. 2019. (ENG.). 54p. (J). pap. 6.99 *(978-1-7931-9679-8(6))* Independently Published.

—My First Name Is Nevaeh: Personalized Primary Name Tracing Workbook for Kids Learning How to Write Their First Name, Practice Paper with 1 Ruling Designed for Children in Preschool & Kindergarten. Button, Big Red. 2019. (ENG.). 54p. (J). pap. 6.99 *(978-1-7932-0953-5(7))* Independently Published.

—My First Name Is Oliver: Personalized Primary Name Tracing Workbook for Kids Learning How to Write Their First Name, Practice Paper with 1 Ruling Designed for Children in Preschool & Kindergarten. Button, Big Red. 2019. (ENG.). 54p. (J). pap. 6.99 *(978-1-7946-1281-5(5))* Independently Published.

—My First Name Is Rafael: Personalized Primary Name Tracing Workbook for Kids Learning How to Write Their First Name, Practice Paper with 1 Ruling Designed for Children in Preschool & Kindergarten. Button, Big Red. 2019. (ENG.). 54p. (J). pap. 6.99 *(978-1-0925-4332-3(5))* Independently Published.

—My First Name Is Riley: Personalized Primary Name Tracing Workbook for Kids Learning How to Write Their First Name, Practice Paper with 1 Ruling Designed for Children in Preschool & Kindergarten. Button, Big Red. 2019. (ENG.). 54p. (J). pap. 6.99 *(978-1-7932-0954-2(5))* Independently Published.

—My First Name Is Serenity: Personalized Primary Name Tracing Workbook for Kids Learning How to Write Their First Name, Practice Paper with 1 Ruling Designed for Children in Preschool & Kindergarten. Button, Big Red. 2019. (ENG.). 54p. (J). pap. 6.99 *(978-1-7946-1371-3(4))* Independently Published.

Douglas, Karlon. My First Name Is Stephanie: Fun Walrus Themed Personalized Primary Name Tracing Workbook for Kids Learning How to Write Their First Name, Practice Paper with 1 Ruling Designed for Children in Preschool & Kindergarten. Button, Big Red. 2019. (ENG.). 54p. (J). pap. 6.99 ***(978-1-6910-3338-6(3))*** Independently Published.

Douglas, Karlon. My First Name Is Yaretzi: Personalized Primary Name Tracing Workbook for Kids Learning How to Write Their First Name, Practice Paper with 1 Ruling Designed for Children in Preschool & Kindergarten. Button, Big Red. 2019. (ENG.). 54p. (J). pap. 6.99 *(978-1-0932-8366-2(1))* Independently Published.

—My First Name Is Zooey: Fun Walrus Themed Personalized Primary Name Tracing Workbook for Kids Learning How to Write Their First Name, Practice Paper with 1 Ruling Designed for Children in Preschool & Kindergarten. Button, Big Red. 2019. (ENG.). 54p. (J). pap. 6.99 *(978-1-0793-0086-4(4))* Independently Published.

—My Last Name Is Allen: Personalized Primary Name Tracing Workbook for Kids Learning How to Write Their Last Name, Practice Paper with 1 Ruling Designed for Children in Preschool & Kindergarten. Button, Big Red. 2019. (ENG.). 54p. (J). pap. 6.99 *(978-1-7931-3466-0(9))* Independently Published.

Douglas, Karlon. My Last Name Is Gomez: Personalized Primary Name Tracing Workbook for Kids Learning How to Write Their Last Name, Practice Paper with 1 Ruling Designed for Children in Preschool & Kindergarten. Button, Big Red. 2019. (ENG.). 54p. (J). pap. 6.99 ***(978-1-6971-9454-8(0))*** Independently Published.

Douglas, Karlon. My Last Name Is Jackson: Personalized Primary Name Tracing Workbook for Kids Learning How to Write Their Last Name, Practice Paper with 1 Ruling Designed for Children in Preschool & Kindergarten. Button, Big Red. 2019. (ENG.). 54p. (J). pap. 6.99 *(978-1-7931-4614-4(4))* Independently Published.

—My Last Name Is Lopez: Personalized Primary Name Tracing Workbook for Kids Learning How to Write Their Last Name, Practice Paper with 1 Ruling Designed for Children in Preschool & Kindergarten. Button, Big Red. 2019. (ENG.). 54p. (J). pap. 6.99 *(978-1-7931-4774-5(4))* Independently Published.

—My Last Name Is Miller: Personalized Primary Name Tracing Workbook for Kids Learning How to Write Their Last Name, Practice Paper with 1 Ruling Designed for Children in Preschool & Kindergarten. Button, Big Red. 2019. (ENG.). 54p. (J). pap. 6.99 *(978-1-7931-4827-8(9))* Independently Published.

—My Last Name Is Perez: Personalized Primary Name Tracing Workbook for Kids Learning How to Write Their Last Name, Practice Paper with 1 Ruling Designed for Children in Preschool & Kindergarten. Button, Big Red. 2019. (ENG.). 54p. (J). pap. 6.99 *(978-1-7931-4824-7(4))* Independently Published.

Douglas, Karlon. My Last Name Is Phillips: Personalized Primary Name Tracing Workbook for Kids Learning How to Write Their Last Name, Practice Paper with 1 Ruling Designed for Children in Preschool & Kindergarten. Button, Big Red. 2019. (ENG.). 54p. (J). pap. 6.99 ***(978-1-6971-9455-5(9))*** Independently Published.

Douglas, Karlon. My Last Name Is Soler: Personalized Primary Name Tracing Workbook for Kids Learning How to Write Their Last Name, Practice Paper with 1 Ruling Designed for Children in Preschool & Kindergarten. Button, Big Red. 2019. (ENG.). 54p. (J). pap. 6.99 *(978-1-0932-8370-9(X))* Independently Published.

—My Last Name Is Thompson: Personalized Primary Name Tracing Workbook for Kids Learning How to Write Their Last Name, Practice Paper with 1 Ruling Designed for Children in Preschool & Kindergarten. Button, Big Red. 2019. (ENG.). 54p. (J). pap. 6.99 *(978-1-7931-8142-8(X))* Independently Published.

—My Last Name Is Torres: Personalized Primary Name Tracing Workbook for Kids Learning How to Write Their Last Name, Practice Paper with 1 Ruling Designed for Children in Preschool & Kindergarten. Button, Big Red. 2019. (ENG.). 54p. (J). pap. 6.99 *(978-1-7931-8143-5(8))* Independently Published.

—My Last Name Is Walker: Personalized Primary Name Tracing Workbook for Kids Learning How to Write Their Last Name, Practice Paper with 1 Ruling Designed for Children in Preschool & Kindergarten. Button, Big Red. 2019. (ENG.). 54p. (J). pap. 6.99 *(978-1-7931-8282-1(5))* Independently Published.

—My Name Is Abigail: Personalized Primary Tracing Workbook for Kids Learning How to Write Their Name, Practice Paper with 1 Ruling Designed for Children in Preschool & Kindergarten. Button, Big Red. 2018. (ENG.). 54p. (J). pap. 6.99 *(978-1-7916-7192-1(6))* Independently Published.

—My Name Is Adam: Fun Mad Scientist Themed Personalized Primary Name Tracing Workbook for Kids Learning How to Write Their First Name, Practice Paper with 1 Ruling Designed for Children in Preschool & Kindergarten. Button, Big Red. 2019. (ENG.). 54p. (J). pap. 6.99 *(978-1-0932-8685-4(7))* Independently Published.

Douglas, Karlon. My Name Is Adan: 2 Workbooks in 1! Personalized Primary Name & Letter Tracing Book for Kids Learning How to Write Their First Name & the Alphabet with Cute Dinosaur Theme, Handwriting Practice Paper Designed for Children in Pre-K & Kindergarten. Button, Big Red. 2019. (ENG.). 108p. (J). pap. 9.99 ***(978-1-0864-7740-5(5))*** Independently Published.

Douglas, Karlon. My Name Is Aiden: Personalized Primary Tracing Workbook for Kids Learning How to Write Their Name, Practice Paper with 1 Ruling Designed for Children in Preschool & Kindergarten. Button, Big Red. 2018. (ENG.). 54p. (J). pap. 6.99 *(978-1-7915-0957-6(6))* Independently Published.

—My Name Is Alexa: 2 Workbooks in 1! Personalized Primary Name & Letter Tracing Workbook for Kids Learning How to Write Their First Name & the Alphabet, Practice Paper with 1 Ruling Designed for Children in Preschool & Kindergarten. Button, Big Red. 2019. (ENG.). 108p. (J). pap. 9.99 *(978-1-0924-8898-3(7))* Independently Published.

Douglas, Karlon. My Name Is Alicia: 2 Workbooks in 1! Personalized Primary Name & Letter Tracing Book for Kids Learning How to Write Their First Name & the Alphabet with Cute Dinosaur Theme, Handwriting Practice Paper Designed for Children in Pre-K & Kindergarten. Button, Big Red. 2019. (ENG.). 108p. (J). pap. 9.99 ***(978-1-0864-7744-3(8))*** Independently Published.

Douglas, Karlon. My Name Is Angel: 2 Workbooks in 1! Personalized Primary Name & Letter Tracing Workbook for Kids Learning How to Write Their First Name & the Alphabet, Practice Paper with 1 Ruling Designed for Children in Preschool & Kindergarten. Button, Big Red. 2019. (ENG.). 108p. (J). pap. 9.99 *(978-1-0921-2018-0(1))* Independently Published.

—My Name Is Angela: 2 Workbooks in 1! Personalized Primary Name & Letter Tracing Book for Kids Learning How to Write Their First Name & the Alphabet with Cute Dinosaur Theme, Handwriting Practice Paper Designed for Children in Pre-K & Kindergarten. Button, Big Red. 2019. (ENG.). 108p. (J). pap. 9.99 *(978-1-0811-8669-2(0))* Independently Published.

D

Douglas, Karlon. My Name Is Aria: 2 Workbooks in 1! Personalized Primary Name & Letter Tracing Book for Kids Learning How to Write Their First Name & the Alphabet with Cute Dinosaur Theme, Handwriting Practice Paper Designed for Children in Pre-K & Kindergarten. Button, Big Red. 2020. (ENG.). 108p. (J). pap. 5.99 ***(978-1-6613-8464-7(1))*** Independently Published.

Douglas, Karlon. My Name Is Ava: Personalized Primary Tracing Workbook for Kids Learning How to Write Their Name, Practice Paper with 1 Ruling Designed for Children in Preschool & Kindergarten. Button, Big Red. 2018. (ENG.). 54p. (J). pap. 6.99 *(978-1-7916-7193-8(4))* Independently Published.

Douglas, Karlon. My Name Is Averie: 2 Workbooks in 1! Personalized Primary Name & Letter Tracing Book for Kids Learning How to Write Their First Name & the Alphabet with Cute Dinosaur Theme, Handwriting Practice Paper Designed for Children in Pre-K & Kindergarten. Button, Big Red. 2019. (ENG.). 108p. (J). pap. 9.99 ***(978-1-0867-6118-4(9))*** Independently Published.

—My Name Is Ayla: 2 Workbooks in 1! Personalized Primary Name & Letter Tracing Book for Kids Learning How to Write Their First Name & the Alphabet with Cute Dinosaur Theme, Handwriting Practice Paper Designed for Children in Pre-K & Kindergarten. Button, Big Red. 2019. (ENG.). 108p. (J). pap. 9.99 ***(978-1-0867-6121-4(9))*** Independently Published.

Douglas, Karlon. My Name Is Blake: 2 Workbooks in 1! Personalized Primary Name & Letter Tracing Workbook for Kids Learning How to Write Their First Name & the Alphabet, Practice Paper with 1 Ruling Designed for Children in Preschool & Kindergarten. Button, Big Red. 2019. (ENG.). 108p. (J). pap. 9.99 *(978-1-0921-2025-8(4))* Independently Published.

Douglas, Karlon. My Name Is Braylon: 2 Workbooks in 1! Personalized Primary Name & Letter Tracing Book for Kids Learning How to Write Their First Name & the Alphabet with Cute Dinosaur Theme, Handwriting Practice Paper Designed for Children in Pre-K & Kindergarten. Button, Big Red. 2019. (ENG.). 108p. (J). pap. 9.99 ***(978-1-0867-6137-5(5))*** Independently Published.

Douglas, Karlon. My Name Is Brody: Fun Mad Scientist Themed Personalized Primary Name Tracing Workbook for Kids Learning How to Write Their First Name, Practice Paper with 1 Ruling Designed for Children in Preschool & Kindergarten. Button, Big Red. 2019. (ENG.). 54p. (J). pap. 6.99 *(978-1-0932-8686-1(5))* Independently Published.

—My Name Is Brooklyn: Personalized Primary Tracing Workbook for Kids Learning How to Write Their Name, Practice Paper with 1 Ruling Designed for Children in Preschool & Kindergarten. Button, Big Red. 2018. (ENG.). 54p. (J). pap. 6.99 *(978-1-7916-8869-1(1))* Independently Published.

Douglas, Karlon. My Name Is Camille: 2 Workbooks in 1! Personalized Primary Name & Letter Tracing Workbook for Kids Learning How to Write Their First Name & the Letters of the Alphabet, Practice Paper with 1 Ruling Designed for Children in Preschool & Kindergarten. Button, Big Red. 2019. (ENG.). 108p. (J). pap. 9.99 ***(978-1-6956-7836-1(2))*** Independently Published.

Douglas, Karlon. My Name Is Chase: 2 Workbooks in 1! Personalized Primary Name & Letter Tracing Workbook for Kids Learning How to Write Their First Name & the Alphabet, Practice Paper with 1 Ruling Designed for Children in Preschool & Kindergarten. Button, Big Red. 2019. (ENG.). 108p. (J). pap. 9.99 *(978-1-0727-2251-9(8))* Independently Published.

—My Name Is Chase: Fun Mad Scientist Themed Personalized Primary Name Tracing Workbook for Kids Learning How to Write Their First Name, Practice Paper with 1 Ruling Designed for Children in Preschool & Kindergarten. Button, Big Red. 2019. (ENG.). 54p. (J). pap. 6.99 *(978-1-0932-8689-2(X))* Independently Published.

Douglas, Karlon. My Name Is Daleyza: Fun Mad Scientist Themed Personalized Primary Name Tracing Workbook for Kids Learning How to Write Their First Name, Handwriting Practice Paper with 1 Ruling Designed for Children in Preschool & Kindergarten. Button, Big Red. 2019. (ENG.). 54p. (J). pap. 6.99 ***(978-1-6952-1733-1(0))*** Independently Published.

Douglas, Karlon. My Name Is Dean: 2 Workbooks in 1! Personalized Primary Name & Letter Tracing Book for Kids Learning How to Write Their First Name & the Alphabet with Cute Dinosaur Theme, Handwriting Practice Paper Designed for Children in Pre-K & Kindergarten. Button, Big Red. 2019. (ENG.). 108p. (J). pap. 9.99 *(978-1-0809-7006-3(1))* Independently Published.

—My Name Is Derrick: 2 Workbooks in 1! Personalized Primary Name & Letter Tracing Book for Kids Learning How to Write Their First Name & the Alphabet with Cute Dinosaur Theme, Handwriting Practice Paper Designed for Children in Pre-K & Kindergarten. Button, Big Red. 2019. (ENG.). 108p. (J). pap. 9.99 *(978-1-0827-4719-9(X))* Independently Published.

—My Name Is Desmond: 2 Workbooks in 1! Personalized Primary Name & Letter Tracing Book for Kids Learning How to Write Their First Name & the Alphabet with Cute Dinosaur Theme, Handwriting Practice Paper Designed for Children in Pre-K & Kindergarten. Button, Big Red. 2019. (ENG.). 108p. (J). pap. 9.99 *(978-1-0827-4721-2(1))* Independently Published.

Douglas, Karlon. My Name Is Diana: 2 Workbooks in 1! Personalized Primary Name & Letter Tracing Workbook for Kids Learning How to Write Their First Name & the Letters of the Alphabet, Practice Paper with 1 Ruling Designed for Children in Preschool & Kindergarten. Button, Big Red. 2020. (ENG.). 108p. (J). pap. 5.99 ***(978-1-6619-5836-7(2))*** Independently Published.

Douglas, Karlon. My Name Is Ellie: 2 Workbooks in 1! Personalized Primary Name & Letter Tracing Workbook for Kids Learning How to Write Their First Name & the Alphabet, Practice Paper with 1 Ruling Designed for Children in Preschool & Kindergarten. Button, Big Red. 2019. (ENG.). 108p. (J). pap. 9.99 *(978-1-0924-8916-4(9))* Independently Published.

—My Name Is Elliot: 2 Workbooks in 1! Personalized Primary Name & Letter Tracing Book for Kids Learning How to Write Their First Name & the Alphabet with Cute Dinosaur Theme, Handwriting Practice Paper Designed for Children in Pre-K & Kindergarten. Button, Big Red. 2019. (ENG.). 108p. (J). pap. 9.99 *(978-1-0811-6234-4(1))* Independently Published.

—My Name Is Emilio: Fun Dino Monsters Themed Personalized Primary Name Tracing Workbook for Kids Learning How to Write Their First Name, Practice Paper with 1 Ruling Designed for Children in Preschool & Kindergarten. Button, Big Red. 2019. (ENG.). 54p. (J). pap. 6.99 *(978-1-0976-7075-8(9))* Independently Published.

—My Name Is Emily: Personalized Primary Tracing Workbook for Kids Learning How to Write Their Name, Practice Paper with 1 Ruling Designed for Children in Preschool & Kindergarten. Button, Big Red. 2018. (ENG.). 54p. (J). pap. 6.99 *(978-1-7916-7461-8(5))* Independently Published.

Douglas, Karlon. My Name Is Erin: 2 Workbooks in 1! Personalized Primary Name & Letter Tracing Book for Kids Learning How to Write Their First Name & the Alphabet with Cute Dinosaur Theme, Handwriting Practice Paper Designed for Children in Pre-K & Kindergarten. Button, Big Red. 2019. (ENG.). 108p. (J). pap. 9.99 ***(978-1-6923-7100-5(2))*** Independently Published.

—My Name Is Esteban: 2 Workbooks in 1! Personalized Primary Name & Letter Tracing Book for Kids Learning How to Write Their First Name & the Alphabet with Cute Dinosaur Theme, Handwriting Practice Paper Designed for Children in Pre-K & Kindergarten. Button, Big Red. 2019. (ENG.). 108p. (J). pap. 9.99 ***(978-1-0863-8423-9(7))*** Independently Published.

Douglas, Karlon. My Name Is Eva: Fun Mad Scientist Themed Personalized Primary Name Tracing Workbook for Kids Learning How to Write Their First Name, Practice Paper with 1 Ruling Designed for Children in Preschool & Kindergarten. Button, Big Red. 2019. (ENG.). 54p. (J). pap. 6.99 *(978-1-0933-1083-2(9))* Independently Published.

—My Name Is Ezra: Personalized Primary Name Tracing Workbook for Kids Learning How to Write Their First Name, Practice Paper with 1 Ruling Designed for Children in Preschool & Kindergarten. Button, Big Red. 2019. (ENG.). 54p. (J). pap. 6.99 *(978-1-0917-2562-1(4))* Independently Published.

—My Name Is Faith: Fun Mad Scientist Themed Personalized Primary Name Tracing Workbook for Kids Learning How to Write Their First Name, Practice Paper with 1 Ruling Designed for Children in Preschool & Kindergarten. Button, Big Red. 2019. (ENG.). 54p. (J). pap. 6.99 *(978-1-0933-1081-8(2))* Independently Published.

—My Name Is Genesis: 2 Workbooks in 1! Personalized Primary Name & Letter Tracing Workbook for Kids Learning How to Write Their First Name & the Alphabet, Practice Paper with 1 Ruling Designed for Children in Preschool & Kindergarten. Button, Big Red. 2019. (ENG.). 108p. (J). pap. 9.99 *(978-1-0925-0025-8(1))* Independently Published.

—My Name Is Gianna: Fun Mad Scientist Themed Personalized Primary Name Tracing Workbook for Kids Learning How to Write Their First Name, Practice Paper with 1 Ruling Designed for Children in Preschool & Kindergarten. Button, Big Red. 2019. (ENG.). 54p. (J). pap. 6.99 *(978-1-0933-1082-5(0))* Independently Published.

—My Name Is Grayson: 2 Workbooks in 1! Personalized Primary Name & Letter Tracing Workbook for Kids Learning How to Write Their First Name & the Alphabet, Practice Paper with 1 Ruling Designed for Children in Preschool & Kindergarten. Button, Big Red. 2019. (ENG.). 108p. (J). pap. 9.99 *(978-1-0727-2252-6(6))* Independently Published.

Douglas, Karlon. My Name Is Henry: 2 Workbooks in 1! Personalized Primary Name & Letter Tracing Book for Kids Learning How to Write Their First Name & the Alphabet with Cute Dinosaur Theme, Handwriting Practice Paper Designed for Children in Pre-K & Kindergarten. Button, Big Red. 2020. (ENG.). 108p. (J). pap. 5.99 ***(978-1-6613-8459-3(5))*** Independently Published.

Douglas, Karlon. My Name Is Ian: Fun Mad Scientist Themed Personalized Primary Name Tracing Workbook for Kids Learning How to Write Their First Name, Practice Paper with 1 Ruling Designed for Children in Preschool & Kindergarten. Button, Big Red. 2019. (ENG.). 54p. (J). pap. 6.99 *(978-1-0932-9085-1(4))* Independently Published.

—My Name Is Jason: 2 Workbooks in 1! Personalized Primary Name & Letter Tracing Workbook for Kids Learning How to Write Their First Name & the Alphabet, Practice Paper with 1 Ruling Designed for Children in Preschool & Kindergarten. Button, Big Red. 2019. (ENG.). 108p. (J). pap. 9.99 *(978-1-0727-2254-0(2))* Independently Published.

—My Name Is Jason: Fun Mad Scientist Themed Personalized Primary Name Tracing Workbook for Kids Learning How to Write Their First Name, Practice Paper with 1 Ruling Designed for Children in Preschool & Kindergarten. Button, Big Red. 2019. (ENG.). 54p. (J). pap. 6.99 *(978-1-0932-9088-2(9))* Independently Published.

Douglas, Karlon. My Name Is Jeffrey: 2 Workbooks in 1! Personalized Primary Name & Letter Tracing Book for Kids Learning How to Write Their First Name & the Alphabet with Cute Dinosaur Theme, Handwriting Practice Paper Designed for Children in Pre-K & Kindergarten. Button, Big Red. 2019. (ENG.). 108p. (J). pap. 9.99 ***(978-1-0870-0077-0(7))*** Independently Published.

Douglas, Karlon. My Name Is Jeremiah: 2 Workbooks in 1! Personalized Primary Name & Letter Tracing Workbook for Kids Learning How to Write Their First Name & the Alphabet, Practice Paper with 1 Ruling Designed for Children in Preschool & Kindergarten. Button, Big Red. 2019. (ENG.). 108p. (J). pap. 9.99 *(978-1-0921-3819-2(6))* Independently Published.

Douglas, Karlon. My Name Is Jett: 2 Workbooks in 1! Personalized Primary Name & Letter Tracing Book for Kids Learning How to Write Their First Name & the Alphabet with Cute Dinosaur Theme, Handwriting Practice Paper Designed for Children in Pre-K & Kindergarten. Button, Big Red. 2019. (ENG.). 108p. (J). pap. 9.99 ***(978-1-0864-1134-8(X))*** Independently Published.

Douglas, Karlon. My Name Is Jocelyn: Fun Mad Scientist Themed Personalized Primary Name Tracing Workbook for Kids Learning How to Write Their First Name, Practice Paper with 1 Ruling Designed for Children in Preschool & Kindergarten. Button, Big Red. 2019. (ENG.). 54p. (J). pap. 6.99 *(978-1-0933-1433-5(8))* Independently Published.

Douglas, Karlon. My Name Is Julio: 2 Workbooks in 1! Personalized Primary Name & Letter Tracing Workbook for Kids Learning How to Write Their First Name & the Letters of the Alphabet, Practice Paper with 1 Ruling Designed for Children in Preschool & Kindergarten. Button, Big Red. 2020. (ENG.). 108p. (J). pap. 5.99 ***(978-1-6619-5840-4(0))*** Independently Published.

Douglas, Karlon. My Name Is Justin: Fun Mad Scientist Themed Personalized Primary Name Tracing Workbook for Kids Learning How to Write Their First Name, Practice Paper with 1 Ruling Designed for Children in Preschool & Kindergarten. Button, Big Red. 2019. (ENG.). 54p. (J). pap. 6.99 *(978-1-0932-9094-3(3))* Independently Published.

Douglas, Karlon. My Name Is Karson: 2 Workbooks in 1! Personalized Primary Name & Letter Tracing Book for Kids Learning How to Write Their First Name & the Alphabet with Cute Dinosaur Theme, Handwriting Practice Paper Designed for Children in Pre-K & Kindergarten. Button, Big Red. 2019. (ENG.). 108p. (J). pap. 9.99 ***(978-1-0893-2684-7(X))*** Independently Published.

Douglas, Karlon. My Name Is Katherine: 2 Workbooks in 1! Personalized Primary Name & Letter Tracing Workbook for Kids Learning How to Write Their First Name & the Alphabet, Practice Paper with 1 Ruling Designed for Children in Preschool & Kindergarten. Button, Big Red. 2019. (ENG.). 108p. (J). pap. 9.99 *(978-1-0727-2245-8(3))* Independently Published.

—My Name Is Kaydence: 2 Workbooks in 1! Personalized Primary Name & Letter Tracing Book for Kids Learning How to Write Their First Name & the Alphabet with Cute Dinosaur Theme, Handwriting Practice Paper Designed for Children in Pre-K & Kindergarten. Button, Big Red. 2019. (ENG.). 108p. (J). pap. 9.99 *(978-1-0827-4726-7(2))* Independently Published.

Douglas, Karlon. My Name Is Kayleigh: 2 Workbooks in 1! Personalized Primary Name & Letter Tracing Book for Kids Learning How to Write Their First Name & the Alphabet with Cute Dinosaur Theme, Handwriting Practice Paper Designed for Children in Pre-K & Kindergarten. Button, Big Red. 2019. (ENG.). 108p. (J). pap. 9.99 ***(978-1-0893-2686-1(6))*** Independently Published.

—My Name Is Keegan: 2 Workbooks in 1! Personalized Primary Name & Letter Tracing Book for Kids Learning How to Write Their First Name & the Alphabet with Cute Dinosaur Theme, Handwriting Practice Paper Designed for Children in Pre-K & Kindergarten. Button, Big Red. 2019. (ENG.). 108p. (J). pap. 9.99 ***(978-1-0893-2687-8(4))*** Independently Published.

—My Name Is Keira: 2 Workbooks in 1! Personalized Primary Name & Letter Tracing Workbook for Kids Learning How to Write Their First Name & the Letters of the Alphabet, Practice Paper with 1 Ruling Designed for Children in Preschool & Kindergarten. Button, Big Red. 2020. (ENG.). 108p. (J). pap. 5.99 ***(978-1-6619-5842-8(7))*** Independently Published.

—My Name Is Keith: 2 Workbooks in 1! Personalized Primary Name & Letter Tracing Book for Kids Learning How to Write Their First Name & the Alphabet with Cute Dinosaur Theme, Handwriting Practice Paper Designed for Children in Pre-K & Kindergarten. Button, Big Red. 2020. (ENG.). 108p. (J). pap. 5.99 ***(978-1-6613-8460-9(9))*** Independently Published.

—My Name Is Kellan: 2 Workbooks in 1! Personalized Primary Name & Letter Tracing Book for Kids Learning How to Write Their First Name & the Alphabet with Cute Dinosaur Theme, Handwriting Practice Paper Designed for Children in Pre-K & Kindergarten. Button, Big Red. 2019. (ENG.). 108p. (J). pap. 9.99 ***(978-1-0893-2690-8(4))*** Independently Published.

—My Name Is Kennedi: 2 Workbooks in 1! Personalized Primary Name & Letter Tracing Book for Kids Learning How to Write Their First Name & the Alphabet with Cute Dinosaur Theme, Handwriting Practice Paper Designed for Children in Pre-K & Kindergarten. Button, Big Red. 2019. (ENG.). 108p. (J). pap. 9.99 ***(978-1-0893-3317-3(X))*** Independently Published.

Douglas, Karlon. My Name Is Kevin: 2 Workbooks in 1! Personalized Primary Name & Letter Tracing Workbook for Kids Learning How to Write Their First Name & the Alphabet, Practice Paper with 1 Ruling Designed for Children in Preschool & Kindergarten. Button, Big Red. 2019. (ENG.). 108p. (J). pap. 9.99 *(978-1-0921-3823-9(4))* Independently Published.

—My Name Is Khloe: 2 Workbooks in 1! Personalized Primary Name & Letter Tracing Workbook for Kids Learning How to Write Their First Name & the Alphabet, Practice Paper with 1 Ruling Designed for Children in Preschool & Kindergarten. Button, Big Red. 2019. (ENG.). 108p. (J). pap. 9.99 *(978-1-0727-2246-5(1))* Independently Published.

Douglas, Karlon. My Name Is Leila: 2 Workbooks in 1! Personalized Primary Name & Letter Tracing Workbook for Kids Learning How to Write Their First Name & the Letters of the Alphabet, Practice Paper with 1 Ruling Designed for Children in Preschool & Kindergarten. Button, Big Red. 2019. (ENG.). 108p. (J). pap. 9.99 ***(978-1-6956-7844-6(3))*** Independently Published.

Douglas, Karlon. My Name Is Lexi: Fun Dino Monsters Themed Personalized Primary Name Tracing Workbook for Kids Learning How to Write Their First Name, Practice Paper with 1 Ruling Designed for Children in Preschool & Kindergarten. Button, Big Red. 2019. (ENG.). 54p. (J). pap. 6.99 *(978-1-0955-9753-8(1))* Independently Published.

Douglas, Karlon. My Name Is Logan: 2 Workbooks in 1! Personalized Primary Name & Letter Tracing Book for Kids Learning How to Write Their First Name & the Alphabet with Cute Dinosaur Theme, Handwriting Practice Paper Designed for Children in Pre-K & Kindergarten. Button, Big Red. 2019. (ENG.). 108p. (J). pap. 9.99 ***(978-1-6923-8228-5(4))*** Independently Published.

—My Name Is Lukas: 2 Workbooks in 1! Personalized Primary Name & Letter Tracing Book for Kids Learning How to Write Their First Name & the Alphabet with Cute Dinosaur Theme, Handwriting Practice Paper Designed for Children in Pre-K & Kindergarten. Button, Big Red. 2019. (ENG.). 108p. (J). pap. 9.99 ***(978-1-6943-6368-8(6))*** Independently Published.

Douglas, Karlon. My Name Is Lydia: Fun Mad Scientist Themed Personalized Primary Name Tracing Workbook for Kids Learning How to Write Their First Name, Practice Paper with 1 Ruling Designed for Children in Preschool & Kindergarten. Button, Big Red. 2019. (ENG.). 54p. (J). pap. 6.99 *(978-1-0933-1440-3(0))* Independently Published.

—My Name Is Madison: Personalized Primary Tracing Workbook for Kids Learning How to Write Their Name, Practice Paper with 1 Ruling Designed for Children in Preschool & Kindergarten. Button, Big Red. 2018. (ENG.). 54p. (J). pap. 6.99 *(978-1-7916-7464-9(X))* Independently Published.

—My Name Is Makayla: Fun Mad Scientist Themed Personalized Primary Name Tracing Workbook for Kids Learning How to Write Their First Name, Practice Paper with 1 Ruling Designed for Children in Preschool & Kindergarten. Button, Big Red. 2019. (ENG.). 54p. (J). pap. 6.99 *(978-1-0933-1442-7(7))* Independently Published.

Douglas, Karlon. My Name Is Makenna: 2 Workbooks in 1! Personalized Primary Name & Letter Tracing Book for Kids Learning How to Write Their First Name & the Alphabet with Cute Dinosaur Theme, Handwriting Practice Paper Designed for Children in Pre-K & Kindergarten. Button, Big Red. 2019. (ENG.). 108p. (J). pap. 9.99 ***(978-1-0864-1145-4(5))*** Independently Published.

—My Name Is Mckinley: 2 Workbooks in 1! Personalized Primary Name & Letter Tracing Book for Kids Learning How to Write Their First Name & the Alphabet with Cute Dinosaur Theme, Handwriting Practice Paper Designed for Children in Pre-K & Kindergarten. Button, Big Red. 2019. (ENG.). 108p. (J). pap. 9.99 ***(978-1-6956-8437-9(0))*** Independently Published.

—My Name Is Miriam: 2 Workbooks in 1! Personalized Primary Name & Letter Tracing Book for Kids Learning How to Write Their First Name & the Alphabet with Cute Dinosaur Theme, Handwriting Practice Paper Designed for Children in Pre-K & Kindergarten. Button, Big Red. 2019. (ENG.). 108p. (J). pap. 9.99 ***(978-1-0864-1907-8(3))*** Independently Published.

Douglas, Karlon. My Name Is Morgan: Fun Mad Scientist Themed Personalized Primary Name Tracing Workbook for Kids Learning How to Write Their First Name, Practice Paper with 1 Ruling Designed for Children in Preschool & Kindergarten. Button, Big Red. 2019. (ENG.). 54p. (J). pap. 6.99 *(978-1-0933-7760-6(7))* Independently Published.

—My Name Is Naliyah: Personalized Primary Name Tracing Workbook for Kids Learning How to Write Their First Name, Practice Paper with 1 Ruling Designed for Children in Preschool & Kindergarten. Button, Big Red. 2019. (ENG.). 54p. (J). pap. 6.99 *(978-1-0916-7040-2(4))* Independently Published.

Douglas, Karlon. My Name Is Nina: 2 Workbooks in 1! Personalized Primary Name & Letter Tracing Book for Kids Learning How to Write Their First Name & the Alphabet with Cute Dinosaur Theme, Handwriting Practice Paper Designed for Children in Pre-K & Kindergarten. Button, Big Red. 2019. (ENG.). 108p. (J). pap. 9.99 ***(978-1-6930-5144-9(3))*** Independently Published.

—My Name Is Noelle: 2 Workbooks in 1! Personalized Primary Name & Letter Tracing Book for Kids Learning How to Write Their First Name & the Alphabet with Cute Dinosaur Theme, Handwriting Practice Paper Designed for Children in Pre-K & Kindergarten. Button, Big Red. 2019. (ENG.). 108p. (J). pap. 9.99 ***(978-1-0867-6934-0(1))*** Independently Published.

Douglas, Karlon. My Name Is Peyton: 2 Workbooks in 1! Personalized Primary Name & Letter Tracing Workbook for Kids Learning How to Write Their First Name & the Alphabet, Practice Paper with 1 Ruling Designed for Children in Preschool & Kindergarten. Button, Big Red. 2019. (ENG.). 108p. (J). pap. 9.99 *(978-1-0925-0041-8(3))* Independently Published.

Douglas, Karlon. My Name Is Phoebe: 2 Workbooks in 1! Personalized Primary Name & Letter Tracing Book for Kids Learning How to Write Their First Name & the Alphabet with Cute Dinosaur Theme, Handwriting Practice Paper Designed for Children in Pre-K & Kindergarten. Button, Big Red. 2019. (ENG.). 108p. (J). pap. 9.99 ***(978-1-0867-6932-6(5))*** Independently Published.

Douglas, Karlon. My Name Is Prince: 2 Workbooks in 1! Personalized Primary Name & Letter Tracing Book for Kids Learning How to Write Their First Name & the Alphabet with Cute Dinosaur Theme, Handwriting Practice Paper Designed for Children in Pre-K & Kindergarten. Button, Big Red. 2019. (ENG.). 108p. (J). pap. 9.99 *(978-1-0827-4734-2(3))* Independently Published.

Douglas, Karlon. My Name Is Quinn: 2 Workbooks in 1! Personalized Primary Name & Letter Tracing Book for Kids Learning How to Write Their First Name & the Alphabet with Cute Dinosaur Theme, Handwriting Practice Paper Designed for Children in Pre-K & Kindergarten. Button, Big Red. 2019. (ENG.). 108p. (J). pap. 9.99 ***(978-1-6956-8442-3(7))*** Independently Published.

—My Name Is Raegan: 2 Workbooks in 1! Personalized Primary Name & Letter Tracing Book for Kids Learning How to Write Their First Name & the Alphabet with Cute Dinosaur Theme, Handwriting Practice Paper Designed for Children in Pre-K & Kindergarten. Button, Big Red. 2019. (ENG.). 108p. (J). pap. 9.99 ***(978-1-6930-5150-0(8))*** Independently Published.

—My Name Is Reed: 2 Workbooks in 1! Personalized Primary Name & Letter Tracing Book for Kids Learning How to Write Their First Name & the Alphabet with Cute Dinosaur Theme, Handwriting Practice Paper Designed for Children in Pre-K & Kindergarten. Button, Big Red. 2019. (ENG.). 108p. (J). pap. 9.99 ***(978-1-6936-4310-1(3))*** Independently Published.

—My Name Is Remington: 2 Workbooks in 1! Personalized Primary Name & Letter Tracing Book for Kids Learning How to Write Their First Name & the Alphabet with Cute Dinosaur Theme, Handwriting Practice Paper Designed for Children in Pre-K & Kindergarten. Button, Big Red. 2019. (ENG.). 108p. (J). pap. 9.99 ***(978-1-0862-6699-3(4))*** Independently Published.

—My Name Is Ricardo: 2 Workbooks in 1! Personalized Primary Name & Letter Tracing Book for Kids Learning How to Write Their First Name & the Alphabet with Cute Dinosaur Theme, Handwriting Practice Paper Designed for Children in Pre-K & Kindergarten. Button, Big Red. 2019. (ENG.). 108p. (J). pap. 9.99 ***(978-1-0867-6923-4(6))*** Independently Published.

—My Name Is Ronan: 2 Workbooks in 1! Personalized Primary Name & Letter Tracing Book for Kids Learning How to Write Their First Name & the Alphabet with Cute Dinosaur Theme, Handwriting Practice Paper Designed for Children in Pre-K & Kindergarten. Button, Big Red. 2019. (ENG.). 108p. (J). pap. 9.99 ***(978-1-6936-4318-7(9))*** Independently Published.

—My Name Is Rylan: 2 Workbooks in 1! Personalized Primary Name & Letter Tracing Workbook for Kids Learning How to Write Their First Name & the Letters of the Alphabet, Practice Paper with 1 Ruling Designed for Children in Preschool & Kindergarten. Button, Big Red. 2020. (ENG.). 108p. (J). pap. 5.99 ***(978-1-6619-5843-5(5))*** Independently Published.

Douglas, Karlon. My Name Is Sadie: 2 Workbooks in 1! Personalized Primary Name & Letter Tracing Workbook for Kids Learning How to Write Their First Name & the Alphabet, Practice Paper with 1 Ruling Designed for Children in Preschool & Kindergarten. Button, Big Red. 2019. (ENG.). 108p. (J). pap. 9.99 *(978-1-0925-0492-8(3))* Independently Published.

—My Name Is Samuel: Personalized Primary Name Tracing Workbook for Kids Learning How to Write Their First Name, Practice Paper with 1 Ruling Designed for Children in Preschool & Kindergarten. Button, Big Red. 2018. (ENG.). 54p. (J). pap. 6.99 *(978-1-7929-7740-4(9))* Independently Published.

—My Name Is Serenity: 2 Workbooks in 1! Personalized Primary Name & Letter Tracing Workbook for Kids Learning How to Write Their First Name & the Alphabet, Practice Paper with 1 Ruling Designed for Children in Preschool & Kindergarten. Button, Big Red. 2019. (ENG.). 108p. (J). pap. 9.99 *(978-1-0925-0493-5(1))* Independently Published.

Douglas, Karlon. My Name Is Shawn: 2 Workbooks in 1! Personalized Primary Name & Letter Tracing Book for Kids Learning How to Write Their First Name & the Alphabet with Cute Dinosaur Theme, Handwriting Practice Paper Designed for Children in Pre-K & Kindergarten. Button, Big Red. 2019. (ENG.). 108p. (J). pap. 9.99 ***(978-1-0862-6694-8(3))*** Independently Published.

Douglas, Karlon. My Name Is Sloane: 2 Workbooks in 1! Personalized Primary Name & Letter Tracing Book for Kids Learning How to Write Their First Name & the Alphabet with Cute Dinosaur Theme, Handwriting Practice Paper Designed for Children in Pre-K & Kindergarten. Button, Big Red. 2019. (ENG.). 108p. (J). pap. 9.99 *(978-1-0827-3076-4(9))* Independently Published.

Douglas, Karlon. My Name Is Solomon: 2 Workbooks in 1! Personalized Primary Name & Letter Tracing Book for Kids Learning How to Write Their First Name & the Alphabet with Cute Dinosaur Theme, Handwriting Practice Paper Designed for Children in Pre-K & Kindergarten. Button, Big Red. 2019. (ENG.). 108p. (J). pap. 9.99 ***(978-1-0827-3074-0(2))*** Independently Published.

Douglas, Karlon. My Name Is Stella: 2 Workbooks in 1! Personalized Primary Name & Letter Tracing Workbook for Kids Learning How to Write Their First Name & the Alphabet, Practice Paper with 1 Ruling Designed for Children in Preschool & Kindergarten. Button, Big Red. 2019. (ENG.). 108p. (J). pap. 9.99 *(978-1-0925-0495-9(8))* Independently Published.

Douglas, Karlon. My Name Is Stephen: 2 Workbooks in 1! Personalized Primary Name & Letter Tracing Book for Kids Learning How to Write Their First Name & the Alphabet with Cute Dinosaur Theme, Handwriting Practice Paper Designed for Children in Pre-K & Kindergarten. Button, Big Red. 2020. (ENG.). 108p. (J). pap. 5.99 ***(978-1-6613-8462-3(5))*** Independently Published.

Douglas, Karlon. My Name Is Taylor: 2 Workbooks in 1! Personalized Primary Name & Letter Tracing Workbook for Kids Learning How to Write Their First Name & the Alphabet, Practice Paper with 1 Ruling Designed for Children in Preschool & Kindergarten. Button, Big Red. 2019. (ENG.). 108p. (J). pap. 9.99 *(978-1-0925-0496-6(6))* Independently Published.

—My Name Is Thiago: 2 Workbooks in 1! Personalized Primary Name & Letter Tracing Book for Kids Learning How to Write Their First Name & the Alphabet with Cute Dinosaur Theme, Handwriting Practice Paper Designed for Children in Pre-K & Kindergarten. Button, Big Red. 2019. (ENG.). 108p. (J). pap. 9.99 *(978-1-0824-9161-0(6))* Independently Published.

—My Name Is Trenton: 2 Workbooks in 1! Personalized Primary Name & Letter Tracing Book for Kids Learning How to Write Their First Name & the Alphabet with Cute Dinosaur Theme, Handwriting Practice Paper Designed for Children in Pre-K & Kindergarten. Button, Big Red. 2019. (ENG.). 108p. (J). pap. 9.99 *(978-1-0824-9151-1(9))* Independently Published.

—My Name Is Trevor: 2 Workbooks in 1! Personalized Primary Name & Letter Tracing Book for Kids Learning How to Write Their First Name & the Alphabet with Cute Dinosaur Theme, Handwriting Practice Paper Designed for Children in Pre-K & Kindergarten. Button, Big Red. 2019. (ENG.). 108p. (J). pap. 9.99 *(978-1-0824-9150-4(0))* Independently Published.

Douglas, Karlon. My Name Is Trevor: 2 Workbooks in 1! Personalized Primary Name & Letter Tracing Workbook for Kids Learning How to Write Their First Name & the Letters of the Alphabet, Practice Paper with 1 Ruling Designed for Children in Preschool & Kindergarten. Button, Big Red. 2020. (ENG.). 108p. (J). pap. 5.99 ***(978-1-6619-5845-9(1))*** Independently Published.

Douglas, Karlon. My Name Is Tyler: 2 Workbooks in 1! Personalized Primary Name & Letter Tracing Workbook for Kids Learning How to Write Their First Name & the Alphabet, Practice Paper with 1 Ruling Designed for Children in Preschool & Kindergarten. Button, Big Red. 2019. (ENG.). 108p. (J). pap. 9.99 *(978-1-0921-4024-9(7))* Independently Published.

—My Name Is Valeigh: Personalized Primary Name Tracing Workbook for Kids Learning How to Write Their First Name, Practice Paper with 1 Ruling Designed for Children in Preschool & Kindergarten. Button, Big Red. 2019. (ENG.). 54p. (J). pap. 6.99 *(978-1-7964-8164-8(5))* Independently Published.

—My Name Is Victoria: Personalized Primary Tracing Workbook for Kids Learning How to Write Their Name, Practice Paper with 1 Ruling Designed for Children in Preschool & Kindergarten. Button, Big Red. 2018. (ENG.). 54p. (J). pap. 6.99 *(978-1-7916-8991-9(4))* Independently Published.

—My Name Is Walker: 2 Workbooks in 1! Personalized Primary Name & Letter Tracing Book for Kids Learning How to Write Their First Name & the Alphabet with Cute Dinosaur Theme, Handwriting Practice Paper Designed for Children in Pre-K & Kindergarten. Button, Big Red. 2019. (ENG.). 108p. (J). pap. 9.99 *(978-1-0824-9143-6(8))* Independently Published.

—Natalie: Personalized Ima Gonna Color My Happy Easter Coloring Book for Kids. Art, Black River. 2019. (ENG.). 52p. (J). pap. 6.99 *(978-1-0918-3836-9(4))* Independently Published.

—Reed's Writing Tablet: Personalized Book for Kids, Primary Writing Tablet with 65 Sheets of Blank Lined Practice Paper with 1 Ruling Designed for Children Learning How to Write in Pre-K, Kindergarten or First Grade. Button, Big Red. 2019. (ENG.). 68p. (J). pap. 6.99 *(978-1-0814-0169-6(9))* Independently Published.

—Sloane's Writing Tablet: Personalized Book for Kids, Primary Writing Tablet with 65 Sheets of Blank Lined Practice Paper with 1 Ruling Designed for Children Learning How to Write in Pre-K, Kindergarten or First Grade. Button, Big Red. 2019. (ENG.). 68p. (J). pap. 6.99 *(978-1-0814-0526-7(0))* Independently Published.

—Sophia: Personalized Ima Gonna Color My Happy Easter Coloring Book for Kids. Art, Black River. 2019. (ENG.). 52p. (J). pap. 6.99 *(978-1-0918-3841-3(0))* Independently Published.

—Victoria: Personalized Ima Gonna Color My Happy Easter Coloring Book for Kids. Art, Black River. 2019. (ENG.). 52p. (J). pap. 6.99 *(978-1-0919-1365-3(X))* Independently Published.

—Walter's Writing Tablet: Personalized Primary Writing Tablet for Kids, 65 Sheets of Blank Lined Practice Paper with 1 Ruling Designed for Children Learning How to Write in Preschool, Kindergarten or First Grade. Button, Big Red. 2019. (ENG.). 68p. (J). pap. 6.99 *(978-1-0812-4554-2(9))* Independently Published.

—Zoey: Personalized Ima Gonna Color My Happy Easter Coloring Book for Kids. Art, Black River. 2019. (ENG.). 52p. (J). pap. 6.99 *(978-1-0919-1368-4(4))* Independently Published.

Douglas, Karlon. Alles Gute Zum 10. Geburtstag: Süße Schwein Skizzenbuch Für Kinder Perfekt Für Doodling, Zeichnung und Skizzieren. Vergessen Sie Die Geburtstagskarte und Erhalten Sie Stattdessen ein Geburtstagsbuch! Douglas, Karlon. Designs, Level Up. 2019. (GER.). 102p. (J). pap. 5.99 *(978-1-0802-0924-8(7))* Independently Published.

—Alles Gute Zum 11. Geburtstag: 11 Jahre Geliebt, Zeigen Sie Ihre Liebe Mit Diesem Süßen Geburtstagsbuch, das Als Tagebuch Oder Notebook Verwendet Werden Kann. Besser Als eine Geburtstagskarte! Douglas, Karlon. Designs, Level Up. 2019. (GER.). 108p. (J). pap. 5.99 *(978-1-0987-9515-3(6))* Independently Published.

—Alles Gute Zum 11. Geburtstag: Niedliches, Schwein Entworfenes Geburtstagsbuch, das Als Tagebuch Oder Notebook Verwendet Werden Kann. Besser Als eine Geburtstagskarte! Douglas, Karlon. Designs, Level Up. 2019. (GER.). 108p. (J). pap. 5.99 *(978-1-0957-1432-4(5))* Independently Published.

—Alles Gute Zum 12. Geburtstag: Niedliches, Schwein Entworfenes Geburtstagsbuch, das Als Tagebuch Oder Notebook Verwendet Werden Kann. Besser Als eine Geburtstagskarte! Douglas, Karlon. Designs, Level Up. 2019. (GER.). 108p. (J). pap. 5.99 *(978-1-0957-1433-1(3))* Independently Published.

—Alles Gute Zum 14. Geburtstag: Niedliches, Schwein Entworfenes Geburtstagsbuch, das Als Tagebuch Oder Notebook Verwendet Werden Kann. Besser Als eine Geburtstagskarte! Douglas, Karlon. Designs, Level Up. 2019. (GER.). 108p. (J). pap. 5.99 *(978-1-0957-1436-2(8))* Independently Published.

—Alles Gute Zum 15. Geburtstag: Niedliches, Schwein Entworfenes Geburtstagsbuch, das Als Tagebuch Oder Notebook Verwendet Werden Kann. Besser Als eine Geburtstagskarte! Douglas, Karlon. Designs, Level Up. 2019. (GER.). 108p. (J). pap. 5.99 *(978-1-0957-1437-9(6))* Independently Published.

—Alles Gute Zum 6. Geburtstag: 6 Jahre Geliebt, Dieses Sketchbook Wurde Für Kinder Entwickelt und Eignet Sich Perfekt Zum Doodling, Zeichnen und Skizzieren. Vergessen Sie Die Geburtstagskarte und Erhalten Sie Stattdessen ein Geburtstagsbuch! Douglas, Karlon. Designs, Level Up. 2019. (GER.). 102p. (J). pap. 5.99 *(978-1-0809-9494-6(7))* Independently Published.

—Alles Gute Zum 7. Geburtstag: 7 Jahre Geliebt, Dieses Sketchbook Wurde Für Kinder Entwickelt und Eignet Sich Perfekt Zum Doodling, Zeichnen und Skizzieren. Vergessen Sie Die Geburtstagskarte und Erhalten Sie Stattdessen ein Geburtstagsbuch! Douglas, Karlon. Designs, Level Up. 2019. (GER.). 102p. (J). pap. 5.99 *(978-1-0809-9495-3(5))* Independently Published.

—Alles Gute Zum 7. Geburtstag: Süße Schwein Skizzenbuch Für Kinder Perfekt Für Doodling, Zeichnung und Skizzieren. Vergessen Sie Die Geburtstagskarte und Erhalten Sie Stattdessen ein Geburtstagsbuch! Douglas, Karlon. Designs, Level Up. 2019. (GER.). 102p. (J). pap. 5.99 *(978-1-0802-0919-4(0))* Independently Published.

—Alles Gute Zum 9. Geburtstag: 9 Jahre Geliebt, Zeigen Sie Ihre Liebe Mit Diesem Süßen Geburtstagsbuch, das Als Tagebuch Oder Notebook Verwendet Werden Kann. Besser Als eine Geburtstagskarte! Douglas, Karlon. Designs, Level Up. 2019. (GER.). 108p. (J). pap. 5.99 *(978-1-0987-9513-9(X))* Independently Published.

—Happy 10th Birthday: 10歳の誕生日おめでとう Cute Pig Themed Birthday Book That Can Be Used As a Diary or Notebook. Better Than a Birthday Card! Douglas, Karlon. Designs, Level Up. 2019. (ENG.). 108p. (J). pap. 5.99 *(978-1-0996-4059-9(8))* Independently Published.

—Happy 13th Birthday: 13歳の誕生日おめでとう Cute Pig Themed Birthday Book That Can Be Used As a Diary or Notebook. Better Than a Birthday Card! Douglas, Karlon. Designs, Level Up. 2019. (ENG.). 108p. (J). pap. 5.99 *(978-1-0996-4062-9(8))* Independently Published.

—Happy 18th Birthday: 18歳の誕生日おめでとう Cute Pig Themed Birthday Book That Can Be Used As a Diary or Notebook. Better Than a Birthday Card! Douglas, Karlon. Designs, Level Up. 2019. (ENG.). 108p. (J). pap. 5.99 *(978-1-0996-6878-4(6))* Independently Published.

—Happy 19th Birthday: 19 Years Loved, Say Happy Birthday & Show Your Love All in One Sweet Birthday Book to Use As a Journal or Notebook. Better Than a Birthday Card! Douglas, Karlon. Designs, Level Up. 2019. (ENG.). 108p. (J). pap. 5.99 *(978-1-7951-3482-8(8))* Independently Published.

—Happy 19th Birthday: 19歳の誕生日おめでとう Cute Pig Themed Birthday Book That Can Be Used As a Diary or Notebook. Better Than a Birthday Card! Douglas, Karlon. Designs, Level Up. 2019. (ENG.). 108p. (J). pap. 5.99 *(978-1-0996-6880-7(8))* Independently Published.

—Happy 20th Birthday: 20 Years Loved, Say Happy Birthday & Show Your Love All in One Sweet Birthday Book to Use As a Journal or Notebook. Better Than a Birthday Card! Douglas, Karlon. Designs, Level Up. 2019. (ENG.). 108p. (J). pap. 5.99 *(978-1-7951-3483-5(6))* Independently Published.

—Happy 20th Birthday: Better Than a Birthday Card! Cute Piggy Designed Birthday Book with 105 Lined Pages That Can Be Used As a Journal or Notebook. Douglas, Karlon. Designs, Level Up. 2019. (ENG.). 108p. (J). pap. 5.99 *(978-1-7934-3953-6(2))* Independently Published.

—Happy 32nd Birthday: 32歳の誕生日おめでとう Cute Pig Themed Birthday Book That Can Be Used As a Diary or Notebook. Better Than a Birthday Card! Douglas, Karlon. Designs, Level Up. 2019. (ENG.). 108p. (J). pap. 5.99 *(978-1-0998-9658-3(4))* Independently Published.

—Happy 46th Birthday: Give That Special Someone a Glimpse into Their Future with This Funny Password Book. Way Better Than a Birthday Card! Douglas, Karlon. Designs, Level Up. l.t. ed. 2019. (ENG.). 100p. (J). pap. 5.99 *(978-1-7963-8700-1(2))* Independently Published.

—Happy 46th Birthday: Wish Them Happy Birthday with This Book, That Can Be Used As a Journal or Notebook, Adorned with the Bible Verse Numbers 6:24. Better Than a Birthday Card! Douglas, Karlon. Designs, Level Up. 2019. (ENG.). 108p. (J). pap. 6.99 *(978-1-0965-4665-8(5))* Independently Published.

—Happy 48th Birthday: Better Than a Birthday Card! Gay Pride Flag Themed Book That Can Be Used As a Journal or Notebook. Douglas, Karlon. Designs, Level Up. 2019. (ENG.). 108p. (J). pap. 5.99 *(978-1-7988-5483-9(X))* Independently Published.

Douglas, Karlon. Happy 48th Birthday: For That Special Someone Whose Balls Hang Low, This Funny Birthday Book That Can Be Used As a Journal or Notebook Makes the Perfect Gift. Way Better Than a Birthday Card! Douglas, Karlon. Designs, Level Up. 2019. (ENG.). 108p. (J). pap. 6.99 ***(978-1-0964-1681-4(6))*** Independently Published.

Douglas, Karlon. Happy 48th Birthday: Give That Special Someone a Glimpse into Their Future with This Funny Birthday Book That Can Be Used As a Journal or Notebook. Way Better Than a Birthday Card! Douglas, Karlon. Designs, Level Up. 2019. (ENG.). 108p. (J). pap. 5.99 *(978-1-0994-7310-4(1))* Independently Published.

—Happy 49th Birthday: Better Than a Birthday Card! Gay Pride Flag Themed Book That Can Be Used As a Journal or Notebook. Douglas, Karlon. Designs, Level Up. 2019. (ENG.). 108p. (J). pap. 5.99 *(978-1-7988-5484-6(8))* Independently Published.

—Happy 50th Birthday: Wish Them Happy Birthday with This Book, That Can Be Used As a Journal or Notebook, Adorned with the Bible Verse Numbers 6:24. Better Than a Birthday Card! Douglas, Karlon. Designs, Level Up. 2019. (ENG.). 108p. (J). pap. 6.99 *(978-1-0965-4669-6(8))* Independently Published.

—Happy 6th Birthday: Better Than a Birthday Card! American Flag Themed Birthday Book with 105 Lined Pages That Can Be Used As a Journal or Notebook. Douglas, Karlon. Designs, Level Up. 2019. (ENG.). 108p. (J). pap. 5.99 *(978-1-7942-3925-8(1))* Independently Published.

—Happy 6th Birthday: Better Than a Birthday Card! Cute Piggy Designed Birthday Book with 105 Lined Pages That Can Be Used As a Journal or Notebook. Douglas, Karlon. Designs, Level Up. 2019. (ENG.). 108p. (J). pap. 5.99 *(978-1-7933-9758-4(9))* Independently Published.

—Happy 7th Birthday: Better Than a Birthday Card! Cute Piggy Designed Birthday Book with 105 Lined Pages That Can Be Used As a Journal or Notebook. Douglas, Karlon. Designs, Level Up. 2019. (ENG.). 108p. (J). pap. 5.99 *(978-1-7933-9759-1(7))* Independently Published.

—Happy 8th Birthday: 8 Years Loved, Say Happy Birthday & Show Your Love All in One Sweet Birthday Book to Use As a Journal or Notebook. Better Than a Birthday Card! Douglas, Karlon. Designs, Level Up. 2019. (ENG.). 108p. (J). pap. 5.99 *(978-1-7951-3071-4(7))* Independently Published.

—Happy 9th Birthday: 9 Years Loved, Say Happy Birthday & Show Your Love All in One Sweet Birthday Book to Use As a Journal or Notebook. Better Than a Birthday Card! Douglas, Karlon. Designs, Level Up. 2019. (ENG.). 108p. (J). pap. 5.99 *(978-1-7951-3085-1(7))* Independently Published.

—Happy 9th Birthday: 9歳の誕生日おめでとう Cute Pig Themed Birthday Book That Can Be Used As a Diary or Notebook. Better Than a Birthday Card! Douglas, Karlon. Designs, Level Up. 2019. (ENG.). 108p. (J). pap. 5.99 *(978-1-0996-4058-2(X))* Independently Published.

—Joyeux 10e Anniversaire: Livre d'anniversaire Qui Peut être Utilisé Comme un Journal Ou un Cahier Avec la Conception Mignonne de Cochon. Mieux Qu'une Carte D'anniversaire! Douglas, Karlon. Designs, Level Up. 2019. (FRE.). 108p. (J). pap. 5.99 *(978-1-0956-9068-0(X))* Independently Published.

—Joyeux 11e Anniversaire: Livre d'anniversaire Qui Peut être Utilisé Comme un Journal Ou un Cahier Avec la Conception Mignonne de Cochon. Mieux Qu'une Carte D'anniversaire! Douglas, Karlon. Designs, Level Up. 2019. (FRE.). 108p. (J). pap. 5.99 *(978-1-0956-9070-3(1))* Independently Published.

—Joyeux 12e Anniversaire: Livre d'anniversaire Qui Peut être Utilisé Comme un Journal Ou un Cahier Avec la Conception Mignonne de Cochon. Mieux Qu'une Carte D'anniversaire! Douglas, Karlon. Designs, Level Up. 2019. (FRE.). 108p. (J). pap. 5.99 *(978-1-0956-9071-0(X))* Independently Published.

—Joyeux 15e Anniversaire: Livre d'anniversaire Qui Peut être Utilisé Comme un Journal Ou un Cahier Avec la Conception Mignonne de Cochon. Mieux Qu'une Carte D'anniversaire! Douglas, Karlon. Designs, Level Up. 2019. (FRE.). 108p. (J). pap. 5.99 *(978-1-0956-9077-2(9))* Independently Published.

Douglas, Keith Cartoon Man. A Woolly Mammoth on Amelia Street: Read Aloud Poems4Kids (and Grownups Too!) St. Pierre, Todd-Michael. 2003. 164p. (J). mass mkt. 15.95 *(978-0-9742602-0-4(7))* Prytania Pr.

Douglas, Punchye. Safari Oklahoma Presents: The Magic of Christmas Around the World. Douglas, Bettye. Douglas, Bettye, ed. (Multicultural). 16p. (J). (gr. k-6). 5.00 *(978-0-9703183-4-3(0))* Douglas, Bettye Forum, Inc., The.

—Safari Oklahoma Presents Operation Safe 2000: Halloween Coloring Book. (Safari Oklahoma Presents). 16p. (J). (gr. k-6). 5.00 *(978-0-9703183-2-9(4))* Douglas, Bettye Forum, Inc., The.

D

Douglas, Vannick. Syler & the Sandpaper Towel. Shinno, Stephanie. 2012. 32p. 24.95 *(978-1-4626-6677-5(9))* America Star Bks.

Douglass, Ralph. Baby Jack & Jumping Jack Rabbit. Tireman, Loyd. 2015. (Mesaland Ser.). (ENG.). 48p. (J). 12.95 *(978-0-8263-5604-8(4))* Univ. of New Mexico Pr.

—Big Fat. Tireman, Loyd. 2015. (Mesaland Ser.). (ENG.). 48p. (J). 12.95 *(978-0-8263-5605-5(2))* Univ. of New Mexico Pr.

—Cocky. Tireman, Loyd. 2015. (Mesaland Ser.). (ENG.). 48p. (J). 12.95 *(978-0-8263-5606-2(0))* Univ. of New Mexico Pr.

—Dumbee. Tireman, Loyd. 2015. (Mesaland Ser.). (ENG.). 48p. (J). 12.95 *(978-0-8263-5607-9(9))* Univ. of New Mexico Pr.

—Hop-a-Long: Stories. Tireman, Loyd. 2015. (Mesaland Ser.). (ENG.). 48p. (J). 12.95 *(978-0-8263-5608-6(7))* Univ. of New Mexico Pr.

—Quills. Tireman, Loyd. 2015. (Mesaland Ser.). (ENG.). 48p. (J). 12.95 *(978-0-8263-5609-3(5))* Univ. of New Mexico Pr.

—3 Toes. Tireman, Loyd. 2015. (Mesaland Ser.). (ENG.). 48p. (J). 12.95 *(978-0-8263-5610-9(9))* Univ. of New Mexico Pr.

Douglass, Ryan. A Little Netherton Book: Mario the Goldfish. Netherton, Mary Ann. 2019. (Little Netherton Bks.: Vol. 1). (ENG.). 30p. (J). 19.99 *(978-1-949609-86-8(3))* Pen It! Pubns., LLC.

Doungploy, Nattanan. Katrina Cantina: Katch-A-Kan Cannery. Adams, Isaac Edward. 2016. (ENG.). (J). (gr. 2-4). 20.00 *(978-0-692-80001-0(8))* Edward, Isaac Adams.

Dousias, Spiro. Master Stitchum & the Moon. Maher, Mickle Brandt. 2003. (J). 19.99 *(978-1-932188-01-1(0))* Bollix Bks.

Doutsiopoulos, George. Mamie on the Mound: A Woman in Baseball's Negro Leagues. Henderson, Leah. 2020. (ENG.). 32p. (J). (gr. 3-5). 18.95 *(978-1-68446-023-6(9)*, 139306, Capstone Editions) Capstone.

Dove, Emily. Catch the Sky. Heidbreder, Robert. 2020. 40p. (J). (gr. -1-4). 17.95 ***(978-1-77164-631-4(4)**,* Greystone Bks.) Greystone Books Ltd. CAN. Dist: Publishers Group West (PGW).

Dove, Emily. Hello Honeybees. Rogge, Hannah. 2019. (ENG.). 14p. (J). (gr. -1 — 1). bds. 11.99 *(978-1-4521-6892-0(X))* Chronicle Bks. LLC.

Dove, Emily. Little Love Bug: Finger Puppet Book. Chronicle Books. 2020. (ENG.). 12p. (J). (gr. -1 — 1). bds. 7.99 ***(978-1-4521-8174-5(8))*** Chronicle Bks. LLC.

Dove, Emily. Spencer & Vincent, the Jellyfish Brothers. Johnston, Tony. 2019. (ENG.). 40p. (J). (gr. -1-3). 18.99 *(978-1-5344-1208-8(5)*, Simon & Schuster/Paula Wiseman Bks.) Simon & Schuster/Paula Wiseman Bks.

Dove, Jason. First Graphics: Dinosaurs. Clay, Kathryn et al. 2012. (First Graphics: Dinosaurs Ser.). (ENG.). 24p. (gr. 1-2). pap. 142.80 *(978-1-4296-8369-2(4))* Capstone.

—Stegosaurus: Armored Defender, 1 vol. Clay, Kathryn. 2012. (First Graphics: Dinosaurs Ser.). (ENG.). 24p. (J). (gr. k-3). lib. bdg. 24.65 *(978-1-4296-7604-5(3))* Capstone.

—Stegosaurus: Armored Defender. Clay, Kathryn. 2012. (First Graphics: Dinosaurs Ser.). (ENG.). 24p. (gr. 1-2). pap. 35.70 *(978-1-4296-8364-7(3))* Capstone.

—Triceratops: Three-Horned Giant, 1 vol. Bolte, Mari. 2012. (First Graphics: Dinosaurs Ser.). (ENG.). 24p. (J). (gr. k-3). lib. bdg. 24.65 *(978-1-4296-7601-4(9))*; (gr. 1-2). pap. 35.70 *(978-1-4296-8365-4(1))* Capstone.

—Tyrannosaurus Rex: Mighty Meat-Eater. Hammer, Sheila. 2012. (First Graphics: Dinosaurs Ser.). (ENG.). 24p. (gr. 1-2). pap. 35.70 *(978-1-4296-8366-1(X))* Capstone.

—Velociraptor: Clawed Hunter. Kolpin, Molly. 2012. (First Graphics: Dinosaurs Ser.). (ENG.). 24p. (gr. 1-2). pap. 35.70 *(978-1-4296-8367-8(8))* Capstone.

Dove, Sean. BroBots & the Mecha Malarkey!, Vol. 2. Torres, J. 2017. (BroBots Ser.: 2). (ENG.). 40p. (J). 12.99 *(978-1-62010-424-8(5)*, 9781620104248, Lion Forge) Oni Pr., Inc.

—BroBots And the Shoujo Shenanigans! Torres, J. 2018. (BroBots Ser.: 3). (ENG.). 40p. (J). 12.99 *(978-1-62010-521-4(7)*, Lion Forge) Oni Pr., Inc.

Dow, Danica, jt. illus. see Dow, Kathy.

Dow, Kathy & Dow, Danica. Low-Down Dirty Words. 2004. 28p. (J). *(978-0-9749886-0-3(X))* KayStar Publishing.

Dow, S. B. A Day with Shapes. Heinze, Monica Bacon. 2004. (J). *(978-0-9761710-0-3(7))* Paisley Publishing.

—The Lion's Deceit. Otukile, Mpho. 2011. (ENG.). 32p. (J). pap. *(978-0-9867460-0-0(2))* Village Life Bks.

—Orville Oak & Friends. Hilgendorf, L. B. 2005. 26p. (gr. -1-1). bds. 11.95 *(978-1-58275-149-8(8))* Black Forest Pr.

Dowell, Ashley E. My Spots. Parker, Kimberly. 2020. (ENG.). 26p. (J). (gr. k-6). pap. 12.99 ***(978-0-578-67839-9(X)**,* Pierre Publishing) Carol J. Pierre, LLC.

Dowell, Larry. The Ghost of Hampton Court. Hannah, Martha. 2006. 32p. (J). 17.95 *(978-0-9779808-0-2(4))* CicadaSun.

Dowley, Coco. The Wonderful Happens. Rylant, Cynthia. 2003. (ENG.). 40p. (J). (gr. -1-3). pap. 8.99 *(978-0-689-86355-4(1)*, Simon & Schuster Bks. For Young Readers) Simon & Schuster Bks. For Young Readers.

Dowling, Audrey. Reindeer Down! An Irish Christmas Tale. Mac a'Bháird, Natasha. 2019. (ENG.). 32p. 19.99 *(978-1-78849-099-3(1))* O'Brien Pr., Ltd., The IRL. Dist: Casemate Pubs. & Bk. Distributors, LLC.

Dowling, Kaylynne. Biju Silver Lining. Vine, Mary. 2018. (ENG.). 28p. (J). pap. 9.95 *(978-0-9998957-3-3(7))* Melland Publishing, LLC.

Dowling, Kaylynne. Dragon Gilby. Vine, Mary. 2020. (ENG.). 26p. (J). pap. 9.95 ***(978-1-952447-02-0(X))*** Windtree Pr.

Dowling, Victor J. Joey Goes to Sea. Villiers, Alan. 2005. (Maritime Ser.). (ENG.). 70p. (J). (gr. 4-7). pap. 9.95 *(978-0-939511-10-5(X))* Mystic Seaport Museum, Inc.

Down, Alan. Beowulf: An Anglo-Saxon Epic. 2004. (J). (CZE & ENG.). 30p. pap. *(978-1-84444-114-3(8))*; 30p. pap. *(978-1-84444-113-6(X))*; (SER & ENG.). 30p. pap. *(978-1-84444-112-9(1))*; 30p. pap. *(978-1-84444-110-5(5))*; 30p. pap. *(978-1-84444-109-9(1))*; (TUR & ENG.). 30p. pap. *(978-1-84444-033-7(8))*; 30p. pap. *(978-1-84444-032-0(X))*; 32p. pap. *(978-1-84444-031-3(1))*; 30p. pap. *(978-1-84444-030-6(3))*; (PAN.). 30p. pap. *(978-1-84444-029-0(X))*; 30p. pap. *(978-1-84444-028-3(1))*; 30p. pap. *(978-1-84444-027-6(3))*; 30p. pap. *(978-1-84444-026-9(5))*; 32p. pap. *(978-1-84444-023-8(0))*; 32p. pap. *(978-1-84444-022-1(2))* Mantra Lingua.

—Beowulf: An Anglo-Saxon Epic. Barkow, Henriette. 2003. (J). (URD & ENG.). 32p. pap. 12.95 *(978-1-84444-034-4(6))*; (CHI & ENG.). 30p. pap. 12.95 *(978-1-84444-025-2(7))*; (BEN & ENG.). 30p. pap. 12.95 *(978-1-84444-024-5(9))* Mantra Lingua GBR. Dist: Chinasprout, Inc.

Down, Becky. The Case of the Lost Cat. Minden, Cecilia. 2019. (Little Blossom Stories Ser.). (ENG.). 16p. (J). (gr. -1-2). pap. 11.36 *(978-1-5341-3909-1(5)*, 212477, Cherry Blossom Press) Cherry Lake Publishing.

—The Case of the Lost Frog. Minden, Cecilia. 2019. (Little Blossom Stories Ser.). (ENG.). 16p. (J). (gr. -1-2). pap. 11.36 *(978-1-5341-3910-7(9)*, 212480, Cherry Blossom Press) Cherry Lake Publishing.

—The Case of the Lost Hen. Minden, Cecilia. 2019. (Little Blossom Stories Ser.). (ENG.). 16p. (J). (gr. -1-2). pap. 11.36 *(978-1-5341-3911-4(7)*, 212483, Cherry Blossom Press) Cherry Lake Publishing.

—The Case of the Lost Pig. Minden, Cecilia. 2019. (Little Blossom Stories Ser.). (ENG.). 16p. (J). (gr. -1-2). pap. 11.36 *(978-1-5341-3912-1(5)*, 212486, Cherry Blossom Press) Cherry Lake Publishing.

—The Case of the Lost Pup. Minden, Cecilia. 2019. (Little Blossom Stories Ser.). (ENG.). 16p. (J). (gr. -1-2). pap. 11.36 *(978-1-5341-3913-8(3)*, 212489, Cherry Blossom Press) Cherry Lake Publishing.

—Piper & Emma. Minden, Cecilia. 2020. (Little Blossom Stories Ser.). (ENG.). 16p. (J). (gr. -1-2). pap. 11.36 *(978-1-5341-6090-3(6)*, 214372, Cherry Blossom Press) Cherry Lake Publishing.

—Piper at the Vet. Minden, Cecilia. 2020. (Little Blossom Stories Ser.). (ENG.). 16p. (J). (gr. -1-2). pap. 11.36 *(978-1-5341-6091-0(4)*, 214375, Cherry Blossom Press) Cherry Lake Publishing.

—Piper Has a Birthday. Minden, Cecilia. 2020. (Little Blossom Stories Ser.). (ENG.). 16p. (J). (gr. -1-2). pap. 11.36 *(978-1-5341-6093-4(0)*, 214381, Cherry Blossom Press) Cherry Lake Publishing.

—Piper in the Park. Minden, Cecilia. 2020. (Little Blossom Stories Ser.). (ENG.). 16p. (J). (gr. -1-2). pap. 11.36 *(978-1-5341-6092-7(2)*, 214378, Cherry Blossom Press) Cherry Lake Publishing.

—Piper on a Plane. Minden, Cecilia. 2020. (Little Blossom Stories Ser.). (ENG.). 16p. (J). (gr. -1-2). pap. 11.36 *(978-1-5341-6094-1(9)*, 214384, Cherry Blossom Press) Cherry Lake Publishing.

Downard, Barry. Carla's Famous Traveling Feather & Fur Show. Downard, Barry. 2006. (ENG.). 32p. (J). (gr. 4-7). 16.95 *(978-1-59687-171-7(7))* IBks., Inc.

—The Race of the Century. Downard, Barry. 2008. (ENG.). 40p. (J). (gr. -1-3). 17.99 *(978-1-4169-2509-5(0)*, Simon & Schuster Bks. For Young Readers) Simon & Schuster Bks. For Young Readers.

Downer, Maggie. Freddie & Flossie & the Easter Egg Hunt. Hope, Laura Lee. 2006. (Ready-To-Read Pre-Level 1 Ser.). (ENG.). 32p. (J). (gr. -1-1). 16.19 *(978-1-4169-1029-9(8))* Simon & Schuster, Inc.

—The Lion, the Witch & the Wardrobe: Tea with Mr. Tumnus. Frantz, Jennifer. 2005. (Festival Reader Ser.). 32p. (J). 14.99 *(978-0-06-079117-9(9))* Zonderkidz.

—The Little Christmas Tree: With an Advent Calendar Just for You! Andersen, Hans. 2015. (ENG.). 10p. (J). (gr. k-3). bds. 7.99 *(978-1-86147-291-5(9)*, Armadillo) Anness Publishing GBR. Dist: National Bk. Network.

—Noah: My First Storybook. 2016. 48p. (J). (gr. -1-12). bds. 9.99 *(978-1-86147-776-7(7)*, Armadillo) Anness Publishing GBR. Dist: National Bk. Network.

—The Secret of Cliff Castle: 3 Great Adventure Stories. Blyton, Enid. 2013. (ENG.). 288p. (J). 16.50 *(978-1-84135-588-7(7))* Award Pubns. Ltd. GBR. Dist: Parkwest Pubns., Inc.

Downer, Romeo. Rosa's Paw-Paw Tree: An inspiring tale about a daughter's deep love for her Mother. Callender, Simone. 2011. 24p. pap. 8.99 *(978-1-4575-0596-6(7))* Dog Ear Publishing, LLC.

Downes, Belinda. Baby Days: A Quilt of Rhymes & Pictures. Downes, Belinda. 2006. (ENG.). 32p. (J). (— 1). 14.99 *(978-0-7636-2786-7(0))* Candlewick Pr.

Downey, Dagney. The Cool Story Behind Snow. Rao, Joe. 2015. (Science of Fun Stuff Ser.). (ENG.). 48p. (J). (gr. 1-3). pap. 3.99 *(978-1-4814-4413-2(1)*, Simon Spotlight) Simon Spotlight.

—The Innings & Outs of Baseball. Brown, Jordan D. 2015. (Science of Fun Stuff Ser.). (ENG.). 48p. (J). (gr. 1-3). pap. 4.99 *(978-1-4814-2861-3(6)*, Simon Spotlight) Simon Spotlight.

Downey, Dagney, jt. illus. see Kennedy, Kelly.

Downey, Lisa. Blackberry Banquet, 1 vol. Pierce, Terry. 2008. (ENG.). 32p. (J). (gr. -1-3). pap. 9.95 *(978-1-934359-28-0(9))* Arbordale Publishing.

—Blackberry Banquet in Chinese. Pierce, Terry. Shuqi, Yang, tr. 2019. (CHI.). 32p. (J). (gr. k-3). pap. 11.95 *(978-1-60718-438-6(9))* Arbordale Publishing.

—Happy Birthday to Whooo? A Baby Animal Riddle Book, 1 vol. Fisher, Doris. 2006. (ENG.). 32p. (J). (gr. -1-3). 15.95 *(978-0-9768823-1-2(0))*; pap. 8.95 *(978-1-934359-06-8(8))* Arbordale Publishing.

—Julie the Rockhound, 1 vol. Karwoski, Gail Langer. 2007. (ENG.). 32p. (J). (gr. k-4). 15.95 *(978-0-9764943-7-9(X))* Arbordale Publishing.

Downey, Lisa. The Pirates of Plagiarism. Downey, Lisa. Fox, Kathleen. 2010. 32p. (J). (gr. 1-4). lib. bdg. 17.95 *(978-1-60213-053-1(1)*, Upstart Bks.) Highsmith Inc.

Downey, William. Deadly Ants. Simon, Seymour. 2012. (Dover Children's Science Bks.). (ENG.). 64p. (J). (gr. 3-5). pap. 5.99 *(978-0-486-48468-6(8)*, 484688) Dover Pubns., Inc.

—Poisonous Snakes. Simon, Seymour. 2012. (Dover Children's Science Bks.). (ENG.). 80p. (J). (gr. 3-5). pap. 5.99 *(978-0-486-48470-9(X)*, 48470X) Dover Pubns., Inc.

Downie, Christopher. The Hungry Cat. Nadimi, Suzan. l.t. ed. 2005. (PER.). 32p. 5.95 net. *(978-0-9764947-0-6(1))* Nur Pubns.

Downing, Jacari. Little Brown Girls with Melanin & Curls. Downing, Ashley L. 2019. (ENG.). 26p. (J). pap. 9.50 ***(978-1-6964-7859-5(6))*** Independently Published.

Downing, Jade. Noah, der Kindergartenneuling. Nuttall, Carl D. Hieksch, Ute, tr. 2019. (GER.). 66p. (J). pap. 5.99 *(978-1-0962-2369-6(4))* Independently Published.

—Petites Histoires Pour les Enfants: Encore Plus d'Aventures d'Incroyables Animaux. Nuttall, Carl D. Fourcadier, Emilie Rigault-, tr. 2019. (French Ser.: Vol. 4). (FRE.). 76p. (J). pap. 6.49 *(978-1-0723-8683-4(6))* Independently Published.

Downing, Johnette. My Aunt Came Back from Louisiane, 1 vol. Downing, Johnette, adapted by. 2008. (ENG.). 32p. (J). (gr. 1-3). 16.99 *(978-1-58980-607-8(7)*, Pelican Publishing) Arcadia Publishing.

—There Was an Old Lady Who Swallowed Some Bugs, 1 vol. Downing, Johnette, adapted by. 2010. (ENG.). 32p. (J). (gr. k-3). 16.99 *(978-1-58980-858-4(4)*, Pelican Publishing) Arcadia Publishing.

Downing, Johnette. Why the Crawfish Lives in the Mud, 1 vol. Downing, Johnette. 2009. (ENG.). 32p. (J). (gr. k-3). 16.99 *(978-1-58980-678-8(6)*, Pelican Publishing) Arcadia Publishing.

Downing, Julie. All the Ways I Love You. Wang, Dorothea DePrisco & Imperato, Teresa. 2005. (ENG.). 10p. (J). bds. 8.95 *(978-1-58117-190-7(0)*, Intervisual/Piggy Toes) Bendon, Inc.

—All the Ways I Love You (bilingual Edition) 2005. (SPA & ENG.). 10p. (J). 8.95 *(978-1-58117-335-2(0)*, Intervisual/Piggy Toes) Bendon, Inc.

—All the Way's I Love You Mini. Piggy Toes Press Staff. 2005. (ENG.). 10p. (J). 4.95 *(978-1-58117-437-3(3)*, Intervisual/Piggy Toes) Bendon, Inc.

—Cabbage Rose. Helldorfer, M. C. 2013. (ENG.). 32p. (J). (gr. -1-3). 16.99 *(978-1-4814-2156-0(5)*, Atheneum Bks. for Young Readers) Simon & Schuster Children's Publishing.

—The Christmas Story. Chancellor, Deborah. 12p. (J). (gr. -1-18). bds. 6.95 *(978-0-8294-1480-6(0))* Loyola Pr.

—Cubs in the Tub: The True Story of the Bronx Zoo's First Woman Zookeeper. Fleming, Candace. 2020. (ENG.). 48p. (J). (gr. -1-3). 18.99 *(978-0-8234-4318-5(3)*, Neal Porter Bks) Holiday Hse., Inc.

—Don't Turn the Page. Burk, Rachelle. 2014. (ENG.). 32p. (J). (gr. -1-3). 16.95 *(978-1-939547-06-4(7))* Creston Bks.

—The Firekeeper's Son. Park, Linda Sue. 2009. (ENG.). 40p. (J). (gr. -1-3). pap. 7.99 *(978-0-547-23769-5(3)*, 1083886) Houghton Mifflin Harcourt Publishing Co.

—A First Book of Fairy Tales. Hoffman, Mary. 2006. (ENG.). 80p. (J). (gr. 3-7). pap. 9.99 *(978-0-7566-2107-0(0)*, DK Children) Dorling Kindersley Publishing, Inc.

—First Mothers. Gherman, Beverly. 2016. (ENG.). 64p. (J). (gr. 1-4). 6.99 *(978-0-544-66839-3(1)*, 1625440, HMH Books For Young Readers) Houghton Mifflin Harcourt Publishing Co.

—Ice Cream King. Metzger, Steve. 2011. (ENG.). 32p. (J). (gr. -1-2). 15.95 *(978-1-58925-096-3(6))*; pap. 7.95 *(978-1-58925-427-5(9))* Tiger Tales.

—Lullaby & Good Night: Songs for Sweet Dreams. 2014. (ENG.). 32p. (J). (gr. -1-3). 16.99 *(978-1-4814-2528-5(5)*, Simon & Schuster Bks. For Young Readers) Simon & Schuster Bks. For Young Readers.

—Spooky Friends. Feder, Jane. 2013. (ENG.). 40p. (J). (gr. k-2). 16.99 *(978-0-545-47815-1(4)*, Scholastic Pr.) Scholastic, Inc.

—Tessa Takes Wing. Jackson, Richard. 2018. (ENG.). 40p. (J). 17.99 *(978-1-62672-439-6(3)*, 900157253) Roaring Brook Pr.

Downing, Julie. The Night Before Christmas. Downing, Julie. 2013. (ENG.). 32p. (J). (gr. -1-3). 16.99 *(978-1-4814-2151-5(4)*, Simon & Schuster Bks. For Young Readers) Simon & Schuster Bks. For Young Readers.

—Where Is My Mommy? Downing, Julie. 2003. (ENG.). 32p. (J). (gr. -1-18). 15.99 *(978-0-688-17824-6(3))* HarperCollins Pubs.

Downing, Sue. Coding with Python. Scrivano, Álvaro. 2019. (Ready, Set, Code! Ser.). (ENG.). 32p. (J). (gr. 2-5). pap. 9.99 *(978-1-5415-4667-7(9))*; lib. bdg. 29.32 *(978-1-5415-3876-4(5)*, Lerner Pubns.) Lerner Publishing Group.

—Coding with ScratchJr. Scrivano, Álvaro. 2019. (Ready, Set, Code! Ser.). (ENG.). 32p. (J). (gr. 2-5). 29.32 *(978-1-5415-3875-7(7)*, Lerner Pubns.) Lerner Publishing Group.

—The Unofficial Guide to Coding with Minecraft. Scrivano, Álvaro. 2019. (Ready, Set, Code! Ser.). (ENG.). 32p. (J). (gr. 2-5). pap. 9.99 *(978-1-5415-4666-0(0))*; lib. bdg. 29.32 *(978-1-5415-3877-1(3)*, Lerner Pubns.) Lerner Publishing Group.

Downs, Braden. The Treasures of Christmas. Holthaus, Abbey. 2008. 126p. pap. 19.95 *(978-1-60672-152-0(6))* America Star Bks.

Downs, Dorothy. Canoe Back in Time. Downs, Dorothy. 2017. (ENG.). (J). (gr. 1-6). 70p. 20.00 *(978-1-5154-3909-7(7))*; pap. 16.95 *(978-1-5154-1709-5(3))* Wilder Pubns., Corp.

Doyel, Ginger. Gertrude the Albino Frog & Her Friend Rupert the Turtle. Silvermetz, Marcia A. 2003. 48p. (J). (gr. 2-3). 19.95 *(978-0-9718724-0-0(6))* Hiccup Cottage Pubns.

Doyle, Adam S. Fat & Bones: And Other Stories. Theule, Larissa. 2014. (ENG.). 112p. (J). (gr. 4-12). lib. bdg. 16.95 *(978-1-4677-0825-8(9)*, 9781467708258, Carolrhoda Bks.) Lerner Publishing Group.

Doyle, Amanda. Zim: The Lazy Goldfish. Whyte, Anne. 2020. (ENG.). 26p. (J). pap. 9.13 ***(978-1-7201-4184-6(3))*** Independently Published.

Doyle, Beverly. Aliens from Earth: When Animals & Plants Invade Other Ecosystems, 1 vol. Batten, Mary. rev. ed. 2016. (ENG.). 36p. (J). (gr. 3-6). 16.95 *(978-1-56145-900-1(3))* Peachtree Publishing Co. Inc.

—Extinct! Creatures of the Past. Batten, Mary. 2004. (J). pap. *(978-0-375-82554-5(1))*; lib. bdg. *(978-0-375-92554-2(6))* Random Hse. Children's Bks. (Random Hse. Bks. for Young Readers).

Doyle, Ed. Buddy the Drone. St George-Smith, Ronald. 2018. (Buddy the Drone Ser.: Vol. 1). (ENG.). 66p. (J). pap. *(978-1-912639-43-4(2))* Terence, Michael Publishing.

Doyle, Evan Brain. Evan Brain's Christmas List & Other Shenanigans: Boy Warrior Fights Evil. Doyle, Evan Brain. Becker-Doyle, Eve. 2008. (ENG.). 64p. pap. 15.95 *(978-0-9794716-3-6(X))* BDA Publishing.

Doyle, Lizzy. Colors. Rainstorm Publishing, ed. 2019. (Look & Learn Ser.). (ENG.). 20p. (J). bds. 7.99 ***(978-1-926444-55-0(8))*** Rainstorm Pr.

Doyle, Lizzy. I Love Pluto. Ferrie, Chris & Maynard-Casely, Helen. 2020. 18p. (J). bds. 10.99 *(978-1-7282-0524-3(7))* Sourcebooks, Inc.

—It's Time to Build a Snowman! Acampora, Courtney. 2018. (Christmas Gift Tags Ser.). (ENG.). 12p. (J). (— 1). bds. 4.99 *(978-1-68412-384-1(4)*, Silver Dolphin Bks.) Printers Row Publishing Group.

—Kaleidoscope: Too Cute! Coloring. Editors of Silver Dolphin Books. 2019. (Kaleidoscope Ser.). (ENG.). 64p. (J). (gr. 1-3). pap. 14.99 *(978-1-68412-697-2(5)*, Silver Dolphin Bks.) Printers Row Publishing Group.

Doyle, Lizzy. Numbers. Rainstorm Publishing, ed. 2019. (Look & Learn Ser.). (ENG.). 20p. (J). bds. 7.99 ***(978-1-926444-54-3(X))*** Rainstorm Pr.

—Planes, Trains, & Animobiles. Rainstorm Publishing, ed. 2019. (ENG.). 20p. (J). bds. 7.99 ***(978-1-926444-91-8(4))*** Rainstorm Pr.

Doyle, Lizzy. This Book. Allen, Kathryn Madeline. 2018. (ENG.). 24p. (J). (— 1). bds. 9.99 *(978-0-8075-7881-0(9)*, 807578819) Whitman, Albert & Co.

—8 Little Planets. Ferrie, Chris. 2018. 18p. (J). bds. 10.99 *(978-1-4926-7124-4(X)*, Sourcebooks Jabberwocky) Sourcebooks, Inc.

Doyle, Ming. Kieren's Story. Smith, Cynthia Leitich. 2011. (Tantalize Ser.: 5). (ENG.). 192p. (YA). (gr. 9). pap. 19.99 *(978-0-7636-4114-6(6))* Candlewick Pr.

Doyle, Ming, et al. Tomorrow's Avengers. Bendis, Brian Michael. 2015. (Guardians of the Galaxy Ser.). (ENG.). 36p. (J). (gr. 3-6). 27.07 *(978-1-61479-392-2(1)*, 18223, Marvel Age) Spotlight.

Doyle, Patrick H. T. Edgar Font's Hunt for a House to Haunt: Adventure Two: the Fakersville Power Station. Doyle, Patrick H. T. 2007. (Edgar Font's Hunt for a House to Haunt Ser.). 303p. (J). (gr. 4-7). per. 7.99 *(978-0-9786132-1-1(X))* Armadillo Bks.

Doyle, Richard. Jack the Giant Killer. Doyle, Richard. 2004. 96p. (J). reprint ed. 19.00 *(978-0-7567-7478-3(0))* DIANE Publishing Co.

Doyle, Sandra. Bone Collection: Skulls. Colson, Rob Scott & de la Bédoyère, Camilla. 2014. (ENG.). 96p. (J). (gr. 3-7). pap. 14.99 *(978-0-545-72457-9(0)*, Scholastic Paperbacks) Scholastic, Inc.

Doyle, Tommy. Busy Noisy Construction. Crowe, Carmen. Cottage Door Press, ed. 2020. (Interactive Early Bird Children's Song Book with 10 Sing-Along Tunes Ser.). (ENG.). 10p. (J). (gr. -1-1). bds. 18.99 *(978-1-68052-839-8(4)*, 1005500) Cottage Door Pr.

—Leon the Raccoon: Explores the Arctic. Papineau, Lucie. 2017. (ENG.). 32p. (J). (gr. -1). 14.95 *(978-2-7338-5045-9(8))* Auzou, Philippe Editions FRA. Dist: Consortium Bk. Sales & Distribution.

—Silly Animal Stories. Winget, Rosie. Cottage Door Press, ed. 2019. (Early Bird Learning Ser.). (ENG.). 16p. (J). (gr. -1-2). bds. 12.99 *(978-1-68052-308-9(2)*, 1002830) Cottage Door Pr.

Doyon, Patrick. The Poisoned Cake. Marois, André & Norman, Taylor. 2017. (J). *(978-1-4521-4660-7(8))* Chronicle Bks. LLC.

—The Sandwich Thief. Marois, Andre. 2016. (ENG.). 160p. (J). (gr. 1-4). 14.99 *(978-1-4521-4659-1(4))* Chronicle Bks. LLC.

Dozerdraws. Lumberjanes Vol. 13. Leyh, Kat. 2019. (Lumberjanes Ser.: 13). (ENG.). 112p. (J). pap. 14.99 *(978-1-68415-450-0(2))* Boom! Studios.

Dozier, Ashlyn & Dozier, Makenna Joy. The Confused Tooth Fairy. Dozier, Kim. 2005. (ENG.). 28p. (J). 10.00 *(978-0-9745839-3-8(6)*, Fun to Read Bks. with Royally Good Morals) MKADesigns.

Dozier, Ashlyn McCauley. The Ear-Less Kingdom. Dozier, Kim. l.t. ed. 2003. (ENG.). 24p. (J). 7.50 *(978-0-9745839-1-4(X)*, Fun to Read Bks. with Royally Good Morals) MKADesigns.

—The Forgetful Princess. Dozier, Kim. 2nd l.t. ed. 2003. (ENG.). 24p. (J). 10.00 *(978-0-9745839-0-7(1)*, Fun to Read Bks. with Royally Good Morals) MKADesigns.

—Where's Dwight Dragon. Dozier, Kim. l.t. ed. 2004. (ENG.). 32p. (J). 10.00 *(978-0-9745839-2-1(8)*, Fun to Read Bks. with Royally Good Morals) MKADesigns.

Dozier, Ashlyn McCauley & Dozier, Makenna Joy. The Backwards Wizard. Dozier, Kim. l.t. ed. 2005. (ENG.). 28p. (J). 10.00 *(978-0-9745839-4-5(4)*, Fun to Read Bks. with Royally Good Morals) MKADesigns.

Dozier, Brendan, et al, photos by. A Book Your Baby Can Read! Titzer, Robert C. 2003. (Early Language Development Ser.: Vol. 2). 14p. (J). pap. 7.95 *(978-0-9657510-5-6(8)*, 0-9657510-5-8) Infant Learning Co., The.

—A Book Your Baby Can Read! Review: Early Language Development Series. Titzer, Robert C. 2003. (Early Language Development Ser.). 14p. (J). pap. 7.95

(978-1-931026-04-8(1), 1-931026-04-1) Infant Learning Co., The.

Dozier, Lisa, et al, photos by. A Book Your Baby Can Read! Early Language Development Series. Titzer, Robert C. 2003. (Early Language Development Ser.: Vol. 3). 14p. (J). pap. 7.95 *(978-0-9657510-9-4(0)*, 0-9657510-9-0) Infant Learning Co., The.

—A Book Your Baby Can Read! Starter: Early Language Development Series, 1, Starter Book. Titzer, Robert C. 2003. (Book Your Baby Can Read!: Starter Book). 14p. (J). pap. 7.95 *(978-1-931026-03-1(3)*, 1-931026-03-3) Infant Learning Co., The.

Dozier, Makenna Joy, jt. illus. see Dozier, Ashlyn McCauley.

Dozier, Makenna Joy, jt. illus. see Dozier, Ashlyn.

Drage, Robyn. Matson the Mouse. O'Brien, Duncan. 2011. (J). *(978-0-9686734-2-3(2))* Pier 10 Media.

Drago, Flavia Z. Gustavo, el Fantasmita Tímido. Drago, Flavia Z. 2020. (SPA.). 40p. (J). (gr. -1-2). 16.99 ***(978-1-5362-1414-7(0))*** Candlewick Pr.

—Gustavo, the Shy Ghost. Drago, Flavia Z. 2020. (ENG.). 40p. (J). (gr. -1-2). 16.99 ***(978-1-5362-1114-6(1))*** Candlewick Pr.

Dragony, Barbara. Hacer la Compra. Yannone, Deborah. 2014.Tr. of Grocery Shopping. (SPA.). 16p. (gr. k-1). pap. 7.95 *(978-1-61181-153-7(8)*, Kaeden Bks.) Kaeden Corp.

—My Tiger Cat. Frankford, Marilyn. Kaeden Corp. Staff, ed. 2006. (ENG.). 12p. (gr. k-2). pap. 7.95 *(978-1-879835-52-8(5)*, Kaeden Bks.) Kaeden Corp.

Dragony, Barbara. Olive Ann. Stanley, Sharon P. I.t. ed. 2019. (ENG.). 24p. (J). (gr. k-1). pap. 10.95 ***(978-1-61633-999-9(3))*** Guardian Angel Publishing, Inc.

—Why Are the Donkeys Dirty? Stanley, Sharon P. 2020. (ENG.). 16p. (J). (gr. k-3). pap. 9.95 ***(978-1-951545-05-5(2))*** Guardian Angel Publishing, Inc.

Dragos, Bujdei. Pink the Painter. Blum, Ingo. 2019. (Pink the Hedgehog Ser.: Vol. 1). (ENG.). 80p. (J). (gr. 1-3). ***(978-3-947410-86-6(7))*** Blum, Ingo Planet-Oh Concepts.

Dragt, Tonke. The Letter for the King. Dragt, Tonke. Watkinson, Laura, tr. 2018. (ENG.). 512p. (J). (gr. 3-7). pap. 15.95 *(978-1-78269-081-8(6)*, Pushkin Children's Bks.) Steerforth Pr.

—The Letter for the King (Netflix Original Series Tie-In) Dragt, Tonke. Watkinson, Laura, tr. ed. 2020. (ENG.). 512p. (J). (gr. 3-7). pap. 15.95 *(978-1-78269-259-1(2)*, Pushkin Children's Bks.) Steerforth Pr.

—The Secrets of the Wild Wood. Dragt, Tonke. Watkinson, Laura, tr. 2018. (ENG.). 512p. (J). (gr. 3-7). pap. 15.95 *(978-1-78269-195-2(2)*, Pushkin Children's Bks.) Steerforth Pr.

—The Song of Seven. Dragt, Tonke. Watkinson, Laura, tr. 2018. (ENG.). 352p. (J). (gr. 3-7). pap. 15.95 *(978-1-78269-142-6(1)*, Pushkin Children's Bks.) Steerforth Pr.

Drake, Lana. Woody Acorn. Drake, Lana. Clauson, Marilyn. 2012. 48p. 24.95 *(978-1-4626-9647-5(3))*; pap. 24.95 *(978-1-4626-7946-1(3))* America Star Bks.

Drake, Malarie. Carletto. Licari, Violetta Anna. 2019. (Children of the World Ser.: Vol. 2). (ENG.). 42p. (J). pap. 7.99 ***(978-1-0783-0173-2(5))*** Independently Published.

Drake, Marybeth. Sundancer. Peterson, Shelley. rev. ed. 2007. (ENG.). 264p. (YA). (gr. 7-12). pap. 7.95 *(978-1-55263-842-2(1))* Leaf Storm Pr.

Drape, Kaitlin. Slowpoke the Turtle & Company. Finally, Lil Rose. 2005. (J). pap. 8.00 *(978-0-8059-6778-4(8))* Dorrance Publishing Co., Inc.

Draper, Richard. Bugs. Parker, Steve. 2010. (I Love Animals Ser.). (ENG.). 24p. (J). (gr. 1-5). pap. 8.15 *(978-1-61533-252-6(9))*; lib. bdg. 25.60 *(978-1-61533-246-5(4))* Windmill Bks.

—Spiders. Parker, Steve. 2010. (I Love Animals Ser.). (ENG.). 24p. (J). (gr. 1-5). pap. 8.15 *(978-1-61533-256-4(1))*; lib. bdg. 25.60 *(978-1-61533-250-2(2))* Windmill Bks.

—10 Things You Should Know about Spiders. Parker, Steve. Gallagher, Belinda & Borton, Paula, eds. 2004. (10 Things You Should Know Ser.). 24p. (J). 6.99 *(978-1-84236-122-1(8))* Miles Kelly Publishing, Ltd. GBR. Dist: Independent Pubs. Group.

Draper, Richard, jt. illus. see Dennis, Peter.

Draper, Rochelle. The Stone Wall Dragon. Draper, Rochelle. ed. 2007. (ENG.). 32p. (J). (gr. 1-17). 15.95 *(978-0-89272-690-5(3))* Down East Bks.

Drashner, Diane. Grandma & Grandpa Visit Denali. Richter, Bernd & Richter, Susan. 2008. 48p. (J). pap. 9.95 *(978-1-931353-33-5(6))* Saddle Pal Creations, Inc.

Draven, Shelly. Care for Creation. Baldwin, Christy. 2010. (ENG.). 32p. (J). lib. bdg. 16.95 *(978-0-9822565-6-5(6))* Tribute Bks.

Drawlish. Crash! Bang! Oooooo. Christie, Sherry. 2018. (ENG.). 34p. (J). (gr. k-1). pap. *(978-1-9996577-6-5(4))* Little Goblins' Bks.

Drawson, Blair. Arachne Speaks. Hovey, Kate. 2014. (ENG.). 40p. (J). (gr. 5). 13.99 *(978-1-4814-5069-0(7)*, McElderry, Margaret K. Bks.) McElderry, Margaret K. Bks.

—Island of the Minotaur: The Greek Myths of Ancient Crete. Oberman, Sheldon. 2003. (ENG.). 96p. (J). 19.95 *(978-1-56656-531-8(6)*, Crocodile Bks.) Interlink Publishing Group, Inc.

Dray, Matt. Dougal, the Garbage Dump Bear. Dray, Matt. 2005. 32p. (J). pap. *(978-0-14-350097-1(X))* Penguin Publishing Group.

Draycott, Michelle. Daisy Wants to Go Riding, 1 vol. Dale, Jay. 2012. (Wonder Words Ser.). (ENG.). 32p. (gr. k-2). pap. 5.99 *(978-1-4296-8920-5(X)*, Capstone Pr.) Capstone.

—Here I Go, 1 vol. Dale, Jay. 2012. (Wonder Words Ser.). (ENG.). 32p. (gr. k-2). pap. 5.99 *(978-1-4296-8892-5(0)*, Capstone Pr.) Capstone.

—Pippa & the Flowers, 1 vol. Dale, Jay. 2012. (Wonder Words Ser.). (ENG.). 32p. (gr. k-2). pap. 5.99 *(978-1-4296-8908-3(0)*, Capstone Pr.) Capstone.

Drayton, Adrienne. Mindful Messages Mentoring Workbook: Healing Thoughts for the Hip & Hop Descendants from the Motherland. Day, Deborah A. Patterson, L. Kahlil, ed. 2nd I.t. ed. 2004. 192p. (YA). per. 14.95 *(978-0-9704048-2-4(4))* Ashay by the Bay.

Dreaming Tortoise Staff. Alioramus on the Hunt. Dreaming Tortoise Staff. 2017. (When Dinosaurs Ruled the Earth Ser.). (ENG.). 32p. (J). (gr. k-3). lib. bdg. 27.99 *(978-1-925235-19-7(X)*, Big and SMALL) ChoiceMaker Pty. Ltd., The AUS. Dist: Lerner Publishing Group.

—Armored Ankylosaurus. Dreaming Tortoise Staff. 2017. (When Dinosaurs Ruled the Earth Ser.). (ENG.). 32p. (J). (gr. k-3). lib. bdg. 27.99 *(978-1-925235-20-3(3)*, Big and SMALL) ChoiceMaker Pty. Ltd., The AUS. Dist: Lerner Publishing Group.

—Restless Iguanodon. Dreaming Tortoise Staff. 2017. (When Dinosaurs Ruled the Earth Ser.). (ENG.). 32p. (J). (gr. k-3). lib. bdg. 27.99 *(978-1-925235-22-7(X)*, Big and SMALL) ChoiceMaker Pty. Ltd., The AUS. Dist: Lerner Publishing Group.

Dreams, 91. Alien Invasion Part 1. McCaw, Charley & Awesome. 2019. (Alien Invasion Part 1 Ser.: Vol. 1). (ENG.). 46p. (J). pap. 12.00 *(978-1-0908-6626-4(7))* Independently Published.

Dreany, E. Joseph. Annie Oakley, Sharpshooter. Verral, Charles Spain. 2011. 28p. pap. 35.95 *(978-1-258-06762-5(5))* Literary Licensing, LLC.

—The Lone Ranger. Fletcher, Steffi. 2013. (Little Golden Book Ser.). 24p. (J). (-k). 4.99 *(978-0-449-81793-3(8)*, Golden Bks.) Random Hse. Children's Bks.

Dreidemy, Joëlle, et al. Adventure Homes. Bailey, Gerry. 2013. (ENG.). 32p. (J). *(978-0-7787-0287-0(1))*; pap. *(978-0-7787-0291-7(X))* Crabtree Publishing Co.

Dreidemy, Joëlle. Cinderella: The Terrible Truth. North, Laura. 2014. (Race Ahead with Reading Ser.). (ENG.). 32p. (J). (gr. 2-2). *(978-0-7787-1326-5(1))* Crabtree Publishing Co.

—The Disastrous Magical Wishes of Classroom 13. Lee, Honest & Gilbert, Matthew J. 2017. (Classroom 13 Ser.: 2). (ENG.). 128p. (J). (gr. 1-5). pap. 5.99 *(978-0-316-46456-7(2))* Little, Brown Bks. for Young Readers.

—Dragons Do Eat Homework. Jones, Marcia & Dadey, Debbie. 2007. 64p. (J). *(978-0-545-00234-9(6))* Scholastic, Inc.

—The Fantastic & Terrible Fame of Classroom 13. Lee, Honest & Gilbert, Matthew J. 2017. (Classroom 13 Ser.: 3). 128p. (J). (gr. 1-5). 15.99 *(978-0-316-46457-4(0))*; (ENG.). pap. 5.99 *(978-0-316-46458-1(9))* Little, Brown Bks. for Young Readers.

—Ghosts Do Splash in Puddles. Jones, Marcia & Dadey, Debbie. 2006. 64p. (J). pap. *(978-0-439-87629-2(X))* Scholastic, Inc.

—The Happy & Heinous Halloween of Classroom 13. Lee, Honest & Gilbert, Matthew J. 2018. (Classroom 13 Ser.: 5). 128p. (J). (gr. 1-5). pap. 9.99 *(978-0-316-50115-6(8))* Little Brown & Co.

Dreidemy, Joëlle. Interrupting Cow. Yolen, Jane. 2020. (Interrupting Cow Ser.). (ENG.). 32p. (J). (gr. k-2). 17.99 ***(978-1-5344-5424-8(1))***; pap. 4.99 ***(978-1-5344-5423-1(3))*** Simon Spotlight. (Simon Spotlight).

—The Lamb Who Came for Dinner. Smallman, Steve. (Favorite Stories Ser.). 32p. (J). (gr. -1-2). 2020. (ENG.). lib. bdg. 23.99 ***(978-1-68010-224-6(9))***; 2007. 15.95 *(978-1-58925-067-3(2))* Tiger Tales.

Dreidemy, Joëlle. My Explosive Diary. Gale, Emily. 2014. (Eliza Boom Ser.: 1). (ENG.). 128p. (J). (gr. 1-4). 15.99 *(978-1-4814-0650-5(7)*, Simon & Schuster/Paula Wiseman Bks.) Simon & Schuster/Paula Wiseman Bks.

—My Super-Spy Diary. 2014. (Eliza Boom Ser.: 2). (ENG.). 128p. (J). (gr. 1-4). pap. 5.99 *(978-1-4814-0652-9(3)*, Aladdin) Simon & Schuster Children's Publishing.

—Press Play. Fine, Anne. 2nd ed. 2016. (Reading Ladder Ser.). (ENG.). 48p. (J). (gr. k-2). pap. 7.99 *(978-1-4052-8242-0(8))* Egmont Bks., Ltd. GBR. Dist: Independent Pubs. Group.

Dreidemy, Joelle. The Princess & the Frozen Peas. North, Laura. 2014. (Tadpoles: Fairytale Twists Ser.). (ENG.). 32p. (J). (gr. 1-2). *(978-0-7787-0446-1(7))*; pap. *(978-0-7787-0481-2(5))* Crabtree Publishing Co.

Dreidemy, Joëlle. Smelly Peter: The Great Pea Eater. Smallman, Steve. 2008. 32p. (J). (gr. 4-7). 15.95 *(978-1-58925-076-5(1))* Tiger Tales.

—The Super Awful Superheroes of Classroom 13. Lee, Honest & Gilbert, Matthew J. 2018. (Classroom 13 Ser.: 4). 128p. (J). (gr. 1-5). (ENG.). 22.00 *(978-0-316-50109-5(3))*; pap. 5.99 *(978-0-316-50112-5(3))* Little, Brown Bks. for Young Readers.

—The Unlucky Lottery Winners of Classroom 13. Lee, Honest & Gilbert, Matthew J. 2017. (Classroom 13 Ser.: 1). (ENG.). 128p. (J). (gr. 1-5). pap. 5.99 *(978-0-316-46462-8(7))* Little, Brown Bks. for Young Readers.

—The Usborne Healthy Cookbook. Allman, Howard, photos by. Patchett, Fiona. 2008. (Children's Cooking Ser.). (ENG.). 64p. (J). (gr. 4-7). pap. 16.99 *(978-0-7945-2062-5(6)*, Usborne) EDC Publishing.

—The Witch with a Twitch. Marlow, Layn. (Tiger Tales Ser.). (J). (gr. -1-2). 2006. 28p. pap. 6.95 *(978-1-58925-400-8(7))*; 2005. 32p. 15.95 *(978-1-58925-052-9(4))* Tiger Tales.

—Wizards Do Roast Turkeys. Jones, Marcia & Dadey, Debbie. 2007. 64p. (J). pap. *(978-0-545-00235-6(4))* Scholastic, Inc.

Dreidemy, Joëlle, et al. Working Homes. Bailey, Gerry. 2013. (ENG.). 32p. (J). *(978-0-7787-0290-0(1))* Crabtree Publishing Co.

Dreidemy, Joëlle & Bigwood, John. Sneezy Alien Attack. Collins, Tim. 2014. (Cosmic Colin Ser.: 2). (ENG.). 128p. (J). (gr. 4-6). pap. 9.99 *(978-1-78055-242-2(4))* O'Mara, Michael Bks., Ltd. GBR. Dist: Independent Pubs. Group.

Dreidemy, Joëlle, jt. illus. see Radford, Karen.

Dreiling, Katrin. Bedtime Daddy! Giltrow, Sharon. 2020. (ENG.). 32p. (J). (gr. -1-2). 18.99 *(978-1-925820-38-6(6)*, 335031, EK Bks.) Exisle Publishing Pty Ltd. AUS. Dist: Hachette UK Distribution.

Dreisbach, Kristin Wolf & Foreman, Austin Lee. Winston the Duck & His Big Orange Bill. Dreisbach, Kristin Wolf. 2013. 20p. pap. 13.97 *(978-1-62212-897-6(4)*, Strategic Bk. Publishing) Strategic Book Publishing & Rights Agency (SBPRA).

Dreistadt, Becky. Capture Creatures. Gibson, Frank. 2018. (ENG.). 128p. (J). (gr. 3). pap. 14.99 *(978-1-60886-798-1(6))* Boom! Studios.

Drescher, Daniela. An Illustrated Treasury of Grimm's Fairy Tales: Cinderella, Sleeping Beauty, Hansel & Gretel & Many More Classic Stories, 10 vols. Grimm, The Brothers. 2013. Orig. Title: Die 100 Schönsten Märchen der Brüder Grimm. (ENG.). 224p. (J). 24.95 *(978-0-86315-947-3(8))* Floris Bks. GBR. Dist: Consortium Bk. Sales & Distribution.

Drescher, Heather. You & Me Make Three. Stephens, Edna Cucksey et al. 2008. (Build-A-Bear Workshop Ser.). 32p. (J). (gr. -1-3). 0.00 *(978-0-9798088-0-7(4))* EDCO Publishing, Inc.

—You & Me Make Three & Accompanying Plush B. B. the Bear. Stephens, Edna Cucksey et al. 2008. 32p. (J). 35.00 *(978-0-9798088-2-1(0))* EDCO Publishing, Inc.

Drescher, Henrick. The Fool & the Flying Ship. Metaxas, Eric. 2007. (Rabbit Ears-A Classic Tale Ser.). (ENG.). 36p. (J). (gr. 2-6). 28.50 *(978-1-59961-308-6(5)*, 12961, Picture Bk.) Spotlight.

Drescher, Henrik. The Story of Brer Rabbit & the Wonderful Tar Baby, 1 vol. Harris, Joel Chandler. 2004. (Rabbit Ears-A Classic Tale Ser.). (ENG.). 52p. (J). (gr. 2-6). 28.50 *(978-1-59197-761-2(4)*, 12922, Picture Bk.) Spotlight.

Drescher, Joan. A Journey in the Moon Balloon: When Images Speak Louder Than Words. Drescher, Joan. 2015. (ENG.). 72p. (J). 19.95 *(978-1-84905-730-1(3)*, 693781) Kingsley, Jessica Pubs. GBR. Dist: Hachette UK Distribution.

Dresen, Kris. A Book in Four Languages: My Colors. Broderick, Kathy. 2019. (ENG.). 20p. (J). bds. *(978-1-5037-4702-9(6)*, addde9e2-8dd8-4b5f-9ab0-dc651cb3016a, p i kids) Phoenix International Publications, Inc.

—A Book in Four Languages: My Numbers. Winslow, Claire. de Alba, Arlette et al, trs. 2019. (ENG.). 20p. (J). bds. *(978-1-5037-4701-2(8)*, 375af6a4-5adb-42de-a48e-d7fdc88ae281, p i kids) Phoenix International Publications, Inc.

Dress, Robert. The Art Contest: No Cheating Allowed! Banks, Steven. 2006. (SpongeBob SquarePants Ser.: 12). (ENG.). 24p. (J). (gr. -1-3). pap. 3.99 *(978-1-4169-0667-4(3)*, Simon Spotlight/Nickelodeon) Simon Spotlight/Nickelodeon.

—Class Confusion. Willson, Sarah. 2006. (SpongeBob SquarePants Ser.: 11). (ENG.). 24p. (J). (gr. -1-3). pap. 3.99 *(978-1-4169-1239-2(8)*, Simon Spotlight/Nickelodeon) Simon Spotlight/Nickelodeon.

—Highway Robbery. Thompson, Kate. 2009. (ENG.). 128p. (J). (gr. 5-18). 15.99 *(978-0-06-173034-4(3)*, Greenwillow Bks.) HarperCollins Pubs.

—Mother Knows Best. Willson, Sarah. 2006. (SpongeBob SquarePants Chapter Bks.: Vol. 11). (ENG.). 64p. (J). (gr. 3-7). pap. 4.99 *(978-1-4169-0793-0(9)*, Simon Spotlight/Nickelodeon) Simon Spotlight/Nickelodeon.

Dress, Robert & Markowitz, Dan. Drew & the Camp Color War (Drew Pendous #1) Sterling Children's, Sterling et al. 2019. (Drew Pendous Ser.: 1). 96p. (J). (gr. k-4). pap. 6.95 *(978-1-4549-3107-2(8))* Sterling Publishing Co., Inc.

—Drew Travels to Ancient Egypt (Drew Pendous #2) Sterling Children's, Sterling et al. 2019. (Drew Pendous Ser.: 2). 96p. (J). (gr. k-4). pap. 6.95 *(978-1-4549-3109-6(4))* Sterling Publishing Co., Inc.

Dressen-McQueen, Stacey. Boxes for Katje. Fleming, Candace. 2003. (ENG.). 40p. (J). (gr. -1-3). 18.99 *(978-0-374-30922-0(1)*, 9780374309220, Farrar, Straus & Giroux (BYR)) Farrar, Straus & Giroux.

—Boxes for Katje. Fleming, Candace. 2004. (YA). 27.95 incl. audio *(978-0-8045-6930-9(4)*, SAC6930) Spoken Arts, Inc.

Drew, Benjamin. Grandma's Adventures with Benjamin. Drew, Joyce. 2013. 16p. pap. 24.95 *(978-1-63004-098-7(3))* America Star Bks.

Drew-Brook, Deborah & Cormack, Allan. Volcanoes Inside & Out. Souza, D. M. 2006. (On My Own Science Ser.). (ENG.). 48p. (J). (gr. 2-4). per. 7.99 *(978-1-57505-853-5(7)*, First Avenue Editions) Lerner Publishing Group.

Drew-Brook, Deborah, jt. illus. see Cormack, Allan.

Drewes, Dan. The Case of the Missing Peanut Butter: The Adventures of Peanut Butter Bob. Seykora, Teresa. 2010. 32p. 12.99 *(978-1-4520-2678-7(5))* AuthorHouse.

—Hair Like That. Wimberly, Nikisha. 2010. 24p. 13.00 *(978-1-4520-0177-7(4))* AuthorHouse.

—Lilith Celebrates Lammas. Manderly, Lorin. 2010. 36p. pap. 15.50 *(978-1-4520-2689-3(0))* AuthorHouse.

—"You're a Meany!" Douglas, Rachel. 2011. 13p. pap. 10.19 *(978-1-4567-8643-4(1))* AuthorHouse.

Drewett, Trudi. Stinky Goldfish. Manne, Joy. 2016. (ENG.). (J). (gr. 1-5). pap. *(978-2-9701092-3-5(9))* Manne, Joy.

Drewitz, Paul Aaron. Baby's Counting Book. Drewitz, Jessica Erin & Law, Susan L. Krevitsky, eds. 2019. (ENG.). 28p. (J). pap. 9.95 *(978-1-0723-3503-0(4))* Independently Published.

Drews, Judith. Lily Loves. Luftner, Kai. 2012. (ENG.). 32p. (J). (gr. -1-3). 16.95 *(978-1-897476-94-9(9))* Simply Read Bks. CAN. Dist: Ingram Publisher Services.

Dreyer, Laura. The ABC Bible Verse Book. Scherm, Deedra. 2007. (ENG.). 26p. (J). (gr. -1-3). bds. 8.99 *(978-1-934789-04-9(6))* Lemon Vision Productions.

—Cinco Panes y un Par de Peces: Una Historia de la Fe y de Dar. Scherm, Deedra. 2008. (SPA.). 20p. (J). (gr. -1-3). bds. 7.99 *(978-1-934789-06-3(2))* Lemon Vision Productions.

—Five Loaves & a Couple of Fish: A Story of Faith & Giving. Scherm, Deedra. 2007. (ENG.). 20p. 7.99 *(978-1-934789-01-8(1))* Lemon Vision Productions.

—Only One Me: A Sweet Little Rhyme to Help Your Light Shine. Scherm, Deedra. 2008. (ENG.). 22p. (J). (gr. -1-3). 7.99 *(978-1-934789-02-5(X))* Lemon Vision Productions.

—Solo uno Como Yo: Una Rima Dulce y Pequenita para Ayudar Hacer Brillar Tu Lucecita. Scherm, Deedra. 2008. (SPA.). 22p. (J). (gr. -1-3). 7.99 *(978-1-934789-05-6(4))* Lemon Vision Productions.

—The Whale & Jonah: A Story of Obedience & Forgiveness. Scherm, Deedra. 2007. (ENG.). 20p. 7.99 *(978-1-934789-00-1(3))* Lemon Vision Productions.

Driedemy, Joëlle. The Wolves Who Came for Dinner. Smallman, Steve. 2019. (ENG.). 32p. (J). (gr. -1-2). 17.99 *(978-1-68010-159-1(5))* Tiger Tales.

Driessen, Anita. The Night after Christmas. Hebler, Michael. 2010. (ENG.). 28p. (J). 8.99 *(978-0-615-39525-8(2)*, Night After Night Pubns., Inc.) Hebler, Michael.

Dringova, Irina. Mommys Are People, Too. Movitz, Katina. 2019. (ENG.). 26p. (J). pap. 13.99 *(978-1-0922-2364-5(9))* Independently Published.

Driver, Audrey. Timmy Turtle Teaches. Takara, Kathryn Waddell. 2012. 54p. pap. 29.95 *(978-0-9840204-3-0(8))* Pacific Raven Pr.

Drmacich-Ryan, Judy. Cefa's Big Adventure. Caton, Cristine. 2019. (Adventures of Cefa the Cat Ser.: Vol. 3). (ENG.). 42p. (J). pap. 9.95 *(978-1-0726-4011-0(2))* Independently Published.

Drogaitseva, Anastasia. The Freckle Monster. Caswell, Erika-Elizabeth. Faludi-Harpell, Julie, ed. 2015. (Freckles the Bunny Ser.: Vol. 6). (ENG.). 48p. (J). pap. ***(978-0-9920306-0-5(9))*** Caswell, Vickianne.

Drogaitseva, Anastasia. Freckles & the Cost of Popularity. Caswell, Vickianne. Faludi-Harpell, Julie, ed. 2016. (ENG.). (J). pap. *(978-1-988345-34-5(0))* Caswell, Vickianne.

—Freckles & the True Meaning of Christmas. Caswell, Vickianne. Faludi-Harpell, Julie, ed. 2016. (Freckles the Bunny Ser.: Vol. 4). (ENG.). (J). (gr. 1-4). pap. *(978-1-988345-35-2(9))* Caswell, Vickianne.

—Freckles Lends a Paw. Caswell, Vickianne. 4 Paws Games and Publishing, ed. 2016. (Freckles the Bunny Ser.: Vol. 3). (ENG.). (J). (gr. 1-4). pap. *(978-1-988345-36-9(7))* Caswell, Vickianne.

Droney, John. The Ghost Hunter & the Ghost of the Amazon Warrior. Kline, Trish & Donev, Mary. 2003. 96p. (J). per. 7.50 *(978-0-9717234-1-2(9))* Ghost Hunter Productions.

Dronsfield, Paul. The Bulldozer. 2009. (My Shiny Little Truck Bks.). (ENG.). 10p. (J). bds. 3.95 *(978-1-58117-858-6(1)*, Intervisual/Piggy Toes) Bendon, Inc.

—The Concrete Mixer. 2009. (My Shiny Little Truck Bks.). (ENG.). 10p. (J). bds. 3.95 *(978-1-58117-859-3(X)*, Intervisual/Piggy Toes) Bendon, Inc.

—The Digger. 2009. (My Shiny Little Truck Bks.). (ENG.). 10p. (J). bds. 3.95 *(978-1-58117-860-9(3)*, Intervisual/Piggy Toes) Bendon, Inc.

—The Dump Truck. 2009. (My Shiny Little Truck Bks.). (ENG.). 10p. (J). bds. 3.95 *(978-1-58117-861-6(1)*, Intervisual/Piggy Toes) Bendon, Inc.

—Pilot Your Own Deep-Sea Submarine. Trowell, Michelle. 2007. 22p. (J). (gr. -1-3). *(978-1-84666-352-9(0)*, Tide Mill Pr.) Top That! Publishing PLC.

—Rescue Helicopter. Top That Publishing Staff, ed. 2007. (Story Book Ser.). (ENG.). 33p. (J). (gr. -1). bds. *(978-1-84666-179-2(X)*, Tide Mill Pr.) Top That! Publishing PLC.

Dronzek, Laura. Birds. Henkes, Kevin. 2009. (ENG.). 32p. (J). (gr. -1-k). 17.99 *(978-0-06-136304-7(9))*; lib. bdg. 18.89 *(978-0-06-136305-4(7))* HarperCollins Pubs. (Greenwillow Bks.).

—Birds Board Book. Henkes, Kevin. 2017. (ENG.). 32p. (J). (gr. -1 — 1). bds. 7.99 *(978-0-06-257305-6(5)*, Greenwillow Bks.) HarperCollins Pubs.

—In the Middle of Fall. Henkes, Kevin. (ENG.). 40p. (J). (gr. -1-3). 2019. pap. 8.99 *(978-0-06-274724-2(X))*; 2017. 17.99 *(978-0-06-257311-7(X))* HarperCollins Pubs. (Greenwillow Bks.).

—In the Middle of Fall Board Book. Henkes, Kevin. 2018. (ENG.). 36p. (J). (gr. -1 — 1). bds. 8.99 *(978-0-06-274726-6(6)*, Greenwillow Bks.) HarperCollins Pubs.

—It Is Night. Rowand, Phyllis. 2014. (ENG.). 32p. (J). (gr. -1-3). 16.99 *(978-0-06-225024-7(8)*, Greenwillow Bks.) HarperCollins Pubs.

—Summer Song. Henkes, Kevin. 2020. (ENG.). 40p. (J). (gr. -1-3). 18.99 *(978-0-06-286613-4(3))*; lib. bdg. 19.89 *(978-0-06-286614-1(1))* HarperCollins Pubs. (Greenwillow Bks.).

—Tippy-Toe Chick, Go! Shannon, George. 2003. (ENG.). 32p. (J). (gr. -1-3). 17.99 *(978-0-06-029823-4(5)*, Greenwillow Bks.) HarperCollins Pubs.

—When Spring Comes. Henkes, Kevin. (ENG.). 40p. (J). (gr. -1-3). 2019. pap. 8.99 *(978-0-06-274167-7(5))*; 2016. 18.89 *(978-0-06-233140-3(X))* HarperCollins Pubs. (Greenwillow Bks.).

—When Spring Comes Board Book. Henkes, Kevin. 2018. (ENG.). 36p. (J). (gr. -1-k). bds. 7.99 *(978-0-06-274166-0(7)*, Greenwillow Bks.) HarperCollins Pubs.

—White Is for Blueberry. Shannon, George. 2005. 40p. (J). (gr. -1). lib. bdg. 17.89 *(978-0-06-029276-8(8))*; (ENG.). 17.99 *(978-0-06-029275-1(X)*, Greenwillow Bks.) HarperCollins Pubs.

—Winter Is Here. Henkes, Kevin. 2018. (ENG.). 40p. (J). (gr. -1-3). 17.99 *(978-0-06-274718-1(5))*; lib. bdg. 18.89 *(978-0-06-274719-8(3))* HarperCollins Pubs. (Greenwillow Bks.).

—Winter Is Here Board Book. Henkes, Kevin. 2019. (ENG.). 36p. (J). (gr. -1 — 1). bds. 8.99 *(978-0-06-274721-1(5)*, Greenwillow Bks.) HarperCollins Pubs.

Droop, Constanza. Felix & the Flying Suitcase Adventure. Langen, Annette. 2003. 47p. (J). 14.99 *(978-1-59384-035-8(7))* Parklane Publishing.

—Felix Explores Planet Earth. Langen, Annette. 2004. (Perfect for Earth Day Promotions! Ser.). 47p. (J). 14.99 *(978-1-59384-030-3(6))* Parklane Publishing.

D

—Felix Travels Back in Time. Langen, Annette. 2004. 40p. (J). 14.99 *(978-1-59384-032-7(2))* Parklane Publishing.

—Felix's Christmas Around the World. Langen, Annette. 2003. 40p. (J). 14.99 *(978-1-59384-036-5(5))* Parklane Publishing.

—Jesus Is Risen. Krenzer, Rolf. Maloney, Linda M., tr. from GER. 2005. 24p. (gr. -1-3). 14.95 *(978-0-8146-2764-8(1))* Liturgical Pr.

—Letters from Felix: A Little Rabbit on a World Tour. Langen, Annette. 2003. 47p. (J). 14.99 *(978-1-59384-034-1(9))* Parklane Publishing.

Droop, Constanza. Que? Como? Por Que?: Las Estaciones del Ano. Droop, Constanza. Caballero, D., tr. 2007. (Junior (Silver Dolphin) Ser.). 16p. (J). (gr. -1). *(978-970-718-492-3(2)*, Silver Dolphin en Español) Advanced Marketing, S. de R. L. de C. V.

Drotar. Eloy the Elk & His Desert Friends. Clapp. Clapp, ed. 2009. (J). pap. 9.95 *(978-0-9825181-0-6(2))* Arizona Elk Society.

Drotleff, David J. The Littlest Elf: Marvin Mcgee & the Candle of Fate. Snedeker, Erin. 2010. 44p. pap. 15.50 *(978-1-60911-194-6(X)*, Eloquent Bks.) Strategic Book Publishing & Rights Agency (SBPRA).

Drouin, Julie Saint-Onge, jt. illus. see Arseneau, Philippe.

Drouot, Lucile Danis. Philadelphia Monsters: A Search & Find Book. 2018. (ENG.). 22p. (J). (gr. -1). bds. 9.99 *(978-2-924734-09-4(6))* City Monsters Bks. CAN. Dist: Publishers Group West (PGW).

Drouot, Lucile Danis, jt. illus. see Mackay, Stephanie.

Drown, Eleanor J. The Wheelchair Adventures of Jeannie & the Wallpaper Children. Kraemer, Lillian Rosa. 2011. 150p. 40.95 *(978-1-258-08936-8(X))* Literary Licensing, LLC.

Drozd, Jerzy & Colon, Ernie. Warren Commission Report: A Graphic Investigation into the Kennedy Assassination. Mishkin, Dan. 2014. (ENG.). 160p. 29.95 *(978-1-4197-1230-2(6))*; pap. 17.95 *(978-1-4197-1231-9(4))* Abrams, Inc. (Abrams ComicArts).

Drucker, Susan. Kunu's Basket: A Story of Indian Island, 1 vol. Francis, Lee DeCora. 2012. (ENG.). 32p. (J). 16.95 *(978-0-88448-330-4(4))* Tilbury Hse. Pubs.

Druckman, Joan. Memory Emory & His Hiding Places. Druckman, Michael. 2006. 24p. (gr. -1-3). per. 10.99 *(978-1-59858-060-0(4))* Dog Ear Publishing, LLC.

Drummond, Allan. The Journey That Saved Curious George: The True Wartime Escape of Margret & H. A. Rey. Borden, Louise & Borden, Louise W. 2005. (Curious George Ser.). (ENG.). 80p. (J). (gr. 3-7). 17.99 *(978-0-618-33924-2(8)*, 581802) Houghton Mifflin Harcourt Publishing Co.

—The Journey That Saved Curious George: The True Wartime Escape of Margret & H. A. Rey. Borden, Louise W. 2010. (Curious George Ser.). (ENG.). 80p. (J). (gr. 3-7). pap. 8.99 *(978-0-547-41746-2(2)*, 1430026) Houghton Mifflin Harcourt Publishing Co.

—The Journey That Saved Curious George Young Readers Edition: The True Wartime Escape of Margret & H. A. Rey. Borden, Louise. 2016. (Curious George Ser.). (ENG.). 96p. (J). (gr. 3-7). pap. 7.99 *(978-0-544-76345-6(9)*, 1635105, HMH Books For Young Readers) Houghton Mifflin Harcourt Publishing Co.

—A Sporting Chance: How Paralympics Founder Ludwig Guttmann Saved Lives with Sports. Alexander, Lori. 2020. (ENG.). 128p. (J). (gr. 3-7). 17.99 *(978-1-328-58079-5(2)*, 1728624, HMH Books For Young Readers) Houghton Mifflin Harcourt Publishing Co.

Drummond, Allan. Energy Island. Drummond, Allan. 2015. (ENG.). (J). (gr. 1-5). lib. bdg. 18.60 *(978-1-62765-710-5(X))* Perfection Learning Corp.

—Energy Island: How One Community Harnessed the Wind & Changed Their World. Drummond, Allan. 2011. (ENG.). 40p. (J). (gr. 1-5). 18.99 *(978-0-374-32184-0(1)*, 900065067, Farrar, Straus & Giroux (BYR)) Farrar, Straus & Giroux.

—Energy Island: How One Community Harnessed the Wind & Changed Their World. Drummond, Allan. 2015. (ENG.). 40p. (J). (gr. 1-5). 8.99 *(978-1-250-05676-4(4)*, 900139047) Square Fish.

Drummond, Sarah. Raven & the Red Ball. 2013. (ENG.). 28p. (J). 9.95 *(978-0-7649-6609-5(X))* Pomegranate Communications, Inc.

Drummond, V. H. Carbonel: The King of the Cats. Sleigh, Barbara. (ENG.). 192p. (J). (gr. 4-7). 2018. pap. 9.99 *(978-1-68137-305-8(X)*, NYRB Kids); 2004. reprint ed. 16.95 *(978-1-59017-126-4(8)*, NYR Children's Collection) New York Review of Bks., Inc., The.

Drumond, Sergio. Little Dhonte Learns the Power of Believing in Himself. Heard, Linda. 2020. (ENG.). 56p. (J). pap. 12.00 ***(978-1-948747-69-1(3))*** J2B Publishing LLC.

Drumond, Sergio. Little Me. Crowder, Rebecca Stanley. 2019. (ENG.). 26p. (J). pap. 9.99 *(978-1-948747-37-0(5))* J2B Publishing LLC.

—Little Me. Crowder, Rebecca Stanley. 2019. (ENG.). 26p. (J). 18.99 *(978-1-948747-38-7(3))* J2B Publishing LLC.

—Pinto the Chisholm Pony: 150th Chisholm Trail Edition. Dutton, Stella. anniv. collector's ed. 2017. (ENG.). 62p. (J). (gr. -1-6). 39.99 *(978-0-9790832-9-7(X))* 405 Pubns.

Drumond, Sergio. Trudy Matoody: Espanol. Franco, Natalia, tr. 2020. (Trudy Matoody Espanol Ser.: Vol. 1). (SPA.). 36p. (J). pap. 10.95 ***(978-1-7097-0937-1(5))*** Independently Published.

Drumond, Sergio. Trudy Matoody Coloring & Activity Book. Ashford, Marcia McGee. 2019. (ENG.). 38p. (J). pap. 6.99 *(978-1-0746-4305-8(4))* Independently Published.

Druschel, Bob. Finny the Friendly Shark. Janacone, Matt. 2005. 40p. (J). per. 20.99 *(978-1-58939-655-5(3))* Virtualbookworm.com Publishing, Inc.

Druvert, Hélène. The Phantom of the Opera: Based on the Novel by Gaston Leroux. Amaury. Rosner, Gillian, tr. 2016. (ENG.). 40p. (J). (gr. k-2). 19.95 *(978-1-4197-2086-4(4)*, Abrams Bks. for Young Readers) Abrams, Inc.

Dry, Roland. The Pied Piper. Barkow, Henriette. 2004. 32p. (J). (ENG.). *(978-1-85269-990-1(6))*; (SOM & ENG.). pap. *(978-1-85269-995-6(7))*; (ENG & POR.). pap. *(978-1-85269-980-2(9))*; (ENG & POL.). pap. *(978-1-85269-975-8(2))*; (PAN & ENG.). pap. *(978-1-85269-970-3(1))*; (ENG & ITA.). pap. *(978-1-85269-965-9(5))*; (ENG & GUJ.). pap. *(978-1-85269-955-0(8))*; (ENG & GER.). pap. *(978-1-85269-950-5(7))*; (FRE & ENG.). pap. *(978-1-85269-945-1(0))*; (ENG & PER.). pap. *(978-1-85269-940-6(X))*; (ENG & CZE.). pap. *(978-1-85269-935-2(3))*; (ENG & ARA.). pap. *(978-1-85269-920-8(5))*; (URD & ENG.). pap. *(978-1-85269-916-1(7))*; (ENG & ALB.). pap. *(978-1-85269-915-4(9))*; (TUR & ENG.). pap. *(978-1-85269-911-6(6))*; (ENG & TAM.). pap. *(978-1-85269-906-2(X))*; (ENG & SPA.). pap. *(978-1-85269-901-7(9))* Mantra Lingua.

—Pied Piper. 2004. (J). E-Book incl. cd-rom *(978-1-84444-466-3(X))* Mantra Lingua.

Drzewiecki, Paul. Just Like Dad. Hiris, Monica. l.t. ed. 2003. (ENG.). 8p. (gr. k-1). pap. 7.95 *(978-1-879835-76-4(2)*, Kaeden Bks.) Kaeden Corp.

—My Native American School. Gould, Carol. l.t. ed. 2003. (ENG.). 16p. (gr. k-2). pap. 7.95 *(978-1-879835-77-1(0)*, Kaeden Bks.) Kaeden Corp.

—Snake Hunts for Lunch. Hoenecke, Karen. l.t. ed. 2005. (ENG.). 12p. (gr. k-2). pap. 7.95 *(978-1-57874-006-2(1)*, Kaeden Bks.) Kaeden Corp.

du Bois, William Pène. The Mousewife. Godden, Rumer. 2009. (ENG.). 56p. (J). (gr. -1-2). 16.95 *(978-1-59017-310-7(4)*, NYR Children's Collection) New York Review of Bks., Inc., The.

du Bois, William Pène. Twenty-One Balloons. du Bois, William Pène. 2005. 180p. (J). lib. bdg. 15.00 *(978-1-4242-2270-4(2))* Fitzgerald Bks.

du Fay, Laure. El Pedo Más Grande Del Mundo. Ordonez Cuadrado, Rafael. 2017. (SPA.). 48p. (J). (gr. -1-4). 16.95 *(978-84-945971-5-2(9))* NubeOcho Ediciones ESP. Dist: Consortium Bk. Sales & Distribution.

—The World's Biggest Fart. Ordonez Cuadrado, Rafael. 2017. (ENG.). 48p. (J). (gr. -1-4). 16.95 *(978-84-945971-4-5(0))* NubeOcho Ediciones ESP. Dist: Consortium Bk. Sales & Distribution.

Du Houx, E. M. Cornell. Seasons. Kroner, David & Du Houx, Ramona. 2007. 70p. (J). per. 6.95 *(978-1-882190-54-6(8))* Polar Bear & Co.

—Two Birds in a Box. Ouilette, K. T. Valliere-Denis. 2006. 59p. (J). per. 6.95 *(978-1-882190-55-3(6))* Polar Bear & Co.

—Wisdom of Bear. Barry, Holly et al. 2006. 63p. (J). per. 6.95 *(978-1-882190-50-8(5))* Polar Bear & Co.

du Houx, Emily. Madalynn the Monarch Butterfly & Her Quest to Michoacan. Haque, Mary Baca. Jones, Francisco Lancaster, tr. from ENG. 2003. (ENG & SPA.). 64p. pap. 14.00 *(978-1-882190-52-2(1))* Polar Bear & Co.

—A Voice for the Redwoods. Halter, Loretta. 2003. 64p. pap. 14.00 *(978-1-882190-66-9(1))* Polar Bear & Co.

du Houx, Emily C. Millicent the Magnificent. Hoffmann, Burton R. 2004. 64p. pap. 12.00 *(978-1-882190-68-3(8))* Polar Bear & Co.

du Houx, Ramona. Women Who Walk with the Sky. Levesque, Dawn Renee. 2003. 64p. pap. 14.00 *(978-1-882190-12-6(2))* Polar Bear & Co.

du Houx, Ramona & Cornell du Houx, Emily. Manitou, a Mythological Journey in Time. du Houx, Ramona et al. Cornell du Houx, Alex et al. unabr. ed. 2003. 224p. pap. 12.00 *(978-1-882190-77-5(7))* Polar Bear & Co.

Du, Jane. Finn & Remy Explore Dallas: An Illustrated Guidebook. Du, Jane. Rosamond, Jonathan. 2018. (ENG.). 56p. (J). 35.00 *(978-1-7322788-0-6(6))* Finn & Remy, LLC.

du Plessis, David. When Bat Was a Bird: And Other Animal Tales from Africa. Greaves, Nick. 2005. (ENG.). 144p. per. 11.50 *(978-1-86872-998-2(2))* Penguin Random House South Africa ZAF. Dist: Casemate Pubs. & Bk. Distributors, LLC.

Du Pont, Brittany. Chosen Last. Oehmichen, Ariel. 2012. 28p. pap. 9.99 *(978-1-937165-26-0(4))* Orange Hat Publishing.

—Invincible Me. Schmidt, Shawntay. 2013. 24p. pap. 8.99 *(978-1-937165-61-1(2))* Orange Hat Publishing.

Duarte, Amy. We Are the Trees. Taylor, Marian S. 2017. (ENG.). 36p. pap. 16.95 *(978-1-5043-7422-4(3)*, Balboa Pr.) Author Solutions, Inc.

Duarte, Gustavo. Dear Justice League. Northrop, Michael. 2019. (ENG.). 136p. (J). (gr. 2). pap. 9.99 *(978-1-4012-8413-8(2)*, DC Zoom) DC Comics.

Duarte, Gustavo. Monsters! & Other Stories. Duarte, Gustavo. Hahn, Sierra, ed. 2014. (ENG.). 152p. pap. 12.99 *(978-1-61655-309-8(X))* Dark Horse Comics.

Duarte, Gustavo, jt. illus. see Bustos, Natacha.

Duarte, Javier. El Carrito Del Pony. Gritts, Gail. 2020. (Reba & Katherine Ser.: Vol. 3). (ENG.). 44p. (J). pap. 9.99 ***(978-1-951772-06-2(7))*** Kids Bk. Pr.

—Hubert to the Rescue. Kocot, L. E. 2019. (ENG.). 70p. (J). pap. 11.00 ***(978-1-68111-339-5(2))*** Wasteland Pr.

Duarte, Javier. The Insomniant: A Human Holiday Story. Wooten, Neal. 2017. (ENG.). (J). pap. 3.99 *(978-1-61225-389-3(X))* Mirror Publishing.

Duarte, Javiera Andrea. La Obra de Arte M�s Hermosa. Mendez Gatica, Patricia. Nunez, Miguel Angel, ed. 2019. (SPA.). 48p. (J). pap. 12.99 ***(978-1-0869-1719-2(7))*** Independently Published.

Duarte-Oskrdal, Jasmine. Chuck the Ninja GOD: The Adventures of Charles the Cat with the Question Mark Tail. Singleton, Elaine Florence. Eckert, David W., ed. 2020. (Adventures of Charles the Cat with the Questio Ser.: Vol. 3). (ENG.). 48p. (J). ***(978-0-2288-2542-5(3))***; pap. ***(978-0-2288-2541-8(5))*** Tellwell Talent.

—More of the Adventures of Charles the Cat with the Question Mark Tail. Singleton, Elaine Florence. Eckert, David W., ed. 2020. (ENG.). 48p. (J). ***(978-0-2288-2465-7(6))***; pap. ***(978-0-2288-2464-0(8))*** Tellwell Talent.

Duarte, Pamela. An Egg-Stra Special Easter! (Barbie) Random House Staff. 2014. (ENG.). 48p. (J). (gr. -1-2). pap. 3.99 *(978-0-385-37319-7(8)*, Random Hse. Bks. for Young Readers) Random Hse. Children's Bks.

—Pink-Tastic! (Barbie) Man-Kong, Mary. 2016. (ENG.). 128p. (J). (gr. -1-2). pap. 5.99 *(978-1-101-93248-3(1)*, Golden Bks.) Random Hse. Children's Bks.

Duarte, Pamela, jt. illus. see Golden Books Staff.

Dub Leffler. Rocky & Louie. Walleystack, Phillip & Caisley, Raewyn. 2020. (ENG.). 32p. (J). (gr. -1-k). 24.99 ***(978-0-14-378652-8(0)***, Puffin) Penguin Random Hse. AUS. Dist: Independent Pubs. Group.

Dubac, Debra. The Itchy Little Musk Ox. Brown, Tricia. 2006. (ENG.). 32p. (J). (gr. -1-3). pap. 11.99 *(978-0-88240-614-5(0)*, Alaska Northwest Bks.) West Margin Pr.

—Musher's Night Before Christmas, 1 vol. Brown, Tricia. 2011. (Night Before Christmas Ser.). (ENG.). 32p. (J). (gr. k-3). 16.99 *(978-1-58980-843-0(6)*, Pelican Publishing) Arcadia Publishing.

Dubin, Jill. The Biggest Leaf Pile. Metzger, Steve. 2003. (J). *(978-0-439-55657-6(0))* Scholastic, Inc.

—I Can Cooperate! Parker, David. 2004. (J). *(978-0-439-62812-9(1))* Scholastic, Inc.

—I Can Share! Parker, David. 2005. (J). *(978-0-439-73587-2(4))* Scholastic, Inc.

—Over in a River: Flowing Out to the Sea, 1 vol. Berkes, Marianne. 2013. (ENG.). 32p. (J). (gr. -1-3). 16.95 *(978-1-58469-329-1(0))*; pap. 8.95 *(978-1-58469-330-7(4))* Sourcebooks, Inc. (Dawn Pubns.).

—Over in Australia: Amazing Animals down Under, 1 vol. Berkes, Marianne. 2011. (Over- Dawn Pub Ser.). (ENG.). 32p. (J). (gr. -1-1). 24.94 *(978-1-58469-135-8(2))* Dawn Pubns.

—Over in Australia: Amazing Animals down Under, 1 vol. Berkes, Marianne. 2011. (ENG.). 32p. (J). (gr. -1-2). pap. 8.99 *(978-1-58469-136-5(0)*, Dawn Pubns.) Sourcebooks, Inc.

—Over in the Arctic: Where the Cold Winds Blow, 1 vol. Berkes, Marianne. 2008. (ENG.). 32p. (J). (gr. -1-2). pap. 8.95 *(978-1-58469-110-5(7)*, Dawn Pubns.) Sourcebooks, Inc.

—Over in the Forest: Come & Take a Peek, 1 vol. Berkes, Marianne. 2012. (ENG.). 32p. (J). 16.95 *(978-1-58469-162-4(X))* Dawn Pubns.

—Over in the Forest: Come & Take a Peek. Berkes, Marianne. 2012. (ENG.). 32p. (J). (-2). pap. 8.95 *(978-1-58469-163-1(8)*, Dawn Pubns.) Sourcebooks, Inc.

—Over in the Grasslands: On an African Savanna, 1 vol. Berkes, Marianne. 2016. (ENG.). 32p. (J). (gr. -1-2). 16.95 *(978-1-58469-567-7(6)*, Dawn Pubns.) Sourcebooks, Inc.

—Over on a Desert: Somewhere in the World, 1 vol. Berkes, Marianne. 2018. (ENG.). 32p. (J). (-3). 16.95 *(978-1-58469-629-2(X)*, Dawn Pubns.) Sourcebooks, Inc.

—Over on a Mountain: Somewhere in the World, 1 vol. Berkes, Marianne. 2015. (ENG.). 32p. (J). (gr. -1-3). 16.95 *(978-1-58469-518-9(8)*, Dawn Pubns.) Sourcebooks, Inc.

—Samantha Stays Safe. Mishica, Clare. 2012. 32p. (J). pap. 8.00 *(978-1-935014-40-9(4))* Hutchings, John Pubs.

Dubisch, Michael. Blue Bay Mystery, 1 vol. Warner, Gertrude Chandler. 2009. (Boxcar Children Graphic Novels Ser.). (ENG.). 32p. (J). (gr. 3-8). 29.93 *(978-1-60270-591-3(7)*, 3674, Graphic Planet - Fiction) Magic Wagon.

—The Boxcar Children, 1 vol. Denton, Shannon Eric & Warner, Gertrude Chandler. 2009. (Boxcar Children Graphic Novels Ser.). (ENG.). 32p. (J). (gr. 3-8). lib. bdg. 29.93 *(978-1-60270-586-9(0)*, 3669, Graphic Planet - Fiction) Magic Wagon.

—Freya. Long, Christopher E. 2010. (Short Tales Norse Myths Ser.). (ENG.). 32p. (J). (gr. 1-4). 27.07 *(978-1-60270-565-4(8)*, 13459, Short Tales) Magic Wagon.

—The Lion & the Mouse. Denton, Shannon Eric & Aesop Enterprise Inc. Staff. 2010. (Short Tales Fables Ser.). (ENG.). 32p. (J). (gr. 1-4). 27.07 *(978-1-60270-554-8(2)*, 13409, Short Tales) Magic Wagon.

—Mike's Mystery, 1 vol. Warner, Gertrude Chandler. 2009. (Boxcar Children Graphic Novels Ser.). (ENG.). 32p. (J). (gr. 3-8). 29.93 *(978-1-60270-590-6(9)*, 3673, Graphic Planet - Fiction) Magic Wagon.

—Mystery Ranch, 1 vol. Warner, Gertrude Chandler. 2009. (Boxcar Children Graphic Novels Ser.). (ENG.). 32p. (J). (gr. 3-8). 29.93 *(978-1-60270-589-0(5)*, 3672, Graphic Planet - Fiction) Magic Wagon.

—Surprise Island, 1 vol. Worley, Rob M. & Warner, Gertrude Chandler. 2009. (Boxcar Children Graphic Novels Ser.). (ENG.). 32p. (J). (gr. 3-8). 29.93 *(978-1-60270-587-6(9)*, 3670, Graphic Planet - Fiction) Magic Wagon.

—Tyr. Long, Christopher E. 2010. (Short Tales Norse Myths Ser.). (ENG.). 32p. (J). (gr. 1-4). 27.07 *(978-1-60270-570-8(4)*, 13469, Short Tales) Magic Wagon.

—The Yellow House Mystery, 1 vol. Warner, Gertrude Chandler. 2009. (Boxcar Children Graphic Novels Ser.). (ENG.). 32p. (J). (gr. 3-8). 29.93 *(978-1-60270-588-3(7)*, 3671, Graphic Planet - Fiction) Magic Wagon.

Dubisch, Mike. Aladdin & the Magic Lamp. Denton, Shannon Eric. 2008. (Short Tales Fairy Tales Ser.). (ENG.). 32p. (J). (gr. 2-5). 27.07 *(978-1-60270-126-7(1)*, 590, Short Tales) Magic Wagon.

—The Amusement Park Mystery, 1 vol. Denton, Shannon Eric & Warner, Gertrude Chandler. 2010. (Boxcar Children Graphic Novels Ser.). (ENG.). 32p. (J). (gr. 3-8). 29.93 *(978-1-60270-718-4(9)*, 3679, Graphic Planet - Fiction) Magic Wagon.

—The Castle Mystery. Denton, Shannon Eric & Warner, Gertrude Chandler. 2010. (Boxcar Children Graphic Novels Ser.). (ENG.). 32p. (J). (gr. 3-8). 29.93 *(978-1-60270-720-7(0)*, 3681, Graphic Planet - Fiction) Magic Wagon.

—The Haunted Cabin Mystery. 2009. (Boxcar Children Graphic Novels Ser.: 9). (ENG.). 32p. (J). (gr. 1-5). pap. 6.99 *(978-0-8075-3180-8(4)*, 807531804) Whitman, Albert & Co.

—Medusa. Worley, Rob M. 2008. (Short Tales Greek Myths Ser.). (ENG.). 32p. (J). (gr. 3-6). 27.07 *(978-1-60270-137-3(7)*, 13439, Short Tales) Magic Wagon.

—Mike's Mystery, No. 5. 2009. (Boxcar Children Graphic Novels Ser.). (ENG.). 32p. (J). (gr. 2-5). 6.99 *(978-0-8075-2871-6(4))* Whitman, Albert & Co.

—The Pizza Mystery, 1 vol. Worley, Rob M. & Warner, Gertrude Chandler. 2010. (Boxcar Children Graphic Novels Ser.). (ENG.). 32p. (J). (gr. 3-8). 29.93 *(978-1-60270-719-1(7)*, 3680, Graphic Planet - Fiction) Magic Wagon.

—Puss in Boots. Worley, Rob M. 2008. (Short Tales Fairy Tales Ser.). (ENG.). 32p. (J). (gr. 2-5). 27.07 *(978-1-60270-130-4(X)*, 598, Short Tales) Magic Wagon.

—Sleeping Beauty. Denton, Shannon Eric. 2008. (Short Tales Fairy Tales Ser.). (ENG.). 32p. (J). (gr. 2-5). 27.07 *(978-1-60270-131-1(8)*, 600, Short Tales) Magic Wagon.

—Snowbound Mystery. Warner, Gertrude Chandler. 2009. (Boxcar Children Graphic Novels Ser.: 7). (ENG.). 32p. (J). (gr. 5-5). pap. 6.99 *(978-0-8075-7515-4(1)*, 807575151) Whitman, Albert & Co.

—Snowbound Mystery, 1 vol. Warner, Gertrude Chandler. 2010. (Boxcar Children Graphic Novels Ser.). (ENG.). 32p. (J). (gr. 3-8). 29.93 *(978-1-60270-715-3(4)*, 3676, Graphic Planet - Fiction) Magic Wagon.

—Tree House Mystery. 2009. (Boxcar Children Graphic Novels Ser.: 8). (ENG.). 32p. (J). (gr. 1-5). pap. 6.99 *(978-0-8075-8088-2(0)*, 807580880) Whitman, Albert & Co.

—The Wonderful Wizard of Oz: The Cyclone. Baum, L. Frank. 2008. (Short Tales Classics Ser.). (ENG.). 32p. (J). (gr. 2-6). 27.07 *(978-1-60270-124-3(5)*, 13399, Short Tales) Magic Wagon.

—The Yellow House Mystery, No. 3. Warner, Gertrude Chandler. 2009. (Boxcar Children Graphic Novels Ser.). (ENG.). 32p. (J). (gr. 2-5). 6.99 *(978-0-8075-2869-3(2))* Whitman, Albert & Co.

DuBois, Claude. The Old Man. V, Sarah. 2018. (ENG.). 72p. (J). (gr. k-5). 16.99 *(978-1-77657-191-8(6))* Gecko Pr. NZL. Dist: Lerner Publishing Group.

DuBois, Claude K. Me Quieres O No Me Quieres? Norac, Carl. 2007. (SPA.). 32p. (J). (gr. -1-k). 12.99 *(978-84-8470-155-2(7))* Corimbo, Editorial S.L. ESP. Dist: Lectorum Pubns., Inc.

Dubois, Claude K. Still My Grandma. Van Den Abeele, Veronique. 2007. (ENG.). 28p. (J). (gr. -1-5). 16.00 *(978-0-8028-5323-3(4)*, Eerdmans Bks For Young Readers) Eerdmans, William B. Publishing Co.

Dubois, Gérard. The Amazing Collection of Joey Cornell: Based on the Childhood of a Great American Artist. Fleming, Candace. 2018. 40p. (J). (gr. -1-3). 17.99 *(978-0-399-55238-0(3)*, Schwartz & Wade Bks.) Random Hse. Children's Bks.

Dubois, Gerard. Dorothea's Eyes: Dorothea Lange Photographs the Truth. Rosenstock, Barb. 2016. (ENG.). 40p. (J). (gr. 3-7). 17.99 *(978-1-62979-208-8(X)*, Calkins Creek) Boyds Mills Pr.

DuBois, Gérard. L' Ecuyere. Gingras, Charlotte. 2004. (Picture Bks.). (FRE.). 32p. (J). (gr. -1). *(978-2-89021-666-2(7))*; pap. *(978-2-89021-665-5(9))* Diffusion du livre Mirabel (DLM).

—Monsieur Marceau: Actor Without Words. Schubert, Leda. 2012. (ENG.). 40p. (J). (gr. -1-3). 17.99 *(978-1-59643-529-2(1)*, 900060853) Roaring Brook Pr.

Dubois, Lisa Lewis. Rugrats Vol. 1. Brown, Box & Naujokaitis, Pranas. Leopard, Whitney, ed. 2018. (ENG.). 112p. (J). (gr. 3). pap. 14.99 *(978-1-68415-176-9(7))* Boom! Studios.

Dubois, Liz Goulet. Abraham Lincoln. Bauer, Marion Dane. 2012. (My First Biography Ser.). (ENG.). 32p. (J). (gr. -1-k). pap. 3.99 *(978-0-545-34294-0(5))* Scholastic, Inc.

Dubois, Liz Goulet. Aaron's Bar Mitzvah. Dubois, Liz Goulet, tr. Rouss, Sylvia A. 2003. (J). 14.95 *(978-0-8246-0447-9(4))* David, Jonathan Pubs., Inc.

DuBois, Marc. Yala & Sunnie Meet Sam: A Gender Neutral Story in a New Age World. Watkin, Vikki. 2019. (ENG.). 24p. (J). ***(978-0-2288-2520-3(2))***; pap. ***(978-0-2288-2137-3(1))*** Tellwell Talent.

Dubois, Marie Thérèse. Agha the Eight-Mile Monster. Wilson-Timmons, Karen. rev. ed. 2012. (ENG.). 32p. (J). (gr. -1). 16.99 *(978-1-60887-124-7(X))* Mandala Publishing.

DuBosque, D. C. Draw Animals: Ocean - Rainforest - Desert - Grassland. 2015. 321p. (J). pap. *(978-1-943158-00-3(2)*, Blackbirch Pr., Inc.) Peel Productions, Inc.

Dubowski, Cathy East, et al. A Horse Named Seabiscuit. Dubowski, Cathy East & Dubowski, Mark. 2003. (All Aboard Reading: Station Stop 3 Ser.). (ENG.). 48p. (J). (gr. 2-4). 16.19 *(978-0-448-43342-4(7))* Penguin Young Readers Group.

Dubrovin, Barbara. Fantasy Fair: Bright Stories of Imagination. Dubrovin, Barbara. 2007. 128p. (J). pap. 17.50 *(978-0-9638339-6-9(0))* Storycraft Publishing.

Dubuc, Marianne. Mr. Postmouse's Rounds. Dubuc, Marianne. 2015. (ENG.). 24p. (J). (gr. -1-2). 17.95 *(978-1-77138-572-5(3))* Kids Can Pr., Ltd. CAN. Dist: Hachette Bk. Group.

DuBurke, Randy. The Bravest Girls in the World. George, Olivia. 2004. 32p. (J). lib. bdg. 15.00 *(978-1-4242-0241-6(8))* Fitzgerald Bks.

Duburke, Randy. Catching the Moon: The Story of a Young Girl's Baseball Dream, 1 vol. Hubbard, Crystal. 2005. (ENG.). 32p. (J). (gr. 1-5). 16.95 *(978-1-58430-243-8(7))* Lee & Low Bks., Inc.

DuBurke, Randy. Catching the Moon: The Story of a Young Girl's Baseball Dream, 1 vol. Hubbard, Crystal. 2005. (ENG.). 32p. (J). (gr. 1-5). pap. 10.95 *(978-1-60060-572-7(9)*, 4b1e4e62-3430-49d7-ad94-b8de2a1abf78) Lee & Low Bks., Inc.

—Game Changer: John Mclendon & the Secret Game. Coy, John. 2015. (ENG.). 32p. (J). (gr. 2-5). 17.99 *(978-1-4677-2604-7(4)*, 9781467726047); E-Book 27.99

(978-1-4677-8810-6(4)) Lerner Publishing Group. (Carolrhoda Bks.).
—Game Changer: John McLendon & the Secret Game. Coy, John. ed. 2015. (ENG.). 32p. (J). (gr. 2-5). E-Book 27.99 *(978-1-4677-9055-0(9)*, 9781467790550); E-Book 9.99 *(978-1-4677-9056-7(7)*, 9781467790567) Lerner Publishing Group. (Carolrhoda Bks.).
Duc, Nhan. Moon Moon Who Are You? Hose, Roxanne Samuels. 2019. (ENG.). 30p. (J). pap. 9.95 *(978-1-5333-9922-9(0))* CreateSpace Independent Publishing Platform.
Duchateau. The Fascinating Madame Tussaud. Follet, René. 2008. (Expresso Collection). (ENG.). 104p. pap. 19.95 *(978-1-905460-36-6(8))* CineBook GBR. Dist: National Bk. Network.
Duchess, Olivia. Who's Your Daddy? Discovering the Awesomest Daddy Ever. Harper, Lisa. 2018. (ENG.). 32p. (J). (gr. -1-2). 14.99 *(978-1-5359-0601-2(4)*, 005803938, B&H Kids) B&H Publishing Group.
Duck Egg Blue (Firm) Staff, et al. Colours & Shapes: Touch & Trace Early Learning Fun! Hewett, Angela. 2014. (ENG.). 26p. (J). bds. 13.50 *(978-1-84135-945-8(9))* Award Pubns. Ltd. GBR. Dist: Parkwest Pubns., Inc.
Ducker Signs Plus. Fisherman Jack Meets the River Creatures, 1 vol. Wilson, Elaine Moody. 2009. 40p. pap. 24.95 *(978-1-60836-967-6(6))* PublishAmerica, Inc.
Duckworth, Jeffrey. The Wonderful World of Cupcakes. Wise-Douglas, Terri. 2011. 28p. pap. 24.95 *(978-1-4626-3570-2(9))* America Star Bks.
Duckworth, Michelle. The Moon Throws a Birthday Party. Fischer, Kelly. 2011. 32p. (J). 19.50 *(978-1-58385-237-8(9))* ktf-writers-studio.
—The Most Beautiful Color of All. Fischer, Kelly. 2011. 36p. (J). 19.50 *(978-1-58385-281-1(6))* ktf-writers-studio.
Duckworth, Ruth. Saints Adrian & Natalie. Seco, Nina S. & Pilutik, Anastasia D. Date not set. (Cloud of Witnesses Ser.). (Orig.). (J). (gr. -1-1). pap. *(978-0-913026-29-8(8))* St. Nectarios Pr.
Duckworth, Tami Hohman. The Little Angel with Glasses. Naville, Tim. 2020. (ENG.). 36p. (J). pap. 12.95 ***(978-1-6747-7975-1(5))*** Independently Published.
Ducommon, Barbara. Nosy Noodles: The Curious Cow. Purkapile, Susan. 2006. 15p. (J). (gr. k-5). 13.95 *(978-1-930596-34-4(0))* Amherst Pr.
Ducommun, Barbara. Mumbles the Bumble Bee: The Bee Who Couldn't Buzz. Purkapile, Susan & Peck, Amy. 2008. (J). *(978-1-930596-87-0(1))* Amherst Pr.
Ducornet, Rikki. The Blue Rock Collection. Gander, Forrest. 2004. (ENG.). 128p. pap. 14.95 *(978-1-84471-045-4(9))* Salt Publishing GBR. Dist: SPD-Small Pr. Distribution.
Ducote, Billie Seaon. The Adventures of Artie Eco Part One: The Problem with Greed, 2 vols, Vol. 1. Ducote, Billie Seaon. 2007. (ENG.). 26p. (J). 18.95 *(978-0-9787597-5-9(3))* PureLight Pubns.
—The Adventures of Artie Eco Part Two: The Problem with Greed Artie Eco Goes to Dirtyville, 2 vols., Vol. 2. Ducote, Billie Seaon. 2007. 26p. (J). act. bk. ed. 18.95 *(978-0-9787597-1-1(0))* PureLight Pubns.
duCray, Belle Crow. Sparkle & the Light. Sullivan, Ayn Cates. 2013. (ENG.). (J). (gr. 1-4). 19.99 *(978-0-9884537-0-8(3))* Infinite Light Publishing.
Ducrest, Olivier. Love Is in the Air. Sam, Amélie & Trouillot, Virgile. 2009. (Groove High Ser.). 112p. (YA). (gr. 5-8). 15.75 *(978-1-60754-212-4(9)*, 1293915); pap. 15.25 *(978-1-60754-213-1(7)*, 1293915) Windmill Bks.
Ducy, George. Where Is Your Name? Ms. Sue. 2009. 24p. pap. 24.95 *(978-1-60672-711-9(7))* America Star Bks.
Duda, Jenny. Big Sister to an Angel. Hunt, Holly. 2019. (ENG.). 36p. (J). pap. *(978-1-7750123-1-3(X))* Pier 44 Pr.
Dudás, Gergely. Fox & Rabbit Make Believe (Fox & Rabbit Book #2) Ferry, Beth. 2020. (ENG.). 96p. (J). (gr. 1-4). 12.99 ***(978-1-4197-4687-1(1)*** , 1274601, Amulet Bks.) Abrams, Inc.
Dudás, Gergely. Bear's Merry Book of Hidden Things: Christmas Seek-And-Find. Dudás, Gergely. 2017. (ENG.). 32p. (J). (gr. -1-3). 14.99 *(978-0-06-257078-9(1))* HarperCollins Pubs.
—Bear's Spooky Book of Hidden Things: Halloween Seek-And-Find. Dudás, Gergely. 2018. (ENG.). 32p. (J). (gr. -1-3). pap. 8.99 *(978-0-06-257079-6(X))* HarperCollins Pubs.
—Bear's Springtime Book of Hidden Things. Dudás, Gergely. 2019. (ENG.). 32p. (J). (gr. -1-3). pap. 8.99 *(978-0-06-257080-2(3))* HarperCollins Pubs.
Duddle, Jonny. The Billionaire's Curse. Newsome, Richard. 2011. (Archer Legacy Ser.). (ENG.). 384p. (J). (gr. 3-7). pap. 7.99 *(978-0-06-194491-8(2)*, Waldon Pond Pr.) HarperCollins Pubs.
—The Emerald Casket. Newsome, Richard. 2012. (Archer Legacy Ser.). (ENG.). 384p. (J). (gr. 3-7). pap. 6.99 *(978-0-06-194493-2(9)*, Waldon Pond Pr.) HarperCollins Pubs.
—The Mask of Destiny, 3. Newsome, Richard. 2013. (Archer Legacy Ser.). (ENG.). 384p. (J). (gr. 3-7). pap. 6.99 *(978-0-06-194495-6(5))* HarperCollins Pubs.
—El Salteador de Caminos/Highway Robbery. Thompson, Kate. Acevedo, Adriana, tr. 2009. (SPA.). 100p. (J). (gr. 3-5). pap. *(978-84-263-7270-3(8))* Vives, Luis Editorial (Edelvives).
—We Give a Squid a Wedgie, 3. London, C. Alexander. 2013. (Accidental Adventure Ser.: 3). 400p. (J). (gr. 4-6). 22.44 *(978-0-14-242475-9(7)*, Puffin) Penguin Publishing Group.
—Will Gallows & the Rock Demon's Blood. Keilty, Derek. 2013. 288p. (J). (gr. 4-6). pap. 13.99 *(978-1-84939-535-9(7))* Andersen Pr. GBR. Dist: Independent Pubs. Group.
Duddle, Jonny. Gigantosaurus. Duddle, Jonny. 2014. (Gigantosaurus Ser.). (ENG.). 32p. (J). (gr. -1-2). 17.99 *(978-0-7636-7131-0(2)*, Templar) Candlewick Pr.
—The Jolley-Rogers & the Cave of Doom. Duddle, Jonny. 2016. (Jolley-Rogers Ser.). (ENG.). 160p. (J). (gr. 1-4). 6.99 *(978-0-7636-8909-4(2)*, Templar) Candlewick Pr.
—The Jolley-Rogers & the Ghostly Galleon. Duddle, Jonny. 2016. (Jolley-Rogers Ser.). (ENG.). 160p. (J). (gr. 1-4). pap. 6.99 *(978-0-7636-8910-0(6)*, Templar) Candlewick Pr.
—The Jolley-Rogers & the Monster's Gold. Duddle, Jonny. 2017. (Jolley-Rogers Ser.). (ENG.). 160p. (J). (gr. 1-4). pap. 6.99 *(978-0-7636-9292-6(1)*, Templar) Candlewick Pr.
Duddle, Jonny. The Jolley-Rogers & the Pirate Piper. Duddle, Jonny. 2020. (Jolley-Rogers Ser.). (ENG.). 160p. (J). (gr. 1-4). pap. 7.99 ***(978-1-5362-1236-5(9)***, Templar) Candlewick Pr.
Duddle, Jonny. King of Space. Duddle, Jonny. 2013. (ENG.). 44p. (J). (gr. -1-2). 15.99 *(978-0-7636-6435-0(9)*, Templar) Candlewick Pr.
—The Pirates of Scurvy Sands. Duddle, Jonny. 2018. (ENG.). 44p. (J). (gr. 1-4). 16.99 *(978-0-7636-9293-3(X)*, Templar) Candlewick Pr.
Dudek, Ilene. Little Ant & the Ice Cream Mystery. Dudek, Ilene. 2018. (ENG.). 28p. (J). (gr. -1-2). pap. 10.00 *(978-0-578-40624-4(1))* Dudek, Ilene.
Dudley, Dick, jt. illus. see Ely, Paul.
Dudley, Peter. Bungee down Under. Ford, Sally. 2004. 40p. (J). 14.95 *(978-1-931807-26-5(4))* Randall, Peter E. Pub.
Dudley, Rebecca, photos by. Hank Finds an Egg. Dudley, Rebecca. 2013. (ENG.). 40p. (J). 16.99 *(978-1-4413-1158-0(0))* Peter Pauper Pr. Inc.
—Hank Has a Dream. Dudley, Rebecca. 2014. (ENG., 32p. (J). 16.99 *(978-1-4413-1572-4(1)*, 9781441315724) Peter Pauper Pr. Inc.
Dudok de Wit, Michael. Oscar & Hoo. Theo. 2003. 32p. (J). (gr. -1-2). 17.99 *(978-0-00-710793-3(5)*, HarperCollins Children's Bks.) HarperCollins Pubs. Ltd. GBR. Dist: Trafalgar Square Publishing.
Dudziuk, Kasia. Catch It, Jess! & Cat Nap. Dale, Katie. 2020. (Early Bird Readers — Red (Early Bird Stories (tm)) Ser.). (ENG.). 32p. (J). (gr. -1-2). pap. 7.99 *(978-1-5415-8729-8(4)*, Lerner Pubns.) Lerner Publishing Group.
—The Nutcracker. Hay, Sam. 2017. (3D Colouring & Activity Ser.). (ENG.). 24p. (J). (gr. 1-4). pap. 11.99 *(978-1-4052-7912-3(5))* Egmont Bks., Ltd. GBR. Dist: Independent Pubs. Group.
Duendes Del Sur. Read & Learn Bible. American Bible Society. 2005. (American Bible Society Ser.). (ENG.). 544p. (J). (gr. -1-3). 14.99 *(978-0-439-65126-4(3))* Scholastic, Inc.
Duendes Del Sur Staff. Chill Out, Scooby-Doo!, 1 vol. Sander, Sonia. 2011. (Scooby-Doo! Ser.: No. 2). (ENG.). 32p. (J). (gr. k-4). lib. bdg. 27.07 *(978-1-59961-865-4(6)*, 13243, Picture Bk.) Spotlight.
—Fall Fright. Herman, Gail. 2005. (Hello Reader! Ser.). 32p. (J). pap. *(978-0-439-78358-3(5))* Scholastic, Inc.
—Lee y Aprende: La Biblia. Scholastic, Inc. Staff & American Bible Society Staff. Navarro, Carmen, tr. 2007. (American Bible Society Ser.). (SPA.). 544p. (J). (gr. -1-3). 14.99 *(978-0-545-00339-1(3)*, Scholastic en Espanol) Scholastic, Inc.
—Mean Green Mystery Machine: Junior Chapter Book. Gelsey, James. 2004. (Scooby Doo Ser.: Vol. 2). 48p. (J). mass mkt. 3.99 *(978-0-439-55711-5(9)*, Scholastic Paperbacks) Scholastic, Inc.
—Mi Primera Biblia. Scholastic, Inc. Staff & American Bible Society Staff. American Bible Society Staff, ed. 2008. (American Bible Society Ser.). (SPA.). 19p. (J). (gr. -1-k). bds. 9.99 *(978-0-545-05656-4(X)*, Scholastic en Espanol) Scholastic, Inc.
—My First Read & Learn Book of Prayers. Simon, Mary Manz. 2007. (American Bible Society Ser.). (ENG.). 40p. (J). (gr. -1-k). bds. 9.99 *(978-0-439-90632-6(6))* Scholastic, Inc.
—Scooby-Doo & the Hungry Ghost. Cunningham, Scott. 2005. (Scooby Doo Ser.). (ENG.). 12p. (J). (gr. -1-3). 8.99 *(978-0-439-74882-7(8))* Scholastic, Inc.
—Scooby-Doo & the Thanksgiving Terror, 1 vol. Balaban, Mariah. 2011. (Scooby-Doo! Ser.: No. 2). (ENG.). 24p. (J). (gr. k-4). lib. bdg. 27.07 *(978-1-59961-870-8(2)*, 13248, Picture Bk.) Spotlight.
—A Scooby-Rific Reader. Herman, Gail. 2005. (Scooby Doo Ser.). 290p. (J). *(978-0-681-15349-3(0))* Scholastic, Inc.
Duezakin, Akin. Questions Asked. Gaarder, Jostein. Bartlett, Don, tr. 2017. (ENG.). 72p. (J). (gr. -1-2). 14.00 *(978-0-914671-66-4(9)*, Elsewhere Editions) Steerforth Pr.
DuFalla, Anita. Alex in Numberland. Howard, Annabelle. ed. 2004. (Reader's Theater Ser.). (J). pap. *(978-1-4108-2303-8(2)*, A23032) Benchmark Education Co.
—Angry. Collins, Savina. 2017. (I Have Feelings Ser.). (ENG.). 24p. (gr. -1-1). 29.93 *(978-1-68342-141-2(8)*, 9781683421412); pap. 8.95 *(978-1-68342-183-2(3)*, 9781683421832) Rourke Educational Media.
—A Bad Case of Tattle Tongue. Cook, Julia. 2008. 32p. (J). (gr. -1). pap. 9.95 *(978-1-931636-86-5(9))* National Ctr. For Youth Issues.
—Best Birthday. Cleland, JoAnn. 2011. (Little Birdie Readers Ser.). (ENG.). 24p. (gr. k-1). 29.93 *(978-1-61741-798-6(X)*, 9781617417986) Rourke Educational Media.
—Blackout. Pugliano-Martin, Carol. ed. 2004. (Reader's Theater Ser.). (J). pap. *(978-1-4108-2298-7(2)*, A22982) Benchmark Education Co.
—But That Rule Doesn't Apply to Me. Cook, Julia. 2016. (Responsible Me! Ser.: Vol. 3). (ENG.). 32p. (J). 10.95 *(978-1-934490-98-3(9))* Boys Town Pr.
—Cliques Just Don't Make Cents. Cook, Julia. 2012. (ENG.). 32p. (J). pap. 10.95 *(978-1-934490-39-6(3))* Boys Town Pr.
—Five Little Monkeys (Cinco Monitos) Wallace, Rhea. 2016. (Nursery Rhymes Ser.). (ENG & SPA.). 12p. (gr. -1-k). bds. 5.95 *(978-1-68342-015-6(2)*, 9781683420156) Rourke Educational Media.
—Gas Happens! What to Do When It Happens to You. Cook, Julia. 2015. (ENG.). 32p. (J). pap. 10.95 *(978-1-934490-76-1(8)*, 1387428) Boys Town Pr.
—Grandpa Comes to First Grade. Robertson, J. Jean. 2011. (Little Birdie Readers Ser.). (ENG.). 24p. (gr. k-1). 29.93 *(978-1-61741-800-6(5)*, 9781617418006); pap. 8.95 *(978-1-61236-004-1(1)*, 9781612360041) Rourke Educational Media.
DuFalla, Anita. Grief Is Like a Snowflake. Cook, Julia. 2011. (ENG.). (J). (gr. k-3). 9.95 ***(978-1-931636-78-0(8))*** National Ctr. For Youth Issues.
DuFalla, Anita. Happy. Collins, Savina. 2017. (I Have Feelings Ser.). (ENG.). 24p. (gr. -1-1). 29.93 *(978-1-68342-143-6(4)*, 9781683421436); pap. 8.95 *(978-1-68342-185-6(X)*, 9781683421856) Rourke Educational Media.
—How Many Bites? Robertson, J. Jean. ed. 2011. (Little Birdie Readers Ser.). (ENG.). 24p. (gr. k-1). pap. 8.95 *(978-1-61236-005-8(X)*, 9781612360058) Rourke Educational Media.
—I Want to Be the Only Dog! Cook, Julia. 2015. (ENG.). 32p. (J). pap. 10.95 *(978-1-934490-86-0(5))* Boys Town Pr.
—If You're Happy & You Know It (Si Te Sientes Bien Contento) Wallace, Rhea. 2016. (Nursery Rhymes Ser.). (ENG & SPA.). 12p. (gr. -1-k). bds. 5.95 *(978-1-68342-009-5(8)*, 9781683420095) Rourke Educational Media.
—I'm the Boss. Williams, Sam. 2012. (Little Birdie Bks.). (ENG.). 24p. (gr. k-1). pap. 8.95 *(978-1-61810-297-3(4)*, 9781618102973) Rourke Educational Media.
—It's My Turn. Williams, Sam. 2012. (Little Birdie Bks.). (ENG.). 24p. (gr. k-1). pap. 8.95 *(978-1-61810-296-6(6)*, 9781618102966) Rourke Educational Media.
—It's You & Me Against the Pee... & the Poop, Too! Cook, Julia & Jana, Laura. 2011. 32p. (gr. -1). pap. 9.95 *(978-1-931636-75-9(3))* National Ctr. For Youth Issues.
Dufalla, Anita. The Judgmental Flower. Cook, Julia. 2016. (ENG.). 32p. (J). pap. 10.95 *(978-1-944882-05-1(7))* Boys Town Pr.
DuFalla, Anita. Keep Your Chin Up. Hord, Colleen. 2012. (Little Birdie Bks.). (ENG.). 24p. (gr. 1-2). pap. 8.95 *(978-1-61810-315-4(6)*, 9781618103154) Rourke Educational Media.
—The King's New Crown. Howard, Annabelle. ed. 2004. (Reader's Theater Ser.). (J). pap. *(978-1-4108-2296-3(6)*, A22966) Benchmark Education Co.
—Monkey Business. Robertson, J. Jean. 2012. (Little Birdie Bks.). (ENG.). 24p. (gr. 2-3). pap. 8.95 *(978-1-61810-322-2(9)*, 9781618103222) Rourke Educational Media.
—My Name Is Not... Robertson, J. Jean. 2012. (Little Birdie Bks.). (ENG.). 24p. (gr. 1-2). pap. 8.95 *(978-1-61810-320-8(2)*, 9781618103208) Rourke Educational Media.
Dufalla, Anita. The Pattern Hike, 6 vols. Romer, Ruth. ed. 2004. (Reader's Theater Ser.). (J). pap. *(978-1-4108-2290-1(7)*, A22907) Benchmark Education Co.
DuFalla, Anita. Peer Pressure Gauge. Cook, Julia. 2013. (ENG.). 32p. (J). pap. 10.95 *(978-1-934490-48-8(2))* Boys Town Pr.
—The Porch Swing. Butler, Dori Hillestad. Flounders, Anne, ed. ed. 2004. (Reader's Theater Ser.). (J). pap. *(978-1-4108-2246-8(X)*, A2246X) Benchmark Education Co.
Dufalla, Anita. The Procrastinator, no. 5. Cook, Julia. 2017. (Responsible Me! Ser.: 5). (ENG.). 32p. (J). pap. 10.95 *(978-1-944882-09-9(X))* Boys Town Pr.
DuFalla, Anita. Sad. Collins, Savina. 2017. (I Have Feelings Ser.). (ENG.). 24p. (gr. -1-1). 29.93 *(978-1-68342-142-9(6)*, 9781683421429); pap. 8.95 *(978-1-68342-184-9(1)*, 9781683421849) Rourke Educational Media.
—Scared. Collins, Savina. 2017. (I Have Feelings Ser.). (ENG.). 24p. (gr. -1-1). 29.93 *(978-1-68342-140-5(X)*, 9781683421405); pap. 8.95 *(978-1-68342-182-5(5)*, 9781683421825) Rourke Educational Media.
—Sumac & the Magic Lake. ed. 2004. (Reader's Theater Ser.). (J). pap. *(978-1-4108-2291-8(5)*, A22915) Benchmark Education Co.
—Swim for It! Greve, Meg. 2011. (Little Birdie Readers Ser.). (ENG.). 24p. (gr. k-1). 29.93 *(978-1-61741-805-1(6)*, 9781617418051) Rourke Educational Media.
—Table Talk: A Book about Table Manners. Cook, Julia. 2016. (Building Relationships Ser.: Vol. 7). (ENG.). 32p. (J). pap. 10.95 *(978-1-934490-97-6(0))* Boys Town Pr.
—Table Wars! Steinkraus, Kyla. 2012. (Little Birdie Bks.). (ENG.). 24p. (gr. 2-3). pap. 8.95 *(978-1-61810-330-7(X)*, 9781618103307) Rourke Educational Media.
—Tease Monster: (a Book about Teasing vs. Bullying) Cook, Julia. 2013. (Building Relationships Ser.). (ENG.). 32p. (J). pap. 10.95 *(978-1-934490-47-1(4))* Boys Town Pr.
—Technology Tail: A Digital Footprint Story. Cook, Julia. 2017. (ENG.). 32p. (J). (gr. 1-6). pap. 10.95 *(978-1-944882-13-6(8))* Boys Town Pr.
Dufalla, Anita. Thanks for the Feedback, I Think. Cook, Julia. 2013. (ENG.). 32p. (J). pap. 10.95 *(978-1-934490-49-5(0))* Boys Town Pr.
DuFalla, Anita. That's Not Fair! Reed, Jennifer. 2012. (Little Birdie Bks.). (ENG.). 24p. (gr. 1-2). pap. 8.95 *(978-1-61810-309-3(1)*, 9781618103093); lib. bdg. 29.93 *(978-1-61810-176-1(5)*, 9781618101761) Rourke Educational Media.
Dufalla, Anita. Well, I Can Top That! Cook, Julia. 2014. (ENG.). 32p. (J). pap. 10.95 *(978-1-934490-57-0(1))* Boys Town Pr.
DuFalla, Anita. Who's Right. Picou, Lin. 2012. (Little Birdie Bks.). (ENG.). 24p. (gr. 2-3). pap. 8.95 *(978-1-61810-323-9(7)*, 9781618103239) Rourke Educational Media.
DuFalla, Anita, jt. illus. see Heiser, Aline.
Dufey, Alexandra. What Great Music! Classical Selections to Hear & to See. Apostoli, Andrea, ed. 2011. (ENG.). 48p. (J). (-1). pap. 19.95 *(978-1-57999-841-7(0))* G I A Pubns., Inc.
Duffek, Kim Kanoa. Victor el Zopilote Renuente! Hanson, Jonathan. 2012. 36p. (J). pap. 16.95 *(978-1-886679-46-7(0))* Arizona Sonora Desert Museum Pr.
Duffour, Jean-Pierre, jt. illus. see Avril, Francois.
Dufft, Sanne. Bear Child, 30 vols. Mead, Geoff. 2018. (ENG.). 32p. (J). 17.95 *(978-1-78250-476-4(1))* Floris Bks. GBR. Dist: Consortium Bk. Sales & Distribution.
—The Sand Elephant, 40 vols. Hermann, Rinna. 2020. (ENG.). 28p. (J). 17.95 *(978-1-78250-615-7(2))* Floris Bks. GBR. Dist: Consortium Bk. Sales & Distribution.
—The Shepherd Boy & the Christmas Gifts, 44 vols. Hilberts, Aly. 2017. Orig. Title: Nathan, de Kleine Herder. (ENG.). 32p. (J). 17.95 *(978-1-78250-438-2(9))* Floris Bks. GBR. Dist: Consortium Bk. Sales & Distribution.
Dufft, Sanne. The Night Lion. Dufft, Sanne. 2018. Orig. Title: Magnus und der Nachtlöwe. (ENG.). 32p. (J). (gr. -1-k). 15.95 *(978-1-77278-041-3(3))* Pajama Pr. CAN. Dist: Ingram Publisher Services.
Duffy, Bunny. Die Dohlen Vom Dannebergpark: Das Kleine Mädchen, das Nicht Sprechen Wollte. Platzer, Kathryn. 2018. (GER.). 44p. (J). 25.95 *(978-1-942209-51-5(7))* Bellastoria Pr.
—The Jackdaws of Danneberg Park: The Little Girl Who Wouldn't Speak. Platzer, Kathryn. 2018. (ENG.). 44p. (J). 25.95 *(978-1-942209-50-8(9))* Bellastoria Pr.
Duffy, Ciaran. Gulliver's Travels. Ladybird Books Staff & Swift, Jonathan. 2015. (Ladybird Classics Ser.). 72p. (J). (gr. 1-3). 10.99 *(978-1-4093-1127-0(9))* Penguin Bks., Ltd. GBR. Dist: Independent Pubs. Group.
Duffy, Jackie. A Broom for Ma. Cable, Rhonda. 2019. (ENG.). 30p. (J). (gr. k-6). 14.99 *(978-0-578-52955-4(6))* Monday Creek Publishing.
Duffy, Katherine. Twinkle, Twinkle Little Star. Taylor, Jane. 2016. (ENG.). 32p. (J). (gr. -1-k). pap. 9.99 *(978-1-5324-0073-5(X))* Xist Publishing.
Duffy, Spencer. Daddy's Wish. Smith, Brent. 2019. (ENG.). 52p. (J). pap. *(978-1-5255-4175-9(7))* FriesenPress.
Duforu, Sebastian. El Nino Envuelto. Bornemann, Elsa. 2003. (SPA.). 176p. (YA). (gr. 5-8). pap. 13.95 *(978-950-511-623-2(3))* Alfaguara S.A. de Ediciones ARG. Dist: Santillana USA Publishing Co., Inc.
DuFulla, Anita. Decibella & Her 6-Inch Voice. Cook, Julia. 2014. (ENG.). 32p. (J). pap. 10.95 *(978-1-934490-58-7(X))* Boys Town Pr.
—Hygiene... You Stink! Cook, Julia. 2014. (ENG.). 32p. (J). pap. 10.95 *(978-1-934490-62-4(8))* Boys Town Pr.
Dugan, Alan. Grandma Can You Tell Me. Butcher, A D. 2007. 16p. per. 10.95 *(978-1-4327-1316-4(7))* Outskirts Pr., Inc.
Dugan, Karen. Camping with the President. Wadsworth, Ginger. 2009. (ENG.). 32p. (J). (gr. 4-7). 16.99 *(978-1-59078-497-6(9)*, Calkins Creek) Boyds Mills Pr.
—Christmas USA. Lankford, Mary D. 2006. 48p. (J). (gr. 3-7). 16.99 *(978-0-688-15012-9(8)*, Collins) HarperCollins Pubs.
—In the Spin of Things: Poetry of Motion. Dotlich, Rebecca Kai. 2010. (ENG.). 32p. (J). (gr. k-2). pap. 11.95 *(978-1-59078-828-8(1)*, Wordsong) Boyds Mills Pr.
—Marie Curie, Brave Scientist. Mattern, Joanne & Brandt, Keith. 2005. 45p. (J). *(978-0-439-80153-9(2))* Scholastic, Inc.
—Mazes Around the World. Lankford, Mary D. 2008. 26p. (J). *(978-0-688-16519-2(2)*, Collins) HarperCollins Pubs. Ltd.
—When Riddles Come Rumbling: Poems to Ponder. Dotlich, Rebecca Kai. 2013. (ENG.). 32p. (J). (gr. 1-4). pap. 7.95 *(978-1-62091-031-3(4)*, Wordsong) Boyds Mills Pr.
Dugan, Karen. Always Blue for Chicu. Dugan, Karen. 2010. (ENG.). 32p. (J). (gr. k-2). 16.95 *(978-0-940719-09-5(6))* Gryphon Pr., The.
Duggan, John M. The Action-Packed Book of Adventure Doodles: 187 Fun & Exciting Drawings You Can Finish Yourself. 2009. (ENG.). 192p. (J). (gr. -1-3). pap. 12.95 *(978-1-56975-724-6(0))* Ulysses Pr.
Duggan, Micheal. Mi & Two. Soto, Manuel. 2008. 27p. pap. 24.95 *(978-1-60610-877-2(8))* America Star Bks.
Duggins, Peat. Grendel Gander the Sinister Goose. Homan, Michael. 2012. 48p. pap. 14.95 *(978-1-60808-049-6(8)*, WriteLife Publishing) Boutique of Quality Books Publishing Co., Inc.
Dugin, Andrei, jt. illus. see Dugina, Olga.
Dugina, Olga & Dugin, Andrei. Dragon Feathers, 20 vols. 2010. Orig. Title: Die Drachenfedern. (ENG.). 24p. (J). (gr. k-3). 17.95 *(978-0-86315-774-5(2))* Floris Bks. GBR. Dist: Consortium Bk. Sales & Distribution.
Duhameau, Élodie. Christmas Countdown Gift Set: Storybook & Elf Plush Toy. Thompson, Kim. 2018. (ENG.). 48p. (J). (gr. -1). 19.99 *(978-2-924786-72-7(X)*, CrackBoom! Bks.) Chouette Publishing CAN. Dist: Publishers Group West (PGW).
—Santa's Countdown to Christmas: 24 Days of Stories. 2017. 56p. (J). (gr. -1). 14.95 *(978-2-924786-05-5(3)*, CrackBoom! Bks.) Chouette Publishing CAN. Dist: Publishers Group West (PGW).
Duhig, Lee & Weltjens, Jochen, photos by. Posefile, Vol. 1. 2003. (ENG., 192p. (YA). pap. 22.95 *(978-0-9728978-1-5(X)*, a0780cb0-70da-4cb8-8e0c-a0bd8d08468b) Antarctic Pr., Inc.
Duis, Laura. Jasper. Groce, Michelle. 2003. 174p. (J). 17.95 *(978-0-9708972-6-8(X))* Novello Festival Pr.
Duivenvoorden, Yvonne, photos by. What's for Lunch?, 1 vol. Curtis, Andrea. 2012. (ENG.). 40p. (J). (gr. 6-8). pap. 12.95 *(978-0-88995-482-3(8)*, 3da1f673-0880-4ae7-a1d4-37982aa5ff88) Trifolium Bks., Inc. CAN. Dist: Firefly Bks., Ltd.
Duke, Barbara, jt. illus. see Phillips-Duke, Barbara Jean.
Duke, Jenny. Where Did You Go Today? Duke, Jenny. 2019. (Child's Play Library). 32p. (J). *(978-1-78628-201-9(1))*; pap., pap. *(978-1-78628-200-2(3))* Child's Play International Ltd.
Duke, Kate. Mr. Big Brother. Hooks, William H. 2015. (ENG.). 34p. (J). pap. 11.95 *(978-1-899694-58-7(7)*, ipicturebooks) ibooks, Inc.
—One Saturday Evening. Baker, Barbara. 2007. (J). *(978-0-525-47850-8(7)*, Dutton Juvenile) Penguin Publishing Group.
Duke, Kate. In the Rainforest. Duke, Kate. 2014. (Let's-Read-And-Find-Out Science 2 Ser.). (ENG.). 40p. (J). (gr. -1-3). pap. 5.99 *(978-0-06-445197-0(6))* HarperCollins Pubs.

D

Duke, Marion. The Pipeline C. Y. O'Connor Built. LeFroy, Joy & Frylinck, Diana. 2003. 40p. 22.50 *(978-1-920731-60-1(1))* Fremantle Pr. AUS. Dist: Independent Pubs. Group.

—Trumpet's Kittens. Polizzotto, Carolyn & Spinks, Sarah. 2003. 32p. (YA). 22.50 *(978-1-86368-331-9(3))* Fremantle Pr. AUS. Dist: Independent Pubs. Group.

Dukes, Rachel & Yan, Edison. Summer Brain Quest: Between Grades 1 And 2. Butler, Megan et al. 2017. (Summer Brain Quest Ser.). (ENG.). 160p. (J). (gr. 1-2). pap. 12.95 *(978-0-7611-8917-6(3)*, 18917) Workman Publishing Co., Inc.

Dulac, Edmund. Aladdin & the Wonderful Lamp. Housman, Laurence. 2019. (ENG.). 96p. (J). (gr. 1-6). 19.95 *(978-0-486-83241-8(4))* Dover Pubns., Inc.

—Dulac's Fairy Tale Illustrations in Full Color. Menges, Jeff A., ed. 2004. (Dover Fine Art, History of Art Ser.). (ENG.). 64p. pap. 12.95 *(978-0-486-43669-2(1))* Dover Pubns., Inc.

—The Sleeping Beauty & Other Fairy Tales. 2011. (Calla Editions Ser.). (ENG.). 208p. 35.00 *(978-1-60660-019-1(2))* Dover Pubns., Inc.

—The Snow Queen. Andersen, Hans. 2012.Tr. of ??????? ????????. (J). *(978-1-59583-459-1(1))* Laughing Elephant.

Dulaney, Debbie, jt. illus. see Evans, Rose Grier.

Dulemba, Elizabeth. Crow Not Crow. 1 vol. Yolen, Jane & Stemple, Adam. 2018. (ENG.). 36p. (J). (gr. k-5). 15.95 *(978-1-943645-31-2(0)*, 9ee82963-2c8c-462b-af8e-8af0b8342159, Cornell Lab Publishing Group, The) WunderMill, Inc.

Dulemba, Elizabeth O. Glitter Girl & the Crazy Cheese. Hollon, Frank Turner et al. 2006. (ENG.). 32p. (J). (gr. -1-3). *(978-1-59692-137-5(4))* MacAdam/Cage Publishing, Inc.

—Merbaby's Lullaby. Yolen, Jane. 2019. (ENG.). 24p. (J). (— 1). bds. 9.99 *(978-1-5344-4317-4(7)*, Little Simon) Little Simon.

—The Prince's Diary. Ting, Renee. 2005. (Prince's Diary Ser.). 32p. (J). (gr. -1-3). 16.95 *(978-1-885008-27-5(9)*, Shen's Bks.) Lee & Low Bks., Inc.

—The Twelve Days of Christmas in Georgia. Spain, Susan Rosson. (Twelve Days of Christmas in America Ser.). (J). (-k). 2018. 22p. bds. 7.95 *(978-1-4549-2995-6(2))*; 2010. 40p. 12.95 *(978-1-4027-7008-1(1))* Sterling Publishing Co., Inc.

Dulemba, Elizabeth O. Soap, Soap, Soap. Dulemba, Elizabeth O. 2010. (ENG.). 32p. (J). (gr. -1-3). pap. 7.95 *(978-1-934960-65-3(9)*, Raven Tree Pr.,Csi) Continental Sales, Inc.

Dulin, Dorothy. The Fairy Babies. Smith, Laura Rountree. 2011. 126p. 40.95 *(978-1-258-09063-0(5))* Literary Licensing, LLC.

Dull, Dennis Stanley. Baby Basics & Beyond: ABC's, 123's & Shapes. Dull, Dennis Stanley. 2nd ed. 2004. (J). *(978-0-9717475-4-8(7))* Laurel Valley Graphics, Inc.

Dullaghan, Penelope. Max Attacks. Appelt, Kathi. 2019. (ENG.). 40p. (J). (gr. -1-3). 18.99 *(978-1-4814-5146-8(4)*, Atheneum/Caitlyn Dlouhy Books) Simon & Schuster Children's Publishing.

Dumas, Philippe. Adam & Thomas. Appelfeld, Aharon. Green, Jeffrey M., tr. 2017. 160p. (J). (gr. 3-7). pap. 14.95 *(978-1-60980-744-3(8)*, Triangle Square) Seven Stories Pr.

Dumas, Ryan. Art of the Ninja: Earth. Perkins, T. J. 2011. (Shadow Legacy Ser.: 1). (YA). 19.95 *(978-1-60975-039-8(X))* Silver Leaf Bks., LLC.

Dumm, Brian. Henry & Hala Build a Haiku. Higgins, Nadia. 2011. (Poetry Builders Ser.). 32p. (J). (gr. 2-4). lib. bdg. 25.27 *(978-1-59953-435-0(5))* Norwood Hse. Pr.

—The Little Runaway. Hillert, Margaret. 21st ed. 2016. (BeginningtoRead Ser.). (ENG.). 32p. (J). (gr. -1-2). pap. 11.94 *(978-1-60357-942-1(7))*; (gr. k-2). 22.60 *(978-1-59953-801-3(6))* Norwood Hse. Pr.

—Piper the Elf Trains Santa. Driscoll, Colleen. 2012. (ENG.). 32p. (J). 16.95 *(978-0-938467-56-4(5))* Headline Bks., Inc.

Dumm, Brian Caleb. April, 1 vol. Kesselring, Mari. 2009. (Months of the Year Ser.). (ENG.). 24p. (J). (gr. k-2). 27.07 *(978-1-60270-631-6(X)*, 11569, Looking Glass Library) Magic Wagon.

—Firefighters at Work, 1 vol. Kenney, Karen L. 2009. (Meet Your Community Workers Ser.). (ENG.). 32p. (J). (gr. k-4). 28.50 *(978-1-60270-648-4(4)*, 11404, Looking Glass Library) Magic Wagon.

—The Legend of Bigfoot, 1 vol. Troupe, Thomas Kingsley. 2010. (Legend Has It Ser.). (ENG.). 32p. (J). (gr. 2-4). lib. bdg. 27.99 *(978-1-4048-6032-2(0)*, Picture Window Bks.) Capstone.

—Librarians at Work, 1 vol. Kenney, Karen Latchana. 2009. (Meet Your Community Workers Ser.). (ENG.). 32p. (J). (gr. k-4). 28.50 *(978-1-60270-649-1(2)*, 11406, Looking Glass Library) Magic Wagon.

—Life on the Mayflower, 1 vol. Gunderson, Jessica. 2011. (Thanksgiving Ser.). (ENG.). 24p. (J). (gr. k-3). pap. 7.95 *(978-1-4048-6719-2(8)*, Picture Window Bks.) Capstone.

—Mail Carriers at Work, 1 vol. Kenney, Karen Latchana. 2009. (Meet Your Community Workers Ser.). (ENG.). 32p. (J). (gr. k-4). 28.50 *(978-1-60270-650-7(6)*, 11408, Looking Glass Library) Magic Wagon.

—March, 1 vol. Kesselring, Mari. 2009. (Months of the Year Ser.). (ENG.). 24p. (J). (gr. k-2). 27.07 *(978-1-60270-630-9(1)*, 11567, Looking Glass Library) Magic Wagon.

—May, 1 vol. Kesselring, Mari. 2009. (Months of the Year Ser.). (ENG.). 24p. (J). (gr. k-2). 27.07 *(978-1-60270-632-3(8)*, 11571, Looking Glass Library) Magic Wagon.

—Nurses at Work, 1 vol. Kenney, Karen L. 2009. (Meet Your Community Workers Ser.). (ENG.). 32p. (J). (gr. k-4). 28.50 *(978-1-60270-651-4(4)*, 11410, Looking Glass Library) Magic Wagon.

—Okie the Wonder Dog. Schwartz, Anna L. 2016. 62p. (J). pap. *(978-1-63293-111-5(7))* Sunstone Pr.

—Police Officers at Work, 1 vol. Kenney, Karen L. 2009. (Meet Your Community Workers Ser.). (ENG.). 32p. (J). (gr. k-4). 28.50 *(978-1-60270-652-1(2)*, 11412, Looking Glass Library) Magic Wagon.

—Teachers at Work, 1 vol. Kenney, Karen L. 2009. (Meet Your Community Workers Ser.). (ENG.). 32p. (J). (gr. k-4). 28.50 *(978-1-60270-653-8(0)*, 11414, Looking Glass Library) Magic Wagon.

Dumont, Daniel. Les Jumeaux Bulle Series. Gauthier, Bertrand. 2004. (FRE.). 64p. (J). (gr. 1-4). pap. *(978-2-89021-684-6(5))* Diffusion du livre Mirabel (DLM).

Dumont, Jean-françois. Edgar Wants to Be Alone. Mathews, Leslie. 2015. (ENG.). 26p. (J). 16.00 *(978-0-8028-5457-5(5)*, Eerdmans Bks For Young Readers) Eerdmans, William B. Publishing Co.

—I Am a Bear. Mathews, Leslie. 2015. (ENG.). 34p. (J). 16.00 *(978-0-8028-5447-6(8)*, Eerdmans Bks For Young Readers) Eerdmans, William B. Publishing Co.

—The Sheep Go on Strike. Mathews, Leslie. 2014. (ENG.). 34p. (J). 16.00 *(978-0-8028-5470-4(2)*, Eerdmans Bks For Young Readers) Eerdmans, William B. Publishing Co.

Dumont, Madeleine. Jaune. Averous, Helene. 2013. 38p. pap. *(978-981-07-5312-2(8))* MHC Asia Group.

—Yellow. Averous, Helene. 2013. 38p. pap. *(978-981-07-5311-5(X))* MHC Asia Group.

Dumont, Yves. Our Environment: Everything You Need to Know. Pasquet, Jacques. Tanaka, Shelley, tr. from FRE. 2020. Orig. Title: Notre Environnement. (ENG.). 56p. (J). (gr. 3-6). 18.95 *(978-1-77147-389-7(4))* Owlkids Bks. Inc. CAN. Dist: Publishers Group West (PGW).

Dumortier, Marjorie. Did Dinosaurs Eat People? And Other Questions Kids Have about Dinosaurs, 1 vol. Bowman, Donna H. 2009. (Kids' Questions Ser.). (ENG.). 24p. (J). (gr. k-2). lib. bdg. 27.32 *(978-1-4048-5527-4(0)*, Picture Window Bks.) Capstone.

—Zoe & Her Zany Animals. 2006. (ENG.). 32p. (J). (gr. -1-3). 14.99 *(978-0-7145-3306-3(8))* Boyars, Marion Pubs., Ltd. GBR. Dist: Consortium Bk. Sales & Distribution.

Dunaway, Nancy. I Scream, You Scream: A Feast of Food Rhymes. Morrison, Lillian. 2005. (Story Cove Ser.). (ENG.). 96p. (J). (gr. -1-3). 12.95 *(978-0-87483-495-6(3))* August Hse. Pubs., Inc.

Dunbar, Eddie, photos by. Insects of Wente Scout Reservation: Mendocino County, California. 2005th ed. 2005. cd-rom 10.00 *(978-0-9764454-3-2(3)*, Exploring California Insects) Insect Sciences Museum of California.

Dunbar, Geoff. High in the Clouds. Ardagh, Philip. 2007. 93p. (J). 20.00 *(978-1-4223-6720-9(7))* DIANE Publishing Co.

Dunbar, Max, et al. Legends of Marvel: X-Men. 2020. (ENG.). 112p. (YA). (gr. 8-17). pap. 15.99 *(978-1-302-92194-1(0))* Marvel Worldwide, Inc.

Dunbar, Polly. The Boy Who Climbed into the Moon. Almond, David. 2010. (ENG.). 128p. (J). (gr. 3-7). 15.99 *(978-0-7636-4217-4(7))* Candlewick Pr.

—Buster & the Baby. Hest, Amy. 2017. (ENG.). 32p. (J). (-k). 15.99 *(978-0-7636-8787-8(1))* Candlewick Pr.

—Here's a Little Poem: A Very First Book of Poetry. 2007. 112p. (J). (gr. k-12). 21.99 *(978-0-7636-3141-3(8))* Candlewick Pr.

—The Hug. McLaughlin, Eoin. 2019. (ENG.). 56p. (J). 15.95 *(978-0-571-34875-6(0)*, Faber & Faber Children's Bks.) Faber & Faber, Inc.

—My Dad's a Birdman. Almond, David. 2011. (ENG.). 115p. (J). (gr. 2-4). 24.94 *(978-0-7636-3667-8(3))* Candlewick Pr.

—Pat-A-Cake Baby. Dunbar, Joyce. 2015. (ENG.). 40p. (J). (-k). 15.99 *(978-0-7636-7577-6(6))* Candlewick Pr.

Dunbar, Polly. While We Can't Hug. McLaughlin, Eoin. 2020. (ENG.). 32p. (J). 15.95 ***(978-0-571-36558-6(2))*** Faber & Faber, Inc.

Dunbar, Polly. Arthur's Dream Boat. Dunbar, Polly. 2012. (ENG.). 40p. (J). (gr. -1-k). 15.99 *(978-0-7636-5867-0(7))* Candlewick Pr.

—Goodnight, Tiptoe. Dunbar, Polly. 2009. (Tilly & Friends Ser.). (ENG.). 32p. (J). (gr. -1-2). 12.99 *(978-0-7636-4328-7(9))* Candlewick Pr.

—A Lion Is a Lion. Dunbar, Polly. 2018. (ENG.). 40p. (J). (gr. -1-2). 15.99 *(978-0-7636-9731-0(1))* Candlewick Pr.

—Penguin. Dunbar, Polly. 2010. (ENG.). 40p. (J). (gr. -1-3). pap. 6.99 *(978-0-7636-4972-2(4))* Candlewick Pr.

—Pretty Pru: A Tilly & Friends Book. Dunbar, Polly. 2009. (Tilly & Friends Ser.). (ENG.). 32p. (J). (gr. -1-2). 12.99 *(978-0-7636-4272-3(X))* Candlewick Pr.

Duncan, Aura Velez. Bow Wow Woof Woof Bark Bark. Abdallah, Mustafaa. 2019. (ENG.). 30p. (J). pap. 9.99 *(978-1-7943-2061-1(X))* Independently Published.

Duncan, Beverly. Unseen Rainbows, Silent Songs: The World of Animal Senses. Goodman, Susan E. 2008. (ENG.). 40p. (J). (gr. 4-6). 12.99 *(978-1-4169-7575-5(6)*, Aladdin) Simon & Schuster Children's Publishing.

Duncan, Christa. The Story of the H Brothers. 2007. (J). 7.99 *(978-0-9792897-0-5(X))* Smartypants Publishing.

Duncan, Dan. Teenage Mutant Ninja Turtles Volume 1: Change Is Constant. Waltz, Tom & Eastman, Kevin. 2012. (Teenage Mutant Ninja Turtles Ser.: 1). (ENG.). 104p. pap. 17.99 *(978-1-61377-139-6(8)*, 9781613771396) Idea & Design Works, LLC.

—Teenage Mutant Ninja Turtles Volume 1: Change Is Constant Deluxe Edition. Waltz, Tom & Eastman, Kevin. 2012. (Teenage Mutant Ninja Turtles Ser.). (ENG.). 192p. 49.99 *(978-1-61377-233-1(5)*, 9781613772331) Idea & Design Works, LLC.

—Teenage Mutant Ninja Turtles Volume 3: Shadows of the Past, Vol. 3. Waltz, Tom & Eastman, Kevin. 2016. (Teenage Mutant Ninja Turtles Ser.: 3). (ENG.). 104p. pap. 17.99 *(978-1-61377-405-2(2)*, 9781613774052) Idea & Design Works, LLC.

Duncan, Dan & Santolouco, Mateus. Teenage Mutant Ninja Turtles Volume 2: Enemies Old, Enemies New. Waltz, Tom & Eastman, Kevin. 2016. (Teenage Mutant Ninja Turtles Ser.: 2). (ENG.). 104p. pap. 17.99 *(978-1-61377-288-1(2)*, 9781613772881) Idea & Design Works, LLC.

Duncan, Dan, jt. illus. see Santolouco, Mateus.

Duncan, Daniel. The Adventures of Henry Whiskers. Priebe, Gigi. 2017. (Adventures of Henry Whiskers Ser.: 1). (ENG.). 160p. (J). (gr. 2-5). pap. 5.99 *(978-1-4814-6574-8(0)*, Simon & Schuster/Paula Wiseman Bks.) Simon & Schuster/Paula Wiseman Bks.

Duncan, Daniel. The Candy Mafia. Tidhar, Lavie. 2020. (ENG.). 256p. (J). (gr. 3-7). 16.99 ***(978-1-68263-197-3(4))*** Peachtree Publishing Co. Inc.

Duncan, Daniel. The Long Way Home. Priebe, Gigi. 2017. (Adventures of Henry Whiskers Ser.: 2). (ENG.). 160p. (J). (gr. 2-5). 17.99 *(978-1-4814-6578-6(3))*; pap. 5.99 *(978-1-4814-6577-9(5))* Simon & Schuster Children's Publishing. (Aladdin).

—Mr. Posey's New Glasses. Kooser, Ted. 2019. 40p. (J). (gr. 1-4). 16.99 *(978-0-7636-9609-2(9))* Candlewick Pr.

Duncan, Daniel. Russell Wrestles the Relatives. Johnson, Cindy Chambers. (ENG.). 40p. (J). (gr. -1-3). 2020. 7.99 ***(978-1-5344-4422-5(X))***; 2018. 18.99 *(978-1-4814-9159-4(8))* Simon & Schuster Children's Publishing. (Aladdin).

Duncan, Daniel. Shark Nate-O. Luebbe, Tara & Cattie, Becky. 2018. (ENG.). 40p. (J). (gr. -1-3). 17.99 *(978-1-4998-0496-6(2))* Little Bee Books Inc.

—When Wilma Rudolph Played Basketball. Weakland, Mark. 2016. (Leaders Doing Headstands Ser.). (ENG.). 32p. (J). (gr. 1-4). pap. 7.95 *(978-1-5158-0136-8(5))*; lib. bdg. 28.65 *(978-1-4795-9684-3(1))* Capstone. (Picture Window Bks.).

—When Wilma Rudolph Played Basketball. Weakland, Mark. 2017. 32p. (J). *(978-1-5158-0140-5(3)*, Picture Window Bks.) Capstone.

—Who Wants to Be a Pirate? What It Was Really Like in the Golden Age of Piracy. Heos, Bridget. 2019. (ENG.). 32p. (J). 17.99 *(978-0-8050-9770-2(8)*, 900118849, Holt, Henry & Co. Bks. For Young Readers) Holt, Henry & Co.

Duncan, Karen & Stringle, Sam. The Story of Armadillo. Robb, Jackie & Stringle, Berny. 2003. (Bang on the Door Ser.). 32p. (YA). pap. *(978-1-85602-337-5(0)*, Pavilion Children's Books) Pavilion Bks.

—The Story of Bat. Robb, Jackie & Stringle, Berny. 2003. (Bang on the Door Ser.). 32p. (YA). pap. *(978-1-85602-316-0(8)*, Pavilion Children's Books) Pavilion Bks.

—The Story of Cat. Robb, Jackie & Stringle, Berny. 2004. (Bang on the Door Ser.). 32p. (YA). pap. *(978-1-85602-314-6(1)*, Pavilion Children's Books) Pavilion Bks.

—The Story of Dog. Robb, Jackie & Stringle, Berny. 2004. (Bang on the Door Ser.). 32p. (YA). pap. *(978-1-85602-315-3(X)*, Pavilion Children's Books) Pavilion Bks.

—The Story of Pea Brain. Robb, Jackie & Stringle, Berny. 2004. (Bang on the Door Ser.). 32p. (YA). pap. *(978-1-85602-383-2(4)*, Pavilion Children's Books) Pavilion Bks.

—The Story of Plankton. Robb, Jackie & Stringle, Berny. 2004. (Bang on the Door Ser.). 32p. (YA). pap. *(978-1-85602-336-8(2)*, Pavilion Children's Books) Pavilion Bks.

—The Story of Slug. Robb, Jackie & Stringle, Berny. 2004. (Bang on the Door Ser.). 32p. (YA). pap. *(978-1-85602-317-7(6)*, Pavilion Children's Books) Pavilion Bks.

—The Story of Spider. Robb, Jackie & Stringle, Berny. 2004. (Bang on the Door Ser.). 32p. (YA). pap. *(978-1-85602-318-4(4)*, Pavilion Children's Books) Pavilion Bks.

Duncan Ph D, Hall. Perry's Big Dig & Other Poems. Hoppes, Virginia. 2016. (ENG.). 36p. (J). pap. 6.99 *(978-0-9820466-0-9(X))* Humor & Communication.

Duncan Ph D, Hall & Gaeddert, Margaret. Noah's Ark & Other Bible Poems. Hoppes, Virginia. 2016. (ENG.). (J). pap. 9.89 *(978-0-9820466-7-8(7))* Humor & Communication.

Duncan, Teil. Ordinary Love. Barber, Morgan. 2020. (ENG.). 34p. (J). (gr. -1-k). 15.99 ***(978-1-64111-608-4(0)***, Vertel Publishing) Nextone Inc.

Dungan, Julia. ABC Exercise with Me. Gomes, Julie. 2005. (J). per. 7.50 *(978-0-9770207-0-6(3))* JCCJ Pr.

Dungey, Thomas. Nimble the Thimble Mouse. 1. Meek, Jeffrey/K. 2007. 21p. (J). 9.95 *(978-0-9794522-0-8(1))* Thimble Mouse Publishing, Inc.

Dunham Akiyama, Laine. Mr. Lincoln's Gift: A Civil War Story. Stewart, Whitney. 2008. 32p. (J). 19.95 *(978-0-9754917-4-4(1))* Friends of Hildene, Inc.

Dunk, Sarah. The Greenhouse Effect. Reiter, David P. 2nd ed. 2009. (Project Earth-Mend Ser.: Bk. 1). (ENG.). 200p. (J). pap. 14.95 *(978-1-921479-25-0(6)*, IP Kidz) Interactive Pubns. Pty, Ltd. AUS. Dist: Ingram Content Group.

Dunlap, Hope. The Pied Piper of Hamelin, Illustrated by Hope Dunlap. Browning, Robert. 2008. 52p. pap. 12.95 *(978-1-59915-265-3(7))* Yesterday's Classics.

Dunlap, Joan, jt. illus. see Bennett, Michele.

Dunlap, Lana. Angel in the Alley: An Oklahoma Story of Fur, Friendship, & Finding Family. Conover McKinnis, Sara. 2018. (ENG.). 48p. (J). (gr. k-5). pap. 16.00 *(978-0-692-15641-4(0))* Mot de Mere Publishing.

Dunlavey, Rob. Counting Crows. Appelt, Kathi. 2015. (ENG.). 40p. (J). (gr. -1-3). 17.99 *(978-1-4424-2327-5(7))* Simon & Schuster Children's Publishing.

—In the Woods. Elliott, David. 2020. 40p. (J). (gr. -1-2). 17.99 *(978-0-7636-9783-9(4))* Candlewick Pr.

—Over in the Wetlands: A Hurricane-On-the-Bayou Story. Rose, Caroline Starr. 2015. (ENG.). 40p. (J). (gr. -1-3). 17.99 *(978-0-449-81016-3(X)*, Schwartz & Wade Bks.) Random Hse. Children's Bks.

Dunlavey, Ryan. Action Presidents #1: George Washington! Van Lente, Fred. 2020. (Action Presidents Ser.: 1). 128p. (J). (gr. 3-7). 22.99 *(978-0-06-289118-1(9))* HarperCollins Pubs.

Dunmeyer, Vernell, photos by. Try'umsee's Wings. Bee, Patricia. 2007. (ENG.). 44p. pap. 17.99 *(978-1-4257-0920-4(6))* Xlibris Corp.

Dunn, Anna. My Rainbow Surprise. Sklansky, Amy E. 2018. (ENG.). 14p. (J). (— 1). 8.99 *(978-1-338-11098-2(5)*, Cartwheel Bks.) Scholastic, Inc.

—Sweet Hearts. Sklansky, Amy E. 2017. 14p. (J). (— 1). bds. 8.99 *(978-1-338-11099-9(3)*, Cartwheel Bks.) Scholastic, Inc.

Dunn, Anthony. Completely Magi-CaLL: The TRUE Secrets of Magic: A Study of the Magician's Art. Gunther, Chat, photos by. 2009. 346p. (YA). pap. 29.95 *(978-0-9729546-8-6(6))* SMC Pubns., LLC.

Dunn, Ben. The Adventure of Abbey Grange. 2010. (Graphic Novel Adventures of Sherlock Holmes Ser.). (ENG.). 48p. (J). (gr. 3-8). 31.35 *(978-1-60270-722-1(7)*, 415, Graphic Planet - Fiction) Magic Wagon.

—The Adventure of the Blue Carbuncle, 1 vol. Goodwin, Vincent. 2012. (Graphic Novel Adventures of Sherlock Holmes Ser.). (ENG.). 48p. (J). (gr. 3-8). lib. bdg. 31.35 *(978-1-61641-891-5(5)*, 9110, Graphic Planet - Fiction) Magic Wagon.

—The Adventure of the Cardboard Box, 1 vol. Goodwin, Vincent. 2013. (Graphic Novel Adventures of Sherlock Holmes Ser.). (ENG.). 48p. (J). (gr. 3-8). lib. bdg. 31.35 *(978-1-61641-971-4(7)*, 9124, Graphic Planet - Fiction) Magic Wagon.

—The Adventure of the Copper Beeches, 1 vol. Goodwin, Vincent. 2012. (Graphic Novel Adventures of Sherlock Holmes Ser.). (ENG.). 48p. (J). (gr. 3-8). lib. bdg. 31.35 *(978-1-61641-892-2(3)*, 9112, Graphic Planet - Fiction) Magic Wagon.

—The Adventure of the Dancing Men. 2010. (Graphic Novel Adventures of Sherlock Holmes Ser.). (ENG.). 48p. (J). (gr. 3-8). 31.35 *(978-1-60270-723-8(5)*, 417, Graphic Planet - Fiction) Magic Wagon.

—The Adventure of the Dying Detective, 1 vol. Goodwin, Vincent. 2013. (Graphic Novel Adventures of Sherlock Holmes Ser.). (ENG.). 48p. (J). (gr. 3-8). lib. bdg. 31.35 *(978-1-61641-972-1(5)*, 9126, Graphic Planet - Fiction) Magic Wagon.

—The Adventure of the Empty House. 2010. (Graphic Novel Adventures of Sherlock Holmes Ser.). (ENG.). 48p. (J). (gr. 3-8). 31.35 *(978-1-60270-724-5(3)*, 419, Graphic Planet - Fiction) Magic Wagon.

—The Adventure of the Engineer's Thumb, 1 vol. Goodwin, Vincent. 2012. (Graphic Novel Adventures of Sherlock Holmes Ser.). (ENG.). 48p. (J). (gr. 3-8). lib. bdg. 31.35 *(978-1-61641-893-9(1)*, 9114, Graphic Planet - Fiction) Magic Wagon.

—The Adventure of the Norwood Builder. 2010. (Graphic Novel Adventures of Sherlock Holmes Ser.). (ENG.). 48p. (J). (gr. 3-8). 31.35 *(978-1-60270-725-2(1)*, 421, Graphic Planet - Fiction) Magic Wagon.

—The Adventure of the Priory School, 1 vol. Goodwin, Vincent. 2013. (Graphic Novel Adventures of Sherlock Holmes Ser.). (ENG.). 48p. (J). (gr. 3-8). lib. bdg. 31.35 *(978-1-61641-973-8(3)*, 9128, Graphic Planet - Fiction) Magic Wagon.

—The Adventure of the Red Circle, 1 vol. Goodwin, Vincent. 2013. (Graphic Novel Adventures of Sherlock Holmes Ser.). (ENG.). 48p. (J). (gr. 3-8). lib. bdg. 31.35 *(978-1-61641-974-5(1)*, 9130, Graphic Planet - Fiction) Magic Wagon.

—The Adventure of the Red-Headed League. 2010. (Graphic Novel Adventures of Sherlock Holmes Ser.). (ENG.). 48p. (J). (gr. 3-8). 31.35 *(978-1-60270-726-9(X)*, 423, Graphic Planet - Fiction) Magic Wagon.

—The Adventure of the Second Stain, 1 vol. Goodwin, Vincent. 2013. (Graphic Novel Adventures of Sherlock Holmes Ser.). (ENG.). 48p. (J). (gr. 3-8). lib. bdg. 31.35 *(978-1-61641-975-2(X)*, 9132, Graphic Planet - Fiction) Magic Wagon.

—The Adventure of the Six Napoleons, 1 vol. Goodwin, Vincent. 2013. (Graphic Novel Adventures of Sherlock Holmes Ser.). (ENG.). 48p. (J). (gr. 3-8). lib. bdg. 31.35 *(978-1-61641-976-9(8)*, 9134, Graphic Planet - Fiction) Magic Wagon.

—The Adventure of the Solitary Cyclist, 1 vol. Goodwin, Vincent. 2012. (Graphic Novel Adventures of Sherlock Holmes Ser.). (ENG.). 48p. (J). (gr. 3-8). lib. bdg. 31.35 *(978-1-61641-894-6(X)*, 9116, Graphic Planet - Fiction) Magic Wagon.

—The Adventure of the Speckled Band. 2010. (Graphic Novel Adventures of Sherlock Holmes Ser.). (ENG.). 48p. (J). (gr. 3-8). 31.35 *(978-1-60270-727-6(8)*, 425, Graphic Planet - Fiction) Magic Wagon.

—The Adventure of the Three Students, 1 vol. Goodwin, Vincent. 2012. (Graphic Novel Adventures of Sherlock Holmes Ser.). (ENG.). 48p. (J). (gr. 3-8). lib. bdg. 31.35 *(978-1-61641-895-3(8)*, 9118, Graphic Planet - Fiction) Magic Wagon.

—The Adventure of Wisteria Lodge, 1 vol. Goodwin, Vincent. 2012. (Graphic Novel Adventures of Sherlock Holmes Ser.). (ENG.). 48p. (J). (gr. 3-8). lib. bdg. 31.35 *(978-1-61641-896-0(6)*, 9120, Graphic Planet - Fiction) Magic Wagon.

—Amelia Earhart, 1 vol. Dunn, Joeming W. 2008. (Bio-Graphics Ser.). (ENG.). 32p. (J). (gr. 3-8). 29.93 *(978-1-60270-173-1(3)*, 3585, Graphic Planet - Fiction) Magic Wagon.

—Armistice Day. Dunn, Joeming. 2015. (Graphic Warfare Ser.). 32p. (J). (gr. 3-8). 29.93 *(978-1-61641-978-3(4)*, 19202, Graphic Planet - Fiction) Magic Wagon.

—The California Gold Rush, 1 vol. Dunn, Joe & National Geographic Learning Staff. 2007. (Graphic History Ser.). (ENG.). 32p. (J). (gr. 3-8). 29.93 *(978-1-60270-076-5(1)*, 9038, Graphic Planet - Fiction) Magic Wagon.

—Crossfire: Police Story Christian Comicbook: Bonus Origin Back Story, Little Soldier of the Cross: the Girl with Super-Faith. Hartley, Al. 2017. (ENG.). 47p. (YA). 4.99 *(978-1-888092-33-2(5)*, 73c29ca8-c833-4bc7-b20e-6be2670b67d4) Nordskog Publishing, Inc.

—Fallujah. Dunn, Joeming. 2015. (Graphic Warfare Ser.). 32p. (J). (gr. 3-8). 29.93 *(978-1-61641-980-6(6)*, 19206, Graphic Planet - Fiction) Magic Wagon.

—Gettysburg. Dunn, Joeming W. 2015. (Graphic Warfare Ser.). 32p. (J). (gr. 3-8). 29.93 *(978-1-61641-981-3(4)*, 19208, Graphic Planet - Fiction) Magic Wagon.
—Hamlet, 1 vol. Dunn, Rebecca. 2008. (Graphic Shakespeare Ser.). (ENG.). 48p. (J). (gr. 5-10). 31.35 *(978-1-60270-188-5(1)*, 9138, Graphic Planet - Fiction) Magic Wagon.
—The Lighthouse Mystery. Dunn, Joeming. 2010. (Boxcar Children Graphic Novels Ser.: 14). (ENG.). 32p. (J). (gr. 1-5). pap. 6.99 *(978-0-8075-4547-8(3)*, 807545473) Whitman, Albert & Co.
—The Lighthouse Mystery, 1 vol., Bk. 14. Dunn, Joeming & Warner, Gertrude Chandler. 2011. (Boxcar Children Graphic Novels Ser.). (ENG.). 32p. (J). (gr. 2-8). 29.93 *(978-1-61641-122-0(8)*, 3684, Graphic Planet - Fiction) Magic Wagon.
—The Merry Adventures of Robin Hood, 1 vol. Pyle, Howard. 2007. (Graphic Classics Ser.). (ENG.). 32p. (J). (gr. 3-8). 29.93 *(978-1-60270-053-6(2)*, 9024, Graphic Planet - Fiction) Magic Wagon.
—Miracle on Ice, 1 vol. Dunn, Joe. 2007. (Graphic History Ser.). (ENG.). 32p. (J). (gr. 3-8). 29.93 *(978-1-60270-077-2(X)*, 9040, Graphic Planet - Fiction) Magic Wagon.
—Mountain Top Mystery, 1 vol., Bk. 15. Dunn, Joeming & Warner, Gertrude Chandler. 2011. (Boxcar Children Graphic Novels Ser.). (ENG.). 32p. (J). (gr. 3-8). 29.93 *(978-1-61641-123-7(6)*, 3685, Graphic Planet - Fiction) Magic Wagon.
—Mystery in the Sand, 1 vol., Bk. 18. Dunn, Joeming & Warner, Gertrude Chandler. 2011. (Boxcar Children Graphic Novels Ser.). (ENG.). 32p. (J). (gr. 3-8). 29.93 *(978-1-61641-126-8(0)*, 3688, Graphic Planet - Fiction) Magic Wagon.
—Peter Pan, 1 vol. Barrie, J. M. 2007. (Graphic Classics Ser.). (ENG.). 32p. (J). (gr. 3-8). 29.93 *(978-1-60270-052-9(4)*, 9022, Graphic Planet - Fiction) Magic Wagon.
—Tet Offensive. Dunn, Joeming. 2015. (Graphic Warfare Ser.). 32p. (J). (gr. 3-8). 29.93 *(978-1-61641-983-7(0)*, 19212, Graphic Planet - Fiction) Magic Wagon.
—The Time Machine, 1 vol. Wells, H. G. 2007. (Graphic Classics Ser.). (ENG.). 32p. (J). (gr. 3-8). 29.93 *(978-1-60270-054-3(0)*, 9026, Graphic Planet - Fiction) Magic Wagon.
—The Woodshed Mystery. Dunn, Joeming. 2010. (Boxcar Children Graphic Novels Ser.: 13). (ENG.). 32p. (J). (gr. 1-5). pap. 6.99 *(978-0-8075-9208-3(0)*, 807592080) Whitman, Albert & Co.
—The Woodshed Mystery, 1 vol., Bk. 13. Dunn, Joeming & Warner, Gertrude Chandler. 2011. (Boxcar Children Graphic Novels Ser.). (ENG.). 32p. (J). (gr. 3-8). 29.93 *(978-1-61641-121-3(X)*, 3683, Graphic Planet - Fiction) Magic Wagon.
—The Wright Brothers, 1 vol. Dunn, Joe. 2007. (Bio-Graphics Ser.). (ENG.). 32p. (J). (gr. 3-8). 29.93 *(978-1-60270-071-0(0)*, 3575, Graphic Planet - Fiction) Magic Wagon.
Dunn, Ben, jt. illus. see Dunn, Joeming W.
Dunn, Fiona W. & Skeate, Sarah. Martin Luther King, Jr: Graphic Biographies. Ruiz, Rachel. 2019. (Great Lives Ser.). (ENG.). 128p. (J). (gr. 4-7). pap. 12.99 *(978-1-4380-1205-6(5)*, B.E.S. Publishing) Peterson's.
Dunn, Gary. Johnny Catbiscuit & the Stolen Secrets! Cox, Michael. 2008. (Johnny Catbiscuit Ser.). (ENG.). 160p. (J). (gr. 2-4). pap. 9.95 *(978-1-4052-3739-0(2))* Egmont Bks., Ltd. GBR. Dist: Independent Pubs. Group.
—Stop That Robot!: Band 00/Lilac (Collins Big Cat) Sage, Alison. 2007. (Collins Big Cat Ser.). (ENG.). 16p. (J). (gr. -1-k). pap. 6.99 *(978-0-00-718678-5(9))* HarperCollins Pubs. Ltd. GBR. Dist: Independent Pubs. Group.
Dunn, Joeming W. & Dunn, Ben. Bicycle Mystery, 1 vol., Bk. 17. Warner, Gertrude Chandler. 2011. (Boxcar Children Graphic Novels Ser.). (ENG.). 32p. (J). (gr. 3-8). 29.93 *(978-1-61641-125-1(2)*, 3687, Graphic Planet - Fiction) Magic Wagon.
—D-Day. Dunn, Joeming W. & Dunn, Ben. 2015. (Graphic Warfare Ser.). 32p. (J). (gr. 3-8). 29.93 *(978-1-61641-979-0(2)*, 19204, Graphic Planet - Fiction) Magic Wagon.
—Houseboat Mystery, 1 vol., Bk. 16. Warner, Gertrude Chandler. 2011. (Boxcar Children Graphic Novels Ser.). (ENG.). 32p. (J). (gr. 3-8). 29.93 *(978-1-61641-124-4(4)*, 3686, Graphic Planet - Fiction) Magic Wagon.
Dunn Jr., Howard Alfred. The Light of the Moon. Dunn, Layne. 2012. 16p. pap. 24.95 *(978-1-4626-5501-4(7))* America Star Bks.
Dunn, Mary C. Summer Vacation. Leckenby, Nicole M. Bindas, Rachael, ed. 2019. (ENG.). 44p. (J). pap. 15.00 ***(978-1-7006-7110-3(3))*** Independently Published.
Dunn, Phoebe. Guess Who I Am... gif. ed. 2005. 10p. (J). (gr. -1). per., bds. 7.99 *(978-1-57791-175-3(X))* Brighter Minds Children's Publishing.
Dunn, Phoebe. The Little Duck. Dunn, Phoebe, photos by. Dunn, Judy, photos by. 2017. (Step into Reading Ser.). 32p. (J). (gr. -1-1). pap. 3.99 *(978-0-553-53352-1(5)*, Random Hse. Bks. for Young Readers) Random Hse. Children's Bks.
Dunn, Phoebe, photos by. The Little Duck. Dunn, Judy. 2014. (ENG., 14p. (J). (— 1). bds. 6.99 *(978-0-385-38521-3(8)*, Random Hse. Bks. for Young Readers) Random Hse. Children's Bks.
—The Little Rabbit. Dunn, Judy. 2016. (Step into Reading Ser.). 32p. (J). (gr. -1-1). pap. 3.99 *(978-0-553-53354-5(1)*, Random Hse. Bks. for Young Readers) Random Hse. Children's Bks.
Dunn, Robert. Little Women. Alcott, Louisa May. 2013. 46p. (J). *(978-1-4351-4813-0(4))* Barnes & Noble, Inc.
—The Littlest Bunny: An Easter Adventure. Jacobs, Lily. 2015. (ENG.). 32p. (J). (-3). 9.99 *(978-1-4926-1012-0(7)*, Sourcebooks Jabberwocky) Sourcebooks, Inc.
—The Littlest Bunny in Albuquerque: An Easter Adventure. Jacobs, Lily. 2015. (ENG.). 32p. (J). (-3). 9.99 *(978-1-4926-1021-2(6)*, Sourcebooks Jabberwocky) Sourcebooks, Inc.
—The Littlest Bunny in Austin. Jacobs, Lily. 2016. (ENG.). 32p. (J). (-7). 9.99 *(978-1-4926-3347-1(X)*, 9781492633471, Sourcebooks Jabberwocky) Sourcebooks, Inc.
—The Littlest Bunny in Buffalo. Jacobs, Lily. 2016. (ENG.). 32p. (J). (-7). 9.99 *(978-1-4926-3346-4(1)*, 9781492633464, Sourcebooks Jabberwocky) Sourcebooks, Inc.
—The Littlest Bunny in Calgary: An Easter Adventure. Jacobs, Lily. 2015. (ENG.). 32p. (J). (-3). 9.99 *(978-1-4926-1039-7(9)*, Sourcebooks Jabberwocky) Sourcebooks, Inc.
—The Littlest Bunny in California: An Easter Adventure. Jacobs, Lily. 2015. (ENG.). 32p. (J). (-3). 9.99 *(978-1-4926-1042-7(9)*, Sourcebooks Jabberwocky) Sourcebooks, Inc.
—The Littlest Bunny in Canada: An Easter Adventure. Jacobs, Lily. 2015. (ENG.). 32p. (J). (-3). 9.99 *(978-1-4926-1045-8(3)*, Sourcebooks Jabberwocky) Sourcebooks, Inc.
—The Littlest Bunny in Cincinnati: An Easter Adventure. Jacobs, Lily. 2015. (ENG.). 32p. (J). (-3). 9.99 *(978-1-4926-1054-0(2)*, Sourcebooks Jabberwocky) Sourcebooks, Inc.
—The Littlest Bunny in Cleveland. Jacobs, Lily. 2016. (ENG.). 32p. (J). (-7). 9.99 *(978-1-4926-3353-2(4)*, 9781492633532, Sourcebooks Jabberwocky) Sourcebooks, Inc.
—The Littlest Bunny in Delaware: An Easter Adventure. Jacobs, Lily. 2015. (ENG.). 32p. (J). (-3). 9.99 *(978-1-4926-1063-2(1)*, Sourcebooks Jabberwocky) Sourcebooks, Inc.
—The Littlest Bunny in Edmonton: An Easter Adventure. Jacobs, Lily. 2015. (ENG.). 32p. (J). (-3). 9.99 *(978-1-4926-1066-3(6)*, Sourcebooks Jabberwocky) Sourcebooks, Inc.
—The Littlest Bunny in Florida: An Easter Adventure. Jacobs, Lily. 2015. (ENG.). 32p. (J). (-3). 9.99 *(978-1-4926-1069-4(0)*, Sourcebooks Jabberwocky) Sourcebooks, Inc.
—The Littlest Bunny in Illinois: An Easter Adventure. Jacobs, Lily. 2015. (ENG.). 32p. (J). (-3). 9.99 *(978-1-4926-1081-6(X)*, Sourcebooks Jabberwocky) Sourcebooks, Inc.
—The Littlest Bunny in Indiana: An Easter Adventure. Jacobs, Lily. 2015. (ENG.). 32p. (J). (-3). 9.99 *(978-1-4926-1084-7(4)*, Sourcebooks Jabberwocky) Sourcebooks, Inc.
—The Littlest Bunny in Kansas City: An Easter Adventure. Jacobs, Lily. 2015. (ENG.). 32p. (J). (-3). 9.99 *(978-1-4926-1093-9(3)*, Sourcebooks Jabberwocky) Sourcebooks, Inc.
—The Littlest Bunny in Kentucky: An Easter Adventure. Jacobs, Lily. 2015. (ENG.). 32p. (J). (-3). 9.99 *(978-1-4926-1096-0(8)*, Sourcebooks Jabberwocky) Sourcebooks, Inc.
—The Littlest Bunny in Maryland: An Easter Adventure. Jacobs, Lily. 2015. (ENG.). 32p. (J). (-3). 9.99 *(978-1-4926-1111-0(5)*, Sourcebooks Jabberwocky) Sourcebooks, Inc.
—The Littlest Bunny in Michigan: An Easter Adventure. 2015. (ENG.). 32p. (J). (-3). 9.99 *(978-1-4926-1117-2(4)*, Sourcebooks Jabberwocky) Sourcebooks, Inc.
—The Littlest Bunny in Minnesota: An Easter Adventure. Jacobs, Lily. 2015. (ENG.). 32p. (J). (-3). 9.99 *(978-1-4926-1120-2(4)*, Sourcebooks Jabberwocky) Sourcebooks, Inc.
—The Littlest Bunny in Mississippi: An Easter Adventure. Jacobs, Lily. 2015. (ENG.). 32p. (J). (-3). 9.99 *(978-1-4926-1123-3(9)*, Sourcebooks Jabberwocky) Sourcebooks, Inc.
—The Littlest Bunny in Missouri: An Easter Adventure. Jacobs, Lily. 2015. (ENG.). 32p. (J). (-3). 9.99 *(978-1-4926-1126-4(3)*, Sourcebooks Jabberwocky) Sourcebooks, Inc.
—The Littlest Bunny in Montana: An Easter Adventure. Jacobs, Lily. 2015. (ENG.). 32p. (J). (-3). 9.99 *(978-1-4926-1129-5(8)*, Sourcebooks Jabberwocky) Sourcebooks, Inc.
—The Littlest Bunny in Nashville. Jacobs, Lily. 2016. (ENG.). 32p. (J). (-7). 9.99 *(978-1-4926-3351-8(8)*, 9781492633518, Sourcebooks Jabberwocky) Sourcebooks, Inc.
—The Littlest Bunny in Nebraska: An Easter Adventure. Jacobs, Lily. 2015. (ENG.). 32p. (J). (-3). 9.99 *(978-1-4926-1132-5(8)*, Sourcebooks Jabberwocky) Sourcebooks, Inc.
—The Littlest Bunny in Nevada: An Easter Adventure. Jacobs, Lily. 2015. (ENG.). 32p. (J). (-3). 9.99 *(978-1-4926-1135-6(2)*, Sourcebooks Jabberwocky) Sourcebooks, Inc.
—The Littlest Bunny in New England: An Easter Adventure. Jacobs, Lily. 2015. (ENG.). 32p. (J). (-3). 9.99 *(978-1-4926-1138-7(7)*, Sourcebooks Jabberwocky) Sourcebooks, Inc.
—The Littlest Bunny in New Hampshire: An Easter Adventure. Jacobs, Lily. 2015. (ENG.). 32p. (J). (-3). 9.99 *(978-1-4926-1141-7(7)*, Sourcebooks Jabberwocky) Sourcebooks, Inc.
—The Littlest Bunny in New Jersey: An Easter Adventure. Jacobs, Lily. 2015. (ENG.). 32p. (J). (-3). 9.99 *(978-1-4926-1144-8(1)*, Sourcebooks Jabberwocky) Sourcebooks, Inc.
—The Littlest Bunny in New Mexico: An Easter Adventure. Jacobs, Lily. 2015. (ENG.). 32p. (J). (-3). 9.99 *(978-1-4926-1147-9(6)*, Sourcebooks Jabberwocky) Sourcebooks, Inc.
—The Littlest Bunny in New Orleans. Jacobs, Lily. 2016. (ENG.). 32p. (J). (-7). 9.99 *(978-1-4926-3350-1(X)*, 9781492633501, Sourcebooks Jabberwocky) Sourcebooks, Inc.
—The Littlest Bunny in New York: An Easter Adventure. Jacobs, Lily. 2015. (ENG.). 32p. (J). (-3). 9.99 *(978-1-4926-1150-9(6)*, Sourcebooks Jabberwocky) Sourcebooks, Inc.
—The Littlest Bunny in New York City: An Easter Adventure. Jacobs, Lily. 2015. (ENG.). 32p. (J). (-3). 9.99 *(978-1-4926-1153-0(0)*, Sourcebooks Jabberwocky) Sourcebooks, Inc.
—The Littlest Bunny in Newfoundland. Jacobs, Lily. 2016. (ENG.). 32p. (J). (-7). 9.99 *(978-1-4926-3352-5(6)*, 9781492633525, Sourcebooks Jabberwocky) Sourcebooks, Inc.
—The Littlest Bunny in North Carolina: An Easter Adventure. Jacobs, Lily. 2015. (ENG.). 32p. (J). (-3). 9.99 *(978-1-4926-1156-1(5)*, Sourcebooks Jabberwocky) Sourcebooks, Inc.
—The Littlest Bunny in North Dakota: An Easter Adventure. Jacobs, Lily. 2015. (ENG.). 32p. (J). (-3). 9.99 *(978-1-4926-1159-2(X)*, Sourcebooks Jabberwocky) Sourcebooks, Inc.
—The Littlest Bunny in Ohio: An Easter Adventure. Jacobs, Lily. 2015. (ENG.). 32p. (J). (-3). 9.99 *(978-1-4926-1162-2(X)*, Sourcebooks Jabberwocky) Sourcebooks, Inc.
—The Littlest Bunny in Oklahoma: An Easter Adventure. Jacobs, Lily. 2015. (ENG.). 32p. (J). (-3). 9.99 *(978-1-4926-1165-3(4)*, Sourcebooks Jabberwocky) Sourcebooks, Inc.
—The Littlest Bunny in Omaha: An Easter Adventure. Jacobs, Lily. 2015. (ENG.). 32p. (J). (-3). 9.99 *(978-1-4926-1168-4(9)*, Sourcebooks Jabberwocky) Sourcebooks, Inc.
—The Littlest Bunny in Oregon: An Easter Adventure. Jacobs, Lily. 2015. (ENG.). 32p. (J). (-3). 9.99 *(978-1-4926-1171-4(9)*, Sourcebooks Jabberwocky) Sourcebooks, Inc.
—The Littlest Bunny in Ottawa: An Easter Adventure. Jacobs, Lily. 2015. (ENG.). 32p. (J). (-3). 9.99 *(978-1-4926-1174-5(3)*, Sourcebooks Jabberwocky) Sourcebooks, Inc.
—The Littlest Bunny in Pennsylvania: An Easter Adventure. Jacobs, Lily. 2015. (ENG.). 32p. (J). (-3). 9.99 *(978-1-4926-1177-6(8)*, Sourcebooks Jabberwocky) Sourcebooks, Inc.
—The Littlest Bunny in Philadelphia: An Easter Adventure. Jacobs, Lily. 2015. (ENG.). 32p. (J). (-3). 9.99 *(978-1-4926-1180-6(8)*, Sourcebooks Jabberwocky) Sourcebooks, Inc.
—The Littlest Bunny in Pittsburgh: An Easter Adventure. Jacobs, Lily. 2015. (ENG.). 32p. (J). (-3). 9.99 *(978-1-4926-1183-7(2)*, Sourcebooks Jabberwocky) Sourcebooks, Inc.
—The Littlest Bunny in Portland: An Easter Adventure. Jacobs, Lily. 2015. (ENG.). 32p. (J). (-3). 9.99 *(978-1-4926-1186-8(7)*, Sourcebooks Jabberwocky) Sourcebooks, Inc.
—The Littlest Bunny in Rhode Island: An Easter Adventure. 2015. (ENG.). 32p. (J). (-3). 9.99 *(978-1-4926-1189-9(1)*, Sourcebooks Jabberwocky) Sourcebooks, Inc.
—The Littlest Bunny in San Diego. Jacobs, Lily. 2016. (ENG.). 32p. (J). (-7). 9.99 *(978-1-4926-3348-8(8)*, 9781492633488, Sourcebooks Jabberwocky) Sourcebooks, Inc.
—The Littlest Bunny in San Francisco: An Easter Adventure. Jacobs, Lily. 2015. (ENG.). 32p. (J). (-3). 9.99 *(978-1-4926-1192-9(1)*, Sourcebooks Jabberwocky) Sourcebooks, Inc.
—The Littlest Bunny in South Carolina: An Easter Adventure. Jacobs, Lily. 2015. (ENG.). 32p. (J). (-3). 9.99 *(978-1-4926-1195-0(6)*, Sourcebooks Jabberwocky) Sourcebooks, Inc.
—The Littlest Bunny in South Dakota: An Easter Adventure. Jacobs, Lily. 2015. (ENG.). 32p. (J). (-3). 9.99 *(978-1-4926-1198-1(0)*, Sourcebooks Jabberwocky) Sourcebooks, Inc.
—The Littlest Bunny in St. Louis: An Easter Adventure. Jacobs, Lily. 2015. (ENG.). 32p. (J). (-3). 9.99 *(978-1-4926-1201-8(4)*, Sourcebooks Jabberwocky) Sourcebooks, Inc.
—The Littlest Bunny in Tampa Bay: An Easter Adventure. Jacobs, Lily. 2015. (ENG.). 32p. (J). (-3). 9.99 *(978-1-4926-1204-9(9)*, Sourcebooks Jabberwocky) Sourcebooks, Inc.
—The Littlest Bunny in Tennessee: An Easter Adventure. Jacobs, Lily. 2015. (ENG.). 32p. (J). (-3). 9.99 *(978-1-4926-1207-0(3)*, Sourcebooks Jabberwocky) Sourcebooks, Inc.
—The Littlest Bunny in Texas: An Easter Adventure. Jacobs, Lily. 2015. (ENG.). 32p. (J). (-3). 9.99 *(978-1-4926-1210-0(3)*, Sourcebooks Jabberwocky) Sourcebooks, Inc.
—The Littlest Bunny in Toronto: An Easter Adventure. Jacobs, Lily. 2015. (ENG.). 32p. (J). (-3). 9.99 *(978-1-4926-1213-1(8)*, Sourcebooks Jabberwocky) Sourcebooks, Inc.
—The Littlest Bunny in Tulsa: An Easter Adventure. Jacobs, Lily. 2015. (ENG.). 32p. (J). (-3). 9.99 *(978-1-4926-1216-2(2)*, Sourcebooks Jabberwocky) Sourcebooks, Inc.
—The Littlest Bunny in Utah: An Easter Adventure. Jacobs, Lily. 2015. (ENG.). 32p. (J). (-3). 9.99 *(978-1-4926-1219-3(7)*, Sourcebooks Jabberwocky) Sourcebooks, Inc.
—The Littlest Bunny in Vancouver: An Easter Adventure. Jacobs, Lily. 2015. (ENG.). 32p. (J). (-3). 9.99 *(978-1-4926-1222-3(7)*, Sourcebooks Jabberwocky) Sourcebooks, Inc.
—The Littlest Bunny in Vermont: An Easter Adventure. Jacobs, Lily. 2015. (ENG.). 32p. (J). (-3). 9.99 *(978-1-4926-1225-4(1)*, Sourcebooks Jabberwocky) Sourcebooks, Inc.
—The Littlest Bunny in Virginia: An Easter Adventure. Jacobs, Lily. 2015. (ENG.). 32p. (J). (-3). 9.99 *(978-1-4926-1228-5(6)*, Sourcebooks Jabberwocky) Sourcebooks, Inc.
—My First Santa's Coming to Michigan. Smallman, Steve et al. 2015. (ENG.). 18p. (J). bds. 9.99 *(978-1-4926-2873-6(5)*, Sourcebooks Jabberwocky) Sourcebooks, Inc.
—My First Santa's Coming to Minnesota. Smallman, Steve et al. 2015. (ENG.). 18p. (J). bds. 9.99 *(978-1-4926-2879-8(4)*, Sourcebooks Jabberwocky) Sourcebooks, Inc.
—My First Santa's Coming to New Jersey. Smallman, Steve et al. 2015. (ENG.). 18p. (J). bds. 9.99 *(978-1-4926-2882-8(4)*, Sourcebooks Jabberwocky) Sourcebooks, Inc.
—My First Santa's Coming to Ohio. Smallman, Steve et al. 2015. (ENG.). 18p. (J). bds. 9.99 *(978-1-4926-2876-7(X)*, Sourcebooks Jabberwocky) Sourcebooks, Inc.
—My First Santa's Coming to Texas. Smallman, Steve et al. 2015. (ENG.). 18p. (J). bds. 9.99 *(978-1-4926-2870-5(0)*, Sourcebooks Jabberwocky) Sourcebooks, Inc.
—My First Santa's Coming to My House. Smallman, Steve et al. 2015. (ENG.). 18p. (J). bds. 9.99 *(978-1-4926-2885-9(9)*, Sourcebooks Jabberwocky) Sourcebooks, Inc.
—Santa Is Coming to Alabama. Smallman, Steve. 2nd ed. 2019. (Santa Is Coming... Ser.). (ENG.). 40p. (J). (-3). 12.99 *(978-1-7282-0041-5(5))* Sourcebooks, Inc.
—Santa Is Coming to Alaska. Smallman, Steve. 2nd ed. 2019. (Santa Is Coming... Ser.). (ENG.). 40p. (J). (-3). 12.99 *(978-1-7282-0042-2(3))* Sourcebooks, Inc.
—Santa Is Coming to Arizona. Smallman, Steve. 2nd ed. 2019. (Santa Is Coming... Ser.). (ENG.). 40p. (J). (-3). 12.99 *(978-1-7282-0043-9(1))* Sourcebooks, Inc.
—Santa Is Coming to Arkansas. Smallman, Steve. 2nd ed. 2019. (Santa Is Coming... Ser.). (ENG.). 40p. (J). (-3). 12.99 *(978-1-7282-0044-6(X))* Sourcebooks, Inc.
—Santa Is Coming to Boston. Smallman, Steve. 2nd ed. 2019. (Santa Is Coming... Ser.). (ENG.). 40p. (J). (-3). 12.99 *(978-1-7282-0045-3(8))* Sourcebooks, Inc.
—Santa Is Coming to Buffalo. Smallman, Steve. 2nd ed. 2019. (Santa Is Coming... Ser.). (ENG.). 40p. (J). (-3). 12.99 *(978-1-7282-0046-0(6))* Sourcebooks, Inc.
—Santa Is Coming to Calgary. Smallman, Steve. 2nd ed. 2019. (Santa Is Coming... Ser.). (ENG.). 40p. (J). (-3). 12.99 *(978-1-7282-0047-7(4))* Sourcebooks, Inc.
—Santa Is Coming to California. Smallman, Steve. (ENG.). (J). (-3). 2012. 32p. 9.99 *(978-1-4022-7515-9(3)*, Sourcebooks Jabberwocky); 2nd ed. 2019. 40p. 12.99 *(978-1-7282-0048-4(2))* Sourcebooks, Inc.
—Santa Is Coming to Canada. Smallman, Steve. 2nd ed. 2019. (Santa Is Coming... Ser.). (ENG.). 40p. (J). (-3). 12.99 *(978-1-7282-0049-1(0))* Sourcebooks, Inc.
—Santa Is Coming to Chicago. Smallman, Steve. 2nd ed. 2019. (Santa Is Coming... Ser.). (ENG.). 40p. (J). (-3). 12.99 *(978-1-7282-0050-7(4))* Sourcebooks, Inc.
—Santa Is Coming to Cincinnati. Smallman, Steve. 2nd ed. 2019. (Santa Is Coming... Ser.). (ENG.). 40p. (J). (-3). 12.99 *(978-1-7282-0051-4(2))* Sourcebooks, Inc.
—Santa Is Coming to Colorado. Smallman, Steve. 2013. (ENG.). 32p. (J). (-3). 9.99 *(978-1-4022-8815-9(8)*, Sourcebooks Jabberwocky) Sourcebooks, Inc.
—Santa Is Coming to Colorado. Smallman, Steve. 2nd ed. 2019. (Santa Is Coming... Ser.). (ENG.). 40p. (J). (-3). 12.99 *(978-1-7282-0052-1(0))* Sourcebooks, Inc.
—Santa Is Coming to Connecticut. Smallman, Steve. 2nd ed. 2019. (Santa Is Coming... Ser.). (ENG.). 40p. (J). (-3). 12.99 *(978-1-7282-0053-8(9))* Sourcebooks, Inc.
—Santa Is Coming to Dallas. Smallman, Steve. 2nd ed. 2019. (Santa Is Coming... Ser.). (ENG.). 40p. (J). (-3). 12.99 *(978-1-7282-0054-5(7))* Sourcebooks, Inc.
—Santa Is Coming to Delaware. Smallman, Steve. 2nd ed. 2019. (Santa Is Coming... Ser.). (ENG.). 40p. (J). (-3). 12.99 *(978-1-7282-0055-2(5))* Sourcebooks, Inc.
—Santa Is Coming to Edmonton. Smallman, Steve. 2nd ed. 2019. (Santa Is Coming... Ser.). (ENG.). 40p. (J). (-3). 12.99 *(978-1-7282-0056-9(3))* Sourcebooks, Inc.
—Santa Is Coming to Florida. Smallman, Steve. (ENG.). (J). (-3). 2012. 32p. 9.99 *(978-1-4022-7527-2(7)*, Sourcebooks Jabberwocky); 2nd ed. 2019. 40p. 12.99 *(978-1-7282-0057-6(1))* Sourcebooks, Inc.
—Santa Is Coming to Georgia. Smallman, Steve. 2013. (ENG.). 32p. (J). (-3). 9.99 *(978-1-4022-8794-7(1)*, Sourcebooks Jabberwocky) Sourcebooks, Inc.
—Santa Is Coming to Georgia. Smallman, Steve. 2nd ed. 2019. (Santa Is Coming... Ser.). (ENG.). 40p. (J). (-3). 12.99 *(978-1-7282-0058-3(X))* Sourcebooks, Inc.
—Santa Is Coming to Hawaii. Smallman, Steve. 2nd ed. 2019. (Santa Is Coming... Ser.). (ENG.). 40p. (J). (-3). 12.99 *(978-1-7282-0059-0(8))* Sourcebooks, Inc.
—Santa Is Coming to Idaho. Smallman, Steve. 2nd ed. 2019. (Santa Is Coming... Ser.). (ENG.). 40p. (J). (-3). 12.99 *(978-1-7282-0060-6(1))* Sourcebooks, Inc.
—Santa Is Coming to Illinois. Smallman, Steve. 2nd ed. 2019. (Santa Is Coming... Ser.). (ENG.). 40p. (J). (-3). 12.99 *(978-1-7282-0061-3(X))* Sourcebooks, Inc.
—Santa Is Coming to Indiana. Smallman, Steve. 2nd ed. 2019. (Santa Is Coming... Ser.). (ENG.). 40p. (J). (-3). 12.99 *(978-1-7282-0062-0(8))* Sourcebooks, Inc.
—Santa Is Coming to Iowa. Smallman, Steve. 2nd ed. 2019. (Santa Is Coming... Ser.). (ENG.). 40p. (J). (-3). 12.99 *(978-1-7282-0063-7(6))* Sourcebooks, Inc.
—Santa Is Coming to Kansas. Smallman, Steve. 2nd ed. 2019. (Santa Is Coming... Ser.). (ENG.). 40p. (J). (-3). 12.99 *(978-1-7282-0064-4(4))* Sourcebooks, Inc.
—Santa Is Coming to Kansas City. Smallman, Steve. 2nd ed. 2019. (Santa Is Coming... Ser.). (ENG.). 40p. (J). (-3). 12.99 *(978-1-7282-0065-1(2))* Sourcebooks, Inc.
—Santa Is Coming to Kentucky. Smallman, Steve. 2nd ed. 2019. (Santa Is Coming... Ser.). (ENG.). 40p. (J). (-3). 12.99 *(978-1-7282-0066-8(0))* Sourcebooks, Inc.
—Santa Is Coming to Louisiana. Smallman, Steve. 2nd ed. 2019. (Santa Is Coming... Ser.). (ENG.). 40p. (J). (-3). 12.99 *(978-1-7282-0067-5(9))* Sourcebooks, Inc.
—Santa Is Coming to Maine. Smallman, Steve. 2nd ed. 2019. (Santa Is Coming... Ser.). (ENG.). 40p. (J). (-3). 12.99 *(978-1-7282-0068-2(7))* Sourcebooks, Inc.
—Santa Is Coming to Maryland. Smallman, Steve. 2nd ed. 2019. (Santa Is Coming... Ser.). (ENG.). 40p. (J). (-3). 12.99 *(978-1-7282-0069-9(5))* Sourcebooks, Inc.

—Santa Is Coming to Massachusetts. Smallman, Steve. 2nd ed. 2019. (Santa Is Coming... Ser.). (ENG.). 40p. (J). (-3). 12.99 *(978-1-7282-0070-5(9))* Sourcebooks, Inc.

—Santa Is Coming to Michigan. Smallman, Steve. (ENG.). (J). (-3). 2012. 32p. 9.99 *(978-1-4022-7539-5(0),* Sourcebooks Jabberwocky); 2nd ed. 2019. 40p. 12.99 *(978-1-7282-0071-2(7))* Sourcebooks, Inc.

—Santa Is Coming to Minnesota. Smallman, Steve. (ENG.). (J). (-3). 2012. 32p. 9.99 *(978-1-4022-7530-2(7),* Sourcebooks Jabberwocky); 2nd ed. 2019. 40p. 12.99 *(978-1-7282-0072-9(5))* Sourcebooks, Inc.

—Santa Is Coming to Mississippi. Smallman, Steve. 2nd ed. 2019. (Santa Is Coming... Ser.). (ENG.). 40p. (J). (-3). 12.99 *(978-1-7282-0073-6(3))* Sourcebooks, Inc.

—Santa Is Coming to Missouri. Smallman, Steve. 2nd ed. 2019. (Santa Is Coming... Ser.). (ENG.). 40p. (J). (-3). 12.99 *(978-1-7282-0074-3(1))* Sourcebooks, Inc.

—Santa Is Coming to Montana. Smallman, Steve. 2nd ed. 2019. (Santa Is Coming... Ser.). (ENG.). 40p. (J). (-3). 12.99 *(978-1-7282-0075-0(X))* Sourcebooks, Inc.

—Santa Is Coming to My House. Smallman, Steve. (ENG.). (J). (-3). 2012. 32p. 11.99 *(978-1-4022-7775-7(X),* Sourcebooks Jabberwocky); 2nd ed. 2019. 40p. 12.99 *(978-1-7282-0076-7(8))* Sourcebooks, Inc.

—Santa Is Coming to Nashville. Smallman, Steve. 2nd ed. 2019. (Santa Is Coming... Ser.). (ENG.). 40p. (J). (-3). 12.99 *(978-1-7282-0077-4(6))* Sourcebooks, Inc.

—Santa Is Coming to Nebraska. Smallman, Steve. 2nd ed. 2019. (Santa Is Coming... Ser.). (ENG.). 40p. (J). (-3). 12.99 *(978-1-7282-0078-1(4))* Sourcebooks, Inc.

—Santa Is Coming to Nevada. Smallman, Steve. 2nd ed. 2019. (Santa Is Coming... Ser.). (ENG.). 40p. (J). (-3). 12.99 *(978-1-7282-0079-8(2))* Sourcebooks, Inc.

—Santa Is Coming to New Hampshire. Smallman, Steve. 2nd ed. 2019. (Santa Is Coming... Ser.). (ENG.). 40p. (J). (-3). 12.99 *(978-1-7282-0080-4(6))* Sourcebooks, Inc.

—Santa Is Coming to New Jersey. Smallman, Steve. 2013. (ENG.). 32p. (J). (-3). 9.99 *(978-1-4022-8797-8(6),* Sourcebooks Jabberwocky) Sourcebooks, Inc.

—Santa Is Coming to New Jersey. Smallman, Steve. 2nd ed. 2019. (Santa Is Coming... Ser.). (ENG.). 40p. (J). (-3). 12.99 *(978-1-7282-0081-1(4))* Sourcebooks, Inc.

—Santa Is Coming to New Mexico. Smallman, Steve. 2nd ed. 2019. (Santa Is Coming... Ser.). (ENG.). 40p. (J). (-3). 12.99 *(978-1-7282-0082-8(2))* Sourcebooks, Inc.

—Santa Is Coming to New York. Smallman, Steve. 2nd ed. 2019. (Santa Is Coming... Ser.). (ENG.). 40p. (J). (-3). 12.99 *(978-1-7282-0083-5(0))* Sourcebooks, Inc.

—Santa Is Coming to New York City. Smallman, Steve. 2nd ed. 2019. (Santa Is Coming... Ser.). (ENG.). 40p. (J). (-3). 12.99 *(978-1-7282-0084-2(9))* Sourcebooks, Inc.

—Santa Is Coming to Newfoundland. Smallman, Steve. 2nd ed. 2019. (Santa Is Coming... Ser.). (ENG.). 40p. (J). (-3). 12.99 *(978-1-7282-0085-9(7))* Sourcebooks, Inc.

—Santa Is Coming to North Carolina. Smallman, Steve. 2nd ed. 2019. (Santa Is Coming... Ser.). (ENG.). 40p. (J). (-3). 12.99 *(978-1-7282-0086-6(5))* Sourcebooks, Inc.

—Santa Is Coming to North Dakota. Smallman, Steve. 2nd ed. 2019. (Santa Is Coming... Ser.). (ENG.). 40p. (J). (-3). 12.99 *(978-1-7282-0087-3(3))* Sourcebooks, Inc.

—Santa Is Coming to Nova Scotia. Smallman, Steve. 2nd ed. 2019. (Santa Is Coming... Ser.). (ENG.). 40p. (J). (-3). 12.99 *(978-1-7282-0088-0(1))* Sourcebooks, Inc.

—Santa Is Coming to Ohio. Smallman, Steve. 2nd ed. 2019. (Santa Is Coming... Ser.). (ENG.). 40p. (J). (-3). 12.99 *(978-1-7282-0089-7(X))* Sourcebooks, Inc.

—Santa Is Coming to Oklahoma. Smallman, Steve. 2nd ed. 2019. (Santa Is Coming... Ser.). (ENG.). 40p. (J). (-3). 12.99 *(978-1-7282-0090-3(3))* Sourcebooks, Inc.

—Santa Is Coming to Oregon. Smallman, Steve. 2nd ed. 2019. (Santa Is Coming... Ser.). (ENG.). 40p. (J). (-3). 12.99 *(978-1-7282-0091-0(1))* Sourcebooks, Inc.

—Santa Is Coming to Ottawa. Ventura, Steve & Smallman, Steve. 2nd ed. 2019. (Santa Is Coming... Ser.). (ENG.). 40p. (J). (-3). 12.99 *(978-1-7282-0092-7(X))* Sourcebooks, Inc.

—Santa Is Coming to Pennsylvania. Smallman, Steve. 2nd ed. 2019. (Santa Is Coming... Ser.). (ENG.). 40p. (J). (-3). 12.99 *(978-1-7282-0093-4(8))* Sourcebooks, Inc.

—Santa Is Coming to Philadelphia. Smallman, Steve. 2nd ed. 2019. (Santa Is Coming... Ser.). (ENG.). 40p. (J). (-3). 12.99 *(978-1-7282-0094-1(6))* Sourcebooks, Inc.

—Santa Is Coming to Pittsburgh. Smallman, Steve. 2nd ed. 2019. (Santa Is Coming... Ser.). (ENG.). 40p. (J). (-3). 12.99 *(978-1-7282-0095-8(4))* Sourcebooks, Inc.

—Santa Is Coming to Portland. Smallman, Steve. 2nd ed. 2019. (Santa Is Coming... Ser.). (ENG.). 40p. (J). (-3). 12.99 *(978-1-7282-0096-5(2))* Sourcebooks, Inc.

—Santa Is Coming to Rhode Island. Smallman, Steve. 2nd ed. 2019. (Santa Is Coming... Ser.). (ENG.). 40p. (J). (-3). 12.99 *(978-1-7282-0097-2(0))* Sourcebooks, Inc.

—Santa Is Coming to San Diego. Smallman, Steve. 2nd ed. 2019. (Santa Is Coming... Ser.). (ENG.). 40p. (J). (-3). 12.99 *(978-1-7282-0098-9(9))* Sourcebooks, Inc.

—Santa Is Coming to San Francisco. Smallman, Steve. 2nd ed. 2019. (Santa Is Coming... Ser.). (ENG.). 40p. (J). (-3). 12.99 *(978-1-7282-0099-6(7))* Sourcebooks, Inc.

—Santa Is Coming to South Carolina. Smallman, Steve. 2nd ed. 2019. (Santa Is Coming... Ser.). (ENG.). 40p. (J). (-3). 12.99 *(978-1-7282-0100-9(4))* Sourcebooks, Inc.

—Santa Is Coming to South Dakota. Smallman, Steve. 2nd ed. 2019. (Santa Is Coming... Ser.). (ENG.). 40p. (J). (-3). 12.99 *(978-1-7282-0101-6(2))* Sourcebooks, Inc.

—Santa Is Coming to St. Louis. Smallman, Steve. 2nd ed. 2019. (Santa Is Coming... Ser.). (ENG.). 40p. (J). (-3). 12.99 *(978-1-7282-0102-3(0))* Sourcebooks, Inc.

—Santa Is Coming to Tennessee. Smallman, Steve. 2nd ed. 2019. (Santa Is Coming... Ser.). (ENG.). 40p. (J). (-3). 12.99 *(978-1-7282-0103-0(9))* Sourcebooks, Inc.

—Santa Is Coming to Texas. Smallman, Steve. (ENG.). (J). (-3). 2012. 32p. 9.99 *(978-1-4022-7512-8(9),* Sourcebooks Jabberwocky); 2nd ed. 2019. 40p. 12.99 *(978-1-7282-0104-7(7))* Sourcebooks, Inc.

—Santa Is Coming to Toronto. Smallman, Steve. 2nd ed. 2019. (Santa Is Coming... Ser.). (ENG.). 40p. (J). (-3). 12.99 *(978-1-7282-0105-4(5))* Sourcebooks, Inc.

—Santa Is Coming to Tulsa. Smallman, Steve. 2nd ed. 2019. (Santa Is Coming... Ser.). (ENG.). 40p. (J). (-3). 12.99 *(978-1-7282-0106-1(3))* Sourcebooks, Inc.

—Santa Is Coming to Utah. Smallman, Steve. 2nd ed. 2019. (Santa Is Coming... Ser.). (ENG.). 40p. (J). (-3). 12.99 *(978-1-7282-0107-8(1))* Sourcebooks, Inc.

—Santa Is Coming to Vancouver. Smallman, Steve. 2nd ed. 2019. (Santa Is Coming... Ser.). (ENG.). 40p. (J). (-3). 12.99 *(978-1-7282-0108-5(X))* Sourcebooks, Inc.

—Santa Is Coming to Vermont. Smallman, Steve. 2nd ed. 2019. (Santa Is Coming... Ser.). (ENG.). 40p. (J). (-3). 12.99 *(978-1-7282-0109-2(8))* Sourcebooks, Inc.

—Santa Is Coming to Virginia. Smallman, Steve. 2013. (ENG.). 32p. (J). (-3). 9.99 *(978-1-4022-8800-5(X),* Sourcebooks Jabberwocky) Sourcebooks, Inc.

—Santa Is Coming to Virginia. Smallman, Steve. 2nd ed. 2019. (Santa Is Coming... Ser.). (ENG.). 40p. (J). (-3). 12.99 *(978-1-7282-0110-8(1))* Sourcebooks, Inc.

—Santa Is Coming to Washington. Smallman, Steve. (ENG.). (J). (-3). 2012. 32p. 9.99 *(978-1-4022-7524-1(2),* Sourcebooks Jabberwocky); 2nd ed. 2019. 40p. 12.99 *(978-1-7282-0111-5(X))* Sourcebooks, Inc.

—Santa Is Coming to Washington, D. C. Smallman, Steve. 2nd ed. 2019. (Santa Is Coming... Ser.). (ENG.). 40p. (J). (-3). 12.99 *(978-1-7282-0112-2(8))* Sourcebooks, Inc.

—Santa Is Coming to West Virginia. Smallman, Steve. 2nd ed. 2019. (Santa Is Coming... Ser.). (ENG.). 40p. (J). (-3). 12.99 *(978-1-7282-0113-9(6))* Sourcebooks, Inc.

—Santa Is Coming to Wisconsin. Smallman, Steve. (ENG.). (J). (-3). 2012. 32p. 9.99 *(978-1-4022-7533-3(1),* Sourcebooks Jabberwocky); 2nd ed. 2019. 40p. 12.99 *(978-1-7282-0114-6(4))* Sourcebooks, Inc.

—Santa Is Coming to Wyoming. Smallman, Steve. 2nd ed. 2019. (Santa Is Coming... Ser.). (ENG.). 40p. (J). (-3). 12.99 *(978-1-7282-0115-3(2))* Sourcebooks, Inc.

—Santa's Sleigh Is on Its Way to Alabama: A Christmas Adventure. James, Eric. 2015. (ENG.). 32p. (J). (-2). 12.99 *(978-1-4926-2763-0(1),* Sourcebooks Jabberwocky) Sourcebooks, Inc.

—Santa's Sleigh Is on Its Way to Alaska: A Christmas Adventure. James, Eric. 2016. (ENG.). 32p. (J). (-2). 12.99 *(978-1-4926-4314-2(9),* 9781492643142, Sourcebooks Jabberwocky) Sourcebooks, Inc.

—Santa's Sleigh Is on Its Way to Albuquerque: A Christmas Adventure. James, Eric. 2016. (ENG.). 32p. (J). (-2). 12.99 *(978-1-4926-4315-9(7),* 9781492643159, Sourcebooks Jabberwocky) Sourcebooks, Inc.

—Santa's Sleigh Is on Its Way to Arizona: A Christmas Adventure. James, Eric. 2016. (ENG.). 32p. (J). (-2). 12.99 *(978-1-4926-4316-6(5),* 9781492643166, Sourcebooks Jabberwocky) Sourcebooks, Inc.

—Santa's Sleigh Is on Its Way to Arkansas: A Christmas Adventure. James, Eric. 2016. (ENG.). 32p. (J). (-2). 12.99 *(978-1-4926-4317-3(3),* 9781492643173, Sourcebooks Jabberwocky) Sourcebooks, Inc.

—Santa's Sleigh Is on Its Way to Boise: A Christmas Adventure. James, Eric. 2016. (ENG.). 32p. (J). (-2). 12.99 *(978-1-4926-4318-0(1),* 9781492643180, Sourcebooks Jabberwocky) Sourcebooks, Inc.

—Santa's Sleigh Is on Its Way to Boston: A Christmas Adventure. James, Eric. 2016. (ENG.). 32p. (J). (-2). 12.99 *(978-1-4926-4319-7(X),* 9781492643197, Sourcebooks Jabberwocky) Sourcebooks, Inc.

—Santa's Sleigh Is on Its Way to Calgary: A Christmas Adventure. James, Eric. 2016. (ENG.). 32p. (J). (-2). 12.99 *(978-1-4926-4320-3(3),* 9781492643203, Sourcebooks Jabberwocky) Sourcebooks, Inc.

—Santa's Sleigh Is on Its Way to California: A Christmas Adventure. James, Eric. 2015. (ENG.). 32p. (J). (-2). 12.99 *(978-1-4926-2747-0(X),* Sourcebooks Jabberwocky) Sourcebooks, Inc.

—Santa's Sleigh Is on Its Way to Canada: A Christmas Adventure. James, Eric. 2016. (ENG.). 32p. (J). (-2). 12.99 *(978-1-4926-4321-0(1),* 9781492643210, Sourcebooks Jabberwocky) Sourcebooks, Inc.

—Santa's Sleigh Is on Its Way to Charleston: A Christmas Adventure. James, Eric. 2016. (ENG.). 32p. (J). (-2). 12.99 *(978-1-4926-4322-7(X),* 9781492643227, Sourcebooks Jabberwocky) Sourcebooks, Inc.

—Santa's Sleigh Is on Its Way to Chicago: A Christmas Adventure. James, Eric. 2016. (ENG.). 32p. (J). (-2). 12.99 *(978-1-4926-4323-4(8),* 9781492643234, Sourcebooks Jabberwocky) Sourcebooks, Inc.

—Santa's Sleigh Is on Its Way to Cincinnati: A Christmas Adventure. James, Eric. 2016. (ENG.). 32p. (J). (-2). 12.99 *(978-1-4926-4324-1(6),* 9781492643241, Sourcebooks Jabberwocky) Sourcebooks, Inc.

—Santa's Sleigh Is on Its Way to Colorado: A Christmas Adventure. James, Eric. 2015. (ENG.). 32p. (J). (-2). 12.99 *(978-1-4926-2756-2(9),* Sourcebooks Jabberwocky) Sourcebooks, Inc.

—Santa's Sleigh Is on Its Way to Connecticut: A Christmas Adventure. James, Eric. 2016. (ENG.). 32p. (J). (-2). 12.99 *(978-1-4926-4325-8(4),* 9781492643258, Sourcebooks Jabberwocky) Sourcebooks, Inc.

—Santa's Sleigh Is on Its Way to Delaware: A Christmas Adventure. James, Eric. 2016. (ENG.). 32p. (J). (-2). 12.99 *(978-1-4926-4326-5(2),* 9781492643265, Sourcebooks Jabberwocky) Sourcebooks, Inc.

—Santa's Sleigh Is on Its Way to Edmonton: A Christmas Adventure. James, Eric. 2016. (ENG.). 32p. (J). (-2). 12.99 *(978-1-4926-4327-2(0),* 9781492643272, Sourcebooks Jabberwocky) Sourcebooks, Inc.

—Santa's Sleigh Is on Its Way to Florida: A Christmas Adventure. James, Eric. 2015. (ENG.). 32p. (J). (-2). 12.99 *(978-1-4926-2743-2(7),* Sourcebooks Jabberwocky) Sourcebooks, Inc.

—Santa's Sleigh Is on Its Way to Georgia: A Christmas Adventure. James, Eric. 2015. (ENG.). 32p. (J). (-2). 12.99 *(978-1-4926-2744-9(5),* Sourcebooks Jabberwocky) Sourcebooks, Inc.

—Santa's Sleigh Is on Its Way to Hawaii: A Christmas Adventure. James, Eric. 2016. (ENG.). 32p. (J). (-2). 12.99 *(978-1-4926-4328-9(9),* 9781492643289, Sourcebooks Jabberwocky) Sourcebooks, Inc.

—Santa's Sleigh Is on Its Way to Illinois: A Christmas Adventure. James, Eric. 2015. (ENG.). 32p. (J). (-2). 12.99 *(978-1-4926-2746-3(1),* Sourcebooks Jabberwocky) Sourcebooks, Inc.

—Santa's Sleigh Is on Its Way to Indiana: A Christmas Adventure. James, Eric. 2015. (ENG.). 32p. (J). (-2). 12.99 *(978-1-4926-2753-1(4),* Sourcebooks Jabberwocky) Sourcebooks, Inc.

—Santa's Sleigh Is on Its Way to Iowa: A Christmas Adventure. James, Eric. 2015. (ENG.). 32p. (J). (-2). 12.99 *(978-1-4926-2749-4(6),* Sourcebooks Jabberwocky) Sourcebooks, Inc.

—Santa's Sleigh Is on Its Way to Kansas: A Christmas Adventure. James, Eric. 2016. (ENG.). 32p. (J). (-2). 12.99 *(978-1-4926-4330-2(0),* 9781492643302, Sourcebooks Jabberwocky) Sourcebooks, Inc.

—Santa's Sleigh Is on Its Way to Kansas City: A Christmas Adventure. James, Eric. 2016. (ENG.). 32p. (J). (-2). 12.99 *(978-1-4926-4331-9(9),* 9781492643319, Sourcebooks Jabberwocky) Sourcebooks, Inc.

—Santa's Sleigh Is on Its Way to Kentucky: A Christmas Adventure. James, Eric. 2015. (ENG.). 32p. (J). (-2). 12.99 *(978-1-4926-2761-6(5),* Sourcebooks Jabberwocky) Sourcebooks, Inc.

—Santa's Sleigh Is on Its Way to Las Vegas: A Christmas Adventure. James, Eric. 2016. (ENG.). 32p. (J). (-2). 12.99 *(978-1-4926-4332-6(7),* 9781492643326, Sourcebooks Jabberwocky) Sourcebooks, Inc.

—Santa's Sleigh Is on Its Way to Los Angeles: A Christmas Adventure. James, Eric. 2016. (ENG.). 32p. (J). (-2). 12.99 *(978-1-4926-4333-3(5),* 9781492643333, Sourcebooks Jabberwocky) Sourcebooks, Inc.

—Santa's Sleigh Is on Its Way to Louisiana: A Christmas Adventure. James, Eric. 2015. (ENG.). 32p. (J). (-2). 12.99 *(978-1-4926-2762-3(3),* Sourcebooks Jabberwocky) Sourcebooks, Inc.

—Santa's Sleigh Is on Its Way to Maine: A Christmas Adventure. James, Eric. 2016. (ENG.). 32p. (J). (-2). 12.99 *(978-1-4926-4334-0(3),* 9781492643340, Sourcebooks Jabberwocky) Sourcebooks, Inc.

—Santa's Sleigh Is on Its Way to Maryland: A Christmas Adventure. James, Eric. 2016. (ENG.). 32p. (J). (-2). 12.99 *(978-1-4926-4335-7(1),* 9781492643357, Sourcebooks Jabberwocky) Sourcebooks, Inc.

—Santa's Sleigh Is on Its Way to Massachusetts: A Christmas Adventure. James, Eric. 2016. (ENG.). 32p. (J). (-2). 12.99 *(978-1-4926-4336-4(X),* 9781492643364, Sourcebooks Jabberwocky) Sourcebooks, Inc.

—Santa's Sleigh Is on Its Way to Michigan: A Christmas Adventure. James, Eric. 2015. (ENG.). 32p. (J). (-2). 12.99 *(978-1-4926-2741-8(0),* Sourcebooks Jabberwocky) Sourcebooks, Inc.

—Santa's Sleigh Is on Its Way to Minnesota: A Christmas Adventure. James, Eric. 2015. (ENG.). 32p. (J). (-2). 12.99 *(978-1-4926-2748-7(8),* Sourcebooks Jabberwocky) Sourcebooks, Inc.

—Santa's Sleigh Is on Its Way to Mississippi: A Christmas Adventure. James, Eric. 2016. (ENG.). 32p. (J). (-2). 12.99 *(978-1-4926-4337-1(8),* 9781492643371, Sourcebooks Jabberwocky) Sourcebooks, Inc.

—Santa's Sleigh Is on Its Way to Missouri: A Christmas Adventure. James, Eric. 2015. (ENG.). 32p. (J). (-2). 12.99 *(978-1-4926-2759-3(3),* Sourcebooks Jabberwocky) Sourcebooks, Inc.

—Santa's Sleigh Is on Its Way to Montana: A Christmas Adventure. James, Eric. 2016. (ENG.). 32p. (J). (-2). 12.99 *(978-1-4926-4338-8(6),* 9781492643388, Sourcebooks Jabberwocky) Sourcebooks, Inc.

—Santa'S Sleigh Is on Its Way to My House: A Christmas Adventure. James, Eric. 2015. (ENG.). 32p. (J). (-2). 12.99 *(978-1-4926-2740-1(2),* Sourcebooks Jabberwocky) Sourcebooks, Inc.

—Santa's Sleigh Is on Its Way to Nebraska: A Christmas Adventure. James, Eric. 2016. (ENG.). 32p. (J). (-2). 12.99 *(978-1-4926-4339-5(4),* 9781492643395, Sourcebooks Jabberwocky) Sourcebooks, Inc.

—Santa's Sleigh Is on Its Way to Nevada: A Christmas Adventure. James, Eric. 2016. (ENG.). 32p. (J). (-2). 12.99 *(978-1-4926-4340-1(8),* 9781492643401, Sourcebooks Jabberwocky) Sourcebooks, Inc.

—Santa's Sleigh Is on Its Way to New England: A Christmas Adventure. James, Eric. 2016. (ENG.). 32p. (J). (-2). 12.99 *(978-1-4926-4341-8(6),* 9781492643418, Sourcebooks Jabberwocky) Sourcebooks, Inc.

—Santa's Sleigh Is on Its Way to New Hampshire: A Christmas Adventure. James, Eric. 2016. (ENG.). 32p. (J). (-2). 12.99 *(978-1-4926-4342-5(4),* 9781492643425, Sourcebooks Jabberwocky) Sourcebooks, Inc.

—Santa's Sleigh Is on Its Way to New Jersey: A Christmas Adventure. James, Eric. 2015. (ENG.). 32p. (J). (-2). 12.99 *(978-1-4926-2758-6(5),* Sourcebooks Jabberwocky) Sourcebooks, Inc.

—Santa's Sleigh Is on Its Way to New Mexico: A Christmas Adventure. James, Eric. 2016. (ENG.). 32p. (J). (-2). 12.99 *(978-1-4926-4343-2(2),* 9781492643432, Sourcebooks Jabberwocky) Sourcebooks, Inc.

—Santa's Sleigh Is on Its Way to New York: A Christmas Adventure. James, Eric. 2015. (ENG.). 32p. (J). (-2). 12.99 *(978-1-4926-2751-7(8),* Sourcebooks Jabberwocky) Sourcebooks, Inc.

—Santa's Sleigh Is on Its Way to New York City: A Christmas Adventure. James, Eric. 2016. (ENG.). 32p. (J). (-2). 12.99 *(978-1-4926-4344-9(0),* 9781492643449, Sourcebooks Jabberwocky) Sourcebooks, Inc.

—Santa's Sleigh Is on It's Way to Newfoundland: A Christmas Adventure. James, Eric. 2016. (ENG.). 32p. (J). (-2). 12.99 *(978-1-4926-4505-4(2),* 9781492645054, Sourcebooks Jabberwocky) Sourcebooks, Inc.

—Santa's Sleigh Is on Its Way to North Carolina: A Christmas Adventure. James, Eric. 2015. (ENG.). 32p. (J). (-2). 12.99 *(978-1-4926-2750-0(X),* Sourcebooks Jabberwocky) Sourcebooks, Inc.

—Santa's Sleigh Is on Its Way to North Dakota: A Christmas Adventure. James, Eric. 2016. (ENG.). 32p. (J). (-2). 12.99 *(978-1-4926-4345-6(9),* 9781492643456, Sourcebooks Jabberwocky) Sourcebooks, Inc.

—Santa's Sleigh Is on It's Way to Nova Scotia: A Christmas Adventure. James, Eric. 2016. (ENG.). 32p. (J). (-2). 12.99 *(978-1-4926-4508-5(7),* 9781492645085, Sourcebooks Jabberwocky) Sourcebooks, Inc.

—Santa's Sleigh Is on Its Way to Ohio: A Christmas Adventure. James, Eric. 2015. (ENG.). 32p. (J). (-2). 12.99 *(978-1-4926-2742-5(9),* Sourcebooks Jabberwocky) Sourcebooks, Inc.

—Santa's Sleigh Is on Its Way to Oklahoma: A Christmas Adventure. James, Eric. 2016. (ENG.). 32p. (J). (-2). 12.99 *(978-1-4926-4346-3(7),* 9781492643463, Sourcebooks Jabberwocky) Sourcebooks, Inc.

—Santa's Sleigh Is on Its Way to Omaha: A Christmas Adventure. James, Eric. 2016. (ENG.). 32p. (J). (-2). 12.99 *(978-1-4926-4347-0(5),* 9781492643470, Sourcebooks Jabberwocky) Sourcebooks, Inc.

—Santa's Sleigh Is on Its Way to Pennsylvania: A Christmas Adventure. James, Eric. 2015. (ENG.). 32p. (J). (-2). 12.99 *(978-1-4926-2745-6(3),* Sourcebooks Jabberwocky) Sourcebooks, Inc.

—Santa's Sleigh Is on Its Way to Philadelphia: A Christmas Adventure. James, Eric. 2016. (ENG.). 32p. (J). (-2). 12.99 *(978-1-4926-4350-0(5),* 9781492643500, Sourcebooks Jabberwocky) Sourcebooks, Inc.

—Santa's Sleigh Is on Its Way to Pittsburgh: A Christmas Adventure. James, Eric. 2016. (ENG.). 32p. (J). (-2). 12.99 *(978-1-4926-4351-7(3),* 9781492643517, Sourcebooks Jabberwocky) Sourcebooks, Inc.

—Santa's Sleigh Is on Its Way to Portland: A Christmas Adventure. James, Eric. 2016. (ENG.). 32p. (J). (-2). 12.99 *(978-1-4926-4352-4(1),* 9781492643524, Sourcebooks Jabberwocky) Sourcebooks, Inc.

—Santa's Sleigh Is on Its Way to Rhode Island: A Christmas Adventure. James, Eric. 2016. (ENG.). 32p. (J). (-2). 12.99 *(978-1-4926-4353-1(X),* 9781492643531, Sourcebooks Jabberwocky) Sourcebooks, Inc.

—Santa's Sleigh Is on Its Way to San Francisco: A Christmas Adventure. James, Eric. 2016. (ENG.). 32p. (J). (-2). 12.99 *(978-1-4926-4354-8(8),* 9781492643548, Sourcebooks Jabberwocky) Sourcebooks, Inc.

—Santa's Sleigh Is on Its Way to South Carolina: A Christmas Adventure. James, Eric. 2015. (ENG.). 32p. (J). (-2). 12.99 *(978-1-4926-2757-9(7),* Sourcebooks Jabberwocky) Sourcebooks, Inc.

—Santa's Sleigh Is on Its Way to South Dakota: A Christmas Adventure. James, Eric. 2016. (ENG.). 32p. (J). (-2). 12.99 *(978-1-4926-4355-5(6),* 9781492643555, Sourcebooks Jabberwocky) Sourcebooks, Inc.

—Santa's Sleigh Is on Its Way to St. Louis: A Christmas Adventure. James, Eric. 2016. (ENG.). 32p. (J). (-2). 12.99 *(978-1-4926-4356-2(4),* 9781492643562, Sourcebooks Jabberwocky) Sourcebooks, Inc.

—Santa's Sleigh Is on Its Way to Tampa Bay: A Christmas Adventure. James, Eric. 2016. (ENG.). 32p. (J). (-2). 12.99 *(978-1-4926-4357-9(2),* 9781492643579, Sourcebooks Jabberwocky) Sourcebooks, Inc.

—Santa's Sleigh Is on Its Way to Tennessee: A Christmas Adventure. James, Eric. 2015. (ENG.). 32p. (J). (-2). 12.99 *(978-1-4926-2752-4(6),* Sourcebooks Jabberwocky) Sourcebooks, Inc.

—Santa's Sleigh Is on Its Way to Texas: A Christmas Adventure. James, Eric. 2015. (ENG.). 32p. (J). (-2). 12.99 *(978-1-4926-2739-5(9),* Sourcebooks Jabberwocky) Sourcebooks, Inc.

—Santa's Sleigh Is on Its Way to Tulsa: A Christmas Adventure. James, Eric. 2016. (ENG.). 32p. (J). (-2). 12.99 *(978-1-4926-4359-3(9),* 9781492643593, Sourcebooks Jabberwocky) Sourcebooks, Inc.

—Santa's Sleigh Is on Its Way to Utah: A Christmas Adventure. James, Eric. 2016. (ENG.). 32p. (J). (-2). 12.99 *(978-1-4926-4360-9(2),* 9781492643609, Sourcebooks Jabberwocky) Sourcebooks, Inc.

—Santa's Sleigh Is on Its Way to Vermont: A Christmas Adventure. James, Eric. 2016. (ENG.). 32p. (J). (-2). 12.99 *(978-1-4926-4362-3(9),* 9781492643623, Sourcebooks Jabberwocky) Sourcebooks, Inc.

—Santa's Sleigh Is on Its Way to Virginia: A Christmas Adventure. James, Eric. 2015. (ENG.). 32p. (J). (-2). 12.99 *(978-1-4926-2754-8(2),* Sourcebooks Jabberwocky) Sourcebooks, Inc.

—Santa's Sleigh Is on Its Way to Washington: A Christmas Adventure. James, Eric. 2015. (ENG.). 32p. (J). (-2). 12.99 *(978-1-4926-2760-9(7),* Sourcebooks Jabberwocky) Sourcebooks, Inc.

—Santa's Sleigh Is on Its Way to Washington, D. C. A Christmas Adventure. James, Eric. 2016. (ENG.). 32p. (J). (-2). 12.99 *(978-1-4926-4363-0(7),* 9781492643630, Sourcebooks Jabberwocky) Sourcebooks, Inc.

—Santa's Sleigh Is on Its Way to West Virginia: A Christmas Adventure. James, Eric. 2016. (ENG.). 32p. (J). (-2). 12.99 *(978-1-4926-4364-7(5),* 9781492643647, Sourcebooks Jabberwocky) Sourcebooks, Inc.

—Santa's Sleigh Is on Its Way to Wisconsin: A Christmas Adventure. James, Eric. 2015. (ENG.). 32p. (J). (-2). 12.99 *(978-1-4926-2755-5(0),* Sourcebooks Jabberwocky) Sourcebooks, Inc.

—Santa's Sleigh Is on Its Way to Wyoming: A Christmas Adventure. James, Eric. 2016. (ENG.). 32p. (J). (-2). 12.99 *(978-1-4926-4365-4(3),* 9781492643654, Sourcebooks Jabberwocky) Sourcebooks, Inc.

—The Three Musketeers. Dumas, Alexandre. 2013. 46p. (J). *(978-1-4351-4812-3(6))* Barnes & Noble, Inc.

—When Day Is Done, Vol. Creech, Natalee. 2019. (ENG.). 32p. (J). (gr. -1-k). 16.99 *(978-1-5064-4772-8(4),* Beaming Books) Augsburg Fortress, Pubs.

—Your Magnificent Chooser. Ortberg, John. 2017. (ENG.). 40p. (J). 14.99 *(978-1-4964-1742-8(9),* 20_27850, Tyndale Kids) Tyndale Hse. Pubs.

Dunn, Robert. There's Only One Scruffle. Dunn, Robert. 2017. (Story Corner Ser.). (ENG.). 24p. (J). (gr. -1-k). lib. bdg. 19.99 *(978-1-68297-187-1(2))* QEB Publishing Inc.

Dunn, Robert & Jessell, Tim. The Boardwalk Mystery. 2013. (Boxcar Children Mysteries Ser.: 131). (ENG.). 144p. (J). (gr. 1-5). pap. 5.99 *(978-0-8075-0803-9(9),* 807508039);131. 15.99 *(978-0-8075-0802-2(0),* 807508020) Whitman, Albert & Co.

Dunn, Robert & Piwowarski, Marcin. California Books for Kids Gift Set. Jacobs, Lily et al. 2020. (ENG.). (J). 29.99 ***(978-1-7282-4189-0(8))*** Sourcebooks, Inc.

—Florida Books for Kids Gift Set. Jacobs, Lily et al. 2020. (ENG.). (J). (-3). 29.99 ***(978-1-7282-4191-3(X))*** Sourcebooks, Inc.

—Illinois Books for Kids Gift Set. Jacobs, Lily et al. 2020. (ENG.). (J). (-3). 29.99 ***(978-1-7282-4193-7(6))*** Sourcebooks, Inc.

Dunn, Robert & Poole, Helen. New Jersey Books for Kids Gift Set. Ashford, Rachel et al. 2020. (ENG.). (J). bds. 20.00 ***(978-1-7282-4198-2(7))*** Sourcebooks, Inc.

—Ohio Books for Kids Gift Set. Ashford, Rachel et al. 2020. (ENG.). (J). bds. 20.00 ***(978-1-7282-4196-8(0))*** Sourcebooks, Inc.

—Texas Books for Kids Gift Set. Ashford, Rachel et al. 2020. (ENG.). (J). bds. 20.00 ***(978-1-7282-4195-1(2))*** Sourcebooks, Inc.

Dunn, Robert, jt. illus. see Piwowarski, Marcin.

Dunn, Robert, jt. illus. see Poole, Helen.

Dunn, Robert, jt. illus. see West, Karl.

Dunn, Robert A. The Littlest Bunny in Washington, DC: An Easter Adventure. Jacobs, Lily. 2015. (ENG.). 32p. (J). (-3). 9.99 *(978-1-4926-1234-6(0),* Sourcebooks Jabberwocky) Sourcebooks, Inc.

Dunn, Sandy. The Hen House: A True Story of Growing up on a Maine Farm. Dean, Carol. 2003. (ENG.). 32p. (J). (gr. -1-17). 15.95 *(978-0-89272-609-7(1))* Down East Bks.

Dunne, Kathleen. Hide & Seek Monsters. Williams, Rozanne Lanczak. 2005. (Reading for Fluency Ser.). 16p. (J). pap. 3.49 *(978-1-59198-154-1(9),* 4254) Creative Teaching Pr., Inc.

Dunne, Tom. Dude: Fun with Dude & Betty. Pliscou, Lisa. 2011. (ENG.). 40p. (J). (gr. 1-3). 14.99 *(978-0-06-175690-0(3))* HarperCollins Pubs.

Dunnick, Regan. Bad Astrid. Brennan, Eileen. 2013. 40p. (J). (gr. -1-2). 15.99 *(978-0-375-85580-1(7),* Random Hse. Bks. for Young Readers) Random Hse. Children's Bks.

—Bad Astrid: Read & Listen Edition. Brennan, Eileen. ed. 2013. (ENG.). 40p. (J). (gr. -1-2). E-Book *(978-0-449-81427-7(0),* Random Hse. Bks. for Young Readers) Random Hse. Children's Bks.

—Creak! Said the Bed. Root, Phyllis. 2015. 32p. (J). (gr. -1-3). 6.99 *(978-0-7636-7969-9(0))* Candlewick Pr.

—The Louds Move In!, 1 vol. Crimi, Carolyn. 2006. (ENG.). 32p. (J). (gr. -1-3). 14.95 *(978-0-7614-5221-8(4))* Marshall Cavendish Corp.

Dunnier, Tina. Grandpa's a Martian. Wehrman, Tom. 2013. 28p. pap. 8.99 *(978-1-938768-27-9(2))* Gypsy Pubns.

—Mousekabitz. Fisher, Meaghan. 2013. (ENG.). 32p. (J). pap. 8.99 *(978-1-938768-31-6(0))* Gypsy Pubns.

Dunnigan, Stefanie. Travel Tails: All Bark & No Bite. Dunnigan, Stefanie. Traina, Tina. 2017. (Travel Tails Ser.: 1). (ENG.). (J). (gr. k-5). pap. 7.95 *(978-0-9962796-0-4(1))* Dunnigan, Stefanie and Tina Traina.

Dunningham, Jo. Michael & the Elf. Sullivan, Kathryn. 2nd ed. 2012. 24p. pap. 10.95 *(978-1-61633-356-0(1))* Guardian Angel Publishing, Inc.

Dunnington, Tom. Animal Babies. Hamsa, Bobbie. 2011. (Rookie Ready to Learn Ser.). 40p. (J). (gr. -1-k). (ENG.). pap. 5.95 *(978-0-531-26800-1(4));* lib. bdg. 23.00 *(978-0-531-25640-4(5))* Scholastic Library Publishing. (Children's Pr.).

—The Great Bug Hunt. Dobkin, Bonnie. 2011. (Rookie Ready to Learn — Animals Ser.). 40p. (J). (gr. -1-k). lib. bdg. 25.00 *(978-0-531-26415-7(7));* pap. 5.95 *(978-0-531-26696-0(6))* Scholastic Library Publishing. (Children's Pr.).

—Help Dress Priscilla: A Talk-along Book. Punnett, Dick. 2nd ed. 2005. (Talk-Along Bks.). 32p. (J). pap. 6.99 *(978-0-9657211-3-4(2))* Tomoka Pr.

—Help Jumbo Escape: A Talk-along Book. Punnett, Dick. 2nd ed. 2005. (Talk-Along Bks.). 32p. (J). pap. 6.99 *(978-0-9657211-2-7(4))* Tomoka Pr.

Dunrea, Olivier. Gossie & Gertie. Dunrea, Olivier. 2007. (Gossie & Friends Ser.). (ENG.). 16p. (J). (gr. -1 — 1). bds. 6.99 *(978-0-618-74793-1(1),* 484929) Houghton Mifflin Harcourt Publishing Co.

—Ollie. Dunrea, Olivier. 2003. (Gossie & Friends Ser.). (ENG.). 32p. (J). (gr. -1 — 1). tchr. ed. 9.95 *(978-0-618-33928-0(0),* 584931) Houghton Mifflin Harcourt Publishing Co.

Dunstan, David. Chester the Crab. Tovey, Peter. Hinkler Books Staff, ed. 2010. (Wiggly Eyes Ser.). 12p. (J). (gr. -1). 12.99 *(978-1-74185-405-3(9),* Ideal Pubns.) Worthy Publishing.

—Max the Monster. Cuthbert, Kate. Hinkler Books Staff, ed. 2010. (Wiggly Eyes Ser.). 12p. (J). (gr. -1). 12.99 *(978-1-74185-404-6(0),* Ideal Pubns.) Worthy Publishing.

Dunton, Blair. Where the Animals Are King: Ranthambore National Park. Dunton, Blair. 2016. (ENG.). (J). 12.95 *(978-1-934159-29-3(8))* ThingsAsian Pr.

Dunton, Trevor. Get the Fruit: Band 00/Lilac (Collins Big Cat) Shipton, Paul. 2004. (Collins Big Cat Ser.). (ENG.). 16p. (J). (gr. -1-k). pap. 6.99 *(978-0-00-718529-0(4))* HarperCollins Pubs. Ltd. GBR. Dist: Independent Pubs. Group.

—In the Boat: Band 01A/Pink a (Collins Big Cat) Shipton, Paul. 2007. (Collins Big Cat Ser.). (ENG.). 16p. (J). (gr. -1-k). pap. 6.99 *(978-0-00-718646-4(0))* HarperCollins Pubs. Ltd. GBR. Dist: Independent Pubs. Group.

—Lion Is Worried. Graves, Sue. 2016. (Behavior Matters Ser.). (ENG.). 32p. (J). (gr. 3-2). lib. bdg. 27.25 *(978-1-4994-8084-9(9),* Windmill Bks.) Rosen Publishing Group, Inc., The.

Duntze, Dorothee. Hansel & Gretel. Grimm, Jacob & Grimm, Wilhelm K. 2006. 24p. (J). (gr. k-4). reprint ed. 17.00 *(978-1-4223-5008-9(8))* DIANE Publishing Co.

—The Twelve Dancing Princesses. Brothers Grimm. 2013. 32p. (J). (gr. -1-2). 17.95 *(978-0-7358-4121-5(7))* North-South Bks., Inc.

Dünzinger, Eva. The Black Bull: Band 14/Ruby (Collins Big Cat) McCombie, Karen. 2016. (Collins Big Cat Ser.). (ENG.). 48p. (J). pap. 10.95 *(978-0-00-814717-4(5))* HarperCollins Pubs. Ltd. GBR. Dist: Independent Pubs. Group.

Dupasquier, Philippe. Billy y el Vestido Rosa. Fine, Anne. 2003.Tr. of Bill's New Frock. (SPA.). 100p. (J). (gr. 3-5). pap. 8.95 *(978-958-24-0175-7(3))* Santillana USA Publishing Co., Inc.

—Bombs & Blackberries: A World War Two Play. Donaldson, Julia. (ENG.). 48p. (YA). *(978-0-7502-4124-3(1),* Wayland) Hachette Children's Group.

—The Sandal. Bradman, Tony. 32p. (J). (gr. 1-3). pap. 9.99 *(978-0-86264-843-5(2))* Andersen Pr. GBR. Dist: Trafalgar Square Publishing.

Dupeyron, Sarah. The ABC's of Vermont Coloring Book. 2007. 32p. (J). 4.95 *(978-0-9793790-0-0(8))* Howard Printing, Inc.

Dupon-Martinez, Christopher. Ian's Bad Choices Turned His Life Around. Carson, Shonette. 2011. 24p. pap. 24.95 *(978-1-4560-0965-6(6))* America Star Bks.

DuPont, Brittany. Little Mouse Finds a New Home. Silvola, Liz. 2013. 24p. pap. 9.99 *(978-1-937165-42-0(6))* Orange Hat Publishing.

Dupont, Lindsay Harper. Lizzy's Ups & Downs: NOT an Ordinary School Day. Harper, Jessica. 2004. 32p. (J). (gr. -1-3). 15.99 *(978-0-06-052063-2(9))* HarperCollins Pubs.

Dupre, Kelly. The Best Part of a Sauna, 1 vol. Peterson, Sheryl. 2013. 32p. (J). (gr. 1-2). 17.95 *(978-0-9883508-0-9(7));* (ENG.). pap. 9.95 *(978-0-9883508-1-6(5))* Raven Productions, Inc.

—How Coyote Stole the Summer: [a Native American Folktale]. Krensky, Stephen. 2009. (On My Own Folklore Ser.). (ENG.). 48p. (J). (gr. 2-4). pap. 7.99 *(978-1-58013-848-2(9),* First Avenue Editions) Lerner Publishing Group.

—The Lion's Share/Qayb Libaax: A Somali Folktale. Ahmed, Said Salah. 2006. 32p. (J). (gr. -1-3). pap. 7.95 *(978-1-931016-13-1(5))* Minnesota Humanities Ctr.

—The Littlest Christmas Kitten. Jackson, Leona Novy. 2005. (ENG.). 32p. (J). 16.00 *(978-0-930643-18-8(6),* 1250560) Images Unlimited Publishing.

Dupree, Bruce. The Wild Texas Stampede!, 1 vol. McManis, Margaret. 2008. (ENG.). 32p. (J). (gr. 1-3). 16.99 *(978-1-58980-568-2(2),* Pelican Publishing) Arcadia Publishing.

Dupuis, Karina, et al. Caillou, Sweet Dreams: Nightlight Book. Publishing, Chouette & Paradis, Anne. 2016. (Nightlight Book Ser.). (ENG.). 14p. (J). (gr. -1-k). 12.99 *(978-2-89718-336-3(5))* Caillouet, Gerry.

Dupuis, Karina. Caillou Tries New Foods. Patenaude, Danielle & L'Heureux, Christine. 2018. (Caillou's Essentials Ser.). (ENG.). 24p. (J). (gr. -1-k). bds. 7.99 *(978-2-89718-439-1(6))* Caillouet, Gerry.

—Goodnight Around the World: A Nightlight Book. 2018. (Nightlight Book Ser.). 14p. (J). (gr. -1-k). 12.99 *(978-2-924786-55-0(X),* CrackBoom! Bks.) Chouette Publishing CAN. Dist: Publishers Group West (PGW).

—Michigan Monsters: A Search & Find Book. 2018. (ENG.). 22p. (J). (gr. -1). bds. 9.99 *(978-2-924734-10-0(X))* City Monsters Bks. CAN. Dist: Publishers Group West (PGW).

Dupuis, Karina & Boudreau, Chantale. Big Book of Colors, Shapes, Numbers & Opposites: With Flaps to Lift & Grooves to Trace. 2019. (ENG.). 20p. (J). (gr. -1). bds. 12.99 *(978-2-924786-96-3(7),* CrackBoom! Bks.) Chouette Publishing CAN. Dist: Publishers Group West (PGW).

Dupuis, Karina & Epic Games Staff. It's Time to Dream: a Lift-The-Flap Book. Branca, Valeria. Egar, Joann, tr. 2019. 10p. (J). (gr. -1). bds. 7.99 *(978-2-924786-93-2(2),* CrackBoom! Bks.) Chouette Publishing CAN. Dist: Publishers Group West (PGW).

Dupuis, Karina, jt. illus. see Allard, Mario.

Dupuis, Karina, jt. illus. see Bangson Books Inc., Staff.

Dupuis, Karina, jt. illus. see Baretti, Sonia.

Dupuis, Karina, jt. illus. see Kary.

Dupuis, Karina, jt. illus. see Miller, Jonathan.

Dupuis, Karina, jt. illus. see Nelvana Ltd. Staff.

Dupuis, Karina, jt. illus. see Nelvana Ltd., Staff.

Dupuis, Karina, jt. illus. see Nelvana Ltd. Staff.

Dupuis, Karina, jt. illus. see ROI Visual Staff.

Dupuis, Karina, jt. illus. see Schofield, Jayne.

Dupuis, Karina, jt. illus. see Sevigny, Eric.

Dupuis, Karina, jt. illus. see Sevingy, Eric.

Dupuis, Karina, jt. illus. see Tremblay, Danielle.

Duquennoy, Jacques. Las Cataratas del Niagara. Duquennoy, Jacques. 2007. (Pandilla Fantasma Ser.). (SPA.). 27p. (J). (gr. -1). 8.95 *(978-84-263-5228-6(6))* Vives, Luis Editorial (Edelvives) ESP. Dist: Ediciones Urano S. A.

Duquet, Guy J. The Perfect Little Pumpkin. Waters, George T. I.t. ed. 2006. 30p. (J). per. 14.95 *(978-1-59879-286-7(5))* Lifevest Publishing, Inc.

Duran, Jesus. De la Tierra a la Luna. Verne, Julio. 2017. (SPA.). 116p. (J). (gr. 4). pap. *(978-9978-18-360-1(4))* Radmandi Editorial, Compania Ltd.

Duran, Jesus. Moby Dick: Ilustrado. Tayupanta, Jonathan, ed. 2020. (Ariel Juvenil Ilustrada Ser.: Vol. 52). (SPA.). 136p. (J). pap. ***(978-9978-18-564-3(X))*** Radmandi Editorial, Compania Ltd.

—Veinte Mil Leguas de Viaje Submarino. Rodriguez de Flores, Aldo. 2017. (Ariel Juvenil Ilustrada Ser.: Vol. 31). (SPA.). 110p. (J). pap. ***(978-9978-18-361-8(2))*** Radmandi Editorial, Compania Ltd.

Duran, Teresa. El Rey Ignacio. Tort, Pep & Josep, Tort. 2006. (Montana Encantada Ser.). (SPA.). 47p. (J). per. *(978-84-241-8558-9(7))* Everest Editora.

Duranceau, Suzanne. Follow the Moon Book & CD. Weeks, Sarah. 2003. (ENG.). 32p. (J). (gr. -1-3). 17.99 *(978-0-06-055744-7(3))* HarperCollins Pubs.

—Without You. Weeks, Sarah. 40p. (J). (gr. -1-2). 2007. (ENG.). pap. 7.99 *(978-0-06-113998-7(X));* 2003. 16.99 *(978-0-06-027816-8(1),* Geringer, Laura Book) HarperCollins Pubs.

Durand, Aurelia. This Book Is Anti-Racist: 20 Lessons on How to Wake up, Take Action, & Do the Work. Jewell, Tiffany. 2020. (ENG.). 160p. (J). (gr. 6-10). pap. 14.99 ***(978-0-7112-4521-1(5),*** Frances Lincoln Children's Bks.) Quarto Publishing Group UK GBR. Dist: Hachette Bk. Group.

Durand, Delphine. Al Pha's Bet. Rosenthal, Amy Krouse. 2011. 32p. (J). (gr. -1-k). 16.99 *(978-0-399-24601-2(0),* G.P. Putnam's Sons Books for Young Readers) Penguin Young Readers Group.

—The House That Jill Built: A Pop-up Book. Root, Phyllis. 2007. 18p. (J). reprint ed. 16.00 *(978-1-4223-6756-8(8))* DIANE Publishing Co.

—Welcome to Cuckooville. Chandler, Susan. 2012. (ENG.). 24p. (J). (gr. k-3). 16.95 *(978-1-61608-665-7(3),* 608665, Sky Pony Pr.) Skyhorse Publishing Co., Inc.

Durand, Élodie. Felix from Berlin. Feuchter, Anke. 2014. (AV2 Fiction Readalong Ser.: Vol. 126). (ENG.). 32p. (J). (gr. -1-3). lib. bdg. 34.28 *(978-1-4896-2277-8(2),* AV2 by Weigl) Weigl Pubs., Inc.

Durber, Matt. First ABC. 2007. (Usborne Look & Say Ser.). 22p. (J). (gr. -1-k). bds. 14.99 *(978-0-7945-1435-8(9),* Usborne) EDC Publishing.

—First Colors. Allman, Howard & MMStudios, photos by. 2006. (Usborne Look & Say Ser.). 18p. (J). (gr. -1-k). bds. 14.99 *(978-0-7945-1348-1(4),* Usborne) EDC Publishing.

Durber, Matt & Jones, Stephanie. First Picture Nature. MMStudios, photos by. 2007. (First Picture Board Bks). 16p. (J). (gr. -1-k). bds. 11.99 *(978-0-7945-1751-9(X),* Usborne) EDC Publishing.

Durfey, James Harvey. Magicopoli's Surprise: An Elephant in the Backyard. Durfey, James Harvey. 2019. (ENG.). 48p. (J). pap. 10.98 *(978-1-7288-3762-8(6))* Independently Published.

Durie, Sally. The Magic of the Dark Ravine. Wendling, Peter. 2011. 36p. pap. 13.95 *(978-1-60976-933-8(3),* Eloquent Bks.) Strategic Book Publishing & Rights Agency (SBPRA).

Durk, Jim. Apple-Picking Day! Brooke, Samantha. 2007. (Clifford's Puppy Days Ser.). (J). *(978-0-545-02841-7(8))* Scholastic, Inc.

—Backpack Puppy. Fisch, Sarah & Bridwell, Norman. 2005. (J). pap. *(978-0-439-73379-3(0))* Scholastic, Inc.

—Brave Little Engines (Thomas & Friends) Awdry, W. 2014. (ENG.). 128p. (J). (gr. -1-2). pap. 7.99 *(978-0-385-38510-7(2),* Golden Bks.) Random Hse. Children's Bks.

—Graduation Party. Kosara, Victoria. 2010. (J). pap. *(978-0-545-23400-9(X))* Scholastic, Inc.

—Mr. Potato Head: the Busy Day. Onish, Liane B. 2008. (Storytime Stickers Ser.). 16p. (J). (gr. -1-k). pap. 5.95 *(978-1-4027-5354-1(3))* Sterling Publishing Co., Inc.

—Pirate Treasure. Awdry, W. 2015. (ENG.). 48p. (J). (gr. -1-2). pap. 4.99 *(978-0-553-52478-9(X),* Golden Bks.) Random Hse. Children's Bks.

—Puppy Love. Marsoli, Lisa Ann. 2003. pap. *(978-0-439-61116-9(4))* Scholastic, Inc.

—Puppy Mind. Nance, Andrew Jordan. 2016. 22p. (J). (gr. -1-2). 16.95 *(978-1-941529-44-7(5),* Plum Blossom Bks.) Parallax Pr.

—Rudolph the Red-Nosed Reindeer Pencil Toppers. 2018. (Pencil Toppers Ser.). (ENG.). 64p. (J). (gr. 1-3). pap. 9.99 *(978-1-68412-379-7(8),* Silver Dolphin Bks.) Printers Row Publishing Group.

—The Secret of the Mine. Awdry, Wilbert V. 2013. (Glow-In-the-Dark Sticker Book Ser.). (ENG.). 48p. (J). (gr. -1-2). pap. 3.99 *(978-0-449-81711-7(3),* Golden Bks.) Random Hse. Children's Bks.

—Skating with Friends. Fisch, Sarah. 2007. (Little Red Reader Ser.). (J). pap. *(978-0-439-90898-6(1))* Scholastic, Inc.

—The Smallest Snowman. Fisch, Sarah. 2006. (J). *(978-0-439-81616-8(5))* Scholastic, Inc.

—Thomas & Friends 6-Movie Coloring Collection. Golden Books. 2016. (ENG.). 224p. (J). (gr. -1-2). pap. 5.99 *(978-1-101-94019-8(0),* Golden Bks.) Random Hse. Children's Bks.

—Thomas & Friends: the Holiday Express. Long, Susan Hill. 2017. (Lift-The-Flap Ser.). (ENG.). 10p. (J). (gr. -1 — 1). bds. 8.99 *(978-0-7944-4028-2(2),* Reader's Digest Children's Bks.) Studio Fun International.

—Thomas' Christmas Star. Awdry, Wilbert V. 2013. (ENG.). 48p. (J). (gr. -1-2). pap. 3.99 *(978-0-449-81880-0(2),* Golden Bks.) Random Hse. Children's Bks.

—Thomas' Giant Puzzle Book (Thomas & Friends) Awdry, Wilbert V. 2012. (ENG.). 40p. (J). (gr. -1-2). pap. 9.99 *(978-0-307-97690-1(4),* Golden Bks.) Random Hse. Children's Bks.

—Thomas' Halloween Delivery (Thomas & Friends) Awdry, W. 2011. (Glow-In-the-Dark Sticker Book Ser.). (ENG.). 48p. (J). (gr. -1-2). pap. 3.99 *(978-0-375-87229-7(9),* Golden Bks.) Random Hse. Children's Bks.

—Thomas Takes a Vacation (Thomas & Friends) Golden Books. 2015. (ENG.). 64p. (J). (gr. -1-2). pap. 4.99 *(978-0-553-50846-8(6),* Golden Bks.) Random Hse. Children's Bks.

—Thomas' Valentine Party. Awdry, Wilbert V. 2011. (ENG.). 32p. (J). (gr. -1-2). pap. 3.99 *(978-0-375-86815-3(1),* Golden Bks.) Random Hse. Children's Bks.

Durk, Jim, jt. illus. see Golden Books Staff.

Durkee, Noura. The Fall of the Giant. Durkee, Noura. 2007. (ENG.). 26p. (J). (gr. k-5). 16.00 *(978-1-879402-63-8(7))* Tahrike Tarsile Quran, Inc.

—The King, the Prince & the Naughty Sheep. Durkee, Noura. 2007. (ENG.). 24p. (J). (gr. k-5). 16.00 *(978-1-879402-58-4(0))* Tahrike Tarsile Quran, Inc.

—Yunus & the Whale. Durkee, Noura. 2007. (ENG.). 28p. (J). (gr. k-5). 16.00 *(978-1-879402-60-7(2))* Tahrike Tarsile Quran, Inc.

Durland DeSaix, Deborah. Peter's War: A Boy's True Story of Survival in World War II Europe. Ruelle, Karen Gray. 2020. 40p. (J). (gr. 2). 18.99 *(978-0-8234-2416-0(2))* Holiday Hse., Inc.

Durland, Maud. How the Sea Came to Marissa. Renaud, Anne. 2006. 32p. (J). *(978-1-58270-129-5(6))* Beyond Words Publishing, Inc.

Durley, Natasha. Jungle Pops. 2019. (ENG.). 30p. (J). (gr. k-2). 12.99 *(978-1-78055-536-2(9))* O'Mara, Michael Bks., Ltd. GBR. Dist: Independent Pubs. Group.

—Scratch & Learn Animals: With 7 Interactive Spreads. Brownridge, Lucy. 2019. (Scratch & Learn Ser.). (ENG.). 16p. (J). (gr. -1-2). bds. 17.99 *(978-1-78603-795-4(5),* Wide Eyed Editions) Quarto Publishing Group UK GBR. Dist: Hachette Bk. Group.

Durley, Natasha. Creature Features. Durley, Natasha. 2020. (ENG.). 24p. (J). (gr. -1-2). bds. 17.99 *(978-1-5362-1043-9(9),* Big Picture Press) Candlewick Pr.

Durr, Carol Atkinson. Tico's Book. Conure, Lunatico. 2008. 36p. (J). 15.00 *(978-0-9717047-8-7(3))* Bay Media, Inc.

Durrell, Julie. I Am Creative! Parker, David. 2005. (J). *(978-0-439-73586-5(6))* Scholastic, Inc.

—Jesus Rose on Easter Morn: A Listen! Look! Book. Stockstill, Gloria McQueen. 2004. 20p. (J). bds. 5.49 *(978-0-7586-0143-8(3))* Concordia Publishing Hse.

—The Night Before Kindergarten. Wing, Natasha. 2014. (Night Before Ser.). 32p. (J). (gr. -1-k). 12.99 *(978-0-448-48255-2(X),* Grosset & Dunlap) Penguin Young Readers Group.

—To the Town of Bethlehem. Stockstill, Gloria McQueen. 2004. 20p. (J). bds. 5.49 *(978-0-7586-0051-6(8))* Concordia Publishing Hse.

Durst, Kathryn. Arlo, Mrs. Ogg, & the Dinosaur Zoo. Hemming, Alice. 2020. (Class X Ser.). (ENG.). 144p. (J). (gr. 2-5). lib. bdg. 15.99 *(978-1-84886-468-9(X))* Maverick Arts Publishing GBR. Dist: Lerner Publishing Group.

—Float, Flutter. Singer, Marilyn. 2019. (Ready-To-Reads Ser.). (ENG.). 32p. (J). (gr. -1-k). pap. 4.99 *(978-1-5344-2129-5(7),* Simon Spotlight) Simon Spotlight.

—Gulp, Gobble: Ready-To-Read Pre-Level 1. Singer, Marilyn. 2019. (Ready-To-Reads Ser.). (ENG.). 32p. (J). (gr. -1-k). 17.99 *(978-1-5344-2134-9(3));* pap. 4.99 *(978-1-5344-2133-2(5))* Simon Spotlight. (Simon Spotlight).

—Hey Grandude! McCartney, Paul. 2019. (ENG.). 32p. (J). (gr. -1-1). 17.99 *(978-0-525-64867-3(4));* lib. bdg. 20.99 *(978-0-525-64868-0(2))* Random Hse. Children's Bks. (Random Hse. Bks. for Young Readers).

—Life with My Family. Hooker, Renee & Jones, Karl. 2018. 32p. (J). (gr. -1-2). 17.99 *(978-1-5247-8937-4(2),* Penguin Workshop) Penguin Young Readers Group.

—Merry Christmas, Mary Christmas! Friedman, Laurie. 2017. (ENG.). 32p. (J). (gr. -1-3). lib. bdg. 17.99 *(978-1-4677-9261-5(6),* 9781467792615, Carolrhoda Bks.) Lerner Publishing Group.

Dusan, Lakicevic. Adventure Steve in the Atlantic (for 8-13 Year Olds) Shanly, Stephen. 2019. (ENG.). 84p. (J). pap. ***(978-1-78623-675-3(3))*** Grosvenor Hse. Publishing Ltd.

Dusekove, Maja. Santa Claus & the Christmas Surprise, 30 vols. Lachner, Dorothea. 2018. Orig. Title: Ein Geschenk Vom Nikolaus. (ENG.). 28p. (J). 17.95 *(978-1-78250-543-3(1))* Floris Bks. GBR. Dist: Consortium Bk. Sales & Distribution.

Dusikovaa, Maja. Advent Storybook: 24 Stories to Share Before Christmas. Schneider, Antonie. Miller, Marisa, tr. 2005. 64p. (J). (gr. -1-3). 17.95 *(978-0-7358-1963-4(7))* North-South Bks., Inc.

—Sleeping Beauty. Grimm, Brothers. 2012. 32p. (J). (gr. -1-3). 17.95 *(978-0-7358-4087-4(3))* North-South Bks., Inc.

Dussling, Deborah & Melmon, Deborah. If the Shoe Fits: Nonstandard Units of Measurement. Dussling, Jennifer. 2015. (Mouse Math ® Ser.). (ENG.). 32p. (J). (gr. -1-1). lib. bdg. 22.65 *(978-1-57565-800-1(3))* Astra Publishing Hse.

Dustin, Michael. There's a Rainbow in Me. Cooke, Pam. 2004. 30p. (J). pap. 12.95 *(978-1-892343-39-0(8))* Oak Tree Publishing.

Duta, H'Upahu & Win, Zitkada Zi. Adventures of Keya. Duta, H'Upahu. 2020. (ENG.). 70p. (J). ***(978-0-2288-2167-0(3));*** pap. ***(978-0-2288-2166-3(5))*** Tellwell Talent.

Dutchak, Shelly. Onami: The Great Wave. Sterner, Nathan. 2007. (J). per. *(978-0-9795529-0-8(7))* 716 Productions.

Dutcher, Kieren. Chinese & English Nursery Rhymes: Little Mouse & Other Charming Chinese Rhymes (Audio Disc in Chinese & English Included) Wu, Faye-Lynn. ed. 2018. 32p. (J). (gr. -1-3). 12.99 *(978-0-8048-4999-9(4))* Tuttle Publishing.

Dutertre, Charles. Meet the Woolly Mammoth. Philippo, Sophie. 2005. (ENG.). 45p. (J). (gr. 4-7). 15.95 *(978-1-58728-521-9(5))* Cooper Square Publishing Llc.

Dutertre, Sophie. Sagesses et Malices de la Tradition Juive. Bloch, Muriel. 2004. (A. M. Sag Malice Ser.). (FRE.). 188p. (J). *(978-2-226-11863-9(2))* Albin-Michel, Editions.

Dutkiewicz, Michal. The Last Realm Dragonscarpe. McNamara, Pat & Turner, Gary. 2007. (Last Realm Ser.: Bk. 1). 320p. (YA). *(978-982-9109-01-9(1))* Angel Phoenix Publishing.

Dutrait, Vincent. The Queen's Pirate - Francis Drake. Courtauld, Sarah. 2008. (Usborne Young Reading: Series Three Ser.). 64p. (J). 8.99 *(978-0-7945-2048-9(0),* Usborne) EDC Publishing.

—The Story of Pirates. Jones, Rob Lloyd. 2007. (Young Reading Series 3 Gift Bks). 63p. (J). (gr. 4-7). 8.99 *(978-0-7945-1618-5(1),* Usborne) EDC Publishing.

Dutta, Dipali. Dinosaur Adventure: A Field Trip to Remember. Santana-Banks, Kelly. 2016. (Let's Learn While Playing Ser.: Vol. 2). (ENG.). (J). (gr. k-3). pap. 7.99 *(978-0-9977530-1-1(3))* RBTB Publishing.

Dutta, Dipali, jt. illus. see Smith, Jennifer.

Dutton, John. Tiger's Island. Dutton, John. unabr. ed. Date not set. (Dreamguard Ser.: Vol. 2). viii, 245p. (J). pap. 12.95 *(978-0-9577556-1-1(9))* Samara Pr.

Dutton, Mike. Donovan's Big Day. Newman, Lesléa. 2011. (ENG.). 32p. (J). (gr. -1-2). 17.99 *(978-1-58246-332-2(8),* Tricycle Pr.) Random Hse. Children's Bks.

—Food Truck Fest! Penfold, Alexandra. 2018. (ENG.). 40p. (J). 17.99 *(978-0-374-30318-1(5),* 900154880, Farrar, Straus & Giroux (BYR)) Farrar, Straus & Giroux.

D

Duufek, Kim Kanoa. Victor, the Reluctant Vulture. Hanson, Jonathan. 2012. 36p. (J). pap. 16.95 *(978-1-886679-45-0(2))* Arizona Sonora Desert Museum Pr.

Duursema, Jan. Episode II Vol. 1: Attack of the Clones, 1 vol. Gilroy, Henry. 2009. (Star Wars Ser.: No. 1). (ENG.). 40p. (J). (gr. 6-12). 27.07 *(978-1-59961-612-4(2))*, 13768, Graphic Novels) Spotlight.

—Episode II Vol. 3: Attack of the Clones. Gilroy, Henry. 2009. (Star Wars Ser.: No. 1). (ENG.). 40p. (J). (gr. 6-12). 27.07 *(978-1-59961-614-8(9))*, 13770, Graphic Novels) Spotlight.

—Episode II Vol. 4: Attack of the Clones. Gilroy, Henry. 2009. (Star Wars Ser.: No. 1). (ENG.). 40p. (J). (gr. 6-12). 27.07 *(978-1-59961-615-5(7))*, 13771, Graphic Novels) Spotlight.

—Episode II - Attack of the Clones, Vol. 2. Gilroy, Henry. 2009. (Star Wars Ser.: No. 1). (ENG.). 40p. (J). (gr. 6-12). 27.07 *(978-1-59961-613-1(0))*, 13769, Graphic Novels) Spotlight.

Duursema, Jan, et al. Star Wars Legends Epic Collection: the Clone Wars Vol. 3. 2020. (ENG.). 424p. (YA). (gr. 4-17). pap. 39.99 *(978-1-302-92376-1(5))* Marvel Worldwide, Inc.

—Star Wars Legends Epic Collection: the Menace Revealed Vol. 2. 2019. (ENG.). 144p. (YA). (gr. 4-17). pap. 39.99 *(978-1-302-92033-3(2))* Marvel Worldwide, Inc.

—X-Men Milestones: Phalanx Covenant. 2019. (ENG.). 488p. (YA). (gr. 4-17). pap. 39.99 *(978-1-302-92054-8(5))* Marvel Worldwide, Inc.

DuVall, Sara. The Bridge: How the Roeblings Connected Brooklyn to New York. Tomasi, Peter J. 2018. (ENG.). 208p. 24.99 *(978-1-4197-2852-5(0)*, Abrams ComicArts) Abrams, Inc.

DuVall, Sara, et al. Bridge: How the Roeblings Connected Brooklyn to New York. Tomasi, Peter J. 2019. (ENG.). 208p. (gr. 8-17). pap. 18.99 *(978-1-4197-3616-2(7)*, Abrams ComicArts) Abrams, Inc.

Duverne, Evelyne. Rules of the Net, 1 vol. McKerley, Jennifer Guess. 2009. (Read-It! Readers: Character Education Ser.). (ENG.). 32p. (J). (gr. k-2). 21.32 *(978-1-4048-5240-2(9)*, Picture Window Bks.) Capstone.

Duvoisin, Roger. A Doll for Marie. Fatio, Louise. 2015. (ENG.). 32p. (J). (gr. -1-2). 16.99 *(978-0-385-75596-2(1)*, Knopf Bks. for Young Readers) Random Hse. Children's Bks.

—Happy Hunter. 2016. (ENG.). 40p. (J). (gr. -1-3). 16.95 *(978-1-59270-205-3(8))* Enchanted Lion Bks., LLC.

—The Happy Lion. Fatio, Louise. (J). (gr. -1-2). 2015. 32p. 7.99 *(978-0-553-50850-5(4)*, Dragonfly Bks.); 2010. (ENG.). 40p. pap. 7.99 *(978-0-553-11364-8(X)*, Dragonfly Bks.); 2004. 40p. 16.99 *(978-0-375-82759-4(5)*, Knopf Bks. for Young Readers) Random Hse. Children's Bks.

Düzakin, Akin. I'm Right Here. Ørbeck-Nilssen, Constance. 2015. (ENG.). 28p. (J). 16.00 *(978-0-8028-5455-1(9)*, Eerdmans Bks For Young Readers) Eerdmans, William B. Publishing Co.

—Vanishing Colors. Ørbeck-Nilssen, Constance. 2019. (ENG.). 40p. (J). *(978-0-8028-5518-3(0)*, Eerdmans Bks For Young Readers) Eerdmans, William B. Publishing Co.

Dvorák, Jaroslav. Bobek, the Cat with a Pompon Tail. Dvok, Eduard & Dvorák, Eduard. 2010. 52p. pap. 17.00 *(978-1-60911-734-4(4)*, Eloquent Bks.) Strategic Book Publishing & Rights Agency (SBPRA).

Dwight, Laura, photos by. How Many? (English/Haitian Creole), 1 vol. Christian, Cheryl. 2005. (ENG., 12p. (J). 5.95 *(978-1-59572-024-5(3))* Star Bright Bks., Inc.

—How Many? (English/Russian), 1 vol. Christian, Cheryl. 2005. (Photo Flap Bks.). (RUS & ENG., 12p. (J). 5.95 *(978-1-932065-88-6(1))* Star Bright Bks., Inc.

—How Many? (Korean), 1 vol. Christian, Cheryl. Choi, Jin, tr. 2004. (KOR & ENG., 12p. (J). 5.95 *(978-1-932065-82-4(2))* Star Bright Bks., Inc.

—How Many? (Portuguese/English), 1 vol. Christian, Cheryl. 2009. (ENG & POR., 12p. (J). 5.95 *(978-1-59572-190-7(8))* Star Bright Bks., Inc.

—How Many? (Simplified Mandarin), 1 vol. Christian, Cheryl. 2004. (CHI & ENG., 12p. (J). 5.95 *(978-1-932065-70-1(9))* Star Bright Bks., Inc.

—How Many? (Traditional Cantonese) Christian, Cheryl. 2004. (CHI., 12p. (J). bds. 5.95 *(978-1-932065-64-0(4))* Star Bright Bks., Inc.

—How Many? (Vietnamese) Christian, Cheryl. 2004. (VIE., 12p. (J). bds. 5.95 *(978-1-932065-76-3(8))* Star Bright Bks., Inc.

—Toby & Tutter Therapy Dogs. DeBear, Kirsten. 2012. (ENG., 32p. (J). 17.95 *(978-0-9847812-0-1(X))* Toby & Tutter Publishing.

—What Happens Next? (Haitian Creole/English), 1 vol. Christian, Cheryl. 2005. (ENG & HAT., 12p. (J). (gr. -1). 5.95 *(978-1-59572-025-2(1))* Star Bright Bks., Inc.

—What Happens Next? (Korean), 1 vol. Christian, Cheryl. Choi, Jin, tr. 2004. (KOR & ENG., 12p. (J). 5.95 *(978-1-932065-81-7(4))* Star Bright Bks., Inc.

—What Happens Next? (Russian/English), 1 vol. Christian, Cheryl. 2005. (Photo Flap Bks.). (RUS & ENG., 12p. (J). 5.95 *(978-1-932065-87-9(3))* Star Bright Bks., Inc.

—What Happens Next? (Simplified Mandarin), 1 vol. Christian, Cheryl. 2004. (CHI & ENG., 12p. (J). 5.95 *(978-1-932065-69-5(5))* Star Bright Bks., Inc.

—What Happens Next? (Traditional Cantonese) Christian, Cheryl. 2004. (CHI., 12p. (J). bds. 5.95 *(978-1-932065-63-3(6))* Star Bright Bks., Inc.

—What Happens Next? (Vietnamese), 1 vol. Christian, Cheryl. 2004. (VIE & ENG., 12p. (J). 5.95 *(978-1-932065-75-6(X))* Star Bright Bks., Inc.

—What Happens Next (Spanish/English) Bilingual Edition, 1 vol. Christian, Cheryl. 2004. (Photoflaps Ser.). (ENG & SPA., 32p. (J). bds. 5.50 *(978-1-932065-57-2(1)*, 718-784-9112) Star Bright Bks., Inc.

—Where Does It Go? (Haitian Creole/English), 1 vol. Christian, Cheryl. 2005. (CRP & ENG., 12p. (J). 5.95 *(978-1-59572-026-9(X))* Star Bright Bks., Inc.

—Where Does It Go? (Korean), 1 vol. Christian, Cheryl. Choi, Jin, tr. from ENG. 2004. (Photo Flap Bks.). (KOR & ENG., 12p. (J). 5.95 *(978-1-932065-83-1(0))* Star Bright Bks., Inc.

—Where Does It Go? (Russian/English), 1 vol. Christian, Cheryl. 2005. (Photo Flap Bks.). (RUS & ENG., 12p. (J). 5.95 *(978-1-932065-89-3(X))* Star Bright Bks., Inc.

—Where Does It Go? (Simplified Mandarin), 1 vol. Christian, Cheryl. 2004. (CHI & ENG., 12p. (J). 5.95 *(978-1-932065-71-8(7))* Star Bright Bks., Inc.

—Where Does It Go? (Traditional Cantonese) Christian, Cheryl. 2004. (CHI., 12p. (J). bds. 5.95 *(978-1-932065-65-7(2))* Star Bright Bks., Inc.

—Where Does It Go? (Vietnamese) Christian, Cheryl. 2004. (VIE., 12p. (J). bds. 5.95 *(978-1-932065-77-0(6))* Star Bright Bks., Inc.

—Where's the Baby? (Haitian Creole/English), 1 vol. Christian, Cheryl. 2005. (Photoflaps Ser.). (HAT & ENG., 12p. (J). (gr. -1). 5.95 *(978-1-59572-027-6(8))* Star Bright Bks., Inc.

—Where's the Baby? (Korean) Christian, Cheryl. Choi, Jin, tr. 2004. (KOR., 12p. (J). bds. 5.95 *(978-1-932065-80-0(6))* Star Bright Bks., Inc.

—Where's the Baby? (Russian/English), 1 vol. Christian, Cheryl. 2005. (Photoflaps Ser.). (RUS & ENG., 24p. (J). (gr. -1). bds. 5.95 *(978-1-932065-86-2(5))* Star Bright Bks., Inc.

—Where's the Baby? (Simplified Mandarin) Christian, Cheryl. 2004. (CHI., 12p. (J). bds. 5.95 *(978-1-932065-68-8(7))* Star Bright Bks., Inc.

—Where's the Baby? (Spanish/English) Bilingual Edition, 1 vol. Christian, Cheryl. Fiol, Maria A., tr. 2004. (SPA & ENG., 12p. (J). 5.95 *(978-1-932065-56-5(3))* Star Bright Bks., Inc.

—Where's the Baby? (Traditional Cantonese) Christian, Cheryl. 2004. (CHI., 12p. (J). bds. 5.95 *(978-1-932065-62-6(8))* Star Bright Bks., Inc.

—Where's the Baby? (Vietnamese) Christian, Cheryl. 2004. (VIE., 12p. (J). bds. 5.50 *(978-1-932065-74-9(1))* Star Bright Bks., Inc.

—Where's the Kitten? (Haitian Creole/English), 1 vol. Christian, Cheryl. 2005. (Photoflaps Ser.). (HAT & ENG., 12p. (J). (gr. -1). 5.95 *(978-1-59572-028-3(6))* Star Bright Bks., Inc.

—Where's the Kitten? (Korean), 1 vol. Christian, Cheryl. Choi, Jin, tr. 2004. (KOR & ENG., 12p. (J). 5.95 *(978-1-932065-78-7(4))* Star Bright Bks., Inc.

—Where's the Kitten? (Russian/English), 1 vol. Christian, Cheryl. 2004. (RUS & ENG., 12p. (J). 5.95 *(978-1-932065-84-8(9))* Star Bright Bks., Inc.

—Where's the Kitten? (Simplified Mandarin) Christian, Cheryl. 2004. (CHI., 12p. (J). bds. 5.95 *(978-1-932065-66-4(0))* Star Bright Bks., Inc.

—Where's the Kitten? (Spanish/English) Bilingual Edition, 1 vol. Christian, Cheryl. Fiol, Maria A., tr. 2004. (SPA & ENG., 32p. (J). bds. 5.50 *(978-1-932065-54-1(7)*, 718-784-9112) Star Bright Bks., Inc.

—Where's the Kitten? (Traditional Cantonese), 1 vol. Christian, Cheryl. 2004. (CHI & ENG., 12p. (J). 5.95 *(978-1-932065-60-2(1))* Star Bright Bks., Inc.

—Where's the Kitten? (Vietnamese) Christian, Cheryl. 2004. (VIE., 12p. (J). bds. 5.95 *(978-1-932065-72-5(5))* Star Bright Bks., Inc.

—Where's the Puppy? (Haitian Creole/English), 1 vol. Christian, Cheryl. 2005. (Photoflaps Ser.). (HAT & ENG., 12p. (J). (gr. -1). 5.95 *(978-1-59572-029-0(4))* Star Bright Bks., Inc.

—Where's the Puppy? (Korean), 1 vol. Christian, Cheryl. Choi, Jin, tr. 2004. (KOR & ENG., 12p. (J). 5.95 *(978-1-932065-79-4(2))* Star Bright Bks., Inc.

—Where's the Puppy? (Russian/English), 1 vol. Christian, Cheryl. 2005. (Photo Flap Bks.). (RUS & ENG., 12p. (J). 5.95 *(978-1-932065-85-5(7))* Star Bright Bks., Inc.

—Where's the Puppy? (Simplified Mandarin), 1 vol. Christian, Cheryl. 2004. (CHI & ENG., 12p. (J). 5.95 *(978-1-932065-67-1(9))* Star Bright Bks., Inc.

—Where's the Puppy? (Traditional Cantonese) Christian, Cheryl. 2004. (CHI., 12p. (J). bds. 5.95 *(978-1-932065-61-9(X))* Star Bright Bks., Inc.

—Where's the Puppy? (Vietnamese) Christian, Cheryl. 2004. (VIE., 12p. (J). bds. 5.50 *(978-1-932065-73-2(3))* Star Bright Bks., Inc.

—Where's the Puppy (Spanish/English) Bilingual Edition, 1 vol. Christian, Cheryl. Fiol, Maria A., tr. 2004. (Photoflaps Ser.). (ENG & SPA., 32p. (J). bds. 5.95 *(978-1-932065-55-8(5)*, 718-784-9112) Star Bright Bks., Inc.

Dwight, Laura, photos by. We Can Do It!, 1 vol. Dwight, Laura. 2005. (ENG., 32p. (J). pap. 5.95 *(978-1-59572-033-7(2))* Star Bright Bks., Inc.

Dworkin, Doug. Chain Letter. Day, Lucille. 2005. 32p. (J). (gr. 3-7). 14.95 *(978-1-59714-011-9(2))* Heyday.

Dwyer, Corinne, et al. Okay, Riders, Set 'Em Up: A Nate Walker BMX Adventure. Wielkiewicz, Richard M. 2005. 140p. (J). pap. 12.95 *(978-0-9774129-0-7(3))* Main Event Pr.

Dwyer, Jenny. Footsteps in Bay de Verde: A Mysterious Tale, 1 vol. Cotter, Charis. 2020. (ENG.). 36p. (J). (gr. 4-7). 19.95 ***(978-1-927917-28-2(X))*** Running the Goat, Bks. & Broadsides CAN. Dist: Orca Bk. Pubs. USA.

Dwyer, Kerry. Rhett's Colorful Campus Tour- Boston University A-Z. 2004. (J). 9.99 *(978-1-933069-03-6(1))* Odd Duck Ink, Inc.

Dwyer, Kieron. Plants vs. Zombies Volume 16: the Garden Path. Tobin, Paul. 2020. (ENG.). 88p. (J). (gr. 3-7). 10.99 ***(978-1-5067-1306-9(8)***, Dark Horse Books) Dark Horse Comics.

Dwyer, Michael. Barnyard Bash. Dwyer, Mary. 2006. (J). spiral bd. incl. cd-rom *(978-1-933843-00-1(4))* That's Me Publishing, LLC.

Dwyer, Mindy. Alaska's Three Little Pigs. Laverde, Arlene. 2015. (Paws IV Ser.). (ENG.). 20p. (J). (— 1). bds. 8.99 *(978-1-57061-974-8(3)*, Little Bigfoot) Sasquatch Bks.

—Chia & the Fox Man: An Alaskan Dena'ina Fable. 2020. (ENG.). 32p. (J). (gr. k-2). 16.99 *(978-1-5132-6267-3(X)*, Alaska Northwest Bks.) West Margin Pr.

Dwyer, Mindy. How Raven Got His Crooked Nose: An Alaskan Dena'ina Fable. 2020. (ENG.). 32p. (J). (gr. k-3). pap. 11.99 ***(978-1-5132-6439-4(7)***, Alaska Northwest Bks.) West Margin Pr.

Dwyer, Mindy. Kayak Girl. Devine, Monica. 2012. (ENG.). 32p. (J). pap. 12.95 *(978-1-60223-188-7(5))* Univ. of Alaska Pr.

—Knitting with Gigi. Thalcker, Karen. 2007. (ENG.). 32p. 24.95 *(978-1-56477-816-1(9))* Martingale & Co.

Dwyer, Mindy. Alaska's Sleeping Beauty. Dwyer, Mindy. 2014. (Paws IV Ser.). 32p. (J). (gr. k-3). pap. 10.99 *(978-1-57061-872-7(0)*, Little Bigfoot) Sasquatch Bks.

Dyan, Penelope. Be Who You Are! Dyan, Penelope D. l.t. ed. 2019. (ENG.). 34p. (J). pap. 12.60 ***(978-1-61477-436-5(6))*** Bellissima Publishing, LLC.

Dyan, Penelope. Bunny Ears. Dyan, Peneope. 2011. 34p. pap. 11.95 *(978-1-935630-68-5(7))* Bellissima Publishing, LLC.

Dyan, Penelope. Apologize! Dyan, Penelope. l.t. ed. 2019. (ENG.). 34p. (J). pap. 12.60 *(978-1-61477-388-7(2))* Bellissima Publishing, LLC.

—Arianna's Shoes. Dyan, Penelope. 2008. 44p. pap. 11.95 *(978-1-935118-33-6(1))* Bellissima Publishing, LLC.

—Ayes & Nays. Dyan, Penelope. l.t. ed. 2018. (ENG.). 34p. (J). (gr. k-4). pap. 12.60 *(978-1-61477-358-0(0))* Bellissima Publishing, LLC.

—Ba-Ba-Ba-Bad — -The Story of One Mean Moose. Dyan, Penelope. 2012. 34p. pap. 11.95 *(978-1-61477-053-4(0))* Bellissima Publishing, LLC.

—Bake a Cake, Make Two — -and Let Them Eat Cake. Dyan, Penelope. 2008. 44p. pap. 11.95 *(978-1-935118-18-3(8))* Bellissima Publishing, LLC.

—Baylee's Giraffes! Sometimes Only a Giraffe Will Do. Dyan, Penelope. 2013. 34p. pap. 11.95 *(978-1-61477-085-5(9))* Bellissima Publishing, LLC.

—Ben's Adventures — -Proof Positive That Boys Will Be Boys. Dyan, Penelope. 2008. 44p. pap. 11.95 *(978-1-935118-40-4(4))* Bellissima Publishing, LLC.

—The Big Mikey & Me Workbook. Dyan, Penelope. 2011. 48p. pap. 11.95 *(978-1-935630-72-2(5))* Bellissima Publishing, LLC.

—Blake the Cat & His Very Loose Tooth! Dyan, Penelope. 2011. 34p. pap. 10.95 *(978-1-935630-77-7(6))* Bellissima Publishing, LLC.

—Bubble Trouble — -for Boys Only ®. Dyan, Penelope. 2011. 34p. pap. 11.95 *(978-1-935630-92-0(X))* Bellissima Publishing, LLC.

—Bunny Love! a Book about Home & Bunnies. Dyan, Penelope. 2013. 34p. pap. 11.95 *(978-1-61477-084-8(0))* Bellissima Publishing, LLC.

—The Carousel. Dyan, Penelope. 2010. 34p. pap. 11.95 *(978-1-935630-26-5(1))* Bellissima Publishing, LLC.

—Changes! Dyan, Penelope. 2013. 34p. (J). pap. 11.95 *(978-1-61477-097-8(2))* Bellissima Publishing, LLC.

—The Christmas Flamingo. Dyan, Penelope. 2013. 34p. pap. 11.95 *(978-1-61477-121-0(9))* Bellissima Publishing, LLC.

—Christmas Is — -A Time to Remember, to Smile & to Share. Dyan, Penelope. 2009. 44p. pap. 11.95 *(978-1-935118-46-6(3))* Bellissima Publishing, LLC.

—Classy Nancy — A One of a Kind Girl. Dyan, Penelope. 2009. 48p. pap. 11.95 *(978-1-935118-45-9(5))* Bellissima Publishing, LLC.

—Compromise! Dyan, Penelope. l.t. ed. 2019. (ENG.). 34p. (J). (gr. k-4). pap. 12.60 *(978-1-61477-387-0(4))* Bellissima Publishing, LLC.

—Courtney's Beach. Dyan, Penelope. 2008. 44p. pap. 11.95 *(978-1-935118-35-0(8))* Bellissima Publishing, LLC.

—The Day an Elephant Flies! Dyan, Penelope. 2013. 34p. pap. 11.95 *(978-1-61477-113-5(8))* Bellissima Publishing, LLC.

—Dear God, Thank-You! Dyan, Penelope. 2013. 34p. pap. 11.95 *(978-1-61477-072-5(7))* Bellissima Publishing, LLC.

—Don't Wake up the Bear! Dyan, Penelope. 2013. 34p. pap. 11.95 *(978-1-61477-094-7(8))* Bellissima Publishing, LLC.

—Eve. Dyan, Penelope. 2011. 34p. pap. 11.95 *(978-1-935630-95-1(4))* Bellissima Publishing, LLC.

—The Fish That Got Away — -for Boys Only®. Dyan, Penelope. 2010. 34p. pap. 11.95 *(978-1-935630-29-6(6))* Bellissima Publishing, LLC.

—Frugal Frannie — and the Big Room Cleaning Day. Dyan, Penelope. 2009. 44p. pap. 11.95 *(978-1-935118-47-3(1))* Bellissima Publishing, LLC.

—Gabriela's Dogs — -Because Happiness Really Is a Warm Puppy! Dyan, Penelope. 2008. 44p. pap. 11.95 *(978-1-935118-37-4(4))* Bellissima Publishing, LLC.

—Gettin' Dirty! for Boys Only R. Dyan, Penelope. 2013. 34p. pap. 11.95 *(978-1-61477-083-1(2))* Bellissima Publishing, LLC.

—A Girl Named Dot. Dyan, Penelope. 2013. 34p. pap. 11.95 *(978-1-61477-102-9(2))* Bellissima Publishing, LLC.

—Go Far Star Car — Even Though Cars Are Not People. Dyan, Penelope. 2008. 44p. pap. 11.95 *(978-1-935118-12-1(9))* Bellissima Publishing, LLC.

—Go Run, Have Fun — -Because Everyone Likes Fun. Dyan, Penelope. 2008. 44p. pap. 11.95 *(978-1-935118-15-2(3))* Bellissima Publishing, LLC.

—Go to Rat House, Go to Cat House — Even Though Houses Are Not People. Dyan, Penelope. 2008. 44p. pap. 11.95 *(978-1-935118-14-5(5))* Bellissima Publishing, LLC.

—Good Luck Chuck! Dyan, Penelope. 2013. 34p. pap. 11.95 *(978-1-61477-098-5(0))* Bellissima Publishing, LLC.

—Good Night! Dyan, Penelope. 2013. 34p. pap. 11.95 *(978-1-61477-089-3(1))* Bellissima Publishing, LLC.

—Grandma's Suitcase — -Where a Kid Can Always Find a Surprise! Dyan, Penelope. 2008. 44p. pap. 11.95 *(978-1-935118-36-7(6))* Bellissima Publishing, LLC.

—Great Grandma Is Getting Old. Dyan, Penelope. 2010. 42p. pap. 11.95 *(978-1-935118-97-8(8))* Bellissima Publishing, LLC.

—Hair We Are! Dyan, Penelope. 2009. 44p. pap. 11.95 *(978-1-935118-61-9(7))* Bellissima Publishing, LLC.

—Happy Birthday! a Book about Birthdays, Dreams & Wishes. Dyan, Penelope. 2009. 42p. pap. 11.95 *(978-1-935118-73-2(0))* Bellissima Publishing, LLC.

—Happy Birthday Usa! Dyan, Penelope. 2010. 32p. pap. 11.95 *(978-1-935630-15-9(6))* Bellissima Publishing, LLC.

—The Hatchling, the Story of Stegi Stegosaurus. Dyan, Penelope. 2010. 42p. pap. 11.95 *(978-1-935630-08-1(3))* Bellissima Publishing, LLC.

—Hello Doctor! Dyan, Penelope. 2013. 34p. pap. 11.95 *(978-1-61477-096-1(4))* Bellissima Publishing, LLC.

—Hooray 4 Five! Dyan, Penelope. 2013. 34p. pap. 11.95 *(978-1-61477-103-6(0))* Bellissima Publishing, LLC.

—I Am a Monster! Dyan, Penelope. 2010. 34p. pap. 11.95 *(978-1-935630-24-1(5))* Bellissima Publishing, LLC.

—I Am Eight! Dyan, Penelope. 2010. 34p. pap. 11.95 *(978-1-935630-17-3(2))* Bellissima Publishing, LLC.

—I Am There! Dyan, Penelope. 2011. 34p. pap. 11.95 *(978-1-935630-98-2(9))* Bellissima Publishing, LLC.

—I Am Three! Dyan, Penelope. 2011. 34p. pap. 11.95 *(978-1-935630-97-5(0))* Bellissima Publishing, LLC.

—I Can't Stand the Rain! Dyan, Penelope. 2012. 34p. pap. 11.95 *(978-1-61477-040-4(9))* Bellissima Publishing, LLC.

—I Did It, & I Hid It! a Book about Taking Responsibility. Dyan, Penelope. 2009. 44p. pap. 11.95 *(978-1-935118-68-8(4))* Bellissima Publishing, LLC.

—I Like Football — for Boys Only®. Dyan, Penelope. 2010. 34p. pap. 11.95 *(978-1-935630-27-2(X))* Bellissima Publishing, LLC.

—I Love You! Dyan, Penelope. 2012. 34p. pap. 11.95 *(978-1-61477-050-3(6))* Bellissima Publishing, LLC.

—If You Snooze! Dyan, Penelope. 2012. 34p. pap. 11.95 *(978-1-61477-059-6(X))* Bellissima Publishing, LLC.

—In Gracie's Yard! Dyan, Penelope. 2012. 34p. pap. 11.95 *(978-1-61477-067-1(0))* Bellissima Publishing, LLC.

—In My Attic. Dyan, Penelope. 2010. 34p. pap. 11.95 *(978-1-935630-23-4(7))* Bellissima Publishing, LLC.

—Introducing Fabulous Marie, a Girl with a Good Head on Her Shoulders. Dyan, Penelope. 2009. 44p. pap. 11.95 *(978-1-935118-55-8(2))* Bellissima Publishing, LLC.

—Jordan's Hair — -the Big Dilemm. Dyan, Penelope. 2008. 44p. pap. 11.95 *(978-1-935118-34-3(X))* Bellissima Publishing, LLC.

—Jump Frog, Funny Frog — -Because Frogs Are Funny. Dyan, Penelope. 2008. 44p. pap. 11.95 *(978-1-935118-19-0(6))* Bellissima Publishing, LLC.

—Just Look Out the Window! Dyan, Penelope. 2010. 34p. pap. 11.95 *(978-1-935630-25-8(3))* Bellissima Publishing, LLC.

—Ladies First, Please! a Kid's Most Important & Fun Guide to Good Manners. Dyan, Penelope. 2009. 106p. pap. 8.95 *(978-1-935118-67-1(6))* Bellissima Publishing, LLC.

—Life in the Pits. Dyan, Penelope. 2010. 34p. pap. 11.95 *(978-1-935630-18-0(0))* Bellissima Publishing, LLC.

—Life Is a Dream! Dyan, Penelope. 2013. 34p. pap. 11.95 *(978-1-61477-091-6(3))* Bellissima Publishing, LLC.

—Little Miss Chris & the Incredible Red Shoes. Dyan, Penelope. 2009. 44p. pap. 11.95 *(978-1-935118-49-7(8))* Bellissima Publishing, LLC.

—A Lot of Snot, a for Boys Only Book. Dyan, Penelope. 2008. 44p. pap. 11.95 *(978-1-935118-23-7(4))* Bellissima Publishing, LLC.

—Lovely Libby. Dyan, Penelope. 2010. 34p. pap. 11.95 *(978-1-935630-28-9(8))* Bellissima Publishing, LLC.

—Mama Says. Dyan, Penelope. l.t. ed. 2018. (ENG.). 34p. (J). (gr. k-4). pap. 12.60 *(978-1-61477-343-6(2))* Bellissima Publishing, LLC.

—Mermaids & Wishes for Tails Like Fishes. Dyan, Penelope. 2009. 44p. pap. 11.95 *(978-1-935118-50-3(1))* Bellissima Publishing, LLC.

—Mikey & Me & the Bees, the Continuing Story of a Girl & Her Dog. Dyan, Penelope. 2010. 48p. pap. 14.95 *(978-1-935118-90-9(0))* Bellissima Publishing, LLC.

—Mikey & Me & the Fly — -the Continuing Story of a Girl & Her Dog. Dyan, Penelope. 2010. 50p. pap. 14.95 *(978-1-935118-94-7(3))* Bellissima Publishing, LLC.

—Mikey & Me & the Frogs — -the Continuing Story of a Girl & Her Dog. Dyan, Penelope. 2010. 50p. pap. 14.95 *(978-1-935118-93-0(5))* Bellissima Publishing, LLC.

—Mikey & Me & the Spider — -the Continuing Story of a Girl & Her Dog. Dyan, Penelope. 2010. 50p. pap. 14.95 *(978-1-935118-95-4(1))* Bellissima Publishing, LLC.

—Mikey & Me & the Valentines — -the Continuing Story of a Girl & Her Dog. Dyan, Penelope. 2010. 50p. pap. 14.95 *(978-1-935118-96-1(X))* Bellissima Publishing, LLC.

—Molly Moose Is on the Loose. Dyan, Penelope. 2012. 34p. pap. 11.95 *(978-1-61477-025-1(5))* Bellissima Publishing, LLC.

—The Musical Family — Sometimes a Song Says It All. Dyan, Penelope. 2009. 42p. pap. 11.95 *(978-1-935118-81-7(1))* Bellissima Publishing, LLC.

—My Grandpa Had Bypass Surgery. Dyan, Penelope. l.t. ed. 2019. (ENG.). 34p. (J). (gr. k-4). pap. 12.60 *(978-1-61477-400-6(5))* Bellissima Publishing, LLC.

—My Mother Always Says. Dyan, Penelope. 2010. 42p. pap. 11.95 *(978-1-935118-98-5(6))* Bellissima Publishing, LLC.

—A New Bag! Dyan, Penelope. 2012. 34p. pap. 11.95 *(978-1-61477-054-1(9))* Bellissima Publishing, LLC.

—New Shoes for Hand Me down Rose. Dyan, Penelope. 2012. 34p. pap. 11.95 *(978-1-61477-041-1(7))* Bellissima Publishing, LLC.

—A Nose by Any Other Name Is Still a Nose! Dyan, Penelope. 2009. 44p. pap. 11.95 *(978-1-935118-62-6(5))* Bellissima Publishing, LLC.

—Off to School. Dyan, Penelope. 2010. 34p. pap. 11.95 *(978-1-935630-21-0(0))* Bellissima Publishing, LLC.

—Olympic Gold — Because Everyone Loves a Winner! Dyan, Penelope. 2008. 44p. pap. 11.95 *(978-1-935118-20-6(X))* Bellissima Publishing, LLC.

—Out of Deepest Africa — -Another of Ben's Big Adventures — -for Boys Only ®. Dyan, Penelope. 2010. 34p. pap. 11.95 *(978-1-935630-13-5(X))* Bellissima Publishing, LLC.

—Pink Patti Pinkerton. Dyan, Penelope. 2009. 44p. pap. 11.95 *(978-1-935118-63-3(3))* Bellissima Publishing, LLC.

—Respect! Dyan, Penelope. 2012. 34p. pap. 11.95 *(978-1-61477-058-9(1))* Bellissima Publishing, LLC.

—Smile! Dyan, Penelope. 2012. 34p. pap. 11.95 *(978-1-61477-028-2(X))* Bellissima Publishing, LLC.

—Speak up! but Don't Forget to Dance! Dyan, Penelope. l.t. ed. 2019. (ENG.). 34p. (J). (gr. k-4). pap. 12.60 *(978-1-61477-390-0(4))* Bellissima Publishing, LLC.

—Sticks — -Because Sticks Are Also People. Dyan, Penelope. 2008. 52p. pap. 11.95 *(978-1-935118-07-7(2))* Bellissima Publishing, LLC.
—Sticks — the for Boys Only Version — Because Sticks Are Also People. Dyan, Penelope. 2008. 52p. pap. 11.95 *(978-1-935118-13-8(7))* Bellissima Publishing, LLC.
—The Story of Snagatooth — -Who Is Commonly Known As the Tooth Fairy. Dyan, Penelope. 2008. 44p. pap. 11.95 *(978-1-935118-42-8(0))* Bellissima Publishing, LLC.
—The Sunny Side! Dyan, Penelope. 2012. 34p. pap. 11.95 *(978-1-61477-057-2(3))* Bellissima Publishing, LLC.
—Sunny the Bunny. Dyan, Penelope. l.t. ed. 2018. (ENG.). 34p. (J). (gr. k-3). pap. 12.60 *(978-1-61477-313-9(0))* Bellissima Publishing, LLC.
—Tammy's Left Shoe — -As Opposed to Her Right. Dyan, Penelope. 2008. 44p. pap. 11.95 *(978-1-935118-41-1(2))* Bellissima Publishing, LLC.
—Ted E Bearæs Most Unfortunate Experience to Date. Dyan, Penelope. 2009. 44p. pap. 11.95 *(978-1-935118-44-2(7))* Bellissima Publishing, LLC.
—Teeth! Dyan, Penelope. 2012. 34p. pap. 11.95 *(978-1-61477-060-2(3))* Bellissima Publishing, LLC.
—That Fat Elephant — -Because Everyone Likes Elephants. Dyan, Penelope. 2008. 44p. pap. 11.95 *(978-1-935118-16-9(1))* Bellissima Publishing, LLC.
—That Fat Rat Family — Because All Families Aren't Rats. Dyan, Penelope. 2008. 44p. pap. 11.95 *(978-1-935118-17-6(X))* Bellissima Publishing, LLC.
—There Are Bees in My Trees! Dyan, Penelope. 2009. 44p. pap. 11.95 *(978-1-935118-59-6(5))* Bellissima Publishing, LLC.
—There Are No Ants in My Pants! for Boys Only®. Dyan, Penelope. 2010. 32p. pap. 11.95 *(978-1-935630-16-6(4))* Bellissima Publishing, LLC.
—There's a Chicken in My Kitchen! Dyan, Penelope. 2009. 44p. pap. 11.95 *(978-1-935118-60-2(9))* Bellissima Publishing, LLC.
—There's a Flea in My Te. Dyan, Penelope. 2012. 34p. pap. 11.95 *(978-1-61477-047-3(6))* Bellissima Publishing, LLC.
—There's a Racoon in My House! Dyan, Penelope. 2009. 44p. pap. 11.95 *(978-1-935118-58-9(7))* Bellissima Publishing, LLC.
—There's a Skunk in My Trunk. Dyan, Penelope. 2012. 34p. pap. 11.95 *(978-1-61477-045-9(X))* Bellissima Publishing, LLC.
—There's a Teddy Bear in My Heart! Dyan, Penelope. 2012. 34p. pap. 11.95 *(978-1-61477-048-0(4))* Bellissima Publishing, LLC.
—There's an Alligator in My Closet! Dyan, Penelope. 2009. 44p. pap. 11.95 *(978-1-935118-64-0(1))* Bellissima Publishing, LLC.
—There's No Business Like Bartholomew Bunny's Business. Dyan, Penelope. 2009. 44p. pap. 11.95 *(978-1-935118-54-1(4))* Bellissima Publishing, LLC.
—This Means War! for Boys Only. Dyan, Penelope. 2009. 44p. pap. 11.95 *(978-1-935118-65-7(X))* Bellissima Publishing, LLC.
—Thou Shalt Not Covet! Dyan, Penelope. 2012. 34p. pap. 11.95 *(978-1-61477-042-8(5))* Bellissima Publishing, LLC.
—A Thousand Stars. Dyan, Penelope. 2012. 34p. pap. 11.95 *(978-1-61477-049-7(2))* Bellissima Publishing, LLC.
—Three Strikes — -Doesn't Really Mean You Are Out. Dyan, Penelope. 2008. 44p. pap. 11.95 *(978-1-935118-39-8(0))* Bellissima Publishing, LLC.
—To See or Not to See — -the Story of Kourtney's Glasses. Dyan, Penelope. 2008. 44p. pap. 11.95 *(978-1-935118-38-1(2))* Bellissima Publishing, LLC.
—Today I Am 4! Dyan, Penelope. 2012. 34p. pap. 11.95 *(978-1-61477-043-5(3))* Bellissima Publishing, LLC.
—Today I Am Two! I Am Two Years Old Today! Dyan, Penelope. 2010. 34p. pap. 11.95 *(978-1-935630-14-2(8))* Bellissima Publishing, LLC.
—Tony Pickleloni, a Boy Full of Baloney. Dyan, Penelope. 2009. 44p. pap. 11.95 *(978-1-935118-52-7(8))* Bellissima Publishing, LLC.
—Vita Mccafee Mckay, Cat Rescuer. Dyan, Penelope. 2009. 44p. pap. 11.95 *(978-1-935118-53-4(6))* Bellissima Publishing, LLC.
—What Is a Telephant? Dyan, Penelope. 2013. 34p. pap. 11.95 *(978-1-61477-112-8(X))* Bellissima Publishing, LLC.
—What Is Truth? Dyan, Penelope. 2011. 34p. pap. 11.95 *(978-1-935630-96-8(2))* Bellissima Publishing, LLC.
—When Touching Is Bad. Dyan, Penelope. 2013. 34p. pap. 11.95 *(978-1-61477-088-6(3))* Bellissima Publishing, LLC.
—Where Is Lucy? Dyan, Penelope. 2013. 34p. pap. 11.95 *(978-1-61477-120-3(0))* Bellissima Publishing, LLC.
—The White Elephant No One Wants. Dyan, Penelope. 2012. 34p. pap. 11.95 *(978-1-61477-024-4(7))* Bellissima Publishing, LLC.
—Who Cut the Cheese? a for Boys Only Book. Dyan, Penelope. 2008. 44p. pap. 11.95 *(978-1-935118-22-0(6))* Bellissima Publishing, LLC.
—Who Deserves a Giant Chocolate Chip Cookie? Dyan, Penelope. 2009. 44p. pap. 11.95 *(978-1-935118-56-5(0))* Bellissima Publishing, LLC.
—Who's the Fairest of Them All? Dyan, Penelope. 2010. 34p. pap. 11.95 *(978-1-935630-20-3(2))* Bellissima Publishing, LLC.
—Why Angels Sing! Dyan, Penelope. 2012. 34p. pap. 11.95 *(978-1-61477-065-7(4))* Bellissima Publishing, LLC.
—Woolly Bully! Dyan, Penelope. 2013. 34p. pap. 11.95 *(978-1-61477-069-5(7))* Bellissima Publishing, LLC.
—Work It Out! Dyan, Penelope. 2012. 34p. pap. 11.95 *(978-1-61477-056-5(5))* Bellissima Publishing, LLC.
—You Are Okay! Dyan, Penelope. 2013. 34p. pap. 11.95 *(978-1-61477-070-1(0))* Bellissima Publishing, LLC.
Dyan, Penelope, photos by. Wonderful, Wonderful Copenhagen! a Kid's Guide to Copenhagen, Denmark. Weigand, John D. 2011. 34p. pap. 11.95 *(978-1-935630-62-3(8))* Bellissima Publishing, LLC.
Dyan, Penwlope. Eileen Green the Recycling Queen. Dyan, Penelope. 2009. 44p. pap. 11.95 *(978-1-935118-51-0(X))* Bellissima Publishing, LLC.
D'yans, Masha. Flower Talk: How Plants Use Color to Communicate. Levine, Sara. 2019. (ENG.). 32p. (J). (gr. 2-5). 19.99 *(978-1-5415-1928-2(0))*, Millbrook Pr.) Lerner Publishing Group.
—Parrots, Pugs, & Pixie Dust: A Book about Fashion Designer Judith Leiber. Blumenthal, Deborah. 2019. (ENG.). 40p. (J). (gr. k-4). 17.99 *(978-1-4998-0898-8(4))* Little Bee Books Inc.
—A Poem As Big As New York City: Little Kids Write about the Big Apple. Teachers Writers Collaborative Staff, ed. 2012. (ENG.). 38p. (J). (gr. k-4). 19.95 *(978-0-7893-2083-4(5))* Universe Publishing.
—Polka Dot Parade: A Book about Bill Cunningham. Blumenthal, Deborah. 2018. (ENG.). 40p. (J). (gr. -1-3). 17.99 *(978-1-4998-0664-9(7))* Little Bee Books Inc.
Dybing, Michelle. Carlos & the Puppies, 1 vol. Dale, Jay. 2012. (Wonder Words Ser.). (ENG.). 32p. (gr. k-2). pap. 5.99 *(978-1-4296-8902-1(1)*, Capstone Pr.) Capstone.
—Gran & Me, 1 vol. Dale, Jay. 2012. (Wonder Words Ser.). (ENG.). 32p. (gr. k-2). pap. 5.99 *(978-1-4296-8898-7(X)*, Capstone Pr.) Capstone.
—I Am in the Park. Dale, Jay. 2012. (Wonder Words Ser.). (ENG.). 32p. (gr. k-2). pap. 5.99 *(978-1-4296-8890-1(4)*, Capstone Pr.) Capstone.
—I Go up & Down. Dale, Jay. 2012. (Wonder Words Ser.). (ENG.). 32p. (gr. k-2). pap. 5.99 *(978-1-4296-8894-9(7)*, Capstone Pr.) Capstone.
—To the Moon, 1 vol. Dale, Jay. 2012. (Wonder Words Ser.). (ENG.). 32p. (gr. k-2). pap. 5.99 *(978-1-4296-8904-5(8)*, Capstone Pr.) Capstone.
Dye, Jerel. Any Two Can Be Twindollicious. Danna, Natasha. 2013. 32p. (J). 17.95 *(978-1-60131-154-2(0)*, Castlebridge Bks.) Big Tent Bks.
Dyen, Don. Benjamin & the Word: Benjamín y la Palabra. Olivas, Daniel. Baeza Ventura, Gabriela, tr. 2011. 32p. (J). pap. 7.95 *(978-1-55885-687-5(0)*, Piñata Books) Arte Publico Pr.
Dyer, Brooke. Mama Always Comes Home. Wilson, Karma. 32p. (J). (gr. -1-1). 2007. (ENG.). pap. 6.99 *(978-0-06-057507-6(7)*, Harper Trophy); 2005. 15.99 *(978-0-06-057505-2(0))* HarperCollins Pubs.
—Sleep, Black Bear, Sleep. Yolen, Jane & Stemple, Heidi E. Y. 2007. 32p. (J). (gr. -1-1). (ENG.). 15.99 *(978-0-06-081560-8(4))*; lib. bdg. 16.89 *(978-0-06-081561-5(2))* HarperCollins Pubs.
Dyer, Brooke, jt. illus. see Dyer, Jane.
Dyer, Colin. Searching for Truth: The Illustrated Gospel. Chaffey, Tim. 2017. (ENG.). 70p. (YA). pap. 15.99 *(978-1-68344-033-8(1)*, Master Books) New Leaf Publishing Group.
Dyer, Jacqueline. Storms of Assiral. Morecambe, Annie. 2nd ed. 2018. (Legend of Greywinds Ser.: Vol. 5). (ENG.). 316p. (J). (gr. 3-6). pap. 11.99 *(978-1-936748-24-2(X))* Lake 'n Moor, Ltd.
Dyer, Jane. All We Know. Ashman, Linda. 2016. (ENG.). 40p. (J). (gr. -1-3). 17.99 *(978-0-06-168958-1(0))* HarperCollins Pubs.
—A Band of Babies. Gerber, Carole. 2017. (ENG.). 32p. (J). (gr. -1-3). 17.99 *(978-0-06-168955-0(6))* HarperCollins Pubs.
—Blue Moon Soup: A Family Cookbook. Goss, Gary. 2013. 72p. (J). (gr. 1-1). 16.95 *(978-1-62087-990-0(5)*, 620990, Sky Pony Pr.) Skyhorse Publishing Co., Inc.
—Christmas Cookies: Bite-Size Holiday Lessons. Rosenthal, Amy Krouse. 2008. 40p. (J). (gr. k-5). lib. bdg. 13.89 *(978-0-06-058025-4(9))*; (ENG.). 12.99 *(978-0-06-058024-7(0))* HarperCollins Pubs.
—Cookies: Bite-Size Life Lessons. Rosenthal, Amy Krouse. 2006. (ENG.). 40p. (J). (gr. -1-1). 12.99 *(978-0-06-058081-0(X))* HarperCollins Pubs.
—Cookies Board Book: Bite-Size Life Lessons. Rosenthal, Amy Krouse. 2016. (ENG.). 36p. (J). (gr. -1 — 1). bds. 7.99 *(978-0-06-242739-7(3)*, HarperFestival) HarperCollins Pubs.
—Cracked Corn & Snow Ice Cream: A Family Almanac. Willard, Nancy. 2005. 56p. (YA). (gr. 4-8). 18.00 *(978-0-7567-8835-3(8))* DIANE Publishing Co.
—Goodnight Goodnight Sleepyhead. Krauss, Ruth. 2004. 32p. (J). (gr. -1-1). lib. bdg. 16.89 *(978-0-06-028895-2(7))* HarperCollins Pubs.
—Goodnight Goodnight Sleepyhead Board Book. Krauss, Ruth. 2007. (ENG.). 32p. (J). (gr. -1-3). bds. 7.99 *(978-0-694-01501-6(6)*, HarperFestival) HarperCollins Pubs.
—Lucky & Squash. Birdsall, Jeanne. 2012. (ENG.). 32p. (J). (gr. -1-2). 16.99 *(978-0-06-083150-9(2))* HarperCollins Pubs.
—Move over, Rover! Beaumont, Karen. (ENG.). 40p. (J). (gr. -1-3). 2016. 7.99 *(978-0-544-80900-0(9)*, 1641299, HMH Books For Young Readers); 2006. 16.99 *(978-0-15-201979-2(0)*, 1191451) Houghton Mifflin Harcourt Publishing Co.
—Move over, Rover! (board Book) Beaumont, Karen. 2019. (ENG.). 32p. (J). (— 1). bds. 7.99 *(978-1-328-60635-8(X)*, 1732552, HMH Books For Young Readers) Houghton Mifflin Harcourt Publishing Co.
—Oh My Baby, Little One. Appelt, Kathi. (ENG.). 32p. (J). (gr. -1 — 1). 2006. pap. 4.99 *(978-0-15-206031-2(6)*, 1198114); 2005. reprint ed. pap. 6.99 *(978-0-15-205242-3(9)*, 1195792) Houghton Mifflin Harcourt Publishing Co.
—Once There Was a Story: Tales from Around the World, Perfect for Sharing. Yolen, Jane. 2017. (ENG.). 160p. (J). (gr. -1-3). 19.99 *(978-1-4169-7172-6(6)*, Simon & Schuster/Paula Wiseman Bks.) Simon & Schuster/Paula Wiseman Bks.
—Roly Poly. Birdsall, Jeanne, photos by. Fox, Mem. 2019. (ENG.). 40p. (J). (gr. -1-3). 17.99 *(978-1-4814-4556-6(1)*, Beach Lane Bks.) Beach Lane Bks.
—Sophie's Masterpiece: A Spider's Tale. Spinelli, Eileen. 2004. (ENG.). 32p. (J). (gr. -1-2). reprint ed. 7.99 *(978-0-689-86680-7(1)*, Simon & Schuster Bks. For Young Readers) Simon & Schuster Bks. For Young Readers.
—Time for Bed. Fox, Mem. 2010. (ENG.). 28p. (J). (gr. k — 1). bds. 8.99 *(978-0-547-40856-9(0)*, 1428814) Houghton Mifflin Harcourt Publishing Co.
—Time for Bed: Lap-Sized Board Book. Fox, Mem. 2005. (ENG.). 28p. (J). (gr. k — 1). bds. 12.99 *(978-0-15-205349-9(2)*, 1196112) Houghton Mifflin Harcourt Publishing Co.
—Time for Bed (Es Hora de Dormir) Fox, Mem. 2012. (ENG.). 28p. (J). (gr. k — 1). bds. 6.99 *(978-0-547-71907-8(8)*, 1481834) Houghton Mifflin Harcourt Publishing Co.
—Wee Rhymes: Baby's First Poetry Book. Yolen, Jane. 2013. (ENG.). 112p. (J). (gr. -1-3). 19.99 *(978-1-4169-4898-8(8)*, Simon & Schuster/Paula Wiseman Bks.) Simon & Schuster/Paula Wiseman Bks.
—Where Did You Come from, Baby Dear? MacDonald, George. 2018. (ENG.). 32p. (J). (gr. -1-2). 17.99 *(978-0-553-50919-9(5))*; lib. bdg. 20.99 *(978-0-553-50920-5(9))* Random Hse. Children's Bks. (Random Hse. Bks. for Young Readers).
—A Woman for President: The Story of Victoria Woodhull. Krull, Kathleen. 2006. (J). (gr. 2-7). 14.60 *(978-0-7569-8179-2(4))* Perfection Learning Corp.
Dyer, Jane & Dyer, Brooke. One Smart Cookie: Bite-Size Lessons for the School Years & Beyond. Rosenthal, Amy Krouse. 2010. (ENG.). 40p. (J). (gr. k-5). 12.99 *(978-0-06-142970-5(8))* HarperCollins Pubs.
—Santa Claus & the Three Bears, Vol. Modugno, Maria. 2013. (ENG.). 40p. (J). (gr. -1-3). 17.99 *(978-0-06-170023-1(1))* HarperCollins Pubs.
—Sugar Cookies: Sweet Little Lessons on Love. Rosenthal, Amy Krouse. 2009. (ENG.). 40p. (J). (gr. k-5). 12.99 *(978-0-06-174072-5(1))* HarperCollins Pubs.
Dyer, Sarah. Double Trouble. 2020. (ENG.). 32p. (J). (gr. -1-17). 16.99 *(978-1-84976-659-3(2))* Tate Publishing, Ltd. GBR. Dist: Hachette Bk. Group.
Dyer, Sarah. Princess for a Day: A Clementine & Mungo Story. Dyer, Sarah. 32p. (J). (gr. -1-k). 2009. pap. 12.95 *(978-0-7475-8891-7(0))*; 2007. 22.95 *(978-0-7475-8753-8(1))* Bloomsbury Publishing Plc GBR. Dist: Independent Pubs. Group.
Dykes, John S. Funny Boy Meets the Airsick Alien from Andromeda. Gutman, Dan. 2012. (Funny Boy Ser.). (ENG.). 136p. (J). (gr. 2-5). pap. 10.99 *(978-1-4532-9527-4(5))* Open Road Integrated Media, Inc.
Dynamo Limited. Blazing Shapes! (Blaze & the Monster Machines) Random House. 2017. (ENG.). 24p. (J). (— 1). bds. 6.99 *(978-1-5247-1716-2(9)*, Random Hse. Bks. for Young Readers) Random Hse. Children's Bks.
—Fix That Truck! Steele, Michael Anthony. 2012. (LEGO City Ser.). (ENG.). 24p. (J). (gr. -1-3). pap. 3.99 *(978-0-545-47061-2(7))* Scholastic, Inc.
—Let's Build a Snowman (Barbie) Depken, Kristen L. 2017. (Step into Reading Ser.). (ENG.). 24p. (J). (gr. -1-1). lib. bdg. 12.99 *(978-1-5247-6481-4(7)*, Random Hse. Bks. for Young Readers) Random Hse. Children's Bks.
—Let's Build a Snowman! (Barbie) Depken, Kristen L. 2017. (Step into Reading Ser.). (ENG.). 24p. (J). (gr. -1-1). pap. 4.99 *(978-1-5247-6480-7(9)*, Random Hse. Bks. for Young Readers) Random Hse. Children's Bks.
—Let's Pick Apples! (Barbie) Random House. 2017. (Step into Reading Ser.). (ENG.). 24p. (J). (gr. -1-1). pap. 4.99 *(978-1-5247-6477-7(9))*; lib. bdg. 12.99 *(978-1-5247-6478-4(7))* Random Hse. Children's Bks. (Random Hse. Bks. for Young Readers).
—A Monster Machine Christmas (Blaze & the Monster Machines) Berrios, Frank. 2016. (Big Golden Book Ser.). (ENG.). 32p. (J). (gr. -1-2). 9.99 *(978-0-399-55353-0(3)*, Golden Bks.) Random Hse. Children's Bks.
—Monster Phonics (Blaze & the Monster Machines) 12 Step into Reading Books. Liberts, Jennifer. 2016. (Step into Reading Ser.). (ENG.). 144p. (J). (gr. -1-1). pap. 12.99 *(978-1-101-94026-6(3)*, Random Hse. Bks. for Young Readers) Random Hse. Children's Bks.
—Rainbow Magic Special Edition: Lindsay the Luck Fairy. Meadows, Daisy. 2013. (Rainbow Magic Special Edition Ser.). (ENG.). 192p. (J). (gr. 2-5). pap. 6.99 *(978-0-545-48492-3(8)*, Scholastic Paperbacks) Scholastic, Inc.
—Rusty's Robot Rescue (Rusty Rivets) Golden Books. 2017. (ENG.). 48p. (J). (gr. -1-2). pap. 4.99 *(978-1-5247-1675-2(8)*, Golden Bks.) Random Hse. Children's Bks.
Dynamo Limited Staff, jt. illus. see Makuc, Lucy.
Dynamo Limited Staff, jt. illus. see Random House Disney Staff.
Dynamo Limited Staff, jt. illus. see Random House.
Dynes, Katy. More Than Just a Star. Clarke, E. J. 2018. (ENG.). 28p. (J). (gr. k-3). 18.99 *(978-1-78719-788-6(3))*; pap. 12.99 *(978-1-78719-787-9(5))* New Generation Publishing GBR. Dist: Independent Pubs. Group.
—Percy the Pebble. Wokes, Paul & Cummings, Delphine. 2016. (ENG.). (J). (gr. k-2). pap. *(978-1-78719-152-5(4))* Authors OnLine, Ltd.
—Poddle's First Flight. Wokes, Paul & Cummings, Delphine. 2017. (ENG.). (J). (gr. k-2). pap. *(978-1-78719-312-3(8))* Authors OnLine, Ltd.
Dyoni, Upit. Imagine Me in Jannah! Bashir, Rabia. 2020. (ENG.). 38p. (J). (gr. k-3). ***(978-1-913677-00-8(1))***; pap. ***(978-1-9997432-5-3(3))*** Precious Bees.
Dyro, Janniche. Forever Dancing. 32p. (J). (gr. 4-18). 16.00 *(978-0-9675413-8-9(7))* Libros, Encouraging Cultural Literacy.
Dyrud, Chris Wold. The Song of Christmas. Clark, Lisa. 2014. (Arch Bks.). (ENG.). 16p. (J). (gr. k-4). pap. 2.49 *(978-0-7586-4605-7(4))* Concordia Publishing Hse.
Dyrud, Chris Wold & Quackenbush, Marcia. Periodo: Guina de una Joven. Loulan, Joann & Worthen, Bonnie. 4th ed. 2003. (Lansky, Vicki Ser.). (SPA.). 92p. pap. 9.99 *(978-0-916773-99-1(X))* Book Peddlers.
Dysinger, Stephen. William. Dysinger, Stephen. 2007. 28p. (J). (gr. -1-3). per. 12.99 *(978-1-59879-297-3(0))* Lifevest Publishing, Inc.
Dyson, Nikki. Dinosaurs Don't Have Bedtimes! Knapman, Timothy. 2016. (ENG.). 32p. (J). (gr. -1-2). 15.99 *(978-0-7636-8927-8(0))* Candlewick Pr.
—Flip Flap Dogs. Nosy Crow. 2018. (Flip Flap Bks.). (ENG.). 28p. (J). (gr. -1-2). 11.99 *(978-1-5362-0258-8(4)*, Nosy Crow) Candlewick Pr.
—How to Be a Pirate. Fliess, Sue. 2014. (Little Golden Book Ser.). 24p. (J). (-k). 4.99 *(978-0-449-81309-6(6)*, Golden Bks.) Random Hse. Children's Bks.
—How to Be a Superhero. Fliess, Sue. 2014. (Little Golden Book Ser.). 24p. (J). (-k). 4.99 *(978-0-385-38737-8(7)*, Golden Bks.) Random Hse. Children's Bks.
—A Mighty Bitey Creature. Armitage, Ronda. 2018. (ENG.). 40p. (J). (gr. -1-2). 15.99 *(978-0-7636-9878-2(4))* Candlewick Pr.
—Oscar the Hungry Unicorn. Carter, Lou. 2020. (Oscar the Hungry Unicorn Ser.). 24p. (J). (gr. -1-k). bds. 10.99 *(978-1-4083-5953-2(7)*, Orchard Bks.) Hachette Children's Group GBR. Dist: Hachette Bk. Group.
—Pirate Stew. Carter, Lou. 2018. 32p. (J). (gr. -1-k). pap. 9.99 *(978-1-4083-3921-3(8)*, Orchard Bks.) Hachette Children's Group GBR. Dist: Hachette Bk. Group.
—1,000 Things to Eat. 2015. (1,000 Pictures Ser.). (ENG.). 34p. (J). (gr. k-5). 14.99 *(978-0-7945-3406-6(6)*, Usborne) EDC Publishing.
Dzama, Marcel, jt. illus. see Ozama, Marcel.
Dzidrums, Joseph. Superhero Siblings. Dzidrums, Christine. 2016. (ENG.). 46p. (J). pap. 9.99 *(978-1-938438-68-4(X))* Creative Media Publishing.
Dzidrums, Joseph, photos by. Cutters Don't Cry. Dzidrums, Christine. Allison, Elizabeth, ed. 2010. 132p. (YA). 24.99 *(978-0-9826435-2-5(7))*; pap. 14.99 *(978-0-9826435-1-8(9))* Creative Media Publishing.
—Jennie Finch: Softball Superstar. Dzidrums, Christine & Rendon, Leah. 2013. (ENG., 72p. (J). pap. 9.99 *(978-1-938438-13-4(2))* Creative Media Publishing.
—Mike Trout: Baseball Sensation. Dzidrums, Christine. 2013. 64p. pap. 9.99 *(978-1-938438-28-8(0))* Creative Media Publishing.
Dzidrums, Joseph, et al, photos by. Yuna Kim: Ice Queen. Dzidrums, Christine. Rendon, Leah, ed. 2011. (Skate Stars Ser.: Vol. 2). 72p. (YA). pap. 10.99 *(978-0-9826435-9-4(4))* Creative Media Publishing.
Dzidrums, Joseph, jt. illus. see Lopez, Lyle.
Dzierzawska, Zosia. Doctor Esperanto & the Language of Hope. Rockliff, Mara. 2019. 40p. (J). (gr. 2-4). 16.99 *(978-0-7636-8915-5(7))* Candlewick Pr.
Dzioba, Wes, jt. illus. see Silva, Leandro Ricardo da.
Dziuba, Nell. Ellie's Rainy Day. Pollack, Barry. 2019. (Zayde Book Ser.: Vol. 7). (ENG.). 26p. (J). pap. 9.99 ***(978-1-7133-1386-1(3))*** Independently Published.
Dziubak, Emilia. The House of Lost & Found, 30 vols. Widmark, Martin. 2018. Orig. Title: Huset Som Vaknade. (ENG.). 40p. (J). 17.95 *(978-1-78250-542-6(3))* Floris Bks. GBR. Dist: Consortium Bk. Sales & Distribution.
—Little Pearl, 28 vols. Widmark, Martin. 2020. (ENG.). 32p. (J). 17.95 *(978-1-78250-599-0(7))* Floris Bks. GBR. Dist: Consortium Bk. Sales & Distribution.
—The Lost Rainforest #1: Mez's Magic. Schrefer, Eliot. 2018. (ENG.). (J). (gr. 3-7). 384p. pap. 6.99 *(978-0-06-249113-8(X))*; 368p. 16.99 *(978-0-06-249107-7(5))* HarperCollins Pubs. (Tegen, Katherine Bks).
—The Lost Rainforest #2: Gogi's Gambit. Schrefer, Eliot. 2019. (ENG.). (J). (gr. 3-7). 368p. pap. 6.99 *(978-0-06-249115-2(6))*; 352p. 16.99 *(978-0-06-249111-4(3))* HarperCollins Pubs. (Tegen, Katherine Bks).
—The Lost Rainforest #3: Rumi's Riddle. Schrefer, Eliot. 2020. (ENG.). 320p. (J). (gr. 3-7). 17.99 *(978-0-06-249120-6(2)*, Tegen, Katherine Bks) HarperCollins Pubs.
—Secret Life of a Tiger. Wechterowicz, Przemyslaw. 2017. (ENG.). 32p. (J). (gr. -1-2). 17.95 *(978-1-68297-154-3(6)*, Words & Pictures) Quarto Publishing Group UK GBR. Dist: Hachette Bk. Group.
Dzuiba, Nell. Le Jour de Pluie D'Ellie. Pollack, Barry. 2019. (FRE.). 26p. (J). pap. 9.13 ***(978-1-6795-3449-2(1))*** Independently Published.

E

E

Eachus, Jennifer. I'm Sorry. McBratney, Sam. 2006. (ENG.). 32p. (J). (gr. -1-2). pap. 7.99 *(978-0-06-079927-4(7))* HarperCollins Pubs.
Eaddy, Susan. First Look at Aircraft. Galvin, Laura Gates. 2008. (ENG.). 16p. (J). (gr. -1-k). bds. 6.95 *(978-1-59249-862-8(0))* Soundprints.
—First Look at Rescue Vehicles. Galvin, Laura Gates. 2009. (ENG.). 16p. (J). (gr. -1-k). 6.95 *(978-1-60727-106-2(0))*; bds. 6.95 *(978-1-60727-093-5(5))* Soundprints.
—First Look at Trucks. Galvin, Laura Gates. 2008. (ENG.). 16p. (J). (gr. -1-k). 6.95 *(978-1-59249-861-1(2))* Soundprints.
—Papa Fish's Lullaby. Hubbell, Patricia. 2007. (ENG.). 32p. (J). (gr. -1-1). 16.95 *(978-1-55971-965-0(6))* Cooper Square Publishing Llc.
Eadie, Eleanor O. Through Four Seasons. Patch, Edith M. & Howe, Harrison E. 2018. (Nature & Science Readers Ser.: Vol. 4). (ENG.). 266p. (J). (gr. 4-6). pap. 12.95 *(978-1-63334-102-9(X))* Yesterday's Classics.
Eadie, Inger Sommer, jt. illus. see Grimm, Debi.
Eagle, Joy. The African Bush Fire & the Elephant: Green Kids Club. Medina, Sylvia M. & Landen, Kelly. 2016. (ENG.). 35p. (J). (gr. k-3). pap. 9.95 *(978-1-939871-22-0(0))* Green Kids Club, Inc.
Eagle, Joy. The Belize Trash Monster - Hardback. Medina, Sylvia M. & Bowen, Dixie. 2020. (ENG.). 43p. (J). (gr. k-3). 21.50 ***(978-1-939871-97-8(2))*** Green Kids Club, Inc.

—The Belize Trash Monster - Paperback. Medina, Sylvia M. & Bowen, Dixie. 2020. (ENG.). 43p. (J). (gr. k-3). pap. 11.50 ***(978-1-939871-98-5(0))*** Green Kids Club, Inc.

Eagle, Joy. Chewoo in Nut Sweet Nut. Medina, Sylvia M. 2017. (Green Kids Club / Yoohoo & Firends Ser.: Vol. 4). (ENG.). 28p. (J). (gr. k-2). pap. 9.99 *(978-1-939871-57-2(3))* Green Kids Club, Inc.

—Chilean Mines. Ballock-Dixon, Saige J. & Medina, Sylvia M. 2013. 35p. pap. 11.49 *(978-1-939871-00-8(X))* Green Kids Club, Inc.

—Desert Mirage. Medina, Sylvia M. & Ballock-Dixon, Saige J. 2012. 32p. pap. 11.59 *(978-0-9836602-6-2(3))* Green Kids Club, Inc.

—Gorilla's Roar. Medina, Sylvia M. & B allock-Dixon, Saige J. 2012. 36p. pap. 11.49 *(978-0-9836602-5-5(5))* Green Kids Club, Inc.

—Green Springs Junior. Medina, Sylvia M. & Ballock-Dixon, Saige J. 2013. 35p. 11.59 *(978-0-9836602-7-9(1))* Green Kids Club, Inc.

—Jade Elephant. Medina, Sylvia M. & Ballock-Dixon, Saige J. 2012. 36p. pap. 11.49 *(978-0-9836602-4-8(7))* Green Kids Club, Inc.

—The Monk Seal & the Mermaid. Medina, Sylvia M. 2018. (Green Kids Club Ser.). (ENG.). 35p. (J). (gr. k-3). pap. 9.95 *(978-1-939871-43-5(3))* Green Kids Club, Inc.

—Ringring in the Great Panda Escape. Medina, Sylvia M. Crandall, Natasca N., ed. 2017. (Green Kids Club / Yoohoo & Friends Ser.: Vol. 5). (ENG.). (J). (gr. k-2). pap. 9.99 *(978-1-939871-58-9(1))* Green Kids Club, Inc.

—The Shark & the Volcano - Third Edition Paperback. Medina, Sylvia M. Hill, Krista, ed. 3rd ed. 2019. (ENG.). 36p. (J). (gr. k-3). pap. 10.50 *(978-1-939871-66-4(2))* Green Kids Club, Inc.

—Shooga to the Rescue. Medina, Sylvia M. 2017. (Green Kids Club / Yoohoo & Firends Ser.: Vol. 6). (ENG.). 28p. (J). (gr. k-2). pap. 9.99 *(978-1-939871-59-6(X))* Green Kids Club, Inc.

—Sparkee & the Stinky Treasure: Green Kids Club. Medina, Sylvia & Matheny, Bill. 2016. (Green Kids Club Ser.). (ENG.). 27p. (J). (gr. k-2). pap. 9.95 *(978-1-939871-21-3(2))* Green Kids Club, Inc.

—Sparkee & the Stinky Treasure - Paperback US 2nd. Matheny, Bill & Medina, Sylvia M. 2nd ed. 2019. (ENG.). 28p. (J). (gr. k-3). pap. 9.99 *(978-1-939871-84-8(0))* Green Kids Club, Inc.

—Tiago Meets Coco in Nawi* (*Nature's Ancient World, Imagined) Medina, Sylvia M. 2017. (Green Kids Club Ser.). (ENG.). 20p. (J). (gr. k-2). pap. 9.95 *(978-1-939871-47-3(6))* Green Kids Club, Inc.

—Tinee Wanta a Mudbath. Medina, Sylvia M. 2017. (Green Kids Club / Yoohoo & Firends Ser.: Vol. 7). (ENG.). 28p. (J). (gr. k-2). pap. 9.99 *(978-1-939871-61-9(1))* Green Kids Club, Inc.

Eagle, Joy & Tavcar, Samantha. Chewoo in Nut Sweet Nut - Paperback US 2nd. Medina, Sylvia M. 2nd ed. 2019. (ENG.). 28p. (J). (gr. k-3). pap. 9.99 *(978-1-939871-82-4(4))* Green Kids Club, Inc.

Eagle, Mike. Coronado's Golden Quest. Weisberg, Barbara & Haley, Alex. 2009. (Steck-Vaughn Stories of America Ser.). (ENG.). 88p. (gr. 3-8). pap. 14.20 *(978-0-8114-8072-7(0))* Houghton Mifflin Harcourt Publishing Co.

Eaglesham, Dale, et al. Perdition's Gate, Vol. 6. Dixon, Chuck. 2004. (Sigil Ser.: Vol. 6). 160p. (YA). pap. 15.95 *(978-1-59314-048-9(7))* CrossGeneration Comics, Inc.

—Steve Rogers: Super-Soldier - the Complete Collection. 2017. (ENG.). 216p. (YA). (gr. 8-17). pap. 24.99 *(978-1-302-90873-7(1))* Marvel Worldwide, Inc.

Eakins, Bonny Mae & Hoffbauer, Wyng. Wonder Island. Eakins, Bonny Mae. 2nd ed. 2013. 80p. pap. 14.95 *(978-1-893660-26-7(5))* Ravenhawk Bks.

Eakle, Tayah. 3 A's & 3 B's All the Way to Z, 1 vol. Eakle, Janice. 2009. 36p. pap. 24.95 *(978-1-60813-739-8(2))* America Star Bks.

Eargle, Ben. Fame: Jennifer Lawrence. Davis, Darren G. Troy, Michael, ed. 2017. (Fame Ser.). (ENG.). (YA). (gr. 8-12). pap. 5.99 *(978-1-948216-41-8(8))* TidalWave.

Earlenbaugh, Dennis. Puzzling over Sherlock. Senuta, Michael. 2003. (Fact-Based Bks.). 32p. (YA). (gr. 4-12). pap. 8.00 *(978-0-934468-54-1(0))* Gaslight Pubns.

—Second Thoughts about Sherlock Holmes. Senuta, Michael. 2003. (Novels, Novelas, Short Stories Ser.). 32p. (YA). (gr. 4-12). pap. 8.00 *(978-0-934468-55-8(9))* Gaslight Pubns.

Earley, Anna. Thieves of Weirdwood. Shivering, William & Heidicker, Christian McKay. 2020. (Thieves of Weirdwood Ser.: 1). (ENG.). 352p. (J). 16.99 *(978-1-250-30288-5(9))*, 900197000, Holt, Henry & Co. Bks. For Young Readers) Holt, Henry & Co.

Earley, Catherine M., photos by. God Makes Beautiful Things. Earley, Catherine M. 2005. 48p. (YA). per. 11.00 *(978-0-9769589-0-1(2))* Naynay Bks.

Earnest, Terri. Hoppin' Hankaroo. Earnest-Jenkins, Janet. 2016. (ENG.). 26p. (J). pap. 15.00 *(978-1-4835-8306-8(6))* BookBaby.

Easey, Chris. Toulouse Tangled up in Lights. Thompson, Kimberly. 2011. 64p. (J). 19.95 *(978-0-9818976-1-5(4))* Little Pigeon Bks.

Easler, Kris. The Day the Mustache Came Back. Katz, Alan. 2016. (Mustache Ser.: 2). 224p. (J). 13.99 *(978-1-61963-560-9(7))*, 900140626, Bloomsbury USA Childrens) Bloomsbury Publishing USA.

—The Day the Mustache Took Over. Katz, Alan. 2015. (Mustache Ser.: 1). 208p. (YA). (gr. 2-4). 13.99 *(978-1-61963-558-6(5))*, 900140624, Bloomsbury USA Childrens) Bloomsbury Publishing USA.

Eason, D. M. The Goodwill Vultures Club. Willard, Hugh. Holjes, Kerry, ed. 2013. 122p. pap. 9.99 *(978-1-935711-26-1(1))* Peak City Publishing, LLC.

—The Goodwill Vultures Club: No Time for Play. Willard, Hugh. Holjes, Kerry, ed. 2013. 140p. pap. 9.99 *(978-1-935711-30-8(X))* Peak City Publishing, LLC.

—The Goodwill Vultures Club: The Gift of the Vulture. Willard, Hugh. Dozier, Dolly, ed. 2013. 128p. pap. 9.99 *(978-1-935711-34-6(2))* Peak City Publishing, LLC.

—The Rusty Bucket Kids, A Behind the Scenes Look at the Rusty Bucket Kids, Lincoln, Journey To 16. Demers, Roxanna. 2010. (ENG.). 82p. (J). pap. 19.99 *(978-1-935711-04-9(0))* Peak City Publishing, LLC.

Eason, Rohan. Oblibion. Kaaberbøl, Lene. Barslund, Charlotte, tr. from DAN. 2016. (Wildwitch Ser.). (ENG.). 160p. (J). (gr. 4-7). pap. 9.99 *(978-1-78269-084-9(0))*, Pushkin Children's Bks.) Steerforth Pr.

—Wildfire. Kaaberbøl, Lene. Barslund, Charlotte, tr. 2016. (Wildwitch Ser.: 1). (ENG.). 160p. (J). (gr. 4-7). pap. 9.99 *(978-1-78269-083-2(2))*, Pushkin Children's Bks.) Steerforth Pr.

Eason, Rohan Daniel. Benice: An Adventure of Love & Friendship. Karayaka, Metin. 2018. (ENG.). 216p. (J). (gr. 3-7). 24.99 *(978-0-9989640-5-8(0))* Yunka Publishing.

—Bloodling. Kaaberbøl, Lene & Barslund, Charlotte. 2017. (Wildwitch Ser.: 4). (ENG.). 200p. (J). (gr. 3-7). pap. 9.99 *(978-1-78269-086-3(7))*, Pushkin Children's Bks.) Steerforth Pr.

—Brave Red, Smart Frog: A New Book of Old Tales. Jenkins, Emily. 2017. 104p. (J). (gr. 3-7). 17.99 *(978-0-7636-6558-6(4))* Candlewick Pr.

—Life Stealer. Kaaberbøl, Lene. Barslund, Charlotte, tr. 2017. (Wildwitch Ser.: 3). (ENG.). 160p. (J). (gr. 4-7). pap. 9.99 *(978-1-78269-085-6(9))*, Pushkin Children's Bks.) Steerforth Pr.

East, Jacqueline. Adeline Porcupine. Ghigna, Charles. 2015. (Tiny Tales Ser.). (ENG.). 64p. (J). (gr. -1-2). lib. bdg. 23.99 *(978-1-4795-6530-6(X))*, Picture Window Bks.) Capstone.

—All the Ways I Love You. Larkin, Susan. 2014. (J). *(978-1-4351-5821-4(0))* Barnes & Noble, Inc.

—Always in My Heart. Landes, Andi. 2018. (ENG.). 20p. (J). (gr. -1-k). bds. 6.99 *(978-1-68412-585-2(5))*, Silver Dolphin Bks.) Printers Row Publishing Group.

—Baby Dinosaur Can Play, 1 vol. Dale, Jay. 2012. (Engage Literacy Red Ser.). (ENG.). 32p. (gr. k-2). pap. 5.99 *(978-1-4296-8936-6(6))*, Capstone Pr.) Capstone.

—Baby Dinosaur Is Hiding, 1 vol. Dale, Jay. 2012. (Engage Literacy Yellow Ser.). (ENG.). 32p. (gr. k-2). pap. 5.99 *(978-1-4296-8952-6(8))*, Capstone Pr.) Capstone.

—Baby Dinosaur Is Lost, 1 vol. Dale, Jay. 2012. (Engage Literacy Blue Ser.). (ENG.). 32p. (gr. k-2). pap. 5.99 *(978-1-4296-8972-4(2))*, Capstone Pr.) Capstone.

—Bobby Bear. Ghigna, Charles. 2015. (Tiny Tales Ser.). (ENG.). 64p. (J). (gr. -1-2). lib. bdg. 23.99 *(978-1-4795-6531-3(8))*, Picture Window Bks.) Capstone.

—Bunnies Are for Kissing. Zobel-Nolan, Allia. 2009. 24p. (J). (gr. -1-k). 7.95 *(978-1-58925-842-6(8))* Tiger Tales.

—Bunny Blessings, 1 vol. Washburn, Kim. 2018. (ENG.). 18p. (J). bds. 8.99 *(978-0-310-76209-6(X))* Zonderkidz.

—The Children's Book of Manners. Giles, Sophie et al. 2014. (ENG.). 32p. (J). pap. 10.00 *(978-1-84135-971-7(8))* Award Pubns. Ltd. GBR. Dist: Parkwest Pubns., Inc.

—Cuddle Bunny. Ghigna, Charles. 2015. (Tiny Tales Ser.). (ENG.). 64p. (J). (gr. -1-2). lib. bdg. 23.99 *(978-1-4795-6528-3(8))*, Picture Window Bks.) Capstone.

—Easter Hop. 2008. (ENG.). 16p. (gr. -1-k). bds. 5.95 *(978-1-58117-686-5(4))*, Intervisual/Piggy Toes) Bendon, Inc.

—Five Naughty Kittens. Beardsley, Martyn. 2005. (Reading Corner Ser.). 24p. (J). (gr. k-3). lib. bdg. 22.80 *(978-1-59771-006-0(7))* Sea-To-Sea Pubns.

—The Flying Monkey, 6 pack. Holden, Pam. 2009. (Red Rocket Readers Ser.). 16p. (gr. -1-1). pap. *(978-1-877363-29-0(4))*, Red Rocket Readers) Flying Start Bks.

—Grumpy Old Bear, 1 vol. Dale, Jay. 2012. (Wonder Words Ser.). (ENG.). 32p. (gr. k-2). pap. 5.99 *(978-1-4296-8918-2(8))*, Capstone Pr.) Capstone.

East, Jacqueline, et al. Hickory Dickory Dock: And Other Silly-Time Rhymes. 2005. (Mother Goose Rhymes Ser.). (ENG.). 36p. (J). (gr. -1-k). 12.95 *(978-1-59249-463-7(3))*, 1D019) Soundprints.

East, Jacqueline. Learn Good Habits with Jessica: Above All, Don't Behave Like Zoe!, 1 vol. 2008. (ENG.). 28p. (J). (gr. -1-3). 6.95 *(978-1-59496-163-2(8))* Teora USA LLC.

—Learn Good Manners with Charles: Above All, Don't Behave Like Trevor!, 1 vol. 2008. (ENG.). 28p. (J). (gr. -1-3). 6.95 *(978-1-59496-162-5(X))* Teora USA LLC.

—Little Zebra, 1 vol. Dale, Jay. 2012. (Wonder Words Ser.). (ENG.). 32p. (gr. k-2). pap. 5.99 *(978-1-4296-8906-9(4))*, Capstone Pr.) Capstone.

—Look at My Home, 6 vols. Holden, Pam. 2009. (Red Rocket Readers Ser.). 16p. (gr. -1-1). pap. *(978-1-877363-04-7(9))*, Red Rocket Readers) Flying Start Bks.

—Lots of Love, 1 vol. Washburn, Kim. 2016. (ENG.). 18p. (J). bds. 8.99 *(978-0-310-75861-7(0))* Zonderkidz.

—Lucy Goose. Ghigna, Charles. 2015. (Tiny Tales Ser.). (ENG.). 64p. (J). (gr. -1-2). lib. bdg. 23.99 *(978-1-4795-6529-0(6))*, Picture Window Bks.) Capstone.

—Max Monkey, 6 pack. Holden, Pam. 2009. (Red Rocket Readers Ser.). 16p. (gr. -1-1). pap. *(978-1-877363-24-5(3))*, Red Rocket Readers) Flying Start Bks.

—Monkey. Elliot, Rachel. 2009. (Wiggle-Waggles Bks.). (ENG.). 8p. (J). (gr. -1). bds. 4.99 *(978-0-7641-6238-1(1))*, B.E.S. Publishing) Peterson's.

—My Good Night Bible (Padded) Lingo, Susan. 2017. (ENG.). 192p. (J). (gr. -1-k). 12.99 *(978-1-4627-4273-8(4))*, 005793371, B&H Kids) B&H Publishing Group.

—Peter Cottontail's Busy Day. 2009. 10p. 5.95 *(978-1-58117-862-3(X))*, Intervisual/Piggy Toes) Bendon, Inc.

—Princess Palace: A Three-Demensional Playset. 2006. 8p. (J). (gr. -1-3). 22.95 *(978-1-58117-492-2(6))*, Intervisual/Piggy Toes) Bendon, Inc.

—Pumpkin Patch Blessings, 1 vol. Washburn, Kim. 2016. (ENG.). 18p. (J). bds. 8.99 *(978-0-310-75819-8(X))* Zonderkidz.

—Puppy Love. Barad, Alexis. 2013. (J). *(978-0-545-47733-8(6))* Scholastic, Inc.

—See Me Ride, 6 pack. Holden, Pam. 2009. (Red Rocket Readers Ser.). 16p. (gr. -1-1). pap. *(978-1-877363-30-6(8))*, Red Rocket Readers) Flying Start Bks.

—Stickybeak the Parrot, 6 pack. Holden, Pam. 2009. (Red Rocket Readers Ser.). 16p. (gr. -1-1). pap. *(978-1-877363-28-3(6))*, Red Rocket Readers) Flying Start Bks.

—Ten Little Mermaids. Williams, Becky. 2007. (Story Book Ser.). 22p. (J). (gr. -1). bds. *(978-1-84666-375-8(X))*, Tide Mill Pr.) Top That! Publishing PLC.

—Three Billy Goats' Stuff!, 1 vol. Hartman, Bob. 2009. 32p. (J). 14.95 *(978-0-8254-7853-6(7))*, Lion Children's) Lion Hudson PLC GBR. Dist: Kregel Pubns.

—The Town Mouse & the Country Mouse. 2007. (Picture Book Classics Ser.). (J). (gr. -1-3). 24p. 9.99 *(978-0-7945-1877-6(X))*; 48p. 8.99 *(978-0-7945-1613-0(0))* EDC Publishing. (Usborne).

—When I Grow Up. Holden, Pam. 2009. (Red Rocket Readers Ser.). 16p. (gr. -1-1). pap. *(978-1-877363-06-1(5))*, Red Rocket Readers) Flying Start Bks.

East, Matt. Tommy Cat & the Giant Chickens. East, Bob. 2008. 24p. per. 24.95 *(978-1-4241-9242-7(0))* America Star Bks.

East, Nick. Chicken Little. Tiger Tales. 2016. (My First Fairy Tales Ser.). (ENG.). 32p. (J). (gr. -1-2). pap. 7.99 *(978-1-58925-476-3(7))* Tiger Tales.

East, Nick. Christopher Pumpkin. Hendra, Sue & Linnet, Paul. 2020. (ENG.). (J). (gr. -1 — 1). 30p. bds. 8.99 ***(978-0-316-42756-2(X))***; 32p. 17.99 ***(978-0-316-42755-5(1))*** Little, Brown Bks. for Young Readers.

East, Nick. Do Not Wash This Bear. Hay, Sam. 2016. (J). *(978-1-4351-6399-7(0))* Barnes & Noble, Inc.

—Ellie's Magical Wellies. Sparkes, Amy. 2017. (ENG.). 32p. (J). (gr. -1-k). pap. 10.99 *(978-1-4052-7379-4(8))* Egmont Bks., Ltd. GBR. Dist: Independent Pubs. Group.

—Goodnight Santa: The Perfect Bedtime Book. Robinson, Michelle. 2015. (Goodnight Ser.). (ENG.). 32p. (gr. -1 — 1). pap. 7.99 *(978-1-4380-0660-4(8))*, B.E.S. Publishing) Peterson's.

—Goodnight Spaceman: The Perfect Bedtime Book! Robinson, Michelle. 2017. (Goodnight Ser.). (ENG.). 32p. (J). (gr. -1 — 1). pap. 7.99 *(978-1-4380-1086-1(9))*, B.E.S. Publishing) Peterson's.

—Harry & the Monster. Mongredien, Sue. 2013. (ENG.). 32p. (J). (gr. -1-2). 14.99 *(978-1-58925-146-5(6))* Tiger Tales.

—Simon Sock. Hendra, Sue. 2019. 32p. (J). (gr. -1-k). pap. 9.99 *(978-1-4449-3681-0(6))* Hachette Children's Group GBR. Dist: Hachette Bk. Group.

East, Stella. The Paint Box, 1 vol. Trottier, Maxine. 2004. (ENG.). 32p. (J). (gr. 1-4). pap. 8.95 *(978-1-55041-808-8(4))*, ce1e514c-386f-47f8-a586-91d1cccd34c9) Trifolium Bks., Inc. CAN. Dist: Firefly Bks., Ltd.

Easthope, Kevin. Dipnetting with Dad. Sellars, Willie. 2014. (ENG.). 48p. (J). (gr. 1-7). bds. 19.95 *(978-1-927575-53-6(2))* Caitlin Pr., Inc. CAN. Dist: Independent Pubs. Group.

Eastland, Sue. Little Red Ruthie. Koster, Gloria. 2017. (ENG.). 32p. (J). (gr. -1-3). 16.99 *(978-0-8075-4646-8(1))*, 807546461) Whitman, Albert & Co.

—The Ugly Duckling. Tiger Tales. 2017. (My First Fairy Tales Ser.). (ENG.). 32p. (J). (gr. -1-2). pap. 7.99 *(978-1-58925-497-8(X))* Tiger Tales.

Eastley, Melanie. Scott the Starfish - an Unexpected Adventure! Fraser, Jennifer. 2012. 32p. pap. *(978-0-9868776-4-3(6))* MW Bk. Pubs.

Eastman, Dianne. One Splendid Tree. Helmer, Marilyn. 2007. 32p. (J). (gr. -1-3). 6.95 *(978-1-55453-166-0(7))* Kids Can Pr., Ltd. CAN. Dist: Hachette Bk. Group.

Eastman, Dianne & Hobbs, Dan. Wow Canada! Exploring This Land from Coast to Coast to Coast. Bowers, Vivien. 2nd ed. 2010. (Wow Canada! Ser.). (ENG.). 160p. (J). (gr. 3-6). pap. 24.95 *(978-1-897349-83-0(1))*, Owlkids) Owlkids Bks. Inc. CAN. Dist: Publishers Group West (PGW).

Eastman, P. D. Go, Dog. Go! Eastman, P. D. 2008. (ENG.). 64p. pap. *(978-0-00-722546-0(6))* HarperCollins Pubs. Ltd.

Eastman, P. D. & Eastman, Tony. Big Dog... Little Dog. Eastman, P. D. 2003. (Beginner Books(R) Ser.). (ENG.). 48p. (J). (gr. -1-2). 9.99 *(978-0-375-82297-1(6))*, Random Hse. Bks. for Young Readers) Random Hse. Children's Bks.

Eastman, Peter. Fred & Ted Like to Fly. Eastman, Peter. 2007. (Beginner Books(R) Ser.). 48p. (J). (gr. -1-2). 9.99 *(978-0-375-84064-7(8))*, Random Hse. Bks. for Young Readers) Random Hse. Children's Bks.

Eastman, Tony, jt. illus. see Eastman, P. D.

Easton, Grace. Good Dog, Mctavish. Rosoff, Meg. 2019. (Mctavish Stories Ser.: 1). (ENG.). 112p. (J). (gr. 2-5). 15.99 *(978-1-5362-0058-4(1))* Candlewick Pr.

Easton, Grace, et al. In Focus: Cities. Walden, Libby. 2017. (ENG.). 28p. (J). (gr. 1-4). 22.99 *(978-1-944530-08-2(8))*, 360 Degrees) Tiger Tales.

Easton, Grace. McTavish Goes Wild. Rosoff, Meg. 2020. (Mctavish Stories Ser.). (ENG.). 96p. (J). (gr. 2-5). 15.99 *(978-1-5362-0331-8(9))* Candlewick Pr.

Easton, Mark. The Monster Book of Banana Jokes. Bailey, Bee. 2019. (Monster Book of Jokes Ser.: Vol. 2). (ENG.). 118p. (J). pap. 6.95 ***(978-1-6937-1161-9(3))*** Independently Published.

Easton, Susan. Punkinhead's Veggie Adventure: And the Strange Contraption in the Kitchen. Rosenbaum, Elizabeth, photos by. Trooboff, Rhoda. 2013. (ENG.). 56p. (J). (gr. -1). pap. 15.00 *(978-0-9773536-7-5(2))* Tenley Circle Pr.

Easton, W. G. The Mysterious Shin Shira. Farrow, George Edward. 2007. 120p. per. *(978-1-4065-1690-6(2))* Dodo Pr.

Eastwood, John. Annie Saves the Day. Lindsay, Elizabeth. 2003. 92p. (J). *(978-0-439-44651-8(1))* Scholastic, Inc.

—The Catlady. King-Smith, Dick. 2007. (ENG.). 80p. (J). (gr. 1-4). 5.99 *(978-0-440-42031-6(8))*, Yearling) Random Hse. Children's Bks.

—Funny Frank. King-Smith, Dick. 2003. (ENG.). 112p. (J). (gr. 1-4). 6.99 *(978-0-440-41880-1(1))*, Yearling) Random Hse. Children's Bks.

—Titus Rules! King-Smith, Dick. 2004. (ENG.). 96p. (J). (gr. 1-4). reprint ed. 5.99 *(978-0-440-42000-2(8))*, Yearling) Random Hse. Children's Bks.

Eaton, Matthew. How to Capture a Monster. Frome, Annie. 2020. (Backpack Ser.: 1). (ENG.). 24p. (J). pap. 11.11 ***(978-0-692-19582-6(3))*** BookBaby.

Eaton, Maxwell, III. The Truth about Bears: Seriously Funny Facts about Your Favorite Animals. Eaton, Maxwell, III. 2018. (Truth about Your Favorite Animals Ser.). (ENG.). 32p. (J). 15.99 *(978-1-62672-666-6(3))*, 900169980) Roaring Brook Pr.

—The Truth about Butterflies. Eaton, Maxwell, III. 2020. (Truth about Your Favorite Animals Ser.: 1). (ENG.). 32p. (J). 16.99 *(978-1-250-23253-3(8))*, 900209867) Roaring Brook Pr.

—The Truth about Crocodiles: Seriously Funny Facts about Your Favorite Animals. Eaton, Maxwell, III. 2019. (Truth about Your Favorite Animals Ser.). (ENG.). 32p. (J). 16.99 *(978-1-250-19844-0(5))*, 900194595) Roaring Brook Pr.

—The Truth about Dolphins: Seriously Funny Facts about Your Favorite Animals. Eaton, Maxwell, III. 2018. (Truth about Your Favorite Animals Ser.). (ENG.). 32p. (J). 15.99 *(978-1-62672-668-0(X))*, 900169985) Roaring Brook Pr.

Eaton, Scot, et al. Sigil, Vol. 5. Dixon, Chuck. 2003. (Sigil Ser.: Vol. 5). 160p. (YA). pap. 15.95 *(978-1-931484-83-1(X))* CrossGeneration Comics, Inc.

Eaton, Scot & Barreiro, Mike. Leonard Nimoy's Primortals Vol. 1, No. 1: Origins. Nimoy, Leonard. Chambers, James et al, eds. 36p. (Orig.). (YA). pap. 2.25 *(978-0-9645175-1-6(5))* Big Entertainment, Inc.

Eaton, Scot, jt. illus. see Abnett, Dan.

Eaves, Ed. How to Catch a Dragon. Hart, Caryl. 2014. (ENG.). 32p. pap. 8.99 *(978-0-85707-959-6(X))*, Simon & Schuster Children's) Simon & Schuster, Ltd. GBR. Dist: Simon & Schuster, Inc.

—How to Save a Superhero. Hart, Caryl. 2018. (ENG.). 32p. (J). (gr. -1). 7.99 *(978-1-4711-4478-3(X))*, Simon & Schuster Children's) Simon & Schuster, Ltd. GBR. Dist: Simon & Schuster, Inc.

Eaves, Ed. You Can't Cuddle a Crocodile. Hendry, Diana. 2020. 32p. (J). (gr. -1-k). 18.99 ***(978-1-4449-2454-1(0))***; pap. 10.99 ***(978-1-4449-2455-8(9))*** Hachette Children's Group GBR. Dist: Hachette Bk. Group.

Eaves, Edward. Say Goodnight to the Sleepy Animals! Whybrow, Ian. 2017. (J). *(978-1-4351-6510-6(1))* Barnes & Noble, Inc.

—Say Hello to the Baby Animals! Whybrow, Ian. 2017. (J). *(978-1-4351-6513-7(6))* Barnes & Noble, Inc.

—Say Hello to the Jungle Animals! Whybrow, Ian. 2017. (J). *(978-1-4351-6511-3(X))* Barnes & Noble, Inc.

—Say Hello to the Snowy Animals! Whybrow, Ian. 2012. (J). *(978-0-7607-9675-7(0))* Barnes & Noble, Inc.

Ebbeler, Jeff. Don't Forget! A Responsibility Story, 1 vol. Suen, Anastasia. 2008. (Main Street School~ Kids with Character Ser.). (ENG.). 32p. (J). (gr. k-4). 28.50 *(978-1-60270-269-1(1))*, 11273, Looking Glass Library) Magic Wagon.

—Game Over: Dealing with Bullies, 1 vol. Suen, Anastasia. 2008. (Main Street School~ Kids with Character Ser.). (ENG.). 32p. (J). (gr. k-4). 28.50 *(978-1-60270-270-7(5))*, 11275, Looking Glass Library) Magic Wagon.

—Girls Can, Too! A Tolerence Story, 1 vol. Suen, Anastasia. 2008. (Main Street School~ Kids with Character Ser.). (ENG.). 32p. (J). (gr. k-4). 28.50 *(978-1-60270-271-4(3))*, 11277, Looking Glass Library) Magic Wagon.

—Laugh Out Loud. Patterson, James & Grabenstein, Chris. 2017. (ENG.). 304p. (J). (gr. 3-7). 13.99 *(978-0-316-43146-0(X))*, Jimmy Patterson) Little Brown & Co.

—Stone Soup: Lap Book Edition. Smith, Carrie. 2016. (My First Reader's Theater Tales Ser.). (J). (gr. k). *(978-1-5021-5508-5(7))* Benchmark Education Co.

—Stone Soup: Small Book Edition. Smith, Carrie. 2016. (My First Reader's Theater Tales Ser.). (J). (gr. k). *(978-1-5021-5513-9(3))* Benchmark Education Co.

—Trust Me: A Loyalty Story, 1 vol. Suen, Anastasia. 2008. (Main Street School~ Kids with Character Ser.). (ENG.). 32p. (J). (gr. k-4). 28.50 *(978-1-60270-273-8(X))*, 11281, Looking Glass Library) Magic Wagon.

—Vote for Isaiah! A Citizenship Story, 1 vol. Suen, Anastasia. 2008. (Main Street School~ Kids with Character Ser.). (ENG.). 32p. (J). (gr. k-4). 28.50 *(978-1-60270-274-5(8))*, 11283, Looking Glass Library) Magic Wagon.

—A Warrior Prince for God Curriculum Leader's Guide. Chapman, Kelly. 2009. pap. 12.99 *(978-0-7369-2899-1(5))* Harvest Hse. Pubs.

—Your Life As a Pharaoh in Ancient Egypt, 1 vol. Gunderson, Jessica Sarah. 2012. (Way It Was Ser.). (ENG.). 32p. (J). (gr. 2-5). pap. 8.95 *(978-1-4048-7744-3(4))*, Picture Window Bks.) Capstone.

—Your Life As a Pharaoh in Ancient Egypt, 1 vol. Gunderson, Jessica. 2012. (Way It Was Ser.). (ENG.). 32p. (J). (gr. 2-5). lib. bdg. 27.32 *(978-1-4048-7371-1(6))*, Picture Window Bks.) Capstone.

Ebbeler, Jeffrey. Cinco de Mouse-O! Cox, Judy. (Adventures of Mouse Ser.: 2). (ENG.). 32p. (J). (gr. -1-3). 2011. pap. 7.99 *(978-0-8234-2328-6(X))*; 2010. 16.95 *(978-0-8234-2194-7(5))* Holiday Hse., Inc.

—Cutting in Line Isn't Fair!, 1 vol. Suen, Anastasia. 2007. (Main Street School~ Kids with Character Ser.). (ENG.). 32p. (J). (gr. -1-4). 28.50 *(978-1-60270-029-1(X))*, 11259, Looking Glass Library) Magic Wagon.

—Eli's Lie-O-Meter: A Story about Telling the Truth. Levins, Sandra. 2010. 32p. (J). (gr. -1-3). 14.95 *(978-1-4338-0735-0(1))*; pap. 9.95 *(978-1-4338-0736-7(X))* American Psychological Assn. (Magination Pr.).

—Feast of Peas. Sheth, Kashmira. 2020. (ENG.). 32p. (J). (gr. -1-3). 17.99 *(978-1-68263-135-5(4))* Peachtree Publishing Co. Inc.

—A Good Team: A Cooperation Story, 1 vol. Suen, Anastasia. 2008. (Main Street School~ Kids with Character Ser.).

(ENG.). 32p. (J). (gr. k-4). 28.50 *(978-1-60270-272-1(1)*, 11279, Looking Glass Library) Magic Wagon.
—Hanukkah Cookies with Sprinkles. Adler, David A. 2015. (J). *(978-0-87441-918-4(2))*; Vol. (ENG.). *(978-1-68115-500-5(1))* Behrman Hse., Inc.
—Helping Sophia, 1 vol. Suen, Anastasia. 2007. (Main Street School~ Kids with Character Ser.). (ENG.). 32p. (J). (gr. -1-4). 28.50 *(978-1-60270-030-7(3)*, 11261, Looking Glass Library) Magic Wagon.
—Lights Out Shabbat, Vol. Shulimson, Sarene. 2012. (ENG.). 32p. (J). (gr. -1-2). pap. 7.95 *(978-0-7613-7565-4(1)*, 9780761375654, Kar-Ben Publishing) Lerner Publishing Group.
Ebbeler, Jeffrey. Mouse's Thanksgiving. Cox, Judy. 2020. (Adventures of Mouse Ser.: 1). 30p. (J). (— 1). bds. 7.99 ***(978-0-8234-4826-5(6))*** Holiday Hse., Inc.
Ebbeler, Jeffrey. One Is a Feast for Mouse: A Thanksgiving Tale. Cox, Judy. 2009. (Adventures of Mouse Ser.: 1). (ENG.). 32p. (J). (gr. -1-3). pap. 7.99 *(978-0-8234-2231-9(3))* Holiday Hse., Inc.
—The Only Alex Addleston in All These Mountains. Solheim, James. 2014. (ENG.). 32p. (J). (gr. -1-3). lib. bdg. 17.95 *(978-1-4677-0346-8(X)*, 9781467703468, Carolrhoda Bks.) Lerner Publishing Group.
—Raising the Flag, 1 vol. Suen, Anastasia. 2007. (Main Street School~ Kids with Character Ser.). (ENG.). 32p. (J). (gr. -1-4). 28.50 *(978-1-60270-031-4(1)*, 11263, Looking Glass Library) Magic Wagon.
—Scissors, Paper & Sharing, 1 vol. Suen, Anastasia. 2007. (Main Street School~ Kids with Character Ser.). (ENG.). 32p. (J). (gr. -1-4). 28.50 *(978-1-60270-032-1(X)*, 11265, Looking Glass Library) Magic Wagon.
—Scout Moore, Junior Ranger: Yellowstone, Vol. Howell, Theresa. 2019. (ENG.). 32p. (J). (gr. 2-7). 15.95 *(978-1-63076-345-9(4))* Muddy Boots Pr.
—Show Some Respect, 1 vol. Suen, Anastasia. 2007. (Main Street School~ Kids with Character Ser.). (ENG.). 32p. (J). (gr. -1-4). 28.50 *(978-1-60270-033-8(8)*, 11267, Looking Glass Library) Magic Wagon.
—Snow Day for Mouse. Cox, Judy. 2013. (Adventures of Mouse Ser.: 4). (ENG.). 32p. (J). (gr. -1-3). pap. 7.99 *(978-0-8234-2913-4(X))* Holiday Hse., Inc.
—The Table & the Chair. Lear, Edward. 2011. (Poetry for Children Ser.). (ENG.). 24p. (J). (gr. k-3). 27.07 *(978-1-60973-156-4(5)*, 201185) Child's World, Inc., The.
Ebbeler, Jeffrey. There Was a Young Rabbi: A Hanukkah Tale. Wolfe, Suzanne. 2020. (ENG.). 24p. (J). (gr. -1-3). 17.99 ***(978-1-5415-7607-0(1)***, Kar-Ben Publishing) Lerner Publishing Group.
Ebbeler, Jeffrey. Tiger in My Soup, 1 vol. Sheth, Kashmira. (ENG.). 32p. (J). (gr. -1-3). 2015. pap. 7.95 *(978-1-56145-890-5(2))*; 2013. 15.95 *(978-1-56145-696-3(9))* Peachtree Publishing Co. Inc.
—Times Tables Cheat, 1 vol. Suen, Anastasia. 2007. (Main Street School~ Kids with Character Ser.). (ENG.). 32p. (J). (gr. -1-4). 28.50 *(978-1-60270-034-5(6)*, 11269, Looking Glass Library) Magic Wagon.
—The Twelve Days of Christmas in Illinois. Bellisario, Gina. (Twelve Days of Christmas in America Ser.). (J). (-k). 2018. 22p. bds. 7.95 *(978-1-4549-2928-4(6))*; 2012. 40p. 12.95 *(978-1-4027-9733-0(8))* Sterling Publishing Co., Inc.
—The Twelve Days of Christmas in Ohio. Gerber, Carole. (Twelve Days of Christmas in America Ser.). (J). (-k). 2017. 22p. bds. 7.95 *(978-1-4549-2794-5(1))*; 2014. 40p. 12.95 *(978-1-4549-0890-6(4))* Sterling Publishing Co., Inc.
—We Both Read Bilingual Edition-The Mouse in My House/un Raton en Mi Casa. Orshoski, Paul. Canetti, Yanitzia, tr. from ENG. 2014. (We Both Read - Level 1 (Quality) Ser.). (ENG & SPA.). 44p. (J). (gr. 1). pap. 4.99 *(978-1-60115-056-1(3))* Treasure Bay, Inc.
—We Both Read-My Sitter Is a T-Rex! (Level 1-2) Orshoski, Paul. 2011. (ENG.). 44p. (J). 9.95 *(978-1-60115-253-4(1))*; pap. 4.99 *(978-1-60115-254-1(X))* Treasure Bay, Inc.
—We Both Read-The Mouse in My House. Orshoski, Paul. 2012. 44p. (J). pap. 4.99 *(978-1-60115-258-9(2))* Treasure Bay, Inc.
—We Read Phonics-Ant in Her Pants. Orshoski, Paul. 2010. (ENG.). 32p. (J). pap. 4.99 *(978-1-60115-328-9(7))* Treasure Bay, Inc.
—We Read Phonics-Dad Does It All. Orshoski, Paul. 2011. 32p. (J). 9.95 *(978-1-60115-341-8(4))*; (YA). pap. 4.99 *(978-1-60115-342-5(2))* Treasure Bay, Inc.
—We Read Phonics-I Do Not Like Greens! Orshoski, Paul. 2011. (We Read Phonics: Level 4 Ser.). (ENG.). 32p. (J). (gr. 1-3). 17.44 *(978-1-60115-331-9(7))* Treasure Bay, Inc.
—We Read Phonics-Robot Man. Orshoski, Paul. 2010. (We Read Phonics Ser.). 32p. (J). (gr. 1-5). 9.95 *(978-1-60115-329-6(5))*; pap. 4.99 *(978-1-60115-330-2(9))* Treasure Bay, Inc.
—We Read Phonics-Sports Dream. Orshoski, Paul. 2011. (We Read Phonics: Level 5-6 Ser.). 32p. (J). (ENG.). (gr. k-3). 17.44 *(978-1-60115-335-7(X))*; (gr. 1-3). pap. 4.99 *(978-1-60115-336-4(8))* Treasure Bay, Inc.
—When Bill Gates Memorized an Encyclopedia. Weakland, Mark. 2018. (Leaders Doing Headstands Ser.). (ENG.). 32p. (J). (gr. 1-4). lib. bdg. 28.65 *(978-1-5158-3040-5(3)*, 138680, Picture Window Bks.) Capstone.
—Your Life As an Explorer on a Viking Ship. Troupe, Thomas Kingsley. 2012. (Way It Was Ser.). (ENG.). 32p. (J). (gr. 2-5). pap. 8.95 *(978-1-4048-7252-3(3))*; lib. bdg. 27.32 *(978-1-4048-7160-1(8))* Capstone. (Picture Window Bks.).
Ebensperger, Michael. The Girl with the Dinosaur Tooth. Reynolds, Joey. 2020. (Girl with the Dinosaur Tooth Ser.: Vol. 1). (ENG.). 44p. (J). (gr. k-4). 19.99 ***(978-1-7348462-0-1(8))*** Scribble Scholars.
Eberbach, Andrea. Ame the Elephant: Terrorized by Evil Mice. Louthain, J. A. 2nd l.t. ed. 2003. 48p. (J). 12.97 *(978-0-9679416-2-2(8)*, 0-9679416-2-8) Alexie Bks.
Eberhart, Donald G. Grizzly Bear Family. Fraggalosch, Audrey M. (Soundprints' Amazing Animal Adventures! Ser.). (ENG.). (J). 2005. 36p. (gr. -1-2). 8.95 *(978-1-59249-395-1(5)*, SC7103); 2005. 32p. (gr. 2-2). 19.95 *(978-1-59249-394-4(7)*, BC7103); 2003. 36p. (gr. -1-3). 9.95 *(978-1-59249-059-2(X)*, PS7153); 2003. 36p. (gr. -1-k). pap. 2.95 *(978-1-59249-050-9(6)*, S7153) Soundprints.
Eberle, Lis. Lilly Grace's Conversation: Monday Is Getting It Done Day. Russell, Tamlyn. 2016. (ENG.). (J). (gr. k-6). pap. 9.95 *(978-1-61314-360-5(5))* Innovo Publishing, LLC.
Ebert, Anne. La Granja. Caballero, D., tr. 2006. (Junior (Silver Dolphin) Ser.). (SPA.). 16p. (J). (gr. -1). 9.95 *(978-970-718-345-2(4))* Readerlink Distribution Services, LLC.
Ebert, Len. All about Sports with Inspector McQ. Mullins, Patty Rutland. 2004. (Treasure Tree Ser.). 32p. (J). *(978-0-7166-1645-0(9))* World Bk., Inc.
—An Amusement Park Mystery in Ohio. Wilsdon, Christina. 2006. 26p. (J). 7.99 *(978-1-59939-013-0(2))* Cornerstone Pr.
—The Easter Cave. Wedeven, Carol. 2004. 32p. (J). (gr. -1-2). 10.49 *(978-0-570-07135-8(6))* Concordia Publishing Hse.
—The Fisherman & His Wife: A Tale about Being Happy & Satisfied. Grimm, Jacob & Grimm, Wilhelm K. 2006. (J). *(978-1-59939-097-0(3)*, Reader's Digest Young Families, Inc.) Studio Fun International.
—It's Called Kibud Av Va'Eim: A Story about Honoring Parents. Rosenfeld, Dina. 2014. 20p. (J). 10.95 *(978-1-929628-78-0(1))* Hachai Publishing.
—Joseph's Christmas Story. Dreyer, Nicole E. 2004. (ENG.). 16p. (J). 1.99 *(978-0-570-07577-6(7))* Concordia Publishing Hse.
—Off to Bed. Albee, Sarah. 2006. (Step-By-Step Readers Ser.). (J). pap. *(978-1-59939-060-4(4)*, Reader's Digest Young Families, Inc.) Studio Fun International.
—The Selfish Giant: A Tale about Being Unselfish. Wilde, Oscar. 2006. (J). *(978-1-59939-085-7(X)*, Reader's Digest Young Families, Inc.) Studio Fun International.
—Thomas Jefferson: A Founding Father of the United States of America, 1 vol. Mortensen, Lori. 2008. (Biographies Ser.). (ENG.). 24p. (J). (gr. k-3). lib. bdg. 27.32 *(978-1-4048-3729-4(9)*, Picture Window Bks.) Capstone.
Ebert, Roey. Mommies & Daddies Are Nurses. Wasson, E. & Strausser, A. 2011. 32p. pap. 15.99 *(978-1-4634-3451-9(0))* AuthorHouse.
Ebert, Roey. Pumpkin Pie Surprise. Ebert, Roey. l.t. ed. 2016. (ENG.). (J). (gr. k-2). 19.95 *(978-1-61633-788-9(5))*; pap. 10.95 *(978-1-61633-789-6(3))* Guardian Angel Publishing, Inc.
Ebertsch, Ted. The Fail Free Zone. Barden, Laura. 2010. 100p. pap. 10.49 *(978-1-4520-0857-8(4))* AuthorHouse.
Eberz, Robert. Splat the Cat & the Quick Chicks. Scotton, Rob. 2016. 30p. (J). *(978-1-4844-7139-5(3))* Harper & Row Ltd.
Eberz, Robert, jt. illus. see Farley, Rick.
Ebin, Matthew. The Wonderfully Ridiculous Alphabet Book. 2007. 27p. (J). 10.00 *(978-0-9787628-0-3(0))* MEAR LLC.
Ebiwok, Cecil. Jake the Snowflake. Devereux, Dorothy. 2018. (ENG.). 36p. (J). pap. 14.95 *(978-1-7913-9413-4(2))* Independently Published.
Eccles, Jane. The Baking Life of Amelie Day. Curtis, Vanessa. 2015. (Middle-Grade Novels Ser.). (ENG.). 176p. (J). (gr. 4-7). lib. bdg. 25.27 *(978-1-4965-2216-0(8)*, Stone Arch Bks.) Capstone.
—What I Like! Poems for the Very Young. Phinn, Gervase. 2004. (Poetry Ser.). 32p. (J). (gr. 2-3). pap. *(978-1-904550-12-9(6))* Child's Play International Ltd.
Eccles, Jane & Blake, Quentin. Collins Musicals - Roald Dahl's Cinderella (Book + CD/CD-ROM) MacGregor, Helen et al. 2008. (and C Black Musicals Ser.). (ENG.). 64p. (J). (gr. 2-6). pap. 42.95 incl. cd-rom *(978-0-7136-8195-6(0))* HarperCollins Pubs. Ltd. GBR. Dist: Independent Pubs. Group.
—Collins Musicals - Roald Dahl's Goldilocks & the Three Bears: an Impeccably Judged Musical. Dahl, Roald et al. Baiton, Janice & Daley, Michelle, eds. 2005. (and C Black Musicals Ser.). (ENG.). 56p. (J). (gr. 2-6). pap. 42.95 *(978-0-7136-7085-1(1))* HarperCollins Pubs. Ltd. GBR. Dist: Independent Pubs. Group.
—Collins Musicals - Roald Dahl's Little Red Riding Hood & the Wolf: a Howling Hilarious Musical. White, Matthew et al. Baiton, Janice & Daley, Michelle, eds. 2005. (and C Black Musicals Ser.). (ENG.). 56p. (J). (gr. 2-6). pap. 42.95 incl. cd-rom *(978-0-7136-6958-9(6))* HarperCollins Pubs. Ltd. GBR. Dist: Independent Pubs. Group.
Echavez, Alejandro. Beastronauts. Jolley, D. A. 2017. (ENG.). (J). (gr. k-6). 17.99 *(978-1-365-86195-6(3))*; pap. 13.99 *(978-1-365-86197-0(X))*; 32p. pap. 13.99 *(978-1-64372-228-3(X)*, Huskies Pub) Lulu Pr., Inc.
—Beastronauts. Jolley, D. A. ed. 2017. (ENG.). 32p. (J). (gr. k-6). 17.99 *(978-1-64372-017-3(1)*, Huskies Pub) MacLaren-Cochrane Publishing, Inc.
—Beastronauts Dyslexic Edition: Dyslexic Font. Jolley, D. A. ed. 2017. (ENG.). 34p. (J). (gr. k-6). 19.99 *(978-1-64372-229-0(8))*; pap. 15.99 *(978-1-64372-230-6(1))* MacLaren-Cochrane Publishing, Inc.
—Beastronauts Dyslexic Font. Jolley, Da. 2017. (ENG.). 34p. (J). (gr. k-6). 21.99 *(978-1-365-86196-3(1))*; pap. 15.99 *(978-1-365-86198-7(8))* Lulu Pr., Inc.
—Why I Need a Dinosaur. Derby, T. L. 2019. (ENG.). 26p. (J). (gr. k-3). 17.99 *(978-1-387-59858-8(9))* Lulu Pr., Inc.
Echavez, Alejandro. Why I Need a Dinosaur. Derby, T. L. ed. 2019. (ENG.). 28p. (J). (gr. k-3). 17.99 ***(978-1-64372-289-4(1))***; pap. 13.99 ***(978-1-64372-290-0(5))*** MacLaren-Cochrane Publishing, Inc. (Huskies Pub).
—Why I Need a Dinosaur Dyslexic Edition: Dyslexic Font. Derby, T. L. ed. 2019. (ENG.). 28p. (J). (gr. k-3). 19.99 ***(978-1-64372-033-3(3))***; pap. 15.99 ***(978-1-64372-288-7(3))*** MacLaren-Cochrane Publishing, Inc.
Echevarria, Mina. Kitty Alone. Feierabend, John M. 2018. (First Steps in Music Ser.). (ENG.). 32p. (J). (gr. -1-k). 17.95 *(978-1-62277-283-4(0))* G I A Pubns., Inc.
Echeverri, Catalina. A Box of Socks. Brandon, Amanda. 2019. (Early Bird Readers — Orange (Early Bird Stories (tm)) Ser.). (ENG.). 32p. (J). (gr. k-3). 27.99 *(978-1-5415-4220-4(7)*, 9781541542204); pap. 7.99 *(978-1-5415-7412-0(5)*, 9781541574120) Lerner Publishing Group. (Lerner Pubns.).
—The Christmas Promise Board Book. Mitchell, Alison. 2019. (Tales That Tell the Truth Ser.). (ENG.). 16p. (J). bds. *(978-1-78498-439-7(6))* Good Bk. Co., The.
—The Friend Who Forgives: A True Story about How Peter Failed & Jesus Forgave. DeWitt, Daniel. 2018. (Tales That Tell the Truth Ser.). (ENG.). 24p. (J). *(978-1-78498-302-4(0))* Good Bk. Co., The.
—God's Very Good Idea - Coloring & Activity Book. 2018. (Tales That Tell the Truth Ser.). (ENG.). 32p. (J). pap. *(978-1-78498-271-3(7))* Good Bk. Co., The.
—Goodbye to Goodbyes Colouring & Activity Book: Packed with Puzzles & Activities. Chandler, Lauren. 2019. (Tales That Tell the Truth Ser.). (ENG.). (J). pap. *(978-1-78498-386-4(1))* Good Bk. Co., The.
—How Do You Say Good Night?, 1 vol. 2018. (ENG.). 20p. (J). bds. 8.99 *(978-1-4002-0911-8(0))* Nelson, Thomas Inc.
—I Want to Be a Doctor. Driscoll, Laura. 2018. 31p. (J). *(978-1-5444-0496-7(4))* Harper & Row Ltd.
—I Want to Be a Doctor. Driscoll, Laura. 2018. (I Can Read Level 1 Ser.). (ENG.). 32p. (J). (gr. -1-3). 16.99 *(978-0-06-243241-4(9))* HarperCollins Pubs.
—I Want to Be a Doctor. Driscoll, Laura. 2018. (I Can Read Level 1 Ser.). (ENG.). 32p. (J). (gr. -1-3). pap. 4.99 *(978-0-06-243240-7(0)*, HarperCollins) HarperCollins Pubs. Ltd. GBR. Dist: HarperCollins Pubs.
—I Want to Be a Pilot. Driscoll, Laura. 2019. (I Can Read Level 1 Ser.). (ENG.). 32p. (J). (gr. -1-3). 16.99 *(978-0-06-243250-6(8))*; pap. 4.99 *(978-0-06-243249-0(4))* HarperCollins Pubs.
—I Want to Be a Police Officer. Driscoll, Laura. 2018. (I Can Read Level 1 Ser.). (ENG.). 32p. (J). (gr. -1-3). 16.99 *(978-0-06-243245-2(1))*; pap. 4.99 *(978-0-06-243243-8(5))* HarperCollins Pubs.
—I Want to Be a Veterinarian. Driscoll, Laura. 2018. (I Can Read Level 1 Ser.). (ENG.). 32p. (J). (gr. -1-3). 16.99 *(978-0-06-243247-6(8))*; pap. 4.99 *(978-0-06-243261-2(3))* HarperCollins Pubs.
—Jesus & the Lions' Den: A True Story about How Daniel Points Us to Jesus. Mitchell, Alison. 2019. (Tales That Tell the Truth Ser.). (ENG.). 32p. (J). *(978-1-78498-433-5(7))* Good Bk. Co., The.
Echeverri, Catalina. Jesus & the Lions' Den Colouring & Activity Book: Colouring, Puzzles, Mazes & More. Mitchell, Alison. 2020. (Tales That Tell the Truth Ser.). (ENG.). (J). ***(978-1-78498-435-9(3))*** Good Bk. Co., The.
—Jesus & the Very Big Surprise: A True Story about Jesus, His Return, & How to Be Ready. Goodgame, Randall. 2020. (Tales That Tell the Truth Ser.). (ENG.). (J). ***(978-1-78498-441-0(8))*** Good Bk. Co., The.
Echeverri, Catalina. The One o'Clock Miracle Coloring Book. 2017. (Tales That Tell the Truth Ser.). (ENG.). (J). pap. *(978-1-78498-220-1(2))* Good Bk. Co., The.
Echeverri, Catalina. The Prisoners, the Earthquake & the Midnight Song: A True Story about How God Uses People to Save People. Hartman, Bob. 2020. (Tales That Tell the Truth Ser.). (ENG.). (J). ***(978-1-78498-440-3(X))*** Good Bk. Co., The.
Echeverri, Catalina. A Royal Mess. Lyon, Rachel. 2019. (Early Bird Readers — Purple (Early Bird Stories (tm)) Ser.). (ENG.). 32p. (J). (gr. k-3). 27.99 *(978-1-5415-4228-0(2)*, 9781541542280); pap. 7.99 *(978-1-5415-7420-5(6)*, 9781541574205) Lerner Publishing Group. (Lerner Pubns.).
—A Scarf & a Half. Brandon, Amanda. 2019. (Early Bird Readers — Orange (Early Bird Stories (tm)) Ser.). (ENG.). 32p. (J). (gr. k-3). 27.99 *(978-1-5415-4222-8(3)*, 9781541542228); pap. 7.99 *(978-1-5415-7415-1(X)*, 9781541574151) Lerner Publishing Group. (Lerner Pubns.).
—The Storm That Stopped Colouring & Activity Book. 2017. (Tales That Tell the Truth Ser.). (ENG.). (J). pap. *(978-1-78498-177-8(X))* Good Bk. Co., The.
Echeverria Gyorkos, Charmaine. The EGGbees. Echeverria-Bis, Olivia. 2009. (ENG & SPA.). 32p. (J). (gr. -1-3). 16.95 *(978-1-55885-529-8(7)*, Piñata Books) Arte Publico Pr.
Eck, Bernhard. Saga de la Mariposa. Martin, Ivonne. l.t. ed. 2003. (SPA.). 80p. (YA). pap. *(978-1-931481-25-0(3))* LiArt-Literature & Art.
Eckel, Jessie. How to Be a Princess in 7 Days or Less. 2005. (How to be A Ser.). 32p. (J). (gr. 3-5). 12.95 *(978-0-7534-5921-8(3)*, Kingfisher) Roaring Brook Pr.
—I Heart Easter. 2019. (ENG.). 128p. (J). (gr. 1-5). pap. 8.99 *(978-1-78055-577-5(6))* O'Mara, Michael Bks., Ltd. GBR. Dist: Independent Pubs. Group.
—I Heart Elves. 2019. (I Heart Ser.: 5). (ENG.). 128p. (J). (gr. 1-3). pap. 12.95 *(978-1-4549-3811-8(0))* Sterling Publishing Co., Inc.
Eckerson, Margaret. The Admirable Tinker: Child of the World. Jepson, Edgar. 2007. 204p. per. *(978-1-4065-2736-0(X))* Dodo Pr.
Eckert, Charles, photos by. Eternal Spring Chi Kung. Chu, C. K. Borrelli, James, ed. 2003. 56p. 24.95 *(978-0-9616586-4-9(9))* Sunflower Pr.
Eckert, Julieth. My Parents Are Fighting Again: Dealing with the Feelings. Camden Psy D, Marian Louise. 2019. (ENG.). 42p. (J). pap. 15.00 *(978-1-9795-6118-1(4))* CreateSpace Independent Publishing Platform.
Eckhardt, Jason C. Capitol Cat & Watch Dog Unite Lady Freedoms. Law, Janice. 2008. 64p. (J). *(978-1-934645-71-0(0)*, Eakin Pr.) Eakin Pr.
—The Legend of the China Poblana. 2003. (J). 10.95 *(978-1-57168-731-9(9)*, Eakin Pr.) Eakin Pr.
—Mystery at Jacob's Well. Bennett, Marcia Allen. 2003. 160p. (J). (gr. -1). per. 12.95 *(978-1-57168-641-1(X))* Eakin Pr.
—Paisano Pete: Snake-Killer Bird. Komechak, Marilyn Gilbert. 2003. 100p. (J). (gr. 3-7). per. 11.95 *(978-1-57168-770-8(X)*, Eakin Pr.) Eakin Pr.
Eckl-Shear, Veronica. What Is It All About? Eckl, Joseph J. & Eckl, Theresa R. 2003. (YA). (gr. 7-12). pap. 14.95 *(978-0-9746686-0-4(5)*, 100103) Eckl, Joseph J.
Eckman, Jeff. The Forgotten Trolley. Weaver, Mary Ruth. 2020. (ENG.). 52p. (J). 33.95 ***(978-1-7283-6143-7(5))***; pap. 20.95 ***(978-1-7283-6141-3(9))*** AuthorHouse.
Eckstein, Caitlyn. Agatha Cyprus: Not So Fast, Mom! Steele, Jerilynn & Steele, Alan. 2018. (ENG.). 28p. (J). 22.95 *(978-1-64003-604-8(0))* Covenant Bks.
Eckstein, Joe. Twee' Caron, Susie. 2013. 24p. (J). pap. 12.99 *(978-0-9889113-0-7(2))* Coda Grove Publishing.
—The Ultimate Friend Book: More Than Your Average Address Book for Kids. Eckstein, Kristen. 2004. 112p. (J). per. *(978-0-9761317-0-0(6))* Imagine! Studios.
—The Ultimate Friend Book: More Than Your Average Address Book for Teens. Eckstein, Kristen. 2004. 112p. (YA). per. *(978-0-9761317-1-7(4))* Imagine! Studios.
Eckstrom, Nathaniel. Bird on a Wire. Gordon, Kate. 2020. (ENG.). 24p. (J). (gr. -1-k). 18.99 ***(978-1-76012-858-6(9))*** Little Hare Bks. AUS. Dist: Independent Pubs. Group.
Eckstrom, Nathaniel. The Dress-Up Box. Guest, Patrick. 2018. (ENG.). 32p. (J). (gr. -1-k). 19.99 *(978-1-76012-492-2(3))* Little Hare Bks. AUS. Dist: Independent Pubs. Group.
—Duck! McKinlay, Meg. 2019. (ENG.). 32p. (J). (gr. k-4). 15.99 *(978-1-5362-0422-3(6))* Candlewick Pr.
—The Hair Ball. Lee, Spider. 2012. (ENG.). 32p. (J). 23.49 *(978-0-9873586-9-1(3))* JoJo Publishing AUS. Dist: Baker & Taylor Publisher Services (BTPS).
—The Ricker Racker Club. Guest, Patrick. 2017. (ENG.). 32p. (J). (gr. -1-k). 18.99 *(978-1-76012-292-8(0))* Little Hare Bks. AUS. Dist: Independent Pubs. Group.
—The Road Trip. Parker, Danny. 2017. (ENG.). 48p. (J). (gr. -1-k). 19.99 *(978-1-76012-740-4(X))* Little Hare Bks. AUS. Dist: Independent Pubs. Group.
Ecob, Simon. Boys Only: How to Survive Anything! Oliver, Martin. 2012. (Best at Everything Ser.). (ENG.). 64p. (J). (gr. 3-7). pap. 6.99 *(978-0-545-43096-8(8)*, Scholastic Paperbacks) Scholastic, Inc.
Ecob, Simon, jt. illus. see Geremia, Daniela.
Edblom, Erika. Ayden's Choice. Felix, Sam. 2016. (ENG.). (J). pap. *(978-3-9524716-0-9(7))* Felixideas GmbH.
Eddy, Randon T. Dillo - A Baby Armadillo's Adventure on Sanibel Island. Miller, Kyle Linda. l.t. ed. 2005. (ENG.). 64p. (J). 16.95 *(978-0-9769332-0-5(9))* Jungle Hse. Pubns.
—DILLO the Coloring Book. 2006. 53p. (J). pap. 6.95 *(978-0-9769332-1-2(7))* Jungle Hse. Pubns.
Eddy, Randon T. The Mysterious Creature. Eddy, Randon T. 2007. 32p. (J). per. 15.95 *(978-0-9769332-2-9(5))* Jungle Hse. Pubns.
Ede, Lara. Bob the Booger Fairy. Make Believe Ideas Ltd & Cox, Xander. 2020. (ENG.). 32p. (J). (gr. -1-7). pap. ***(978-1-78947-773-3(5))***; pap. ***(978-1-78947-775-7(1))*** Make Believe Ideas.
—Coral & the Rainbow Reef. Make Believe Ideas Ltd & Greening, Rosie. 2020. (ENG.). 32p. (J). (gr. -1-7). pap. ***(978-1-78947-772-6(7))***; pap. ***(978-1-78947-834-1(0))*** Make Believe Ideas.
—Don't You Dare Brush My Hair! Make Believe Ideas Ltd & Greening, Rosie. 2020. (ENG.). 32p. (J). (gr. -1-7). ***(978-1-78947-383-4(7))*** Make Believe Ideas.
—Don't You Dare Brush My Hair! Greening, Rosie. 2020. (ENG.). 12p. (J). bds. ***(978-1-78947-430-5(2))*** Make Believe Ideas.
Ede, Lara. Just Narwhal. Make Believe Ideas Ltd. 2019. (Two-Way Sequin Picture Bks.). (ENG.). 32p. (J). (gr. -1-3). *(978-1-78843-754-7(3))*; pap. *(978-1-78843-666-3(0))* Make Believe Ideas.
Ede, Lara. Just Narwhal. Make Believe Ideas Ltd. 2020. (ENG.). 32p. (J). (gr. -1-7). ***(978-1-78947-558-6(9))*** Make Believe Ideas.
—Little Owl's Big Surprise. Make Believe Ideas Ltd. 2020. (ENG.). 10p. (J). bds. ***(978-1-78947-735-1(2))*** Make Believe Ideas.
Ede, Lara. The Magic Purse. Make Believe Ideas Ltd. 2019. (ENG.). 12p. (J). bds. *(978-1-78947-008-6(0))* Make Believe Ideas.
—Meghan Sparkle & the Royal Baby. Greening, Rosie. 2019. (ENG.). 32p. (J). (gr. -1-7). *(978-1-78947-023-9(4))*; pap. *(978-1-78947-022-2(6))*; pap. *(978-1-78947-024-6(2))* Make Believe Ideas.
—Mermaids Activity Book. Make Believe Ideas Ltd. 2019. (ENG.). 36p. (J). pap. *(978-1-78947-034-5(X))* Make Believe Ideas.
—My Easter Basket. Down, Hayley & Make Believe Ideas Staff. 2014. (ENG.). 12p. (J). (gr. -1). bds. 8.99 *(978-1-78235-074-3(8))* Make Believe Ideas GBR. Dist: Nelson, Thomas Inc.
Ede, Lara. My Pink & Powerful Alphabet. Make Believe Ideas Ltd. 2020. (ENG.). 20p. (J). (gr. -1-7). ***(978-1-78947-763-4(8))*** Make Believe Ideas.
Ede, Lara. My Pretty Pink Bible Sticker Purse. Make Believe Ideas Ltd. 2020. (ENG.). 48p. (J). (gr. -1-7). pap. *(978-1-78947-289-9(X))* Make Believe Ideas.
Ede, Lara. The Naughty List. Lansley, Holly. 2019. (ENG.). 26p. (J). (gr. -1-7). bds. ***(978-1-78843-927-5(9))*** Make Believe Ideas.
Ede, Lara. Oh No, Narwhal. Make Believe Ideas Ltd. 2019. (Oh No Narwhal Ser.). (ENG.). 12p. (J). bds. *(978-1-78843-649-6(0))* Make Believe Ideas.
—Sophia Sparks. Best, Elanor. 2019. (Story Book Ser.). (ENG.). 32p. (J). (gr. -1-7). *(978-1-78843-665-6(2))*; pap. *(978-1-78843-664-9(4))* Make Believe Ideas.
—The Story of Jesus. Boon, Fiona. 2014. (ENG.). 22p. (J). bds. *(978-1-78235-883-1(8))* Make Believe Ideas.
Ede, Lara. Ten Little Pumpkins. Make Believe Ideas Ltd & Greening, Rosie. 2018. (ENG.). 32p. (J). ***(978-1-78843-359-4(9))*** Make Believe Ideas.
—Unicorns & Mermaids Activity Book. Make Believe Ideas Ltd. 2020. (Scratch & Sparkle Ser.). (ENG.). 68p. (J). pap. ***(978-1-78947-505-0(8))*** Make Believe Ideas.

Ede, Lara. The Very Hungry Worry Monsters. Make Believe Ideas Ltd & Greening, Rosie. 2020. (ENG.). 12p. (J). (gr. -1-3). bds. (978-1-78947-741-2(7)) Make Believe Ideas.

Ede, Lara. The Very Hungry Worry Monsters. Make Believe Ideas Ltd. 2019. (ENG.). 32p. (J). (gr. -1-7). (978-1-78947-012-3(9)) Make Believe Ideas.

Edelmann, Heinz. The Beatles Yellow Submarine. Gardner, Charlie. 2006. 37p. (J). (gr. 4-8). reprint ed. 18.00 (978-1-4223-5184-0(X)) DIANE Publishing Co.

—Yellow Submarine. Beatles, The. 2018. (ENG.). 40p. (J). (gr. k-12). 9.99 (978-1-5362-0145-1(6)) Candlewick Pr.

—Yellow Submarine: A Panorama Pop. Beatles, The. 2018. (Panorama Pops Ser.). (ENG.). 30p. (J). (gr. k-4). 8.99 (978-1-5362-0146-8(4)) Candlewick Pr.

Edelson, Wendy. The Baker's Dozen: A Saint Nicholas Tale. Shepard, Aaron. 2016. (ENG.). (J). (gr. k-6). pap. 10.00 (978-1-62035-503-9(5), Skyhook Pr.) Shepard Pubns.

—The Baker's Dozen: A Saint Nicholas Tale, with Bonus Cookie Recipe & Pattern for St. Nicholas Christmas Cookies (25th Anniversary Edition) Shepard, Aaron. 2018. (ENG.). 40p. (J). (gr. k-6). 24.00 (978-1-62035-572-5(8)); pap. 12.00 (978-1-62035-571-8(X)) Shepard Pubns. (Skyhook Pr.).

—The Baker's Dozen: A Saint Nicholas Tale, with Bonus Cookie Recipe & Pattern for St. Nicholas Christmas Cookies (Special Edition) Shepard, Aaron. 2018. (ENG.). 40p. (J). (gr. k-6). 24.00 (978-1-62035-579-4(5)); pap. 12.00 (978-1-62035-578-7(7)) Shepard Pubns. (Skyhook Pr.).

—The Best Part of the Day. Ban Breathnach, Sarah. 2014. (ENG.). 40p. (J). (-k). 16.99 (978-1-62157-252-7(8), Regnery Kids) Regnery Publishing, Inc., An Eagle Publishing Co.

—The Christmas Story. Pingry, Patricia A. 2004. (ENG.). 26p. (J). bds. 6.95 (978-0-8249-6549-5(3), Ideal Pubns.) Worthy Publishing.

—Christmas Truce: A Story of World War 1. Shepard, Aaron. 2016. (ENG.). (J). (gr. 3-6). pap. 10.00 (978-1-62035-505-3(1), Skyhook Pr.) Shepard Pubns.

—Easter Bunnies. Cosgrove, Stephen. 32p. (J). pap. 4.95 (978-0-8249-5371-3(1), Ideal Pubns.) Worthy Publishing.

—Fiddler T. Bear. Cosgrove, Stephen. 2015. (Barely There Ser.). (ENG.). 32p. (J). (gr. k-4). pap. 7.95 (978-1-941437-44-5(3)) Heritage Builders, LLC.

—Gabriel Faintheart. Cosgrove, Stephen. 2015. (Barely There Ser.). (ENG.). 32p. (J). (gr. k-4). pap. 7.95 (978-1-941437-46-9(X)) Heritage Builders, LLC.

—GrandPa Sam. Cosgrove, Stephen. 2015. (Barely There Ser.). (ENG.). 32p. (J). (gr. k-4). pap. 7.95 (978-1-941437-48-3(6)) Heritage Builders, LLC.

—I Believe in Genevieve. Craig, Jenny. 2013. (ENG.). 40p. (J). (gr. -1-3). 16.95 (978-1-62157-085-1(1), Regnery Kids) Regnery Publishing, Inc., An Eagle Publishing Co.

—One Baby Jesus/Un Nino Dios. Pingry, Patricia A. & Urbano, Aide. 2003. (ENG & SPA.). 30p. (J). pap. 3.95 (978-0-8249-5472-7(6), Ideal Pubns.) Worthy Publishing.

—Pretty, Pretty Prettina. Cosgrove, Stephen. 2015. (Barely There Ser.). (ENG.). 32p. (J). (gr. k-4). pap. 7.95 (978-1-941437-50-6(8)) Heritage Builders, LLC.

—Quackling: A Feathered Fairy Tale. Shepard, Aaron. 2019. (ENG.). 26p. (J). (gr. k-3). 24.00 (978-1-62035-585-5(X)); pap. 12.00 (978-1-62035-584-8(1)) Shepard Pubns. (Skyhook Pr.).

—Quackling: A Very Loud Fairy Tale. Shepard, Aaron. 2018. (J). 28p. (gr. -1-4). lib. bdg. 24.00 (978-1-62035-575-6(2)); (ENG.). 26p. (gr. k-3). pap. 10.00 (978-1-62035-574-9(4)) Shepard Pubns. (Skyhook Pr.).

—Saturn for My Birthday, 1 vol. McGranaghan, John. 2008. (ENG.). 32p. (J). (gr. -1-4). 16.95 (978-1-934359-13-6(0)); pap. 8.95 (978-1-934359-27-3(0)) Arbordale Publishing.

Edelstein, Racheli. Goodbye, Pacifier! Licht, S. 2013. 24p. (J). 10.95 (978-1-60091-284-9(2)) Israel Bookshop Pubns.

—Goodbye, Thumb-Sucking! Licht, S. 2013. 24p. 10.95 (978-1-60091-266-5(4)) Israel Bookshop Pubns.

Eden, David. The Potter's Wheel Story & Activity Book. Eden, David. 2011. (ENG.). 48p. (J). pap. 16.95 (978-0-9841658-6-5(X), Ignition Pr.) Publishing Services @ Thomson-Shore.

Edgar, Barrie. Up the Wooden Hill: Bedtime Stories for Little Ones. Trotter, Bob. 2011. 98p. pap. 17.99 (978-1-60976-139-4(1), Eloquent Bks.) Strategic Book Publishing & Rights Agency (SBPRA).

Edgar, Scott. Adventurous Abbie. Harris, Fiona & Rippin, Sally. 2018. (Super Moopers Ser.). (ENG.). 48p. (J). (gr. k-2). pap. 10.99 (978-1-76068-045-9(1)) Bonnier Publishing GBR. Dist: Independent Pubs. Group.

—Nervous Nellie. Harris, Fiona & Rippin, Sally. 2017. (Super Moopers Ser.). (ENG.). 48p. (J). pap. 9.99 (978-1-76040-649-3(X)) Bonnier Publishing GBR. Dist: Independent Pubs. Group.

—Quiet Quinn. Harris, Fiona & Rippin, Sally. 2018. (Super Moopers Ser.). (ENG.). 48p. (J). (gr. k-2). pap. 10.99 (978-1-76068-046-6(X)) Bonnier Publishing GBR. Dist: Independent Pubs. Group.

Edge, Elizabeth. A Blessing from Above. Henderson, Patti & Golden Books Staff. 2004. (Little Golden Book Ser.). 32p. (J). (gr. -1-2). 4.99 (978-0-375-82866-9(4), Golden Bks.) Random Hse. Children's Bks.

Edgerley, Ross. The Legend of Ross the Reader: A Story of How a Smart Cowboy Saved the Prairie One Book at a Time. Dailey, Reid. 2007. 32p. per. 15.95 (978-1-59858-483-7(9)) Dog Ear Publishing, LLC.

—Ross the Reader & the Adventure of the Pirate's Treasure. Dailey, Reid. 2009. 44p. pap. 16.95 (978-1-59858-900-9(8)) Dog Ear Publishing, LLC.

Edgerton, Sean Vidal. Inside of a Dog — Young Readers Edition: What Dogs See, Smell, & Know. Horowitz, Alexandra. (ENG.). (J). (gr. 3-7). 2017. 272p. pap. 7.99 (978-1-4814-5094-2(8)); 2016. 256p. 16.99 (978-1-4814-5093-5(X)) Simon & Schuster Bks. For Young Readers. (Simon & Schuster Bks. For Young Readers).

Edgson, Alison. Bear & Turtle & the Great Lake Race. Fusek Peters, Andrew. (Traditional Tales with a Twist Ser.). 32p. (J). 2010. (gr. -1-2). (978-1-84643-347-4(9)); 2005. (gr. 2-2). per. (978-1-904550-91-4(6)) Child's Play International Ltd.

—Bear's House of Books. Bishop, Poppy. 2017. (ENG.). 32p. (J). (gr. -1-2). 16.99 (978-1-68010-038-9(6)) Tiger Tales.

—The Elves & the Shoemaker. 2007. (Flip-Up Fairy Tales Ser.). 24p. (J). (978-1-84643-142-5(5)); (gr. 2-2). (978-1-84643-076-3(3)) Child's Play International Ltd.

—The Emperor's New Clothes. (Flip-Up Fairy Tales Ser.). 24p. (J). 2007. (gr. -1-2). (978-1-84643-093-0(3)); 2006. (gr. 2-2). (978-1-84643-020-6(8)) Child's Play International Ltd.

—Grandma Loves You! McLean, Danielle. 2018. (ENG.). 28p. (J). (gr. -1-k). bds. 7.99 (978-1-68010-546-9(9)) Tiger Tales.

—I Love You, Mommy. Little Bee Books. 2017. (ENG.). 12p. (J). (gr. -1-k). bds. 8.99 (978-1-4998-0546-8(2)) Little Bee Books Inc.

—I Want My Mommy! Corderoy, Tracey. 2014. (ENG.). 32p. (J). (gr. -1-k). mass mkt. 3.99 (978-1-58925-453-4(8)) Tiger Tales.

—The Magician's Apprentice. 2011. (Flip-Up Fairy Tales Ser.). 24p. (J). (gr. 2-2). (978-1-84643-370-2(3)) Child's Play International Ltd.

—Me & My Dad! Ritchie, Alison. 2007. (J). pap. (978-0-545-02064-0(6)) Scholastic, Inc.

—Me & My Grandma! Ritchie, Alison. 2018. (ENG.). 32p. (J). (gr. -1-2). 16.99 (978-1-68010-079-2(3)) Tiger Tales.

—No Time for Bed! Rusling, Annette. 2014. (ENG.). 18p. (J). (gr. -1-k). 12.99 (978-1-58925-529-6(1)) Tiger Tales.

—Pirates Aren't Afraid of the Dark! Powell-Tuck, Maudie. 2014. (ENG.). 32p. (J). (gr. -1-2). 16.99 (978-1-58925-165-6(2)) Tiger Tales.

—Three Billy Goats Gruff. (Flip-Up Fairy Tales Ser.). 24p. (J). 2007. (gr. -1-2). (978-1-84643-089-3(5)); 2006. (ENG.). (gr. 1-2). (978-1-904550-72-3(X)) Child's Play International Ltd.

—To Mom, with Love. 2018. (Special Delivery Bks.). (ENG.). 8p. (J). (— 1). bds. 6.49 (978-1-68412-268-4(6), Silver Dolphin Bks.) Printers Row Publishing Group.

—Waiting for Santa. Metzger, Steve. 2015. (J). (978-0-545-89992-5(3)) Scholastic, Inc.

—Waiting for Santa. Metzger, Steve. 2015. (ENG.). 32p. (J). (gr. -1-2). 16.99 (978-1-58925-199-1(7)) Tiger Tales.

Edgson, Allison. I Love You All the Same, 1 vol. Keith, Donna. 2014. (ENG.). 20p. (J). bds. 9.99 (978-0-529-10204-1(8)) Nelson, Thomas Inc.

—I Love You Even When, 1 vol. Keith, Donna. 2015. (ENG.). 20p. (J). bds. 9.99 (978-0-7180-3644-7(1)) Nelson, Thomas Inc.

Edgson, Alison. Te Amo Aún Cuando, 1 vol. Keith, Donna. 2018. (SPA.). 20p. (J). bds. 9.99 (978-1-4185-9921-8(2)) Grupo Nelson.

—Te Amo Igual, 1 vol. Keith, Donna. 2018. (SPA.). 20p. (J). bds. 9.99 (978-1-4185-9896-9(8)) Grupo Nelson.

—Te Amo Porque Sí, 1 vol. Keith, Donna. 2018. (SPA.). 20p. (J). bds. 9.99 (978-1-4185-9876-1(3)) Grupo Nelson.

Edith. Tom's Midnight Garden Graphic Novel. Pearce, Philippa. 2018. (ENG.). 100p. (J). (gr. 3-7). 22.99 (978-0-06-269657-1(2)); pap. 10.99 (978-0-06-269656-4(4)) HarperCollins Pubs. (Greenwillow Bks.).

Editorial El Antillano. Tai Juega Pelota. Editorial El Antillano. 2008. (J). 4.00 (978-0-9793026-2-6(5)) Editorial El Antillano, Inc.

—Tai va de Pesca. Editorial El Antillano. 2005. (SPA.). (J). 4.00 (978-0-9755661-9-0(9)) Editorial El Antillano, Inc.

Edlund, Bambi. What a Waste: Where Does Garbage Go? Eamer, Claire. 2017. (ENG.). 96p. (J). (gr. 3-7). pap. 12.95 (978-1-55451-918-7(7)) Annick Pr., Ltd. CAN. Dist: Publishers Group West (PGW).

—What a Waste: Where Does Our Garbage Go? Eamer, Claire. 2017. (ENG.). 96p. (J). (gr. 3-7). 22.95 (978-1-55451-919-4(5)) Annick Pr., Ltd. CAN. Dist: Publishers Group West (PGW).

Edmonds, Andrea. Visiting You. Sharpe Shelberg, Rebecka. 2018. (ENG.). 32p. (J). (gr. -1-3). 17.99 (978-1-925335-66-8(6), EK Bks.) Exisle Publishing Pty Ltd. AUS. Dist: Hachette Bk. Group.

Edmonds, Sarah. Discovery Globe: Build-Your-Own Globe Kit. Gray, Leon. 2018. (ENG.). 48p. (J). (gr. 3-7). 22.99 (978-0-7636-9748-8(6)) Candlewick Pr.

Edmondson, Brad. Mr. Frank's Magic School Bus: Rainbow's End Adventure. Edmondson, Frank. 2007. 20p. per. 24.95 (978-1-4241-8617-4(X)) America Star Bks.

—Mr. Frank's Magic School Bus: Rainbow's End Adventure, 1 vol. Edmondson, Frank. 2010. 20p. 24.95 (978-1-4512-1042-2(6)) PublishAmerica, Inc.

Edmonson, Tim. Enrique Speaks with His Hands. Fudge, Benjamin. 2008. (ENG.). 32p. (J). (gr. -1-3). 16.95 (978-0-9800649-3-3(7)) Hilton Publishing Co.

Edmunds, Kate. Dry Bones. (Classic Books with Holes Big Book Ser.). (J). 2009. 16p. (gr. -1-1). spiral bd. (978-1-84643-210-1(3)); 2009. (ENG.). 16p. pap. incl. audio compact disk (978-1-84643-259-0(6)); 2007. 14p. (gr. -1-1). spiral bd. (978-1-84643-112-8(3)); 2007. 16p. (gr. 1-1). pap. (978-1-84643-108-1(5)) Child's Play International Ltd.

Edmunds, Kirstie. The Monster Who Lost His Mean. Strelitz Haber, Tiffany. 2012. (ENG.). 40p. (J). (gr. -1-3). 18.99 (978-0-8050-9375-9(3), 900073740, Holt, Henry & Co. Bks. For Young Readers) Holt, Henry & Co.

Edrington, Greg Q., jt. illus. see Caprio-Scalera, Jill.

Edsall, Steven. The Story of Peabo, 1 vol. Prince-Stokes, Cathy. 2009. 35p. pap. 24.95 (978-1-61582-732-9(3)) America Star Bks.

Edson, Anharad. Little One... Good Night: A Lullaby from Vermont. Vaughan, Kathryn Mademann. 2004. (J). per. 19.95 incl. audio compact disk (978-0-9747447-0-4(0)) Chaser Media LLC.

Eduar, Gilles. Here Comes Doctor Hippo: A Little Hippo Story. London, Jonathan. 2013. (Little Hippo Ser.). (ENG.). 32p. (J). (gr. -1-k). pap. 6.95 (978-1-62091-595-0(2)) Boyds Mills Pr.

Edward, Aaron. Calvin Can - Be Happy. Edward, Judy. 2012. 32p. pap. (978-1-4602-0097-1(7)) FriesenPress.

Edward J Russell Elementary School Students. Oliver Bean, Doctors Aren't Mean! Bacon, Joy. 2007. (ENG.). 32p. (J). (gr. 4-7). pap. 8.95 (978-0-9792371-1-9(4)) Keene Publishing.

Edward, Linda. This Little Piggy. O'Brien, Eileen. Tyler, Jenny, ed. 2004. (Carry-Me Bks.). 16p. (J). 5.95 (978-0-7945-0125-9(7), Usborne) EDC Publishing.

Edwards, Cedric. Damaged Goods. Wheeler, Tonika Yvonne. Attaway, Anelda, ed. 2013. 100p. pap. 13.99 (978-0-9892656-0-7(9)) Jazzy Kitty Pubns.

Edwards, Daniel Taylor. The Amelia Limited... Finest Train in America: Pride of the Clarkton Central Railroad. Edwards, Daniel Taylor. 2019. (ENG.). 30p. (J). pap. 9.95 (978-1-7943-2276-9(0)) Independently Published.

Edwards, Daniel Taylor. Grandpa's Fish House: And How Things Were in down East Carteret County Long Ago. Edwards, Daniel Taylor. 2020. (ENG.). 28p. (J). pap. 10.95 (978-1-7294-1240-4(8)) Independently Published.

Edwards, Dennis. Bibleman & the Baton of Friendship (board Book) P23 Entertainment Inc., P23. 2018. (Bibleman Ser.). (ENG.). 24p. (J). (-k). bds. 7.99 (978-1-5359-0250-2(7), 005803448, B&H Kids) B&H Publishing Group.

—Bibleman & the Wish-A-Prayer Machine (board Book) P23 Entertainment Inc., P23. 2018. (Bibleman Ser.). (ENG.). 24p. (J). (gr. -1-1). bds. 7.99 (978-1-4627-7824-9(0), 005799216, B&H Kids) B&H Publishing Group.

Edwards, Frank. Is the Spaghetti Ready?, 1 vol. Bianchi, John. 2008. (New Reader Ser.). (ENG.). 32p. (J). (978-1-894323-35-2(1)) Bungalo Bks.

Edwards, George Wharton. Travels & Adventures of Little Baron Trump & His Wonderful Dog Bulger (Illustrated Edition) Lockwood, Ingersoll. 2019. (ENG.). 220p. (J). pap. (978-1-4068-9073-0(1)) Echo Library.

Edwards, Gina. When Cats Had No Tails. Phillippe, Steve. 2019. (ENG.). 36p. (J). 23.95 (978-1-64471-960-2(6)); pap. 13.95 (978-1-64471-959-6(2)) Covenant Bks.

Edwards, Gunvor & Felstead, Cathie. Abracadabra Piano, Bk. 1. Sebba, Jane. (ENG.). 48p. (J). pap. (978-0-7136-3724-3(2), 93113, A&C Black) Bloomsbury Publishing Plc.

Edwards, Heather. Featherpaws the Trilogy: The Trilogy. Edwards, Heather. 2017. (ENG.). 520p. (J). pap. (978-1-9999347-0-5(9)) Owl Crest Pubns.

Edwards, I. I. Eugene. Say Something Ana. McBayne, Lj. 2019. (ENG.). 32p. (J). (gr. 2-6). 14.99 (978-1-7341058-8-9(7)); (gr. 3-6). pap. 9.99 (978-1-7341058-7-2(9)) Pecan Tree Publishing.

Edwards, Jeff. The Moon, 1 vol. Oxlade, Chris. 2012. (Astronaut Travel Guides). (ENG.). 48p. (J). (gr. 3-6). lib. bdg. 33.32 (978-1-4109-4572-3(3), Raintree) Capstone.

Edwards, Jim. Bartholomule's Blessing. Taylor, Sandra J. 2018. (ENG.). 28p. (J). pap. 12.95 (978-1-64003-546-1(X)) Covenant Bks.

Edwards, Jo. All Families Invited. Goodman, Kathleen. 2019. (ENG.). 34p. (J). (gr. -1-3). 19.95 (978-1-7336080-1-5(X)) Goodman, Kathleen.

Edwards, Karl. Slow & Steady Wins the Race, Vol. 4260. Williams, Rozanne Lanczak. 2005. (Reading for Fluency Ser.). 16p. (J). pap. 3.49 (978-1-59198-158-9(1), 4260) Creative Teaching Pr., Inc.

—You Can't Catch Me. Williams, Rozanne Lanczak. 2005. (Reading for Fluency Ser.). 8p. (J). pap. 3.49 (978-1-59198-150-3(6), 4250) Creative Teaching Pr., Inc.

Edwards, Karl Newsom. The Hugely-Wugely Spider. Berlin, Ethan T. 2018. (ENG.). 40p. (J). 17.99 (978-0-374-30616-8(8), 900174319, Farrar, Straus & Giroux (BYR)) Farrar, Straus & Giroux.

—Stewart's Best Pen. Martin, Stephen W. 2018. (ENG.). 32p. (J). (gr. -1-3). 17.99 (978-0-544-86773-4(4), 1648800, Clarion Bks.) Houghton Mifflin Harcourt Trade & Reference Pubs.

Edwards, Ken. Princess Party Paint Book. Simon-Kerr, Julia. 2005. (My Little Pony Ser.). 32p. (J). 3.99 (978-0-06-074699-5(8), HarperFestival) HarperCollins Pubs.

Edwards, Ken, jt. illus. see Middleton, Gayle.

Edwards, Kristen. Santa's First Stop. Reynolds, Cecelia. 2020. (ENG.). 24p. pap. 13.95 (978-1-4808-8902-6(4)) Archway Publishing.

Edwards, Laurie J. & Britt, Joanna. Stakeout. Doerr, Bonnie J. 2011. 310p. pap. 12.99 (978-1-61603-007-0(0)) Leap Bks.

Edwards, Laurie J., jt. illus. see Britt, Joanna.

Edwards, Linda. Animal Picture Atlas. Maskell, Hazel. 2008. (Atlases Ser.). 48p. (J). 12.99 (978-0-7945-2083-0(9), Usborne) EDC Publishing.

—La Biblia para Ninos. Amery, Heather, ed. 2004.Tr. of Children's Bible. (SPA.). 144p. (J). (gr. -1-4). 19.95 (978-0-7460-3674-7(4)) EDC Publishing.

—Greek Myths for Young Children. Amery, Heather. 2004. (Greek Myths for Young Children Ser.). 128p. (J). (gr. -1-3). lib. bdg. 26.95 (978-1-58086-261-5(6)); 7.99 (978-0-7945-0141-9(9), Usborne) EDC Publishing.

—Stories from Around the World. Amery, Heather. 2004. (Stories for Young Children Ser.). (SPA.). 128p. (J). (gr. -1-3). lib. bdg. 24.95 (978-1-58086-330-8(2)) EDC Publishing.

—Stories of Dragons. Doherty, Gillian. Milbourne, Anna, ed. 2007. (Stories for Young Children Ser.). 96p. (J). 16.99 (978-0-7945-1465-5(0), Usborne) EDC Publishing.

—Stories of Wizards. Doherty, Gillian. 2008. (Stories for Young Children Ser.). 95p. (J). (gr. 1). 16.99 (978-0-7945-1915-5(6), Usborne) EDC Publishing.

—Usborne Children's Picture Atlas. Brocklehurst, Ruth. 2004. (Children's Picture Atlas Ser.). 48p. (J). 12.95 (978-0-7945-0640-7(2), Usborne) EDC Publishing.

—Usborne Greek Myths Jigsaw Book. Amery, Heather. 2006. (Usborne Jigsaw Bks.). 14p. (J). bds. 14.99 (978-0-7945-1183-8(X), Usborne) EDC Publishing.

Edwards, Mark. Colossal Clubs: Activities-Based Curriculum for School-Age Programs. Martinez, Kathleen & Edwards, Sue. 2006. per. 29.95 (978-0-917505-39-3(5), School Age Notes) Gryphon Hse., Inc.

—Moving Day. Pedder, Pamela a. Hardcastle, E. Rachael, ed. 2019. (Amazing Adventures of Berty Bee Ser.: Vol. 1). (ENG.). 36p. (J). pap. 8.99 (978-1-9161342-0-1(3), Curious Cat Bks.) Legacy Bound.

Edwards, Mark & Moss, Chris. The Queen's Visit. Pedder, Pamela a. 2019. (Amazing Adventures of Berty Bee Ser.: Vol. 2). (ENG.). 38p. (J). pap. 8.99 (978-1-9161342-1-8(1), Curious Cat Bks.) Legacy Bound.

Edwards, Mat. How to Draw Amazing Airplanes & Spacecraft. McCurry, Kristen. 2012. (Smithsonian Drawing Bks.). (ENG.). 64p. (gr. 3-4). pap. 41.70 (978-1-4296-9449-0(1)) Capstone.

—Julius Caesar, 1 vol. Hunter, Nick. 2013. (Hero Journals). (ENG.). 48p. (J). (gr. 4-6). pap. 9.95 (978-1-4109-5363-6(7), Raintree) Capstone.

—Magnificent Book of Reptiles & Amphibians. Jackson, Tom. 2019. (Magnificent Book Of Ser.). (ENG.). 80p. (J). (gr. 3-7). 18.99 (978-1-68412-297-4(X), Silver Dolphin Bks.) Printers Row Publishing Group.

—Smithsonian Drawing Books. McCurry, Kristen. 2012. (Smithsonian Drawing Bks.). (ENG.). 64p. (gr. 3-4). pap. 83.40 (978-1-4296-9453-7(X)) Capstone.

Edwards, Mat, et al. Smithsonian Drawing Books. McCurry, Kristen. (Smithsonian Drawing Bks.). (ENG.). 64p. (gr. 3-4). 2013. pap. 166.80 (978-1-62065-732-4(5)); 2012. (J). pap., pap., pap. 21.57 (978-1-62065-731-7(7)) Capstone.

Edwards, Mat & Pyke, Jeremy. Megafast Cars. Farndon, John. 2016. (Megafast Ser.). (ENG.). 32p. (J). (gr. 3-6). lib. bdg. 27.99 (978-1-4677-9363-6(9), 9781467793636, Hungry Tomato ®) Lerner Publishing Group.

—Megafast Planes. Farndon, John. 2016. (Megafast Ser.). (ENG.). 32p. (J). (gr. 3-6). lib. bdg. 27.99 (978-1-4677-9365-0(5), 9781467793650, Hungry Tomato ®) Lerner Publishing Group.

—Megafast Trucks. Farndon, John. 2016. (Megafast Ser.). (ENG.). 32p. (J). (gr. 3-6). lib. bdg. 27.99 (978-1-4677-9366-7(3), 9781467793667, Hungry Tomato ®) Lerner Publishing Group.

Edwards, Neil, et al. X-Men: Summers & Winter. 2019. (ENG.). 112p. (YA). (gr. 8-17). pap. 14.99 (978-1-302-91942-9(3)) Marvel Worldwide, Inc.

Edwards, Nick. Galaxy's Most Wanted. Kloepfer, John. 2014. (Galaxy's Most Wanted Ser.: 1). (ENG.). 224p. (J). (gr. 3-7). 12.99 (978-0-06-223101-7(4)) HarperCollins Pubs.

—Galaxy's Most Wanted #2: into the Dorkness. Kloepfer, John. (Galaxy's Most Wanted Ser.: 2). (ENG.). (J). (gr. 3-7). 2016. 272p. pap. 6.99 (978-0-06-223109-3(X)); 2015. 256p. 12.99 (978-0-06-223104-8(9)) HarperCollins Pubs.

—Galaxy's Most Wanted #3: Starship Bloopers. Kloepfer, John. 2016. (Galaxy's Most Wanted Ser.: 3). (ENG.). 240p. (J). (gr. 3-7). 12.99 (978-0-06-223106-2(5)) HarperCollins Pubs.

Edwards, Paul. It's My Birthday. Haworth, Margaret. 2003. 31p. (J). (gr. -1-3). pap. 10.00 (978-0-9740313-0-9(5)) Haworth, Margaret.

—The New Kid: Rusty Book. Haworth, Margaret. l.t. ed. 2003. (Books That Help Ser.: Vol. 3). 34p. (J). (gr. k-6). pap. 9.95 (978-0-9740313-3-0(X)) Haworth, Margaret.

—When Daddy Goes Away: Rusty Books. Haworth, Margaret. l.t. ed. 2003. (Books That Help Ser.: Vol. 2). 34p. (J). (gr. -1-5). pap. 9.95 (978-0-9740313-1-6(3)) Haworth, Margaret.

Edwards, Rebecca. Revenge. Richardson, Duncan. 2005. 30p. (J). pap. (978-1-876682-69-9(8)) Post Pressed.

Edwards, Tommy Lee. I Am Superman! Sudduth, Brent. 2006. (Superman Returns Ser.). 24p. (J). (gr. 4-7). pap. 3.99 (978-0-696-22905-3(6)) Meredith Bks.

Edwards, W M. Booger Boogie. 2007. (Playdate Kids Musical Ser.). 27p. (J). (gr. -1-3). 14.95 incl. audio compact disk (978-1-933721-13-2(8)) Playdate Kids Publishing.

—Chloe Loses Her Pet. Thiel, Annie. 2007. (Playdate Kids: Let's Be Friends! Ser.). 26p. (J). per. 6.95 (978-1-933721-21-7(9)) Playdate Kids Publishing.

—Danny's Secret. Thiel, Annie. 2007. (Playdate Kids: Let's Be Friends! Ser.). 27p. (J). (gr. -1-3). per. 6.95 (978-1-933721-22-4(7)) Playdate Kids Publishing.

—The I Like Me Dance! Friedlander, Tim. 2007. (Playdate Kids Musical Ser.). 27p. (J). (gr. -1-3). 14.95 incl. audio compact disk (978-1-933721-07-1(3)) Playdate Kids Publishing.

—Island Potty Party. 2007. (Playdate Kids Musical Ser.). 27p. (J). (gr. -1-3). 14.95 incl. audio compact disk (978-1-933721-15-6(4)) Playdate Kids Publishing.

Edwards, Wallace. Mixed Beasts. Cox, Kenyon. 2013. (ENG.). 32p. (J). (gr. 1-6). pap. 9.95 (978-1-77138-035-5(7)) Kids Can Pr., Ltd. CAN. Dist: Hachette Bk. Group.

—You Are the Earth: Know Your World So You Can Help Make It Better. Suzuki, David & Vanderlinden, Kathy. 2nd rev. ed. 2010. 144p. (gr. k-7). pap. 18.95 (978-1-55365-476-6(5)) Greystone Books Ltd. CAN. Dist: Publishers Group West (PGW).

Edwards, Wallace. Alphabeasts. Edwards, Wallace. 2008. (ENG.). 32p. (J). (gr. 1-4). pap. 9.95 (978-1-55453-227-8(2)) Kids Can Pr., Ltd. CAN. Dist: Hachette Bk. Group.

—The Extinct Files: My Science Project. Edwards, Wallace. 2006. (ENG.). 32p. (J). (gr. k-3). 17.95 (978-1-55337-971-3(3)) Kids Can Pr., Ltd. CAN. Dist: Hachette Bk. Group.

—Monkey Business. Edwards, Wallace. 2004. 32p. (J). (gr. 1-6). 18.95 (978-1-55337-462-6(2)) Kids Can Pr., Ltd. CAN. Dist: Hachette Bk. Group.

—Woodrow at Sea. Edwards, Wallace. 2018. (ENG.). 32p. (J). (gr. -1-k). 16.95 (978-1-77278-029-1(4)) Pajama Pr. CAN. Dist: Ingram Publisher Services.

Edwards, William M. Cosmos' Blended Family. Thiel, Annie. 2007. (Playdate Kids: Let's Be Friends! Ser.). 27p. (J). (gr. -1-3). per. 6.95 *(978-1-933721-23-1(5))* Playdate Kids Publishing.

—Dakota Gets Lost. Thiel, Annie & Fanning, Tena. 2007. (Playdate Kids: Let's Be Friends! Ser.). 27p. (J). (gr. -1-3). per. 6.95 *(978-1-933721-20-0(0))* Playdate Kids Publishing.

—Danny Is Moving. Thiel, Annie. 2006. (Playdate Kids Ser.). 32p. (J). (gr. -1-3). 14.95 *(978-1-933721-02-6(2))* Playdate Kids Publishing.

Edwards, William M. & Marjoribanks, Karen. Cosmos' Mom & Dad Are Moving Apart. Thiel, Annie. 2006. (Playdate Kids Ser.). 32p. (J). (gr. -1-3). 14.95 *(978-1-933721-04-0(9))* Playdate Kids Publishing.

—Dakota's Mom Goes to the Hospital. Thiel, Annie. 2006. (Playdate Kids Ser.). 32p. (J). (gr. -1-3). 14.95 *(978-1-933721-03-3(0))* Playdate Kids Publishing.

Edwards, William M., jt. illus. see Marjoribanks, Karen.

Edwin, Kimberly. Freddie the Fox & Peter the Cheetah. Ford, Carole S. 30p. (J). (gr. -1). pap. 4.95 *(978-1-891533-03-7(7))* Calvin Partnership, LLC.

—Timothy Turtle & Sammy Scallop. Ford, Carole S. 30p. (J). (gr. -1-k). pap. 4.95 *(978-1-891533-02-0(9))* Calvin Partnership, LLC.

Ee, Jeanne. Bark in the Dark. Nott, Kelly a. 2019. (ENG.). 40p. (J). 19.99 *(978-0-578-41938-1(6))* Living Breathing Story Pubns.

Effler, Jim. A Home for Panda. Nagda, Ann Whitehead. (Amazing Animal Adventures Ser.). (ENG.). 36p. (J). 2005. (gr. -1-2). 15.95 *(978-1-59249-045-5(X)*, B7102); 2005. (gr. -1-2). pap. 6.95 *(978-1-59249-046-2(8)*, S7102); 2005. (gr. 2-2). 19.95 *(978-1-59249-392-0(0)*, BC7102); 2005. (gr. 2-2). 8.95 *(978-1-59249-393-7(9)*, SC7102); 2003. (gr. -1-3). 2.95 *(978-1-59249-047-9(6)*, S7152) Soundprints.

—A Home for Panda. Nagda, Ann Whitehead. 2003. (ENG.). 36p. (J). (gr. -1-3). 9.95 *(978-1-59249-058-5(1)*, PS7152) Soundprints.

Egan, Caroline, jt. illus. see RH Disney Staff.

Egan, Lynn. Good Night, Grace. Egan, Lynn. Gaer, Sarah W. 2020. (ENG.). 30p. (J). pap. 12.99 ***(978-1-6789-9954-4(7))*** Independently Published.

Egan, Tim. Dodsworth in London. Egan, Tim. 2010. (Dodsworth Book Ser.). (ENG.). 48p. (J). (gr. 1-4). pap. 4.99 *(978-0-547-41440-9(4)*, 1429469) Houghton Mifflin Harcourt Publishing Co.

—Dodsworth in New York. Egan, Tim. 2007. (Dodsworth Ser.). (ENG.). 48p. (J). (gr. 1-3). 17.44 *(978-0-618-77708-2(3))* Houghton Mifflin Harcourt Publishing Co.

—Dodsworth in Paris. Egan, Tim. (Dodsworth Ser.). 48p. (J). (gr. 1-3). 2011. 16.19 *(978-0-618-98062-8(8))*; 2010. (ENG.). pap. 4.99 *(978-0-547-33192-8(4)*, 1417441) Houghton Mifflin Harcourt Publishing Co.

—Dodsworth in Tokyo. Egan, Tim. 2014. (Dodsworth Book Ser.). (ENG.). 48p. (J). (gr. 1-4). pap. 4.99 *(978-0-544-33915-6(0)*, 1584486, HMH Books For Young Readers) Houghton Mifflin Harcourt Publishing Co.

Egbert, Corey. The Atonement of Jesus Christ Is for Me. Wilson, Sierra. 2018. (ENG.). 32p. (J). (gr. k-3). 14.99 *(978-1-4621-2194-6(2))* Cedar Fort, Inc./CFI Distribution.

—The Holy Ghost Is Like a Blanket. Hall, Annalisa. 2014. 12.99 *(978-1-4621-1419-1(9)*, Horizon Pubs.); 2014. (ENG.). (J). (gr. -1-2). bds. 12.99 *(978-1-4621-2117-5(9))*; 2013. (ENG.). 32p. (J). (gr. 3-7). 14.99 *(978-1-4621-1229-6(3))* Cedar Fort, Inc./CFI Distribution.

—I Want to Be Baptized. Hall, Annalisa. 2015. (J). 10.99 *(978-1-4621-1670-6(1)*, Horizon Pubs.); 2014. 14.99 *(978-1-4621-1461-0(X))* Cedar Fort, Inc./CFI Distribution.

—The Sleeping Beauty: My First Ballet Book, 1 vol. Adams, Jennifer. 2019. 22p. (J). (gr. -1-1). bds. 9.99 *(978-1-4236-5259-5(2))* Gibbs Smith, Publisher.

—Stars, Stockings, & Shepherds. Chabot, Shersta. 2014. 14.99 *(978-1-4621-1462-7(8)*, Horizon Pubs.) Cedar Fort, Inc./CFI Distribution.

Eger, Caroline Ruth. The Modern Story Book. Wadsworth, Wallace. 2010. (Dover Read & Listen Ser.). (ENG.). 112p. (J). (gr. 1-5). pap. 14.99 incl. audio compact disk *(978-0-486-47844-9(0))* Dover Pubns., Inc.

Eggbert, Corey. I Can Pray Every Day. Christensen, Catherine. 2015. (J). 14.99 *(978-1-4621-1646-1(9)*, Horizon Pubs.) Cedar Fort, Inc./CFI Distribution.

Eggenschwiler, Byron. Beastly Puzzles: A Brain-Boggling Animal Guessing Game. Poliquin, Rachel. 2019. (ENG.). 32p. (J). (gr. 2-5). 16.99 *(978-1-77138-913-6(3))* Kids Can Pr., Ltd. CAN. Dist: Hachette Bk. Group.

Eggenschwiler, Byron. The Little Ghost Who Was a Quilt. Nason, Riel. 2020. (ENG.). 40p. (J). (gr. -1-2). 17.99 ***(978-0-7352-6447-2(3)***, Tundra Bks.) Tundra Bks. CAN. Dist: Penguin Random Hse. LLC.

Egger, Virginie. Anton. Egger, Emmanuelle. 2004. (ENG.). 32p. (J). (gr. -1 — 1). *(978-2-89021-664-8(0))*; pap. *(978-2-89021-663-1(2))* Editions de la Courte Echelle, Inc.

—My Cat Isis. Austen, Catherine. 2011. 32p. (J). (gr. -1-2). 16.95 *(978-1-55453-413-5(5))* Kids Can Pr., Ltd. CAN. Dist: Hachette Bk. Group.

Eggers, James, jt. illus. see Bartram, Bob.

Eggink, Aimee. La Grande Bataille des Rois Ronron et Oro. Lecomte, Serge. 2019. (FRE.). 38p. (J). pap. 10.99 ***(978-1-68160-651-4(8))*** Crimson Cloak Publishing.

—The Nose-Ear War. Lecomte, Serge. 2019. (ENG.). 42p. (J). pap. 10.99 ***(978-1-68160-322-3(5))*** Crimson Cloak Publishing.

Eggleton, Bob. If Dinosaurs Lived in My Town. Plumridge, Marianne. 2013. (ENG.). 56p. (J). (gr. -1-3). 16.95 *(978-1-62636-176-8(2)*, 263176, Sky Pony Pr.) Skyhorse Publishing Co., Inc.

—Years in the Making: The Time Travel Stories of L. Sprague de Camp. de Camp, L. Sprague. Olson, Mark L., ed. 2005. (NESFA's Choice Ser.: 28). 384p. (YA). 25.00 *(978-1-886778-47-4(7)*, NESFA Pr.) New England Science Fiction Assn., Inc.

Egielski, Richard. The End. LaRochelle, David. 2006. (J). 16.99 *(978-0-439-64012-1(1)*, Levine, Arthur A. Bks.) Scholastic, Inc.

—The Fabulous Feud of Gilbert & Sullivan. Winter, Jonah. 2009. (J). pap. *(978-0-439-93051-2(0)*, Levine, Arthur A. Bks.) Scholastic, Inc.

—The Fierce Yellow Pumpkin. Brown, Margaret Wise. (ENG.). 32p. (J). (gr. -1-1). 2003. 16.99 *(978-0-06-024479-8(8))*; 2006. reprint ed. pap. 6.99 *(978-0-06-443534-5(2))* HarperCollins Pubs.

—Gumption! Broach, Elise. 2010. (ENG.). 40p. (J). (gr. k-3). 19.99 *(978-1-4169-1628-4(8)*, Atheneum Bks. for Young Readers) Simon & Schuster Children's Publishing.

Egielski, Richard. Itsy Bitsy Spider. Egielski, Richard. 2012. (ENG.). 12p. (J). (gr. -1-1). 19.99 *(978-1-4169-9895-2(0)*, Atheneum Bks. for Young Readers) Simon & Schuster Children's Publishing.

—Slim & Jim. Egielski, Richard. 2005. 37p. (J). (gr. k-4). reprint ed. 16.00 *(978-0-7567-8936-7(2))* DIANE Publishing Co.

Egitim, Hasan. The All-Merciful Master: The Beautiful Names of God. Ergün, Erol. 2009. 127p. (J). pap. *(978-1-59784-223-5(0)*, Tughra Bks.) Blue Dome, Inc.

Eglitis, Anna, jt. illus. see Brim, Warren.

Egmont, Hardie Grant. Lucky Jars & Broken Promises. Perry, Chrissie. 2017. (Penelope Perfect Ser.: 3). (ENG.). 144p. (J). (gr. 2-5). 16.99 *(978-1-4814-9088-7(5))*; pap. 5.99 *(978-1-4814-9087-0(7))* Simon & Schuster Children's Publishing. (Aladdin).

—The Truly Terrible Mistake. Perry, Chrissie. 2018. (Penelope Perfect Ser.: 4). (ENG.). 144p. (J). (gr. 2-5). 16.99 *(978-1-4814-9085-6(0))*; pap. 5.99 *(978-1-4814-9084-9(2))* Simon & Schuster Children's Publishing. (Aladdin).

Egmont, Hardie Grant, jt. illus. see Kissi, Marta.

Egneus, Daniel. Grandpa S Top Threes. Meddour, Wendy. 2019. (ENG.). 32p. (J). (-k). 16.99 *(978-1-5362-1125-2(7))* Candlewick Pr.

Egnéus, Daniel. Lubna & Pebble. Meddour, Wendy. 2019. (ENG.). 32p. (J). (gr. -1-3). 17.99 *(978-0-525-55416-5(5)*, Dial Bks) Penguin Young Readers Group.

—Moth. Thomas, Isabel. 2019. (ENG.). 48p. (J). 18.99 *(978-1-5476-0020-5(9)*, 900195004, Bloomsbury Children's Bks.) Bloomsbury Publishing USA.

Egneus, Daniel. The Thing. Puttock, Simon. 2019. (ENG.). 32p. (J). (gr. -1-k). pap. 9.99 *(978-1-4052-8371-7(8))* Egmont Bks., Ltd. GBR. Dist: Independent Pubs. Group.

Egremont, Maddie. Where's My Bear? Bray, Amy. 2019. (ENG.). 28p. (J). pap. *(978-1-910565-98-8(9))* Britain's Next Bestseller.

Eguiguren, A. R., jt. illus. see Eguiguren, India J.

Eguiguren, India J. & Eguiguren, A. R. Boris: The Bengal Tiger. Jones, Thomas Rumsey. 2013. 46p. pap. 5.99 *(978-1-883378-81-3(8))* Sun on Earth Bks.

Ehlert, Lois. Chica Chica Bum Bum ABC. Martin, Bill, Jr. & Archambault, John. 2011. (SPA.). 16p. (J). (gr. -1-1). bds. 7.99 *(978-1-4424-2292-6(0)*, Libros Para Ninos) Libros Para Ninos.

—Chica Chica Bum Bum (Chicka Chicka Boom Boom) Martin Jr, Bill & Archambault, John. 2018. (Chicka Chicka Book Ser.). (SPA.). 36p. (J). (gr. -1 — 1). bds. 7.99 *(978-1-5344-1837-0(7)*, Libros Para Ninos) Libros Para Ninos.

Ehlert, Lois. Chica Chica uno Dos Tres (Chicka Chicka 1 2 3) Martin Jr, Bill & Sampson, Michael. 2020. (Chicka Chicka Book Ser.). (SPA.). 36p. (J). (— 1). bds. 7.99 ***(978-1-5344-7347-8(5)***, Libros Para Ninos) Libros Para Ninos.

Ehlert, Lois. Chicka Chicka 1, 2, 3. Martin, Bill, Jr. & Sampson, Michael. 2017. (Chicka Chicka Book Ser.). (ENG.). 36p. (J). (gr. -1 — 1). bds. 7.99 *(978-1-4814-0056-5(8)*, Little Simon) Little Simon.

—Chicka Chicka 1, 2, 3. Martin, Bill, Jr. & Sampson, Michael. 2004. (Chicka Chicka Book Ser.). (ENG.). 40p. (J). (gr. -1-2). 17.99 *(978-0-689-85881-9(7)*, Simon & Schuster Bks. For Young Readers) Simon & Schuster Bks. For Young Readers.

—Chicka Chicka 1, 2, 3. Martin, Bill, Jr. & Sampson, Michael. 2005. (J). (gr. -1-3). 29.95 *(978-0-439-76677-7(X)*, WHCD669) Weston Woods Studios, Inc.

—Chicka Chicka 1, 2, 3: Lap Edition. Martin, Bill, Jr. & Sampson, Michael. 2013. (Chicka Chicka Book Ser.). (ENG.). 36p. (J). (gr. -1-1). bds. 12.99 *(978-1-4424-6613-5(8)*, Little Simon) Little Simon.

—Chicka Chicka ABC. Archambault, John & Martin, Bill, Jr. 2005. (Chicka Chicka Book Ser.). (ENG.). 16p. (J). (gr. -1 — 1). bds. 9.99 *(978-0-689-87820-6(6)*, Little Simon) Little Simon.

—Chicka Chicka ABC: Lap Edition. Martin, Bill, Jr. & Archambault, John. 2009. (Chicka Chicka Book Ser.). (ENG.). 16p. (J). (gr. -1-1). bds. 10.99 *(978-1-4169-8447-4(X)*, Little Simon) Little Simon.

—Chicka Chicka ABCs & 123s Collection: Chicka Chicka ABC; Chicka Chicka 1, 2, 3; Words. Martin Jr, Bill et al. ed. 2018. (Chicka Chicka Book Ser.). (ENG.). 66p. (J). (gr. -1 — 1). bds. 21.99 *(978-1-5344-2520-0(9)*, Little Simon) Little Simon.

—Chicka Chicka Boom Boom. Martin, Bill, Jr. et al. 2008. (J). 13.99 *(978-1-59319-935-7(X))* LeapFrog Enterprises, Inc.

—Chicka Chicka Boom Boom. Martin, Bill, Jr. & Archambault, John. 2012. (Classic Board Bks.). 36p. (J). (gr. -1 — 1). bds. 7.99 *(978-1-4424-5070-7(3)*, Little Simon) Little Simon.

—Chicka Chicka Boom Boom: Anniversary Edition. Martin, Bill, Jr. & Archambault, John. anniv. ed. 2009. (Chicka Chicka Book Ser.). (ENG.). 40p. (J). (gr. -1-3). 18.99 *(978-1-4169-9091-8(7)*, Beach Lane Bks.) Beach Lane Bks.

—Chicka Chicka Boom Boom: Book & CD. Martin, Bill, Jr. & Archambault, John. 2006. (Chicka Chicka Book Ser.). (ENG.). 40p. (J). (gr. -1-3). 10.99 *(978-1-4169-2718-1(2)*, Little Simon) Little Simon.

Ehlert, Lois. Chicka Chicka Boom Boom: Classroom Edition. Martin, Bill, Jr. & Archambault, John. 2020. (Chicka Chicka Book Ser.). (ENG.). 40p. (J). (gr. -1-3). 29.99 ***(978-1-5344-5711-9(9)***, Simon & Schuster Bks. For Young Readers) Simon & Schuster Bks. For Young Readers.

Ehlert, Lois. Chicka Chicka Boom Boom: Lap Edition. Martin, Bill, Jr. & Archambault, John. 2010. (Chicka Chicka Book Ser.). (ENG.). 36p. (J). (gr. -1-1). bds. 12.99 *(978-1-4169-9999-7(X)*, Little Simon) Little Simon.

—Chicka Chicka Box Box! Chicka Chicka Boom Boom; Chicka Chicka 1, 2, 3. Martin, Bill, Jr. et al. ed. 2013. (Chicka Chicka Book Ser.). (ENG.). 80p. (J). (gr. -1-3). 35.99 *(978-1-4814-0223-1(4)*, Beach Lane Bks.) Beach Lane Bks.

—Mice. Fyleman, Rose. 2012. (ENG.). 40p. (J). (gr. -1-k). 16.99 *(978-1-4424-5684-6(1)*, Beach Lane Bks.) Beach Lane Bks.

—A Pair of Socks. Murphy, Stuart J. 2006. (MathStart 1 Ser.: Level 1). (ENG.). 40p. (J). (gr. -1-3). 5.99 *(978-0-06-446703-2(1))* Perfection Learning Corp.

—Ten Little Caterpillars. Martin, Bill, Jr. 2011. (ENG.). 40p. (J). (gr. -1-3). 18.99 *(978-1-4424-3385-4(X)*, Beach Lane Bks.) Beach Lane Bks.

Ehlert, Lois. Boo to You! Ehlert, Lois. 2009. (ENG.). 42p. (J). (gr. -1-2). 19.99 *(978-1-4169-8625-6(1)*, Beach Lane Bks.) Beach Lane Bks.

—Heart to Heart. Ehlert, Lois. 2017. (ENG.). 72p. (J). (gr. -1-3). 9.99 *(978-1-4814-8087-1(1)*, Beach Lane Bks.) Beach Lane Bks.

—Holey Moley. Ehlert, Lois. 2015. (ENG.). 40p. (J). (gr. -1-3). 17.99 *(978-1-4424-9301-8(1)*, Beach Lane Bks.) Beach Lane Bks.

—Lots of Spots. Ehlert, Lois. 2010. (ENG.). 40p. (J). (gr. -1-3). 19.99 *(978-1-4424-0289-8(X)*, Beach Lane Bks.) Beach Lane Bks.

—Lots of Spots. Ehlert, Lois. 2014. (Classic Board Bks.). (ENG.). 40p. (J). (gr. -1 — 1). bds. 7.99 *(978-1-4424-8927-1(8)*, Little Simon) Little Simon.

—Planting a Rainbow. Ehlert, Lois. 2003. (ENG.). 32p. (J). (gr. k — 1). bds. 7.99 *(978-0-15-204633-0(X)*, 1193956) Houghton Mifflin Harcourt Publishing Co.

—Rain Fish. Ehlert, Lois. 2016. (ENG.). 40p. (J). (gr. -1-3). 18.99 *(978-1-4814-6152-8(4)*, Beach Lane Bks.) Beach Lane Bks.

—RRRalph. Ehlert, Lois. 2011. (ENG.). 40p. (J). (gr. -1-1). 19.99 *(978-1-4424-1305-4(0)*, Beach Lane Bks.) Beach Lane Bks.

—RRRalph. Ehlert, Lois. 2016. (Classic Board Bks.). (ENG.). 36p. (J). (gr. -1 — 1). bds. 7.99 *(978-1-4814-5211-3(8)*, Little Simon) Little Simon.

—The Scraps Book: Notes from a Colorful Life. Ehlert, Lois. 2014. (ENG.). 72p. (J). (gr. k-5). 17.99 *(978-1-4424-3571-1(2))* Simon & Schuster Children's Publishing.

Eichelberger, Jennifer. Monday I Was a Monkey: A "Tale" of Reverence. McClain, Jennie. 2011. (J). *(978-1-60861-243-7(0))* Covenant Communications.

Eichenberg, Fritz. Mistress Masham's Repose. White, T. H. 2004. (ENG.). 260p. (J). (gr. 4-7). 19.95 *(978-1-59017-103-5(9)*, NYR Children's Collection) New York Review of Bks., Inc., The.

Eid, Jean-Paul. The Smelly Story of Hazel the Weasel. Chartrand, Lili. 2009. (Rainy Day Readers Ser.). 32p. (J). (gr. -1-3). 25.60 *(978-1-60754-379-4(6))*; pap. 10.55 *(978-1-60754-380-0(X))* Windmill Bks.

Eide, Tarjei Rypdal. The Iceberg Family. Lippert, Audbjorg Gjerde. Rypdal, Olla, ed. 2019. (ENG.). 48p. (J). ***(978-82-690941-6-9(1))*** Olla Forlag.

Eilat, Eyal. Ron & Rona Fight the Corona. Starinsky, Ron & Mizrahi, Amit. 2020. (ENG.). 26p. (J). ***(978-1-922439-42-0(8))***; pap. ***(978-1-922439-41-3(X))*** Tablo Publishing.

Eimann, Céline. The Sky Dreamer / Le Bateau de Reves. Eimann, Céline, tr. Morgan, Anne. 2011.Tr. of Sky Dreamer. (FRE.). 36p. pap. *(978-1-921869-60-0(7)*, IP Kidz) Interactive Pubns. Pty, Ltd.

Einarson, Earl. The Moccasins, 1 vol. Einarson, Earl. ed. 2004. (ENG.). 16p. (J). (gr. -1-k). pap. 10.95 *(978-1-894778-14-5(6))* Theytus Bks., Ltd. CAN. Dist: Orca Bk. Pubs. USA.

Einberg, Indrek Silver. Awesome Jokes That Every 7 Year Old Should Know! Waugh, Mat. 2018. (Awesome Jokes Ser.: Vol. 3). (ENG.). 104p. (J). (gr. 2-3). pap. ***(978-1-9999147-3-8(2))*** Big Red Button Bks.

—Awesome Jokes That Every 8 Year Old Should Know! Waugh, Mat. 2018. (Awesome Jokes Ser.: Vol. 4). (ENG.). 104p. (J). (gr. 3-4). pap. ***(978-1-9999147-4-5(0))*** Big Red Button Bks.

Einstein, Susan. Baseball Treasures. Wong, Stephen. 2007. 58p. (J). (gr. 4-7). lib. bdg. 17.89 *(978-0-06-114473-8(8))* HarperCollins Pubs.

Eisby, Lizzy. Pini the Pitcher: A Story for Hanukkah. Osterbach, Batya Kirshenbaum. 2005. 32p. (J). (gr. 1-4). 16.95 *(978-1-932687-50-7(5)*, Devora Publishing) Simcha Media Group.

Eiseman, Joan. Ricardo & the Fisherman. Eiseman, Joan. 2007. 32p. (J). per. 12.95 *(978-0-9786745-4-0(5))* Marble Hse. Editions.

Eisen, Nancy. Runaway Piggy Bank. Peck, Judith. 2003. 32p. (J). pap. 13.99 *(978-0-9746119-1-4(3))* Imagination Arts Pubns.

Eisenberg, Linda. Toying Around with Science: The Physics Behind Toys & Gags. Friedhoffer, Bob. 2019. (ENG.). 94p. (J). pap. 9.99 *(978-1-0723-1928-3(4))* Independently Published.

Eisenberg, Serge. The Ladybug & Me. Soler, Michael. 2007. 24p. (J). per. 8.99 *(978-0-9795469-0-7(7))* Soler, Michael.

Eisenbraun, Patty. The Small Sports Take the Field! Damman, Matthew. 2nd ed. 2013. (ENG.). 32p. (J). 15.99 *(978-0-9856967-0-2(2))* MAP Creative LLC.

Eisenfeld, Candice. The Crimson Fish. Robbins, Neal. 58p. (Orig.). (J). (gr. 1-18). pap. 4.00 *(978-1-884993-02-2(8))* Koldarana Pubns.

Eisenreich, David. Remember the Dormouse: Follow Alice. Matson, Faye. 2018. (ENG.). 84p. (J). pap. 5.85 *(978-1-7307-9001-0(1))* Independently Published.

Eisenring, Rahel Nicole. Kiki. Schuler, Christoph. 2009. 32p. (J). (gr. -1-3). 14.95 *(978-0-7358-2202-3(6))* North-South Bks., Inc.

Eisner, Will. Cities of the Fantastic: Brusel. Melville, Herman. 2003. (Cities of the Fantastic Ser.). (ENG.). 120p. 19.95 *(978-1-56163-291-6(0))* NBM Publishing Co.

—Moby Dick. Melville, Herman. 2003. (ENG.). 32p. (J). (gr. 4-7). 15.95 *(978-1-56163-293-0(7))* NBM Publishing Co.

Eisner, Will. The Princess & the Frog. Eisner, Will. 2003. (ENG.). 30p. (J). (gr. k-4). 15.95 *(978-1-56163-244-2(9))* NBM Publishing Co.

Eisner, Will. Sundiata: A Legend of Africa. Eisner, Will, retold by. 2003. (ENG.). 32p. (gr. k-3). 15.95 *(978-1-56163-332-6(1))* NBM Publishing Co.

Eitzen, Allan. The Christmas Surprise. Moore, Ruth Nulton. 2007. (Princeton Theological Monograph Ser.: Vol. 151). (ENG.). 162p. (J). (gr. 4-7). 40.00 ***(978-1-5326-6696-4(9))*** Resource Pubns., Inc.

Eitzen, Allan. The Christmas Surprise. Moore, Ruth Nulton. 2007. 160p. (gr. 4-7). pap. 20.00 *(978-1-55635-418-2(5)*, Resource Pubns.(OR)) Wipf & Stock Pubs.

—Corduroy Makes a Cake. Inches, Alison. 2018. (Corduroy Ser.). 32p. (J). (gr. 1-2). 14.99 *(978-1-5247-8864-3(3))*; pap. 3.99 *(978-1-5247-8863-6(5))* Penguin Young Readers Group. (Penguin Young Readers).

—Corduroy Writes a Letter. Inches, Alison. 2018. (Corduroy Ser.). 32p. (J). (gr. 1-2). 14.99 *(978-1-5247-8866-7(X))*; pap. 4.99 *(978-1-5247-8865-0(1))* Penguin Young Readers Group. (Penguin Young Readers).

—Corduroy's Garden. Inches, Alison & Freeman, Don. 2019. (Corduroy Ser.). (ENG.). 32p. (J). (gr. 1-3). 15.99 *(978-1-5247-9085-1(0))*; pap. 4.99 *(978-1-5247-9084-4(2))* Penguin Young Readers Group. (Penguin Young Readers).

—Corduroy's Hike. Freeman, Don & Inches, Alison. 2019. (Corduroy Ser.). 32p. (J). (gr. 1-3). 15.99 *(978-1-5247-9087-5(7))*; pap. 4.99 *(978-1-5247-9086-8(9))* Penguin Young Readers Group. (Penguin Young Readers).

—Costa Rica ABCs: A Book about the People & Places of Costa Rica, 1 vol. Cooper, Sharon Katz. 2007. (Country ABCs Ser.). (ENG.). 32p. (J). (gr. k-5). lib. bdg. 28.65 *(978-1-4048-2249-8(6)*, Picture Window Bks.) Capstone.

—Deadly Snakes. McCourt, Lisa. *(978-0-439-65544-6(7)*, Scholastic) Scholastic, Inc.

—Key to the Prison. Vernon, Louise A. 2nd ed. (Louise A. Vernon Ser.). (ENG.). (YA). (gr. 4-9). 2007. 144p. pap. 8.99 *(978-0-8361-1813-1(8))*; 2003. 146p. pap. 8.99 *(978-0-8361-1698-4(4))* Herald Pr.

—Loose Tooth. Suen, Anastasia. 2004. 28p. (gr. -1-3). 14.00 *(978-0-7569-1955-9(X))* Perfection Learning Corp.

—Verdadero Cuento de Navidad. Navillus, Nell. Alvarez, Lourdes, tr. 2005. (SPA.). 28p. (J). 12.95 *(978-1-58173-250-4(3))* Sweetwater Pr.

Ekmanis, Rena. Hawaii's Animals Do the Most Amazing Things! Coste, Marion. 2014. (ENG.). 48p. 15.99 *(978-0-8248-3962-8(5)*, 1507, Latitude 20) Univ. of Hawaii Pr.

Eko-Burgess, Carrie. The Construction Crew. Meltzer, Lynn. 2011. (ENG.). 40p. (J). (gr. -1-k). 16.99 *(978-0-8050-8884-7(9)*, 9780805088847, Holt, Henry & Co. Bks. For Young Readers) Holt, Henry & Co.

El Fathi, Mickael. Peace & Me: Inspired by the Lives of Nobel Peace Prize Laureates. Winter, Ali. 2018. (ENG.). 40p. (J). (gr. 2-5). 17.99 *(978-1-911373-28-5(5))* Lantana Publishing GBR. Dist: Lerner Publishing Group.

El Fisgsn. El Profesor Ziper y la Fabulosa Guitarra Electrica. Villoro, Juan. 2005. (Infantil Ser.). (SPA.). 96p. (J). (gr. 5-8). pap. 9.95 *(978-968-19-0206-3(8))* Santillana USA Publishing Co., Inc.

El Moisés, El. Owl in a Straw Hat: El Tecolote Del Sombrero de Paja. Anaya, Rudolfo. Lamadrid, Enrique R., tr. 2017. (ENG & SPA.). 44p. (J). 16.95 *(978-0-89013-630-0(0))* Museum of New Mexico Pr.

El Wakil, Mohamed. The Last Night of Ramadan, 1 vol. Hamed, Maissa. 2007. (ENG.). (J). (gr. -1-3). *(978-0-88010-586-6(0)*, Bell Pond Bks.) SteinerBooks, Inc.

Eladwi, Maha. The Magical Crevice an Egyptian Tale Bedtime Stories. Abolrous, Sam. Husseiny, Abdo a, tr. 2020. (ENG.). 48p. (J). pap. 16.50 ***(978-1-6606-8506-6(0))*** Independently Published.

Elam, Brock. Naughty Nello & the Sleds. Puccinelli, Joanne. 2012. 34p. (J). pap. 12.95 *(978-1-938707-00-1(1))* Stoneydale Pr. Publishing Co.

Elden, Christian. Petunia Pepper's Picture Day. Breisacher, Cathy. 2010. 32p. (J). 14.99 *(978-1-59317-397-5(0))* Warner Pr., Inc.

Elder, Harold. The Green Bay Area in History & Legend. Foley, Betsy, ed. 2004. xiii, 322p. 29.95 *(978-0-9641499-9-1(0))* Brown County Historical Society.

Elder, Jennifer & Thomas, Marc. Autistic Planet. Elder, Jennifer. 2007. (ENG.). 48p. (gr. -1-k). 21.95 *(978-1-84310-842-9(9)*, 692610) Kingsley, Jessica Pubs. GBR. Dist: Hachette UK Distribution.

—Different Like Me: My Book of Autism Heroes. Elder, Jennifer. 2005. (ENG.). 48p. 16.95 *(978-1-84310-815-3(1)*, 692276) Kingsley, Jessica Pubs. GBR. Dist: Hachette UK Distribution.

Eldred, David. Elizabeth Anne: Goodness Girl & Her Green-Eyed Monster. Hoffmaster, Casey. 2018. (ENG.). 36p. (J). pap. 17.99 *(978-0-692-13484-9(0))* Hoffmaster, Casey Camille.

Eldredge, Ernie. A Is for Alabama. Sullivan, E. J. 2006. (State Alphabet Bks.). 24p. (J). *(978-1-58173-523-9(5))* Sweetwater Pr.

—Bubba the Redneck Reindeer. Sullivan, E. J. 2007. 32p. (J). (gr. 4-7). 12.95 *(978-1-60261-008-8(8))* Cliff Road Bks.

—F Is for Florida. Sullivan, E. J. 2006. (State Alphabet Bks.). 24p. (J). *(978-1-58173-525-3(1))* Sweetwater Pr.

—How Santa Got His Elves. Sullivan, E. J. 2006. (J). (gr. -1-3). 9.95 *(978-1-58173-308-2(9))* Sweetwater Pr.

—N Is for North Carolina. Sullivan, E. J. 2007. (State Alphabet Bks.). 20p. *(978-1-58173-625-0(8))* Sweetwater Pr.

—The North Carolina Night Before Christmas. Sullivan, Ellen. 2006. (J). *(978-1-60261-163-4(7))* Sweetwater Pr.

—S Is for South Carolina. Sullivan, E. J. 2007. (State Alphabet Bks.). 20p. *(978-1-58173-626-7(6))* Sweetwater Pr.

E

—V Is for Virginia. Sullivan, E. J. 2006. 24p. (J). lib. bdg. *(978-1-58173-526-0(X))* Sweetwater Pr.

Eldredge, Larry. The Night Before Christmas. Moore, Clement C. 2006. (Night Before Christmas Ser.). 32p. (J). 9.95 *(978-1-58173-306-8(2))*; 26p. bds. 9.95 *(978-1-58173-300-6(3))* Sweetwater Pr.

—La Nochebuena, 1. Moore, Clement C. Alvarez, Lourdes, tr. 2005.Tr. of Twas the Night Before Christmas. (SPA.). 28p. (J). bds. 12.95 *(978-1-58173-257-3(0))* Sweetwater Pr.

—The Tennessee Night Before Christmas. Sullivan, E. J. 2005. (Night Before Christmas Ser.). (J). (gr. -1-3). 12.95 *(978-1-58173-395-2(X))* Sweetwater Pr.

Eldridge, Crystal. When My Mommy Cries: A Story to Help Families Cope with Sadness. LaPoint, Crystal Godfrey. 2012. (ENG.). 32p. (gr. k-6). pap. 19.99 *(978-1-4525-4241-6(4),* 7529fdad-44ef-45a0-9351-f4e3e18c4d7c, Balboa Pr.) Author Solutions, Inc.

Eldridge, Jim. Atlantis & Other Lost Cities. Shone, Rob. 2006. (Graphic Mysteries Ser.). (ENG.). 48p. (YA). (gr. 5-8). lib. bdg. 35.45 *(978-1-4042-0794-3(5))* Rosen Publishing Group, Inc., The.

—Who Was Sitting Bull? Spinner, Stephanie & Who HQ. 2014. (Who Was? Ser.). 112p. (J). (gr. 3-7). 5.99 *(978-0-448-47965-1(6),* Penguin Workshop) Penguin Young Readers Group.

—Who Was Sojourner Truth? McDonough, Yona Zeldis & Who HQ. 2015. (Who Was? Ser.). 112p. (J). (gr. 3-7). 5.99 *(978-0-448-48678-9(4),* Penguin Workshop) Penguin Young Readers Group.

—Who Was Steve Irwin? Anastasio, Dina & Who HQ. 2015. (Who Was? Ser.). 112p. (J). (gr. 3-7). 5.99 *(978-0-448-48838-7(8),* Penguin Workshop) Penguin Young Readers Group.

Eldridge, Lauren. Sleep Train. London, Jonathan. 2018. 32p. (J). (-k). 17.99 *(978-0-451-47303-5(5),* Viking Books for Young Readers) Penguin Young Readers Group.

Eldridge, Les & Casey, James. Santa's Cat. Eldridge, Les. 2003. 24p. (J). *(978-1-877338-03-8(6))* Steele Roberts Aotearoa Ltd.

Eldridge, Lucy. A House Without Walls. Laird, Elizabeth. 2019. (ENG.). 288p. (J). (gr. 4-6). 16.99 ***(978-1-5098-8072-0(0)***, Macmillan Children's Bks.) Pan Macmillan GBR. Dist: Independent Pubs. Group.

Eldridge, Lucy. If a Horse Had Words. Cooper, Kelly. 2018. (ENG.). 48p. (J). (gr. -1-3). 17.99 *(978-1-101-91872-2(1),* Tundra Bks.) Tundra Bks. CAN. Dist: Penguin Random Hse. LLC.

Eldridge, Marion. Mommy & Daddy Are Always Supposed to Say Yes — Aren't They? Rothenberg, B. Annye. 2007. 40p. (J). pap. 9.95 *(978-0-9790420-0-3(3))* Perfecting Parenting Pr.

—Shante Keys & the New Year's Peas. Piernas-Davenport, Gail. (ENG.). 32p. (J). (gr. 9-3). 2017. pap. 7.99 *(978-0-8075-7331-0(0),* 807573310); 2007. lib. bdg. 16.99 *(978-0-8075-7330-3(2),* 807573302) Whitman, Albert & Co.

Eldridge-Murray, Lauren. Twevven & the Horrible Big Bigger Biggest Baby Burp. Burns, Ian. 2012. 52p. pap. *(978-0-9806606-5-4(3))* Greybold Investing Pty Ltd.

Electronic Arts Inc., Staff. The Big Book of Apex Legends: The Ultimate Guide to Dominate the Arena. Davis, Michael. 2019. (ENG.). 112p. (J). (gr. 7). 12.99 *(978-2-89802-136-7(9),* CrackBoom! Bks.) Chouette Publishing CAN. Dist: Publishers Group West (PGW).

Elejalde, Eliana. The Adventures of Valeria Veterinarian: Las Aventuras de Valeria Veterinaria, 1. Graziani, Maria. l.t. ed. 2004. (SPA.). 23p. (J). 7.00 *(978-0-9762361-0-8(9))* Ed. Acespanish S.A.C.- Lima, Peru.

—A Black Cat on Halloween: Un Gato Negro en Dia de Brujas. Graziani, Maria. l.t. ed. 2004. (SPA.). 23p. (J). 7.00 *(978-0-9762361-1-5(7))* Ed. Acespanish S.A.C.- Lima, Peru.

Elena, Horacio. El Superzorro. Dahl, Roald. 2003.Tr. of Fantastic Mr Fox. (SPA.). 96p. (J). (gr. 5-8). pap. 9.95 *(978-968-19-0719-8(1))* Santillana USA Publishing Co., Inc.

Elena, Horacio. Experimentos Sencillos con la Luz y el Sonido. Elena, Horacio, tr. Vecchione, Glen. 2004. (Juego de la Ciencia Ser.). (SPA.). 124p. 10.99 *(978-84-9754-043-8(3),* 87814) Ediciones Oniro S.A. ESP. Dist: Lectorum Pubns., Inc.

Eleven. Spirit Comes to Earth: Renewing Your Heart's Mission. Eleven. 2005. 128p. (YA). per. 13.95 *(978-0-9743540-0-2(7),* By title) Peace Love Karma Publishing.

Elfast, Rebecca. Power to the Period (wt) A Menstruation Manifesto. Okamoto, Nadya. 2018. (ENG.). 368p. (YA). (gr. 7). 19.99 *(978-1-5344-3021-1(0))*; pap. 12.99 *(978-1-5344-3020-4(2))* Simon & Schuster Bks. For Young Readers. (Simon & Schuster Bks. For Young Readers).

Elfezzani, Thierry. Six Chicks. Branford, Henrietta. 2004. (ENG.). 32p. (J). (gr. k-k). pap. 8.99 *(978-0-00-664767-6(7),* HarperCollins Children's Bks.) HarperCollins Pubs. Ltd. GBR. Dist: Independent Pubs. Group.

Elgin, Kathleen. In the Steps of the Great American Entomologist. Pallister, John C. 2014. (ENG.). 128p. (J). (gr. 2-6). pap. 11.95 *(978-1-59077-364-2(0))* Evans, M. & Co., Inc.

Eli, Jessica. I Love to Dance with Jesus. Eli, Jessica. 2019. (ENG.). 32p. (J). pap. 9.99 *(978-1-7958-2529-0(4))* Independently Published.

Eliana, Blanchard. Ellie's Stories: Kindergarten & 1st Grade. Eliana, Blanchard. 2016. (ENG.). (J). pap. 34.00 *(978-0-692-78442-6(X))* KidsCanPublish.Org.

Eliasian, Serineh. Clementine Can't Wait. Gliane, Alquin. 2019. (ENG.). 26p. (J). pap. 9.99 *(978-1-0808-4329-9(9))* Independently Published.

Elio. What's Inside My Lunch Box? A Lift-The-Flap Book. Eliot, Hannah. 2018. (ENG.). 12p. (J). (gr. -1 — 1). bds. 7.99 *(978-1-5344-1594-2(7),* Little Simon) Little Simon.

Eliopolous, Chris. Bach to the Rescue!!! How a Rich Dude Who Couldn't Sleep Inspired the Greatest Music Ever. Angleberger, Tom. 2019. (ENG.). 40p. (J). (gr. -1-3). 17.99 *(978-1-4197-3164-8(5),* Abrams Bks. for Young Readers) Abrams, Inc.

—I Lost My Sock! A Matching Mystery. Roberts, P. J. 2017. (ENG.). 24p. (J). (gr. -1-k). 12.95 *(978-1-4197-2301-8(4),* Abrams Appleseed) Abrams, Inc.

Eliopoulos, Chris. Bun, Onion, Burger. Mandel, Peter. 2010. (ENG.). 40p. (J). (gr. -1-1). 12.99 *(978-1-4169-2466-1(3),* Simon & Schuster Bks. For Young Readers) Simon & Schuster Bks. For Young Readers.

—Chameleon Cage Match! Lemke, Donald B. 2013. (Lucha Lizards Ser.). (ENG.). 48p. (J). (gr. 3-5). pap. 5.95 *(978-1-4342-3874-0(1))*; lib. bdg. 23.99 *(978-1-4342-3285-4(9))* Capstone. (Stone Arch Bks.).

—I Am...: a Journal for Extraordinary Kids. Meltzer, Brad. 2019. (Ordinary People Change the World Ser.). 40p. (J). (gr. k-3). 14.99 *(978-0-525-57700-3(9),* Clarkson Potter) Crown Publishing Group, The.

Eliopoulos, Chris. Does a Great Job, 1 vol. Eliopoulos, Chris. 2013. (Mr. Puzzle Ser.). (ENG.). 40p. (J). (gr. 2-5). lib. bdg. 23.99 *(978-1-4342-6025-3(9),* Stone Arch Bks.) Capstone.

—Mr. Puzzle. Eliopoulos, Chris. 2013. (Mr. Puzzle Ser.). (ENG.). 40p. (J). (gr. 2-5). lib. bdg., lib. bdg., lib. bdg. 95.96 *(978-1-4342-6347-6(9),* Stone Arch Bks.) Capstone.

—Mr. Puzzle Super Collection!, 1 vol. Eliopoulos, Chris. 2013. (Mr. Puzzle Ser.). (ENG.). 128p. (J). (gr. 3-6). pap. 7.95 *(978-1-62370-035-5(3),* Capstone Young Readers) Capstone.

—No Instructions Needed, 1 vol. Eliopoulos, Chris. 2013. (Mr. Puzzle Ser.). (ENG.). 40p. (J). (gr. 2-5). lib. bdg. 23.99 *(978-1-4342-6026-0(7),* Stone Arch Bks.) Capstone.

—A Perfect Fit, 1 vol. Eliopoulos, Chris. 2013. (Mr. Puzzle Ser.). (ENG.). 40p. (J). (gr. 2-5). lib. bdg. 23.99 *(978-1-4342-6024-6(0),* Stone Arch Bks.) Capstone.

—Piece by Piece, 1 vol. Eliopoulos, Chris. 2013. (Mr. Puzzle Ser.). (ENG.). 40p. (J). (gr. 2-5). lib. bdg. 23.99 *(978-1-4342-6027-7(5),* Stone Arch Bks.) Capstone.

Eliopoulos, Christopher. I Am Abraham Lincoln. Meltzer, Brad. 2014. (Ordinary People Change the World Ser.). (ENG.). 40p. (J). (gr. k-3). 15.99 *(978-0-8037-4083-9(2),* Dial Bks) Penguin Young Readers Group.

—I Am Albert Einstein. Meltzer, Brad. 2014. (Ordinary People Change the World Ser.). (ENG.). 40p. (J). (gr. k-3). 15.99 *(978-0-8037-4084-6(0),* Dial Bks) Penguin Young Readers Group.

—I Am Amelia Earhart. Meltzer, Brad. 2014. (Ordinary People Change the World Ser.). (ENG.). 40p. (J). (gr. k-3). 15.99 *(978-0-8037-4082-2(4),* Dial Bks) Penguin Young Readers Group.

—I Am Billie Jean King. Meltzer, Brad. 2019. (Ordinary People Change the World Ser.). 40p. (J). (gr. k-3). 15.99 *(978-0-7352-2874-0(4),* Dial Bks) Penguin Young Readers Group.

—I Am Brave: A Little Book about Martin Luther King, Jr. Meltzer, Brad. 2019. (Ordinary People Change the World Ser.). 12p. (J). (-k). bds. 7.99 *(978-1-9848-1424-1(9),* Dial Bks) Penguin Young Readers Group.

—I Am Caring: A Little Book about Jane Goodall. Meltzer, Brad. 2019. (Ordinary People Change the World Ser.). 12p. (J). (-k). bds. 7.99 *(978-1-9848-1425-8(7),* Dial Bks) Penguin Young Readers Group.

—I Am Curious: A Little Book about Albert Einstein. Meltzer, Brad. 2020. (Ordinary People Change the World Ser.). 12p. (J). (-k). bds. 7.99 *(978-0-593-11007-2(2),* Dial Bks) Penguin Young Readers Group.

—I Am George Washington. Meltzer, Brad. 2016. (Ordinary People Change the World Ser.). (ENG.). 40p. (J). (gr. k-3). 15.99 *(978-0-525-42848-0(8),* Dial Bks) Penguin Young Readers Group.

—I Am Harriet Tubman. Meltzer, Brad. 2018. (Ordinary People Change the World Ser.). (ENG.). 40p. (J). (gr. k-3). 15.99 *(978-0-7352-2871-9(X),* Dial Bks) Penguin Young Readers Group.

—I Am Helen Keller. Meltzer, Brad. 2015. (Ordinary People Change the World Ser.). 40p. (J). (gr. k-3). 15.99 *(978-0-525-42851-0(8),* Dial Bks) Penguin Young Readers Group.

—I Am Jackie Robinson. Meltzer, Brad. 2015. (Ordinary People Change the World Ser.). (ENG.). 40p. (J). (gr. k-3). 15.99 *(978-0-8037-4086-0(7),* Dial Bks) Penguin Young Readers Group.

—I Am Jane Goodall. Meltzer, Brad. 2016. (Ordinary People Change the World Ser.). 40p. (J). (gr. k-3). 15.99 *(978-0-525-42849-7(6),* Dial Bks) Penguin Young Readers Group.

—I Am Jim Henson. Meltzer, Brad. 2017. (Ordinary People Change the World Ser.). 40p. (J). (gr. k-3). 14.99 *(978-0-525-42850-3(X),* Dial Bks) Penguin Young Readers Group.

—I Am Kind: A Little Book about Abraham Lincoln. Meltzer, Brad. 2019. (Ordinary People Change the World Ser.). 12p. (J). (-k). bds. 7.99 *(978-0-525-55295-6(2),* Dial Bks) Penguin Young Readers Group.

—I Am Leonardo Da Vinci. Meltzer, Brad. 2020. (Ordinary People Change the World Ser.). 32p. (J). (gr. k-3). 15.99 *(978-0-525-55588-9(9),* Dial Bks) Penguin Young Readers Group.

—I Am Lucille Ball. Meltzer, Brad. 2015. (Ordinary People Change the World Ser.). 40p. (J). (gr. k-3). 15.99 *(978-0-525-42855-8(0),* Dial Bks) Penguin Young Readers Group.

—I Am Marie Curie. Meltzer, Brad. 2019. (Ordinary People Change the World Ser.). (ENG.). 40p. (J). (gr. k-3). 15.99 *(978-0-525-55585-8(4),* Dial Bks) Penguin Young Readers Group.

—I Am Martin Luther King, Jr. Meltzer, Brad. 2016. (Ordinary People Change the World Ser.). 40p. (J). (gr. k-3). 15.99 *(978-0-525-42852-7(6),* Dial Bks) Penguin Young Readers Group.

—I Am Neil Armstrong. Meltzer, Brad. 2018. (Ordinary People Change the World Ser.). (ENG.). 40p. (J). (gr. k-3). 15.99 *(978-0-7352-2872-6(8),* Dial Bks) Penguin Young Readers Group.

—I Am Rosa Parks. Meltzer, Brad. 2014. (Ordinary People Change the World Ser.). (ENG.). 40p. (J). (gr. k-3). 15.99 *(978-0-8037-4085-3(9),* Dial Bks) Penguin Young Readers Group.

—I Am Sacagawea. Meltzer, Brad. 2017. (Ordinary People Change the World Ser.). 40p. (J). (gr. k-3). 15.99 *(978-0-525-42853-4(4),* Dial Bks) Penguin Young Readers Group.

—I Am Sonia Sotomayor. Meltzer, Brad. 2018. (Ordinary People Change the World Ser.). 40p. (J). (gr. k-3). 14.99 *(978-0-7352-2873-3(6),* Dial Bks) Penguin Young Readers Group.

—I Am Strong: A Little Book about Rosa Parks. Meltzer, Brad. 2020. (Ordinary People Change the World Ser.). 12p. (J). (-k). bds. 7.99 *(978-0-593-11010-2(2),* Dial Bks) Penguin Young Readers Group.

—I Am Unstoppable: A Little Book about Amelia Earhart. Meltzer, Brad. 2019. (Ordinary People Change the World Ser.). 12p. (J). (-k). bds. 7.99 *(978-0-525-55293-2(6),* Dial Bks) Penguin Young Readers Group.

—I Am Walt Disney. Meltzer, Brad. 2019. (Ordinary People Change the World Ser.). 40p. (J). (gr. k-3). 15.99 *(978-0-7352-2875-7(2),* Dial Bks) Penguin Young Readers Group.

—Ordinary People Change the World Sticker Activity Book. Meltzer, Brad. 2017. (Ordinary People Change the World Ser.). 48p. (J). (gr. k-3). pap. 9.99 *(978-0-515-15964-6(6),* Grosset & Dunlap) Penguin Young Readers Group.

—Strong Girls Gift Set, 4 vols. Meltzer, Brad. 2018. (Ordinary People Change the World Ser.). 160p. (J). (gr. k-3). 50.00 *(978-0-525-55304-5(5),* Dial Bks) Penguin Young Readers Group.

Eliopoulos, Christopher. Cosmic Commandos. Eliopoulos, Christopher. (J). (gr. 3-7). 2020. 192p. pap. 9.99 *(978-1-101-99447-4(9))*; 2017. 176p. 13.99 *(978-1-101-99448-1(7))* Penguin Young Readers Group. (Dial Bks).

—Monster Mayhem. Eliopoulos, Christopher. (J). (gr. 3-7). 2020. 216p. pap. 9.99 *(978-0-593-11003-4(X))*; 2018. 196p. 15.99 *(978-0-7352-3124-5(9))* Penguin Young Readers Group. (Dial Bks).

—The Yawns Are Coming! Eliopoulos, Christopher. 2020. 32p. (J). (gr. -1-3). 17.99 *(978-1-9848-1630-6(6),* Dial Bks) Penguin Young Readers Group.

Eliou, Lewis. They Came from near & Afar: The Saga of Recca ND Tony Terrific. Porter, Virginia. 2018. (Georgette & George Adventures Ser.: Vol. 3). (ENG.). 56p. (J). pap. 11.59 *(978-1-7312-5565-5(9))* Independently Published.

Eliou, Lewis M. A George & Georgette & Friends Adventure: Tony Terrific Goes Shopping. Porter, Judith Ann. 2019. (ENG.). 48p. (J). pap. 10.49 ***(978-1-6923-0742-4(8))*** Independently Published.

Eliseev, Sergey. My Princess Bible. Holmes, Andy. 2010. (ENG.). 66p. (J). bds. 12.99 *(978-1-4143-3324-3(2),* 4602314) Tyndale Hse. Pubs.

—Princess Stories: Real Bible Stories of God's Princesses. Larsen, Carolyn. 2012. (ENG.). 128p. (J). 14.99 *(978-1-4143-4811-7(8),* 4603801, Tyndale Kids) Tyndale Hse. Pubs.

Elissambura. Alligator Seder, Vol. Hickman, Jessica. 2020. (ENG.). 12p. (J). (gr. -1 — 1). bds. 6.99 *(978-1-5415-6041-3(8),* Kar-Ben Publishing) Lerner Publishing Group.

—Who's Got the Etrog? Kohuth, Jane. 2018. (ENG.). 32p. (J). (gr. -1-2). 17.99 *(978-1-5415-0966-5(8),* Kar-Ben Publishing) Lerner Publishing Group.

Elissambura, Elissambura. God Grows Our World. Bower, Gary. 2018. (God Our Maker Ser.). 20p. (J). (gr. -1-k). bds. 6.99 *(978-0-8249-1671-8(9))* Worthy Publishing.

Elizabeth, Megan. The Travel Adventures of Pj Mouse: In Italy. Page, Gwyneth Jane. 2018. (Travel Adventures of Pj Mouse Ser.: Vol. 5). (ENG.). 74p. (J). (gr. k-5). pap. *(978-0-9959661-4-7(1))* Gwyneth Jane Page.

Elizabeth Mobley. My First Ride with Isaiah. Cooper, Wendy. 2006. 18p. (J). 11.95 *(978-0-9772964-8-4(2))* Kingdom Publishing Group, Inc.

Elizabeth, Pratt. If It's No Trouble... a Big Polar Bear, 1 vol. Dalrymple, Lisa. 2012. (ENG.). 32p. (J). (gr. k-3). *(978-1-897174-95-1(0))* Breakwater Bks., Ltd.

Elizalde, Marcelo. Harry's Hats. Tompert, Ann. 2004. (Rookie Readers Ser.). 31p. (J). 19.50 *(978-0-516-23613-1(X),* Children's Pr.) Scholastic Library Publishing.

—The Space Program. Metzger, Joanna. 2006. 142p. (J). *(978-1-59336-695-7(7))* Mondo Publishing.

Elizarova, Mariya. Your Thoughts Matter: Negative Self-Talk, Growth Mindset. Cordova, Esther Pia. 2019. (Growth Mindset Ser.: Vol. 4). (ENG.). 40p. (J). pap. ***(978-3-948298-08-1(4))*** Cordova, Esther Pia Power Of Yet.

Elkerton, Andy. ABC. Watt, Fiona. 2009. (Luxury Touchy-Feely Board Bks). 10p. (J). (gr. -1). bds. 15.99 *(978-0-7945-2094-6(4),* Usborne) EDC Publishing.

—The Candies Save Christmas. Patterson, James. 2017. (Candies Ser.). (ENG.). 24p. (J). (gr. -1 — 1). bds. 7.99 *(978-0-316-43576-5(7),* Jimmy Patterson) Little Brown & Co.

—Collins Big Cat Phonics for Letters & Sounds - Zip & Zigzag: Band 02A/Red A, Bd. 2A. Coe, Catherine. 2018. (Collins Big Cat Phonics Ser.). (ENG.). 16p. (J). (gr. -1-k). pap. 6.99 *(978-0-00-825143-7(6))* HarperCollins Pubs. Ltd. GBR. Dist: Independent Pubs. Group.

—The Dinosaur Next Door. Stimson, Joan. 2009. (Tadpoles Ser.). (ENG.). (J). (gr. k-k). lib. bdg. 17.55 *(978-1-61383-948-5(0))* Perfection Learning Corp.

—The Dinosaur Who Lost His Roar. Punter, Russell. 2007. (Usborne First Reading: Level 3 Ser.). 48p. (J). 8.99 *(978-0-7945-1547-8(9),* Usborne) EDC Publishing.

—Do Not Bring Your Dragon to Recess. Gassman, Julie. 2018. (Fiction Picture Bks.). (ENG.). 32p. (J). (gr. -1-2). lib. bdg. 21.32 *(978-1-5158-2843-3(3),* 138276, Picture Window Bks.) Capstone.

—Do Not Bring Your Dragon to the Last Day of School. Gassman, Julie. 2020. (ENG.). 32p. (J). (gr. -1-2). 16.95 *(978-1-68446-067-0(0),* 140524, Capstone Editions) Capstone.

—Do Not Bring Your Dragon to the Library. Gassman, Julie. 2016. (Fiction Picture Bks.). (ENG.). 32p. (J). (gr. -1-2). lib. bdg. 21.32 *(978-1-4795-9175-6(0),* Picture Window Bks.) Capstone.

—Do Not Bring Your Dragon to the Library. Gassman, Julie. (Fiction Picture Bks.). (ENG.). 32p. (J). (gr. -1-2). 2018. pap. 7.95 *(978-1-5158-3897-5(8),* 139671, Picture Window Bks.); 2016. 14.95 *(978-1-62370-651-7(3),* Capstone Young Readers) Capstone.

—Do Not Take Your Dragon on a Field Trip. Gassman, Julie. 2019. (ENG.). 32p. (J). (gr. -1-2). lib. bdg. 16.95 *(978-1-68446-059-5(X),* 140409, Capstone Editions) Capstone.

—Do Not Take Your Dragon to Dinner. Gassman, Julie. 2017. (Fiction Picture Bks.). (ENG.). 32p. (J). (gr. -1-2). lib. bdg. 21.32 *(978-1-4795-9888-5(7),* 135339, Picture Window Bks.) Capstone.

—Ella Power & the Sun Puppies: A Power Families Adventure. Moore, Suse. 2011. (ENG.). 40p. (J). 17.99 *(978-0-9837863-2-0(1))* Jack Hook Publishing.

—Good Night Coral Reef. Gamble, Adam & Jasper, Mark. 2019. (Good Night Our World Ser.). 20p. (J). (— 1). bds. 9.95 *(978-1-60219-776-3(8))* Good Night Bks.

—Good Night Great Barrier Reef. Gamble, Adam & Jasper, Mark. 2020. (Good Night Our World Ser.). (ENG.). 20p. (J). (— 1). bds. 9.95 *(978-1-60219-806-7(3))* Good Night Bks.

—Good Night Solar System. Gamble, Adam & Jasper, Mark. 2019. (Good Night Our World Ser.). (ENG.). 20p. (J). (— 1). bds. 9.95 *(978-1-60219-823-4(3))* Good Night Bks.

—How to Catch a Dinosaur. Wallace, Adam. 2019. (How to Catch Ser.: 0). 40p. (J). (-5). 10.99 *(978-1-4926-8052-9(4))* Sourcebooks, Inc.

—How to Catch a Dragon. Wallace, Adam. 2019. (How to Catch Ser.: 0). 40p. (J). (-5). 10.99 *(978-1-4926-9369-7(3),* Sourcebooks Jabberwocky) Sourcebooks, Inc.

—How to Catch a Leprechaun. Wallace, Adam. 2016. (How to Catch Ser.). 32p. (J). (-6). 10.99 *(978-1-4926-3291-7(0),* 9781492632917, Sourcebooks Jabberwocky) Sourcebooks, Inc.

—How to Catch a Mermaid. Wallace, Adam & Wallace, Adam. 2018. (How to Catch Ser.: 0). 40p. (J). (-5). 10.99 *(978-1-4926-6247-1(X),* Sourcebooks Jabberwocky) Sourcebooks, Inc.

—How to Catch a Monster. Wallace, Adam & Wallace, Adam. 2017. (How to Catch Ser.: 0). 40p. (J). (-3). 10.99 *(978-1-4926-4894-9(9),* Sourcebooks Jabberwocky) Sourcebooks, Inc.

—How to Catch a Snowman. Wallace, Adam. 2018. (How to Catch Ser.). (ENG.). 40p. (J). (-5). 17.99 *(978-1-4926-8055-0(9))* Sourcebooks, Inc.

—How to Catch a Turkey. Wallace, Adam & Wallace, Adam. 2018. (How to Catch Ser.: 0). 40p. (J). (-6). 10.99 *(978-1-4926-6435-2(9),* Sourcebooks Jabberwocky) Sourcebooks, Inc.

—How to Catch a Unicorn. Wallace, Adam. 2019. (How to Catch Ser.: 0). 40p. (J). (-6). 10.99 *(978-1-4926-6973-9(3),* Sourcebooks Jabberwocky) Sourcebooks, Inc.

Elkerton, Andy. How to Catch a Yeti. Wallace, Adam. 2020. (How to Catch Ser.). 40p. (J). (-5). 10.99 ***(978-1-7282-1674-4(5))*** Sourcebooks, Inc.

—How to Catch an Elf. Wallace, Adam. (J). 2020. ***(978-1-7282-2274-5(5))***; 2016. 32p. 10.99 *(978-1-4926-4631-0(8),* 9781492646310, Sourcebooks Jabberwocky) Sourcebooks, Inc.

Elkerton, Andy. How to Catch the Easter Bunny. Wallace, Adam. 2017. (How to Catch Ser.). 40p. (J). (-6). 10.99 *(978-1-4926-3817-9(X),* 9781492638179, Sourcebooks Jabberwocky) Sourcebooks, Inc.

—How to Catch the Tooth Fairy. Wallace, Adam & Wallace, Adam. 2016. (How to Catch Ser.: 0). 32p. (J). (-6). 10.99 *(978-1-4926-3733-2(5),* 9781492637332, Sourcebooks Jabberwocky) Sourcebooks, Inc.

—Jungle. Watt, Fiona. 2009. (Luxury Touchy-Feely Board Bks). 10p. (J). (gr. -1). bds. 15.99 *(978-0-7945-2433-3(8),* Usborne) EDC Publishing.

—Let's Go to the Zoo!/Vamos Al Zoologico! Rosa-Mendoza, Gladys. 2007. (English Spanish Foundations Ser.). (ENG & SPA.). 20p. (J). (gr. -1-k). bds. 6.95 *(978-1-931398-20-6(8))* Me+Mi Publishing.

—Liberty Saves the Day! Heald, Robin. 2017. (J). *(978-0-87935-290-5(6))* Colonial Williamsburg Foundation.

—No Lleves Tu Dragón a la Biblioteca. Gassman, Julie. (Cuentos Ilustrados de Ficción Ser.).Tr. of Do Not Bring Your Dragon to the Library. (SPA.). 32p. (J). (gr. -1-2). 2020. pap. 7.95 *(978-1-5158-6086-0(8),* 142362); 2019. lib. bdg. 21.32 *(978-1-5158-4667-3(9),* 141304) Capstone. (Picture Window Bks.).

—No Lleves Tu Dragón Al Recreo. Gassman, Julie. 2019. (Cuentos Ilustrados de Ficción Ser.). (SPA.). 32p. (J). (gr. -1-2). lib. bdg. 21.32 *(978-1-5158-4666-6(0),* 141303, Picture Window Bks.) Capstone.

—Stinky! Bryant, Ann. 2014. (Race Ahead with Reading Ser.). (ENG.). 32p. (J). (gr. 2-2). *(978-0-7787-1289-3(3))* Crabtree Publishing Co.

—Three Cheers for Liberty! Trumbore, Cindy. 2016. 126p. (J). pap. *(978-0-87935-287-5(6))* Colonial Williamsburg Foundation.

—We Both Read - Changing Places. Panec, D. J. 2017. (ENG.). 41p. (J). 9.95 *(978-1-60115-297-8(3))* Treasure Bay, Inc.

—When You're Feeling Sick. Bowles, Coy. 2017. 32p. (J). (gr. -1-2). 12.99 *(978-0-399-55286-1(3),* Doubleday Bks. for Young Readers) Random Hse. Children's Bks.

Elkina, Ekaterina. Animal World: 9 Mini Board Book Box Set. Clever Publishing. 2019. (Clever Mini Board Bks.). (ENG.). 54p. (J). (gr. -1 — 1). bds. 16.99 *(978-1-948418-52-2(5),* 321906) Clever Media Group.

—Clever Baby: 9 Mini Board Book Box Set. Clever Publishing. 2019. (Clever Mini Board Bks.). (ENG.). 54p. (J). (gr. -1 —

1). bds. 16.99 *(978-1-948418-51-5(7),* 321907) Clever Media Group.

—Riddle Cards: Memory Flash Cards. Clever Publishing. 2018. (Clever Big Box Of Ser.). (ENG.). 20p. (J). (gr. -1 — 1). 14.99 *(978-1-948418-44-7(4))* Clever Media Group.

Elkorek, Alexander. The Forgotten Daughter. Snedeker, Caroline Dale. 2005. 206p. (J). per. 14.95 *(978-0-9667067-6-5(5))* American Home-School Publishing, LLC.

—The Spartan. Snedeker, Caroline Dale. 2005. (YA). per. 15.95 *(978-0-9667067-8-9(1))* American Home-School Publishing, LLC.

—Twelve Bright Trumpets. 2004. 198p. (J). per. 14.95 *(978-0-9667067-5-8(7))* American Home-School Publishing, LLC.

Ella, Peter Leo. Isiumanu & Manubada. Baia, Edward. 2013. 30p. pap. *(978-9980-86-493-2(1))* Univ. of Papua New Guinea Pr.

Ella, Peter Leo. Class Party on the Big Yellow School Bus. Ella, Peter Leo. 2013. 28p. pap. *(978-9980-86-513-7(X))* Univ. of Papua New Guinea Pr.

Ella, Peter Leo, jt. illus. see Mape, Michael.

Ellams, Victoria. Grumpy Ted: The Teds Volume One. Whitley-Kinzett, Sara. 2009. 16p. pap. 10.65 *(978-1-4251-0051-3(1))* Trafford Publishing.

Ellenbogen, Keith. The Octopus Scientists. Montgomery, Sy. 2015. (Scientists in the Field Ser.). (ENG.). 80p. (J). (gr. 5-7). 18.99 *(978-0-544-23270-9(4),* 1564095, HMH Books For Young Readers) Houghton Mifflin Harcourt Publishing Co.

Ellenbogen, Keith, photos by. Amazon Adventure: How Tiny Fish Are Saving the World's Largest Rainforest. Montgomery, Sy. 2017. (Scientists in the Field Ser.). (ENG.). 80p. (J). (gr. 5-7). 18.99 *(978-0-544-35299-5(8),* 1586365, HMH Books For Young Readers) Houghton Mifflin Harcourt Publishing Co.

Eller, Jerod R. My Grandfather's Farm. West, Stephen Earl. 2011. 20p. pap. 24.95 *(978-1-4560-6628-4(5))* America Star Bks.

Eller, Sydney. Where Do Socks Go? McCord, Joseph Lennon. 2012. 32p. pap. 24.95 *(978-1-4626-6624-9(8))* America Star Bks.

Ellerby, Marc. Love the Way You Love. Rich, Jamie S. 2006. (J). *(978-1-932664-52-2(1))* Oni Pr., Inc.

Ellery, Amanda, jt. illus. see Ellery, Tom.

Ellery, Tom. If I Had a Dragon. Ellery, Amanda. 2006. (ENG.). 40p. (J). (gr. -1-3). 19.99 *(978-1-4169-0924-8(9),* Simon & Schuster Bks. For Young Readers) Simon & Schuster Bks. For Young Readers.

—If I Were a Jungle Animal. Ellery, Amanda. 2009. (ENG.). 40p. (J). (gr. -1-3). 19.99 *(978-1-4169-3778-4(1),* Simon & Schuster Bks. For Young Readers) Simon & Schuster Bks. For Young Readers.

Ellery, Tom & Ellery, Amanda. If I Had a Dragon/Si Yo Tuviera un Dragon. Mlawer, Teresa. 2006. (ENG & SPA.). (J). (gr. -1-3). per. 3.99 *(978-1-933032-17-7(0));* 32p. (gr. 5-6). 12.99 *(978-1-933032-16-0(2))* Lectorum Pubns., Inc.

Ellie, Colton. The Lullabible Storybook. Elkins, Stephen. 2006. (Lulla-Bible Ser.). 37p. (J). (gr. -1). 14.99 incl. audio compact disk *(978-0-8054-4185-7(9))* B&H Publishing Group.

Ellie, Norton. Rainbow Neigh Neigh. Friedman, Joyce Miriam. 2017. (ENG.). 34p. (J). pap. 8.99 *(978-0-578-48355-9(6))* Joyce Miriam Friedman.

Elling, Lars. The Dream Factory Starring Anna & Henry. Sortland, Bjorn. Christianson, Emily V. & Hedin, Robert, trs. from NOR. 2003. (Picture Bks.). 40p. (J). (gr. -1-3). 15.95 *(978-0-87614-009-3(6),* Carolrhoda Bks.) Lerner Publishing Group.

—The Story of the Search for the Story. Sortland, Bjorn. 2003. (Picture Bks.). 40p. (J). (gr. -1-3). 15.95 *(978-1-57505-375-2(6),* Carolrhoda Bks.) Lerner Publishing Group.

Ellingsworth, Colleen. Sam's Harvest Party, 1 vol. Farrell, Connie. 2009. 29p. pap. 24.95 *(978-1-60813-937-8(9))* America Star Bks.

Elliot, David. High Rhulain. Jacques, Brian. 2007. (Redwall Ser.). 320p. (gr. 3-7). 18.00 *(978-0-7569-7763-4(0))* Perfection Learning Corp.

—The Sable Quean. Jacques, Brian. ed. 2012. (Redwall Ser.: 21). lib. bdg. 19.65 *(978-0-606-23646-1(5))* Turtleback.

—The Smell of Powder: A History of Duelling in New Zealand. Kerr, Donald. 2006. 160p. pap. *(978-1-86941-813-7(1))* Random Hse. New Zealand.

Elliot, David. Henry's Map. Elliot, David. 2013. (ENG.). 40p. (J). (gr. -1-3). 17.99 *(978-0-399-16072-1(8),* Philomel Bks.) Penguin Young Readers Group.

—Henry's Stars. Elliot, David. 2015. (ENG.). 40p. (J). (gr. k-3). 16.99 *(978-0-399-17116-1(9),* Philomel Bks.) Penguin Young Readers Group.

—Oink. Elliot, David. 2019. (ENG.). 32p. (J). (gr. -1-k). 16.99 *(978-1-77657-214-4(9))* Gecko Pr. NZL. Dist: Lerner Publishing Group.

Elliot, David & Schoenherr, Ian. The Angel's Command. Jacques, Brian. 2005. (Castaways of the Flying Dutchman Ser.). (ENG.). 384p. (J). (gr. 3-7). 7.99 *(978-0-14-240285-6(0),* Firebird) Penguin Young Readers Group.

Elliot, Enid. And Some Who Dream: A Tale of Tiny Bats. Justice, Wanda E. Justice, Clive L., ed. 2016. (ENG.). 32p. (J). (gr. k-6). pap. *(978-0-9920461-6-3(5))* BC Bigleaf Maple Book ltd.

Elliot, Lee, photos by. I Am Beautiful, for All the Children of the World, 1 vol. Brown, Ayanna. 2010. 20p. pap. 24.95 *(978-1-4489-8112-0(3))* PublishAmerica, Inc.

Elliot, Mark. Yukon: Sled Dog, 0 vols. Presnall, Judith Janda. 2013. (ENG.). 32p. (J). (gr. 1-8). 17.99 *(978-1-4778-1731-5(X),* 9781477817315, Two Lions) Amazon Publishing.

Elliot, Rebecca. My Daddy. Hubery, Julia. 2014. (J). *(978-1-4351-5507-7(6))* Barnes & Noble, Inc.

Elliot, Thomas. Good Night Sleepy Caterpillar. Hegarty, Patricia. 2018. (ENG.). 22p. (J). (gr. -1 — 1). bds. 7.99 *(978-1-68412-248-6(1),* Silver Dolphin Bks.) Printers Row Publishing Group.

Elliott, Ann T. Barn Mouse, Farm House. Smith, Kirsten a. 2018. (ENG.). 34p. (J). pap. 12.99 *(978-0-692-18507-0(0))* Elliott, Ann T.

Elliott, Gertrude. Two Little Gardeners. Hurd, Edith Thacher & Brown, Margaret Wise. 2006. (Little Golden Book Ser.). 32p. (J). (gr. -1-2). 4.99 *(978-0-375-83529-2(6),* Golden Bks.) Random Hse. Children's Bks.

Elliott, Helen. Paradise Found. Milton, John. 2019. (ENG.). 36p. (J). (gr. k-4). E-Book 11.99 *(978-1-912213-64-1(8))* Graffeg Limited GBR. Dist: Independent Pubs. Group.

Elliott, Jane. Dog's Christmas Present. MacGregor, Cynthia. 2018. (ENG.). 28p. (J). (gr. 1-6). pap. 9.99 *(978-1-68160-634-7(8))* Crimson Cloak Publishing.

Elliott, John. Pope Pius XII: Bilingual Coloring Book. Marchione, Margherita. 2004. (SPA & ENG.). 32p. 1.00 *(978-0-8091-6721-0(2),* 6721-2) Paulist Pr.

Elliott, Joyce L. Heroes Were Made On 9/11, 1 vol. Rodriguez, Cindy L. 2010. 26p. 24.95 *(978-1-4489-6070-5(3))* PublishAmerica, Inc.

Elliott, Judith. Arcadia. Ighamre, Odiri. 2018. (ENG.). 44p. (J). pap. *(978-1-912092-59-8(X))* Arkbound.

Elliott, Julia. Where Did God Come From? Elliott, Julia. 2005. (J). 15.95 *(978-0-9764129-0-8(X))* Rain Tree Bks.

Elliott, Luke. Jeffrey's Great Day. Henkel, Pat. 2012. 16p. pap. 24.95 *(978-1-4626-7993-5(5))* America Star Bks.

Elliott, Mark. About Average. Clements, Andrew. (ENG.). (J). (gr. 3-7). 2014. 144p. pap. 7.99 *(978-1-4169-9725-2(3));* 2012. 128p. 16.99 *(978-1-4169-9724-5(5))* Simon & Schuster Children's Publishing. (Atheneum Bks. for Young Readers).

—Dexter the Tough. Haddix, Margaret Peterson. 2008. (ENG.). 144p. (J). (gr. 2-5). pap. 6.99 *(978-1-4169-1170-8(7));* 2007. 141p. pap. 7.99 *(978-0-15-377020-3(1));* 2007. (ENG.). 144p. (J). (gr. 2-5). 17.99 *(978-1-4169-1159-3(6))* Simon & Schuster Bks. For Young Readers. (Simon & Schuster Bks. For Young Readers).

—Extra Credit. Clements, Andrew. (ENG.). (J). (gr. 3-7). 2011. 224p. pap. 7.99 *(978-1-4169-4931-2(3));* 2009. 192p. 18.99 *(978-1-4169-4929-9(1))* Simon & Schuster Children's Publishing. (Atheneum Bks. for Young Readers).

—Grandpa Has a Great Big Face. Hanson, Warren. 2006. 32p. (J). (gr. -1-3). 17.89 *(978-0-06-078776-9(7),* Geringer, Laura Book) HarperCollins Pubs.

—I Am Helen Keller. Norwich, Grace. 2012. (I Am Ser.: 3). (ENG.). 128p. (J). (gr. 3-5). pap. 5.99 *(978-0-545-44779-9(8))* Scholastic, Inc.

—Little Joe. Neil Wallace, Sandra. 2011. 192p. (J). (gr. 3-7). 6.99 *(978-0-375-85450-7(9),* Yearling) Random Hse. Children's Bks.

—Lost & Found. Clements, Andrew. (ENG.). (J). (gr. 3-7). 2010. 192p. pap. 7.99 *(978-1-4169-0986-6(9));* 2008. 176p. 16.99 *(978-1-4169-0985-9(0))* Simon & Schuster Children's Publishing. (Atheneum Bks. for Young Readers).

—No Talking. Clements, Andrew. (ENG.). 160p. (J). (gr. 3-7). 2009. pap. 7.99 *(978-1-4169-0984-2(2));* 2007. 19.99 *(978-1-4169-0983-5(4))* Simon & Schuster Children's Publishing. (Atheneum Bks. for Young Readers).

—No Talking. Clements, Andrew. l.t. ed. 2007. (Literacy Bridge Middle Reader Ser.). 155p. (J). (gr. 3-7). 23.95 *(978-1-4104-0294-3(0))* Thorndike Pr.

—The Princess Tales, Volume 2, No. 2. Levine, Gail Carson. 2004. (Princess Tales Ser.). (ENG.). 256p. (J). (gr. 2-7). pap. 9.99 *(978-0-06-056043-0(6),* HarperCollins) HarperCollins Pubs. Ltd. GBR. Dist: HarperCollins Pubs.

—Room One: A Mystery or Two. Clements, Andrew. (ENG.). (J). (gr. 3-7). 2008. 192p. pap. 7.99 *(978-0-689-86687-6(9));* 2006. 176p. 19.99 *(978-0-689-86686-9(0))* Simon & Schuster Children's Publishing. (Atheneum Bks. for Young Readers).

—Thomas Jefferson: A Day at Monticello. Chew, Elizabeth V. 2014. (ENG.). 56p. (J). (gr. 3-7). 18.95 *(978-1-4197-0541-0(5),* Abrams Bks. for Young Readers) Abrams, Inc.

—Troublemaker. Clements, Andrew. (ENG.). (J). (gr. 3-7). 2013. 176p. pap. 7.99 *(978-1-4169-4932-9(1));* 2011. 160p. lib. bdg. 16.99 *(978-1-4169-4930-5(5))* Simon & Schuster Children's Publishing. (Atheneum Bks. for Young Readers).

—What Sank the World's Biggest Ship? And Other Questions About... The Titanic. Carson, Mary Kay. 2012. (Good Question! Ser.). 32p. (J). pap. 5.95 *(978-1-4027-8733-1(2))* Sterling Publishing Co., Inc.

—When Jackie & Hank Met, 0 vols. Fishman, Cathy Goldberg. 2012. (ENG.). 40p. (J). (gr. 2-5). 17.99 *(978-0-7614-6140-1(X),* 9780761461401, Two Lions) Amazon Publishing.

Elliott, Mark & Hunt, Robert. Did It All Start with a Snowball Fight? And Other Questions about... The American Revolution. Carson, Mary Kay. 2012. (Good Question! Ser.). 32p. (J). pap. 5.95 *(978-1-4027-8734-8(0))* Sterling Publishing Co., Inc.

Elliott, Neil. Can You Crack Them? Bentel, Erica & Bentel Family Trust Staff. 2012. 32p. pap. *(978-0-9753548-0-3(9))* Palm Publishing LLC.

Elliott, Rebecca, et al. Five Little Monkeys: And Other Counting Rhymes. 2004. (Mother Goose Ser.). (ENG.). 36p. (J). 15.95 *(978-1-59249-523-8(0),* 1D026) Soundprints.

—Five Little Monkeys: And Other Counting Rhymes. Studio Mouse Staff. rev. ed. 2007. (ENG.). 24p. (J). (gr. -1-k). 4.99 *(978-1-59069-608-8(5))* Studio Mouse LLC.

Elliott, Rebecca. I Can Learn Times Tables: With Magnetic Numbers to Use Again & Again! Baxter, Nicola. 2013. (ENG.). 16p. (J). (gr. -1-7). bds. 17.99 *(978-1-84322-986-5(2),* Armadillo) Anness Publishing GBR. Dist: National Bk. Network.

—Kaleidoscope Book: My First Book of Learning. Baxter, Nicola. 2013. (ENG.). 16p. bds. 16.99 *(978-1-84322-930-8(7),* Armadillo) Anness Publishing GBR. Dist: National Bk. Network.

—Learn about Our World. Baxter, Nicola. 2013. (ENG.). 16p. (J). (gr. k-2). bds. 17.99 *(978-1-84322-985-8(4),* Armadillo) Anness Publishing GBR. Dist: National Bk. Network.

—Learn to Count. Baxter, Nicola. 2013. (ENG.). 16p. (J). (gr. -1-2). bds. 17.99 *(978-1-84322-984-1(6),* Armadillo) Anness Publishing GBR. Dist: National Bk. Network.

—Learn to Tell Time: With Magnets to Use Again & Again! Baxter, Nicola. 2013. (ENG.). 16p. (J). (gr. -1-12). bds. 17.99 *(978-1-84322-638-3(3),* Armadillo) Anness Publishing GBR. Dist: National Bk. Network.

—Millie the Millipede: Collects Colors as She Munches Her Way Through the Pages. Top That Publishing Staff, ed. 2007. (Story Book Ser.). 20p. (J). (gr. -1). bds. *(978-1-84666-274-4(5),* Tide Mill Pr.) Top That! Publishing PLC.

—Monkey Tumbles. Wang, Margaret. 2007. (ENG.). 10p. (gr. -1-k). bds. 9.95 *(978-1-58117-501-1(9),* Intervisual/Piggy Toes) Bendon, Inc.

—My Nativity Jigsaw Book, 1 vol. Goodings, Christina. 2009. 12p. (J). bds. 9.99 *(978-0-8254-7888-8(X),* Lion Children's) Lion Hudson PLC GBR. Dist: Kregel Pubns.

—Who Ate All the Lettuce? Munton, Gill. Top That Publishing Staff, ed. 2007. 12p. (gr. -1-k). bds. *(978-1-84666-177-8(3),* Tide Mill Pr.) Top That! Publishing PLC.

Elliott, Rebecca. Baxter Is Missing - A Branches Book. Elliott, Rebecca. 2017. (Owl Diaries: 6). (ENG.). 80p. (J). (gr. k-2). pap. 4.99 *(978-1-338-04284-9(X))* Scholastic, Inc.

—Baxter Is Missing: a Branches Book (Owl Diaries #6) Elliott, Rebecca. 2017. (Owl Diaries: 6). (ENG.). 80p. (J). (gr. k-2). lib. bdg. 15.99 *(978-1-338-04285-6(8))* Scholastic, Inc.

—Bo the Brave: a Branches Book. Elliott, Rebecca. 2020. (Unicorn Diaries: 3). (ENG.). 80p. (J). (gr. k-2). pap. 4.99 *(978-1-338-32342-9(3))* Scholastic, Inc.

—Una Boda en el Bosque. Elliott, Rebecca. 2017. (Diario de una Lechuza Ser.: 3). (SPA.). 80p. (J). (gr. k-2). pap. 4.99 *(978-1-338-15905-9(4));* lib. bdg. 15.99 *(978-1-338-18790-8(2))* Scholastic, Inc. (Scholastic en Espanol).

—El Día de Corazones Cálidos. Elliott, Rebecca. 2018. (Diario de una Lechuza Ser.: 5). Orig. Title: Owl Diaries #5: Warm Hearts Day. (SPA.). 80p. (J). (gr. 2-5). pap. 4.99 *(978-1-338-15906-6(2))* Scholastic, Inc.

—Diario de una Lechuza #8: Eva y el Poni Perdido: Un Libro de la Serie Branches. Elliott, Rebecca. 2019. (Diario de una Lechuza Ser.: 8). (SPA.). 80p. (J). (gr. k-2). pap. 4.99 *(978-1-338-60120-6(2),* Scholastic en Espanol) Scholastic, Inc.

—Eva & Baby Mo. Elliott, Rebecca. 2019. (Owl Diaries: 10). (ENG.). 80p. (J). (gr. k-2). pap. 4.99 *(978-1-338-29857-4(7));* lib. bdg. 24.99 *(978-1-338-29858-1(5))* Scholastic, Inc.

—Eva & the Lost Pony. Elliott, Rebecca. 2018. (Owl Diaries: 8). (ENG.). 80p. (J). (gr. k-2). lib. bdg. 24.99 *(978-1-338-16304-9(3))* Scholastic, Inc.

—Eva & the Lost Pony: A Branches Book. Elliott, Rebecca. 2018. (Owl Diaries: 8). (ENG.). 80p. (J). (gr. k-2). pap. 4.99 *(978-1-338-16303-2(5))* Scholastic, Inc.

—Eva & the New Owl. Elliott, Rebecca. 2016. (Owl Diaries: 4). (ENG.). 80p. (J). (gr. k-2). pap. 4.99 *(978-0-545-82559-7(8))* Scholastic, Inc.

—Eva Sees a Ghost. Elliott, Rebecca. 2015. (Owl Diaries: 2). (ENG.). 80p. (J). (gr. k-2). 15.99 *(978-0-545-78784-0(X));* pap. 4.99 *(978-0-545-78783-3(1))* Scholastic, Inc.

—Eva y la Nueva Lechuza. Elliott, Rebecca. 2017. (Diario de una Lechuza Ser.: 4). (SPA.). 80p. (J). (gr. -1-3). pap. 4.99 *(978-1-338-18792-2(9));* (gr. k-2). lib. bdg. 15.99 *(978-1-338-23346-9(7))* Scholastic, Inc.

—Eva's Big Sleepover. Elliott, Rebecca. 2018. (Owl Diaries: 9). (ENG.). 80p. (J). (gr. k-2). pap. 4.99 *(978-1-338-16306-3(X))* Scholastic, Inc.

—Eva's Treetop Festival, Bk. 1. Elliott, Rebecca. 2015. (Owl Diaries: 1). (ENG.). 80p. (J). (gr. k-2). pap. 4.99 *(978-0-545-68362-3(9))* Scholastic, Inc.

—Gastón Ha Desaparecido. Elliott, Rebecca. 2018. (Diario de una Lechuza Ser.: 6). (SPA.). 80p. (J). (gr. k-2). pap. 4.99 *(978-1-338-32973-5(1),* Scholastic en Espanol) Scholastic, Inc.

—God Bless This Starry Night, 1 vol. Elliott, Rebecca. ed. 2016. (ENG.). 10p. (J). (— 1). bds. 7.99 *(978-0-7459-6558-1(X))* Lion Hudson PLC GBR. Dist: Kregel Pubns.

—God Loves Little Me, 1 vol. Elliott, Rebecca. ed. 2016. (ENG.). 10p. (J). (— 1). bds. 7.99 *(978-0-7459-6559-8(8))* Lion Hudson PLC GBR. Dist: Independent Pubs. Group.

—Missing Jack. Elliott, Rebecca. ed. 2015. (ENG.). 32p. (J). (gr. -1-k). 12.99 *(978-0-7459-6502-4(4))* Lion Hudson PLC GBR. Dist: Independent Pubs. Group.

—Noah's Noisy Animals, 1 vol. Elliott, Rebecca. ed. 2016. (ENG.). 5p. (J). (— 1). bds. 7.99 *(978-0-7459-6561-1(X))* Lion Hudson PLC GBR. Dist: Independent Pubs. Group.

—La Pastelería del Bosque Salvaje. Elliott, Rebecca. 2019. (Diario de una Lechuza Ser.: 7). (SPA.). 80p. (J). (gr. k-2). pap. 4.99 *(978-1-338-35914-5(2),* Scholastic en Espanol) Scholastic, Inc.

—Sometimes. Elliott, Rebecca. (ENG.). 32p. (J). (gr. k-2). 2012. 14.99 *(978-0-7459-6297-9(1));* 2011. pap. 7.99 *(978-0-7459-6269-6(6))* Lion Hudson PLC GBR. Dist: Independent Pubs. Group.

—Warm Hearts Day: A Branches Book. Elliott, Rebecca. 2016. (Owl Diaries: 5). (ENG.). 80p. (J). (gr. k-2). pap. 4.99 *(978-1-338-04280-1(7))* Scholastic, Inc.

—The Wildwood Bakery. Elliott, Rebecca. 2017. (Owl Diaries: 7). (ENG.). 80p. (J). (gr. k-2). pap. 4.99 *(978-1-338-16300-1(0));* lib. bdg. 15.99 *(978-1-338-16301-8(9))* Scholastic, Inc.

—A Woodland Wedding. Elliott, Rebecca. 2016. (Owl Diaries: 3). (ENG.). 80p. (J). (gr. k-2). 24.99 *(978-0-545-82558-0(X))* Scholastic, Inc.

—Zoo Girl. Elliott, Rebecca. (ENG.). 32p. (J). (gr. k-2). 2012. 14.99 *(978-0-7459-6323-5(4));* 2011. pap. 7.99 *(978-0-7459-6270-2(X))* Lion Hudson PLC GBR. Dist: Independent Pubs. Group.

Elliott, Ruth. Little Blossom, 1 disc. Elliott, Ruth. Culiquipuma, Diana y. Jose, tr. 2008. (ENG & SPA.). 26p. (J). per. 12.99 incl. DVD *(978-0-9795017-2-2(5))* Edu Designs.

—The Night Princess, 1 disc. Elliott, Ruth. 2007. (SPA.). (J). per. 12.99 incl. DVD *(978-0-9795017-1-5(7))* Edu Designs.

—The Richest Kid in the Poor House. Elliott, Ruth. Elliott, David. 2008. (J). pap. *(978-0-9795017-4-6(1))* Edu Designs.

—See What You're Looking At. Elliott, Ruth. 2008. (J). 27.00 *(978-0-9795017-0-8(9))* Edu Designs.

Elliott, Thomas. Baby 101: Anatomy for Babies. Litton, Jonathan. 2018. (Baby 101 Ser.). (ENG.). 22p. (J). (— 1). bds. 8.99 *(978-0-525-64877-2(1),* Doubleday Bks. for Young Readers) Random Hse. Children's Bks.

—Baby 101: Architecture for Babies. Litton, Jonathan. 2018. (Baby 101 Ser.). (ENG.). 22p. (J). (— 1). bds. 8.99 *(978-0-525-64880-2(1),* Doubleday Bks. for Young Readers) Random Hse. Children's Bks.

—Baby 101: Botany for Babies. Litton, Jonathan. 2018. (Baby 101 Ser.). (ENG.). 22p. (J). (— 1). bds. 8.99 *(978-0-525-64878-9(X),* Doubleday Bks. for Young Readers) Random Hse. Children's Bks.

—Baby 101: Zoology for Babies. Litton, Jonathan. 2018. (Baby 101 Ser.). (ENG.). 22p. (J). (— 1). bds. 8.99 *(978-0-525-64879-6(8),* Doubleday Bks. for Young Readers) Random Hse. Children's Bks.

—Good Night Farm. Hegarty, Patricia. 2016. (ENG.). 18p. (J). (gr. -1-k). bds. 12.99 *(978-1-58925-233-2(0))* Tiger Tales.

—I Love You, Little One. Hegarty, Patricia. 2017. (ENG.). 18p. (J). (gr. -1-k). bds. 12.99 *(978-1-58925-241-7(1))* Tiger Tales.

—Night Night, Dino-Snores. Edwards, Nicola. 2018. (ENG.). 22p. (J). (gr. -1-k). bds. 12.99 *(978-1-68010-548-3(5))* Tiger Tales.

Elliott, Tori. The Phlunk's Worldwide Symphony. Rhodes, Lou. 2014. (ENG.). 32p. (J). pap. *(978-0-9573690-2-3(6))* Strata Bks.

Elliott, Victoria Grace. Ellen Degeneres. Little Bee Books. 2020. (People of Pride Ser.). (ENG.). 22p. (J). (gr. -1-k). bds. 6.99 *(978-1-4998-1015-8(6))* Little Bee Books Inc.

Elliott, Victoria Grace. Harvey Milk. Little Bee Books. 2020. (People of Pride Ser.). (ENG.). 22p. (J). (gr. -1-k). bds. 6.99 ***(978-1-4998-1016-5(4))*** Little Bee Books Inc.

Ellis, Amy. Job-O E: Elementary. Ferry, Francis. 3rd ed. 2003. (Job-O Ser.). (J). *(978-1-887481-43-4(5))* CFKR Career Materials, Inc.

Ellis, Andy. Just for You! Leeson, Christine. (Tiger Tales Ser.). (J). 2008. 24p. (gr. -1-2). pap. 6.95 *(978-1-58925-408-4(2));* 2004. 32p. tchr. ed. 15.95 *(978-1-58925-042-0(7))* Tiger Tales.

—The Midnight Mouse. Baglio, Ben M. 2003. 59p. (J). *(978-0-439-41916-1(6))* Scholastic, Inc.

Ellis, Brendan. A Day to Remember at the Giant's Causeway. Carville, Declan. 29p. (J). (gr. 2-5). pap. 7.95 *(978-0-9538222-0-1(6))* Discovery Pubns. GBR. Dist: Irish Bks. & Media, Inc.

Ellis, Carson. The Beautiful Stories of Life: Six Greek Myths, Retold. Rylant, Cynthia. 2009. (ENG.). 88p. (J). (gr. 5-7). 17.99 *(978-0-15-206184-5(3),* 1098959) Houghton Mifflin Harcourt Publishing Co.

—The Composer Is Dead. Snicket, Lemony. 2009. (ENG.). 40p. (J). (gr. k-5). 17.99 *(978-0-06-123627-3(6))* HarperCollins Pubs.

—The Mysterious Benedict Society. Stewart, Trenton Lee. (Mysterious Benedict Society Ser.: 1). (ENG.). (J). (gr. 3-7). 2008. 512p. pap. 9.99 *(978-0-316-00395-7(6));* 2007. 496p. 19.00 *(978-0-316-05777-6(0),* Tingley, Megan Bks.) Little, Brown Bks. for Young Readers.

—The Mysterious Benedict Society. Stewart, Trenton Lee. ed. 2008. (Mysterious Benedict Society Ser.: 1). 485p. (J). (gr. 3-7). lib. bdg. 19.65 *(978-1-4178-1817-4(4))* Turtleback.

—The Mysterious Benedict Society: 10th Anniversary Edition. Stewart, Trenton Lee. 2017. (Mysterious Benedict Society Ser.: 1). (ENG.). 528p. (J). (gr. 3-7). 18.99 *(978-0-316-46491-8(0))* Little, Brown Bks. for Young Readers.

—The Shortest Day. Cooper, Susan. 2019. (ENG.). 32p. (J). (gr. k-12). 17.99 *(978-0-7636-8698-7(0))* Candlewick Pr.

—Under Wildwood. Meloy, Colin. (Wildwood Chronicles Ser.: 2). (ENG.). (J). (gr. 3). 2013. 592p. pap. 9.99 *(978-0-06-202473-2(6));* 2012. 576p. 17.99 *(978-0-06-202471-8(X))* HarperCollins Pubs. (Balzer & Bray).

—The Whiz Mob & the Grenadine Kid. Meloy, Colin. (ENG.). 432p. (J). (gr. 3-7). 2019. pap. 8.99 *(978-0-06-234246-1(0));* 2017. 17.99 *(978-0-06-234245-4(2))* HarperCollins Pubs. (Balzer & Bray).

—Wildwood. Meloy, Colin. (Wildwood Chronicles Ser.: 1). (ENG.). (J). (gr. 3). 2012. 576p. pap. 9.99 *(978-0-06-202470-1(1));* 2011. 560p. 19.99 *(978-0-06-202468-8(X))* HarperCollins Pubs. (Balzer & Bray).

—Wildwood. Meloy, Colin. ed. 2012. (Wildwood Chronicles Ser.: 1). (J). lib. bdg. 20.85 *(978-0-606-26864-6(2))* Turtleback.

—Wildwood Imperium. Meloy, Colin. (Wildwood Chronicles Ser.: 3). (ENG.). 592p. (J). (gr. 3). 2015. pap. 9.99 *(978-0-06-202476-3(0));* 2014. 17.99 *(978-0-06-202474-9(4))* HarperCollins Pubs. (Balzer & Bray).

Ellis, Carson. Du Iz Tak? Ellis, Carson. 2016. (ENG.). 48p. (J). (gr. -1-3). 16.99 *(978-0-7636-6530-2(4))* Candlewick Pr.

—Hogar. Ellis, Carson. 2020. (SPA.). 40p. (J). (gr. -1-3). 17.99 *(978-1-5362-1067-5(6));* 7.99 *(978-1-5362-1068-2(4))* Candlewick Pr.

—Home. Ellis, Carson. 2015. 40p. (J). (gr. -1-3). 17.99 *(978-0-7636-6529-6(0))* Candlewick Pr.

Ellis, Christina, jt. illus. see Joyce, William.

Ellis, Elina. Jesus Loves the Little Children, 1 vol. 2019. (Sing-Along Book Ser.). (ENG.). 20p. (J). bds. 8.99 *(978-0-310-75928-7(5))* Zonderkidz.

E

—Joseph's Dreamcoat & Other Stories. David, Juliet. ed. 2019. (ENG.). 48p. (J). (gr. -1-k). 6.99 (978-1-78128-356-1(7)) Lion Hudson PLC GBR. Dist: Independent Pubs. Group.

—Little Boost en Espanol. Jones, Christianne C. 2019. (Pasito a Pasito Ser.). (SPA.). (J). (gr. -1-2). 47.98 (978-1-5158-4690-1(3), 197181, Picture Window Bks.) Capstone.

—Luis Barros, el Chismoso. Jones, Christianne C. 2019. (Pasito a Pasito Ser.). (SPA.). 32p. (J). (gr. -1-2). lib. bdg. 23.99 (978-1-5158-4654-3(7), 141255, Picture Window Bks.) Capstone.

—Miles Mchale, Tattletale. Jones, Christianne C. 2017. (Little Boost Ser.). (ENG.). 32p. (J). (gr. -1-2). lib. bdg. 23.99 (978-1-5158-0752-0(5), Picture Window Bks.) Capstone.

—My Little Picture Bible, 1 vol. David, Juliet. ed. 2015. (ENG.). 160p. (J). (gr. -1-k). 9.99 (978-1-78128-176-5(9), Candle Bks.) Lion Hudson PLC GBR. Dist: Independent Pubs. Group.

Ellis, Elina. Pasito a Pasito. Jones, Christianne C. 2020. (Pasito a Pasito Ser.).Tr. of Little Boost. (SPA.). (J). (gr. -1-1). 95.96 **(978-1-5158-7205-4(X)**, 200726); pap., pap., pap. 29.85 **(978-1-5158-7339-6(0)**, 201796) Capstone. (Picture Window Bks.).

Ellis, Elina. The Reptile Club. Fergus, Maureen. 2018. (ENG.). 32p. (J). (gr. -1-2). 16.99 (978-1-77138-655-5(X)) Kids Can Pr., Ltd. CAN. Dist: Hachette Bk. Group.

—Stories of Jesus. David, Juliet. ed. 2019. (ENG.). 48p. (J). (gr. -1-k). 6.99 (978-1-78128-357-8(5)) Lion Hudson PLC GBR. Dist: Independent Pubs. Group.

—There Was an Old Giant Who Swallowed a Clock. Davies, Becky. 2018. (ENG.). 32p. (J). (gr. -1-2). 16.99 (978-1-68010-076-1(9)) Tiger Tales.

Ellis, Elina. This Is the Path the Wolf Took. Farina, Laura. 2020. (ENG.). 40p. (J). (gr. -1-2). 18.99 **(978-1-5253-0153-7(5))** Kids Can Pr., Ltd. CAN. Dist: Hachette Bk. Group.

—99 Prayers for Children. David, Juliet. ed. 2020. (ENG.). 108p. (J). (gr. -1). 7.99 **(978-1-78128-405-6(9)**, Candle Bks.) Lion Hudson PLC GBR. Dist: Independent Pubs. Group.

—99 Stories from the Bible. David, Juliet. ed. 2020. (ENG.). 196p. (J). (gr. -1-k). 12.99 **(978-1-78128-387-5(7)**, Candle Bks.) Lion Hudson PLC GBR. Dist: Independent Pubs. Group.

Ellis, Gerry. Chimpanzees. Ellis, Gerry, photos by. Kane, Karen. 2004. (Early Bird Nature Bks.). (ENG.). 48p. (gr. 2-5). 26.60 (978-0-8225-2418-2(X), Lerner Pubns.) Lerner Publishing Group.

Ellis, Jan Davey. It's Back to School We Go! First Day Stories Fro Around the World. Jackson, Ellen B. 2003. 32p. lib. bdg. 23.90 (978-0-7613-2562-8(X), Millbrook Pr.) Lerner Publishing Group.

—It's Back to School We Go! First Day Stories from Around the World. Jackson, Ellen. 2003. (ENG.). 32p. (J). (gr. k-3). 19.99 (978-0-7613-1948-1(4), Millbrook Pr.) Lerner Publishing Group.

—Skillet Bread, Sourdough, & Vinegar Days: Cooking in Pioneer Days. Ichord, Loretta Frances & Millbrook Press. 2005. 64p. (J). (gr. 4-8). per. 8.95 (978-0-7613-9521-8(0), First Avenue Editions) Lerner Publishing Group.

—Turn of the Century: Eleven Centuries of Children & Change. Jackson, Ellen. 2003. 32p. (J). (gr. k-3). pap. 8.95 (978-0-88106-370-7(3)) Charlesbridge Publishing, Inc.

—The Winter Solstice. Jackson, Ellen. 2003. (Traditions of the Seasons Ser.). (ENG.). 32p. (J). (gr. 3-6). pap. 8.99 (978-0-7613-0297-1(2), First Avenue Editions) Lerner Publishing Group.

Ellis, Jessica. The Gifts of the Spirit, 6 vols. Walters, David. 2005. 64p. (J). pap. 8.95 (978-1-888081-68-8(6)) Good News Fellowship Ministries.

Ellis, Joey. Magic Smells Awful. Manning, Matthew K. 2018. (Xander & the Rainbow-Barfing Unicorns Ser.). (ENG.). 128p. (J). (gr. 3-5). pap. 7.95 (978-1-4965-5719-3(0), 136708); lib. bdg. 22.65 (978-1-4965-5715-5(8), 136704) Capstone. (Stone Arch Bks.).

—Return to Pegasia. Manning, Matthew K. 2018. (Xander & the Rainbow-Barfing Unicorns Ser.). (ENG.). 128p. (J). (gr. 3-5). pap. 7.95 (978-1-4965-5718-6(2), 136707); lib. bdg. 22.65 (978-1-4965-5714-8(X), 136703) Capstone. (Stone Arch Bks.).

—Revenge of the One-Trick Pony. Manning, Matthew K. 2018. (Xander & the Rainbow-Barfing Unicorns Ser.). (ENG.). 128p. (J). (gr. 3-5). pap. 7.95 (978-1-4965-5716-2(6), 136705); lib. bdg. 22.65 (978-1-4965-5712-4(3), 136701) Capstone. (Stone Arch Bks.).

—The Search for Stalor. Manning, Matthew K. 2018. (Xander & the Rainbow-Barfing Unicorns Ser.). (ENG.). 128p. (J). (gr. 3-5). pap. 7.95 (978-1-4965-5717-9(4), 136706); lib. bdg. 22.65 (978-1-4965-5713-1(1), 136702) Capstone. (Stone Arch Bks.).

—A Winter's Dream. Dunn, Hunter S. 2004. 65p. (J). 19.95 (978-0-9761732-0-5(4)) Dunn, Hunter.

—Xander & the Rainbow-Barfing Unicorns, 4 vols. Manning, Matthew K. 2018. (Xander & the Rainbow-Barfing Unicorns Ser.). (ENG.). 128p. (J). (gr. 3-5). 90.60 (978-1-4965-5732-2(8), 27383, Stone Arch Bks.) Capstone.

—Xander & the Rainbow-Barfing Unicorns, 4 vols. Manning, Matthew K. 2018. (Xander & the Rainbow-Barfing Unicorns Ser.). (ENG.). 128p. (J). (gr. 3-5). pap., pap., pap. 31.80 (978-1-4965-5733-9(6), 27384, Stone Arch Bks.) Capstone.

Ellis, Kim & Schulz, Charles. Let's Fly a Kite, Charlie Brown! (Peanuts) Verr, Harry Coe. 2015. (Little Golden Book Ser.). (ENG.). 24p. (J). (gr. -1-1). 4.99 (978-1-101-93519-4(7), Golden Bks.) Random Hse. Children's Bks.

Ellis, Kim, jt. illus. see Schulz, Charles.

Ellis, Lauren. Magnetic Play Fairies. George, Joshua. 2018. (Magnetic Play Ser.). (ENG.). 12p. (J). (gr. -1-1). 12.99 (978-1-78700-261-6(6)) Top That! Publishing PLC GBR. Dist: Independent Pubs. Group.

—Play Felt Magical Unicorns. George, Joshua. 2020. (Soft Felt Play Bks.). (ENG.). 10p. (J). (gr. -1-k). bds. 12.99 (978-1-78958-420-2(5)) Top That! Publishing PLC GBR. Dist: Independent Pubs. Group.

—Princesses. Linn, Susie. 2017. (Search & Find Ser.). (ENG.). 48p. (J). (gr. k-2). pap. 6.99 (978-1-78700-034-6(6)) Top That! Publishing PLC GBR. Dist: Independent Pubs. Group.

—Ten Little Mermaids. Linn, Susie. 2018. (Counting to Ten Bks.). (ENG.). 20p. (J). (gr. -1-1). 9.99 (978-1-78700-375-0(2)) Top That! Publishing PLC GBR. Dist: Independent Pubs. Group.

Ellis, Libby. Riggeldy Jiggeldy Joggeldy Jam: Can You Guess Who I Am? Nelson, Esther & Hirsch, Davida. 2003. (J). bds. 5.95 (978-0-7607-3278-6(7)) Barnes & Noble, Inc.

—Riggeldy Jiggeldy Joggeldy Roo: Can You Guess What I Do? Nelson, Esther & Hirsch, Davida. 2003. (J). bds. 5.95 (978-0-7607-3279-3(5)) Barnes & Noble, Inc.

Ellis, Melissa Martin, photos by. The Redwood Review Summer 2003, 2. Van Gruisen, Janette van de Geest et al. 2003. 183p. (YA). per. 0.00 (978-0-9708317-3-6(0)) Timshel Literature.

Ellis, Steve. The Only Living Girl #1: The Island at the Edge of Infinity. Gallaher, David. 2019. (Only Living Girl Ser.: 1). (ENG.). 72p. (J). 13.99 (978-1-5458-0203-8(3), 900198496); pap. 8.99 (978-1-5458-0202-1(5), 900198497) Papercutz.

—The Only Living Girl #2: Beneath the Unseen City. Gallaher, David. 2020. (Only Living Girl Ser.: 2). (ENG.). 72p. (J). 13.99 (978-1-62991-056-7(2), 900138259); pap. 8.99 (978-1-62991-055-0(4), 900138258) Papercutz.

Ellison, Chris. The Christmas Tree Ship. Crane, Carol. 2011. (ENG.). 32p. (J). (gr. k-6). 15.95 (978-1-58536-285-1(9)) Sleeping Bear Pr.

—Let Them Play. Raven, Margot Theis. 2005. (ENG.). 32p. (J). (gr. 1-4). 17.99 (978-1-58536-260-8(3), 202075) Sleeping Bear Pr.

—The Lucky Star. Young, Judy. 2008. (Tales of Young Americans Ser.). (ENG.). 40p. (J). (gr. 1-4). 17.95 (978-1-58536-348-3(0), 202135) Sleeping Bear Pr.

—M Is for Mom: A Child's Alphabet. Riehle, Mary Ann McCabe. 2009. (ENG.). 32p. (J). (gr. k-6). 17.95 (978-1-58536-458-9(4)) Sleeping Bear Pr.

—Pappy's Handkerchief. Scillian, Devin. rev. ed. 2007. (Tales of Young Americans Ser.). (ENG.). 40p. (J). (gr. 1-4). 17.95 (978-1-58536-316-2(2), 202120) Sleeping Bear Pr.

—Rudy Rides the Rails: A Depression Era Story. Mackall, Dandi Daley. rev. ed. 2007. (Tales of Young Americans Ser.). (ENG.). 40p. (J). (gr. 1-4). 17.95 (978-1-58536-286-8(7), 202097) Sleeping Bear Pr.

—Saint Nicholas: The Real Story of the Christmas Legend. Stiegemeyer, Julie. (J). 2007. 32p. (gr. -1). per. 7.49 (978-0-7586-1341-7(5)); 2005. 16p. (gr. -1-17). bds. 7.49 (978-0-7586-0688-4(5)); 2003. 32p. 13.49 (978-0-7586-0376-0(2)) Concordia Publishing Hse.

—That's My Colt: An Easter Tale. Mackall, Dandi Daley. 2008. 24p. (J). (gr. -1). 13.49 (978-0-7586-1423-0(3)) Concordia Publishing Hse.

Ellison, Chris, et al. Westward Journeys. Scillian, Devin & Young, Judy. 2013. (American Adventures Ser.). (ENG.). 96p. (J). (gr. 3-6). pap. 6.99 (978-1-58536-860-0(1), 202367) Sleeping Bear Pr.

Ellison, Chris & Benny, Mike. America's White Table. Raven, Margot Theis. 2005. (ENG.). 48p. (J). (gr. k-6). 16.95 (978-1-58536-216-5(6)) Sleeping Bear Pr.

Ellithorpe, Chris. Developing Reading Fluency Grade 1: Using Modeled Reading, Phrasing, & Repeated Oral Reading. Callella, Trisha. Fisch, Teri L., ed. 2003. (Developing Reading Fluency Ser.). 96p. (gr. 1-2). per. 14.99 (978-1-57471-994-9(7), 2247) Creative Teaching Pr., Inc.

Ellithorpe, Chris, jt. illus. see Hilliam, Corbin.

Ells, Marcia Louise. Glips, Snodagers & Wallywogs. Ells, Marcia Louise. l.t. ed. 2006. 44p. (J). 6.99 (978-0-9777359-0-7(7)) Marcia's Menagerie.

Ellsworth, Jayden. Gabby's Gumball Garden. Rozumowicz, Sue. 2017. (ENG.). 24p. (J). pap. 10.99 (978-1-948365-01-7(4)) Orange Hat Publishing.

—Three Royal Moons. Rozumowicz, Sue. 2018. (ENG.). 26p. (J). (gr. 3-6). pap. 10.99 (978-1-948365-54-3(5)) Orange Hat Publishing.

Ellwand, David. Twinkle Twinkle Little Star: David Ellwand's Bears. Ellwand, David. 2018. (ENG.). 14p. (J). (— 1). bds. 6.99 (978-1-5362-0220-5(7)) Candlewick Pr.

Ellwand, David. The Mystery of the Fool & the Vanisher. Ellwand, David, photos by. Ellwand, Ruth. 2008. (ENG.). 104p. (J). (gr. 5). 18.99 (978-0-7636-2096-7(3)) Candlewick Pr.

Ellwand, David, photos by. Cinderlily: A Floral Fairy Tale. Ellwand, David, ed. Tagg, Christine. 2006. 26p. (J). (gr. k-4). reprint ed. 17.00 (978-1-4223-5558-9(6)) DIANE Publishing Co.

Ellwell, Tristan. A Wolf at the Door. Datlow, Ellen. Windling, Terri, ed. 2013. (ENG.). 192p. (J). (gr. 4-9). pap. 13.99 (978-1-4814-0167-8(X), Simon & Schuster Bks. For Young Readers) Simon & Schuster Bks. For Young Readers.

Ellwood, Christine Jc. Fred the Alien Visits Earth. Ellwood, Christine Jc. 2019. (ENG.). 50p. (J). pap. 11.11 **(978-1-6861-9922-6(8))** Independently Published.

Elmore, Larry. Penguin Comes Home. Young, Louise O. 2005. (Amazing Animal Adventures Ser.). (ENG.). 36p. (J). (gr. -1-2). 2.95 (978-1-59249-325-8(4), S7158) Soundprints.

—Penguin Comes Home. Young, Louise. 2005. (Soundprints' Amazing Animal Adventures! Ser.). (ENG.). 32p. (J). (gr. -1-2). 9.95 (978-1-59249-329-6(7), PS7158) Soundprints.

—Penguin Comes Home. Young, Louise O. (Amazing Animal Adventures Ser.). (ENG.). (J). (gr. -1-2). 2005. 36p. 15.95 (978-1-59249-324-1(6), B7108); 2005. 32p. 19.95 (978-1-59249-327-2(0), BC7108); 2004. 36p. pap. 6.95 (978-1-59249-326-5(2), S7108) Soundprints.

élo. Birds of a Color. élo. 2018. (ENG.). 20p. (J). (-k). bds. 12.00 (978-1-5362-0063-8(8)) Candlewick Pr.

—Contrary Dogs. élo. 2018. (ENG.). 20p. (J). (-k). bds. 12.00 (978-1-5362-0062-1(X)) Candlewick Pr.

Elphinstone, Katy. Moby Dick. Melville, Herman. 2014. (Travel & Adventure Ser.). (ENG.). 64p. pap. 6.95 (978-1-906230-72-2(2)) Real Reads Ltd. GBR. Dist: Casemate Pubs. & Bk. Distributors, LLC.

—Robinson Crusoe. Dafoe, Daniel. 2014. (Travel & Adventure Ser.). (ENG.). 64p. pap. 6.95 (978-1-906230-71-5(4)) Real Reads Ltd. GBR. Dist: Casemate Pubs. & Bk. Distributors, LLC.

Elsammak, Ariane. House Thirty-One. Melhoff, D. 2014. (ENG.). 62p. (J). pap. (978-0-9921331-5-3(7)) Bellwoods Publishing.

—Noodlehead Stories: World Tales Kids Can Read & Tell. Hamilton, Martha & Weiss, Mitch. 2006. (ENG.). 96p. (J). (gr. 1-6). 24.95 (978-0-87483-584-7(4)) August Hse. Pubs., Inc.

—The Toymaker. Melhoff, D. 2018. (ENG.). 58p. (J). pap. (978-0-9921331-9-1(X)) Bellwoods Publishing.

Elsayed, Sousann. What Is a Muslim? Elsayed, Ali. 2018. (ENG.). 32p. (J). (gr. k-6). 20.00 (978-1-7321600-0-2(7)) Itsy Bitsy Muslims.

Elsby, Lizzy. Pini the Pitcher: A Story for Hanukkah. Osterbach, Batya. 2005. 32p. (J). (gr. 1-4). per. 9.95 (978-1-932687-51-4(3), Devora Publishing) Simcha Media Group.

Elschner, Géraldine. Saint Francis of Assisi. Elschner, Géraldine. 2018. (ENG.). 32p. (J). (gr. k-2). 17.99 (978-988-8341-44-3(8), Minedition) Neugebauer, Michael (Publishing) Limited HKG. Dist: Penguin Random Hse. LLC.

Else, Somebody. Grateful Jill & the Giant. Wilkins, Benjamin. 2019. (ENG.). (J). pap. (978-0-9979086-3-3(7)) Wilson Boulevard Pr.

Elsen, Janis A. As Constant As the Stars. Nees, Diane L. 2012. 36p. 24.95 (978-1-4626-6886-1(0)); pap. 12.99 (978-1-4626-7919-5(6)) America Star Bks.

Elsie, Ralston. The Valley of Hearts: Meditations for Children. Graugaard, Gitte Winter. Harbsmeier, Helle Selma, ed. 2019. (Valley of Hearts Ser.: Vol. 1). (ENG.). 74p. (J). pap. (978-87-93210-26-4(4)) Room for Reflection.

Elsmore, Robert. I Heard a Noise: (... in Our Backyard) McIntosh, Tamey. 2018. (ENG.). 28p. (J). (978-1-5255-2781-4(9)); pap. (978-1-5255-2782-1(7)) FriesenPress.

Elsom, Clare. Animal Family Albums. Guillain, Charlotte & Mason, Paul. 2013. (Animal Family Albums Ser.). (ENG.). 32p. (gr. 2-4). (J). pap., pap., pap. 31.96 (978-1-4109-4944-8(3)); lib. bdg. 125.28 (978-1-4109-4939-4(7)) Capstone. (Raintree).

—Bring on Spring! Katschke, Judy. 2015. 32p. (J). pap. (978-0-545-82337-1(4)) Scholastic, Inc.

—Cats. Guillain, Charlotte. 2013. (Animal Family Albums Ser.). (ENG.). 32p. (J). (gr. 2-4). pap. 8.29 (978-1-4109-4940-0(0)); 31.32 (978-1-4109-4935-6(4)) Capstone. (Raintree).

—Dealing with Feeling... Angry. Thomas, Isabel. 2013. (Dealing with Feeling... Ser.). (ENG.). 24p. (J). (gr. 1-2). pap. 6.79 (978-1-4329-7112-0(3), Heinemann) Capstone.

—Dealing with Feeling... Caring. Thomas, Isabel. 2013. (Dealing with Feeling... Ser.). (ENG.). 24p. (J). (gr. 1-2). pap. 6.79 (978-1-4329-7113-7(1)); lib. bdg. 23.99 (978-1-4329-7104-5(2)) Capstone. (Heinemann).

—Dealing with Feeling Happy, 1 vol. Thomas, Isabel. 2013. (Dealing with Feeling... Ser.). (ENG.). 24p. (J). (gr. 1-2). pap. 6.79 (978-1-4329-7114-4(X), Heinemann) Capstone.

—Dealing with Feeling... Happy. Thomas, Isabel. 2013. (Dealing with Feeling... Ser.). (ENG.). 24p. (J). (gr. 1-2). lib. bdg. 23.99 (978-1-4329-7105-2(0), Heinemann) Capstone.

—Dealing with Feeling... Jealous. Thomas, Isabel. 2013. (Dealing with Feeling... Ser.). (ENG.). 24p. (J). (gr. 1-2). pap. 6.79 (978-1-4329-7115-1(8)); lib. bdg. 23.99 (978-1-4329-7106-9(9)) Capstone. (Heinemann).

—Dealing with Feeling... Proud. Thomas, Isabel. 2013. (Dealing with Feeling... Ser.). (ENG.). 24p. (J). (gr. 1-2). pap. 6.79 (978-1-4329-7116-8(6), Heinemann) Capstone.

—Dealing with Feeling... Sad. Thomas, Isabel. 2013. (Dealing with Feeling... Ser.). (ENG.). 24p. (J). (gr. 1-2). pap. 6.79 (978-1-4329-7117-5(4)); lib. bdg. 23.99 (978-1-4329-7108-3(5)) Capstone. (Heinemann).

—Dealing with Feeling... Shy. Thomas, Isabel. 2013. (Dealing with Feeling... Ser.). (ENG.). 24p. (J). (gr. 1-2). pap. 6.79 (978-1-4329-7118-2(2)); lib. bdg. 23.99 (978-1-4329-7109-0(3)) Capstone. (Heinemann).

—Dealing with Feeling... Worried. Thomas, Isabel. 2013. (Dealing with Feeling... Ser.). (ENG.). 24p. (J). (gr. 1-2). pap. 6.79 (978-1-4329-7119-9(0)); lib. bdg. 23.99 (978-1-4329-7110-6(7)) Capstone. (Heinemann).

—Dogs. Mason, Paul. 2013. (Animal Family Albums Ser.). (ENG.). 32p. (J). (gr. 2-4). pap. 8.29 (978-1-4109-4941-7(9)); 31.32 (978-1-4109-4936-3(2)) Capstone. (Raintree).

—Firefighters to the Rescue! Katschke, Judy. 2016. 32p. (J). pap. (978-0-545-89203-2(1)) Scholastic, Inc.

—First Grade Feast!/By Judy Katschke; Illustrated by Clare Elsom. Katschke, Judy. 2014. 32p. (J). pap. (978-0-545-75844-4(0)) Scholastic, Inc.

—George the Knight. Read, Leon. 2011. (Tadpoles Ser.). (ENG.). (J). (gr. -1-3). lib. bdg. 17.55 (978-1-61383-940-9(5)) Perfection Learning Corp.

—Hooray for the 100th Day! Katschke, Judy. 2015. 32p. (J). (978-0-545-77607-3(4)) Scholastic, Inc.

—Horses & Ponies. Mason, Paul. 2013. (Animal Family Albums Ser.). (ENG.). 32p. (J). (gr. 2-4). pap. 8.29 (978-1-4109-4942-4(7)); 31.32 (978-1-4109-4937-0(0)) Capstone. (Raintree).

—The Last Chocolate Chip Cookie. Rix, Jamie. 2015. (ENG.). 32p. (J). (gr. -1-2). 16.99 (978-1-4998-0086-9(X)) Little Bee Books Inc.

—Our Funny Valentine. Katschke, Judy. 2015. 32p. (J). (978-0-545-77605-9(8)) Scholastic, Inc.

—Rabbits. Guillain, Charlotte. 2013. (Animal Family Albums Ser.). (ENG.). 32p. (J). (gr. 2-4). 31.32 (978-1-4109-4938-7(9), Raintree) Capstone.

—Rabbits - Animal Family Albums. Guillain, Charlotte. 2013. (Animal Family Albums Ser.). (ENG.). 32p. (J). (gr. 2-4). pap. 8.29 (978-1-4109-4943-1(5), Raintree) Capstone.

—Ready, Set, Boo! Katschke, Judy. 2014. 32p. (J). pap. (978-0-545-75843-7(2)) Scholastic, Inc.

—Second Grade Rocks! Katschke, Judy. 2015. 32p. (J). (978-0-545-82338-8(2)) Scholastic, Inc.

Elson, Richard. The Battle of Midway: The Destruction of the Japanese Fleet. Abnett, Dan. 2007. (Graphic Battles of World War II Ser.). (ENG.). 48p. (YA). (gr. 4-7). lib. bdg. 35.45 (978-1-4042-0783-7(X)) Rosen Publishing Group, Inc., The.

Elston, James W. Battling Bigfoot. Simonson, Louise. 2007. (Extreme Monsters Ser.). 94p. (J). (gr. 2-5). per. 3.99 (978-1-57791-275-0(6), Penny Candy Pr.) Brighter Minds Children's Publishing.

—Meet Mr. Hydeous, Vol. 3. Simonson, Louise. gif. ed. 2006. (Extreme Monsters Ser.). 96p. (J). per. 3.99 (978-1-57791-255-2(1)) Brighter Minds Children's Publishing.

—What's with Wulf? Simonson, Louise. gif. ed. 2005. (Extreme Monsters Ser.). 96p. (J). (gr. 2-5). per. 3.99 (978-1-57791-179-1(2)) Brighter Minds Children's Publishing.

Elwell, Ellen Banks & Turk, Caron. The Toddler's Songbook. 2009. (J). (978-1-4335-0597-3(5)) Crossway.

—The Toddler's Songbook. Elwell, Ellen Banks. 2009. (ENG.). 48p. (J). 14.99 incl. audio compact disk (978-1-4335-0595-9(9)) Crossway.

Elwell, Peter. My Mother Is Mine. Bauer, Marion Dane. 2009. (Classic Board Bks.). (ENG.). 36p. (J). (gr. -1-k). bds. 8.99 (978-1-4169-6090-4(2), Little Simon) Little Simon.

—My Mother Is Mine. Bauer, Marion Dane. 2004. (ENG.). 40p. (J). (gr. -1-k). reprint ed. 7.99 (978-0-689-86695-1(X), Simon & Schuster Bks. For Young Readers) Simon & Schuster Bks. For Young Readers.

Elwell, Peter. A Most Remarkable Bear. Elwell, Peter. Date not set. 32p. (J). (gr. k-3). 15.95 (978-0-7614-5008-5(4)) Marshall Cavendish Corp.

Elwell, Telva. Ellasense Misses the Train. Elwell, Telva. Kelley, Barbara. 2004. 48p. (J). per. 12.95 (978-0-9754591-0-2(4)) Cubby Hole Tales.

Elwell, Tristan. Kingdom Keepers III: Disney in Shadow. Pearson, Ridley. 3rd ed. 2010. (Kingdom Keepers Ser.: Bk. 3). (ENG.). 560p. (J). (gr. 5-9). 17.99 (978-1-4231-2899-1(0)) Hyperion Pr.

—Kingdom Keepers (Kingdom Keepers) Disney after Dark. Pearson, Ridley. 2009. (Kingdom Keepers Ser.: 1). (ENG.). 336p. (J). (gr. 5-9). pap. 8.99 (978-1-4231-2311-8(5)) Hyperion Pr.

Elworthy, Antony. Have You Ever?: Band 02A/Red a (Collins Big Cat) Pym, Tasha. 2007. (Collins Big Cat Ser.). (ENG.). 16p. (J). (gr. -1-k). pap. 6.99 (978-0-00-718654-9(1)) HarperCollins Pubs. Ltd. GBR. Dist: Independent Pubs. Group.

—What Are You Making?: Band 02B/Red B (Collins Big Cat) Hawes, Alison. 2007. (Collins Big Cat Ser.). (ENG.). 16p. (J). (gr. -1-k). pap. 6.99 (978-0-00-718657-0(6)) HarperCollins Pubs. Ltd. GBR. Dist: Independent Pubs. Group.

Ely, Dave. Maggie's Christmas Miracle. Pohl, Dora & Kremer, Kevin. 2010. 78p. (J). pap. 4.99 (978-0-9824611-2-9(7)) Snow In Sarasota Publishing.

—Santa's Our Substitute Teacher. Kremer, Kevin. 2006. 150p. (gr. 4-7). per. 5.99 (978-0-9663335-4-1(3), 703-001) Snow In Sarasota Publishing.

Ely, Donald, jt. illus. see Minter, Daniel.

Ely, Jennifer W. If You Were a Kid Building a Pyramid. Schimel, Lawrence. 2017. (If You Were a Kid Ser.). (ENG.). 32p. (J). (gr. 2-4). pap. 7.95 (978-0-531-23949-0(7)); lib. bdg. 26.00 (978-0-531-23748-9(6)) Scholastic Library Publishing. (Children's Pr.).

Ely, Paul & Dudley, Dick. Eerie Feary Feeling: A Hairy Scary Pop-up Book. Hulme, Joy N. 2006. 12p. (J). (gr. k-4). reprint ed. 14.00 (978-1-4223-5171-0(8)) DIANE Publishing Co.

Élyum Studio. The Planet of the Night Globes: Book 6, Bk. 6. Gonnard, Christel. 2013. (Little Prince Ser.: 6). (ENG.). 56p. (J). (gr. 4-8). pap. 7.95 (978-1-4677-0738-1(4), 9781467707381, Graphic Universe™) Lerner Publishing Group.

Élyum Studio Staff. The Planet of Gehom, No. 16. Gaudin, Thierry. Smith, Anne & Smith, Owen, trs. 2014. (Little Prince Ser.: 16). (ENG.). 48p. (J). (gr. 4-8). lib. bdg. 26.65 (978-0-7613-8766-4(8), 9780761387664, Graphic Universe™) Lerner Publishing Group.

—The Planet of the Giant, No. 9. Adrien, Gilles & Broders, Alain. 2013. (Little Prince Ser.: 9). (ENG.). 56p. (J). (gr. 4-8). lib. bdg. 26.65 (978-0-7613-8759-6(5), 9780761387596, Graphic Universe™) Lerner Publishing Group.

—The Planet of the Grand Buffoon, No. 14. Cerami, Matteo et al. Smith, Anne & Smith, Owen, trs. 2014. (Little Prince Ser.: 14). (ENG.). 48p. (J). (gr. 4-8). lib. bdg. 26.65 (978-0-7613-8764-0(1), 9780761387640, Graphic Universe™) Lerner Publishing Group.

—The Star Snatcher's Planet, No. 5. Barichella, Thomas. 2013. (Little Prince Ser.: 5). 56p. (J). (gr. 4-8). lib. bdg. 26.65 (978-0-7613-8755-8(2), 9780761387558, Graphic Universe™) Lerner Publishing Group.

Elzbieta & Hawcock, David. Mimi's Scary Theater: A Play in Nine Scenes for Seven Characters & an Egg. Elzbieta. 2004. 20p. (J). (gr. -1-3). reprint ed. 15.00 (978-0-7567-8299-3(6)) DIANE Publishing Co.

Em, Mary. Armadillo Tamarillo. Katay, Katie. 2019. (Fruit Tree Neighbourhood Ser.: Vol. 1). (ENG.). 134p. (J). (gr. 3-4). pap. (978-0-473-43037-5(1)) Inko Junior.

Em, Mary. My Unruly Mop of Hair. Katay, Katie. 2020. (ENG.). 36p. (J). (gr. k-1). **(978-0-9951332-1-1(2))** Sunsmile Bks.

—My Unruly Mop of Hair Activity & Colouring Book: 2-N-1 Flip Book. Katay, Katie. 2019. (ENG.). 34p. (J). (gr. k-1). pap. **(978-0-9951238-2-3(9))** Sunsmile Bks.

Em, Mary. Princess Peach & the Precious Pearl: A Princess Peach Story. Em, Mary. 2020. (Princess Peach Ser.: Vol. 2). (ENG.). 104p. (J). pap. **(978-0-9951196-3-5(5))** Silversmith Publishing.

Em, Vickers. The Life of a Rodeo Clown. Drews, Ann. 2018. (Rodeo Ser.: Vol. 1). (ENG.). 24p. (J). pap. 12.99 (978-1-948390-92-7(2)) Pen It! Pubns., LLC.

Emabat, Lionel. Elijah & His Invisible Friend. Bishop, Sabrena & Bishop, Elijah. 2018. (Madison & Elijah Ser.: Vol. 1). (ENG.). 34p. (J). (gr. k-5). 19.99 (978-1-948071-34-5(7)) Lauren Simone Publishing Hse.

Emanuel, Effie Ann. The Way to Go! Phillips, Cynthia. 2008. 17p. pap. 24.95 (978-1-60610-455-2(1)) America Star Bks.

Ember, Dave. Alaska's Wildlife. Compton, Carrie. 2005. (Alaska Mini Book Gift Ser.). 80p. 5.95 (978-0-9727921-6-5(3)) WW West, Inc.

Ember, Kathi. Don't Talk to Strangers. Mehlhaff, Christine. 2007. (J). (978-0-545-00103-8(X)) Scholastic, Inc.

—A Father's Day Thank You. Nolan, Janet. 2013. (AV2 Fiction Readalong Ser.: Vol. 79). (ENG.). (J). (gr. -1-2). 34.28 (978-1-62127-862-7(X), AV2 by Weigl) Weigl Pubs., Inc.

—A Father's Day Thank You. Nolan, Janet. 2011. (ENG.). 32p. (J). (gr. -1-1). lib. bdg. 21.19 (978-0-8075-2291-2(0)) Whitman, Albert & Co.

—I Can Show Respect. Burch, Regina G. & Donovan Guntly, Jenette. 2004. (Doing the Right Thing Ser.). 16p. (gr. -1-2). lib. bdg. 21.00 (978-0-8368-4248-7(0), Gareth Stevens Learning Library) Stevens, Gareth Publishing LLLP.

—Mighty Ants: Exploring an Ant Colony. Boynton, Alice & Blevins, Wiley. 2017. (Imagine That! Ser.). (ENG.). 32p. (J). (gr. 2-4). pap. 7.99 (978-1-63440-276-7(6)); lib. bdg. 26.65 (978-1-63440-274-3(X), 9781634402743) Red Chair Pr.

—Squirrel's New Year's Resolution. Miller, Pat. 2012. (J). 34.28 (978-1-61913-135-4(8)) Weigl Pubs., Inc.

—Squirrel's New Year's Resolution. Miller, Pat. (ENG.). 32p. (J). (gr. -1-3). 2017. pap. 7.99 (978-0-8075-7592-5(5), 807575925); 2010. 16.99 (978-0-8075-7591-8(7), 807575917) Whitman, Albert & Co.

—Substitute Groundhog. Miller, Pat. 2012. (J). (978-1-61913-133-0(1)) Weigl Pubs., Inc.

—Substitute Groundhog, 1 vol. Miller, Pat. 2010. (ENG.). 32p. (J). (gr. -1-3). pap. 6.99 (978-0-8075-7644-1(1), 807576441) Whitman, Albert & Co.

Ember, Kathi, jt. illus. see Yamada, Jane.

Emberley, Barbara & Ed. The Moon Seems to Change. Branley, Franklyn M. 2015. (Let's-Read-And-Find-Out Science 2 Ser.). (ENG.). 32p. (J). (gr. -1-3). pap. 6.99 (978-0-06-238206-1(3)) HarperCollins Pubs.

Emberley, Ed. The Ant & the Grasshopper. Emberley, Rebecca. 2012. (ENG.). 28p. (J). (gr. -1-2). 18.99 (978-1-59643-493-6(7), 900057378) Roaring Brook Pr.

—Chicken Little. Emberley, Rebecca. 2009. (ENG.). 34p. (J). (gr. -1-2). 19.99 (978-1-59643-464-6(3), 900055508) Roaring Brook Pr.

—The Crocodile & the Scorpion. Emberley, Rebecca. 2013. (ENG.). 32p. (J). (gr. -1-2). 17.99 (978-1-59643-494-3(5), 900057379) Roaring Brook Pr.

—The Lion & the Mice. Emberley, Rebecca. 2012. (I Like to Read Ser.). (ENG.). 24p. (J). (gr. -1-3). pap. 7.99 (978-0-8234-2641-6(6)) Holiday Hse., Inc.

—Mice on Ice. Emberley, Rebecca. 2013. (I Like to Read Ser.). (ENG.). 24p. (J). (gr. -1-3). pap. 7.99 (978-0-8234-2908-0(3)) Holiday Hse., Inc.

—There Was an Old Monster! Emberley, Rebecca & Emberley, Adrian. 2009. (ENG.). 32p. (J). (gr. -1-k). 17.99 (978-0-545-10145-5(X), Orchard Bks.) Scholastic, Inc.

Emberley, Ed. Bye-Bye, Big Bad Bullybug! Emberley, Ed. 2007. (ENG.). 32p. (J). (gr. -1-3). 16.99 (978-0-316-01762-6(0)) Little, Brown Bks. for Young Readers.

—Ed Emberley's Big Green Drawing Book. Emberley, Ed. 2005. (ENG.). 96p. (J). (gr. 2-17). pap. 12.99 (978-0-316-78976-9(3)) Little, Brown Bks. for Young Readers.

—Ed Emberley's Big Purple Drawing Book. Emberley, Ed. 2005. (ENG.). 96p. (J). (gr. 2-17). pap. 12.99 (978-0-316-78973-8(9)) Little, Brown Bks. for Young Readers.

—Ed Emberley's Drawing Book: Make a World. Emberley, Ed. 2006. (ENG.). 32p. (J). (gr. 2-17). pap. 8.99 (978-0-316-78972-1(0)) Little, Brown Bks. for Young Readers.

—Ed Emberley's Drawing Book of Faces (REPACKAGED) Emberley, Ed. 2006. (ENG.). 32p. (J). (gr. 2-17). pap. 8.99 (978-0-316-78970-7(4)) Little, Brown Bks. for Young Readers.

—Ed Emberley's Drawing Book of Trucks & Trains. Emberley, Ed. 2005. (ENG.). 32p. (J). (gr. 2-17). pap. 8.99 (978-0-316-78967-7(4)) Little, Brown Bks. for Young Readers.

—Ed Emberley's Fingerprint Drawing Book. Emberley, Ed. 2005. 48p. (J). (gr. 2-17). pap., pap. 10.99 (978-0-316-78969-1(0)) Little, Brown Bks. for Young Readers.

—Ed Emberley's Great Thumbprint Drawing Book. Emberley, Ed. 2005. 48p. (J). (gr. 2-17). per. 8.99 (978-0-316-78968-4(2)) Little, Brown Bks. for Young Readers.

—Ed Emberley's Picture Pie. Emberley, Ed. 2006. (ENG.). 48p. (J). (gr. 2-17). pap. 10.99 (978-0-316-78982-0(8)) Little, Brown Bks. for Young Readers.

—Ed Emberley's Picture Pie Two Vol. 2. Emberley, Ed. 2005. (ENG.). 32p. (J). (gr. 2-17). pap. 10.99 (978-0-316-78980-6(1)) Little, Brown Bks. for Young Readers.

—If You're a Monster & You Know It... Emberley, Ed. Emberley, Rebecca. 2010. (ENG.). 32p. (J). (gr. -1-k). 17.99 (978-0-545-21829-0(2), Orchard Bks.) Scholastic, Inc.

Emberley, Edward R., jt. illus. see Emberley, Rebecca.

Emberley, Michael. Baby's Firsts. Day, Nancy Raines. 2018. 32p. (J). (— 1). lib. bdg. 14.99 (978-1-58089-774-7(6)) Charlesbridge Publishing, Inc.

—David Dinosaur-Rrr! What It's Like to Be 3. Harris, Robie H. 2005. (Growing up Stories Ser.). (ENG.). 40p. (J). 16.95 (978-0-689-83260-4(5), McElderry, Margaret K. Bks.) McElderry, Margaret K. Bks.

—Forget-Me-Nots: Poems to Learn by Heart. Hoberman, Mary Ann. 2012. (ENG.). 144p. (J). (gr. -1-3). 20.99 (978-0-316-12947-3(X), Tingley, Megan Bks.) Little, Brown Bks. for Young Readers.

—It's Not the Stork! A Book about Girls, Boys, Babies, Bodies, Families & Friends. Harris, Robie H. (Family Library). (ENG.). 64p. (J). (gr. -1-3). 2008. pap. 12.99 (978-0-7636-3331-8(3)); 2006. 17.99 (978-0-7636-0047-1(4)) Candlewick Pr.

—It's So Amazing! A Book about Eggs, Sperm, Birth, Babies, & Families. Harris, Robie H. 2014. (Family Library). (ENG.). 88p. (J). (gr. 2-5). 22.99 (978-0-7636-6873-0(7)) Candlewick Pr.

—Maybe a Bear Ate It (a StoryPlay Book) Harris, Robie H. 2017. (StoryPlay Ser.). (ENG.). 40p. (J). (gr. -1-k). 5.99 (978-1-338-16110-6(5), Cartwheel Bks.) Scholastic, Inc.

—Miss Brooks Loves Books! Bottner, Barbara. 2010. 32p. (J). (gr. -1-2). 17.99 (978-0-375-84682-3(4), Knopf Bks. for Young Readers) Random Hse. Children's Bks.

—Miss Brooks Loves Books (and I Don't) Bottner, Barbara. 2018. (ENG.). 32p. (J). (gr. -1-2). 7.99 (978-1-9848-5210-6(8), Dragonfly Bks.) Random Hse. Children's Bks.

—Miss Brooks' Story Nook (Where Tales Are Told & Ogres Are Welcome) Bottner, Barbara. 2014. 40p. (J). (gr. k-4). 16.99 (978-0-449-81328-7(2), Knopf Bks. for Young Readers) Random Hse. Children's Bks.

—Priscilla Gorilla. Bottner, Barbara. 2017. (ENG.). 40p. (J). (gr. -1-2). 17.99 (978-1-4814-5897-9(3), Atheneum/Caitlyn Dlouhy Books) Simon & Schuster Children's Publishing.

—The Ultimate Guide to Grandmas & Grandpas! Lloyd-Jones, Sally. 2008. (ENG.). 32p. (J). (gr. -1-3). 14.99 (978-0-06-075687-1(X)) HarperCollins Pubs.

—Very Short Mother Goose Tales to Read Together. Hoberman, Mary Ann. 3rd ed. 2012. (You Read to Me, I'll Read to You Ser.). 32p. (J). (gr. -1-3). pap. 8.99 (978-0-316-20715-7(2)) Little, Brown Bks. for Young Readers.

—Very Short Scary Tales to Read Together No. 2. Hoberman, Mary Ann. 2009. (You Read to Me, I'll Read to You Ser.). 32p. (J). (gr. -1-3). pap. 8.99 (978-0-316-04351-9(6)) Little Brown & Co.

—Very Short Stories to Read Together. Hoberman, Mary Ann. 2006. (You Read to Me, I'll Read to You Ser.). 32p. (J). (gr. -1-3). pap. 8.99 (978-0-316-01316-1(1), Tingley, Megan Bks.) Little, Brown Bks. for Young Readers.

—Very Short Tall Tales to Read Together. Hoberman, Mary Ann. 2014. (You Read to Me, I'll Read to You Ser.). (ENG.). 32p. (J). (gr. -1-3). 17.99 (978-0-316-18329-1(6)) Little Brown & Co.

—Very Short Tall Tales to Read Together. Hoberman, Mary Ann. 2019. (You Read to Me, I'll Read to You Ser.). 32p. (J). (gr. -1-3). pap. 8.99 (978-0-316-53140-5(5)) Little, Brown Bks. for Young Readers.

—You Read to Me, I'll Read to You: Very Short Stories to Read Together. Hoberman, Mary Ann. 2006. 28p. (gr. -1-1). 17.00 (978-0-7569-6581-5(0)) Perfection Learning Corp.

—You Read to Me, I'll Read to You: Very Short Fables to Read Together. Hoberman, Mary Ann. 2010. (You Read to Me, I'll Read to You Ser.). (ENG.). 32p. (J). (gr. -1-3). 17.99 (978-0-316-04117-1(3)) Little Brown & Co.

—You Read to Me, I'll Read to You: Very Short Fables to Read Together. Hoberman, Mary Ann. 2013. (You Read to Me, I'll Read to You Ser.). 32p. (J). (gr. -1-3). 8.99 (978-0-316-21847-4(2)) Little, Brown Bks. for Young Readers.

—(3) Very Short Fairy Tales to Read Together. Hoberman, Mary Ann. 2004. (You Read to Me, I'll Read to You Ser.). (ENG.). 32p. (J). (gr. -1-3). 18.99 (978-0-316-14611-1(0)) Little, Brown Bks. for Young Readers.

Emberley, Rebecca & Emberley, Edward R. Mice on Ice. Emberley, Rebecca & Emberley, Edward R. 2012. (I Like to Read Ser.). (ENG.). 24p. (J). (gr. -1-3). 14.95 (978-0-8234-2576-1(2)) Holiday Hse., Inc.

Embleton, Christopher. Is This My Tail? 2017. (J). (978-1-62885-286-8(0)) Kidsbooks, LLC.

Embleton-Hall, Chris. My Toddler Bible, 1 vol. David, Juliet. ed. 2016. (ENG.). 224p. (J). (gr. -1-k). 12.99 (978-1-78128-241-0(2), Candle Bks.) Lion Hudson PLC GBR. Dist: Independent Pubs. Group.

—Pull-Out Jonah & the Big Fish, 1 vol. Edwards, Josh. ed. 2014. (Candle Pull-Out Ser.). (ENG.). 10p. (J). (gr. -1-k). bds. 11.99 (978-1-85985-998-8(4), Candle Bks.) Lion Hudson PLC GBR. Dist: Independent Pubs. Group.

Embry, Stacey. Somebody Stole My Yawn! Jones, Bryan E. 2009. 28p. pap. 24.95 (978-1-60749-877-3(4)) America Star Bks.

Emelyanova, Tanya. My First Big Book of Princesses. Little Bee Books. 2019. (My First Big Book of Coloring Ser.). (ENG.). 192p. (J). (gr. -1-k). 8.99 (978-1-4998-0913-8(1)) Little Bee Books Inc.

—My First Big Book of Trucks. Little Bee Books. 2019. (My First Big Book of Coloring Ser.). (ENG.). 192p. (J). (gr. -1-k). 8.99 (978-1-4998-0914-5(X)) Little Bee Books Inc.

—The Super Cute Drawing Book: Step-By-step Kawaii Creatures! Potter, William. 2020. (ENG.). 96p. (J). pap. 9.99 (978-1-83857-605-9(3), c2b0abc2-806b-4275-9fb7-ee0293fe7237) Arcturus Publishing GBR. Dist: Baker & Taylor Publisher Services (BTPS).

Emerling, Dorothy. The Lost Seal. McKnight, Diane. 2006. (Long Term Ecological Research Ser.). (ENG.). 40p. (J). (gr. 4-7). 19.95 (978-0-9723422-7-8(3)) Taylor Trade Publishing.

—My Water Comes from the Rocky Mountains. Fourment, Tiffany. 2009. (Long Term Ecological Research Ser.). (ENG.). 32p. (J). (gr. 1-5). pap. 9.95 (978-0-9817700-1-7(0)) Taylor Trade Publishing.

—My Water Comes from the San Juan Mountains. Fourment, Tiffany & Gianniny, Gary. 2009. (ENG.). 32p. (J). (gr. 4-7). pap. 9.95 (978-0-9817700-3-1(7)) Taylor Trade Publishing.

Emerson, Emily. God's Garden of Blessings. Puffinton, Brick. Cottage Door Press, ed. 2020. (Little Sunbeams Finger Puppet Board Book Ser.). (ENG.). 12p. (J). (gr. -1-k). bds. 6.99 (978-1-68052-816-9(5), 1005290) Cottage Door Pr.

—God's Love Is a Rainbow. Puffinton, Brick. Cottage Door Press, ed. 2020. (Little Sunbeams Finger Puppet Board Book Ser.). (ENG.). 12p. (J). (gr. -1 — 1). bds. 6.99 (978-1-68052-817-6(3), 1005300) Cottage Door Pr.

Emerson, Hunt, et al. Fight the Power! A Visual History of Protest among the English Speaking Peoples. Wilson, Sean Michael & Dickson, Benjamin. 2013. (ENG.). 192p. pap. 19.95 (978-1-60980-492-3(9)) Seven Stories Pr.

Emerson, Hunt. Graphic Classics - Jack London, Vol. 5. London, Jack. Pomplun, Tom, ed. 2003. (ENG.). 144p. (gr. 7-18). pap. 9.95 (978-0-9712464-5-4(9), 8cb800d4-ac0b-401c-8c15-c6e5601ccac2) Eureka Productions.

Emerson, Marcus. Bad Guy Is a Two-Word Word. 2017. 149p. (J). (978-1-5490-0441-4(7)) Roaring Brook Pr.

Emerson, Marcus. Ben Braver & the Incredible Exploding Kid. Emerson, Marcus. 2019. (Ben Braver Ser.: 2). (ENG.). 336p. (J). 13.99 (978-1-62672-711-3(2), 900171428) Roaring Brook Pr.

—Ben Braver & the Incredible Exploding Kid. Emerson, Marcus. 2020. (Ben Braver Ser.: 2). (ENG.). 352p. (J). pap. 7.99 (978-1-250-23341-7(0), 900180486) Square Fish.

—Ben Braver & the Vortex of Doom. Emerson, Marcus. 2020. (Ben Braver Ser.: 3). (ENG.). 320p. (J). 13.99 (978-1-62672-712-0(0), 900171429) Roaring Brook Pr.

—Recess Warriors: Hero Is a Four Letter Word. Emerson, Marcus. 2017. (Recess Warriors Ser.). (ENG.). 144p. (J). pap. 12.99 (978-1-62672-708-3(2), 9781626727083) Roaring Brook Pr.

—Recess Warriors 2: Bad Guy Is a Two-Word Word. Emerson, Marcus. 2017. (Recess Warriors Ser.: 2). (ENG.). 160p. (J). pap. 12.99 (978-1-62672-709-0(0), 900171422) Roaring Brook Pr.

—The Super Life of Ben Braver. Emerson, Marcus. 2019. (Ben Braver Ser.: 1). (ENG.). 336p. (J). pap. 7.99 (978-1-250-29434-0(7), 900180484) Square Fish.

Emery, Jennifer. Sheila Says We're Weird, 1 vol. Smalley, Ruth Ann. 2011. (ENG.). 32p. (J). 16.95 (978-0-88448-326-7(6)) Tilbury Hse. Pubs.

Emili, Awele. Between My Best Friends & the School Bullies. Emili, Cynthia. 2019. (ENG.). 42p. (J). pap. 9.99 (978-1-7987-4618-9(2)) Independently Published.

Emilio, Urberuaga & Urberuaga, Emilio. Manolito Four-Eyes, 0 vols. Lindo, Elvira. 2010. (Manolito Four-Eyes Ser.: 1). (ENG.). 155p. (J). (gr. 3-7). pap. 9.99 (978-0-7614-5729-9(1), 9780761457299, Two Lions) Amazon Publishing.

Emily, Bolam. Animals Go. Tiger Tales Staff, ed. 2010. (Touch, Look, & Learn! Ser.). (ENG.). 10p. (J). (gr. -1). bds. 5.95 (978-1-58925-854-9(1)) Tiger Tales.

—Animals Talk. Tiger Tales Staff, ed. 2010. (Touch, Look, & Learn! Ser.). (ENG.). 10p. (J). (gr. -1). bds. 5.95 (978-1-58925-855-6(X)) Tiger Tales.

Eminence Systems. The Adventures of Quint the Bookmobile: The Big Move to Roneyville. Quinton, Kathleen a. Carr, Kim, ed. 2018. (Adventures of Quint the Bookmobile Ser.: Vol. 1). (ENG.). 28p. (J). (gr. k-3). 16.99 (978-1-5136-3611-5(1)) Quintessential Productions.

—Wise Tales: A Collection of Nigerian Folk Tales: Volume 1. Akinleye-Atinmo, Titilope. 2016. (ENG.). (J). 16.99 (978-0-9983312-0-1(1)) Akinleye, Titilope.

Emison, Patricia A. & Feldman Emison, Chloë. Growing with the Grain: Dynamic Families Shaping History from Ancient Times to the Present. 2005. xix, 321p. (YA). 44.95 (978-0-9765572-0-3(7)) Lady Illyria Pr.

Emma. The Adventures of Blue Flamingo. Emma. 2018. (Adventures of Blue Flamingo Ser.). (ENG.). 26p. (J). (gr. 1-3). pap. 6.99 (978-1-63529-973-1(X)) Caliber Comics.

Emmerich, Peter. A Is for Audra: Broadway's Leading Ladies from a to Z. Allman, John Robert. 2019. 48p. (J). (gr. -1-2). 18.99 (978-0-525-64540-5(3)); (ENG.). lib. bdg. 21.99 (978-0-525-64541-2(1)) Random Hse. Children's Bks. (Doubleday Bks. for Young Readers).

Emmerichs, Bern. William Bligh: A Stormy Story of Tempestuous Times. Sedunary, Michael. 2016. (ENG.). 54p. (J). (gr. 4). 24.95 (978-0-9942895-3-7(7)) Berbay Publishing AUS. Dist: Independent Pubs. Group.

Emmerson, Michael. Dump Truck Day, 1 vol. Meister, Cari. (My First Graphic Novel Ser.). (ENG.). 32p. (J). (gr. k-2). 2010. pap. 6.25 (978-1-4342-2288-6(8)); 2009. 24.65 (978-1-4342-1621-2(7)) Capstone. (Stone Arch Bks.).

Emmerson, Michael. Thank You, Helpers: Doctors, Nurses, Teachers, Grocery Workers, & More Who Care for Us. Hegarty, Patricia. 2020. (ENG.). 32p. (J). (gr. -1-3). pap. 7.99 **(978-0-593-37338-5(3)**, Random Hse. Bks. for Young Readers) Random Hse. Children's Bks.

Emmitt, Randy, photos by. Butterflies of the Carolinas & Virginias. Emmitt, Randy. 2005. (YA). cd-rom 19.95 (978-0-9767239-0-5(5)) Metalmark Pr.

Emmons, Loretta. Alive by God's Grace: The True Life Adventures of an African Boy. Emmons, Loretta, ed. Emmons, Erik, ed. 2018. (ENG.). 100p. (J). pap. 7.99 (978-1-7312-4906-7(3)) Independently Published.

Emms, Sarah Frushour. I Love You. Ulshafer, Katherine S. 2018. (ENG.). 36p. (J). 22.95 (978-1-64028-326-8(9)); pap. 13.95 (978-1-64191-615-8(X)) Christian Faith Publishing.

Empson, Jo. Little Home Bird. Empson, Jo. 2016. (Child's Play Library). (ENG.). 36p. (J). (978-1-84643-889-9(6)) Child's Play International Ltd.

—Never Ever. Empson, Jo. 2013. (Child's Play Library). (ENG.). 32p. (J). (978-1-84643-552-2(8)) Child's Play International Ltd.

—Rabbityness. Empson, Jo. 2012. (Child's Play Library). 32p. (J). (ENG.). (978-1-84643-492-1(0)); (978-1-84643-482-2(3)) Child's Play International Ltd.

Emroca Flores, Jose. The Room of Woe: An Up2U Horror Adventure, 1 vol. Wallace, Rich. 2015. (Up2U Adventures Ser.). (ENG.). 80p. (J). (gr. 2-5). 29.93 (978-1-62402-094-0(1), 17357, Calico Chapter Bks.) ABDO Publishing Co.

Emslie, Peter. The Sorcerer's Apprentice (Disney Classic) Ferguson, Don. 2018. (Little Golden Book Ser.). (ENG.). 24p. (J). (-k). 4.99 (978-0-7364-3868-1(8), Golden/Disney) Random Hse. Children's Bks.

Ende, Michael. Momo. Ende, Michael. 2004. (SPA.). 256p. (YA). (gr. 8-12). pap. 10.95 (978-968-19-0255-1(6)) Santillana USA Publishing Co., Inc.

Endelman, David. The Big Squeal: A Wild, True, & Twisted Tail, Vol. Scaglione, Joanne & Small, Gail. 2005. (ENG.). 56p. pap. 39.00 (978-1-57886-256-6(6)) Rowman & Littlefield Education.

Endersby, Frank. The First Snow. Butler, M. Christina. 2012. (J). (978-1-4351-4320-3(5)) Barnes & Noble, Inc.

—Grandma Prays for You, 1 vol. Fischer, Jean. 2019. (ENG.). 20p. (J). bds. 9.99 (978-1-4002-1209-5(X)) Nelson, Thomas Inc.

—Just Because You're Mine. Lloyd-Jones, Sally. 2011. (ENG.). 32p. (J). (gr. -1-2). 16.99 (978-0-06-201476-4(5)) HarperCollins Pubs.

—Love You, Hug You, Read to You! Rabe, Tish. 2015. (ENG.). 32p. (J). (gr. -1 — 1). bds. 7.99 (978-1-101-93655-9(X), Random Hse. Bks. for Young Readers) Random Hse. Children's Bks.

—Maths Problem Solving: Year 1, 6 vols. Yemm, Caterhine. 2005. 106p. pap. (978-1-903853-74-0(5)) Brilliant Pubns.

—Maths Problem Solving: Year 2, 6 vols. Yemm, Caterhine. 2005. 106p. pap. (978-1-903853-75-7(3)) Brilliant Pubns.

—Maths Problem Solving: Year 3, 6 vols. Yemm, Caterhine. 2005. 80p. pap. (978-1-903853-76-4(1)) Brilliant Pubns.

—Maths Problem Solving: Year 4, 6 vols. Yemm, Caterhine. 2005. 80p. pap. (978-1-903853-77-1(X)) Brilliant Pubns.

—Maths Problem Solving: Year 5, 6 vols. Yemm, Caterhine. 2005. 80p. pap. (978-1-903853-78-8(8)) Brilliant Pubns.

—Maths Problem Solving: Year 6, 6 vols. Yemm, Caterhine. 2006. 80p. pap. (978-1-903853-79-5(6)) Brilliant Pubns.

—My Christmas Prayer, 1 vol. Parker, Amy. 2017. (ENG.). 12p. (J). bds. 8.99 (978-0-7180-9952-7(4)) Nelson, Thomas Inc.

—My First Book of Opposites. Brown, Janet Allison. 2004. (Early Learning Ser.). 18p. (J). bds. 5.99 (978-1-85854-530-1(7)) Brimax Books Ltd. GBR. Dist: Byeway Bks.

—¡Te Amo, Te Abrazo, Leo Contigo!/Love You, Hug You, Read to You! Rabe, Tish. 2015. (ENG.). 32p. (J). (gr. -1 — 1). bds. 7.99 (978-1-101-93657-3(6), Random Hse. Bks. for Young Readers) Random Hse. Children's Bks.

—A Treasury for Little Ones: Hours of Fun for Babies & Toddlers - Stories & Rhymes, Puzzles to Solve, & Things to Make & Do. Baxter, Nicola & Birkinshaw, Marie. 2014. 80p. (J). (gr. -1-6). 14.99 (978-1-86147-368-4(0), Armadillo) Anness Publishing GBR. Dist: National Bk. Network.

—You're My Dream Come True, 1 vol. Fischer, Jean. 2020. (ENG.). 20p. (J). bds. 9.99 (978-1-4002-1615-4(X)) Nelson, Thomas Inc.

Endersby, Frank, jt. illus. see Hartung, Susan Kathleen.

Endersly, Frank, jt. illus. see Hartung, Susan Kathleen.

Endicott, Lou. The Day Jake Ran Out of Hugs. Hjort, A. Nicky. 2018. (ENG.). 38p. (J). pap. 10.99 (978-1-7216-7445-9(4)) CreateSpace Independent Publishing Platform.

Endle, Kate. Augie to Zebra: An Alphabet Book! Babypants, Caspar. 2012. 32p. (J). (gr. -1-2). 16.99 (978-1-57061-750-8(3), Little Bigfoot) Sasquatch Bks.

—Big Earth, Little Me. Wiley, Thom. 2009. 16p. (J). pap. (978-0-545-22335-5(0)) Scholastic, Inc.

—My Woodland Wish. Babypants, Caspar & Ballew, Chris. 2011. (ENG.). 32p. (J). (gr. -1-2). 17.99 (978-1-57061-748-5(1), Little Bigfoot) Sasquatch Bks.

—Ocean Motions. Babypants, Caspar. 2018. 20p. (J). (— 1). bds. 9.99 (978-1-63217-131-3(7), Little Bigfoot) Sasquatch Bks.

—Old Manhattan Has Some Farms: (E-I-E-I-Grow!) Lendroth, Susan. 2014. 32p. (J). (gr. -1-2). lib. bdg. 16.95 (978-1-58089-572-9(7)) Charlesbridge Publishing, Inc.

—Penguin on a Scooter. Babypants, Caspar. 2018. 20p. (J). (— 1). bds. 9.99 (978-1-63217-130-6(9), Little Bigfoot) Sasquatch Bks.

—Trout Are Made of Trees. Sayre, April Pulley. 2008. 32p. (J). (gr. -1-3). 7.99 (978-1-58089-138-7(1)) Charlesbridge Publishing, Inc.

—Trout Are Made of Trees. Sayre, April Pulley & National Geographic Learning Staff. 2008. (Rise & Shine Ser.). (ENG.). 32p. (C). (gr. k-3). 21.19 (978-1-58089-137-0(3)) Charlesbridge Publishing, Inc.

Endoh, Minari. Dazzle, Vol. 1. Endoh, Minari. 2006. (Dazzle Ser.). 200p. (gr. 8-18). pap. 9.99 (978-1-59816-092-5(3)) TOKYOPOP, Inc.

Endres, Patrick J., photos by. Alaska. Gill, Shelley. 2007. 32p. (J). (gr. 1-4). pap. 7.99 (978-0-88106-293-9(6)) Charlesbridge Publishing, Inc.

—Grizzly Bears of Alaska: Explore the Wild World of Bears. Miller, Debbie S. 2014. (Paws IV Ser.). 32p. (J). (gr. k-3). pap. 10.99 (978-1-57061-932-8(8), Little Bigfoot) Sasquatch Bks.

Endres, Sharlene Duggan, jt. illus. see Schmitt, Nannette Toups.

Enecio, Jeremy. U. S. Special Forces: Ghosts of the Night. Manning, Matthew K. 2016. (U. S. Special Ops Ser.). (ENG.). 96p. (J). (gr. 3-6). lib. bdg. 26.65 (978-1-4965-3475-0(1), Stone Arch Bks.) Capstone.

—U.S. Special Forces: Ghosts of the Night. Manning, Matthew K. 2016. (U. S. Special Ops Ser.). (ENG.). 96p. (gr. 3-4). E-Book 26.65 (978-1-4965-3477-4(8), Stone Arch Bks.) Capstone.

E

Enersen, Adele. When My Baby Dreams. Enersen, Adele. 2012. (ENG.). 48p. (J). (gr. -1-3). 14.99 (978-0-06-207175-0(0)) HarperCollins Pubs.

—When My Baby Dreams of Fairy Tales. Enersen, Adele. 2013. (ENG.). 48p. (J). (gr. -1-k). 15.99 (978-0-06-207177-4(7)) HarperCollins Pubs.

Eng, Gee Fan. Frida Kahlo Doll & Book Set: For the Littlest Dreamers. Sanchez Vegara, Maria Isabel. ed. 2020. (Little People, Big Dreams Ser.: Vol. 45). (ENG.). 24p. (J). (gr. -1). bds. **(978-0-7112-4886-1(9))** Frances Lincoln Childrens Bks.

Engel, Bali. Nature's Lullaby Fills the Night. Leone, Dee. 2018. 40p. (J). (gr. -1). 16.95 (978-1-4549-2139-4(0)) Sterling Publishing Co., Inc.

Engel, Christiane. Astronauts. 2018. (First Explorers Ser.). (ENG.). 10p. (J). (— 1). bds. 8.95 (978-1-4549-2940-6(5)) Sterling Publishing Co., Inc.

—Baby's First Words. Blackstone, Stella & Scribens, Sunny. 2017. (ENG.). 30p. (J). (gr. -1-k). bds. 14.99 (978-1-78285-321-3(9)) Barefoot Bks., Inc.

—Bath! Bath! Bath! Florian, Douglas. 2018. (ENG.). 18p. (J). (gr. -1-1). bds. 6.99 (978-1-4998-0485-0(7)) Little Bee Books Inc.

—Curious Kids: Explore the Meadow. Marx, Jonny. 2020. (ENG.). 16p. (J). (gr. 1-3). 12.99 (978-1-68010-618-3(X)) Tiger Tales.

—Curious Kids: Explore the Shore. Marx, Jonny. 2020. (ENG.). 16p. (J). (gr. 1-3). 12.99 (978-1-68010-619-0(8)) Tiger Tales.

—Dump Truck Disco. Silver, Skye. 2018. (ENG.). 32p. (J). (gr. -1-2). 16.99 (978-1-78285-407-4(X)) Barefoot Bks., Inc.

—The Earth Gives More. Fliess, Sue. 2019. (ENG.). 32p. (J). (gr. -1-3). 16.99 (978-0-8075-7710-3(3), 807577103) Whitman, Albert & Co.

—From Here to There. Fliess, Sue. 2016. (ENG.). 32p. (J). (gr. -1-3). 16.99 (978-0-8075-2622-4(3), 807526223) Whitman, Albert & Co.

—The Mitzvah Magician. Marshall, Linda Elovitz. 2012. (ENG.). 24p. (J). (gr. -1-2). lib. bdg. 7.95 (978-0-7613-5655-4(X), 9780761356554, Kar-Ben Publishing) Lerner Publishing Group.

—Photos Pink a Band. Hawes, Alison. 2017. (Cambridge Reading Adventures Ser.). (ENG.). 16p. pap. 7.37 (978-1-108-40066-4(3)) Cambridge Univ. Pr.

—Play! Play! Play! Florian, Douglas. 2018. (ENG.). 18p. (J). (gr. -1-1). bds. 6.99 (978-1-4998-0484-3(9)) Little Bee Books Inc.

Engel, Christiane. Ready, Set, Go! Sports of All Sorts. Cortright, Celeste. 2020. (J). **(978-1-78285-985-7(3))**; (ENG.). pap. **(978-1-78285-991-8(8))** Barefoot Bks., Inc.

Engel, Christiane. What Do You Celebrate? Holidays & Festivals Around the World. Stewart, Whitney. 2019. 40p. (J). (gr. k-4). 16.95 (978-1-4549-3213-0(9)) Sterling Publishing Co., Inc.

—What's on Your Plate? Exploring the World of Food. Stewart, Whitney. 2018. 40p. (J). (gr. k-4). 16.95 (978-1-4549-2672-6(4)) Sterling Publishing Co., Inc.

Engel, Christiane. You're So Brave, 1 vol. Marrs, Carrie. 2020. (Little Faithfuls Ser.). (ENG.). 32p. (J). 14.99 **(978-1-4002-1898-1(5))** Nelson, Thomas Inc.

—You're So Kind, 1 vol. Marrs, Carrie. 2020. (Little Faithfuls Ser.). (ENG.). 32p. (J). 14.99 **(978-1-4002-1924-7(8))** Nelson, Thomas Inc.

Engel, Christiane. Knick Knack Paddy Whack. Engel, Christiane. Songs, Steve. 2011. 24p. (J). (gr. -1-2). 9.99 (978-1-84686-659-3(6)) Barefoot Bks., Inc.

Engel, Elizabeth. The Adventures of Charlie Chameleon: School Days. Buikema, Ellen L. 2016. (ENG.). (J). pap. 8.95 (978-0-9908979-6-5(6)) Running Horse Pr.

Engel, Tonya. Our Lady of Guadalupe, 0 vols. Bernier-Grand, Carmen T. 2012. (ENG.). 32p. (J). (gr. 1-3). 17.99 (978-0-7614-6135-7(3), 9780761461357, Two Lions) Amazon Publishing.

—Rise! From Caged Bird to Poet of the People, Maya Angelou, 1 vol. Hegedus, Bethany. 2019. (ENG.). 48p. (J). (gr. 2-5). 20.95 (978-1-62014-587-6(1), c0924e44-1134-4019-b508-7a7a4ad9320a) Lee & Low Bks., Inc.

Engelbreit, Mary. The Bedtime Book, 1 vol. 2018. (ENG.). 24p. (J). (gr. -1-3). bds. 9.99 (978-0-310-76618-6(4)) Zonderkidz.

—A Little Princess. Burnett, Frances Hodgson. 2007. (Mary Engelbreit's Classic Library). (ENG.). 304p. (J). (gr. 3-7). 9.99 (978-0-06-008137-9(6), HarperFestival) HarperCollins Pubs.

—The Night Before Christmas, Set. Moore, Clement C. gif. ed. 2007. (ENG.). 40p. (J). (gr. -1-3). 25.00 (978-0-06-136495-2(9), HarperFestival) HarperCollins Pubs.

—The Night Before Christmas. Moore, Clement C. (ENG.). 40p. (J). (gr. -1-3). 2020. 9.99 (978-0-06-208944-1(7)); 2006. 17.99 (978-0-06-008160-7(0)) HarperCollins Pubs. Ltd. GBR. (HarperCollins). Dist: HarperCollins Pubs.

Engelbreit, Mary. Baby Booky: Honey Bunny. Engelbreit, Mary. 2004. (ENG.). 14p. (J). (gr. -1-18). 6.99 (978-0-06-008135-5(X), HarperFestival) HarperCollins Pubs.

—Mary Engelbreit's 5-Minute Fairy Tales: Includes 12 Nursery & Fairy Tales! Engelbreit, Mary. 2018. (ENG.). 192p. (J). (gr. -1-3). 12.99 (978-0-06-266326-9(7)) HarperCollins Pubs.

—Mary Engelbreit's A Merry Little Christmas: Celebrate from A to Z. Engelbreit, Mary. 2006. 40p. (J). (gr. -1-3). lib. bdg. 17.89 (978-0-06-074159-4(7)) HarperCollins Pubs.

—Mary Engelbreit's a Merry Little Christmas: Celebrate from a to Z, Vol. Engelbreit, Mary. 2010. (ENG.). 40p. (J). (gr. -1-3). pap. 7.99 (978-0-06-074160-0(0)) HarperCollins Pubs.

—Mary Engelbreit's a Merry Little Christmas Board Book: Celebrate from a to Z. Engelbreit, Mary. 2019. (ENG.). 32p. (J). (gr. -1 — 1). bds. 7.99 (978-0-06-074161-7(9), HarperFestival) HarperCollins Pubs.

—Mary Engelbreit's Color ME Christmas Book of Postcards. Engelbreit, Mary. 2017. (ENG.). 20p. (J). (gr. -1). pap. 9.99 (978-0-06-266327-6(5)) HarperCollins Pubs.

—Mary Engelbreit's Color ME Christmas Coloring Book. Engelbreit, Mary. 2016. (ENG.). 96p. (J). (gr. -1-3). pap. 15.99 (978-0-06-256260-9(6)) HarperCollins Pubs.

—Mary Engelbreit's Color ME Coloring Book: Coloring Book for Adults & Kids to Share. Engelbreit, Mary. 2015. (ENG.). 96p. (J). (gr. -1-3). pap. 15.99 (978-0-06-244561-2(8)) HarperCollins Pubs.

—Mary Engelbreit's Color ME Too Coloring Book: Coloring Book for Adults & Kids to Share. Engelbreit, Mary. 2016. (ENG.). 96p. (J). (gr. -1-3). pap. 15.99 (978-0-06-256258-6(4)) HarperCollins Pubs.

—Mary Engelbreit's Fairy Tales: Twelve Timeless Treasures. Engelbreit, Mary. 2010. (ENG.). 128p. (J). 19.99 (978-0-06-088583-0(1)) HarperCollins Pubs.

—Mary Engelbreit's Greeting Card Book: 24 Cards, 24 Envelopes, Plus Stickers! Engelbreit, Mary. 2018. (ENG.). 74p. (J). (gr. -1-3). pap. 12.99 (978-0-06-280375-7(1), HarperFestival) HarperCollins Pubs.

—Mary Engelbreit's Mother Goose: One Hundred Best-Loved Verses. Engelbreit, Mary. 2005. (ENG.). 128p. (J). (gr. -1-k). 19.99 (978-0-06-008171-3(6)) HarperCollins Pubs.

—Mary Engelbreit's Mother Goose Board Book. Engelbreit, Mary. 2018. (ENG.). 36p. (J). (gr. -1-3). bds. 7.99 (978-0-06-274223-0(X), HarperFestival) HarperCollins Pubs.

—Mary Engelbreit's Nursery & Fairy Tales Collection. Engelbreit, Mary. 2014. (ENG.). 192p. (J). (gr. -1-3). 11.99 (978-0-06-228707-6(9)) HarperCollins Pubs.

—Mary Engelbreit's Nursery & Fairy Tales Storybook Favorites: Includes 20 Stories Plus Stickers! Engelbreit, Mary. 2020. (ENG.). 192p. (J). (gr. -1-3). 13.99 (978-0-06-294266-1(2), HarperCollins) HarperCollins Pubs. Ltd. GBR. Dist: HarperCollins Pubs.

—Mary Engelbreit's Nursery Tales: A Treasury of Children's Classics. Engelbreit, Mary. 2008. (ENG.). 136p. (J). (gr. 4-7). 19.99 (978-0-06-073168-7(0)) HarperCollins Pubs.

—Mary Engelbreit's Nutcracker. Engelbreit, Mary. (ENG.). 40p. (J). (gr. -1-3). 2014. 9.99 (978-0-06-222417-0(4)); 2011. 17.99 (978-0-06-088579-3(3)) HarperCollins Pubs.

—Mary Engelbreit's the World Is Yours. Engelbreit, Mary. 2019. (ENG.). 48p. (J). (gr. -1-3). 12.99 (978-0-06-288994-2(X)) HarperCollins Pubs.

—Queen of Christmas. Engelbreit, Mary. 2003. (Ann Estelle Stories Ser.). (J). 32p. 16.99 (978-0-06-058608-9(7)); 159.90 (978-0-06-056902-0(6)); 127.92 (978-0-06-056903-7(4)) HarperCollins Pubs.

—Queen of Easter. Engelbreit, Mary. 2009. (Ann Estelle Stories Ser.). (ENG.). 32p. (J). (gr. -1-3). pap. 7.99 (978-0-06-008186-7(4)) HarperCollins Pubs.

—Queen of Halloween. Engelbreit, Mary. 2008. 32p. (J). (gr. -1-3). lib. bdg. 17.89 (978-0-06-008191-1(0)); (ENG.). 17.99 (978-0-06-008190-4(2)) HarperCollins Pubs.

—Queen of Hearts. Engelbreit, Mary. 2008. (Ann Estelle Stories Ser.). (ENG.). 32p. (J). (gr. -1-3). pap. 6.99 (978-0-06-008183-6(X)) HarperCollins Pubs.

—Queen of the Class. Engelbreit, Mary. 2007. 24p. (J). 16.00 (978-1-4223-6705-6(3)) DIANE Publishing Co.

Engelhart, Ann. Bambinelli Sunday: A Christmas Blessing. Welborn, Amy. 2013. (ENG.). 32p. (J). (gr. k-2). 16.99 (978-1-61636-649-0(4), B36649) Franciscan Media.

Engelhart, Ann Kissane. Adventures in Assisi: on the Path with St. Francis: On the Path with St. Francis. Welborn, Amy. 2014. (ENG.). 32p. (J). (gr. k-3). 15.99 (978-1-61636-650-6(8), B36650) Franciscan Media.

Engelking, Esther Rebecca. Mister Meow on Holiday. Engelking, Esther Rebecca. 2018. (ENG.). 42p. (J). pap. 10.00 (978-1-7915-3546-9(1)) Independently Published.

Engell, Mette. Christmas Makes Me Feel Pine Green! A Scratch-And-Sniff Holiday Story. Hastings, Ximena. 2020. (Crayola Ser.). (ENG.). 14p. (J). (gr. -1-k). bds. 8.99 **(978-1-5344-7088-0(3)**, Simon Spotlight) Simon Spotlight.

Engell, Mette. I'm Feeling Outrageous Orange: A Halloween Book. Gallo, Tina. 2019. (Crayola Ser.). (ENG.). 14p. (J). (gr. -1-k). bds. 5.99 (978-1-5344-4019-7(4), Simon Spotlight) Simon Spotlight.

—Matzah Belowstairs. Meyer, Susan Lynn. 2019. (ENG.). 24p. (J). (gr. -1-2). 17.99 (978-1-5415-2168-1(4), Kar-Ben Publishing) Lerner Publishing Group.

—Snow Day. Gates, Margo. 2019. (Let's Look at Weather (Pull Ahead Readers — Fiction) Ser.). (ENG.). 16p. (J). (gr. -1-1). pap. 6.99 (978-1-5415-7318-5(8), 9781541573185, Lerner Pubns.) Lerner Publishing Group.

—Up the Tree. Gates, Margo. 2019. (Let's Look at Animal Habitats (Pull Ahead Readers — Fiction) Ser.). (ENG.). 16p. (J). (gr. -1-1). 22.65 (978-1-5415-5868-7(5), 9781541558687, Lerner Pubns.) Lerner Publishing Group.

Engels, Christiane. Knick Knack Paddy Whack. Engel, Christiane. 2008. 24p. (J). (gr. -1-k). 16.99 (978-1-84686-144-4(6)) Barefoot Bks., Inc.

England, Katy. I Love You As Much. Loder, Mari. (ENG.). (J). 2018. 34p. 22.95 (978-1-64299-534-3(7)); 2017. pap. 12.95 (978-1-64028-046-5(4)) Christian Faith Publishing.

Engle, Amber Lena. The Life of Riley: A Solve-It Book: Repetitive Edition. O'Brien-Palmer, Michelle. 2018. (ENG.). 38p. (J). (gr. k-4). pap. 9.99 (978-1-879235-09-0(9)) Seattle Review Pr.

—The Life of Riley: A Solve-It Book, Repetitive Version. O'Brien-Palmer, Michelle. 2018. (ENG.). 38p. (J). (gr. k-4). 21.99 (978-1-879235-08-3(0)) Seattle Review Pr.

Engle, Jason. Samurai. Stowell, Louie. 2007. (Young Reading Series 3 Gift Bks). 58p. (J). (gr. 2-5). 8.99 (978-0-7945-1719-9(6), Usborne) EDC Publishing.

Engle, Jenny. Big Brothers & Big Sisters Are VIP's (Very Important Persons) A Color Me Book. Palmore, Julie. III, 56p. (J). (gr. -1-1). spiral bd. 9.95 (978-0-9722653-0-0(9)) Palmore, Julie.

Engle, Mette. Huggle Wuggle Bedtime Snuggle, Vol. Ferreri, Della Ross. 2019. (ENG.). 26p. (J). (gr. -1 — 1). 7.99 (978-1-5064-4858-9(5), Beaming Books) Augsburg Fortress, Pubs.

Englebrecht, Patti. Just Be There. Sheridan, Colleen M. 2019. (ENG.). 18p. (J). pap. 9.99 **(978-0-578-61833-3(8))** sheridan, colleen.

Engledow, Dave. The Little Girl Who Didn't Want to Go to Bed. Engledow, Dave. 2017. (ENG.). 40p. (J). (gr. -1-3). 17.99 (978-0-06-242537-9(4)) HarperCollins Pubs.

—The Little Girl Who Wanted to Be Big. Engledow, Dave. 2018. (ENG.). 40p. (J). (gr. -1-3). 17.99 (978-0-06-242539-3(0)) HarperCollins Pubs.

Engleheart, Phil. Choreographing the Stage Musical. Sunderland, Margot & Pickering, Ken. 2003. (Musical Theatre Ser.). 152p. (YA). (gr. 4-12). pap. 20.00 (978-0-85343-586-0(3)) Miller, J. Garnet Ltd. GBR. Dist: Empire Publishing Service.

Engler, Lori. Tiny Takes a Trip. Kennedy, Geno. 2011. 24p. pap. 24.95 (978-1-4560-8523-0(9)) America Star Bks.

English, Sarah Jane. Secrets in Stone: All about Maya Hieroglyphs. Coulter, Lavrie. 2003. 48p. (gr. 4-8). 18.00 (978-0-7567-9000-4(X)) DIANE Publishing Co.

Englund, Jonathon. Infaeter. Brett, James. 2nd ed. 2013. 238p. pap. (978-1-908462-03-9(5)) New Dawn Pubs.

Engman, Camilla. The Voyage, 1 vol. Salinas, Veronica. Eirheim, Jeanne, tr. 2013. (ENG.). 40p. (J). (gr. -1-2). 16.95 (978-1-55498-386-5(X)) Groundwood Bks. CAN. Dist: Publishers Group West (PGW).

Enik, Ted. The Cat in the Hat Flips His Lid. Brooke, Susan Rich & Seuss, Dr. 2003. (J). (978-0-7853-8446-5(4)) Publications International, Ltd.

—Curiosity, with a Capital S. Trimble, Tonya. 2011. 144p. (J). pap. 9.95 (978-0-9816453-9-1(9)); 16.95 (978-0-9829421-5-4(X)) Tell Me Pr., LLC.

—Fancy Nancy: Bubbles, Bubbles, & More Bubbles! O'Connor, Jane. 2018. 32p. (J). (978-1-5444-0218-5(X)) Harper & Row Ltd.

—It's Backward Day! O'Connor, Jane & Glasser, Robin Preiss. 2016. 32p. (J). (978-1-4806-9929-8(2)) Harper & Row Ltd.

—The Magic School Bus Gets Caught in a Web. Lane, Jeanette et al. 2007. (Scholastic Reader Ser.). (J). (978-0-545-03587-3(2)) Scholastic, Inc.

—Wee Witches, 1 vol. Roth, Beth. 2019. (ENG.). 32p. (J). (gr. -1-3). 14.99 (978-0-7643-5798-5(0), 16251, Red Feather) Schiffer Publishing, Ltd.

Enik, Ted, jt. illus. see Glasser, Robin Preiss.

Enik, Ted, jt. illus. see Wenzel, Paul.

Enjary, Raphaële, jt. illus. see Philipponneau, Olivier.

Enoki, Hiro. Tourette Syndrome: A Survival Kit. Murphy, Tara & Millar, Damon. 2019. (ENG.). 208p. (J). 17.95 **(978-1-78592-359-3(5)**, 696612) Kingsley, Jessica Pubs. GBR. Dist: Hachette UK Distribution.

Enos, Daryl. Farmer Brown & His Little Red Truck. Cochran, Jean M. 2009. (ENG.). 32p. (J). (gr. -1-k). 16.95 (978-0-9792035-0-3(3)) Pleasant St. Pr.

Enos, Randall. Inchworm & a Half. Pinczes, Elinor J. 2003. (ENG.). 32p. (J). pap. 7.99 (978-0-618-31101-9(7), 493403) Houghton Mifflin Harcourt Publishing Co.

—Mocha Dick: the Legend & Fury. Heinz, Brian. 2014. (ENG.). 32p. (J). (gr. 1-3). 18.99 (978-1-56846-242-4(5), Creative Editions) Creative Co., The.

Enos, Randall. Jibber-Jabber. Enos, Randall. 2018. 14p. (J). (gr. -1-k). bds. 8.99 (978-1-56846-315-5(4), Creative Editions) Creative Co., The.

Enos, Solomon. Akua Hawaii: Hawaiian Gods & Their Stories. Armitage, Kimo. 2005. 72p. (J). 16.95 (978-1-58178-042-0(7)) Bishop Museum Pr.

Enright, Amanda. Animal Antics, 1 vol. Virr, Paul. 2019. (Just Kidding! Ser.). (ENG.). 32p. (J). (gr. 1-2). 27.25 (978-1-5383-9120-4(1)); pap. 10.00 (978-1-7253-9300-4(X)) Rosen Publishing Group, Inc., The. (Windmill Bks.).

—Animals in Fall: Preparing for Winter. Rustad, Martha E. H. 2011. (Fall's Here! Ser.). pap. 39.62 (978-0-7613-8643-8(2)); (ENG.). 24p. (J). pap. 8.99 (978-0-7613-8506-6(1), 9780761385066); (ENG.). 24p. (J). lib. bdg. 25.32 (978-0-7613-5066-8(7), 9780761350668) Lerner Publishing Group. (Millbrook Pr.).

—Bow! Wow! Meow! Townsend, John. ed. 2020. (Booktacular Ser.). 36p. (J). (— 1). 9.95 (978-1-912904-97-6(7), Scribblers) Book Hse. GBR. Dist: Sterling Publishing Co., Inc.

—Collins Big Cat Phonics for Letters & Sounds - I Spy Nursery Rhymes: Band 00/Lilac. Guille-Marrett, Emily & Raby, Charlotte. 2018. (Collins Big Cat Phonics Ser.). (ENG.). 16p. (J). pap. 6.99 (978-0-00-825123-9(1)) HarperCollins Pubs. Ltd. GBR. Dist: Independent Pubs. Group.

—Diversión con Animales en Otoño. Rustad, Martha E. H. 2019. (Diversión en Otoño (Fall Fun) (Early Bird Stories (tm) en Español) Ser.). (SPA.). 24p. (J). (gr. k-2). 27.99 (978-1-5415-4079-8(4), Ediciones Lerner) Lerner Publishing Group.

—Diversión con Calabazas en Otoño (Fall Pumpkin Fun) Rustad, Martha E. H. 2019. (Diversión en Otoño (Fall Fun) (Early Bird Stories (tm) en Español) Ser.). (SPA.). 24p. (J). (gr. k-2). pap. 7.99 (978-1-5415-4539-7(7)); lib. bdg. 27.99 (978-1-5415-4083-5(2)) Lerner Publishing Group. (Ediciones Lerner).

—Diversión con la Cosecha de Otoño. Rustad, Martha E. H. & Becerra-Cárdenas, José. 2019. (Diversión en Otoño (Fall Fun) (Early Bird Stories (tm) en Español) Ser.). (SPA.). 24p. (J). (gr. k-2). 27.99 (978-1-5415-4081-1(6), Ediciones Lerner) Lerner Publishing Group.

—Diversión con Las Hojas de Otoño. Rustad, Martha E. H. 2019. (Diversión en Otoño (Fall Fun) (Early Bird Stories (tm) en Español) Ser.). (SPA.). 24p. (J). (gr. k-2). 27.99 (978-1-5415-4082-8(4), 9781541540828, Ediciones Lerner) Lerner Publishing Group.

—Diversión con Manzanas en Otoño. Rustad, Martha E. H. 2019. (Diversión en Otoño (Fall Fun) (Early Bird Stories (tm) en Español) Ser.). (SPA.). 24p. (J). (gr. k-2). 27.99 (978-1-5415-4080-4(8), Ediciones Lerner) Lerner Publishing Group.

—Diversión en el Clima de Otoño. Rustad, Martha E. H. 2019. (Diversión en Otoño (Fall Fun) (Early Bird Stories (tm) en Español) Ser.). (SPA.). 24p. (J). (gr. k-2). 27.99 (978-1-5415-4084-2(0), Ediciones Lerner) Lerner Publishing Group.

—Fall Animal Fun. Rustad, Martha E. H. 2018. (Fall Fun (Early Bird Stories (tm)) Ser.). (ENG.). 24p. (J). (gr. k-2). 27.99 (978-1-5415-2000-4(9), Lerner Pubns.) Lerner Publishing Group.

—Fall Apple Fun. Rustad, Martha E. H. 2018. (Fall Fun (Early Bird Stories (tm)) Ser.). (ENG.). 24p. (J). (gr. k-2). 27.99 (978-1-5415-2001-1(7), Lerner Pubns.) Lerner Publishing Group.

—Fall Apples: Crisp & Juicy. Rustad, Martha E. H. 2011. (Fall's Here! Ser.). pap. 39.62 (978-0-7613-8644-5(0)); (ENG.). 24p. (J). pap. 8.99 (978-0-7613-8507-3(X), 9780761385073); (ENG.). 24p. (J). lib. bdg. 25.32 (978-0-7613-5064-4(0), 9780761350644) Lerner Publishing Group. (Millbrook Pr.).

—Fall Harvest Fun. Rustad, Martha E. H. 2018. (Fall Fun (Early Bird Stories (tm)) Ser.). (ENG.). 24p. (J). (gr. k-2). 27.99 (978-1-5415-2002-8(5), Lerner Pubns.) Lerner Publishing Group.

—Fall Harvests: Bringing in Food. Rustad, Martha E. H. 2011. (Fall's Here! Ser.). pap. 39.62 (978-0-7613-8645-2(9)); (ENG.). 24p. (J). lib. bdg. 25.32 (978-0-7613-5067-5(5), 9780761350675) Lerner Publishing Group. (Millbrook Pr.).

—Fall Leaves: Colorful & Crunchy. Rustad, Martha E. H. 2011. (Fall's Here! Ser.). pap. 39.62 (978-0-7613-8646-9(7)); (ENG.). 24p. (J). pap. 8.99 (978-0-7613-8505-9(3), 9780761385059) Lerner Publishing Group. (Millbrook Pr.).

—Fall Leaves Fun. Rustad, Martha E. H. 2018. (Fall Fun (Early Bird Stories (tm)) Ser.). (ENG.). 24p. (J). (gr. k-2). pap. 7.99 (978-1-5415-2720-1(8)); lib. bdg. 27.99 (978-1-5415-2003-5(3), Lerner Pubns.) Lerner Publishing Group.

—Fall Pumpkin Fun. Rustad, Martha E. H. 2018. (Fall Fun (Early Bird Stories (tm)) Ser.). (ENG.). 24p. (J). (gr. k-2). pap. 7.99 (978-1-5415-2721-8(6)); lib. bdg. 27.99 (978-1-5415-2004-2(1), Lerner Pubns.) Lerner Publishing Group.

—Fall Pumpkins: Orange & Plump. Rustad, Martha E. H. 2011. (Fall's Here! Ser.). pap. 39.62 (978-0-7613-8647-6(5)); (ENG.). 24p. (J). pap. 8.99 (978-0-7613-8509-7(6), 9780761385097); (ENG.). 24p. (J). lib. bdg. 25.32 (978-0-7613-5065-1(9), 9780761350651) Lerner Publishing Group. (Millbrook Pr.).

—Fall Weather: Cooler Temperatures. Rustad, Martha E. H. 2011. (Fall's Here! Ser.). pap. 39.62 (978-0-7613-8648-3(3)); (ENG.). 24p. (J). pap. 8.99 (978-0-7613-8510-3(X), 9780761385103) Lerner Publishing Group. (Millbrook Pr.).

—Fall Weather Fun. Rustad, Martha E. H. 2018. (Fall Fun (Early Bird Stories (tm)) Ser.). (ENG.). 24p. (J). (gr. k-2). pap. 7.99 (978-1-5415-2722-5(4)); lib. bdg. 27.99 (978-1-5415-2005-9(X), Lerner Pubns.) Lerner Publishing Group.

—The Girls' Book: How to Be the Best at Everything. Foster, Juliana. Wingate, Philippa, ed. 2007. (Best at Everything Ser.). (ENG.). 128p. (J). (gr. 3-7). 9.99 (978-0-545-01629-2(0), Scholastic Pr.) Scholastic, Inc.

—Hoppity! Cheep! Quack! Townsend, John. ed. 2020. (Booktacular Ser.). (ENG.). 30p. (J). (— 1). 9.95 (978-1-912904-96-9(9), Scribblers) Book Hse. GBR. Dist: Sterling Publishing Co., Inc.

—I Want to Be A... Fairy. Eaton, Kait. 2014. (J). (978-1-4351-5499-5(1)) Barnes & Noble, Inc.

—Kitchen Capers, 1 vol. Virr, Paul. 2019. (Just Kidding! Ser.). (ENG.). 32p. (J). (gr. 1-2). 27.25 (978-1-5383-9122-8(8)); pap. 10.00 (978-1-5081-9793-5(8)) Rosen Publishing Group, Inc., The. (Windmill Bks.).

—Monster Laughs, 1 vol. Virr, Paul. 2019. (Just Kidding! Ser.). (ENG.). 32p. (J). (gr. 1-2). 27.25 (978-1-5383-9126-6(0)); pap. 10.00 (978-1-5383-9124-2(4)) Rosen Publishing Group, Inc., The. (Windmill Bks.).

Enright, Amanda. My Little Bible & Prayers. ed. 2020. (ENG.). 208p. (J). (gr. -1-k). 12.99 **(978-1-78128-388-2(5)**, Candle Bks.) Lion Hudson PLC GBR. Dist: Independent Pubs. Group.

Enright, Amanda. My Little Bible Memory Game, 1 vol. Williaon, Karen. ed. 2014. (ENG.). 80p. (J). (gr. -1-1). 9.99 (978-1-85985-986-5(0), Candle Bks.) Lion Hudson PLC GBR. Dist: Kregel Pubns.

—My Little Life of Jesus, 1 vol. Williamson, Karen. ed. 2014. (ENG.). 68p. (J). (gr. -1-k). 8.99 (978-1-78128-131-4(9), Candle Bks.) Lion Hudson PLC GBR. Dist: Kregel Pubns.

—No More Pacifiers! With Disappearing Pacifiers! O'Brien, Melanie. 2008. (ENG.). 18p. (J). (gr. -1-k). 10.95 (978-1-58117-684-1(8), Intervisual/Piggy Toes) Bendon, Inc.

—Noisy Touch & Feel: Cow Says Moo. Walden, Libby. 2016. (Noisy Touch & Feel Ser.). (ENG.). 12p. (J). bds. 14.99 (978-1-62686-575-4(2), Silver Dolphin Bks.) Readerlink Distribution Services, LLC.

—Noisy Touch & Feel: Owl Says Hoot. Walden, Libby. 2016. (Noisy Touch & Feel Ser.). (ENG.). 12p. (J). bds. 14.99 (978-1-62686-576-1(0), Silver Dolphin Bks.) Readerlink Distribution Services, LLC.

—Pride & Prejudice. 2017. (Seek & Find Classics Ser.). (ENG.). 48p. (J). (gr. 2). 9.99 (978-1-4998-0625-0(6)) Little Bee Books Inc.

—Silly Stories, 1 vol. Virr, Paul. 2019. (Just Kidding! Ser.). (ENG.). 32p. (J). (gr. 1-2). 27.25 (978-1-5383-9130-3(9)); pap. 10.00 (978-1-5383-9128-0(7)) Rosen Publishing Group, Inc., The. (Windmill Bks.).

Enright, Amanda. Wild Bios: Edgar Allan Crow. Acampora, Courtney & Fischer, Maggie. 2020. (Wild Bios Ser.). (ENG.). 16p. (J). (— 1). bds. 7.99 **(978-1-64517-227-7(9)**, Silver Dolphin Bks.) Printers Row Publishing Group.

Enright, Amanda & Pigott, Louise. Seek & Find: A Christmas Carol. Dickens, Charles & Cooper, Gemma. 2017. (Seek & Find Classics Ser.). (ENG.). 48p. (J). 9.99 (978-1-4998-0624-3(8)) Little Bee Books Inc.

Enright, Elizabeth. The Four-Story Mistake. Enright, Elizabeth. 3rd ed. 2008. (Melendy Quartet Ser.: 2). (ENG.). 208p. (J). (gr. 3-7). per. 9.99 (978-0-312-37599-7(9), 900048318) Square Fish.

—The Saturdays. Enright, Elizabeth. 3rd ed. 2008. (Melendy Quartet Ser.: 1). (ENG.). 192p. (J). (gr. 3-7). per. 7.99 *(978-0-312-37598-0(0)*, 900048317) Square Fish.
—Spiderweb for Two: A Melendy Maze. Enright, Elizabeth. 3rd ed. 2008. (Melendy Quartet Ser.: 4). (ENG.). 224p. (J). (gr. 3-7). per. 10.99 *(978-0-312-37601-7(4)*, 900048320) Square Fish.
—Then There Were Five. Enright, Elizabeth. 3rd ed. 2008. (Melendy Quartet Ser.: 3). (ENG.). 272p. (J). (gr. 3-7). per. 9.99 *(978-0-312-37600-0(6)*, 900048319) Square Fish.
—Thimble Summer. Enright, Elizabeth. 2008. (ENG.). 144p. (J). (gr. 3-7). pap. 7.99 *(978-0-312-38002-1(X)*, 900050525) Square Fish.
Enright, Kameron, jt. illus. see Bouchelion, Anastasia.
Enright, Vicky. Crafts to Make in the Fall. Ross, Kathy. 2003. (Crafts for All Seasons Ser.). (ENG.). 64p. (J). (gr. k-3). pap. 9.95 *(978-0-7613-0335-0(9)*, First Avenue Editions) Lerner Publishing Group.
—Crafts to Make in the Summer. Ross, Kathy. 2003. (Crafts for All Seasons Ser.: 3). (ENG.). 64p. (gr. k-3). pap. 9.95 *(978-0-7613-0334-3(0)*, First Avenue Editions) Lerner Publishing Group.
—It's a Beautiful Day! Haddon, Jean. 2005. (Silly Millies Ser.). 32p. (J). per. 5.95 *(978-0-7613-2397-6(X)*, First Avenue Editions) Lerner Publishing Group.
—Read Anything Good Lately? Allen, Susan & Lindaman, Jane. 32p. 2006. (ENG.). (J). (gr. k-3). per. 7.99 *(978-0-8225-6470-6(X)*, First Avenue Editions); 2003. 22.90 *(978-0-7613-2322-8(8)*, Millbrook Pr.); 2003. (J). (gr. -1-3). 14.95 *(978-0-7613-1889-7(5)*, Millbrook Pr.) Lerner Publishing Group.
—Used Any Numbers Lately? Allen, Susan & Lindaman, Jane. 2008. 32p. (J). (gr. k-4). 16.95 *(978-0-8225-8658-6(4)*, Millbrook Pr.) Lerner Publishing Group.
—Written Anything Good Lately? Allen, Susan & Lindaman, Jane. (J). 2010. (ENG.). 32p. (gr. k-3). pap. 7.99 *(978-0-7613-5477-2(8)*, First Avenue Editions); 2006. 31p. (gr. 3-7). lib. bdg. 15.95 *(978-0-7613-2426-3(7)*, Millbrook Pr.) Lerner Publishing Group.
Enright, Vicky. It's a Beautiful Day! Enright, Vicky, tr. Haddon, Jean. 2005. (Silly Millies Level 2 Ser.). (ENG.). 32p. (J). (gr. 1-3). lib. bdg. 21.27 *(978-0-7613-2834-6(3)*, Millbrook Pr.) Lerner Publishing Group.
Enright, Walter J. King Arthur & His Knights (Yesterday's Classics) Warren, Maude Radford. 2006. (J). per. 9.95 *(978-1-59915-194-6(4))* Yesterday's Classics.
Enrique, Sanchez. Big Enough Bastante Grande. Ofelia, Dumas Lachtman. 2008. 32p. (J). pap. 7.95 *(978-1-55885-239-6(5))* Arte Publico Pr.
Enriquez, Bea. La Playa de Los Inútiles. Nogués, Alex. 2020. (SPA.). 88p. (J). (gr. 4-7). pap. 17.95 *(978-84-17440-32-9(1))* Akiara Bks. ESP. Dist: Independent Pubs. Group.
Enroc Illustrations. The Golden Egg: A Story about Adoption. Thrasher, Jenny & Thrasher, Phil. 2006. (ENG.). 24p. per. 10.95 *(978-1-59800-468-7(9))* Outskirts Pr., Inc.
Ensikat, Klaus. The Life & Times of Martin Luther. Roth-Beck, Meike. 2017. (ENG.). 44p. (J). *(978-0-8028-5495-7(8)*, Eerdmans Bks For Young Readers) Eerdmans, William B. Publishing Co.
Ensor, Barbara. Cinderella (As If You Didn't Already Know the Story) Ensor, Barbara. 2011. 128p. (J). (gr. 2-5). 5.99 *(978-0-375-87387-4(2)*, Yearling) Random Hse. Children's Bks.
Entertainment One, Entertainment. Peppa Pig's Princess Pop-Up Castle. Candlewick Press Staff. 2017. (Peppa Pig Ser.). (ENG.). 6p. (J). (gr. -1-2). 24.99 *(978-0-7636-9734-1(6)*, Candlewick Entertainment) Candlewick Pr.
Entertainment, Premise. Elena of Avalor: Isabel's School Adventure. Miller, Sara & Valle, Mercedes. 2019. (World of Reading Level 1 Ser.). (ENG.). 32p. (J). (gr. -1-3). lib. bdg. 27.07 *(978-1-5321-4399-1(0)*, 33804) Spotlight.
—Henry Hugglemonster: The Huggleball Game. Scollon, Bill & Redeker, Kent. 2018. (World of Reading Level Pre-1 Ser.). (ENG.). 32p. (J). (gr. -1-2). lib. bdg. 27.07 *(978-1-5321-4179-9(3)*, 28526) Spotlight.
—Henry Hugglemonster: Snow Day. Scollon, Bill & Tyrrell, Colm. 2018. (World of Reading Level Pre-1 Ser.). (ENG.). 32p. (J). (gr. -1-2). lib. bdg. 27.07 *(978-1-5321-4180-5(7)*, 31061) Spotlight.
—The Lion Guard: Bunga the Wise. Behling, Steve & Loy, John. 2018. (World of Reading Level 1 Ser.). (ENG.). 32p. (J). (gr. -1-3). lib. bdg. 27.07 *(978-1-5321-4190-4(4)*, 28532) Spotlight.
—The Lion Guard: Unlikely Friends. Gold, Gina & Hopps, Kevin. 2018. (World of Reading Level Pre-1 Ser.). (ENG.). 32p. (J). (gr. -1-2). lib. bdg. 27.07 *(978-1-5321-4181-2(5)*, 28527) Spotlight.
Entertainment, Premise and Team. Puppy Dog Pals: Meet A. R. F. Olson, Michael & Smiley, Bob. 2019. (World of Reading Level Pre-1 Ser.). (ENG.). 32p. (J). (gr. -1-2). lib. bdg. 27.07 *(978-1-5321-4394-6(X)*, 33799) Spotlight.
Entner, Phyllis Defabrizio. How Almost Saved the Baby. Saul, Shura. Schaffer, Rita Tiero, tr. 2020. (Almost Ser.: Vol. 2). (ENG.). 32p. (J). pap. 11.95 ***(978-1-6551-3450-0(7))*** Independently Published.
Eone. Around the World with Peppa. 2018. (Scholastic Reader, Level 1 Ser.). (ENG.). 32p. (J). (gr. -1-k). pap. 4.99 *(978-1-338-32773-1(9))* Scholastic, Inc.
—Bedtime for Peppa. 2018. (Peppa Pig Ser.). (ENG.). 24p. (J). (gr. -1-k). pap. 4.99 *(978-1-338-32774-8(7))* Scholastic, Inc.
—Best Friends (Peppa Pig) Scholastic, Inc. Staff. 2015. (Peppa Pig Ser.). (ENG.). 32p. (J). (gr. -1-k). 8.99 *(978-0-545-84232-7(8))* Scholastic, Inc.
—Christmas Adventure. 2017. (Ben & Holly's Little Kingdom Ser.). (ENG.). 24p. (J). (gr. -1-k). pap. 4.99 *(978-1-338-22813-7(7))* Scholastic, Inc.
—Christmas with Peppa. 2017. (Peppa Pig Ser.). (ENG.). 16p. (J). (gr. -1-k). bds. 7.99 *(978-1-338-15898-4(8))* Scholastic, Inc.
—¡Compartir Es Genial! Rusu, Meredith. 2018. (Peppa Pig Ser.). (SPA.). 24p. (J). (gr. -1-k). pap. 4.99 *(978-1-338-29954-0(9))* Scholastic, Inc.
—Cuentos de Peppa en 5 Minutos. 2017. (Cerdita Peppa Ser.). (SPA.). 192p. (J). (gr. -1-k). 12.99 *(978-1-338-18789-2(9)*, Scholastic en Espanol) Scholastic, Inc.
—Doctors to the Rescue. Rusu, Meredith. 2019. (Peppa Pig Ser.). (ENG.). 32p. (J). (gr. -1-k). pap. 4.99 *(978-1-338-30762-7(2))* Scholastic, Inc.
EOne. Easter Surprise (Peppa Pig) Scholastic. 2017. (Peppa Pig Ser.). (ENG.). 10p. (J). (gr. -1-k). bds. 7.99 *(978-1-338-21028-6(9))* Scholastic, Inc.
Eone. Family Trip. 2018. (Peppa Pig Ser.). (ENG.). 24p. (J). (gr. -1-k). pap. 4.99 *(978-1-338-22875-5(7))* Scholastic, Inc.
—Five-Minute Peppa Stories (Peppa Pig) 2016. (Peppa Pig Ser.). (ENG.). 192p. (J). (gr. -1-k). 12.99 *(978-1-338-05804-8(5))* Scholastic, Inc.
EOne. Fun at the Fair: a Sticker Storybook (Peppa Pig) Scholastic. 2016. (Peppa Pig Ser.). (ENG.). 24p. (J). (gr. -1-k). pap. 7.99 *(978-1-338-03281-9(X))* Scholastic, Inc.
—George Catches a Cold. Scholastic. 2018. (Peppa Pig Ser.). (ENG.). 24p. (J). (gr. -1-k). pap. 4.99 *(978-1-338-32777-9(1))* Scholastic, Inc.
Eone. George Se Resfría. 2017. (Cerdita Peppa Ser.). (SPA.). 24p. (J). (gr. -1-k). pap. 3.99 *(978-1-338-23349-0(1))* Scholastic, Inc.
—George's New Dinosaur. 2018. (Peppa Pig Ser.). (ENG.). 24p. (J). (gr. -1-k). pap. 4.99 *(978-1-338-32778-6(X))* Scholastic, Inc.
EOne. I Can Be Anything! Auerbach, Annie. 2018. (Peppa Pig Ser.). (ENG.). 16p. (J). (gr. -1-k). bds. 7.99 *(978-1-338-22883-0(8))* Scholastic, Inc.
Eone. La Jornada Escolar de Peppa Peppa's School Day. Rusu, Meredith. 2018. (Peppa Pig Ser.). (SPA & ENG.). 32p. (J). (gr. k-2). pap. 3.99 *(978-1-338-15902-8(X)*, Scholastic en Espanol) Scholastic, Inc.
EOne. Learning to Share (Peppa Pig) Rusu, Meredith. 2017. (Peppa Pig Ser.). (ENG.). 24p. (J). (gr. -1-k). pap. 4.99 *(978-1-338-21026-2(2))* Scholastic, Inc.
Eone. The Lost Egg (Ben & Holly's Little Kingdom: Level 1 Reader) 2017. (Ben & Holly's Little Kingdom Ser.). (ENG.). 32p. (J). (gr. -1-k). pap. 4.99 *(978-1-338-23034-5(4))* Scholastic, Inc.
—Magic School. 2017. (Ben & Holly's Little Kingdom Ser.). (ENG.). 24p. (J). (gr. -1-k). pap. 4.99 *(978-1-338-22814-4(5))* Scholastic, Inc.
—The Magical Tale of Ben & Holly. Astley, Neville & Baker, Mark. 2017. (Ben & Holly's Little Kingdom Ser.). (ENG.). 32p. (J). (gr. -1-k). 8.99 *(978-1-338-22353-8(4))* Scholastic, Inc.
—My Daddy. 2018. (Peppa Pig Ser.). (ENG.). 16p. (J). (gr. -1-k). bds. 7.99 *(978-1-338-22878-6(1))* Scholastic, Inc.
EOne. Night Creatures: A Lift-the-Flap Book. Scholastic. 2018. (Peppa Pig Ser.). (ENG.). 14p. (J). (gr. -1-k). bds. 10.99 *(978-1-338-22879-3(X))* Scholastic, Inc.
—Peppa & Pals. Scholastic. 2019. (Peppa Pig Ser.). (ENG.). 10p. (J). (gr. -1-k). bds. 12.99 *(978-1-338-30764-1(9))* Scholastic, Inc.
Eone. Peppa & the Big Train (Peppa Pig) 2017. (Peppa Pig Ser.). (ENG.). 16p. (J). (gr. -1-k). bds. 7.99 *(978-1-338-05420-0(1))* Scholastic, Inc.
—Peppa en el Espacio. 2019. (Cerdita Peppa Ser.). (SPA.). 24p. (J). (gr. -1-k). pap. 4.99 *(978-1-338-60123-7(7)*, Scholastic en Espanol) Scholastic, Inc.
—Peppa Gives Thanks. 2018. (Peppa Pig Ser.). (ENG.). 24p. (J). (gr. -1-k). pap. 4.99 *(978-1-338-22876-2(5))* Scholastic, Inc.
—Peppa Goes Apple Picking. Rusu, Meredith. 2018. (Peppa Pig Ser.). (ENG.). 24p. (J). (gr. -1-k). pap. 4.99 *(978-1-338-32781-6(X))* Scholastic, Inc.
—Peppa Goes Swimming. 2018. (Peppa Pig Ser.). (ENG.). 24p. (J). (gr. -1-k). pap. 4.99 *(978-1-338-32783-0(6))* Scholastic, Inc.
EOne. Peppa Goes to the Zoo. Scholastic. 2019. (Peppa Pig Ser.). (ENG.). 10p. (J). (gr. -1-k). bds. 8.99 *(978-1-338-30763-4(0))* Scholastic, Inc.
Eone. Peppa Pig. Auerbach, Annie. 2019. (Peppa Pig Ser.). (SPA.). 24p. (J). (gr. -1-k). pap. 3.99 *(978-1-338-35918-3(5)*, Scholastic en Espanol) Scholastic, Inc.
EOne. Peppa Pig: Hide-And-Seek: Scratch Magic. Rusu, Meredith. 2020. (Peppa Pig Ser.). (ENG.). 64p. (J). (gr. -1-k). pap. 12.99 *(978-1-338-60343-9(4))* Scholastic, Inc.
—Peppa Pig: Peppa's Magical Unicorn. 2019. (Peppa Pig Ser.). (ENG.). 24p. (J). (gr. -1-k). pap. 4.99 *(978-1-338-58400-4(6))* Scholastic, Inc.
—Peppa Pig: Peppa's Valentine's Day. Carbone, Courtney. 2017. (Peppa Pig Ser.). (ENG.). 24p. (J). (gr. -1-k). pap. 4.99 *(978-1-338-15897-7(X))* Scholastic, Inc.
—Peppa Pig: Play Ball! 2019. (Peppa Pig Ser.). (ENG.). 32p. (J). (gr. -1-k). pap. 4.99 *(978-1-338-58445-5(6))* Scholastic, Inc.
—Peppa Plays Soccer (Peppa Pig: 8x8) Scholastic. 2016. (Peppa Pig Ser.). (ENG.). 24p. (J). (gr. -1-k). pap. 4.99 *(978-1-338-03279-6(8))* Scholastic, Inc.
—Peppa's Busy Day Magnet Book (Peppa Pig) Scholastic. 2016. (Peppa Pig Ser.). (ENG.). 10p. (J). (gr. -1-k). 12.99 *(978-0-545-92545-7(2))* Scholastic, Inc.
—Peppa's Chinese New Year. 2018. (Peppa Pig Ser.). (ENG.). 24p. (J). (gr. -1-3). pap. 4.99 *(978-1-338-54115-1(3))* Scholastic, Inc.
—Peppa's Easter Egg Hunt. Scholastic. 2019. (Peppa Pig Ser.). (ENG.). 24p. (gr. -1-k). 4.99 *(978-1-338-32784-7(4))* Perfection Learning Corp.
Eone. Peppa's First 100 Words. 2018. (Peppa Pig Ser.). (ENG.). 14p. (J). (gr. -1-k). 9.99 *(978-1-338-22877-9(3))* Scholastic, Inc.
—Peppa's First Colors (Peppa Pig) Scholastic. 2017. (Peppa Pig Ser.). (ENG.). 10p. (J). (gr. -1-k). bds. 7.99 *(978-1-338-18257-6(9))* Scholastic, Inc.
—Peppa's First Sleepover. 2018. (Peppa Pig Ser.). (ENG.). 24p. (J). (gr. -1-k). pap. 4.99 *(978-1-338-32776-2(3))* Scholastic, Inc.
—Peppa's Giant Pumpkin. Lizzio, Samantha. 2019. (Peppa Pig Ser.). (ENG.). 10p. (J). (gr. -1-k). bds. 7.99 *(978-1-338-33922-2(2))* Scholastic, Inc.
—Peppa's Halloween Party. 2016. (Peppa Pig Ser.). (ENG.). 24p. (J). (gr. -1-k). 4.99 *(978-0-545-92543-3(6))* Scholastic, Inc.
EOne. Peppa's Mermaid (Peppa Pig) 2020. (Peppa Pig Ser.). (ENG.). 24p. (J). (gr. -1-k). pap. 4.99 *(978-1-338-61174-8(7))* Scholastic, Inc.
Eone. Peppa's School Day. Rusu, Meredith. 2018. (Peppa Pig Ser.). (ENG.). 32p. (J). (gr. -1-k). pap. 4.99 *(978-1-338-32785-4(2))* Scholastic, Inc.
—Play Time for Peppa & George (Peppa Pig) Rusu, Meredith. 2016. (Peppa Pig Ser.). (ENG.). 32p. (J). (gr. -1-k). 8.99 *(978-1-338-03280-2(1))* Scholastic, Inc.
—Princess Peppa. Auerbach, Annie. 2017. (Peppa Pig Ser.). (ENG.). 32p. (J). (gr. -1-k). 8.99 *(978-0-545-62786-3(9))* Scholastic, Inc.
—The Pumpkin Contest. Rusu, Meredith. 2018. (Peppa Pig Ser.). (ENG.). 32p. (J). (gr. -1-k). pap. 4.99 *(978-1-338-22881-6(1))* Scholastic, Inc.
—The Safety First! Carbone, Courtney. 2018. (Peppa Pig Ser.). (ENG.). 32p. (J). (gr. -1-k). pap. 4.99 *(978-1-338-22882-3(X))* Scholastic, Inc.
—Sweet Dreams. Auerbach, Annie. 2019. (Peppa Pig Ser.). (ENG.). 32p. (J). (gr. -1-k). 17.99 *(978-1-338-26835-5(X))* Scholastic, Inc.
—When I Grow up. Easton, Marilyn & LeVine, Nicole. 2018. (Peppa Pig Ser.). (ENG.). 32p. (J). (gr. -1-3). 8.99 *(978-1-338-22880-9(3))* Scholastic, Inc.
Epelbaum, Mariano. Beware of the Giant Brain! Young, Mark. 2020. (Franken-Sci High Ser.: 4). (ENG.). 176p. (J). (gr. 3-7). 17.99 ***(978-1-4814-9140-2(7))***; pap. 6.99 ***(978-1-4814-9139-6(3))*** Simon Spotlight. (Simon Spotlight).
Epelbaum, Mariano. Celebrate Hanukkah with Bubbe's Tales. Flor Ada, Alma. Hayes, Joe & Franco, Sharon, trs. from SPA. 2007. (Cuentos para Celebrar / Stories to Celebrate Ser.). 30p. (J). (gr. k-6). per. 11.95 *(978-1-59820-134-5(4))* Santillana USA Publishing Co., Inc.
Epelbaum, Mariano. The Creature in Room #YTH-125. Young, Mark. 2020. (Franken-Sci High Ser.: 5). (ENG.). 176p. (J). (gr. 3-7). 17.99 ***(978-1-4814-9143-3(1))***; pap. 6.99 ***(978-1-4814-9142-6(3))*** Simon Spotlight. (Simon Spotlight).
Epelbaum, Mariano. The Creeping Clown: A Tale of Terror. Gunderson, Jessica. 2018. (Michael Dahl Presents: Phobia Ser.). (ENG.). 72p. (J). (gr. 4-6). pap. 5.95 *(978-1-4965-7348-3(X)*, 138935); lib. bdg. 25.32 *(978-1-4965-7344-5(7)*, 138931) Capstone. (Stone Arch Bks.).
—The Cursed Stage. Terrell, Brandon. 2017. (Snoops, Inc Ser.). (ENG.). 112p. (J). (gr. 4-8). lib. bdg. 26.65 *(978-1-4965-4346-2(7)*, Stone Arch Bks.) Capstone.
—Cyber Poser. Kesselring, Mari. 2014. (ENG.). 64p. (J). *(978-1-63235-036-7(X)*, 12-Story Library) Bookstaves, LLC.
—Digital Reveal. Kesselring, Mari. 2015. (ENG.). 64p. (J). *(978-1-63235-040-4(8)*, 12-Story Library) Bookstaves, LLC.
—Dinosaurs Can't Roar. Beason, Layla. 2020. 40p. (J). (-3). 17.99 *(978-1-4926-9365-9(0))* Sourcebooks, Inc.
—Dolls of Doom: A Tale of Terror. Brezenoff, Steve. 2018. (Michael Dahl Presents: Phobia Ser.). (ENG.). 72p. (J). (gr. 4-6). lib. bdg. 25.32 *(978-1-4965-7342-1(0)*, 138929, Stone Arch Bks.) Capstone.
—Don't Look Down: A Tale of Terror. Terrell, Brandon. 2019. (Michael Dahl Presents: Phobia Ser.). (ENG.). 72p. (J). (gr. 4-6). lib. bdg. 25.32 *(978-1-4965-7912-6(7)*, 139617, Stone Arch Bks.) Capstone.
—Drone Detective. Kesselring, Mari. 2015. (ENG.). 64p. (J). *(978-1-63235-041-1(6)*, 12-Story Library) Bookstaves, LLC.
—Fitness Crash. Kesselring, Mari. 2015. (ENG.). 64p. (J). *(978-1-63235-042-8(4)*, 12-Story Library) Bookstaves, LLC.
—The Frog Prince: An Interactive Fairy Tale Adventure. Hoena, Blake. 2020. (You Choose: Fractured Fairy Tales Ser.). (ENG.). 112p. (J). (gr. 3-7). pap. 6.95 *(978-1-4966-5812-8(4)*, 142244); lib. bdg. 32.65 *(978-1-5435-9012-8(8)*, 141368) Capstone.
—How to Catch a Dino Thief. Dare, Will. 2017. (Dino Riders Ser.: 4). (ENG.). 128p. (J). (gr. 2-5). pap. 5.99 *(978-1-4926-3623-6(1)*, Sourcebooks Jabberwocky) Sourcebooks, Inc.
—How to Hog-Tie a T-Rex. Dare, Will. 2017. (Dino Riders Ser.: 3). (ENG.). 128p. (J). (gr. 2-5). pap. 6.99 *(978-1-4926-3626-7(6)*, Sourcebooks Jabberwocky) Sourcebooks, Inc.
—How to Live Like a Roman Gladiator. Ganeri, Anita. 2015. (How to Live Like ... Ser.). (ENG.). 32p. (J). (gr. 3-6). lib. bdg. 27.99 *(978-1-4677-6355-4(1)*, 9781467763554, Hungry Tomato ®) Lerner Publishing Group.
—How to Live Like a Stone-Age Hunter. Ganeri, Anita. 2015. (How to Live Like ... Ser.). (ENG.). 32p. (J). (gr. 3-6). lib. bdg. 27.99 *(978-1-4677-6352-3(7)*, 9781467763523, Hungry Tomato ®) Lerner Publishing Group.
—How to Live Like a Viking Warrior. Ganeri, Anita. 2015. (How to Live Like ... Ser.). (ENG.). 32p. (J). (gr. 3-6). lib. bdg. 27.99 *(978-1-4677-6354-7(3)*, 9781467763547, Hungry Tomato ®) Lerner Publishing Group.
—How to Scare a Stegosaurus. Dare, Will. 2018. (Dino Riders Ser.: 6). (ENG.). 128p. (J). (gr. 2-5). pap. 5.99 *(978-1-4926-6812-1(5)*, Sourcebooks Jabberwocky) Sourcebooks, Inc.
—How to Track a Pterodactyl. Dare, Will. 2018. (Dino Riders Ser.: 5). (ENG.). 128p. (J). (gr. 2-5). pap. 5.99 *(978-1-4926-6809-1(5)*, Sourcebooks Jabberwocky) Sourcebooks, Inc.
—The Little Mermaid: An Interactive Fairy Tale Adventure. Braun, Eric Mark. 2020. (You Choose: Fractured Fairy Tales Ser.). (ENG.). 112p. (J). (gr. 3-7). pap. 6.95 *(978-1-4966-5813-5(2)*, 142245); lib. bdg. 32.65 *(978-1-5435-9013-5(6)*, 141369) Capstone.
—Little Red Riding Hood: An Interactive Fairy Tale Adventure. Braun, Eric. 2015. (You Choose: Fractured Fairy Tales Ser.). (ENG.). 112p. (J). (gr. 3-7). pap. 6.95 *(978-1-4914-5929-4(8)*, Capstone Pr.) Capstone.
—The Monster in the Mirror: A Tale of Terror. Wacholtz, Anthony. 2018. (Michael Dahl Presents: Phobia Ser.). (ENG.). 72p. (J). (gr. 4-6). lib. bdg. 25.32 *(978-1-4965-7341-4(2)*, 138928, Stone Arch Bks.) Capstone.
—No Escape: A Tale of Terror. Terrell, Brandon. 2019. (Michael Dahl Presents: Phobia Ser.). (ENG.). 72p. (J). (gr. 4-6). lib. bdg. 25.32 *(978-1-4965-7911-9(9)*, 139616, Stone Arch Bks.) Capstone.
—Phantom of the Library. Terrell, Brandon. 2017. (Snoops, Inc Ser.). (ENG.). 112p. (J). (gr. 4-8). lib. bdg. 26.65 *(978-1-4965-5060-6(9)*, 135986, Stone Arch Bks.) Capstone.
—The Robot Who Knew Too Much. Young, Mark. 2020. (Franken-Sci High Ser.: 3). (ENG.). 176p. (J). (gr. 3-7). 17.99 *(978-1-4814-9137-2(7))*; pap. 6.99 *(978-1-4814-9136-5(9))* Simon Spotlight. (Simon Spotlight).
—Science Fair Sabotage. Terrell, Brandon. 2017. (Snoops, Inc Ser.). (ENG.). 112p. (J). (gr. 4-8). lib. bdg. 26.65 *(978-1-4965-4347-9(5)*, Stone Arch Bks.) Capstone.
—Selfie Sabotage. Kesselring, Mari. 2014. (ENG.). 64p. (J). *(978-1-63235-037-4(8)*, 12-Story Library) Bookstaves, LLC.
—Sleeping Beauty: An Interactive Fairy Tale Adventure. Gunderson, Jessica. 2018. (You Choose: Fractured Fairy Tales Ser.). (ENG.). 112p. (J). (gr. 3-7). lib. bdg. 32.65 *(978-1-5435-3006-3(0)*, 138603, Capstone Pr.) Capstone.
—Techie Cheater. Kesselring, Mari. 2014. (ENG.). 64p. (J). *(978-1-63235-038-1(6)*, 12-Story Library) Bookstaves, LLC.
—Three Blind Mice Team up with the Three Little Pigs. Harrison, Paul. 2016. (Fairy Tale Mix-Ups Ser.). (ENG.). 24p. (J). (gr. k-2). lib. bdg. 23.99 *(978-1-4109-8301-5(3)*, Raintree) Capstone.
—Tracking Champ. Terrell, Brandon. 2017. (Snoops, Inc Ser.). (ENG.). 112p. (J). (gr. 4-8). lib. bdg. 26.65 *(978-1-4965-4348-6(3)*, Stone Arch Bks.) Capstone.
—The Undercover Cheerleader. Terrell, Brandon. 2017. (Snoops, Inc Ser.). (ENG.). 112p. (J). (gr. 4-8). lib. bdg. 26.65 *(978-1-4965-5061-3(7)*, 135988, Stone Arch Bks.) Capstone.
—The Vanishing Treasure. Terrell, Brandon. 2017. (Snoops, Inc Ser.). (ENG.). 112p. (J). (gr. 4-8). lib. bdg. 26.65 *(978-1-4965-4345-5(9)*, Stone Arch Bks.) Capstone.
Epelbaum, Mariano. Pixel Perfection. Epelbaum, Mariano. Kesselring, Mari. 2015. (ENG.). 64p. (J). pap. 8.95 *(978-1-63235-103-6(X))* RiverStream Publishing.
—Tuned Out. Epelbaum, Mariano. Kesselring, Mari. 2015. (ENG.). 64p. (J). pap. 8.95 *(978-1-63235-099-2(8))* RiverStream Publishing.
Epic Games Staff, jt. illus. see Dupuis, Karina.
Epps, Joesph, jt. illus. see Sith, Robert.
Epps, SArah. Alphabet for Young Eckists. Giordano, Jean. 2nd ed. 2007. (J). pap. *(978-1-57043-245-3(7))* Eckankar.
Epps, Spencer. ¿Abuelita, de Qué Están Hechos Los Ositos? Un Cuento de Amor. Newth, Midge & Cruz, Ruth. 2019. (SPA.). 32p. (J). pap. 9.99 *(978-0-9967949-3-0(X))* Thunder Child Productions LLC. dba PuppyDucks Publishing.
Epstein, Eugene. Arthur. Gould, Robert, photos by. Duey, Kathleen. (Time Soldiers Ser.: Vol. 4). (ENG.). (J). (gr. k-2). 2005. 96p. per. 5.95 *(978-1-929945-56-6(6))*; 2004. 48p. 15.95 *(978-1-929945-05-4(1))* Big Guy Bks., Inc.
—Bugs, Vol. 7. Gould, Robert. 2009. (Big Stuff Ser.: 7 vols.). (ENG.). 16p. (J). bds. 7.95 *(978-1-929945-66-5(3))* Big Guy Bks., Inc.
—Leonardo. Duey, Kathleen. 2009. (Time Soldiers Ser.). (ENG.). (J). (gr. k-2). 95p. 9.95 *(978-1-929945-89-4(2))*;Bk. 8. 48p. 15.95 *(978-1-929945-88-7(4))* Big Guy Bks., Inc.
—Rex. Gould, Robert, photos by. Duey, Kathleen & Gould, Robert. Windler-Cheren, Victoria, tr. 2003. (Time Soldiers Ser.: Bk. 1). (SPA & ENG.). 48p. (J). (gr. k-4). pap. 8.95 *(978-1-929945-35-1(3))* Big Guy Bks., Inc.
—Rex. Gould, Robert, photos by. Duey, Kathleen. 2003. (Time Soldiers Ser.: Bk. 1). (ENG.). 48p. (J). (gr. k-2). pap. 7.95 *(978-1-929945-20-7(5))* Big Guy Bks., Inc.
—Rex. Duey, Kathleen. 2006. (Time Soldiers Ser.: Bk. 1). 96p. (J). (gr. -1-7). lib. bdg. 24.21 *(978-1-59961-227-0(5))* Spotlight.
—Rex 2. Gould, Robert, photos by. Duey, Kathleen. 2003. (Time Soldiers Ser.: Bk. 2). (ENG.). 48p. (J). (gr. k-2). pap. 8.95 *(978-1-929945-27-6(2))* Big Guy Bks., Inc.
—Rex 2. Gould, Robert, photos by. Duey, Kathleen & Gould, Robert. 2003. (Soldados de Tiempo Libro: Vol. 2). (SPA & ENG.). 48p. (J). (gr. k-4). pap. 8.95 *(978-1-929945-36-8(1))* Big Guy Bks., Inc.
—Rex2. Gould, Robert, photos by. Duey, Kathleen & Gould, Robert. 2003. (Time Soldiers Ser.). 48p. (J). (gr. 4-7). 17.10 *(978-0-7569-3472-9(9))* Perfection Learning Corp.
—Samurai. Duey, Kathleen. l.t. ed. 2006. (Time Soldiers Ser.: Bk. 6). (ENG.). 48p. (J). (gr. k-2). 15.95 *(978-1-929945-62-7(0))* Big Guy Bks., Inc.
—Time Soldiers, Set. Gould, Robert, photos by. Duey, Kathleen. gif. ed. 2003. (Time Soldiers Ser.). (ENG.). 144p. (J). (gr. k-2). 32.95 *(978-1-929945-23-8(X))* Big Guy Bks., Inc.
—Time Soldiers - Mummy. Gould, Robert, photos by. Duey, Kathleen. 2005. (Time Soldiers Ser.: 5). (ENG.). (J). (gr. k-2). 48p. 15.95 *(978-1-929945-50-4(7))*; 96p. per. 5.95 *(978-1-929945-57-3(4))* Big Guy Bks., Inc.
—Time Soldiers - Patch. Gould, Robert, photos by. Duey, Kathleen. (Time Soldiers Ser.: Bk. 3). (ENG.). (J). (gr. k-2). 2005. 96p. per. 5.95 *(978-1-929945-55-9(8))*; 2003. 48p. pap. 8.95 *(978-1-929945-28-3(0))*; 2003. 48p. 15.95 *(978-1-929945-02-3(7))* Big Guy Bks., Inc.
—Time Soldiers - Rex. Gould, Robert, photos by. Gould, Robert & Duey, Kathleen. 2005. (Time Soldiers Ser.: Bk. 1). (ENG.). 96p. (J). (gr. k-2). per. 5.95

(978-1-929945-53-5(1)); per. 5.95 *(978-1-929945-54-2(X))* Big Guy Bks., Inc.

Epstein, Gabriela. Pierre's Stupendous Birthday Bash. Lammers, Elizabeth A. & McKinney, Dan. 2011. 48p. pap. 24.95 *(978-1-4560-4294-3(7))* America Star Bks.

—The Tale of the Black Igloo: Another Adventure of Pepe & Pierre, 1 vol. Lammers, Elizabeth A. & McKinney, Dan. 2010. 26p. pap. 24.95 *(978-1-60610-433-0(0))* PublishAmerica, Inc.

Epstein, Len. An Illustrated Timeline of U. S. Presidents, 1 vol. Englar, Mary. 2012. (Visual Timelines in History Ser.). (ENG.). 32p. (J). (gr. 2-4). pap. 7.49 *(978-1-4048-7254-7(X))*; lib. bdg. 29.32 *(978-1-4048-7161-8(6))* Capstone. (Picture Window Bks.).

Epstein, Len. The Lion Picture Puzzle Bible. Martin, Peter. ed. (ENG.). 32p. (J). (gr. k-2). 2020. pap. 8.99 ***(978-0-7459-7714-0(6)***, Lion Children's); 2016. 12.99 *(978-0-7459-6545-1(8))* Lion Hudson PLC GBR. Dist: Independent Pubs. Group, Kregel Pubns.

Epstein, Len. Ted Saw an Egg. Schmauss, Judy Kentor. 2006. (Barron's Reader's Clubhouse Level 1 Ser.). (ENG.). 24p. (J). (gr. k-3). 16.19 *(978-0-7641-3283-4(0)*, B.E.S. Publishing) Peterson's.

—Yes I Can. Kviat, Hindy & Lefkowitz, Chaya. 2018. (ENG.). 28p. (J). 10.95 *(978-1-945560-05-7(3))* Hachai Publishing.

Epstein, Len & Smith, Simon. Seek It Out. Kalz, Jill. 2013. (Seek It Out Ser.). (ENG.). 32p. (J). (gr. k-3). lib. bdg., lib. bdg., lib. bdg. 81.96 *(978-1-4048-7945-4(5)*, Picture Window Bks.) Capstone.

Epstein, Len, jt. illus. see Smith, Simon.

Epting, Steve, et al. Avengers Epic Collection: the Gatherers Strike! 2019. (ENG.). 488p. (YA). (gr. 4-17). pap. 39.99 *(978-1-302-92063-0(4))* Marvel Worldwide, Inc.

Epting, Steve, et al. Avengers: Live Kree or Die. 2020. (ENG.). 216p. (YA). (gr. 8-17). pap. 24.99 ***(978-1-302-92318-1(8))*** Marvel Worldwide, Inc.

Epting, Steve. Captain America Vol. 2: The Death of Captain America Volume 2 - the Burden of Dreams. 2008. (ENG.). 160p. (YA). (gr. 8-17). pap. 14.99 *(978-0-7851-2424-5(1))* Marvel Worldwide, Inc.

—Captain America: Winter Soldier Marvel Select Edition. 2020. 304p. (YA). (gr. 8-17). 29.99 *(978-1-302-92123-1(1))* Marvel Worldwide, Inc.

Epting, Steve, et al. Crux, Vol. 4. Dixon, Chuck. 2003. (Crux Ser.: Vol. 4). 160p. (YA). pap. 15.95 *(978-1-931484-99-2(6))* CrossGeneration Comics, Inc.

—Strangers in Atlantis, Vol. 3. Dixon, Chuck. 2003. (Crux Ser.: Vol. 3). 160p. (YA). (gr. 7-18). pap. 7.95 *(978-1-931484-63-3(5))* CrossGeneration Comics, Inc.

—X-Men: The Complete Age of Apocalypse Epic - Book 2. 2006. (ENG.). 376p. (YA). (gr. 8-17). 29.99 *(978-0-7851-1874-9(8))* Marvel Worldwide, Inc.

Epting, Steve & D'Armata, Frank. Blood Red Sea. Dixon, Chuck. 2004. (Cazador Ser.: Vol. 1). 160p. (YA). pap. 9.95 *(978-1-59314-058-8(4))* CrossGeneration Comics, Inc.

Er, Jiu. The Moose of Ewenki. Blackcrane, Gerelchimeg. Mixter, Helen, tr. 2019. 68p. (J). (gr. k-4). 19.95 *(978-1-77164-538-6(5)*, Greystone Bks.) Greystone Books Ltd. CAN. Dist: Publishers Group West (PGW).

Erb, Amanda. Look Out, T-Ball! Pryor, Shawn. 2020. (Kids' Sports Stories Ser.). (ENG.). 32p. (J). (gr. k-2). pap. 5.95 *(978-1-5158-5880-5(4)*, 142136); lib. bdg. 21.32 *(978-1-5158-4810-3(8)*, 141422) Capstone. (Picture Window Bks.).

—Tae Kwon Do Test. Oxtra, Cristina. 2020. (Kids' Sports Stories Ser.). (ENG.). 32p. (J). (gr. k-2). pap. 5.95 *(978-1-5158-5878-2(2)*, 142134); lib. bdg. 21.32 *(978-1-5158-4806-6(X)*, 141420) Capstone. (Picture Window Bks.).

Erb, Amanda & Kote, Geneviève. Kids' Sports Stories. Meister, Cari et al. 2020. (Kids' Sports Stories Ser.). (ENG.). (J). (gr. k-2). 170.56 ***(978-1-5158-7137-8(1)***, 199565); pap., pap., pap. 47.60 ***(978-1-5158-7780-6(9)***, 203143); 85.28 *(978-1-5158-4812-7(4)*, 29775); pap., pap., pap. 23.80 *(978-1-5158-5892-8(8)*, 29950) Capstone. (Picture Window Bks.).

Ercolini, David. It's a Moose! Rosoff, Meg. 2020. 40p. (J). (gr. -1-2). 17.99 *(978-0-399-16664-8(5)*, G.P. Putnam's Sons Books for Young Readers) Penguin Young Readers Group.

—The Night Before Christmas. Moore, Clement C. 2015. (ENG.). 32p. (J). (gr. -1-k). 16.99 *(978-0-545-39112-2(1)*, Orchard Bks.) Scholastic, Inc.

Erdelji, Darka. Polly MacCauley's Finest, Divinest, Wooliest Gift of All: A Yarn for All Ages, 1 vol. Fitch, Sheree. 2017. (ENG.). 68p. (J). (gr. 4-7). 16.95 ***(978-1-927917-10-7(7))*** Running the Goat, Bks. & Broadsides CAN. Dist: Orca Bk. Pubs. USA.

—The Queen of Paradise's Garden, 1 vol. Jones, Andy. 2009. (Jack Tale Ser.: 1). (ENG.). 44p. (J). (gr. 4-7). pap. 12.95 ***(978-0-9737578-3-5(3))*** Running the Goat, Bks. & Broadsides CAN. Dist: Orca Bk. Pubs. USA.

Erdogan, Buket. Mouse Loves Fall. Thompson, Lauren. 2018. (Mouse Ser.). (ENG.). 32p. (J). (gr. -1-k). 17.99 *(978-1-5344-2147-9(5))*; pap. 4.99 *(978-1-5344-2146-2(7))* Simon Spotlight. (Simon Spotlight).

—Mouse Loves Love. Thompson, Lauren. 2018. (Mouse Ser.). (ENG.). 32p. (J). (gr. -1-k). 17.99 *(978-1-5344-2150-9(5))*; pap. 4.99 *(978-1-5344-2149-3(1))* Simon Spotlight. (Simon Spotlight).

—Mouse Loves School. Thompson, Lauren. 2011. (Mouse Ser.). (ENG.). 24p. (J). (gr. -1-k). pap. 3.99 *(978-1-4424-2898-0(8))*; lib. bdg. 16.99 *(978-1-4424-2899-7(6))* Simon Spotlight. (Simon Spotlight).

—Mouse Loves Snow. Thompson, Lauren. 2017. (Mouse Ser.). (ENG.). 32p. (J). (gr. -1-k). 17.99 *(978-1-5344-0182-2(2))*; pap. 4.99 *(978-1-5344-0181-5(4))* Simon Spotlight. (Simon Spotlight).

—Mouse Loves Spring. Thompson, Lauren. 2018. (Mouse Ser.). (ENG.). 32p. (J). (gr. -1-k). 17.99 *(978-1-5344-0185-3(7))*; pap. 4.99 *(978-1-5344-0184-6(9))* Simon Spotlight. (Simon Spotlight).

—Mouse Loves Summer. Thompson, Lauren. 2018. (Mouse Ser.). (ENG.). 32p. (J). (gr. -1-k). 17.99 *(978-1-5344-2057-1(6))*; pap. 4.99 *(978-1-5344-2056-4(8))* Simon Spotlight. (Simon Spotlight).

—Mouse's First Christmas. Thompson, Lauren. 2003. (ENG.). 32p. (J). (gr. -1-3). 7.99 *(978-0-689-86348-6(9)*, Simon & Schuster Bks. For Young Readers) Simon & Schuster Bks. For Young Readers.

—Mouse's First Christmas. Thompson, Lauren. ed. 2003. (gr. -1-1). lib. bdg. 18.40 *(978-0-613-91039-2(7))* Turtleback.

—Mouse's First Day of School. Thompson, Lauren. 2010. (Mouse Ser.). (ENG.). 34p. (J). (gr. -1 — 1). bds. 7.99 *(978-1-4169-9476-3(9)*, Little Simon) Little Simon.

—Mouse's First Day of School. Thompson, Lauren & Jackson, Livia. 2003. (Mouse Ser.). (ENG.). 32p. (J). (gr. -1-3). 17.99 *(978-0-689-84727-1(0)*, Simon & Schuster Bks. For Young Readers) Simon & Schuster Bks. For Young Readers.

—Mouse's First Fall. Thompson, Lauren. 2010. (Classic Board Bks.). (ENG.). 34p. (J). (gr. -1 — 1). bds. 8.99 *(978-1-4169-9477-0(7)*, Little Simon) Little Simon.

—Mouse's First Halloween. Thompson, Lauren. 2003. (Classic Board Bks.). (ENG.). 34p. (J). (gr. -1 — 1). bds., bds. 7.99 *(978-0-689-85584-9(2)*, Little Simon) Little Simon.

—Mouse's First Snow. Thompson, Lauren. 2011. (Classic Board Bks.). (ENG.). 34p. (J). (gr. -1 — 1). bds. 7.99 *(978-1-4424-2651-1(9)*, Little Simon) Little Simon.

—Mouse's First Snow. Thompson, Lauren. 2005. (ENG.). 32p. (J). (gr. -1-3). 16.99 *(978-0-689-85836-9(1)*, Simon & Schuster Bks. For Young Readers) Simon & Schuster Bks. For Young Readers.

—Mouse's First Spring. Thompson, Lauren. 2012. (Classic Board Bks.). (ENG.). 34p. (J). (gr. -1-3). bds. 7.99 *(978-1-4424-3431-8(7)*, Little Simon) Little Simon.

—Mouse's First Spring. Thompson, Lauren. 2005. (ENG.). 32p. (J). (gr. -1-3). 17.99 *(978-0-689-85838-3(8)*, Simon & Schuster Bks. For Young Readers) Simon & Schuster Bks. For Young Readers.

—Mouse's First Summer. Thompson, Lauren. 2013. (Classic Board Bks.). (ENG.). 34p. (J). (gr. -1 — 1). bds. 7.99 *(978-1-4424-5842-0(9)*, Little Simon) Little Simon.

—Mouse's First Summer. Thompson, Lauren. 2014. (J). *(978-1-4351-5506-0(8))* Simon & Schuster.

—Mouse's First Summer. Thompson, Lauren. 2004. (ENG.). 32p. (J). (gr. -1-3). 19.99 *(978-0-689-85835-2(3)*, Simon & Schuster Bks. For Young Readers) Simon & Schuster Bks. For Young Readers.

—Mouse's First Valentine. Thompson, Lauren. 2013. (J). *(978-1-4351-5014-0(7))* Barnes & Noble, Inc.

—Mouse's First Valentine. Thompson, Lauren. 2004. (Classic Board Bks.). (ENG.). 34p. (J). (gr. -1 — 1). bds. 7.99 *(978-0-689-85585-6(0)*, Little Simon) Little Simon.

—On the Go with Mouse! Mouse Loves Summer; Mouse Loves Fall; Mouse Loves Snow; Mouse Loves Spring; Mouse Loves School, Mouse Loves Love. Thompson, Lauren. ed. 2019. (Mouse Ser.). (ENG.). 184p. (J). (gr. -1-k). pap. 17.99 *(978-1-5344-4021-0(6)*, Simon Spotlight) Simon Spotlight.

—Trick or Treat, Calico! Wilson, Karma. 2014. (J). *(978-1-4351-5610-4(2)*, Little Simon) Little Simon.

Erdrich, Lise. Bears Make Rock Soup. Fifield, Lisa. 2013. (ENG.). 32p. (J). pap. 9.95 *(978-0-89239-300-8(9)*, Children's Book Press) Lee & Low Bks., Inc.

Erdrich, Louise. Chickadee. Erdrich, Louise. (Birchbark House Ser.: 4). (ENG.). (J). (gr. 3-7). 2013. 224p. pap. 7.99 *(978-0-06-057792-6(4))*; 2012. 208p. 16.99 *(978-0-06-057790-2(8))*; 2012. 208p. lib. bdg. 17.89 *(978-0-06-057791-9(6))* HarperCollins Pubs.

—Makoons. Erdrich, Louise. (Birchbark House Ser.: 5). (ENG.). (J). (gr. 3-7). 2018. 192p. pap. 6.99 *(978-0-06-057795-7(9))*; 2016. 176p. 16.99 *(978-0-06-057793-3(2))* HarperCollins Pubs.

—The Porcupine Year. Erdrich, Louise. (Birchbark House Ser.: 3). (ENG.). (J). (gr. 3-7). 2010. 224p. pap. 7.99 *(978-0-06-441030-4(7))*; 2008. 208p. 16.99 *(978-0-06-029787-9(5))* HarperCollins Pubs.

Eremeyev, Margarita. Mama, Don't! Merrick, Laurie K. 2008. 20p. per. 24.95 *(978-1-4241-9868-9(2))* America Star Bks.

Erfanian, Banafsheh. A Cage Went in Search of a Bird, 1 vol. Fagan, Cary. 2017. (ENG.). 32p. (J). (gr. -1-2). 18.95 *(978-1-55498-861-7(6))* Groundwood Bks. CAN. Dist: Publishers Group West (PGW).

Eric, F. Rowe. Las Minas del Rey Salomon. Haggard, H. Rider. 5th ed. (Coleccion Clasicos en Accion).Tr. of King Solomon's Mines. (SPA.). 80p. (YA). (gr. 5-8). 12.76 *(978-84-241-5779-1(6))* Everest Editora ESP. Dist: Lectorum Pubns., Inc.

—El Último Mohicano. Cooper, James Fenimore. 6th ed. (Coleccion Clasicos en Accion). (SPA.). 76p. (YA). (gr. 5-8). 15.95 *(978-84-241-5780-7(X)*, EV0655) Everest Editora ESP. Dist: Lectorum Pubns., Inc.

Eric, Kincaid. Puss in Boots. Claire, Black. 2004. 30p. pap. *(978-1-84577-074-7(9))* Berryland Bks.

Eric, Whitfield. The Gift of the Magic: And Other Enchanting Character-Building Stories for Smart Teenage Girls Who Want to Grow up to Be Strong Women. Showstack, Richard. 2004. 156p. (YA). per. 14.95 *(978-1-888725-64-3(8)*, BeachHouse Bks.) Science & Humanities Pr.

Ericksen, Barb, et al. Time at the Top & All in Good Time: Two Novels. Ormondroyd, Edward. 2011. (ENG.). 379p. (J). (gr. 4-7). pap. 12.95 *(978-1-930900-55-4(4))* Purple Hse. Pr.

Ericksen, Barbara. Time at the Top. Ormondroyd, Edward. 40th anniv. ed. 2003. 191p. (J). 17.95 *(978-1-930900-19-6(8))* Purple Hse. Pr.

Erickson, Darren. Caterpillarology. Grogan, Brian, photos by. Ross, Michael Elsohn. 2003. (Backyard Buddies Ser.). 48p. (YA). (gr. 3-5). 6.95 *(978-1-57505-434-6(5)*, Carolrhoda Bks.) Lerner Publishing Group.

—Ladybugology. Grogan, Brian, photos by. Ross, Michael Elsohn. 2005. (Backyard Buddies Ser.). 48p. (gr. 3-6). 19.93 *(978-1-57505-435-3(3))* Lerner Publishing Group.

—Millipedeology. Grogan, Brian, photos by. Ross, Michael Elsohn. 2005. (Backyard Buddies Ser.). 48p. (gr. 3-6). lib. bdg. 19.93 *(978-1-57505-398-1(5))* Lerner Publishing Group.

—Millipedology. Grogan, Brian, photos by. Ross, Michael Elsohn. 2003. (Backyard Buddies Ser.). 48p. (YA). (gr. 3-5). 6.95 *(978-1-57505-436-0(1)*, Carolrhoda Bks.) Lerner Publishing Group.

—Snailology. Grogan, Brian, photos by. Ross, Michael Elsohn. 2003. (Backyard Buddies Ser.). 48p. (YA). (gr. 3-5). 6.95 *(978-1-57505-437-7(X)*, Carolrhoda Bks.) Lerner Publishing Group.

—Spiderology. Grogan, Brian, photos by. Ross, Michael Elsohn. (Backyard Buddies Ser.). 48p. (gr. 3-6). 2005. lib. bdg. 19.93 *(978-1-57505-387-5(X))*; 2003. (YA). 6.95 *(978-1-57505-438-4(8)*, Carolrhoda Bks.) Lerner Publishing Group.

Erickson, David. Brothers of the Falls. Emery, Joanna. 2004. (Adventures in America Ser.). (gr. 4). 14.95 *(978-1-893110-37-3(0))* Silver Moon Pr.

—Easter Around the World. Zemlicka, Shannon. 2005. (On My Own Holidays Ser.). 48p. (J). (gr. k-3). pap. 6.95 *(978-1-57505-765-1(4))* Lerner Publishing Group.

—Easter Around the World. Knudsen, Shannon. 2005. (On My Own Holidays Ser.). (ENG.). 48p. (gr. 2-4). 25.26 *(978-1-57505-655-5(0))* Lerner Publishing Group.

—Grandpa, Is There a Heaven? Bohlmann, Katharine. 2008. 32p. pap. 7.49 *(978-0-7586-1478-0(0))* Concordia Publishing Hse.

—Tell Me about God. Henley, Karyn. 2005. 24p. (J). 9.99 *(978-1-59185-616-0(7)*, Charisma Kids) Charisma Media.

Erickson, David L. Hablame de Dios. Henley, Karyn. 2005. 20p. (J). (gr. 4-7). 8.99 *(978-1-59185-825-6(9)*, Charisma Kids) Charisma Media.

—La Pascua en Todo el Mundo. Knudsen, Shannon. 2007. (Yo Solo - Festividades (on My Own - Holidays) Ser.). 48p. (J). (gr. k-5). (SPA.). lib. bdg. 25.26 *(978-0-8225-7791-7(7))*; per. 6.95 *(978-0-8225-7794-2(1))* Lerner Publishing Group.

Erickson, John & Holmes, Gerald L. The Case of the Prowling Bear. 2013. 126p. (J). *(978-1-59188-261-9(3))*; pap. *(978-1-59188-161-2(7))* Maverick Bks.

Erickson, John & Klofkorn, Lisa. Color Analyzers: Investigating Light & Color. Hoyt, Richard, photos by. Erickson, John & Willard, Carolyn. rev. ed. 2005. (Great Explorations in Math & Science Ser.). 96p. (J). pap., instr.'s gde. ed. 21.00 *(978-0-924886-89-8(7)*, GEMS) Univ. of California, Berkeley, Lawrence Hall of Science.

Erickson, Lindsey. The Knock: A Collection of Childhood Memories. Watkins, Carolyn. 2020. (ENG.). 50p. (J). 16.99 ***(978-1-7334732-3-1(8))*** Mindstir Media.

Erickson, Melissa. When the Tooth Fairy Comes... Erickson, Melissa. 2007. 15p. (J). (gr. -1-3). 10.99 *(978-1-59879-369-7(1))* Lifevest Publishing, Inc.

Erickson, Sue Ann. Grammy Grammy & the Magic Hat. Hoffmann, Mary Byrne. 2019. (ENG.). 38p. (J). (gr. k-2). 15.99 ***(978-1-7325265-5-6(9))*** Dayton Publishing.

Erickson, Terri. April Is Born: Adventures of a New Quarter Horse Filly. Hawkins, Al. l.t. ed. 2004. 24p. (J). pap. 9.50 *(978-0-9640056-5-5(4))* Arrowhead Publishing.

Erickson, Timothy Ronald. Death's Whisper Recoil, 2. Erickson, Timothy Ronald. 2003. (YA). pap. 14.95 *(978-1-59492-001-1(X))* Erickson, Tim.

Ericson, Lisa. Dill & Bizzy: An Odd Duck & a Strange Bird. Ericson, Nora. 2016. (ENG.). 40p. (J). (gr. -1-3). 17.99 *(978-0-06-230452-0(6))* HarperCollins Pubs.

—Dill & Bizzy: Opposite Day. Ericson, Nora. 2017. (ENG.). 40p. (J). (gr. -1-3). 17.99 *(978-0-06-230453-7(4))* HarperCollins Pubs.

Ericsson, Annie Beth. What's in My Garden? A Book of Colors. Christian, Cheryl. 2009. 16p. (J). (gr. -1). bds. 6.25 *(978-1-59572-166-2(5))* Star Bright Bks., Inc.

—What's in My Toybox: A Book of Shapes, 1 vol. Christian, Cheryl. 2009. (ENG.). 32p. (J). (gr. -1). bds. 6.25 *(978-1-59572-164-8(9))* Star Bright Bks., Inc.

Eriksen, Tone. I Love You Little One. Deprisco Wang, Dorothea. 2007. (Story Book Ser.). 10p. (J). (gr. -1). bds. *(978-1-84666-173-0(0)*, Tide Mill Pr.) Top That! Publishing PLC.

Eriksson, Eva. All's Happy That Ends Happy. Lagercrantz, Rose. 2020. (My Happy Life Ser.). (ENG.). 224p. (J). (gr. k-3). 18.99 ***(978-1-77657-292-2(0))*** Gecko Pr. NZL. Dist: Lerner Publishing Group.

Eriksson, Eva. A Day with Dad. Holmberg, Bo R. 2008. (ENG.). 32p. (J). (gr. -1-3). 15.99 *(978-0-7636-3221-2(X))* Candlewick Pr.

—Julia Wants a Pet. Lindgren, Barbro. Dyssegaard, Elisabeth Kallick, tr. 2003. 32p. (J). (gr. -1 — 1). 15.00 *(978-91-29-65940-5(X))* R & S Bks. SWE. Dist: Macmillan.

—Little Sister Rabbit & the Fox, 46 vols. Nilsson, Ulf. Beard, Susan, tr. 2017. Orig. Title: Nar Lilla Syster Kanin Blev Jagad Av en Rav. (ENG.). 32p. (J). 17.95 *(978-1-78250-378-1(1))* Floris Bks. GBR. Dist: Consortium Bk. Sales & Distribution.

—Little Sister Rabbit Gets Lost, 46 vols. Nilsson, Ulf. Beard, Susan, tr. 2017. Orig. Title: Nar Lilla Syster Kanin Gick Alldeles Vilse. (ENG.). 32p. (J). 17.95 *(978-1-78250-377-4(3))* Floris Bks. GBR. Dist: Consortium Bk. Sales & Distribution.

—The Midsummer Tomte & the Little Rabbits: A Day-By-day Summer Story in Twenty-one Short Chapters, 14 vols. Stark, Ulf. Beard, Susan, tr. 2016. Orig. Title: Sommar i Stora Skogen. (ENG.). 120p. (J). 24.95 *(978-1-78250-244-9(0))* Floris Bks. GBR. Dist: Consortium Bk. Sales & Distribution.

—My Happy Life. Lagercrantz, Rose. 2013. (My Happy Life Ser.). (ENG.). 136p. (J). (gr. k-3). 16.95 *(978-1-877579-35-6(1)*, 9781877579356) Gecko Pr. NZL. Dist: Lerner Publishing Group.

—See You When I See You. Lagercrantz, Rose. 2017. (My Happy Life Ser.). (ENG.). 152p. (J). (gr. k-3). 16.99 *(978-1-77657-129-1(0)*, 9781776571291) Gecko Pr. NZL. Dist: Lerner Publishing Group.

—When I Am Happiest. Lagercrantz, Rose. 2015. (My Happy Life Ser.). (ENG.). 128p. (J). (gr. k-3). 16.99 *(978-1-927271-90-2(8)*, 9781927271902) Gecko Pr. NZL. Dist: Lerner Publishing Group.

—Where Dani Goes, Happy Follows. Lagercrantz, Rose. 2019. (My Happy Life Ser.). (ENG.). 196p. (J). (gr. k-3). 17.99 *(978-1-77657-225-0(4))* Gecko Pr. NZL. Dist: Lerner Publishing Group.

—The Yule Tomte & the Little Rabbits, 15 vols. Stark, Ulf. Beard, Susan, tr. 2014. (ENG.). 104p. (J). 24.95 *(978-1-78250-136-7(3))* Floris Bks. GBR. Dist: Consortium Bk. Sales & Distribution.

Erimu. Imaginary Aquarium Stackable Crayon Activity Book. 2019. (Kawaii Kids Club Ser.). (ENG.). 120p. (J). pap. 12.99 *(978-4-05-621105-4(1))* Gakken Plus Co., Ltd. JPN. Dist: Simon & Schuster, Inc.

Ering, Timothy Basil. The Children & the Wolves. Rapp, Adam. 2012. 160p. (YA). (gr. 9). 16.99 *(978-0-7636-5337-8(3))* Candlewick Pr.

—Don't Let the Peas Touch! Blumenthal, Deborah. 2004. (J). *(978-0-439-29733-2(8)*, Levine, Arthur A. Bks.) Scholastic, Inc.

—Finn Throws a Fit! Elliott, David. 32p. (J). 2011. (gr. k-k). pap. 6.99 *(978-0-7636-5604-1(6))*; 2009. (gr. -1-k). 16.99 *(978-0-7636-2356-2(3))* Candlewick Pr.

—Mr. & Mrs. God in the Creation Kitchen. Wood, Nancy. 2006. (ENG.). 32p. (J). (gr. k-4). 16.99 *(978-0-7636-1258-0(8))* Candlewick Pr.

—Snook Alone. Nelson, Marilyn. 2012. 48p. (J). (gr. -1-1). (ENG.). 21.19 *(978-0-7636-2667-9(8))*; pap. 7.99 *(978-0-7636-6120-5(1))* Candlewick Pr.

—The Tale of Despereaux: Being the Story of a Mouse, a Princess, Some Soup & a Spool of Thread. Dicamillo, Kate. 2013. 296p. (J). *(978-0-7636-7205-8(X))* Candlewick Pr.

—The Tale of Despereaux: Being the Story of a Mouse, a Princess, Some Soup & a Spool of Thread. Dicamillo, Kate. 2003. pap. *(978-0-439-70167-9(8)*, Scholastic) Scholastic, Inc.

—The Tale of Despereaux: Being the Story of a Mouse, a Princess, Some Soup, & a Spool of Thread. Dicamillo, Kate. 2003. (ENG.). 272p. (J). (gr. 2-5). 19.99 *(978-0-7636-1722-6(9))* Candlewick Pr.

—The Tale of Despereaux: Being the Story of a Mouse, a Princess, Some Soup, & a Spool of Thread. DiCamillo, Kate. 2015. 272p. (J). (gr. 2-5). pap. 8.99 *(978-0-7636-8089-3(3))* Candlewick Pr.

—The Tale of Despereaux: Being the Story of a Mouse, a Princess, Some Soup & a Spool of Thread. Dicamillo, Kate. abr. ed. 2008. (ENG.). 272p. (J). (gr. 2-5). 29.99 *(978-0-7636-2928-1(6))* Candlewick Pr.

—The Tale of Despereaux: Being the Story of a Mouse, a Princess, Some Soup & a Spool of Thread. Dicamillo, Kate. l.t. ed. 2004. (Thorndike Literacy Bridge Ser.). (ENG.). 247p. (J). pap. 11.95 *(978-1-4104-1527-1(9))* Thorndike Pr.

—33 Snowfish. Rapp, Adam. 2006. (ENG.). 192p. (YA). (gr. 9-12). per. 7.99 *(978-0-7636-2917-5(0))* Candlewick Pr.

Ering, Timothy Basil. The Almost Fearless Hamilton Squidlegger. Ering, Timothy Basil. 2014. (ENG.). 48p. (J). (gr. -1-2). 16.99 *(978-0-7636-2357-9(1))* Candlewick Pr.

—The Story of Frog Belly Rat Bone. Ering, Timothy Basil. 2013. (ENG.). 48p. (J). (gr. -1-3). 18.99 *(978-0-7636-6661-3(0))* Candlewick Pr.

—The Unexpected Love Story of Alfred Fiddleduckling. Ering, Timothy Basil. 2017. (ENG.). 48p. (J). (-k). 16.99 *(978-0-7636-6432-9(4))* Candlewick Pr.

Eriza, Gustavo. A Princess Alphabet: The ABCs of Royalty! Jaycox, Jaclyn. 2016. (Alphabet Connection Ser.). (ENG.). 32p. (J). (gr. -1-2). lib. bdg. 27.99 *(978-1-4795-6885-7(6)*, Picture Window Bks.) Capstone.

Erkas, Sinem. The Girl Guide. Ibrahim, Marawa. 2018. 214p. (J). *(978-1-5490-6729-7(X))* HarperCollins Pubs.

—The Girl Guide: 50 Ways to Learn to Love Your Changing Body. Ibrahim, Marawa. 2018. (ENG.). 224p. (J). (gr. 3-7). pap. 14.99 *(978-0-06-283943-5(8))* HarperCollins Pubs.

Erkas, Sinem. Work It, Girl: Mae Jemison: Blast off into Space, Like. Moss, Caroline. 2020. (Work It, Girl Ser.). (ENG.). 64p. (J). (gr. 2-6). 15.99 ***(978-0-7112-4514-3(2)***, 327178, Frances Lincoln Children's Bks.) Quarto Publishing Group UK GBR. Dist: Hachette UK Distribution.

—Work It, Girl: Michelle Obama. Moss, Caroline. 2020. (Work It, Girl Ser.). (ENG.). 64p. (J). (gr. 2-6). 15.99 ***(978-0-7112-4517-4(7)***, 327184, Frances Lincoln Children's Bks.) Quarto Publishing Group UK GBR. Dist: Hachette UK Distribution.

—Work It, Girl: Michelle Obama: Become a Leader Like. Moss, Caroline. 2020. (Work It, Girl Ser.). (ENG.). 64p. (J). (gr. 3-7). 15.99 ***(978-0-7112-4518-1(5)***, Frances Lincoln Children's Bks.) Quarto Publishing Group UK GBR. Dist: Hachette Bk. Group.

Erker, Robert. The Secret of the Bounce-Back Mom. Pohlmann-Eden, Bernd. Hofer, Klaus C., tr. 2013. 34p. pap. *(978-1-897462-27-0(1))* Glen Margaret Publishing.

Erkkinen, Joel. ABC Death. Hawley, Shane. 2018. (Button Poetry Picture Bks.). (ENG.). 72p. 16.00 *(978-1-943735-46-4(8))* Button Poetry.

Erkocak, Sahin. King Arthur & the Sword in the Stone, 1 vol. Meister, Cari. 2008. (Read-It! Readers: Legends Ser.). (ENG.). 32p. (J). (gr. k-3). 21.32 *(978-1-4048-4837-5(1)*, Picture Window Bks.) Capstone.

—No Snow for Christmas, 1 vol. Kalz, Jill. 2013. (Pfeffernut County Ser.). (ENG.). 32p. (J). (gr. k-2). 8.99 *(978-1-4795-2158-6(2)*, Picture Window Bks.) Capstone.

Erlbruch, Wolf. The Bear Who Wasn't There & the Fabulous Forest. Lavie, Oren. 2016. (ENG.). 48p. (J). (gr. -1-2). 17.95 *(978-1-61775-490-6(0)*, Black Sheep) Akashic Bks.

—The King & the Sea. Janisch, Heinz. 2015.Tr. of Der Koenig und das Meer. (ENG.). 48p. (J). (gr. 2-4). 16.99 *(978-1-877579-94-3(7))* Gecko Pr. NZL. Dist: Lerner Publishing Group.
—The Story of the Little Mole Sound Book. Holzwarth, Werner. 2012. 24p. (J). (gr. -1-k). 17.99 *(978-1-84365-132-1(7)*, Pavilion Children's Books) Pavilion Bks. GBR. Dist: Penguin Random Hse. LLC.
Erlbruch, Wolf. Duck, Death & the Tulip. Erlbruch, Wolf. (ENG.). 38p. 2016. (YA). (gr. 4-12). 16.99 *(978-1-877467-14-1(6))*; 2011. (J). 17.95 *(978-1-877579-02-8(5))* Gecko Pr. NZL. Dist: Lerner Publishing Group.
Erlich, Esther. Jonathon's Thongs. Kliman, Susie. 2013. 35p. pap. *(978-0-9875296-1-9(7))* Aly's Bks.
Ermos, George. Alexander Hamilton: American Hero. Lowell, Barbara. 2018. (Penguin Young Readers, Level 4 Ser.). (ENG.). 32p. (J). (gr. 1-3). pap. 3.99 *(978-1-5247-8773-8(6)*, Penguin Young Readers) Penguin Young Readers Group.
—April Fiendish. Singleton, Linda Joy. 2019. (Haunted Holidays Ser.). (ENG.). 48p. (J). (gr. 3-7). lib. bdg. 29.93 *(978-1-5321-3661-0(7)*, 33768, Spellbound) Magic Wagon.
Ermos, George. A Beast C: From Alien to Zombie. Turner, Katie. Cottage Door Press, ed. 2020. (ENG.). 26p. (J). (gr. -1-1). 14.99 ***(978-1-68052-925-8(0)***, 1005670) Cottage Door Pr.
Ermos, George. Dough Knights & Dragons. Leone, Dee. 2017. 40p. (J). (gr. k). 16.95 *(978-1-4549-2141-7(2))* Sterling Publishing Co., Inc.
—The End of Something Wonderful: A Practical Guide to a Backyard Funeral. Lucianovic, Stephanie V. W. 2019. 32p. (J). (gr. -1-3). 16.95 *(978-1-4549-3211-6(2))* Sterling Publishing Co., Inc.
—Fright of July. Singleton, Linda Joy. 2019. (Haunted Holidays Ser.). (ENG.). 48p. (J). (gr. 3-7). lib. bdg. 29.93 *(978-1-5321-3662-7(5)*, 33770, Spellbound) Magic Wagon.
—Haunted Holidays (Set), 4 vols. Singleton, Linda Joy. 2019. (Haunted Holidays Ser.). (ENG.). 48p. (J). (gr. 3-7). lib. bdg. 119.72 *(978-1-5321-3660-3(9)*, 33766, Spellbound) Magic Wagon.
—Spin. Janni, Rebecca. 2017. (ENG.). 32p. (J). (-k). pap. 3.99 *(978-0-448-48948-3(1)*, Grosset & Dunlap) Penguin Young Readers Group.
—Trick or Terror. Singleton, Linda Joy. 2019. (Haunted Holidays Ser.). (ENG.). 48p. (J). (gr. 3-7). lib. bdg. 29.93 *(978-1-5321-3663-4(3)*, 33772, Spellbound) Magic Wagon.
—Valenterror. Singleton, Linda Joy. 2019. (Haunted Holidays Ser.). (ENG.). 48p. (J). (gr. 3-7). lib. bdg. 29.93 *(978-1-5321-3664-1(1)*, 33774, Spellbound) Magic Wagon.
Ernst, Clara, jt. illus. see Madan, Fredric C.
Ernst, Clara, jt. illus. see Mingo, Norman.
Ernst, Lisa Campbell. Boots for Beth. Moran, Alex. 2003. (Green Light Readers Level 2 Ser.). (ENG.). 24p. (J). (gr. -1-3). pap. 3.95 *(978-0-15-204838-9(3)*, 1194610) Houghton Mifflin Harcourt Publishing Co.
—The Chick That Wouldn't Hatch. Daniel, Claire. 2003. (Green Light Readers Level 2 Ser.). (ENG.). 24p. (J). (gr. -1-3). pap. 3.95 *(978-0-15-204831-0(6)*, 1194589) Houghton Mifflin Harcourt Publishing Co.
—Come Here, Tiger! Moran, Alex. 2003. (Green Light Readers Level 1 Ser.). (ENG.). 24p. (J). (gr. -1-3). pap. 4.99 *(978-0-15-204860-0(X)*, 1194677) Houghton Mifflin Harcourt Publishing Co.
—Lucy's Quiet Book. Medearis, Angela Shelf. 2004. (Green Light Readers Level 2 Ser.). (ENG.). 24p. (J). (gr. -1-3). pap. 3.95 *(978-0-15-205143-3(0)*, 1195521) Houghton Mifflin Harcourt Publishing Co.
—Lucy's Quiet Book. Medearis, Angela Shelf. 2004. (Green Light Readers Level 2 Ser.). (gr. k-2). 13.95 *(978-0-7569-4310-3(8))* Perfection Learning Corp.
Ernst, Lisa Campbell. The Gingerbread Girl. Ernst, Lisa Campbell. 2009. 32p. (J). (gr. -1-k). pap. 6.99 *(978-0-14-241448-4(4)*, Puffin) Penguin Publishing Group.
—The Gingerbread Girl. Ernst, Lisa Campbell. 2006. (ENG.). 32p. (J). (gr. -1-k). 17.99 *(978-0-525-47667-2(9)*, Dutton Books for Young Readers) Penguin Young Readers Group.
—Goldilocks Returns. Ernst, Lisa Campbell. 2003. (ENG.). 40p. (J). (gr. -1-3). pap. 7.99 *(978-0-689-85705-8(5)*, Simon & Schuster Bks. For Young Readers) Simon & Schuster Bks. For Young Readers.
—El Pollito Que No Quería Salir del Huevo. Ernst, Lisa Campbell. Daniel, Claire. Flor Ada, Alma & Campoy, F. Isabel, trs. 2009. (Green Light Readers Level 2 Ser.).Tr. of Chick That Wouldn't Hatch. (ENG.). 28p. (J). (gr. -1-3). pap. 3.99 *(978-0-15-206446-4(X)*, 1099024) Houghton Mifflin Harcourt Publishing Co.
—The Turn-Around, Upside-Down Alphabet Book. Ernst, Lisa Campbell. 2004. (ENG.). 32p. (J). (gr. -1-3). 19.99 *(978-0-689-85685-3(7)*, Simon & Schuster Bks. For Young Readers) Simon & Schuster Bks. For Young Readers.
—Wake up, It's Spring! Ernst, Lisa Campbell. 2004. (ENG.). 40p. (J). (gr. -1-3). 16.99 *(978-0-06-008985-6(7))* HarperCollins Pubs.
Ernst, Nikki. Djeaneautha the Terrible: DJ the Terrible. Nemeth, Samantha. 2019. (ENG.). 130p. (J). pap. ***(978-1-989506-07-3(0))*** Pandamonium Publishing Hse.
Ernst, Sara. The Small Grey Goat: A Weathered Tale of the Heart. Ernst, Sara. 2019. (ENG.). 36p. (J). pap. 14.00 *(978-1-7928-3964-1(2))* Independently Published.
Ernt, Clara, jt. illus. see Mingo, Norman.
Ero, Aguilar. I Love My Mama. Zapple, Elias. 2020. (I Love... Ser.: Vol. 1). (ENG.). 32p. (J). (gr. k). pap. ***(978-1-912704-34-7(X))*** Heads or Tales Pr.
Erps, Yitzy. Tell Me a Tale: 8 Great Stories. 2005. 64p. (J). *(978-1-4226-0018-4(1))* Mesorah Pubns., Ltd.
Errington, Rachael. Count Grumpula & the Wood Witch. Blackhurst, Rebecca. 2013. 18p. *(978-0-473-24899-4(9))* Cobble Creep Productions.
Erskine, Gary, et al. Star Wars Legends Epic Collection: the New Republic Vol. 3. 2017. (ENG.). 472p. (J). (gr. 4-17). pap. 39.99 *(978-1-302-90797-6(2))* Marvel Worldwide, Inc.
Ersoz, Sahin. The Mad Mysterious Mansion: Izzy & Daisy. Ersoz, Isabella. 2013. 40p. pap. 12.95 *(978-0-9912023-4-8(1))* Pep & Olie Publishing.
—Mr. Kite & the Perilous Flight: Izzy & Daisy. Lebost, Diana. 2013. 88p. pap. 18.95 *(978-0-9912023-5-5(X))* Pep & Olie Publishing.
Ertel, Susan. A Day in D. C. with the Forest Friends. Earnhart, Hugh. 2016. (ENG.). (J). 16.95 *(978-1-939710-53-6(7))* Orange Frazer Pr.
Ervin, Keith. Charlie & Chu Chu's Day of Adventure. Ervin, Imogene. 2005. (J). 7.00 *(978-0-9771549-0-6(4))* Finer Moments.
Erwert, Scott. How to Be a Vampire: A Fangs-On Guide for the Newly Undead. Gray, Amy. 2009. (ENG.). 144p. (YA). (gr. 7-18). 14.99 *(978-0-7636-4915-9(5))* Candlewick Pr.
Erwin, Steve, et al. The Battle of Gettysburg, 1 vol. Burgan, Michael & Hoena, Blake A. 2006. (Graphic History Ser.). (ENG.). 32p. (J). (gr. 3-9). 31.32 *(978-0-7368-5491-7(6)*, Capstone Pr.) Capstone.
—The Battle of Gettysburg. Burgan, Michael. 2006. (Graphic History Ser.). (ENG.). 32p. (J). (gr. 3-9). per. 8.10 *(978-0-7368-6880-8(1)*, Capstone Pr.) Capstone.
—Convergence. Friedman, Michael Jan et al. 2008. (Titan Star Trek Collections). (ENG.). 176p. pap. 14.95 *(978-1-84576-320-6(3)*, Titan Bks.) Titan Bks. Ltd. GBR. Dist: Penguin Random Hse. LLC.
Erwin, Steve. A Crash Course in Forces & Motion with Max Axiom, Super Scientist. Sohn, Emily. 2016. (Graphic Science Ser.). (ENG.). 32p. (J). (gr. 3-9). pap. 8.10 *(978-1-5157-4638-6(0))* Capstone.
—A Crash Course in Forces & Motion with Max Axiom Super Scientist: 4D an Augmented Reading Science Experience. Sohn, Emily. 2018. (Graphic Science 4D Ser.). (ENG.). 32p. (J). (gr. 3-9). lib. bdg. 34.65 *(978-1-5435-2945-6(3)*, 138534, Capstone Pr.) Capstone.
—A Crash Course in Forces & Motion with Max Axiom Super Scientist: An Augmented Reading Science Experience. Sohn, Emily. 2018. (Graphic Science 4D Ser.). (ENG.). 32p. (J). (gr. 3-9). pap. 7.95 *(978-1-5435-2956-2(9)*, 138556, Capstone Pr.) Capstone.
Erwin, Steve, et al. The Hindenburg Disaster, 1 vol. Doeden, Matt. 2006. (Disasters in History Ser.). (ENG.). 32p. (J). (gr. 3-9). 31.32 *(978-0-7368-5481-8(9)*, Capstone Pr.) Capstone.
—The Story of Jamestown, 1 vol. Braun, Eric. 2005. (Graphic History Ser.). (ENG.). 32p. (J). (gr. 3-9). 31.32 *(978-0-7368-4967-8(X)*, Capstone Pr.) Capstone.
Erwin, Steve. The Wright Brothers & the Airplane, 1 vol. Niz, Xavier W. & Barnett, Charles, III. 2007. (Inventions & Discovery Ser.). (ENG.). 32p. (J). (gr. 3-9). per. 8.10 *(978-0-7368-7897-5(1)*, Capstone Pr.) Capstone.
—The Z-Boys & Skateboarding, 1 vol. Anderson, Jameson. 2007. (Inventions & Discovery Ser.). (ENG.). 32p. (J). (gr. 3-9). 31.32 *(978-1-4296-0150-4(7)*, Capstone Pr.) Capstone.
Erwin, Steve & Barnett, Charles, III. Mother Jones: Labor Leader, 1 vol. Miller, Connie Colwell. 2006. (Graphic Biographies Ser.). (ENG.). 32p. (J). (gr. 3-9). per. 8.10 *(978-0-7368-9662-7(7)*, Capstone Pr.) Capstone.
Esberger, Trudi. The Boy Who Lost His Bumble. Esberger, Trudi. (Child's Play Library). 32p. (J). 2016. *(978-1-84643-661-1(3))*; 2015. (ENG.). *(978-1-84643-662-8(1))* Child's Play International Ltd.
Escabasse, Sophie. Shelly Struggles to Shine (the Derby Daredevils Book #2) Rosewater, Kit. 2020. (Derby Daredevils Ser.). (ENG.). 176p. (J). (gr. 3-7). 14.99 ***(978-1-4197-4685-7(5)***, 1289601, Amulet Bks.) Abrams, Inc.
Escalante, Rachel. After the Rain: A New Day Dawns for Kids with Disabilities. Berman, Michael. Neal, Linda, ed. 2019. (ENG.). 32p. (J). pap. 11.99 ***(978-1-6952-1562-7(1))*** Independently Published.
—After the Rain - Despues de la Lluvia: A New Day Dawns for Kids with Disabilities (English/Espanol) Neal, Linda, ed. Travieso, Liz, tr. 2019. (SPA.). 32p. (J). pap. 11.99 ***(978-1-6952-6129-7(1))*** Independently Published.
Escandell, Victor. Sleuth & Solve: 20+ Mind-Twisting Mysteries: (Mystery Book for Kids & Adults, Puzzle & Brain Teaser Book for All Ages) 2019. (ENG.). 64p. (J). (gr. 3-7). 17.99 *(978-1-4521-7713-7(9))* Chronicle Bks. LLC.
Escandell, Victor. Sleuth & Solve: History: 20+ Mind-Twisting Mysteries. Gallo, Ana. 2020. (ENG.). 60p. (J). (gr. 3-7). 18.99 ***(978-1-4521-8007-6(5))*** Chronicle Bks. LLC.
Escher, M. C. TIDELOG 2003 Graphic Almanac for Southeastern States: Covering the Entire South Carolina Coast, North to Wilmington NC, & South to Brunswick, Ga. Born, Mark Alan. 2004. 144p. spiral bd. 14.95 *(978-1-933120-05-8(3))* Pacific Pubs.
Escobar, Antonio Rocha. El Misterio de la Casa Chueca (y el Bulto Color Mugre) The Mystery of the Crooked House. Anza, Ana Luisa. rev. ed. 2006. (Castillo de la Lectura Naranja Ser.). (SPA & ENG.). 120p. (J). (gr. 4-7). pap. 7.95 *(978-970-20-0200-0(1))* Castillo, Ediciones, S. A. de C. V. MEX. Dist: Macmillan.
—La Videocasetera YA No Esta a Dieta. Garcia, Juan Carlos Quezadas et al. rev. ed. 2007. (Castillo de la Lectura Naranja Ser.). (SPA & ENG.). 120p. (J). (gr. 4-7). pap. 7.95 *(978-970-20-0307-6(5))* Castillo, Ediciones, S. A. de C. V. MEX. Dist: Macmillan.
Escobar, Chris. The Adventures of Chupacabra Charlie. Aldama, Frederick Luis. 2020. (Latinographix Ser.). (ENG.). 36p. (J). pap. 9.95 *(978-0-8142-5586-5(8)*, Mad Creek Bks.) Ohio State Univ. Pr.
Escobar, Paola. Pages & Co.: the Bookwanderers. James, Anna. (ENG.). 304p. (J). (gr. 3-7). 2020. pap. 8.99 ***(978-1-9848-3714-1(1)***, Puffin Books); 2019. (Pages & Co Ser.: 1). 16.99 *(978-1-9848-3712-7(5)*, Philomel Bks.) Penguin Young Readers Group.
Escobar, Paola. Pages & Co.: the Lost Fairy Tales. James, Anna. 2020. (Pages & Co Ser.: 2). (ENG.). 288p. (J). (gr. 3-7). 16.99 *(978-1-9848-3729-5(X)*, Philomel Bks.) Penguin Young Readers Group.
Escobar, Paola. Pages & Co.: the Map of Stories. James, Anna. 2020. (Pages & Co Ser.: 3). (ENG.). 336p. (J). (gr. 4-7). 16.99 ***(978-1-9848-3732-5(X)***, Philomel Bks.) Penguin Young Readers Group.
Escobar, Paola. Planting Stories: the Life of Librarian & Storyteller Pura Belpré. Denise, Anika Aldamuy. 2019. (ENG.). 40p. (J). (gr. -1-3). 17.99 *(978-0-06-274868-3(8)*, HarperCollins) HarperCollins Pubs. Ltd. GBR. Dist: HarperCollins Pubs.
Escobar, Paola. Queen of Tejano Music: Selena. López, Silvia. 2020. (ENG.). 48p. (J). (gr. k-4). 18.99 ***(978-1-4998-1142-1(X))*** Little Bee Books Inc.
—Rescatando Palabras (Digging for Words Spanish Edition) José Alberto Gutiérrez y la Biblioteca Que Creó. Kunkel, Angela Burke. 2020. 40p. (J). (gr. -1-3). 17.99 ***(978-0-593-18170-6(0))***; (SPA.). lib. bdg. 20.99 ***(978-0-593-18171-3(9))*** Random Hse. Children's Bks. (Schwartz & Wade Bks.).
—Selena, Reina de la Música Tejana. López, Silvia. 2020. (ENG.). 48p. (J). (gr. k-4). 18.99 ***(978-1-4998-1143-8(8))*** Little Bee Books Inc.
Escobar, Paola. Sembrando Historias: Pura Belpré: Bibliotecaria y Narradora de Cuentos: Planting Stories: the Life of Librarian & Storyteller Pura Belpre (Spanish Edition), 1 vol. Denise, Anika Aldamuy. 2019. (SPA.). 40p. (J). (gr. -1-3). 17.99 *(978-1-4002-1264-4(2))* HarperCollins Español.
Escott, Esther. The Clockmaker of Mullen. Escott, Jamison. 2004. 24p. (J). pap. 8.95 *(978-1-57733-127-8(3)*, Papillon Publishing) Blue Dolphin Publishing, Inc.
Escriva, Ana Lopez. La Familia de Mic. Pacheco, Miguel Angel. 2003. (SPA.). (J). *(978-970-690-761-5(0))* Planeta Mexicana Editorial S. A. de C. V.
—Please Do Feed the Bears. Naylor, Phyllis Reynolds. 2007. (ENG.). 40p. (J). (gr. -1-2). 11.99 *(978-1-4169-6750-7(8)*, Simon & Schuster/Paula Wiseman Bks.) Simon & Schuster/Paula Wiseman Bks.
—El Viejo Reloj. Alonso, Fernando & Fernando, Alonso. (SPA.). 48p. (J). *(978-84-392-8114-6(5))* Gaviota Ediciones ESP. Dist: Lectorum Pubns., Inc.
Escriva, Sandra Lopez. Ratoncito Prez, Cartero. Flor Ada, Alma & Campoy, F. Isabel. 2015. (Santillana USA Ser.).Tr. of New Job for Pérez, the Mouse. (SPA.). 32p. (J). (gr. 6-6). pap. 15.95 *(978-1-63113-547-7(3)*, Santillana) Santillana USA Publishing Co., Inc.
Escriva, Vivi. Muu, Moo! Rimas de Animales/Animal Nursery Rhymes: Bilingual Spanish-English. Campoy, F. Isabel & Ada, Alma Flor. 2010. (ENG.). 48p. (J). (gr. -1-3). lib. bdg. 17.89 *(978-0-06-134614-9(4)*, HarperCollins Español) HarperCollins Christian Publishing.
—Muu, Moo! Rimas de Animales/Animal Nursery Rhymes: Bilingual Spanish-English Children's Book. Campoy, F. Isabel & Ada, Alma Flor. 2010. (ENG.). 48p. (J). (gr. -1-3). 16.99 *(978-0-06-134613-2(6)*, HarperCollins Español) HarperCollins Christian Publishing.
—My Grandma/Mi Abuelita: Bilingual Spanish-English Children's Book. Guy, Ginger Foglesong. 2007.Tr. of My Grandma. (ENG.). 24p. (J). (gr. -1-k). 16.99 *(978-0-06-079098-1(9)*, Rayo) HarperCollins Pubs.
Escrivá, Viví. El Patio de Mi Casa y Otras Canciones Infantiles. Puncel, Maria. 2003. (SPA.). 32p. 4.95 *(978-84-372-8018-9(4))* Altea, Ediciones, S.A. - Grupo Santillana ESP. Dist: Santillana USA Publishing Co., Inc.
Escriva, Vivi. Pio Peep! Traditional Spanish Nursery Rhymes: Bilingual Spanish-English. Ada, Alma Flor et al. 2003. (SPA.). 64p. (J). (gr. -1-1). 16.99 *(978-0-688-16019-7(0)*, HarperCollins Español) HarperCollins Christian Publishing.
—Pio Peep! Traditional Spanish Nursery Rhymes: Bilingual Spanish-English. Campoy, F. Isabel et al. 2019. (ENG.). 64p. (J). (gr. -1-1). pap. 7.99 *(978-0-06-443868-1(6))* HarperCollins Español.
—Pio Peep! Traditional Spanish Nursery Rhymes Book & CD: Bilingual Spanish-English. Campoy, F. Isabel et al. 2006. (ENG.). 64p. (J). (gr. -1-1). audio compact disk 16.99 *(978-0-06-111666-7(1)*, Rayo) HarperCollins Pubs.
Escrivá, Viví. Tainos. Dorris, Michael. 97th ed. 2003.Tr. of Morning Girl. (SPA.). 112p. (gr. 5-8). pap. 26.30 *(978-84-204-4757-5(9)*, AF1929) Harcourt Schl. Pubs.
Escudero, Jesús. Do You Know a Superhero? duopress labs. 2018. (ENG.). 22p. (J). (— 1). bds. 7.95 *(978-1-947458-24-6(8)*, 805824, Duo Pr. Llc (US)) Duo Pr. LLC.
EsDesignStudio, jt. illus. see Bates, Delphine Branon.
Esham, Barbara. If You're So Smart, How Come You Can't Spell Mississippi? Esham, Barbara. 2008. 32p. (J). (gr. k-18). 16.95 *(978-1-60336-448-5(X)*, Adventures of Everyday Geniuses, The) Mainstream Connections Publishing.
Eshbach, Ariel. Charity Prays for Rain. Krahn, Maria. 2014. 32p. (J). *(978-0-7399-2475-4(3))* Rod & Staff Pubs., Inc.
Eshbaugh, Rick. Two Countries, Three Friends. Kanter, Raejean. 2020. (Grandma Book's World Ser.). (ENG.). 36p. (J). 16.99 ***(978-1-64538-113-6(7))***; pap. 10.00 ***(978-1-64538-112-9(9))*** Orange Hat Publishing.
Eskandari, Elmira, jt. illus. see oliver, juanbjuan.
Eslava, Jennifer. What Happens When They Believe a Lie Is True? Farhat, Mary. 2019. (ENG.). 50p. (J). 25.95 ***(978-1-64471-906-0(1))***; pap. 15.95 ***(978-1-64559-075-0(5))*** Covenant Bks.
Espadaler, Rosa. Then It Rained. Stranaghan, Crystal J. 2007. 24p. (J). *(978-0-9784047-8-9(5))* Pays et Terroirs.
Espanol, Frances. The Cat Named Bud. Thoma EdD, Gwen Beaudean. 2017. (ENG.). 40p. pap. 21.99 *(978-1-5434-1487-5(7))* Xlibris Corp.
—Johanna the Iguana & Her Limousine Load of Shoes: A Call of Change. Facey, Paulet. 2019. (ENG.). 24p. (J). pap. 15.99 *(978-1-7960-2191-2(1))* Xlibris Corp.
Espanol, Frances. Let's Bother Father. Colton, Richard D. 2020. (ENG.). 26p. (J). pap. 21.99 ***(978-1-7960-8349-1(6))*** Xlibris Corp.
Esparra, Veronica. Heaven Is All Around You. Esparra, Lydia. 2012. 28p. pap. 12.95 *(978-1-61244-071-2(1))* Halo Publishing International.
Esparza, Andres, et al. Attack of the Zom-Bees! Sonnebom, Scott. 2013. (Tiger Moth Ser.). (ENG.). 48p. (J). (gr. 3-5). pap. 6.19 *(978-1-4342-3871-9(7)*, Stone Arch Bks.) Capstone.
—A Midsummer Night's Dream, 1 vol. Maese, Fares & Shakespeare, William. 2011. (Shakespeare Graphics Ser.). (ENG.). 88p. (J). (gr. 5-9). pap. 7.15 *(978-1-4342-3449-0(5)*, Stone Arch Bks.) Capstone.
—Power at the Plate, 1 vol. Ciencin, Scott. 2011. (Sports Illustrated Kids Graphic Novels Ser.). (ENG.). 56p. (J). (gr. 3-8). pap. 7.19 *(978-1-4342-3400-1(2)*, Stone Arch Bks.) Capstone.
—Power at the Plate, 1 vol. Ciencin, Scott & Cano, Fernando. 2011. (Sports Illustrated Kids Graphic Novels Ser.). (ENG.). 56p. (J). (gr. 3-8). lib. bdg. 26.65 *(978-1-4342-2239-8(X)*, Stone Arch Bks.) Capstone.
—Snowboard Standoff, 1 vol. Ciencin, Scott et al. 2011. (Sports Illustrated Kids Graphic Novels Ser.). (ENG.). 56p. (J). (gr. 3-8). pap. 7.19 *(978-1-4342-3403-2(7)*, Stone Arch Bks.) Capstone.
Esparza, Andres. Tiger Moth: Attack of the Zom-Bees!, 1 vol. Sonnebom, Scott. 2013. (Tiger Moth Ser.). (ENG.). 48p. (J). (gr. 3-5). lib. bdg. 23.99 *(978-1-4342-3283-0(2)*, Stone Arch Bks.) Capstone.
Esparza, Andres & Aburto, Jesus. BMX Blitz, 1 vol. Ciencin, Scott & Maese, Fares. 2011. (Sports Illustrated Kids Graphic Novels Ser.). (ENG.). 56p. (J). (gr. 3-8). lib. bdg. 26.65 *(978-1-4342-2222-0(5)*, Stone Arch Bks.) Capstone.
Esparza, Andres, jt. illus. see Aburto, Jesus.
Esparza, Bob, photos by. Hadas. Haab, Rachel. Esteve, Laura, tr. 2005. (SPA., 38p. (J). spiral bd. 20.95 *(978-987-1078-27-1(7))* Klutz Latino MEX. Dist: Independent Pubs. Group.
Esper, Dwain. The Mystery of the Vanishing Pony. Butler, Bonnie. 2019. (ENG.). 34p. (J). pap. 20.17 ***(978-1-7283-9707-8(3))*** AuthorHouse.
Esperanta Delmat & Frito Bastien. The Whispering Benches. Kreilick, Cynthia. 2020. (ENG.). 42p. (J). (gr. 1-4). 17.95 ***(978-0-578-65314-3(1))*** morning circle media.
Esperanza, Charles George. Jackie & Me: A Very Special Friendship. Grossinger, Tania. (ENG.). 32p. (J). (gr. -1-k). 2017. 6.99 *(978-1-5107-1270-6(4))*; 2013. 16.95 *(978-1-62087-683-1(3)*, 620683) Skyhorse Publishing Co., Inc. (Sky Pony Pr.).
—Red, Yellow, Blue (and a Dash of White, Too!) 2015. (ENG.). 40p. (J). (gr. -1-k). 16.99 *(978-1-62914-624-9(2)*, Sky Pony Pr.) Skyhorse Publishing Co., Inc.
Espin, Salva. Age of X-Man: Apocalypse & the X-Tracts. 2019. (ENG.). 112p. (YA). (gr. 8-17). pap. 15.99 *(978-1-302-91580-3(0))* Marvel Worldwide, Inc.
—Deadpool: Secret Agent Deadpool. 2019. 136p. (gr. 10-17). pap. 14.99 *(978-1-302-91343-4(3))* Marvel Worldwide, Inc.
—Guardians of the Galaxy: Telltale Games. 2018. (ENG.). 112p. (YA). (gr. 8-17). pap. 15.99 *(978-1-302-90939-0(8))* Marvel Worldwide, Inc.
Espin, Salvador & Henry, Clayton. The Last Knights of Wundagore. Van Lente, Fred. 2009. (Wolverine: First Class Ser.). (ENG.). 24p. (J). (gr. 2-6). Pt. 1. lib. bdg. 27.07 *(978-1-59961-671-1(8)*, 15319); Pt. 2. lib. bdg. 27.07 *(978-1-59961-672-8(6)*, 15320) Spotlight. (Marvel Age).
—Little Girls. Van Lente, Fred. 2009. (Wolverine: First Class Ser.). (ENG.). 24p. (J). (gr. 2-6). lib. bdg. 27.07 *(978-1-59961-673-5(4)*, 15321, Marvel Age) Spotlight.
Espina, Vito. Sometimes Boxes Make the Best Forts. Rawlings, John S. 2006. (J). pap. 15.00 *(978-0-8059-7181-1(5))* Dorrance Publishing Co., Inc.
Espinola, Nicole & Nealon, Eve. Danny & the Detention Demons. Webb, Mack H., Jr. I.t. ed. 2007. 52p. (J). per. 15.95 *(978-0-9779576-2-0(4))* Pilinut Pr., Inc.
Espinosa, Chris. The Spaniel Family Goes to the State Fair. Ellsberry, Sharon. 2004. 24p. (J). 9.00 *(978-0-9724637-2-0(0))* Sky Rocket Pr.
Espinosa, Chris. Rocket Megabyte's Texas Adventure. Espinosa, Chris. Rawlett, Robert. 2004. 68p. (J). 14.00 *(978-0-9724637-1-3(2))* Sky Rocket Pr.
Espinosa, Génie, et al. Little Bird Stories: Red Hen, Goldilocks, & Jack & the Beanstalk: Small Padded Board Book 3 Pack. Redd, R. I. & Crowe, Carmen. 2017. (Little Bird Stories Ser.). (ENG.). 15p. (J). (gr. -1-k). bds., bds., bds. 20.97 *(978-1-68052-245-7(0)*, 9000790) Cottage Door Pr.
Espinosa, Genie. My Peekaboo Farm. Marx, Jonny. 2019. (ENG.). 12p. (J). (gr. 2-k). bds. 10.99 *(978-1-68010-592-6(2))* Tiger Tales.
Espinosa, Leo. Goldfish on Vacation. Lloyd-Jones, Sally. 2018. (ENG.). 40p. (J). (gr. -1-3). 17.99 *(978-0-385-38611-1(7)*, Schwartz & Wade Bks.) Random Hse. Children's Bks.
—Islandborn. Díaz, Junot. 2018. (ENG.). 48p. (J). (gr. k-3). 17.99 *(978-0-7352-2986-0(4)*, Dial Bks) Penguin Young Readers Group.
—Jackrabbit Mccabe & the Electric Telegraph. Rozier, Lucy Margaret. 2015. 40p. (J). (gr. -1-3). 17.99 *(978-0-385-37843-7(2)*, Schwartz & Wade Bks.) Random Hse. Children's Bks.
—Kitchen Chaos. Levine, Deborah A. & Riley, JillEllyn. 2015. (Saturday Cooking Club Ser.: 1). (ENG.). 336p. (J). (gr. 4-9). 17.99 *(978-1-4424-9939-3(7)*, Aladdin) Simon & Schuster Children's Publishing.
—Lola: Edición en Español de ISLANDBORN. Díaz, Junot. 2018. (SPA.). 48p. (J). (gr. k-3). 17.99 *(978-0-525-55281-9(2)*, Dial Bks) Penguin Young Readers Group.
Espinosa, Leo. Our Subway Baby. Mercurio, Peter. 2020. 40p. (J). (gr. -1-3). 17.99 ***(978-0-525-42754-4(6)***, Dial Bks) Penguin Young Readers Group.
Espinosa, Nuri. Perseo: El Joven que Venció a Medusa. Róman, Pedro. 2006. (SPA.). 32p. *(978-958-30-1958-6(5))* Panamericana Editorial.

E

Espinosa, Patrick, photos by. Graphing Favorite Things. Marrewa, Jennifer. 2008. (Math in Our World: Level 2 Ser.). 24p. (gr. 1-4). lib. bdg. 23.00 (978-0-8368-9008-2(6), Weekly Reader Leveled Readers) Stevens, Gareth Publishing LLLP.

Espinosa, Rod. Abraham Lincoln, 1 vol. Dunn, Joe. 2007. (Bio-Graphics Ser.). (ENG.). 32p. (J). (gr. 3-8). 29.93 (978-1-60270-064-2(8), 3561, Graphic Planet - Fiction) Magic Wagon.

—Barack Obama: 44th U. S. President, 1 vol. Dunn, Joeming. 2011. (Presidents of the United States Bio-Graphics Ser.). (ENG.). 32p. (J). (gr. 3-6). 29.93 (978-1-61641-648-5(3), 12788, Graphic Planet - Fiction) Magic Wagon.

—Building the Transcontinental Railroad, 1 vol. Dunn, Joeming W. 2008. (Graphic History Ser.). (ENG.). 32p. (J). (gr. 3-8). 29.93 (978-1-60270-180-9(6), 9052, Graphic Planet - Fiction) Magic Wagon.

—Cesar Chavez, 1 vol. Dunn, Joeming W. 2008. (Bio-Graphics Ser.). (ENG.). 32p. (J). (gr. 3-8). 29.93 (978-1-60270-172-4(5), 3583, Graphic Planet - Fiction) Magic Wagon.

—Clara Barton, 1 vol. Dunn, Joeming W. 2008. (Bio-Graphics Ser.). (ENG.). 32p. (J). (gr. 3-8). 29.93 (978-1-60270-170-0(9), 3579, Graphic Planet - Fiction) Magic Wagon.

—The Comedy of Errors: Graphic Novel, 1 vol. Shakespeare, William. 2010. (Graphic Shakespeare Ser.). (ENG.). 48p. (J). (gr. 5-10). 31.35 (978-1-60270-762-7(6), 9158, Graphic Planet - Fiction) Magic Wagon.

—The Eyes: A Graphic Novel Tour, 1 vol. Dunn, Joeming. 2009. (Graphic Adventures: the Human Body Ser.). (ENG.). 32p. (J). (gr. 3-8). 29.93 (978-1-60270-684-2(0), 9006, Graphic Planet - Fiction) Magic Wagon.

—Jackie Robinson, 1 vol. Dunn, Joe. 2007. (Bio-Graphics Ser.). (ENG.). 32p. (J). (gr. 3-8). 29.93 (978-1-60270-068-0(0), 3569, Graphic Planet - Fiction) Magic Wagon.

—The Kidneys: A Graphic Novel Tour, 1 vol. Dunn, Joeming. 2009. (Graphic Adventures: the Human Body Ser.). (ENG.). 32p. (J). (gr. 3-8). 29.93 (978-1-60270-686-6(7), 9010, Graphic Planet - Fiction) Magic Wagon.

—The Liver: A Graphic Novel Tour, 1 vol. Dunn, Joeming. 2009. (Graphic Adventures: the Human Body Ser.). (ENG.). 32p. (J). (gr. 3-8). 29.93 (978-1-60270-687-3(5), 9012, Graphic Planet - Fiction) Magic Wagon.

—The Lungs: A Graphic Novel Tour, 1 vol. Dunn, Joeming. 2009. (Graphic Adventures: the Human Body Ser.). (ENG.). 32p. (J). (gr. 3-8). 29.93 (978-1-60270-688-0(3), 9014, Graphic Planet - Fiction) Magic Wagon.

—A MidSummer Night's Dream, 1 vol. Connor, Daniel. 2008. (Graphic Shakespeare Ser.). (ENG.). 48p. (J). (gr. 5-10). 31.35 (978-1-60270-191-5(1), 9144, Graphic Planet - Fiction) Magic Wagon.

—Moby Dick, 1 vol. Melville, Herman. 2007. (Graphic Classics Ser.). (ENG.). 32p. (J). (gr. 3-8). 29.93 (978-1-60270-051-2(6), 9020, Graphic Planet - Fiction) Magic Wagon.

Espinosa, Rod, et al. Moon Landing, 1 vol. Dunn, Joe. 2007. (Graphic History Ser.). (ENG.). 32p. (J). (gr. 3-8). 29.93 (978-1-60270-078-9(8), 9042, Graphic Planet - Fiction) Magic Wagon.

Espinosa, Rod. Phantom of the Opera, 1 vol. Leroux, Gaston. 2009. (Graphic Horror Ser.). (ENG.). 32p. (J). (gr. 5-8). 29.93 (978-1-60270-679-8(4), 9088, Graphic Planet - Fiction) Magic Wagon.

—Reaching the North Pole, 1 vol. Dunn, Joeming W. 2008. (Graphic History Ser.). (ENG.). 32p. (J). (gr. 3-8). 29.93 (978-1-60270-185-4(7), 9062, Graphic Planet - Fiction) Magic Wagon.

—Romeo & Juliet, 1 vol. Dunn, Joeming. 2008. (Graphic Shakespeare Ser.). (ENG.). 48p. (J). (gr. 5-10). 31.35 (978-1-60270-193-9(8), 9148, Graphic Planet - Fiction) Magic Wagon.

—Sacagawea, 1 vol. Dunn, Joeming W. 2008. (Bio-Graphics Ser.). (ENG.). 32p. (J). (gr. 3-8). 29.93 (978-1-60270-176-2(8), 3591, Graphic Planet - Fiction) Magic Wagon.

—Thomas Jefferson, 1 vol. Dunn, Joeming. 2008. (Bio-Graphics Ser.). (ENG.). 32p. (J). (gr. 3-8). 29.93 (978-1-60270-174-8(1), 3587, Graphic Planet - Fiction) Magic Wagon.

—The Winter's Tale: Graphic Novel, 1 vol. Shakespeare, William. 2010. (Graphic Shakespeare Ser.). (ENG.). 48p. (J). (gr. 5-10). 31.35 (978-1-60270-768-9(5), 9170, Graphic Planet - Fiction) Magic Wagon.

Espinosa, Rod. The Battle of the Alamo, 1 vol. Espinosa, Rod. 2007. (Graphic History Ser.). (ENG.). 32p. (J). (gr. 3-8). 29.93 (978-1-60270-073-4(7), 9032, Graphic Planet - Fiction) Magic Wagon.

—Benjamin Franklin, 1 vol. Espinosa, Rod. 2007. (Bio-Graphics Ser.). (ENG.). 32p. (J). (gr. 3-8). 29.93 (978-1-60270-066-6(4), 3565, Graphic Planet - Fiction) Magic Wagon.

—The Boston Tea Party, 1 vol. Espinosa, Rod. 2007. (Graphic History Ser.). (ENG.). 32p. (J). (gr. 3-8). 29.93 (978-1-60270-075-8(3), 9036, Graphic Planet - Fiction) Magic Wagon.

—The Brain: A Graphic Novel Tour, 1 vol. Espinosa, Rod. Dunn, Joeming. 2009. (Graphic Adventures: the Human Body Ser.). (ENG.). 32p. (J). (gr. 3-8). 29.93 (978-1-60270-683-5(2), 9004, Graphic Planet - Fiction) Magic Wagon.

—The Courageous Princess: The Dragon Queen. Espinosa, Rod. 2015. (Courageous Princess Ser.). (ENG.). 180p. (J). (gr. 3-7). 19.99 (978-1-61655-724-9(9)) Dark Horse Comics.

—Courageous Princess Vol. 1: Beyond the Hundred Kingdoms. Espinosa, Rod. 3rd ed. 2015. (ENG.). 250p. (J). (gr. 3-7). 19.99 (978-1-61655-722-5(2)) Dark Horse Comics.

—Courageous Princess Volume 1. Espinosa, Rod. 2019. (ENG.). 240p. (J). (gr. 3-7). pap. 14.99 (978-1-5067-1446-2(3)) Dark Horse Comics.

—George Washington, 1 vol. Espinosa, Rod. 2007. (Bio-Graphics Ser.). (ENG.). 32p. (J). (gr. 3-8). 29.93 (978-1-60270-067-3(2), 3567, Graphic Planet - Fiction) Magic Wagon.

—The Heart: A Graphic Novel Tour, 1 vol. Espinosa, Rod. Dunn, Joeming. 2009. (Graphic Adventures: the Human Body Ser.). (ENG.). 32p. (J). (gr. 3-8). 29.93 (978-1-60270-685-9(9), 9008, Graphic Planet - Fiction) Magic Wagon.

—Lewis & Clark, 1 vol. Espinosa, Rod. 2007. (Bio-Graphics Ser.). (ENG.). 32p. (J). (gr. 3-8). 29.93 (978-1-60270-069-7(9), 3571, Graphic Planet - Fiction) Magic Wagon.

—Patrick Henry, 1 vol. Espinosa, Rod. 2007. (Bio-Graphics Ser.). (ENG.). 32p. (J). (gr. 3-8). 29.93 (978-1-60270-070-3(2), 3573, Graphic Planet - Fiction) Magic Wagon.

—The Unremembered Lands. Espinosa, Rod. 2015. (ENG.). 166p. (J). (gr. 3-7). 19.99 (978-1-61655-723-2(0)) Dark Horse Comics.

Espinosa, Rod & Hutchison, David. Graphic Horror Set 3, 6 vols. 2014. (Graphic Horror Ser.: 6). 32p. (J). (gr. 5-8). lib. bdg. 179.58 (978-1-62402-012-4(7), 9094, Graphic Planet - Fiction) Magic Wagon.

Espinosa, Rod, jt. illus. see Wight, Joseph.

EspinoZa, Carlota D., jt. illus. see Espinoza, Gabbi.

Espinoza, Gabbi & EspinoZa, Carlota D. God Made a Very Big Big Bang! Espinoza, Carlota D. 2011. 32p. pap. 24.95 (978-1-4560-9582-6(X)) America Star Bks.

Espinoza, Ramon. Jungle Scout: A Vietnam War Story, 1 vol. Hoppey, Tim. 2008. (Historical Fiction Ser.). (ENG.). 56p. (J). (gr. 3-6). pap. 6.25 (978-1-4342-0846-0(X), Stone Arch Bks.) Capstone.

Espiritu, Selina. Brave Chef Brianna. Sykes, Sam. 2017. (ENG.). 112p. (J). (gr. 3). pap. 14.99 (978-1-68415-050-2(7)) Boom! Studios.

Espluga, Maria. Fabulame un Fabula. Duran, Teresa. 2003. (SPA.). 96p. (978-84-480-1638-8(6), TM30428) Timun Mas, Editorial S.A. ESP. Dist: Lectorum Pubns., Inc.

—Ricitos de Oro y Los Tres Osos. Bailer, Darice & Domínguez, Madelca. 2007. (SPA & ENG.). 28p. (J). (978-0-545-02447-1(1)) Scholastic, Inc.

Esplugas, Sonia. Magic Train Ride. Crabtree, Sally. (J). 2012. 32p. (gr. -1-2). 9.99 (978-1-84686-657-9(X)); 2007. (ENG.). 32p. (gr. -1-k). pap. 9.99 (978-1-905236-91-6(3)); 2006. 0032p. 16.99 (978-1-905236-52-7(2)) Barefoot Bks., Inc.

Esplugas, Sonia & Espulgas, Sonia. Magic Train Ride. Crabtree, Sally. 2007. (ENG.). 32p. (J). (gr. -1-k). 6.99 (978-1-84686-132-1(2)) Barefoot Bks., Inc.

Espulgas, Sonia, jt. illus. see Esplugas, Sonia.

Espy, Lauren. Tiny World: Crochet! Espy, Lauren. Odd Dot. 2020. (Tiny World Ser.: 5). (ENG.). 32p. (J). pap. 14.99 (978-1-250-20816-3(5), 900203025, Odd Dot) St. Martin's Pr.

Esquinaldo, Virginia. My Book of Prayers. 2006. 48p. (J). 3.95 (978-0-8198-4843-7(3)) Pauline Bks. & Media.

—My First Missal. Dateno, Maria Grace. 2006. 48p. (J). pap. 3.95 (978-0-8198-4842-0(5)) Pauline Bks. & Media.

—Saint John Neumann: Missionary to Immigrants. Brown, Laura Rhoderica. 2016. 144p. (J). pap. (978-0-8198-9066-5(9)) Pauline Bks. & Media.

Esquinaldo, Virginia. What Did Baby Jesus Do? Esquinaldo, Virginia. 2006. 12p. (J). bds. 6.95 (978-0-8198-8310-0(7)) Pauline Bks. & Media.

Esquinaldo, Virginia. Saint Therese of Lisieux: The Way of Love. Esquinaldo, Virginia, tr. Glavich, Mary Kathleen. 2003. (Encounter the Saints Ser.). 132p. (J). pap. 5.95 (978-0-8198-7074-2(9), 332-370) Pauline Bks. & Media.

Esquivel, Isidro. Miss Taqui. González, Catalina. 2014. (SPA.). 98p. (J). (gr. 4-7). pap. 7.95 (978-607-8237-28-9(4)) Nostra Ediciones MEX. Dist: Independent Pubs. Group.

Esquivel, Isidro R. Entre Nosches y Fantasmas. Tario, Francisco. 2016. (SPA.). 120p. (YA). 13.99 (978-607-16-4268-4(X)) Fondo de Cultura Economica USA.

Este, James. Tres Porculi. Williams, Rose. L and L Enterprises, ed. 2006. (LAT.). spiral bd. 18.00 (978-0-9760046-5-3(8)) L & L Enterprises.

Estep, Emone. Tess Ivy's Very Fairy Surprise. Hope, Jaimie. 2018. (ENG.). 44p. (J). pap. 9.50 (978-1-7278-1475-0(4)) CreateSpace Independent Publishing Platform.

Estep, Joanna. Roadsong, Vol. 1. 2006. 200p. pap. 9.99 (978-1-59816-398-8(1)) TOKYOPOP, Inc.

Esterman, Sophia. Now for My Next Number! Songs for Multiplying Fun. Park, Margaret. 2007. (ENG.). 48p. (J). (gr. 1-2). 16.95 (978-0-915556-38-0(3)) Great River Bks.

Estes, John & MacNeil, Colin. Avengers: Tales to Astonish. 2018. 224p. (YA). (gr. 8-17). pap. 24.99 (978-1-302-90804-1(9)) Marvel Worldwide, Inc.

Estes, Margaret. Benny, the Crow: A Tale of the Everglades. Sutton, Ben & Sutton, Sue. 2019. (ENG.). 26p. (J). 22.95 (978-1-68456-688-4(6)) Page Publishing Inc.

Esteves, Kika. A Day with Lady: A Day with Lady/un Dia con Lady, a Picture Book in English & Spanish. Getz, Shari & Sen, C. 2010. (ENG.). 42p. (J). (gr. -1-2). pap. 9.50 (978-0-9830781-2-8(2)) My Kinda Bks.

Esteves, Margarida, et al. Amazing Women of the Middle East: 25 Stories from Ancient Times to Present Day. Wafa', Tarnowska. 2020. (ENG.). 112p. (J). 19.95 (978-1-62371-870-1(8), Crocodile Bks.) Interlink Publishing Group, Inc.

Estill, Amy. Abby & the Helping Mommy. Mathisen, Michael. 2009. 28p. pap. 13.99 (978-1-4389-5327-4(5)) AuthorHouse.

Estoquia, Jonathan T. Butete: The Sotry of a Remarkable Fish. Gundaya, Asela Hazel Z. 2009. 45p. (J). (978-1-4415-4909-9(9)) Xlibris Corp.

Estrada, Ixchel. El Arbol del Tiempo: Para Que Sirven las Genealogias. Otero, Armando Lenero. rev. ed. 2006. (Otra Escalera Ser.). (SPA & ENG.). 24p. (J). (gr. 2-4). pap. 9.95 (978-968-5920-67-4(2)) Castillo, Ediciones, S. A. de C. V. MEX. Dist: Macmillan.

—Barriga Llena. Olivera, Martin Bonfil. rev. ed. 2006. (Otra Escalera Ser.). (SPA & ENG.). 24p. (J). (gr. 2-4). pap. 9.95 (978-968-5920-60-5(5)) Castillo, Ediciones, S. A. de C. V. MEX. Dist: Macmillan.

—Cuentos Escritos a Maquina. Rodari, Gianni. 2017. (Serie Naranja Ser.). (SPA.). 288p. (J). (gr. 4-7). pap. 11.95 (978-1-64101-228-7(5)) Santillana USA Publishing Co., Inc.

Estrada, Jomar. A Frog Named Sandy. Tapora, Lorrie. 2018. (ENG.). 42p. (J). pap. (978-9980-900-23-4(7)) Library For All Limited.

Estrada, Pau. Little Red Riding Hood: Caperucita Roja. Grimm, Jacob & Grimm, Wilhelm K. Surges, James, tr. 2006. 22p. (J). (gr. k-4). reprint ed. 15.00 (978-0-7567-9994-6(5)) DIANE Publishing Co.

—El Mejor Novio del Mundo. (SPA.). 24p. 12.95 (978-84-246-1983-1(8)) Baker & Taylor Bks.

—Pedro's Burro. Capucilli, Alyssa Satin. 2008. (My First I Can Read Ser.). (ENG.). 32p. (J). (gr. -1 — 1). pap. 4.99 (978-0-06-056033-1(9)) HarperCollins Pubs.

—Pippo the Fool. Fern, Tracey E. 48p. (J). (gr. k-3). 2011. pap. 7.95 (978-1-57091-793-6(0)); 2009. 15.95 (978-1-57091-655-7(1)) Charlesbridge Publishing, Inc.

—Princess & the Pea (La Princesa y el Guisante) Andersen, Hans. 2013. (Bilingual Fairy Tales Ser.). (SPA & ENG.). 32p. (J). (gr. 1-4). lib. bdg. 28.50 (978-1-60753-357-3(X)) Amicus Publishing.

—Princess & the Pea/la Princesa y el Guisante. Boada, Francesc. 2004. (Bilingual Fairy Tales Ser.: BILI). (ENG.). 32p. (J). (gr. -1-7). pap. 6.99 (978-0-8118-4452-9(8)) Chronicle Bks. LLC.

—Soccer Counts! McGrath, Barbara Barbieri & Alderman, Peter. 2003. 32p. (J). (gr. -1-3). pap. 7.95 (978-1-57091-554-3(7)) Charlesbridge Publishing, Inc.

—Soccer Counts! (El Fútbol Cuenta!) McGrath, Barbara Barbieri & Alderman, Peter. ed. 2011. (SPA & ENG.). 32p. (J). (gr. -1-3). 22.44 (978-1-57091-795-0(7)) Charlesbridge Publishing, Inc.

Estrada, Pau. Pedro's Burro. Estrada, Pau. 2007. (My First I Can Read Bks.). 32p. (J). (gr. -1-k). lib. bdg. 16.89 (978-0-06-056032-4(0)) HarperCollins Pubs.

Estrada, Ric. I'm a Healthy Eater. Pappas, Diane H. & Covey, Richard D. 2007. (J). (978-0-545-01424-3(7)) Scholastic, Inc.

—It's Good to Be Clean. Pappas, Diane H. & Covey, Richard D. 2007. (J). pap. (978-0-545-01430-4(1)) Scholastic, Inc.

—My Healthy Food Pyramid. Pappas, Diane H. & Covey, Richard D. 2007. (J). pap. (978-0-545-01429-8(8)) Scholastic, Inc.

—My Trip to the Dentist. Pappas, Diane H. et al. 2007. (J). pap. (978-0-545-01425-0(5)) Scholastic, Inc.

—Why I Need Exercise. Pappas, Diane H. et al. 2007. (J). pap. (978-0-545-01428-1(X)) Scholastic, Inc.

—Why I Need My Sleep. Pappas, Diane H. & Covey, Richard D. 2007. (J). pap. (978-0-545-01427-4(1)) Scholastic, Inc.

Estrella, Al. The Boy & the Lone Mango Tree. Lopez, Mark J. M. 2017. (ENG.). (J). pap. (978-1-5255-0280-4(8)) FriesenPress.

Estudio Haus. The Colors of a Sunset: An Algonquin Nature Myth. Yasuda, Anita. 2012. (Short Tales Native American Myths Ser.). (ENG.). 32p. (J). (gr. 3-6). lib. bdg. 27.07 (978-1-61641-879-3(6), 13445, Short Tales) Magic Wagon.

—Stolen Fire: A Seminole Trickster Myth. Yasuda, Anita. 2012. (Short Tales Native American Myths Ser.). (ENG.). 32p. (J). (gr. 3-6). lib. bdg. 27.07 (978-1-61641-883-0(4), 13453, Short Tales) Magic Wagon.

Estudio, Pulsar, jt. illus. see Saichann, Alberto.

Eterno, Nacho. Totem: Spirit Animals of Ancient Civilizations. Cassany, Mia. 2019. (ENG.). 36p. (J). (gr. k-4). 14.95 (978-3-7913-7401-7(X)) Prestel Verlag GmbH & Co KG. DEU. Dist: Penguin Random Hse. LLC.

Ether, Judy. My Daily Prayer Journal. Ether, Judy. 2019. (ENG.). 108p. (J). pap. 5.95 (978-1-7068-2397-1(5)) Independently Published.

Etheridge, Katy, jt. illus. see Villaloz, ChiChi.

Ethier, Vicki. I Know My Nana Rosa Is an Alien. Ethier, Vicki. 2003. 20p. (J). 6.00 (978-1-928972-10-5(1)) Critter Pubns.

—Papa & the Hen. Ethier, Vicki. 2004. 36p. (J). 7.00 (978-1-928972-12-9(8)) Critter Pubns.

Etorma, Crisanto. Amo a Dios. Zapple, Elias & Teran. 2020. (Cuentos para Dormir Ser.: Vol. 3). (SPA.). 36p. (J). pap. (978-1-912704-69-9(2)) Heads or Tales Pr.

—Amo a MIS Mamás. Zapple, Elias. Terán, Camila Ayala, tr. 2020. (Cuentos para Dormir Ser.: Vol. 5). (SPA.). 32p. (J). pap. (978-1-912704-59-0(5)) Heads or Tales Pr.

—I Love God. Zapple, Elias. 2020. (I Love Bedtime Stories Ser.: Vol. 3). (ENG.). 36p. (J). pap. (978-1-912704-39-2(0)) Heads or Tales Pr.

—I Love My Big Brother. Zapple, Elias. 2020. (I Love Bedtime Stories Ser.: Vol. 2). (ENG.). 32p. (J). pap. (978-1-912704-40-8(4)) Heads or Tales Pr.

—I Love My Mamas. Zapple, Elias. 2020. (I Love Bedtime Stories Ser.: Vol. 5). (ENG.). 32p. (J). (gr. k). pap. (978-1-912704-57-6(9)) Heads or Tales Pr.

—J'aime Dieu. Zapple, Elias. Kalbfeis, Blanche, tr. 2020. (J'Aime les Contes du Soir Ser.: Vol. 3). (FRE.). 36p. (J). pap. (978-1-912704-67-5(6)) Heads or Tales Pr.

—わたしはおかあさんがすき Zapple, Elias. Kondo, Katsunori, tr. 2020. (わたしは ものがたりがす Ser.: Vol. 5). (JPN.). 32p. (J). pap. (978-1-912704-58-3(7)) Heads or Tales Pr.

—わたしはかみさまがすき Zapple, Elias. Kondo, Katsunori, tr. 2020. (わたしは ものがたりがす Ser.: Vol. 3). (JPN.). 36p. (J). pap. (978-1-912704-70-5(6)) Heads or Tales Pr.

—我爱我的哥哥 Zapple, Elias. 刘全国, tr. 2020. (CHI.). 32p. (J). pap. (978-1-912704-73-6(0)) Heads or Tales Pr.

—我爱我的妈妈 Zapple, Elias. 刘全国, tr. 2020. (我喜欢睡前故事 Ser.: Vol. 5). (CHI.). 32p. (J). pap. (978-1-912704-75-0(7)) Heads or Tales Pr.

Etorma, Crisanto, jt. illus. see Zapple, Elias.

Ets, Marie Hall. Just Me. Ets, Marie Hall. unabr. ed. (J). (gr. k-3). pap., stu. ed. 33.95 (978-0-941078-74-0(4)); pap. 15.95 incl. audio (978-0-941078-73-3(6)) Live Oak Media.

Ettinger, Charles. Andy the Ant in Precious Cargo. Blackwell, Nancy. 2011. 40p. pap. 14.99 (978-1-937129-03-3(9)) Faithful Life Pubs.

—Jasper & Jesus at the Well. Sharpe, Charlotte. 2012. 16p. pap. 11.99 (978-1-937129-33-0(0)) Faithful Life Pubs.

Ettinger, Dorris. The Mystery of the Ancient Anchor. Price, Matt. 2010. 56p. (J). (978-0-8341-2490-5(4)) Beacon Hill Pr. of Kansas City.

Ettinger, Bill Farnsworth, et al. Westward Journeys. Scillian, Devin & Young, Judy. 2013. (American Adventures Ser.). (ENG.). (J). (gr. 3-6). lib. bdg. 18.10 (978-1-62765-946-8(3)) Perfection Learning Corp.

Ettlinger, Doris. Abe Lincoln Loved Animals. Jackson, Ellen. 2013. (AV2 Fiction Readalong Ser.: Vol. 56). (ENG.). 32p. (J). 34.28 (978-1-62127-864-1(6), AV2 by Weigl) Weigl Pubs., Inc.

—Aim for the Skies: Jerrie Mock & Joan Merriam Smith's Race to Complete Amelia Earhart's Quest. Bissonette, Aimee. 2018. (ENG.). 32p. (J). (gr. 1-4). 16.99 (978-1-58536-381-0(2), 204581) Sleeping Bear Pr.

—A Book for Black-Eyed Susan. Young, Judy. 2011. (Tales of Young Americans Ser.). (ENG.). 32p. (J). (gr. 1-4). lib. bdg. 16.95 (978-1-58536-463-3(0), 202185) Sleeping Bear Pr.

—Catholic Book of Bible Stories, 1 vol. Knowlton, Laurie Lazzaro et al. 2004. (ENG.). 224p. (J). 16.99 (978-0-310-70505-5(3)) Zonderkidz.

—G Is for Garden State: A New Jersey Alphabet. Cameron, Eileen. 2004. (Discover America State by State Ser.). (ENG.). 40p. (J). 17.95 (978-1-58536-152-6(6)) Sleeping Bear Pr.

—Hazelle Boxberg. Goodman, Susan E. 2004. (Brave Kids Ser.). (ENG.). 64p. (J). (gr. 1-4). pap. 5.99 (978-0-689-84982-4(6), Simon & Schuster/Paula Wiseman Bks.) Simon & Schuster/Paula Wiseman Bks.

—The Legend of Sea Glass. Noble, Trinka Hakes. 2016. (Myths, Legends, Fairy & Folktales Ser.). (ENG.). 32p. (J). (gr. 1-4). 17.99 (978-1-58536-611-8(0), 204027) Sleeping Bear Pr.

—Lost in the Snow. Baglio, Ben M. 2007. 153p. (J). (978-0-439-87144-0(1)) Scholastic, Inc.

—Memories of the Manger. Adams, Michelle Medlock. 2005. (J). (978-0-8249-5484-0(X), Ideal Pubns.) Worthy Publishing.

—The Orange Shoes. Noble, Trinka Hakes. rev. ed. 2007. (ENG.). 40p. (J). (gr. k-6). 16.95 (978-1-58536-277-6(8)) Sleeping Bear Pr.

—Pigeon Hero! Redmond, Shirley Raye. 2005. (Ready-to-Read Ser.). 31p. (gr. k-2). 14.00 (978-0-7569-5560-1(2)) Perfection Learning Corp.

—Pigeon Hero! Redmond, Shirley Raye. 2003. (Ready-To-Reads Ser.). (ENG.). 32p. (J). lib. bdg. 11.89 (978-0-689-85487-3(0), Aladdin Library) Simon & Schuster Children's Publishing.

—Pigeon Hero! Redmond, Shirley Raye. 2003. (Ready-To-Reads Ser.). (ENG.). 32p. (J). (gr. k-2). pap. 4.99 (978-0-689-85486-6(2), Simon Spotlight) Simon Spotlight.

—Robert Henry Hendershot. Goodman, Susan E. 2003. (Brave Kids Ser.). (ENG.). 64p. (J). (gr. 1-4). pap. 6.99 (978-0-689-84980-0(X), Simon & Schuster/Paula Wiseman Bks.) Simon & Schuster/Paula Wiseman Bks.

—Rupert's Parchment: Story of Magna Carta. Cameron, Eileen. 2015. (ENG.). (J). (gr. -1-3). 17.95 (978-1-62086-984-0(5)) Mascot Bks., Inc.

—S Is for Sea Glass: A Beach Alphabet. Michelson, Richard. 2014. (ENG.). 32p. (J). (gr. 2-5). 15.95 (978-1-58536-862-4(8), 203010) Sleeping Bear Pr.

—T Is for Teacher: A School Alphabet. Layne, Steven L. & Layne, Deborah Dover. 2007. (ENG.). 40p. (J). (gr. 1-4). per. 7.95 (978-1-58536-331-5(6), 202294) Sleeping Bear Pr.

—T Is for Teachers: A School Alphabet. Layne, Steven L. et al. 2005. (ENG.). 40p. (J). (gr. 1-4). 16.95 (978-1-58536-159-5(3), 202019) Sleeping Bear Pr.

—T Is for Teachers: A School Alphabet. Layne, Deborah & Layne, Stephen L. rev. ed. 2005. (ENG.). 40p. (J). (gr. k-6). 14.95 (978-1-58536-266-0(2)) Sleeping Bear Pr.

—Vanishing Point. Baglio, Ben M. 2007. 158p. (J). pap. (978-0-439-87145-7(X)) Scholastic, Inc.

—Welcome to America, Champ. Stier, Catherine. 2013. (Tales of the World Ser.). (ENG.). 32p. (J). (gr. 1-4). 17.95 (978-1-58536-606-4(4), 202360) Sleeping Bear Pr.

Ettlinger, Doris & Layne, Deborah. Number 1 Teacher: A School Counting Book. Layne, Steven L. 2008. (ENG.). 40p. (J). (gr. k-6). 17.95 (978-1-58536-307-0(3)) Sleeping Bear Pr.

Eubank, Patricia Reeder. Natalia's Favorite Color. Dude, Rosanna Eubank. 2008. (ENG.). 32p. (J). (gr. -1-3). 12.99 (978-0-8249-5523-6(4), Ideal Pubns.) Worthy Publishing.

Eubank, Patricia Reeder. ABCs of Halloween. Eubank, Patricia Reeder. 2020. 26p. (J). (gr. -1 — 1). 7.99 (978-1-5460-1485-0(3), Worthy Kids/Ideals) Worthy Publishing.

Eubank, Patricia Reeder. The Princess & the Snarls. Eubank, Patricia Reeder. 2006. (ENG.). 32p. (J). (gr. k-3). 16.95 (978-0-8249-5536-6(6), Ideal Pubns.) Worthy Publishing.

Eubank, Patti Reeder. Just Where You Belong. 2004. 32p. (J). 8.95 (978-0-8249-5481-9(5), Ideal Pubns.) Worthy Publishing.

Eubanks, Charles. Alphabet Puke: Monsters' Medicine A-Z. Cole, Quinn. 2013. 32p. pap. 6.99 (978-1-936214-94-5(6)) Wyatt-MacKenzie Publishing.

Eudes-Pascal, Elisabeth. Monkey in the Mud. Poulin, Andree. 2009. (Rainy Day Readers Ser.). 32p. (J). (gr. -1-3). pap. 10.55 (978-1-60754-371-8(0)) Windmill Bks.

—Raffi's Animal Rescue. Meunier, Sylvain. Cummins, Sarah, tr. 2007. (ENG.). 64p. (J). (gr. 2-5). *(978-0-88780-742-8(9))* Formac Publishing Co., Ltd.

—Raffi's Animal Rescue, 1 vol. Meunier, Sylvain. Cummins, Sarah, tr. 2007. (Formac First Novels Ser.). (ENG.). 64p. (J). (gr. 2-5). 4.95 *(978-0-88780-740-4(2),* 740) Formac Publishing Co., Ltd. CAN. Dist: Formac Lorimer Bks. Ltd.

—Raffi's Island Adventure, 1 vol. Meunier, Sylvain. Cummins, Sarah, tr. 2008. (Formac First Novels Ser.). (ENG.). 64p. (J). (gr. 2-5). 5.95 *(978-0-88780-755-8(0),* 755) Formac Publishing Co., Ltd. CAN. Dist: Formac Lorimer Bks. Ltd.

Eugene, Karryl. Max the Blue Jay Helps His New Friend. Housen, Karlin L. 2018. (ENG.). 58p. (J). (gr. k-3). 14.95 *(978-0-692-12500-7(0))* Brooklyn Publishing.

—Max the Blue Jay Is Not Fitting In. Housen, Karlin. 2017. (Max the Blue Jay Ser.: Vol. 2). (ENG.). (J). (gr. k-4). 14.95 *(978-0-692-96601-3(3))* Brooklyn Publishing.

Eugene, Karryl. Out of the Woodwork: If Those Walls Could Talk. Nolan, K. D. 2019. (ENG.). 40p. (J). (gr. k-5). 17.95 ***(978-0-578-60438-1(8))*** Brooklyn Publishing.

Eugênia, Maria. Cruiser & the Night Noises. Johnston, Jan. 2009. (ENG.). 20p. 12.99 *(978-1-934706-51-0(5))* Blue Apple Bks.

Euvremer, Teryl. Toby, Who Are You? Steig, William. 2004. 32p. (J). (gr. -1-3). lib. bdg. 15.89 *(978-0-06-000706-5(0),* Cotler, Joanna Books) HarperCollins Pubs.

Eva, Kamila. The Day the Tea Party Traveled. Gunderson, Lisa. 2018. (ENG.). 42p. (J). (gr. k-4). 17.99 *(978-0-692-12699-8(6),* Tea Time Socials, LLC) Gunderson, Lisa M.

Eva, Sassin. Building Site Sticker Book. Channing, Margot. ed. 2019. (Scribblers Fun Activity Ser.). (ENG.). 32p. (J). (gr. -1). pap. 5.95 *(978-1-912537-78-5(8),* Scribblers) Book Hse. GBR. Dist: Sterling Publishing Co., Inc.

Evangelista, Galina. The Legend of the Wishing Pearl. Salvati, Urbano. 2016. (ENG.). (J). (gr. k-6). pap. 19.95 *(978-1-68181-716-3(0))* Strategic Book Publishing & Rights Agency (SBPRA).

—The Number Jungle. Salvati, Urbano. 2018. (ENG.). 26p. (J). (gr. 3-6). pap. 12.95 *(978-1-946540-68-3(4))* Strategic Book Publishing & Rights Agency (SBPRA).

Evangelista, Mauro. Alice's Adventures in Wonderland. Carroll, Lewis. 2006. 63p. (J). (gr. 2). 8.99 *(978-0-7945-1239-2(9),* Usborne) EDC Publishing.

—The Wizard of Oz. Baum, L. Frank. (Usborne Young Reading: Series Two Ser.). 64p. (J). 2010. 6.99 *(978-0-7945-2826-3(0));* 2007. (gr. 3-7). 8.99 *(978-0-7945-1457-0(X),* Usborne) EDC Publishing.

Evans, Anna. Grandma Ugogo's Zulu Hut. Benzie-Morgan, Patricia. 2020. (ENG.). 22p. (J). ***(978-1-922409-22-5(7));*** pap. ***(978-1-922409-21-8(9))*** Vivid Publishing.

Evans, Antony. Brick Builder's Illustrated Bible: Over 35 Bible Stories for Kids, 1 vol. Dammer, Emily. 2018. (ENG.). 224p. (J). 17.99 *(978-0-310-75437-4(2))* Zonderkidz.

—Don't Give up! Lap Book. Giachetti, Julia. 2014. (MySELF Ser.). (J). (gr. -1-k). 27.00 *(978-1-4788-0517-5(X))* Newmark Learning LLC.

—Dylan's Questions Lap Book. Daniel, Claire. 2014. (MySELF Ser.). (J). (gr. -1-k). 27.00 *(978-1-4788-0519-9(6))* Newmark Learning LLC.

—I Am a Star! Lap Book. Garcia, Ellen. 2014. (MySELF Ser.). (J). (gr. -1-k). 27.00 *(978-1-4788-0516-8(1))* Newmark Learning LLC.

—I Can Make a Plan. Garcia, Ellen. 2014. (J). (gr. -1). 3.99 *(978-1-4788-0478-9(5))* Newmark Learning LLC.

—I Can Make a Plan Lap Book. Garcia, Ellen. 2014. (MySELF Ser.). (J). (gr. -1-k). 27.00 *(978-1-4788-0515-1(3))* Newmark Learning LLC.

—I Will Find a Way. Linde, Barbara M. 2014. (J). (gr. -1). 3.99 *(978-1-4788-0483-3(1))* Newmark Learning LLC.

—I Will Find a Way Lap Book. Linde, Barbara M. 2014. (MySELF Ser.). (J). (gr. -1-k). 27.00 *(978-1-4788-0520-5(X))* Newmark Learning LLC.

—Let's Get It Started. Sparks, Stacey. 2014. (J). (gr. -1). 3.99 *(978-1-4788-0481-9(5))* Newmark Learning LLC.

—Let's Get It Started Lap Book. Sparks, Stacey. 2014. (MySELF Ser.). (J). (gr. -1-k). 27.00 *(978-1-4788-0518-2(8))* Newmark Learning LLC.

Evans, Ashley. Welcome to the Party. Union, Gabrielle. 2020. (ENG.). 32p. (J). (gr. -1-3). 18.99 *(978-0-06-297861-5(6),* HarperCollins) HarperCollins Pubs. Ltd. GBR. Dist: HarperCollins Pubs.

Evans, Belinda. London Folk Tales for Children. JOHNSON / TOWNSEND et al. 2019. (ENG.). 192p. (J). (gr. 2-6). pap. 16.99 *(978-0-7509-8689-2(1))* History Pr. Ltd.,The GBR. Dist: Independent Pubs. Group.

Evans, Cambria. Part-Time Princess. Underwood, Deborah. 2013. (Part-Time Ser.). 40p. (J). (gr. -1-k). 16.99 *(978-1-4231-2485-6(5))* Hyperion Pr.

Evans, Carol. A West Coast Summer. Woodward, Caroline. 2018. (ENG.). 32p. (J). *(978-1-55017-843-2(1))* Harbour Publishing Co., Ltd.

Evans, Casey. Pip, Veronica & the Harmonica. Krinsky, Ed. 2013. 32p. pap. 13.00 *(978-1-62516-945-7(0),* Strategic Bk. Publishing) Strategic Book Publishing & Rights Agency (SBPRA).

Evans, Chadrick Michael. Johnny Lumpkin Wants a Friend. Evans, Rhonda Boone. 2007. 32p. per. 24.95 *(978-1-4241-8614-3(5))* America Star Bks.

Evans, Claire. The Three Little Superpigs. Evans, Claire. 2018. (ENG.). 40p. (J). (gr. -1-k). 14.99 *(978-1-338-24545-5(7),* Scholastic Pr.) Scholastic, Inc.

—The Three Little Superpigs: Once upon a Time. Evans, Claire. 2019. (ENG.). 40p. (J). (gr. -1-k). 14.99 *(978-1-338-24548-6(1),* Scholastic Pr.) Scholastic, Inc.

Evans, Dianne. Adventures of Miss Patty's Goose & Other Friends. Christison, Ken, photos by. Gibson, Trudy. 2018. (ENG.). 84p. 29.00 *(978-0-692-18817-0(7))* BookBaby.

Evans, Dustin. Chasing Whales Aboard the Charles W. Morgan, 1 vol., Bk. 2. Specter, Baron. 2010. (Ghostly Graphic Adventures Ser.). (ENG.). 32p. (J). (gr. 3-6). 29.93 *(978-1-60270-771-9(5),* 8840, Graphic Planet - Fiction) Magic Wagon.

—Costume Craziness, 1 vol. 2013. (Mystical Pencil Ser.). (ENG.). 32p. (J). (gr. 3-6). 29.93 *(978-1-61641-926-4(1),* 11708, Graphic Planet - Fiction) Magic Wagon.

—Dinosaur Drama, 1 vol. 2013. (Mystical Pencil Ser.). (ENG.). 32p. (J). (gr. 3-6). 29.93 *(978-1-61641-927-1(X),* 11710, Graphic Planet - Fiction) Magic Wagon.

—Dodging Danger on the Dartmouth, 1 vol., Bk. 1. Specter, Baron. 2010. (Ghostly Graphic Adventures Ser.). (ENG.). 32p. (J). (gr. 3-6). 29.93 *(978-1-60270-770-2(7),* 8838, Graphic Planet - Fiction) Magic Wagon.

—Drama at Dungeon Rock: #6, 1 vol. Specter, Baron. 2010. (Ghostly Graphic Adventures Ser.). (ENG.). 32p. (J). (gr. 3-6). 29.93 *(978-1-60270-775-7(8),* 8848, Graphic Planet - Fiction) Magic Wagon.

—The Lighthouse of Terror, 1 vol., Bk. 3. Specter, Baron. 2010. (Ghostly Graphic Adventures Ser.). (ENG.). 32p. (J). (gr. 3-6). 29.93 *(978-1-60270-772-6(3),* 8842, Graphic Planet - Fiction) Magic Wagon.

—A Medieval Mess, 1 vol. 2013. (Mystical Pencil Ser.). (ENG.). 32p. (J). (gr. 3-6). 29.93 *(978-1-61641-928-8(8),* 11712, Graphic Planet - Fiction) Magic Wagon.

—Raging Robots, 1 vol. 2013. (Mystical Pencil Ser.). (ENG.). 32p. (J). (gr. 3-6). 29.93 *(978-1-61641-929-5(6),* 11714, Graphic Planet - Fiction) Magic Wagon.

—The Spooky Short Sands Shipwreck: #4, 1 vol. Specter, Baron. 2010. (Ghostly Graphic Adventures Ser.). (ENG.). 32p. (J). (gr. 3-6). 29.93 *(978-1-60270-773-3(1),* 8844, Graphic Planet - Fiction) Magic Wagon.

—The Star Island Spirits: #5, 1 vol. Specter, Baron. 2010. (Ghostly Graphic Adventures Ser.). (ENG.). 32p. (J). (gr. 3-6). 29.93 *(978-1-60270-774-0(X),* 8846, Graphic Planet - Fiction) Magic Wagon.

Evans, Elise. Can I Tell You about Self-Harm? A Guide for Friends, Family & Professionals. Knightsmith, Pooky. 2018. (Can I Tell You About...? Ser.). (ENG.). 72p. (J). pap. 14.95 *(978-1-78592-428-6(1),* 696716) Kingsley, Jessica Pubs. GBR. Dist: Hachette UK Distribution.

Evans, Fran, et al. Green Isles of the Ocean. Francis, Marnie et al. 2005. (ENG.). 32p. pap. 12.95 *(978-1-84323-421-0(1))* Beekman Bks., Inc.

Evans, Gabriel. Oh, Rats! Seidler, Tor. 2020. (ENG.). 336p. (J). (gr. 3-7). pap. 7.99 *(978-1-5344-2685-6(X),* Atheneum Bks. for Young Readers) Simon & Schuster Children's Publishing.

—Pick-a-WooWoo - Born to Love Frogs: All children have a Gift!, 16 vols., Vol. 8. Nicholl, Jacqueline. 2009. 32p. pap. *(978-0-9803669-7-6(6))* Pick-a-Woo Woo Pubs.

—Pick-a-WooWoo - Herbie & the Tune: Deep within every moment, there is pure Joy. Kyle, Bradley. 2011. (ENG.). 32p. pap. *(978-1-921883-02-6(2))* Pick-a-Woo Woo Pubs.

—Pick-a-WooWoo - Oceans Calling: An enlightening journey to the lost city of Atlantis. Nicoll, Jacqueline. 2010. 32p. pap. *(978-0-9806520-1-7(4))* Pick-a-Woo Woo Pubs.

—Pick-a-WooWoo - the Star Who Lost Her Sparkle: Sprinkle here & Sparkle ther. We work with love because we Care. Lee, Patricia Mary. 2011. (ENG.). 28p. pap. *(978-1-921883-03-3(0))* Pick-a-Woo Woo Pubs.

—Silly Gilly Gil - Gay L-U-V. Frantz, Donna. 2013. 30p. pap. *(978-1-921883-38-5(3),* MBS Pr.) Pick-a-Woo Woo Pubs.

Evans, Gabriel. Ollie & Augustus. Evans, Gabriel. 2020. (ENG.). 40p. (J). (gr. -1-2). 16.99 *(978-1-5362-0967-9(8))* Candlewick Pr.

Evans, Graham. Daddies & Baddies. Waugh, Mat. 2019. (ENG.). 34p. (J). (gr. k-2). ***(978-1-912883-15-8(5));*** pap. ***(978-1-912883-14-1(7))*** Big Red Button Bks.

—What's the Magic Word? Waugh, Mat. 2018. (ENG.). 34p. (J). (gr. k-3). pap. ***(978-1-9999147-7-6(5))*** Big Red Button Bks.

—When I Grow Up. Bird, Bronwyn. 2020. (ENG.). 28p. (J). pap. ***(978-1-922374-90-5(3))*** Library For All Limited.

Evans, Jessica Linn. Solar the Polar. Constantinescu, Kim. 2017. (ENG.). (J). (gr. k-6). 17.99 *(978-1-365-86182-6(1));* pap. 13.99 *(978-1-365-86184-0(8))* Lulu Pr., Inc.

Evans, Jessica Linn. Solar the Polar. Constantinescu, Kim. ed. 2017. (ENG.). 26p. (J). (gr. k-6). 17.99 ***(978-1-64372-025-8(2));*** pap. 13.99 ***(978-1-64372-260-3(3))*** MacLaren-Cochrane Publishing, Inc. (Huskies Pub).

—Solar the Polar Dyslexic Font. Constantinescu, Kim. ed. 2017. (ENG.). 26p. (J). (gr. k-6). 19.99 ***(978-1-64372-261-0(1));*** pap. 15.99 ***(978-1-64372-262-7(X))*** MacLaren-Cochrane Publishing, Inc.

Evans, Jessica Linn. Solar the Polar Dyslexic Font. Constantinescu, Kim. 2017. (ENG.). 28p. (J). (gr. k-6). 21.99 *(978-1-365-86183-3(X));* pap. 15.99 *(978-1-365-86185-7(6))* Lulu Pr., Inc.

Evans, Kate. Vincent's Starry Night & Other Stories: A Children's History of Art. Bird, Michael. 2016. (ENG.). 336p. (J). (gr. 4-8). 29.99 *(978-1-78067-615-9(8),* King, Laurence Publishing) Orion Publishing Group, Ltd. GBR. Dist: Hachette Bk. Group.

Evans, Kevin. The Elves of Owl's Head Mountain. Sutliff, Jamie. Blumberg, Christine A., ed. 2007. 280p. (gr. 8-12). 26.95 *(978-0-9712867-7-1(9))* Cold River Pubns.

Evans, Kevin C. The Land of Nen-Us-Yok. Sutliff, Jamie. Blumberg, Christine A., ed. 2007. 256p. pap. 10.95 *(978-0-9712867-4-0(4));* 26.95 *(978-0-9712867-6-4(0))* Cold River Pubns.

Evans, Laura. A Castle at the Straits. Panagopoulos, Janie Lynn. 2003. 48p. (J). (gr. 1-6). *(978-0-911872-83-5(3))* Mackinac State Historic Parks.

—Home to Mackinac: The Tale of Young Jack Murphy's Discovery of Loyalty, Family, & Forgiveness. Cory, Kim Delmar. 2007. (ENG.). 175p. (J). (gr. 3-7). per. 9.95 *(978-0-911872-87-3(6))* Mackinac State Historic Parks.

Evans, Leslie. At the Sea Floor Café: Odd Ocean Critter Poems, 1 vol. Bulion, Leslie. (ENG.). 48p. (J). (gr. 3-6). 2016. pap. 7.95 *(978-1-56145-920-9(8));* 2011. 14.95 *(978-1-56145-565-2(2))* Peachtree Publishing Co. Inc.

—Faces of the Moon. Crelin, Bob. 2009. 36p. (J). (gr. 1-4). 16.95 *(978-1-57091-785-1(X))* Charlesbridge Publishing, Inc.

—Hey There, Stink Bug! Bulion, Leslie. 48p. (J). (gr. 2-5). 2008. per. 5.95 *(978-1-58089-340-4(6));* 2006. lib. bdg. 12.95 *(978-1-58089-304-6(X))* Charlesbridge Publishing, Inc.

—Leaf Jumpers. Gerber, Carole. (J). 2017. 28p. (— 1). bds. 7.99 *(978-1-58089-782-2(7));* 2006. 32p. (gr. -1-2). per. 7.95 *(978-1-57091-498-0(2))* Charlesbridge Publishing, Inc.

—Spring Blossoms. Gerber, Carole. 32p. (J). (gr. -1-3). 2015. pap. 7.95 *(978-1-58089-413-5(5));* 2013. lib. bdg. 16.95 *(978-1-58089-412-8(7))* Charlesbridge Publishing, Inc.

—You Have to Be Smart If You're Going to Be Tall/Tienes Que Ser Inteligente Si Vas a Ser Alta. 2006. 46p. (J). (gr. -1-3). per. 16.99 *(978-1-59879-217-1(2))* Lifevest Publishing, Inc.

Evans, Lisa. The Flower. Light, John. (Child's Play Library). (ENG.). 32p. (J). 2011. *(978-1-84643-070-1(4));* 2007. (gr. 1-2). *(978-1-84643-072-5(0))* Child's Play International Ltd.

Evans, Lisa, jt. illus. see Braun, Sebastien.

Evans, Lisa M. Rich Man's Song. Evans, Lisa M. 2019. 36p. (J). pap. 7.99 *(978-0-9745264-2-3(8))* Marquise Publishing.

Evans, Margaret. Tad, the Sad Tadpole, 1 vol. Shorty. 2009. 29p. pap. 19.95 *(978-1-4489-2458-5(8))* PublishAmerica, Inc.

Evans, Mark & Vue, Tou. Claws in the Snow. Dahl, Michael. 2009. (Dragonblood Ser.). (ENG.). 40p. (J). (gr. 4-8). 23.99 *(978-1-4342-1262-7(9),* Stone Arch Bks.) Capstone.

Evans, Melvyn. Once I Was a Cardboard Box... But Now I'm a Book about Polar Bears. Poitier, Anton. 2010. 24p. (J). (gr. k-3). 7.99 *(978-0-8416-7200-0(8))* Hammond World Atlas Corp.

—Once I Was a Comic... But Now I'm a Book about Tigers. Poitier, Anton. 2010. 24p. (J). (gr. k-3). 7.99 *(978-0-8416-7201-7(6))* Hammond World Atlas Corp.

Evans, Michael. Over in the Meadow. 2004. (Classic Books with Holes 8x8 Ser.). (ENG.). 16p. (J). pap. *(978-0-85953-692-9(0))* Child's Play International Ltd.

—Songbooks - Tom Thumb's Musical Maths: Developing Maths Skills with Simple Songs. MacGregor, Helen. Sanderson, Ana, ed. 2005. (Songbooks Ser.). (ENG.). 64p. (J). pap. 22.95 *(978-0-7136-7295-4(1))* HarperCollins Pubs. Ltd. GBR. Dist: Independent Pubs. Group.

Evans, Michael. Poggle & the Treasure. Evans, Michael. 2011. (Poggle Ser.). (ENG.). 32p. (J). (gr. k — 1). pap. 8.99 *(978-1-4052-4812-9(2))* Egmont Bks., Ltd. GBR. Dist: Independent Pubs. Group.

Evans, Michael, Jr. & Evans, Michael. Over in the Meadow. 2007. (Classic Books with Holes 8x8 Ser.). (ENG.). 16p. (J). (gr. -1-1). pap. *(978-1-84643-136-4(0))* Child's Play International Ltd.

Evans, Michael, jt. illus. see Evans, Michael, Jr.

Evans, Nancy. Flutter Your Wings. Sikes, Jan. 2017. (ENG.). (J). pap. 9.95 *(978-0-9906179-8-3(X))* RiJan Publishing.

Evans, Neil. The Creature in the Crystal. Darke, J. A. 2018. (Spine Shivers Ser.). (ENG.). 128p. (J). (gr. 4-6). lib. bdg. 26.65 *(978-1-4965-6433-7(2),* 138273, Stone Arch Bks.) Capstone.

—Do Not Watch. Darke, J. A. 2016. (Spine Shivers Ser.). (ENG.). 128p. (J). (gr. 4-6). lib. bdg. 26.65 *(978-1-4965-3071-4(3),* Stone Arch Bks.) Capstone.

—Fade to Black. Darke, J. A. 2016. (Spine Shivers Ser.). (ENG.). 128p. (J). (gr. 4-6). lib. bdg. 26.65 *(978-1-4965-3070-7(5),* Stone Arch Bks.) Capstone.

Evans, Neil. The Medusa Doll. Brezenoff, Steve. 2020. (Michael Dahl Presents: Scary Stories Ser.). (ENG.). 72p. (J). (gr. 3-5). pap. 5.95 ***(978-1-4965-9891-2(1),*** 201253); lib. bdg. 25.32 ***(978-1-4965-9715-1(X),*** 199343) Capstone. (Stone Arch Bks.).

—The Nightmare Gnomes of Neary Heights. Atwood, Megan. 2020. (Michael Dahl Presents: Scary Stories Ser.). (ENG.). 72p. (J). (gr. 3-5). pap. 5.95 ***(978-1-4965-9892-9(X),*** 201255); lib. bdg. 25.32 ***(978-1-4965-9716-8(8),*** 199344) Capstone. (Stone Arch Bks.).

Evans, Neil. Sasquatch Island. Darke, J. A. & Terrell, Brandon. 2018. (Spine Shivers Ser.). (ENG.). 128p. (J). (gr. 4-6). lib. bdg. 26.65 *(978-1-4965-6432-0(4),* 138272, Stone Arch Bks.) Capstone.

—Spine Shivers. 2016. (Spine Shivers Ser.). (ENG.). 128p. (gr. 3-4). pap. 13.90 *(978-1-4965-3083-7(7),* Stone Arch Bks.) Capstone.

Evans, Neil. The Watchers of Whitmore Way. Atwood, Megan. 2020. (Michael Dahl Presents: Scary Stories Ser.). (ENG.). 72p. (J). (gr. 3-5). pap. 5.95 ***(978-1-4965-9893-6(8),*** 201254); lib. bdg. 25.32 ***(978-1-4965-9718-2(4),*** 199347) Capstone. (Stone Arch Bks.).

—Werewolf Hotel. Brezenoff, Steve. 2020. (Michael Dahl Presents: Scary Stories Ser.). (ENG.). 72p. (J). (gr. 3-5). pap. 5.95 ***(978-1-4965-9894-3(6),*** 201256); lib. bdg. 25.32 ***(978-1-4965-9717-5(6),*** 199346) Capstone. (Stone Arch Bks.).

Evans, Nicola, et al. Little Bird Greetings: Special Delivery, Bless Child, Little Girls: Keepsake Greeting Card Board Book 3 Pack. Birdsong, Minnie. 2015. (Little Bird Greetings Ser.). (ENG.). 16p. (J). (gr. -1-k). bds., bds., bds. 20.97 *(978-1-68052-248-8(5),* 9000820) Cottage Door Pr.

Evans, Nicola. Special Delivery: Keepsake Greeting Card Board Book. Birdsong, Minnie. ed. 2017. (Little Bird Greetings Ser.). (ENG.). 8p. (J). (gr. -1-k). bds. 6.99 *(978-1-68052-209-9(4),* 1000451) Cottage Door Pr.

Evans, Pat K. Methuselah. Evans, Pat K. Preece, Murray. 2018. (ENG.). 52p. (J). pap. 12.00 *(978-1-7903-0742-5(2))* Independently Published.

Evans, Pat K. Raccoons: A New Idea. Evans, Pat K. Preece, Murray. 2019. (ENG.). 60p. (J). pap. 12.99 ***(978-1-6897-9726-9(6))*** Independently Published.

Evans, Rebecca, et al. Facing Feelings & Fears Picture Book Set: Social Emotional Books for Kids. Ingalls, Ann et al. 2020. (ENG.). (J). (-6). pap. 47.75 ***(978-1-7282-4200-2(2),*** Dawn Pubns.) Sourcebooks, Inc.

Evans, Rebecca. Finding the Speed of Light, 1 vol. Weston, Mark. 2019. (ENG.). 32p. (J). (gr. 5-7). E-Book 9.99 *(978-0-88448-547-6(1),* 884547) Tilbury Hse. Pubs.

—If You Played Hide-And-Seek with a Chameleon, 1 vol. Wise, Bill. 2019. (ENG.). 32p. (J). (gr. k-6). 16.95 *(978-1-58469-650-6(8));* pap. 8.95 *(978-1-58469-651-3(6))* Sourcebooks, Inc. (Dawn Pubns.).

—Jeannie Houdini: A Hamster's Tale. Stouck, Mary-Ann. 2019. (ENG.). 25p. (J). 17.95 *(978-0-940719-40-8(1))* Gryphon Pr., The.

—Masterpiece Robot: And the Ferocious Valerie Knick Knack!, 1 vol. Tra, Frank. 2018. (ENG.). 36p. (J). (gr. 2-6). 17.95 *(978-0-88448-518-6(8),* 884518) Tilbury Hse. Pubs.

—Why Should I Walk? I Can Fly! Ingalls, Ann. 2019. (ENG.). 32p. (J). (gr. -1-3). 16.95 *(978-1-58469-638-4(9),* Dawn Pubns.) Sourcebooks, Inc.

Evans, Rose. Madame Cat. Dow, Richard. 2016. (ENG.). (J). pap. 12.99 *(978-0-9983859-0-7(5))* Madame Cat Publishing.

Evans, Rose Grier. Madame Cat. Dow, Richard. 2017. (ENG.). (J). 17.99 *(978-0-9983859-1-4(3))* Madame Cat Publishing.

—Mumford the Manatee. Mountcastle, Dee. 2018. (ENG.). 38p. (J). 21.95 *(978-0-9992073-1-4(8))* Mountcastle, Deirdre D. PA.

Evans, Rose Grier & Dulaney, Debbie. The Memory Tree. Reed, Elizabeth. 2018. (ENG.). (J). 42p. 21.95 *(978-0-9993012-0-3(9));* 48p. pap. 14.95 *(978-0-9993012-1-0(7))* MeAgain Publishing.

Evans, Rowena. Brumbies. Boer, Paula. 2011. (ENG.). 148p. pap. 14.99 *(978-0-615-56093-9(8))* IFWG Publishing Inc.

Evans, Ruth Todd. The Panda Who Would Not Eat. Evans, Ruth Todd. 2007. 32p. (J). (gr. -1-3). per. 9.95 *(978-0-932653-84-0(7))* Sunbelt Pubns., Inc.

Evans, Shane. Bintou's Braids. Diouf, Sylvianne. 2004. (ENG.). 40p. (J). (gr. -1-7). pap. 6.99 *(978-0-8118-4629-5(6))* Chronicle Bks. LLC.

—My Brother Charlie. Peete, Holly Robinson & Peete, Ryan Elizabeth. 2010. (ENG.). 40p. (J). (gr. 2-5). 17.99 *(978-0-545-09466-5(6),* Scholastic Pr.) Scholastic, Inc.

—My Cold Plum Lemon Pie Bluesy Mood. Brown, Tameka Fryer. 2013. (ENG.). 32p. (J). (gr. -1-2). 17.99 *(978-0-670-01285-5(8),* Viking Books for Young Readers) Penguin Young Readers Group.

Evans, Shane W. Art from Her Heart: Folk Artist Clementine Hunter. Whitehead, Kathy. 2008. (ENG.). 32p. (J). (gr. 1-3). 16.99 *(978-0-399-24219-9(8),* G.P. Putnam's Sons Books for Young Readers) Penguin Young Readers Group.

—The Banana-Leaf Ball: How Play Can Change the World. Milway, Katie Smith. 2017. (CitizenKid Ser.). (ENG.). 32p. (J). (gr. 3-7). 18.99 *(978-1-77138-331-8(3))* Kids Can Pr., Ltd. CAN. Dist: Hachette Bk. Group.

—Big Papa & the Time Machine. Bernstrom, Daniel. 2020. (ENG.). 40p. (J). (gr. -1-3). 17.99 *(978-0-06-246331-9(4),* HarperCollins) HarperCollins Pubs. Ltd. GBR. Dist: HarperCollins Pubs.

—Black Jack: The Ballad of Jack Johnson. Smith, Charles R., Jr. 2010. (ENG.). 40p. (J). (gr. -1-1). 18.99 *(978-1-59643-473-8(2),* 900055762) Roaring Brook Pr.

—Chocolate Me! Diggs, Taye. (ENG.). (J). 2019. 32p. bds. 7.99 *(978-1-250-20785-2(1),* 900201772); 2011. 40p. (gr. -1-3). 18.99 *(978-0-312-60326-7(6),* 900064334) Feiwel & Friends.

—Chocolate Me! Book & CD Storytime Set. Diggs, Taye. unabr. ed. 2019. (ENG.). 1p. (J). 12.99 *(978-1-250-22256-5(7),* 900208043) Feiwel & Friends.

—Did I Tell You I Love You Today? Jordan, Deloris. 2004. (ENG.). 32p. (J). (gr. -1-3). 19.99 *(978-0-689-85271-8(1),* Simon & Schuster/Paula Wiseman Bks.) Simon & Schuster/Paula Wiseman Bks.

—Free at Last! Stories & Songs of Emancipation. Rappaport, Doreen. 2006. (ENG.). 64p. (J). (gr. 4-7). pap. 9.99 *(978-0-7636-3147-5(7))* Candlewick Pr.

—Hands Up! McDaniel, Breanna J. 2019. (ENG.). 32p. (J). (gr. -1-3). 17.99 *(978-0-525-55231-4(6),* Dial Bks) Penguin Young Readers Group.

—Homemade Love [Board Book]. Hooks, Bell. 2017. (ENG.). 28p. (J). (gr. -1 — 1). bds. 7.99 *(978-1-4847-9935-2(6),* Jump at the Sun) Hyperion Bks. for Children.

—Hosea Plays On. Blasi, Kathleen M. 2020. (ENG.). 32p. (J). (gr. -1-4). 16.95 *(978-1-4549-2683-2(X))* Sterling Publishing Co., Inc.

—I Love You More Than ... Diggs, Taye. 2018. (ENG.). 32p. (J). 17.99 *(978-1-250-13534-6(6),* 900178264) Feiwel & Friends.

—Li'l Rabbit's Kwanzaa. Washington, Donna L. 2010. (ENG.). 32p. (J). (gr. -1-2). 12.99 *(978-0-06-072816-8(7),* Tegen, Katherine Bks) HarperCollins Pubs.

—Lillian's Right to Vote: A Celebration of the Voting Rights Act Of 1965. Winter, Jonah. 2015. (ENG.). 40p. (J). (gr. k-4). 17.99 *(978-0-385-39028-6(9),* Schwartz & Wade Bks.) Random Hse. Children's Bks.

—Mixed Me! Diggs, Taye. 2015. (ENG.). 40p. (J). (gr. -1-3). 17.99 *(978-1-250-04719-9(6),* 900132069) Feiwel & Friends.

—No More! Stories & Songs of Slave Resistance. Rappaport, Doreen. 2005. (ENG.). 64p. (J). (gr. 4-7). reprint ed. pap. 9.99 *(978-0-7636-2876-5(X))* Candlewick Pr.

—Nobody Gonna Turn Me 'Round: Stories & Songs of the Civil Rights Movement. Rappaport, Doreen. 2006. (ENG.). 64p. (J). (gr. 4-7). 19.99 *(978-0-7636-1927-5(2))* Candlewick Pr.

—Nobody Gonna Turn Me 'Round: Stories & Songs of the Civil Rights Movement. Rappaport, Doreen. 2008. (ENG.). 64p. (J). (gr. 4-7). pap. 9.99 *(978-0-7636-3892-4(7))* Candlewick Pr.

—The Red Pencil. Pinkney, Andrea Davis. (J). (gr. 4-17). 2015. 192p. pap. 8.99 *(978-0-316-24782-5(0));* 2014. (ENG.). 336p. 17.99 *(978-0-316-24780-1(4))* Little, Brown Bks. for Young Readers.

—Shanna's Ballerina Show. Marzollo, Jean. 2003. (Shanna Show Ser.). (ENG.). 24p. (J). (gr. -1-1). pap. 16.19 *(978-0-7868-1758-0(5))* Hyperion Bks. for Children.

E

—The Way a Door Closes. Smith, Hope Anita. 2011. (ENG.). 64p. (J). (gr. 3-7). pap. 10.99 *(978-0-312-66169-4(X),* 900070773) Square Fish.

—When Harriet Met Sojourner. Clinton, Catherine. 2007. (ENG.). 32p. (J). (gr. k-2). 16.99 *(978-0-06-050425-0(0),* Tegen, Katherine Bks) HarperCollins Pubs.

—28 Days: Moments in Black History That Changed the World. Smith, Charles R., Jr. 2015. (ENG.). 56p. (J). (gr. -1-5). 18.99 *(978-1-59643-820-0(7),* 900087175) Roaring Brook Pr.

Evans, Shane W. Underground. Evans, Shane W. 2015. (ENG.). (J). (gr. -1-3). lib. bdg. 19.60 *(978-1-62765-768-6(1))* Perfection Learning Corp.

—Underground: Finding the Light to Freedom. Evans, Shane W. 2011. (ENG.). 32p. (J). (gr. -1-3). 16.99 *(978-1-59643-538-4(0),* 900061339) Roaring Brook Pr.

—We March. Evans, Shane W. 2012. (ENG.). 32p. (J). (gr. -1-3). 18.99 *(978-1-59643-539-1(9),* 900061341) Roaring Brook Pr.

Evans, Sherri. Nana & the Jabbywalker, 1 vol. Helbig-Miller, Theresa. 2008. (ENG.). 30p. 24.95 *(978-1-60703-567-1(7))* America Star Bks.

Evans, Steve. Adding up (Collins Children's Poster) Collins Kids, Collins. 2018. (ENG.). 1p. (J). (-4). ring bd. 9.99 *(978-0-00-830477-5(7))* HarperCollins Pubs. Ltd. GBR. Dist: Independent Pubs. Group.

—Alphabet (Collins Children's Poster) Collins Kids, Collins. 2018. (ENG.). 1p. (J). (-4). ring bd. 9.99 *(978-0-00-830469-0(6))* HarperCollins Pubs. Ltd. GBR. Dist: Independent Pubs. Group.

—Collins Children's Picture Atlas. Collins Kids, Collins. 3rd rev. ed. 2019. (ENG.). 48p. (J). (gr. 3-7). 16.95 *(978-0-00-832032-4(2))* HarperCollins Pubs. Ltd. GBR. Dist: Independent Pubs. Group.

—First Phonics (Collins Children's Poster) Collins Kids, Collins. 2018. (ENG.). 1p. (J). (-4). ring bd. 9.99 *(978-0-00-830472-0(6))* HarperCollins Pubs. Ltd. GBR. Dist: Independent Pubs. Group.

—First Words (Collins Children's Poster) Collins Kids, Collins. 2018. (ENG.). 1p. (J). (-4). ring bd. 9.99 *(978-0-00-830470-6(X))* HarperCollins Pubs. Ltd. GBR. Dist: Independent Pubs. Group.

—Flags (Collins Children's Poster) Collins Kids, Collins. 2018 (ENG.). 1p. (J). (-4). ring bd. 9.99 *(978-0-00-830479-9(3))* HarperCollins Pubs. Ltd. GBR. Dist: Independent Pubs. Group.

—Human Body (Collins Children's Poster) Collins Kids, Collins. 2018. (ENG.). 1p. (J). (-4). ring bd. 9.99 *(978-0-00-830481-2(5))* HarperCollins Pubs. Ltd. GBR. Dist: Independent Pubs. Group.

—Numbers 1 - 100 (Collins Children's Poster) Collins Kids, Collins. 2018. (ENG.). 1p. (J). (-4). ring bd. 9.99 *(978-0-00-830474-4(2))* HarperCollins Pubs. Ltd. GBR. Dist: Independent Pubs. Group.

—Numbers 1 - 20 (Collins Children's Poster) Collins Kids, Collins. 2018. (ENG.). 1p. (J). (-4). ring bd. 9.99 *(978-0-00-830473-7(4))* HarperCollins Pubs. Ltd. GBR. Dist: Independent Pubs. Group.

Evans, Steve, et al. Pupil Book 3B, Bk. 3B. Mumford, Jeanette et al. 2014. (Busy Ant Maths Ser.). (ENG.). 16p. (gr. 2). pap., stu. ed. 13.99 *(978-0-00-756238-1(1))* HarperCollins Pubs. Ltd. GBR. Dist: Independent Pubs. Group.

—Pupil Book 5A, Bk. 5A. Mumford, Jeanette et al. ed. 2014. (Busy Ant Maths Ser.). (ENG.). 128p. (gr. 4). pap. 12.95 *(978-0-00-756833-8(9))* HarperCollins Pubs. Ltd. GBR. Dist: Independent Pubs. Group.

—Pupil Book 5B, Bk. 5B. Mumford, Jeanette et al. ed. 2014. (Busy Ant Maths Ser.). (ENG.). 128p. (gr. 4). pap. 14.95 *(978-0-00-756834-5(7))* HarperCollins Pubs. Ltd. GBR. Dist: Independent Pubs. Group.

—Pupil Book 5C, Bk. 5C. Mumford, Jeanette et al. ed. 2014. (Busy Ant Maths Ser.). (ENG.). 128p. (gr. 4). pap. 14.99 *(978-0-00-756835-2(5))* HarperCollins Pubs. Ltd. GBR. Dist: Independent Pubs. Group.

—Pupil Book 6A, Bk. 6A. Mumford, Jeanette et al. ed. 2014. (Busy Ant Maths Ser.). (ENG.). 128p. (gr. 4). pap. 14.95 *(978-0-00-756836-9(3))* HarperCollins Pubs. Ltd. GBR. Dist: Independent Pubs. Group.

—Pupil Book 6B, Bk. 6B. Mumford, Jeanette et al. ed. 2014. (Busy Ant Maths Ser.). (ENG.). 128p. (gr. 4). pap. 14.95 *(978-0-00-756837-6(1))* HarperCollins Pubs. Ltd. GBR. Dist: Independent Pubs. Group.

—Pupil Book 6C, Bk. 6C. Mumford, Jeanette et al. ed. 2014. (Busy Ant Maths Ser.). (ENG.). 128p. (gr. 4). pap. 14.99 *(978-0-00-756838-3(X))* HarperCollins Pubs. Ltd. GBR. Dist: Independent Pubs. Group.

Evans, Steve. Solar System (Collins Children's Poster) Collins Kids, Collins. 2018. (ENG.). 1p. (J). (-4). ring bd. 9.99 *(978-0-00-830480-5(7))* HarperCollins Pubs. Ltd. GBR. Dist: Independent Pubs. Group.

—Telling the Time (Collins Children's Poster) Collins Kids, Collins. 2018. (ENG.). 1p. (J). (-4). ring bd. 9.99 *(978-0-00-830476-8(9))* HarperCollins Pubs. Ltd. GBR. Dist: Independent Pubs. Group.

—Times Tables (Collins Children's Poster) Collins Kids, Collins. 2018. (ENG.). 1p. (J). (-4). ring bd. 9.99 *(978-0-00-830478-2(5))* HarperCollins Pubs. Ltd. GBR. Dist: Independent Pubs. Group.

Evans, Vince. Tyrannosaurus Ralph. Evans, Nate. 2017. (ENG.). 144p. (J). pap. 9.99 *(978-1-4494-7208-5(7))* Andrews McMeel Publishing.

Evans, Wynne. Albie's First Word: A Tale Inspired by Albert Einstein's Childhood. Tourville, Jacqueline. 2014. 40p. (J). (gr. -1-3). 17.99 *(978-0-307-97893-6(1),* Schwartz & Wade Bks.) Random Hse. Children's Bks.

Evanson, Ashley. London: A Book of Opposites. Evanson, Ashley. 2015. (Hello, World Ser.). 14p. (J). (— 1). bds. 7.99 *(978-0-448-48916-2(3),* Penguin Workshop) Penguin Young Readers Group.

—New York: A Book of Colors. Evanson, Ashley. 2015. (Hello, World Ser.). 14p. (J). (— 1). bds. 7.99 *(978-0-448-48913-1(9),* Penguin Workshop) Penguin Young Readers Group.

—Paris: A Book of Shapes. Evanson, Ashley. 2015. (Hello, World Ser.). 14p. (J). (— 1). bds. 7.99 *(978-0-448-48915-5(5),* Penguin Workshop) Penguin Young Readers Group.

—Rio de Janeiro: A Book of Sounds. Evanson, Ashley. 2019. (Hello, World Ser.). 14p. (J). (-k). bds. 7.99 *(978-1-5247-9235-0(7),* Penguin Workshop) Penguin Young Readers Group.

—San Francisco: A Book of Numbers. Evanson, Ashley. 2015. (Hello, World Ser.). 14p. (J). (— 1). bds. 7.99 *(978-0-448-48914-8(7),* Penguin Workshop) Penguin Young Readers Group.

—Tokyo: A Book of Senses. Evanson, Ashley. 2019. (Hello, World Ser.). 14p. (J). (-k). bds. 7.99 *(978-1-5247-9233-6(0),* Penguin Workshop) Penguin Young Readers Group.

Eve Cravens Nawahine. Not Too Close. Esther Cravens Schwalger. 2009. 16p. pap. 8.49 *(978-1-4389-6987-9(2))* AuthorHouse.

Eve, Lealand. Dolly Goes on Vacation. Herman, Alison & Grossman, Lynne. 2007. 22p. (J). 24.95 *(978-0-9746153-2-5(3))* DMH Pr., Inc.

—Dolly Goes to the Beach. Herman, Alison & Grossman, Lynne. 2007. 24p. (J). 24.95 *(978-0-9746153-1-8(5))* DMH Pr., Inc.

—Dolly Goes to the Supermarket. Herman, Alison & Grossman, Lynne. 2007. 22p. (J). 24.96 *(978-0-9746153-0-1(7))* DMH Pr., Inc.

—Liberty's Journey: The Story of Our Freedom. Weigman, Matthew. 2004. 31p. (J). 16.95 *(978-0-9747981-0-3(X))* Fahnestock Pr.

Eveland, Erin. Farmer Frank & the Fuel Can. Taylor, Kendall. 2019. (ENG.). 26p. (J). pap. 10.00 *(978-1-0962-3206-3(5))* Independently Published.

Even Or, Anat. No More Monsters under Your Bed! Chouteau, Jordan. 2019. 32p. (J). (gr. -1-1). 16.99 *(978-0-316-45388-2(9),* Jimmy Patterson) Little Brown & Co.

Evens, Kevin C. The Elves of Owl's Head Mountain. Sutliff, Jamie. Blumberg, Christine A., ed. 2007. 276p. pap. 10.95 *(978-0-9712867-8-8(7))* Cold River Pubns.

Evenwel, Patricia L. Pierogies with the Pope: A Tribute to Pope John Paul II, & New Beginnings with Pope Benedict XVI for Young Readers, 1 vol. Barry, Todd J. 2009. 58p. pap. 16.95 *(978-1-60836-325-4(2))* America Star Bks.

—Shoofly Pie with the Pastor: A Journey Through Pennsylvania Dutch Country. Barry, Todd J. 2013. 70p. pap. 17.95 *(978-1-62709-944-8(1))* America Star Bks.

Everett, Amy. A Ballerina Saurus. Knight, Andy. 2019. (ENG.). 36p. (J). pap. 9.99 ***(978-1-0975-7544-2(6))*** Independently Published.

Everett-Hawkes, Bonnie. Blue Paint. Maher, Liam. 2012. 20p. pap. 9.95 *(978-1-61633-290-7(5))* Guardian Angel Publishing, Inc.

—Have You Ever Heard of a Rainbow Farm. Cousineau-Peiffer, Trisha. 2006. 32p. (J). 12.95 *(978-0-9792084-1-6(6))* Dream Ridge Pr.

—Have You Ever Heard of a Rainbow Farm: The Missing Color Kittens. Cousineau-Peiffer, Trisha. 2007. 48p. (J). per. 15.95 *(978-0-9792084-2-3(4))* Dream Ridge Pr.

Everett, J. H. Doxie. Pickell, Sammy. 2013. (ENG.). (J). 18.99 *(978-0-9827972-3-5(0))* MMJ Foundation.

—No! No! No! Nicholas, Shelby & Nicholas, Shelby. 2013. (ENG.). (J). 18.99 *(978-0-9827972-2-8(2))* MMJ Foundation.

Everett, J. H. & Scott-Waters, Marilyn. Haunted Histories: Creepy Castles, Dark Dungeons, & Powerful Palaces. Everett, J. H. & Scott-Waters, Marilyn. 2013. (ENG.). 160p. (J). (gr. 4-7). pap. 14.99 *(978-1-250-02726-9(8),* 900098298) Square Fish.

Evergreen, Nelson. Attack of the Mud Creatures. Darke, J. A. 2015. (Spine Shivers Ser.). (ENG.). 128p. (J). (gr. 4-6). lib. bdg. 26.65 *(978-1-4965-0220-9(5),* Stone Arch Bks.) Capstone.

—Death Sentence. Dahl, Michael. 2015. (Library of Doom: the Final Chapters Ser.). (ENG.). 40p. (J). (gr. 4-8). 23.99 *(978-1-4342-9678-8(4),* Stone Arch Bks.) Capstone.

—The Grin in the Dark. Darke, J. A. 2015. (Spine Shivers Ser.). (ENG.). 128p. (J). (gr. 4-6). lib. bdg. 26.65 *(978-1-4965-0217-9(5),* Stone Arch Bks.) Capstone.

—The House of Memories. Hulme-Cross, Benjamin. 2015. (Dark Hunter Ser.). (ENG.). 64p. (J). (gr. 4-8). pap. 4.99 *(978-1-4677-8085-8(5),* 9781467780858, Darby Creek) Lerner Publishing Group.

—John Henry - Hammerin' Hero. Stone Arch Books Staff. 2010. (Graphic Spin Ser.). (ENG.). 40p. (J). (gr. 3-6). pap. 5.95 *(978-1-4342-2265-7(9),* Stone Arch Bks.) Capstone.

—John Henry - Hammerin' Hero. Capstone Press Staff. 2010. (Graphic Spin Ser.). (ENG.). 40p. (J). (gr. 3-6). lib. bdg. 25.32 *(978-1-4342-1898-8(8),* Stone Arch Bks.) Capstone.

—The Lost Page. Dahl, Michael. 2015. (Library of Doom: the Final Chapters Ser.). (ENG.). 40p. (J). (gr. 4-8). 23.99 *(978-1-4342-9679-5(2),* Stone Arch Bks.) Capstone.

—The Marsh Demon. Hulme-Cross, Benjamin. ed. 2015. (Dark Hunter Ser.). (ENG.). 64p. (J). (gr. 4-8). E-Book 34.65 *(978-1-4677-8658-4(6),* Darby Creek) Lerner Publishing Group.

—The Screaming Bridge. Darke, J. A. 2015. (Spine Shivers Ser.). (ENG.). 128p. (J). (gr. 4-6). lib. bdg. 26.65 *(978-1-4965-0219-3(1),* Stone Arch Bks.) Capstone.

—Ship of Death. Hulme-Cross, Benjamin. 2015. (Dark Hunter Ser.). (ENG.). 64p. (J). (gr. 4-8). pap. 4.99 *(978-1-4677-8090-2(1),* 9781467780902, Darby Creek) Lerner Publishing Group.

—The Spine Tingler. Dahl, Michael. 2015. (Library of Doom: the Final Chapters Ser.). (ENG.). 40p. (J). (gr. 4-8). 23.99 *(978-1-4342-9680-1(6),* Stone Arch Bks.) Capstone.

—The Stone Witch. Hulme-Cross, Benjamin. 2015. (Dark Hunter Ser.). (ENG.). 64p. (J). (gr. 4-8). pap. 4.99 *(978-1-4677-8089-6(8),* 9781467780896, Darby Creek) Lerner Publishing Group.

—Tech Fury. Darke, J. A. 2015. (Spine Shivers Ser.). (ENG.). 128p. (J). (gr. 4-6). lib. bdg. 26.65 *(978-1-4965-0218-6(3),* Stone Arch Bks.) Capstone.

—Tome Raider. Dahl, Michael. 2015. (Library of Doom: the Final Chapters Ser.). (ENG.). 40p. (J). (gr. 4-8). 23.99 *(978-1-4342-9677-1(6),* Stone Arch Bks.) Capstone.

Evergreen, Nelson & Kendall, Bradford. The Demon Card, 1 vol. Strange, Jason. 2012. (Jason Strange Ser.). (ENG.). 72p. (J). (gr. 3-6). pap. 6.25 *(978-1-4342-3884-9(9));* lib. bdg. 25.32 *(978-1-4342-3296-0(4))* Capstone. (Stone Arch Bks.).

—The Graveyard Plot, 1 vol. Strange, Jason. 2012. (Jason Strange Ser.). (ENG.). 72p. (J). (gr. 3-6). pap. 6.25 *(978-1-4342-3886-3(5),* Stone Arch Bks.) Capstone.

—Strays, 1 vol. Strange, Jason. 2012. (Jason Strange Ser.). (ENG.). 72p. (J). (gr. 3-6). pap. 6.25 *(978-1-4342-3883-2(0));* lib. bdg. 25.32 *(978-1-4342-3295-3(6))* Capstone. (Stone Arch Bks.).

—23 Crow's Perch, 1 vol. Strange, Jason. 2012. (Jason Strange Ser.). (ENG.). 72p. (J). (gr. 3-6). pap. 6.25 *(978-1-4342-3885-6(7));* lib. bdg. 25.32 *(978-1-4342-3297-7(2))* Capstone. (Stone Arch Bks.).

Everhart, Adelaide. The Christmas Porringer (Yesterday's Classics) Stein, Evaleen. 2006. (J). per. 7.95 *(978-1-59915-193-9(6))* Yesterday's Classics.

Everidge, Channing. Catie Conrad: Faith, Friendship & Fashion Disasters. Spady, Angie. 2014. (Desperate Diva Diaries Ser.). (ENG.). 304p. (gr. 3-7). 12.99 *(978-1-4336-8460-9(8),* 005673920, B&H Kids) B&H Publishing Group.

Everitt, Betsy. Popcorn. Moran, Alex. 2003. (Green Light Readers Level 1 Ser.). (ENG.). 24p. (J). (gr. -1-3). pap. 4.99 *(978-0-15-204861-7(8),* 1194679) Houghton Mifflin Harcourt Publishing Co.

Everitt-Stewart, Andrew. Our Baby, 1 vol. Dale, Jay. 2012. (Engage Literacy Green Ser.). (ENG.). 32p. (gr. k-2). pap. 5.99 *(978-1-4296-9023-2(2),* Capstone Pr.) Capstone.

—Our Special Rock Pool, 1 vol. Dale, Jay. 2012. (Engage Literacy Green Ser.). (ENG.). 32p. (gr. k-2). pap. 5.99 *(978-1-4296-9009-6(7),* Capstone Pr.) Capstone.

Everitt-Stewart, Andy. All Grown Up. Burlingham, Abi. 2009. (Stories to Grow with Ser.). 24p. (J). (gr. -1-2). 25.60 *(978-1-60754-469-2(5));* pap. 8.15 *(978-1-60754-470-8(9))* Windmill Bks.

—Best Friends. Burlingham, Abi. 2009. (Stories to Grow with Ser.). 24p. (J). (gr. -1-2). 25.60 *(978-1-60754-475-3(X));* pap. 8.15 *(978-1-60754-476-0(8))* Windmill Bks.

—Five Christmas Reindeer: A Slide & Count Book. Rivers-Moore, Debbie. 2015. (ENG.). 10p. (J). (gr. -1 — 1). bds. 8.99 *(978-1-4998-0169-9(6))* Little Bee Books Inc.

—Five Little Snowmen: A Slide & Count Book. Rivers-Moore, Debbie. 2015. (ENG.). 10p. (J). (gr. -1 — 1). bds. 8.99 *(978-1-4998-0170-5(X))* Little Bee Books Inc.

—Scaredy Bear. Nash, Sarah. 2009. (Stories to Grow with Ser.). 24p. (J). (gr. -1-2). 25.60 *(978-1-60754-472-2(5))* Windmill Bks.

—Smelly Blanket. Nash, Sarah. 2009. (Stories to Grow with Ser.). 24p. (J). (gr. -1-2). 25.60 *(978-1-60754-466-1(0));* pap. 8.15 *(978-1-60754-467-8(9))* Windmill Bks.

—3-Minute Animal Stories. Baxter, Nicola. 2013. (ENG.). 80p. (J). (gr. -1-k). pap. 9.99 *(978-1-84322-978-0(1),* Armadillo) Anness Publishing GBR. Dist: National Bk. Network.

Everson, Andy. I am Raven. Bouchard, David. 2nd ed. 2008. 28p. (J). *(978-0-9784327-0-6(3))* More Than Words Bks., Inc.

Everson, Mya. Ole Mackerel. Jacobsen, Annie. 2012. 32p. (J). 9.98 *(978-0-9778276-5-7(8))* Pickled Herring Pr.

Eves, Mickey. Pugs Are People, Too. Ramsay, Connie. 2018. (ENG.). 26p. (J). pap. *(978-1-988071-87-9(9))* Hasmark Services Publishing.

Evgeniya, Erokhina. There's a New Baby at My Place. Hosking, M. I. M. 2019. (Children of the World Ser.: Vol. 1). (ENG.). 28p. (J). pap. ***(978-0-6485494-0-6(2))*** Tranquility Rise.

Evrard, Gaetan. Let's Get to Work!/Vamos a Trabajar! Anderson, Jill, ed. 2005. (Word Play/Juegos con Pala Ser.). (ENG & SPA.). 20p. (J). (gr. -1-17). bds. 6.95 *(978-1-58728-512-7(6))* Cooper Square Publishing Llc.

Ewald, Chris. Hildie Bitterpickles Needs Her Sleep. Newman, Robin. 2016. (ENG.). 32p. (J). (gr. k-2). 16.99 *(978-1-939547-23-1(7))* Creston Bks.

—No Peacocks! A Feathered Tale of Three Mischievous Foodies. Newman, Robin. 2018. (ENG.). 32p. (J). (gr. -1-3). 16.99 *(978-1-5107-1480-9(4),* Sky Pony Pr.) Skyhorse Publishing Co., Inc.

—Sweet Dreams, Sarah. Kirkfield, Vivian. 2019. (ENG.). 32p. (J). (gr. 2-5). 17.99 *(978-1-939547-31-6(8))* Creston Bks.

Ewart, Claire. The Green Musician. Shahegh, Mahvash. 2015. 36p. (J). (gr. k-3). 16.95 *(978-1-937786-42-7(0),* Wisdom Tales) World Wisdom, Inc.

—The Olive Tree, Vol. Marston, Elsa. 2014. 32p. (J). (gr. -1-2). 16.95 *(978-1-937786-29-8(3),* Wisdom Tales) World Wisdom, Inc.

—The Seagoing Cowboy. Miller, Peggy Reiff. 2016. 39p. (J). *(978-0-87178-212-0(X))* Brethren Pr.

Ewen, Diane. Coming to England. Benjamin, Floella. 2020. (ENG.). 32p. (J). (gr. -1-k). 19.99 ***(978-1-5290-0941-5(3),*** Macmillan Children's Bks.) Pan Macmillan GBR. Dist: Independent Pubs. Group.

—Save the Animals. Chancellor, Deborah. 2020. 32p. (J). ***(978-0-7787-7285-9(3))*** Crabtree Publishing Co.

Ewen, Eileen R. Mr. Mcginty's Monarchs. Heyden, Linda Vander. 2016. (ENG.). 32p. (J). (gr. 1-4). 16.99 *(978-1-58536-612-5(9),* 204034) Sleeping Bear Pr.

Ewen, Eileen Ryan. The Gwen Frostic Story. McDivitt, Lindsey. 2018. (ENG.). 32p. (J). (gr. 1-4). 16.99 *(978-1-58536-405-3(3),* 204585) Sleeping Bear Pr.

—Miss Colfax's Light. Bissonette, Aimee. 2016. (ENG.). 32p. (J). (gr. 1-4). 16.99 *(978-1-58536-955-3(1),* 204029) Sleeping Bear Pr.

—A Symphony of Cowbells. Preusser, Heather. 2017. (ENG.). 32p. (J). (gr. k-3). 16.99 *(978-1-58536-968-3(3),* 204233) Sleeping Bear Pr.

Ewers, Joe. The Monsters on the Bus (Sesame Street) Albee, Sarah. 2013. (Little Golden Book Ser.). (ENG.). 24p. (J). (-k). 4.99 *(978-0-307-98058-8(8),* Golden Bks.) Random Hse. Children's Bks.

—The Pied Piper: A Tale about Promises. 2006. (J). 6.99 *(978-1-59939-004-8(3))* Cornerstone Pr.

—Splish-Splash Spring! (Sesame Street) Alexander, Liza. 2016. (Pictureback(R) Ser.). (ENG.). 24p. (J). (gr. -1-3). 4.99 *(978-1-101-93429-6(8),* Random Hse. Bks. for Young Readers) Random Hse. Children's Bks.

Ewing, Al. Immortal Hulk Vol. 6: We Believe in Bruce Banner. 2020. (ENG.). 112p. (YA). (gr. 8-17). pap. 15.99 *(978-1-302-92050-0(2))* Marvel Worldwide, Inc.

Ewing, John. Dezzer the Gasser. Lorraine, Florido. Shami, Susan & Crossman, Keith, eds. 2009. 32p. (J). 15.99 *(978-0-9818449-0-9(1))* Thinkus Pubs.

—Hugo the Punk. Florido, Lorraine. Shami, Susan, ed. 2013. 108p. (YA). pap. 9.98 *(978-0-9818449-6-1(0))* Thinkus Pubs.

Ewing, Richard. Spanking Shakespeare. Wizner, Jake. 2008. (ENG.). 304p. (YA). (gr. 9). pap. 8.99 *(978-0-375-85594-8(7),* Ember) Random Hse. Children's Bks.

Exelby, Ilana. Going to Town. Channing, Margot. ed. 2018. (Little Learners Ser.). (ENG.). 32p. (J). (gr. -1-k). pap. 5.95 *(978-1-912233-31-1(2),* Scribblers) Book Hse. GBR. Dist: Sterling Publishing Co., Inc.

—Learn to Go on an Adventure. Channing, Margot. ed. 2018. (Little Learners Ser.). (ENG.). 32p. (J). (gr. -1-k). pap. 5.95 *(978-1-912537-14-3(1),* Scribblers) Book Hse. GBR. Dist: Sterling Publishing Co., Inc.

—Learn to Put on a Show. Channing, Margot. ed. 2018. (Little Learners Ser.). (ENG.). 32p. (J). (gr. -1-k). pap. 5.95 *(978-1-912537-15-0(X),* Scribblers) Book Hse. GBR. Dist: Sterling Publishing Co., Inc.

—Learn with Me! Colors. 2017. (ENG.). 18p. (J). (-k). bds. 8.95 *(978-1-912006-25-0(1),* Scribblers) Book Hse. GBR. Dist: Sterling Publishing Co., Inc.

—Lift-The-Flap Colors. Channing, Margot. 2018. (ENG.). 32p. (J). (-k). bds. 9.95 *(978-1-912233-66-3(5),* Scribblers) Book Hse. GBR. Dist: Sterling Publishing Co., Inc.

—Lift-The-Flap Shapes. Channing, Margot. ed. 2018. 14p. (J). (-k). bds. 9.95 *(978-1-912233-41-0(X),* Scribblers) Book Hse. GBR. Dist: Sterling Publishing Co., Inc.

—Shabbat Hiccups. Newman, Tracy. 2016. (ENG.). 32p. (J). (gr. -1-3). 16.99 *(978-0-8075-7312-9(4),* 807573124) Whitman, Albert & Co.

Exes. Tales from the Crypt, 2. Todd, Mort et al. 2nd rev. ed. 2007. (Tales from the Crypt Ser.: 2). (ENG.). 112p. (J). (gr. 5-11). 22.44 *(978-1-59707-085-0(8),* 9781597070850) Papercutz.

Exley, A. L. The Runestone Guardians: Secrets of Sølvefalske. Exley, A. L. 2020. (Runestone Guardians Ser.: Vol. 1). (ENG.). 238p. (YA). pap. 9.99 ***(978-1-6539-3342-6(9))*** Independently Published.

Exley, William. Bugs! Forshaw, Nick. 2018. (Explorer Ser.). (ENG.). 46p. (J). (gr. 1-5). 14.95 *(978-0-9955770-6-0(4))* What on Earth Bks GBR. Dist: Ingram Publisher Services.

—Mammals! Forshaw, Nick. 2019. (Explorer Ser.). (ENG.). 38p. (J). 14.95 *(978-0-9955770-7-7(2))* What on Earth Bks GBR. Dist: Ingram Publisher Services.

—North America: A Fold-Out Graphic History. Albee, Sarah. 2019. (Fold-Out Graphic History Ser.). (ENG.). 22p. (J). (gr. 3-8). 19.99 *(978-1-9999679-2-5(5))* What on Earth Books.

—Plants! Forshaw, Nick. 2019. (Explorer Ser.). (ENG.). 38p. (J). 14.95 *(978-0-9955770-8-4(0))* What on Earth Bks GBR. Dist: Ingram Publisher Services.

Experts, Epublishing. Will of the Hill: Up, up & Around. Cobb, Marshall. 2018. (ENG.). 196p. (J). pap. 10.00 *(978-1-7267-0877-7(2))* Independently Published.

Eyckerman, Merel. The Ant & the Grasshopper. 2013. (Usborne First Reading: Level 1 Ser.). (ENG.). 32p. (J). (gr. -1-3). 6.99 *(978-0-7945-2257-5(2),* Usborne) EDC Publishing.

—Qué Es Ese Ruido? Benjamin, A. H. 2019. (SPA.). 32p. (J). 15.95 *(978-84-17123-54-3(7))* NubeOcho Ediciones ESP. Dist: Consortium Bk. Sales & Distribution.

—What's That Terrible Growl? Benjamin, A. H. 2019. (ENG.). 32p. (J). 15.95 *(978-84-17123-55-0(5))* NubeOcho Ediciones ESP. Dist: Consortium Bk. Sales & Distribution.

Eyolfson, Norman. First Spy Case. Richler, Mordecai. 2003. (Jacob Two-Two Ser.). (ENG.). 144p. (J). (gr. 3-7). pap. 6.95 *(978-0-88776-694-7(3))* Tundra Bks. CAN. Dist: Random Hse., Inc.

—Jacob Two-Two & the Dinosaur. Richler, Mordecai. 2004. (Jacob Two-Two Ser.). (ENG.). 96p. (J). (gr. 3-7). pap. 6.95 *(978-0-88776-712-8(5))* Tundra Bks. CAN. Dist: Random Hse., Inc.

Eyre, Jane. Tyler's Halloween Horror, 1 vol. Beraducci, Deborah. 2009. 22p. pap. 24.95 *(978-1-4489-2133-1(3))* America Star Bks.

Eyre, Jane. Creatures of the New Jersey Pine Barrens Coloring Book, 1 vol. Eyre, Jane. 2004. 36p. spiral bd. 6.00 *(978-0-9762483-0-9(1))* Fun Fitness Publishing.

Eyuboglu, Melisa. Angel in a Bubble. Eyuboglu, Melisa, . 2007. 28p. (J). 10.95 *(978-1-933090-48-1(0))* Guardian Angel Publishing, Inc.

Ezhik, Nina. Autumn Song: A Day in the Life of a Kid. Kotowicz, Anetta. 2019. (Day in the Life of a Kid Ser.: Vol. 1). (ENG.). 32p. (J). pap. 11.98 *(978-1-7321862-8-6(6))* ArtsKindred.

—Spring Song. Kotowicz, Anetta. 2019. (Day in the Life of a Kid Ser.). (ENG.). 32p. (J). (gr. k-2). 16.98 *(978-1-7321862-0-0(0))* ArtsKindred.

—Summer Song. Kotowicz, Anetta. 2019. (Day in the Life of a Kid Ser.). (ENG.). 32p. (J). (gr. k-2). 16.98 *(978-1-7321862-1-7(9))* ArtsKindred.

F

Faas, Linde. The Birthday Surprise. Lootens, Ann. 2013. (Wild Woods Ser.). (ENG.). 32p. (J). (gr. -1-k). 15.95 *(978-1-60537-147-4(5))* Clavis Publishing.

Faassen, Louis. A Guide to the CMMI: Interpreting the Capability Maturity Model Integration. Dymond, Kenneth. Dymond, Detta, ed. 2004. spiral bd. 20.00 *(978-0-9646008-4-3(6))* Process Transition International, Inc.

Fabbian, Frederica. Trey, the Chef. Parris-Moore, Kira. 2019. (ENG.). 30p. (J). 18.99 *(978-1-64096-763-2(X))* Newman Springs Publishing, Inc.

Fabbretti, Valerio. Alexander Hamilton: from Orphan to Founding Father. Kulling, Monica. 2017. (Step into Reading Ser.). (ENG.). 48p. (J). (gr. k-3). pap. 4.99 *(978-1-5247-1698-1(7)*, Random Hse. Bks. for Young Readers) Random Hse. Children's Bks.

—Eliza Hamilton: Founding Mother. Kulling, Monica. 2018. (Step into Reading Ser.). (ENG.). 48p. (J). (gr. k-3). pap. 4.99 *(978-1-5247-7232-1(1)*, Random Hse. Bks. for Young Readers) Random Hse. Children's Bks.

—Fearless Flyers, Dazzle Painters, & Code Talkers! World War I. Dennis, Elizabeth. 2018. (Secrets of American History Ser.). (ENG.). 48p. (J). (gr. 1-3). 16.99 *(978-1-5344-1052-7(X))*; pap. 4.99 *(978-1-5344-1051-0(1))* Simon Spotlight. (Simon Spotlight).

—Ghost Light Burning: An Up2U Mystery Adventure, 1 vol. Fields, Jan. 2015. (Up2U Adventures Ser.). (ENG.). 80p. (J). (gr. 2-5). 29.93 *(978-1-62402-092-6(5)*, 17353, Calico Chapter Bks.) ABDO Publishing Co.

—Hamster Holmes: A Mystery Comes Knocking. Sadar, Albin. 2015. (Hamster Holmes Ser.: 1). (ENG.). 32p. (J). (gr. k-2). 16.99 *(978-1-4814-2037-2(2)*, Simon Spotlight) Simon Spotlight.

—Hamster Holmes, a Big-Time Puzzle. Sadar, Albin. 2019. (Hamster Holmes Ser.). (ENG.). 32p. (J). (gr. k-2). 17.99 *(978-1-5344-2198-1(X))*; pap. 4.99 *(978-1-5344-2197-4(1))* Simon Spotlight. (Simon Spotlight).

—Hamster Holmes, a Bit Stumped. Sadar, Albin. 2019. (Hamster Holmes Ser.). (ENG.). 32p. (J). (gr. k-2). 17.99 *(978-1-5344-2192-9(0))*; pap. 4.99 *(978-1-5344-2191-2(2))* Simon Spotlight. (Simon Spotlight).

—Hamster Holmes, a Mystery Comes Knocking. Sadar, Albin. 2015. (Hamster Holmes Ser.: 1). (ENG.). 32p. (J). (gr. k-2). pap. 4.99 *(978-1-4814-2036-5(4)*, Simon Spotlight) Simon Spotlight.

—Hamster Holmes, Afraid of the Dark? Sadar, Albin. 2019. (Hamster Holmes Ser.). (ENG.). 32p. (J). (gr. k-2). 17.99 *(978-1-5344-2195-0(5))*; pap. 4.99 *(978-1-5344-2194-3(7))* Simon Spotlight. (Simon Spotlight).

Fabbretti, Valerio. Hamster Holmes Box of Mysteries: Hamster Holmes, a Mystery Comes Knocking; Hamster Holmes, Combing for Clues; Hamster Holmes, on the Right Track; Hamster Holmes, a Bit Stumped; Hamster Holmes, Afraid of the Dark?; Hamster Holmes, a Big-Time Puzzle. Sadar, Albin. ed. 2020. (Hamster Holmes Ser.). (ENG.). 192p. (J). (gr. k-2). pap. 17.99 ***(978-1-5344-6548-0(0)**, Simon Spotlight)* Simon Spotlight.

Fabbretti, Valerio. Hamster Holmes, Combing for Clues. Sadar, Albin. 2015. (Hamster Holmes Ser.: 2). (ENG.). 32p. (J). (gr. k-2). pap. 4.99 *(978-1-4814-2039-6(9)*, Simon Spotlight) Simon Spotlight.

—Hamster Holmes, on the Right Track. Sadar, Albin. 2016. (Hamster Holmes Ser.). (ENG.). 32p. (J). (gr. k-2). pap. 4.99 *(978-1-4814-2042-6(9)*, Simon Spotlight) Simon Spotlight.

—Heroes Who Risked Everything for Freedom: Civil War. Lakin, Patricia. 2017. (Secrets of American History Ser.). (ENG.). 48p. (J). (gr. 1-3). 16.99 *(978-1-4814-9973-6(4))*; pap. 4.99 *(978-1-4814-9972-9(6))* Simon Spotlight. (Simon Spotlight).

—Mount Rushmore's Hidden Room & Other Monumental Secrets: Monuments & Landmarks. Calkhoven, Laurie. 2018. (Secrets of American History Ser.). (ENG.). 48p. (J). (gr. 1-3). 17.99 *(978-1-5344-2925-3(5))*; pap. 4.99 *(978-1-5344-2924-6(7))* Simon Spotlight. (Simon Spotlight).

—P Is for President. Lewison, Wendy Cheyette. 2016. 32p. (J). (-k). pap. 3.99 *(978-1-101-99611-9(0)*, Grosset & Dunlap) Penguin Young Readers Group.

—Secrets of American History Collection: The Founding Fathers Were Spies!; Secret Agents! Sharks! Ghost Armies!; Heroes Who Risked Everything for Freedom; Fearless Flyers, Dazzle Painters, & Code Talkers!; You Can't Bring a Sandwich to the Moon; Mount Rushmore's Hidden Room & Other Monuments. ed. 2018. (Secrets of American History Ser.). (ENG.). 288p. (J). (gr. 1-3). pap. 17.99 *(978-1-5344-3661-9(8)*, Simon Spotlight) Simon Spotlight.

—You Can't Bring a Sandwich to the Moon ... & Other Stories about Space! Space Age. Calkhoven, Laurie. 2018. (Secrets of American History Ser.). (ENG.). 48p. (J). (gr. 1-3). 17.99 *(978-1-5344-1781-6(8))*; pap. 4.99 *(978-1-5344-1780-9(X))* Simon Spotlight. (Simon Spotlight).

Fabbri, Daniele. Do You Really Want to Meet a Badger? Heos, Bridget. 2017. (Do You Really Want to Meet... Wild Animals? Ser.). (ENG.). 24p. (J). (gr. 1-3). pap. 8.99 *(978-1-68152-115-2(6))* Amicus.

—Do You Really Want to Meet a Badger? Heos, Bridget. 2016. (Do You Really Want to Meet... Wild Animals? Ser.). (ENG.). 24p. (J). (gr. k-3). 20.95 *(978-1-60753-944-5(6))* Amicus Publishing.

—Do You Really Want to Meet a Camel? Heos, Bridget. 2017. (Do You Really Want to Meet... Wild Animals? Ser.). (ENG.). 24p. (J). (gr. 1-3). pap. 8.99 *(978-1-68152-116-9(4))* Amicus.

—Do You Really Want to Meet a Camel? Heos, Bridget. 2016. (Do You Really Want to Meet... Wild Animals? Ser.). (ENG.). 24p. (J). (gr. k-3). 20.95 *(978-1-60753-945-2(4))* Amicus Publishing.

—Do You Really Want to Meet a Cape Buffalo? Meister, Cari. 2015. (Do You Really Want to Meet ... ? Ser.). (ENG.). 24p. (J). (gr. 1-3). 19.95 *(978-1-60753-738-0(9))* Amicus Publishing.

—Do You Really Want to Meet a Cheetah? Meister, Cari. 2019. (J). lib. bdg. *(978-1-68151-390-4(0))* Amicus Publishing.

—Do You Really Want to Meet a Chimpanzee? Meister, Cari. 2019. (J). lib. bdg. *(978-1-68151-391-1(9))* Amicus Publishing.

—Do You Really Want to Meet a Crocodile? Meister, Cari. 2015. (Do You Really Want to Meet... ? Ser.). 24p. (J). 27.10 *(978-1-60753-457-0(6))* Amicus Publishing.

—Do You Really Want to Meet a Fox? Meister, Cari. 2019. (J). lib. bdg. *(978-1-68151-392-8(7))* Amicus Publishing.

—Do You Really Want to Meet a Hippopotamus? Heos, Bridget. 2017. (Do You Really Want to Meet... Wild Animals? Ser.). (ENG.). 24p. (J). (gr. 1-3). pap. 8.99 *(978-1-68152-117-6(2))* Amicus.

—Do You Really Want to Meet a Hippopotamus? Heos, Bridget. 2016. (Do You Really Want to Meet... Wild Animals? Ser.). (ENG.). 24p. (J). (gr. k-3). 20.95 *(978-1-60753-946-9(2))* Amicus Publishing.

—Do You Really Want to Meet a Kangaroo? Meister, Cari. 2015. (Do You Really Want to Meet ... ? Ser.). (ENG.). 24p. (J). (gr. 1-3). 19.95 *(978-1-60753-734-2(6))* Amicus Publishing.

—Do You Really Want to Meet a Lion? Meister, Cari. 2015. (Do You Really Want to Meet ... ? Ser.). (ENG.). 24p. (J). (gr. 1-3). 19.95 *(978-1-60753-735-9(4))* Amicus Publishing.

—Do You Really Want to Meet a Monkey? Meister, Cari. 2015. (Do You Really Want to Meet... ? Ser.). 24p. (J). 27.10 *(978-1-60753-456-3(8))* Amicus Publishing.

—Do You Really Want to Meet a Moose? Meister, Cari. 2015. (Do You Really Want to Meet ... ? Ser.). (ENG.). 24p. (J). (gr. 1-3). 19.95 *(978-1-60753-736-6(2))* Amicus Publishing.

—Do You Really Want to Meet a Platypus? Meister, Cari. 2014. (Do You Really Want to Meet... ? Ser.). (ENG.). 24p. (J). (gr. 1-4). 27.10 *(978-1-60753-460-0(6))* Amicus Publishing.

—Do You Really Want to Meet a Polar Bear? Aboff, Marcie. 2015. (Do You Really Want to Meet... ? Ser.). 24p. (J). 27.10 *(978-1-60753-455-6(X))* Amicus Publishing.

—Do You Really Want to Meet a Pterosaur? Pimentel, Annette Bay. 2017. (Do You Really Want to Meet a Dinosaur? Ser.). (ENG.). 24p. (J). (gr. 1-4). 20.95 *(978-1-68151-113-9(4))* Amicus Publishing.

—Do You Really Want to Meet a Shark? Meister, Cari. 2015. (Do You Really Want to Meet ... ? Ser.). (ENG.). 24p. (J). (gr. 1-3). 19.95 *(978-1-60753-737-3(0))* Amicus Publishing.

—Do You Really Want to Meet a Stegosaurus? Pimentel, Annette Bay. 2017. (Do You Really Want to Meet a Dinosaur? Ser.). (ENG.). 24p. (J). (gr. 1-4). 20.95 *(978-1-68151-114-6(2))* Amicus Publishing.

—Do You Really Want to Meet a Swan? Meister, Cari. 2014. (Do You Really Want to Meet... ? Ser.). (ENG.). 24p. (J). (gr. 1-4). 27.10 *(978-1-60753-458-7(4))* Amicus Publishing.

—Do You Really Want to Meet a Tiger? Meister, Cari. 2015. (Do You Really Want to Meet... ? Ser.). 24p. (J). 27.10 *(978-1-60753-459-4(2))* Amicus Publishing.

—Do You Really Want to Meet a Weasel? Meister, Cari. 2019. (J). lib. bdg. *(978-1-68151-393-5(5))* Amicus Publishing.

—Do You Really Want to Meet a Wolf? Heos, Bridget. 2017. (Do You Really Want to Meet... Wild Animals? Ser.). (ENG.). 24p. (J). (gr. 1-3). pap. 8.99 *(978-1-68152-120-6(2))* Amicus.

—Do You Really Want to Meet a Wolf? Heos, Bridget. 2016. (Do You Really Want to Meet... Wild Animals? Ser.). (ENG.). 24p. (J). (gr. k-3). 20.95 *(978-1-60753-949-0(7))* Amicus Publishing.

—Do You Really Want to Meet Allosaurus? Pimentel, Annette Bay. 2020. (J). lib. bdg. *(978-1-68151-708-7(6))* Amicus Publishing.

—Do You Really Want to Meet an Anteater? Meister, Cari. 2019. (J). lib. bdg. *(978-1-68151-394-2(3))* Amicus Publishing.

—Do You Really Want to Meet an Elephant? Meister, Cari. 2015. (Do You Really Want to Meet ... ? Ser.). (ENG.). 24p. (J). (gr. 1-3). 19.95 *(978-1-60753-733-5(8))* Amicus Publishing.

—Do You Really Want to Meet an Octopus? Meister, Cari. 2019. (J). lib. bdg. *(978-1-68151-395-9(1))* Amicus Publishing.

—Do You Really Want to Meet an Orca? Heos, Bridget. 2017. (Do You Really Want to Meet... Wild Animals? Ser.). (ENG.). 24p. (J). (gr. 1-3). pap. 8.99 *(978-1-68152-118-3(0))* Amicus.

—Do You Really Want to Meet an Orca? Heos, Bridget. 2016. (Do You Really Want to Meet... Wild Animals? Ser.). (ENG.). 24p. (J). (gr. k-3). 20.95 *(978-1-60753-947-6(0))* Amicus Publishing.

—Do You Really Want to Meet an Owl? Heos, Bridget. 2017. (Do You Really Want to Meet... Wild Animals? Ser.). (ENG.). 24p. (J). (gr. 1-3). pap. 8.99 *(978-1-68152-119-0(9))* Amicus.

—Do You Really Want to Meet Ankylosaurus? Pimentel, Annette Bay. 2020. (J). lib. bdg. *(978-1-68151-709-4(4)*, Amicus Illustrated) Amicus Publishing.

—Do You Really Want to Meet Apatosaurus? Pimentel, Annette Bay. 2017. (Do You Really Want to Meet a Dinosaur? Ser.). (ENG.). 24p. (J). (gr. 1-4). 20.95 *(978-1-68151-112-2(6))* Amicus Publishing.

—Do You Really Want to Meet Diplodocus. Pimentel, Annette Bay. 2020. (J). lib. bdg. *(978-1-68151-706-3(X))* Amicus Publishing.

—Do You Really Want to Meet Edmontosaurus? Pimentel, Annette Bay. 2020. (J). lib. bdg. *(978-1-68151-710-0(8)*, Amicus Illustrated) Amicus Publishing.

—Do You Really Want to Meet Iguanodon? Pimentel, Annette Bay. 2019. (Do You Really Want to Meet a Dinosaur? Ser.). (ENG.). 24p. (J). (gr. 1-3). pap. 9.99 *(978-1-68152-497-9(X))* Amicus.

—Do You Really Want to Meet Spinosaurus? Pimentel, Annette Bay. 2019. (Do You Really Want to Meet a Dinosaur? Ser.). (ENG.). 24p. (J). (gr. 1-3). pap. 9.99 *(978-1-68152-493-1(7))* Amicus.

—Do You Really Want to Meet Triceratops? Pimentel, Annette Bay. 2017. (Do You Really Want to Meet a Dinosaur? Ser.). (ENG.). 24p. (J). (gr. 1-4). 20.95 *(978-1-68151-115-3(0))* Amicus Publishing.

—Do You Really Want to Meet Tyrannosaurus Rex? Pimentel, Annette Bay. 2017. (Do You Really Want to Meet a Dinosaur? Ser.). (ENG.). 24p. (J). (gr. 1-4). 20.95 *(978-1-68151-116-0(9))* Amicus Publishing.

—Do You Really Want to Meet Velociraptor? Pimentel, Annette Bay. 2017. (Do You Really Want to Meet a Dinosaur? Ser.). (ENG.). 24p. (J). (gr. 1-4). 20.95 *(978-1-68151-117-7(7))* Amicus Publishing.

—Do You Really Want to Visit a Coral Reef? Heos, Bridget. 2014. (Do You Really Want to Visit... ? Ser.). (ENG.). 24p. (J). (gr. 1-4). 27.10 *(978-1-60753-449-5(5))* Amicus Publishing.

—Do You Really Want to Visit a Prairie? Heos, Bridget. 2014. (Do You Really Want to Visit... ? Ser.). (ENG.). 24p. (J). (gr. 1-4). lib. bdg. 27.10 *(978-1-60753-452-5(5))* Amicus Publishing.

—Do You Really Want to Visit a Temperate Forest? Heos, Bridget. 2014. (Do You Really Want to Visit... ? Ser.). (ENG.). 24p. (J). (gr. 1-4). lib. bdg. 27.10 *(978-1-60753-451-8(7))* Amicus Publishing.

—Do You Really Want to Visit a Wetland? Heos, Bridget. 2014. (Do You Really Want to Visit... ? Ser.). (ENG.). 24p. (J). (gr. 1-4). lib. bdg. 27.10 *(978-1-60753-454-9(1))* Amicus Publishing.

—Do You Really Want to Visit Mars? Adamson, Thomas K. 2013. (Do You Really Want to Visit... ? Ser.). (ENG.). 24p. (gr. 1-4). 27.10 *(978-1-60753-198-2(4))* Amicus Publishing.

—Do You Really Want to Visit Mercury? Adamson, Thomas K. 2013. (Do You Really Want to Visit... ? Ser.). (ENG.). 24p. (gr. 1-4). 27.10 *(978-1-60753-195-1(X))* Amicus Publishing.

—Do You Really Want to Visit Neptune? Heos, Bridget. 2013. (Do You Really Want to Visit... ? Ser.). (ENG.). 24p. (gr. 1-4). 27.10 *(978-1-60753-201-9(8))* Amicus Publishing.

—Do You Really Want to Visit Saturn? Heos, Bridget. 2013. (Do You Really Want to Visit... ? Ser.). (ENG.). 24p. (gr. 1-4). 27.10 *(978-1-60753-200-2(X))* Amicus Publishing.

—Do You Really Want to Visit the Moon? Adamson, Thomas K. 2013. (Do You Really Want to Visit... ? Ser.). (ENG.). 24p. (gr. 1-4). 27.10 *(978-1-60753-197-5(6))* Amicus Publishing.

—Do You Really Want to Visit Uranus? Heos, Bridget. 2013. (Do You Really Want to Visit... ? Ser.). (ENG.). 24p. (gr. 1-4). 27.10 *(978-1-60753-202-6(6))* Amicus Publishing.

—Do You Really Want to Visit Venus? Adamson, Thomas K. 2013. (Do You Really Want to Visit... ? Ser.). (ENG.). 24p. (gr. 1-4). 27.10 *(978-1-60753-196-8(8))* Amicus Publishing.

Fabbri, Daniele. In Search of Dinosaurs: Find the Fossils: Identify the Dinosaurs. Dixon, Dougal. 2019. (ENG.). 44p. (J). (gr. k-2). 17.95 ***(978-1-78603-549-3(9)**, Words & Pictures)* Quarto Publishing Group UK GBR. Dist: Hachette Bk. Group.

Fabbri, Daniele. My First Arabic Phrases, 1 vol. Kalz, Jill. TransPerfect Translations Staff, tr. 2012. (Speak Another Language! Ser.). (ENG.). 32p. (J). (gr. k-3). lib. bdg. 27.32 *(978-1-4048-7517-3(4)*, Picture Window Bks.) Capstone.

—My First French Phrases, 1 vol. Kalz, Jill. Translations.com Staff, tr. 2012. (Speak Another Language! Ser.). (ENG.). 32p. (J). (gr. k-3). pap. 8.95 *(978-1-4048-7244-8(2))*; lib. bdg. 27.32 *(978-1-4048-7153-3(5))* Capstone. (Picture Window Bks.).

—My First German Phrases, 1 vol. Mayesky & Kalz, Jill. Translations.com Staff, tr. 2012. (Speak Another Language! Ser.). (ENG.). 32p. (J). (gr. k-3). lib. bdg. 27.32 *(978-1-4048-7154-0(3)*, Picture Window Bks.) Capstone.

—My First Japanese Phrases, 1 vol. Kalz, Jill. TransPerfect Translations Staff, tr. 2012. (Speak Another Language! Ser.). (ENG.). 32p. (J). (gr. k-3). lib. bdg. 27.32 *(978-1-4048-7514-2(X)*, Picture Window Bks.) Capstone.

—My First Mandarin Chinese Phrases, 1 vol. Kalz, Jill. Advocate-Art Staff & Translations.com Staff, trs. 2012. (Speak Another Language! Ser.). (ENG.). 32p. (J). (gr. k-3). pap. 8.95 *(978-1-4048-7246-2(9)*, Picture Window Bks.) Capstone.

—My First Mandarin Chinese Phrases, 1 vol. Kalz, Jill. Translations.com Staff, tr. 2012. (Speak Another Language! Ser.). (ENG.). 32p. (J). (gr. k-3). lib. bdg. 27.32 *(978-1-4048-7155-7(1)*, Picture Window Bks.) Capstone.

—My First Russian Phrases, 1 vol. Kalz, Jill. TransPerfect Translations Staff, tr. 2012. (Speak Another Language! Ser.). (ENG.). 32p. (J). (gr. k-3). lib. bdg. 27.32 *(978-1-4048-7515-9(8)*, Picture Window Bks.) Capstone.

—My First Spanish Phrases, 1 vol. Kalz, Jill. Advocate-Art Staff & Translations.com Staff, trs. 2012. (Speak Another Language! Ser.). (ENG.). 32p. (J). (gr. k-3). lib. bdg. 27.32 *(978-1-4048-7152-6(7)*, Picture Window Bks.) Capstone.

—So You Want to Grow a Pie? Heos, Bridget. 2015. (Grow Your Food Ser.). (ENG.). 24p. (gr. 1-3). 19.95 *(978-1-60753-739-7(7))* Amicus Publishing.

—So You Want to Grow a Pizza? Heos, Bridget. 2015. (Grow Your Food Ser.). (ENG.). 24p. (gr. 1-3). 19.95 *(978-1-60753-740-3(0))* Amicus Publishing.

—So You Want to Grow a Salad? Heos, Bridget. 2015. (Grow Your Food Ser.). (ENG.). 24p. (gr. 1-3). 19.95 *(978-1-60753-741-0(9))* Amicus Publishing.

—So You Want to Grow a Taco? Heos, Bridget. 2015. (Grow Your Food Ser.). (ENG.). 24p. (gr. 1-3). 19.95 *(978-1-60753-742-7(7))* Amicus Publishing.

—Who Are You? Korba, Joanna & Benchmark Education Co., LLC. 2014. (Text Connections Ser.). (J). (gr. 3). *(978-1-4509-9664-8(7))* Benchmark Education Co.

—Who Are YOU? Set Of 6. Korba, Joanna. 2014. (Text Connections Ser.). (J). (gr. 3). 49.00 net. *(978-1-4900-0140-1(9))* Benchmark Education Co.

—Why Do Tractors Have Such Big Tires? Shand, Jennifer. Paiva, Johannah Gilman, ed. 2014. (ENG.). 20p. (J). (gr. k-4). 8.99 *(978-1-4867-0382-1(8))* Flowerpot Children's Pr. Inc. CAN. Dist: Cardinal Pubs. Group.

—The World Needs Beautiful Things. Berkowitz, Leah Rachel. 2018. (ENG.). 32p. (J). (gr. -1-2). 17.99 *(978-1-5124-4448-3(0)*, Kar-Ben Publishing) Lerner Publishing Group.

Fabbri, Davide. The Empire Strikes Back, 1 vol. Land, David. 2011. (Star Wars: Infinites Ser.). (ENG.). 24p. (J). (gr. 6-12). 27.07 *(978-1-59961-849-4(4)*, 13815); Vol. 2. 27.07 *(978-1-59961-850-0(8)*, 13818); Vol. 3. 27.07 *(978-1-59961-851-7(6)*, 13816); Vol. 4. 27.07 *(978-1-59961-852-4(4)*, 13817) Spotlight. (Graphic Novels).

Fabbrucci, Fabiano, jt. illus. see Stalio, Ivan.

Faber, Jules. The Awesome Book of Rap, Rhyme & Putrid Poetry. Jones, Andy. 2017. 272p. 6.99 *(978-0-7333-3566-2(7))* ABC Bks. AUS. Dist: HarperCollins Pubs.

—Leo Da Vinci! vs the Furniture Overlord. Pryor, Michael. 2016. (Leo Da Vinci Ser.: 2). 192p. (J). (gr. 4-6). pap. 8.99 *(978-0-85798-839-3(5))* Random Hse. Australia AUS. Dist: Independent Pubs. Group.

—Leo Da Vinci vs the Ice-Cream Domination League. Pryor, Michael. 2015. (Leo Da Vinci Ser.). 192p. (J). (gr. 4-7). 8.99 *(978-0-85798-837-9(9))* Random Hse. Australia AUS. Dist: Independent Pubs. Group.

Faber, Rudy. Darling Doll. Troupe, Thomas Kingsley. 2016. (Hauntiques Ser.). (ENG.). 128p. (J). (gr. 4-6). lib. bdg. 25.32 *(978-1-4965-3548-1(0)*, Stone Arch Bks.) Capstone.

—Ghostly Goalie. Troupe, Thomas Kingsley. 2016. (Hauntiques Ser.). (ENG.). 128p. (J). (gr. 4-6). lib. bdg. 25.32 *(978-1-4965-3544-3(8)*, Stone Arch Bks.) Capstone.

—Hauntiques, 4 vols. Troupe, Thomas Kingsley. 2016. (Hauntiques Ser.). (ENG.). 128p. (J). (gr. 4-6). lib. bdg., lib. bdg., lib. bdg. 101.28 *(978-1-4965-3561-0(8)*, Stone Arch Bks.) Capstone.

—Phantom's Favorite. Troupe, Thomas Kingsley. 2016. (Hauntiques Ser.). (ENG.). 128p. (J). (gr. 4-6). lib. bdg. 25.32 *(978-1-4965-3546-7(4)*, Stone Arch Bks.) Capstone.

—Rebel with a Cause: The Daring Adventure of Dicey Langston, Girl Spy of the American Revolution. Kudlinski, Kathleen V. 2015. (Encounter: Narrative Nonfiction Picture Bks.). (ENG.). 40p. (J). (gr. 3-6). lib. bdg. 29.32 *(978-1-4914-6073-3(3)*, Capstone Young Readers) Capstone.

—Wandering Wagon. Troupe, Thomas Kingsley. 2016. (Hauntiques Ser.). (ENG.). 128p. (J). (gr. 4-6). lib. bdg. 25.32 *(978-1-4965-3547-4(2)*, Stone Arch Bks.) Capstone.

Fabian, Gabriella. Wishes. Morrison, Julia. 2013. 42p. pap. 10.00 *(978-1-883651-65-7(4))* Winters Publishing.

Fabiani, Federico. Tallulah the Tooth Fairy CEO. Pizzoli, Tamara. 2019. (ENG.). 40p. (J). 17.99 *(978-0-374-30919-0(1)*, 900189989, Farrar, Straus & Giroux (BYR)) Farrar, Straus & Giroux.

Fabicka, Patrycja. Boo Books. Bird, Benjamin et al. 2020. (Boo Bks.). (ENG.). (J). (gr. k-2). 213.20 ***(978-1-5158-7111-8(8)**, 199210, Picture Window Bks.)* Capstone.

Fabicka, Patrycja. Campfire Vampire. Sazaklis, John. 2019. (Boo Bks.). (ENG.). 32p. (J). (gr. k-2). lib. bdg. 21.32 *(978-1-5158-4485-3(4)*, 140581, Picture Window Bks.) Capstone.

Fabicka, Patrycja. Clowns from Outer Space. Dahl, Michael. 2020. (Boo Bks.). (ENG.). 32p. (J). (gr. k-2). lib. bdg. 21.32 ***(978-1-5158-7109-5(6)**, 199207, Picture Window Bks.)* Capstone.

—Game Over. Bird, Benjamin. 2020. (Boo Bks.). (ENG.). 32p. (J). (gr. k-2). lib. bdg. 21.32 ***(978-1-5158-7107-1(X)**, 199206, Picture Window Bks.)* Capstone.

—Slime Time! Sazaklis, John. 2020. (Boo Bks.). (ENG.). 32p. (J). (gr. k-2). lib. bdg. 21.32 ***(978-1-5158-7108-8(8)**, 199205, Picture Window Bks.)* Capstone.

—Swamp Creature Teacher. Sazaklis, John. 2020. (Boo Bks.). (ENG.). 32p. (J). (gr. k-2). lib. bdg. 21.32 ***(978-1-5158-7110-1(X)**, 199208, Picture Window Bks.)* Capstone.

Fabicka, Patrycja, jt. illus. see Cotroneo, Marilisa.

Fabiniak, Manya. Aurora's Greatest Discovery. Fabiniak, Manya. (ENG.). 2020. 148p. (YA). (gr. 7-12). pap. 24.95 ***(978-1-7340139-8-6(2))**;* 2017. (J). 29.95 *(978-0-9977996-2-0(5))* Primedia eLaunch LLC.

Fabio, Valerio. Una Antica Soffitta: Con Illustrazioni in Bianco e Nero. Fasanaro, Massimo. 2019. (ITA.). 68p. (J). pap. 6.00 *(978-1-7970-2458-5(2))* Independently Published.

—Una Antica Soffitta: Edizione a Colori. Fasanaro, Massimo. 2019. (ITA.). 68p. (J). pap. 15.00 *(978-1-7970-1764-8(0))* Independently Published.

Fabiola. Song Bird. Briscoe, Nicole. 2016. (ENG.). (J). pap. 9.00 *(978-0-578-17838-7(9))* Briscoe, Nicole .

FableVision, jt. illus. see Reynolds, Peter H.

Fabrega, Marta. Do You Have a Secret? Moore-Mallinos, Jennifer. 2005. (Let's Talk about It! Ser.). 32p. (J). (gr. -1-2). pap. 7.99 *(978-0-7641-3170-7(2)*, B.E.S. Publishing) Peterson's.

—I Am Deaf. Moore-Mallinos, Jennifer. 2009. (Live & Learn Ser.). (ENG.). 36p. (J). (gr. -1-2). pap. 7.99 *(978-0-7641-4179-9(1)*, B.E.S. Publishing) Peterson's.

—I Can't Sit Still! Living with ADHD. Pollack, Pam & Belviso, Meg. 2009. (Live & Learn Ser.). (ENG.). 36p. (J). (gr. k-3). 21.19 *(978-0-7641-4419-6(7)*, B.E.S. Publishing) Peterson's.

—Mi Mama Tiene Cancer! My Mom Has Cancer! (Spanish-Language Edition) Moore-Mallinos, Jennifer &

F

Roca, Nuria. 2008. (Hablemos de Esto! / Let's Talk about It! Ser.). (SPA.). 32p. (J). (gr. k-3). 22.44 *(978-0-7641-4075-4(2),* B.E.S. Publishing) Peterson's.

—Mis Abuelitos son Especiales: Spanish Edition of My Grandparents are Special. Moore-Mallinos, Jennifer & Roca, Nuria. 2006. (Hablemos de Esto! / Let's Talk about It! Ser.). (SPA.). 32p. (J). (gr. k-3). 22.44 *(978-0-7641-3507-1(4),* B.E.S. Publishing) Peterson's.

—My Brother Is Autistic. Moore-Mallinos, Jennifer & Roca, Nuria. 2008. (Let's Talk about It! Ser.). 32p. (J). (gr. k-2). pap. 7.99 *(978-0-7641-4044-0(2),* B.E.S. Publishing) Peterson's.

—New Kid on the Block. Moore-Mallinos, Jennifer. 2009. (Live & Learn Ser.). (ENG.). 32p. (J). (gr. k-3). 21.19 *(978-0-7641-4181-2(3),* B.E.S. Publishing) Peterson's.

—¡No Puedo Estar Quieto! Mi Vida con ADHD. Pollack, Pam & Belviso, Meg. 2009. (Vive y Aprende Libros Ser.). (SPA.). 36p. (J). (gr. k-2). pap. 6.99 *(978-0-7641-4420-2(0),* B.E.S. Publishing) Peterson's.

—Winning Isn't Everything! Moore-Mallinos, Jennifer. 2007. (Live & Learn Ser.). (ENG.). 36p. (J). (gr. k-3). 21.19 *(978-0-7641-3791-4(3),* B.E.S. Publishing) Peterson's.

—1, 2, 3 Suddenly in Brazil: The Ribbons of Bonfim. Maldonado, Cristina Falcon. 2011. (1, 2, 3 Suddenly In... Ser.). (ENG.). 35p. (J). (gr. 1-3). 22.44 *(978-0-7641-4582-7(7),* B.E.S. Publishing) Peterson's.

Fabretti, Valerio. Blue in the Face: A Story of Risk, Rhyme, & Rebellion. Swallow, Gerry. (Magnificent Tales of Misadventure Ser.). (J). 2017. 336p. pap. 7.99 *(978-1-61963-489-3(9),* 900138578); 2016. 320p. 16.99 *(978-1-61963-487-9(2),* 301160) Bloomsbury Publishing USA. (Bloomsbury USA Childrens).

—Long Live the Queen: A Blue in the Face Novel. Swallow, Gerry. 2017. (Magnificent Tales of Misadventure Ser.). 288p. (J). 16.99 *(978-1-61963-490-9(2),* 900138579, Bloomsbury USA Childrens) Bloomsbury Publishing USA.

Fabri, Nathalie. Brainy Boo: And the Discovery of Taste. Gianjorio, Orietta. 2019. (ENG.). 100p. (J). pap. 22.00 *(978-1-7920-5530-0(7))* Independently Published.

Fabrizio, Cinzia. Wild Africa ABC: An ABC Children's Picture Book of African Animals. Fabrizio, Cinzia. 2019. (My ABC Ser.: Vol. 1). (ENG.). 78p. (J). pap. 15.43 ***(978-1-7062-6180-3(2))*** Independently Published.

Fabul, J. C. & Calero, Dennis. The Pit & the Pendulum, 1 vol. Tulien, Sean & Poe, Edgar Allen. 2013. (Edgar Allan Poe Graphic Novels Ser.). (ENG.). 72p. (J). (gr. 5-9). pap. 6.10 *(978-1-4342-4260-0(9));* lib. bdg. 27.99 *(978-1-4342-4024-8(X))* Capstone. (Stone Arch Bks.).

Facchini, Vittoria. Uno Y 7. Rodari, Gianni. 2018. (Buenas Noches Ser.). (SPA.). 32p. (J). pap. ***(978-958-04-9853-7(9))*** Norma Ediciones, S.A.

Facciotto, Giuseppe, et al. My Autosaurus Will Win! Stilton, Geronimo & Heim, Julia. 2016. 113p. (J). *(978-1-5182-0304-6(3))* Scholastic, Inc.

Facciotto, Giuseppe & Costa, Alessandro. Attack of the Dragons. Stilton, Geronimo & Clement, Emily. 2016. 115p. (J). *(978-0-605-93525-9(4))* Scholastic, Inc.

—Get the Scoop, Geronimo! Stilton, Geronimo et al. 2015. 113p. (J). *(978-1-5182-0417-3(1))* Scholastic, Inc.

—The Helmet Holdup. Stilton, Geronimo & Schaffer, Andrea. 2017. 112p. (J). *(978-1-5379-5611-4(6))* Scholastic, Inc.

Facciotto, Giuseppe & Verzini, Daniele. Beware! Space Junk!, 7. Stilton, Geronimo & Heim, Julia. 2016. (Geronimo Stilton: Spacemice Ser.). (ENG.). 128p. (J). (gr. 2-4). 22.44 *(978-1-4844-8016-8(3))* Scholastic, Inc.

—Rescue Rebellion, 5. Stilton, Geronimo & Tramontozzi, Lidia Morson. 2015. (Geronimo Stilton: Spacemice Ser.). (ENG.). 128p. (J). (gr. 2-4). 21.19 *(978-1-4844-6251-5(3))* Scholastic, Inc.

—The Underwater Planet. Stilton, Geronimo & Pizzelli, Anna. 2016. 113p. (J). *(978-1-5182-0303-9(5))* Scholastic, Inc.

Fach, Gernot, jt. illus. see Zengin-Karaian, Alex.

Facio, Sebastian. Swamp Sting!, 1 vol. Hoena, Blake A. 2011. (Graphic Sparks Ser.). (ENG.). 40p. (J). (gr. 2-4). pap. 5.95 *(978-1-4342-3065-2(1));* lib. bdg. 23.99 *(978-1-4342-2960-1(2))* Capstone. (Stone Arch Bks.).

Facklam, Paul. Snow Dance, 1 vol. Thomas, Peggy. 2008. (ENG.). 32p. (J). (gr. 1-3). 16.99 *(978-1-58980-478-4(3),* Pelican Publishing) Arcadia Publishing.

Fadden, David. When the Shadbush Blooms, 1 vol. Messinger, Carla & Katz, Susan. 2020. (ENG.). 32p. (J). (gr. 3-3). pap. 10.95 ***(978-1-64379-201-9(6),*** 6c8ec686-6fec-4a65-aaba-c491914b6437) Lee & Low Bks., Inc.

Faddoul, Maia. Canadian Women Now & Then: More Than 100 Stories of Fearless Trailblazers. MacLeod, Elizabeth. 2020. (ENG.). 80p. (J). (gr. 4-7). 19.99 *(978-1-5253-0061-5(X))* Kids Can Pr., Ltd. CAN. Dist: Hachette Bk. Group.

Fae, Sylva. Tales from Ridgeway Furrow: Book 1 - Save the Stream!: a Chapter Book for 7-10 Year Olds. Fae, Sylva. K, Ng. 2020. (Harry the Happy Mouse Ser.: Vol. 6). (ENG.). 170p. (J). (gr. 5-6). pap. ***(978-1-9160811-2-3(6))*** ngk media.

Faerber, Jeff. Bad Bananas: A Story Cookbook for Kids. Beckstrand, Karl. 2017. (ENG.). (J). 23.95 *(978-0-9776065-4-2(6))* Premio Publishing & Gozo Bks., LLC.

Fagan, Kirbi. Blizzard - A Tale of Snow-Blind Survival. Troupe, Thomas Kingsley. 2016. (Survive! Ser.). (ENG.). 56p. (J). (gr. 4-8). lib. bdg. 25.32 *(978-1-4965-2554-3(X),* Stone Arch Bks.) Capstone.

—Fire & Ice: A Mermaid's Journey. Gilbert, Julie. 2017. (Dark Waters Ser.). (ENG.). 160p. (J). (gr. 5-9). lib. bdg. 26.65 *(978-1-4965-4168-0(5),* Stone Arch Bks.) Capstone.

—Into the Storm: A Mermaid's Journey. Gilbert, Julie. 2017. (Dark Waters Ser.). (ENG.). 160p. (J). (gr. 5-9). lib. bdg. 26.65 *(978-1-4965-4171-0(5),* Stone Arch Bks.) Capstone.

—Lost - A Wild Tale of Survival. Troupe, Thomas Kingsley. 2016. (Survive! Ser.). (ENG.). 56p. (J). (gr. 4-8). lib. bdg. 25.32 *(978-1-4965-2557-4(4),* Stone Arch Bks.) Capstone.

—Neptune's Trident: A Mermaid's Journey. Gilbert, Julie. 2017. (Dark Waters Ser.). (ENG.). 160p. (J). (gr. 5-9). lib. bdg. 26.65 *(978-1-4965-4169-7(3),* Stone Arch Bks.) Capstone.

—The Sighting: A Mermaid's Journey. Gilbert, Julie. 2017. (Dark Waters Ser.). (ENG.). 160p. (J). (gr. 5-9). lib. bdg. 26.65 *(978-1-4965-4170-3(7),* Stone Arch Bks.) Capstone.

—Tornado - A Twisting Tale of Survival. Troupe, Thomas Kingsley. 2016. (Survive! Ser.). (ENG.). 56p. (J). (gr. 4-8). lib. bdg. 25.32 *(978-1-4965-2556-7(6),* Stone Arch Bks.) Capstone.

—Volcano - A Fiery Tale of Survival. Troupe, Thomas Kingsley. 2016. (Survive! Ser.). (ENG.). 56p. (J). (gr. 4-8). lib. bdg. 25.32 *(978-1-4965-2555-0(8),* Stone Arch Bks.) Capstone.

Fagan, Martin. Lamhainni Glasa. Ghlinn, Aine Ni. 2004. (Sraith Sos Ser.: 11). (GLE.). 10p. (J). pap. 11.00 *(978-0-86278-901-5(X))* O'Brien Pr., Ltd., The IRL. Dist: Casemate Pubs. & Bk. Distributors, LLC.

—Mo Mhadra Beoga. Deeley, Patrick. 2005. (Sraith Sos Ser.: 12). (GLE.). 64p. (J). pap. 11.00 *(978-0-86278-942-8(7))* O'Brien Pr., Ltd., The IRL. Dist: Casemate Pubs. & Bk. Distributors, LLC.

—A Pasear Perros. Lindeen, Mary. 2016. (Early Rising Readers Ser.). (SPA.). (J). (gr. -1). 6.67 *(978-1-4788-3671-1(7))* Newmark Learning LLC.

—Ponte a Reir! Lindeen, Mary. 2016. (Early Rising Readers Ser.). (SPA.). 16p. (J). (gr. 1-1). 6.67 *(978-1-4788-4170-8(2))* Newmark Learning LLC.

—Put on Smiles! Lindeen, Mary. 2015. (Early Rising Readers Ser.). (J). (gr. -1-k). 5.83 *(978-1-4788-2135-9(3))* Newmark Learning LLC.

—The Secret Life of Wally Smithers. Jenkins, Amanda & Benchmark Education Co., LLC. 2014. (Text Connections Ser.). (J). (gr. 3). *(978-1-4509-9656-3(6))* Benchmark Education Co.

—The Secret Life of Wally Smithers: Set Of 6. Jenkins, Amanda. 2014. (Text Connections Ser.). (J). (gr. 3). 49.00 net. *(978-1-4900-0132-6(8))* Benchmark Education Co.

—A Trip to Washington, D. C. A Capital Idea. Turnage, Cyndy. 2013. (Reader's Theater Word Plays Ser.). (J). (gr. 1-2). *(978-1-4509-8941-1(1))* Benchmark Education Co.

—Wally Smithers Tames the River. Jenkins, Amanda. 2017. (Text Connections Guided Close Reading Ser.). (J). (gr. 2). *(978-1-4900-1842-3(5))* Benchmark Education Co.

—Wolfgran Returns. O'Connor, Finbar. 2004. (ENG.). 96p. (J). pap. 10.95 *(978-0-86278-884-1(6))* O'Brien Pr., Ltd., The IRL. Dist: Dufour Editions, Inc.

Faganello, Keilan. A Soggy, Soaky, Rainy Day. Faganello, Kim. 2019. (ENG.). 36p. (J). pap. 9.99 ***(978-1-6523-8064-1(7))*** Independently Published.

Fagernes, Annelin. Free As a Bird / Libre Como una Ave. Fagernes, Annelin. 2018. (Xist Kids Bilingual Spanish English Ser.). (ENG & SPA.). 32p. (J). (gr. -1-3). pap. 9.99 *(978-1-5324-0101-5(9))* Xist Publishing.

—Libre Como una Ave. Fagernes, Annelin. 2018. (Xist Kids Spanish Bks.). (SPA.). 32p. (J). (gr. -1-3). pap. 9.99 *(978-1-5324-0123-7(X))* Xist Publishing.

Fahim, Pranto, jt. illus. see Sayekti, Sri.

Fahringer, Sarah. Lessons from the Vine Second Grade Spring Quarter. Thompson, Kathy. 2012. 170p. pap. 35.00 *(978-1-935014-31-7(5),* Lessons From The Vine) Hutchings, John Pubs.

Fahy, Emer. Oh God, Where Are You? Resman, Michael. 2018. (Whispers of the Holy Spirit Ser.: Vol. 4). (ENG.). 40p. (J). pap. *(978-976-8273-04-8(6))* Producciones de la Hamaca.

Faiai, Iosefa L. Rhiney Goes to School. Smith, Nicholas. 2019. (Life of Rhiney the Rhino Ser.: Vol. 1). (ENG.). 26p. (J). pap. 12.99 ***(978-1-6890-0413-8(4))*** Independently Published.

—Rhiney Goes to the Dentist. Smith, Nicholas. 2019. (Life of Rhiney the Rhino Ser.: Vol. 2). (ENG.). 26p. (J). pap. 12.99 ***(978-1-7062-4979-5(9))*** Independently Published.

Failla, Marco. Age of X-Man: the Marvelous X-Men. 2019. (ENG.). 112p. (YA). (gr. 8-17). pap. 24.99 *(978-1-302-91575-9(4))* Marvel Worldwide, Inc.

Failla, Marco & Bustos, Natacha. Moon Girl & Devil Dinosaur Vol. 2: Cosmic Cooties. 2017. (ENG.). 136p. (J). (gr. 4-17). pap. 17.99 *(978-1-302-90208-7(3))* Marvel Worldwide, Inc.

Fain, Cheryl. Rosa: A German Woman on the Texas Frontier. Crawford, Ann Fears. I.t. ed. 2003. 60p. (J). (gr. 3-8). 16.95 *(978-1-931823-09-8(X))* Halcyon Pr.

Faino, Mary. Rome a Day: Scenes from the Eternal City. Kelly, S. D. 2018. (ENG.). 34p. (J). pap. 14.99 *(978-1-7322085-0-6(6))* Paper Mermaid, The.

Fair, Anton. Aphids Attack. Schwaegerle, Owen. 2018. (Frutopia Valley a Short Story Ser.: Vol. 1). (ENG.). 26p. (J). pap. 9.99 *(978-1-7201-5885-1(1))* Independently Published.

Fair, Patricia Anne. Paddle Tail's First Winter Adventure. Legrand, H J, III. 2006. 64p. (J). per. 7.95 *(978-1-59466-082-5(4),* Growing Years) Port Town Publishing.

Fairbanks, Letitia. Princess April Morning-Glory: What Kind of a World Would You Create, If You Had to Do Three Dood Deeds to Make Ii Home Again? Fairbanks, Letitia. 2013. (ENG.). 66p. pap. 24.00 *(978-0-9887848-0-2(7))* Sandramantos Publishing.

Fairbanks, Mark. Mikey. Pinto, Mindee & Cohen, Judy. 2013. 32p. pap. 9.99 *(978-1-937165-41-3(8))* Orange Hat Publishing.

Fairchild, Vincent. Are You There? Fairchild, Dianne. 2007. 32p. (J). pap. 16.00 *(978-0-8059-7535-2(7))* Dorrance Publishing Co., Inc.

Fairclough, Chris. Camping Trip. Chancellor, Deborah. 2005. (Reading Corner Ser.). 24p. (J). (gr. k-3). lib. bdg. 22.80 *(978-1-59771-010-7(5))* Sea-To-Sea Pubns.

Fairclough, Chris, photos by. How to Make a Card. Humphrey, Paul. 2007. (Crafty Kids Ser.). 24p. (J). (gr. -1-3). lib. bdg. 24.25 *(978-1-59771-100-5(4))* Sea-To-Sea Pubns.

—How to Make a Mask. Humphrey, Paul. 2007. (Crafty Kids Ser.). 24p. (J). (gr. -1-3). lib. bdg. 24.25 *(978-1-59771-101-2(2))* Sea-To-Sea Pubns.

—How to Make a Present. Humphrey, Paul. 2007. (Crafty Kids Ser.). 24p. (J). (gr. -1-3). lib. bdg. 24.25 *(978-1-59771-103-6(9))* Sea-To-Sea Pubns.

—Mumbai. Green, Jen. 2007. (Global Cities Ser.). 61p. (gr. 5-8). lib. bdg. 30.00 *(978-0-7910-8851-7(0),* Chelsea Hse.) Facts On File, Inc.

—New York. Garrington, Sally. 2006. (Global Cities Ser.). 61p. (gr. 5-8). lib. bdg. 30.00 *(978-0-7910-8853-1(7))* Facts On File, Inc.

Fairgray, Richard & Jones, Terry. My Grandpa Is a Dinosaur. 2016. (ENG.). 32p. (J). (gr. -1-k). 16.99 *(978-1-63450-632-8(4),* Sky Pony Pr.) Skyhorse Publishing Co., Inc.

—That's Not the Monster We Ordered. Black, Tara. 2016. (ENG.). 32p. (J). (gr. -1-k). 16.99 *(978-1-5107-1136-5(8),* Sky Pony Pr.) Skyhorse Publishing Co., Inc.

Fairhurst, Carol. One Shining Day. Dorling, Anna et al. 2011. (Purple Elephant Tales). 66p. (J). pap. *(978-1-921883-15-6(4),* MBS Pr.) Pick-a-Woo Woo Pubs.

Fairhurst, Joanne. Archie & the Red Wool. Fairhurst, Joanne. 2011. 16p. pap. *(978-1-908341-21-1(1))* Paragon Publishing, Rothersthorpe.

Fairman, Jennifer. El Cuerpo Humano. Beck, Paul. 2007. (SPA.). 48p. (J). (gr. k-5). *(978-970-718-436-7(1),* Silver Dolphin en Español) Advanced Marketing, S. de R. L. de C. V.

Fairman, Jennifer, jt. illus. see Desrocher, Jack.

Fairy, Meg. The Three Ants & Mother Bird. Ives, Bob. Deskov, Vladimir, ed. 2004. 40p. (J). *(978-1-920832-06-3(8))* Four Heads Publishing Group Pty, Ltd.

—The Three Ants & the Cat. Ives, Bob. 2003. 40p. (J). *(978-1-920832-07-0(6))* Four Heads Publishing Group Pty, Ltd.

Fajardo, Kat. The Isle of the Lost: the Graphic Novel (a Descendants Novel) Venditti, Robert & de la Cruz, Melissa. 2018. (Descendants Ser.). (ENG.). 128p. (J). (gr. 3-7). pap. 12.99 *(978-1-368-04051-8(9))* Hyperion Bks. for Children.

—The Isle of the Lost: the Graphic Novel (the Descendants Series) Venditti, Robert & de la Cruz, Melissa. 2018. (Descendants Ser.). (ENG.). 128p. (J). (gr. 3-7). 21.99 *(978-1-368-03981-9(2))* Hyperion Bks. for Children.

Fajardo, Ruben Carral & Zamyslov, Ivan. Sommerferien! Andi, Julia und der Keltenschatz. Meschnark, Eva-Maria. 2019. (Sommerferien! Ser.: Vol. 3). (GER.). 132p. (J). pap. 8.39 *(978-1-0768-3750-9(6))* Independently Published.

Falbo, K. J. Pig-A-Boo. Falbo, K. J. 2018. (ENG.). 34p. (J). pap. *(978-1-989161-19-7(7))* Hasmark Services Publishing.

Falcone, Fernando. The Big Book of Vampires. Despeyroux, Denise. 2012. (ENG.). 112p. (J). (gr. 4-7). 17.95 *(978-1-77049-371-1(9),* Tundra Bks.) Tundra Bks. CAN. Dist: Penguin Random Hse. LLC.

Falconer, Ian. Olivia Se Prepara para la Navidad. Mlawer, Teresa, tr. from ENG. 2008.Tr. of Olivia Helps with Christmas. (SPA.). 58p. (J). (gr. k-1). 16.99 *(978-1-933032-42-9(1))* Lectorum Pubns., Inc.

Falconer, Ian. Olivia: Book & CD. Falconer, Ian. 2009. (ENG.). 40p. (J). (gr. -1-3). 14.99 *(978-1-4169-8034-6(2),* Atheneum Bks. for Young Readers) Simon & Schuster Children's Publishing.

—Olivia ... & the Missing Toy. Falconer, Ian. 2003. (ENG.). 42p. (J). (gr. -1-3). 19.99 *(978-0-689-85291-6(6),* Atheneum Bks. for Young Readers) Simon & Schuster Children's Publishing.

—Olivia & the Fairy Princesses. Falconer, Ian. 2012. (ENG.). 40p. (J). (gr. -1-3). 19.99 *(978-1-4424-5027-1(4),* Atheneum Bks. for Young Readers) Simon & Schuster Children's Publishing.

—Olivia Forma una Banda. Falconer, Ian. Mlawer, Teresa, tr. from ENG. 2007. (SPA.). 39p. (J). (gr. -1-3). 17.99 *(978-1-933032-23-8(5))* Lectorum Pubns., Inc.

—Olivia Forms a Band. Falconer, Ian. 2006. (ENG.). 50p. (J). (gr. -1-3). 19.99 *(978-1-4169-2454-8(X),* Atheneum Bks. for Young Readers) Simon & Schuster Children's Publishing.

—Olivia Forms a Band: Book & CD. Falconer, Ian. 2009. (ENG.). 50p. (J). (gr. -1-3). 12.99 *(978-1-4169-8037-7(7),* Atheneum Bks. for Young Readers) Simon & Schuster Children's Publishing.

—Olivia Goes to Venice. Falconer, Ian. 2010. (ENG.). 48p. (J). (gr. -1-2). 17.99 *(978-1-4169-9674-3(5),* Atheneum Bks. for Young Readers) Simon & Schuster Children's Publishing.

—Olivia Helps with Christmas. Falconer, Ian. (Classic Board Bks.). (ENG.). (J). (gr. -1-2). 2013. 40p. bds. 7.99 *(978-1-4424-9446-6(8));* 2007. 58p. 19.99 *(978-1-4169-0786-2(6))* Simon & Schuster Children's Publishing. (Atheneum Bks. for Young Readers).

—Olivia Saves the Circus. Falconer, Ian. 2010. (Classic Board Bks.). (ENG.). 36p. (J). (gr. -1-2). bds. 8.99 *(978-1-4424-1287-3(9),* Atheneum Bks. for Young Readers) Simon & Schuster Children's Publishing.

—Olivia: the Essential Latin Edition. Falconer, Ian. High, Amy, tr. 2007. (LAT.). 40p. (J). (gr. 3-7). 17.99 *(978-1-4169-4218-4(1),* Atheneum Bks. for Young Readers) Simon & Schuster Children's Publishing.

—Olivia the Spy. Falconer, Ian. 2017. (ENG.). 40p. (J). (gr. -1-3). 17.99 *(978-1-4814-5795-8(0),* Atheneum/Caitlyn Dlouhy Books) Simon & Schuster Children's Publishing.

—Olivia y el Juguete Desaparecido. Falconer, Ian. Mlawer, Teresa, tr. from ENG. 2004. (Olivia Ser.).Tr. of Olivia & the Missing Toy. (SPA.). 30p. (J). 16.95 *(978-1-930332-71-3(8))* Lectorum Pubns., Inc.

—Teatro Olivia: Swan Lake; Romeo & Juliet; Turandot. Falconer, Ian. 2004. (Olivia Ser.). 10p. (J). 19.95 *(978-0-689-87816-9(8))* Simon & Schuster, Inc.

Falconer, Sam. Life Cycles: Everything from Start to Finish. DK. 2020. (ENG.). 144p. (J). (gr. 2-4). 19.99 ***(978-1-4654-9744-4(7),*** DK Children) Dorling Kindersley Publishing, Inc.

Falk, Cathy Kennerson. Love Stories for Children. Kennerson, Vern. 2013. (ENG.). 67p. (YA). pap. 17.95 *(978-1-4787-1665-5(7))* Outskirts Pr., Inc.

Falkenstern, Lisa. The Busy Tree, 0 vols. Ward, Jennifer. 2009. (ENG.). 32p. (J). (gr. k-3). 17.99 *(978-0-7614-5550-9(7),* 9780761455509, Two Lions) Amazon Publishing.

Falkenstern, Lisa. A Dragon Moves In. Falkenstern, Lisa. 2018. (ENG.). 33p. (J). (gr. -1-3). pap. 9.99 *(978-1-5420-9204-3(3),* 9781542092043, Two Lions) Amazon Publishing.

Fall, Brandon. The President Looks Like Me, Vol. 2. Michelle, Tanya. 2nd I.t. ed. 2010. (ENG.). 25p. (J). *(978-0-615-57799-9(7))* Bee's Ink Publishing.

Fall, Brandon & Nishio, Kimiyo. The Bicycle Fence. Noll, Tom. ed. 2014. (Trash to Treasure Ser.: 1). (ENG.). 32p. (J). lib. bdg. 17.99 *(978-1-939377-50-0(1))* Green Kids Pr., LLC.

Fallahee, Kate. I Want an Ostrich: Coloring Book. Song, Sonya Annita. 2019. (ENG.). 24p. (J). pap. *(978-1-989381-11-3(1))* Chinchilla Bks.

—My Teacher Dad. Song, Sonya Annita. 2019. (ENG.). 32p. (J). *(978-1-9995402-6-5(3));* (My Teacher Dad Ser.: Vol. 1). pap. *(978-1-9995402-7-2(1))* Chinchilla Bks.

Fallahee, Kate. The Vegetarian Leopard. Baker, Patrick. 2019. (ENG.). 44p. (J). pap. ***(978-0-473-49382-0(9))*** HookMedia Co. Ltd.

Faller, Regis. The Adventures of Polo. Faller, Regis. 2006. (Adventures of Polo Ser.). (ENG.). 80p. (J). (gr. -1-3). 21.99 *(978-1-59643-160-7(1),* 900038103) Roaring Brook Pr.

Fallon, Lisa. Miss Olivia, the Little Red Poodle: Her First Big Adventure. Kaminski, Tom. 2006. (J). pap. 16.00 *(978-0-8059-7253-5(6))* Dorrance Publishing Co., Inc.

Falorsi, Ilaria. Right for Me. Munton, Gill. 2014. (Traditional Tales Ser.). (ENG.). 16p. (J). (gr. k-1). pap. 6.95 *(978-1-62521-596-3(7),* Capstone Classroom) Capstone.

Falorsi, Ilaria. Who Does What? A Slide-And-Learn Book. Babin, Stephanie. 2020. (Slide-And-Learn Ser.: 4). (ENG.). 14p. (J). (gr. -1-k). bds. 14.99 ***(978-2-408-01970-9(2))*** Editions Tourbillon FRA. Dist: Hachette Bk. Group.

Falsini, Camilla. 5 Wild Shapes. 2019. (ENG.). 10p. (J). (gr. -1 — 1). bds. 14.95 *(978-0-7112-4088-9(4),* 308394, Words & Pictures) Quarto Publishing Group UK GBR. Dist: Hachette UK Distribution.

Falwell, Cathryn. Butterflies for Kiri. Falwell, Cathryn. 2003. (ENG.). 32p. (J). *(978-1-58430-100-4(7))* Lee & Low Bks., Inc.

—Los Dibujos de David. Falwell, Cathryn. de La Vega, Eida, tr. from ENG. 2005. (SPA.). 32p. (J). (gr. -1-5). pap. 10.95 *(978-1-58430-258-2(5))* Lee & Low Bks., Inc.

—Feast for 10, 1 vol. Falwell, Cathryn. (ENG.). (J). (gr. -1-3). 2008. 32p. 10.99 *(978-0-547-06431-4(4),* 1040021); 2003. 28p. bds. 6.99 *(978-0-618-38226-2(7),* 100339) Houghton Mifflin Harcourt Publishing Co.

—Gobble, Gobble, 1 vol. Falwell, Cathryn. 2012. (ENG.). 32p. (J). (-3). 16.95 *(978-1-58469-148-8(4));* pap. 8.95 *(978-1-58469-149-5(2))* Sourcebooks, Inc. (Dawn Pubns.).

—Mystery Vine. Falwell, Cathryn. 2009. 32p. (J). lib. bdg. 17.89 *(978-0-06-177197-2(X),* Greenwillow Bks.) HarperCollins Pubs.

—Rainbow Stew, 1 vol. Falwell, Cathryn. 2013. (ENG.). 32p. (J). 17.95 *(978-1-60060-847-6(7))* Lee & Low Bks., Inc.

—Turtle Splash! Countdown at the Pond. Falwell, Cathryn. 2008. (ENG.). 32p. (J). (gr. -1-3). pap. 7.99 *(978-0-06-142927-9(9),* Greenwillow Bks.) HarperCollins Pubs.

Fan, Eric & Fan, Terry. The Scarecrow. Ferry, Beth. 2019. (ENG.). 40p. (J). (gr. -1-3). 18.99 *(978-0-06-247576-3(2))* HarperCollins Pubs.

Fan, Eric, jt. illus. see Fan, Terry.

Fan, Terry. Rooftoppers. Rundell, Katherine. 2013. (ENG.). 288p. (J). (gr. 3-7). 18.99 *(978-1-4424-9058-1(6),* Simon & Schuster Bks. For Young Readers) Simon & Schuster Bks. For Young Readers.

Fan, Terry & Fan, Eric. The Antlered Ship. Slater, Dashka. 2017. (ENG.). 48p. (J). (gr. -1-3). 17.99 *(978-1-4814-5160-4(X),* Beach Lane Bks.) Beach Lane Bks.

—The Night Gardener. Fan, Terry & Fan, Eric. 2016. (ENG.). 48p. (J). (gr. -1-3). 17.99 *(978-1-4814-3978-7(2))* Simon & Schuster, Inc.

—Ocean Meets Sky. Fan, Terry & Fan, Eric. 2018. (ENG.). 48p. (J). (gr. -1-3). 17.99 *(978-1-4814-7037-7(X),* Simon & Schuster Bks. For Young Readers) Simon & Schuster Bks. For Young Readers.

Fan, Terry, jt. illus. see Fan, Eric.

Fancher, Lou & Johnson, Steve. All God's Creatures. Hill, Karen. 2005. (ENG.). 14p. (J). (gr. -1 — 1). 9.99 *(978-0-689-87819-0(2),* Little Simon) Little Simon.

—Bambi: A Life in the Woods. Salten, Felix. Chambers, Whittaker, tr. 2014. (Scribner Classics Ser.). (ENG.). 192p. (J). (gr. 5). 29.99 *(978-1-4424-9345-2(3),* Atheneum Bks. for Young Readers) Simon & Schuster Children's Publishing.

—Dolley Madison: Parties Can Be Patriotic! Krull, Kathleen. 2015. (Women Who Broke the Rules Ser.). (ENG.). 48p. (J). (gr. 1-4). 16.99 *(978-0-8027-3793-9(5),* 9780802737939, Bloomsbury USA Childrens) Bloomsbury Publishing USA.

—For the Love of Music: The Remarkable Story of Maria Anna Mozart. Rusch, Elizabeth. 2011. (ENG.). 32p. (J). (gr. k-3). 16.99 *(978-1-58246-326-1(3),* Tricycle Pr.) Random Hse. Children's Bks.

—Silver Seeds. Paolilli, Paul & Brewer, Dan. 2003. (ENG.). 32p. (J). (gr. k-4). pap. 6.99 *(978-0-14-250010-1(0),* Puffin Books) Penguin Young Readers Group.

—Sofia's Stoop Story: 18th Street, Brooklyn: 18th Street, Brooklyn. Bohrer, Maria. 2014. 32p. (J). 17.95 *(978-0-9885295-2-6(1))* Blue Marlin Pubns.

—With My Hands: Poems about Making Things. VanDerwater, Amy Ludwig. 2018. (ENG.). 32p. (J). (gr. -1-3). 17.99 *(978-0-544-31340-8(2),* 1581615, Clarion Bks.) Houghton Mifflin Harcourt Trade & Reference Pubs.

Fancher, Lou, jt. illus. see Johnson, Steve.

Fandos, Mar. A Christmas Adventure: The Adventures of Petey Pots & Pans. Curtis, Chasity L. & Small, Evelyn Robin, eds. 2018. (Adventures of Petey Pots & Pans Ser.: Vol. 5). (ENG.). 40p. (J). pap. 9.99 *(978-1-7308-3702-9(6))* Independently Published.

Fandos, Mar. Letter from Santa Claus. Jones, Robin. 2nd ed. 2019. (ENG.). 48p. (J). ***(978-1-5255-5141-3(8))***; pap. ***(978-1-5255-5142-0(6))*** FriesenPress.

—Magnus o'Meere, Mind Pioneer. Pierce, Kristin S. 2019. (ENG.). 40p. (J). (gr. k-3). ***(978-1-9990881-0-1(7))*** Inner Compass Bks.

—Mayva o'Meere, Creationeer. Pierce, Kristin. 2018. (ENG.). 44p. (J). (gr. k-3). pap. ***(978-1-77370-548-4(2))***; ***(978-1-77370-549-1(0))*** Inner Compass Bks.

Fanelli, Sara. Pinocchio: Candlewick Illustrated Classic. Collodi, Carlo. Rose, Emma, tr. 2010. (Candlewick Illustrated Classics Ser.). (ENG.). 192p. (J). (gr. 2-5). pap. 12.99 *(978-0-7636-4731-5(4))* Candlewick Pr.

Fanelli, Sara. My Map Book. Fanelli, Sara. 2019. (ENG.). 32p. (J). (gr. -1-3). 17.99 *(978-0-06-289887-6(6))* HarperCollins Pubs.

Fang, Jade. The Twelve Days of Christmas. Accord Publishing Staff. 2011. (ENG.). 26p. (J). 17.99 *(978-1-4494-0361-4(1))* Andrews McMeel Publishing.

—The Twelve Days of Christmas. Andrews McMeel Publishing Staff. 2015. (ENG.). 24p. (J). bds. 9.99 *(978-1-4494-6001-3(1))* Andrews McMeel Publishing.

Fang, Susan Chen & Disney Storybook Art Team. Disney It's a Small World Around-The-World Safari. Glass, Calliope & Disney Book Group. 2013. (ENG.). 24p. (J). (gr. -1-1). pap. 17.44 *(978-1-4231-6233-9(1))* Disney Pr.

Fann, Linsey. Puppy Love. Fann, Linsey. Abdulai, David, ed. Date not set. 32p. (J). (gr. 4-6). pap. 19.95 *(978-0-9647012-6-7(X)*, Dawn of a New Day Pubns., The) Konkori International.

Fannon, Chris. Eddie, the Elf Who Would Be Elvis. Guiffre, William A. 2011. (ENG.). 40p. (J). 17.95 *(978-0-9830172-0-2(4))*; pap. 9.95 *(978-0-9830172-1-9(2))* Guiffre Bk. Publishing.

Fanny. A Daycare for Connor. Cochard, Nadège. 2009. (My First Stories Ser.). 24p. (J). (gr. -1-3). 25.60 *(978-1-60754-353-4(2))*; pap. 8.15 *(978-1-60754-354-1(0))* Windmill Bks.

—Grandma & Grandpa Visit Connor. Cochard, Nadège. 2009. (My First Stories Ser.). 24p. (J). (gr. -1-3). 25.60 *(978-1-60754-357-2(5))* Windmill Bks.

—Grandma & Grandpa Visit Connor. Cochard, Nadège. 2009. (My First Stories Ser.). 24p. (J). (gr. -1-3). pap. 8.15 *(978-1-60754-356-5(7))* Windmill Bks.

—Up Cat. Hutchins, Hazel. 2nd ed. 2012. (ENG.). 26p. (J). (gr. -1-k). bds. 7.99 *(978-1-55451-388-8(X)*, 9781554513888) Annick Pr., Ltd. CAN. Dist: Publishers Group West (PGW).

—Up Dog. Hutchins, Hazel. 2nd ed. 2012. (ENG.). 26p. (J). (gr. -1-k). bds. 6.95 *(978-1-55451-389-5(8)*, 9781554513895) Annick Pr., Ltd. CAN. Dist: Publishers Group West (PGW).

Fanny, Nanny. The New Girl in Town: A Children's Book. Fanny, Nanny. 2013. 32p. pap. 12.99 *(978-1-62516-179-6(4)*, Strategic Bk. Publishing) Strategic Book Publishing & Rights Agency (SBPRA).

Fanti, Rosemary. The Glamorous Life of Josie Marie: Hollywood 1957. Olszewski, Angie M. 2nd ed. 2019. (1 Ser.: Vol. 1). (ENG.). 50p. (J). (gr. k-6). pap. 12.00 ***(978-0-578-59324-1(6))*** Olszewski, Angie.

Faragher, Rosie. Astrid & the Sky Calf. Faragher, Rosie. 2019. (Child's Play Library). 32p. (J). *(978-1-78628-354-2(9))*; pap. *(978-1-78628-353-5(0))* Child's Play International Ltd.

Farah, Jackie, jt. illus. see Scott, Ruby.

Faraone, Andrea. Dalla Terra Alla Luna (Illustrato) Trajet Direct en 97 Heures 20 Minutes. Verne, Jules. Pizzigoni, Giuseppina, tr. 2019. (ITA.). 416p. (J). pap. 16.99 *(978-1-7966-5919-1(3))* Independently Published.

Farcas, Fabiana, jt. illus. see Grey, Elizabeth.

Fardell, John. Jeremiah Jellyfish Flies High! Fardell, John. 2011. 32p. (J). (gr. -1-k). pap. 13.99 *(978-1-84939-147-4(5))* Andersen Pr. GBR. Dist: Independent Pubs. Group.

Fargo, Lisa J. Touched by an Angel's Tear. Santora, L. Steven. Connors, Clare & Szitas, Kathie, eds. 2008. 32p. (J). lib. bdg. 15.95 *(978-0-9818622-0-0(9))* Guilin City Publishing.

Fargo, Todd. A Charm for Jo. Brady, Bill & Brady, Laurie. I.t. ed. 2005. (Turtle Bks.). (ENG.). 32p. (J). (gr. 2-5). pap. 9.95 *(978-0-944727-47-8(6))* Jason & Nordic Pubs.

—It's Time. Mammay, Judith. I.t. ed. 2007. 32p. (J). pap. 9.95 *(978-0-944727-20-1(4))*; lib. bdg. 15.95 *(978-0-944727-21-8(2))* Jason & Nordic Pubs. (Turtle Bks.).

—Me, Hailey. Plucker, Sheri. 2005. (Turtle Books). 32p. (J). (gr. k-3). pap. 9.95 *(978-0-944727-49-2(2))*; lib. bdg. 15.95 *(978-0-944727-50-8(6)*, Turtle Bks.) Jason & Nordic Pubs.

—Peter & Friends at Camp. Scott, Rosanna. I.t. ed. 2006. (Turtle Books). 32p. (J). (gr. k-4). pap. 9.95 *(978-0-944727-51-5(4))*; lib. bdg. 15.95 *(978-0-944727-52-2(2))* Jason & Nordic Pubs. (Turtle Bks.).

—Ryan's Victory. Mammay, Judith. 2009. 32p. (J). pap. 9.95 *(978-0-944727-53-9(0))*; lib. bdg. 15.95 *(978-0-944727-54-6(9))* Jason & Nordic Pubs. (Turtle Bks.).

—Two Tracks in the Snow. Bryant, Louella. I.t. ed. 2004. (Turtle Bks.). 32p. (J). lib. bdg. 15.95 *(978-0-944727-46-1(8))*; per. 9.95 *(978-0-944727-45-4(X))* Jason & Nordic Pubs. (Turtle Bks.).

Faria, Remy. The Magic Mirror. Costa, Natalia. 2019. (ENG.). 58p. (J). pap. 12.00 *(978-1-7962-5021-3(X))* Independently Published.

Faria, Rosana. El Libro Negro de los Colores. Cottin, Menena. Amado, Elisa, tr. 2008. (SPA.). (J). (gr. k-5). 20.99 *(978-970-825-019-1(8))* Tecolote, Ediciones, S.A. de C.V. MEX. Dist: Lectorum Pubns., Inc.

—Splash! Pantin, Yolanda. 2003. (SPA.). 16p. (J). (gr. -1-1). *(978-980-6437-19-7(5))* Playco Editores, C.A.

—Tiririca, Jararaca y Perereca. MacHado, Ana Maria. 2003. 28p. pap. *(978-980-257-283-0(7))* Ekare, Ediciones.

Faria, Rosana & Faria, Rosana. The Black Book of Colors. Cottin, Menena. Amado, Elisa, tr. 2008. (ENG.). 24p. (J). (gr. k-5). 17.95 *(978-0-88899-873-6(2))* Groundwood Bks. CAN. Dist: Publishers Group West (PGW).

Faria, Rosana, jt. illus. see Faria, Rosana.

Farias, Carolina, et al. Caperucita Roja: 3 Cuentos Predliectos de Alrededor Del Mundo. Gunderson, Jessica. 2020. (Cuentos Multiculturales Ser.).Tr. of Little Red Riding Hood Stories Around the World. (SPA.). 32p. (J). (gr. k-2). pap. 6.95 *(978-1-5158-6070-9(1)*, 142291); lib. bdg. 27.99 *(978-1-5158-5712-9(3)*, 142073) Capstone. (Picture Window Bks.).

Farias, Carolina. Sing-Along Nursery Rhymes. Lewis, Anthony. 2016. (Rookie Nursery Rhymes Ser.). (ENG.). 32p. (J). (gr. -1-k). 25.00 *(978-0-531-22876-0(2)*, Children's Pr.) Scholastic Library Publishing.

—The Truth about Fairies, 1 vol. Johnson, J. Angelique. 2010. (Fairy-Tale Superstars Ser.). (ENG.). 32p. (J). (gr. 1-3). lib. bdg. 27.99 *(978-1-4048-5746-9(X)*, Picture Window Bks.) Capstone.

Farias, Carolina. Twinkle, Twinkle Little Star. Rhatigan, Joe. 2017. (Classic Nursery Rhymes Retold Ser.). (ENG.). 32p. (J). (gr. -1-k). 12.95 *(978-1-63322-237-3(3)*, Moondance) Quarto Publishing Group USA.

—When Christmas Feels Like Home. Griffith, Gretchen. 2014. (AV2 Fiction Readalong Ser.: Vol. 119). (ENG.). 32p. (J). (gr. k-3). lib. bdg. 34.28 *(978-1-4896-2392-8(2)*, AV2 by Weigl) Weigl Pubs., Inc.

Farias, Carolina & Lewis, Anthony. Sing-Along Nursery Rhymes. 2017. (Rookie Read-Aloud Ser.). (ENG.). 32p. (J). (gr. -1-k). pap. 12.00 *(978-0-531-23048-0(1)*, Children's Pr.) Scholastic Library Publishing.

Farias, Susan Norberg. Think for Yourself: A Kid's Guide to Solving Life's Dilemmas & Other Sticky Problems. MacGregor, Cynthia. 2004. (ENG.). 96p. (J). (gr. 4-7). pap. 7.95 *(978-1-894222-73-0(3))* Lobster Pr. CAN. Dist: Univ. of Toronto Pr.

Faricy, Patrick. Cabin in the Snow. Hopkinson, Deborah. ed. 2005. 74p. (J). lib. bdg. 15.00 *(978-1-59054-896-7(5))* Fitzgerald Bks.

—Our Kansas Home. Hopkinson, Deborah. ed. 2005. 64p. (J). lib. bdg. 15.00 *(978-1-59054-910-0(4))* Fitzgerald Bks.

—Our Kansas Home. Hopkinson, Deborah. 2003. (Prairie Skies Ser.). 69p. (J). 11.65 *(978-0-7569-3448-4(6))* Perfection Learning Corp.

—Pioneer Summer. Hopkinson, Deborah. ed. 2005. 74p. (J). lib. bdg. 15.00 *(978-1-59054-911-7(2))* Fitzgerald Bks.

—Robert Smalls: The Boat Thief. Kennedy, Robert F., Jr. 2008. (Robert F. Kennedy, Jr.'s American Heroes Ser.). (ENG.). 48p. (gr. 5-8). 16.99 *(978-1-4231-0802-3(7))* Hyperion Pr.

—Teddy Kennedy: Lion of the Senate. Stanley, George E. 2010. (Childhood of Famous Americans Ser.). (ENG.). 224p. (J). (gr. 3-7). pap. 5.99 *(978-1-4169-9041-3(0)*, Simon & Schuster/Paula Wiseman Bks.) Simon & Schuster/Paula Wiseman Bks.

Faricy, Patrick, jt. illus. see Patrick, Jean L. S.

Farina, Kathy. Three Colors of Katie. Washington, Kathy. 2010. (J). (gr. k-2). pap. 9.95 *(978-1-932514-18-6(X))* College of DuPage Pr.

Farina, Katy. Steven Universe: Warp Tour (Vol. 1) Gillman, Melanie. 2017. (Steven Universe Ser.: 1). (ENG.). 112p. (J). (gr. 4-7). pap. 14.99 *(978-1-68415-033-5(7))* Boom! Studios.

Farina, Katy & Leth, Kate. The Amazing World of Gumball: after School Special Vol. 1. 2017. (Amazing World of Gumball Ser.: 1). (ENG.). 128p. (J). (gr. 4-7). pap. 14.99 *(978-1-68415-017-5(5))* Boom! Studios.

Farinas, Ulises. Star Wars Deluxe Where's the Wookiee? Pallant, Katrina. 2019. (Star Wars Where's the Wookiee? Ser.). (ENG.). 80p. (J). (gr. 1-3). 12.99 *(978-0-7944-4366-5(4)*, Studio Fun International) Printers Row Publishing Group.

Farinas, Ulises. Star Wars: Where's the Wookiee? the Search Continues... Editors of Studio Fun International. 2020. (Star Wars Where's the Wookiee? Ser.). (ENG.). 32p. (J). (gr. 1-3). 9.99 ***(978-0-7944-4412-9(1)***, Studio Fun International) Printers Row Publishing Group.

Faris, Eva. The Three Little Kittens. Stephenson, Nancy. I.t. ed. 2003. 30p. (J). per. 7.99 *(978-1-932338-13-3(6))* Lifevest Publishing, Inc.

Fariss, Michelle. The Sad Saint. Becker, Curt. 2009. 36p. pap. 14.95 *(978-1-60844-161-7(X))* Dog Ear Publishing, LLC.

Farkas, Levente. Rigby the Sled Dog's Christmas Story. Byiers, Raymond P. 2019. (ENG.). 24p. (J). ***(978-1-5255-5390-5(9))***; pap. ***(978-1-5255-5391-2(7))*** FriesenPress.

Farkus, Ruldolf & Love, Mike. Discovering Dinosaurs. Chapman, Simon. 2014. 32p. *(978-1-4351-6432-1(6))* Barnes & Noble, Inc.

Farley, Andrew, jt. illus. see Hull, Biz.

Farley, Brianne. Building Books. Lloyd, Megan Wagner. 2018. 32p. (J). (gr. -1-2). 17.99 *(978-1-5247-7367-0(0))*; (ENG.). lib. bdg. 20.99 *(978-1-5247-7368-7(9))* Random Hse. Children's Bks. (Knopf Bks. for Young Readers).

—Charlotte the Scientist Finds a Cure. Andros, Camille. 2019. (Charlotte the Scientist Ser.). (ENG.). 40p. (J). (gr. -1-3). 17.99 *(978-0-544-81376-2(6)*, 1642033, Clarion Bks.) Houghton Mifflin Harcourt Trade & Reference Pubs.

—Charlotte the Scientist Is Squished. Andros, Camille. 2017. (Charlotte the Scientist Ser.). (ENG.). 40p. (J). (gr. -1-3). 17.99 *(978-0-544-78583-0(5)*, 1638581) Houghton Mifflin Harcourt Publishing Co.

Farley, Brianne. Ike's Incredible Ink. Farley, Brianne. 2013. (ENG.). 32p. (J). (gr. -1-3). 17.99 *(978-0-7636-6296-7(8))* Candlewick Pr.

—Secret Tree Fort. Farley, Brianne. 2016. (ENG.). 32p. (J). (gr. -1-3). 16.99 *(978-0-7636-6297-4(6))* Candlewick Pr.

Farley, Erin. Emily Windsnap & the Falls of Forgotten Island. Kessler, Liz. (Emily Windsnap Ser.: 7). (ENG.). 320p. (J). (gr. 3-7). 2019. pap. 6.99 *(978-1-5362-0635-7(0))*; 2018. 15.99 *(978-0-7636-9574-3(2))* Candlewick Pr.

—Emily Windsnap & the Pirate Prince. Kessler, Liz. (Emily Windsnap Ser.). (ENG.). 288p. (J). (gr. 3-7). 2020. pap. 6.99 *(978-1-5362-1312-6(8))*; 2019. 15.99 *(978-1-5362-0299-1(1))* Candlewick Pr.

—Emily Windsnap & the Tides of Time. Kessler, Liz. 2020. (Emily Windsnap Ser.: 9). (ENG.). 272p. (J). (gr. 3-7). 16.99 *(978-1-5362-0969-3(4))* Candlewick Pr.

Farley, Jason, jt. illus. see Seiler, Jason.

Farley, Jennifer. Shooting for the Stars: My Journey to Become Ireland's First Astronaut. Patten, Norah. 2019. (ENG.). 44p. 24.99 *(978-1-78849-100-6(9))* O'Brien Pr., Ltd., The IRL. Dist: Casemate Pubs. & Bk. Distributors, LLC.

Farley, Katherine. Hope Music. Powell, Amy. 2006. 32p. (J). (gr. -1-3). per. 12.00 *(978-0-9773608-4-0(9))* Shiny Red Ball Publishing.

Farley, Rick, et al. Batman Phonics Fun! Rosen, Lucy. 2011. (My First I Can Read Ser.). (ENG.). 36p. (J). (gr. -1-3). pap. 14.99 *(978-0-06-188542-6(8))* HarperCollins Pubs.

Farley, Rick. I Am Superman. Teitelbaum, Michael. 2009. (I Can Read Level 2 Ser.). (ENG.). 32p. (J). (gr. -1-3). pap. 3.99 *(978-0-06-187857-2(X))* HarperCollins Pubs.

—Paint Book. Jacobs, Lana. 2006. (Charlotte's Web Ser.). 32p. (J). 4.99 *(978-0-06-088277-8(8))* HarperCollins Pubs.

Farley, Rick & Eberz, Robert. Splat the Cat & the Big Secret. Scotton, Rob. 2016. (J). *(978-1-4844-8600-9(5))* Publishers Quality Library Service.

Farmer, Charlotte. Make Buildings. Harrisson, Christopher. 2016. (ENG.). 112p. (J). pap. 11.99 *(978-1-61067-410-2(3))* Kane Miller.

Farmer, Charlotte. Histor: A World of History to Colour. Farmer, Charlotte. 2018. (Map Colouring Bks.). (ENG.). 48p. (J). (gr. 3). pap. 15.99 *(978-1-78055-431-0(1))* O'Mara, Michael Bks., Ltd. GBR. Dist: Independent Pubs. Group.

Farmer, Hilary. Cedar Island Dreams. Radcliffe, Tj. 2020. (Inner Islands Trilogy Ser.: Vol. 1). (ENG.). 164p. (J). (gr. 3-6). pap. ***(978-0-9937543-4-0(1))*** Siduri Pr.

Farmer, Jonathan, photos by. Every You, Every Me. Levithan, David. ed. 2012. lib. bdg. 20.85 *(978-0-606-26816-5(2))* Turtleback.

Farmer, Jonathan, jt. photos by see Levithan, David.

Farmer, Libby. Polly Possum's Wandering Path. Miner, Ann. 2013. 20p. (J). pap. 12.95 *(978-1-4575-1849-2(X))* Dog Ear Publishing, LLC.

Farmer, Suzanne. Graeme Goes Home. Pitkethly, Maggie. 2008. 32p. pap. 12.00 *(978-0-9791402-8-0(5))* Stewart, R. J. Bks.

Farmer, Zoe. The Jewel in the Attic & the Adventures of Tiger. Kimmons, Janet M. 2007. 108p. (J). (gr. 1-3). pap. *(978-1-58690-028-1(5))* Mould, Paul Publishing.

—The Magnificent Six. Bellis, Jill. 2007. 52p. pap. *(978-1-904959-47-2(4))* Mould, Paul Publishing.

—The Return of the Magnificent Six: A Christmas Adventure. Bellis, Jill. 2008. (The Magnificent Six: Vol. 2). 62p. pap. 14.00 *(978-1-58690-073-1(0))* Players Pr., Inc.

Farmer, Zoe. Practice Makes Perfect. Farmer, Zoe. 2007. 74p. (gr. -1-k). pap. *(978-1-58690-029-8(3))* Mould, Paul Publishing.

Farnsworth, Bill. Big-Enough Anna: The Little Sled Dog Who Braved the Arctic. Flowers, Pam. 2003. (ENG.). 32p. (J). (gr. 1-3). 15.95 *(978-0-88240-577-3(2))*; pap. 11.99 *(978-0-88240-580-3(2))* West Margin Pr. (Alaska Northwest Bks.).

—Buffalo Song. Bruchac, Joseph. (J). 2014. (ENG.). 40p. pap. 11.95 *(978-1-60060-990-9(2))*; 2008. Lee & Low Bks., Inc.

—By the Sword. Castrovilla, Selene. 2007. (ENG.). 40p. (J). (gr. 1-4). 17.95 *(978-1-59078-427-3(8)*, Calkins Creek) Boyds Mills Pr.

—Eli Remembers. Vander Zee, Ruth & Sneider, Marian. 2007. (ENG.). 32p. (J). (gr. -1-3). 18.00 *(978-0-8028-5309-7(9)*, Eerdmans Bks For Young Readers) Eerdmans, William B. Publishing Co.

—Ellie's Long Walk: The True Story of Two Friends on the Appalachian Trail. Flowers, Pam. 2012. (ENG.). 32p. (J). (gr. k-3). pap. 11.99 *(978-0-88240-885-9(2)*, West Winds Pr.) West Margin Pr.

—The Flag with Fifty-Six Stars: A Gift from the Survivors of Mauthausen. Rubin, Susan Goldman. (ENG.). 40p. (J). (gr. 1-5). 2005. 17.95 *(978-0-8234-1653-0(4))*; 2006. reprint ed. 6.95 *(978-0-8234-2019-3(1))* Holiday Hse., Inc.

—Grandpa's Music. Acheson, Alison. 2013. (AV2 Fiction Readalong Ser.). (ENG.). (J). (gr. 3-7). 34.28 *(978-1-62127-878-8(6)*, AV2 by Weigl) Weigl Pubs., Inc.

—The Great Stone Face. 2005. 32p. (J). pap. 8.00 *(978-0-8028-5292-2(0))* Eerdmans, William B. Publishing Co.

—Heroes for Civil Rights. Adler, David A. 2007. (ENG.). 32p. (J). (gr. 1-4). 17.95 *(978-0-8234-2008-7(6))* Holiday Hse., Inc.

—The Hunter's Promise: An Abenaki Tale, Vol. Bruchac, Joseph. 2015. 32p. (J). (gr. k-3). 16.95 *(978-1-937786-43-4(9)*, Wisdom Tales) World Wisdom, Inc.

—Irena Sendler & the Children of the Warsaw Ghetto. Rubin, Susan Goldman. (ENG.). 40p. (J). (gr. 1-4). 2016. pap. 8.99 *(978-0-8234-2595-2(9))*; 2011. 18.95 *(978-0-8234-2251-7(8))* Holiday Hse., Inc.

—The Long Trail. Hopkinson, Deborah. ed. 2005. 2004p. (J). lib. bdg. 15.00 *(978-1-59054-904-9(X))* Fitzgerald Bks.

—Louis Sockalexis: Native American Baseball Pioneer, 1 vol. Wise, Bill. 2007. (ENG.). 32p. (J). (gr. 1-7). 16.95 *(978-1-58430-269-8(0))* Lee & Low Bks., Inc.

—Miles of Smiles: The Story of Roxey, the Long Island Rail Road Dog. Worthington, Heather Hill. 2010. (J). *(978-0-9792918-4-5(4))*; pap. *(978-0-9792918-8-3(7))* Blue Marlin Pubns.

—Mingo, 1 vol. Strohmeier, Lenice. 2003. (ENG.). 32p. (J). 16.95 *(978-0-7614-5111-2(0))* Marshall Cavendish Corp.

—Minnow & Rose: An Oregon Trail Story. Young, Judy. 2009. (Tales of Young Americans Ser.). (ENG.). 32p. (J). (gr. 1-4). 17.95 *(978-1-58536-421-3(5)*, 202156) Sleeping Bear Pr.

—One Fine Day: A Radio Play. Van Steenwyk, Elizabeth. 2004. 32p. (J). (gr. 3-5). 16.00 *(978-0-8028-5234-2(3))* Eerdmans, William B. Publishing Co.

—Our Flag Was Still There: The Story of the Star-Spangled Banner. Craven, Tracy Leininger. 2004. (J). *(978-0-9724287-3-6(9))* Vision Forum, Inc., The.

—Prairie School. Avi. 2003. (I Can Read Level 4 Ser.). (ENG.). 48p. (J). (gr. 3-4). pap. 4.99 *(978-0-06-051318-4(7))* HarperCollins Pubs.

—Prairie School. Avi. 2003. (I Can Read Bks.). 47p. (gr. 3-7). 14.00 *(978-0-7569-1452-3(3))* Perfection Learning Corp.

—Railroad!, Level 3: A Story of the Transcontinental Railroad. Bailer, Darice. 3rd ed. 2004. (Soundprints' Read-and-Discover Ser.). (ENG.). 48p. (J). (gr. 1-4). pap. 3.95 *(978-1-59249-017-2(4)*, S2007) Soundprints.

—Sailing for Gold. Hopkinson, Deborah. ed. 2005. 76p. (J). lib. bdg. 15.00 *(978-1-59054-915-5(5))* Fitzgerald Bks.

—Sojo: Memoirs of a Reluctant Sled Dog. Flowers, Pam. 2016. (ENG.). 120p. (J). (gr. 3-7). 23.99 *(978-1-943328-55-0(2))*; pap. 12.99 *(978-1-943328-53-6(6))* West Margin Pr. (Alaska Northwest Bks.).

—Tenth Avenue Cowboy. High, Linda Oatman. 2008. 32p. (J). (gr. 4-7). 17.00 *(978-0-8028-5330-1(7)*, Eerdmans Bks For Young Readers) Eerdmans, William B. Publishing Co.

—The Wheat Doll, 1 vol. Randall, Alison L. 2008. (ENG.). 32p. (J). (gr. k-3). 16.95 *(978-1-56145-456-3(7))* Peachtree Publishing Co. Inc.

—When Abraham Talked to the Trees. Van Steenwyk, Elizabeth. 2004. 32p. (J). (gr. 2-5). 16.00 *(978-0-8028-5191-8(6))*; pap. 8.00 *(978-0-8028-5233-5(5))* Eerdmans, William B. Publishing Co.

Farnsworth, Lauren, jt. illus. see Richards, Steve.

Farooq, Faiza. Good Morning Matty! Davis Jr, Christopher. 2019. (ENG.). 38p. (J). (gr. k-5). 22.00 *(978-0-578-45747-5(4))* Christopher Davis, Jr.

—Good Morning Matty! Davis Jr, Christopher. 2019. (ENG.). 36p. (J). pap. 14.99 *(978-1-7909-6783-4(X))* Independently Published.

Farquharson, Alexander. The White House Is Burning: August 24 1814. Sutcliffe, Jane. 2014. 128p. (J). (gr. 4-7). 19.95 *(978-1-58089-656-6(1))* Charlesbridge Publishing, Inc.

—The White House Is Burning: August 24 1814. Sutcliffe, Jane. 2020. 128p. (J). (gr. 4-7). pap. 12.99 *(978-1-58089-657-3(X))* Charlesbridge Publishing, Inc.

Farr, Rich. And Then It Rained on Malcolm. Feurer, Paige. 2015. 40p. (J). (gr. -1-k). 16.99 *(978-1-63450-150-7(0)*, Sky Pony Pr.) Skyhorse Publishing Co., Inc.

Farrar, David. The Day the Strangers Came. Dwyer, Tony. 2019. (ENG.). 150p. (J). pap. 6.99 *(978-1-0713-8241-7(1))* Independently Published.

Farré, Lluís. If You Were a Kid at the First Thanksgiving Dinner. Samo, Melissa. 2017. (If You Were a Kid Ser.). (ENG.). 32p. (J). (gr. 2-4). pap. 7.95 *(978-0-531-23097-8(X)*, Children's Pr.) Scholastic Library Publishing.

Farrell, Alison. Runaway Signs. Holub, Joan. 2020. 32p. (J). (gr. -1-2). 17.99 *(978-0-399-17225-0(4)*, Nancy Paulsen Books) Penguin Young Readers Group.

Farrell, Amy. William Wobbly & the Very Bad Day: A Story about When Feelings Become Too Big. Naish, Sarah & Jefferies, Rosie. 2016. (Therapeutic Parenting Bks.). (ENG.). 32p. (C). pap. 15.95 *(978-1-78592-151-3(7)*, 696303) Kingsley, Jessica Pubs. GBR. Dist: Hachette UK Distribution.

Farrell, Jordy. The Adventures of Gracie & Monkeybear: Book 2: Winter. O'Kelly, C. S. Callahan, Tricia, ed. 2017. (Adventures of Gracie & Monkeybear Ser.: Vol. 2). (ENG.). 34p. (J). (gr. k-4). pap. 9.99 *(978-1-946807-05-2(2)*, MonkeyBear Publishing) LORE Mountain Productions.

—Las Aventuras de Gracie y OsoMono: Libro 1: Verano. O'Kelly, C. S. Callahan, Tricia, ed. Calvo, Irma, tr. 2017.Tr. of Adventures of Gracie & MonkeyBear. 48p. (J). (gr. -1-5). 17.99 *(978-0-9970294-6-8(3)*, MonkeyBear Publishing) LORE Mountain Productions.

Farrell, Lauren. Doodle Cat Wears a Cape. Patrick, Kat. 2019. (ENG.). 32p. (J). (gr. -1-2). 16.99 *(978-1-947534-98-8(X))* Scribe Pubns. AUS. Dist: Consortium Bk. Sales & Distribution.

Farrell Racette, Sherry. Wisahkecahk Flies to the Moon, 1 vol. Ahenakew, Freda. 2015. (ENG.). 32p. (J). 10.95 *(978-0-921827-57-3(1)*, 5be135dd-f3a9-455b-b6a7-acc4698cf248) Pemmican Pubns., Inc. CAN. Dist: Firefly Bks., Ltd.

Farrell, Russell. Horses & Ponies: Step-by-Step Insructions for 25 Different Breads. 2011. (Learn to Draw Ser.). 32p. (J). (gr. 1-4). *(978-1-936309-16-0(5))* Quarto Publishing Group USA.

—How to Draw Horses & Ponies: Step-By-step Instructions for 20 Different Breeds. Walter Foster Jr. Creative Team. 2018. (Learn to Draw Ser.). (ENG.). 32p. (J). (gr. 1-3). pap. 5.99 *(978-1-63322-748-4(0)*, Walter Foster Jr) Quarto Publishing Group USA.

—How to Draw Sea Creatures: Step-By-step Instructions for 20 Ocean Animals. Walter Foster Jr. Creative Team. 2018. (Learn to Draw Ser.). (ENG.). 32p. (J). (gr. 1-3). pap. 5.99 *(978-1-63322-756-9(1)*, Walter Foster Jr) Quarto Publishing Group USA.

—Sea Creatures: Step-by-Step Insructions for 25 Ocean Animals. Walter Foster Creative Team. 2011. (Learn to Draw Ser.). 32p. (J). (gr. 1-4). 28.50 *(978-1-936309-19-1(X))* Quarto Publishing Group USA.

Farrell, Russell & Fisher, Diana. All about Drawing Sea Creatures & Animals. 2010. (All about Drawing Ser.). 80p. (J). 34.25 *(978-1-936309-08-5(4))* Quarto Publishing Group USA.

Farrell, Triona, jt. illus. see Wijngaard, Caspar.

Farrelly, Linda & Hopkins, Simon. Elliot's Amazing Adventures Number 1. Farrelly, Linda. 2013. 52p. pap. *(978-0-9560331-5-4(6))* Children' Story Pubs.

Farrington, Susan. What I Love About You. Farrington, Susan. 2016. (ENG.). 32p. (J). (gr. -1-3). 17.99 *(978-0-06-239353-1(7))* HarperCollins Pubs.

F

Farrington, Teresa. Dragon Talk. Huxman, K. D. l.t. ed. 2006. 24p. (J). pap. 14.99 *(978-0-9765786-7-3(0))* Dragonfly Publishing, Inc.

Farris, Cat. Emily & the Strangers Volume 2: Breaking the Record, Vol. 2. Reger, Rob. 2015. (Emily & the Strangers Ser.: 2). (ENG.). 1p. (J). (gr. 5-12). 12.99 *(978-1-61655-598-6(X))* Dark Horse Comics.

—Plants vs. Zombies Volume 13: Snow Thanks. Tobin, Paul. 2019. (ENG.). 88p. (J). (gr. 3-7). 10.99 *(978-1-5067-0839-3(0),* Dark Horse Books) Dark Horse Comics.

Farris, Kim. The Happy Angel: A Fractured Fairy Tale. Cantrell, Pete. 2010. (ENG.). 32p. (J). 9.95 *(978-1-61005-010-4(X))* BookLogix.

Farris, Michael. Mr Boo Bear. Farris, Judy. 2009. 24p. pap. 15.49 *(978-1-4389-4553-8(1))* AuthorHouse.

Farrow Milner, Susan. Izzy Asks Why? Farrow Milner, Susan. 2017. (ENG.). 44p. (J). (gr. 4-6). *(978-1-77354-047-4(5))* PageMaster Publication Services, Inc.

Farrow, Simon. How I Lost My Ear (Grandpa Gristle's Bedtime Tales) Beck, Adam. 2018. (ENG.). 382p. (J). (gr. 3-6). pap. *(978-4-908629-03-7(X))* Bilingual Adventures.

Farrow, T. C. The Dragon in the Cliff: A Novel Based on the Life of Mary Anning. Cole, Sheila. 2016. (ENG.). 228p. (gr. 5-10). pap. 12.99 *(978-1-5040-3301-5(9))* Open Road Integrated Media, Inc.

Faruqi, Sultan. Time to Speak: Anecdotes from Sadi Shirazi. Sardar, Ziauddin. Abu Turab, Ashraf, ed. 2007. (ENG.). 32p. pap. 3.95 *(978-0-9503954-3-2(9))* Revival Pubns. GBR. Dist: Consortium Bk. Sales & Distribution.

Fasbinder, George. Get Ready. Fasbinder, Susie. 2019. (ENG.). 30p. (J). pap. 12.95 ***(978-1-0886-9336-0(9))*** Independently Published.

Faschi, Silvia. The Adventures of Simba the Frisky Feline. McLean, Linda. 2012. (J). 14.95 *(978-1-937406-24-0(5))* Mascot Bks., Inc.

Fasolino, Peter. Attack of the Toy Eating Veggie Monsters. Mulley, Brad. 2017. (ENG.). 30p. (J). pap. 9.99 *(978-0-9996420-0-9(6))* Mulley, Bradley.

Fast, Suellen M., photos by. America's Daughters. Fast, Suellen M. 100p. (Orig.). (J). (gr. k-18). pap. 19.00 *(978-0-935281-13-2(4))* Daughter Culture Pubns.

Fastner, Steve, jt. illus. see Pierard, John.

Fatus, Sophie. The Abominable Snowman: A Story from Nepal. Parnell, Fran. 2011. (Monster Stories Ser.). 48p. (J). (gr. 1-5). pap. 8.99 *(978-1-84686-558-9(1))* Barefoot Bks., Inc.

—Algarabia en la Granja. MacDonald, Margaret Read. 2009. (J). 9.99 *(978-1-84686-282-3(5))* Barefoot Bks., Inc.

—The Barefoot Book of Monsters! Parnell, Fran. 2003. 64p. (J). 19.99 *(978-1-84148-178-4(5))* Barefoot Bks., Inc.

—Build a Story Cards Community Helpers. Books, Barefoot. 2019. (Build a Story Cards Ser.). (ENG.). 36p. (J). (gr. -1-5). ring bd. *(978-1-78285-740-2(0))* Barefoot Bks., Ltd.

—The Farmyard Jamboree. MacDonald, Margaret Read. 2009. (ENG.). (J). 16.99 *(978-1-84686-290-8(6))* Barefoot Bks., Inc.

—The Feathered Ogre: A Story from Italy, 1. Parnell, Fran. 2011. (Monster Stories Ser.). 30p. (J). (gr. 1-3). pap. 22.44 *(978-1-84686-562-6(X))* Barefoot Bks., Ltd. GBR. Dist: Children's Plus, Inc.

Fatus, Sophie. Fun & Games: Everyday Play. Cortright, Celeste. 2020. (ENG.). 24p. (J). pap. ***(978-1-64686-054-8(3))*** Barefoot Bks., Inc.

Fatus, Sophie. A Hen, a Chick & a String Guitar. 2005. 32p. (J). 17.99 incl. audio compact disk *(978-1-84148-796-0(1))* Barefoot Bks., Inc.

—Here We Go Round the Mulberry Bush. Penner, Fred. 24p. (J). 2011. (gr. -1-2). 9.99 *(978-1-84686-656-2(1))*; 2008. (ENG.). 9.99 *(978-1-84686-079-9(2))*; 2008. (ENG.). 6.99 *(978-1-84686-189-5(6))* Barefoot Bks., Inc.

—If You're Happy & You Know It. McQuinn, Anna. 2011. (ENG.). 80p. (J). pap. 6.99 *(978-1-84686-434-6(8))* Barefoot Bks., Inc.

—The Journey Home from Grandpa's. Lumley, Jemima. 2012. 24p. (J). (gr. -1-2). 16.99 *(978-1-84686-898-6(X))* Barefoot Bks., Inc.

—The Journey Home from Grandpa's. Lumley, Jemima & Penner, Fred. 2011. 24p. (J). (gr. -1-2). 9.99 *(978-1-84686-658-6(8))* Barefoot Bks., Inc.

—The Journey Home from Grandpa's. Lumley, Jemima. 2006. (ENG.). 24p. (J). 6.99 *(978-1-84686-029-4(6))*; (gr. -1-k). 9.99 *(978-1-84686-026-3(1))*; (gr. -1-3). 16.99 *(978-1-905236-37-4(9))* Barefoot Bks., Inc.

—The Journey Home from Grandpa's. Lumley, Jemima. 2010. 16p. (J). (gr. -1-3). pap. 5.99 *(978-1-84686-277-9(9))* Barefoot Bks., Inc.

—The Mother of Monsters: A Story from South Africa. Parnell, Fran. 2011. (Monster Stories Ser.). 48p. (J). (gr. 1-5). pap. 8.99 *(978-1-84686-560-2(3))* Barefoot Bks., Inc.

—My Daddy Is a Pretzel: Yoga for Parents & Kids. Baptiste, Baron. 48p. (J). 2012. (gr. k-3). pap. 9.99 *(978-1-84686-899-3(8))*; 2004. (ENG.). (gr. -1-2). 16.99 *(978-1-84148-151-7(3))* Barefoot Bks., Inc.

Fatus, Sophie. Night & Day. Porcella, Teresa. 2020. (ENG.). (J). bds. ***(978-1-78285-974-1(8))*** Barefoot Bks., Inc.

Fatus, Sophie. One More Friend. Flor Ada, Alma. 2007. 24p. (J). *(978-0-15-206278-1(5))* Harcourt Trade Pubs.

—Una Princesa Real: Un Cuento Matemagico. Williams, Brenda & Barefoot Books Staff. 2014. 40p. (J). (gr. k-4). pap. 8.99 *(978-1-78285-078-6(3))* Barefoot Bks., Inc.

—The Real Princess. Williams, Brenda. 2008. (ENG.). 40p. (J). (gr. -1-3). 16.99 *(978-1-905236-88-6(3))* Barefoot Bks., Inc.

—Real Princess. Williams, Brenda. 2019. (ENG.). 40p. (J). (gr. -1-2). pap. *(978-1-78285-786-0(9))* Barefoot Bks., Ltd.

—Riddle Me This! Riddles & Stories to Challenge Your Mind. Lupton, Hugh. 2003. 64p. (J). 19.99 *(978-1-84148-169-2(6))* Barefoot Bks., Inc.

—Riddle Me This! Riddles & Stories to Sharpen Your Wits. Lupton, Hugh. 2007. (ENG.). 64p. (J). pap. 12.99 *(978-1-905236-92-3(1))* Barefoot Bks., Inc.

—Riddles. Lupton, Hugh. 2016. (ENG.). 64p. (J). (gr. 1-5). pap. 14.99 *(978-1-78285-280-3(8))* Barefoot Bks., Inc.

—The Story Tree. Lupton, Hugh. 2009. (ENG.). 64p. (J). 19.99 *(978-1-84686-301-1(5))* Barefoot Bks., Inc.

—The Story Tree. Lupton, Hugh. 2019. (ENG.). 64p. (J). (gr. -1-2). pap. *(978-1-78285-421-0(5))* Barefoot Bks., Ltd.

—The Story Tree: Tales to Read Aloud. Lupton, Hugh. 2005. 64p. (J). (gr. -1-2). 16.99 *(978-1-905236-13-8(1))* Barefoot Bks., Inc.

—The Story Tree Artist Card Portfolio. (J). 12.99 *(978-1-84148-543-0(8))* Barefoot Bks., Inc.

Fatus, Sophie. Grim, Grunt & Grizzle-Tail: A Story from Chile. Fatus, Sophie. Parnell, Fran. 2013. (Monster Stories Ser.: 6). 48p. (J). (gr. 1-4). pap. 8.99 *(978-1-84686-910-5(2))* Barefoot Bks., Inc.

—Here We Go Round the Mulberry Bush. Fatus, Sophie. Penner, Fred. 2007. (ENG.). 24p. (J). (gr. -1-2). 16.99 *(978-1-84686-035-5(0))* Barefoot Bks., Inc.

—If You're Happy & You Know It! Fatus, Sophie. McQuinn, Anna. 2011. 24p. (J). (gr. -1-2). 9.99 *(978-1-84686-619-7(7))* Barefoot Bks., Inc.

—Journey Home from Grandpa's. Fatus, Sophie. 2012. (J). (gr. -1-1). 14.99 *(978-1-84686-745-3(2))* Barefoot Bks., Inc.

—My Big Barefoot Book of Wonderful Words. Fatus, Sophie. Barefoot Books. 2014. 48p. (J). (gr. -1-1). 19.99 *(978-1-78285-092-2(9))* Barefoot Bks., Inc.

—The Real Princess. Fatus, Sophie. Williams, Brenda. 2009. 40p. (J). (gr. k-4). 10.99 *(978-1-84686-393-6(7))* Barefoot Bks., Inc.

—Rona Long-Teeth: A Story from Tahiti. Fatus, Sophie. Parnell, Fran. 2013. (Monster Stories Ser.: 5). 48p. (J). (gr. 1-5). pap. 8.99 *(978-1-84686-908-2(0))* Barefoot Bks., Inc.

—Yoga Pretzels: 50 Fun Yoga Activities for Kids & Grownups. Fatus, Sophie. Kalish, Leah & Guber, Tara. 2005. (ENG.). 50p. (J). (gr. k-5). 14.99 *(978-1-905236-04-6(2))* Barefoot Bks., Inc.

Fatus, Sophie, jt. illus. see Bell, Siobhan.

Faucher, Marilyn. All the Little Fathers. Brown, Margaret Wise. (Margaret Wise Brown Classics Ser.). (ENG.). (J). (gr. -1-k). 2020. 28p. bds. 7.99 *(978-1-68412-968-3(0))*; 2019. 32p. 12.99 *(978-1-68412-750-4(5))* Printers Row Publishing Group. (Silver Dolphin Bks.).

—My Bright Friend. Boulerice, Simon. 2019. Orig. Title: Un Ami Lumineux. (ENG.). 32p. (J). (gr. -1-k). 19.95 *(978-1-4598-2189-7(0))* Orca Bk. Pubs. USA.

Faucher, Marylin. Animals Do, Too! How They Behave Just Like You. Kaner, Etta. 2017. (ENG.). 32p. (J). (gr. -1-2). 16.95 *(978-1-77138-569-5(3))* Kids Can Pr., Ltd. CAN. Dist: Hachette Bk. Group.

Faucher, Wayne. Rogue War. Johns, Geoff. rev. ed. 2006. (Flash (DC Comics) Ser.). (ENG.). 208p. (YA). pap. 17.99 *(978-1-4012-0924-7(6))* DC Comics.

Faul, Tara, jt. illus. see Lamoureux, Hampton.

Faulkner, Keith, et al. Time's Up! Faulkner, Keith & Tyger, Rory. 2003. (J). *(978-0-439-56155-6(8))* Scholastic, Inc.

Faulkner, Keith & Holmes, Stephen. Animal ? Math. Faulkner, Keith & Holmes, Stephen. 2003. (J). *(978-0-439-62755-9(9))* Scholastic, Inc.

Faulkner, Matt. Because I Could Not Stop My Bike: And Other Poems. Shapiro, Karen Jo. 2005. 32p. (J). (gr. 2-5). pap. 7.95 *(978-1-58089-105-9(5))* Charlesbridge Publishing, Inc.

—Don't Know Much about American History. Davis, Kenneth C. 2003. (Don't Know Much About Ser.). (ENG.). 224p. (J). (gr. 3-7). pap. 6.99 *(978-0-06-440836-3(1))* HarperCollins Pubs.

—Elizabeth Started All the Trouble. Rappaport, Doreen. 2016. (ENG.). 40p. (J). (gr. -1-3). 17.99 *(978-0-7868-5142-3(2))* Disney Pr.

—Groundhog's Dilemma. Remenar, Kristen. 2015. 32p. (J). (gr. -1-2). lib. bdg. 17.99 *(978-1-58089-600-9(6))* Charlesbridge Publishing, Inc.

—Independent Dames: What You Never Knew about the Women & Girls of the American Revolution. Anderson, Laurie Halse. 2008. (ENG.). 40p. (J). (gr. 1-5). 18.99 *(978-0-689-85808-6(6),* Simon & Schuster Bks. For Young Readers) Simon & Schuster Bks. For Young Readers.

—The Monster Who Ate My Peas, 1 vol. Schnitzlein, Danny. 2010. (ENG.). 32p. (J). pap. 7.95 *(978-1-56145-533-1(4))* Peachtree Publishing Co. Inc.

—The Night Henry Ford Met Santa. Hagen, Carol L. 2006. (ENG.). 32p. (J). (gr. k-6). 17.95 *(978-1-58536-132-8(1))* Sleeping Bear Pr.

—Stand Tall, Abe Lincoln. St. George, Judith. 2015. (ENG.). 48p. (J). (gr. 2-4). 8.99 *(978-0-14-751447-9(9),* Puffin Books) Penguin Young Readers Group.

—Thank You, Sarah: The Woman Who Saved Thanksgiving. Anderson, Laurie Halse. 2005. (ENG.). 40p. (J). (gr. k-3). 7.99 *(978-0-689-85143-8(X),* Simon & Schuster Bks. For Young Readers) Simon & Schuster Bks. For Young Readers.

—Trick or Treat on Monster Treat, 1 vol. Schnitzlein, Danny. 2008. (ENG.). 32p. (J). (gr. k-3). 16.95 *(978-1-56145-465-5(6))* Peachtree Publishing Co. Inc.

—What's the Big Deal about Americans. Shamir, Ruby. (J). 2020. 64p. (gr. 1-4). 5.99 *(978-0-593-11636-4(4))*; 2020. 64p. (gr. 1-4). 13.99 *(978-0-593-11639-5(9))*; 2019. (What's the Big Deal About Ser.: 4). 32p. (gr. -1-3). 17.99 *(978-1-5247-3803-7(4))* Penguin Young Readers Group. (Philomel Bks.).

Faulkner, Matt. What's the Big Deal about Elections. Shamir, Ruby. (J). 2020. 64p. (gr. 1-4). 5.99 ***(978-0-593-11640-1(2))***; 2020. 64p. (gr. 1-4). 13.99 ***(978-0-593-11643-2(7))***; 2018. 32p. (gr. -1-3). 17.99 *(978-1-5247-3807-5(7))* Penguin Young Readers Group. (Philomel Bks.).

Faulkner, Matt. What's the Big Deal about First Ladies. Shamir, Ruby. (What's the Big Deal About Ser.). (J). 2020. 64p. (gr. 1-4). 5.99 *(978-0-593-11483-4(3))*; 2020. 64p. (gr. 1-4). 13.99 *(978-0-593-11486-5(8))*; 2017. 32p. (gr. -1-3). 17.99 *(978-0-399-54724-9(X))* Penguin Young Readers Group. (Philomel Bks.).

—What's the Big Deal about Freedom. Shamir, Ruby. (What's the Big Deal About Ser.). (J). 2020. 64p. (gr. 1-4). 5.99 *(978-0-593-11487-2(6))*; 2020. 64p. (gr. 1-4). 13.99 *(978-0-593-11490-2(6))*; 2017. 32p. (gr. -1-3). 17.99 *(978-0-399-54728-7(2))* Penguin Young Readers Group. (Philomel Bks.).

Faulkner, Matt. A Taste of Colored Water. Faulkner, Matt. 2008. (ENG.). 48p. (J). (gr. 1-3). 18.99 *(978-1-4169-1629-1(6),* Simon & Schuster Bks. For Young Readers) Simon & Schuster Bks. For Young Readers.

Faulkner, Matt & Bunting, Matt. S Is for Shamrock: An Ireland Alphabet. Bunting, Eve. rev. ed. 2007. (Discover the World Ser.). (ENG.). 40p. (J). (gr. -1-3). 17.95 *(978-1-58536-290-5(5))* Sleeping Bear Pr.

Faure, Florence. Geronimo, 1 vol. Spilsbury, Richard. 2013. (Hero Journals). (ENG.). 48p. (J). (gr. 4-6). pap. 9.95 *(978-1-4109-5367-4(X),* Raintree) Capstone.

Fausone, Flavio, jt. illus. see Ferrario, Giuseppe.

Faust Kalscheur, Jann, photos by. ABC's Naturally: A Child's Guide to the Alphabet Through Nature. Faust Kalscheur, Jann. Smith, Lynn. 2003. (J). 16.95 *(978-1-931599-27-6(0),* Trails Bks.) Bower Hse.

Faust, Laurie. A New Home for Honey. 2006. (Adventures of Honey Ser.). (J). pap. 9.95 *(978-0-9789227-0-2(0))* Weeping Willow Publishing.

—Pinky's Rainy Day: Pinky Padooka takes a trip to Imaginationville. Damschroder, Scott. 2004. 36p. (J). lib. bdg. 19.95 *(978-0-9754728-0-4(1))* Big Ransom Studio.

—Small Dog, Small Dog, Small, Small, Dog. Damschroder, Scott. 2004. 24p. (J). lib. bdg. 19.95 *(978-0-9754728-2-8(8))* Big Ransom Studio.

Faust, Laurie A. Cow Cake. Solomon, Michelle & Pereira, Lavinia. 2009. (ENG.). 26p. pap. 10.96 *(978-1-4251-8951-8(2))* Trafford Publishing.

—The Day the Trash Came Out to Play. Beadle, David M. 2004. 32p. (J). 16.95 *(978-0-9727855-0-1(7))* Ezra's Earth Publishing.

—Honey's Peanut Butter Adventure. Greer, Tom C. 2007. (Adventures of Honey Ser.). (J). pap. 9.95 *(978-0-9789227-1-9(9))* Weeping Willow Publishing.

—The Magical Tree & Musical Wind. The Library Fairy. 2008. 32p. pap. 16.95 *(978-1-59858-604-6(1))* Dog Ear Publishing, LLC.

—Too Big! Solomon, Michelle & Pereira, Lavinia. 2009. 24p. pap. 10.96 *(978-1-4251-8949-5(0))* Trafford Publishing.

—Uh - Oh! Solomon, Michelle & Pereira, Lavinia. 2009. (ENG.). 26p. pap. 10.96 *(978-1-4251-8950-1(4))* Trafford Publishing.

—Why Is Mommy Sad? A Child's Guide to Parental Depression. Chan, Paul D. 2006. 12p. (J). pap. 6.99 *(978-1-929622-71-9(6))* Current Clinical Strategies Publishing.

Fautsch, Jackie. Catie Corn & the Corn Cops. Watson, Gayle. l.t. ed. 22p. (J). 2006. 15.99 *(978-1-59879-098-6(6))*; 2005. per. 9.99 *(978-1-59879-079-5(X))* Lifevest Publishing, Inc.

Fauvel, Claire. Catherine's War. Billet, Julia. Hahnenberger, Ivanka, tr. 2020. (ENG.). 176p. (J). (gr. 3-7). 21.99 *(978-0-06-291560-3(6))*; pap. 12.99 *(978-0-06-291559-7(2))* HarperCollins Pubs.

Favereau, Beatrice. Christmas with Norky the Adventure Begins... Algeier, Steve. 2007. (ENG.). 36p. (J). 17.99 *(978-0-9769209-0-8(5))* NORKY AMERICA.

Favreau, Luc. Los Volcanes, Montañas Vivientes / Volcanoes: Living Mountains. Krafft, Maurice. 2018. (Altea Benjamín Ser.). (SPA.). 32p. (J). (gr. 3-7). pap. 10.99 *(978-1-947783-59-1(9),* Altea) Penguin Random House Grupo Editorial ESP. Dist: Penguin Random Hse. LLC.

Favreau, Marie-Claude. Un Dromadaire Chez Marilou Polaire. Plante, Raymond. 2003. (Premier Roman Ser.). (FRE.). 64p. (J). (gr. 1-4). pap. *(978-2-89021-608-2(X))* Diffusion du livre Mirabel (DLM).

—Le Grand Role de Marilou Polaire. Plante, Raymond. 2003. (Premier Roman Ser.). (FRE.). 64p. (J). (gr. 2-5). pap. *(978-2-89021-288-6(2))* Diffusion du livre Mirabel (DLM).

—Marilou Forecasts the Future, 1 vol. Plante, Raymond. Cummins, Sarah, tr. 2003. (Formac First Novels Ser.: 49). (ENG.). 64p. (J). (gr. 1-5). 4.95 *(978-0-88780-614-8(7),* 614); (gr. 2-5). 14.95 *(978-0-88780-615-5(5),* 615) Formac Publishing Co., Ltd. CAN. Dist: Formac Lorimer Bks. Ltd.

—Marilou Keeps a Camel. Plante, Raymond. 2004. 61p. (J). lib. bdg. 12.00 *(978-1-4242-1232-3(4))* Fitzgerald Bks.

—Marilou Keeps a Camel, 1 vol. Plante, Raymond. Cummins, Sarah, tr. 2004. (Formac First Novels Ser.: 50). (ENG.). 64p. (J). (gr. 1-5). 4.95 *(978-0-88780-634-6(1),* 634); 14.95 *(978-0-88780-635-3(X),* 635) Formac Publishing Co., Ltd. CAN. Dist: Formac Lorimer Bks. Ltd.

—Otis & Alice, 1 vol. Bertouille, Ariane. 2013. (ENG.). 32p. (J). (gr. -1-k). 18.95 *(978-1-55455-294-8(X),* ee91b326-3b75-46b6-b640-7e73fcb25770) Trifolium Bks., Inc. CAN. Dist: Firefly Bks., Ltd.

Fawcett, Vicki. My Arctic Circle of Friends. Belair, Brenda Brousseau, photos by. Doupe, Pauline Wood. 2009. 24p. pap. 16.98 *(978-1-4251-8097-3(3))* Trafford Publishing.

Fawkes, Glynnis. Charlotte Brontë Before Jane Eyre. Fawkes, Glynnis. 2019. (Center for Cartoon Studies Presents Ser.). 112p. (J). (gr. 5-9). 17.99 ***(978-1-368-02329-0(0))***; pap. 12.99 ***(978-1-368-04582-7(0))*** Little, Brown Bks. for Young Readers.

Fay. The Collective Coffin. Nya. 2014. (ENG.). 36p. (J). pap. 11.99 *(978-0-9894691-5-9(8))* Happy Woods Pr.

—The Colossal Club. Nya. 2014. (ENG.). 36p. (J). pap. 11.99 *(978-0-9894691-4-2(X))* Happy Woods Pr.

—A Hazardous Holiday. Nya. 2014. (ENG.). 36p. (J). pap. 11.99 *(978-0-9894691-7-3(4))* Happy Woods Pr.

—A Muddy Mess. Nya. 2014. (ENG.). 36p. (J). pap. 11.99 *(978-0-9894691-6-6(6))* Happy Woods Pr.

Fay, Claire. L' Anti-Livre de Lecture. Brami, Elisabeth. 2008. (A. M. Divers Ser.). (FRE.). (J). *(978-2-226-17768-1(X))* Albin-Michel, Editions.

Fay, Claire. Color, Snap, App! My First Animated Coloring Book. Fay, Claire. 2017. (ENG.). 32p. (J). (gr. k-4). pap. 9.99 *(978-0-7636-9347-3(2))* Candlewick Pr.

Faye, Jackson. Our Funny Dunny. Moncrieff, Celia. 2018. (ENG.). 34p. (J). (gr. k-6). pap. *(978-0-6483558-1-6(0))* Bobbin Bks.

—Twimble & Twomble. Moncrieff, Celia. 2019. (ENG.). 48p. (J). (gr. k-6). pap. *(978-0-6483559-7-7(7))* Bobbin Bks.

Fayolle, Diane & Benoit, Jérôme. The Planet of the Firebird, Bk. 2. Dorison, Guillaume et al. 2012. (Little Prince Ser.: 2). 56p. (J). (gr. 4-8). lib. bdg. 26.65 *(978-0-7613-8752-7(8),* 9780761387527, Graphic Universe™) Lerner Publishing Group.

Fazel, Vahid. Feelu: Explore Your Feelings. Shafiei, Niloufar. 2020. (ENG.). 50p. (J). ***(978-0-2288-2150-2(9))***; pap. ***(978-0-2288-2149-6(5))*** Tellwell Talent.

Fazio, Michael. The Remarkable David Wordsworth. Kopley, Richard. 2013. 30p. (J). pap. *(978-1-936172-67-2(4))* Eifrig Publishing.

Fazlalizadeh, Tatyana. Libba: The Magnificent Musical Life of Elizabeth Cotten. Veirs, Laura. 2018. (ENG.). 48p. (J). (gr. k-3). 17.99 *(978-1-4521-4857-1(0))* Chronicle Bks. LLC.

Feagan, Alice. School Days Around the World. Ruurs, Margriet. (ENG.). 40p. (J). 2020. pap. 8.99 ***(978-1-5253-0560-3(3))***; 2015. (gr. -1-2). 18.95 *(978-1-77138-047-8(0))* Kids Can Pr., Ltd. CAN. Dist: Hachette Bk. Group.

Feagin, Renwick Paul. Life Lessons for Youth: How to Avoid the Pitfalls of Making Bad Choices. Johnson Jr, Victor. 2018. (ENG.). 64p. (J). pap. 14.99 *(978-1-7268-4427-7(7))* Independently Published.

Fearing, Mark. Ben Franklin's in My Bathroom! Fleming, Candace. 2017. (History Pals Ser.). (ENG.). 272p. (J). (gr. 2-5). 13.99 *(978-1-101-93406-7(9))*; lib. bdg. 16.99 *(978-1-101-93407-4(7))* Random Hse. Children's Bks. (Schwartz & Wade Bks.).

—The Book That Eats People. Perry, John. 2009. 38p. (J). (gr. -1-2). 16.99 *(978-1-58246-268-4(2),* Tricycle Pr.) Random Hse. Children's Bks.

—Chicken Story Time. Asher, Sandy. 2016. (ENG.). 40p. (J). (-k). 17.99 *(978-0-8037-3944-4(3),* Dial Bks) Penguin Young Readers Group.

—Eleanor Roosevelt's in My Garage! Fleming, Candace. 2018. (History Pals Ser.). (ENG.). 336p. (J). (gr. 2-5). 13.99 *(978-1-5247-6786-0(7))*; lib. bdg. 16.99 *(978-1-5247-6787-7(5))* Random Hse. Children's Bks. (Schwartz & Wade Bks.).

—The Frightful Ride of Michael Mcmichael. Becker, Bonny. 2018. 32p. (J). (gr. -1-3). 16.99 *(978-0-7636-8150-0(4))* Candlewick Pr.

—Great, Now We've Got Barbarians! Eaton, Jason Carter. 2017. 40p. (J). (gr. -1-3). 16.99 *(978-0-7636-6827-3(3))* Candlewick Pr.

—How Martha Saved Her Parents from Green Beans. LaRochelle, David. 2013. (ENG.). 32p. (J). (gr. k-3). 16.99 *(978-0-8037-3766-2(1),* Dial Bks) Penguin Young Readers Group.

—Middle School Bites. Banks, Steven. 2020. (Middle School Bites Ser.: 1). 304p. (J). (gr. 3-7). 13.99 *(978-0-8234-4543-1(7))* Holiday Hse., Inc.

Fearing, Mark. Middle School Bites: Tom Bites Back. Banks, Steven. 2020. (Middle School Bites Ser.: 2). 304p. (J). (gr. 3-7). 13.99 ***(978-0-8234-4615-5(8))*** Holiday Hse., Inc.

Fearing, Mark. Superhero Instruction Manual. Dempsey, Kristy. 2016. 40p. (J). (gr. k-3). 16.99 *(978-0-385-75534-4(1),* Knopf Bks. for Young Readers) Random Hse. Children's Bks.

—The Three Little Aliens & the Big Bad Robot. McNamara, Margaret. 2011. (ENG.). 40p. (J). (gr. -1-3). 16.99 *(978-0-375-86689-0(2),* Schwartz & Wade Bks.) Random Hse. Children's Bks.

—The Three Little Aliens & the Big Bad Robot. McNamara, Margaret. 2018. (ENG.). 36p. (J). (-k). bds. 8.99 *(978-0-525-57885-7(4),* Schwartz & Wade Bks.) Random Hse. Children's Bks.

—A Very Witchy Spelling Bee. Shannon, George. 2013. (ENG.). 32p. (J). (gr. -1-3). 16.99 *(978-0-15-206696-3(9),* 1199789) Houghton Mifflin Harcourt Publishing Co.

Fearing, Mark. Giant Pants. Fearing, Mark. 2017. 40p. (J). (gr. -1-2). 16.99 *(978-0-7636-8984-1(X))* Candlewick Pr.

—The Great Thanksgiving Escape. Fearing, Mark. 32p. (J). (gr. k-3). 2017. 6.99 *(978-0-7636-9511-8(4))*; 2014. 15.99 *(978-0-7636-6306-3(9))* Candlewick Pr.

Fearn, Katrina. Christmas fairy things to make & Do. Gilpin, Rebecca. 2004. 34p. (J). pap. 6.95 *(978-0-7945-0835-7(9),* Usborne) EDC Publishing.

—The Usborne Big Book of Christmas Things to Make & Do. Watt, Fiona & Gilpin, Rebecca. 2005. 99p. (J). *(978-0-439-81506-2(1))* Scholastic, Inc.

Fearn, Katrina. First Dot-To-Dot Dinosaurs. Fearn, Katrina, des. ed. 2013. (First Dot-To-Dot Ser.). 16p. (J). pap. 5.99 *(978-0-7945-3341-0(8),* Usborne) EDC Publishing.

—First Dot-To-Dot Pirates. Fearn, Katrina, des. ed. 2013. (First Dot-To-Dot Ser.). 16p. (J). pap. 5.99 *(978-0-7945-3393-9(0),* Usborne) EDC Publishing.

Fearn, Katrina & Hussain, Nelupa. Fairy Things to Stitch & Sew. Watt, Fiona. 2006. (Usborne Activities Ser.). 32p. (J). (gr. 1-4). pap. 6.99 *(978-0-7945-1235-4(6),* Usborne) EDC Publishing.

Fearnley, Jan. Never Too Little to Love. Willis, Jeanne. 2013. (ENG.). 32p. (J). (gr. -1-2). 9.99 *(978-0-7636-6656-9(4))* Candlewick Pr.

Fearnley, Jan. Billy Tibble Moves Out! Fearnley, Jan. 2006. 29p. (J). (gr. k-4). reprint ed. 16.00 *(978-1-4223-5557-2(8))* DIANE Publishing Co.

—Little Robin's Christmas. Fearnley, Jan. 2019. (ENG.). 32p. (J). (-k). 16.99 *(978-1-5362-0825-2(6),* Nosy Crow) Candlewick Pr.

—Mr Wolf & the Enormous Turnip. Fearnley, Jan. 2005. (ENG.). 40p. (J). (gr. k-2). pap. 10.99 *(978-1-4052-1580-0(1))* Egmont Bks., Ltd. GBR. Dist: Independent Pubs. Group.

Fearns, Georgie. Willow Tree Wood Book 2 - Little Deer & the Dragon. Betts, J. S. 2020. (Willow Tree Wood Ser.). (ENG.). 104p. (J). pap. 4.99 ***(978-1-78958-320-5(9))*** Willow Tree Bks. GBR. Dist: Independent Pubs. Group.

—Willow Tree Wood Book 3 - Little Squirrel & the Mermaid. Betts, J. S. 2020. (Willow Tree Wood Ser.: 3). (ENG.).

104p. (J). (gr. 2-4). 4.99 (978-1-78958-566-7(X)) Willow Tree Bks. GBR. Dist: Independent Pubs. Group.
—Willow Tree Wood Book 4 - Little Owl & the Unicorn. Betts, J. S. 2020. (Willow Tree Wood Ser.: 4). (ENG.). 104p. (J). pap. 4.99 (978-1-78958-632-9(1)) Willow Tree Bks. GBR. Dist: Independent Pubs. Group.
Fearns, Georgie. Dress up One Direction. Fearns, Georgie. Buster Books Staff. 2013. (ENG.). 34p. (J). (gr. 1-3). pap. 7.99 (978-1-78055-162-3(2)) O'Mara, Michael Bks., Ltd. GBR. Dist: Independent Pubs. Group.
Fearon, Merrill. Canadian Poems for Canadian Kids. Hamilton, Jen, ed. 2005. (ENG.). 64p. pap. 14.95 (978-0-9736675-0-9(8)) Subway Bks. CAN. Dist: Univ. of Toronto Pr.
Feazell, Matt. The Amazing Cynicalman, Vol. 2. Feazell, Matt. l.t. ed. 2013. 160p. (YA). pap. 14.95 (978-0-9744767-1-1(4), Not Available Books) Not Available Comics.
Febirana, Putri. On the Plane Activity Book: Includes Puzzles, Mazes, Dot-To-dots & Drawing Activities. Alexander, Heather. 2019. (ENG.). 64p. (J). (gr. -1-1). pap. 12.99 (978-1-78240-740-9(5), Ivy Kids) Ivy Group, The GBR. Dist: Hachette Bk. Group.
Fecchi, Massimo, jt. illus. see Cavazzano, Giorgio.
Fedatova, Marina. The 12 Elves: A New Christmas Tradition. 2010. (ENG.). 18p. (J). (gr. -1-k). bds. 12.99 (978-1-4424-1684-0(X), Little Simon) Little Simon.
Fedele, Chiara. The Brave Cyclist: The True Story of A Holocaust Hero. Hoffman, Amalia. 2019. (ENG.). 40p. (J). (gr. 3-4). lib. bdg. 17.95 (978-1-68446-063-2(8), 140522, Capstone Editions) Capstone.
—A Fall Ball for All. Swenson, Jamie A. 2018. (ENG.). 32p. (J). (gr. k-2). 19.99 (978-1-5124-9803-5(3), Millbrook Pr.) Lerner Publishing Group.
—When Rosa Parks Went Fishing. Ruiz, Rachel. 2017. (Leaders Doing Headstands Ser.). (ENG.). 32p. (J). (gr. 1-4). lib. bdg. 28.65 (978-1-5158-1574-7(9), 136244, Picture Window Bks.) Capstone.
—Yaffa & Fatima: Shalom, Salaam. Gilani-Williams, Fawzia. 2017. (ENG.). 24p. (J). (gr. -1-3). 17.99 (978-1-4677-8938-7(0), 9781467789387, Kar-Ben Publishing) Lerner Publishing Group.
Federman, Cassandra. This Is a Sea Cow. Federman, Cassandra. 2019. (ENG.). 32p. (J). (gr. -1-3). 16.99 (978-0-8075-7874-2(6), 807578746) Whitman, Albert & Co.
Federman, Cassandra. This Is a Seahorse. Federman, Cassandra. 2020. (ENG.). 32p. (J). (gr. -1-4). 16.99 (978-0-8075-7860-5(6), 0807578606) Whitman, Albert & Co.
Fedhar. Como Dibujar Personajes Magicos. Fedhar. 2003. (SPA.). 160p. (J). (gr. 4-8). pap. (978-987-550-281-9(2)) Longseller S.A. ARG. Dist: Bilingual Pubns. Co., The.
Fedigan-Linton, Katherine V. Electrum. Froimowitz, Michael P. 2003. 44p. 5.00 (978-0-9717796-2-4(7), Mystic Night Bks.) Pink Stucco Pr.
Fedorava, Marianna. Deeper & Deeper (Tetun Edition) - Nani Iha Tasi. Rumbam, Stella. 2020. (TET.). 26p. (J). pap. (978-1-922331-53-3(8)) Library For All Limited.
Fedorov, Valentin. Moscow Ballet Great Russian Nutcracker. Herman, Mark & Apter, Ronnie, trs. from RUS. 2003. 32p. (J). (978-0-9743082-0-3(X)) Sports Marketing International, Inc.
Fedotova, Marina. Who's My Cupcake? Guest, Elissa Haden. 2011. (ENG.). 16p. (J). (gr. -1 — 1). bds. 6.99 (978-1-4424-2051-9(0), Little Simon) Little Simon.
Fee, Jim. Bad Fads. Long, Mark A. 2005. 119p. (YA). reprint ed. pap. 24.00 (978-0-7567-9409-5(9)) DIANE Publishing Co.
Feek, Cathy. The Oglin: A Hero's Journey Across Africa... Towards the Tomorrows. Richardson, Dick. 2004. 417p. (J). 24.95 (978-0-9759440-3-5(7)) Savanna Pr.
Feelings, Tom. Moja Means One: A Swahili Counting Book. Feelings, Muriel L. 2004. 20p. (J). (gr. k-4). reprint ed. pap. 5.00 (978-0-7567-7108-9(0)) DIANE Publishing Co.
—To Be a Slave. Lester, Julius. 2005. (Puffin Modern Classics Ser.). (ENG.). 176p. (J). (gr. 3-7). 7.99 (978-0-14-240386-0(5), Puffin Books) Penguin Young Readers Group.
Feeney, Betsy Franco. Amoeba Hop. Lavin, Christine. 2003. 36p. (J). (gr. 2-3). 19.95 incl. audio compact disk (978-0-9726487-4-5(7)) Puddle Jump Pr., Ltd.
Feeney, Siri Weber. Sequoyah & His Talking Leaves: A Play about the Cherokee Syllabary. Coleman, Wim & Perrin, Pat. 2014. (Setting the Stage for Fluency Ser.). (ENG.). 40p. (J). (gr. 3-5). pap. 8.99 (978-1-939656-35-3(4)) Red Chair Pr.
—Suffrage Sisters: The Fight for Liberty. Mead, Maggie. 2015. (Setting the Stage for Fluency Ser.). (ENG.). 40p. (J). (gr. 3-5). lib. bdg. 27.99 (978-1-939656-68-1(0)) Red Chair Pr.
Feeney, Tatyana. Snobby Cat. Deeley, Patrick. 2005. (Pandas Ser.: 32). (ENG.). 64p. (J). pap. 11.00 (978-0-86278-946-6(X)) O'Brien Pr., Ltd., The IRL. Dist: Dufour Editions, Inc.
Feezell, Karis. Asylum. Whitener, K. R. & Marsh, H. G. 2018. (ENG.). 268p. (J). pap. 10.99 (978-1-9777-8289-2(2)) CreateSpace Independent Publishing Platform.
Feher, Joseph & Kane, Herb K. Hawai'i. 2010. (ENG.). 72p. pap. (978-1-59700-839-6(7)) Island Heritage Publishing.
Fehlau, Dagmar, et al. Mother Goose & Her Animal Friends. Hopkins, Lee Bennett. 2005. (Lee Bennett Hopkins Mother Goose Ser.). (YA). (gr. -1-1). 76.50 (978-0-8215-0470-3(3)) Sadlier, William H. Inc.
—Mother Goose & Her Children. Hopkins, Lee Bennett. 2005. (Lee Bennett Hopkins Mother Goose Ser.). (YA). (gr. -1-1). 76.50 (978-0-8215-0460-4(6)) Sadlier, William H. Inc.
—Mother Goose Around the World. Hopkins, Lee Bennett. 2005. (Lee Bennett Hopkins Mother Goose Ser.). (YA). (gr. -1-1). 76.50 (978-0-8215-0490-1(8)); suppl. ed. 57.00 (978-0-8215-0494-9(0)) Sadlier, William H. Inc.
—Mother Goose Through the Seasons. Hopkins, Lee Bennett. 2005. (Lee Bennett Hopkins Mother Goose Ser.). (YA). (gr. -1-1). 76.50 (978-0-8215-0480-2(0)) Sadlier, William H. Inc.
Fehlau, Dagmar. My Robot. Bunting, Eve. 2006. (Green Light Readers Level 2 Ser.). (ENG.). 24p. (J). (gr. -1-3). pap. 3.95 (978-0-15-205617-9(3), 1196894) Houghton Mifflin Harcourt Publishing Co.
—My Robot. Bunting, Eve. 2006. (Green Light Readers Level 2 Ser.). (gr. k-2). lib. bdg. 13.95 (978-0-7569-7211-0(6)) Perfection Learning Corp.
—Snowbear's Winter Day: A Winter Wonder Book. DePrisco, Dorothea. 2005. 18p. (J). (gr. -1). 9.95 (978-1-58117-133-4(1), Intervisual/Piggy Toes) Bendon, Inc.
Fehling, Leslie. What Would You Do? A Kid's Guide to Staying Safe in a World of Strangers. Ridenour, Melissa Harker. 2011. (J). (978-0-938467-11-3(5)) Headline Bks., Inc.
Fehr, Molly. My Jolly Christmas. Herrera, Mariana. 2020. (My Little Holiday Ser.). 18p. (J). (gr. -1 — 1). bds. 7.99 (978-0-06-291599-3(1), HarperFestival) HarperCollins Pubs.
—My Spooky Halloween. Herrera, Mariana. 2020. (My Little Holiday Ser.). 18p. (J). (gr. -1 — 1). bds. 7.99 (978-0-06-291598-6(3), HarperFestival) HarperCollins Pubs.
Fehrl, Kathrin. Hop. Garnett, Jaye. Cottage Door Press, ed. 2019. (Peek-A-Flap Board Book Ser.). (ENG.). 12p. (J). (gr. -1-1). bds. 8.99 (978-1-68052-779-7(7), 1005020) Cottage Door Pr.
Fehrl, Kathrin. A Little Unicorn. Puffinton, Brick. Cottage Door Press, ed. 2020. (Finger Puppet Board Book Ser.). (ENG.). 12p. (J). (gr. -1 — 1). bds. 6.99 (978-1-68052-933-3(1), 1005750) Cottage Door Pr.
Fehrl, Kathrin. Somebunny Loves You: Large Little Bird Greetings. Birdsong, Minnie. Cottage Door Press, ed. 2018. (Little Bird Greetings Keepsake Book Ser.). (ENG.). 10p. (J). (gr. -1-2). bds. 6.99 (978-1-68052-379-9(1), 1003440) Cottage Door Pr.
—Somebunny Loves You: Little Bird Greetings. Birdsong, Minnie. Cottage Door Press, ed. 2019. (ENG.). 8p. (J). (gr. -1-k). bds. 6.99 (978-1-68052-479-6(8), 1003600) Cottage Door Pr.
Fei, Shen. The Crushing Crystals. Dahl, Michael. 2019. (Escape from Planet Alcatraz Ser.). (ENG.). 40p. (J). (gr. 3-6). lib. bdg. 23.99 (978-1-4965-8316-1(7), 140491, Stone Arch Bks.) Capstone.
—Flaming Fields of Death. Dahl, Michael. 2019. (Escape from Planet Alcatraz Ser.). (ENG.). 40p. (J). (gr. 3-6). lib. bdg. 23.99 (978-1-4965-8313-0(2), 140488, Stone Arch Bks.) Capstone.
—Prisoners of the Poison Sea. Dahl, Michael. 2019. (Escape from Planet Alcatraz Ser.). (ENG.). 40p. (J). (gr. 3-6). lib. bdg. 23.99 (978-1-4965-8312-3(4), 140487, Stone Arch Bks.) Capstone.
Fei, Shen, jt. illus. see Clarey, Patricio.
Fei, Wang, jt. illus. see Louis, Catherine.
Feiffer, Jules. The Annotated Phantom Tollbooth. Juster, Norton. 2011. (ENG.). 320p. (J). (gr. 3-7). 29.99 (978-0-375-85715-7(X), Knopf Bks. for Young Readers) Random Hse. Children's Bks.
—The Birthday Ball. Lois, Lowry. 2011. 192p. (J). (gr. 4-6). 21.19 (978-0-547-23869-2(X)); (ENG.). (gr. 5-7). pap. 7.99 (978-0-547-57710-4(9), 1458458) Houghton Mifflin Harcourt Publishing Co.
—Henry the Dog with No Tail. Feiffer, Kate. 2007. (ENG.). 32p. (J). (gr. -1-3). 19.99 (978-1-4169-1614-7(8), Simon & Schuster/Paula Wiseman Bks.) Simon & Schuster/Paula Wiseman Bks.
—Jacob's Eye Patch. Shaw, Jacob & Kobliner, Beth. 2013. (ENG.). 32p. 17.00 (978-1-4767-3732-4(0)) Simon & Schuster.
—My Side of the Car. Feiffer, Kate. 2011. (ENG.). 32p. (J). (gr. -1-3). 16.99 (978-0-7636-4405-5(6)) Candlewick Pr.
—No Go Sleep! Feiffer, Kate. 2012. (ENG.). 32p. (J). (gr. -1-2). 16.99 (978-1-4424-1683-3(1), Simon & Schuster/Paula Wiseman Bks.) Simon & Schuster/Paula Wiseman Bks.
—The Odious Ogre. Juster, Norton. 2010. 32p. (J). (gr. -1-2). 17.95 (978-0-545-16202-9(5), Di Capua, Michael) Scholastic, Inc.
—The Phantom Tollbooth. Juster, Norton. 2004. (ENG.). 255p. (J). (gr. 1). pap. 16.40 (978-0-618-43624-8(3)) Houghton Mifflin Harcourt Trade & Reference Pubs.
—The Phantom Tollbooth. Juster, Norton. 2003. (J). mass mkt. 5.99 (978-0-440-23808-9(0), Laurel) Random House Publishing Group.
—The Phantom Tollbooth. Juster, Norton. 256p. (J). pap. 4.99 (978-0-8072-1400-8(0), Listening Library) Random Hse. Audio Publishing Group.
—Some Things Are Scary. Heide, Florence Parry. 2011. (ENG.). 40p. (J). (gr. -1-2). pap. 8.99 (978-0-7636-5590-7(2)) Candlewick Pr.
—Which Puppy? Feiffer, Kate. 2009. (ENG.). 32p. (J). (gr. -1-3). 16.99 (978-1-4169-9147-2(6), Simon & Schuster/Paula Wiseman Bks.) Simon & Schuster/Paula Wiseman Bks.
Feiffer, Jules. The House Across the Street. Feiffer, Jules. 2003. 28p. (J). (gr. 1-4). reprint ed. 16.00 (978-0-7567-6845-4(4)) DIANE Publishing Co.
—I'm Not Bobby! Feiffer, Jules. 2006. 28p. (J). (gr. k-4). reprint ed. 16.00 (978-0-7567-9853-6(1)) DIANE Publishing Co.
—A Room with a Zoo. Feiffer, Jules. (ENG.). 192p. (gr. 2-7). 2007. per. 7.99 (978-0-7868-3703-8(9)); 2005. 16.95 (978-0-7868-3702-1(0)) Hyperion Bks. for Children. (di Capua, Michael Bks.).
—Rupert Can Dance. Feiffer, Jules. 2014. (ENG.). 32p. (J). (gr. -1-1). 17.95 (978-0-374-36363-5(3), 9780374363635, Farrar, Straus & Giroux (BYR)) Farrar, Straus & Giroux.
—Smart George. Feiffer, Jules. 2020. 40p. (J). (gr. -1-3). 17.99 (978-0-06-279099-6(4), HarperCollins) HarperCollins Pubs. Ltd. GBR. Dist: HarperCollins Pubs.
Feiffer, Jules, jt. illus. see Chast, Roz.
Feil, Denise J. Praze B. a Growing, Loving Day: Forgiveness & Responsibility. Feil, Denise J. 2004. (J). per. 5.50 (978-0-9741588-0-8(1)) Feil.
Fein, Sheila. Mama Graciela's Secret Dyslexic Edition: Dyslexic Font. Calvani, Mayra. 2017. (ENG.). 34p. (J). (gr. k-6). 19.99 (978-1-64372-258-0(1)); pap. 15.99 (978-1-64372-259-7(X)) MacLaren-Cochrane Publishing, Inc.
Feinberg, Betsy. Shorty's Christmas Present. Harold, Don. 2018. (ENG.). 84p. (J). (gr. k-6). pap. 13.95 (978-1-68454-986-3(8)) Primedia eLaunch LLC.
Feinberg, Betsy Hoyt. Gamer Giraffe's Birthday. Wesolowski, Mary Cay. 2018. (Gamer Giraffe Ser.: Vol. 2). (ENG.). 42p. (J). (gr. k-6). pap. 8.55 (978-1-945604-06-5(9)) Primedia eLaunch LLC.
Feinberg, Xeth. City of Hamburgers. Reiss, Mike. 2008. 32p. (J). 14.95 (978-1-59299-346-8(X)) Inkwater Pr.
Feiner, Beck. My First Jewish Baby Book: Almost Everything You Need to Know about Being Jewish — From Afikomen to Zayde. Merberg, Julie. 2018. (ENG.). 20p. (J). bds. 10.99 (978-1-941367-60-5(7)) Downtown Bookworks.
Feinman, Anthony, et al. Escape in a Dirigible: Or to Make the World Safe for Tea. Feinman, Myke, photos by. Feinman, Anthony & Hall, Andrew. 2004. (J). pap. (978-0-9664974-5-8(7)) Ink & Feathers Comics.
Feito, Luciana. The Nutcracker, 1 vol. 2020. (Stories of Christmas Ser.). (ENG.). 24p. (J). (gr. 1-2). lib. bdg. 24.60 (978-1-4994-8595-0(6)); pap. 8.25 (978-1-4994-8593-6(X)) Rosen Publishing Group, Inc., The. (Windmill Bks.).
Fekete, Hédi. Ashley Small & Ashlee Tall. Jakubowski, Michele. (Ashley Small & Ashlee Tall Ser.). (ENG.). 64p. (J). (gr. 1-3). 2017. pap., pap., pap. 19.80 (978-1-5158-0022-4(9), 24642); 2016. lib. bdg., lib. bdg., lib. bdg. 82.60 (978-1-5158-0021-7(0)) Capstone. (Picture Window Bks.).
—Best Friends Forever? Jakubowski, Michele. 2016. (Ashley Small & Ashlee Tall Ser.). (ENG.). 64p. (J). (gr. 1-3). lib. bdg. 20.65 (978-1-4795-9191-6(2), Picture Window Bks.) Capstone.
—Brushes & Basketballs. Jakubowski, Michele. 2016. (Ashley Small & Ashlee Tall Ser.). (ENG.). 64p. (J). (gr. 1-3). lib. bdg. 20.65 (978-1-5158-0010-1(5), Picture Window Bks.) Capstone.
—The Grass Is Always Greener. Jakubowski, Michele. (Ashley Small & Ashlee Tall Ser.). (ENG.). 64p. (J). (gr. 1-3). 2017. pap. 4.95 (978-1-5158-0016-3(4)); 2016. lib. bdg. 20.65 (978-1-5158-0012-5(1)) Capstone. (Picture Window Bks.).
—Sleepover. Jakubowski, Michele. (Ashley Small & Ashlee Tall Ser.). (ENG.). 64p. (J). (gr. 1-3). 2017. pap. 4.95 (978-1-5158-0015-6(6)); 2016. lib. bdg. 20.65 (978-1-5158-0011-8(3)) Capstone. (Picture Window Bks.).
Fekete, Lucy. A Dragon Called Wilbur: How a Fire-Breathing Dragon Made Friends. Heeney, Bronwyn. 2012. 40p. pap. 16.97 (978-1-61204-803-1(X), Strategic Bk. Publishing) Strategic Book Publishing & Rights Agency (SBPRA).
Feldman Emison, Chloë, jt. illus. see Emison, Patricia A.
Feldman, Kathryn J. Mission to Space. Gross, Jamie Feldman. 2019. (Adventures of Emily Ser.: Vol. 3). (ENG.). 44p. (J). pap. 11.00 (978-1-0792-2943-1(4)) Independently Published.
Feldman, Luke. Beauty & the Beast: The Graphic Novel, 1 vol. Stone Arch Books Staff. 2008. (Graphic Spin Ser.). (ENG.). 40p. (J). (gr. 3-6). pap. 5.95 (978-1-4342-0861-3(3), Stone Arch Bks.) Capstone.
—La Bella y la Bestia: La Novela Grafica, 1 vol. Andersen, Hans & Stone Arch Books Staff. 2010. (Graphic Spin en Español Ser.). (SPA.). 40p. (J). (gr. 3-6). pap. 5.95 (978-1-4342-2269-5(1), Stone Arch Bks.) Capstone.
—La Bella y la Bestia: La Novela Grafica. Andersen, Hans & Capstone Press Editors. 2010. (Graphic Spin en Español Ser.). (SPA.). 40p. (J). (gr. 3-6). lib. bdg. 25.32 (978-1-4342-1899-5(6), Stone Arch Bks.) Capstone.
—Chaff n' Skaffs: Mai & the Lost Moskivvy. Chin, Amanda. 2009. (ENG.). 36p. (J). (gr. -1-3). 15.95 (978-1-59702-013-8(3)) Immedium.
—Pet's Playground: Playing Safe in a Dog-And-Cat World. Chin, Amanda. 2009. 104p. (J). pap. 11.95 (978-1-58326-115-6(X)) American Animal Hospital Assn. Pr.
Feldmeier Sims, Julie & Hartman, John. Oscar's First Flight. Zimmerman, Kathleen. 2005. 44p. (J). per. 16.95 (978-0-9744330-0-4(4)) Kat Tales Publishing.
Feliciano, Jose. La Sopa. Lindeen, Mary. 2016. (Early Rising Readers Ser.). (SPA.). 16p. (J). (gr. 1-1). 6.67 (978-1-4788-4211-8(3)) Newmark Learning LLC.
Feliciano, Misti. Grandpa's Christmas Tree Story. Zoldak, J. William. 2019. (ENG.). 24p. (J). 22.00 (978-1-948018-61-6(6)); pap. 10.00 (978-1-948018-48-7(9)) Stonehedges.
Felipe, Ugalde Alcántara, jt. illus. see Ugalde, Felipe.
Felix, Gloria. The Dramatic Life of Azaleah Lane. Smith, Nikki Shannon. 2020. (Azaleah Lane Ser.). (ENG.). 112p. (J). (gr. k-2). 14.95 (978-1-5158-4465-5(X), 186484, Picture Window Bks.) Capstone.
Félix, Gloria. Nuestra América: 30 Inspiring Latinas/Latinos Who Have Shaped the United States. Vourvoulias, Sabrina. 2020. 128p. (J). (gr. 3-7). 17.99 (978-0-7624-9747-8(5), Running Pr. Kids) Running Pr.
Félix, Lucie. Give & Take. Félix, Lucie. 2016. (Old Barn Bks.). (ENG.). 16p. (J). (gr. -1-2). bds. 19.99 (978-0-7636-9011-3(2)) Candlewick Pr.
Felix, Monique. Chicken Wants a Nap. Marchini, Tracy. 2017. (ENG.). 24p. (J). (gr. 1-3). 17.99 (978-1-56846-308-7(1), Creative Editions) Creative Co., The.
—Dream Song. de la Mare, Walter. 2019. (ENG.). 16p. (J). (gr. 1-3). 14.99 (978-1-56846-337-7(5), Creative Editions) Creative Co., The.
—Good Ship Crocodile. Lewis, J. Patrick. 2013. (ENG.). 32p. (J). (gr. 1-3). 18.99 (978-1-56846-238-7(7), Creative Editions) Creative Co., The.
—In the Garden. Riggs, Kate. 2020. (ENG.). 12p. (J). (gr. -1 — 1). bds. 9.99 (978-1-56846-335-3(9), Creative Editions) Creative Co., The.
—Let's Go Outside. Riggs, Kate. 2018. (ENG.). 14p. (J). (gr. -1-k). bds. 8.99 (978-1-56846-316-2(2), Creative Editions) Creative Co., The.
—Tuba Lessons. Bartlett, T. C. (ENG.). 32p. (J). (gr. 1-17). 2011. pap. 9.95 (978-0-89812-522-1(7), Creative Paperbacks); 2009. 17.95 (978-1-56846-209-7(3)) Creative Co., The.
—The Velveteen Rabbit. Williams, Margery. 40p. 2013. (ENG.). (J). (gr. 1-3). pap. 8.99 (978-0-89812-831-4(5), Creative Paperbacks); 2005. pap. 8.95 (978-0-89812-383-8(6)) Creative Co., The.
—Wake up, Weather. Marshall, Rita. 2016. (ENG.). 14p. (J). (gr. -1-k). bds. 8.99 (978-1-56846-286-8(7), Creative Editions) Creative Co., The.
—Where Do I End & You Begin? Oppenheim, Shulamith. 2015. (ENG.). 32p. (J). (gr. 1-3). 17.99 (978-1-56846-274-5(3), Creative Editions) Creative Co., The.
Felix, Monique. The Alphabet. Felix, Monique. 2012. (Mouse Book Ser.). (ENG.). 32p. (J). (gr. -1-k). 12.99 (978-1-56846-226-4(3), Creative Editions) Creative Co., The.
—Mouse Book: the Colors. Felix, Monique. 2013. (ENG.). 32p. (J). (gr. -1-k). 12.99 (978-1-56846-234-9(4), Creative Editions) Creative Co., The.
—Mouse Book: the Numbers. Felix, Monique. 2013. (ENG.). 32p. (J). (gr. -1-k). 12.99 (978-1-56846-235-6(2), Creative Editions) Creative Co., The.
—Mouse Book: the Valentine. Felix, Monique. 2013. (Mouse Book Ser.). (ENG.). 32p. (J). (gr. -1-k). 12.99 (978-1-56846-247-9(6), Creative Editions) Creative Co., The.
—The Rumor. Felix, Monique. 2011. (ENG.). 24p. (J). (gr. 1-3). 19.99 (978-1-56846-219-6(0), Creative Editions) Creative Co., The.
—The Wind. Felix, Monique. 2012. (Mouse Book Ser.). (ENG.). 32p. (J). (gr. -1-k). 12.99 (978-1-56846-227-1(1), Creative Editions) Creative Co., The.
Fell, H. Granville & Millar, H. R. The Book of Dragons. Nesbit, E. unabr. ed. 2004. (Dover Children's Classics Ser.). (ENG.). 176p. (gr. 3-5). pap. 8.95 (978-0-486-43648-7(9)) Dover Pubns., Inc.
Fell, Jenny. Second Thoughts. Nuttall, Neil & Hawkins, Andy, eds. 2004. (ENG.). 64p. pap. 14.95 (978-1-84323-046-5(1)) Beekman Bks., Inc.
Fellers, Cody. Toby & the Alien: In the Adventures of the Unusual Toys, 1 vol. Fellers, Tina. 2009. 28p. pap. 24.95 (978-1-60672-195-7(X)) America Star Bks.
Fellows, Stan. The Horse's Haiku. Rosen, Michael J. 2018. 48p. (J). (gr. 1-4). 17.99 (978-0-7636-8916-2(5)) Candlewick Pr.
—John Muir. Lasky, Kathryn. 2014. (Candlewick Biographies Ser.). (ENG.). (J). (gr. 3-7). lib. bdg. 15.60 (978-1-62765-551-4(4)) Perfection Learning Corp.
Felmang, Romano. Egyptian Myths. Jeffrey, Gary. 2006. (Graphic Mythology Ser.). (ENG.). 48p. (J). (gr. 4-7). lib. bdg. 35.45 (978-1-4042-0800-1(3)); (gr. 5-8). pap. 14.05 (978-1-4042-0812-4(7)) Rosen Publishing Group, Inc., The.
—A Tale of Two Cities. Dickens, Charles. 2018. (Classic Graphic Fiction Ser.). (ENG.). 48p. (J). (gr. 4). pap. 7.95 (978-1-912233-59-5(2), Scribo) Book Hse. GBR. Dist: Sterling Publishing Co., Inc.
Felsen, Holly. Rag Top. Felsen, Henry Gregor. 2013. 212p. pap. 15.00 (978-1-62272-001-9(6)) Felsen Ink.
Felstead, Cathie. Earthshake: Poems from the Ground Up. Peters, Lisa Westberg. 2003. (ENG.). 32p. (J). (gr. k-5). 17.99 (978-0-06-029265-2(2), Greenwillow Bks.) HarperCollins Pubs.
—Family Lullaby. Shapiro, Jody Fickes. 2007. 40p. (J). (gr. -1). lib. bdg. 17.89 (978-0-06-051483-9(3)) HarperCollins Pubs.
—An Island Grows. Schaefer, Lola M. 2006. (ENG.). 40p. (J). (gr. -1-3). 17.99 (978-0-06-623930-9(3), Greenwillow Bks.) HarperCollins Pubs.
Felstead, Cathie, jt. illus. see Edwards, Gunvor.
Felten, Ross. Ava the Monster Slayer. Maggiore, Lisa. 2015. (Ava the Monster Slayer Ser.: 1). (ENG.). 36p. (J). (gr. -1-k). 16.99 (978-1-63450-151-4(9), Sky Pony Pr.) Skyhorse Publishing Co., Inc.
—Ava the Monster Slayer: Cousin Power. Maggiore, Lisa. 2019. (Ava the Monster Slayer Ser.: 2). (ENG.). 44p. (J). (gr. -1-1). 16.99 (978-1-5107-4810-1(5), Sky Pony Pr.) Skyhorse Publishing Co., Inc.
Felter & Butterworth & Heath. Glaucia the Greek Slave: A Tale of Athens in the First Century. Leslie, Emma. 2007. 308p. per. 14.95 (978-1-934671-01-6(0)) Salem Ridge Press LLC.
Felter and Gunston & Butterworth and Heath. Out of the Mouth of the Lion: Or, the Church in the Catacombs. Leslie, Emma. 2007. 296p. 24.95 (978-1-934671-04-7(5)); per. 14.95 (978-1-934671-05-4(3)) Salem Ridge Press LLC.
Feltes, Tess. Why Does It Rain? Jango-Cohen, Judith. (On My Own Science Ser.). 2006. 47p. (J). (gr. k-3). per. 6.95 (978-1-57505-854-2(5)); 2005. (ENG.). 48p. (gr. 2-4). lib. bdg. 25.26 (978-1-57505-762-0(X)) Lerner Publishing Group. (Millbrook Pr.).
Feltman, Ryan, jt. illus. see Carola, Dominic.
Felton, Richard. Poor Dan. Williams, Lorraine. 2008. 36p. per. 24.95 (978-1-60441-170-6(8)) America Star Bks.
Felts, Shirley. Sweet & Sour: Tales from China. Kendall, Carol & Li, Yao-Wen. 2007. (ENG.). 114p. (J). (gr. 5-7). per. 8.95 (978-0-618-75245-4(5), 100527) Houghton Mifflin Harcourt Publishing Co.
Feltus, Helena. The Alphabet Book of Lowercase Letters. Feltus, Helena. 2018. (ENG.). 36p. (J). (gr. k-1). 22.00 (978-1-7320292-0-0(2)) Qum.
Fendel, Ronald. The Fortunate Fairy. Fendel, Michele. 2014. (ENG.). 32p. (J). pap. (978-0-9924684-2-2(6)) Sandler, David.
Fenderson, David. Mommy, Why Is the Sky So Blue? Fenderson, Shani. 2009. 24p. pap. 24.95 (978-1-60749-550-5(3)) America Star Bks.

F

Fendy, Sasha. The Little Bee Family / the Happy Beast's Pool Party. Carlisle, Bella and Bailey. 2019. (ENG.). 26p. (J). pap. 9.99 (978-1-0906-8516-2(5)) Independently Published.

Fenech, Liza. Max Explores Chicago. Laberje, Reji. 2014. (Max Explores Ser.). (ENG.). 20p. (J). (— 1). bds. 9.95 (978-1-62937-003-3(7)) Triumph Bks.

—Max Explores New York. Laberje, Reji. 2014. (Max Explores Ser.). (ENG.). 20p. (J). (— 1). bds. 9.95 (978-1-62937-004-0(5)) Triumph Bks.

—Max Explores San Francisco. Laberje, Reji. 2014. (Max Explores Ser.). (ENG.). 20p. (J). (— 1). bds. 9.95 (978-1-62937-005-7(3)) Triumph Bks.

—Max Explores Seattle. Laberje, Reji. 2015. (Max Explores Ser.). (ENG.). 20p. (J). (— 1). bds. 9.95 (978-1-62937-103-0(3)) Triumph Bks.

—Max Explores the Beach. Laberje, Reji. 2015. (Max Explores Ser.). (ENG.). 20p. (J). (— 1). bds. 9.95 (978-1-62937-101-6(7)) Triumph Bks.

Feng, Katherine. Panda Kindergarten. Ryder, Joanne. (ENG.). 32p. (J). (gr. -1-3). 2015. pap. 7.99 (978-0-06-057852-7(1), Collins); 2009. 17.99 (978-0-06-057850-3(5)) HarperCollins Pubs.

Feng, Katherine, photos by. Panda Kindergarten. Ryder, Joanne. 2014. 32p. pap. 8.00 (978-1-61003-332-9(9)) Center for the Collaborative Classroom.

Feng, Lisk. The Ant & the Grasshopper. Hoena, Blake. 2018. (Classic Fables in Rhythm & Rhyme Ser.). (ENG.). 24p. (C). (gr. k-2). lib. bdg. 33.99 (978-1-68410-386-7(X), 140358) Cantata Learning.

Feng, Lisk, et al. Classic Fables in Rhythm & Rhyme. Hoena, Blake. 2019. (Classic Fables in Rhythm & Rhyme Ser.). (ENG.). (C). (gr. k-2). pap., pap., pap. 47.70 (978-1-4966-2030-9(5), 29709); pap., pap., pap. 87.45 (978-1-4966-1947-1(1), 29281) Cantata Learning.

Feng, Lisk. Everest. Francis, Angela. 2018. (ENG.). 80p. (J). (gr. 3-7). 24.00 (978-1-911171-99-7(2)) Flying Eye Bks. GBR. Dist: Penguin Random Hse. LLC.

—A Hug Is for Holding Me. Wheeler, Lisa. 2018. (ENG.). 24p. (J). (gr. -1-k). 14.99 (978-1-4197-2826-6(1), Abrams Appleseed) Abrams, Inc.

Fenimore, Kristina. My Picnic Basket: And How God Is Always Near. Simon, Mary Manz. 2013. (ENG.). 14p. (J). (gr. -1-k). bds. 9.99 (978-0-7847-3699-9(5), B&H Kids) B&H Publishing Group.

Fennell, Clare. Big Book about Being Big. Paratore, Coleen Murtagh. 2019. 40p. (J). (-2). 17.99 (978-1-4926-9684-1(6), Little Pickle Pr.) Sourcebooks, Inc.

—Big Shark, Little Shark. Make Believe Ideas Ltd. 2019. (ENG.). 14p. (J). bds. (978-1-78947-000-0(5)) Make Believe Ideas.

—Board Book I Can Count To 10. Make Believe Ideas Ltd. 2019. (ENG.). 14p. (J). bds. (978-1-78843-650-2(4)) Make Believe Ideas.

—Farm Families. 2017. (Push & Pull Bks.). (ENG.). 8p. (J). (gr. -1 — 1). bds. 5.99 (978-0-7641-6888-8(6), B.E.S. Publishing) Peterson's.

—Five Nosy Reindeer. Make Believe Ideas Ltd. 2019. (ENG.). 12p. (J). (gr. -1-7). bds. (978-1-78843-923-7(6)) Make Believe Ideas.

—Forest Homes. 2017. (Push & Pull Bks.). (ENG.). 8p. (J). (gr. -1 — 1). bds. 5.99 (978-0-7641-6891-8(6), B.E.S. Publishing) Peterson's.

—Goldilocks & the Three Bears. Make Believe Ideas Ltd. 2019. (ENG.). 10p. (J). (gr. -1-7). (978-1-78947-064-2(1)) Make Believe Ideas.

—I Can Count To 100. Make Believe Ideas Ltd. 2019. (I Can Count To 100 Ser.). (ENG.). 14p. (J). (gr. -1-7). bds. (978-1-78843-652-6(0)) Make Believe Ideas.

—Jingle Bells, Something Smells! Make Believe Ideas Ltd. 2019. (ENG.). 14p. (J). (gr. -1-7). bds. (978-1-78947-051-2(X)) Make Believe Ideas.

—Noisy Jungle. 2017. (Push & Pull Bks.). (ENG.). 8p. (J). (gr. -1 — 1). bds. 5.99 (978-0-7641-6889-5(4), B.E.S. Publishing) Peterson's.

—Playtime Pond. 2017. (Push & Pull Bks.). (ENG.). 8p. (J). (gr. -1 — 1). bds. 5.99 (978-0-7641-6890-1(8), B.E.S. Publishing) Peterson's.

—Ten Tiny Dinosaurs. Walden, Libby. 2020. (ENG.). 26p. (J). (-k). pap. 4.99 (978-1-68010-465-3(9)) Tiger Tales.

—Touch & Feel Baby Animals. Make Believe Ideas Ltd. 2019. (Touch & Feel Ser.). (ENG.). 12p. (J). bds. (978-1-78843-539-0(7)) Make Believe Ideas.

Fennell, Clare. The Unicorns Are Coming to Town. Make Believe Ideas Ltd & Robinson, Alexandra. 2020. (ENG.). 32p. (J). **(978-1-78947-766-5(2))** Make Believe Ideas.

Fennell, Kristen & Petruccelli, Jessica. A World of Hope: Written by Hope's Parents Laurie & Mike. l.t. ed. 2005. 18p. (J). per. 9.99 (978-1-59879-069-6(2)) Lifevest Publishing, Inc.

Fennell, Tracy. The Qur'an & Islam. Ganeri, Anita. 2003. 30p. (J). lib. bdg. 24.25 (978-1-58340-241-2(1)) Black Rabbit Bks.

Fennell, Tracy, jt. illus. see Morgan, Richard.

Fennewald, Joseph Grant. Wonderful White Wintery Day: The Marvelous Misadventure of Katy Bear, 1 vol. Matherly, Ashley Page. 2009. 43p. pap. 24.95 (978-1-61546-323-7(2)) PublishAmerica, Inc.

Fenoglio, Chris. Goosebumps: Horrors of the Witch House. Tipton, Denton J. & Smith, Matthew Dow. 2019. (Goosebumps Ser.: 3). 80p. (J). (gr. 4-7). 12.99 (978-1-68405-539-5(3)) Idea & Design Works, LLC.

—Goosebumps: Monsters at Midnight. Lambert, Jeremy. 2018. (Goosebumps Ser.). (ENG.). 72p. (J). (gr. 2-5). 12.99 (978-1-68405-155-7(X)) Idea & Design Works, LLC.

Fenoughty, Charles. Beautiful Games. Hamley, Dennis. 2004. 104p. per. (978-1-904529-13-2(5), Back to Front) Solidus.

—Haunted United. Hamley, Dennis. 2004. 148p. per. (978-1-904529-11-8(9), Back to Front) Solidus.

Fenske, Jonathan. After Squidnight. Fenske, Jonathan E. 2020. 32p. (J). (gr. -1-3). 12.99 **(978-1-5247-9308-1(6),** Penguin Workshop) Penguin Young Readers Group.

Fenske, Jonathan. I Will Race You Through This Book! Fenske, Jonathan E. 2019. 32p. (J). (gr. -1-3). 4.99 (978-1-5247-9196-4(2), Penguin Workshop) Penguin Young Readers Group.

—I Will Race You Through This Book! 2019. 32p. (J). (gr. -1-3). 9.99 (978-1-5247-9195-7(4), Penguin Workshop) Penguin Young Readers Group.

Fenske, Jonathan. Barnacle Is Bored. Fenske, Jonathan. 2016. (ENG.). 40p. (J). (gr. -1-k). 14.99 (978-0-545-86504-3(2), Scholastic Pr.) Scholastic, Inc.

—Guppy Up! Fenske, Jonathan. 2013. (Penguin Young Readers, Level 1 Ser.). 32p. (J). (gr. k-1). mass mkt. 4.99 (978-0-448-49646-7(1), Penguin Young Readers) Penguin Young Readers Group.

—Hello, Crabby! Fenske, Jonathan. 2019. (Crabby Book Ser.: 1). (ENG.). 48p. (J). (gr. -1-1). pap. 4.99 (978-1-338-28150-7(X)) Scholastic, Inc.

—¡Hola, Cangrejito! Un Libro de la Serie Acorn. Fenske, Jonathan. 2019. (Libro de Cangrejito Ser.: 1). (SPA.). 48p. (J). (gr. -1-1). pap. 4.99 (978-1-338-35911-4(8), Scholastic en Espanol) Scholastic, Inc.

—I'm Fun, Too! Fenske, Jonathan. 2018. (Lego Ser.). 32p. (J). (gr. -1-3). 16.99 (978-1-338-26097-7(9)) Scholastic, Inc.

—Love Is in the Air. Fenske, Jonathan. 2012. (Penguin Young Readers, Level 2 Ser.). (ENG.). 32p. (J). (gr. 1-2). mass mkt. 3.99 (978-0-448-49647-4(X), Penguin Young Readers) Penguin Young Readers Group.

—A Pig, a Fox, & a Box. Fenske, Jonathan. Bader, Bonnie. 2015. (Penguin Young Readers, Level 2 Ser.). (ENG.). 32p. (J). (gr. 1-2). pap. 4.99 (978-0-448-48510-2(9), Penguin Young Readers) Penguin Young Readers Group.

—Plankton Is Pushy. Fenske, Jonathan. 2017. 40p. (J). (gr. -1-k). pap. 14.99 (978-1-338-09896-9(9), Scholastic Pr.) Scholastic, Inc.

—Please, No More Nuts! Fenske, Jonathan. 2018. (Penguin Young Readers, Level 2 Ser.). 32p. (J). (gr. 1-2). pap. 4.99 (978-0-515-15965-3(4), Penguin Young Readers) Penguin Young Readers Group.

—We Need More Nuts! Fenske, Jonathan. 32p. (J). (gr. 1-2). 2019. (ENG.). 4.99 (978-0-593-09599-7(5), Penguin Workshop); 2017. (ENG.). 14.99 (978-0-515-15914-1(X), Penguin Young Readers); 2017. pap. 4.99 (978-0-515-15913-4(1), Penguin Young Readers) Penguin Young Readers Group.

—Woodward & Mctwee. Fenske, Jonathan. 32p. (J). (gr. 1-2). 2019. 4.99 (978-0-593-09598-0(7), Penguin Workshop); 2014. pap. 3.99 (978-0-448-47991-0(5), Penguin Young Readers) Penguin Young Readers Group.

Fenton, Joe. Boo! Fenton, Joe. 2010. (ENG.). 32p. (J). (gr. -1-1). 12.99 (978-1-4169-7936-4(0), Simon & Schuster Bks. For Young Readers) Simon & Schuster Bks. For Young Readers.

—What's under the Bed? Fenton, Joe. 2008. (ENG.). 32p. (J). (gr. -1-2). 18.99 (978-1-4169-4943-5(7), Simon & Schuster Bks. For Young Readers) Simon & Schuster Bks. For Young Readers.

Fenton, Mary Frances & Kostecke, Nancy. Worms Eat Our Garbage: Classroom Activities for a Better Environment. Appelhof, Mary et al. Harris, Barbara Loss et al. 2004. 232p. (Orig.). (gr. 4-18). pap., stu. ed. 22.95 (978-0-942256-05-5(0)) Flowerfield Enterprises.

Fenton, Tanya. The Granimal. Alexander, Christian. 2016. 155p. (J). (gr. -1-3). pap. 11.99 (978-1-907432-22-4(1)) Hogs Back Bks. GBR. Dist: Independent Pubs. Group.

Fenton, Tanya. Three Silly Chickens. Fenton, Tanya. 2015. 32p. (J). (gr. -1-1). pap. 8.99 (978-1-907432-11-8(6)) Hogs Back Bks. GBR. Dist: Independent Pubs. Group.

Fentz, Mike. Garfield & the Santa Spy. Teitelbaum, Michael. 2004. 92p. (J). (978-0-439-70543-1(6)) Scholastic, Inc.

—Monster Trouble. Nickel, Scott. 2004. (Scholastic Reader Ser.). 22p. (J). pap. (978-0-439-66977-1(4)) Scholastic, Inc.

Fentz, Mike & Barker, Lori. Egg Hunt. Nickel, Scott. 2005. 22p. (J). (978-0-439-67211-5(2)) Scholastic, Inc.

Fenwick, Ray. The Great & Only Barnum: the Tremendous, Stupendous Life of Showman P. T. Barnum. Fleming, Candace. 2009. 160p. (J). (gr. 3-7). 19.99 (978-0-375-84197-2(0), Schwartz & Wade Bks.) Random Hse. Children's Bks.

Fequiere, Christopher. Taiwo & Kehinde: The Wedding Trip. Beckles, Darrion & Ajayi, Lola and Dupe. 2018. (ENG.). 304p. (J). pap. 12.99 (978-1-5439-5669-6(6)) BookBaby.

Ferchaud, Steve. Glen Robbie: A Scottish Fairy Tale. ed. 2006. (J). 22.95 (978-1-58478-013-7(4), Highland Children's Pr.) Heather & Highlands Publishing.

—Gracie's Big Adventure... with Augustine the Beaver. Cobb, Debbie. 2006. (J). per. 10.95 (978-0-9787376-0-3(1)) Laurob Pr.

—The Man Who Spoke with Cats. 2006. (ENG.). 48p. (J). 18.95 (978-1-58478-019-9(3), Highland Children's Pr.) Heather & Highlands Publishing.

—Mom Can I Have a Dragon? Watson, T. E. 2018. (ENG.). 38p. (J). (gr. -1-3). pap. (978-1-58478-072-4(X), Highland Pr.) Paw Print Pr.

—The Mountain. Watson, T. E. 2014. (ENG.). (J). pap. (978-1-58478-046-5(0), Highland Pr.) Paw Print Pr.

Ferchaud, Steve. Princess Yellow Boots Finds a Friend. Elliott, Lynn H. & Elliott, Dani. 2019. (ENG.). 34p. (YA). pap. 8.95 **(978-1-935807-48-3(X))** Stansbury Publishing.

Ferchaud, Steve. Santa's Hat. Claus, Nancy. 2006. (J). (978-0-9746747-6-6(1)) Cypress Bay Publishing.

—Santa's Prize. Claus, Nancy. 2006. (J). (978-0-9746747-5-9(3)) Cypress Bay Publishing.

Ferenc, Bill. The Good Samaritan & Other Bible Stories. Glaser, Rebecca. 2015. (Holy Moly Bible Storybooks Ser.). (ENG.). 32p. (J). (gr. k-3). 12.99 (978-1-5064-0251-2(8), Sparkhouse Family) Augsburg Fortress, Pubs.

—The Holy Moly Christmas Story, Vol. Glaser, Rebecca. 2015. (Holy Moly Bible Storybooks Ser.). (ENG.). 32p. (J). (gr. k-3). 12.99 (978-1-5064-0257-4(7), Sparkhouse Family) Augsburg Fortress, Pubs.

—The Holy Moly Easter Story, Vol. Glaser, Rebecca. 2016. (Holy Moly Bible Storybooks Ser.). (ENG.). 32p. (J). (gr. k-3). 12.99 (978-1-5064-0256-7(9), Sparkhouse Family) Augsburg Fortress, Pubs.

—Jesus Feeds 5,000 & Other Bible Stories. Glaser, Rebecca. 2015. (Holy Moly Bible Storybooks Ser.). (ENG.). 32p. (J). (gr. k-3). 12.99 (978-1-5064-0252-9(6), Sparkhouse Family) Augsburg Fortress, Pubs.

—Saul Meets Jesus & Other Bible Stories. Glaser, Rebecca. 2016. (Holy Moly Bible Storybooks Ser.). (ENG.). 32p. (J). (gr. k-3). 12.99 (978-1-5064-0255-0(0), Sparkhouse Family) Augsburg Fortress, Pubs.

Ferenic, Bill. The Holy Moly Story Bible: Exploring God's Awesome Word, Vol. Glaser, Rebecca. 2015. (ENG.). 352p. (J). (gr. k-3). 22.99 (978-1-4514-9988-9(4), Sparkhouse Family) Augsburg Fortress, Pubs.

Fereyra, Lucas. Penguins of Madagascar, Vol. 1. Matthews, Alex. 2015. (Penguins of Madagascar Ser.: 1). 64p. (J). (gr. 1-4). pap. 6.99 (978-1-78276-251-5(5)) Titan Bks. Ltd. GBR. Dist: Penguin Random Hse. LLC.

Ferguson, Ben. The Five Needs of Animal Welfare. Gothard, Nicola. 2016. (ENG.). (J). (gr. 1-6). pap. (978-0-9934631-6-7(9)) Generation 2050.

Ferguson, C. Brent. Buffy the Vampire Slayer Roleplaying Game: Slayer's Handbook. Carella, C. J. et al. 2006. (Buffy RPG Ser.). 156p. 30.00 (978-1-891153-89-1(7)) Eden Studios, Inc.

Ferguson, Chaveevah Banks. Henry the Farsighted Heron. Barbatti, Joyce. 2008. (ENG.). 24p. (J). 7.00 (978-0-9818219-0-0(1)) BaHar Publishing, L.C.

—Travis, It's NOT Your Birthday! Hickey, Joshalyn M. 2006. (ENG.). 34p. (J). pap. 13.00 (978-0-9718939-5-5(0)) BaHar Publishing, L.C.

Ferguson Fuller, Sandy. The Bunny Poets. Toboni, Barbara. 2018. (ENG.). 36p. (J). (gr. k-6). 17.99 (978-1-365-86137-6(6)); pap. 13.99 (978-1-365-86139-0(2)) Lulu Pr., Inc.

Ferguson Fuller, Sandy. The Bunny Poets. Toboni, Barbara. ed. 2018. (ENG.). 36p. (J). (gr. k-6). pap. 13.99 **(978-1-64372-271-9(9));** 17.99 **(978-1-64372-028-9(7))** MacLaren-Cochrane Publishing, Inc. (Huskies Pub).

—The Bunny Poets Dyslexic Edition: Dyslexic Font. Toboni, Barbara. ed. 2018. (ENG.). 36p. (J). (gr. k-6). 19.99 **(978-1-64372-272-6(7));** pap. 15.99 **(978-1-64372-273-3(5))** MacLaren-Cochrane Publishing, Inc.

Ferguson Fuller, Sandy. The Bunny Poets Dyslexic Font. Toboni, Barbara. 2018. (ENG.). 36p. (J). (gr. k-6). 21.99 (978-1-365-86138-3(4)); pap. 15.99 (978-1-365-86140-6(6)) Lulu Pr., Inc.

Ferguson, Jessica. The Black Hole. Robertson, Christi. 2019. (ENG.). 78p. (J). (gr. 3-5). 12.99 (978-0-578-51065-1(0)) Clear Wind Publishing.

Ferguson, Lee. Batgirl Classic: on the Case! Marsham, Liz. 2018. (I Can Read Level 2 Ser.). 32p. (J). (gr. -1-3). pap. 4.99 (978-0-06-236095-3(7)) HarperCollins Pubs.

—Batgirl, on the Case! Marsham, Liz. 2018. 30p. (J). (978-1-5364-3013-4(7)) Harper & Row Ltd.

—I Am an Amazon Warrior. Marston, William Moulton. 2017. 31p. (J). (978-1-5182-4342-4(8)) Harper & Row Ltd.

—Superman - A Giant Attack. Lemke, Donald. 2015. (I Can Read Level 2 Ser.). (ENG.). 32p. (J). (gr. -1-3). pap. 3.99 (978-0-06-234488-5(9)) HarperCollins Pubs.

—Wonder Woman Classic: Maze of Magic. Marsham, Liz. 2017. (I Can Read Level 2 Ser.). 32p. (J). (gr. -1-3). pap. 3.99 (978-0-06-236093-9(0)) HarperCollins Pubs.

Ferguson, Peter. The Anybodies. Bode, N. E. 2005. (ENG.). 288p. (J). (gr. 5-8). reprint ed. pap. 7.99 (978-0-06-055737-9(0)) HarperCollins Pubs.

—The Boy Who Cried Fabulous. Newman, Lesléa. 2007. 32p. (J). (gr. -1-2). pap. 7.99 (978-1-58246-224-0(0), Tricycle Pr.) Random Hse. Children's Bks.

—The Council of Mirrors (the Sisters Grimm #9) 10th Anniversary Edition. Buckley, Michael. 10th ed. 2018. (ENG.). 304p. (J). (gr. 3-7). pap. 8.99 (978-1-4197-2009-3(0), Amulet Bks.) Abrams, Inc.

—The Everafter War (the Sisters Grimm #7) 10th Anniversary Edition. Buckley, Michael. 10th ed. 2018. (ENG.). 272p. (J). (gr. 3-7). pap. 8.99 (978-1-4197-2011-6(2), Amulet Bks.) Abrams, Inc.

—The Fairy-Tale Detectives: And the Unusual Suspects. Buckley, Michael. 2012. 580p. (J). (978-1-4351-4487-3(2), Amulet Bks.) Abrams, Inc.

—Fairy-Tale Detectives (the Sisters Grimm #1) 10th Anniversary Edition. Buckley, Michael. 10th anniv. ed. 2017. (ENG.). 288p. (J). (gr. 3-7). pap. 8.95 (978-1-4197-2005-5(8), Amulet Bks.) Abrams, Inc.

—The Guide to the Territories of Halla. MacHale, D. J. 2005. (Pendragon Ser.). (ENG.). 48p. (J). (gr. 5-9). pap. 12.99 (978-1-4169-0014-6(4), Aladdin) Simon & Schuster Children's Publishing.

—Magic & Other Misdemeanors (the Sisters Grimm #5) 10th Anniversary Edition. Buckley, Michael. 10th ed. 2017. (ENG.). 280p. (J). (gr. 3-7). pap. 8.99 (978-1-4197-2010-9(4), Amulet Bks.) Abrams, Inc.

—My Havana: Memories of a Cuban Boyhood. Wells, Rosemary et al. 2010. 72p. (J). (gr. 2-5). 17.99 (978-0-7636-4305-8(X)) Candlewick Pr.

—Once upon a Crime (the Sisters Grimm #4) 10th Anniversary Edition. Buckley, Michael. 10th anniv. ed. 2017. (ENG.). 272p. (J). (gr. 2-8). pap. 8.99 (978-1-4197-2007-9(4), Amulet Bks.) Abrams, Inc.

—Problem Child (the Sisters Grimm #3) 10th Anniversary Edition. Buckley, Michael. 10th ed. 2017. (ENG.). 288p. (J). (gr. 3-7). pap. 8.95 (978-1-4197-2004-8(X), Amulet Bks.) Abrams, Inc.

—The Red Ghost. Bauer, Marion Dane. 2009. (Stepping Stone Book(TM) Ser.). 96p. (J). (gr. 1-4). 4.99 (978-0-375-84082-1(6), Random Hse. Bks. for Young Readers) Random Hse. Children's Bks.

—The Sisters Grimm: Book #7: the Everafter War. Buckley, Michael. (ENG.). (J). (gr. 3-7). 2010. (Sisters Grimm Ser.: Bk. 7). 336p. pap. 8.95 (978-0-8109-8429-5(6)); Bk. 7. 2009. (Sisters Grimm Ser.). 304p. 16.95 (978-0-8109-8355-7(9)) Abrams, Inc. (Amulet Bks.).

—The Sisters Grimm Book 6: Tales from the Hood. Buckley, Michael. 2008. (ENG.). 288p. (J). (gr. 3-7). 16.95 (978-0-8109-9478-2(X), Amulet Bks.) Abrams, Inc.

—Tales from the Hood (the Sisters Grimm #6) 10th Anniversary Edition. Buckley, Michael. 10th ed. 2017. (ENG.). 256p. (J). (gr. 3-7). pap. 8.99 (978-1-4197-2012-3(0), Amulet Bks.) Abrams, Inc.

—Unusual Suspects (the Sisters Grimm #2) 10th Anniversary Edition. Buckley, Michael. 10th anniv. ed. 2017. (ENG.). 288p. (J). (gr. 3-7). pap. 8.95 (978-1-4197-2008-6(2), Amulet Bks.) Abrams, Inc.

—A Very Grimm Guide. Buckley, Michael. 2011. (ENG.). 128p. (J). (gr. 3-7). 16.95 (978-1-4197-0201-3(7), Amulet Bks.) Abrams, Inc.

—Working Myself to Pieces & Bits. Kelly, Katy. 2008. (Lucy Rose Ser.: 4). (ENG.). 208p. (J). (gr. 3-7). 6.99 (978-0-440-42186-3(1), Yearling) Random Hse. Children's Bks.

Ferguson, Rachel C. Growing up Supremely: The Women of the U. S. Supreme Court. Gutgold, Nichola D. & Armstrong, Jessica L. 2020. (ENG.). 34p. (J). (gr. k-5). pap. 9.99 **(978-1-63233-218-9(3))** Elfrig Publishing.

Ferguson, Sandra. Where the Bigglebob Grows. Ferguson, Charles J. 2019. (ENG.). 30p. (J). 25.95 **(978-1-64471-818-6(9));** pap. 15.95 **(978-1-64471-817-9(0))** Covenant Bks.

Ferguson, Simon. The Star of the Yshan Kings. Davies, Michael. 2018. (Yshan Kings Trilogy Ser.: Vol. 1). (ENG.). 130p. (J). (gr. 4-6). pap. (978-0-6484702-1-2(0)) Dalton, Mickie Foundation, The.

Ferguson, Tamara. Did Noah Have Whales on the Ark? Hairston, Angelica. l.t. ed. 2004. 44p. (J). (978-0-9716136-1-4(3)) Broadcast Quality Productions, Inc.

Ferguson, Teresa. I Am an Aspie Girl: A Book for Young Girls with Autism Spectrum Conditions. Bulhak-Paterson, Danuta. 2015. (ENG.). 32p. 15.95 (978-1-84905-634-2(X), 693794) Kingsley, Jessica Pubs. GBR. Dist: Hachette UK Distribution.

Fern, Jim, et al. Wolverine Epic Collection: Inner Fury. 2020. (ENG.). 464p. (YA). (gr. 8-17). pap. 39.99 (978-1-302-92390-7(0)) Marvel Worldwide, Inc.

Fernanda Heredia, Maria. Por Si No Te lo He Dicho. Fernanda Heredia, Maria. 2015. (Serie Verde / Album Ilustrado Ser.). (SPA.). 24p. (J). pap. 12.95 (978-9942-19-337-7(5)) Santillana USA Publishing Co., Inc.

Fernandes, Eugenie. Beyond Old McDonald: Funny Poems from down on the Farm. Hoce, Charley. 2005. (ENG.). 32p. (J). (gr. k-2). 16.95 (978-1-59078-312-2(3), Wordsong) Boyds Mills Pr.

Fernandes, Eugenie. Earth Magic. Brand, Dionne. 2020. (ENG.). 32p. (J). (gr. 5-9). pap. 10.99 **(978-1-5253-0458-3(5))** Kids Can Pr., Ltd. CAN. Dist: Hachette Bk. Group.

Fernandes, Eugenie. Hope Springs. Walters, Eric. 2014. (ENG.). 32p. (J). (gr. 1-4). 17.99 (978-1-77049-530-2(4), Tundra Bks.) Tundra Bks. CAN. Dist: Penguin Random Hse. LLC.

—A Likkle Miss Lou: How Jamaican Poet Louise Bennett Coverley Found Her Voice. Hohn, Nadia L. 2019. (ENG.). 32p. (J). (gr. k-5). 16.95 (978-1-77147-350-7(9)) Owlkids Bks. Inc. CAN. Dist: Publishers Group West (PGW).

—Mermaid in the Bathtub, 1 vol. Peetoom, Laura. 2006. (First Flight Level 4 Ser.). (ENG.). 104p. (J). (gr. 4-7). pap. 4.95 (978-1-55041-362-5(7)) Fitzhenry & Whiteside, Ltd. CAN. Dist: F&W Media, Inc.

—Mimi's Village: And How Basic Health Care Transformed It. Milway, Katie Smith. 2012. (CitizenKid Ser.). (ENG.). 32p. (J). (gr. 3-7). 18.99 (978-1-55453-722-8(3)) Kids Can Pr., Ltd. CAN. Dist: Hachette Bk. Group.

—My Name Is Blessing. Walters, Eric. 2013. (ENG.). 208p. (J). (gr. 1-4). 17.95 (978-1-77049-301-8(8), Tundra Bks.) Tundra Bks. CAN. Dist: Penguin Random Hse. LLC.

—One Hen: How One Small Loan Made a Big Difference. Milway, Katie Smith. (CitizenKid Ser.). (ENG.). 32p. (J). (gr. 3-7). 2020. pap. 10.99 (978-1-894786-09-6(2)); 2008. 18.99 (978-1-55453-028-1(8)) Kids Can Pr., Ltd. CAN. Dist: Hachette Bk. Group.

—Polar Bear, Arctic Hare: Poems of the Frozen North. Spinelli, Eileen. 2007. (ENG.). 32p. (J). (gr. -1-k). 16.95 (978-1-59078-344-3(1), Wordsong) Boyds Mills Pr.

—There's a Barnyard in My Bedroom. Suzuki, David. 2010. (ENG.). 64p. (gr. -1-3). pap. 10.95 (978-1-55365-532-9(X)) Greystone Books Ltd. CAN. Dist: Publishers Group West (PGW).

—Today Is the Day. Walters, Eric. 2015. (ENG.). 36p. (J). (gr. 1-4). 16.99 (978-1-77049-648-4(3), Tundra Bks.) Tundra Bks. CAN. Dist: Penguin Random Hse. LLC.

Fernandes, Eugenie. Kitten's Autumn. Fernandes, Eugenie. 2010. (ENG.). 24p. (J). (gr. -1 — 1). 14.95 (978-1-55453-341-1(4)) Kids Can Pr., Ltd. CAN. Dist: Hachette Bk. Group.

—Kitten's Spring. Fernandes, Eugenie. 2010. (ENG.). 24p. (J). (gr. -1 — 1). 14.95 (978-1-55453-340-4(6)) Kids Can Pr., Ltd. CAN. Dist: Hachette Bk. Group.

—Kitten's Summer. Fernandes, Eugenie. (ENG.). 24p. (J). (gr. -1 — 1). 2013. bds. 7.95 (978-1-55453-721-1(5)); 2011. 14.95 (978-1-55453-342-8(2)) Kids Can Pr., Ltd. CAN. Dist: Hachette Bk. Group.

—Kitten's Winter. Fernandes, Eugenie. 2011. (ENG.). 24p. (J). (gr. -1 — 1). 14.95 (978-1-55453-343-5(0)) Kids Can Pr., Ltd. CAN. Dist: Hachette Bk. Group.

Fernandes, Kim. One Gray Mouse. Burton, Katherine. 2006. (ENG.). 24p. (J). (gr. -1 — 1). bds. 7.95 (978-1-55453-026-7(1)) Kids Can Pr., Ltd. CAN. Dist: Hachette Bk. Group.

—Une Souris Grise. Burton, Katherine.Tr. of Souris Grise. (FRE.). 24p. (J). pap. 6.99 (978-0-590-16023-0(0)) Scholastic, Inc.

Fernandez, Carina. Lily's Rainbow. Giacomo, Renee San. 2013. 28p. pap. 24.95 (978-1-63004-174-8(2)) America Star Bks.

Fernandez, Daniel. The Knight & the Firefly: A Boy, a Bug, & a Lesson in Bravery. Jenkins, Amanda & Reeves, Tara McClary. 2017. (Firefly Chronicles Ser.). (ENG.). 32p. (J). (gr. -1-3). pap. 3.99 *(978-1-4627-4519-7(9)*, 005793882, B&H Kids) B&H Publishing Group.

—What's So Wonderful about Webster? Kendrick, Stephen & Kendrick, Alex. 2019. (ENG.). 32p. (J). (gr. -1-3). 12.99 *(978-1-5359-4986-6(4)*, 005813513, B&H Kids) B&H Publishing Group.

Fernandez, Elizabeth & De La Torre, Eric. Tommy & Tammy the Firefighting Children. Kennedy, By Firefighting Tim. 2017. (Tommy & Tammy the Firefighting Children Ser.). (ENG.). (J). pap. *(978-1-4602-8723-1(1))* FriesenPress.

—Tommy & Tammy the Firefighting Children: Save the Environment. Kennedy, Firefighting Tim. 2018. (ENG.). 40p. (J). *(978-1-5255-2323-6(6))*; pap. *(978-1-5255-2324-3(4))* FriesenPress.

Fernandez Garcia, Marta. Las Aventuras de Álex Y Álvaro. Salazar Calle, Javier. 2019. (SPA.). 70p. (J). pap. 9.95 *(978-1-5172-6779-7(X))* CreateSpace Independent Publishing Platform.

Fernandez, Laura & Jacobson, Rick. Little Dog Moon, 1 vol. Trottier, Maxine. 2006. (ENG.). 24p. (J). (gr. 1-4). 7.95 *(978-1-55005-160-5(1)*, 4e40b252-6693-4dac-bd01-e48fb557632e) Fitzhenry & Whiteside, Ltd. CAN. Dist: Firefly Bks., Ltd.

—Vivaldi's Ring of Mystery. Cowling, Douglas. 2004. (ENG.). 44p. (J). *(978-0-439-96904-8(2)*, North Winds Pr) Scholastic Canada, Ltd.

Fernandez, Laura, jt. illus. see Jacobson, Rick.

Fernandez, Leandro, et al. New Mutants by Abnett & Lanning: the Complete Collection Vol. 2. 2019. (ENG.). 240p. (YA). pap. 34.99 *(978-1-302-91143-0(0))* Marvel Worldwide, Inc.

Fernandez, Leandro. Punisher Max - Volume 5: The Slavers. 2006. (ENG.). 144p. (gr. 13-17). 15.99 *(978-0-7851-1899-2(3))* Marvel Worldwide, Inc.

Fernandez, Leo. Incredible Hulk, Vol. 3. Jones, Bruce. Youngquist, Jeff, ed. 2004. (Hulk Ser.). 272p. 29.99 *(978-0-7851-1237-2(5))* Marvel Worldwide, Inc.

Fernandez, Lucia. Milagros en la Biblia. de Sturtz, Maria Ester H. 2007. (Manos a la Obra Ser.). 32p. (J). (gr. -1-4). per. 7.99 *(978-0-7586-1458-2(6))* Concordia Publishing Hse.

Fernandez, Luciana. Monstruos de Visita. Repún, Graciela. 2006. (SPA.). 24p. (J). (gr. k-2). pap. 7.50 *(978-987-1296-09-5(6))* Unaluna Ediciones ARG. Dist: Lectorum Pubns., Inc.

Fernandez, Maria Xose. A Cazar Palabras. Cáccamo, Pepe. (SPA.). 142p. (J). (gr. k-2). *(978-84-95123-36-7(3)*, KA1393) Kalandraka Editora, S.L. ESP. Dist: Lectorum Pubns., Inc.

Fernández, Pablo. Chat Natacha chat (Edición Especial) Pescetti, Luis Mariá. 2008. (Natacha Ser.). (SPA.). 124p. (gr. 3-5). pap. 12.95 *(978-970-58-0449-6(4))* Ediciones Alfaguara ESP. Dist: Santillana USA Publishing Co., Inc.

Fernandez, Pablo. Padrisimo, Natacha! Pescetti, Luis Mariá. 2008. (Natacha! Ser.). (SPA.). 138p. (J). (gr. 2-7). pap. 12.95 *(978-970-58-0495-3(8))* Ediciones Alfaguara ESP. Dist: Santillana USA Publishing Co., Inc.

—Padrisimo, Natacha! Maria Pescetti, Luis. 2009. (Serie Naranja / Natacha Ser.). (SPA.). 144p. (J). pap. 12.95 *(978-607-01-3627-6(6))* Santillana USA Publishing Co., Inc.

—Querido Diario (Natacha) Maria Pescetti, Luis. 2017. (Serie Naranja / Natacha Ser.). (SPA.). 144p. (J). pap. 12.95 *(978-607-01-3578-1(4))* Santillana USA Publishing Co., Inc.

Fernandez, Raul. Breakout. Bedard, Tony. 2005. (Spider-Man Legends Ser.). 120p. (YA). pap. 13.99 *(978-0-7851-1807-7(1))* Marvel Worldwide, Inc.

Fernandez, Raul, jt. illus. see Santacruz, Juan.

Fernandez, Victoria. Scratch & Learn Space: With 7 Interactive Spreads. Brownridge, Lucy. 2019. (Scratch & Learn Ser.). (ENG.). 16p. (J). (gr. -1-2). bds. 17.99 *(978-1-78603-794-7(7)*, Wide Eyed Editions) Quarto Publishing Group UK GBR. Dist: Hachette Bk. Group.

Fernando, jt. illus. see Denise.

Fernihough, Jo. Bathtime & Bedtime (Iggy Iguanadon: Time to Read, Level 2) MacDonald, Maryann. 2020. (Time to Read Ser.). (ENG.). 48p. (J). (gr. k-2). 12.99 ***(978-0-8075-3641-4(5)***, 0807536415) Whitman, Albert & Co.

—Playtime & Mealtime (Iggy Iguanadon: Time to Read, Level 2) MacDonald, Maryann. 2020. (Time to Read Ser.). (ENG.). 48p. (J). (gr. k-2). 12.99 ***(978-0-8075-3642-1(3)***, 0807536423) Whitman, Albert & Co.

Ferns, Kevin. The Spuds - the Fancy Dress Party. Haydon, David J. 2011. 20p. pap. *(978-1-908341-08-2(4))* Paragon Publishing, Rothersthorpe.

—The Spuds - the Windy Day. Haydon, David J. 2010. 20p. pap. *(978-1-907611-11-7(8))* Paragon Publishing, Rothersthorpe.

Ferone, Sarah. Top This! the Ice Cream Game. 2019. (ENG.). 4p. (J). (gr. -1-3). 16.99 *(978-1-4521-7164-7(5))* Chronicle Bks. LLC.

Ferraby, Teagan. Flora Jean & the Money Mix-Up. Perrine, Niccole. 2019. (Joy Ser.: Vol. 2). (ENG.). 62p. (J). pap. 6.91 ***(978-1-6934-2788-6(5))*** Independently Published.

Ferran, Daniel. Macbeth, 1 vol. Shakespeare, William. 2011. (Shakespeare Graphics Ser.). (ENG.). 88p. (J). (gr. 5-9). lib. bdg. 27.99 *(978-1-4342-2506-1(2)*, Stone Arch Bks.) Capstone.

Ferran, Daniel, jt. illus. see Pérez, Daniel.

Ferrándiz, Elena. Mis Primeras 1000 Palabras/My First 1,000 Words. 2004. (ENG & SPA.). 72p. (J). (gr. -1-2). 15.95 *(978-1-58394-100-3(2)*, Frog Children's Bks.) North Atlantic Bks.

Ferrando, Carol. Cabbages & Queens. Sullivan, Maureen. 2010. 57p. (J). pap. *(978-0-9820381-3-0(5))* MoJo InkWorks.

Ferrara, Eduardo. 8-Bit Baseball, 1 vol. Terrell, Brandon. 2014. (Sports Illustrated Kids Graphic Novels Ser.). (ENG.). 72p. (J). (gr. 3-8). 26.65 *(978-1-4342-4164-1(5)*, Stone Arch Bks.) Capstone.

Ferrara, Eduardo, jt. illus. see Garcia, Eduardo.

Ferrara, Madeleine. The Story of Cardinal George: The Boy Who Wanted to be a Priest. the God Who Wanted Him to be a Prince. Keusal, Eugene L. 2004. 33p. (J). 5.00 *(978-0-9786605-0-5(1))* Dooley Bks., Ltd.

Ferrari, Antongionata. Apollo. Colloredo, Sabino. 2009. (Hotel Olympus Ser.). 128p. (J). (gr. 3-6). 34.95 *(978-1-60754-710-5(4))* Windmill Bks.

—Athena. Colloredo, Sabino. 2009. (Hotel Olympus Ser.). 128p. (J). (gr. 3-6). 34.95 *(978-1-60754-709-9(0))* Windmill Bks.

—Hercules. Colloredo, Sabino. 2009. (Hotel Olympus Ser.). 128p. (J). (gr. 3-6). 34.95 *(978-1-60754-708-2(2))* Windmill Bks.

—No Honking Allowed. Calmenson, Stephanie. 2017. (ENG.). 40p. (J). (gr. -1-2). 16.95 *(978-0-8234-3672-9(1))* Holiday Hse., Inc.

—Zeus. Colloredo, Sabino. 2009. (Hotel Olympus Ser.). 128p. (J). (gr. 3-6). 34.95 *(978-1-60754-707-5(4))* Windmill Bks.

—50 Adventures to Have Before You Turn 14. Baccalario, Pierdomenico & Percivale, Tommaso. Hauber, Sara, tr. 2019. (ENG.). 176p. (YA). (gr. 5-8). pap. 14.99 *(978-1-4926-7155-8(X)*, Sourcebooks Jabberwocky) Sourcebooks, Inc.

Ferrario, Giuseppe, et al. Cyber-Thief Showdown. Stilton, Geronimo & Pizzelli, Anna. 2018. 107p. (J). *(978-1-5490-0240-3(6))* Scholastic, Inc.

Ferrario, Giuseppe & Fausone, Flavio. The Treasure of Easter Island, 60. Stilton, Geronimo & Tramontozzi, Lidia Morson. 2015. (Geronimo Stilton Ser.). (ENG.). 128p. (J). (gr. 2-4). 22.44 *(978-1-4844-5770-2(6))* Scholastic, Inc.

Ferraro Close, Laura. Storytime Stickers: Farm Follies. Plourde, Lynn. 2010. (Storytime Stickers Ser.). 16p. (J). (gr. k-2). pap. 5.95 *(978-1-4027-7127-9(4))* Sterling Publishing Co., Inc.

Ferraro-Oster, Margaret. Freddie Q. Freckle. Messinger, Midge. Messinger, Robert, ed. unabr. ed. 2003. 40p. (gr. -1-2). 12.95 *(978-1-893237-00-1(1))* Little Mai Pr.

Ferraz, Mayhara. The Little Blue Dinosaur. Rawandzi, Kardason. 2020. (ENG.). 30p. (J). pap. ***(978-0-2288-2357-5(9))*** Tellwell Talent.

Ferree, Rebecca Ann. Stella's Journey. Ferree, Rebecca Ann. 2018. (Stella Steller Jay Ser.: Vol. 1). (ENG.). 32p. (J). (gr. k-3). pap. 12.00 *(978-0-692-07066-6(4))* Ferree, Rebecca Ann.

Ferreira, Marcelo. Morbius Vol. 1: Old Wounds. 2020. 112p. (YA). (gr. 8-17). pap. 15.99 ***(978-1-302-92099-9(5))*** Marvel Worldwide, Inc.

Ferreira, Melissa. Bear's All-Night Party. Harley, Bill. 2005. (ENG.). 32p. (J). (gr. -1-2). 15.95 *(978-0-87483-572-4(0))* August Hse. Pubs., Inc.

Ferrenburg, Susie. There's Only One I in Charlie. Snyder, Sandy. 2011. 48p. pap. 24.95 *(978-1-4626-4086-7(9))* America Star Bks.

Ferrer, Heather. Hogan's Hope: Finding a Forever Home of Love & Acceptance. Bombaci, Connie. 2020. (ENG.). 36p. (J). 17.99 ***(978-1-935258-67-4(2))*** Husky Trail Pr. LLC.

Ferrer, Marianne. The Invisible Garden, 1 vol. Picard, Valérie. 2019. (ENG.). 64p. (J). (gr. -1-k). 19.95 *(978-1-4598-2211-5(0))* Orca Bk. Pubs. USA.

—Mel & Mo's Marvelous Balancing Act. Winstanley, Nicola. 2019. (ENG.). 32p. (J). (gr. -1-2). 18.95 *(978-1-77321-324-8(5))* Annick Pr., Ltd. CAN. Dist: Publishers Group West (PGW).

—Un Pique-Nique Au Soleil: Les Aventures Extraordinaires de la Bande � B�bert. Duchesne, Christiane. 2020. (ENG.). 48p. (J). (gr. k-2). 16.95 *(978-2-924774-59-5(4))* Secret Mountain CAN. Dist: Independent Pubs. Group.

Ferrero, Mar. The Wooden Sheep. Mezquita, Roberto. 2019. (ENG.). 36p. (J). (gr. -1-k). 16.95 *(978-84-16566-98-3(4))* Ediciones La Fragatina ESP. Dist: Independent Pubs. Group.

Ferrerya, Lucas. Penguins Collection 2. Scott, Cavan & Matthews, Alex. 2016. (Penguins of Madagascar Ser.: 2). 112p. (gr. 1-4). pap. 12.99 *(978-1-78585-316-6(3))* Titan Bks. Ltd. GBR. Dist: Penguin Random Hse. LLC.

Ferreyra, Lucas. Penguins of Madagascar Volume 4. Scott, Cavan. 2016. (Penguins of Madagascar Ser.: 4). 64p. (J). (gr. 1-4). 6.99 *(978-1-78276-254-6(X))* Titan Bks. Ltd. GBR. Dist: Penguin Random Hse. LLC.

Ferri, Francesca. Good Night, Teddy. 2003. (ENG.). 8p. (J). (gr. -1). 16.99 *(978-0-7641-2595-9(8)*, B.E.S. Publishing) Peterson's.

Ferri, Giuliano. Ant & Grasshopper. Gray, Luli. 2011. (ENG.). 32p. (J). (gr. -1-2). 17.99 *(978-1-4169-5140-7(7)*, McElderry, Margaret K. Bks.) McElderry, Margaret K. Bks.

—Best Friends. Hao, K. T. Kung, Annie, tr. 2008. (ENG.). 32p. (J). (gr. -1). 15.95 *(978-1-933327-38-9(3))*; lib. bdg. 16.50 *(978-1-933327-39-6(1))* Purple Bear Bks., Inc.

—Illustrated Stories from Aesop. 2014. (ENG.). 272p. (J). 19.99 *(978-0-7945-2917-8(8)*, Usborne) EDC Publishing.

—Jonah's Whale. Spinelli, Eileen. 2012. (ENG.). 32p. (J). 16.00 *(978-0-8028-5382-0(X)*, Eerdmans Bks For Young Readers) Eerdmans, William B. Publishing Co.

—The Legend of Saint Nicholas. Grün, Anselm et al. 2014. (ENG.). 26p. (J). 16.00 *(978-0-8028-5434-6(6)*, Eerdmans Bks For Young Readers) Eerdmans, William B. Publishing Co.

—The Magic Book. Hao, K. T. 2008. (ENG.). 32p. (J). (gr. -1). 16.50 *(978-1-933327-44-0(8))*; 15.95 *(978-1-933327-43-3(X))* Purple Bear Bks., Inc.

—The Story of Daniel in the Lions' Den. McCarthy, Michael. 2003. 32p. (J). (gr. 1-3). 16.99 *(978-1-84148-209-5(9))* Barefoot Bks., Inc.

—The 100th Customer. Kim, Byung-Gyu & Hao, K. T. 2005. (ENG.). 32p. (J). (gr. -1-17). 15.95 *(978-1-933327-03-7(0))* Purple Bear Bks., Inc.

Ferri, Giuliano. I See, I Touch ... Ferri, Giuliano. 2018. (ENG.). 24p. (J). (— 1). bds. 9.99 *(978-988-8341-56-6(1)*, Minedition) Neugebauer, Michael (Publishing) Limited HKG. Dist: Penguin Random Hse. LLC.

—Let's Play Soccer! Ferri, Giuliano. 2019. (ENG.). 14p. (J). (gr. -1-k). bds. 8.99 *(978-988-8341-85-6(5)*, Minedition) Neugebauer, Michael (Publishing) Limited HKG. Dist: Penguin Random Hse. LLC.

—Manny Loses His Fangs. Ferri, Giuliano. 2019. (ENG.). 32p. (J). (gr. k-2). 17.99 *(978-988-8341-83-2(9)*, Minedition) Neugebauer, Michael (Publishing) Limited HKG. Dist: Penguin Random Hse. LLC.

Ferri, Guiliano. I Do It Myself. Adam, Luisa. 2016. (ENG.). 24p. (J). (gr. -1-k). *(978-1-925386-55-4(4)*, Brolly Bks.) Borghesi & Adam Pubs. Pty Ltd.

Ferrier, Katherine. The Ghosts in the Clouds, No. 4. Ferrier, Katherine. Ferrier, Florian & Burrell, Carol klio. 2017. (Hotel Strange Ser.: 4). 40p. (J). (gr. 2-5). 26.65 *(978-1-4677-8587-7(3)*, 9781467785877, Graphic Universe™) Lerner Publishing Group.

—The Ghosts in the Clouds: Book 4. Ferrier, Katherine. Ferrier, Florian. ed. 2017. (Hotel Strange Ser.: 4). (ENG.). 40p. (J). (gr. 2-5). E-Book 39.99 *(978-1-5124-2704-2(7)*, 9781512427042, Graphic Universe™) Lerner Publishing Group.

—The Ghosts in the Clouds: Book 4, No. 4. Ferrier, Katherine. Ferrier, Florian. 2017. (Hotel Strange Ser.: 4). (ENG.). 40p. (J). (gr. 2-5). 11.99 *(978-1-5124-3066-0(8)*, 9781512430660, Graphic Universe™) Lerner Publishing Group.

—His Royal Majesty of the Mushrooms, No. 3. Ferrier, Katherine. Ferrier, Florian. 2016. (Hotel Strange Ser.: 3). 40p. (J). (gr. 2-5). lib. bdg. 26.65 *(978-1-4677-8586-0(5)*, 9781467785860, Graphic Universe™) Lerner Publishing Group.

—Wake Up, Spring, Bk. 1. Ferrier, Katherine. Ferrier, Florian & Burrell, Carol klio. 2015. (Hotel Strange Ser.). 40p. (J). (gr. 2-5). 26.65 *(978-1-4677-8584-6(9)*, 9781467785846, Graphic Universe™) Lerner Publishing Group.

Ferrigno, Angela. Hope's Garden. Jane, Sarah. 2008. (ENG.). 32p. (J). (gr. -1-2). lib. bdg. 16.95 *(978-0-9790962-0-4(0))* Tri Valley Children's Publishing.

Ferris, Carole Anne. Donkey & the Racehorse. Johnson, Joanne Gail. 2011. (ENG.). 48p. pap. 12.00 *(978-0-230-02552-3(8)*, Macmillan) Pan Macmillan GBR. Dist: Macmillan.

Ferro, Elisa. Daddies Do. Evans, Lezlie. 2018. (ENG.). 32p. (J). (gr. -1). 16.95 *(978-1-4549-2171-4(4))* Sterling Publishing Co., Inc.

Ferrone, John M. Gus & the Golden Dragon. Ferrone, John M. Date not set. 36p. (gr. -1-5). pap. 16.95 *(978-1-928811-02-2(7))* Story Stuff, Inc.

—Gus & the Pirate Treasure. Ferrone, John M. Date not set. 36p. (J). (gr. -1-5). pap. 16.95 *(978-1-928811-01-5(9))* Story Stuff, Inc.

—Margo Goes on Safari. Ferrone, John M. Date not set. 36p. (J). (gr. -1-5). pap. 16.95 *(978-1-928811-04-6(3))* Story Stuff, Inc.

Ferrone, John M., photos by. Margo & the Secret Pond. Ferrone, John M. Date not set. 36p. (J). (gr. -1-5). pap. 16.95 *(978-1-928811-03-9(5))* Story Stuff, Inc.

—Margo & the Trail Ride. Ferrone, John M. Date not set. 36p. (J). (gr. -1-5). pap. 16.95 *(978-1-928811-05-3(1))* Story Stuff, Inc.

Ferry, Pasqual, et al. X-Men Milestones: Onslaught. 2020. (ENG.). 488p. (YA). (gr. 8-17). pap. 39.99 *(978-1-302-92192-7(4))* Marvel Worldwide, Inc.

Fesseha, Zewditu. Lakech One: Amharic Ethiopian Script. Fesseha, Zewditu, photos by. Mammo, Rebecca et al, eds. 2005. (Lakech Two Ser.: Vol. 3). (YA). 25.00 *(978-0-9758877-0-7(X))* Orange, Michael Nicholas.

Feterl, Bill. Henry's Adventure at the Franklin Hotel. Cartwright, Nancy & Jones, Joanna. 2011. (YA). lib. bdg. *(978-0-913062-44-9(8))* Fenwyn Pr.

Fetherston, Catherine & Miller, Tom. Texas Roundup: Jake the Beagle's Crazy Adventures. Hernandez, Regina. Woods, Carol, ed. 2003. (Jake the Beagle Crazy Adventure Ser.: 2). 90p. (J). pap. 5.99 *(978-0-9727771-2-4(1))* Regal Enterprises.

Fetter-Vorm, Jonathan. Battle Lines: A Graphic History of the Civil War. Fetter-Vorm, Jonathan. Kelman, Ari. 2015. (ENG.). 224p. 26.00 *(978-0-8090-9474-5(6)*, 900076226, Hill & Wang) Farrar, Straus & Giroux.

Fetz, Ingrid. Maurice's Room. Fox, Paula. 2010. (ENG.). 64p. (J). (gr. 2-5). pap. 6.99 *(978-1-4424-1678-9(5)*, Simon & Schuster/Paula Wiseman Bks.) Simon & Schuster/Paula Wiseman Bks.

Feuti, Norm. Do You Like My Bike? An Acorn Book. Feuti, Norm. 2019. (Hello, Hedgehog! Ser.: 1). (ENG.). 48p. (J). (gr. -1-1). pap. 4.99 *(978-1-338-28138-5(0))*; lib. bdg. 15.99 *(978-1-338-28139-2(9))* Scholastic, Inc.

Feyh, Alexa & Deghand, Tim. Does God Have a Remote Control? Feyh, Janelle. l.t. ed. 2003. 66p. (J). per. 11.95 *(978-1-932344-26-4(8))* Thornton Publishing, Inc.

Feynman, Drew. Awesome Minds: the Creators of the IPhone®. Ventura, Marne. 2017. (Awesome Minds Ser.). (ENG.). 56p. (J). (gr. 1-5). 14.99 *(978-1-938093-77-7(1)*, 809377, Duo Pr. Llc (US)) Duo Pr. LLC.

Fiadzigbey, Setor. Breakaway. Sabino, David. 2019. (Game Day Ser.). (ENG.). 40p. (J). (gr. k-2). 17.99 *(978-1-5344-3935-1(8))*; pap. 4.99 *(978-1-5344-3934-4(X))* Simon Spotlight. (Simon Spotlight).

Fiadzigbey, Setor. Dive In. Sabino, David. 2020. (Game Day Ser.). (ENG.). 40p. (J). (gr. k-2). 17.99 ***(978-1-5344-6544-2(8))***; pap. 4.99 ***(978-1-5344-6543-5(X))*** Simon Spotlight. (Simon Spotlight).

Fiadzigbey, Setor. Epic Athletes: Lebron James. Wetzel, Dan. 2019. (Epic Athletes Ser.: 5). (ENG.). 176p. (J). 16.99 *(978-1-250-29580-4(7)*, 900195494, Holt, Henry & Co. Bks. For Young Readers) Holt, Henry & Co.

—Match Point. Sabino, David. 2020. (Game Day Ser.). (ENG.). 40p. (J). (gr. k-2). 17.99 *(978-1-5344-5392-0(X))*; pap. 4.99 *(978-1-5344-5391-3(1))* Simon Spotlight. (Simon Spotlight).

—Slap Shot. Sabino, David. 2019. (Game Day Ser.). (ENG.). 40p. (J). (gr. k-2). 17.99 *(978-1-5344-4442-3(4))*; pap. 4.99 *(978-1-5344-4441-6(6))* Simon Spotlight. (Simon Spotlight).

Fiala, Émilie. ¿cómo Nací Yo? Curtiss, Dominique. Rodriguez, Guadalupe, tr. 2015. (SPA.). 42p. (J). pap. *(978-2-89687-524-5(7))* chouetteditions.com.

—Sag Wie Kam Ich Auf Die Welt? Curtiss, Dominique. Lusser, Walpurga, tr. 2015. (GER.). 42p. (J). pap. *(978-2-89687-479-8(8))* chouetteditions.com.

—Where Do I Come From? Curtiss, Dominique. Hill, Rowland, tr. 2013. 42p. pap. *(978-2-89687-245-9(0))* chouetteditions.com.

Fiammenghi, Gioia. Chocolate Fever. Smith, Robert Kimmel. 2006. 96p. (J). (gr. 3-7). 5.99 *(978-0-14-240595-6(7)*, Puffin Books) Penguin Young Readers Group.

—Una Coleccion para Kate (A Collection for Kate) deRubertis, Barbara. 2007. (Math Matters Ser.). (SPA.). 29p. (J). (gr. -1-3). pap. 5.95 *(978-1-57565-240-5(4))* Astra Publishing Hse.

—A Collection for Kate: Addition. deRubertis, Barbara. 2006. (Math Matters ® Ser.). (ENG.). 32p. (J). (gr. k-2). pap. 5.95 *(978-1-57565-089-0(4))* Astra Publishing Hse.

—I Accept You As You Are! Parker, David. 2004. (J). *(978-0-439-62811-2(3))* Scholastic, Inc.

—I Show Respect! Parker, David. 2004. (J). pap. *(978-0-439-62809-9(1))* Scholastic, Inc.

—It's about Time, Max! Time. Richards, Kitty. 2006. (Math Matters ® Ser.). (ENG.). 32p. (J). (gr. k-3). pap. 5.95 *(978-1-57565-088-3(6))* Astra Publishing Hse.

—Play Date: Calendar. Santos, Rosa. 2006. (Math Matters ® Ser.). (ENG.). 32p. (J). (gr. k-2). pap. 5.95 *(978-1-57565-105-7(X))* Astra Publishing Hse.

—¿Quién Tiene Manchas? (Who's Got Spots?) Tallies & Graphs. Williams Aber, Linda. 2007. (Math Matters en Español Ser.). (SPA.). 32p. (J). (gr. 1-3). pap. 5.95 *(978-1-57565-251-1(X))* Astra Publishing Hse.

—Slowpoke: Elapsed Time. Penner, Lucille Recht. 2006. (Math Matters ® Ser.). (ENG.). 32p. (J). (gr. k-3). pap. 5.95 *(978-1-57565-108-8(4))* Astra Publishing Hse.

—Who's Got Spots? Tallies & Graphs. Williams Aber, Linda. 2006. (Math Matters ® Ser.). (ENG.). 32p. (J). (gr. k-3). pap. 5.95 *(978-1-57565-099-9(1))* Astra Publishing Hse.

Fiammetta, Dogi. Crowds of Creatures. Riggs, Kate. 2017. (ENG.). 14p. (J). (gr. -1 — 1). bds. 7.99 *(978-1-56846-301-8(4)*, Creative Education) Creative Co., The.

Fick, K. A. & Fick, M. Ormsby Otter River Tales: First Spring. Fick, Twig. 2020. (ENG.). 50p. (J). pap. 17.95 ***(978-1-9736-9008-5(X)***, WestBow Pr.) Author Solutions, Inc.

Fick, Kalie. Escape to Ninothia. Kores, M. T. Zander, Christian, ed. 2016. (ENG.). (J). (gr. 3-6). 24.99 *(978-0-692-78763-2(1))* Kores, Michelle.

Fick, M., jt. illus. see Fick, K. A.

Fickling, Phillip. Fillmore & Geary Take Off! The Adventures of a Robot Boy & a Boy Boy. Shulman, Mark. 2004. (ENG.). 40p. (J). (gr. -1-7). 14.95 *(978-1-58717-256-4(9)*, SeaStar Bks.) Chronicle Bks. LLC.

Ficorilli, Francesca. Rebecca Rides for Freedom: An American Revolution Survival Story. Berne, Emma Carlson. 2020. (Girls Survive Ser.). (ENG.). 112p. (J). (gr. 3-6). pap. 7.95 ***(978-1-4965-9910-0(1)***, 201321); lib. bdg. 25.99 ***(978-1-4965-9690-1(0)***, 199285) Capstone. (Stone Arch Bks.).

—Tara & the Towering Wave: An Indian Ocean Tsunami Survival Story. Oxtra, Cristina. 2020. (Girls Survive Ser.). (ENG.). 112p. (J). (gr. 3-6). pap. 7.95 ***(978-1-4965-9911-7(X)***, 201322); lib. bdg. 25.99 ***(978-1-4965-9691-8(9)***, 199286) Capstone. (Stone Arch Bks.).

Fidawi, Maya. Alya & the Three Cats. Retnani, Mehdi, tr. from ARA. 2020. (ENG.). 32p. (J). (gr. -1). 15.95 *(978-2-89802-236-4(5)*, CrackBoom! Bks.) Chouette Publishing CAN. Dist: Publishers Group West (PGW).

—My Brother & I. Najjar, Taghreed & Dupuis, Karina. Hartman, Michelle, tr. 2019. (ENG.). 32p. (J). (gr. -1). 15.95 *(978-2-89802-013-1(3)*, CrackBoom! Bks.) Chouette Publishing CAN. Dist: Publishers Group West (PGW).

—Watermelon Madness. Najjar, Taghreed & Dupuis, Karina. Hartman, Michelle, tr. 2018. 32p. (J). (gr. -1). 15.95 *(978-2-924786-22-2(3)*, CrackBoom! Bks.) Chouette Publishing CAN. Dist: Publishers Group West (PGW).

Fiddy, Samantha Lane. Mr. Astley's Blueberries. Lin, Kelly Jenkins. 2012. 36p. pap. 12.95 *(978-0-615-67849-8(1))* Three Flower Farm Pr.

Fiebiger, John. The Knee Bender: Drill Sergeant Bear Volume 3, 1 vol. Hand, Reuben. 2009. 17p. pap. 24.95 *(978-1-61582-706-0(4))* America Star Bks.

—The Push Up: Drill Sergeant Bear Volume 2. Hand, Reuben. 2009. 20p. pap. 24.95 *(978-1-61546-234-6(1))* America Star Bks.

—The Turn & Bounce, 1 vol. Hand, Reuben. 2010. 18p. 24.95 *(978-1-4489-5185-7(2))* PublishAmerica, Inc.

Fiedler, Joseph Daniel. Hard Labor: The First African Americans 1619. McKissack, Patricia C. & McKissack, Fredrick L., Jr. 2004. (Milestone Ser.). (ENG.). 64p. (J). (gr. 2-5). pap. 6.99 *(978-0-689-86149-9(4)*, Simon & Schuster/Paula Wiseman Bks.) Simon & Schuster/Paula Wiseman Bks.

—Juan Verdades: The Man Who Couldn't Tella Lie. Hayes, Joe. 2011. (ENG & SPA.). (J). (gr. 3-6). lib. bdg. 20.05 *(978-1-61383-080-2(7))* Perfection Learning Corp.

—Juan Verdades - El Hombre Que No Sabía Mentir. Hayes, Joe. 2011.Tr. of Juan Verdades/The Man Who Couldn't Tell a Lie. (ENG.). 32p. (J). (gr. 3-6). pap. 8.95 *(978-1-933693-70-5(3))* Cinco Puntos Pr.

Fiegenschuh, Emily & Lewis-MacDougall, Patricia Ann. How Things Came to Be: Inuit Stories of Creation, 1 vol. Qitsualik-Tinsley, Rachel & Qitsualik-Tinsley, Sean. 2019. (ENG.). 80p. (J). pap. 12.95 *(978-1-77227-259-8(0))* Inhabit Media Inc. CAN. Dist: Consortium Bk. Sales & Distribution.

Fiegenschuh, Emily & MacDougall, Larry. The Shadows That Rush Past: A Collection of Frightening Inuit Folktales. Qitsualik-Tinsley, Rachel. 2018. (ENG.). 48p. (J). (gr. 3-6). pap. 10.95 *(978-1-77227-218-5(3))* Inhabit Media Inc. CAN. Dist: Consortium Bk. Sales & Distribution.

Fiegenshuh, Emily. Key to the Griffon's Lair. Ransom, Candice. 2005. (Knights of the Silver Dragon Ser.: Bk. 9). 182p. (J). *(978-1-4156-3032-7(1),* Mirrorstone) Wizards of the Coast.

—The Silver Spell. Banerjee, Anjali. 2005. (Knights of the Silver Dragon Ser.: Bk. 8). 174p. (J). *(978-1-4156-1645-1(0),* Mirrorstone) Wizards of the Coast.

Fieger, Grace, jt. illus. see Hovda, Lily.

Field, Conrad. Alaska Ocean ABCs. Field, Conrad. 2008. 32p. (J). pap. 9.95 *(978-0-9797442-2-8(9))* Alaska Independent Pubs.

Field, Elaine. Ahora Me Toca a Mi! Bedford, David. (SPA.). 32p. (J). *(978-84-8418-051-7(4))* Corimbo, Editorial S.L. ESP. Dist: Lectorum Pubns., Inc.

Field, Fiona. Can I Tell You about Eating Disorders? A Guide for Friends, Family & Professionals. Lask, Bryan & Watson, Lucy. 2014. (Can I Tell You About... ? Ser.). (ENG.). 56p. pap. 14.95 *(978-1-84905-421-8(5),* 694419) Kingsley, Jessica Pubs. GBR. Dist: Hachette UK Distribution.

Field, James. The Awesome Book of Duckbills & Boneheads. Benton, Michael. Paiva, Johannah Gilman, ed. 2014. (ENG.). 32p. (J). (gr. 3-7). 7.99 *(978-1-4867-0343-2(7))* Flowerpot Children's Pr. Inc. CAN. Dist: Cardinal Pubs. Group.

—The Awesome Book of Flesh-Eaters. Benton, Michael. Paiva, Johannah Gilman, ed. 2014. (ENG.). 32p. (J). (gr. 3-7). 7.99 *(978-1-4867-0341-8(0))* Flowerpot Children's Pr. Inc. CAN. Dist: Cardinal Pubs. Group.

—A Cool Kid's Field Guide to Dinosaurs. Crosbie, Duncan. 2009. (Cool Kid's Field Guide Ser.). 26p. (J). (gr. 1-3). spiral bd. 6.99 *(978-0-8416-7145-4(1))* Hammond World Atlas Corp.

—Defying Death in the Wilderness. Shone, Rob. 2010. (Graphic Survival Stories Ser.). 48p. (YA). 58.50 *(978-1-4488-0068-1(4));* (ENG.). pap. 14.05 *(978-1-61532-865-9(3));* (gr. 5-8). 35.45 *(978-1-4358-3531-3(X))* Rosen Publishing Group, Inc., The. (Rosen Reference).

—Dinosaurs: Discover the Awesome Lost World of the Dinosaur. Eason, Sarah. 2014. 64p. (J). (gr. -1-4). 14.99 *(978-1-86147-364-6(8),* Armadillo) Anness Publishing GBR. Dist: National Bk. Network.

—Diplodocus: The Whip-Tailed Dinosaur. Shone, Rob. 2008. (Graphic Dinosaurs Ser.). (ENG.). 32p. (J). 50.50 *(978-1-61532-137-7(3),* PowerKids Pr.); (gr. 2-5). lib. bdg. 28.50 *(978-1-4358-2504-8(7))* Rosen Publishing Group, Inc., The.

—Fighter Pilots. West, David. 2008. (Graphic Careers Ser.). (ENG.). 48p. (gr. 5-8). per. 14.05 *(978-1-4042-1456-9(9));* (YA). lib. bdg. 35.45 *(978-1-4042-1455-2(0))* Rosen Publishing Group, Inc., The.

—Real Ninja: Over 20 Stories of Japan's Secret Assassins. Turnbull, Stephen & Tulloch, Coral. 2009. (Real Adventurers Ser.). (ENG.). 48p. (gr. 3-3). 23.79 *(978-1-59270-081-3(0))* Cavendish Square Publishing LLC.

—Real Samurai: Over 20 True Stories about the Knights of Old Japan! Turnbull, Stephen. 2009. (Real Adventurers Ser.). (ENG.). 48p. (gr. 3-3). 23.79 *(978-1-59270-060-8(8))* Cavendish Square Publishing LLC.

—Stegosaurus: The Plated Dinosaur. Jeffrey, Gary. (Graphic Dinosaurs Ser.). (ENG.). 32p. 2009. (gr. 2-5). pap. 12.30 *(978-1-4042-7713-7(7),* PowerKids Pr.); 2008. (J). 50.50 *(978-1-61532-136-0(5),* PowerKids Pr.); 2008. (J). (gr. 2-5). lib. bdg. 28.50 *(978-1-4358-2503-1(9))* Rosen Publishing Group, Inc., The.

—Tyrannosaurus: The Tyrant Lizard. Shone, Rob. 2007. (Graphic Dinosaurs Ser.). (ENG.). 32p. (J). (gr. 2-5). lib. bdg. 26.50 *(978-1-4042-3897-8(2))* Rosen Publishing Group, Inc., The.

—Velociraptor: The Speedy Thief. West, David. (Graphic Dinosaurs Ser.). (ENG.). 32p. (gr. 2-5). 2008. pap. 12.30 *(978-1-4042-9628-2(X),* Rosen Classroom); 2007. (J). lib. bdg. 28.50 *(978-1-4042-3898-5(0))* Rosen Publishing Group, Inc., The.

Field, James & Weston, Steve. Iguanodon & Other Leaf-Eating Dinosaurs, 1 vol. 2009. (Dinosaur Find Ser.). (ENG.). 24p. (J). (gr. k-3). 27.32 *(978-1-4048-5174-0(7),* Picture Window Bks.) Capstone.

Field, James, jt. illus. see Shone, Rob.

Field, James, jt. illus. see Weston, Steve.

Field, Jim. Cats Ahoy! Bently, Peter. 2019. (ENG.). 32p. (J). (gr. -1-k). pap. 10.99 ***(978-1-5290-1607-9(X),*** Macmillan Children's Bks.) Pan Macmillan GBR. Dist: Independent Pubs. Group.

Field, Jim. Dog on a Frog? Gray, Kes & Gray, Claire. 2017. (ENG.). 32p. (J). (gr. -1-k). 17.99 *(978-1-338-11695-3(9),* Scholastic Pr.) Scholastic, Inc.

—Frog on a Log? Gray, Kes. 2015. (ENG.). 32p. (J). (gr. -1-k). 16.99 *(978-0-545-68791-1(8),* Scholastic Pr.) Scholastic, Inc.

—The Koala Who Could. Bright, Rachel. 2017. (ENG.). 32p. (J). (gr. -1-k). 16.99 *(978-1-338-13908-2(8))* Scholastic, Inc.

—The Lion Inside. Bright, Rachel. 2016. (ENG.). 32p. (J). (gr. -1-k). 16.99 *(978-0-545-87350-5(9),* Scholastic Pr.) Scholastic, Inc.

—Oi Cat! Gray, Kes. 2019. (Oi Frog & Friends Ser.). 32p. (J). (gr. -1-k). 16.99 *(978-1-4449-3251-5(9));* pap. 9.99 *(978-1-4449-3252-2(7))* Hachette Children's Group GBR. Dist: Hachette Bk. Group.

—Oi Duck-Billed Platypus! Gray, Kes. 2019. (Oi Frog & Friends Ser.). 32p. (J). (gr. -1-1). 16.99 *(978-1-4449-3732-9(4))* Hachette Children's Group GBR. Dist: Hachette Bk. Group.

—Pull-Back Busy Train. Watt, Fiona. ed. 2013. (Pull-Back Bks). 10p. (J). ring bd. 24.99 *(978-0-7945-3333-5(7),* Usborne) EDC Publishing.

—Rabbit & Bear: Attack of the Snack. Gough, Julian. 2020. (Rabbit & Bear Ser.: 3). (ENG.). 112p. (J). (gr. 1-3). 9.99 *(978-1-68412-617-0(7),* Silver Dolphin Bks.) Printers Row Publishing Group.

—Rabbit & Bear: Rabbit's Bad Habits. Gough, Julian. 2019. (Rabbit & Bear Ser.: 1). (ENG.). 112p. (J). (gr. 1-3). 9.99 *(978-1-68412-588-3(X),* Silver Dolphin Bks.) Printers Row Publishing Group.

—Rabbit & Bear: the Pest in the Nest. Gough, Julian. 2019. (Rabbit & Bear Ser.: 2). (ENG.). 112p. (J). (gr. 1-3). 9.99 *(978-1-68412-589-0(8),* Silver Dolphin Bks.) Printers Row Publishing Group.

—There's a Lion in My Cornflakes. Robinson, Michelle. 2015. (ENG.). 32p. (J). (gr. -1-1). 16.99 *(978-0-8027-3836-3(2),* 900142746, Bloomsbury USA Childrens) Bloomsbury Publishing USA.

—The Way Home for Wolf. Bright, Rachel. 2019. (ENG.). 32p. (J). (gr. -1-k). 16.99 *(978-1-338-59274-0(2),* Scholastic Pr.) Scholastic, Inc.

Field, Lisa. A Charmed Life / una Vida con Suerte. Barbieri, Gladys. 2016. (MUL, ENG & SPA.). 32p. (J). (gr. k-3). 17.95 *(978-1-55885-827-5(X),* Piñata Books) Arte Publico Pr.

Field, Mandy & Pearson, Maria. First Stories from the Bible. Doherty, Gillian, ed. 2007. (Bible Tales Readers Ser.). 143p. (J). (gr. -1-k). 17.99 *(978-0-7945-1668-0(8),* Usborne) EDC Publishing.

Field, Sabra. Where Do They Go? Alvarez, Julia. 2016. (ENG.). 24p. (J). (gr. -1-2). 18.95 *(978-1-60980-670-5(0),* Triangle Square) Seven Stories Pr.

Field, Susan. The O'Brien Book of Irish Fairy Tales & Legends. Leavy, Una. 2012. (ENG.). 96p. (J). pap. 21.00 *(978-1-84717-313-3(6))* O'Brien Pr., Ltd., The IRL. Dist: Casemate Pubs. & Bk. Distributors, LLC.

Fielder, John, photos by. Do You See What I See? 2006. (J). 14.99 *(978-1-56579-554-9(7))* Fielder, John Publishing.

Fielder, Simon D. Am I Bad: Stories of Autism. Miller, Brandy. 2017. (ENG.). 26p. (J). (gr. k-5). pap. *(978-1-9998896-0-9(6))* Miller, Brandy.

Fieldhouse, Vicky. My Favorite Run. Richards, Katherine. 2013. (ENG.). 32p. (J). 16.99 *(978-0-9895095-2-7(4))* Fit Kids Publishing.

Fielding, Grace. Bilby & the Bushfire. Crawford, Joanne. 2007. 28p. (J). pap. *(978-1-921248-30-6(0))* Magabala Bks.

—Bip the Snapping Bungaroo. McRobbie, Narelle. 2nd ed. 2010. (ENG.). 36p. (J). (gr. 2-4). pap. 19.95 *(978-1-921248-07-8(6))* Magabala Bks. AUS. Dist: Independent Pubs. Group.

—A Home for Bilby. Crawford, Joanne. 2004. 28p. (J). pap. *(978-1-875641-91-8(2))* Magabala Bks.

Fields, Coy. Adventures in Cottontail Pines: The Summer Princess. Wade, T. K. 2017. (Adventures in Cottontail Pines Ser.: Vol. 1). (ENG.). 28p. (J). (gr. 2-6). pap. 11.99 *(978-0-692-04699-9(2))* Wade, T.K.

Fields, Laura & Walters, Bob. Velociraptor up Close: Swift Dinosaur. Dodson, Peter & Library Association Staff. 2011. (Zoom in on Dinosaurs! Ser.). 24p. (J). (gr. k-2). 23.95 *(978-0-7660-3337-5(6))* Enslow Publishing, LLC.

Fields, Laura, jt. illus. see Marshall, Todd.

Fields, Lisa. Barreling over Niagara Falls, 1 vol. Allen, Nancy Kelly. 2013. (ENG.). 40p. (J). (gr. k-3). 17.99 *(978-1-4556-1766-1(0),* Pelican Publishing) Arcadia Publishing.

—Grandma's Chocolate/El Chocolate de Abuelita. Price, Mara & Ventura, Gabriela Baeza. 2010. (SPA.). 32p. (J). (gr. -1-3). 16.95 *(978-1-55885-587-8(4),* Piñata Books) Arte Publico Pr.

—Lewis Tewanima: Born to Run, 1 vol. Solomon, Sharon. 2014. (ENG.). 32p. (J). (gr. k-3). 16.99 *(978-1-4556-1941-2(8),* Pelican Publishing) Arcadia Publishing.

—Sofia & the Purple Dress / Sofía y el Vestido Morado. Gonzales Bertrand, Diane. Baeza Ventura, Gabriela, tr. 2012. (SPA & ENG.). (J). 17.95 *(978-1-55885-701-8(X),* Piñata Books) Arte Publico Pr.

—Too Perfect. Ludwig, Trudy. 2009. 32p. (J). (gr. 1-4). 15.99 *(978-1-58246-258-5(5),* Tricycle Pr.) Random Hse. Children's Bks.

Fields, Lisa, jt. illus. see Corpi, Lucha.

Fienieg, Annette. In Our Street. Meinderts, Koos. 2013. (ENG.). 32p. (J). (gr. -1). 12.95 *(978-1-935954-24-8(5),* 9781935954248) Lemniscaat USA.

—The Man in the Clouds. Meinderts, Koos. 2012. (ENG.). 38p. (J). (gr. 1). 16.95 *(978-1-935954-13-2(X),* 9781935954132) Lemniscaat USA.

Fierle, Sarah. Be Kind to Your Mind: An Adventure in Mindfulness from A-Z. Abbott, Lisa. 2019. (ENG.). 32p. (J). (gr. k-6). pap. 10.99 ***(978-0-578-49757-0(3))*** Abbott, Lisa.

Fife, Jay. Ten Dollar Words for Kids. Kennedy, Kevin. 2013. 26p. pap. 11.95 *(978-1-61244-244-0(7))* Halo Publishing International.

Figert, Anya & Roberts, Megan. Sea Billows. Glassco, Jill Watson. 2018. (ENG.). 96p. (J). pap. 9.50 *(978-1-939535-29-0(8))* Deep Sea Publishing.

Figg, Non, et al. Big Book of Things to Draw. Allman, Howard, photos by. Watt, Fiona et al. 2007. (Art Ideas Drawing School Ser.). 96p. (J). (gr. 4-7). pap. 15.99 *(978-0-7945-1328-3(X),* Usborne) EDC Publishing.

—Dibujos Paso A Paso Dinosaurios. Watt, Fiona. 2007. (Titles in Spanish Ser.). 31p. (J). 8.99 *(978-0-7460-8373-4(4),* Usborne) EDC Publishing.

Figg, Non. How to Draw Animals. Pratt, Leonie & Stowell, Louie. 2006. (Usborne Activities Ser.). 32p. (J). (gr. 1-4). pap. 8.99 *(978-0-7945-1241-5(0),* Usborne) EDC Publishing.

Figg, Non, et al. How to Draw Dinosaurs. Watt, Fiona. 2005. (Usborne Activities Ser.). 31p. (J). (gr. -1-3). pap. 8.95 *(978-0-7945-1056-5(6),* Usborne) EDC Publishing.

Figg, Non, jt. illus. see Miller, Antonia.

Figg, Non Et Al. Making Cards. Watt, Fiona. 2007. 64p. (J). pap. 14.99 *(978-0-7945-1356-6(5),* Usborne) EDC Publishing.

Figueroa, Nicolas Ramirez. El Sueño de un Llavero. Gatica, Patricia Mendez. Nunez, Miguel Angel, ed. 2019. (SPA.). 50p. (J). pap. 12.99 *(978-1-0908-7624-9(6))* Independently Published.

Figus, Valentina. Coding for Kids: Create Your Own Video Games with Scratch. Aludden, Johan et al. 2017. (ENG.). 96p. (J). (gr. 3-7). 12.95 *(978-88-544-1188-3(4))* White Star ITA. Dist: Sterling Publishing Co., Inc.

Fil, et al. Le Petit Frere du Chaperon Rouge. Tremblay, Marc. 2004. (était une Fois Ser.). (FRE.). 24p. (J). (gr. -1). pap. *(978-2-89021-698-3(5))* Diffusion du livre Mirabel (DLM).

Fil & Julie. La Loi du Talion. Charest, Jocelyne. 2004. (FRE.). 145p. (YA). 8.95 *(978-2-922565-85-0(8))* Editions de la Paix CAN. Dist: World of Reading, Ltd.

Fil and Julie Staff. A Duck in New York City. Kaldor, Connie. 2005. (ENG.). 36p. (J). (gr. -1-2). 16.95 *(978-2-923163-02-4(8))* La Montagne Secrete CAN. Dist: Independent Pubs. Group.

—A Poodle in Paris. Kaldor, Connie. 2006. (ENG.). 36p. (J). (gr. -1-2). 16.95 *(978-2-923163-12-3(5))* La Montagne Secrete CAN. Dist: Independent Pubs. Group.

Fil et, Julie. Graindsel et Bretel. Meunier, Sylvain & Lapierre, Steeve. 2004. (était une Fois Ser.). (FRE.). 24p. (J). (gr. -1). pap. *(978-2-89021-699-0(3))* Diffusion du livre Mirabel (DLM).

Filella, Luis. La Arañita. Schmauss, Judy Kentor. 2016. (Early Rising Readers Ser.). (SPA.). (J). (gr. -1). 6.67 *(978-1-4788-3676-6(8))* Newmark Learning LLC.

—La Caminata. Schmauss, Judy Kentor. 2016. (Early Rising Readers Ser.). (SPA.). (J). (gr. -1). 6.67 *(978-1-4788-3693-3(8))* Newmark Learning LLC.

—Mi Gráfico. Schmauss, Judy Kentor. 2016. (Early Rising Readers Ser.). (SPA.). (J). (gr. -1). 6.67 *(978-1-4788-3672-8(5))* Newmark Learning LLC.

—Mira Mi Jardin. Schmauss, Judy Kentor. 2016. (Early Rising Readers Ser.). (SPA.). 16p. (J). (gr. 1-1). 6.67 *(978-1-4788-4167-8(2))* Newmark Learning LLC.

—The Spider. Schmauss, Judy Kentor. 2015. (Early Rising Readers Ser.). (J). (gr. -1-k). 5.83 *(978-1-4788-1598-3(1))* Newmark Learning LLC.

—The Walk. Schmauss, Judy Kentor. 2015. (Early Rising Readers Ser.). (J). (gr. -1-k). 5.83 *(978-1-4788-1585-3(X))* Newmark Learning LLC.

Filgate, Leonard. Counting Animals/Contando Animales: An English/Spanish Number Book. Filgate, Susan Yost. 2018. (ENG.). 32p. (J). pap. 12.00 *(978-0-9978819-4-3(1))* America Hispanic Consulting Group Inc.

—Los Animales Me Hacen Feliz: Un Libro Del Abecedario. America Hispanic Consulting Group. 2016. (SPA.). (J). pap. 12.00 *(978-0-9978819-3-6(3))* America Hispanic Consulting Group Inc.

—Rip Squeak & His Friends. Yost-Filgate, Susan. 2004. 32p. (J). 16.95 *(978-1-59384-058-7(6))* Parklane Publishing.

Filice, Annette. My Yosemite: A Guide for Young Adventurers. Graf, Mike. 2012. (J). *(978-1-59714-170-3(4))* Heyday.

—My Yosemite: A Guide for Young Adventurers. Graf, Mike. 2012. (ENG.). 176p. (gr. 4). pap. 12.95 *(978-1-930238-30-5(4))* Yosemite Conservancy.

Fililla, Luis. My Garden. Schmauss, Judy Kentor. 2015. (Early Rising Readers Ser.). (J). (gr. -1-k). 5.83 *(978-1-4788-2168-7(X))* Newmark Learning LLC.

Filipak, Christine & Vargo, Joseph. Madame Endora's Fortune Cards. 2003. 17.99 *(978-0-9675756-3-6(X))* Monolith Graphics.

Filipczak, Sylwia. Collins Big Cat Phonics for Letters & Sounds - Six of Us: Band 02A/Red A. Belcher, Angie. 2020. (Collins Big Cat Phonics for Letters & Sounds Ser.). (ENG.). 16p. (J). (gr. -1-k). pap. 6.99 *(978-0-00-835766-5(8))* HarperCollins Pubs. Ltd. GBR. Dist: Independent Pubs. Group.

Filipina, Monika. I Say Shehechiyanu. Rocklin, Joanne. ed. 2015. (ENG.). 24p. (J). (gr. -1-2). E-Book 23.99 *(978-1-4677-6203-8(2),* Kar-Ben Publishing) Lerner Publishing Group.

—Liam's Pets. Mellion, Nicole. 2017. (Text Connections Guided Close Reading Ser.). (J). (gr. 1). *(978-1-4900-1802-7(6))* Benchmark Education Co.

—Look at Me! Set Of 6. Parkes, Brenda. 2014. (Shared Reading Foundations Ser.). (J). (gr. 1). 36.00 net. *(978-1-4900-0025-1(9))* Benchmark Education Co.

—Look at Me! Book Set. Parkes, Brenda. 2014. (Shared Reading Foundations Ser.). (J). (gr. 1). 72.00 net. *(978-1-4509-9995-3(6))* Benchmark Education Co.

Filipina, Monika, et al. Mark Sees the Stars - a Night Hunt for Food - Red Bird Chirps: BuildUp Unit 8 Lap Book. Flynn, Cam et al. 2015. (Build up Core Phonics Ser.). (J). (gr. 1). *(978-1-4900-2607-7(X))* Benchmark Education Co.

—Pop! Pop! Pop! - Cat in a Cap - Hot, Hot, Hot: StartUp Unit 4 Lap Book. Lee, Kim et al. 2015. (Start up Core Phonics Ser.). (J). (gr. k). *(978-1-4900-2593-3(6))* Benchmark Education Co.

Filipina, Monika. All about Cats. Filipina, Monika. 2017. (Child's Play Library). 32p. (J). (ENG.). *(978-1-84643-934-6(5));* pap. *(978-1-84643-933-9(7))* Child's Play International Ltd.

Filippi, Mirko. Mog. van der Peijl, Liza Rebecca. 2019. (SPA.). 64p. (J). (gr. -1-3). 9.95 *(978-607-748-141-6(6),* Uranito) Ediciones Urano de México MEX. Dist: Spanish Pubs., LLC.

Filippone, Nicole. Aiden Mcgee Gets a Case of the Actuallys. McGinley, Aaron. Fisher, Wyatt, ed. 2019. (ENG.). 30p. (J). (gr. k-3). pap. 12.00 *(978-1-7330859-2-2(0))* McGinley, Aaron.

Filippucci, Laura. Cinderella. Brothers Grimm. 2017. (ENG.). 32p. (J). (gr. -1-3). 17.95 *(978-0-7358-4294-6(9))* North-South Bks., Inc.

Filippucci, Laura Francesca. The Hidden Bestiary of Marvelous, Mysterious, & (Maybe Even) Magical Creatures. Young, Judy. 2009. (ENG.). 32p. (J). (gr. 1-4). 16.95 *(978-1-58536-433-6(9),* 1299753) Sleeping Bear Pr.

Fillbach. Clone Wars Adventures, 7. Fillbach. 2013. (Star Wars Digests Ser.). (ENG.). 80p. (J). (gr. 3-8). lib. bdg. 29.93 *(978-1-61479-058-7(2),* 13761, Graphic Novels) Spotlight.

—Star Wars: Clone Wars Adventures. Fillbach. 2013. (Star Wars Digests Ser.). (ENG.). 80p. (J). (gr. 3-8). lib. bdg. 29.93 *(978-1-61479-059-4(0),* 13762, Graphic Novels) Spotlight.

Fillion, Susan. Pizza in Pienza. Fillion, Susan. 2013. (ENG.). 32p. (J). 17.95 *(978-1-56792-459-6(X))* Godine, David R. Pub.

Finch, Avis. Country Music Hoedown! Kris. 2018. (ENG.). 20p. (J). (gr. -1-k). bds. 8.99 *(978-1-4998-0557-4(8))* Little Bee Books Inc.

Finch, David. Avengers Disassembled. 2006. 176p. (YA). (gr. 8-17). pap. 15.99 *(978-0-7851-1482-6(3))* Marvel Worldwide, Inc.

—New Avengers: Breakout Marvel Select Edition. 2020. (ENG.). 160p. (YA). (gr. 4-17). 24.99 *(978-1-302-91907-8(5))* Marvel Worldwide, Inc.

Finch, Jonathan. Moo! on the Farm. George, Joshua. 2017. (Stick & Learn Ser.). (ENG.). 36p. (J). (gr. -1-1). pap. 5.99 *(978-1-78700-193-0(8))* Top That! Publishing PLC GBR. Dist: Independent Pubs. Group.

—Vroom! Things That Go. George, Joshua. 2017. (Stick & Learn Ser.). (ENG.). 36p. (J). (gr. -1-1). pap. 5.99 *(978-1-78700-192-3(X))* Top That! Publishing PLC GBR. Dist: Independent Pubs. Group.

Fincher, Kathryn Andrews. Charlene's Grumpy Day: A Scoozie Tale about Patience. Carlson, Melody. Date not set. 32p. (J). 9.99 *(978-0-7369-0734-7(3))* Harvest Hse. Pubs.

—Grover Tells a Whopper: A Scoozie Tale about Honesty. Carlson, Melody. Date not set. 32p. (J). 9.99 *(978-0-7369-0733-0(5))* Harvest Hse. Pubs.

Fincher, Kathy. Baby's First Christmas. 2006. 8p. (gr. -1-k). bds. 7.95 *(978-0-88271-705-0(7))* Regina Pr., Malhame & Co.

—A Catholic's Baby's First Prayer Book. 2006. 16p. (gr. -1-k). bds. 9.95 *(978-0-88271-706-7(5))* Regina Pr., Malhame & Co.

—My Child: Boy. Waller, Steven H. 2008. 37p. (J). 11.95 *(978-0-88271-172-0(5))* Regina Pr., Malhame & Co.

—My Child: Girl. Waller, Steven H. 2009. 37p. (J). 11.95 *(978-0-88271-173-7(3))* Regina Pr., Malhame & Co.

—Remembrance of My First Holy Communion Boy. Hoagland, Victor & Theola Zimmerman, Mary. 2010. (ENG.). 126p. (J). 12.95 *(978-0-88271-184-3(9))* Regina Pr., Malhame & Co.

Findley, Judy. Sarah's Christmas Crown. Grimes, Marty. 2020. (ENG.). 32p. (J). 16.95 ***(978-1-941247-77-8(6))*** 3G Publishing, Inc.

Findley, Kelly. Puckster's First Hockey Tournament. Nicholson, Lorna Schultz. 2012. (Puckster Ser.). (ENG.). 24p. (J). (gr. -1-3). pap. 6.99 *(978-1-77049-457-2(X),* Fenn-Tundra) Tundra Bks. CAN. Dist: Penguin Random Hse. LLC.

—Puckster's First Hockey Tryout. Nicholson, Lorna Schultz. 2013. (Puckster Ser.). (ENG.). 24p. (J). (gr. -1-3). pap. 6.99 *(978-1-77049-596-8(7),* Fenn-Tundra) Tundra Bks. CAN. Dist: Penguin Random Hse. LLC.

Findley School Students. Butterfly: In English & Afaan Oromo. Ready Set Go Books. Gemeda, Ahmed Dedo, tr. 2019. (ENG.). 34p. (J). pap. 9.99 ***(978-1-6773-3071-3(6))*** Independently Published.

Fine, Alex. 50 Things about My Father (Fill-In Gift Book) A Celebration. Abrams Noterie. 2018. (ENG.). 96p. 12.99 *(978-1-4197-2977-5(2),* Abrams Noterie) Abrams, Inc.

Fine, Aron. Milly & Her Kittens. Wilson, Barbara. 2012. (ENG.). 16p. (gr. k-3). pap. 9.00 *(978-1-56778-542-5(5))* Wilson Language Training.

—Mrs. Hen & Her Six Chicks. Wilson, Barbara. 2012. (ENG.). 16p. (gr. k-3). pap. 9.00 *(978-1-56778-543-2(3))* Wilson Language Training.

Fine, Howard. All Aboard the Dinotrain. Lund, Deb. (ENG.). (J). (gr. -1 — 1). 2011. 30p. bds. 7.99 *(978-0-547-55415-0(X),* 1452006); 2009. 40p. pap. 7.99 *(978-0-547-24825-7(3),* 1100733) Houghton Mifflin Harcourt Publishing Co.

—Dinosailors. Lund, Deb. 2008. (ENG.). 36p. (J). (gr. -1-3). pap. 7.99 *(978-0-15-206124-1(X),* 1198391) Houghton Mifflin Harcourt Publishing Co.

—Hampire! Bardhan-Quallen, Sudipta. 2011. (ENG.). 32p. (J). (gr. -1-3). 16.99 *(978-0-06-114239-0(5))* HarperCollins Pubs.

—Piggie Pie!, 1 vol. Palatini, Margie. 2008. (ENG.). 32p. (J). (gr. -1-3). 10.99 *(978-0-547-18178-3(7),* 1055919) Houghton Mifflin Harcourt Publishing Co.

Finethy, Buddy. Arrowheads, Inc. Powell, Sammy. 2019. (Fox Tree Chronicles Ser.: Vol. 3). (ENG.). 92p. (J). (gr. 1-6). pap. 6.99 ***(978-1-946637-04-8(1))*** Brent Darnell International.

Finethy, Buddy. Little John's Secret. Powell, Sammy. 2017. (Fox Tree Chronicles Ser.: Vol. 2). (ENG.). 88p. (J). (gr. 1-6). pap. 6.99 *(978-0-9970445-8-4(6))* Brent Darnell International.

Fingerman, Bob. MySpace Dark Horse Presents, 6 vols., Vol. 1. Whedon, Joss et al. Allie, Scott & Hahn, Sierra, eds. 2008. (MySpace Dark Horse Presents Ser.: 1). (ENG.). 168p. (gr. 7-18). pap. 19.95 *(978-1-59307-998-7(2))* Dark Horse Comics.

Fink, Sam. The Declaration of Independence. Fink, Sam. 2007. (ENG.). 160p. (J). (gr. 3-6). 29.94 *(978-0-439-70315-4(8))* Scholastic, Inc.

—The Declaration of Independence: The Words That Made America. Fink, Sam. 2007. 160p. (YA). (gr. 7). 19.65 *(978-0-7569-8187-7(5))* Perfection Learning Corp.

Finkbeiner, Kevin. Tommy Tablet at Niagara Falls. Prantera, Julie. 2017. (ENG.). (J). pap. 12.99 *(978-1-62586-064-4(1))* Credo Hse. Pubs.

Finkelstein, Jeff. Mazel Tov! It's a Boy: Mazel Tov! It's a Girl. Finkelstein, Jeff, photos by. Korngold, Jamie S. 2015. (J). 6.99 *(978-1-4677-6206-9(7),* Kar-Ben Publishing) Lerner Publishing Group.

Finkle, Lindy. Have You Heard of Me ABC. Laura, Abigail. 2019. (ENG.). 44p. (J). 24.95 ***(978-1-64559-760-5(1));*** pap. 14.95 ***(978-1-64559-759-9(8))*** Covenant Bks.

Finlay, Lizzie. Buri & the Marrow. Barkow, Henriette. 2004. (ENG & FRE.). 24p. (J). pap. *(978-1-85269-583-5(8))* Mantra Lingua.

—Buri & the Marrow. 2004. 24p. (J). pap. *(978-1-85269-587-3(0));* pap. *(978-1-85269-590-3(0));*

(ENG & TUR.). pap. (978-1-85269-591-0(9)) Mantra Lingua.
—Buri & the Marrow. Barkow, Henriette. 2004. (ENG & ARA.). 24p. (J). pap. (978-1-85269-579-8(X)); pap. (978-1-85269-581-1(1)); pap. (978-1-85269-582-8(X)); pap. (978-1-85269-584-2(6)); pap. (978-1-85269-585-9(4)); pap. (978-1-85269-588-0(9)); pap. (978-1-85269-589-7(7)); pap. (978-1-85269-592-7(7)) Mantra Lingua.
—Buri & the Marrow: Buri Dhe Kungulli. Barkow, Henriette. 2004. (ENG & ALB.). 24p. (J). pap. (978-1-85269-578-1(1)) Mantra Lingua.
—Pony-Crazed Princess: Princess Ellie's Mystery. Kimpton, Diana. 3rd rev. ed. 2006. (ENG.). 96p. (gr. 1-4). pap. 3.99 (978-0-7868-4872-0(3)) Hyperion Pr.
—Pony-Crazed Princess Super Special: Princess Ellie's Summer Vacation. Kimpton, Diana. 2007. (ENG.). 144p. (gr. 1-4). pap. 4.99 (978-1-4231-0616-6(4)) Hyperion Pr.
—Princess Ellie Solves a Mystery. Kimpton, Diana. 8th rev. ed. 2007. (ENG.). 96p. (gr. 1-4). pap. 3.99 (978-1-4231-0901-3(5)) Hyperion Pr.
—Princess Ellie to the Rescue. Kimpton, Diana. 2006. (ENG.). 96p. (gr. 1-4). pap. 3.99 (978-0-7868-4870-6(7)) Hyperion Pr.
—Princess Ellie's Royal Jamboree No. 11. Kimpton, Diana. 11th ed. 2008. (ENG.). 96p. (gr. 1-4). pap. 3.99 (978-1-4231-1531-1(7)) Hyperion Pr.
—Princess Ellie's Secret No. 2. Kimpton, Diana. 2nd rev. ed. 2006. (ENG.). 96p. (gr. 1-4). pap. 3.99 (978-0-7868-4871-3(5)) Hyperion Pr.
—Princess Ellie's Snowy Ride. Kimpton, Diana. 2007. (Pony-Crazed Princess Ser.). 90p. (J). 11.65 (978-0-7569-8352-9(5)) Perfection Learning Corp.
—Princess Ellie's Snowy Ride No. 9. Kimpton, Diana. 9th rev. ed. 2007. (ENG.). 96p. (gr. 1-4). pap. 3.99 (978-1-4231-0902-0(3)) Hyperion Pr.
—Princess Ellie's Treasure Hunt No. 10. Kimpton, Diana. 10th ed. 2008. (ENG.). 96p. (gr. -1-3). pap. 3.99 (978-1-4231-1414-7(0)) Hyperion Pr.
—Sam's First Day. Mills, David. 2004. 24p. (J). (978-1-85269-630-6(3)); (978-1-85269-631-3(1)); (978-1-85269-635-1(4)); (978-1-85269-636-8(2)); (978-1-85269-637-5(0)); (978-1-85269-639-9(7)) (ENG.). (978-1-85269-640-5(0)); (978-1-85269-642-9(7)); (978-1-85269-643-6(5)); (978-1-85269-645-0(1)); (978-1-85269-646-7(X)); (978-1-85269-702-0(4)); (TUR & ENG.). (978-1-85269-644-3(3)); (978-1-84444-166-2(0)); 2nd ed. (PER & ENG.). (978-1-85269-634-4(6)) Mantra Lingua.
—A Surprise for Princess Ellie. Kimpton, Diana. 6th rev. ed. 2006. (ENG.). 96p. (gr. 1-4). pap. 3.99 (978-0-7868-4875-1(8)) Hyperion Pr.
Finlayson, Luke. Ninja Meerkats (#1): the Clan of the Scorpion, 1. Jones, Gareth P. 2013. (Ninja Meerkats Ser.: 1). (ENG.). 128p. (J). (gr. 2-4). pap. 6.99 (978-1-250-01664-5(9), 900087078) Square Fish.
—Ninja Meerkats (#3): Escape from Ice Mountain, 3. Jones, Gareth P. 2013. (Ninja Meerkats Ser.: 3). (ENG.). 128p. (J). (gr. 2-4). pap. 5.99 (978-1-250-02931-7(7), 900118543) Square Fish.
—Ninja Meerkats (#4): Hollywood Showdown, 4. Jones, Gareth P. 2013. (Ninja Meerkats Ser.: 4). (ENG.). 128p. (J). (gr. 2-4). pap. 18.69 (978-1-250-02932-4(5), 9781250029324) Square Fish.
—Ninja Meerkats (#5): the Tomb of Doom. Jones, Gareth P. 2013. (Ninja Meerkats Ser.: 5). (ENG.). 128p. (J). (gr. 2-4). pap. 8.99 (978-1-250-03402-1(7), 9781250034021) Square Fish.
—Ninja Meerkats (#6): Big City Bust-Up. Jones, Gareth P. 2013. (Ninja Meerkats Ser.: 6). (ENG.). 128p. (J). (gr. 2-4). pap. 14.99 (978-1-250-03403-8(5), 900120573) Square Fish.
—Ninja Meerkats (#7) the Ultimate Dragon Warrior. Jones, Gareth P. 2014. (Ninja Meerkats Ser.: 7). (ENG.). 128p. (J). (gr. 2-4). pap. 16.99 (978-1-250-04665-9(3), 9781250046659) Square Fish.
—Ninja Meerkats (#8) Outback Attack. Jones, Gareth P. 2014. (Ninja Meerkats Ser.: 8). (ENG.). 128p. (J). (gr. 2-4). pap. 16.99 (978-1-250-04667-3(X), 9781250046673) Square Fish.
Finlayson, Luke & Davis, Jacqui. How the Stars Got into the Sky - Two Native American Pourquoi Tales. Hayes, Joe. 2014. (Text Connections Ser.). (J). (gr. 4). pap. (978-1-4900-0073-2(9)) Benchmark Education Co.
Finley, Shawn, jt. illus. see Dean Kleven Studios.
Finley, Thomas Murray. Danger Dolphin. Kernan, Martin James. 2012. 28p. pap. 14.95 (978-1-4675-2428-5(X)) Independent Pub.
—Entertaining Elephant. Kernan, Martin James. 2012. (ENG.). 28p. (J). pap. 9.95 (978-1-4675-4149-7(4)) Independent Pub.
Finn, Ann-Marie. Gus, the Asparagus. 2017. (ENG.). (J). pap. (978-0-9945570-6-3(X)) Yellow Brick Bks.
—Start of the Ocean. Worthington, Michelle. 2013. 32p. pap. (978-0-9874160-1-8(4)) Wybble Publishing.
Finn, Ann-Marie. Captain Kieron. Finn, Ann-Marie. 2013. 32p. pap. (978-0-9874160-3-2(0)) Wybble Publishing.
Finn, Christine. Little Mozarts Go to Hollywood, Pop Book 1 And 2: 10 Favorites from TV, Movies & Radio. Barden, Christine H. et al. 2008. (Music for Little Mozarts Ser.: Bk 1-2). (ENG.). 24p. (J). pap. 8.99 (978-0-7390-5013-2(3)) Alfred Publishing Co., Inc.
Finn, Jenny. Tales from Hallowed Hollow: Karma. Watt, Marg. 2012. 34p. (YA). pap. (978-0-9872715-8-7(X)) Moonra Pubns.
Finn, Rebecca. Airport. Sterling Children's, Sterling. 2015. (Busy Bks.). (ENG.). 10p. (J). (— 1). bds. 8.95 (978-1-4549-1732-8(6)) Sterling Publishing Co., Inc.
—Bedtime Lullabies: Fall Asleep to Your Free Cd. Baxter, Nicola. 2014. 12p. (J). (gr. -1-12). bds. 14.99 (978-1-86147-360-8(5), Armadillo) Anness Publishing GBR. Dist: National Bk. Network.
—Builders. Sterling Children's, Sterling. 2015. (Busy Bks.). (ENG.). 10p. (J). (— 1). bds. 8.95 (978-1-4549-1733-5(4)) Sterling Publishing Co., Inc.
—Busy Beach. 2016. (Busy Bks.). (ENG.). 10p. (J). (gr. -1). bds. 8.95 (978-1-4549-1941-4(8), 1402428) Sterling Publishing Co., Inc.
—Busy Fire Station. 2016. (Busy Bks.). (ENG.). 10p. (J). (gr. -1). bds. 8.95 (978-1-4549-1942-1(6), 1402425) Sterling Publishing Co., Inc.
—Christmas Lullabies for Children. Baxter, Nicola, ed. 2014. (ENG.). 12p. (J). (gr. k-5). bds. 14.99 incl. audio compact disk (978-1-84322-931-5(5), Armadillo) Anness Publishing GBR. Dist: National Bk. Network.
—First Sticker Book Princesses. Greenwall, Jessica. ed. 2013. (First Sticker Bks). 16p. (J). pap. 6.99 (978-0-7945-3357-1(4), Usborne) EDC Publishing.
—Garage. Sterling Publishing Co., Inc. Staff. 2015. (Busy Bks.). (ENG.). 10p. (J). (— 1). bds. 8.95 (978-1-4549-1734-2(2)) Sterling Publishing Co., Inc.
—Jolly Snowman. 2005. (Cuddly Cuffstm Ser.). 6p. (J). (gr. -1-13). 6.95 (978-1-58925-754-2(5)) Tiger Tales.
—Little Bunny. (Cuddly Cuffstm Ser.). 6p. (J). 6.95 (978-1-58925-767-2(7)) Tiger Tales.
—Little Ducky. (Cuddly Cuffstm Ser.). 6p. (J). 6.95 (978-1-58925-766-5(9)) Tiger Tales.
—Little Kitty. (Cuddly Cuffstm Ser.). 6p. (J). 6.95 (978-1-58925-764-1(2)) Tiger Tales.
—Little Puppy. (Cuddly Cuffstm Ser.). 6p. (J). 6.95 (978-1-58925-765-8(0)) Tiger Tales.
—My Fairy Glade. Prasadam, Smriti. 2008. (Peep Through Play Bks.). 12p. (J). (gr. k-k). bds. 7.95 (978-0-7475-8809-2(0)) Bloomsbury Publishing Plc GBR. Dist: Independent Pubs. Group.
—Ponies (First Sticker Book) Patchett, Fiona. ed. 2011. (First Sticker Book Ser.). 24p. (J). pap. 6.99 (978-0-7945-2921-5(6), Usborne) EDC Publishing.
—Santa's Day. 2005. (Cuddly Cuffstm Ser.). 6p. (J). (gr. -1-13). 6.95 (978-1-58925-755-9(3)) Tiger Tales.
—Sing-Along Songs for Children: Join in with Your Free CD. Baxter, Nicola. 2014. (ENG.). 12p. (J). (gr. -1-k). bds. 14.99 (978-1-84322-892-9(0), Armadillo) Anness Publishing GBR. Dist: National Bk. Network.
—Toys (Cuddly Cuffs W/Hang Tag) Field, Elaine. (Cuddly Cuffs Ser.). 12p. (J). tchr. ed. 5.95 (978-1-58925-709-2(X)) Tiger Tales.
Finn, Rebecca, jt. illus. see Richards, Lucy.
Finnegan, Marco. Lizard in a Zoot Suit. Finnegan, Marco. 2020. (ENG.). 144p. (YA). (gr. 7-12). pap. 12.99 (978-1-5415-8695-6(6), Graphic Universe™) Lerner Publishing Group.
Finnegan, Marco, jt. illus. see Magallanes, Marco.
Finnegan, Molly. Ben the Tractor & Friends: For the Ben Moon Testimonial Year. #BackingBen. Ben Moon Testimonial Year. 2019. (ENG.). 34p. pap. 9.00 **(978-1-4463-0821-9(9))** David & Charles Pubs. GBR. Dist: Two Rivers Distribution.
Finnell-Acosta, B. C. The Search for the Missing Ball: Norman G. Bear. Pwob. 2010. 64p. pap. 25.49 (978-1-4520-3952-7(6)) AuthorHouse.
Finnell, Cyndy, jt. illus. see Stephens, Sherry.
Finney, Kathryn. Little Louie. 2014. 32p. (J). (gr. -1-k). 16.95 (978-1-62914-615-7(3), Sky Pony Pr.) Skyhorse Publishing Co., Inc.
Finney, Kathryn Kunz. Rising above the Storm Clouds: What It's Like to Forgive. Enright, Robert D. 2004. 32p. (J). 14.95 (978-1-59147-075-5(7)); pap. 9.95 (978-1-59147-076-2(5)) American Psychological Assn. (Magination Pr.).
Finney, Simone. My Daddy Is A Deputy Sheriff. Beckler, Bruce. l.t. ed. 2004. 14p. (J). per. 5.59 (978-0-9745210-4-6(3)) Myers Publishing Co.
—My Daddy Is a Police Officer: My Daddy Wears a Star. Beckler, Bruce. l.t. ed. 2004. 14p. (J). per. 5.59 (978-0-9745210-3-9(5)) Myers Publishing Co.
—My Daddy Is A Police Officer: Wears A Badge, 8 bks. Beckler, Bruce. l.t. ed. 2004. 14p. (J). per. 5.59 (978-0-9745210-2-2(7)) Myers Publishing Co.
—My Mommy Is A Deputy Sheriff. Beckler, Bruce. l.t. ed. 2004. 14p. (J). 5.59 (978-0-9745210-7-7(8)) Myers Publishing Co.
—My Mommy Is A Police Officer: My Mommy Wears A Badge. Beckler, Bruce. l.t. ed. 2004. 14p. (J). per. 5.59 (978-0-9745210-5-3(1)) Myers Publishing Co.
—My Mommy Is A Police Officer: My Mommy Wears A Star. Beckler, Bruce. l.t. ed. 2004. 14p. (J). 5.59 (978-0-9745210-6-0(X)) Myers Publishing Co.
Finni-Price, Isabel. Friends on the Spectrum. Lowry, Lorraine. 2018. (ENG.). 24p. (J). (978-1-5255-2311-3(2)); pap. (978-1-5255-2312-0(0)) FriesenPress.
Fino, Roberto. Awake in the Dark! McMillan, Dawn. 2009. (Rigby PM Stars Bridge Bks.). (ENG.). 24p. (gr. 2-3). pap. 8.70 (978-1-4190-5527-0(5)) Rigby Education.
Fiore, Peter M. Henry David's House. Schnur, Steven. 2007. (ENG.). 32p. (J). (gr. k-3). pap. 7.95 (978-0-88106-117-8(4)) Charlesbridge Publishing, Inc.
—When Washington Crossed the Delaware: A Wintertime Story for Young Patriots. Cheney, Lynne. 2012. (ENG.). 40p. (J). (gr. k-4). 7.99 (978-1-4424-4423-2(1), Simon & Schuster/Paula Wiseman Bks.) Simon & Schuster/Paula Wiseman Bks.
Fiore, Peter M. Touching the Sky: The Flying Adventures of Wilbur & Orville Wright. Fiore, Peter M. Borden, Louise & Marx, Trish. 2003. (ENG.). 64p. (J). (gr. k-3). 19.99 (978-0-689-84876-6(5), McElderry, Margaret K. Bks.) McElderry, Margaret K. Bks.
Fiore, Rob. First Fairytales. Zakarin, Debra Mostow. 2010. 10p. 9.95 (978-1-60747-746-4(7), Pickwick Pr.) Phoenix Bks., Inc.
Fiorentino, Chiara. Bad Rex! Rosen, Robert. 2017. (Play Time Ser.). (ENG.). 24p. (gr. -1-2). 29.93 (978-1-68342-730-8(0), 9781683427308); pap. 8.95 (978-1-68342-782-7(3), 9781683427827) Rourke Educational Media.
—Billy's Camping Trip. Ko, Hannah. 2017. (Family Time Ser.). (ENG.). 24p. (gr. -1-2). 29.93 (978-1-68342-738-4(6), 9781683427384); pap. 8.95 (978-1-68342-790-2(4), 9781683427902) Rourke Educational Media.
—Dust Everywhere. Rosen, Robert. 2017. (I Help My Friends Ser.). (ENG.). 24p. (gr. -1-2). 29.93 (978-1-68342-720-9(3), 9781683427209) Rourke Educational Media.
—Saving Water. Walters, Abby. 2017. (I Help My Friends Ser.). (ENG.). 24p. (gr. -1-2). 29.93 (978-1-68342-744-5(0), 9781683427445) Rourke Educational Media.
—Summer Fruits. Newman, Constance. 2017. (Seasons Around Me Ser.). (ENG.). 24p. (gr. -1-2). pap. 8.95 (978-1-68342-753-7(X), 9781683427537) Rourke Educational Media.
—A Year of Fun. Nino, Carl. 2017. (Family Time Ser.). (ENG.). 24p. (gr. -1-2). pap. 8.95 (978-1-68342-759-9(9), 9781683427599) Rourke Educational Media.
Fiorentino, Fabrizio, et al. Master Class, Vol. 5. Bedard, Tony. 2003. (Mystic Ser.: Vol. 5). 160p. (YA). (gr. 7-18). pap. 9.95 (978-1-931484-79-4(1)) CrossGeneration Comics, Inc.
—Out All Night, Vol. 4. Bedard, Tony. 2003. (Mystic Ser.: Vol. 4). 160p. (YA). (gr. 7-18). pap. 7.95 (978-1-931484-46-6(5)) CrossGeneration Comics, Inc.
Fioretti, Angelina P. The Princess & the Sisters. Fioretti, Angelina P. Fioretti, B. J., ed. 2016. (ENG.). 30p. (J). pap. (978-0-9952979-0-6(8)) Fioretti, Brenda.
Fiorillo, Gabriella. Endangered Species Series, Elephants. Scott, Russell & Petrone Miller, Patti. 2017. (ENG.). 54p. (J). 21.28 (978-1-5380-3470-5(0)) Barnes & Noble Pr.
Fiorin, Fabiano. Big Book of Dinosaurs Internet Referenced. Frith, Alex. 2010. (Big Bks.). 16p. (J). bds. 13.99 (978-0-7945-2770-9(1), Usborne) EDC Publishing.
—Hide-and-Seek Dragons. Watt, Fiona. 2007. (Touchy-Feely Flap Bks). 10p. (J). (gr. -1-k). bds. 16.99 (978-0-7945-1590-4(8), Usborne) EDC Publishing.
—Noisy Books. Harrison, Paul. 2009. (Get Ready (Windmill Books) Ser.). 32p. (J). (gr. k-2). lib. bdg. 25.60 (978-1-60754-258-2(7)) Windmill Bks.
—Planeta Dinosaurio. Orme, David. 2005. (Lectores Relampago / Lightning Readers: Level 3 Ser.). (SPA.). 32p. (J). (gr. 1-2). 16.19 (978-0-7696-4071-6(0)) School Specialty, Incorporated.
—Stories of Cowboys. Punter, Russell. 2008. (Usborne Young Reading: Series One Ser.). 48p. (J). 8.99 (978-0-7945-1822-6(2), Usborne) EDC Publishing.
—The Usborne Big Book of Big Monsters. Stowell, Louie. 2013. (Usborne Big Book Of... Ser.). (ENG.). 16p. (J). (gr. -1-3). 14.99 (978-0-7945-3025-9(7), Usborne) EDC Publishing.
—Wanted: Prince Charming. Benjamin, A. H. 2014. (Race Ahead with Reading Ser.). (ENG.). 32p. (J). (gr. 2-2). (978-0-7787-1313-5(X)) Crabtree Publishing Co.
Fiorin, Fabioano. My Key Verse Bible, 1 vol. Carroll, Vanessa & Fodor, Cecilie. 2018. 92p. (J). (gr. -1-2). 12.99 (978-0-8254-4582-8(5)) Kregel Pubns.
Fiorini, Nancy. Leyendas Sobre Aparecidos. Sanabria Santaliz, Edgardo. 2007. (Leyendas de Puerto Rico Ser.). (SPA.). 32p. (J). pap. 7.95 (978-1-63113-916-1(9)) Santillana USA Publishing Co., Inc.
—La Nube Traicionera. Walsh, Maria Elena. 2003. (SPA.). 88p. (YA). (gr. 5-8). 14.95 (978-950-511-616-4(0)) Alfaguara S.A. de Ediciones ARG. Dist: Santillana USA Publishing Co., Inc.
Fiorito, Marcio. Marvel Action: Avengers: the Fear Eaters (Book Three) Manning, Matthew K. 2020. (Marvel Action: Avengers Ser.: 3). 80p. (J). (gr. 4-7). pap. 9.99 (978-1-68405-581-4(4)) Idea & Design Works, LLC.
Firebrace, Francis. More Stories from the Billabong. Marshall, James Vance. 2013. (ENG.). 80p. (J). (978-1-921720-48-2(4)) Walker Bks. Australia Pty, Ltd.
—Stories from the Billabong. Marshall, James Vance. 2010. (ENG.). 64p. (J). (gr. k-3). pap. 9.99 (978-1-84780-124-1(2), Frances Lincoln Children's Bks.) Quarto Publishing Group UK GBR. Dist: Hachette Bk. Group.
Firehammer, Karla. The Flea's Sneeze. Downey, Lynn. 2005. (ENG.). 32p. (J). (gr. -1-1). reprint ed. pap. 8.99 (978-0-8050-7756-8(7), 900028855) Square Fish.
Firenze, Inklink. A Day in the Life of a Knight. Hopkins, Andrea. 2007. (Day in the Life Ser.: Vol. 4). 32p. (J). (gr. 4-7). lib. bdg. 27.25 (978-1-4042-3851-0(4)) Rosen Publishing Group, Inc., The.
—A Day in the Life of a Native American. Helbrough, Emma. 2007. (Day in the Life Ser.: Vol. 4). 32p. (J). (gr. 3-7). lib. bdg. 27.25 (978-1-4042-3854-1(9)) Rosen Publishing Group, Inc., The.
—A Day in the Life of a Pirate. Helbrough, Emma. 2007. (Day in the Life Ser.: Vol. 4). 32p. (J). (gr. 3-7). lib. bdg. 27.25 (978-1-4042-3853-4(0)) Rosen Publishing Group, Inc., The.
—Medieval world - internet Linked. Bingham, Jane. rev. ed. 2004. 96p. (J). pap. 14.95 (978-0-7945-0815-9(4), Usborne) EDC Publishing.
—The Usborne Internet-Linked Prehistoric World. Chandler, Fiona et al. 2005. 96p. (J). pap. (978-0-439-78504-4(9)) Scholastic, Inc.
Firenze, Inklink, jt. illus. see Galante, Studio.
Firm, Amb Publishing. When I Grow Up. Britt, Shelby L. 2019. (ENG.). 30p. (J). pap. 9.15 **(978-1-0990-4224-9(0))** Independently Published.
Firmansyah, Alti. The Unstoppable Wasp: Unlimited Vol. 2. 2019. (Unstoppable Wasp: Unlimited Ser.: 2). (ENG.). 112p. (YA). (gr. 8-17). pap. 15.99 (978-1-302-91427-1(8)) Marvel Worldwide, Inc.
Firmansyah, Miralti, jt. illus. see Leach, Garry.
Firmin, Hannah. Prayers for Your Confirmation. Rock, Lois. ed. 2007. (ENG.). 48p. (J). (gr. 4). 9.95 (978-0-7459-6045-6(6)) Lion Hudson PLC GBR. Dist: Independent Pubs. Group.
Firmin, Peter. Then & Now. Amery, Heather. 2008. (Then & Now Ser.). 24p. (J). (gr. -1-3). pap. 4.99 (978-0-7945-2211-7(4), Usborne) EDC Publishing.
Firos, Daphne. Square Bear Meets Round Hound: A Fairytale of Shapes. Penn, M. W. 2012. (ENG.). 38p. (J). pap. 11.95 (978-0-9840425-8-6(X)) MathWord Pr., LLC.
—A Tangram ABC: Shaping the Alphabet from an Ancient Chinese Puzzle. McKay, Chelsea. 2013. 60p. (J). pap. 13.95 (978-1-939431-04-2(2)) MathWord Pr., LLC.
—2 Lines. Penn, M. W. 2011. (ENG.). 32p. (J). pap. 11.95 (978-0-9840425-0-0(4)) MathWord Pr., LLC.
Firpo, Ethan. Custer Brown in Marshmallow Madness. Costley, Kirk. 2012. 34p. pap. 15.95 (978-1-893075-85-6(0)) Spirit Pr., LLC.
Firsova, Yuliya. Why Mommy Is a Democrat. Zilber, Jeremy. 2005. 28p. (J). pap. 8.00 (978-0-9786688-0-8(4)) Zilber, Jeremy.
First Choice Productions Staff, photos by. Almost There: A Series of Monologues. Darnell, Yolanda. 2003. 51p. (YA). (gr. 8-18). pap. 12.99 (978-1-884429-13-2(0)) Papillon Pr.
Firth, Barbara. Bears in the Forest: Read & Wonder. Wallace, Karen. 2009. (Read & Wonder Ser.). (ENG.). 32p. (J). (gr. -1-3). pap. 6.99 (978-0-7636-4522-9(2)) Candlewick Pr.
—Can't You Sleep, Little Bear?: Candlewick Storybook Animations. Waddell, Martin. 2008. (Candlewick Storybook Animations Ser.). (ENG.). 32p. (J). (gr. k-k). 14.99 (978-0-7636-3537-4(5)) Candlewick Pr.
Firtl, Mary Meehan. The Broken Doll. Zuber, Diane C. 2006. (ENG.). 32p. (J). (gr. -1-3). incl. audio compact disk (978-0-9785551-1-5(2)) Zuber Publishing.
Fischer, Chuck. Great American Houses & Gardens: A Pop-up Book. Fischer, Chuck. 2005. 12p. (J). (gr. 4-8). reprint ed. 40.00 (978-0-7567-9193-3(6)) DIANE Publishing Co.
Fischer, Hans. In Fairyland: The Finest of Tales by the Brothers Grimm. Brothers Grimm, Brothers. 2019. (ENG.). 144p. (J). (gr. -1-2). 30.00 (978-0-7358-4339-4(2)) North-South Bks., Inc.
Fischer, Jeff. Johnny Appleseed. 2006. (Famous Fables Ser.). (J). 6.99 (978-1-59939-028-4(0)) Cornerstone Pr.
Fischer, Kate Elizabeth. Your Angel Army: A Book of Hope. Fischer, Kate Elizabeth. 2019. (ENG.). 34p. (J). (gr. k-6). 24.99 **(978-0-578-55307-8(4))** Little Fisch.
Fischer, Sandi. Where the Leprechauns Hide. Hoyt, Charlene. 2007. (ENG.). 40p. per. 12.99 (978-0-9792258-9-5(2)) Bezalel Bks.
Fischer, Scott M. Animals Anonymous. Michelson, Richard. 2008. (ENG.). 96p. (YA). (gr. 9-18). 14.99 (978-1-4169-1424-2(2), Simon & Schuster Bks. For Young Readers) Simon & Schuster Bks. For Young Readers.
—The Bronze Key. Black, Holly & Clare, Cassandra. 2017. (Magisterium Ser.: 3). (ENG.). 256p. (J). (gr. 3-7). pap. 7.99 (978-0-545-52232-8(3), Scholastic Pr.) Scholastic, Inc.
—Lottie Paris & the Best Place. Johnson, Angela. 2013. (ENG.). 32p. (J). (gr. k-4). 17.99 (978-0-689-87378-2(6), Simon & Schuster Bks. For Young Readers) Simon & Schuster Bks. For Young Readers.
—Lottie Paris Lives Here. Johnson, Angela. 2011. (ENG.). 32p. (J). (gr. k-4). 16.99 (978-0-689-87377-5(8), Simon & Schuster Bks. For Young Readers) Simon & Schuster Bks. For Young Readers.
Fischer, Scott M., et al. Mars Trilogy: A Princess of Mars - The Gods of Mars - The Warlord of Mars. Burroughs, Edgar Rice. 2012. (ENG.). 704p. (gr. 7). pap. 16.99 (978-1-4424-2387-9(0), Simon & Schuster Bks. For Young Readers) Simon & Schuster Bks. For Young Readers.
Fischer, Scott M. Peter Pan in Scarlet. McCaughrean, Geraldine. (ENG.). 320p. (J). (gr. 4-9). 2008. pap. 6.99 (978-1-4169-1809-7(4)); 2006. 19.99 (978-1-4169-1808-0(6)) McElderry, Margaret K. Bks. (McElderry, Margaret K. Bks.).
—Scary School. Ghost, Derek The. (Scary School Ser.: 1). (ENG.). (J). (gr. 3-7). 2012. 272p. pap. 6.99 (978-0-06-196094-9(2)); 2011. 256p. 16.99 (978-0-06-196092-5(6)) HarperCollins Pubs.
—Scary School #2: Monsters on the March. Ghost, Derek The. (Scary School Ser.: 2). (ENG.). (J). (gr. 3-7). 2013. 272p. pap. 6.99 (978-0-06-196097-0(7)); 2012. 256p. 15.99 (978-0-06-196095-6(0)) HarperCollins Pubs.
—Scary School #3: the Northern Frights. Ghost, Derek The. 2013. (Scary School Ser.: 3). (ENG.). 272p. (J). (gr. 3-7). 16.99 (978-0-06-196098-7(5)) HarperCollins Pubs.
—Secrets of Dripping Fang, Book One: The Onts. Greenburg, Dan. 2005. (Secrets of Dripping Fang Ser.: Bk. 1). (ENG.). 144p. (J). (gr. 3-7). 12.99 (978-0-15-205457-1(X), 1196419) Houghton Mifflin Harcourt Publishing Co.
—Secrets of Dripping Fang, Book Two: Treachery & Betrayal at Jolly Days. Greenburg, Dan. 2006. (Secrets of Dripping Fang Ser.: Bk. 2). (ENG.). 144p. (J). (gr. 3-7). 12.99 (978-0-15-205463-2(4), 1196437) Houghton Mifflin Harcourt Publishing Co.
—The Shluffmuffin Boy Is History, Bk. 5. Greenburg, Dan. 2006. (Secrets of Dripping Fang Ser.: Bk. 5). (ENG.). 176p. (J). (gr. 3-7). 12.99 (978-0-15-206035-0(9), 1198126) Houghton Mifflin Harcourt Publishing Co.
—The Vampire's Curse, Bk. 3. Greenburg, Dan & Diterlizzi, Angela. 2006. (Secrets of Dripping Fang Ser.: Bk. 3). (ENG.). 144p. (J). (gr. 3-7). 12.99 (978-0-15-205469-4(3), 1196455) Houghton Mifflin Harcourt Publishing Co.
Fischer, Scott M. Jump! Fischer, Scott M. 2010. (ENG.). 32p. (J). (gr. -1-3). 17.99 (978-1-4169-7884-8(4), Simon & Schuster Bks. For Young Readers) Simon & Schuster Bks. For Young Readers.
Fischer, Shan. The Back Alley Pupsters: Zac & Roxie for the Win. Layne, Casey & Jordan, Cedar. 2013. (ENG.). (J). (gr. -1-3). 14.95 (978-1-62086-300-8(6)) Mascot Bks., Inc.
Fish, John Freeman. Goodland: The Best Medicine of All. Fish, Ross. 2019. (My Granny Rose Ser.: Vol. 1). (ENG.). 28p. (J). pap. 7.92 (978-1-0797-2918-4(6)) Independently Published.
Fish, Lori Flying. One Shining Starfish. Fish, Lori Flying. 2010. 16p. pap. 9.95 (978-1-936343-12-6(6)) Peppertree Pr., The.
Fish, Mister. Snerfy Cat Meets Prancy Finch. Fish, Mister, . 2007. 80p. (J). 14.99 (978-0-9794753-0-6(9)) Children's Classic Book Pubs.

F

Fish, Veronica. Avengers: Endgame the Pirate Angel, the Talking Tree, & Captain Rabbit. Behling, Steve. 2019. (ENG.). 208p. (J). (gr. 3-7). 13.99 (978-1-368-04695-4(9), Marvel Pr.) Disney Publishing Worldwide.

—Spider-Woman: Shifting Gears Vol. 3: Scare Tactics. 2017. (ENG.). 112p. (YA). (gr. 8-17). pap. 15.99 (978-1-302-90330-5(6)) Marvel Worldwide, Inc.

Fishback, Richard. Do Fleas Sneeze? Buster & Frankie Lu, Story 1. Lashier, Scott. 2017. (ENG.). 18p. (J). 24.95 (978-1-4787-8084-7(3)) Outskirts Pr., Inc.

Fisher, Alyssa. I Love You to the North Pole & Back. Almeida, Mariana. 2018. (ENG.). 30p. (J). pap. 12.00 (978-1-7199-2152-7(0)) Independently Published.

Fisher, Bonnie & Wolski, Bobbi. Charles Gordon Willingham. Whitlow, Crystal K. 2006. per. (978-0-9777361-0-2(5)) Day3 Productions, Inc.

Fisher, Brenda Beck. The White Horse. Goodman, Eli. 2016. (ENG.). 68p. (J). pap. 12.95 (978-1-63047-932-9(2)) Morgan James Publishing.

Fisher, Carolyn. Good Night, World. Perlman, Willa. 2011. (ENG.). 40p. (J). (gr. -1-k). 16.99 (978-1-4424-0197-6(4), Beach Lane Bks.) Beach Lane Bks.

—Good Night, World. Perlman, Willa. 2019. (Classic Board Bks.). (ENG.). 40p. (J). (gr. -1 — 1). bds. 7.99 (978-1-5344-4384-6(3), Little Simon) Little Simon.

Fisher, Carolyn. Summer Feet, 1 vol. Fitch, Sheree. 2020. (ENG.). 32p. (J). 16.95 **(978-1-77108-854-1(0)**, d7293f36-9599-4450-aed6-7aaea1d52ed1) Nimbus Publishing, Ltd. CAN. Dist: Baker & Taylor Publisher Services (BTPS).

Fisher, Carolyn. Two Old Potatoes & Me. Coy, John. 2013. (ENG.). (J). (gr. k-3). pap. 7.99 (978-1-935666-46-2(0)) Nodin Pr.

—Weeds Find a Way. Jenson-Elliott, Cindy. 2014. (ENG.). 40p. (J). (gr. -1-3). 17.99 (978-1-4424-1260-6(7)) Simon & Schuster Children's Publishing.

Fisher, Carolyn. Cells: An Owner's Handbook. Fisher, Carolyn. 2019. (ENG.). 48p. (J). (gr. -1-3). 17.99 (978-1-5344-5185-8(4), Beach Lane Bks.) Beach Lane Bks.

Fisher, Cathy. Flying Free. Davies, Nicola. 2019. (Country Tales Ser.). (ENG.). 36p. (J). (gr. 4-7). pap. 12.99 (978-1-912654-09-3(1)) Graffeg Limited GBR. Dist: Independent Pubs. Group.

—Little Mistake. Davies, Nicola. 2019. (Country Tales Ser.). (ENG.). 36p. (J). (gr. k-2). pap. 12.99 (978-1-912654-08-6(3)) Graffeg Limited GBR. Dist: Independent Pubs. Group.

—The Pond. Davies, Nicola. 2017. (ENG.). 32p. (J). (gr. k-2). 16.99 (978-1-912050-70-3(6)) Graffeg Limited GBR. Dist: Independent Pubs. Group.

Fisher, Chris. Ballet Magic, Vol. 1. Castor, Harriet. (ENG.). 64p. (J). pap. 7.95 (978-0-14-038479-6(0)) Penguin Publishing Group.

—Mountain Mona: Band 09/Gold (Collins Big Cat) French, Vivian. 2006. (Collins Big Cat Ser.). (ENG.). 24p. (J). (gr. 2-2). pap. 8.99 (978-0-00-718700-3(9)) HarperCollins Pubs. Ltd. GBR. Dist: Independent Pubs. Group.

—Royston Knapper: Return of the Rogue. Phinn, Gervase. 2005. (Child's Play Library - First Chapter Bks.). 126p. (J). (978-0-85953-024-8(8)) Child's Play International Ltd.

—The Snow Dragon. French, Vivian. 2003. (ENG.). 32p. (J). pap. 11.99 (978-0-552-54595-2(3)) Transworld Publishers Ltd. GBR. Dist: Trafalgar Square Publishing.

Fisher, Cynthia. Friends, Like You. Griswold, Melissa. 2007. (J). 24.95 (978-0-9797287-2-3(X)); 32p. 15.00 (978-0-9797287-3-0(8)) Mainstream Ctr., Schl. for the Deaf, The.

—Friends, Like You: Children's Activity Book. Griswold, Melissa. 2007. 16p. (J). (978-0-9797287-4-7(6)) Mainstream Ctr., Schl. for the Deaf, The.

Fisher, Cynthia. The Night Before Halloween Activity Book. Wing, Natasha. 2020. (Night Before Ser.). 24p. (J). (gr. -1-2). pap. 5.99 **(978-0-593-09558-4(8)**, Grosset & Dunlap) Penguin Young Readers Group.

Fisher, Cynthia, jt. illus. see Holub, Joan.

Fisher, Diana. Animals: Step-by-Step Instructions for 26 Captivating Creatures. Walter Foster Creative Team. 2011. (Learn to Draw Ser.). 32p. (J). (gr. 1-4). 28.50 (978-1-936309-20-7(3)) Quarto Publishing Group USA.

—Dogs & Puppies: Step-by-Step Insructions for 25 Different Breeds. Walter Foster Creative Team. 2011. (Learn to Draw Ser.). 32p. (J). (gr. 1-4). 28.50 (978-1-936309-18-4(1)) Quarto Publishing Group USA.

—Dolphins, Whales, Fish & More: A Step-By-step Drawing & Story Book. Winterberg, Jenna. 2006. (Watch Me Draw Ser.). (ENG.). 24p. (J). (gr. -1-3). pap. 4.95 (978-1-56010-949-5(1), 1560109491) Quarto Publishing Group USA.

—I Love Cats! Activity Book: Meow-Velous Stickers, Trivia, Step-by-step Drawing Projects, & More for the Cat Lover in You! Walter Foster Creative Team. 2011. (I Love Activity Bks.). (ENG.). 112p. (J). (gr. 1-3). pap. 14.99 (978-1-60058-224-0(9), 1600582249) Quarto Publishing Group USA.

—I Love Dogs! Activity Book: Pup-Tacular Stickers, Trivia, Step-by-step Drawing Projects, & More for the Dog Lover in You! Walter Foster Creative Team. 2011. (I Love Activity Bks.). (ENG.). 112p. (J). (gr. 1-3). pap., act. bk. ed. 12.95 (978-1-60058-225-7(7), 1600582257) Quarto Publishing Group USA.

—Learn to Draw Cats & Kittens. 2012. (J). (978-1-936309-51-1(3)) Quarto Publishing Group USA.

—Learn to Draw Reptiles & Amphibians. 2012. (J). (978-1-936309-50-4(5)) Quarto Publishing Group USA.

—The Monsters under My Bed. Razo, Rebecca J. 2014. (Watch Me Draw Ser.). (ENG.). 24p. (J). (gr. k-2). 23.99 (978-1-939581-37-2(0), Walter Foster Jr) Quarto Publishing Group USA.

—Watch Me Draw a Boy's Adventure. Winterberg, Jenna. 2014. (Watch Me Draw Ser.). (ENG.). 24p. (J). (gr. k-2). 23.99 (978-1-936309-79-5(3), Walter Foster Jr) Quarto Publishing Group USA.

—Watch Me Draw a Magical Fairy World. Fitzgerald, Stephanie. 2014. (Watch Me Draw Ser.). (ENG.). 24p. (J). (gr. k-2). 23.99 (978-1-936309-91-7(2), Walter Foster Jr) Quarto Publishing Group USA.

—Watch Me Draw Dinosaurs. Winterberg, Jenna. 2014. (Watch Me Draw Ser.). (ENG.). 24p. (J). (gr. k-2). 23.99 (978-1-936309-89-4(0), Walter Foster Jr) Quarto Publishing Group USA.

—Watch Me Draw Disney's Little Einsteins Amazing Missions. 2012. (J). (978-1-936309-43-6(2)) Quarto Publishing Group USA.

—Watch Me Draw Favorite Pets. 2012. 24p. (J). (978-1-936309-77-1(7)) Quarto Publishing Group USA.

—Watch Me Draw Things Girls Love. 2012. (J). (978-1-936309-78-8(5)) Quarto Publishing Group USA.

Fisher, Diana & Shelly, Jeff. All about Dinosaurs & Reptiles. 2010. (All about Drawing Ser.). 80p. (J). 34.25 (978-1-936309-07-8(6)) Quarto Publishing Group USA.

Fisher, Diana, jt. illus. see Cerato, Mattia.

Fisher, Diana, jt. illus. see Farrell, Russell.

Fisher, Diana, jt. illus. see Ho, Jannie.

Fisher, Douglas W., jt. illus. see Fisher, Phyllis Mae Richardson.

Fisher, Eric Scott. The Adventures of Robinson Crusoe. Dafoe, Daniel. 2010. (Calico Illustrated Classics Ser.: No. 1). (ENG.). 112p. (J). (gr. 2-5). 29.93 (978-1-60270-703-0(0), 3959, Calico Chapter Bks.) ABDO Publishing Co.

—Frankenstein, 1 vol. Shelley, Mary. 2010. (Calico Illustrated Classics Ser.: No. 1). (ENG.). 112p. (J). (gr. 2-5). 29.93 (978-1-60270-705-4(7), 3963, Calico Chapter Bks.) ABDO Publishing Co.

—The Invisible Man. Wells, H. G. 2011. (Calico Illustrated Classics Ser.: No. 3). (ENG.). 112p. (J). (gr. 2-5). 29.93 (978-1-61641-103-9(1), 4013, Calico Chapter Bks.) ABDO Publishing Co.

—A Journey to the Center of the Earth, 1 vol. Verne, Jules. 2011. (Calico Illustrated Classics Ser.: No. 3). (ENG.). 112p. (J). (gr. 2-5). 29.93 (978-1-61641-104-6(X), 4015, Calico Chapter Bks.) ABDO Publishing Co.

—Kidnapped, 1 vol. Stevenson, Robert Louis. 2011. (Calico Illustrated Classics Ser.: No. 3). (ENG.). 112p. (J). (gr. 2-5). 29.93 (978-1-61641-105-3(8), 4017, Calico Chapter Bks.) ABDO Publishing Co.

—Moby Dick, 1 vol. Melville, Herman. 2010. (Calico Illustrated Classics Ser.: No. 1). (ENG.). 112p. (J). (gr. 2-5). 29.93 (978-1-60270-709-2(X), 3971, Calico Chapter Bks.) ABDO Publishing Co.

—The Picture of Dorian Gray, 1 vol. Wilde, Oscar. 2011. (Calico Illustrated Classics Ser.: No. 4). (ENG.). 112p. (J). (gr. 2-5). 29.93 (978-1-61641-618-8(1), 4051, Calico Chapter Bks.) ABDO Publishing Co.

—The War of the Worlds, 1 vol. Wells, H. G. 2011. (Calico Illustrated Classics Ser.: No. 3). (ENG.). 112p. (J). (gr. 2-5). 29.93 (978-1-61641-111-4(2), 4029, Calico Chapter Bks.) ABDO Publishing Co.

—20,000 Leagues under the Sea, 1 vol. Verne, Jules. 2011. (Calico Illustrated Classics Ser.: No. 3). (ENG.). 112p. (J). (gr. 2-5). 29.93 (978-1-61641-110-7(4), 4027, Calico Chapter Bks.) ABDO Publishing Co.

Fisher, Fox. Are You a Boy or Are You a Girl? Savage, Sarah. 2017. (ENG.). 32p. (J). 16.95 (978-1-78592-267-1(X), 696461) Kingsley, Jessica Pubs. GBR. Dist: Hachette UK Distribution.

Fisher, G. W., jt. illus. see Malbrough, Michael.

Fisher, Henry. Away in My Airplane. Brown, Margaret Wise. 2019. (Margaret Wise Brown Classics Ser.). (ENG.). 32p. (J). (gr. -1-k). 12.99 (978-1-68412-753-5(X), Silver Dolphin Bks.) Printers Row Publishing Group.

—The Night Before Christmas. Clement C., Moore. Cottage Door Press, ed. 2018. (ENG.). 32p. (J). (gr. -1-3). 9.99 (978-1-68052-456-7(9), 2000550) Cottage Door Pr.

Fisher, Henry. ABC Dreams. Fisher, Henry. 2014. (ENG.). 12p. (J). (gr. -1-k). 7.99 (978-1-78244-535-7(8)) Top That! Publishing PLC GBR. Dist: Independent Pubs. Group.

—When I Dream of ABC. Fisher, Henry. 2018. (Picture Storybooks Ser.). (ENG.). 26p. (J). (gr. -1-1). bds. 9.99 (978-1-78700-258-6(6)) Top That! Publishing PLC GBR. Dist: Independent Pubs. Group.

Fisher, Henry, jt. illus. see Orkrania, Alexia.

Fisher, Jeff. A Picture Book of Amelia Earhart. Adler, David A. 2015. 32p. pap. 8.00 (978-1-61003-403-6(1)) Center for the Collaborative Classroom.

—A Picture Book of Amelia Earhart. Adler, David A. 2018. (Picture Book Biography Ser.). 32p. (J). (gr. -1-3). pap. 7.99 (978-0-8234-4056-6(7)) Holiday Hse., Inc.

Fisher, Jessie, jt. illus. see Santy, Elizabeth.

Fisher-Johnson, Paul. Can You Survive an Alien Invasion? An Interactive Doomsday Adventure. Hoena, B. A. 2015. (You Choose: Doomsday Ser.). (ENG.). 112p. (J). (gr. 3-7). lib. bdg. 32.65 (978-1-4914-5853-2(4), Capstone Pr.) Capstone.

—Can You Survive an Artificial Intelligence Uprising? An Interactive Doomsday Adventure. Doeden, Matt. 2016. (You Choose: Doomsday Ser.). (ENG.). 112p. (J). (gr. 3-7). lib. bdg. 32.65 (978-1-4914-8107-3(2), Capstone Pr.) Capstone.

Fisher, Leonard Everett. A Horse Named Justin Morgan. Felton, Harold W. 2011. 162p. 41.95 (978-1-258-07855-3(4)) Literary Licensing, LLC.

—The Military History of Civil War Land Battles. Dupuy, Trevor Nevitt. 2011. 98p. 38.95 (978-1-258-07607-8(1)); 38.95 (978-1-258-01405-6(X)) Literary Licensing, LLC.

—The Queen's Most Honorable Pirate. Wood, James Playsted. 2011. 192p. 42.95 (978-1-258-09722-6(2)) Literary Licensing, LLC.

Fisher, Leonard Everett. William Tell. Fisher, Leonard Everett. 2006. 28p. (J). reprint ed. 16.00 (978-0-7567-9880-2(9)) DIANE Publishing Co.

Fisher, Leonard Everett & Waltrip, Mildred. The First Book of the Indian Wars. Morris, Richard B. 2011. 94p. 38.95 (978-1-258-01128-4(X)) Literary Licensing, LLC.

Fisher, Marianne. The Last Pacifier. Oliveri, Lisa L. 2013. 36p. pap. 24.95 (978-1-62709-860-1(7)) America Star Bks.

Fisher, Megan. Puppy Love! (Sunny Day) Lewman, David. 2017. (Big Golden Book Ser.). (ENG.). 32p. (J). (gr. -1-2). 10.99 (978-1-5247-6876-8(6), Golden Bks.) Random Hse. Children's Bks.

Fisher, Pat. Walk a Mile in Our Shoes. Fisher, Pat, photos by. Fisher, D. H., photos by. Fisher, D. H., ed. l.t. ed. 2005. 288p. reprint ed. pap. 20.00 (978-0-9677231-4-3(0)) ITSMEEE Industries.

Fisher, Patrica A. I Want to Live. Fisher, Patrica A. Fisher, Patrica A., ed. 2004. 200p. (YA). 20.00 (978-0-9677231-5-0(9)) ITSMEEE Industries.

Fisher, Phyllis Mae Richardson. Chrissy (#1 in the 1989 Family Friends Paper Doll Set) l.t. ed. 2004. 24p. (J). 10.00 (978-0-9745615-5-4(X)) PJs Corner.

—Janae, #3 in the 1989 Family Friends Paper Doll Set, Vol. 3. l.t. ed. 2003. 24p. (J). 10.00 (978-0-9745615-7-8(6)) PJs Corner.

—Melly, #2 in the 1989 Family Friends Paper Doll Set, Vols. 3, Vol. 2. l.t. ed. 2004. 24p. (J). 10.00 (978-0-9745615-6-1(8)) PJs Corner.

—Natasha, an International Friends Paper Doll from Russia. 2004. 15p. (J). 10.00 (978-0-9745615-8-5(4)) PJs Corner.

—Tess, an International Friends Paper Doll from Africa. 2004. (J). 10.00 (978-0-9745615-9-2(2)) PJs Corner.

Fisher, Phyllis Mae Richardson. Rueben & Rachel's Paper Doll Coloring Book. Fisher, Phyllis Mae Richardson, . 2003. (J). 8.00 (978-0-9745615-0-9(9)) PJs Corner.

Fisher, Phyllis Mae Richardson & Fisher, Douglas W. Twiglet the Little Christmas Tree. Fisher, Phyllis Mae Richardson. 2003. (J). 30.00 (978-0-9745615-1-6(7), Twiglet The Little Christmas Tree); 186p. 12.00 (978-0-9745615-4-7(1)) PJs Corner.

Fisher, Rachael. Under the Sea: Earth Designs: Black & White & Red Book (from Two Months) Whiteley, Iya & Whiteley, Graham. 2017. (ENG.). (J). pap. (978-1-912490-00-4(5)) Cosmic Baby Bks.

Fisher, Sandy. The Adventures of CJ & Angel; the Scary Helicopter Ride. 2008. 24p. (J). (978-0-9779072-1-2(X)) Creative Life Publishing.

Fisher, Scott. The Count of Monte Cristo, 1 vol. Dumas, Alexandre. 2010. (Calico Illustrated Classics Ser.). (ENG.). 112p. (J). (gr. 2-5). 29.93 (978-1-60270-744-3(8), 3989, Calico Chapter Bks.) ABDO Publishing Co.

—The House of the Seven Gables, 1 vol. Hawthorne, Nathaniel. 2010. (Calico Illustrated Classics Ser.). (ENG.). 112p. (J). (gr. 2-5). 29.93 (978-1-60270-746-7(4), 3993, Calico Chapter Bks.) ABDO Publishing Co.

—The Phantom of the Opera, 1 vol. Leroux, Gaston. 2010. (Calico Illustrated Classics Ser.). (ENG.). 112p. (J). (gr. 2-5). 29.93 (978-1-60270-749-8(9), 3999, Calico Chapter Bks.) ABDO Publishing Co.

—The Strange Case of Dr. Jekyll & Mr. Hyde, 1 vol. Stevenson, Robert Louis. 2010. (Calico Illustrated Classics Ser.). (ENG.). 112p. (J). (gr. 2-5). 29.93 (978-1-60270-750-4(2), 4001, Calico Chapter Bks.) ABDO Publishing Co.

Fisher, Sean, jt. illus. see Menking, Amanda.

Fisher, Takako. A Little Horse. Puffinton, Brick. Cottage Door Press, ed. 2020. (Finger Puppet Board Book Ser.). (ENG.). 12p. (J). (gr. -1 — 1). bds. 6.99 (978-1-68052-786-5(X), 1005090) Cottage Door Pr.

—Mommy Wishes: Padded Board Book. Bunting, Rose. Cottage Door Press, ed. 2019. (Love You Always Ser.). (ENG.). 18p. (J). (gr. -1-1). bds. 9.99 (978-1-68052-373-7(2), 1003380) Cottage Door Pr.

—Springtime Babies. Smith, Danna. 2018. (Little Golden Book Ser.). 24p. (J). (-k). 4.99 (978-1-5247-1516-8(6), Golden Bks.) Random Hse. Children's Bks.

Fisher, Takako. When I Grow Up. Redwing, Jack. Cottage Door Press, ed. 2020. (John Deere Sound Book Ser.). (ENG.). 10p. (J). (gr. -1-k). bds. 9.99 **(978-1-68052-930-2(7)**, 1005720) Cottage Door Pr.

Fisher, Takako. Where Do Kisses Come From? Fleming, Maria. 2019. (Little Golden Book Ser.). 24p. (J). (-k). 4.99 (978-1-9848-5247-2(7), Golden Bks.) Random Hse. Children's Bks.

Fisher, Todd. The Snake with a Bellyache. Schwartz, Jean. 2007. 20p. per. 10.95 (978-1-934246-41-2(7)) Peppertree Pr., The.

Fisher, Valorie. Moxy Maxwell Does Not Love Writing Thank-You Notes. Gifford, Peggy. 2009. (Moxy Maxwell Ser.: 2). (ENG.). 192p. (J). (gr. 2-5). 6.99 (978-0-375-84343-3(4), Yearling) Random Hse. Children's Bks.

Fisher, Valorie. Ellsworth's Extraordinary Electric Ears & Other. Fisher, Valorie. 2009. (ENG.). 36p. (J). (gr. -1-3). 10.99 (978-1-4424-0658-2(5), Atheneum Bks. for Young Readers) Simon & Schuster Children's Publishing.

—Everything I Need to Know Before I'm Five. Fisher, Valorie. 2011. 40p. (J). (gr. k-k). 17.99 (978-0-375-86865-8(8), Schwartz & Wade Bks.) Random Hse. Children's Bks.

—Now You Know How It Works. Fisher, Valorie. 2018. (ENG.). 40p. (J). (gr. -1-1). 17.99 (978-1-338-21545-8(0), Orchard Bks.) Scholastic, Inc.

—Now You Know What You Eat. Fisher, Valorie. 2019. (ENG.). 40p. (J). (gr. -1-2). 17.99 (978-1-338-21546-5(9), Orchard Bks.) Scholastic, Inc.

Fisher, Valorie. Moxy Maxwell Does Not Love Practicing the Piano: (But She Does Love Being in Recitals) Fisher, Valorie, photos by. Gifford, Peggy Elizabeth. 2009. (Moxy Maxwell Ser.). (ENG.). 192p. (J). (gr. 4-6). lib. bdg. 21.19 (978-0-375-96688-0(9), Yearling) Random Hse. Children's Bks.

—Moxy Maxwell Does Not Love Writing Thank-You Notes. Fisher, Valorie, photos by. Gifford, Peggy Elizabeth. 2008. (Moxy Maxwell Ser.). (ENG.). 176p. (J). (gr. 4-6). lib. bdg. 18.69 (978-0-375-94552-6(0), Yearling) Random Hse. Children's Bks.

Fisher, Valorie, photos by. Moxy Maxwell Does Not Love Stuart Little. Gifford, Peggy. 2008. (Moxy Maxwell Ser.: 1). (ENG., 112p. (J). (gr. 2-5). 6.99 (978-0-440-42230-3(2), Yearling) Random Hse. Children's Bks.

Fisher, Valorie, photos by. My Big Sister. Fisher, Valorie. 2003. (ENG., 40p. (J). (gr. -1-3). 17.99 (978-0-689-85479-8(X), Atheneum Bks. for Young Readers) Simon & Schuster Children's Publishing.

Fisher-Wright, Blanche. The Real Mother Goose. Fisher-Wright, Blanche. Scholastic, Inc. Staff. Maccarone, Grace, ed. anniv. ed. 2006. (ENG.). 144p. (J). (gr. 3-7). 10.99 (978-0-439-85875-5(5), Cartwheel Bks.) Scholastic, Inc.

Fishline. Moose the Mouse, Kitty the Kitten, & the Clown Who Frowns. M, J. "E", ed. 2019. (Moose the Mouse Ser.: Vol. 1). (ENG.). 36p. (J). pap. 15.95 **(978-1-947656-23-9(6))** Butterfly Typeface, The.

—St. Nicholas: Patron & Protector of Children. Segars, Marion "butch". Williams, Iris M., ed. 2019. (ENG.). 38p. (J). pap. 15.00 **(978-1-947656-82-6(1))** Butterfly Typeface, The.

Fisinger, Barbara. Samantha Spinner & the Super-Secret Plans. Ginns, Russell. 2018. (Samantha Spinner Ser.: 1). 272p. (J). (gr. 3-7). 7.99 (978-1-5247-2003-2(8), Yearling) Random Hse. Children's Bks.

—Wedgie & Gizmo. Selfors, Suzanne. 2017. (Wedgie & Gizmo Ser.: 1). (ENG.). 176p. (J). (gr. 3-7). 12.99 (978-0-06-244763-0(7), Tegen, Katherine Bks) HarperCollins Pubs.

—Wedgie & Gizmo vs. the Great Outdoors. Selfors, Suzanne. 2018. (Wedgie & Gizmo Ser.: 3). (ENG.). 176p. (J). (gr. 3-7). 12.99 (978-0-06-244775-3(0), Tegen, Katherine Bks) HarperCollins Pubs.

—Wedgie & Gizmo vs. the Toof. Selfors, Suzanne. 2018. (Wedgie & Gizmo Ser.: 2). (ENG.). 192p. (J). (gr. 3-7). 12.99 (978-0-06-244765-4(3), Tegen, Katherine Bks) HarperCollins Pubs.

Fisk, David. Hooga Booga Presents the Little Pumpkin. Fisk, Cindy. 2013. 28p. pap. 11.95 (978-1-938743-02-3(4)) Reimann Bks.

—Melvin Pickles. Fisk, Cindy. 2013. 26p. pap. 11.95 (978-1-938743-03-0(2)) Reimann Bks.

Fiske, Anna. How Do You Make a Baby? Fiske, Anna. 2020. (ENG.). 80p. (J). (gr. 4-7). 18.99 **(978-1-77657-285-4(8))** Gecko Pr. NZL. Dist: Lerner Publishing Group.

Fiss, Matthew. The Squeezor Is Coming! Benishek, Becky. 2018. (ENG.). 42p. (J). (gr. k-6). 17.99 (978-1-387-02173-4(7)); pap. 13.99 (978-1-387-02174-1(5)) Lulu Pr., Inc.

—The Squeezor Is Coming! Dyslexic Edition: Dyslexic Font. Benishek, Becky. ed. 2018. (ENG.). 42p. (J). (gr. k-6). pap. 15.99 (978-1-64372-067-8(8)) MacLaren-Cochrane Publishing, Inc.

Fitch, Jada. A Blanding's Turtle Story, 1 vol. Kim, Melissa. 2016. (Wildlife on the Move Ser.). (ENG.). 24p. (J). bds. 10.95 (978-1-939017-92-5(0), 9781939017925) Islandport Pr., Inc.

—A Little Brown Bat Story, 1 vol. Kim, Melissa. 2015. (ENG.). 24p. (J). bds. 10.95 (978-1-939017-70-3(X), 9781939017703) Islandport Pr., Inc.

—Ten Days in the North Woods: A Kids' Hiking Guide to the Katahdin Region. Rowan, Hope. 2019. (ENG.). 104p. (J). pap. 12.95 (978-1-944762-64-3(7), 74d6f162-df8f-4839-bc6e-4e44bc0600cb) Islandport Pr., Inc.

Fitch, Rik. Hershel the Dog. Tysseland, Elsie. 2008. (ENG.). 32p. pap. 12.99 (978-1-4389-2130-3(6)) AuthorHouse.

Fithian, Catherine. The Magical Merry-Go-Round. 2008. (ENG.). (J). lib. bdg. (978-0-9754867-2-6(1)) Snodgrass, Ruth M.

Fitterling, Michael. The Elson Readers. Newcomer, Mary Jane et al. 2005. (ENG.). (J). (gr. -1-12). Bk. 4. 193p. tchr. ed., per. 19.99 (978-1-890623-28-9(8)); Bk. 5. 267p. tchr. ed., per. 20.99 (978-1-890623-29-6(6)) Lost Classic Bks.

Fitterling, Michael A., jt. illus. see Burgess, H.

Fitterling, Michael A., jt. illus. see Shute, A. B.

Fitts, Seth. Birds I've Met Through the Alphabet. Tietjen, Amy. 2013. 32p. pap. 17.95 (978-1-938230-33-2(7)) Vabella Publishing.

—Bugs I've Met Through the Alphabet. Tietjen, Amy. 2018. (ENG.). 32p. (J). pap. 16.95 (978-1-942766-49-0(1)) Vabella Publishing.

Fitzgerald, Anita. Dancing in the Moonlight. Fitzgerald, Kevin. 2005. (J). (978-0-9765987-4-9(4)) Foundation, Pr. The.

—The EGG-Cellent Adventure. Fitzgerald, Kevin. 2005. (J). (978-0-9765987-3-2(6)) Foundation, Pr. The.

Fitzgerald, Anne. Being Mad: A Book about Anger... Just for Me! Wigand, Molly. 2012. 32p. (J). pap. 7.95 (978-0-87029-502-7(0)) Abbey Pr.

—Being Sad When Someone Dies: A Book about Grief... Just for Me! Mundy, Linus. 2012. 32p. (J). pap. 7.95 (978-0-87029-501-0(2)) Abbey Pr.

—How to Be a Friend: A Book about Friendship... Just for Me! Wigand, Molly. 2012. 32p. (J). pap. 7.95 (978-0-87029-503-4(9)) Abbey Pr.

—Making Good Choices: Just for Me Book. Engelhardt, Lisa O. 2012. 32p. (J). pap. 7.95 (978-0-87029-514-0(4)) Abbey Pr.

—My Family Is Changing: A Book about Divorce. Menéndez-Aponte, Emily. 2013. 32p. (J). pap. 7.95 (978-0-87029-555-3(1)) Abbey Pr.

—Sometimes I'm Afraid: A Book about Fear... Just for Me! Mundy, Michaelene. 2012. 32p. (J). pap. 7.95 (978-0-87029-500-3(4)) Abbey Pr.

—We Are Different & Alike: A Book about Diversity. Geisen, Cynthia. 2013. 32p. (J). 7.95 (978-0-87029-557-7(8)) Abbey Pr.

—What Is God Like? Just for Me Book. Geisen, Cynthia. 2012. 32p. (J). pap. 7.95 (978-0-87029-516-4(0)) Abbey Pr.

Fitzgerald, Brian. The Boy & the Fish. Mannion, Mary. 2010. 52p. pap. (978-1-907276-62-0(9)) Lapwing Pubns.

—My Dad Loves Me This Much. Fitzpatrick, Joe. 2017. (ENG.). 32p. (J). (gr. k-2). 16.99 (978-1-4867-1318-9(1), e82b2eae-55f7-41e9-9a4e-961ae2d799c9) Flowerpot Pr.

—Roaring Rory. Mannion, Mary. 2010. 68p. pap. (978-1-907276-63-7(7)) Lapwing Pubns.

—Some Pigs Can Fly. Mannion, Mary. 2016. (ENG.). (J). (gr. 4-6). pap. 10.00 (978-1-937260-27-9(5)) Sleepytown Pr.

Fitzgerald, Deborah. Sadie's Smile. Fitzgerald, Deborah. Monahan, Frank, ed. 2017. (ENG.). (J). (gr. k-6). 19.99 *(978-1-945355-92-9(1))* Rocket Science Productions, LLC.

FitzGerald, Emma. EveryBody's Different on EveryBody Street, 1 vol. Fitch, Sheree. 2018. (ENG.). 32p. (J). (gr. 1-3). 22.95 *(978-1-77108-600-4(9),* e21593a4-afce-430f-9927-49c9d4ae402b) Nimbus Publishing, Ltd. CAN. Dist: Baker & Taylor Publisher Services (BTPS).

—A Pocket of Time: The Poetic Childhood of Elizabeth Bishop, 1 vol. Bishop, Elizabeth & Wilson, Rita. 2019. (ENG.). 40p. (J). 18.95 *(978-1-77108-809-1(5),* fc6959db-b14f-424c-8a6a-964eb1d515a6) Nimbus Publishing, Ltd. CAN. Dist: Baker & Taylor Publisher Services (BTPS).

Fitzgerald, Gerald. Flying over Brooklyn, 1 vol. Uhlberg, Myron. 2003. (ENG.). 32p. (J). (gr. k-3). pap. 7.95 *(978-1-56145-294-1(7))* Peachtree Publishing Co. Inc.

Fitzgerald, Jennifer. Marley's Treasure. Yerrid, Gable. 2007. 28p. (J). (gr. -1-3). 15.95 *(978-0-9767442-6-9(0))* Yorkville Pr.

Fitzgerald, Joanne. Emily's House, 1 vol. Scharer, Niko. 2010. (ENG.). 24p. (J). (gr. k — 1). bds. 7.95 *(978-0-88899-831-6(7))* Groundwood Bks. CAN. Dist: Publishers Group West (PGW).

Fitzgerald, Joanne. Este Soy Yo y lo Que Me Rodea, 1 vol. Fitzgerald, Joanne. Garay, Luis, tr. 2008. (SPA.). 32p. (J). (gr. -1-k). pap. 7.95 *(978-1-55455-108-8(0),* f681344f-e277-4f64-81f7-eba68e68c514) Fitzhenry & Whiteside, Ltd. CAN. Dist: Firefly Bks., Ltd.

Fitzgerald, Royce. The Super Sluggers: Slumpbuster. Markey, Kevin. 2010. (Super Sluggers Ser.). (ENG.). 208p. (J). (gr. 3-7). pap. 6.99 *(978-0-06-115220-7(X))* HarperCollins Pubs.

Fitzgerald, Royce & Jessell, Tim. Knights of the Ruby Wand, 36. Abbott, Tony. 2010. (Secrets of Droon Ser.: 36). (ENG.). 128p. (J). (gr. 2-4). 17.44 *(978-0-545-09886-1(6))* Scholastic, Inc.

Fitzgerald, Royce, jt. illus. see Jessell, Tim.

Fitzgerald, Susan. The Adventures of Blade & Rye. Terrell, P. M. 2018. (ENG.). 44p. (J). pap. 11.99 *(978-1-935970-42-2(9))* Drake Valley Pr.

Fitzl, Richelle Kristi. Grandma's Garden. 2004. (J). *(978-0-9741657-1-4(9))* Galaxia Publishing Group, LLC.

Fitzpatrick, Audrey. Jamaal's Lucky Day. Little, Robert. 2003. 32p. (J). (gr. 2-6). 15.95 *(978-0-9701863-4-8(7))* Relde Publishing.

Fitzpatrick, Brad. Cansada de Esperar, 1 vol. Meachen Rau, Dana. Ruíz, Carlos, tr. 2006. (Read-It! Readers en Español: Story Collection).Tr. of Tired of Waiting. (SPA.). 32p. (J). (gr. -1-3). 21.32 *(978-1-4048-1695-4(X),* Picture Window Bks.) Capstone.

—In the Money: A Book about Banking, 1 vol. Loewen, Nancy. 2010. (Money Matters Ser.). (ENG.). 32p. lib. bdg. 9.95 *(978-1-4048-6036-0(3),* Picture Window Bks.) Capstone.

—Taxes, Taxes! Where the Money Goes. Loewen, Nancy. 2005. (Money Matters Ser.). (ENG.). 24p. (J). (gr. 1-3). lib. bdg. 27.32 *(978-1-4048-1158-4(3),* Picture Window Bks.) Capstone.

Fitzpatrick, Brad & Jensen, Brian. Lemons & Lemonade: A Book about Supply & Demand. Loewen, Nancy. 2005. (Money Matters Ser.). (ENG.). 24p. (J). (gr. 1-3). 27.32 *(978-1-4048-0956-7(2),* Picture Window Bks.) Capstone.

—Save, Spend, or Donate? A Book about Managing Money. Loewen, Nancy. 2005. (Money Matters Ser.). (ENG.). 24p. (gr. 1-3). 25.99 *(978-1-4048-0952-9(X),* Picture Window Bks.) Capstone.

Fitzpatrick, Marie-Louise. Owl Bat Bat Owl. Fitzpatrick, Marie-Louise. 2017. (ENG.). 32p. (J). (gr. -1-2). 15.99 *(978-0-7636-9161-5(5))* Candlewick Pr.

—There. Fitzpatrick, Marie-Louise. 2009. (ENG.). 32p. (J). (gr. -1-2). 18.99 *(978-1-59643-087-7(7),* 900031312) Roaring Brook Pr.

Fitzpatrick, Meg & Ravenhill, John A. The World of Bridgett & Emily. Friederich, Uve. 2004. 41p. (J). mass mkt. 8.95 *(978-0-9747532-4-9(6))* Taylor-Dth Publishing.

Fitzpatrick, Tammi. The Swamp Ninja: Swamp Chronicle Book Two. Fitzpatrick, Tammi. 2019. (Swamp Chronicles Ser.: Vol. 2). (ENG.). 26p. (J). (gr. 3-5). pap. ***(978-1-987852-24-0(9))*** Wood Islands Prints.

Fitzsimmons, Catherine. A Jewel on Sapphire. Fitzsimmons, Catherine. 2019. (Adventures in Space Ser.: Vol. 1). (ENG.). 96p. (J). (gr. 1-4). pap. ***(978-1-928011-27-9(6))*** Brain Lag.

Fiume, Cosimo & Alrubaye, Salim. Woody. Fiume, Cosimo. 2018. (ENG.). 36p. (J). (gr. 2-6). pap. 9.99 *(978-1-68160-701-6(8))* Crimson Cloak Publishing.

Five Mile Press Staff. Renaissance Artists. deluxe ed. 2007. *(978-1-74178-336-0(4))* Five Mile Australia.

—The Seven Continents of the World. Mappin, Jennifer. 2008. 12p. (J). (gr. -1-3). *(978-1-74124-473-1(0))* Five Mile Australia.

Fix, Philippe. Seraphin. Fix, Philippe. Nicholson-Smith, Donald, tr. 2019. (ENG.). 28p. (J). (gr. k-3). pap. 18.00 *(978-1-939810-25-0(6),* Elsewhere Editions) Steerforth Pr.

Fizer Coleman, Stephanie. ABC Ready for School: An Alphabet of Social Skills. Delaney, Celeste. 2018. (ENG.). 40p. (J). (gr. -1-1). 15.99 *(978-1-63198-174-6(9))* Free Spirit Publishing, Inc.

—Acorn to Oak Tree. Tonkin, Rachel. 2019. (Follow the Life Cycle Ser.). (ENG.). 24p. (J). (gr. 2-2). pap. *(978-0-7787-6387-1(0),* 22aed180-f6c3-48a2-bb06-864c1a75e594); lib. bdg. *(978-0-7787-6379-6(X),* 06b16217-d63a-45d9-8e8e-0f2fa8128f8d) Crabtree Publishing Co.

—Egg to Butterfly. Tonkin, Rachel. 2019. (Follow the Life Cycle Ser.). (ENG.). 24p. (J). (gr. 2-2). pap. *(978-0-7787-6395-6(1),* 6958f327-c87c-4857-9eb5-f99fa204056f); lib. bdg. *(978-0-7787-6384-0(6),* 630ed18a-3f47-4f47-8fe1-a6763438316f) Crabtree Publishing Co.

—Egg to Chicken. Tonkin, Rachel. 2019. (Follow the Life Cycle Ser.). (ENG.). 24p. (J). (gr. 2-2). pap. *(978-0-7787-6396-3(X),* ee6e78b4-bfb0-4b31-aaa1-982e3dacb9d1); lib. bdg. *(978-0-7787-6385-7(4),* 770e5ae3-e994-4bce-af7f-99ee75d8dcbd) Crabtree Publishing Co.

—Egg to Frog. Tonkin, Rachel. 2019. (Follow the Life Cycle Ser.). (ENG.). 24p. (J). (gr. 2-2). pap. *(978-0-7787-6397-0(8),* fcef0923-86ca-4245-b28b-668bd4ddcb12); lib. bdg. *(978-0-7787-6386-4(2),* f4073435-d8a2-40e4-84c1-cb89728d0ef7) Crabtree Publishing Co.

Fizer-Coleman, Stephanie. Let's Go to Our Zoo. Feldman, Thea. Cottage Door Press, ed. 2019. (Smithsonian Kids Ser.). (ENG.). 12p. (J). (gr. -1-1). bds. 12.99 *(978-1-68052-603-5(0),* 1004140) Cottage Door Pr.

—Mindful Moments at Bedtime: Tall Trade Format. Rossa, Paloma. Cottage Door Press, ed. 2019. (ENG.). 24p. (J). (gr. -1-3). 14.99 *(978-1-68052-368-3(6),* 1003330) Cottage Door Pr.

Flack, Marjorie. The Country Bunny & the Little Gold Shoes 75th Anniversary Edition. Heyward, DuBose. 2014. (ENG.). 56p. (J). (gr. -1-3). 17.99 *(978-0-544-25197-7(0),* 1566548, HMH Books For Young Readers) Houghton Mifflin Harcourt Publishing Co.

—Happy Easter, Country Bunny. Heyward, DuBose. 2018. (ENG.). 18p. (J). (— 1). bds. 8.99 *(978-1-328-68394-6(X),* 1670548, HMH Books For Young Readers) Houghton Mifflin Harcourt Publishing Co.

Flaherty, Tom, photos by. Continuing the Passion. Bowyer, Clifford B. 2009. 360p. (J). 18.95 *(978-0-9787782-6-2(X))* Silver Leaf Bks., LLC.

Flamand, Keiron J. Little Metis & the Metis Sash, 1 vol. Falk, Deborah L. & Delaronde, Deborah L. 2015. (ENG.). 32p. (J). (gr. 2-3). mass mkt. 13.95 *(978-1-894717-02-1(3),* aa123702-115a-450d-8a74-cc3c9236492b) Pemmican Pubns., Inc. CAN. Dist: Firefly Bks., Ltd.

Flamini, Lorella. The Bible for Little Ones. Prestofillipo, Mary Nazarene, tr. 2004. 38p. (J). 9.95 *(978-0-8198-1166-0(1),* 332-029) Pauline Bks. & Media.

—Growing in Love: Virtues for Little Ones. 2006. 40p. (J). (gr. -1-k). bds. 11.95 *(978-0-8198-3105-7(0))* Pauline Bks. & Media.

—The Story of Creation. Prestofillipo, Mary Nazarene, tr. 2005. Orig. Title: Piccola storia della Creazione. (ITA.). 36p. (J). pap. 12.95 *(978-0-8198-7093-3(5))* Pauline Bks. & Media.

—The Story of Noah's Ark. Prestofillopo, Mary Nazarene, tr. 2003. 38p. (J). 9.95 *(978-0-8198-7084-1(6),* 332-380) Pauline Bks. & Media.

—Thank You Dear God! Prayers for Little Ones. 2006. 40p. (J). (gr. -1-k). bds. 11.95 *(978-0-8198-7417-7(5))* Pauline Bks. & Media.

Flanagan, Jeff. Pass It On. Fantasia, Kathryn. 2009. 28p. pap. 18.65 *(978-1-4415-5446-8(7))* Xlibris Corp.

Flanigan, Ruth. Hagamos una Obra. Hillert, Margaret. 2020. (Beginning-To-Read: Spanish Easy Stories Ser.). (SPA.). 32p. (J). (-2). 22.60 ***(978-1-68450-876-1(2))***; pap. 11.94 ***(978-1-68404-538-9(X))*** Norwood Hse. Pr.

Flanigan, Ruth. Let's Have a Play. Hillert, Margaret. 2016. (BeginningtoRead Ser.). (ENG.). 32p. (J). (gr. -1-2). pap. 11.94 *(978-1-60357-980-3(X))*; (gr. k-2). 22.60 *(978-1-59953-818-1(0))* Norwood Hse. Pr.

Flannery, Alex & Yianolatos, Michael. The Fairy Trail Room: Crystal City Series, Book 8. Yianolatos, Linda. 2018. (Crystal City Ser.: Vol. 8). (ENG.). 40p. (J). pap. 9.99 *(978-1-7288-2805-3(8))* Independently Published.

Flass, E. C. The Turkey Doll. Gates, Josephine Scribner. 2007. 62p. (J). lib. bdg. 59.00 *(978-1-60304-016-7(1))* Dollworks.

Flaterud, Morghie. A Year of Holidays with Papa Hein. Grand, Karen. 2017. (ENG.). (J). *(978-1-5255-1321-3(4))*; pap. *(978-1-5255-1322-0(2))* FriesenPress.

Flath, Regina. Emily Grace & the What Ifs: A Story for Children about Nighttime Fears. Gehring, Lisa B. 2016. 32p. (J). *(978-1-4338-2106-6(0),* Magination Pr.) American Psychological Assn.

Flather, Lisa. Caribou Journey. French, Vivian. 2003. (Fantastic Journeys Ser.). 32p. (J). *(978-1-84089-216-1(1))* Zero to Ten, Ltd.

Flaviano. Black Widow: No Restraints Play. 2019. (ENG.). 112p. (YA). (gr. 8-17). pap. 15.99 *(978-1-302-91673-2(4))* Marvel Worldwide, Inc.

Flavin, Teresa. All Families Are Special. Simon, Norma. 2013. (AV2 Fiction Readalong Ser.: Vol. 59). (ENG.). 32p. (J). (gr. k-3). 34.28 *(978-1-62127-867-2(0),* AV2 by Weigl) Weigl Pubs., Inc.

—All Families Are Special. Simon, Norma. 2003. (ENG.). 32p. (J). (gr. -1-3). 16.99 *(978-0-8075-2175-5(2),* 807521752) Whitman, Albert & Co.

—Fly High! The Story of Bessie Coleman. Borden, Louise & Kroeger, Mary Kay. 2004. (ENG.). 40p. (J). (gr. 3-7). 8.99 *(978-0-689-86462-9(0),* Simon & Schuster/Paula Wiseman Bks.) Simon & Schuster/Paula Wiseman Bks.

—The Old Cotton Blues. England, Linda. 2011. (ENG.). 32p. (J). (gr. -1-2). 14.99 *(978-1-4424-2945-1(3),* McElderry, Margaret K. Bks.) McElderry, Margaret K. Bks.

—Pushing up the Sky. Bruchac, Joseph. 2015. 96p. pap. 10.00 *(978-1-61003-552-1(6))* Center for the Collaborative Classroom.

—Pushing up the Sky: Seven Native American Plays for Children. Bruchac, Joseph. 2019. (ENG.). 96p. (J). (gr. 2-5). pap. 9.99 *(978-1-9848-1483-8(4),* Puffin Books) Penguin Young Readers Group.

Fleck, Jay. Black Belt Bunny. Davis, Jacky. 2017. 40p. (J). (-k). 16.99 *(978-0-525-42902-9(6),* Dial Bks) Penguin Young Readers Group.

—The Diamond & the Boy: The Creation of Diamonds & the Life of H. Tracy Hall. Holt, Hannah. 2018. (ENG.). 40p. (J). (gr. -1-3). 17.99 *(978-0-06-265903-3(0),* Balzer & Bray) HarperCollins Pubs.

—Double Take! A New Look at Opposites. Hood, Susan. 2017. (ENG.). 32p. (J). (gr. -1-2). 16.99 *(978-0-7636-7291-1(2))* Candlewick Pr.

—Everything You: A Board Book. McPike, Elizabeth. 2019. (ENG.). 32p. (J). bds. 7.99 *(978-0-374-31193-3(5),* 900196708, Farrar, Straus & Giroux (BYR)) Farrar, Straus & Giroux.

—Haunted Halloween. Fliess, Sue. 2018. (ENG.). 18p. (J). (gr. -1 — 1). 6.99 *(978-1-338-04533-8(4),* Cartwheel Bks.) Scholastic, Inc.

—The Three Little Yogis & the Wolf Who Lost His Breath: A Fairy Tale to Help You Feel Better. Verde, Susan. 2020. (Feel-Good Fairy Tales Ser.). (ENG.). 32p. (J). (gr. -1-3). 16.99 *(978-1-4197-4103-6(9),* 1218301, Abrams Bks. for Young Readers) Abrams, Inc.

—Tiny T. Rex & the Impossible Hug (Dinosaur Books, Dinosaur Books for Kids, Dinosaur Picture Books, Read Aloud Family Books, Books for Young Children) Stutzman, Jonathan. 2019. (ENG.). 48p. (J). (gr. -1-k). 15.99 *(978-1-4521-7033-6(9))* Chronicle Bks. LLC.

—Two Brothers, One Tail. Morris, Richard T. 2019. 32p. (J). (gr. -1-2). 17.99 *(978-1-5247-4085-6(3),* Philomel Bks.) Penguin Young Readers Group.

—We're Going on a Treasure Hunt. DiPucchio, Kelly. (ENG.). 32p. (J). 2020. bds. 7.99 *(978-0-374-31414-9(4),* 900225662); 2019. 17.99 *(978-0-374-30641-0(9),* 900175838) Farrar, Straus & Giroux. (Farrar, Straus & Giroux (BYR)).

Fleecs, Tony, et al. Cutie Mark Crusaders & Discord, 1 vol. Whitley, Jeremy. 2016. (My Little Pony: Friends Forever Ser.). (ENG.). 24p. (J). (gr. 1-8). 27.07 *(978-1-61479-506-3(1),* 21412, Graphic Novels) Spotlight.

Fleecs, Tony. Fluttershy, 1 vol. Kesel, Barbara Randall. 2015. (My Little Pony Ser.). (ENG.). 24p. (J). (gr. 1-8). 27.07 *(978-1-61479-332-8(8),* 17154, Graphic Novels) Spotlight.

Fleecs, Tony, et al. Fluttershy & Zecora, 1 vol. Zahler, Thom. 2016. (My Little Pony: Friends Forever Ser.). (ENG.). 24p. (J). (gr. 1-8). 27.07 *(978-1-61479-507-0(X),* 21413, Graphic Novels) Spotlight.

—Granny & the Flim Flam Brothers. Rice, Christina. 2018. (My Little Pony: Friends Forever Ser.). (ENG.). 24p. (J). (gr. 1-8). lib. bdg. 27.07 *(978-1-5321-4237-6(4),* 28565, Graphic Novels) Spotlight.

Fleecs, Tony. My Little Pony: Feats of Friendship. Flynn, Ian. 2020. 80p. (J). (gr. 4-7). pap. 9.99 *(978-1-68405-671-2(3))* Idea & Design Works, LLC.

Fleecs, Tony, et al. My Little Pony: Friends Forever Omnibus, Vol. 3, Vol. 3. Whitley, Jeremy & Rice, Christina. 2018. (MLP FF Omnibus Ser.: 3). 144p. (J). (gr. 4-7). pap. 24.99 *(978-1-68405-050-5(2))* Idea & Design Works, LLC.

Fleecs, Tony. My Little Pony: Legends of Magic, Vol. 2. Whitley, Jeremy. 2018. (MLP Legends of Magic Ser.: 2). 144p. (J). (gr. 4-7). pap. 19.99 *(978-1-68405-158-8(4))* Idea & Design Works, LLC.

Fleecs, Tony, et al. Pinkie Pie & Princess Luna, 1 vol. Whitley, Jeremy. 2016. (My Little Pony: Friends Forever Ser.). (ENG.). 24p. (J). (gr. 1-8). 27.07 *(978-1-61479-509-4(6),* 21415, Graphic Novels) Spotlight.

Fleecs, Tony. Rainbow Dash, 1 vol. Lindsay, Ryan K. 2015. (My Little Pony Ser.). (ENG.). 24p. (J). (gr. 1-8). 27.07 *(978-1-61479-334-2(4),* 17156, Graphic Novels) Spotlight.

Fleecs, Tony & Garbowska, Agnes. My Little Pony: Friendship Is Magic Volume 11, Vol. 11. Zahler, Thom & Anderson, Ted. 2017. (My Little Pony Ser.: 11). 120p. (J). (gr. 4-7). pap. 19.99 *(978-1-63140-815-1(1),* 9781631408151) Idea & Design Works, LLC.

Fleecs, Tony, jt. illus. see Hickey, Brenda.

Fleecs, Tony, jt. illus. see Price, Andy.

Fleet, Julie. A Day with Yayah. Campbell, Nicola I. 2017. (J). *(978-1-56656-041-2(1),* Crocodile Bks.) Interlink Publishing Group, Inc.

Fleischaker, John. Addie Sinclair: In the Moon Room. Clarke, Kimberley S. 2016. (ENG.). (J). pap. *(978-0-9865001-3-8(5))* Pink Wig Publishing.

Fleischman, Brandon. All Those Risks. Fleischman, Justin. 2019. (ENG.). 226p. (J). pap. 11.99 ***(978-1-4991-2627-3(1))*** CreateSpace Independent Publishing Platform.

Fleishman, Seymour. Babe Ruth. Van Riper Jr., Guernsey. 2015. (History's All-Stars Ser.). (ENG.). 208p. (J). (gr. 3-7). pap. 6.99 *(978-1-4814-2507-0(2),* Aladdin) Simon & Schuster Children's Publishing.

—Gus & the Baby Ghost. Thayer, Jane. 2018. (Gus the Ghost Ser.). (ENG.). 32p. (J). 17.95 *(978-1-948959-05-6(4))* Purple Hse. Pr.

Fleitas, Luciano. Fae Captive. Wilson, Sarah K. L. 2020. (Tangled Fae Ser.: Vol. 2). (ENG.). 198p. (YA). ***(978-1-9992872-4-5(X))*** Wilson, Sarah K. L.

Fleites, Juan. Red As Blue. Strangeway, Ji. 2018. (ENG.). 294p. (YA). (gr. 9-12). pap. 24.98 *(978-0-9988778-0-8(8))* GYATRi Media.

Fleming, Christopher. Wires, 1 vol. Long, Tyler. 2009. 28p. pap. 24.95 *(978-1-60836-217-2(5))* America Star Bks.

Fleming, Denise. Alphabet under Construction. Fleming, Denise. 2006. (ENG.). 32p. (J). (gr. -1-k). reprint ed. pap. 7.99 *(978-0-8050-8112-1(7),* 900039580) Square Fish.

—The Cow Who Clucked. Fleming, Denise. rev. ed. 2006. (ENG.). 40p. (J). (gr. -1-2). 18.99 *(978-0-8050-7265-5(9),* 900038949, Holt, Henry & Co. Bks. For Young Readers) Holt, Henry & Co.

—The Everything Book. Fleming, Denise. rev. ed. 2004. (ENG.). 26p. (J). (— 1). bds. 8.99 *(978-0-8050-7709-4(X),* 900026642, Holt, Henry & Co. Bks. For Young Readers) Holt, Henry & Co.

—The First Day of Winter. Fleming, Denise. 2013. (ENG.). 32p. (J). (gr. k-3). pap. 18.69 *(978-0-312-37138-8(1),* 9780312371388) Square Fish.

—Go, Shapes, Go! Fleming, Denise. 2014. (ENG.). 40p. (J). (gr. -1-3). 18.99 *(978-1-4424-8240-1(0),* Beach Lane Bks.) Beach Lane Bks.

—In the Small, Small Pond. Fleming, Denise. 2007. (ENG.). 32p. (J). (gr. -1-k). pap. 27.99 *(978-0-8050-8117-6(8),* 900039664, Holt, Henry & Co. Bks. For Young Readers) Holt, Henry & Co.

—Lunch. Fleming, Denise. 2019. (ENG.). 32p. (J). 18.99 *(978-1-250-23228-1(7),* 900209664, Holt, Henry & Co. Bks. For Young Readers) Holt, Henry & Co.

—Pumpkin Eye. Fleming, Denise. rev. ed. 2005. (ENG.). 32p. (J). (gr. -1-k). reprint ed. pap. 7.99 *(978-0-8050-7635-6(2),* 9780805076356) Square Fish.

—This Is the Nest That Robin Built. Fleming, Denise. 2018. (ENG.). 32p. (J). (gr. -1-3). 17.99 *(978-1-4814-3083-8(1),* Beach Lane Bks.) Beach Lane Bks.

—UnderGROUND. Fleming, Denise. 2012. (ENG.). 40p. (J). (gr. -1-3). 17.99 *(978-1-4424-5882-6(8),* Beach Lane Bks.) Beach Lane Bks.

—5 Little Ducks. Fleming, Denise. 2016. (ENG.). 40p. (J). (gr. -1-3). 17.99 *(978-1-4814-2422-6(X),* Beach Lane Bks.) Beach Lane Bks.

Fleming, Diana Trucks. Nine Goldfish in David's Pond. Calvert, Ellen Hasenecz. 2013. 36p. pap. 14.99 *(978-1-936745-18-0(6))* Nuevo Bks.

Fleming, Garry. Hello Wild Animals! A First Book of Animal Facts & Sounds. Adam, Luisa. 2019. (ENG.). 24p. (J). bds. *(978-0-6484571-0-7(9),* Brolly Bks.) Borghesi & Adam Pubs. Pty Ltd.

—Look at the Animals, 1 vol. Dale, Jay. 2012. (Engage Literacy Magenta Ser.). (ENG.). 32p. (gr. k-2). pap. 5.99 *(978-1-4296-8880-2(7),* Capstone Pr.) Capstone.

—The School Garden, 1 vol. Giulieri, Anne. 2012. (Engage Literacy Yellow Ser.). (ENG.). 32p. (gr. k-2). pap. 5.99 *(978-1-4296-8958-8(7),* Capstone Pr.) Capstone.

Fleming, Garry. The Cassowary's Egg. Fleming, Garry. 2016. (ENG.). 244p. (J). (gr. k-2). pap. *(978-0-9775720-6-9(4),* Brolly Bks.) Borghesi & Adam Pubs. Pty Ltd.

Fleming, Jesse, jt. illus. see Matsunaga, Judd.

Fleming, Kerri Hicks. Thank You Lord for Little Feet. Jimenez, Dawn. 2017. (ENG.). 26p. (J). pap. 11.99 *(978-1-945620-33-1(1))* Hear My Heart Publishing.

Fleming, Kim. Something Very Sad Happened: A Toddler's Guide to Understanding Death. Zucker, Bonnie. 2016. 32p. (J). 14.95 *(978-1-4338-2266-7(0),* Magination Pr.) American Psychological Assn.

Fleming, Kye. The Friendship Seed. Hull, Bunny. 2007. (Young Masters Ser.). 28p. (J). (gr. -1-2). per. 13.95 incl. audio compact disk *(978-0-9721478-6-6(1),* Dream A World) BrassHeart Music.

—The Hidden Treasure. Bunny, Hull. 2007. (Young Masters Ser.). (J). (gr. -1). 13.95 incl. audio compact disk *(978-0-9721478-8-0(8))* BrassHeart Music.

—Young Masters: The Magic Eye. Hull, Bunny. 2007. (Young Masters Ser.). (J). (gr. -1). 13.95 incl. audio compact disk *(978-0-9721478-7-3(X))* BrassHeart Music.

Fleming, Kyle. Hockey Wars 2: The New Girl. Lawrence, Sam & Jackson, Ben. 2019. (Hockey Wars Ser.: Vol. 2). (ENG.). 172p. (J). (gr. 3-7). pap. 10.99 *(978-1-988656-27-4(3))* Indie Publishing Group.

Fleming, Kyle. Hockey Wars 3: The Tournament. Lawrence, Sam & Jackson, Ben. 2019. (Hockey Wars Ser.: Vol. 3). (ENG.). 136p. (J). pap. 10.99 ***(978-1-988656-32-8(X))*** Indie Publishing Group.

Fleming, Lucy. All the Love in the World. Salzano, Tammi. 2019. (ENG.). 22p. (J). (-k). bds. 9.99 *(978-1-68010-603-9(1))* Tiger Tales.

—Babies Are Love: Crochet Rattle & Book Boxed Set. Finch, Rusty. 2015. (Knitty Bitty Rattle Set Ser.). (ENG.). 10p. (J). (gr. -1-2). bds. 14.99 *(978-1-68052-068-2(7),* 1000430) Cottage Door Pr.

Fleming, Lucy. Dark Tricks. Chapman, Linda. 2020. (Star Friends Ser.: 4). (ENG.). 160p. (J). (gr. 1-4). 16.99 ***(978-1-68010-216-1(8))***; pap. 6.99 ***(978-1-68010-469-1(1))*** Tiger Tales.

Fleming, Lucy. Dios, Sé Que Estás Allí, 1 vol. Jensen, Bonnie Rickner. ed. 2020. (SPA.). 24p. (J). bds. 9.99 *(978-1-4041-1060-1(7))* Grupo Nelson.

Fleming, Lucy. Eenie Meenie Halloweenie. Eaddy, Susan. 2020. (ENG.). 32p. (J). (gr. -1-3). 15.99 ***(978-0-06-269167-5(8)***, HarperCollins) HarperCollins Pubs. Ltd. GBR. Dist: HarperCollins Pubs.

Fleming, Lucy. For the Beauty of the Earth, Vol. Pierpoint, Folliott Sandford & Kocher, Conrad. 2017. (ENG.). (J). 16.99 *(978-1-5064-2183-4(0),* Sparkhouse Family) Augsburg Fortress, Pubs.

—Ghosts & Gummy Worms: A Readers' Theater Script & Guide, 1 vol. Wallace, Nancy K. 2015. (Readers' Theater: How to Put on a Production Ser.). 32p. (J). (gr. 3-6). 28.50 *(978-1-62402-113-8(1),* 18168, Looking Glass Library) Magic Wagon.

—God, I Know You're There, 1 vol. Jensen, Bonnie Rickner. 2019. 24p. (J). bds. 9.99 *(978-1-4002-0922-4(6))* Nelson, Thomas Inc.

—Groundhogs & Guinea Pigs: A Readers' Theater Script & Guide, 1 vol. Wallace, Nancy K. 2015. (Readers' Theater: How to Put on a Production Ser.). 32p. (J). (gr. 3-6). 28.50 *(978-1-62402-114-5(X),* 18170, Looking Glass Library) Magic Wagon.

—Hello, Fall! Diesen, Deborah. 2018. (ENG.). 32p. (J). 16.99 *(978-0-374-30754-7(7),* 900180736, Farrar, Straus & Giroux (BYR)) Farrar, Straus & Giroux.

—Mirror Magic. Chapman, Linda. 2020. (Star Friends Ser.: 1). (ENG.). 160p. (J). (gr. 1-4). 18.99 *(978-1-68010-182-9(X))*; pap. 6.99 *(978-1-68010-458-5(6))* Tiger Tales.

—Molly Discovers Magic (Then Wants to un-Discover It) Atwood, Megan. 2016. (Dear Molly, Dear Olive Ser.). (ENG.). 96p. (J). (gr. 1-3). lib. bdg. 21.99 *(978-1-4795-8694-3(3),* Picture Window Bks.) Capstone.

—Molly Discovers Magic (Then Wants to Un-Discover It) Atwood, Megan. 2017. (Dear Molly, Dear Olive Ser.). (ENG.). 96p. (J). (gr. 1-3). pap. 5.95 *(978-1-62370-616-6(5),* Capstone Young Readers) Capstone.

—Molly Meets Trouble (Whose Real Name Is Jenna) Atwood, Megan. 2016. (Dear Molly, Dear Olive Ser.). (ENG.). 96p. (J). (gr. 1-3). lib. bdg. 21.99 *(978-1-4795-8696-7(X),* Picture Window Bks.) Capstone.

—Most Wonderful Gift in the World. Sperring, Mark. 2019. (ENG.). 32p. (J). (gr. -1-2). 17.99 *(978-1-68010-173-7(0))* Tiger Tales.

—Olive Finds Treasure (of the Most Precious Kind) Atwood, Megan. (Dear Molly, Dear Olive Ser.). (ENG.). 96p. (J). (gr. 1-3). 2017. pap. 5.95 *(978-1-62370-615-9(7),* Capstone Young Readers); 2016. lib. bdg. 21.99 *(978-1-4795-8693-6(5),* Picture Window Bks.) Capstone.

—Olive Spins a Tale (and It's a Doozy!) Atwood, Megan. 2016. (Dear Molly, Dear Olive Ser.). (ENG.). 96p. (J). (gr. 1-3). lib. bdg. 21.99 *(978-1-4795-8695-0(1)*, Picture Window Bks.) Capstone.

—One Big Heart: A Celebration of Being More Alike Than Different, 1 vol. Davis, Linsey. 2019. (ENG.). 32p. (J). 17.99 *(978-0-310-76785-5(7))* Zonderkidz.

—Pickles & Parks: A Readers' Theater Script & Guide, 1 vol. Wallace, Nancy K. 2015. (Readers' Theater: How to Put on a Production Ser.). 32p. (J). (gr. 3-6). 28.50 *(978-1-62402-116-9(6)*, 18174, Looking Glass Library) Magic Wagon.

—Piper Morgan in Charge! Faris, Stephanie. 2016. (Piper Morgan Ser.: 2). (ENG.). 112p. (J). (gr. 1-4). pap. 5.99 *(978-1-4814-5711-8(X)*, Aladdin) Simon & Schuster Children's Publishing.

—Piper Morgan in Charge! Faris, Stephanie. 2016. (Piper Morgan Ser.: 2). (ENG.). 112p. (J). (gr. 1-4). 16.99 *(978-1-4814-5712-5(8)*, Simon & Schuster/Paula Wiseman Bks.) Simon & Schuster/Paula Wiseman Bks.

—Piper Morgan Joins the Circus. Faris, Stephanie. 2016. (Piper Morgan Ser.: 1). (ENG.). 112p. (J). (gr. 1-4). pap. 5.99 *(978-1-4814-5708-8(X)*, Aladdin) Simon & Schuster Children's Publishing.

—Piper Morgan Joins the Circus. Faris, Stephanie. 2016. (Piper Morgan Ser.: 1). (ENG.). 112p. (J). (gr. 1-4). 16.99 *(978-1-4814-5709-5(8)*, Simon & Schuster/Paula Wiseman Bks.) Simon & Schuster/Paula Wiseman Bks.

—Piper Morgan Makes a Splash. Faris, Stephanie. 2017. (Piper Morgan Ser.: 4). (ENG.). 96p. (J). (gr. 1-4). pap. 5.99 *(978-1-4814-5717-0(9)*, Simon & Schuster/Paula Wiseman Bks.) Simon & Schuster/Paula Wiseman Bks.

—Piper Morgan Plans a Party. Faris, Stephanie. 2017. (Piper Morgan Ser.: 5). (ENG.). 96p. (J). (gr. 1-4). 16.99 *(978-1-5344-0386-4(8))*; pap. 5.99 *(978-1-5344-0385-7(X))*;5. 18.69 *(978-1-5364-2740-0(3))* Simon & Schuster Children's Publishing. (Aladdin).

—Piper Morgan Summer of Fun Collection Books 1-4: Piper Morgan Joins the Circus; Piper Morgan in Charge!; Piper Morgan to the Rescue; Piper Morgan Makes a Splash. Faris, Stephanie. ed. 2017. (Piper Morgan Ser.). (ENG.). 432p. (J). (gr. 1-4). pap. 23.99 *(978-1-4814-9978-1(5)*, Aladdin) Simon & Schuster Children's Publishing.

—Piper Morgan to the Rescue. Faris, Stephanie. 2016. (Piper Morgan Ser.: 3). (ENG.). 112p. (J). (gr. 1-4). pap. 5.99 *(978-1-4814-5714-9(4)*, Aladdin) Simon & Schuster Children's Publishing.

—Piper Morgan to the Rescue. Faris, Stephanie. 2016. (Piper Morgan Ser.: 3). (ENG.). 112p. (J). (gr. 1-4). 16.99 *(978-1-4814-5715-6(2)*, Simon & Schuster/Paula Wiseman Bks.) Simon & Schuster/Paula Wiseman Bks.

—Pippa's Night Parade. Robinson, Lisa. 2019. (ENG.). 32p. (J). (gr. -1-2). 17.99 *(978-1-5420-9300-2(7)*, 9781542093002, Two Lions) Amazon Publishing.

—Princess Snowbelle. Frost, Libby. 2017. (ENG.). 32p. (J). 16.99 *(978-1-68119-690-9(5)*, 900182161, Bloomsbury USA Childrens) Bloomsbury Publishing USA.

—River Rose & the Magical Christmas. Clarkson, Kelly. 2017. (J). *(978-0-06-274098-4(9))* Harper & Row Ltd.

—River Rose & the Magical Christmas. Clarkson, Kelly. 2017. (ENG.). 32p. (J). (gr. -1-3). 19.99 *(978-0-06-269764-6(1))* HarperCollins Pubs.

—A Royal Ride: Catherine the Great's Great Invention. Fulton, Kristen. 2019. (ENG.). 40p. (J). (gr. -1-3). 17.99 *(978-1-4814-9657-5(3)*, McElderry, Margaret K. Bks.) McElderry, Margaret K. Bks.

Fleming, Lucy. Secret Spell. Chapman, Linda. 2020. (Star Friends Ser.: 3). (ENG.). 160p. (J). (gr. 1-4). 16.99 ***(978-1-68010-215-4(X))***; pap. 6.99 ***(978-1-68010-468-4(3))*** Tiger Tales.

Fleming, Lucy. The Snow Queen. Pirotta, Saviour. 2017. (Once upon a Time ... Ser.). (ENG.). 24p. (J). (gr. -1-k). lib. bdg. 19.99 *(978-1-68297-172-7(4))* QEB Publishing Inc.

—Turkey & Take-Out: A Readers' Theater Script & Guide, 1 vol. Wallace, Nancy K. 2015. (Readers' Theater: How to Put on a Production Ser.). 32p. (J). (gr. 3-6). 28.50 *(978-1-62402-117-6(4)*, 18176, Looking Glass Library) Magic Wagon.

—Wish Trap. Chapman, Linda. 2020. (Star Friends Ser.: 2). (ENG.). 160p. (J). (gr. 1-4). 18.99 *(978-1-68010-183-6(8))*; pap. 6.99 *(978-1-68010-459-2(4))* Tiger Tales.

—The World Is Awake: A Celebration of Everyday Blessings, 1 vol. Davis, Linsey. 2018. (ENG.). 32p. (J). 17.99 *(978-0-310-76203-4(0))* Zonderkidz.

Fleming, Michael. Ten Eggs in a Nest. Sadler, Marilyn. 2014. (Bright & Early Books(R) Ser.). (ENG.). 48p. (J). (gr. -1-2). lib. bdg. 13.99 *(978-0-375-97151-8(3)*, Random Hse. Bks. for Young Readers) Random Hse. Children's Bks.

—Time for School, Little Dinosaur. Herman, Gail. 2017. (Step into Reading Ser.). 32p. (J). (gr. -1-1). pap. 4.99 *(978-0-399-55645-6(1)*, Random Hse. Bks. for Young Readers) Random Hse. Children's Bks.

—Twinky the Dinky Dog. Klimo, Kate. 2013. (Step into Reading Ser.). 48p. (J). (gr. k-3). pap. 4.99 *(978-0-307-97667-3(X)*, Random Hse. Bks. for Young Readers) Random Hse. Children's Bks.

—10 Busy Brooms. Gerber, Carole. (J). 2018. (ENG.). 26p. (— 1). bds. 7.99 *(978-1-5247-6899-7(5))*; 2016. 32p. (gr. -1-2). 12.99 *(978-0-553-53341-5(X))* Random Hse. Children's Bks. (Doubleday Bks. for Young Readers).

Fleming, Yvonne B. Going Home with Jesus, 1 vol. Fleming, Theresa. 2009. 22p. pap. 24.95 *(978-1-60813-703-9(1))* America Star Bks.

Flener, Sheila S. Sidney's Bedtime Stories. Flener, Bettie D. 2011. 44p. pap. 24.95 *(978-1-4560-3226-5(7))* America Star Bks.

Flesher, Vivienne. East of the Sun, West of the Moon, 1 vol. MacHale, D. J. 2007. (Rabbit Ears-A Classic Tale Ser.). (ENG.). 36p. (J). (gr. 2-6). 28.50 *(978-1-59961-306-2(9)*, 12959, Picture Bk.) Spotlight.

Flesher, Vivienne. Alfred's Nose. Flesher, Vivienne. 2008. 32p. (J). (gr. -1-2). lib. bdg. 17.89 *(978-0-06-084314-4(4))* HarperCollins Pubs.

Fletcher, Beth. God Loves You, Little One. Make Believe Ideas Ltd. 2020. (ENG.). 26p. (J). bds. ***(978-1-78947-839-6(1))*** Make Believe Ideas.

Fletcher, Bob. I Grew up on a Farm. Lewis, Alan K. 2005. (ENG.). 32p. (J). (gr. -1-3). 19.95 *(978-0-9766805-2-9(1))* Keene Publishing.

Fletcher, Claire. Painting Pepette. Lodding, Linda Ravin. 2016. (ENG.). 40p. (J). (gr. -1-3). 17.99 *(978-1-4998-0136-1(X))* Little Bee Books Inc.

Fletcher, Corina, jt. illus. see Roberts, David.

Fletcher, Lyn. Merry Christmas, Rarity! Shepherd, Jodie. 2006. (My Little Pony Ser.). 32p. (J). (gr. -1-1). pap., act. bk. ed. 3.99 *(978-0-06-079472-9(0)*, HarperFestival) HarperCollins Pubs.

Fletcher, Neil & Williamson, Katie, photos by. Penguin. Ling, Mary & Dorling Kindersley Publishing Staff. 2007. (See How They Grow Ser.). (ENG., 24p. (J). (gr. k-3). 16.19 *(978-0-7566-3371-4(0))* Dorling Kindersley Publishing, Inc.

Fletcher, Robert A. Jeeps at War. Fletcher, Robert A. Naples, Thomas R. et al, eds. 2008. 36p. (J). 19.95 *(978-0-9722961-1-3(5))* Iron Mountain Pr.

Fletcher, Rusty. God Bless America. Beveridge, Amy. 2006. 16p. (J). pap. 1.99 *(978-0-7847-1509-3(2)*, 22136) Standard Publishing.

—God Made Dinosaurs. Head, Heno. 2013. (Happy Day Ser.). (ENG.). 16p. (J). pap. 2.49 *(978-1-4143-9296-7(6)*, 4608286) Tyndale Hse. Pubs.

—Ice Skating. Weil, Ann. 2004. (Elements of Reading: Phonics Ser.). 16p. pap. 40.00 *(978-0-7398-9010-3(7))* Houghton Mifflin Harcourt Supplemental Pubs.

—My Pink Piggy Bank. Williams, Rozanne Lanczak. 2005. (Reading for Fluency Ser.). 8p. (J). pap. 2.49 *(978-1-59198-144-2(1)*, 4244) Creative Teaching Pr., Inc.

—Thank You, God, for This Day. Bowman, Crystal. 2014. (Happy Day Ser.). (ENG.). 16p. (J). pap. 2.49 *(978-1-4143-9486-2(1)*, 4608476) Tyndale Hse. Pubs.

—The Weather. George, Olivia. 2005. (My First Reader Ser.). (ENG.). 32p. (J). (gr. k-1). lib. bdg. 18.50 *(978-0-516-24880-6(4)*, Children's Pr.) Scholastic Library Publishing.

Flett, Julie. Dolphin Sos, 1 vol. Miki, Roy & Miki, Slavia. 2014. (ENG.). 32p. (J). (gr. 1-3). 16.95 *(978-1-896580-76-0(9))* Tradewind Bks. CAN. Dist: Orca Bk. Pubs. USA.

—Dragonfly Kites, 1 vol. Highway, Tomson. 2019. (Songs of the North Wind Ser.). (ENG.). 32p. (J). (gr. -1-8). 14.95 *(978-1-897252-64-2(1)*, 27f40354-5546-488b-88c0-291c526a6183) Fifth Hse. Pubs. CAN. Dist: Firefly Bks., Ltd.

Flett, Julie. Ekospi Ka Ki Pekowak/When We Were Alone. Robertson, David A. Leask, Alderick, tr. ed. 2020. (ENG & CRE.). 32p. (J). (gr. k-3). ***(978-1-55379-905-4(4)***, HighWater Pr.) Portage & Main Pr.

Flett, Julie. Johnny's Pheasant. Minnema, Cheryl. 2019. (ENG.). 32p. (J). (gr. -1-3). 16.95 *(978-1-5179-0501-9(X))* Univ. of Minnesota Pr.

—Little You, 1 vol. Van Camp, Richard. 2013. (ENG.). 24p. (J). (gr. -1 — 1). bds. 10.95 *(978-1-4598-0248-3(9))* Orca Bk. Pubs. USA.

—Little You / Nīya-K'apisīsisīyân, 1 vol. Van Camp, Richard. Collins, Mary, tr. ed. 2018. (CRE & ENG.). 24p. (J). (gr. -1-k). 6.95 *(978-1-4598-2006-7(1))* Orca Bk. Pubs. USA.

—My Heart Fills with Happiness, 1 vol. Gray Smith, Monique. 2016. (ENG.). 24p. (J). (gr. -1 — 1). bds. 10.95 *(978-1-4598-0957-4(2))* Orca Bk. Pubs. USA.

—My Heart Fills With Happiness / Sâkaskinêw Nitêh Miywêyihtamowin Ohci, 1 vol. Gray Smith, Monique. Collins, Mary, tr. ed. 2018. (CRE & ENG.). 24p. (J). (gr. -1-k). 6.95 *(978-1-4598-2018-0(5))* Orca Bk. Pubs. USA.

—Owls See Clearly at Night/Lii Yiiboo Nayaapiwak Lii Swer: A Michif Alphabet/l'Alfabet Di Michif. 2010.Tr. of Owls See Clearly at Night - A Michif Alphabet. (ENG.). 56p. (J). (gr. -1-3). 16.95 *(978-1-897476-28-4(0))* Simply Read Bks. CAN. Dist: Ingram Publisher Services.

—We Sang You Home, 1 vol. Van Camp, Richard. 2016. (ENG.). 26p. (J). (gr. -1 — 1). bds. 10.95 *(978-1-4598-1178-2(X))* Orca Bk. Pubs. USA.

—We Sang You Home / Ka Kîweh Nikâmôstamâtinân, 1 vol. Van Camp, Richard. Collins, Mary, tr. ed. 2018. (CRE & ENG.). 26p. (J). (gr. -1-k). 6.95 *(978-1-4598-2014-2(2))* Orca Bk. Pubs. USA.

—When We Were Alone, 1 vol. Robertson, David A. 2017. (ENG.). 25p. (J). (gr. 1-3). 18.95 *(978-1-55379-673-2(X)*, HighWater Pr.) Portage & Main Pr. CAN. Dist: Orca Bk. Pubs. USA.

—Zoe & the Fawn. Jameson, Catherine. ed. 2006. (ENG.). 32p. pap. 11.95 *(978-1-894778-43-5(X))* Theytus Bks., Ltd. CAN. Dist: Univ. of Toronto Pr.

Flett, Julie. Birdsong. Flett, Julie. 2019. 48p. (J). (gr. -1-3). 17.95 *(978-1-77164-473-0(7)*, Greystone Bks.) Greystone Books Ltd. CAN. Dist: Publishers Group West (PGW).

Fletter, Sharon Sofia. My Guardian Angel. Fletter, Sharon Sofia. l.t. ed. 2007.Tr. of Mi Angel Guardian, il Mio Angelo, Meu Anjo Da Guarda, Mein Schutzengel, Mon Ange Guardian. (SPA, ITA, POR, GER & FRE.). 44p. (J). per. 17.95 *(978-0-9793113-0-7(6))* SoulSong Publishing.

Flinn, Hannah. Dashing Duke & His Dodgy Adventures. Albuquerque, Blossom. 2011. 36p. pap. 13.95 *(978-1-60911-743-6(3)*, Strategic Bk. Publishing) Strategic Book Publishing & Rights Agency (SBPRA).

Flint, Christopher. 100 Words on the Go: Tiered Shaped Board Book. Byrd, Redd. Cottage Door Press, ed. 2017. (Discover & Learn Ser.). (ENG.). 12p. (J). (gr. -1-1). bds. 12.99 *(978-1-68052-181-8(0)*, 1001790) Cottage Door Pr.

Flint, Gillian. Balletball. Dionne, Erin. 2020. 32p. (J). (gr. -1-3). lib. bdg. 16.99 *(978-1-58089-939-0(0))* Charlesbridge Publishing, Inc.

—Be Still. O'Brien, Kathryn. (My First Bible Memory Bks.). (ENG.). (J). 2018. 32p. bds. 7.99 *(978-1-4964-2780-9(7)*, 20_30669); 2016. 40p. 14.99 *(978-1-4964-1116-7(1)*, 4612791) Tyndale Hse. Pubs.

—Give Thanks. O'Brien, Kathryn. 2018. (My First Bible Memory Bks.). (ENG.). 32p. (J). bds. 7.99 *(978-1-4964-2781-6(5)*, 20_30670, Tyndale Kids) Tyndale Hse. Pubs.

—Hugga Bugga Love. Ohanesian, Diane. (ENG.). (J). (gr. -1-k). 2018. 26p. bds. 7.99 *(978-1-4998-0744-8(9))*; 2017. 32p. 16.99 *(978-1-4998-0395-2(8))* Little Bee Books Inc.

—I Can. O'Brien, Kathryn. (My First Bible Memory Bks.). (ENG.). (J). 2018. 32p. bds. 7.99 *(978-1-4964-2782-3(3)*, 20_30674, Tyndale Kids); 2016. 40p. 14.99 *(978-1-4964-1117-4(X)*, 4612792) Tyndale Hse. Pubs.

—Lady Miss Penny Goes to Lunch. Rodale, Maya. 2020. (Lady Miss Penny Ser.: 1). 32p. (J). (gr. -1-3). 17.99 *(978-1-63565-229-1(4)*, 9781635652291, Rodale Kids) Random Hse. Children's Bks.

—Love You Always. Spinelli, Eileen. (J). (gr. -1-k). 2018. 22p. bds. 7.99 *(978-0-8249-1667-1(0))*; 2017. 32p. 15.99 *(978-0-8249-5686-8(9))* Worthy Publishing.

—My First Book of Prayers. WorthyKids/Ideals. 2018. (ENG.). 20p. (J). (gr. -1-k). bds. 6.99 *(978-0-8249-1683-1(2))* Worthy Publishing.

Flint, Russ. Christian Reader's Theater. Ewald, Thomas. 2005. 64p. (J). per. 8.99 *(978-1-59441-077-2(1)*, CD-204004) Carson-Dellosa Publishing, LLC.

—Taking Godly Care of My Money: Stewardship Lessons in Money Matters, Grades 2-5. Sharp, Anna Layton. 2005. (Resource Bks.). 80p. (J). (gr. 2-5). per. 9.99 *(978-1-59441-082-6(8)*, CD-204009) Carson-Dellosa Publishing, LLC.

Flint, Stacie. Ten Pigs Fiddling. Atlas, Ron. 2006. (ENG.). 32p. (J). (gr. -1-k). 16.00 *(978-0-9630243-8-1(8)*, 1249130) Amberwood Pr.

—Ten Pigs Fiddling. Atlas, Ron. 2nd rev. ed. 2006. (ENG.). 32p. (J). (gr. -1-k). 17.95 *(978-0-9630243-3-6(7))* Amberwood Pr.

Flintham, Thomas. Doodle Spots, 1 vol. Webb, Christina & Lonely Planet Kids. 2016. (ENG.). 100p. (J). (gr. 1-3). pap. 12.99 *(978-1-76034-346-0(3)*, 5343) Lonely Planet Global Ltd. IRL. Dist: Hachette Bk. Group.

—Mesmerizing Math. Litton, Jonathan. 2013. (ENG.). 16p. (J). (gr. 2-5). 18.99 *(978-0-7636-6881-5(8)*, Templar) Candlewick Pr.

Flintham, Thomas. Animal Noises. Flintham, Thomas. 2016. (ENG.). 24p. (J). (gr. -1 — 1). bds. 7.99 *(978-1-4814-6935-7(5)*, Little Simon) Little Simon.

—Animal Numbers. Flintham, Thomas. 2016. (ENG.). 24p. (J). (gr. -1 — 1). bds. 7.99 *(978-1-4814-6937-1(1)*, Little Simon) Little Simon.

—¡Fin del Juego, Súper Chico Conejo! Flintham, Thomas. 2017. (¡Presiona Empezar! Ser.: 1). (SPA.). 80p. (J). (gr. k-2). pap. 4.99 *(978-1-338-15907-3(0))*; lib. bdg. 15.99 *(978-1-338-18791-5(0))* Scholastic, Inc. (Scholastic en Espanol).

—Game over, Super Rabbit Boy! a Branches Book (Press Start! #1) Flintham, Thomas. 2016. (Press Start! Ser.: 1). (ENG.). 80p. (J). (gr. k-2). pap. 4.99 *(978-1-338-03471-4(5))* Scholastic, Inc.

—Robo-Rabbit Boy, Go! Flintham, Thomas. 2019. (Press Start! Ser.: 7). (ENG.). 80p. (J). (gr. k-2). pap. 4.99 *(978-1-338-23981-2(3))* Scholastic, Inc.

—Super Rabbit Boy Blasts Off! Flintham, Thomas. 2018. (Press Start! Ser.: 5). (ENG.). 80p. (J). (gr. k-2). pap. 4.99 *(978-1-338-23962-1(7))* Scholastic, Inc.

—Super Rabbit Boy Powers up! a Branches Book (Press Start! #2) Flintham, Thomas. 2017. (Press Start! Ser.: 2). (ENG.). 80p. (J). (gr. k-2). pap. 4.99 *(978-1-338-03473-8(1))* Scholastic, Inc.

—Super Rabbit Boy vs. Super Rabbit Boss!: a Branches Book (Press Start! #4) Flintham, Thomas. 2018. (Press Start! Ser.: 4). (ENG.). 80p. (J). (gr. k-2). pap. 4.99 *(978-1-338-03475-2(8))* Scholastic, Inc.

—Super Rabbit Boy vs. Super Rabbit Boss! a Branches Book (Press Start! #4) Flintham, Thomas. 2018. (Press Start! Ser.: 4). (ENG.). 80p. (J). (gr. k-2). lib. bdg. 15.99 *(978-1-338-03476-9(6))* Scholastic, Inc.

—Super Rabbit Racers! Flintham, Thomas. 2017. (Press Start! Ser.: 3). (ENG.). 80p. (J). (gr. k-2). 15.99 *(978-1-338-03479-0(0))* Scholastic, Inc.

—The Super Side-Quest Test! Flintham, Thomas. 2018. (Press Start! Ser.: 6). (ENG.). 80p. (J). (gr. k-2). lib. bdg. 15.99 *(978-1-338-23979-9(1))* Scholastic, Inc.

—The Super Side-Quest Test! Flintham, Thomas. 2018. (Press Start! Ser.: 6). (ENG.). 80p. (J). (gr. k-2). pap. 4.99 *(978-1-338-23978-2(3))* Scholastic, Inc.

Flintham, Thomas & Mansfield, Andy. One Lonely Fish. Mansfield, Andy. 2017. 22p. (J). 15.99 *(978-1-68119-201-7(2)*, 900162817, Bloomsbury USA Childrens) Bloomsbury Publishing USA.

Flintman, Thomas. Super Science: Matter Matters! Adams, Tom. 2012. (ENG.). 18p. (J). (gr. 2-5). 18.99 *(978-0-7636-6096-3(5)*, Templar) Candlewick Pr.

Flintoft, Anthony. My First Day at Nursery School. Edwards, Becky. 2004. (ENG.). 32p. (J). (gr. -1-1). pap. 7.99 *(978-1-58234-909-1(6)*, 900024733, Bloomsbury USA Childrens) Bloomsbury Publishing USA.

Flisak, Jerzy. Detective Nosegoode & the Kidnappers. Orton, Marian. Marciniak, Eliza, tr. 2018. (ENG.). 96p. (J). (gr. 3-7). pap. 13.95 *(978-1-78269-157-0(X)*, Pushkin Children's Bks.) Steerforth Pr.

Flo, Maria. Cornelia & the Fancy Lunch. Stapler, Jodi. Vitale, Brooke, ed. 2020. (Cornelia Chronicles Ser.: Vol. 2). (ENG.). 66p. (J). pap. 9.99 ***(978-1-948256-28-5(2))*** Willow Moon Publishing.

Flo, Maria. Cornelia Needs a Space of Her Own. Stapler, Jodi. 2019. (Cornelia Chronicles Ser.: Vol. 1). (ENG.). 68p. (J). pap. 9.99 *(978-1-948256-26-1(6))* Willow Moon Publishing.

Floca, Brian. Ballet for Martha: Making Appalachian Spring. Greenberg, Jan & Jordan, Sandra. 2010. (ENG.). 48p. (J). (gr. 1-5). 19.99 *(978-1-59643-338-0(8)*, 900048498) Roaring Brook Pr.

—Billy & the Rebel: Based on a True Civil War Story. Hopkinson, Deborah. 2005. 44p. (J). lib. bdg. 15.00 *(978-1-4242-1148-7(4))* Fitzgerald Bks.

—Billy & the Rebel: Based on a True Civil War Story. Hopkinson, Deborah. 2006. (Ready-to-Read Ser.). 44p. (gr. 1-3). 14.00 *(978-0-7569-6390-3(7))* Perfection Learning Corp.

—Billy & the Rebel: Based on a True Civil War Story. Hopkinson, Deborah. (Ready-To-Reads Ser.). (ENG.). 48p. (J). (gr. 1-3). 2006. pap. 4.99 *(978-0-689-83396-0(2))*; 2005. 17.99 *(978-0-689-83964-1(2))* Simon Spotlight. (Simon Spotlight).

—City of Light, City of Dark. Avi. 2013. (ENG.). 192p. (J). (gr. 3-7). 19.99 *(978-0-545-54256-2(1))*; pap. 12.99 *(978-0-545-39880-0(0))* Scholastic, Inc. (Graphix).

—Elizabeth, Queen of the Seas. Cox, Lynne. 2014. 48p. (J). (gr. -1-3). 17.99 *(978-0-375-85888-8(1)*, Schwartz & Wade Bks.) Random Hse. Children's Bks.

—Ereth's Birthday. Avi. 2020. (Poppy Ser.: 5). (ENG.). 224p. (J). (gr. 3-7). pap. 7.99 *(978-0-380-80490-0(5)*, HarperCollins) HarperCollins Pubs. Ltd. GBR. Dist: HarperCollins Pubs.

—Ethan Out & about Big Book: Brand New Readers. Hurwitz, Johanna. 2010. (Brand New Readers Ser.). 48p. (J). (gr. -1-3). pap. 24.99 *(978-0-7636-4811-4(6))* Candlewick Pr.

—From Slave to Soldier: Based on a True Civil War Story. Hopkinson, Deborah. (Ready-To-Reads Ser.). (ENG.). 48p. (J). (gr. 1-3). 2007. pap. 3.99 *(978-0-689-83966-5(9))*; 2005. 16.99 *(978-0-689-83965-8(0))* Simon Spotlight. (Simon Spotlight).

—The Hinky-Pink: An Old Tale. 2008. (ENG.). 48p. (J). (gr. -1-3). 16.99 *(978-0-689-87558-5(6)*, Atheneum/Richard Jackson Bks.) Simon & Schuster Children's Publishing.

—Marty McGuire, 1. Messner, Kate. 2011. (ENG.). 160p. (J). (gr. 2-5). pap. 5.99 *(978-0-545-14246-5(6))* Scholastic, Inc.

—Marty McGuire Digs Worms! Messner, Kate. 2012. (ENG.). 176p. (J). (gr. -1-3). pap. 5.99 *(978-0-545-14247-2(4)*, Scholastic Pr.) Scholastic, Inc.

—Marty McGuire Has Too Many Pets! Messner, Kate. 2015. (Marty Mcguire Ser.). (ENG.). 176p. (J). (gr. -1-3). pap. 5.99 *(978-0-545-53560-1(3)*, Scholastic Pr.) Scholastic, Inc.

—Max & Mo Go Apple Picking. Lakin, Patricia. 2007. (Max & Mo Ser.). (ENG.). 32p. (J). (gr. -1-1). pap. 4.99 *(978-1-4169-2535-4(X)*, Simon Spotlight) Simon Spotlight.

—Max & Mo Make a Snowman. Lakin, Patricia. 2007. (Max & Mo Ser.). (ENG.). 32p. (J). (gr. -1-1). pap. 4.99 *(978-1-4169-2537-8(6)*, Simon Spotlight) Simon Spotlight.

—Max & Mo's First Day at School. Lakin, Patricia. 2007. (Max & Mo Ser.). (ENG.). 32p. (J). (gr. -1-1). pap. 4.99 *(978-1-4169-2533-0(3)*, Simon Spotlight) Simon Spotlight.

—Max & Mo's First Day at School. Lakin, Patricia. 2007. (Ready-To-Read - Level 1 (Quality) Ser.). (ENG.). (J). (gr. -1-1). lib. bdg. 14.60 *(978-1-62765-854-6(8))* Perfection Learning Corp.

—Max & Mo's Halloween Surprise. Lakin, Patricia. 2008. (Max & Mo Ser.). (ENG.). 32p. (J). (gr. -1-1). pap. 3.99 *(978-1-4169-2539-2(2)*, Simon Spotlight) Simon Spotlight.

—The Mayor of Central Park. Avi. 2003. tchr. ed. *(978-0-06-057254-9(X))*; 2003. (ENG.). 208p. (J). (gr. 3-6). 15.99 *(978-0-06-000682-2(X))*; 2005. (ENG.). 208p. (J). (gr. 3-7). reprint ed. pap. 6.99 *(978-0-06-051557-7(0))* HarperCollins Pubs.

—The Mayor of Central Park. Avi. 2005. 193p. (J). (gr. 3-7). 13.65 *(978-0-7569-5125-2(9))* Perfection Learning Corp.

—Old Wolf. Avi. 2015. (ENG.). 160p. (J). (gr. 3-7). 17.99 *(978-1-4424-9921-8(4))* Simon & Schuster Children's Publishing.

—Poppy. Avi. 2020. (Poppy Ser.: 3). (ENG.). 192p. (J). (gr. 3-7). pap. 7.99 *(978-0-380-72769-8(2)*, HarperCollins) HarperCollins Pubs. Ltd. GBR. Dist: HarperCollins Pubs.

—Poppy & Ereth. Avi. 2020. (Poppy Ser.: 7). (ENG.). 240p. (J). (gr. 3-7). pap. 7.99 *(978-0-06-111971-2(7))* HarperCollins Pubs.

—Poppy & Rye. Avi. 2020. (Poppy Ser.: 4). (ENG.). 240p. (J). (gr. 3-7). pap. 6.99 *(978-0-380-79717-2(8)*, HarperCollins) HarperCollins Pubs. Ltd. GBR. Dist: HarperCollins Pubs.

—Poppy & Rye. Avi. ed. 2006. (Poppy Stories Ser.: 3). 182p. (J). (gr. 3-7). lib. bdg. 17.20 *(978-0-613-17447-3(X))* Turtleback.

—Poppy's Return. Avi. 2005. (Poppy Stories Ser.). 240p. (J). lib. bdg. 16.89 *(978-0-06-000013-4(9))* HarperCollins Pubs.

—Poppy's Return. Avi. 2020. (Poppy Ser.: 6). (ENG.). 256p. (J). (gr. 3-7). pap. 7.99 *(978-0-06-000014-1(7)*, HarperCollins) HarperCollins Pubs. Ltd. GBR. Dist: HarperCollins Pubs.

—Princess Cora & the Crocodile. Schlitz, Laura Amy. 80p. (J). (gr. -1-3). 2019. pap. 7.99 *(978-1-5362-0878-8(7))*; 2017. 16.99 *(978-0-7636-4822-0(1))* Candlewick Pr.

—Ragweed. Avi. 2020. (Poppy Ser.: 1). (ENG.). 224p. (J). (gr. 3-7). pap. 7.99 *(978-0-380-80167-1(1)*, HarperCollins) HarperCollins Pubs. Ltd. GBR. Dist: HarperCollins Pubs.

—Ragweed & Poppy. Avi. 2020. (Poppy Ser.: 2). (ENG.). 272p. (J). (gr. 3-7). 16.99 *(978-0-06-267134-9(0))*; lib. bdg. 17.89 *(978-0-06-267135-6(9))* HarperCollins Pubs. Ltd. GBR. (HarperCollins). Dist: HarperCollins Pubs.

—Tomfoolery: Randolph Caldecott & the Rambunctious Coming-Of-Age of Children's Books. Markel, Michelle. 2018. (J). *(978-0-8118-7923-1(2))* Chronicle Bks. LLC.

—The True Gift. MacLachlan, Patricia. 2013. (ENG.). 112p. (J). (gr. 2-6). pap. 6.99 *(978-1-4424-8858-8(1)*, Atheneum Bks. for Young Readers) Simon & Schuster Children's Publishing.

—The True Gift: A Christmas Story. MacLachlan, Patricia. 2009. (ENG.). 96p. (J). (gr. 2-6). 14.99 *(978-1-4169-9081-9(X)*, Atheneum Bks. for Young Readers) Simon & Schuster Children's Publishing.

—Uncles & Antlers. Wheeler, Lisa. 2014. (ENG.). 40p. (J). (gr. -1-3). 17.99 *(978-1-4814-3018-0(1)*, Atheneum Bks. for Young Readers) Simon & Schuster Children's Publishing.

Floca, Brian. Five Trucks. Floca, Brian. 2014. (ENG.). 32p. (J). (gr. -1-3). 17.99 *(978-1-4814-0593-5(4)*, Atheneum Bks. for Young Readers) Simon & Schuster Children's Publishing.

—The Frightful Story of Harry Walfish. Floca, Brian. 2004. 26p. (J). (gr. k-4). reprint ed. pap. *(978-0-7567-7852-1(2))* DIANE Publishing Co.

—Lightship. Floca, Brian. 2007. (ENG.). 48p. (J). (gr. -1-3). 19.99 *(978-1-4169-2436-4(1)*, Atheneum/Richard Jackson Bks.) Simon & Schuster Children's Publishing.

—Locomotive. Floca, Brian. 2013. (ENG.). 64p. (J). (gr. -1-5). 19.99 *(978-1-4169-9415-2(7)*, Atheneum/Richard Jackson Bks.) Simon & Schuster Children's Publishing.

—Moonshot: The Flight of Apollo 11. Floca, Brian. 2019. (ENG.). 56p. (J). (gr. -1-5). 19.99 *(978-1-5344-4030-2(5)*, Atheneum/Richard Jackson Bks.) Simon & Schuster Children's Publishing.

Flocco, Gervasio Benítez. Zombis, Fuerzas y Movimiento. Weakland, Mark Andrew. 2019. (Ciencias Monstruosas Ser.). (SPA.). 32p. (J). (gr. 3-9). lib. bdg. 31.32 *(978-1-5435-8262-8(1)*, 141272) Capstone.

Floerchinger, Jeremy. Ocean of Dreams. Floerchinger, Lori Liddic. 2008. 36p. pap. 24.95 *(978-1-60703-003-4(9))* America Star Bks.

Floeter, Nell. A Year in the Life of the Kingwood Bunnies. Wood, David. 2010. 54p. pap. 15.95 *(978-1-936343-07-2(X))* Peppertree Pr., The.

Floethe, Richard. The Avion My Uncle Flew. Fisher, Cyrus. 2018. (J). pap. *(978-1-948959-00-1(3))* Purple Hse. Pr.

Flood, Ciara. There's a Walrus in My Bed! Flood, Ciara. 2017. (ENG.). 32p. (J). (gr. -1-3). 17.99 *(978-1-5124-8122-8(X)*, 9781512481228) Lerner Publishing Group.

Flood, Joe. Dinosaurs: Fossils & Feathers. Reed, M. K. 2016. (Science Comics Ser.). (ENG.). 128p. (J). (gr. 4-6). 31.19 *(978-1-4844-7999-5(8))* Roaring Brook Pr.

—Science Comics: Dinosaurs: Fossils & Feathers. Reed, M. K. 2016. (Science Comics Ser.). (ENG.). 128p. (J). pap. 12.99 *(978-1-62672-143-2(2)*, 900140354, First Second Bks.) Roaring Brook Pr.

Flood, Joe. Science Comics: Sharks: Nature's Perfect Hunter. Flood, Joe. 2018. (Science Comics Ser.). (ENG.). 128p. (J). 19.99 *(978-1-62672-787-8(2)*, 900173583); pap. 12.99 *(978-1-62672-788-5(0)*, 900173584) Roaring Brook Pr. (First Second Bks.).

Flood, Jordyn. Adventures of the Super Hero Sisters: Case #16 - Lucy's Missing Toy. Ramsay, Ty M. 2018. (ENG.). 26p. (J). pap. 9.99 *(978-1-7177-2922-4(3))* Independently Published.

Flood, Jordyn. Adventures of the Super Hero Sisters! Case #22 - What Does Mommy Do? Ramsay, Ty. 2020. (ENG.). 26p. (J). pap. 11.99 ***(978-1-0952-0863-2(2))*** Independently Published.

Flook, Helen. Beatrice More & the Perfect Party, 1 vol. Hughes, Alison. 2019. (Orca Echoes Ser.). (ENG.). 104p. (J). (gr. 1-3). pap. 6.95 *(978-1-4598-1709-8(5))* Orca Bk. Pubs. USA.

—Beatrice More Moves In, 1 vol. Hughes, Alison. 2015. (Orca Echoes Ser.). (ENG.). 80p. (J). (gr. 1-3). pap. 6.95 *(978-1-4598-0761-7(8))* Orca Bk. Pubs. USA.

—Black Gold, 1 vol. Cassidy, Sara. 2017. (Orca Echoes Ser.). (ENG.). 96p. (J). (gr. 1-3). pap. 6.95 *(978-1-4598-1422-6(3))* Orca Bk. Pubs. USA.

—Bruno for Real, 1 vol. Adderson, Caroline. 2009. (Orca Echoes Ser.). (ENG.). 64p. (J). (gr. 1-3). pap. 6.95 *(978-1-55469-023-7(4))* Orca Bk. Pubs. USA.

—I, Bruno, 1 vol. Adderson, Caroline. 2007. (Orca Echoes Ser.). (ENG.). 64p. (J). (gr. 1-3). per. 6.95 *(978-1-55143-501-5(2))* Orca Bk. Pubs. USA.

—Silas' Seven Grandparents, 1 vol. Horrocks, Anita. ed. 2017. (ENG.). 32p. (J). (gr. -1-k). 10.95 *(978-1-4598-1640-4(4))* Orca Bk. Pubs. USA.

Floor, Guus. The Bombing of Pearl Harbor. Uschan, Michael V. & Goff, Elizabeth Hudson. 2006. (Graphic Histories Ser.). 32p. (gr. 5-8). lib. bdg. 28.00 *(978-0-8368-6206-5(6))* Stevens, Gareth Publishing LLLP.

—The California Gold Rush. Goff, Elizabeth Hudson et al. 2006. (Graphic Histories Ser.). 32p. (gr. 5-8). lib. bdg. 28.00 *(978-0-8368-6202-7(3))* Stevens, Gareth Publishing LLLP.

Floor, Guus & Spay, Anthony. The First Moon Landing. Anderson, Dale & Goff, Elizabeth Hudson. 2006. (Graphic Histories Ser.). 32p. (gr. 5-8). lib. bdg. 27.00 *(978-0-8368-6203-4(1))* Stevens, Gareth Publishing LLLP.

Flor Ada, Alma, jt. illus. see López, Rafael.

Flor, Martina. The Selection Coloring Book. Cass, Kiera. 2016. (ENG.). 96p. (J). (gr. 8). pap. 15.99 *(978-0-06-264114-4(X)*, HarperTeen) HarperCollins Pubs.

Florean, Arianna. Dragons - Defenders of Berk Vol. 1: The Endless Night. Furman, Simon. 2016. (FBI Profiler Novel Ser.: 1). 64p. (J). (gr. 3-7). pap. 6.99 *(978-1-78276-214-0(0))* Titan Bks. Ltd. GBR. Dist: Penguin Random Hse. LLC.

—Marvel Action: Black Panther: Rise Together (Book Two) Ayala, Vita. 2020. (Marvel Action: Black Panther Ser.: 2). 80p. (J). (gr. 4-7). pap. 9.99 *(978-1-68405-523-4(7))* Idea & Design Works, LLC.

—Star Wars Adventures Vol. 6: Flight of the Falcon. Moreci, Michael. 2019. (Star Wars Adventures Ser.: 6). (ENG.). 80p. (J). (gr. 5-9). pap. 9.99 *(978-1-68405-499-2(0))* Idea & Design Works, LLC.

Florean, Arianna & Matera, Adele. Rey. Houser, Jody. 2018. (Star Wars: Forces of Destiny Ser.). (ENG.). 24p. (J). (gr. 4-9). lib. bdg. 27.07 *(978-1-5321-4295-6(1)*, 31121, Graphic Novels) Spotlight.

Florendo, Rm. Joe & the Magic Apple. Ash, Leon Terrell. 2019. (ENG.). 34p. (J). pap. 20.00 ***(978-1-6509-0256-2(5))*** Independently Published.

—Tia Lee & Her Family. Ash, Leon Terrell. 2020. (ENG.). 34p. (J). pap. 14.99 ***(978-1-6539-3882-7(X))*** Independently Published.

—Tim Tim Spell a Word. Ash, Leon Terrell. 2019. (ENG.). 36p. (J). pap. 12.50 ***(978-1-6509-1913-3(1))*** Independently Published.

Florendo, Ronaldo. Cuac, Cuac, Quinceañera. Kelley, Joseph. Cellini, Don, tr. 2019. (SPA.). 44p. (J). pap. 12.99 *(978-1-0783-1126-7(9))* Independently Published.

Florendo, Ronaldo. Donna & Blitzen. McWood, Allison. 2019. (ENG.). 28p. (J). pap. ***(978-1-9994377-8-7(0))*** Annelid Pr.

Flores, Carolyn Dee. Dale, Dale, Dale / Hit It, Hit It, Hit It: Una Fiesta de Numeros / a Fiesta of Numbers. Saldana, Rene. 2014. (ENG & SPA.). (J). 17.95 *(978-1-55885-782-7(6)*, Piñata Books) Arte Publico Pr.

—Daughters of Two Nations. Caravantes, Peggy. 2013. 144p. (J). pap. 14.00 *(978-0-87842-610-2(8))* Mountain Pr. Publishing Co., Inc.

—A Surprise for Teresita / una Sorpresa para Teresita. Sánchez-Korrol, Virginia. 2016. (ENG & SPA.). 32p. (J). (gr. k-3). 17.95 *(978-1-55885-831-2(8)*, Piñata Books) Arte Publico Pr.

Flores, Carolyn Dee. Amazing Watercolor Fish, the / el Asombroso Pez Acuarela. Flores, Carolyn Dee. 2018. (ENG & SPA.). 32p. (J). (gr. -1-2). 17.95 *(978-1-55885-873-2(3)*, Piñata Books) Arte Publico Pr.

—Canta, Rana, Canta. Flores, Carolyn Dee. Rosales-Yeomans, Natalia, tr. from SPA. 2013.Tr. of Sing, Froggie, Sing. (ENG & SPA.). 32p. (J). 16.95 *(978-1-55885-764-3(8)*, Piñata Books) Arte Publico Pr.

Flores, Catty. Compagnons de Voyage: French Edition of Traveling Companions. Pere, Tuula. Girval, Edith, tr. 2018. (Nepal Ser.: Vol. 1). (FRE.). 32p. (J). (gr. k-4). *(978-952-357-053-5(6))*; pap. *(978-952-357-051-1(X))* Wickwick oy.

—De Uil en de Herdersjongen: Dutch Edition of the Owl & the Shepherd Boy. Pere, Tuula. Van Eekelen, Mariken, tr. 2018. (Nepal Ser.: Vol. 3). (DUT.). 32p. (J). (gr. k-4). *(978-952-357-045-0(5))*; pap. *(978-952-357-044-3(7))* Wickwick oy.

—Gered Uit de Vlammen: Dutch Edition of Saved from the Flames. Pere, Tuula. Van Eekelen, Mariken, tr. 2018. (Nepal Ser.: Vol. 2). (DUT.). 32p. (J). (gr. k-4). *(978-952-357-043-6(9))*; pap. *(978-952-357-042-9(0))* Wickwick oy.

—Helmi, Perhosemme: Finnish Edition of Pearl, Our Butterfly. Pere, Tuula. 2019. (Helmi Ser.: Vol. 3). (FIN.). 32p. (J). (gr. k-4). pap. *(978-952-357-071-9(4))* Wickwick oy.

—Helmin Elämää: Finnish Edition of Pearl's Life. Pere, Tuula. 2019. (Helmi Ser.: Vol. 2). (FIN.). 32p. (J). (gr. k-4). *(978-952-357-066-5(8))*; pap. *(978-952-357-065-8(X))* Wickwick oy.

Flores, Catty. Hurjat Hampaat: Finnish Edition of Terrific Teeth. Pere, Tuula. 2019. (Little Fears Ser.: Vol. 1). (FIN.). 32p. (J). (gr. k-2). pap. ***(978-952-357-296-6(2))*** Wickwick oy.

—Hurjat Hampaat: Finnish Edition of Terrific Teeth. Pere, Tuula. Korman, Susan, ed. 2019. (Little Fears Ser.: Vol. 1). (FIN.). 32p. (J). (gr. k-2). ***(978-952-357-295-9(4))*** Wickwick oy.

—Kauheat K��rmeet: Finnish Edition of the Scary Snakes. Pere, Tuula. 2019. (Little Fears Ser.: Vol. 2). (FIN.). 32p. (J). (gr. k-2). ***(978-952-357-301-7(2))***; pap. ***(978-952-357-302-4(0))*** Wickwick oy.

Flores, Catty. Matkakaverukset: Finnish Edition of Traveling Companions. Pere, Tuula. 2018. (Nepal Ser.: Vol. 1). (FIN.). 32p. (J). (gr. k-4). pap. *(978-952-5878-24-0(4))* Wickwick oy.

—Les Misérables. Hugo, Victor. adapted ed. 2014. (ENG.). 64p. pap. 6.95 *(978-1-906230-79-1(X))* Real Reads Ltd. GBR. Dist: Casemate Pubs. & Bk. Distributors, LLC.

—The Owl & the Shepherd Boy. Pere, Tuula. Korman, Susan, ed. 2018. (Nepal Ser.: Vol. 3). (ENG.). 32p. (J). (gr. k-4). pap. *(978-952-5878-47-9(3))* Wickwick oy.

—Pearl, Our Butterfly. Pere, Tuula. Korman, Susan, ed. 2019. (Pearl Ser.: Vol. 3). (ENG.). 32p. (J). (gr. k-4). *(978-952-357-070-2(6))*; pap. *(978-952-357-069-6(2))* Wickwick oy.

—Pearl's Life. Pere, Tuula. Korman, Susan, ed. 2019. (Pearl Ser.: Vol. 2). (ENG.). 32p. (J). (gr. k-4). *(978-952-357-064-1(1))*; pap. *(978-952-357-063-4(3))* Wickwick oy.

—Perla, Vår Fjäril: Swedish Edition of Pearl, Our Butterfly. Pere, Tuula. Angelika, Nikolowski-Bogomoloff, tr. 2019. (Perla Ser.: Vol. 3). (SWE.). 32p. (J). (gr. k-4). pap. *(978-952-357-073-3(0))* Wickwick oy.

—Perlas LIV: Swedish Edition of Pearl's Life. Pere, Tuula. Angelika, Nikolowski-Bogomoloff, ed. 2019. (Perla Ser.: Vol. 2). (SWE.). 32p. (J). (gr. k-4). *(978-952-357-068-9(4))*; pap. *(978-952-357-067-2(6))* Wickwick oy.

—Pöllö Ja Paimenpoika: Finnish Edition of the Owl & the Shepherd Boy. Pere, Tuula. 2018. (Nepal Ser.: Vol. 3). (FIN.). 32p. (J). (gr. k-4). pap. *(978-952-5878-51-6(1))* Wickwick oy.

—Räddad Ur Lågorna: Swedish Edition of Saved from the Flames. Pere, Tuula. Torstensson, Elisabeth, tr. 2018. (Nepal Ser.: Vol. 2). (SWE.). 32p. (J). (gr. k-4). pap. *(978-952-5878-75-2(9))* Wickwick oy.

—Reddet Fra Flammerne: Danish Edition of Saved from the Flames. Pere, Tuula. Lundbeck, Merete, tr. 2018. (Nepal Ser.: Vol. 2). (DAN.). 32p. (J). (gr. k-4). *(978-952-357-034-4(X))*; pap. *(978-952-325-273-8(9))* Wickwick oy.

—Reisgenoten: Dutch Edition of Traveling Companions. Pere, Tuula. Van Eekelen, Mariken, tr. 2018. (Nepal Ser.: Vol. 1). (DUT.). 32p. (J). (gr. k-4). *(978-952-357-041-2(2))*; pap. *(978-952-357-040-5(4))* Wickwick oy.

—Rejsekammerater: Danish Edition of Traveling Companions. Pere, Tuula. Lundbeck, Merete, tr. 2018. (Nepal Ser.: Vol. 1). (DAN.). 32p. (J). *(978-952-357-033-7(1))*; pap. *(978-952-325-260-8(7))* Wickwick oy.

—Reskamraterna: Swedish Edition of Traveling Companions. Pere, Tuula. Torstensson, Elisabeth, tr. 2018. (Nepal Ser.: Vol. 1). (SWE.). 32p. (J). (gr. k-4). pap. *(978-952-5878-25-7(2))* Wickwick oy.

—Sauvés des Flammes: French Edition of Saved from the Flames. Pere, Tuula. Girval, Edith, tr. 2018. (Nepal Ser.: Vol. 2). (FRE.). 32p. (J). (gr. k-4). *(978-952-357-054-2(4))*; pap. *(978-952-357-052-8(8))* Wickwick oy.

—Saved from the Flames. Pere, Tuula. Korman, Susan, ed. 2018. (Nepal Ser.: Vol. 2). (ENG.). 32p. (J). (gr. k-4). pap. *(978-952-5878-73-8(2))* Wickwick oy.

Flores, Catty. The Scary Snakes. Pere, Tuula. Korman, Susan, ed. 2019. (Little Fears Ser.: Vol. 2). (ENG.). 32p. (J). (gr. k-2). ***(978-952-357-298-0(9))***; pap. ***(978-952-357-299-7(7))*** Wickwick oy.

—Terrific Teeth. Pere, Tuula. Korman, Susan, ed. 2019. (Little Fears Ser.: Vol. 1). (ENG.). 32p. (J). (gr. k-2). ***(978-952-357-292-8(X))***; pap. ***(978-952-357-293-5(8))*** Wickwick oy.

Flores, Catty. Tervetuloa Kotiin, Helmi: Finnish Edition of Welcome Home, Pearl. Pere, Tuula. 2019. (Helmi Ser.: Vol. 1). (FIN.). 32p. (J). (gr. k-4). *(978-952-357-060-3(9))*; pap. *(978-952-357-059-7(5))* Wickwick oy.

—Traveling Companions. Pere, Tuula. Korman, Susan, ed. 2018. (Nepal Ser.: Vol. 1). (ENG.). 32p. (J). (gr. k-4). pap. *(978-952-5878-23-3(6))* Wickwick oy.

—Tulesta Turvaan: Finnish Edition of Saved from the Flames. Pere, Tuula. 2018. (Nepal Ser.: Vol. 2). (FIN.). 32p. (J). (gr. k-4). pap. *(978-952-5878-74-5(0))* Wickwick oy.

—Ugglan Och Herdepojken: Swedish Edition of the Owl & the Shepherd Boy. Pere, Tuula. Torstensson, Elisabeth, tr. 2018. (Nepal Ser.: Vol. 3). (SWE.). 32p. (J). (gr. k-4). pap. *(978-952-5878-52-3(X))* Wickwick oy.

—Uglen Og Gedehyrden: Danish Edition of the Owl & the Shepherd Boy. Pere, Tuula. Lundbeck, Merete, tr. 2018. (Nepal Ser.: Vol. 3). (DAN.). 32p. (J). (gr. k-4). *(978-952-357-035-1(8))*; pap. *(978-952-325-292-9(5))* Wickwick oy.

—Välkommen Hem, Perla: Swedish Edition of Welcome Home, Pearl. Pere, Tuula. Angelika, Nikolowski-Bogomoloff, ed. 2019. (Perla Ser.: Vol. 1). (SWE.). 32p. (J). (gr. k-4). *(978-952-357-062-7(5))*; pap. *(978-952-357-061-0(7))* Wickwick oy.

Flores, Catty. Villi Vauhti: Finnish Edition of the Wild Waves. Pere, Tuula. 2019. (Little Fears Ser.: Vol. 3). (FIN.). 32p. (J). (gr. k-2). ***(978-952-357-307-9(1))***; pap. ***(978-952-357-308-6(X))*** Wickwick oy.

Flores, Catty. Welcome Home, Pearl. Pere, Tuula. Korman, Susan, ed. 2019. (Pearl Ser.: Vol. 1). (ENG.). 32p. (J). (gr. k-4). *(978-952-357-058-0(7))*; pap. *(978-952-357-057-3(9))* Wickwick oy.

Flores, Catty. The Wild Waves. Pere, Tuula. Korman, Susan, ed. 2019. (Little Fears Ser.: Vol. 3). (ENG.). 32p. (J). (gr. k-2). ***(978-952-357-304-8(7))***; pap. ***(978-952-357-305-5(5))*** Wickwick oy.

Flores, Catty & Swartz, Karen. The Amazing Captain K: A Special Needs Space Pirate Adventure. Schulze, Christine E. 2019. (Special Needs Heroes Ser.: Vol. 3). (ENG.). 54p. (J). pap. 12.99 ***(978-1-0795-4490-9(9))*** Independently Published.

Flores, Christine P. Alex's Adventures in Wonderland: I Wonder about My Family. Bebelia, Lia. Adams, Matt, ed. 2018. (ENG.). 34p. (J). (gr. k-2). pap. *(978-1-9999298-0-0(2))* Lia Bebelia Publishing.

—Alex's Adventures in Wonderland: I Wonder about the Tooth Fairy. Bebelia, Lia. McAlister, Rufus, ed. 2018. (978-1-9999298-2-4 Ser.). (ENG.). 38p. (J). (gr. k-2). pap. *(978-1-9999298-2-4(9))* Lia Bebelia Publishing.

Flores, Christine P. Aventurile Lui Alex in Ţara Minunilor: Mă Minunez de Coronavirus (şi Alte Virusuri, Bacterii şi Germeni) Bebelia, Lia. 2020. (RUM.). 88p. (J). pap. ***(978-1-9999298-6-2(1))*** Lia Bebelia Publishing.

Flores, Cory. Bugs on Parade: A Counting Book. 2006. 8p. (J). *(978-1-58970-400-8(2))* Lakeshore Learning Materials.

Flores, Enrique. The Harvest Birds: Los Pajaros de la Cosecha. de Mariscal, Blanca Lopez. 2014. (ENG & SPA.). 32p. (J). (gr. 1-18). pap. 10.95 *(978-0-89239-169-1(3)*, Children's Book Press) Lee & Low Bks., Inc.

Flores, Hemerson Maury. Alicia Nel Belpaese. Pirolo, Antonella. 2016. (ITA.). 44p. (J). pap. *(978-88-909981-7-1(2))* Fraleighe.

Flores, Heyliana. Entre Amigos. Chimal, Monica Genis. rev. ed. 2006. (Otra Escalera Ser.). (SPA & ENG.). 24p. (J). (gr. 2-4). pap. 9.95 *(978-968-5920-65-0(6))* Castillo, Ediciones, S. A. de C. V. MEX. Dist: Macmillan.

Flores, Joe, et al. Math Bridge Enriching Classroom Skills: 4th Grade. Moore, Jennifer et al. Willie, Kirsten et al, eds. 2004. (Math & Reading Bridge Ser.). 96p. (gr. 4-18). wbk. ed. 9.95 *(978-1-887923-16-3(0))* Rainbow Bridge Publishing.

—Math Bridge Enriching Classroom Skills: 5th Grade. Moore, Jennifer et al. Willie, Kirsten et al, eds. 2004. (Math & Reading Bridge Ser.). 96p. (gr. 5-18). wbk. ed. 9.95 *(978-1-887923-17-0(9))* Rainbow Bridge Publishing.

—Math Bridge Enriching Classroom Skills: 6th Grade. Dankberg, Tracy & Graham, Leland. Willie, Kirsten et al, eds. 2004. (Math & Reading Bridge Ser.). 96p. (gr. 6-18). wbk. ed. 9.95 *(978-1-887923-18-7(7))* Rainbow Bridge Publishing.

—Math Bridge Enriching Classroom Skills: 8th Grade. Dankberg, Tracy & Graham, Leland. Willie, Kirsten et al, eds. 2004. (Math & Reading Bridge Ser.). 96p. (gr. 8-18). wbk. ed. 9.95 *(978-1-887923-20-0(9))* Rainbow Bridge Publishing.

—Reading Bridge Enriching Classroom Skills: 5th Grade. Moore, Jennifer. Willie, Kirsten et al, eds. 2004. (Math & Reading Bridge Ser.). 96p. (gr. 5-18). wbk. ed. 9.95 *(978-1-887923-12-5(8))* Rainbow Bridge Publishing.

—Reading Bridge Enriching Classroom Skills: 6th Grade. Ledbetter, Darril & Graham, Leland. Willie, Kirsten et al, eds. 2004. (Math & Reading Bridge Ser.). 96p. (gr. 6-18). wbk. ed. 9.95 *(978-1-887923-13-2(6))* Rainbow Bridge Publishing.

—Reading Bridge Enriching Classroom Skills: 7th Grade. Ledbetter, Darril & Graham, Leland. Willie, Kirsten et al, eds. 2004. (Math & Reading Bridge Ser.). 96p. (gr. 7-18). wbk. ed. 9.95 *(978-1-887923-14-9(4))* Rainbow Bridge Publishing.

—Reading Bridge Enriching Classroom Skills: 8th Grade. Ledbetter, Darril & Graham, Leland. Willie, Kirsten et al, eds. 2004. (Math & Reading Bridge Ser.). 96p. (gr. 8-18). wbk. ed. 9.95 *(978-1-887923-15-6(2))* Rainbow Bridge Publishing.

Flores, Justin. Henry & Dale. Schwinn, Ruth E. 2010. (ENG.). 24p. (J). 14.95 *(978-0-578-04719-5(5)*, 9780578047195) PRF Pubs.

Flores, Lupita. La Vida Util de Pillo Polilla. Manzur, Vivian Mansour & Mansour, Vivian. rev. ed. 2005. (Castillo de la Lectura Naranja Ser.). (SPA & ENG.). 112p. (J). (gr. -1-7). pap. 7.95 *(978-970-20-0129-4(3))* Castillo, Ediciones, S. A. de C. V. MEX. Dist: Macmillan.

Flores, María. Little Pencil Finds His Forever Friends: A Rhyming Pencil Grip Picture Book. Calabrese, Christine. 2018. (Early Childhood Skills Ser.: Vol. 1). (ENG.). 36p. (J). (gr. k-3). 18.99 *(978-0-9995220-0-4(0))* Calabrese, Christine.

Flores, Maria Victoria. Little Pencil Finds His Forever Friends: A Rhyming Pencil Grip Picture Book. Calabrese, Christine. 2018. (Early Childhood Skills Ser.: Vol. 1). (ENG.). 36p. (J). (gr. k-2). pap. 9.99 *(978-0-9995220-2-8(7))* Calabrese, Christine.

Flores, Mariana. Tommy's ABCs. Heimerman, Jrenee. 2019. (ENG.). 34p. (J). (gr. k-4). 15.95 *(978-1-7324186-7-7(5))*; pap. 9.95 *(978-1-7324186-6-0(7))* Fabulicity Lifestyle Creations.

Flores, Martha, jt. illus. see Diego, Rapi.

Flores, Olvier. Mexicas: Los Indígenas de Mesoamérica II. Romero, José Rubén. 2019. (Historias de Verdad Ser.). (SPA.). 80p. (J). (gr. 4-7). pap. 12.00 *(978-607-8469-55-0(X))* Nostra Ediciones MEX. Dist: Independent Pubs. Group.

Flores, Valeria R. ¿Como Se Metieron Ahi?/How'd They Get in There? Flores, Valeria R. 2012. (ENG.). 28p. pap. 21.99 *(978-1-4653-0884-9(9))* Xlibris Corp.

Floresguerra, Angel. La Oscuridad y Yo: Darkness & I. Flores-Figueroa, Sylvia. 2019. (SPA.). 34p. (J). pap. 8.99 *(978-1-64086-327-9(3))* ibukku, LLC.

Florian, Douglas. Autumnblings. Florian, Douglas. 2003. (ENG.). 48p. (J). (gr. k-5). 16.99 *(978-0-06-009278-8(5)*, Greenwillow Bks.) HarperCollins Pubs.

—Dinothesaurus: Prehistoric Poems & Paintings. Florian, Douglas. 2009. (ENG.). 56p. (J). (gr. 1-5). 17.99 *(978-1-4169-7978-4(6)*, Beach Lane Bks.) Beach Lane Bks.

—Friends & Foes: Poems about Us All. Florian, Douglas. 2018. (ENG.). 48p. (J). (gr. -1-5). 17.99 *(978-1-4424-8795-6(X)*, Beach Lane Bks.) Beach Lane Bks.

—How to Draw a Dragon. Florian, Douglas. 2015. (ENG.). 42p. (J). (gr. -1-3). 17.99 *(978-1-4424-7399-7(1)*, Beach Lane Bks.) Beach Lane Bks.

—Laugh-Eteria. Florian, Douglas. 2008. (ENG.). 160p. (J). (gr. 1-4). pap. 8.99 *(978-0-15-206148-7(7)*, 1198460) Houghton Mifflin Harcourt Publishing Co.

—Pig Is Big on Books. Florian, Douglas. 2015. (I Like to Read Ser.). (ENG.). 24p. (J). (gr. -1-3). 7.99 *(978-0-8234-3424-4(9))* Holiday Hse., Inc.

—Poetrees. Florian, Douglas. 2010. (ENG.). 48p. (J). (gr. 1-5). 17.99 *(978-1-4169-8672-0(3)*, Beach Lane Bks.) Beach Lane Bks.

—UnBEElievables: Honeybee Poems & Paintings. Florian, Douglas. 2012. (ENG.). 32p. (J). (gr. k-3). 17.99 *(978-1-4424-2652-8(7)*, Beach Lane Bks.) Beach Lane Bks.

Florian, Douglas & Taplinger, Lee, photos by. See for Your Self. Florian, Douglas. 2005. (Meet the Author Ser.). (ENG., 32p. (J). 14.95 *(978-1-57274-821-7(4)*, 731, Meet the Author) Owen, Richard C. Pubs., Inc.

Florian, Melanie. Emma, the Extra Ordinary Princess. Rennert, Laura Joy. 2009. (J). *(978-0-525-42152-8(1)*, Dutton Juvenile) Penguin Publishing Group.

Florian, Mélanie. Princess Addison Gets Angry, 1 vol. Martin, Molly. 2013. (Princess Heart Ser.). (ENG.). 24p. (J). (gr. -1-1). lib. bdg. 22.65 *(978-1-4048-7851-8(3)*, Picture Window Bks.) Capstone.

—Princess Harper Gets Happy, 1 vol. Martin, Molly. 2013. (Princess Heart Ser.). (ENG.). 24p. (J). (gr. -1-1). 6.95 *(978-1-4048-8108-2(5))*; lib. bdg. 22.65 *(978-1-4048-7852-5(1))* Capstone. (Picture Window Bks.).

—Princess Heart. Martin, Molly. 2013. (Princess Heart Ser.). (ENG.). 24p. (J). (gr. -1-1). lib. bdg., lib. bdg., lib. bdg. 90.60 *(978-1-4048-8056-6(9)*, Picture Window Bks.) Capstone.

—Princess Sophia Gets Scared, 1 vol. Martin, Molly. 2013. (Princess Heart Ser.). (ENG.). 24p. (J). (gr. -1-1). 6.95 *(978-1-4048-8110-5(7))*; lib. bdg. 22.65 *(978-1-4048-7854-9(8))* Capstone. (Picture Window Bks.).

—Princess Stella Gets Sad, 1 vol. Martin, Molly. 2013. (Princess Heart Ser.). (ENG.). 24p. (J). (gr. -1-1). 6.95 *(978-1-4048-8109-9(3))*; lib. bdg. 22.65 *(978-1-4048-7853-2(X))* Capstone. (Picture Window Bks.).

Florian, Melanie. Royal Princess Academy: Dragon Dreams. Rennert, Laura Joy. 2012. (Royal Princess Academy Ser.). (ENG.). 112p. (J). (gr. 1-4). 18.69 *(978-0-8037-3750-1(5))* Penguin Young Readers Group.

Florian, Mélanie. School Lunch Pink B Band. Franklin, Glen & Bodman, Sue. 2017. (Cambridge Reading Adventures Ser.). (ENG.). 16p. (J). pap. 5.62 *(978-1-108-43963-3(2))* Cambridge Univ. Pr.

—Sleepy Little Caterpillar, 1 vol. Giulieri, Anne. 2012. (Engage Literacy Red Ser.). (ENG.). 32p. (gr. k-2). pap. 5.99 *(978-1-4296-8932-8(3)*, Capstone Pr.) Capstone.

—To the Shops, 1 vol. Giulieri, Anne. 2012. (Engage Literacy Magenta Ser.). (ENG.). 32p. (gr. k-2). pap. 5.99 *(978-1-4296-8882-6(3)*, Capstone Pr.) Capstone.

Florio, Gianfranco. DISNEY·PIXAR Toy Story Adventures (Graphic Novel) Sisti, Alessandro et al. 2019. (ENG.). 240p. (J). (gr. 3-7). pap. 10.99 *(978-1-5067-1266-6(5)*, Dark Horse Books) Dark Horse Comics.

—Disney PIXAR Toy Story Adventures Volume 2 (Graphic Novel) Ferrari, Alessandro et al. 2019. (ENG.). 240p. (J). (gr. 3-7). pap. 10.99 *(978-1-5067-1451-6(X)*, Dark Horse Books) Dark Horse Comics.

Florio, Gianfranco, et al. DuckTales: Mischief & Miscreants. Behling, Steve & Caramagna, Joe. 2019. (Duck Tales Ser.: 6). (ENG.). 72p. (J). (gr. 4-7). pap. 9.99 *(978-1-68405-559-3(8))* Idea & Design Works, LLC.

—DuckTales: Quests & Quacks. Caramagna, Joe & Cavalieri, Joey. 2018. (Duck Tales Ser.: 3). 80p. (J). (gr. 2-5). pap. 9.99 *(978-1-68405-319-3(6))* Idea & Design Works, LLC.

Florio, Gianfranco. DuckTales: Treasure Trove. Caramagna, Joe & Cavalieri, Joey. 2018. (Duck Tales Ser.: 1). 80p. (J). (gr. 4-7). pap. 9.99 (978-1-68405-208-0(4)) Idea & Design Works, LLC.

Florio, Gianfranco & Urbano, Emilio. DuckTales: Monsters & Mayhem. Behling, Steve et al. 2019. (Duck Tales Ser.: 5). (ENG.). 72p. (J). (gr. 4-7). pap. 9.99 (978-1-68405-490-9(7)) Idea & Design Works, LLC.

Flory, Jane. The Too Little Fire Engine. Flory, Jane. dePaola, Tomie. 2015. (G&d Vintage Ser.). 24p. (J). (gr. -1-k). bds. 7.99 (978-0-448-48217-0(7), Grosset & Dunlap) Penguin Young Readers Group.

Flotte, Eddie. Angkat: The Cambodian Cinderella. Coburn, Jewell Reinhart. 2014. (ENG.). 32p. (J). pap. 10.95 (978-1-885008-42-8(2), Shen's Bks.) Lee & Low Bks., Inc.

Flournoy, L. Diana. Learning Through Symbolism & Celebrations. Love, Mary A. 2nd rev. ed. 2011. (ENG.). 168p. pap. 24.00 (978-1-929548-00-2(1)) Love's Creative Resources.

Flower, Alexis. Gabriel Entre Chien et Loup. Tougas, Janine. 2017. (Collection Voyages Ser.). (FRE.). 192p. (J). (gr. 4-6). pap. (978-1-897328-93-4(1)) Apprentissage Illimite, Inc.

—Henri et le Cheval Noir. Tougas, Janine. 2016. (Collection Voyages Ser.). (FRE.). 224p. (J). (gr. 2-6). pap. (978-1-77222-304-0(2)) Apprentissage Illimite, Inc.

—Sylvianne Aux Couleurs du Corbeau. Tougas, Janine. 2016. (Collection Voyages Ser.). (FRE.). 294p. (J). (gr. 4-6). pap. (978-1-77222-306-4(9)) Apprentissage Illimite, Inc.

Flower, Amelia. Wilma Rudolph. Sanchez Vegara, Maria Isabel. 2019. (Little People, Big Dreams Ser.: Vol. 27). (ENG.). 32p. (J). (gr. -1-2). **978-1-78603-751-0(3))** Frances Lincoln Childrens Bks.

—Wilma Rudolph: My First Wilma Rudolph. Sanchez Vegara, Maria Isabel. 2020. (Little People, BIG DREAMS Ser.: 27). (ENG.). 24p. (J). (— 1). bds. 9.99 **(978-0-7112-4626-3(2)**, 330273, Frances Lincoln Children's Bks.) Quarto Publishing Group UK GBR. Dist: Hachette UK Distribution.

Flowers, Luke. A Is for Ark. Bowman, Crystal & McKinley, Teri. 2017. (Our Daily Bread for Little Hearts Ser.). (ENG.). 18p. (J). (— 1). bds. 9.99 (978-1-62707-599-2(2)) Discovery Hse. Pubs.

—Adam & Eve's 1-2-3s. Bowman, Crystal & McKinley, Teri. 2017. (Our Daily Bread for Little Hearts Ser.). (ENG.). 18p. (J). (— 1). bds. 9.99 (978-1-62707-600-5(X)) Discovery Hse. Pubs.

—Balloon Blast! (Rusty Rivets) Matheis, Mickie. 2017. (Little Golden Book Ser.). (ENG.). 24p. (J). (-k). 4.99 (978-1-5247-1672-1(3), Golden Bks.) Random Hse. Children's Bks.

—A Beautiful Day in the Neighborhood: The Poetry of Mister Rogers. Rogers, Fred. 2019. (Mister Rogers Poetry Bks.: 1). 144p. (J). (gr. 1-3). 19.99 (978-1-68369-113-6(X)) Quirk Bks.

—Deep Dive! (Minecraft Woodsword Chronicles #3) Eliopulos, Nick. 2019. (Stepping Stone Book(TM) Ser.). (ENG.). 144p. (J). (gr. 1-4). 12.99 (978-1-9848-5052-2(0)); 9.99 (978-1-9848-5051-5(2)) Random Hse. Children's Bks. (Random Hse. Bks. for Young Readers).

—Fourth of July. Berne, Emma Carlson. 2018. (Holidays in Rhythm & Rhyme Ser.). (ENG.). 24p. (gr. k-2). lib. bdg. 33.99 (978-1-68410-391-1(6), 140364); lib. bdg. 33.99 incl. audio compact disk (978-1-68410-125-2(5), 31841) Cantata Learning.

Flowers, Luke. It's You I Like: A Mister Rogers Poetry Book. Rogers, Fred. 2020. (Mister Rogers Poetry Bks.: 3). 32p. (J). (-k). bds. 9.99 **(978-1-68369-201-0(2))** Quirk Bks.

Flowers, Luke. Little Bo Peep & Her Bad, Bad Sheep: A Mother Goose Hullabaloo. Wegwerth, A. L. 2016. (Fiction Picture Bks.). (ENG.). 40p. (J). (gr. -1-2). lib. bdg. 22.65 (978-1-4795-6483-5(4), Picture Window Bks.) Capstone.

—The Llamas in the Field. Fronis, Aly. 2020. (ENG.). 16p. (J). (-k). bds. 6.99 (978-1-4998-1005-9(9)) Little Bee Books Inc.

—Move! Hopwood, Lolly & Kusters, YoYo. 2016. (ENG.). 32p. (J). (gr. -1-1). bds. 12.95 (978-0-7611-8733-2(2), 18733) Workman Publishing Co., Inc.

—Night of the Bats! (Minecraft Woodsword Chronicles #2) Eliopulos, Nick. 2019. (Stepping Stone Book(TM) Ser.). (ENG.). 144p. (J). (gr. 1-4). 9.99 (978-1-9848-5048-5(2), Random Hse. Bks. for Young Readers) Random Hse. Children's Bks.

—One More Dino on the Floor. Lyons, Kelly Starling. 2016. (ENG.). 32p. (J). (gr. -1-3). 16.99 (978-0-8075-1598-3(1), 807515981) Whitman, Albert & Co.

—Pirate Treasure Hunt! (Rusty Rivets) Berrios, Frank. 2018. (Little Golden Book Ser.). (ENG.). 24p. (J). (-k). 4.99 (978-1-5247-6795-2(6), Golden Bks.) Random Hse. Children's Bks.

—Ready, Set, Sail! Fleming, Meg. 2018. (ENG.). 32p. (J). (gr. -1-3). 16.99 (978-1-4998-0533-8(0)) Little Bee Books Inc.

—A Subir la Colina. Schmauss, Judy Kentor. 2016. (Early Rising Readers Ser.). (SPA.). 16p. (J). (gr. 1-1). 6.67 (978-1-4788-3735-0(7)) Newmark Learning LLC.

—The Tale of Paul Bunyan. Houran, Lori Haskins. 2020. (Little Golden Book Ser.). 24p. (J). (-k). 4.99 (978-1-9848-5179-6(9), Golden Bks.) Random Hse. Children's Bks.

—This Little Bunny. Fronis, Aly. 2019. (ENG.). 16p. (J). (gr. -1-k). bds. 5.99 (978-1-4998-0777-6(5)) Little Bee Books Inc.

—This Little Pumpkin. Fronis, Aly. 2018. (ENG.). 16p. (J). (gr. -1-k). bds. 5.99 (978-1-4998-0645-8(0)) Little Bee Books Inc.

—This Little Reindeer. Fronis, Aly. 2017. (ENG.). 16p. (J). (gr. -1-k). bds. 5.99 (978-1-4998-0525-3(X)) Little Bee Books Inc.

—Unicorn Day. Murray, Diana. 2019. 32p. (J). (-3). 17.99 (978-1-4926-6722-3(6), Sourcebooks Jabberwocky) Sourcebooks, Inc.

—Up a Big Hill. Schmauss, Judy Kentor. 2015. (Early Rising Readers Ser.). (J). (gr. -1-k). 5.83 (978-1-4788-1679-9(1)) Newmark Learning LLC.

Flowers, Luke. Won't You Be My Neighbor? A Mister Rogers Poetry Book. Rogers, Fred. 2020. (Mister Rogers Poetry Bks.: 2). 32p. (J). (-k). bds. 9.99 **(978-1-68369-199-0(7))** Quirk Bks.

Flowers, Luke. Ninja at the Firehouse. Flowers, Luke. 2018. (Scholastic Reader, Level 1 Ser.). (ENG.). 32p. (J). (gr. -1-3). pap. 3.99 (978-1-338-25611-6(4)); lib. bdg. 16.99 (978-1-338-25612-3(2)) Scholastic, Inc.

—Ninja at the Pet Shop (Scholastic Reader, Level 1: Moby Shinobi) Flowers, Luke. 2017. (Scholastic Reader, Level 1 Ser.). (ENG.). 32p. (J). (gr. -1-1). pap. 3.99 (978-1-338-18726-7(0)) Scholastic, Inc.

—Ninja in the Kitchen. Flowers, Luke. 2017. (Scholastic Reader, Level 1 Ser.). (ENG.). 32p. (J). (gr. -1-1). pap. 3.99 (978-0-545-93534-0(2)) Scholastic, Inc.

—Ninja on the Farm. Flowers, Luke. 2016. (Scholastic Reader, Level 1 Ser.). (ENG.). 32p. (J). (gr. -1-3). pap. 3.99 (978-0-545-93537-1(7)) Scholastic, Inc.

—Ninja on the Job. Flowers, Luke. 2018. (Scholastic Reader, Level 1 Ser.). (ENG.). 32p. (J). (gr. -1-1). lib. bdg. 16.99 (978-1-338-25615-4(7)); pap. 3.99 (978-1-338-25614-7(9)) Scholastic, Inc.

Flowers, Luke, jt. illus. see Golden Books.

Flowers, Tony. The Battle for the Golden Egg. Falk, Nick. 2015. (Samurai vs Ninja Ser.: 1). 96p. (J). (gr. 1-3). pap. 7.99 (978-0-85798-605-4(8)) Random Hse. Australia AUS. Dist: Independent Pubs. Group.

—Curse of the Oni. Falk, Nick. 2016. (Samurai vs Ninja Ser.: 4). 96p. (J). (gr. 1-3). pap. 7.99 (978-0-85798-640-5(6)) Random Hse. Australia AUS. Dist: Independent Pubs. Group.

—Day of the Dreadful Undead. Falk, Nick. 2016. (Samurai vs Ninja Ser.: 3). 96p. (J). (gr. 1-3). pap. 7.99 (978-0-85798-638-2(4)) Random Hse. Australia AUS. Dist: Independent Pubs. Group.

—Eaten Alive! Falk, Nick. 2014. (Billy Is a Dragon Ser.: 4). 160p. (J). (gr. 1-3). pap. 11.99 (978-0-85798-317-6(2)) Random Hse. Australia AUS. Dist: Independent Pubs. Group.

—The Race for the Shogun's Treasure. Falk, Nick. 2015. (Samurai vs Ninja Ser.: 2). 96p. (J). (gr. 1-3). pap. 7.99 (978-0-85798-636-8(8)) Random Hse. Australia AUS. Dist: Independent Pubs. Group.

—Shadow Shifter. Falk, Nick. 2014. 144p. (J). (gr. 1-3). 11.99 (978-0-85798-315-2(6)) Random Hse. Australia AUS. Dist: Independent Pubs. Group.

—Werewolves Beware! Falk, Nick. 2014. 144p. (J). (gr. 1-3). 12.99 (978-0-85798-307-7(5)) Random Hse. Australia AUS. Dist: Independent Pubs. Group.

Floyd, Claire. Stupid Alabama: A Laugh-So-Hard-You-Will-Snot about Growing up to Discover Not All Things Are Stupid but a Lot of Them Are. Wines, Michael P. Gierhart, Steve, ed. 2013. (ENG.). 244p. (gr. 5-12). pap. 19.95 (978-1-938667-13-8(1)) Ardent Writer Pr., LLC, The.

Floyd, Darneice. My Little Brown Boy. Rush, Hailey H. 2017. (ENG.). 18p. (J). 19.95 (978-0-692-99626-3(5)) Rush, Hailey.

Floyd, John, Jr. A Bedtime Lullaby. Heath, Beverly C. 2006. 9p. (J). (gr. -1). bds. 5.95 (978-0-9752860-1-2(3)) OurRainbow Pr., LLC.

—Counting with Colors. Heath, Beverly C. 2005. 8p. (J). (gr. -1). bds. 5.95 (978-0-9752860-0-5(5)) OurRainbow Pr., LLC.

—I Like Dressing Up. Collins, Elaine Banks. 2005. (J). bds. 5.95 (978-0-9752860-5-0(6)) OurRainbow Pr., LLC.

—Let's Potty! Lewis, Bisa. 2006. (J). bds. 6.99 (978-1-934214-12-1(4)) OurRainbow Pr., LLC.

—My Parts Equal Me! Heath, Beverly C. 2005. 15p. (J). (gr. -1). bds. 5.95 (978-0-9752860-2-9(1)) OurRainbow Pr., LLC.

—Neeko's Angel: A Story about Kindness. Mims, Melanie. 2006. (Fruit of the Spirit Ser.). 24p. (J). (gr. -1-1). 6.95 (978-0-9752860-7-4(2)) OurRainbow Pr., LLC.

—Not All Angels Have Wings. Mims, Melanie. 2006. (Fruit of the Spirit Ser.). 24p. (J). (gr. -1-1). 6.95 (978-0-9752860-6-7(4)) OurRainbow Pr., LLC.

—Opposites. Heath, Beverly C. 2006. 8p. (J). (gr. -1). bds. 5.95 (978-0-9752860-3-6(X)) OurRainbow Pr., LLC.

—See What I Can Do. Collins, Elaine Banks. 2006. 10p. (J). (gr. -1). bds. 5.95 (978-0-9752860-4-3(8)) OurRainbow Pr., LLC.

Fluckiger, Kory. The Legend of Re-Run. Behunin, Keith & Ericksen, Mike. I.t. ed. 2020. (ENG.). 24p. (J). (gr. k-3). 19.95 **(978-1-61633-964-7(0))**; pap. 10.95 **(978-1-61633-963-0(2))** Guardian Angel Publishing, Inc.

Fluharty, Kristi & Fluharty, T. Lively. Fool Moon Rising. Fluharty, Kristi & Fluharty, T. Lively. 2009. (ENG.). 40p. (J). 16.99 (978-1-4335-0682-6(3)) Crossway.

Fluharty, T. Lively. The Barber Who Wanted to Pray. Sproul, R. C. 2011. (ENG.). 40p. (J). 17.99 (978-1-4335-2703-6(0)) Crossway.

Fluharty, T. Lively, jt. illus. see Fluharty, Kristi.

Flusin, Marie. My Prayer Book. Tertrais, Gaelle. 2017. (ENG.). 96p. (J). (gr. 1-5). 14.99 (978-1-62164-178-0(3)) Ignatius Pr.

Flynn, Cathy Summar. La Estrellita Solitaria: Nuestras Diferencias Nos Ayudan a Descubrir Nuestro Destino. Flynn, Cathy Summar. (Estrellita Solitaria Ser.: Vol. 1).Tr. of Lonely Little Star. (SPA.). (J). 2019. 32p. (gr. k-5). pap. 14.99 (978-0-9962188-7-0(4)); 2017. (gr. -1-5). 21.90 (978-0-9962188-4-9(X)) — High Art Forms, LLC.

—The Lonely Little Star: Our Differences May Help Us Discover Our Destiny. Flynn, Cathy Summar. (Lonely Little Star Ser.: Vol. 1).Tr. of Estrellita Solitaria. (ENG.). 32p. (J). 2019. (gr. k-5). pap. 14.99 (978-0-9962188-6-3(6)); 2nd ed. 2017. (gr. -1-5). 21.90 (978-0-9962188-2-5(3)) — High Art Forms, LLC.

Flynn, Noel. Summer Dance of the Fireflies. Connolly, Ed. 2003. 44p. per. 18.95 (978-1-888996-64-7(1)) Red Hen Pr.

Flynn, Samantha. Friends in a Storm. Seymour, Mary Sue. 2013. 20p. pap. 9.95 (978-1-61633-376-8(6)) Guardian Angel Publishing, Inc.

Foa, Maryclare. Myths of the Vikings: Odin's Family & Other Tales of the Norse Gods. Philip, Neil. 2018. 128p. (J). (gr. 3-7). 13.99 (978-1-86147-860-3(7), Armadillo) Anness Publishing GBR. Dist: National Bk. Network.

Fochesato, Giorgio. Untold. Brennan, Sarah Rees. 2013. (Lynburn Legacy Ser.: Bk. 2). (ENG.). 384p. (YA). (gr. 7). 18.99 (978-0-375-87042-2(3), Random Hse. Bks. for Young Readers) Random Hse. Children's Bks.

Fochtman, Omra Jo. What's on the Other Side of the Rainbow? The Secret of the Golden Mirror. Masterson, Carla Jo. 2006. 40p. (J). 24.95 (978-1-59975-228-0(X)) Father & Son Publishing.

Fodi, Lee Edward. Gwynne, Fair & Shining. Tara, Stephanie L. 2006. (J). (gr. -1-3). 16.95 (978-1-933285-62-7(1)) Brown Books Publishing Group.

—Martha Ann's Quilt for Queen Victoria. Hicks, Kyra E. 2006. 28p. (J). (gr. -1-3). 16.95 (978-1-933285-59-7(1)) Brown Books Publishing Group.

Födi, Lee Edward. Martha Ann's Quilt for Queen Victoria. Hicks, Kyra E. 2012. 32p. (J). pap. 12.95 (978-0-9824796-8-1(9)) Black Threads Pr.

Fodi, Lee Edward. Kendra Kandlestar & the Box of Whispers. Fodi, Lee Edward. 2005. 227p. (J). (gr. 2). 16.95 (978-1-933285-10-8(9)); per. 8.95 (978-1-933285-11-5(7)) Brown Books Publishing Group.

—Kendra Kandlestar & the Crack in Kazah. Fodi, Lee Edward. 2011. (ENG.). 282p. (J). (gr. 4-7). 16.95 (978-1-61254-018-4(X)) Brown Books Publishing Group.

—Kendra Kandlestar & the Shard from Greeve. Fodi, Lee Edward. 2009. 304p. (J). (gr. 3-18). 16.95 (978-1-934812-37-2(4)) Brown Books Publishing Group.

Fogarty, Alexandria, jt. illus. see Little Airplane Productions.

Fogden, Katherine, photos by. Meet Christopher: An Osage Indian Boy from Oklahoma. Simermeyer, Genevieve. 2008. (My World — Young Native Americans Today Ser.). (ENG., 48p. (J). 15.95 (978-1-57178-217-5(6)) Council Oak Bks.

Fogel, Seymour. Among the River Pirates. Lloyd, Hugh. 2011. 204p. 44.95 (978-1-258-06703-8(X)) Literary Licensing, LLC.

—Held for Ransom: A Skippy Dare Mystery Story. Lloyd, Hugh. 2011. 228p. 46.95 (978-1-258-07879-9(1)) Literary Licensing, LLC.

Fogg, Paul. He Leads Me. 2008. 24p. pap. 9.95 (978-0-9814878-1-6(5)) Little Hands Bk. Co., LLC.

—Jesus Said. 2008. 36p. pap. 10.95 (978-0-9814878-2-3(3)) Little Hands Bk. Co., LLC.

Fogle, Christina Melato. Museum Mouse. 2017. (J). pap. (978-1-5393-7488-6(2)) CreateSpace Independent Publishing Platform.

Foglio, Phil. Girl Genius: The Second Journey of Agatha Heterodyne Volume 5: Queens & Pirates. Foglio, Phil. Foglio, Kaja. 2020. (ENG.). 128p. (YA). (gr. 9-12). pap. 25.00 (978-1-890856-69-4(X), 102d2dd9-e84b-4e0a-b367-207ab91f2122) Studio Foglio, LLC.

Folch, Sergio. Good-bye Diaper! Geis, Patricia. 2009. (Good Habits with Coco & Tula Ser.). 16p. (J). (gr. -1-k). bds. 11.40 (978-1-60754-404-3(0)) Windmill Bks.

—Good-bye Pacifier! Geis, Patricia. 2009. (Good Habits with Coco & Tula Ser.). 16p. (J). (gr. -1-k). bds. 11.40 (978-1-60754-405-0(9)) Windmill Bks.

—Let's Eat! Geis, Patricia. 2009. (Good Habits with Coco & Tula Ser.). 16p. (J). (gr. -1-k). bds. 11.40 (978-1-60754-411-1(3)) Windmill Bks.

—Let's Get Dressed! Geis, Patricia. 2009. (Good Habits with Coco & Tula Ser.). 16p. (J). (gr. -1-k). bds. 11.40 (978-1-60754-409-8(1)) Windmill Bks.

—Let's Get Well! Geis, Patricia. 2009. (Good Habits with Coco & Tula Ser.). 16p. (J). (gr. -1-k). bds. 11.40 (978-1-60754-407-4(5)) Windmill Bks.

—Let's Go to Sleep! Geis, Patricia. 2009. (Good Habits with Coco & Tula Ser.). 16p. (J). (gr. -1-k). bds. 11.40 (978-1-60754-408-1(3)) Windmill Bks.

—Let's Help! Geis, Patricia. 2009. (Good Habits with Coco & Tula Ser.). 16p. (J). (gr. -1-k). bds. 11.40 (978-1-60754-406-7(7)) Windmill Bks.

—Let's Wash Up! Geis, Patricia. 2009. (Good Habits with Coco & Tula Ser.). 16p. (J). (gr. -1-k). bds. 11.40 (978-1-60754-410-4(5)) Windmill Bks.

Foley, Greg. Kat Keeps the Beat. Foley, Greg. 2019. (ENG.). 18p. (J). (gr. -1 — 1). bds. 7.99 (978-1-5344-0682-7(4), Little Simon) Little Simon.

Foley, Greg. Kat Needs a Nap. Foley, Greg. 2020. (ENG.). 20p. (J). (gr. -1-k). bds. 7.99 **(978-1-5344-0684-1(0)**, Little Simon) Little Simon.

Foley, Greg. Kat Writes a Song. Foley, Greg. 2018. (ENG.). 40p. (J). (gr. -1-2). 14.99 (978-1-5344-0680-3(8), Little Simon) Little Simon.

—Thank You Bear Board Book. Foley, Greg. 2012. (ENG.). 28p. (J). (gr. -1-k). bds. 6.99 (978-0-670-78507-0(5), Viking Books for Young Readers) Penguin Young Readers Group.

—Willoughby & the Lion. Foley, Greg. 2009. 40p. (J). (gr. -1-2). 17.99 (978-0-06-154750-8(6)) HarperCollins Pubs.

Foley, James. Fully Booked. Harris, Tim. 2019. (Toffle Towers Ser.: 1). (ENG.). 272p. (J). (gr. 3-5). 14.99 **(978-0-14-379542-1(2)**, Puffin) Penguin Random Hse. AUS. Dist: Independent Pubs. Group.

Foley, James. Last Viking. Jorgensen, Norman. 2018. 32p. (J). (gr. -1-k). 12.95 (978-1-925163-15-5(6)) Fremantle Pr. AUS. Dist: Independent Pubs. Group.

—Last Viking Returns. Jorgensen, Norman. 2018. (Last Viking Ser.). 32p. (J). (gr. -1-k). 12.95 (978-1-925163-16-2(4)) Fremantle Pr. AUS. Dist: Independent Pubs. Group.

Foley, Niki. Blaze & the Monster Machines Little Golden Book. Berrios, Frank. 2016. (Little Golden Book Ser.). (ENG.). 24p. (J). (-k). 4.99 (978-0-399-55351-6(7), Golden Bks.) Random Hse. Children's Bks.

—Blaze of Glory (Blaze & the Monster Machines) Random House Staff. 2015. (Pictureback(R) Ser.). (ENG.). 16p. (J). (gr. -1-2). 4.99 (978-0-553-52457-4(7), Random Hse. Bks. for Young Readers) Random Hse. Children's Bks.

—DuckTales: Solving Mysteries & Rewriting History! Renzetti, Rob & Vine, Rachel. 2018. (ENG.). 160p. (J). (gr. 3-7). 12.99 (978-1-368-00841-9(0)) Disney Pr.

—Rootin' Tootin' Racetrack! (Blaze & the Monster Machines) Berrios, Frank. 2017. (Little Golden Book Ser.). (ENG.). 24p. (J). (-k). 4.99 (978-1-5247-1668-4(5), Golden Bks.) Random Hse. Children's Bks.

—Zeg & the Egg. Tillworth, Mary. 2016. 18p. (J). (978-1-4806-9878-9(4)) Random Hse., Inc.

—Zeg & the Egg (Blaze & the Monster Machines) Tillworth, Mary. 2016. (Step into Reading Ser.). (ENG.). 24p. (J). (gr. -1-1). 4.99 (978-0-553-53935-6(3), Random Hse. Bks. for Young Readers) Random Hse. Children's Bks.

Foley, Tim. The Age of Exploration: Totally Getting Lost (Epic Fails #4) Thompson, Ben & Slader, Erik. 2019. (Epic Fails Ser.: 4). (ENG.). 160p. (J). 16.99 (978-1-250-15054-7(X), 900182541); pap. 7.99 (978-1-250-15053-0(1), 900182542) Roaring Brook Pr.

—The Bambino: The Story of Babe Ruth's Legendary 1927 Season, 1 vol. Yomtov, Nelson. 2010. (American Graphic Ser.). (ENG.). 32p. (J). (gr. 3-9). lib. bdg. 31.32 (978-1-4296-5473-9(2)) Capstone.

—The Bambino: The Story of Babe Ruth's Legendary 1927 Season, 1 vol. Yomtov, Nel. 2011. (American Graphic Ser.). (ENG.). 32p. (gr. 3-9). (J). pap. 8.10 (978-1-4296-6265-9(4)); pap. 47.70 (978-1-4296-6433-2(9), Capstone Pr.) Capstone.

—Bringing down a President: The Watergate Scandal. Balis, Andrea & Levy, Elizabeth. 2019. (ENG.). 240p. (J). 19.99 (978-1-250-17679-0(4), 900189617) Roaring Brook Pr.

—The Cross & the Switchblade: The True Story of One Man's Fearless Faith. Wilkerson, David et al. 2018. (ENG.). 208p. (J). pap. 9.99 (978-0-8007-9879-6(1)) Chosen Bks.

—God's Smuggler. Andrew et al. 2017. (ENG.). 224p. (J). pap. 9.99 (978-0-8007-9805-5(8)) Chosen Bks.

—Not-So-Great Presidents: Commanders in Chief (Epic Fails #3) Thompson, Ben & Slader, Erik. 2019. (Epic Fails Ser.: 3). (ENG.). 160p. (J). pap. 6.99 (978-1-250-15059-2(0), 900182548) Roaring Brook Pr.

—The Race to Space: Countdown to Liftoff (Epic Fails #2) Thompson, Ben & Slader, Erik. 2018. (Epic Fails Ser.: 2). (ENG.). 160p. (J). 15.99 (978-1-250-15061-5(2), 900182550); pap. 6.99 (978-1-250-15062-2(0), 900182551) Roaring Brook Pr.

—What Are the Ten Commandments? McDonough, Yona Zeldis & Who HQ. 2017. (What Was? Ser.). 112p. (J). (gr. 3-7). 5.99 (978-0-515-15723-9(6)); lib. bdg. 15.99 (978-0-515-15725-3(2)) Penguin Young Readers Group. (Penguin Workshop).

—What Is the Constitution? Demuth, Patricia Brennan & Who HQ. 2018. (What Was? Ser.). (ENG.). 112p. (J). (gr. 3-7). 5.99 (978-1-5247-8609-0(8)); lib. bdg. 15.99 (978-1-5247-8611-3(X)) Penguin Young Readers Group. (Penguin Workshop).

—What Is the Panama Canal? Pascal, Janet B. & Who HQ. 2014. (What Was? Ser.). 112p. (J). (gr. 3-7). 5.99 (978-0-448-47899-9(4), Penguin Workshop) Penguin Young Readers Group.

—What Was the Bombing of Hiroshima? Who HQ & Brallier, Jess. 2020. (What Was? Ser.). 112p. (J). (gr. 3-7). (ENG.). 5.99 (978-1-5247-9265-7(9)); 15.99 (978-1-5247-9266-4(7)) Penguin Young Readers Group. (Penguin Workshop).

—What Was the Great Chicago Fire? Pascal, Janet B. & Who HQ. 2016. (What Was? Ser.). 112p. (J). (gr. 3-7). 5.99 (978-0-399-54158-2(6), Penguin Workshop) Penguin Young Readers Group.

—What Was the Lewis & Clark Expedition? St. George, Judith & Who HQ. 2014. (What Was? Ser.). (ENG.). 112p. (J). (gr. 3-7). pap. 5.99 (978-0-448-47901-9(X), Penguin Workshop) Penguin Young Readers Group.

—What Was the Vietnam War? Who HQ & O'Connor, Jim. 2019. (What Was? Ser.). 112p. (J). (gr. 3-7). 5.99 (978-1-5247-8977-0(1)); 15.99 (978-1-5247-8978-7(X)) Penguin Young Readers Group. (Penguin Workshop).

—Where Is Area 51? Manzanero, Paula K. & Who HQ. 2018. (Where Is? Ser.). 112p. (J). (gr. 3-7). 5.99 (978-1-5247-8641-0(1)); lib. bdg. 15.99 (978-1-5247-8642-7(X)) Penguin Young Readers Group. (Penguin Workshop).

—Where Is Hollywood? Anastasio, Dina & Who HQ. 2019. (Where Is? Ser.). 112p. (J). (gr. 3-7). 5.99 (978-1-5247-8644-1(6)); lib. bdg. 15.99 (978-1-5247-8645-8(4)) Penguin Young Readers Group. (Penguin Workshop).

—Where Is Niagara Falls? Stine, Megan & Who HQ. 2015. (Where Is? Ser.). (ENG.). 112p. (J). (gr. 3-7). 5.99 (978-0-448-48425-9(0), Penguin Workshop) Penguin Young Readers Group.

—Where Is the Bermuda Triangle? Stine, Megan & Who HQ. 2018. (Where Is? Ser.). 112p. (J). (gr. 3-7). (ENG.). 5.99 (978-1-5247-8626-7(8)); lib. bdg. 15.99 (978-1-5247-8628-1(4)) Penguin Young Readers Group. (Penguin Workshop).

—Where Is the Eiffel Tower? Anastasio, Dina & Who HQ. 2017. (Where Is? Ser.). 112p. (J). (gr. 3-7). pap. 5.99 (978-0-451-53384-5(4), Penguin Workshop) Penguin Young Readers Group.

—Who Was Edgar Allan Poe? Gigliotti, Jim. 2015. (Who Was-? Chapters Ser.). (ENG.). 112p. (J). (gr. 4-6). 18.69 (978-1-4844-6178-5(9)) Penguin Young Readers Group.

—Who Was Isaac Newton? Pascal, Janet B. & Who HQ. 2014. (Who Was? Ser.). (ENG.). 112p. (J). (gr. 3-7). pap. 5.99 (978-0-448-47913-2(3), Penguin Workshop) Penguin Young Readers Group.

—Who Was Julius Caesar? Medina, Nico & Who HQ. 2014. (Who Was? Ser.). (ENG.). 112p. (J). (gr. 3-7). pap. 5.99 (978-0-448-48083-1(2), Penguin Workshop) Penguin Young Readers Group.

—Who Was Laura Ingalls Wilder? Demuth, Patricia Brennan & Who HQ. 2013. (Who Was? Ser.). (ENG.). 112p. (J). (gr. 3-7). 5.99 (978-0-448-46706-1(2), Penguin Workshop) Penguin Young Readers Group.

—Who Was Milton Bradley? Anderson, Kirsten & Who HQ. 2016. (Who Was? Ser.). 112p. (J). (gr. 3-7). 15.99

(978-0-399-54236-7(1), Penguin Workshop) Penguin Young Readers Group.

—Who Was Robert Ripley? Anderson, Kirsten & Who HQ. 2015. (Who Was? Ser.). 112p. (J). (gr. 3-7). 5.99 *(978-0-448-48298-9(3)*, Penguin Workshop) Penguin Young Readers Group.

—Who Were the Wright Brothers? Buckley, James, Jr. et al. 2014. (Who Was? Ser.). 112p. (J). (gr. 3-7). 5.99 *(978-0-448-47951-4(6)*, Penguin Workshop) Penguin Young Readers Group.

—Who Were the Wright Brothers? Buckley, James. 2014. 106p. (J). *(978-1-101-99527-3(0))* Penguin Publishing Group.

—The Wright Brothers: Nose-Diving into History (Epic Fails #1) Thompson, Ben & Slader, Erik. 2018. (Epic Fails Ser.: 1). (ENG.). 128p. (J). 15.99 *(978-1-250-15055-4(8)*, 900182544); pap. 6.99 *(978-1-250-15056-1(6)*, 900182545) Roaring Brook Pr.

Foli, Gianluca. Wild in the City, 1 vol. Lonely Planet Kids & Baker, Kate. 2019. (ENG.). 112p. (J). (gr. 4-7). 18.99 *(978-1-78868-491-0(5))* Lonely Planet Global Ltd. IRL. Dist: Hachette Bk. Group.

Folkard, Charles. Pinocchio, As First Translated into English by M a Murray & Illustrated by Charles Folkard. Murray, M. A., tr. 2009. 280p. pap. 11.95 *(978-1-59915-177-9(4))* Yesterday's Classics.

Folkerts, Jason. The Mystery of the Round Rocks. Meierhenry, Mark V. & Volk, David. 2007. 44p. (J). (gr. 2-5). 13.95 *(978-0-9777955-3-6(5)*, South Dakota State Historical Society Pr.) South Dakota Historical Society Pr.

—The Mystery of the Tree Rings. Meierhenry, Mark V. & Volk, David. 2008. 44p. (J). 13.95 *(978-0-9798940-0-8(X)*, South Dakota State Historical Society Pr.) South Dakota State Historical Society Pr.

Follath, Isabelle. Aggie Morton, Mystery Queen: Peril at Owl Park. Jocelyn, Marthe. 2020. (Aggie Morton, Mystery Queen Ser.: 2). (ENG.). 400p. (J). (gr. 5). 15.99 ***(978-0-7352-6549-3(6)***, Tundra Bks.) Tundra Bks. CAN. Dist: Penguin Random Hse. LLC.

Follath, Isabelle. Aggie Morton, Mystery Queen: the Body under the Piano. Jocelyn, Marthe. 2020. (Aggie Morton, Mystery Queen Ser.: 1). (ENG.). 256p. (J). (gr. 5). 15.99 *(978-0-7352-6546-2(1)*, Tundra Bks.) Tundra Bks. CAN. Dist: Penguin Random Hse. LLC.

Follette, Serina. Nimiyw�yiht�n: I Feel Great. Whiskeyjack, Lana. Eaglespeaker, Jason, ed. 2019. (ENG.). 28p. (J). pap. 11.99 ***(978-1-0898-6855-2(3))*** Independently Published.

Folley, John. Mr. Mehan's Mildly Amusing Mythical Mammals. Mehan, Matthew. 2018. (ENG.). 140p. (J). (gr. 3-7). 24.95 *(978-1-5051-1249-8(4)*, 2756) TAN Bks.

Folmsbee, Patricia. Happy Anderson & Connie Clam. Custureri, Mary. 2006. 36p. (J). spiral bd. 24.95 *(978-1-933190-00-6(0))* HighPoint Publishing, Inc.

Foltz-Gray, Matthew. Warm for Winter. Purchase, Elizabeth. 2016. (ENG.). (J). pap. *(978-0-9949564-2-2(8))* Elizabeth Purchase.

Foltz, Susan Convery. Jan Napjus & the Ghost. Foltz, Sharon Terpstra. 2009. 24p. (J). 15.99 *(978-1-4415-5097-2(6))* Xlibris Corp.

Fomenko, Margarita. The Magical Hands of Zalatimo: How a Resilient Young Man Created the World's Tastiest Treats! Zalatimo, Salah Akram. 2018. (ENG.). 40p. (J). pap. 9.99 *(978-1-7261-4052-2(0))* CreateSpace Independent Publishing Platform.

Fomin, A. The Matter of the May Mouse. Brewer Gant, Kirsten. 2019. (ENG.). 48p. (J). pap. 11.99 ***(978-1-6969-2614-0(9))*** Independently Published.

—The Matter of the May Mouse. Brewer Gant, Kirsten. 2019. (ENG.). 48p. (J). 16.99 ***(978-1-948256-27-8(4))*** Willow Moon Publishing.

Fong, Lee Kow. Musical Adventures with Quek Quek: Discover the Sounds of the Chinese Orchestra. Chinese, the Singapore. 2016. (ENG.). 96p. pap. 25.00 incl. cd-rom *(978-981-4677-23-3(X))* Marshall Cavendish International (Asia) Private Ltd. SGP. Dist: National Bk. Network.

Fong, William. Jesus Heals a Man on a Stretcher. Brookes, Dawn. 2017. (ENG.). 37p. (J). pap. *(978-0-9955561-3-3(X))* Brookes, Dawn Publishing.

Fonseca-Hughes, Sarah. The Grape Escape: Call 9-1-1, the Grapes Are on the Run! Debowksi, Sharon. 2007. 32p. (J). 14.95 *(978-0-60227-472-3(X))* Above the Clouds Publishing.

Font, Ignasi. Everything Is Connected. Gruhl, Jason. 2019. (ENG.). 36p. (J). (gr. -1-3). 16.95 *(978-1-61180-631-1(3)*, Bala Kids) Shambhala Pubns., Inc.

Fontabona, Virginia, jt. illus. see Golina-Sagetelian, Irina.

Fontana, Ugo. The Rabbit Catcher & Other Fairy Tales. Bechstein, Ludwig. Jarrell, Randall, tr. 2011. 42p. 35.95 *(978-1-258-08375-5(2))* Literary Licensing, LLC.

Fontanez, Edwin. En esta hermosa Isla. Fontanez, Edwin. 2nd rev. ed. 2005. (SPA.). 32p. (J). 16.95 *(978-0-9640868-7-6(5))* Exit Studio.

—Hadas, Sirenas y Sapos: Un ramito de poemas Encantados. Fontanez, Edwin. 2008. (SPA.). 32p. (J). lib. bdg. 19.99 *(978-0-9640868-8-3(3))* Exit Studio.

—On This Beautiful Island. Fontanez, Edwin. l.t. ed. 2004. 32p. (J). 16.95 *(978-0-9640868-6-9(7)*, 1241077) Exit Studio.

Fontano, Jay. Gilly's Treasure. Murphy, Julie. 2016. (ENG.). 14.99 *(978-1-4621-1845-8(3)*, Sweetwater Bks.) Cedar Fort, Inc./CFI Distribution.

Fonts, José Colomer. Disney a Christmas Carol, Starring Scrooge Mcduck (Graphic Novel) Martina, Guido. 2019. (ENG.). 80p. (J). (gr. 3-7). pap. 10.99 *(978-1-5067-1215-4(0)*, Dark Horse Books) Dark Horse Comics.

Foo, Rachel. Spooky Little Kitten. VonFeder, Rosa. Cottage Door Press, ed. 2020. (ENG.). 10p. (J). (gr. -1-k). bds. 4.99 ***(978-1-68052-927-2(7)***, 1005690) Cottage Door Pr.

Foote, Dan. Jack Hayford Presenta Hechos una Historia de la Biblia. Hayford, Jack W. 2005. 60p. (J). (gr. -1-5). 9.99 *(978-1-59185-487-6(3)*, Charisma Kids) Charisma Media.

—The Land of Havala. Moores, Katie. 2006. (ENG.). 64p. pap. 6.99 *(978-1-59185-910-9(7)*, 9107, Creation Hse.) Charisma Media.

Foote, David. Modern Fairies, Dwarves, Goblins, & Other Nasties: A Practical Guide by Miss Edythe McFate. Blume, Lesley M. M. 2010. (ENG.). 256p. (J). (gr. 3-7). 16.99 *(978-0-375-86203-8(X)*, Knopf Bks. for Young Readers) Random Hse. Children's Bks.

—The Wondrous Journals of Dr. Wendell Wellington Wiggins. Blume, Lesley M. M. 2013. (ENG.). 256p. (J). (gr. 3-7). pap. 8.99 *(978-0-375-87218-1(3)*, Knopf Bks. for Young Readers) Random Hse. Children's Bks.

Foott, Jeff, photos by. A Pod of Killer Whales: The Mysterious Life of the Intelligent Orca. León, Vicki. 2nd ed. 2006. (Jean-Michel Cousteau Presents Ser.). 48p. (J). (gr. 4-9). pap. 9.95 *(978-0-9766134-7-3(6))* London Town Pr.

For Women, Prayer Journal. Prayer Journal: A Creative Christian Prayer Journal for Girls & Ladies, 8 X 10 Inches 134 Pages. Design, Prayer Journal. 2019. (Prayer Journal Bible Study Notebook Ser.: Vol. 7). (ENG.). 136p. (J). pap. 6.20 ***(978-1-7001-9732-0(0))*** Independently Published.

Forberg, Ati. Samurai of Gold Hill. Uchida, Yoshiko. 2005. 119p. (J). (gr. 2). per. 8.95 *(978-1-59714-015-7(5))* Heyday.

Forbes, Ashley. Pet Preacher. Forbes, Ashley. 2003. 20p. pap. 5.95 *(978-0-9711564-6-3(8))* Pendleton Publishing, Inc.

Forbes, Justin. Under the Faithful Watch of the River Hawk. Forbes, J. L. 2013. 20p. pap. 24.95 *(978-1-62709-899-1(2))* America Star Bks.

Forbush, Lisa. A Is for Alaska: An ABC Book. Forbush, Kyle & Forbush, Kyle. 2004. (J). bds. 6.95 *(978-1-57833-287-8(7))* Todd Communications.

—Alaska's Wild Animals Coloring Book. Forbush, Kyle. 2003. (J). 3.95 *(978-1-57833-232-8(X))* Todd Communications.

—Balto: The Dog Hero. Forbush, Kyle. 2004. (J). pap. 14.95 *(978-1-57833-267-0(2))* Todd Communications.

—The Sourdoughs' Five Children. Forbush, Kyle. 2004. (J). bds. 6.95 *(978-1-57833-258-8(3))* Todd Communications.

—Who Is Alaska's Favorite Bear? Forbush, Kyle. 2003. (J). bds. 6.95 *(978-1-57833-211-3(7))* Todd Communications.

Forcada, Adiela & Giron, Elizabeth. Lambyro. Olesen, Demetria Vassiliou. 2011. (ENG.). 32p. (J). 19.00 *(978-0-615-47664-3(3))* Elissian Publishing Co.

Ford, A. G. Barack. Winter, Jonah. 32p. (J). (gr. -1-2). 2010. (ENG.). pap. 7.99 *(978-0-06-170396-6(6)*, Tegen, Katherine Bks); 2008. lib. bdg. 18.89 *(978-0-06-170393-5(1))* HarperCollins Pubs.

—A Big Day for Baseball. Osborne, Mary Pope. 2019. (Magic Tree House (R) Ser.: 29). (ENG.). 96p. (J). (gr. 1-4). 5.99 *(978-1-5247-1311-9(2)*, Random Hse. Bks. for Young Readers) Random Hse. Children's Bks.

—The Big Move. Leavitt, Lindsey. 2016. (Commander in Cheese Ser.: 1). (ENG.). 112p. (J). (gr. 2-5). 4.99 *(978-1-101-93112-7(4)*, Random Hse. Bks. for Young Readers) Random Hse. Children's Bks.

—Birthday Suit. Leavitt, Lindsey. 2017. (Commander in Cheese Ser.: 4). 96p. (J). (gr. 2-5). 4.99 *(978-1-101-93121-9(3)*, Random Hse. Bks. for Young Readers) Random Hse. Children's Bks.

—Brown Baby Lullaby. Brown, Tameka Fryer. 2020. (ENG.). 32p. (J). 16.99 *(978-0-374-30752-3(0)*, 900180735, Farrar, Straus & Giroux (BYR)) Farrar, Straus & Giroux.

—Construction Site on Christmas Night. Rinker, Sherri Duskey. 2018. (ENG.). 40p. (J). (gr. -1-k). 16.99 *(978-1-4521-3911-1(3))* Chronicle Bks. LLC.

Ford, A. G. Cookiesaurus Christmas. Evans, Nate & Fellner Dominy, Amy. 2018. (Cookiesaurus Rex Ser.: 2). 40p. (J). (gr. -1-3). 16.99 ***(978-1-4847-6745-0(4))*** Little, Brown Bks. for Young Readers.

—Cookiesaurus Rex. Fellner Dominy, Amy. 2018. (Cookiesaurus Rex Ser.: 1). (ENG.). 32p. (J). (gr. -1-3). bds. 7.99 ***(978-1-368-01906-4(4))*** Little, Brown Bks. for Young Readers.

—Cookiesaurus Rex. Evans, Nate & Fellner Dominy, Amy. 2017. (Cookiesaurus Rex Ser.: 1). 40p. (J). (gr. -1-3). 16.99 ***(978-1-4847-6744-3(6))*** Little, Brown Bks. for Young Readers.

Ford, A. G. Desmond & the Very Mean Word. Tutu, Desmond. 2012. (ENG.). 32p. (J). (gr. 1-4). 17.99 *(978-0-7636-5229-6(6))* Candlewick Pr.

—Goal! Javaherbin, Mina. 2012. 40p. (J). (gr. 1-4). pap. 7.99 *(978-0-7636-5822-9(7))* Candlewick Pr.

—Have a Mice Flight! Commander In Cheese #3. Leavitt, Lindsey. 2016. (Commander in Cheese Ser.: 3). 96p. (J). (gr. 2-5). 5.99 *(978-1-101-93118-9(3)*, Random Hse. Bks. for Young Readers) Random Hse. Children's Bks.

—Hello, I'm Johnny Cash. Neri, G. 2014. 40p. (J). (gr. 4-7). 17.99 *(978-0-7636-6245-5(3))* Candlewick Pr.

Ford, A. G. Hurricane Heroes in Texas. Osborne, Mary Pope. (Magic Tree House (R) Ser.: 30). (J). (gr. 1-4). 2020. 128p. 5.99 ***(978-1-5247-1315-7(5))***; 2018. 112p. 13.99 *(978-1-5247-1312-6(0))*; 2018. (ENG.). 112p. lib. bdg. 16.99 *(978-1-5247-1313-3(9))* Random Hse. Children's Bks. (Random Hse. Bks. for Young Readers).

Ford, A. G. JFK. Winter, Jonah. 2013. (ENG.). 32p. (J). (gr. -1-3). 17.99 *(978-0-06-176807-1(3))* HarperCollins Pubs.

Ford, A. G. Late Lunch with Llamas. Osborne, Mary Pope. 2020. (Magic Tree House (R) Ser.: 34). (J). (gr. 1-4). 128p. 13.99 ***(978-0-525-64840-6(2))***; (ENG.). 112p. lib. bdg. 16.99 ***(978-0-525-64841-3(0))*** Random Hse. Children's Bks. (Random Hse. Bks. for Young Readers).

Ford, A. G. Littles: And How They Grow. DiPucchio, Kelly. 2017. (ENG.). 32p. (J). (gr. -1 — 1). lib. bdg. 20.99 *(978-0-399-55527-5(7)*, Doubleday Bks. for Young Readers) Random Hse. Children's Bks.

—Littles: & How They Grow. DiPucchio, Kelly. (J). 2019. 26p. (— 1). bds. 7.99 *(978-1-9848-2985-6(8))*; 2017. 32p. (gr. -1 — 1). 17.99 *(978-0-399-55526-8(9))* Random Hse. Children's Bks. (Doubleday Bks. for Young Readers).

—Malcolm Little: The Boy Who Grew up to Become Malcolm X. Shabazz, Ilyasah. 2014. (ENG.). 48p. (J). (gr. 1-5). 19.99 *(978-1-4424-1216-3(X))* Simon & Schuster Children's Publishing.

—Michelle. Hopkinson, Deborah. 2009. 32p. (J). (gr. -1-2). 17.99 *(978-0-06-182739-6(8))* HarperCollins Pubs.

—Mouse Rushmore. Leavitt, Lindsey. 2017. (Commander in Cheese Ser.: 1). (ENG.). 128p. (J). (gr. 2-5). lib. bdg. 12.99 *(978-1-5247-2049-0(6)*, Random Hse. Bks. for Young Readers) Random Hse. Children's Bks.

—Mouse Rushmore: Commander In Cheese Super Special #1. Leavitt, Lindsey. 2017. (Commander in Cheese Ser.: 1). 112p. (J). (gr. 2-5). 5.99 *(978-1-5247-2047-6(X)*, Random Hse. Bks. for Young Readers) Random Hse. Children's Bks.

—My Daddy, Dr. Martin Luther King, Jr. King, Martin Luther, III. (ENG.). 32p. (J). (gr. -1-3). 2018. pap. 6.99 *(978-0-06-446209-9(9))*; 2013. 17.99 *(978-0-06-028075-8(1))*; 2013. 18.89 *(978-0-06-028076-5(X))* HarperCollins Pubs. (Amistad).

—Narwhal on a Sunny Night. Osborne, Mary Pope. 2020. (Magic Tree House (R) Ser.: 33). (ENG.). 112p. (J). (gr. 1-4). 13.99 *(978-0-525-64836-9(4))*; lib. bdg. 16.99 *(978-0-525-64837-6(2))* Random Hse. Children's Bks. (Random Hse. Bks. for Young Readers).

—Oval Office Escape. Leavitt, Lindsey. 2016. (Commander in Cheese Ser.: 2). (ENG.). 112p. (J). (gr. 2-5). 4.99 *(978-1-101-93115-8(9)*, Random Hse. Bks. for Young Readers) Random Hse. Children's Bks.

—Roc & Roe's Twelve Days of Christmas. Cannon, Nick & Carey, Mariah. 2014. (ENG.). 32p. (J). (gr. -1-k). 17.99 *(978-0-545-51950-2(0)*, Orchard Bks.) Scholastic, Inc.

—Summer Jackson: Grown Up. Harris, Teresa. 2011. (ENG.). 32p. (J). (gr. -1-2). 16.99 *(978-0-06-185757-7(2)*, Tegen, Katherine Bks) HarperCollins Pubs.

—Three Cheers for Kid McGear! Rinker, Sherri Duskey. 2019. (ENG.). 40p. (J). (gr. -1-k). 17.99 *(978-1-4521-5582-1(8))* Chronicle Bks. LLC.

—To the Future, Ben Franklin! Osborne, Mary Pope. 2019. (Magic Tree House (R) Ser.: 32). (ENG.). 112p. (J). (gr. 1-4). lib. bdg. 16.99 *(978-0-525-64833-8(X)*, Random Hse. Bks. for Young Readers) Random Hse. Children's Bks.

—Warriors in Winter. Osborne, Mary Pope. 2019. (Magic Tree House (R) Ser.: 31). 112p. (J). (gr. 1-4). 13.99 *(978-0-525-64764-5(3))*; (ENG.). lib. bdg. 16.99 *(978-0-525-64765-2(1))* Random Hse. Children's Bks. (Random Hse. Bks. for Young Readers).

Ford, A. G., jt. illus. see Boos, Ben.

Ford, A. G., jt. illus. see Murdocca, Sal.

Ford, Christina. A Button for a Crown. Lawrence, Ava. l.t. ed. 2003. 84p. (J). 14.95 *(978-0-9651048-4-5(2))* Papillon Publishing.

Ford, Christopher. An Epic Doodle, Bk. 1. Ford, Christopher. 2011. (Stickman Odyssey Ser.: 1). (ENG.). 208p. (J). (gr. 3-7). 12.99 *(978-0-399-25426-0(9)*, Philomel Bks.) Penguin Young Readers Group.

—The Wrath of Zozimos, 2 vols., Bk. 2. Ford, Christopher. 2012. (Stickman Odyssey Ser.: 2). (ENG.). 240p. (J). (gr. 3-7). 12.99 *(978-0-399-25427-7(7)*, Philomel Bks.) Penguin Young Readers Group.

Ford, David. Power Reading: Chapter/Sci-Fi/Dr. Little 2. Cole, Bob. 2005. 25p. (J). (gr. 3-4). vinyl bd. 39.95 *(978-1-883186-76-0(5)*, PPSF4) National Reading Styles Institute, Inc.

—Power Reading: Chapter/Sci-Fi/Superhero. Cole, Bob. 2004. 25p. (J). (gr. 3-4). vinyl bd. 39.95 *(978-1-883186-62-3(5)*, PPSF2) National Reading Styles Institute, Inc.

—Power Reading: Chapter/Sci-Fi/Time Warp. Cole, Bob. 2004. 25p. (J). (gr. 4-18). vinyl bd. 39.95 *(978-1-883186-60-9(9)*, PPSF3) National Reading Styles Institute, Inc.

—Power Reading: Chapter/Sci-Fi/Time Warp 2. Cole, Bob. 2005. 52p. (J). (gr. 4-18). vinyl bd. 39.95 *(978-1-883186-75-3(7)*, PPSF5) National Reading Styles Institute, Inc.

—Power Reading: Comic Book/Superhero. Cole, Bob. 2005. 34p. (J). (gr. 2-4). vinyl bd. 29.95 *(978-1-883186-79-1(X)*, PPSFC2) National Reading Styles Institute, Inc.

—Power Reading: Comic Book/Time Warp. Cole, Bob. 2005. 36p. (J). (gr. 3-4). vinyl bd. 29.95 *(978-1-883186-69-2(2)*, PPSFC3) National Reading Styles Institute, Inc.

—Power Reading: Comic Book/Time Warp 2. Cole, Bob. 2005. 36p. (J). (gr. 3-4). vinyl bd. 29.95 *(978-1-933533-01-8(3)*, PPSFC3A) National Reading Styles Institute, Inc.

Ford, E. Little Lion: In English & Amharic. Ready Set Go Books & Laporte, T. 2019. (ENG.). 34p. (J). pap. 11.99 ***(978-1-6876-0068-4(6))*** Independently Published.

Ford, Emily. Jesus Loves Trucks. Haluska, David. 2014. 32p. (J). 7.99 *(978-0-8280-2719-9(6))* Review & Herald Publishing Assn.

Ford, George. Paul Robeson, 1 vol. Greenfield, Eloise. 2009. (ENG.). 40p. (J). (gr. 3-6). pap. 11.95 *(978-1-60060-262-7(2)*, 5e793d3a-2517-425d-966b-e807cdbbad05) Lee & Low Bks., Inc.

—The Story of Ruby Bridges. Coles, Robert. 50th anniv. ed. 2010. (ENG.). 32p. (J). (gr. -1-3). pap. 6.99 *(978-0-439-47226-5(1)*, Scholastic Paperbacks) Scholastic, Inc.

Ford, Geraint. Harry Houdini (the First Names Series) Poskitt, Kjartan. (First Names Ser.). (ENG.). (J). (gr. 3-7). 2020. 176p. pap. 6.99 *(978-1-4197-4090-9(3)*, 1279203); 2019. 160p. 9.99 *(978-1-4197-3862-3(3))* Abrams, Inc. (Abrams Bks. for Young Readers).

Ford, Gilbert. Alice Across America: The Story of the First Women's Cross-Country Road Trip. Marsh, Sarah Glenn. 2020. (ENG.). 40p. (J). 18.99 *(978-1-250-29702-0(8)*, 900195861, Holt, Henry & Co. Bks. For Young Readers) Holt, Henry & Co.

—Itch! Everything You Didn't Want to Know about What Makes You Scratch. Sanchez, Anita. 2018. (ENG.). 80p. (J). (gr. 3-7). 17.99 *(978-0-544-81101-0(1)*, 1641759, HMH Books For Young Readers) Houghton Mifflin Harcourt Publishing Co.

—Moonpenny Island. Springstubb, Tricia. (ENG.). (J). (gr. 3-7). 2016. 320p. pap. 6.99 *(978-0-06-211294-1(5)*, Balzer & Bray); 2015. 304p. 16.99 *(978-0-06-211293-4(7))* HarperCollins Pubs.

—Mr. Ferris & His Wheel. Davis, Kathryn Gibbs. 2014. (ENG.). 40p. (J). (gr. -1-3). 17.99 *(978-0-547-95922-1(2)*, 1520242, HMH Books For Young Readers) Houghton Mifflin Harcourt Publishing Co.

—Poker Night: All You Need to Bet, Bluff, & Win. Ford, McNeely. 2004. (ENG.). 56p. (gr. 8-17). 24.95 *(978-0-8118-4381-2(5))* Chronicle Bks. LLC.

—Rotten! Vultures, Beetles, Slime, & Nature's Other Decomposers. Sanchez, Anita. 2019. (ENG.). 96p. (J). (gr. 3-7). 17.99 *(978-1-328-84165-0(0)*, 1691746, HMH Books For Young Readers) Houghton Mifflin Harcourt Publishing Co.

—Soldier Song: A True Story of the Civil War. Levy, Debbie. 2017. 80p. (J). (gr. 3-7). 18.99 *(978-1-4847-2598-6(0))* Disney Pr.

—Twelve Days of New York. Bolden, Tonya. 2013. (ENG.). 32p. (J). (gr. -1-k). 17.95 *(978-1-4197-0542-7(3)*, Abrams Bks. for Young Readers) Abrams, Inc.

Ford, Gilbert. How the Cookie Crumbled: The True (and Not-So-True) Stories of the Invention of the Chocolate Chip Cookie. Ford, Gilbert. 2017. (ENG.). 40p. (J). (gr. -1-3). 18.99 *(978-1-4814-5067-6(0))* Simon & Schuster Children's Publishing.

Ford, H. J. The Book of Romance. Lang, Andrew, ed. 2004. reprint ed. pap. 34.95 *(978-1-4179-1718-1(0))* Kessinger Publishing, LLC.

—The Book of Saints & Heroes. Lang, Leonora Blanche. Lang, Andrew, ed. 2012. 344p. pap. 13.50 *(978-1-936639-18-2(1))* St. Augustine Academy Pr.

—Fairy Tales from Around the World. 2014. 736p. lthr. *(978-1-4351-4482-8(1))* Barnes & Noble, Inc.

—Tales of Troy & Greece. Lang, Andrew. 2006. (Dover Children's Classics Ser.). (ENG.). 336p. (gr. 9-12). per. 9.95 *(978-0-486-44917-3(3))* Dover Pubns., Inc.

—The Yellow Fairy Book - Illustrated by H. J. Ford. Lang, Andrew. 2016. (ENG.). (J). *(978-1-4733-3534-9(5))* Read Bks.

Ford, H. J. The Tale of the Cid: And Other Stories of Knights & Chivalry. Ford, H. J. Lang, Andrew. 2007. (Dover Children's Classics Ser.). (ENG.). 208p. (J). (gr. 4-7). per. 9.95 *(978-0-486-45470-2(3))* Dover Pubns., Inc.

Ford, Henry J. The Blue Fairy Book: Complete & Unabridged. Lang, Andrew. 2019. (Andrew Lang Fairy Book Ser.: 1). 384p. (J). (gr. 3-8). 14.99 *(978-1-63158-276-9(3)*, Racehorse Publishing) Skyhorse Publishing Co., Inc.

—The Gray Fairy Book: Complete & Unabridged. Lang, Andrew. 2020. (Andrew Lang Fairy Book Ser.: 6). 360p. (J). (gr. 2-8). 14.99 *(978-1-63158-569-2(X)*, Racehorse Publishing) Skyhorse Publishing Co., Inc.

—The Green Fairy Book: Complete & Unabridged. Lang, Andrew. 2020. (Andrew Lang Fairy Book Ser.: 3). 436p. (J). (gr. 3-8). 14.99 *(978-1-63158-563-0(0)*, Racehorse Publishing) Skyhorse Publishing Co., Inc.

—The Pink Fairy Book: Complete & Unabridged. Lang, Andrew. 2020. (Andrew Lang Fairy Book Ser.: 5). 360p. (J). (gr. 2-8). 14.99 *(978-1-63158-567-8(3)*, Racehorse Publishing) Skyhorse Publishing Co., Inc.

—The Red Book of Animal Stories 1899. Lang, Andrew, ed. 2004. reprint ed. pap. 34.95 *(978-1-4179-8249-3(7))* Kessinger Publishing, LLC.

—The Red Fairy Book: Complete & Unabridged. Lang, Andrew. 2019. (Andrew Lang Fairy Book Ser.: 2). 384p. (J). (gr. 3-8). 14.99 *(978-1-63158-277-6(1)*, Racehorse Publishing) Skyhorse Publishing Co., Inc.

—The Yellow Fairy Book: Complete & Unabridged. Lang, Andrew. 2020. (Andrew Lang Fairy Book Ser.: 4). 408p. (J). (gr. 3-8). 14.99 *(978-1-63158-565-4(7)*, Racehorse Publishing) Skyhorse Publishing Co., Inc.

Ford, Isabelle. Ed (or Fred) the Indecisive Donkey. Bryer, Josh. 2019. (ENG.). 24p. (J). (gr. -1-1). pap. ***(978-0-6487204-2-3(X))*** Agency23.

Ford, Jessie. Mrs. Peanuckle's Bird Alphabet. Peanuckle. 2018. (Mrs. Peanuckle's Alphabet Ser.: 3). 24p. (J). (— 1). bds. 7.99 *(978-1-62336-937-8(1)*, 9781623369378, Rodale Kids) Random Hse. Children's Bks.

—Mrs. Peanuckle's Bug Alphabet. Peanuckle. 2018. (Mrs. Peanuckle's Alphabet Ser.: 4). 24p. (J). (— 1). bds. 7.99 *(978-1-62336-939-2(8)*, 9781623369392, Rodale Kids) Random Hse. Children's Bks.

—Mrs. Peanuckle's Flower Alphabet. Peanuckle. 2018. (Mrs. Peanuckle's Alphabet Ser.: 3). 24p. (J). (— 1). bds. 7.99 *(978-1-62336-941-5(X)*, 9781623369415, Rodale Kids) Random Hse. Children's Bks.

—Mrs. Peanuckle's Tree Alphabet. Peanuckle. 2018. (Mrs. Peanuckle's Alphabet Ser.: 5). 24p. (J). (— 1). 7.99 *(978-1-62336-943-9(6)*, 9781623369439, Rodale Kids) Random Hse. Children's Bks.

—Mrs. Peanuckle's Vegetable Alphabet. Peanuckle. 2017. (Mrs. Peanuckle's Alphabet Ser.: 1). 28p. (J). (— 1). bds. 7.99 *(978-1-62336-870-8(7)*, 9781623368708, Rodale Kids) Random Hse. Children's Bks.

Ford, Kate. How to Be a Wizard at Grammer. Yates, Irene. 48p. (J). (gr. 3-6). pap. *(978-1-876367-29-9(6))* Wizard Bks.

—How to Be a Wizard at Nursery Rhymes. Laurence, Jo. 48p. (J). (gr. 1-3). pap. *(978-1-876367-28-2(8))* Wizard Bks.

—How to Be Brilliant at Science Investigations. Hughes, Colin & Wade, Winnie. 2004. 48p. pap. 30.00 *(978-1-897675-11-3(9))* Brilliant Pubns. GBR. Dist: Parkwest Pubns., Inc.

—How to Be Brilliant at Writing Poetry. Yates, Irene Dorothy. 2004. 48p. pap. 30.00 *(978-1-897675-01-4(1))* Brilliant Pubns. GBR. Dist: Parkwest Pubns., Inc.

—How to Sparkle at Assessing Science. Burton, Neil. 2004. 48p. pap. 30.00 *(978-1-897675-20-5(8))* Brilliant Pubns. GBR. Dist: Parkwest Pubns., Inc.

Ford, Louise. The Adventures of Meyrick the Mouse: A Story Book for Young Children Based on the Adventures of a Little Mouse Named Meyrick. There Is a Coloring Book to Accompany This Storybook for Those That Love to Color. Meakin, Nigel J. & Crystal Coloring Books. 2019. (Meyrick Adventures Ser.: Vol. 1). (ENG.). 36p. (J). pap. 9.99 ***(978-1-7125-1388-0(5))*** Independently Published.

F

Ford, Melissa & Tilley, Shiho. The Adventures of Violet & Dash: Super Sleuths (Disney/Pixar the Incredibles 2) Francis, Suzanne. 2018. (ENG.). 128p. (J). (gr. 1-4). 6.99 *(978-0-7364-3942-8(0))*; lib. bdg. 12.99 *(978-0-7364-3943-5(9))* Random Hse. Children's Bks. (RH/Disney).

Ford, Noelle Boucher. The Blanket & the Bear: A Whimsical Story of the Endless Possibilities of Love. Stewart, Buffy Ford. 2018. (ENG.). 50p. (J). 19.95 *(978-1-7328172-0-3(0))* WhatAboutABoo Productions.

Ford, Sandy Lee. Gullah, the Nawleans Cat Meets Katrina. 2007. 32p. (J). *(978-0-9793637-0-2(5))* Hart Street Pubs.

Ford, Stephanie. Nadine, My Funny & Trusty Guide Dog, 1 vol. Fleischman, Carol. 2015. (ENG.). 32p. 16.99 *(978-1-4556-1927-6(2)*, Pelican Publishing) Arcadia Publishing.

—Tad Lucas: Trick-Riding Rodeo Cowgirl, 1 vol. Edge, Laura. 2017. (ENG.). 32p. (J). (gr. k-3). 16.99 *(978-1-4556-2277-1(X)*, Pelican Publishing) Arcadia Publishing.

—Willy the Texas Longhorn, 1 vol. Elliott, Alan. 2013. (ENG.). 32p. (J). (gr. k-3). 16.99 *(978-1-4556-1870-5(5)*, Pelican Publishing) Arcadia Publishing.

Ford, Stephanie. Gunpowder on Their Skirts: Military Heroines for the Blue & Gray, 1 vol. Ford, Stephanie. 2018. (ENG.). 96p. (gr. 4-8). pap. 10.95 *(978-1-4556-2435-5(7)*, Pelican Publishing) Arcadia Publishing.

Ford, Yvonne. Farm Days A-Z Coloring Book. Marsh, Carole. 2009. 28p. (J). 5.99 *(978-0-635-07421-8(4))* Gallopade International.

Fordham, Fred. The Adventures of John Blake: Mystery of the Ghost Ship. Pullman, Philip. (ENG.). 160p. (J). (gr. 3-7). 2018. pap. 12.99 *(978-1-338-14911-1(3))*; 2017. 19.99 *(978-1-338-14912-8(1))* Scholastic, Inc. (Graphix).

—The Adventures of John Blake: Mystery of the Ghost Ship. Pullman, Philip. ed. 2017. lib. bdg. 33.05 *(978-0-606-40195-1(4))* Turtleback.

Fore, Elizabeth. Maude, the Flop-Eared Mule. Wilson, Douglas. 2012. 38p. 24.95 *(978-1-4626-7455-8(0))* America Star Bks.

Fore, Emma. The Sleepover: A Stellyn Story. Martin, Molly K. 2018. (ENG.). 40p. (J). pap. 9.99 *(978-1-7223-7556-0(6))* CreateSpace Independent Publishing Platform.

Foreman, A. Skeeter Sneeter Doodlebop. Smith, C. Michelle. 2009. 24p. pap. 15.63 *(978-1-934840-54-2(8))* Nimble Bks. LLC.

—Skeeter Uses Manners. Smith, C. Michelle. 2010. 28p. pap. 17.36 *(978-1-60888-017-1(6))* Nimble Bks. LLC.

Foreman, Austin Lee, jt. illus. see Dreisbach, Kristin Wolf.

Foreman, Gabe. Halifax Hal. Thran, Nick. 2013. (ENG.). 46p. (YA). (gr. 5). pap. 9.95 *(978-1-897411-77-3(4))* Bayeux Arts, Inc. CAN. Dist: Chicago Distribution Ctr.

Foreman, Michael. Bedtime Stories. Jones, Terry & Newman, Nanette. 2007. (ENG.). 192p. (J). (gr. 2-4). pap. 16.99 *(978-1-84458-477-2(1))* Pavilion Bks. GBR. Dist: Independent Pubs. Group.

—Beowulf. Morpurgo, Michael. 2015. (ENG.). 160p. (J). (gr. 3-7). pap. 6.99 *(978-0-7636-7297-3(1))* Candlewick Pr.

—Billy the Kid. Morpurgo, Michael. (ENG.). 80p. (J). 2013. (gr. 4-7). pap. 11.99 *(978-1-84365-260-1(9)*, Pavilion Children's Books); 2nd ed. 2006. (gr. 2-4). pap. 13.95 *(978-1-84458-366-9(X))* Pavilion Bks. GBR. Dist: Penguin Random Hse. LLC, Independent Pubs. Group.

—El Caballo de Arena. Turnbull, Ann. (Barril Sin Fondo Ser.).Tr. of Sand Horse. (SPA.). (J). (gr. 3-5). pap. *(978-968-6465-00-6(6))* Casa de Estudios de Literatura y Talleres Artisticos Amaquemecan A.C. MEX. Dist: Lectorum Pubns., Inc.

—A Child's Garden of Verses. Stevenson, Robert Louis. rev. ed. 2017. (ENG.). 128p. (J). (gr. k-5). 24.99 *(978-1-910959-10-7(3))* Otter-Barry Bks. GBR. Dist: Independent Pubs. Group.

—El Delfín de Luis. Morpurgo, Michael. 2004.Tr. of Dolphin Boy. (SPA.). 32p. (J). (gr. 1-2). 19.99 *(978-84-261-3401-1(7)*, JV32953) Juventud, Editorial ESP. Dist: Lectorum Pubns., Inc.

—Dolphin Boy. Morpurgo, Michael. 2005. (ENG.). 32p. (J). 14.99 *(978-1-84270-320-5(X))* Andersen Pr. GBR. Dist: Trafalgar Square Publishing.

—Dolphin Boy. Morpurgo, Michael. 2019. 32p. (J). (gr. -1-k). pap. 9.99 *(978-1-78344-750-3(8))* Penguin Random Hse. AUS. Dist: Independent Pubs. Group.

—Farm Boy. Morpurgo, Michael. 2007. (ENG.). 76p. (J). (gr. 4-7). pap. 15.99 *(978-1-84365-090-4(8))* Pavilion Bks. GBR. Dist: Independent Pubs. Group.

—The General. Charters, Janet. 2010. (ENG.). 48p. (J). (gr. k-12). 16.99 *(978-0-7636-4875-6(2)*, Templar) Candlewick Pr.

—Gentle Giant. Morpurgo, Michael. 2006. 28p. (J). reprint ed. (gr. k-4). pap. 12.00 *(978-1-4223-5667-8(1))*; (gr. 4-8). 19.00 *(978-1-4223-5398-1(2))* DIANE Publishing Co.

—Gentle Giant. Morpurgo, Michael. 2003. (ENG.). 32p. (J). 16.95 *(978-0-00-711064-3(2)*, HarperCollins Children's Bks.) HarperCollins Pubs. Ltd. GBR. Dist: Trafalgar Square Publishing.

—Kaspar the Titanic Cat. Morpurgo, Michael. 2012. (ENG.). 208p. (J). (gr. 3-7). 16.99 *(978-0-06-200618-9(5))* HarperCollins Pubs.

—Leon Garfield's Shakespeare Stories. Garfield, Leon. 2015. (ENG.). 576p. (J). (gr. 5). 27.95 *(978-1-59017-931-4(5)*, NYR Children's Collection) New York Review of Bks., Inc., The.

—The Little Ships: The Heroic Rescue at Dunkirk in World War II. Borden, Louise. 2003. (ENG.). 32p. (J). (gr. 4-7). 7.99 *(978-0-689-85396-8(3)*, McElderry, Margaret K. Bks.) McElderry, Margaret K. Bks.

—Long Neck & Thunder Foot. Piers, Helen. 2013. 32p. (J). (gr. -1-k). pap. 8.99 *(978-1-84939-482-6(2))* Andersen Pr. GBR. Dist: Independent Pubs. Group.

—Michael Foreman's the Wonderful Wizard of Oz. Baum, L. Frank. 2010. (ENG.). 160p. (J). (gr. k-2). 19.99 *(978-1-84365-157-4(2)*, Pavilion Children's Books) Pavilion Bks. GBR. Dist: Penguin Random Hse. LLC.

—Not Bad for a Bad Lad. Morpurgo, Michael. 2016. (ENG.). 128p. (J). (gr. 2-4). pap. 9.99 *(978-1-84812-471-4(6))* Bonnier Publishing GBR. Dist: Independent Pubs. Group.

—Peter Pan & Wendy. Barrie, J. M. 2003. (Chrysalis Childrens Classics Ser.). 176p. (YA). pap. *(978-1-84365-039-3(8)*, Pavilion Children's Books) Pavilion Bks.

—Peter Pan & Wendy. Barrie, J. M. 2010. (ENG.). 160p. (J). (gr. 2-7). 19.99 *(978-1-84365-136-9(X)*, Pavilion Children's Books) Pavilion Bks. GBR. Dist: Independent Pubs. Group.

—Robin of Sherwood. Morpurgo, Michael. 2018. (ENG.). 192p. (J). (gr. 4-7). 24.99 *(978-1-78675-046-4(5))* Palazzo Editions, Ltd. GBR. Dist: Independent Pubs. Group.

—The Saga of Erik the Viking. Jones, Terry. 2017. 168p. (YA). (gr. 7-7). pap. 14.99 *(978-1-84365-314-1(1)*, Pavilion Children's Books) Pavilion Bks. GBR. Dist: Penguin Random Hse. LLC.

—Say Hello. Foreman, Jack. 2012. (ENG.). (J). (gr. -1-1). 32p. 21.19 *(978-0-7636-3657-9(6))*; 40p. pap. 6.99 *(978-0-7636-6087-1(6))* Candlewick Pr.

—Toro! Toro! Morpurgo, Michael. 2007. (ENG.). 128p. (J). (gr. 4-7). pap. 8.99 *(978-0-00-710718-6(8)*, HarperCollins Children's Bks.) HarperCollins Pubs. Ltd. GBR. Dist: HarperCollins Pubs.

—The White Horse of Zennor & Other Stories. Morpurgo, Michael. 2015. (ENG.). 176p. (J). (gr. 2-4). pap. 10.99 *(978-1-4052-7301-5(1))* Egmont Bks., Ltd. GBR. Dist: Independent Pubs. Group.

—White Owl, Barn Owl: Read & Wonder. Davies, Nicola. 2009. (Read & Wonder Ser.). (ENG.). 32p. (J). (gr. -1-3). pap. 7.99 *(978-0-7636-4143-6(X))* Candlewick Pr.

—White Owl, Barn Owl with Audio, Peggable. Davies, Nicola. 2009. (Read, Listen, & Wonder Ser.). (ENG.). 32p. (J). (gr. -1-3). pap. 9.99 *(978-0-7636-4194-8(4))* Candlewick Pr.

Foreman, Michael. After the War Was Over. Foreman, Michael. 2007. (ENG.). 96p. (J). (gr. 4-7). pap. 16.99 *(978-1-84365-088-1(6))* Pavilion Bks. GBR. Dist: Independent Pubs. Group.

—Cat & Dog. Foreman, Michael. 2014. (ENG.). 32p. (J). (gr. -1-3). 16.95 *(978-1-4677-5124-7(3)*, 9781467751247) Lerner Publishing Group.

—Fortunately, Unfortunately. Foreman, Michael. 2011. (ENG.). 32p. (J). (gr. -1-3). 17.99 *(978-0-7613-7460-2(4)*, 9780761374602) Lerner Publishing Group.

—I Didn't Do It! Foreman, Michael. 2020. (ENG.). 32p. (J). (gr. -1-3). 17.99 *(978-1-5415-9629-0(3))* Lerner Publishing Group.

—I Love You, Too! Foreman, Michael. 2014. (ENG.). 32p. (J). (gr. -1-3). 16.95 *(978-1-4677-3451-6(9)*, 9781467734516) Lerner Publishing Group.

—Jamal's Journey. Foreman, Michael. 2017. (ENG.). 32p. (J). (gr. -1-3). 17.99 *(978-1-5124-3949-6(5))* Lerner Publishing Group.

—The Little Bookshop & the Origami Army! Foreman, Michael. (Origami Girl Ser.). 32p. (J). 2017. (-k). pap. 9.99 *(978-1-78344-208-9(5))*; 2015. (gr. -1-k). 16.99 *(978-1-78344-120-4(8))* Andersen Pr. GBR. Dist: Independent Pubs. Group.

—Moose. Foreman, Michael. 2015. 32p. (J). (gr. -1-k). pap. 9.99 *(978-1-78344-101-3(1))* Andersen Pr. GBR. Dist: Independent Pubs. Group.

—Newspaper Boy & Origami Girl! Foreman, Michael. 2013. (Origami Girl Ser.). (ENG.). 32p. (J). (gr. -1-k). 20.99 *(978-1-84939-451-2(2))* Andersen Pr. GBR. Dist: Independent Pubs. Group.

—Norman's Ark. Foreman, Michael. 2006. (Tiger Tales Ser.). 24p. (J). (gr. -1-3). pap. 6.95 *(978-1-58925-401-5(5))* Tiger Tales.

—Oh! If Only... Foreman, Michael. 2013. (ENG.). 32p. (J). (gr. -1-3). 16.95 *(978-1-4677-1213-2(2)*, 9781467712132) Lerner Publishing Group.

—Seal Surfer. Foreman, Michael. 2007. 36p. (J). (gr. k-4). pap. 12.99 *(978-1-84270-578-0(4))* Andersen Pr. GBR. Dist: Independent Pubs. Group.

—The Seeds of Friendship. Foreman, Michael. 2015. (ENG.). 32p. (J). (gr. -1-3). 16.99 *(978-0-7636-7834-0(1))* Candlewick Pr.

—Superfrog & the Big Stink! Foreman, Michael. 2014. (ENG.). 32p. (J). (gr. -1-k). pap. 9.99 *(978-1-78344-030-6(9))* Andersen Pr. GBR. Dist: Independent Pubs. Group.

—Tufty. Foreman, Michael. 2016. (ENG.). 32p. (J). (gr. -1-3). 17.99 *(978-1-5124-0425-8(X)*, 9781512404258); E-Book 27.99 *(978-1-5124-0448-7(9))* Lerner Publishing Group.

—Wonder Goal! Foreman, Michael. 2010. (ENG.). 32p. (J). (gr. k-2). pap. 12.99 *(978-1-84270-934-4(8))* Andersen Pr. GBR. Dist: Independent Pubs. Group.

Foreman, Michael. Fairy Tales & Fantastic Stories. Foreman, Michael, tr. Jones, Terry. 10th anniv. ed. 2003. 256p. (YA). *(978-1-84365-055-3(X)*, Pavilion Children's Books) Pavilion Bks.

Foreman, Travel, et al. Black Cat Vol. 1: Grand Theft Marvel. 2020. (ENG.). 152p. (YA). (gr. 4-17). pap. 15.99 *(978-1-302-91920-7(2))* Marvel Worldwide, Inc.

Foreman, Travel. Black Cat Vol. 2: On the Run. 2020. (ENG.). 112p. (J). (gr. 8-17). pap. 15.99 ***(978-1-302-91921-4(0))*** Marvel Worldwide, Inc.

Foreman, Travel. Ultimates 2 Vol. 1: Troubleshooters. 2017. (ENG.). 112p. (YA). (gr. 8-17). pap. 17.99 *(978-1-302-90675-7(5))* Marvel Worldwide, Inc.

—Ultimates 2 Vol. 2: Eternity War, Vol. 2. 2017. (ENG.). 160p. (YA). (gr. 8-17). pap. 15.99 *(978-1-302-90676-4(3))* Marvel Worldwide, Inc.

Forest, Crista. Let's Explore, Moose! Fraggalosch, Audrey. (ENG.). 32p. (J). (gr. -1-1). 2005. pap. 3.95 *(978-1-59249-151-3(0)*, S2017); 2003. 12.95 *(978-1-59249-152-0(9)*, PS2017) Soundprints.

Forester, Liz. Connect the Dots: Awesome Animals. Acampora, Courtney. 2018. (ENG.). 32p. (J). (gr. -1 — 1). pap. 12.99 *(978-1-62686-937-0(5)*, Silver Dolphin Bks.) Printers Row Publishing Group.

—Hey, Diddle Diddle & Other Classic Nursery Rhymes. Editors of Silver Dolphin Books. 2018. (ENG.). 12p. (J). (gr. -1 — 1). bds. 8.99 *(978-1-68412-349-0(6)*, Silver Dolphin Bks.) Printers Row Publishing Group.

Foresti, Sara. The President Wears Pink. Vetto, Mandana. 2020. (ENG.). 26p. (J). (gr. -1-3). 18.99 ***(978-0-578-59679-2(2))*** Mach Media LLC.

Foresti, Sara. Treasure of the Gold Dragon. West, Tracey. 2018. (Dragon Masters Ser.: 12). (ENG.). 96p. (J). (gr. 1-3). pap. 4.99 *(978-1-338-26368-8(4))* Scholastic, Inc.

Forgas-Davis, Melissa. After Dark. Forgas, Christine. 2004. 17p. (J). (gr. 1-6). pap. *(978-1-930200-27-2(7))* Martell Publishing Co.

Forget-Eminizer, Christine. Pourquoi Je Suis Diff�rent: Comprendre L'autisme. Eminizer, Don. Doyen, Gilles, ed. 2019. (FRE.). 24p. (J). pap. 10.99 ***(978-1-6960-6104-9(0))*** Independently Published.

—Why I'm Different: Understanding Autism. Eminizer, Don. 2018. (ENG.). 24p. (J). pap. 10.99 ***(978-1-5136-4037-2(2))*** Litmocracy Pubns.

Forgo, Ivana. Dem Bones. Weane, Holly. 2019. (Flowerpot Holiday Ser.). (ENG.). 20p. (J). (gr. -1-1). bds. 7.99 *(978-1-4867-1674-6(1)*, 57ec6aba-feb4-4d5a-b016-8517d6a15a41) Flowerpot Pr.

—Horsey, Horsey. Everett, Melissa. 2017. (ENG.). 24p. (J). (gr. -1-2). *(978-1-4867-1263-2(0))* Flowerpot Children's Pr. Inc.

—5 Very Little Pumpkins. Weane, Holly. 2019. (Flowerpot Holiday Ser.). (ENG.). 20p. (J). (gr. -1-1). bds. 7.99 *(978-1-4867-1673-9(3)*, 6270ecdb-050e-4586-9096-b8018e4a19e8) Flowerpot Pr.

Forkuo, Fleance. Perfect As I Am. Serwaa, Maame. 2018. (ENG.). 30p. (J). pap. 9.99 *(978-1-62676-800-0(5)*, Melanin Origins, LLC) Grivante Pr.

Forlati, Anna. Yoga for Kids: Simple Animal Poses for Any Age. Pajalunga, Lorena V. 2015. (ENG.). 32p. (J). (gr. -1-3). 16.99 *(978-0-8075-9172-7(6)*, 807591726) Whitman, Albert & Co.

Formelio, Lorri. If You Sleep with a Cat on Your Head. Starling, Landa. 2008. 27p. pap. 24.95 *(978-1-60703-318-9(6))* America Star Bks.

Formica, Paola. Barefoot Books Incredible Animals. Rahwan, Dunia. 2020. (ENG.). 64p. (J). ***(978-1-64686-066-1(7))*** Barefoot Bks., Inc.

Formosa, Natasha. Potato Boy. Rate, Kristina. 2005. 32p. (J). (gr. -1). per. *(978-0-9549372-0-1(1))* Fastback TV Ltd.

Fornari, Giuliano. Panoramas Human Body. 2006. (J). *(978-0-7607-8155-5(9))* backpackbook.

Fornarni, Giuliano. The Body Atlas: A Pictorial Guide to the Human Body. DK. 2020. (ENG.). 64p. (J). (gr. 4-7). 20.00 ***(978-1-4654-9096-4(5)***, DK Children) Dorling Kindersley Publishing, Inc.

Forney, Ellen. The Absolutely True Diary of a Part-Time Indian. Alexie, Sherman. 2008. 230p. 25.00 *(978-1-60686-072-4(0))* Perfection Learning Corp.

—The Absolutely True Diary of a Part-Time Indian. Alexie, Sherman. l.t. ed. 2008. (Thorndike Literacy Bridge Ser.). (ENG.). 302p. (YA). (gr. 7-12). 23.95 *(978-1-4104-0499-2(4))* Thorndike Pr.

Forney, Ellen. Monkey Food: The Complete I was Seven in '75 Collection. Forney, Ellen. 2005. 142p. (YA). reprint ed. pap. 13.00 *(978-0-7567-8610-6(X))* DIANE Publishing Co.

Forrest, A. S. Our Island Story (Yesterday's Classics) Marshall, H. E. l.t. ed. 2006. 676p. (J). per. 19.95 *(978-1-59915-009-3(3))* Yesterday's Classics.

Forrest, Chris. One-Eyed Jack. Miller, Paula. (J). 2007. (ENG.). 133p. (gr. 2-7). pap. 8.95 *(978-0-9769417-0-5(8))*; 2006. 144p. 13.95 *(978-0-9718348-8-0(1))* Blooming Tree Pr.

Forrest, Genevieve. Pick-a-WooWoo -the Happy Little Spirit: Each of us has a Spirit but what is it & where did it come From?, 16 vols., Vol. 2. Harper, Julie Ann. 2008. 32p. (J). pap. *(978-0-9803669-1-4(7))* Pick-a-Woo Woo Pubs.

Forrest, Grace Metzger. Mary & the Fireflies. Davis, Mary Perrone. Williams, Nancy E., ed. 2018. (ENG.). 24p. (J). (gr. k-3). pap. 14.98 *(978-1-943523-51-1(7))* Laurus Co., Inc., The.

Forrest, Grace Metzger. Mary & the Little Lamb. Davis, Mary Perrone. Williams, Nancy E., ed. 2019. (ENG.). 24p. (J). (gr. k-6). pap. 14.98 ***(978-1-943523-80-1(0))*** Laurus Co., Inc., The.

Forrest, Grace Metzger. Mary Loves to Sing. Davis, Mary Perrone. 2018. (ENG.). 24p. (J). (gr. k-3). pap. 14.98 *(978-1-943523-69-6(X))* Laurus Co., Inc., The.

—Mary Visits a Farm. Davis, Mary Perrone. Williams, Nancy E., ed. 2019. (ENG.). 24p. (J). (gr. k-3). pap. 14.98 *(978-1-943523-71-9(1))* Laurus Co., Inc., The.

—Mary's Butterfly Garden. Davis, Mary Perrone. Williams, Nancy E., ed. 2017. (ENG.). 24p. (J). (gr. k-1). pap. 14.98 *(978-1-943523-42-9(8))* Laurus Co., Inc., The.

—Morris Plunkett, Extraordinary Hero. Ratliff, Barbara Tiffany. Williams, Nancy E., ed. 2016. (Extraordinary Hero Ser.: Vol. 2). (ENG.). (J). (gr. k-6). pap. 17.98 *(978-1-943523-22-1(3))* Laurus Co., Inc., The.

—Shelby's Collection Day. Dixon, Dallas L. Williams, Nancy E., ed. 2013. 24p. (J). pap. 12.98 *(978-1-938526-54-1(6))* Laurus Co., Inc., The.

—Shelby's Seasons. Dixon, Dallas L. Williams, Nancy E., ed. 5th ed. 2018. (Shelby Ser.: Vol. 5). (ENG.). 24p. (J). (gr. k-6). pap. 18.98 *(978-1-943523-54-2(1))* Laurus Co., Inc., The.

—Silas Watts: The Highly Electric Lightning Bug. Barnes, Brenda J. Williams, Nancy E., ed. 2013. 28p. (J). pap. 17.98 *(978-1-938526-36-7(8))* Roxby Media Ltd. GBR. Dist: Laurus Co., The.

Forrest, James. Eric & the Angrrry Frog, Vol. 2. Sprecher, John. l.t. ed. Date not set. (Special Kids "Special Message" Book Ser.). 32p. (J). (gr. k-4). pap. 10.00 *(978-1-892186-01-0(2))* Anythings Possible, Inc.

—Tori & Cassandra & the Pelican in Peril. Sprecher, John. l.t. ed. Date not set. (Special Kids "Special Message" Book Ser.: Vol. 3). 32p. (J). (gr. k-4). pap. 10.00 *(978-1-892186-02-7(0))* Anythings Possible, Inc.

—Zoe & the Very Unmerry Bear. Sprecher, John. l.t. ed. Date not set. (Special Kids "Special Message" Book Ser.). 32p. (J). (gr. k-4). pap. 10.00 *(978-1-892186-03-4(9)*, SKPB4) Anythings Possible, Inc.

Forrest, Nancy. What Is Beautiful? Boritzer, Etan. 2004. (gr. -1-5). 40p. 14.95 *(978-0-9637597-6-4(0))*; 32p. pap. *(978-0-9637597-7-1(9))* Lane, Veronica Bks.

—What Is Death? Boritzer, Etan. 2004. (What Is? Ser.). 40p. (J). (gr. k-5). pap. 6.95 *(978-0-9637597-5-7(2))* Lane, Veronica Bks.

Forrest, Teri. Red the Pasta Pig: Book Four RED Travels West. McDonald, Caro. 2019. (Red Travels West Ser.: Vol. 4). (ENG.). (J). 42p. pap. 15.00 *(978-1-0968-7406-5(7))*; 40p. pap. 15.00 *(978-1-0967-9523-0(X))* Independently Published.

Forrester, Anne Marie. Wild Girls: The Path of the Young Goddess. Monaghan, Patricia & Managhan, Patricia. 2nd exp. ed. 2005. (ENG.). 258p. pap. 15.95 *(978-0-9760604-1-3(8))* Crosby Advanced Medical Systems Inc.

Forrester Baldy, Sherri. Daria Rose & the Day She Chose. Capitelli, Yvonne. 2008. (ENG.). 32p. (J). 16.95 *(978-0-9818366-0-7(7))* ASunnyDay Publishing.

Forrester, Kate. Adventures with Waffles. Parr, Maria. (ENG.). 240p. (J). (gr. 2-5). 2018. pap. 7.99 *(978-1-5362-0366-0(1))*; 2015. 16.99 *(978-0-7636-7281-2(5))* Candlewick Pr.

Forsey, Chris. Martin Luther King Jr: The Life of a Civil Rights Leader. Jeffrey, Gary. 2007. (Graphic Nonfiction Biographies Ser.). (ENG.). 48p. (YA). (gr. 4-7). lib. bdg. 35.45 *(978-1-4042-0858-2(5))* Rosen Publishing Group, Inc., The.

—War Correspondents. Shone, Rob. 2008. (Graphic Careers Ser.). (ENG.). 48p. (J). (gr. 5-8). lib. bdg. 35.45 *(978-1-4042-1449-1(6))*; per. 14.05 *(978-1-4042-1450-7(X))* Rosen Publishing Group, Inc., The.

Forsey, Christopher. Martin Luther King Jr: The Life of a Civil Rights Leader. Jeffrey, Gary. 2007. (Graphic Biographies Ser.). (ENG.). 48p. (gr. 5-8). pap. 14.05 *(978-1-4042-0921-3(2))* Rosen Publishing Group, Inc., The.

Forshall, Rose. Pirate Gran. Durrant, Geraldine. 2009. 32p. (J). 19.95 *(978-0-948065-96-5(6))* National Maritime Museum GBR. Dist: Independent Pubs. Group.

Forshaw, Andy. Absolutely Everything!: A History of Earth, Dinosaurs, Rulers, Robots & Other Things Too Numerous to Mention. Lloyd, Christopher. 2018. (ENG.). 352p. (J). (gr. 4-7). 21.99 *(978-1-9998028-3-7(7))* What on Earth Books.

—The Big History Timeline Posterbook: Unfold the History of the Universe — From the Big Bang to the Present Day! Lloyd, Christopher. 2017. (ENG.). 10p. (J). pap. 49.95 *(978-0-9954820-3-6(9))* What on Earth Bks GBR. Dist: Ingram Publisher Services.

—The Big History Timeline Stickerbook: From the Big Bang to the Present Day; 14 Billion Years on One Amazing Timeline! Lloyd, Christopher. 2017. (ENG.). 18p. (J). pap. 9.95 *(978-0-9955766-5-0(3))* What on Earth Bks GBR. Dist: Ingram Publisher Services.

—The Big History Timeline Wallbook: Unfold the History of the Universe — From the Big Bang to the Present Day! Lloyd, Christopher. 2017. (ENG.). 24p. (J). (gr. 1-9). 19.95 *(978-0-9932847-2-4(8))* What on Earth Bks GBR. Dist: Ingram Publisher Services.

—Dinosaurs! Forshaw, Nick. 2018. (Explorer Ser.). (ENG.). 46p. (J). (gr. 1-5). 14.95 *(978-0-9955770-5-3(6))* What on Earth Bks GBR. Dist: Ingram Publisher Services.

—¿en Qué Mundo Vives? Libromural. Cronología de la Naturaleza. Lloyd, Christopher. 2017. (SPA.). 26p. (J). (gr. 2-4). pap. 28.95 *(978-84-942689-5-3(3))* Ediciones Rodeno ESP. Dist: Independent Pubs. Group.

—The Magna Carta Chronicle: A Young Person's Guide to 800 Years in the Fight for Freedom. Lloyd, Christopher & Skipworth, Patrick. 2015. 32p. (gr. 3-9). pap. 12.99 *(978-0-9930199-1-3(9))* What on Earth Books.

—The Nature Timeline Posterbook: Unfold the Story of Nature — From the Dawn of Life to the Present Day! Lloyd, Christopher. 2017. (ENG.). 10p. (J). pap. 49.95 *(978-0-9954820-4-3(7))* What on Earth Bks GBR. Dist: Ingram Publisher Services.

—The Nature Timeline Stickerbook: From Bacteria to Humanity: the Story of Life on Earth in One Epic Timeline! Lloyd, Christopher. 2017. (ENG.). 18p. (J). pap. 9.95 *(978-0-9955766-6-7(1))* What on Earth Bks GBR. Dist: Ingram Publisher Services.

—The Nature Timeline Wallbook: Unfold the Story of Nature — From the Dawn of Life to the Present Day! Lloyd, Christopher. 2017. (ENG.). 24p. (J). 19.95 *(978-0-9932847-3-1(6))* What on Earth Bks GBR. Dist: Ingram Publisher Services.

—The Posterbook Timeline Collection. Lloyd, Christopher. 2017. (ENG.). 10p. (J). pap. 199.00 *(978-0-9954820-9-8(8))* What on Earth Bks GBR. Dist: Ingram Publisher Services.

—The Science Timeline Posterbook: Unfold the Story of Inventions — From the Stone Age to the Present Day! Lloyd, Christopher. 2017. (ENG.). 10p. (J). pap. 49.95 *(978-0-9954820-6-7(3))* What on Earth Bks GBR. Dist: Ingram Publisher Services.

—The Science Timeline Stickerbook: The Story of Science from the Stone Ages to the Present Day! Lloyd, Christopher. 2017. (ENG.). 18p. (J). pap. 9.95 *(978-0-9955766-7-4(X))* What on Earth Bks GBR. Dist: Ingram Publisher Services.

—The Science Timeline Wallbook: Unfold the Story of Inventions — From the Stone Age to the Present Day! Lloyd, Christopher. 2017. (ENG.). 24p. (J). 19.95 *(978-0-9932847-5-5(2))* What on Earth Bks GBR. Dist: Ingram Publisher Services.

—The Shakespeare Timeline Posterbook: Unfold the Complete Plays of Shakespeare — One Theater, Thirty-Eight Dramas! Lloyd, Christopher. 2017. (ENG.). 10p. (J). pap. 49.95 *(978-0-9954820-8-1(X))* What on Earth Bks GBR. Dist: Ingram Publisher Services.

—The Shakespeare Timeline Stickerbook: See All the Plays of Shakespeare Being Performed at Once in the Globe Theatre! Lloyd, Christopher & Walton, Nick. 2017. (ENG.).

72p. (J). pap. 9.95 *(978-0-9955766-8-1(8))* What on Earth Bks GBR. Dist: Ingram Publisher Services.

—The Shakespeare Timeline Wallbook: Unfold the Complete Plays of Shakespeare — One Theater, Thirty-Eight Dramas! Lloyd, Christopher & Walton, Nick. 2017. (ENG.). 24p. (J). 19.95 *(978-0-9932847-6-2(0))* What on Earth Bks GBR. Dist: Ingram Publisher Services.

—The Sports Timeline Posterbook: Unfold the Story of Sport — from the Ancient Olympics to the Present Day! Lloyd, Christopher. 2017. (ENG.). 10p. (J). pap. 49.95 *(978-0-9954820-7-4(1))* What on Earth Bks GBR. Dist: Ingram Publisher Services.

—The Stickerbook Timeline Collection. 2017. (ENG.). 30p. (J). pap. 24.95 *(978-0-9955766-9-8(6))* What on Earth Bks GBR. Dist: Ingram Publisher Services.

—The Wallbook Timeline Collection. Lloyd, Christopher. 2017. (ENG.). 72p. (J). 54.95 *(978-0-9955770-0-8(5))* What on Earth Bks GBR. Dist: Ingram Publisher Services.

Forshaw, John. The Beast of Didley Dale. Popper, Garry. 2004. (Bret the Vet Ser.). 40p. 7.00 *(978-1-84161-024-5(0))* Ravette Publishing, Ltd. GBR. Dist: Parkwest Pubns., Inc.

—High Noon in Didley Pidley. Popper, Garry. 2004. (Bret the Vet Ser.). 40p. 7.00 *(978-1-84161-013-9(5))* Ravette Publishing, Ltd. GBR. Dist: Parkwest Pubns., Inc.

—Scary Monkeys: Going Ape. Popper, Garry. 2004. 48p. 9.00 *(978-1-84161-014-6(3))* Ravette Publishing, Ltd. GBR. Dist: Parkwest Pubns., Inc.

—Worm's Eye View: A Witch's Tale. Popper, Garry. 2004. 48p. 7.00 *(978-1-84161-025-2(9))* Ravette Publishing, Ltd. GBR. Dist: Parkwest Pubns., Inc.

Forshaw, Louise. Brachiosaurus: The Nosy Dinosaur, 1 vol. Veitch, Catherine. 2020. (Dinosaur Adventures Ser.). (ENG.). 24p. (gr. 1-2). pap. 8.25 ***(978-1-4994-8489-2(5))***; lib. bdg. 24.60 ***(978-1-4994-8491-5(7))*** Rosen Publishing Group, Inc., The. (Windmill Bks.).

Forshaw, Louise. Dinosaur Safari. 2014. (ENG.). 10p. (J). 14.99 *(978-1-4711-2121-0(6)*, Simon & Schuster Children's) Simon & Schuster, Ltd. GBR. Dist: Simon & Schuster, Inc.

—I Can Get It & Hop In! Jinks, Jenny. 2020. (Early Bird Readers — Pink (Early Bird Stories (tm)) Ser.). (ENG.). 32p. (J). (gr. -1-2). pap. 7.99 *(978-1-5415-8726-7(X)*, Lerner Pubns.) Lerner Publishing Group.

—Izzy! Wizzy! Dale, Elizabeth. 2019. (Early Bird Readers — Yellow (Early Bird Stories (tm)) Ser.). (ENG.). 32p. (J). (gr. -1-2). 27.99 *(978-1-5415-4168-9(5)*, Lerner Pubns.) Lerner Publishing Group.

—Little Explorers: Scottish Castles (Push, Pull & Slide), 20 vols. 2019. (ENG.). 12p. (J). 14.95 *(978-1-78250-562-4(8)*, Kelpies) Floris Bks. GBR. Dist: Consortium Bk. Sales & Distribution.

—Please & Thank You. Charlesworth, Liza. 2017. 16p. (J). *(978-1-338-18029-9(0))* Scholastic, Inc.

—Velociraptor: The Speedy Tale, 1 vol. Bromage, Fran. 2019. (Dinosaur Adventures Ser.). (ENG.). 24p. (J). (gr. 1-2). 24.60 *(978-1-7253-9521-3(5))*; pap. 8.25 *(978-1-7253-9519-0(3))* Rosen Publishing Group, Inc., The. (Windmill Bks.).

Forshay, Christina. Goodnight Baseball. Dahl, Michael. 2013. (Sports Illustrated Kids Bedtime Bks.). (ENG.). 32p. (J). (gr. -1-2). pap. 6.95 *(978-1-4795-4975-7(4))*; lib. bdg. 22.60 *(978-1-4048-7979-9(X))* Capstone. (Picture Window Bks.).

—Goodnight Hockey. Dahl, Michael. 2015. (Sports Illustrated Kids Bedtime Bks.). (ENG.). 32p. (J). (gr. -1-2). lib. bdg. 22.60 *(978-1-4795-6526-9(1)*, Picture Window Bks.) Capstone.

—A Morning with Gong Gong. Liu, Sylvia. 2016. (ENG.). 32p. (J). (gr. -1-3). 17.95 *(978-1-62014-192-2(2))* Lee & Low Bks., Inc.

Forshay, Christina. A Morning with Grandpa, 1 vol. Liu, Sylvia. 2020. (ENG.). 32p. (J). (gr. k-3). pap. 10.95 ***(978-1-64379-422-8(1)***, c00ece66-26d9-4d6b-bc09-05815057efe1) Lee & Low Bks., Inc.

Forshay, Christina. The Really Groovy Story of the Tortoise & the Hare. Crow, Kristyn & Aesop, Aesop. 2012. (J). *(978-1-61913-128-6(5))* Weigl Pubs., Inc.

Forshay, Christina E. Goodnight Baseball, 1 vol. Dahl, Michael. 2013. (Sports Illustrated Kids Bedtime Bks.). (ENG.). 32p. (J). (gr. -1-2). 14.95 *(978-1-62370-000-3(0)*, Picture Window Bks.) Capstone.

—Goodnight Soccer. Dahl, Michael. 2018. (Sports Illustrated Kids Bedtime Bks.). (ENG.). 32p. (J). (gr. -1-2). lib. bdg. 21.93 *(978-1-5158-0870-1(X)*, 134393, Capstone Young Readers) Capstone.

—Sports Illustrated Kids Bedtime Books. Dahl, Michael. (Sports Illustrated Kids Bedtime Bks.). (ENG.). (J). (gr. -1-2). 2018. 32p. 89.73 *(978-1-5158-0871-8(8)*, 25930); 2016. pap., pap., pap. 20.85 *(978-1-4795-8262-4(X)*, Picture Window Bks.) Capstone.

Forss, Ian. Un Año del Arco Iris. Perez, Marlene. enl. ed. 2004. (SPA.). (J). pap. 26.00 *(978-1-4108-2367-0(9)*, 23679) Benchmark Education Co.

—Apúrate, Teddy: Fiction-to-Fact Big Book. Holl, Robert. enl. ed. 2004. (SPA.). (J). pap. 26.00 *(978-1-4108-2362-5(8)*, 23628) Benchmark Education Co.

Forster, Gregor. Build the Train. Steele, Philip. 2020. (Build The... Ser.). (ENG.). 32p. (J). (gr. 3-7). pap. 19.99 *(978-1-68412-337-7(2)*, Silver Dolphin Bks.) Printers Row Publishing Group.

Forsyth, Brett. Alphie the Albino Polar Bear. Forsyth, C. Michael. 2018. (ENG.). 32p. (J). pap. 7.99 *(978-0-9884780-8-4(0))*; 15.00 *(978-0-9884780-5-3(6))* Freedom's Hammer.

Forsyth, Matt. American Indian Mythology. Clark, Anthony. 2017. (Mythology Marvels Ser.). (ENG.). 32p. (gr. 3-5). pap. 9.95 *(978-1-68342-895-4(1)*, 9781683428954) Rourke Educational Media.

—Carrie & the Great Storm: A Galveston Hurricane Survival Story. Gunderson, Jessica. 2019. (Girls Survive Ser.). (ENG.). 112p. (J). (gr. 3-7). pap. 7.95 *(978-1-4965-8447-2(3)*, 140972); lib. bdg. 25.99 *(978-1-4965-8385-7(X)*, 140681) Capstone. (Stone Arch Bks.).

—Daisy & the Deadly Flu: A 1918 Influenza Survival Story. Gilbert, Julie Kathleen. 2020. (Girls Survive Ser.). (ENG.). 112p. (J). (gr. 3-7). pap. 7.95 *(978-1-4965-9215-6(8)*, 142247); lib. bdg. 25.99 *(978-1-4965-8712-1(X)*, 141519) Capstone. (Stone Arch Bks.).

—Egyptian Mythology. Palmer, Erin. 2017. (Mythology Marvels Ser.). (ENG.). 32p. (gr. 3-5). pap. 9.95 *(978-1-68342-894-7(3)*, 9781683428947) Rourke Educational Media.

Forsyth, Matt. Girls Survive. Berne, Emma Carlson et al. (Girls Survive Ser.). (ENG.). (J). (gr. 3-6). 2020. 415.84 ***(978-1-4965-9767-0(2)***, 199571); 2019. 207.92 *(978-1-4965-8388-8(4)*, 29356); 2019. pap., pap., pap. 63.60 *(978-1-4965-8492-2(9)*, 29567) Capstone. (Stone Arch Bks.).

Forsyth, Matt. Greek Mythology. Palmer, Erin. 2017. (Mythology Marvels Ser.). (ENG.). 32p. (gr. 3-5). pap. 9.95 *(978-1-68342-892-3(7)*, 9781683428923) Rourke Educational Media.

—Mary & the Trail of Tears: A Cherokee Removal Survival Story. Rogers, Andrea L. 2020. (Girls Survive Ser.). (ENG.). 112p. (J). (gr. 3-7). pap. 7.95 *(978-1-4965-9216-3(6)*, 142248); lib. bdg. 25.99 *(978-1-4965-8714-5(6)*, 141520) Capstone. (Stone Arch Bks.).

—Ruth & the Night of Broken Glass: A World War II Survival Story. Berne, Emma Carlson. 2019. (Girls Survive Ser.). (ENG.). 112p. (J). (gr. 3-7). pap. 7.95 *(978-1-4965-8449-6(X)*, 140974); lib. bdg. 25.99 *(978-1-4965-8387-1(6)*, 140683) Capstone. (Stone Arch Bks.).

Forsyth, Matt & Trunfio, Alessia. Girls Survive. Bybee, Veeda et al. 2020. (Girls Survive Ser.). (ENG.). (J). (gr. 3-6). pap., pap., pap. 127.20 ***(978-1-4965-9927-8(6)***, 201361); 311.88 *(978-1-4965-8720-6(0)*, 29792); pap., pap., pap. 95.40 *(978-1-4965-9273-6(5)*, 29970) Capstone. (Stone Arch Bks.).

Forsyth, Matt, jt. illus. see Trunfio, Alessia.

Forsyth, Robert. A Song of Life 1922. Morley, Margaret Warner. 2004. reprint ed. pap. 21.95 *(978-1-4179-7842-7(2))* Kessinger Publishing, LLC.

Forsythe, Matthew. The Bad Mood & the Stick. Snicket, Lemony. 2017. (ENG.). 48p. (J). (gr. -1-3). 17.99 *(978-0-316-39278-5(2))* Little, Brown Bks. for Young Readers.

—The Brilliant Deep: Rebuilding the World's Coral Reefs. Messner, Kate. 2018. (ENG.). 48p. (J). (gr. k-3). 17.99 *(978-1-4521-3350-8(6))* Chronicle Bks. LLC.

—The Gold Leaf. Hall, Kirsten. 2017. 48p. (J). (gr. -1-3). 18.95 *(978-1-59270-214-5(7))* Enchanted Lion Bks., LLC.

—My Name Is Elizabeth! Dunklee, Annika. 2011. (ENG.). 24p. (J). (gr. -1-2). 14.95 *(978-1-55453-560-6(3))* Kids Can Pr., Ltd. CAN. Dist: Hachette Bk. Group.

—Please, Open This Book! 2015. (ENG.). 40p. (J). (gr. -1-3). 18.99 *(978-1-4424-5071-4(1)*, Simon & Schuster/Paula Wiseman Bks.) Simon & Schuster/Paula Wiseman Bks.

—Warning: Do Not Open This Book! Lehrhaupt, Adam. 2013. (ENG.). 40p. (J). (gr. -1-3). 17.99 *(978-1-4424-3582-7(8)*, Simon & Schuster Bks. For Young Readers) Simon & Schuster Bks. For Young Readers.

Forsythe, Matthew. Pokko & the Drum. Forsythe, Matthew. 2019. (ENG.). 64p. (J). (gr. -1-3). 17.99 *(978-1-4814-8039-0(1)*, Simon & Schuster/Paula Wiseman Bks.) Simon & Schuster/Paula Wiseman Bks.

Forte, Helen. Minimus Secundus Pupil's Book: Moving on in Latin. Bell, Barbara. 2004. (Minimus Ser.). (ENG.). 96p. pap., stu. ed. 35.82 *(978-0-521-75545-0(X))* Cambridge Univ. Pr.

—Minimus Secundus Teacher's Resource Book: Moving on in Latin. Bell, Barbara. 2004. (Minimus Ser.). (ENG.). 95p. tchr. ed., spiral bd. 102.46 *(978-0-521-75546-7(8))* Cambridge Univ. Pr.

Fortenberry, Julie. Pirate Boy. Bunting, Eve. (ENG.). (J). 2018. 28p. (— 1). bds. 7.99 *(978-0-8234-3979-9(8))*; 2012. 32p. (gr. -1-3). pap. 7.99 *(978-0-8234-2546-4(0))*; 2011. 32p. (gr. -1-3). 16.95 *(978-0-8234-2321-7(2))* Holiday Hse., Inc.

—Sadie & Ori & the Blue Blanket. Korngold, Jamie. 2015. (ENG.). 32p. (J). (gr. -1-2). 9.99 *(978-1-4677-1191-3(8)*, 9781467711913, Kar-Ben Publishing) Lerner Publishing Group.

—Sadie's Almost Marvelous Menorah. Korngold, Jamie S. 2013. (Hanukkah Ser.). 24p. (J). (gr. -1-1). lib. bdg. 17.95 *(978-0-7613-6493-1(5)*, Kar-Ben Publishing) Lerner Publishing Group.

—Sadie's Almost Marvelous Menorah. Korngold, Jamie. ed. 2013. (ENG.). 24p. (J). (gr. -1-1). E-Book 27.99 *(978-1-4677-0051-1(7))*; Vol. 7.95 *(978-0-7613-6495-5(1)*, 9780761364955) Lerner Publishing Group. (Kar-Ben Publishing).

—Sadie's Lag Ba'Omer Mystery, Vol. Korngold, Jamie. 2014. (ENG.). 32p. (J). (gr. -1-3). 7.95 *(978-0-7613-9048-0(0)*, 9780761390480, Kar-Ben Publishing) Lerner Publishing Group.

—Sadie's Snowy Tu B'Shevat. Korngold, Jamie. 2017. (ENG.). 32p. (J). (gr. -1-1). 17.99 *(978-1-5124-2677-9(6)*, 9781512426779, Kar-Ben Publishing) Lerner Publishing Group.

—Sadie's Sukkah Breakfast. Korngold, Jamie S. 2011. (Sukkot & Simchat Torah Ser.). (ENG.). 24p. (J). (gr. -1-1). lib. bdg. 16.95 *(978-0-7613-5647-9(9)*, Kar-Ben Publishing) Lerner Publishing Group.

Fortenberry, Julie. Pearl Goes to Preschool. Fortenberry, Julie. 2020. (ENG.). 32p. (J). (-k). 16.99 *(978-1-5362-0743-9(8))* Candlewick Pr.

Fortier, Natali & Brenier, Claire. Half & Half-A Doctor for the Animals. Moncomble, Gerard & Van den Dries, Sidonie. 2008. (J). 32p. pap. 4.99 *(978-1-60115-204-6(3))*; (ENG.). 29p. 17.44 *(978-1-60115-203-9(5))* Treasure Bay, Inc.

Fortnum, Peggy. More about Paddington. Bond, Michael. 2015. (Paddington Ser.). (ENG.). 176p. (J). (gr. 3-7). 9.99 *(978-0-06-231220-4(0))* HarperCollins Pubs.

—Paddington Abroad. Bond, Michael. 2015. (Paddington Ser.). (ENG.). 176p. (J). (gr. 3-7). 9.99 *(978-0-06-231222-8(7))* HarperCollins Pubs.

—Paddington at Large. Bond, Michael. 2016. (Paddington Ser.). (ENG.). 176p. (J). (gr. 3-7). 9.99 *(978-0-06-231224-2(3))* HarperCollins Pubs.

—Paddington at Work. Bond, Michael. (Paddington Ser.). (ENG.). 176p. (J). (gr. 3-7). 2018. pap. 6.99 *(978-0-06-243312-1(1))*; 2017. 9.99 *(978-0-06-231226-6(X))* HarperCollins Pubs.

—Paddington Goes to Town. Bond, Michael. (Paddington Ser.). (ENG.). 176p. (J). (gr. 3-7). 2018. pap. 6.99 *(978-0-06-243313-8(X))*; 2017. 9.99 *(978-0-06-231228-0(6))* HarperCollins Pubs.

—Paddington Goes to Town. Bond, Michael. 2003. (Paddington Bear Adventures Ser.). 136p. (J). (gr. 3-7). 12.60 *(978-0-8124-2266-5(X))* Perfection Learning Corp.

—Paddington Helps Out. Bond, Michael. 2015. (Paddington Ser.). (ENG.). 160p. (J). (gr. 3-7). 9.99 *(978-0-06-231230-3(8))* HarperCollins Pubs.

—Paddington Marches On. Bond, Michael. 2016. (Paddington Ser.). (ENG.). 176p. (J). (gr. 3-7). 9.99 *(978-0-06-231232-7(4))* HarperCollins Pubs.

—Paddington on Top. Bond, Michael. 2018. (Paddington Ser.). (ENG.). 176p. (J). (gr. 3-7). pap. 6.99 *(978-0-06-243314-5(8))*; 9.99 *(978-0-06-231234-1(0))* HarperCollins Pubs.

—Paddington Takes the Air. Bond, Michael. 2018. (Paddington Ser.). (ENG.). 176p. (J). (gr. 3-7). 9.99 *(978-0-06-231238-9(3))* HarperCollins Pubs.

—Paddington Takes the Air. Bond, Michael. 2019. (Paddington Ser.). (ENG.). 176p. (J). (gr. 3-7). pap. 6.99 *(978-0-06-243315-2(6))* HarperCollins Pubs.

—Paddington Takes the Test. Bond, Michael. (Paddington Ser.). (ENG.). 176p. (J). (gr. 3-7). 2017. pap. 5.99 *(978-0-06-243307-7(5))*; 2016. 9.99 *(978-0-06-231240-2(5))* HarperCollins Pubs.

Fortnum, Peggy & Alley, R. W. Love from Paddington. Bond, Michael. (Paddington Ser.). (ENG.). 144p. (J). (gr. 3-7). 2016. pap. 5.99 *(978-0-06-242526-3(9))*; 2014. 9.99 *(978-0-06-236816-4(8))* HarperCollins Pubs.

—Paddington Races Ahead. Bond, Michael. (Paddington Ser.). (ENG.). 192p. (J). (gr. 3-7). 2019. pap. 6.99 *(978-0-06-243316-9(4))*; 2018. 9.99 *(978-0-06-231236-5(7))* HarperCollins Pubs.

—Paddington's Finest Hour. Bond, Michael. 2017. (Paddington Ser.). (ENG.). 144p. (J). (gr. 3-7). 9.99 *(978-0-06-266972-8(9))* HarperCollins Pubs.

Fortuna, Ilya. M�s All� Del Mar. Antoine, Kimone. Antoine, Keisha, tr. 2019. (Aventuras de Reciclaje Ser.: Vol. 1). (SPA.). 36p. (J). pap. 11.99 ***(978-1-6563-1242-6(5))*** Independently Published.

Fortune, Eric. Bunnicula Meets Edgar Allan Crow. Howe, James. (Bunnicula & Friends Ser.). (ENG.). 160p. (J). (gr. 3-7). 2008. pap. 7.99 *(978-1-4169-1473-0(0))*; 2006. 17.99 *(978-1-4169-1458-7(7))* Simon & Schuster Children's Publishing. (Atheneum Bks. for Young Readers).

—Magickeepers: The Eternal Hourglass. Kirov, Erica. 2010. (ENG.). 256p. (J). (gr. 4-7). pap. 10.99 *(978-1-4022-3855-0(X)*, Sourcebooks Jabberwocky) Sourcebooks, Inc.

—The Shadow Thieves. Ursu, Anne. 2007. (Cronus Chronicles Ser.: 1). (ENG.). 432p. (J). (gr. 3-7). pap. 9.99 *(978-1-4169-0588-2(X)*, Atheneum Bks. for Young Readers) Simon & Schuster Children's Publishing.

—The Siren Song. Ursu, Anne. (Cronus Chronicles Ser.: 2). (ENG.). (J). (gr. 3-7). 2008. 464p. pap. 9.99 *(978-1-4169-0590-5(1))*; 2007. 448p. 19.99 *(978-1-4169-0589-9(8))* Simon & Schuster Children's Publishing. (Atheneum Bks. for Young Readers).

Fortune, Leslie. Petey the Pigasaurus. Nordquist, Donna M. 2011. 32p. pap. 24.95 *(978-1-4560-6051-0(1))* America Star Bks.

Fortuny, Liliana. Alex & the Monsters: Here Comes Mr. Flat! Copons, Jaume & Dupuis, Karina. Warriner, David, tr. 2018. 136p. (J). (gr. 1). 9.99 *(978-2-924786-09-3(6)*, CrackBoom! Bks.) Chouette Publishing CAN. Dist: Publishers Group West (PGW).

—Alex & the Monsters: Restaurant Rescue! Copons, Jaume & Dupuis, Karina. Warriner, David, tr. 2018. 136p. (J). (gr. 1). 9.99 *(978-2-924786-10-9(X)*, CrackBoom! Bks.) Chouette Publishing CAN. Dist: Publishers Group West (PGW).

Forward, Max. The Legend of Baeoh: How Baeoh Got His Stripes. Lee, Lucas Taekwon. 2007. (ENG.). 36p. (J). (gr. 1-7). 17.95 *(978-1-931741-88-0(3))* Reed, Robert D. Pubs.

Fosdike, David. Izzy Folau 3: Pushed to the Limit. Harding, David. 2016. (Izzy Folau Ser.: 3). 176p. (J). (gr. 4-7). pap. 9.99 *(978-0-85798-665-8(1))* Random Hse. Australia AUS. Dist: Independent Pubs. Group.

—Standing Tall: Izzy Folau 4. Harding, David. 2016. (Izzy Folau Ser.: 4). 176p. (J). (gr. 4-7). pap. 9.99 *(978-0-85798-667-2(8))* Random Hse. Australia AUS. Dist: Independent Pubs. Group.

Fosdike, James. Chance of a Lifetime: Izzy Folau 1. Harding, David. 2015. (Izzy Folau Ser.: 1). 176p. (J). (gr. 4-7). pap. 9.99 *(978-0-85798-661-0(9))* Random Hse. Australia AUS. Dist: Independent Pubs. Group.

—Reality Check: Izzy Folau 2. Harding, David. 2015. (Izzy Folau Ser.: 2). 176p. (J). (gr. 4-7). pap. 9.99 *(978-0-85798-663-4(5))* Random Hse. Australia AUS. Dist: Independent Pubs. Group.

Fosgitt, Jay, et al. My Little Pony: Friends Forever Omnibus, Vol. 2, Vol. 2. Whitley, Jeremy & Rice, Christina. 2017. (MLP FF Omnibus Ser.: 2). 147p. (J). (gr. 4-7). pap. 24.99 *(978-1-63140-882-3(8)*, 9781631408823) Idea & Design Works, LLC.

—Rainbow Dash & Spitfire. Anderson, Ted. 2018. (My Little Pony: Friends Forever Ser.). (ENG.). 24p. (J). (gr. 1-8). lib. bdg. 27.07 *(978-1-5321-4240-6(4)*, 28568, Graphic Novels) Spotlight.

Fosgitt, Joy & Garbowska, Agnes. My Little Pony: Friendship Is Magic Volume 8. Anderson, Ted et al. 2015. (My Little Pony Ser.: 8). 120p. (J). (gr. 4-7). pap. 19.99 *(978-1-63140-446-7(6)*, 9781631404467) Idea & Design Works, LLC.

Foss, Timothy. Rocks & the People Who Love Them, 1 vol. Yomtov, Nel. 2012. (Adventures in Science Ser.). (ENG.). 32p. (gr. 3-9). (J). pap. 8.10 *(978-1-4296-7988-6(3))*; pap. 47.70 *(978-1-4296-8466-8(6))* Capstone. (Capstone Pr.).

Foster, Alex. God Counts: Numbers in His Word & His World. Sun, Irene & Sun, Irene. 2017. (ENG.). 32p. (J). 15.99 *(978-1-945270-79-6(9))* New Growth Pr.

Foster, Brad W. & Simmons, Mark. Flight to Freedom! Nickolas Flux & the Underground Railroad, 1 vol. Bolte, Mari. 2014. (Nickolas Flux History Chronicles Ser.). (ENG.). 32p. (J). (gr. 3-9). lib. bdg. 31.32 *(978-1-4914-0254-2(7))* Capstone.

Foster, Dara, photos by. Now You See It! Pupstyle Red Carpet Pups. Foster, Dara. 2013. (ENG., 64p. (J). (gr. 2-5). pap. 5.99 *(978-0-545-53245-7(0))* Scholastic, Inc.

Foster, Frank. Run Farrah Run: Detecting, Ditching & Dealing with Dating Dopes. Taylor, Paula. von Seeburg, Kate, ed. 2004. 128p. (YA). pap. 12.95 *(978-0-9749173-0-6(3))* Tea Party Pr.

Foster, Jack. The Adventures of Firebolt. Pearl, Debbie & Lewis, Brittany Nicole. 2020. (Furtastic Ser.: Vol. 1). (ENG.). 38p. (J). 14.99 ***(978-0-578-22846-4(7))*** Dream Fetchers.

Foster, Jack. All Time Hero. Bangert-Wood, Susan. l.t. ed. 2017. (ENG.). (J). (gr. k-5). pap. 10.95 *(978-1-61633-894-7(6))* Guardian Angel Publishing, Inc.

—Amos Faces His Bully. Malandrinos, Cheryl. l.t. ed. 2018. (ENG.). 20p. (J). (gr. k-4). pap. 10.95 *(978-1-61633-909-8(8))* Guardian Angel Publishing, Inc.

—The Apple Tree. Finch, Jane. 2018. (Chickens Laugh Out Loud Ser.: Vol. 2). (ENG.). 36p. (J). (gr. k-4). pap. 9.99 *(978-1-68160-620-0(8))* Crimson Cloak Publishing.

Foster, Jack. Born in My Heart. Phillips, Dixie & Coles, Charlotte. 2020. (ENG.). 16p. (J). (gr. k-4). pap. 9.95 ***(978-1-951545-07-9(9))*** Guardian Angel Publishing, Inc.

Foster, Jack. The Chicken Farm. Finch, Jane. 2018. (Chickens Laugh Out Loud Ser.: Vol. 1). (ENG.). 38p. (J). (gr. k-4). pap. 9.99 *(978-1-68160-611-8(9))* Crimson Cloak Publishing.

—Cobbledom's Curse. Kennedy, J. Aday. 2012. 20p. pap. 9.95 *(978-1-61633-265-5(4))* Guardian Angel Publishing, Inc.

—Come Inside the Ark. Harrah, Judith. 2012. (J). pap. 17.99 *(978-1-937331-12-2(1))* ShadeTree Publishing, LLC.

—Doodle Girl. Reed, Jennifer Bond. 2012. 20p. pap. 9.95 *(978-1-61633-341-6(3))* Guardian Angel Publishing, Inc.

Foster, Jack. Five Minutes, Alfie. Walters, Lily Mae. 2020. (ENG.). 60p. (J). pap. 11.99 ***(978-1-68160-707-8(7))*** Crimson Cloak Publishing.

Foster, Jack. The Giving Plate. Tietz, Heather. l.t. ed. 2019. (ENG.). 16p. (J). (gr. k-3). pap. 9.95 *(978-1-61633-969-2(1))* Guardian Angel Publishing, Inc.

Foster, Jack. Happy Haiku. Crocket, Elizabeth. 2019. (ENG.). 36p. (J). pap. 9.99 ***(978-1-68160-692-7(5))*** Crimson Cloak Publishing.

Foster, Jack. Harriet's Heartbroken Heart. Belcastro, Lainie & Belcastro, Nika. l.t. ed. 2017. (ENG.). (J). (gr. -1-2). 10.95 *(978-1-61633-886-2(5))* Guardian Angel Publishing, Inc.

—Itcha Itcha Goo Goo Blues. Kennedy, J. Aday. 2012. 20p. pap. 10.95 *(978-1-61633-294-5(8))* Guardian Angel Publishing, Inc.

—Little Isaac's Big Adventure. Helixon, Tracy Schuldt. 2012. 16p. pap. 9.95 *(978-1-61633-321-8(9))* Guardian Angel Publishing, Inc.

—Lonnie the Lawnmower. Phillips, Dixie & Nolt, Rachel. l.t. ed. 2018. (ENG.). 16p. (J). pap. 9.95 *(978-1-61633-960-9(8))* Guardian Angel Publishing, Inc.

—One in a Buzzillion. Schreiber, Hannah & Hartsock, Conner. 2011. 16p. pap. 9.95 *(978-1-61633-154-2(2))* Guardian Angel Publishing, Inc.

—Ridiculously Ridiculous. Tucker, Susan K. 2012. 16p. pap. 9.95 *(978-1-61633-346-1(4))* Guardian Angel Publishing, Inc.

—Sh Sh Sh Let the Baby Sleep. Stemke, Kathy. 2011. 20p. pap. 10.95 *(978-1-61633-156-6(9))* Guardian Angel Publishing, Inc.

—Shoo Cat. Lyle-Soffe, Shari. 2010. 16p. pap. 9.95 *(978-1-61633-033-0(3))* Guardian Angel Publishing, Inc.

—Stella, the Fire Farting Dragon. Kennedy, J. Aday. 2011. 20p. pap. 10.95 *(978-1-61633-149-8(6))* Guardian Angel Publishing, Inc.

—Tootsie Mcpeezalot. Stanley, Sharon. l.t. ed. 2017. (ENG.). (J). pap. 9.95 *(978-1-61633-831-2(8))* Guardian Angel Publishing, Inc.

—Unbridled Joy. Stewart, Beth. 2018. (ENG.). 32p. (J). (gr. k-3). 18.99 *(978-0-9909447-3-7(5))*; pap. 15.99 *(978-0-9909447-1-3(9))* Bethstewartministries.

—You Ought to Be in Pig-Tures. Branning, Debe. l.t. ed. 2016. (Adventures of Chickolet Pigolet Ser.: Vol. 3). (ENG.). (J). (gr. 3-6). pap. 9.95 *(978-1-61633-813-8(X))* Guardian Angel Publishing, Inc.

—Zippy y Las Rayas de Valor. Sullivan, Candida. 2013. 40p. pap. 13.99 *(978-1-937331-51-1(2))* ShadeTree Publishing, LLC.

Foster, Janet. Elmer the Elf & the Magical Jingle Bells, 1 vol. Robinson, George. 2008. (ENG.). 33p. 24.95 *(978-1-60610-606-8(6))* America Star Bks.

Foster, jonathan. Sleep, 1 vol. Spiritworks. 2010. 18p. 24.95 *(978-1-4489-4930-4(0))* PublishAmerica, Inc.

Foster, Marcia Lane. Canadian Fairy Tales: [Illustrated Edition]. MacMillan, Cyrus. 2019. (ENG.). 234p. (J). (gr. k-4). pap. *(978-605-7876-32-4(6))* Uhrayoglu, Murat E Kitap Projesi.

Foster, Marcia Lane. Canadian Fairy Tales: [Illustrated Edition]. MacMillan, Cyrus. 2019. (ENG.). 234p. (J). (gr. k-4). ***(978-605-7748-56-0(5))*** Uhrayoglu, Murat E Kitap Projesi.

F

Foster, Michael K. The Donkey in the Living Room: A Tradition That Celebrates the Real Meaning of Christmas. Cunningham, Sarah. 2014. (ENG.). 32p. (J). (gr. -1-3). 14.99 *(978-1-4336-8317-6(2)*, 005615710, B&H Kids) B&H Publishing Group.

—The Donkey in the Living Room Nativity Set: A Tradition That Celebrates the True Meaning of Christmas. Cunningham, Sarah. 2014. (ENG.). 32p. (J). (gr. -1-3). 29.99 *(978-1-4336-8448-7(9)*, 005671261, B&H Kids) B&H Publishing Group.

Foster, Peggy. Wild Logging: Sustainable Forestry among Western Woodlot Owners. Foster, Bryan. rev. ed. 161p. (J). (gr. 4). pap. *(978-0-87842-448-1(2)*, 335) Mountain Pr. Publishing Co., Inc.

Foster, Ron. I Like Rain. 2007. 28p. (J). (gr. 1-4). *(978-1-929039-39-5(5))* Ambassador Bks., Inc.

—I Like Snow! 2006. 28p. (J). (gr. -1-3). *(978-1-929039-37-1(9))* Ambassador Bks., Inc.

—I Like Sunshine! O'Day, Joseph E. 2007. (J). *(978-1-929039-41-8(7))* Ambassador Bks., Inc.

—I Like Wind! Joseph, O'Day E. 2007. 28p. (J). (gr. -1-3). *(978-1-929039-42-5(5))* Ambassador Bks., Inc.

Foster, Teresa. Let's Learn French. Watson, Carol & Moyle, Philippa. 2003. (Let's Learn Ser.). (ENG.). 32p. pap. 9.95 *(978-0-7818-1014-2(0))* Hippocrene Bks., Inc.

Foster, Trista, photos by. Animals of the Ark: (for a boy named Clay) Reynolds, Loralyn & Caldwell, Christiana Marie Melvin. 2011. 36p. pap. 15.14 *(978-1-4634-3328-4(X))* AuthorHouse.

Foster, William. Nonsense Drolleries: The Owl & the Pussy-Cat, the Duck & the Kangaroo. Lear, Edward. 2007. 32p. pap. 10.95 *(978-1-60355-050-5(X))* Juniper Grove.

Foston, Desirae. The Hawaiian Hiatus of Herkimer Street. Foston, Desirae. 2013. 24p. 24.00 *(978-1-940021-00-3(6))* Bliss Group.

Fotheringham, Ed. Tony Baloney: Buddy Trouble. Ryan, Pam Muñoz. 2013. 38p. (J). pap. *(978-0-545-48170-0(8))* Scholastic, Inc.

—Tony Baloney: Pen Pal. Ryan, Pam Muñoz. 2014. 39p. (J). pap. *(978-0-545-69227-4(X)*, Scholastic Pr.) Scholastic, Inc.

—Yo Ho Ho, Halloween! Ryan, Pam Muñoz. 2015. 39p. (J). pap. *(978-0-545-91590-8(2))* Scholastic, Inc.

Fotheringham, Edwin. Big Sister, Little Monster. Rosenbaum, Andria Warmflash. 2017. (ENG.). 40p. (J). (gr. -1-3). 17.99 *(978-0-545-83192-5(X)*, Scholastic Pr.) Scholastic, Inc.

—Blue Grass Boy: The Story of Bill Monroe, Father of Bluegrass Music. Rosenstock, Barb. 2018. (ENG.). 40p. (J). (gr. 4-7). 17.95 *(978-1-62979-439-6(2)*, Calkins Creek) Boyds Mills Pr.

—The Extraordinary Mark Twain (According to Susy) Kerley, Barbara. 2010. 48p. (J). (gr. 2-6). 17.99 *(978-0-545-12508-6(1)*, Scholastic Pr.) Scholastic, Inc.

—The "Extrodinary" Mark Twain (According to Susy) Kerley, Barbara. 2010. (J). *(978-0-545-12509-3(X)*, Scholastic Pr.) Scholastic, Inc.

—Full of Beans: Henry Ford Grows a Car. Thomas, Peggy. 2019. (ENG.). 48p. (J). (gr. 2-5). 18.99 *(978-1-62979-639-0(5)*, Calkins Creek) Boyds Mills Pr.

—A Home for Mr. Emerson. Kerley, Barbara. 2014. (ENG.). 48p. (J). (gr. 3-7). 18.99 *(978-0-545-35088-4(3)*, Scholastic Pr.) Scholastic, Inc.

—Monkey & Duck Quack Up! Hamburg, Jennifer. 2015. (ENG.). 32p. (J). (gr. -1-3). 17.99 *(978-0-545-64514-0(X)*, Scholastic Pr.) Scholastic, Inc.

Fotheringham, Edwin. Most Wanted: The Revolutionary Partnership of John Hancock & Samuel Adams. Marsh, Sarah Jane. 2020. 80p. (J). (gr. 1-5). 19.99 ***(978-1-368-02683-3(4))*** Little, Brown Bks. for Young Readers.

Fotheringham, Edwin. Rescuing the Declaration of Independence: How We Almost Lost the Words That Built America. Redding, Anna Crowley. 2020. (ENG.). 40p. (J). (gr. -1-3). 18.99 *(978-0-06-274032-8(6)*, HarperCollins) HarperCollins Pubs. Ltd. GBR. Dist: HarperCollins Pubs.

—Those Rebels, John & Tom. Kerley, Barbara. 2012. (ENG.). 48p. (J). (gr. 2-5). 17.99 *(978-0-545-22268-6(0)*, Scholastic Pr.) Scholastic, Inc.

—Tony Baloney. Ryan, Pam Muñoz. 2011. (Tony Baloney Ser.). (ENG.). 40p. (J). (gr. -1-k). 17.99 *(978-0-545-23135-0(3)*, Scholastic Pr.) Scholastic, Inc.

—Tony Baloney: School Rules. Ryan, Pam Muñoz. 2012. (J). pap. *(978-0-545-48167-0(8))* Scholastic, Inc.

—Tony Baloney Yo Ho Ho, Halloween! Ryan, Pam Muñoz. 2016. (Tony Baloney Ser.). (ENG.). 40p. (J). (gr. k-2). 6.99 *(978-0-545-90885-6(X)*, Scholastic Pr.) Scholastic, Inc.

—What to Do about Alice? How Alice Roosevelt Broke the Rules, Charmed the World, & Drove Her Father Teddy Crazy! Kerley, Barbara. 2008. (ENG.). 48p. (J). (gr. 2-6). 16.99 *(978-0-439-92231-9(3)*, Scholastic Pr.) Scholastic, Inc.

Foti, Anthony J. Emma's New Beginning. Gunderson, Jessica. 2015. (U. S. Immigration in The 1900s Ser.). (ENG.). 96p. (J). (gr. 3-6). pap. 7.95 *(978-1-4965-0501-9(8)*, Stone Arch Bks.) Capstone.

—Mars for Humanity. Terrell, Brandon. 2015. (Exploring Space & Beyond Ser.). (ENG.). 96p. (J). (gr. 3-6). lib. bdg. 26.65 *(978-1-4965-0502-6(6)*, Stone Arch Bks.) Capstone.

Foti, Tony. Journey to Star Wars: the Rise of Skywalker Force Collector. Shinick, Kevin. 2019. (ENG.). 384p. (YA). (gr. 7-17). 17.99 *(978-1-368-04558-2(8)*, Disney Lucasfilm Press) Disney Publishing Worldwide.

Fotos, Jay, jt. illus. see Moreno, Chris.

Fougasse. J. Smith. Fougasse. 2015. (ENG.). 152p. (J). (gr. 5). 25.00 *(978-0-7636-7763-3(9))* Candlewick Pr.

Foulke, Nancy. How Many Spots Have I Got? McCabe, Lauren A. 2005. (J). 16.00 *(978-1-893516-02-1(4))* Our Child Pr.

Foulkes, Fiona, et al. Period Costume for Stage & Screen Vol. 5: Dominos, Dolmans, Coats, Pelisses, Spencers, Callashes, Hoods & Bonnets. Hunnisett, Jean. 2003. 176p. (gr. 8-12). 59.00 *(978-0-88734-670-5(7))* Players Pr., Inc.

Found, M. Tails of the Caygeon Cats. Coulter, Lynn. 2018. (ENG.). 54p. (J). pap. 12.95 *(978-1-7193-2002-3(0))* CreateSpace Independent Publishing Platform.

Found, Melina. Harry & Buster Go to the Cottage. Callingham, Darlene. 2019. (ENG.). 20p. (J). ***(978-1-5255-4949-6(9))***; pap. ***(978-1-5255-4950-2(2))*** FriesenPress.

Fountain, John. Birthday Wishes. Phillips, Leigh Hope. 2005. (J). pap. *(978-1-933156-10-1(4))*; per. *(978-1-933156-03-3(1))* GSVQ Publishing. (VisionQuest Kids).

Fouquier, Elsa. My First Book of Gymnastics: Movement Exercises for Young Children. Ouerghi, Rida. 2018. (My First Book of ... Ser.). (ENG.). 36p. (J). (gr. -1-1). 16.95 *(978-1-63322-629-6(8)*, Walter Foster Jr) Quarto Publishing Group USA.

—My First Book of Pilates: Pilates for Children. Ouerghi, Rida. 2018. (My First Book of ... Ser.). (ENG.). 30p. (J). (gr. -1-1). bds. 16.95 *(978-1-63322-589-3(5)*, Walter Foster Jr) Quarto Publishing Group USA.

Fournier, Laure. A Church for All. Pitman, Gayle E. 2018. (ENG.). 32p. (J). (gr. -1-k). 16.99 *(978-0-8075-1179-4(X)*, 080751179X) Whitman, Albert & Co.

—The Merchant & the Thief: A Folktale from India, 1 vol. Zacharias, Ravi. (ENG.). 32p. (J). 2020. pap. 10.99 *(978-0-310-76999-6(X))*; 2012. 15.99 *(978-0-310-71636-5(5))* Zonderkidz.

—Wake up, City! Silverman, Erica. 2016. (ENG.). 32p. (J). (gr. -1-3). 16.99 *(978-1-4998-0173-6(4))* Little Bee Books Inc.

Fowkes, Charlie. Harry the Clever Spider at School: Band 07/Turquoise (Collins Big Cat) Jarman, Julia. 2007. (Collins Big Cat Ser.). (ENG.). 24p. (J). (gr. 1-2). pap. 6.99 *(978-0-00-718670-9(3))* HarperCollins Pubs. Ltd. GBR. Dist: Independent Pubs. Group.

Fowler, Charlie, photos by. Mountain Star: A Story about a Mountaineer That Will Teach You How to Draw a Star! Fowler Hicks, Ginny. 2008. 24p. (J). 18.95 *(978-0-9763309-3-6(8))* Mountain World Media LLC.

Fowler, Claire. My Sister Saarah. Talhah, Abu & Books, Greenbird. 2013. 30p. pap. *(978-0-9576379-6-2(9))* Greenbird Bks.

Fowler, Eleri. Bold Springtime to Color: Coloring Book for Adults & Kids to Share. Fowler, Eleri. 2017. (ENG.). 96p. (J). (gr. -1). pap. 15.99 *(978-0-06-256996-7(1))* HarperCollins Pubs.

—My Mother, My Heart: A Joyful Book to Color. Fowler, Eleri. 2016. (ENG.). 96p. (J). (gr. -1). pap. 15.99 *(978-0-06-247938-9(5))* HarperCollins Pubs.

—Words of Love to Color: Sweet Thoughts to Live & Color By. Fowler, Eleri. 2016. (ENG.). 96p. (J). (gr. -1). pap. 15.99 *(978-0-06-256608-9(3))* HarperCollins Pubs.

Fowler, Elizabeth. Luke & Nana, 1 vol. Whitby, Rozene. 2010. 16p. 24.95 *(978-1-4489-3826-1(0))* PublishAmerica, Inc.

Fowler, Faith. Sissy Goes to Washington. Goguen, Martha. 2013. 36p. pap. *(978-1-897435-59-5(2))* Agio Publishing Hse.

Fowler, Jason. Meet Mutzie. Parrish, Amanda. 2018. (ENG.). 28p. (J). (gr. k-4). 24.95 *(978-1-61493-599-5(8))* Peppertree Pr., The.

Fowler, Jim. Arctic Aesop's Fables: Twelve Retold Tales. Fowler, Susi Gregg. 2013. (Paws IV Ser.). 32p. (J). (gr. 1-4). pap. 10.99 *(978-1-57061-861-1(5)*, Little Bigfoot) Sasquatch Bks.

—Patsy Ann of Alaska: The True Story of a Dog. Brown, Tricia. 2011. (Paws IV Ser.). 32p. (J). (gr. -1-2). pap. 10.99 *(978-1-57061-697-6(3)*, Little Bigfoot) Sasquatch Bks.

Fowler, Richard. The Toy Cupboard. Wood, David. 2005. 14p. (J). (gr. -1-3). 14.95 *(978-1-58117-103-7(X)*, Intervisual/Piggy Toes) Bendon, Inc.

Fowler, Romana, jt. illus. see Martins, Ann-Kathrin.

Fowler, Rosamund. Home for a Tiger, Home for a Bear. Williams, Brenda. (ENG.). 32p. (J). 2017. (gr. -1-1). pap. 8.99 *(978-1-78285-343-5(X))*; 2009. pap. 7.99 *(978-1-84686-353-0(8))* Barefoot Bks., Inc.

Fowler, Tom. Hulk: Incredible Origins. 2019. (ENG.). 136p. (YA). (gr. 8-17). pap. 15.99 *(978-0-7851-6392-3(1))* Marvel Worldwide, Inc.

Fowles, Shelley. The Most Magnificent Mosque. Jungman, Ann. 2007. (ENG.). 32p. (J). (gr. 1-4). 8.99 *(978-1-84507-085-4(2)*, Frances Lincoln Children's Bks.) Quarto Publishing Group UK GBR. Dist: Hachette Bk. Group.

Fowlkes, Christopher M. Waves of Darkness. Logan, Maggie. 2020. (ENG.). 84p. (YA). ***(978-1-5255-5704-0(1))***; pap. ***(978-1-5255-5705-7(X))*** FriesenPress.

Fox, Carolyn a. Ruby & Ralph Take a Chance. Reeser, Anna Mae. 2013. (ENG.). 38p. (J). pap. 15.00 ***(978-0-9831191-6-6(3))*** Learning Line Media, The.

Fox, Charles Philip, photos by. Sweet Sue's Adventures. Campbell, Sam. 2010. 119p. reprint ed. pap. 10.95 *(978-1-57258-210-1(3))* TEACH Services, Inc.

Fox, Christyan. Cat & Dog's Alphabet. Fox, Diane. 2020. (ENG.). 32p. (J). (gr. -1-3). 16.99 ***(978-0-8075-1096-4(3)***, 807510963) Whitman, Albert & Co.

Fox, Christyan. The Cat, the Dog, Little Red, the Exploding Eggs, the Wolf, & Grandma. Fox, Diane. 2014. (ENG.). 32p. (J). (gr. -1-3). 16.99 *(978-0-545-69481-0(7)*, Scholastic Pr.) Scholastic, Inc.

—Cats & Kittens. Burton, Jane, photos by. Starke, Katherine & Watt, Fiona. 2006. 30p. (J). pap. *(978-0-439-78492-4(1))* Scholastic, Inc.

—Creaky Castle. Clarke, Jane. 2013. *(978-1-4351-4951-9(3))* Barnes & Noble, Inc.

—Dogs & Puppies. Starke, Katherine & Watt, Fiona. 2004. 31p. (J). *(978-0-439-78715-4(7))* Scholastic, Inc.

—Farm Animals. Daynes, Katie. 2006. (Beginners Nature: Level 1 Ser.). 32p. (J). (gr. k-2). 4.99 *(978-0-7945-1396-2(4)*, Usborne) EDC Publishing.

—Firefighters. Daynes Katie et al. 2006. (Usborne Beginners Ser.). 32p. (J). *(978-0-439-88992-6(8))* Scholastic, Inc.

—Firefighters. Daynes, Katie. 2007. (Beginners Social Studies). 32p. (J). (gr. -1-3). 4.99 *(978-0-7945-1658-1(0)*, Usborne) EDC Publishing.

—Gerbils. Burton, Jane, photos by. Howell, Laura. 2005. (Usborne First Pets Ser.). 32p. (J). (gr. k-4). pap. 5.95 *(978-0-7945-1116-6(3)*, Usborne) EDC Publishing.

—Guinea Pigs. Burton, James, photos by. Howell, Laura. 2005. (Usborne First Pets Ser.). 32p. (J). (gr. k-4). pap. 5.95 *(978-0-7945-1115-9(5)*, Usborne) EDC Publishing.

—Hamsters. Meredith, Susan et al. 2004. 30p. (J). *(978-0-439-78698-0(3))* Scholastic, Inc.

—Pirate Adventures. Punter, Russell. 2007. (Usborne Young Reading: Series One Ser.). 48p. (J). (gr. 2). 13.99 *(978-1-58086-985-0(8))*; (gr. 4-7). pap. 5.99 *(978-0-7945-1447-1(2))* EDC Publishing. (Usborne).

—Trash & Recycling. Turnbull, Stephanie. 2006. (Beginners Science: Level 2 Ser.). 32p. (J). (gr. 1-3). 4.99 *(978-0-7945-1400-6(6)*, Usborne) EDC Publishing.

—Understanding Your Brain - Internet Linked. Treays, Rebecca. rev. ed. 2004. (Science for Beginners Ser.). 32p. (J). pap. 7.95 *(978-0-7945-0853-1(7)*, Usborne) EDC Publishing.

—Understanding Your Muscles & Bones: Internet-Linked. Treays, Rebecca. rev. ed. 2006. (Usborne Science for Beginners Ser.). 32p. (J). (gr. 3-7). per. 7.99 *(978-0-7945-0813-5(8)*, Usborne) EDC Publishing.

—Understanding Your Senses - Internet Linked. Treays, Rebecca. rev. ed. 2004. (Science for Beginners Ser.). 32p. (J). pap. 7.95 *(978-0-7945-0852-4(9)*, Usborne) EDC Publishing.

—Wind-Up Pirate Ship. Stowell, Louie. 2010. (Wind-up Bks). 13p. (J). bds. 29.99 *(978-0-7945-2835-5(X)*, Usborne) EDC Publishing.

Fox, Christyan & Fox, Diane. Enzo the Racing Car. Fox, Christyan & Fox, Diane. 2008. (Wheelyworld Ser.). (ENG.). 32p. (J). (gr. -1-k). pap. 8.95 *(978-1-4052-2742-1(7))* Egmont Bks., Ltd. GBR. Dist: Independent Pubs. Group.

—Monty the Rally Car. Fox, Christyan & Fox, Diane. 2008. (Wheelyworld Ser.). (ENG.). 32p. (J). (gr. -1-k). pap. 8.95 *(978-1-4052-2743-8(5))* Egmont Bks., Ltd. GBR. Dist: Independent Pubs. Group.

Fox, Christyan & Pang, Alex. Life in Space. Daynes, Katie & Wray, Zoe. 2008. (Usborne Beginners Ser.). 32p. (J). *(978-0-545-06963-2(7))* Scholastic, Inc.

—Living in Space. Daynes, Katie. 2003. (Usborne Beginners Ser.). 32p. (J). (gr. 1). lib. bdg. 12.99 *(978-1-58086-930-0(0)*, Usborne) EDC Publishing.

Fox, Christyan, jt. illus. see Donaera, Patrizia.

Fox, Christyan, jt. illus. see Wray, Zoe.

Fox, Culpeo. A Tangle of Brungles. Viswanath, Shobha. 2018. (ENG.). 34p. (J). 15.95 *(978-81-8190-360-0(9))* Karadi Tales Co. Pvt. Ltd. IND. Dist: Consortium Bk. Sales & Distribution.

Fox-Davies, Sarah. Bat Loves the Night. Davies, Nicola. 2008. (Read, Listen, & Wonder Ser.). (ENG.). 32p. (J). (gr. -1-3). pap. 8.99 *(978-0-7636-3863-4(3))* Candlewick Pr.

—Bat Loves the Night. Davies, Nicola. 2006. (Read & Wonder Ser.). 17.00 *(978-0-7569-6561-7(6))* Perfection Learning Corp.

—Bat Loves the Night: Read & Wonder. Davies, Nicola. 2004. (Read & Wonder Ser.). (ENG.). 32p. (J). (gr. -1-3). pap. 7.99 *(978-0-7636-2438-5(1))* Candlewick Pr.

—Walk with a Wolf: Read, Listen & Wonder. Howker, Janni. 2008. (Read, Listen, & Wonder Ser.). (ENG.). 32p. (J). (gr. -1-3). pap. 8.99 *(978-0-7636-3875-7(7))* Candlewick Pr.

Fox, Diane, jt. illus. see Fox, Christyan.

Fox, Emily. Fabio the World's Greatest Flamingo Detective: Mystery on the Ostrich Express. James, Laura. 2020. (ENG.). 128p. (J). 16.99 *(978-1-5476-0459-3(X)*, 900223954); pap. 6.99 *(978-1-5476-0458-6(1)*, 900223951) Bloomsbury Publishing USA. (Bloomsbury Children's Bks.).

—Fabio the World's Greatest Flamingo Detective: the Case of the Missing Hippo. James, Laura. 2019. (ENG.). 144p. (J). 16.99 *(978-1-5476-0217-9(1)*, 900203642); pap. 6.99 *(978-1-5476-0216-2(3)*, 900203643) Bloomsbury Publishing USA. (Bloomsbury Children's Bks.).

Fox, Heather. Don't Feed the Coos! Stutzman, Jonathan. 2020. (ENG.). 48p. (J). 17.99 *(978-1-250-30318-9(4)*, 900197053, Holt, Henry & Co. Bks. For Young Readers) Holt, Henry & Co.

—Llama Destroys the World. Stutzman, Jonathan. 2019. (Llama Book Ser.: 1). (ENG.). 40p. (J). 17.99 *(978-1-250-30317-2(6)*, 900197052, Holt, Henry & Co. Bks. For Young Readers) Holt, Henry & Co.

—Llama Unleashes the Alpacalypse. Stutzman, Jonathan. 2020. (Llama Book Ser.: 2). (ENG.). 40p. (J). 18.99 *(978-1-250-22285-5(0)*, 900208101, Holt, Henry & Co. Bks. For Young Readers) Holt, Henry & Co.

Fox, Heather. Santa Baby. Stutzman, Jonathan. 2020. (ENG.). 48p. (J). 18.99 ***(978-1-250-25561-7(9)***, 900219014, Holt, Henry & Co. Bks. For Young Readers) Holt, Henry & Co.

Fox, Holly, photos by. The Cookie Book of Colors. 2020. (ENG., 14p. (J). (-k). bds. 7.99 *(978-0-593-09319-1(4)*, Penguin Workshop) Penguin Young Readers Group.

Fox, Jim. Babies Nurse. Fox, Phoebe. 2018. (ENG.). 32p. (J). (gr. -1-2). 14.95 *(978-1-930775-61-9(X))*; pap. 9.95 *(978-1-930775-71-8(7))* Platypus Media, L.L.C.

—Babies Nurse / Así Se Alimentan Los Bebés. Fox, Phoebe. Geating, Karen Rivera, tr. 2018. (ENG.). 32p. (J). (gr. -1-2). 14.95 *(978-1-930775-73-2(3))*; pap. 9.95 *(978-1-930775-72-5(5))* Platypus Media, L.L.C.

Fox, Kat. Alphabet Job Buddies. Weaver, Karen. 2019. (ENG.). 32p. (J). pap. *(978-0-6485378-1-6(1))*; *(978-0-9954104-0-4(2))* Serenity Press.

—Minky Monkey Meets Alex the Astronaut. Weaver, Karen. 2019. (ENG.). 20p. (J). pap. *(978-0-6485891-4-3(5))* Serenity Press.

Fox, Kat. Minky Monkey Meets Barney the Brickie. Weaver, Karen. 2019. (ENG.). 20p. (J). pap. ***(978-0-6485378-0-9(3))*** Serenity Press.

Fox, Lisa. Josie the Giraffe & the Starry Night. Baxter, Nicola. 2016. (ENG.). 16p. (J). (gr. -1-12). 7.99 *(978-0-85723-526-8(5)*, Armadillo) Anness Publishing GBR. Dist: National Bk. Network.

—Noah's Ark. McCombs, Margi. 2014. (ENG.). 10p. (J). (gr. -1-k). bds. 7.99 *(978-0-545-60557-1(1)*, Little Shepherd) Scholastic, Inc.

—You Go Away. Corey, Dorothy. 2010. (ENG.). 16p. (J). (gr. -1 — 1). bds. 7.99 *(978-0-8075-9440-7(7)*, 807594407) Whitman, Albert & Co.

Fox, Matt. Color Your Own Dinosaur! Fox, Matt. Photography, Northridge. 2018. (ENG.). 40p. (J). pap. 8.98 *(978-1-7920-6177-6(3))* Independently Published.

—Yeti & the Mountaineer. Fox, Matt. 2018. (ENG.). 70p. (J). pap. 14.98 *(978-1-7201-3523-4(1))* Independently Published.

Fox, Nathan. Dogs of War. Keenan, Sheila. 2013. 176p. (J). (gr. 3-7). pap. 14.99 *(978-0-545-12888-9(9)*, Graphix) Scholastic, Inc.

Fox, Peter, photos by. Insectos Insolitos. Hutnick, Theresa & Phillips, Karen. 2005. (SPA., 38p. (J). spiral bd. 17.95 *(978-987-1078-43-1(9))* Klutz Latino MEX. Dist: Independent Pubs. Group.

Fox, Rebecca. Circle. Smallwood, Sally & Jones, Bryony. 2011. (Shapes Are Fun Ser.). (ENG.). 24p. (J). (gr. k — 1). bds. *(978-1-84089-610-7(8))* Zero to Ten, Ltd.

—Rectangle. Smallwood, Sally & Jones, Bryony. 2011. (Shapes Are Fun Ser.). (ENG.). 14p. (J). (gr. k — 1). bds. *(978-1-84089-613-8(2))* Zero to Ten, Ltd.

—Square. Smallwood, Sally & Jones, Bryony. 2011. (Shapes Are Fun Ser.). (ENG.). 14p. (J). (gr. k — 1). bds. *(978-1-84089-612-1(4))* Zero to Ten, Ltd.

—Triangle. Smallwood, Sally & Jones, Bryony. 2011. (Shapes Are Fun Ser.). (ENG.). 14p. (J). (gr. k — 1). bds. *(978-1-84089-611-4(6))* Zero to Ten, Ltd.

Fox, Tahna Desmond. The Gift. Kritz, Khristian. 2020. (ENG.). 40p. (J). 24.00 ***(978-1-938505-50-8(6))*** Lionheart Group Publishing.

—The Gift. Kritz, Khristian. 2020. (ENG.). 40p. (J). pap. 14.42 ***(978-1-938505-51-5(4))*** Lionheart Group Publishing.

Fox, Tahna Desmond. What Does a Hero Look Like? Linhart, Sandra Miller. 2016. (ENG.). 53p. (J). (gr. -1-6). 16.05 *(978-1-938505-02-7(6))* Lionheart Group Publishing.

Fox, Tom Paul. Bullying Is Wrong. Anderson, Georgia Lee. 2012. (ENG.). 26p. pap. 14.95 *(978-1-57258-882-0(9)*, Aspect Bk.) TEACH Services, Inc.

Fox, Will. Bertie Bolt. Fox, Will. 2013. (ENG.). 20p. (J). pap. 6.04 *(978-1-908865-20-5(2))* Beecroft Publishing GBR. Dist: Ingram Content Group.

—Billy Brush. Fox, Will. 2013. (ENG.). 20p. (J). pap. 6.04 *(978-1-908865-25-0(3))* Beecroft Publishing GBR. Dist: Ingram Content Group.

—Hector Hacksaw. Fox, Will. 2013. (ENG.). 20p. (J). pap. 6.04 *(978-1-908865-28-1(8))* Beecroft Publishing GBR. Dist: Ingram Content Group.

—Molly Mallet. Fox, Will. 2013. (ENG.). 20p. (J). pap. 6.04 *(978-1-908865-27-4(X))* Beecroft Publishing GBR. Dist: Ingram Content Group.

—Peggy Peg. Fox, Will. 2013. (ENG.). 20p. (J). pap. 6.04 *(978-1-908865-22-9(9))* Beecroft Publishing GBR. Dist: Ingram Content Group.

—Rusty Nail. Fox, Will. 2013. (ENG.). 20p. (J). pap. 6.04 *(978-1-908865-21-2(0))* Beecroft Publishing GBR. Dist: Ingram Content Group.

—Sally Screw. Fox, Will. 2013. (ENG.). 20p. (J). pap. 6.04 *(978-1-908865-23-6(7))* Beecroft Publishing GBR. Dist: Ingram Content Group.

—Spiky Saw. Fox, Will. 2013. (ENG.). 16p. (J). pap. 6.04 *(978-1-908865-26-7(1))* Beecroft Publishing GBR. Dist: Ingram Content Group.

—Suzy Scissors. Fox, Will. 2013. (ENG.). 20p. (J). pap. 6.04 *(978-1-908865-29-8(6))* Beecroft Publishing GBR. Dist: Ingram Content Group.

—Twisty Drill. Fox, Will. 2013. (ENG.). 16p. (J). pap. 6.04 *(978-1-908865-24-3(5))* Beecroft Publishing GBR. Dist: Ingram Content Group.

Fox, Woody. Alice Again. Curtin, Judi. 2006. (ENG.). 240p. (J). pap. 12.95 *(978-0-86278-956-5(7))* O'Brien Pr., Ltd., The IRL. Dist: Dufour Editions, Inc.

—Alice & Megan Forever. Curtin, Judi. 2nd rev. ed. 2015. (Alice & Megan Ser.: 6). (ENG.). 288p. (J). pap. 14.00 *(978-1-84717-690-5(9))* O'Brien Pr., Ltd., The IRL. Dist: Casemate Pubs. & Bk. Distributors, LLC.

—Alice in the Middle. Curtin, Judi. (ENG.). 256p. (J). 2007. pap. 12.95 *(978-1-84717-038-5(2))*; 2nd rev. ed. 2014. (Alice & Megan Ser.: 4). 14.00 *(978-1-84717-673-8(9))* O'Brien Pr., Ltd., The IRL. Dist: Dufour Editions, Inc., Casemate Pubs. & Bk. Distributors, LLC.

—Alice Next Door. Curtin, Judi. 2005. (ENG.). 208p. (J). pap. 12.95 *(978-0-86278-898-8(6))* O'Brien Pr., Ltd., The IRL. Dist: Dufour Editions, Inc.

—Alice to the Rescue. Curtin, Judi. 2015. (Alice & Megan Ser.: 7). (ENG.). 272p. (J). pap. 14.00 *(978-1-84717-691-2(7))* O'Brien Pr., Ltd., The IRL. Dist: Casemate Pubs. & Bk. Distributors, LLC.

—Bonjour Alice. Curtin, Judi. 2015. (Alice & Megan Ser.: 5). (ENG.). 256p. (J). pap. 14.00 *(978-1-84717-689-9(5))* O'Brien Pr., Ltd., The IRL. Dist: Casemate Pubs. & Bk. Distributors, LLC.

—Collins Big Cat Phonics for Letters & Sounds - Where Did My Dingo Go?: Band 05/Green, Bd. 5. Clarke, Jane. 2018. (Collins Big Cat Phonics Ser.). (ENG.). 24p. (J). (gr. k-1). pap. 6.99 *(978-0-00-825168-0(1))* HarperCollins Pubs. Ltd. GBR. Dist: Independent Pubs. Group.

—Don't Ask Alice. Curtin, Judi. (ENG.). 256p. (J). 2007. pap. 12.95 *(978-1-84717-023-1(4))*; 2nd rev. ed. 2014. (Alice & Megan Ser.: 3). 14.00 *(978-1-84717-672-1(0))* O'Brien Pr., Ltd., The IRL. Dist: Dufour Editions, Inc., Casemate Pubs. & Bk. Distributors, LLC.

—Emma Says Boo. Donovan, Anna. 2003. (Panda Cubs Ser.: 03). (ENG.). 48p. (J). pap. 9.95 *(978-0-86278-795-0(5))* O'Brien Pr., Ltd., The IRL. Dist: Dufour Editions, Inc.

—Emma Says Oops! Donovan, Anna. 2004. (Panda Cubs Ser.: 04). (ENG.). 48p. (J). pap. 9.95 *(978-0-86278-902-2(8))* O'Brien Pr., Ltd., The IRL. Dist: Dufour Editions, Inc.

—Eva & the Hidden Diary. Curtin, Judi. 2013. (Eva Ser.: 4). (ENG.). 240p. (J). pap. 15.00 *(978-1-84717-588-5(0))*

O'Brien Pr., Ltd., The IRL. Dist: Casemate Pubs. & Bk. Distributors, LLC.
—A One-Octopus Band. Boelts, Maribeth. 2016. (Spring Forward Ser.). (J). (gr. 1). *(978-1-4900-9379-6(6))* Benchmark Education Co.
—What Do Rabbits Think? And Other Fun Poems for Kids. Reddin, Brian. 2006. (ENG.). 64p. (J). pap. 17.95 *(978-1-85635-517-9(9))* Mercier Pr., Ltd., The IRL. Dist: Dufour Editions, Inc.
Foy, Denis. Dear God, Are There Any Flies in Heaven? Gallina, Danielle. 2013. (ENG.). (J). 15.98 *(978-1-62086-380-0(4))* Mascot Bks., Inc.
Foye, Jon. I Got This Hat. Temple, Jol & Temple, Kate. 2015. 32p. (J). 17.99 *(978-0-7333-3206-7(4))* ABC Children's Bks. AUS. Dist: HarperCollins Pubs.
Foye, Lloyd. Basketball Showdown. Arena, Jacqueline. 2005. (Girlz Rock! Ser.). (J). pap. *(978-1-59336-704-6(X))* Mondo Publishing.
—Bowling Buddies. Dinbergs, Holly Smith. 2005. (Girlz Rock! Ser.). (J). pap. *(978-1-59336-699-5(X))* Mondo Publishing.
—The Sleepover. Mullins, Julie. 2005. (Girlz Rock! Ser.). (J). pap. *(978-1-59336-707-7(4))* Mondo Publishing.
Fra, Irene. Los Inventores de Cuentos. García-Castellano, Ana. 2009. (SPA.). 76p. (J). (gr. 3-6). pap. *(978-607-11-0102-0(6))* Aguilar, Altea, Taurus, Alfaguara, S.A. de C.V.
Fragakis, Katie. The Hanger Family: A New Day. Mengarelli, Tom. 2020. (ENG.). 44p. (J). pap. 10.00 ***(978-1-7036-2772-5(5))*** Independently Published.
Fraggalosch, Crista. Northern Refuge: A Story of a Canadian Boreal Forest. Fraggalosch, Audrey. 2005. (Soundprints' Wild Habitats Ser.). (ENG.). 36p. (J). (gr. 1-4). 8.95 *(978-1-59249-100-1(6),* SC7012) Soundprints.
Fragoso, Jose. La Princesa Sara No Para. del Mazo, Margarita. 2020. (SPA.). 40p. (J). 16.95 *(978-84-17123-82-6(2))* NubeOcho Ediciones ESP. Dist: Consortium Bk. Sales & Distribution.
—Princess Jill Never Sits Still. del Mazo, Margarita. 2020. (ENG.). 40p. (J). 16.95 *(978-84-17123-83-3(0))* NubeOcho Ediciones ESP. Dist: Consortium Bk. Sales & Distribution.
Frahm, Paul. A Staten Island Ferry Tale. St Jean, Catherine Avery. 2006. 32p. (J). per. 26.99 *(978-1-4134-0262-9(3))* Xlibris Corp.
Fraizer, Pam. Body Talk. Combs, Lisa. 2019. (ENG.). 38p. (J). pap. 9.95 ***(978-1-7229-4910-5(4))*** CreateSpace Independent Publishing Platform.
Fraizer, Pam. Think Like a Yeti. Combs, Lisa. 2019. (ENG.). 32p. (J). pap. 9.95 *(978-1-7278-2789-7(9))* CreateSpace Independent Publishing Platform.
Frake, Barbara. Tales from Falmac Farm. Falcone, Karen. 2005. (ENG.). 47p. (J). per. *(978-1-933002-08-8(5))* PublishingWorks.
Framestore. The Creature Department. Weston, Robert Paul. 2014. (Creature Department Ser.: 1). (ENG.). 352p. (J). (gr. 3-7). pap. 8.99 *(978-1-59514-684-7(9),* Razorbill) Penguin Young Readers Group.
Frampton, David. At Jerusalem's Gate: Poems of Easter. Grimes, Nikki. 2005. 48p. (J). 20.00 *(978-0-8028-5183-3(5))* Eerdmans, William B. Publishing Co.
—The Song of Francis & the Animals. Mora, Pat. 2005. 32p. (J). (gr. -1-2). 16.00 *(978-0-8028-5253-3(X))* Eerdmans, William B. Publishing Co.
Frampton, David. Beastie ABC. Frampton, David. Date not set. 32p. (J). (gr. -1-1). pap. 5.99 *(978-0-06-443653-3(5))* HarperCollins Pubs.
—Mr. Ferlinghetti's Poem. Frampton, David. 2006. 32p. (J). (gr. k-4). 18.00 *(978-0-8028-5290-8(4),* Eerdmans Bks For Young Readers) Eerdmans, William B. Publishing Co.
—The Whole Night Through. Frampton, David. Date not set. 32p. (J). (gr. -1-1). pap. 5.99 *(978-0-06-443652-6(7))* HarperCollins Pubs.
—The Whole Night Through: A Lullaby. Frampton, David. 2004. 30p. (J). (gr. k-4). reprint ed. *(978-0-7567-7723-4(2))* DIANE Publishing Co.
Frampton, Otis. Beauty & the Dreaded Sea Beast: A Graphic Novel. Simonson, Louise. 2019. (Far Out Fairy Tales Ser.). (ENG.). 40p. (J). (gr. 3-6). pap. 5.95 *(978-1-4965-8442-7(2),* 140967); lib. bdg. 25.32 *(978-1-4965-8393-2(0),* 140684) Capstone. (Stone Arch Bks.).
Frampton, Otis, et al. Far Out Fairy Tales. Simonson, Louise et al. 2016. (Far Out Fairy Tales Ser.). (ENG.). 176p. (J). (gr. 3-6). pap. 12.95 *(978-1-4965-2511-6(6),* Stone Arch Bks.) Capstone.
Frampton, Otis. The Ginger-Red Caterpillar: A Graphic Novel. Harper, Benjamin. 2020. (Far Out Fairy Tales Ser.). (ENG.). 40p. (J). (gr. 3-6). pap. 5.95 ***(978-1-4965-9905-6(5),*** 201316); lib. bdg. 25.32 ***(978-1-4965-9683-3(8),*** 199248) Capstone. (Stone Arch Bks.).
Frampton, Otis. Paul Bunyan & Babe the Blue Whale: A Graphic Novel. Gruber, Penelope. 2019. (Far Out Folktales Ser.). (ENG.). 40p. (J). (gr. 3-6). lib. bdg. 25.32 *(978-1-4965-7842-6(2),* 139308, Stone Arch Bks.) Capstone.
—Soul Mates. Downer, Denise. 2013. (Tombstone Twins Ser.). (ENG.). 48p. (J). (gr. 3-5). lib. bdg. 23.99 *(978-1-4342-2248-0(9),* Stone Arch Bks.) Capstone.
—Tombstone Twins: Soul Mates, 1 vol. Downer, Denise. 2013. (Tombstone Twins Ser.). (ENG.). 48p. (J). (gr. 3-5). pap. 5.95 *(978-1-4342-3873-3(3),* Stone Arch Bks.) Capstone.
—Tombstone Twins Package: Soul Mates. Downer, Denise. 2013. (ENG.). 41p. (J). (gr. 2-4). pap. 35.70 *(978-1-4342-3955-6(1),* Stone Arch Bks.) Capstone.
—The Ugly Dino Hatchling: A Graphic Novel. Peters, Stephanie. 2017. (Far Out Fables Ser.). (ENG.). 40p. (J). (gr. 3-6). pap. 4.95 *(978-1-4965-5423-9(X),* 136356); lib. bdg. 25.32 *(978-1-4965-5419-2(1),* 136352) Capstone. (Stone Arch Bks.).
—Walt Disney: the Magical Innovator! Shulman, Mark. 2020. (Show Me History! Ser.). (ENG.). 96p. (J). (gr. 3-7). 12.99 *(978-1-64517-075-4(6),* Portable Pr.) Printers Row Publishing Group.
Frampton, Otis. Caperuza Roja, la Superheroína: Una Novela Gráfica. Frampton, Otis. 2020. (Cuentos de Hadas Futuristas Ser.).Tr. of Red Riding Hood, Superhero: a Graphic Novel. (SPA.). 40p. (J). (gr. 3-6). pap. 5.95 ***(978-1-4965-9959-9(4),*** 201605); lib. bdg. 25.32 ***(978-1-4965-9813-4(X),*** 200701) Capstone. (Stone Arch Bks.).
Frampton, Otis. Red Riding Hood, Superhero: A Graphic Novel. Frampton, Otis. 2015. (Far Out Fairy Tales Ser.). (ENG.). 40p. (J). (gr. 3-6). lib. bdg. 25.32 *(978-1-4342-9650-4(4),* Stone Arch Bks.) Capstone.
Frampton, Otis & Lozano, Omar. Cuentos de Hadas Futuristas. Comeau, Joey & Frampton, Otis. 2020. (Cuentos de Hadas Futuristas Ser.).Tr. of Far Out Fairy Tales. (SPA.). (J). (gr. 3-6). 101.28 ***(978-1-4965-9829-5(6),*** 200729); pap., pap., pap. 23.80 ***(978-1-5158-7349-5(8),*** 201806) Capstone. (Stone Arch Bks.).
Francavilla, Francesco. Cry of the Banshee! Ciencin, Scott. 2008. 48p. (J). pap. *(978-0-545-03981-9(9))* Scholastic, Inc.
—Escape from Blackbeard's Curse! Ciencin, Scott. 2007. 48p. (J). pap. *(978-0-545-03767-9(0))* Scholastic, Inc.
Francavilla, Francesco, et al. Star Wars Adventures: Return to Vader's Castle. Scott, Cavan. 2020. (Star Wars Adventures Ser.). (ENG.). 120p. (J). (gr. 4-7). pap. 14.99 *(978-1-68405-667-5(5))* Idea & Design Works, LLC.
France, Mark. The Horsosaurus. Stanley, Dean. 2008. 32p. pap. 14.62 *(978-1-4251-8158-1(9))* Trafford Publishing.
Francey, Amanda. That Christmas Feeling. Wilkinson, Lili. 2018. (ENG.). 32p. (J). (gr. -1). 17.99 *(978-1-76029-496-0(9))* Allen & Unwin AUS. Dist: Independent Pubs. Group.
Francine Ngardab, Riches. What Makes a Tree Smile? Pitt, Tamina & Terri, Janke. 2003. (Uupababa Ser.). 24p. (J). pap. *(978-1-875641-80-2(7))* Magabala Bks.
Francis, Amber Rose. Jeanettie Is Called Retard, 1 vol. Blackmore, Charlotte Lozano. 2010. 34p. 24.95 *(978-1-4489-4096-7(6))* PublishAmerica, Inc.
Francis, Cheryl. Gratitude Journal & Coloring Book for Kids: A Few Minutes a Day to Create the Habit & Attitude of Gratitude. Change, Journal for. 2020. (ENG.). 168p. (J). pap. 7.99 ***(978-1-6541-8075-1(0))*** Independently Published.
Francis, Cheryl. Journal: Lots of Ideas Lined Paper Blank Pages (Notebook, Diary) Francis, Cheryl. 2018. (ENG.). 122p. (J). pap. 8.99 *(978-1-7294-4973-8(5))* Independently Published.
Francis, Chris. Poopy Patinski's Green Egg Adventure. Graham, Scott. 2018. (ENG.). 114p. (J). *(978-1-5255-3032-6(1));* pap. *(978-1-5255-3033-3(X))* FriesenPress.
Francis, David. A Rat in a Stripy Sock. Watts, Frances. 2018. 24p. pap. 6.99 *(978-0-7333-3460-3(1))* ABC Bks. AUS. Dist: HarperCollins Pubs.
Francis, Dwight. La Fresa. Nunez, Jaclyn. 2016. (Early Rising Readers Ser.). (SPA.). 16p. (J). (gr. 1-1). 6.67 *(978-1-4788-4201-9(6))* Newmark Learning LLC.
—Pecos Bill y Sluefoot Sue. Blane, Antonio. 2016. (Jump into Genre Ser.). (SPA.). (J). (gr. 3). 5.25 *(978-1-4788-3617-9(2))* Newmark Learning LLC.
—La Piloto Annie Hace Justicia. Blane, Antonio. 2016. (Jump into Genre Ser.). (SPA.). (J). (gr. 3). 5.25 *(978-1-4788-3616-2(4))* Newmark Learning LLC.
Francis, Guy. The Alien, the Giant, & Rocketman. Perry, Phyllis Jean. 2006. (J). pap. *(978-1-59336-723-7(6))* Mondo Publishing.
—Betsy Ross's Star, 8. Deutsch, Stacia & Cohon, Rhody. 2006. (Blast to the Past Ser.: 8). (ENG.). 121p. (J). (gr. 3-6). 16.19 *(978-1-4169-3388-5(3))* Simon & Schuster, Inc.
—Betsy Ross's Star. Deutsch, Stacia & Cohon, Rhody. 2015. (Blast to the Past Ser.: 8). (ENG.). 128p. (J). (gr. 2-5). pap. 6.99 *(978-1-4424-9541-8(3),* Simon & Schuster/Paula Wiseman Bks.) Simon & Schuster/Paula Wiseman Bks.
—Clark the Shark. Hale, Bruce. 2013. (Clark the Shark Ser.). (ENG.). 32p. (J). (gr. -1-3). 17.99 *(978-0-06-219226-4(4))* HarperCollins Pubs.
—Clark the Shark: Afraid of the Dark. Hale, Bruce. 2015. (Clark the Shark Ser.). (ENG.). 32p. (J). (gr. -1-3). 17.99 *(978-0-06-237450-9(8))* HarperCollins Pubs.
—Clark the Shark & the Big Book Report. Hale, Bruce. 2017. 32p. (J). *(978-1-5182-4609-8(5))* HarperCollins Pubs.
—Clark the Shark & the Big Book Report. Hale, Bruce. 2017. (I Can Read Level 1 Ser.). (ENG.). 32p. (J). (gr. -1-3). pap. 4.99 *(978-0-06-227912-5(2),* HarperCollins) HarperCollins Pubs. Ltd. GBR. Dist: HarperCollins Pubs.
—Clark the Shark Dares to Share. Hale, Bruce. 2013. (Clark the Shark Ser.). (ENG.). 32p. (J). (gr. -1-3). 17.99 *(978-0-06-227905-7(X),* HarperCollins) HarperCollins Pubs. Ltd. GBR. Dist: HarperCollins Pubs.
—Clark the Shark: Lost & Found. Hale, Bruce. 2016. (I Can Read Level 1 Ser.). (ENG.). 32p. (J). (gr. -1-3). pap. 4.99 *(978-0-06-227910-1(6))* HarperCollins Pubs.
—Clark the Shark Loves Christmas. Hale, Bruce. 2016. (Clark the Shark Ser.). (ENG.). 32p. (J). (gr. -1-3). 17.99 *(978-0-06-237452-3(4))* HarperCollins Pubs.
—Clark the Shark Takes Heart. Hale, Bruce. 2014. (Clark the Shark Ser.). (ENG.). 32p. (J). (gr. -1-3). 17.99 *(978-0-06-219227-1(2))* HarperCollins Pubs.
—Clark the Shark: Too Many Treats. Hale, Bruce. 2019. (I Can Read Level 1 Ser.). (ENG.). 32p. (J). (gr. -1-3). 16.99 *(978-0-06-227917-0(3));* pap. 4.99 *(978-0-06-227916-3(5))* HarperCollins Pubs.
—Clark the Shark: Tooth Trouble. Hale, Bruce. 2014. (I Can Read Level 1 Ser.). (ENG.). 32p. (J). (gr. -1-3). 16.99 *(978-0-06-227908-8(4))* HarperCollins Pubs.
—Clark the Shark: Tooth Trouble. Hale, Bruce. 2014. (I Can Read Level 1 Ser.). (ENG.). 32p. (J). (gr. -1-3). pap. 4.99 *(978-0-06-227906-4(8),* HarperCollins) HarperCollins Pubs. Ltd. GBR. Dist: HarperCollins Pubs.
—Dance by the Light of the Moon. Ryder, Joanne. 2006. (ENG.). 40p. (gr. -1-1). 15.99 *(978-0-7868-1820-4(4))* Hyperion Pr.
—Guys & Ghouls. Jones, Marcia & Dadey, Debbie. 2006. (Ghostville Elementary Ser.: Bk. 13). 81p. *(978-0-439-79402-2(1))* Scholastic, Inc.
—Knock Knock. Sauer, Tammi. 2018. (ENG.). 40p. (J). (gr. -1-k). 16.99 *(978-1-338-11694-6(0),* Scholastic Pr.) Scholastic, Inc.
—Mason Dixon: Basketball Disasters. Mills, Claudia. 2013. (Mason Dixon Ser.: 3). 176p. (J). (gr. 2-5). pap. 6.99 *(978-0-375-87276-1(0),* Yearling) Random Hse. Children's Bks.
—Mason Dixon: Fourth-Grade Disasters. Mills, Claudia. 2012. (Mason Dixon Ser.: 2). 176p. (J). (gr. 4-7). 6.99 *(978-0-375-87275-4(2),* Yearling) Random Hse. Children's Bks.
—Mason Dixon: Pet Disasters. Mills, Claudia. 2012. (Mason Dixon Ser.: 1). 176p. (J). (gr. 4-7). 6.99 *(978-0-375-87274-7(4),* Yearling) Random Hse. Children's Bks.
—Never Ever Talk to Strangers. Pace, Anne Marie. 2010. (J). *(978-0-545-24229-5(0))* Scholastic, Inc.
—Pet Disasters, 1. Mills, Claudia. 2012. (Mason Dixon Ser.). (ENG.). 176p. (J). (gr. 4-6). lib. bdg. 21.19 *(978-0-375-96873-0(3),* Knopf Bks. for Young Readers) Random Hse. Children's Bks.
—The Pup Who Cried Wolf. Kurtz, Chris. 2010. (ENG.). 144p. (YA). (gr. 2-4). 15.99 *(978-1-59990-497-9(7),* 9781599904979); pap. 5.99 *(978-1-59990-492-4(6),* 9781599904924) Bloomsbury Publishing USA. (Bloomsbury USA Childrens).
—Red, White, & Boo! Jones, Marcia & Dadey, Debbie. 2007. (Ghostville Elementary Ser.: Bk. 16). 64p. (J). *(978-0-439-88364-1(4))* Scholastic, Inc.
—The Top Secret Toys. Kehoe, Tim. 2013. (Vincent Shadow Ser.: 2). 272p. (J). (gr. 3-7). pap. 6.99 *(978-0-316-05668-7(5))* Little, Brown Bks. for Young Readers.
—The View at the Zoo. Bostrom, Kathleen Long. 2019. (ENG.). 26p. (J). (gr. -1-1). bds. 7.99 *(978-0-8249-1690-9(5),* Worthy Kids/Ideals) Worthy Publishing.
—Washington's War. Deutsch, Stacia & Cohon, Rhody. 2015. (Blast to the Past Ser.: 7). (ENG.). 128p. (J). (gr. 2-5). pap. 6.99 *(978-1-4424-9540-1(5),* Simon & Schuster/Paula Wiseman Bks.) Simon & Schuster/Paula Wiseman Bks.
—We're Going on a Spooky Ghost Hunt. Geist, Ken. 2017. (StoryPlay Ser.). (ENG.). 32p. (J). (gr. -1 — 1). 5.99 *(978-1-338-14189-4(9),* Cartwheel Bks.) Scholastic, Inc.
Francis, Guy & Wohnoutka, Mike. Vincent Shadow: Toy Inventor. Kehoe, Tim. 2011. (Vincent Shadow Ser.: 1). (ENG.). 224p. (J). (gr. 3-7). pap. 13.99 *(978-0-316-05666-3(9))* Little Brown & Co.
Francis II, Rodger C. Patty Penguin's Favorite Days of the Year. Grogan, Kathy. Reese, Rachelle, ed. 2018. (ENG.). 32p. (J). pap. 10.00 *(978-1-7909-2484-4(7))* Independently Published.
Francis II, Rodger C. What Patty Penguin Loves about Christmas. Grogan, Kathy. Reese, Rachelle, ed. 2019. (Patty Penguin Ser.: Vol. 4). (ENG.). 36p. (J). pap. 10.00 ***(978-1-7031-2325-8(5))*** Independently Published.
Francis, Jamie, et al. Big Keep Books- Spanish Caption Books: Dinosaurios; Camiones; ¿Qué Es lo Que Veo?; el Tráfico; Globos; la Granja, 8 bks., Set. deLeon Diaz, Rosa et al. deLeon Diaz, Rosa et al, trs. enl. ed. 2005.Tr. of Caption Books. (SPA.). 8p. (J). 20.00 *(978-1-893986-41-1(1))* Keep Bks.
Francis, John. My Big Dinosaur World. Mugford, Simon. 2008. 60p. (J). *(978-1-84332-594-9(2),* Priddy Bks.) St. Martin's Pr.
—Prehistoric Animals. Franklin, Carolyn. 2013. (World of Wonder Ser.). (ENG.). 32p. (gr. 1-3). lib. bdg. 31.35 *(978-1-904642-65-7(9))* Book Hse. GBR. Dist: Black Rabbit Bks.
Francis, John, et al. Scary Creatures of the River. Cheshire, Gerard. 2009. (Scary Creatures Ser.). (ENG.). 32p. (J). (gr. 2-4). 27.00 *(978-0-531-21823-5(6),* Watts, Franklin); pap. 8.95 *(978-0-531-22228-7(4),* Children's Pr.) Scholastic Library Publishing.
Francis, John. The Truth about Animal Communication. Stonehouse, Bernard & Bertram, Esther. 2003. (Animals Exposed! Ser.). 48p. (J). 11.99 *(978-0-439-54329-3(0))* Scholastic, Inc.
Francis, John & Scott, Kimberley. Wolves. MacLaine, James. 2013. (Usborne Beginners Ser.). (ENG.). 32p. (J). 4.99 *(978-0-7945-3402-8(3),* Usborne) EDC Publishing.
Francis, John & Testar, Sue. Dogs Sticker Book. Glover, Harry. 2007. (Spotter's Guides Sticker Books - New Format Ser.). 24p. (J). (gr. -1-3). pap. 8.99 *(978-0-7945-1690-1(4),* Usborne) EDC Publishing.
Francis, Lauren. Hannah's Sunday Hats. Yoxen, Jackie. l.t. ed. 2006. 32p. (J). 19.95 *(978-1-59879-184-6(2))* Lifevest Publishing, Inc.
Francis, Michael Harlowe, photos by. Watching Yellowstone & Grand Teton Wildlife. Wilkinson, Todd. 2008. (ENG., 96p. per. 12.95 *(978-1-931832-27-4(7))* Riverbend Publishing.
Francis, Peter. The Big Island Burglary. Keene, Carolyn. 2020. (Nancy Drew Clue Book Ser.: 14). (ENG.). 112p. (J). (gr. 1-4). 17.99 ***(978-1-5344-4268-9(5));*** pap. 5.99 ***(978-1-5344-4267-2(7))*** Simon & Schuster Children's Publishing. (Aladdin).
Francis, Peter. Big Top Flop. Keene, Carolyn. 2016. (Nancy Drew Clue Book Ser.: 4). (ENG.). 96p. (J). (gr. 1-4). pap. 5.99 *(978-1-4814-3752-3(6),* Aladdin) Simon & Schuster Children's Publishing.
—Boo Crew. Keene, Carolyn. 2018. (Nancy Drew Clue Book Ser.: 10). (ENG.). 112p. (J). (gr. 1-4). 16.99 *(978-1-5344-1389-4(8));* pap. 5.99 *(978-1-5344-1388-7(X))* Simon & Schuster Children's Publishing. (Aladdin).
—Butterfly Blues. Keene, Carolyn. 2015. (Nancy Drew & the Clue Crew Ser.: 40). (ENG.). 96p. (J). (gr. 1-4). pap. 5.99 *(978-1-4814-1470-8(4),* Aladdin) Simon & Schuster Children's Publishing.
—Candy Kingdom Chaos. Keene, Carolyn. 2017. (Nancy Drew Clue Book Ser.: 7). (ENG.). 96p. (J). (gr. 1-4). 16.99 *(978-1-4814-5827-6(2));* pap. 5.99 *(978-1-4814-5826-9(4))* Simon & Schuster/Paula Wiseman Bks. (Simon & Schuster/Paula Wiseman Bks.).
—God Bless America, 1 vol. 2016. (Land That I Love Book Ser.). (ENG.). 18p. (J). bds. 9.99 *(978-0-310-75347-6(3))* Zonderkidz.
—God Bless Florida, 1 vol. 2016. (Land That I Love Book Ser.). (ENG.). 18p. (J). bds. 9.99 *(978-0-310-75348-3(1))* Zonderkidz.
—God Bless Texas, 1 vol. 2016. (Land That I Love Book Ser.). (ENG.). 18p. (J). bds. 9.99 *(978-0-310-75343-8(0))* Zonderkidz.
—Last Lemonade Standing. Keene, Carolyn. 2015. (Nancy Drew Clue Book Ser.: 2). (ENG.). 96p. (J). (gr. 1-4). pap. 5.99 *(978-1-4814-3748-6(8),* Aladdin) Simon & Schuster Children's Publishing.
—Movie Madness. Keene, Carolyn. 2016. (Nancy Drew Clue Book Ser.: 5). (ENG.). 96p. (J). (gr. 1-4). pap. 5.99 *(978-1-4814-5820-7(5),* Aladdin) Simon & Schuster Children's Publishing.
—Movie Madness. Keene, Carolyn. 2016. (Nancy Drew Clue Book Ser.: 5). (ENG.). 96p. (J). (gr. 1-4). 16.99 *(978-1-4814-5821-4(3),* Simon & Schuster/Paula Wiseman Bks.) Simon & Schuster/Paula Wiseman Bks.
—Pets on Parade. Keene, Carolyn. 2016. (Nancy Drew Clue Book Ser.: 6). (ENG.). 96p. (J). (gr. 1-4). pap. 5.99 *(978-1-4814-5823-8(X),* Aladdin) Simon & Schuster Children's Publishing.
—Pool Party Puzzler. Keene, Carolyn. 2015. (Nancy Drew Clue Book Ser.: 1). (ENG.). 96p. (J). (gr. 1-4). 16.99 *(978-1-4814-3896-4(4),* Aladdin) Simon & Schuster Children's Publishing.
—Puppy Love Prank. Keene, Carolyn. 2020. (Nancy Drew Clue Book Ser.: 13). (ENG.). 112p. (J). (gr. 1-4). 16.99 *(978-1-5344-3134-8(9),* Simon & Schuster/Paula Wiseman Bks.) Simon & Schuster/Paula Wiseman Bks.
—Springtime Crime. Keene, Carolyn. 2018. (Nancy Drew Clue Book Ser.: 9). (ENG.). 112p. (J). (gr. 1-4). 16.99 *(978-1-4814-9954-5(8));* pap. 5.99 *(978-1-4814-9953-8(X))* Simon & Schuster Children's Publishing. (Aladdin).
—A Star Witness. Keene, Carolyn. 2015. (Nancy Drew Clue Book Ser.: 3). (ENG.). 96p. (J). (gr. 1-4). 16.99 *(978-1-4814-3998-5(7),* Aladdin) Simon & Schuster Children's Publishing.
—The Tortoise & the Scare. Keene, Carolyn. 2019. (Nancy Drew Clue Book Ser.: 11). (ENG.). 96p. (J). (gr. 1-4). 16.99 *(978-1-5344-1483-9(5));* pap. 5.99 *(978-1-5344-1482-2(7))* Simon & Schuster Children's Publishing. (Aladdin).
—Turkey Trot Plot. Keene, Carolyn. 2019. (Nancy Drew Clue Book Ser.: 12). (ENG.). 112p. (J). (gr. 1-4). pap. 5.99 *(978-1-5344-3129-4(2),* Simon & Schuster/Paula Wiseman Bks.) Simon & Schuster/Paula Wiseman Bks.
—World Record Mystery. Keene, Carolyn. 2017. (Nancy Drew Clue Book Ser.: 8). (ENG.). 96p. (J). (gr. 1-4). 16.99 *(978-1-4814-5836-8(1));* pap. 5.99 *(978-1-4814-5835-1(3))* Simon & Schuster Children's Publishing. (Aladdin).
Francis, Tracy-Ann L. If the Shoe Won't Fit Journal Colouring Book. Francis, Tracy-Ann L. 2018. (ENG.). 226p. (J). pap. 8.99 *(978-1-7929-8323-8(9))* Independently Published.
Francis Yu, Leinil, et al. Dawn of X Vol. 1. Hickman, Jonathan et al. 2020. 280p. (YA). (gr. 8-17). pap. 24.99 ***(978-1-302-92156-9(8))*** Marvel Worldwide, Inc.
—Dawn of X Vol. 2. Hickman, Jonathan et al. 2020. 176p. (YA). (gr. 8-17). pap. 17.99 ***(978-1-302-92157-6(6))*** Marvel Worldwide, Inc.
—Dawn of X Vol. 3. Hickman, Jonathan et al. 2020. (ENG.). 176p. (YA). (gr. 8-17). pap. 17.99 ***(978-1-302-92158-3(4))*** Marvel Worldwide, Inc.
—Dawn of X Vol. 4. Hickman, Jonathan et al. 2020. 176p. (gr. 10-17). pap. 17.99 ***(978-1-302-92159-0(2))*** Marvel Worldwide, Inc.
—Dawn of X Vol. 5. Hickman, Jonathan et al. 2020. 176p. (gr. 10-17). pap. 17.99 ***(978-1-302-92160-6(6))*** Marvel Worldwide, Inc.
Francisco, David, jt. illus. see Vialva, Clivia.
Francisco, Manny. Learn Filipino: Book One, Book One. Romero, Victor Eclar. 2004. 384p. per. 29.95 *(978-1-932956-41-2(7))* Magsimba Pr.
Francisco, Tina, et al. Jake Maddox Graphic Novels. Maddox, Jake. 2020. (Jake Maddox Graphic Novels Ser.). (ENG.). (J). (gr. 3-6). 426.40 ***(978-1-4965-9772-4(9),*** 199577); pap., pap., pap. 111.20 ***(978-1-4965-9929-2(2),*** 201363); 319.80 *(978-1-4965-8379-6(5),* 29355); pap., pap., pap. 83.40 *(978-1-4965-9249-1(2),* 29958) Capstone. (Stone Arch Bks.).
Francisco, Tina. Running Overload. Maddox, Jake. 2020. (Jake Maddox Graphic Novels Ser.). (ENG.). 72p. (J). (gr. 3-8). pap. 6.95 *(978-1-4965-8456-4(2),* 140981); lib. bdg. 26.65 *(978-1-4965-8377-2(9),* 140676) Capstone. (Stone Arch Bks.).
Francisco, Wendy. Animal Alphabet: On the Land, in the Sky or Sea, Meet God's Creatures from a to Z. Hopkins, Mary Rice. 2003. 32p. (J). (gr. -1-1). 12.99 *(978-0-89107-968-2(8))* Crossway.
—David & His Giant Battle, 5 vols. Hansen, Janis. 2003. (Bible Adventure Club Ser.). 36p. wbk. ed. 19.99 incl. audio, cd-rom *(978-1-58134-321-2(3))* Crossway.
—Jesus: The Birthday of the King, 5 vols. Hansen, Janis. 2003. (Bible Adventure Club Ser.). 36p. wbk. ed. 19.99 incl. audio, cd-rom *(978-1-58134-331-1(0))* Crossway.
—Jonah & His Amazing Voyage, 5 vols. Hansen, Janis. 2003. (Bible Adventure Club Ser.). 36p. wbk. ed. 19.99 incl. audio, cd-rom *(978-1-58134-326-7(4))* Crossway.
—Noah & the Incredible Flood, 5 vols. Carlson, Melody. 2003. (Bible Adventure Club Ser.). 36p. wbk. ed. 19.99 incl. audio, cd-rom *(978-1-58134-336-6(1))* Crossway.
—Stella's Secret. Du Toit, Lydia. 2017. (ENG.). (J). (gr. 1-6). *(978-0-9922236-0-1(1));* pap. *(978-0-9922236-1-8(X))* Mirror Word Publishing.
Franco, Betsy, jt. illus. see Franco, Tom.

F

Franco-Feeney, Betsy. Hole in the Bottom of the Sea. Franco-Feeney, Betsy. Lavin, Christine. McHugh, Patricia & Feeney, Kathryn, eds. 2012. (ENG.). 32p. (J). 18.95 incl. audio compact disk (978-0-9726487-8-3(X)) Puddle Jump Pr., Ltd.

Franco, Franco, et al. Dino-Mike & the Lunar Showdown. Franco, Franco & Aureliani, Franco. 2016. (Dino-Mike! Ser.). (ENG.). 128p. (J). (gr. 2-3). lib. bdg. 25.32 (978-1-4965-2492-8(6), Stone Arch Bks.) Capstone.

Franco, George. La Historia de la Sra. Inez. Wolfe, Madeline. 2020. (SPA.). 40p. (J). pap. 16.99 **(978-1-6784-9078-2(4))** Zadok Supply, LLC.

Franco, Liliana. Cogito Pt. 1: Antoine & Liliana, the Separation. Franco, Liliana. Bacha, Antoine. 2007. 293p. pap. 24.95 (978-0-9794618-1-1(2)) AJL Publishers.

Franco, Mauricio. Cuentos para Ninos de la Candelaria. Mzjica, Elisa. 2004. (Literatura Juvenil (Panamericana Editorial) Ser.). (SPA.). 125p. (YA). (gr. 4-7). pap. (978-958-30-0303-5(4)) Panamericana Editorial.

Franco, Paula. Amigos de la Granja (Farmyard Friends) (Set), 4 vols. Mullarkey, Lisa. 2019. (Amigos de la Granja (Farmyard Friends) Ser.). 32p. (J). (gr. -1-3). lib. bdg. 108.28 (978-1-5321-3610-8(2), 31959, Calico Chapter Bks) Magic Wagon.

—Ashley Goes Viral. Jones, Jen. 2015. (Sleepover Girls Ser.). (ENG.). 128p. (J). (gr. 3-5). pap. 6.95 (978-1-62370-306-6(9), Capstone Young Readers) Capstone.

—Awesome Recipes You Can Make & Share, 1 vol. Bolte, Mari. 2014. (Sleepover Girls Crafts Ser.). (ENG.). 32p. (J). (gr. 2-5). 28.65 (978-1-4914-1733-1(1), Capstone Young Readers) Capstone.

—Battle of the Bunks, 1 vol. Mullarkey, Lisa. 2016. (Storm Cliff Stables Ser.). (ENG.). 112p. (J). (gr. 2-5). lib. bdg. 29.93 (978-1-62402-162-6(X), 21541, Calico Chapter Bks.) ABDO Publishing Co.

—Carly. Mullarkey, Lisa. (Chicas Poni (Pony Girls) Ser.).Tr. of Carly. 112p. (J). 2016. (SPA.). (gr. 1-4). lib. bdg. 29.93 (978-1-61479-621-3(1), 25052); 2015. (ENG.). (gr. 2-5). 29.93 (978-1-62402-127-5(1), 19375) ABDO Publishing Co. (Calico Chapter Bks.).

—Charlie. Mullarkey, Lisa. 2019. (Pony Girls Ser.). (ENG.). 112p. (J). (gr. 2-5). lib. bdg. 29.93 (978-1-5321-3646-7(3), 33738, Calico Chapter Bks.) ABDO Publishing Co.

—Colorful Creations You Can Make & Share, 1 vol. Bolte, Mari. 2014. (Sleepover Girls Crafts Ser.). (ENG.). 32p. (J). (gr. 2-5). 28.65 (978-1-4914-1734-8(X)) Capstone.

—Daisy la Vaca (Daisy the Cow) Mullarkey, Lisa. 2019. (Amigos de la Granja (Farmyard Friends) Ser.). (SPA.). 32p. (J). (gr. -1-3). lib. bdg. 28.50 (978-1-5321-3611-5(0), 31961, Calico Chapter Bks) Magic Wagon.

—Daisy the Cow. Mullarkey, Lisa. 2017. (Farmyard Friends Ser.). (ENG.). 32p. (J). (gr. -1-3). 49.94 (978-1-62402-990-5(6), 26386); lib. bdg. 28.50 (978-1-5321-4043-3(6), 25514) Magic Wagon. (Calico Chapter Bks).

—Daniela. Mullarkey, Lisa. (Chicas Poni (Pony Girls) Ser.).Tr. of Daniela. 112p. (J). 2016. (SPA.). (gr. 1-4). lib. bdg. 29.93 (978-1-61479-622-0(X), 25054); 2015. (ENG.). (gr. 2-5). 29.93 (978-1-62402-128-2(X), 19377) ABDO Publishing Co. (Calico Chapter Bks.).

—Delaney vs. the Bully. Jones, Jen. 2015. (Sleepover Girls Ser.). (ENG.). 128p. (J). (gr. 3-5). lib. bdg. 22.65 (978-1-4965-0541-5(7), Stone Arch Bks.) Capstone.

—Dog Days for Delaney. Jones, Jen. 2014. (Sleepover Girls Ser.). (ENG.). 128p. (J). (gr. 3-5). 22.65 (978-1-4342-9756-3(X), Stone Arch Bks.) Capstone.

—Dora la Gallina (Golden Girl the Chicken) Mullarkey, Lisa. 2019. (Amigos de la Granja (Farmyard Friends) Ser.). (SPA.). 32p. (J). (gr. -1-3). lib. bdg. 28.50 (978-1-5321-3614-6(5), 31967, Calico Chapter Bks) Magic Wagon.

—Fab Fashions You Can Make & Share, 1 vol. Bolte, Mari. 2014. (Sleepover Girls Crafts Ser.). (ENG.). 32p. (J). (gr. 2-5). lib. bdg. 28.65 (978-1-4914-1735-5(8)) Capstone.

—Farmyard Friends Set 2 (Set), 4 vols. Mullarkey, Lisa. 2019. (Farmyard Friends Ser.). 32p. (J). (gr. -1-3). lib. bdg. 108.28 (978-1-5321-3485-2(1), 31889, Calico Chapter Bks) Magic Wagon.

—A Feast of Fun, 1 vol. Mullarkey, Lisa. 2016. (Storm Cliff Stables Ser.). (ENG.). 112p. (J). (gr. 2-5). lib. bdg. 29.93 (978-1-62402-163-3(8), 21543, Calico Chapter Bks.) ABDO Publishing Co.

—A Filming Fiasco, 1 vol. Mullarkey, Lisa. 2016. (Storm Cliff Stables Ser.). (ENG.). 112p. (J). (gr. 2-5). lib. bdg. 29.93 (978-1-62402-164-0(6), 21545, Calico Chapter Bks.) ABDO Publishing Co.

—Freckles the Pig. Mullarkey, Lisa. 2017. (Farmyard Friends Ser.). (ENG.). 32p. (J). (gr. -1-3). lib. bdg. 28.50 (978-1-5321-4044-0(4), 25516, Calico Chapter Bks) Magic Wagon.

—Gabriela, 4 vols. Mullarkey, Lisa. (Chicas Poni (Pony Girls) Ser.).Tr. of Gabriela. 112p. (J). 2016. (SPA.). (gr. 1-4). lib. bdg. 114.00 (978-1-61479-620-6(3), 25050); 2016. (SPA.). (gr. 1-4). lib. bdg. 29.93 (978-1-61479-623-7(8), 25056); 2015. (ENG.). (gr. 2-5). 29.93 (978-1-62402-129-9(8), 19379) ABDO Publishing Co. (Calico Chapter Bks.).

—Gastón la Cabra (Gaston the Goat) Mullarkey, Lisa. 2019. (Amigos de la Granja (Farmyard Friends) Ser.). (SPA.). 32p. (J). (gr. -1-3). lib. bdg. 28.50 (978-1-5321-3613-9(7), 31965, Calico Chapter Bks) Magic Wagon.

—Gaston the Goat. Mullarkey, Lisa. 2017. (Farmyard Friends Ser.). (ENG.). 32p. (J). (gr. -1-3). lib. bdg. 28.50 (978-1-5321-4045-7(2), 25518, Calico Chapter Bks) Magic Wagon.

—Golden Girl the Chicken. Mullarkey, Lisa. 2017. (Farmyard Friends Ser.). (ENG.). 32p. (J). (gr. -1-3). lib. bdg. 28.50 (978-1-5321-4046-4(0), 25520, Calico Chapter Bks) Magic Wagon.

—Gracie. Mullarkey, Lisa. 2019. (Pony Girls Ser.). (ENG.). 112p. (J). (gr. 2-5). lib. bdg. 29.93 (978-1-5321-3647-4(1), 33740, Calico Chapter Bks.) ABDO Publishing Co.

—The Great Jewelled Egg Mystery Turquoise Band. Pritchard, Gabby. 2016. (Cambridge Reading Adventures Ser.). (ENG.). 16p. pap. 7.37 (978-1-107-57614-8(8)) Cambridge Univ. Pr.

—Hopes in Hiding, 1 vol. Mullarkey, Lisa. 2016. (Storm Cliff Stables Ser.). (ENG.). 112p. (J). (gr. 2-5). lib. bdg. 29.93 (978-1-62402-165-7(4), 21547, Calico Chapter Bks.) ABDO Publishing Co.

—Kianna. Mullarkey, Lisa. (Chicas Poni (Pony Girls) Ser.).Tr. of Kianna. 112p. (J). 2016. (SPA.). (gr. 1-4). lib. bdg. 29.93 (978-1-61479-624-4(6), 25058); 2015. (ENG.). (gr. 2-5). 29.93 (978-1-62402-130-5(1), 19381) ABDO Publishing Co. (Calico Chapter Bks.).

—Maren Loves Luke Lewis. Jones, Jen. 2014. (Sleepover Girls Ser.). (ENG.). 128p. (J). (gr. 3-5). lib. bdg. 22.65 (978-1-4342-9755-6(1), Stone Arch Bks.) Capstone.

—Maren's New Family. Jones, Jen. 2015. (Sleepover Girls Ser.). (ENG.). 128p. (J). (gr. 3-5). lib. bdg. 22.65 (978-1-4965-0540-8(9), Stone Arch Bks.) Capstone.

—The New Ashley. Jones, Jen. 2014. (Sleepover Girls Ser.). (ENG.). 128p. (J). (gr. 3-5). lib. bdg. 22.65 (978-1-4342-9758-7(6), Stone Arch Bks.) Capstone.

Franco, Paula. The Newspaper Club. Vrabel, Beth. 2020. (Newspaper Club Ser.: 1). 208p. (J). (gr. 3-7). pap. 7.99 **(978-0-7624-9686-0(X))**; 16.99 (978-0-7624-9685-3(1)) Running Pr. (Running Pr. Kids).

Franco, Paula. Paisley. Mullarkey, Lisa. 2019. (Pony Girls Ser.). (ENG.). 112p. (J). (gr. 2-5). lib. bdg. 29.93 (978-1-5321-3648-1(X), 33742, Calico Chapter Bks.) ABDO Publishing Co.

—Patches the Cat. Mullarkey, Lisa. 2019. (Farmyard Friends Ser.). (ENG.). 32p. (J). (gr. -1-3). lib. bdg. 28.50 (978-1-5321-3486-9(X), 31891, Calico Chapter Bks) Magic Wagon.

—Pecas el Cerdo (Freckles the Pig) Mullarkey, Lisa. 2019. (Amigos de la Granja (Farmyard Friends) Ser.). (SPA.). 32p. (J). (gr. -1-3). lib. bdg. 28.50 (978-1-5321-3612-2(9), 31963, Calico Chapter Bks) Magic Wagon.

—Pip & Squeak the Miniature Horses. Mullarkey, Lisa. 2019. (Farmyard Friends Ser.). (ENG.). 32p. (J). (gr. -1-3). lib. bdg. 28.50 (978-1-5321-3487-6(8), 31893, Calico Chapter Bks) Magic Wagon.

—Pony Girls Set 2 (Set), 4 vols. Mullarkey, Lisa. 2019. (Pony Girls Ser.). (ENG.). 112p. (J). (gr. 2-5). lib. bdg. 119.72 (978-1-5321-3645-0(5), 33736, Calico Chapter Bks.) ABDO Publishing Co.

—Silo the Dog. Mullarkey, Lisa. 2019. (Farmyard Friends Ser.). (ENG.). 32p. (J). (gr. -1-3). lib. bdg. 28.50 (978-1-5321-3488-3(6), 31895, Calico Chapter Bks) Magic Wagon.

—Sleepover Girls Crafts: Amazing Recipes You Can Make & Share. Bolte, Mari. 2014. (Sleepover Girls Crafts Ser.). (ENG.). 64p. (J). (gr. 2-5). pap. 9.95 (978-1-62370-197-0(X), Capstone Young Readers) Capstone.

—Sleepover Girls Crafts: Colorful Creations You Can Make & Share. Bolte, Mari. 2014. (Sleepover Girls Crafts Ser.). (ENG.). 64p. (J). (gr. 2-5). pap. 9.95 (978-1-62370-198-7(8)) Capstone.

—Sleepover Girls Crafts: Fab Fashions You Can Make & Share. Bolte, Mari. 2014. (Sleepover Girls Crafts Ser.). (ENG.). 64p. (J). (gr. 2-5). pap. 9.95 (978-1-62370-199-4(6)) Capstone.

—Sleepover Girls Crafts: Spa Projects You Can Make & Share. Bolte, Mari. 2014. (Sleepover Girls Crafts Ser.). (ENG.). 64p. (J). (gr. 2-5). pap. 9.95 (978-1-62370-200-7(3)) Capstone.

—Spa Projects You Can Make & Share, 1 vol. Bolte, Mari. 2014. (Sleepover Girls Crafts Ser.). (ENG.). 32p. (J). (gr. 2-5). lib. bdg. 28.65 (978-1-4914-1736-2(6)) Capstone.

—Storm Cliff Stables, 4 vols. ABDO Publishing Company Staff & Mullarkey, Lisa. 2014. (Storm Cliff Stables Ser.: 4). 112p. (J). (gr. 2-5). lib. bdg. 114.00 (978-1-62402-048-3(8), 1663, Calico Chapter Bks.) ABDO Publishing Co.

—Storm Cliff Stables Set 2, 4 vols. Mullarkey, Lisa. 2016. (Storm Cliff Stables Ser.). (ENG.). 112p. (J). (gr. 2-5). lib. bdg. 114.00 (978-1-62402-161-9(1), 21539, Calico Chapter Bks.) ABDO Publishing Co.

—Sweet Pea the Sheep. Mullarkey, Lisa. 2019. (Farmyard Friends Ser.). (ENG.). 32p. (J). (gr. -1-3). lib. bdg. 28.50 (978-1-5321-3489-0(4), 31897, Calico Chapter Bks) Magic Wagon.

—Willow's: Spring Break Adventure. Jones, Jen. 2015. (Sleepover Girls Ser.). (ENG.). 128p. (J). (gr. 3-5). pap. 6.95 (978-1-62370-305-9(0), Capstone Young Readers) Capstone.

—Willow's Boy-Crazy Birthday. Jones, Jen. 2014. (Sleepover Girls Ser.). (ENG.). 128p. (J). (gr. 3-5). lib. bdg. 22.65 (978-1-4342-9757-0(8), Stone Arch Bks.) Capstone.

—Zoey. Mullarkey, Lisa. 2019. (Pony Girls Ser.). (ENG.). 112p. (J). (gr. 2-5). lib. bdg. 29.93 (978-1-5321-3649-8(8), 33744, Calico Chapter Bks.) ABDO Publishing Co.

Franco, Tom & Franco, Betsy. Metamorphosis: Junior Year. Franco, Betsy. 2009. 128p. (YA). (gr. 9-18). 16.99 (978-0-7636-3765-1(3)) Candlewick Pr.

Francois, Andre. Little Boy Brown. Harris, Isobel. 2013. (ENG.). 48p. (J). (gr. -1-3). 15.95 (978-1-59270-135-3(3)) Enchanted Lion Bks., LLC.

—Roland. Stephane, Nelly. 2016. (ENG.). 36p. (J). (gr. -1-3). 17.95 (978-1-59270-204-6(X)) Enchanted Lion Bks., LLC.

Francour, Kathleen. Charmed. Book Company Staff. 2003. (Stationery Ser.). (J). bds. 19.95 (978-1-74047-380-4(9)) Book Co. Publishing Pty, Ltd., The AUS. Dist: Penton Overseas, Inc.

—Flitterbyes Photo Frames. Book Company Staff. 2003. (Stationery Ser.). (J). 9.95 (978-1-74047-354-5(X)) Book Co. Publishing Pty, Ltd., The AUS. Dist: Penton Overseas, Inc.

—Friends Forever. 2003. (Puzzles Ser.). (J). bds. 10.95 (978-1-74047-342-2(6)) Book Co. Publishing Pty, Ltd., The AUS. Dist: Penton Overseas, Inc.

—Little Treasures. Book Company Staff. 2003. (Stationery Ser.). (J). 14.95 (978-1-74047-311-8(6)) Book Co. Publishing Pty, Ltd., The AUS. Dist: Penton Overseas, Inc.

Francour, Kathleen, photos by. The Friends in My Garden. Appel, Dee. Date not set. (Tiny Times Board Book Ser.). 10p. (J). bds. 5.99 (978-0-7369-0564-0(2)) Harvest Hse. Pubs.

—Let's Play Dress Up. Appel, Dee. Date not set. (Tiny Times Board Book Ser.). 10p. (J). bds. 5.99 (978-0-7369-0563-3(4)) Harvest Hse. Pubs.

Francq, Philippe. The Heir. Van Hamme, Jean. 2008. (Largo Winch Ser.: 1). (ENG.). 96p. pap. 19.95 (978-1-905460-48-9(1)) CineBook GBR. Dist: National Bk. Network.

Franfou. Melvin & Hockey Night in the Town of Shinny (Hardcover) Burke, Christina. 2018. (Melvin the Mouse Ser.: Vol. 3). (ENG.). 60p. (J). (gr. 1-6). (978-1-7753404-0-9(6)) Stars Aligned Publishing.

—Melvin & Hockey Night in the Town of Shinny (Softcover) Burke, Christina. 2018. (Melvin the Mouse Ser.: Vol. 3). (ENG.). 60p. (J). (gr. k-6). pap. (978-1-7753404-1-6(4)) Stars Aligned Publishing.

—Melvin et le Grand Match de Hockey. Burke, Christina. Minguet, Anne, tr. 2013. 52p. (978-0-9918561-3-8(9)); pap. (978-0-9918561-2-1(0)) Stars Aligned Publishing.

Franfou Studio. The Color of People. Labuda, Scott A. 2011. (ENG.). 34p. (J). (gr. -1-3). 15.95 (978-1-935268-94-9(5)) Halo Publishing International.

Frangouli, Rena. My Greek Reader. Papaloizos, Theodore C. 2004. (GRE & ENG.). 124p. (Orig.). (YA). (gr. 2). pap. (978-0-932416-46-9(2)) Papaloizos Pubns., Inc.

Frank, Dave. I Went to the Party in Kalamazoo. Shankman, Ed. 2013. (ENG.). 40p. pap. 12.95 (978-1-938700-22-4(8), Commonwealth Editions) Applewood Bks.

Frank, Gary, et al. Incredible Hercules: the Complete Collection Vol. 1. 2019. (ENG.). 464p. (YA). (gr. 8-17). pap. 39.99 (978-1-302-91866-8(4)) Marvel Worldwide, Inc.

Frank, Kevin. Scurvy Dogs. Frank, Kevin. 2017. (ENG.). 96p. (J). pap. 5.99 (978-1-61067-459-1(6)) Kane Miller.

Frank, Rebecca. Council of Magic: Urban Fantasy Series. Hendricks, J. L. Reddell, Rebecca, ed. 2018. (Voodoo Dolls Ser.: Vol. 3). (ENG.). 264p. (J). pap. 10.99 (978-0-9974915-8-6(2)) Hendricks, J. L.

Frank, Remkiewicz, jt. illus. see Remkiewicz, Frank.

Frankel, Alona. Once upon a Potty - - Girl. Frankel, Alona. 2007. (Once upon a Potty Ser.). (ENG.). 40p. (J). (gr. -1 — 1). 7.95 (978-1-55407-284-2(0), 1fdbf638-8413-4bd5-a175-7a3bf02e0b20) Firefly Bks., Ltd.

—Once upon a Potty - Boy. Frankel, Alona. 2007. (Once upon a Potty Ser.). (ENG.). 40p. (J). (gr. -1 — 1). 7.95 (978-1-55407-283-5(2), 38a7fe84-0bc6-41f2-b5ac-b29af9cb8bd8) Firefly Bks., Ltd.

Frankenberg, Robert. Fire Canoe. Falk, Elsa. 2012. 188p. 42.95 (978-1-258-23680-9(X)); pap. 27.95 (978-1-258-24375-3(X)) Literary Licensing, LLC.

Frankenhuyzen, Gijsbert van. Challenger: America's Favorite Eagle. Raven, Margot Theis. 2005. (ENG.). 40p. (J). (gr. k-6). 17.95 (978-1-58536-261-5(1)) Sleeping Bear Pr.

—H Is for Horse: An Equestrian Alphabet. Ulmer, Michael. 2015. (Av2 Fiction Readalong 2016 Ser.). (ENG.). (J). (gr. 1-4). lib. bdg. 34.28 (978-1-4896-3750-5(8), AV2 by Weigl) Weigl Pubs., Inc.

—I Love You Just Enough. Frankenhuyzen, Robbyn Smith van. 2014. (Hazel Ridge Farm Stories Ser.). (ENG.). 36p. (J). (gr. 1-4). 16.95 (978-1-58536-839-6(3), 203009) Sleeping Bear Pr.

—S Is for Sleeping Bear Dunes: A National Lakeshore Alphabet. Wargin, Kathy-jo. 2015. (ENG.). 32p. (J). (gr. 2-4). 16.99 (978-1-58536-917-1(9), 203818) Sleeping Bear Pr.

—S Is for Smithsonian: America's Museum Alphabet. Smith, Roland & Smith, Marie. 2010. (Sleeping Bear Alphabets Ser.). (ENG.). 32p. (J). (gr. 1-5). 17.95 (978-1-58536-314-8(6)) Sleeping Bear Pr.

—Saving Moon Bears. Robinson, Jill & Bekoff, Marc. 2013. (ENG.). 40p. (J). (gr. 1-4). 16.99 (978-1-58536-798-6(2), 202359) Sleeping Bear Pr.

—The Skydiving Beavers of Idaho: A True Tale. Wood, Susan. 2017. (ENG.). 32p. (J). (gr. 1-4). 16.99 (978-1-58536-994-2(2), 204229) Sleeping Bear Pr.

Frankenhuyzen, Gijsbert van, et al. Voices for Freedom. Swain, Gwenyth. 2013. (American Adventures Ser.). (ENG.). 72p. (J). (gr. 3-6). 6.99 (978-1-58536-886-0(5), 202900) Sleeping Bear Pr.

Frankenhuyzen, Gijsbert van. W Is for Woof: A Dog Alphabet. Strother, Ruth. 2009. (ENG.). 40p. (J). (gr. k-6). pap. 7.95 (978-1-58536-477-0(0)) Sleeping Bear Pr.

Frankfeldt, Gwen & Morrow, Glenn. Dateline - Troy. Frankfeldt, Gwen & Fleischman, Paul. ed. 2006. 80p. (J). (gr. 7-10). pap. 8.99 (978-0-7636-3084-3(5)) Candlewick Pr.

Frankland, David. Highway Cats. Lisle, Janet Taylor. 2008. (ENG.). 112p. (J). (gr. 4-6). 21.19 (978-0-399-25070-5(0)) Penguin Young Readers Group.

—Kingdom Keepers: Disney after Dark. Pearson, Ridley. 2005. (Kingdom Keepers Ser.). (ENG.). 336p. (J). (gr. 5-9). 17.99 (978-0-7868-5444-8(8), Disney Editions) Disney Pr.

Frankland, Martha. Animal Adventures at Rainbow Cottage. Salthouse, Betty. 2018. (ENG.). 114p. (J). (gr. k-3). pap. (978-1-911223-27-6(5)) Hawkesbury Pr.

Franklin, Carolyn. How a Caterpillar Grows into a Butterfly. Kant, Tanya. 2008. (Amaze Ser.). (ENG.). 32p. (J). (gr. -1-3). pap. 8.95 (978-0-531-23800-4(8)); (gr. k-3). 27.00 (978-0-531-24046-5(0)) Scholastic Library Publishing. (Children's Pr.).

—How a Seed Grows into a Sunflower. Stewart, David. 2008. (Amaze Ser.). (ENG.). 32p. (J). (gr. k-3). 27.00 (978-0-531-20442-9(1), Children's Pr.) Scholastic Library Publishing.

—How a Tadpole Grows into a Frog. Stewart, David. 2008. (Amaze Ser.). (ENG.). 32p. (J). (gr. k-3). pap. 8.95 (978-0-531-20454-2(5)); 24.94 (978-0-531-20443-6(X)) Scholastic Library Publishing. (Children's Pr.).

—How an Egg Grows into a Chicken. Kant, Tanya. (Amaze Ser.). (ENG.). 32p. (J). 2009. (gr. k-3). 24.94 (978-0-531-24047-2(9)); 2008. (gr. -1-3). pap. 8.95 (978-0-531-23801-1(6)) Scholastic Library Publishing. (Children's Pr.).

—How Your Body Works: A Good Look Inside You Insides. Stewart, David. 2008. (Amaze Ser.). (ENG.). 32p. (J). (gr. k-3). pap. 8.95 (978-0-531-20455-9(3), Children's Pr.) Scholastic Library Publishing.

—How Your Body Works: A Good Look Inside Your Insides. Stewart, David. 2008. (Amaze Ser.). (ENG.). 32p. (J). (gr. k-3). 27.00 (978-0-531-20444-3(8), Children's Pr.) Scholastic Library Publishing.

—The Migration of a Butterfly. Kant, Tanya. 2008. (Amaze Ser.). (ENG.). 32p. (J). (gr. -1-3). pap. 8.95 (978-0-531-23802-8(4), Children's Pr.); (gr. k-3). 27.00 (978-0-531-24048-9(7)) Scholastic Library Publishing.

—Rain Forest Animals. 2013. (World of Wonder Ser.). 32p. (gr. 1-3). 31.35 (978-1-904642-67-1(5)) Book Hse. GBR. Dist: Black Rabbit Bks.

—World of Myths & Legends. Morley, Jacqueline & Salariya, David. 2013. (Mythology Ser.). 64p. (gr. 3-6). 41.35 (978-1-908973-93-1(5)) Book Hse. GBR. Dist: Black Rabbit Bks.

Franklin, Carolyn. Ocean Life. Franklin, Carolyn. 2013. (World of Wonder Ser.). 32p. (gr. 1-3). 31.35 (978-1-904642-63-3(2)) Book Hse. GBR. Dist: Black Rabbit Bks.

—Ocean Life. Franklin, Carolyn. Stewart, David. 2008. (World of Wonder Ser.). (ENG.). 32p. (J). (gr. 1-4). 29.00 (978-0-531-20451-1(0), Children's Pr.) Scholastic Library Publishing.

—Rain Forest Animals. Franklin, Carolyn. Stewart, David. 2008. (World of Wonder Ser.). (ENG.). 32p. (J). (gr. 1-4). 29.00 (978-0-531-20452-8(9), Children's Pr.) Scholastic Library Publishing.

Franklin, Mark. Color Yourself Smart: Geography. Cowling, Dan. 2012. (Color Yourself Smart Ser.). (ENG.). 128p. 19.95 (978-1-60710-216-8(1), Thunder Bay Pr.) Readerlink Distribution Services, LLC.

Franko, Sviatoslav. Rocket the Dachsund. Carter, Laura J. 2020. (ENG.). 42p. (J). pap. **(978-1-6599-9184-0(6))** Wobbly Pr.

Franks, C. J. The Virginia Night Before Christmas. Sullivan, Ellen & Moore, Clement C. 2005. (J). (978-1-58173-392-1(5)) Sweetwater Pr.

Franscisco, Tina. Yo-Kai Watch. Esquivel, Eric M. 2017. (ENG.). 72p. (J). (gr. 4-7). 12.99 (978-1-63140-993-6(X)) Idea & Design Works, LLC.

Franscisco, Tina & Hao, Mae. Volume 5: Food Truck Frenzy. Ball, Georgia. 2017. (Strawberry Shortcake Ser.). (ENG.). 24p. (J). (gr. 2-8). lib. bdg. 27.07 (978-1-5321-4033-4(9), 25465, Graphic Novels) Spotlight.

Franscisco, Tina & Pinto, Valentina. Volume 6: Market Yourself. Ball, Georgia. 2017. (Strawberry Shortcake Ser.). (ENG.). 24p. (J). (gr. 2-8). lib. bdg. 27.07 (978-1-5321-4034-1(7), 25466, Graphic Novels) Spotlight.

Fransisco, Wendy. Creation: God's Wonderful Gift, 5 vols. Hansen, Janis. 2003. (Bible Adventure Club Ser.). 36p. wbk. ed. 19.99 incl. audio, cd-rom (978-1-58134-292-5(6)) Crossway.

Franson, Leanne. Best Wishes for Eddie. Nayer, Judy. 2012. (First Chapters: Set 2 Ser.: Vol. 8). (ENG.). 64p. (J). (gr. 2-3). pap. 9.50 (978-0-7652-0884-2(9)) Modern Curriculum Pr.

—Flood Warning, 1 vol. Pearce, Jacqueline. 2012. (Orca Echoes Ser.). (ENG.). 64p. (J). (gr. 1-3). pap. 6.95 (978-1-4598-0068-7(0)) Orca Bk. Pubs. USA.

—The Girl Who Hated Books, 1 vol. Pawagi, Manjusha. 24p. (J). 2010. (ENG.). (gr. 1-3). pap. 7.95 (978-1-896764-09-2(6)); 2005. 12.95 (978-1-896764-11-5(8)) Second Story Pr. CAN. Dist: Orca Bk. Pubs. USA.

—It's a Baby, Andy Russell. Adler, David A. 2006. (Andy Russell Ser.: Bk. 6). (ENG.). 128p. (J). (gr. 1-4). pap. 9.95 (978-0-15-205610-0(6), 1196873) Houghton Mifflin Harcourt Publishing Co.

—Not Wanted by the Police. Adler, David A. 2005. (Andy Russell Ser.: Bk. 5). (ENG.). 128p. (J). (gr. 1-4). pap. 7.99 (978-0-15-216719-6(6), 1201719) Houghton Mifflin Harcourt Publishing Co.

—Ripley's Believe It or Not! Awesome Collection. Packard, Mary, ed. 361p. (J). pap. (978-0-681-15435-3(7)) Scholastic, Inc.

—Ripley's Believe It or Not! Bizarre Collection. Packard, Mary. 2004. 361p. (J). pap. 3.99 (978-0-681-02479-3(8)) Scholastic, Inc.

—Totally Gross. Packard, Mary. 2004. 85p. (J). (978-0-439-71739-7(6)) Scholastic, Inc.

Fransoy, Monse. Cinderella (Cenicienta) Perrault, Charles. 2013. (Bilingual Fairy Tales Ser.). (ENG & SPA.). 32p. (gr. 1-4). lib. bdg. 28.50 (978-1-60753-356-6(1)) Amicus Publishing.

Franssen, Angie. Activiteiten Boek 1 Creative Coaching: Een Maatje Bij Het Ontdekken Van Vormen en Kleuren Voor Kinderen. Franssen, Angie. 2019. (Creative Coaching Ser.: Vol. 7). (DUT.). 52p. (J). pap. 11.95 **(978-1-6752-2053-5(0))** Independently Published.

Franta, Jiří. The Big Book of the Dark. Harastová, Helena. ed. 2017. (ENG.). 24p. (J). (gr. 2). 14.95 (978-1-911242-99-4(7), Scribblers) Book Hse. GBR. Dist: Sterling Publishing Co., Inc.

Franz, Lauren. Zoo Avenue: The Sleepover. Franz, Brian. 2016. (Zoo Avenue Ser.: Vol. 3). (ENG.). (J). (gr. k-3). 19.95 (978-0-9905402-6-7(X)); pap. 12.95 (978-0-9905402-7-4(8)) Sweet Grin Bks.

Franzen, Sean, photos by. Busy Kitties. Schindel, John. 2004. (Busy Book Ser.). 20p. (J). (— 1). bds. 6.99 (978-1-58246-130-4(9), Knopf Bks. for Young Readers) Random Hse. Children's Bks.

Franzese, Nora Tapp. I Want to Learn to Dance. Wigden, Susan. 2012. 36p. pap. 11.99 (978-1-60820-725-1(0)) MLR Pr., LLC.

Franzke, Michael. Opa, Wo Kommt der Honig Her. Falk, Wolfgang Peter. 2019. (GER.). 28p. (J). pap. 12.00 *(978-1-7945-4420-8(8))* Independently Published.

Frare, Michela. Dumbo. Ferrari, Alessandro. 2020. (Disney Classics Ser.). (ENG.). 52p. (J). (gr. 2-6). lib. bdg. 28.50 ***(978-1-5321-4536-0(5)***, 35183, Graphic Novels) Spotlight.

Frasca, Simone. Awa Teaches Numbers: Young Awa Teaches Numbers to Her Village. Giusti, Enrico. 101translations, tr. 2019. (In the World of Numbers Ser.: Vol. 1). (ENG.). 46p. (J). pap. ***(978-0-9541723-6-7(1))*** Adverbage, Ltd.

Fraser-Allen, Johnny. The Squickerwonkers. Lilly, Evangeline. 2014. 42p. (gr. k-3). 16.99 *(978-1-78329-545-6(7)*, Titan Bks.) Titan Bks. Ltd. GBR. Dist: Penguin Random Hse. LLC.

Fraser, Betty. The Llama Who Had No Pajama: 100 Favorite Poems. Hoberman, Mary Ann. 2006. (ENG.). 68p. (J). (gr. 1-4). pap. 8.99 *(978-0-15-205571-4(1)*, 1196756); (gr. k-3). 24.94 *(978-0-15-200111-7(5))* Houghton Mifflin Harcourt Publishing Co.

—Sounds Are High, Sounds Are Low: I Wonder Why. Lowery, Lawrence F. 2014. (I Wonder Why Ser.). (ENG.). 36p. (J). (gr. k-3). pap. 11.95 *(978-1-941316-04-7(2))* National Science Teachers Assn.

Fraser, Frank. Bearista: A Grand Adventure. Fraser, Frank. 2003. (J). pap. 14.95 *(978-0-9726394-0-8(3))* Starbucks Coffee Co.

—Before I Was Me. Fraser, Frank. 2018. (ENG.). (J). pap. 10.95 *(978-1-62282-606-3(X))* Sophia Institute Pr.

Fraser, Jess. Gleedus the Happy Grasshopper. Wright, Bill, Sr. 2006. (J). cd-rom 9.99 *(978-0-9795190-6-2(3))* Color & Learn.

—Henry's New Home. Fraser, Lynne. 2007. (J). cd-rom 9.99 *(978-0-9795190-9-3(8))* Color & Learn.

—Jungle Jingles. 2007. (J). cd-rom 9.99 *(978-0-9795190-8-6(X))* Color & Learn.

—The Legend of the Cosmic Cowboy. 2007. (J). cd-rom 12.99 *(978-0-9795190-7-9(1))* Color & Learn.

Fraser, John. The Jindo & the Mailman. Palumbo, Nancy L. 2019. (ENG.). 24p. (J). (gr. -1-2). pap. 12.95 *(978-1-59152-248-5(X)*, Sweetgrass Bks.) Farcountry Pr.

Fraser, Kara-Anne. Brave Dave & the Dragons. Reed, Janet. 2009. 12p. (J). *(978-0-545-16142-8(8))* Scholastic, Inc.

Fraser, Kay. Finn Reeder, Flu Fighter: How I Survived a Worldwide Pandemic, the School Bully, & the Craziest Game of Dodge Ball Ever. Stevens, Eric. 2009. (Finn Reeder Ser.). (ENG.). 80p. (J). (gr. 3-8). lib. bdg. 26.65 *(978-1-4342-2450-7(3)*, Stone Arch Bks.) Capstone.

—Flu Fighter: How I Survived a Worldwide Pandemic, the School Bully, & the Craziest Game of Dodge Ball Ever. Stevens, Eric. 2010. (Finn Reeder Ser.). (ENG.). 80p. (J). (gr. 3-8). 9.99 *(978-1-4342-2562-7(3)*, Stone Arch Bks.) Capstone.

Fraser, Kevin. Ants? in My Pants? An Antimated Tale. Bahz, Kahanni. 2005. 72p. (J). (gr. k-4). reprint ed. 22.00 *(978-0-7567-8705-9(X))* DIANE Publishing Co.

Fraser, MacKenzie. Ladybug, Ladybug. Kelley, 'lizbeth. 2019. (Anya & Bugs of Summer Ser.: Vol. 1). (ENG.). 24p. (J). (gr. k-2). 15.99 *(978-1-5092-2499-9(8))* Wild Rose Pr., Inc., The.

Fraser, Mary Ann. Down Comes the Rain. Branley, Franklyn M. 2017. (Let's-Read-And-Find-Out Science 2 Ser.). (ENG.). 40p. (J). (gr. -1-3). pap. 6.99 *(978-0-06-238663-2(8))* HarperCollins Pubs.

—Life with Mammoth, 0 vols. Fraser, Ian. (Ogg & Bob Ser.: 2). (ENG.). 64p. (J). (gr. k-3). 2013. pap. 9.99 *(978-1-4778-1615-8(1)*, 9781477816158); 2010. 14.99 *(978-0-7614-5722-0(4)*, 9780761457220) Amazon Publishing. (Two Lions).

—Meet Mammoth, 0 vols. Fraser, Ian. 2013. (Ogg & Bob Ser.: 1). (ENG.). 64p. (J). (gr. 1-3). pap. 9.99 *(978-1-4778-1617-2(8)*, 9781477816172, Two Lions) Amazon Publishing.

—No Yeti Yet. 2015. (ENG.). 32p. (J). 16.99 *(978-1-4413-0855-9(5)*, 9781441308559) Peter Pauper Pr. Inc.

—Papa Bear's Page Fright. Bradford, Wade. 2018. (J). *(978-1-4413-2598-3(0))* Peter Pauper Pr. Inc.

Fraser, Mary Ann. Alexander Graham Bell Answers the Call. Fraser, Mary Ann. 2017. 32p. (J). (gr. 1-4). lib. bdg. 16.99 *(978-1-58089-721-1(5))* Charlesbridge Publishing, Inc.

—Milton & Odie & the Bigger-Than-Bigmouth Bass. Fraser, Mary Ann. 2019. 32p. (J). (gr. -1-3). lib. bdg. 16.99 *(978-1-62354-098-2(4))* Charlesbridge Publishing, Inc.

Fraser, Richard M. The Boy Who Saved a Cape Cod Town: And Other Cape Cod Stories. Clark, Admont G. 2006. 56p. (J). (gr. 6-12). per. 12.95 *(978-0-9785766-0-8(8))* On Cape Pubns.

Fraser, Sigmund. Smile Bright. Wallace, Jazey. 2012. 24p. pap. 11.50 *(978-1-61897-755-7(5)*, Strategic Bk. Publishing) Strategic Book Publishing & Rights Agency (SBPRA).

Frasier, Debra. A Fabulous Fair Alphabet. Frasier, Debra. 2010. (ENG.). 40p. (J). (gr. k-6). 16.99 *(978-1-4169-9817-4(9)*, Beach Lane Bks.) Beach Lane Bks.

—Miss Alaineus: A Vocabulary Disaster. Frasier, Debra. 2007. (ENG.). 40p. (J). (gr. -1-3). pap. 7.99 *(978-0-15-206053-4(7)*, 1198181) Houghton Mifflin Harcourt Publishing Co.

—Spike: Ugliest Dog in the Universe. Frasier, Debra. 2013. (ENG.). 40p. (J). (gr. -1-3). 16.99 *(978-1-4424-1452-5(9)*, Beach Lane Bks.) Beach Lane Bks.

Frattino, Andre. A Land Remembered: the Graphic Novel, Vol. Smith, Patrick D. 2018. (ENG.). 320p. (J). (gr. 3-7). pap. 14.95 *(978-1-68334-021-8(3))* Pineapple Pr., Inc.

Fraunfelter, Brad. Affinity for War. Morin, Frank. Essoe, Joshua, ed. 2018. (Petralist Ser.: Vol. 4). (ENG.). 478p. (YA). (gr. 7-12). 29.99 *(978-1-946910-05-9(8))* Whipsaw Pr.

Fravel, Harold. Fellsmere the Pirate, Chipley's Adventure. Fravel, Gale. 2011. 28p. pap. 12.95 *(978-1-936343-79-9(7))* Peppertree Pr., The.

Frawley, Keith. Rollo's Many Coats. Duncan, Reed. 2020. (Rollo Ser.). 32p. (J). (gr. 1-2). 9.99 *(978-1-5247-9249-7(7)*, Penguin Workshop) Penguin Young Readers Group.

—Super Schnoz & the Invasion of the Snore Snatchers. Urey, Gary. 2014. (Super Schnoz Ser.: 2). (ENG.). 160p. (J). (gr. 3-7). 14.99 *(978-0-8075-7557-4(7)*, 807575577) Whitman, Albert & Co.

—Uh-Oh, Rollo! Duncan, Reed. (Rollo Ser.). 32p. (J). (gr. 1-2). 2020. 4.99 *(978-1-5247-9244-2(6))*; 2019. 9.99 *(978-1-5247-9243-5(8))* Penguin Young Readers Group. (Penguin Workshop).

—Where's Rollo? Duncan, Reed. (Rollo Ser.). 32p. (J). (gr. 1-2). 2020. 4.99 *(978-1-5247-9247-3(0))*; 2019. 9.99 *(978-1-5247-9246-6(2))* Penguin Young Readers Group. (Penguin Workshop).

Frawley, Keith, jt. illus. see Long, Ethan.

Frazao, Catia. The Story of Señor Pico. Guatemala, Anne. 2007.Tr. of Historia del Señor Pico. (ENG & SPA.). 32p. (J). pap. 17.00 *(978-0-8059-7818-6(6))* Dorrance Publishing Co., Inc.

Frazee, Marla. All the World. Scanlon, Liz Garton. 2009. (ENG.). 40p. (J). (gr. -1-3). 18.99 *(978-1-4169-8580-8(8)*, Beach Lane Bks.) Beach Lane Bks.

—All the World. Scanlon, Liz Garton. 2015. (Classic Board Bks.). (ENG.). 44p. (J). (gr. -1-k). bds. 7.99 *(978-1-4814-3121-7(8)*, Little Simon) Little Simon.

—All the World. Scanlon, Liz Garton. 2011. (J). (gr. -1-2). 29.95 *(978-0-545-32716-9(4))* Weston Woods Studios, Inc.

—Clementine. Pennypacker, Sara. (Clementine Ser.: 1). (ENG.). (J). (gr. 1-5). 2008. 160p. pap. 5.99 *(978-0-7868-3883-7(3))*; 2006. 144p. 14.99 *(978-0-7868-3882-0(5))* Hyperion Pr.

—Clementine & the Family Meeting. Pennypacker, Sara. (Clementine Ser.: 5). (ENG.). 176p. (J). (gr. 1-5). 2012. pap. 5.99 *(978-1-4231-2436-8(7))*; 2011. 14.99 *(978-1-4231-2356-9(5))* Hyperion Pr.

—Clementine & the Spring Trip. Pennypacker, Sara. 2013. (Clementine Ser.: 6). (ENG.). 160p. (J). (gr. 1-5). 14.99 *(978-1-4231-2357-6(3))* Hyperion Pr.

—Clementine Friend of the Week. Pennypacker, Sara. (Clementine Ser.: 4). (ENG.). 176p. (J). (gr. 1-5). 2011. pap. 5.99 *(978-1-4231-1560-1(0))*; 2010. 14.99 *(978-1-4231-1355-3(1))* Hyperion Pr.

—Clementine's Letter. Pennypacker, Sara. 2009. (Clementine Ser.: 3). (ENG.). 160p. (J). (gr. 1-5). pap. 5.99 *(978-0-7868-3885-1(X))* Hyperion Pr.

Frazee, Marla. Completely Clementine. Pennypacker, Sara. (Clementine Ser.: 7). (ENG.). (J). (gr. 1-5). 2016. 208p. pap. 5.99 ***(978-1-4231-2438-2(3))***; 2015. 192p. 14.99 ***(978-1-4231-2358-3(1))*** Little, Brown Bks. for Young Readers.

Frazee, Marla. Everywhere Babies. Meyers, Susan. (ENG.). 30p. (J). 2016. (— 1). bds. 8.99 *(978-0-544-79120-6(7)*, 1639294, HMH Books For Young Readers); 2011. (gr. -1 — 1). bds. 11.99 *(978-0-547-51074-3(8)*, 1443771) Houghton Mifflin Harcourt Publishing Co.

—Everywhere Babies. Meyers, Susan. 2004. (ENG.). 30p. (J). (gr. k — 1). bds. 7.99 *(978-0-15-205315-4(8)*, 1196012) Houghton Mifflin Harcourt Publishing Co.

—God Got a Dog. Rylant, Cynthia. 2013. (ENG.). 48p. (J). (gr. 5-5). 17.99 *(978-1-4424-6518-3(2)*, Beach Lane Bks.) Beach Lane Bks.

—Harriet, You'll Drive Me Wild! Fox, Mem. 2003. (ENG.). 32p. (J). (gr. -1-3). pap. 7.99 *(978-0-15-204598-2(8)*, 1193846) Houghton Mifflin Harcourt Publishing Co.

—Is Mommy? Chang, Victoria. 2015. (ENG.). 40p. (J). (gr. -1-k). 15.99 *(978-1-4814-0292-7(7)*, Beach Lane Bks.) Beach Lane Bks.

—It Takes a Village: Picture Book. Clinton, Hillary Rodham. 2017. (ENG.). 40p. (J). (gr. -1-3). 19.99 *(978-1-4814-3087-6(4)*, Simon & Schuster/Paula Wiseman Bks.) Simon & Schuster/Paula Wiseman Bks.

—Mrs. Biddlebox: Her Bad Day & What She Did about It. Smith, Linda. Date not set. 32p. (J). (gr. -1-3). pap. 5.99 *(978-0-06-443620-5(9))* HarperCollins Pubs.

—On the Mom of Mayfest. Silverman, Erica. 2011. (ENG.). 32p. (J). (gr. -1-2). pap. 13.99 *(978-1-4424-4341-9(3)*, Simon & Schuster Bks. For Young Readers) Simon & Schuster Bks. For Young Readers.

—The Seven Silly Eaters. Hoberman, Mary Ann. ed. 2004. (J). (gr. k-3). spiral bd. *(978-0-616-14576-0(4))* Canadian National Institute for the Blind/Institut National Canadien pour les Aveugles.

—Stars. Ray, Mary Lyn. 2011. (ENG.). 40p. (J). (gr. -1-3). 18.99 *(978-1-4424-2249-0(1)*, Beach Lane Bks.) Beach Lane Bks.

—Stars. Ray, Mary Lyn. 2017. (Classic Board Bks.). (ENG.). 36p. (J). (gr. -1-k). bds. 7.99 *(978-1-5344-0662-9(X)*, Little Simon) Little Simon.

Frazee, Marla, et al. Sweet Stories for Baby Gift Set. Meyers, Susan & Fox, Mem. 2015. (ENG.). 128p. (J). (— 1). 16.99 *(978-0-544-53121-5(3)*, 1607942, HMH Books For Young Readers) Houghton Mifflin Harcourt Publishing Co.

Frazee, Marla. The Talented Clementine. Pennypacker, Sara. (Clementine Ser.: 2). (ENG.). (J). (gr. 1-5). 2008. 160p. pap. 5.99 *(978-0-7868-3871-4(X))*; 2007. 144p. 14.99 *(978-0-7868-3870-7(1))* Hyperion Pr.

Frazee, Marla. Waylon! Even More Awesome. Pennypacker, Sara. 2018. (Waylon! Ser.: 2). (ENG.). 224p. (J). (gr. 1-5). pap. 5.99 ***(978-1-4847-8237-8(2))*** Little, Brown Bks. for Young Readers.

—Waylon! One Awesome Thing. Pennypacker, Sara. 2017. (Waylon! Ser.: 1). (ENG.). 224p. (J). (gr. 1-5). pap. 5.99 ***(978-1-4847-7821-0(9))*** Little, Brown Bks. for Young Readers.

—Waylon! the Most Awesome of All. Pennypacker, Sara. 2019. (Waylon! Ser.: 3). (ENG.). 160p. (J). (gr. 1-5). pap. 15.99 ***(978-1-4847-0154-6(2))*** Little, Brown Bks. for Young Readers.

Frazee, Marla. Boot & Shoe. Frazee, Marla. 2012. (ENG.). 40p. (J). (gr. -1-3). 18.99 *(978-1-4424-2247-6(5)*, Beach Lane Bks.) Beach Lane Bks.

—The Boss Baby. Frazee, Marla. (ENG.). 40p. (J). (gr. -1-3). 2016. pap. 7.99 *(978-1-4814-6981-4(9))*; 2010. 17.99 *(978-1-4424-0167-9(2))* Beach Lane Bks. (Beach Lane Bks.).

—The Boss Baby. Frazee, Marla. 2013. (Classic Board Bks.). (ENG.). 36p. (J). (gr. -1 — 1). bds. 7.99 *(978-1-4424-8779-6(8)*, Little Simon) Little Simon.

—The Bossier Baby. Frazee, Marla. 2016. (ENG.). 40p. (J). (gr. -1-3). 17.99 *(978-1-4814-7162-6(7)*, Beach Lane Bks.) Beach Lane Bks.

Frazee, Marla. The Farmer & the Monkey. Frazee, Marla. 2020. (Farmer Bks.). (ENG.). 32p. (J). (gr. -1-3). 17.99 ***(978-1-5344-4619-9(2)***, Beach Lane Bks.) Beach Lane Bks.

Frazee, Marla. Little Brown. Frazee, Marla. 2018. (ENG.). 40p. (J). (gr. -1-3). 17.99 *(978-1-4814-2522-3(6)*, Beach Lane Bks.) Beach Lane Bks.

—Roller Coaster. Frazee, Marla. 2003. (ENG.). 32p. (J). (gr. -1-3). 17.99 *(978-0-15-204554-8(6)*, 1193714) Houghton Mifflin Harcourt Publishing Co.

—Walk On! A Guide for Babies of All Ages. Frazee, Marla. 2006. (ENG.). 40p. (J). (gr. -1-k). 16.99 *(978-0-15-205573-8(8)*, 1196762) Houghton Mifflin Harcourt Publishing Co.

Frazee, Marla & Pedersen, Janet. Bully Buster. Clements, Andrew. 2008. (Jake Drake Ser.: Bk. 1). 67p. (gr. 2-5). 15.00 *(978-0-7569-9001-5(7))* Perfection Learning Corp.

—Jake Drake, Know-It-All. Clements, Andrew. 2007. (Jake Drake Ser.: Bk. 2). 88p. (gr. 2-5). 15.00 *(978-0-7569-8212-6(X))* Perfection Learning Corp.

Frazer, Andrew. Drawn Onward. McKinlay, Meg. 2018. 32p. (J). (gr. 6). 14.99 *(978-1-925164-84-8(5))* Fremantle Pr. AUS. Dist: Independent Pubs. Group.

Frazier, Craig. The Tiny Brown Seed. Frazier, Daniele. 2003. 24p. (J). (gr. -1-1). 14.95 *(978-1-932026-11-5(8))* Graphis, U.S., Inc.

—Trucks Roll! Lyon, George Ella. 2007. (ENG.). 40p. (J). (gr. -1-2). 19.99 *(978-1-4169-2435-7(3)*, Atheneum/Richard Jackson Bks.) Simon & Schuster Children's Publishing.

—Tyler Makes a Birthday Cake! Florence, Tyler. 2014. (J). lib. bdg. *(978-0-06-204761-8(2))* Harper & Row Ltd.

—Tyler Makes a Birthday Cake! Florence, Tyler. 2014. (ENG.). 40p. (J). (gr. -1-3). 17.99 *(978-0-06-204760-1(4))* HarperCollins Pubs.

—Tyler Makes Pancakes! Florence, Tyler. 2012. (ENG.). 40p. (J). (gr. -1-2). 16.99 *(978-0-06-204752-6(3))* HarperCollins Pubs.

—Tyler Makes Spaghetti! Florence, Tyler. 2013. (ENG.). 40p. (J). (gr. -1-3). 17.99 *(978-0-06-204756-4(6))* HarperCollins Pubs.

Frazier, Craig. Going Board Book. Frazier, Craig. 2019. (ENG.). 32p. (J). (gr. -1 — 1). bds. 7.99 *(978-0-06-279629-5(1)*, HarperFestival) HarperCollins Pubs.

—Sitting Board Book. Frazier, Craig. 2019. (ENG.). 32p. (J). (gr. -1 — 1). bds. 7.99 *(978-0-06-279630-1(5)*, HarperFestival) HarperCollins Pubs.

Frazier, James J. Pennsylvania Fireside Tales Volume V Vol. V: Origins & Foundations of Pennsylvania Mountains Folktales, Legends, & Folklore. Frazier, Jeffrey R. 2003. (ENG.). 250p. 15.00 *(978-0-9652351-6-7(5))* Egg Hill Pubns.

Freccero, Andrea & De Lorenzi, Paolo. Donald Quest: Hammer of Magic. Ambrosio, Stefano et al. 2017. (Donald Duck Ser.). 160p. (J). (gr. 4-7). pap. 14.99 *(978-1-63140-912-7(3))* Idea & Design Works, LLC.

Fred, Ana. The Suspended Castle: A Philemon Adventure. Fred, Ana. Kutner, Richard. 2016. (Toon Graphics Ser.). (ENG.). 56p. (J). (gr. 3-6). lib. bdg. 29.93 *(978-1-61479-501-8(0)*, 21437, Graphic Novels) Spotlight.

Freda, AnnMarie. Moody Moon. Fox, Mary Ann. 2019. (ENG.). 34p. (J). pap. 9.95 *(978-1-0809-4699-0(3))* Independently Published.

Frederick-Frost, Alexis. Explore Spring! 25 Great Ways to Learn about Spring. Anderson, Maxine & Berkenkamp, Lauri. 2007. (Explore Your World Ser.). 96p. (J). (gr. k-4). per. 12.95 *(978-0-9785037-4-1(0)*, abbb5766-b2db-4f54-b6cb-d6e63d34876f) Nomad Pr.

—Explore Winter! 25 Great Ways to Learn about Winter. Anderson, Maxine. 2007. (Explore Your World Ser.). 96p. (J). (gr. k-4). pap. 12.95 *(978-0-9785037-5-8(9)*, 4a74a618-5ae6-4d64-80ef-8d9f98a1617a) Nomad Pr.

Frederick, Jayde. Who Is Nyla Nova? The Stemsation. Washington, Nakeisha. 2019. (ENG.). 38p. (J). 31.99 *(978-1-7960-2914-7(9))*; pap. 21.99 *(978-1-7960-2913-0(0))* Xlibris Corp.

Frederick, Sarah. School is Not for Me, Jeremy James Conor McGee. Mahony, Mary. 2009. (J). pap. 7.95 *(978-0-9658879-4-6(4))* Redding Pr.

Fredericks, John. Pepperson Pat & the TV Star. Fredericks, John. 2019. (ENG.). 36p. (J). pap. 9.99 *(978-1-7933-8257-3(3))* Independently Published.

Fredericks, Rob. The Adventures of Tyler the Dinosaur, 1 vol. Fredericks, Eleanor. 2009. 31p. pap. 24.95 *(978-1-61546-233-9(3))* America Star Bks.

Fredi, Peg Richie. Jojo's Christmas. Spain, George. 2017. (ENG.). (J). 29.95 *(978-1-62880-129-3(8))*; pap. 17.95 *(978-1-62880-128-6(X))* Published by Westview, Inc.

Fredrich, Volker. Rechtschreibtraining fuer die 1. Klasse. (Duden-Lemminuten Ser.). (GER.). 32p. (J). wbk. ed. *(978-3-411-70831-4(X))* Bibliographisches Institut & F. A. Brockhaus AG DEU. Dist: International Bk. Import Service, Inc.

—Rechtschreibtraining fuer die 1. und 2. Klasse. (Duden-Lemminuten Ser.). (GER.). 32p. (J). wbk. ed. *(978-3-411-70841-3(7))* Bibliographisches Institut & F. A. Brockhaus AG DEU. Dist: International Bk. Import Service, Inc.

Freeberg, Eric. Animal Stories. 2010. (Classic Starts® Ser.). 160p. (J). (gr. 2-4). 6.95 *(978-1-4027-6646-6(7))* Sterling Publishing Co., Inc.

—Great Expectations. Dickens, Charles. 2010. (Classic Starts® Ser.). 160p. (J). (gr. 2-4). 6.95 *(978-1-4027-6645-9(9))* Sterling Publishing Co., Inc.

—Greek Myths. 2011. (Classic Starts® Ser.). 160p. (J). (gr. 2-4). 6.95 *(978-1-4027-7312-9(9))* Sterling Publishing Co., Inc.

—Grimm's Fairy Tales. Grimm, Jakob & Grimm, Wilhelm K. 2011. (Classic Starts® Ser.). 160p. (J). (gr. 2-4). 6.95 *(978-1-4027-7311-2(0))* Sterling Publishing Co., Inc.

—I Am America Set 2 (Set Of 2) 2019. (I Am America Set 2 (Set Of 2) Ser.). (ENG.). 320p. (J). pap. 17.98 *(978-1-63163-368-3(6)*, 1631633686); lib. bdg. 57.00 *(978-1-63163-367-6(8)*, 1631633678) North Star Editions. (Jolly Fish Pr.).

—I Am America (Set Of 4) 2019. (I Am America Ser.). (ENG.). 640p. (J). pap. 35.96 *(978-1-63163-268-6(X)*, 163163268X); lib. bdg. 114.00 *(978-1-63163-267-9(1)*, 1631632671) North Star Editions. (Jolly Fish Pr.).

—If the Fire Comes: A Story of Segregation During the Great Depression. Daley, Tracy. 2019. (I Am America Set 2 (Set Of 2) Ser.). (ENG.). 160p. (J). pap. 8.99 *(978-1-63163-372-0(4)*, 1631633724); lib. bdg. 28.50 *(978-1-63163-371-3(6)*, 1631633716) North Star Editions. (Jolly Fish Pr.).

—The Iliad. Homer. 2014. (Classic Starts® Ser.). 160p. (J). (gr. 2-4). 6.95 *(978-1-4549-0612-4(X))* Sterling Publishing Co., Inc.

—Journey to a Promised Land: A Story of the Exodusters. Lassieur, Allison. 2019. (I Am America Ser.). (ENG.). 160p. (J). pap. 8.99 *(978-1-63163-276-1(0)*, 1631632760); lib. bdg. 28.50 *(978-1-63163-275-4(2)*, 1631632752) North Star Editions. (Jolly Fish Pr.).

—Journey to the Center of the Earth. Verne, Jules. 2011. (Classic Starts® Ser.). 160p. (J). (gr. 2-4). 6.95 *(978-1-4027-7313-6(7))* Sterling Publishing Co., Inc.

—Lines We Draw: A Story of Imprisoned Japanese Americans. Lee, Camellia. 2019. (I Am America Ser.). (ENG.). 160p. (J). pap. 8.99 *(978-1-63163-280-8(9)*, 1631632809); lib. bdg. 28.50 *(978-1-63163-279-2(5)*, 1631632795) North Star Editions. (Jolly Fish Pr.).

—Moby-Dick. Melville, Herman. 2010. (Classic Starts® Ser.). (ENG.). 160p. (J). (gr. 2-4). 6.95 *(978-1-4027-6644-2(0))* Sterling Publishing Co., Inc.

—The Odyssey. Homer. 2011. (Classic Starts® Ser.). 160p. (J). (gr. 2-4). 6.95 *(978-1-4027-7334-1(X))* Sterling Publishing Co., Inc.

—Roman Myths. Namm, Diane. 2014. (Classic Starts® Ser.). 160p. (J). (gr. 2-4). 6.95 *(978-1-4549-0611-7(1))* Sterling Publishing Co., Inc.

—United to Strike: A Story of the Delano Grape Workers. Zenk, Molly. 2019. (I Am America Set 2 (Set Of 2) Ser.). (ENG.). 160p. (J). pap. 8.99 *(978-1-63163-284-6(1)*, 1631632841); lib. bdg. 28.50 *(978-1-63163-283-9(3)*, 1631632833) North Star Editions. (Jolly Fish Pr.).

Freeborn, Andrew J. Colorways: For Days. abr. ed. 2005. 32p. pap. *(978-0-9769575-0-8(7))* N8TIVE.

Freedman, Claire. Candle Bible & Prayers for Kids, 1 vol. David, Juliet. ed. 2016. (ENG.). 528p. (J). 24.99 *(978-1-78128-274-8(9)*, Candle Bks.) Lion Hudson PLC GBR. Dist: Kregel Pubns.

Freedman, Deborah. This House, Once. Freedman, Deborah. 2017. (ENG.). 40p. (J). (gr. -1-3). 17.99 *(978-1-4814-4284-8(8))* Simon & Schuster Children's Publishing.

Freel, Mirle. Zigzag the Rocking Roadrunner. O'Toole-Freel, Judy. 2012. 40p. 24.95 *(978-1-4626-9970-4(7))* America Star Bks.

Freeland, Devon & Contreras-Freeland, Gina. A Boy & His Wizard. Smith, M. a. & Smith, M. A. 2009. 32p. pap. 8.95 *(978-1-60076-152-2(6))* StoneGarden.net Publishing.

Freeland, Margi. Inspire. Grimes, Cassandra. 2019. (ENG.). 26p. (J). pap. 12.99 ***(978-1-951178-02-4(5))*** Hydra Productions Online LLC.

Freeland, Rose. La Gallina Amarilla y el Zorro Rojo. McClain, Minnie Rimmer. 2019. (SPA.). 40p. (J). pap. 12.95 ***(978-1-7095-0602-4(4))*** Independently Published.

Freeman, Angela. Just Inn Time. Angelo, Tony. 2011. 24p. pap. 24.95 *(978-1-4560-6828-8(8))* America Star Bks.

Freeman, Don. The Day Is Waiting, 1 vol. Zuckerman, Linda. 2015. (ENG.). 32p. (J). 9.99 *(978-0-310-74054-4(1))* Zonderkidz.

Freeman, Don. Corduroy 40th Anniversary Edition. Freeman, Don. 40th anniv. ed. 2008. (Corduroy Ser.). (ENG.). 48p. (J). (gr. -1-k). 19.99 *(978-0-670-06336-9(3)*, Viking Books for Young Readers) Penguin Young Readers Group.

—Earl the Squirrel. Freeman, Don. 2008. (J). (gr. -1-2). pap. 16.95 incl. audio *(978-1-4301-0411-7(2))* Live Oak Media.

—Fly High, Fly Low. Freeman, Don. (ENG.). 64p. (J). (gr. -1-k). 2004. reprint ed. 16.99 *(978-0-670-03685-1(4)*, Viking Books for Young Readers); 50th anniv. ed. 2007. 7.99 *(978-0-14-240817-9(4)*, Puffin Books) Penguin Young Readers Group.

—Fly High, Fly Low. Freeman, Don. 2007. 56p. (gr. -1-3). 18.00 *(978-0-7569-8001-6(1))* Perfection Learning Corp.

—Gregory's Shadow. Freeman, Don. 2003. pap. 39.95 incl. audio compact disk *(978-1-59112-536-5(7))*; (J). 25.95 incl. audio *(978-1-59112-238-8(4))*; (J). pap. 37.95 incl. audio *(978-1-59112-239-5(2))* Live Oak Media.

Freeman, Don & McCue, Lisa. Corduroy Series Boxed Set: Corduroy; A Pocket for Corduroy; Corduroy's Busy Street; Corduroy Goes to the Doctor; Corduroy's Day; Corduroy's Party, Set. Freeman, Don & McCue, Lisa. (Corduroy Ser.). (J). (gr. k-1). pap. 30.95 incl. audio *(978-0-87499-471-1(3))* Live Oak Media.

Freeman, Eve. The Thorn & the Pocket. Freeman, Eve. 2019. (ENG.). 38p. (J). (gr. k-4). 20.00 ***(978-0-578-55800-4(9))*** Freeman Bks.

Freeman, Gary. Battles of the American Revolution: Bridges Edition. Burgan, Michael. 2015. (Prime Plus Ser.). (YA). (gr. 6-8). pap. *(978-1-4900-1943-7(X))* Benchmark Education Co.

—Battles of the American Revolution: Bridges Edition Set of 6 with Common Core Indicators. Burgan, Michael. 2015. (Prime Plus Ser.). (YA). (gr. 6-8). 69.00 net. *(978-1-4900-2039-6(X))* Benchmark Education Co.

—Causes of the American Revolution: Bridges Edition. Reisfeld, Randi & Jackie Robb. 2015. (Prime Plus Ser.). (YA). (gr. 6-8). pap. *(978-1-4900-1942-0(1))* Benchmark Education Co.

—Causes of the American Revolution: Bridges Edition Set of 6 with Common Core Indicators. Reisfeld, Randi & Jackie

F

Robb. 2015. (Prime Plus Ser.). (YA). (gr. 6-8). 69.00 net. *(978-1-4900-2038-9(1))* Benchmark Education Co.
—Earth's Freshwater Bodies: Bridges Edition, Set Of 10. Hirschmann, Kris. 2013. (Prime Plus Ser.). (J). (gr. 6-8). 99.00 net. *(978-1-4509-9936-6(0))* Benchmark Education Co.
—Earth's Freshwater Bodies: Prime Bridges Edition. Hirschmann, Kris. 2013. (Prime Ser.). (YA). (gr. 6-8). pap. *(978-1-4509-9687-7(6))* Benchmark Education Co.
—Earth's Freshwater Bodies: Set Of 10. Hirschmann, Kris. 2013. (Prime Plus Ser.). (J). (gr. 6-8). 99.00 net. *(978-1-4509-9912-0(3))* Benchmark Education Co.
—Earth's Hydrosphere: Bridges Edition, Set Of 10. Worth, Richard. 2013. (Prime Plus Ser.). (J). (gr. 6-8). 99.00 net. *(978-1-4509-9934-2(4))* Benchmark Education Co.
—Earth's Hydrosphere: Prime Bridges Edition. Worth, Richard. 2013. (Prime Ser.). (YA). (gr. 6-8). pap. *(978-1-4509-9685-3(X))* Benchmark Education Co.
—Earth's Hydrosphere: Set Of 10. Worth, Richard. 2013. (Prime Plus Ser.). (J). (gr. 6-8). 99.00 net. *(978-1-4509-9910-6(7))* Benchmark Education Co.
—Earth's Oceans: Bridges Edition, Set Of 10. Hirschmann, Kris. 2013. (Prime Plus Ser.). (J). (gr. 6-8). 99.00 net. *(978-1-4509-9935-9(2))* Benchmark Education Co.
—Earth's Oceans: Prime Bridges Edition. Hirschmann, Kris. 2013. (Prime Ser.). (YA). (gr. 6-8). pap. *(978-1-4509-9686-0(8))* Benchmark Education Co.
—Earth's Oceans: Set Of 10. Hirschmann, Kris. 2013. (Prime Plus Ser.). (J). (gr. 6-8). 99.00 net. *(978-1-4509-9911-3(5))* Benchmark Education Co.
—Faces of the American Revolution: Bridges Edition. Reisfeld, Randi & Jackie Robb. 2015. (Prime Plus Ser.). (YA). (gr. 6-8). pap. *(978-1-4900-1944-4(8))* Benchmark Education Co.
—Faces of the American Revolution: Bridges Edition Set of 6 with Common Core Indicators. Reisfeld, Randi & Jackie Robb. 2015. (Prime Plus Ser.). (YA). (gr. 6-8). 69.00 net. *(978-1-4900-2040-2(3))* Benchmark Education Co.
—Kanchil y Los Cocodrilos. Fuerst, Jeffrey B. 2016. (Jump into Genre Ser.). (SPA.). (J). (gr. 3). 5.25 *(978-1-4788-3622-3(9))* Newmark Learning LLC.
Freeman, Julie. Le Cheval Magique: French-Arabic Edition. Shah, Idries. 2018. (Hoopoe Teaching-Stories Ser.). (FRE.). 40p. (J). (gr. 3-6). pap. 9.99 ***(978-1-949358-48-3(8)***, Hoopoe Bks.) I S H K.
Freeman, Julie. In the Garden with the LittleWeeds: A Counting Book for Little Ones. Weisenfluh, C. C. 2004. 26p. (J). 11.95 *(978-0-9746782-0-7(1))* B'Squeak Productions.
—The Magic Horse: English-Dari Edition. Shah, Idries. 2017. (Hoopoe Teaching-Stories Ser.). (ENG.). (J). (gr. k-6). pap. 9.99 *(978-1-946270-14-6(8)*, Hoopoe Bks.) I S H K.
—The Magic Horse: English-Pashto Edition. Shah, Idries. 2017. (Hoopoe Teaching-Stories Ser.). (ENG & PUS.). (J). (gr. 2-6). pap. 9.99 *(978-1-944493-59-2(X)*, Hoopoe Bks.) I S H K.
—The Magic Horse: English-Urdu Bilingual Edition. Shah, Idries. 2016. (URD & ENG.). (J). (gr. k-6). pap. 9.99 *(978-1-942698-76-0(3)*, Hoopoe Bks.) I S H K.
Freeman, Kathryn S. Loon Chase, 1 vol. Diehl, Jean Heilprin. 2006. (ENG.). 32p. (J). (gr. 1-5). 15.95 *(978-0-9764943-8-6(8))* Arbordale Publishing.
Freeman, Laura. Althea Gibson: the Story of Tennis' Fleet-Of-Foot Girl. Reid, Megan. 2020. (ENG.). 40p. (J). (gr. -1-3). 17.99 *(978-0-06-285109-3(8)*, Balzer & Bray) HarperCollins Pubs.
—Biddy Mason Speaks Up. White, Arisa & Atkins, Laura. 2019. (Fighting for Justice Ser.: 2). (ENG.). 112p. (J). 18.00 *(978-1-59714-403-2(7))* Heyday.
—Birthday Blues, Bk. 2. English, Karen. 2010. (Nikki & Deja Ser.: 2). (ENG.). 96p. (J). (gr. 1-4). pap. 5.99 *(978-0-547-24893-6(8)*, 1100905) Houghton Mifflin Harcourt Publishing Co.
—Días de Perros: Crónicas de la Primaria Carver, Libro 1. English, Karen. Humaran, Aurora & Monge, Leticia, trs. 2020. (Carver Chronicles Ser.). (SPA.). 128p. (J). (gr. 1-4). pap. 5.99 *(978-0-358-21370-3(3)*, 1765786, Clarion Bks.) Houghton Mifflin Harcourt Trade & Reference Pubs.
—Dog Days. English, Karen. 2014. (Carver Chronicles Ser.). (ENG.). 128p. (J). (gr. 1-4). pap. 6.99 *(978-0-544-33912-5(6)*, 1584483, HMH Books For Young Readers) Houghton Mifflin Harcourt Publishing Co.
—Don't Feed the Geckos! The Carver Chronicles, Book Three. English, Karen. 2016. (Carver Chronicles Ser.). (ENG.). 144p. (J). (gr. 1-4). pap. 6.99 *(978-0-544-81083-9(X)*, 1641525, HMH Books For Young Readers) Houghton Mifflin Harcourt Publishing Co.
—Dream Builder: The Story of Architect Philip Freelon, 1 vol. Lyons, Kelly Starling. 2020. (ENG.). 40p. (J). (gr. 3-5). 19.95 *(978-1-62014-955-3(9)*, 6ba3cd90-2766-4979-aa73-21d94826823a) Lee & Low Bks., Inc.
—Fancy Party Gowns: The Story of Fashion Designer Ann Cole Lowe. Blumenthal, Deborah. 2017. (ENG.). 40p. (J). (gr. -1-3). 17.99 *(978-1-4998-0239-9(0))* Little Bee Books Inc.
—Fiesta de Patinetas: Crónicas de la Primaria Carver, Libro 2. English, Karen. Humaran, Aurora & Monge, Leticia, trs. 2020. (Carver Chronicles Ser.: 2). (SPA.). 128p. (J). (gr. 1-4). pap. 5.99 *(978-0-358-24434-9(X)*, 1767923, Clarion Bks.) Houghton Mifflin Harcourt Trade & Reference Pubs.
Freeman, Laura. Fiesta de Pizzas: Crónicas de la Primaria Carver, Libro 6. English, Karen. Humaran, Aurora & Monge, Leticia, trs. 2020. (Carver Chronicles Ser.: 6). (SPA.). 144p. (J). (gr. 1-4). pap. 5.99 ***(978-0-358-25200-9(8)***, 1770097, Clarion Bks.) Houghton Mifflin Harcourt Trade & Reference Pubs.
Freeman, Laura. Hidden Figures: The True Story of Four Black Women & the Space Race. Shetterly, Margot Lee. 2018. (ENG.). 40p. (J). (gr. -1-3). 17.99 *(978-0-06-274246-9(9))* HarperCollins Pubs.
Freeman, Laura. Kamala Harris: Rooted in Justice. Grimes, Nikki. 2020. (ENG.). 40p. (J). (gr. -1-3). 17.99 ***(978-1-5344-6267-0(8)***, Atheneum Bks. for Young Readers) Simon & Schuster Children's Publishing.
Freeman, Laura. The New Kid: The Carver Chronicles, Book Five. English, Karen. 2018. (Carver Chronicles Ser.: 5). (ENG.). 128p. (J). (gr. 1-4). pap. 6.99 *(978-1-328-49797-0(6)*, 1717851, HMH Books For Young Readers) Houghton Mifflin Harcourt Publishing Co.
—The Newsy News Newsletter, Bk. 3. English, Karen. 2011. (Nikki & Deja Ser.: 3). (ENG.). 96p. (J). (gr. 1-4). pap. 6.99 *(978-0-547-40626-8(6)*, 1428504) Houghton Mifflin Harcourt Publishing Co.
—Nikki & Deja. English, Karen. 2009. (Nikki & Deja Ser.: 1). (ENG.). 80p. (J). (gr. -1-3). pap. 6.99 *(978-0-547-13362-1(6)*, 1048763) Houghton Mifflin Harcourt Publishing Co.
—Nikki & Deja. English, Karen. 2007. (Nikki & Deja Ser.). 76p. (J). (gr. 2-4). 16.19 *(978-0-618-75238-6(2)*, Clarion Bks.) Houghton Mifflin Harcourt Trade & Reference Pubs.
—Nikki & Deja: Substitute Trouble. English, Karen. 2014. (Nikki & Deja Ser.). (ENG.). 112p. (J). (gr. 1-4). pap. 6.99 *(978-0-544-22388-2(8)*, 1563368, HMH Books For Young Readers) Houghton Mifflin Harcourt Publishing Co.
Freeman, Laura. El niño Nuevo: Crónicas de la Primaria Carver, Libro 5. English, Karen. Humaran, Aurora & Monge, Leticia, trs. 2020. (Carver Chronicles Ser.: 5). (SPA.). 144p. (J). (gr. 1-4). pap. 5.99 ***(978-0-358-25199-6(0)***, 1770096, Clarion Bks.) Houghton Mifflin Harcourt Trade & Reference Pubs.
Freeman, Laura. ¡No Alimentes a Los Gecos! Crónicas de la Primaria Carver, Libro 3. English, Karen. Humaran, Aurora & Monge, Leticia, trs. 2020. (Carver Chronicles Ser.: 3). (SPA.). 160p. (J). (gr. 1-4). pap. 5.99 *(978-0-358-21486-1(6)*, 1765787, Clarion Bks.) Houghton Mifflin Harcourt Trade & Reference Pubs.
—Pies from Nowhere: How Georgia Gilmore Sustained the Montgomery Bus Boycott. Romito, Dee. 2018. (ENG.). 40p. (J). (gr. k-4). 17.99 *(978-1-4998-0720-2(1))* Little Bee Books Inc.
—Pizza Party: The Carver Chronicles, Book Six. English, Karen. 2019. (Carver Chronicles Ser.: 6). (ENG.). 128p. (J). (gr. 1-4). pap. 7.99 *(978-0-358-09747-1(9)*, 1747602, HMH Books For Young Readers) Houghton Mifflin Harcourt Publishing Co.
Freeman, Laura. Problemas en la Casa de Al Lado: Crónicas de la Primaria Carver, Libro 4. English, Karen. Humaran, Aurora & Monge, Leticia, trs. 2020. (Carver Chronicles Ser.: 4). (SPA.). 160p. (J). (gr. 1-4). pap. 5.99 ***(978-0-358-25197-2(4)***, 1770095, Clarion Bks.) Houghton Mifflin Harcourt Trade & Reference Pubs.
Freeman, Laura. Trouble Next Door. English, Karen. 2016. (Carver Chronicles Ser.: 4). (ENG.). 144p. (J). (gr. 1-4). 15.99 *(978-0-544-80127-1(X)*, 1640323) Houghton Mifflin Harcourt Publishing Co.
—Trouble Next Door: The Carver Chronicles, Book Four. English, Karen. 2018. (Carver Chronicles Ser.). (ENG.). 144p. (J). (gr. 1-4). pap. 6.99 *(978-1-328-90011-1(8)*, 1700039, HMH Books For Young Readers) Houghton Mifflin Harcourt Publishing Co.
—A Voice Named Aretha. Russell-Brown, Katheryn. 2020. 40p. (J). 17.99 *(978-1-68119-850-7(9)*, 900189371, Bloomsbury Children's Bks.) Bloomsbury Publishing USA.
—Wedding Drama. English, Karen. 2013. (Nikki & Deja Ser.). (ENG.). 112p. (J). (gr. 1-4). pap. 5.99 *(978-0-544-00324-8(1)*, 1526366) Houghton Mifflin Harcourt Publishing Co.
Freeman, Lynda. The Clock That Lost Its Tick & Other Tales. Watson, Terry H. 2016. (ENG.). (J). pap. *(978-0-9956807-0-8(1))* Ramoan Pr.
Freeman, Mark. Santa's Precious Secret: The Best Gift of All. Bartlett, William. 2016. (ENG.). (J). pap. *(978-0-473-37711-3(X))* William Bartlett Global Publishing.
Freeman, Melita. The Knight of Lord Greengate's Castle. Freeman, Melita. 2012. 28p. pap. 10.00 *(978-1-936750-90-0(2))* Yorkshire Publishing Group.
Freeman, Mike, photos by. Rocks & Minerals Spotter's Guide: With Internet Links. Woolley, Alan. rev. ed. 2007. (Spotter's Guides). 64p. (J). pap. 5.99 *(978-0-7945-1304-7(2)*, Usborne) EDC Publishing.
Freeman, Mike & Julings, Emma, photos by. Usborne Rocks & Minerals Sticker Book. Miles, Lisa. Khan, Sarah & Armstrong, Carrie, eds. rev. ed. 2006. (Spotter's Guides Sticker Books - New Format Ser.). 16p. (J). (gr. 2-5). pap. 8.99 *(978-0-7945-1413-6(8)*, Usborne) EDC Publishing.
Freeman, Patricia. Where Is God? Stevens, Sherri. 2005. 24p. (YA). 15.95 *(978-0-9769541-0-1(9)*, 2005-1) Enlightened Bks.
Freeman, T. R. The Lark in the Morn. Vipont, Elfrida. 2007. (Young Adult Historical Bookshelf Ser.). (ENG.). 196p. (J). (gr. 7-9). pap. 12.95 *(978-1-932350-22-7(5))* Ignatius Pr.
—The Lark on the Wing. Vipont, Elfrida. 2008. 233p. (J). pap. 12.95 *(978-1-932350-11-1(X))* Bethlehem Bks.
Freeman, Tina. Ten Little Monkeys Jumping on the Bed. (Classic Books with Holes 8x8 with CD Ser.). (ENG.). 16p. (J). 2007. (gr. -1-1). pap. incl. audio compact disk *(978-1-904550-67-9(3))*; 2004. bds. *(978-0-85953-450-5(2))*; 2003. pap. *(978-0-85953-137-5(6))* Child's Play International Ltd.
Freeman, Tor. The B on Your Thumb: 60 Poems to Boost Reading & Spelling. Hiller, Colette. ed. 2020. (ENG.). 80p. (J). (gr. -1-3). 19.99 ***(978-0-7112-5460-2(5)***, Frances Lincoln Children's Bks.) Quarto Publishing Group UK GBR. Dist: Hachette Bk. Group.
Freeman, Tor. Colin the Cart Horse. Puckett, Gavin. 2018. (Fables from the Stables Ser.). (ENG.). 80p. (J). 8.95 *(978-0-571-31543-7(7))* Faber & Faber, Inc.
—Hayley the Hairy Horse. Puckett, Gavin. 2019. (Fables from the Stables Ser.). (ENG.). 80p. pap. 8.95 *(978-0-571-33780-4(5)*, Faber & Faber Children's Bks.) Faber & Faber, Inc.
—Hendrix the Rocking Horse. Puckett, Gavin. 2018. (Fables from the Stables Ser.). (ENG.). 96p. (J). 8.95 *(978-0-571-31540-6(2)*, Faber & Faber Children's Bks.) Faber & Faber, Inc.
—Murray the Race Horse. Puckett, Gavin. 2018. (Fables from the Stables Ser.). (ENG.). 80p. (J). pap. 8.95 *(978-0-571-33468-1(7))* Faber & Faber, Inc.
—Poppy the Police Horse: Fables from the Stables Book 4. Puckett, Gavin. 2018. (Fables from the Stables Ser.). (ENG.). 80p. 8.95 *(978-0-571-33778-1(3)*, Faber & Faber Children's Bks.) Faber & Faber, Inc.
—Ten Fat Sausages. Robinson, Michelle. 2020. (ENG.). 32p. (J). (gr. -1-2). 10.99 *(978-1-5247-9329-6(9)*, Penguin Workshop) Penguin Young Readers Group.
—Turtle & Me. Harris, Robie. 2015. (ENG.). 40p. (J). (gr. -1-3). 16.99 *(978-1-4998-0046-3(0))* Little Bee Books Inc.
—The Wind in the Willows. Grahame, Kenneth. 2017. (Alma Junior Classics Ser.). (ENG.). 192p. (J). pap. 9.99 *(978-1-84749-638-6(5)*, 351540) Alma Classics GBR. Dist: Bloomsbury Publishing Plc.
Freeman, Tor. Olive & the Bad Mood. Freeman, Tor. 2013. (ENG.). 32p. (J). (gr. -1-3). 15.99 *(978-0-7636-6657-6(2)*, Templar) Candlewick Pr.
—Olive & the Big Secret. Freeman, Tor. 2012. (ENG.). 32p. (J). (gr. -1-3). 15.99 *(978-0-7636-6149-6(X)*, Templar) Candlewick Pr.
—Olive & the Embarrassing Gift. Freeman, Tor. 2014. (ENG.). 32p. (J). (gr. -1-3). 15.99 *(978-0-7636-7406-9(0)*, Templar) Candlewick Pr.
Freeman, Troy. All Dried Out. Brodland, Rita, ed. l.t. ed. 2006. (WeWrite Kids! Ser.: 50). 68p. (J). pap. 11.95 *(978-1-57635-063-8(0))* WeWrite LLC.
Freepik. Journal Intime Licorne: Carnet de Notes Original, Format A5 13,97x21,59 Cm Pour �criture Journal Intime, Bullet Journal, 100 Pages Avec Lignes, Id�e Cadeau Enfant Fille. Licorne, Journal Intime. 2019. (FRE.). 102p. (J). pap. 8.00 ***(978-1-6707-0392-7(4))*** Independently Published.
Freeswick, Jill. Making Mouth Sounds All Day Long. Clayton, Darcy M. 2013. 36p. pap. 9.95 *(978-1-889131-90-0(3)*, Castlebridge Bks.) Big Tent Bks.
Frega, Muriel. Amorcitos Sub-14. Bornemann, Elsa. 2015. (Serie Azul Ser.). (SPA.). 128p. (J). (gr. 4-7). pap. 11.95 *(978-950-46-4510-8(0))* Santillana USA Publishing Co., Inc.
Fregoe, Douglas. Ronnie the Rattler. Hartigan, Tina. 2019. (ENG.). 34p. (J). pap. 12.99 *(978-1-0735-6594-8(7))* Independently Published.
Freire, Carlos. Jan's Awesome Party, 1 vol. Hughes, Monica. 2016. (Formac First Novels Ser.: 18). (ENG.). 57p. (J). (gr. 1-5). 5.95 *(978-0-88780-532-5(9)*, 44625186-67d7-42d6-8741-b6ae999a14b6) Formac Publishing Co., Ltd. CAN. Dist: Lerner Publishing Group.
Freisager, Katrin, photos by. The Seventh Generation: Images of the Lakota Today. Seals, David. 2005. 144p. (gr. 1-18). 45.00 *(978-1-57687-031-0(6)*, powerHouse Bks.) powerHse. Bks.
Freitag, Charles. The Christmas Tractor. Aumann, Jane & Ladage, Cindy. 2003. 30p. (J). (gr. k-4). pap. 8.95 *(978-0-9703319-2-2(4))* Roots & Wings.
French, David. Dear God, Will You Give Me A Dog?, 1 vol. Pierro, Rita. 2009. 35p. pap. 19.95 *(978-1-61582-589-9(4))* PublishAmerica, Inc.
—The Duck Who Couldn't Swim, 1 vol. Pierro, Rita. 2010. 26p. 24.95 *(978-1-4489-6405-5(9))* PublishAmerica, Inc.
—A Horse in the House, 1 vol. Pierro, Rita. 2009. 29p. pap. 24.95 *(978-1-60836-410-7(0))* America Star Bks.
French, Felicity. Gift Boxes to Decorate & Make: Easter. Nosy Crow. 2018. (ENG.). 50p. (J). (gr. 3-7). pap. 15.99 *(978-0-7636-9638-2(2)*, Nosy Crow) Candlewick Pr.
—The Lion Bible Verses Colouring Book, 1 vol. ed. 2017. (ENG.). 32p. (J). (gr. 2-4). pap. 6.99 *(978-0-7459-7689-1(1)*, Lion Books) Lion Hudson PLC GBR. Dist: Independent Pubs. Group.
—The Lion Nativity Colouring Book. Jackson, Antonia. ed. 2016. (ENG.). 32p. (J). (gr. 2-4). pap. 9.99 *(978-0-7459-7617-4(4))* Lion Hudson PLC GBR. Dist: Independent Pubs. Group.
—The Lion Psalms Colouring Book, 1 vol. Jackson, Antonia. ed. 2016. (ENG.). 32p. (J). (gr. 2-4). pap. 7.99 *(978-0-7459-7618-1(2))* Lion Hudson PLC GBR. Dist: Independent Pubs. Group.
French, Fiona. Anancy & Mr Dry-Bone. 2005. (ENG.). 32p. (J). (gr. -1-2). 7.95 *(978-1-84507-164-6(6)*, Frances Lincoln Children's Bks.) Quarto Publishing Group UK GBR. Dist: Hachette Bk. Group.
French, Martin. Stompin' at the Savoy: The Story of Norma Miller. 2006. (ENG.). 64p. (J). (gr. 4-7). 17.99 *(978-0-7636-2244-2(3))* Candlewick Pr.
French, Phyllis. The Chocolate Chip Ghost. Peifer, Meighan. 2004. (J). 14.95 *(978-1-58597-245-6(2))* Leathers Publishing.
French, Renee. Barry's Best Buddy. French, Renee. 2013. (ENG.). 32p. (J). (gr. -1-3). 12.95 *(978-1-935179-21-4(7))* TOON Books / RAW Junior, LLC.
—The Soap Lady. French, Renee. 2005. 111p. (J). (gr. 4-8). reprint ed. 20.00 *(978-0-7567-9419-4(6))* DIANE Publishing Co.
Frenkel, Yetti. Andre the Famous Harbor Seal. Hodgkins, Fran. 2003. (ENG.). 32p. (J). (gr. k-17). 16.95 *(978-0-89272-594-6(X))* Down East Bks.
Frenkel, Yetti. The Big, Blue Lump. Frenkel, Yetti. 2004. 32p. (J). 16.95 *(978-0-9749006-0-5(5))* Snow Tree Bks.
—Libby & the Cat. Frenkel, Yetti. 2005. 32p. (J). 16.95 *(978-0-9749006-2-9(1))* Snow Tree Bks.
—Trudy & the Captain's Cat. Frenkel, Yetti. 2005. 32p. (J). 16.95 *(978-0-9749006-1-2(3))* Snow Tree Bks.
Frenna, Federica. The Jungle Book. Kipling, Rudyard. 2018. (Seek & Find Classics Ser.). (ENG.). 48p. (J). (gr. 2). 9.99 *(978-1-4998-0685-4(X))* Little Bee Books Inc.
—Rapunzel: An Interactive Fairy Tale Adventure. Jakubowski, Michele. 2017. (You Choose: Fractured Fairy Tales Ser.). (ENG.). 112p. (J). (gr. 3-7). pap. 6.95 *(978-1-5157-8778-5(8)*, 136329); lib. bdg. 32.65 *(978-1-5157-8776-1(1)*, 136327) Capstone. (Capstone Pr.).
Frenz, Ron, et al. Thor Epic Collection: the Black Galaxy. 2019. (ENG.). 488p. (YA). (gr. 4-17). pap. 39.99 *(978-1-302-91850-7(8))* Marvel Worldwide, Inc.
Frenz, Ron & Buscema, Sal. G. I. Joe Vol. 6: A Real American Hero. Hama, Larry et al. 2013. (G. I. Joe Rah Ser.: 6). 128p. pap. 19.99 *(978-1-61377-582-0(2)*, 9781613775820) Idea & Design Works, LLC.
Frenz, Ron & Olliffe, Pat. Spider-Girl: the Complete Collection Vol. 2. 2019. (ENG.). 432p. (YA). (gr. 4-17). pap. 39.99 *(978-1-302-91844-6(3))* Marvel Worldwide, Inc.
Freschet, Gina. Beto & the Bone Dance. Freschet, Gina. 2005. 30p. (J). (gr. 4-8). reprint ed. 16.00 *(978-0-7567-8933-6(8))* DIANE Publishing Co.
Freshman, Floris R., jt. illus. see James, Larry W.
Fresson, Robert G. Flying Colors: A Guide to Flags from Around the World! Jacobs, Robin. 2018. (ENG.). 122p. (J). (gr. k-7). 22.95 *(978-1-908714-46-6(8))* Cicada Bks. GBR. Dist: Consortium Bk. Sales & Distribution.
Fretczak-Rodak, Monika. Jungle. Miedzybrodzka, Wiktoria. 2014. (Mommy & Me Bath Bks.). (ENG.). 6p. (J). (gr. -1 — 1). 4.99 *(978-1-4380-7485-6(9)*, B.E.S. Publishing) Peterson's.
Frey, Ben. My Friend Jamal. McQuinn, Anna. 2008. (ENG.). 32p. (J). (gr. -1-2). 17.95 *(978-1-55451-123-5(2)*, 9781554511235) Annick Pr., Ltd. CAN. Dist: Publishers Group West (PGW).
—Runaway Alphabet. Winters, Kari-Lynn. 2010. (ENG.). 32p. (J). (gr. -1-3). 17.95 *(978-1-897476-24-6(8))* Simply Read Bks. CAN. Dist: Ingram Publisher Services.
Frey, Daniel. Jacy Meets Betsy: Jacy's Search for Jesus Book 2. Edwards, Carol. 2006. 32p. (J). 15.95 *(978-0-9755314-1-9(7))* Majestic Publishing, LLC.
Frey, Daniel J. Jacy Faces Evil: Jacy's Search for Jesus Book III. Edwards, Carol. 2008. 32p. (J). 15.95 *(978-0-9755314-3-3(3))* Majestic Publishing, LLC.
—Jacy's Coloring & Activity Book. 2006. 32p. (J). 3.00 *(978-0-9755314-2-6(5))* Majestic Publishing, LLC.
—Jacy's Search for Jesus. Edwards, Carol. 2005. 31p. (J). (gr. -1-3). 15.95 *(978-0-9755314-0-2(9))* Majestic Publishing, LLC.
Frey, Kathryn. Carlos Goes to Preschool. Wood, Zach. 2018. (ENG.). 36p. (J). pap. 15.00 *(978-1-7287-3659-4(5))* Independently Published.
Freya Blackwood & Joyner, Andrew. Boo! Wild, Margaret. 2019. (ENG.). 24p. (J). (— 1). 19.99 ***(978-0-670-07807-3(7)***, Puffin) Penguin Random Hse. AUS. Dist: Independent Pubs. Group.
Freymann, Saxton. Foods with Moods: a First Book of Feelings. Freymann, Saxton. Elffers, Joost. 2018. 18p. (J). (— 1). bds. 7.99 *(978-1-338-19441-8(0)*, Levine, Arthur A. Bks.) Scholastic, Inc.
—How Are You Peeling? Foods with Moods. Freymann, Saxton. Elffers, Joost. 2004. (Scholastic Bookshelf Ser.). (ENG.). 48p. (J). (gr. -1-3). reprint ed. pap. 7.99 *(978-0-439-59841-5(9)*, Scholastic Paperbacks) Scholastic, Inc.
Freysinger, Karen. Adventures of Countess Pigula Her Royal Imagination. Freysinger, Karen. 2006. (J). 15.95 *(978-0-9786729-0-4(9))* Aha! Elora Danan Productions.
freysinger, karen. Adventures of Countess Pigula up, up & Away. freysinger, karen. 2009. 32p. (J). 16.99 *(978-0-9786729-1-1(7))* Aha! Elora Danan Productions.
Freytag, Lorna. My Humongous Hamster Goes to School. Freytag, Lorna. 2015. (My Humongous Hamster Ser.). (ENG.). 32p. (J). (gr. -1-3). 16.99 *(978-1-62779-140-3(X)*, 9781627791403, Holt, Henry & Co. Bks. For Young Readers) Holt, Henry & Co.
Friar, Joanne. Freedom Quilt. Helmso, Candy Grant. 2003. (Books for Young Learners). (ENG.). 16p. (J). 5.75 net. *(978-1-57274-529-2(0)*, 2744, Bks. for Young Learners) Owen, Richard C. Pubs., Inc.
—My Favorite Place. Heller, Maryellen. 2005. (ENG.). 16p. (J). 5.75 *(978-1-57274-535-3(5)*, 2771, Bks. for Young Learners) Owen, Richard C. Pubs., Inc.
—My Mom's Apron. O'Brien, Claudia Moore. 2005. (ENG.). 12p. (J). 5.75 *(978-1-57274-753-1(6)*, 2772, Bks. for Young Learners) Owen, Richard C. Pubs., Inc.
—Nathan of Yesteryear & Michael of Today. Heinz, Brian J. 2006. (Exceptional Social Studies Titles for Intermediate Grades). (ENG.). 32p. (J). (gr. 3-6). lib. bdg. 22.60 *(978-0-7613-2893-3(9)*, Millbrook Pr.) Lerner Publishing Group.
—O Christmas Tree: Its History & Holiday Traditions. Farmer, Jacqueline. 2010. 32p. (J). (gr. k-3). pap. 7.95 *(978-1-58089-239-1(6))* Charlesbridge Publishing, Inc.
—A Place for Elijah. Ruben, Kelly Easton. 2016. (ENG.). 32p. (J). (gr. k-4). 9.99 *(978-1-4677-7841-1(9)*, 9781467778411, Kar-Ben Publishing) Lerner Publishing Group.
Fricker, Steve. Como Funcionan los Animales. Ganeri, Anita. (Coleccion Como Funcionan). (SPA.). 30p. (J). (gr. 1-3). 18.95 *(978-84-272-4092-6(9)*, ML30534) Molino, Editorial ESP. Dist: Lectorum Pubns., Inc.
Fricker, Steve & Holder, John. Como Funcionan los Huesos y Otras Partes del Cuerpo. Ganeri, Anita. (Coleccion Como Funcionan). (SPA.). 30p. (J). (gr. 1-3). *(978-84-272-4091-9(0)*, ML30533) Molino, Editorial ESP. Dist: Lectorum Pubns., Inc.
Friday, Arthur. Peter Pan: An Illustrated Classic for Kids & Young Readers (Excellent for Bedtime & Young Readers) Barrie, J. M. eMusic, Tom, ed. 2013. 38p. pap. 6.99 *(978-1-62321-067-0(4))* Tommye-music Corp. DBA Tom eMusic.
Fridell, Pat. Thar She Blows! Whaling in The 1860s. Kassirer, Sue. 2007. 32p. (J). 15.00 *(978-1-4223-6721-6(5))* DIANE Publishing Co.
Fridolfs, Derek. Fantastic Four: The Chameleon Strikes! Dezago, Todd. 2006. (Spider-Man Team Up Ser.). (ENG.). 24p. (J). (gr. 2-6). lib. bdg. 27.07 *(978-1-59961-005-4(1)*, 13645, Marvel Age) Spotlight.
Fried, Janice. A Mezuzah on the Door. Meltzer, Amy. 2007. (Jewish Identity Ser.). 32p. (J). (gr. -1-3). 17.95 *(978-1-58013-249-7(9))*; Vol. (ENG.). 7.95 *(978-1-58013-251-0(0))* Lerner Publishing Group. (Kar-Ben Publishing).
—Where Is Grandpa Dennis? Abraham, Michelle Shapiro. 2009. (J). *(978-0-8074-1083-7(7))* URJ Pr.
Friedel, Charles J. Hi It's Me! I Have ADHD. Mabry, Katelyn. 2020. (ENG.). 28p. (J). (gr. k-4). pap. 9.99 ***(978-1-948604-38-3(8)***, Purple Butterfly Pr.) Kat Biggie Pr.

Friedel, J. Charles. Hi, It's Me! I Have ADHD. Mabry, Katelyn. 2020. (ENG.). 28p. (J). (gr. k-3). 19.99 ***(978-1-948604-37-6(X)**, Purple Butterfly Pr.) Kat Biggie Pr.

Friedericy Dolls. Into the Woods: Favorite Fairy Tales from the World of Friedericy Dolls. Greer, Rob, photos by. 2009. 74p. (J). *(978-0-9824812-0-2(9))* POCEE Publishing.

Friedlander, Randolyn. The Mystery at Area 51. Marsh, Carole. 2011. (Carole Marsh Mysteries Ser.). 32p. pap. 7.99 *(978-0-635-07961-9(5)*, Marsh, Carole Mysteries) Gallopade International.

—The Mystery at Cape Cod. Marsh, Carole. 2010. (Real Kids, Real Places Teacher Guides). 32p. (J). pap. 7.99 *(978-0-635-07600-7(4))* Gallopade International.

—The Mystery at Fort Sumter. Marsh, Carole. 2010. (Real Kids, Real Places Ser.). 32p. (J). pap. 7.99 *(978-0-635-07432-4(X)*, Marsh, Carole Mysteries) Gallopade International.

—The Mystery at Motown. Marsh, Carole. 2011. (Carole Marsh Mysteries Ser.). 32p. pap. 7.99 *(978-0-635-07962-6(3)*, Marsh, Carole Mysteries) Gallopade International.

—The Mystery at Mount Vernon. Marsh, Carole. 2010. (Real Kids, Real Places Ser.). 32p. pap. 7.99 *(978-0-635-07444-7(3)*, Marsh, Carole Mysteries) Gallopade International.

—The Mystery in Hawaii. Marsh, Carole. 2010. (Real Kids, Real Places Ser.). 32p. pap. 7.99 *(978-0-635-07447-8(8)*, Marsh, Carole Mysteries) Gallopade International.

—The Mystery on the Oregon Trail. Marsh, Carole. 2010. (Real Kids, Real Places Ser.). 32p. pap. 7.99 *(978-0-635-07441-6(9)*, Marsh, Carole Mysteries) Gallopade International.

Friedman, Judith. Aidan of Oren: The Journey Begins. St. Jean, Alan. 2004. (ENG.). 208p. (J). (gr. 4-7). 19.95 *(978-0-9724853-5-7(X))* Keene Publishing.

—One Incredible Dog! Boone. Williams, Christopher. 2005. (One Incredible Dog! Ser.). (ENG.). 32p. (J). (gr. -1-3). lib. bdg. 15.95 *(978-0-9724853-9-5(2))* Keene Publishing.

—One Incredible Dog! Kizzy. Williams, Christopher. 2006. (One Incredible Dog! Ser.). (ENG.). 32p. (J). (gr. -1-3). lib. bdg. 15.95 *(978-0-9766805-5-0(6))* Keene Publishing.

—One Incredible Dog! Lady. Williams, Christopher. 2004. (ENG.). 32p. (J). (gr. -1-3). 15.95 *(978-0-9724853-3-3(3)*, 845-987-7750) Keene Publishing.

Friedman, Laura. Henry the Steinway a Star Is Born. Coveleskie, Sally & Peter, Goodrich. 2003. (Henry the Steinway Ser.: Vol. 2). 32p. (J). (gr. k-3). *(978-0-9729427-1-3(8))* Yorkville Pr.

—Henry the Steinway & the Piano Recital. Coveleskie, Sally et al. 2003. (Henry the Steinway Ser.: Vol. 1). 32p. (J). (gr. k-3). *(978-1-931721-05-9(X))* Night Heron Media.

—Henry the Steinway Tours the World. Coveleskie, Sally & Goodrich, Peter. 2005. (Henry the Steinway Ser.: 3). 32p. (J). (gr. -1-3). 15.95 *(978-0-9729427-8-2(5))* Yorkville Pr.

Friedman, Michael (Myk). Echoes of the Lost Boys of Sudan, 4 vols., Vol. 1. Clark, Susan, ed. 2nd l.t. ed. 2004. 36p. (YA). 4.95 *(978-0-9759995-0-9(8))* Echoes Joint Venture.

Friend, Alison. Bear's Book. Freedman, Claire. 2019. (ENG.). 34p. (J). (gr. -1-2). 16.99 *(978-1-5362-0571-8(0)*, Templar) Candlewick Pr.

—Bramble & Maggie: Give & Take. Haas, Jessie. 2013. 56p. (J). (gr. k-3). 14.99 *(978-0-7636-5021-6(8))* Candlewick Pr.

—Bramble & Maggie Give & Take. Haas, Jessie. 2015. (Candlewick Sparks Ser.). 56p. (J). (gr. k-4). pap. 4.99 *(978-0-7636-7787-9(6))* Candlewick Pr.

—Bramble & Maggie: Horse Meets Girl. Haas, Jessie. 2013. (Candlewick Sparks Ser.). 56p. (J). (gr. k-3). pap. 4.99 *(978-0-7636-6251-6(8))* Candlewick Pr.

—Bramble & Maggie: Snow Day. Haas, Jessie. (Candlewick Sparks Ser.). 56p. (J). (gr. k-4). 2017. pap. 4.99 *(978-0-7636-9780-8(X))*; 2016. 14.99 *(978-0-7636-7364-2(1))* Candlewick Pr.

—Bramble & Maggie Spooky Season. Haas, Jessie. 2016. (Candlewick Sparks Ser.). 56p. (J). (gr. k-3). pap. 5.99 *(978-0-7636-8743-4(X))* Candlewick Pr.

—Making a Friend. Sauer, Tammi. 2018. (ENG.). 40p. (J). (gr. -1-3). 17.99 *(978-0-06-227893-7(2))* HarperCollins Pubs.

—Scrawny Cat. Root, Phyllis. 2011. 40p. (J). (gr. -1-3). 16.99 *(978-0-7636-4164-1(2))* Candlewick Pr.

—The Secret Life of Figgy Mustardo. Chall, Marsha Wilson. 2016. (ENG.). 40p. (J). (gr. -1-3). 17.99 *(978-0-06-228582-9(3)*, Tegen, Katherine Bks) HarperCollins Pubs.

—That Bear Can't Babysit. Quayle, Ruth. 2018. (ENG.). 32p. (J). (gr. -1-2). 16.99 *(978-0-7636-9952-9(7))*, Nosy Crow) Candlewick Pr.

—What Color Is Caesar? Kumin, Maxine. 2010. (ENG.). 56p. (J). (gr. -1-k). 16.99 *(978-0-7636-3432-2(8))* Candlewick Pr.

Friend, Alison. Freddy & Frito & the Clubhouse Rules. Friend, Alison. 2015. (ENG.). 40p. (J). (gr. -1-3). 17.99 *(978-0-06-228580-5(7))* HarperCollins Pubs.

Friend, Bonnie. The Little Carrot, 1 vol. Waxman, Melanie Brown. 2009. 39p. pap. 24.95 *(978-1-61546-046-5(2))* America Star Bks.

Friend, David Michael. Blueberry Mouse. Friend, David Michael, tr. Low, Alice. 2004. (J). 15.95 *(978-1-59336-111-2(4))*; pap. *(978-1-59336-112-9(2))* Mondo Publishing.

Friesen, Alex. Okapi Jack & Me. Paetkau, Alia. 2017. (ENG.). (J). (gr. k-3). pap. *(978-1-4866-1529-2(5))* Word Alive Pr.

Friesen, Anni. A Big Change, 1 vol. Unrau, Adela. 2010. 16p. pap. 24.95 *(978-1-4489-7672-0(3))* PublishAmerica, Inc.

—That Was a Nice Surprise, 1 vol. Unrau, Adela. 2010. 16p. 24.95 *(978-1-4489-5744-6(3))* PublishAmerica, Inc.

Friesen, Ippiksaut. Only in My Hometown, 1 vol. Friesen, Angnakuluk. Kusugak, Jean, tr. ed. 2017. (ENG.). 24p. (J). (gr. -1-2). 18.95 *(978-1-55498-883-9(7))* Groundwood Bks. CAN. Dist: Publishers Group West (PGW).

Friesen, Wayne. Dino Treasure Hunt, 1 vol. Henry, LaTosha. 2010. 16p. 24.95 *(978-1-4489-3966-4(6))* PublishAmerica, Inc.

Friet, Sarah. Primary Potions. Hunter, Chelsea. 2019. (Color Coven Collection: Vol. 1). (ENG.). 30p. (J). pap. 10.00 *(978-1-0741-7805-5(X))* Independently Published.

Frigeri, Juan. Age of X-Man: the Amazing Nightcrawler. 2019. (ENG.). 112p. (YA). (gr. 8-17). pap. 15.99 *(978-1-302-91577-3(0))* Marvel Worldwide, Inc.

Frigeri, Juan, et al. Spider-Verse: Spider-Zero. 2020. (ENG.). 136p. (J). (gr. 4-17). pap. 17.99 ***(978-1-302-92026-5(X))*** Marvel Worldwide, Inc.

Frigeri, Juan. Star Wars: Darth Maul - Son of Dathomir. 2017. 136p. (J). (gr. 4-17). pap. 15.99 *(978-1-302-90846-1(4))* Marvel Worldwide, Inc.

Friis, Karen. Ethan's Butterflies: A Spiritual Book for Parents & Young Children after a Baby's Passing. Jonas-Simpson, Christine. 2009. (ENG.). 24p. pap. 9.95 *(978-1-4120-8850-3(X))* Trafford Publishing.

Frink, Josh, jt. illus. see Sawvel, Gennai.

Frink, Phil, photos by. What's the Difference? Costa, David. 2004. 24p. (J). per. 26.99 *(978-1-4134-4855-9(0))* Xlibris Corp.

Frischeteau, Gérard. Water's Children: Celebrating the Resource That Unites Us All. Delaunois, Angèle. Woods, Erin, tr. from FRE. 2017. (ENG.). 32p. (J). (gr. k-3). 16.95 *(978-1-77278-015-4(4))* Pajama Pr. CAN. Dist: Ingram Publisher Services.

Frisk, Maria, jt. illus. see Perkins, Nicole.

Fristoe Sr, John. Trevor & the T's. Nemec, Gale. 2019. (ENG.). 32p. (J). pap. 10.00 *(978-1-5086-8920-1(2))* CreateSpace Independent Publishing Platform.

—Trevor & the T's. Nemec, Gale. 2019. (ENG.). 32p. (J). pap. 10.00 *(978-1-947608-12-2(6))* Nemec LLC.

Frith, Michael. Coming to England. Benjamin, Floella. 2017. (ENG.). 144p. (J). (gr. 4-6). 9.99 *(978-1-5098-3549-2(0))* Pan Macmillan GBR. Dist: Independent Pubs. Group.

Frith, Nicholas John. Beavers. Poliquin, Rachel. (Superpower Field Guide Ser.). (ENG.). 96p. (J). (gr. 3-7). 2020. pap. 8.99 *(978-0-358-27257-1(2)*, 1771928); 2018. 18.99 *(978-0-544-94987-4(0)*, 1659964) Houghton Mifflin Harcourt Publishing Co. (HMH Books For Young Readers).

—Moles. Poliquin, Rachel. (Superpower Field Guide Ser.). (ENG.). 96p. (J). (gr. 3-7). 2020. pap. 8.99 *(978-0-358-27259-5(9)*, 1771930); 2019. 18.99 *(978-0-544-95107-5(7)*, 1659965) Houghton Mifflin Harcourt Publishing Co. (HMH Books For Young Readers).

—Ostriches. Poliquin, Rachel. (Superpower Field Guide Ser.). (ENG.). 96p. (J). (gr. 3-7). 2020. pap. 8.99 *(978-0-358-27266-3(1)*, 1771931); 2019. 18.99 *(978-0-544-95040-5(2)*, 1659969) Houghton Mifflin Harcourt Publishing Co. (HMH Books For Young Readers).

Frith, Nicholas John. Hector & Hummingbird. Frith, Nicholas John. 2016. (ENG.). 32p. (J). (gr. -1-3). 17.99 *(978-0-545-85701-7(5))* Scholastic, Inc.

—Hello, Mr. Dodo! Frith, Nicholas John. 2017. (ENG.). 32p. (J). (gr. -1-3). 17.99 *(978-1-338-08939-4(0))* Scholastic, Inc.

Frito Bastien, jt. illus. see Esperanta Delmat.

Fritz, C. S. Good Night Tales: A Family Treasury of Read-Aloud Stories. Fritz, C. S. 2017. (ENG.). 176p. (J). 19.99 *(978-1-63146-556-7(2)*, 20_11823) NavPress Publishing Group.

Fritz, Jack P. One of My Favorite Things to Do. Caprio Scalera, Jill S. 2019. (ENG.). 30p. (J). pap. 9.99 *(978-1-7192-0895-6(6))* CreateSpace Independent Publishing Platform.

Fritz, Kathleen Cheney. Tears of Mother Bear. Lewis, Anne Margaret. 2012. 32p. (J). (gr. -1-3). pap. 8.95 *(978-1-934133-62-0(0)*, Mackinac Island Press, Inc.) Charlesbridge Publishing, Inc.

Fritz Perry, Marie. I Love Seeds. Smithwick, Julie. 2018. (ENG.). 32p. (J). pap. *(978-1-988071-83-1(6))* Hasmark Services Publishing.

Fritz, Ron. Sam y Sus Cuadrados de Zapatos (Sam's Sneaker Squares) Measuring: Area. Gabriel, Nat. 2009. (Math Matters en Español Ser.). (SPA.). 32p. (J). (gr. 1-3). pap. 5.95 *(978-1-57565-276-4(5))* Astra Publishing Hse.

—Sam's Sneaker Squares: Measuring: Area. Gabriel, Nat. 2006. (Math Matters ® Ser.). (ENG.). 32p. (J). (gr. k-3). pap. 5.95 *(978-1-57565-114-9(9))* Astra Publishing Hse.

Fritz, Siegfried. Katie's Day. Iverson, Gregory. 2006. 48p. (J). *(978-0-9755184-1-0(0))* Sandbox Bks.

—Tyler's Big Blue Truck. Iverson, Gregory. 2006. 40p. (J). *(978-0-9755184-0-3(2))* Sandbox Bks.

Froehlich, Cindy. Legend of the Star Runner: A Timmi Tobbson Adventure. Wagner, J. I. Hall, Bradley, ed. 2018. 168p. (YA). pap. 12.99 *(978-3-96326-777-2(1))* Upper Room Bks.

Froehlich, Marie. Brave Little Black Bear. Froehlich, Frances. 2018. (ENG.). 40p. (J). pap. 14.95 *(978-1-64299-530-5(4))* Christian Faith Publishing.

Froese, Tom. Whose Boat? Buzzeo, Toni. 2018. (ENG.). 16p. (J). (gr. -1 — 1). bds. 9.99 *(978-1-4197-2835-8(0)*, Abrams Appleseed) Abrams, Inc.

Fröhlich, Lorenz & Pedersen, Vilhelm. Hans Andersen's Fairy Tales: A Selection. Andersen, Hans. Kingsland, L. W., tr. 2009. (Oxford World's Classics Ser.). (ENG.). 384p. pap. 10.95 *(978-0-19-955585-7(0))* Oxford Univ. Pr., Inc.

Frongia, Daniela. The Adventures of Camellia N. The Arctic. Wideroe, Debra L. 2016. (Adventures of Camellia N. Ser.: 1). (ENG.). 36p. (J). (gr. -1-2). 16.95 *(978-0-9970851-1-2(8))* Notable Kids Publishing.

—The Adventures of Camellia N.; the Rainforest. Wideroe, Debra. 2018. (Adventures of Camellia N. Ser.: 3). (ENG.). 40p. (J). (gr. k-3). 16.95 *(978-0-9970851-4-3(2))* Notable Kids Publishing.

—Allah's Gifts. Nazeer, Tasnim & Publishing, Greenbirdbooks Childrens. 2012. 26p. pap. *(978-0-9562141-7-1(7))* Greenbird Bks.

—A Beautiful Husky Needs a Home. Orcutt, Cherie. 2012. 32p. pap. 21.00 *(978-1-4685-7156-1(7))* AuthorHouse.

Frongia, Daniela. The Magic Glasses. Sands, Shannon & Verstraelen, Marcus. 2019. (ENG.). 34p. (J). pap. 11.99 ***(978-1-0804-7852-1(3))*** Independently Published.

Frongia, Daniela. Mister D. Stevens, Elizabeth. 2012. 24p. (J). 16.95 *(978-1-60131-114-6(1))* Big Tent Bks.

—Otto the Otter's Muddy Puddle. Rafter, Chez. 2018. (Rubbish Rebellion Ser.: Vol. 2). (ENG.). 40p. (J). *(978-0-6484070-1-0(2))* Aurora House.

—What Made Ben Happy. Nyanzi, Sarah Kiki. 2018. (ENG.). 40p. (J). pap. 10.69 *(978-1-948581-30-1(2))* Lincross Publishing.

Front, Charles. Carbonel & Calidor: Being the Further Adventures of a Royal Cat. Sleigh, Barbara. 2009. (Carbonel Ser.). (ENG.). 224p. (J). (gr. 4-7). 17.95 *(978-1-59017-333-6(3)*, NYR Children's Collection) New York Review of Bks., Inc., The.

Fronty, Aurélia. Animals of the Bible. Delval, Marie-Hélène. 2010. (ENG.). 88p. (J). (gr. -1-3). 16.50 *(978-0-8028-5376-9(5)*, Eerdmans Bks For Young Readers) Eerdmans, William B. Publishing Co.

—Hilo de Hada. Lechermeier, Philippe. Rozarena, P., tr. from FRE. 2009. (SPA.). 89p. (J). (gr. 4-7). *(978-84-263-7257-4(0))* Vives, Luis Editorial (Edelvives).

—I Have the Right to Be a Child, 1 vol. Serres, Alain. Mixter, Helen, tr. 2012. (ENG.). 48p. (J). (gr. -1-2). 18.95 *(978-1-55498-149-6(2))* Groundwood Bks. CAN. Dist: Publishers Group West (PGW).

—Malala: Activist for Girls' Education. Frier, Raphaële. 2017. 45p. (J). *(978-1-63289-592-9(7))* Charlesbridge Publishing, Inc.

—Malala: Activist for Girls' Education. Frier, Raphaële. 2017. (ENG.). 48p. (J). (gr. 1-4). 17.99 *(978-1-58089-785-3(1))* Charlesbridge Publishing, Inc.

—One City, Two Brothers. Smith, Chris. 2007. (ENG.). 32p. (J). (gr. -1-3). 16.99 *(978-1-84686-042-3(3))* Barefoot Bks., Inc.

—One City, Two Brothers: A Story from Jerusalem. Smith, Chris & Barefoot Books. 2015. (ENG.). 32p. (J). (gr. 1-4). pap. 9.99 *(978-1-78285-252-0(2))* Barefoot Bks., Inc.

—Songs from a Journey with a Parrot: Lullabies & Nursery Rhymes from Portugal & Brazil. Lerasle, Magdeleine. 2013. (POR & ENG.). 52p. (J). (gr. -1-k). 16.95 *(978-2-923163-99-4(0))* La Montagne Secrete CAN. Dist: Independent Pubs. Group.

—Sube y Baja Por Los Andes: Un Cuento de un Festival Peruano. Krebs, Laurie. 2011. 32p. (J). (gr. 1-6). pap. 7.99 *(978-1-84686-548-0(4))* Barefoot Bks., Inc.

—Up & down the Andes. Krebs, Laurie. 2011. (ENG.). 32p. (J). (gr. k-1). pap. 8.99 *(978-1-84686-468-1(2))* Barefoot Bks., Inc.

—Up & down the Andes: A Peruvian Festival Tale. Krebs, Laurie. 2008. 32p. (J). (gr. -1-5). 16.99 *(978-1-84686-203-8(5))* Barefoot Bks., Inc.

Frossard, Claire. Emma's Journey. Frossard, Etienne, photos by. 2010. (ENG.). 56p. (J). (gr. -1-3). 17.95 *(978-1-59270-099-8(3))* Enchanted Lion Bks., LLC.

—Little Mole, Please Open the Door! Lallemand, Orianne. 2018. (ENG.). 32p. (J). 14.95 *(978-2-7338-6146-2(8))* Auzou, Philippe Editions FRA. Dist: Consortium Bk. Sales & Distribution.

—A Surprise for Little Mole. Lallemand, Orianne. 2019. (ENG.). 30p. (J). 14.95 *(978-2-7338-6732-7(6))* Auzou, Philippe Editions FRA. Dist: Consortium Bk. Sales & Distribution.

Frost, Adam. Paw Prints in the Snow. Grindley, Sally. 2012. 105p. (J). (gr. 3-5). pap. 11.99 *(978-1-4088-1945-6(7)*, 900086973, Bloomsbury Children's Bks.) Bloomsbury Publishing USA.

Frost, Bruno, et al. A World of Friends Coloring Book: The Story of the Tower of Babel. 2019. (St. Jerome Library Coloring Bks.: Vol. 17). (ENG.). 26p. (J). pap. 7.95 *(978-1-0728-0350-8(X))* Independently Published.

Frost, Julian. Do Not Lick This Book. Ben-barak, Idan. 2018. (ENG.). 40p. (J). 16.99 *(978-1-250-17536-6(4)*, 900189389) Roaring Brook Pr.

Frost, Julian. There's a Skeleton Inside You! Ben-Barak, Idan. 2020. (ENG.). 40p. (J). 16.99 ***(978-1-250-17537-3(2)**, 900189390) Roaring Brook Pr.

Frost, Justine. Squeaks Narrow Squeaks. Davey, Keith Peter. 2009. 32p. pap. 14.62 *(978-1-4120-4402-8(2))* Trafford Publishing.

Frost, Maddie. The Adventures of Chatterer the Red Squirrel. Burgess, Thornton W. 2017. (Thornton Burgess Library). (ENG.). 128p. (J). (gr. -1-2). pap. 9.95 *(978-1-63322-369-1(8)*, Seagrass) Quarto Publishing Group USA.

—The Adventures of Paddy the Beaver. Burgess, Thornton W. 2018. (Thornton Burgess Library). (ENG.). 128p. (J). (gr. -1-2). pap. 9.95 *(978-1-63322-554-1(2)*, Seagrass) Quarto Publishing Group USA.

—Alfie & Bet's ABC. 2018. (J). 12.99 *(978-1-61067-647-2(5))* Kane Miller.

—The Amazing Life Cycle of Butterflies. Barnham, Kay. 2018. (Look & Wonder Ser.). (ENG.). 32p. (J). (gr. k-3). 10.99 *(978-1-4380-5042-3(9)*, B.E.S. Publishing) Peterson's.

—The Amazing Life Cycle of Plants. Barnham, Kay. 2018. (Look & Wonder Ser.). (ENG.). 32p. (J). (gr. k-3). 10.99 *(978-1-4380-5043-0(7)*, B.E.S. Publishing) Peterson's.

—Candy Apple Blessings, 1 vol. 2018. (Sweet Blessings Ser.). (ENG.). 20p. (J). bds. 8.99 *(978-1-4003-1779-0(7))* Nelson, Thomas Inc.

—Everybody Needs a Buddy. Jackson, Ellen. 2019. (ENG.). 26p. (J). (gr. -1 — 1). bds. 7.99 *(978-1-5344-3971-9(4)*, Little Simon) Little Simon.

—The Great Big Water Cycle Adventure. Barnham, Kay. 2018. (Look & Wonder Bks.). (ENG.). 32p. (J). (gr. k-3). 10.99 *(978-1-4380-5044-7(5)*, B.E.S. Publishing) Peterson's.

—Indestructibles: Busy City. 2018. (Indestructibles Ser.). (ENG.). 12p. (J). pap. 5.95 *(978-1-5235-0468-8(4)*, 100468) Workman Publishing Co., Inc.

—Indestructibles: Hello, Farm! 2018. (Indestructibles Ser.). (ENG.). 12p. (J). pap. 5.95 *(978-1-5235-0467-1(6)*, 100467) Workman Publishing Co., Inc.

—Indestructibles: ¡Hola, Granja! / Hello, Farm! 2020. (Indestructibles Ser.). (SPA.). 12p. (J). (— 1). pap. 5.95 *(978-1-5235-0989-8(9)*, 100989) Workman Publishing Co., Inc.

—Indestructibles: My Neighborhood. 2018. (Indestructibles Ser.). (ENG.). 12p. (J). pap. 5.95 *(978-1-5235-0469-5(2)*, 100469) Workman Publishing Co., Inc.

—It's Not the Baby. Lewis, J. Patrick & Lewis, Leigh. 2017. 14p. (J). (gr. -1 — 1). bds. 9.99 *(978-1-68152-194-7(6))* Amicus.

—It's Not the Puppy. Lewis, J. Patrick & Lewis, Leigh. 2019. 14p. (J). (gr. -1-k). bds. 9.99 *(978-1-68152-409-2(0))* Amicus.

—Jelly Bean Blessings, 1 vol. 2019. (Sweet Blessings Ser.). (ENG.). 20p. (J). bds. 8.99 *(978-1-4002-0932-3(3))* Nelson, Thomas Inc.

—Little Hugs from Little Loves. Sperring, Mark. 2019. (ENG.). 24p. (J). (gr. -1 — 1). bds. 7.99 *(978-0-316-48433-6(4))* Little, Brown Bks. for Young Readers.

—The Littlest Things Give the Loveliest Hugs. Sperring, Mark. 2018. (ENG.). 32p. (J). (gr. -1-3). 17.99 *(978-0-316-48434-3(2))* Little, Brown Bks. for Young Readers.

—Peekaboo Baby Animals. Tiger Tales. 2017. (ENG.). 12p. (J). (gr. -1-k). bds. 7.99 *(978-1-68010-514-8(0))* Tiger Tales.

—The Snowflake Mistake. Treleaven, Lou. 2018. (ENG.). 32p. (J). (gr. -1-3). 17.99 *(978-1-84886-312-5(8))* Maverick Arts Publishing GBR. Dist: Lerner Publishing Group.

—A Stroll Through the Seasons. Barnham, Kay. 2018. (Look & Wonder Ser.). (ENG.). 32p. (J). (gr. k-3). 10.99 *(978-1-4380-5041-6(0)*, B.E.S. Publishing) Peterson's.

—What Makes a Blizzard? Zoehfeld, Kathleen Weidner. 2018. (Let's-Read-And-Find-Out Science 2 Ser.). (ENG.). 40p. (J). (gr. -1-3). 17.99 *(978-0-06-248473-4(7))*; pap. 6.99 *(978-0-06-248472-7(9))* HarperCollins Pubs.

Frost, Maddie. Once upon a Zzzz. Frost, Maddie. 2018. (ENG.). 40p. (J). (gr. -1-k). 16.99 *(978-0-8075-6064-8(2)*, 807560642) Whitman, Albert & Co.

Frost, Michael, photos by. Boo Who? A Foldout Halloween Adventure. Schaefer, Lola M. 2009. (ENG., 12p. (J). (gr. -1-k). bds. 7.99 *(978-1-4169-5911-3(4)*, Little Simon) Little Simon.

—Private Killer: Book Two in the Killer Mystery Trilogy, Bk. 2. 2010. (Hardy Boys (All New) Undercover Brothers Ser.: 32). (ENG., 160p. (J). (gr. 3-7). pap. 5.99 *(978-1-4169-8697-3(9)*, Aladdin) Simon & Schuster Children's Publishing.

—The Vincent Brothers. Glines, Abbi. 2012. (ENG., 304p. (YA). (gr. 11). 17.99 *(978-1-4424-8529-7(9)*, Simon Pulse) Simon Pulse.

Frost, Tom. The Greatest Opposites Book on Earth. Singh, Lee. 2017. (ENG.). 16p. (J). (gr. -1-2). bds. 18.99 *(978-0-7636-9554-5(8)*, Big Picture Press) Candlewick Pr.

—Under Threat: An Album of Endangered Animals. Jenkins, Martin. 2019. (ENG.). 64p. (J). (gr. 4-7). 19.99 *(978-1-5362-0543-5(5))* Candlewick Pr.

Froud, Brian. Chelsea Morning. 2004. (ENG.). 32p. (J). (gr. -1-3). 17.95 *(978-1-59687-178-6(4))* IBks., Inc.

—Chelsea Morning. 2004. 32p. (J). *(978-0-689-03593-7(4)*, Milk & Cookies) ibooks, Inc.

—Shadows of the Dark Crystal #1. Lee, J. M. 2016. (Jim Henson's the Dark Crystal Ser.: 1). (ENG.). 272p. (YA). (gr. 7). 17.99 *(978-0-448-48289-7(4)*, Grosset & Dunlap) Penguin Young Readers Group.

Froud, Brian & Godbey, Cory. Shadows of the Dark Crystal #1. Lee, J. M. 2019. (Jim Henson's the Dark Crystal Ser.: 1). 288p. (YA). (gr. 7). pap. 9.99 *(978-1-5247-9097-4(4)*, Penguin Workshop) Penguin Young Readers Group.

Froud, Wendy. Midsummer Night's Faery Tale. Jones, John Lawrence, photos by. Windling, Terri. 2005. 52p. (J). (gr. k-4). reprint ed. 18.00 *(978-0-7567-8759-2(9))* DIANE Publishing Co.

Fruchter, Jason. The Baby Is Here! 2015. (Daniel Tiger's Neighborhood Ser.). (ENG.). 24p. (J). (gr. -1-2). pap. 4.99 *(978-1-4814-3013-5(0)*, Simon Spotlight) Simon Spotlight.

—Big Brother Daniel. Santomero, Angela C. 2015. (Daniel Tiger's Neighborhood Ser.). (ENG.). 14p. (J). (gr. -1-k). bds. 6.99 *(978-1-4814-3172-9(2)*, Simon Spotlight) Simon Spotlight.

—Big Enough to Help. 2015. (Daniel Tiger's Neighborhood Ser.). (ENG.). 24p. (J). (gr. -1-1). pap. 5.99 *(978-1-4814-2942-9(6)*, Simon Spotlight) Simon Spotlight.

—The Big Pony Race. David, Erica. 2006. 27p. (J). *(978-0-7172-9869-3(8))* Scholastic, Inc.

—Books Are the Best. 2019. (Daniel Tiger's Neighborhood Ser.). (ENG.). 32p. (J). (gr. -1-k). 17.99 *(978-1-5344-5491-0(8))*; pap. 4.99 *(978-1-5344-5490-3(X))* Simon Spotlight. (Simon Spotlight).

—A Busy Day in the Neighborhood. Spinner, Cala. 2017. (Daniel Tiger's Neighborhood Ser.). (ENG.). 12p. (J). (gr. -1-k). bds. 14.99 *(978-1-4814-8583-8(0)*, Simon Spotlight) Simon Spotlight.

—Calm at the Restaurant. 2019. (Daniel Tiger's Neighborhood Ser.). (ENG.). 16p. (J). (gr. -1-2). pap. 6.99 *(978-1-5344-5193-3(5)*, Simon Spotlight) Simon Spotlight.

—Christmas Countdown (Team Umizoomi) Golden Books. 2013. (ENG.). 48p. (J). (gr. -1-2). pap. 3.99 *(978-0-449-81853-4(5)*, Golden Bks.) Random Hse. Children's Bks.

—Christmas Wishes. 2018. (PJ Masks Ser.). (ENG.). 26p. (J). (gr. -1-2). 12.99 *(978-1-5344-2059-5(2)*, Simon Spotlight) Simon Spotlight.

—Daniel & the Nutcracker. Santomero, Angela C. 2018. (Daniel Tiger's Neighborhood Ser.). (ENG.). 20p. (J). (gr. -1 — 1). bds. 6.99 *(978-1-5344-2206-3(4)*, Simon Spotlight) Simon Spotlight.

—Daniel & the Nutcracker. 2015. (Daniel Tiger's Neighborhood Ser.). (ENG.). 26p. (J). (gr. -1-2). 12.99 *(978-1-4814-4345-6(3)*, Simon Spotlight) Simon Spotlight.

—Daniel Can Dance. Finnegan, Delphine. 2018. (Daniel Tiger's Neighborhood Ser.). (ENG.). 32p. (J). (gr. -1-k). 17.99 *(978-1-5344-3041-9(5))*; pap. 4.99 *(978-1-5344-3040-2(7))* Simon Spotlight. (Simon Spotlight).

—Daniel Chooses to Be Kind. 2017. (Daniel Tiger's Neighborhood Ser.). (ENG.). 24p. (J). (gr. -1-2). pap. 4.99

F

(978-1-5344-0130-3(X), Simon Spotlight) Simon Spotlight.
—Daniel Feels Left Out. 2015. (Daniel Tiger's Neighborhood Ser.). (ENG.). 32p. (J). (gr. -1-k). 16.99 (978-1-4814-3836-0(0), Simon Spotlight) Simon Spotlight.
—Daniel Finds a New Friend. Testa, Maggie. 2018. (Daniel Tiger's Neighborhood Ser.). (ENG.). 32p. (J). (gr. -1-k). 17.99 (978-1-5344-2938-3(7)); pap. 4.99 (978-1-5344-2937-6(9)) Simon Spotlight. (Simon Spotlight).
—Daniel Gets His Hair Cut. 2019. (Daniel Tiger's Neighborhood Ser.). (ENG.). 24p. (J). (gr. -1-2). pap. 4.99 (978-1-5344-4327-3(4), Simon Spotlight) Simon Spotlight.
—Daniel Gets Scared. 2015. (Daniel Tiger's Neighborhood Ser.). (ENG.). 32p. (J). (gr. -1-k). pap. 3.99 (978-1-4814-5257-1(6), Simon Spotlight) Simon Spotlight.
Fruchter, Jason. Daniel Goes Camping! 2020. (Daniel Tiger's Neighborhood Ser.). (ENG.). 32p. (J). (gr. -1-k). 17.99 **(978-1-5344-6424-7(7))**; pap. 4.99 **(978-1-5344-6423-0(9))** Simon Spotlight. (Simon Spotlight).
Fruchter, Jason. Daniel Goes Out for Dinner. 2015. (Daniel Tiger's Neighborhood Ser.). (ENG.). 32p. (J). (gr. -1-k). 16.99 (978-1-4814-2872-9(1), Simon Spotlight) Simon Spotlight.
—Daniel Goes to School. 2014. (Daniel Tiger's Neighborhood Ser.). (ENG.). 24p. (J). (gr. -1-7). pap. 3.99 (978-1-4814-0318-4(4), Simon Spotlight) Simon Spotlight.
—Daniel Goes to the Carnival. 2017. (Daniel Tiger's Neighborhood Ser.). (ENG.). 24p. (J). (gr. -1-2). pap. 4.99 (978-1-4814-7808-3(7), Simon Spotlight) Simon Spotlight.
—Daniel Goes to the Dentist. 2019. (Daniel Tiger's Neighborhood Ser.). (ENG.). 24p. (J). (gr. -1-2). pap. 4.99 (978-1-5344-4909-1(4), Simon Spotlight) Simon Spotlight.
—Daniel Goes to the Playground. 2015. (Daniel Tiger's Neighborhood Ser.). (ENG.). 24p. (J). (gr. -1-2). pap. 3.99 (978-1-4814-5198-7(7), Simon Spotlight) Simon Spotlight.
—Daniel Has an Allergy. 2017. (Daniel Tiger's Neighborhood Ser.). (ENG.). 24p. (J). (gr. -1-2). pap. 4.99 (978-1-5344-0905-7(X), Simon Spotlight) Simon Spotlight.
—Daniel Learns to Ride a Bike. 2018. (Daniel Tiger's Neighborhood Ser.). (ENG.). 32p. (J). (gr. -1-2). pap. 4.99 (978-1-5344-3086-0(5), Simon Spotlight) Simon Spotlight.
—Daniel Learns to Share. 2016. (Daniel Tiger's Neighborhood Ser.). (ENG.). 32p. (J). (gr. -1-k). pap. 4.99 (978-1-4814-6751-3(4), Simon Spotlight) Simon Spotlight.
—Daniel Loves Fall! 2017. (Daniel Tiger's Neighborhood Ser.). (ENG.). 12p. (J). (gr. -1-k). bds. 5.99 (978-1-5344-0453-3(8), Simon Spotlight) Simon Spotlight.
—Daniel Loves Playtime! Cassel Schwartz, Alexandra. 2019. (Daniel Tiger's Neighborhood Ser.). (ENG.). 16p. (J). (gr. -1-2). pap. 6.99 (978-1-5344-5709-6(7), Simon Spotlight) Simon Spotlight.
—Daniel Loves to Explore. 2020. (Daniel Tiger's Neighborhood Ser.). (ENG.). 14p. (J). (gr. -1-2). bds. 5.99 (978-1-5344-5555-9(8), Simon Spotlight) Simon Spotlight.
—Daniel Loves You. To Be Announced & Cassel, Alexandra. 2018. (Daniel Tiger's Neighborhood Ser.). (ENG.). 14p. (J). (gr. -1-k). bds. 5.99 (978-1-5344-3750-0(9), Simon Spotlight) Simon Spotlight.
—Daniel Meets the New Neighbors. 2018. (Daniel Tiger's Neighborhood Ser.). (ENG.). 32p. (J). (gr. -1-2). pap. 4.99 (978-1-5344-2962-8(X), Simon Spotlight) Simon Spotlight.
—Daniel Plays at School. 2016. (Daniel Tiger's Neighborhood Ser.). (ENG.). 32p. (J). (gr. -1-k). pap. 3.99 (978-1-4814-6102-3(8), Simon Spotlight) Simon Spotlight.
Fruchter, Jason. Daniel Plays in a Gentle Way. 2020. (Daniel Tiger's Neighborhood Ser.). (ENG.). 24p. (J). (gr. -1-2). pap. 4.99 **(978-1-5344-6448-3(4)**, Simon Spotlight) Simon Spotlight.
Fruchter, Jason. Daniel Tiger's 3-Minute Bedtime Stories. 2018. (Daniel Tiger's Neighborhood Ser.). (ENG.). 144p. (J). (gr. -1-2). 12.99 (978-1-5344-2859-1(3), Simon Spotlight) Simon Spotlight.
—Daniel Tiger's Day & Night. 2017. (Daniel Tiger's Neighborhood Ser.). (ENG.). 16p. (J). (gr. -1-1). 5.99 (978-1-5344-1176-0(3), Simon Spotlight) Simon Spotlight.
—Daniel Tiger's Treasury of Stories. 2018. (Daniel Tiger's Neighborhood Ser.). (ENG.). 30p. (J). (gr. -1-2). bds. 11.99 (978-1-5344-3312-0(0), Simon Spotlight) Simon Spotlight.
—Daniel Tries a New Food. 2015. (Daniel Tiger's Neighborhood Ser.). (ENG.). 24p. (J). (gr. -1-2). pap. 4.99 (978-1-4814-4170-4(1), Simon Spotlight) Simon Spotlight.
—Daniel Will Pack a Snack. Gallo, Tina. 2017. (Daniel Tiger's Neighborhood Ser.). (ENG.). 32p. (J). (gr. -1-k). 16.99 (978-1-5344-1118-0(6)); pap. 4.99 (978-1-5344-1117-3(8)) Simon Spotlight. (Simon Spotlight).
Fruchter, Jason. Daniel's Apple-Picking Adventure: A Scratch-&-Sniff Book. 2020. (Daniel Tiger's Neighborhood Ser.). (ENG.). 14p. (J). (gr. -1-1). bds. 8.99 **(978-1-5344-6587-9(1)**, Simon Spotlight) Simon Spotlight.
Fruchter, Jason. Daniel's Bath Time. 2019. (Daniel Tiger's Neighborhood Ser.). (ENG.). 22p. (J). (— 1). bds. 6.99 (978-1-5344-5553-5(1), Simon Spotlight) Simon Spotlight.
—Daniel's First Babysitter. 2018. (Daniel Tiger's Neighborhood Ser.). (ENG.). 24p. (J). (gr. -1-2). pap. 4.99 (978-1-5344-1655-0(2), Simon Spotlight) Simon Spotlight.
Fruchter, Jason. Daniel's First Day of School. 2020. (Daniel Tiger's Neighborhood Ser.). (ENG.). 16p. (J). (gr. -1-2). 6.99 **(978-1-5344-6306-6(2)**, Simon Spotlight) Simon Spotlight.
Fruchter, Jason. Daniel's First Fireworks. 2016. (Daniel Tiger's Neighborhood Ser.). (ENG.). 24p. (J). (gr. -1-2). pap. 3.99 (978-1-4814-6053-8(6), Simon Spotlight) Simon Spotlight.
—Daniel's First Sleepover. 2015. (Daniel Tiger's Neighborhood Ser.). (ENG.). 24p. (J). (gr. -1-2). pap. 4.99 (978-1-4814-2893-4(4), Simon Spotlight) Simon Spotlight.
Fruchter, Jason. Daniel's Little Songs for Big Feelings. 2020. (Daniel Tiger's Neighborhood Ser.). (ENG.). 112p. (J). (gr. -1-2). 12.99 **(978-1-5344-7090-3(5)**, Simon Spotlight) Simon Spotlight.
Fruchter, Jason. Daniel's New Friend. 2015. (Daniel Tiger's Neighborhood Ser.). (ENG.). 24p. (J). (gr. -1-2). pap. 4.99 (978-1-4814-3543-7(4), Simon Spotlight) Simon Spotlight.
—Daniel's Potty Time. 2019. (Daniel Tiger's Neighborhood Ser.). (ENG.). 16p. (J). (gr. -1-2). pap. 5.99 (978-1-5344-5175-9(7), Simon Spotlight) Simon Spotlight.
—Daniel's Ugga Mugga Box: Daniel Loves You, I Like to Be with My Family, Won't You Be My Neighbor? ed. 2019. (Daniel Tiger's Neighborhood Ser.). (ENG.). 42p. (J). (gr. -1-k). bds. 18.99 (978-1-5344-6112-3(4), Simon Spotlight) Simon Spotlight.
—Daniel's Winter Adventure. Friedman, Becky. ed. 2016. (Daniel Tiger's Neighborhood 8X8 Ser.). (ENG.). 24p. (gr. -1-2). 13.55 (978-0-606-39247-1(5)) Turtleback.
—Un Dia en la Playa. Silverhardt, Lauryn. Ziegler, Argentina Palacios, tr. 2004. (Dora la Exploradora Ser.).Tr. of Day at the Beach. (SPA.). 22p. (J). bds. 4.99 (978-0-689-86976-1(2), Libros Para Ninos) Libros Para Ninos.
—Dora Goes for a Ride. Beinstein, Phoebe. 2004. (Dora the Explorer Ser.). (ENG.). 22p. (J). bds. 4.99 (978-0-689-86372-1(1), Simon Spotlight/Nickelodeon) Simon Spotlight/Nickelodeon.
—Dora's Nursery Rhyme Adventure. Ricci, Christine. 2005. (Dora the Explorer Ser.). (J). (978-0-7172-9819-8(1)) Scholastic, Inc.
—A Duckling for Daniel. 2016. (Daniel Tiger's Neighborhood Ser.). (ENG.). 14p. (J). (gr. -1-k). bds. 5.99 (978-1-4814-5781-1(0), Simon Spotlight) Simon Spotlight.
—Fairy Magic (Dora the Explorer) Golden Books Staff. 2012. (ENG.). 48p. (J). (gr. -1-2). pap. 3.99 (978-0-307-93030-9(0), Golden Bks.) Random Hse. Children's Bks.
—Farm Alarm! (Team Umizoomi) Random House. 2014. (Step into Reading Ser.). (ENG.). 24p. (J). (gr. -1-1). pap. 3.99 (978-0-385-38508-4(0), Random Hse. Bks. for Young Readers) Random Hse. Children's Bks.
—Five Little Ninjalinos: A Halloween Story. 2018. (PJ Masks Ser.). (ENG.). 14p. (J). (gr. -1-2). bds. 6.99 (978-1-5344-1783-0(4), Simon Spotlight) Simon Spotlight.
—Friends Are the Best! Testa, Maggie. 2014. (Daniel Tiger's Neighborhood Ser.). (ENG.). 12p. (J). (gr. -1-k). bds. 5.99 (978-1-4424-9547-0(2), Simon Spotlight) Simon Spotlight.
—Friends Ask First! A Book about Sharing. 2019. (Daniel Tiger's Neighborhood Ser.). (ENG.). 14p. (J). (gr. -1-k). bds. 5.99 (978-1-5344-4052-4(6), Simon Spotlight) Simon Spotlight.
—Friends Help Each Other. 2014. (Daniel Tiger's Neighborhood Ser.). (ENG.). 32p. (J). (gr. -1-k). pap. 3.99 (978-1-4814-0366-5(4), Simon Spotlight) Simon Spotlight.
—Grow & Go with Daniel! No Red Sweater for Daniel; Tiger Family Trip; Daniel Goes to the Carnival; Daniel Chooses to Be Kind; Daniel's First Babysitter; Daniel Has an Allergy. ed. 2019. (Daniel Tiger's Neighborhood Ser.). (ENG.). 144p. (J). (gr. -1-2). pap. 17.99 (978-1-5344-5079-0(3), Simon Spotlight) Simon Spotlight.
—Happy Halloween, Daniel Tiger! A Lift-The-Flap Book. Santomero, Angela C. 2014. (Daniel Tiger's Neighborhood Ser.). (ENG.). 14p. (J). (gr. -1-2). bds. 6.99 (978-1-4814-0429-7(6), Simon Spotlight) Simon Spotlight.
—Happy Love Day, Daniel Tiger! A Lift-The-Flap Book. 2015. (Daniel Tiger's Neighborhood Ser.). (ENG.). 14p. (J). (gr. -1-2). bds. 6.99 (978-1-4814-4855-0(2), Simon Spotlight) Simon Spotlight.
—The Helpers in Your Neighborhood. Cassel, Alexandra. 2019. (Daniel Tiger's Neighborhood Ser.). (ENG.). 32p. (J). (gr. -1-2). pap. 7.99 (978-1-5344-5208-4(7)); 12.99 (978-1-5344-4322-8(3)) Simon Spotlight. (Simon Spotlight).
—Hey, Buddy! Miller, Mona. 2010. (ENG.). 96p. (J). (gr. -1-2). pap. 3.99 (978-0-375-86155-0(6), Golden Bks.) Random Hse. Children's Bks.
—How Is Daniel Feeling? 2015. (Daniel Tiger's Neighborhood Ser.). (ENG.). 14p. (J). (gr. -1-k). bds. 12.99 (978-1-4814-3856-8(5), Simon Spotlight) Simon Spotlight.
—I Like to Be with My Family. Kalban, Rachel. 2016. (Daniel Tiger's Neighborhood Ser.). (ENG.). 26p. (J). (gr. -1-k). bds. 8.99 (978-1-4814-6100-9(1), Simon Spotlight) Simon Spotlight.
—I Love You, Dad. 2015. (Daniel Tiger's Neighborhood Ser.). (ENG.). 26p. (J). (gr. -1-k). bds. 8.99 (978-1-4814-5736-1(5), Simon Spotlight) Simon Spotlight.
—I'm Feeling Happy. Shaw, Natalie. 2016. (Daniel Tiger's Neighborhood Ser.). (ENG.). 14p. (J). (gr. -1 — 1). bds. 5.99 (978-1-4814-6178-8(8), Simon Spotlight) Simon Spotlight.
—I'm Feeling Mad. Shaw, Natalie. 2016. (Daniel Tiger's Neighborhood Ser.). (ENG.). 14p. (J). (gr. -1 — 1). bds. 6.99 (978-1-4814-6176-4(1), Simon Spotlight) Simon Spotlight.
—I'm Feeling Thankful. Shaw, Natalie. 2017. (Daniel Tiger's Neighborhood Ser.). (ENG.). 14p. (J). (gr. -1 — 1). bds. 5.99 (978-1-4814-8009-3(X), Simon Spotlight) Simon Spotlight.
—I'M Feeling Silly. Shaw, Natalie. 2016. (Daniel Tiger's Neighborhood Ser.). (ENG.). 14p. (J). (gr. -1 — 1). bds. 5.99 (978-1-4814-6815-2(4), Simon Spotlight) Simon Spotlight.
—Kai-Lan's Carnival. 2010. (Ni Hao, Kai-Lan Ser.). (ENG.). 24p. (J). (gr. -1-1). 16.19 (978-1-4424-0177-8(X)) Simon & Schuster, Inc.
—King Daniel the Kind. 2017. (Daniel Tiger's Neighborhood Ser.). (ENG.). 12p. (J). (gr. -1-k). bds. 5.99 (978-1-5344-0373-4(6), Simon Spotlight) Simon Spotlight.
—Kite Riders! (Team Umizoomi) Golden Books Staff. 2012. (ENG.). 48p. (J). (gr. -1-2). pap. 3.99 (978-0-375-86119-2(X), Golden Bks.) Random Hse. Children's Bks.
—Lalaloopsy: Halloween Surprise. Cecil, Lauren. 2012. (Lalaloopsy Ser.). (ENG.). 24p. (J). (gr. -1-3). pap. 3.99 (978-0-545-43388-4(6)) Scholastic, Inc.
—Let's Dance! Golden Books Staff. 2005. (ENG.). 32p. (J). (gr. -1-2). pap. 3.99 (978-0-375-83478-3(8), Golden Bks.) Random Hse. Children's Bks.
—Look for the Helpers. 2018. (Daniel Tiger's Neighborhood Ser.). (ENG.). 32p. (J). (gr. -1-2). pap. 4.99 (978-1-5344-2629-0(9), Simon Spotlight) Simon Spotlight.
—Lovestruck! Lewman, David. 2004. (Fairly Oddparents Ser.). (J). (gr. -1-3). 11.15 (978-0-7569-1992-4(4)) Perfection Learning Corp.
—Magic Carpet Race! (Shimmer & Shine) Finnegan, Delphine. 2017. (Step into Reading Ser.). (ENG.). 24p. (J). (gr. -1-1). pap. 4.99 (978-1-5247-1690-5(1)); lib. bdg. 12.99 (978-1-5247-1691-2(X)) Random Hse. Children's Bks. (Random Hse. Bks. for Young Readers).
—Mama Travels for Work. 2019. (Daniel Tiger's Neighborhood Ser.). (ENG.). 16p. (J). (gr. -1-2). pap. 5.99 (978-1-5344-4176-7(X), Simon Spotlight) Simon Spotlight.
—Merry Christmas, Daniel Tiger! A Lift-The-Flap Book. Santomero, Angela C. 2015. (Daniel Tiger's Neighborhood Ser.). (ENG.). 14p. (J). (gr. -1-2). bds. 6.99 (978-1-4814-4660-0(6), Simon Spotlight) Simon Spotlight.
—Mighty Adventures (Team Umizoomi) Golden Books. 2012. (ENG.). 96p. (J). (gr. -1-2). pap. 3.99 (978-0-307-93085-9(8), Golden Bks.) Random Hse. Children's Bks.
—Mom Tiger's New Job. 2019. (Daniel Tiger's Neighborhood Ser.). (ENG.). 24p. (J). (gr. -1-2). pap. 4.99 (978-1-5344-5347-0(4), Simon Spotlight) Simon Spotlight.
Fruchter, Jason. More Daniel Tiger 5-Minute Stories. 2020. (Daniel Tiger's Neighborhood Ser.). (ENG.). 192p. (J). (gr. -1-2). 12.99 **(978-1-5344-7114-6(6)**, Simon Spotlight) Simon Spotlight.
Fruchter, Jason. Moving to the Neighborhood. 2018. (Daniel Tiger's Neighborhood Ser.). (ENG.). 14p. (J). (gr. -1-k). bds. 5.99 (978-1-5344-3194-2(2), Simon Spotlight) Simon Spotlight.
—Munch Your Lunch! 2018. (Daniel Tiger's Neighborhood Ser.). (ENG.). 16p. (J). (gr. -1-2). pap. 5.99 (978-1-5344-1778-6(8), Simon Spotlight) Simon Spotlight.
Fruchter, Jason. My Family Is Special. 2020. (Daniel Tiger's Neighborhood Ser.). (ENG.). 32p. (J). (gr. -1-k). 17.99 **(978-1-5344-6982-2(6))**; pap. 4.99 **(978-1-5344-6981-5(8))** Simon Spotlight. (Simon Spotlight).
Fruchter, Jason. My First 100 Neighborhood Words. Testa, Maggie. 2018. (Daniel Tiger's Neighborhood Ser.). (ENG.). 26p. (J). (gr. -1-k). bds. 7.99 (978-1-5344-2526-2(8), Simon Spotlight) Simon Spotlight.
—My Heart Is Happy! Golden Books Staff. 2009. (Holographic Sticker Book Ser.). (ENG.). 48p. (J). (gr. -1-2). pap. 3.99 (978-0-375-85723-2(0), Golden Bks.) Random Hse. Children's Bks.
Fruchter, Jason. Naptime in the Neighborhood. 2020. (Daniel Tiger's Neighborhood Ser.). (ENG.). 24p. (J). (gr. -1-2). pap. 4.99 **(978-1-5344-6903-7(6)**, Simon Spotlight) Simon Spotlight.
Fruchter, Jason. No Red Sweater for Daniel. 2016. (Daniel Tiger's Neighborhood Ser.). (ENG.). 24p. (J). (gr. -1-k). pap. 3.99 (978-1-4814-6768-1(9), Simon Spotlight) Simon Spotlight.
—No Red Sweater for Daniel. Friedman, Becky. ed. 2016. (Daniel Tiger's Neighborhood 8X8 Ser.). (ENG.). 24p. (gr. -1-k). 13.55 (978-0-606-39246-4(7)) Turtleback.
—Outer-Space Chase (Team Umizoomi) Random House Staff. 2013. (Step into Reading Ser.). (ENG.). 32p. (J). (gr. -1-1). 3.99 (978-0-449-81890-9(X), Random Hse. Bks. for Young Readers) Random Hse. Children's Bks.
—Remembering Blue Fish. 2017. (Daniel Tiger's Neighborhood Ser.). (ENG.). 24p. (J). (gr. -1-2). pap. 4.99 (978-1-5344-0095-5(8), Simon Spotlight) Simon Spotlight.
—The Science Project. McCann, Jesse Leon. 2003. 61p. (J). (978-0-439-56271-3(6)) Scholastic, Inc.
—Silly Costume Contest (Team Umizoomi) Golden Books. 2014. (ENG.). 48p. (J). (gr. -1-2). pap. 3.99 (978-0-385-38413-1(0), Golden Bks.) Random Hse. Children's Bks.
—Space Race. 2017. (J). (978-1-5182-2283-2(8), Golden Bks.) Random Hse. Children's Bks.
—The Spooky Cabin. 2017. 22p. (J). (978-1-5182-4358-5(4)) Random Hse., Inc.
—The Spooky Cabin (PAW Patrol) Random House. 2017. (Step into Reading Ser.). (ENG.). 24p. (J). (gr. -1-1). pap. 4.99 (978-1-5247-1694-3(4)); lib. bdg. 12.99 (978-1-5247-1695-0(2)) Random Hse. Children's Bks. (Random Hse. Bks. for Young Readers).
Fruchter, Jason. A Starry Night in the Neighborhood: A Count-The-Stars Bedtime Book. Gallo, Tina. 2020. (Daniel Tiger's Neighborhood Ser.). (ENG.). 14p. (J). (— 1). bds. 8.99 **(978-1-5344-7577-9(X)**, Simon Spotlight) Simon Spotlight.
Fruchter, Jason. Tigertastic Stories with Daniel: Daniel Gets Scared; Daniel Learns to Share; Daniel Plays at School; Who Can? Daniel Can!; Daniel Will Pack a Snack; Trolley Ride! ed. 2018. (Daniel Tiger's Neighborhood Ser.). (ENG.). 192p. (J). (gr. -1-k). pap. 17.99 (978-1-5344-3777-7(0), Simon Spotlight) Simon Spotlight.
—Time to Fly! (Disney Junior: Sheriff Callie's Wild West) Posner-Sanchez, Andrea. 2015. (Little Golden Book Ser.). (ENG.). 24p. (J). (-k). 4.99 (978-0-7364-3362-4(7), Golden/Disney) Random Hse. Children's Bks.
—Trolley Ride! Spinner, Cala. 2018. (Daniel Tiger's Neighborhood Ser.). (ENG.). 32p. (J). (gr. -1-k). 17.99 (978-1-5344-1627-7(7)); pap. 4.99 (978-1-5344-1626-0(9)) Simon Spotlight. (Simon Spotlight).
—Truck or Treat! (Blaze & the Monster Machines) Lewman, David. 2017. (Big Golden Book Ser.). (ENG.). 48p. (J). (gr. -1-2). 9.99 (978-1-5247-1669-1(3), Golden Bks.) Random Hse. Children's Bks.
—¡Vámonos! / Let's Go! Beinstein, Phoebe. Ziegler, Argentina Palacios, tr. 2007. (Dora la Exploradora Ser.). (SPA & ENG.). 14p. (J). bds. 4.99 (978-1-4169-3367-0(0), Libros Para Ninos) Libros Para Ninos.
—A Very Merry Day in the Neighborhood. Cassel, Alexandra. 2019. (Daniel Tiger's Neighborhood Ser.). (ENG.). 22p. (J). (— 1). bds. 6.99 (978-1-5344-5052-3(1), Simon Spotlight) Simon Spotlight.
—We Can Ride down the Slide. Testa, Maggie. 2019. (Daniel Tiger's Neighborhood Ser.). (ENG.). 32p. (J). (gr. -1-k). 17.99 (978-1-5344-4938-1(8)); pap. 4.99 (978-1-5344-4937-4(X)) Simon Spotlight. (Simon Spotlight).
—We Love Halloween! Golden Books Staff. 2010. (Glow-In-the-Dark Sticker Book Ser.). (ENG.). 48p. (J). (gr. -1-2). pap. 3.99 (978-0-375-86513-8(6), Golden Bks.) Random Hse. Children's Bks.
—What Is Daniel Wearing? Friedman, Becky. 2015. (Daniel Tiger's Neighborhood Ser.). (ENG.). 14p. (J). (gr. -1 — 1). 8.99 (978-1-4814-2899-6(3), Simon Spotlight) Simon Spotlight.
—What Time Is It, Daniel Tiger? 2016. (Daniel Tiger's Neighborhood Ser.). (ENG.). 14p. (J). (gr. -1-k). bds. 10.99 (978-1-4814-6934-0(7), Simon Spotlight) Simon Spotlight.
—Who Can? Daniel Can! Testa, Maggie. 2017. (Daniel Tiger's Neighborhood Ser.). (ENG.). 32p. (J). (gr. -1-k). pap. 4.99 (978-1-4814-9518-9(6), Simon Spotlight) Simon Spotlight.
—Wild in Africa! (Wild Kratts) Kratt, Chris & Kratt, Martin. 2016. (Little Golden Book Ser.). (ENG.). 24p. (J). (-k). 4.99 (978-1-101-93862-1(5), Golden Bks.) Random Hse. Children's Bks.
Fruchter, Jason. You Can Do It! (Top Wing) Stephens, Elle. 2020. (Step into Reading Ser.). (ENG.). 24p. (J). (gr. -1-1). 5.99 **(978-1-9848-4775-1(9))**; 14.99 **(978-0-593-17460-9(7))** Random Hse. Children's Bks. (Random Hse. Bks. for Young Readers).
Fruchter, Jason. You're Still You! 2016. (Daniel Tiger's Neighborhood Ser.). (ENG.). 12p. (J). (gr. -1-k). bds. 5.99 (978-1-4814-6743-8(3), Simon Spotlight) Simon Spotlight.
Fruchter, Jason, jt. illus. see RH Disney Staff.
Fruisen, Catherine Myler. Alice & Her Fabulous Teeth! Maconie, Robin. 2004. 32p. (J). per. (978-1-893974-21-0(9), Design Pr. Bks.) Savannah College of Art & Design Exhibitions.
—Rick & Rocky. Wallace, Paula S. 2004. 32p. (J). pap. (978-1-893974-22-7(7), Design Pr. Bks.) Savannah College of Art & Design Exhibitions.
Frullo, Samuel. The Adventures of Jack Rascal. Bingham, Priscilla. 2018. (ENG.). 34p. (J). (gr. k-2). 16.99 (978-1-78955-184-6(6)); pap. 10.99 (978-1-78719-786-2(7)) New Generation Publishing GBR. Dist: Independent Pubs. Group.
Fry, Debbie. Donkeywise & Otherwise: The Story of Daisy Doo & Dudley Duz. 2004. 44p. (J). (978-0-9759647-0-5(4), 1238040) Fry, Debbie.
Fry, Kelly. But I Don't Eat Ants. Marvin, Dan. 2017. (ENG.). 32p. (J). (gr. -1-2). 16.99 (978-1-57687-837-8(6), powerHouse Bks.) powerHse. Bks.
Fry, Michael. Bobbie Mendoza Saves the World (Again) Fry, Michael. Jackson, Bradley. 2018. (ENG.). 272p. (J). (gr. 3-7). 12.99 (978-0-06-265193-8(5)) HarperCollins Pubs.
—The Naughty List. Fry, Michael. Jackson, Bradley. 2015. (ENG.). 240p. (J). (gr. 3-7). 12.99 (978-0-06-235475-4(2)) HarperCollins Pubs.
Fry, Michael. The Naughty List. Fry, Michael. Jackson, Bradley. 2020. (ENG.). 240p. (J). (gr. 3-7). pap. 7.99 **(978-0-06-304275-9(4)**, HarperCollins) HarperCollins Pubs. Ltd. GBR. Dist: HarperCollins Pubs.
Fry, Rosalie K. Secret of the Ron Mor Skerry. Fry, Rosalie K. 2017. 104p. (J). (gr. 3-7). 15.95 (978-1-68137-166-5(9), NYR Children's Collection) New York Review of Bks., Inc., The.
Frye, Paige Billin. The Giant Jellybean Jar. Aboff, Marcie. 2004. (Penguin Young Readers, Level 3 Ser.). 32p. (J). (gr. 1-3). mass mkt. 4.99 (978-0-14-240049-4(1), Penguin Young Readers) Penguin Young Readers Group.
Fryer, Chervelle. Bones: an Inside Look at the Animal Kingdom. Howard, Jules. 2020. (ENG.). 80p. (J). (gr. 2-5). 19.99 (978-1-5362-1041-5(2), Big Picture Press) Candlewick Pr.
Fryer, Joshua. Lost. Fryer, Joshua. Fryer, Rebekah, ed. 2019. (Big Boots Publisher Ser.: Vol. 2). (ENG.). 32p. (J). **(978-0-473-48596-2(6))** Big Boots Pub.
Fryer, Joshua Stephen. Little Rumble. Fryer, Joshua Stephen. 2018. (ENG.). 32p. (J). pap. (978-0-473-44945-2(5)) Big Boots Pub.
FT, Genevieve, et al. Garfield: Homecoming. Nickel, Scott. 2019. (Garfield Ser.). (ENG.). 112p. (J). (gr. 1-3). pap. 9.99 (978-1-68415-309-1(3)) Boom! Studios.
Fu, Fenny. Child of Light, Divine You Are. Hart, Stefanie. 2020. (ENG.). 48p. (J). pap. 14.99 **(978-1-6629-0111-9(9))** Gatekeeper Pr.
Fu, Sherwin, jt. illus. see Abboreno, Joseph F.
Fuchs, Bernie. The Wolves. Heinz, Brian. 2005. 32p. (J). lib. bdg. 15.99 (978-0-936335-11-7(4)) Ballyhoo BookWorks, Inc.
Fuchs, Kaitlyn. Puppies & Poems. Sack, Nancy. 2012. (ENG.). 32p. (J). 19.95 (978-1-4327-8470-6(6)) Outskirts Pr., Inc.
Fuchs, Laura. Clara the Rhino. Hirt, Katrin. 2020. (ENG.). 48p. (J). (gr. -1-2). 18.95 (978-0-7358-4395-0(3)) North-South Bks., Inc.
Fučíková, Renata. Madame Butterfly. Puccini, Giacomo. 2005. (ENG.). 40p. (Orig.). (J). 15.95 (978-1-933327-04-4(9)) Purple Bear Bks., Inc.
Fucile, Tony. Best Friends Forever. Dicamillo, Kate & Mcghee, Alison. 2013. (Bink & Gollie Ser.). 96p. (J). (gr. 1-4). 16.99 (978-0-7636-3497-1(2)) Candlewick Pr.
—Bink & Gollie. Dicamillo, Kate & Mcghee, Alison. (Bink & Gollie Ser.). (ENG.). (J). (gr. 1-4). 2012. 88p. pap. 6.99 (978-0-7636-6954-7(1)); 2010. 96p. 16.99 (978-0-7636-3266-3(X)) Candlewick Pr.
—Bink & Gollie: Best Friends Forever. DiCamillo, Kate & McGhee, Alison. 2014. (Bink & Gollie Ser.). (ENG.). 88p. (J). (gr. 1-4). pap. 6.99 (978-0-7636-7092-4(8)) Candlewick Pr.
—Bink & Gollie: the Completely Marvelous Collection. DiCamillo, Kate & McGhee, Alison. 2014. (Bink & Gollie Ser.). (J). (gr. 1-4). 19.99 (978-0-7636-7536-3(9)) Candlewick Pr.
—Bink & Gollie: Two for One. DiCamillo, Kate & McGhee, Alison. (Bink & Gollie Ser.). 96p. (J). (gr. 1-4). 2013. pap.

6.99 (978-0-7636-6445-9(6)); 2012. (ENG.). 16.99 (978-0-7636-3361-5(5)) Candlewick Pr.

—Mitchell Goes Bowling. Durand, Hallie. 2013. (Mitchell Goes Ser.). (ENG.). 40p. (J). (gr. -1-2). 15.99 (978-0-7636-6049-9(3)) Candlewick Pr.

—Mitchell Goes Driving. Durand, Hallie. 2013. (Mitchell Goes Ser.). 40p. (J). (gr. -1-2). pap. 6.99 (978-0-7636-6737-5(4)) Candlewick Pr.

—Mitchell's License. Durand, Hallie. 2011. (Mitchell Goes Ser.). (ENG.). 40p. (J). (gr. -1-2). 15.99 (978-0-7636-4496-3(X)) Candlewick Pr.

Fucile, Tony. Out & about with Mitchell & Dad. Durand, Hallie. 2020. 72p. (J). (gr. k-4). 12.99 **(978-1-5362-1304-1(7))**; pap. 4.99 **(978-1-5362-1167-2(2))** Candlewick Pr.

Fucile, Tony. Let's Do Nothing! Fucile, Tony. 2012. 40p. (J). (gr. -1-3). pap. 7.99 (978-0-7636-5269-2(5)) Candlewick Pr.

—Poor Louie. Fucile, Tony. 2017. (ENG.). 40p. (J). (gr. -1-2). 16.99 (978-0-7636-5828-1(6)) Candlewick Pr.

Fuenmayor, Morella. Rosaura en Bicicleta. Barbot, Daniel. 2005. (SPA.). 23p. (J). (gr. -1-2). reprint ed. pap. 14.00 (978-0-7567-8947-3(8)) DIANE Publishing Co.

Fuentes, Benny & Tortosa, Wilson. Escuadrón de la Sombra. Bowen, Carl. 2019. (Escuadrón de la Sombra Ser.). (SPA.). (J). (gr. 4-8). 106.60 (978-1-4965-8572-1(0), 29721, Stone Arch Bks.) Capstone.

—Operación Ancla. Bowen, Carl. 2019. (Escuadrón de la Sombra Ser.). (SPA.). 112p. (J). (gr. 4-8). lib. bdg. 26.65 (978-1-4965-8548-6(8), 141297, Stone Arch Bks.) Capstone.

Fuentes, Benny, jt. illus. see Tortosa, Wilson.

Fuentes, Mikel. How You Were Born. Calaf, Monica. 2014. 48p. (J). (gr. -1-3). 9.99 (978-1-78066-125-4(8)) Pinter & Martin Ltd. GBR. Dist: National Bk. Network.

Fuert, L. A. & Woodbury et al, Charles H. Fresh Fields. Burroughs, John. 2008. 196p. pap. (978-1-4099-2065-6(8)) Dodo Pr.

Fuertes, Louis Agassiz. The Burgess Animal Book for Children. Burgess, Thornton W. 2008. 284p. (gr. 4-7). pap. (978-1-4099-2052-6(6)) Dodo Pr.

—The Burgess Animal Book for Children. Burgess, Thornton W. 2011. 478p. 52.95 (978-1-169-84273-1(9)); 2010. 478p. 42.36 (978-1-163-21392-6(6)); 2010. 478p. pap. 30.36 (978-1-162-64734-0(5)); 2004. 476p. (gr. 4-7). 52.95 (978-1-4326-2165-0(3)); 2004. reprint ed. pap. 37.95 (978-1-4179-2978-8(2)) Kessinger Publishing, LLC.

—The Burgess Animal Book for Children (Yesterday's Classics) Burgess, Thornton W. 2006. (J). per. 13.95 (978-1-59915-171-7(5)) Yesterday's Classics.

—The Burgess Bird Book for Children. Burgess, Thornton W. 2008. 168p. (gr. -1-7). pap. 7.99 (978-1-4209-3052-8(4)) Digireads.com Publishing.

—The Burgess Bird Book for Children. Burgess, Thornton W. 2003. (Dover Children's Classics Ser.). (ENG.). 272p. (J). (gr. 3-8). pap. 11.95 (978-0-486-42840-6(0), 428400) Dover Pubns., Inc.

—The Burgess Bird Book for Children (Yesterday's Classics) Burgess, Thornton W. 2006. (J). per. 13.95 (978-1-59915-170-0(7)) Yesterday's Classics.

—Citizen Bird: Scenes from Bird-Life in Plain English for Beginners. Wright, Mabel Osgood & Coues, Elliott. 2009. 386p. pap. (978-1-4099-8625-6(X)) Dodo Pr.

—Citizen Bird: Scenes from Bird Life in Plain English for Beginners (1897) Wright, Mabel Osgood & Coues, Elliott. 2010. 446p. 41.56 (978-1-164-42138-2(7)); 2010. 446p. pap. 29.56 (978-1-164-13374-2(8)); 2008. 444p. 51.95 (978-1-4366-1564-8(X)); 2008. (ENG.). 448p. per. 36.95 (978-0-548-81704-9(9)) Kessinger Publishing, LLC.

Fuge, Charles. Gilbert the Great. Clarke, Jane. 2016. (Gilbert Ser.). (ENG.). 32p. (J). (gr. -1-1). lib. bdg. 21.19 (978-1-4844-7982-7(3)) Sterling Publishing Co., Inc.

—I Love It When You Smile. McBratney, Sam. 2012. (ENG.). 32p. (J). (gr. -1-3). 9.99 (978-0-06-222133-9(7)) HarperCollins Pubs.

—A Lullaby for Little One. Casey, Dawn. (ENG.). (J). (-k). 2017. 20p. bds. 8.99 (978-0-7636-8661-1(1)); 2015. 32p. 12.99 (978-0-7636-7608-7(X)) Candlewick Pr. (Nosy Crow).

—Who Will You Meet on Scary Street? Nine Pop-up Nightmares! Tagg, Christine. 2004. 20p. (J). reprint ed. 15.00 (978-0-7567-8003-6(9)) DIANE Publishing Co.

—Who Woke the Baby? Clarke, Jane. 2016. (ENG.). (J). (gr. -1-2). 12.99 (978-0-7636-8662-8(X), Nosy Crow) Candlewick Pr.

Fuglestad, R. A. Over the Rainbow with Joey. Acopiado, Ginger. I.t. ed. 2004. 22p. (J). bds. 8.99 (978-0-9729093-0-3(3)) Tike Time, Inc.

Fuhr, Ute & Sautai, Raoul. Los Indios. Fuhr, Ute & Sautai, Raoul. Jeunesse, Gallimard. (Coleccion Mundo Maravilloso). (SPA.). 86p. (J). (gr. 2-4). (978-84-348-4654-8(3), SM6992) SM Ediciones ESP. Dist: Lectorum Pubns., Inc.

Fuhriman, Raphael Scott. Jake the Puppy & Emma the Cat. Oakes, Krista Ralston. 2012. 36p. (J). 19.99 (978-0-9838321-2-6(9)) Higher Ground Pr.

Fuijkschot, Edo. I Can. Cartwright, Amanda. 2017. (ENG.). 18p. (J). (gr. k-1). pap. (978-0-9935596-2-4(X)) Cartwright, Amanda.

Fujikawa, Gyo. A Child's Book of Poems. 2007. 128p. (J). (gr. -1-2). 12.95 (978-1-4027-5061-8(7)) Sterling Publishing Co., Inc.

—A Child's Garden of Verses: A Collection of Scriptures, Prayers & Poems. Stevenson, Robert Louis. 2007. 104p. (J). (gr. -1-2). 12.95 (978-1-4027-5062-5(5)) Sterling Publishing Co., Inc.

—Fairy Tales & Fables. 2008. 128p. (J). (gr. -1-2). 12.95 (978-1-4027-5698-6(4)) Sterling Publishing Co., Inc.

—Let's Play. 2010. 20p. (J). (gr. k-k). bds. 5.95 (978-1-4027-6821-7(4)) Sterling Publishing Co., Inc.

—Mother Goose. 2007. (ENG.). 130p. (J). (gr. -1-2). 12.95 (978-1-4027-5064-9(1)) Sterling Publishing Co., Inc.

—The Night Before Christmas. Moore, Clement C. 2007. 32p. (J). (gr. -1-2). 9.95 (978-1-4027-5065-6(X)) Sterling Publishing Co., Inc.

—Sleepy Time. 2011. 20p. (J). (gr. k-k). bds. 7.95 (978-1-4027-6820-0(6)) Sterling Publishing Co., Inc.

Fujikawa, Gyo. Baby Animals. Fujikawa, Gyo. 2008. 24p. (J). (gr. -1-2). bds. 7.95 (978-1-4027-5701-3(8)) Sterling Publishing Co., Inc.

—Sunny Books - Four-Favorite Tales, 4 bks., Set. Fujikawa, Gyo. (J). (gr. -1). reprint ed. (978-1-55987-042-9(7), Sunny Bks.) J B Communications, Inc.

Fujisawa, Mizuho. Jesus, I Love You: My First Words to Pray to God. Gadient, Augustine. 2020. (My First Words Ser.). (ENG.). 20p. (J). (gr. -1-k). bds. 12.99 **(978-1-62164-357-9(3))** Ignatius Pr.

Fujisawa, Tohru. GTO: Great Teacher Onizuka, 25 vols., Vol. 21. Fujisawa, Tohru, compiled by. rev. ed. 2004. 192p. pap. 9.99 (978-1-59182-455-8(9), Tokyopop Adult) TOKYOPOP, Inc.

Fujishima, Kosuke. Oh My Goddess! Volume 43. Fujishima, Kosuke. Horn, Carl Gustav, ed. 2013. (ENG.). 176p. pap. 12.99 (978-1-61655-082-0(1)) Dark Horse Comics.

Fujita, Artur, jt. illus. see Hart, Sam.

Fujita, Goro. Battle of the Bots. Richards, C. J. 2015. (Robots Rule Ser.: 3). (ENG.). 240p. (J). (gr. 3-7). 13.99 (978-0-544-33932-3(0), 1584503, HMH Books For Young Readers) Houghton Mifflin Harcourt Publishing Co.

—The Junkyard Bot, Bk. 7. Richards, C. J. 2014. (Robots Rule Ser.: 1). (ENG.). 208p. (J). (gr. 5-7). 13.99 (978-0-544-33936-1(3), 1584507, HMH Books For Young Readers) Houghton Mifflin Harcourt Publishing Co.

—The Junkyard Bot: Robots Rule, Book 1. Richards, C. J. 2016. (Robots Rule Ser.). (ENG.). 208p. (J). (gr. 5-7). pap. 7.99 (978-0-544-66843-0(X), 1625458, HMH Books For Young Readers) Houghton Mifflin Harcourt Publishing Co.

—Lots of Bots. Richards, C. J. (Robots Rule Ser.: 2). (ENG.). 224p. (J). (gr. 3-7). 2016. pap. 6.99 (978-0-544-81082-2(1), 1641524); 2015. 13.99 (978-0-544-33934-7(7), 1584505) Houghton Mifflin Harcourt Publishing Co. (HMH Books For Young Readers).

Fujita, Goro. Your Alien. Sauer, Tammi. (J). (gr. -1). 2020. 28p. bds. 7.95 **(978-1-4549-4211-5(8))**; 2015. 40p. 14.95 (978-1-4549-1129-6(8)) Sterling Publishing Co., Inc.

Fujita, Goro. Your Alien Returns. Sauer, Tammi. 2016. 40p. (J). (gr. -1). 14.95 (978-1-4549-1130-2(1)) Sterling Publishing Co., Inc.

Fujita, Mikiko. Strange Light Afar: Tales of the Supernatural from Old Japan, 1 vol. Umezawa, Rui. 2015. (ENG.). 144p. (J). (gr. 6). 18.95 (978-1-55498-723-8(7)) Groundwood Bks. CAN. Dist: Publishers Group West (PGW).

Fujita, Rima. The Day the Buddha Woke Up. Miller, Andrea. 2018. (ENG.). 18p. (J). (gr. -1-1). bds. 10.95 (978-1-61429-450-4(X)) Wisdom Pubns.

Fujiwara, Kim. My Name is Leona. Harris, Carol Gahara. 2013. 24p. (J). 19.95 (978-0-9860324-0-0(9)) Snowy Night Pub.

Fuka, Vladimír. New York: A Mod Portrait of the City. Mahler, Zdenek. 2014. (ENG.). 128p. 24.95 (978-0-7893-2727-7(9)) Universe Publishing.

Fukuda, Toyofumi, photos by. Life-Size Zoo: From Tiny Rodents to Gigantic Elephants, an Actual Size Animal Encyclopedia. Earhart, Kristin, ed. 2009. (ENG., 48p. (gr. -1). 17.95 (978-1-934734-20-9(9)) Seven Footer Pr.

Fukuda, Yukihiro, photos by. Bunny Island. Kennard, Philippa. 2015. (ENG., 32p. (J). (gr. -1-1). pap. 4.99 (978-1-77085-657-8(9), 71fc889c-443f-45a5-bf20-df3a99f661f1) Firefly Bks., Ltd.

Fukuoka, Aki. The Bad Butterfly. Rippin, Sally. 2012. 44p. (J). (978-1-61067-132-3(5)) Kane Miller.

—The Bad Butterfly: Billie B. Brown. Rippin, Sally. 2013. (ENG.). 48p. (J). pap. 4.99 (978-1-61067-095-1(7)) Kane Miller.

—The Best Project. Rippin, Sally. 2014. 43p. (J). (978-1-61067-292-4(5)) Kane Miller.

—The Birthday Mix-Up. Rippin, Sally. 2013. 43p. (J). (978-1-61067-232-0(1)) Kane Miller.

—Code Breakers. Rippin, Sally. 2014. 92p. (J). (978-1-61067-333-4(6)) Kane Miller.

—The Copycat Kid. Rippin, Sally. 2015. 42p. (J). (978-1-61067-449-2(9)) Kane Miller.

—The Copycat Kid: Billie B. Brown. Rippin, Sally. 2016. (ENG.). 48p. (J). pap. 4.99 (978-1-61067-389-1(1)) Kane Miller.

—The Deep End. Rippin, Sally. 2016. (ENG.). 48p. (J). pap. 4.99 (978-1-61067-390-7(5)) Kane Miller.

—The Little Lie. Rippin, Sally. 2014. 43p. (J). (978-1-61067-291-7(7)) Kane Miller.

—The Midnight Feast. Rippin, Sally. (J). 2013. (ENG.). 48p. pap. 4.99 (978-1-61067-097-5(3)); 2012. 44p. (978-1-61067-134-7(1)) Kane Miller.

—The Night Fright. Rippin, Sally. 2015. 43p. (J). (978-1-61067-451-5(0)) Kane Miller.

—The Night Fright: Billie B Brown. Rippin, Sally. 2016. (ENG.). 48p. (J). pap. 4.99 (978-1-61067-391-4(3)) Kane Miller.

—The Soccer Star. Rippin, Sally. (J). 2013. (ENG.). 48p. pap. 4.99 (978-1-61067-096-8(5)); 2012. 44p. (978-1-61067-133-0(3)) Kane Miller.

—Spooky House. Rippin, Sally. 2014. 89p. (J). (978-1-61067-332-7(8)) Kane Miller.

—The Spotty Vacation. Rippin, Sally. 2013. 43p. (J). (978-1-61067-233-7(X)) Kane Miller.

—Treasure Hunt: A Billie B. Mystery. Rippin, Sally. 2016. (ENG.). 96p. (J). pap. 4.99 (978-1-61067-464-5(2)) Kane Miller.

Fulcher, Roz. Baptism Promises. Wehrheim, Carol A. 2018. (ENG.). 18p. (J). bds. 8.00 (978-1-947888-03-6(X), Flyaway Bks.) Westminster John Knox Pr.

Fulcher, Roz. Dedication Promises. Wehrheim, Carol A. 2021. (ENG.). 18p. (J). bds. 10.00 **(978-1-947888-29-6(3)**, 1947888293, Flyaway Bks.) Westminster John Knox Pr.

Fulcher, Roz. First Look at Farm Animals. Galvin, Laura Gates. 2009. (ENG.). 16p. bds. 6.95 (978-1-59249-999-1(6)) Soundprints.

—First Look at Zoo Animals. Galvin, Laura Gates. 2009. (ENG.). 16p. (J). bds. 6.95 (978-1-59249-998-4(8)) Studio Mouse LLC.

—Months of the Year. Scelsa, Greg. Faulkner, Stacey, ed. 2006. (J). pap. 2.99 (978-1-59198-320-0(7)) Creative Teaching Pr., Inc.

Fulco, Haley. Elephant Hips Are Expensive! A Tale of the Sooner State. Hudson, Marilyn A. 2007. 50p. (J). per. (978-0-9778850-2-2(X), WhorlBooks Thumbprints) Whorl Bks.

Fulford, Jason & Shopsin, Tamara. This Equals That. Fulford, Jason & Shopsin, Tamara. 2014. (ENG.). 80p. (J). (gr. 3-7). 19.95 (978-1-59711-288-8(7), e7e22b10-8d87-4780-b06b-4ca20d91302b) Aperture Foundation, Inc.

Fulford, Jason & Shopsin, Tamara. This Equals That (signed Edition) Fulford, Jason & Shopsin, Tamara. 2014. (ENG.). 80p. (J). (gr. 3-7). 19.95 **(978-1-68395-020-2(8)**, Aperture) Aperture Foundation, Inc.

Fuller Baldwin, Fran. What Animal Needs a Wig?, 1 vol. Wollman, Neil & Fuller, Abigail. 2014. (ENG.). 32p. (J). pap. 6.99 (978-1-59572-677-3(2)) Star Bright Bks., Inc.

Fuller, Bob. The Costume Trunk. 2011. (J). (978-1-936169-01-6(0)) Paddywhack Lane LLC.

Fuller, Bob. Lauren & the Leaky Pail. Fuller, Bob. 2010. 32p. (J). (gr. -1-3). 15.99 (978-1-936169-00-9(2)) Paddywhack Lane LLC.

Fuller, Cari. Bobby Dog & the Flying Frog. Pepin, Rebecca. 2004. (J). (gr. 4-18). 16.99 (978-0-9760684-0-2(0)); pap. 11.99 (978-0-9760684-1-9(9)) FullofPep Pubns.

Fuller, Elizabeth. Mrs. Wishy-Washy's Farm. Cowley, Joy. (ENG.). 32p. (J). (gr. -1-k). 2006. 7.99 (978-0-14-240299-3(0), Puffin Books); 2003. 16.99 (978-0-399-23872-7(7), Philomel Bks.) Penguin Young Readers Group.

Fuller, Harvey. Tommy & the Island. Fuller, Harvey. 2007. (J). pap. 18.95 (978-0-9773725-7-7(X)) Flat Hammock Pr.

Fuller, India. Posy's Hiccups. Ward, Hayley. 2019. (ENG.). 26p. (J). pap. 9.99 **(978-1-6888-2909-1(1))** Independently Published.

Fuller, Jeremy. Puff Flies. Grindley, Sally. 2011. (My Phonics Readers: Level 3 Ser.). 24p. (J). (gr. -1-1). 24.25 (978-1-84898-514-8(2)) Sea-To-Sea Pubns.

Fuller, Laurie. Who Goes with That Nose? The Wild Adventures of Juicy Coppertoes. Kobert, Michael Gilead & Donato, Dona. 2005. 40p. (J). per. 9.95 (978-0-9770700-0-8(X)) Giggling Gorilla Productions, LLC.

Fuller, Michael J. Busy Beekeeper Bob. Fuller, Lisa. 2018. (ENG.). 38p. (J). pap. 12.00 (978-1-7202-4387-8(5)) Independently Published.

—Dragons in the Mailbox 3: A Long Visit. Fuller, Lisa. 2018. (ENG.). 148p. (J). pap. 10.00 (978-1-7267-7216-7(0)) Independently Published.

—Dragons in the Mailbox 3: A Long Visit: Reading Workbook Companion. Fuller, Lisa. 2018. (ENG.). 44p. (J). pap. 15.00 (978-1-7288-7185-1(9)) Independently Published.

—Dragons in the Mailbox 4: A New Home. Fuller, Lisa. 2018. (ENG.). 146p. (J). pap. 10.00 (978-1-7906-5597-7(8)) Independently Published.

—Dragons in the Mailbox 4: A New Home: Reading Workbook Companion. Fuller, Lisa. 2018. (ENG.). 38p. (J). pap. 15.00 (978-1-7928-2980-2(9)) Independently Published.

—Jimmy Lives in a Castle. Fuller, Lisa. 2019. (ENG.). 60p. (J). pap. 15.00 (978-1-0989-2881-0(4)) Independently Published.

—The Journaling Queen: April Files. Fuller, Lisa. 2019. (Journaling Queen Ser.: Vol. 5). (ENG.). 82p. (J). pap. 10.00 (978-1-0918-8700-8(4)) Independently Published.

—The Journaling Queen: December Files. Fuller, Lisa. 2018. (Journaling Queen Ser.: Vol. 1). (ENG.). 84p. (J). pap. 12.00 (978-1-7292-7209-1(6)) Independently Published.

—The Journaling Queen: February Files. Fuller, Lisa. 2019. (ENG.). 84p. (J). pap. 10.00 (978-1-7943-2700-9(2)) Independently Published.

—The Journaling Queen: January Files. Fuller, Lisa. 2018. (ENG.). 74p. (J). pap. 10.00 (978-1-7907-8298-7(8)) Independently Published.

—The Journaling Queen: May Files. Fuller, Lisa. 2019. (Journaling Queen Ser.: Vol. 6). (ENG.). 72p. (J). pap. 10.00 (978-1-0959-1415-1(4)) Independently Published.

Fuller, Michael J. Rainbow's Promise. Dalton, Mary. 2019. (Rainbow's Promise Ser.: Vol. 1). (ENG.). 50p. (J). pap. 13.50 **(978-1-6910-4107-7(6))** Independently Published.

Fuller, Rachel. All Kinds of Festivals. Safran, Sheri. 2012. (ENG.). 12p. (J). (gr. -1). 12.99 (978-1-60887-162-9(2)) Insight Editions.

—Esperando Al Bebé/Waiting for Baby. Mlawer, Teresa, tr. ed. 2018. (New Baby Spanish/English Edition Ser.: 4). 12p. (J). (978-1-78628-150-0(3)) Child's Play International Ltd.

—Let's Dress! Safran, Sheri. 2011. (ENG.). 20p. (J). (gr. -1-2). 18.99 (978-1-85707-725-4(3)) Tango Bks. GBR. Dist: Independent Pubs. Group.

—Look at Me! 2009. (New Baby Ser.). 12p. (J). (gr. -1). spiral bd. (978-1-84643-278-1(2)) Child's Play International Ltd.

—Mi Nuevo Bebé/My New Baby. Mlawer, Teresa, tr. ed. 2018. (New Baby Spanish/English Edition Ser.: 4). 12p. (J). bds. (978-1-78628-151-7(1)) Child's Play International Ltd.

—¡Mírame!/Look at Me! Mlawer, Teresa, tr. ed. 2018. (New Baby Spanish/English Edition Ser.: 4). 12p. (J). bds. (978-1-78628-152-4(X)) Child's Play International Ltd.

—My New Baby. 2009. (New Baby Ser.). 12p. (J). (gr. -1). spiral bd. (978-1-84643-276-7(6)) Child's Play International Ltd.

—Tú y Yo/You & Me. Mlawer, Teresa, tr. ed. 2018. (New Baby Spanish/English Edition Ser.: 4). 12p. (J). bds. (978-1-78628-153-1(8)) Child's Play International Ltd.

—Waiting for Baby. 2009. (New Baby Ser.). 12p. (J). (gr. -1). spiral bd. (978-1-84643-275-0(8)) Child's Play International Ltd.

—You & Me! 2009. (New Baby Ser.). 12p. (J). (gr. -1). spiral bd. (978-1-84643-277-4(4)) Child's Play International Ltd.

Fuller, Rachel. You & Me Board Book Set Of 4. 2020. (Social & Emotional Learning Sets Ser.). (ENG.). 56p. (J). bds., bds., bds. **(978-1-78628-529-4(0))** Child's Play International Ltd.

Fuller, Sandy Ferguson. Hannah & the Perfect Picture Pony: A Story of the Great Depression. Zimet, Sara Goodman. 2005. 24p. (J). lib. bdg. 16.95 (978-0-9645159-2-5(X)) Discovery Pr. Pubns., Inc.

Fuller, Sarah H. What in the World Did Winter Do? Fuller, Sarah H. 2019. (ENG.). 44p. (J). pap. 9.89 **(978-1-7055-9567-1(7))** Independently Published.

Fullerton, Alma. Community Soup. Fullerton, Alma. 2019. (ENG.). 32p. (J). (gr. -1-3). pap. 11.95 (978-1-77278-070-3(7)) Pajama Pr. CAN. Dist: Ingram Publisher Services.

Fullerton, Gavin. BAGS (or a Story Thereof) McHale, Patrick. 2019. (ENG.). 96p. (J). pap. 12.99 (978-1-68415-409-8(X)) Boom! Studios.

Fulleylove, John & Baikie, Constance N. Peeps at Many Lands: Ancient Greece (Yesterday's Classics) Baikie, James. 2008. 128p. pap. 8.95 (978-1-59915-289-9(4)) Yesterday's Classics.

Fullgraf, Eric Von. The Book, the Key, & the Magic Fire. Montgomery, Harriet Huntley. Levenhagen, Macey, ed. 2018. (SPA.). 110p. (J). pap. 10.95 (978-1-7904-2158-9(6)) Independently Published.

Fulmer, Patrick. My Angel Next Door. Holt, Madeline. Kovalevich, Denise, ed. 2003. 20p. 10.00 (978-0-9740016-0-9(0)) Holt Enterprise, LLC.

Fulton, Parker. Small One's Adventure. Mueller, Doris. 2004. 32p. (J). (gr. k-5). 16.95 (978-0-9710278-1-7(1)) All About Kids Publishing.

Fulvimari, Jeffrey. The English Roses. Madonna, Madonna. 10th ed. 2017. (English Roses Ser.: 1). (ENG.). 48p. (J). (gr. 3-5). 24.95 (978-0-935112-10-8(3)) Callaway Arts & Entertainment.

—Friends for Life! New Full-Color Edition. Madonna. 2018. (English Roses Ser.: 1). (ENG.). 96p. (J). (gr. 3-7). 14.95 (978-0-935112-68-9(5)) Callaway Arts & Entertainment.

—Goodbye, Grace? New Full-Color Edition. Madonna. 2018. (English Roses Ser.: 2). (ENG.). 144p. (J). (gr. 3-7). 14.95 (978-0-935112-70-2(7)) Callaway Arts & Entertainment.

Fumizuki, Kou. Ai Yori Aoshi, 9 vols. Fumizuki, Kou, creator. rev. ed. Vol. 6. 2004. 196p. pap. 9.99 (978-1-59182-650-7(0)); Vol. 9. 2005. 192p. pap. 9.99 (978-1-59532-372-9(4)) TOKYOPOP, Inc.

Funck, Diego. Aim High. Pryor, Shawn. 2020. (Kids' Sports Stories Ser.). (ENG.). 32p. (J). (gr. k-2). pap. 5.95 **(978-1-5158-7284-9(X)**, 201309); lib. bdg. 21.32 **(978-1-5158-7095-1(2)**, 199191) Capstone. (Picture Window Bks.).

Funck, Diego. The Color Factory. Telchin, Eric. 2018. (ENG.). 40p. (J). (gr. -1-3). 17.99 (978-1-4998-0556-7(X)) Little Bee Books Inc.

Funck, Diego. Hockey Hero. Smith, Elliott. 2020. (Kids' Sports Stories Ser.). (ENG.). 32p. (J). (gr. k-2). pap. 5.95 **(978-1-5158-7286-3(6)**, 201311); lib. bdg. 21.32 **(978-1-5158-7098-2(7)**, 199193) Capstone. (Picture Window Bks.).

Funck, Diego. When Sparks Fly: The True Story of Robert Goddard, the Father of US Rocketry. Fulton, Kristen. 2018. (ENG.). 40p. (J). (gr. -1-3). 17.99 (978-1-4814-6098-9(6), McElderry, Margaret K. Bks.) McElderry, Margaret K. Bks.

Funderburk, Tony. Dreamtown Dilly Dally. Funderburk, Tony. 2012. (ENG.). 34p. (J). pap. 7.00 (978-1-5441-8722-8(X)) CreateSpace Independent Publishing Platform.

Fundora, Yolanda V. My Brain Won't Float Away / Mi cerebro no va a salir Flotando. Perez, Annette. Herranz Brooks, Jacqueline, tr. 2007. (ENG & SPA.). 32p. (J). 19.95 (978-0-9725611-2-9(9), Campanita Bks.) Editorial Campana.

—Sand, Sea & Poetry. Moolenaar Bernier, Ashley-Ruth. 2014. (J). pap. (978-1-934370-35-3(5)) Editorial Campana.

—A Very Smart Cat: Una Gata Muy Inteligente. Picayo, Mario. 2008. (SPA & ENG.). 32p. (J). (978-1-934370-00-1(2)) Editorial Campana.

Funk, Clotilde Embree. Flowers & Their Travels. Fox, Frances Margaret. 2011. 230p. 46.95 (978-1-258-07400-5(1)) Literary Licensing, LLC.

—The Three Tripps. Moore, Margaret & Moore, John Travers. 2011. 158p. 41.95 (978-1-258-08478-3(3)) Literary Licensing, LLC.

Funk, Debbie. My Dog, Eddie. Holzer, Angela. 2009. 36p. (J). lib. bdg. 8.99 (978-0-9821563-5-3(9)) Good Sound Publishing.

Funke, Cornelia. Ghosthunters & the Muddy Monster of Doom! Funke, Cornelia. 2007. (Ghosthunters Ser.: 4). (ENG.). 165p. (J). (gr. 3-6). 17.44 (978-0-439-86269-1(8)) Scholastic, Inc.

—Igraine the Brave. Funke, Cornelia. Bell, Anthea, tr. I.t. ed. 2008. (Thorndike Literacy Bridge Middle Reader Ser.). 259p. (J). (gr. 4-7). 23.95 (978-1-4104-0341-4(6)) Thorndike Pr.

Funke, Peggy. Ellie Saves the Day, 1 vol. Johnson, Gerald J. J. 2009. 12p. pap. 24.95 (978-1-60836-709-2(6)) America Star Bks.

Funnell, Eve. Flying Fiona & Baby Emma at the Dentist: Flying Fiona y la Beb� Emma. O'Leary, Jessica. Larsson Perfect, Marla, tr. 2019. (Flying Fiona Ser.: Vol. 2). (ENG.). 30p. (J). pap. 10.99 **(978-1-64538-099-3(8))** Orange Hat Publishing.

Funnell, Sonja. Timmy the Goat: Spelunking Adventure. Anderson, Henry Morgan. Falk, Wendy & Makepeace, Jonathan, eds. 2011. (Adventures of Henry Ser.). 48p. 14.99 (978-1-936813-00-1(9)) Adventures of Henry, LLC.

Fur, Emil. Ronny. Vujadinovic, Nenad. 2007. (POL & ENG.). 32p. (J). pap. 12.95 (978-1-60195-105-2(1)) International Step by Step Assn.

Furchgott, Eve. Naughty Elepaio. Kruger, Malia. 2008. 32p. 14.95 (978-0-87336-158-3(X)) Kamehameha Publishing.

F

Furie, Matt. The Night Riders. 48p. (J). 2013. (ENG.). (gr. -1-3). 8.95 *(978-1-938073-72-4(X),* 0dfeb182-81b2-47bf-9539-7a36721afcaa); 2012. 17.95 *(978-1-936365-56-2(1),* 491737cc-4253-4f1e-88fb-f59a829a4d82) McSweeney's Publishing.

Furlong, Frank. Not Yet: Poems for Kids Five & Up. 2011. 24p. pap. 14.95 *(978-1-4575-0467-9(7))* Dog Ear Publishing, LLC.

—Pop Pop's Magic Chair. 2010. 24p. pap. 12.95 *(978-1-60844-658-2(1))* Dog Ear Publishing, LLC.

Furlotti, Marco. Hickory Dickory Dock. Bell, Lucy. 2017. (ENG.). 20p. (J). (gr. -1-1). bds. *(978-1-4867-1244-1(4))* Flowerpot Children's Pr. Inc.

—The Peace Dragon. Ragsdale, Linda. (Peace Dragon Tales Ser.). (ENG.). 32p. (J). (gr. k-3). 2019. 7.99 *(978-1-4867-1773-6(X),* ebfabe35-564e-4d92-a24d-bf56fc00c0c7); 2018. 16.99 *(978-1-4867-1466-7(8),* 4680207e-fe11-4791-9423-3fb22963ec45) Flowerpot Pr.

—Whisper. Fitzpatrick, Joe. 2017. (ENG.). 32p. (J). (gr. -1-2). *(978-1-4867-1266-3(5))* Flowerpot Children's Pr. Inc.

—Yesterday I Found an A. Blossom, Maggie. 2017. (ENG.). 32p. (J). (gr. -1-3). 16.99 *(978-1-4867-1201-4(0),* 9ca6adea-ecf6-4b31-980d-0699898cdb6d) Flowerpot Pr.

Furlow Jr., James. Chicka Poo. Ross, Jada. 2020. (ENG.). 40p. (J). 31.99 ***(978-1-6641-3281-8(3))***; pap. 21.99 ***(978-1-7960-6876-4(4))*** Xlibris Corp.

Furman, Jane Christine. Sam the Clam: Adventures under the Jetty. Dougherty, Lindsey Furman. 2020. (ENG.). 58p. (J). pap. 19.99 ***(978-1-7944-4176-7(X))*** Independently Published.

Furniss, Harry. Sylvie & Bruno / Sylvie & Bruno Concluded: (Complete: Vol. 1 & 2 - Illustrated & Annotated) Carroll, Lewis. Barry, ed. annot. ed. 2020. (ENG.). 704p. (J). pap. 49.95 ***(978-1-6543-9948-1(5))*** Independently Published.

Furniss, Harry. Sylvie & Bruno Concluded. Carroll, Lewis. 462p. 2010. 42.36 *(978-1-167-13605-4(5))*; 2010. pap. 30.36 *(978-1-167-01946-3(6))*; 2009. 52.95 *(978-1-120-84142-1(9))*; 2009. pap. 37.95 *(978-1-120-71925-6(9))* Kessinger Publishing, LLC.

Furniss, Harry. Sylvie & Bruno (Illustrated & Annotated) Carroll, Lewis. Barry, ed. annot. ed. 2019. (Sylvie & Bruno Ser.: Vol. 1). (ENG.). 474p. (J). pap. 39.95 ***(978-1-7033-4139-3(2))*** Independently Published.

Furnival, Keith. Introduction to Weather & Climate Change. Howell, Laura. 2004. (Geography Ser.). 96p. (J). (gr. 5). lib. bdg. 22.95 *(978-1-58086-613-2(1),* Usborne) EDC Publishing.

—The Usborne Internet-Linked Mysteries & Marvels of Science. Clarke, Phillip et al. 2005. 96p. (J). *(978-0-439-81568-0(1))* Scholastic, Inc.

Furnival, Keith, jt. illus. see Scott, Peter David.

Furukawa, Masumi, et al. Baby & Toddler Treasury. Davidson, Susanna. 2007. (Baby & Toddler Treasury Ser.). 95p. (J). (gr. -1-k). 19.99 *(978-0-7945-1150-0(3),* Usborne) EDC Publishing.

Furukawa, Masumi. Bears. Courtauld, Sarah. 2010. (First Reading Level 2 Ser.). 32p. (J). 6.99 *(978-0-7945-2735-8(3),* Usborne) EDC Publishing.

Furukawa, Masumi. Everybody Loves Butterflies. Taylor, Tanis. 2014. (J). ***(978-1-4351-5246-5(8))*** Barnes & Noble, Inc.

Furukawa, Masumi. Let's Be Friends. Choi, SeoYun. rev. ed. 2014. (MySELF Bookshelf Ser.). (ENG.). 32p. (J). (gr. k-2). pap. 11.94 *(978-1-60357-658-1(4))*; lib. bdg. 25.27 *(978-1-59953-649-1(8))* Norwood Hse. Pr.

—The Moon Followed Me Home. Bewley, Elizabeth. 2007. (ENG.). 6p. (J). (gr. -1-3). 12.95 *(978-1-58117-598-1(1),* Intervisual/Piggy Toes) Bendon, Inc.

—This Is My Monster. Taplin, Sam. 2008. (Noisy Touchy-Feely Board Bks). 10p. (J). bds. 16.99 *(978-0-7945-2353-4(6),* Usborne) EDC Publishing.

—The Ugly Duckling. (Flip-Up Fairy Tales Ser.). 24p. (J). 2007. (gr. -1-2). *(978-1-84643-095-4(X))*; 2006. (gr. 2-2). pap. *(978-1-84643-022-0(4))* Child's Play International Ltd.

—The Usborne Book of Poems for Little Children. Taplin, Sam. 2007. 47p. (J). 11.99 *(978-0-7945-1426-6(X),* Usborne) EDC Publishing.

Furuya, Michael. The Adventures of Gary & Harry: A Tale of Two Turtles. Matsumoto, Lisa. 2006. (J). 16.95 *(978-0-9647491-4-6(9))* Lehua, Inc.

—Keoni's Special Gift. 2009. (J). *(978-1-56647-915-8(0))* Mutual Publishing LLC.

Furuya, Usamaru. Short Cuts, Vol. 2. Furuya, Usamaru. 2003. (Short Cuts Ser.: 2). (ENG.). 128p. pap. 12.95 *(978-1-59116-069-4(3))* Viz Media.

Furuzono, Carlos, jt. illus. see Lima, Dijjo.

Fusco, Michael Vincent. My Mom Is a Nurse. Campbell, Candy. 2017. (ENG.). 34p. (J). 14.95 *(978-0-9842385-9-0(X))* Peripatetic Productions, LLC.

—My Mom Is a Nurse. Campbell, Candy. Imura, Toshiyoshi, tr. 2017. (JPN.). (J). pap. 14.95 *(978-0-9842385-4-5(9))* Peripatetic Productions, LLC.

Fusi, Alessandra. Collins Big Cat Phonics for Letters & Sounds - the Dragon King's Daughter: Band 07/Turquoise, Bd. 7. Raby, Charlotte. 2018. (Collins Big Cat Phonics Ser.). (ENG.). 24p. (J). pap. 6.99 *(978-0-00-825153-6(3))* HarperCollins Pubs. Ltd. GBR. Dist: Independent Pubs. Group.

—Legendary Goddesses. Gagne, Tammy et al. 2019. (Legendary Goddesses Ser.). (ENG.). (J). (gr. 3-9). 229.20 *(978-1-5435-7420-3(3),* 29360); pap., pap., pap. 63.60 *(978-1-5435-8246-8(X),* 29702); 114.60 *(978-1-5435-5459-5(8),* 28797) Capstone.

Futaki, Attila & Gaspar, Tamas. Percy Jackson & the Olympians Sea of Monsters, the: the Graphic Novel. Riordan, Rick & Venditti, Robert. 2013. (Percy Jackson & the Olympians Ser.). (ENG.). 128p. (J). (gr. 5-9). pap. 12.99 *(978-1-4231-4550-9(X))* Hyperion Pr.

Futaki, Attila & Guilhaumond, Gregory. Percy Jackson & the Olympians the Titan's Curse: the Graphic Novel. Riordan, Rick & Venditti, Robert. 2013. (Percy Jackson & the Olympians Ser.). (ENG.). 128p. (J). (gr. 5-9). pap. 12.99 *(978-1-4231-4551-6(8))* Hyperion Pr.

—Percy Jackson & the Olympians the Titan's Curse: the Graphic Novel. Venditti, Robert & Riordan, Rick. 2013. (Percy Jackson & the Olympians Ser.: 3). (ENG.). 128p. (J). (gr. 5-9). 19.99 *(978-1-4231-4530-1(5))* Disney Pr.

Futaki, Attila & Villarrubia, Jose. Percy Jackson & the Olympians the Lightning Thief: the Graphic Novel. Riordan, Rick & Venditti, Robert. 2010. (Percy Jackson & the Olympians Ser.). (ENG.). 128p. (J). (gr. 5-9). 21.99 *(978-1-4231-1696-7(8))*; pap. 12.99 *(978-1-4231-1710-0(7))* Hyperion Pr.

Futterer, Ralf. Emile. Futterer, Kurt. Gray, Bronwen et al, trs. from GER. 2004. (ENG.). 32p. (J). *(978-1-931561-95-2(8))* MacAdam/Cage Publishing, Inc.

Fuyuyuki. How a Realist Hero Rebuilt the Kingdom (Light Novel) Vol. 1. Dojyomaru. 2018. (How a Realist Hero Rebuilt the Kingdom (Light Novel) Ser.: 1). (ENG.). 250p. (YA). pap. 13.99 *(978-1-62692-907-4(6),* 900195555) Seven Seas Entertainment, LLC.

—How a Realist Hero Rebuilt the Kingdom (Light Novel) Vol. 2. Dojyomaru. 2019. (How a Realist Hero Rebuilt the Kingdom (Light Novel) Ser.: 2). (ENG.). 250p. (YA). pap. 13.99 *(978-1-62692-981-4(5),* 900197853) Seven Seas Entertainment, LLC.

Fyffe, Brian. Christmas Counting: Count & Create with 42 Holiday Stickers. 2003. 10p. (J). (gr. -1-18). bds. 4.99 *(978-1-57151-722-7(7))* Playhouse Publishing.

—Easter Colors Sticker Book. Mackall, Dandi Daley. 2004. 10p. (J). (gr. -1-18). bds. 4.99 *(978-1-57151-723-4(5))* Playhouse Publishing.

Fylling, Marni. Curious Kids Nature Guide: Explore the Amazing Outdoors of the Pacific Northwest. Cohen, Fiona. 2017. 96p. (J). (gr. k-4). 19.99 *(978-1-63217-083-5(3),* Little Bigfoot) Sasquatch Bks.

F¿lix, Gloria. Nuestra América: 30 Latinas/latinos Inspiradores Que Han Forjado la Historia de Los Estados Unidos. Vourvoulias, Sabrina. 2020. (ENG.). 128p. (J). 17.99 ***(978-0-7624-7175-1(1),*** Running Pr. Kids) Running Pr.

G

G., Ashley. Critter Colors. G., Ashley. 2015. (ENG.). 28p. (J). (gr. -1-k). bds. 7.99 *(978-1-4814-4218-3(X),* Little Simon) Little Simon.

G., Ashley R. Mona Whine'ona: (the List) Green, Melissa J. & G., Melissa J. 2007. 20p. per. 24.95 *(978-1-4241-8451-4(7))* PublishAmerica, Inc.

G, Brandi. Kaleb Did It! G, Brandi. 2018. (Mykaleb Ser.: Vol. 1). (ENG.). 32p. (J). pap. 10.99 *(978-1-7200-2016-5(7))* Independently Published.

G, D. ADHD & Me: (Oh Look a Squirrel!) Hundrieser, Julie. 2019. (ENG.). 26p. (J). pap. 14.99 *(978-1-0952-0506-8(4))* Independently Published.

—The Sore Loser: (don't Be One!) Reese, Nia Mya. 2018. (ENG.). 36p. (J). (gr. k-4). pap. 10.99 *(978-0-9980271-1-1(1))* Ladd-Reese Group, LLC, The.

—The Sore Loser (Don't Be One!) Coloring Book. Reese, Nia Mya. 2018. (ENG.). 36p. (J). (gr. k-4). pap. 7.00 *(978-0-9980271-2-8(X))* Ladd-Reese Group, LLC, The.

G!, Holly. Best of Sabrina the Teenage Witch. Golliher, Bill. 2011. (Archie & Friends All-Stars Ser.: 15). (ENG.). 128p. (J). (gr. 4-7). pap. 9.95 *(978-1-879794-75-7(6))* Archie Comic Pubns., Inc.

Gaash, Elisheva. My Middos World: Dina-dee Is a Goody, 4. Beckerman, Menucha. 2003. (My Middos World Ser.: Vol. 4). 24p. (J). (gr. k-5). 11.95 *(978-1-931681-03-2(1))* Israel Bookshop Pubns.

—My Middos World: Dina-dee Loves Shabbos, 5. Beckerman, Menucha. 2003. (My Middos World Ser.: Vol. 5). 24p. (J). (gr. k-5). 11.95 *(978-1-931681-04-9(X))* Israel Bookshop Pubns.

—My Middos World: Why Did Dina-dee's Face Shine, 6. Beckerman, Menucha. 2003. (My Middos World Ser.: Vol. 6). 24p. (J). (gr. k-5). 11.95 *(978-1-931681-05-6(8))* Israel Bookshop Pubns.

Gaban, Jesus. A la Sombra del Maestro. Farias, Juan. 2003. (SPA.). 108p. (J). (gr. 5-8). pap. 9.95 *(978-84-204-4872-5(9))* Santillana USA Publishing Co., Inc.

—El Libro de Don Quijote para niños / the Don Quixote Book for Children. Cervantes, Miguel de. 2016. (SPA.). 112p. (J). (gr. 4-7). 20.95 *(978-84-16075-98-0(0),* B De Blook) Ediciones B ESP. Dist: Penguin Random Hse. LLC.

Gabàn, Jesús. Moon Boy: Level 2. Brenner, Barbara. 2020. (ENG.). 34p. (J). pap. 9.95 ***(978-1-876965-73-0(8))*** ibooks, Inc.

Gaban, Jesus. No Somos Irrompibles. Bornemann, Elsa. (SPA.). 117p. (YA). (gr. 5-8). pap. *(978-84-207-4249-6(X),* GS5807) Grupo Anaya, S.A. ESP. Dist: Lectorum Pubns., Inc.

Gabán, Jesús. Cuentos de Risa: El Perro Picatoste. Gabán, Jesús, tr. Fuertes, Gloria. 2003. (SPA.). 124p. *(978-84-305-8308-9(4),* SU5206) Susaeta Ediciones, S.A. ESP. Dist: Lectorum Pubns., Inc.

Gabbey, Terry. Daily Life on a Southern Plantation. Slingsby, Miki, photos by. Erickson, Paul. 2006. 48p. (J). (gr. 2-5). reprint ed. pap. 8.00 *(978-1-4223-5727-9(9))* DIANE Publishing Co.

Gabby, Hammaker. Christmas with Marco: A Chesapeake Bay Adventure. Freland, Cindy. 2016. (ENG.). (J). (gr. 1-4). 18.00 *(978-1-941927-87-8(4))*; pap. 12.00 *(978-1-941927-86-1(6))* Maryland Secretarial Services, Inc.

Gabel, Deborah Boudreau. Deep in the Woods. Aiosssa, Janet M. l.t. ed. 2005. 24p. (J). lib. bdg. 16.95 *(978-0-9769360-0-8(3),* 0503) Adam Hill Pubns.

Gaber, Susan. Angel Coming. Henson, Heather. 2011. (ENG.). 40p. (J). (gr. -1-1). pap. 16.99 *(978-1-4424-3077-8(X),* Atheneum Bks. for Young Readers) Simon & Schuster Children's Publishing.

—The Baker's Dozen. Forest, Heather. 2013. (ENG.). 32p. (J). (gr. -1-3). 8.95 *(978-1-939160-70-6(7))* August Hse. Pubs., Inc.

—The Contest Between the Sun & the Wind: An Aesop's Fable. Forest, Heather. 2013. (ENG.). 32p. (J). (gr. -1-3). pap. 8.95 *(978-1-939160-66-9(9))* August Hse. Pubs., Inc.

—The Finest Horse in Town. Martin, Jacqueline Briggs. (J). 2016. (ENG.). pap. 8.99 *(978-1-930900-82-0(1))*; 2003. 32p. 17.95 *(978-1-930900-27-1(9))* Purple Hse. Pr.

—The Little Red Hen: An Old Fable. 2015. (ENG.). 32p. (J). (gr. -1-3). pap. 8.95 *(978-1-939160-97-3(9))* August Hse. Pubs., Inc.

—Ten Sleepy Sheep. Root, Phyllis. 2009. 12p. (J). (-k). bds. 7.99 *(978-0-7636-4142-9(1))* Candlewick Pr.

—The Very First Thanksgiving Day. Greene, Rhonda Gowler. 2006. (ENG.). 32p. (J). (gr. -1-1). 7.99 *(978-1-4169-1916-2(3),* Atheneum Bks. for Young Readers) Simon & Schuster Children's Publishing.

—The Woman Who Flummoxed the Fairies. Forest, Heather. 2013. (ENG.). 32p. (J). (gr. -1-3). 8.95 *(978-1-939160-71-3(5))* August Hse. Pubs., Inc.

Gaber, Susan & Greenstein, Susan. A Big Quiet House: A Yiddish Folktale. Forest, Heather. 2005. (ENG.). 32p. (J). (gr. k-3). pap. 7.95 *(978-0-87483-604-2(2))* August Hse. Pubs., Inc.

Gabert, Cassidy. Fin the Fern. Flodin, Samantha. 2019. (ENG.). 24p. (J). 19.95 ***(978-0-578-52582-2(8))*** Flodin, Samantha.

Gable, Brian. A-B-a-B-A: A Book of Pattern Play. Cleary, Brian P. 2010. (Math Is CATegorical ® Ser.). (ENG.). 32p. (J). (gr. k-3). lib. bdg. 16.95 *(978-0-8225-7880-2(8))* Lerner Publishing Group.

—A-B-A-B-a — a Book of Pattern Play. Cleary, Brian P. 2012. (Math Is CATegorical ® Ser.). (ENG.). 32p. (J). (gr. k-3). pap. 7.99 *(978-0-7613-8502-8(9),* Millbrook Pr.) Lerner Publishing Group.

—The Action of Subtraction. Cleary, Brian P. (Math Is CATegorical ® Ser.). (ENG.). 32p. (J). (gr. k-3). 2008. pap. 7.99 *(978-1-58013-843-7(8),* 9781580138437); 2006. lib. bdg. 16.95 *(978-0-7613-9461-7(3),* 9780761394617) Lerner Publishing Group. (Millbrook Pr.).

—Backyard Beasties: Jokes to Snake You Smile. Burns, Diane L. et al. 2004. (Make Me Laugh! Ser.). 32p. (J). (gr. k-3). lib. bdg. 19.93 *(978-1-57505-646-3(1))* Lerner Publishing Group.

—Breezier, Cheesier, Newest, & Bluest: What Are Comparatives & Superlatives? Cleary, Brian P. (Words Are CATegorical ® Ser.). (ENG.). 32p. (J). (gr. 2-5). 2015. pap. 7.99 *(978-1-4677-6078-2(1),* 9781467760782); 2013. lib. bdg. 16.95 *(978-0-7613-5362-1(3),* 9780761353621) Lerner Publishing Group. (Millbrook Pr.).

—But & for, yet & Nor: What Is a Conjunction? Cleary, Brian P. (Words Are CATegorical ® Ser.). (ENG.). 32p. (gr. 2-5). 2012. (J). pap. 7.99 *(978-0-7613-8503-5(7),* 9780761385035, Millbrook Pr.); 2010. pap. 39.62 *(978-0-7613-9205-7(X),* Millbrook Pr.); 2010. lib. bdg. 16.95 *(978-0-8225-9153-5(7))* Lerner Publishing Group.

—Cool! Whoa! Ah & Oh! What Is an Interjection? Cleary, Brian P. (Words Are CATegorical ® Ser.). (ENG.). 32p. (J). (gr. 2-5). 2013. pap. 7.99 *(978-1-4677-0900-2(X))*; 2011. 16.95 *(978-1-58013-594-8(3))* Lerner Publishing Group. (Millbrook Pr.).

—Dearly, Nearly, Insincerely: What Is an Adverb? Cleary, Brian P. (Words Are CATegorical ® Ser.). (ENG.). 32p. (J). (gr. 2-5). 2005. per. 7.99 *(978-1-57505-919-8(3))*; 2003. 16.95 *(978-0-87614-924-9(7))* Lerner Publishing Group. (Millbrook Pr.).

—Dearly, Nearly, Insincerely: What Is an Adverb? Cleary, Brian P. 2006. (Words Are Categorical Ser.). (gr. k-2). 17.00 *(978-0-7569-6881-6(X))* Perfection Learning Corp.

—A Dollar, a Penny, How Much & How Many? Cleary, Brian P. (Math Is CATegorical ® Ser.). (ENG.). 32p. (gr. k-3). 2014. (J). pap. 7.99 *(978-1-4677-2629-0(X),* 9781467726290); 2012. lib. bdg. 16.95 *(978-0-8225-7882-6(4))* Lerner Publishing Group. (Millbrook Pr.).

—Don't Kid Yourself: Relatively Great (Family) Jokes. Schultz, Sam. 2004. (Make Me Laugh! Ser.). 32p. (J). (gr. k-3). lib. bdg. 19.93 *(978-1-57505-641-8(0))* Lerner Publishing Group.

—Feet & Puppies, Thieves & Guppies: What Are Irregular Plurals? Cleary, Brian P. (Words Are CATegorical ® Ser.). (ENG.). 32p. (J). (gr. 2-5). 2014. pap. 7.99 *(978-1-4677-2627-6(3),* 9781467726276); 2012. lib. bdg. 16.95 *(978-0-7613-4918-1(9))* Lerner Publishing Group. (Millbrook Pr.).

—Foul Play: Sports Jokes That Won't Strike Out. Walton, Rick & Walton, Ann. 2005. (Make Me Laugh! Ser.). 32p. (J). (gr. k-3). lib. bdg. 19.93 *(978-1-57505-666-1(6))* Lerner Publishing Group.

—A Fraction's Goal — Parts of a Whole. Cleary, Brian P. 2013. (Math Is CATegorical ® Ser.). (ENG.). 32p. (J). (gr. k-3). pap. 7.99 *(978-1-4677-1380-1(5),* Millbrook Pr.) Lerner Publishing Group.

—Game-Time Gigglers: Winning Jokes to Score Some Laughs. Schultz, Sam. 2004. (Make Me Laugh! Ser.). 32p. (J). (gr. k-3). lib. bdg. 19.93 *(978-1-57505-644-9(5))* Lerner Publishing Group.

—Grin & Bear It: Zoo Jokes to Make You Roar. Friedman, Sharon. 2005. (Make Me Laugh! Ser.). 32p. (J). (gr. k-3). lib. bdg. 19.93 *(978-1-57505-660-9(7))* Lerner Publishing Group.

—Holiday Howlers: Jokes for Punny Parties. Roop, Peter & Roop, Connie. 2004. (Make Me Laugh! Ser.). 32p. (J). (gr. k-3). lib. bdg. 19.93 *(978-1-57505-645-6(3))* Lerner Publishing Group.

—Horsing Around: Jokes to Make Ewe Smile. Burns, Diane L. 2005. (Make Me Laugh! Ser.). 32p. (J). (gr. k-3). lib. bdg. 19.93 *(978-1-57505-662-3(3))* Lerner Publishing Group.

—Horsing Around: Jokes to Make Ewe Smile. Burns, Diane L. & Scholten, Dan. 2004. (Make Me Laugh! Ser.). 32p. (J). (gr. -1-3). per. 4.95 *(978-1-57505-737-8(9))* Lerner Publishing Group.

—How Long or How Wide? A Measuring Guide. Cleary, Brian P. 2009. (Math Is CATegorical ® Ser.). (ENG.). 32p. (J). (gr. k-3). pap. 7.99 *(978-1-58013-844-4(6),* Millbrook Pr.) Lerner Publishing Group.

—How Much Can a Bare Bear Bear? Cleary, Brian P. 2004. (Words Are CATegorical ® Ser.). (ENG.). (gr. 2-5). pap. 39.62 *(978-0-8225-9899-2(X))* Lerner Publishing Group.

—How Much Can a Bare Bear Bear? What Are Homonyms & Homophones? Cleary, Brian P. (Words Are CATegorical ® Ser.). (ENG.). 32p. (J). (gr. 2-5). 2007. per. 7.99 *(978-0-8225-6710-3(5))*; 2005. lib. bdg. 16.95 *(978-1-57505-824-5(3))* Lerner Publishing Group. (Millbrook Pr.).

—I & You & Don't Forget Who: What Is a Pronoun? Cleary, Brian P. (Words Are CATegorical ® Ser.). (ENG.). 32p. (J). (gr. 2-5). 2006. per. 7.99 *(978-0-8225-6469-0(6))*; 2004. 16.95 *(978-1-57505-596-1(1))* Lerner Publishing Group. (Millbrook Pr.).

—I & You & Don't Forget Who: What Is a Pronoun? Cleary, Brian P. 2006. (Words Are Categorical Ser.). (gr. 2-4). 17.00 *(978-0-7569-6728-4(7))* Perfection Learning Corp.

—I'm & Won't, They're & Don't: What's a Contraction? Cleary, Brian P. (Words Are CATegorical ® Ser.). (ENG.). 32p. (J). (gr. 2-5). 2012. pap. 7.99 *(978-0-7613-8504-2(5))*; 2010. lib. bdg. 16.95 *(978-0-8225-9155-9(3))* Lerner Publishing Group. (Millbrook Pr.).

—Ivan to Make You Laugh: Jokes about Novel, Nifty, & Notorious Names. Schultz, Sam. 2005. (Make Me Laugh! Ser.). 32p. (J). (gr. k-3). lib. bdg. 19.93 *(978-1-57505-659-3(3))* Lerner Publishing Group.

—Jordan in Pictures. Burns, Diane L. et al. 2nd ed. 2005. (Visual Geography Series, Second Ser.). (ENG.). 80p. (gr. 5-12). 31.93 *(978-0-8225-1173-1(8))* Lerner Publishing Group.

—Lazily, Crazily, Just a Bit Nasally: More about Adverbs. Cleary, Brian P. (Words Are CATegorical ® Ser.). (ENG.). 32p. (J). (gr. 2-5). 2010. pap. 7.99 *(978-1-58013-937-3(X))*; 2008. lib. bdg. 16.95 *(978-0-8225-7848-2(4))* Lerner Publishing Group. (Millbrook Pr.).

—Let the Fun Begin: Nifty Knock-Knocks, Playful Puns, & More. Peterson, Scott K. 2005. (Make Me Laugh! Ser.). 32p. (J). (gr. k-3). lib. bdg. 19.93 *(978-1-57505-661-6(5))* Lerner Publishing Group.

—A Lime, a Mime, a Pool of Slime: More about Nouns. Cleary, Brian P. 2008. (Words Are CATegorical ® Ser.). (ENG.). 32p. (J). (gr. 2-5). pap. 7.99 *(978-1-58013-934-2(5),* Millbrook Pr.) Lerner Publishing Group.

—Madam & Nun And 1001: What Is a Palindrome? Cleary, Brian P. (Words Are CATegorical ® Ser.). (ENG.). 32p. (J). (gr. 2-5). 2014. pap. 7.99 *(978-1-4677-2628-3(1),* 9781467726283); 2012. lib. bdg. 16.95 *(978-0-7613-4919-8(7),* 9780761349198) Lerner Publishing Group. (Millbrook Pr.).

—Magical Mischief: Jokes That Shock & Amaze. Walton, Rick & Walton, Ann. 2005. (Make Me Laugh! Ser.). 32p. (J). (gr. k-3). lib. bdg. 19.93 *(978-1-57505-664-7(X))* Lerner Publishing Group.

—The Mission of Addition. Cleary, Brian P. (Math Is CATegorical ® Ser.). (ENG.). 32p. (gr. k-3). 2007. (J). pap. 7.99 *(978-0-8225-6695-3(8))*; 2005. lib. bdg. 16.95 *(978-1-57505-859-7(6))* Lerner Publishing Group. (Millbrook Pr.).

—Monster Mayhem: Jokes to Scare You Silly. Schultz, Sam. 2004. (Make Me Laugh! Ser.). 32p. (J). (gr. k-3). lib. bdg. 19.93 *(978-1-57505-642-5(9))* Lerner Publishing Group.

—On the Scale, a Weighty Tale. Cleary, Brian P. (Math Is CATegorical ® Ser.). (ENG.). 32p. (gr. k-3). 2010. (J). pap. 7.99 *(978-1-58013-845-1(4),* Millbrook Pr.); 2008. 16.95 *(978-0-8225-7851-2(4))* Lerner Publishing Group.

—Pitch & Throw, Grasp & Know: What Is a Synonym? Cleary, Brian P. (Words Are CATegorical ® Ser.). (ENG.). 32p. (J). (gr. 2-5). 2007. pap. 7.99 *(978-0-8225-6877-3(2))*; 2005. 16.95 *(978-1-57505-796-5(4))* Lerner Publishing Group. (Millbrook Pr.).

—Punny Places: Jokes That Go the Extra Mile. Swanson, June. 2004. (Make Me Laugh! Ser.). 32p. (J). (gr. k-3). lib. bdg. 19.93 *(978-1-57505-647-0(X))* Lerner Publishing Group.

—Quirky, Jerky, Extra Perky: More about Adjectives. Cleary, Brian P. (Words Are CATegorical ® Ser.). (ENG.). 32p. (J). (gr. 2-5). 2009. pap. 7.99 *(978-1-58013-936-6(1))*; 2007. lib. bdg. 16.95 *(978-0-8225-6709-7(1))* Lerner Publishing Group. (Millbrook Pr.).

—Real Classy: Silly School Jokes. Walton, Rick et al. 2005. (Make Me Laugh! Ser.). 32p. (J). (gr. k-3). lib. bdg. 19.93 *(978-1-57505-665-4(8))* Lerner Publishing Group.

—Schoolyard Snickers: Classy Jokes That Make the Grade. Schultz, Sam. 2004. (Make Me Laugh! Ser.). (ENG.). 32p. (J). (gr. k-3). lib. bdg. 17.44 *(978-1-57505-643-2(7),* Lerner Pubns.) Lerner Publishing Group.

—A Second, a Minute, a Week with Days in It: A Book about Time. Cleary, Brian P. 2015. (Math Is CATegorical ® Ser.). (ENG.). 32p. (J). (gr. k-3). pap. 7.99 *(978-1-4677-2050-2(X),* Millbrook Pr.) Lerner Publishing Group.

—Skin Like Milk, Hair of Silk: What Are Similes & Metaphors? Cleary, Brian P. (Words Are CATegorical ® Ser.). (ENG.). (gr. 2-5). 2011. 32p. (J). pap. 7.99 *(978-0-7613-3945-8(0))*; 2009. 32p. (J). 16.95 *(978-0-8225-9151-1(0))*; 2007. pap. 39.62 *(978-0-7613-8361-1(1))* Lerner Publishing Group. (Millbrook Pr.).

—The Sky's the Limit: Naturally Funny Jokes. Walton, Rick. 2005. (Make Me Laugh! Ser.). 32p. (J). (gr. k-3). lib. bdg. 19.93 *(978-1-57505-663-0(1))* Lerner Publishing Group.

—Slide & Slurp, Scratch & Burp: More about Verbs. Cleary, Brian P. (Words Are CATegorical ® Ser.). (ENG.). (gr. 2-5). 2009. 32p. (J). pap. 7.99 *(978-1-58013-935-9(3),* Millbrook Pr.); 2007. 32p. (J). lib. bdg. 16.95 *(978-0-8225-6207-8(3),* Millbrook Pr.); 2006. pap. 39.62 *(978-0-7613-4815-3(8))* Lerner Publishing Group.

—Stop & Go, Yes & No. Cleary, Brian P. 2009. (Words Are CATegorical ® Ser.). (ENG.). (gr. 2-5). pap. 39.62 (978-0-8225-9904-3(X)) Lerner Publishing Group.
—Stop & Go, Yes & No: What Is an Antonym? Cleary, Brian P. 2008. (Words Are CATegorical ® Ser.). (ENG.). 32p. (J). (gr. 2-5). per. 7.99 (978-0-8225-9025-5(5), Millbrook Pr.) Lerner Publishing Group.
—Straight & Curvy, Meek & Nervy: More about Antonyms. Cleary, Brian P. (Words Are CATegorical ® Ser.). (ENG.). 32p. (gr. 2-5). 2011. (J). pap. 7.99 (978-1-58013-939-7(6), Millbrook Pr.); 2009. 16.95 (978-0-8225-7878-9(6)); 2008. pap. 39.62 (978-0-7613-7605-7(4), Millbrook Pr.) Lerner Publishing Group.
—Stroll & Walk, Babble & Talk: More about Synonyms. Cleary, Brian P. (Words Are CATegorical ® Ser.). (ENG.). 32p. (J). (gr. 2-5). 2010. pap. 7.99 (978-1-58013-938-0(8)); 2008. 16.95 (978-0-8225-7850-5(6)) Lerner Publishing Group. (Millbrook Pr.).
—Thumbtacks, Earwax, Lipstick, Dipstick: What Is a Compound Word? Cleary, Brian P. (Words Are CATegorical ® Ser.). (ENG.). 32p. (J). (gr. 2-5). 2013. pap. 7.99 (978-1-4677-1379-5(1), 9781467713795); 2011. lib. bdg. 16.95 (978-0-7613-4917-4(0), 9780761349174) Lerner Publishing Group. (Millbrook Pr.).
—Under, over, by the Clover: What Is a Preposition? Cleary, Brian P. 2003. (Words Are CATegorical ® Ser.). (ENG.). 32p. (J). (gr. 2-5). pap. 7.99 (978-1-57505-201-4(6), Millbrook Pr.) Lerner Publishing Group.
—Under, over, by the Clover: What Is a Preposition? Cleary, Brian P. 2006. (Words Are Categorical Ser.). (gr. 2-4). 16.95 (978-0-7569-6885-4(2)) Perfection Learning Corp.
—Windows, Rings, & Grapes — a Look at Different Shapes. Cleary, Brian P. (Math Is CATegorical ® Ser.). (ENG.). 32p. (J). (gr. k-3). 2011. pap. 7.99 (978-1-58013-846-8(2)); 2009. 16.95 (978-0-8225-7879-6(4)) Lerner Publishing Group. (Millbrook Pr.).
—Windows, Rings, & Grapes - A Look at Different Shapes. Cleary, Brian P. 2011. (Math Is CATegorical Ser.). pap. 39.62 (978-0-7613-8360-4(3), Millbrook Pr.) Lerner Publishing Group.

Gabler, Michael. The Saint Vincent Coloring Book. Boosel, Brian D. 2005. 36p. (J). 9.99 (978-0-9708216-7-6(0)) St. Vincent Archabbey Pubns.

Gabriel, Andrea. Alguien Ha Estado Aquí, Alguien lo Ha Hecho: Descifrando Las Señales de Los Animales, 1 vol. Weber, Jen Funk. 2016. (SPA.). 32p. (J). (gr. k-3). pap. 11.95 (978-1-62855-741-1(9)) Arbordale Publishing.
—Been There, Done That: Reading Animal Signs, 1 vol. Weber, Jen Funk. 2016. (ENG & SPA.). 32p. (J). (gr. k-3). 17.95 (978-1-62855-727-5(3)) Arbordale Publishing.
—Daytime Nighttime, All Through the Year, 1 vol. Lang, Diane. 2017. (ENG.). 32p. (J). (gr. -1-3). 16.95 (978-1-58469-606-3(0)); pap. 8.95 (978-1-58469-607-0(9)) Sourcebooks, Inc. (Dawn Pubns.).
—Grandes Migraciones de la Ballena Gris, 1 vol. Lindsey, Marta. 2015. (SPA.). 32p. (J). (gr. k-3). pap. 11.95 (978-1-62855-468-7(1)) Arbordale Publishing.
—He's Your Daddy: Ducklings, Joeys, Kits, & More, 1 vol. Profiri, Charline. 2018. (ENG.). 32p. (J). (-3). 16.95 (978-1-58469-625-4(7), Dawn Pubns.) Sourcebooks, Inc.
—Little Gray's Great Migration, 1 vol. Lindsey, Marta. 2015. (ENG.). 32p. (J). (gr. k-3). 17.95 (978-1-62855-452-6(5)) Arbordale Publishing.
—Magia con Imanes, 1 vol. Jennings, Terry Catasús. 2016. (SPA.). 32p. (J). (gr. k-3). pap. 11.95 (978-1-62855-863-0(6)) Arbordale Publishing.
—Magnetic Magic, 1 vol. Jennings, Terry Catasús. 2016. (ENG & SPA.). 32p. (J). (gr. k-3). 17.95 (978-1-62855-861-6(X)) Arbordale Publishing.
—Sequoyah & the Cherokee Alphabet. Townsend, Dana E. 2005. (Voices Reading Ser.). 32p. (J). (978-0-7367-2953-6(4)) Zaner-Bloser, Inc.
—Where Do I Sleep? A Pacific Northwest Lullaby. Blomgren, Jennifer. (J). (— 1). 2015. 20p. bds. 9.99 (978-1-63217-019-4(1)); 2008. 32p. pap. 10.99 (978-1-57061-593-1(4)) Sasquatch Bks. (Little Bigfoot).
—Where Would I Be in an Evergreen Tree? Blomgren, Jennifer. 2011. 32p. (J). (gr. -1-2). pap. 10.99 (978-1-57061-753-9(8), Little Bigfoot) Sasquatch Bks.
—Why Do I Sing? Animal Songs of the Pacific Northwest. Blomgren, Jennifer. (J). 2015. 20p. (— 1). bds. 9.99 (978-1-63217-020-0(5)); 2013. 32p. (gr. -1-2). 16.99 (978-1-57061-845-1(3)) Sasquatch Bks. (Little Bigfoot).
—The Zoopendous Surprise! Hensel, Boots. 2009. (ENG.). 32p. (J). (gr. -1-k). 16.95 (978-0-9792035-5-8(4)) Pleasant St. Pr.

Gabriel, Andrea. My Favorite Bear. Gabriel, Andrea. 2004. 32p. (J). (-k). pap. 7.95 (978-1-58089-039-7(3)) Charlesbridge Publishing, Inc.

Gabriel, Annie. Arabella's Tree. Larter, Maureen. 2019. (ENG.). 26p. (J). (gr. k-1). pap. (978-0-6484695-4-4(9)) Sweetfields Publishing.

Gabriel, Annie. Bridget Bilby & the Blue Button. Larter, Maureen. 2019. (Alphabet Animals of Australia Ser.). (ENG.). 28p. (J). (gr. k-3). pap. (978-0-6485076-3-5(7)) Sweetfields Publishing.
—Broken Wing. Larter, Maureen. 2018. (Fairies of Aurora Village Ser.: Vol. 1). (ENG.). 82p. (J). (gr. 3-6). pap. (978-0-9873500-9-1(9)) Sweetfields Publishing.
—Dinosaur Dreaming. Larter, Maureen. 2019. (ENG.). 26p. (J). (gr. k-4). pap. (978-0-6485076-4-2(5)) Sweetfields Publishing.

Gabriel, Annie. Iggy Ibis Is Important: In the Series 'alphabet Animals of Australia'. Larter, Maureen. 2018. (ENG.). 28p. (J). pap. 12.00 (978-1-9856-5054-1(0)) CreateSpace Independent Publishing Platform.

Gabriel, Annie. In Search of the Elusive Panda: The Green Peak Canyon Expedition. Larter, Maureen. 2018. (Kathy Edwards Adventure Ser.: Vol. 1). (ENG.). 92p. (J). (gr. 4-6). pap. (978-0-9876393-9-4(0)) Sweetfields Publishing.
—Rosferado - Wizard Banished. Larter, Maureen. 2020. (Rosferado Wizard Ser.: Vol. 2). (ENG.). 100p. (J). (gr. 4-6). pap. (978-0-6485076-9-7(6)) Sweetfields Publishing.

Gabriel, Annie. Rosferado - Wizard Extraordinaire. Larter, Maureen. 2019. (ENG.). 130p. (J). (gr. 4-6). pap. (978-0-6484695-6-8(5)) Sweetfields Publishing.

Gabriel, Annie. Spiders, Lizards & Flies. Larter, Maureen. 2018. (Fairies of Aurora Village Ser.: Vol. 2). (ENG.). 102p. (J). pap. (978-0-9876393-0-1(7)) Sweetfields Publishing.
—Tania, the Tasmanian Devil. Larter, Maureen. 2020. (Alphabet Animals of Australia Ser.). (ENG.). 22p. (J). (gr. 1-5). pap. (978-0-6485076-8-0(8)) Sweetfields Publishing.

Gabriel, Evette. Buck's Bad Dreams. Scotto, Michael. 2009. (J). (978-1-935193-46-3(5)) Lincoln Learning Solutions.
—Build a the Re-Bicycler. Scotto, Michael. 2009. (J). (978-1-935193-22-7(8)) Lincoln Learning Solutions.

Gabriel, Evette, et al. Just Flash. Scotto, Michael. 2009. (J). (978-1-935193-50-0(3)) Lincoln Learning Solutions.

Gabriel, Evette. Sweet Tooth Bun. Scotto, Michael. 2009. (J). (978-1-935193-48-7(1)) Lincoln Learning Solutions.

Gabrili, Alexandra. Nicholas Wins the Prize 1: Young Nicholas Experiences the Sacrament of Confession. Iakovos-Dalalakis, Helen. 2003. (ENG.). 24p. (J). (gr. 2-6). 15.95 (978-1-880971-82-6(8)) Light & Life Publishing Co.

Gadd, Maxine. Kandide & the Secret of the Mists. Zimmerman, Diana S. 2008. (Calabiyau Chronicles Ser.: Bk. 1). 296p. (YA). (gr. 5-18). 17.99 (978-0-9794328-3-5(9));Bk. 1. 290p. (J). (gr. 4-7). pap. 9.99 (978-0-9794328-2-8(0)) Noesis Publishing.

Gade, Satwik. The Boy Who Asked Why: The Story of Bhimrao Ambedkar. Rajendran, Sowmya. 2018. (ENG.). 40p. (J). (gr. k-6). 19.95 (978-0-9995476-0-1(7)); pap. 11.95 (978-0-9995476-1-8(5)) KitaabWorld.Com, LLC.

Gadeselli, Natalie. Curiosity. Philips, Lyn D. 2013. 32p. pap. (978-1-904928-27-0(7)) Copeland & Wickson.

Gadra, Jessica. Sneaking Treats. McRoberts, Eddison. 2013. 48p. pap. 9.95 (978-1-62137-298-1(7)) Virtualbookworm.com Publishing, Inc.
—Sneaking Treats: A Halloween Hunt. McRoberts, Eddison. 2012. 48p. 19.95 (978-1-62137-136-6(0)) Virtualbookworm.com Publishing, Inc.
—Top Leaf. Gold, Jennifer. 2017. (ENG.). (J). (gr. k-2). 19.00 (978-0-9978741-3-6(9)) Buffalo Arts Publishing.
—Yes! I Knew the Queen. Gold, Jennifer. 2018. (ENG.). 34p. (J). (gr. 1-4). pap. 14.00 (978-1-950006-03-8(4)); 21.00 (978-0-9978741-8-1(X)) Buffalo Arts Publishing.

Gadtan Jean Louis, Rosley. Michael's First Word! Beach, Linda M. 2009. 20p. pap. 12.49 (978-1-4389-0766-6(4)) AuthorHouse.

Gadzińska, Anita. Blessed Is the Spot Coloring & Activity Book. 2019. (ENG.). 48p. (J). pap. 8.95 (978-1-947485-03-7(2)) InnerPrize Group, LLC.

Gaeddert, Margaret, jt. illus. see Duncan Ph D, Hall.

Gaffney, Ellen. Wings for a Flower. Gaffney, Ellen. 2013. 32p. 16.95 (978-0-9882212-6-0(8)) Three Bean Pr.

Gág, Flavia. The Wily Woodchucks. Travers, Georgia. 2009. (Fesler-Lampert Minnesota Heritage Ser.). (ENG.). 32p. 14.95 (978-0-8166-6548-8(6)) Univ. of Minnesota Pr.

Gág, Wanda. Gone Is Gone: Or the Story of a Man Who Wanted to Do Housework. Gág, Wanda. 2003. (Fesler-Lampert Minnesota Heritage Ser.). (ENG.). 64p. 14.95 (978-0-8166-4243-4(5)) Univ. of Minnesota Pr.
—Millions of Cats. Gág, Wanda. 2006. (gr. -1-3). 18.00 (978-0-7569-6785-7(6)) Perfection Learning Corp.
—Millions of Cats (Gift Edition) Gág, Wanda. gif. ed. 2006. (ENG.). 32p. (J). (gr. -1-k). pap. 8.99 (978-0-14-240708-0(9), Puffin Books) Penguin Young Readers Group.
—More Tales from Grimm. Gág, Wanda. Grimm, Wilhelm K. & Grimm, Jacob. 2006. (Fesler-Lampert Minnesota Heritage Ser.). (ENG.). 272p. (gr. 4-7). per. 16.95 (978-0-8166-4938-9(3)) Univ. of Minnesota Pr.

Gág, Wanda. Tales from Grimm. Gág, Wanda, tr. Grimm, Wilhelm K. & Grimm, Jacob. 2006. (Fesler-Lampert Minnesota Heritage Ser.). (ENG.). 256p. (gr. 4-7). per. 16.95 (978-0-8166-4936-5(7)) Univ. of Minnesota Pr.

Gage, Amy Glaser & McIntyre, Connie. Upside Downside Inside Out: Poems about Being a Kid. Gage, Amy Glaser & McIntyre, Connie. 2nd rev. ed. 2003. 49p. (J). per. 9.95 (978-0-9677685-4-0(3)) Grannie Annie Family Story Celebration, The.

Gage, Kathryn. Wow, I'm a Big Brother. 2011. 48p. (J). spiral bd. 6.25 net. (978-1-890703-44-8(3)) Penny Laine Papers, Inc.
—Wow, I'm a Big Sister. 2011. 48p. (J). spiral bd. 6.25 net. (978-1-890703-45-5(1)) Penny Laine Papers, Inc.

Gaggelli, Pascal. Suzy's Smile: Suzy Dogfish Gets Braces. Dot, Momma. 2015. (ENG.). 34p. (J). pap. 11.34 (978-0-9967667-2-2(3)) Momma Dot Publishing LLC.

Gaggiotti, Lucia. Frankie's Food Truck. Educational Insights. 2019. (ENG.). 12p. (J). (— 1). bds. 9.99 (978-1-5362-0687-6(3), Candlewick Entertainment) Candlewick Pr.
—Hoppy Floppy's Carrot Hunt. Educational Insights. 2020. (ENG.). 12p. (J). (— 1). bds. 9.99 (978-1-5362-1231-0(8), Candlewick Entertainment) Candlewick Pr.
—How Did That Get in My Lunchbox? The Story of Food. Butterworth, Christine. 2011. (Exploring the Everyday Ser.). (ENG.). 32p. (J). (gr. k-3). 12.99 (978-0-7636-5005-6(6)) Candlewick Pr.
—How Did That Get in My Lunchbox? The Story of Food. Butterworth, Chris. 2013. (Exploring the Everyday Ser.). (ENG.). 32p. (J). (gr. k-3). 6.99 (978-0-7636-6503-6(7)) Candlewick Pr.

Gaggiotti, Lucia. How Does My Home Work? Butterworth, Chris. (Exploring the Everyday Ser.). (ENG.). 32p. (J). (gr. k-3). 2020. 6.99 (978-1-5362-1594-6(5)); 2017. 14.99 (978-0-7636-9594-1(7)) Candlewick Pr.

Gaggiotti, Lucia. I Really Want the Cake. Philip, Simon. 2020. (ENG.). 40p. (J). (gr. -1-k). 17.99 (978-1-338-58941-2(5), Orchard Bks.) Scholastic, Inc.
—Shelby's Snack Shack. Educational Insights. 2018. 12p. (J). (— 1). bds. 9.99 (978-0-7636-9873-7(3), Candlewick Entertainment) Candlewick Pr.
—The Sneaky, Snacky Squirrel. Educational Insights. 2017. (ENG.). 12p. (J). (— 1). bds. 9.99 (978-0-7636-9465-4(7), Candlewick Entertainment) Candlewick Pr.
—Where Did My Clothes Come From? Butterworth, Chris. 2015. (Exploring the Everyday Ser.). (ENG.). 32p. (J). (gr. k-3). 12.99 (978-0-7636-7750-3(7)) Candlewick Pr.
—Where Did My Clothes Come From? Butterworth, Christine. 2017. (Exploring the Everyday Ser.). (ENG.). 32p. (J). (gr. k-3). 6.99 (978-0-7636-9518-7(1)) Candlewick Pr.

Gagliardo, Lucy. Giving Back to the Earth: Teacher's Guide to Project Puffin & Other Seabird Studies. Salmansohn, Pete & Kress, Stephen W. 2010. (National Audubon Society Book). 80p. (Orig.). (gr. 3-6). pap., tchr. ed. 9.95 (978-0-88448-172-0(7)) Tilbury Hse. Pubs.

Gagne, Alexandra. Les Aventures de Couki et Broni: Le Grand Départ. Valt, Cindy. 2018. (FRE.). 28p. (J). pap. (978-2-9557516-1-9(8)) Cindy, Valt.

Gagne, Alexandra. Les Aventures de Couki et Broni: Une Journ�e � la P�che. Valt, Cindy. 2019. (Aventures de Couki et Broni Ser.: Vol. 2). (FRE.). 28p. (J). pap. (978-2-9557516-4-0(2)) Cindy, Valt.

Gagnon, Celeste, et al. Franklin & the Cookies. Jennings, Sharon. 2005. 32p. (J). lib. bdg. 15.38 (978-1-4242-1167-8(0)) Fitzgerald Bks.
—Franklin & the Scooter. Jennings, Sharon. 2004. 32p. (J). lib. bdg. 15.38 (978-1-4242-1169-2(7)) Fitzgerald Bks.

Gagnon, Céleste. Franklin the Detective. Jennings, Sharon et al. 2004. 32p. (J). pap. (978-0-439-41822-5(4)) Scholastic, Inc.

Gagnon, Celeste, et al. Franklin the Detective. Jennings, Sharon. 2004. 32p. (J). lib. bdg. 15.38 (978-1-4242-1171-5(9)) Fitzgerald Bks.

Gagnon, Céleste. Franklin's Library Book. Jennings, Sharon et al. 2005. 32p. (J). (978-0-439-82297-8(1)) Scholastic, Inc.

Gagnon, Celeste, jt. illus. see Gagnon, Cileste.

Gagnon, Cileste & Gagnon, Celeste. Knotting: Make Your Own Basketball Nets, Guitar Straps, Sports Bags & More. Sadler, Judy Ann & Sadler, Judy. 2006. (Kids Can Do It Ser.). 40p. (J). (gr. 3-7). 6.95 (978-1-55337-834-1(2)) Kids Can Pr., Ltd. CAN. Dist: Hachette Bk. Group.

Gago, Noel. Fabien the Alien. Gago, Noel. 2016. (ENG.). (J). (gr. k-6). 21.35 (978-0-692-72531-3(8)) Gago, Noel.

Gahng, Hwa-kyeong. I Am a Little Monk: Thailand. Joo, Mi-hwa. 2015. (Global Kids Storybooks Ser.). (ENG.). 32p. (J). (gr. 1-4). pap. 8.99 (978-1-925233-47-6(2), Big and SMALL) ChoiceMaker Pty. Ltd., The AUS. Dist: Lerner Publishing Group.
—I Am a Little Monk: Thailand. Joo, Mi-hwa. Cowley, Joy, ed. 2015. (Global Kids Storybooks Ser.). (ENG.). 32p. (J). (gr. 1-4). 26.65 (978-1-925246-06-3(X)); 26.65 (978-1-925246-32-2(9)); 7.99 (978-1-925246-58-2(2)) ChoiceMaker Pty. Ltd., The AUS. (Big and SMALL). Dist: Lerner Publishing Group.

Gahng, In. Crayon Road: Imagination - Lines. Jeong, Jini. Cowley, Joy, ed. 2015. (Step up - Creative Thinking Ser.). (ENG.). 32p. (gr. -1-2). 26.65 (978-1-925246-10-0(8)); 26.65 (978-1-925246-36-0(1)); 7.99 (978-1-925246-62-9(0)) ChoiceMaker Pty. Ltd., The AUS. (Big and SMALL). Dist: Lerner Publishing Group.

Gail M Nelson. The Recycling Project. Mazzitelli, Donna. 2018. (ENG.). 50p. (J). pap. 10.00 (978-1-939919-57-1(6)) Merry Dissonance Pr.

Gaillard, Jason. Running Shoes. Lipp, Frederick. 2008. 32p. (J). (gr. 2-5). 16.95 (978-1-58089-175-2(6)); pap. 7.95 (978-1-58089-176-9(4)) Charlesbridge Publishing, Inc.

Gaillard, Jason. Bread Song. Gaillard, Jason, tr. Lipp, Frederick J. 2004. (J). 15.95 (978-1-59336-000-9(2)); pap. (978-1-59336-001-6(0)) Mondo Publishing.

Gaines, Lynn. A Child's Introduction to African American History: The Experiences, People, & Events That Shaped Our Country. Asim, Jabari. 2018. (Child's Introduction Ser.). 96p. (J). (gr. 3-7). 19.99 (978-0-316-43642-7(9), Black Dog & Leventhal Pubs. Inc.) Hachette Bks.

Gaisey, Christopher. Pop Goes the Weasel: A Silly Song Book. Auerbach, Annie. 2005. 12p. (J). (gr. -1-3). 12.95 (978-1-58117-426-7(8), Intervisual/Piggy Toes) Bendon, Inc.

Gait, Darlene. Secret of the Dance, 1 vol. Spalding, Andrea & Scow, Alfred. 2009. (ENG.). 32p. (J). (gr. -1-k). 10.95 (978-1-55469-129-6(X)) Orca Bk. Pubs. USA.
—Soapstone Porcupine, 1 vol. Pinkney, Jeffrey R. 2018. (Orca Echoes Ser.). (ENG.). 88p. (J). (gr. 1-3). pap. 6.95 (978-1-4598-1472-1(X)) Orca Bk. Pubs. USA.
—Soapstone Signs, 1 vol. Pinkney, Jeff. 2014. (Orca Echoes Ser.). (ENG.). 64p. (J). (gr. 1-3). pap. 6.95 (978-1-4598-0400-5(7)) Orca Bk. Pubs. USA.

Gal, Laszlo. Tiktala, 1 vol. Shaw-MacKinnon, Margaret. 2005. (ENG.). 32p. (J). (gr. 1-4). per. 9.95 (978-1-55005-143-8(1), e1d19284-7c03-4f56-a262-c414345d9bdb) Fitzhenry & Whiteside, Ltd. CAN. Dist: Firefly Bks., Ltd.

Gal, Susan. Here Is the World: A Year of Jewish Holidays. Newman, Lesléa & Newman, Lesléa. 2014. (ENG.). 48p. (J). (gr. -1-2). 18.95 (978-1-4197-1185-5(7)) Abrams, Inc.
—Hocus Pocus, It's Fall! O'Brien, Anne Sibley. 2016. (ENG.). 24p. (J). (gr. -1-k). 12.95 (978-1-4197-2125-0(9), Abrams Appleseed) Abrams, Inc.
—Welcoming Elijah: A Passover Tale with a Tail. Newman, Lesléa. 2020. 32p. (J). (gr. k-3). lib. bdg. 16.99 (978-1-58089-882-9(3)) Charlesbridge Publishing, Inc.
—A World of Cookies for Santa: Follow Santa's Tasty Trip Around the World. Furman, M. E. 2017. (ENG.). 48p. (J). (gr. -1-3). 16.99 (978-0-544-22620-3(8), 1563497, HMH Books For Young Readers) Houghton Mifflin Harcourt Publishing Co.

Galán, Gema. Busy Book of Search & Find: Amazing Animals. 2021. (ENG.). 32p. (J). 14.95 (978-1-5319-1483-7(7)) Sellers Publishing, Inc.

Galán, Manny. The Great Big Poop Party. Berger, Samantha. 2020. (ENG.). 40p. (J). 14.99 (978-1-250-23787-3(4), 900210828, Holt, Henry & Co. Bks. For Young Readers) Holt, Henry & Co.

Galan-Robles, Francisco. Wee Dragonslayers. Harrar, Frank W. 2008. 45p. pap. 24.95 (978-1-60610-851-2(4)) America Star Bks.

Galante, Ashley. There Are Monsters Here! Cimorelli, Amber. 2013. 40p. pap. 24.95 (978-1-62709-064-3(9)) America Star Bks.

Galante, Studio & Firenze, Inklink. The Great Dinosaur Search. Heywood, Rosie. Wingate, Philippa, ed. rev. ed. 2005. (Great Searches - New Format Ser.). 32p. (J). (gr. -1). pap. 7.99 (978-0-7945-1046-6(9), Usborne) EDC Publishing.

Galaska, Taylor, jt. illus. see Paglia, Rhonda.

Galbany, Montse. Junko Tabei Masters the Mountains. Rebel Girls. 2020. (Good Night Stories for Rebel Girls Chapter Book Ser.). (ENG.). 128p. (J). (gr. 2-5). 12.99 (978-1-7333292-0-0(X), Rebel Girls) Timbuktu Labs, Inc.

Galbraith, Alison L. Coco's Vineyard Vacation: Double Fun on Martha's Vineyard. Kelly, Sharon L. C. M. 2005. 40p. (J). 16.95 (978-0-9766283-0-9(9)) Secret Garden Bookworks.

G

Galdone, Paul. Adventures of Homer Fink. Offit, Sidney. 2016. (ENG.). 192p. pap. 11.99 (978-1-5040-3621-4(2)) Open Road Integrated Media, Inc.
—Basil & the Cave of Cats. Titus, Eve. 2016. (Great Mouse Detective Ser.: 2). (ENG.). 112p. (J). (gr. 1-4). pap. 5.99 (978-1-4814-6404-8(3), Aladdin) Simon & Schuster Children's Publishing.
—Basil & the Lost Colony. Titus, Eve. 2017. (Great Mouse Detective Ser.: 5). (ENG.). 96p. (J). (gr. 1-4). pap. 5.99 (978-1-4814-6413-0(2), Aladdin) Simon & Schuster Children's Publishing.
—Basil in Mexico. Titus, Eve. 2016. (Great Mouse Detective Ser.: 3). (ENG.). 112p. (J). (gr. 1-4). pap. 5.99 (978-1-4814-6407-9(8), Aladdin) Simon & Schuster Children's Publishing.
—Basil in Mexico. Titus, Eve. 2016. (Great Mouse Detective Ser.: 3). (ENG.). 112p. (J). (gr. 1-4). 16.99 (978-1-4814-6408-6(6), Simon & Schuster/Paula Wiseman Bks.) Simon & Schuster/Paula Wiseman Bks.
—Basil of Baker Street. Titus, Eve. 2016. (Great Mouse Detective Ser.: 1). (ENG.). 112p. (J). (gr. 1-4). 16.99 (978-1-4814-6402-4(7)); pap. 5.99 (978-1-4814-6401-7(9)) Simon & Schuster Children's Publishing. (Aladdin).
—Space Cat. Todd, Ruthven. 2018. (ENG.). 80p. (gr. 1-5). 16.95 (978-0-486-82272-3(9), 822729) Dover Pubns., Inc.
—Space Cat & the Kittens. Todd, Ruthven. 2018. (ENG.). 96p. (gr. 1-5). 16.95 (978-0-486-82275-4(3), 822753) Dover Pubns., Inc.
—Space Cat Meets Mars. Todd, Ruthven. 2018. (ENG.). 80p. (gr. 1-5). 16.95 (978-0-486-82274-7(5), 822745) Dover Pubns., Inc.
—Space Cat Visits Venus. Todd, Ruthven. 2018. (ENG.). 96p. (gr. 1-5). 16.95 (978-0-486-82273-0(7), 822737) Dover Pubns., Inc.
—The Three Bears. 2011. (J). pap. (978-0-547-86831-8(6)) Harcourt.

Galdone, Paul. The Gingerbread Boy, 1 vol. Galdone, Paul. 2008. (Paul Galdone Classics Ser.). (ENG.). 40p. (J). (gr. -1-3). 10.99 (978-0-618-89498-7(5), 100587) Houghton Mifflin Harcourt Publishing Co.
—The Little Red Hen. Galdone, Paul. (J). (gr. -1-k). pap. 12.95 incl. audio Weston Woods Studios, Inc.
—The Three Billy Goats Gruff, 1 vol. Galdone, Paul. 2008. (Paul Galdone Classics Ser.). (ENG.). 32p. (J). (gr. -1-3). 10.99 (978-0-618-89499-4(3), 100588) Houghton Mifflin Harcourt Publishing Co.
—Three Little Kittens, 1 vol. Galdone, Paul. 2007. (Paul Galdone Classics Ser.). (ENG.). 32p. (J). (gr. -1-3). 10.99 (978-0-618-85285-7(9), 416198) Houghton Mifflin Harcourt Publishing Co.
—The Three Little Pigs, 1 vol. Galdone, Paul. 2006. (Paul Galdone Classics Ser.). (ENG.). 48p. (J). (gr. -1-3). 10.99 (978-0-618-73277-7(2), 100519) Houghton Mifflin Harcourt Publishing Co.

Galdone, Paul & Mottram, David. The Great Mouse Detective Mastermind Collection Books 1-8: Basil of Baker Street; Basil & the Cave of Cats; Basil in Mexico; Basil in the Wild West; Basil & the Lost Colony; Basil & the Big Cheese Cook-Off; Basil & the Royal Dare; Basil & the Library Ghost. Titus, Eve & Hapka, Cathy. ed. 2020. (Great Mouse Detective Ser.). (ENG.). 832p. (J). (gr. 1-4). pap. 47.99 (978-1-5344-6307-3(0), Aladdin) Simon & Schuster Children's Publishing.

Gale - Budol, Louise. Life Skills Series - Learning to Claim or Being a Dolphin. Shani, Asaf. 2019. (Children's Life Skills Ser.: Vol. 11). (ENG.). 26p. (J). pap. 10.99 (978-1-6916-1894-1(2)) Independently Published.

Gale Budol, Louise. Learning Gratitude or Quieting the Rough Sea. Shani, Asaf. 2018. (Jade's Life Skills Ser.: Vol. 8). (ENG.). 24p. (J). pap. 10.99 (978-1-7199-8733-2(5)) Independently Published.
—Learning Persistence or Yes I Can! Shani, Asaf. 2018. (Jades's Life Skills Ser.: Vol. 7). (ENG.). 26p. (J). pap. 10.99 (978-1-7199-8955-8(9)) Independently Published.
—Letting Go of Yucky Feelings or Drop the Lemons. Shani, Asaf. 2018. (Jade's Life Skills Ser.: Vol. 3). (ENG.). 24p. (J). pap. 10.99 (978-1-7199-8862-9(5)) Independently Published.

Gale Budol, Louise. Life Skills Series - Meaning Attribution or Keeping It Sunny. Shani, Asaf. 2019. (Children's Life Skills Ser.: Vol. 5). (ENG.). 26p. (J). pap. 10.99 (978-1-0874-0691-6(9)) Independently Published.
—Life Skills Series - Mental Flexibility or Move the Picture. Shani, Asaf. 2019. (Children's Life Skills Ser.: Vol. 6). (ENG.). 28p. (J). pap. 10.99 (978-1-6907-1186-5(8)) Independently Published.
—Life Skills Series - Problem Solving or Don't Push. Shani, Asaf. 2019. (Children's Life Skills Ser.: Vol. 10). (ENG.). 26p. (J). pap. 10.99 (978-1-6912-1706-9(9)) Independently Published.

Gale, Cathy. Mary Is Scary. Cottringer, Anne. (Bloomsbury Paperbacks Ser.). 32p. (J). 2007. (gr. k-2). pap. 9.99 (978-0-7475-7927-4(X)); 2005. (gr. -1-3). 19.99 (978-0-7475-6464-5(7)) Bloomsbury Publishing Plc GBR. Dist: Independent Pubs. Group.

Galea, Jose' Angel. A Spoiled Little Pony. Pfeiffer, Ingrid E. 2019. (ENG.). 34p. (J). pap. 10.00 (978-1-7307-9650-0(8)) Independently Published.

Galea, Ryan & Taliana, Philip. The Gozo Cat Detectives: Trilogy 2. Springham, Sarah. 2018. (ENG.). 88p. (J). (gr. 2-6). pap. *(978-99957-48-84-5(3))* Faraxa Publishing.

Galeano, Martha. The Letters Danced for Cara. Sansone, Angela. 2019. (ENG.). 26p. (J). pap. 9.25 ***(978-1-7100-6145-1(6))*** Independently Published.

Galego, Ane M. Leprechaun Magic. Whittle, J. Robert & Sandilands, Joyce. 2004. 64p. (J). *(978-0-9685061-2-7(7))* Whitlands Publishing, Ltd.

Galer, Jeffrey. The Big Red Barn. Galer, Jeffrey. Galer, Christa. 2003. 40p. (J). 11.49 *(978-0-9706491-0-2(X))* Purple Crayon Studios.

Galeron, Henri. El Dinosaurio. Galeron, Henri. Prunier, Jameâs et al. Prunier, Jameâs & Barroso, Paz, trs. 7th ed. (Coleccion Mundo Maravilloso). (SPA.). 40p. (J). (gr. 2-4). *(978-84-348-3725-6(0),* DI9915) SM Ediciones.

Galeron, Henri, jt. illus. see Prunier, James.

Galetto, Florencia. Baby Dragon ABC's - Handwriting Practice & Coloring Pages for 3-5 Year Olds. Books, Baby Dragon. 2019. (Baby Dragon Bks.: Vol. 1). (ENG.). 124p. (J). pap. 7.99 *(978-1-0733-6783-2(5))* Independently Published.

Galey, Chuck. The Fat Stock Stampede at the Houston Livestock Show & Rodeo, 1 vol. Enderle, Dotti. 2008. (ENG.). 32p. (J). (gr. 1-3). 16.99 *(978-1-58980-443-2(0),* Pelican Publishing) Arcadia Publishing.

—Favorite Bible Heroes: Ages 2&3. Pelfrey, Wanda B. & Kuhn, Pamela J. 2005. 96p. (J). pap. 11.95 *(978-0-937282-22-9(7),* RB36196) Rainbow Pubs. & Legacy Pr.

—Favorite Bible Heroes: Ages 4&5. Sanders, Nancy I. & Kuhn, Pamela J. 2005. 96p. (J). (gr. -1-k). pap. 11.95 *(978-0-937282-23-6(5),* RB36197) Rainbow Pubs. & Legacy Pr.

—Favorite Bible Heroes: Grades 1&2. Domelj, Scoti & Kuhn, Pamela J. 2005. 96p. (J). (gr. 1-2). pap. 11.95 *(978-0-937282-24-3(3),* RB36198) Rainbow Pubs. & Legacy Pr.

—Favorite Bible Heroes: Grades 3&4. Pearson, Mary R. & Kuhn, Pamela J. 2005. 96p. (J). (gr. 3-4). pap. 11.95 *(978-0-937282-25-0(1),* RB36199) Rainbow Pubs. & Legacy Pr.

—Five-Minute Sunday School Activities for Preschoolers: Bible Adventures. Davis, Mary J. 2005. 96p. (J). pap. 11.95 *(978-1-58411-046-0(5))* Rainbow Pubs. & Legacy Pr.

—Five-Minute Sunday School Activities for Preschoolers: Jesus Shows Me. Davis, Mary J. 2005. 96p. (J). pap. 11.95 *(978-1-58411-047-7(3))* Rainbow Pubs. & Legacy Pr.

—Fun Day in Mrs. Walker's Class. Little, Robert. 2005. 32p. (J). *(978-0-9701863-6-2(3))* Relde Publishing.

—Jay & the Bounty of Books, 1 vol. Ivey, Randall. 2007. (ENG.). 32p. (J). (gr. k-3). 16.99 *(978-1-58980-372-5(8),* Pelican Publishing) Arcadia Publishing.

—My Brother Dan's Delicious, 1 vol. Layne, Steven L. 2003. (ENG.). 32p. (J). (gr. k-3). 16.99 *(978-1-58980-071-7(0),* Pelican Publishing) Arcadia Publishing.

—Rock 'n' Roll Dogs, 1 vol. Davis, David. 2006. (ENG.). 32p. (J). (gr. k-3). 16.99 *(978-1-58980-349-7(3),* Pelican Publishing) Arcadia Publishing.

Galey, Chuck. Un Aliento de Esperanza. Galey, Chuck. Kittinger, Jo S. & Mlawer, Teresa. 2013. (SPA.). (J). *(978-1-61438-868-5(7))* American Bar Assn.

Galey, Chuck & Winn, Chris. Teaching Children Memory Verses: Ages 2&3. Davis, Mary. 2005. 96p. (J). pap. 11.95 *(978-1-58411-063-7(5))* Rainbow Pubs. & Legacy Pr.

—Teaching Children Memory Verses: Grades 1&2. Davis, Mary. 2005. 96p. (J). pap. 11.95 *(978-1-58411-065-1(1))* Rainbow Pubs. & Legacy Pr.

—Teaching Children Memory Verses: Grades 3&4. Davis, Mary. 2005. 96p. (J). pap. 11.95 *(978-1-58411-066-8(X))* Rainbow Pubs. & Legacy Pr.

Gali, Mercè. Everything I Know about Poop. Copons, Jaume. 2018. (ENG.). 28p. (J). (gr. k-2). 12.95 *(978-0-2281-0083-6(6),* 945d4ce9-d64d-45ce-8c97-2db7a1d7d1e7) Firefly Bks., Ltd.

Galicia, Diana. Mi Cabello Se Llama Bella. Onwuemene, Toyosi. 2018.Tr. of My Hair Is Beauty. (SPA.). 32p. (J). 21.98 *(978-1-948960-07-6(9))* Onwuemene Publishing Group.

Galih, Adit. Little Linguists' Library, Book One (French) Où Est Mon Ballon ? Collier, William. 2018. (Little Linguists' Library (French) Ser.: Vol. 1). (ENG.). 32p. (J). (gr. k-1). pap. *(978-1-9164703-0-9(0))* Cocoa Bean Pr.

—Little Linguists' Library, Book One (Spanish) ¿dónde Está Mi Globo? Collier, William. 2018. (Little Linguists' Library (Spanish) Ser.: Vol. 1). (ENG.). 32p. (J). (gr. k-1). *(978-1-9164703-3-0(5))*; pap. *(978-1-9164703-2-3(7))* Cocoa Bean Pr.

—Prickle. Litwin, April. 2018. (ENG.). 34p. (J). (gr. k-4). 17.99 *(978-0-692-18539-1(9))* Litwin, April Lynn.

—Sophia's Stories. Bourgeau, Kim. 2016. (ENG.). (J). pap. 9.50 *(978-1-61704-261-4(7))* River Styx Publishing Co.

Galindo, Alejandro. The Party for Papá Luis/La Fiesta para Papá Luis. Bertrand, Diane Gonzales & Ventura, Gabriela Baeza. 2010. (ENG.). 32p. (J). (gr. -1-3). 16.95 *(978-1-55885-532-8(7))* Arte Publico Pr.

Galindo, Diego & Sharma, Lalit Kumar. Disney Aladdin: Four Tales of Agrabah (Graphic Novel) Bechko, Corinna. 2019. (ENG.). 72p. (J). (gr. 3-7). pap. 10.99 *(978-1-5067-1267-3(3))* Dark Horse Comics.

Galindo, Felipe. My Teacher Can Teach... Anyone! Nikola-Lisa, W. 2004. (ENG.). 32p. (J). (gr. -1-2). 16.95 *(978-1-58430-163-9(5))*; pap. 11.95 *(978-1-60060-276-4(2))* Lee & Low Bks., Inc.

Galindo, Renata. The Cherry Thief. Galindo, Renata. (Child's Play Library). 32p. (J). 2016. *(978-1-84643-651-2(6))*; 2014. *(978-1-84643-652-9(4))* Child's Play International Ltd.

Galindro, Paulo. El Tibur�n en la Ba�era. Machado, David. 2019. (Torre Roja Ser.). (SPA.). 48p. (J). pap. ***(978-958-00-0208-6(8))*** Norma Ediciones, S.A.

Galkin, Simon. Favorite Russian Fairy Tales. Ransome, Arthur. 2011. (Dover Children's Thrift Classics Ser.). (ENG.). 96p. (J). (gr. 3-8). pap. 4.00 *(978-0-486-28632-7(0),* 286320) Dover Pubns., Inc.

—The Firebird & Other Russian Fairy Tales. Ransome, Arthur. 2004. (ENG.). (J). (gr. 3-6). lib. bdg. 16.55 *(978-1-61383-696-5(1))* Perfection Learning Corp.

Gall, Chris. America the Beautiful. Bates, Katharine Lee. 2010. (ENG.). 32p. (J). (gr. -1-3). pap. 7.99 *(978-0-316-08338-6(0))* Little, Brown Bks. for Young Readers.

—Little Red's Riding 'Hood. Stein, Peter. 2015. (ENG.). 40p. (J). (gr. -1-k). 16.99 *(978-0-545-60969-2(0))* Scholastic, Inc.

—The Ninjabread Man. Leigh, C. J. 2016. (ENG.). 40p. (J). (gr. -1-k). 16.99 *(978-0-545-81430-0(8))* Scholastic, Inc.

Gall, Chris. Go for the Moon: A Rocket, a Boy, & the First Moon Landing. Gall, Chris. 2019. (ENG.). 48p. (J). 19.99 *(978-1-250-15579-5(7),* 900184774) Roaring Brook Pr.

—Jumbo: The Making of the Boeing 747. Gall, Chris. 2020. (ENG.). 48p. (J). 19.99 *(978-1-250-15580-1(0),* 900184775) Roaring Brook Pr.

Gallagher-Cole, Mernie. Bed, Bats, & Beyond. Holub, Joan. (Darby Creek Exceptional Titles Ser.). 64p. (J). 2010. (ENG.). (gr. 1-3). pap. 6.95 *(978-0-7613-6451-1(X))*; 2008. (gr. -1-1). 14.95 *(978-1-58196-077-8(8),* Darby Creek) Lerner Publishing Group.

—Birthday Crafts. Trueit, Trudi Strain. 2016. (Holiday Crafts Ser.). (ENG.). 24p. (J). (gr. k-3). 28.50 *(978-1-5038-0815-7(7),* 210651) Child's World, Inc., The.

—Christmas Crafts. Miller, Mirella S. 2016. (Holiday Crafts Ser.). (ENG.). 24p. (J). (gr. k-3). 28.50 *(978-1-5038-0816-4(5),* 210652) Child's World, Inc., The.

—Cuddle-Up Prayers. Adams, Michelle Medlock. 2020. 26p. (J). (gr. -1 — 1). bds. 9.99 *(978-1-5460-1429-4(2),* Worthy Kids/Ideals) Worthy Publishing.

—Easter Crafts. Yasuda, Anita. 2016. (Holiday Crafts Ser.). (ENG.). 24p. (J). (gr. k-3). 28.50 *(978-1-5038-0817-1(3),* 210653) Child's World, Inc., The.

—Go Fly a Kite! (and Other Sayings We Don't Really Mean) Klingel, Cynthia Fitterer & Klingel, Cynthia. 2007. (Sayings & Phrases Ser.). (ENG.). 24p. (J). (gr. 2-5). 14.21 *(978-1-59296-904-3(6),* 200788) Child's World, Inc., The.

—Halloween Crafts. Yasuda, Anita. 2016. (Holiday Crafts Ser.). (ENG.). 24p. (J). (gr. k-3). 28.50 *(978-1-5038-0820-1(3),* 210656) Child's World, Inc., The.

—I'm All Thumbs! (and Other Odd Things We Say) Amoroso, Cynthia. 2011. (Sayings & Phrases Ser.). (ENG.). 24p. (J). (gr. 2-5). lib. bdg. 14.21 *(978-1-60253-682-1(1),* 200781) Child's World, Inc., The.

—It's a Long Shot! (and Other Strange Sayings) Amoroso, Cynthia. 2011. (Sayings & Phrases Ser.). (ENG.). 24p. (J). (gr. 2-5). lib. bdg. 14.21 *(978-1-60253-683-8(X),* 200782) Child's World, Inc., The.

—El Lugar de Luis, 1 vol. Blackaby, Susan. Ruiz, Carlos, tr. 2006. (Read-It! Readers en Español: Story Collection).Tr. of Place for Mike. (SPA.). 24p. (J). (gr. -1-3). 21.32 *(978-1-4048-1688-6(7),* Picture Window Bks.) Capstone.

—Max Celebra el Ano Nuevo Chino, 1 vol. Klein, Adria F. Robledo, Sol, tr. 2007. (Read-It! Readers en Español: la Vida de Max Ser.). (SPA.). 24p. (J). (gr. -1-3). lib. bdg. 21.32 *(978-1-4048-3794-2(9),* Picture Window Bks.) Capstone.

—Max Celebrates Cinco de Mayo, 1 vol. Worsham, Adria F. 2008. (Read-It! Readers: the Life of Max Ser.). (ENG.). 24p. (J). (gr. -1-2). lib. bdg. 21.32 *(978-1-4048-4759-0(6),* Picture Window Bks.) Capstone.

—Max Come Al Aire Libre, 1 vol. Klein, Adria F. Robledo, Sol, tr. 2007. (Read-It! Readers en Español: la Vida de Max Ser.). (SPA.). 24p. (J). (gr. -1-3). lib. bdg. 21.32 *(978-1-4048-3795-9(7),* Picture Window Bks.) Capstone.

—Max Goes to School. Klein, Adria F. 2007. (Read-It! Readers: the Life of Max Ser.). (ENG.). 24p. (J). (gr. -1-2). per. 3.95 *(978-1-4048-3059-2(6),* Picture Window Bks.) Capstone.

—Max Goes to the Barber. Klein, Adria F. 2007. (Read-It! Readers: the Life of Max Ser.). (ENG.). 24p. (J). (gr. -1-2). per. 3.95 *(978-1-4048-3060-8(X),* Picture Window Bks.) Capstone.

—Max Goes to the Dentist. Klein, Adria F. 2007. (Read-It! Readers: the Life of Max Ser.). (ENG.). 24p. (J). (gr. -1-2). per. 3.95 *(978-1-4048-3061-5(8),* Picture Window Bks.) Capstone.

—Max Goes to the Doctor, 1 vol. Klein, Adria F. 2007. (Read-It! Readers: the Life of Max Ser.). (ENG.). 24p. (J). (gr. -1-2). lib. bdg. 21.32 *(978-1-4048-3680-8(2))*; per. 3.95 *(978-1-4048-3686-0(1),* 1274408) Capstone. (Picture Window Bks.).

—Max Goes to the Farmers' Market, 1 vol. Klein, Adria F. 2009. (Read-It! Readers: the Life of Max Ser.). (ENG.). 24p. (J). (gr. -1-2). 21.32 *(978-1-4048-5263-1(8),* Picture Window Bks.) Capstone.

—Max Goes to the Fire Station, 1 vol. Klein, Adria F. 2009. (Read-It! Readers: the Life of Max Ser.). (ENG.). 24p. (J). (gr. -1-2). 21.32 *(978-1-4048-5266-2(2),* Picture Window Bks.) Capstone.

—Max Goes to the Library. Klein, Adria F. (Read-It! Readers: the Life of Max Ser.). (ENG.). 24p. (J). (gr. -1-2). 2007. per. 3.95 *(978-1-4048-3062-2(6))*; 2005. lib. bdg. 21.32 *(978-1-4048-1182-9(6))* Capstone. (Picture Window Bks.).

—Max Goes to the Nature Center, 1 vol. Klein, Adria F. 2009. (Read-It! Readers: the Life of Max Ser.). (ENG.). 24p. (J). (gr. -1-2). 21.32 *(978-1-4048-5269-3(7),* Picture Window Bks.) Capstone.

—Max Goes to the Recycling Center, 1 vol. Klein, Adria F. 2009. (Read-It! Readers: the Life of Max Ser.). (ENG.). 24p. (J). (gr. -1-2). 21.32 *(978-1-4048-5272-3(7),* Picture Window Bks.) Capstone.

—Max Goes to the Zoo. Klein, Adria F. 2007. (Read-It! Readers: the Life of Max Ser.). (ENG.). 24p. (J). (gr. -1-2). per. 3.95 *(978-1-4048-3683-9(7),* Picture Window Bks.) Capstone.

—Max Va a la Biblioteca, 1 vol. Klein, Adria F. Lozano, Clara, tr. 2007. (Read-It! Readers en Español: la Vida de Max Ser.). (SPA.). 24p. (J). (gr. -1-3). per. 3.95 *(978-1-4048-3036-3(7),* Picture Window Bks.) Capstone.

—Max Va a la Escuela, 1 vol. Klein, Adria F. Lozano, Clara, tr. 2007. (Read-It! Readers en Español: la Vida de Max Ser.). (SPA.). 24p. (J). (gr. -1-3). per. 3.95 *(978-1-4048-3037-0(5),* Picture Window Bks.) Capstone.

—Max Va a la Peluqueria, 1 vol. Klein, Adria F. Lozano, Clara, tr. 2007. (Read-It! Readers en Español: la Vida de Max Ser.). (SPA.). 24p. (J). (gr. -1-3). per. 3.95 *(978-1-4048-3038-7(3),* Picture Window Bks.) Capstone.

—Max Va Al Dentista, 1 vol. Klein, Adria F. Lozano, Clara, tr. 2007. (Read-It! Readers en Español: la Vida de Max Ser.). (SPA.). 24p. (J). (gr. -1-3). per. 3.95 *(978-1-4048-3039-4(1),* Picture Window Bks.) Capstone.

—Max Va Al Doctor. Klein, Adria F. Lozano, Clara, tr. 2008. (Read-It! Readers en Español: la Vida de Max Ser.). (SPA.). 24p. (J). (gr. -1-3). per. 3.95 *(978-1-4048-4584-8(4),* Picture Window Bks.) Capstone.

—Max's Fun Day, 1 vol. Klein, Adria F. 2007. (Read-It! Readers: the Life of Max Ser.). (ENG.). 24p. (J). (gr. -1-2). lib. bdg. 21.32 *(978-1-4048-3150-6(9),* 1265797, Picture Window Bks.) Capstone.

—Mother's Day Crafts. Trueit, Trudi Strain. 2016. (Holiday Crafts Ser.). (ENG.). 24p. (J). (gr. k-3). 28.50 *(978-1-5038-0819-5(X),* 210655) Child's World, Inc., The.

—Mousekin's Special Day: A Book about Special Days. Moncure, Jane Belk. 2013. (Magic Castle Readers Ser.). (ENG.). 32p. (J). (gr. -1-2). 14.21 *(978-1-62323-586-4(3),* 206321) Child's World, Inc., The.

—Rev up Your Writing in Blogs. Owings, Lisa. 2015. (Rev up Your Writing Ser.). (ENG.). 24p. (J). (gr. 2-5). 28.50 *(978-1-63407-061-4(5),* 208896) Child's World, Inc., The.

—Rev up Your Writing in Fictional Stories. Pearson, Yvonne. 2015. (Rev up Your Writing Ser.). (ENG.). 24p. (J). (gr. 2-5). 28.50 *(978-1-63407-062-1(3),* 208897) Child's World, Inc., The.

—Rev up Your Writing in Informational Texts. Garstecki, Julia. 2015. (Rev up Your Writing Ser.). (ENG.). 24p. (J). (gr. 2-5). 28.50 *(978-1-63407-063-8(1),* 208898) Child's World, Inc., The.

—Rev up Your Writing in Letters & E-Mails. Simons, Lisa M. Bolt. 2015. (Rev up Your Writing Ser.). (ENG.). 24p. (J). (gr. 2-5). 28.50 *(978-1-63407-064-5(X),* 208899) Child's World, Inc., The.

—Rev up Your Writing in Nonfiction Narratives. Garstecki, Julia. 2015. (Rev up Your Writing Ser.). (ENG.). 24p. (J). (gr. 2-5). 28.50 *(978-1-63407-065-2(8),* 208900) Child's World, Inc., The.

—Rev up Your Writing in Opinion Pieces. Simons, Lisa M. Bolt. 2015. (Rev up Your Writing Ser.). (ENG.). 24p. (J). (gr. 2-5). 28.50 *(978-1-63407-066-9(6),* 208901) Child's World, Inc., The.

—Rev up Your Writing in Procedural Texts. Zee, Amy Van. 2015. (Rev up Your Writing Ser.). (ENG.). 24p. (J). (gr. 2-5). 28.50 *(978-1-63407-067-6(4),* 208902) Child's World, Inc., The.

—St. Patrick's Day Crafts. Malaspina, Ann. 2016. (Holiday Crafts Ser.). (ENG.). 24p. (J). (gr. k-3). 28.50 *(978-1-5038-0818-8(1),* 210654) Child's World, Inc., The.

—Super Apostrophe Saves the Day! Higgins, Nadia. 2012. (PunctuationBooks Ser.). (ENG.). 24p. (J). (gr. k-3). 27.07 *(978-1-61473-265-5(5),* 204962) Child's World, Inc., The.

—Super Colon Saves the Day! Lynette, Rachel. 2012. (PunctuationBooks Ser.). (ENG.). 24p. (J). (gr. k-3). 27.07 *(978-1-61473-266-2(3),* 204963) Child's World, Inc., The.

—Super Comma Saves the Day! Higgins, Nadia. 2012. (PunctuationBooks Ser.). (ENG.). 24p. (J). (gr. k-3). 27.07 *(978-1-61473-267-9(1),* 204964) Child's World, Inc., The.

—Super Exclamation Point Saves the Day! Higgins, Nadia. 2012. (PunctuationBooks Ser.). (ENG.). 24p. (J). (gr. k-3). 27.07 *(978-1-61473-268-6(X),* 204965) Child's World, Inc., The.

—Super Parentheses Saves the Day! Lynette, Rachel. 2012. (PunctuationBooks Ser.). (ENG.). 24p. (J). (gr. k-3). 27.07 *(978-1-61473-269-3(8),* 204966) Child's World, Inc., The.

—Super Period Saves the Day! Higgins, Nadia. 2012. (PunctuationBooks Ser.). (ENG.). 24p. (J). (gr. k-3). 27.07 *(978-1-61473-270-9(1),* 204967) Child's World, Inc., The.

—Super Question Mark Saves the Day! Higgins, Nadia. 2012. (PunctuationBooks Ser.). (ENG.). 24p. (J). (gr. k-3). 27.07 *(978-1-61473-271-6(X),* 204968) Child's World, Inc., The.

—Super Quotation Marks Saves the Day! Higgins, Nadia. 2012. (PunctuationBooks Ser.). (ENG.). 24p. (J). (gr. k-3). 27.07 *(978-1-61473-272-3(8),* 204969) Child's World, Inc., The.

—Thanksgiving Crafts. Gulati, Annette. 2016. (Holiday Crafts Ser.). (ENG.). 24p. (J). (gr. k-3). 28.50 *(978-1-5038-0821-8(1),* 210657) Child's World, Inc., The.

—That's the Last Straw! (And Other Weird Things We Say) Amoroso, Cynthia. 2011. (Sayings & Phrases Ser.). (ENG.). 24p. (J). (gr. 2-5). lib. bdg. 14.21 *(978-1-60954-230-6(4),* 200783) Child's World, Inc., The.

—Valentine's Day Crafts. Mathiowetz, Claire. 2016. (Holiday Crafts Ser.). (ENG.). 24p. (J). (gr. k-3). 28.50 *(978-1-5038-0822-5(X),* 210658) Child's World, Inc., The.

—What Can We Play Today? A Book about Community Helpers. Moncure, Jane Belk. 2013. (Magic Castle Readers Ser.). (ENG.). 32p. (J). (gr. -1-2). 14.21 *(978-1-62323-587-1(1),* 206322) Child's World, Inc., The.

—What Do You Do with a Grumpy Kangaroo? A Book about Feelings. Moncure, Jane Belk. 2013. (Magic Castle Readers Ser.). (ENG.). 32p. (J). (gr. -1-2). 14.21 *(978-1-62323-589-5(8),* 206324) Child's World, Inc., The.

—What Do You Say When a Monkey Acts This Way? A Book about Manners. Moncure, Jane Belk. 2013. (Magic Castle Readers Ser.). (ENG.). 32p. (J). (gr. -1-2). 14.21 *(978-1-62323-590-1(1),* 206325) Child's World, Inc., The.

—The Witch Who Went for a Walk. Hillert, Margaret. 2016. (BeginningtoRead Ser.). (ENG.). 32p. (J). (gr. -1-2). pap. 11.94 *(978-1-60357-951-3(6))*; (gr. 1-2). 22.60 *(978-1-59953-810-5(5))* Norwood Hse. Pr.

Gallagher-Cole, Mernie, jt. illus. see Cole, Mernie.

Gallagher, Denise. Jean le Chasseur et Ses Chiens, 1 vol. Ancelet, Barry Jean. 2016. (FRE & ENG.). 32p. (J). pap. *(978-1-935754-81-7(5))* Univ. of Louisiana at Lafayette Pr.

Gallagher, Denise. Peg Bearskin: A Traditional Newfoundland Tale, 1 vol. Dinn, Philip & Jones, Andy. 2nd ed. 2019. (ENG.). 44p. (J). (gr. 4-7). pap. 12.95 ***(978-1-927917-19-0(0))*** Running the Goat, Bks. & Broadsides CAN. Dist: Orca Bk. Pubs. USA.

Gallagher, Denise. A Tip Tap Tale. 2017. (J). *(978-1-946160-09-6(1))* Univ. of Louisiana at Lafayette Pr.

Gallagher, Jack, jt. illus. see Garbot, Dave.

Gallagher, Terry. Murdo's Story: A Legend from Northern Manitoba, 1 vol. Scribe, Murdo. Beardy, Ruby, tr. 2015. (ENG.). 44p. (J). (gr. 2-3). pap. 9.95 *(978-0-921827-02-3(4),* 3d822663-56d2-49ad-bab2-c630f5786f21) Pemmican Pubns., Inc. CAN. Dist: Firefly Bks., Ltd.

—Murdo's Story: A Legend from Northern Manitoba. Dejarlais, Cecil & Painter, Florence, trs. 2015. (ENG.). 22p. (J). pap. 9.95 *(978-0-921827-01-6(6),* 94c5713e-4248-40e5-8ffd-50d942bc0e5e) Pemmican Pubns., Inc. CAN. Dist: Firefly Bks., Ltd.

Gallanosa, Primo. Hey, Who Made This Mess? Gallanosa, Primo. 2020. 32p. (J). (-k). 16.99 *(978-0-525-51736-8(7),* G.P. Putnam's Sons Books for Young Readers) Penguin Young Readers Group.

Gallant, S. DreamWorks Classics Vol 3, Vol. 3. Abnett, Dan. 2016. (DreamWorks Classics Ser.: 3). 64p. (J). (gr. 3-7). pap. 6.99 *(978-1-78276-248-5(5))* Titan Bks. Ltd. GBR. Dist: Penguin Random Hse. LLC.

Gallant, S. L., jt. illus. see Dalton, Alex.

Gallardo, Jesús. Cece Saves the Planet. Keller, Ashley. 2020. (ENG.). 34p. (J). pap. 10.97 ***(978-1-7345680-5-9(4),*** Fig Factor Media LLC) JJR Marketing Consultants LLC.

Gallardo, Mary. The Tiny Little Raindrop. Gallardo, Mary, as told by. 2007. 32p. (J). 15.99 *(978-0-9779763-0-0(0))* Blue Cat Bks.

Gallego, Benito. El Dragon de Diego, Segundo Libro: Los Dragones de la Grieta Oscura. Gerard, Kevin. Bonis, Lucia, tr. 2018. (SPA.). 234p. (J). pap. 14.49 *(978-0-9859802-9-0(X))* Crying Cougar Pr.

Gallego, James, jt. illus. see Laguna, Fabio.

Gallego, Pablo. The Great Inventor. Pritchard, Gabby. 2016. (Cambridge Reading Adventures Ser.). (ENG.). 16p. pap. 7.37 *(978-1-316-50083-5(7))* Cambridge Univ. Pr.

Gallego, Pablo. Sybil Ludington Rides to the Rescue: Courageous Kid of the American Revolution. Gunderson, Jessica. 2020. (Courageous Kids Ser.). (ENG.). 32p. (J). (gr. 3-5). pap. 7.95 ***(978-1-4966-8804-0(X),*** 201689); lib. bdg. 31.32 ***(978-1-4966-8503-2(2),*** 200559) Capstone. (Capstone Pr.).

Gallegos, Benito. Diego's Dragon, Book Three: Battle at Tenochtitlan. Gerard, Kevin. Dreadfuls, Penny, ed. 2013. 298p. pap. 14.99 *(978-0-9859802-3-8(0))* Crying Cougar Pr.

Gallegos, Lauren. The Circus Thief. Adams, Alane. 2018. (ENG.). 32p. (J). (gr. 1-2). 15.00 *(978-1-943006-75-5(X))* SparkPr. (a Bks.parks Imprint).

—The Coal Thief. Adams, Alane. 2015. (ENG.). 32p. (J). 15.00 *(978-1-940716-27-5(6))* SparkPr. (a Bks.parks Imprint).

—Kobee Manatee: Heading Home to Florida. Thayer, Robert Scott. Korman, Susan, ed. 2013. (Kobee Manatee Ser.). (ENG.). 32p. (J). (gr. k-2). 16.99 *(978-0-9883269-2-7(2))* Thompson Mill Pr.

—Kobee Manatee: Shipwreck Sea Friends. Thayer, Robert Scott. Korman, Susan, ed. 2017. (ENG.). 32p. (J). (gr. k-2). 16.99 *(978-0-9971239-3-7(1))* Thompson Mill Pr.

—On the Day Love Was Born. Cerrito, Dana. 2011. 24p. (J). pap. 10.95 *(978-0-9835048-0-1(6))* Little Hill Pubs.

—Rubio & Julienne: A Sweet & Cheesy Tale, 1 vol. Paley, Dan. 2018. (ENG.). 32p. (J). (gr. -1-3). 16.95 *(978-0-88448-487-5(4),* 884487) Tilbury Hse. Pubs.

—The Santa Thief. Adams, Alane. 2017. (ENG.). 32p. (J). (gr. -1-3). 15.00 *(978-1-940716-86-2(1))* SparkPr. (a Bks.parks Imprint).

—Vulture Verses: Love Poems for the Unloved. Lang, Diane. 2015. (ENG.). 32p. (J). (gr. -1-2). pap. 9.95 *(978-1-938849-64-0(7))* Prospect Park Bks., LLC.

Gallegos, Sheyla. Akiti the Hunter II - Akiti Falls in Love: Part II of the Akiti the Hunter Series. Ajayi, Bolaji. 2017. (Akiti the Hunyer Ser.: Vol. 2). (ENG.). 58p. (J). (gr. k-6). pap. *(978-1-910882-88-7(7))* Abela Publishing.

Gallenson, Ann, jt. illus. see Heins, Tanya.

Gallenson, Ann, jt. illus. see Morgan, Mark.

Gallet, Karl. Joe E, 1 vol. Mistretta, Jay. 2009. 19p. pap. 24.95 *(978-1-60749-850-6(2))* America Star Bks.

Galletti, Chiara. Fright School. Lawler, Janet. 2018. (ENG.). 32p. (J). (gr. -1-3). 16.99 *(978-0-8075-2553-1(7),* 807525537) Whitman, Albert & Co.

—Seek-And-Circle Bible Journeys. B&H Kids Editorial Staff. 2019. (One Big Story Ser.). (ENG.). 14p. (J). (gr. -1-3). bds. 12.99 *(978-1-5359-4633-9(4),* 005812560, B&H Kids) B&H Publishing Group.

Galley, Lauren. Pocket Rocket. Story, Jj. 2019. (ENG.). 28p. (J). pap. 10.00 ***(978-1-6772-3033-4(9))*** Independently Published.

Galligan, Gale. Dawn & the Impossible Three. Martin, Ann M. 2017. (Baby-Sitters Club Graphix Ser.: 5). 160p. (J). (gr. 3-7). 10.99 *(978-1-338-06711-8(7))*; (ENG.). 24.99 *(978-1-338-06730-9(3))* Scholastic, Inc. (Graphix).

—Kristy's Big Day. Martin, Ann M. 2018. (Baby-Sitters Club Graphic Novel Ser.: 6). 160p. (J). (gr. 3-7). (ENG.). 24.99 *(978-1-338-06768-2(0))*; pap. 10.99 *(978-1-338-06761-3(3))* Scholastic, Inc. (Graphix).

Galligher, John, jt. illus. see Jourdan, Diego.

Gallinger, Jared. Life Is Fragile: One Girl's Story of the Bath School Disaster. Spencer, Betty. 2007. 68p. per. 19.95 *(978-1-60441-772-2(2))* America Star Bks.

Gallion, Taylor. Goodnight, Knight: Long Vowel I Sound. Bunt, Stephanie Marie. 2019. (ENG.). 44p. (J). pap. 10.95 ***(978-1-948863-25-4(1))*** Bunt, Stephanie.

Gallion, Taylor. Kit the Pit. Bunt, Stephanie Marie. 2018. (ENG.). 30p. (J). pap. 10.95 *(978-1-948863-84-1(7))* Bunt, Stephanie.

Gallion, Taylor. Learn to Read Books for Kids 5-7: Decodable Words. Bunt, Stephanie Marie. 2020. (Long Vowel Sounds Ser.: Vol. 1). (ENG.). 206p. (J). pap. 39.95 ***(978-1-948863-54-4(5))*** Bunt, Stephanie.

Gallion, Taylor. Yog the Hog: Phonics (Short Vowel O) Bunt, Stephanie Marie. 2018. (ENG.). 36p. (J). pap. 10.95 *(978-1-948863-51-3(0))* Bunt, Stephanie.

Gallion, Taylor. 5 Phonics Books In 1: Short Vowel Sounds. Bunt, Stephanie Marie. 2019. (ENG.). 160p. (J). pap. 34.95 ***(978-1-948863-95-7(2))*** Bunt, Stephanie.

Gallo, Valeria. Valija de Cuentos Familiares. Segura, Judith. 2019. (Torre Azul Ser.). (SPA.). 96p. (J). pap. ***(978-607-13-0204-5(8))*** Norma Ediciones, S.A.

Gallow, Robyn. Can I Tell You about Selective Mutism? A Guide for Friends, Family & Professionals. Johnson, Maggie & Wintgens, Alison. 2012. (Can I Tell You About...? Ser.). (ENG.). 56p. pap. 13.95 *(978-1-84905-289-4(1),* 694659) Kingsley, Jessica Pubs. GBR. Dist: Hachette UK Distribution.

Galloway, Fiona. ABC Alphabet Sticker Book. Tiger Tales. 2014. (My Little World Ser.). (ENG.). 14p. (J). (gr. -1-k). pap. 3.99 *(978-1-58925-445-9(7))* Tiger Tales.

—Babies Love Colors: Small Board Lift-A-Flap. Rhodes-Conway, Michelle. Cottage Door Press, ed. 2018. (Babies Love Ser.). (ENG.). 12p. (J). (gr. -1 — 1). bds. 7.99 *(978-1-68052-320-1(1),* 1002961) Cottage Door Pr.

—Big Fish Little Fish. Litton, Jonathan. 2016. (My Little World Ser.). (ENG.). 16p. (J). (gr. -1-k). bds. 7.99 *(978-1-58925-215-8(2))* Tiger Tales.

—Boo! Litton, Jonathan. 2015. (My Little World Ser.). (ENG.). 16p. (J). (-k). bds. 7.99 *(978-1-68010-501-8(9))* Tiger Tales.

—Busy Day Sticker Book. 2014. (My Little World Ser.). (ENG.). 14p. (J). pap. 3.99 *(978-1-58925-446-6(5))* Tiger Tales.

—Colores: Libro con Solapas. Rhodes-Conway, Michelle. Cottage Door Press, ed. 2019. (Babies Love Ser.). (SPA.). 12p. (J). (gr. -1 — 1). bds. 7.99 *(978-1-68052-841-1(6),* 1002960-SLA) Cottage Door Pr.

—Dino. Litton, Jonathan. 2016. (My Little World Ser.). (ENG.). 24p. (J). (gr. -1-k). mass mkt. 3.99 *(978-1-58925-485-5(6))* Tiger Tales.

—Fall Is Here! 2015. (ENG.). 16p. (J). (gr. -1 — 1). bds. 5.99 *(978-1-4998-0110-1(6))* Little Bee Books Inc.

—Finding First Animals & More! Walden, Libby. 2016. (My Little World Ser.). (ENG.). 12p. (J). (gr. -1-k). bds. 12.99 *(978-1-58925-229-5(2))* Tiger Tales.

—Finding First Words & More! Walden, Libby. 2016. (My Little World Ser.). (ENG.). 12p. (J). (gr. -1-k). bds. 12.99 *(978-1-58925-218-9(7))* Tiger Tales.

—Fire Engine. 2016. (J). *(978-1-62885-168-7(6))* Kidsbooks, LLC.

—Flamingo. Hegarty, Patricia. 2019. (My Little World Ser.). (ENG.). 16p. (J). (gr. 2-k). bds. 8.99 *(978-1-68010-598-8(1))* Tiger Tales.

—Follow Me: Animal Faces. 2016. (ENG.). 10p. (J). (gr. -1 — 1). bds. 7.99 *(978-1-4998-0268-9(4))* Little Bee Books Inc.

—Follow Me: Bedtime. 2016. (ENG.). 10p. (J). (gr. -1 — 1). bds. 7.99 *(978-1-4998-0267-2(6))* Little Bee Books Inc.

—Hoot. Litton, Jonathan. 2014. (My Little World Ser.). (ENG.). 16p. (J). (gr. -1-k). bds. 7.99 *(978-1-58925-595-1(X))* Tiger Tales.

—I Like to Squeak! How Do You Speak? Litton, Jonathan. 2015. (My Little World Ser.). (ENG.). 10p. (J). (-k). bds. 12.99 *(978-1-68010-505-6(1))* Tiger Tales.

—I Love My Daddy. Litton, Jonathan. 2016. (My Little World Ser.). (ENG.). 16p. (J). (gr. -1-k). bds. 7.99 *(978-1-58925-217-2(9))* Tiger Tales.

—I Love My Mommy. Litton, Jonathan. 2016. (My Little World Ser.). (ENG.). 16p. (J). (gr. -1-k). bds. 7.99 *(978-1-58925-216-5(0))* Tiger Tales.

—I Love My Mommy: A Story Full of Cuddly, Snuggly Fun. Joyce, Melanie. 2016. (ENG.). 16p. (J). bds. 7.95 *(978-1-78557-586-0(4))* Igloo Bks. GBR. Dist: Simon & Schuster, Inc.

—I Spy Learn & Go. Litton, Jonathan. 2015. (My Little World Ser.). (ENG.). 48p. (J). (gr. -1-2). 9.99 *(978-1-58925-313-1(2))* Tiger Tales.

—I Spy on the Farm. Litton, Jonathan. 2015. (My Little World Ser.). (ENG.). 48p. (J). (gr. -1-2). 9.99 *(978-1-58925-312-4(4))* Tiger Tales.

—Love from Me to You. Hegarty, Patricia. 2019. (ENG.). 20p. (J). (gr. -1-k). bds. 7.99 *(978-1-68412-696-5(7),* Silver Dolphin Bks.) Printers Row Publishing Group.

—Moo. Litton, Jonathan. 2016. (My Little World Ser.). (ENG.). 24p. (J). (gr. -1-k). mass mkt. 3.99 *(978-1-58925-484-8(8))* Tiger Tales.

—Moo: A First Book of Counting. 2016. (J). *(978-1-5182-3185-8(3))* Tiger Tales.

—Noisy Noisy Digger. Litton, Jonathan. 2017. (My Little World Ser.). (ENG.). 10p. (J). (gr. -1-k). bds. 12.99 *(978-1-58925-242-4(X))* Tiger Tales.

—Nursery Rhymes. Tiger Tales. 2015. (My Little World Ser.). (ENG.). 14p. (J). (gr. -1-k). 3.99 *(978-1-58925-452-7(X))* Tiger Tales.

—Roar. Litton, Jonathan. 2014. (My Little World Ser.). (ENG.). 16p. (J). (-k). bds. 7.99 *(978-1-58925-593-7(3))* Tiger Tales.

—Snap. Hegarty, Patricia. 2020. (My Little World Ser.). (ENG.). 16p. (J). (-k). bds. 8.99 *(978-1-68010-625-1(2))* Tiger Tales.

—Snap: A Peek-Through Book of Shapes. Litton, Jonathan. 2014. (My Little World Ser.). (ENG.). 16p. (J). (gr. -1-k). bds. 7.99 *(978-1-58925-566-1(6))* Tiger Tales.

—Surprise: A Book of Christmas Shapes. Litton, Jonathan. 2014. (ENG.). 16p. (J). (gr. -1-k). bds. 7.99 *(978-1-58925-567-8(4))* Tiger Tales.

—Tall & Short. Litton, Jonathan. 2014. (My Little World Ser.). (ENG.). 16p. (J). (gr. -1-k). bds. 7.99 *(978-1-58925-565-4(8))* Tiger Tales.

—Ten Tiny Gingerbread Men. Tiger Tales. 2015. (ENG.). 24p. (J). (gr. -1-k). pap. 4.99 *(978-1-58925-470-1(8))* Tiger Tales.

—Touch-And-Feel 123. Litton, Jonathan. 2017. (My Little World Ser.). (ENG.). 10p. (J). (gr. -1-k). bds. 8.99 *(978-1-68010-511-7(6))* Tiger Tales.

—Touch-And-Feel Colors. Litton, Jonathan. 2017. (My Little World Ser.). (ENG.). 10p. (J). (gr. -1-k). bds. 8.99 *(978-1-68010-510-0(8))* Tiger Tales.

—Touch-And-Feel First Words. Walden, Libby. 2017. (My Little World Ser.). (ENG.). 10p. (J). (gr. -1-k). bds. 8.99 *(978-1-68010-521-6(3))* Tiger Tales.

—Unicorn. Hegarty, Patricia. 2019. (My Little World Ser.). (ENG.). 16p. (J). (gr. 2-k). bds. 8.99 *(978-1-68010-597-1(3))* Tiger Tales.

—Where's the Pumpkin? 2015. (ENG.). 16p. (J). (gr. -1 — 1). bds. 5.99 *(978-1-4998-0097-5(5))* Little Bee Books Inc.

—123 Counting Sticker Book. Tiger Tales. 2014. (My Little World Ser.). (ENG.). 14p. (J). (gr. -1-k). pap. 3.99 *(978-1-58925-444-2(9))* Tiger Tales.

Galloway, Fhiona & Hogan, Martina. Babies Love Learning: Slipcase 4-Pack Including Babies Love Colors, Babies Love First Words, Babies Love Things That Go, & Babies Love Animals. Rhodes-Conway, Michelle & Wing, Scarlett. Cottage Door Press, ed. 2018. (ENG.). 48p. (J). (gr. -1-k). bds., bds., bds. 24.99 *(978-1-68052-339-3(2),* 9001190) Cottage Door Pr.

Galloway, Ruth. Fidgety Fish & Friends. Bright, Paul. 2008. (Tiger Tales Ser.). 24p. (J). (gr. -1-2). pap. 6.95 *(978-1-58925-409-1(0))* Tiger Tales.

—How Do You Say That in French? 1000 Words & Phrases for Kids. Delaney, Sally & Richards, Wendy. 2014. 64p. (J). (gr. 2-6). 12.99 *(978-1-84322-915-5(3),* Armadillo) Anness Publishing GBR. Dist: National Bk. Network.

—Ten Busy, Whizzy Bugs. 2017. (J). *(978-1-84857-561-5(0))* Little Tiger Pr. Group.

—Ten Little Lovebugs. Tiger Tales. 2018. (ENG.). 26p. (J). (gr. -1-k). mass mkt. 4.99 *(978-1-68010-417-2(9))* Tiger Tales.

Galloway, Ruth. Clumsy Crab. Galloway, Ruth. (Ocean Adventures Ser.). 32p. (J). (gr. -1-2). 2018. (ENG.). 23.99 *(978-1-68010-086-0(6));* 2007. pap. 6.95 *(978-1-58925-402-2(3));* 2005. 15.95 *(978-1-58925-050-5(8))* Tiger Tales.

—Fidgety Fish. Galloway, Ruth. (Ocean Adventures Ser.). (J). 2017. (ENG.). 32p. (gr. -1-2). 23.99 *(978-1-68010-055-6(6));* 2006. 16p. bds. 6.95 *(978-1-58925-772-6(3));* 2003. 32p. pap. 6.95 *(978-1-58925-377-3(9))* Tiger Tales.

—Smiley Shark. Galloway, Ruth. 32p. (J). 2005. 6.95 *(978-1-58925-391-9(4));* 2003. tchr. ed. 15.95 *(978-1-58925-028-4(1))* Tiger Tales.

—Tickly Octopus. Galloway, Ruth. (Ocean Adventures Ser.). 2018. (ENG.). 32p. (J). (gr. -1-2). 23.99 *(978-1-68010-087-7(4));* 2007. 15.95 *(978-1-58925-064-2(8))* Tiger Tales.

—The Very Fidgety Fish. Galloway, Ruth. 2014. (ENG.). 32p. (J). (gr. -1-2). 6.99 *(978-1-58925-509-8(7))* Tiger Tales.

Gallup, Tracy. My First Book of Haiku Poetry: A Picture, a Poem, a Dream. Ramirez-Christensen, Esperanza. 2019. 48p. (J). (gr. k-4). 16.99 *(978-4-8053-1515-6(6))* Tuttle Publishing.

Galluzzo, Madeline. The Belly Garden. Story, Rita. 2008. 23p. pap. 24.95 *(978-1-60610-035-6(1))* America Star Bks.

Galouchko, Annouchka. The Nutmeg Princess. Keens-Douglas, Richardo. 2nd rev. ed. 2014. (ENG.). 32p. (J). (gr. 1-4). pap. 9.95 *(978-1-55451-599-8(8),* 9781554515998) Annick Pr., Ltd. CAN. Dist: Publishers Group West (PGW).

—The Walking Stick, 1 vol. Trottier, Maxine. 2012. (ENG.). 24p. (J). (gr. 1-2). pap. 9.95 *(978-1-55455-239-9(7),* 1373a2b3-2841-4305-b792-93f270f5cd5b) Fitzhenry & Whiteside, Ltd. CAN. Dist: Firefly Bks., Ltd.

Galouchko, Annouchka Gravel & Daigle, Stephan. The Birdman. Charles, Veronika Martenova. 2006. 32p. (J). (gr. k-3). 17.95 *(978-0-88776-740-1(0),* Tundra Bks.) Tundra Bks. CAN. Dist: Penguin Random Hse. LLC.

Galsterer, Lynne. Making Friends, 2. Haller, Reese. 2nd ed. 2006. (Fred the Mouse Ser.). 112p. (J). per. 4.97 *(978-0-9772321-0-9(7))* Personal Power Pr.

Galt, Daniel. Galactic Space Bully. Galt, Daniel. 2017. (ENG.). (J). (gr. 2-6). pap. 9.97 *(978-0-9992257-0-7(7))* GALT, DANIEL Bks., LLC.

Galusha, Tadd. Cretaceous. Galusha, Tadd. 2019. (ENG.). 160p. (J). pap. 14.99 *(978-1-62010-565-8(9),* Lion Forge) Oni Pr., Inc.

Galvani, Maureen. Make & Play Airplanes. Holzer, David. 2005. (Fun Kits (Top That!) Ser.). 48p. (J). (gr. -1-3). *(978-1-84510-549-5(4))* Top That! Publishing PLC.

Galvao, Elder. Boa Noite, Bicho Papao. Taufick, Roberto. 2018. (POR.). 58p. (J). pap. *(978-85-924256-0-9(3))* Taufick, R.D. Oliveira Lima.

Galvez, Daniel. It Doesn't Have to Be This Way, 1 vol. Rodriguez, Luis J. 2013. (ENG & SPA.). 32p. (J). (gr. 2-6). pap. 10.95 *(978-0-89239-203-2(7),* eb1a6a4b-a6e3-446b-ad5d-e2076b21b19c) Lee & Low Bks., Inc.

Galvin, Jennifer. My Catholic School Holiday: Reproducible Sheets for Home & School. Galvin, Jennifer. 2005. 32p. act. bk. ed. 6.95 *(978-0-8091-6724-1(7),* 6724-7) Paulist Pr.

Galy, Paul. The Cat & the Convict. Cross, Judie. 2017. (ENG.). (J). *(978-0-6481315-9-5(9))* Beck Shnidman & Alexa Publishing Pty, Ltd.

Galyon, Stephanie. The Unusual Zoo. Doll, Danette Lea. ed. 2019. (ENG.). 32p. (J). (gr. k-6). 17.99 *(978-1-64372-195-8(X),* Huskies Pub) MacLaren-Cochrane Publishing, Inc.

—The Unusual Zoo Dyslexic Edition: Level 3 - Hold My Hand: Dyslexic Font. Doll, Danette Lea. ed. 2019. (ENG.). 32p. (J). (gr. k-4). 19.99 *(978-1-64372-198-9(4));* pap. 15.99 *(978-1-64372-199-6(2))* MacLaren-Cochrane Publishing, Inc.

Gam do, Rin Bo. Insects & Spiders. Cowley, Joy, ed. 2015. (Science Storybooks Ser.). (ENG.). 32p. (gr. k-3). 26.65 *(978-1-925246-23-0(X))* ChoiceMaker Pty. Ltd., The AUS. Dist: Lerner Publishing Group.

Gama, Esperanza. Abuelo Vivia Solo/Grandpa Used to Live Alone. Costales, Amy. 2010. (ENG.). 32p. (J). (gr. -1-3). 16.95 *(978-1-55885-531-1(9))* Arte Publico Pr.

Gambino, Alisha Ann Guadalupe. Sunflowers/Girasoles. Zepeda, Gwendolyn & Ventura, Gabriela Baeza. 2009. (SPA & ENG.). 32p. (J). (gr. -1-2). 16.95 *(978-1-55885-267-9(0),* Piñata Books) Arte Publico Pr.

Gamble, Ed. Why Do I Love Millie? Bennett, Betty J. 2018. (ENG.). 36p. (J). 25.95 *(978-1-4808-5675-2(4));* pap. 16.95 *(978-1-4808-5674-5(6))* Archway Publishing.

Gamble, Gael. Milly Feather. Darragh, Jill. 2013. 64p. pap. *(978-0-473-26560-1(5))* Rangitawa Publishing.

Gamble, Kent. And Nobody Got Hurt! The World's Weirdest, Wackiest True Sports Stories. Berman, Len. 2005. (ENG.). 128p. (J). (gr. 3-7). per. 9.99 *(978-0-316-01029-0(4))* Little, Brown Bks. for Young Readers.

Gamble, Kim. The Adventures of Mouse Deer. Shepard, Aaron. 2005. 48p. (J). (gr. -1-4). pap. 10.00 *(978-0-938497-32-5(4),* Skyhook Pr.) Shepard Pubns.

—The Adventures of Mouse Deer: Favorite Tales of Southeast Asia. Shepard, Aaron. (ENG.). (J). (gr. k-3). 2018. 50p. 24.00 *(978-1-62035-561-9(2));* 2017. pap. 10.00 *(978-1-62035-525-1(6))* Shepard Pubns. (Skyhook Pr.).

—Minton Goes! Underwater & Home at Last. Fienberg, Anna. 2008. (Minton Ser.). (ENG.). 64p. (J). (gr. -1-k). mass mkt. 9.99 *(978-1-74175-429-2(1))* Allen & Unwin AUS. Dist: Independent Pubs. Group.

—Once Tashi Met a Dragon. Fienberg, Anna & Fienberg, Barbara. 2014. (Tashi Ser.). (ENG.). 32p. (J). (gr. k-2). 16.99 *(978-1-74175-887-0(4))* Allen & Unwin AUS. Dist: Independent Pubs. Group.

—Tashi & the Dancing Shoes. Fienberg, Anna & Fienberg, Barbara. 8th ed. 2007. (Tashi Ser.). (ENG.). 64p. (Orig.). (J). (gr. k-2). pap. 8.99 *(978-1-74114-972-2(X))* Allen & Unwin AUS. Dist: Independent Pubs. Group.

—Tashi & the Forbidden Room. Fienberg, Anna & Fienberg, Barbara. 12th ed. 2007. (Tashi Ser.: 12). (ENG.). 64p. (J). (gr. k-2). pap. 8.99 *(978-1-74114-964-7(9))* Allen & Unwin AUS. Dist: Independent Pubs. Group.

—Tashi & the Golem. Fienberg, Anna & Fienberg, Barbara. 2010. (Tashi Ser.: 16). (ENG.). 64p. (J). (gr. k-2). pap. 8.99 *(978-1-74175-792-7(4))* Allen & Unwin AUS. Dist: Independent Pubs. Group.

—Tashi & the Haunted House. Fienberg, Anna & Fienberg, Barbara. 9th ed. 2007. (Tashi Ser.). (ENG.). 64p. (Orig.). (J). (gr. k-2). pap. 8.99 *(978-1-74114-953-1(3))* Allen & Unwin AUS. Dist: Independent Pubs. Group.

—Tashi & the Mixed-Up Monster. Fienberg, Anna & Fienberg, Barbara. 2008. (Tashi Ser.: 14). (ENG.). 64p. (J). (gr. k-2). pap. 8.99 *(978-1-74175-191-8(8))* Allen & Unwin AUS. Dist: Independent Pubs. Group.

—Tashi & the Phoenix. Fienberg, Anna & Fienberg, Barbara. 2009. (Tashi Ser.: 15). (ENG.). 64p. (J). (gr. k-2). mass mkt. 9.99 *(978-1-74175-474-2(7))* Allen & Unwin AUS. Dist: Independent Pubs. Group.

—Tashi & the Royal Tomb. Fienberg, Anna & Fienberg, Barbara. 10th ed. 2007. (Tashi Ser.: 10). (ENG.). 64p. (Orig.). (J). (gr. k-2). pap. 8.99 *(978-1-74114-973-9(8))* Allen & Unwin AUS. Dist: Independent Pubs. Group.

—Tashi & the Stolen Bus. Fienberg, Anna & Fienberg, Barbara. 2007. (Tashi Ser.: 13). (ENG.). 64p. (Orig.). (J). (gr. k-2). pap. 8.99 *(978-1-74114-877-0(4))* Allen & Unwin AUS. Dist: Independent Pubs. Group.

—Tashi Lost in the City. Fienberg, Anna & Fienberg, Barbara. 11th ed. 2007. (Tashi Ser.: 11). (ENG.). 64p. (J). (gr. k-2). pap. 8.99 *(978-1-74114-963-0(0))* Allen & Unwin AUS. Dist: Independent Pubs. Group.

—Tashi Storybook. Fienberg, Anna. 2018. (Tashi Ser.). (ENG.). 256p. (J). (gr. k-3). 23.99 *(978-1-76029-568-4(X))* Allen & Unwin AUS. Dist: Independent Pubs. Group.

Gamble, Kim & Axelsen, Stephen. Monsters. Fienberg, Anna. 2018. (ENG.). 32p. (J). (gr. k-3). 20.99 *(978-1-76029-336-9(9))* Allen & Unwin AUS. Dist: Independent Pubs. Group.

Gamble, Paul. How to Draw Monsters & Other Scary Stuff. Gamble, Paul. 2020. (ENG.). 128p. (J). pap. 12.99 *(978-1-78950-957-1(2),* 3fb29f22-941f-4416-aea3-b75f2c22ad32) Arcturus Publishing GBR. Dist: Baker & Taylor Publisher Services (BTPS).

Gamble, Penel. Forgetting to Remember. Tayleur, Karen. 2004. iv, 36p. (J). pap. *(978-0-7608-6746-4(1))* Sundance/Newbridge Educational Publishing.

Gamboa, Ricardo. Just One More. Silvano, Wendi. 2007. (ENG.). 36p. (J). reprint ed. pap. 11.95 *(978-0-9744446-5-9(0))* All About Kids Publishing.

Gambrioli, Bianca Camilla. Poppy Is Lost in the Garden. Stevens, Hazel. 2019. (Poppy Ser.: Vol. 2). (ENG.). 28p. (J). (gr. k-2). pap. *(978-1-911424-74-1(2))* Black Wolf Edition & Publishing Ltd.

Gamdo & Do, Gam. Insects & Spiders. Rin, Bo. Cowley, Joy, ed. 2015. (Science Storybooks Ser.). (ENG.). 32p. (J). (gr. k-4). 10.00 *(978-1-925233-61-2(8),* Big and SMALL) ChoiceMaker Pty. Ltd., The AUS. Dist: Lerner Publishing Group.

Gamlen, Pete. You Smell! (and So Does Everything Else!) (an Educational Humor Book about Smelly Things) Gifford, Clive. 2019. (ENG.). 48p. (J). (gr. 2-6). 17.99 *(978-1-78627-393-2(4),* King, Laurence Publishing) Orion Publishing Group, Ltd. GBR. Dist: Hachette Bk. Group.

Gammage, Dana. Wisdom for Young Hearts Volume 2 - Applications of Wisdom. Delea, Pattie. 2011. 126p. pap. 20.00 *(978-1-61286-058-9(3))* Avid Readers Publishing Group.

Gammelgaard, Leslie. Andi's Fair Surprise, 1 vol. Marlow, Susan K. 2011. (Circle C Beginnings Ser.). 80p. (J). (gr. 1-3). pap. 5.99 *(978-0-8254-4184-4(6))* Kregel Pubns.

—Andi's Indian Summer, 1 vol. Marlow, Susan K. 2010. (Circle C Beginnings Ser.). 80p. (J). (gr. 1-3). pap. 5.99 *(978-0-8254-4182-0(X))* Kregel Pubns.

—Andi's Pony Trouble, 1 vol. Marlow, Susan K. 2010. (Circle C Beginnings Ser.). 80p. (J). (gr. 1-3). pap. 5.99 *(978-0-8254-4181-3(1))* Kregel Pubns.

—Andi's Scary School Days, 1 vol. Marlow, Susan K. 2011. (Circle C Beginnings Ser.). 80p. (J). (gr. 1-3). pap. 5.99 *(978-0-8254-4183-7(8))* Kregel Pubns.

Gammell, Stephen. Humble Pie. Donnelly, Jennifer. 2007. (ENG.). 32p. (J). (gr. -1-2). 13.99 *(978-1-4169-6751-4(6),* Aladdin) Simon & Schuster Children's Publishing.

—Laugh-Out-Loud Baby. Johnston, Tony. 2012. (ENG.). 32p. (J). (gr. -1-3). 16.99 *(978-1-4424-1380-1(8),* Simon & Schuster Bks. For Young Readers) Simon & Schuster/Paula Wiseman Bks.

—More Scary Stories to Tell in the Dark. 80p. (J). (gr. 4-6). pap. 4.95 *(978-0-8072-1424-4(8),* Listening Library) Random Hse. Audio Publishing Group.

—More Scary Stories to Tell in the Dark. Schwartz, Alvin. 2017. (Scary Stories Ser.: 2). (ENG.). 112p. (J). (gr. 3-7). pap. 7.99 *(978-0-06-268285-7(7))* HarperCollins Pubs.

—More Scary Stories to Tell in the Dark Movie Tie-In Edition. Schwartz, Alvin. 2019. (Scary Stories Ser.: 2). (ENG.). 112p. (J). (gr. 3-7). pap. 7.99 *(978-0-06-296130-3(6))* HarperCollins Pubs.

—My Friend, the Starfinder. Lyon, George Ella. 2008. (ENG.). 40p. (J). (gr. -1-2). 19.99 *(978-1-4169-2738-9(7),* Atheneum/Richard Jackson Bks.) Simon & Schuster Children's Publishing.

—The Old Banjo. Haseley, Dennis. 2013. (ENG.). 32p. (J). (gr. -1-3). 16.99 *(978-1-4424-8879-3(4),* Simon & Schuster Bks. For Young Readers) Simon & Schuster Bks. For Young Readers.

—Scary Stories 3: More Tales to Chill Your Bones. Schwartz, Alvin. 2017. (Scary Stories Ser.: 3). (ENG.). 128p. (J). (gr. 3-7). pap. 7.99 *(978-0-06-268287-1(3))* HarperCollins Pubs.

—Scary Stories 3: More Tales to Chill Your Bones. Schwartz, Alvin. 2005. pap. *(978-0-590-13589-4(9))* Scholastic, Inc.

—Scary Stories 3-Book Box Set Movie Tie-In Edition: Scary Stories to Tell in the Dark, More Scary Stories to Tell in the Dark, Scary Stories 3. Schwartz, Alvin. 2019. (Scary Stories Ser.). (ENG.). 368p. (J). (gr. 3-7). pap. 23.97 *(978-0-06-296132-7(2))* HarperCollins Pubs.

—Scary Stories 3 Movie Tie-In Edition: More Tales to Chill Your Bones. Schwartz, Alvin. 2019. (Scary Stories Ser.: 3). (ENG.). 128p. (J). (gr. 3-7). pap. 7.99 *(978-0-06-296131-0(4))* HarperCollins Pubs.

—Scary Stories Paperback Box Set: The Complete 3-Book Collection with Classic Art by Stephen Gammell. Schwartz, Alvin. 2017. (Scary Stories Ser.). (ENG.). 368p. (J). (gr. 3-7). pap. 23.97 *(978-0-06-268289-5(X))* HarperCollins Pubs.

—Scary Stories to Tell in the Dark. Schwartz, Alvin. (Scary Stories Ser.: 1). 128p. (J). (gr. 3-7). 2075. 12.99 *(978-0-06-296683-4(9));* 2017. (ENG.). pap. 7.99 *(978-0-06-268282-6(2))* HarperCollins Pubs.

—Scary Stories to Tell in the Dark Movie Tie-In Edition. Schwartz, Alvin. 2019. (Scary Stories Ser.: 1). (ENG.). 128p. (J). (gr. 3-7). pap. 7.99 *(978-0-06-296128-0(4))* HarperCollins Pubs.

—Scary Stories to Tell in the Dark: Three Books to Chill Your Bones: All 3 Scary Stories Books with the Original Art! Schwartz, Alvin. 2019. (Scary Stories Ser.). (ENG.). 368p. (J). (gr. 3-7). 19.99 *(978-0-06-296897-5(1))* HarperCollins Pubs.

—The Scary Stories Treasury: Three Books to Chill Your Bones. Schwartz, Alvin. *(978-0-7607-3418-6(6))* Barnes & Noble, Inc.

—The Secret Science Project That Almost Ate the School. Sierra, Judy. 2006. (ENG.). 32p. (J). (gr. 1-4). 19.99 *(978-1-4169-1175-3(8),* Simon & Schuster/Paula Wiseman Bks.) Simon & Schuster/Paula Wiseman Bks.

—Song & Dance Man. Ackerman, Karen. 2015. 32p. pap. 8.00 *(978-1-61003-554-5(2))* Center for the Collaborative Classroom.

—Song & Dance Man. Ackerman, Karen. 2003. 32p. (J). (gr. -1-2). 15.95 *(978-0-394-89330-3(1),* Knopf Bks. for Young Readers) Random Hse. Children's Bks.

—Where the Buffaloes Begin. Baker, Olaf. 2019. (ENG.). 48p. (J). (gr. 1-4). 16.95 *(978-0-486-83283-8(X))* Dover Pubns., Inc.

Gammil, Kerry, et al. X-Men: Fallen Angels. 2019. (ENG.). 208p. (YA). (gr. 8-17). pap. 19.99 *(978-1-302-92400-3(1))* Marvel Worldwide, Inc.

Ganapathy, Kalyani. Great Jataka Tales. 2018. (ENG.). 122p. (J). (gr. 2-6). pap. *(978-93-88326-64-3(4))* Speaking Tiger Publishing.

Gandini, Vero, jt. illus. see Kesinger, Brian.

Gandy, Jamie R. This Ocean Is Weird. Gandy, Jamie R. ed. 2017. (ENG.). (J). (gr. k-5). pap. 12.80 *(978-0-692-92150-0(8))* Pandality Bks.

Ganeri, Anita, jt. illus. see West, David.

Ganeshan, Sahana. Si Sa at Treasure Peninsula. Ganeshan, Raji. 2018. (Si Sa Ser.: Vol. 1). (ENG.). 28p. (J). (gr. k-6). 17.00 *(978-0-692-14768-9(3))* Ganeshan, Rajeshwari Iyer.

Gang, Jobie. Pookie Lookie: The Pink Spotted Panda Bear. Shealeya, Mildred. 2007. 32p. (J). per. 12.95 *(978-0-9669595-7-4(4))* SMS Cos., Inc.

Gang, MinJeong. Who's Coming Tonight? Choi, JeongIm. rev. ed. 2014. (MySELF Bookshelf Ser.). (ENG.). 32p. (J). (gr. k-2). lib. bdg. 25.27 *(978-1-59953-653-8(6))* Norwood Hse. Pr.

Gangelhoff, Gene. A Walk Through the Minnesota Zoo. Gangelhoff, Jeanne M. & Belk, Bradford. 32p. (J). 9.95 *(978-0-9635006-1-8(9))* G J & B Publishing.

Gangian, Linda M. The Movement Game: New Edition. Lambertson, Andrea. 2020. (ENG.). 24p. (J). pap. 8.99 ***(978-1-64550-973-8(7))*** Matchstick Literary.

Gangloff, Hope. Rocky Road Trip. Stamper, Judith Bauer. 2004. (Magic School Bus Science Chapter Bks.). 89p. (gr. 2-5). lib. bdg. 15.00 *(978-0-7569-3093-6(6))* Perfection Learning Corp.

Gannett, Ruth. My Father's Dragon. Gannett, Ruth Stiles. 2018. (ENG.). 92p. (J). (gr. 3-6). pap. 4.35 *(978-1-68422-196-7(X))* Martino Fine Bks.

Gannett, Ruth Chrisman. The Dragons of Blueland. Gannett, Ruth Stiles. (Tales of My Father's Dragon Ser.: Bk. 3). 88p. (J). (gr. 3-6). pap. 4.99 incl. audio *(978-0-8072-1287-5(3)*, Listening Library) Random Hse. Audio Publishing Group.

—Elmer & the Dragon. Gannett, Ruth Stiles. (Tales of My Father's Dragon Ser.: Bk. 2). 87p. (J). (gr. 3-6). pap. 4.99 incl. audio *(978-0-8072-1288-2(1)*, Listening Library) Random Hse. Audio Publishing Group.

—My Father's Dragon. Gannett, Ruth Stiles. 2014. (ENG.). 96p. (J). (gr. 1-4). pap. 5.99 *(978-0-486-49283-4(4))* Dover Pubns., Inc.

—My Father's Dragon. Gannett, Ruth Stiles. 2005. (My Father's Dragon Ser.: 1). (ENG.). 96p. (J). (gr. 3-7). 6.99 *(978-0-440-42121-4(7)*, Yearling) Random Hse. Children's Bks.

Gannon, Ned. The Man & the Vine. Meyer, Jane G. 2006. (ENG.). 32p. (J). 18.00 *(978-0-88141-315-1(1))* St. Vladimir's Seminary Pr.

—Time to Pray. Addasi, Maha. 2010. (ENG.). 32p. (J). (gr. 2-4). 17.95 *(978-1-59078-611-6(4))* Boyds Mills Pr.

—The White Nights of Ramadan. Addasi, Maha. (ENG.). 32p. (J). (gr. 2-4). 2017. pap. 7.95 *(978-1-62979-846-2(0))*; 2008. 16.95 *(978-1-59078-523-2(1))* Boyds Mills Pr.

Gannon, Ned, jt. illus. see Meyer, Jane G.

Gannon, Nicholas. Bob. Mass, Wendy & Stead, Rebecca. 2018. (ENG.). 208p. (J). 16.99 *(978-1-250-16662-3(4)*, 900187289) Feiwel & Friends.

—Bob. Mass, Wendy & Stead, Rebecca. 2019. (ENG.). 224p. (J). pap. 7.99 *(978-1-250-30869-6(0)*, 900187290) Square Fish.

Gannon, Nicholas. The Doldrums & the Helmsley Curse. Gannon, Nicholas. (ENG.). 384p. (J). (gr. 3-7). 2018. pap. 8.99 *(978-0-06-232098-8(X))*; 2017. 17.99 *(978-0-06-232097-1(1))* HarperCollins Pubs. (Greenwillow Bks.).

Gant, Linda G. Readers Are Leaders. Gant, Linda G. Date not set. (J). (gr. -1-3). *(978-0-9673625-0-2(4))* Readers Are Leaders.

Gant, Robert. My Big Box of Addition & Subtraction. gif. ed. 2005. 64p. (J). cd-rom 24.95 *(978-1-57791-196-8(2))* Brighter Minds Children's Publishing.

—My Big Box of Letters. gif. ed. 2005. 64p. (J). cd-rom 24.95 *(978-1-57791-193-7(8))* Brighter Minds Children's Publishing.

—My Big Box of Numbers. gif. ed. 2005. 64p. (J). cd-rom 24.95 *(978-1-57791-194-4(6))* Brighter Minds Children's Publishing.

—My Big Box of Reading. gif. ed. 2005. 64p. (J). cd-rom 24.95 *(978-1-57791-195-1(4))* Brighter Minds Children's Publishing.

Gantschev, Ivan. Santa's Favorite Story: Santa Tells the Story of the First Christmas. Aoki, Hisako. 2007. (ENG.). 28p. (J). (gr. -1-3). 9.99 *(978-1-4169-5029-5(X)*, Simon & Schuster Bks. For Young Readers) Simon & Schuster Bks. For Young Readers.

Gantt, Amy. Journey Through the Unified Field, 1 vol. Barlow, Cassie & Norrod, Sue. 2019. (ENG.). 128p. (J). (gr. 3-7). pap. 9.95 *(978-1-4556-2478-2(0)*, Pelican Publishing) Arcadia Publishing.

Ganucheau, Paulina, et al. Legend of the Fire Princess (She-Ra Graphic Novel #1) Gigi D.G., Paulina. 2020. (She-Ra Ser.: 1). (ENG.). 128p. (J). (gr. 3-5). 24.99 *(978-1-338-62716-9(3))* Scholastic, Inc.

Ganucheau, Paulina. Snoballs for All, 1 vol. McConduit, Alexander Brian. 2015. (ENG.). 32p. (J). (gr. k-3). pap. 8.99 *(978-1-4556-2002-9(5)*, Pelican Publishing) Arcadia Publishing.

Ganucheau, Savanna. Bloom. Panetta, Kevin. 2019. (ENG.). 368p. (YA). 24.99 *(978-1-250-19691-0(4)*, 900194268); pap. 17.99 *(978-1-62672-641-3(8)*, 900164146) Roaring Brook Pr. (First Second Bks.).

Ganz, Andreas. Cheyanne: And Other Tales from Underground. Schreyer, Casia. 2019. (Underground Ser.: Vol. 8). (ENG.). 112p. (J). pap. ***(978-1-988853-37-6(0))*** Schreyer Ink Publishing.

Ganz, Andreas. Separation. Schreyer, Casia. 2017. (ENG.). (J). pap. *(978-1-988853-06-2(0))* Schreyer Ink Publishing.

Ganz, Andreas. Sunlight. Schreyer, Casia. 2019. (Underground Ser.: Vol. 7). (ENG.). 118p. (J). pap. ***(978-1-988853-40-6(0))*** Schreyer Ink Publishing.

Ganz, Cristina Milián. El Alfabeto Cubano. Otero, Eduardo A. 2006. (SPA.). 40p. (J). pap. 16.95 *(978-0-9779124-0-7(X))* Cristal Publishing Co.

Ganzer, Theresa. Llama Tails: Ricky's Adventure. Ganzer, Diane & St. Croix, Sammy. 2008. 172p. pap. 9.99 *(978-0-9801438-7-4(X))* Avid Readers Publishing Group.

Gao, Gloria. The Alphabet Book for Children of the Heavenly Way: A Parent Read- along Book. Wu, Amelia. 2018. (ENG.). 64p. (J). 26.95 *(978-1-64258-222-2(0))* Christian Faith Publishing.

Gapaillard, Laurent. The Long Tall Journey. Wahl, Jan. 2015. (ENG.). 48p. (J). (gr. 1-3). 18.99 *(978-1-56846-230-1(1)*, Creative Editions) Creative Co., The.

—The York. Santini, Bertrand. 2018. (ENG.). 80p. (J). (gr. 3-5). 16.99 *(978-1-77657-171-0(1))* Gecko Pr. NZL. Dist: Lerner Publishing Group.

Garafalo, Beatrice. Sadie's Wish: Three Little Elves. Addino, Victoria. 2012. 32p. (-18). pap. 24.95 *(978-1-4626-9907-0(3))* America Star Bks.

Garafano, Marie. Te Extraño Hasta Cuando Estas Dormido. Feist, Robert Churchill. 2019. (SPA.). 30p. (J). pap. 12.18 *(978-1-0918-7821-1(8))* Independently Published.

Garage, Design. Jon Scieszka's Trucktown, 6 vols. Scieszka, Jon. 2015. (Jon Scieszka's Trucktown Ser.: Vol. 6). (ENG.). 24p. (J). (gr. -1-2). 162.42 *(978-1-61479-393-9(X)*, 18178) Spotlight.

Garamella, Joyce Orchard. What Makes a Good Teacher? Here's What the Kids Say! Whyte, Donna. 2003. 32p. (J). 6.95 *(978-1-884548-59-8(8)*, Crystal Springs Bks.) Staff Development for Educators.

Garand, Jeff, jt. illus. see Garand, Robin.

Garand, Robin & Garand, Jeff. Kringle the Cat & the Magic Door. Garand, Robin. 2019. (ENG.). 30p. (J). pap. 10.79 ***(978-1-9733-8638-4(0))*** Independently Published.

Garay, Ester. Albie Newton. Funk, Josh. 2018. (ENG.). 32p. (J). (gr. k-4). 16.95 *(978-1-4549-2258-2(3))* Sterling Publishing Co., Inc.

Garay, Luis. Alfredito Flies Home, 1 vol. Argueta, Jorge. Amado, Elisa, tr. 2007. (ENG.). 36p. (J). (gr. -1-4). 17.95 *(978-0-88899-585-8(7))* Groundwood Bks. CAN. Dist: Publishers Group West (PGW).

—Popol Vuh: A Sacred Book of the Maya, 1 vol. Montejo, Victor. Unger, David, tr. 2009. (ENG.). 88p. (J). (gr. 3-4). pap. 14.95 *(978-0-88899-921-4(6))* Groundwood Bks. CAN. Dist: Publishers Group West (PGW).

—Primas, 1 vol. Amado, Elisa. Iribarren, Elena & Iribarren, Leopoldo, trs. 2004. (SPA.). 32p. (J). 16.95 *(978-0-88899-548-3(2))* Groundwood Bks. CAN. Dist: Publishers Group West (PGW).

—Un Puñado de Semillas. Hughes, Monica & Hughes, Mónica. 2007. (SPA.). 36p. (gr. 1-3). pap. 10.99 *(978-980-257-243-4(8)*, EK8796) Ekare, Ediciones VEN. Dist: Lectorum Pubns., Inc.

Garay, Nicole. The Wooden Bowl/El Bol de Madera. Moreno Winner, Ramona. 2009. (ENG & SPA.). (J). (gr. k-3). 15.95 *(978-0-9651174-3-2(X))* BrainStorm 3000.

Garbett, Lee. Captain Marvel Vol. 3: The Last Avenger. 2020. 112p. (YA). (gr. 8-17). pap. 17.99 ***(978-1-302-92308-2(0))*** Marvel Worldwide, Inc.

Garbett, Lee. Immortal Hulk Vol. 2: The Green Door. 2019. (Immortal Hulk Ser.: 2). 112p. (YA). (gr. 8-17). pap. 15.99 *(978-1-302-91256-7(9))* Marvel Worldwide, Inc.

Garboski, Tanya. Zephyr the Dragonslayer. Doran, Christine Thomas. 2020. (ENG.). 106p. (J). pap. 14.95 ***(978-1-950768-17-2(1))***; 19.95 ***(978-1-950768-18-9(X))*** ProsePress.

Garbot, Dave. Easter Bunny on the Loose! A Seek & Solve Mystery! Wax, Wendy. 2013. (ENG.). 32p. (J). (gr. -1-3). 7.99 *(978-0-06-223709-5(8))* HarperCollins Pubs.

—First Dog of 1600 Pooch'Lvania Avenue: My First Year in Arf, Arf Office!! Grant, Ron & Ovadia, Ron. 2010. 34p. pap. 13.95 *(978-1-59858-995-5(4))* Dog Ear Publishing, LLC.

—Hurry Up! Murray, Carol. 2003. (Rookie Readers Ser.). (ENG.). 32p. (J). 19.50 *(978-0-516-22585-2(5)*, Children's Pr.) Scholastic Library Publishing.

—Map Mania: Discovering Where You Are & Getting to Where You Aren't. Dispenzio, Michael A. 2006. 80p. (J). (gr. 4-8). reprint ed. 20.00 *(978-0-7567-9893-2(0))* DIANE Publishing Co.

—Santa on the Loose! A Seek & Solve Mystery! Hale, Bruce. 2012. (ENG.). 32p. (J). (gr. -1-3). 7.99 *(978-0-06-202262-2(8))* HarperCollins Pubs.

—Super Science Experiments. Mandell, Muriel. 2005. (No-Sweat Science® Ser.). 128p. (J). (gr. 3-7). per. 5.95 *(978-1-4027-2149-6(8))* Sterling Publishing Co., Inc.

Garbot, Dave. Mashup Mania: Learn to Draw More Than 20 Laughable, Loony Characters. Garbot, Dave. 2016. (Cartooning for Kids Ser.). (ENG.). 64p. (J). (gr. k-5). 33.32 *(978-1-939581-92-1(3)*, Walter Foster Jr) Quarto Publishing Group USA.

—Silly Sports: Learn to Draw More Than 20 Amazingly Awesome Athletes. Garbot, Dave. 2016. (Cartooning for Kids Ser.). (ENG.). 64p. (J). (gr. k-5). 33.32 *(978-1-939581-93-8(1)*, Walter Foster Jr) Quarto Publishing Group USA.

—Space Aliens. Garbot, Dave. 2016. (Cartooning for Kids Ser.). (ENG.). 64p. (J). (gr. k-5). 33.32 *(978-1-939581-94-5(X)*, Walter Foster Jr) Quarto Publishing Group USA.

—Spectacular Superheroes. Garbot, Dave. 2016. (Cartooning for Kids Ser.). (ENG.). 64p. (J). (gr. k-5). 33.32 *(978-1-939581-95-2(8)*, Walter Foster Jr) Quarto Publishing Group USA.

Garbot, Dave & Gallagher, Jack. Amazing Science Experiments. Churchill, E. Richard. 2005. (No-Sweat Science Ser.). (ENG.). 128p. (J). (gr. 3-6). 18.69 *(978-1-4027-2331-5(8))* Sterling Publishing Co., Inc.

Garbowska, Agata. Gandy & Parker Escape the Zoo: An Illustrated Adventure. Garbowska, Agata. Mardon, Austin A. & Mardon, Catherine A. 2013. 97p. pap. *(978-1-897472-82-8(X))* Golden Meteorite Pr.].

Garbowska, Agnes. Care Bears: Unlock the Magic. Erman, Matthew & Shammas, Nadia. 2020. 72p. (J). (gr. 4-7). pap. 9.99 *(978-1-68405-622-4(5))* Idea & Design Works, LLC.

—DC Super Hero Girls: Powerless. Wolfram, Amy. 2020. 144p. (J). (gr. 3-7). pap. 9.99 *(978-1-4012-9361-1(1))* DC Comics.

Garbowska, Agnes, et al. My Little Pony: Friends Forever Volume 9, Vol. 9. Rice, Christina & Zahler, Thom. 2017. (MLP Friends Forever Ser.: 9). 120p. (J). (gr. 4-7). pap. 19.99 *(978-1-63140-918-9(2))* Idea & Design Works, LLC.

—My Little Pony: Friendship Is Magic Volume 13, Vol. 13. Rice, Christina & Zahler, Thom. 2017. (My Little Pony Ser.: 13). 145p. (J). (gr. 4-7). pap. 17.99 *(978-1-68405-029-1(4))* Idea & Design Works, LLC.

—My Little Pony: Friendship Is Magic Volume 14, Vol. 14. Anderson, Ted & Rice, Christina. 2018. (My Little Pony Ser.: 14). 128p. (J). (gr. 4-7). pap. 17.99 *(978-1-68405-246-2(7))* Idea & Design Works, LLC.

—My Little Pony: Friendship Is Magic Volume 6. Anderson, Ted & Whitley, Jeremy. 2015. (My Little Pony Ser.: 6). 104p. (J). (gr. 4-7). pap. 17.99 *(978-1-63140-203-6(X)*, 9781631402036) Idea & Design Works, LLC.

—My Little Pony Omnibus Volume 4. Rice, Christina & Anderson, Ted. 2018. (My Little Pony OMNIBUS Ser.: 4). 288p. (J). (gr. 2-5). pap. 24.99 *(978-1-68405-141-0(X))* Idea & Design Works, LLC.

—My Little Pony Omnibus Volume 5. Rice, Christina & Zahler, Thom. 2020. (My Little Pony OMNIBUS Ser.: 5). 336p. (J). (gr. 4-7). pap. 24.99 *(978-1-68405-588-3(1))* Idea & Design Works, LLC.

Garbowska, Agnes. My Little Pony: Ponyville Mysteries. Rice, Christina. 2019. (My Little Pony Ser.). (ENG.). 120p. (J). (gr. 2-5). pap. 17.99 *(978-1-68405-393-3(5))* Idea & Design Works, LLC.

—Past Times at Super Hero High. Fontana, Shea. 2017. (ENG.). 132p. (J). (gr. 3-7). pap. 9.99 *(978-1-4012-7383-5(1)*, DC Zoom) DC Comics.

Garbowska, Agnes, et al. Princess Luna & Spike. Whitley, Jeremy. 2018. (My Little Pony: Friends Forever Ser.). (ENG.). 24p. (J). (gr. 1-8). lib. bdg. 27.07 *(978-1-5321-4239-0(0)*, 28567, Graphic Novels) Spotlight.

—Rarity & Babs Seed. Whitley, Jeremy. 2018. (My Little Pony: Friends Forever Ser.). (ENG.). 24p. (J). (gr. 1-8). lib. bdg. 27.07 *(978-1-5321-4241-3(2)*, 28569, Graphic Novels) Spotlight.

Garbowska, Agnes. Spaced Out. Fontana, Shea. 2019. (ENG.). 128p. (J). (gr. 2-5). pap. 9.99 *(978-1-4012-8256-1(3)*, DC Zoom) DC Comics.

Garbowska, Agnes & Hickey, Brenda. My Little Pony: Friendship Is Magic Volume 10, Vol. 10. Cook, Katie et al. 2016. (My Little Pony Ser.: 10). 124p. (J). (gr. 4-7). pap. 19.99 *(978-1-63140-688-1(4)*, 9781631406881) Idea & Design Works, LLC.

Garbowska, Agnes & Labat, Yancey. DC Super Hero Girls. Fontana, Shea. 2020. (DC Super Hero Girls Ser.). (ENG.). (J). (gr. 2-6). 191.94 ***(978-1-5158-7438-6(9)*** 202145, Stone Arch Bks.) Capstone.

Garbowska, Agnes & Uyetake, Neil. Fluttershy & Iron Will. Rice, Christina. 2018. (My Little Pony: Friends Forever Ser.). (ENG.). 24p. (J). (gr. 1-8). lib. bdg. 27.07 *(978-1-5321-4236-9(6)*, 28564, Graphic Novels) Spotlight.

—Princess Celestia & Spike. Anderson, Ted. 2016. (My Little Pony: Friends Forever Ser.). (ENG.). 24p. (J). (gr. 1-8). 27.07 *(978-1-61479-510-0(X)*, 21416, Graphic Novels) Spotlight.

—Rainbow Dash & Trixie, 1 vol. Zahler, Thom. 2016. (My Little Pony: Friends Forever Ser.). (ENG.). 24p. (J). (gr. 1-8). 27.07 *(978-1-61479-511-7(8)*, 21417, Graphic Novels) Spotlight.

Garbowska, Agnes, jt. illus. see DiChiara, Marcelo.

Garbowska, Agnes, jt. illus. see Fleecs, Tony.

Garbowska, Agnes, jt. illus. see Fosgitt, Joy.

Garbutt, Chris. Commas Say Take a Break. Dahl, Michael. 2019. (Word Adventures: Punctuation Ser.). (ENG.). 32p. (J). (gr. k-3). lib. bdg. 27.99 *(978-1-5158-3861-6(7)*, 139586, Picture Window Bks.) Capstone.

—Exclamation Points Say Wow! Dahl, Michael. 2019. (Word Adventures: Punctuation Ser.). (ENG.). 32p. (J). (gr. k-3). lib. bdg. 27.99 *(978-1-5158-3863-0(3)*, 139587, Picture Window Bks.) Capstone.

—Periods Say Stop. Dahl, Michael. 2019. (Word Adventures: Punctuation Ser.). (ENG.). 32p. (J). (gr. k-3). pap. 7.95 *(978-1-5158-4054-1(9)*, 140048, Picture Window Bks.) Capstone.

—Question Marks Say What? Dahl, Michael. 2019. (Word Adventures: Punctuation Ser.). (ENG.). 32p. (J). (gr. k-3). pap. 7.95 *(978-1-5158-4056-5(5)*, 140050, Picture Window Bks.) Capstone.

Garbutt, Lisa. When I Am an Old Woman: Stationery. Martz, Sandra, ed. 2nd rev. ed. 2006. (C). pap. 7.95 *(978-1-57601-085-3(6))* Nodin Pr.

Garc. Pap. Garc. 2018. (Ficci Ser.: Vol. 38). (SPA.). 34p. (J). pap. 9.13 *(978-1-7198-3823-8(2))* Independently Published.

Garchinsky, Kate. Belle's Journey: An Osprey Takes Flight. Bierregaard, Rob. 2018. 112p. (J). (gr. 2-5). 18.99 *(978-1-58089-792-1(4))* Charlesbridge Publishing, Inc.

—The Secret Life of the Little Brown Bat. Pringle, Laurence. 2018. (Secret Life Ser.). 32p. (J). (gr. 1-4). 17.95 *(978-1-62979-601-7(8))* Boyds Mills Pr.

—The Secret Life of the Red Fox. Pringle, Laurence. 2017. (Secret Life Ser.). (ENG.). 32p. (J). (gr. 1-4). 16.99 *(978-1-62979-260-6(8))* Boyds Mills Pr.

—The Secret Life of the Skunk. Pringle, Laurence. 2019. (Secret Life Ser.). 32p. (J). (gr. 1-4). 17.99 *(978-1-62979-877-6(0))* Boyds Mills Pr.

Garcia. La Perrita Que le Encantaban las Tortillas. Saenz, Benjamin Alire. 2009. (Little Diego Book Ser.).Tr. of Dog Who Loved Tortillas. (ENG.). 40p. (J). (gr. 1-4). 17.95 *(978-1-933693-54-5(1))* Cinco Puntos Pr.

Garcia, Adriana M. All Around Us. Gonzalez, Xelena. 2017. (ENG.). 32p. (J). (gr. -1-2). 17.95 *(978-1-941026-76-2(1))* Cinco Puntos Pr.

—A Nuestro Alrededor. Gonzalez, Xelena. 2019. (SPA.). 32p. (J). 17.95 *(978-1-947627-25-3(2))* Cinco Puntos Pr.

Garcia Bernal, Victor. Andrea Se Viste de Rojo. Munoz Ledo Carrasco, Norma. 2016. (Cuentamelo Otra Vez Ser.). (SPA.). 24p. (J). 16.95 *(978-1-68165-263-4(3))* Trialtea USA, LLC.

—Versos Que Se Cuentan y Se Cantan. Angel Lome, Emilio. 2015. (Serie Morada Ser.). (SPA.). 116p. (J). pap. 11.95 *(978-1-64101-179-2(3))* Santillana USA Publishing Co., Inc.

Garcia, Brianna. Holiday Treats! (Butterbean's Café) Random House. 2019. (ENG.). 22p. (J). (gr. -1-2). bds. 6.99 *(978-1-9848-9441-0(2)*, Random Hse. Bks. for Young Readers) Random Hse. Children's Bks.

Garcia, Camille Rose. Alice's Adventures in Wonderland. Carroll, Lewis. 2010. (ENG.). 160p. 16.99 *(978-0-06-188657-7(2)*, Harper Design) HarperCollins Pubs.

Garcia, Christina. Why Did Sergeant Stubby Go to War? Werling, Cathy. 2018. (Children's Unsung Heroes Book Ser.: Vol. 2). (ENG.). 28p. (J). (gr. k-5). pap. 9.95 *(978-0-9988266-2-2(6))* Lowell Milken Ctr. for Unsung Heroes.

García-Cortés, Ester. Alice in Wonderland. Carroll, Lewis & Ladybird Books Staff. 2015. (Ladybird Classics Ser.). 72p. (J). (gr. k-3). 10.99 *(978-1-4093-1123-2(6))* Penguin Bks., Ltd. GBR. Dist: Independent Pubs. Group.

Garcia, Daniel. Am I Honest. Lanning, Steve. 2019. (Ibook Series - Core Values for Kids Ser.: Vol. 1). (ENG.). 26p. (J). pap. 9.99 *(978-1-0986-4444-4(1))* Independently Published.

—Am I Kind. Lanning, Steve. 2019. (Ibook Series - Core Values for Kids Ser.: Vol. 2). (ENG.). 26p. (J). pap. 9.99 *(978-1-0730-3097-2(0))* Independently Published.

—Am I Rich. Lanning, Steve. 2019. (Ibook Series - Core Values for Kids Ser.: Vol. 3). (ENG.). 30p. (J). pap. 9.99 *(978-1-0730-3379-9(1))* Independently Published.

—Am I Right. Lanning, Steve. 2019. (Ibook Series - Core Values for Kids Ser.: Vol. 4). (ENG.). 26p. (J). pap. 9.99 *(978-1-0730-3576-2(X))* Independently Published.

Garcia, Deborah. Visiting Ted in Heaven. McGee, Janet. 2018. (ENG.). 32p. (J). 16.95 *(978-1-59298-749-8(4))* Beaver's Pond Pr., Inc.

Garcia, Eduardo. Beastly Basketball, 1 vol. Johnson, Lauren. 2014. (Sports Illustrated Kids Graphic Novels Ser.). (ENG.). 72p. (J). (gr. 3-8). lib. bdg. 26.65 *(978-1-4342-6490-9(4)*, Stone Arch Bks.) Capstone.

—Calling His Shot: Babe Ruth's Legendary Home Run. Terrell, Brandon. 2018. (Greatest Sports Moments Ser.). (ENG.). 32p. (J). (gr. 3-9). lib. bdg. 31.32 *(978-1-5435-2868-8(6)*, 138371, Capstone Pr.) Capstone.

—Carrera Extrema. Maddox, Jake. 2020. (Jake Maddox Novelas Gráficas Ser.).Tr. of Gear Hero. (SPA.). 72p. (J). (gr. 3-8). pap. 6.95 *(978-1-4965-9313-9(8)*, 142343); lib. bdg. 26.65 *(978-1-4965-9178-4(X)*, 142087) Capstone. (Stone Arch Bks.).

Garcia, Eduardo. Catch Soccer's Beat. Maddox, Jake. 2020. (Jake Maddox Graphic Novels Ser.). (ENG.). 72p. (J). (gr. 3-6). pap. 6.95 ***(978-1-4965-9922-3(5)***, 201333); lib. bdg. 26.65 ***(978-1-4965-9712-0(5)***, 199335) Capstone. (Stone Arch Bks.).

Garcia, Eduardo. Cycling Champion, 1 vol. Maddox, Jake. 2012. (Jake Maddox Sports Stories Ser.). (ENG.). 72p. (J). (gr. 3-6). pap. 5.95 *(978-1-4342-3904-4(7))*; lib. bdg. 25.32 *(978-1-4342-3290-8(5))* Capstone. (Stone Arch Bks.).

—The Death of Baldur. Simonson, Louise. 2016. (Norse Myths: a Viking Graphic Novel Ser.). (ENG.). 56p. (J). (gr. 4-8). lib. bdg. 27.99 *(978-1-4965-3488-0(3)*, Stone Arch Bks.) Capstone.

—Defying Hitler: Jesse Owens' Olympic Triumph. Yomtov, Nel. 2018. (Greatest Sports Moments Ser.). (ENG.). 32p. (J). (gr. 3-9). lib. bdg. 31.32 *(978-1-5435-2865-7(1)*, 138368, Capstone Pr.) Capstone.

—Faceoff Fall Out. Maddox, Jake & Fuentes, Benny. 2018. (Jake Maddox Graphic Novels Ser.). (ENG.). 72p. (J). (gr. 3-8). lib. bdg. 26.65 *(978-1-4965-6043-8(4)*, 137412, Stone Arch Bks.) Capstone.

—The Fisherman & the Genie, 1 vol. Fein, Eric. 2010. (Classic Fiction Ser.). (ENG.). 72p. (J). (gr. 5-9). 27.99 *(978-1-4342-2134-6(2))*; pap. 7.15 *(978-1-4342-2777-5(4))* Capstone. (Stone Arch Bks.).

—Gear Hero. Terrell, Brandon. 2018. (Jake Maddox Graphic Novels Ser.). (ENG.). 72p. (J). (gr. 3-8). pap. 6.95 *(978-1-4965-6049-0(3)*, 137430, Stone Arch Bks.) Capstone.

—Gear Hero. Maddox, Jake. 2018. (Jake Maddox Graphic Novels Ser.). (ENG.). 72p. (J). (gr. 3-8). lib. bdg. 26.65 *(978-1-4965-6045-2(0)*, 137426, Stone Arch Bks.) Capstone.

Garcia, Eduardo, et al. Gods & Thunder: A Graphic Novel of Old Norse Myths. Bowen, Carl et al. 2017. (ENG.). 208p. (J). (gr. 4-7). pap. 14.95 *(978-1-62370-848-1(6)*, Capstone Young Readers) Capstone.

Garcia, Eduardo. Gold Medal Swim, 1 vol. Maddox, Jake. 2012. (Jake Maddox Sports Stories Ser.). (ENG.). 72p. (J). (gr. 3-6). pap. 5.95 *(978-1-4342-3902-0(0))*; lib. bdg. 25.32 *(978-1-4342-3288-5(3))* Capstone. (Stone Arch Bks.).

—In the Red Zone. Maddox, Jake. 2020. (Jake Maddox Graphic Novels Ser.). (ENG.). 72p. (J). (gr. 3-8). pap. 6.95 *(978-1-4965-8455-7(4)*, 140980); lib. bdg. 26.65 *(978-1-4965-8376-5(0)*, 140675) Capstone. (Stone Arch Bks.).

—Julius Caesar, 1 vol. Shakespeare, William. 2011. (Shakespeare Graphics Ser.). (ENG.). 88p. (J). (gr. 5-9). pap. 7.15 *(978-1-4342-3450-6(9))*; lib. bdg. 27.99 *(978-1-4342-2631-0(X))* Capstone. (Stone Arch Bks.).

—Lake Placid Miracle: When U. S. Hockey Stunned the World. Hoena, Blake. 2018. (Greatest Sports Moments Ser.). (ENG.). 32p. (J). (gr. 3-9). lib. bdg. 31.32 *(978-1-5435-2867-1(8)*, 138370, Capstone Pr.) Capstone.

—Pase Completo. Maddox, Jake. 2019. (Jake Maddox Novelas Gráficas Ser.). (SPA.). 72p. (J). (gr. 3-8). pap. 6.95 *(978-1-4965-8588-2(7)*, 141329); lib. bdg. 26.65 *(978-1-4965-8576-9(3)*, 141310) Capstone. (Stone Arch Bks.).

—Quarterback Rush, 1 vol. Bowen, Carl. 2014. (Sports Illustrated Kids Graphic Novels Ser.). (ENG.). 72p. (J). (gr. 3-8). 26.65 *(978-1-4342-6489-3(0)*, Stone Arch Bks.) Capstone.

—Relay Race Breakdown, 1 vol. Maddox, Jake. 2012. (Jake Maddox Sports Stories Ser.). (ENG.). 72p. (J). (gr. 3-6). pap. 5.95 *(978-1-4342-3903-7(9))*; lib. bdg. 25.32 *(978-1-4342-3289-2(1))* Capstone. (Stone Arch Bks.).

—Rivalidad Sobre el Hielo. Maddox, Jake. 2020. (Jake Maddox Novelas Gráficas Ser.).Tr. of Faceoff Fall Out. (SPA.). 72p. (J). (gr. 3-8). pap. 6.95 *(978-1-4965-9311-5(1)*, 142341); lib. bdg. 26.65 *(978-1-4965-9176-0(3)*, 142086) Capstone. (Stone Arch Bks.).

—Soccer Showdown: U. S. Women's Stunning 1999 World Cup Win. Terrell, Brandon. 2019. (Greatest Sports Moments Ser.). (ENG.). 32p. (J). (gr. 3-9). pap. 7.95 *(978-1-5435-4222-6(0)*, 139120); lib. bdg. 31.32 *(978-1-5435-4220-2(4)*, 139118) Capstone.

—Thor vs. the Giants: A Viking Graphic Novel. Bowen, Carl. 2016. (Norse Myths: a Viking Graphic Novel Ser.). (ENG.). 56p. (J). (gr. 4-8). pap. 5.95 *(978-1-4965-3491-0(3))*; lib. bdg. 27.99 *(978-1-4965-3487-3(5))* Capstone. (Stone Arch Bks.).

—Track & Field Takedown, 1 vol. Maddox, Jake. 2012. (Jake Maddox Sports Stories Ser.). (ENG.). 72p. (J). (gr. 3-6). pap. 5.95 *(978-1-4342-3901-3(2))*; lib. bdg. 25.32 *(978-1-4342-3287-8(5))* Capstone. (Stone Arch Bks.).

—Twilight of the Gods: A Viking Graphic Novel. Dahl, Michael. 2016. (Norse Myths: a Viking Graphic Novel Ser.). (ENG.). 56p. (J). (gr. 4-8). lib. bdg. 27.99 *(978-1-4965-3489-7(1)*, Stone Arch Bks.) Capstone.

—A Win for Women: Billie Jean King Takes down Bobby Riggs. Terrell, Brandon. 2019. (Greatest Sports Moments Ser.). (ENG.). 32p. (J). (gr. 3-9). pap. 7.95

(978-1-5435-4221-9(2), 139119); lib. bdg. 31.32 *(978-1-5435-4219-6(0)*, 139117) Capstone.

Garcia, Eduardo & Ferrara, Eduardo. Caught in a Pickle, 1 vol. Jacobson, Ryan. 2011. (B-Team Ser.). (ENG.). 40p. (J). (gr. 2-4). lib. bdg. 23.99 *(978-1-4342-2606-8(9)*, Stone Arch Bks.) Capstone.

Garcia, Eduardo, jt. illus. see Aureliani, Franco.

Garcia, Eduardo, jt. illus. see Max, Iman.

Garcia, Eduardo, jt. illus. see Smith, Tod.

Garcia, Edwin. Doogie's Dad. Dyches, Richard W. Hudson, Edward K., ed. 2016. (ENG.). (J). (gr. k-3). pap. 7.95 *(978-0-9829203-1-2(8))* Children Left Behind.

Garcia, Geronimo. A Gift from Papa Diego: Un Regalo de Papa Diego. Saenz, Benjamin Alire. 2008. (Little Diego Book Ser.). (SPA.). 40p. (J). pap. 10.95 *(978-0-938317-33-3(4))* Cinco Puntos Pr.

Garcia, Gustavo. Braydon the Red. DeBoer, Heidi a. 2018. (ENG.). 26p. (J). pap. 12.95 *(978-1-7904-3574-6(9))* Independently Published.

Garcia, Helena. Brownie Quest: Follow the Trails... of the ELF Adventure & the Three Keys. Redpath, Ann & Tuchman, Laura. 2008. 73p. (J). pap. *(978-0-88441-711-8(5))* Girl Scouts of the USA.

—A World of Girls. Welsh, Anne Marie & Tuchman, Laura. 2010. 40p. (J). *(978-0-88441-750-7(6))* Girl Scouts of the USA.

—Wow! Wonders of Water. Welsh, Anne Marie & Fenly, Leigh. 2009. 112p. (J). pap. *(978-0-88441-732-3(8))* Girl Scouts of the USA.

García, Helena Pérez. How the Finch Got His Colors. Riley Guertin, Annemarie. 2018. (ENG.). 32p. (J). 16.99 *(978-1-945547-77-5(4)*, 554777) Familius LLC.

Garcia, Helena Perez. Meet the Artist: the Pre-Raphaelites: An Art Activity Book. 2019. (ENG.). 32p. (J). (gr. k-2). pap. 12.95 *(978-1-84976-591-6(X))* Tate Publishing, Ltd. GBR. Dist: Hachette Bk. Group.

Garcia, Helena Pérez. Sophie & the Heidelberg Cat. Wilson, Andrew. 2019. (ENG.). 36p. 12.99 *(978-1-4335-6418-5(1))* Crossway.

García, Helena Pérez. Why Evergreens Keep Their Leaves. Riley Guertin, Annemarie. 2019. (ENG.). 32p. (J). 16.99 *(978-1-64170-158-7(7)*, 550158) Familius LLC.

Garcia, Humberto. Animales Entreversos. Lozano, Juan Antonio. rev. ed. 2007. (Castillo de la Lectura Blanca Ser.). (SPA & ENG.). 43p. (J). (gr. k). pap. 6.95 *(978-970-20-0341-0(5))* Castillo, Ediciones, S. A. de C. V. MEX. Dist: Macmillan.

García, José. Truckus Maximus. Peterson, Scott. 2019. (ENG.). 288p. (J). 23.99 *(978-1-250-19696-5(5)*, 900194275); pap. 16.99 *(978-1-59643-814-9(2)*, 900086788) Roaring Brook Pr. (First Second Bks.).

Garcia, Juan F. Team 002: The Abduction of the Queen. Hildebrand, Jens. 2013. 224p. pap. *(978-3-929892-46-8(4))* Hildebrand, Jutta Warped Tomato Publishing.

—Team 002 und das Utopia-Element. Hildebrand, Jens. 2013. 270p. pap. *(978-3-929892-39-0(1))* Hildebrand, Jutta Warped Tomato Publishing.

—Team 002 und Die Entführung der Queen. Hildebrand, Jens. 2013. 240p. pap. *(978-3-929892-37-6(5))* Hildebrand, Jutta Warped Tomato Publishing.

García Maciá, Raquel. Jumping Jenny. Bari, Ellen. 2011. (ENG.). 32p. (J). (gr. k-3). pap. 7.95 *(978-0-7613-5143-6(4)*, 9780761351436, Kar-Ben Publishing) Lerner Publishing Group.

Garcia, Manuel. Come Out & Fight Like a (Molecule) Man. Parker, Jeff. 2007. (Fantastic Four Ser.: No. 2). (ENG.). 24p. (J). (gr. 2-6). 27.07 *(978-1-59961-388-8(3)*, 7226, Marvel Age) Spotlight.

—Finding Zemo. Parker, Jeff. 2007. (Avengers Ser.: No. 1). (ENG.). 24p. (J). (gr. 2-6). 27.07 *(978-1-59961-383-3(2)*, 23, Marvel Age) Spotlight.

—Law of the Jungle. Parker, Jeff. 2007. (Fantastic Four Ser.: No. 2). (ENG.). 24p. (J). (gr. 2-6). 27.07 *(978-1-59961-390-1(5)*, 7228, Marvel Age) Spotlight.

—The Leader Has a Big Head. Parker, Jeff. 2007. (Avengers Ser.: No. 1). (ENG.). 24p. (J). (gr. 2-6). 27.07 *(978-1-59961-384-0(0)*, 24, Marvel Age) Spotlight.

Garcia, Manuel, et al. Marvel-Verse: Black Panther. 2020. 128p. (J). (gr. 5-9). pap. 9.99 *(978-1-302-92360-0(9))* Marvel Worldwide, Inc.

Garcia, Manuel. The Masters of Evil. Parker, Jeff. Paniccia, Mark, ed. 2007. (Avengers Ser.: No. 1). (ENG.). 24p. (J). (gr. 2-6). 27.07 *(978-1-59961-385-7(9)*, 25, Marvel Age) Spotlight.

—Noble Vol. 3: No One Man. Thomas, Brandon. 2019. (ENG.). 144p. (YA). pap. 14.99 *(978-1-941302-84-2(X)*, 94dc6b33-4661-45b8-9a8c-73f05118f665, Lion Forge) Oni Pr., Inc.

—The Replacements. Parker, Jeff. Paniccia, Mark, ed. 2007. (Avengers Ser.: No. 1). (ENG.). 24p. (J). (gr. 2-6). 27.07 *(978-1-59961-386-4(7)*, 26, Marvel Age) Spotlight.

—4 Titles, 4 vols. ABDO Publishing Company Staff & Parker, Jeff. 2007. (Avengers Ser.: 4). (ENG.). 24p. (J). (gr. 2-6). lib. bdg. 108.28 *(978-1-59961-382-6(4)*, 22, Marvel Age) Spotlight.

Garcia, Marc Khayam. The Adventures of Billy Butterfly. Lehnert, R. B. 2003. (J). per. *(978-0-9747628-2-1(2))* BKB Group, Inc., The.

—Color Me & My Pals: The Adventures of Billy Butterfly Coloring Book. 2003. (J). 3.95 *(978-0-9747628-3-8(0))* BKB Group, Inc., The.

Garcia, Michael Satoshi, photos by. I Am Hapa. Smith, Crystal. 2016. (J). *(978-0-9973947-0-2(6))* East West Discovery Pr.

García, Miguel Ángel. Relic of the Dragon. BENATAR, ADRIÁN. 2018. (ENG.). 56p. (J). (gr. 2-5). 9.99 *(978-1-68405-215-8(7))* Idea & Design Works, LLC.

Garcia, Nasario & Aragon, Dolores. Grandpa Lolo's Matanza: A New Mexican Tradition = la Matanza de Abuelito Lolo: Una Tradición Nuevo Mexicana. 2015. (SPA & ENG.). 70p. (J). *(978-1-936744-47-3(3)*, Rio Grande Bks.) LPD Pr.

Garcia, Nelson. Brave Jack the Flying Squirrel in Wings of Courage. Fez, Uncle. 2009. (ENG.). 54p. pap. 30.50 *(978-1-4120-2548-5(6))* Trafford Publishing.

GARCIA ORIHUELA, Luis. The Army of Words. Garcia Orihuela, Luis & DIVINCENZO, Sofia & Yoselem. 2012. 24p. pap. 19.99 *(978-1-61196-934-4(4))* Pintos, Yoselem G.

Garcia, Patricio E. The Eyes of the Weaver: Los Ojos Del Tejedor. Ortega, Cristina. 2006. (ENG.). 64p. (J). 19.95 *(978-0-8263-3990-4(5))* Univ. of New Mexico Pr.

Garcia Piza, Mariana. Meow Cello. Halverson, Kristen. 2019. (ENG.). 32p. (J). (gr. 2-4). 24.99 ***(978-1-0878-0179-7(6))*** The Tale of Noel: The Holiday Horse Angel, The.

—Sienna Rose: The Dancing Swan. Halverson, Kristen. 2019. (ENG.). 38p. (J). (gr. k-5). 24.99 ***(978-0-578-51603-5(9))*** The Tale of Noel: The Holiday Horse Angel, The.

Garcia, R. a. A Fairy Princess. McLellan, T. S. 2019. (Faircraft Ser.: Vol. 1). (ENG.). 134p. (J). pap. 7.99 ***(978-1-7103-1223-2(8))*** Independently Published.

Garcia Sanchez, Sergio. Lost in NYC: A Subway Adventure. Spiegelman, Nadja. 2015. (ENG.). 52p. (J). (gr. 2-7). 16.95 *(978-1-935179-81-8(0))* TOON Books / RAW Junior, LLC.

Garcia, Segundo. Driving Force! (Blaze & the Monster Machines) Random House. 2016. (Pictureback(R) Ser.). (ENG.). 24p. (J). (gr. -1-2). 4.99 *(978-0-553-53889-2(6)*, Random Hse. Bks. for Young Readers) Random Hse. Children's Bks.

—A Stroke of Magic (Shimmer & Shine) Golden Books. 2016. (ENG.). 128p. (J). (gr. -1-2). pap. 7.99 *(978-0-553-52363-8(5)*, Golden Bks.) Random Hse. Children's Bks.

Garcia, Victor Manuel Gut. De la Vez Que Tino Perdio Su Par. Ochoa, Minerva. rev. ed. 2006. (Castillo de la Lectura Blanca Ser.). (SPA & ENG.). 88p. (J). (gr. k-2). pap. 6.95 *(978-970-20-0196-6(X))* Castillo, Ediciones, S. A. de C. V. MEX. Dist: Macmillan.

Garcia, Victor Manuel Gut, jt. illus. see Garcia, Victor Manuel Gutierrez.

Garcia, Victor Manuel Gutierrez & Garcia, Victor Manuel Gut. Espartaco y Yo. Parada, Enrique. rev. ed. 2006. (Castillo de la Lectura Verde Ser.). (SPA & ENG.). 68p. (J). (gr. 2). pap. 7.95 *(978-968-5920-90-2(7))* Castillo, Ediciones, S. A. de C. V. MEX. Dist: Macmillan.

Gardie, Amandine. Drawmaster Princess & Unicorn: Super Stencil Kit: 4 Easy Steps to Draw Your Heroes. 2019. (Drawmaster Ser.). (ENG.). 24p. (J). (gr. k). 11.99 *(978-2-89802-095-7(8)*, CrackBoom! Bks.) Chouette Publishing CAN. Dist: Publishers Group West (PGW).

Gardie, Amandine & Legdani, Sanaa. Everything Princess: A Carry along Book. 2017. 24p. (J). (gr. -1-1). bds. 7.99 *(978-2-924786-03-1(7)*, CrackBoom! Bks.) Chouette Publishing CAN. Dist: Publishers Group West (PGW).

Gardiner, Lindsey. Abuelita, te Acuerdas? Langston, Laura. 2004.Tr. of Mile High Apple Pie. (SPA.). (J). 18.99 *(978-84-488-1911-8(X))* Beascoa, Ediciones S.A. ESP. Dist: Lectorum Pubns., Inc.

—If You're Happy & You Know It! Ormerod, Jan. 2003. 32p. (J). (gr. -1-3). 15.95 *(978-1-932065-07-7(5))*; pap. 5.95 *(978-1-932065-10-7(5))* Star Bright Bks., Inc.

—Trosclair & the Alligator, 1 vol. Huggins, Peter. (ENG.). 32p. (J). 2013. pap. 7.95 *(978-1-59572-640-7(3))*; 2005. (gr. -1-3). 15.95 *(978-1-932065-98-5(9))* Star Bright Bks., Inc.

Gardiner, Lisa M. Crazy Critters. Paiva, Johannah Gilman, ed. 2013. (Big Padded Lift-The-Flap Ser.). (ENG.). 20p. (J). (gr. -1-2). 8.99 *(978-1-77093-630-0(0))* Flowerpot Children's Pr. Inc. CAN. Dist: Cardinal Pubs. Group.

—Farm Find. Paiva, Johannah Gilman, ed. 2013. 20p. (J). (gr. -1-1). 8.99 *(978-1-77093-688-1(2))* Flowerpot Children's Pr. Inc. CAN. Dist: Cardinal Pubs. Group.

—Now I Lay Me down to Sleep. Flowerpot Press. 2016. (ENG.). 32p. (J). (gr. k-2). bds. 10.99 *(978-1-4867-0847-5(1)*, 41ce3a4e-39b5-488a-b06f-5571d47c1286) Flowerpot Pr.

—The People That I Meet. Gilman, Savannah, ed. 2017. (ENG.). 24p. (J). (gr. -1-1). *(978-1-4867-1261-8(4))* Flowerpot Children's Pr. Inc.

—Things That Go. Gilman, Savannah, ed. 2017. (ENG.). 24p. (J). (gr. -1-1). *(978-1-4867-1262-5(2))* Flowerpot Children's Pr. Inc.

Gardiner, Nancy. Tap Shoes & Horse Shoes. Macy, Tana. 2011. 50p. pap. 18.00 *(978-1-60976-086-1(7)*, Eloquent Bks.) Strategic Book Publishing & Rights Agency (SBPRA).

Gardner, David C. Ticktock Banneker's Clock. Keller, Shana. 2016. (ENG.). 32p. (J). (gr. 1-4). 16.99 *(978-1-58536-956-0(X)*, 204114) Sleeping Bear Pr.

—Write on, Irving Berlin! Kimmelman, Leslie. 2018. (ENG.). 32p. (J). (gr. 1-4). 16.99 *(978-1-58536-380-3(4)*, 204405) Sleeping Bear Pr.

Gardner, David G. Rettie & the Ragamuffin Parade: A Thanksgiving Story. Noble, Trinka Hakes. 2017. (Tales of Young Americans Ser.). (ENG.). 32p. (J). (gr. 1-4). 17.95 *(978-1-58536-960-7(8)*, 204322) Sleeping Bear Pr.

Gardner, Louise. Five Little Easter Eggs. (ENG.). 10p. (J). 2009. (gr. -1). 5.95 *(978-1-58117-849-4(2))*; 2008. 9.95 *(978-1-58117-682-7(1))* Bendon, Inc. (Intervisual/Piggy Toes).

—The Gingerbread Family: A Scratch-And-Sniff Book. Maccarone, Grace. 2010. (ENG.). 14p. (J). (gr. -1-k). bds. 7.99 *(978-1-4424-0678-0(X)*, Little Simon) Little Simon.

—Good Night Princesses. Gamble, Adam & Jasper, Mark. 2016. (Good Night Our World Ser.). (ENG.). 20p. (J). (— 1). bds. 9.95 *(978-1-60219-225-6(1))* Good Night Bks.

Gardner, Louise. Let's Go to School. Burroughs, Caleb. 2020. (ENG.). 18p. (J). bds. ***(978-1-64269-253-2(0)***, 7e4c1943-2e26-4e82-8876-49fdd69c2db1, Sequoia Publishing & Media LLC) Phoenix International Publications, Inc.

Gardner, Louise. Old MacDonald. 2004. 24p. (J). bds. 6.99 *(978-1-85854-901-9(9))* Brimax Books Ltd. GBR. Dist: Byeway Bks.

Gardner, Louise, et al. Old MacDonald & Other Sing-along Rhymes. 2006. (Mother Goose Ser.). (ENG.). 36p. (J). 12.95 *(978-1-59249-525-2(7)*, 1D028) Soundprints.

Gardner, Marjory. Hedgeburners: An A-Z PI Mystery. Alexander, Goldie. 2009. 184p. (YA). pap. 13.95 *(978-1-921479-26-7(4)*, IP Kidz) Interactive Pubns. Pty, Ltd. AUS. Dist: CreateSpace Independent Publishing Platform.

—The Present 6 Packs. KinderConcepts. Wallace, Jessica. (Kinderstarters Ser.). 8p. (gr. -1-1). 21.00 *(978-0-7635-8720-8(5))* Rigby Education.

Gardner, Rita. One Day the Animals Talked: Short Stories. MacDonald, Bernell. 2005. (ENG.). 84p. (J). pap. *(978-0-9686034-5-1(9)*, Lion's Head Pr.) Chipmunk Bks.

Gardner, Stephen. Childs Play: Positive Affirmations for Children to Sing & Dramatize. Kulsa, Wha. Date not set. 30p. (J). (gr. 1-7). pap. *(978-1-886942-08-0(0))* White Lion Pr.

Gardner, Whitney. Becoming RBG: Ruth Bader Ginsburg's Journey to Justice. Levy, Debbie. 2019. (ENG.). 208p. (J). (gr. 5). 19.99 *(978-1-5344-2456-2(3))*; pap. 12.99 *(978-1-5344-2455-5(5))* Simon & Schuster Bks. For Young Readers. (Simon & Schuster Bks. For Young Readers).

Gardner, Whitney. Fake Blood. Gardner, Whitney. 2018. (ENG.). 336p. (J). (gr. 5). 21.99 *(978-1-4814-9556-1(9))*; pap. 14.99 *(978-1-4814-9557-8(7))* Simon & Schuster Bks. For Young Readers. (Simon & Schuster Bks. For Young Readers).

Garfano, Marie. I Even Miss You While You're Sleeping. Feist, Robert Churchill. 2019. (ENG.). 30p. (J). pap. 12.18 *(978-1-0917-0302-5(7))* Independently Published.

Garg, Lovyaa. A Fish Name Fred. Neal, Tamara. 2018. (ENG.). 34p. (J). (gr. k-3). pap. 11.97 *(978-0-9909379-2-0(5))* Tamara's Bks.

Garland, Lynn Rockwell, jt. illus. see Venema, Lisa J.

Garland, Michael. Animal School: What Class Are You? Lord, Michelle. 2014. (ENG.). 32p. (J). (gr. -1-3). 16.95 *(978-0-8234-3045-1(6))* Holiday Hse., Inc.

—The Best Book to Read. Bertram, Debbie & Bloom, Susan. 2011. 32p. (J). (gr. -1-2). pap. 7.99 *(978-0-375-87300-3(7)*, Dragonfly Bks.) Random Hse. Children's Bks.

—The Best Place to Read. Bloom, Susan & Bertram, Debbie. 2007. 32p. (J). (gr. -1-2). pap. 7.99 *(978-0-375-83757-9(4)*, Dragonfly Bks.) Random Hse. Children's Bks.

—Diary of a Drummer Boy. Brill, Marlene Targ. 2018. (ENG.). 50p. (J). (gr. 4-6). pap. 9.99 *(978-1-7320276-4-0(1))* Golden Alley Pr.

Garland, Michael. Herman Jiggle, Say Hello! How to Talk to People When Your Words Get Stuck. Cook, Julia. 2020. (ENG.). 32p. (J). (gr. k-3). pap. 10.95 ***(978-1-944882-51-8(0))*** Boys Town Pr.

Garland, Michael. I'd Be Your Princess: A Royal Tale of Godly Character. O'Brien, Kathryn. 2007. 28p. (J). (gr. -1-3). 6.99 *(978-0-7847-1964-0(0))* Standard Publishing.

—The Night Santa Got Lost: How NORAD Saved Christmas. Keane, Michael. ed. 2015. (ENG.). 28p. (J). (gr. -1). 16.99 *(978-1-62157-398-2(2)*, Regnery Kids) Regnery Publishing, Inc., An Eagle Publishing Co.

—Pooch on the Loose: A Christmas Adventure, 0 vols. Kroll, Steven. 2013. (ENG.). 40p. (J). (gr. -1-3). pap. 9.99 *(978-0-7614-5443-4(8)*, 9780761454434, Two Lions) Amazon Publishing.

—Pooch on the Loose: A Christmas Adventure, 1 vol. Kroll, Steven & Droll. 2005. (ENG.). 32p. (J). (gr. -1-3). 14.95 *(978-0-7614-5239-3(7))* Marshall Cavendish Corp.

—SantaKid. Patterson, James. 2004. (ENG.). 48p. (J). (gr. -1-1). 17.99 *(978-0-316-00061-1(2)*, Jimmy Patterson) Little Brown & Co.

Garland, Michael. Daddy Played the Blues, 1 vol. Garland, Michael. 2017. (ENG.). 48p. (J). (gr. 1-5). 17.95 *(978-0-88448-588-9(9)*, 884588) Tilbury Hse. Pubs.

—Hooray José!, 1 vol. Garland, Michael. 2007. (ENG.). 32p. (J). (gr. -1-3). 16.99 *(978-0-7614-5345-1(8))* Marshall Cavendish Corp.

—King Puck. Garland, Michael. 32p. (J). (gr. -1-3). 2009. (ENG.). pap. 7.99 *(978-0-06-084811-8(1))*; 2007. (ENG.). 16.99 *(978-0-06-084809-5(X))*; 2007. lib. bdg. 18.99 *(978-0-06-084810-1(3))* HarperCollins Pubs.

—Last Night at the Zoo. Garland, Michael. 2003. (ENG.). 32p. (J). (gr. k-2). pap. 10.95 *(978-1-59078-167-8(8))* Boyds Mills Pr.

—Miss Smith Reads Again! Garland, Michael. 2008. (ENG.). 32p. (J). (gr. -1-2). 6.99 *(978-0-14-241140-7(X)*, Puffin Books) Penguin Young Readers Group.

—Miss Smith's Incredible Storybook. Garland, Michael. 2005. 32p. (J). (gr. -1-2). pap. 7.99 *(978-0-14-240282-5(6)*, Puffin Books) Penguin Young Readers Group.

—Oh, What a Christmas! Garland, Michael. 2011. (ENG.). 40p. (J). (gr. -1-3). 16.99 *(978-0-545-24210-3(X)*, Scholastic Pr.) Scholastic, Inc.

Garland, Nicholas. Mommy Daddy Evan Sage. McHenry, Eric. 2011. (ENG.). 72p. (J). pap. 18.00 *(978-1-904130-45-1(3))* Waywiser Pr., The GBR. Dist: SPD-Small Pr. Distribution.

Garland, Sally. Eres Extraordinario, 1 vol. Johnson, Craig & Johnson, Samantha. ed. 2020. (SPA.). 32p. (J). 14.99 *(978-1-4002-1839-4(X))* Grupo Nelson.

—Little Mole Finds Hope. Nellist, Glenys. 2020. (Little Mole Ser.). (ENG.). 32p. (J). (gr. k-3). 17.99 *(978-1-5064-4874-9(7)*, Beaming Books) Augsburg Fortress, Pubs.

—The Little Pink Rosebud. 2019. (ENG.). 32p. (J). (gr. k-2). 16.99 *(978-1-4867-1555-8(9)*, d4e4f3ea-8253-41d1-b647-68c0a8e27904) Flowerpot Pr.

—The Magic in a Year. Boylan, Frank. 2017. (ENG.). 32p. (J). (gr. k-2). 16.99 *(978-1-4867-1319-6(X)*, b1fdd83e-24ea-48fe-a339-3b9ddfccddf4) Flowerpot Pr.

—Un Monstruo en los Manglares (Monster in the Mangroves) Everett, Reese. 2017. (Beginning Chapter Bks.). (SPA.). 48p. (gr. k-3). pap. 8.95 *(978-1-68342-248-8(1)*, 9781683422488) Rourke Educational Media.

—La Pandilla Manada de Lobos Esta Fuera de Vista (Wolfpack Gang Is Outta Sight) Everett, Reese. 2017. (Beginning Chapter Bks.). (SPA.). 48p. (gr. k-3). pap. 8.95 *(978-1-68342-250-1(3)*, 9781683422501) Rourke Educational Media.

Garland, Sally. This Drop of Water. Claybourne, Anna. 2019. (ENG.). 48p. (J). (gr. 2-4). ***(978-1-4451-6365-9(9)***, Franklin Watts) Hachette Children's Group.

Garland, Sally. You Are Extraordinary, 1 vol. Johnson, Samantha. 2019. (ENG.). 32p. (J). 16.99 *(978-1-4002-0913-2(7))* Nelson, Thomas Inc.

—You Are Extraordinary, 1 vol. 2019. (ENG.). 26p. (J). bds. 9.99 *(978-1-4002-0915-6(3))* Nelson, Thomas Inc.

Garlick, Mark A. Astronomy, Set. Garlick, Mark A. 2004. (gr. 9-12). 23.95 *(978-0-86717-676-6(8)*, ES3010, Lifepac) Alpha Omega Pubns., Inc.

Garner, Essex. A Children's Book of Barack Obama Our 44th President. Garner, Lama. 2009.Tr. of Children's Book of Barack Obama Our 44th President. 24p. pap. 7.95 *(978-0-615-31464-8(3))* Art Of Essex Fine Art, The.

Garner, James. Bob & the River of Time. Garner, James. 2016. (ENG.). 72p. (C). pap. 16.95 *(978-1-78583-112-6(7))* Crown Hse. Publishing LLC.

Garney, Ron, et al. Hulk: the Dogs of War. 2019. 832p. (YA). (gr. 8-17). 100.00 *(978-1-302-91594-0(0))* Marvel Worldwide, Inc.

—Silver Surfer Epic Collection: Inner Demons. 2019. (ENG.). 464p. (YA). (gr. -1-17). pap. 39.99 *(978-1-302-91813-2(3))* Marvel Worldwide, Inc.

—Thor by Jason Aaron: the Complete Collection Vol. 1. 2019. 432p. (YA). (gr. -1-17). pap. 39.99 *(978-1-302-91810-1(9))* Marvel Worldwide, Inc.

—X-Men: Unstoppable. 2019. (ENG.). 440p. (YA). (gr. 8-17). pap. 39.99 *(978-1-302-91612-1(2))* Marvel Worldwide, Inc.

Garns, Allen. Twisters! Penner, Lucille Recht. 2009. (Step into Reading Ser.). 48p. (J). (gr. k-3). pap. 4.99 *(978-0-375-86224-3(2)*, Random Hse. Bks. for Young Readers) Random Hse. Children's Bks.

Garnsey, Wayne. Math 8 X-treme Review: Concise Training for NYS Math Intermediate Assessment. Milanese, Celestine Marie & Peck, Carolyn. Stich, Paul, ed. 2007. 160p. per. 13.95 *(978-0-935487-85-5(9)*, X-treme Reviews) N&N Publishing Co., Inc.

Garnu, Elena. Don't Ask Me Where I'm From. De Leon, Jennifer. 2020. (ENG.). 336p. (YA). (gr. 9). 18.99 ***(978-1-5344-3824-8(6)***, Atheneum/Caitlyn Dlouhy Books) Simon & Schuster Children's Publishing.

Garnvin, Rebecka. Eli - the Bi-Polar Bear. Liddle, Sharon. Maximilian Press Staff, ed. deluxe ed. 2003. 76p. (J). (gr. 1-4). 29.95 *(978-1-930211-49-0(X))* Maximilian Pr. Pubs.

Garoche, Camille. Pillowland. Berkner, Laurie. 2017. (ENG.). 32p. (J). (gr. -1-3). 17.99 *(978-1-4814-6467-3(1)*, Simon & Schuster Bks. For Young Readers) Simon & Schuster Bks. For Young Readers.

Garofalo, Gianluca. Hurricane Hunters & Tornado Chasers. Jeffrey, Gary. 2008. (Graphic Careers Ser.). (ENG.). 48p. (gr. 5-8). per. 14.05 *(978-1-4042-1459-0(3))*; (YA). lib. bdg. 35.45 *(978-1-4042-1458-3(5))* Rosen Publishing Group, Inc., The.

Garofoli, Viviana. Are You Living? A Song about Living & Nonliving Things, 1 vol. Salas, Laura Purdie. 2009. (Science Songs Ser.). (ENG.). 24p. (J). (gr. 1-3). lib. bdg. 27.32 *(978-1-4048-5302-7(2)*, Picture Window Bks.) Capstone.

—Ducks Go Vroom. Kohuth, Jane. 2011. (Step into Reading Ser.). 32p. (J). (gr. -1-1). pap. 4.99 *(978-0-375-86560-2(8)*, Random Hse. Bks. for Young Readers) Random Hse. Children's Bks.

—Firefighters! Speeding! Spraying! Saving!, 0 vols. Hubbell, Patricia. (ENG.). 32p. (J). (gr. -1-2). 2012. pap. 7.99 *(978-0-7614-6245-3(7)*, 9780761462453); 2009. bds. 7.99 *(978-0-7614-5615-5(5)*, 9780761456155) Amazon Publishing. (Two Lions).

—Hanukkah Is Coming!, Vol. Newman, Tracy. 2015. (ENG.). 12p. (J). (gr. -1 — 1). bds. 5.99 *(978-1-4677-5241-1(X)*, 9781467752411, Kar-Ben Publishing) Lerner Publishing Group.

—Havdalah Is Coming!, Vol. Newman, Tracy. 2020. (ENG.). 12p. (J). (gr. -1 — 1). bds. 6.99 *(978-1-5415-2163-6(3)*, Kar-Ben Publishing) Lerner Publishing Group.

—Home on the Earth: A Song about Earth's Layers, 1 vol. Salas, Laura Purdie. 2009. (Science Songs Ser.). (ENG.). 24p. (J). (gr. 1-3). lib. bdg. 27.32 *(978-1-4048-5296-9(4)*, Picture Window Bks.) Capstone.

—I Can Save the Earth! One Little Monster Learns to Reduce, Reuse, & Recycle. Inches, Alison. 2008. (Little Green Bks.). (ENG.). 24p. (J). (gr. -1-1). pap. 4.99 *(978-1-4169-6789-7(3)*, Little Simon) Little Simon.

—I Can Save the Ocean! The Little Green Monster Cleans up the Beach. Inches, Alison. 2010. (Little Green Bks.). (ENG.). 24p. (J). (gr. -1-1). 9.99 *(978-1-4169-9514-2(5)*, Little Simon) Little Simon.

—Ma! There's Nothing to Do Here! A Word from Your Baby-in-Waiting. Park, Barbara. 2008. (Picture Book Ser.). (ENG.). 40p. (J). (gr. -1-2). 15.99 *(978-0-375-83852-1(X)*, Random Hse. Bks. for Young Readers) Random Hse. Children's Bks.

—Meet Einstein. Kleiner, Mariela. 2011. 28p. (J). (gr. -1-1). lib. bdg. *(978-0-615-31579-9(8))* Meet Bks., LLC.

—My Big Rig, 0 vols. London, Jonathan. 2013. (ENG.). 32p. (J). (gr. -1-3). pap. 9.99 *(978-1-4778-1673-8(9)*, 9781477816738, Two Lions) Amazon Publishing.

—My Little Golden Book about Abraham Lincoln. Bader, Bonnie. 2016. (Little Golden Book Ser.). 24p. (J). (-k). 4.99 *(978-1-101-93971-0(0)*, Golden Bks.) Random Hse. Children's Bks.

—My Little Golden Book about George Washington. Houran, Lori Haskins. 2016. (Little Golden Book Ser.). 24p. (J). (-k). 4.99 *(978-1-101-93969-7(9)*, Golden Bks.) Random Hse. Children's Bks.

—My Little Golden Book about the Statue of Liberty. Arena, Jen. 2018. (Little Golden Book Ser.). 24p. (J). (-k). 4.99 *(978-1-5247-7033-4(7)*, Golden Bks.) Random Hse. Children's Bks.

—My Race into Space! A Water Wonder Book. Auerbach, Annie. 2005. 18p. (J). 9.95 *(978-1-58117-351-2(2)*, Intervisual/Piggy Toes) Bendon, Inc.

—Night Night Sleep Tight. Wolf, Jackie. 2004. 10p. (J). (gr. -1-18). bds. 5.99 *(978-1-57151-734-0(0))* Playhouse Publishing.

Garófoli, Viviana. Ouch Moments: When Words Hurt. Genhart, Michael. 2015. 32p. (J). *(978-1-4338-1961-2(9),* Magination Pr.) American Psychological Assn.

Garofoli, Viviana. Passover Is Coming! Newman, Tracy. ed. 2016. (ENG.). 12p. (J). (gr. -1 — 1). E-Book 23.99 *(978-1-4677-9610-1(7));* Vol. bds. 5.99 *(978-1-4677-5242-8(8),* 9781467752428) Lerner Publishing Group. (Kar-Ben Publishing).

—Purim Is Coming! Newman, Tracy. ed. 2017. (ENG.). 12p. (J). (gr. -1 — 1). E-Book 23.99 *(978-1-5124-2725-7(X),* 9781512427257); Vol. bds. 5.99 *(978-1-5124-0827-0(1),* 9781512408270) Lerner Publishing Group. (Kar-Ben Publishing).

—Rosh Hashanah Is Coming! Newman, Tracy. ed. 2016. (ENG.). 12p. (J). (gr. -1 — 1). E-Book 23.99 *(978-1-5124-0945-1(6));* Vol. bds., bds. 5.99 *(978-1-4677-7988-3(1),* 9781467779883) Lerner Publishing Group. (Kar-Ben Publishing).

—Shabbat Is Coming!, Vol. Newman, Tracy. 2014. (ENG.). 12p. (J). (gr. -1 — 1). bds. 5.99 *(978-1-4677-1367-2(8),* 9781467713672, Kar-Ben Publishing) Lerner Publishing Group.

—Simchat Torah Is Coming!, Vol. Newman, Tracy. 2018. (ENG.). 12p. (J). (gr. -1 — 1). bds. 5.99 *(978-1-5124-2100-2(6),* Kar-Ben Publishing) Lerner Publishing Group.

—The Spooky Smells of Halloween. Man-Kong, Mary. 2005. (Scented Storybook Ser.). 32p. (J). (gr. -1-2). 8.99 *(978-0-375-83285-7(8),* Golden Bks.) Random Hse. Children's Bks.

—Sukkot Is Coming!, Vol. Newman, Tracy. 2017. (ENG.). 12p. (J). (gr. -1 — 1). bds. 5.99 *(978-1-5124-0828-7(X),* 9781512408287, Kar-Ben Publishing) Lerner Publishing Group.

—Tu B'Shevat Is Coming!, Vol. Newman, Tracy. 2017. (ENG.). 12p. (J). (gr. -1 — 1). bds. 5.99 *(978-1-5124-2676-2(8),* 9781512426762, Kar-Ben Publishing) Lerner Publishing Group.

—The White House. Arena, Jen. 2019. (Little Golden Book Ser.). 24p. (J). (-k). 4.99 *(978-0-525-58233-5(9),* Golden Bks.) Random Hse. Children's Bks.

Garófoli, Viviana. Why Am I Blue? A Story about Being Yourself. Dakos, Kalli. 2017. 32p. (J). 15.95 *(978-1-4338-2734-1(4),* Magination Pr.) American Psychological Assn.

Garofoli, Viviana. Zoom, Zoom, Zoom. Hall, Kirsten. 2004. (My First Reader Ser.). (ENG.). 32p. (J). (gr. k-1). pap. 3.95 *(978-0-516-25509-5(6),* Children's Pr.) Scholastic Library Publishing.

Garratt, Richard. Agricultural & Urban Areas. Moore, Peter D. 2006. (Biomes of the Earth Ser.). 240p. (gr. 6-12). 39.50 *(978-0-8160-5326-1(X))* Facts On File, Inc.

—Atmosphere: A Scientific History of Air, Weather, & Climate. Allaby, Michael. 2009. (Discovering the Earth Ser.). 242p. (C). (gr. 9-18). 39.95 *(978-0-8160-6098-6(3))* Facts On File, Inc.

—Deserts. Allaby, Michael. 2006. (Biomes of the Earth Ser.). 272p. (gr. 6-12). 39.50 *(978-0-8160-5320-9(0))* Facts On File, Inc.

—Earth Science: A Scientific History of the Solid Earth. Allaby, Michael. 2009. (Discovering the Earth Ser.). 224p. (C). (gr. 9-18). 39.95 *(978-0-8160-6097-9(5))* Facts On File, Inc.

—Ecology: Plants, Animals, & the Environment. Allaby, Michael. 2009. (Discovering the Earth Ser.). 256p. (C). (gr. 9-18). 39.95 *(978-0-8160-6100-6(9))* Facts On File, Inc.

—Grasslands. Allaby, Michael. 2006. (Biomes of the Earth Ser.). 288p. (gr. 6-12). 39.50 *(978-0-8160-5323-0(5))* Facts On File, Inc.

—Lakes & Rivers. Day, Trevor. 2006. (Biomes of the Earth Ser.). 272p. (gr. 6-12). 39.50 *(978-0-8160-5328-5(6))* Facts On File, Inc.

—Oceans. Day, Trevor. 2006. (Biomes of the Earth Ser.). 272p. (gr. 6-12). 39.50 *(978-0-8160-5327-8(8))* Facts On File, Inc.

—Oceans: A Scientific History of Oceans & Marine Life. Allaby, Michael. 2009. (Discovering the Earth Ser.). 208p. (J). (gr. 9-18). 39.95 *(978-0-8160-6099-3(1))* Facts On File, Inc.

—Plants. Allaby, Michael. 2010. (Discovering the Earth Ser.). 240p. (C). (gr. 9-18). 39.95 *(978-0-8160-6102-0(5))* Facts On File, Inc.

—Taiga. Day, Trevor. 2006. (Biomes of the Earth Ser.). 240p. (gr. 6-12). 39.50 *(978-0-8160-5329-2(4))* Facts On File, Inc.

—Temperate Forests. Allaby, Michael. 2006. (Biomes of the Earth Ser.). 288p. (J). (gr. 6-12). 39.50 *(978-0-8160-5321-6(9))* Facts On File, Inc.

—Tropical Forests. Allaby, Michael. 2006. (Biomes of the Earth Ser.). 288p. (gr. 6-12). 39.50 *(978-0-8160-5322-3(7))* Facts On File, Inc.

—Tundra. Moore, Peter D. (Ecosystems Ser.). 2007. 224p. (C). (gr. 9). 70.00 *(978-0-8160-5933-1(0));* 2006. 240p. (gr. 6-12). 39.50 *(978-0-8160-5325-4(1))* Facts On File, Inc.

—Wetlands. Moore, Peter D. (Biomes of the Earth Ser.). 2006. 240p. (gr. 6-12). 39.50 *(978-0-8160-5324-7(3));* 2nd rev. ed. 2007. 256p. (C). (gr. 9-12). 70.00 *(978-0-8160-5931-7(4))* Facts On File, Inc.

Garraway, Kym. A Mississippi Summer on Bluebird Hill: A True Story about Our Little Farm in the Hills of Southern Mississippi. Remson, Billie. 2005. (J). pap. 12.95 *(978-1-59571-073-4(6))* Word Association Pubs.

—A Mississippi Winter on Bluebird Hill: A True Story about Our Little Farm in the Hills of Southern Mississippi. Remson, Billie. 2004. (J). per. 12.95 *(978-1-59571-044-4(2))* Word Association Pubs.

Garraway, Kym W. A Mississippi Spring on Bluebird Hill. Remson, Billie. 2004. per. 12.95 *(978-1-59571-004-8(3))* Word Association Pubs.

Garren, Kathy. Me & My Goose. Guthrie, Arlo. 2014. (ENG.). (J). 15.00 *(978-0-9915370-6-8(8))* Rising Son International, Ltd.

Garres, Rafa & Dauterman, Russell. Mighty Thor Vol. 2: Lords of Midgard. 2017. (ENG.). 160p. (YA). (gr. 8-17). pap. 19.99 *(978-0-7851-9966-3(7))* Marvel Worldwide, Inc.

Garretson, Jerri & Dollar, Diane A. Kansas Tall Tales: Tenth Anniversary Anthology. Garretson, Jerri. 2008. 106p. (J). pap. 19.95 *(978-0-9659712-7-0(9))* Ravenstone Pr.

Garrett, Caroline S. Mushroom's Day Away. Ledbetter, Penny S. 2005. 32p. (J). 9.95 *(978-1-933251-19-6(0))* Parkway Pubs., Inc.

Garrett, Caroline S. Jeremiah. Garrett, Caroline S., tr. Underhill, Marjorie Fay. 2003. (J). 12.00 *(978-1-887905-75-6(8))* Parkway Pubs., Inc.

Garrett, De'coriyanna & Hope, Marie. Learning from Rose: (Rose Teaches Bully a Lesson) 2019. (Learning from Rose Ser.: Vol. 1). (ENG.). 42p. (J). pap. 9.99 ***(978-1-7245-1041-9(X))*** CreateSpace Independent Publishing Platform.

Garrett, Jooce. Basel's Hidden Stories: A Child's Active Guide to Basel's Old Town. Darling, Jeanne. 2017. (ENG.). 47p. (J). 21.00 *(978-3-03869-004-7(X))* Bergli Bks. CHE. Dist: ISD.

Garrett, Keith. Hooty & Pig: The Missing Christmas Pudding. Williams, Mark. 2013. 24p. pap. *(978-1-78132-133-1(7))* SilverWood Bks.

Garrett, Myers. Meet the Super Sisters. Moore, Mykela. 2013. (J). 9.99 *(978-0-9852746-9-6(7))* Hope of Vision Publishing.

—Theo the Thief with Zoom-Boom & Buttons the Bullfrog. Brown, Joel. 2018. (Zoom-Boom & the Scarecrow & Friends Ser.: 7). (ENG.). 30p. (J). (gr. k-3). pap. 12.95 *(978-1-946683-20-5(5));* 17.99 *(978-1-946683-12-0(4))* Rapier Publishing Co., LLC.

Garrett, Scott. Always Watch Out for the Flying Potato Salad! #9. Winkler, Henry & Oliver, Lin. 2017. (Here's Hank Ser.: 9). 128p. (J). (gr. 1-3). 5.99 *(978-1-101-99583-9(1),* Penguin Workshop) Penguin Young Readers Group.

Garrett, Scott. The Anti-Boredom Book of Brilliant Outdoor Things to Do: Games, Crafts, Puzzles, Jokes, Riddles, & Trivia for Hours of Fun. Seed, Andy. 2020. (Anti-Boredom Bks.). (ENG.). 160p. (J). pap. 7.99 ***(978-1-5107-5483-6(0),*** Sky Pony Pr.) Skyhorse Publishing Co., Inc.

Garrett, Scott. The Anti-Boredom Book of Brilliant Things to Do: Games, Crafts, Puzzles, Jokes, Riddles, & Trivia for Hours of Fun. Seed, Andy. 2020. (Anti-Boredom Bks.). (ENG.). 160p. (J). pap. 7.99 *(978-1-5107-5484-3(9),* Sky Pony Pr.) Skyhorse Publishing Co., Inc.

—The Anti-Boredom Christmas Book: Games, Crafts, Puzzles, Jokes, Riddles, & Carols for Hours of Family Fun. Seed, Andy. 2019. (Anti-Boredom Bks.). (ENG.). 168p. (J). pap. 7.99 *(978-1-5107-5470-6(9),* Sky Pony Pr.) Skyhorse Publishing Co., Inc.

—Bookmarks Are People Too! #1. Winkler, Henry & Oliver, Lin. 2014. (Here's Hank Ser.: 1). (ENG.). 128p. (J). (gr. 1-3). 14.99 *(978-0-448-48239-2(8),* Grosset & Dunlap);No. 1. 5.99 *(978-0-448-47997-2(4),* Penguin Workshop) Penguin Young Readers Group.

—Everybody Is Somebody #12. Winkler, Henry & Oliver, Lin. 2019. (Here's Hank Ser.: 12). 128p. (J). (gr. 1-3). (ENG.). 6.99 *(978-0-515-15719-2(8));* 14.99 *(978-0-515-15720-8(1))* Penguin Young Readers Group. (Penguin Workshop).

—Fake Snakes & Weird Wizards #4. Winkler, Henry & Oliver, Lin. 2015. (Here's Hank Ser.: 4). (ENG.). 128p. (J). (gr. 1-3). 6.99 *(978-0-448-48252-1(5),* Penguin Workshop) Penguin Young Readers Group.

—Hooray! My Butt Left the Bench! #10. Winkler, Henry & Oliver, Lin. 2017. (Here's Hank Ser.: 10). 128p. (J). (gr. 1-3). 5.99 *(978-1-101-99586-0(6));* 14.99 *(978-1-101-99587-7(4))* Penguin Young Readers Group. (Penguin Workshop).

Garrett, Scott. How Can I Help the World? Inspiring Stories & Practical Ideas to Help You Join in with Saving Our Planet. Alexander, Jenny. 2019. (ENG.). 134p. (J). pap. ***(978-1-910300-27-5(6))*** Five Lanes Pr.

Garrett, Scott. How to Hug an Elephant #6. Winkler, Henry & Oliver, Lin. 2015. (Here's Hank Ser.: 6). 128p. (J). (gr. 1-3). bds. 14.99 *(978-0-448-48657-4(1));* bds. 5.99 *(978-0-448-48656-7(3))* Penguin Young Readers Group. (Grosset & Dunlap).

—A Short Tale about a Long Dog #2. Winkler, Henry & Oliver, Lin. 2014. (Here's Hank Ser.: 2). (ENG.). 128p. (J). (gr. 1-3). 14.99 *(978-0-448-48240-8(1),* Grosset & Dunlap);No. 2. 5.99 *(978-0-448-47998-9(2),* Penguin Workshop) Penguin Young Readers Group.

—The Silly Book of Sidesplitting Stuff. Seed, Andy. 2015. (ENG.). 160p. (J). (gr. 2-4). pap. 9.99 *(978-1-61963-794-8(4),* 900148772, Bloomsbury Activity Bks.) Bloomsbury Publishing USA.

—The Soggy, Foggy Campout #8, Vol. 8. Winkler, Henry & Oliver, Lin. 2016. (Here's Hank Ser.: 8). 128p. (J). (gr. 1-3). 5.99 *(978-0-448-48660-4(1),* Grosset & Dunlap) Penguin Young Readers Group.

—Stop That Frog! #3. Winkler, Henry & Oliver, Lin. 2014. (Here's Hank Ser.: 3). 128p. (J). (gr. 1-3). 5.99 *(978-0-448-48152-4(9),* Penguin Workshop); 14.99 *(978-0-448-48241-5(X),* Grosset & Dunlap) Penguin Young Readers Group.

—There's a Zombie in My Bathtub #5. Oliver, Lin & Winkler, Henry. 2015. (Here's Hank Ser.: 5). (ENG.). 128p. (J). (gr. 1-3). 5.99 *(978-0-448-48512-6(5),* Grosset & Dunlap) Penguin Young Readers Group.

—You Can't Drink a Meatball Through a Straw #7. Winkler, Henry & Oliver, Lin. 2016. (Here's Hank Ser.: 7). 128p. (J). (gr. 1-3). 6.99 *(978-0-448-48658-1(X),* Grosset & Dunlap) Penguin Young Readers Group.

Garrett, Toni. The Last Voyage of the Dan-D. Alston, E. B. l.t. ed. 2003. 47p. (J). per. 8.00 *(978-0-9747735-0-6(6))* Righter Publishing Co., Inc.

Garrigue, Roland. How to Defeat Dragons. Leblanc, Catherine. 2014. (ENG.). 32p. (J). (gr. -1). pap. 8.99 *(978-1-60887-412-5(5))* Insight Editions.

—How to Demolish Dinosaurs. Leblanc, Catherine. 2013. (ENG.). 32p. (J). (gr. -1). 14.99 *(978-1-60887-191-9(6))* Insight Editions.

—How to Get Rid of Ghosts. Leblanc, Catherine. 2013. (ENG.). 32p. (J). (gr. -1). 14.99 *(978-1-60887-195-7(9))* Insight Editions.

—How to Mash Monsters. Leblanc, Catherine. 2013. (ENG.). 32p. (J). (gr. -1). 14.99 *(978-1-60887-190-2(8))* Insight Editions.

—How to Outwit Witches. Leblanc, Catherine. 2013. (ENG.). 32p. (J). (gr. -1). 14.99 *(978-1-60887-193-3(2))* Insight Editions.

—How to Pulverize Pirates. Leblanc, Catherine. 2013. (ENG.). 32p. (J). (gr. -1). 14.99 *(978-1-60887-192-6(4))* Insight Editions.

—How to Ward off Wolves. Leblanc, Catherine. 2013. (ENG.). 32p. (J). (gr. -1). 14.99 *(978-1-60887-194-0(0))* Insight Editions.

—Mother Ghost: Nursery Rhymes for Little Monsters. Kolar, Rachel. 2018. (ENG.). 32p. (J). (gr. k-2). 16.99 *(978-1-58536-392-6(8),* 204588) Sleeping Bear Pr.

—My Monster-Mashing Activity Book. Leblanc, Catherine. 2016. (ENG.). 80p. (J). (gr. -1). pap., act. bk. ed. 14.99 *(978-1-60887-710-2(8))* Insight Editions.

Garrigue, Roland. Princess Kevin. Escoffier, Michaël. 2020. (ENG.). 32p. (J). (gr. -1-2). 18.99 ***(978-0-7112-5435-0(4),*** Frances Lincoln Children's Bks.) Quarto Publishing Group UK GBR. Dist: Hachette Bk. Group.

Garris, Norma. The Story of Christmas. 2013. (Happy Day Ser.). (ENG.). 16p. (J). pap. 2.49 *(978-1-4143-9524-1(8),* 4608514) Tyndale Hse. Pubs.

Garrison, Barbara. Another Celebrated Dancing Bear. Scheffrin-Falk, Gladys. (J). 2007. 32p. (gr. -1-3). 18.95 *(978-1-930900-35-6(X));* 20th ed. 2011. 28p. 18.95 *(978-1-930900-50-9(3))* Purple Hse. Pr.

Garrison, Betty. Mike Mascot of the Marines. Alvarez, Gene. 2018. (ENG.). 46p. (J). (gr. k-6). pap. 11.95 *(978-1-61493-612-1(9))* Peppertree Pr., The.

Garrison, Carri. Making the Message Mine. Morgan, Marlo. Grimme, Jeannette, ed. Date not set. 115p. (Orig.). (YA). pap. *(978-1-883473-01-3(2))* MM Co.

Garrison, Ron, jt. illus. see Bohn, Ken.

Garrison, Sue. Willy: The Little Jeep Who Wanted to Be a Fire Truck. Estes, Don. 2003. 46p. (J). lib. bdg. 14.95 *(978-1-883551-47-6(1),* ASP-471, Attic Studio Pr.) Attic Studio Publishing Hse.

Garrity-Riley, Kelsey. Born to Ride: A Story about Bicycle Face. Theule, Larissa. 2019. (ENG.). 32p. (J). (gr. -1-3). 17.99 *(978-1-4197-3412-0(1),* Abrams Bks. for Young Readers) Abrams, Inc.

—Goldie Takes a Stand! Golda Meir's First Crusade. Krasner, Barbara. 2014. (ENG.). 32p. (J). (gr. k-4). 17.95 *(978-1-4677-1200-2(0))* Lerner Publishing Group.

—Goldie Takes a Stand: Golda Meir's First Crusade, Vol. Krasner, Barbara. 2014. (ENG.). 32p. (J). (gr. k-4). 7.95 *(978-1-4677-1201-9(9),* 9781467712019, Kar-Ben Publishing) Lerner Publishing Group.

Garrity-Riley, Kelsey. You Are a Beautiful Beginning. Laden, Nina. 2020. (ENG.). 40p. (J). 18.99 ***(978-1-250-31183-2(7),*** 900199041) Roaring Brook Pr.

Garron, Javier. Ant-Man & the Wasp: Lost & Found. 2018. (Ant-Man & the Wasp (2018) Ser.: 1). (ENG.). 112p. (YA). (gr. 8-17). pap. 15.99 *(978-0-7851-9462-0(2))* Marvel Worldwide, Inc.

—Miles Morales: Spider-Man Vol. 1: Straight Out of Brooklyn. 2019. 136p. (YA). (gr. 4-17). pap. 17.99 *(978-1-302-91478-3(2))* Marvel Worldwide, Inc.

Garron, Javier. Miles Morales: Spider-Man Vol. 3: Family Business. 2020. (ENG.). 136p. (J). (gr. 4-17). pap. 15.99 ***(978-1-302-92016-6(2))*** Marvel Worldwide, Inc.

Garron, Javier. Secret Warriors Vol. 1: Secret Empire, Vol. 1. 2017. (ENG.). 112p. (YA). (gr. 8-17). pap. 15.99 *(978-1-302-90692-4(5))* Marvel Worldwide, Inc.

Garrow, Linda. Planets, Moons, & Stars. Evert, Laura. 2003. (Take along Guides). (ENG.). 48p. (J). (gr. 2-5). pap. 7.95 *(978-1-55971-842-4(0))* Cooper Square Publishing Llc.

Garry, Jerilynn. Little Purple Gets Lost. Coryell, Kelly. 2016. (ENG.). (J). (gr. 1-3). pap. 11.95 *(978-0-9855233-4-3(4))* Sunshine53 Pr.

—Little Purple Helps a Friend. Coryell, Kelly. 2017. (ENG.). 26p. (J). 24.95 *(978-1-4958-1390-0(8))* Infinity Publishing.

—Little Purple Plays Soccer. Coryell, Kelly. 2016. (Adventures of Little Purple Ser.: Vol. 3). (ENG.). (J). (gr. k-2). pap. 19.99 *(978-0-9855233-1-2(X))* Sunshine53 Pr.

Garson, Sarah. Alfie's Angels. Barkow, Henriette. 2004. 32p. (J). (FRE & ENG.). pap. *(978-1-85269-977-2(9));* (ENG & PAN.). pap. *(978-1-85269-997-0(3))* Mantra Lingua.

—Alfie's Angels: Big Book English Only. Barkow, Henriette. 2004. 30p. (J). *(978-1-84444-119-8(9))* Mantra Lingua.

Garson, Sarah. One, Two, Cockatoo! Garson, Sarah. 2012. 32p. (J). (gr. k — 1). pap. 10.99 *(978-1-84270-944-3(5))* Andersen Pr. GBR. Dist: Independent Pubs. Group.

Gartier, Monica & Sulik, Alberta. Molly & Tim's Zooventure. Mancuso, Kathleen. 2018. (ENG.). 32p. (J). pap. 12.95 *(978-1-7324191-5-5(9))* No Frills Buffalo.

Gartner, Kathleen. Uncle Willy's Tickles: A Child's Right to Say No. Aboff, Marcie. 2nd ed. 2003. 32p. (J). 14.95 *(978-1-55798-998-7(2));* pap. 9.95 *(978-1-55798-999-4(0))* American Psychological Assn. (Magination Pr.).

Garton, Michael. Ava & the Big Ouch: A Book about Feeling Better, Vol. Bell, Lucy. 2018. (Frolic First Faith Ser.). (ENG.). 32p. (J). (gr. -1-3). 12.99 *(978-1-5064-2504-7(6),* Sparkhouse Family) Augsburg Fortress, Pubs.

—Ava y el Picnic Raquitico. Carr, Elias. 2016. (SPA.). (J). *(978-1-5064-2095-0(8))* Augsburg Fortress, Pubs.

Garton, Michael. Dino Potty: Learn to Potty with Dino. Conway, Sara. 2019. (ENG.). 18p. (J). (gr. -1-k). bds. 7.99 ***(978-1-926444-50-5(7))*** Rainstorm Pr.

Garton, Michael. Dios No Creo Todos. McCurry, Kristen & Hilton, Jennifer. 2016. (SPA.). (J). *(978-1-5064-2092-9(3))* Augsburg Fortress, Pubs.

—Hal & the Prickle Problem: A Book about Doing Your Part, Vol. Bell, Lucy. 2018. (Frolic First Faith Ser.). (ENG.). 32p. (J). (gr. -1-3). 12.99 *(978-1-5064-3970-9(5),* Sparkhouse Family) Augsburg Fortress, Pubs.

—Hal y el Nuevo Compañero. Carr, Elias. 2016. (SPA.). (J). *(978-1-5064-2098-1(2))* Augsburg Fortress, Pubs.

—Harry & the Horse. Graves, Sue. 2011. (Tadpoles Ser.). (ENG.). (J). (gr. -1-3). lib. bdg. 17.55 *(978-1-61383-944-7(8))* Perfection Learning Corp.

—Jo & the Not-So-Little Lie: A Book about Telling the Truth, Vol. Bell, Lucy. 2018. (Frolic First Faith Ser.). (ENG.). 32p. (J). (gr. -1-3). 12.99 *(978-1-5064-2503-0(8),* Sparkhouse Family) Augsburg Fortress, Pubs.

—Jo y la Sopa Lenta. Carr, Elias. 2016. (SPA.). (J). *(978-1-5064-2097-4(4),* Sparkhouse Pr.) Spark Hse.

—Ora a Dios. Hilton, Jennifer Sue & McCurry, Kristen. 2016. (SPA.). (J). *(978-1-5064-2093-6(1))* Augsburg Fortress, Pubs.

—Rufus & the Scary Storm: A Book about Being Brave, Vol. Bell, Lucy. 2018. (Frolic First Faith Ser.). (ENG.). 32p. (J). (gr. -1-3). 12.99 *(978-1-5064-3971-6(3),* Sparkhouse Family) Augsburg Fortress, Pubs.

—Rufus Loses His Cape: A Book about Asking for Help, Vol. Bell, Lucy J. 2017. (ENG.). (J). 12.99 *(978-1-5064-1788-2(4),* Sparkhouse Family) Augsburg Fortress, Pubs.

—Rufus y Su Cola Enojada. Carr, Elias. 2016. (SPA.). (J). *(978-1-5064-2096-7(6))* Augsburg Fortress, Pubs.

—Uri & the Busy Day: A Book about Feeling Overwhelmed, Vol. Bell, Lucy J. 2017. (ENG.). (J). 12.99 *(978-1-5064-1787-5(6),* Sparkhouse Family) Augsburg Fortress, Pubs.

—Whose Nose? Tarsky, Sue. 2019. (Whose Are These? Ser.). (ENG.). 24p. (J). (gr. -1-3). 15.99 *(978-0-8075-9046-1(0),* 807590460) Whitman, Albert & Co.

—Whose Tail? Tarsky, Sue. 2019. (Whose Are These? Ser.). (ENG.). 24p. (J). (gr. -1-3). 15.99 *(978-0-8075-9045-4(2),* 807590452) Whitman, Albert & Co.

Garton, Sam. Otter: Hello, Sea Friends! 2016. 32p. (J). *(978-1-5182-2257-3(9),* Balzer & Bray) HarperCollins Pubs.

—Otter: Let's Go Swimming! 2017. 32p. (J). *(978-1-5182-4207-6(3),* Balzer & Bray) HarperCollins Pubs.

Garton, Sam. I Am Otter. Garton, Sam. 2014. (ENG.). 32p. (J). (gr. -1-3). 16.99 *(978-0-06-224775-9(1))* HarperCollins Pubs.

—I Am Otter Board Book. Garton, Sam. 2016. (ENG.). 34p. (J). (gr. -1 — 1). bds. 7.99 *(978-0-06-240908-9(5))* HarperCollins Pubs.

—Otter Goes to School. Garton, Sam. 2016. (ENG.). 32p. (J). (gr. -1-3). 17.99 *(978-0-06-235225-5(3))* HarperCollins Pubs.

—Otter: Hello, Sea Friends! Garton, Sam. 2016. (My First I Can Read Ser.). (ENG.). 32p. (J). (gr. -1-3). pap. 4.99 *(978-0-06-236660-3(2),* Balzer & Bray) HarperCollins Pubs.

—Otter: I Love Books! Garton, Sam. 2019. (My First I Can Read Ser.). (ENG.). 32p. (J). (gr. -1-3). 16.99 *(978-0-06-284508-5(X),* Balzer & Bray) HarperCollins Pubs.

—Otter in Space. Garton, Sam. 2015. (ENG.). 32p. (J). (gr. -1-3). 16.99 *(978-0-06-224776-6(X))* HarperCollins Pubs.

—Otter: Let's Go Swimming! Garton, Sam. 2017. (My First I Can Read Ser.). (ENG.). 32p. (J). (gr. -1-3). pap. 4.99 *(978-0-06-236663-4(7))* HarperCollins Pubs.

—Otter Loves Easter! Garton, Sam. 2017. (ENG.). 32p. (J). (gr. -1-3). 9.99 *(978-0-06-236667-2(X))* HarperCollins Pubs.

—Otter Loves Halloween! Garton, Sam. 2015. (ENG.). 32p. (J). (gr. -1-3). 9.99 *(978-0-06-236666-5(1),* Balzer & Bray) HarperCollins Pubs.

—Otter: Oh No, Bath Time! Garton, Sam. 2016. (My First I Can Read Ser.). (ENG.). 32p. (J). (gr. -1-3). pap. 4.99 *(978-0-06-236657-3(2),* Balzer & Bray) HarperCollins Pubs.

—Otter: the Best Job Ever! Garton, Sam. 2016. (My First I Can Read Ser.). (ENG.). 32p. (J). (gr. -1-3). pap. 4.99 *(978-0-06-236654-2(8),* Balzer & Bray) HarperCollins Pubs.

—Otter: What Pet Is Best? Garton, Sam. 2019. (My First I Can Read Ser.). (ENG.). 32p. (J). (gr. -1-3). 16.99 *(978-0-06-284513-9(6));* pap. 4.99 *(978-0-06-284512-2(8))* HarperCollins Pubs. (Balzer & Bray).

Garvey, Brann. Advice about Family: Claudia Cristina Cortez Uncomplicates Your Life. Gallagher, Diana G. 2010. (Claudia Cristina Cortez Ser.). (ENG.). 80p. (J). (gr. 4-8). pap. 6.10 *(978-1-4342-2250-3(0),* Stone Arch Bks.) Capstone.

—Advice about Friends: Claudia Cristina Cortez Uncomplicates Your Life. Gallagher, Diana G. 2010. (Claudia Cristina Cortez Ser.). (ENG.). 80p. (J). (gr. 4-8). pap. 6.10 *(978-1-4342-2251-0(9),* Stone Arch Bks.) Capstone.

—Advice about School: Claudia Cristina Cortez Uncomplicates Your Life. Gallagher, Diana G. 2010. (Claudia Cristina Cortez Ser.). (ENG.). 80p. (J). (gr. 4-8). pap. 6.10 *(978-1-4342-2252-7(7));* 26.65 *(978-1-4342-1905-3(4))* Capstone. (Stone Arch Bks.).

—Advice about Work & Play: Claudia Cristina Cortez Uncomplicates Your Life. Gallagher, Diana G. 2010. (Claudia Cristina Cortez Ser.). (ENG.). 80p. (J). (gr. 4-8). pap. 6.10 *(978-1-4342-2253-4(5),* Stone Arch Bks.) Capstone.

—¿Amigas para Siempre? La Complicada Vida de Claudia Cristina Cortez. Gallagher, Diana G. 2019. (Claudia Cristina Cortez en Español Ser.). (SPA.). 88p. (J). (gr. 4-8). pap. 6.95 *(978-1-4965-8585-1(2),* 141318); lib. bdg. 26.65 *(978-1-4965-8544-8(5),* 141293) Capstone. (Stone Arch Bks.).

—Beach Blues: The Complicated Life of Claudia Cristina Cortez, 1 vol. Gallagher, Diana G. 2008. (Claudia Cristina Cortez Ser.). (ENG.). 88p. (J). (gr. 4-8). pap. 6.10 *(978-1-4342-0869-9(9),* Stone Arch Bks.) Capstone.

—Beware! The Complicated Life of Claudia Cristina Cortez, 1 vol. Gallagher, Diana G. 2009. (Claudia Cristina Cortez

Ser.). (ENG.). 88p. (J). (gr. 4-8). 26.65 *(978-1-4342-1575-8(X)*, Stone Arch Bks.) Capstone.
—Boy Trouble: The Complicated Life of Claudia Cristina Cortez. Gallagher, Diana G. 2009. (Claudia Cristina Cortez Ser.). (ENG.). 88p. (J). (gr. 4-8). pap. 6.10 *(978-1-4342-1757-8(4)*, Stone Arch Bks.) Capstone.
—Camp Can't: The Complicated Life of Claudia Cristina Cortez, 1 vol. Gallagher, Diana G. 2007. (Claudia Cristina Cortez Ser.). (ENG.). 88p. (J). (gr. 4-8). per. 6.10 *(978-1-59889-878-1(7)*, Stone Arch Bks.) Capstone.
Garvey, Brann. Campamento lo Siento: La Complicada Vida de Claudia Cristina Cortez. Gallagher, Diana G. 2020. (Claudia Cristina Cortez en Español Ser.).Tr. of Camp Can't: the Complicated Life of Claudia Cristina Cortez. (SPA.). 88p. (J). (gr. 4-8). pap. 6.95 ***(978-1-4965-9968-1(3)***, 201661); lib. bdg. 26.65 ***(978-1-4965-9806-6(7)***, 200694) Capstone. (Stone Arch Bks.).
—Claudia Cristina Cortez en Español. Gallagher, Diana G. (Claudia Cristina Cortez en Español Ser.).Tr. of Claudia Cristina Cortez. (SPA.). (J). (gr. 4-8). 2020. 213.20 ***(978-1-4965-9828-8(8)***, 200728); 2020. pap., pap., pap. 55.60 ***(978-1-5158-7347-1(1)***, 201804); 2019. 106.60 *(978-1-4965-8570-7(4)*, 29719); 2019. pap., pap., pap. 27.80 *(978-1-4965-8595-0(X)*, 29735) Capstone. (Stone Arch Bks.).
—El Club ¡lo Que Sea! La Complicada Vida de Claudia Cristina Cortez. Gallagher, Diana G. 2020. (Claudia Cristina Cortez en Español Ser.).Tr. of Whatever!: the Complicated Life of Claudia Cristina Cortez. (SPA.). 88p. (J). (gr. 4-8). pap. 6.95 ***(978-1-4965-9967-4(5)***, 201660); lib. bdg. 26.65 ***(978-1-4965-9805-9(9)***, 200691) Capstone. (Stone Arch Bks.).
Garvey, Brann. ¡Cuidado! La Complicada Vida de Claudia Cristina Cortez. Gallagher, Diana G. 2019. (Claudia Cristina Cortez en Español Ser.). (SPA.). 88p. (J). (gr. 4-8). pap. 6.95 *(978-1-4965-8584-4(4)*, 141317); lib. bdg. 26.65 *(978-1-4965-8546-2(1)*, 141295) Capstone. (Stone Arch Bks.).
—The Curse of the Wendigo: An Agate & Buck Adventure, 1 vol. Welvaert, Scott R. & Jungman, Ann. 2006. (Vortex Bks.). (ENG.). 112p. (J). (gr. 5-9). pap. 7.19 *(978-1-59889-282-6(7)*, Stone Arch Bks.) Capstone.
—Dama de la Mala Suerte: La Complicada Vida de Claudia Cristina Cortez. Gallagher, Diana G. 2019. (Claudia Cristina Cortez en Español Ser.). (SPA.). 88p. (J). (gr. 4-8). pap. 6.95 *(978-1-4965-8583-7(6)*, 141316); lib. bdg. 26.65 *(978-1-4965-8545-5(3)*, 141294) Capstone. (Stone Arch Bks.).
—Dance Trap: The Complicated Life of Claudia Cristina Cortez, 1 vol. Gallagher, Diana G. 2007. (Claudia Cristina Cortez Ser.). (ENG.). 88p. (J). (gr. 4-8). per. 6.10 *(978-1-59889-879-8(5)*, Stone Arch Bks.) Capstone.
Garvey, Brann. El Dilema Del Baile: La Complicada Vida de Claudia Cristina Cortez. Gallagher, Diana G. 2020. (Claudia Cristina Cortez en Español Ser.).Tr. of Dance Trap: the Complicated Life of Claudia Cristina Cortez. (SPA.). 88p. (J). (gr. 4-8). pap. 6.95 ***(978-1-4965-9969-8(1)***, 201662); lib. bdg. 26.65 ***(978-1-4965-9807-3(5)***, 200693) Capstone. (Stone Arch Bks.).
Garvey, Brann. Excuses! Survive & Succeed with David Mortimore Baxter. Tayleur, Karen. 2007. (David Mortimore Baxter Ser.). (ENG.). 88p. (J). (gr. 4-8). per. 6.05 *(978-1-59889-205-5(3)*, Stone Arch Bks.) Capstone.
—Famous (Scholastic) The Awesome Life of David Mortimore Baxter. Tayleur, Karen. 2009. (David Mortimore Baxter Ser.). 88p. pap. 0.80 *(978-1-4342-2503-0(8)*, Stone Arch Bks.) Capstone.
—Friends Forever? The Complicated Life of Claudia Cristina Cortez, 1 vol. Gallagher, Diana G. 2008. (Claudia Cristina Cortez Ser.). (ENG.). 88p. (J). (gr. 4-8). pap. 6.10 *(978-1-4342-0868-2(0))*; lib. bdg. 26.65 *(978-1-4342-0772-2(2))* Capstone. (Stone Arch Bks.).
—Guilty! The Complicated Life of Claudia Cristina Cortez, 1 vol. Gallagher, Diana G. 2007. (Claudia Cristina Cortez Ser.). (ENG.). 88p. (J). (gr. 4-8). per. 6.10 *(978-1-59889-881-1(7)*, Stone Arch Bks.) Capstone.
—Liar! The True Story of David Mortimore Baxter. Tayleur, Karen. 2007. (David Mortimore Baxter Ser.). (ENG.). 80p. (J). (gr. 4-8). per. 6.05 *(978-1-59889-206-2(1)*, Stone Arch Bks.) Capstone.
—Manners! Staying Out of Trouble with David Mortimore Baxter. Tayleur, Karen. 2007. (David Mortimore Baxter Ser.). (ENG.). 88p. (J). (gr. 4-8). per. 6.05 *(978-1-59889-207-9(X)*, Stone Arch Bks.) Capstone.
—The Mosquito King: An Agate & Buck Adventure, 1 vol. Welvaert, Scott R. (Vortex Bks.). (ENG.). 112p. 2008. (gr. 2-3). pap. 6.95 *(978-1-59889-923-8(6))*; 2007. (J). (gr. 5-9). 26.65 *(978-1-59889-857-6(4))* Capstone. (Stone Arch Bks.).
—Party! The Complicated Life of Claudia Cristina Cortez, 1 vol. Gallagher, Diana G. 2008. (Claudia Cristina Cortez Ser.). (ENG.). 88p. (J). (gr. 4-8). pap. 6.10 *(978-1-4342-0867-5(2))*; lib. bdg. 26.65 *(978-1-4342-0771-5(4))* Capstone. (Stone Arch Bks.).
—The Pirate, Big Fist, & Me, 1 vol. MacPhail, C. & Cosson, M. J. 2006. (Vortex Bks.). (ENG.). 112p. (J). (gr. 5-9). 7.19 *(978-1-59889-279-6(7)*, Stone Arch Bks.) Capstone.
—The Pirate, Big Fist, & Me, 1 vol. Cosson, M. J. 2006. (Vortex Bks.). (ENG.). 112p. (J). (gr. 5-9). 26.65 *(978-1-59889-068-6(9)*, Stone Arch Bks.) Capstone.
—Pool Problem: The Complicated Life of Claudia Cristina Cortez, 1 vol. Gallagher, Diana G. 2009. (Claudia Cristina Cortez Ser.). (ENG.). 88p. (J). (gr. 4-8). 26.65 *(978-1-4342-1577-2(6))*; pap. 6.10 *(978-1-4342-1758-5(2))* Capstone. (Stone Arch Bks.).
Garvey, Brann. El Problema con la Piscina: La Complicada Vida de Claudia Cristina Cortez. Gallagher, Diana G. 2020. (Claudia Cristina Cortez en Español Ser.).Tr. of Pool Problem: the Complicated Life of Claudia Cristina Cortez. (SPA.). 88p. (J). (gr. 4-8). pap. 6.95 ***(978-1-4965-9966-7(7)***, 201659); lib. bdg. 26.65 ***(978-1-4965-9804-2(0)***, 200692) Capstone. (Stone Arch Bks.).
Garvey, Brann. Promises! Vote for David Mortimore Baxter. Tayleur, Karen. 2007. (David Mortimore Baxter Ser.). (ENG.). 96p. (J). (gr. 4-8). per. 6.05 *(978-1-59889-208-6(8)*, Stone Arch Bks.) Capstone.
—The Truth! David Mortimore Baxter Comes Clean, 1 vol. Tayleur, Karen. 2006. (David Mortimore Baxter Ser.). (ENG.). 96p. (J). (gr. 4-8). lib. bdg. 26.65 *(978-1-59889-078-5(6)*, Stone Arch Bks.) Capstone.
—¡Vota! La Complicada Vida de Claudia Cristina Cortez. Gallagher, Diana G. 2019. (Claudia Cristina Cortez en Español Ser.). (SPA.). 88p. (J). (gr. 4-8). pap. 6.95 *(978-1-4965-8586-8(0)*, 141319); lib. bdg. 26.65 *(978-1-4965-8543-1(7)*, 141292) Capstone. (Stone Arch Bks.).
—Vote! The Complicated Life of Claudia Cristina Cortez, 1 vol. Gallagher, Diana G. 2008. (Claudia Cristina Cortez Ser.). (ENG.). 88p. (J). (gr. 4-8). pap. 6.10 *(978-1-4342-0866-8(4))*; lib. bdg. 26.65 *(978-1-4342-0770-8(6))* Capstone. (Stone Arch Bks.).
—Whatever! The Complicated Life of Claudia Cristina Cortez, 1 vol. Gallagher, Diana G. 2007. (Claudia Cristina Cortez Ser.). (ENG.). 88p. (J). (gr. 4-8). pap. 6.10 *(978-1-59889-880-4(9))*; lib. bdg. 26.65 *(978-1-59889-839-2(6))* Capstone. (Stone Arch Bks.).
Garvey, Brann & O'Connor, Niamh. The Ghost's Revenge, 1 vol. Peschke, Marci & Townson, H. 2006. (Vortex Bks.). (ENG.). 112p. (J). (gr. 5-9). 7.19 *(978-1-59889-283-3(5)*, Stone Arch Bks.) Capstone.
Garvey, Brian, jt. illus. see Greenan, Amy.
Garvey, Tara. Mary Chilton Winslow: Survivor of the Mayflower Voyage. Prince, Joyce. 2019. (ENG.). 68p. (J). (gr. k-6). pap. 14.95 ***(978-1-60571-466-0(6)***, Shires Press) Northshire Pr.
Garvin, Elaine. All-Girl Crafts. Ross, Kathy. 2005. (Girl Crafts Ser.). (ENG.). 48p. (gr. 2-5). lib. bdg. 26.60 *(978-0-7613-2776-9(2)*, Millbrook Pr.); per. 7.95 *(978-0-7613-2391-4(0)*, First Avenue Editions) Lerner Publishing Group.
—Babe Ruth & the Ice Cream Mess. Gutman, Dan. 2004. (Ready-To-read COFA Ser.). (ENG.). 32p. (J). (gr. k-2). pap. 4.99 *(978-0-689-85529-0(X)*, Simon Spotlight) Simon Spotlight.
—Jackie Robinson & the Big Game. Gutman, Dan. 2006. 32p. (J). lib. bdg. 15.00 *(978-1-4242-0957-6(9))* Fitzgerald Bks.
—Jackie Robinson & the Big Game. Gutman, Dan. 2006. (Ready-To-read COFA Ser.). (ENG.). 32p. (J). (gr. k-2). pap. 3.99 *(978-0-689-86239-7(3)*, Simon & Schuster/Paula Wiseman Bks.) Simon & Schuster/Paula Wiseman Bks.
—The Little Elephant with the Big Earache. Cowan, Charlotte. 2007. (Dr. Hippo Ser.). (ENG.). 32p. (J). (gr. -1-3). 17.95 *(978-0-9753516-0-4(5))* Hippocratic Pr., The.
—Play Fair, Little Bear. Allan-Meyer, Kathleen. 2003. (Little Bear Adventure Ser.: Vol. 7). 28p. (J). (gr. -1-1). pap. 6.49 *(978-1-57924-887-1(X))* BJU Pr.
—Things to Make for Your Doll. Ross, Kathy. (Girl Crafts Ser.). 48p. 2005. (ENG.). (gr. 2-5). lib. bdg. 26.60 *(978-0-7613-2861-2(0)*, Millbrook Pr.); 2003. (J). (gr. k-2). pap. 7.95 *(978-0-7613-1781-4(3)*, First Avenue Editions) Lerner Publishing Group.
Garvin, Sheri. Little Rhymes for Quiet Times. Franck, Charlotte. 2006. 29p. per. 15.95 *(978-1-60002-116-9(6)*, 4029) Mountain Valley Publishing, LLC.
Garwood, Gord. Thank You Day. 2014. (Daniel Tiger's Neighborhood Ser.). (ENG.). 24p. (J). (gr. -1-k). pap. 3.99 *(978-1-4424-9833-4(1)*, Simon Spotlight) Simon Spotlight.
—Welcome to the Neighborhood! Friedman, Becky. 2014. (Daniel Tiger's Neighborhood Ser.). (ENG.). 24p. (J). (gr. -1-1). pap. 4.99 *(978-1-4424-9741-2(6)*, Simon Spotlight) Simon Spotlight.
Gary, Glenn. The Lost Lighthouse. VanRiper, Justin & VanRiper, Gary. 2003. (Adirondack Kids Ser.: Vol. 3). 82p. (J). (gr. 2-7). pap. 9.95 *(978-0-9707044-2-9(9)*, ADK3) Adirondack Kids Pr.
Gary, Ken. The Fire Stealers: A Hopi Story. Gary, Ken, tr. 2003. (J). 15.95 *(978-1-885772-13-8(0))* Kiva Publishing, Inc.
Gary, McCluskey. The Christmas Cats Care for the Bear. Wilson, Constance Corcoran. 2016. (Christmas Cats Ser.: Vol. 5). (ENG.). (J). (gr. k-4). pap. 6.99 *(978-0-9863898-2-5(X))* Quad City Pr.
Gary Ripper. Princess Maddy & Her Blankie. Brice, Ginny. 2011. 20p. pap. 24.95 *(978-1-4560-7745-7(7))* America Star Bks.
Garza, Carmen Lomas. Cuadros de Familia.Tr. of Family Pictures. (ENG & SPA.). 32p. (J). 2nd anniv. ed. 2013. pap. 10.95 *(978-0-89239-207-0(X))*; 15th anniv. ed. 2005. (gr. -1-17). 16.95 *(978-0-89239-206-3(1))* Lee & Low Bks., Inc.
—Magic Windows: Ventanas Magicas. 2013. (ENG & SPA.). 32p. (J). pap. 10.95 *(978-0-89239-183-7(9)*, Children's Book Press) Lee & Low Bks., Inc.
—Making Magic Windows. 2014. (ENG & SPA.). 32p. (J). (gr. 4-7). pap. 11.95 *(978-0-89239-159-2(6))* Lee & Low Bks., Inc.
Garza, Fabiola. Coco. 2017. (J). *(978-1-5379-5892-7(5)*, Golden Bks.) Random Hse. Children's Bks.
Garza, Fabiola. The Story of Saint John Paul II: A Boy Who Became Pope. Garza, Fabiola. 2014. (J). 15.95 *(978-0-8198-9013-9(8))* Pauline Bks. & Media.
Garza, Rosa Maria. Peanut Butter & Jam: Bootsy Gets a Sister. Davis, Natrix. 2019. (Peanut Butter & Jam Ser.: Vol. 2). (ENG.). 68p. (J). pap. 19.99 ***(978-0-9997822-2-4(3))*** Davis, Nathaniel.
Garza, Xavier. The Great & Mighty Nikko. 2015. (ENG.). 32p. (J). pap. 7.95 *(978-1-935955-83-2(7))*; (gr. -1-4). 16.95 *(978-1-935955-82-5(9))* Cinco Puntos Pr.
—Maximilian & the Bingo Rematch: A Lucha Libre Sequel. 2013. (Max's Lucha Libre Adventures Ser.). (ENG.). 208p. (J). 19.95 *(978-1-935955-59-7(4))* Cinco Puntos Pr.
—Maximilian & the Lucha Libre Club. 2016. (Max's Lucha Libre Adventures Ser.). (ENG.). 208p. (J). (gr. 2-7). 19.95 *(978-1-941026-40-3(0))* Cinco Puntos Pr.
—Maximilian & the Mystery of the Guardian Angel. 2011. (Max's Lucha Libre Adventures Ser.). (ENG.). 160p. (J). (gr. 5-8). pap. 12.95 *(978-1-933693-98-9(3))* Cinco Puntos Pr.
Garza, Xavier. Zulema & the Witch Owl/Zulema y la Bruja Lechuza. Garza, Xavier. Villarroel, Carolina. 2009. (SPA & ENG.). 32p. (J). (gr. -1-4). 16.95 *(978-1-55885-515-1(7)*, Piñata Books) Arte Publico Pr.
Gas, Toma Feizo. Kiviuq & the Bee Woman. McDermott, Noel. 2019. (ENG.). 36p. (J). (gr. 4-7). 16.95 *(978-1-77227-215-4(9))* Inhabit Media Inc. CAN. Dist: Consortium Bk. Sales & Distribution.
—Kiviuq & the Mermaids, 1 vol. McDermott, Noel. 2016. (ENG.). 40p. (J). (gr. 4-7). 16.95 *(978-1-77227-082-2(2))* Inhabit Media Inc. CAN. Dist: Consortium Bk. Sales & Distribution.
—Those Who Dwell Below. Johnston, Aviaq. 2019. (ENG.). 208p. (J). pap. 13.95 *(978-1-77227-235-2(3))* Inhabit Media Inc. CAN. Dist: Consortium Bk. Sales & Distribution.
—Why the Monster, 1 vol. Qitsualik-Tinsley, Rachel & Qitsualik-Tinsley, Sean. 2017. (ENG.). 248p. (YA). (gr. 7). pap. 13.95 *(978-1-77227-141-6(1))* Inhabit Media Inc. CAN. Dist: Consortium Bk. Sales & Distribution.
Gasal, Ben. Boxy: A Tree of the Prairie. Daugherty, Doug. 2008. 24p. pap. 24.95 *(978-1-60610-808-6(5))* PublishAmerica, Inc.
Gascoigne, Martin. The Call of the Wild. Gascoigne, Martin. London, Jack. 2008. (Puffin Classics Ser.). 160p. (J). (gr. 3-7). 6.99 *(978-0-14-132105-9(9)*, Puffin Books) Penguin Young Readers Group.
Gascon, Jose. Grandpa's Magical Forest. Robinson, Tina. 2019. (ENG.). 38p. (J). (gr. 2-6). ***(978-1-9992973-1-2(8))*** Robinson, Tina.
Gaspar, Tamas, jt. illus. see Futaki, Attila.
Gast, Daniela. Little Fox & the Rainsticks. Sylva, Rowan. 2019. (Adventures of Little Fox Ser.: Vol. 1). (ENG.). 76p. (J). pap. *(978-0-9951165-1-1(2))* Lasavia Publishing Ltd.
Gast, Linda, photos by. So What, Saw-Whet? Frank, Rochelle. 2004. (J). per. 9.95 *(978-0-9746792-0-4(8))* Hummingbird Mountain Pr.
Gastaldo, Walter. El Cocodrilo Lloron. Barsy, Kalman. 2004. (Yellow Ser.). (SPA.). 31p. (J). (gr. k-3). pap. 5.95 *(978-1-57581-433-9(1))* Santillana USA Publishing Co., Inc.
Gastaut, Charlotte. Thumbelina. Gresham, Xanthe. 2016. (ENG.). 48p. (J). (gr. 1-5). pap. 9.99 *(978-1-78285-276-6(X))* Barefoot Bks., Inc.
Gaston, Carter J. How Do You Know When It's Time to Go to Bed? Gaston, P. J. 2008. (ENG.). 28p. (J). 10.00 *(978-0-9675574-2-7(9))* "How Do You Know".
gaston, carter j. How Do You Know When It's Time to Go to Bed? 2008. 28p. (J). pap. 8.00 *(978-0-9675574-3-4(7))* "How Do You Know".
Gaston, Francesco & Broccardo, Andrea. Monsters Unleashed Vol. 2: Learning Curve. 2018. (ENG.). 136p. (J). (gr. 4-17). pap. 19.99 *(978-0-7851-9637-2(4))* Marvel Worldwide, Inc.
Gaston, Keith A. Call Me Madame President. Pyatt, Sue. 2003. 31p. (J). 17.00 *(978-0-9742575-0-1(8))* Imagination Station Pr.
Gaston, Sierra. Grandma, Do Angels Have Wings?, 1 vol. Wiedeman, Connie. 2010. 40p. 24.95 *(978-1-4512-1054-5(X))* PublishAmerica, Inc.
Gatagan, T. Las Preguntas de Bingo Brown. Byars, Betsy. 2nd ed. 2003. (Espasa Juvenil Ser.: Vol. 15).Tr. of Burning Questions of Bingo Brown. (SPA.). 186p. (J). (gr. 7-18). *(978-84-239-8862-4(7)*, EC4398) Espasa Calpe, S.A. ESP. Dist: Lectorum Pubns., Inc.
Gatagan, Tino. Poesia Espanola para Ninos. Pelegrin (Compiler), Ana. 2015. (Serie Naranja Ser.). (SPA.). 152p. (J). pap. 10.95 *(978-1-64101-236-2(6))* Santillana USA Publishing Co., Inc.
Gatagán, Tino. Poesía Española para Niños. Gatagán, Tino, tr. 2nd ed. 2015. (SPA.). 152p. 10.95 *(978-84-204-4899-2(0))* Ediciones Alfaguara ESP. Dist: Santillana USA Publishing Co., Inc.
Gate, Darren. The Dangerous Lives of the Jacobites: Fact-Tastic Stories from Scotland's History, 34 vols. Strachan, Linda. 2019. (Fact-Tastic Stories from Scotland's History Ser.). (ENG.). 136p. (J). pap. 9.95 *(978-1-78250-596-9(2)*, Kelpies) Floris Bks. GBR. Dist: Consortium Bk. Sales & Distribution.
Gate, Darren. Hank's New Shoes. Gallagher, Chris. 2019. (ENG.). 34p. (J). 24.99 ***(978-0-578-56238-4(3))*** Gallagher, Chris.
Gate, Darren. A Secret Diary of the First World War: Fact-Tastic Stories from Scotland's History, 60 vols. Arbuthnott, Gill. 2018. (Fact-Tastic Stories from Scotland's History Ser.: 1). (ENG.). 144p. (J). pap. 6.95 *(978-1-78250-527-3(X)*, Kelpies) Floris Bks. GBR. Dist: Consortium Bk. Sales & Distribution.
Gateley, Edwina. God Goes on Vacation. Gateley, Edwina. 2009. 32p. (Orig.). (J). pap. 9.95 *(978-0-8091-6747-0(6))* Paulist Pr.
Gateley, Edwina. God Goes to School. Gateley, Edwina, text. 2009. 32p. (J). pap. 9.95 *(978-0-8091-6748-7(4))* Paulist Pr.
Gates, Donald. Hoggle's Christmas. Shelton, Rick. 2007. (ENG.). 79p. (J). pap. 11.95 *(978-1-60306-026-4(X)*, NewSouth Bks.) NewSouth, Inc.
Gates, Leslie. Buttercup: Poodles on Parade. Williams, Kristy. 2018. (ENG.). 32p. (J). pap. 12.95 *(978-1-64191-360-7(6))* Christian Faith Publishing.
Gathigo, Cyrus Ngatia. Lilana Ageiraü. Resman, Michael. Cayetano, Eldred Roy, tr. 2013. 40p. pap. *(978-976-8142-50-4(2))* Producciones de la Hamaca.
—The Villagers. Resman, Michael. Senelwa, Fred, tr. 2012. 40p. pap. *(978-976-8142-41-2(3))* Producciones de la Hamaca.
Gatlin, Lee. Monster School. Coombs, Kate. 2018. (ENG.). 40p. (J). (gr. k-3). 16.99 *(978-1-4521-2938-9(X))* Chronicle Bks. LLC.
—Shout Out for the Fitzgerald-Trouts. Spalding, Esta. 2019. (Fitzgerald-Trouts Ser.). (ENG.). 352p. (J). (gr. 3-7). 16.99 *(978-0-7352-6451-9(1)*, Tundra Bks.) Tundra Bks. CAN. Dist: Penguin Random Hse. LLC.
Gatt, Elizabeth. Sea Otter Pup, 1 vol. Miles, Victoria. (ENG.). (J). (gr. -1 — 1). 2017. 28p. 6.95 *(978-1-4598-1506-3(8))*; 2013. 26p. bds. 10.95 *(978-1-4598-0467-8(8))* Orca Bk. Pubs. USA.
Gatto, Horacio. George & Will Have a Baby: The Gift of Family. Celcer, Iréné. 2018. (J). pap. *(978-1-938313-24-0(0))* Graphite Pr.
—The Gift. Celcer, Irene. 2009. (J). pap. *(978-0-9755810-6-3(6))* Graphite Pr.
—The Gift of Adoption. Celcer, Irene. 2009. (J). pap. *(978-0-9755810-5-6(8))* Graphite Pr.
—The Gift of Egg Donation. Celcer, Irene. 2007. (Hope & Will Have a Baby Ser.). 32p. (J). (gr. k-3). pap. 19.95 *(978-0-9755810-1-8(5)*, 9780975581018) Graphite Pr.
—The Gift of Embryo Donation. Celcer, Irene. 2007. (Hope & Will Have a Baby Ser.). 32p. (J). (gr. k-3). pap. 19.95 *(978-0-9755810-2-5(3)*, 9780975581025) Graphite Pr.
—The Gift of Sperm Donation. Celcer, Irene. 2007. (Hope & Will Have a Baby Ser.). 32p. (J). (gr. k-3). pap. 19.95 *(978-0-9755810-3-2(1)*, 9780975581032) Graphite Pr.
—The Gift of Surrogacy. Celcer, Irene. 2007. (Hope & Will Have a Baby Ser.). 32p. (J). (gr. k-3). pap. 19.95 *(978-0-9755810-4-9(X)*, 9780975581049) Graphite Pr.
—Hope & Rosie Have a Baby: The Gift of Family. Celcer, Iréné. 2018. (J). pap. *(978-1-938313-22-6(4))* Graphite Pr.
—Hope Has a Baby: The Gift of Family. Celcer, Iréné. 2018. (J). pap. *(978-1-938313-20-2(8))* Graphite Pr.
Gatto, Kim. K Is for Kite: God's Springtime Alphabet, 1 vol. Wargin, Kathy-jo. 2010. (ENG.). 40p. (J). (gr. -1-2). 15.99 *(978-0-310-71662-4(4))* Zonderkidz.
Gau Family Studio. The Little Girl Who Lied: The Importance of Honesty. Carty, Amy. Williams, Nancy E., ed. 2013. 40p. (J). pap. 16.98 *(978-1-938526-69-5(4))* Laurus Co., Inc., The.
Gaudard, Elliot. Adventures of a Creeper: an Unofficial Minecraft Diary. Kid, Books. 2019. (Minecraft Ser.: 1). (ENG.). 144p. (J). (gr. 3-7). pap. 7.99 *(978-1-68412-922-5(2)*, Silver Dolphin Bks.) Printers Row Publishing Group.
—Adventures of a Slime: an Unofficial Minecraft Diary. Kid, Books. 2019. (Minecraft Ser.: 2). (ENG.). 144p. (J). (gr. 3-7). pap. 7.99 *(978-1-68412-921-8(4)*, Silver Dolphin Bks.) Printers Row Publishing Group.
Gaudenzi, Giacinto. Los Caballeros - Internet Linked. Firth, Rachel. 2004. (Titles in Spanish Ser.). (SPA.). 48p. (J). pap. 8.95 *(978-0-7460-5083-5(6)*, Usborne) EDC Publishing.
—Roman Britain: Internet-Linked. Brocklehurst, Ruth. Chisholm, Jane, ed. 2006. (Usborne History of Britain Ser.). 48p. (J). (gr. 4-7). per. 8.99 *(978-0-7945-1232-3(1)*, Usborne) EDC Publishing.
Gaudenzi, Giacinto & Haggerty, Tim. Horses & Ponies. Milbourne, Anna. 2006. (Beginners Nature: Level 1 Ser.). 32p. (J). (gr. k-2). 4.99 *(978-0-7945-1397-9(2)*, Usborne) EDC Publishing.
Gaudenzi, Giacinto & Montgomery, Lee. Knights & Armor. Firth, Rachel. 2006. 95p. (J). (gr. 4-7). 17.99 *(978-0-7945-1279-8(8)*, Usborne) EDC Publishing.
Gaudet, Christine. Donkey Oatie's Field Trip. Rath, Tom H. 2013. 26p. pap. *(978-0-9918033-4-7(5))* Wood Islands Prints.
Gaudiamo, Adi Darda. Berlin Breakout, 1 vol. Avery, Ben. 2008. (Z Graphic Novels / TimeFlyz Ser.). (ENG.). 160p. (J). (gr. 4-7). pap. 6.99 *(978-0-310-71363-0(3))* Zondervan.
—Pyramid Peril, 1 vol., 1. Avery, Ben G. 2007. (TimeFlyz Ser.). (ENG.). 160p. (J). (gr. 4-6). 21.19 *(978-0-310-71361-6(7))* Zonderkidz.
—Tunnel Twist-Up, 1 vol., 4. Avery, Ben. 2008. (TimeFlyz Ser.). (ENG.). 160p. (J). (gr. 4-6). 21.19 *(978-0-310-71364-7(1))* Zondervan.
—Turtle Trouble, 1 vol., 2. Avery, Ben G. 2007. (TimeFlyz Ser.). (ENG.). 160p. (J). (gr. 4-6). 21.19 *(978-0-310-71362-3(5))* Zondervan.
Gauguin, Paul René. Little Parsley. Hagerup, Inger. Crook, Becky L., tr. 2019. (J). 17.95 *(978-1-59270-286-2(4))* Enchanted Lion Bks., LLC.
—That Summer. Hagerup, Inger. Crook, Becky L., tr. 2019. 40p. (J). 17.95 *(978-1-59270-277-0(5))* Enchanted Lion Bks., LLC.
Gauld, Tom. The Three Musketeers: (Penguin Classics Deluxe Edition) Dumas, Alexandre. Pevear, Richard, tr. 2007. (Penguin Classics Deluxe Edition Ser.). (ENG.). 736p. (gr. 12-18). 20.00 *(978-0-14-310500-8(0)*, Penguin Classics) Penguin Publishing Group.
Gauldie, Matt. The Tale of the Anzac Tortoise. Riddell, Shona. 2019. (ENG.). 36p. (J). (gr. -1-3). pap. 12.99 *(978-0-473-31894-9(6))* Exisle Publishing Pty Ltd. AUS. Dist: Hachette Bk. Group.
Gausden, Vicki. Happy Birthday to You, Pirate. Robinson, Michelle. 2019. (ENG.). 32p. (J). pap. 6.99 *(978-0-00-824220-6(8)*, HarperCollins Children's Bks.) HarperCollins Pubs. Ltd. GBR. Dist: HarperCollins Pubs.
—Happy Birthday to You, Princess. Robinson, Michelle. 2019. (ENG.). 32p. (J). pap. 6.99 *(978-0-00-824221-3(6)*, HarperCollins Children's Bks.) HarperCollins Pubs. Ltd. GBR. Dist: HarperCollins Pubs.
Gauss, Rose. Callie & the Stepmother. Meyers, Susan A. I.t. ed. 2005. (ENG.). 64p. (J). (gr. -1-3). pap. 6.95 *(978-0-9718348-0-4(6))* Blooming Tree Pr.
Gautam, Anamika, jt. illus. see Shrestha, Sudesha.
Gauthier, Clayton. The Salmon Run, 1 vol. 2016. (Schchechmala Children's Ser.). (ENG.). 20p. (J). (gr. 1-3). 9.95 ***(978-1-926886-44-2(5))*** Theytus Bks., Ltd. CAN. Dist: Orca Bk. Pubs. USA.
Gauthier, Elizabeth. A Bald Chimpanzee, an Adventure in ABC's. Gauthier, Elizabeth. 2010. (ENG.). 40p. (J). (gr. -1-4). 16.95 *(978-0-9820812-2-8(7)*, Frog Legs Ink) Gauthier Pubns. Inc.
Gauthier, Elizabeth & Bonney, Joan. A Bald Chimpanzee: An Adventure in ABCs. Gauthier, Elizabeth. 2012. (ENG.). 40p. (J). pap. 12.99 *(978-0-9833593-5-7(0)*, Frog Legs Ink) Gauthier Pubns. Inc.
Gauthier, Glenn G. The A to Z Book. Gauthier, Glenn G. 2006. 32p. (J). 16.95 *(978-1-887542-42-5(6))* Bk. Pubs. Network.

G

Gauthier, Manon. Marcel Marceau: Master of Mime. Spielman, Gloria. 2011. (ENG.). 32p. (J). (gr. 3-5). lib. bdg. 17.95 *(978-0-7613-3961-8(2)*, 9780761339618); Vol. pap. 7.95 *(978-0-7613-3962-5(0)*, 9780761339625) Lerner Publishing Group. (Kar-Ben Publishing).

—Wash On! Marineau, Michèle. 2018. (ENG.). 40p. (J). (gr. k-2). 16.95 *(978-1-77278-018-5(9))* Pajama Pr. CAN. Dist: Ingram Publisher Services.

Gauvin, Matthew. A Cloudy Day. Da Puzzo, Allegra & Da Puzzo, Jackson. 2012. 24p. pap. *(978-0-9843477-5-9(5))* Roxby Media Ltd.

Gavarni & Johannot, Tony. Le COMTE de MONTE-CRISTO (Edition Illustrée) Barry, ed. 2019. (Comte de Monte-Cristo. Edition Intégrale Illustrée en Deux Volumes Ser.: Vol. 1). (FRE.). 704p. (J). pap. 33.33 *(978-1-0807-2686-8(1))* Independently Published.

—Le COMTE de MONTE-CRISTO (Illustré) Dumas (Pere), Alexandre. 2019. (Edition Intégrale Illustrée en Deux Volumes Ser.: Vol. 2). (FRE.). 678p. (J). pap. 33.33 *(978-1-0808-8604-3(4))* Independently Published.

Gavet, Nathalie. Meeting My Cas. Robe, Adam D. Robe, Kim A., ed. 2009. 16p. pap. 11.99 *(978-0-9817403-5-5(9))* Robe Communications, Inc.

—Moving to Another Foster Home. Robe, Adam D. Robe, Kim A., ed. 2009. 16p. pap. 11.99 *(978-0-9817403-4-8(0))* Robe Communications, Inc.

—Robbie's Trail Through Adoption. Robe, Adam D. Robe, Kim A., ed. 2010. 44p. pap. 23.99 *(978-1-935831-03-7(8))* Robe Communications, Inc.

—Robbie's Trail Through Adoption — Activity Book. Robe, Adam D. Robe, Kim A., ed. 2010. 36p. pap. 16.99 *(978-1-935831-04-4(6))* Robe Communications, Inc.

—Robbie's Trail Through Adoption — Adult Guide. Robe, Adam D. Robe, Kim A., ed. 2010. 28p. pap. 16.99 *(978-1-935831-05-1(4))* Robe Communications, Inc.

—Robbie's Trail Through Divorce. Robe, Kim. 2012. 40p. (-18). pap. 23.99 *(978-1-935831-11-2(9))* Robe Communications, Inc.

—Robbie's Trail Through Divorce - Activity Book. Robe, Kim. 2012. 28p. (-18). pap. 16.99 *(978-1-935831-12-9(7))* Robe Communications, Inc.

—Robbie's Trail Through Divorce - Adult Guide. Robe, Kim. 2012. 28p. (-18). pap. 16.99 *(978-1-935831-13-6(5))* Robe Communications, Inc.

—Robbie's Trail Through Foster Care. Robe, Adam D. Robe, Kim A., ed. 2010. 40p. pap. 23.99 *(978-1-935831-00-6(3))* Robe Communications, Inc.

—Robbie's Trail Through Foster Care — Activity Book. Robe, Adam D. Robe, Kim A., ed. 2010. 36p. pap. 16.99 *(978-1-935831-01-3(1))* Robe Communications, Inc.

—Robbie's Trail Through Foster Care — Adult Guide. Robe, Adam D. Robe, Kim A., ed. 2010. 28p. pap. 16.99 *(978-1-935831-02-0(X))* Robe Communications, Inc.

—Robbie's Trail Through Open Adoption. Robe, Adam D. Robe, Kim A., ed. 2010. 44p. pap. 23.99 *(978-1-935831-06-8(2))* Robe Communications, Inc.

—Wanting to Belong. Robe, Adam D. Robe, Kim A., ed. 2009. 16p. pap. 11.99 *(978-0-9817403-6-2(7))* Robe Communications, Inc.

Gavin, Carolyn. Nature All Around: Birds. Hickman, Pamela. 2020. (ENG.). 32p. (J). (gr. 2-5). 18.99 ***(978-1-77138-818-4(8))*** Kids Can Pr., Ltd. CAN. Dist: Hachette Bk. Group.

Gavin, Carolyn. Nature All Around: Bugs. Hickman, Pamela. 2019. (ENG.). 1p. (J). (gr. 2-5). 17.99 *(978-1-77138-820-7(X))* Kids Can Pr., Ltd. CAN. Dist: Hachette Bk. Group.

—Nature All Around: Plants. Hickman, Pamela. 2020. (ENG.). 32p. (J). (gr. 2-5). 18.99 *(978-1-77138-819-1(6))* Kids Can Pr., Ltd. CAN. Dist: Hachette Bk. Group.

—Nature All Around: Trees. Hickman, Pamela. 2019. (ENG.). 32p. (J). (gr. 2-5). 18.99 *(978-1-77138-804-7(8))* Kids Can Pr., Ltd. CAN. Dist: Hachette Bk. Group.

Gavin, Carolyn, et al. 24 Mini Book Block! p i kids. 2013. (ENG.). 240p. (J). bds., bds. *(978-1-4508-7482-3(7)*, 256b8fc7-4ea1-4abf-9054-bbb84a68f781, p i kids) Phoenix International Publications, Inc.

Gavin, Rebecca Thompson. The Adventures of Oakey Dokey Acorn: Oakey & Ivy. Gavin, Rebecca Thompson. 2003. 64p. (J). *(978-1-57579-255-2(9))* Pine Hill Pr.

Gavioli, Gino. Candido, el Limpiador de Chimeneas. Gavioli, Gino. Gavoili, G. Brignole, Giancarla, tr. rev. ed. 2006. (Fabulas De Familia Ser.). (SPA & ENG.). 32p. (J). (gr. k-4). pap. 6.95 *(978-970-20-0264-2(8))* Castillo, Ediciones, S. A. de C. V. MEX. Dist: Macmillan.

Gaviraghi, Giuditta. Good Night, Cow. Cottage Door Press & Parragon Books, eds. ed. 2019. (Peek-A-Boo Board Bks.). (ENG.). 10p. (J). (gr. -1 — 1). bds. 5.99 *(978-1-68052-535-9(2)*, 2000960, Parragon Books) Cottage Door Pr.

—Hello, Hedgehog. Cottage Door Press & Parragon Books, eds. ed. 2019. (Peek-A-Boo Bks.). (ENG.). 10p. (J). (gr. -1 — 1). bds. 5.99 *(978-1-68052-534-2(4)*, 2000950, Parragon Books) Cottage Door Pr.

—Peek-A-Boo Penguin. Cottage Door Press & Parragon Books, eds. 2019. (Peek-A-Boo Bks.). (ENG.). 10p. (J). (gr. -1 — 1). bds. 5.99 *(978-1-68052-790-2(8)*, 2002970, Parragon Books) Cottage Door Pr.

Gaviraghi, Giuditta, jt. illus. see Abbot, Judi.

Gaviro Ortega, Manuel Antonio. Plut�n Quiere Ser Estrella. Baquedano Mengual, Laura. 2019. (SPA.). 36p. (J). pap. 13.20 ***(978-1-7067-7857-8(0))*** Independently Published.

Gavish, Boaz. MIA & the Rocket Ship Tree. Gavish, Boaz. 2018. (ENG.). 44p. (J). *(978-1-9997532-1-4(6))*; pap. *(978-1-9997532-2-1(4))* Koalabo Publishing.

Gavrilovskiy, Olga. Car Key Elves. Hunter, T. H. 2008. 32p. (J). 16.95 *(978-0-9788085-1-8(7))* Tetoca Pr.

—Elf Night: A Christmas Story. Hunter, Todd H. 2006. 52p. (J). (gr. -1-7). 16.95 *(978-0-9788085-0-1(9))* Tetoca Pr.

Gawron, Gay. The New Hampshire Coloring Book. 2008. 40p. (YA). pap. 8.95 *(978-0-9801672-0-7(5))* Hobblebush Bks.

Gawthrop, Shaughn. Be Happy. D'Arcy, Megan. 2011. 32p. (J). 14.95 *(978-1-879094-95-6(9))* Momentum Bks., LLC.

Gay-Kassel, Doreen. Big Machines. Jones, Melanie Davis. 2003. (Rookie Reader Ser.). (ENG.). 24p. (J). (gr. k-2). pap. 4.95 *(978-0-516-27829-2(0)*, Children's Pr.) Scholastic Library Publishing.

Gay, Maria T. Sweet Little Girl. Hankey, Sandy. 2004. 20p. pap. 24.95 *(978-1-4137-3329-7(8))* PublishAmerica, Inc.

Gay, Marie-Louise. The Christmas Orange, 1 vol. Gillmore, Don. 2003. (ENG.). 32p. (J). (gr. 1-4). pap. 9.95 *(978-1-55005-075-2(3)*, 566d0f70-a6ed-402e-a820-2be3f6d7161e) Fitzhenry & Whiteside, Ltd. CAN. Dist: Firefly Bks., Ltd.

—The Fabulous Song. Gillmor, Don. 2003. 32p. (J). pap. 7.95 *(978-1-929132-48-5(4))* Kane Miller.

—The Fabulous Song. Gillmor, Don et al. 2006. (ENG.). 44p. (J). (gr. -1-2). 16.95 *(978-2-923163-17-8(6))* La Montagne Secrete CAN. Dist: Independent Pubs. Group.

—Houndsley & Catina. Howe, James. 40p. (J). (gr. k-4). 2013. (Candlewick Sparks Ser.). pap. 4.99 *(978-0-7636-6638-5(6))*; 2006. (Houndsley & Catina Ser.: 1). (ENG.). 15.99 *(978-0-7636-2404-0(7))* Candlewick Pr.

—Houndsley & Catina. Howe, James. 2007. 36p. (J). (gr. k-2). lib. bdg. 12.65 *(978-0-7569-8141-9(7))* Perfection Learning Corp.

—Houndsley & Catina & Cousin Wagster. Howe, James. 2018. (Houndsley & Catina Ser.: 5). 48p. (J). (gr. k-3). 15.99 *(978-0-7636-4709-4(8))* Candlewick Pr.

—Houndsley & Catina & the Birthday Surprise. Howe, James. 2006. (Houndsley & Catina Ser.: 2). (ENG.). 48p. (J). (gr. k-4). 15.99 *(978-0-7636-2405-7(5))* Candlewick Pr.

—Houndsley & Catina & the Birthday Surprise: Candlewick Sparks. Howe, James. 2013. (Candlewick Sparks Ser.). (ENG.). 48p. (J). (gr. k-4). pap. 4.99 *(978-0-7636-6639-2(4))* Candlewick Pr.

—Houndsley & Catina & the Quiet Time. Howe, James. 2008. (Houndsley & Catina Ser.: 3). 48p. (J). (gr. k-4). 15.99 *(978-0-7636-3384-4(4))* Candlewick Pr.

—Houndsley & Catina & the Quiet Time: Candlewick Sparks. Howe, James. 2013. (Candlewick Sparks Ser.). 48p. (J). (gr. k-4). pap. 4.99 *(978-0-7636-6863-1(X))* Candlewick Pr.

Gay, Marie Louise. Houndsley & Catina at the Library. Howe, James. 2020. (Houndsley & Catina Ser.). 48p. (J). (gr. k-3). 15.99 *(978-0-7636-9662-7(5))* Candlewick Pr.

Gay, Marie-Louise. Houndsley & Catina Plink & Plunk. Howe, James. 2013. (Candlewick Sparks Ser.). (ENG.). 48p. (J). (gr. k-4). pap. 4.99 *(978-0-7636-6640-8(8))* Candlewick Pr.

Gay, Marie Louise. Houndsley & Catina Through the Seasons. Howe, James. 2018. (Houndsley & Catina Ser.: 7). 184p. (J). (gr. k-3). pap. 9.99 *(978-1-5362-0326-4(2))* Candlewick Pr.

Gay, Marie-Louise. Maddie on TV. Leblanc, Louise. Cummins, Sarah, tr. 2003. (Formac First Novels Ser.: 48). (ENG.). 64p. (J). (gr. 2-5). 14.95 *(978-0-88780-613-1(9)*, 613) Formac Publishing Co., Ltd. CAN. Dist: Formac Lorimer Bks. Ltd.

—Maddie Stands Tall. Leblanc, Louise. Cummins, Sarah, tr. 2005. (Formac First Novels Ser.: 54). (ENG.). 64p. (J). (gr. 2-5). 14.95 *(978-0-88780-683-4(X)*, 683) Formac Publishing Co., Ltd. CAN. Dist: Formac Lorimer Bks. Ltd.

—Maddie Stands Tall, 1 vol. Leblanc, Louise. Cummins, Sarah, tr. 2005. (Formac First Novels Ser.: 54). (ENG.). 64p. (J). (gr. 2-5). 4.95 *(978-0-88780-682-7(1)*, 682) Formac Publishing Co., Ltd. CAN. Dist: Formac Lorimer Bks. Ltd.

—Maddie Surfs for Cyber-Pals. Leblanc, Louise. 2004. 64p. (J). lib. bdg. 12.00 *(978-1-4242-1226-2(X))* Fitzgerald Bks.

—Maddie Surfs for Cyber-Pals. Leblanc, Louise. Cummins, Sarah, tr. 2004. (Formac First Novels Ser.: 52). (ENG.). 64p. (gr. 2-5). 14.95 *(978-0-88780-639-1(2)*, 639) Formac Publishing Co., Ltd. CAN. Dist: Formac Lorimer Bks. Ltd.

—Maddie Surfs for Cyber Pals, 1 vol. Leblanc, Louise. Cummins, Sarah, tr. 2004. (Formac First Novels Ser.: 52). (ENG.). 64p. (J). (gr. 2-5). 4.95 *(978-0-88780-638-4(4)*, 638) Formac Publishing Co., Ltd. CAN. Dist: Formac Lorimer Bks. Ltd.

—Maddie's Big Test. Leblanc, Louise. Cummins, Sarah, tr. 2006. (Formac First Novels Ser.: 58). (ENG.). 64p. (J). (gr. 2-5). 14.95 *(978-0-88780-718-3(6)*, 718) Formac Publishing Co., Ltd. CAN. Dist: Formac Lorimer Bks. Ltd.

—Maddie's Big Test, 1 vol. Leblanc, Louise. Cummins, Sarah, tr. 2006. (Formac First Novels Ser.). (ENG.). 64p. (J). (gr. 2-5). 4.95 *(978-0-88780-714-5(3)*, 714) Formac Publishing Co., Ltd. CAN. Dist: Formac Lorimer Bks. Ltd.

—On the Road Again! More Travels with My Family. Gay, Homel D. 2008. (Travels with My Family Ser.). (ENG.). 120p. (J). (gr. 1-5). 15.95 *(978-0-88899-846-0(5))* Groundwood Bks. CAN. Dist: Publishers Group West (PGW).

—Please, Louise!, 1 vol. Wishinsky, Frieda. 2007. (ENG.). 32p. (J). (gr. k-k). 17.95 *(978-0-88899-796-8(5))* Groundwood Bks. CAN. Dist: Publishers Group West (PGW).

—Plink & Plunk. Howe, James. 2009. (Houndsley & Catina Ser.: 4). 48p. (J). (gr. k-4). 15.99 *(978-0-7636-3385-1(2))* Candlewick Pr.

—Stella, Queen of the Snow. braille ed. 2004. (J). (gr. -1-1). spiral bd. *(978-0-616-08492-2(7))* Canadian National Institute for the Blind/Institut National Canadien pour les Aveugles.

—Tiger & Badger. Jenkins, Emily. 2016. 32p. (J). (-k). 15.99 *(978-0-7636-6604-0(1))* Candlewick Pr.

—Yuck, a Love Story. Gillmor, Don. ed. 2004. (J). (gr. k-3). spiral bd. *(978-0-616-07238-7(4))*; spiral bd. *(978-0-616-08494-6(3))* Canadian National Institute for the Blind/Institut National Canadien pour les Aveugles.

—Yuck, a Love Story, 1 vol. Gillmor, Don. 2010. (ENG.). 32p. (J). (gr. k-2). pap. 9.95 *(978-1-55455-172-9(2)*, 22c06c67-ac15-4283-b0c3-cb6c296fd01e) Trifolium Bks., Inc. CAN. Dist: Firefly Bks., Ltd.

Gay, Marie-Louise. On the Road Again!, 1 vol. Gay, Marie-Louise. Homel, David. 2011. (ENG.). 144p. (J). (gr. 1-5). pap. 8.95 *(978-1-55498-087-1(9))* Groundwood Bks. CAN. Dist: Publishers Group West (PGW).

—Princess Pistachio, 1 vol. Gay, Marie-Louise. Homel, Jacob, tr. from FRE. 2015. Orig. Title: Princesse Pistache. (ENG.). 48p. (J). (gr. k-3). 10.95 *(978-1-927485-69-9(X))* Pajama Pr. CAN. Dist: Ingram Publisher Services.

—Summer in the City, 1 vol. Gay, Marie-Louise. Homel, David. 2012. (Travels with My Family Ser.). (ENG.). 152p. (J). (gr. 1-5). 15.95 *(978-1-55498-177-9(8))* Groundwood Bks. CAN. Dist: Publishers Group West (PGW).

Gayle, Vandercook. Mr. Blair's Labyrinth. Robert, Lytle. 2011. (J). 10.95 *(978-0-9798088-4-5(7))* EDCO Publishing, Inc.

Gaylor, Kyra, jt. illus. see Merrifield, Teagan Trif.

Gaylor, Terence. Cutie's Big Adventures - Cutie Saves Miss Bunny. Di John, Felicia. 2017. (Cutie's Big Adventures Ser.: Vol. 2). (ENG.). (J). (gr. k-6). 18.95 *(978-0-9987568-2-0(2))* Cutie Series Co., The.

Gaylord, Penelope R. Battle on the Moon (Marvel Avengers) Sazaklis, John. 2019. (Little Golden Book Ser.). (ENG.). 24p. (J). (-k). 4.99 *(978-1-9848-4786-7(4)*, Golden Bks.) Random Hse. Children's Bks.

—Captain Marvel Little Golden Book (Marvel) Sazaklis, Athena Maria. 2019. (Little Golden Book Ser.). (ENG.). 24p. (J). (-k). 4.99 *(978-1-5247-6870-6(7)*, Golden Bks.) Random Hse. Children's Bks.

Gaytan, Julio. Always Angel: A Coloring Storybook. Eisendrath, Kimberly. 2016. (J). (gr. k-6). (SPA.). pap. 8.95 *(978-0-9861864-7-9(3))*; (ENG.). pap. 8.95 *(978-0-9861864-5-5(7))* Silver Thread Publishing.

Gazarik, Rebecca Renee. The Caribbean Caribou's Ancient Discovery. Gazarik, Rebecca Renee. Patterson, Aaron James, ed. 2012. 36p. (J). *(978-0-9802258-2-2(5))* Gazarik, Rebecca.

Gazzaneo, Lucia. El Gigante y el Mar. Brignole, Giancarla, tr. (Fabulas De Familia Ser.). (SPA.). 32p. *(978-970-20-0268-0(0))* Castillo, Ediciones, S. A. de C. V.

Gazzetta, Katherine Cutchin. Love from a Star. Gazzetta, Katherine Cutchin. 2015. (ENG.). 32p. (J). (gr. -1-k). 14.99 *(978-1-58536-950-8(0)*, 204017) Sleeping Bear Pr.

Gazzola, Ronny. Red. Doering, Amanda. 2018. (Sing Your Colors! Ser.). (ENG.). 24p. (J). (gr. -1-2). lib. bdg. 33.99 *(978-1-68410-319-5(3)*, 140865); lib. bdg. 33.99 incl. audio compact disk *(978-1-68410-128-3(X)*, 31848) Cantata Learning.

Gbala, Deswin R. Rock University: A Collection of Short Stories & Poems. Gbala, Deswin R. Date not set. 51p. (Orig.). (J). (gr. 3-10). pap. 8.50 *(978-0-9650629-2-3(9))* Coulee Region Pubns., Inc.

Gear, Linnea. Brooding YA Hero: Becoming a Main Character (Almost) As Awesome As Me. McHottiepants, Broody & DiRisio, Carrie. 2017. (ENG.). 352p. (J). (gr. 7-12). 17.99 *(978-1-5107-2666-6(7)*, Sky Pony Pr.) Skyhorse Publishing Co., Inc.

Gearbox. Laugh-Out-Loud Awesome Jokes for Kids. Elliott, Rob. 2017. (Laugh-Out-Loud Jokes for Kids Ser.). (ENG.). 128p. (J). (gr. 1-5). pap. 4.99 *(978-0-06-249795-6(2))* HarperCollins Pubs.

—Laugh-Out-Loud Christmas Jokes for Kids. Elliott, Rob. 2016. (Laugh-Out-Loud Jokes for Kids Ser.). (ENG.). 144p. (J). (gr. 1-5). pap. 5.99 *(978-0-06-249791-8(X))* HarperCollins Pubs.

—Laugh-Out-Loud Holiday Jokes for Kids: 2-In-1 Collection of Spooky Jokes & Christmas Jokes. Elliott, Rob. 2016. (Laugh-Out-Loud Jokes for Kids Ser.). (ENG.). 272p. (J). (gr. 1-5). 10.99 *(978-0-06-256976-9(7))* HarperCollins Pubs.

—Laugh-Out-Loud Road Trip Jokes for Kids. Elliott, Rob. 2017. (Laugh-Out-Loud Jokes for Kids Ser.). (ENG.). 128p. (J). (gr. 1-5). pap. 4.99 *(978-0-06-249793-2(6))* HarperCollins Pubs.

—Laugh-Out-Loud Ultimate Jokes for Kids: 2-In-1 Collection of Awesome Jokes & Road Trip Jokes. Elliott, Rob. 2017. (Laugh-Out-Loud Jokes for Kids Ser.). (ENG.). 256p. (J). (gr. 1-5). 10.99 *(978-0-06-256977-6(5))* HarperCollins Pubs.

Geary, Steve. Beginnings Vol. 2: Tales of the Mandrasaurs, Volume the Second. Everson, Chance. 2004. cd-rom 9.95 *(978-0-9760303-1-7(4))* R.A.R.E. TALES.

—Discoveries: Tales of the Mandrasaurs, Volume the Third. Everson, Chance. 2004. cd-rom 9.95 *(978-0-9760303-2-4(2))* R.A.R.E. TALES.

—Forever & a Day Vol. 1: Tales of the Mandrasaurs, Volume the First. Everson, Chance. 2004. cd-rom 9.95 *(978-0-9760303-0-0(6))* R.A.R.E. TALES.

—Verlin's Magical Blunder: Tales of the Mandrasaurs, Volume the Seventh. Everson, Chance. 2004. cd-rom 9.95 *(978-0-9760303-6-2(5))* R.A.R.E. TALES.

GEbhard, Andy. Exaggeration Aggravation. BAtey, Kathey. 2006. (J). 8.00 *(978-0-9790017-0-3(6))* Spirited Presentations.

Gebhardt-Gayler, Winnie. The Little Water-Sprite. Preussler, Otfried. Bell, Anthea, tr. from GER. 2015. (ENG.). 136p. (J). (gr. k-4). 15.95 *(978-1-59017-933-8(1)*, NYR Children's Collection) New York Review of Bks., Inc., The.

—The Little Witch. Preussler, Otfried. Bell, Anthea, tr. 2015. (ENG.). 144p. (J). (gr. k-4). 16.95 *(978-1-59017-934-5(X)*, NYR Children's Collection) New York Review of Bks., Inc., The.

Gebr, Jaroslav. Jackie Winquackey & Her 43 Cats Go to Hollywood. Frees, Jessie Lynch. 2005. 32p. (J). 14.99 *(978-0-9760553-0-3(9))* Tizbit Books, LLC.

Geddes, Anne, photos by. Opposites. 2010. (ENG., 14p. (J). (gr. k — 1). bds. 5.99 *(978-1-921652-10-3(1))* Geddes, Anne Publishing AUS. Dist: Two Rivers Distribution.

Geddes, Hannah. Drawing Zentangle Animals. Ard, Catherine. 2017. (How to Draw Zentangle Art Ser.). 32p. (gr. 3-3). pap. 63.00 *(978-1-5382-0705-5(2))* Stevens, Gareth Publishing LLLP.

—Drawing Zentangle Birds. Ard, Catherine. 2017. (How to Draw Zentangle Art Ser.). 32p. (gr. 3-3). pap. 63.00 *(978-1-5382-0706-2(0))* Stevens, Gareth Publishing LLLP.

—Drawing Zentangle Bugs & Butterflies. Ard, Catherine. 2017. (How to Draw Zentangle Art Ser.). 32p. (gr. 3-3). pap. 10.50 *(978-1-5382-0840-3(7))* Stevens, Gareth Publishing LLLP.

—Drawing Zentangle Fantasy Worlds. Ard, Catherine. 2017. (How to Draw Zentangle Art Ser.). 32p. (gr. 3-3). pap. 63.00 *(978-1-5382-0708-6(7))* Stevens, Gareth Publishing LLLP.

—Drawing Zentangle Holidays. Ard, Catherine. 2017. (How to Draw Zentangle Art Ser.). 32p. (gr. 3-3). pap. 63.00 *(978-1-5382-0709-3(5))* Stevens, Gareth Publishing LLLP.

—Drawing Zentangle Sea Life. Ard, Catherine. 2017. (How to Draw Zentangle Art Ser.). 32p. (gr. 3-3). pap. 63.00 *(978-1-5382-0710-9(9))* Stevens, Gareth Publishing LLLP.

Geddes, Serena. Birthday Bonanza: The Fabulous Diary of Persephone Pinchgut. Darlison, Aleesah. 2016. (Totally Twins Ser.: 4). (ENG.). 192p. (J). 8.99 *(978-1-78226-298-5(9)*, b512c408-325b-43e2-a8d2-022357598ffa) Sweet Cherry Publishing GBR. Dist: Baker & Taylor Publisher Services (BTPS).

—Blow Me a Kiss. Collum, Karen. 2012. (J). *(978-1-4351-4513-9(5))* Barnes & Noble, Inc.

—Buttercup Mystery. Earhart, Kristin. 2015. (Marguerite Henry's Misty Inn Ser.: 2). (ENG.). 128p. (J). (gr. 2-5). pap. 5.99 *(978-1-4814-1416-6(X)*, Aladdin) Simon & Schuster Children's Publishing.

—The Fabulous Diary of Persephone Pinchgut. Darlison, Aleesah. 2016. (Totally Twins Ser.). (ENG.). 666p. (J). 8.99 *(978-1-78226-299-2(7)*, f248cfd4-4972-4ec3-b367-1baab5da4c62) Sweet Cherry Publishing GBR. Dist: Baker & Taylor Publisher Services (BTPS).

—Finding Luck. Earhart, Kristin. 2016. (Marguerite Henry's Misty Inn Ser.: 4). (ENG.). 128p. (J). (gr. 2-5). pap. 5.99 *(978-1-4814-1422-7(4)*, Aladdin) Simon & Schuster Children's Publishing.

—Home at Last. Katschke, Judy. 2018. (Marguerite Henry's Misty Inn Ser.: 8). (ENG.). 144p. (J). (gr. 2-5). 16.99 *(978-1-4814-6995-1(9))*; pap. 5.99 *(978-1-4814-6994-4(0))* Simon & Schuster Children's Publishing. (Aladdin).

—Lulu Bell & the Arabian Nights. Murrell, Belinda. 2015. (Lulu Bell Ser.). 96p. (J). (gr. 1-3). pap. 7.99 *(978-0-85798-558-3(2))* Random Hse. Australia AUS. Dist: Independent Pubs. Group.

—Lulu Bell & the Birthday Unicorn. Murrell, Belinda. 2014. (Lulu Bell Ser.: 1). 96p. (J). (gr. 1-3). 8.99 *(978-1-74275-875-6(4))* Random Hse. Australia AUS. Dist: Independent Pubs. Group.

—Lulu Bell & the Christmas Elf. Murrell, Belinda. 2020. (Lulu Bell Ser.: 8). (ENG.). 128p. (J). (gr. 2-4). 9.99 *(978-1-76089-220-3(3)*, Puffin) Penguin Random Hse. AUS. Dist: Independent Pubs. Group.

—Lulu Bell & the Christmas Elf. Murrell, Belinda. 2015. (Lulu Bell Ser.). (ENG.). 128p. (J). (gr. 2-4). 9.99 *(978-0-85798-503-3(5))* Random Hse. Australia AUS. Dist: Independent Pubs. Group.

—Lulu Bell & the Circus Pup. Murrell, Belinda. 2015. (Lulu Bell Ser.: 5). 96p. (J). (gr. 1-3). 8.99 *(978-0-85798-199-8(4))* Random Hse. Australia AUS. Dist: Independent Pubs. Group.

—Lulu Bell & the Fairy Penguin. Murrell, Belinda. 2014. (Lulu Bell Ser.: 2). 96p. (J). (gr. 1-3). 8.99 *(978-1-74275-877-0(0))* Random Hse. Australia AUS. Dist: Independent Pubs. Group.

—Lulu Bell & the Moon Dragon. Murrell, Belinda. 2014. (Lulu Bell Ser.: 4). (ENG.). 96p. (J). (gr. 1-3). 7.99 *(978-1-74275-881-7(9))* Random Hse. Australia AUS. Dist: Independent Pubs. Group.

—Lulu Bell & the Pyjama Party. Murrell, Belinda. 2020. (Lulu Bell Ser.: 7). 96p. (J). (gr. 2-5). 9.99 *(978-1-76089-228-9(9)*, Puffin) Penguin Random Hse. AUS. Dist: Independent Pubs. Group.

—Lulu Bell & the Pyjama Party. Murrell, Belinda. 2015. (Lulu Bell Ser.). (ENG.). 96p. (J). (gr. 2-4). 8.99 *(978-0-85798-303-9(2))* Random Hse. Australia AUS. Dist: Independent Pubs. Group.

—Lulu Bell & the Tiger Cub. Murrell, Belinda. 2020. (Lulu Bell Ser.: 9). (ENG.). 96p. (J). (gr. 2-5). 9.99 *(978-1-76089-230-2(0)*, Puffin) Penguin Random Hse. AUS. Dist: Independent Pubs. Group.

—Lulu Bell & the Tiger Cub. Murrell, Belinda. 2015. (Lulu Bell Ser.). (ENG.). 96p. (J). (gr. 2-4). 7.99 *(978-0-85798-301-5(6))* Random Hse. Australia AUS. Dist: Independent Pubs. Group.

—Lulu Bell's Amazing Animal Adventures. Murrell, Belinda. 2020. (Lulu Bell Ser.). 384p. (J). (gr. 2-5). 19.99 *(978-1-76089-101-5(0)*, Puffin) Penguin Random Hse. AUS. Dist: Independent Pubs. Group.

—Lulu Bell's Best Friends Ever. Murrell, Belinda. 2020. (Lulu Bell Ser.). 384p. (J). (gr. 2-5). 19.99 *(978-1-76089-102-2(9)*, Puffin) Penguin Random Hse. AUS. Dist: Independent Pubs. Group.

—Lulu Bell's Fantastic Holiday Fun. Murrell, Belinda. 2020. (Lulu Bell Ser.). (ENG.). 384p. (J). (gr. 2-5). 19.99 *(978-1-76089-157-2(6)*, Puffin) Penguin Random Hse. AUS. Dist: Independent Pubs. Group.

—Marguerite Henry's Misty Inn Treasury Books 1-8: Welcome Home!; Buttercup Mystery; Runaway Pony; Finding Luck; a Forever Friend; Pony Swim; Teacher's Pet; Home at Last. Earhart, Kristin & Katschke, Judy. ed. 2018. (Marguerite Henry's Misty Inn Ser.). (ENG.). 1088p. (J). (gr. 2-5). pap. 47.99 *(978-1-5344-2215-5(3)*, Aladdin) Simon & Schuster Children's Publishing.

—Model Mania: The Fabulous Diary of Persephone Pinchgut. Darlison, Aleesah. 2016. (Totally Twins Ser.: 2). (ENG.). 160p. (J). 8.99 *(978-1-78226-296-1(2)*, a2909597-5deb-4c2f-87f5-40be68d9e7b3) Sweet Cherry Publishing GBR. Dist: Baker & Taylor Publisher Services (BTPS).

—Runaway Pony. Earhart, Kristin. 2015. (Marguerite Henry's Misty Inn Ser.: 3). (ENG.). 128p. (J). (gr. 2-5). pap. 5.99 *(978-1-4814-1419-7(4)*, Aladdin) Simon & Schuster Children's Publishing.

—Teacher's Pet. Katschke, Judy. 2017. (Marguerite Henry's Misty Inn Ser.: 7). (ENG.). 128p. (J). (gr. 2-5). pap. 5.99 *(978-1-4814-6991-3(6)*, Aladdin) Simon & Schuster Children's Publishing.

—Tropical Trouble: The Fabulous Diary of Persephone Pinchgut. Darlison, Aleesah. 2016. (Totally Twins Ser.: 3).

(ENG.). 160p. (J). 8.99 *(978-1-78226-297-8(0)*, 736025fb-1232-4385-8c87-bfb2710261fa) Sweet Cherry Publishing GBR. Dist: Baker & Taylor Publisher Services (BTPS).

—Welcome Home! Earhart, Kristin. 2015. (Marguerite Henry's Misty Inn Ser.: 1). (ENG.). 128p. (J). (gr. 2-5). 16.99 *(978-1-4814-1414-2(3)*, Aladdin) Simon & Schuster Children's Publishing.

—Why I Love My Mom. Reynolds, Alison. 2015. (ENG.). 22p. (J). (gr. -1-1). 9.99 *(978-1-4998-0020-3(7))* Little Bee Books Inc.

Geddes, Serena. Rosie & Rasmus. Geddes, Serena. 2019. (Rosie & Rasmus Ser.). (ENG.). 48p. (J). (gr. -1-3). 17.99 *(978-1-4814-9874-6(6)*, Aladdin) Simon & Schuster Children's Publishing.

Geddes, Serena. Where the Dragons Live. Geddes, Serena. 2020. (Rosie & Rasmus Ser.). (ENG.). 48p. (J). (gr. -1-3). 17.99 ***(978-1-4814-9876-0(2)***, Aladdin) Simon & Schuster Children's Publishing.

Geddy, Iman, jt. illus. see Jamieson, Victoria.

Gedeon, Gloria. Bandages: 6 Copies, 6 vols. Moskowitz, Ellen. 2006. (ENG.). 16p. (gr. k-2). pap. 7.95 *(978-1-879835-71-9(1)*, Kaeden Bks.) Kaeden Corp.

—In the Hen House. Oppenlander, Meredith. I.t. ed. 2006. (ENG.). 12p. (gr. k-2). pap. 7.95 *(978-1-57874-003-1(7)*, Kaeden Bks.) Kaeden Corp.

—Little Mouse. Hoenecke, Karen. I.t. ed. 2005. (ENG.). 12p. (gr. k-2). pap. 7.95 *(978-1-57874-023-9(1)*, Kaeden Bks.) Kaeden Corp.

—Little Rabbit Is Sad. Williams, Deborah. I.t. ed. 2005. (ENG.). 12p. (Orig.). (gr. k-1). pap. 7.95 *(978-1-879835-99-3(1)*, Kaeden Bks.) Kaeden Corp.

—Moose's Loose Tooth. Spinelle, Nancy Louise. I.t. ed. 2005. (ENG.). 16p. (gr. k-2). pap. 7.95 *(978-1-57874-032-1(0)*, Kaeden Bks.) Kaeden Corp.

—Nickels & Pennies. Williams, Deborah. I.t. ed. 2005. (ENG.). 12p. (gr. k-1). pap. 7.95 *(978-1-879835-87-0(8)*, Kaeden Bks.) Kaeden Corp.

—Sammy. Urmston, Kathleen. 2005. (ENG.). 16p. (gr. k-1). pap. 7.95 *(978-1-57874-089-5(4)*, Kaeden Bks.) Kaeden Corp.

Gedovius, Juan. Ana, Verdad? Hinojosa, Francisco. 2003. (Coleccion Derechos Del Nino Ser.). (SPA.). 32p. (J). (gr. 3-5). pap. 7.95 *(978-84-204-5824-3(4))* Santillana USA Publishing Co., Inc.

—Busca un Magico Lunar. Macias, Elva. 2003. (SPA.). 32p. (J). (gr. k-3). pap. 7.95 *(978-968-19-0744-0(2))* Santillana USA Publishing Co., Inc.

Gedovius, Juan. Un Cuento �grrr! Bialet, Graciela. 2018. (Buenas Noches Ser.). (SPA.). 38p. (J). pap. ***(978-958-776-011-8(5))*** Norma Ediciones, S.A.

Gedovius, Juan. From the Vine. Gedovius, Juan. 24p. (J). (gr. k-6). 14.95 *(978-968-19-1053-2(2))* Santillana USA Publishing Co., Inc.

—Purple Cubed. Gedovius, Juan. 32p. (J). (gr. k-6). 13.95 *(978-968-19-0751-8(5))* Santillana USA Publishing Co., Inc.

Gedrich, Colleen. A Different Kind of Hero. Evans, Leah Beth. 2007. 40p. (J). per. 14.95 *(978-0-9795045-2-5(X))* Tribute Bks.

—Stanley Seagull. Mazur, Cathy. 2011. 32p. (J). 16.95 *(978-0-9837418-1-7(6))*; pap. 7.95 *(978-0-9837418-0-0(8))* Tribute Bks.

Gedzyk, Emily. Paleo Cooking for Cavekids. 2012. (ENG.). 102p. (J). pap. 19.75 *(978-0-9855541-2-5(6))* Firestorm Editions.

Gee, Bonnie. How to Draw Icky Bugs. Pallotta, Jerry. 2003. (J). mass mkt. *(978-0-439-38916-7(X))* Scholastic, Inc.

Gee, Isybilla. Issy Books Set 1, 5 bks. Calfee, Pat. 2013. 60p. (J). pap. 24.95 *(978-1-938406-13-3(3)*, Compass) Raphel Marketing, Inc.

—Issy Books Set 2, 5 bks. Calfee, Pat. 2013. 60p. (J). pap. 24.95 *(978-1-938406-14-0(1)*, Compass) Raphel Marketing, Inc.

—Issy Books Set 3, 10 books. Calfee, Pat. 2013. 120p. (J). pap. 39.95 *(978-1-938406-15-7(X)*, Compass) Raphel Marketing, Inc.

Gee, Kimberly. The Class. Ashburn, Boni. 2016. (ENG.). 40p. (J). (gr. -1-3). 17.99 *(978-1-4424-2248-3(3)*, Beach Lane Bks.) Beach Lane Bks.

Gee, Kimberly. Glad, Glad Bear! Gee, Kimberly. 2020. (Bear's Feelings Ser.). (ENG.). 40p. (J). (-3). 17.99 *(978-1-5344-5269-5(9)*, Beach Lane Bks.) Beach Lane Bks.

—Mad, Mad Bear! Gee, Kimberly. 2018. (Bear's Feelings Ser.). (ENG.). 40p. (J). (gr. -1-3). 17.99 *(978-1-4814-4971-7(0)*, Beach Lane Bks.) Beach Lane Bks.

—Up, up, up, Down! Gee, Kimberly. 2019. (ENG.). 32p. (J). (— 1). 16.99 *(978-0-525-51733-7(2)*, G.P. Putnam's Sons Books for Young Readers) Penguin Young Readers Group.

Geehan, Wayne. Multiplying Menace: The Revenge of Rumpelstiltskin. Calvert, Pam. 2006. (Charlesbridge Math Adventures Ser.). 32p. (J). (gr. 2-5). per. 7.95 *(978-1-57091-890-2(2))* Charlesbridge Publishing, Inc.

—The Multiplying Menace Divides! Calvert, Pam. 2011. (Charlesbridge Math Adventures Ser.). 32p. (J). (gr. 2-5). pap. 7.95 *(978-1-57091-782-0(5))* Charlesbridge Publishing, Inc.

—Sir Cumference & All the King's Tens. Neuschwander, Cindy. 2009. (Sir Cumference Ser.). 32p. (J). (gr. 3-7). 16.95 *(978-1-57091-727-1(2))* Charlesbridge Publishing, Inc.

—Sir Cumference & the Fracton Faire. Neuschwander, Cindy. 2017. (Sir Cumference Ser.). 32p. (J). (gr. 2-5). lib. bdg. 16.99 *(978-1-57091-771-4(X))* Charlesbridge Publishing, Inc.

—Sir Cumference & the Isle of Immeter. Neuschwander, Cindy. 2006. (Sir Cumference Ser.). 32p. (J). (gr. 3-7). per. 7.99 *(978-1-57091-681-6(0))* Charlesbridge Publishing, Inc.

—Sir Cumference & the off-The-Charts Dessert. Neuschwander, Cindy. 2013. (Sir Cumference Ser.). 32p. (J). (gr. 3-7). pap. 7.95 *(978-1-57091-199-6(1))* Charlesbridge Publishing, Inc.

—Sir Cumference & the Roundabout Battle. Neuschwander, Cindy. 2015. (Sir Cumference Ser.). 32p. (J). (gr. 3-7). lib. bdg. 16.95 *(978-1-57091-765-3(5))* Charlesbridge Publishing, Inc.

—Sir Cumference & the Sword in the Cone. Neuschwander, Cindy. 2003. (Sir Cumference Ser.). 32p. (J). (gr. 3-7). pap. 7.95 *(978-1-57091-601-4(2))* Charlesbridge Publishing, Inc.

—Sir Cumference & the Viking's Map. Neuschwander, Cindy. 2012. (Sir Cumference Ser.). 32p. (J). (gr. 3-7). 16.95 *(978-1-57091-791-2(4))*; pap. 7.95 *(978-1-57091-792-9(2))* Charlesbridge Publishing, Inc.

—Sir Cumference & the Viking's Map. Neuschwander, Cindy. ed. 2012. (Sir Cumference Ser.). lib. bdg. 18.40 *(978-0-606-26445-7(0))* Turtleback.

Geer, Charles. The Big Chunk of Ice: The Last Known Adventure of the Mad Scientists' Club. Brinley, Bertrand R. 2005. (Mad Scientist Club Ser.). 275p. (J). (gr. 3-7). 18.95 *(978-1-930900-29-5(5))* Purple Hse. Pr.

—The Big Kerplop! The Original Adventure of the Mad Scientist's Club. Brinley, Bertrand R. 2003. 238p. (J). 17.95 *(978-1-930900-22-6(8))* Purple Hse. Pr.

—The Biggest (And Best) Flag That Ever Flew, 1 vol. Jones, Rebecca C. 2009. (ENG.). 30p. (J). (gr. -1-3). 8.99 *(978-0-87033-440-5(9))*, 3594, Cornell Maritime Pr./Tidewater Pubs.) Schiffer Publishing, Ltd.

—Ginger Box. Foster, Martha S. 2011. 126p. 40.95 *(978-1-258-06588-1(6))* Literary Licensing, LLC.

—Horse Stories: Young Readers. Furman, A. L., ed. 2011. 192p. 42.95 *(978-1-258-09836-0(9))* Literary Licensing, LLC.

—Indian Stories. Furman, A. L., ed. 2011. 190p. 42.95 *(978-1-258-09304-4(9))* Literary Licensing, LLC.

—The Mad Scientists' Club. Brinley, Bertrand R. 50th ed. 2011. (J). 18.95 *(978-1-930900-53-0(8))* Purple Hse. Pr.

—The Mad Scientists' Club Complete Collection. Brinley, Bertrand R. 2010. 619p. (YA). pap. 29.99 *(978-1-930900-51-6(1))* Purple Hse. Pr.

—The Marvelous Inventions of Alvin Fernald. Hicks, Clifford B. 119p. (J). (gr. 3-7). 2013. (ENG.). pap. 7.99 *(978-1-930900-72-1(4))*; 2006. 16.95 *(978-1-930900-21-9(X))* Purple Hse. Pr.

—Pioneer Stories: Young Readers. Furman, A. L., ed. 2011. 190p. 42.95 *(978-1-258-09907-7(1))* Literary Licensing, LLC.

—Plain Girl. Sorensen, Virginia. 2003. (ENG.). 176p. (J). (gr. 3-7). pap. 7.99 *(978-0-15-204725-2(5)*, 1194243) Houghton Mifflin Harcourt Publishing Co.

—Sauncey & Mr. King's Gallery, 1 vol. Simmons, Clara Ann. 2009. (ENG.). 30p. (J). (gr. 1-4). 10.95 *(978-0-87033-498-6(0)*, 9780870334986, Cornell Maritime Pr./Tidewater Pubs.) Schiffer Publishing, Ltd.

—Wild Life Stories: Young Readers. Furman, A. L., ed. 2011. 192p. 42.95 *(978-1-258-10201-2(3))* Literary Licensing, LLC.

—Young Visitor to Mars. Elam Jr., Richard M. 2011. 256p. 47.95 *(978-1-258-09909-1(8))* Literary Licensing, LLC.

Geer, Charles H. Detective Stories: Young Readers. Coombs, Charles. 2011. 194p. 42.95 *(978-1-258-10586-0(1))* Literary Licensing, LLC.

—Indoor Sports Stories. Coombs, Charles Ira. 2011. 190p. 42.95 *(978-1-258-09130-9(5))* Literary Licensing, LLC.

—Railroad Stories: Young Readers. Coombs, Charles. 2011. 194p. 42.95 *(978-1-258-10208-1(0))* Literary Licensing, LLC.

—Young Crow Raider: Young Heroes Library. Kroll, Francis Lynde. 2011. 186p. 42.95 *(978-1-258-09906-0(3))* Literary Licensing, LLC.

—Young Infield Rookie. Coombs, Charles. 2011. 190p. 42.95 *(978-1-258-10529-7(2))* Literary Licensing, LLC.

—Young Sand Hills Cowboy: Young Heroes Library. Kroll, Francis Lynde. 2011. 188p. 42.95 *(978-1-258-09908-4(X))* Literary Licensing, LLC.

—Young Sioux Warrior. Kroll, Francis Lynde. 2011. 188p. 42.95 *(978-1-258-10209-8(9))* Literary Licensing, LLC.

Geer, William J. Nicky Jones & the Roaring Rhinos. Grambling, Lois G. 2004. 32p. (J). 6.95 *(978-1-877810-14-5(2))* Rayve Productions, Inc.

Geeson, Andrew & Veldhoven, Marijke. Save the Orangutan. Eason, Sarah. 2009. (Save the... Ser.). 32p. (J). (gr. 2-5). lib. bdg. 27.25 *(978-1-4358-2811-7(9))* Rosen Publishing Group, Inc., The.

—Save the Panda. Eason, Sarah. 2009. (Save the... Ser.). 32p. (J). (gr. 2-5). lib. bdg. 27.25 *(978-1-4358-2812-4(7))* Rosen Publishing Group, Inc., The.

—Save the Polar Bear. Eason, Sarah. 2009. (Save the... Ser.). 32p. (J). (gr. 2-5). lib. bdg. 27.25 *(978-1-4358-2810-0(0))* Rosen Publishing Group, Inc., The.

—Save the Tiger. Eason, Sarah. 2009. (Save the... Ser.). 32p. (J). (gr. 2-5). lib. bdg. 27.25 *(978-1-4358-2813-1(5))* Rosen Publishing Group, Inc., The.

Gehr, Mary. Surprise Island. Warner, Gertrude Chandler. 2020. (Boxcar Children Ser.). (ENG.). 184p. (J). (gr. 2-6). lib. bdg. 27.07 ***(978-1-5321-4480-6(6)***, 35170, Chapter Bks.) Spotlight.

Gehr, Mary. We're Going to Town! Aldis, Dorothy Keeley. 2011. 58p. 36.95 *(978-1-258-08388-5(4))* Literary Licensing, LLC.

Gehr, Mary. The Yellow House Mystery. Warner, Gertrude Chandler. 2020. (Boxcar Children Ser.). (ENG.). 192p. (J). (gr. 2-6). lib. bdg. 27.07 ***(978-1-5321-4482-0(2)***, 35172, Chapter Bks.) Spotlight.

Gehrmann, Katja. Goose the Bear. 2014. (ENG.). 40p. (J). (gr. -1-3). 16.95 *(978-1-62636-384-7(6)*, Sky Pony Pr.) Skyhorse Publishing Co., Inc.

Geiken, Brenda. Free to Be Me: The Eskimo Way. Amundson, Susan. 2003. 56p. lib. bdg. 16.95 *(978-1-883477-65-3(4)*, Lone Oak Pr., Ltd.) Finney Co., Inc.

Geiken, Brenda Joy. Three Little Lambs — Somewhere. Amundson, Susan D. 2006. 40p. (J). *(978-1-59984-002-4(2))* Bluedoor, llc.

Geis, Alissa Imre. Our Friendship Rules, 1 vol. Moss, Peggy. 2007. (ENG.). 32p. (J). (gr. 2-6). 16.95 *(978-0-88448-291-8(X)*, 884291) Tilbury Hse. Pubs.

Geis Conti, Patricia. Las Meninas. 2010. (SPA.). (J). (gr. 2-6). *(978-84-9825-487-7(6))* Combel Editorial, S.A.

Geis, Patricia. Paca Lamar. Geis, Patricia. 2004. (Mi Ciudad Ser.). (SPA & ENG.). 24p. (J). (gr. -1-k). 6.95 *(978-84-7864-797-2(X))* Combel Editorial, S.A. ESP. Dist: Independent Pubs. Group.

—Pascual Midón. Geis, Patricia. 2004. (Mi Ciudad Ser.). (SPA & ENG.). 24p. (J). (gr. -1-k). 6.95 *(978-84-7864-799-6(6))* Combel Editorial, S.A. ESP. Dist: Independent Pubs. Group.

—Pepa Pas. Geis, Patricia. 2004. (Mi Ciudad Ser.). (SPA & ENG.). 24p. (J). (gr. -1-k). 6.95 *(978-84-7864-796-5(1))* Combel Editorial, S.A. ESP. Dist: Independent Pubs. Group.

Geisler, Dagmar. The Creation of the World. Natus, Uwe. 2016. (ENG.). 28p. (J). (gr. -1-3). 14.99 *(978-1-5064-0883-5(4)*, Sparkhouse Family) Augsburg Fortress, Pubs.

Geisler, Dagmar. I Can Be Brave: Overcoming Fear, Finding Confidence, & Asserting Yourself. Kreul, Holde. 2020. (Safe Child, Happy Parent Ser.). 36p. (J). (gr. -1-1). 16.99 ***(978-1-5107-4661-9(7)***, Sky Pony Pr.) Skyhorse Publishing Co., Inc.

Geisler, Dagmar. I Can Build Confidence. Zöller, Elisabeth. 2019. (Safe Child, Happy Parent Ser.). (ENG.). 32p. (J). (gr. -1-1). 16.99 *(978-1-5107-4651-0(X)*, Sky Pony Pr.) Skyhorse Publishing Co., Inc.

—My Body Belongs to Me from My Head to My Toes. 2014. (Safe Child, Happy Parent Ser.). 36p. (J). (gr. -1-k). 16.95 *(978-1-62636-345-8(5)*, 263345, Sky Pony Pr.) Skyhorse Publishing Co., Inc.

—My Feelings & Me. Kreul, Holde. 2018. (Safe Child, Happy Parent Ser.). (ENG.). 32p. (J). (gr. -1-k). 16.99 *(978-1-5107-3533-0(X)*, Sky Pony Pr.) Skyhorse Publishing Co., Inc.

—Sometimes People Fight — Even When They Love Each Other. 2019. (Safe Child, Happy Parent Ser.). 32p. (J). (gr. -1-1). 16.99 *(978-1-5107-4654-1(4)*, Sky Pony Pr.) Skyhorse Publishing Co., Inc.

—When Boys & Girls Become Men & Women: Everything You Need to Know about Growing Up. Müller, Jörg. 2020. (Safe Child, Happy Parent Ser.). 96p. (YA). (gr. 2-6). 19.99 *(978-1-5107-4656-5(0)*, Sky Pony Pr.) Skyhorse Publishing Co., Inc.

Geist, Hans. And Heaven Stood Silent. Billiot, Christopher. 2009. 36p. pap. 15.49 *(978-1-4389-5894-1(3))* AuthorHouse.

Geister, David. B Is for Battle Cry: A Civil War Alphabet. Bauer, Patricia. 2009. (History Ser.). (ENG.). 40p. (J). (gr. 2-5). 17.95 *(978-1-58536-356-8(1))* Sleeping Bear Pr.

—The Legend of Minnesota. Wargin, Kathy-jo. 2006. (Legend (Sleeping Bear) Ser.). (ENG.). 40p. (J). (gr. 3-7). 17.95 *(978-1-58536-262-2(X))* Sleeping Bear Pr.

—Riding to Washington. Swain, Gwenyth. 2007. (Tales of Young Americans Ser.). (ENG.). 40p. (J). (gr. 1-4). 17.95 *(978-1-58536-324-7(3)*, 202128) Sleeping Bear Pr.

—S Is for Scientists: A Discovery Alphabet. Verstraete, Larry. 2010. (Science Alphabet Ser.). (ENG.). 40p. (J). (gr. 1-4). 16.95 *(978-1-58536-470-1(3)*, 202189) Sleeping Bear Pr.

—Storm's Coming! Preus, Margi. 2016. (ENG.). 32p. (J). 16.95 *(978-1-68134-018-0(6))* Minnesota Historical Society Pr.

—T Is for Twin Cities: A Minneapolis/St. Paul Alphabet. Carlson, Nancy & McCool, Barry. 2012. (City Alphabet Ser.). (ENG.). 32p. (J). (gr. 1-5). 16.95 *(978-1-58536-583-8(1))* Sleeping Bear Pr.

Geister, David, et al. Voices for Freedom. Whelan, Gloria & Swain, Gwenyth. 2013. (American Adventures Ser.). (ENG.). (J). (gr. 3-6). lib. bdg. 18.10 *(978-1-62765-945-1(5))* Perfection Learning Corp.

Geister, David & Van Frankenhuyzen, Gijsbert. The Voyageur's Paddle. Wargin, Kathy-jo. rev. ed. 2007. (Myths, Legends, Fairy & Folktales Ser.). (ENG.). 40p. (J). (gr. 1-4). 19.99 *(978-1-58536-007-9(4)*, 201942) Sleeping Bear Pr.

Gelev, Penko. Dr. Jekyll & Mr. Hyde. Stevenson, Robert Louis. 2017. (Classic Graphic Fiction Ser.). (ENG.). 48p. (J). (gr. 4). pap. 7.95 *(978-1-912006-01-4(4))* Book Hse. GBR. Dist: Sterling Publishing Co., Inc.

—Dracula. Stoker, Bram. 2017. (Classic Graphic Fiction Ser.). (ENG.). 48p. (J). (gr. 4). pap. 7.95 *(978-1-912006-02-1(2))* Book Hse. GBR. Dist: Sterling Publishing Co., Inc.

—Frankenstein. Shelley, Mary. 2017. (Classic Graphic Fiction Ser.). (ENG.). 48p. (J). (gr. 4). pap. 7.95 *(978-1-912006-22-9(7))* Book Hse. GBR. Dist: Sterling Publishing Co., Inc.

—Treasure Island. Stevenson, Robert Louis. 2006. (Graphic Classics Ser.). (ENG.). 48p. (J). (gr. 5-8). 24.94 *(978-0-7641-5976-3(3)*, B.E.S. Publishing) Peterson's.

Gelev, Penko & Sidong, Li. The Odyssey. Homer. 2009. (Barron's Graphic Classics Ser.). (ENG.). (J). (gr. 5-11). lib. bdg. 21.10 *(978-1-62765-645-0(6))* Perfection Learning Corp.

Gelhardt, Rob. The Adventures of Shuster: The Very Special Rooster. Roberts, H. Donald. 2017. (ENG.). 36p. (J). (gr. 2-4). pap. 12.99 *(978-0-692-05085-9(X))* Roberts, Hebard D. Bks.

Gellatly, Michael. The 5 Year-Old Lawyer & Her Frog. Kadry Parra, Gloria Elizabeth. 2020. (ENG.). 38p. (J). (gr. k-1). 19.95 ***(978-1-7324511-9-3(2))*** Something Or Other Publishing.

Gelsinger, Dona. All Things Bright & Beautiful. 2007. (ENG.). 10p. bds. 6.99 *(978-1-4037-3411-2(9)*, Spirit Pr.) Bendon, Inc.

Gemal, Gerald. Puddle Bubble Trouble. Hatt, Pat. 2018. (ENG.). 34p. (J). pap. 9.99 *(978-1-7237-3378-9(4))* Independently Published.

Gen, Pixels. Emma's Special Tummy. 2018. (J). pap. 11.95 *(978-1-7322513-0-4(4))* Lancaster, Paula.

Gendi, Bishoy. A Lamb Called Love. Bennitt-Young, Milly. 2nd ed. 2018. (ENG.). 30p. (J). *(978-0-9946974-5-5(7))* Seraph Creative.

Gendler, Robert, photos by. The Little Moon Phase Book. Grice, Noreen. 2005. 12p. (J). spiral bd. 23.95 *(978-0-9773285-0-5(3))* Ozone Publishing, Corp.

Gendron, Cathy. The Nutcracker Comes to America: How Three Ballet-Loving Brothers Created a Holiday Tradition. Barton, Chris. 2015. (ENG.). 36p. (J). (gr. 2-5). 19.99 *(978-1-4677-2151-6(4)*, 9781467721516); E-Book 30.65 *(978-1-4677-8848-9(1))* Lerner Publishing Group. (Millbrook Pr.).

—Trees Make Perfect Pets. Czajak, Paul. 2020. 32p. (J). (-3). 17.99 *(978-1-4926-6473-4(1)*, Sourcebooks Jabberwocky) Sourcebooks, Inc.

Gendron, Sabrina. Badir & the Beaver, 1 vol. Stewart, Shannon. 2019. (Orca Echoes Ser.). (ENG.). 104p. (J). (gr. 1-3). pap. 6.95 *(978-1-4598-1727-2(3))* Orca Bk. Pubs. USA.

—High & Dry. Walters, Eric. 2020. (Orca Echoes Ser.). (ENG.). 96p. (J). (gr. 1-3). pap. 7.95 *(978-1-4598-2310-5(9))* Orca Bk. Pubs. USA.

Genest, Micah. Wonder: A Story about a Boy & His Loss. Genest, Micah. 2018. (ENG.). 52p. (J). pap. ***(978-1-7753721-8-9(9))*** Mortar and Pestle Publishing.

Geneva B, Geneva. The Dragon Thief. Elliott, Zetta. 2019. (Dragons in a Bag Ser.: 2). (ENG.). 176p. (J). (gr. 3-7). 16.99 *(978-1-5247-7049-5(3)*, Random Hse. Bks. for Young Readers) Random Hse. Children's Bks.

—Dragons in a Bag. Elliott, Zetta. 2018. (Dragons in a Bag Ser.: 1). (ENG.). 160p. (J). (gr. 3-7). 16.99 *(978-1-5247-7045-7(0))*; lib. bdg. 19.99 *(978-1-5247-7046-4(9))* Random Hse. Children's Bks. (Random Hse. Bks. for Young Readers).

Gennari, Joel. The Best-Selling App, 1 vol. Furgang, Adam. 2020. (Power Coders Ser.). (ENG.). 32p. (J). (gr. 5-5). 26.25 *(978-1-7253-0770-4(7))*; pap. 10.60 *(978-1-7253-0768-1(5))* Rosen Publishing Group, Inc., The. (PowerKids Pr.).

—Build Your Algorithm Skills, 1 vol. Harris, Christopher. 2019. (Unplugged Activities for Future Coders Ser.). (ENG.). 48p. (gr. 5-5). 27.93 *(978-1-9785-1074-6(8))* Enslow Publishing, LLC.

—Build Your Computational Thinking Skills, 1 vol. Harris, Christopher. 2019. (Unplugged Activities for Future Coders Ser.). (ENG.). 48p. (gr. 5-5). pap. 11.70 *(978-1-9785-1061-6(6))* Enslow Publishing, LLC.

—Build Your Computer Security Skills, 1 vol. Furgang, Adam & Harris, Christopher. 2019. (Unplugged Activities for Future Coders Ser.). (ENG.). 48p. (gr. 5-5). pap. 11.70 *(978-1-9785-1064-7(0))* Enslow Publishing, LLC.

—Build Your Debugging Skills, 1 vol. Furgang, Kathy & Harris, Christopher. 2019. (Unplugged Activities for Future Coders Ser.). (ENG.). 48p. (gr. 5-5). pap. 11.70 *(978-1-9785-1067-8(5))* Enslow Publishing, LLC.

—The Chat Bot Mystery. McKay, C. R. 2018. (Power Coders Ser.). 32p. (J). (gr. 9-11). 26.25 *(978-1-5383-4009-7(7)*, PowerKids Pr.) Rosen Publishing Group, Inc., The.

—A Peculiar Sequence of Events. Vink, Amanda. 2018. (Power Coders Ser.). 32p. (gr. 9-11). 26.25 *(978-1-5383-4029-5(1)*, PowerKids Pr.) Rosen Publishing Group, Inc., The.

—The Secret of the Five Bugs. McKay, C. R. 2018. (Power Coders Ser.). 32p. (gr. 9-11). 26.25 *(978-1-5383-4013-4(5))*; pap. 10.60 *(978-1-5383-4014-1(3))* Rosen Publishing Group, Inc., The. (PowerKids Pr.).

—The Simulated Friend. Vink, Amanda. 2018. (Power Coders Ser.). 32p. (gr. 9-11). 26.25 *(978-1-5383-4017-2(8)*, PowerKids Pr.) Rosen Publishing Group, Inc., The.

Gennari, Joel, jt. illus. see Antal, Lara.

Genolet, Andres. Runaways by Rainbow Rowell Vol. 4: But You Can't Hide. Rowell, Rainbow. 2019. (Runaways by Rainbow Rowell Ser.: 4). (ENG.). 144p. (YA). (gr. 8-17). pap. 17.99 *(978-1-302-91801-9(X))* Marvel Worldwide, Inc.

—Runaways by Rainbow Rowell Vol. 5: Canon Fodder. Rowell, Rainbow. 2020. 136p. (YA). (gr. 8-17). pap. 19.99 *(978-1-302-92028-9(6))* Marvel Worldwide, Inc.

Genovés, Graciela. Jorge Luis Borges. Genovés, Graciela. Lázaro León, Georgina. 2009. (Cuando los Grandes Eran Pequenos Ser.). (SPA.). 32p. (J). (gr. 4-6). 14.99 *(978-1-933032-40-5(5))* Lectorum Pubns., Inc.

Genovese, Karen Marie. Child of the Wind. Wander, Sharon Lee. Even, William C., ed. 2018. (ENG.). 36p. (J). (gr. k-6). pap. 12.95 *(978-0-9971276-4-5(3))* Media Hatchery.

Genth, Christina. The Messy Monkey Tea Party. Deich, Cheri Bivin. 2007. 32p. (J). (gr. -1-3). 15.95 *(978-1-60108-006-6(9))* Red Cygnet Pr.

Gentieu, Penny. Baby Signs for Animals. Acredolo, Linda & Goodwyn, Susan. 2003. (ENG.). 14p. (J). (gr. -1 — 1). bds. 6.99 *(978-0-06-009075-3(8)*, HarperFestival) HarperCollins Pubs.

Gentieu, Penny, photos by. Knots in My Yo-Yo Strong. Spinelli, Jerry. 2014. 158p. pap. 11.00 *(978-1-61003-375-6(2))* Center for the Collaborative Classroom.

Gentieu, Penny, photos by. You & Me, Baby. Reiser, Lynn. 2008. (ENG., 32p. (J). (— 1). bds. 6.99 *(978-0-375-84420-1(1)*, Knopf Bks. for Young Readers) Random Hse. Children's Bks.

Gentile, Christopher. The Little Bitty Story of Austin Q. Peapot, 1 vol. Boie, Kristen. 2009. 20p. pap. 24.95 *(978-1-60749-548-2(1))* America Star Bks.

Gentry, Beatrice. Piep. Gentry, Beatrice. 2016. (ENG.). 36p. (J). *(978-1-78222-453-2(X))* Paragon Publishing, Rothersthorpe.

Gentry, Debra. Jeremy & the Wappo. Elwell, Sharon. 126p. (Orig.). (J). (gr. 3-4). pap. 10.50 *(978-0-9626210-0-0(5))* Rattle OK Pubns.

Gentry, Kyle. The Adventures of Sammy Snowflake, Vol. 1. Becker, Brooke. 2007. (ENG.). 64p. (gr. 4-7). 19.95 *(978-0-9795260-0-8(0))* Courtyard Publishing, LLC.

Gentry, Lauren. Scotland 123. Day, Anna. 2015. (ENG.). (J). pap. 10.95 *(978-0-9575456-2-5(2))* Playroom Pr.

Gentry, Marita. Beware, Beware of the Big Bad Bear!, 1 vol. de Las Casas, Dianne. 2012. (ENG.). 32p. (J). (gr. k-3). 16.99 *(978-1-4556-1690-9(7)*, Pelican Publishing) Arcadia Publishing.

—The Cajun Cornbread Boy, 1 vol. de Las Casas, Dianne. 2008. (Cajun Tall Tales Ser.). (ENG.). 32p. (J). (gr. k-3). 16.99 *(978-1-58980-224-7(1),* Pelican Publishing) Arcadia Publishing.
—The Cajun Cornbread Boy & the Buttermilk Biscuit Girl, 1 vol. de Las Casas, Dianne. 2017. (Cajun Tall Tales Ser.). (ENG.). 32p. (J). (gr. k-3). 16.99 *(978-1-4556-2311-2(3),* Pelican Publishing) Arcadia Publishing.
—Dinosaur Mardi Gras, 1 vol. de Las Casas, Dianne. 2011. (ENG.). 32p. (J). (gr. k-3). 17.99 *(978-1-58980-966-6(1),* Pelican Publishing) Arcadia Publishing.
—The Gigantic Sweet Potato, 1 vol. de Las Casas, Dianne. 2010. (ENG.). 32p. (J). (gr. k-3). 16.99 *(978-1-58980-755-6(3),* Pelican Publishing) Arcadia Publishing.
—Madame Poulet & Monsieur Roach, 1 vol. de Las Casas, Dianne. 2009. (ENG.). 32p. (J). (gr. k-3). 16.99 *(978-1-58980-686-3(7),* Pelican Publishing) Arcadia Publishing.
—New Orleans Mother Goose, 1 vol. Adam, Ryan. 2014. (Mother Goose Ser.). (ENG.). 40p. (J). 17.99 *(978-1-4556-1953-5(1),* Pelican Publishing) Arcadia Publishing.
—There's a Dragon in the Library, 1 vol. de Las Casas, Dianne. 2011. (ENG.). 32p. (J). (gr. k-3). 16.99 *(978-1-58980-844-7(4),* Pelican Publishing) Arcadia Publishing.
Gentry, Susana, photos by. What Should I Eat? Sly, Stacey. 2010. 26p. pap. 12.95 *(978-1-60911-432-9(9),* Eloquent Bks.) Strategic Book Publishing & Rights Agency (SBPRA).
Gentry, T. Kyle. Grandpa for Sale. Enderle, Dotti & Sansum, Vicki. 2007. (ENG.). 32p. (J). (gr. k-3). 17.95 *(978-0-9729225-8-6(X))* Flashlight Pr.
—Hidden, 1 vol. Enderle, Dotti. 2007. (ENG.). 104p. (J). (gr. 3-7). per. 8.95 *(978-1-58980-481-4(3),* Pelican Publishing) Arcadia Publishing.
—Koala Koala, I'm Not a Bear, I'm a Koala. Earl, David G. 2009. 32p. pap. 12.95 *(978-1-936051-22-9(2))* Peppertree Pr., The.
Genzo, John Paul. Islands of Ice: The Story of a Harp Seal. Hollenbeck, Kathleen M. (Smithsonian Oceanic Collection Ser.). (ENG.). 32p. (J). (gr. -1-3). 2011. 19.95 *(978-1-60727-652-4(6));* 2005. 4.95 *(978-1-56899-966-1(6),* B4071); 2005. 19.95 *(978-1-56899-967-8(4),* BC4021); 2005. 9.95 *(978-1-56899-970-8(4),* PB4071); 2005. 15.95 *(978-1-56899-965-4(8),* B4021) Soundprints.
Geoffrey, Beaulieu, jt. illus. see Vecchio, Luciano.
Geoffroi, Remie. The Dreadful Truth: Canadian Crime. Staunton, Ted. 2006. (Dreadful Truth Ser.). (ENG.). 104p. (J). (gr. 3-8). *(978-0-88780-705-3(4))* Formac Publishing Co., Ltd.
—Gold Rush. Staunton, Ted. 2008. (Dreadful Truth Ser.). (ENG.). 104p. (YA). (gr. 3-8). *(978-0-88780-747-3(X))* Formac Publishing Co., Ltd.
—Money: Deal with It or Pay the Price, 1 vol. Mototsune, Kat. 2016. (Lorimer Deal with It Ser.). (ENG.). 32p. (J). (gr. 4-9). pap. 12.95 *(978-1-55028-958-9(6),* 998bbdab-fc6f-44aa-88b0-7b7f3edeabee) James Lorimer & Co. Ltd., Pubs. CAN. Dist: Lerner Publishing Group.
—Teasing: Before the Joke's on You, 1 vol. Slavens, Elaine & Pitt, Steve. 2016. (Lorimer Deal with It Ser.). (ENG.). 32p. (J). (gr. 4-9). 24.95 *(978-1-55277-497-7(X),* 076b9f36-3433-4fa0-ab3a-dd75377b592b) James Lorimer & Co. Ltd., Pubs. CAN. Dist: Lerner Publishing Group.
—Teasing: Deal with It Before the Joke's on You, 1 vol. Pitt, Steve. 2007. (Lorimer Deal with It Ser.). (ENG.). 32p. (J). (gr. 4-8). pap., instr.'s gde. ed. 12.95 *(978-1-55028-946-6(2),* 9781550289466) James Lorimer & Co. Ltd., Pubs. CAN. Dist: Orca Bk. Pubs. USA.
George, Alex. The Magic Flower. Hemmingway, Tracy Hayden. 2003. (ENG.). 24p. pap. 9.00 *(978-1-4120-0984-3(7))* Trafford Publishing.
George, Audra. Vagabonding. George, Audra. 2006. 32p. (J). (gr. -1-3). 17.95 *(978-1-60108-010-3(7))* Red Cygnet Pr.
George, Boy. I Hear... 2013. 36p. (J). (gr. -1-k). 12.99 *(978-1-908473-07-3(X))* PatrickGeorge GBR. Dist: Independent Pubs. Group.
George, Chris. Blast from the Past. Beechen, Adam. 2004. (Fairly OddParents (8x8) Ser.: Vol. 1). (ENG.). (J). (gr. k-3). lib. bdg. 14.10 *(978-0-7569-1970-2(3))* Perfection Learning Corp.
George, Hannah. The Baby Deer Rescue (Animal Adventure Club 1), 50 vols. Sloan, Michelle. 2019. (Animal Adventure Club Ser.). (ENG.). 104p. (J). 6.95 *(978-1-78250-556-3(3),* Kelpies) Floris Bks. GBR. Dist: Consortium Bk. Sales & Distribution.
—The Baby Otter Rescue (Animal Adventure Club 2), 50 vols. Sloan, Michelle. 2019. (Animal Adventure Club Ser.). (ENG.). 112p. (J). 6.95 *(978-1-78250-592-1(X))* Floris Bks. GBR. Dist: Consortium Bk. Sales & Distribution.
—It's a Dog's Life. Morpurgo, Michael. 2016. (Reading Ladder Ser.). (ENG.). 48p. (J). (gr. k-2). pap. 7.99 *(978-1-4052-8256-7(8))* Egmont Bks., Ltd. GBR. Dist: Independent Pubs. Group.
George, John, 3rd. Moving Day. Pope, Amy. 2004. (J). bds. 9.99 *(978-1-4183-0010-4(1))* Christ Inspired, Inc.
George Jr, Robert. If I Were A... Walters, Danna J. 2019. (ENG.). 30p. (J). (gr. k-2). 19.40 ***(978-0-578-57249-9(4))*** walters, danna j. author.
George, Karen. Freddie & the Fairy, 7. Donaldson, Julia. 4th ed. 2012. (ENG.). 32p. (J). (gr. -1-k). 10.99 *(978-0-330-51118-6(1))* Pan Macmillan GBR. Dist: Independent Pubs. Group.
—Wake up Do, Lydia Lou!, 2. Donaldson, Julia. 2nd ed. 2015. (ENG.). 24p. (J). (gr. -1-k). pap. 10.99 *(978-1-4472-0957-7(5))* Pan Macmillan GBR. Dist: Independent Pubs. Group.
George, Leonard, Jr. Eyes, Ears, Nose & Mouth. Olson, Karen W. (ENG.). 20p. 2005. (J). pap. 10.95 *(978-1-894778-34-3(0));* 2009. pap. 9.95 *(978-1-894778-52-7(9))* Theytus Bks., Ltd. CAN. Dist: Univ. of Toronto Pr.
—Living Safe, Playing Safe. Olson, Karen W. ed. 2009. (Caring for Me Ser.). (ENG.). 20p. (J). (gr. -1-k). pap. 9.95 *(978-1-894778-51-0(0))* Theytus Bks., Ltd. CAN. Dist: Orca Bk. Pubs. USA.
George, Lindsay Barrett. Pick, Pull, Snap! Where Once a Flower Bloomed. Schaefer, Lola M. 2003. (ENG.). 32p. (J). (gr. k-5). 17.99 *(978-0-688-17834-5(0),* Greenwillow Bks.) HarperCollins Pubs.
George, Lindsay Barrett. In the Garden: Who's Been Here? George, Lindsay Barrett. 2006. (ENG.). 48p. (J). (gr. -1-3). 17.99 *(978-0-06-078762-2(7),* Greenwillow Bks.) HarperCollins Pubs.
—Inside Mouse, Outside Mouse. George, Lindsay Barrett. (ENG.). 40p. (J). (gr. -1-3). 2004. 17.99 *(978-0-06-000466-8(5));* 2006. reprint ed. pap. 7.99 *(978-0-06-000468-2(1))* HarperCollins Pubs. (Greenwillow Bks.).
—Maggie's Ball. George, Lindsay Barrett. 2010. (ENG.). 32p. (J). (gr. -1-k). 16.99 *(978-0-06-172166-3(2),* Greenwillow Bks.) HarperCollins Pubs.
—The Secret. George, Lindsay Barrett. 2005. 32p. (J). 16.89 *(978-0-06-029600-1(3))* HarperCollins Pubs.
—That Pup! George, Lindsay Barrett. 2011. (ENG.). 32p. (J). (gr. -1-k). 16.99 *(978-0-06-200413-0(1),* Greenwillow Bks.) HarperCollins Pubs.
George, Patrick. I Taste... George, Patrick. 2013. 36p. (J). (gr. -1-k). 12.99 *(978-1-908473-06-6(1))* PatrickGeorge GBR. Dist: Independent Pubs. Group.
—I Touch .. George, Patrick. 2013. 36p. (J). (gr. -1-k). 12.99 *(978-1-908473-08-0(8))* PatrickGeorge GBR. Dist: Independent Pubs. Group.
George, Peter. Davy Crockett & the Great Mississippi Snag, 1 vol. Meister, Cari. 2014. (American Folk Legends Ser.). (ENG.). 32p. (J). (gr. k-2). lib. bdg. 27.99 *(978-1-4795-5431-7(6),* Picture Window Bks.) Capstone.
Georgelli, Clair. Who Stole the Sun? Georgelli, Clair. 2020. 32p. (J). (gr. -1-k). 17.99 ***(978-1-913060-00-8(4))*** Faros Bks. GBR. Dist: Independent Pubs. Group.
Georger, Lucie. Don't Be Afraid to Say No! Lammertink, Ilona. 2013. (ENG.). 32p. (J). (gr. k-2). 15.95 *(978-1-60537-148-1(3))* Clavis Publishing.
Georgetta. What Can You Do with a Mud Pie? Thompson, Connie J. 2018. (ENG.). 30p. (J). (gr. k-2). 17.95 *(978-0-9998139-0-4(0))* Front Porch Publishing.
Georgieva-Gode, Dolly. Beautiful, Wonderful, Strong Little Me! Dias, Hannah. 2018. (ENG.). 34p. (J). (gr. k-5). pap. 9.99 *(978-1-63233-169-4(1))* Elfrig Publishing.
Geraci, Drew. Tower of Babel, Vol. 7. Waid, Mark et al. rev. ed. 2005. (Justice League Adventures Ser.: Bk. 7). (ENG.). 160p. (YA). pap. 12.99 *(978-1-56389-727-6(X))* DC Comics.
—The Travelling Circus. Watson, Mark. 2016. (ENG.). (J). pap. *(978-0-9956448-0-9(2))* Watson, Mark Bks.
Geraghty, Paul. Hoppameleon. Geraghty, Paul. 2014. 32p. (J). (gr. -1-k). pap. 9.99 *(978-1-84939-773-5(2))* Andersen Pr. GBR. Dist: Independent Pubs. Group.
Geran, Chad. Crazy for Science with Carmelo the Science Fellow. Piazza, Carmelo & Buckley, James. 2015. (ENG.). 98p. (J). (gr. 1-4). 19.95 *(978-1-57687-682-4(9),* powerHouse Bks.) powerHse. Bks.
—Still a Gorilla! Norman, Kim. 2016. (ENG.). 32p. (J). (gr. -1-k). 16.99 *(978-0-545-75791-1(6))* Scholastic, Inc.
Gerard, Justin. Beowulf Bk. 1: Grendel the Ghastly. 2007. 32p. (J). (gr. 4-6). 17.95 *(978-0-9797183-0-4(9))* Portland Studios, Inc.
—Keeping Holiday. Meade, Starr et al. 2008. (ENG.). 192p. (gr. k). pap. 14.99 *(978-1-4335-0142-5(2))* Crossway.
—The Lightlings. Sproul, R. C., Jr. 2006. (ENG.). 40p. (J). (gr. 3-7). lib. bdg. 18.00 *(978-1-56769-078-1(5),* Reformation Trust Publishing) Ligonier Ministries.
—The Priest with Dirty Clothes. Sproul, R. C. 2nd ed. 2011. (ENG.). 45p. (J). (gr. 3-7). 18.00 *(978-1-56769-210-5(9),* Reformation Trust Publishing) Ligonier Ministries.
—The Prince's Poison Cup. Sproul, R. C. 2008. (ENG.). 35p. (J). (gr. 3-7). 18.00 *(978-1-56769-104-7(8),* Reformation Trust Publishing) Ligonier Ministries.
—Secrets of a Christmas Box. Hornby, Steven. 2009. 248p. (J). (gr. 2-5). 18.95 *(978-0-9815883-0-8(1))* Ecky Thump Bks., Inc.
—Through the Skylight. Baucom, Ian. (ENG.). 400p. (J). (gr. 4-8). 2014. pap. 6.99 *(978-1-4424-8167-1(6));* 2013. 17.99 *(978-1-4169-1777-9(2))* Simon & Schuster Children's Publishing. (Atheneum Bks. for Young Readers).
—Twelve Dancing Unicorns. Heyman, Alissa. 2014. 32p. (J). (gr. -1-2). 14.95 *(978-1-4027-8732-4(4))* Sterling Publishing Co., Inc.
Gerard, Justin, jt. illus. see Grosvenor, Charles.
Gerard, Karla. The Girl from over There: The Hopeful Story of a Young Jewish Immigrant. Rechter, Sharon. 2020. 112p. (J). (gr. 2-8). 16.99 ***(978-1-5107-5367-9(2),*** Sky Pony Pr.) Skyhorse Publishing Co., Inc.
Gerardi, Jan. Andrew Lost #11: with the Dinosaurs. Greenburg, J. C. 2005. (Andrew Lost Ser.: 11). (ENG.). 96p. (J). (gr. 1-4). 4.99 *(978-0-375-82951-2(2),* Random Hse. Bks. for Young Readers) Random Hse. Children's Bks.
—Andrew Lost #14: with the Bats. Greenburg, J. C. 2006. (Andrew Lost Ser.: 14). (ENG.). 96p. (J). (gr. 1-4). 4.99 *(978-0-375-83563-6(6),* Random Hse. Bks. for Young Readers) Random Hse. Children's Bks.
—Green Eggs & Ham: a Magnetic Play Book. Seuss. 2019. (ENG.). 8p. (J). (gr. -1-2). bds. 12.99 *(978-1-5247-7345-8(X),* Random Hse. Bks. for Young Readers) Random Hse. Children's Bks.
—Happy Birthday, Baby! Seuss, Dr. 2009. (Dr. Seuss Nursery Collection). (ENG.). 12p. (J). (— 1). 11.99 *(978-0-375-84621-2(2),* Random Hse. Bks. for Young Readers) Random Hse. Children's Bks.
—In the Deep. Greenburg, J. C. 2004. (Andrew Lost Ser.: 8). (ENG.). 96p. (J). (gr. 1-4). 4.99 *(978-0-375-82526-2(6),* Random Hse. Bks. for Young Readers) Random Hse. Children's Bks.
—In the Desert. Greenburg, J. C. 2008. (Andrew Lost Ser.: 17). (ENG.). 96p. (J). (gr. 1-4). per. 4.99 *(978-0-375-84667-0(0),* Random Hse. Bks. for Young Readers) Random Hse. Children's Bks.
—In the Garbage. Greenburg, J. C. 2006. (Andrew Lost Ser.: 13). (ENG.). 96p. (J). (gr. 1-4). 4.99 *(978-0-375-83562-9(8),* Random Hse. Bks. for Young Readers) Random Hse. Children's Bks.
—In the Ice Age. Greenburg, J. C. 2005. (Andrew Lost Ser.: 12). 96p. (J). (gr. 1-4). 4.99 *(978-0-375-82952-9(0),* Random Hse. Bks. for Young Readers) Random Hse. Children's Bks.
—In Time. Greenburg, J. C. 2004. (Andrew Lost Ser.: 9). 96p. (J). (gr. 1-4). 4.99 *(978-0-375-82949-9(0),* Random Hse. Bks. for Young Readers) Random Hse. Children's Bks.
—In Uncle Al, No. 16. Greenburg, J. C. 2007. (Andrew Lost Ser.: 16). (ENG.). 96p. (J). (gr. 1-4). 4.99 *(978-0-375-83565-0(2),* Random Hse. Bks. for Young Readers) Random Hse. Children's Bks.
—A Little Book about 123s (Leo Lionni's Friends) Lionni, Leo. 2020. (Leo Lionni's Friends Ser.). (ENG.). 28p. (J). (— 1). bds. 8.99 *(978-0-525-58230-4(4),* Random Hse. Bks. for Young Readers) Random Hse. Children's Bks.
—The Lorax Deluxe Doodle Book. Golden Books Staff. 2013. (ENG.). 256p. (J). (gr. -1-2). pap. 9.99 *(978-0-449-81061-3(5),* Golden Bks.) Random Hse. Children's Bks.
—The Lorax Doodle Book. Golden Books Staff. 2012. (ENG.). 128p. (J). (gr. -1-2). pap. 5.99 *(978-0-307-92982-2(5),* Golden Bks.) Random Hse. Children's Bks.
—Oh, Baby! Go, Baby! Seuss, Dr. 2010. (Dr. Seuss Nursery Collection). (ENG.). 14p. (J). (gr. k — 1). 11.99 *(978-0-375-85738-6(9),* Random Hse. Bks. for Young Readers) Random Hse. Children's Bks.
—Oh, the Places I'll Go! by ME, Myself. Seuss, Dr. 2016. (ENG.). 64p. (J). (gr. -1-3). 16.99 *(978-0-553-52058-3(X),* Random Hse. Bks. for Young Readers) Random Hse. Children's Bks.
—On Earth, 10. Greenburg, J. C. 2005. (Andrew Lost Ser.: Bk. 10). (ENG.). 90p. (J). (gr. 3-6). lib. bdg. 16.19 *(978-0-375-92950-2(9))* Random House Publishing Group.
—On Earth. Greenburg, J. C. 10th ed. 2005. (Andrew Lost Ser.: 10). 96p. (J). (gr. 1-4). 4.99 *(978-0-375-82950-5(4),* Random Hse. Bks. for Young Readers) Random Hse. Children's Bks.
—A Tree for Me! Golden Books Staff. 2012. (ENG.). 48p. (J). (gr. k — 1). pap. 3.99 *(978-0-307-92981-5(7),* Golden Bks.) Random Hse. Children's Bks.
—With the Frogs, 18. Greenburg, J. C. 2008. (Andrew Lost Ser.: No. 18). (ENG.). 86p. (J). (gr. 3-6). lib. bdg. 16.19 *(978-0-375-94668-4(3))* Random House Publishing Group.
—With the Frogs. Greenburg, J. C. 2008. (Andrew Lost Ser.: 18). (ENG.). 96p. (J). (gr. 1-4). 4.99 *(978-0-375-84668-7(9),* Random Hse. Bks. for Young Readers) Random Hse. Children's Bks.
Gerardi, Jan, jt. illus. see Lionni, Leo.
Gerardi, Jan, jt. illus. see Reed, Mike.
Gerber, Kathryn. Iraq in a Nutshell. Roraback, Amanda. 2003. (Nutshell Notes). 36p. 5.95 *(978-0-9702908-5-4(3))* Enisen Publishing.
Gerber, Mary Jane. A Pioneer Alphabet. Downie, Mary Alice. 2009. (ABC Our Country Ser.). 32p. (J). (gr. k-3). pap. 7.95 *(978-0-88776-961-0(6),* Tundra Bks.) Tundra Bks. CAN. Dist: Penguin Random Hse. LLC.
—Sky, 1 vol. Porter, Pamela. 2005. (ENG.). 104p. (J). (gr. 3-5). pap. 9.95 *(978-0-88899-607-7(1),* Libros Tigrillo) Groundwood Bks. CAN. Dist: Publishers Group West (PGW).
—Tuk & the Whale, 1 vol. Rivera, Raquel. 2009. (ENG.). 96p. (J). (gr. 2-5). pap. 7.95 *(978-0-88899-891-0(0))* Groundwood Bks. CAN. Dist: Publishers Group West (PGW).
Gerber, Patric. This Is the Hill. Lasater, Amy. 2005. (J). *(978-1-59156-720-2(3))* Covenant Communications.
Gerber, Pesach. Shadow Play: A True Story of Tefillah. Shollar, Leah Pearl. 2006. 32p. (J). 11.95 *(978-1-929628-21-6(8))* Hachai Publishing.
Gerbolez Rondon, Alid Nail. La Verdad Perdida. Rebull Leon, Loreley. 2019. (SPA.). 24p. (J). pap. 24.50 ***(978-1-6745-0781-1(X))*** Independently Published.
Gere, C. M. Russian Fairy Tales: From the Skazki of Polevoi. Bain, R. Nisbet. 2019. (ENG.). 218p. (J). (gr. k-4). ***(978-605-7748-61-4(1));*** pap. *(978-605-7876-39-3(3))* Uhrayoglu, Murat E Kitap Projesi.
Gerecke, Bretta. Maximilian's Mistake. Christenson, Jonathan. 2012. (ENG.). 42p. (J). pap. 9.95 *(978-1-897411-35-3(9))* Bayeux Arts, Inc. CAN. Dist: Chicago Distribution Ctr.
Geremia, Daniela. Lightning Rod Faces the Cyclops Queen. Beakman, Onk. 2014. 155p. (J). *(978-1-4242-6276-2(3),* Grosset & Dunlap) Penguin Publishing Group.
—The Mask of Power: Eruptor Meets the Nightmare King. Beakman, Onk. 2016. 157p. (J). *(978-1-5182-2804-9(6),* Grosset & Dunlap) Penguin Publishing Group.
—Mask of Power: Trigger Happy Targets the Evil Kaos. Beakman, Onk. 2016. 150p. (J). *(978-1-5182-2805-6(4),* Grosset & Dunlap) Penguin Publishing Group.
Geremia, Daniela & Ecob, Simon. Girls Only: How to Survive Anything! Stride, Lottie & Oliver, Martin. 2012. (Best at Everything Ser.). (ENG.). 64p. (J). (gr. 3-7). pap. 6.99 *(978-0-545-43095-1(X),* Scholastic Paperbacks) Scholastic, Inc.
Gergely, Tibor. Animal Gym. Hoffman, Beth Greiner. 2009. (Little Golden Book Ser.). 32p. (J). (gr. -1-2). 4.99 *(978-0-375-84751-6(0),* Golden Bks.) Random Hse. Children's Bks.
—Daddies. Frank, Janet & Golden Books Staff. 2011. (Little Golden Book Ser.). (ENG.). 24p. (J). (gr. -1-2). 4.99 *(978-0-375-86130-7(0),* Golden Bks.) Random Hse. Children's Bks.
—The Fire Engine Book. Golden Books. 2015. 26p. (J). (-k). bds. 7.99 *(978-0-553-52224-2(8),* Golden Bks.) Random Hse. Children's Bks.
—The Happy Man & His Dump Truck. Miryam. 2005. (Little Golden Book Ser.). 32p. (J). (gr. -1-k). 4.99 *(978-0-375-83207-9(6),* Golden Bks.) Random Hse. Children's Bks.
—The Jolly Barnyard. North Bedford, Annie. 2004. (Little Golden Book Ser.). 32p. (J). (gr. -1-2). 4.99 *(978-0-375-82842-3(7),* Golden Bks.) Random Hse. Children's Bks.
Gergely, Tibor, et al. Little Golden Book Daddy Stories. Frank, Janet et al. 2015. 80p. (J). (gr. -1-1). 6.99 *(978-0-553-49762-5(6),* Golden Bks.) Random Hse. Children's Bks.
Gergely, Tibor. Little Golden Book Train Stories. Crampton, Gertrude et al. 2014. 80p. (J). (-k). 7.99 *(978-0-385-37862-8(9),* Golden Bks.) Random Hse. Children's Bks.
—The Merry Shipwreck. Duplaix, Georges & Golden Books Staff. 2011. (Little Golden Book Ser.). 32p. (J). (gr. -1-2). 4.99 *(978-0-375-86800-9(3),* Golden Bks.) Random Hse. Children's Bks.
—Scuffy the Tugboat. Crampton, Gertrude. deluxe ed. Date not set. (J). (gr. -1-2). reprint ed. *(978-1-929566-59-4(X))* Cronies.
—Scuffy the Tugboat: Classic Edition. Crampton, Gertrude. Date not set. (J). reprint ed. *(978-1-929566-52-5(2))* Cronies.
—Tootle. Golden Books Staff, photos by. deluxe ed. Date not set. (J). (gr. -1-2). reprint ed. *(978-1-929566-58-7(1))* Cronies.
—Tootle: Classic Edition. Crampton, Gertrude. Date not set. 21p. (J). (gr. -1-1). *(978-1-929566-53-2(0))* Cronies.
Gergely, Tibor & Wilkin, Eloise. 75 Years of Little Golden Books: 1942-2017: A Commemorative Set of 12 Best-Loved Books. Williams, Garth & Wise Brown, Margaret. 2017. (Little Golden Book Ser.). (ENG.). 24p. (J). (-k). 59.88 *(978-0-399-55951-8(5),* Golden Bks.) Random Hse. Children's Bks.
Gergely, Tibor, jt. illus. see Rojankovsky, Feodor.
Gerhart, Cortlee. Ian Greets the World. Klein, Toni. 2019. (ENG.). 38p. (J). pap. 16.99 ***(978-1-5320-8404-1(8))*** iUniverse, Inc.
Gerin, Etienne. Dino Moon. de Cadier, Morgane. 2018. (ENG.). 32p. (J). (gr. -1-1). lib. bdg. 17.99 *(978-1-57565-966-4(2),* StarBerry) Astra Publishing Hse.
Gerke, Jeff. The Maiden & the Toad. Busch, Melinda K. 2017. (ENG.). 28p. (J). 15.00 *(978-0-692-99192-3(1))* Busch, Melinda K.
Gerlings, Rebecca. Diva Delores & the Opera House Mouse. Sassi, Laura. 2018. 32p. (J). (gr. -1). 16.95 *(978-1-4549-2200-1(1))* Sterling Publishing Co., Inc.
—If Pluto Was a Pea. Prendergast, Gabrielle. 2019. (ENG.). 40p. (J). (gr. -1-3). 17.99 *(978-1-5344-0435-9(X),* McElderry, Margaret K. Bks.) McElderry, Margaret K. Bks.
Gerlings, Rebecca. Enormouse! Gerlings, Rebecca. 2011. (ENG.). 32p. (J). (gr. -1-k). pap. 8.99 *(978-1-4052-4832-7(7))* Egmont Bks., Ltd. GBR. Dist: Independent Pubs. Group.
Gerlyng, Marlene. Into the Arctic. Long, Matthew. 2020. 32p. (J). (gr. 2-3). 14.95 ***(978-1-76036-085-6(6),*** 5ac5e57e-858a-4ff8-8a64-ccf2e523cbcd) Starfish Bay Publishing Pty Ltd. AUS. Dist: Baker & Taylor Publisher Services (BTPS).
Germain, Daniella. That's What Wings Are For. Guest, Patrick. 2018. (ENG.). 32p. (J). (gr. -1-k). pap. 9.99 *(978-1-76050-147-1(6))* Little Hare Bks. AUS. Dist: Independent Pubs. Group.
Germain, Philippe. Une Maison dans la Baleine. Hébert, Marie-Francine. 2003. (Premier Roman Ser.). (FRE.). 64p. (J). (gr. 2-5). pap. *(978-2-89021-240-4(8))* Diffusion du livre Mirabel (DLM).
Germain-Therrien, Chloé & Chloloula. Mama Bird Lost an Egg. Fournier, Evelyne. Penn, Nathaniel, tr. 2019. (ENG.). 32p. (J). (gr. -1). 15.95 *(978-2-89802-082-7(6),* CrackBoom! Bks.) Chouette Publishing CAN. Dist: Publishers Group West (PGW).
Germano, Nicholas. Dugan Peckles & the Keepers of the Crystal Flame. Pepper, Sly. 2006. 229p. per. 5.99 *(978-0-9747668-1-2(X))* MindMaze Publishing Co.
Germeau, Hannah. A Rattlesnake's Story: The Story of a Young Snake Who Discovers the Sad Truth about Rattlesnake Roundups. Taracka, Grace. 2018. (ENG.). 28p. (J). pap. 11.95 *(978-1-7312-4078-1(3))* Independently Published.
Gernhart, Carlie. The Adventures of Gertrude Mccluck, Chicken in Charge Vol. 1: The Missing Eggs, 4 vols. Gernhart, Cyndi. l.t. ed. 2005. 32p. (J). 8.00 *(978-0-9778240-1-4(2))* Prairie Winds Publishing.
—The Adventures of Gertrude Mccluck, Chicken in Charge Vol. 2: The Great Crate Mystery, 4 vols. Gernhart, Cyndi. l.t. ed. 2005. 40p. (J). 8.00 *(978-0-9778240-2-1(0))* Prairie Winds Publishing.
—The Adventures of Gertrude Mccluck, Chicken in Charge Vol. 3: The Yellow-Eyed Pond Monster, 4 vols. Gernhart, Cyndi. l.t. ed. 2005. 52p. (J). 8.00 *(978-0-9778240-3-8(9))* Prairie Winds Publishing.
—The Adventures of Gertrude Mccluck, Chicken in Charge Vol. 4: A Midwinter Light's Dream, 4 vols. Gernhart, Cyndi. l.t. ed. 2006. 52p. (J). 8.00 *(978-0-9778240-4-5(7))* Prairie Winds Publishing.
Gernhart, Cyndi, et al. Gertrude Sees... On the Farm. Gernhart, Cyndi. l.t. ed. 2006. 20p. (J). 8.00 *(978-0-9778240-0-7(4))* Prairie Winds Publishing.
Gerrell, Spike. Max Archer, Kid Detective: The Case of the Recurring Stomachaches. Bennett, Howard J. 2012. 48p. (J). 14.95 *(978-1-4338-1130-2(8));* pap. 9.95 *(978-1-4338-1129-6(4))* American Psychological Assn. (Magination Pr.).
—Max Archer, Kid Detective: The Case of the Wet Bed. Bennett, Howard J. 2011. 48p. (J). (gr. 1-5). 14.95 *(978-1-4338-0953-8(2),* Magination Pr.) American Psychological Assn.
—Soccer School Season 1: Where Soccer Explains (Rules) the World. Bellos, Alex & Lyttleton, Ben. (Soccer School Ser.). (ENG.). 208p. (J). (gr. 2-5). 2019. pap. 7.99 *(978-1-5362-0835-1(3));* 2018. 15.99 *(978-1-5362-0435-3(8))* Candlewick Pr.

—Soccer School Season 2: Where Soccer Explains (Saves) the World. Bellos, Alex & Lyttleton, Ben. 2019. (Soccer School Ser.). (ENG.). 208p. (J). (gr. 2-5). pap. 7.99 *(978-1-5362-0875-7(2))* Candlewick Pr.

—Soccer School Season 3: Where Soccer Explains the World. Bellos, Alex & Lyttleton, Ben. 2019. (Soccer School Ser.). (ENG.). 176p. (J). (gr. 2-5). 15.99 *(978-1-5362-0695-1(4))* Candlewick Pr.

—La Teoría de Los Muchos Mundos / the Many Worlds of Albie Bright. Edge, Christopher. 2017. (SPA.). 232p. (YA). (gr. 8-12). pap. 17.95 *(978-84-16712-54-0(9),* B De Blook) Ediciones B ESP. Dist: Penguin Random Hse. LLC.

—Where Soccer Explains (Saves) the World. Bellos, Alex & Lyttleton, Ben. 2018. (Soccer School Ser.). (ENG.). 208p. (J). (gr. 2-5). 15.99 *(978-1-5362-0436-0(6))* Candlewick Pr.

Gershator, Phillis. Little Lenty. 2014. (J). pap. *(978-1-934370-48-3(7))* Editorial Campana.

—Where Did the Baby Go? Gershator, David. 2016. (J). pap. *(978-1-934370-57-5(6))* Editorial Campana.

Gershman, Jo. Mommy, Daddy, I Had a Bad Dream! Pieper, Martha Heineman. 2012. 32p. (J). 18.99 *(978-0-9838664-0-4(6))* Smart Love Pr., LLC.

—Nutcracker Ballet: A Book, Theater, & Paper Doll Foldout Play Set. Conlon, Mara. 2007. (Foldout Playset Ser.). 30p. (J). 17.99 *(978-1-59359-885-3(8))* Peter Pauper Pr. Inc.

Gershman, Jo, jt. illus. see Chang, Tara Larsen.

Gerstein, Mordecai. The Camping Trip That Changed America: Theodore Roosevelt, John Muir, & Our National Parks. Rosenstock, Barb. 2012. 32p. (J). (gr. 1-3). 17.99 *(978-0-8037-3710-5(6),* Dial Bks) Penguin Young Readers Group.

Gerstein, Mordicai. A Hare-Raising Tale. Levy, Elizabeth. unabr. ed. 2006. (First Chapter Bks.). (J). (gr. 2-4). pap. 17.95 incl. audio *(978-1-59519-704-7(4));* pap. 20.95 incl. audio compact disk *(978-1-59519-705-4(2))* Live Oak Media.

—I Am Arachne: Fifteen Greek & Roman Myths. Spires, Elizabeth. 2009. (ENG.). 112p. (J). (gr. 3-7). pap. 9.99 *(978-0-312-56125-3(3),* 900058860) Square Fish.

—The Principal's on the Roof. Levy, Elizabeth. ed. 2005. 74p. (J). lib. bdg. 15.00 *(978-1-59054-912-4(0))* Fitzgerald Bks.

—The Principal's on the Roof. Levy, Elizabeth. unabr. ed. 2006. (First Chapter Bks.). (J). (gr. 2-4). pap. 17.95 incl. audio *(978-1-59519-698-9(6));* pap. 20.95 incl. audio compact disk *(978-1-59519-699-6(4))* Live Oak Media.

—Three Samurai Cats: A Story from Japan. 2004. (J). *(978-0-439-69256-4(3))* Scholastic, Inc.

Gerstein, Mordicai. The Boy & the Whale. Gerstein, Mordicai. 2017. (ENG.). 40p. (J). 18.99 *(978-1-62672-505-8(5),* 900159303) Roaring Brook Pr.

—How to Bicycle to the Moon to Plant Sunflowers: A Simple but Brilliant Plan in 24 Easy Steps. Gerstein, Mordicai. 2013. (ENG.). 40p. (J). (gr. -1-2). 17.99 *(978-1-59643-512-4(7),* 900058922) Roaring Brook Pr.

—The Man Who Walked Between the Towers. Gerstein, Mordicai. rev. ed. 2003. (ENG.). 44p. (J). (gr. k-3). 21.99 *(978-0-7613-1791-3(0),* 900029456) Roaring Brook Pr.

—The Man Who Walked Between the Towers. Gerstein, Mordicai. 2007. (ENG.). 44p. (J). (gr. k-3). per. 8.99 *(978-0-312-36878-4(X),* 900042726) Square Fish.

—Mountains of Tibet. Gerstein, Mordicai. 2013. (ENG.). 32p. (J). (gr. k-5). 14.99 *(978-1-78285-047-2(3))* Barefoot Bks., Inc.

—The Sleeping Gypsy. Gerstein, Mordicai. 2016. (ENG.). 32p. (J). (gr. -1-3). 16.95 *(978-0-8234-2142-8(2))* Holiday Hse., Inc.

—What Charlie Heard. Gerstein, Mordicai. pap. 18.95 incl. audio compact disk *(978-1-59112-277-7(5));* pap. incl. audio *(978-1-59112-279-1(1));* pap. 16.95 incl. audio *(978-1-59112-484-9(0));* pap. incl. audio compact disk *(978-1-59112-525-9(1))* Live Oak Media.

—You Can't Have Too Many Friends! Gerstein, Mordicai. 2014. (ENG.). 32p. (J). (gr. -1-2). 16.95 *(978-0-8234-2393-4(X))* Holiday Hse., Inc.

Gerstein, Mordicai & Coville, Katherine. The Dragon of Doom. Levy, Elizabeth & Coville, Bruce. ed. 2005. 71p. (J). lib. bdg. 15.00 *(978-1-59054-903-2(1))* Fitzgerald Bks.

Gerstein, Yoni. Effy Helps Out. Kugel, Bruriah. 2008. 26p. (J). (gr. -1). 14.99 *(978-1-58330-942-1(X))* Feldheim Pubs.

Gerszak, Rafal, photos by. Thunder over Kandahar. McKay, Sharon. 3rd ed. 2010. 264p. (YA). (gr. 7-12). pap. 12.95 *(978-1-55451-266-9(2),* 9781554512669) Annick Pr., Ltd. CAN. Dist: Publishers Group West (PGW).

Gerth, Melanie, jt. illus. see Diaz, James.

Gervais, Ross. She Shoots... She Scores! Barnes, Charlene. 2017. (ENG.). (J). pap. *(978-1-5255-1006-9(1))* FriesenPress.

Gervasi, Christine. Poems from the Playground & Other Places. McKenzie, Richard. 2004. (J). 12.00 *(978-0-9725901-0-5(2))* Lekha Pubs., LLC.

Gervasio. Vampires & Light, 1 vol. Shaffer, Jody Jensen. 2013. (Monster Science Ser.). (ENG.). 32p. (gr. 3-9). (J). pap. 8.10 *(978-1-62065-820-8(8));* 47.70 *(978-1-62065-821-5(6));* (J). lib. bdg. 31.32 *(978-1-4296-9928-0(0))* Capstone. (Capstone Pr.).

—Zombies & Forces & Motion, 1 vol. Weakland, Mark. 2011. (Monster Science Ser.). (ENG.). 32p. (J). (gr. 3-9). lib. bdg. 31.32 *(978-1-4296-6577-3(7),* Capstone Pr.) Capstone.

Gervasio & Aón, Carlos. Monster Science. Weakland, Mark et al. 2013. (Monster Science Ser.). (ENG.). 32p. (gr. 3-4). pap. 381.60 *(978-1-62065-826-0(7),* Capstone Pr.) Capstone.

Gervasio, jt. illus. see Mallea, Cristian.

Gestin, Muriel. C'Est l'Heure du Bain, Lou ! - Lou It's Time to Wash. Curtiss, Dominique. Prokofyev, Dmitry, tr. 2018. (Lou & Teddy Ser.: Vol. 2). (FRE.). 44p. (J). (gr. k-3). pap. *(978-2-89687-753-9(3))* chouetteditions.com.

—I'm Afraid of the Dark. Curtiss, Dominique. 2018. (ENG.). 30p. (J). (gr. k-2). pap. *(978-2-89687-744-7(4))* chouetteditions.com.

—I'm Afraid of the Dark. - Chi So Bong Toi. (Bilingual Book in English - Vietnamese) Hill, Rowland & Tong, Thi Khanh Huyen, trs. 2018. (ENG.). 30p. (J). pap. *(978-2-89687-743-0(6))* chouetteditions.com.

—I'm Afraid of the Dark. - Nan Eodum-I Museowo. (Bilingual Book in English - Korean.) Hill, Rowland & Lee, Hyonhee, trs. 2018. (ENG.). 30p. (J). pap. *(978-2-89687-747-8(9))* chouetteditions.com.

Gestin, Muriel. It's Bath Time, Lou! - Лу пора мыться! Curtiss, Dominique. Prokofyev, Dmitry, tr. 2019. (ENG.). 42p. (J). (gr. k-4). ***(978-2-89687-822-2(X))*** chouetteditions.com.

Gestin, Muriel. J'Ai Peur du Noir - Ich Habe Angst VOR der Dunkelheit: Livre Bilingue en Français - Allemand. Curtiss, Dominique. Lusser, Walpurga, tr. 2018. (FRE.). 30p. (J). pap. *(978-2-89687-749-2(5))* chouetteditions.com.

—J'Ai Peur du Noir. - Tengo Miedo a la Oscuridad. (Livre Bilingue Fran. Curtiss, Dominique. Rodriguez, Guadalupe, tr. 2018. (FRE.). 30p. (J). pap. *(978-2-89687-746-1(0))* chouetteditions.com.

—J'Ai Peur du Noir. - YA Boyus' Temnoty. Curtiss, Dominique. Dmitry, Prokofyev, tr. 2018. (FRE.). 30p. (J). (gr. k-2). pap. *(978-2-89687-748-5(7))* chouetteditions.com.

Gestin, Muriel. Los Fabulosos Sombreros de Margot - les Fabuleux Chapeaux de Margaux. Curtiss, Dominique. Rodr�guez, Guadalupe, tr. 2020. (SPA.). 50p. (J). (gr. 1-5). ***(978-2-89687-828-4(9))*** chouetteditions.com.

—Margot's Fabulous Hats - Невероятные шляпы Марго Curtiss, Dominique. Prokofyev, Dmitry, tr. 2019. (ENG.). 50p. (J). (gr. 1-5). ***(978-2-89687-818-5(1))*** chouetteditions.com.

—Margot's Fabulous Hats - les Fabuleux Chapeaux de Margaux. Curtiss, Dominique. Hill, Rowland, tr. 2019. (ENG.). 50p. (J). (gr. 1-5). ***(978-2-89687-824-6(6))*** chouetteditions.com.

—Margot's Fabulous Hats - Los Fabulosos Sombreros de Margot. Curtiss, Dominique. Hill, Rowland, tr. 2019. (ENG.). 50p. (J). (gr. 1-5). ***(978-2-89687-826-0(2))*** chouetteditions.com.

—The Most Beautiful Fables of la Fontaine - les Plus Belles Fables de la Fontaine. La Fontaine, Jean. Hill, Rowland, tr. 2019. (ENG.). 60p. (J). (gr. 1-5). ***(978-2-89687-812-3(2))*** chouetteditions.com.

Gestin, Muriel. Où Te Caches-Tu, Nounours ? - 어디어디 숨었니, 곰돌아? Curtiss, Dominique. Lee, Hyonhee, tr. 2019. (FRE.). 44p. (J). (gr. k-3). pap. *(978-2-89687-758-4(4))* chouetteditions.com.

Gestin, Muriel. Rotk�ppchen - 赤ずきんちゃん Perrault, Charles. Nakatsu, Masaya, tr. 2020. (GER.). 28p. (J). (gr. k-5). pap. ***(978-2-89687-831-4(9))*** chouetteditions.com.

—Where Are You Hiding, Teddy? - Где ты прячешься, Мишка? Curtiss, Dominique. Prokofyev, Dmitry, tr. 2020. (ENG.). 40p. (J). (gr. 1-3). ***(978-2-89687-819-2(X))*** chouetteditions.com.

—Where Are You Hiding, Teddy? - 어디어디 숨었니, 곰돌아? Curtiss, Dominique. Hill, Rowland, tr. 2019. (ENG.). 42p. (J). (gr. k-3). ***(978-2-89687-816-1(5))*** chouetteditions.com.

—Wo Bist du Nur, Teddyb�r? - 어디어디 숨었니, 곰돌아? Curtiss, Dominique. Lusser, Walpurga, tr. 2019. (GER.). 42p. (J). (gr. 1-3). ***(978-2-89687-817-8(3))*** chouetteditions.com.

—Невероятные шляпы Марго; Curtiss, Dominique. Prokofyev, Dmitry, tr. 2019. (RUS.). 50p. (J). (gr. 1-5). pap. ***(978-2-89687-827-7(0))*** chouetteditions.com.

—ヌヌルス、どこにいるの？- o� Te Caches-Tu, Nounours ? Curtiss, Dominique. Nakatsu, Masaya, tr. 2020. (JPN.). 42p. (J). (gr. k-3). ***(978-2-89687-825-3(4))*** chouetteditions.com.

Gesue, Lynn. That's the Way the Cookie Crumbles. Mazer, Anne. 2005. (Amazing Days of Abby Hayes Ser.: 16). (ENG.). 119p. (J). (gr. 2-4). 18.69 *(978-0-439-68067-7(0))* Scholastic, Inc.

Gettner, Helen E. The Enchanted Tower Garden: Tower Garden by Juice Plus+(r) Mohr, Julie & Leon, Noel. 2016. (ENG.). (J). (gr. k-6). pap. 12.00 *(978-1-68181-539-8(7))* Strategic Book Publishing & Rights Agency (SBPRA).

Getty, jt. illus. see Suwanda, Teguh.

Getty, Spud, jt. illus. see Suwanda, Teguh.

Gettys, Katherine. Kavaldo & His Diamond Pills. Ferrier, Paul Eugene. 2013. (ENG.). 72p. pap. 12.99 *(978-1-940395-07-4(0))* Yawn's Bks. & More, Inc.

Gevry, Christine. My Baby. Deprisco Wang, Dorothea. 2007. (Story Book Ser.). 10p. (J). (gr. -1). *(978-1-84666-263-8(X),* Tide Mill Pr.) Top That! Publishing PLC.

Gevry, Claudine. Baby's Carry along Bible, Vol. Lloyd-Jones, Sally. 2020. (ENG.). 24p. (J). (gr. -1 — 1). bds. 12.99 *(978-0-06-296123-5(3),* HarperFestival) HarperCollins Pubs.

—Baby's Hug-A-Bible. Lloyd-Jones, Sally. 2010. (ENG.). 24p. (J). (gr. -1 — 1). bds. 15.99 *(978-0-06-156621-9(7),* HarperFestival) HarperCollins Pubs.

Gévry, Claudine. The Big Book of Bible Fish Tales. Finbarr, Desmond. 2003. 10p. (J). bds. 8.99 *(978-0-8254-5514-8(6))* Kregel Pubns.

—Caterpillar Spring, Butterfly Summer. Hood, Susan. 2003. (ENG.). 10p. (J). (gr. k-3). bds. 12.99 *(978-0-7944-0149-8(X))* Reader's Digest Assn., Inc., The.

—Little School of Fish. DePrisco, Dorothea. 2006. 12p. (gr. -1-k). 10.95 *(978-1-58117-485-4(3),* Intervisual/Piggy Toes) Bendon, Inc.

Gevry, Claudine. Mi Pequena Historia de la Pascua (My Little Easter Story) Goodings, Christina. 2014. (ENG & SPA.). (J). (gr. -1-1). 6.99 *(978-1-55883-170-4(3))* Libros Desafio.

—My Christmas Stocking: Filled with God's Love, 1 vol. Bowman, Crystal. 2015. (ENG.). 14p. (J). bds. 6.99 *(978-0-310-73823-7(7))* Zonderkidz.

Gévry, Claudine. One Little Bear & Her Friends. Ranson, Erin. 2007. 10p. (J). (gr. -1-k). bds. *(978-1-84666-354-3(7),* Tide Mill Pr.) Top That! Publishing PLC.

—One Little Penguin & His Friends: A Pushing, Turning, Counting Book. Top That Publishing Staff. ed. 2007. 10p. (J). (gr. -1-3). bds. *(978-1-84666-268-3(0),* Tide Mill Pr.) Top That! Publishing PLC.

Gevry, Claudine. One Little Penguin & His Friends: A Pushing, Turning, Counting Book. 2012. (ENG.). 10p. (J). bds. *(978-1-84956-027-6(7))* Top That! Publishing PLC.

—One, Two... Boo! Depken, Kristen L. 2009. 12p. (J). (gr. -1 — 1). 3.99 *(978-0-375-84418-8(X),* Golden Bks.) Random Hse. Children's Bks.

—Play Felt Roarsome Dinosaurs! Graham, Oakley. 2020. (Soft Felt Play Bks.). (ENG.). 10p. (J). (gr. -1-k). bds. 12.99 *(978-1-78958-422-6(1))* Top That! Publishing PLC GBR. Dist: Independent Pubs. Group.

Gévry, Claudine. Snack, Snooze, Skedaddle: How Animals Get Ready for Winter. Salas, Laura Purdie. 2019. (ENG.). 32p. (J). (gr. k-3). 19.99 *(978-1-5415-2900-7(6),* Millbrook Pr.) Lerner Publishing Group.

—Spin & Spell: A Book & Game in One! Perez, Jessica. 2005. 12p. (J). 14.95 *(978-1-58117-332-1(6),* Intervisual/Piggy Toes) Bendon, Inc.

Gevry, Claudine. A Star for Jesus, 1 vol. Bowman, Crystal. 2014. (ENG.). 14p. (J). bds. 6.99 *(978-0-310-73826-8(1))* Zonderkidz.

Gévry, Claudine. When I Grow Up: A Touch & Feel Book. Wang, Margaret C. 2005. (ENG.). 12p. (J). bds. 10.95 *(978-1-58117-423-6(3),* Intervisual/Piggy Toes) Bendon, Inc.

—1,2,3 Octopus & Me. Rovetch, L. Bob. 2006. (J). *(978-1-58987-011-6(5))* Kindermusik International.

Gévry, Claudine & Gévry, Claudine. Spin the Dreidel!, Vol. Cooper, Alexandra. 2004. (ENG.). 14p. (J). (gr. -1-2). bds. 8.99 *(978-0-689-86430-8(2),* Little Simon) Little Simon.

Gévry, Claudine, jt. illus. see Gévry, Claudine.

Geyer, Kim. Go to Sleep, Monty! Geyer, Kim. 2015. (ENG.). 32p. (J). (gr. -1-3). 17.99 *(978-1-4677-9311-7(6),* 9781467793117) Lerner Publishing Group.

Geyer, Mark Edward. The Inquisitor's Apprentice. Moriarty, Chris. 2013. (ENG.). 352p. (J). (gr. 5-7). pap. 7.99 *(978-0-547-85084-9(0),* 1501042) Houghton Mifflin Harcourt Publishing Co.

—Secrets of Shakespeare's Grave, Bk. 1. Hicks, Deron R. 2013. (Shakespeare Mysteries Ser.: 1). (ENG.). 320p. (J). (gr. 3-7). pap. 7.99 *(978-0-544-10504-1(4),* 1540806) Houghton Mifflin Harcourt Publishing Co.

—Secrets of Shakespeare's Grave. Hicks, Deron R. 2013. (Shakespeare Mysteries Ser.: Vol. 1). (ENG.). (J). (gr. 2-5). lib. bdg. 18.60 *(978-1-68065-134-8(X))* Perfection Learning Corp.

—Tower of the Five Orders: The Shakespeare Mysteries, Book 2. Hicks, Deron R. 2014. (Shakespeare Mysteries Ser.). (ENG.). 320p. (J). (gr. 5-7). pap. 7.99 *(978-0-544-33630-8(5),* 1584176, HMH Books For Young Readers) Houghton Mifflin Harcourt Publishing Co.

—The Watcher in Shadows. Moriarty, Chris. 2014. (Inquisitor's Apprentice (Quality) Ser.). (ENG.). (J). (gr. 5-7). lib. bdg. 18.60 *(978-1-62765-542-2(5))* Perfection Learning Corp.

—The Watcher in the Shadows. Moriarty, Chris. 2014. (ENG.). 336p. (J). (gr. 5-7). pap. 18.99 *(978-0-544-22776-7(X),* 1563388, HMH Books For Young Readers) Houghton Mifflin Harcourt Publishing Co.

—Who Was Charles Dickens? Belviso, Meg et al. 2014. (Who Was? Ser.). 112p. (J). (gr. 3-7). pap. 5.99 *(978-0-448-47967-5(2),* Penguin Workshop) Penguin Young Readers Group.

—Who Was Ulysses S. Grant? Stine, Megan & Who HQ. 2014. (Who Was? Ser.). 112p. (J). (gr. 3-7). 5.99 *(978-0-448-47894-4(3),* Penguin Workshop) Penguin Young Readers Group.

G'Fellers, Jeanne. Rhea Wells Boy of Jonesborough. G'Fellers, Brenda. 2017. (ENG.). 32p. (J). pap. 9.95 *(978-0-692-98919-7(6))* Mountain Gap Bks.

Ghaderi, Simin & Rezaei, Heidi. Come Count with Happy Campers! Rezaei, Heidi P. 2018. (ENG.). 24p. (J). *(978-1-5255-3248-1(0));* pap. *(978-1-5255-3249-8(9))* FriesenPress.

Ghahremani, Susie. Little Muir's Song. 2019. (ENG.). 14p. (J). bds. 8.99 *(978-1-930238-89-3(4))* Yosemite Conservancy.

—She Wanted to Be Haunted. Ewert, Marcus. 2020. (ENG.). 40p. (J). 17.99 *(978-1-68119-791-3(X),* 900187075, Bloomsbury Children's Bks.) Bloomsbury Publishing USA.

—What Will Grow? Ward, Jennifer. 2017. 40p. (J). 17.99 *(978-1-68119-030-3(3),* 900156309, Bloomsbury USA Childrens) Bloomsbury Publishing USA.

—What Will Hatch? Ward, Jennifer. 2013. (ENG.). 40p. (J). (gr. -1-1). 14.99 *(978-0-8027-2311-6(X),* 900075834, Bloomsbury USA Childrens) Bloomsbury Publishing USA.

Ghazwah, Sura. Aladdin & His Magic Lamp: From the One Thousand & One Nights. 2016. (ENG.). 64p. pap. 6.95 *(978-1-911091-00-4(X))* Real Reads Ltd. GBR. Dist: Casemate Pubs. & Bk. Distributors, LLC.

—Ali Baba & the Forty Thieves: From the One Thousand & One Nights. 2016. (ENG.). 64p. pap. 6.95 *(978-1-911091-01-1(8))* Real Reads Ltd. GBR. Dist: Casemate Pubs. & Bk. Distributors, LLC.

—Sinbad the Sailor: From the One Thousand & One Nights. 2016. (ENG.). 64p. pap. 6.95 *(978-1-911091-02-8(6))* Real Reads Ltd. GBR. Dist: Casemate Pubs. & Bk. Distributors, LLC.

Ghervase, Alina & Balcan, Ioana. Pickles & His Island. Amazing, Rosie. 2020. (ENG.). 28p. (J). pap. ***(978-1-7771360-6-2(7))*** Annelid Pr.

Ghiuselev, Iassen. Alice's Adventures in Wonderland. Carroll, Lewis. rev. ed. 2012. 120p. (J). (gr. 3). 29.95 *(978-1-897476-42-0(6))* Simply Read Bks. CAN. Dist: Ingram Publisher Services.

—The King of the Golden River. Ruskin, John. 2005. (ENG.). 65p. (J). (gr. k). 19.95 *(978-1-894965-15-6(9))* Simply Read Bks. CAN. Dist: Ingram Publisher Services.

—The Queen Bee. Brothers Grimm, Brothers. James, Elizabeth, tr. 2003. (ENG.). 24p. (J). 16.95 *(978-0-9688768-4-8(6))* Simply Read Bks. CAN. Dist: Ingram Publisher Services.

Gholizadeh, Fariba. What in the World Is Wrong with Gisbert? Weeber, Jochen. 2018. (ENG.). 32p. (J). (gr. -1-3). 16.00 *(978-1-947888-02-9(1),* Flyaway Bks.) Westminster John Knox Pr.

Ghosh, Premola. Ten Timeless Tales. 2005. 38p. (J). *(978-81-89013-35-6(1))* Zubaan.

Ghosh, Ronojoy. Are You My Bottom? Temple, Kate & Temple, Jol. 2019. (ENG.). 32p. (J). (gr. -1-k). 16.99 *(978-1-76063-164-2(7))* Allen & Unwin AUS. Dist: Independent Pubs. Group.

—I'm an Immigrant Too: An Australian Story. Fox, Mem. 2018. (ENG.). 40p. (J). (gr. -1-3). 17.99 *(978-1-5344-3602-2(2),* Beach Lane Bks.) Beach Lane Bks.

Ghostbot and Hasbro, Ghostbot &. Star Wars Forces of Destiny: Meet the Heroes. Patrick, Ella. 2019. (World of Reading Level 2 Ser.). (ENG.). 32p. (J). (gr. k-3). lib. bdg. 27.07 *(978-1-5321-4415-8(6),* 33820) Spotlight.

Giacobbe, Beppe. Clang! Clang! Beep! Beep! Listen to the City. Burleigh, Robert. 2009. (ENG.). 32p. (J). (gr. -1-2). 19.99 *(978-1-4169-4052-4(9),* Simon & Schuster/Paula Wiseman Bks.) Simon & Schuster/Paula Wiseman Bks.

—Nobody's Diggier Than a Dog. Bartoletti, Susan Campbell. 2005. (ENG.). 40p. (gr. -1-17). 15.99 *(978-0-7868-1824-2(7))* Hyperion Pr.

Giacobino, Sebastian. A Dark Descent. Fiedler, Lisa. 2018. (Ages of Oz Ser.). (ENG.). 368p. (J). (gr. 3-7). 17.99 *(978-1-4814-6974-6(6),* McElderry, Margaret K. Bks.) McElderry, Margaret K. Bks.

—A Fiery Friendship. Fiedler, Lisa. 2017. (Ages of Oz Ser.). (ENG.). 432p. (J). (gr. 3-7). 17.99 *(978-1-4814-6971-5(1),* McElderry, Margaret K. Bks.) McElderry, Margaret K. Bks.

—A Fiery Friendship. Fiedler, Lisa. 2018. (Ages of Oz Ser.). (ENG.). 448p. (J). (gr. 3-7). pap. 8.99 *(978-1-4814-6972-2(X),* McElderry, Margaret K. Bks.) McElderry, Margaret K. Bks.

Giacomini, Amanda. Mo Smells Blue: A Scentsational Journey. Hyde, Margaret. 3rd ed. 2010. (Mo's Nose Ser.). (ENG.). 24p. (J). (gr. k-k). 17.95 *(978-0-9816255-4-6(1))* Mo's Nose, LLC.

—Mo Smells Christmas: A Scentsational Journey. Hyde, Margaret. 4th ed. 2010. (Mo's Nose Ser.). (ENG.). 24p. (J). (gr. k-k). 17.95 *(978-0-9816255-6-0(8))* Mo's Nose, LLC.

—Mo Smells Green: A Scentsational Journey. Hyde, Margaret. 2009. (Mo's Nose Ser.). (ENG.). 16p. (J). (gr. k-k). 17.95 *(978-0-9816255-2-2(5))* Mo's Nose, LLC.

—Mo Smells Pink: A Scentsational Journey. Hyde, Margaret. 5th ed. 2011. (Mo's Nose Ser.). (ENG.). 24p. (J). (gr. k-k). 17.95 *(978-0-9816255-5-3(X))* Mo's Nose, LLC.

—Mo Smells the Holidays: A Scentsational Journey. Hyde, Margaret. 2009. (Mo's Nose Ser.). (ENG.). 24p. (J). (gr. k-k). 17.95 *(978-0-9816255-3-9(3))* Mo's Nose, LLC.

Giacomo, Kris Di. When a Wolf Is Hungry. Naumann-villemin, Christine. 2017. (ENG.). 34p. (J). 16.00 *(978-0-8028-5482-7(6),* Eerdmans Bks For Young Readers) Eerdmans, William B. Publishing Co.

Giallongo, Zack. Science Comics: Polar Bears: Survival on the Ice. Viola, Jason. 2018. (Science Comics Ser.). (ENG.). (J). 128p. 19.99 *(978-1-62672-823-3(2),* 900174976); 384p. pap. 12.99 *(978-1-62672-824-0(0),* 900174977) Roaring Brook Pr. (First Second Bks.).

—The Stratford Zoo Midnight Revue Presents Macbeth. Lendler, Ian. 2014. (Stratford Zoo Ser.). (ENG.). 80p. (J). (gr. 2-5). pap. 12.99 *(978-1-59643-915-3(7),* 9781596439153, First Second Bks.) Roaring Brook Pr.

—Tricky Rabbit Tales. Schweizer, Chris. 2011. (Tricky Journeys Ser.: 2). (ENG.). (J). (gr. 2-4). pap. 39.62 *(978-0-7613-8626-1(2))* Lerner Publishing Group.

Giallongo, Zack. Star Wars Doodles. Giallongo, Zack. 2015. (Doodle Book Ser.). (ENG.). 128p. (J). (gr. 1-3). pap. 12.99 *(978-1-4847-0684-8(6),* Disney Lucasfilm Press) Disney Publishing Worldwide.

Gianassi, Sara. Have You Ever Heard a Unicorn's Song? Lift & Listen Adventure. Birdsong, Minnie. 2018. (ENG.). 12p. (J). (gr. -1-2). bds. 16.99 *(978-1-68052-325-6(2),* 1003010) Cottage Door Pr.

—My Merry Christmas (padded Board Book) Lloyd-Jones, Sally. 2017. (ENG.). 20p. (J). (gr. -1-k). bds. 12.99 *(978-1-4336-4895-3(4),* 005790558, B&H Kids) B&H Publishing Group.

—The Night Before Christmas. Moore, Clement. Cottage Door Press, ed. 2019. (ENG.). 26p. (J). (gr. -1-3). 14.99 *(978-1-68052-703-2(7),* 1004360) Cottage Door Pr.

Giancanelli, Candace. The Adventures of Beezer. Gard, Don. 2006. 100p. per. 12.95 *(978-1-59858-157-7(0))* Dog Ear Publishing, LLC.

Giaquinta, Maria. Forever Friends. Fabbella, Teresa. 2010. 26p. pap. 9.95 *(978-1-60911-366-7(7),* Eloquent Bks.) Strategic Book Publishing & Rights Agency (SBPRA).

Giarrusso, Chris. Encounter Vol. 1: Out of This World. Baltazar, Art & Franco. 2018. (ENG.). 136p. (J). pap. 12.99 *(978-1-5493-0270-1(1),* cf2f2f92-4425-4179-9471-936c2c8dff06, Lion Forge) Oni Pr., Inc.

—Freezer Burned, 2. Bell, Jake. 2010. (Amazing Adventures of Nate Banks Ser.: 2). (ENG.). 176p. (J). (gr. 4-6). 18.69 *(978-0-545-15670-7(X))* Scholastic, Inc.

G

—Secret Identity Crisis, 1. Bell, Jake. 2010. (Amazing Adventures of Nate Banks Ser.: 1). 176p. (J). (gr. 3-7). 5.99 *(978-0-545-15669-1(6))* Scholastic, Inc.
Gibala-Broxholm, Scott. City Witch, Country Switch, 0 vols. Wax, Wendy. 2013. (ENG.). 42p. (J). (gr. -1-3). pap. 9.99 *(978-1-4778-1676-9(3)*, 9781477816769, Two Lions) Amazon Publishing.
Gibala-Broxholm, Scott. Maddie's Monster Dad, 0 vols. Gibala-Broxholm, Scott. 2011. (ENG.). 40p. (J). (gr. -1-3). 16.99 *(978-0-7614-5846-3(8)*, 9780761458463, Two Lions) Amazon Publishing.
Gibault, Thomas. Hotel Fantastic. Gibault, Thomas. 2018. (ENG.). 32p. (J). (gr. -1-2). 16.99 *(978-1-77138-992-1(3))* Kids Can Pr., Ltd. CAN. Dist: Hachette Bk. Group.
Gibb, Sarah. Beauty & the Beast. Jones, Ursula. 2014. (ENG.). 32p. (J). (gr. -1-3). 16.99 *(978-0-8075-0600-4(1)*, 807506001) Whitman, Albert & Co.
—Emily Windsnap & the Monster from the Deep. Kessler, Liz. 2012. (Emily Windsnap Ser.: 2). (ENG.). 240p. (J). (gr. 3-7). pap. 6.99 *(978-0-7636-6018-5(3))* Candlewick Pr.
—Emily Windsnap & the Ship of Lost Souls. Kessler, Liz. 2015. (Emily Windsnap Ser.: 6). (ENG.). 288p. (J). (gr. 3-7). 15.99 *(978-0-7636-7688-9(8))* Candlewick Pr.
—Emily Windsnap: Two Magical Mermaid Tales. Kessler, Liz. 2014. (Emily Windsnap Ser.). (ENG.). 464p. (J). (gr. 3-7). pap. 9.99 *(978-0-7636-7452-6(4))* Candlewick Pr.
—Princess Charlotte & the Enchanted Rose. French, Vivian. 2007. (Tiara Club Ser.: No. 7). 80p. (J). (gr. 1-4). pap. 3.99 *(978-0-06-112441-9(9)*, Tegen, Katherine Bks) HarperCollins Pubs.
—Princess Georgia & the Shimmering Pearl. French, Vivian. 2008. (Tiara Club Ser.: No. 3). (ENG.). 80p. (J). (gr. 1-4). pap. 3.99 *(978-0-06-143486-0(8)*, Harper Trophy) HarperCollins Pubs.
—Princess Katie & the Silver Pony. French, Vivian. 2007. (Tiara Club Ser.: No.2). 80p. (J). (gr. 1-4). 15.99 *(978-0-06-112432-7(X)*, Tegen, Katherine Bks) HarperCollins Pubs.
—Straw into Gold: Fairy Tales Re-Spun. McKay, Hilary. 2019. (ENG.). 304p. (J). (gr. 3-7). 17.99 *(978-1-5344-3284-0(1)*, McElderry, Margaret K. Bks.) McElderry, Margaret K. Bks.
—The Tail of Emily Windsnap. Kessler, Liz. 2012. (Emily Windsnap Ser.: 1). (ENG.). 224p. (J). (gr. 3-7). pap. 6.99 *(978-0-7636-6020-8(5))* Candlewick Pr.
Gibb, Sarah. Sleeping Beauty: Based on the Original Story by the Brothers Grimm. Gibb, Sarah. 2015. (ENG.). 32p. (J). (gr. -1-3). 16.99 *(978-0-8075-7351-8(5)*, 807573515) Whitman, Albert & Co.
Gibb, Sarah & Ledwidge, Natacha. Four Sparkling Underwater Adventures. Kessler, Liz. 2012. (Emily Windsnap Ser.). (ENG.). (J). (gr. 3-7). pap. 23.96 *(978-0-7636-6295-0(X))* Candlewick Pr.
Gibb, Sarah, jt. illus. see Ledwidge, Natacha.
Gibbins, Amy. To Magiko Ftero. Ouzoun-Andreou, Calliope. 2019. (GRE.). 38p. (J). pap. *(978-618-5318-60-4(1))* Fylatos, Ekdoseis.
Gibbon, Rebecca. The Bee Who Spoke: The Wonderful World of Belle & the Bee. Maccuish, Al. 2014. (ENG.). 32p. (J). (gr. k-2). 14.95 *(978-0-500-65027-1(6)*, 565027) Thames & Hudson.
—Elizabeth Leads the Way: Elizabeth Cady Stanton & the Right to Vote. Stone, Tanya Lee. 2008. (ENG.). 32p. (J). (gr. 1-5). 18.99 *(978-0-8050-7903-6(3)*, 9780805079036, Holt, Henry & Co. Bks. For Young Readers) Holt, Henry & Co.
—Elizabeth Leads the Way: Elizabeth Cady Stanton & the Right to Vote. Stone, Tanya Lee. 2010. (ENG.). 32p. (J). (gr. 1-5). pap. 8.99 *(978-0-312-60236-9(7)*, 900064232) Square Fish.
—The Great Spruce. Duvall, John. 2016. 40p. (J). (gr. k-3). 17.99 *(978-0-399-16084-4(1)*, G.P. Putnam's Sons Books for Young Readers) Penguin Young Readers Group.
—The Homesick Club, 502 vols. Martinez, Libby. 2020. 32p. (J). (gr. -1-2). 17.95 *(978-1-77306-164-1(X))* Groundwood Bks. CAN. Dist: Publishers Group West (PGW).
Gibbon, Rebecca. Marjory Saves the Everglades: The Story of Marjory Stoneman Douglas. Wallace, Sandra Neil. 2020. (ENG.). 56p. (J). (gr. -1-3). 18.99 ***(978-1-5344-3154-6(3)***, Simon & Schuster/Paula Wiseman Bks.) Simon & Schuster/Paula Wiseman Bks.
Gibbon, Rebecca. Players in Pigtails. Corey, Shana. 2006. 28p. (YA). (gr. 8-11). reprint ed. 17.00 *(978-1-4223-5848-1(8))* DIANE Publishing Co.
Gibbons, Cassandra. Ride the Potato Train. Selig, Josh. 2013. 30p. (J). *(978-1-4844-0420-1(3)*, Planet Dexter) Penguin Publishing Group.
—The Small Potatoes Go Camping. Selig, Josh. 2013. (Small Potatoes Ser.). (ENG.). 32p. (J). (gr. -1-3). lib. bdg. 16.19 *(978-1-4844-0111-8(5))* Penguin Young Readers Group.
Gibbons, Dave. All Star Comics, Vol. 3. Thomas, Roy et al. Kahan, Bob, ed. rev. ed. 2005. (DC Archive Editions Ser.). (ENG.). 240p. (YA). 49.99 *(978-1-56389-370-4(3))* DC Comics.
Gibbons, Deanna, jt. illus. see Wilson, Raylene Jenee.
Gibbons, Gail. Coral Reefs. Gibbons, Gail. 2009. (ENG.). 32p. (J). (gr. -1-3). pap. 7.99 *(978-0-8234-2278-4(X))* Holiday Hse., Inc.
—Corn. Gibbons, Gail. 2008. (ENG.). 32p. (J). (gr. -1-3). 16.95 *(978-0-8234-2169-5(4))* Holiday Hse., Inc.
—Cowboys & Cowgirls. Gibbons, Gail. ed. 2003. (J). (gr. 1-4). 18.45 *(978-0-613-71749-6(X))* Turtleback.
—Elephants of Africa. Gibbons, Gail. 2008. (ENG.). 32p. (J). (gr. -1-3). 16.95 *(978-0-8234-2168-8(6))* Holiday Hse., Inc.
—From Seed to Plant. Gibbons, Gail. 2012. audio compact disk 18.95 *(978-1-4301-1079-8(1))* Live Oak Media.
—Gorillas. Gibbons, Gail. 2011. (ENG.). 32p. (J). (gr. -1-3). 17.95 *(978-0-8234-2236-4(4))* Holiday Hse., Inc.
—Grizzly Bears. Gibbons, Gail. 2003. (ENG.). 32p. (J). (gr. -1-3). tchr. ed. 17.95 *(978-0-8234-1793-3(X))* Holiday Hse., Inc.
—Hurricanes! Gibbons, Gail. 2010. (ENG.). 32p. (J). (gr. -1-3). pap. 7.99 *(978-0-8234-2297-5(6))* Holiday Hse., Inc.
—It's Raining! Gibbons, Gail. (ENG.). 32p. (J). (gr. -1-3). 2015. 7.99 *(978-0-8234-3303-2(X))*; 2014. 17.95 *(978-0-8234-2924-0(5))* Holiday Hse., Inc.
—It's Snowing! Gibbons, Gail. 2012. (ENG.). 32p. (J). (gr. -1-3). pap. 7.99 *(978-0-8234-2545-7(2))* Holiday Hse., Inc.
—Ladybugs. Gibbons, Gail. 2013. (ENG.). 32p. (J). (gr. -1-3). pap. 7.99 *(978-0-8234-2760-4(9))* Holiday Hse., Inc.
—The Quilting Bee. Gibbons, Gail. 2004. (ENG.). 32p. (J). (gr. k-5). 17.99 *(978-0-688-16397-6(1)*, HarperCollins) HarperCollins Pubs. Ltd. GBR. Dist: HarperCollins Pubs.
—Snakes. Gibbons, Gail. 2010. (ENG.). 32p. (J). (gr. -1-3). pap. 7.99 *(978-0-8234-2300-2(X))* Holiday Hse., Inc.
—Surrounded by Sea: Life on a New England Fishing Island. Gibbons, Gail. 2006. (ENG.). 32p. (J). (gr. -1-3). 7.99 *(978-0-8234-2021-6(3))* Holiday Hse., Inc.
—Tornadoes! Gibbons, Gail. 2009. (ENG.). 32p. (J). (gr. -1-3). pap. 7.99 *(978-0-8234-2274-6(7))* Holiday Hse., Inc.
Gibbons, Myla, jt. illus. see Walker, Sherry.
Gibbons, Timothy M. Finding Utopia. Sutherland, Paul H. 2006. 44p. (J). (gr. k-7). 20.00 *(978-0-9661060-4-6(0))* Utopia Pr.
—Mani & Pitouee: The Truee Legend of Sleeping Bear Dunes. Sutherland, Paul H. 2006. 36p. (J). (gr. -1-3). 20.00 *(978-0-9661060-3-9(2))* Utopia Pr.
Gibbons, Tony. The Dodo: Extinct Species. Green, Tamara. 2007. 24p. (J). reprint ed. 15.00 *(978-1-4223-6677-6(4))* DIANE Publishing Co.
Gibbs, Andrew. Pantone: Color Cards: 18 Oversized Flash Cards. Pantone. 2013. (ENG.). 20p. (J). (gr. -1 — 1). 15.95 *(978-1-4197-0626-4(8)*, Abrams Appleseed) Abrams, Inc.
Gibbs, Bryan. Mundo Hostil. Fields, Michael S. 2017. (SPA.). 492p. (J). pap. 20.00 *(978-1-0988-8838-1(3))* Independently Published.
Gibbs, Edward. I Spy in the Sky. Gibbs, Edward. 2014. (ENG.). 32p. (J). (-k). 14.99 *(978-0-7636-6840-2(0)*, Templar) Candlewick Pr.
—I Spy on the Farm. Gibbs, Edward. 2016. (ENG.). 22p. (J). (gr. -1-k). bds. 7.99 *(978-0-7636-8530-0(5)*, Templar) Candlewick Pr.
—I Spy under the Sea. Gibbs, Edward. 2012. (ENG.). 32p. (J). (gr. k-k). 14.99 *(978-0-7636-5952-3(5)*, Templar) Candlewick Pr.
—I Spy with My Little Eye. Gibbs, Edward. 2014. (ENG.). 22p. (J). (-k). bds. 7.99 *(978-0-7636-7163-1(0)*, Templar) Candlewick Pr.
Gibbs, Rebecca. Apples, Pears, & Pirate Underwear: The Magnificent Muffin Adventures of Princess Beans & Sir Boogie Boog. Fisher, Ronnie. 2017. (ENG.). 26p. (J). pap. ***(978-0-473-42681-1(1))*** Kingfisher Publishing.
Gibbs, Tracy. The Magic Fair. Morgan, Sally. 2010. (Waarda Series for Young Readers Ser.: Bk. 5). 48p. (J). (gr. 2-4). pap. 7.00 *(978-1-921696-12-1(5))* Fremantle Pr. AUS. Dist: Independent Pubs. Group.
Giberson, Kim. The Dinosocks. McWood, Allison. 2018. (ENG.). 44p. (J). pap. *(978-0-9782729-3-7(5))* Annelid Pr.
—The Super Special Panda Egg. McWood, Allison. 2018. (ENG.). 36p. (J). pap. *(978-0-9782729-5-1(1))* Annelid Pr.
Gibert, Jean Claude & Gray, J. M. L. Babar: Four Stories to Read & Share. Weiss, Ellen. 2006. (J). 9.99 *(978-0-8109-9308-2(2)*, Abrams Bks. for Young Readers) Abrams, Inc.
Gibie. Timo: Le Porte-Bonheur. Vincent, Durham. 2018. (FRE.). 94p. (J). pap. 10.74 *(978-1-7918-5251-1(3))* Independently Published.
Giblin, Sheri, jt. photos by see Van Vynckt, Virginia.
Gibson, Barbara. Chester Raccoon & the Acorn Full of Memories. Penn, Audrey. 2009. (Kissing Hand Ser.). (ENG.). 32p. (J). (gr. -1-3). 16.95 *(978-1-933718-29-3(3))* Tanglewood Pr.
—Chester Raccoon & the Almost Perfect Sleepover. Penn, Audrey. 2017. (Kissing Hand Ser.). (ENG.). 32p. (J). (gr. -1-3). 16.95 *(978-1-939100-11-5(9))* Tanglewood Pr.
—Chester Raccoon & the Big Bad Bully. Penn, Audrey. 2008. (Kissing Hand Ser.). (ENG.). 32p. (J). (gr. -1-3). 16.95 *(978-1-933718-15-6(3))* Tanglewood Pr.
—Chester Raccoon & the Big Bad Bully [with CD]. Penn, Audrey. 2008. (Kissing Hand Ser.). (ENG.). 32p. (J). (gr. -1-3). pap. 12.95 incl. audio compact disk *(978-1-933718-30-9(7))* Tanglewood Pr.
—Chester the Brave. Penn, Audrey. 2012. (Kissing Hand Ser.). (ENG.). 32p. (J). (gr. -1-3). 16.99 *(978-1-933718-79-8(X))* Tanglewood Pr.
—A Color Game for Chester Raccoon. Penn, Audrey. 2012. (Kissing Hand Ser.). (ENG.). 14p. (J). (gr. -1-2). bds. 7.95 *(978-1-933718-58-3(7))* Tanglewood Pr.
—Exploring Capitol Hill: A Kid's Guide to the U. S. Capitol & Congress. Dodge, Andrew. Wasniewski, Matthew, ed. 12p. (J). pap. 1.95 *(978-0-916200-25-1(6))* U. S. Capitol Historical Society.
—A Kiss Goodbye. Penn, Audrey. 2007. (Kissing Hand Ser.). (ENG.). 32p. (J). (gr. -1-3). 16.99 *(978-1-933718-04-0(8))* Tanglewood Pr.
—A Kissing Hand for Chester Raccoon. Penn, Audrey. 2014. (Kissing Hand Ser.). (ENG.). 14p. (J). (gr. -1-2). bds. 7.99 *(978-1-933718-77-4(3))* Tanglewood Pr.
—The Whistling Tree. Penn, Audrey. 2003. 32p. 16.95 *(978-0-87868-852-4(8)*, 8528, Child & Family Pr.) Child Welfare League of America, Inc.
—The Whistling Tree. Penn, Audrey. 2006. (ENG.). 32p. (J). (gr. -1-4). 16.95 *(978-0-9749303-9-8(3))* Tanglewood Pr.
Gibson, Barbara Leonard. The Dragonfly Door. rev. ed. 2007. (ENG.). 40p. (J). (gr. k-5). 17.95 *(978-1-934066-12-6(5))* Feather Rock Bks., Inc.
—N Is for our Nation's Capital: A Washington, DC Alphabet. Smith, Marie et al. 2005. (Discover America State by State Ser.). (ENG.). 40p. (J). 17.95 *(978-1-58536-148-9(8))* Sleeping Bear Pr.
—A Pocket Full of Kisses. Penn, Audrey. 2004. (New Child & Family Press Titles Ser.). 32p. (gr. -1-1). 16.95 *(978-0-87868-894-4(3)*, 8943, Child & Family Pr.) Child Welfare League of America, Inc.
Gibson, Bridget. Fold-Up Fortune-Tellers: Tear Out, Fold up, Find Your Future! Manzanero, Paula K. 2020. 24p. (J). (gr. 2). pap. 7.99 *(978-0-593-09367-2(4)*, Penguin Workshop) Penguin Young Readers Group.
—Life Sucks: How to Deal with the Way Life Is, Was, & Will Always Be Unfair. Bennett, Michael & Bennett, Sarah. 2019. (ENG.). 240p. (YA). (gr. 7). 17.99 *(978-1-5247-8790-5(6)*, Penguin Workshop) Penguin Young Readers Group.
Gibson, Christine. Sam & the Biggest Bubble. Blade, Brendon. 2017. (ENG.). 30p. (J). (gr. k-5). pap. *(978-0-473-38433-3(7))* Maake Ltd.
Gibson, Dave. Davy D's Dog: 3-in-1 Package. Eggleton, Jill. (Sails Literacy Ser.). 24p. (gr. k-18). 57.00 *(978-0-7578-8615-7(9))* Rigby Education.
—Davy D's Dog: 6 Small Books. Eggleton, Jill. (Sails Literacy Ser.). 24p. (gr. k-18). 25.00 *(978-0-7578-7728-5(1))* Rigby Education.
—Davy D's Dog: Big Book Only. Eggleton, Jill. (Sails Literacy Ser.). 24p. (gr. k-18). 27.00 *(978-0-7578-6198-7(9))* Rigby Education.
Gibson, Gregory V. Latawnya the Naughty Horse Two, 1 vol. Gibson, Sylvia Scott & Gibson, James E. 2010. 22p. 24.95 *(978-1-4489-7859-5(9))* PublishAmerica, Inc.
—Ricky the Skating Worm & Friends, 1 vol. Gibson, Sylvia Scott. 2009. 21p. pap. 24.95 *(978-1-60836-473-2(9))* America Star Bks.
—Treetoe the Space Monster, 1 vol. Gibson, James E. & Gibson, Sylvia Scott. 2010. 28p. 24.95 *(978-1-4489-4896-3(7))* PublishAmerica, Inc.
Gibson, Ian, et al. Star Wars Legends Epic Collection: the Empire Vol. 5. 2019. (ENG.). 480p. (YA). (gr. -1-17). pap. 39.99 *(978-1-302-91809-5(5))* Marvel Worldwide, Inc.
Gibson, James C. Hey, God! Listen! Gibson, Roxie C. 2007. (ENG.). 64p. (J). (gr. -1-3). 7.99 *(978-1-887654-59-3(3))* Premium Pr. America.
—Hey God! What Is Christmas? Gibson, Roxie C. 2007. (ENG.). 64p. (J). (gr. 4-7). 7.99 *(978-1-887654-95-1(X))* Premium Pr. America.
—Hey, God! What Makes You Happy? Gibson, Roxie C. 2007. (ENG.). 64p. (J). 7.99 *(978-1-933725-78-9(8))* Premium Pr. America.
—Hey God, Where Are You? Gibson, Roxie Cawood. 2007. (ENG.). 64p. 7.99 *(978-1-887654-63-0(1))* Premium Pr. America.
Gibson, Jessica. Babies Love Kittens. Wing, Scarlett. Cottage Door Press, ed. 2020. (Babies Love Ser.). (ENG.). 12p. (J). (gr. -1-k). bds. 7.99 *(978-1-68052-782-7(7)*, 1005050) Cottage Door Pr.
—Babies Love Puppies. Wing, Scarlett. Cottage Door Press, ed. 2020. (Babies Love Ser.). (ENG.). 12p. (J). (gr. -1-k). bds. 7.99 *(978-1-68052-781-0(9)*, 1005040) Cottage Door Pr.
—Bumble B. Mission Fun. Qualey, Marsha. ed. 2018. (Bumble B. Ser.). (ENG.). 96p. (J). (gr. k-2). pap. 7.95 *(978-1-68436-016-1(1)*, 137804, Picture Window Bks.) Capstone.
—Four Little Pigs. Crowe, Carmen. 2018. (Little Bird Stories Ser.). (ENG.). 12p. (J). (gr. -1-2). bds. 6.99 *(978-1-68052-153-5(5)*, 1001470) Cottage Door Pr.
—Mission Farmers' Market. Qualey, Marsha. 2018. (Bumble B. Ser.). (ENG.). 40p. (J). (gr. k-2). 22.65 *(978-1-4965-6183-1(X)*, 137798, Picture Window Bks.) Capstone.
—Mission Lost Cat. Qualey, Marsha. 2018. (Bumble B. Ser.). (ENG.). 40p. (J). (gr. k-2). 22.65 *(978-1-4965-6182-4(1)*, 137797, Picture Window Bks.) Capstone.
—Mission Science Club. Qualey, Marsha. 2018. (Bumble B. Ser.). (ENG.). 40p. (J). (gr. k-2). 22.65 *(978-1-4965-6184-8(8)*, 137799, Picture Window Bks.) Capstone.
—Mission Super Halloween. Qualey, Marsha. 2018. (Bumble B. Ser.). (ENG.). 40p. (J). (gr. k-2). 22.65 *(978-1-4965-6181-7(3)*, 137796, Picture Window Bks.) Capstone.
—Ready to Fly: How Sylvia Townsend Became the Bookmobile Ballerina. Lyon, Lea & LaFaye, Alexandria. 2020. (ENG.). 40p. (J). (gr. -1-3). 18.99 *(978-0-06-288878-5(1)*, HarperCollins) HarperCollins Pubs. Ltd. GBR. Dist: HarperCollins Pubs.
Gibson, Jessica. Time to Roar. Cole, Olivia A. 2020. (ENG.). 32p. (J). 17.99 ***(978-1-5476-0370-1(4)***, 900215085, Bloomsbury Children's Bks.) Bloomsbury Publishing USA.
Gibson, Jessica. Very Lulu: The (Mostly) True Story of a Training School Dropout. Campisi, Stephanie. 2019. 32p. (J). (-3). 17.99 *(978-1-4926-7321-7(8)*, Sourcebooks Jabberwocky) Sourcebooks, Inc.
—Welcome to Jazz: A Swing-Along Celebration of America's Music, Featuring When the Saints Go Marching In. Sloan, Carolyn. 2019. (ENG.). 32p. (J). (gr. -1-3). 24.95 *(978-1-5235-0688-0(1)*, 100688) Workman Publishing Co., Inc.
Gibson, Jim. Talking with God. Gibson, Roxie. 2007. (ENG.). 24p. (J). (gr. -1-3). 7.99 *(978-1-933725-75-8(3))* Premium Pr. America.
Gibson, Maria. The Dinohumes. Welton, Darlene. 2017. (ENG.). 48p. (J). (gr. k-6). *(978-0-9949425-6-2(7))* Credit River Critters.
—Rufus, the Rac. Welton, Darlene. 2019. (ENG.). 48p. (J). (gr. k-6). *(978-0-9949425-8-6(3))* Credit River Critters.
Gibson, Mary. Buried Treasure. 2007. 12p. (J). 5.95 *(978-0-9801269-0-7(8))* Scribe's Closet Pubns., The.
Gibson, Nichoel. Grandma Loves Her Harley Too. Vogl, Nancy & Strange, David. ed. 2006. (J). per. 16.95 *(978-0-9772771-1-7(9))* Cherry Tree Pr. LLC.
Gibson, Sabina. Friendsgiving. Siscoe, Nancy. 2020. 40p. (J). (gr. -1-3). 17.99 ***(978-0-06-295676-7(0)***, Balzer & Bray) HarperCollins Pubs.
Gibson, Sabina. Snow Much Fun! Siscoe, Nancy. 2019. (ENG.). 40p. (J). (gr. -1-3). 17.99 *(978-0-06-274112-7(8)*, Balzer & Bray) HarperCollins Pubs.
Gibson, Sabina. Unicorn Magic. Gibson, Sabina. 2018. (ENG.). 32p. (J). (gr. -1-3). 17.99 *(978-0-545-81331-0(X)*, Scholastic Pr.) Scholastic, Inc.
Gibson, Silas. Some Monsters Look Like This. Gibson, Silas. 2018. (ENG.). 32p. (J). pap. 9.99 *(978-1-7314-4595-7(4))* Independently Published.
Gibson, Taylor. The Golden Knight #1: The Boy Is Summoned. Clark, Steven & Clark, Justin. 2011. (ENG.). 80p. (J). pap. 5.99 *(978-0-9647933-9-2(3))* New Horizons Pr.
Gibson, Valerie. Ebba Exactly. Frank, Gertie. 2017. (ENG.). (J). (gr. 3-6). 28.95 *(978-1-935186-88-5(4))*; pap. 14.95 *(978-1-935186-87-8(6))* Waldenhouse Pubs., Inc.
Giddens, Jake. Hoops. Leipold, Judith. 2013. 24p. 23.95 *(978-1-61493-223-9(9))* Peppertree Pr., The.
Giebfried, Rosemary. Sea Soup: Discovering the Watery World of Phytoplankton. Stevens, Betsy T. 2010. 96p. (gr. 3-7). pap., tchr. ed., tchr.'s training gde. ed. 9.95 *(978-0-88448-209-3(X))* Tilbury Hse. Pubs.
—Shelterwood: Discovering the Forest. Markowsky, Judy Kellogg. 2010. 80p. (gr. 3-6). pap., tchr. ed., tchr.'s training gde. ed. 9.95 *(978-0-88448-211-6(1))* Tilbury Hse. Pubs.
Giella, Joe, jt. illus. see Infantino, Carmine.
Giese, Daniel, jt. illus. see Amaquq-Baril, Alethea.
Giessl, Janet. Creation Story Coloring & Drawing Book. Giessl, Janet. 2020. (ENG.). 236p. (J). pap. 9.99 ***(978-1-6554-3311-5(3))*** Independently Published.
—Nativity Activity Book: Bible-Based Activities That Tell the Story of the Miracle of Jesus' Birth. Giessl, Janet. 2019. (ENG.). 168p. (J). pap. 8.99 ***(978-1-7116-4037-2(9))*** Independently Published.
—Nativity Tracing & Handwriting Practice Book: Bible-Based Nativity Tracing, Coloring, & Handwriting Practice Activities. Giessl, Janet. 2019. (ENG.). 170p. (J). pap. 8.99 ***(978-1-7104-5713-1(9))*** Independently Published.
Giffen, Keith, et al. Fantastic Four: the World's Greatest Comic Magazine. 2018. (ENG.). 280p. (J). (gr. 4-17). pap. 24.99 *(978-1-302-91337-3(9))* Marvel Worldwide, Inc.
Giffin, Brelyn. The Tale of Noodle the Uncurly Poodle. Lerner, Katherine. 2019. (ENG.). 46p. (J). pap. 9.95 ***(978-1-6724-4883-3(2))*** Independently Published.
Giffin, Noelle. Courtney Saves Christmas. Chand, Emlyn. 2012. 60p. 21.95 *(978-1-62253-114-1(0))* Evolved Publishing.
—Izzy the Inventor: A Bird Brain Book. Chand, Emlyn. l.t. ed. 2013. (ENG.). 56p. (gr. k-3). 21.95 *(978-1-62253-123-3(X))*; pap. 10.95 *(978-1-62253-122-6(1))* Evolved Publishing.
—Larry the Lonely: A Bird Brain Book. Chand, Emlyn. l.t. ed. 2013. (ENG.). 62p. (gr. k-3). pap. 10.95 *(978-1-62253-128-8(0))* Evolved Publishing.
—Ricky the Runt: A Bird Brain Book. Chand, Emlyn. l.t. ed. 2013. (ENG.). 52p. (gr. k-3). pap. 10.95 *(978-1-62253-125-7(6))* Evolved Publishing.
—Valentina & the Haunted Mansion (Valentina's Spooky Adventures - 1) Verstraete, Majanka. l.t. ed. 2013. (ENG.). 48p. 21.95 *(978-1-62253-057-1(8))*; pap. 10.95 *(978-1-62253-056-4(X))* Evolved Publishing.
—Valentina & the Whackadoodle Witch: Valentina's Spooky Adventures. Verstraete, Majanka. l.t. ed. 2013. (ENG.). 46p. (gr. k-4). pap. 10.95 *(978-1-62253-059-5(4))* Evolved Publishing.
—Vicky Finds a Valentine: Bird Brain Books. Chand, Emlyn. ed. 2013. (ENG.). 50p. (gr. k-1). pap. 10.95 *(978-1-62253-116-5(7))*; 21.95 *(978-1-62253-117-2(5))* Evolved Publishing.
Gifford, Lucinda. The Fourteenth Summer of Angus Jack. Storer, Jen. 2020. 336p. 7.99 *(978-0-7333-3443-6(1))* ABC Bks. AUS. Dist: HarperCollins Pubs.
Gigena, Florencia. The Titanosaur. Pol, Diego & Carballido, Jose Luis. 2019. (ENG.). 40p. (J). (gr. k-2). 18.99 *(978-1-338-20739-2(3)*, Orchard Bks.) Scholastic, Inc.
Gigi Bousidan, Inbal. Shimri's Big Idea: A Story of Ancient Jerusalem. Weber, Elka. 2019. (J). *(978-1-68115-541-8(9)*, Apples & Honey Pr.) Behrman Hse., Inc.
Gigot, Jami. Imagination Vacation. Gigot, Jami. 2019. (ENG.). 32p. (J). (gr. -1-3). 16.99 *(978-0-8075-3619-3(9)*, 807536199) Whitman, Albert & Co.
—Mae & the Moon. Gigot, Jami. 2015. (ENG.). 36p. (J). (gr. k-2). 17.99 *(978-0-9913866-2-8(0))* Ripple Grove Pr.
—Seb & the Sun. Gigot, Jami. 2018. (ENG.). 36p. (J). (gr. k-2). 17.99 *(978-0-9990249-0-4(6))* Ripple Grove Pr.
Gil, Alicja. The Band Together Family. Semerano, Frank. 2019. (ENG.). 26p. (J). pap. 9.95 *(978-1-0740-3005-6(2))* Independently Published.
—Sneaky Petey Penguin. Semerano, Frank. 2018. (ENG.). 56p. (J). pap. 11.99 *(978-1-7262-6093-0(3))* CreateSpace Independent Publishing Platform.
Gil, Alicja, jt. illus. see Ignaczak, Alicja.
Gil, Cristina. Look at Me! Castellanos, Graciela. 2019. (ENG.). 28p. (J). pap. 9.50 ***(978-1-6921-8744-6(9))*** Independently Published.
Gil, Ismael & Tolutis, Vytenis. Niall & the Stone of Destiny: Book I. MacNeill, Lance Joseph. 2016. (ENG.). (J). (gr. 5-6). 29.99 *(978-0-692-75992-9(1))* McNeill, Lance.
Gil, Jesús Enrique. H2o. Rodríguez Morales, Enrique Adonis. 2016. (SPA.). 112p. (J). (gr. 4-7). pap. 7.95 *(978-607-8237-89-0(6))* Nostra Ediciones MEX. Dist: Independent Pubs. Group.
Gil, Maca. Anti/Hero. Quinn, Kate Karyus & Lunetta, Demitria. 2020. 144p. (J). (gr. 3-7). pap. 9.99 *(978-1-4012-9325-3(5))* DC Comics.
Gil, Rodolpho. Mr. Meme. Goza, Shelly. 2005. (J). bds. 9.99 *(978-1-4183-0077-7(2))* Christ Inspired, Inc.
Gilbert, Anne Yvonne. Dracula. Stoker, Bram. 2010. (ENG.). 96p. (YA). (gr. 7-18). 19.99 *(978-0-7636-4793-3(4)*, Templar) Candlewick Pr.
Gilbert, Anne Yvonne, et al. Ghostology: A True Revelation of Spirits, Ghouls, & Hauntings. Curtie, Lucinda & Steer, Dugald A. 2020. (Ologies Ser.). (ENG.). 30p. (J). (gr. 5). 27.99 ***(978-1-5362-0915-0(5))*** Candlewick Pr.
Gilbert, Anne Yvonne. Jesus Is Born. Piper, Sophie. 2016. (ENG.). 32p. (J). (gr. -1-3). 16.99 *(978-1-68099-187-1(6)*, Good Bks.) Skyhorse Publishing Co., Inc.
—Robin Hood: The Classic Adventure Tale. Raven, Nicky. 2019. 104p. (J). (gr. 3-7). 14.99 *(978-1-63158-271-4(2)*, Racehorse Publishing) Skyhorse Publishing Co., Inc.
Gilbert, Anne Yvonne & Andrew, Ian. Children's Stories from the Bible. Pirotta, Saviour. 2009. (ENG.). 304p. (J). (gr. k-12). 19.99 *(978-0-7636-4551-9(6)*, Templar) Candlewick Pr.

Gilbert, Anne Yvonne & Powers, Gretchen Ellen. The Boxcar Children. Warner, Gertrude Chandler. ed. 2017. (Boxcar Children Mysteries Ser.). (ENG.). 168p. (J). (gr. 1-5). 34.99 *(978-0-8075-0925-8(6),* 807509256) Whitman, Albert & Co.
Gilbert, Cecilia. Jammin' Jerone! The lamb who played the Saxaphone. Bey, Angelique. 2008. (ENG.). 34p. pap. 12.99 *(978-1-4196-8093-9(5))* CreateSpace Independent Publishing Platform.
Gilbert, Douglas R., photos by. Bob Dylan: Unscripted. Rojas Cardona, Javier, ed. 2005. 40p. 14.95 *(978-0-9663572-2-6(1))* Tango Latin.
Gilbert, Elizabeth T. Watch Me Draw Tiggerific Tales. 2013. (Watch Me Draw Ser.). 24p. (gr. -1-2). 25.65 *(978-1-936309-87-0(4))* Quarto Publishing Group USA.
Gilbert, Elizabeth T., jt. illus. see Tucker, Marianne.
Gilbert, Elliott. Lizzie! Kumin, Maxine. 2014. 160p. (J). (gr. 4-7). 21.95 *(978-1-60980-518-0(6),* Triangle Square) Seven Stories Pr.
Gilbert, John. Soldiers & Sailors (Illustrated Edition) Mogridge (Old Humphrey), George. 2018. (ENG.). 192p. (J). pap. *(978-1-4068-8937-6(7))* Echo Library.
Gilbert, Michael. The Day of the Ness. Gilbert, Michael. Norton, Andre. 2020. (ENG.). 102p. (J). pap. 7.99 ***(978-1-68068-012-6(9))*** Ethan Ellenberg Literary Agency.
Gilbert, Rob. It's Raining, It's Pouring. Eagle, Kin. 2006. (Iza Trapani's Extended Nursery Rhymes Ser.). (ENG.). 32p. (gr. -1-k). 7.95 *(978-1-879085-71-8(2))* Perfection Learning Corp.
Gilbert, Rob, jt. illus. see Davenier, Christine.
Gilbert, Yvonne. Goodnight, My Angel: A Lullabye. Joel, Billy. 2004. (J). pap. *(978-0-439-55378-0(4))* Scholastic, Inc.
—Off the Page. Picoult, Jodi & van Leer, Samantha. 2015. (YA). lib. bdg. *(978-0-553-53557-0(9),* Delacorte Pr) Random House Publishing Group.
—Off the Page. Picoult, Jodi & van Leer, Samantha. (ENG.). (YA). (gr. 7). 2016. 368p. pap. 9.99 *(978-0-553-53559-4(5),* Ember); 2015. 384p. 19.99 *(978-0-553-53556-3(0),* Delacorte Pr.) Random Hse. Children's Bks.
—Per & the Dala Horse. Hickox, Rebecca. 2003. 32p. (J). pap. 8.95 *(978-1-57534-034-0(8))* Skandisk, Inc.
—Princess of the Wild Swans. Zahler, Diane. 2013. (ENG.). 240p. (J). (gr. 3-7). pap. 6.99 *(978-0-06-200495-6(6))* HarperCollins Pubs.
—The Wild Swans. Andersen, Hans. Lewis, Naomi, tr. from DAN. 2005. 48p. (J). 17.99 *(978-1-84148-164-7(5))* Barefoot Bks., Inc.
Gilboa, Rinat. Sing-Along Alef Bet. Vol. Thomas, Doni Zasloff & Lindberg, Eric. 2016. (ENG.). (J). *(978-1-68115-509-8(5))* Behrman Hse., Inc.
Gilchrist, Jan Spivey. Brothers & Sisters: Family Poems. Greenfield, Eloise. 2008. (ENG.). 32p. (J). (gr. k-4). 17.99 *(978-0-06-056284-7(6),* Amistad) HarperCollins Pubs.
—The Friendly Four. Greenfield, Eloise. 2006. (ENG.). 48p. (J). (gr. -1-3). 17.99 *(978-0-06-000759-1(1),* Amistad) HarperCollins Pubs.
—The Girl Who Buried Her Dreams in a Can. Trent, Tererai. 2015. (ENG.). 40p. (J). (gr. 1-3). 17.99 *(978-0-670-01654-9(3),* Viking Books for Young Readers) Penguin Young Readers Group.
—The Great Migration: Journey to the North. Greenfield, Eloise. 2010. (ENG.). 32p. (J). (gr. -1-3). 16.99 *(978-0-06-125921-0(7),* Amistad) HarperCollins Pubs.
Gilchrist, Jan Spivey. The Great Migration: Journey to the North. Greenfield, Eloise. 2020. 32p. (J). (gr. -1-3). pap. 8.99 ***(978-0-06-125923-4(3),*** Amistad) HarperCollins Pubs.
Gilchrist, Jan Spivey. Honey, I Love. Greenfield, Eloise. 2016. (ENG.). 32p. (J). (gr. -1-3). pap. 7.99 *(978-0-06-009125-5(8),* Amistad) HarperCollins Pubs.
—In the Land of Words: New & Selected Poems. Greenfield, Eloise. (ENG.). 48p. (J). (gr. -1-3). 2016. pap. 7.99 *(978-0-06-443692-2(6));* 2003. 17.99 *(978-0-06-028993-5(7))* HarperCollins Pubs. (Amistad).
—Me & Neesie. Greenfield, Eloise. anniv. ed. 2005. (Amistad Ser.). 32p. (J). (gr. -1-3). 15.99 *(978-0-06-000701-0(X),* Amistad) HarperCollins Pubs.
—We Are Shining. Brooks, Gwendolyn. 2017. (ENG.). 32p. (J). (gr. -1-3). 17.99 *(978-0-06-257066-6(8))* HarperCollins Pubs.
—When the Horses Ride By: Children in the Times of War. Greenfield, Eloise. 2006. (ENG.). 40p. (J). pap. 12.95 *(978-1-60060-454-6(4));* (gr. 4-7). 17.95 *(978-1-58430-249-0(6))* Lee & Low Bks., Inc.
—Yafi's Family: An Ethiopian Boy's Journey of Love, Loss, & Adoption. Pettitt, Linda & Darrow, Sharon. 2010. (J). (gr. -1-2). 17.95 *(978-0-9797481-4-1(3))* Amharic Kids.
Gildea, Shir. Loving All the Colors. Gildea, Shir. 2009. 24p. pap. 10.95 *(978-1-4269-0713-5(3))* Trafford Publishing.
Gilderdale, Alan. The Little Yellow Digger Goes to School. Gilderdale, Betty. 2005. 32p. (J). *(978-1-86943-686-5(5))* Scholastic New Zealand Ltd.
Gildersleeve, Owen. My Amazing Body Machine: A Colorful Visual Guide to How Your Body Works. Winston, Robert. 2017. (ENG.). 128p. (J). (gr. 2-4). 19.99 *(978-1-4654-6185-8(X),* DK Children) Dorling Kindersley Publishing, Inc.
Giles, Mike. Halloween Is Fun! 2009. (Yo Gabba Gabba! Ser.). (ENG.). 16p. (J). (gr. -1-1). pap. 6.99 *(978-1-4169-7824-4(0),* Simon Spotlight) Simon Spotlight.
Giles, Mike, jt. illus. see Ruiz, Aristides.
Giles, Mike, jt. illus. see Spaziante, Patrick.
Giles, Susan. Caribbean Cats. Giles, Susan. 2003. (Meet the Author Ser.). (ENG.). 16p. (J). pap. 5.75 net. *(978-1-57274-662-6(9),* 2728, Bks. for Young Learners) Owen, Richard C. Pubs., Inc.
Gilgannon-Collins, Denise. The Rabbit Who Lost His Hop: A Story about Self-Control. Nass, Marcia Shoshana. 2004. (Early Prevention Ser.: 5). (J). per. 19.95 *(978-1-58815-061-5(5),* 66525) Childswork/Childsplay.
Gili, Phillida. Cinderella: A Pop-up Book. Gili, Phillida. 2007. 12p. (J). 25.00 *(978-1-4223-9031-3(4))* DIANE Publishing Co.
Giliewe, Unada. God Provides Victory Through Gideon. Bader, Joanne. 2004. (Arch Bks.). 16p. (J). 1.99 *(978-0-7586-0673-0(7))* Concordia Publishing Hse.
Gill, Bob. A Balloon for Blunderbuss. 2008. (ENG.). 36p. (gr. -1-3). 14.95 *(978-0-7148-4873-0(5))* Phaidon Pr., Inc.
—Supposing. Reid, Alastair. 2010. 48p. (J). (gr. -1-3). 15.95 *(978-1-59017-369-5(4),* NYR Children's Collection) New York Review of Bks., Inc., The.
Gill, Brandewyn. The Coffee-Drinking Reindeer. Dipert, E. S. 2018. (ENG.). 30p. (J). pap. 9.77 ***(978-1-7313-0434-6(X))*** Independently Published.
Gill, Deirdre, jt. illus. see Rosenbaum, Andria Warmflash.
Gill, Jacqueline Paske. The Treasure-Hunt Friends Discover Autistic Trends. Martin, Brenda Damley. 2016. (ENG.). (J). pap. 11.95 *(978-0-9903034-2-8(X))* BrenMar Communications.
Gill, Jacqueline Paske. The Monster in the Basement. Gill, Jacqueline Paske. 2011. 32p. pap. 12.95 *(978-1-61493-003-7(1))* Peppertree Pr., The.
Gill, Olivia Lomenech. Fantastic Beasts & Where to Find Them. Rowling, J. K. 2017. (Harry Potter Ser.). (ENG.). 160p. (J). (gr. 3). 175.00 *(978-1-338-23269-1(X))* Scholastic, Inc.
—Fantastic Beasts & Where to Find Them. Rowling, J. K. & Scamander, Newt. 2017. (Harry Potter Ser.). (ENG.). 160p. (J). (gr. 3-3). 34.99 *(978-1-338-21679-0(1),* Levine, Arthur A. Bks.) Scholastic, Inc.
Gill, Robert & Asrar, Mahmud. The Totally Awesome Hulk Vol. 4: My Best Friends Are Monsters. 2018. (Totally Awesome Hulk (2016) Ser.: 4). (ENG.). 136p. (J). (gr. 4-17). pap. 17.99 *(978-1-302-90576-7(7))* Marvel Worldwide, Inc.
Gill, Tim. Santa's Toys. Williams, Sam. 2003. 14p. bds. *(978-1-85602-274-3(9),* Pavilion Children's Books) Pavilion Bks.
Gillain, Dominique. Troy. Geras, Adèle. 2017. (ENG.). 368p. (YA). (gr. 9). pap. 9.99 *(978-0-544-92546-5(7),* 1656861, HMH Books For Young Readers) Houghton Mifflin Harcourt Publishing Co.
Gillard, Jason. You May Just Be a Dinosaur, 1 vol. Macht, Heather. 2015. (ENG.). 32p. (J). (gr. k-3). 16.99 *(978-1-4556-2040-1(8),* Pelican Publishing) Arcadia Publishing.
Gilleard, James. Dinosaur Atlas, 1 vol. Rooney, Anne & Lonely Planet Kids. 2017. (ENG.). 32p. (J). (gr. 4-7). 18.99 *(978-1-78657-719-1(4),* 5652) Lonely Planet Global Ltd. IRL. Dist: Hachette Bk. Group.
—Disney Parks Presents the Haunted Mansion. Baker, Buddy. 2018. (Disney Parks Presents Ser.). (ENG.). 32p. (J). (gr. -1-k). 16.99 *(978-1-368-04898-9(6))* Disney Pr.
Gillen, Lisa P. Brians Garden. Williams, Heather L. l.t. ed. 2004. (HRL Little Book Ser.). (J). (gr. -1-1). pap. 10.95 *(978-1-57332-300-0(4));* pap. 10.95 *(978-1-57332-299-7(7))* Carson-Dellosa Publishing, LLC. (HighReach Learning, Incorporated).
—Caillou Finds Colors. Howard-Parham, Pam. l.t. ed. 2005. (HRL Board Book Ser.). (J). (gr. -1-k). bds. 10.95 *(978-1-57332-313-0(6),* HighReach Learning, Incorporated) Carson-Dellosa Publishing, LLC.
—Caillou Finds Shapes. Mullican, Judy & Crowell, Knox. l.t. ed. 2005. (HRL Board Book Ser.). (J). (gr. -1-k). bds. 10.95 *(978-1-57332-312-3(8),* HighReach Learning, Incorporated) Carson-Dellosa Publishing, LLC.
—Caillou Gets in Shape. Howard-Parham, Pam. l.t. ed. 2006. (HRL Board Book Ser.). (J). (gr. k-18). pap. 10.95 *(978-1-57332-331-4(4),* HighReach Learning, Incorporated) Carson-Dellosa Publishing, LLC.
—Caillou's Trip to the Harbor. Hensley, Sarah M. l.t. ed. 2004. (HRL Board Book Ser.). (J). (gr. -1-1). pap. 10.95 *(978-1-57332-290-4(3),* HighReach Learning, Incorporated) Carson-Dellosa Publishing, LLC.
—Let's Take a Ride. Mullican, Judy. l.t. ed. 2004. (HRL Big Book Ser.). (J). (gr. -1-k). pap. 10.95 *(978-1-57332-318-5(7));* pap. 10.95 *(978-1-57332-319-2(5))* Carson-Dellosa Publishing, LLC. (HighReach Learning, Incorporated).
—When I Take a Bath. Parham, Pam H. l.t. ed. 2005. (HRL Board Book Ser.). 12p. (J). (gr. -1-1). pap. 10.95 *(978-1-57332-284-3(9),* HighReach Learning, Incorporated) Carson-Dellosa Publishing, LLC.
—Why Have Rules? Black, Jessica L. l.t. ed. 2003. (HRL Little Book Ser.). 8p. (J). (gr. -1). pap. 10.95 *(978-1-57332-271-3(7));* pap. 10.95 *(978-1-57332-270-6(9))* Carson-Dellosa Publishing, LLC. (HighReach Learning, Incorporated).
Gillen, Lisa P. Spring Time. Gillen, Lisa P. l.t. ed. 2006. 12p. (J). (gr. -1-k). pap. 10.95 *(978-1-57332-351-2(9),* HighReach Learning, Incorporated) Carson-Dellosa Publishing, LLC.
Gillen, Lisa P., jt. illus. see Storch, Ellen N.
Gillen, Rosemarie. Albert & Freddie. Thyroff, Brad. 2013. 24p. pap. 9.99 *(978-1-61286-190-6(3))* Avid Readers Publishing Group.
—Alicia's Blended Family. Powell, Angela. 2013. 24p. pap. 9.99 *(978-1-61286-153-1(9))* Avid Readers Publishing Group.
—Blessed Jacint: Patron for Children for Tummy Troubles. Lagneau, Mary. 2012. 20p. pap. 7.50 *(978-1-61286-134-0(2))* Avid Readers Publishing Group.
—The Bonds. Gainey, Gary. 2012. 150p. pap. 9.99 *(978-1-937260-12-5(7))* Sleepytown Pr.
—Dandylion the Duck. Gober, Thomas. 2012. 26p. (J). 16.95 *(978-1-60131-126-9(5),* Castlebridge Bks.) Big Tent Bks.
—Funny Jimmy. Lee, Vanessa Rose. 2011. (ENG.). 28p. pap. 21.00 *(978-1-4567-2347-7(2))* AuthorHouse.
—Grammy & Her Lambies: Chicken Puddles. Dewald, Mike. 2018. (Grammy & Her Lambies Ser.: Vol. 1). (ENG.). 28p. (J). pap. 9.13 *(978-1-7298-2224-1(X))* CreateSpace Independent Publishing Platform.
—The Haunted House of Riddles. Lee, Vanessa Rose. 2011. 28p. pap. 7.99 *(978-1-61286-053-4(2))* Avid Readers Publishing Group.
—I Used to Be a Fairy... A True Story by Granny. Obrien, Cynthia Kern. 2019. (ENG.). 30p. (J). (gr. k-4). pap. 10.99 *(978-1-61286-360-3(4))* Avid Readers Publishing Group.
—The Lamb Who Counted Clouds. Jolivert, Immaculine. 2013. 24p. pap. 13.75 *(978-1-937260-91-0(7))* Sleepytown Pr.
—Little Al, the Angel. Salerno, Anthony Vincent. 2016. (ENG.). (J). pap. 12.95 *(978-1-61286-314-6(0))* Avid Readers Publishing Group.
—Movember with My Doggy. Bucklaschuk, Angela. 2013. 32p. pap. 11.95 *(978-1-61286-188-3(1))* Avid Readers Publishing Group.
—The Queen's Jewels. Carroll, Jacquie Lund. 2013. 26p. pap. 9.99 *(978-1-61286-147-0(4))* Avid Readers Publishing Group.
—Tyler & the Spider. Lancaster, Melinda. 2010. 32p. (J). pap. 9.95 *(978-1-935706-08-3(X))* Wiggles Pr.
—A Voice in the Night. Dail, Ernestine. 2012. 46p. pap. 9.99 *(978-1-61286-099-2(0))* Avid Readers Publishing Group.
—When the Lights Go Out at Grandma's. Benages, Patricia Dial. 2017. (ENG.). (J). (gr. k-3). 18.00 *(978-0-692-94388-5(9))* White Hare Publishing LLC.
—Where Is God, Grandfather. O'Donnell, Candy. 2008. 28p. pap. 12.95 *(978-0-9814532-1-7(X))* Living Waters Publishing Co.
Gillenardo-Goudreau, Christian. Plants vs. Zombies Volume 15: Better Homes & Guardens. Tobin, Paul. 2020. (ENG.). 88p. (J). (gr. 3-7). 9.99 *(978-1-5067-1305-2(X),* Dark Horse Books) Dark Horse Comics.
Gilles, Alice. Meditation for Kids: How to Clear Your Head & Calm Your Mind. Dupeyrat, Laurent & Bernard, Johanne. 2019. (ENG.). 96p. (J). (gr. 2-5). pap. 16.95 *(978-1-61180-620-5(8),* Bala Kids) Shambhala Pubns., Inc.
Gilles-Gray, Carolyn. Emu Can't Fly. Taylor, Helen. 2013. 24p. pap. *(978-1-921883-39-2(1),* MBS Pr.) Pick-a-Woo Woo Pubs.
Gillespie, Greg G. A Kid's Guide to Being a Winner. Shelton, C. H. & Shelton, C. H. 2011. 38p. (J). (gr. 2-8). 9.99 *(978-0-9841910-4-8(6))* Choice PH.
Gillespie, Lisa Mulvaney. Botts's Dots: Not Just a Bump in the Road. Silva, Roz. 2018. (Who Invented That? Ser.: Vol. 1). (ENG.). 32p. (J). (gr. 2-6). pap. 6.99 *(978-1-7325265-0-1(8))* Dayton Publishing.
Gillespie, Martin. A Jelly Fish Bit My Bum. Whitehead, Russell. 2019. (ENG.). 42p. (J). pap. ***(978-0-6485812-0-8(9))*** Whitehead, Russell.
Gillett, Hallie. Spinner McClock & the Christmas Visit. Dacey, Richard. 2004. 32p. (J). 13.95 *(978-1-929039-24-1(7))* Ambassador Bks., Inc.
Gillette, Henry S. Benjamin Franklin, Man of Science: A First Biography. Eberle, Irmengarde. 2011. 156p. 41.95 *(978-1-258-08044-0(3))* Literary Licensing, LLC.
Gillette, Richard, photos by. Sonoma: The Ultimate Winery Guide. Cusick-Dickerson, Heidi H. 2nd rev. ed. 2005. (ENG., 120p. (gr. 8-17). pap. 19.95 *(978-0-8118-4200-6(2))* Chronicle Bks. LLC.
Gillette, Tim. Baby Bible Board Books Collection No. 1: Stories of Jesus, 4 vols. Bolme, Edward Sarah. l.t. ed. 2003. 20p. (J). bds. 23.99 *(978-0-9725546-4-0(5))* CREST Pubns.
—Jesus Feeds the People. Bolme, Edward Sarah. l.t. ed. 2003. 20p. (J). bds. 6.99 *(978-0-9725546-0-2(2))* CREST Pubns.
—Jesus Heals a Little Girl. Bolme, Edward Sarah. l.t. ed. 2003. 20p. (J). bds. 6.99 *(978-0-9725546-1-9(0))* CREST Pubns.
—Jesus Helps a Blind Man. Bolme, Edward Sarah. l.t. ed. 2003. 20p. (J). bds. 6.99 *(978-0-9725546-2-6(9))* CREST Pubns.
—Jesus Stops a Storm. Bolme, Edward Sarah. l.t. ed. 2003. 20p. (J). bds. 6.99 *(978-0-9725546-3-3(7))* CREST Pubns.
Gilliam, David. Gingertown. Gillam, David. 2012. 216p. (J). 29.99 *(978-1-60131-122-1(2))* Big Tent Bks.
Gillies, Chuck. The Song of the King. Lucado, Max. ed. 2014. (ENG.). 32p. (J). 17.99 *(978-1-4335-4290-9(0))* Crossway.
Gilligan, Paul. King of the Mole People (Book 1) Gilligan, Paul. 2019. (King of the Mole People Ser.: 1). (ENG.). 272p. (J). 13.99 *(978-1-250-17134-4(2),* 900188283, Holt, Henry & Co. Bks. For Young Readers) Holt, Henry & Co.
Gilligan, Paul. King of the Mole People: Rise of the Slugs. Gilligan, Paul. 2020. (King of the Mole People Ser.: 2). (ENG.). 288p. (J). 13.99 ***(978-1-250-17136-8(9),*** 900188289, Holt, Henry & Co. Bks. For Young Readers) Holt, Henry & Co.
Gilliland, Grant. Theo. Lim, Kenny. 2019. (ENG.). 56p. (J). pap. 14.99 *(978-1-9737-8041-0(0))* CreateSpace Independent Publishing Platform.
Gilliland, Jillian Hulme. How the Devil Got His Cat & Other Multicultural Folktales for Children. Downie, Mary Alice & Zola, Mequido. 144p. (J). pap. 16.95 *(978-1-55082-100-0(8))* Quarry Pr. CAN. Dist: LPC/InBook.
Gillingham, Sara. The Doll Hospital. George, Kallie. 2018. (ENG.). 32p. (J). (gr. -1-3). 17.99 *(978-1-5344-0121-1(0))* Simon & Schuster Children's Publishing.
—I Am So Brave! Krensky, Stephen. 2014. (ENG.). 12p. (J). (gr. -1 — 1). bds. 7.99 *(978-1-4197-0937-1(2),* Abrams Appleseed) Abrams, Inc.
—I Can Do It Myself! Krensky, Stephen. 2012. (ENG.). 12p. (J). (gr. -1 — 1). bds. 6.95 *(978-1-4197-0400-0(1),* Abrams Appleseed) Abrams, Inc.
—I Know a Lot! Krensky, Stephen. 2013. (ENG.). 12p. (J). (gr. -1 — 1). bds. 7.99 *(978-1-4197-0938-8(0),* Abrams Appleseed) Abrams, Inc.
—Love Is a Truck. Novesky, Amy. 2016. (ENG.). 24p. (J). (gr. -1-1). 12.95 *(978-1-937359-86-7(7),* Cameron Kids) Cameron + Co.
—Love Is a Tutu. Novesky, Amy. 2016. (ENG.). 24p. (J). (gr. -1-k). pap. 12.95 *(978-1-937359-81-2(6),* Cameron Kids) Cameron + Co.
—Now I Am Big! Krensky, Stephen. 2012. (ENG.). 12p. (J). (gr. -1 — 1). bds. 6.95 *(978-1-4197-0416-1(8),* Abrams Appleseed) Abrams, Inc.
—Snuggle the Baby. 2014. (ENG.). 12p. (J). (gr. -1 — 1). bds. 12.99 *(978-1-4197-1124-4(5),* Abrams Appleseed) Abrams, Inc.
Gillis, Bonnie. Baby Moses. Melania, Mother. 2008. (Old Testament Stories for Children Ser.). (ENG.). 28p. (gr. -1-3). pap. 8.95 *(978-1-888212-97-6(7))* Ancient Faith Publishing.
—The Entrance of the Theotokos into the Temple. Elayne. 2003. (Twelve Great Feasts for Children Ser.). (ENG.). 24p. (J). pap. 5.95 *(978-1-888212-40-2(3))* Ancient Faith Publishing.
—Jonah's Journey to the Deep. Melania, Mother. 2009. (Old Testament Stories for Children Ser.). (ENG.). 28p. (J). pap. 8.95 *(978-1-888212-59-4(4))* Ancient Faith Publishing.
Gillis, Emily R. The Ashport Archives: Cage of the Karura. Gillis, Stephanie a. M, Halah, ed. 2018. (Ashport Archives Ser.: Vol. 3). (ENG.). 378p. (J). pap. 14.99 *(978-1-7263-3286-6(1))* CreateSpace Independent Publishing Platform.
Gillis, Jane. Dead End. Frenette, Liza. 2005. x, 65p. (J). *(978-1-59531-001-9(0))* North Country Bks., Inc.
Gillman, Melanie. Stage Dreams. 2019. 104p. (YA). (gr. 8-12). 29.32 *(978-1-5124-4000-3(0),* Graphic Universe™) Lerner Publishing Group.
Gillmore, Jean. Dewey Doo-It Feeds a Friend. Wenger, Brahm & Green, Alan. 2004. (J). *(978-0-9745143-0-7(6))* RandallFraser Publishing.
Gillmore, Karen. Explore the Rocky Shore with Sam & Crystal, 1 vol. Snively, Gloria. 2018. (Explore with Sam & Crystal Ser.: 2). (ENG.). 64p. (J). (gr. 4-7). 18.95 *(978-1-77203-236-9(0))* Heritage Hse. CAN. Dist: Orca Bk. Pubs. USA.
—Explore the Wild Coast with Sam & Crystal, 1 vol. Snively, Gloria. 2018. (Explore with Sam & Crystal Ser.: 1). (ENG.). 64p. (J). (gr. 4-7). 18.95 *(978-1-77203-167-6(4))* Heritage Hse. CAN. Dist: Orca Bk. Pubs. USA.
Gillmore, Karen. High Tide, Low Tide: A Shoreline Activity Book. Snively, Gloria. 2020. (ENG.). 56p. (J). (gr. 1-3). pap. 16.95 ***(978-1-77203-321-2(9))*** Heritage Hse. CAN. Dist: Orca Bk. Pubs. USA.
Gillogly, Duane. Tortillas for Trina. Bates, Elizabeth A. 2006. (ENG.). 36p. (YA). 21.99 *(978-1-4257-3049-9(3))* Xlibris Corp.
Gilman, Phoebe. Once upon a Golden Apple: 25th Anniversary Edition. Little, Jean & de Vries, Maggie. 25th ed. 2016. (ENG.). 26p. (J). (— 1). bds. 7.99 *(978-0-670-07007-7(6),* Puffin Canada) PRH Canada Young Readers CAN. Dist: Penguin Random Hse. LLC.
Gilman, Sara. Melvin: A True Story with a Happy Ending. Mayfield, Holly. 2013. 38p. pap. 9.99 *(978-0-9892711-9-6(6))* Mindstir Media.
Gilmour, Karen. I Am Your Emotions. McNulty John. 2006. 32p. (J). *(978-0-9769580-4-8(X))* I Am Your Playground LLC.
—I Am Your Imagination. McNulty John. 2006. 32p. *(978-0-9769580-3-1(1))* I Am Your Playground LLC.
—I Am Your Self-Esteem. McNulty John. 2006. 32p. (J). *(978-0-9769580-5-5(8))* I Am Your Playground LLC.
Gilpin, Stephen. Attack of the Growling Eyeballs. Oliver, Lin. 2009. (Who Shrunk Daniel Funk? Ser.: 1). (ENG.). 160p. (J). (gr. 3-7). pap. 7.99 *(978-1-4169-0958-3(3),* Simon & Schuster Bks. For Young Readers) Simon & Schuster Bks. For Young Readers.
—Bear Country: Bearly a Misadventure. Cronin, Doreen. (Chicken Squad Ser.: 6). (ENG.). 112p. (J). (gr. 2-5). 2019. pap. 7.99 *(978-1-5344-0575-2(5));* 2018. 12.99 *(978-1-5344-0574-5(7),* Atheneum/Caitlyn Dlouhy Books) Simon & Schuster Children's Publishing.
—The Big Hairy Secret, 1 vol. Troupe, Thomas Kingsley. 2013. (Furry & Flo Ser.). (ENG.). 128p. (J). (gr. 2-3). lib. bdg. 25.32 *(978-1-4342-3858-0(X),* Stone Arch Bks.) Capstone.
—Cronus the Titan Tells All: Tricked by the Kids, 1 vol. Braun, Eric. 2014. (Other Side of the Myth Ser.). (ENG.). 32p. (J). (gr. -1-3). 27.99 *(978-1-4795-2184-5(1),* Picture Window Bks.) Capstone.
—Dark Shadows: Yes, Another Misadventure. Cronin, Doreen. 2017. (Chicken Squad Ser.: 4). (ENG.). 128p. (J). (gr. 2-5). 12.99 *(978-1-4814-5049-2(2),* Atheneum/Caitlyn Dlouhy Books) Simon & Schuster Children's Publishing.
—Eoin Colfer Artemis Fowl: the Graphic Novel. Moreci, Michael & Colfer, Eoin. 2019. (Artemis Fowl Ser.). (ENG.). 128p. (J). (gr. 3-7). 21.99 *(978-1-368-04314-4(3))* Disney Pr.
—Escape of the Mini-Mummy. Oliver, Lin. 2009. (Who Shrunk Daniel Funk? Ser.: 2). (ENG.). 160p. (J). (gr. 3-7). pap. 8.99 *(978-1-4169-0960-6(5),* Simon & Schuster Bks. For Young Readers) Simon & Schuster Bks. For Young Readers.
—Even Firefighters Go to the Potty: A Potty Training Lift-The-Flap Story. Wax, Wendy & Wax, Naomi. 2008. (ENG.). 22p. (J). (gr. -1-k). 8.99 *(978-1-4169-2720-4(4),* Little Simon) Little Simon.
—The Extraordinary Adventures of Ordinary Boy, Book 1: the Hero Revealed. Boniface, William. 2008. (Extraordinary Adventures of Ordinary Boy Ser.: 1). (ENG.). 320p. (J). (gr. 3-7). pap. 6.99 *(978-0-06-077466-0(5))* HarperCollins Pubs.
—The Extraordinary Adventures of Ordinary Boy, Book 2: the Return of Meteor Boy? Boniface, William. 2008. (Extraordinary Adventures of Ordinary Boy Ser.: 2). (ENG.). 368p. (J). (gr. 3-7). pap. 6.99 *(978-0-06-077469-1(X))* HarperCollins Pubs.
—The Extraordinary Adventures of Ordinary Boy, Book 3: the Great Powers Outage Bk. 3. Boniface, William. 2010. (Extraordinary Adventures of Ordinary Boy Ser.: 3). (ENG.). 352p. (J). (gr. 3-7). pap. 7.99 *(978-0-06-077472-1(X))* HarperCollins Pubs.
—Fart Squad. Pilger, Seamus. 2015. (Fart Squad Ser.: 1). (ENG.). 112p. (J). (gr. 1-5). pap. 4.99 *(978-0-06-229045-8(2),* HarperFestival) HarperCollins Pubs.
—Fart Squad #2: Fartasaurus Rex. Pilger, Seamus. 2015. (Fart Squad Ser.: 2). (ENG.). 112p. (J). (gr. 1-5). 15.99

(978-0-06-236632-0(7)); pap. 4.99 *(978-0-06-229047-2(9))* HarperCollins Pubs.

—Fart Squad #3: Unidentified Farting Objects. Pilger, Seamus. 2016. (Fart Squad Ser.: 3). (ENG.). 112p. (J). (gr. 1-5). pap. 4.99 *(978-0-06-229049-6(5))* HarperCollins Pubs.

—Fart Squad #4: the Toilet Vortex. Pilger, Seamus. 2016. (Fart Squad Ser.: 4). (ENG.). 112p. (J). (gr. 1-5). pap. 4.99 *(978-0-06-229051-9(7))* HarperCollins Pubs.

—Fart Squad #5: Underpantsed! Pilger, Seamus. 2016. (Fart Squad Ser.: 5). (ENG.). 112p. (J). (gr. 1-5). pap. 4.99 *(978-0-06-229053-3(3))* HarperCollins Pubs.

—Fart Squad #6: Blast from the Past. Pilger, Seamus. 2017. (Fart Squad Ser.: 6). (ENG.). 128p. (J). (gr. 1-5). pap. 4.99 *(978-0-06-229055-7(X))* HarperCollins Pubs.

—Felix Takes the Stage. Lasky, Kathryn. (ENG.). 144p. (J). (gr. 2-5). 2011. pap. 5.99 *(978-0-545-11730-2(5),* Scholastic Paperbacks); 2010. 15.99 *(978-0-545-11681-7(3),* Scholastic Pr.) Scholastic, Inc.

—The Gecko & Sticky: Sinister Substitute. Van Draanen, Wendelin. 2011. (Gecko & Sticky Ser.: 3). (ENG.). 224p. (J). (gr. 3-7). 7.99 *(978-0-440-42244-0(2),* Yearling) Random Hse. Children's Bks.

—The Gecko & Sticky: the Greatest Power. Van Draanen, Wendelin. 2011. (Gecko & Sticky Ser.: 2). (ENG.). 208p. (J). (gr. 3-7). 7.99 *(978-0-440-42243-3(4),* Yearling) Random Hse. Children's Bks.

—The Gecko & Sticky: the Power Potion. Van Draanen, Wendelin. 2011. (Gecko & Sticky Ser.: 4). (ENG.). 240p. (J). (gr. 3-7). 7.99 *(978-0-440-42245-7(0),* Yearling) Random Hse. Children's Bks.

—The Gecko & Sticky: Villain's Lair. Van Draanen, Wendelin. 2011. (Gecko & Sticky Ser.: 1). (ENG.). 208p. (J). (gr. 3-7). pap. 7.99 *(978-0-440-42242-6(6),* Yearling) Random Hse. Children's Bks.

—Gimme Shelter: Misadventures & Misinformation. Cronin, Doreen. (Chicken Squad Ser.: 5). (ENG.). (J). (gr. 2-5). 2018. 144p. pap. 7.99 *(978-1-5344-0572-1(0),* Atheneum Bks. for Young Readers); 2017. 128p. 12.99 *(978-1-5344-0571-4(2),* Atheneum/Caitlyn Dlouhy Books) Simon & Schuster Children's Publishing.

—Hair-Pocalypse. Herbach, Geoff. 2017. (Fiction Picture Bks.). (ENG.). 32p. (J). (gr. k-3). lib. bdg. 23.32 *(978-1-5158-1411-5(4),* 135243, Picture Window Bks.) Capstone.

—Helen of Troy Tells All: Blame the Boys, 1 vol. Loewen, Nancy. 2014. (Other Side of the Myth Ser.). (ENG.). 32p. (J). (gr. -1-3). 27.99 *(978-1-4795-2182-1(5),* Picture Window Bks.) Capstone.

—Into the Wild: Yet Another Misadventure. Cronin, Doreen. (Chicken Squad Ser.: 3). (ENG.). 112p. (J). (gr. 2-5). 2017. pap. 7.99 *(978-1-4814-5047-8(6))*; 2016. 12.99 *(978-1-4814-5046-1(8),* Atheneum/Caitlyn Dlouhy Books) Simon & Schuster Children's Publishing.

—Librarian on the Roof! King, M. G. 2010. (ENG.). 32p. (J). (gr. 1-3). 16.99 *(978-0-8075-4512-6(0),* 807545120) Whitman, Albert & Co.

—Librarian on the Roof: A True Story. King, M. G. 2012. (J). *(978-1-61913-147-7(1))* Weigl Pubs., Inc.

—Los Tres Cabritos, 0 vols. Kimmel, Eric A. 2012. (SPA.). 32p. (J). (gr. k-2). 22.44 *(978-0-7614-5961-3(8),* 9780761459613, Amazon Children's Publishing) Amazon Publishing.

—Matthew & His Funky Fabulous Machine (W. T.) Naylor, Phyllis Reynolds. 2017. (ENG.). 176p. (J). (gr. 2-6). 16.99 *(978-1-4814-3779-0(8),* Atheneum/Caitlyn Dlouhy Books) Simon & Schuster Children's Publishing.

—Medea Tells All: A Mad, Magical Love, 1 vol. Braun, Eric. 2014. (Other Side of the Myth Ser.). (ENG.). 32p. (J). (gr. -1-3). pap. 6.95 *(978-1-4795-2940-7(0),* Picture Window Bks.) Capstone.

—Medusa Tells All: Beauty Missing, Hair Hissing, 1 vol. Fjelland Davis, Rebecca. 2014. (Other Side of the Myth Ser.). (ENG.). 32p. (J). (gr. -1-3). pap. 6.95 *(978-1-4795-2942-1(7),* Picture Window Bks.) Capstone.

—The Misplaced Mummy, 1 vol. Troupe, Thomas Kingsley. 2014. (Furry & Flo Ser.). (ENG.). 128p. (J). (gr. 2-3). 25.32 *(978-1-4342-6396-4(7),* Stone Arch Bks.) Capstone.

—Pirate Mom. Underwood, Deborah. 2006. (Step into Reading Ser.: Vol. 3). 48p. (J). (gr. k-3). per. 4.99 *(978-0-375-83323-6(4),* Random Hse. Bks. for Young Readers) Random Hse. Children's Bks.

—Pirates, Ho!, 0 vols. Thomson, Sarah L. 2012. (ENG.). 32p. (J). (gr. k-3). pap. 7.99 *(978-0-7614-6247-7(3),* 9780761462477, Two Lions) Amazon Publishing.

—Pottymouth & Stoopid. Patterson, James & Grabenstein, Chris. 2019. (ENG.). 336p. (J). (gr. 3-7). pap. 7.99 *(978-0-316-51498-9(5),* Jimmy Patterson) Little Brown & Co.

—Pottymouth & Stoopid. Patterson, James. 2017. (ENG.). 336p. (J). (gr. 3-7). 13.99 *(978-0-316-34963-5(1))* Little Brown & Co.

—The Problems with Goblins, 1 vol. Troupe, Thomas Kingsley. 2013. (Furry & Flo Ser.). (ENG.). 128p. (J). (gr. 2-3). lib. bdg. 25.32 *(978-1-4342-5042-1(3),* Stone Arch Bks.) Capstone.

—Revenge of the Itty-Bitty Brothers. Oliver, Lin. 2010. (Who Shrunk Daniel Funk? Ser.: 3). (ENG.). 176p. (J). (gr. 3-7). pap. 6.99 *(978-1-4169-0962-0(1),* Simon & Schuster Bks. For Young Readers) Simon & Schuster Bks. For Young Readers.

—Revenge of the Itty-Bitty Brothers, 3. Oliver, Lin. 2009. (Who Shrunk Daniel Funk? Ser.: 3). (ENG.). 112p. (J). (gr. 2-4). 21.19 *(978-1-4169-0961-3(3))* Simon & Schuster, Inc.

—Secret of the Super-Small Superstar. Oliver, Lin. 2010. (Who Shrunk Daniel Funk? Ser.: 4). (ENG.). 160p. (J). (gr. 3-7). 14.99 *(978-1-4169-0963-7(X),* Simon & Schuster Bks. For Young Readers) Simon & Schuster Bks. For Young Readers.

—Sir Fartsalot Hunts the Booger. Bolger, Kevin. 2009. (ENG.). 224p. (J). (gr. 3-7). 7.99 *(978-1-59514-284-9(3))*; (gr. 4-6). 18.69 *(978-1-59514-176-7(6))* Penguin Young Readers Group. (Razorbill).

—The Skeletons in City Park, 1 vol. Troupe, Thomas Kingsley. 2014. (Furry & Flo Ser.). (ENG.). 128p. (J). (gr. 2-3). 25.32 *(978-1-4342-6397-1(5),* Stone Arch Bks.) Capstone.

—Snowball Trouble. Howard, Kate. 2015. (ANG.). 40p. (J). pap. *(978-0-545-75839-0(4))* Scholastic, Inc.

—The Solemn Golem. Troupe, Thomas Kingsley. 2015. (Furry & Flo Ser.). (ENG.). 128p. (J). (gr. 2-3). lib. bdg. 25.32 *(978-1-4342-9646-7(6),* Stone Arch Bks.) Capstone.

—Spiders on the Case, Bk. 2. Lasky, Kathryn. 2011. (ENG.). 176p. (J). (gr. 2-5). 15.99 *(978-0-545-11682-4(1),* Scholastic Pr.) Scholastic, Inc.

—That Stinks! A Punny Show-and-Tell. Katz, Alan. 2016. (ENG.). 32p. (J). (gr. -1-3). 17.99 *(978-1-4169-7880-0(1),* Simon & Schuster Bks. For Young Readers) Simon & Schuster Bks. For Young Readers.

—The Three Cabritos, 0 vols. Kimmel, Eric A. 2012. (ENG.). 32p. (J). (gr. -1-3). pap. 7.99 *(978-0-7614-6309-2(7),* 9780761463092, Two Lions) Amazon Publishing.

—Uncle Si, the Christmas Elf: Work Hard, Nap Hard. Robertson, Si & Nelson, Ashley Howard. 2014. (ENG.). 48p. (J). (gr. -1-3). 29.99 *(978-1-4814-1821-8(1),* Simon & Schuster Bks. For Young Readers) Simon & Schuster Bks. For Young Readers.

—The Voiceless Vampire. Troupe, Thomas Kingsley. 2015. (Furry & Flo Ser.). (ENG.). 128p. (J). (gr. 2-3). lib. bdg. 25.32 *(978-1-4342-9645-0(8),* Stone Arch Bks.) Capstone.

—What If I Pulled This Thread. Hall, John. 2006. 48p. 12.99 *(978-1-59379-067-7(8))* White Stone Bks.

—What to Do When You're Sent to Your Room. Stott, Ann. 2014. 32p. (J). (gr. -1-3). 15.99 *(978-0-7636-6052-9(3))* Candlewick Pr.

—Wires & Nerve, Volume 2: Gone Rogue. Meyer, Marissa. 2018. (Wires & Nerve Ser.: 2). (ENG.). 336p. (YA). 21.99 *(978-1-250-07828-5(8),* 900153574) Feiwel & Friends.

—Wires & Nerve, Volume 2: Gone Rogue. Meyer, Marissa. 2019. (Wires & Nerve Ser.: 2). (ENG.). 336p. (YA). pap. 17.99 *(978-1-250-07829-2(6),* 900153575) Square Fish.

—100 Snowmen, 0 vols. Arena, Jen. 2013. (ENG.). 24p. (J). (gr. k-3). 14.99 *(978-1-4778-4703-9(0),* 9781477847039, Two Lions) Amazon Publishing.

Gilpin, Stephen, jt. illus. see Cornell, Kevin.

Gilson, David. Drago 4: Red Romper Specials. Crawford, Macy. 2020. (ENG.). 26p. (J). pap. 16.99 ***(978-1-7283-4986-2(9))*** AuthorHouse.

—Drago 5: A New School Year. Crawford, Macy. 2020. (ENG.). 24p. (J). pap. 16.99 ***(978-1-7283-4998-5(2))*** AuthorHouse.

—Drago 6: The Test. Crawford, Macy. 2020. (ENG.). 30p. (J). pap. 16.99 ***(978-1-7283-6406-3(X))*** AuthorHouse.

—Drago 7: The School Dance. Crawford, Macy. 2020. (ENG.). 26p. (J). pap. 16.99 ***(978-1-7283-6404-9(3))*** AuthorHouse.

—Drago 8: The Lunch Room. Crawford, Macy. 2020. (ENG.). 24p. (J). pap. 16.99 ***(978-1-7283-6408-7(6))*** AuthorHouse.

Gilson, Heather, photos by. Up to No Good: The Rascally Things Boys Do. Harmon, Kitty. Harmon, Kitty, ed. 2005. (ENG., 108p. (gr. 8-17). pap. 9.95 *(978-0-8118-4840-4(X))* Chronicle Bks. LLC.

Gilsvik, David. The Complete Book of Trapping. Gilsvik, Bob. 172p. (J). (gr. 7). reprint ed. 14.95 *(978-0-936622-29-3(6))* A.R. Harding Publishing Co.

Gilvan-Cartwright, Chris. Who's in the Jungle? DePrisco, Dorothea. 2006. (ENG.). 10p. (J). bds. 4.95 *(978-1-58117-507-3(8),* Intervisual/Piggy Toes) Bendon, Inc.

—Who's in the Jungle? Lift-the-Flap 'n' Learn. Gondek, Heather. 2005. (Fun with Animals Ser.). 10p. (J). 9.95 *(978-1-58117-075-7(0),* Intervisual/Piggy Toes) Bendon, Inc.

—Who's in the Ocean? 2005. (Lift-The-Flap 'n' Learn Ser.). 10p. (J). 9.95 *(978-1-58117-213-3(3),* Intervisual/Piggy Toes) Bendon, Inc.

—Who's in the Ocean? DePrisco, Dorothea. 2006. (ENG.). 10p. (gr. -1-k). bds. 4.95 *(978-1-58117-509-7(4),* Intervisual/Piggy Toes) Bendon, Inc.

—Who's on the Farm? DePrisco, Dorothea. 2006. (ENG.). 10p. (gr. -1-k). bds. 4.95 *(978-1-58117-508-0(6),* Intervisual/Piggy Toes) Bendon, Inc.

—Who's on the Farm? Lift-the-Flap 'n' Learn Book. Gondek, Heather J. 2005. (Fun with Animals Ser.). 10p. (J). (gr. -1-k). act. bk. ed. 9.95 *(978-1-58117-143-3(9),* Intervisual/Piggy Toes) Bendon, Inc.

Gim, jt. illus. see Romeo Pallar.

Gimbergsson, Sara. The Rabbit Who Couldn't Find His Daddy. Edvall, Lilian. 2006. 32p. (J). (gr. -1-3). 15.00 *(978-91-29-66429-4(2))* R & S Bks. SWE. Dist: Macmillan.

—The Rabbit Who Didn't Want to Go to Sleep. Edvall, Lilian. Dyssegaard, Elisabeth Kallick, tr. from SWE. 2004. 32p. (J). 15.00 *(978-91-29-66001-2(7))* R & S Bks. SWE. Dist: Macmillan.

Gimlin, Mihaela. The Old Man's Daughter & the Old Woman's Daughter / Fata Babei Si Fata Mosneagului. Creanga, Ion. Todd Kaplan, Delia Angelescu, tr. 2013. 42p. pap. 17.95 *(978-1-936629-30-5(5))* Reflection Publishing.

Ginerva, Dante. The King & the Cobbler: A Tale from Afghanistan. Brereton, Libby. 2016. 24p. (J). pap. 9.95 *(978-1-927244-63-0(3))* Flying Start Bks. NZL. Dist: Flying Start Bks.

—The King & the Cobbler (Big Book Edition) A Tale from Afghanistan. Brereton, Libby. 2016. 24p. (J). pap. *(978-1-927244-73-9(0))* Flying Start Bks.

—The Roaring 20s & the Great Depression: Bridges Edition. Reisfeld, Randi. 2015. (Prime Plus Ser.). (YA). (gr. 6-8). pap. *(978-1-4900-1951-2(0))* Benchmark Education Co.

—The Roaring 20s & the Great Depression: Bridges Edition Set of 6 with Common Core Indicators. Reisfeld, Randi. 2015. (Prime Plus Ser.). (YA). (gr. 6-8). 69.00 net. *(978-1-4900-2047-1(0))* Benchmark Education Co.

—Theodore Roosevelt & the Progressive Era: Bridges Edition. Walker, Paul Robert. 2015. (Prime Plus Ser.). (YA). (gr. 6-8). pap. *(978-1-4900-1949-9(9))* Benchmark Education Co.

—Theodore Roosevelt & the Progressive Era: Bridges Edition Set of 6 with Common Core Indicators. Walker, Paul Robert. 2015. (Prime Plus Ser.). (YA). (gr. 6-8). 69.00 net. *(978-1-4900-2045-7(4))* Benchmark Education Co.

—The United States Becomes a World Power: 1890-1918: Bridges Edition. Worth, Richard. 2015. (Prime Plus Ser.). (YA). (gr. 6-8). pap. *(978-1-4900-1950-5(2))* Benchmark Education Co.

—The United States Becomes a World Power: 1890-1918: Bridges Edition Set of 6 with Common Core Indicators. Worth, Richard. 2015. (Prime Plus Ser.). (YA). (gr. 6-8). 69.00 net. *(978-1-4900-2046-4(2))* Benchmark Education Co.

Ginesin, Zack. Prince Jack, the Little Artist. Ginesin, Lucia. 2009. 28p. pap. 11.99 *(978-1-59858-983-2(0))* Dog Ear Publishing, LLC.

Ginevra, Dante. Arrested for Witchcraft! Nickolas Flux & the Salem Witch Trials, 1 vol. Bolte, Marissa. 2014. (Nickolas Flux History Chronicles Ser.). (ENG.). (J). (gr. 3-9). 40p. pap. 7.95 *(978-1-4765-5151-7(0))*; 32p. lib. bdg. 31.32 *(978-1-4765-3947-8(2))* Capstone. (Capstone Pr.).

—Behind Enemy Lines: The Escape of Robert Grimes with the Comet Line. Chandler, Matt. 2017. (Great Escapes of World War II Ser.). (ENG.). 32p. (J). (gr. 3-9). lib. bdg. 31.32 *(978-1-5157-3530-4(3),* Capstone Pr.) Capstone.

—Defend until Death! Nickolas Flux & the Battle of the Alamo, 1 vol. Yomtov, Nel. 2014. (Nickolas Flux History Chronicles Ser.). (ENG.). 32p. (J). (gr. 3-9). lib. bdg. 31.32 *(978-1-4765-3945-4(6),* Capstone Pr.) Capstone.

—Night of Rebellion! Nickolas Flux & the Boston Tea Party, 1 vol. Yomtov, Nel. 2014. (Nickolas Flux History Chronicles Ser.). (ENG.). 32p. (J). (gr. 3-9). lib. bdg. 31.32 *(978-1-4765-3946-1(4))* Capstone.

—Stake a Claim! Nickolas Flux & the California Gold Rush, 1 vol. Collins, Terry. 2014. (Nickolas Flux History Chronicles Ser.). (ENG.). 32p. (J). (gr. 3-9). lib. bdg. 31.32 *(978-1-4765-3944-7(8))* Capstone.

—The Sword in the Stone: Band 11 Lime/Band 16 Sapphire (Collins Big Cat Progress) Hoffman, Mary. 2014. (Collins Big Cat Progress Ser.). (ENG.). 32p. (J). (gr. 4-5). pap. 9.99 *(978-0-00-751935-4(4))* HarperCollins Pubs. Ltd. GBR. Dist: Independent Pubs. Group.

Ginevra, Dante Luis. The Assassination of Martin Luther King, Jr: April 4 1968, 1 vol. Collins, Terry. 2014. (24-Hour History Ser.). (ENG.). 48p. (J). (gr. 3-9). pap. 8.95 *(978-1-4329-9302-3(X))*; lib. bdg. 33.99 *(978-1-4329-9296-5(1))* Capstone. (Heinemann).

Ginger Illustration. Four Square: The Personal Writing Coach, Grades 4-6. Gould, Judith S. & Burke, Mary F. 2005. 112p. (J). pap. 12.95 *(978-1-57310-447-0(7))* Teaching & Learning Co.

Ginger Illustrations Staff. Discovering Differentiation: Strategies for Success in the Language Arts Classroom. Tuszynski, Kathy & Yarber, Angela. Mitchell, Judy, ed. 2004. 80p. (J). pap. 9.95 *(978-1-57310-423-4(X))* Teaching & Learning Co.

—Storytime Discoveries: Math. Enderle, Dotti. 2004. 64p. (J). pap. 9.95 *(978-1-57310-440-1(X))* Teaching & Learning Co.

Ginsberg, Dvora. Feivel the Falafel Ball Who Wanted to Do a Mitzvah. Yerushalmi, Miriam. 2007. 28p. (J). 16.50 *(978-0-911643-37-4(0))* Aura Printing, Inc.

—Menachem Saves the Day. Yerushalmi, Miriam. 2019. (Feivel the Falafel Ball Ser.). (ENG.). 40p. (J). 20.00 *(978-0-578-45069-8(0))* Sane.

Ginsberg, Dvorah. Feivel the Falafel Ball Who Wanted to Do a Mitzvah (Hebrew) Yerushalmi, Miriam. 2018. (HEB.). 30p. (J). 20.00 *(978-0-692-15473-1(6))* Sane.

Ginsburg, David, photos by. Menorah under the Sea. Heller, Esther Susan. 2009. (Hanukkah Ser.). 32p. (J). (gr. k-2). 17.95 *(978-0-8225-7386-9(5),* Kar-Ben Publishing) Lerner Publishing Group.

Ginukov, Valentin. A Great Time: Children's Poems in Russian & English. Shurin, Masha. Morris, Brian, ed. Barton, Alica, tr. 2007. (RUS & ENG.). 32p. (J). 19.95 *(978-0-9792583-2-9(4))* White Stag Pr.

Gioffre-Suzuki, Luisa. Many Colored Coats. Lockwood, Penny. 2016. (ENG.). (J). (gr. k-2). pap. 11.99 *(978-1-940310-54-1(7))* 4RV Pub.

—Missing Pinky. Williams, Juliet. 2019. (ENG.). 34p. (J). pap. 14.99 *(978-1-0962-4627-5(9))* Independently Published.

—Willard Dragon: Camp Dragon-Fire. Cordatos, Suzanne. 2016. (Willard the Dragon Ser.: Vol. 2). (ENG.). (J). (gr. k-2). 20.99 *(978-1-940310-53-4(9))* 4RV Pub.

Gionet Landry, Noemie, et al. My Feelings, My Choices. Arrow, Emily. 2019. (My Feelings, My Choices Ser.). (ENG.). (J). (gr. -1-2). 135.96 *(978-1-68410-413-0(0),* 29713) Cantata Learning.

Giordana, D., et al. Worlds' End, BK. 8. Gaiman, Neil. Kahan, Bob, ed. rev. ed. 2006. (Sandman Ser.: Vol. 8). (ENG.). 168p. pap. 19.99 *(978-1-56389-171-7(9))* DC Comics.

Giordano. A Warm & Fuzzy Christmas. Beilenson, Evelyn. 2013. (ENG.). 80p. 5.95 *(978-1-4413-1358-4(3))* Peter Pauper Pr. Inc.

Giordano, Joseph. I Have a Secret: A First Counting Book. Memling, Carl. 2019. (Little Golden Book Ser.). 24p. (J). (-k). 4.99 *(978-1-5247-7338-0(7),* Golden Bks.) Random Hse. Children's Bks.

Giordano, Philip. Stay, Little Seed. Valentini, Cristiana. 2020. 28p. (J). (gr. -1-3). 17.95 ***(978-1-77164-646-8(2),*** Greystone Bks.) Greystone Books Ltd. CAN. Dist: Publishers Group West (PGW).

Giordano, Philip. I Ate Sunshine for Breakfast. Holland, Michael. 2020. (ENG.). 128p. (J). (gr. 2-4). 19.95 *(978-1-912497-74-4(3))* Flying Eye Bks. GBR. Dist: Penguin Random Hse. LLC.

Giovannini, Jody. Grandma Battles the Mouse. Jones, Carroll. 2007. 52p. pap. 16.95 *(978-0-9774260-1-0(7))* Omdee Omnimedia, Inc.

Giovine, Sergio. A Bundle of Trouble: A Rebecca Mystery. Reiss, Kathryn. 2011. (American Girl Mysteries Ser.). (ENG.). 192p. (YA). (gr. 4-6). pap. 21.19 *(978-1-59369-754-9(6))* American Girl Publishing, Inc.

—The Cameo Necklace: A Cecile Mystery. Coleman, Evelyn. 2012. (American Girl Mysteries Ser.). (ENG.). 192p. (J). (gr. 4-6). pap. 18.69 *(978-1-59369-900-0(X))* American Girl Publishing, Inc.

—Clue in the Castle Tower: A Samantha Mystery. Buckey, Sarah Masters. Ross, Peg, ed. 2011. (American Girl Mysteries Ser.). (ENG.). 184p. (YA). (gr. 4-6). pap. 21.19 *(978-1-59369-752-5(X))* American Girl Publishing, Inc.

Giovine, Sergio, jt. illus. see Bernstein, Galia.

Giraffe, Red & Doughty, Clare. Volcano Alert! Team Mission: A Pop-up Book. Hayler, Kate. 2006. 10p. (J). (gr. k-4). reprint ed. 19.00 *(978-1-4223-5075-1(4))* DIANE Publishing Co.

Girard, Alexander. Alexander Girard Coloring Book. 2014. (ENG.). 30p. pap. 9.95 *(978-1-934429-86-0(4))* AMMO Bks., LLC.

Girard, Félix. That's Not Hockey! Poulin, Andrée. 2018. (ENG.). 32p. (J). (gr. k-3). 17.95 *(978-1-77321-051-3(3))* Annick Pr., Ltd. CAN. Dist: Publishers Group West (PGW).

Girard, Philippe. Gustave et le Capitaine Planète. Girard, Philippe. 2004. (Mon Roman Ser.). (FRE.). 96p. (J). (gr. 2). pap. *(978-2-89021-649-5(7))* Diffusion du livre Mirabel (DLM).

—Gustave et les Sosies du Capitaine Planète. Girard, Philippe. 2004. (Mon Roman Ser.). (FRE.). 96p. (J). (gr. 2). pap. *(978-2-89021-707-2(8))* Diffusion du livre Mirabel (DLM).

Girard, Thomas. Space: Planets, Moons, Stars, & More! Rhatigan, Joe. 2016. (Step into Reading Ser.). 48p. (J). (gr. k-3). 4.99 *(978-0-553-52316-4(3),* Random Hse. Bks. for Young Readers) Random Hse. Children's Bks.

—Sybil Ludington's Revolutionary War Story. Marsico, Katie. 2018. (Narrative Nonfiction: Kids in War Ser.). (ENG.). 32p. (J). (gr. 2-4). pap. 9.99 *(978-1-5415-1194-1(8))*; lib. bdg. 27.99 *(978-1-5124-5676-9(4),* Lerner Pubns.) Lerner Publishing Group.

—Tillie Pierce's Civil War Story. Marsico, Katie. 2018. (Narrative Nonfiction: Kids in War Ser.). (ENG.). 32p. (J). (gr. 2-4). 27.99 *(978-1-5124-5677-6(2),* Lerner Pubns.) Lerner Publishing Group.

Girard, Thomas. The Nameless Treasure. Girard, Thomas. 2013. 58p. pap. *(978-0-9918736-0-9(2))* Bric-a-brac Bks.

Girard, Thomas P. Tillie Pierce's Civil War Story. Marsico, Katie. 2018. (Narrative Nonfiction: Kids in War Ser.). (ENG.). 32p. (J). (gr. 2-4). pap. 9.99 *(978-1-5415-1195-8(6))* Lerner Publishing Group.

Girasole, Alessia. Our Den. Pritchard, Gabby. 2016. (Cambridge Reading Adventures Ser.). (ENG.). 16p. pap. 7.37 *(978-1-316-50078-1(0))* Cambridge Univ. Pr.

—The Stinky Giant. Weiss, Ellen & Friedman, Mel. ed. 2012. (Step into Reading Level 3 Ser.). lib. bdg. 13.55 *(978-0-606-23858-8(1))* Turtleback.

—Under the Apple Tree. Metzger, Steve. 2009. (J). *(978-0-545-14200-7(8))* Scholastic, Inc.

—365 Classic Bedtime Bible Stories: Inspired by Jesse Lyman Hurlbut's Story of the Bible. Hurlbut, Jesse Lyman. Partner, Daniel, ed. 2017. (ENG.). 384p. (J). (gr. -1). 19.99 *(978-1-63058-380-4(4))* Barbour Publishing, Inc.

Giraud, Teresa, jt. illus. see Allen, Kd.

Girel, Stephane. A Bird in Winter: A Children's Book Inspired by Pieter Breugel. 2011. (ENG.). 32p. (J). (gr. -1-3). 14.95 *(978-3-7913-7080-4(4))* Prestel Verlag GmbH & Co KG. DEU. Dist: Penguin Random Hse. LLC.

—Where Is the Frog? A Children's Book Inspired by Claude Monet. 2013. (Children's Books Inspired by Famous Artworks Ser.). (ENG.). 32p. (J). (gr. -1-3). 14.95 *(978-3-7913-7139-9(8))* Prestel Verlag GmbH & Co KG. DEU. Dist: Penguin Random Hse. LLC.

Girgenti, Antonio. The Fox & the Castle. Volpe, Julia. 2019. (ENG.). 48p. (J). pap. ***(978-1-4600-1021-1(3),*** Epic Pr.) Essence Publishing.

Girmay, Aracelis. Changing, Changing: Story & Collages. Girmay, Aracelis. 2005. (ENG.). 48p. (J). (gr. 1-17). 19.95 *(978-0-8076-1553-9(6),* 761553) Braziller, George Inc.

Giron, Elizabeth, jt. illus. see Forcada, Adiela.

Giron, Maria. Yoga Storytime: Breathe - Stretch - Be Calm, 1 vol. Raventos, Miriam. 2018. (ENG.). 40p. (J). 16.99 *(978-1-4236-4935-9(4))* Gibbs Smith, Publisher.

Girouard, Patricia L. The Blind Man by the Road. Stockstill, Gloria McQueen. 2003. (Listen! Look! Ser.). 20p. (J). bds. 5.49 *(978-0-7586-0144-5(1))* Concordia Publishing Hse.

Girouard, Patrick. Austin & Alex Learn about Adjectives. Bailer, Darice. 2014. (Language Builders Ser.). (ENG.). 32p. (J). (gr. 2-4). pap. 11.94 *(978-1-60357-703-8(3))*; lib. bdg. 25.27 *(978-1-59953-668-2(4))* Norwood Hse. Pr.

—Basket in the River. Stockstill, Gloria McQueen. 2004. 20p. (J). bds. 5.49 *(978-0-7586-0052-3(6))* Concordia Publishing Hse.

—The Bears Upstairs: A Book of Creative Dramatics. Moncure, Jane Belk. 2013. (Magic Castle Readers Ser.). (ENG.). 32p. (J). (gr. -1-2). 14.21 *(978-1-62323-564-2(2),* 206302) Child's World, Inc., The.

—The Birthday Car. Hillert, Margaret. 2016. (BeginningtoRead Ser.). (ENG.). 32p. (J). (gr. -1-2). pap. 11.94 *(978-1-60357-936-0(2))*; (gr. k-2). 22.60 *(978-1-59953-795-5(8))* Norwood Hse. Pr.

—A Color Clown Comes to Town: A Book about Recognizing Colors. Moncure, Jane Belk. 2013. (Magic Castle Readers Ser.). (ENG.). 32p. (J). (gr. -1-2). 14.21 *(978-1-62323-565-9(0),* 206299) Child's World, Inc., The.

—Drive Along, 1 vol. Crow, Melinda Melton. 2010. (Truck Buddies Ser.). (ENG.). 32p. (J). (gr. -1-1). pap. 6.25 *(978-1-4342-2296-1(9))*; lib. bdg. 22.65 *(978-1-4342-1866-7(X))* Capstone. (Stone Arch Bks.).

—Five Little Monkeys Jumping on the Bed. Thompson, Kim Mitzo. 2010. (Padded Board Book W/CD Ser.). 8p. (J). (gr. k-2). bds. 10.99 incl. audio compact disk *(978-1-59922-581-4(6))* Twin Sisters IP, LLC.

—Getting Ready for Christmas. Browne, Yolanda. 2005. 32p. (gr. -1-3). 7.49 *(978-0-7586-0860-4(8))* Concordia Publishing Hse.

—Hop-Skip-Jump-a-Roo Zoo: A Book about Imitating. Moncure, Jane Belk. 2013. (Magic Castle Readers Ser.).

(ENG.). 32p. (J). (gr. -1-2). 14.21 (978-1-62323-566-6(9), 206300) Child's World, Inc., The.

—Little Wheels, 1 vol. Crow, Melinda Melton. 2010. (Truck Buddies Ser.). (ENG.). 32p. (J). (gr. -1-1). pap. 6.25 (978-1-4342-2297-8(7)); lib. bdg. 22.65 (978-1-4342-1865-0(1)) Capstone. (Stone Arch Bks.).

—Nanny Goat's Boat: A Book of Rhyming. Moncure, Jane Belk. 2013. (Magic Castle Readers Ser.). (ENG.). 32p. (J). (gr. -1-2). 14.21 (978-1-62323-567-3(7), 206301) Child's World, Inc., The.

—Old MacDonald Had a Farm. Thompson, Kim Mitzo. 2010. (Padded Board Book W/CD Ser.). 8p. (J). (gr. k-2). bds. 10.99 incl. audio compact disk (978-1-59922-579-1(4)) Twin Sisters IP, LLC.

—Ride & Seek, 1 vol. Crow, Melinda Melton. 2010. (Truck Buddies Ser.). (ENG.). 32p. (J). (gr. -1-1). pap. 6.25 (978-1-4342-2298-5(5), Stone Arch Bks.) Capstone.

—Sherlock Chick & Bunny Watson: The Mislaid Egg. Herz, Henry. 2019. 32p. (J). (978-1-4556-2433-1(0), Pelican Publishing) Arcadia Publishing.

—Teach Me Everyday English V1, 2 bks & 2 cd's, Vol 1. Mahoney, Judy. 2008. (ENG.). 32p. (J). (gr. -1). 19.95 (978-1-59972-108-8(2)) Teach Me Tapes, Inc.

—Teach Me Everyday French Vol 1, Vol 1. Mahoney, Judy. 2008. (FRE & ENG.). 32p. (J). (gr. -1). 19.95 (978-1-59972-101-9(5)) Teach Me Tapes, Inc.

—Teach Me Everyday German V. 1, Vol 1. Mahoney, Judy. 2008. (ENG.). 32p. (J). (gr. -1). 19.95 (978-1-59972-103-3(1), 1286054) Teach Me Tapes, Inc.

—Teach Me Everyday Italian: Celebrating the Seasons, 22 vols., Vol. 2. Mahoney, Judy. adapted ed. 2010. (ENG.). 32p. (J). 19.95 (978-1-59972-207-8(0), 1286051) Teach Me Tapes, Inc.

—Teach Me Everyday Japanese V 1, Vol 1. Mahoney, Judy. 2008. (JPN & ENG.). 32p. (J). (gr. -1). 19.95 (978-1-59972-104-0(X)) Teach Me Tapes, Inc.

—Teach Me Everyday Spanish: Celebrating the Seasons, 22 vols., Vol. 2. Mahoney, Judy. adapted ed. 2009. (SPA & ENG.). 32p. (J). (gr. -1-2). lib. bdg. 19.95 incl. audio compact disk (978-1-59972-202-3(X)) Teach Me Tapes, Inc.

—Teach Me Everyday Spanish Vol 1, Volume 1. Mahoney, Judy. 2008. (SPA & ENG.). 32p. (J). (gr. -1). 19.95 (978-1-59972-102-6(3)) Teach Me Tapes, Inc.

—The Tiger & the General. Millhouse, Jackie. 2007. (J). (978-1-932911-32-9(4)) World Tribune Pr.

—Tired Trucks, 1 vol. Crow, Melinda Melton. 2010. (Truck Buddies Ser.). (ENG.). 32p. (J). (gr. -1-1). pap. 6.25 (978-1-4342-2299-2(3)); lib. bdg. 22.65 (978-1-4342-1864-3(3)) Capstone. (Stone Arch Bks.).

—Yikes — Lice! Caffey, Donna. 2013. (AV2 Fiction Readalong Ser.: Vol. 95). (ENG.). (J). (gr. -1-3). 32.71 (978-1-62127-912-9(X), AV2 by Weigl) Weigl Pubs., Inc.

—5 Steps to Drawing Dinosaurs. Hall, Pamela. 2018. (5 Steps to Drawing Ser.). (ENG.). 32p. (J). (gr. k-3). 29.93 (978-1-5038-2477-5(2), 212237) Child's World, Inc., The.

—5 Steps to Drawing Monsters. StJohn, Amanda. 2018. (5 Steps to Drawing Ser.). (ENG.). 32p. (J). (gr. k-3). 29.93 (978-1-5038-2483-6(7), 212243) Child's World, Inc., The.

Girourard, Patrick. Nina & Nolan Build a Nonsense Poem. Bullard, Lisa. 2011. (Poetry Builders Ser.). 32p. (J). (gr. 2-4). lib. bdg. 25.27 (978-1-59953-437-4(1)) Norwood Hse. Pr.

Gisler, Carol. I Have My Baby, My Baby Has Me. Mortensen, Josh. 2018. (ENG.). 30p. (J). pap. 12.99 (978-1-7321012-0-3(5)) Magpie Children's Bks.

Gisser, George H., et al. Happy Kappy-The Flying Kangaroo(Who couldn't hop!) Bk. 1: "Without Our Tails" Gisser, George H. 2011. 30p. (J). pap. 12.99 (978-0-615-45522-8(0)) Happy Kappy Karacters.

Gitego, Peter. A City of Only Children. Warugaba, Christine. 2017. (ENG.). 26p. (J). pap. (978-99977-772-6-3(3)) FURAHA Pubs. Ltd.

—Fruit Kingdom. Warugaba, Christine. 2017. (ENG.). 24p. (J). pap. (978-99977-772-4-9(7)) FURAHA Pubs. Ltd.

—Furaha. Warugaba, Christine. 2017. (ENG.). 24p. (J). pap. 9.50 (978-1-7931-7831-2(3)) Independently Published.

—Go Away Dust! Warugaba, Christine. 2017. (ENG.). 24p. (J). pap. (978-99977-773-6-2(0)) FURAHA Pubs. Ltd.

—The Good Squirrel. Murangwa, Bonny Bruno. 2016. (ENG.). 28p. (J). pap. (978-99977-770-9-6(3)) FURAHA Pubs. Ltd.

—Gorillas in Mishanana. Warugaba, Christine. 2018. (ENG.). 28p. (J). pap. (978-99977-772-5-6(5)) FURAHA Pubs. Ltd.

—Grandpa's Hat. Warugaba, Christine. 2018. (ENG.). 26p. (J). pap. (978-99977-772-9-4(8)) FURAHA Pubs. Ltd.

—The Green Village. Warugaba, Christine. 2018. (ENG.). 26p. (J). pap. (978-99977-772-7-0(1)) FURAHA Pubs. Ltd.

—The Kind Bee. Murangwa, Bonny Bruno. 2016. (ENG.). 24p. (J). pap. (978-99977-771-1-9(5)) FURAHA Pubs. Ltd.

—The Magic Shoe & the Kind Man. Warugaba, Christine. 2017. (ENG.). 28p. (J). pap. (978-99977-772-3-2(9)) FURAHA Pubs. Ltd.

—Nyiraneza the Albino Child. Mbabazi, Mary G. 2017. (ENG.). 26p. (J). pap. (978-99977-771-4-0(X)) FURAHA Pubs. Ltd.

—Smile! Warugaba, Christine. 2017. (ENG.). 26p. (J). pap. (978-99977-772-2-5(0)) FURAHA Pubs. Ltd.

Giuliani, Mady & Cangialosi, Ciro. Crack-Up Comics Collection (Bendy) Vannotes. 2020. (ENG.). 160p. (J). (gr. 5-5). pap. 12.99 **(978-1-338-65206-2(0))** Scholastic, Inc.

Givens, R. The Eight Ball Bible: A Guide to Bar Table Play. Givens, R. 2004. 288p. (YA). per. 29.95 (978-0-9747273-7-0(7), 415-776-1596) 8-Ball Express, Inc.

Gizicki-Lipson, Coryn. An Angel in the Sky. Gizicki-Lipson, Coryn. Gizicki, Carlie. 2003. (ENG.). 32p. (J). 14.95 (978-0-9740438-0-7(X)) In the Sky Publishing.

Gladfelter, Allen. Cars: Route 66 Dash! Porter, Alan J. 2010. (Cars Ser.). (ENG.). 112p. (J). (gr. 3-6). pap. 9.99 (978-1-60886-585-7(1)) Boom! Studios.

Gladfelter, Allen & Zazo. Hotel Transylvania Graphic Novel Vol. 2: My Little Monster-Sitter. Petrucha, Stefan. 2019. (Hotel Transylvania Ser.: 2). (ENG.). 64p. (J). pap. 7.99 (978-1-62991-854-9(7), 900185409) Papercutz.

—Hotel Transylvania Graphic Novel Vol. 2: My Little Monster-Sitter. Petrucha, Stefan. 2018. (Hotel Transylvania Ser.: 2). (ENG.). 64p. (J). 12.99 (978-1-62991-855-6(5), 900185408) Papercutz.

Gladfelter, Scott, et al. Be the One! The Todd Beamer Story an Adaptation of Let's Roll! by Lisa Beamer & Todd Anderson. 2005. 52p. (J). pap. (978-1-933206-00-4(4), 5010) Bible Visuals International, Inc.

Gladnick, Anke. An Incredible Journey. Keefe, Alicia. NOAA Fisheries, West Coast Region (U.S.), ed. 2018. (ENG.). 47p. (J). (gr. 2). pap. 13.00 (978-0-16-094604-2(2), 003-017-0573-9, National Marine Fisheries Service) United States Government Printing Office.

Glanville, Caroline. African & Caribbean Celebrations, 24 vols. Johnson, Gail & Grell, Jane. Green, Toby, ed. 2008. (Crafts, Festivals & Family Activities Ser.). (ENG.). 224p. pap. (978-1-903458-00-6(5)) Hawthorn Pr. GBR. Dist: SteinerBooks, Inc.

Glanzman, Louis. The Space Pioneers: A Tom Corbett Space Cadet Adventure. Rockwell, Carey & Ley, Willy. 2011. 220p. 44.95 (978-1-258-10097-1(5)) Literary Licensing, LLC.

—Treachery in Outer Space: A Tom Corbett Space Cadet Adventure. Rockwell, Carey & Ley, Willy. 2011. 220p. 44.95 (978-1-258-09685-4(4)) Literary Licensing, LLC.

Glanzman, Louis S. The Wish-Tree. Ciardi, John. 2015. (ENG.). 96p. (J). pap. 9.99 (978-0-486-79618-5(3)) Dover Pubns., Inc.

Glanzman, Sam. The Unauthorized Tarzan. Gill, Joe & Dark Horse Comics Staff. Wright, Brendan, ed. 2013. (ENG.). 128p. 29.99 (978-1-61655-070-7(8)) Dark Horse Comics.

Glasbergen, Randy. Yes, Your Parents Are Crazy! A Teen Survival Handbook. Bradley, Michael J. 2004. (ENG.). 432p. pap. 14.95 (978-0-936197-48-7(X)) Harbor Pr., Inc.

Glaser, Byron & Higashi, Sandra. Zolocolor! Doodling Between Black & White. Glaser, Byron & Higashi, Sandra. 2011. (ENG.). 96p. (J). 7.99 (978-1-4424-2261-2(0), Little Simon) Little Simon.

—Zolocolor! Christmas Doodling. Glaser, Byron & Higashi, Sandra. 2012. (ENG.). 96p. (J). (gr. -1). pap. 7.99 (978-1-4424-4592-5(0), Little Simon) Little Simon.

—Zolocolor! Doodle Canoodle. 2013. (ENG.). 96p. (J). (gr. -1). 7.99 (978-1-4424-6848-1(3), Little Simon) Little Simon.

—Zolocolor! Toodle-Oo Doodle-oo. 2013. (ENG.). 96p. (J). (gr. -1). 7.99 (978-1-4424-6847-4(5), Little Simon) Little Simon.

Glaser, Milton. The Alphazeds. Glaser, Shirley. 2005. 32p. (J). (gr. k-4). reprint ed. 20.00 (978-0-7567-9367-8(X)) DIANE Publishing Co.

—If Apples Had Teeth. Glaser, Shirley. 2017. 40p. (J). (-3). 16.95 (978-1-59270-226-8(0)) Enchanted Lion Bks., LLC.

—The Smallest Elephant in the World. Tresselt, Alvin. 2019. 40p. (J). 16.95 (978-1-59270-261-9(9)) Enchanted Lion Bks., LLC.

Glass, Andrew. The Booford Summer. Smith, Susan Mathias. 2004. (ENG.). 144p. (J). (gr. 5-7). pap. 10.95 (978-0-618-43245-5(0), 100357) Houghton Mifflin Harcourt Publishing Co.

—Lavender. Hesse, Karen. 2010. (ENG.). 48p. (J). (gr. 2-4). pap. 9.99 (978-0-312-37609-3(X), 900048338) Square Fish.

—The Wish Giver: Three Tales of Coven Tree. Brittain, Bill. 2019. (Trophy Bk.). (ENG.). 192p. (J). (gr. 3-7). pap. 6.99 (978-0-06-440168-5(5), HarperCollins) HarperCollins Pubs. Ltd. GBR. Dist: HarperCollins Pubs.

Glass, Andrew. The Wondrous Whirligig: The Wright Brothers¿ First Flying Machine. Glass, Andrew. 2007. 30p. (J). reprint ed. 17.00 (978-1-4223-6765-0(7)) DIANE Publishing Co.

Glass, Andrew, photos by. Thank You Very Much, Captain Ericsson! Wooldridge, Connie N. & Wooldridge, Connie Nordhielm. 2004. (ENG., 32p. (J). (gr. k-3). tchr. ed. 16.95 (978-0-8234-1626-4(7)) Holiday Hse., Inc.

Glass, Eric. Willy & Friends traveling through the Seasons: The continuing story of Willy the little fire Jeep. Estes, Don. 2006. (J). (978-1-883551-75-9(7), Maple Corners Press) Attic Studio Publishing Hse.

Glass, Hilary Ann Love. A Different Kind of Safari. Hipp, Helen C. Diaco, Paula Tedford, ed. 2013. 32p. 17.95 (978-0-9890134-0-6(5)) A Different Kind of Safari LLC.

Glass House Graphics. Marvel Spider-Man: Spider-Man Steals the Show. Padgett, JoAnn. 2019. (ENG.). 14p. (J). (gr. 1-3). 10.99 (978-0-7944-4280-4(3), Studio Fun International) Printers Row Publishing Group.

Glass House Graphics, Glass House, jt. illus. see Kirschner, Rafael.

Glass House Graphics Staff. Alien Snow, 1 vol. Dahl, Michael. 2011. (Good vs Evil Ser.). (ENG.). 48p. (J). (gr. 5-9). pap. 6.29 (978-1-4342-3444-5(4), Stone Arch Bks.) Capstone.

—Survival Logbook. Cawthon, Scott. 2017. (Five Nights at Freddy's Ser.). (ENG.). 112p. (YA). (gr. 7-7). 12.99 (978-1-338-22930-1(3)) Scholastic, Inc.

Glass, Roger. The M & M's® Brand Color Pattern Book. McGrath, Barbara Barbieri. 2004. 32p. (J). 16.95 (978-1-57091-416-4(8)); pap. 6.95 (978-1-57091-417-1(6)) Charlesbridge Publishing, Inc.

—The M & M's® Brand Counting Book. McGrath, Barbara Barbieri. rev. ed. 2004. 32p. (J). 16.95 (978-1-57091-367-9(6)); pap. 6.95 (978-1-57091-368-6(4)) Charlesbridge Publishing, Inc.

—Mas Matematicas con los Chocolates de M & M's Brand. McGrath, Barbara Barbieri. Mlawer, Teresa, tr. 2004. (SPA.). 32p. (J). pap. 6.95 (978-1-57091-481-2(8), CH30498) Charlesbridge Publishing, Inc.

Glass, V. V. At the End of Your Tether. Smith, Adam. 2020. (ENG.). 144p. (YA). pap. 19.99 (978-1-62010-731-7(7), Lion Forge) Oni Pr., Inc.

Glassby, Cathie. Dads: A Field Guide. Ractliffe, Justin. 32p. (J). (gr. -1-k). 2013. 16.99 (978-1-74275-549-6(6)); 2nd ed. 2014. 9.99 (978-1-74275-551-9(8)) Random Hse. Australia AUS. Dist: Independent Pubs. Group.

Glasser, Robin Preiss. A Is for Abigail: An Almanac of Amazing American Women. Cheney, Lynne. 2003. (ENG.). 48p. (J). (gr. 1-7). 19.99 (978-0-689-85819-2(1), Simon & Schuster Bks. For Young Readers) Simon & Schuster Bks. For Young Readers.

—Alexander, Who's Not (Do You Hear Me? I Mean It!) Going to Move. Viorst, Judith. 2015. 32p. pap. 9.00 (978-1-61003-597-2(6)) Center for the Collaborative Classroom.

—Escape Goat. Patchett, Ann . 2020. (ENG.). 32p. (J). (gr. -1-3). 18.99 (978-0-06-288339-1(9), HarperCollins) HarperCollins Pubs. Ltd. GBR. Dist: HarperCollins Pubs.

—Fancy Nancy. O'Connor, Jane. 2005. (Fancy Nancy Ser.). (ENG.). 32p. (J). (gr. -1-3). 17.89 (978-0-06-054210-8(1)); 17.99 (978-0-06-054209-2(8)) HarperCollins Pubs.

—Fancy Nancy: Bonjour, Butterfly. O'Connor, Jane. 2008. (Fancy Nancy Ser.). (J). 203.88 (978-0-06-158245-5(X)) HarperCollins Pubs.

—Fancy Nancy: 5-Minute Fancy Nancy Stories. O'Connor, Jane. 2015. (Fancy Nancy Ser.). (ENG.). 192p. (J). (gr. -1-3). 12.99 (978-0-06-241216-4(7), HarperFestival) HarperCollins Pubs.

—Fancy Nancy: a Flutter of Butterflies Reusable Sticker Book. O'Connor, Jane. 2010. (Fancy Nancy Ser.). (ENG.). 12p. (J). (gr. -1-2). pap. 6.99 (978-0-06-170387-4(7), HarperFestival) HarperCollins Pubs.

—Fancy Nancy & the Boy from Paris. O'Connor, Jane. 2008. (I Can Read Level 1 Ser.). (ENG.). 32p. (J). (gr. -1-3). 16.99 (978-0-06-123610-5(1)); pap. 4.99 (978-0-06-123609-9(8)) HarperCollins Pubs.

—Fancy Nancy & the Dazzling Jewels. O'Connor, Jane. 2017. (Fancy Nancy Ser.). (ENG.). 24p. (J). (gr. -1-3). pap. 4.99 (978-0-06-237793-7(0), HarperFestival) HarperCollins Pubs.

—Fancy Nancy & the Delectable Cupcakes. O'Connor, Jane. 2010. (I Can Read Level 1 Ser.). (ENG.). 32p. (J). (gr. -1-3). 16.99 (978-0-06-188269-2(0)) HarperCollins Pubs.

—Fancy Nancy & the Delectable Cupcakes. O'Connor, Jane. 2010. (I Can Read Level 1 Ser.). (ENG.). 32p. (J). (gr. -1-3). pap. 4.99 (978-0-06-188268-5(2), HarperCollins) HarperCollins Pubs. Ltd. GBR. Dist: HarperCollins Pubs.

—Fancy Nancy & the Fabulous Fashion Boutique. O'Connor, Jane. 2010. (Fancy Nancy Ser.). (ENG.). 32p. (J). (gr. -1-3). 17.99 (978-0-06-123592-4(X)); lib. bdg. 18.89 (978-0-06-123593-1(8)) HarperCollins Pubs.

—Fancy Nancy & the Fall Foliage. O'Connor, Jane. 2014. (Fancy Nancy Ser.). (ENG.). 24p. (J). (gr. -1-3). pap. 4.99 (978-0-06-208630-3(8), HarperFestival) HarperCollins Pubs.

—Fancy Nancy & the Late, Late, LATE Night. O'Connor, Jane. 2010. (Fancy Nancy Ser.). (ENG.). 24p. (J). (gr. -1-3). pap. 3.99 (978-0-06-170377-5(X), HarperFestival) HarperCollins Pubs.

—Fancy Nancy & the Mean Girl. O'Connor, Jane. 2011. (I Can Read Level 1 Ser.). (ENG.). 32p. (J). (gr. -1-3). 16.99 (978-0-06-200178-8(7)); pap. 4.99 (978-0-06-200177-1(9)) HarperCollins Pubs.

—Fancy Nancy & the Mermaid Ballet. O'Connor, Jane. 2012. (Fancy Nancy Ser.). (ENG.). 32p. (J). (gr. -1-2). 17.99 (978-0-06-170381-2(8)) HarperCollins Pubs.

—Fancy Nancy & the Missing Easter Bunny. O'Connor, Jane. 2017. (Fancy Nancy Ser.). (ENG.). 24p. (J). (gr. -1-3). pap. 4.99 (978-0-06-237792-0(2), HarperFestival) HarperCollins Pubs.

—Fancy Nancy & the Posh Puppy. O'Connor, Jane. (Fancy Nancy Ser.). (ENG.). 32p. (J). (gr. -1-2). 2012. 9.99 (978-0-06-221052-4(1)); 2007. 17.99 (978-0-06-054213-9(6)); 2007. lib. bdg. 18.89 (978-0-06-054215-3(2)) HarperCollins Pubs.

—Fancy Nancy & the Quest for the Unicorn: Includes over 30 Stickers! O'Connor, Jane. 2018. (Fancy Nancy Ser.). (ENG.). 24p. (J). (gr. -1-3). pap. 4.99 (978-0-06-237794-4(9), HarperFestival) HarperCollins Pubs.

Glasser, Robin Preiss, et al. Fancy Nancy & the Sensational Babysitter. O'Connor, Jane. 2010. (Fancy Nancy Ser.). (ENG.). 24p. (J). (gr. -1-3). pap. 3.99 (978-0-06-170378-2(8), HarperFestival) HarperCollins Pubs.

Glasser, Robin Preiss. Fancy Nancy & the Too-Loose Tooth. O'Connor, Jane. 2012. (I Can Read Level 1 Ser.). (ENG.). 32p. (J). (gr. -1-3). 16.99 (978-0-06-208301-2(5)) HarperCollins Pubs.

—Fancy Nancy & the Too-Loose Tooth. O'Connor, Jane. 2012. (I Can Read Level 1 Ser.). (ENG.). 32p. (J). (gr. -1-3). pap. 4.99 (978-0-06-208302-9(3), HarperCollins) HarperCollins Pubs. Ltd. GBR. Dist: HarperCollins Pubs.

—Fancy Nancy & the Wedding of the Century. O'Connor, Jane. 2014. (Fancy Nancy Ser.). (ENG.). 32p. (J). (gr. -1-3). 17.99 (978-0-06-208319-7(8)); lib. bdg. 18.89 (978-0-06-208320-3(1)) HarperCollins Pubs.

—Fancy Nancy: Apples Galore! O'Connor, Jane. 2013. (I Can Read Level 1 Ser.). (ENG.). 32p. (J). (gr. -1-3). 16.99 (978-0-06-208311-1(2)); pap. 4.99 (978-0-06-208310-4(4)) HarperCollins Pubs.

—Fancy Nancy: Aspiring Artist. O'Connor, Jane. 2011. (Fancy Nancy Ser.). (ENG.). 32p. (J). (gr. -1-2). 12.99 (978-0-06-191526-0(2)) HarperCollins Pubs.

—Fancy Nancy at the Museum. O'Connor, Jane & Harper Collins / LeapFrog. 2008. (Fancy Nancy Ser.). (J). 13.99 (978-1-59319-940-1(6)) LeapFrog Enterprises, Inc.

—Fancy Nancy at the Museum. O'Connor, Jane. 2008. (I Can Read Level 1 Ser.). (ENG.). 32p. (J). (gr. -1-3). 16.99 (978-0-06-123608-2(X)); pap. 4.99 (978-0-06-123607-5(1)) HarperCollins Pubs.

—Fancy Nancy: Best Reading Buddies. O'Connor, Jane. 2016. (I Can Read Level 1 Ser.). (ENG.). 32p. (J). (gr. -1-3). pap. 4.99 (978-0-06-237783-8(3), HarperCollins) HarperCollins Pubs. Ltd. GBR. Dist: HarperCollins Pubs.

—Fancy Nancy Big Book. O'Connor, Jane. 2009. (Fancy Nancy Ser.). (ENG.). 32p. (J). (gr. -1-3). 24.99 (978-0-06-171944-8(7), HarperFestival) HarperCollins Pubs.

—Fancy Nancy: Bonjour, Butterfly. O'Connor, Jane. (Fancy Nancy Ser.). (ENG.). 32p. (J). (gr. -1-2). 2012. 9.99 (978-0-06-221053-1(X)); 2008. 17.99 (978-0-06-123588-7(1)) HarperCollins Pubs.

—Fancy Nancy: Bubbles, Bubbles, & More Bubbles! O'Connor, Jane. 2018. (I Can Read Level 1 Ser.). (ENG.). 32p. (J). (gr. -1-3). pap. 4.99 (978-0-06-237789-0(2)) HarperCollins Pubs.

—Fancy Nancy: Budding Ballerina. O'Connor, Jane. 2013. (Fancy Nancy Ser.). (ENG.). 24p. (J). (gr. -1-3). pap. 3.99 (978-0-06-208628-0(6), HarperFestival) HarperCollins Pubs.

—Fancy Nancy: Candy Bonanza. O'Connor, Jane. 2015. (Fancy Nancy Ser.). (ENG.). 24p. (J). (gr. -1-3). pap. 4.99 (978-0-06-226958-4(5), HarperFestival) HarperCollins Pubs.

—Fancy Nancy Collector's Quintet. O'Connor, Jane. 2009. (I Can Read Level 1 Ser.). (ENG.). (J). (gr. k-3). pap. 16.99 (978-0-06-171905-9(6)) HarperCollins Pubs.

Glasser, Robin Preiss, et al. Fancy Nancy: Every Day Is Earth Day. O'Connor, Jane. 2010. (I Can Read Level 1 Ser.). (ENG.). 32p. (J). (gr. -1-3). 16.99 (978-0-06-187327-0(6)); pap. 4.99 (978-0-06-187326-3(8)) HarperCollins Pubs.

Glasser, Robin Preiss. Fancy Nancy: Explorer Extraordinaire! O'Connor, Jane. 2009. (Fancy Nancy Ser.). (ENG.). 32p. (J). (gr. -1-2). 12.99 (978-0-06-168486-9(4)) HarperCollins Pubs.

—Fancy Nancy: Express Yourself! A Doodle & Draw Book. O'Connor, Jane. 2011. (Fancy Nancy Ser.). (ENG.). 64p. (J). (gr. -1-3). pap. 6.99 (978-0-06-188281-4(X), HarperFestival) HarperCollins Pubs.

—Fancy Nancy: Fanciest Doll in the Universe. O'Connor, Jane. 2013. (Fancy Nancy Ser.). (ENG.). 32p. (J). (gr. -1-3). 17.99 (978-0-06-170384-3(2)); lib. bdg. 18.89 (978-0-06-170385-0(0)) HarperCollins Pubs.

—Fancy Nancy: Fancy Day in Room 1-A. O'Connor, Jane. 2012. (I Can Read Level 1 Ser.). (ENG.). 32p. (J). (gr. -1-3). 16.99 (978-0-06-208305-0(8)); pap. 4.99 (978-0-06-208304-3(X)) HarperCollins Pubs.

—Fancy Nancy: Fashionista: a Coloring & Activity Book. O'Connor, Jane. 2011. (Fancy Nancy Ser.). (ENG.). 32p. (J). (gr. -1-3). pap., act. bk. ed. 4.99 (978-0-06-188266-1(6), HarperFestival) HarperCollins Pubs.

—Fancy Nancy: Hair Dos & Hair Don'ts. O'Connor, Jane. 2011. (I Can Read Level 1 Ser.). (ENG.). 32p. (J). (gr. -1-3). 16.99 (978-0-06-200180-1(9)); pap. 4.99 (978-0-06-200179-5(5)) HarperCollins Pubs.

—Fancy Nancy: Halloween... or Bust! O'Connor, Jane. 2009. (Fancy Nancy Ser.). (ENG.). 24p. (J). (gr. -1-3). pap. 4.99 (978-0-06-123595-5(4), HarperFestival) HarperCollins Pubs.

—Fancy Nancy: Heart to Heart: With Fancy Stickers! O'Connor, Jane. 2009. (Fancy Nancy Ser.). (ENG.). 24p. (J). (gr. -1-3). pap. 4.99 (978-0-06-123596-2(2), HarperFestival) HarperCollins Pubs.

—Fancy Nancy: It's Backward Day! O'Connor, Jane. 2016. (I Can Read Level 1 Ser.). (ENG.). 32p. (J). (gr. -1-3). pap. 4.99 (978-0-06-226981-2(X), HarperCollins) HarperCollins Pubs. Ltd. GBR. Dist: HarperCollins Pubs.

—Fancy Nancy: Jojo & Daddy Bake a Cake. O'Connor, Jane. 2017. (My First I Can Read Ser.). (ENG.). 32p. (J). (gr. -1-3). 16.99 (978-0-06-237802-6(3)); pap. 4.99 (978-0-06-237801-9(5)) HarperCollins Pubs.

—Fancy Nancy: Jojo & the Big Mess. O'Connor, Jane. 2017. (My First I Can Read Ser.). (ENG.). 32p. (J). (gr. -1-3). pap. 4.99 (978-0-06-237798-2(1)) HarperCollins Pubs.

—Fancy Nancy: Jojo & the Magic Trick. O'Connor, Jane. 2017. (My First I Can Read Ser.). (ENG.). 32p. (J). (gr. -1-3). pap. 4.99 (978-0-06-237795-1(7)) HarperCollins Pubs.

—Fancy Nancy: Jojo & the Twins. O'Connor, Jane. 2018. (My First I Can Read Ser.). (ENG.). 32p. (J). (gr. -1-3). 16.99 (978-0-06-237805-7(8)); pap. 4.99 (978-0-06-237804-0(X)) HarperCollins Pubs.

—Fancy Nancy: Just My Luck! O'Connor, Jane. 2013. (I Can Read Level 1 Ser.). (ENG.). 32p. (J). (gr. -1-3). 16.99 (978-0-06-208314-2(7)); pap. 4.99 (978-0-06-208313-5(9)) HarperCollins Pubs.

—Fancy Nancy Loves! Loves!! Loves!!! Reusable Sticker Book. O'Connor, Jane. 2007. (Fancy Nancy Ser.). (ENG.). 12p. (J). (gr. -1-2). pap. 6.99 (978-0-06-123599-3(7), HarperFestival) HarperCollins Pubs.

—Fancy Nancy: My Family History. O'Connor, Jane. 2010. (I Can Read Level 1 Ser.). (ENG.). 32p. (J). (gr. -1-3). 16.99 (978-0-06-188270-8(4)); pap. 4.99 (978-0-06-188271-5(2)) HarperCollins Pubs.

—Fancy Nancy: Nancy Clancy Bind-Up: Books 1 And 2: Super Sleuth & Secret Admirer. O'Connor, Jane. 2015. (Nancy Clancy Ser.). (ENG.). 256p. (J). (gr. 1-5). 12.99 (978-0-06-240364-3(8)) HarperCollins Pubs.

—Fancy Nancy: Nancy Clancy Bind-Up: Books 3 And 4: Sees the Future & Secret of the Silver Key. O'Connor, Jane. 2015. (Nancy Clancy Ser.). (ENG.). 256p. (J). (gr. 1-5). 12.99 (978-0-06-240365-0(6)) HarperCollins Pubs.

—Fancy Nancy: Nancy Clancy, Late-Breaking News! O'Connor, Jane. (Nancy Clancy Ser.: 8). (ENG.). 144p. (J). (gr. 1-5). 2018. pap. 5.99 (978-0-06-226972-0(0)); 2017. 9.99 (978-0-06-226973-7(9)) HarperCollins Pubs.

—Fancy Nancy: Nancy Clancy: My Secret Diary. O'Connor, Jane. 2015. (Nancy Clancy Ser.). (ENG.). 144p. (J). (gr. 1-5). pap. 11.99 (978-0-06-234983-5(X)) HarperCollins Pubs.

—Fancy Nancy: Nancy Clancy, Secret Admirer. O'Connor, Jane. 2013. (Nancy Clancy Ser.: 2). (ENG.). (J). (gr. 1-5). 144p. pap. 5.99 (978-0-06-208420-0(8)); 128p. 9.99 (978-0-06-208295-4(7)) HarperCollins Pubs.

—Fancy Nancy: Nancy Clancy, Secret of the Silver Key. O'Connor, Jane. (Nancy Clancy Ser.: 4). (ENG.). (J). (gr. 1-5). 2015. 144p. pap. 5.99 (978-0-06-208422-4(4)); 2014. 128p. 9.99 (978-0-06-208299-2(X)) HarperCollins Pubs.

—Fancy Nancy: Nancy Clancy Sees the Future. O'Connor, Jane. (Nancy Clancy Ser.: 3). (ENG.). (J). (gr. 1-5). 2014. 144p. pap. 5.99 (978-0-06-208421-7(6)); 2013. 128p. 9.99 (978-0-06-208297-8(3)) HarperCollins Pubs.

—Fancy Nancy: Nancy Clancy, Soccer Mania. O'Connor, Jane. (Nancy Clancy Ser.: 6). (ENG.). (J). (gr. 1-5). 2016. 144p. pap. 4.99 *(978-0-06-226966-9(6))*; 2015. 128p. 9.99 *(978-0-06-226967-6(4))* HarperCollins Pubs.

—Fancy Nancy: Nancy Clancy, Star of Stage & Screen. O'Connor, Jane. (Nancy Clancy Ser.: 5). (ENG.). (J). (gr. 1-5). 2016. 144p. pap. 4.99 *(978-0-06-226963-8(1))*; 2015. 128p. 9.99 *(978-0-06-226964-5(X))* HarperCollins Pubs.

—Fancy Nancy: Nancy Clancy, Super Sleuth. O'Connor, Jane. (Nancy Clancy Ser.: 1). (ENG.). (J). (gr. 1-5). 2013. 144p. pap. 5.99 *(978-0-06-208419-4(4))*; 2012. 128p. 9.99 *(978-0-06-208293-0(0))* HarperCollins Pubs.

—Fancy Nancy: Nancy Clancy's Astounding Chapter Book Quartet: Books 5-8. O'Connor, Jane. 2019. (Nancy Clancy Ser.). (ENG.). 592p. (J). (gr. 1-5). pap. 20.96 *(978-0-06-297959-9(0))* HarperCollins Pubs.

—Fancy Nancy: Nancy Clancy's Tres Charming Chapter Book Box Set: Books 1-3, 3 vols., Set. O'Connor, Jane. 2013. (Nancy Clancy Ser.). (ENG.). 384p. (J). (gr. 1-5). 24.99 *(978-0-06-227793-0(6))* HarperCollins Pubs.

—Fancy Nancy: Nancy Clancy's Ultimate Chapter Book Quartet: Books 1 Through 4. O'Connor, Jane. 2015. (Nancy Clancy Ser.). (ENG.). 576p. (J). (gr. 1-5). pap. 23.96 *(978-0-06-242273-6(1))* HarperCollins Pubs.

—Fancy Nancy: Oodles of Kittens. O'Connor, Jane. 2018. (Fancy Nancy Ser.). (ENG.). 32p. (J). (gr. -1-3). 17.99 *(978-0-06-226987-4(9))* HarperCollins Pubs.

—Fancy Nancy: Ooh la la! It's Beauty Day. O'Connor, Jane. 2010. (Fancy Nancy Ser.). (ENG.). 40p. (J). (gr. -1-2). 12.99 *(978-0-06-191525-3(4))* HarperCollins Pubs.

—Fancy Nancy: Our Thanksgiving Banquet. O'Connor, Jane. 2011. (Fancy Nancy Ser.). (ENG.). 24p. (J). (gr. -1-3). pap. 4.99 *(978-0-06-123598-6(9)*, HarperFestival) HarperCollins Pubs.

Glasser, Robin Preiss, et al. Fancy Nancy: Pajama Day. O'Connor, Jane. 2009. (I Can Read Level 1 Ser.). (ENG.). 32p. (J). (gr. -1-3). 16.99 *(978-0-06-170371-3(0))* HarperCollins Pubs.

—Fancy Nancy: Pajama Day. O'Connor, Jane. 2009. (I Can Read Level 1 Ser.). (ENG.). 32p. (J). (gr. -1-3). pap. 4.99 *(978-0-06-170370-6(2)*, HarperCollins) HarperCollins Pubs. Ltd. GBR. Dist: HarperCollins Pubs.

Glasser, Robin Preiss. Fancy Nancy: Peanut Butter & Jellyfish. O'Connor, Jane. 2015. (I Can Read Level 1 Ser.). (ENG.). 32p. (J). (gr. -1-3). 16.99 *(978-0-06-226976-8(3))*; pap. 4.99 *(978-0-06-226975-1(5))* HarperCollins Pubs.

—Fancy Nancy Petite Library: 4 Mini Books. O'Connor, Jane. 2010. (Fancy Nancy Ser.). (ENG.). 32p. (J). (gr. k-3). 14.99 *(978-0-06-191527-7(0)*, HarperFestival) HarperCollins Pubs.

—Fancy Nancy: Poet Extraordinaire! O'Connor, Jane. 2010. (Fancy Nancy Ser.). (ENG.). 32p. (J). (gr. -1-2). 12.99 *(978-0-06-189643-9(8))* HarperCollins Pubs.

—Fancy Nancy: Poison Ivy Expert. O'Connor, Jane. 2008. (I Can Read Level 1 Ser.). (ENG.). 32p. (J). (gr. -1-3). 16.99 *(978-0-06-123614-3(4))*; pap. 4.99 *(978-0-06-123613-6(6))* HarperCollins Pubs.

—Fancy Nancy: Puppy Party. O'Connor, Jane. 2013. (Fancy Nancy Ser.). (ENG.). 24p. (J). (gr. -1-3). pap. 3.99 *(978-0-06-208627-3(8)*, HarperFestival) HarperCollins Pubs.

—Fancy Nancy: Puzzle-Palooza. O'Connor, Jane. 2011. (Fancy Nancy Ser.). (ENG.). 32p. (J). (gr. -1-3). pap. 4.99 *(978-0-06-188267-8(4)*, HarperFestival) HarperCollins Pubs.

—Fancy Nancy: Sand Castles & Sand Palaces. O'Connor, Jane. 2014. (Fancy Nancy Ser.). (ENG.). 24p. (J). (gr. -1-3). pap. 4.99 *(978-0-06-226954-6(2)*, HarperFestival) HarperCollins Pubs.

—Fancy Nancy: Saturday Night Sleepover. O'Connor, Jane. 2016. (Fancy Nancy Ser.). (ENG.). 32p. (J). (gr. -1-3). 17.99 *(978-0-06-226985-0(2))* HarperCollins Pubs.

—Fancy Nancy Sees Stars. O'Connor, Jane. (I Can Read Level 1 Ser.). (ENG.). (J). (gr. -1-3). 2017. 40p. 9.99 *(978-0-06-257275-2(X))*; 2008. 32p. 16.99 *(978-0-06-123612-9(8))*; 2008. 32p. pap. 4.99 *(978-0-06-123611-2(X))* HarperCollins Pubs.

—Fancy Nancy: Spectacular Spectacles. O'Connor, Jane. 2010. (I Can Read Level 1 Ser.). (ENG.). 32p. (J). (gr. -1-3). 16.99 *(978-0-06-188263-0(1))*; pap. 4.99 *(978-0-06-188264-7(X))* HarperCollins Pubs.

—Fancy Nancy: Splendid Speller. O'Connor, Jane. 2011. (I Can Read Level 1 Ser.). (ENG.). 32p. (J). (gr. -1-3). 16.99 *(978-0-06-200176-4(0))*; pap. 4.99 *(978-0-06-200175-7(2))* HarperCollins Pubs.

—Fancy Nancy: Splendiferous Christmas. O'Connor, Jane. (Fancy Nancy Ser.). (ENG.). 32p. (J). (gr. -1-3). 2018. 9.99 *(978-0-06-284726-3(0))*; 2009. lib. bdg. 18.89 *(978-0-06-123591-7(1))* HarperCollins Pubs.

—Fancy Nancy: Splendiferous Christmas. O'Connor, Jane. 2011. (Fancy Nancy Ser.). (ENG.). 32p. (J). (gr. -1-2). 17.99 *(978-0-06-123590-0(3)*, HarperCollins) HarperCollins Pubs. Ltd. GBR. Dist: HarperCollins Pubs.

—Fancy Nancy: Spring Fashion Fling. O'Connor, Jane. 2015. (Fancy Nancy Ser.). (ENG.). 24p. (J). (gr. -1-3). pap. 4.99 *(978-0-06-226956-0(9)*, HarperFestival) HarperCollins Pubs.

—Fancy Nancy: Stellar Stargazer! O'Connor, Jane. 2011. (Fancy Nancy Ser.). (ENG.). 32p. (J). (gr. -1-2). 12.99 *(978-0-06-191523-9(8))* HarperCollins Pubs.

—Fancy Nancy Storybook Favorites. O'Connor, Jane. 2020. (Fancy Nancy Ser.). (ENG.). 192p. (J). (gr. -1-3). 13.99 *(978-0-06-291548-1(7)*, HarperCollins) HarperCollins Pubs. Ltd. GBR. Dist: HarperCollins Pubs.

—Fancy Nancy Storybook Treasury. O'Connor, Jane. 2013. (Fancy Nancy Ser.). (ENG.). 192p. (J). (gr. -1-3). 11.99 *(978-0-06-211978-0(8)*, HarperFestival) HarperCollins Pubs.

—Fancy Nancy: Super Secret Surprise Party. O'Connor, Jane. 2015. (I Can Read Level 1 Ser.). (ENG.). 32p. (J). (gr. -1-3). 16.99 *(978-0-06-226979-9(8))*; pap. 4.99 *(978-0-06-226978-2(X))* HarperCollins Pubs.

—Fancy Nancy: Tea for Two. O'Connor, Jane. 2012. (Fancy Nancy Ser.). (ENG.). 24p. (J). (gr. -1-3). pap. 3.99 *(978-0-06-123597-9(0)*, HarperFestival) HarperCollins Pubs.

—Fancy Nancy: Tea Parties. O'Connor, Jane. 2009. (Fancy Nancy Ser.). (ENG.). 40p. (J). (gr. -1-2). 12.99 *(978-0-06-180174-7(7)*, HarperCollins) HarperCollins Pubs. Ltd. GBR. Dist: HarperCollins Pubs.

—Fancy Nancy: the 100th Day of School. O'Connor, Jane. 2009. (I Can Read Level 1 Ser.). (ENG.). 32p. (J). (gr. -1-3). 16.99 *(978-0-06-170375-1(3))*; pap. 4.99 *(978-0-06-170374-4(5))* HarperCollins Pubs.

—Fancy Nancy: the Dazzling Book Report. O'Connor, Jane. 2009. (I Can Read Level 1 Ser.). (ENG.). 32p. (J). (gr. -1-3). 16.99 *(978-0-06-170369-0(9))*; pap. 4.99 *(978-0-06-170368-3(0))* HarperCollins Pubs.

—Fancy Nancy: the Show Must Go On. O'Connor, Jane. 2009. (I Can Read Level 1 Ser.). (ENG.). 32p. (J). (gr. -1-3). 16.99 *(978-0-06-170373-7(7))*; pap. 4.99 *(978-0-06-170372-0(9))* HarperCollins Pubs.

—Fancy Nancy: the Worst Secret Keeper Ever. O'Connor, Jane. 2016. (Fancy Nancy Ser.). (ENG.). 24p. (J). (gr. -1-3). pap. 4.99 *(978-0-06-226960-7(7)*, HarperFestival) HarperCollins Pubs.

—Fancy Nancy: There's No Day Like a Snow Day. O'Connor, Jane. 2012. (Fancy Nancy Ser.). (ENG.). 24p. (J). (gr. -1-3). pap. 4.99 *(978-0-06-208629-7(4)*, HarperFestival) HarperCollins Pubs.

—Fancy Nancy: Time for Puppy School. O'Connor, Jane. 2017. (I Can Read Level 1 Ser.). (ENG.). 32p. (J). (gr. -1-3). pap. 4.99 *(978-0-06-237786-9(8))* HarperCollins Pubs.

—Fancy Nancy: Too Many Tutus. O'Connor, Jane. 2012. (I Can Read Level 1 Ser.). (ENG.). 32p. (J). (gr. -1-3). 16.99 *(978-0-06-208308-1(2))*; pap. 4.99 *(978-0-06-208307-4(4))* HarperCollins Pubs.

—Fancy Nancy's 12-Book Fantastic Phonics Fun! Includes 12 Mini-Books Featuring Short & Long Vowel Sounds, 12 vols. O'Connor, Jane. 2013. (My First I Can Read Ser.). (ENG.). 120p. (J). (gr. -1-3). pap. 14.99 *(978-0-06-208633-4(2)*, HarperCollins) HarperCollins Pubs. Ltd. GBR. Dist: HarperCollins Pubs.

—Fancy Nancy's Absolutely Stupendous Sticker Book. O'Connor, Jane. 2009. (Fancy Nancy Ser.). (ENG.). 100p. (J). (gr. -1-2). pap. 12.99 *(978-0-06-172563-0(3)*, HarperFestival) HarperCollins Pubs.

—Fancy Nancy's Elegant Easter. O'Connor, Jane. 2009. (Fancy Nancy Ser.). (ENG.). 16p. (J). (gr. -1-3). pap. 6.99 *(978-0-06-170379-9(6)*, HarperFestival) HarperCollins Pubs.

—Fancy Nancy's Fabulous Fall Storybook Collection. O'Connor, Jane. 2014. (Fancy Nancy Ser.). (ENG.). 192p. (J). (gr. -1-3). 11.99 *(978-0-06-228884-4(9))* HarperCollins Pubs.

—Fancy Nancy's Fabulously Fancy Treasury. O'Connor, Jane. 2012. (Fancy Nancy Ser.). (ENG.). 25p. (J). (gr. -1-3). 15.99 *(978-0-06-218804-5(6)*, HarperFestival) HarperCollins Pubs.

—Fancy Nancy's Fashion Parade! Reusable Sticker Book. O'Connor, Jane. 2008. (Fancy Nancy Ser.). (ENG.). 12p. (J). (gr. -1-2). pap. 6.99 *(978-0-06-123601-3(2)*, HarperFestival) HarperCollins Pubs.

—Fancy Nancy's Favorite Fancy Words: From Accessories to Zany. O'Connor, Jane. 2008. (Fancy Nancy Ser.). (ENG.). 32p. (J). (gr. -1-2). 12.99 *(978-0-06-154923-6(1))* HarperCollins Pubs.

—Fancy Nancy's Gloriously Gigantic Sticker-Tivity Book. O'Connor, Jane. 2010. (Fancy Nancy Ser.). (ENG.). 100p. (J). (gr. -1-2). pap. 12.99 *(978-0-06-197931-6(7)*, HarperFestival) HarperCollins Pubs.

—Fancy Nancy's Haunted Mansion: a Reusable Sticker Book for Halloween. O'Connor, Jane. 2011. (Fancy Nancy Ser.). (ENG.). 12p. (J). (gr. -1-2). pap. 6.99 *(978-0-06-170388-1(5)*, HarperFestival) HarperCollins Pubs.

—Fancy Nancy's Marvelous Mother's Day Brunch. O'Connor, Jane. 2011. (Fancy Nancy Ser.). (ENG.). 16p. (J). (gr. -1-3). pap. 6.99 *(978-0-06-170380-5(X)*, HarperFestival) HarperCollins Pubs.

—Fancy Nancy's Perfectly Pink Playtime Purse. O'Connor, Jane. 2015. (Fancy Nancy Ser.). (ENG.). 80p. (J). (gr. -1-3). 9.99 *(978-0-06-226962-1(3)*, HarperFestival) HarperCollins Pubs.

—Fancy Nancy's Perfectly Posh Paper Doll Book. O'Connor, Jane. 2009. (Fancy Nancy Ser.). (ENG.). 16p. (J). (gr. -1-3). pap. 6.99 *(978-0-06-187328-7(4)*, HarperFestival) HarperCollins Pubs.

—Lambslide. Patchett, Ann. 2019. (ENG.). 32p. (J). (gr. -1-3). 18.99 *(978-0-06-288338-4(0))* HarperCollins Pubs.

—LeapReader Book, Fancy Nancy Explorer Extraordinaire! O'Connon, Jane & Harper Collins/Leap Frog. 2017. (J). (gr. -1-7). pap. 13.99 *(978-1-60685-272-9(8))* LeapFrog Enterprises, Inc.

—Nancy Clancy, Soccer Mania. O'Connor, Jane. ed. 2016. (Nancy Clancy Ser.: 6). (ENG.). 144p. (J). (gr. 1-5). 14.75 *(978-0-606-39270-9(X))* Turtleback.

—Nancy la Elegante: Fancy Nancy (Spanish Edition), 1 vol. O'Connor, Jane. 2008. (Fancy Nancy Ser.). (SPA.). 32p. (J). (gr. -1-3). 17.99 *(978-0-06-143528-7(7)*, HarperCollins Español) HarperCollins Christian Publishing.

—Nancy la Elegante y la Perrita Popoff: Fancy Nancy & the Posh Puppy (Spanish Edition), 1 vol. O'Connor, Jane. 2011. (Fancy Nancy Ser.). (SPA.). 32p. (J). (gr. -1-3). 16.99 *(978-0-06-179961-7(0)*, HarperCollins Español) HarperCollins Christian Publishing.

—Our 50 States: A Family Adventure Across America. Cheney, Lynne. 2006. (ENG.). 74p. (J). (gr. 2-5). 19.99 *(978-0-689-86717-0(4)*, Simon & Schuster/Paula Wiseman Bks.) Simon & Schuster/Paula Wiseman Bks.

—A Sock Is a Pocket for Your Toes: A Pocket Book. Scanlon, Elizabeth Garton. 2004. (ENG.). 32p. (J). (gr. -1-2). 16.99 *(978-0-06-029526-4(0))* HarperCollins Pubs.

—Super-Completely & Totally the Messiest. Viorst, Judith. 2004. (ENG.). 32p. (J). (gr. -1-2). 7.99 *(978-0-689-86617-3(8)*, Atheneum Bks. for Young Readers) Simon & Schuster Children's Publishing.

—Super-Completely & Totally the Messiest! Viorst, Judith. 2006. (ENG.). 32p. (J). (gr. -1-2). 16.99 *(978-1-4169-4200-9(9)*, Atheneum Bks. for Young Readers) Simon & Schuster Children's Publishing.

—Tea for Ruby. Ferguson, Sarah. 2008. (ENG.). 40p. (J). (gr. -1-3). 18.99 *(978-1-4169-5419-4(8)*, Simon & Schuster/Paula Wiseman Bks.) Simon & Schuster/Paula Wiseman Bks.

—Tea for Ruby. Ferguson, Sarah. 2012. (ENG.). 40p. (J). (gr. -1-3). pap. 8.99 *(978-1-4169-5420-0(1)*, Simon & Schuster/Paula Wiseman Bks.) Simon & Schuster/Paula Wiseman Bks.

—Tea for Two. O'Connor, Jane. ed. 2012. (Fancy Nancy Picture Bks.). (J). lib. bdg. 13.55 *(978-0-606-23577-8(9))* Turtleback.

—You Made Me a Mother. Sala, Laurenne. 2016. (ENG.). 32p. (J). (gr. -1-3). 15.99 *(978-0-06-235886-8(3))* HarperCollins Pubs.

Glasser, Robin Preiss & Bracken, Carolyn. Fancy Nancy: Nancy Clancy Seeks a Fortune. O'Connor, Jane. 2016. (Nancy Clancy Ser.: 7). (ENG.). 144p. (J). (gr. 1-5). 9.99 *(978-0-06-226969-0(0))* HarperCollins Pubs.

Glasser, Robin Preiss & Enik, Ted. Fancy Nancy: The Dazzling Book Report. O'Connor, Jane. 2009. (Fancy Nancy Ser.). 32p. lib. bdg. 14.00 *(978-1-60686-531-6(5))* Perfection Learning Corp.

—Poison Ivy Expert. O'Connor, Jane. ed. 2008. (Fancy Nancy - I Can Read! Ser.). 32p. (J). lib. bdg. 13.55 *(978-1-4364-5050-8(0))* Turtleback.

—Time for Puppy School. O'Connor, Jane. 2017. 32p. (J). *(978-1-5182-3869-7(6))* Harper & Row Ltd.

Glasser, Robin Preiss & Ivanov, Olga. Fancy Nancy: Girl on the Go: A Doodle & Draw Book. O'Connor, Jane. 2012. (Fancy Nancy Ser.). (ENG.). 64p. (J). (gr. -1-3). pap. 6.99 *(978-0-06-188282-1(8)*, HarperFestival) HarperCollins Pubs.

Glastetter, KC & Hollman, Jeremie, photos by. Yellowstone Natl Park Abc Adv. 2010. 64p. (J). pap. 12.00 *(978-0-87842-572-3(1))* Mountain Pr. Publishing Co., Inc.

Glazier, Garth, jt. illus. see Zapater Oliva, Carlos.

Gleason, Patrick & Bazaldua, Oscar. Amazing Spider-Man: 2099 (Vol. 7) 2020. 136p. (J). (gr. 4-17). pap. 17.99 ***(978-1-302-92022-7(7))*** Marvel Worldwide, Inc.

Gledhill, Carly. The Bedtime Book. Marendaz, S. 2020. (ENG.). 32p. (J). (gr. -1-2). 17.99 *(978-1-68010-186-7(2))* Tiger Tales.

—Jack & the Beanstalk. 2020. (Penguin Bedtime Classics Ser.). 18p. (J). (— 1). bds. 7.99 *(978-0-593-11543-5(0)*, Viking Books for Young Readers) Penguin Young Readers Group.

—The Nutcracker. Hoffmann, E. T. A. 2019. (Penguin Bedtime Classics Ser.). (ENG.). 18p. (J). (— 1). bds. 7.99 *(978-0-593-11324-0(1)*, Viking Books for Young Readers) Penguin Young Readers Group.

—The Three Little Pigs. 2020. (Penguin Bedtime Classics Ser.). 18p. (J). (— 1). bds. 7.99 *(978-0-593-11545-9(7)*, Viking Books for Young Readers) Penguin Young Readers Group.

—Time for Bed, Little Puppy. 2018. (ENG.). 12p. (J). (gr. -1 — 1). 12.99 *(978-1-68412-190-8(6)*, Silver Dolphin Bks.) Printers Row Publishing Group.

—The Wizard of Oz. Baum, L. Frank. 2020. (Penguin Bedtime Classics Ser.). (ENG.). 18p. (J). (— 1). bds. 7.99 *(978-0-593-11475-9(2)*, Viking Books for Young Readers) Penguin Young Readers Group.

Gledhill, Carly & Ross, Tony. Alice's Adventures in Wonderland. Carroll, Lewis. 2019. (Penguin Bedtime Classics Ser.). (ENG.). 18p. (J). (— 1). bds. 7.99 *(978-0-593-11325-7(X)*, Viking Books for Young Readers) Penguin Young Readers Group.

Gledhill, Sarah. The Alligator Wrestler: A Girls Can Do Anything Book. Petro, Carmen. 2019. (ENG.). 38p. (J). (gr. 2-6). pap. 12.99 ***(978-1-64633-087-4(0))*** Primedia eLaunch LLC.

Gledhill, Sarah. Buttons. Pickrell, Karen & Ambrosio, Laura E. 2017. (ENG.). 32p. (J). pap. 9.99 *(978-0-9993482-0-8(5))* Pickrell, Karen.

—Carpenters & Catapults: A Girls Can Do Anything Book. Petro, Carmen. 2019. (Girls Can Do Anything Ser.: Vol. 2). (ENG.). 36p. (J). (gr. 2-6). pap. 12.99 *(978-1-64516-660-3(0))* Primedia eLaunch LLC.

—Gone Fishing: A Girls Can Do Anything Book. Petro, Carmen. 2019. (Girls Can Do Anything Ser.: Vol. 1). (ENG.). 36p. (J). (gr. 2-6). pap. 12.99 *(978-1-64467-219-8(7))* Primedia eLaunch LLC.

Gledhill, Sarah. The Magpie & the Turtle: A Native American-Inspired Folk Tale. Yeahquo, Timothy. 2019. (ENG.). 26p. (J). (gr. k-5). pap. 12.99 ***(978-1-64633-089-8(7))*** Primedia eLaunch LLC.

—Odo & the Stranger. Johnson, Mark. 2020. (ENG.). 36p. (J). (gr. k-5). pap. 12.99 ***(978-1-64826-123-7(X))*** Primedia eLaunch LLC.

Gledhill, Sarah. Shooting Stars: A Girls Can Do Anything Book. Petro, Carmen. 2019. (Girls Can Do Anything Ser.: Vol. 2). (ENG.). 38p. (J). (gr. 2-6). pap. 12.99 *(978-1-64606-832-6(7))* Primedia eLaunch LLC.

—That Scarlett Bacon. Johnson, Mark. 2018. (ENG.). 36p. (J). (gr. k-5). pap. 9.99 *(978-1-64204-922-0(0))* Primedia eLaunch LLC.

Gleeson, J. M. & Bransom, Paul. Just So Stories. Kipling, Rudyard. 2009. 208p. pap. 9.95 *(978-1-59915-172-4(3))* Yesterday's Classics.

Gleeson, J. M., jt. illus. see Bransom, Paul.

Gleeson, Joseph M. Just So Stories. 2013. 250p. pap. *(978-1-909302-29-7(5))* Abela Publishing.

—Just So Stories. Kipling, Rudyard. 2018. (ENG.). 168p. (J). pap. 14.00 *(978-1-7310-9752-1(2))* Independently Published.

—Just So Stories - Illustrated by Joseph M. Gleeson. Kipling, Rudyard. 2016. (ENG.). (J). *(978-1-4733-3519-6(1))* Read Bks.

Gleich, Jacky. Martes Peludo. Pez, Alberto. (SPA.). (J). 8.95 *(978-958-04-5092-4(7))* Norma S.A. COL. Dist: Distribuidora Norma, Inc.

—La Pequena Nina Grande. Orlev, Uri. (Buenas Noches Ser.). (SPA.). (J). 8.95 *(978-958-04-4902-7(3))* Norma S.A. COL. Dist: Distribuidora Norma, Inc.

Glenn, Ebony. Beacon to Freedom: The Story of a Conductor on the Underground Railroad. Glatzer, Jenna. 2017. (Encounter: Narrative Nonfiction Picture Bks.). (ENG.). 40p. (J). (gr. 1-5). lib. bdg. 29.32 *(978-1-5157-3496-3(X)*, Capstone Pr.) Capstone.

—Brave Ballerina: The Story of Janet Collins. Meadows, Michelle. 2019. (Who Did It First? Ser.). (ENG.). 32p. (J). 17.99 *(978-1-250-12773-0(4)*, 900175518, Holt, Henry & Co. Bks. For Young Readers) Holt, Henry & Co.

—Mommy's Khimar. Thompkins-Bigelow, Jamilah. 2018. (ENG.). 40p. (J). (gr. -1-3). 17.99 *(978-1-5344-0059-7(1)*, Salaam Reads) Simon & Schuster Bks. For Young Readers.

—Not Quite Snow White. Franklin, Ashley. 2019. (ENG.). 32p. (J). (gr. -1-3). 17.99 *(978-0-06-279860-2(X))* HarperCollins Pubs.

—The Starving Ghost: An Up2U Mystery Adventure. Rogers, Kelly. 2017. (Up2U Adventures Set 3 Ser.). (ENG.). 80p. (J). (gr. 2-5). lib. bdg. 29.93 *(978-1-5321-3031-1(7)*, 25510, Calico Chapter Bks.) ABDO Publishing Co.

—The Unstoppable Garrett Morgan: Inventor, Entrepreneur, Hero, 1 vol. DiCicco, Joan. 2019. (ENG.). 40p. (J). (gr. 2-7). 19.95 *(978-1-62014-564-7(2)*, 444d6d40-8524-467d-9e96-3a559e975b01) Lee & Low Bks., Inc.

Glenn, Emily & Groothuis, Maya Rose. Peace in Our World. Groothuis, Paula. 2019. (ENG.). 26p. (J). pap. 10.00 *(978-1-0796-9378-2(5))* Independently Published.

Glenn, Lumsden. Is There Anybody up There? The Smart Kid's Guide to God. Daly, Bruce R. 2017. (ENG.). (J). (gr. 1-5). *(978-0-9806020-0-5(9))* Dalten Media Pty Ltd.

Glennon, Michelle. Duncan the Circus Dinosaur. Glennon, Michelle. 2008. 21p. (J). 16.95 *(978-0-9796625-5-3(9))* GDG Publishing.

—My Big Green Teacher: Don't Rock the Boat: Saving Our Oceans. Glennon, Michelle. 2008. 32p. (J). 19.95 *(978-0-9796625-2-2(4))* GDG Publishing.

—My Big Green Teacher: Please Turn off the Lights. Glennon, Michelle. 2008. (ENG.). 32p. (J). 19.95 *(978-0-9796625-3-9(2))* GDG Publishing.

—My Big Green Teacher: Seven Generations from Now. Glennon, Michelle. 2008. (J). 19.95 *(978-0-9797952-1-3(4))* GDG Publishing.

—My Big Green Teacher: Take a Deep Breath: Saving Our Rainforests. Glennon, Michelle. 2008. (ENG.). 32p. (J). 19.95 *(978-0-9797952-0-6(6))* GDG Publishing.

—My Big Green Teacher: Taking the Green Road. Glennon, Michelle. 2008. 32p. (J). 19.95 *(978-0-9796625-7-7(5))* GDG Publishing.

—My Big Green Teacher: Recycling: It's Easy Being Green. Glennon, Michelle. 2007. 32p. (J). 19.95 *(978-0-9796625-6-0(7))* GDG Publishing.

Glick, Sharon. Perros! Perros!/Dogs! Dogs! Bilingual Spanish-English Children's Book. Guy, Ginger Foglesong. 2006. (ENG.). 32p. (J). (gr. -1-3). 16.99 *(978-0-06-083574-3(5)*, Greenwillow Bks.) HarperCollins Pubs.

Glick, Shifra. Shikufitsky, Vol. 2. Glick, Shifra. 100p. (J). 19.99 *(978-1-58330-640-6(4))* Feldheim Pubs.

Glienke, Amelie. El Pequeno Vampiro. Sommer-Bodenburg, Angela. 2003. (SPA.). 192p. (J). (gr. 3-5). pap. 11.95 *(978-968-19-0673-3(X))* Santillana USA Publishing Co., Inc.

Gliori, Debi. Amazing Alphabets. Bruce, Lisa. 2003. (ENG.). 24p. (J). pap. 9.95 *(978-0-7112-2129-1(4))* Fleming, Randall.

—Side by Side. Bright, Rachel. 2015. (ENG.). 32p. (J). (gr. -1-k). 17.99 *(978-0-545-81326-6(3)*, Scholastic Pr.) Scholastic, Inc.

—Tell Me Something Happy Before I Go to Sleep. Dunbar, Joyce. 2013. (Lullaby Lights Ser.). (ENG.). 24p. (J). (— 1). bds. 11.99 *(978-0-547-94059-5(9)*, 1516931) Houghton Mifflin Harcourt Publishing Co.

—Tell Me Something Happy Before I Go to Sleep (padded Board Book) Dunbar, Joyce. 2018. (Lullaby Lights Ser.). (ENG.). 24p. (J). (— 1). bds. 8.99 *(978-1-328-91068-4(7)*, 1701812, HMH Books For Young Readers) Houghton Mifflin Harcourt Publishing Co.

Gliori, Debi. All the Way Home. Gliori, Debi. 2017. 32p. (J). 17.99 *(978-1-4088-7207-9(2)*, 900189198, Bloomsbury Children's Bks.) Bloomsbury Publishing USA.

—Goodnight World. Gliori, Debi. (ENG.). (J). 2018. 26p. bds. 7.99 *(978-1-68119-789-0(8)*, 900186961, Bloomsbury Children's Bks.); 2017. 32p. 16.99 *(978-1-68119-363-2(9)*, 900171540, Bloomsbury USA Childrens) Bloomsbury Publishing USA.

—Witch Baby & Me on Stage. Gliori, Debi. Hurst, Kelly. 2011. 336p. (J). (gr. 2-4). pap. 7.99 *(978-0-552-55679-8(3))* Transworld Publishers Ltd. GBR. Dist: Independent Pubs. Group.

Gloade, Gerald. Juji'jk: Mi'kmaw Insects, 1 vol. 2019. (ENG & MIC.). 40p. (J). pap. 10.95 ***(978-1-77108-757-5(9)***, 0d598230-bdc0-4fc1-a11a-47be703f721a) Nimbus Publishing, Ltd. CAN. Dist: Baker & Taylor Publisher Services (BTPS).

Glon, Nancy. Silent Knife, Holy Knife. Magness, Robert. 2003. 345p. 10.00 *(978-0-9774577-0-0(2))* Magness, Robert Pubns., LLC.

Glover, Anna-Maria. The Goblin of the East Hill. Evans, Huw M. A. 2018. (ENG.). 118p. (J). pap. *(978-1-9996031-2-0(5))* Living Lantern.

Glover, Maria Robinson. Who Do I Want to Be? Contemporary Black Women from A to Z. Glover, Maria Robinson. 2006. (J). 16.95 *(978-0-9787940-0-2(1))* HotComb Pr.

Glover, Matt R. Shapes, Lines & Dots: Amazing Animals from Around the World (Volume 3) Glover, Matt R. 2017. (Shapes, Lines & Dots Ser.: Vol. 3). (ENG.). (J). (gr. k-6). pap. *(978-0-9953613-2-4(0))* Glover, Matt.

—Shapes, Lines & Dots: Dragons, Dinosaurs & Other Incredible Creatures (Volume 2) Glover, Matt R. 2017. (Shapes, Lines & Dots Ser.: Vol. 2). (ENG.). (J). pap. *(978-0-9953613-1-7(2))* Glover, Matt.

—Shapes, Lines & Dots: Wheels, Wings & Moving Things (Volume 4) Glover, Matt R. 2018. (Shapes, Lines & Dots Ser.: Vol. 4). (ENG.). 90p. (J). (gr. k-6). pap. *(978-0-9953613-3-1(9))* Glover, Matt.

Glover, Peter. Catch That Plane! (Giant Size) A First Reading Adventure Book. Baxter, Nicola. 2016. (ENG.). 24p. (J). (gr. -1-12). pap. 6.99 *(978-1-86147-755-2(4)*, Armadillo) Anness Publishing GBR. Dist: National Bk. Network.

—Chase That Car! A First Reading Adventure Book. Baxter, Nicola. 2016. (ENG.). 24p. (J). (gr. -1-12). pap. 6.99 *(978-1-86147-756-9(2)*, Armadillo) Anness Publishing GBR. Dist: National Bk. Network.

—Follow That Fire Engine! A First Reading Adventure Book. Baxter, Nicola. 2016. (ENG.). 24p. (J). (gr. -1-12). pap. 6.99 *(978-1-86147-757-6(0)*, Armadillo) Anness Publishing GBR. Dist: National Bk. Network.

—Stop That Tractor! Baxter, Nicola. 2016. 24p. (J). (gr. -1-12). pap. 6.99 *(978-1-86147-758-3(9)*, Armadillo) Anness Publishing GBR. Dist: National Bk. Network.

Glover, Robert. A Boy Scout's Handbook of Madcap Tales. Nuttbucket, Oliver S., III. 2003. 48p. (YA). per. 7.95 *(978-0-9741310-0-9(8)*, 0-9741310-0-8) Lost Scout Pr.

Glyn, Chris. Behind You! Glyn, Chris, tr. Morgan, Ruth. 2003. (ENG.). 48p. pap. 11.95 *(978-1-84323-269-8(3))* Beekman Bks., Inc.

Glynn, Chris. Byd Llawn Hud. Hopwood, Mererid et al. 2005. (WEL.). 32p. pap. 4.99 *(978-1-84323-342-8(8))*; pap. 12.99 *(978-1-84323-343-5(6))* Gomer Pr. GBR. Dist: Gomer Pr.

—Dim Mwnci'n y Dosbarth. Lewis, Siân. 2005. (WEL.). 64p. pap. 4.99 *(978-1-84323-427-2(0))* Gomer Pr. GBR. Dist: Gomer Pr.

—One Busy Book. Kay, Francesca. 2004. (ENG.). 32p. pap. 12.95 *(978-1-84323-344-2(4))* Beekman Bks., Inc.

Glynn, Dylan. Be Amazing: A History of Pride. Napoles, Desmond. 2020. (ENG.). 40p. (J). 18.99 *(978-0-374-31258-9(3)*, 900201262, Farrar, Straus & Giroux (BYR)) Farrar, Straus & Giroux.

Gnoli, Domenico. Alberic the Wise & Other Journeys. Juster, Norton. 2010. (ENG.). 96p. (J). (gr. 2-4). lib. bdg. 18.69 *(978-0-375-96699-6(4))* Random House Publishing Group.

—Alberic the Wise & Other Journeys. Juster, Norton. 2010. (ENG.). 96p. (J). (gr. 3-7). 5.99 *(978-0-375-86699-9(X)*, Yearling) Random Hse. Children's Bks.

Goade, Michaela. Encounter. Luby, Brittany. 2019. 40p. (J). (gr. -1-3). 18.99 *(978-0-316-44918-2(0))* Little Brown & Co.

—We Are Water Protectors. Lindstrom, Carole. 2020. (ENG.). 48p. (J). 17.99 *(978-1-250-20355-7(4)*, 900200518) Roaring Brook Pr.

Gobillot, Romane. Les Contes du Grand Chêne. Greffe, Elodie. 2019. (Contes des Deux Comtés Ser.: Vol. 3). (FRE.). 254p. (J). pap. *(978-2-490647-04-0(0))* Les Lutins de Kelach.

Goble, Dale Nigel. Summer Days Fall Days, 1 vol. Colley, Kate. 2019. (ENG.). 26p. (J). (gr. -1 — 1). bds. 10.95 *(978-1-4598-2106-4(8))* Orca Bk. Pubs. USA.

—Winter Days Spring Days, 1 vol. Colley, Kate. 2019. (ENG.). 26p. (J). (gr. -1 — 1). bds. 10.95 *(978-1-4598-2109-5(2))* Orca Bk. Pubs. USA.

Goble, Faith. Gander Press Review: Fall/Winter 2008. Goble, Faith, ed. Zimny, Stan, photos by. Goble, Brant, ed. 2008. (ENG.). pap. 8.95 *(978-0-9820991-0-0(X))* Loosey Goosey Pr.

Goble, Paul. Mystic Horse. Goble, Paul. 2003. (ENG.). 40p. (J). (gr. k-5). 17.99 *(978-0-06-029813-5(8))* HarperCollins Pubs.

—Song of Creation. Goble, Paul. 2004. (ENG.). 32p. (J). 17.00 *(978-0-8028-5271-7(8))* Eerdmans, William B. Publishing Co.

—Walking Along: Plains Indian Trickster Stories. Goble, Paul. 2011. 72p. (J). 19.95 *(978-0-9845041-5-2(X)*, South Dakota State Historical Society Pr.) South Dakota State Historical Society Pr.

Goble, Warwick. The Water Babies: A Fairy Tale for a Land-Baby. Kingsley, Charles. ed. 2006. (Dover Children's Classics Ser.). (ENG.). 160p. (J). (gr. 3-6). per. 14.95 *(978-0-486-45000-1(7))* Dover Pubns., Inc.

Gocotano, Cecil. Adventure Day: A Children's Book about Hiking & Chasing Waterfalls. Dowd, Dineo. 2019. (ENG.). 26p. (J). (gr. k). 17.99 ***(978-1-0878-5159-4(9))*** dineo dowd.

Godbey, Corey. Sammy & His Shepherd. Hunt, Susan. 2008. (ENG.). 56p. (J). (gr. 3-7). 17.00 *(978-1-56769-109-2(9)*, Reformation Trust Publishing) Ligonier Ministries.

Godbey, Cory. The Big God Story, 1 vol. Anthony, Michelle. ed. 2010. (ENG.). 36p. (J). 12.99 *(978-1-4347-6454-6(0)*, 106521) Cook, David C.

—Flames of the Dark Crystal #4. Lee, J. M. 2019. (Jim Henson's the Dark Crystal Ser.: 4). (J). (gr. 7). 328p. pap. 9.99 *(978-0-593-09538-6(3))*; 272p. 17.99 *(978-0-399-53987-9(5))* Penguin Young Readers Group. (Penguin Workshop).

—Jamie's Journey: The Mountain. Ebbers, Susan M. 2019. (ENG.). 46p. (J). (gr. k-4). 22.00 *(978-1-939054-88-3(5))*; pap. 12.00 *(978-1-939054-89-0(3))* Rowe Publishing.

—Jamie's Journey: The Savannah. Ebbers, Susan M. 2012. 38p. 17.99 *(978-0-9833971-8-2(X))*; pap. 9.99 *(978-0-9833971-9-9(8))* Rowe Publishing.

—Jim Henson's Fraggle Rock Omnibus. Brown, Jeffrey et al. 2018. (Fraggle Rock Ser.: 1). (ENG.). 240p. (gr. 3). pap. 19.99 *(978-1-68415-118-9(X)*, Archaia Entertainment) Boom! Studios.

—The Night Knights. Sterer, Gideon. 2018. (ENG.). 40p. (J). (gr. -1-3). 17.99 *(978-1-4197-2846-4(6)*, Abrams Bks. for Young Readers) Abrams, Inc.

—Song of the Dark Crystal #2. Lee, J. M. (Jim Henson's the Dark Crystal Ser.: 2). 272p. (gr. 7). 2019. (J). pap. 9.99 *(978-0-593-09537-9(5)*, Penguin Workshop); 2017. (YA). 17.99 *(978-0-399-53981-7(6)*, Grosset & Dunlap) Penguin Young Readers Group.

—Tides of the Dark Crystal #3. Lee, J. M. 2019. (Jim Henson's the Dark Crystal Ser.: 3). 296p. (YA). (gr. 7). pap. 9.99 *(978-0-399-53985-5(9)*, Penguin Workshop) Penguin Young Readers Group.

Godbey, Cory, jt. illus. see Froud, Brian.

Godbey, Cory, jt. illus. see Wolski, Igor.

Godbey, Courtney. Barking Bella. Kim, Carol. 2020. (Doggie Daycare Set 2 Ser.). (ENG.). 48p. (J). pap. 6.99 ***(978-1-63163-457-4(7)***, 1631634577); lib. bdg. 24.27 ***(978-1-63163-456-7(9)***, 1631634569) North Star Editions. (Jolly Fish Pr.).

—Doggie Daycare Set 2 (Set Of 4) Kim, Carol. 2020. (Doggie Daycare Set 2 Ser.). (ENG.). 192p. (J). pap. 27.96 ***(978-1-63163-454-3(2)***, 1631634542); lib. bdg. 97.08 ***(978-1-63163-453-6(4)***, 1631634534) North Star Editions. (Jolly Fish Pr.).

—Muddy Mutt. Kim, Carol. 2020. (Doggie Daycare Set 2 Ser.). (ENG.). 48p. (J). pap. 6.99 ***(978-1-63163-461-1(5)***, 1631634615); lib. bdg. 24.27 ***(978-1-63163-460-4(7)***, 1631634607) North Star Editions. (Jolly Fish Pr.).

—One Trick Puppy. Kim, Carol. 2020. (Doggie Daycare Set 2 Ser.). (ENG.). 48p. (J). pap. 6.99 ***(978-1-63163-465-9(8)***, 1631634658); lib. bdg. 24.27 ***(978-1-63163-464-2(X)***, 163163464X) North Star Editions. (Jolly Fish Pr.).

—Tank's Forever Home. Kim, Carol. 2020. (Doggie Daycare Set 2 Ser.). (ENG.). 48p. (J). pap. 6.99 ***(978-1-63163-469-7(0)***, 1631634690); lib. bdg. 24.27 ***(978-1-63163-468-0(2)***, 1631634682) North Star Editions. (Jolly Fish Pr.).

Godbout, Geneviève. Goodnight, Anne: Inspired by Anne of Green Gables. George, Kallie. 2018. (ENG.). 40p. (J). (gr. -1-2). 17.99 *(978-1-77049-926-3(1)*, Tundra Bks.) Tundra Bks. CAN. Dist: Penguin Random Hse. LLC.

—If I Couldn't Be Anne. George, Kallie. 2020. (ENG.). 40p. (J). (gr. -1-2). 17.99 *(978-1-77049-928-7(8)*, Tundra Bks.) Tundra Bks. CAN. Dist: Penguin Random Hse. LLC.

Godbout, Genevieve. Joseph Fipps. Robert, Nadine. 2014. (ENG.). 64p. (J). (gr. -1-2). 16.95 *(978-1-59270-117-9(5))* Enchanted Lion Bks., LLC.

Godbout, Geneviève. Kindergarten Luck. Borden, Louise. 2015. (ENG.). 32p. (J). (gr. -1-k). 16.99 *(978-1-4521-1394-4(7))* Chronicle Bks. LLC.

Godbout, Genevieve. Mary Poppins (picture Book) Travers, P. L. 2018. (Mary Poppins Ser.). (ENG.). 32p. (J). (gr. -1-3). 17.99 *(978-1-328-91677-8(4)*, 1702240, HMH Books For Young Readers) Houghton Mifflin Harcourt Publishing Co.

Godbout, Geneviève. My Little Golden Book about Johnny Appleseed. Houran, Lori Haskins. 2017. (Little Golden Book Ser.). 24p. (J). (-k). 4.99 *(978-0-399-55590-9(0)*, Golden Bks.) Random Hse. Children's Bks.

—Searching for Sleep. Dube, Pierrette. 2019. (ENG.). 40p. (J). (gr. -1-3). 16.95 *(978-1-77229-021-9(1))* Simply Read Bks. CAN. Dist: Ingram Publisher Services.

—When Santa Was a Baby. Bailey, Linda. (ENG.). (J). 2017. 30p. (— 1). bds. 9.99 *(978-1-101-91916-3(7))*; 2015. 36p. (gr. -1-2). 16.99 *(978-1-77049-556-2(8))* Tundra Bks. CAN. (Tundra Bks.). Dist: Penguin Random Hse. LLC.

Goddard, Brenda & Haskett, Dan. Grandma's House (Dora the Explorer) Golden Books Staff & Carbone, Courtney. 2013. (Little Golden Book Ser.). (ENG.). 24p. (J). (-k). 3.99 *(978-0-307-98105-9(3)*, Golden Bks.) Random Hse. Children's Bks.

Goddard-Laurence, Brenda & Haskett, Dan. The Dragon Bully (Nella the Princess Knight) Matheis, Mickie. 2017. (Little Golden Book Ser.). (ENG.). 24p. (J). (-k). 4.99 *(978-1-5247-1676-9(6)*, Golden Bks.) Random Hse. Children's Bks.

Goddard-Laurence, Brenda, jt. illus. see Haskett, Dan.

Goddard, Stephanie. De'Marcus & the Dinosaur. Green, Stella. 2017. (ENG.). 28p. (J). pap. *(978-0-9937118-6-2(3))* Green, Stella Mary.

Godeassi, Anna. We Are Brothers. Oh, DaYun. 2014. (MySELF Bookshelf Ser.). (ENG.). 32p. (J). (gr. k-2). pap. 11.94 *(978-1-60357-692-5(4))*; lib. bdg. 25.27 *(978-1-59953-657-6(9))* Norwood Hse. Pr.

Godenir, Jo-Ann. What Do You Do with a Feeling? Your Guide to Becoming a Feelings Expert. Belix, Tasha. 2019. (ENG.). 52p. (J). ***(978-1-5255-3536-9(6))***; pap. ***(978-1-5255-3537-6(4))*** FriesenPress.

Godfrey, Arthur Dwayne. Tongue Turning Tales for the Classroom. McCarroll, Barbara. 2008. 36p. pap. 24.95 *(978-1-60703-254-0(6))* America Star Bks.

Godfrey, Neshelle & Kurshid, Nida. Pheobe the Super Hero! Hero! Hero! Godfrey, Neshelle. 2020. (ENG.). 28p. (J). (gr. 3-6). pap. 12.00 ***(978-0-9974404-4-7(9))*** Ware Resources.

Godi. Ducoboo: In the Corner! Zidrou. 2007. (Ducoboo Ser.: 2). (ENG.). 48p. (J). (gr. 4-7). pap. 9.99 *(978-1-905460-26-7(0))* CineBook GBR. Dist: National Bk. Network.

—Ducoboo No. 3: Your Answers or Your Life! Zidrou. 2008. (Ducoboo Ser.: 3). (ENG.). 48p. pap. 11.95 *(978-1-905460-28-1(7))* CineBook GBR. Dist: National Bk. Network.

Godi & Grobet, Veronique. Ducoboo: The Class Struggle. Zidrou. Spear, Luke, tr. 2010. (Ducoboo Ser.: 4). (ENG.). 46p. (J). (gr. 3-17). pap. 11.95 *(978-1-84918-031-3(8))* CineBook GBR. Dist: National Bk. Network.

Godkin, Celia. Skydiver: Saving the Fastest Bird in the World. Godkin, Celia. (ENG.). 32p. (J). (gr. 1-3). 2014. 17.95 *(978-1-927485-61-3(4))*; 2020. 13.95 ***(978-1-77278-186-1(X))*** Pajama Pr. CAN. Dist: Ingram Publisher Services.

—What about Ladybugs? Godkin, Celia. 2015. (ENG.). 40p. (J). (gr. -1-3). pap. 7.95 *(978-0-87156-921-9(3)*, 7c323d30-37de-4474-b653-ed16060c1451) Fitzhenry & Whiteside, Ltd. CAN. Dist: Firefly Bks., Ltd.

—When the Giant Stirred: Legend of a Volcanic Island, 1 vol. Godkin, Celia. 2005. (ENG.). 40p. (J). (gr. k-2). pap. 12.95 *(978-1-55041-965-8(X)*, 8960d0e3-a69f-46f8-8607-a9bda3fe5456) Fitzhenry & Whiteside, Ltd. CAN. Dist: Firefly Bks., Ltd.

—Wolf Island, 1 vol. Godkin, Celia. 2006. (ENG.). 32p. (J). (gr. k-3). pap. 11.95 *(978-1-55455-008-1(4)*, 81b2d9d3-31fc-4a3e-ad04-fe9ddbe8f98f) Fitzhenry & Whiteside, Ltd. CAN. Dist: Firefly Bks., Ltd.

—The Wolves Return. Godkin, Celia. 2017. (ENG.). 32p. (J). (gr. 1-3). 17.95 *(978-1-77278-011-6(1))* Pajama Pr. CAN. Dist: Ingram Publisher Services.

Godkin, Celia. Amber: The Story of a Fox, 1 vol. Godkin, Celia, tr. Woods, Shirley E. 2005. (ENG.). 96p. (J). (gr. 3-5). pap. 8.95 *(978-1-55041-810-1(6)*, 29d2e526-d3ab-4ddf-9e4e-28c2779ffc78) Trifolium Bks., Inc. CAN. Dist: Firefly Bks., Ltd.

Godon, Ingrid. I Wish. Tellegen, Toon. Colmer, David, tr. 2020. (ENG.). 105p. (J). (gr. 3-7). 22.00 *(978-1-939810-32-8(9)*, Elsewhere Editions) Steerforth Pr.

—My Daddy Is a Giant: For Everyone Who Has the Best Daddy in the World. Norac, Carl. 2004. 32p. (J). (ENG & GLE.). pap. *(978-1-84444-719-0(7))*; (YOR & ENG.). pap. *(978-1-84444-379-6(5))*; (ENG & VIE.). pap. *(978-1-84444-378-9(7))*; (ENG & URD.). pap. *(978-1-84444-377-2(9))*; (ENG & TWI.). pap. *(978-1-84444-376-5(0))*; (ENG & TGL.). pap. *(978-1-84444-373-4(6))*; (SPA & ENG.). pap. *(978-1-84444-372-7(8))*; (SOM & ENG.). pap. *(978-1-84444-371-0(X))*; (ENG & SNA.). pap. *(978-1-84444-370-3(1))*; (ENG & RUS.). pap. *(978-1-84444-369-7(8))*; (ENG & PAN.). pap. *(978-1-84444-366-6(3))*; (ENG & KUR.). pap. *(978-1-84444-365-9(5))*; (ENG & JPN.). pap. *(978-1-84444-364-2(7))*; (ITA & ENG.). pap. *(978-1-84444-363-5(9))*; (FRE & ENG.). pap. *(978-1-84444-359-8(0))*; (ENG & HRV.). pap. *(978-1-84444-357-4(4))*; (ENG & CHI.). pap. *(978-1-84444-356-7(6))*; (ENG & CHI.). pap. *(978-1-84444-355-0(8))*; (ENG & BUL.). pap. *(978-1-84444-354-3(X))*; (ENG & BEN.). pap. *(978-1-84444-353-6(1))*; (ALB & ENG.). pap. *(978-1-84444-351-2(5))*; (ENG & KOR.). pap. *(978-1-84444-300-0(0))* Mantra Lingua.

—My Daddy Is a Giant: For Everyone Who Has the Best Daddy in the World. Norac, Carl. 2005. (ENG.). 32p. (J). pap. 14.95 *(978-1-4050-2168-5(3)*, Macmillan Children's Bks.) Pan Macmillan GBR. Dist: Trans-Atlantic Pubns., Inc.

—Something Big. Neeman, Sylvie. 2013. (ENG.). 40p. (J). (gr. -1-3). 16.95 *(978-1-59270-140-7(X))* Enchanted Lion Bks., LLC.

—What Shall We Do with the Boo Hoo Baby? Cowell, Cressida. 2004. (J). (SER & ENG.). 25p. *(978-1-85269-862-1(4))*; (GER & ENG.). 25p. *(978-1-85269-799-0(7))*; 25p. *(978-1-85269-795-2(4))*; (CZE & ENG.). 25p. *(978-1-85269-794-5(6))*; (ALB & ENG.). 25p. *(978-1-85269-790-7(3))*; 25p. *(978-1-85269-679-5(6))*; (VIE & ENG.). 25p. *(978-1-85269-276-6(6))*; 25p. *(978-1-85269-274-2(X))*; (TUR & ENG.). 25p. *(978-1-85269-273-5(1))*; 25p. *(978-1-85269-272-8(3))*; (ENG & SPA.). 25p. *(978-1-85269-271-1(5))*; (SOM & ENG.). 25p. *(978-1-85269-270-4(7))*; (ITA & ENG.). 25p. *(978-1-85269-256-8(1))*; 25p. *(978-1-85269-255-1(3))*; (POR & ENG.). 25p. *(978-1-85269-254-4(5))*; (POL & ENG.). 32p. pap. *(978-1-85269-683-2(4))*; (ENG & PAN.). 32p. pap. *(978-1-85269-258-2(8))*; (ENG & BEN.). 32p. pap. *(978-1-85269-792-1(X))*; (ENG & CHI.). 32p. pap. *(978-1-85269-793-8(8))*; (FRE & ENG.). 32p. pap. *(978-1-85269-796-9(2))*; (ENG & ARA.). 32p. pap. *(978-1-85269-791-4(1))* Mantra Lingua.

Godwin, Frank. The Blue Fairy Book. Lang, Andrew. 2019. (ENG.). 280p. (J). (gr. 3-8). pap. 9.99 *(978-1-4209-6223-9(X))* Digireads.com Publishing.

Goeddaeus, Donna & Panske, Andy. Heirloom Antics: A Collection of Short Stories. Rippel, Marie & LaTulippe, Renée. 2014. 243p. (J). *(978-1-935197-55-3(X))* All About Learning Pr.

Goedde, Steve Diet, photos by. Steve Diet Goedde - Kumi Postcard Collection. 2008. (ENG., 8p. (YA). 10.00 *(978-1-890836-07-8(9))* Steve Diet Goedde.

—Steve Diet Goedde - Masuimi Max Postcard Collection. 2008. (ENG., 10p. (YA). 10.00 *(978-1-890836-00-9(1))* Steve Diet Goedde.

Goede, Irene. Creepy Crawlies. Post, Hans. 2006. (ENG.). 32p. (J). (gr. -1-3). 16.95 *(978-1-932425-65-9(9))* Lemniscaat USA.

—Sparrows. Post, Hans & Heij, Kees. 2008. (ENG.). 32p. (J). (gr. -1-3). 16.95 *(978-1-59078-570-6(3))* Lemniscaat USA.

Goedeken, Kathy. Sasha Cohen: Autobiography of a Champion Figure Skater. Cohen, Sasha. 2005. (ENG.). 192p. (J). (gr. 3-18). pap. 9.99 *(978-0-06-072489-4(7))* HarperCollins Pubs.

Goegebuer, Jade. Jingle Bells. Pierpont, James. 2018. (ENG.). 32p. (J). (gr. k-3). pap. 9.99 *(978-1-5324-0818-2(8))* Xist Publishing.

—We Play: Level 1 Reader. Streza, Katrina. 2014. (Discover Reading Ser.). (ENG.). 32p. (J). (gr. k-3). pap. 9.99 *(978-1-62395-454-3(1))* Xist Publishing.

Goembel, Ponder. Castaway Cats. Wheeler, Lisa. 2006. (ENG.). 32p. (J). (gr. -1-2). 17.99 *(978-0-689-86232-8(6)*, Atheneum/Richard Jackson Bks.) Simon & Schuster Children's Publishing.

—Cotter Otter in Treasure Water. Bleu, Kennedy. 2014. (ENG.). 24p. (J). pap. 24.95 *(978-1-63004-814-3(3))* America Star Bks.

—Dinosnores. DiPucchio, Kelly. 2005. 32p. (J). (gr. -1 — 1). 17.99 *(978-0-06-051577-5(5))*; lib. bdg. 16.89 *(978-0-06-051578-2(3))* HarperCollins Pubs.

—Mr. Mosquito Put on His Tuxedo. Morrow, Barbara Olenyik. 2009. (ENG.). 32p. (J). (gr. -1-3). 16.95 *(978-0-8234-2072-8(8))* Holiday Hse., Inc.

—Old Cricket. Wheeler, Lisa. 2006. 28p. (gr. -1-1). 18.00 *(978-0-7569-6795-6(3))* Perfection Learning Corp.

—Old Cricket. Wheeler, Lisa. 2006. (ENG.). 32p. (J). (gr. -1-2). reprint ed. 7.99 *(978-1-4169-1855-4(8)*, Atheneum Bks. for Young Readers) Simon & Schuster Children's Publishing.

Goembel, Ponder. Animal Fair, 0 vols. Goembel, Ponder. (ENG.). 24p. (J). (gr. -1 — 1). 2012. bds. 7.99 *(978-0-7614-6205-7(8)*, 9780761462057); 2010. 12.99 *(978-0-7614-5642-1(2)*, 9780761456421) Amazon Publishing. (Two Lions).

Goering, Ellemae. Too Brave: In English & Tigrinya. Goering, Noh & Ready Set Go Books. 2019. (ENG.). 32p. (J). pap. 9.99 *(978-1-0800-4115-2(X))* Independently Published.

Goes, Peter. Follow Finn: A Search-And-Find Maze Book. Goes, Peter. 2018. (ENG.). 32p. (J). (gr. k-5). 16.99 *(978-1-77657-185-7(1))* Gecko Pr. NZL. Dist: Lerner Publishing Group.

—Rivers: A Visual History from River to Sea. Goes, Peter. 2018. (ENG.). 80p. (J). (gr. 2-6). 29.99 *(978-1-77657-216-8(5))* Gecko Pr. NZL. Dist: Lerner Publishing Group.

—Timeline: A Visual History of Our World. Goes, Peter. 2016. (ENG.). 80p. (J). (gr. 5-12). 29.99 *(978-1-77657-069-0(3))* Gecko Pr. NZL. Dist: Lerner Publishing Group.

Goettling, Nickalas, jt. illus. see Dabney, Undra.

Goetzinger, Jason. I Am a Kitty. Goetzinger, Cherie. 2019. (Taryn Amelia Ser.). (ENG.). 32p. (J). ***(978-1-5255-3524-6(2))***; pap. ***(978-1-5255-3525-3(0))*** FriesenPress.

Goetzl, Robert F. Many Nations. Goetzl, Robert F. Bruchac, Joseph. 2004. (ENG.). 32p. (J). (gr. 5-9). pap. 6.99 *(978-0-439-63590-5(X))* Scholastic, Inc.

Goff, Brian. The Dreadful Truth: Building the Railway. Staunton, Ted. 2005. (Dreadful Truth Ser.). (ENG.). 80p. (J). (gr. 3-8). *(978-0-88780-690-2(2))* Formac Publishing Co., Ltd.

Goffe, Toni. Big or Little? Stinson, Kathy. 2nd rev. ed. 2009. (ENG.). 32p. (J). (gr. -1-1). pap. 6.95 *(978-1-55451-168-6(2)*, 1297424) Annick Pr., Ltd. CAN. Dist: Publishers Group West (PGW).

—The Jesus Book: 40 Bible Stories. Neff, LaVonne. 2004. (Life of Christ for Children Ser.). 84p. (gr. -1-k). 9.95 *(978-0-8294-1373-1(1))* Loyola Pr.

—Knights & Castles. Hindley, Judy. Wheatley, Abigail, ed. 2006. (Time Traveler Ser.). 32p. (J). (gr. 3). lib. bdg. 14.95 *(978-1-58086-554-8(2))* EDC Publishing.

—The Legend of Lightning Larry. Shepard, Aaron. (J). (gr. k-6). 2018. (ENG.). 50p. 24.00 *(978-1-62035-560-2(4))*; 2017. (ENG.). pap. 10.00 *(978-1-62035-524-4(8))*; 2005. 48p. pap. 10.00 *(978-0-938497-28-8(6))* Shepard Pubns. (Skyhook Pr.).

—Where Did Dinosaurs Go? Unwin, Mike. Evans, Cheryl, ed. 2006. (Usborne Starting Point Science Ser.). 24p. (J). (gr. 2). lib. bdg. 12.99 *(978-1-58086-937-9(8)*, Usborne) EDC Publishing.

Gogolewski, Kathe. Tato. 2008. (J). *(978-0-9800064-2-1(2))* Red Engine Pr.

Goh, Douglas. Sarah's BFF (Best Friend Forever) Beale, Madeline. 2017. 947p. 10.00 *(978-981-4751-87-2(1))* Marshall Cavendish International (Asia) Private Ltd. SGP. Dist: National Bk. Network.

—Sarah's Favourite Food. Beale, Madeline. 2017. 919p. 10.00 *(978-981-4751-85-8(5))* Marshall Cavendish International (Asia) Private Ltd. SGP. Dist: National Bk. Network.

—Sarah's Great Adventures. Beale, Madeline. 2017. 109p. 10.00 *(978-981-4751-86-5(3))* Marshall Cavendish International (Asia) Private Ltd. SGP. Dist: National Bk. Network.

—Sarah's Happy Holidays. Beale, Madeline. 2017. 872p. 10.00 *(978-981-4751-88-9(X))* Marshall Cavendish International (Asia) Private Ltd. SGP. Dist: National Bk. Network.

Goh, Tai Hwa. Hello Baldwin! Aryal, Aimee. 2004. 24p. (J). 19.95 *(978-1-932888-13-3(6))* Mascot Bks., Inc.

—Hello, Testudo! Aryal, Aimee. 2004. 24p. (J). 18.95 *(978-0-9743442-1-8(4))* Mascot Bks., Inc.

Gohda, Hiroaki, jt. illus. see Uon, Taraku.

Goins, Heather Lea. Ivy Tales: The First Irish Fairy. Goodnight, Lora. 2012. 28p. pap. 24.95 *(978-1-4626-9484-6(5))* America Star Bks.

Golaboff, Laura J. Goofball the Golf Ball. Golaboff, Laura J. 2013. (ENG.). 30p. (J). (gr. 1-3). 19.95 *(978-0-9996184-0-0(7))* Golaboff, Laura J.

—Goofball the Golf Ball: Lost in Discovery. Golaboff, Laura J. 2017. (ENG.). 38p. (J). (gr. 1-3). 21.95 *(978-0-9996184-1-7(5))* Golaboff, Laura J.

Golant, Evgenia. Play Checkers with Me. Golant, Galina & Grant, Lisa. 2003. 32p. (J). pap. 6.95 *(978-1-932133-01-1(1))* Writers' Collective, The.

Gold, Alexandra. A Boy Named Tuck: Tuck & His Magical Stick. Rodney, Reea. Pierre, Anne D., ed. 2018. (ENG.). 38p. (J). 17.99 *(978-1-7321362-1-2(1))* Dara Publishing LLC.

—I Am Uniquely Made & Exceptionally Awesome: Self-Esteem Workbook. Rodney, Reea. 2017. (ENG.). 26p. (J). pap. 12.99 *(978-0-9975059-7-9(4))* Dara Publishing LLC.

—Juniper & Rose: Sisters First, & Best Friends Forever. Rodney, Reea. 2016. (ENG.). (J). pap. 12.99 *(978-0-9975059-0-0(7))* Dara Publishing LLC.

—Juniper y Rose: Primero Hermanas y Mejores Amigas Por Siempre. Rodney, Reea. 2016. (SPA.). (J). pap. 12.99 *(978-0-9975059-2-4(3))* Dara Publishing LLC.

Gold, D. Goylemiks. 2017. (YID.). 59p. *(978-1-68091-171-8(6))* Kinder Shpiel USA, Inc.

Gold, D., jt. illus. see Got, Eli.

Gold, Ethel. Outdoor Things. (Picture Bks.: No. S8817-3). 28p. (J). (gr. -1). pap. 3.95 *(978-0-7214-5142-8(X)*, Dutton Juvenile) Penguin Publishing Group.

—Things That Go. (Picture Bks.: No. S8817-1). 28p. (J). (gr. -1). pap. 3.95 *(978-0-7214-5140-4(3)*, Dutton Juvenile) Penguin Publishing Group.

Gold, Michael, photos by. Fireworks. Cobb, Vicki. 2005. (Where's the Science Here? Ser.). 48p. (J). (gr. 3-7). lib. bdg. 23.93 *(978-0-7613-2771-4(1)*, Millbrook Pr.) Lerner Publishing Group.

—Junk Food. Cobb, Vicki. 2005. (Where's the Science Here? Ser.). (ENG., 48p. (gr. 3-5). 23.93 *(978-0-7613-2773-8(8)*, Millbrook Pr.) Lerner Publishing Group.

G

—On Stage. Cobb, Vicki. 2005. (Where's the Science Here? Ser.). (ENG., 48p. (gr. 3-5). lib. bdg. 23.93 *(978-0-7613-2774-5(6),* Millbrook Pr.) Lerner Publishing Group.

Gold, Nelson. Caroline, a Princess of Prayer. Konow, Heidi. 2019. (Princesses of the Lord Ser.: Vol. 1). (ENG.). 62p. (J). pap. 6.00 *(978-1-0906-9954-1(9))* Independently Published.

Gold, Suzanne. The Fish & the Magic Light: A Mystical Journey. R.B. Schron/I.M. Heer. 2005. (ENG.). 46p. pap. 17.99 *(978-1-4134-8443-4(3))* Xlibris Corp.

Goldberg, Barry. Bubble Blowers, Beware! 2004. (SpongeBob SquarePants Ser.). (ENG.). 24p. (J). pap. 3.99 *(978-0-689-86862-7(6),* Simon Spotlight/Nickelodeon) Simon Spotlight/Nickelodeon.

—Halloween Howl. Herman, Gail & Bridwell, Norman. 2004. (Clifford's Puppy Days Ser.). (ENG.). 24p. (J). (gr. -1-k). 3.99 *(978-0-439-58353-4(5),* Cartwheel Bks.) Scholastic, Inc.

—I Can Help Thomas Sliding Sound Book. Awdry, W. 2012. 12p. (J). bds. *(978-1-4508-3099-7(4))* Publications International, Ltd.

—The Little Blue Easter Egg. Fisch, Sarah & Bridwell, Norman. 2006. (Clifford's Puppy Days Ser.). 23p. (J). *(978-0-439-81617-5(3))* Scholastic, Inc.

—Sesame Street: Big Bird's Road Trip. Winslow, Claire. 2019. (ENG.). 40p. (J). *(978-1-5037-5187-3(2),* 4c55286a-7a02-4688-9adc-b46f606fccd8, p i kids) Phoenix International Publications, Inc.

—Thomas & Friends: Sound Storybook Treasury. 2012. (Play-A-Sound Ser.). (ENG.). 36p. (J). bds. *(978-1-4508-3709-5(3),* 4d75c904-9348-413f-a8d7-ce1a852a7616, p i kids) Phoenix International Publications, Inc.

—Watch Me Draw SpongeBob's Underwater Escapades. 2012. (J). *(978-1-936309-75-7(0))* Quarto Publishing Group USA.

Goldberg, Enid. Wicked History: Vlad the Impaler: The Real Count Dracula. Goldberg, Enid A. & Itzkowitz, Norman. 2008. (Wicked History Ser.). (ENG.). 128p. (J). (gr. 8-13). 18.69 *(978-0-531-12599-1(8),* Watts, Franklin) Scholastic Library Publishing.

Goldberg, Stan, et al. Marvel Visionaries: Roy Thomas. 2019. (ENG.). 352p. (YA). (gr. 4-17). pap. 34.99 *(978-1-302-91840-8(0))* Marvel Worldwide, Inc.

Goldberger, Dylan. Tony the Ferry Riding Pigeon. Palmer, Priscilla & Hoffman, Don. 2016. (ENG.). 32p. (J). (gr. k-2). pap. 3.99 *(978-1-943154-05-0(8))* Peek-A-Boo Publishing.

Goldblatt, Rob. The Boy Who Didn't Want to Be Sad. 2004. 32p. (J). 14.95 *(978-1-59147-134-9(6),* Magination Pr.) American Psychological Assn.

Goldeen, Bill, photos by. Alef-Bet Yoga for Kids. Goldeen, Bill. Goldeen, Ruth. 2009. (Israel Ser.). (ENG., 32p. (J). (gr. -1-2). 15.95 *(978-0-8225-8756-9(4),* Kar-Ben Publishing) Lerner Publishing Group.

Goldeen, Bill, jt. photos by see Goldeen, Ruth.

Goldeen, Ruth & Goldeen, Bill, photos by. Alef-Bet Yoga for Kids. Goldeen, Ruth & Goldeen, Bill. 2009. (ENG., 32p. (J). (gr. -1-2). pap. 7.95 *(978-0-7613-4506-0(X),* Kar-Ben Publishing) Lerner Publishing Group.

Goldemberg, Ana. Baba Yaga. Bradman, Tony. 2014. (Traditional Tales Ser.). (ENG.). 32p. (J). (gr. 1-2). pap. 7.95 *(978-1-62521-534-5(7),* Capstone Classroom) Capstone.

Golden Books. The ABC Book (Pokémon) Foxe, Steve. 2020. (Little Golden Book Ser.). (ENG.). 24p. (J). (gr. -1-2). 4.99 ***(978-1-9848-4927-4(1),*** Golden Bks.) Random Hse. Children's Bks.

Golden Books. Apples Everywhere! (Sunny Day) Matheis, Mickie. 2018. (Little Golden Book Ser.). (ENG.). 24p. (J). (-k). 4.99 *(978-0-525-57754-6(8),* Golden Bks.) Random Hse. Children's Bks.

—Avengers Little Golden Book Favorites (Marvel) 2018. (Little Golden Book Ser.). (ENG.). 80p. (J). (gr. -1-2). 7.99 *(978-0-525-57786-7(6),* Golden Bks.) Random Hse. Children's Bks.

—Barbie 9 Favorite Fairy Tales (Barbie) 2013. (ENG.). 224p. (J). (-k). 10.99 *(978-0-449-81861-9(6),* Golden Bks.) Random Hse. Children's Bks.

—Better Together! (Shimmer & Shine) Chlebowski, Rachel. 2017. (ENG.). 128p. (J). (gr. -1-2). pap. 9.99 *(978-0-399-55793-4(8),* Golden Bks.) Random Hse. Children's Bks.

—The Big Book of DC Super Friends (DC Super Friends) Berrios, Frank. 2015. (Big Golden Book Ser.). (ENG.). 48p. (J). (gr. k-4). 9.99 *(978-0-553-50773-7(7),* Golden Bks.) Random Hse. Children's Bks.

—The Big Book of Small to Tall Pokémon (Pokémon) Foxe, Steve. 2018. (Big Golden Book Ser.). (ENG.). 48p. (J). (gr. -1-2). 10.99 *(978-1-5247-7257-4(7),* Golden Bks.) Random Hse. Children's Bks.

—The Big Book of the Alola Region (Pokémon) Foxe, Steve. 2017. (Big Golden Book Ser.). (ENG.). 48p. (J). (gr. -1-2). 10.99 *(978-1-5247-7009-9(4),* Golden Bks.) Random Hse. Children's Bks.

—Big Heroes! (DC Super Friends) Wrecks, Billy. 2011. (Little Golden Book Ser.). (ENG.). 24p. (J). (gr. -1-2). 4.99 *(978-0-375-87237-2(X),* Golden Bks.) Random Hse. Children's Bks.

—Big Monster Machines! (Blaze & the Monster Machines) Berrios, Frank. 2016. (Big Coloring Book Ser.). (ENG.). 48p. (J). (gr. -1-2). pap. 6.99 *(978-0-399-55691-3(5),* Golden Bks.) Random Hse. Children's Bks.

—Blast to the Past! Linsley, Paul. 2015. (Big Golden Book Ser.). (ENG.). 32p. (J). (gr. -1-2). 9.99 *(978-1-101-93464-7(6),* Golden Bks.) Random Hse. Children's Bks.

—Blaze & the Monster Machines Little Golden Book Library (Blaze & the Monster Machines) Five of Nickelodeon's Blaze & the Monster Machines Little Golden Books, 5 vols. 2017. (Little Golden Book Ser.). (ENG.). 120p. (J). (-k). 24.95 *(978-1-5247-6410-4(8),* Golden Bks.) Random Hse. Children's Bks.

—Blaze Takes the Lead! (Blaze & the Monster Machines) Berrios, Frank. 2017. (ENG.). 128p. (J). (gr. -1-2). pap. 9.99 *(978-0-399-55794-1(6),* Golden Bks.) Random Hse. Children's Bks.

—Blue Mountain Mystery. Awdry, W. 2012. (Little Golden Book Ser.). (ENG.). 24p. (J). (gr. k-k). 4.99 *(978-0-307-97590-4(8),* Golden Bks.) Random Hse. Children's Bks.

—Branch's Bunker Birthday (DreamWorks Trolls) Lewman, David. 2018. (Little Golden Book Ser.). 24p. (J). (-k). 4.99 *(978-1-5247-7260-4(7),* Golden Bks.) Random Hse. Children's Bks.

—Christmas Parade! (Frosty the Snowman) Man-Kong, Mary. 2015. (ENG.). 48p. (J). (gr. -1-2). pap. 6.99 *(978-0-553-52273-0(6),* Golden Bks.) Random Hse. Children's Bks.

Golden Books, et al. Classroom Surprise! (Nella the Princess Knight) James, Hollis. 2018. (Little Golden Book Ser.). (ENG.). 24p. (J). (-k). 4.99 *(978-0-525-57753-9(X),* Golden Bks.) Random Hse. Children's Bks.

Golden Books. The Complete Skywalker Saga: Little Golden Book Library (Star Wars), 9 vols. 2020. (Little Golden Book Ser.). (ENG.). 216p. (J). (-k). 44.91 ***(978-0-7364-4088-2(7),*** Golden Bks.) Random Hse. Children's Bks.

Golden Books. DC Super Friends Little Golden Book Favorites #2 (DC Super Friends) 2016. (ENG.). 80p. (J). (-k). 7.99 *(978-1-101-94023-5(9),* Golden Bks.) Random Hse. Children's Bks.

—DC Super Friends Little Golden Book Favorites (DC Super Friends) 2013. (Little Golden Book Favorites Ser.). (ENG.). 80p. (J). (-k). 6.99 *(978-0-449-81621-9(4),* Golden Bks.) Random Hse. Children's Bks.

—DC Super Friends Little Golden Book Library (DC Super Friends) Superman; Batman; Green Lantern; Wonder Woman, 5 vols. 2015. (Little Golden Book Ser.). (ENG.). 120p. (J). (-k). 24.95 *(978-0-553-50897-0(0),* Golden Bks.) Random Hse. Children's Bks.

—Disney Classics Little Golden Book Library (Disney Classic) Lady & the Tramp; 101 Dalmatians; the Lion King; Alice in Wonderland; the Jungle Book, 5 vols. 2013. (Little Golden Book Ser.). (ENG.). 24p. (J). (-k). 24.95 *(978-0-7364-3149-1(7),* Golden/Disney) Random Hse. Children's Bks.

—Disney Junior Little Golden Book Library (Disney Junior) Doc Mcstuffins; Sofia the First; Minnie Mouse Bow-Tique; Jake & the Never Land Pirates, 5 vols. 2013. (Little Golden Book Ser.). (ENG.). 120p. (J). (-k). 24.95 *(978-0-7364-3076-0(8),* Golden/Disney) Random Hse. Children's Bks.

Golden Books, et al. Doctor Strange Little Golden Book (Marvel: Doctor Strange) Kaplan, Arie. 2017. (Little Golden Book Ser.). (ENG.). 24p. (J). (-k). 4.99 *(978-1-101-93865-2(X),* Golden Bks.) Random Hse. Children's Bks.

Golden Books. Easter Surprises! Man-Kong, Mary. 2015. 96p. (J). (gr. -1-2). pap. 3.99 *(978-0-553-50820-8(2),* Golden Bks.) Random Hse. Children's Bks.

—A Friend Like Pikachu! (Pokémon) Chlebowski, Rachel. 2019. (Little Golden Book Ser.). (ENG.). 24p. (J). (gr. -1-2). 4.99 *(978-1-9848-4817-8(8),* Golden Bks.) Random Hse. Children's Bks.

—Frosty the Snowman (Frosty the Snowman) Muldrow, Diane. 2013. (Big Golden Board Book Ser.). (ENG.). 22p. (J). (-k). bds. 10.99 *(978-0-385-37870-3(X),* Golden Bks.) Random Hse. Children's Bks.

—Frozen 2 Little Golden Book (Disney Frozen) 2019. (Little Golden Book Ser.). (ENG.). 24p. (J). (-k). 4.99 *(978-0-7364-4020-2(8),* Golden/Disney) Random Hse. Children's Bks.

—Gone Fishing! (Disney Junior: Mickey & the Roadster Racers) Stoner, Sherri. 2018. (Little Golden Book Ser.). (ENG.). 24p. (J). (-k). 4.99 *(978-0-7364-3844-5(0),* Golden/Disney) Random Hse. Children's Bks.

Golden Books. Happy Birthday, Blue! (Blue's Clues & You) Roth, Megan. 2020. (Little Golden Book Ser.). (ENG.). 24p. (J). (-k). 4.99 ***(978-0-593-12393-5(X),*** Golden Bks.) Random Hse. Children's Bks.

Golden Books. Happy, Jolly Fun! (Frosty the Snowman) Man-Kong, Mary. 2014. (ENG.). 48p. (J). (gr. -1-2). pap. 3.99 *(978-0-385-38723-1(7),* Golden Bks.) Random Hse. Children's Bks.

Golden Books, et al. The Haunted Hot Rod (Disney Junior: Mickey & the Roadster Racers) Liberts, Jennifer. 2018. (Little Golden Book Ser.). (ENG.). 24p. (J). (-k). 4.99 *(978-0-7364-3902-2(1),* Golden/Disney) Random Hse. Children's Bks.

Golden Books. Here Come the Bit Police! (Rusty Rivets) Berrios, Frank. 2018. (Little Golden Book Ser.). (ENG.). 24p. (J). (-k). 4.99 *(978-1-5247-7241-3(0),* Golden Bks.) Random Hse. Children's Bks.

—I Can Be a Rock Star (Barbie) Man-Kong, Mary. 2010. (Pictureback(R) Ser.). (ENG.). 16p. (J). (gr. -1-2). pap. 3.99 *(978-0-375-86545-9(4),* Golden Bks.) Random Hse. Children's Bks.

—Justice for All! (DC Super Friends) Berrios, Frank. 2016. (ENG.). 64p. (J). (gr. -1-2). pap. 9.99 *(978-1-101-93151-6(5),* Golden Bks.) Random Hse. Children's Bks.

—Kung Fu Panda. Scollon, Bill. 2017. (Little Golden Book Ser.). 24p. (J). (-k). 4.99 *(978-1-5247-6772-3(7),* Golden Bks.) Random Hse. Children's Bks.

—The Littlest Vampire (Disney Junior Vampirina) Forte, Lauren. 2018. (Little Golden Book Ser.). (ENG.). 24p. (J). (-k). 4.99 *(978-0-7364-3781-3(9),* Golden/Disney) Random Hse. Children's Bks.

—Madagascar. Frolick, Billy. 2017. (Little Golden Book Ser.). 24p. (J). (-k). 4.99 *(978-1-5247-6768-6(9),* Golden Bks.) Random Hse. Children's Bks.

—Magical Misadventures! (Shimmer & Shine) Chlebowski, Rachel. 2017. (ENG.). 64p. (J). (gr. -1-2). pap. 9.99 *(978-0-399-55890-0(X),* Golden Bks.) Random Hse. Children's Bks.

—Marvel Little Golden Book Library (Marvel Super Heroes) Spider-Man; Hulk; Iron Man; Captain America; the Avengers, 5 vols. 2016. (Little Golden Book Ser.). (ENG.). 24p. (J). (-k). 24.95 *(978-0-449-81735-3(0),* Golden Bks.) Random Hse. Children's Bks.

—Mickey & the Beanstalk (Disney Classic) Anastasio, Dina. 2018. (Little Golden Book Ser.). (ENG.). 24p. (J). (-k). 4.99 *(978-0-7364-3785-1(1),* Golden/Disney) Random Hse. Children's Bks.

—Mighty Pup Power! (PAW Patrol) James, Hollis. 2018. (Little Golden Book Ser.). (ENG.). 24p. (J). (-k). 4.99 *(978-0-525-57772-0(6),* Golden Bks.) Random Hse. Children's Bks.

—The Mighty Thor (Marvel: Thor) Wrecks, Billy. 2016. (Little Golden Book Ser.). (ENG.). 24p. (J). (gr. -1-k). 4.99 *(978-0-307-93051-4(3),* Golden Bks.) Random Hse. Children's Bks.

—Mister Rogers' Neighborhood: Henrietta Meets Someone New. Rogers, Fred. 2019. (Little Golden Book Ser.). (ENG.). 24p. (J). (-k). 4.99 *(978-0-593-11997-6(5),* Golden Bks.) Random Hse. Children's Bks.

—Monster Mayhem! (Teenage Mutant Ninja Turtles) Lewman, David. 2017. (Big Golden Book Ser.). (ENG.). 48p. (J). (gr. -1-2). 9.99 *(978-1-5247-1670-7(7),* Golden Bks.) Random Hse. Children's Bks.

—My Little Pony: Pinkie Pie's Big Baking Bonanza. May, Tallulah. 2018. (Little Golden Book Ser.). (ENG.). 24p. (J). (-k). 4.99 *(978-1-5247-6978-9(9),* Golden Bks.) Random Hse. Children's Bks.

—My Little Pony: the Movie Big Golden Book (My Little Pony) Sisler, Celeste & Ventura, Bonnie. 2017. (Big Golden Book Ser.). (ENG.). 32p. (J). (gr. -1-1). 10.99 *(978-1-5247-6964-2(9),* Golden Bks.) Random Hse. Children's Bks.

—Nickelodeon Little Golden Book Library (Nickelodeon), 5 vols. 2015. (Little Golden Book Ser.). (ENG.). 120p. (J). (-k). 24.95 *(978-0-553-50797-3(4),* Golden Bks.) Random Hse. Children's Bks.

Golden Books. Nickelodeon Little Golden Book Library (Nickelodeon) Mighty Pup Power!; Happy Birthday, Blue!; Time to Be Kind; Sleepover Surprise; My Heart Is Bright!, 5 vols. 2020. (Little Golden Book Ser.). (ENG.). 120p. (J). (-k). 24.95 ***(978-0-593-17903-1(X),*** Golden Bks.) Random Hse. Children's Bks.

Golden Books. Nine Marvel Super Hero Tales (Marvel) 2017. (ENG.). 224p. (J). (-k). 12.99 *(978-1-5247-1783-4(5),* Golden Bks.) Random Hse. Children's Bks.

—Nine Nickelodeon Tales (Nickelodeon) 2016. (ENG.). 224p. (J). (-k). 12.99 *(978-0-399-55350-9(9),* Golden Bks.) Random Hse. Children's Bks.

—No Job Is Too Big! (PAW Patrol) Huntley, Tex. 2015. (ENG.). 48p. (J). (gr. -1-2). pap. 6.99 *(978-0-553-52276-1(0),* Golden Bks.) Random Hse. Children's Bks.

—Ono the Tickbird (Disney Junior: the Lion Guard) Lagonegro, Melissa. 2018. (Little Golden Book Ser.). (ENG.). 24p. (J). (-k). 4.99 *(978-0-7364-3838-4(6),* Golden/Disney) Random Hse. Children's Bks.

—PAW Patrol Little Golden Book Library (PAW Patrol) Itty-Bitty Kitty Rescue; Puppy Birthday!; Pirate Pups; All-Star Pups!; Jurassic Bark!, 5 vols. 2017. (Little Golden Book Ser.). (ENG.). 120p. (J). (-k). 24.95 *(978-1-5247-6412-8(4),* Golden Bks.) Random Hse. Children's Bks.

—Peppa's Egg-Citing Easter! (Peppa Pig) Carbone, Courtney. 2020. (ENG.). 48p. (J). (gr. -1-2). pap. 7.99 *(978-0-593-12266-2(6),* Golden Bks.) Random Hse. Children's Bks.

—Poppy's Paint Party! (DreamWorks Trolls) Chlebowski, Rachel. 2019. (ENG.). 128p. (J). (gr. -1-2). pap. 7.99 *(978-1-9848-5060-7(1),* Golden Bks.) Random Hse. Children's Bks.

—Puppies in Paris (Disney Junior: Puppy Dog Pals) Olson, Michael. 2018. (Big Golden Book Ser.). (ENG.). 32p. (J). (gr. -1-2). 10.99 *(978-0-7364-3842-1(4),* Golden/Disney) Random Hse. Children's Bks.

—Purr-Fect Valentine! (Barbie) Man-Kong, Mary. 2012. (ENG.). 128p. (J). (gr. -1-2). pap. 7.99 *(978-0-307-98210-0(6),* Golden Bks.) Random Hse. Children's Bks.

—Ready, Set, Tow! (Blaze & the Monster Machines) Tillworth, Mary. 2018. (Little Golden Book Ser.). (ENG.). 24p. (J). (-k). 4.99 *(978-1-5247-6843-0(X),* Golden Bks.) Random Hse. Children's Bks.

—Rock & Rule. Tillworth, Mary. 2012. (ENG.). 48p. (J). (gr. -1-2). pap. 3.99 *(978-0-307-97620-8(3),* Golden Bks.) Random Hse. Children's Bks.

—Rockin' Rainbow! (DreamWorks Trolls World Tour) Clauss, Lauren. 2020. (ENG.). 128p. (J). (gr. -1-2). pap. 7.99 *(978-0-593-12233-4(X),* Golden Bks.) Random Hse. Children's Bks.

—Skate Like a Ninja! (Teenage Mutant Ninja Turtles) Tillworth, Mary. 2017. (Little Golden Book Ser.). (ENG.). 24p. (J). (-k). 4.99 *(978-0-399-55796-5(2),* Golden Bks.) Random Hse. Children's Bks.

—Sparkle & Smile! (Frosty the Snowman) Man-Kong, Mary. 2017. (ENG.). 64p. (J). (gr. -1-2). pap. 5.99 *(978-1-5247-6405-0(1),* Golden Bks.) Random Hse. Children's Bks.

—Spider-Man Little Golden Book Library (Marvel) Spider-Man!; Trapped by the Green Goblin; the Big Freeze!; High Voltage!; Night of the Vulture!, 5 vols. 2017. (Little Golden Book Ser.). (ENG.). 120p. (J). (-k). 24.95 *(978-1-5247-6409-8(4),* Golden Bks.) Random Hse. Children's Bks.

—Star Wars: I Am A... Little Golden Book Library (Star Wars) I Am a Pilot; I Am a Jedi; I Am a Sith; I Am a Droid; I Am a Princess, 5 vols. 2016. (Little Golden Book Ser.). (ENG.). 120p. (J). (-k). 24.95 *(978-0-7364-3638-0(3),* Golden Bks.) Random Hse. Children's Bks.

—The Star Wars Little Golden Book Library (Star Wars) The Phantom Menace; Attack of the Clones; Revenge of the Sith; a New Hope; the Empire Strikes Back; Return of the Jedi, 6 vols. 2015. (Little Golden Book Ser.). (ENG.). 144p. (J). (-k). 29.94 *(978-0-7364-3470-6(4),* Golden Bks.) Random Hse. Children's Bks.

—The Super Hero Sticker Collection! (DC Super Hero Girls) Chlebowski, Rachel. 2018. (ENG.). 48p. (J). (gr. 2-4). pap. 9.99 *(978-1-5247-1727-8(4),* Golden Bks.) Random Hse. Children's Bks.

—The Sweetest Valentine (Peppa Pig) Man-Kong, Mary. 2019. (ENG.). 48p. (J). (gr. -1-2). pap. 7.99 *(978-0-593-12092-7(2),* Golden Bks.) Random Hse. Children's Bks.

—Teenage Mutant Ninja Turtles Little Golden Book Library (Teenage Mutant Ninja Turtles), 5 vols. 2017. (Little Golden Book Ser.). (ENG.). 120p. (J). (-k). 24.95 *(978-1-5247-6411-1(6),* Golden Bks.) Random Hse. Children's Bks.

Golden Books, et al. Tiana Is My Babysitter (Disney Princess) Jordan, Apple. 2018. (Little Golden Book Ser.). (ENG.). 24p. (J). (-k). 4.99 *(978-0-7364-3783-7(5),* Golden/Disney) Random Hse. Children's Bks.

Golden Books. Trolls World Tour Little Golden Book (DreamWorks Trolls World Tour) Lewman, David. 2020. (Little Golden Book Ser.). (ENG.). 24p. (J). (-k). 4.99 *(978-0-593-12239-6(9),* Golden Bks.) Random Hse. Children's Bks.

—Trouble with Trix (Winx Club), 2. Reisfeld, Randi. 2012. (Winx Club: Chapter Bks.). (ENG.). 128p. (J). (gr. 2-5). 17.44 *(978-0-307-97995-7(4))* Random House Publishing Group.

Golden Books. Unicorns, Mermaids, & More! (Peppa Pig) Man-Kong, Mary. 2020. (ENG.). 48p. (J). (gr. -1-2). pap. 6.99 ***(978-0-593-12767-4(6),*** Golden Bks.) Random Hse. Children's Bks.

Golden Books. Vee's First Day of School (Disney Junior: Vampirina) Beyl, Chelsea. 2018. (Big Golden Book Ser.). (ENG.). 32p. (J). (gr. -1-2). 10.99 *(978-0-7364-3843-8(2),* Golden/Disney) Random Hse. Children's Bks.

—A Very Busy Coloring Book (the World of Eric Carle) Miller, Mona. 2013. (ENG.). 224p. (J). (gr. -1-2). pap. 5.99 *(978-0-449-81609-7(5),* Golden Bks.) Random Hse. Children's Bks.

—Welcome to Alfea, 1. Reisfeld, Randi. 2012. (Winx Club: Chapter Bks.). (ENG.). 128p. (J). (gr. 2-5). 17.44 *(978-0-307-97994-0(6))* Random House Publishing Group.

—Who You Gonna Call? Sazaklis, John. 2016. (Little Golden Book Ser.). 24p. (J). (gr. -1-2). 4.99 *(978-1-5247-1491-8(7),* Golden Bks.) Random Hse. Children's Bks.

Golden Books. Adventures with Peppa (Peppa Pig) Golden Books. 2020. (ENG.). 224p. (J). (gr. -1-2). pap. 5.99 *(978-0-593-12275-4(5),* Golden Bks.) Random Hse. Children's Bks.

—The Art of the Ninja (Teenage Mutant Ninja Turtles) Golden Books. 2014. (ENG.). 128p. (J). (gr. -1-2). pap. 5.99 *(978-0-385-37851-2(3),* Golden Bks.) Random Hse. Children's Bks.

—The Big Book of Ninja Turtles (Teenage Mutant Ninja Turtles) Golden Books. 2014. (Big Golden Book Ser.). (ENG.). 48p. (J). (gr. -1-2). 9.99 *(978-0-553-50769-0(9),* Golden Bks.) Random Hse. Children's Bks.

—The Big Book of Paw Patrol (Paw Patrol) Golden Books. 2014. (Big Golden Book Ser.). (ENG.). 32p. (J). (gr. -1-2). 9.99 *(978-0-553-51276-2(5),* Golden Bks.) Random Hse. Children's Bks.

—A Big Easter Adventure (Peter Cottontail) Golden Books. 2012. 48p. (J). (gr. -1-2). pap. 6.99 *(978-0-375-86557-2(8),* Golden Bks.) Random Hse. Children's Bks.

—The Big Golden Book of Starships, Speeders, & Space Stations (Star Wars) Golden Books. 2017. (Big Golden Book Ser.). (ENG.). 48p. (J). (gr. -1-2). 10.99 *(978-0-7364-3693-9(6),* Golden Bks.) Random Hse. Children's Bks.

—Blaze & the Monster Machines Awesome Sticker Collection (Blaze & the Monster Machines) Golden Books. 2017. (ENG.). 64p. (J). (gr. -1-2). pap. 12.99 *(978-1-5247-1683-7(9),* Golden Bks.) Random Hse. Children's Bks.

—Blaze & the Monster Machines Color Plus Cardstock & Stickers. Golden Books. 2016. (ENG.). 32p. (J). (gr. -1-2). pap. 5.99 *(978-0-399-55303-5(7),* Golden Bks.) Random Hse. Children's Bks.

—Blaze Little Golden Book Favorites (Blaze & the Monster Machines) Golden Books. 2017. (ENG.). 80p. (J). (-k). 7.99 *(978-0-399-55891-7(8),* Golden Bks.) Random Hse. Children's Bks.

Golden Books. Blue's Big Coloring Book (Blue's Clues & You) Golden Books. 2020. (ENG.). 48p. (J). (gr. -1-2). pap. 6.99 ***(978-0-593-30776-2(3),*** Golden Bks.) Random Hse. Children's Bks.

Golden Books. Bubble Bonanza! (Bubble Guppies) Golden Books. 2013. (Color & Paint Plus Stickers Ser.). (ENG.). 128p. (J). (gr. -1-2). pap. 9.99 *(978-0-449-81948-7(5),* Golden Bks.) Random Hse. Children's Bks.

—Bubble Guppies Little Golden Book Favorites (Bubble Guppies) Golden Books. 2015. (Little Golden Book Favorites Ser.). (ENG.). 80p. (J). (gr. -1-2). 7.99 *(978-0-553-52115-3(2),* Golden Bks.) Random Hse. Children's Bks.

—Cadets Stick Together! (Top Wing) Golden Books. 2019. (ENG.). 64p. (J). (gr. -1-2). pap. 9.99 *(978-1-9848-4943-4(3),* Golden Bks.) Random Hse. Children's Bks.

—Calling All Cadets! (Top Wing) Golden Books. 2018. (ENG.). 128p. (J). (gr. -1-2). pap. 7.99 *(978-0-525-64579-5(9),* Golden Bks.) Random Hse. Children's Bks.

—Championship Colors! (Blaze & the Monster Machines) Golden Books. 2017. (ENG.). 224p. (J). (gr. -1-2). pap. 6.99 *(978-1-5247-6558-3(9),* Golden Bks.) Random Hse. Children's Bks.

—Christmas Magic! (Frosty the Snowman) Golden Books. 2016. (ENG.). 128p. (J). (gr. -1-2). pap. 9.99 *(978-0-399-55224-3(3),* Golden Bks.) Random Hse. Children's Bks.

—Clash with the Kraang! (Teenage Mutant Ninja Turtles) Golden Books. 2013. (Deluxe Reusable Sticker Book Ser.). (ENG.). 24p. (J). (gr. -1-2). pap. 6.99 *(978-0-449-81883-1(7),* Golden Bks.) Random Hse. Children's Bks.

—Coco Big Golden Book (Disney/Pixar Coco) Golden Books. 2017. (Big Golden Book Ser.). (ENG.). 48p. (J). (gr. -1-2). 10.99 *(978-0-7364-3694-6(4),* Golden/Disney) Random Hse. Children's Bks.

Golden Books. Coco Little Golden Board Book (Disney/Pixar Coco) Golden Books. 2020. (Little Golden Book Ser.). (ENG.). 26p. (J). (— 1). bds. 7.99 ***(978-0-7364-4117-9(4),*** Golden/Disney) Random Hse. Children's Bks.

Golden Books. Color Caper! (DC Super Hero Girls) Golden Books. 2018. (ENG.). 128p. (J). (gr. -1-2). pap. 7.99 *(978-1-5247-6603-0(8),* Golden Bks.) Random Hse. Children's Bks.

—Color, Color, Everywhere! (Thomas & Friends) Golden Books. 2018. (ENG.). 128p. (J). (gr. -1-2). pap. 7.99 *(978-0-525-57798-0(X),* Golden Bks.) Random Hse. Children's Bks.

—Combine It & Design It! (Rusty Rivets) Golden Books. 2018. (ENG.). 64p. (J). (gr. -1-2). pap. 5.99 *(978-1-5247-6793-8(X),* Golden Bks.) Random Hse. Children's Bks.

—Cute Christmas! (Peppa Pig) Golden Books. 2019. (ENG.). 128p. (J). (gr. -1-2). pap. 7.99 *(978-0-593-11895-5(2),* Golden Bks.) Random Hse. Children's Bks.

—The Dark Crystal (Little Golden Book) Golden Books. 2019. (Little Golden Book Ser.). 24p. (J). (-k). 4.99 *(978-0-593-12080-4(9),* Golden Bks.) Random Hse. Children's Bks.

—A Dash of Color! (Butterbean's Cafe) Golden Books. 2020. (ENG.). 128p. (J). (gr. -1-2). pap. 7.99 *(978-0-593-12398-0(0),* Golden Bks.) Random Hse. Children's Bks.

Golden Books. DC Super Friends Little Golden Book Treasury (DC Super Friends) Golden Books. 2020. (Little Golden Book Ser.). (ENG.). 176p. (J). (gr. -1-2). 11.99 ***(978-0-593-17848-5(3),*** Golden Bks.) Random Hse. Children's Bks.

Golden Books. Disney Princess Babysitter Stories (Disney Princess) Golden Books. 2018. (Little Golden Book Ser.). (ENG.). 128p. (J). (-k). 9.99 *(978-0-7364-3779-0(7),* Golden/Disney) Random Hse. Children's Bks.

—Doodle Adventures! (PAW Patrol) Golden Books. 2019. (ENG.). 48p. (J). (gr. -1-2). pap. 9.99 *(978-1-9848-4893-2(3),* Golden Bks.) Random Hse. Children's Bks.

—Dream Big! (Shimmer & Shine) Golden Books. 2016. (ENG.). 48p. (J). (gr. -1-2). pap. 6.99 *(978-1-101-93673-3(8),* Golden Bks.) Random Hse. Children's Bks.

—The Epic Trolls. Golden Books. 2016. (4 Color Plus 1,000 Stickers Ser.). (ENG.). 64p. (J). (gr. -1-2). pap. 12.99 *(978-0-399-55901-3(9),* Golden Bks.) Random Hse. Children's Bks.

—Flying Colors! (Shimmer & Shine) Golden Books. 2017. (ENG.). 224p. (J). (gr. -1-2). pap. 6.99 *(978-1-5247-6541-5(4),* Golden Bks.) Random Hse. Children's Bks.

—Friends for Life. Golden Books. 2016. 64p. (J). (gr. -1-2). pap. 5.99 *(978-0-399-55488-9(2),* Golden Bks.) Random Hse. Children's Bks.

—Friends Stick Together (Sunny Day) Golden Books. 2019. (ENG.). 64p. (J). (gr. -1-2). pap. 9.99 *(978-0-525-64850-5(X),* Golden Bks.) Random Hse. Children's Bks.

—Full Speed Ahead! (Blaze & the Monster Machines) Golden Books. 2015. (ENG.). 48p. (J). (gr. -1-2). pap. 4.99 *(978-0-553-52455-0(0),* Golden Bks.) Random Hse. Children's Bks.

—Genie Magic! (Shimmer & Shine) Golden Books. 2016. (ENG.). 48p. (J). (gr. -1-2). pap. 4.99 *(978-0-553-52205-1(1),* Golden Bks.) Random Hse. Children's Bks.

—Giant Adventures. Golden Books. 2015. (ENG.). 48p. (J). (gr. -1-2). pap. 6.99 *(978-0-553-52292-1(2),* Golden Bks.) Random Hse. Children's Bks.

—Glam in the Garden! (Sunny Day) Golden Books. 2018. (ENG.). 48p. (J). (gr. -1-2). pap. 4.99 *(978-1-5247-6853-9(7),* Golden Bks.) Random Hse. Children's Bks.

—Grumpy Cat. Golden Books. 2018. (Little Golden Book Ser.). 80p. (J). (-k). 7.99 *(978-1-5247-6777-8(8),* Golden Bks.) Random Hse. Children's Bks.

—Grumpy Cat's First Worst Christmas (Grumpy Cat) Golden Books. 2017. (Big Golden Book Ser.). 32p. (J). (gr. -1-1). 10.99 *(978-1-5247-6969-7(X),* Golden Bks.) Random Hse. Children's Bks.

—Have a Very Peppa Christmas! (Peppa Pig) Golden Books. 2019. (ENG.). 48p. (J). (gr. -1-2). pap. 4.99 *(978-0-593-11894-8(4),* Golden Bks.) Random Hse. Children's Bks.

—Here Comes Peter Cottontail Big Golden Book (Peter Cottontail) Golden Books. 2017. (Big Golden Book Ser.). (ENG.). 32p. (J). (gr. -1-2). 9.99 *(978-0-399-55785-9(7),* Golden Bks.) Random Hse. Children's Bks.

—Here Comes Peter Cottontail Little Golden Book (Peter Cottontail) Golden Books. 2014. (Little Golden Book Ser.). 24p. (J). (-k). 4.99 *(978-0-385-37839-0(4),* Golden Bks.) Random Hse. Children's Bks.

—Heroes & Villains Little Golden Book Collection (Star Wars) Golden Books. 2017. (ENG.). 176p. (J). (-k). 12.99 *(978-0-7364-3698-4(7),* Golden Bks.) Random Hse. Children's Bks.

—Hooray for Dora! (Dora the Explorer) Golden Books. 2012. (ENG.). 416p. (J). (gr. -1-2). pap. 10.99 *(978-0-307-93093-4(9),* Golden Bks.) Random Hse. Children's Bks.

—Hugs & Happiness (DreamWorks Trolls) Golden Books. 2017. (ENG.). 48p. (J). (gr. -1-2). pap. 9.99 *(978-0-399-55843-6(8),* Golden Bks.) Random Hse. Children's Bks.

—I Am a Hero (Star Wars) Golden Books. 2017. (Little Golden Book Ser.). (ENG.). 24p. (J). (-k). 4.99 *(978-0-7364-3587-1(5),* Golden Bks.) Random Hse. Children's Bks.

—I Am a Wookiee (Star Wars) Golden Books. 2018. (Little Golden Book Ser.). (ENG.). 24p. (J). (-k). 4.99 *(978-0-7364-3796-7(7),* Golden Bks.) Random Hse. Children's Bks.

—I Am the Beast (Disney Beauty & the Beast) Golden Books. 2017. (Little Golden Book Ser.). (ENG.). 24p. (J). (-k). 4.99 *(978-0-7364-3907-7(2),* Golden/Disney) Random Hse. Children's Bks.

—It's Time for Christmas! (Bubble Guppies) Golden Books. 2014. (ENG.). 48p. (J). (gr. -1-2). pap. 6.99 *(978-0-385-38409-4(2),* Golden Bks.) Random Hse. Children's Bks.

—Join the Team! (Team Umizoomi) Golden Books. 2012. (Big Coloring Book Ser.). (ENG.). 48p. (J). (gr. -1-2). pap. 6.99 *(978-0-307-93138-2(2),* Golden Bks.) Random Hse. Children's Bks.

—Jumbo Coloring Adventures! (Nickelodeon) Golden Books. 2015. (ENG.). 416p. (J). (gr. -1-2). pap. 10.99 *(978-0-553-52087-3(3),* Golden Bks.) Random Hse. Children's Bks.

—Just Yelp for Help! (PAW Patrol) Golden Books. 2015. (ENG.). 40p. (J). (gr. -1-2). pap. 9.99 *(978-0-553-53386-6(X),* Golden Bks.) Random Hse. Children's Bks.

—Kingdom of Colors (Nella the Princess Knight) Golden Books. 2018. (ENG.). 128p. (J). (gr. -1-2). pap. 7.99 *(978-0-525-58016-4(6),* Golden Bks.) Random Hse. Children's Bks.

—Love Is in the Hair! Golden Books. Chlebowski, Rachel. 2016. (ENG.). 48p. (J). (gr. -1-2). pap. 7.99 *(978-0-399-55892-4(6),* Golden Bks.) Random Hse. Children's Bks.

—Mega-Mutations! (Teenage Mutant Ninja Turtles) Golden Books. 2014. (ENG.). 224p. (J). (gr. -1-2). pap. 5.99 *(978-0-385-38504-6(8),* Golden Bks.) Random Hse. Children's Bks.

—Mutants Rule! (Teenage Mutant Ninja Turtles) Golden Books. Berrios, Frank. 2013. (ENG.). 128p. (J). (gr. -1-2). pap. 9.99 *(978-0-449-81952-4(3),* Golden Bks.) Random Hse. Children's Bks.

—Nella's Sticker Adventure! (Nella the Princess Knight) Golden Books. 2018. (ENG.). 64p. (J). (gr. -1-2). pap. 5.99 *(978-1-5247-6886-7(3),* Golden Bks.) Random Hse. Children's Bks.

—Nine Disney Classics (Disney Classic) Golden Books. 2018. (Little Golden Book Ser.). (ENG.). 224p. (J). (-k). 12.99 *(978-0-7364-3788-2(6),* Golden/Disney) Random Hse. Children's Bks.

—Numbers, Letters, & More! (PAW Patrol) Golden Books. 2017. (ENG.). 64p. (J). (gr. -1-2). pap. 6.99 *(978-1-5247-6930-7(4),* Golden Bks.) Random Hse. Children's Bks.

—The Official Ninja Turtle Handbook (Teenage Mutant Ninja Turtles) Golden Books. 2014. (ENG.). 64p. (J). (gr. 2-4). pap. 6.99 *(978-0-553-50768-3(0),* Random Hse. Bks. for Young Readers) Random Hse. Children's Bks.

—On the Ball! Golden Books. Chlebowski, Rachel. 2016. (ENG.). 128p. (J). (gr. -1-2). pap. 7.99 *(978-0-399-55494-0(7),* Golden Bks.) Random Hse. Children's Bks.

—One Sparkly Christmas (Shimmer & Shine) Golden Books. 2016. (ENG.). 64p. (J). (gr. -1-2). pap. 4.99 *(978-0-399-55298-4(7),* Golden Bks.) Random Hse. Children's Bks.

—Oscar's Book (Sesame Street) Golden Books. 2018. (Little Golden Book Ser.). (ENG.). 24p. (J). (-k). 4.99 *(978-0-525-57840-6(4),* Golden Bks.) Random Hse. Children's Bks.

—Paint with Peppa! (Peppa Pig) Golden Books. 2019. (ENG.). 128p. (J). (gr. -1-2). pap. 7.99 *(978-0-593-11890-0(1),* Golden Bks.) Random Hse. Children's Bks.

—PAW Patrol Awesome Sticker Collection (PAW Patrol) Golden Books. 2017. (ENG.). 64p. (J). (gr. -1-2). pap. 12.99 *(978-1-5247-1682-0(0),* Golden Bks.) Random Hse. Children's Bks.

—PAW Patrol LGB Collection (PAW Patrol) Golden Books. 2019. (Little Golden Book Ser.). (ENG.). 176p. (J). (gr. -1-2). 12.99 *(978-0-525-64796-6(1),* Golden Bks.) Random Hse. Children's Bks.

—PAW Patrol Little Golden Book Favorites, Volume 2 (PAW Patrol) Golden Books. 2018. (Little Golden Book Ser.). (ENG.). 80p. (J). (-k). 7.99 *(978-1-5247-7272-7(0),* Golden Bks.) Random Hse. Children's Bks.

—PAW Patrol Super Sticker Fun! (Paw Patrol) Golden Books. 2018. (ENG.). 48p. (J). (gr. -1-2). pap. 9.99 *(978-0-525-57788-1(2),* Golden Bks.) Random Hse. Children's Bks.

—Peeps Full-Color Activity Book (Peeps) Golden Books. 2017. (ENG.). 48p. (J). (gr. -1-2). pap. 5.99 *(978-1-5247-1909-8(9),* Golden Bks.) Random Hse. Children's Bks.

Golden Books. Peppa Pig: My First Coloring Book (Peppa Pig) Golden Books. 2020. (ENG.). 192p. (J). (— 1). pap. 9.99 ***(978-0-593-30852-3(2),*** Golden Bks.) Random Hse. Children's Bks.

—Peppa Pig Paper Doll Book (Peppa Pig) Golden Books. 2020. (ENG.). 24p. (J). (gr. -1-2). pap. 9.99 ***(978-0-593-12768-1(4),*** Golden Bks.) Random Hse. Children's Bks.

Golden Books. Peppa Pig Super Sticker Book (Peppa Pig) Golden Books. 2019. (ENG.). 64p. (J). (gr. -1-2). pap. 12.99 *(978-0-593-11893-1(6),* Golden Bks.) Random Hse. Children's Bks.

—Peppa's Colorful World (Peppa Pig) Golden Books. 2019. (ENG.). 128p. (J). (gr. -1-2). pap. 9.99 *(978-0-593-11891-7(X),* Golden Bks.) Random Hse. Children's Bks.

—Peppa's Happy Halloween! (Peppa Pig) Golden Books. 2019. (ENG.). 48p. (J). (gr. -1-2). pap. 5.99 *(978-0-593-11846-7(4),* Golden Bks.) Random Hse. Children's Bks.

—Pet in the City. Golden Books. Chlebowski, Rachel. 2016. (ENG.). 48p. (J). (gr. -1-2). pap. 4.99 *(978-0-399-55489-6(0),* Golden Bks.) Random Hse. Children's Bks.

—Plank-Ton's Big Plan! Golden Books. movie tie-in ed. 2015. (ENG.). 48p. (J). (gr. -1-2). pap. 6.99 *(978-0-553-50827-7(X),* Golden Bks.) Random Hse. Children's Bks.

—Power Play! (DC Super Hero Girls) Golden Books. 2017. (ENG.). 24p. (J). (gr. 1-4). pap. 9.99 *(978-1-5247-6394-7(2),* Golden Bks.) Random Hse. Children's Bks.

—Pump up the Volume (DreamWorks Trolls World Tour) Golden Books. 2020. (ENG.). 32p. (J). (gr. -1-2). pap. 9.99 *(978-0-593-12783-4(8),* Golden Bks.) Random Hse. Children's Bks.

—Puppy Love! (Bubble Guppies) Golden Books. 2012. (ENG.). 32p. (J). (gr. -1-2). pap. 3.99 *(978-0-307-98197-4(5),* Golden Bks.) Random Hse. Children's Bks.

—Pups Stick Together! (PAW Patrol) Golden Books. 2018. (ENG.). 64p. (J). (gr. -1-2). pap. 5.99 *(978-1-5247-6877-5(4),* Golden Bks.) Random Hse. Children's Bks.

—Puptacular Rescues! (Paw Patrol) Golden Books. 2016. (ENG.). 224p. (J). (gr. -1-2). pap. 5.99 *(978-0-553-53905-9(1),* Golden Bks.) Random Hse. Children's Bks.

—Race Across Gotham City. Golden Books. 2016. (Big Golden Book Ser.). (ENG.). 48p. (J). (-k). 9.99 *(978-0-399-55013-3(5),* Golden Bks.) Random Hse. Children's Bks.

—Rainbow Adventures! (Top Wing) Golden Books. 2020. (ENG.). 128p. (J). (gr. -1-2). pap. 7.99 *(978-0-593-12190-0(2),* Golden Bks.) Random Hse. Children's Bks.

Golden Books. Rainbow Riders! (Corn & Peg) Golden Books. 2020. (ENG.). 128p. (J). (gr. -1-2). pap. 7.99 ***(978-0-593-12429-1(4),*** Golden Bks.) Random Hse. Children's Bks.

Golden Books. Ready to Roll! (Paw Patrol) Golden Books. 2015. (ENG.). 64p. (J). (gr. -1-2). pap. 9.99 *(978-0-553-50795-9(8),* Golden Bks.) Random Hse. Children's Bks.

—Really Spaced Out! (Teenage Mutant Ninja Turtles) Golden Books. 2016. (Little Golden Book Ser.). (ENG.). 24p. (J). (-k). 4.99 *(978-1-101-93694-8(0),* Golden Bks.) Random Hse. Children's Bks.

Golden Books. The Rise of Skywalker (Star Wars) Golden Books. 2020. (Little Golden Book Ser.). (ENG.). 24p. (J). (-k). 4.99 ***(978-0-7364-4076-9(3),*** Golden Bks.) Random Hse. Children's Bks.

Golden Books. Ruff-Ruff Rescues! (Paw Patrol) Golden Books. 2015. (ENG.). 128p. (J). (gr. -1-2). pap. 9.99 *(978-0-553-52080-4(6),* Golden Bks.) Random Hse. Children's Bks.

—Rusty Rivets Super Sticker Fun! Golden Books. 2018. (ENG.). 48p. (J). (gr. -1-2). pap. 9.99 *(978-1-5247-7243-7(7),* Golden Bks.) Random Hse. Children's Bks.

Golden Books. Santa's Toy Shop Little Golden Board Book (Disney Classic) Golden Books. 2020. (ENG.). 26p. (J). (-k). bds. 7.99 ***(978-0-7364-4111-7(5),*** Golden/Disney) Random Hse. Children's Bks.

Golden Books. SCOOB! Best Friends Activity Book (Scooby-Doo) Golden Books. 2020. (ENG.). 48p. (J). (gr. -1-2). pap. 6.99 *(978-0-593-17868-3(8),* Random Hse. Bks. for Young Readers) Random Hse. Children's Bks.

—Scooby-Doo & the Pirate Treasure (Scooby-Doo) Golden Books. 2020. (Little Golden Book Ser.). (ENG.). 24p. (J). (-k). 4.99 *(978-0-593-17869-0(6),* Golden Bks.) Random Hse. Children's Bks.

—Shimmer & Shine Awesome Sticker Collection (Shimmer & Shine) Golden Books. 2017. (4 Color Plus 1,000 Stickers Ser.). (ENG.). 64p. (J). (gr. -1-2). pap. 12.99 *(978-1-5247-1680-6(4),* Golden Bks.) Random Hse. Children's Bks.

—Shimmer & Shine Little Golden Book Favorites (Shimmer & Shine) Golden Books. 2017. (ENG.). 80p. (J). (gr. -1-2). 7.99 *(978-1-5247-1720-9(7),* Random Hse. Bks. for Young Readers) Random Hse. Children's Bks.

—Small & Mighty! Golden Books. 2019. (Little Golden Book Ser.). (ENG.). 24p. (J). (-k). 4.99 *(978-1-9848-5193-2(4),* Golden Bks.) Random Hse. Children's Bks.

—Smiles & Giggles (Peppa Pig) Golden Books. 2019. (ENG.). 48p. (J). (gr. -1-2). pap. 4.99 *(978-0-593-11838-2(3),* Golden Bks.) Random Hse. Children's Bks.

—Snoopy & Friends. Golden Books. 2015. (Little Golden Book Ser.). (ENG.). 24p. (J). (gr. -1-1). 4.99 *(978-1-101-93515-6(4),* Golden Bks.) Random Hse. Children's Bks.

—Snow Wonder! (Frosty the Snowman) Golden Books. 2013. (ENG.). 128p. (J). (gr. -1-2). pap. 7.99 *(978-0-385-37179-7(9),* Golden Bks.) Random Hse. Children's Bks.

—Sparkle with Love! (Shimmer & Shine) Golden Books. 2016. (ENG.). 64p. (J). (gr. -1-2). pap. 4.99 *(978-0-399-55791-0(1),* Golden Bks.) Random Hse. Children's Bks.

—SpongeBob SquarePants 400th Episode Big Golden Book (SpongeBob SquarePants) Golden Books. 2017. (Big Golden Book Ser.). (ENG.). 32p. (J). (gr. -1-2). 9.99 *(978-1-5247-1430-7(5),* Golden Bks.) Random Hse. Children's Bks.

—SpongeBob's Best Days! (SpongeBob SquarePants) Golden Books. 2010. (ENG.). 224p. (J). (gr. -1-2). pap. 6.99 *(978-0-375-86351-6(6),* Golden Bks.) Random Hse. Children's Bks.

—Star Wars Little Golden Book Collection (Star Wars) Golden Books. 2016. (ENG.). 176p. (J). (-k). 12.99 *(978-0-7364-3609-0(X),* Golden Bks.) Random Hse. Children's Bks.

—Starships, Speeders & Space Stations. Golden Books. 2019. (Little Golden Book Ser.). (ENG.). 24p. (J). (-k). 4.99 *(978-1-9848-4833-8(X),* Golden Bks.) Random Hse. Children's Bks.

—Start Your Engines! (Bubble Guppies) Golden Books. 2015. (ENG.). 48p. (J). (gr. -1-2). pap. 4.99 *(978-0-553-49764-9(2),* Golden Bks.) Random Hse. Children's Bks.

—Stick Together! (Rusty Rivets) Golden Books. 2017. (ENG.). 64p. (J). (gr. -1-2). pap. 9.99 *(978-1-5247-2071-1(2),* Golden Bks.) Random Hse. Children's Bks.

—Sticker Celebration! (Nickelodeon) Golden Books. 2015. (ENG.). 64p. (J). (gr. -1-2). pap. 9.99 *(978-0-553-52271-6(X),* Golden Bks.) Random Hse. Children's Bks.

Golden Books. Sticker Magic! (Butterbean's Cafe) Golden Books. 2020. (ENG.). 32p. (J). (gr. -1-2). pap. 9.99 ***(978-0-593-17273-5(6),*** Golden Bks.) Random Hse. Children's Bks.

Golden Books. Teenage Mutant Ninja Turtles: Out of the Shadows. Golden Books. 2016. (ENG.). 48p. (J). (gr. -1-2). pap. 4.99 *(978-1-101-94030-3(1),* Golden Bks.) Random Hse. Children's Bks.

—Teenage Mutant Ninja Turtles Holiday. Golden Books. 2016. (Big Golden Book Ser.). (ENG.). 32p. (J). (gr. -1-2). 9.99 *(978-0-399-55119-2(0),* Golden Bks.) Random Hse. Children's Bks.

—Teenage Mutant Ninja Turtles Little Golden Book Favorites (Teenage Mutant Ninja Turtles) Golden Books. 2016. (Little Golden Book Favorites Ser.). (ENG.). 80p. (J). (-k). 7.99 *(978-0-399-55359-2(2),* Golden Bks.) Random Hse. Children's Bks.

—Toca Life Doodle Book (Toca Boca) Golden Books. 2018. (Toca Boca Ser.). (ENG.). 96p. (J). (gr. 1-4). pap. 12.99 *(978-1-5247-7078-5(7),* Random Hse. Bks. for Young Readers) Random Hse. Children's Bks.

—Toca Life Sticker Collection (Toca Boca) Golden Books. 2018. (Toca Boca Ser.). (ENG.). 64p. (J). (gr. 1-4). pap. 14.99 *(978-1-5247-7077-8(9),* Random Hse. Bks. for Young Readers) Random Hse. Children's Bks.

—Troll Time! Golden Books. 2015. (ENG.). 48p. (J). (gr. -1-2). pap. 4.99 *(978-0-385-38769-9(5),* Golden Bks.) Random Hse. Children's Bks.

—Trolls Paper Doll Playset. Golden Books. 2017. (ENG.). 24p. (J). (gr. 1-4). pap. 9.99 *(978-1-5247-6396-1(9),* Golden Bks.) Random Hse. Children's Bks.

—The World of Barbie. Golden Books. 50th anniv. ed. 2012. (Little Golden Book Ser.). (ENG.). 24p. (J). (gr. -1-2). 4.99 *(978-0-307-98090-8(1),* Golden Bks.) Random Hse. Children's Bks.

Golden Books. 150 Things to Make & Do with Peppa (Peppa Pig) Golden Books. 2020. (ENG.). 160p. (J). (gr. -1-2). pap. 15.99 ***(978-0-593-37406-1(1),*** Golden Bks.) Random Hse. Children's Bks.

Golden Books & Aikins, David. Umi Egg Hunt (Team Umizoomi) Golden Books. 2013. (ENG.). 32p. (J). (gr. -1-2). pap. 3.99 *(978-0-307-98211-7(4),* Golden Bks.) Random Hse. Children's Bks.

Golden Books & Batson, Alan. Ghostbusters/Ghostbusters 2016 Big Golden Book. Sazaklis, John. 2016. (Big Golden Book Ser.). (ENG.). 48p. (J). (gr. -1-2). 9.99 *(978-1-5247-1487-1(9),* Golden Bks.) Random Hse. Children's Bks.

—I Am Belle (Disney Beauty & the Beast) Golden Books & Posner-Sanchez, Andrea. 2017. (Little Golden Book Ser.). (ENG.). 24p. (J). (-k). 4.99 *(978-0-7364-3905-3(6),* Golden/Disney) Random Hse. Children's Bks.

Golden Books & Cartobaleno Staff. Magical Manners! (Shimmer & Shine) Tillworth, Mary. 2019. (Little Golden Book Ser.). (ENG.). 24p. (J). (-k). 4.99 *(978-1-5247-7246-8(1),* Golden Bks.) Random Hse. Children's Bks.

Golden Books & Cespedes-Alicea, Marcela. Halloween Tricks & Treats! (Nella the Princess Knight) James, Hollis. 2018. (ENG.). 22p. (J). (-k). bds. 6.99 *(978-0-525-57769-0(6),* Random Hse. Bks. for Young Readers) Random Hse. Children's Bks.

Golden Books & Chen, Helen. Wreck-It Ralph 2 Little Golden Book (Disney Wreck-It Ralph 2) Golden Books & Parent, Nancy. 2018. (Little Golden Book Ser.). (ENG.). 24p. (J). (-k). 4.99 *(978-0-7364-3845-2(9),* Golden/Disney) Random Hse. Children's Bks.

Golden Books & Flowers, Luke. Cupcake Catapult! (Rusty Rivets) Berrios, Frank. 2017. (Little Golden Book Ser.). (ENG.). 24p. (J). (-k). 4.99 *(978-1-5247-6540-8(6),* Golden Bks.) Random Hse. Children's Bks.

Golden Books & Jackson, Mike. Marshall to the Rescue! (Paw Patrol) Golden Books. 2016. (Big Golden Book Ser.). (ENG.). 32p. (J). (gr. -1-2). 9.99 *(978-1-101-93847-8(1),* Golden Bks.) Random Hse. Children's Bks.

Golden Books & Kennett, Chris. Aliens, Creatures, & Beasts. Thomas, Richard & Macri, Thomas. 2018. (Big Golden Book Ser.). (ENG.). 48p. (J). (gr. -1-2). 10.99 *(978-0-7364-3691-5(X),* Golden Bks.) Random Hse. Children's Bks.

Golden Books & Lovett, Nate. Howl for Halloween! (PAW Patrol) Golden Books. 2016. (Big Golden Book Ser.). (ENG.). 32p. (J). (gr. -1-2). 9.99 *(978-0-399-55873-3(X),* Golden Bks.) Random Hse. Children's Bks.

Golden Books & Meurer, Caleb. SpongeBob Squarepants Movie Tie-In. Golden Books. 2015. (Little Golden Book Ser.). (ENG.). 24p. (J). (-k). 4.99 *(978-0-553-49775-5(8),* Golden Bks.) Random Hse. Children's Bks.

Golden Books & Persico, Zoe. Rainbow Dash Reading Rainboom! May, Tallulah. 2018. (Little Golden Book Ser.). (ENG.). 24p. (J). (-k). 4.99 *(978-0-525-57789-8(0),* Golden Bks.) Random Hse. Children's Bks.

—Twilight Sparkle: Best Aunt Ever! (My Little Pony) Sisler, Celeste & May, Tallulah. 2017. (Little Golden Book Ser.). (ENG.). 24p. (J). (-k). 4.99 *(978-1-5247-6962-8(2),* Golden Bks.) Random Hse. Children's Bks.

Golden Books & Pixel Mouse House Staff. Monster in the Forest! (Blaze & the Monster Machines) Golden Books & Chlebowski, Rachel. 2016. (ENG.). 64p. (J). (gr. -1-2). pap. 4.99 *(978-1-101-93700-6(9),* Golden Bks.) Random Hse. Children's Bks.

Golden Books & Random House Staff. Jurassic World. Golden Books & Chlebowski, Rachel. 2018. (ENG.). 48p. (J). (gr. -1-2). pap. 5.99 *(978-0-525-58086-7(7)*, Random Hse. Bks. for Young Readers) Random Hse. Children's Bks.

—Ninja Challenges! (Rise of the Teenage Mutant Ninja Turtles) Golden Books & Random House Staff. 2019. (ENG.). 48p. (J). (gr. -1-2). pap. 8.99 *(978-0-525-64858-1(5)*, Random Hse. Bks. for Young Readers) Random Hse. Children's Bks.

Golden Books Staff. Barbie: A Fairy Secret. Man-Kong, Mary. 2011. (Little Golden Book Ser.). (ENG.). 24p. (J). (gr. -1-2). 3.99 *(978-0-375-86540-4(3)*, Golden Bks.) Random Hse. Children's Bks.

—Barbie & the Diamond Castle. Man-Kong, Mary. 2008. (Pictureback(R) Ser.). (ENG.). 24p. (J). (gr. -1-2). pap. 3.99 *(978-0-375-87505-2(0)*, Golden Bks.) Random Hse. Children's Bks.

—Barbie in a Mermaid Tale. Man-Kong, Mary. 2010. (Pictureback(R) Ser.). (ENG.). 16p. (J). (gr. -1-2). pap. 3.99 *(978-0-375-85735-5(4)*, Random Hse. Bks. for Young Readers) Random Hse. Children's Bks.

—The Courageous Captain America. Wrecks, Billy. 2016. (Little Golden Book Ser.). (ENG.). 24p. (J). (gr. -1-k). 4.99 *(978-0-307-93050-7(5)*, Golden Bks.) Random Hse. Children's Bks.

—Day of the Diesels. Awdry, Wilbert V. 2012. (Little Golden Book Ser.). (ENG.). 24p. (J). (gr. k-k). 4.99 *(978-0-307-92989-1(2)*, Golden Bks.) Random Hse. Children's Bks.

Golden Books Staff, et al. Dinosaurs A to Z. Posner-Sanchez, Andrea. 2011. (ENG.). 28p. (J). (gr. -1 — 1). bds. 11.99 *(978-0-375-87143-6(8)*, Random Hse. Bks. for Young Readers) Random Hse. Children's Bks.

Golden Books Staff. Egg in the Hole. Scarry, Richard. 2011. (ENG.). 20p. (J). (gr. k — 1). bds. 8.99 *(978-0-375-86291-5(9)*, Golden Bks.) Random Hse. Children's Bks.

—A Fin-Tastic Journey! Man-Kong, Mary. 2012. (ENG.). 48p. (J). (gr. k-k). pap. 3.99 *(978-0-307-92978-5(7)*, Golden Bks.) Random Hse. Children's Bks.

—Hero of the Rails (Thomas & Friends) Awdry, W. 2010. (Little Golden Book Ser.). (ENG.). 24p. (J). (gr. -1-k). 4.99 *(978-0-375-85950-2(0)*, Golden Bks.) Random Hse. Children's Bks.

Golden Books Staff, et al. High Voltage! (Marvel: Spider-Man) Berrios, Frank. 2016. (Little Golden Book Ser.). (ENG.). 24p. (J). (-k). 4.99 *(978-0-385-37427-9(5)*, Golden Bks.) Random Hse. Children's Bks.

Golden Books Staff. Misty Island Rescue. Awdry, W. 2011. (Little Golden Book Ser.). (ENG.). 24p. (J). (gr. -1-k). 4.99 *(978-0-375-87212-9(4)*, Golden Bks.) Random Hse. Children's Bks.

—My Fabulous Friends! Man-Kong, Mary. 2009. (Pictureback(R) Ser.). (ENG.). 16p. (J). (gr. -1-2). pap. 3.99 *(978-0-375-85789-8(3)*, Random Hse. Bks. for Young Readers) Random Hse. Children's Bks.

—A Perfect Christmas (Barbie) Man-Kong, Mary & Tillworth, Mary. 2011. (Pictureback(R) Ser.). (ENG.). 16p. (J). (gr. -1-2). pap. 3.99 *(978-0-375-87363-8(5)*, Random Hse. Bks. for Young Readers) Random Hse. Children's Bks.

—Princess Charm School (Barbie) Man-Kong, Mary & Tillworth, Mary. 2011. (Little Golden Book Ser.). (ENG.). 24p. (J). (gr. -1-2). 3.99 *(978-0-375-87361-4(9)*, Golden Bks.) Random Hse. Children's Bks.

—Rolling on the Rails. Awdry, Wilbert V. 2011. (Thomas & Friends Ser.). (ENG.). 12p. (J). (gr. k — 1). bds. 8.99 *(978-0-375-87304-1(X)*, Golden Bks.) Random Hse. Children's Bks.

—Sensational Style Barbie. Man-Kong, Mary. 2010. (ENG.). 48p. (J). (gr. -1-2). pap. 6.99 *(978-0-375-86490-2(3)*, Golden Bks.) Random Hse. Children's Bks.

—Snowman Surprise (Disney Junior: Doc Mcstuffins) Posner-Sanchez, Andrea & Random House Staff. 2013. (Little Golden Book Ser.). (ENG.). 24p. (J). (-k). 4.99 *(978-0-7364-3142-2(X)*, Golden/Disney) Random Hse. Children's Bks.

—Somebunny Special (SpongeBob SquarePants) Carbone, Courtney. 2013. (ENG.). 48p. (J). (gr. -1-2). pap. 3.99 *(978-0-307-98104-2(5)*, Golden Bks.) Random Hse. Children's Bks.

—Tales of Discovery. Awdry, Wilbert V. 2011. (ENG.). 30p. (J). (gr. k — 1). bds. 11.99 *(978-0-375-87192-4(6)*, Golden Bks.) Random Hse. Children's Bks.

—Thomas' Colorful Ride (Thomas & Friends) Awdry, Wilbert V. & Awdry, Rev. W. 2011. (ENG.). 128p. (J). (gr. -1-2). pap. 7.99 *(978-0-375-87248-8(5)*, Golden Bks.) Random Hse. Children's Bks.

—Thumbelina. Man-Kong, Mary. 2009. (Barbie 8 X 8 Ser.). (ENG.). 16p. (J). (gr. -1-1). 16.19 *(978-0-375-84596-3(8))* Random House Publishing Group.

—Toy Story Little Golden Book Favorites. Random House Disney Staff. 2019. (Little Golden Book Ser.). (ENG.). 80p. (J). (gr. -1-k). 7.99 *(978-0-7364-2752-4(X)*, Golden/Disney) Random Hse. Children's Bks.

Golden Books Staff, et al. Trolls Big Golden Book (DreamWorks Trolls) Golden Books Staff. 2016. (Big Golden Book Ser.). 48p. (J). (gr. -1-2). 9.99 *(978-0-399-55895-5(0)*, Golden Bks.) Random Hse. Children's Bks.

Golden Books Staff. Beautiful Barbie. Golden Books Staff. 2009. (ENG.). 64p. (J). (gr. -1-2). pap. 12.99 *(978-0-375-85553-5(X)*, Golden Bks.) Random Hse. Children's Bks.

—Bunny's Garden. Golden Books Staff. 2010. 12p. (J). (gr. -1 — 1). 7.99 *(978-0-375-85788-1(5)*, Golden Bks.) Random Hse. Children's Bks.

—Cars. Golden Books Staff. 2009. (ENG.). 16p. (J). (gr. -1-2). 5.99 *(978-0-375-84597-0(6)*, Golden Bks.) Random Hse. Children's Bks.

—Catch a Wave! Golden Books Staff. 2009. (ENG.). 48p. (J). (gr. -1-2). pap. 3.99 *(978-0-375-85107-0(0)*, Golden Bks.) Random Hse. Children's Bks.

—Easter Deliveries. Golden Books Staff. 2010. 48p. (J). (gr. -1-2). pap. 3.99 *(978-0-375-85747-8(8)*, Golden Bks.) Random Hse. Children's Bks.

—Let's Get Happy! Golden Books Staff. 2016. (ENG.). 64p. (J). (gr. -1-2). pap. 9.99 *(978-1-101-93848-5(X)*, Golden Bks.) Random Hse. Children's Bks.

—A Need for Speed! (Blaze & the Monster Machines) Golden Books Staff. 2016. (ENG.). 64p. (J). (gr. -1-2). pap. 9.99 *(978-0-553-53890-8(X)*, Golden Bks.) Random Hse. Children's Bks.

—Trainloads of Fun. Golden Books Staff. 2010. (ENG.). 224p. (J). (gr. -1-2). pap. 5.99 *(978-0-375-86363-9(X)*, Golden Bks.) Random Hse. Children's Bks.

Golden Books Staff & Aikins, Dave. Show Your Love! (Shimmer & Shine) Tillworth, Mary. 2016. (Big Golden Book Ser.). (ENG.). 32p. (J). (gr. -1-2). 9.99 *(978-1-5247-1603-5(0)*, Golden Bks.) Random Hse. Children's Bks.

—SpongeBob for President! (SpongeBob SquarePants) Golden Books Staff. 2012. (Color Plus Chunky Crayons Ser.). (ENG.). 48p. (J). (gr. -1-2). pap. 3.99 *(978-0-307-97634-5(3)*, Golden Bks.) Random Hse. Children's Bks.

Golden Books Staff & An, Jiyoung. I Can Be... Anything I Want to Be. Man-Kong, Mary. 2011. (ENG.). 32p. (J). (gr. -1-2). pap. 5.49 *(978-0-375-87260-0(4)*, Golden Bks.) Random Hse. Children's Bks.

Golden Books Staff & Duarte, Pamela. Pop Star Dreams (Barbie) Man-Kong, Mary. 2013. (ENG.). 48p. (J). (gr. -1-2). pap. 3.99 *(978-0-449-81611-0(7)*, Golden Bks.) Random Hse. Children's Bks.

—The Sweetest Halloween (Barbie) Man-Kong, Mary. 2012. (Glow-In-the-Dark Sticker Book Ser.). (ENG.). 48p. (J). (gr. -1-2). pap. 3.99 *(978-0-307-93115-3(3)*, Golden Bks.) Random Hse. Children's Bks.

Golden Books Staff & Durk, Jim. Up, up & Away! Awdry, Wilbert V. 2013. (ENG.). 48p. (J). (gr. -1-1). pap. 3.99 *(978-0-307-98199-8(1)*, Golden Bks.) Random Hse. Children's Bks.

Golden Books Staff & Hand, Jason. Disney Planes. RH Disney Staff & Hall, Klay. 2013. (Little Golden Book Ser.). (ENG.). 24p. (J). (-k). 4.99 *(978-0-7364-2974-0(3)*, Golden/Disney) Random Hse. Children's Bks.

Golden Books Staff & Kellman, Craig. Secret Life of Pets. Lewman, David. 2016. (Big Golden Book Ser.). (ENG.). 32p. (J). (gr. -1-2). 9.99 *(978-0-399-55477-3(7)*, Golden Bks.) Random Hse. Children's Bks.

Golden Books Staff & Laguna, Fabio. Rainbow Party! Golden Books Staff. 2016. (ENG.). 128p. (J). (gr. -1-2). pap. 7.99 *(978-0-399-55902-0(7)*, Golden Bks.) Random Hse. Children's Bks.

Golden Books Staff & Lambe, Steve. Green vs. Mean (Teenage Mutant Ninja Turtles) Golden Books Staff & Smith, Geof. 2015. (Little Golden Book Ser.). (ENG.). 24p. (J). (-k). 4.99 *(978-1-101-93465-4(4)*, Golden Bks.) Random Hse. Children's Bks.

—Mighty Monster Machines (Blaze & the Monster Machines) Golden Books Staff. 2015. (Little Golden Book Ser.). (ENG.). 24p. (J). (-k). 4.99 *(978-0-553-52456-7(9)*, Golden Bks.) Random Hse. Children's Bks.

Golden Books Staff & Lovett, Nate. Puppy Hugs & Kisses! Golden Books Staff. 2016. (ENG.). 64p. (J). (gr. -1-2). pap. 4.99 *(978-0-399-55878-8(0)*, Golden Bks.) Random Hse. Children's Bks.

—Puppy Power! (Paw Patrol) Golden Books Staff. 2014. (ENG.). 48p. (J). (gr. -1-2). pap. 3.99 *(978-0-385-38445-2(9)*, Golden Bks.) Random Hse. Children's Bks.

Golden Books Staff & Lovett, Nathaniel. Rubble on the Double! (Paw Patrol) Golden Books Staff. 2016. (ENG.). 48p. (J). (gr. -1-2). pap. 4.99 *(978-1-101-93699-3(1)*, Golden Bks.) Random Hse. Children's Bks.

Golden Books Staff & Random House Staff. Enter the Lair (Teenage Mutant Ninja Turtles) Golden Books Staff & Random House Staff. 2013. (Pictureback(R) Ser.). (ENG.). 16p. (J). (gr. -1-2). pap. 4.99 *(978-0-449-81385-0(1)*, Random Hse. Bks. for Young Readers) Random Hse. Children's Bks.

Golden Books Staff & Riley, Kellee. I Can Be a Teacher (Barbie) Man-Kong, Mary. 2011. (Step into Reading Ser.). (ENG.). 32p. (J). (gr. -1-1). pap. 4.99 *(978-0-375-86927-3(1)*, Random Hse. Bks. for Young Readers) Random Hse. Children's Bks.

Golden Books Staff & Sciarrone, Claudio. Half-Shell Heroes! (Teenage Mutant Ninja Turtles) Carbone, Courtney. 2013. (ENG.). 48p. (J). (gr. -1-2). pap. 3.99 *(978-0-307-98233-9(5)*, Golden Bks.) Random Hse. Children's Bks.

Golden Books Staff, jt. illus. see Random House Editors.

Golden Books Staff, jt. illus. see Scarry, Richard.

Golden Books Staff, jt. illus. see Walt Disney Company Staff.

Golden, Christopher. Omnibus, 7 vols., Vol. 4. Golden, Christopher. 2008. (Buffy the Vampire Slayer Ser.). (ENG.). 408p. pap. 24.95 *(978-1-59307-968-0(0))* Dark Horse Comics.

Golden, Emily. Let's Draw Bugs & Critters with Crayola ®! Allen, Kathy. 2019. (Let's Draw with Crayola ®! Ser.). (ENG.). 32p. (J). (gr. -1-3). pap. 6.99 *(978-1-5415-4607-3(5)*, Lerner Pubns.) Lerner Publishing Group.

—Let's Draw Bugs & Critters with Crayola®! Allen, Kathy. 2019. (Let's Draw with Crayola ®! Ser.). (ENG.). 32p. (J). (gr. -1-3). 27.99 *(978-1-5415-1101-9(8)*, Lerner Pubns.) Lerner Publishing Group.

—Let's Draw Robots with Crayola! Allen, Kathy. 2018. (Let's Draw with Crayola ®! Ser.). (ENG.). 32p. (J). (gr. -1-3). 27.99 *(978-1-5124-3296-1(2)*, Lerner Pubns.) Lerner Publishing Group.

Golden, Harriet. The Ugly Duckling & Other Fairy Tales. Andersen, Hans. ed. 2012. (Dover Children's Thrift Classics Ser.). (ENG.). 96p. (Orig.). (J). (gr. 3-8). pap. 3.00 *(978-0-486-27081-4(5))* Dover Pubns., Inc.

Golden, Jess. My Little Golden Book about Dogs. Houran, Lori Haskins. 2018. (Little Golden Book Ser.). 24p. (J). (-k). 4.99 *(978-0-399-55813-9(6)*, Golden Bks.) Random Hse. Children's Bks.

—Pilar's Worries. Sanchez, Victoria M. 2018. (ENG.). 32p. (J). 16.99 *(978-0-8075-6546-9(6)*, 807565466) Whitman, Albert & Co.

—Sam Visits the School Library. Rustad, Martha. 2017. (Cloverleaf Books (tm) — off to School Ser.). (ENG.). 24p. (J). (gr. k-2). lib. bdg. 25.32 *(978-1-5124-3938-0(X)*, 9781512439380, Millbrook Pr.) Lerner Publishing Group.

—Scuba Dog. Stephens, Ann Marie. 2016. (ENG.). 40p. (J). (gr. -1-3). 17.99 *(978-1-4998-0143-9(2))* Little Bee Books Inc.

—Snow Dog, Sand Dog. Singleton, Linda Joy. 2014. (AV2 Fiction Readalong Ser.: Vol. 150). (ENG.). (J). (gr. -1-2). lib. bdg. 34.28 *(978-1-4896-2377-5(9)*, AV2 by Weigl) Weigl Pubs., Inc.

—Soccer with Mom. Berrios, Frank. 2016. (Little Golden Book Ser.). 24p. (J). (-k). 4.99 *(978-0-553-53854-0(3)*, Golden Bks.) Random Hse. Children's Bks.

—The Twelve Days of Christmas in North Dakota. Salonen, Roxane Beauclair. 2018. (Twelve Days of Christmas in America Ser.). 22p. (J). (gr. k). bds. 7.95 *(978-1-4549-3091-4(8))* Sterling Publishing Co., Inc.

—The Wheels on the Tuk Tuk. Sehgal, Kabir & Sehgal, Surishtha. 2016. (ENG.). 40p. (J). (gr. -1-k). 18.99 *(978-1-4814-4831-4(5)*, Beach Lane Bks.) Beach Lane Bks.

Golden, Jessica. The Twelve Days of Christmas in North Dakota. Salonen, Roxane Beauclair. 2017. (Twelve Days of Christmas in America Ser.). 40p. (J). (gr. k). 12.95 *(978-1-4549-2008-3(4))* Sterling Publishing Co., Inc.

Golden, John Ashton. Numbering the Crime: Forensic Mathematics, 11 vols. McIntosh, Kenneth. 2007. (Crime Scene Club Ser.). 144p. (YA). (gr. 9-12). lib. bdg. 24.95 *(978-1-4222-0257-9(7))* Mason Crest.

—A Stranger's Voice: Forensic Speech Identification, 9 vols. McIntosh, Kenneth. 2007. (Crime Scene Club Ser.). 144p. (YA). (gr. 9-12). lib. bdg. 24.95 *(978-1-4222-0255-5(0))* Mason Crest.

—Things Fall Apart: Forensic Engineering, 10 vols. McIntosh, Kenneth. 2007. (Crime Scene Club Ser.). 144p. (YA). (gr. 9-12). lib. bdg. 24.95 *(978-1-4222-0256-2(9))* Mason Crest.

Golden, Kathleen M. Cleopatra's Big Birthday BBQ. Golden, Kathleen M. 2003. 18p. (J). (gr. -1-k). mass mkt. 14.95 *(978-0-9726418-0-7(7))* Happyland Media.

Golden, Lilly. See Mom Run. Thom, Kara Douglass. 2003. (ENG.). 32p. (J). 15.00 *(978-1-891369-40-7(7))* Breakaway Bks.

Golden, Rayna. Ali & the Magic Ball. Edwards, Wayne. 2009. 24p. pap. 12.50 *(978-1-60860-367-1(9)*, Eloquent Bks.) Strategic Book Publishing & Rights Agency (SBPRA).

Golden, Shyama. Llamanoes. Chronicle Books Staff. 2018. (ENG.). 28p. (J). (gr. -1-k). 12.99 *(978-1-4521-6371-0(5))* Chronicle Bks. LLC.

Goldfinger, Jennifer P. I Need Glasses. Thomas, Charlie. 2005. (Rookie Readers Ser.). (ENG.). 32p. (J). (gr. k-2). lib. bdg. 19.50 *(978-0-516-24863-9(4)*, Children's Pr.) Scholastic Library Publishing.

Goldfinger, Jennifer P. Hello, My Name Is Tiger. Goldfinger, Jennifer P. 2016. (ENG.). 40p. (J). (gr. -1-3). 17.99 *(978-0-06-239951-9(9))* HarperCollins Pubs.

Goldin, David. Baxter, the Pig Who Wanted to Be Kosher. Snyder, Laurel. 2010. (ENG.). 32p. (J). (gr. -1-2). 15.99 *(978-1-58246-315-5(8)*, Tricycle Pr.) Random Hse. Children's Bks.

Golding, J. C. A Bird's Day at Yaquina Head. Monroe, Guy. Monroe, Karol, ed. 2003. 52p. 7.95 *(978-0-9742443-0-3(9))* Monroe, Guy.

Goldman, Garnet. His Dogness Finds a Blue Heart. Underwood, Ralph Kim. 2004. 32p. (J). 16.95 *(978-0-89587-304-0(4))* Blair.

—The Wonderful World of Sparkle Girl & Doobins. Underwood, Kim. 2009. 48p. (J). pap. 16.95 *(978-0-89587-373-6(7))* Blair.

Goldman, Linda Sarah. From Pie Town to Yum Yum: Weird & Wacky Place Names Across the United States. Herman, Debbie. ed. 2011. (ENG.). 120p. (J). pap. 10.99 *(978-1-935279-79-2(3))* Kane Miller.

Goldner, Rita. Spring! Time to Build a Nest, a Story about Trumpeter Swans. Renner, Barbara. 2019. (ENG.). 48p. (J). (gr. k-4). pap. 14.95 *(978-0-9990586-3-3(0))* Renner Writes.

Golds, Alexandra Kimla. I Love My Mommy. Kimla, Lenka J. 2008. 22p. pap. 24.95 *(978-1-60703-126-0(4))* America Star Bks.

Goldsberry, Ryan. Create Your Own Secret Language: Invent Codes, Ciphers, Hidden Messages, & More. Peterson, David J. & Odd Dot. 2020. (ENG.). 144p. (J). pap. 12.99 *(978-1-250-22232-9(X)*, 900207987, Odd Dot) St. Martin's Pr.

Goldsborough, June. Dark As a Shadow. Lowery, Lawrence F. 2014. (I Wonder Why Ser.). (ENG.). 36p. (J). (gr. k-3). pap. 11.95 *(978-1-941316-06-1(9))* National Science Teachers Assn.

Goldsmith, Tom. Ben & Zip: Two Short Friends. Linden, Joanne. 2014. (ENG.). 32p. (J). (gr. -1-k). 16.95 *(978-1-936261-28-4(6))* Flashlight Pr.

—The Pocket Mommy. Eugster, Rachel. 2013. 32p. (J). (gr. -1-1). 16.95 *(978-1-77049-300-1(X)*, Tundra Bks.) Tundra Bks. CAN. Dist: Penguin Random Hse. LLC.

Goldsmith, Wallace. The Canterville Ghost: Annotated. Wilde, Oscar. 2019. (ENG.). 92p. (J). pap. 10.00 ***(978-1-6937-7701-1(0))*** Independently Published.

Goldsmith, William. Wildheart: The Daring Adventures of John Muir. Bertagna, Julie. 2019. (ENG.). 128p. (J). 17.99 *(978-1-930238-94-7(0))* Yosemite Conservancy.

Goldstein, A. Nancy. Behind the Bedroom Wall. Williams, Laura E. 2005. (Historical Fiction for Young Readers Ser.). (ENG.). 184p. (J). (gr. 3-7). per. 8.00 *(978-1-57131-658-5(2))* Milkweed Editions.

—Behind the Bedroom Wall. Williams, Laura E. 2006. 169p. (gr. -1-7). 17.45 *(978-0-7569-6389-7(3))* Perfection Learning Corp.

Goldstein, Lauren. A Peek under the Big Top. Beaule, Nancy. 2019. (Chompy & the Munchy Bunch Ser.: Vol. 5). (ENG.). 26p. (J). pap. 9.99 ***(978-1-6960-8909-8(3))*** Independently Published.

Goldstone, Bruce. Great Estimations. Goldstone, Bruce. rev. ed. 2006. (ENG.). 32p. (J). (gr. 2-5). 18.99 *(978-0-8050-7446-8(5)*, 900037959, Holt, Henry & Co. Bks. For Young Readers) Holt, Henry & Co.

—Great Estimations. Goldstone, Bruce. 2010. (ENG.). 32p. (J). (gr. 2-5). pap. 8.99 *(978-0-312-60887-3(X)*, 900065182) Square Fish.

—I See a Pattern Here. Goldstone, Bruce. 2015. (ENG.). 32p. (J). (gr. 2-5). 17.99 *(978-0-8050-9209-7(9)*, 900066056, Holt, Henry & Co. Bks. For Young Readers) Holt, Henry & Co.

—100 Ways to Celebrate 100 Days. Goldstone, Bruce. 2010. (ENG.). 48p. (J). (gr. -1-3). 16.99 *(978-0-8050-8997-4(7)*, 900058872, Holt, Henry & Co. Bks. For Young Readers) Holt, Henry & Co.

—100 Ways to Celebrate 100 Days. Goldstone, Bruce. 2013. (ENG.). 48p. (J). (gr. -1-3). 8.99 *(978-1-250-03369-7(1)*, 900120168) Square Fish.

Goldstone, Bruce, photos by. Awesome Autumn: All Kinds of Fall Facts & Fun. Goldstone, Bruce. 2012. (Season Facts & Fun Ser.). (ENG., 48p. (J). (gr. -1-3). 18.99 *(978-0-8050-9210-3(2)*, 900066057, Holt, Henry & Co. Bks. For Young Readers) Holt, Henry & Co.

Goldstrom, Robert. Dream Away. Durango, Julia & Trupiano, Katie Belle. 2011. (ENG.). 32p. (J). (gr. -1-3). 16.99 *(978-1-4169-8702-4(9)*, Simon & Schuster Bks. For Young Readers) Simon & Schuster Bks. For Young Readers.

Golen, Jessica. Smitty Moose, Petey & Me - Episode One, the Witch. Plourde, Paulette. l.t. ed. 2005. 32p. (J). per. 9.95 *(978-1-59879-038-2(2))* Lifevest Publishing, Inc.

Golert, Amanda. Kidpower Children's Safety Comics Color Edition: Use Your Power to Stay Safe! 2020. (ENG.). 78p. (J). pap. 20.00 ***(978-1-6523-6891-5(4))*** Independently Published.

Golert, Amanda. Kidpower Safety Comics: An Introduction to "People Safety" for Young Children Ages 3 to 10 & Their Adults. van der Zande, Irene. 2011. 44p. (J). pap. *(978-0-9796191-4-4(9))* van der Zande, Irene.

Goley, Jonathon & Alvarenga, Angela. It Starts with a Raindrop: Comienza con una Gota de Lluvia. Smith, Michael. 2016. (ENG & SPA.). 33p. (J). *(978-0-9973947-1-9(4))* East West Discovery Pr.

Goliger, Janet, photos by. I Need to Be SAFE I'm Worth It! How to Protect Your Child from Danger. Goliger, Janet. Bond, Amy, ed. 2006. 144p. (J). per. 19.95 *(978-0-9768273-2-0(8)*, 705-002, CLASS Publications) Children Learning Awareness, Safety & Self-Defense.

Golina-Sagetelian, Irina & Fontabona, Virginia. Mind-Boggling Maze Games. Phillips, Dave & Regan, Lisa. 2018. (ENG.). 96p. (J). (gr. 2-5). pap. 7.99 *(978-1-4380-1129-5(6)*, B.E.S. Publishing) Peterson's.

Golino, Mirto. The Little Chapel That Stood. Curtiss, A. B. l.t. ed. 2005. (ENG.). 36p. (J). (gr. -1-3). 18.95 *(978-0-932529-77-0(1))* Oldcastle Publishing.

Gollan, Stewart. I Want to Be a Cricketer. Carbon, Sally & Langer, Justin. 2008. 32p. (J). pap. 16.95 *(978-1-921361-24-1(7))* Fremantle Pr. AUS. Dist: Independent Pubs. Group.

Golliher, Bill & Vaughan, Jack. Webber Interactive WH Questions Level 2: Whcd22. 2006. (J). cd-rom 49.99 *(978-1-58650-647-6(1))* Super Duper Pubns.

Golliher, Bill, jt. illus. see Ink, Bruce.

Golondrina, Juanita. Barney the Boring Barumbus. Elliott Jr, Daryl. 2019. (ENG.). 26p. (J). pap. 9.99 ***(978-1-7043-8421-4(4))*** Independently Published.

Golubeva, Evgenia. As Quiet As a Mouse. Owen, Karen. 2019. (Early Bird Readers — Purple (Early Bird Stories (tm)) Ser.). (ENG.). 32p. (J). (gr. k-3). pap. 7.99 *(978-1-5415-7421-2(4)*, 9781541574212, Lerner Pubns.) Lerner Publishing Group.

—Shh ... Shh ... Shabbat. Marshall, Linda Elovitz. ed. 2016. (ENG.). 12p. (J). (gr. -1 — 1). E-Book 23.99 *(978-1-4677-9615-6(8))*; Vol. bds. 5.99 *(978-1-4677-5873-4(6)*, 9781467758734) Lerner Publishing Group. (Kar-Ben Publishing).

Golubeva, Evgenia. I'm NOT a Mouse! Golubeva, Evgenia. 2020. (Child's Play Library). 32p. (J). ***(978-1-78628-464-8(2))*** Child's Play International Ltd.

Golubeva, Evgeniia. As Quiet As a Mouse. Owen, Karen. 2019. (Early Bird Readers — Purple (Early Bird Stories (tm)) Ser.). (ENG.). 32p. (J). (gr. k-3). 27.99 *(978-1-5415-4224-2(X)*, 9781541542242, Lerner Pubns.) Lerner Publishing Group.

Gombert, Bobby. PageLand: A Story about Love & Sharing & Working Together. Hutchens, David. 2004. (gr. 4-8). 14.99 *(978-0-8054-2726-4(0))* B&H Publishing Group.

Gombinski, Rita, jt. illus. see Baker, Syd.

Gomer, William. I am Not a Flying Elephant Fish! A Children's Science Book on the Butterfly. Bronson, Cary. l.t. ed. 2004. 32p. (J). lib. bdg. 14.95 *(978-0-9746094-0-9(4))* Connect With Your Kid Bks.

Gomes, John. La Camada con Suerte: Cachorros de Lobo Rescatados de un Incendio Forestal, 1 vol. Curtis, Jennifer Keats. 2015. (ENG & SPA.). 32p. (J). (gr. 2-5). pap. 9.95 *(978-1-62855-720-6(6))* Arbordale Publishing.

Gomes, John. L' Histoire de Kali: le Sauvetage d'un Ourson Blanc Orphelin: (kali's Story: an Orphaned Polar Bear Rescue in French) Curtis, Jennifer Keats. Troff, Sophie, tr. 2019. (FRE.). 32p. (J). (gr. 2-3). 11.95 ***(978-1-64351-733-9(3))*** Arbordale Publishing.

Gomes, John. La Historia de Kali: El Rescate de un Oso Polar Huérfano. Curtis, Jennifer Keats. 2014.Tr. of Kali's Story: an Orphaned Polar Bear Rescue. (SPA.). 32p. (J). (gr. 1-4). pap. 11.95 *(978-1-62855-226-3(3))* Arbordale Publishing.

—The Lucky Litter: Wolf Pups Rescued from Wildfire, 1 vol. Curtis, Jennifer Keats. 2015. (ENG.). 32p. (J). (gr. 2-5). 17.95 *(978-1-62855-718-3(4))* Arbordale Publishing.

G

Gomes, John, photos by. Kali's Story: An Orphaned Polar Bear Rescue, 1 vol. Curtis, Jennifer Keats. 2014. (ENG., 32p. (J). (gr. 1-4). 17.95 *(978-1-62855-208-9(5))* Arbordale Publishing.
Gomes, Tania. The Mango Tree. Smith, Brooke. 2018. (ENG.). 42p. (J). 21.95 ***(978-0-578-41819-3(3))*** Wonder Storm Productions, LLC.
Gomes, Tania. The Tortoise & the Flair. Smith, Brooke. 2018. (ENG.). 38p. (J). pap. 11.48 *(978-1-9863-0720-8(4))* CreateSpace Independent Publishing Platform.
Gomes, Tania. The Tortoise & the Flair. Smith, Brooke. 2018. (ENG.). 38p. (J). (gr. 1-4). 21.95 ***(978-0-578-41824-7(X))*** Wonder Storm Productions, LLC.
Gomez. Daniela & the Pirate Girls. Isern, Susanna. 2020. (ENG.). 44p. (J). 16.95 *(978-84-17673-27-7(X))* NubeOcho Ediciones ESP. Dist: Consortium Bk. Sales & Distribution.
GOMEZ. Daniela Pirata. Isern, Susanna. 2018. (SPA.). 44p. (J). 16.95 *(978-84-17123-11-6(3))* NubeOcho Ediciones ESP. Dist: Consortium Bk. Sales & Distribution.
—Daniela the Pirate. Isern, Susanna. Dawlatly, Ben, tr. 2018. (ENG.). 44p. (J). 16.95 *(978-84-17123-12-3(1))* NubeOcho Ediciones ESP. Dist: Consortium Bk. Sales & Distribution.
Gomez. Daniela y Las Chicas Pirata. Isern, Susanna. 2020. (SPA.). 44p. (J). 16.95 *(978-84-17673-26-0(1))* NubeOcho Ediciones ESP. Dist: Consortium Bk. Sales & Distribution.
—El Dedo en la Nariz. Merlan, Paula. 2019. (ENG.). 44p. (J). 16.95 *(978-84-17123-77-2(6))* NubeOcho Ediciones ESP. Dist: Consortium Bk. Sales & Distribution.
GOMEZ. Discover the Rain. Albo, Pablo. 2019. (ENG.). 36p. (J). 14.95 *(978-84-946551-9-7(1))* NubeOcho Ediciones ESP. Dist: Consortium Bk. Sales & Distribution.
—Erizo y Conejo - Descubriendo la Lluvia. Albo, Pablo. 2019. (SPA.). 36p. (J). 14.95 *(978-84-946551-8-0(3))* NubeOcho Ediciones ESP. Dist: Consortium Bk. Sales & Distribution.
—Erizo y Conejo. el Susto Del Viento (Junior Library Guild Selection) Albo, Pablo. 2017. (SPA.). 32p. (J). (gr. -1-k). 14.95 *(978-84-945971-6-9(7))* NubeOcho Ediciones ESP. Dist: Consortium Bk. Sales & Distribution.
—Erizo y Conejo. la Nube Cabezota. Albo, Pablo. 2017. (SPA.). 32p. (J). (gr. -1-k). 14.95 *(978-84-945971-8-3(3))* NubeOcho Ediciones ESP. Dist: Consortium Bk. Sales & Distribution.
Gomez. Federico & All His Families. Hernandez, Mili. 2020. (ENG.). 18p. (J). bds. 9.95 *(978-84-17673-56-7(3))* NubeOcho Ediciones ESP. Dist: Consortium Bk. Sales & Distribution.
—Federico y Sus Familias. Hernandez, Mili. 2020. (SPA.). 18p. (J). bds. 9.95 *(978-84-17673-48-2(2))* NubeOcho Ediciones ESP. Dist: Consortium Bk. Sales & Distribution.
GOMEZ. Hedgehog & Rabbit: the Scary Wind (Junior Library Guild Selection) Albo, Pablo. 2017. (ENG.). 32p. (J). (gr. -1-k). 14.95 *(978-84-945971-7-6(5))* NubeOcho Ediciones ESP. Dist: Consortium Bk. Sales & Distribution.
—Hedgehog & Rabbit: the Stubborn Cloud. Albo, Pablo. 2017. (ENG.). 32p. (J). (gr. -1-k). 14.95 *(978-84-945971-9-0(1))* NubeOcho Ediciones ESP. Dist: Consortium Bk. Sales & Distribution.
Gomez. I'm a Zcary Vampire. Andres, Jose Carlos. 2020. (ENG.). 40p. (J). 16.95 ***(978-84-17673-85-7(7))*** NubeOcho Ediciones ESP. Dist: Consortium Bk. Sales & Distribution.
Gomez, Ana. A Campfire Tale. Marsh, Sarah Glenn. 2018. (ENG.). 40p. (J). (gr. -1). 16.95 *(978-1-4549-1993-3(0))* Sterling Publishing Co., Inc.
Gómez, Ana. Fairness Comes First. Harimann, Sierra. 2016. 32p. (J). pap. *(978-1-338-03339-7(5))* Scholastic, Inc.
Gomez, Ana. Food Fight Fiesta: A Tale about la Tomatina. Kyle, Tracey. 2018. (ENG.). 32p. (J). (gr. k-3). 16.99 *(978-1-5107-3215-5(2)*, Sky Pony Pr.) Skyhorse Publishing Co., Inc.
Gómez, Ana. A Friend to Trust. Simon, Jenne. 2016. 32p. (J). pap. *(978-1-338-03337-3(9))* Scholastic, Inc.
Gomez, Bella. 5 Wild Numbers. words&pictures. 2018. (ENG.). 10p. (J). (gr. -1 — 1). bds. 14.95 ***(978-1-910277-60-7(6)***, Words & Pictures) Quarto Publishing Group UK GBR. Dist: Hachette Bk. Group.
Gomez, Blanca. Are We Still Friends? Horowitz, Ruth. 2017. 40p. (J). (gr. -1-3). 16.99 *(978-0-545-64521-8(2)*, Scholastic Pr.) Scholastic, Inc.
Gómez, Blanca. Cerca / Close. Herrera, Juan Felipe. 2019. (ENG & SPA.). 14p. (J). (-k). bds. 7.99 *(978-0-7636-9062-5(7))* Candlewick Pr.
—City Moon. Cole, Rachael. 2017. 40p. (J). (gr. -1-2). 17.99 *(978-0-553-49707-6(3))*; (ENG.). lib. bdg. 20.99 *(978-0-553-49708-3(1))* Random Hse. Children's Bks. (Schwartz & Wade Bks.).
—Lejos / Far. Herrera, Juan Felipe. 2019. 14p. (J). (-k). bds. 7.99 *(978-0-7636-9063-2(5))* Candlewick Pr.
Gomez, Blanca. One Family. Shannon, George. 2015. (ENG.). 32p. (J). (gr. -1-3). 18.99 *(978-0-374-30003-6(8)*, 900127481, Farrar, Straus & Giroux (BYR)) Farrar, Straus & Giroux.
Gómez, Blanca. Red House, Tree House, Little Bitty Brown Mouse. Godwin, Jane. 2019. (ENG.). 40p. (J). (-k). 16.99 *(978-0-525-55381-6(9)*, Dial Bks) Penguin Young Readers Group.
Gomez, Carlos. Amazing Mary Jane: Down in Flames, up in Smoke. 2020. 112p. (YA). (gr. 4-17). pap. 15.99 *(978-1-302-92027-2(8))* Marvel Worldwide, Inc.
Gomez, Carlos, jt. illus. see Villa, Carlos.
Gomez, Eddie Martinez. Amigos del Otro Lado. Anza, Ana Luisa. rev. ed. 2004. (Castillo de la Lectura Naranja Ser.). (SPA & ENG.). 136p. (J). pap. 7.95 *(978-970-20-0130-0(7))* Castillo, Ediciones, S. A. de C. V. MEX. Dist: Macmillan.
Gomez, Elena. Creation Song. Scott-Brown, Anna. 2008. 32p. (J). (gr. k-2). 12.99 *(978-0-8254-6263-4(0))* Kregel Pubns.
—Shy Shark. Morgan, Michaela. 2005. (ENG.). 24p. (J). lib. bdg. 23.65 *(978-1-59646-722-4(3))* Dingles & Co.
—Through the Heart of the Jungle. Emmett, Jonathan. 2003. 32p. (J). tchr. ed. 15.95 *(978-1-58925-029-1(X))*; pap. 5.95 *(978-1-58925-380-3(9))* Tiger Tales.
—A World of Prayers. 2006. (ENG.). 32p. (J). (gr. k). 16.00 *(978-0-8028-5265-4(8)*, Eerdmans Bks For Young Readers) Eerdmans, William B. Publishing Co.
Gómez, Elizabeth. Moony Luna, 1 vol. Argueta, Jorge. 2014.Tr. of Luna, Lunita Lunera. (ENG & SPA.). 32p. (J). (gr. 2-4). pap. 10.95 *(978-0-89239-306-0(8)*, 4896c7f8-6820-4114-8645-00b75dfe45c5, Children's Book Press) Lee & Low Bks., Inc.
Gomez, Elizabeth. Moony Luna: Luna, Lunita Lunera. Argueta, Jorge & Alvarez, Cecilia Concepcion. 2005. (ENG & SPA.). 32p. (J). 16.95 *(978-0-89239-205-6(3))* Lee & Low Bks., Inc.
Gómez, Elizabeth. The Upside down Boy, 1 vol. Herrera, Juan Felipe. 2013.Tr. of Nino de Cabeza. (ENG & SPA.). 32p. (J). (gr. 1-5). per. 10.95 *(978-0-89239-217-9(7)*, f6db27be-04ba-4c53-a4cf-2bd4dd7f622f, Children's Book Press) Lee & Low Bks., Inc.
Gomez, Elizabeth & Gómez, Elizabeth. Una Pelicula en Mi Almohada. Argueta, Jorge. 2013.Tr. of Movie in My Pillow. (ENG & SPA.). 32p. (J). (gr. k). pap. 9.95 *(978-0-89239-219-3(3))* Lee & Low Bks., Inc.
Gómez, Elizabeth, jt. illus. see Gomez, Elizabeth.
Gómez, Isabel. Mapuches. Navarrete, Federico. 2014. (SPA.). 88p. (J). (gr. 4-7). pap. 11.95 *(978-607-8237-49-4(7))* Nostra Ediciones MEX. Dist: Independent Pubs. Group.
Gomez, Lorena Alvarez. Lights, Camera, Carmen! Denise, Anika. 2018. (ENG.). 32p. (J). (gr. k-2). 16.99 *(978-1-4197-3169-3(6)*, Abrams Bks. for Young Readers) Abrams, Inc.
Gomez, Marce. Hush Little Baby. Goose, Mother. 2020. (ENG.). 32p. (J). (gr. k-1). 12.99 *(978-1-5324-1564-7(8))*; pap. 12.99 *(978-1-5324-1540-1(0))* Xist Publishing.
Gomez, Marcela. Un día Caluroso. Corriols, Carmen. 2016. (Early Rising Readers Ser.). (SPA.). (J). (gr. -1). 6.67 *(978-1-4788-3698-8(9))* Newmark Learning LLC.
—Frogs on a Log. Koons, Linda. 2015. (Early Rising Readers Ser.). (J). (gr. -1-k). 5.83 *(978-1-4788-1595-2(7))* Newmark Learning LLC.
—The Hot Day. Corriols, Carmen. 2015. (Early Rising Readers Ser.). (J). (gr. -1-k). 5.83 *(978-1-4788-1699-7(6))* Newmark Learning LLC.
—The No-Tech Day of Play. Parkes, Brenda & Fuerst, Jeffrey B. 2015. (Shared Reading Contemporary Tales Ser.). (J). (gr. k-1). *(978-1-4900-2116-4(7))* Benchmark Education Co.
—The No-Tech Day of Play: Big Book Edition. Parkes, Brenda & Fuerst, Jeffrey B. 2015. (Shared Reading Contemporary Tales Ser.). (J). (gr. k-1). *(978-1-4900-2111-9(6))* Benchmark Education Co.
—Ranitas Sobre un Tronco. Koons, Linda. 2016. (Early Rising Readers Ser.). (SPA.). (J). (gr. -1). 6.67 *(978-1-4788-3675-9(X))* Newmark Learning LLC.
Gomez, Marcela & Silva, David. Celebra el Cinco de Mayo con un Jarabe Tapatío. Flor Ada, Alma. 2006. (Cuentos para Celebrar / Stories to Celebrate Ser.). 30p. (gr. k-6). per. 11.95 *(978-1-59820-118-5(2))* Ediciones Alfaguara ESP. Dist: Santillana USA Publishing Co., Inc.
Gómez Morin, Mauricio. Belle Bestioles: Initiation à la Musique Classique. Gerhard, Ana. 2020. (ENG.). 72p. (J). (gr. 2-4). 16.95 *(978-2-924774-57-1(8))* Secret Mountain CAN. Dist: Independent Pubs. Group.
Gómez Morin, Mauricio. Little Creatures: An Introduction to Classical Music. Gerhard, Ana. 2019. (ENG.). 62p. (J). (gr. 2-3). 16.95 *(978-2-924774-55-7(1))* La Montagne Secrete CAN. Dist: Independent Pubs. Group.
Gomez, Obed. Mis Papitos: Heroes de la Cosecha. Caraballo, Samuel. 2005. (ENG & SPA.). 32p. (J). (gr. -1-3). 16.95 *(978-1-55885-450-5(9)*, Piñata Books) Arte Publico Pr.
Gomez, Patricio. Gatico-Gatico. Sarduy, Severo. (Literary Encounters Ser.). (SPA.). (J). (gr. 3-5). pap. *(978-968-494-062-8(9)*, CI1124) Centro de Informacion y Desarrollo de la Comunicacion y la Literatura MEX. Dist: Lectorum Pubns., Inc.
Gomez, Patricio & Villagomez, Raul. Me Gusta Jugar Con los Libros. Santirso, Liliana. (SPA.). (J). (gr. k-1). pap. *(978-968-6465-48-8(0))* Casa de Estudios de Literatura y Talleres Artisticos Amaquemecan A.C. MEX. Dist: Lectorum Pubns., Inc.
Gomez, Sebastián. If You Were a Kid in a Medieval Castle. Gregory, Josh. 2017. (If You Were a Kid Ser.). (ENG.). 32p. (J). (gr. 2-4). lib. bdg. 26.00 *(978-0-531-22385-7(X)*, Children's Pr.) Scholastic Library Publishing.
Gómez Silván, Sergio. J. K. Rowling's Wizarding World: a Pop-Up Gallery of Curiosities. 2016. (J. K. Rowling's Wizarding World Ser.). (ENG.). 10p. (J). (gr. 3-7). 27.99 *(978-0-7636-9588-0(2))* Candlewick Pr.
Gompper, Gail. Every Day by the Bay. Gompper, Gail. 2011. (ENG.). 24p. (J). bds. 9.95 *(978-0-9726487-7-6(1))* Puddle Jump Pr., Ltd.
Gon, Adriano. The Magic Backpack. Jarman, Julia. 2003. (Flying Foxes Ser.). (ENG.). 48p. (J). lib. bdg. *(978-0-7787-1487-3(X))* Crabtree Publishing Co.
—The Magic Backpack. Jarman, Julia. 2004. (Flying Foxes Ser.). (ENG.). (J). (gr. 1-1). lib. bdg. 16.05 *(978-0-7569-3018-9(9))* Perfection Learning Corp.
Gonçalves da Silva, Fabio. Ariela Aparecida E O Vale Da Neblina Da Cachoeir. Janesh, Ron. 2012. 56p. pap. 20.50 *(978-1-60976-925-3(2)*, Strategic Bk. Publishing) Strategic Book Publishing & Rights Agency (SBPRA).
Goncalves, Edison. The Little Brown Turkey. Wilborn, Beth G. 2016. (ENG.). (J). pap. 12.95 *(978-1-68197-740-9(0))* Christian Faith Publishing.
Goncalves, Iasmim. The Adventures of Gus & Flynn. Tamburello, Samantha. 2019. (ENG.). 26p. (J). pap. 9.50 *(978-1-0996-0547-5(4))* Independently Published.
Goncalves, Iasmim. Tea for Two. Chan, Anna. 2020. (Toychest Stories Ser.: Vol. 1). (ENG.). 190p. (J). pap. 8.95 ***(978-1-6576-7838-5(5))*** Independently Published.
Goncharov, Oleg. Skazki Volshebnogo Lesa. Karpova, Natal'ia. 2017. (RUS.). 19p. (J). bds. *(978-5-4335-0562-9(6))* NIGMA.
Goneau, Martin. A Bat Cannot Bat, a Stair Cannot Stare: More about Homonyms & Homophones. Cleary, Brian P. 2014. (Words Are CATegorical ® Ser.). (ENG.). 32p. (J). (gr. 2-5). lib. bdg. 16.95 *(978-0-7613-9032-9(4)*, 9780761390329, Millbrook Pr.) Lerner Publishing Group.
—A Bat Cannot Bat, a Stair Cannot Stare: More about Homonyms & Homophones. Cleary, Brian P. 2016. (Words Are CATegorical ® Ser.). (ENG.). 32p. (J). (gr. 2-5). pap. 7.99 *(978-1-5124-1799-9(8)*, 9781512417999, Millbrook Pr.) Lerner Publishing Group.
—Black Beans & Lamb, Poached Eggs & Ham: What Is in the Meat & Beans Group? Cleary, Brian P. & Nelson, Jennifer K. 2010. (Food Is CATegorical (tm) Ser.). (ENG.). 32p. (J). (gr. k-3). lib. bdg. 25.32 *(978-1-58013-591-7(9)*, Millbrook Pr.) Lerner Publishing Group.
—Bugs That Make Your Computer Crawl: What Are Computer Bugs? Cleary, Brian P. 2019. (Coding Is CATegorical (tm) Ser.). (ENG.). 24p. (J). (gr. k-3). pap. 8.99 *(978-1-5415-4560-1(5))*; 27.99 *(978-1-5415-3309-7(7))* Lerner Publishing Group. (Millbrook Pr.).
—Butterfly, Flea, Beetle, & Bee: What Is an Insect? Cleary, Brian P. 2012. (Animal Groups Are CATegorical (tm) Ser.). (ENG.). 32p. (J). (gr. k-3). lib. bdg. 26.65 *(978-0-7613-6208-1(8)*, 9780761362081, Millbrook Pr.) Lerner Publishing Group.
—Catfish, Cod, Salmon, & Scrod: What Is a Fish? Cleary, Brian P. 2012. (Animal Groups Are CATegorical (tm) Ser.). (ENG.). 32p. (J). (gr. k-3). lib. bdg. 26.65 *(978-0-7613-6211-1(8)*, 9780761362111, Millbrook Pr.) Lerner Publishing Group.
—Chips & Cheese & Nana's Knees: What Is Alliteration? Cleary, Brian P. 2015. (Words Are CATegorical ® Ser.). (ENG.). 32p. (J). (gr. 2-5). lib. bdg. 17.95 *(978-1-4677-2649-8(4)*, 9781467726498, Millbrook Pr.) Lerner Publishing Group.
—Chips & Cheese & Nana's Knees: What Is Alliteration? Cleary, Brian P. 2017. (Words Are CATegorical ® Ser.). (ENG.). 32p. (J). (gr. 2-5). 7.99 *(978-1-5124-3421-7(3)*, 9781512434217, Millbrook Pr.) Lerner Publishing Group.
—Ful & -Less, -Er And -Ness: What Is a Suffix? Cleary, Brian P. (Words Are CATegorical ® Ser.). (ENG.). 32p. (J). (gr. 2-5). 2016. pap. 7.99 *(978-1-5124-0088-5(2)*, 9781512400885); 2014. lib. bdg. 16.95 *(978-1-4677-0610-0(8)*, 9781467706100) Lerner Publishing Group. (Millbrook Pr.).
—Nothing Loopy about This: What Are Loops & Conditionals? Cleary, Brian P. 2019. (Coding Is CATegorical (tm) Ser.). (ENG.). 24p. (J). (gr. k-3). pap. 8.99 *(978-1-5415-4558-8(3))*; 27.99 *(978-1-5415-3307-3(0))* Lerner Publishing Group. (Millbrook Pr.).
—Oils (Just a Bit) to Keep Your Body Fit: What Are Oils? Cleary, Brian P. 2011. (Food Is CATegorical (tm) Ser.). (ENG.). 32p. (J). (gr. k-3). pap. 7.95 *(978-0-7613-6389-7(0)*, Millbrook Pr.) Lerner Publishing Group.
—Pre- & Re-, Mis- & Dis- What Is a Prefix? Cleary, Brian P. 2015. (Words Are CATegorical ® Ser.). (ENG.). 32p. (J). (gr. 2-5). pap. 7.99 *(978-1-4677-9383-4(3)*, 9781467793834, Millbrook Pr.) Lerner Publishing Group.
—Salamander, Frog, & Polliwog: What Is an Amphibian? Cleary, Brian P. 2012. (Animal Groups Are CATegorical (tm) Ser.). (ENG.). 32p. (J). (gr. k-3). pap. 7.95 *(978-1-4677-0339-0(7)*, 9781467703390); lib. bdg. 26.65 *(978-0-7613-6209-8(6)*, 9780761362098) Lerner Publishing Group. (Millbrook Pr.).
—Sparrow, Eagle, Penguin, & Seagull: What Is a Bird? Cleary, Brian P. 2012. (Animal Groups Are CATegorical (tm) Ser.). (ENG.). 32p. (J). (gr. k-3). pap. 7.95 *(978-1-4677-0340-6(0)*, 9781467703406); lib. bdg. 26.65 *(978-0-7613-6207-4(X)*, 9780761362074) Lerner Publishing Group. (Millbrook Pr.).
—This Python Isn't a Snake: What Are Languages & Syntax? Cleary, Brian P. 2019. (Coding Is CATegorical (tm) Ser.). (ENG.). 24p. (J). (gr. k-3). 27.99 *(978-1-5415-3306-6(2)*, Millbrook Pr.) Lerner Publishing Group.
—Tortoise, Tree Snake, Gator, & Sea Snake: What Is a Reptile? Cleary, Brian P. 2012. (Animal Groups Are CATegorical (tm) Ser.). (ENG.). 32p. (J). (gr. k-3). lib. bdg. 26.65 *(978-0-7613-6210-4(X)*, 9780761362104, Millbrook Pr.) Lerner Publishing Group.
—You Can't Dance to These Rhythms: What Are Algorithms? Cleary, Brian P. 2019. (Coding Is CATegorical (tm) Ser.). (ENG.). 24p. (J). (gr. k-3). pap. 8.99 *(978-1-5415-4559-5(1))*; 27.99 *(978-1-5415-3308-0(9))* Lerner Publishing Group. (Millbrook Pr.).
Gonina, Luba. The Owls of the Enchanted Forest. Harary, Keith. 2008. 52p. (J). pap. 15.88 *(978-0-9799196-8-8(1))* Owl Pals.
—The Owls of the Enchanted Forest - 2007 Special Collector's Edition. Harary, Keith. 2007. 50p. (J). 50.00 incl. DVD *(978-0-9799196-3-3(0))* Owl Pals.
Gonne, Maud. Celtic Wonder-Tales. Young, Ella. 2014. (J). *(978-0-486-78065-8(1))* Dover Pubns., Inc.
Gonsalves, Andy, et al. Gravity Falls: Journal 3. Renzetti, Rob & Hirsch, Alex. 2016. (ENG.). 288p. (J). (gr. 3-7). 19.99 *(978-1-4847-4669-1(4))* Disney Pr.
Gonsalves, Rob. Imagine a Day. Thomson, Sarah L. 2005. (Imagine A... Ser.). (ENG.). 40p. (J). (gr. -1-3). 19.99 *(978-0-689-85219-0(3)*, Atheneum Bks. for Young Readers) Simon & Schuster Children's Publishing.
—Imagine a Night. Thomson, Sarah L. 2003. (Imagine A... Ser.). (ENG.). 40p. (J). (gr. -1-3). 19.99 *(978-0-689-85218-3(5)*, Atheneum Bks. for Young Readers) Simon & Schuster Children's Publishing.
—Imagine a Place. Thomson, Sarah L. 2008. (Imagine A... Ser.). (ENG.). 40p. (J). (gr. -1-6). 19.99 *(978-1-4169-6802-3(4)*, Atheneum Bks. for Young Readers) Simon & Schuster Children's Publishing.
Gonsalves, Rob. Imagine a World. Gonsalves, Rob. 2015. (Imagine A... Ser.). (ENG.). 48p. (J). (gr. -1-3). 17.99 *(978-1-4814-4973-1(7))* Simon & Schuster Canada CAN. Dist: Simon & Schuster, Inc.
Gonyea, Mark. One Little Monster. Gonyea, Mark. 2018. (ENG.). 40p. (J). (gr. -1-3). 17.99 *(978-1-5344-0674-2(3)*, Aladdin) Simon & Schuster Children's Publishing.
Gonzales, Chuck. Emoji Phantom of the Opera: Epic Tales in Tiny Texts. Furman, Katherine & Leroux, Gaston. 2017. (Condensed Classics Ser.). (ENG.). 160p. 12.99 *(978-1-63106-428-9(2)*, Race Point Publishing) Quarto Publishing Group USA.
—Fashionista! Barbo, Maria S. 2009. (ENG.). 128p. (J). (gr. 2-6). pap. 16.99 *(978-0-312-59607-1(3)*, 9780312596071) Feiwel & Friends.
—The Gigantic, Genuine Genie. Williams, Suzanne. 2007. (Princess Power Ser.: No. 6). 128p. (J). 15.99 *(978-0-06-078309-9(5))* HarperCollins Pubs.
—The Mysterious, Mournful Maiden. Williams, Suzanne. 2007. 112p. (J). 15.99 *(978-0-06-078305-1(2))* HarperCollins Pubs.
—Rock Star! Barbo, Maria S. 2009. (ENG.). 128p. (J). (gr. 2-6). pap. 16.99 *(978-0-312-59606-4(5)*, 9780312596064) Feiwel & Friends.
Gonzales, Laura. Collins Big Cat Phonics for Letters & Sounds - Number Fun: Band 00/Lilac. Guille-Marrett, Emily & Raby, Charlotte. 2018. (Collins Big Cat Phonics Ser.). (ENG.). 16p. (J). (gr. -1-k). pap. 6.99 *(978-0-00-825122-2(3))* HarperCollins Pubs. Ltd. GBR. Dist: Independent Pubs. Group.
Gonzales, Nana. The Sock Thief. Crespo, Ana. 2015. (ENG.). 32p. (J). (gr. -1-3). 16.99 *(978-0-8075-7538-3(0)*, 807575380) Whitman, Albert & Co.
Gonzales, Sharon. Airport Explorers: 2008 Activity Book. 2008. 32p. (J). 6.95 *(978-0-9745294-2-4(7))* San Diego County Regional Airport Authority.
Gonzalez, Alvaro. The Big Thing: Brave Bea Finds Silver Linings with the Help of Family & Friends During a Global Pandemic. Meng, Angela & Friedman, Alexander. 2020. 30p. (J). (ENG.). 15.99 ***(978-0-578-68357-7(1))***; (SPA.). 15.99 ***(978-0-578-68866-4(2))*** Asymmetry LLC.
Gonzalez, Amanda. A Different Me. Mickens, Erica. 2018. (ENG.). 44p. (J). pap. 14.99 *(978-1-7210-9346-5(X))* CreateSpace Independent Publishing Platform.
González, Ana Ramírez. Kamala & Maya's Big Idea. Harris, Meena. 2020. (ENG.). 32p. (J). (gr. -1-3). 18.99 *(978-0-06-293740-7(5)*, Balzer & Bray) HarperCollins Pubs.
González, Ángel Luis. Mujercitas. González, Ángel Luis, tr. Luna, Sagrario & Alcott, Louisa May. (SPA.). 92p. (J). (gr. 5-8). pap. 9.95 *(978-84-204-5748-2(5))* Santillana USA Publishing Co., Inc.
Gonzalez, Ashley. Magic of Masara. Kagna, Barbara. 2010. 24p. pap. 12.50 *(978-1-4490-5651-3(2))* AuthorHouse.
Gonzalez, Carlos F. Roundy & Friends - Russia: Soccertowns Book Series. Varela, Andres. 2018. (ENG.). 32p. (J). (gr. k-5). 19.99 *(978-1-943255-49-8(0))* Soccertowns LLC.
González Chico, Norberto. Rebelión en Celestya. Ortiz Bello, Frank Joseph & Ortiz Bello, Mayra a, eds. 2020. (SPA.). 314p. (J). pap. 30.00 ***(978-1-881741-91-6(5))*** Ediciones Eleos.
Gonzalez de Echavarri, Jesus & Vaquero, Pilar. S�ptimo y Porquito: El Nuevo Patito Feo. Plaza Garcia-Navas, David, ed. 2019. (Cuentilandia Ser.: Vol. 1). (SPA.). 48p. (J). pap. 15.98 ***(978-1-7130-8896-7(7))*** Independently Published.
Gonzalez, Enrique. Hershey Finds a Home. Gonzalez, Dorothy. 2018. (ENG.). 20p. (J). pap. 9.95 *(978-1-64096-130-2(5))* Newman Springs Publishing, Inc.
Gonzalez, Francisco. El Coyote Tonto. Garrido, Felipe. 2003. (Infantil Alfaguara Ser.).Tr. of Dumb Coyote. (SPA.). 60p. (J). (gr. 3-5). pap. 8.95 *(978-968-19-0277-3(7))* Santillana USA Publishing Co., Inc.
Gonzalez, Henry. Aviador Santiago. Nino, Jairo Anibal. 2003. (Literatura Juvenil (Panamericana Editorial) Ser.). (SPA.). 138p. (YA). (gr. -1-7). pap. *(978-958-30-0297-7(6))* Panamericana Editorial.
—La Casa del Abuelo. Buitrago, Fanny. 2003. (Literatura Juvenil (Panamericana Editorial) Ser.). (SPA.). 71p. (YA). (gr. -1-7). per. *(978-958-30-0338-7(7))* Panamericana Editorial.
—La Casa del Arco Iris: Una Novela de la Infancia. Buitrago, Fanny. 2003. (Literatura Juvenil (Panamericana Editorial) Ser.). (SPA.). 186p. (YA). (gr. -1-7). pap. *(978-958-30-0334-9(4))* Panamericana Editorial.
—Las Cosas de la Casa. Roman, Celso. 2003. (Literatura Juvenil (Panamericana Editorial) Ser.). (SPA.). 87p. (YA). (gr. -1-7). per. *(978-958-30-0296-0(8))* Panamericana Editorial.
—El Maravilloso Viaje de Rosendo Bucuru. Roman, Celso. 2003. (Coleccion Corcel Ser.). (SPA.). 109p. (J). (gr. -1-7). pap. *(978-958-30-0343-1(3))* Panamericana Editorial.
—Preguntario. Niqo, Jairo Anmbal. 2007. (Literatura Juvenil (Panamericana Editorial) Ser.). (SPA.). 188p. (gr. 5-7). pap. 18.99 *(978-958-30-0497-1(9)*, PV30461) Panamericana Editorial COL. Dist: Lectorum Pubns., Inc.
—Primitivos Relatos Contados Otra Vez: Heroes y Mitos Amazonicos. Niño, Hugo. 2004. (Literatura Juvenil (Panamericana Editorial) Ser.). (SPA.). 160p. (YA). (gr. 4-7). pap. *(978-958-30-0365-3(4))* Panamericana Editorial.
Gonzalez, Henry & Granada, Nancy. Como el Leopardo Obtuvo Sus Manchas: Y Otros Cuentos de Animales. Kipling, Rudyard. Calderon, Catalina, tr. 2004. (Cajon de Cuentos Ser.). (SPA.). 165p. (J). (gr. -1-7). *(978-958-30-0328-8(X))* Panamericana Editorial.
Gonzalez III, Raul. Lowriders Blast from the Past. Camper, Cathy. 2018. (Lowriders Ser.: 3). (ENG.). 128p. (J). (gr. 3-7). pap. 9.99 *(978-1-4521-6316-1(2))* Chronicle Bks. LLC.
Gonzalez, Ile. Super Sons: the PolarShield Project. Pearson, Ridley. 2019. (ENG.). 160p. (gr. 3-7). pap. 9.99 *(978-1-4012-8639-2(9)*, DC Zoom) DC Comics.
Gonzalez, Ileana. The Foxglove Mission. Pearson, Ridley. 2019. 160p. (J). (gr. 3-7). pap. 9.99 *(978-1-4012-8640-8(2)*, DC Zoom) DC Comics.
Gonzalez, Javier A. Friday, 1 vol. Lindeen, Mary. 2008. (Days of the Week Ser.). (ENG.). 24p. (J). (gr. k-2). 27.07 *(978-1-60270-101-4(6)*, 5103, Looking Glass Library) Magic Wagon.
—Monday, 1 vol. Lindeen, Mary. 2008. (Days of the Week Ser.). (ENG.). 24p. (J). (gr. k-2). 27.07

(978-1-60270-097-0(4)), 5095, Looking Glass Library) Magic Wagon.
—Saturday, 1 vol. Lindeen, Mary. 2008. (Days of the Week Ser.). (ENG.). 24p. (J). (gr. k-2). 27.07 *(978-1-60270-102-1(4))*, 5105, Looking Glass Library) Magic Wagon.
—Sunday, 1 vol. Lindeen, Mary. 2008. (Days of the Week Ser.). (ENG.). 24p. (J). (gr. k-2). 27.07 *(978-1-60270-096-3(6))*, 5093, Looking Glass Library) Magic Wagon.
—Thursday, 1 vol. Lindeen, Mary. 2008. (Days of the Week Ser.). (ENG.). 24p. (J). (gr. k-2). 27.07 *(978-1-60270-100-7(8))*, 5101, Looking Glass Library) Magic Wagon.
—Tuesday, 1 vol. Lindeen, Mary. 2008. (Days of the Week Ser.). (ENG.). 24p. (J). (gr. k-2). 27.07 *(978-1-60270-098-7(2))*, 5097, Looking Glass Library) Magic Wagon.
—Wednesday, 1 vol. Lindeen, Mary. 2008. (Days of the Week Ser.). (ENG.). 24p. (J). (gr. k-2). 27.07 *(978-1-60270-099-4(0))*, 5099, Looking Glass Library) Magic Wagon.
—The Week, 1 vol. Lindeen, Mary. 2008. (Days of the Week Ser.). (ENG.). 24p. (J). (gr. k-2). 27.07 *(978-1-60270-103-8(2))*, 5107, Looking Glass Library) Magic Wagon.
Gonzalez, Jerry. The Big Sketch Book SKETCH SKETCH SKETCH: A Large Sketch Book with Lots of Pages to Draw On! Gonzalez, Jerry. 2019. (ENG.). 202p. (J). pap. 9.99 *(978-1-0756-4425-2(9))* Independently Published.
Gonzalez, Jerry. Christmas Coloring Book for Kids: 25 Fun Christmas Designs to Color! Gonzalez, Jerry. 2019. (ENG.). 52p. (J). pap. 8.99 ***(978-1-6885-8151-7(0))*** Independently Published.
—Composition Notebook: Back to School Apple Theme Ruled Lined Notebook for Kids, Teens & Teachers. Gonzalez, Jerry. 2019. (ENG.). 122p. (J). pap. 7.99 ***(978-1-0858-5840-3(5))*** Independently Published.
Gonzalez, Jerry. Composition Notebook: Back to School Basketball Dog Theme Notebook / Journal / Diary for Kids & Teens. Gonzalez, Jerry. 2019. (ENG.). 122p. (J). pap. 7.99 *(978-1-0776-4061-0(7))* Independently Published.
—Composition Notebook: Back to School Composition Pirate Dog Theme Notebook for Kids & Teens. Gonzalez, Jerry. 2019. (ENG.). 122p. (J). pap. 7.99 *(978-1-0790-1703-8(8))* Independently Published.
—Composition Notebook: Back to School Funny Car Wearing a Baseball Cap College Ruled Lined Notebook / Journal / Diary. Gonzalez, Jerry. 2019. (ENG.). 122p. (J). pap. 7.99 *(978-1-0772-9780-7(7))* Independently Published.
—Composition Notebook: Back to School Funny Fang Car Theme Notebook for Kids & Teens. Gonzalez, Jerry. 2019. (ENG.). 122p. (J). pap. 7.99 *(978-1-0802-4857-5(9))* Independently Published.
Gonzalez, Jerry. Composition Notebook: Back to School Hot Dog Theme Ruled Lined Notebook for Kids & Teens. Gonzalez, Jerry. 2019. (ENG.). 122p. (J). pap. 7.99 ***(978-1-0859-8283-2(1))*** Independently Published.
—Composition Notebook: Back to School Ice Cream Cone Theme Ruled Lined Notebook for Kids & Teens. Gonzalez, Jerry. 2019. (ENG.). 122p. (J). pap. 7.99 ***(978-1-0859-7504-9(5))*** Independently Published.
Gonzalez, Jerry. Composition Notebook: Back to School Pizza Ruled Lined Notebook. Gonzalez, Jerry. 2019. (ENG.). 122p. (J). pap. 7.99 *(978-1-0737-2487-1(5))* Independently Published.
—Composition Notebook: Back to School Reading Cat Theme Ruled Lined Notebook - Great Notebook for Kids - Notebook for Cat Lovers. Gonzalez, Jerry. 2019. (ENG.). 122p. (J). pap. 7.99 *(978-1-0750-0892-4(1))* Independently Published.
—Composition Notebook: Back to School Rule Lined Music Boombox Theme Notebook for Boys & Girls. Gonzalez, Jerry. 2019. (ENG.). 122p. (J). pap. 7.99 *(978-1-0774-4509-3(1))* Independently Published.
—Composition Notebook: Back to School Rule Lined Soccer Theme Notebook for Boys & Girls. Gonzalez, Jerry. 2019. (ENG.). 122p. (J). pap. 7.99 *(978-1-0752-6197-8(X))* Independently Published.
—Composition Notebook: Back to School Singing Ice Cream Theme Ruled Lined Notebook - Great Notebook for Kids. Gonzalez, Jerry. 2019. (ENG.). 122p. (J). pap. 6.99 *(978-1-0749-7277-6(5))* Independently Published.
Gonzalez, Jerry. Composition Notebook: Back to School Soccer Ball College Ruled Lined Notebook / Journal / Diary. Gonzalez, Jerry. 2019. (ENG.). 122p. (J). pap. 7.99 ***(978-1-0859-4246-1(5))*** Independently Published.
Gonzalez, Jerry. Composition Notebook: Back to School Soccer Theme Composition Notebook for Kids & Teens. Gonzalez, Jerry. 2019. (ENG.). 122p. (J). pap. 7.99 *(978-1-0795-2311-9(1))* Independently Published.
—Composition Notebook: Back to School Space Car Theme Ruled Lined Notebook / Journal / Diary / for Students. Gonzalez, Jerry. 2019. (ENG.). 122p. (J). pap. 7.99 *(978-1-0782-1863-4(3))* Independently Published.
—Composition Notebook: Back to School Spooky Car with Fangs Theme Ruled Lined Notebook for Kids & Teens. Gonzalez, Jerry. 2019. (ENG.). 122p. (J). pap. 7.99 *(978-1-0794-7110-6(3))* Independently Published.
—Composition Notebook: Back to School UFO Theme Ruled Lined Notebook / Journal for Students. Gonzalez, Jerry. 2019. (ENG.). 122p. (J). pap. 7.99 *(978-1-0773-9766-8(6))* Independently Published.
Gonzalez, Jerry. Composition Notebook: Notebook for Home Schoolers, Kids, Teens & Teachers. Gonzalez, Jerry. 2019. (ENG.). 122p. (J). pap. 7.99 ***(978-1-0870-9762-6(2))*** Independently Published.
Gonzalez, Jerry. Composition Notebook: Pumpkin Halloween Theme Ruled Lined Notebook for Kids & Teens. Gonzalez, Jerry. 2019. (ENG.). 122p. (J). pap. 7.99 *(978-1-0754-3000-8(3))* Independently Published.
—Composition Notebook: The Funny Pumpkins Halloween Theme Notebook for Kids or Teens. Gonzalez, Jerry. 2019. (ENG.). 122p. (J). pap. 7.99 *(978-1-0757-2758-0(8))* Independently Published.
—Composition Notebook: The Funny Singing Dog Theme College Ruled Notebook. Gonzalez, Jerry. 2019. (Singing Creatures Ser.: Vol. 2). (ENG.). 122p. (J). pap. 6.99 *(978-1-0821-6590-0(5))* Independently Published.
—Composition Notebook: The Funny Singing Pencil Theme College Ruled Notebook. Gonzalez, Jerry. 2019. (Singing Creatures Ser.: Vol. 1). (ENG.). 122p. (J). pap. 6.99 *(978-1-0821-5108-8(4))* Independently Published.
—Composition Notebook: The UFO / Flying Saucer Ruled Lined Notebook for Kids & Teens. Gonzalez, Jerry. 2019. (ENG.). 122p. (J). pap. 7.99 *(978-1-0755-5800-9(X))* Independently Published.
—Monster Journal Sketchbook: The Blue Monster Theme Combo Notebook for Writing & Drawing. Gonzalez, Jerry. 2019. (Monster Journal Sketchbook Ser.: Vol. 3). (ENG.). 102p. (J). pap. 7.99 *(978-1-0818-8799-5(0))* Independently Published.
—Monster Journal Sketchbook: The Orange Monster Theme Combo Notebook for Writing & Drawing. Gonzalez, Jerry. 2019. (Monster Journal Sketchbook Ser.: Vol. 1). (ENG.). 102p. (J). pap. 7.99 *(978-1-0817-0473-5(X))* Independently Published.
Gonzalez, Jerry. Primary Composition Notebook: Write & Draw Composition Cat Theme Notebook for Kids Grades K-2. Gonzalez, Jerry. 2019. (ENG.). 122p. (J). pap. 6.99 ***(978-1-6882-0672-4(8))*** Independently Published.
González, Jorge. Captain Barbosa & the Pirate Hat Chase. 2019. (ENG.). 32p. (J). (gr. k-3). 26.65 *(978-1-5415-4154-2(5)*, Graphic Universe™) Lerner Publishing Group.
González, Jorge. Captain Barbosa & the Pirate Hat Chase. González, Jorge. 2019. (ENG.). 32p. (J). (gr. k-3). pap. 7.99 *(978-1-5415-4527-4(3)*, Graphic Universe™) Lerner Publishing Group.
Gonzalez, Jorge H., photos by. Arte Ruso Sobre Laminas de Aluminio: El Teatro y los Titeres. Neira, Maria Lia. Panamericana Editorial, ed. 2003. (Manos Maestras Ser.). (SPA., 18p. pap. *(978-958-30-1089-7(8))* Panamericana Editorial.
Gonzalez, Jose Antonio, jt. illus. see Andersen, Flemming.
Gonzalez., Jose L. Slinkie the courageous Snail. Adams, Marlene. 2004. 68p. (J). pap. 25.75 *(978-1-4184-8340-1(0))* AuthorHouse.
Gonzalez, Julian. The Adventures of the Traveling Glasses. Smallman, Michelle. 2018. (ENG.). 20p. (J). (gr. k-6). pap. *(978-1-7753422-0-5(4))* Smallman, Michelle.
—Les Aventures d'une Paire de Lunettes en Voyage. Smallman, Michelle. 2018. (FRE.). 20p. (J). (gr. k-6). pap. *(978-1-7753422-1-2(2))* Smallman, Michelle.
Gonzalez, Laura. Holy Squawkamole! Little Red Hen Makes Guacamole. Wood, Susan. 2019. (ENG.). 40p. (J). (gr. -1). 16.95 *(978-1-4549-2253-7(2))* Sterling Publishing Co., Inc.
—Not a Bean. Martinez, Claudia Guadalupe. 2019. 32p. (J). (gr. -1-2). lib. bdg. 16.99 *(978-1-58089-815-7(7))* Charlesbridge Publishing, Inc.
Gonzalez, Maddi. Welcome to Wanderland. Ball, Jackie. 2019. (ENG.). 112p. (YA). pap. 14.99 *(978-1-68415-472-2(3))* Boom! Studios.
Gonzalez, Marco Chamorro Y. Luis Bencomo. Caminantes Del Sol. Iturralde, Edna. 2003. (SPA.). 163p. (J). (gr. 4-7). pap. 14.95 *(978-9942-19-804-4(0))* Santillana USA Publishing Co., Inc.
Gonzalez, Maya Christina. Angels Ride Bikes & Other Fall Poems: Los Angeles Andan Bicicletas y Otros Poemas de Otoño, 1 vol. Alarcón, Francisco X. 2013. (Cycle of Seasons Ser.). (ENG & SPA.). 32p. (J). (gr. 2-6). per. 10.95 *(978-0-89239-198-1(7)*, 157425f9-c108-4b3c-99ff-fde8e9d03a66) Lee & Low Bks., Inc.
—Animal Poems of the Iguazú: Animalario del Iguazú, 1 vol. Alarcón, Francisco X. 32p. (J). 2014. (ENG & SPA.). (gr. 3-5). pap. 10.95 *(978-0-89239-299-5(1)*, b944dc39-4ac7-4a97-973f-a7b7cf136479, Children's Book Press); 2008. (SPA & ENG.). (gr. k). 16.95 *(978-0-89239-225-4(8))* Lee & Low Bks., Inc.
—Fiesta Femenina. Gerson, Mary-Joan. 2003. (SPA & ENG.). 64p. (J). 19.99 *(978-1-84148-964-3(6))* Barefoot Bks., Inc.
—From the Bellybutton of the Moon & Other Summer Poems: Del Ombligo de la Luna y Otros Poemas de Verano. Alarcón, Francisco X. ed. 2013. (ENG & SPA.). 32p. (J). (gr. 1-4). per. 9.95 *(978-0-89239-201-8(0))* Lee & Low Bks., Inc.
—Iguanas in the Snow & Other Winter Poems: Iguanas en la Nieve y Otros Poemas de Invierno. Alarcón, Francisco X.Tr. of Iguanas in the Snow & Other Winter Poems. (ENG & SPA.). 32p. (J). (gr. 1-4). 2013. per. 10.95 *(978-0-89239-202-5(9))*; 2004. 16.95 *(978-0-89239-168-4(5))* Lee & Low Bks., Inc.
—Laughing Tomatoes & Other Spring Poems: Jitomates Risueños y Otros Poemas de Primavera, 1 vol. Alarcón, Francisco X. 2013. (Cycle of Seasons Ser.). (ENG & SPA.). 32p. (J). (gr. 2-6). per. 10.95 *(978-0-89239-199-8(5)*, 7704f76f-e69b-4cbf-9909-c2ade625b6a8) Lee & Low Bks., Inc.
—Mi Diario de Aquí Hasta Allá. Pérez, Amada Irma. 2013.Tr. of My Diary from Here to There. (ENG & SPA.). 32p. (J). (gr. k). pap. 10.95 *(978-0-89239-230-8(4))* Lee & Low Bks., Inc.
—Nana, Que Sorpresa! Perez, Amada Irma & Children's Book Press Staff. 2007.Tr. of Nana's Big Surprise. (ENG & SPA.). 32p. (J). (gr. k-2). lib. bdg. 16.95 *(978-0-89239-190-5(1))* Lee & Low Bks., Inc.
—Nana's Big Surprise. Pérez, Amada Irma. 2013.Tr. of Nana, ¡Qué Sorpresa!. (ENG & SPA.). 32p. (J). pap. 10.95 *(978-0-89239-307-7(6)*, Children's Book Press) Lee & Low Bks., Inc.
—Prietita & the Ghost Woman: Prietita y la Llorona. Anzaldúa, Gloria. 2013. (ENG & SPA.). 32p. (J). (gr. 1-18). pap. 9.95 *(978-0-89239-167-7(7))* Lee & Low Bks., Inc.
—When We Love Someone We Sing to Them: Cuando Amamos Cantamos. Martinez, Ernesto Javier. Feliciano, Jorge Gabriel Martinez, tr. 2018. (ENG.). 40p. (J). (gr. 2-5). 19.95 *(978-1-945289-14-9(7))* Reflection Pr.
Gonzalez, Maya Christina. My Colors, My World. Gonzalez, Maya Christina. 2013.Tr. of Mis Colores, Mi Mundo. (ENG & SPA.). 32p. (J). pap. 10.95 *(978-0-89239-278-0(9)*, Children's Book Press) Lee & Low Bks., Inc.
Gonzalez, Maya Cjrostoma. Fiesta Femenina. Gerson, Mary-Joan. 2018. (ENG.). 64p. (J). (gr. -1-5). pap. 16.99 *(978-1-78285-425-8(8))* Barefoot Bks., Inc.
Gonzalez, Pedro Julio. Turtles. Huelin, Jodi. 2003. (Penguin Young Readers, Level 2 Ser.). (ENG.). 32p. (J). (gr. 1-2). 4.99 *(978-0-448-43117-8(3)*, Penguin Young Readers) Penguin Young Readers Group.
Gonzalez, Ralfka & Ruiz, Ana. Mi Primer Libro de Dichos, 1 vol. 2014.Tr. of My First Book of Proverbs. (SPA & ENG.). 32p. (J). (gr. k-6). pap. 10.95 *(978-0-89239-200-1(2)*, 246ee8fa-e8da-4b9a-88a7-814485531fdd) Lee & Low Bks., Inc.
Gonzalez, Raul, III, jt. illus. see Raúl, III.
Gonzalez, Roberto. The Caterpillar That Learned to Fly: A Children's Nature Picture Book, a Fun Caterpillar & Butterfly Story for Kids. Clark, Sharon. 2016. (Insect Ser.: Vol. 3). (ENG.). (J). (gr. 1-4). pap. *(978-0-9952303-4-7(X))* Clark, Sharon.
—The Honeybee That Learned to Dance: A Children's Nature Picture Book, a Fun Honeybee Story That Kids Will Love; Clark, Sharon. 2016. (Educational Science (Insect) Ser.: Vol. 1). (ENG.). (J). (gr. 1-5). pap. *(978-0-9938003-9-4(4))* Clark, Sharon.
—How Danny Found His Brave. Orchard, Kerry. 2017. (ENG.). 34p. (J). (gr. k-3). *(978-1-7750357-2-5(7))*; pap. *(978-1-7750357-3-2(5))* Burroughs Manor Pr.
—How to Tame Dragons & Hush Hyenas. Orchard, Kerry. 2017. (ENG.). 34p. (J). (gr. k-4). *(978-1-7750357-0-1(0))*; pap. *(978-1-7750357-1-8(9))* Burroughs Manor Pr.
—The No Trolls Allowed Guidebook. Orchard, Kerry. 2017. (ENG.). 34p. (J). (gr. k-3). *(978-1-7750357-4-9(3))*; pap. *(978-1-7750357-5-6(1))* Burroughs Manor Pr.
—A Strange Guest in an Ant's Nest: A Children's Nature Picture Book, a Fun Ant Story That Kids Will Love. Clark, Sharon. 2nd ed. 2016. (Educational Science (Insect) Ser.: Vol. 2). (ENG.). 26p. (J). (gr. k-4). *(978-0-9952303-3-0(1))* Clark, Sharon.
—9x Fun: A Children's Picture Book That Makes Math Fun, with a Cartoon Story Format to Help Kids Learn the 9x Table. Clark, Sharon. 2014. (Educational Science (Math) Ser.: Vol. 1). (ENG.). (J). (gr. 2-4). pap. *(978-0-9938003-7-5(8))* Clark, Sharon.
Gonzalez, Santiago, et al. Caminantes del Sol. Iturralde, Edna. 2003. (SPA.). 163p. (J). (gr. 5-8). pap. 14.95 *(978-9978-07-431-2(7))* Santillana USA Publishing Co., Inc.
Gonzalez, Sonia. Red Riding Hood (Tales to Grow By) A Story about Bravery. 2020. (Tales to Grow By Ser.). (ENG.). 32p. (J). (gr. k-1). pap. 6.95 *(978-0-531-24622-1(1))*; lib. bdg. 26.00 *(978-0-531-23188-3(7))* Scholastic Library Publishing. (Children's Pr.).
Gonzalez, Tesa. La Ratita Presumida: Adaptacion Teatral. Ballesteros, Jose Manuel & Manuel, Ballesteros Pastor José.Tr. of Conceited Mouse. (SPA.). 48p. (J). (gr. k-3). 5.56 *(978-84-241-7713-3(4))* Everest Editora ESP. Dist: Lectorum Pubns., Inc.
—Tortuga Numero Cien. Javaloyes, Inigo & Íñigo, Javaloyes. 2006. (Montana Encantada Ser.). (SPA.). 60p. (J). (gr. 3-5). pap. 9.50 *(978-84-241-8047-8(X))* Everest Editora ESP. Dist: Lectorum Pubns., Inc.
Gonzalez, Thomas. Countdown: 2979 Days to the Moon. Slade, Suzanne. 2018. (ENG.). 144p. (J). (gr. 5-9). 22.95 *(978-1-68263-013-6(7))* Peachtree Publishing Co. Inc.
González, Thomas. Gandhi: The March to the Sea, 0 vols. McGinty, Alice B. 2013. (ENG.). 40p. (J). (gr. 4-7). 17.99 *(978-1-4778-1644-8(5)*, 9781477816448, Two Lions) Amazon Publishing.
Gonzalez, Thomas. The House on Dirty-Third Street, 1 vol. Kittinger, Jo S. 2012. (ENG.). 32p. (J). 16.95 *(978-1-56145-619-2(5))* Peachtree Publishing Co. Inc.
Gonzalez, Thomas. Life in a Frozen World: Wildlife of Antarctica. Batten, Mary. 2020. (ENG.). 40p. (J). (gr. 1-5). 18.99 ***(978-1-68263-151-5(6))*** Peachtree Publishing Co. Inc.
Gonzalez, Thomas. Seven & a Half of Tons of Steel, 1 vol. Nolan, Janet. 2016. (ENG.). 36p. (J). (gr. 1-5). 17.95 *(978-1-56145-912-4(7))* Peachtree Publishing Co. Inc.
—Sonia Sotomayor (Spanish Edition) Jueza de la Corte Suprema. Bernier-Grand, Carmen. 2018. (SPA.). 48p. (J). (gr. 3-7). pap. 9.99 *(978-1-5039-0510-8(1)*, 9781503905108, Two Lions) Amazon Publishing.
—Toad Weather, 1 vol. Markle, Sandra. 2015. (ENG.). 32p. (J). (gr. 1-3). 16.95 *(978-1-56145-818-9(X))* Peachtree Publishing Co. Inc.
—14 Cows for America, 1 vol. Deedy, Carmen Agra. (ENG.). 36p. (J). (gr. 1-5). 2016. pap. 8.99 *(978-1-56145-961-2(5))*; 2009. 17.95 *(978-1-56145-490-7(7))* Peachtree Publishing Co. Inc.
—14 Cows for America. Deedy, Carmen Agra. ed. 2016. (ENG.). 36p. (J). (gr. -1-3). lib. bdg. 19.60 *(978-0-606-39065-1(0))* Turtleback.
—14 Vacas para América, 1 vol. Deedy, Carmen Agra. 2008.Tr. of 14 Cows for America. (SPA.). 36p. (J). pap. 8.95 *(978-1-56145-555-3(5))*; (gr. 1-5). 17.95 *(978-1-56145-550-8(4))* Peachtree Publishing Co. Inc.
Gonzalez, Tom. Dream of Wings. Gonzalez, Noni. 2013. (ENG.). 40p. (J). pap. 9.99 *(978-1-939337-20-7(8))*; 14.99 *(978-1-939337-71-9(2))* Telemachus Pr., LLC.
—Kubla, a Koi Story. Gonzalez, Noni. 2013. (ENG.). 38p. (J). pap. 9.99 *(978-1-939337-68-9(2))*; 14.99 *(978-1-939337-72-6(0))* Telemachus Pr., LLC.
Gooch, Brianna. Farm Friends. Redwing, Jack. Cottage Door Press, ed. 2020. (John Deere Lift-A-Flap Board Book Ser.). (ENG.). 12p. (J). (gr. -1-k). bds. 7.99 ***(978-1-68052-809-1(2)***, 1005220) Cottage Door Pr.
Gooch, Randall. Traditional Crafts from China. Temko, Florence. 2005. (Culture Crafts Ser.). 64p. (gr. 3-8). 23.93 *(978-0-8225-2939-2(4))* Lerner Publishing Group.
—Traditional Crafts from Japan. Temko, Florence. 2005. (Culture Crafts Ser.). 64p. (gr. 3-8). 23.93 *(978-0-8225-2938-5(6))* Lerner Publishing Group.
Gooch, Thelma. Nobody's Girl: Companion Story to Nobody's Boy. Malot, Hector & Crewe-Jones, Florence. 2006. 220p. (J). pap. *(978-1-894666-76-3(3))* Inheritance Pubns.
Gooch, Thelma & Gruelle, Johnny. Nobody's Boy: Companion Story to Nobody's Girl. Malot, Hector & Crewe-Jones, Florence. 2006. 237p. (J). pap. *(978-1-894666-75-6(5))* Inheritance Pubns.
Good, Karen. Change the World Before Bedtime, 1 vol. Moulton, Mark Kimball & Chalmers, Josh. 2012. (ENG.). 32p. (J). (gr. -1-3). 16.99 *(978-0-7643-4238-7(X)*, 4551) Schiffer Publishing, Ltd.
—Mr Sparrows Merry Fairy Circus. Moulton, Mark. 2004. 24p. 18.00 *(978-0-7412-1940-4(9))* Lang Graphics, Ltd.
Good, Karen H. Miss Sadie Mcgee Who Lived in a Tree. Moulton, Mark Kimball. 2008. (ENG.). 32p. (J). (gr. k-3). 16.95 *(978-0-8249-5152-8(2)*, Ideal Pubns.) Worthy Publishing.
—A Royal Wedding. Moulton, Mark K. 2007. (ENG.). 32p. (J). (gr. k-3). 14.99 *(978-0-8249-8677-3(6)*, Ideal Pubns.) Worthy Publishing.
—Twisted Sistahs. Moulton, Mark Kimball. 2006. (ENG.). 32p. (J). (gr. 2-3). 14.95 *(978-0-8249-8676-6(8)*, Ideal Pubns.) Worthy Publishing.
Good, Karen Hillard. Reindeer Christmas. Moulton, Mark Kimball. 2008. (ENG.). 40p. (J). (gr. -1-3). 15.99 *(978-1-4169-6108-6(9)*, Simon & Schuster/Paula Wiseman Bks.) Simon & Schuster/Paula Wiseman Bks.
—The Very Best Pumpkin. Moulton, Mark Kimball. 2010. (ENG.). 32p. (J). (gr. -1-3). 14.99 *(978-1-4169-8288-3(4)*, Simon & Schuster/Paula Wiseman Bks.) Simon & Schuster/Paula Wiseman Bks.
Goodale, E. B. Here & Now. Denos, Julia. 2019. (ENG.). 40p. (J). (gr. -1-3). 17.99 *(978-1-328-46564-1(0)*, 1713538, HMH Books For Young Readers) Houghton Mifflin Harcourt Publishing Co.
—A Kiss for Akaraka. Jackson, Richard. 2018. (ENG.). 40p. (J). (gr. -1-3). 17.99 *(978-0-06-265196-9(X)*, Greenwillow Bks.) HarperCollins Pubs.
—A Most Unusual Day. Mallery, Sydra. 2018. (ENG.). 40p. (J). (gr. -1-3). 17.99 *(978-0-06-236430-2(8)*, Greenwillow Bks.) HarperCollins Pubs.
—Windows. Denos, Julia. 2017. (ENG.). 32p. (J). (gr. -1-2). 16.99 *(978-0-7636-9035-9(X))* Candlewick Pr.
Goodale, Krystahl. Timothy: A Little Fish with a Big Purpose! Riley, Brad. 2013. 30p. 22.95 *(978-1-62015-341-3(6))*; pap. 14.95 *(978-1-62015-148-8(0))* Booktrope. (Vox Dei).
Goodall, Bob. There's a Nurse in the Purse of Mrs. Demurse. McGill, Heather. 2017. (ENG.). 24p. (J). *(978-1-5255-1698-6(1))*; pap. *(978-1-5255-1699-3(X))* FriesenPress.
Goodall, John. The Christmas Mouse. Read, Miss. (J). lib. bdg. 14.95 *(978-0-8488-1452-6(5))* Amereon Ltd.
Goodall, Matthew Dion. Hickory Dickory Dock - a Counting Rhyme. Goodall, Matthew Dion. 2020. (ENG.). 34p. (J). (gr. k-1). ***(978-0-473-51801-1(5))*** Goodall, Matthew.
Goodberry, Jo. Read with Me Jack & the Beanstalk: Sticker Activity Book. Page, Nick & Page, Claire. 2006. (Read with Me (Make Believe Ideas) Ser.). 12p. (J). (gr. k-2). pap. *(978-1-84610-180-9(8))* Make Believe Ideas.
—Ready to Read Jack & the Beanstalk Sticker Activity Workbook. Page, Nick & Page, Claire. 2006. (Ready-to-Read Sticker Ser.). 12p. (J). (gr. -1-3). pap., wbk. ed., act. bk. ed. *(978-1-84610-127-4(1))* Make Believe Ideas.
Goode, Diane. Baby Face: A Book of Love for Baby. Rylant, Cynthia. 2008. (ENG.). 40p. (J). (gr. -1-3). 17.99 *(978-1-4169-4909-1(7)*, Simon & Schuster/Paula Wiseman Bks.) Simon & Schuster/Paula Wiseman Bks.
—Ballerina Rosie. Ferguson, Sarah. 2012. (ENG.). 32p. (J). (gr. -1-3). 16.99 *(978-1-4424-3066-2(4)*, Simon & Schuster/Paula Wiseman Bks.) Simon & Schuster/Paula Wiseman Bks.
—The Best Mother. Surrisi, Cynthia. 2018. (ENG.). 32p. (J). (gr. -1-2). 16.99 *(978-1-4197-2534-0(3)*, Abrams Bks. for Young Readers) Abrams, Inc.
—But I Wanted a Baby Brother! Feiffer, Kate. 2010. (ENG.). 32p. (J). (gr. -1-3). 16.99 *(978-1-4169-3941-2(5)*, Simon & Schuster/Paula Wiseman Bks.) Simon & Schuster/Paula Wiseman Bks.
—Christmas in the Barn, Vol. Brown, Margaret Wise. 2007. (ENG.). 32p. (J). (gr. -1-3). per. 7.99 *(978-0-06-052636-8(X))* HarperCollins Pubs.
—Cinderella Smith. Barden, Stephanie. (Cinderella Smith Ser.: 1). (ENG.). (J). (gr. 3-7). 2012. 176p. pap. 6.99 *(978-0-06-196425-1(5))*; 2011. 160p. 16.99 *(978-0-06-196423-7(9))* HarperCollins Pubs.
—Cinderella Smith: the Super Secret Mystery, Vol. 3. Barden, Stephanie. 2013. (Cinderella Smith Ser.: 3). (ENG.). 144p. (J). (gr. 1-5). 16.99 *(978-0-06-200443-7(3))* HarperCollins Pubs.
—Founding Mothers: Remembering the Ladies. Roberts, Cokie. 2014. (ENG.). 40p. (J). (gr. 1-5). 17.99 *(978-0-06-078002-9(9))*; lib. bdg. 18.89 *(978-0-06-078003-6(7))* HarperCollins Pubs.
—Louise the Big Cheese: Divine Diva. Primavera, Elise. (ENG.). 40p. (J). (gr. k-3). 2011. 6.99 *(978-1-4424-2066-3(9))*; 2009. 16.99 *(978-1-4169-7180-1(7))* Simon & Schuster/Paula Wiseman Bks. (Simon & Schuster/Paula Wiseman Bks.).
—Louise the Big Cheese & the Back-To-School Smarty-Pants. Primavera, Elise. 2011. (ENG.). 40p. (J). (gr. k-3). 16.99 *(978-1-4424-0600-1(3)*, Simon & Schuster/Paula Wiseman Bks.) Simon & Schuster/Paula Wiseman Bks.
—Louise the Big Cheese & the La-Di-Da Shoes. Primavera, Elise. 2010. (ENG.). 40p. (J). (gr. k-3). 16.99 *(978-1-4169-7181-8(5)*, Simon & Schuster/Paula Wiseman Bks.) Simon & Schuster/Paula Wiseman Bks.
—Louise the Big Cheese & the Ooh-la-La Charm School. Primavera, Elise. 2012. (ENG.). 40p. (J). (gr. k-3). 16.99 *(978-1-4424-0599-8(6)*, Simon & Schuster/Paula Wiseman Bks.) Simon & Schuster/Paula Wiseman Bks.

—My Mom Is Trying to Ruin My Life. Feiffer, Kate. 2009. (ENG.). 32p. (J). (gr. -1-3). 19.99 *(978-1-4169-4100-2(2),* Simon & Schuster/Paula Wiseman Bks.) Simon & Schuster/Paula Wiseman Bks.

—Ninja Baby. Zeltser, David. 2015. (ENG.). 32p. (J). (gr. -1-k). 16.99 *(978-1-4521-3542-7(8))* Chronicle Bks. LLC.

—President Pennybaker. Feiffer, Kate. 2008. (ENG.). 32p. (J). (gr. -1-3). 16.99 *(978-1-4169-1354-2(8))* Simon & Schuster, Inc.

—President Pennybaker. Feiffer, Kate. 2012. (ENG.). 32p. (J). (gr. -1-3). 7.99 *(978-1-4169-1355-9(6),* Simon & Schuster/Paula Wiseman Bks.) Simon & Schuster/Paula Wiseman Bks.

—The Story of the Nutcracker Ballet. Hautzig, Deborah. 2006. (Pictureback(R) Ser.). (ENG.). 32p. (J). (gr. -1-2). pap. 3.99 *(978-0-394-88178-2(8),* Random Hse. Bks. for Young Readers) Random Hse. Children's Bks.

—When I Grow Up. Chen, Julie. 2018. (ENG.). 32p. (J). (gr. -1-3). 17.99 *(978-1-4814-9719-0(7),* Simon & Schuster/Paula Wiseman Bks.) Simon & Schuster/Paula Wiseman Bks.

Goode, Diane. The Most Perfect Spot. Goode, Diane. 2006. (ENG.). 32p. (J). (gr. -1-3). 16.99 *(978-0-06-072697-3(0))* HarperCollins Pubs.

—Thanksgiving Is Here! Goode, Diane. 2005. (ENG.). 32p. (J). (gr. -1-3). pap. 7.99 *(978-0-06-051590-4(2))* HarperCollins Pubs.

Goode, Larry. The Boy with No Heart. Camozzi, Victor. 2016. (ENG.). (J). 18.99 *(978-0-692-75176-3(9))* Camozzi, Victor.

Goodell, Jon. Chicks! Horning, Sandra. 2013. (Step into Reading Ser.). 32p. (J). (gr. -1-1). pap. 4.99 *(978-0-307-93221-1(4),* Random Hse. Bks. for Young Readers) Random Hse. Children's Bks.

—The Gold Miner's Daughter: A Melodramatic Fairy Tale, 1 vol. Hopkins, Jackie Mims. 2006. (ENG.). 32p. (J). (gr. k-3). 15.95 *(978-1-56145-362-7(5))* Peachtree Publishing Co. Inc.

Goodell, Jon, et al. Mother Goose. p i kids, P. i. Publications International Ltd. Staff, ed. 2010. (ENG.). 120p. (J). bds. *(978-0-7853-7395-7(0),* 66b0b688-2a91-477b-a3f8-269c1c9d31df) Phoenix International Publications, Inc.

Goodell, Jon. Mother, Mother, I Want Another. Robbins, Maria Polushkin. 2005. (ENG.). 32p. (J). (gr. -1-1). lib. bdg. 21.19 *(978-0-375-92588-7(0))* Random House Publishing Group.

—The Racers: A Tale about Fairness. Andersen, Hans. 2007. (J). *(978-1-59939-090-1(6),* Reader's Digest Young Families, Inc.) Studio Fun International.

—Twas the Night Before Christmas. Moore, Clement C. 2013. (ENG.). 26p. (J). bds. 9.99 *(978-1-4494-3557-8(2))* Andrews McMeel Publishing.

—Twas the Night Before Christmas. Andrews McMeel Publishing Staff & Moore, Clement C. deluxe ed. 2009. (ENG.). 26p. (J). (gr. -1-3). 19.99 *(978-0-7407-8432-3(3))* Andrews McMeel Publishing.

Goodell, Jon & Clar, David Austin. Fairy Tales. Publications International Ltd. Staff, ed. 2010. 10p. (J). bds. 12.98 *(978-0-7853-7394-0(2))* Phoenix International Publications, Inc.

Goodell, Mary. The Chicken Pox Puppy: Kate & Jen's Daily Adventures. Goodell, Mary. 2007. 29p. (J). per. 11.99 *(978-1-59879-382-6(9))* Lifevest Publishing, Inc.

Gooderham, Andrew. The True Story of Santa Claus. Walters, Eric & Walters, Christina. 2005. 38p. (J). 9.95 *(978-1-894601-11-5(4))* Chestnut Publishing Group CAN. Dist: Hushion Hse. Publishing, Ltd.

Goodfellow, Dan. Snow White's Seven Patches: A Vitiligo Fairy Tale. Kats, Jewel. 2013. 40p. (J). pap. 14.95 *(978-1-61599-206-5(5))* Loving Healing Pr., Inc.

Goodin, Carolyn M. Candy Land. Goodin, Carolyn M. 2007. 38p. (J). per. 14.99 *(978-0-9797879-1-2(2))* Family Legacy Ministries.

Goodings, Christina. Christmas: Fun Things to Make & Do. Goodings, Christina. ed. 2016. (ENG.). 104p. (J). (gr. k-2). spiral bd. 8.99 *(978-0-7459-7616-7(6),* Lion Books) Lion Hudson PLC GBR. Dist: Independent Pubs. Group.

—Easter! Fun Things to Make & Do. Goodings, Christina. ed. 2017. (ENG.). 104p. (J). (gr. k-2). spiral bd. 8.99 *(978-0-7459-7715-7(4))* Lion Hudson PLC GBR. Dist: Independent Pubs. Group.

Goodings, Christina & Meredith, Samantha. 25 Crafts for a Rainy Day. Goodings, Christina. ed. 2016. (ENG.). 32p. (J). (gr. k-2). pap. 7.99 *(978-0-7459-7672-3(7))* Lion Hudson PLC GBR. Dist: Independent Pubs. Group.

Goodman, Heidi. Mei-Mei's Lucky Birthday Noodles: A Loving Story of Adoption, Chinese Culture & a Special Birthday Treat. Chen, Shan-Shan. 2017. (ENG.). 32p. (J). (gr. -1-3). 6.99 *(978-0-8048-4978-4(1))* Tuttle Publishing.

Goodman, Heidi. Mei-Mei's Lucky Birthday Noodles: A Loving Story of Adoption, Chinese Culture & a Special Birthday Treat. Goodman, Heidi. Chen, Shan-Shan. 2014. (ENG.). 32p. (J). (gr. -1-3). 13.95 *(978-0-8048-4461-1(5))* Tuttle Publishing.

Goodman, Jennie. A Boy & a Dog. Millward, Shae. 2019. 32p. (J). (gr. -1-3). 12.99 *(978-1-921024-94-8(1))* New Holland Pubs. Pty, Ltd. AUS. Dist: Independent Pubs. Group.

Goodman, Larry. Grumpy the Grasshopper. Collier, Wayne Evans. 2012. 20p. pap. 24.95 *(978-1-4626-6844-1(5))* America Star Bks.

Goodman, Laura. Lily & Limbo: Where Flowers Go. Vilhelmsen, Leslie. 2020. (ENG.). 50p. (J). pap. 20.95 ***(978-1-9822-4502-3(6),*** Balboa Pr.) Author Solutions, Inc.

Goodman, Marlene. German Picture Dictionary. Passport Books Staff, ed. 2003. (Let's Learn... Picture Ser.). (GER.). (J). (gr. 4-7). pap. 9.95 *(978-0-8442-2167-0(8),* 21678, Passport Bks.) McGraw-Hill Trade.

—Italian Picture Dictionary. Passport Books Staff, ed. 2003. (Let's Learn... Picture Dictionary Ser.). (ITA.). 72p. (J). (gr. 4-7). pap. 9.95 *(978-0-8442-8065-3(8),* 80658) McGraw-Hill Trade.

—Japanese Picture Dictionary: Elementary Through Junior High. Passport Books Staff, ed. 2003. (Let's Learn... Picture Dictionary Ser.). (JPN.). 80p. (J). (gr. 4-7). pap. 11.95 *(978-0-8442-8494-1(7),* 84947) McGraw-Hill Trade.

—Let's Learn American English. Passport Books Staff, ed. 2003. (Let's Learn... Picture Dictionary Ser.). 72p. (J). (gr. 4-7). pap. 9.95 *(978-0-8442-5453-1(3),* 54533, Passport Bks.) McGraw-Hill Trade.

—Let's Learn Hebrew. Passport Books Staff, ed. 2003. (Let's Learn... Picture Dictionary Ser.). (HEB & ENG.). 72p. (J). (gr. 4-7). 11.95 *(978-0-8442-8490-3(4),* 84904, Passport Bks.) McGraw-Hill Trade.

Goodman, Tama. The Seven Species. Biers-Ariel, Matt. 2003. 48p. 19.95 *(978-0-8074-0852-0(2),* 161902) URJ Pr.

Goodnow, Patti. I Tell the Truth! Parker, David. 2004. (J). pap. *(978-0-439-62808-2(3))* Scholastic, Inc.

Goodpaster, Nancy. Find Your Magic. Payne, Sandy. 2013. 50p. pap. 12.95 *(978-1-937508-16-6(1))* Bearhead Publishing, LLC.

Goodreau, Sarah. Hare & Tortoise Race Across Israel. Gehl, Laura & Aesop, Aesop. 2015. (ENG.). 32p. (J). (gr. -1-1). lib. bdg. 17.95 *(978-1-4677-2199-8(9),* Kar-Ben Publishing) Lerner Publishing Group.

—Hare & Tortoise Race Across Israel. Gehl, Laura. ed. 2015. (ENG.). 32p. (J). (gr. -1-1). E-Book 23.99 *(978-1-4677-6202-1(4),* Kar-Ben Publishing) Lerner Publishing Group.

Goodreau, Sarah. The World-Famous Book of Counting. Goodreau, Sarah. 2018. (ENG.). 16p. (J). (gr. -1-2). bds. 18.99 *(978-0-7636-9894-2(6),* Big Picture Press) Candlewick Pr.

Goodrich, Carter. A Creature Was Stirring. Goodrich, Carter. Moore, Clement Clarke. 2006. (ENG.). 40p. (J). (gr. -1-3). 17.99 *(978-0-689-86399-8(3),* Simon & Schuster Bks. For Young Readers) Simon & Schuster Bks. For Young Readers.

—The Hermit Crab. Goodrich, Carter. 2009. (ENG.). 40p. (J). (gr. 1-5). 16.99 *(978-1-4169-3892-7(3),* Simon & Schuster Bks. For Young Readers) Simon & Schuster Bks. For Young Readers.

—Mister Bud Wears the Cone. Goodrich, Carter. 2014. (ENG.). 48p. (J). (gr. -1-3). 16.99 *(978-1-4424-8088-9(2),* Simon & Schuster Bks. For Young Readers) Simon & Schuster Bks. For Young Readers.

—Nobody Hugs a Cactus. Goodrich, Carter. 2019. (ENG.). 48p. (J). (gr. -1-3). 17.99 *(978-1-5344-0090-0(7),* Simon & Schuster Bks. For Young Readers) Simon & Schuster Bks. For Young Readers.

—Say Hello to Zorro! Goodrich, Carter. 2011. (ENG.). 48p. (J). (gr. -1-3). 16.99 *(978-1-4169-3893-4(1),* Simon & Schuster Bks. For Young Readers) Simon & Schuster Bks. For Young Readers.

—We Forgot Brock! Goodrich, Carter. (ENG.). 48p. (J). (gr. -1-3). 2017. 7.99 *(978-1-5344-1433-4(9));* 2015. 17.99 *(978-1-4424-8090-2(4))* Simon & Schuster Bks. For Young Readers. (Simon & Schuster Bks. For Young Readers).

—Zorro Gets an Outfit. Goodrich, Carter. 2012. (ENG.). 48p. (J). (gr. -1-3). 15.99 *(978-1-4424-3535-3(6),* Simon & Schuster Bks. For Young Readers) Simon & Schuster Bks. For Young Readers.

Goodway, Simon. Leelo. Montreuil, Gaetane. 2013. 50p. pap. *(978-1-926633-67-1(9))* Titles on Demand.

—Monkey & Cat: A Day at the Park. Morris, Sheree'. 2018. (ENG.). 30p. (J). pap. 14.99 *(978-1-7174-7962-4(6))* CreateSpace Independent Publishing Platform.

—Pooks & Boots Meet Jesus. Wood, Julie K. 2018. (Pooks, Boots, & Jesus Ser.: Vol. 1). (ENG.). 58p. (J). (gr. k-3). pap. 16.95 *(978-1-64003-710-6(1))* Covenant Bks.

Goodway, Simon. Pooks & Boots Put on the Armor of God. Wood, Julie K. 2019. (Pooks, Boots & Jesus Ser.: Vol. 2). (ENG.). 56p. (J). pap. 12.95 ***(978-1-64559-127-6(1))*** Covenant Bks.

Goodwin, Adrienne Annette. A Day Like Mine. Bridges, Eunice. 2011. 32p. pap. 24.95 *(978-1-4560-5766-4(9))* America Star Bks.

Goodwin, James. Francesca & the Genie of Science. Cross, Mike. 2019. (ENG.). 26p. (J). pap. 9.99 ***(978-1-7331414-1-3(3))*** Cross, Michael John.

Goodwin, Kathy. I Told You So! The Adventures of William & Thomas. Gunning, Mark. 2019. (I Told You So! Ser.: Vol. 1). (ENG.). 112p. (J). pap. *(978-0-9950670-6-6(6))* Itchygooney Bks.

Goodwin, Kathy. I Told You So! The Adventures of William & Thomas. Gunning, Mark. Sims, Stephanie, ed. 2nd ed. 2019. (I Told You So! Ser.: Vol. 1). (ENG.). 112p. (J). (gr. 3-6). ***(978-1-9992007-1-8(3))*** Itchygooney Bks.

Goodwin, Laura. Beckett's Monsters. Sturm, Robin Conrad. 2019. (ENG.). 46p. (J). (gr. k-6). pap. 9.99 ***(978-1-935355-30-4(9))*** New Shelves Bks.

Goodwin, Laura. Luke's Double Turn. Sturm, Robin C. 2018. (ENG.). 46p. (J). pap. 9.99 *(978-1-935355-26-7(0),* GraceNotes Pr.) New Shelves Bks.

Goodwin, Wendy. Cocoa's Collar, 1 vol. Stalick, Garyanna. 2010. 36p. pap. 24.95 *(978-1-4489-1888-1(X))* America Star Bks.

Gooliaff, Angela. Kikitu & the Secrets of Waruk's Lair. Conner, Tommy. 2019. (Kikitu Ser.). (ENG.). 128p. (J). ***(978-1-5255-4796-6(8));*** pap. ***(978-1-5255-4797-3(6))*** FriesenPress.

—Kikitu & the Stolen Children Mystery. Conner, Tommy. 2020. (Kikitu Ser.). (ENG.). 196p. (J). ***(978-1-5255-5405-6(0));*** pap. ***(978-1-5255-5406-3(9))*** FriesenPress.

—The Little Girl Who Stayed up Late. Turner, David. 2020. (ENG.). 32p. (J). ***(978-1-5255-5646-3(0));*** pap. ***(978-1-5255-5647-0(9))*** FriesenPress.

—Our Moggy. Hogan, Michael. 2020. (ENG.). 24p. (J). ***(978-1-5255-6183-2(9));*** pap. ***(978-1-5255-6184-9(7))*** FriesenPress.

Goomas, John. Even the Dead Get up for Milk. Holaves, Chris. 2008.Tr. of Hasta los muertos se levantan por Leche. (ENG & SPA.). 64p. (J). lib. bdg. 15.95 *(978-0-9792991-0-1(1))* Astakos Publishing.

—Running with the Bats: Corriendo con los Murcielagos. Holaves, Chris. Medina, Candace, tr. 2009. (ENG & SPA.). 64p. (J). (gr. 4-6). pap. 15.95 *(978-0-9792991-1-7(X))* Astakos Publishing.

Goonack, Katrina, et al. Scaly-Tailed Possum & Echidna. Goonack, Cathy. 2010. 32p. (J). (gr. k). pap. 10.95 *(978-1-921248-16-0(5))* Magabala Bks. AUS. Dist: Independent Pubs. Group.

Goopymart. Mad Tausig vs the Interplanetary Puzzling Peace Patrol. Tausig, Ben. 2007. (ENG.). 94p. (J). (gr. 4-6). per. 7.95 *(978-0-9741319-4-8(6))* 4N Publishing LLC.

Goosen, Xenia. Who Am I? Book 3 in the Guardian Series. Goosen, Irma. 2019. (ENG.). 88p. (J). pap. ***(978-1-987982-36-7(3))*** Artistic Warrior Publishing.

Goosens, Philippe. ¡Soy un Dragón! Robberecht, Thierry. 2010. (SPA.). (J). (gr. -1-2). *(978-84-263-7383-0(6))* Vives, Luis Editorial (Edelvives).

Goossens, Philippe. Owl Howl. Friester, Paul. 2014. 32p. (J). 15.95 *(978-0-7358-4188-8(8))* North-South Bks., Inc.

—Owl Howl & the BLU-BLU. Friester, Paul. 2016. (ENG.). 32p. (J). 15.95 *(978-0-7358-4246-5(9))* North-South Bks., Inc.

—Owl Howl Board Book. Friester, Paul. 2nd rev. ed. 2016. (ENG.). 26p. (J). bds. 8.95 *(978-0-7358-4234-2(5))* North-South Bks., Inc.

—Superhero School. Robberecht, Thierry. 2012. 30p. (J). (gr. -1-k). 16.95 *(978-1-60537-140-5(8))* Clavis Publishing.

Gorbachev, Kostya. When Someone Is Afraid, 1 vol. Gorbachev, Valeri. (ENG.). 32p. (J). 2012. pap. 6.95 *(978-1-59572-344-4(7));* 2005. (gr. -1-2). 15.95 *(978-1-932065-99-2(7))* Star Bright Bks., Inc.

—When Someone Is Afraid, 1 vol. Gorbachev, Valeri. 2017. (ENG.). 32p. (J). pap. 6.99 *(978-1-59572-797-8(3))* Star Bright Bks., Inc.

Gorbachev, Valeri. All for Pie, Pie for All. Martin, David. 2008. 32p. (J). (gr. -1-2). pap. 6.99 *(978-0-7636-3891-7(9))* Candlewick Pr.

—The Giant Hug. Horning, Sandra. 2008. (ENG.). 40p. (J). (gr. -1-2). pap. 7.99 *(978-0-553-11262-7(7),* Dragonfly Bks.) Random Hse. Children's Bks.

—Goldilocks & the Three Bears. 2015. 40p. (J). 15.95 *(978-0-7358-4211-3(6))* North-South Bks., Inc.

—Group Soup. Ackerman, Tova. (Orig.). pap. 6.95 *(978-0-9720183-0-2(1))* Puppetry in Practice.

—Little Bunny's Sleepless Night. Roth, Carol. 2013. 40p. (J). (gr. -1-2). 17.95 *(978-0-7358-4123-9(3))* North-South Bks., Inc.

—Rufus Blasts Off. Griswell, Kim T. 2017. 40p. (J). (gr. -1). 16.95 *(978-1-4549-2099-1(8))* Sterling Publishing Co., Inc.

—Rufus Goes to School. Griswell, Kim T. 2013. (ENG.). 32p. (J). (gr. -1-1). 16.95 *(978-1-4549-0416-8(X))* Sterling Publishing Co., Inc.

—Squirrel's Fun Day. Moser, Lisa. (Candlewick Sparks Ser.). 48p. (J). (gr. k-4). 2015. pap. 4.99 *(978-0-7636-7789-3(2));* 2013. 14.99 *(978-0-7636-5726-0(3))* Candlewick Pr.

—Squirrel's World. Moser, Lisa. 2013. (Candlewick Sparks Ser.). (ENG.). 48p. (J). (gr. k-4). pap. 4.99 *(978-0-7636-6644-6(0))* Candlewick Pr.

—There Was a Mouse. Blanchard, Patricia & Suhr, Joanne. 2003. (ENG.). 16p. (J). pap. 15.00 *(978-1-57274-702-9(1),* BB2210, Bks. for Young Learners) Owen, Richard C. Pubs., Inc.

—Where Is Bear? Newman, Lesléa. 2006. (ENG.). 44p. (J). (gr. -1 — 1). pap. 7.99 *(978-0-15-205918-7(0),* 1197770) Houghton Mifflin Harcourt Publishing Co.

—Where Is Bear? (padded Board Book) Newman, Lesléa. 2018. (ENG.). 32p. (J). (— 1). bds. 8.99 *(978-1-328-91891-8(2),* 1702525, HMH Books For Young Readers) Houghton Mifflin Harcourt Publishing Co.

—Who Will Tuck Me in Tonight? Roth, Carol. 2006. (Cheshire Studio Book Ser.). (ENG.). 32p. (J). (gr. -1-1). 6.95 *(978-0-7358-1976-4(9))* North-South Bks., Inc.

Gorbachev, Valeri. The Best Cat. Gorbachev, Valeri. 2010. 32p. (J). (gr. -1-2). 15.99 *(978-0-7636-3675-3(4))* Candlewick Pr.

—Un Dia de lluvia. Gorbachev, Valeri. 2007. (SPA.). 40p. (J). (gr. -1-3). pap. 8.95 *(978-958-04-7074-8(X))* Norma S.A. COL. Dist: Distribuidora Norma, Inc.

—How to Be Friends with a Dragon. Gorbachev, Valeri. 2013. (AV2 Fiction Readalong Ser.: Vol. 96). (ENG.). (J). (gr. -1-2). 34.28 *(978-1-62127-881-8(6),* AV2 by Weigl) Weigl Pubs., Inc.

—Me Too! Gorbachev, Valeri. 2014. (I Like to Read Ser.). (ENG.). 24p. (J). (gr. -1-3). 7.99 *(978-0-8234-3179-3(7))* Holiday Hse., Inc.

—Ms. Turtle the Babysitter. Gorbachev, Valeri. 2005. (I Can Read Bks.). 64p. (J). (gr. k-3). (ENG.). 15.99 *(978-0-06-058073-5(9));* lib. bdg. 16.89 *(978-0-06-058074-2(7))* HarperCollins Pubs.

—Not Me! Gorbachev, Valeri. 2016. (I Like to Read Ser.). (ENG.). 24p. (J). (gr. -1-3). 14.95 *(978-0-8234-3546-3(6));* pap. 7.99 *(978-0-8234-3547-0(4))* Holiday Hse., Inc.

—Whose Hat Is It? Gorbachev, Valeri. 2004. (My First I Can Read Bks.). 32p. (J). (gr. -1-18). (ENG.). 14.99 *(978-0-06-053434-9(6));* lib. bdg. 15.89 *(978-0-06-053435-6(4))* HarperCollins Pubs.

—Whose Hat Is It? Gorbachev, Valeri. 2005. (My First I Can Read Ser.). (ENG.). 32p. (J). (gr. -1 — 1). pap. 4.99 *(978-0-06-053436-3(2),* HarperCollins) HarperCollins Pubs. Ltd. GBR. Dist: HarperCollins Pubs.

Gorbatov, Vadim. Fidget's Folly. Patterson, Stacey. 2012. 36p. (J). 18.00 *(978-0-87842-594-5(2))* Mountain Pr. Publishing Co., Inc.

Gordan, Gus. My Very First Art Book. Dickens, Rosie & Courtauld, Sarah. ed. 2011. (Art Ser.). 48p. (J). pap. 12.99 *(978-0-7945-3018-1(4),* Usborne) EDC Publishing.

Gordillo Miletic, Leticia. Una Maravillosa Sorpresa. Nunez, Miguel Angel & Ediciones, Fortaleza, eds. 2019. (SPA.). 46p. (J). pap. 12.00 *(978-1-7943-0472-7(X))* Independently Published.

Gordo, Aleix. En busca de la Paz. Rodriguez-Nora, Tere. 2005. (ENG.). 32p. (J). (gr. 2-4). 13.95 *(978-84-96046-51-1(6))* Ediciones Norte, Inc.

Gordon, Ayala. Happy Purim Night. Simon, Norma. (Festival Series of Picture Storybooks). (J). (gr. -1). vinyl bd. 4.50 *(978-0-8381-0706-5(0),* 10-706) United Synagogue of America Bk. Service.

Gordon, Carl & Gordon, Mike. Do Princesses Have Best Friends Forever?, Vol. Coyle, Carmela Lavigna. 2010. (ENG.). 32p. (J). (gr. -1-3). 15.95 *(978-1-58979-542-6(3))* Taylor Trade Publishing.

Gordon, Carl, jt. illus. see Gordon, Mike.

Gordon, Danny. The Fall & Rise of Abuse-a-Saurus Rex. Smith-Leckie, Nina. 2003. 28p. (YA). (gr. 5-18). pap. 6.95 *(978-0-9725382-0-6(8))* Prairie Arts, Inc.

Gordon, David. Big Tree Down! Lawlor, Laurie. 2018. (ENG.). 32p. (J). (gr. -1-3). 17.95 *(978-0-8234-3661-3(6))* Holiday Hse., Inc.

—Construction Countdown. Olson, K. C. rev. ed. 2004. (ENG.). 24p. (J). (gr. -1-1). 18.99 *(978-0-8050-6920-4(8),* 900021060, Holt, Henry & Co. Bks. For Young Readers) Holt, Henry & Co.

—Dig, Scoop, Ka-Boom! Holub, Joan. 2013. (Step into Reading Ser.). 24p. (J). (gr. -1-1). pap. 4.99 *(978-0-375-86910-5(7),* Random Hse. Bks. for Young Readers) Random Hse. Children's Bks.

Gordon, David, et al. Dizzy Izzy. Scieszka, Jon. 2010. (Jon Scieszka's Trucktown Ser.). (ENG.). 24p. (J). (gr. -1-1). pap. 4.99 *(978-1-4169-4145-3(2),* Simon Spotlight) Simon Spotlight.

—Kat's Mystery Gift. Scieszka, Jon. 2009. (Jon Scieszka's Trucktown Ser.). (ENG.). 24p. (J). (gr. -1-1). pap. 4.99 *(978-1-4169-4143-9(6),* Simon Spotlight) Simon Spotlight.

—Melvin Might? Scieszka, Jon. 2008. (Jon Scieszka's Trucktown Ser.). (ENG.). 44p. (J). (gr. -1-3). 19.99 *(978-1-4169-4134-7(7),* Simon & Schuster Bks. For Young Readers) Simon & Schuster Bks. For Young Readers.

Gordon, David. The Noisy Airplane Ride. Downs, Mike. 2005. 32p. (J). (gr. -1-2). pap. 7.99 *(978-1-58246-157-1(0),* Tricycle Pr.) Random Hse. Children's Bks.

Gordon, David, et al. Pete's Party. Scieszka, Jon. 2008. (Jon Scieszka's Trucktown Ser.). (ENG.). 24p. (J). (gr. -1-k). lib. bdg. 13.89 *(978-1-4169-4149-1(5));* pap. 3.99 *(978-1-4169-4138-5(X))* Simon Spotlight. (Simon Spotlight).

—Race from a to Z, No. 4. Scieszka, Jon. 2014. (Jon Scieszka's Trucktown Ser.). (ENG.). 48p. (J). (gr. -1-3). 19.99 *(978-1-4169-4136-1(3),* Simon & Schuster Bks. For Young Readers) Simon & Schuster Bks. For Young Readers.

—Snow Trucking! Scieszka, Jon. 2008. (Jon Scieszka's Trucktown Ser.). (ENG.). 24p. (J). (gr. -1-1). pap. 3.99 *(978-1-4169-4140-8(1),* Simon Spotlight) Simon Spotlight.

—Take a Trip with Trucktown! Jon Scieszkas Trucktown et al. 2011. (Jon Scieszka's Trucktown Ser.). (ENG.). 24p. (J). (gr. -1-3). pap. 3.99 *(978-1-4169-4181-1(9),* Simon & Schuster Bks. For Young Readers) Simon & Schuster Bks. For Young Readers.

—Trucks Line Up. Scieszka, Jon. 2011. (Jon Scieszka's Trucktown Ser.). (ENG.). 24p. (J). (gr. -1-1). pap. 4.99 *(978-1-4169-4147-7(9),* Simon Spotlight) Simon Spotlight.

Gordon, David. Extremely Cute Animals Operating Heavy Machinery. Gordon, David. 2016. (ENG.). 48p. (J). (gr. -1-3). 17.99 *(978-1-4169-2441-8(8),* Simon & Schuster Bks. For Young Readers) Simon & Schuster Bks. For Young Readers.

—Smitten. Gordon, David. 2007. (ENG.). 40p. (J). (gr. -1-3). 19.99 *(978-1-4169-2440-1(X),* Atheneum Bks. for Young Readers) Simon & Schuster Children's Publishing.

—The Three Little Rigs. Gordon, David. 2005. (ENG.). 32p. (J). (gr. -1-3). 17.99 *(978-0-06-058118-3(2))* HarperCollins Pubs.

—The Ugly Truckling. Gordon, David. 2004. 32p. (J). (gr. -1-2). lib. bdg. 16.89 *(978-0-06-054601-4(8),* Geringer, Laura Book) HarperCollins Pubs.

Gordon, Eric A. & Gordon, Steven E. Batman Classic: Dawn of the Dynamic Duo. Sazaklis, John. 2011. (I Can Read Level 2 Ser.). (ENG.). 32p. (J). (gr. -1-3). pap. 4.99 *(978-0-06-188520-4(7))* HarperCollins Pubs.

—Darkseid's Revenge. Aptekar, Devan. 2012. (ENG.). 24p. (J). (gr. -1-3). pap. 3.99 *(978-0-06-188533-4(9),* HarperFestival) HarperCollins Pubs.

—Darkseid's Revenge. Aptekar, Devan. ed. 2012. (Justice League Classic 8X8 Ser.). (J). lib. bdg. 13.55 *(978-0-606-23566-2(3))* Turtleback.

—Going Ape. Sutton, Laurie S. 2012. (I Can Read Level 2 Ser.). (ENG.). 32p. (J). (gr. -1-3). pap. 3.99 *(978-0-06-188522-8(3))* HarperCollins Pubs.

—Justice League: Meet the Justice League. Rosen, Lucy. 2013. (I Can Read Level 2 Ser.). (ENG.). 32p. (J). (gr. -1-3). pap. 4.99 *(978-0-06-221002-9(5))* HarperCollins Pubs.

Gordon, Eric A., jt. illus. see Gordon, Steven E.

Gordon, F. C. Among the Farmyard People. Pierson, Clara Dillingham. 2008. 176p. pap. 8.95 *(978-1-59915-281-3(9))* Yesterday's Classics.

Gordon, Gus. Basketball Buddies. Arena, Felice & Kettle, Phil. 2004. (J). pap. *(978-1-59336-369-7(9))* Mondo Publishing.

—Battle of the Games. Arena, Felice & Kettle, Phil. 2004. (J). pap. *(978-1-59336-372-7(9))* Mondo Publishing.

—The Catawampus Cat. Eaton, Jason Carter. 2017. (ENG.). 32p. (J). (gr. -1-3). 16.99 *(978-0-553-50971-7(3),* Crown Books For Young Readers) Random Hse. Children's Bks.

—Golf Legends. Arena, Felice & Kettle, Phil. 2004. (J). pap. *(978-1-59336-367-3(2))* Mondo Publishing.

—Halloween Gotcha! Arena, Felice & Kettle, Phil. 2004. (J). pap. *(978-1-59336-373-4(7))* Mondo Publishing.

—My Life & Other Exploding Chickens. Bancks, Tristan. (Tom Weekly Ser.: 4). (J). (gr. 4-7). 2019. 240p. 9.99 *(978-0-14-379011-2(0));* 2016. (ENG.). 192p. 9.99 *(978-0-85798-531-6(0))* Random Hse. Australia AUS. Dist: Independent Pubs. Group.

—My Life & Other Failed Experiments. Bancks, Tristan. 2019. (Tom Weekly Ser.: 6). 240p. (J). (gr. 4-7). 9.99 *(978-0-14-378161-5(8))* Random Hse. Australia AUS. Dist: Independent Pubs. Group.

G

—My Life & Other Massive Mistakes. Bancks, Tristan. 2018. (Tom Weekly Ser.: 3). 240p. (J). (gr. 4-7). 9.99 (978-0-14-379010-5(2)) Random Hse. Australia AUS. Dist: Independent Pubs. Group.

—My Life & Other Stuff I Made Up. Bancks, Tristan. (J). (gr. 4-7). 2018. (Tom Weekly Ser.: 1). 240p. 9.99 (978-0-14-379008-2(0)); 2014. (My Life & Other Stuff... Ser.). (ENG.). 288p. 9.99 (978-0-85798-319-0(9)); 2011. (My Life & Other Stuff... Ser.). (ENG.). 208p. 9.99 (978-1-86471-817-1(X)) Random Hse. Australia AUS. Dist: Independent Pubs. Group.

—My Life & Other Stuff That Went Wrong. Bancks, Tristan. (J). (gr. 4-7). 2018. (Tom Weekly Ser.: 2). 240p. 9.99 (978-0-14-379009-9(9)); 2014. (My Life & Other Stuff... Ser.). (ENG.). 208p. 9.99 (978-0-85798-037-3(8)) Random Hse. Australia AUS. Dist: Independent Pubs. Group.

—My Life & Other Weaponised Muffins. Bancks, Tristan. 2017. (My Life & Other Stuff... Ser.: 5). (ENG.). 208p. (J). (gr. 4-7). 10.99 (978-0-14-378106-6(5)) Random Hse. Australia AUS. Dist: Independent Pubs. Group.

—Park Soccer. Arena, Felice & Kettle, Phil. 2004. (J). (978-1-59336-366-6(4)) Mondo Publishing.

—Rock Star. Arena, Felice & Kettle, Phil. 2004. (J). pap. (978-1-59336-368-0(0)) Mondo Publishing.

—So Festy! Mawter, J. A. 2004. 160p. (978-0-207-19919-6(1)) HarperCollins Pubs. Australia.

—So Grotty! Mawter, J. A. 5th ed. 2004. (So... Ser.: Bk. 5). 160p. (Orig.). (J). (978-0-207-20007-6(6), Angus & Robertson) HarperCollins Pubs. Australia.

—So Sick! Mawter, J. A. 2003. 144p. (Orig.). (978-0-207-19997-4(3)) HarperCollins Pubs. Australia.

—So Stinky! Mawter, J. A. 2005. 160p. (Orig.). (978-0-207-20008-3(4)) HarperCollins Pubs. Australia.

—To the Moon & Back: The Amazing Australians at the Forefront of Space Travel. Sullivan, Bryan & French, Jackie. 2004. 208p. (Orig.). (J). (978-0-207-20009-0(2)) HarperCollins Pubs.

Gordon, Gus. Finding François: A Story about the Healing Power of Friendship. Gordon, Gus. 2020. (ENG.). 40p. (J). (gr. -1-3). 17.99 **(978-0-525-55400-4(9)**, Dial Bks) Penguin Young Readers Group.

Gordon, Gus. The Last Peach. Gordon, Gus. 2019. (ENG.). 40p. (J). 17.99 (978-1-62672-350-4(8), 900153623) Roaring Brook Pr.

—Somewhere Else: A Picture Book. Gordon, Gus. 2017. (ENG.). 40p. (J). 17.99 (978-1-62672-349-8(4), 900153622) Roaring Brook Pr.

Gordon, Gus & Vane, Mitch. Battle of the Games. Arena, Felice et al. 2004. 48p. (J). pap. (978-0-7329-9254-5(0)) Mondo Publishing.

Gordon, Jessica Rae. Families Around the World. Ruurs, Margriet. (Around the World Ser.). (ENG.). 40p. (J). (gr. -1-2). 2017. pap. 8.99 (978-1-77138-807-8(2)); 2014. 18.95 (978-1-894786-57-7(2)) Kids Can Pr., Ltd. CAN. Dist: Hachette Bk. Group.

Gordon, John. Go, Billy, Go! Being Yourself. Blevins, Wiley. 2015. (Funny Bone Readers (tm) — Dealing with Bullies Ser.). (ENG.). 24p. (J). (gr. k-2). lib. bdg. 19.99 (978-1-63440-003-9(8)) Red Chair Pr.

—Meet Teddy Rex! Williams, Bonnie. 2012. (Dino School Ser.). (ENG.). 24p. (J). (gr. -1-1). 17.99 (978-1-4424-4996-1(9)); pap. 3.99 (978-1-4424-4995-4(0)) Simon Spotlight. (Simon Spotlight).

—Pete Can Fly! Williams, Bonnie. 2014. (Dino School Ser.). (ENG.). 24p. (J). (gr. -1-1). pap. 4.99 (978-1-4814-0465-5(2), Simon Spotlight) Simon Spotlight.

—Say Cheese, Teddy Rex! Williams, Bonnie. 2016. (Dino School Ser.). (J). (ENG.). 24p. (gr. -1-1). pap. 4.99 (978-1-4814-6609-7(7)); (978-1-5182-1896-5(2)) Simon Spotlight. (Simon Spotlight).

Gordon-Lucas, Bonnie. Animals Building Character: An Activities Book to Color. Saint Rain, Justice. 2019. (ENG.). 82p. (J). pap. 12.95 **(978-1-888547-39-9(1))** Special Ideas.

Gordon-Lucas, Bonnie. Fun with My First Words: French-Hebrew Picture Dictionary. Peterseil, Shlomo, ed. 2005. (ENG, FRE & HEB.). 12p. (J). bds. 12.95 (978-1-930143-24-1(9), Devora Publishing) Simcha Media Group.

—Fun with My First Words: Hebrew-English - English-Hebrew Dictionary. Peterseil, Shlomo. 2005. (ENG & HEB.). 12p. (J). (gr. -1-1). bds. 12.95 (978-1-930143-22-7(2), Devora Publishing) Simcha Media Group.

—Fun with My First Words: Russian-Hebrew Picture Dictionary. Peterseil, Shlomo, ed. 2005. (ENG, HEB & RUS.). 12p. (J). bds. 12.95 (978-1-930143-26-5(5), Devora Publishing) Simcha Media Group.

—Fun with My First Words: Spanish-Hebrew Picture Dictionary. Peterseil, Shlomo, ed. 2005. (ENG, HEB & SPA.). 12p. (J). bds. 12.95 (978-1-930143-23-4(0), Devora Publishing) Simcha Media Group.

Gordon, Mike. All Wrapped Up. Callahan, Thera S. (Rookie Reader Ser.). 32p. (J). (gr. k-2). 2004. (ENG.). pap. 4.95 (978-0-516-21949-3(9)); 2003. 19.50 (978-0-516-22844-0(7)) Scholastic Library Publishing. (Children's Pr.).

—Bug Brother. Johnson, Pete. 2019. 107p. (J). pap. 4.99 (978-1-61067-742-4(0)) Kane Miller.

—Butterfly Garden. McNamara, Margaret. 2012. (Robin Hill School Ser.). (ENG.). 32p. (J). (gr. -1-1). 17.99 (978-1-4424-3643-5(3)); pap. 4.99 (978-1-4424-3642-8(5)) Simon Spotlight. (Simon Spotlight).

—The Castle That Jack Built. Sims, Lesley. 2007. (Usborne First Reading: Level 3 Ser.). 48p. (J). (gr. -1-3). 8.99 (978-0-7945-1599-7(1), Usborne) EDC Publishing.

—Class Mom. McNamara, Margaret. 2009. (Robin Hill School Ser.). (ENG.). 32p. (J). (gr. -1-1). pap. 4.99 (978-1-4169-5537-5(2), Simon Spotlight) Simon Spotlight.

—Class Picture Day. McNamara, Margaret. 2011. (Robin Hill School Ser.). (ENG.). 32p. (J). (gr. -1-1). 17.99 (978-1-4424-3611-4(5)); pap. 4.99 (978-1-4169-9173-1(5)) Simon Spotlight. (Simon Spotlight).

—Como Nacen los Bebes? Aprender Sobre Sexualidad. Llewellyn, Claire. (SPA.). (J). (gr. k-2). pap. (978-950-24-0944-3(2)) Albatros ARG. Dist: Lectorum Pubns., Inc.

—Counting Race. McNamara, Margaret. 2003. (Robin Hill School Ser.). (ENG.). 32p. (J). (gr. -1-1). pap. 4.99 (978-0-689-85539-9(7), Simon Spotlight) Simon Spotlight.

—The Counting Race. McNamara, Margaret. ed. 2005. 32p. (J). lib. bdg. 15.00 (978-1-59054-967-4(8)) Fitzgerald Bks.

—Croc by the Rock. Robinson, Hilary. 2005. 32p. (J). lib. bdg. 9.00 (978-1-4242-0885-2(8)) Fitzgerald Bks.

—A Croc Shock! Robinson, Hilary. 2009. (Get Set Readers Ser.). 32p. (J). (gr. -1-2). lib. bdg. 25.60 (978-1-60754-265-0(X)) Windmill Bks.

—Dad Goes to School. McNamara, Margaret. 2007. (Robin Hill School Ser.). (ENG.). 32p. (J). (gr. -1-1). pap. 4.99 (978-1-4169-1541-6(9), Simon Spotlight) Simon Spotlight.

—Do Princesses Become Astronauts?, Vol. Coyle, Carmela Lavigna. 2019. (Do Princesses Ser.). (ENG.). 32p. (J). (gr. -1-2). 15.95 (978-1-63076-347-3(0)) Muddy Boots Pr.

—Do Princesses Boogie?, Vol. Coyle, Carmela Lavigna. 2016. (Do Princesses Ser.). (ENG.). 26p. (J). (gr. -1-2). 7.95 (978-1-63076-159-2(1)) Taylor Trade Publishing.

—Do Princesses Make Happy Campers?, Vol. Coyle, Carmela Lavigna. 2015. (Do Princesses Ser.). (ENG.). 32p. (J). (gr. -1-2). 15.95 (978-1-63076-054-0(4)) Taylor Trade Publishing.

—Do Superheroes Have Teddy Bears?, Vol. Coyle, Carmela Lavigna. 2012. (ENG.). 32p. (J). (gr. -1-2). 15.95 (978-1-58979-693-5(4)) Taylor Trade Publishing.

—Earth Day. McNamara, Margaret. 2009. (Robin Hill School Ser.). (ENG.). 32p. (J). (gr. -1-1). pap. 4.99 (978-1-4169-5535-1(6), Simon Spotlight) Simon Spotlight.

—Eating Well. Gogerly, Liz. 2008. (Looking after Me Ser.). (ENG.). 32p. (J). (gr. -1-3). pap. (978-0-7787-4117-6(6)) Crabtree Publishing Co.

—Election Day. McNamara, Margaret. 2008. (Robin Hill School Ser.). (J). (gr. -1-1). pap. 16.95 (978-1-4301-0598-5(4)) Live Oak Media.

—Election Day. McNamara, Margaret. 2004. (Robin Hill School Ser.). (ENG.). 32p. (J). (gr. -1-1). pap. 4.99 (978-0-689-86425-4(6), Simon Spotlight) Simon Spotlight.

—The Emperor's New Clothes. 2006. 24p. (J). (gr. -1-3). 9.99 (978-0-7945-1350-4(6), Usborne) EDC Publishing.

—Estoy Sano? Aprender Sobre Alimentacion y Actividad Fisica. Llewellyn, Claire. (SPA.). (J). (gr. k-2). pap. (978-950-24-0945-0(0)) Albatros ARG. Dist: Lectorum Pubns., Inc.

—Exercise. Gogerly, Liz. 2008. (Looking after Me Ser.). (ENG.). 32p. (J). (gr. -1-3). pap. (978-0-7787-4118-3(4)) Crabtree Publishing Co.

—Fall Leaf Project. McNamara, Margaret. 2006. (Robin Hill School Ser.). (ENG.). 32p. (J). (gr. -1-1). pap. 4.99 (978-1-4169-1537-9(0), Simon Spotlight) Simon Spotlight.

—Family Photo. Rau, Dana Meachen. 2007. (Rookie Reader Skill Set Ser.). (ENG.). 32p. (J). (gr. k-2). pap. 4.95 (978-0-531-12492-5(4), Children's Pr.) Scholastic Library Publishing.

—Feeling Angry! Douglass, Katie. 2017. (Everyday Feelings Ser.). (ENG.). 32p. (J). (gr. k-4). 12.99 (978-1-63198-251-4(6), 82514) Free Spirit Publishing, Inc.

—Feeling Jealous! Barnham, Kay. 2017. (Everyday Feelings Ser.). (ENG.). 32p. (J). (gr. k-4). 12.99 (978-1-63198-252-1(4)) Free Spirit Publishing, Inc.

—Feeling Sad! Barnham, Kay. 2017. (Everyday Feelings Ser.). (ENG.). 32p. (J). (gr. k-4). 12.99 (978-1-63198-253-8(2), 82538) Free Spirit Publishing, Inc.

—Feeling Scared! Barnham, Kay. 2017. (Everyday Feelings Ser.). (ENG.). 32p. (J). (gr. k-4). 12.99 (978-1-63198-254-5(0)) Free Spirit Publishing, Inc.

—Feeling Shy! Barnham, Kay. 2017. (Everyday Feelings Ser.). (ENG.). 32p. (J). (gr. k-4). 12.99 (978-1-63198-256-9(7)) Free Spirit Publishing, Inc.

—Feeling Worried. Barnham, Kay. 2017. (Everyday Feelings Ser.). (ENG.). 32p. (J). (gr. k-4). 12.99 (978-1-63198-255-2(9), 82552) Free Spirit Publishing, Inc.

—The First Day of School. McNamara, Margaret. 2008. (Robin Hill School Ser.). (J). (gr. -1-3). pap. 16.95 (978-1-4301-0604-3(2)) Live Oak Media.

—The First Day of School. McNamara, Margaret. 2005. (Robin Hill School Ser.). (ENG.). 32p. (J). (gr. -1-1). pap. 3.99 (978-0-689-86914-3(2), Simon Spotlight) Simon Spotlight.

—First-Grade Bunny. McNamara, Margaret. 2005. (Ready-To-Read Level 1 Ser.). (ENG.). 32p. (J). (gr. -1-1). lib. bdg. 16.19 (978-0-689-86428-5(0)) Simon & Schuster, Inc.

—First-Grade Bunny. McNamara, Margaret. 2005. (Robin Hill School Ser.). (ENG.). 32p. (J). (gr. -1-1). pap. 4.99 (978-0-689-86427-8(2), Simon Spotlight) Simon Spotlight.

—Fred & Finn. Goodey, Madeline. 2014. (ReadZone Picture Bks.). (ENG.). 32p. (J). (gr. k-3). pap. 8.99 (978-1-78322-421-0(5)) ReadZone Bks. GBR. Dist: Independent Pubs. Group.

—Free Association Where My Mind Goes During Science Class. Esham, Barbara. 2018. (Adventures of Everyday Geniuses Ser.: 0). 32p. (J). (-3). 17.99 (978-1-4926-6995-1(4), Little Pickle Pr.) Sourcebooks, Inc.

—The Frog Prince. rev. ed. 2007. (Young Reading CD Packs Ser.). 48p. (J). (gr. -1-3). 9.99 incl. audio compact disk (978-0-7945-1868-4(0), Usborne) EDC Publishing.

—The Garden Project. McNamara, Margaret. 2010. (Robin Hill School Ser.). (ENG.). 32p. (J). (gr. -1-1). pap. 4.99 (978-1-4169-9171-7(9), Simon Spotlight) Simon Spotlight.

—Goldilocks & the Three Bears. 2007. (First Reading Level 4 Ser.). 48p. (J). (gr. -1-3). 8.99 (978-0-7945-1708-3(0), Usborne) EDC Publishing.

—Groundhog Day. McNamara, Margaret. 2005. (Robin Hill School Ser.). 32p. (J). (gr. -1-3). 11.65 (978-0-7569-7146-5(2)) Perfection Learning Corp.

—Groundhog Day. McNamara, Margaret. 2006. (Robin Hill School Ser.). (ENG.). 32p. (J). (gr. -1-1). pap. 4.99 (978-1-4169-0507-3(3), Simon Spotlight) Simon Spotlight.

—Halloween Fun. McNamara, Margaret. 2008. (Robin Hill School Ser.). (ENG.). 32p. (J). (gr. -1-1). pap. 4.99 (978-1-4169-3496-7(0), Simon Spotlight) Simon Spotlight.

—Happy Graduation! McNamara, Margaret. 2008. (Robin Hill School Ser.). (J). (gr. -1-1). pap. 16.95 (978-1-4301-0610-4(7)) Live Oak Media.

—Happy Graduation! McNamara, Margaret. 2006. (Robin Hill School Ser.). (ENG.). 32p. (J). (gr. -1-1). pap. 4.99 (978-1-4169-0509-7(X), Simon Spotlight) Simon Spotlight.

—If You're So Smart, How Come You Can't Spell Mississippi. Esham, Barbara. 2018. (Adventures of Everyday Geniuses Ser.: 0). 32p. (J). (-3). 17.99 (978-1-4926-6998-2(9), Little Pickle Pr.) Sourcebooks, Inc.

—Keep Your Eye on the Prize. Esham, Barbara. 2018. (Adventures of Everyday Geniuses Ser.: 0). 32p. (J). (-3). 17.99 (978-1-4926-7000-1(6), Little Pickle Pr.) Sourcebooks, Inc.

—Keeping Clean. Gogerly, Liz. 2008. (Looking after Me Ser.). (ENG.). 32p. (J). (gr. -1-3). pap. (978-0-7787-4119-0(2)); lib. bdg. (978-0-7787-4112-1(5)) Crabtree Publishing Co.

—Las Princesas Mueven el Esqueleto? LaVigna, Carmela. 2018. (SPA.). 26p. (J). (gr. -1-3). 16.95 (978-84-9145-159-4(5), Picarona Editorial) Ediciones Obelisco ESP. Dist: Spanish Pubs., LLC.

—Last to Finish: A Story about the Smartest Boy in Math Class. Esham, Barbara. 2008. 32p. (J). (gr. k-18). 16.95 (978-1-60336-456-0(0), Adventures of Everyday Geniuses, The) Mainstream Connections Publishing.

—Last to Finish, a Story about the Smartest Boy in Math Class. Esham, Barbara. 2018. (Adventures of Everyday Geniuses Ser.: 0). 32p. (J). (-3). 17.99 (978-1-4926-6999-9(7), Little Pickle Pr.) Sourcebooks, Inc.

—Little Red Riding Hood. 2007. (Picture Book Classics Ser.). 24p. (J). (gr. 1-4). 9.99 (978-0-7945-1787-8(0), Usborne) EDC Publishing.

—Looking after Me. Gogerly, Liz. 2008. (ENG.). 32p. (J). (gr. -1-3). (978-0-7787-4109-1(5)) Crabtree Publishing Co.

—Martin Luther King Jr. Day. McNamara, Margaret. 2007. (Ready-To-Read Level 1 Ser.). (ENG.). 32p. (J). (gr. -1-1). lib. bdg. 17.44 (978-1-4169-3495-0(2)) Simon & Schuster, Inc.

—Martin Luther King Jr. Day. McNamara, Margaret. 2007. (Robin Hill School Ser.). (ENG.). 32p. (J). (gr. -1-1). pap. 4.99 (978-1-4169-3494-3(4), Simon Spotlight) Simon Spotlight.

—Me Hace Bien o Mal? Aprender Sobre Medicamentos, Drogas y Salud. Llewellyn, Claire. (SPA.). (J). (gr. k-2). pap. (978-950-24-0946-7(9)) Albatros ARG. Dist: Lectorum Pubns., Inc.

—Mrs. Gorski, I Think I Have the Wiggle Fidgets. Esham, Barbaraa. 2008. (ENG, SPA & FRE.). 32p. (J). (gr. k-18). 16.95 (978-1-60336-469-0(2), Adventures of Everyday Geniuses, The) Mainstream Connections Publishing.

—Mrs. Gorski I Think I Have the Wiggle Fidgets. Esham, Barbara. 2018. (Adventures of Everyday Geniuses Ser.: 0). 32p. (J). (-3). 17.99 (978-1-4926-6997-5(0), Little Pickle Pr.) Sourcebooks, Inc.

—My Best Friend. Namm, Diane. 2004. (My First Reader Ser.). (ENG.). 32p. (J). (gr. k-1). pap. 3.95 (978-0-516-25504-0(5), Children's Pr.) Scholastic Library Publishing.

—My Money Choices. Llewellyn, Claire. 2016. (Your Money Ser.). 00024p. (J). (gr. 1-1). pap. 8.25 (978-1-4994-8191-4(8), Windmill Bks.) Rosen Publishing Group, Inc., The.

—Once There Was a Raindrop. Anderson, Judith. 2010. (Nature's Miracles Ser.). (ENG.). 32p. (J). (gr. k-3). 18.69 (978-0-7641-4495-0(2), B.E.S. Publishing) Peterson's.

—Once There Was a Seed. Anderson, Judith. 2010. (Nature's Miracles Ser.). (ENG.). 32p. (J). (gr. k-3). 18.69 (978-0-7641-4493-6(6), B.E.S. Publishing) Peterson's.

—Once There Was a Tadpole. Anderson, Judith. 2010. (Nature's Miracles Ser.). (ENG.). 32p. (J). (gr. k-3). 18.69 (978-0-7641-4496-7(0), B.E.S. Publishing) Peterson's.

—One Hundred Days (Plus One) McNamara, Margaret. 2008. (Robin Hill School Ser.). (J). (gr. -1-3). pap. 16.95 (978-1-4301-0616-6(6)) Live Oak Media.

—One Hundred Days (Plus One) McNamara, Margaret. 2003. (Ready-to-Read Robin Hill School Ser.). 32p. (J). (gr. -1-3). 11.65 (978-0-7569-1805-7(7)) Perfection Learning Corp.

—One Hundred Days (Plus One) McNamara, Margaret. 2003. (Robin Hill School Ser.). (ENG.). 32p. (J). (gr. -1-1). pap. 4.99 (978-0-689-85535-1(4), Simon Spotlight) Simon Spotlight.

—Picking Apples. McNamara, Margaret. 2009. (Robin Hill School Ser.). (ENG.). 32p. (J). (gr. -1-1). pap. 4.99 (978-1-4169-5539-9(9), Simon Spotlight) Simon Spotlight.

—Pirate Brother. Johnson, Pete. 2019. 111p. (J). pap. 4.99 (978-1-61067-745-5(5)) Kane Miller.

—Playground Problem. McNamara, Margaret. 2004. (Robin Hill School Ser.). (ENG.). 32p. (J). (gr. -1-1). pap. 4.99 (978-0-689-85876-5(0), Simon Spotlight) Simon Spotlight.

—Presidents' Day. McNamara, Margaret. 2010. (Robin Hill School Ser.). (ENG.). 32p. (J). (gr. -1-1). pap. 4.99 (978-1-4169-9170-0(0), Simon Spotlight) Simon Spotlight.

—The Princess & the Pea. rev. ed. 2007. (Young Reading CD Packs Ser.). 48p. (J). (gr. -1-3). 9.99 incl. audio compact disk (978-0-7945-1875-2(3), Usborne) EDC Publishing.

—Princess Handbook. Davidson, Susanna. 2006. 80p. (J). (gr. 3-7). 12.99 (978-0-7945-1329-0(8), Usborne) EDC Publishing.

—The Pumpkin Patch. McNamara, Margaret. 2005. (Ready-to-Read Ser.). 32p. (J). lib. bdg. 15.00 (978-1-59054-932-2(5)) Fitzgerald Bks.

—The Pumpkin Patch. McNamara, Margaret. 2008. (Robin Hill School Ser.). (J). (gr. -1-1). pap. 16.95 (978-1-4301-0622-7(0)) Live Oak Media.

—The Pumpkin Patch. McNamara, Margaret. 2003. (Ready-To-Read Level 1 Ser.). (ENG.). 32p. (J). (gr. -1-1). lib. bdg. 17.44 (978-0-689-85875-8(2)) Simon & Schuster, Inc.

—Un Regalo Bien Envuelto: All Wrapped Up. Callahan, Thera S. 2003. (Rookie Readers Spanish Ser.). (SPA.). (J). 19.50 (978-0-516-25885-0(0), Children's Pr.) Scholastic Library Publishing.

—Robin Hill School the Complete Collection: Too Many Valentines; One Hundred Days (Plus One); the Counting Race; the Pumpkin Patch; the Playground Problem; a Tooth Story; Election Day; First-Grade Bunny; the First Day of School; Happy Thanksgiving; Happy Graduation!; Fall Leaf Project, Etc. McNamara, Margaret. ed. 2018. (Robin Hill School Ser.). (ENG.). 896p. (J). (gr. -1-1). pap. 111.99 (978-1-5344-2714-3(7), Simon Spotlight) Simon Spotlight.

—Safety. Gogerly, Liz. 2008. (Looking after Me Ser.). (ENG.). 32p. (J). (gr. -1-3). pap. (978-0-7787-4120-6(6)); lib. bdg. (978-0-7787-4113-8(3)) Crabtree Publishing Co.

—Saving My Money. Llewellyn, Claire. 2017. (Your Money Ser.). (ENG.). 24p. (J). (gr. -1-2). 19.05 (978-1-5311-8629-6(7)) Perfection Learning Corp.

—Saving My Money. Llewellyn, Claire. 2016. (Your Money Ser.). 00024p. (J). (gr. 1-1). pap. 8.25 (978-1-4994-8194-5(2), Windmill Bks.) Rosen Publishing Group, Inc., The.

—Secret Santa. McNamara, Margaret. 2012. (Robin Hill School Ser.). (ENG.). 32p. (J). (gr. -1-1). 15.99 (978-1-4424-3649-7(2)); pap. 4.99 (978-1-4424-3648-0(4)) Simon Spotlight. (Simon Spotlight).

—Snow Day. McNamara, Margaret. 2007. (Robin Hill School Ser.). (ENG.). 32p. (J). (gr. -1-1). pap. 4.99 (978-1-4169-3493-6(6), Simon Spotlight) Simon Spotlight.

—Snug as a Bug, 1 vol. Imbody, Amy E. & Imbody, Amy. 2008. (I Can Read! Ser.). (ENG.). 32p. (J). (gr. -1-1). pap. 4.99 (978-0-310-71575-7(X)) Zonderkidz.

—Spending My Money. Llewellyn, Claire. 2017. (Your Money Ser.). (ENG.). 24p. (J). (gr. -1-2). 19.05 (978-1-5311-8652-4(1)) Perfection Learning Corp.

—Spending My Money. Llewellyn, Claire. 2016. (Your Money Ser.). 00024p. (J). (gr. 1-1). pap. 8.25 (978-1-4994-8197-6(7), Windmill Bks.) Rosen Publishing Group, Inc., The.

—Stacey Coolidge's Fancy Smancy Cursive Handwriting. Esham, Barbara. 2008. 32p. (J). (gr. k-18). 16.95 (978-1-60336-462-1(5), Adventures of Everyday Geniuses, The) Mainstream Connections Publishing.

—Stacey Coolidge's Fancy-Smancy Cursive Handwriting. Esham, Barbara. 2018. (Adventures of Everyday Geniuses Ser.: 0). 32p. (J). (-3). 17.99 (978-1-4926-6996-8(2), Little Pickle Pr.) Sourcebooks, Inc.

—Stories of Princesses. 2006. 144p. (J). (gr. 4-7). 14.99 (978-0-7945-1385-6(9), Usborne) EDC Publishing.

—Summer Treasure. McNamara, Margaret. 2012. (Robin Hill School Ser.). (ENG.). 32p. (J). (gr. -1-1). 17.99 (978-1-4424-3646-6(8)); pap. 4.99 (978-1-4424-3645-9(X)) Simon Spotlight. (Simon Spotlight).

—Taking Medicine. Gogerly, Liz. 2008. (Looking after Me Ser.). (ENG.). 32p. (J). (gr. -1-3). pap. (978-0-7787-4121-3(4)); lib. bdg. (978-0-7787-4114-5(1)) Crabtree Publishing Co.

—Teeth. Gogerly, Liz. 2008. (Looking after Me Ser.). (ENG.). 32p. (J). (gr. -1-3). pap. (978-0-7787-4122-0(2)); lib. bdg. (978-0-7787-4115-2(X)) Crabtree Publishing Co.

—Too Many Valentines. McNamara, Margaret. 2003. (Robin Hill School Ser.). (ENG.). 32p. (J). (gr. -1-1). pap. 4.99 (978-0-689-85537-5(0), Simon Spotlight) Simon Spotlight.

—A Tooth Story. McNamara, Margaret. 2004. (Robin Hill School Ser.). (ENG.). 32p. (J). (gr. -1-1). pap. 4.99 (978-0-689-86423-0(X), Simon Spotlight) Simon Spotlight.

—Vote for Me! How Governments & Elections Work Around the World. Spilsbury, Louise. 2018. (ENG.). 64p. (J). (gr. 3-6). pap. 9.99 (978-1-4380-1142-4(3), B.E.S. Publishing) Peterson's.

—Wash Your Hands! McNamara, Margaret. 2010. (Robin Hill School Ser.). (ENG.). 32p. (J). (gr. -1-1). pap. 4.99 (978-1-4169-9172-4(7), Simon Spotlight) Simon Spotlight.

—Watch Out! Around Town. Llewellyn, Claire. 2006. (Watch Out! Bks.). (ENG.). 32p. (J). (gr. -1-2). pap. 8.99 (978-0-7641-3326-8(8), B.E.S. Publishing) Peterson's.

Gordon, Mike. We Are Thankful. McNamara, Margaret. 2020. (Robin Hill School Ser.). (ENG.). 32p. (J). (gr. -1-1). 17.99 **(978-1-5344-6825-2(0))**; pap. 4.99 **(978-1-5344-6824-5(2))** Simon Spotlight. (Simon Spotlight).

Gordon, Mike. What Are You Waiting For? Copeland, Cynthia L. 2003. (Silly Millies Ser.: 1). 32p. lib. bdg. 17.90 (978-0-7613-2804-9(1), Millbrook Pr.) Lerner Publishing Group.

—What Is Money? Llewellyn, Claire. 2017. (Your Money Ser.). (ENG.). 24p. (J). (gr. -1-2). 19.05 (978-1-5311-8697-5(1)) Perfection Learning Corp.

—What Is Money? Llewellyn, Claire. 2016. (Your Money Ser.). 00024p. (J). (gr. 1-1). pap. 8.25 (978-1-4994-8200-3(0), Windmill Bks.) Rosen Publishing Group, Inc., The.

—When the Teacher Isn't Looking: And Other Funny School Poems. Nesbitt, Kenn. 2005. 80p. (J). (978-0-88166-489-8(8)) Meadowbrook Pr.

—When the Teacher Isn't Looking: And Other Funny School Poems. Nesbitt, Kenn. 2010. (Giggle Poetry Ser.). (ENG.). 80p. (J). (gr. k-7). per. 8.99 (978-0-684-03128-6(0), Running Pr.) Running Pr.

—Why Should I Eat Well? Llewellyn, Claire. 2005. (Why Should I? Bks.). (ENG.). 32p. (J). (gr. -1-2). pap. 7.99 (978-0-7641-3217-9(2), B.E.S. Publishing) Peterson's.

—Why Should I Recycle? Green, Jen. 2005. (Why Should I? Bks.). (ENG.). 32p. (J). (gr. -1-2). pap. 7.99 (978-0-7641-3155-4(9), B.E.S. Publishing) Peterson's.

—Why Should I Save Energy? Green, Jen. 2005. (Why Should I? Bks.). (ENG.). 32p. (J). (gr. -1-2). pap. 7.99 (978-0-7641-3156-1(7), B.E.S. Publishing) Peterson's.

—Why Should I Save Water? Green, Jen. 2005. (Why Should I? Bks.). (ENG.). 32p. (J). (gr. -1-2). pap. 7.99 *(978-0-7641-3157-8(5),* B.E.S. Publishing) Peterson's.
—The Wish Fish. 2007. (First Reading Level 1 Ser.). 32p. (J). (gr. -1-3). 8.99 *(978-0-7945-1697-0(1),* Usborne) EDC Publishing.
Gordon, Mike. My Best Friend. Gordon, Mike, tr. Namm, Diane. 2004. (My First Reader Ser.). (ENG.). 31p. (J). 18.50 *(978-0-516-24416-7(7),* Children's Pr.) Scholastic Library Publishing.
Gordon, Mike & Gordon, Carl. Dinner with Dracula. Lansky, Bruce, ed. 2006. 32p. (J). *(978-0-88166-512-3(6))* Meadowbrook Pr.
—Do Princesses Count? Coyle, Carmela Lavigna. 2006. (ENG.). 24p. (J). (gr. -1-3). bds. 6.95 *(978-0-87358-916-1(5))* Cooper Square Publishing Llc.
—Do Princesses Have Best Friends Forever? Coyle, Carmela Lavigna. 2010. (J). *(978-1-58979-543-3(1))* Taylor Trade Publishing.
—Do Princesses Really Kiss Frogs?, Vol. Coyle, Carmela Lavigna. 2005. (ENG.). 32p. (J). (gr. -1-2). 15.95 *(978-0-87358-880-5(0))* Cooper Square Publishing Llc.
—Do Princesses Wear Hiking Boots? Coyle, Carmela Lavigna. 2003. (Do Princesses Ser.). (ENG.). 32p. (J). (gr. -1-2). 15.95 *(978-0-87358-828-7(2))* Cooper Square Publishing Llc.
—Do Princesses Wear Hiking Boots? Coyle, Carmela Lavigna. 2014. (ENG.). 96p. (J). (gr. -1-2). spiral bd. 15.95 *(978-1-58979-945-5(3))* Taylor Trade Publishing.
—I'm Allergic to School: Funny Poems & Songs about School. Pottle, Robert. 2007. 32p. *(978-0-88166-522-2(3))* Meadowbrook Pr.
—The Magic Porridge Pot. 2008. (Usborne First Reading: Level 3 Ser.). 48p. (J). (gr. -1-3). 8.99 *(978-0-7945-1883-7(4),* Usborne) EDC Publishing.
—The Musicians of Bremen. Davidson, Susanna. 2007. (Usborne First Reading: Level 3 Ser.). 48p. (J). 8.99 *(978-0-7945-1911-7(3),* Usborne) EDC Publishing.
—Revenge of the Lunch Ladies: The Hilarious Book of School Poetry. Nesbitt, Kenn. 2007. 80p. *(978-0-88166-527-7(4))* Meadowbrook Pr.
Gordon, Mike & Lee, Jared. Quite Enough Hot Dogs & Other Silly Stories. Scholastic Library Publishing et al. 2008. (Rookie Reader Treasury Ser.). (ENG.). 128p. (J). (gr. -1-2). 2.99 *(978-0-531-21728-3(0),* Children's Pr.) Scholastic Library Publishing.
Gordon, Mike, jt. illus. see Gordon, Carl.
Gordon-Noy, Aya. Just Like I Wanted. Keller, Elinoar & Peleg-Segal, Naama. 2015. (ENG.). 26p. (J). 17.00 *(978-0-8028-5453-7(2),* Eerdmans Bks For Young Readers) Eerdmans, William B. Publishing Co.
—Nora the Mind Reader. Gidali, Orit. 2012. (ENG.). 32p. (J). (gr. -1-3). 15.95 *(978-1-59270-120-9(5))* Enchanted Lion Bks., LLC.
Gordon, Sallie. A Golden Change. Lewis, Carolyn. 2018. (ENG.). 28p. (J). pap. 11.99 *(978-1-945620-53-9(6))* Hear My Heart Publishing.
Gordon, Steven E., et al. Adventures of Superman. Siegel, Jerry et al. 2013. 125p. (J). *(978-1-4351-5063-8(5))* Barnes & Noble, Inc.
Gordon, Steven E. Batman: Meet the Super Heroes. Teitelbaum, Michael. 2009. (I Can Read Level 2 Ser.). (ENG.). 32p. (J). (gr. -1-3). pap. 4.99 *(978-0-06-187858-9(8))* HarperCollins Pubs.
—Batman & the Toxic Terror. Huelin, Jodi. 2011. (ENG.). 24p. (J). (gr. -1-3). pap. 3.99 *(978-0-06-188530-3(4),* HarperFestival) HarperCollins Pubs.
—Spider-Man 3: Meet the Heroes & Villains. Lime, Harry. 2007. (I Can Read Bks.). 32p. (J). pap. 3.99 *(978-0-06-083721-1(7),* Harper Trophy) HarperCollins Pubs.
—Superman: Escape from the Phantom Zone. Sazaklis, John. 2011. (I Can Read Level 2 Ser.). (ENG.). 32p. (J). (gr. -1-3). pap. 3.99 *(978-0-06-188519-8(3))* HarperCollins Pubs.
—Tools of the Trade. Huelin, Jodi. 2012. (I Can Read Book 2 Ser.). (ENG.). 32p. (J). (gr. k-3). pap. 3.99 *(978-0-06-213223-9(7))* HarperCollins Pubs.
Gordon, Steven E. & Gordon, Eric A. Batman - Who Is Clayface? Lemke, Donald. 2013. (I Can Read Level 2 Ser.). (ENG.). 32p. (J). (gr. -1-3). pap. 3.99 *(978-0-06-188525-9(8))* HarperCollins Pubs.
—Batman - Winter Wasteland. Lemke, Donald. 2014. (I Can Read Level 2 Ser.). (ENG.). 32p. (J). (gr. -1-3). pap. 4.99 *(978-0-06-221004-3(1))* HarperCollins Pubs.
—Batman Versus Man-Bat. Bright, J. E. 2012. (I Can Read Level 2 Ser.). (ENG.). 32p. (J). (gr. -1-3). pap. 3.99 *(978-0-06-188523-5(1))* HarperCollins Pubs.
—Friends & Foes. Rosen, Lucy. 2013. (I Can Read Level 2 Ser.). (ENG.). 32p. (J). (gr. -1-3). pap. 3.99 *(978-0-06-223595-4(8))* HarperCollins Pubs.
—Justice League Classic: I Am Green Lantern. Santos, Ray. 2013. (I Can Read Level 2 Ser.). (ENG.). 32p. (J). (gr. -1-3). pap. 3.99 *(978-0-06-221006-7(8))* HarperCollins Pubs.
—Parasite City. Rosen, Lucy. 2011. (ENG.). 24p. (J). (gr. -1-3). pap. 3.99 *(978-0-06-188532-7(0),* HarperFestival) HarperCollins Pubs.
Gordon, Steven E., jt. illus. see Gordon, Eric A.
Gordon, Susie. Skipingo Home: A Thoroughbred's Second Chance. Lyons, Jane & Bailey, Karen. 2009. (ENG.). 40p. (J). (gr. -1-3). 16.95 *(978-1-58150-205-3(2),* Eclipse Pr.) Blood-Horse, Inc., The.
Gordon, Tamia. The Champion. Greene, Renee. 2019. (Gatekeeper Chronicles Ser.: Vol. 5). (ENG.). 132p. (J). pap. 8.99 *(978-1-0910-8127-7(1))* Independently Published.
—Distress Calls! Greene, Renee. 2019. (Gatekeeper Chronicles Ser.: Vol. 3). (ENG.). 132p. (J). pap. 8.99 *(978-1-0910-7406-4(2))* Independently Published.
Gordon, Tamia. Don't Vandalize Dragons! Greene, Michael. 2020. (Woodcreek Academy Ser.: Vol. 4). (ENG.). 148p. (J). pap. 8.99 ***(978-1-7133-1288-8(3))*** Independently Published.
—The Dungeon! Greene, Renee. 2019. (Gatekeeper Chronicles Ser.: Vol. 6). (ENG.). 132p. (J). pap. 8.99 ***(978-1-0910-8492-6(0))*** Independently Published.
—Ogres Don't Like Lemons! Greene, Michael. 2019. (Woodcreek Academy Ser.: Vol. 1). (ENG.). 144p. (J). pap. 8.99 ***(978-1-9856-5272-9(2))*** CreateSpace Independent Publishing Platform.
Gordon, Tamia. Say Uncle! Greene, Renee. 2019. (Gatekeeper Chronicles Ser.: Vol. 4). (ENG.). 136p. (J). pap. 8.99 *(978-1-0910-7950-2(1))* Independently Published.
Gordon, Tamia. Soccer Is for Humans! Greene, Michael. 2019. (Woodcreek Academy Ser.: Vol. 2). (ENG.). 148p. (J). pap. 8.99 ***(978-1-9865-6939-2(X))*** CreateSpace Independent Publishing Platform.
Gordon, Tamia. Tournament! Greene, Renee. 2019. (Gatekeeper Chronicles Ser.: Vol. 2). (ENG.). 132p. (J). pap. 8.99 *(978-1-0910-7124-7(1))* Independently Published.
Gordon, Xia. A Song for Gwendolyn Brooks. Duncan, Alice Faye. 2019. (People Who Shaped Our World Ser.: 3). 48p. (J). (gr. k). 16.95 *(978-1-4549-3088-4(8))* Sterling Publishing Co., Inc.
Gore, Christine. Me & My Place in Space. Sweeney, Joan. 2019. (ENG.). 32p. (J). (gr. -1-2). 7.99 *(978-1-5247-7366-3(2))* Perfection Learning Corp.
—Me & My Place in Space. Sweeney, Joan. 2018. 32p. (J). (gr. -1-2). 12.99 *(978-1-5247-7363-2(8),* Knopf Bks. for Young Readers) Random Hse. Children's Bks.
Gore, Leonid. And Nick. Gore, Emily. 2015. (ENG.). 40p. (J). (gr. -1-3). 17.99 *(978-1-4169-5506-1(2))* Simon & Schuster Children's Publishing.
—I Am King! Packard, Mary. 2003. (My First Reader Ser.). (ENG.). 32p. (J). 18.50 *(978-0-516-22927-0(3),* Children's Pr.) Scholastic Library Publishing.
—Monarch & Milkweed. Frost, Helen. 2008. (ENG.). 40p. (J). (gr. -1-3). 19.99 *(978-1-4169-0085-6(3),* Atheneum Bks. for Young Readers) Simon & Schuster Children's Publishing.
—The Princess Mouse: A Tale of Finland. Shepard, Aaron. 2008. (ENG.). 40p. (J). (gr. -1-3). 13.99 *(978-1-4169-8969-1(2),* Atheneum Bks. for Young Readers) Simon & Schuster Children's Publishing.
—Saints among the Animals. Zarin, Cynthia. 2012. (ENG.). 96p. (J). (gr. 2-7). pap. 6.99 *(978-1-4424-7296-9(0),* Atheneum Bks. for Young Readers) Simon & Schuster Children's Publishing.
—Voices of the Trojan War. Hovey, Kate. 2012. (ENG.). 128p. (J). (gr. 3-7). pap. 7.99 *(978-1-4424-8880-9(8),* McElderry, Margaret K. Bks.) McElderry, Margaret K. Bks.
Gore, Leonid. Danny's First Snow. Gore, Leonid. 2007. (ENG.). 40p. (J). (gr. -1-3). 19.99 *(978-1-4169-1330-6(0),* Atheneum Bks. for Young Readers) Simon & Schuster Children's Publishing.
—Mommy, Where Are You? Gore, Leonid. 2009. (ENG.). 32p. (J). (gr. -1-2). 18.99 *(978-1-4169-5505-4(4),* Atheneum Bks. for Young Readers) Simon & Schuster Children's Publishing.
Gorenman, Marcelo. Little Green. Rudnick, Arnold. 2012. 32p. (J). pap. 9.99 *(978-0-9815879-7-4(6))* Paraphrase, LLC.
Gorey, Edward. The Adventures of Gremlin. Jones, DuPre. 2013. 112p. 17.95 *(978-0-7649-6605-7(7))* Pomegranate Communications, Inc.
—He Was There from the Day We Moved In. Levine, Rhoda. 2012. (ENG.). 32p. (J). (gr. -1-2). 18.95 *(978-1-59017-515-6(8),* NYR Children's Collection) New York Review of Bks., Inc., The.
—The House with a Clock in Its Walls. Bellairs, John. (Lewis Barnavelt Ser.: Bk. 1). (ENG.). 192p. (J). (gr. 3-7). 2004. pap. 7.99 *(978-0-14-240257-3(5));* 2018. 7.99 *(978-0-451-48128-3(3))* Penguin Young Readers Group. (Puffin Books).
—The House with a Clock in Its Walls. Bellairs, John. 2004. (John Bellairs Mysteries Ser.). 179p. (J). (gr. 3-7). 13.65 *(978-0-7569-5257-0(3))* Perfection Learning Corp.
—Lions & Lobsters & Foxes & Frogs: Fables from Aesop. Rees, Ennis. 2018. (ENG.). 48p. (gr. 2-7). 14.95 *(978-0-486-82017-0(3))* Dover Pubns., Inc.
—The Mansion in the Mist. Bellairs, John. 2004. (Anthony Monday Ser.: No. 4). (ENG.). 176p. (J). (gr. 3-7). 6.99 *(978-0-14-240262-7(1),* Puffin Books) Penguin Young Readers Group.
—Men & Gods: Myths & Legends of the Ancient Greeks. Warner, Rex. 2008. 288p. 19.95 *(978-1-59017-263-6(9),* NYRB Classics) New York Review of Bks., Inc., The.
—Sam & Emma. Nelsen, Donald. 2016. (ENG.). 48p. pap. 14.99 *(978-0-486-80590-0(5))* Dover Pubns., Inc.
—The Spell of the Sorcerer's Skull. Bellairs, John. 2004. 170p. (J). (gr. 4-7). 13.65 *(978-0-7569-4965-5(3))* Perfection Learning Corp.
—Three Ladies Beside the Sea. Levine, Rhoda. 2010. (ENG.). 40p. (J). (gr. k-4). 17.95 *(978-1-59017-354-1(6),* NYR Children's Collection) New York Review of Bks., Inc., The.
—The War of the Worlds. Wells, H. G. 2005. (ENG.). 260p. 18.95 *(978-1-59017-158-5(6),* NYRB Classics) New York Review of Bks., Inc., The.
Gorey, Edward. The Wuggly Ump. Gorey, Edward. 2007. 32p. 12.95 *(978-0-7649-4192-4(5),* A142) Pomegranate Communications, Inc.
Gorey, Edward & Lear, Edward. The Dong with the Luminous Nose. 2010. 48p. 14.95 *(978-0-7649-5427-6(X))* Pomegranate Communications, Inc.
—Jumblies. 2010. 48p. 14.95 *(978-0-7649-5426-9(1))* Pomegranate Communications, Inc.
Gorey, John, jt. illus. see Hayes, Karel.
Gorham, Adam, et al. Acts of Evil. 2020. (ENG.). 264p. (YA). (gr. 8-17). pap. 34.99 *(978-1-302-92154-5(1))* Marvel Worldwide, Inc.
Gorham, Adam. Rocket: the Blue River Score. 2017. (ENG.). 112p. (YA). (gr. 8-17). pap. 17.99 *(978-1-302-90550-7(3))* Marvel Worldwide, Inc.
Goring, Trevor. Night Witches at War: The Soviet Women Pilots of World War II. Berglund, Bruce. 2019. (Amazing World War II Stories Ser.). (ENG.). 32p. (J). (gr. 3-9). pap. 7.95 *(978-1-5435-7550-7(1),* 141082); lib. bdg. 34.65 *(978-1-5435-7315-2(0),* 140620) Capstone.
Goris, Laura. Monkeying Around: Meet Chippey & His Friends. Smith, Kimberly. 2012. 44p. (J). pap. 14.98 *(978-0-9843166-6-3(3))* Artists' Orchard, LLC, The.
Gorissen, Dean. Ten Little Elvi. Henson, Laura J. & Grooms, Duffy. 2004. 30p. (J). (gr. -1-2). 12.99 *(978-1-58246-124-3(4),* Tricycle Pr.) Random Hse. Children's Bks.
Gorman, Kyrsten. Alicia & Policia, 1 vol. Gorman, Patrick. 2010. 24p. 24.95 *(978-1-4489-6425-3(3))* PublishAmerica, Inc.
Gorman, Meg. All Animals Count. Gorman, Meg. 2018. (ENG.). 34p. (J). (gr. k-2). *(978-1-9164530-1-2(5))* Gorman, Meg.
Gorman, Mike. Alien Contact, No. 5. Service, Pamela F. 2011. (Alien Agent Ser.: 5). (ENG.). 144p. (J). (gr. 4-6). pap. 5.95 *(978-0-7613-7297-4(0),* 9780761372974, Darby Creek) Lerner Publishing Group.
—Alien Encounter. Service, Pamela F. 2010. (Alien Agent Ser.: 4). (ENG.). 152p. (J). (gr. 4-6). 16.95 *(978-0-8225-8873-3(0),* Darby Creek) Lerner Publishing Group.
—Alien Envoy. Service, Pamela F. (Alien Agent Ser.). 176p. (J). (gr. 4-6). 2012. pap. 33.92 *(978-0-7613-9208-8(4));* No. 6. 2012. (ENG.). pap. 5.95 *(978-0-7613-7298-1(9),* 9780761372981); No. 6. 2011. (ENG.). 16.95 *(978-0-7613-5364-5(X),* 9780761353645) Lerner Publishing Group. (Darby Creek).
—Escape from Planet Yastol. Service, Pamela F. ed. (Way-Too-Real Aliens Ser.: 1). (ENG.). 112p. (J). (gr. 4-6). 2015. E-Book 53.32 *(978-1-4677-5960-1(0),* 9781467759601, Lerner Digital); No. 1. 2011. pap. 5.95 *(978-0-7613-7921-8(5),* Darby Creek) Lerner Publishing Group.
—My Cousin, the Alien. Service, Pamela F. 2008. (Alien Agent Ser.: 1). (ENG.). 160p. (J). (gr. 4-6). 16.95 *(978-0-8225-7627-3(9),* Carolrhoda Bks.) Lerner Publishing Group.
—The Not-So-Perfect Planet. Service, Pamela F. (Way-Too-Real Aliens Ser.: 2). (ENG.). 120p. (J). (gr. 4-6). 2012. pap. 6.95 *(978-0-7613-7923-2(1),* Darby Creek); 2015. E-Book 53.32 *(978-1-4677-5961-8(9),* 9781467759618, Lerner Digital) Lerner Publishing Group.
—The Wizards of Wyrd World. Service, Pamela F. ed. 2015. (Way-Too-Real Aliens Ser.: 3). (ENG.). 112p. (J). (gr. 4-6). E-Book 53.32 *(978-1-4677-5962-5(7),* 9781467759625, Lerner Digital) Lerner Publishing Group.
—#4 Alien Encounter. Service, Pamela F. 2011. (Alien Agent Ser.). 152p. (J). pap. 33.92 *(978-0-7613-7608-8(9),* Darby Creek) Lerner Publishing Group.
—#5 Alien Contact. Service, Pamela F. 2011. (Alien Agent Ser.). pap. 33.92 *(978-0-7613-8347-5(6),* Darby Creek) Lerner Publishing Group.
Gorman, Stan. Princess Emily & the Secret Library. Balfanz, Mary. 2009. 32p. (J). (gr. -1-3). 16.99 *(978-0-9817636-0-6(X))* Willow Brook Publishing.
Gorman, Zac. Costume Quest. Gorman, Zac. 2018. (ENG.). 56p. (J). (gr. -1-3). pap. 8.99 *(978-1-62010-559-7(4),* Lion Forge) Oni Pr., Inc.
Gorman, Zac, jt. illus. see Henderson, Erica.
Gormand, Caroline. The Little Prince. De Saint-Exupéry, Antoine. Hill, Rowland, tr. 2016.Tr. of Petit Prince. (ENG.). (J). (gr. 3-6). pap. *(978-2-89687-592-4(1))* chouetteditions.com.
—Le Petit Prince. De Saint-Exupéry, Antoine. 2016. (FRE.). (J). (gr. 3-6). pap. *(978-2-89687-593-1(X))* chouetteditions.com.
Gormley, Julia Ann. Science Projects: Book 1. Project Ideas in the Life Sciences, Vol. 1. Neuhaus, Richard A. 2008. (ENG.). 184p. (gr. 7-12). pap. 24.95 *(978-0-9794500-1-3(2))* Gormley Publishing.
—Science Projects: Book 2. Project Ideas in Chemistry & Biochemistry, Vol. 2. Neuhaus, Richard A. 2008. (ENG.). 196p. (gr. 7-12). pap. 24.95 *(978-0-9794500-4-4(7))* Gormley Publishing.
—Science Projects: How to Collect, Analyze, & Present Your Data. Neuhaus, Richard A. 2007. (ENG.). 184p. (gr. 7-12). pap. 24.95 *(978-0-9794500-0-6(4))* Gormley Publishing.
Görrissen, Janina. I Date Dead People, No. 5. Kerns, Ann. 2012. (My Boyfriend Is a Monster Ser.: 5). (ENG.). 128p. (YA). (gr. 7-12). lib. bdg. 29.32 *(978-0-7613-6007-0(7),* 9780761360070, Graphic Universe™) Lerner Publishing Group.
—#01 I Love Him to Pieces. Tsang, Evonne. 2011. (My Boyfriend Is a Monster Ser.). 128p. (YA). pap. 56.72 *(978-0-7613-7602-6(X),* Graphic Universe™) Lerner Publishing Group.
Görrissen, Janina & Görrissen, Janina. I Date Dead People: Book 5, No. 5. Kerns, Ann. 2012. (My Boyfriend Is a Monster Ser.: 5). (ENG.). 128p. (YA). (gr. 7-12). pap. 9.95 *(978-0-7613-8549-3(5),* 9780761385493, Graphic Universe™) Lerner Publishing Group.
Görrissen, Janina, jt. illus. see Görrissen, Janina.
Gorsky, Nadia. Bobby B. Sprout Meets a Bunch of Rotten Veggies. Levinsky, Ilana K. 2019. (ENG.). 36p. (J). pap. 9.95 ***(978-1-6705-0875-1(7))*** Independently Published.
Gorsline, Douglas. Captain Waymouth's Indians. Molloy, Anne Stearns Baker. 2011. 204p. 44.95 *(978-1-258-06802-8(8))* Literary Licensing, LLC.
Gorsline, Douglas, jt. illus. see Moore, Clement C.
Gorsline, Douglas W. The Story of Good Queen Bess. Malkus, Alida Sims. Meadowcroft, Enid Lamonte, ed. 2011. 192p. 42.95 *(978-1-258-09564-2(5))* Literary Licensing, LLC.
Gorstein, Mordicai. The Mixed-Up Mask Mystery: A Fletcher Mystery. Levy, Elizabeth. unabr. ed. 2006. (First Chapter Bks.). (J). (gr. 2-4). pap. 17.95 incl. audio *(978-1-59519-710-8(9));* pap. 20.95 incl. audio compact disk *(978-1-59519-711-5(7))* Live Oak Media.
Gort, Ilse. Silver Batal & the Water Dragon Races. Halbrook, K. D. 2019. (Silver Batal Ser.: 1). (ENG.). 336p. (J). 16.99 *(978-1-250-18107-7(0),* 900190301, Holt, Henry & Co. Bks. For Young Readers) Holt, Henry & Co.
—Silver Batal & the Water Dragon Races. Halbrook, K. D. 2020. (Silver Batal Ser.: 1). (ENG.). 336p. (J). pap. 7.99 *(978-1-250-25054-4(4),* 900190302) Square Fish.
—Silver Batal: Race for the Dragon Heartstone. Halbrook, K. D. 2020. (Silver Batal Ser.: 2). (ENG.). 272p. (J). 16.99 *(978-1-250-18109-1(7),* 900190311, Holt, Henry & Co. Bks. For Young Readers) Holt, Henry & Co.
Gorton, Julia. I Face the Wind. Cobb, Vicki. 2003. (Science Play Ser.). (ENG.). 40p. (J). (gr. -1-3). 16.99 *(978-0-688-17840-6(5))* HarperCollins Pubs.
—I Fall Down. Cobb, Vicki. 2004. (Science Play Ser.). (ENG.). 40p. (J). (gr. -1-3). 17.99 *(978-0-688-17842-0(1))* HarperCollins Pubs.
—Just Like Mama. Newman, Lesléa & Newman, Lesléa. 2010. (ENG.). 32p. (J). (gr. -1-3). 15.95 *(978-0-8109-8393-9(1),* Abrams Bks. for Young Readers) Abrams, Inc.
Gorton, Julia. Sábado de Súper Castillos: Super Sand Castle Saturday (Spanish Edition) Murphy, Stuart J. 2020. (MathStart 2 Ser.). (ENG.). 40p. (J). (gr. -1-3). pap. 5.99 ***(978-0-06-298328-2(8),*** HarperCollins) HarperCollins Pubs. Ltd. GBR. Dist: HarperCollins Pubs.
Gorton, Julia. The Three Little Fish & the Big Bad Shark. Geist, Ken. 2007. (ENG.). 32p. (J). (gr. -1-3). 7.99 *(978-0-439-71962-9(3))* Scholastic, Inc.
Gorton, Steve, jt. illus. see Dann, Geoff.
Goryl, Madeline. The Butterfly Coloring Book. 2015. 80p. (J). (gr. -1). pap. 5.99 *(978-1-63220-523-0(8),* Sky Pony Pr.) Skyhorse Publishing Co., Inc.
—The Garden Flowers Coloring Book. 2015. (Creative Stress Relieving Adult Coloring Ser.). 80p. (J). (gr. -1). pap. 5.99 *(978-1-63220-524-7(6),* Sky Pony Pr.) Skyhorse Publishing Co., Inc.
Goscinny, Tabary. Iznogoud's Nightmares. Goscinny, René. 2017. (Iznogoud Ser.: 14). (ENG.). 56p. pap. 13.95 *(978-1-84918-360-4(0))* CineBook GBR. Dist: National Bk. Network.
Gosier, Phil. Big Trouble: a Friday Barnes Mystery. Spratt, R. A. 2018. (Friday Barnes Mysteries Ser.). (ENG.). 304p. (J). pap. 12.99 *(978-1-250-16560-2(1),* 900163941) Square Fish.
—Friday Barnes, Girl Detective. Spratt, R. A. 2016. (Friday Barnes Mysteries Ser.: Bk. 1). (ENG.). 272p. (J). 13.99 *(978-1-62672-297-2(8),* 9781626722972) Roaring Brook Pr.
—No Rules: a Friday Barnes Mystery. Spratt, R. A. 2018. (Friday Barnes Mysteries Ser.). (ENG.). 272p. (J). pap. 7.99 *(978-1-250-15899-4(0),* 900163944) Square Fish.
—Under Suspicion. Spratt, R. A. 2016. (Friday Barnes Mysteries Ser.). (ENG.). 288p. (J). 13.99 *(978-1-62672-299-6(4),* 9781626722996) Roaring Brook Pr.
Gosier, Phil. Snow Beast Comes to Play. Gosier, Phil. 2017. (ENG.). 32p. (J). 17.99 *(978-1-62672-519-5(5),* 9781626725195) Roaring Brook Pr.
Gosling, Livi. Women Who Dared: 52 Fearless Daredevils, Adventurers, & Rebels. Skeers, Linda. 2017. 128p. (J). (gr. 3-8). 16.99 *(978-1-4926-5327-1(6),* Sourcebooks Jabberwocky) Sourcebooks, Inc.
Gosney, Joy & Harding, Emma. Singing Languages - Singing English (Book + CD): 22 Photocopiable Songs & Chants for Learning English. MacGregor, Helen & Chadwick, Stephen. 2005. (Singing Languages Ser.). (ENG.). 64p. (J). (gr. k-6). pap. 32.95 incl. audio compact disk *(978-0-7136-7361-6(3))* HarperCollins Pubs. Ltd. GBR. Dist: Independent Pubs. Group.
—Singing Languages - Singing French (Book + CD): 22 Photocopiable Songs & Chants for Learning French. Chadwick, Stephen & MacGregor, Helen. 2004. (ENG.). 64p. (J). (gr. k-2). pap. 29.95 incl. audio compact disk *(978-0-7136-6898-8(9))* HarperCollins Pubs. Ltd. GBR. Dist: Independent Pubs. Group.
Gosney, Joy, jt. illus. see Harding, Emma.
Gospodinov, George. Small Enough Tall Enough. Wilson, Barbara E. 2012. 46p. pap. 14.95 *(978-0-9838964-0-1(2))* Simply Silly Stories.
Goss, John. Our Little Norman Cousin of Long Ago. Stein, Evaleen. 2007. 112p. per. 8.95 *(978-1-59915-245-5(2))* Yesterday's Classics.
—The Story of the Red Cross As Told to the Little Colonel. Johnston, Annie Fellows. 2007. 48p. per. *(978-1-4065-3517-4(6))* Dodo Pr.
—A Texas Blue Bonnet (Illustrated Edition) Jacobs, Caroline Emilia. 2016. (ENG.). (J). pap. *(978-1-4068-8116-5(3))* Echo Library.
Goss, Mini. DuckStar & Cyberfarm. Edwards, Hazel & Anketell, Christine. 2nd ed. 2010. 96p. (J). pap. *(978-1-921479-57-1(4),* IP Kidz) Interactive Pubns. Pty, Ltd.
—Operatic Duck & Duck on Tour. Edwards, Hazel & Anketell, Christine. 2010. 96p. (J). pap. *(978-1-921479-80-9(9),* IP Kidz) Interactive Pubns. Pty, Ltd.
Goss, Rebecca, jt. illus. see Pugh, Carson.
Gosser, Larry. Sadie's Search for Home. Moore, Sandy. 2016. (ENG.). (J). 18.99 *(978-1-4984-8939-3(7));* pap. 9.99 *(978-1-4984-8938-6(9))* Salem Author Services.
Goswami, Swati. Little Danny's Dream Bus Atlantis; to the Cities of Goodness! Haave, David Allen. 2018. (Book 1 Of 10 Ser.). (ENG.). 24p. (J). 17.99 *(978-1-7328515-0-4(6));* pap. 10.99 *(978-1-7328515-9-7(X))* Little Danny's Bks. Inc.
Got, Eli & Gold, D. The Cryptic Script. 2018. 74p. (J). *(978-1-68091-257-9(7))* Kinder Shpiel USA, Inc.
Got, Yves. Sam's Pop-up Schoolhouse. Got, Yves. 2004. 6p. (J). (gr. k-4). reprint ed. 17.00 *(978-0-7567-8065-4(9))* DIANE Publishing Co.
Gotelaere, Nicholas. Starry, Starry Night: A Soft Moonlit Starry Night Casts a Veil of Slumber over the Mountain Meadow Animals. Lessnau, Diane. 2020. (ENG.). 24p. (J). 20.99 ***(978-1-6641-2410-3(1));*** pap. 12.99 ***(978-1-6641-2409-7(8))*** Xlibris Corp.

Gotfredson, Kate. Little Red Cuttlefish, 1 vol. Herz, Henry et al. 2016. (ENG.). 32p. (J). (gr. k-3). 16.99 *(978-1-4556-2146-0(3)*, Pelican Publishing) Arcadia Publishing.

Gothard, David. Little Lola. Saab, Julie. 2014. (ENG.). 32p. (J). (gr. -1-3). 16.99 *(978-0-06-227457-1(0)*, Greenwillow Bks.) HarperCollins Pubs.

—Little Lola Saves the Show. Saab, Julie. 2016. (ENG.). 32p. (J). (gr. -1-3). 17.99 *(978-0-06-227453-3(8)*, Greenwillow Bks.) HarperCollins Pubs.

Gotlieb, Jules. Fisherman Jody. Olds, Helen Diehl. 2011. 64p. 36.95 *(978-1-258-07129-5(0))* Literary Licensing, LLC.

Goto, Scott. The Enormous Turnip. Tolstoy, Alexei. 2003. (Green Light Readers Level 2 Ser.). (ENG.). 24p. (J). (gr. -1-3). pap. 4.99 *(978-0-15-204843-3(X)*, 1194624) Houghton Mifflin Harcourt Publishing Co.

—Hawai'i. Gill, Shelley. 2006. (ENG.). 32p. (J). (gr. 2-5). lib. bdg. 16.95 *(978-0-88106-296-0(0))* Charlesbridge Publishing, Inc.

—Wordsworth the Poet. Kakugawa, Francis. 2003. 32p. (J). (gr. -1-3). 10.95 *(978-0-9742672-0-3(1))* Watermark Publishing, LLC.

Goto, Scott. Perfect Sword. Goto, Scott. 2010. 48p. (J). (gr. 1-4). pap. 8.95 *(978-1-57091-698-4(5))* Charlesbridge Publishing, Inc.

Gotsubo, Masaru. Samurai Champloo, Vol. 1. Gotsubo, Masaru. Manglobe. 2005. 184p. pap. 9.99 *(978-1-59182-282-0(3))* TOKYOPOP, Inc.

—Samurai Champloo, Vol. 2. Gotsubo, Masaru. Manglobe. 2nd rev. ed. 2006. 184p. per. 9.99 *(978-1-59816-215-8(2))* TOKYOPOP, Inc.

Gott, Barry. Car Wash Kid. Fishman, Cathy Goldberg. 2003. (Rookie Reader Ser.). (ENG.). 24p. (J). (gr. k-2). pap. 4.95 *(978-0-516-27811-7(8)*, Children's Pr.) Scholastic Library Publishing.

—Carmen's Sticky Scab. Churchill, Ginger. 2007. (ENG.). 32p. (J). (gr. -1-3). 15.95 *(978-1-933718-13-2(7))* Tanglewood Pr.

—Dino-Baseball. Wheeler, Lisa. 2010. (Dino-Sports Ser.). (ENG.). 32p. (J). (gr. k-3). lib. bdg. 17.99 *(978-0-7613-4429-2(2)*, 9780761344292, Carolrhoda Bks.) Lerner Publishing Group.

—Dino-Basketball. Wheeler, Lisa. 2011. (Dino-Sports Ser.). (ENG.). 32p. (J). (gr. k-3). 17.99 *(978-0-7613-6393-4(9)*, 9780761363934, Carolrhoda Bks.) Lerner Publishing Group.

—Dino-Boarding. Wheeler, Lisa. 2014. (Dino-Sports Ser.). (ENG.). 32p. (J). (gr. k-3). lib. bdg. 17.99 *(978-1-4677-0213-3(7)*, 9781467702133, Carolrhoda Bks.) Lerner Publishing Group.

—Dino-Christmas. Wheeler, Lisa. 2018. (Dino-Holidays Ser.). (ENG.). 32p. (J). (gr. k-3). 17.99 *(978-1-5124-0315-2(6)*, Carolrhoda Bks.) Lerner Publishing Group.

—Dino-Dancing. Wheeler, Lisa. 2017. (Dino-Sports Ser.). (ENG.). 32p. (J). (gr. k-3). lib. bdg. 17.99 *(978-1-5124-0316-9(4)*, 9781512403169, Carolrhoda Bks.) Lerner Publishing Group.

—Dino-Football. Wheeler, Lisa. 2012. (Dino-Sports Ser.). (ENG.). 32p. (J). (gr. k-3). lib. bdg. 17.99 *(978-0-7613-6394-1(7)*, 9780761363941, Carolrhoda Bks.) Lerner Publishing Group.

—Dino-Halloween. Wheeler, Lisa. 2019. (Dino-Holidays Ser.). Orig. Title: Dino-Halloween. (ENG.). 32p. (J). (gr. k-3). 17.99 *(978-1-5124-0317-6(2)*, 9781512403176, Carolrhoda Bks.) Lerner Publishing Group.

—Dino-Hockey. Wheeler, Lisa. 2007. (Dino-Sports Ser.). (ENG.). 32p. (J). (gr. k-3). 17.99 *(978-0-8225-6191-0(3)*, Carolrhoda Bks.) Lerner Publishing Group.

—Dino-Racing. Wheeler, Lisa. 2016. (Dino-Sports Ser.). (ENG.). 32p. (J). (gr. k-3). lib. bdg. 17.99 *(978-1-5124-0314-5(8)*, 9781512403145); E-Book 35.99 *(978-1-5124-0886-7(7))* Lerner Publishing Group. (Carolrhoda Bks.).

—Dino-Soccer. Wheeler, Lisa. 2009. (Dino-Sports Ser.). (ENG.). 32p. (J). (gr. k-3). 17.99 *(978-0-8225-9028-6(X)*, Carolrhoda Bks.) Lerner Publishing Group.

—Dino-Swimming. Wheeler, Lisa. 2015. (Dino-Sports Ser.). (ENG.). 32p. (J). (gr. k-3). lib. bdg. 17.99 *(978-1-4677-0214-0(5)*, 9781467702140); E-Book 35.99 *(978-1-4677-8809-0(0))* Lerner Publishing Group. (Carolrhoda Bks.).

Gott, Barry. Dino-Thanksgiving. Wheeler, Lisa. 2020. (Dino-Holidays Ser.). (ENG.). 32p. (J). (gr. k-3). 17.99 ***(978-1-5124-0318-3(0)***, Carolrhoda Bks.) Lerner Publishing Group.

Gott, Barry. Dino-Wrestling. Wheeler, Lisa. 2013. (Dino-Sports Ser.). (ENG.). 32p. (J). (gr. k-3). 17.99 *(978-1-4677-0212-6(9)*, 9781467702126, Carolrhoda Bks.) Lerner Publishing Group.

—Dizzy Dinosaurs: Silly Dino Poems. Hopkins, Lee Bennett. 2011. (I Can Read Level 2 Ser.). (ENG.). 48p. (J). (gr. k-3). 16.99 *(978-0-06-135839-5(8))*; pap. 4.99 *(978-0-06-135841-8(X))* HarperCollins Pubs.

—Head, Shoulders, Knees, & Toes. 2006. (J). *(978-1-58987-056-7(5))* Kindermusik International.

—The Invasion of the Shag Carpet Creature. David, Lawrence. 2004. (Horace Splattly Ser.). 151p. (J). (gr. 4-7). 12.65 *(978-0-7569-2818-6(4))* Perfection Learning Corp.

—It Came from Outer Space: Meteors & Space Debris. Barker, Henry. 2006. (Science Solves It! ® Ser.). (ENG.). 32p. (J). (gr. 1-3). pap. 5.95 *(978-1-57565-122-4(X))* Astra Publishing Hse.

—The Midnight Kid: Sleep. Walker, Nan. 2007. (Science Solves It! ® Ser.). (ENG.). 32p. (J). (gr. 1-3). pap. 5.95 *(978-1-57565-238-2(2))* Astra Publishing Hse.

—El Misterio Del Arco Iris (the Rainbow Mystery) Dussling, Jennifer. 2009. (Science Solves It! ® en Espanol Ser.). (SPA.). (gr. 1-3). pap. 33.92 *(978-0-7613-4798-9(4))* Lerner Publishing Group.

—A Moldy Mystery: Mold. Knudsen, Michelle. 2006. (Science Solves It! ® Ser.). (ENG.). 32p. (J). (gr. 1-3). pap. 5.95 *(978-1-57565-167-5(X))* Astra Publishing Hse.

—My New School. Hall, Kirsten. 2004. (My First Reader Ser.). (ENG.). 32p. (J). (gr. k-1). pap. 3.95 *(978-0-516-25505-7(3)*, Children's Pr.) Scholastic Library Publishing.

—Patches Lost & Found, 0 vols. Kroll, Steven. 2005. (ENG.). 32p. (J). (gr. k-4). pap. 5.95 *(978-0-7614-5217-1(6)*, 9780761452171, Two Lions) Amazon Publishing.

—A Planet Called Home: Eco-Pig's Animal Protection, 1 vol. French, Lisa S. 2009. (Eco-Pig Ser.). (ENG.). 32p. (J). (gr. k-4). 28.50 *(978-1-60270-662-0(X)*, 6237, Looking Glass Library) Magic Wagon.

—The Rainbow Mystery: Rainbows. Dussling, Jennifer. 2006. (Science Solves It! ® Ser.). (ENG.). 32p. (J). (gr. 1-3). pap. 5.95 *(978-1-57565-119-4(X))* Astra Publishing Hse.

—The Real Me: Roles. May, Eleanor. 2006. (Social Studies Connects ® Ser.). (ENG.). 32p. (J). (gr. k-2). pap. 5.95 *(978-1-57565-186-6(6))* Astra Publishing Hse.

—Rock, Brock, & the Savings Shock. Bair, Sheila. 2017. (ENG.). 32p. (J). (gr. -1-3). pap. 7.99 *(978-0-8075-7095-1(8)*, 807570958) Whitman, Albert & Co.

—Santa's Secrets Revealed: All Your Questions Answered about Santa's Super Sleigh, His Flying Reindeer, & Other Wonders. Solheim, James. 2004. (Carolrhoda Picture Books Ser.). 40p. (J). (gr. k-3). 15.95 *(978-1-57505-600-5(3))* Lerner Publishing Group.

—Sidekicks 5: the Brotherhood of Rotten Babysitters. Danko, Dan & Mason, Tom. 5th ed. 2005. (ENG.). 144p. (J). (gr. 3-7). pap. 10.99 *(978-0-316-15895-4(X))* Little, Brown Bks. for Young Readers.

—Super Specs: Number Patterns. Driscoll, Laura. 2006. (Math Matters ® Ser.). (ENG.). 32p. (J). (gr. k-2). pap. 5.95 *(978-1-57565-145-3(9))* Astra Publishing Hse.

—The Terrible Trash Trail: Eco-Pig Stops Pollution, 1 vol. French, Lisa S. 2009. (Eco-Pig Ser.). (ENG.). 32p. (J). (gr. k-4). 28.50 *(978-1-60270-663-7(8)*, 6239, Looking Glass Library) Magic Wagon.

—The Terror of the Pink Dodo Balloons. David, Lawrence. 2003. (Horace Splattly Ser.). 153p. (J). (gr. 4-7). 12.65 *(978-0-7569-2816-2(8))* Perfection Learning Corp.

—Vino Del Espacio (It Came from Outer Space) Barker, Henry. 2009. (Science Solves It! ® en Espanol Ser.). (SPA.). (gr. 1-3). pap. 33.92 *(978-1-58013-771-3(7))* Lerner Publishing Group.

—What Does It Mean to Be Green? Eco-Pig Explains Living Green, 1 vol. French, Lisa S. 2009. (Eco-Pig Ser.). (ENG.). 32p. (J). (gr. k-4). 28.50 *(978-1-60270-665-1(4)*, 6243, Looking Glass Library) Magic Wagon.

—Who Turned up the Heat? Eco-Pig Explains Global Warming, 1 vol. French, Lisa S. 2009. (Eco-Pig Ser.). (ENG.). 32p. (J). (gr. k-4). 28.50 *(978-1-60270-664-4(6)*, 6241, Looking Glass Library) Magic Wagon.

—Whoa! UFO! Objects in the Sky. Larsen, Kirsten. 2009. (Science Solves It! ® Ser.). (ENG.). 32p. (J). (gr. k-2). pap. 5.95 *(978-1-57565-280-1(3))* Astra Publishing Hse.

Gott, Barry. Honk! Splat! Vroom! Gott, Barry. 2018. (ENG.). 32p. (J). (gr. -1-k). lib. bdg. 17.99 *(978-1-5124-4140-6(6)*, Carolrhoda Bks.) Lerner Publishing Group.

Gott, Barry. To Catch a Clownosaurus. Gott, Barry, tr. David, Lawrence. 2003. (Horace Splattly: Cupcaked Crusader Ser.). (ENG.). 150p. (J). (gr. 3-6). 17.44 *(978-0-525-47154-7(5))* Penguin Young Readers Group.

Gottesman, Val. Iraq. 2003. Poffenberger, Nancy. 2003. 32p. (YA). per. 9.95 *(978-0-938293-11-8(7))* Fun Publishing Co.

Gottheil, Shaindy. The Chanukah Candles. Blank, Nechama. Bassan, Malca, ed. 2018. (ENG.). 30p. (J). pap. 15.00 *(978-1-7907-6742-7(3))* Independently Published.

—The Splendid Succos Surprise. Blank, Nechama D. Bassan, Malca, ed. 2018. (ENG.). 38p. (J). pap. 15.00 *(978-1-7907-6689-5(3))* Independently Published.

Götting, Jean-Claude. The Bible for Young Children. Delval, Marie-Hélène. 2010. (ENG.). 96p. (J). (gr. -1-3). 16.50 *(978-0-8028-5383-7(8)*, Eerdmans Bks For Young Readers) Eerdmans, William B. Publishing Co.

Gottlieb, Iris. Who Gives a Poop? Surprising Science from One End to the Other. Montgomery, Heather L. 2020. 192p. (J). 17.99 ***(978-1-5476-0347-3(X)***, 900233520, Bloomsbury Children's Bks.) Bloomsbury Publishing USA.

Gottschalk, Deana. The Three Little Orphan Kittens. Wise, D. Rudd & Wise, Rachel. 2006. (J). 15.95 *(978-0-9786276-0-7(1))* Mentzer Printing Ink.

Gotzen-Beek, Betina. Antonia & the Big Competition: The Rosenburg Riding Stables, Volume 2. Zoller, Elisabeth et al. 2014. (ENG.). 92p. (J). (gr. 2-7). 9.95 *(978-1-62873-597-0(X)*, Sky Pony Pr.) Skyhorse Publishing Co., Inc.

—Antonia, the Horse Whisperer: The Rosenburg Riding Stables, Volume 1. Zöller, Elisabeth et al. 2014. (ENG.). 96p. (J). (gr. 2-7). 9.95 *(978-1-62636-383-0(8)*, Sky Pony Pr.) Skyhorse Publishing Co., Inc.

Goubar, Alex. Panda the Very Bad Cat Farm Frenzy. Bakker, Lacey L. 2019. (ENG.). 34p. (J). pap. ***(978-1-989506-10-3(0))*** Pandamonium Publishing Hse.

Goudeau, Breanna, jt. illus. see Kern, LaSquizzie.

Gouge, Angela. Casper & Catherine Move to America: An Immigrant Family's Adventures, 1849-1850. Gouge, Angela, tr. Hasler, Brian. 2003. 32p. 17.95 *(978-0-87195-168-7(1))* Indiana Historical Society.

Gough, Bryan. My Friend Isabelle. Woloson, Eliza. 2003. (ENG.). 28p. (J). 14.95 *(978-1-890627-50-8(X))* Woodbine Hse.

Goulart, M. J. Genevieve: Fashion Princess. Goulart, M. J. 2016. (ENG.). (J). (gr. k-4). pap. 11.95 *(978-0-9980932-3-9(8))* Goulart-Johnston, Michelle.

—Tutu's Quilt of Adventure: A Hawaiian Tale. Goulart, M. J. 2017. (ENG.). (J). (gr. k-2). pap. 12.95 *(978-0-9980932-5-3(4))* Goulart-Johnston, Michelle.

Gould, Alan, et al. Hot Water & Warm Homes from Sunlight. Sneider, Cary I., photos by. Gould, Alan. rev. ed. 2005. (Great Explorations in Math & Science Ser.). 80p. 13.50 *(978-1-931542-04-3(X)*, GEMS) Univ. of California, Berkeley, Lawrence Hall of Science.

Gould, Nathan John. A Mole Named Cole Dug a Hole. Gould, Nathan John. Gould, Jonathan, ed. 2019. (ENG.). 30p. (J). pap. 9.99 *(978-1-7909-3615-1(2))* Independently Published.

—Mr. Mom's First Day of School. Gould, Nathan John. Gould, Jonathan, ed. 2018. (ENG.). 26p. (J). pap. 9.99 *(978-1-9746-0532-3(9))* CreateSpace Independent Publishing Platform.

Gould, Robert, photos by. Parche, Vol. 3. Big Guy Books Staff & Duey, Kathleen. 2003. (Soldados en el Tiempo: Vol. 3). (SPA & ENG., 48p. (J). (gr. k-4). pap. 8.95 *(978-1-929945-37-5(X))* Big Guy Bks., Inc.

Gould, Robert, photos by. Racers. Gould, Robert. 2005. (Big Stuff Ser.). (ENG., 16p. (J). bds. 7.95 *(978-1-929945-52-8(3))* Big Guy Bks., Inc.

—Rescue Vehicles. Gould, Robert. 2005. (Big Stuff Ser.). (ENG., 16p. (J). bds. 7.95 *(978-1-929945-51-1(5))* Big Guy Bks., Inc.

Gould, Shawn. Giant of the Sea: The Story of a Sperm Whale. Raff, Courtney Granet. 2005. (Smithsonian Oceanic Collection). (ENG.). 32p. (J). (gr. -1-2). 15.95 *(978-1-931465-71-7(1)*, B4023) Soundprints.

—Mystery Fish. Walker, Sally M. 2006. (On My Own Science Ser.). 47p. (J). pap. 6.95 *(978-1-57505-850-4(2)*, First Avenue Editions) Lerner Publishing Group.

Goulding, Celeste. Classic Tales: Thumbelina. Arengo, Sue. 2006. (ENG.). 24p. 5.50 *(978-0-19-422537-3(2))* Oxford Univ. Pr. GBR. Dist: Oxford Univ. Pr., Inc.

Goulding, June. The Great Pirate Adventure: Peek Inside the 3D Windows. Baxter, Nicola. 2012. 12p. (J). (gr. -1-12). 16.99 *(978-1-84322-966-7(8))* Anness Publishing GBR. Dist: National Bk. Network.

—The Mystery of the Haunted House: Dare You Peek Through the 3-D Windows? Baxter, Nicola. 2013. 12p. 16.99 *(978-1-84322-754-0(1))* Anness Publishing GBR. Dist: National Bk. Network.

—Sunny Bunnies. Blumberg, Margie. 2008. (ENG.). 32p. (gr. -1-k). 15.95 *(978-0-9624166-4-4(9))* MB Publishing, LLC.

Goulding, June & Smyth, Iain. Dracula Steps Out. Ratnett, Michael. 2005. 12p. (J). (gr. k-4). reprint ed. 16.00 *(978-0-7567-8585-7(5))* DIANE Publishing Co.

Gouldthorpe, Peter. Queenie: One Elephant's Story. King, Corinne & Fenton, Corinne. 2013. (ENG.). 24p. (J). (gr. k-3). 16.99 *(978-0-7636-6375-9(1))* Candlewick Pr.

Goulevitch, Aure'lie. Le Petit Chaperon Rouge. Perrault, Charles. 2016. (FRE.). (J). (gr. k-1). pap. *(978-2-89687-594-8(8))* chouetteditions.com.

Goum. The Secret Life of Pets Gift Book: The Fast & the Furry. Lapuss, Stephane. ed. 2019. 96p. (J). (gr. 1-4). 14.99 *(978-1-78773-314-5(9))* Titan Bks. Ltd. GBR. Dist: Penguin Random Hse. LLC.

Gourbault, Martine. Once upon a Dragon: Stranger Safety for Kids (and Dragons) Pendziwol, Jean E. 2006. (ENG.). 32p. (J). (gr. -1-2). 11.99 *(978-1-55337-969-0(1))* Kids Can Pr., Ltd. CAN. Dist: Hachette Bk. Group.

—The Tale of Sir Dragon: Dealing with Bullies for Kids (and Dragons) Pendziwol, Jean E. 2007. (ENG.). 32p. (J). (gr. -1-2). 15.95 *(978-1-55453-135-6(7))*; pap. 7.95 *(978-1-55453-136-3(5))* Kids Can Pr., Ltd. CAN. Dist: Hachette Bk. Group.

—A Treasure at Sea for Dragon & Me: Water Safety for Kids (and Dragons) Pendziwol, Jean E. 2006. (ENG.). 32p. (J). (gr. -1-2). 11.99 *(978-1-55337-880-8(6))* Kids Can Pr., Ltd. CAN. Dist: Hachette Bk. Group.

Gourdeau, Brigitte. I'm a Leader Now. Watson, Wayne. 2019. (ENG.). 38p. (J). pap. ***(978-1-9994753-0-7(5))*** W2 Executive Coaching.

—Je Suis un Leader, Mamie. Watson, Wayne. 2019. (FRE.). 38p. (J). pap. ***(978-1-9994753-1-4(3))*** W2 Executive Coaching.

Gourley, Robbin. A House in the Sky. Jenkins, Steve. (ENG.). 32p. (J). (gr. -1-2). 2020. pap. 7.99 ***(978-1-62354-273-3(1))***; 2018. lib. bdg. 16.99 *(978-1-58089-780-8(0))* Charlesbridge Publishing, Inc.

Goux, Nicole. Shadow of the Batgirl. Kuhn, Sarah. 2020. (ENG.). 208p. (YA). (gr. 7-9). pap. 16.99 *(978-1-4012-8978-2(9))* DC Comics.

Gove, Frank Stanley. Bart the Batronaut. Ferris, Margaret Ann. 2011. (ENG.). 32p. (J). pap. 14.95 *(978-0-9837470-2-4(4))*; pap. *(978-0-9832819-8-6(X))* BookCrafters.

Govenar, Alan B., photos by. Extraordinary Ordinary People: Five American Masters of Traditional Arts. Govenar, Alan B. 2006. (ENG., 96p. (J). (gr. 5-7). 22.99 *(978-0-7636-2047-9(5))* Candlewick Pr.

Govoni, Dennis, jt. photos by see Maiden, D. W.

Gowdy, Danni. Teach Your Giraffe to Ski. Elbee, Viviane. 2018. (ENG.). 32p. (J). (gr. -1-3). 16.99 *(978-0-8075-7767-7(7)*, 807577677) Whitman, Albert & Co.

Gowen, Fiona. Deadly Dinosaurs & Prehistoric Creatures. 2016. (How to Draw Ser.). (ENG.). 32p. (J). (gr. 2-6). pap. 4.99 *(978-1-4380-0852-3(X)*, B.E.S. Publishing) Peterson's.

—How to Draw Amazing Animals & Incredible Insects. 2015. (How to Draw Ser.). (ENG.). 32p. (J). (gr. 2-6). pap. 4.99 *(978-1-4380-0583-6(0)*, B.E.S. Publishing) Peterson's.

—How to Draw Amazing Birds: From Songbirds to Birds of Prey. 2017. (How to Draw Ser.). (ENG.). 32p. (J). (gr. 2-6). pap. 4.99 *(978-1-4380-1053-3(2)*, B.E.S. Publishing) Peterson's.

—How to Draw Awesome Vehicles: Land, Sea, & Air. 2015. (How to Draw Ser.). (ENG.). 32p. (J). (gr. 2-6). pap. 4.99 *(978-1-4380-0582-9(2)*, B.E.S. Publishing) Peterson's.

—How to Draw Flying Vehicles. 2018. (How to Draw Ser.). (ENG.). 32p. (J). (gr. 2-6). pap. 4.99 *(978-1-4380-1054-0(0)*, B.E.S. Publishing) Peterson's.

—How to Draw Scary Monsters & Other Mythical Creatures. 2017. (How to Draw Ser.). (ENG.). 32p. (J). (gr. 2-6). pap. 4.99 *(978-1-4380-1055-7(9)*, B.E.S. Publishing) Peterson's.

—How to Draw Ships & Boats. 2018. (How to Draw Ser.). (ENG.). 32p. (J). (gr. 2-6). pap. 4.99 *(978-1-4380-1056-4(7)*, B.E.S. Publishing) Peterson's.

—Incredible Sharks & Other Ocean Giants. 2016. (How to Draw Ser.). (ENG.). 32p. (J). (gr. 2-6). pap. 4.99 *(978-1-4380-0853-0(8)*, B.E.S. Publishing) Peterson's.

Gowens, Kyle & Richmond, Bob. Monsters Have Big Feet. Kennis, Don. 2006. (J). per. 8.95 *(978-0-9788553-0-7(2))* Guppy Publishing LLC.

Gower, Jeremy & Shields, Chris. Earthquakes & Volcanoes. Watt, Fiona. Stockley, Corinne & Brooks, Felicity, eds. rev. ed. 2007. (Geography Ser.). 32p. (YA). (gr. 8-12). pap. 7.99 *(978-0-7945-1531-7(2)*, Usborne) EDC Publishing.

Gower, Jeremy, jt. illus. see Hewetson, Nicholas J.

Gower, Jim. The Elephants in the City of Light: An Elephant Family Adventure. Eschberger, Beverly. 2010. (J). per. 3.99 *(978-1-932926-28-6(3)*, Kinkajou Pr.) Artemesia Publishing, LLC.

—The Elephants in the Land of Enchantment: An Elephant Family Adventure. Eschberger, Beverly. 2009. (Elephant Family Adventure Ser.: 3). (ENG.). 96p. (J). (-1). pap. 3.99 *(978-1-932926-02-6(X))* Artemesia Publishing, LLC.

—The Elephants Tour England: An Elephant Family Adventure. Eschberger, Beverly. 2009. (Elephant Family Adventure Ser.: 2). (ENG.). 104p. (J). (gr. 2-5). per. 3.99 *(978-1-932926-29-3(1))* Artemesia Publishing, LLC.

—The Elephants Visit London: An Elephant Family Adventure. Eschberger, Beverly. l.t. ed. 2007. (Elephant Family Adventure Ser.: 1). (ENG.). 96p. (J). (-1). per. 3.99 *(978-1-932926-30-9(5))* Artemesia Publishing, LLC.

Gower, Teri. Fairyland Jigsaw Bk. Doherty, Gillian. 2007. 14p. (J). bds. 14.99 *(978-0-7945-1430-3(8)*, Usborne) EDC Publishing.

—Starting Gardening. Allman, Howard, photos by. Johnson, Sue & Evans, Cheryl. 2006. (First Skills Ser.). 32p. (J). (gr. 1). lib. bdg. 12.95 *(978-1-58086-543-2(7))* EDC Publishing.

—Stories of Fairies. Lester, Anna. 2006. (Young Reading Series 1 Gift Bks.). 47p. (J). (gr. 2-5). 8.99 *(978-0-7945-1326-9(3)*, Usborne) EDC Publishing.

—The Story of Castles. Sims, Lesley. 2004. (Young Reading Ser.: Vol. 2). 64p. (J). (gr. 2-18). lib. bdg. 13.95 *(978-1-58086-701-6(4)*, Usborne) EDC Publishing.

—The Story of Rome. Dickins, Rosie. 2006. (Usborne Young Reading: Series Two Ser.). 60p. (J). (gr. 2). lib. bdg. 13.99 *(978-1-58086-900-3(9)*, Usborne) EDC Publishing.

—The Usborne Big Book of Things to Spot. Doherty, Gillian et al. 2006. (1001 Things to Spot Ser.). 132p. (J). (gr. 1). lib. bdg. 20.95 *(978-1-58086-496-1(1))* EDC Publishing.

—1001 Animals Que Buscar. Brocklehurst, Ruth. 2003. (Facts & Lists Internet-Linked Ser.). (SPA.). 64p. (J). (gr. 4-7). lib. bdg. 14.95 *(978-1-58086-493-0(7))* EDC Publishing.

—1001 Bugs to Spot. Helbrough, Emma. 2005. 32p. (J). pap. 6.95 *(978-0-7945-1000-8(0)*, Usborne) EDC Publishing.

—1001 Cosas Que Buscar en el Psia de las Hadas. Doherty, Gillian. 2007. (Titles in Spanish Ser.). 32p. (J). 9.99 *(978-0-7460-8346-8(7)*, Usborne) EDC Publishing.

—1001 Pirate Things to Spot. Jones, Rob Lloyd. 2007. (1001 Things to Spot Ser.). 32p. (J). 9.99 *(978-0-7945-1513-3(4)*, Usborne) EDC Publishing.

—1001 Things to Spot in Fairyland. Doherty, Gillian. 2006. (Usborne 1001 Things to Spot Ser.). 32p. (J). (gr. 1-4). 9.99 *(978-0-7945-1220-0(8)*, Usborne) EDC Publishing.

—1001 Things to Spot in the Sea. Daynes, Katie. 2009. (1001 Things to Spot Ser.). 32p. (J). (gr. 1). 9.99 *(978-0-7945-2615-3(2)*, Usborne) EDC Publishing.

—1001 Things to Spot Long Ago. Doherty, Gillian. Brooks, Felicity, ed. 2006. (Usborne 1001 Things to Spot Ser.). 32p. (J). (gr. 1). lib. bdg. 14.99 *(978-1-58086-963-8(7))* EDC Publishing.

—1001 Things to Spot Long Ago. Doherty, Gillian. rev. ed. 2006. (1001 Things to Spot Ser.). 32p. (J). (gr. -1-3). pap. 6.99 *(978-0-7945-0716-9(6)*, Usborne) EDC Publishing.

—1001 Wizard Things to Spot. Doherty, Gillian. 2008. (Usborne 1001 Things to Spot Ser.). 31p. (J). (gr. 4-7). 9.99 *(978-0-7945-1860-8(5)*, Usborne) EDC Publishing.

Gower, Teri, jt. illus. see Lyon, Chris.

Gownley, Jimmy. Amelia & Her Three Kisses, 1 vol. Gownley, Jimmy. 2013. (Amelia Rules! Ser.). (ENG.). 36p. (J). (gr. 2-6). 27.07 *(978-1-61479-068-6(X)*, 2387, Graphic Novels) Spotlight.

—Amelia & the Gym Class System: #2, 1 vol. Gownley, Jimmy. 2010. (Amelia Rules! Ser.). (ENG.). 36p. (J). (gr. 2-6). 27.07 *(978-1-59961-788-6(9)*, 2381, Graphic Novels) Spotlight.

—Amelia & the Other Side of Yuletide: #4, 1 vol. Gownley, Jimmy. 2010. (Amelia Rules! Ser.). (ENG.). 36p. (J). (gr. 2-6). 27.07 *(978-1-59961-790-9(0)*, 2383, Graphic Novels) Spotlight.

—Amelia in Fireflies & Time, 1 vol. Gownley, Jimmy. 2013. (Amelia Rules! Ser.). (ENG.). 36p. (J). (gr. 2-6). 27.07 *(978-1-61479-069-3(8)*, 2388, Graphic Novels) Spotlight.

—Amelia in Heroes & Villains, 1 vol. Gownley, Jimmy. 2013. (Amelia Rules! Ser.). (ENG.). 36p. (J). (gr. 2-6). 27.07 *(978-1-61479-070-9(1)*, 2389, Graphic Novels) Spotlight.

—Amelia in into Graceland, 1 vol. Gownley, Jimmy. 2013. (Amelia Rules! Ser.). (ENG.). 36p. (J). (gr. 2-6). 27.07 *(978-1-61479-071-6(X)*, 2390, Graphic Novels) Spotlight.

—Amelia in Joy & Wonder, 1 vol. Gownley, Jimmy. 2013. (Amelia Rules! Ser.). (ENG.). 36p. (J). (gr. 2-6). 27.07 *(978-1-61479-072-3(8)*, 2391, Graphic Novels) Spotlight.

—Amelia in Loosely in Disguise & Frightened: #3, 1 vol. Gownley, Jimmy. 2010. (Amelia Rules! Ser.). (ENG.). 36p. (J). (gr. 2-6). 27.07 *(978-1-59961-789-3(7)*, 2382, Graphic Novels) Spotlight.

—Amelia in Speak Softee to Me: #5, 1 vol. Gownley, Jimmy. 2010. (Amelia Rules! Ser.). (ENG.). 36p. (J). (gr. 2-6). 27.07 *(978-1-59961-791-6(9)*, 2384, Graphic Novels) Spotlight.

—Amelia in What Makes You Happy: #6, 1 vol. Gownley, Jimmy. 2010. (Amelia Rules! Ser.). (ENG.). 36p. (J). (gr. 2-6). 27.07 *(978-1-59961-792-3(7)*, 2385, Graphic Novels) Spotlight.

—The Amelia Rules! Collection: The Whole World's Crazy; What Makes You Happy; Superheroes; When the Past Is a Present; the Tweenage Guide to Not Being Unpopular; True Things (Adults Don't Want Kids to Know); the Meaning of Life ... & Other Stuff; Her Permanent Record. Gownley, Jimmy. ed. 2016. (Amelia Rules! Ser.). (ENG.). 1392p. (J). (gr. 2-7). pap. 96.99 *(978-1-4814-9755-8(3)*,

Atheneum Bks. for Young Readers) Simon & Schuster Children's Publishing.

—Amelia vs. the Sneeze Barf: #1, 1 vol. Gownley, Jimmy. 2010. (Amelia Rules! Ser.). (ENG.). 36p. (J). (gr. 2-6). 27.07 *(978-1-59961-787-9(0)*, 2380, Graphic Novels) Spotlight.

—Amelia's Life During Wartime, 1 vol. Gownley, Jimmy. 2013. (Amelia Rules! Ser.). (ENG.). 36p. (J). (gr. 2-6). 27.07 *(978-1-61479-073-0(6)*, 2392, Graphic Novels) Spotlight.

—Her Permanent Record. Gownley, Jimmy. 2012. (Amelia Rules! Ser.). (ENG.). 160p. (J). (gr. 2-7). 24.99 *(978-1-4169-8615-7(4))*; pap. 12.99 *(978-1-4169-8614-0(6))* Simon & Schuster Children's Publishing. (Atheneum Bks. for Young Readers).

—The Meaning of Life ... & Other Stuff. Gownley, Jimmy. 2011. (Amelia Rules! Ser.). (ENG.). 160p. (J). (gr. 2-7). 21.99 *(978-1-4169-8613-3(8))*; pap. 12.99 *(978-1-4169-8612-6(X))* Simon & Schuster Children's Publishing. (Atheneum Bks. for Young Readers).

—Superheroes. Gownley, Jimmy. 2010. (Amelia Rules! Ser.). (ENG.). 176p. (J). (gr. 2-7). pap. 12.99 *(978-1-4169-8606-5(5)*, Atheneum Bks. for Young Readers) Simon & Schuster Children's Publishing.

—True Things: Adults Don't Want Kids to Know. Gownley, Jimmy. 2010. (Amelia Rules! Ser.). (ENG.). 176p. (J). (gr. 2-7). 19.99 *(978-1-4169-8611-9(1)*, Atheneum Bks. for Young Readers) Simon & Schuster Children's Publishing.

—True Things (Adults Don't Want Kids to Know) Gownley, Jimmy. 2010. (Amelia Rules! Ser.). (ENG.). 176p. (J). (gr. 2-7). pap. 12.99 *(978-1-4169-8609-6(X)*, Atheneum Bks. for Young Readers) Simon & Schuster Children's Publishing.

—The Tweenage Guide to Not Being Unpopular. Gownley, Jimmy. 2010. (Amelia Rules! Ser.). (ENG.). 192p. (J). (gr. 2-7). pap. 12.99 *(978-1-4169-8608-9(1)*, Atheneum Bks. for Young Readers) Simon & Schuster Children's Publishing.

—A Very Ninja Christmas. Gownley, Jimmy. 2009. (Amelia Rules! Ser.). (ENG.). 80p. (J). (gr. 2-7). pap. 7.99 *(978-1-4169-8959-2(5)*, Atheneum Bks. for Young Readers) Simon & Schuster Children's Publishing.

—What Makes You Happy. Gownley, Jimmy. (Amelia Rules! Ser.). (ENG.). 176p. (J). (gr. 2-7). 2011. 19.99 *(978-1-4424-4539-0(4))*; 2009. pap. 12.99 *(978-1-4169-8605-8(7))* Simon & Schuster Children's Publishing. (Atheneum Bks. for Young Readers).

—When the Past Is a Present. Gownley, Jimmy. (Amelia Rules! Ser.). (ENG.). 176p. (J). (gr. 2-7). 2011. 24.99 *(978-1-4424-4541-3(6))*; 2010. pap. 12.99 *(978-1-4169-8607-2(3))* Simon & Schuster Children's Publishing. (Atheneum Bks. for Young Readers).

—The Whole World's Crazy. Gownley, Jimmy. (Amelia Rules! Ser.). (ENG.). 176p. (J). (gr. 2-7). 2011. 21.99 *(978-1-4424-4538-3(6))*; 2009. pap. 12.99 *(978-1-4169-8604-1(9))* Simon & Schuster Children's Publishing. (Atheneum Bks. for Young Readers).

Grabas, Peter & Parts, Art. The Homeowner's Handbook: A Guide to Getting Your Act Together & Keeping It That Way. Nosek, Jude. 2003. 124p. (YA). pap. 14.95 *(978-0-9726619-6-6(4))* KnackPacks, Inc.

Grabe, Robert, jt. illus. see Timmons, Johnny.

Graber, Jack. The Brave Little Explorer. Graber, Mark. 2015. (ENG.). (J). 16.99 *(978-0-692-43867-1(X))* JourneytimeBks.

Graber, Jesse. Follow the Leader. Byrne, Marlene. 2009. (ENG.). 39p. (J). 14.99 *(978-0-9777135-1-6(2))* Celtic Chicago Inc.

—Ghost in the Graveyard. Byrne, Marlene F. 2010. 57p. (J). pap. 9.99 *(978-0-9777135-4-7(7))* Celtic Chicago Inc.

—Kick the Can. Byrne, Marlene. 2009. 61p. pap. 9.99 *(978-0-9777135-3-0(9))* Celtic Chicago Inc.

—Treasure Hunt. Byrne, Marlene F. 2009. 36p. (J). 14.99 *(978-0-9777135-0-9(4))* Celtic Chicago Inc.

Graber, Lois. A Song in the Storm. 2012. 32p. (J). *(978-0-7399-2445-7(1))* Rod & Staff Pubs., Inc.

Graber, Luke. Good Egg & Bad Apple, 1 vol. Herz, Henry. 2018. (ENG.). 32p. (J). (gr. -1-3). 16.99 *(978-0-7643-5603-2(8)*, 16111) Schiffer Publishing, Ltd.

—How the Squid Got Two Long Arms, 1 vol. Herz, Henry. 2018. (ENG.). 32p. (J). (gr. -1-3). 16.99 *(978-1-4556-2388-4(1)*, Pelican Publishing) Arcadia Publishing.

Graber, Vickie. Great-Grandpa's Chair: A Story about Living & Dying, Shared Between A Great-Grandpa & His 10-year-old Grandson! Bayne, Nancy. l.t. ed. 2005. 22p. (J). per. 9.99 *(978-1-59879-046-7(3))* Lifevest Publishing, Inc.

Grablewski, Alexandra, photos by. Sublime Stitching: Hundreds of Hip Embroidery Patterns & How-To. Hart, Jenny. 2006. (ENG.). 224p. (gr. 8-17). 22.95 *(978-0-8118-5011-7(0))* Chronicle Bks. LLC.

Graboff, Abner. What Can Cats Do? Graboff, Abner. 2018. (ENG.). 48p. 20.00 *(978-1-85124-493-5(X))* Bodleian Library GBR. Dist: Chicago Distribution Ctr.

Grace, Bill. Constantine Goes to School. Rogers Yaeger, Nancy. 2006. 60p. (J). (gr. 2-5). *(978-1-4050-5714-1(9))* Macmillan Caribbean.

Grace, Christy. My Dream Pillow. Morrison, Shannon L. 2018. (ENG.). 26p. (J). pap. 9.99 *(978-1-948563-01-7(0))* La Puerta Pubns.

Grace, Sina. Among the Ghosts. Benson, Amber. 2011. (ENG.). 256p. (J). (gr. 3-7). pap. 6.99 *(978-1-4169-9426-8(2)*, Aladdin) Simon & Schuster Children's Publishing.

—Among the Ghosts. Benson, Amber. 2010. (ENG.). 256p. (J). (gr. 3-7). 15.99 *(978-1-4169-9405-3(X)*, Simon & Schuster/Paula Wiseman Bks.) Simon & Schuster/Paula Wiseman Bks.

Grad, R. H. Peri's Island Adventure: A Peri the Pelican Story. Holzman, E. M. 2018. (Peri the Pelican Bks.: Vol. 4). (ENG.). 60p. (J). pap. 18.95 *(978-1-9816-5389-8(9))* CreateSpace Independent Publishing Platform.

Grad, R. H. Peri's New York City Adventure: A Peri the Pelican Story. Holzman, E. M. 2019. (Peri the Pelican Bks.: Vol. 4). (ENG.). 38p. (J). pap. 15.95 ***(978-1-6977-0995-7(8))*** Independently Published.

Gradisher, Martha. A Class Play with Ms. Vanilla. Linn, Margot. 2005. (I'm Going to Read! Level 3 Ser.: Level 3). (ENG.). 32p. (J). (gr. 1-2). 16.19 *(978-1-4027-2108-3(0))* Sterling Publishing Co., Inc.

—Sparkalot & the Red Stone: Book III the Gate Between the Worlds. Heller, M. E. 2018. (ENG.). 122p. (J). pap. 9.99 *(978-1-64136-002-9(X))* Celestine Pr.

Grady, Kit. Bradybug. Shepherd, Donna J. 2010. 20p. pap. 10.95 *(978-1-61633-071-2(6))* Guardian Angel Publishing, Inc.

—Flutter Bunnies. Mcintyre, Mel. 2008. 24p. pap. 10.95 *(978-1-933090-68-9(5))* Guardian Angel Publishing, Inc.

—Flutter Bunnies Fossil of Fortune. McIntyre, Mel & Mcintyre, Mel. 2011. 20p. pap. 9.95 *(978-1-61633-170-2(4))* Guardian Angel Publishing, Inc.

—Hamster Holidays: Noun & Adjective Adventures. Reeg, Cynthia. 2009. 24p. pap. 10.95 *(978-1-935137-62-7(X))* Guardian Angel Publishing, Inc.

—Humberto, the Bookworm Hamster. Calvani, Mayra. 2009. 20p. pap. 10.95 *(978-1-935137-92-4(1))* Guardian Angel Publishing, Inc.

—Rainbow Nights. Harris, Sally M. 2009. 20p. pap. 9.95 *(978-1-61633-002-6(3))* Guardian Angel Publishing, Inc.

—Rainbow Nights. Harris, Sally M. 2018. (ENG.). 26p. (J). pap. 9.95 *(978-0-9660839-8-9(9))* Top Cat Publishing.

Graef, Renee. B Is for Badger: A Wisconsin Alphabet. Wargin, Kathy-jo. 2004. (Discover America State by State Ser.). (ENG.). 40p. (J). 17.95 *(978-1-58536-135-9(6))* Sleeping Bear Pr.

—B Is for Beacon: A Great Lakes Lighthouse Alphabet. Wilbur, Helen L. 2016. (ENG.). 32p. (J). (gr. 1-4). 16.99 *(978-1-58536-916-4(0)*, 204025) Sleeping Bear Pr.

—B Is for Bookworm: A Library Alphabet. Prieto, Anita C. 2007. (J). (gr. k-7). 16.10 *(978-0-7569-6657-7(4))* Perfection Learning Corp.

—B Is for Bookworm: A Library Alphabet. Prieto, Anita C. 2007. (ENG.). 40p. (J). (gr. 1-4). per. 7.95 *(978-1-58536-326-1(X)*, 202290) Sleeping Bear Pr.

—Bedtime in the Southwest. Hodgson, Mona Gansberg. 2004. (ENG.). 32p. (J). (gr. -1-k). 14.95 *(978-0-87358-871-3(1))* Cooper Square Publishing Llc.

—Beyond the Heather Hills. Wiley, Melissa. 2003. (Little House Ser.). 189p. (J). (gr. 3-7). 14.65 *(978-0-7569-3467-5(2))* Perfection Learning Corp.

—D Is for Dala Horse: A Nordic Countries Alphabet. Wargin, Kathy-jo. 2010. (Discover the World Ser.). (ENG.). 40p. (J). (gr. 1-3). 17.95 *(978-1-58536-510-4(6)*, 202203) Sleeping Bear Pr.

—Four Famous Faces. Patrick, Jean. 2014. 32p. (J). lib. bdg. 16.99 *(978-0-9798823-8-8(9))* Mount Rushmore Bookstores.

—A Girl Named Dan. Mackall, Dandi Daley. 2008. (ENG.). 32p. (J). (gr. k-6). 16.95 *(978-1-58536-351-3(0))* Sleeping Bear Pr.

—Kirsten Story Collection. Shaw, Janet. 2008. 380p. 29.95 *(978-1-59369-454-8(7))* American Girl Publishing, Inc.

—Lidia's Family Kitchen: Nonna's Birthday Surprise. Bastianich, Lidia. 2013. 60p. (J). (gr. -1-17). 16.95 *(978-0-7624-4655-1(2)*, Running Pr. Kids) Running Pr.

—A Little House Picture Book Treasury: Six Stories of Life on the Prairie. Wilder, Laura Ingalls. 2017. (Little House Picture Book Ser.). (ENG.). 208p. (J). (gr. -1-3). 24.99 *(978-0-06-247077-5(9))* HarperCollins Pubs.

Graef, Renée. Milwaukee. Joosse, Barbara. 2018. (Our City Adventures Ser.). (ENG.). 32p. (J). (gr. k-3). 16.99 *(978-1-5341-1017-5(8)*, 204642) Sleeping Bear Pr.

Graef, Renee. My Favorite Things. Rodgers, Richard et al. 2005. (ENG.). 32p. (J). (gr. -1-3). pap. 7.99 *(978-0-06-443627-4(6))* HarperCollins Pubs.

—Nonna Tell Me a Story: Lidia's Egg-Citing Farm Adventure. Bastianich, Lidia. 2015. 60p. (J). (gr. -1-17). 16.95 *(978-0-7624-5126-5(2)*, Running Pr. Kids) Running Pr.

—The Nutcracker: The Untold Story. Schulman, Janet. 2005. 40p. (J). pap. 6.99 *(978-0-06-443790-5(6)*, Harper Trophy) HarperCollins Pubs.

—Sport: Ship Dog of the Great Lakes. Cameron, Pamela. 2019. (ENG.). 32p. (gr. 2-3). 17.95 *(978-0-87020-914-7(0))* Wisconsin Historical Society.

—T Is for a Time. Smith, Marie & Smith, Roland. 2015. (ENG.). 40p. (J). (gr. 2-5). 16.99 *(978-1-58536-512-8(2)*, 203809) Sleeping Bear Pr.

—Therese Makes a Tapestry. Hinrichs, Alexandra S. D. 2016. (ENG.). 40p. (J). 19.95 *(978-1-60606-473-3(8)*, J. Paul Getty Museum) Getty Pubns.

—Who Carved the Mountain? The Story of Mount Rushmore. Patrick, Jean L. S. 2005. 37p. (J). 16.99 *(978-0-9752617-4-3(6))* Mount Rushmore Bookstores.

Graef, Renee, jt. illus. see Lewis, Kim.

Graegin, Stephanie. Better Together. George, Kallie. 2018. (Heartwood Hotel Ser.: 3). 176p. (J). (gr. 2-5). pap. 5.99 ***(978-1-4847-4640-0(6))*** Little, Brown Bks. for Young Readers.

Graegin, Stephanie. Don't Feed the Boy. Latham, Irene. 2014. (ENG.). 304p. (J). (gr. 3-7). pap. 13.99 *(978-1-250-04428-0(6)*, 9781250044280) Square Fish.

—Elvis Presley's Love Me Tender. Presley, Elvis. 2017. (ENG.). 40p. (J). (-k). 17.99 *(978-0-7352-3122-1(2)*, Dial Bks) Penguin Young Readers Group.

—Elvis Presley's Quiéreme con Ternura. Presley, Elvis. 2019. 40p. (J). (-k). pap. 8.99 *(978-1-9848-3557-4(2)*, Puffin Books) Penguin Young Readers Group.

—The Friendship Book. Ray, Mary Lyn. 2019. (ENG.). 32p. (J). (gr. -1-3). 14.99 *(978-1-328-48899-2(3)*, 1716518, HMH Books For Young Readers) Houghton Mifflin Harcourt Publishing Co.

—Goldilocks & the Three Bears. Namm, Diane. 2013. (Silver Penny Stories Ser.). 48p. (J). (gr. -1-1). 4.95 *(978-1-4027-8430-9(9))* Sterling Publishing Co., Inc.

—The Greatest Gift. George, Kallie. 2017. (Heartwood Hotel Ser.: 2). 176p. (J). (gr. 2-5). 14.99 *(978-1-4847-3234-2(0))* Hyperion Bks. for Children.

—Hansel & Gretel. McFadden, Deanna. 2012. (Silver Penny Stories Ser.). 48p. (J). (gr. -1-1). 4.95 *(978-1-4027-8335-7(3))* Sterling Publishing Co., Inc.

—Happy Birthday, Bunny! Scanlon, Liz Garton. 2013. (ENG.). 32p. (J). (gr. -1-3). 16.99 *(978-1-4424-0287-4(3)*, Beach Lane Bks.) Beach Lane Bks.

—Hector the Collector. Beeny, Emily. 2017. (ENG.). 40p. (J). 17.99 *(978-1-62672-296-5(X)*, 9781626722965) Roaring Brook Pr.

—How to Share with a Bear. Pinder, Eric. 2015. (ENG.). 40p. (J). (gr. -1-1). 17.99 *(978-0-374-30019-7(4)*, 9780374300197, Farrar, Straus & Giroux (BYR)) Farrar, Straus & Giroux.

—The Lost Gift: A Christmas Story. George, Kallie. 2016. 40p. (J). (gr. -1-3). 17.99 *(978-0-553-52481-9(X)*, Schwartz & Wade Bks.) Random Hse. Children's Bks.

—Peace Is an Offering. LeBox, Annette. 2015. 34p. (J). (gr. -1-k). 17.99 *(978-0-8037-4091-4(3)*, Dial Bks) Penguin Young Readers Group.

—Sleeping Beauty. McFadden, Deanna et al. 2013. (Silver Penny Stories Ser.). 48p. (J). (gr. -1-1). 4.95 *(978-1-4027-8341-8(8))* Sterling Publishing Co., Inc.

—Super Manny Cleans Up! DiPucchio, Kelly. 2018. (Super Manny Ser.). (ENG.). 40p. (J). (gr. -1-3). 17.99 *(978-1-4814-5962-4(7))* Simon & Schuster Children's Publishing.

—Super Manny Stands Up! DiPucchio, Kelly. 2017. (Super Manny Ser.). (ENG.). 40p. (J). (gr. -1-3). 17.99 *(978-1-4814-5960-0(0))* Simon & Schuster Children's Publishing.

—The Thank You Book. Ray, Mary Lyn. 2018. (ENG.). 32p. (J). (gr. -1-3). 13.99 *(978-0-544-79136-7(3)*, 1639922, HMH Books For Young Readers) Houghton Mifflin Harcourt Publishing Co.

Graegin, Stephanie. The Thank You Book (padded Board Book) Ray, Mary Lyn. 2020. (ENG.). 32p. (J). (— 1). bds. 9.99 ***(978-0-358-36268-5(7)***, 1784605, HMH Books For Young Readers) Houghton Mifflin Harcourt Publishing Co.

Graegin, Stephanie. A True Home. George, Kallie. 2017. (Heartwood Hotel Ser.: 1). 176p. (J). (gr. 2-5). 14.99 *(978-1-4847-3161-1(1))* Disney Pr.

—Water in the Park: A Book about Water & the Times of the Day. Jenkins, Emily. 2013. 40p. (J). (gr. -1-2). 16.99 *(978-0-375-87002-6(4)*, Schwartz & Wade Bks.) Random Hse. Children's Bks.

Graegin, Stephanie. Little Fox in the Forest. Graegin, Stephanie. 2017. 40p. (J). (gr. -1-3). 17.99 *(978-0-553-53789-5(X)*, Schwartz & Wade Bks.) Random Hse. Children's Bks.

Graf, William. Of Course You Can! Educating Children about Money. Sparks, Candi. 2006. (Can I Have Some Money? Ser.). pap. 11.99 *(978-0-9789445-0-6(X))* Sparks Fly.

Grafe, Amanda. Alex & the Magical Flying Coat. Reid, Julia. 2020. (ENG.). 34p. (J). 16.95 ***(978-1-950323-26-5(9))***; pap. 12.95 ***(978-1-950323-27-2(7))*** Leaning Rock Pr.

Grafe, Amanda. The Sneaky Mouse. Grafe, Amanda. 2020. (ENG.). 38p. (J). 16.95 ***(978-1-950323-32-6(3))***; pap. 12.95 ***(978-1-950323-34-0(X))*** Leaning Rock Pr.

Grafe, Max. The Bearskinner: A Tale of the Brothers Grimm. Schlitz, Laura Amy. 2007. (ENG.). 40p. (J). (gr. 4-7). 16.99 *(978-0-7636-2730-0(5))* Candlewick Pr.

—What the Grizzly Knows. Elliott, David. 2008. (ENG.). 32p. (J). (gr. -1-2). 16.99 *(978-0-7636-2778-2(X))* Candlewick Pr.

Graffam, Merle. Boys' Club. Walker, E. G. 2004. (J). (gr. 2-8). pap. 12.95 *(978-0-9716071-5-6(X))* Walker, Esther.

Graham, Adele. Missouri Horses Vol. 1: Gift to a Nation. Gilbert, Joan Sewell. 2005. 530p. (gr. 6-18). pap. 23.50 *(978-0-9712559-1-3(1))* MoGho Bks., LLC.

—More Missouri Ghosts: Fact, Fiction & Folklore. Gilbert, Joan. 2005. 232p. (gr. 6-18). pap. 14.95 *(978-0-615-11888-8(7))* MoGho Bks., LLC.

Graham, Alistair. Full Moon Soup. Graham, Alistair. 2003. (Full Moon Soup & Full Moon Afloat Ser.). 32p. (YA). pap. *(978-1-85602-071-8(1)*, Pavilion Children's Books) Pavilion Bks.

Graham, Andrew S. & Ribeira, Lili. Me Tarzan, You Jane. Graham, Janice Barrett. 2011. 25p. (J). (gr. 1-4). pap. 6.95 *(978-0-9724770-8-6(X))* Tidal Wave Bks.

Graham, Bob. Monsieur Albert Rides to Glory. Smith, Peter. 2015. (ENG.). 32p. (J). (gr. k-2). 11.99 *(978-1-74331-842-3(1))* Allen & Unwin AUS. Dist: Independent Pubs. Group.

—This Is Our House. Rosen, Michael. 2005. (ENG.). 32p. (J). (gr. -1-2). 7.99 *(978-0-7636-2816-1(6))* Candlewick Pr.

—Want to Play Trucks? Stott, Ann. 2018. 32p. (J). (gr. -1-2). 15.99 *(978-0-7636-8173-9(3))* Candlewick Pr.

Graham, Bob. April & Esme Tooth Fairies. Graham, Bob. (ENG.). 40p. (J). (gr. k-4). 2013. 6.99 *(978-0-7636-6347-6(6))*; 2010. 16.99 *(978-0-7636-4683-7(0))* Candlewick Pr.

—A Bus Called Heaven. Graham, Bob. 2012. (ENG.). 40p. (J). (gr. -1-2). 16.99 *(978-0-7636-5893-9(6))* Candlewick Pr.

—A Bus Called Heaven. Graham, Bob. 2018. (ENG.). 40p. (J). (gr. -1-2). 7.99 *(978-1-5362-0294-6(0))* Candlewick Pr.

—Home in the Rain. Graham, Bob. 2017. (ENG.). 32p. (J). (gr. -1-2). 16.99 *(978-0-7636-9269-8(7))* Candlewick Pr.

—How the Sun Got to Coco's House. Graham, Bob. 2015. 40p. (J). (gr. -1-1). 17.99 *(978-0-7636-8109-8(1))* Candlewick Pr.

—How to Heal a Broken Wing. Graham, Bob. 2008. (ENG.). 40p. (J). (gr. -1-2). 17.99 *(978-0-7636-3903-7(6))* Candlewick Pr.

—How to Heal a Broken Wing. Graham, Bob. 2017. (ENG.). 40p. (J). (gr. -1-2). 7.99 *(978-0-7636-9841-6(5))* Candlewick Pr.

—Let's Get a Pup! Said Kate. Graham, Bob. 2003. (ENG.). 32p. (J). (gr. -1-2). pap. 6.99 *(978-0-7636-2193-3(5))* Candlewick Pr.

—The Poesy Ring: A Love Story. Graham, Bob. 2018. (ENG.). 40p. (J). (-k). 16.99 *(978-0-7636-9884-3(9))* Candlewick Pr.

—The Silver Button. Graham, Bob. 2013. (ENG.). 32p. (J). (gr. -1-1). 16.99 *(978-0-7636-6437-4(5))* Candlewick Pr.

—The Silver Button. Graham, Bob. 2018. (ENG.). 32p. (J). (gr. -1-1). 7.99 *(978-1-5362-0144-4(8))* Candlewick Pr.

—Tooth Fairy Story. Graham, Bob. 2019. (ENG.). 40p. (J). (gr. -1-2). 16.99 *(978-1-5362-1112-2(5))* Candlewick Pr.

—Vanilla Ice Cream. Graham, Bob. 2014. (ENG.). 40p. (J). (gr. -1-1). 16.99 *(978-0-7636-7377-2(3))* Candlewick Pr.

Graham, C. E. If I Had A Wish. Dukoff, K. D. 2008. 12p. pap. 24.95 *(978-1-60610-241-1(9))* America Star Bks.

Graham, Carl. Tom's Wish. Williams, Paula. 2013. 24p. pap. *(978-1-909740-80-8(2))* Legend Pr.

Graham, Caylin. My Son the Petunia Patch. Blair, Rebecca. 2019. (ENG.). 28p. (J). (gr. k-2). 18.00 *(978-0-692-17683-2(7))* Blair, Rebecca E.

Graham, Cherizar. Modes of Transportation: ABC Book of Rhymes: Reading at Bedtime Brainy Benefits. Rosenberg, Yael & Mazor, Sarah. 2019. (Science & Technology for Kids Ser.: Vol. 1). (ENG.). 58p. (J). pap. 14.98 *(978-1-7932-5801-4(5))* Independently Published.

Graham, Dennis. The Little Clay Jar: La Vasijita de Barro. Ramos, Peregrina. 2006.Tr. of vasijita de Barro. (SPA & ENG.). (J). per. 15.95 *(978-0-9788381-0-2(6))* Word Gift Pubns.

Graham, Georgia. Here Comes Hortense! Hartt-Sussman, Heather. 2012. (ENG.). 32p. (J). (gr. -1-1). 17.95 *(978-1-77049-221-9(6)*, Tundra Bks.) Tundra Bks. CAN. Dist: Penguin Random Hse. LLC.

—Nana's Getting Married. Hartt-Sussman, Heather. 2010. 32p. (J). (gr. -1-1). 17.95 *(978-0-88776-911-5(X)*, Tundra Bks.) Tundra Bks. CAN. Dist: Penguin Random Hse. LLC.

—Nana's Summer Surprise. Hartt-Sussman, Heather. 2013. 32p. (J). (gr. -1-1). 17.95 *(978-1-77049-324-7(7)*, Tundra Bks.) Tundra Bks. CAN. Dist: Penguin Random Hse. LLC.

—The Saturday Appaloosa, 1 vol. Sharp, Thelma. 2011. (ENG.). 32p. (J). (gr. 1-3). pap. 9.95 *(978-0-88995-467-0(4)*, 11f60386-7921-4b63-a091-9b5d88a9c0ff) Red Deer Pr. CAN. Dist: Firefly Bks., Ltd.

—Saving Thunder the Great: The True Story of a Gerbil¿s Escape from the Fort Mcmurray Wildfire, 1 vol. Shirtliffe, Leanne. 2016. (ENG.). 36p. (J). (gr. 1-3). 21.95 *(978-1-927099-85-8(4)*, d9f9ccfc-cbd0-4400-bb02-f5382c2f35ee) Clockwise Pr. CAN. Dist: Firefly Bks., Ltd.

—Tiger's New Cowboy Boots, 1 vol. Morck, Irene. 2003. (ENG.). 30p. (J). (gr. -1-4). pap. 9.95 *(978-0-88995-181-5(0)*, af6f10dc-604f-448c-a8a0-ca600f847519) Red Deer Pr. CAN. Dist: Firefly Bks., Ltd.

—Tiger's New Cowboy Boots, 1 vol. Morck, Irene. 2003. (ENG.). 30p. (J). (gr. 1-3). 17.95 *(978-0-88995-153-2(5)*, 34f04ffe-15ab-4a13-887b-63847f25de87) Trifolium Bks., Inc. CAN. Dist: Firefly Bks., Ltd.

—Wanda & the Frogs. Azore, Barbara. 32p. (J). (gr. -1-1). 2012. (ENG.). pap. 7.95 *(978-1-77049-307-0(7))*; 2007. 18.95 *(978-0-88776-761-6(3))* Tundra Bks. CAN. (Tundra Bks.). Dist: Penguin Random Hse. LLC.

—Wanda & the Wild Hair. Azore, Barbara. 2005. (ENG.). 32p. (J). (gr. -1-2). 15.95 *(978-0-88776-717-3(6)*, Tundra Bks.) Tundra Bks. CAN. Dist: Penguin Random Hse. LLC.

—Wanda & the Wild Hair. Azore, Barbara. 2012. (ENG.). 32p. (J). (gr. -1-2). pap. 7.95 *(978-1-77049-306-3(9)*, Tundra Bks.) Tundra Bks. CAN. Dist: Penguin Random Hse. LLC.

—Wanda's Freckles. Azore, Barbara. (ENG.). 24p. (J). (gr. -1-2). 2012. pap. 7.95 *(978-1-77049-308-7(5))*; 2009. 19.95 *(978-0-88776-862-0(8))* Tundra Bks. CAN. (Tundra Bks.). Dist: Penguin Random Hse. LLC.

Graham, Georgia. A Team Like No Other, 1 vol. Graham, Georgia. 2004. (ENG.). 32p. (J). (gr. 1-2). 9.95 *(978-0-88995-290-4(6)*, d3dbce51-2cd4-43dd-83f0-8311a06bd57a) Trifolium Bks., Inc. CAN. Dist: Firefly Bks., Ltd.

Graham, Hannah. Ben's Rubbish Day. Webb, Naomi. 2020. (ENG.). 30p. (J). pap. ***(978-1-78830-712-3(7))*** Olympia Publishers.

Graham, Heather, jt. illus. see Hotchkiss, Conrad.

Graham, Jack. Coin Collecting for Kids. Otfinoski, Steve. ed. 2007. (ENG.). 12p. (J). (gr. 2-7). spiral bd. 17.99 *(978-1-58476-624-7(7)*, IKIDS) Innovative Kids.

Graham, Jarred. The Vampire Goes to the Dentist. Mirelez, Gina & Vamp, Jake. 2015. (ENG.). 28p. (J). pap. 14.99 *(978-1-5186-7242-2(6))* CreateSpace Independent Publishing Platform.

Graham, Jerry L., jt. illus. see Allen, S. Joan.

Graham, Lindsay. The Horse Farm. Workman Publishing Company Staff. 2004. (ENG.). 18p. (J). (gr. -1). pap., tchr. ed. 7.95 *(978-1-58017-583-8(X)*, 67583) Storey Publishing, LLC.

Graham, Margaret Bloy. Harry & the Lady Next Door. Zion, Gene. 2003. (I Can Read Level 1 Ser.). (ENG.). 64p. (J). (gr. k-3). pap. 4.99 *(978-0-06-444008-0(7)*, HarperCollins) HarperCollins Pubs. Ltd. GBR. Dist: HarperCollins Pubs.

—Harry & the Lady Next Door. Zion, Gene. 2004. (I Can Read Bks.). 64p. (gr. -1-3). 14.00 *(978-0-7569-3087-5(1))* Perfection Learning Corp.

—Harry, el Perrito Sucio: Harry the Dirty Dog (Spanish Edition), 1 vol. Zion, Gene. 2003. (Harper Arco Iris Ser.).Tr. of Harry the Dirty Dog. (SPA.). 32p. (J). (gr. -1-3). pap. 7.99 *(978-0-06-443443-0(5)*, HC0801, HarperCollins) HarperCollins Pubs. Ltd. GBR. Dist: HarperCollins Pubs.

—Harry the Dirty Dog. Zion, Gene. 50th anniv. ed. 2006. (ENG.). 32p. (J). (gr. -1-3). 17.99 *(978-0-06-026865-7(4))*; pap. 7.99 *(978-0-06-443009-8(X))* HarperCollins Pubs. Ltd. GBR. (HarperCollins). Dist: HarperCollins Pubs.

—Harry the Dirty Dog Board Book. Zion, Gene. 50th ed. 2006. (ENG.). 34p. (J). (gr. -1-3). bds. 7.99 *(978-0-06-084244-4(X)*, HarperFestival) HarperCollins Pubs.

—No Roses for Harry! Board Book. Zion, Gene. 2020. (ENG.). 34p. (J). (gr. -1 — 1). bds. 7.99 *(978-0-06-297276-7(6)*, HarperFestival) HarperCollins Pubs.

Graham, Mark. I Am a Dancer. Collins, Pat Lowery. 2008. (Millbrook Picture Books Ser.). 30p. (J). (gr. 3-7). 22.60 *(978-0-8225-6369-3(X)*, Millbrook Pr.) Lerner Publishing Group.
—Murphy & Kate. Howard, Ellen. 2007. (ENG.). 32p. (J). (gr. -1-2). 13.99 *(978-1-4169-6157-4(7)*, Simon & Schuster/Paula Wiseman Bks.) Simon & Schuster/Paula Wiseman Bks.
—My Father's Hands. Ryder, Joanne. 2014. 32p. pap. 8.00 *(978-1-61003-330-5(2))* Center for the Collaborative Classroom.
—Naughty Cherie! Oates, Joyce Carol. 2008. 32p. (J). (gr. -1-3). lib. bdg. 17.89 *(978-0-06-074359-8(X))* HarperCollins Pubs.
—Waiting for Noel: An Advent Story. Dixon, Ann. 2004. 32p. (J). (gr. -1-5). pap. 8.00 *(978-0-8028-5239-7(4))* Eerdmans, William B. Publishing Co.
—Where Is Little Reynard? Oates, Joyce Carol. 2003. 32p. (J). 16.89 *(978-0-06-029583-7(X))* HarperCollins Pubs.
Graham, Michael. The Adventures of Swami Somewhere-the Supermarket. Greene, Reggie. 2011. 32p. (J). 14.95 *(978-1-60131-095-8(1))* Big Tent Bks.
—Allow Me to Introduce Myself. Ramos, Odalys Q. 2012. 24p. (-18). pap. 12.95 *(978-1-61493-121-8(6))* Peppertree Pr., The.
—The Great Inhibitator. 2006. 44p. (J). *(978-0-9772977-0-2(5))* Bio Rx.
—I am Nate. 2007. 40p. (J). *(978-0-9772977-1-9(3))* Bio Rx.
Graham, Michele. Body: An Interactive & 3-D Exploration. Ring, Susan. 2008. (ENG.). 20p. (J). (gr. 2). 19.95 *(978-1-58117-801-2(8)*, Intervisual/Piggy Toes) Bendon, Inc.
Graham, Noelle, jt. illus. see Santana, Julia.
Grahame, Kenneth & McKowen, Scott. The Wind in the Willows. Grahame, Kenneth. 2005. (Sterling Unabridged Classics Ser.). 208p. (J). (gr. 5-9). 9.95 *(978-1-4027-2505-0(1))* Sterling Publishing Co., Inc.
Grainger, Lesley. My First Spanish Words Sticker Activity Book/Mi Primer Libro de Palabras en Espanol. 2018. (ENG.). 32p. (J). pap. 4.99 *(978-1-68119-614-5(X)*, 900179036, Bloomsbury Activity Bks.) Bloomsbury Publishing USA.
Graire, Virginie. Animals. Little Bee Books. 2015. (ENG.). 12p. (J). (gr. -1 — 1). bds. 6.99 *(978-1-4998-0088-3(6))* Little Bee Books Inc.
—Christmas Tree. Little Bee Books. 2015. (ENG.). 12p. (J). (gr. -1 — 1). 6.99 *(978-1-4998-0147-7(5))* Little Bee Books Inc.
—Colors. Little Bee Books. 2015. (ENG.). 12p. (J). (gr. -1 — 1). bds. 6.99 *(978-1-4998-0089-0(4))* Little Bee Books Inc.
—Snowflake. Little Bee Books. 2015. (ENG.). 12p. (J). (gr. -1 — 1). 6.99 *(978-1-4998-0148-4(3))* Little Bee Books Inc.
—Snowman. 2016. (ENG.). 12p. (J). (gr. -1 — 1). bds. 6.99 *(978-1-4998-0344-0(3))* Little Bee Books Inc.
Grajczyk, Shane. The Most Important Thing. Roth, Rhonda. 2007. (ENG.). 32p. (J). (gr. -1-3). 16.95 *(978-0-9770141-0-1(X)*, Crossing Guard Bks.) Crossing Guard Bks., LLC.
Graley, Sarah, et al. Invader ZIM Vol. 6. Trueheart, Eric & Graley, Sarah. Logan, Sam. 2018. (Invader ZIM Ser.: 6). (ENG.). 128p. (J). pap. 19.99 *(978-1-62010-536-8(5)*, Lion Forge) Oni Pr., Inc.
Graley, Sarah. Glitch. Graley, Sarah. 2019. (ENG.). 192p. (J). (gr. 3-7). 26.99 *(978-1-338-17452-6(5))*; pap. 14.99 *(978-1-338-17451-9(7))* Scholastic, Inc. (Graphix).
Grall, Caanan, et al. Giant Days: Extra Credit. Allison, John. 2018. (Giant Days Ser.). (ENG.). 112p. (gr. 8-12). pap. 14.99 *(978-1-68415-222-3(4))* Boom! Studios.
Gram, Anja. The Adventures of Harun Al-Rashid, Caliph of Baghdad. Harpendore & Townley, Kelley. 2018. (ENG.). 174p. (J). pap. *(978-1-911030-09-6(4))* Harpendore.
—The Enchanted Horse. Harpendore & Townley, Kelley. 2016. (ENG.). 102p. (J). pap. *(978-1-911030-05-8(1))* Harpendore.
—The Seven Voyages of Sinbad the Sailor. Harpendore & Townley, Kelley. 2016. (ENG.). 214p. (J). pap. *(978-1-911030-04-1(3))* Harpendore.
Gram, Gram. Meet Marley Bryan. Brayn, Mark. 2018. (ENG.). 38p. (J). pap. 11.17 *(978-1-7206-1425-8(3))* CreateSpace Independent Publishing Platform.
Gram, Patrick. Stop by a Pond. Nicholas, Melissa. l.t. ed. 2005. (Little Books & Big Bks.: Vol. 3). 8p. (gr. k-2). 23.00 net. *(978-0-8215-7512-3(0))* Sadlier, William H. Inc.
Gramatky, Hardie. Little Toot. Gramatky, Hardie. 2007. (Little Toot Ser.). 104p. (J). (gr. -1-2). 17.99 *(978-0-399-24713-2(0)*, G.P. Putnam's Sons Books for Young Readers) Penguin Young Readers Group.
Gramelspacher, Sarah. Randolph Saves Christmas, 1 vol. Crochet, Pat. 2018. (ENG.). 32p. (J). (gr. -1-3). 16.99 *(978-1-4556-2269-6(9)*, Pelican Publishing) Arcadia Publishing.
Gran, Meredith. Marceline & the Scream Queens. Gran, Meredith. 2013. (Adventure Time Ser.). (ENG.). 128p. (J). (gr. 4-7). pap. 19.99 *(978-1-60886-313-6(1))* Boom! Studios.
Granada, Nancy, jt. illus. see Gonzalez, Henry.
Granados, Lucia. Bemba's Secret Garden. 2006. (ENG.). 57p. (J). per. 16.95 *(978-0-9790110-0-9(0))* Tpprince Esquire International.
Grand, Aurélie. How to Spot a Sasquatch. Torres, J. 2018. (ENG.). 64p. (J). (gr. 1-5). 16.95 *(978-1-77147-277-7(4))* Owlkids Bks. Inc. CAN. Dist: Publishers Group West (PGW).
—West Meadows Detectives: the Case of the Berry Burglars. O'Donnell, Liam. 2020. (West Meadows Detectives Ser.: 3). (ENG.). 160p. (J). (gr. k-5). pap. 9.95 *(978-1-77147-400-9(9))* Owlkids Bks. Inc. CAN. Dist: Publishers Group West (PGW).
—West Meadows Detectives: the Case of the Snack Snatcher. O'Donnell, Liam. 2018. (West Meadows Detectives Ser.: 1). (ENG.). 128p. (J). (gr. 2-5). pap. 9.95 *(978-1-77147-345-3(2))* Owlkids Bks. Inc. CAN. Dist: Publishers Group West (PGW).
Grandelis, Leiah. To Be a Bird. Dickson, Vivian. 2013. 24p. pap. *(978-0-9873438-2-6(3))* Link Spots.
Grandits, John. Blue Lipstick: Concrete Poems. Grandits, John. 2007. (ENG.). 48p. (J). (gr. 5-7). 7.99 *(978-0-618-85132-4(1)*, 100566) Houghton Mifflin Harcourt Publishing Co.
Grandpré, Karen Haus & Grandpré, Karen Haus. Misty's Twilight. Henry, Marguerite. 2007. (ENG.). 144p. (J). (gr. 3-7). pap. 7.99 *(978-1-4169-2787-7(5)*, Aladdin) Simon & Schuster Children's Publishing.
Grandpré, Karen Haus, jt. illus. see Grandpré, Karen Haus.
GrandPre, Mary. All Welcome Here. Preller, James. 2020. (ENG.). 40p. (J). 18.99 *(978-1-250-15588-7(6)*, 900184791) Feiwel & Friends.
GrandPré, Mary. Aunt Claire's Yellow Beehive Hair, 1 vol. Blumenthal, Deborah. 2007. (ENG.). 32p. (J). (gr. k-3). 16.99 *(978-1-58980-491-3(0)*, Pelican Publishing) Arcadia Publishing.
GrandPre, Mary. The Carnival of the Animals. Prelutsky, Jack. 2010. 40p. (J). (gr. k-3). 19.99 *(978-0-375-86458-2(X)*, Knopf Bks. for Young Readers) Random Hse. Children's Bks.
—A Dragon's Guide to Making Your Human Smarter. Yep, Laurence & Ryder, Joanne. 2016. (Dragon's Guide Ser.: 2). (ENG.). 304p. (J). (gr. 3-7). 16.99 *(978-0-385-39232-7(X)*, Crown Books For Young Readers) Random Hse. Children's Bks.
GrandPré, Mary. A Dragon's Guide to the Care & Feeding of Humans. Yep, Laurence & Ryder, Joanne. 2015. (Dragon's Guide Ser.: 1). 160p. (J). (gr. 3-7). 15.99 *(978-0-385-39228-0(1)*, Crown Books For Young Readers) Random Hse. Children's Bks.
—Harry Potter & the Deathly Hallows. Rowling, J. K. (Harry Potter Ser.: 7). (ENG.). 784p. (J). (gr. 5-7). 2009. pap. 14.99 *(978-0-545-13970-0(8)*, Levine, Arthur A. Bks.); 2007. 34.99 *(978-0-545-01022-1(5))* Scholastic, Inc.
—Harry Potter & the Goblet of Fire. Rowling, J. K. l.t. ed. 2003. (Harry Potter Ser.: Vol. 4). (ENG.). 936p. pap. 11.66 *(978-1-59413-003-8(5))* Thorndike Pr.
—Harry Potter & the Half-Blood Prince. Rowling, J. K. 2006. (Harry Potter Ser.: Year 6). (ENG.). 652p. (gr. 4-8). 23.00 *(978-0-7569-6765-9(1))* Perfection Learning Corp.
—Harry Potter & the Half-Blood Prince. Rowling, J. K. (Harry Potter Ser.: 6). (ENG.). 672p. (J). (gr. 5-8). 2005. 29.99 *(978-0-439-78454-2(9))*; 2006. reprint ed. per. 12.99 *(978-0-439-78596-9(0))* Scholastic, Inc. (Levine, Arthur A. Bks.).
—Harry Potter & the Order of the Phoenix. Rowling, J. K. (Harry Potter Ser.: 5). (ENG.). (J). (gr. 5-7). 2004. 896p. mass mkt. 12.99 *(978-0-439-35807-1(8)*, Scholastic Paperbacks); 2003. 870p. 29.99 *(978-0-439-35806-4(X))* Scholastic, Inc.
—Harry Potter & the Order of the Phoenix. Rowling, J. K. l.t. ed. 2003. (Thorndike Young Adult Ser.). (ENG.). 1232p. (J). (gr. 4-7). per. 14.95 *(978-1-59413-112-7(0)*, Large Print Pr.) Thorndike Pr.
—How the Leopard Got His Claws. Achebe, Chinua & Iroaganachi, John. 2011. (ENG.). 32p. (J). (gr. 2-5). 16.99 *(978-0-7636-4805-3(1))* Candlewick Pr.
—How the Leopard Got His Claws. Achebe, Chinua. 2019. (ENG.). 40p. (J). (gr. 2-5). 7.99 *(978-1-5362-0949-5(X))* Candlewick Pr.
—Nancy & Plum. MacDonald, Betty Bard. 2011. 240p. (J). (gr. 3-7). 7.99 *(978-0-375-85986-1(1)*, Yearling) Random Hse. Children's Bks.
—The Noisy Paint Box: The Colors & Sounds of Kandinsky's Abstract Art. Rosenstock, Barb. 2014. 40p. (J). (gr. -1-3). 17.99 *(978-0-307-97848-6(6)*, Knopf Bks. for Young Readers) Random Hse. Children's Bks.
—Plum. Mitton, Tony. 2003. (J). *(978-0-439-36410-2(8)*, Levine, Arthur A. Bks.) Scholastic, Inc.
—The Purple Snerd. Williams, Rozanne Lanczak. 2003. (Green Light Readers Level 2 Ser.). (ENG.). 24p. (J). (gr. -1-3). pap. 4.99 *(978-0-15-204826-6(X)*, 1194574) Houghton Mifflin Harcourt Publishing Co.
—The Tales of Beedle the Bard. Rowling, J. K. 2008. 128p. *(978-0-7475-9987-6(4))* Bloomsbury Publishing Plc.
—The Tales of Beedle the Bard. Rowling, J. K. collector's ed. 2008. 184p. *(978-0-9560109-0-2(3))* Children's High Level Group.
—Through the Window: Views of Marc Chagall's Life & Art. Rosenstock, Barb. 2018. 40p. (J). (gr. -1-3). 17.99 *(978-1-5247-1751-3(7))*; (ENG.). lib. bdg. 20.99 *(978-1-5247-1752-0(5))* Random Hse. Children's Bks. (Knopf Bks. for Young Readers).
—Tickety Tock. Brown, Jason Robert. 2008. 32p. (J). (gr. -1-3). lib. bdg. 18.89 *(978-0-06-078753-0(8)*, Geringer, Laura Book) HarperCollins Pubs.
—Vincent Can't Sleep: Van Gogh Paints the Night Sky. Rosenstock, Barb. 2017. (J). (gr. -1-3). 32p. 17.99 *(978-1-101-93710-5(6))*; (ENG.). 40p. lib. bdg. 20.99 *(978-1-101-93711-2(4))* Random Hse. Children's Bks. (Knopf Bks. for Young Readers).
GrandPré, Mary. Cleonardo, the Little Inventor. GrandPré, Mary. 2016. (ENG.). 48p. (J). (gr. -1-3). 18.99 *(978-0-439-35764-7(0))* Scholastic, Inc.
GrandPré, Mary, jt. illus. see Selznick, Brian.
Grandville, Jean-Jacques. Fables-Livre I: Illustré Par Jean Jacques Grandville (1668-1694) De La Fontaine, Jean. 2019. (Fables Ser.: Vol. 1). (FRE.). 52p. (J). pap. 17.08 *(978-1-7982-3488-4(2))* Independently Published.
—Joyeux Anniversaire Jean Pierre: Fables Complètes de la Fontaine (Volumes. 1 À 12 - Illustrés) La Fontaine, Jean de. Barry, ed. 2018. (FRE.). 578p. (J). pap. 49.80 *(978-1-7928-0838-8(0))* Independently Published.
Granov, Adi. Iron Man: Extremis Marvel Select Edition. 2019. 160p. (YA). (gr. 8-17). 24.99 *(978-1-302-91890-3(7))* Marvel Worldwide, Inc.
—Marvel Monograph: the Art of Adi Granov. 2019. (ENG.). 112p. (YA). (gr. 8-17). pap. 19.99 *(978-1-302-91759-3(5))* Marvel Worldwide, Inc.
Granqvist, Embla. Moon Friends. Smith, Robin J. 2020. (ENG.). 30p. (J). pap. 12.00 ***(978-1-0750-8001-2(0))*** Independently Published.
Granström, Brita. Books! Books! Books! Explore the Amazing Collection of the British Library. Manning, Mick. 2017. (ENG.). 48p. (J). (gr. 3-7). 17.99 *(978-0-7636-9757-0(5))* Candlewick Pr.
—A Chick Called Saturday. Dunbar, Joyce. 2004. 32p. (J). 16.00 *(978-0-8028-5260-1(2))* Eerdmans, William B. Publishing Co.
—Dog Story. Henderson, Kathy. 32p. (J). 2005. pap. 12.99 *(978-0-7475-7133-9(3))*; 2004. 17.95 *(978-0-7475-5071-6(9))* Bloomsbury Publishing Plc GBR. Dist: Independent Pubs. Group.
—Mi Primer Libro de Teatro. Manning, Mick & Brita, Granström.Tr. of Drama School. (SPA.). (J). (gr. 3-5). 15.16 *(978-84-241-7922-9(6))* Everest Editora ESP. Dist: Lectorum Pubns., Inc.
—Que Hay Debajo de la Cama? Manning, Mick. Cortes, Eunice, tr. 2003. (Descubriendo Mi Mundo Ser.). (SPA.). 32p. (J). *(978-970-690-588-8(X))* Planeta Mexicana Editorial S. A. de C. V.
Granstrom, Brita. Seasons Before the War, 1 vol. Morgan, Bernice. 2018. (ENG.). 48p. (J). (gr. 4-7). 25.00 ***(978-1-927917-18-3(2))*** Running the Goat, Bks. & Broadsides CAN. Dist: Orca Bk. Pubs. USA.
Granström, Brita. The Story of Paintings: A History of Art for Children. Manning, Mick. 2017. (ENG.). 88p. (J). (gr. 3-9). 16.95 *(978-1-4549-2702-0(X))* Sterling Publishing Co., Inc.
Granstrom, Brita. William Shakespeare: Scenes from the Life of the World's Greatest Writer. Manning, Mick. 2017. (ENG.). 48p. (J). (gr. 3-7). pap. 11.99 *(978-1-84780-759-5(3)*, Frances Lincoln Children's Bks.) Quarto Publishing Group UK GBR. Dist: Hachette Bk. Group.
—The Yum Yum Tree. Wild, Jonnie. 2019. (Five Flamingos Ser.: 3). (ENG.). 32p. (J). (gr. -1-k). 10.99 *(978-1-910959-83-1(9))* Otter-Barry Bks. GBR. Dist: Independent Pubs. Group.
Granström, Brita & Granström, Brita. Eyes, Nose, Fingers, & Toes: A First Book All about You. Hindley, Judy. 2004. (ENG.). 24p. (J). (gr. k-k). bds. 6.99 *(978-0-7636-2383-8(0))* Candlewick Pr.
Granström, Brita, jt. illus. see Granström, Brita.
Granstrom, Brita, jt. illus. see Manning, Mick.
Grant, Bob, jt. illus. see Porter, Hank.
Grant-Borden, Anna. Fun Street. Campbell, Constance. 2018. (ENG.). 34p. (J). pap. 12.00 *(978-1-7919-9762-5(7))* Independently Published.
Grant, Cheryl. Mitsy & Marty Mouse Visit Grandpa. Byers, Marcella. 2014. (ENG.). 32p. (gr. -1-2). pap. 8.95 *(978-1-61448-740-1(5)*, 9781614487401) Morgan James Publishing.
Grant, Donald. Music. Delafosse, Claude & Jeunesse, Gallimard. Matthews, Sarah, tr. from FRE. ed. 2019. (My First Discoveries Ser.). (ENG.). 36p. (J). (gr. -1-k). spiral bd. 16.99 *(978-1-85103-474-1(9))* Moonlight Publishing, Ltd. GBR. Dist: Independent Pubs. Group.
Grant, Donald. Atlas of Space. Grant, Donald. 2012. (ENG.). 36p. (J). (gr. -1-k). spiral bd. 14.99 *(978-1-85103-407-9(2))* Moonlight Publishing, Ltd. GBR. Dist: Independent Pubs. Group.
—The Desert. Grant, Donald. 2012. (ENG.). 34p. (J). (gr. k-3). spiral bd. 11.99 *(978-1-85103-299-0(1))* Moonlight Publishing, Ltd. GBR. Dist: Independent Pubs. Group.
—Deserts. Grant, Donald. 2013. (ENG.). 34p. (J). (gr. -1-k). spiral bd. 13.99 *(978-1-85103-422-2(6))* Moonlight Publishing, Ltd. GBR. Dist: Independent Pubs. Group.
—Dinosaurs at Large. Grant, Donald. Delafosse, Claude. 2013. (ENG.). 36p. (J). (gr. -1-k). spiral bd. 13.99 *(978-1-85103-415-4(3))* Moonlight Publishing, Ltd. GBR. Dist: Independent Pubs. Group.
—Homes. Grant, Donald. 2012. (ENG.). 38p. (J). (gr. -1-k). spiral bd. 14.99 *(978-1-85103-398-0(X))* Moonlight Publishing, Ltd. GBR. Dist: Independent Pubs. Group.
—In the Sky. Grant, Donald. Delafosse, Claude. 2013. (ENG.). 36p. (J). (gr. -1-k). spiral bd. 14.99 *(978-1-85103-419-2(6))* Moonlight Publishing, Ltd. GBR. Dist: Independent Pubs. Group.
—Let's Look at Dinosaurs. Grant, Donald. Delafosse, Claude. 2012. (ENG.). 38p. (J). (gr. k-3). spiral bd. 11.99 *(978-1-85103-280-8(0))* Moonlight Publishing, Ltd. GBR. Dist: Independent Pubs. Group.
Grant, Donald & Prunier, James. Trains. Prunier, James. 2012. (ENG.). 34p. (J). (gr. -1-k). spiral bd. 15.99 *(978-1-85103-400-0(5))* Moonlight Publishing, Ltd. GBR. Dist: Independent Pubs. Group.
Grant, Douglas. The Tarzan Twins. Burroughs, Edgar Rice. 2011. 126p. 40.95 *(978-1-258-05126-6(5))* Literary Licensing, LLC.
Grant, Gabby. Harris the Hero, 30 vols. Rickards, Lynne. 2013. (ENG.). 32p. (J). pap. 11.95 *(978-0-86315-952-7(4)*, Kelpies) Floris Bks. GBR. Dist: Consortium Bk. Sales & Distribution.
Grant, Irma. The Red Lantern. Grant, Irma. 2017. (ENG.). (J). (gr. k-3). 19.98 *(978-0-9996033-3-8(7))* Grant, Irma.
Grant, Jacob. Owls Are Good at Keeping Secrets. O'Leary, Sara. 2018. 40p. (J). (gr. -1-2). 17.99 *(978-1-5247-1331-7(7)*, Random Hse. Bks. for Young Readers) Random Hse. Children's Bks.
Grant, Keron & Randolph, Khary. New Mutants: Back to School - the Complete Collection. 2018. (ENG.). 336p. (YA). (gr. 8-17). pap. 34.99 *(978-1-302-91032-7(9))* Marvel Worldwide, Inc.
Grant, Margriet. Baby Moses in a Basket. Mahany, Patricia Shely. 2013. (Happy Day Ser.). (ENG.). 16p. (J). pap. 2.49 *(978-1-4143-9297-4(4)*, 4608287) Tyndale Hse. Pubs.
Grant, Melvyn. The Dragon's Eye. Kingsley, Kaza. 2009. (Erec Rex Ser.: 1). (ENG.). 368p. (J). (gr. 5-9). pap. 12.99 *(978-1-4169-7933-3(6)*, Simon & Schuster Bks. For Young Readers) Simon & Schuster Bks. For Young Readers.
—Erec Rex: The Dragon's Eye. Kingsley, Kaza. Payne, John, ed. 2006. 360p. (J). 17.99 *(978-0-9786555-6-3(7))* Firelight Press, Inc.
—The Monsters of Otherness. Kingsley, Kaza. 2009. (Erec Rex Ser.: 2). (ENG.). 352p. (J). (gr. 5-9). pap. 9.99 *(978-1-4169-7934-0(4)*, Simon & Schuster Bks. For Young Readers) Simon & Schuster Bks. For Young Readers.
Grant, Paige. Samson & the Carrot Cake. Garamella, Priscilla. 2018. (ENG.). 36p. (J). pap. 9.50 *(978-0-692-99433-7(5))* Garamella, Priscilla.
Grant, Sarah. Sleeping Bear: The Legend. Lewis, Anne Margaret. 2007. 36p. (J). (gr. -1-2). 16.95 *(978-1-934133-15-6(9)*, Mackinac Island Press, Inc.) Charlesbridge Publishing, Inc.
Grant, Sophia & Noble, Stuart. Eli the Elephant: A Tsunami Story. Donald, Margaret. 2007. (ENG.). 25p. (gr. 3-7). *(978-81-8386-024-6(9))* India Research Pr. IND. Dist: Independent Pubs. Group.
Grantham, Amy. Bottom down, Penelope Brown! Pulliam, April B. 2019. (ENG.). 46p. (J). pap. 12.00 *(978-1-0725-6210-8(3))* Independently Published.
—Strong Is ... Pulliam, April B. 2019. (ENG.). 32p. (J). pap. 10.00 *(978-1-5303-9359-6(0))* CreateSpace Independent Publishing Platform.
Grantham, Melissa. I Am... I Can: The Polar Bear. Chase, Marie. 2019. (ENG.). 24p. (J). pap. 15.99 ***(978-1-7960-6717-0(2))*** Xlibris Corp.
Granville, Brittany. Callaloo: Did You Know: Coloring & Activity Book. Canady, Marjuan, ed. 2016. (Callaloo: Did You Know Ser.: Vol. 1). (ENG.). (J). (gr. k-2). pap. 9.99 *(978-0-692-81373-7(X))* Bilal, Nabeeh.
Graper, Helen. Bingo. 2016. (J). *(978-1-62885-144-1(9))* Kidsbooks, LLC.
Graper, Helen. I Love Daddy. Galvin, Laura Gates. 2018. (Heart-Shaped Board Ser.). (ENG.). 12p. (J). bds. 7.99 ***(978-1-62885-450-3(2))*** Kidsbooks, LLC.
—I Love Grandma. Galvin, Laura Gates. 2018. (Heart-Shaped Board Ser.). (ENG.). 12p. (J). bds. 7.99 ***(978-1-62885-571-5(1))*** Kidsbooks, LLC.
—I Love Mommy. Galvin, Laura Gates. 2018. (Heart-Shaped Board Ser.). (ENG.). 12p. (J). bds. 7.99 ***(978-1-62885-449-7(9))*** Kidsbooks, LLC.
Graphic Manufacture. The Angel with Red Wings. Martinez, Roland. 2008. 27p. pap. 24.95 *(978-1-60672-713-3(3))* America Star Bks.
Graphics Factory. Picture-Word Quizzes Assessment Sheets & Solution Book: For the Children's Picture-Word & Simple Sentence Book. Irving, Harry. 2009. 196p. pap. 17.14 *(978-1-4269-0667-1(6))* Trafford Publishing.
Graphics, Nataly. Jimmy the Squirrel. Taher, Amr. Taher, Layal, ed. 2011. 36p. (J). 14.99 *(978-1-4567-3526-5(8)*, d5c74768-d14d-4986-83ad-42baf688fae2) AuthorHouse.
Graphics, Section. My Body: Explained & Illustrated. 2015. (ENG.). 48p. (J). (gr. 3-7). 24.95 *(978-3-89955-712-1(3))* Die Gestalten Verlag DEU. Dist: Ingram Publisher Services.
Grass, Jeff, photos by. The Emotionally Unavailable Man: A Blueprint for Healing. Henry, Patti. 2008. (ENG., (YA). cd-rom 24.95 *(978-0-9817155-8-2(3))* Henry, Patti.
Grasseschi, Teresa. A Girl's Guide to the Wild: Be an Adventure-Seeking Outdoor Explorer! McConnell, Ruby. 2019. (Girl's Guide to the Wild Ser.). 272p. (J). (gr. 4-7). pap. 17.99 *(978-1-63217-171-9(6)*, Little Bigfoot) Sasquatch Bks.
Grasso, Craig A. & Grasso, Samantha A. Gracie Comes Home: The Adventures of Gracie & Diane. Dike, Diane. 2007. (J). 14.95 *(978-1-932738-45-2(2))* Western Reflections Publishing Co.
Grasso, Samantha A., jt. illus. see Grasso, Craig A.
Graston, Arlene. In Every Moon There Is a Face. Mathes, Charles. 2003. 32p. 15.95 *(978-0-9701907-4-1(3))* Illumination Arts Publishing Co., Inc.
Grately, Sarah. Little Unicorn's Magical Mane. Make Believe Ideas Ltd & Creese, Sarah. 2020. (ENG.). 12p. (J). bds. ***(978-1-78947-733-7(6))*** Make Believe Ideas.
Grater, Lindsay. One Hundred Shining Candles. Lunn, Janet. 2008. 32p. (J). (gr. k-3). 17.95 *(978-0-88776-889-7(X)*, Tundra Bks.) Tundra Bks. CAN. Dist: Penguin Random Hse. LLC.
Gratz, Ali. Rudy Gets A Transplant. 2008. 28p. (J). pap. 10.00 *(978-0-9820983-0-1(8))* Purple Cow Pr.
Grau, Carmi. How to Spot a Witch. Dahl, Roald. 2020. (ENG.). 32p. (J). (gr. 3-7). 9.99 ***(978-0-593-09711-3(4)***, Grosset & Dunlap) Penguin Young Readers Group.
Grau, Ryon. The ABCs of Frederick Maryland: A Historic Coloring Book. Grau, Maritta, ed. 2007. 32p. 8.95 *(978-0-9772559-0-0(5))* Grau, Ryon.
Graudins, Alex. History Comics: the Great Chicago Fire: Rising from the Ashes. Hannigan, Kate. 2020. (History Comics Ser.). (ENG.). 128p. (J). 19.99 *(978-1-250-17425-3(2)*, 900189162); pap. 12.99 *(978-1-250-17426-0(0)*, 900189163) Roaring Brook Pr. (First Second Bks.).
—Science Comics: the Brain: The Ultimate Thinking Machine. Woollcott, Tory. 2018. (Science Comics Ser.). (ENG.). 128p. (J). 19.99 *(978-1-62672-800-4(3)*, 900174303); pap. 12.99 *(978-1-62672-801-1(1)*, 900174304) Roaring Brook Pr. (First Second Bks.).
Graullera, Fabiola. Las Pinatas. Zepeda, Monique.Tr. of Pinatas. (SPA.). 26p. (J). (gr. 3-5). pap. 6.95 *(978-968-19-0612-2(8))* Santillana USA Publishing Co., Inc.
—Poemas de Perros y Gatos. Cordova, Soledad. 2003. (SPA.). 21p. (J). (gr. 3-5). pap. 7.95 *(978-968-19-0987-1(9))* Santillana USA Publishing Co., Inc.
Graullera, Fabiola, jt. illus. see Martinez, Enrique.
Graullera, Fabiola. I Am Rene, the Boy. Laínez, René Colato. 2005.Tr. of Yo Soy Rene, el Nino. (ENG & SPA.). 32p. (J). (gr. -1-2). 16.95 *(978-1-55885-378-2(2)*, Piñata Books) Arte Publico Pr.
Graullera Ramírez, Fabiola, jt. illus. see Laínez, René Colato.
Graux, Amélie. I Love to Eat. Graux, Amélie. deluxe ed. 2012. (FRE.). 12p. (J). (gr. k — 1). bds. 9.99 *(978-0-547-84842-6(0)*, 1500671) Houghton Mifflin Harcourt Publishing Co.
—I Love to Sleep. Graux, Amélie. Dormir, J'aime & Dormir, Me Encanta. deluxe ed. 2012. (FRE.). 12p. (J). (gr. k — 1).

bds. 9.99 *(978-0-547-84843-3(9)*, 1500672) Houghton Mifflin Harcourt Publishing Co.

Gravano, Steven. Quigley's Quest: Story of a Service Dog. Cook, Sue. Williamson, Kris, ed. 2019. (Quigley Ser.: Vol. 1). (ENG.). 26p. (J). pap. 10.00 *(978-1-0905-0371-8(7))* Independently Published.

Gravas, Mark. Noodle Bear. Gravas, Mark. 2020. (ENG.). 32p. (J). (gr. -1-2). 16.99 ***(978-1-5362-1107-8(9))*** Candlewick Pr.

Grave, Vincent. A Big Garden. Clement, Gilles. 2018. (ENG.). 32p. (J). (gr. 1-4). 24.95 *(978-3-7913-7332-4(3))* Prestel Verlag GmbH & Co KG. DEU. Dist: Penguin Random Hse. LLC.

Gravel, Elise. The Cranky Ballerina. Gravel, Elise. 2016. (ENG.). 32p. (J). (gr. -1-3). 17.99 *(978-0-06-235124-1(9)*, Tegen, Katherine Bks) HarperCollins Pubs.

—I Want a Monster! Gravel, Elise. 2016. (ENG.). 40p. (J). (gr. -1-3). 17.99 *(978-0-06-241533-2(6)*, Tegen, Katherine Bks) HarperCollins Pubs.

—Olga & the Smelly Thing from Nowhere. Gravel, Elise. 2017. (Olga Ser.: 1). (ENG.). 176p. (J). (gr. 3-7). 13.99 *(978-0-06-235126-5(5))* HarperCollins Pubs.

—Olga: Out of Control! Gravel, Elise. 2019. (Olga Ser.: 3). (ENG.). 192p. (J). (gr. 3-7). 12.99 *(978-0-06-235132-6(X))* HarperCollins Pubs.

—Olga: We're Out of Here! Gravel, Elise. 2018. (Olga Ser.: 2). (ENG.). 192p. (J). (gr. 3-7). 12.99 *(978-0-06-235129-6(X))* HarperCollins Pubs.

Graves, Amber Dawn. One Alien & Four Furry (Tails) Tales. Formento, Alison Ashley. 2017. (ENG.). (J). pap. 6.99 *(978-0-692-80787-3(X))* RTE Media, LLC.

Graves, Dan. Pparcel's Notebook Presents: The Search for the Giant Stone Monkey Head, Truth, Friends & Strange Food. Graves, Dan. 2004. 48p. lib. bdg. 15.00 *(978-0-9744999-0-1(0))* Love Cultivating Editions.

Graves, Dennis. Fun. Yannone, Deborah. Kaeden Corp. Staff, ed. 2003. (ENG.). 12p. (gr. k-1). pap. 7.95 *(978-1-879835-56-6(8)*, Kaeden Bks.) Kaeden Corp.

—I Have a Watch. Williams, Deborah. l.t. ed. 2003. (ENG.). 12p. (gr. k-1). pap. 7.95 *(978-1-879835-92-4(4)*, Kaeden Bks.) Kaeden Corp.

—I'll Be a Pirate: World of Discovery II. Eifrig, Kate. l.t. ed. 2006. (SPA & ENG.). 12p. (gr. k-2). pap. 7.95 *(978-1-57874-053-6(3)*, Kaeden Bks.) Kaeden Corp.

—Scary Monster. Eifrig, Kate. 2003. (ENG.). 8p. (gr. k-1). pap. 7.95 *(978-1-879835-29-0(0)*, Kaeden Bks.) Kaeden Corp.

—Snowflakes. Urmston, Kathleen & Evans, Karen. Kaeden Corp. Staff, ed. 2006. (ENG.). 12p. (gr. k-1). pap. 7.95 *(978-1-879835-01-6(0)*, Kaeden Bks.) Kaeden Corp.

—Thanksgiving. Evans, Karen & Urmston, Kathleen. Kaeden Corp. Staff, ed. 2006. (ENG.). 12p. (gr. k-2). pap. 7.95 *(978-1-879835-57-3(6)*, Kaeden Bks.) Kaeden Corp.

—Tree House. Hoenecke, Karen. 2005. (ENG.). 12p. (gr. k-1). pap. 7.95 *(978-1-57874-090-1(8)*, Kaeden Bks.) Kaeden Corp.

Graves, Emily. A Winter Tale: How Raven Gave Light to the World. Turner, Mark. 2014. (ENG.). 48p. 20.00 *(978-1-62288-032-4(3))* Austin, Stephen F. State Univ. Pr.

Graves, Jeseca. Bessie Coleman: The Story of an Aviation Pioneer. 2007. 24p. (J). *(978-0-9745294-1-7(9))* San Diego County Regional Airport Authority.

Graves, Kassie. Brave Little Sailboat. Graves, Kassie. 2003. 20p. (J). 14.95 *(978-0-9728019-0-4(1))* Bright Eyes Pr.

Graves, Keith. Boo-Hoo Moo. Palatini, Margie. 2009. 32p. (J). (gr. -1-3). lib. bdg. 18.89 *(978-0-06-114376-2(6))* HarperCollins Pubs.

—Clovis Crawfish & His Friends, 1 vol. Fontenot, Mary Alice. 2009. (Clovis Crawfish Ser.). (ENG.). 32p. (J). (gr. k-3). 16.99 *(978-1-58980-762-4(6)*, Pelican Publishing) Arcadia Publishing.

—Clovis Crawfish & Petit Papillon, 1 vol. Fontenot, Mary Alice. 2009. (Clovis Crawfish Ser.). (ENG.). 32p. (J). (gr. k-3). 16.99 *(978-1-58980-772-3(3)*, Pelican Publishing) Arcadia Publishing.

—Moo Who? Palatini, Margie. 2007. (ENG.). 40p. (J). (gr. -1-2). pap. 7.99 *(978-0-06-000107-0(0)*, Tegen, Katherine Bks) HarperCollins Pubs.

—Too Many Frogs! Asher, Sandy. 2005. 32p. (J). (gr. -1-k). 16.99 *(978-0-399-23978-6(2)*, Philomel Bks.) Penguin Young Readers Group.

—The World's Greatest: Poems. Lewis, J. Patrick. 2008. (ENG.). 36p. (J). (gr. k-4). 16.99 *(978-0-8118-5130-5(3))* Chronicle Bks. LLC.

Graves, Linda. V Is for Von Trapp: A Musical Family Alphabet. Anderson, William. 2010. (ENG.). 32p. (J). (gr. 1-4). 16.95 *(978-1-58536-531-9(9)*, 202214) Sleeping Bear Pr.

Graves, Linda, jt. illus. see Gruber, Michael.

Graves, Linda, jt. illus. see Linda, Graves.

Graves, Linda Dockey. The Renaissance Kids. Weyn, Suzanne. 2003. (ENG.). 56p. (J). (gr. 6-8). pap. 7.97 net. *(978-0-7652-3277-9(4)*, Celebration Pr.) Savvas Learning Co.

Graves, Lisa. Bug & the Bugs. O'Neill, Juliana. 2019. (Reading Stars Ser.). (ENG.). 28p. (J). (gr. -1-2). pap. 16.99 *(978-1-5324-1125-0(1))* Xist Publishing.

—Bug & the Bugs. O'Neill, Juliana. 2019. (Reading Stars Ser.). (ENG.). 28p. (J). (gr. -1-2). 5.99 *(978-1-5324-1126-7(X))* Xist Publishing.

Graves, Lisa. History's Witches. Graves, Lisa. 2013. (Women in History Ser.). (ENG.). 28p. (J). (gr. 5-12). pap. 19.99 *(978-1-62395-516-8(5))* Xist Publishing.

Graves, Lisa. Simple Stories of Strong Women: An a to Z Guide to Girl Power. Graves, Lisa. 2020. (ENG.). 32p. (J). (gr. k-5). 12.99 ***(978-1-5324-1570-8(2))***; pap. 12.99 ***(978-1-5324-1569-2(9))*** Xist Publishing.

Graves, Michelle. Henry the Elf. Williams, Hap. 2012. 28p. pap. 24.95 *(978-1-4626-8999-6(X))* America Star Bks.

Graves, Sharol. The People Shall Continue, 1 vol. Ortiz, Simon J. 40th l.t. ed. 2017. (ENG.). 32p. (J). (gr. 1-8). pap. 10.95 *(978-0-89239-125-7(1)*, b289537b-a56a-4008-ba7f-03ee853fd479) Lee & Low Bks., Inc.

Graves, Sharol. El Pueblo Seguirá, 1 vol. Graves, Sharol. Ortiz, Simon J. 2017. (SPA.). 32p. (J). (gr. 1-5). pap. 10.95 *(978-0-89239-424-1(2)*, a500b483-f689-4697-9d95-0e24ec2aea86, Children's Book Press) Lee & Low Bks., Inc.

Gravett, Emily. The Afterwards. Harrold, A. F. 2019. (ENG.). 208p. (J). 17.99 *(978-1-5476-0044-1(6)*, 900196151, Bloomsbury Children's Bks.) Bloomsbury Publishing USA.

—Cave Baby, 3. Donaldson, Julia. 2nd ed. 2011. (ENG.). 32p. (J). (gr. -1-k). 11.99 *(978-0-330-52276-2(0))* Pan Macmillan GBR. Dist: Independent Pubs. Group.

Gravett, Emily, et al. Draw It! Color It! Creatures. Houghton Mifflin Harcourt Publishing Company Staff & Gryta, Thomas. 2016. (ENG.). 120p. (J). 11.99 *(978-0-544-77979-2(7)*, 1638036, HMH Books For Young Readers) Houghton Mifflin Harcourt Publishing Co.

Gravett, Emily. The Imaginary. Harrold, A. F. 2015. (ENG.). 240p. (YA). (gr. 3-6). 16.99 *(978-0-8027-3811-0(7)*, 900141005, Bloomsbury USA Childrens) Bloomsbury Publishing USA.

Gravett, Emily. Again! Gravett, Emily. 2013. (ENG.). 32p. (J). (gr. -1-3). 19.99 *(978-1-4424-5231-2(5)*, Simon & Schuster Bks. For Young Readers) Simon & Schuster Bks. For Young Readers.

—Bear & Hare — Where's Bear? Gravett, Emily. 2016. (Bear & Hare Ser.). (ENG.). 32p. (J). (gr. -1-3). 16.99 *(978-1-4814-5615-9(6)*, Simon & Schuster Bks. For Young Readers) Simon & Schuster Bks. For Young Readers.

—Bear & Hare Go Fishing. Gravett, Emily. 2015. (Bear & Hare Ser.). (ENG.). 32p. (J). (gr. -1-3). 15.99 *(978-1-4814-2289-5(8)*, Simon & Schuster Bks. For Young Readers) Simon & Schuster Bks. For Young Readers.

—Bear & Hare Share! Gravett, Emily. 2016. (Bear & Hare Ser.). (ENG.). 32p. (J). (gr. -1-3). 16.99 *(978-1-4814-6217-4(2)*, Simon & Schuster Bks. For Young Readers) Simon & Schuster Bks. For Young Readers.

—Bear & Hare Snow! Gravett, Emily. 2015. (Bear & Hare Ser.). (ENG.). 32p. (J). (gr. -1-3). 16.99 *(978-1-4814-4514-6(6)*, Simon & Schuster Bks. For Young Readers) Simon & Schuster Bks. For Young Readers.

—Blue Chameleon. Gravett, Emily. 2011. (ENG.). 32p. (J). (gr. -1-1). 16.99 *(978-1-4424-1958-2(X)*, Simon & Schuster Bks. For Young Readers) Simon & Schuster Bks. For Young Readers.

—Cyril & Pat. Gravett, Emily. 2019. (ENG.). 32p. (J). (gr. -1-3). 17.99 *(978-1-5344-3950-4(1)*, Simon & Schuster Bks. For Young Readers) Simon & Schuster Bks. For Young Readers.

—Dogs. Gravett, Emily. 2010. (ENG.). 32p. (J). (gr. -1-1). 18.99 *(978-1-4169-8703-1(7)*, Simon & Schuster Bks. For Young Readers) Simon & Schuster Bks. For Young Readers.

—Little Mouse's Big Book of Beasts. Gravett, Emily. 2016. (ENG.). 32p. (J). (gr. -1-3). 17.99 *(978-1-4814-3929-9(4)*, Simon & Schuster Bks. For Young Readers) Simon & Schuster Bks. For Young Readers.

—Little Mouse's Big Book of Fears. Gravett, Emily. 2008. (ENG.). 32p. (J). (gr. -1-3). 19.99 *(978-1-4169-5930-4(0)*, Simon & Schuster Bks. For Young Readers) Simon & Schuster Bks. For Young Readers.

—Matilda's Cat. Gravett, Emily. 2014. (ENG.). 32p. (J). (gr. -1-3). 16.99 *(978-1-4424-7527-4(7)*, Simon & Schuster Bks. For Young Readers) Simon & Schuster Bks. For Young Readers.

Gravett, Emily. Meerkat Christmas. Gravett, Emily. 2020. (ENG.). 32p. (J). (gr. -1-3). 19.99 ***(978-1-5344-7679-0(2)***, Simon & Schuster Bks. For Young Readers) Simon & Schuster Bks. For Young Readers.

Gravett, Emily. Meerkat Mail. Gravett, Emily. 2007. (ENG.). 32p. (J). (gr. -1-3). 18.99 *(978-1-4169-3473-8(1)*, Simon & Schuster Bks. For Young Readers) Simon & Schuster Bks. For Young Readers.

—Monkey & Me. Gravett, Emily. 2008. (ENG.). 32p. (J). (gr. -1-3). 18.99 *(978-1-4169-5457-6(0)*, Simon & Schuster Bks. For Young Readers) Simon & Schuster Bks. For Young Readers.

—The Odd Egg. Gravett, Emily. 2009. (ENG.). 32p. (J). (gr. -1-3). 16.99 *(978-1-4169-6872-6(5)*, Simon & Schuster Bks. For Young Readers) Simon & Schuster Bks. For Young Readers.

—Old Hat. Gravett, Emily. 2018. (ENG.). 32p. (J). (gr. -1-3). 17.99 *(978-1-5344-0917-0(3)*, Simon & Schuster Bks. For Young Readers) Simon & Schuster Bks. For Young Readers.

—Orange Pear Apple Bear. Gravett, Emily. 2011. (Classic Board Bks.). (ENG.). 24p. (J). (gr. -1 — 1). bds. 7.99 *(978-1-4424-2003-8(0)*, Little Simon) Little Simon.

—Orange Pear Apple Bear. Gravett, Emily. 2007. (ENG.). 32p. (J). (gr. -1 — 1). 14.99 *(978-1-4169-3999-3(7)*, Simon & Schuster Bks. For Young Readers) Simon & Schuster Bks. For Young Readers.

—The Rabbit Problem. Gravett, Emily. 2010. (ENG.). 32p. (J). (gr. -1-3). 19.99 *(978-1-4424-1255-2(0)*, Simon & Schuster Bks. For Young Readers) Simon & Schuster Bks. For Young Readers.

—Spells. Gravett, Emily. 2009. (ENG.). 32p. (J). (gr. -1-3). 16.99 *(978-1-4169-8270-8(1)*, Simon & Schuster Bks. For Young Readers) Simon & Schuster Bks. For Young Readers.

—Tidy. Gravett, Emily. 2017. (ENG.). 40p. (J). (gr. -1-3). 17.99 *(978-1-4814-8019-2(7)*, Simon & Schuster Bks. For Young Readers) Simon & Schuster Bks. For Young Readers.

—Wolf Won't Bite! Gravett, Emily. 2012. (ENG.). 32p. (J). (gr. -1-1). 16.99 *(978-1-4424-2763-1(9)*, Simon & Schuster Bks. For Young Readers) Simon & Schuster Bks. For Young Readers.

—Wolves. Gravett, Emily. 2006. (ENG.). 40p. (J). (gr. k-3). 19.99 *(978-1-4169-1491-4(9)*, Simon & Schuster Bks. For Young Readers) Simon & Schuster Bks. For Young Readers.

Gravier, Anne. Prayers Around the Crib. Levivier, Juliette. 2012. (ENG.). 48p. (gr. -1-3). 9.99 *(978-1-58617-773-7(7))* Ignatius Pr.

Gravitt, Bill. Rudee Goes Bananas for Manners. Madore, Michele. 2006. (ENG.). 38p. (J). pap. 6.95 *(978-0-615-17967-4(3))* Manners Toy Co., LLC.

Gray, Anderson. The Lonely Dino. McDougall, Bailey. 2017. (ENG.). (J). pap. *(978-0-6482127-8-2(5))* Serenity Press.

—The Lonely Dino: Special Edition Hard Cover. McDougall, Bailey. 2017. (ENG.). (J). *(978-0-6482127-7-5(7))* Serenity Press.

Gray, Andrea. Why Does That Star Follow Me? Harris-Wyrick, Wayne. 2018. (ENG.). 48p. (J). (gr. k-1). 21.99 *(978-1-940310-84-8(9))*; pap. 15.99 *(978-1-940310-83-1(0))* 4RV Pub.

Gray, Andy. The Very Rude Toytoise. Lynas, Peter. 2019. (ENG.). 44p. (J). pap. ***(978-0-9933403-5-2(0)***, Made-Up Books) Lynas, P J.

Gray, Andy S. Lost Property. Baxter, Alison. 2018. (ENG.). 164p. (J). pap. *(978-1-9993466-0-7(2))* Baxter, Alison J.

Gray, Angela M. Things I Wonder. Smith, Jennifer Lynne. Perez, Angela J., ed. 2007. 36p. (J). 14.95 *(978-0-9778328-5-9(6))* His Work Christian Publishing.

Gray-Barnett, Daniel. Albert's Very Unordinary Birthday. Gray-Barnett, Daniel. 2018. (ENG.). 32p. (J). (gr. -1-2). 16.99 *(978-1-5253-0118-6(7))* Kids Can Pr., Ltd. CAN. Dist: Hachette Bk. Group.

Gray, Cindy. Barnabas the Bad-Mannered Bulldog. Gray, Chris. 2018. (ENG.). 32p. (J). pap. 12.99 *(978-1-7323227-1-4(6))* Three Wise Dogs Pr.

Gray, Cissy. Wild Beach, Vol. Coste, Marion. 2005. 32p. (J). pap. 8.25 *(978-0-89317-062-2(3)*, WW-623); lib. bdg. 17.95 *(978-0-89317-061-5(5)*, WW-0615) Finney Co., Inc. (Windward Publishing).

Gray, Dean. Busy Little Engine: Sound Book Wood Button Module. Lobo, Julia. 2015. (Early Bird Sound Bks.). (ENG.). 10p. (J). (gr. -1-k). bds. 12.99 *(978-1-68052-035-4(0)*, 1000360) Cottage Door Pr.

—Dot & Dan & Snack Attack. Dale, Katie. 2020. (Early Bird Readers — Pink (Early Bird Stories (tm)) Ser.). (ENG.). 32p. (J). (gr. -1-2). pap. 7.99 *(978-1-5415-8724-3(3)*, Lerner Pubns.) Lerner Publishing Group.

—Follow That Tiger: Catch Him If You Can! Joyce, Melanie. 2016. (ENG.). 24p. (J). 9.99 *(978-1-78557-526-6(0))* Igloo Bks. GBR. Dist: Simon & Schuster, Inc.

—Little Fish & Big Fish. Treleaven, Lou. 2019. (Early Bird Readers — Yellow (Early Bird Stories (tm)) Ser.). (ENG.). 32p. (J). (gr. -1-2). pap. 7.99 *(978-1-5415-4632-5(6))* Lerner Publishing Group.

—A Moonlight Book: Halloween Hide-And-Seek. Butterfield, Moira & Golding, Elizabeth. 2015. 12p. (J). (gr. -1-17). 10.95 *(978-0-7624-5846-2(1)*, Running Pr. Kids) Running Pr.

—The Sheep Who Wouldn't Sleep. Brooke, Susan Rich. 2020. (ENG.). 40p. (J). *(978-1-5037-5243-6(7)*, ce774e77-7660-4b78-9ed0-e0c26b625227, p i kids) Phoenix International Publications, Inc.

—Under the Sea: Turn & Learn Wood Disc Board Book. Byrd, Redd. Cottage Door Press, ed. 2016. (Turn & Learn Ser.). (ENG.). 8p. (J). (gr. -1-k). bds. 12.99 *(978-1-68052-076-7(8)*, 1000790) Cottage Door Pr.

Gray, Haley. Clarissa Catfish at the Peoria Playhouse Children's Museum. Powers, Elaine A. 2020. (ENG.). 46p. (J). pap. 14.95 ***(978-1-6552-0004-5(6))*** Independently Published.

Gray, Heath. LaDonna Plays Hoops. Gordon Biddle, Kimberly A. 2017. (ENG.). 32p. (J). (gr. 2-6). 19.99 *(978-1-64372-023-4(6))*; pap. 15.99 *(978-1-64372-254-2(9))* MacLaren-Cochrane Publishing, Inc. (Huskies Pub).

—LaDonna Plays Hoops Dyslexic Edition: Dyslexic Font. Gordon Biddle, Kimberly A. 2017. (ENG.). 32p. (J). (gr. 2-6). 19.99 *(978-1-64372-255-9(7))*; pap. 15.99 *(978-1-64372-256-6(5))* MacLaren-Cochrane Publishing, Inc.

Gray, Heath. LaDonna's Easter in Paris Dyslexic Edition: Dyslexic Font. Gordon Biddle, Kimberly A. 2020. (ENG.). 36p. (J). (gr. k-6). 19.99 ***(978-1-64372-395-2(2))*** MacLaren-Cochrane Publishing, Inc.

Gray, Heath. Tilly the Turtle. Derby, Tannya L. 2017. (ENG.). (J). 17.99 *(978-1-365-51627-6(X))* Lulu Pr., Inc.

Gray, Howard. The Goose & the Golden Eggs. Berne, Emma Carlson. 2019. (Classic Fables in Rhythm & Rhyme Ser.). (ENG.). 24p. (J). (gr. -1-2). lib. bdg. 33.99 *(978-1-68410-333-1(9)*, 140253) Cantata Learning.

Gray II, Randy. Come on Out, Baby. Bethel, Toledia. Brown, Alexis Stix, ed. 2017. (ENG.). 28p. (J). pap. 10.00 ***(978-1-5480-6725-0(3))*** CreateSpace Independent Publishing Platform.

Gray, J. M. L., jt. illus. see Gibert, Jean Claude.

Gray, James Newman. The Magical Toy Box. Joyce, Melanie. 2015. (ENG.). 26p. (J). 8.99 *(978-1-78440-813-8(1))* Igloo Bks. GBR. Dist: Simon & Schuster, Inc.

Gray, James Newman. Tales from Christmas Wood. Senior, Suzy & Senior, Suzanne. ed. 2015. (ENG.). 32p. (J). pap. 7.99 ***(978-0-7459-6546-8(6)***, Lion Children's) Lion Hudson PLC GBR. Dist: Independent Pubs. Group.

Gray, James Newman. Tales from Christmas Wood Activity Book. Senior, Suzy & Senior, Suzanne. ed. 2016. (ENG.). 24p. (J). (gr. k-4). 9.99 *(978-0-7459-7694-5(8)*, Lion Books) Lion Hudson PLC GBR. Dist: Independent Pubs. Group.

—Wish upon a Star. Lansley, Holly. 2015. (ENG.). 26p. (J). bds. 8.95 *(978-1-78343-473-2(2))* Igloo Bks. GBR. Dist: Simon & Schuster, Inc.

Gray, Jane. Only Tadpoles Have Tails. Clarke, Jane. 2003. (Flying Foxes Ser.). (ENG.). 48p. (J). lib. bdg. *(978-0-7787-1484-2(5))* Crabtree Publishing Co.

—Only Tadpoles Have Tails. Clarke, Jane. 2004. (Flying Foxes Ser.). (ENG.). (J). (gr. 1-1). lib. bdg. 15.55 *(978-0-7569-3026-4(X))* Perfection Learning Corp.

Gray, Jonathan & Van Horn, William. Uncle Scrooge: Scrooge's Last Adventure. Artibani, Francesco & Perina, Alessandro. 2016. (Uncle Scrooge Ser.). 160p. (J). (gr. 4-7). pap. 14.99 *(978-1-63140-717-8(1)*, 9781631407178) Idea & Design Works, LLC.

Gray, Karen. Pick-a-WooWoo - the Elf That Flew: Love & Joy give you wings to Fly. Mitchell, Lindy. 2011. (ENG.). 28p. pap. *(978-1-921883-07-1(3))* Pick-a-Woo Woo Pubs.

Gray, Leslie. How to Be Nice — & Other Lessons I Didn't Learn. Bowdish, Lynea. 2006. 47p. (J). pap. *(978-1-59336-726-8(0))* Mondo Publishing.

Gray, M. Promethea. Moore, Alan & Cox, Jeromy. 3rd rev. ed. 2003. 160p. pap. 17.99 *(978-1-4012-0094-7(X)*, Wildstorm) DC Comics.

Gray Mayo, Jo Ann. Love: The Book of Love for Kids. Hawkins Harris, Jennifer. 2003. 20p. (J). per. 7.00 *(978-0-9705458-2-4(7))* Royalty Bks. International, Inc.

Gray, Mick. Al B. Mouse's Abecedarium NEW FULL COLOR EDITION: That's Fancy Talk for a B C Book. Gray, Mick. ed. 2016. (ENG.). 30p. (J). (gr. k-6). 19.99 *(978-1-64372-016-6(3)*, Huskies Pub) MacLaren-Cochrane Publishing, Inc.

—Al B. Mouse's Abecedarium NEW FULL COLOR EDITION: That's Fancy Talk for a B C Book: NEW FULL COLOR EDITION. Gray, Mick. ed. 2017. (ENG.). 30p. (J). (gr. k-6). pap. 15.99 *(978-1-64372-225-2(5)*, Huskies Pub) MacLaren-Cochrane Publishing, Inc.

—Al B. Mouse's Abecedarium NEW FULL COLOR EDITION Dyslexic Edition: That's Fancy Talk for a B C Book Dyslexic Font. Gray, Mick. ed. 2017. (ENG.). 32p. (J). (gr. k-6). 19.99 *(978-1-64372-226-9(3))*; pap. 15.99 *(978-1-64372-227-6(1))* MacLaren-Cochrane Publishing, Inc.

Gray, Mike D. Bold Choice: They Say I'm Bad Interactive Book. Bolds, Terri M. 2019. (ENG.). 26p. (J). (gr. 4-6). pap. 14.99 *(978-1-7330563-4-2(3))* Bold Visions Consulting, LLC.

—Bold Love: A Letter to My Young Sisters. Bolds, Terri M. 2016. (ENG.). 62p. (YA). (gr. 7-12). pap. 13.00 *(978-1-7330563-0-4(0))* Bold Visions Consulting, LLC.

—Bold Me: I AM Worthy. Bolds, Terri M. 2018. (ENG.). 28p. (J). (gr. 1-3). pap. 10.00 *(978-1-7330563-2-8(7))* Bold Visions Consulting, LLC.

—Bold Me: I AM Worthy Interactive Book. Bolds, Terri M. 2019. (ENG.). 32p. (J). (gr. 1-3). pap. 14.99 *(978-1-7330563-3-5(5))* Bold Visions Consulting, LLC.

Gray, Miranda & Trotter, Stuart. The Usborne Book of Horses & Ponies. Smith, Lucy. 2006. 32p. (J). pap. *(978-0-439-88983-4(9))* Scholastic, Inc.

Gray, Paula. Signing Fun: American Sign Language Vocabulary, Phrases, Games, & Activities. Warner, Penny. 2006. (ENG.). 192p. (gr. 6-7). per. 21.95 *(978-1-56368-292-6(3))* Gallaudet Univ. Pr.

Gray, Sara. If You Were a Capital Letter, 1 vol. Shaskan, Trisha Speed. 2009. (Word Fun Ser.). (ENG.). 24p. (J). (gr. 2-4). pap. 7.95 *(978-1-4048-5694-3(3)*, Picture Window Bks.) Capstone.

—If You Were a Comma, 1 vol. Blaisdell, Molly. 2009. (Word Fun Ser.). (ENG.). 24p. (J). (gr. 2-4). pap. 7.95 *(978-1-4048-5321-8(9)*, Picture Window Bks.) Capstone.

—If You Were a Comma [LTD Commodities]. Blaisdell, Molly. 2010. (Word Fun Ser.). 24p. pap. 3.50 *(978-1-4048-6251-7(X)*, Picture Window Bks.) Capstone.

—If You Were a Compound Word, 1 vol. Shaskan, Trisha Speed. 2008. (Word Fun Ser.). (ENG.). 24p. (J). (gr. 2-4). 28.65 *(978-1-4048-4771-2(5))*; pap. 7.95 *(978-1-4048-4776-7(6))* Capstone. (Picture Window Bks.).

—If You Were a Conjunction, 1 vol. Loewen, Nancy. 2006. (Word Fun Ser.). (ENG.). 24p. (J). (gr. 2-4). per. 7.95 *(978-1-4048-2389-1(1)*, Picture Window Bks.) Capstone.

—If You Were a Contraction, 1 vol. Shaskan, Trisha Speed. 2008. (Word Fun Ser.). (ENG.). 24p. (J). (gr. 2-4). pap. 7.95 *(978-1-4048-4775-0(8)*, Picture Window Bks.) Capstone.

—If You Were a Homonym or a Homophone, 1 vol. Loewen, Nancy. 2007. (Word Fun Ser.). (ENG.). 24p. (J). (gr. 2-4). per. 7.95 *(978-1-4048-3571-9(7)*, 1265671, Picture Window Bks.) Capstone.

—If You Were a Noun, 1 vol. Dahl, Michael. 2006. (Word Fun Ser.). (ENG.). 24p. (J). (gr. 2-4). 7.95 *(978-1-4048-1980-1(0)*, Picture Window Bks.) Capstone.

—If You Were a Palindrome, 1 vol. Dahl, Michael. 2007. (Word Fun Ser.). (ENG.). 24p. (J). (gr. 2-4). lib. bdg. 28.65 *(978-1-4048-3162-9(2)*, Picture Window Bks.) Capstone.

—If You Were a Period, 1 vol. Healy, Nick & Healy, Nicholas M. 2009. (Word Fun Ser.). (ENG.). 24p. (J). (gr. 2-4). lib. bdg. 28.65 *(978-1-4048-5332-4(4)*, Picture Window Bks.) Capstone.

—If You Were a Period, 1 vol. Healy, Nicholas M. 2009. (Word Fun Ser.). (ENG.). 24p. (J). (gr. 2-4). pap. 7.95 *(978-1-4048-5333-1(2)*, Picture Window Bks.) Capstone.

—If You Were a Period [LTD Commodities]. Healy, Nicholas M. 2010. (Word Fun Ser.). 24p. pap. 3.50 *(978-1-4048-6252-4(8)*, Picture Window Bks.) Capstone.

—If You Were a Plural Word, 1 vol. Shaskan, Trisha Speed. 2009. (Word Fun Ser.). (ENG.). 24p. (J). (gr. 2-4). pap. 7.95 *(978-1-4048-5696-7(X))*; lib. bdg. 28.65 *(978-1-4048-5516-8(5))* Capstone. (Picture Window Bks.).

—If You Were a Prefix, 1 vol. Aboff, Marcie. 2008. (Word Fun Ser.). (ENG.). 24p. (J). (gr. 2-4). pap. 7.95 *(978-1-4048-4777-4(4)*, Picture Window Bks.) Capstone.

—If You Were a Preposition. Loewen, Nancy. 2006. (Word Fun Ser.). (ENG.). 24p. (J). (gr. 2-4). lib. bdg. 28.65 *(978-1-4048-2386-0(7))*; per. 7.95 *(978-1-4048-2390-7(5))* Capstone. (Picture Window Bks.).

—If You Were a Pronoun, 1 vol. Loewen, Nancy. 2006. (Word Fun Ser.). (ENG.). 24p. (J). (gr. 2-4). per. 7.95 *(978-1-4048-2639-7(4)*, Picture Window Bks.) Capstone.

—If You Were a Question Mark, 1 vol. Lyons, Shelly. 2009. (Word Fun Ser.). (ENG.). 24p. (J). (gr. 2-4). pap. 7.95 *(978-1-4048-5324-9(3)*, Picture Window Bks.) Capstone.

G

—If You Were a Question Mark [LTD Commodities]. Lyons, Shelly. 2010. (Word Fun Ser.). 24p. pap. 3.50 *(978-1-4048-6253-1(6)*, Picture Window Bks.) Capstone.

—If You Were a Question Mark [Readers World]. Lyons, Shelly. 2010. (Word Fun Ser.). 24p. pap. 2.72 *(978-1-4048-6705-5(8)*, Picture Window Bks.) Capstone.

—If You Were a Suffix, 1 vol. Aboff, Marcie. 2008. (Word Fun Ser.). (ENG.). 24p. (J). (gr. 2-4). pap. 7.95 *(978-1-4048-4778-1(2)*, Picture Window Bks.) Capstone.

—If You Were a Synonym, 1 vol. Dahl, Michael. 2007. (Word Fun Ser.). (ENG.). 24p. (J). (gr. 2-4). per. 7.95 *(978-1-4048-2391-4(3)*, 1265673, Picture Window Bks.) Capstone.

—If You Were Alliteration. Shaskan, Trisha Speed. 2008. (Word Fun Ser.). (ENG.). 24p. (J). (gr. 2-4). lib. bdg. 28.65 *(978-1-4048-4097-3(4)*, Picture Window Bks.) Capstone.

—If You Were an Adjective, 1 vol. Dahl, Michael. 2006. (Word Fun Ser.). (ENG.). 24p. (J). (gr. 2-4). 7.95 *(978-1-4048-1982-5(7)*, Picture Window Bks.) Capstone.

—If You Were an Adverb, 1 vol. Dahl, Michael. 2006. (Word Fun Ser.). (ENG.). 24p. (J). (gr. 2-4). 28.65 *(978-1-4048-1357-1(8))*; per. 7.95 *(978-1-4048-1983-2(5))* Capstone. (Picture Window Bks.).

—If You Were an Antonym, 1 vol. Loewen, Nancy & Dahl, Michael. 2007. (Word Fun Ser.). (ENG.). 24p. (J). (gr. 2-4). per. 7.95 *(978-1-4048-2388-4(3)*, 1265670, Picture Window Bks.) Capstone.

—If You Were an Apostrophe, 1 vol. Lyons, Shelly & Blaisdell, Molly. 2009. (Word Fun Ser.). (ENG.). 24p. (J). (gr. 2-4). pap. 7.95 *(978-1-4048-5318-8(9)*, Picture Window Bks.) Capstone.

—If You Were an Apostrophe [Readers World]. Lyons, Shelly. 2010. (Word Fun Ser.). 24p. pap. 2.72 *(978-1-4048-6708-6(2)*, Picture Window Bks.) Capstone.

—If You Were an Exclamation Point, 1 vol. Lyons, Shelly. 2009. (Word Fun Ser.). (ENG.). 24p. (J). (gr. 2-4). pap. 7.95 *(978-1-4048-5327-0(8)*, Picture Window Bks.) Capstone.

—If You Were an Exclamation Point [LTD Commodities]. Lyons, Shelly. 2010. (Word Fun Ser.). 24p. pap. 3.50 *(978-1-4048-6254-8(4)*, Picture Window Bks.) Capstone.

—If You Were an Exclamation Point [Readers World]. Lyons, Shelly. 2010. (Word Fun Ser.). 24p. pap. 2.72 *(978-1-4048-6707-9(4)*, Picture Window Bks.) Capstone.

—If You Were an Interjection. Loewen, Nancy. 2006. (Word Fun Ser.). (ENG.). 24p. (J). (gr. 2-4). lib. bdg. 28.65 *(978-1-4048-2636-6(X))*; per. 7.95 *(978-1-4048-2638-0(6))* Capstone. (Picture Window Bks.).

—If You Were Onomatopoeia. Shaskan, Trisha Speed. 2008. (Word Fun Ser.). (ENG.). 24p. (J). (gr. 2-4). lib. bdg. 28.65 *(978-1-4048-4098-0(2)*, Picture Window Bks.) Capstone.

—If You Were Quotation Marks, 1 vol. Blaisdell, Molly. 2009. (Word Fun Ser.). (ENG.). 24p. (J). (gr. 2-4). pap. 7.95 *(978-1-4048-5330-0(8)*, Picture Window Bks.) Capstone.

—If You Were Quotation Marks [LTD Commodities]. Blaisdell, Molly. 2010. (Word Fun Ser.). 24p. pap. 3.50 *(978-1-4048-6255-5(2)*, Picture Window Bks.) Capstone.

—If You Were Quotation Marks [Readers World]. Blaisdell, Molly. 2010. (Word Fun Ser.). 24p. pap. 2.72 *(978-1-4048-6706-2(6)*, Picture Window Bks.) Capstone.

Gray, Stacy A. A Big Mess. Mullican, Judy. l.t. ed. 2003. (HRL Little Book Ser.). 8p. (J). (gr. -1). pap. 10.95 *(978-1-57332-273-7(3)*, HighReach Learning, Incorporated) Carson-Dellosa Publishing, LLC.

—Caillou Is Healthy. Mullican, Judy. l.t. ed. 2004. (HRL Board Book Ser.). (J). (gr. -1-1). pap. 10.95 *(978-1-57332-287-4(3)*, HighReach Learning, Incorporated) Carson-Dellosa Publishing, LLC.

—Caillou's Musical Band. Jarrell, Pamela R. l.t. ed. 2005. (HRL Board Book Ser.). (J). (gr. -1-k). 10.95 *(978-1-57332-311-6(X)*, HighReach Learning, Incorporated) Carson-Dellosa Publishing, LLC.

—Fall on the Farm. Mullican, Judy. l.t. ed. 2005. (Hrl Board Book Ser.). (J). (gr. -1-k). pap. 10.95 *(978-1-57332-323-9(3)*, HighReach Learning, Incorporated) Carson-Dellosa Publishing, LLC.

—I Want to Ride. Hensley, Sarah M. l.t. ed. 2004. (HRL Board Book Ser.). 10p. (J). (gr. -1-1). pap. 10.95 *(978-1-57332-282-9(2)*, HighReach Learning, Incorporated) Carson-Dellosa Publishing, LLC.

—May We Go to the Zoo? Mullican, Judy. l.t. ed. 2004. (HRL Little Book Ser.). (J). (gr. -1-1). pap. 10.95 *(978-1-57332-304-8(7))*; pap. 10.95 *(978-1-57332-303-1(9))* Carson-Dellosa Publishing, LLC. (HighReach Learning, Incorporated).

—What Can It Be? Mullican, Jody. l.t. ed. 2006. 12p. (J). (gr. -1-k). pap. 10.95 *(978-1-57332-352-9(7)*, HighReach Learning, Incorporated) Carson-Dellosa Publishing, LLC.

Gray, Steve. Cow Can't Sleep. Baker, Ken. (ENG.). (J). (gr. -1-3). 2018. 25p. pap. 9.99 *(978-1-5420-9205-0(1)*, 9781542092050); 2012. 24p. 12.99 *(978-0-7614-6198-2(1)*, 9780761461982) Amazon Publishing. (Two Lions).

—Un Diente esta Flojo: A Tooth Is Loose. Trumbauer, Lisa. 2005. (Rookie Reader Español Ser.). (SPA & ENG.). 24p. (gr. k-2). 19.50 *(978-0-516-24449-5(3)*, Children's Pr.) Scholastic Library Publishing.

—The Ravenous Raven. Stephenson, Midji. 2015. (J). *(978-1-934656-70-9(4))* Grand Canyon Conservancy.

—There Was an Old Martian Who Swallowed the Moon, 0 vols. Ward, Jennifer. 2015. (ENG.). 32p. (J). (gr. -1-3). 16.99 *(978-1-4778-2628-7(9)*, 9781477826287, Two Lions) Amazon Publishing.

—There Was an Old Monkey Who Swallowed a Frog, 0 vols. Ward, Jennifer. 2010. (ENG.). 40p. (J). (gr. k-3). 16.99 *(978-0-7614-5580-6(9)*, 9780761455806, Two Lions) Amazon Publishing.

—A Tooth Is Loose. Trumbauer, Lisa. (Rookie Ready to Learn Ser.). (J). 2011. 32p. pap. 5.95 *(978-0-531-26735-6(0))*; 2011. (ENG.). 32p. (gr. -1-1). lib. bdg. 23.00 *(978-0-531-26503-1(X))*; 2005. (ENG.). 24p. (gr. k-2). pap. 4.95 *(978-0-516-25841-6(9))* Scholastic Library Publishing. (Children's Pr.).

Gray, Steve. Un Diente Está Flojo. Gray, Steve. Trumbauer, Lisa. 2011. (Rookie Ready to Learn Español Ser.). (SPA.). 32p. (J). pap. 5.95 *(978-0-531-26785-1(7))*; (gr. -1-1). lib. bdg. 23.00 *(978-0-531-26117-0(4))* Scholastic Library Publishing. (Children's Pr.).

Gray, Steve, jt. illus. see Sullivan, Mary.

Gray, Susan & Messer, Celia. Colorful Ohio! A Bird's Eye View with Worthington Cardinal, 7 bks. Gray, Susan. 2003. 28p. (J). 4.95 *(978-0-9742862-5-9(7))* Two's Company.

Gray, Virginia. Annie & Koos of the Bushveldt. Williams, Elizabeth. 2016. (ENG.). (J). (gr. 1-6). *(978-0-9945552-6-7(1))* Williams, Elizabeth.

Graybar, Shmuel, jt. illus. see Toron, Eli.

Graybill, Joni. Hello Cocky! Aryal, Aimee. 2004. 24p. (J). 19.95 *(978-1-932888-07-2(1))* Mascot Bks., Inc.

—Hello Tiger! Aryal, Aimee. 2004. 24p. (J). 19.95 *(978-1-932888-25-6(X))* Mascot Bks., Inc.

Grayson, Rick. Captain Jack's Journal. Williams, Rozanne Lanczak. 2006. (Learn to Write Ser.). 16p. (J). (gr. k-2). pap. 2.99 *(978-1-59198-303-3(7)*, 6197) Creative Teaching Pr., Inc.

—Captain Jack's Journal. Williams, Rozanne Lanczak. Maio, Barbara, ed. 2006. (J). per. 8.99 *(978-1-59198-361-3(4))* Creative Teaching Pr., Inc.

—Grammar Minutes: 100 Minutes to Better Basic Skills. Jones, Carmen S. Ly, Dorothy, ed. 2009. 112p. (J). pap. 14.99 *(978-1-60689-123-0(5))* Creative Teaching Pr., Inc.

—Grammar Minutes: 100 Minutes to Better Basic Skills. Hex, Kathleen. Kim, Regina Hurh & Snoddy, Gillian, eds. 2009. 112p. (J). pap. 14.99 *(978-1-60689-124-7(3))* Creative Teaching Pr., Inc.

Grayson, Rick & Iosa, Ann. Reading Comprehension 1-3: Activities for Understanding. Flores, Debra et al. Jennett, Pamela, ed. 2004. 96p. (J). pap. 1.99 *(978-1-59198-045-2(3)*, 3384) Creative Teaching Pr., Inc.

—Reading Comprehension 4-6: Activities for Understanding. Flores, Debra et al. Jennett, Pamela, ed. 2004. 96p. (J). pap. 12.99 *(978-1-59198-046-9(1)*, 3385) Creative Teaching Pr., Inc.

Grayson, Rick, jt. illus. see Armstrong, Beverly.

Grayson, Rick, jt. illus. see Armstrong, Bev.

Grayson, Rick, jt. illus. see Brooks, Nan.

Grayson, Rick, jt. illus. see Campbell, Jenny.

Grayson, Rick, jt. illus. see Hillam, Corbin.

Grayson, Rick, jt. illus. see Iosa, Ann W.

Grayson, Rick, jt. illus. see Rojas, Mary.

Grayson, Rick, jt. illus. see Tom, Darcy.

Graziano, John. Roar! Ripley's Entertainment Inc. 2012. (Ripley's Shout Outs Ser.: 1). (ENG.). 96p. (J). (gr. 2-5). pap. 4.99 *(978-0-545-38075-1(8))* Scholastic, Inc.

—Woof! Ripley's Entertainment Inc. 2012. (Ripley's Shout Outs Ser.: 3). (ENG.). 96p. (J). (gr. 2-5). pap. 4.99 *(978-0-545-38077-5(4))* Scholastic, Inc.

—Woof! Funny Pet Stories. 2012. 96p. (J). pap. *(978-0-545-38687-6(X))* Ripley Entertainment, Inc.

—Zoom! Ripley's Entertainment Inc. 2012. (Ripley's Shout Outs Ser.: 2). (ENG.). 96p. (J). (gr. 2-5). pap. 4.99 *(978-0-545-38076-8(6))* Scholastic, Inc.

Grbich, Aaron. Numeros Importantes. Giganti, Paul. (SPA.). (J). (gr. 1-3). pap. 3.16 net. *(978-0-590-48700-9(0)*, Scholastic Pr.) Scholastic, Inc.

Grden, John. Kathie's Dollhouse. Grden, John. Grden, Mary, ed. 2018. (ENG.). 28p. (J). pap. 9.85 *(978-1-7311-4006-7(1))* Independently Published.

—Why Did the Mouse Go to the Moon? Grden, John. Grden, Mary, ed. 2018. (ENG.). 30p. (J). pap. 11.50 *(978-1-7292-5623-7(6))* Independently Published.

Grealy, Andrea. A Dragon Called Môr. Bebbington, Jilly. 2020. (ENG.). (J). pap. 7.99 ***(978-1-78461-799-8(7))*** Y Lolfa GBR. Dist: Casemate Pubs. & Bk. Distributors, LLC.

Greasley, Kal. Hootie the Doll Face Persian Cat. McAlister, Deborah. 2020. (ENG.). 36p. (J). 27.99 ***(978-1-0983-1404-0(2))*** BookBaby.

Greaux, Romea. A Heritage Undone. Quetel, Linda. 33p. (J). (gr. 11). 9.50 *(978-0-9626458-1-5(8))* xbks publishing.

Greaves, Martin. The Enchanted World of Bracken Lea. Race, Esma. 2018. (Fairy Folk of Bracken Lea Wood Ser.: Vol. 2). (ENG.). 100p. (J). (gr. 2-6). pap. 9.99 *(978-1-68160-560-9(0))* Crimson Cloak Publishing.

Greaves, Naomi. Go Away, Foxy Foxy. Hendriks, Karen. 2020. (ENG.). 36p. (J). (gr. k-3). ***(978-0-6486998-5-9(4))***; pap. ***(978-0-6486998-4-2(6))*** Daisy Lane Publishing.

Greaves, Naomi. I Love the Way You Giggle. Sharp, Jennifer. 2018. (ENG.). 22p. (J). *(978-0-6482957-9-2(6))* Serenity Press.

—I'm Just Little. Sharp, Jennifer. 2018. (ENG.). 26p. (J). (gr. k-4). *(978-0-6482202-3-7(0))*; pap. *(978-0-6482202-4-4(9))* Daisy Lane Publishing.

Greaves, Naomi. Imagine. Sharp, Jennifer. 2019. (ENG.). 24p. (J). (gr. k-4). ***(978-0-6482202-7-5(3))*** Daisy Lane Publishing.

Greaves, Naomi. Watch Her Shine. Henry, Deborah. 2nd ed. 2019. (ENG.). 38p. (J). (gr. 2-4). pap. *(978-0-6484892-4-5(8))* Daisy Lane Publishing.

Greban, Quentin. Pinocchio. Collodi, Carlo. 2018. (ENG.). 176p. (J). (gr. -1-2). 25.00 *(978-0-7358-4328-8(7))* North-South Bks., Inc.

—Sarah So Small. Greban, Tanguy. 2004. (ENG.). 32p. (J). (gr. 4-7). 16.95 *(978-1-59687-179-3(2))* iBks., Inc.

—Sarah So Small. Greban, Tanguy. 2004. 32p. (J). 16.95 *(978-0-689-03594-4(2)*, Milk & Cookies) ibooks, Inc.

—Snow White. Grimm, Jacob & Grimm, Wilhelm. 2013. 32p. (J). (gr. -1-3). pap. 7.95 *(978-0-7358-4116-1(0))* North-South Bks., Inc.

Greban, Quentin. Mommy, I Love You. Greban, Quentin. 2005. 32p. *(978-0-689-03922-5(0)*, Milk & Cookies) ibooks, Inc.

Greco, E. D. Tales & Treasures of California's Missions. Reinstedt, Randall A. 2005. 119p. (YA). reprint ed. 22.00 *(978-0-7567-8681-6(9))* DIANE Publishing Co.

Greder, Armin. The Island. Greder, Armin. 2008. Orig. Title: Die Insel. (ENG.). 32p. (J). (gr. 2). 23.95 *(978-1-74175-266-3(3))* Allen & Unwin AUS. Dist: Independent Pubs. Group.

Gree, Alain. Animal Activity Book. 2019. (Alain Grée Activity Book Ser.). (ENG.). 64p. (J). pap. 12.99 *(978-1-78708-019-5(6))* Button Bks. GBR. Dist: Publishers Group West (PGW).

Greef, Heidi-Kate. Little Santa: The Perfect Pet. Seepersad, Nashreen. 2017. (Little Santa Ser.: Vol. 1). (ENG.). 28p. (J). (gr. k-3). pap. *(978-0-620-73502-5(3))* Seepersad, Nashreen.

—Little Santa: The Secret in the Woods. Seepersad, Nashreen. 2017. (Little Santa Ser.: Vol. 2). (ENG.). 30p. (J). (gr. k-5). pap. *(978-0-620-75883-3(X))* Seepersad, Nashreen.

Greeff, Heidi-Kate. How Cheetah Got His Tears. Van der Merwe, Avril. 2017. (ENG.). 16p. pap. 7.00 *(978-1-4859-0034-4(4))* Penguin Random House Grupo Editorial ESP. Dist: Casemate Pubs. & Bk. Distributors, LLC.

—Once upon a Rhinoceros. Van der Merwe, Avril. 2018. (ENG.). 16p. pap. 7.50 *(978-1-4859-0037-5(9))* Penguin Random House South Africa ZAF. Dist: Casemate Pubs. & Bk. Distributors, LLC.

Green, Andy, jt. illus. see Dartez, Cecilia.

Green, Anne Canevari. Baseball's Boneheads, Bad Boys, & Just Plain Crazy Guys. Sullivan, George. 2003. 64p. (J). (gr. 5-8). pap. 8.95 *(978-0-7613-1928-3(X)*, Millbrook Pr.) Lerner Publishing Group.

—Jobs for Kids: A Smart Kid's Q & A Guide. Kiefer, Jeanne. 2003. (Single Titles Ser.). 112p. (gr. 5-8). lib. bdg. 25.90 *(978-0-7613-2611-3(1)*, Millbrook Pr.) Lerner Publishing Group.

Green, Babs Brumer. Take Her Back: An Andy-Bear Tale. 2003. 19p. (J). pap. *(978-0-9753119-0-5(5))* ATU Golden Pubns.

Green, Barry. Animals. James, Noah. 2020. (Drawing for Dorks Ser.). (ENG.). 128p. (J). (gr. 4-7). pap. 7.99 ***(978-1-78958-633-6(X))*** Top That! Publishing PLC GBR. Dist: Independent Pubs. Group.

Green, Barry. Builder's Tool Kit. Gale, Robyn. 2019. (Pop Out & Play Ser.). (ENG.). 10p. (J). (gr. -1). bds. 7.99 *(978-1-78700-988-2(2))* Top That! Publishing PLC GBR. Dist: Independent Pubs. Group.

—Caveman Capers Activity Fun. Regan, Lisa & Webb, Trudi. 2019. (Dover Children's Activity Bks.). (ENG.). 48p. (J). (gr. 1-4). pap. 7.99 *(978-0-486-83291-3(0))* Dover Pubns., Inc.

Green, Barry. Christmas. Elliot, Kit. 2020. (Scratch & Draw Card Wallet Format Ser.). (ENG.). 34p. (J). (gr. k-3). pap. 9.99 ***(978-1-78958-652-7(6))*** Top That! Publishing PLC GBR. Dist: Independent Pubs. Group.

—Cuter-Than-Cute. James, Noah. 2020. (Drawing for Dorks Ser.). (ENG.). 128p. (J). (gr. 4-7). pap. 7.99 ***(978-1-78958-634-3(8))*** Top That! Publishing PLC GBR. Dist: Independent Pubs. Group.

Green, Barry. Funky Junk: Recycle Rubbish into Art! Kings, Gary & Ginger, Richard. 2012. (Dover Children's Activity Bks.). (ENG.). 64p. (J). (gr. 3-5). pap. 9.99 *(978-0-486-49022-9(X))* Dover Pubns., Inc.

—Funny Animals Sticker Fun: Mix & Match the Stickers to Make Funny Animals. Graham, Oakley. 2019. (Dover Children's Activity Bks.). (ENG.). 64p. (J). (gr. -1-3). pap. 9.99 *(978-0-486-83288-3(0))* Dover Pubns., Inc.

—Funny Faces Sticker Fun: Mix & Match the Stickers to Make Funny Faces. Graham, Oakley. 2019. (Dover Children's Activity Bks.). (ENG.). 64p. (J). (gr. -1-3). pap. 9.99 *(978-0-486-83287-6(2))* Dover Pubns., Inc.

—Fuzzy Christmas. Thomson, Kate. 2017. (Soft Felt Play Bks.). (ENG.). 10p. (J). (gr. -1-1). 12.99 *(978-1-78700-249-4(7))* Top That! Publishing PLC GBR. Dist: Independent Pubs. Group.

—Fuzzy Farm. Ranson, Erin. 2017. (Soft Felt Play Bks.). (ENG.). 10p. (J). (gr. -1-k). 12.99 *(978-1-78700-066-7(4))* Top That! Publishing PLC GBR. Dist: Independent Pubs. Group.

—Fuzzy Ocean. Ranson, Erin. 2017. (Soft Felt Play Bks.). (ENG.). 10p. (J). (gr. -1-k). 12.99 *(978-1-78700-084-1(2))* Top That! Publishing PLC GBR. Dist: Independent Pubs. Group.

—Horses & Unicorns. George, Joshua. 2017. (Scratch & Draw Ser.). (ENG.). 56p. (J). (gr. k-2). 12.99 *(978-1-78700-073-5(7))* Top That! Publishing PLC GBR. Dist: Independent Pubs. Group.

—How to Draw 101 Baby Animals. Lambert, Nat. 2017. (How to Draw 101 Ser.). (ENG.). 48p. (J). (gr. k). pap. 4.99 *(978-1-78700-180-0(6))* Top That! Publishing PLC GBR. Dist: Independent Pubs. Group.

—How to Draw 101 Dinosaurs. Lambert, Nat. 2017. (How to Draw 101 Ser.). (ENG.). 48p. (J). (gr. k). pap. 4.99 *(978-1-78700-181-7(4))* Top That! Publishing PLC GBR. Dist: Independent Pubs. Group.

—How to Draw Dinosaurs & Other Cool Stuff! Lambert, Nat. 2015. (404 Things to Draw Ser.). (ENG.). 192p. (J). (gr. k). pap. 12.99 *(978-1-78445-274-2(2))* Top That! Publishing PLC GBR. Dist: Independent Pubs. Group.

—I Can Do It! Times Tables. Lambert, Nat. 2018. (I Can Do It! Ser.). (ENG.). 12p. (J). (gr. k-3). 8.99 *(978-1-78700-383-5(3))* Top That! Publishing PLC GBR. Dist: Independent Pubs. Group.

—I Can Tie My Own Shoelaces. Graham, Oakley. 2014. (I Can Bks.). (ENG.). 12p. (J). (gr. -1). 7.99 *(978-1-78244-824-2(1))* Top That! Publishing PLC GBR. Dist: Independent Pubs. Group.

—I'm Just a Little Cow. Thompson, Kate. 2017. (Googley-Eye Bks.). (ENG.). 12p. (J). (gr. -1-k). bds. 7.99 *(978-1-78445-870-6(8))* Top That! Publishing PLC GBR. Dist: Independent Pubs. Group.

—I'm Just a Little Ghost. George, Joshua. 2017. (Googley-Eye Bks.). (ENG.). 12p. (J). (gr. -1-k). bds. 7.99 *(978-1-78700-077-3(X))* Top That! Publishing PLC GBR. Dist: Independent Pubs. Group.

—I'm Just a Little Horse. Thompson, Kate. 2017. (Googley-Eye Bks.). (ENG.). 12p. (J). (gr. -1-k). bds. 7.99 *(978-1-78445-868-3(6))* Top That! Publishing PLC GBR. Dist: Independent Pubs. Group.

—I'm Just a Little Kitten. Thompson, Kate. 2016. (Googley-Eye Bks.). (ENG.). 12p. (J). (gr. -1-k). bds. 7.99 *(978-1-78445-861-4(9))* Top That! Publishing PLC GBR. Dist: Independent Pubs. Group.

—I'm Just a Little Penguin. Graham, Oakley. 2019. (Googley-Eyed Board Bks.). (ENG.). 12p. (J). (gr. -1-k). bds. 7.99 *(978-1-78700-879-3(7))* Top That! Publishing PLC GBR. Dist: Independent Pubs. Group.

—I'm Just a Little Pig. Thompson, Kate. 2017. (Googley-Eye Bks.). (ENG.). 12p. (J). (gr. -1-k). bds. 7.99 *(978-1-78445-871-3(6))* Top That! Publishing PLC GBR. Dist: Independent Pubs. Group.

—I'm Just a Little Puppy. Thompson, Kate. 2016. (Googley-Eye Bks.). (ENG.). 12p. (J). (gr. -1-k). bds. 7.99 *(978-1-78445-862-1(7))* Top That! Publishing PLC GBR. Dist: Independent Pubs. Group.

Green, Barry. I'm Just a Little Reindeer. George, Joshua. 2020. (Googley-Eyed Board Bks.). (ENG.). 12p. (J). (gr. -1-k). bds. 7.99 ***(978-1-78700-344-6(2))*** Top That! Publishing PLC GBR. Dist: Independent Pubs. Group.

Green, Barry. I'm Just a Little Sheep. Graham, Oakley. 2014. (ENG.). 12p. (gr. -1). *(978-1-78244-591-3(9))* Top That! Publishing PLC.

—I'm Just a Little Sheep. Thompson, Kate. 2017. (Googley-Eye Bks.). (ENG.). 12p. (J). (gr. -1-k). bds. 7.99 *(978-1-78445-869-0(4))* Top That! Publishing PLC GBR. Dist: Independent Pubs. Group.

—I'm Just a Little Snowman. George, Joshua. 2017. (Googley-Eye Bks.). (ENG.). 12p. (J). (gr. -1-k). bds. 7.99 *(978-1-78700-079-7(6))* Top That! Publishing PLC GBR. Dist: Independent Pubs. Group.

—I'm Santa Claus. George, Joshua. 2017. (Googley-Eye Bks.). (ENG.). 12p. (J). (gr. -1-k). bds. 7.99 *(978-1-78700-078-0(8))* Top That! Publishing PLC GBR. Dist: Independent Pubs. Group.

—Loud Proud Lenny Lion. Thomson, Kate. 2017. (Hand Puppet Bks.). (ENG.). 16p. (J). (gr. -1-1). 9.99 *(978-1-78700-256-2(X))* Top That! Publishing PLC GBR. Dist: Independent Pubs. Group.

—Magical Fairies Activity Fun. Regan, Lisa & Webb, Trudi. 2019. (Dover Children's Activity Bks.). (ENG.). 48p. (J). (gr. 1-4). pap. 7.99 *(978-0-486-83292-0(9)*, 832929) Dover Pubns., Inc.

—Mix & Match Animals: Over 100 Animals to Create! Isaacs, Connie. 2019. (Dover Children's Activity Bks.). (ENG.). 12p. (J). (gr. -1-3). bds. 9.99 *(978-0-486-83289-0(9)*, 832899) Dover Pubns., Inc.

—Mix & Match Monsters: Over 100 Monsters to Create! Isaacs, Connie. 2019. (Dover Children's Activity Bks.). (ENG.). 12p. (J). (gr. -1-3). bds. 9.99 *(978-0-486-83290-6(2)*, 832902) Dover Pubns., Inc.

—Pirates Ahoy! Activity Fun. Regan, Lisa & Webb, Trudi. 2019. (Dover Children's Activity Bks.). (ENG.). 48p. (J). (gr. 1-4). pap. 7.99 *(978-0-486-83293-7(7))* Dover Pubns., Inc.

—Playful Ponies Activity Fun. Regan, Lisa & Webb, Trudi. 2019. (Dover Children's Activity Bks.). (ENG.). 48p. (J). (gr. 1-4). pap. 7.99 *(978-0-486-83297-5(X))* Dover Pubns., Inc.

—Scratch & Draw Animals. Lambert, Nat. 2017. (Scratch & Draw Ser.). (ENG.). 56p. (J). (gr. 2-7). 12.99 *(978-1-78700-245-6(4))* Top That! Publishing PLC GBR. Dist: Independent Pubs. Group.

—Scratch & Draw Construction Site. Over, Arthur. 2018. (Scratch & Draw Ser.). (ENG.). 56p. (J). (gr. k). 12.99 *(978-1-78700-610-2(7))* Top That! Publishing PLC GBR. Dist: Independent Pubs. Group.

—Scratch & Draw Dinosaurs. Lambert, Nat. 2018. (Scratch & Draw Ser.). (ENG.). 56p. (J). (gr. 2-7). 12.99 *(978-1-78700-246-3(2))* Top That! Publishing PLC GBR. Dist: Independent Pubs. Group.

—Scratch & Draw Farm Animals. Over, Arthur. 2020. (Scratch & Draw Ser.). (ENG.). 56p. (J). (gr. k). 12.99 *(978-1-78958-415-8(9))* Top That! Publishing PLC GBR. Dist: Independent Pubs. Group.

—Scratch & Draw Mermaids. Isaacs, Connie. 2018. (Scratch & Draw Ser.). (ENG.). 56p. (J). (gr. k). 12.99 *(978-1-78700-609-6(3))* Top That! Publishing PLC GBR. Dist: Independent Pubs. Group.

—Shopping List. Gale, Robyn. 2019. (Pop Out & Play Ser.). (ENG.). 10p. (J). (gr. -1). bds. 7.99 *(978-1-78700-989-9(0))* Top That! Publishing PLC GBR. Dist: Independent Pubs. Group.

—Sneaky Snappy Mr Croc. Thompson, Kate. 2014. (Hand Puppet Bks.). (ENG.). 10p. (J). (gr. -1). 9.99 *(978-1-78244-618-7(4))* Top That! Publishing PLC GBR. Dist: Independent Pubs. Group.

—Sneezy Wheezy Mr Shark. Thompson, Kate. 2014. (Hand Puppet Bks.). (ENG.). 10p. (J). (gr. -1). 9.99 *(978-1-78244-619-4(2))* Top That! Publishing PLC GBR. Dist: Independent Pubs. Group.

—Space. George, Joshua. 2017. (Scratch & Draw Ser.). (ENG.). 56p. (J). (gr. k-2). 12.99 *(978-1-78700-070-4(2))* Top That! Publishing PLC GBR. Dist: Independent Pubs. Group.

—Subtraction. Gale, Robyn. 2020. (I Can Do It! Ser.). (ENG.). 12p. (J). (gr. k-2). 9.99 *(978-1-78958-471-4(X))* Top That! Publishing PLC GBR. Dist: Independent Pubs. Group.

—Under the Sea. Ranson, Erin. 2007. (Magnetic Story & Play Scene Ser.). (ENG.). 8p. (J). (gr. -1-1). 9.99 *(978-1-84666-089-4(0))* Top That! Publishing PLC GBR. Dist: Independent Pubs. Group.

—Utterly Awesome 501 Things to Draw. 2017. (ENG.). 256p. (J). (gr. k-2). pap. 14.99 *(978-1-78700-067-4(2))* Top That! Publishing PLC GBR. Dist: Independent Pubs. Group.

Green, Burt. Sweet Dreams for Sydney: A Book to Help Dissipate Nightmares, 1 vol. Wiley, Jean. 2009. 25p. pap. 24.95 *(978-1-60703-002-7(0))* America Star Bks.

Green, Chris. Bog Hollow Boys. Jones, C. B. 2017. (Bog Hollow Boys Ser.). (ENG.). 72p. (J). (gr. 4-8). 101.28 *(978-1-4965-4063-8(8)*, 25356, Stone Arch Bks.) Capstone.

—The Cats' Meow. Jones, C. B. 2017. (Bog Hollow Boys Ser.). (ENG.). 72p. (J). (gr. 4-8). lib. bdg. 25.32 *(978-1-4965-4057-7(3)*, Stone Arch Bks.) Capstone.

—Gone to the Buzzards. Jones, C. B. 2017. (Bog Hollow Boys Ser.). (ENG.). 72p. (J). (gr. 4-8). lib. bdg. 25.32 *(978-1-4965-4058-4(1),* Stone Arch Bks.) Capstone.
—Kiss of the Snake. Jones, C. B. 2017. (Bog Hollow Boys Ser.). (ENG.). 72p. (J). (gr. 4-8). lib. bdg. 25.32 *(978-1-4965-4056-0(5),* Stone Arch Bks.) Capstone.
—Sleeping with the Fishes. Jones, C. B. 2017. (Bog Hollow Boys Ser.). (ENG.). 72p. (J). (gr. 4-8). lib. bdg. 25.32 *(978-1-4965-4055-3(7),* Stone Arch Bks.) Capstone.
Green, Chris. You Can Do It Emily! Green, Chris. 2016. (ENG.). (J). (gr. k-6). 16.95 *(978-1-61314-361-2(3));* pap. 11.95 *(978-1-61314-362-9(1))* Innovo Publishing, LLC.
Green, D. Jojo & Her Solo. Green, D. 2018. (Picture Book Ser.). (ENG.). 32p. (J). (gr. 1-2). pap. *(978-1-9997407-0-2(X))* Green, D.
Green, Dan. Kane Rules. Mugford, Simon. 2020. (Soccer Superstars Ser.). (ENG.). 128p. (J). (gr. k). pap. 8.95 ***(978-1-78312-583-8(7))*** Welbeck Publishing Group Ltd. GBR. Dist: Two Rivers Distribution.
—Mbappe Rules. Mugford, Simon. 2020. (Soccer Superstars Ser.). (ENG.). 128p. (J). (gr. k). pap. 8.95 ***(978-1-78312-584-5(5))*** Welbeck Publishing Group Ltd. GBR. Dist: Two Rivers Distribution.
—Messi Rules. Mugford, Simon. 2020. (Soccer Superstars Ser.). (ENG.). 128p. (J). (gr. k). pap. 8.95 ***(978-1-78312-577-7(2))*** Welbeck Publishing Group Ltd. GBR. Dist: Two Rivers Distribution.
—Ronaldo Rules. Mugford, Simon. 2020. (Soccer Superstars Ser.). (ENG.). 128p. (J). (gr. k). pap. 8.95 ***(978-1-78312-578-4(0))*** Welbeck Publishing Group Ltd. GBR. Dist: Two Rivers Distribution.
Green, Dan. 101 Fairies. Green, Barry. 2009. (How to Draw 101... Ser.). (ENG.). 48p. (J). (gr. k). pap. 4.99 *(978-1-84666-852-4(2))* Top That! Publishing PLC GBR. Dist: Independent Pubs. Group.
Green, Dianne. Where the Rivers Meet the Sea. Green, Dianne. 2018. (ENG.). 32p. (J). (gr. 2). pap. *(978-1-9997407-1-9(8))* Green, D.
Green, Donna. Merry Christmas: Best - Loved Stories & Carols. Urmy, Deanne, ed. 2004. 90p. (J). (gr. 4-8). reprint ed. 20.00 *(978-0-7567-7580-3(9))* DIANE Publishing Co.
Green, Elizabeth. PomPom's Hot-Dog Homecoming. Green, Elizabeth. 2019. (Charlie & Pompom Storybooks Ser.: Vol. 24). (ENG.). 30p. (J). pap. 9.99 ***(978-1-7094-5483-7(0))*** Independently Published.
Green, Elizabeth. Project Scarecrow. Green, Elizabeth. 2018. (Charlie & Pompom Storybooks Ser.: Vol. 21). (ENG.). 40p. (J). pap. 9.99 *(978-1-7293-0555-3(5))* Independently Published.
—Pumpkin Surprise. Green, Elizabeth. 2018. (Charlie & Pompom Storybooks Ser.: Vol. 22). (ENG.). 40p. (J). pap. 9.99 *(978-1-7311-3403-5(7))* Independently Published.
Green, Ilya. Marre du Rose. Hense, Nathalie. 2009. (A. M. Alb. Ill. C. Ser.). (FRE.). (J). *(978-2-226-18611-9(5))* Albin-Michel, Éditions.
—Yoga Together! Jouane, Elisabeth. 2019. (ENG.). 56p. (J). (gr. -1-k). 15.99 Éditions Tourbillon FRA. Dist: Hachette Bk. Group.
Green, Jackie Fourcade. The Queen & I. McMahon, Bea Prior. 2013. (ENG.). 54p. (YA). pap. 19.95 *(978-1-4327-4522-6(0))* Outskirts Pr., Inc.
Green, Joey. The Jolly President: Or Letters George W. Bush Never Read. Green, Joey. 2006. (ENG.). 36p. 16.95 *(978-0-9772590-1-4(3))* Lunatic Pr.
Green, John. The Call of the Wild. London, Jack. abr. l.t. ed. 2011. (Dover Children's Thrift Classics Ser.). (ENG.). 64p. (J). (gr. 3-8). pap. 3.00 *(978-0-486-40551-3(6))* Dover Pubns., Inc.
—Scottish Fairy Tales. MacKenzie, Donald A. 2011. (Dover Children's Thrift Classics Ser.). (ENG.). 96p. (J). (gr. 3-8). pap. 4.50 *(978-0-486-29900-6(7))* Dover Pubns., Inc.
—Teen Boat! The Race for Boatlantis. Roman, Dave. 2015. (ENG.). 160p. (YA). (gr. 7). 14.99 *(978-0-547-86563-8(5),* 1503607) Houghton Mifflin Harcourt Publishing Co.
—The Three Musketeers. Dumas, Alexandre. abr. ed. 2011. (Dover Children's Thrift Classics Ser.). (ENG.). 96p. (J). (gr. 3-8). pap. 3.00 *(978-0-486-28326-5(7))* Dover Pubns., Inc.
—Who Lives on the Farm? 2004. (Who Lives... Ser.). 12p. (J). bds. 4.99 *(978-1-85854-647-6(8))* Brimax Books Ltd. GBR. Dist: Byeway Bks.
Green, Jonathan. Amadeus: The Leghorn Rooster. Nevils, Delores B. 2015. (Young Palmetto Bks.). (ENG.). 40p. (J). (gr. 4-4). 19.99 *(978-1-61117-556-1(9))* Univ. of South Carolina Pr.
—Amadeus, the Leghorn Rooster. 2004. (J). 17.95 *(978-0-87844-174-7(3))* Sandlapper Publishing Co., Inc.
—The Freedom Ship of Robert Smalls. Meriwether, Louise. 2018. (Young Palmetto Bks.). (ENG.). 32p. (J). 19.99 *(978-1-61117-855-5(X))* Univ. of South Carolina Pr.
Green, Julia. My Very Merry Ugly Christmas Sweater: A Touch-And-Feel Book. Burton, Jeffrey. 2020. (ENG.). 12p. (J). (gr. -1-k). bds. 9.99 ***(978-1-5344-7678-3(4),*** Little Simon) Little Simon.
Green, Julia & Kubinyi, Laszlo. Survivors: the Gathering Darkness #6: the Final Battle. Hunter, Erin. 2019. (Survivors: the Gathering Darkness Ser.: 6). (ENG.). (J). (gr. 3-7). 352p. pap. 7.99 *(978-0-06-234355-0(6));* 336p. 16.99 *(978-0-06-234353-6(X));* 336p. lib. bdg. 17.89 *(978-0-06-234354-3(8))* HarperCollins Pubs.
Green, Julia, jt. illus. see Kubinyi, Laszlo.
Green, K. C. & McGinty, Ian. Rocko's Modern Life Vol. 1. Ferrier, Ryan. 2018. (ENG.). 112p. (J). (gr. 3). pap. 14.99 *(978-1-68415-199-8(6))* Boom! Studios.
Green, Katie May. Hide & Seek. Green, Katie May. 2019. (ENG.). 32p. (J). (gr. k-3). 16.99 *(978-0-7636-9606-1(4))* Candlewick Pr.
—Seen & Not Heard. Green, Katie May. 2015. (ENG.). 32p. (J). (gr. k-3). 15.99 *(978-0-7636-7612-4(8))* Candlewick Pr.
Green, Keri. Collins Big Cat Phonics for Letters & Sounds - a Bee on a Lark: Band 02B/Red B, Bd. 2B. Baugh, Helen. 2018. (Collins Big Cat Phonics Ser.). (ENG.). 16p. (J). pap. 6.99 *(978-0-00-825148-2(7))* HarperCollins Pubs. Ltd. GBR. Dist: Independent Pubs. Group.
Green, Lucyna A. M. Love You Little Brother. 2006. (J). *(978-1-58669-186-8(4)); (978-1-58669-185-1(6))* Childcraft Education Corp.
Green, Matthew. A Secret Sydney. Valenzuela, Kristine. 2013. 44p. (J). pap. *(978-0-9872061-6-9(8))* DoctorZed Publishing.
Green, Megan. The Cookie Man. Bilbrey, Heather. 2008. 20p. pap. 24.95 *(978-1-60703-328-8(3))* America Star Bks.
—Myrtle the Turtle, 1 vol. Paige, Nancy. 2009. 19p. pap. 24.95 *(978-1-60836-085-7(7))* America Star Bks.
Green, Melissa. Lo & Behold: A Christmas Story. Breeze Green, Sally. 2019. (ENG.). 28p. (J). (gr. -1-3). 23.95 ***(978-1-64569-557-8(3))*** Christian Faith Publishing.
Green, Noel. The Safe Touch Book. Robinson, Beth. 2013. 20p. (J). mass mkt. 8.99 *(978-0-9799092-2-1(8))* Robinson, Beth.
—Where Will I Grow Up? Robinson, Beth. 2013. 20p. (J). mass mkt. 8.99 *(978-0-9799092-6-9(0))* Robinson, Beth.
Green, Rebecca. Becoming a Good Creature. Montgomery, Sy. 2020. (ENG.). 40p. (J). (gr. -1-3). 17.99 ***(978-0-358-25210-8(5),*** 1770051, HMH Books For Young Readers) Houghton Mifflin Harcourt Publishing Co.
Green, Rebecca. From Far Away. Munsch, Robert & Askar, Saoussan. 2017. (ENG.). 32p. (J). (gr. k-2). 9.95 *(978-1-55451-939-2(X));* 18.95 *(978-1-55451-940-8(3))* Annick Pr., Ltd. CAN. Dist: Publishers Group West (PGW).
—The Glass Town Game. Valente, Catherynne M. (ENG.). (J). (gr. 5). 2018. 560p. pap. 9.99 *(978-1-4814-7697-3(1));* 2017. 544p. 17.99 *(978-1-4814-7696-6(3))* McElderry, Margaret K. Bks. (McElderry, Margaret K. Bks.).
—Iqbal & His Ingenious Idea: How a Science Project Helps One Family & the Planet. Suneby, Elizabeth. 2018. (CitizenKid Ser.). (ENG.). 32p. (J). (gr. 3-7). 18.99 *(978-1-77138-720-0(3))* Kids Can Pr., Ltd. CAN. Dist: Hachette Bk. Group.
—Madame Saqui: Revolutionary Rope Dancer. Robinson, Lisa. 2020. 40p. (J). (gr. -1-3). 17.99 *(978-0-525-57997-7(4),* Schwartz & Wade Bks.) Random Hse. Children's Bks.
—A Place Called Home: Look Inside Houses Around the World, 1 vol. Lonely Planet Kids & Baker, Kate. 2020. (ENG.). 16p. (J). (gr. -1-k). 12.99 *(978-1-78868-934-2(8),* Lonely Planet Kids) Lonely Planet Global Ltd. IRL. Dist: Hachette Bk. Group.
—The Skylarks' War. McKay, Hilary. 2019. (ENG.). 336p. (J). (gr. 5-9). 17.99 *(978-1-5344-6004-1(7),* McElderry, Margaret K. Bks.) McElderry, Margaret K. Bks.
—The Unicorn in the Barn. Ogburn, Jacqueline. (ENG.). 304p. (J). (gr. 3-7). 2019. pap. 7.99 *(978-1-328-59585-0(4),* 1730758); 2017. 16.99 *(978-0-544-76112-4(X),* 1634613) Houghton Mifflin Harcourt Publishing Co. (HMH Books For Young Readers).
Green, Rich. The Best Book Ever. Logan, Amy. 2018. (ENG.). 34p. (J). pap. 9.99 *(978-1-7249-4043-8(0))* CreateSpace Independent Publishing Platform.
Green, Ruth. Stanley's Plan: The Birthday Surprise. 2015. (ENG.). 32p. (J). (gr. -1-3). 16.95 *(978-1-84976-305-9(4))* Tate Publishing, Ltd. GBR. Dist: Hachette Bk. Group.
Green, Sarah. Anna Strong: A Spy During the American Revolution. Marsh, Sarah Glenn. 2020. (ENG.). 40p. (J). (gr. -1-3). 18.99 *(978-1-4197-3419-9(9),* Abrams Bks. for Young Readers) Abrams, Inc.
—Brave Clara Barton. Murphy, Frank. 2018. (Step into Reading Ser.). (ENG.). 48p. (J). (gr. k-3). pap. 4.99 *(978-1-5247-1557-1(3));* lib. bdg. 12.99 *(978-1-5247-1558-8(1))* Random Hse. Children's Bks. (Random Hse. Bks. for Young Readers).
—Dorothea Lange. Weatherford, Carole Boston. 2017. (ENG.). 32p. (J). (gr. -1-3). 16.99 *(978-0-8075-1699-7(6),* 807516996) Whitman, Albert & Co.
—Elizabeth Warren: Nevertheless, She Persisted. Wood, Susan. 2018. (ENG.). 48p. (J). (gr. 1-4). 18.99 *(978-1-4197-3162-4(9),* Abrams Bks. for Young Readers) Abrams, Inc.
—Fight of the Century: Alice Paul Battles Woodrow Wilson for the Vote. Rosenstock, Barb. 2020. 40p. (J). (gr. 2-5). 18.99 *(978-1-62979-908-7(4),* Calkins Creek) Boyds Mills Pr.
—Papa Put a Man on the Moon. Dempsey, Kristy. 2019. 32p. (J). (gr. -1-3). 17.99 *(978-0-7352-3074-3(9),* Dial Bks) Penguin Young Readers Group.
Green, Sheldon. There Is a Place... Green, Kelly. 2019. (ENG.). 24p. (J). pap. 9.49 *(978-1-7956-5651-1(4))* Independently Published.
Green, Sue. The Little Bear Who Didn't Want to Hibernate. Richter, Bernd & Richter, Susan. 2003. 42p. pap. 9.95 *(978-1-931353-10-6(7))* Saddle Pal Creations, Inc.
Green, Timothy, II, et al. Avengers Undercover: the Complete Collection. 2018. (Avengers Undercover: the Complete Collection: 1). (ENG.). 224p. (YA). (gr. 8-17). pap. 24.99 *(978-1-302-91393-9(X))* Marvel Worldwide, Inc.
Green, Timothy, et al. Trollhunters: Tales of Arcadia — The Felled. del Toro, Guillermo & Hamilton, Richard. 2018. (ENG.). 72p. (J). (gr. 5). pap. 10.99 *(978-1-5067-0290-2(2))* Dark Horse Comics.
Green, Timothy, jt. illus. see Sienkiewicz, Bill.
Green, Yuko. The Boy Who Drew Cats & Other Japanese Fairy Tales. Hearn, Lafcadio et al. 2012. (Dover Children's Thrift Classics Ser.). (ENG.). 64p. (J). (gr. 3-8). pap. 3.00 *(978-0-486-40348-9(3))* Dover Pubns., Inc.
—Winter Is for Whales: A Book of Hawaiian Seasons. Hirschi, Ron. 2007. (ENG.). 36p. (J). (gr. -1-3). *(978-1-59700-504-3(5))* Island Heritage Publishing.
Greenagel, Frank L., photos by. Think Like a Photographer! How to Take Better Pictures Than Anyone in Your Family. 2006. (J). *(978-1-59336-766-4(X))* Mondo Publishing.
Greenan, Amy & Garvey, Brian. The Bell Witch: Ghost of Tennessee. Bougie, Matt. 2016. (American Legends & Folktales Ser.). 32p. (J). (gr. 3-3). pap. 10.58 *(978-1-5026-2220-4(3))* Cavendish Square Publishing LLC.
Greenaway, Frank & Burton, Jane, photos by. Hamster. Rayner, Matthew & BVetMed MRCVS Staff. 2004. (I Am Your Pet Ser.). 32p. (gr. k-4). lib. bdg. 27.00 *(978-0-8368-4104-6(2),* Gareth Stevens Learning Library) Stevens, Gareth Publishing LLLP.
Greenaway, Frank, jt. photos by see Burton, Jane.
Greenaway, Kate. The Pied Piper of Hamelin - Illustrated by Kate Greenaway. Browning, Robert. 2016. (ENG.). (J). (gr. 3-7). *(978-1-4733-3484-7(5))* Read Bks.
Greenaway, Kate. A Apple Pie - Illustrated by Kate Greenaway. Greenaway, Kate. 2016. (ENG.). (J). *(978-1-4733-3499-1(3))* Read Bks.
Greenberg, Isabel. The Ancient Egyptians. Greenberg, Imogen. 2016. (Discover... Ser.). (ENG.). 32p. (J). (gr. 3-7). 14.99 *(978-1-84780-855-4(7),* Frances Lincoln Children's Bks.) Quarto Publishing Group UK GBR. Dist: Hachette Bk. Group.
—A Hundred Billion Trillion Stars. Fishman, Seth. (ENG.). 40p. (J). (gr. -1-3). 2020. pap. 8.99 *(978-0-06-298178-3(1));* 2017. 17.99 *(978-0-06-245578-9(8))* HarperCollins Pubs. (Greenwillow Bks.).
—The Ocean in Your Bathtub. Fishman, Seth. 2020. (ENG.). 40p. (J). (gr. -1-3). 17.99 *(978-0-06-295336-0(2),* Greenwillow Bks.) HarperCollins Pubs.
—Power Up. Fishman, Seth. 2019. (ENG.). 40p. (J). (gr. -1-3). 17.99 *(978-0-06-245579-6(6),* Greenwillow Bks.) HarperCollins Pubs.
—The Secrets of Tutankhamun: Egypt's Boy King & His Incredible Tomb. Cleveland-Peck, Patricia. 2018. (ENG.). 64p. (J). 18.99 *(978-1-68119-712-8(X),* 900182278, Bloomsbury Children's Bks.) Bloomsbury Publishing USA.
Greenberg, Melanie Hope. Americanly. Sutton, Lynn Parrish. 2018. (ENG.). 30p. (J). 11.99 *(978-1-61067-511-6(8))* Kane Miller.
—Down in the Subway, 1 vol. Cohen, Miriam. 2003. (ENG.). 32p. (J). (gr. k-3). pap. 6.95 *(978-1-932065-24-4(5));* 15.95 *(978-1-932065-08-4(3))* Star Bright Bks., Inc.
Greenberg, Melanie Hope. Aunt Lilly's Laundromat. Greenberg, Melanie Hope. 2016. (ENG.). (J). (gr. k-3). pap. 9.99 *(978-1-68186-681-9(1),* StarWalk Kids Media) Isabella Products, Inc.
Greenberg, Nicki. The Naughtiest Reindeer. Greenberg, Nicki. 2014. (ENG.). 32p. (J). (gr. -1-k). 15.99 *(978-1-74331-304-6(7))* Allen & Unwin AUS. Dist: Independent Pubs. Group.
—Teddy Took the Train. Greenberg, Nicki. 2015. (ENG.). 32p. (J). (gr. -1-1). 15.99 *(978-1-76011-213-4(5))* Allen & Unwin AUS. Dist: Independent Pubs. Group.
Greenblatt, C. H. & Reiss, William. Show Me the Bunny! Banks, Steven. 2004. (Spongebob Squarepants Ser.). 32p. (J). 11.65 *(978-0-7569-5643-1(9))* Perfection Learning Corp.
—Show Me the Bunny! Banks, Steven & Hillenburg, Stephen. 2004. (SpongeBob SquarePants Ser.: 3). (ENG.). 32p. (J). pap. 3.99 *(978-0-689-86485-8(X),* Simon Spotlight/Nickelodeon) Simon Spotlight/Nickelodeon.
Greenburg, Nicki. An Octopus Has Deadly Spit. Greenburg, Nicki. 2007. (It's True! Ser.). (ENG.). 96p. (J). (gr. 3-6). 18.69 *(978-1-55451-078-8(3),* 9781554510788) Annick Pr., Ltd. CAN. Dist: Children's Plus, Inc.
Greene, Hamilton. Rin Tin Tin & the Lost Indian. Hill, Monica. 2011. 28p. pap. 35.95 *(978-1-258-00567-2(0))* Literary Licensing, LLC.
Greene, Jarad. Scullion: A Dishwasher's Guide to Mistaken Identity. Greene, Jarad. 2020. (Scullion Ser.). (ENG.). 186p. (YA). pap. 19.99 ***(978-1-62010-753-9(8),*** Lion Forge) Oni Pr., Inc.
Greene, Judybeth. Mommy, Open up the Secrets of the World. 2005. (J). pap. 9.95 *(978-1-932672-76-3(1))* Outskirts Pr., Inc.
Greene, Kelly Evelyn. Oscar, the Inquisitive Spider. Evans, Barbara Greene. 2013. (ENG.). 45p. (J). pap. 24.95 *(978-1-4787-1779-9(3))* Outskirts Pr., Inc.
Greene, Sanford. Amphibians' End (a Kulipari Novel #3) Pryce, Trevor. 2016. (ENG.). 304p. (J). (gr. 3-7). pap. 8.95 *(978-1-4197-2194-6(1),* Amulet Bks.) Abrams, Inc.
—Everything You Read. Dezago, Todd. 2010. (Spider-Man Ser.: No. 4). (ENG.). 24p. (J). (gr. 2-6). lib. bdg. 27.07 *(978-1-59961-776-3(5),* 13636, Marvel Age) Spotlight.
—Playing Hero. Sumerak, Marc. 2010. (Spider-Man Ser.: No. 4). (ENG.). 24p. (J). (gr. 2-6). lib. bdg. 27.07 *(978-1-59961-778-7(1),* 13638, Marvel Age) Spotlight.
—The Rainbow Serpent: A Kulipari Novel. Pryce, Trevor & Naftali, Joel. (ENG.). (J). (gr. 3-7). 2015. 320p. pap. 8.95 *(978-1-4197-1657-7(3));* 2014. 301p. 15.95 *(978-1-4197-1309-5(4))* Abrams, Inc. (Amulet Bks.).
Greene, Sanford & Bondoc, Elmo. Power Man & Iron Fist Vol. 3: Street Magic. 2017. (ENG.). 136p. (YA). (gr. 8-17). pap. 17.99 *(978-1-302-90539-2(2))* Marvel Worldwide, Inc.
Greene, Soukaina Lalla. Samad in the Desert: Bilingual English-Bemba Edition. Umar, Mohammed & Siulapwa, Christopher Kaule. 2020. (Samad in the Desert Ser.). (BEM.). 24p. (J). pap. ***(978-1-912450-29-9(1))*** Salaam Publishing.
—Samad in the Desert: English-Afrikaans Bilingual Edition. Umar, Mohammed. Simes, Wyno, tr. 2020. (Samad in the Desert Ser.). (AFR.). 24p. (J). pap. ***(978-1-912450-37-4(2))*** Salaam Publishing.
—Samad in the Desert: English-Chichewa Bilingual Edition. Umar, Mohammed. Masamba, Maureen Lynda, tr. 2020. (Samad in the Desert Ser.). (NYA.). 24p. (J). pap. ***(978-1-912450-41-1(0))*** Salaam Publishing.
—Samad in the Desert: English-Kinyarwanda Bilingual Edition. Umar, Mohammed. Mudacumura, Fiston, tr. 2020. (Samad in the Desert Ser.). (KIN.). 24p. (J). pap. ***(978-1-912450-39-8(9))*** Salaam Publishing.
—Samad in the Desert: English-Sesotho Bilingual Edition. Umar, Mohammed. Khumalo, Virginia, tr. 2020. (Samad in the Desert Ser.). (SOT.). 24p. (J). pap. ***(978-1-912450-31-2(3))*** Salaam Publishing.
—Samad in the Desert: English-Xhosa Bilingual Edition. Umar, Mohammed. Saliwa-Mogale, Ncebakazi Faith, tr. 2020. (Samad in the Desert Ser.). (XHO.). 24p. (J). pap. ***(978-1-912450-35-0(6))*** Salaam Publishing.
—Samad in the Desert: English-Zulu Bilingual Edition. Umar, Mohammed. Zungu Oshin, Glenrose Nonhlala, tr. 2020. (Samad in the Desert Ser.). (ZUL.). 24p. (J). pap. ***(978-1-912450-33-6(X))*** Salaam Publishing.
Greene, Soukaina Lalla. Samad in the Desert (English - Amharic Bilingual Edition) Umar, Mohammed. Beyene, Brook, tr. 2019. (ENG.). 24p. (J). pap. *(978-1-912450-24-4(0))* Salaam Publishing.
—Samad in the Desert (English - Oromo Bilingual Edition) Umar, Mohammed. Tedla, Berhanu, tr. 2019. (ENG.). 24p. (J). pap. *(978-1-912450-20-6(8))* Salaam Publishing.
—Samad in the Desert (English - Swahili Bilingual Edition) Umar, Mohammed. Rajab, Ahmed, tr. 2019. (ENG.). 24p. (J). pap. *(978-1-912450-26-8(7))* Salaam Publishing.
—Samad in the Desert (English - Tigrinya Bilingual Edition) Umar, Mohammed. Markos, Tewodros, tr. 2019. (ENG.). 24p. (J). pap. *(978-1-912450-22-0(4))* Salaam Publishing.
Greene, Soukaina Lalla. Samad in the Desert. English-Somali Bilingual Edition. Umar, Mohammed. Hassan, Mohammed Sh, tr. 2020. (SOM.). 24p. (J). pap. ***(978-1-912450-60-2(7))*** Salaam Publishing.
—Samad in the Forest: English-Bemba Bilingual Edition. Umar, Mohammed. Siulapwa, Christopher Kaule, tr. 2020. (Samad in the Forest Ser.). (BEM.). 26p. (J). pap. ***(978-1-912450-28-2(3))*** Salaam Publishing.
—Samad in the Forest: English-Luo Bilingual Edition. Umar, Mohammed. Atoh, Fred Ochieng, tr. 2020. (Samad in the Forest Ser.). (LUO.). 26p. (J). pap. ***(978-1-912450-27-5(5))*** Salaam Publishing.
—Samad in the Forest: English-Sesotho Bilingual Edition. Umar, Mohammed. Khumalo, Virginia, tr. 2020. (Samad in the Forest Ser.). (SOT.). 26p. (J). pap. ***(978-1-912450-30-5(5))*** Salaam Publishing.
—Samad in the Forest: English-Somali Bilingual Edition. Umar, Mohammed. Hassan, Mohammed Ali, tr. 2020. (Samad in the Forest Ser.). (SOM.). 26p. (J). pap. ***(978-1-912450-59-6(3))*** Salaam Publishing.
—Samad in the Forest: English-Xhosa Bilingual Edition. Umar, Mohammed. Saliwa-Mogale, Ncebakazi Faith, tr. 2020. (Samad in the Forest Ser.). (XHO.). 26p. (J). pap. ***(978-1-912450-34-3(8))*** Salaam Publishing.
—Samad in the Forest: English-Zulu Bilingual Edition. Umar, Mohammed. Glenrose Nonhlala, Zungu Oshin, tr. 2020. (Samad in the Forest Ser.). (ZUL.). 26p. (J). pap. ***(978-1-912450-32-9(1))*** Salaam Publishing.
Greene, Soukaina Lalla. Samad in the Forest (English - Amharic Bilingual Edition) Umar, Mohammed. Beyene, Brook, tr. 2019. (ENG.). 26p. (J). pap. *(978-1-912450-23-7(2))* Salaam Publishing.
—Samad in the Forest (English - Oromo Bilingual Edition) Umar, Mohammed. Tedla, Berhanu, tr. 2019. (ENG.). 26p. (J). pap. *(978-1-912450-19-0(4))* Salaam Publishing.
—Samad in the Forest (English - Swahili Bilingual Edition) Umar, Mohammed. Rajab, Ahmed, tr. 2019. (ENG.). 26p. (J). pap. *(978-1-912450-25-1(9))* Salaam Publishing.
—Samad in the Forest (English - Tigrinya Bilingual Edition) Umar, Mohammed. Markos, Tewodros, tr. 2019. (ENG.). 26p. (J). pap. *(978-1-912450-21-3(6))* Salaam Publishing.
Greeneish, Susan. Animal Baths: Wild & Wonderful Ways Animals Get Clean! Fielding, Beth. 2009. 48p. (J). (gr. -1-3). 14.95 *(978-0-9797455-2-2(7))* EarlyLight Bks., Inc.
—Animal Eggs: An Amazing Clutch of Mysteries & Marvels. Cusick, Dawn & O'Sullivan, Joanne. 2011. 48p. (J). (gr. -1-3). 14.95 *(978-0-9797455-3-9(5))* EarlyLight Bks., Inc.
Greener, Yvonne M. Hitheranyon the Friendly Dragon: And His Monarch Butterfly Friends. Di Matteo, Argaille a. 2019. (ENG.). 52p. (J). pap. 23.95 ***(978-1-4624-1281-5(5),*** Inspiring Voices) Author Solutions, Inc.
Greenes, Shimra. My Twin Brother. Kleiman, Deanna M. 2012. 24p. pap. 9.13 *(978-0-615-35370-8(3))* TwinsBooks.
Greene's 29 after school art students, K. Lemurs! Marino, Angie. 2013. 46p. pap. 11.99 *(978-0-9892732-0-6(2))* Illustrate to Educate.
Greenfelder, Jill. A Ride on the Monster's Back. Bogel, Rachel Anne. 2008. 28p. pap. 15.99 *(978-1-59858-752-4(8))* Dog Ear Publishing, LLC.
Greenfelder, Jill & Rosado, Veronica. The Matador Who Ran Away from the Spider. Schmickl, Angela. 2015. (ENG.). 26p. (J). (gr. k-4). pap. *(978-0-9925941-0-7(3))* Schmickl, Angela.
Greengaard, Alex. Itty Bitty Birdie. Lister, Tresina. 2006. 20p. (J). per. 12.95 *(978-0-9791171-0-7(0))* Lister, Tresina.
Greenhalgh, Rachel. A Is for Anteater! Cook, Bob. 2011. 36p. pap. 24.95 *(978-1-4626-4035-5(4))* America Star Bks.
Greenhead, Bill. A-Hunting We Will Go. Fuerst, Jeffrey B. 2010. (Rising Readers Ser.). (J). 3.49 *(978-1-60719-684-6(0))* Newmark Learning LLC.
—Adaptation & Biodiversity: Prime Bridges Edition. Worth, Richard. 2013. (Prime Ser.). (YA). (gr. 6-8). pap. *(978-1-4509-9691-4(4))* Benchmark Education Co.
—Adaptations & Biodiversity: Bridges Edition, Set Of 10. Worth, Richard. 2013. (Prime Plus Ser.). (J). (gr. 6-8). 99.00 net. *(978-1-4509-9940-3(9))* Benchmark Education Co.
—Adaptations & Biodiversity: Set Of 10. Worth, Richard. 2013. (Prime Plus Ser.). (J). (gr. 6-8). 99.00 net. *(978-1-4509-9916-8(6))* Benchmark Education Co.
—Androcles & the Lion: Classic Tales Series. Adams, Alison. 2011. (Classic Tales Ser.). (J). *(978-1-936258-60-4(9))* Benchmark Education Co.
—The Baker. Koons, Linda. 2015. (Early Rising Readers Ser.). (J). (gr. -1-k). 5.83 *(978-1-4788-1590-7(6))* Newmark Learning LLC.
—Big Truck. Lindeen, Mary. 2015. (Early Rising Readers Ser.). (J). (gr. -1-k). 5.83 *(978-1-4788-1709-3(7))* Newmark Learning LLC.
—Bingo. Fuerst, Jeffrey B. 2010. (Rising Readers Ser.). (J). 3.49 *(978-1-60719-687-7(5))* Newmark Learning LLC.
—Bingo, Come Home! Fuerst, Jeffrey B. 2009. (Reader's Theater Nursery Rhymes & Songs Set B Ser.). 48p. (J). pap. *(978-1-60859-151-0(4))* Benchmark Education Co.
—Brer Rabbit Hears a Noise: Classic Tales Series. Adams, Alison. 2011. (Classic Tales Ser.). (J). *(978-1-936258-64-2(1))* Benchmark Education Co.

G

—El Camión Grande. Lindeen, Mary. 2016. (Early Rising Readers Ser.). (SPA.). (J). (gr. -1). 6.67 *(978-1-4788-3706-0(3))* Newmark Learning LLC.

—Cell Structure & Function: Bridges Edition, Set Of 10. Montgomery, Heather. 2013. (Prime Plus Ser.). (J). (gr. 6-8). 99.00 net. *(978-1-4509-9938-0(7))* Benchmark Education Co.

—Cell Structure & Function: Prime Bridges Edition. Montgomery, Heather. 2013. (Prime Ser.). (YA). (gr. 6-8). pap. *(978-1-4509-9689-1(2))* Benchmark Education Co.

—Cell Structure & Function: Set Of 10. Montgomery, Heather. 2013. (Prime Plus Ser.). (J). (gr. 6-8). 99.00 net. *(978-1-4509-9914-4(X))* Benchmark Education Co.

—Chuck, Woodchuck, Chuck! Fuerst, Jeffrey B. 2009. (Reader's Theater Nursery Rhymes & Songs Set B Ser.). 48p. (J). pap. *(978-1-60859-152-7(2))* Benchmark Education Co.

—Cinderella: Classic Tales Edition. Smith, Carrie. 2011. (Classic Tales Ser.). (J). *(978-1-936258-77-2(3))* Benchmark Education Co.

—Cinderella - 6 Pack: Set of 6 with Common Core Teacher Materials. 2015. (Classic Tales Ser.). (J). (gr. k-1). 39.00 *(978-1-5125-8330-4(8))* Benchmark Education Co.

—The Crow & the Pitcher: Classic Tales Series. Smith, Carrie. 2011. (Classic Tales Ser.). (J). *(978-1-936258-73-4(0))* Benchmark Education Co.

—Goldilocks & the Three Bears: Classic Tales Edition. Smith, Carrie. 2011. (Classic Tales Ser.). (J). *(978-1-936258-61-1(7))* Benchmark Education Co.

—Hercules & the Stables - 6 Pack: Set of 6 with Common Core Teacher Materials. 2015. (Classic Tales Ser.). (J). (gr. k-1). 39.00 *(978-1-5125-8344-1(8))* Benchmark Education Co.

—Heredity & Genetics: Bridges Edition, Set Of 10. Kestral, Ted. 2013. (Prime Plus Ser.). (J). (gr. 6-8). 99.00 net. *(978-1-4509-9939-7(5))* Benchmark Education Co.

—Heredity & Genetics: Prime Bridges Edition. Kestral, Ted. 2013. (Prime Ser.). (YA). (gr. 6-8). pap. *(978-1-4509-9690-7(6))* Benchmark Education Co.

—Heredity & Genetics: Set Of 10. Kestral, Ted. 2013. (Prime Plus Ser.). (J). (gr. 6-8). 99.00 net. *(978-1-4509-9915-1(8))* Benchmark Education Co.

—Hodja y la Sopa. Fuerst, Jeffrey B. 2016. (Jump into Genre Ser.). (SPA.). (J). (gr. 2). 5.25 *(978-1-4788-3612-4(1))* Newmark Learning LLC.

—How the Turtle Cracked Its Shell: Classic Tales Edition. Adams, Alison. 2011. (Classic Tales Ser.). (J). *(978-1-936258-58-1(7))* Benchmark Education Co.

—The Lion & the Rabbit: Classic Tales Edition. Smith, Carrie. 2011. (Classic Tales Ser.). (J). *(978-1-936258-65-9(X))* Benchmark Education Co.

—Mr. Jitters & the Sleep Machine: Set Of 6. Fuerst, Jeffrey B. 2014. (Shared Reading Foundations Ser.). (J). (gr. 1). 36.00 net. *(978-1-4900-0039-8(9))* Benchmark Education Co.

—Mr. Jitters & the Sleep Machine Book Set. Fuerst, Jeffrey B. 2014. (Shared Reading Foundations Ser.). (J). (gr. 1). 72.00 net. *(978-1-4900-0009-1(7))* Benchmark Education Co.

—The Nature of Life: Bridges Edition, Set Of 10. Simpson, Kathleen. 2013. (Prime Plus Ser.). (J). (gr. 6-8). 99.00 net. *(978-1-4509-9937-3(9))* Benchmark Education Co.

—The Nature of Life: Prime Bridges Edition. Simpson, Kathleen. 2013. (Prime Ser.). (YA). (gr. 6-8). pap. *(978-1-4509-9688-4(4))* Benchmark Education Co.

—The Nature of Life: Set Of 10. Simpson, Kathleen. 2013. (Prime Plus Ser.). (J). (gr. 6-8). 99.00 net. *(978-1-4509-9913-7(1))* Benchmark Education Co.

—Old MacDonald. Fuerst, Jeffrey B. 2010. (Rising Readers Ser.). (J). 3.49 *(978-1-60719-694-5(8))* Newmark Learning LLC.

—The Old Woman Who Lived in a Shoe. Fuerst, Jeffrey B. 2010. (Rising Readers Ser.). (J). 3.49 *(978-1-60719-703-4(0))* Newmark Learning LLC.

—One Frosty Night at the Farm: Set Of 6. Parkes, Brenda. 2014. (Shared Reading Foundations Ser.). (J). (gr. 1). 36.00 net. *(978-1-4900-0047-3(X))* Benchmark Education Co.

—One Frosty Night at the Farm Book Set. Parkes, Brenda. 2014. (Shared Reading Foundations Ser.). (J). (gr. 1). 72.00 net. *(978-1-4900-0017-6(8))* Benchmark Education Co.

—El Panadero. Koons, Linda. 2016. (Early Rising Readers Ser.). (SPA.). (J). (gr. -1). 6.67 *(978-1-4788-3684-1(9))* Newmark Learning LLC.

—Peter Pumpkin Eater. Fuerst, Jeffrey B. 2010. (Rising Readers Ser.). (J). 3.49 *(978-1-60719-705-8(7))* Newmark Learning LLC.

—Peter Pumpkin Eater Loses His Appetite. Fuerst, Jeffrey B. 2009. (Reader's Theater Nursery Rhymes & Songs Set B Ser.). 48p. (J). pap. *(978-1-60859-164-0(6))* Benchmark Education Co.

—Ratón de Ciudad y Ratón de Campo. Swain, Cynthia. 2016. (Jump into Genre Ser.). (SPA.). (J). (gr. 2). 5.25 *(978-1-4788-3611-7(3))* Newmark Learning LLC.

—Super Dog. O'Dea, Lori. 2017. (Text Connections Guided Close Reading Ser.). (J). (gr. k). *(978-1-4900-1770-9(4))* Benchmark Education Co.

—Superheroes of the Constitution: Action & Adventure Stories about Real-Life Heroes. Bedell, J. M. 2017. (ENG.). 112p. (J). pap. 9.99 *(978-1-63158-233-2(X)*, Racehorse Publishing) Skyhorse Publishing Co., Inc.

—The Three Little Pigs: Classic Tales Edition. Adams, Alison. 2011. (Classic Tales Ser.). (J). *(978-1-936258-71-0(4))* Benchmark Education Co.

—Why Mosquitoes Buzz in People's Ears: Classic Tales Edition. Adams, Alison. 2011. (Classic Tales Ser.). (J). *(978-1-936258-69-7(2))* Benchmark Education Co.

—A Wolf, a Girl, & Her Grandma. Adams, Alison. 2014. (Text Connections Ser.). (J). (gr. k-1). *(978-1-4900-1798-3(4))* Benchmark Education Co.

—A Wolf, a Girl, & Her Grandma - 6 Pack: Set of 6 with Teacher Materials Common Core Edition. Adams, Alison. 2017. (Text Connections Guided Close Reading Ser.). (J). (gr. k-1). 40.00 *(978-1-5021-5485-9(4))* Benchmark Education Co.

—The Woman Who Lived in a Shoe. Fuerst, Jeffrey B. 2009. (Reader's Theater Nursery Rhymes & Songs Set B Ser.). 48p. (J). pap. *(978-1-60859-172-5(7))* Benchmark Education Co.

—El Zorro y el Perro Mapache. Swain, Cynthia. 2016. (Jump into Genre Ser.). (SPA.). (J). (gr. 3). 5.25 *(978-1-4788-3621-6(0))* Newmark Learning LLC.

Greenhead, Bill, jt. illus. see Anderson, Nicola.

Greenleaf, Lisa. Women of the Constitution State: 25 Connecticut Women You Should Know. Mayr, Diane & Sisters, Write. 2012. 136p. (J). pap. 16.00 *(978-0-9842549-1-0(9))* Apprentice Shop Bks., LLC.

—Women of the Granite State: 25 New Hampshire Women You Should Know. Buell, Janet & Sisters, Write. 2012. 136p. (J). pap. 16.00 *(978-0-9842549-8-9(6))* Apprentice Shop Bks., LLC.

—Women of the Green Mountain State: 25 Vermont Women You Should Know. Lyman Schremmer, Patty. 2012. 136p. (J). pap. 16.00 *(978-0-9842549-5-8(1))* Apprentice Shop Bks., LLC.

—Women of the Ocean State: 25 Rhode Island Women You Should Know. Brennan, Linda Crotta. 2012. 136p. (J). pap. 16.00 *(978-0-9842549-7-2(8))* Apprentice Shop Bks., LLC.

—Women of the Pine Tree State: 25 Maine Women You Should Know. Murphy, Andrea & Ray, Joyce. 2012. 136p. (J). pap. 16.00 *(978-0-9842549-6-5(X))* Apprentice Shop Bks., LLC.

—Women of the Prairie State: 25 Illinois Women You Should Know. Darragh, Marty & Pitkin, Jo. 2012. 136p. (J). pap. 16.00 *(978-0-9842549-2-7(7))* Apprentice Shop Bks., LLC.

Greenlee, Carolyn Wing. Speaking for Fire. BlueWolf, James Don. 2007. (ENG.). 44p. (gr. 2-7). per. 12.95 *(978-1-887400-31-2(1))* Earthen Vessel Production, Inc.

Greenseid, Diane. And Then It Rained ... ... & Then the Sun Came Out... Dragonwagon, Crescent. 2014. (ENG.). 40p. (J). (gr. -1-3). 19.99 *(978-1-4814-2529-2(3)*, Atheneum Bks. for Young Readers) Simon & Schuster Children's Publishing.

—Barn Storm. Ghigna, Charles & Ghigna, Debra. 2010. (Step into Reading Ser.). 32p. (J). (gr. -1-1). pap. 4.99 *(978-0-375-86114-7(9)*, Random Hse. Bks. for Young Readers) Random Hse. Children's Bks.

—Waynetta & the Cornstalk: A Texas Fairy Tale. Ketteman, Helen. 2012. (J). *(978-1-61913-152-1(8))* Weigl Pubs., Inc.

Greenstein, Elaine. The Mitten Tree. Christiansen, Candace. (ENG.). 32p. 2009. (J). (gr. -1-1). pap. 13.95 *(978-1-55591-733-3(X))*; 2008. pap. 7.95 *(978-1-55591-698-5(8))* Fulcrum Publishing.

Greenstein, Susan. A Big Quiet House: A Yiddish Folktale from Eastern Europe. Forest, Heather. 2005. (ENG.). 32p. (J). (gr. k-3). 15.95 *(978-0-87483-462-8(7))* August Hse. Pubs., Inc.

Greenstein, Susan, jt. illus. see Gaber, Susan.

Greenwalt, Mary. Franz Schubert & his Merry Friends. Wheeler, Opal & Deucher, Sybil. 2008. 128p. (J). pap. 13.95 *(978-1-933573-13-7(9))* Zeezok Publishing, LLC.

—Handel: at the Court of Kings. Wheeler, Opal. 2006. 166p. per. 13.95 *(978-1-933573-03-8(1)*, 4481) Zeezok Publishing, LLC.

—Joseph Haydn: the Merry Little Peasant. Wheeler, Opal & Deucher, Sybil. 2005. 118p. per. 13.95 *(978-1-933573-00-7(7))* Zeezok Publishing, LLC.

—Ludwig Beethoven & the Chiming Tower Bells. Wheeler, Opal. 2005. 166p. per. 13.95 *(978-0-9746505-6-2(0))* Zeezok Publishing, LLC.

—Mozart the Wonder Boy. Wheeler, Opal & Deucher, Sybil. 2005. 127p. per. 13.95 *(978-0-9746505-3-1(6)*, 4355) Zeezok Publishing, LLC.

—Sebastian Bach: the Boy from Thuringia. Wheeler, Opal & Deucher, Sybil. l.t. ed. 2005. 126p. per. 13.95 *(978-0-9746505-1-7(X)*, 4354) Zeezok Publishing, LLC.

Greenway, Kate. The April Baby's Book of Tunes with the Story of How They Came to Be Written: 1900 (the First) Edition, Illustrated. Von Arnim, Elizabeth. 2019. (ENG.). 48p. (J). pap. 10.99 ***(978-1-0751-2187-6(6))*** Independently Published.

Greenwell, Alan. The Proud Hen. Naeem, Rashid. 2016. (Himalayan Tales Ser.: Vol. 3). (ENG.). (J). pap. *(978-0-9935235-2-6(8))* Himalayan Tales Pubns.

—The Sisters & the Giant: Himalayan Tales. Naeem, Rashid. 2018. (Himalayan Tales Ser.: Vol. 4). (ENG.). 36p. (J). pap. *(978-0-9935235-3-3(6))* Himalayan Tales Pubns.

Greenwood, Francesca. Girls & Goddesses: Stories of Heroines from Around the World. Don, Lari. 2016. (World of Stories Ser.). (ENG.). 120p. (J). (gr. 2-6). 26.65 *(978-1-5124-1317-5(8)*, 9781512413175, Darby Creek) Lerner Publishing Group.

—Magic & Misery: Traditional Tales from Around the World. Pearson, Maggie. 2016. (World of Stories Ser.). (ENG.). 176p. (J). (gr. 2-6). 26.65 *(978-1-5124-1319-9(4)*, 9781512413199, Darby Creek) Lerner Publishing Group.

Greenwood, Marion. Ho Fills the Rice Barrel. Sherer, Mary (Huston). 2012. 128p. 40.95 *(978-1-258-25056-0(X))*; pap. 25.95 *(978-1-258-25732-3(7))* Literary Licensing, LLC.

Greenwood, Sarah G. A Selected Collection of Rhymes for Inspection. Thoolen, Jai D. 2017. (ENG.). (J). pap. *(978-0-6482030-2-5(6))* picklepoetry.

Greer, Ana. Jules the Lighthouse Dog, 1. Custard, P. T. 2006. (ENG.). 32p. (J). 12.95 *(978-0-9785317-0-6(1))* Black Plum Bks.

Greer, Caitlin, jt. illus. see Greer, Karen.

Greer, Karen & Greer, Caitlin. The Kingdom of Slumber: Book One: Bedtime Stories for Children of All Ages. Greer, Gregg J. 2019. (Kingdom of Slumber Ser.: Vol. 1). (ENG.). 134p. (J). pap. 9.99 ***(978-1-4802-8302-2(9))*** CreateSpace Independent Publishing Platform.

Greer, Tica. The Lighthouse Summer, Greer, Hannah. 2009. 156p. pap. 24.95 *(978-1-60813-493-9(8))* America Star Bks.

Gregeory, Vicki. There's Nothing Wrong with Boys. Stratton, Erin. 2010. 26p. pap. 12.00 *(978-1-60911-021-5(8)*, Eloquent Bks.) Strategic Book Publishing & Rights Agency (SBPRA).

Gregg, Alayna. Bumble: The Busy Bees. Writers Club, Lake View & Stovall, Holly. 2019. (ENG.). 26p. (J). pap. 11.98 *(978-1-7930-7531-4(X))* Independently Published.

Gregg, Donna. Bloo the Bear Plays Hide & Seek. Gollman, Jen Whitney. 2019. (Bloo the Bear Ser.: Vol. 2). (ENG.). 46p. (J). pap. 12.99 ***(978-1-6983-9274-5(5))*** Independently Published.

Gregg, Sydni. Seagull & Sea Dragon. Gregg, Sydni. 2019. (ENG.). 40p. (J). (gr. -1-3). 17.99 *(978-1-5344-2048-9(7)*, Simon & Schuster/Paula Wiseman Bks.) Simon & Schuster/Paula Wiseman Bks.

Gregoire, Fabian. Los Ninos de la Mina. Gregoire, Fabian. Malagarriga, Carlos Fanlo, tr. 2006. (SPA.). 45p. (J). *(978-84-8470-234-4(0))* Corimbo, Editorial S.L.

Gregor, Cara. Kate & CICI: Build a Sandcastle. Zierenberg-Senge, Cary. 2018. (Kate & CICI Ser.: Vol. 1). (ENG.). 26p. (J). pap. 10.99 *(978-1-7329722-0-9(6))* Emilia, Cara Pr.

Gregor, Terril. Kids from Critter Cove. Dodson, Merilee. 2007. 48p. per. 24.95 *(978-1-4137-2644-2(5))* America Star Bks.

Gregori, Anthony. Meet the Itslts. l.t. ed. 2007. 40p. (J). lib. bdg. 9.99 *(978-0-9769360-1-5(1))* Adam Hill Pubns.

Gregori, Giuliana. Take Care. Rosenberg, Madelyne. 2018. (ENG.). 24p. (J). (gr. k-2). 12.99 *(978-0-8075-7732-5(4)*, 807577324) Whitman, Albert & Co.

Gregorio, Giuliana. Counting Rhymes. Brooks, Felicity. 2010. (Look & Say Board Bks). 12p. (J). bds. 8.99 *(978-0-7945-2779-2(5)*, Usborne) EDC Publishing.

—Finger Rhymes. Brooks, Felicity. 2010. (Rhyming Look & Say Ser.). 12p. (J). bds. 8.99 *(978-0-7945-2780-8(9)*, Usborne) EDC Publishing.

Gregorio, John L. Don't Lose Your Head. Devleeschouwer, Cheryl. 2019. (ENG.). 32p. (J). 14.99 *(978-0-578-47452-6(2))* DeVleeschouwer, Darren.

Gregory, Aaron John. Roaring, Rumbling Tattoo Dinosaurs: 50 Temporary Tattoos That Teach. Roehrig, Artemis. 2020. (Tattoos That Teach Ser.). (ENG.). 20p. (J). pap. 7.95 ***(978-1-63586-319-2(8)***, 626319) Storey Publishing, LLC.

—Super, Strong Tattoo Sharks: 50 Temporary Tattoos That Teach. Roehrig, Artemis. 2020. (Tattoos That Teach Ser.). (ENG.). 20p. (J). pap. 7.95 ***(978-1-63586-318-5(X)***, 626318) Storey Publishing, LLC.

Gregory, Dorothy Lake. The Box-Car Children. Warner, Gertrude Chandler. 2020. (ENG.). 64p. (J). (gr. 2-5). pap. 6.99 ***(978-1-4209-6966-5(8))*** Digireads.com Publishing.

—The Box-Car Children. Warner, Gertrude Chandler. 2019. (ENG.). 88p. (J). (gr. 1-5). 14.99 ***(978-1-5154-4203-5(9))***; pap. 6.49 ***(978-1-5154-4204-2(7))*** Jorge Pinto Bks. (Illustrated Bks.).

Gregory, Dorothy Lake. Jerry & Jean Detectors. Judson, Clara Ingram. 2007. (ENG.). 116p. (J). (gr. 4-7). 34.95 *(978-0-548-03300-5(5))* Kessinger Publishing, LLC.

Gregory, Fran. The Return of Gabriel. Armistead, John. 2004. 218p. (gr. 3-8). 17.45 *(978-0-7569-3460-6(5))* Perfection Learning Corp.

Gregory, Jenn. The Test. Gregory, Jenn. 2020. (ENG.). 24p. (J). pap. 12.99 ***(978-1-62586-174-0(5))*** Credo Hse. Pubs.

Gregory, Jenny. Labrador on the Lawn. Baglio, Ben M. & Daniels, Lucy. 2005. (Animal Ark Hauntings Ser.: No. 38). (ENG.). 144p. (J). (gr. 2-5). 3.99 *(978-0-439-68488-0(9))* Scholastic, Inc.

Gregory, Kosta. Makani & the Tiki Mikis. Leon, Mike P. 2018. (ENG.). 44p. (J). pap. 11.99 *(978-1-64204-919-0(0))* Primedia eLaunch LLC.

—Owlfred the Owl Learns to Fly. Foster, Caleb. 2018. (ENG.). 38p. (J). 22.00 *(978-1-64467-210-5(3))*; pap. 15.00 *(978-1-64467-208-2(1))* Primedia eLaunch LLC.

Gregory, Sally. The Strange Umbrella: And Other Stories. Blyton, Enid. 2013. 192p. (J). 9.95 *(978-1-84135-461-3(9))* Award Pubns. Ltd. GBR. Dist: Parkwest Pubns., Inc.

Greiman, Brett. Gatita y Yo. Wolfman, Judy. 2018. (Xist Kids Spanish Bks.). (SPA.). 32p. (J). (gr. -1-3). pap. 9.99 *(978-1-5324-0711-6(4))* Xist Publishing.

—Kitty & Me. Wolfman, Judy. 2017. (Reading Stars Ser.). (ENG.). 32p. (J). (gr. k-3). pap. 9.99 *(978-1-5324-0194-7(9))* Xist Publishing.

—Kitty & Me / Gatita y Yo. Wolfman, Judy. 2018. (Xist Kids Bilingual Spanish English Ser.). (ENG & SPA.). 32p. (J). (gr. -1-3). pap. 9.99 *(978-1-5324-0669-0(X))* Xist Publishing.

Greiner, Simon. The Short & Curly Guide to Life. Curly, Short & & Beard, Matt. 2018. (ENG.). 192p. (J). (gr. 2). 23.99 ***(978-0-14-379218-5(0)***, Puffin) Penguin Random Hse. AUS. Dist: Independent Pubs. Group.

Gremillion, Barry. Finding Rover. Allberti, Frances C. 2006. (J). per. *(978-0-9785937-1-1(5))* Open Pages Publishing.

Grenier, Daniel. The World of Penguins. Daigle, Evelyne. Wright, Genevieve, tr. from FRE. 2007. (ENG.). 48p. (J). (gr. 4-7). 18.95 *(978-0-88776-799-9(0)*, Tundra Bks.) Tundra Bks. CAN. Dist: Penguin Random Hse. LLC.

—The World of Penguins. Daigle, Evelyne. Wright, Geneviève, tr. from FRE. 2008. (ENG.). 48p. (J). (gr. 4-7). pap. 12.95 *(978-0-88776-947-4(0)*, Tundra Bks.) Tundra Bks. CAN. Dist: Penguin Random Hse. LLC.

Grenier, Denis. Muffy Was Fluffy. DuBois, Rikki Marie. 2019. (ENG.). 28p. (J). ***(978-1-5255-5649-4(5))***; pap. ***(978-1-5255-5650-0(9))*** FriesenPress.

Grepo, Sarah. All the Things You'll Do! Glavin, Kevin. 2012. 80p. 17.95 *(978-0-9825466-3-5(7))* Glavin, Kevin.

Greppi, Andrea. Finding Dory. Ferrari, Alessandro. 2020. (Disney & Pixar Movies Ser.). (ENG.). 52p. (J). (gr. 2-6). lib. bdg. 28.50 ***(978-1-5321-4548-3(9)***, 35195, Graphic Novels) Spotlight.

Gresham, Delia. The Little Brick House. Lael, Anita. 2012. 32p. pap. 24.95 *(978-1-4626-9374-0(1))*; 30p. 24.95 *(978-1-4626-5972-2(1))* America Star Bks.

Gressley, Madge. Emily Louise Boomtwoshiner. Grable, Diann L. 2019. (ENG.). 90p. (J). pap. 10.00 *(978-1-0702-0096-5(4))* Independently Published.

Gressley, Madge H. Lucky Day Tea Room. Meyer, Charleen H. 2019. (ENG.). 36p. (J). pap. 10.00 *(978-1-0923-6205-4(3))* Independently Published.

Greste, Peter, photos by. Owen & Mzee: The Language of Friendship. Hatkoff, Craig et al. 2006. (Owen & Mzee Ser.). (ENG., 40p. (J). (gr. -1-3). 18.99 *(978-0-439-89959-8(1)*, Scholastic Pr.) Scholastic, Inc.

—Owen & Mzee: The True Story of a Remarkable Friendship. Hatkoff, Craig et al. 2006. (Owen & Mzee Ser.). (ENG., 40p. (J). (gr. -1-3). 17.99 *(978-0-439-82973-1(9)*, Scholastic Pr.) Scholastic, Inc.

Gretta, J. Clemens. Flying Blackbirds. Burtis, Thomson. 2011. 256p. 47.95 *(978-1-258-07554-5(7))* Literary Licensing, LLC.

Gretter, J. Clemens. The Hidden Harbor Mystery, No. 14. Dixon, Franklin W. 2003. (Hardy Boys Ser.). (ENG.). 228p. (J). (gr. 4-7). 14.95 *(978-1-55709-272-4(9))* Applewood Bks.

Gretzer, John. A Touch of Magic. Cavanna, Betty. 2011. 188p. 42.95 *(978-1-258-07218-6(1))* Literary Licensing, LLC.

Greve, Hannah K. Move over! Princess Coming Through!, 1 vol. McCusker, Tammy. 2009. 34p. pap. 24.95 *(978-1-60749-803-2(0))* America Star Bks.

Greven, Doris. An Unusual Family: A Romani Folktale. Sijercic, Hedina. 2009. 28p. pap. *(978-0-9781707-7-6(6))* Magoria Bks.

Grey, Ada. I Love You Just the Way You Are. Salzano, Tammi. 2014. (ENG.). 32p. (J). (gr. -1-2). 16.99 *(978-1-58925-161-8(X))* Tiger Tales.

—The Moon Man. Harris, Isabel. 2018. (ENG.). 32p. (J). (gr. -1-2). 16.99 *(978-1-68010-078-5(5))* Tiger Tales.

—Party for Dads. Guillain, Adam & Guillain, Charlotte. 2019. (ENG.). 32p. (J). (gr. -1-k). pap. 12.99 *(978-1-4052-7750-1(5))* Egmont Bks., Ltd. GBR. Dist: Independent Pubs. Group.

—Poo in the Zoo. Smallman, Steve. 2015. (ENG.). 32p. (J). (gr. -1-2). 16.99 *(978-1-58925-197-7(0))* Tiger Tales.

—School for Dads. Adam, Guillain & Guillain, Charlotte. 2016. (ENG.). 32p. (J). (gr. -1-k). pap. 9.99 *(978-1-4052-7749-5(1))* Egmont Bks., Ltd. GBR. Dist: Independent Pubs. Group.

Grey, Ada. The Twelve Unicorns of Christmas. Knapman, Timothy. 2020. (ENG.). 32p. (J). (gr. -1-3). 17.99 ***(978-1-5344-8019-3(6)***, Aladdin) Simon & Schuster Children's Publishing.

Grey, Ada. The World Book Day Monster. Guillain, Adam & Guillain, Charlotte. 2019. (ENG.). 32p. (J). (gr. -1-k). pap. 12.99 *(978-1-4052-9185-9(0))* Egmont Bks., Ltd. GBR. Dist: Independent Pubs. Group.

Grey, Andrew. Max at School. Wells, Rosemary. 2017. (Max & Ruby Ser.). 32p. (J). (gr. 1-2). (ENG.). 14.99 *(978-0-515-15744-4(9))*; pap. 4.99 *(978-0-515-15743-7(0))* Penguin Young Readers Group. (Penguin Young Readers).

—Max's Bug. Wells, Rosemary. 2017. (Max & Ruby Ser.). (ENG.). 32p. (J). (gr. 1-2). pap. 4.99 *(978-0-515-15740-6(6)*, Penguin Young Readers) Penguin Young Readers Group.

—Max's Half Birthday. Wells, Rosemary. 2018. (Max & Ruby Ser.). 32p. (J). (gr. 1-2). 14.99 *(978-0-515-15747-5(3))*; pap. 3.99 *(978-0-515-15746-8(5))* Penguin Young Readers Group. (Penguin Young Readers).

—Max's Lunch. Wells, Rosemary. 2017. (Max & Ruby Ser.). (ENG.). 32p. (J). (gr. 1-2). pap. 3.99 *(978-0-515-15737-6(6)*, Penguin Young Readers) Penguin Young Readers Group.

—Pooh's Cleanup. Cecil, Lauren. 2011. (Disney Classic Pooh Ser.). (ENG.). 24p. (J). (gr. -1-3). 16.19 *(978-0-448-45558-7(7)*, Grosset & Dunlap) Penguin Publishing Group.

—A Rose for My Mother: A Memoir. Canfield, Nancy Lee. 2010. (ENG.). 300p. pap. 21.95 *(978-1-4502-3123-7(3))* iUniverse, Inc.

Grey, Elizabeth & Farcas, Fabiana. Christmas in Ballyyahoo: A Hilarious Fantasy for Children Ages 8-12. Kay, Jessie, ed. 2018. (Another Little Book from Ballyyahoo Ser.: Vol. 5). (ENG.). 86p. (J). pap. 6.99 *(978-1-7315-7263-9(8))* Independently Published.

—The Witch of Ballyyahoo: A Funny Witchy Fantasy Story for Children. Kay, Jessie, ed. 2018. (Another Little Book from Ballyyahoo Ser.: Vol. 3). (ENG.). 82p. (J). pap. 6.99 *(978-1-7904-6888-1(4))* Independently Published.

Grey, Emma. No Fireplace Is Needed. Anderson, Doree L. 2019. (ENG.). 38p. (J). pap. 9.50 ***(978-1-7032-1537-3(0))*** Independently Published.

Grey, Erika. The Alphabet Bears: Spook-Tales Collection. Grey, Erika. 2010. 127p. (YA). pap. 24.95 *(978-0-9790199-3-7(1))* PeDante Pr.

Grey, Mini. Into the Woods. Grey, Mini. Gardner, Lyn. 2009. (Eden Sisters Ser.). (ENG.). 448p. (J). (gr. 3-7). 8.99 *(978-0-440-42223-5(X)*, Yearling) Random Hse. Children's Bks.

Grezina, Margarita. Looks Like Love. Joseph, Terrica. 2018. (ENG.). 34p. (J). (gr. k-2). 16.99 *(978-1-970016-20-8(5))* Fruit Springs, LLC.

Gribbon, Sean & Jael. A Little Princess: With a Discussion of Generosity. Burnett, Frances Hodgson. Gribbon, Sean & Jael, trs. 2003. (Values in Action Illustrated Classics Ser.). (J). *(978-1-59203-050-7(5))* Learning Challenge, Inc.

Gribel, Christiane & Orlando. No Voy a Dormir/I Am Not Going to Sleep. Gribel, Christiane & Orlando. 2009. (ENG & SPA.). 40p. (J). (gr. -1-1). pap. 7.99 *(978-1-933032-51-1(0))* Lectorum Pubns., Inc.

Grice, Steve. Beath Becomes Her. Pike, Matt J. Chant, Lisa, ed. 2017. (Zombie Rizing Ser.: Vol. 5). (ENG.). 80p. (J). (gr. 3-6). pap. 10.00 ***(978-1-64007-651-8(4))*** Primedia eLaunch LLC.

—Beath Defying. Pike, Matt J. Chant, Lisa, ed. 2017. (Zombie Rizing Ser.: Vol. 6). (ENG.). 86p. (J). (gr. 3-6). pap. 10.00 ***(978-1-64007-652-5(2))*** Primedia eLaunch LLC.

—Creeping Beath. Pike, Matt J. Chant, Lisa, ed. 2017. (Zombie Rizing Ser.: Vol. 4). (ENG.). 82p. (J). (gr. 3-6). pap. 10.00 ***(978-1-64007-650-1(6))*** Primedia eLaunch LLC.

—Life & Beath. Pike, Matt J. Chant, Lisa, ed. 2017. (Zombie Rizing Ser.: Vol. 3). (ENG.). 74p. (J). (gr. 3-6). pap. 10.00 **(978-1-64007-649-5(2))** Primedia eLaunch LLC.

—Scared to Beath. Pike, Matt J. Chant, Lisa, ed. 2016. (Zombie Rizing Ser.: Vol. 1). (ENG.). 70p. (J). (gr. 3-6). pap. 10.00 **(978-1-63587-750-2(4))** Primedia eLaunch LLC.

Grieb, Wendy. Monster Needs a Christmas Tree. Czajak, Paul. 2014. (Monster & Me Ser.). (ENG.). 32p. (J). (-k). 16.95 (978-1-938063-46-6(5), Mighty Media Kids) Mighty Media Pr.

—Monster Needs a Costume. Czajak, Paul. (Monster & Me Ser.). (ENG.). 32p. (J). (-k). 2014. 6.99 (978-1-938063-38-1(4)); 2013. 16.95 (978-1-938063-09-1(0)) Mighty Media Pr. (Mighty Media Kids).

—Monster Needs a Party. Czajak, Paul. 2015. (Monster & Me Ser.). (ENG.). 32p. (J). (-k). 16.95 (978-1-938063-55-8(4), Mighty Media Kids) Mighty Media Pr.

—Monster Needs His Sleep. Czajak, Paul. 2014. (Monster & Me Ser.). (ENG.). 32p. (J). (-k). 16.95 (978-1-938063-26-8(0), Mighty Media Kids) Mighty Media Pr.

—Monster Needs Your Vote. Czajak, Paul. 2015. (Monster & Me Ser.). (ENG.). 32p. (J). (gr. -1-3). 16.95 (978-1-938063-63-3(5), Mighty Media Kids) Mighty Media Pr.

Griego, Tony. AddUps Fun for All Seasons! Tuchman, Gail & Gray, Margaret. 2012. (Dover Little Activity Bks.). (ENG.). 32p. (J). (gr. k-3). pap. 1.50 (978-0-486-49860-7(3)) Dover Pubns., Inc.

—AddUps Going Places! Tuchman, Gail & Gray, Margaret. 2012. (Dover Little Activity Bks.). (ENG.). 32p. (J). (gr. k-3). pap. 1.50 (978-0-486-49861-4(1)) Dover Pubns., Inc.

—AddUps My Day! Tuchman, Gail & Gray, Margaret. 2012. (Dover Little Activity Bks.). (ENG.). 32p. (J). (gr. k-3). pap. 1.50 (978-0-486-49862-1(X)) Dover Pubns., Inc.

Grier, Gary. Don't Hit Me! Scholastic, Inc. Staff et al. 2004. (Just for You Ser.). (ENG.). 32p. (gr. k-1). pap. 3.99 (978-0-439-56860-9(9), Teaching Resources) Scholastic, Inc.

Grier, Geoffrey. The Shaman's Revenge: Based on the Arctic Diaries of Vilhjalmur Stefansson. Stefansson, Vilhjalmur & Irwin, Violet. 2011. 306p. 48.95 (978-1-258-05790-9(5)) Literary Licensing, LLC.

Grier, Laura. Flower Girl, 0 vols. Grier, Laura, photos by. Bottner, Barbara. 2012. (ENG.). 32p. (J). (gr. k-3). 16.99 (978-0-7614-6119-7(1), 9780761461197, Two Lions) Amazon Publishing.

Grieve, Walter G., jt. illus. see Noble, Edwin.

Grifalconi, Ann. Julio's Magic. Dorros, Arthur. 2005. (ENG.). 32p. (J). (gr. -1-4). 15.99 (978-0-06-029004-7(8)) HarperCollins Pubs.

—Lubuto Means Light. Williams, Karen Lynn. 2010. (ENG.). 32p. 16.95 (978-1-59078-716-8(1)) Boyds Mills Pr.

—Patrol: An American Soldier in Vietnam. Myers, Walter Dean. 2005. (ENG.). 40p. (J). (gr. 3-7). pap. 7.99 (978-0-06-073159-5(1)) HarperCollins Pubs.

Griff. Lilac Peabody & Bella Bright, No. 2. Dalton, Annie. 2009. (ENG.). 96p. (J). pap. 5.99 (978-0-00-713772-5(9), HarperCollins Children's Bks.) HarperCollins Pubs. Ltd. GBR. Dist: HarperCollins Pubs.

—Lilac Peabody & Charlie Chase, No. 3. Dalton, Annie. 2009. (ENG.). 96p. (J). pap. 5.99 (978-0-00-713773-2(7), HarperCollins Children's Bks.) HarperCollins Pubs. Ltd. GBR. Dist: HarperCollins Pubs.

—Lilac Peabody & Honeysuckle Hope, No. 4. Dalton, Annie. 2009. (ENG.). 96p. (J). (gr. 2-4). pap. 5.99 (978-0-00-713774-9(5), HarperCollins Children's Bks.) HarperCollins Pubs. Ltd. GBR. Dist: HarperCollins Pubs.

—Lilac Peabody & Sam Sparks, No. 1. Dalton, Annie. 2009. (ENG.). 80p. (J). pap. 5.99 (978-0-00-713771-8(0), HarperCollins Children's Bks.) HarperCollins Pubs. Ltd. GBR. Dist: HarperCollins Pubs.

Griffeth, Bunny. Heal of the Hand. Latimer, Kiki. 2012. 44p. (J). pap. 19.50 (978-1-58432-851-3(7)) Educa Vision Inc.

Griffin, Cheri. Snicker & Snore, 1 vol. Batton, Doris. 2010. 40p. pap. 24.95 (978-1-4489-6113-9(0)) PublishAmerica, Inc.

Griffin, Don. The Great Pigeon Race. Gail, Ginnie. 2008. 28p. per. 24.95 (978-1-4241-9457-5(1)) America Star Bks.

Griffin, Georgene. Dinosaurs, Meat-Eaters. 2004. (J). (978-1-59203-086-6(6)) Learning Challenge, Inc.

—Endangered Mammals. 2004. (J). (978-1-59203-089-7(0)) Learning Challenge, Inc.

Griffin, Georgene & Jael. Cool Wheels. 2004. (J). (978-1-59203-087-3(4)) Learning Challenge, Inc.

Griffin, Georgene, jt. illus. see McKee, Karen.

Griffin, Grant. Star Wars Dark Legends. Mann, George. 2020. (ENG.). 224p. (J). (gr. 3-7). 14.99 **(978-1-368-05733-2(0),** Disney Lucasfilm Press) Disney Publishing Worldwide.

Griffin, Grant. Star Wars Myths & Fables. Lucasfilm Press & Mann, George. 2019. (ENG.). 192p. (J). (gr. 3-7). 17.99 (978-1-368-04345-8(3), Disney Lucasfilm Press) Disney Publishing Worldwide.

Griffin, Hedley. How to Draw 101 Super Heroes. Top That!, ed. 2005. (ENG.). 48p. (J). per. (978-1-84510-738-3(1)) Top That! Publishing PLC.

Griffin, Jason. My Name Is Jason. Mine Too: Our Story. Our Way. Griffin, Jason. Reynolds, Jason. 2009. (ENG.). 96p. (J). (gr. 8-18). pap. 12.99 (978-0-06-154788-1(3), HarperTeen) HarperCollins Pubs.

Griffin, Jim. Legend of the Christmas Stocking: An Inspirational Story of a Wish Come True, 1 vol. Osborne, Rick. 2004. (ENG.). 32p. (J). 17.99 (978-0-310-70898-8(2)) Zonderkidz.

Griffin, Lisa. The Garden in My Mind Activity Guide: Lessons for Social Skill & Common Core Development. McCumbee, Stephanie. 2014. (ENG.). 48p. pap. 20.95 (978-1-934490-55-6(5)) Boys Town Pr.

Griffin, Lisa. I'll Never Get All of That Done! A Story about Planning & Prioritizing. Smith, Bryan. 2020. (Executive Function Ser.: 8). (ENG.). 32p. (J). (gr. k-3). pap. 10.95 **(978-1-944882-50-1(2))** Boys Town Pr.

Griffin, Lisa. Mindset Matters. Smith, Bryan. 2017. (Without Limits Ser.: 2). (ENG.). 32p. (J). (gr. k-5). pap. 10.95 (978-1-944882-12-9(X)) Boys Town Pr.

—Nonnie & I/ Nonnie y Yo. Hendricks, Savannah. 2017. (Xist Kids Bilingual Spanish English Ser.). (ENG & SPA.). 32p. (J). (gr. -1-3). pap. 9.99 (978-1-5324-0103-9(5)) Xist Publishing.

—What Were You Thinking? Learning to Control Your Impulses. Smith, Bryan. 2016. (ENG.). 32p. (J). pap. 10.95 (978-1-934490-96-9(2)) Boys Town Pr.

Griffin, Lisa M. Christmas: Jesus Is Born! Monge, Marlyn. 2018. 32p. (J). pap. (978-0-8198-1670-2(1)) Pauline Bks. & Media.

—The Garden in My Mind: Growing Through Positive Choices. McCumbee, Stephie. 2014. (ENG.). 40p. (J). pap. 12.95 (978-1-934490-54-9(7)) Boys Town Pr.

—How Did You Miss That? A Story Teaching Self-Monitoring. Smith, Bryan. 2019. (Executive Function Ser.: 7). (ENG.). 32p. (J). (gr. k-3). pap. 10.95 (978-1-944882-45-7(6)) Boys Town Pr.

—The Raindrop Who Couldn't Fall. Call, Kirsti. l.t. ed. 2018. (ENG.). 34p. (J). pap. 12.95 (978-1-946124-36-4(2)) Mazo Pubs.

—Spacing Out: Discovering the Importance of Completing Tasks. McCumbee, Stephie. 2015. (ENG.). 32p. (J). pap. 10.95 (978-1-934490-77-8(6)) Boys Town Pr.

Griffin, Lisa M. Navidad: Jesús Ha Nacido. Griffin, Lisa M. Monge, Marlyn. 2018. (SPA.). (J). (978-0-8198-5192-5(2)) Pauline Bks. & Media.

Griffin, Marlin. Bucky's Adventures. Cox Gray, Marjorie. 2008. 100p. pap. 28.99 (978-1-4389-2645-2(6)) AuthorHouse.

Griffin, Matt. Hocus Pocus & the All-New Sequel. Jantha, A. W. 2018. (ENG.). 528p. (YA). (gr. 9-17). 12.99 (978-1-368-02003-9(8)) Disney Publishing Worldwide.

—The Kane Chronicles, Book Three the Serpent's Shadow (new Cover) Riordan, Rick. 2018. (Kane Chronicles Ser.: 3). (ENG.). 496p. (J). (gr. 5-9). pap. 9.99 (978-1-368-01357-4(0)) Hyperion Bks. for Children.

—Kane Chronicles, the, Book One the Red Pyramid (the Kane Chronicles, Book One) Riordan, Rick. 2018. (Kane Chronicles Ser.: 1). (ENG.). 576p. (J). (gr. 5-9). pap. 9.99 (978-1-368-01358-1(9)) Hyperion Bks. for Children.

—Kane Chronicles, the, Book Two the Throne of Fire (Kane Chronicles, the, Book Two) Riordan, Rick. 2018. (Kane Chronicles Ser.: 2). (ENG.). 528p. (J). (gr. 5-9). pap. 9.99 (978-1-368-01359-8(7)) Hyperion Bks. for Children.

—Kane Chronicles, the Paperback Box Set (the Kane Chronicles Box Set with Graphic Novel Sampler) Riordan, Rick. 2018. (Kane Chronicles Ser.). (ENG.). 1472p. (J). (gr. 3-7). pap. 27.99 (978-1-368-01361-1(9)) Hyperion Bks. for Children.

—Watch Hollow: the Alchemist's Shadow. Funaro, Gregory. 2020. (Watch Hollow Ser.: 2). (ENG.). 240p. (J). (gr. 3-7). 16.99 (978-0-06-264348-3(7), HarperCollins) HarperCollins Pubs. Ltd. GBR. Dist: HarperCollins Pubs.

Griffin, Matt. A Cage of Roots. Griffin, Matt. 2015. (Ayla Trilogy Ser.: 1). (ENG.). 240p. pap. 11.00 (978-1-84717-681-3(X)) O'Brien Pr., Ltd., The IRL. Dist: Casemate Pubs. & Bk. Distributors, LLC.

—The Spiral Path: Book 3 in the Ayla Trilogy. Griffin, Matt. 2017. (Ayla Trilogy Ser.: 3). (ENG.). 208p. 15.00 (978-1-84717-886-2(3)) O'Brien Pr., Ltd., The IRL. Dist: Casemate Pubs. & Bk. Distributors, LLC.

Griffin, Matthew. Watch Hollow. Funaro, Gregory. 2019. (Watch Hollow Ser.: 1). (ENG.). 256p. (J). (gr. 3-7). 16.99 (978-0-06-264345-2(2)) HarperCollins Pubs.

—Watch Hollow. Funaro, Gregory. 2020. (Watch Hollow Ser.: 1). (ENG.). 272p. (J). (gr. 3-7). pap. 7.99 (978-0-06-264346-9(0), HarperCollins) HarperCollins Pubs. Ltd. GBR. Dist: HarperCollins Pubs.

Griffin, Meadow. Ciaran: And the Troll Bully. Griffin, Meadow. 2017. (Ciaran Ser.: Vol. 1). (ENG.). (J). (gr. k-2). 20.00 (978-0-9996189-0-5(3)) Legends of Erin.

Griffin, Paul. Abc, Adoption & Me. Swift, Gayle H. & Swift, Casey Anne. 2013. 36p. pap. 13.99 (978-0-9856762-8-5(0)) WRB Pub.

Griffin, Rachel. African Tales. Mhlophe, Gcina. 2009. 96p. (J). (gr. 2-9). 19.99 (978-1-84686-118-5(7)) Barefoot Bks., Inc.

—African Tales: A Barefoot Collection. Mhlophe, Gcina. 96p. (J). 2017. (ENG.). (gr. 1-4). pap. 16.99 (978-1-78285-359-6(6)); 2015. (gr. 3-6). pap. 14.99 (978-1-84686-590-9(5)) Barefoot Bks., Inc.

—Celebration Gift Wrap. (J). 4.99 (978-1-84148-985-8(9)) Barefoot Bks., Inc.

—The Fabrics of Fairytale: Stories Spun from Far & Wide. Batt, Tanya Robyn. 2007. (ENG.). 80p. (J). (gr. -1-3). pap. 16.99 (978-1-84686-089-8(X)) Barefoot Bks., Inc.

Griffin-Scott, Janet & Sanderson, Ruth. Elska: Horse Diaries #1. Hapka, Catherine & Hapka, Cathy. 2009. (Horse Diaries: 1). 144p. (J). (gr. 3-7). pap. 7.99 (978-0-375-84732-5(4), Random Hse. Bks. for Young Readers) Random Hse. Children's Bks.

Griffis, David Randolph. Grandma Bunny: The Forest Herbalist. Bliss, Jenifer Victoria. 2018. (ENG.). 64p. (J). pap. 9.00 (978-0-9912102-4-4(7)) Sierra Muses Pr.

Griffith, Andrew. Foundation. Barber, John. 2012. (Transformers: Dark of the Moon Movie Prequel Ser.). (ENG.). 24p. (J). (gr. 2-6). Vol. 2. 27.07 (978-1-59961-972-9(5), 14852); Vol. 4. 27.07 (978-1-59961-974-3(1), 14854) Spotlight. (Graphic Novels).

—Movie Prequel - Foundation. Barber, John. 2012. (Transformers: Dark of the Moon Movie Prequel Ser.). (ENG.). 24p. (J). (gr. 2-6). 27.07 (978-1-59961-971-2(7), 14851, Graphic Novels) Spotlight.

—Transformers: Dark of the Moon - Foundation. Barber, John. 2012. (Transformers: Dark of the Moon Movie Prequel Ser.). (ENG.). 24p. (J). (gr. 2-6). 27.07 (978-1-59961-973-6(3), 14853, Graphic Novels) Spotlight.

Griffith, Elayne. Slime Spewing Vampire Velociraptors. De Falla, Kat. Hashway, Kelly, ed. 2018. (Moto Maddie BMX Portal Ser.: Vol. 2). (ENG.). 96p. (J). pap. 8.99 (978-1-7200-1758-5(1)) Independently Published.

Griffith, Gershom. Let's Celebrate Martin Luther King, Jr. Day. deRubertis, Barbara. ed. 2013. (Holidays & Heroes Ser.). (ENG.). 32p. (J). (gr. 1-4). E-Book 38.65 (978-1-57565-639-7(6)) Astra Publishing Hse.

—Rosa Parks: Freedom Rider. Brandt, Keith & Mattern, Joanne. 2006. 54p. (J). pap. (978-0-439-66045-7(9)) Scholastic, Inc.

Griffith, Indigo, jt. photos by see Bilik-Franklin, MidiAna.

Griffith, John Anthony. The Scientific Golfer: Improving Your Golf Game Through Baselining, 1. Griffith, John Anthony, photos by. 2004. 150p. 39.95 (978-0-9759331-0-7(8)) Rosetta Stone Communications.

Griffith, Krishana. The Inside Story of the Jackrabbit & the Tortoise. Benson, Rachael. 2018. (ENG.). 44p. (J). pap. 13.99 (978-1-949609-78-3(2)) Pen It! Pubns., LLC.

Griffith, Linda Hill. Best Ever Ring Bearer. 2010. 24p. 10.99 (978-1-4022-3818-5(5)) Sourcebooks, Inc.

—Most Special Flower Girl. 2010. 24p. 10.99 (978-1-4022-3817-8(7)) Sourcebooks, Inc.

Griffiths, Alex G. Does It Fart? A Kid's Guide to the Gas Animals Pass. Caruso, Nick & Rabalotti, Dani. 2019. (ENG.). 48p. (J). (gr. -1-3). 17.99 (978-0-316-49104-4(7)) Little, Brown Bks. for Young Readers.

—Huggy the Python Hugs Too Hard. Dyckman, Ame. 2018. (Wee Beasties Ser.). (ENG.). 22p. (J). (gr. -1-k). bds. 8.99 (978-1-5344-1080-0(5), Little Simon) Little Simon.

—Roary the Lion Roars Too Loud. Dyckman, Ame. 2018. (Wee Beasties Ser.). (ENG.). 22p. (J). (gr. -1-k). bds. 8.99 (978-1-5344-1078-7(3), Little Simon) Little Simon.

—Touchy the Octopus Touches Everything. Dyckman, Ame. 2019. (Wee Beasties Ser.). (ENG.). 22p. (J). (gr. -1-k). bds. 8.99 (978-1-5344-1082-4(1), Little Simon) Little Simon.

—True or Poo? A Kid's Guide to Animal Facts & Fakes. Caruso, Nick & Rabalotti, Dani. 2020. (ENG.). 48p. (J). (gr. -1-3). 17.99 (978-0-316-53539-7(7)) Little Brown & Co.

—The Wee Beasties Collection: Huggy the Python Hugs Too Hard; Roary the Lion Roars Too Loud; Touchy the Octopus Touches Everything. Dyckman, Ame. ed. 2019. (Wee Beasties Ser.). (ENG.). 66p. (J). (gr. -1-k). bds. 26.99 (978-1-5344-6275-5(9), Little Simon) Little Simon.

Griffiths, Alex G. The Bug Collector. Griffiths, Alex G. 2020. (ENG.). 32p. (J). (gr. -1-3). 17.99 (978-1-5415-9634-4(X)) Lerner Publishing Group.

Griffiths, Dean. The Big Tree Gang, 1 vol. Bogart, Jo Ellen. 2005. (Orca Echoes Ser.). (ENG.). 64p. (J). (gr. 1-3). per. 6.95 (978-1-55143-345-5(1)) Orca Bk. Pubs. USA.

—The Big Tree Gang. Bogart, Jo Ellen. 2005. 60p. (J). lib. bdg. 20.00 (978-1-4242-1251-4(0)) Fitzgerald Bks.

—La Course-Poursuite des Loups Gris, 1 vol. Brouwer, Sigmund & Gingras, Gaston. 2011. (Loups Gris Ser.: 3). (FRE.). 72p. (J). (gr. 1-3). pap. 6.95 (978-1-4598-0009-0(5)) Orca Bk. Pubs. USA.

—Le Défi des Loups Gris, 1 vol. Brouwer, Sigmund & Gingras, Gaston. 2011. (Loups Gris Ser.: 1). (FRE.). 72p. (J). (gr. 1-3). pap. 6.95 (978-1-55469-812-7(X)) Orca Bk. Pubs. USA.

—Give Maggie a Chance, 1 vol. Wishinsky, Frieda. 2004. (ENG.). 32p. (J). (gr. -1-2). pap. 7.95 (978-1-55041-704-3(5), d0e55ee2-3d5d-4d4b-8518-cb7706a2fc98) Trifolium Bks., Inc. CAN. Dist: Firefly Bks., Ltd.

—Good Pirate. Winters, Kari-Lynn. 2016. (ENG.). 32p. (J). (gr. k-3). 17.95 (978-1-927485-80-4(0)) Pajama Pr. CAN. Dist: Ingram Publisher Services.

—Les Loups Gris à la Chasse, 1 vol. Brouwer, Sigmund & Gingras, Gaston. 2011. (Loups Gris Ser.: 2).Tr. of Timberwolf Hunt. (FRE.). 72p. (J). (gr. 1-3). pap. 6.95 (978-1-55469-814-1(6)) Orca Bk. Pubs. USA.

—Maggie Can't Wait, 1 vol. Wishinsky, Frieda. 2009. (ENG.). 32p. (J). (gr. -1-1). 17.95 (978-1-55455-103-3(X), 5fa7c681-f79a-4575-93fd-191f4e108a65) Fitzhenry & Whiteside, Ltd. CAN. Dist: Firefly Bks., Ltd.

—Only a Cow, 1 vol. Hamilton, Arlene. 2006. (ENG.). 32p. (J). (gr. -1-2). (978-1-55041-871-2(8)) Fitzhenry & Whiteside, Ltd.

—Only a Cow, 1 vol. Hamilton, Arlene. 2008. (ENG.). 32p. (J). (gr. k-3). pap. 7.95 (978-1-55455-088-3(2), 5b8dcd09-7cac-4a24-bd6b-fc986d5c3211) éditeur, Annika Parance CAN. Dist: Firefly Bks., Ltd.

—Out & about with the Big Tree Gang, 1 vol. Bogart, Jo Ellen & Bogart, Jill. 2006. (Orca Echoes Ser.). (ENG.). 64p. (J). (gr. 2-4). 17.44 (978-1-55143-603-6(5)) Orca Bk. Pubs. USA.

Griffiths, Dean. Pencil: A Story with a Point. Ingalls, Ann. 2020. (ENG.). 32p. (J). (gr. 1-3). 12.95 **(978-1-77278-153-3(3));** 2nd ed. 18.95 **(978-1-77278-154-0(1))** Pajama Pr. CAN. Dist: Ingram Publisher Services.

Griffiths, Dean. Perfect Man, 1 vol. Wilson, Troy. 2005. (ENG.). 32p. (J). (gr. 1-3). per. 9.95 (978-1-55143-435-3(0)) Orca Bk. Pubs. USA.

—La Revanche des Loups Gris, 1 vol. Brouwer, Sigmund & Gingras, Gaston. 2011. (Loups Gris Ser.: 4). (FRE.). 72p. (J). (gr. 1-3). pap. 6.95 (978-1-4598-0011-3(7)) Orca Bk. Pubs. USA.

—Timberwolf Challenge, 1 vol. Brouwer, Sigmund. 2008. (Orca Echoes Ser.). (ENG.). 64p. (J). (gr. 1-3). pap. 6.95 (978-1-55143-730-9(9)) Orca Bk. Pubs. USA.

—Timberwolf Chase, 1 vol. Brouwer, Sigmund. 2006. (Orca Echoes Ser.). (ENG.). 64p. (J). (gr. 1-3). per. 6.95 (978-1-55143-548-0(9)) Orca Bk. Pubs. USA.

—Timberwolf Hunt, 1 vol. Brouwer, Sigmund. 2007. (Orca Echoes Ser.). (ENG.). 64p. (J). (gr. 1-3). per. 6.95 (978-1-55143-726-2(0)) Orca Bk. Pubs. USA.

—Timberwolf Revenge, 1 vol. Brouwer, Sigmund. 2006. (Orca Echoes Ser.). (ENG.). 64p. (J). (gr. 1-3). per. 6.95 (978-1-55143-544-2(6)) Orca Bk. Pubs. USA.

—Timberwolf Trap, 1 vol. Brouwer, Sigmund. 2007. (Orca Echoes Ser.). (ENG.). 64p. (J). (gr. 1-3). per. 6.95 (978-1-55143-722-4(8)) Orca Bk. Pubs. USA.

—Timo Goes Camping. Allenby, Victoria. 2018. (ENG.). 48p. (J). (gr. 1-3). 10.95 (978-1-77278-040-6(5)) Pajama Pr. CAN. Dist: Ingram Publisher Services.

—When Emily Carr Met Woo, 1 vol. Kulling, Monica. 2014. (ENG.). 32p. (J). (gr. k-4). 19.95 (978-1-927485-40-8(1)) Pajama Pr. CAN. Dist: Ingram Publisher Services.

Griffiths, Rachel. The Animals in My Brain: A Kid's Guide to Understanding & Controlling Their Behaviour. Joseph, Sarah. 2018. (ENG.). 34p. (J). (978-1-9994994-1-9(7)); pap. **(978-1-9994994-0-2(9))** & Bks.

Griffiths, Shari. Anna's Prayer: The True Story of an Immigrant Girl. Beckstrand, Karl. 2017. (Young American Immigrants Ser.: 1). (ENG.). 30p. (J). (gr. k-5). 22.95 (978-0-9853988-6-6(8)) Premio Publishing & Gozo Bks., LLC.

Griffo, Daniel. Eye of the Earthquake Dragon. West, Tracey. 2019. (Dragon Masters Ser.: 13). (ENG.). 96p. (J). (gr. 1-3). pap. 4.99 (978-1-338-26371-8(4)) Scholastic, Inc.

—Middle School: Escape to Australia. Patterson, James. 2017. (Middle School Ser.: 9). (ENG.). 288p. (J). (gr. 3-7). 13.99 (978-0-316-27262-9(0), Jimmy Patterson) Little Brown & Co.

—Signing in My World: Sign Language for Kids, 1 vol. Clay, Kathryn & Vonne, Mira. 2013. (Time to Sign Ser.). (ENG.). 32p. (J). (gr. -1-2). 27.99 (978-1-62065-054-7(1)) Capstone.

—1-2-3 Va-Va-Vroom! A Counting Book, 0 vols. Lynn, Sarah. 2012. (ENG.). 32p. (J). (gr. -1-3). 16.99 (978-0-7614-6162-3(0), 9780761461623, Two Lions) Amazon Publishing.

Griftner, Rebecca. Si Si the Circus Cat. Pruitt, Kat. 2011. (ENG.). 24p. (J). pap. 12.95 (978-0-9844037-2-1(8)) Pruggus Publishing.

Griggs-Burr, Alexander & Griggs-Burr, Alexander. A Very Small Something. Hickey, David. 2012. (ENG.). 32p. (J). (gr. -1). 15.95 (978-1-926845-37-1(4)) Biblioasis CAN. Dist: Consortium Bk. Sales & Distribution.

Griggs-Burr, Alexander, jt. illus. see Griggs-Burr, Alexander.

Griggs Jr, Larry D. It's a Big World: Take It to the Top, by Giving It All You Got. Johnson, Rosa Pearl. 2016. (ENG.). (J). (978-1-4602-8666-1(9)); pap. (978-1-4602-8667-8(7)) FriesenPress.

Griglak, Loisann. Danny David Delanco Dragon Finds a Friend. Ricke, Briony Ann. Schiller, Irene, ed. 2018. (ENG.). 54p. (J). pap. 12.99 (978-1-7287-4376-9(1)) Independently Published.

Grigni, Noah. It Feels Good to Be Yourself: A Book about Gender Identity. Thorn, Theresa. 2019. (ENG.). 40p. (J). 17.99 (978-1-250-30295-3(1), 900197013, Holt, Henry & Co. Bks. For Young Readers) Holt, Henry & Co.

Grijalva, M. S. Laurah. Seeing the Underwater World with Abby & Josh. Wang, M. S. Rosie. 2018. (ENG.). 28p. pap. (978-0-646-97449-1(1)) arima publishing.

Grill, Gerald. Oh, What a State I'm In: The USA in Rhyme & Riddle, 1 vol. Merrill, Karen Grill. 2010. 48p. pap. 24.95 (978-1-4489-7979-0(X)) PublishAmerica, Inc.

Grill, William. Earth Verse: Haiku from the Ground Up. Walker, Sally M. 2018. (ENG.). 48p. (J). (gr. 2-4). 17.99 (978-0-7636-7512-7(1)) Candlewick Pr.

—Shackleton's Journey. 2014. 80p. (J). (gr. -1-2). 24.00 (978-1-909263-10-9(9)) Flying Eye Bks. GBR. Dist: Penguin Random Hse. LLC.

—The Wolves of Currumpaw. 2016. 80p. (J). (gr. 2-9). 24.00 (978-1-909263-83-3(4)) Flying Eye Bks. GBR. Dist: Penguin Random Hse. LLC.

Grimard, Gabrielle. Le Bateau Magique, 1 vol. Pearson, Kit & Farris, Katherine. Martinez, Rachel, tr. from ENG. 2019. (FRE.). 32p. (J). (gr. -1-k). 19.95 (978-1-4598-2324-2(9)) Orca Bk. Pubs. USA.

—The Brave Young Knight, 1 vol. Kingsbury, Karen. 2011. (ENG.). 40p. (J). (gr. -1-2). 15.99 (978-0-310-71645-7(4)) Zonderkidz.

—La Chasse au Plomb. Pelletier, Maryse. 2004. (Roman Jeunesse Ser.). (FRE.). 96p. (J). (gr. 4-7). pap. (978-2-89021-692-1(6)) Diffusion du livre Mirabel (DLM).

—The Fabulous World of Mr. Fred, 1 vol. Chartrand, Lili. 2014. (ENG.). 32p. (J). (gr. k-2). pap. 10.95 (978-1-55455-346-4(6), 1ea9249a-ec28-4ad4-801a-7bc30d64bcc1) Trifolium Bks., Inc. CAN. Dist: Firefly Bks., Ltd.

—Jesus Gives Us Peace: The Sacrament of Reconciliation. Dumont, Claire & Lacoursiere, Suzanne. Larocque, Gisele, tr. from FRE. 2006. Orig. Title: Conduis Mes Pas Vers la Paix: le Pardon. 48p. pap. 10.95 (978-0-8198-3984-8(1)) Pauline Bks. & Media.

—The Magic Boat, 1 vol. Pearson, Kit & Farris, Katherine. 2019. (ENG.). 32p. (J). (gr. -1-k). 19.95 (978-1-4598-1432-5(0)) Orca Bk. Pubs. USA.

—Maybe Later, 1 vol. Lee, Ingrid. 2008. (Orca Echoes Ser.). (ENG.). 64p. (J). (gr. 1-3). pap. 6.95 (978-1-55143-764-4(3)) Orca Bk. Pubs. USA.

—The Princess & the Three Knights, 1 vol. Kingsbury, Karen. 2009. (ENG.). 40p. (J). (gr. -1-2). 15.99 (978-0-310-71641-9(1)) Zonderkidz.

Grimard, Gabrielle. Snow Doves. Hartry, Nancy. 2020. (ENG.). 32p. (J). (gr. -1-k). 18.95 **(978-1-77260-135-0(7))** Second Story Pr. CAN. Dist: Orca Bk. Pubs. USA.

Grimard, Gabrielle. Stolen Words, 1 vol. Florence, Melanie. 2017. (ENG.). 24p. (J). (gr. 1-3). 17.95 (978-1-77260-037-7(7)) Second Story Pr. CAN. Dist: Orca Bk. Pubs. USA.

—Stolen Words / Kimotinaniwiw Pikiskwewina, 1 vol. Florence, Melanie. Sand, Dolores & Weenie, Gayle, trs. ed. 2019. (CRE & ENG.). 24p. (J). (gr. -1-k). 14.95 (978-1-77260-101-5(2)) Second Story Pr. CAN. Dist: Orca Bk. Pubs. USA.

—Today, Maybe, 1 vol. Demers, Dominique. 2011. (ENG.). 32p. (J). (gr. -1-k). 19.95 (978-1-55469-400-6(0)) Orca Bk. Pubs. USA.

—When I Was Eight. Jordan-Fenton, Christy & Pokiak-Fenton, Margaret-Olemaun. 2nd ed. 2013. (ENG.). 32p. (J). (gr. 1-4). pap. 9.95 (978-1-55451-490-8(8), 9781554514908);1. 26.19 (978-1-55451-491-5(6), 9781554514915) Annick Pr., Ltd. CAN. Dist: Publishers Group West (PGW), Children's Plus, Inc.

Grimball, Meta. Stories Children Love: a Collection of Stories Arranged for Children. Welsh, Charles, ed. 2007. pap. 36.95 *(978-1-4304-5116-7(5))* Kessinger Publishing, LLC.

Grimes, Carly. Travel with Me & See London. Delevoye, Nancy. 2020. (Travel with Me & See Ser.: Vol. 2). (ENG.). 40p. (J). (gr. k-4). 18.99 ***(978-0-9600423-2-6(6))*** Travel With Me & See.

Grimes, Carly. Travel with Me & See Paris. Delevoye, Nancy. (Travel with Me & See Ser.: Vol. 1). (ENG.). 40p. (J). (gr. k-4). 2019. 18.99 *(978-0-9600423-1-9(8))*; 2018. 17.99 *(978-0-9600423-0-2(X))* Travel With Me & See.

Grimes, Kristopher. Drake the Dragon King. Jones, Brittany. 2013. (ENG.). (J). 14.95 *(978-1-62086-360-2(X))* Mascot Bks., Inc.

Grimly, Gris. Boris & Bella. Crimi, Carolyn. 2006. (ENG.). 32p. (J). (gr. -1-3). reprint ed. pap. 7.99 *(978-0-15-205900-2(8)*, 1197714) Houghton Mifflin Harcourt Publishing Co.

—The Bottle Imp of Bright House. Llewellyn, Tom. (ENG.). 224p. (J). (gr. 3-7). 2020. pap. 9.99 *(978-0-8234-4533-2(X))*; 2018. 17.99 *(978-0-8234-3969-0(0))* Holiday Hse., Inc.

—The Dangerous Alphabet. Gaiman, Neil. (ENG.). 32p. (J). (gr. k). 2010. pap. 7.99 *(978-0-06-078335-8(4))*; 2008. 17.99 *(978-0-06-078333-4(8))* HarperCollins Pubs. Ltd. GBR. (HarperCollins). Dist: HarperCollins Pubs.

—Edgar Allan Poe's Tales of Death & Dementia. Poe, Edgar Allan. 2009. (ENG.). 144p. (J). (gr. 6-9). 22.99 *(978-1-4169-5025-7(7)*, Atheneum Bks. for Young Readers) Simon & Schuster Children's Publishing.

—Edgar Allan Poe's Tales of Mystery & Madness. Poe, Edgar Allen. 2004. (ENG.). 144p. (J). (gr. 5-9). 19.99 *(978-0-689-84837-7(4)*, Atheneum Bks. for Young Readers) Simon & Schuster Children's Publishing.

—Grimericks, 0 vols. Pearson, Susan. 2005. (ENG.). 32p. (J). (gr. 1-4). pap. 9.99 *(978-0-7614-5444-1(6)*, 9780761454441, Two Lions) Amazon Publishing.

—Gris Grimly's Frankenstein. Shelley, Mary. 2013. (ENG.). 208p. (YA). (gr. 8). 24.99 *(978-0-06-186297-7(5)*, Balzer & Bray) HarperCollins Pubs.

—Gris Grimly's Frankenstein. Shelley, Mary. 2015. (ENG.). 208p. (YA). (gr. 8). pap. 16.99 *(978-0-06-186298-4(3)*, Balzer & Bray) HarperCollins Pubs.

—Gris Grimly's Tales from the Brothers Grimm. Hunt, Margaret & Grimm, Jacob and Wilhelm. 2016. (ENG.). 288p. (J). (gr. 3-7). 17.99 *(978-0-06-235233-0(4))* HarperCollins Pubs.

—Guys Read: Terrifying Tales. Scieszka, Jon et al. 2015. (Guys Read Ser.: 6). (ENG.). 288p. (J). (gr. 3-7). 16.99 *(978-0-06-238558-1(5))*; pap. 7.99 *(978-0-06-238557-4(7))* HarperCollins Pubs. (Walden Pond Pr.).

—The Tell-Tale Heart & Other Stories. Poe, Edgar Allan. 2011. (ENG.). 144p. (J). (gr. 6-9). pap. 12.99 *(978-1-4169-5026-4(5)*, Atheneum Bks. for Young Readers) Simon & Schuster Children's Publishing.

Grimly, Gris. Gris Grimly's Wicked Nursery Rhymes. Grimly, Gris. Last, First. 2003. (ENG.). 32p. pap. 16.95 *(978-0-9729388-7-7(7))* Baby Tattoo Bks.

—Little Jordan Ray's Muddy Spud. Grimly, Gris. 2005. (ENG.). 40p. pap. 19.95 *(978-0-9729388-6-0(9))* Last Gasp of San Francisco.

—Old MacDonald Had a Farm. Grimly, Gris. 2017. 40p. (J). (gr. -1-k). 17.99 *(978-1-338-11243-6(0)*, Orchard Bks.) Scholastic, Inc.

Grimm, Dave. Mommy, Tell Me a Story about a Car, 2nd Edition. Grimm, Kristi. 2nd ed. 2013. 32p. pap. 13.99 *(978-0-9855699-9-0(9))* Richer Life, LLC.

—Mommy, Tell Me a Story about a Plane, 2nd Edition. Grimm, Kristi. 2nd ed. 2013. 36p. pap. 13.99 *(978-0-9855699-8-3(0))* Richer Life, LLC.

Grimm, Debi & Eadie, Inger Sommer. The Crocodile Song. Siefker, Eunice. 2009. 40p. (J). (gr. -1-3). 19.95 *(978-1-60227-476-1(2))* Above the Clouds Publishing.

Grimm, Lizzy. I See Rainbows. Grimm, Lizzy. Grimm, Lucy. 2019. (E. G. A. D. S. Ser.: Vol. 4). (ENG.). 44p. (J). pap. 6.00 *(978-1-0914-8594-5(1))* Independently Published.

Grimshaw, Kath. Ellie Jelly & the Massive Mum Meltdown. Naish, Sarah. 2018. (ENG.). 32p. (J). 17.95 *(978-1-78592-516-0(4)*, 696827) Kingsley, Jessica Pubs. GBR. Dist: Hachette UK Distribution.

Grimstvedt, Johann Schweder. Quest for the Golden Orchid. Stimson, Roger. 2019. (ENG.). 102p. (J). pap. 23.95 ***(978-1-9845-9144-9(4))*** Xlibris Corp.

Grimwood, Tracie. Reena's Rainbow. White, Dee. 2017. (ENG.). 32p. (J). (gr. -1-3). 17.99 *(978-1-925335-49-1(6)*, EK Bks.) Exisle Publishing Pty Ltd. AUS. Dist: Hachette Bk. Group.

Grinberg, Alex. Origami a Folded Poem. Grinberg, Sarah J. 2018. (ENG.). 28p. (J). pap. 14.99 *(978-1-7219-7451-1(2))* CreateSpace Independent Publishing Platform.

Grindell, Joan & Grindell, Mark. Let's Make Faces. Langeler, Gerard. 2009. (ENG.). 24p. (J). (gr. -1-3). spiral bd. 14.95 *(978-1-932565-63-8(9))* Future Horizons, Inc.

Grindell, Mark, jt. illus. see Grindell, Joan.

Gringhuis, Dirk. Blue Bay Mystery. Warner, Gertrude Chandler. 2020. (Boxcar Children Ser.). (ENG.). 160p. (J). (gr. 2-6). lib. bdg. 27.07 ***(978-1-5321-4472-1(5)***, 35162, Chapter Bks.) Spotlight.

—Mike's Mystery. Warner, Gertrude Chandler. 2020. (Boxcar Children Ser.). (ENG.). 128p. (J). (gr. 2-6). lib. bdg. 27.07 ***(978-1-5321-4476-9(8)***, 35166, Chapter Bks.) Spotlight.

—Mystery Ranch. Warner, Gertrude Chandler. 2020. (Boxcar Children Ser.). (ENG.). 128p. (J). (gr. 2-6). lib. bdg. 27.07 ***(978-1-5321-4477-6(6)***, 35167, Chapter Bks.) Spotlight.

Grinvalsky, Peggy. Heartwood. Burns, Mary E. 2003. (ENG.). 144p. (YA). per. 9.95 *(978-0-9656763-4-2(X))* Manitowish River Pr.

Gripe, Harald. The Glassblower's Children. Gripe, Maria. 2019. (ENG.). 176p. (J). (gr. 3-7). pap. 11.99 *(978-1-68137-378-2(5)*, NYRB Kids) New York Review of Bks., Inc., The.

Gripe, Harold. Elvis Karlsson. Gripe, Maria. 2003. (SPA.). 148p. (J). (gr. 3-5). pap. 9.95 *(978-958-24-0181-8(8))* Santillana USA Publishing Co., Inc.

Griscom, Laura. The Boy Named 27091: A Teenager's Struggle for Survival during the Holocaust. 2007. (J). lib. bdg. 6.95 *(978-0-9633705-4-9(5))* Share Publishing.

Grisham, Betty. Blue Lewis & Sasha the Great. Newell, Carol Donsky. 2005. (J). per. 6.95 *(978-0-9766199-0-1(3))* Cally Pr.

Grisham, Jason. Benjamin P. Blizzard: Welcome to Christmastown. Nivens, Karen. 2007. 48p. (J). per. *(978-0-9798154-1-6(X))* Living Waters Publishing Co.

Griswold, Earleen. A Caribbean Journey from A to Y: (Read & Discover What Happened to the Z) Picayo, Mario. 2007. (ENG & FRE.). 64p. (J). 19.95 *(978-0-9725611-8-1(8)*, Campanita Bks.) Editorial Campana.

Griswold, Phillip. The Circus. Miller, Lindsey Michael. 2005. 32p. (J). (gr. -1-3). 13.95 *(978-0-9709104-8-6(7))* Hickory Tales Publishing.

Gritton, Steve. The Super Dupers. Gritton, Steve. 2013. 30p. pap. 9.29 *(978-0-9795361-8-2(9))* Bad Frog Art/SMG Bks.

Grivina, Oksana, et al. Leaders Doing Headstands. Weakland, Mark. 2016. (Leaders Doing Headstands Ser.). (ENG.). 32p. (gr. 2-3). 114.60 *(978-1-4795-9687-4(6)*, Picture Window Bks.) Capstone.

Grivina, Oksana. When Amelia Earhart Built a Roller Coaster. Weakland, Mark. (J). 2017. 31p. *(978-1-5158-0142-9(X))*; 2016. (ENG.). 32p. (gr. 1-4). pap. 7.95 *(978-1-5158-0138-2(1))*; 2016. (ENG.). 32p. (gr. 1-4). lib. bdg. 28.65 *(978-1-4795-9686-7(8))* Capstone. (Picture Window Bks.).

Grizzle, Deb. Paisley Little: Finding a Masterpiece. Grizzle, Deb. 2018. (Little Artist Ser.: Vol. 1). (ENG.). 28p. (J). (gr. 1-6). pap. 15.95 *(978-1-61314-456-5(3))* Innovo Publishing, LLC.

Grncaroska, Snezana. Mac, the Butterfly Horse. Halverson, Kristen. 2018. (ENG.). 36p. (J). 21.99 *(978-1-64440-710-3(8))* The Tale of Noel: The Holiday Horse Angel, The.

Grob, Anna. Bear: Ch. Glacier's Storm Kloud. Grob, Anna. 2019. (ENG.). 36p. (J). pap. 12.95 ***(978-1-0866-3320-7(2))*** Independently Published.

Grobet, Veronique, jt. illus. see Godi.

Grobler, Piet. Carnival of the Animals. De Vos, Philip. 32p. (J). *(978-0-7981-3823-9(8))* Human & Rousseau.

—Colors! / ¡Colores!, 1 vol. Luján, Jorge. Simon, John Oliver & Parfitt, Rebecca, trs. 2008.Tr. of Colors!. (ENG & SPA.). 36p. (J). (gr. k-4). 18.95 *(978-0-88899-863-7(5))* Groundwood Bks. CAN. Dist: Publishers Group West (PGW).

—Fiddle-Dee-dee. Hofmeyr, Dianne. 2019. (ENG.). 32p. (J). (gr. -1-2). 17.99 *(978-1-910959-75-6(8))* Otter-Barry Bks. GBR. Dist: Independent Pubs. Group.

—The Playgrounds of Babel, 1 vol. Lawson, JonArno. 2019. (ENG.). 32p. (J). (gr. k-3). 18.95 *(978-1-77306-036-1(8))* Groundwood Bks. CAN. Dist: Publishers Group West (PGW).

Grobler, Piet, et al. Rights of a Child. 2005. (ENG & MUL.). 32p. 11.95 *(978-0-7957-0162-7(4))* Kwela Bks. ZAF. Dist: Independent Pubs. Group.

Grobler, Piet. Little Bird's ABC. Grobler, Piet. 2005. (ENG.). 52p. (J). (gr. -1-3). 8.95 *(978-1-932425-52-9(7))* Lemniscaat USA.

Grochalska, Agnieszka. Dewey Fairchild, Parent Problem Solver. Hom, Lorri. (Dewey Fairchild Ser.: 1). (ENG.). 252p. (J). (gr. 4-7). 2018. pap. 7.99 *(978-1-948705-12-7(5))*; 2017. 13.99 *(978-1-944995-16-4(1))* Amberjack Publishing Co.

—The Wonderful Baron Doppleganger Device. Bower, Eric. 2018. (Bizarre Baron Inventions Ser.: 3). (ENG.). 237p. (J). (gr. 4). 15.99 *(978-1-944995-51-5(X))* Amberjack Publishing Co.

—The Wonderful Baron Doppleganger Device. Bower, Eric. 2018. (Bizarre Baron Inventions Ser.: 3). (ENG.). 238p. (J). pap. 7.99 *(978-1-948705-17-2(6))* Amberjack Publishing Co.

Groebner, Dominic. El Gran Libro de Los Castillos - Internet Linked. Sims, Lesley. 2004. (Titles in Spanish Ser.). (SPA.). 104p. (J). pap. 14.95 *(978-0-7460-5089-7(5)*, Usborne) EDC Publishing.

—The Usborne Big Book of Picture Puzzles. Khanduri, Kamini et al. 2006. 173p. (J). (gr. 3-7). per. 18.99 *(978-0-7945-1165-4(1)*, Usborne) EDC Publishing.

—The Usborne Castle Jigsaw Book. Pearcey, Alice. Milbourne, Anna, ed. 2006. (Jigsaw Bks.). 14p. (J). (gr. k-3). bds. 14.95 *(978-0-7945-1137-1(6)*, Usborne) EDC Publishing.

Groenendyk, Doretta. Fiddles & Spoons: Journey of an Acadian Mouse, 1 vol. Hope-Simpson, Lila. 2017. (ENG.). 32p. (J). (gr. 1-3). pap. 14.95 *(978-1-77108-562-5(2)*, c7a17dca-2479-4d77-be28-f9eb1832a0b0) Nimbus Publishing, Ltd. CAN. Dist: Baker & Taylor Publisher Services (BTPS).

—Love You More Than Anything, 1 vol. 2017. (ENG.). 32p. (J). (gr. -1-k). 19.95 *(978-1-927502-93-8(4)*, d6d9a0ad-49dd-4a48-b012-918a9ad3a7d2) Acorn Pr., The CAN. Dist: Baker & Taylor Publisher Services (BTPS).

Groenewald, Frans. The Mighty Elephant in the Land of Kachoo: The Land of Kachoo Series. Scotford, Groenewald & Scotford, Tina. 2014. (Land of Kachoo Ser.). (ENG.). 32p. (J). (gr. k-2). pap. 10.95 *(978-1-4314-0759-0(3))* Jacana Media ZAF. Dist: Independent Pubs. Group.

—Saving the Rhino in the Land of Kachoo: The Land of Kachoo Series. Scotford, Tina. 2014. (Land of Kachoo Ser.). (ENG.). 32p. (J). (gr. k-2). pap. 10.95 *(978-1-4314-0760-6(7))* Jacana Media ZAF. Dist: Independent Pubs. Group.

Groeninik, Chuck. Dear Daisy Dunnington. Stein, Mathilde. 2012. (ENG.). 32p. (J). (gr. 1). 17.95 *(978-1-935954-18-7(0)*, 9781935954187) Lemniscaat USA.

Groenink, Chuck. The Backwards Birthday Party. Forster, John & Chapin, Tom. 2015. (ENG.). 40p. (J). (gr. -1-3). 17.99 *(978-1-4424-6798-9(3)*, Atheneum Bks. for Young Readers) Simon & Schuster Children's Publishing.

Groenink, Chuck. The Friend Ship. Yeh, Kat. 2016. 32p. (J). 16.99 ***(978-1-4847-0726-5(5))*** Little, Brown Bks. for Young Readers.

Groenink, Chuck. Hank's Big Day: The Story of a Bug. Kuhlman, Evan. 2016. 40p. (J). (gr. -1-2). 16.99 *(978-0-553-51150-5(5)*, Schwartz & Wade Bks.) Random Hse. Children's Bks.

—Honey, the Dog Who Saved Abe Lincoln. Swanson, Shari. 2020. (ENG.). 40p. (J). (gr. -1-3). 17.99 *(978-0-06-269900-8(8)*, Tegen, Katherine Bks) HarperCollins Pubs.

—I Am Not a Fox. Wolf, Karina. 2018. 32p. (J). (gr. -1-2). 16.99 *(978-0-399-17450-6(8)*, G.P. Putnam's Sons Books for Young Readers) Penguin Young Readers Group.

—The Land of Lines. Hussenot, Victor. 2015. (ENG.). 44p. (J). (gr. 1-4). 12.99 *(978-1-4521-4282-1(3))* Chronicle Bks. LLC.

—The Library Book. Chapin, Tom & Mark, Michael. 2017. (ENG.). 40p. (J). (gr. -1-3). 17.99 *(978-1-4814-6092-7(7))* Simon & Schuster Children's Publishing.

—Rufus the Writer. Bram, Elizabeth. 2015. 40p. (J). (gr. -1-3). 17.99 *(978-0-385-37853-6(X)*, Schwartz & Wade Bks.) Random Hse. Children's Bks.

—Under a Pig Tree: A History of the Noble Fruit (a Mixed-Up Book) Palatini, Margie. 2015. (ENG.). 40p. (J). (gr. -1-3). 16.95 *(978-1-4197-1488-7(0)*, Abrams Bks. for Young Readers) Abrams, Inc.

—16 Words: William Carlos Williams & the Red Wheelbarrow. Rogers, Lisa. 2019. 40p. (J). (gr. -1-3). 17.99 *(978-1-5247-2016-2(X)*, Schwartz & Wade Bks.) Random Hse. Children's Bks.

Grof, Stanislav. Lilibit's Dream. Sullivan, Melody. 2011. (ENG.). 32p. (J). 19.95 *(978-1-59275-000-9(1))* Hanford Mead Pubs., Inc.

Groff, David. What Is the Super Bowl? Anastasio, Dina & Who HQ. 2015. (What Was? Ser.). (ENG.). 112p. (J). (gr. 3-7). 5.99 *(978-0-448-48695-6(4)*, Penguin Workshop) Penguin Young Readers Group.

—What Was Ellis Island? Demuth, Patricia Brennan & Who HQ. 2014. (What Was? Ser.). (ENG.). 112p. (J). (gr. 3-7). 5.99 *(978-0-448-47915-6(X)*, Penguin Workshop) Penguin Young Readers Group.

—What Was the Alamo? Belviso, Meg et al. 2013. (What Was? Ser.). (ENG.). 112p. (J). (gr. 3-7). 5.99 *(978-0-448-46710-8(0)*, Penguin Workshop) Penguin Young Readers Group.

—What Was the Hindenburg? Pascal, Janet B. & Who HQ. 2014. (What Was? Ser.). 112p. (J). (gr. 3-7). 5.99 *(978-0-448-48119-7(7)*, Penguin Workshop) Penguin Young Readers Group.

—What Was the Ice Age? Medina, Nico & Who HQ. 2017. (What Was? Ser.). 112p. (J). (gr. 3-7). (ENG.). 5.99 *(978-0-399-54389-0(9))*; lib. bdg. 15.99 *(978-0-399-54391-3(0))* Penguin Young Readers Group. (Penguin Workshop).

—Where Is the White House? Stine, Megan & Who HQ. 2015. (Where Is? Ser.). 112p. (J). (gr. 3-7). 5.99 *(978-0-448-48355-9(6)*, Penguin Workshop) Penguin Young Readers Group.

—Who Was Alexander Graham Bell? Bader, Bonnie & Who HQ. 2013. (Who Was? Ser.). (ENG.). 112p. (J). (gr. 3-7). 5.99 *(978-0-448-46460-2(8)*, Penguin Workshop) Penguin Young Readers Group.

—Who Was Alexander Graham Bell? Bader, Bonnie. 2013. (Who Was... ? Ser.). (ENG.). (J). (gr. 3-7). lib. bdg. 16.60 *(978-1-62765-912-3(9))* Perfection Learning Corp.

—Who Was Clara Barton? Spinner, Stephanie. 2014. (Who Was-? Chapters Ser.). (ENG.). 112p. (J). (gr. 4-6). lib. bdg. 18.69 *(978-1-4844-3355-3(6))* Penguin Young Readers Group.

—Who Was Clara Barton? Spinner, Stephanie & Who HQ. 2014. (Who Was? Ser.). (ENG.). 112p. (J). (gr. 3-7). 5.99 *(978-0-448-47953-8(2)*, Penguin Workshop) Penguin Young Readers Group.

—Who Was Mother Teresa? Gigliotti, Jim & Who HQ. 2015. (Who Was? Ser.). 112p. (J). (gr. 3-7). 5.99 *(978-0-448-48299-6(1)*, Penguin Workshop) Penguin Young Readers Group.

Groff, David, jt. illus. see Hinderliter, John.

Grogan, Patrick. Birding for Children. 2007. 44p. (J). 19.95 *(978-0-615-15948-5(6))* Minton, Art.

Grondel, April. From the Desk of a Three-Year-Old. McNeill, Audrey. 2009. 20p. pap. 24.95 *(978-1-60749-476-8(0))* America Star Bks.

Groome, W. H. C. A Sea-Queen's Sailing. Whistler, Charles W. 2011. 346p. 24.95 *(978-1-934671-42-9(8))* Salem Ridge Press LLC.

Grooms, TeMika. Save the Crash-Test Dummies, 1 vol. Swanson, Jennifer. 2019. (ENG.). 104p. (J). (gr. 3-7). 19.95 *(978-1-68263-022-8(6))* Peachtree Publishing Co. Inc.

Groot, Nicole. The Ants Go Marching One by One. O'Connor, Frankie. Paiva, Johannah Gilman, ed. 2014. (ENG.). 32p. (J). (gr. -1-3). 7.99 *(978-1-4867-0004-2(7))* Flowerpot Children's Pr. Inc. CAN. Dist: Cardinal Pubs. Group.

—The Ants Go Marching One by One: Read with Me. O-Connor, Frankie. 2017. (ENG.). 32p. (J). (gr. -1-3). *(978-1-4867-1277-9(0))* Flowerpot Children's Pr. Inc.

Groothuis, Maya Rose, jt. illus. see Glenn, Emily.

Grose, Helen Mason. The Birds' Christmas Carol. Wiggin, Kate Douglas. 2016. (ENG.). (J). pap. 8.99 *(978-1-4794-1747-6(5))* Wildside Pr., LLC.

Groshelle, Dave. Good Night Little Man. Saunders, Helen. 2006. (J). *(978-0-9763143-4-9(7))* Happy Heart Kids Publishing.

Gross-Andrew, Susannah. It's Your Rite: Girls' Coming-of-Age Stories. Coon, Nora E., ed. 2003. 144p. (J). pap. 9.95 *(978-1-58270-074-8(5))* Beyond Words Publishing, Inc.

Gross, Heather. Bedtime for Cranky Crab. Ergunay, Cristina. 2020. (ENG.). 24p. (J). (gr. -1 — 1). bds. 9.99 *(978-1-338-35796-7(4)*, Cartwheel Bks.) Scholastic, Inc.

—The Greatest Treasure. Fields, Stefanie. 2018. (ENG.). 28p. (J). pap. 14.95 *(978-1-7274-2125-5(6))* CreateSpace Independent Publishing Platform.

Gross, Margaret. A Visit up & down Wall Street. Gross, Jen & Hoch, Jen. 2005. 32p. (J). 14.95 *(978-0-9760875-0-2(2))* Harry & Stephanie Bks.

Gross, Sanai. The Multiplication Monster. Gross, Kimberley & Gross, Kaiya. 2013. 84p. pap. 10.95 *(978-0-9886402-3-8(6))* Vision Bks. LLC.

Gross, Scott. Scooby-Doo! a Number Comparisons Mystery: The Case of the Lunchroom Gobbler, 1 vol. Weakland, Mark. 2014. (Solve It with Scooby-Doo!: Math Ser.). (ENG.). 24p. (J). (gr. k-2). lib. bdg. 28.65 *(978-1-4914-1542-9(8)*, Capstone Pr.) Capstone.

—Scooby-Doo! a Subtraction Mystery: The Case of the Disappearing Doughnuts, 1 vol. Weakland, Mark. 2014. (Solve It with Scooby-Doo!: Math Ser.). (ENG.). 24p. (J). (gr. k-2). lib. bdg. 28.65 *(978-1-4914-1540-5(1)*, Capstone Pr.) Capstone.

—Scooby-Doo! an Addition Mystery: The Case of the Angry Adder, 1 vol. Weakland, Mark. 2014. (Solve It with Scooby-Doo!: Math Ser.). (ENG.). 24p. (J). (gr. k-2). lib. bdg. 28.65 *(978-1-4914-1539-9(8)*, Capstone Pr.) Capstone.

—Scooby-Doo! an Even or Odd Mystery: The Case of the Oddzilla, 1 vol. Weakland, Mark. 2014. (Solve It with Scooby-Doo!: Math Ser.). (ENG.). 24p. (J). (gr. k-2). lib. bdg. 28.65 *(978-1-4914-1541-2(X)*, Capstone Pr.) Capstone.

—Scooby-Doo in Keepaway Camp, 1 vol. Sander, Sonia. 2015. (Scooby-Doo! Ser.). (ENG.). 32p. (J). (gr. k-3). lib. bdg. 27.07 *(978-1-61479-407-3(3)*, 19446, Picture Bk.) Spotlight.

Gross, Sue. I'm Going to Be a Big Brother! Bercun, Brenda. 2007. (ENG.). 33p. (J). (gr. -1-k). 15.95 *(978-0-9767198-7-8(8))* Nurturing Your Children Pr.

Gross, Susan. Soul Searching: A Girl's Guide to Finding Herself. Stillman, Sarah. 2012. (ENG.). 176p. (YA). (gr. 7). pap. 9.99 *(978-1-58270-303-9(5))* Simon Pulse/Beyond Words.

Gross-Zuchman, Deborah. Becky's Braids. Weiss, Susan. 2017. (ENG.). 44p. (J). pap. 15.00 *(978-0-692-89939-7(1))* Abingdon Square Publishing, Ltd.

Grosshauser, Peter. Devociones para Niños Chispita. Lafferty, Jill C. 2016. (SPA.). (J). *(978-1-5064-2101-8(6))* Augsburg Fortress, Pubs.

—The First Christmas: A Spark Story Bible Play & Learn Book, Vol. Lafferty, Jill C., ed. 2016. (ENG.). 64p. (J). (gr. -1-3). 9.99 *(978-1-5064-1763-9(9)*, Sparkhouse Family) Augsburg Fortress, Pubs.

—The Life of Jesus: A Spark Story Bible Play & Learn Book, Vol. Lafferty, Jill C., ed. 2016. (ENG.). 80p. (J). (gr. -1-3). 9.99 *(978-1-5064-1764-6(7)*, Sparkhouse Family) Augsburg Fortress, Pubs.

—My Week. 2010. (My World Ser.). (ENG.). 24p. (J). (gr. -1-1). lib. bdg. 25.60 *(978-1-60754-951-2(4))* Windmill Bks.

—My Week. Wesley, Milliana, ed. 2010. (My World Ser.). (ENG.). 24p. (J). (gr. -1-1). pap. 8.15 *(978-1-61533-035-5(6))* Windmill Bks.

—My Week/Mi Semana. Rosa-Mendoza, Gladys. Wesley, Milliana, ed. 2007. (English Spanish Foundations Ser.). (gr. -1-k). bds. 6.95 *(978-1-931398-25-1(9))* Me+Mi Publishing.

—Old Testament Adventures: A Spark Story Bible Play & Learn Book, Vol. Lafferty, Jill C., ed. 2016. (ENG.). 80p. (J). (gr. -1-3). 9.99 *(978-1-5064-1765-3(5)*, Sparkhouse Family) Augsburg Fortress, Pubs.

—The Spark Story Bible: Spark a Journey Through God's Word, Vol. Hetherington, Debra Thorpe, ed. 2015. (ENG.). 456p. (J). (gr. -1-2). 22.99 *(978-1-4514-9978-0(7)*, Sparkhouse Family) Augsburg Fortress, Pubs.

—Spark Story Bible Devotions for Kids, Vol. Lafferty, Jill C. 2016. (ENG.). 216p. (J). (gr. -1-3). 14.99 *(978-1-5064-1766-0(3))* Augsburg Fortress, Pubs.

—Spark Story Bible Psalm Book: Prayers & Poems for Kids, Vol. Beglau, Judy. Krueger, Naomi Joy, ed. 2016. (ENG.). 112p. (J). (gr. -1-3). 14.99 *(978-1-5064-1768-4(X))* Augsburg Fortress, Pubs.

—The Story of Christmas: A Spark Bible Story, Vol. Smith, Martina. 2015. (Spark Bible Stories Ser.). (ENG.). 32p. (J). (gr. -1-2). 12.99 *(978-1-5064-0224-6(0)*, Sparkhouse Family) Augsburg Fortress, Pubs.

—The Story of Easter: A Spark Bible Story, Vol. Smith, Martina. 2016. (Spark Bible Stories Ser.). (ENG.). 32p. (J). (gr. -1-2). 12.99 *(978-1-5064-0230-7(5)*, Sparkhouse Family) Augsburg Fortress, Pubs.

—The Story of King David: A Spark Bible Story. Smith, Martina. 2016. (Spark Bible Stories Ser.). (ENG.). 32p. (J). (gr. -1-2). 12.99 *(978-1-5064-0226-0(7)*, Sparkhouse Family) Augsburg Fortress, Pubs.

—The Story of Noah's Ark: A Spark Bible Story. Rivadeneira, Caryn Dahlstrand. 2016. (Spark Story Bibles Ser.). (ENG.). 32p. (J). (gr. -1-3). 12.99 *(978-1-5064-1767-7(1))* Augsburg Fortress, Pubs.

Grosshauser, Peter & Temple, Ed. La Historia de la Creacion: Un Relato de la Biblia Chispita. Smith, Martina. 2016. (SPA.). (J). *(978-1-5064-2100-1(8))* Augsburg Fortress, Pubs.

—La Historia de la Navidad: Un Relato de la Biblia Chispita. Smith, Martina. 2016. (SPA.). (J). *(978-1-5064-2102-5(4))* Augsburg Fortress, Pubs.

Grossman, Laurie, photos by. Children of Israel. Grossman, Laurie. 2003. 48p. (J). 17.95 *(978-1-58013-072-1(0)*, Kar-Ben Publishing) Lerner Publishing Group.

Grossman, Nancy. Did You Carry the Flag Today, Charley. Caudill, Rebecca. 2007. 96p. (J). pap. 7.95 *(978-0-8050-8141-1(0)*, Holt, Henry & Co. Bks. For Young Readers) Holt, Henry & Co.

Grossmann-Hensel, Katharina. Papa is a Pirate. Grossmann-Hensel, Katharina. 2009. 32p. (J). (gr. -1-3). 16.95 *(978-0-7358-2237-5(9))* North-South Bks., Inc.

Grosvenor, Charles & Gerard, Justin. How to Train Your Dragon: Meet the Dragons. Hapka, Catherine. 2010. (I Can Read Book 1 Ser.). 32p. (J). (gr. k-3). pap. 3.99 *(978-0-06-156733-9(7))* HarperCollins Pubs.

Grotke, Christopher A. The Mysterious Jamestown Suitcase: A Bailey Fish Adventure. Salisbury, Linda G. 2006. (Bailey Fish Adventures Ser.). 191p. (J). (gr. 3-7). per. 8.95 *(978-1-881539-43-8(1))* Tabby Hse. Bks.
—No Sisters Sisters Club: A Bailey Fish Adventure. Salisbury, Linda G. 2005. 188p. (J). per. 8.95 *(978-1-881539-40-7(7))* Tabby Hse. Bks.
—The Thief at Keswick Inn: A Bailey Fish Adventure. Salisbury, Linda G. 2006. (Bailey Fish Adventures Ser.). 191p. (J). (gr. 3-7). per. 8.95 *(978-1-881539-41-4(5))* Tabby Hse. Bks.
Grott, Isabella. Not Yet! Rosen, Robert. 2017. (Play Time Ser.). (ENG.). 24p. (gr. -1-2). pap. 8.95 *(978-1-68342-766-7(1)*, 9781683427667) Rourke Educational Media.
—The Perfect Pet. Nino, Carl. 2017. (Family Time Ser.). (ENG.). 24p. (gr. -1-2). pap. 8.95 *(978-1-68342-755-1(6)*, 9781683427551) Rourke Educational Media.
—Planting Seeds. James, Lauren & Kisloski, Carolyn. 2017. (Seasons Around Me Ser.). (ENG.). 24p. (gr. -1-2). pap. 8.95 *(978-1-68342-789-6(0)*, 9781683427896) Rourke Educational Media.
—Sarah's Day at Kindergarten. Wells, Robin. 2017. (School Days Ser.). (ENG.). 24p. (gr. -1-2). 29.93 *(978-1-68342-723-0(8)*, 9781683427230) Rourke Educational Media.
—Sarah's Day in Kindergarten. Wells, Robin. 2017. (School Days Ser.). (ENG.). 24p. (gr. -1-2). pap. 8.95 *(978-1-68342-775-9(0)*, 9781683427759) Rourke Educational Media.
—Superheroes Without Capes: Discover the Super Powers of 20 Famous People, & Find Your Own, Too! Magrin, Federica. 2019. (ENG.). 96p. (J). (gr. 4). 16.95 *(978-1-4549-3870-5(6))* Sterling Publishing Co., Inc.
—Trick or Treat. Wells, Robin. 2017. (Field Trip Fun Ser.). (ENG.). 24p. (gr. -1-2). 29.93 *(978-1-68342-717-9(3)*, 9781683427179); pap. 8.95 *(978-1-68342-769-8(6)*, 9781683427698) Rourke Educational Media.
—We Have a Box. Wallace, John & Kisloski, Carolyn. 2017. (My Adventures Ser.). (ENG.). 24p. (gr. -1-2). pap. 8.95 *(978-1-68342-760-5(2)*, 9781683427605) Rourke Educational Media.
—What Is Sam Making? Walters, Abby. 2017. (Play Time Ser.). (ENG.). 24p. (gr. -1-2). 29.93 *(978-1-68342-746-9(7)*, 9781683427469) Rourke Educational Media.
Grout, Paul A. Pauline Jaricot: Foundress of the Living Rosary & the Society for the Propagation of the Faith. Windeatt, Mary F. 2009. (ENG.). 256p. (J). (gr. 3-9). reprint ed. pap. 15.95 *(978-0-89555-425-3(9))* TAN Bks.
—Saint Louis de Montfort: The Story of Our Lady's Slave. Windeatt, Mary F. 2009. Orig. Title: Our Lady's Slave: the Story of St. Louis Mary Grignion de Montfort. (ENG.). 211p. (J). (gr. 2-9). reprint ed. pap. 13.95 *(978-0-89555-414-7(3))* TAN Bks.
Grove, Christine. Amanda Panda & the Bigger, Better Birthday. Ransom, Candice. 2018. 32p. (J). (gr. -1-2). 17.99 *(978-1-5247-6819-5(7))*; (ENG.). lib. bdg. 20.99 *(978-1-5247-6820-1(0))* Random Hse. Children's Bks. (Doubleday Bks. for Young Readers).
—Amanda Panda Quits Kindergarten. Ransom, Candice. 2017. 32p. (J). (gr. -1-2). 17.99 *(978-0-399-55455-1(6)*, Doubleday Bks. for Young Readers) Random Hse. Children's Bks.
—Bounce, Bounce, Baby! Bardaus, Anna W. 2013. (J). *(978-0-545-61897-7(5))* Scholastic, Inc.
—Dance, Dance, Baby! Bardaus, Anna W. 2013. (J). *(978-0-545-61899-1(1))* Scholastic, Inc.
—My Mom Has a Job. Snead, Kathi. 2004. (J). *(978-0-9747385-0-5(6))* City of Manassas Department of Social Services.
—Reach, Reach, Baby! Bardaus, Anna W. 2013. (J). *(978-0-545-61900-4(9))* Scholastic, Inc.
—Read, Read, Baby! Bardaus, Anna W. 2013. (J). *(978-0-545-61898-4(3))* Scholastic, Inc.
—Wait! It's Friday. Barash, Chris. 2019. (J). *(978-1-68115-542-5(7)*, Apples & Honey Pr.) Behrman Hse., Inc.
Grove, Gladys. Poudre Canyon. Gonder, Glen W. Gonder, Sharon J., ed. Date not set. (Adventures of Willy Whacker Ser.: Vol. 9). 161p. (YA). (gr. 6-8). lib. bdg. 8.95 *(978-1-58389-004-2(1))* Osage Bend Publishing Co.
Grover, Becky. Snail, I Love You. Platt, Tevah & Willa, Thiel. 2018. (ENG.). 32p. (J). 19.99 *(978-1-947989-18-4(9)*, Fifth Avenue Pr.) Ann Arbor District Library.
Grover, James, et al. Draw Your Own Lettering & Decorative Zendoodles. Huff, Abby. 2017. (Draw Your Own Zendoodles Ser.). (ENG.). 48p. (J). (gr. 4-8). lib. bdg. 31.99 *(978-1-5157-4841-0(3)*, Capstone Pr.) Capstone.
Grover, Nina. A Children's Songbook Companion. Graham, Pat et al. 2005. per. *(978-0-88290-795-6(6)*, Horizon Pubs.) Cedar Fort, Inc./CFI Distribution.
Groves, Julia. Animal Babies in the Forest! 2016. (Animal Babies Ser.: 4). 14p. (J). spiral bd. *(978-1-84643-878-3(0))* Child's Play International Ltd.
—Animal Babies in the Meadow! 2016. (Animal Babies Ser.: 4). 14p. (J). spiral bd. *(978-1-84643-879-0(9))* Child's Play International Ltd.
—Animal Babies in the River! 2016. (Animal Babies Ser.: 4). 14p. (J). spiral bd. *(978-1-84643-880-6(2))* Child's Play International Ltd.
—Animal Babies on the Mountain! 2016. (Animal Babies Ser.: 4). 14p. (J). spiral bd. *(978-1-84643-881-3(0))* Child's Play International Ltd.
—Rainforest. 2018. (Child's Play Library). 36p. (J). (ENG.). *(978-1-84643-936-0(1))*; pap. *(978-1-84643-935-3(3))* Child's Play International Ltd.
Grubb, W. B. Quarterback Hothead. Heyliger, William. 2011. 262p. 47.95 *(978-1-258-09738-7(9))* Literary Licensing, LLC.
Gruber, Michael & Graves, Linda. The Legend of the Brog. Gruber, Michael. 2005. (J). per. 9.95 *(978-0-9770413-0-5(1))* Gruber Enterprises.
Grubman, Steve, photos by. Orangutans Are Ticklish: Fun Facts from an Animal Photographer. Davis, Jill. 2016. (ENG.). 40p. (J). (gr. -1-2). 7.99 *(978-0-553-53393-4(2)*, Dragonfly Bks.) Random Hse. Children's Bks.
Grudina, Paola Bertolina. My Baptism Bible Catholic Edition. Godfrey, Jan. 2012. 144p. (J). 16.95 *(978-0-8198-4907-6(3))* Pauline Bks. & Media.
Grudina, Paola Bertolini. The Christmas Activity Book. Wright, Sally Ann. 2010. 32p. (J). (gr. k-3). 10.95 *(978-0-8198-1584-2(5))* Pauline Bks. & Media.
—The Easter Swallows. Howie, Vicki. 2007. 32p. (J). 10.95 *(978-0-8198-2360-1(0))* Pauline Bks. & Media.
—What Did the Fishermen Catch? And Other Questions. Wright, Sally Ann. 2006. 32p. (J). (gr. -1). 10.95 *(978-0-8091-6732-6(8)*, 6732-8) Paulist Pr.
—Who Built the Ark? And Other Questions. Wright, Sally Ann. 2006. 32p. (J). (gr. -1-3). 10.95 *(978-0-8091-6730-2(1)*, 6730-1) Paulist Pr.
Gruebele, Michelle. Rudy's Incredible Kidney Machine. Waibel, Stacy Raye. 2011. 32p. (J). 10.95 *(978-0-9820983-3-2(2))* Purple Cow Pr.
Gruelle, Johnny. The Complete Fairy Tales of the Brothers Grimm All-New Third Edition. Zipes, Jack, tr. 3rd ed. 2003. 800p. (J). reprint ed. pap. 24.00 *(978-0-553-38216-7(0)*, Bantam) Random House Publishing Group.
Gruelle, Johnny. Raggedy Ann in Cookie Land: (Classic) Gruelle, Johnny. 2010. (Raggedy Ann Ser.). (ENG.). 96p. (J). (gr. k-5). 21.99 *(978-1-4424-2199-8(1)*, Simon & Schuster Bks. For Young Readers) Simon & Schuster Bks. For Young Readers.
—Raggedy Ann's Wishing Pebble - Written & Illustrated by Johnny Gruelle. Gruelle, Johnny. 2014. (ENG.). (J). (gr. -1-3). *(978-1-4733-2110-6(7))*; pap. *(978-1-4733-2109-0(3))* Read Bks.
Gruelle, Johnny, jt. illus. see Gooch, Thelma.
Gruelle, Justin C. Once Round the Sun. Titchenell, Elsa-Brita. 2011. 62p. 36.95 *(978-1-258-03323-1(2))* Literary Licensing, LLC.
Gruen, Chuck. Little Chief Mischief: From Tales of the Menehune. Salter-Mathieson, Nigel C. S. 2011. 44p. pap. 35.95 *(978-1-258-10135-0(1))* Literary Licensing, LLC.
Gruenfelder, Robin. The Naked Cat With The Velvet Paws. Olek, Lisa B. 2011. 40p. (J). 18.95 *(978-1-60131-092-7(7))* Big Tent Bks.
—Yoshka's Journey to Christmas. Olek, Lisa B. 2012. 70p. (J). 21.95 *(978-1-60131-125-2(7)*, Castlebridge Bks.) Big Tent Bks.
Gruger, F. R. & Justice, B. Martin. Letters from a Self-Made Merchant to His Son. Lorimer, George Horace. 2019. (ENG.). 164p. (J). pap. ***(978-1-5287-1346-7(X))*** Freeman Pr.
Grunden, Kimberly. Circle the Moon. Lockhart, Barbara M. 2008. 24p. pap. 10.95 *(978-1-934246-96-2(4))* Peppertree Pr., The.
—I'm a Perfectly Normal Kid Who Happens to Have Diabetes! Morris, Cathy. 2007. 24p. per. 12.95 *(978-1-934246-85-6(9))* Peppertree Pr., The.
Grunduls Design, Anna. Notebook: Abstract 6x9 Dot Grid Journal with Adult Coloring Margins, 100 Pages. Grunduls Colorful Journals, Anna. 2019. (ENG.). 102p. (J). pap. 6.99 *(978-1-0902-8911-7(1))* Independently Published.
Grundy, Jessica. Greystone Valley. Brooks, Charlie. 2013. 166p. 17.99 *(978-1-938821-33-2(5))*; 198p. pap. 9.99 *(978-1-938821-41-7(6))* Grey Gecko Pr.
Grundy, Peter. Information Graphics: Human Body. Rogers, Simon. 2014. (ENG.). 80p. (J). (gr. 1-4). 17.99 *(978-0-7636-7123-5(1)*, Big Picture Press) Candlewick Pr.
Grupczynski, Kelly. Disney Frozen. PI Kids. 2020. (Look & Find Ser.). (ENG.). 18p. (J). ***(978-1-5037-5470-6(7)***, e93d96a5-a318-4b6c-90f1-3f4e95d94a78, p i kids) Phoenix International Publications, Inc.
Gruszka, Chris A. For the Love of Texas: Tell Me about the Colonists. Christian, Betsy & Christian, George. 2013. (ENG.). 114p. (J). (gr. 4-7). 27.99 *(978-1-5402-2214-5(4)*, History Pr., The) Arcadia Publishing.
Grutzik, Becky. #8 the Runaway Puppy: A Mystery with Probability. Barriman, Lydia. 2011. (Manga Math Mysteries Set II Ser.). pap. 39.62 *(978-0-7613-8365-9(4)*, Graphic Universe™) Lerner Publishing Group.
Grutzik, Rebecca Ann. The Runaway Puppy No. 8: A Mystery with Probability. Barriman, Lydia. 2011. (Manga Math Mysteries Ser.: 8). (ENG.). 48p. (J). (gr. 3-5). pap. 6.95 *(978-0-7613-8137-2(6)*, 9780761381372, Graphic Universe™) Lerner Publishing Group.
Grzelak, Kyle. Gravy on My Mashed Potatoes: A Creative Exploration of Special Relationships. Sisler, Stephanie. 2012. 20p. pap. 11.95 *(978-1-61493-123-2(2))* Peppertree Pr., The.
—Matthews Monsters, a Creative Comprehensive Exercise. Sisler, Stephanie. 2011. 32p. pap. 12.95 *(978-1-61493-015-0(5))* Peppertree Pr., The.
—A Peanut Butter & Monster Sandwich. Dooley, Larry. 2013. 24p. pap. 12.95 *(978-1-61493-206-2(9))* Peppertree Pr., The.
Gsell, Nicole. Spit & Sticks: A Chimney Swift Story. Evans, Marilyn Grohoske. 2015. 32p. (J). (gr. -1-2). lib. bdg. 16.95 *(978-1-58089-588-0(3))* Charlesbridge Publishing, Inc.
Guagenti, Wendy. Glowings & Luke. Dati, Glo Dio. 2019. (ENG.). 40p. (J). 23.95 ***(978-1-4808-8222-5(4))***; pap. 13.99 ***(978-1-4808-8221-8(6))*** Archway Publishing.
Guara, Ig, et al. Marvel-Verse: Black Widow. 2020. 112p. (J). (gr. 5-9). pap. 9.99 *(978-1-302-92119-4(3))* Marvel Worldwide, Inc.
Guardino, Sabrina, jt. illus. see Olsen, Lucas.
Guarducci, Ilaria. Guess Which Hand: A Turn-And-Seek Book. Wilhelm, Hans. 2018. (ENG.). 10p. (J). (gr. -1 — 1). bds. 10.99 *(978-1-4521-6359-8(6))* Chronicle Bks. LLC.
Guarducci, Ilaria. Spiky. Guarducci, Ilaria. Watkinson, Laura, tr. 2019. 36p. (J). (gr. k-2). 17.99 *(978-1-5420-4043-3(4)*, 9781542040433, AmazonCrossing) Amazon Publishing.
Guarnaccia, Steven. Anansi. Gleeson, Brian. 2005. (Rabbit Ears-A Classic Tale Ser.). (ENG.). 36p. (J). (gr. 2-6). 28.50 *(978-1-59679-342-2(2)*, 12943, Picture Bk.) Spotlight.
—Knit Your Bit: A World War I Story. Hopkinson, Deborah. 2013. (ENG.). 32p. (J). (gr. k-3). 17.99 *(978-0-399-25241-9(X)*, G.P. Putnam's Sons Books for Young Readers) Penguin Young Readers Group.
Guarnotta, Lucia. We Are Tigers. 2006. (We Are... Ser.). 40p. (gr. -1-k). bds. *(978-2-7641-1456-8(7))* Tormont Pubns.
Guarracino, Nick. Grumpy Dad Shovels Snow. Romita, Tom. 2017. (Grumpy Dad Ser.). (ENG.). 38p. (J). (gr. k-1). pap. 11.99 *(978-0-9995928-0-9(7))* Romita, Tom.
—Kat Mcgee Saves the World: An Earth Day Adventure! Riddick, Kristin. 2019. (Kat Mcgee Adventure Ser.: Vol. 5). (ENG.). 152p. (J). pap. 11.99 *(978-1-0906-1236-6(2))* Independently Published.
Guasp, Sr Joan. Manantis. el Corazón de Leo. Alba Minano, Sra Alycia. La Fabrica de Suenos, ed. 2017. (SPA.). 242p. (J). pap. *(978-84-944449-9-9(9))* La Fabrica De Suenos S.C.
Guay, Rebecca. Bad Girls: Sirens, Jezebels, Murderesses, Thieves & Other Female Villains. Yolen, Jane & Stemple, Heidi E. Y. 2015. (ENG.). 172p. (J). (gr. 4-7). pap. 9.95 *(978-1-58089-186-8(1))* Charlesbridge Publishing, Inc.
—Bad Girls: Sirens, Jezebels, Murderesses, Thieves & Other Female Villains. Yolen, Jane & Stemple, Heidi E. Y. ed. 2015. (Live Oak Media EReadalong Ser.). (ENG.). 172p. (YA). (gr. 7-9). E-Book 29.95 *(978-1-4301-1785-8(0)*, 9781430117858) Live Oak Media.
—The Barefoot Book Stories from the Ballet. Yolen, Jane et al. 2004. (ENG.). 96p. (J). 19.99 *(978-1-84148-229-3(3))* Barefoot Bks., Inc.
—Goddesses: A World of Myth & Magic. Muten, Burleigh. 2003. (ENG.). 80p. (J). 19.99 *(978-1-84148-075-6(4))* Barefoot Bks., Inc.
Guay, Rebecca, jt. illus. see Wilson, Anne.
Gubitosi, Lillian. A Smickamookum Drinks Belly. Blackman, S. A. 2003. 32p. (J). (gr. -1-k). 16.95 incl. audio *(978-1-929409-02-0(8))* Blade Publishing.
Gubler, Matthew Gray. Rumple Buttercup: a Story of Bananas, Belonging, & Being Yourself. Gubler, Matthew Gray. 2019. (ENG.). 136p. (J). (gr. k-12). 14.99 *(978-0-525-64844-4(5))*; lib. bdg. 17.99 *(978-0-525-70763-9(8))* Random Hse. Children's Bks. (Random Hse. Bks. for Young Readers).
Gudeon, Adam. Bedtime at Bessie & Lil's. Sternberg, Julie. 2015. (ENG.). 32p. (J). (gr. -1-2). 16.95 *(978-1-59078-934-6(2))* Boyds Mills Pr.
Gudeon, Adam. Me & Meow. Gudeon, Adam. 2011. (ENG.). 32p. (J). (gr. -1-k). 12.99 *(978-0-06-199821-8(4))* HarperCollins Pubs.
Gudeon, Karla. The Language of Angels: A Story about the Reinvention of Hebrew. Michelson, Richard. 2017. 32p. (J). (gr. k-4). lib. bdg. 16.99 *(978-1-58089-636-8(7))* Charlesbridge Publishing, Inc.
—One Red Apple. Ziefert, Harriet. 2009. 36p. (J). 15.99 *(978-1-934706-46-6(9))* Blue Apple Bks.
Gudsnuk, Kristen. Making Friends. Gudsnuk, Kristen. 2018. (Making Friends Ser.: 1). (ENG.). 272p. (J). (gr. 3-7). 24.99 *(978-1-338-13922-8(3))*; pap. 12.99 *(978-1-338-13921-1(5))* Scholastic, Inc. (Graphix).
Gudsnuk, Kristen. Minecraft: Wither Without You (Graphic Novel) Gudsnuk, Kristen. 2020. (ENG.). 88p. (J). (gr. 3-7). pap. 10.99 ***(978-1-5067-0835-5(8)***, Dark Horse Books) Dark Horse Comics.
Güell, Fernanado. Disney Princess: Princess Pals. Fischer, Maggie. 2018. (ENG.). 12p. (J). (gr. -1-k). bds. 9.99 *(978-0-7944-4202-6(1)*, Studio Fun International) Printers Row Publishing Group.
Guell, Fernando. Disney Fancy Nancy: Fancy in Every Way! Acampora, Courtney. 2020. (ENG.). 10p. (J). (gr. -1-k). bds. 10.99 *(978-0-7944-4478-5(4)*, Studio Fun International) Printers Row Publishing Group.
Guell, Fernando. Disney Fancy Nancy: Let's Make It Fancy! Acampora, Courtney. 2020. (Deluxe Guess Who? Ser.). (ENG.). 12p. (J). (gr. -1-k). bds. 10.99 ***(978-0-7944-4543-0(8)***, Studio Fun International) Printers Row Publishing Group.
Guénette, Geneviève. Lucifer, Mon Grand-Père, Tome 1. Rosseau, Paul. 2004. (Mon Roman Ser.). (FRE.). 160p. (J). (gr. 2). pap. *(978-2-89021-650-1(0))* Diffusion du livre Mirabel (DLM).
Guenette, Genevieve. Lucifer, Mon Grand-Pere: Tome 2. Rousseau, Paul. 2004. (Mon Roman Ser.). (FRE.). 184p. (J). (gr. 2). pap. *(978-2-89021-703-4(5))* Diffusion du livre Mirabel (DLM).
Guenther, Kim. My Back Yard: Poems to Read to Your Children. Schiffner, Frederick A. 2004. 32p. (J). 14.95 *(978-0-9765782-0-8(4))* Schiffner, Frederick A.
Guerin, Yann. Nino: L'Éveil. Savey, Ross. Savignano, Loris, tr. 2018. (Tome Ser.: Vol. 1). (FRE.). 312p. (J). pap. 11.50 *(978-1-7275-1384-4(3))* CreateSpace Independent Publishing Platform.
Guerlais, Gérald. At the Marsh in the Meadow. Mebane, Jeanie. 2016. (ENG.). 32p. (J). (gr. 1-3). 17.99 *(978-1-58536-958-4(6)*, 204028) Sleeping Bear Pr.
—A Catfish Tale: A Bayou Story of the Fisherman & His Wife. Stewart, Whitney. 2014. (AV2 Fiction Readalong Ser.: Vol. 135). (ENG.). (J). (gr. -1-2). lib. bdg. 34.28 *(978-1-4896-2840-4(1)*, AV2 by Weigl) Weigl Pubs., Inc.
Guerlais, Gérald. For Real, I Paraded in My Underpants! The Story of the Emperor's New Clothes As Told by the Emperor. Loewen, Nancy. 2018. (Other Side of the Story Ser.). (ENG.). (J). pap. 41.70 ***(978-1-5158-2331-5(8)***, 27520, Picture Window Bks.) Capstone.
Guerlais, Gérald. Guardians of Island X, 2. Delaney, Rachelle. 2012. (Ship of Lost Souls Ser.). (ENG.). 224p. (J). (gr. 4-6). 22.44 *(978-0-448-45778-9(4)*, Grosset & Dunlap) Penguin Publishing Group.
—Honestly, Red Riding Hood Was Rotten! The Story of Little Red Riding Hood As Told by the Wolf, 1 vol. Shaskan, Trisha Speed. 2013. (Other Side of the Story Ser.). (ENG.). 24p. (J). (gr. -1-3). 9.95 *(978-1-4795-1940-8(5)*, Picture Window Bks.) Capstone.
—Honestly, Red Riding Hood Was Rotten! The Story of Little Red Riding Hood as Told by the Wolf. Shaskan, Trisha Speed. 2011. (Other Side of the Story Ser.). (ENG.). 24p. (J). (gr. -1-3). pap. 6.95 *(978-1-4048-7046-8(6))*; lib. bdg. 27.99 *(978-1-4048-6673-7(6))* Capstone. (Picture Window Bks.).
—The Hunt for the Panther, 3. Delaney, Rachelle. 2013. (Ship of Lost Souls Ser.: 3). (ENG.). 224p. (J). (gr. 4-6). 22.44 *(978-0-448-45780-2(6))* Penguin Young Readers Group.
—Seriously, Cinderella Is So Annoying! The Story of Cinderella as Told by the Wicked Stepmother. Shaskan, Trisha Speed. (Other Side of the Story Ser.). (ENG.). 24p. (J). (gr. -1-3). 2013. 9.95 *(978-1-4795-1941-5(3))*; 2011. pap. 6.95 *(978-1-4048-7048-2(2))*; 2011. lib. bdg. 27.99 *(978-1-4048-6674-4(4))* Capstone. (Picture Window Bks.).
—Seriously, Snow White Was So Forgetful! The Story of Snow White as Told by the Dwarves. Loewen, Nancy. 2013. (Other Side of the Story Ser.). (ENG.). 24p. (J). (gr. -1-3). pap. 6.95 *(978-1-4048-8085-6(2))*; lib. bdg. 27.99 *(978-1-4048-7937-9(4))* Capstone. (Picture Window Bks.).
—Seriously, Snow White Was SO Forgetful! The Story of Snow White As Told by the Dwarves, 1 vol. Loewen, Nancy. 2013. (Other Side of the Story Ser.). (ENG.). 24p. (J). (gr. -1-3). 9.95 *(978-1-4795-1943-9(X)*, Picture Window Bks.) Capstone.
—The Ship of Lost Souls #1, 1. Delaney, Rachelle. 2012. (Ship of Lost Souls Ser.). (ENG.). 256p. (J). (gr. 4-6). 22.44 *(978-0-448-45776-5(8)*, Grosset & Dunlap) Penguin Publishing Group.
—The Story of Orion: A Roman Constellation Myth, 1 vol. 2012. (Night Sky Stories Ser.). (ENG.). 24p. (J). (gr. 2-4). pap. 8.95 *(978-1-4048-7718-4(5)*, Picture Window Bks.) Capstone.
—The Story of Ursa Major & Ursa Minor: A Roman Constellation Myth, 1 vol. 2012. (Night Sky Stories Ser.). (ENG.). 24p. (J). (gr. 2-4). pap. 8.95 *(978-1-4048-7720-7(7)*, Picture Window Bks.) Capstone.
—Truthfully, Something Smelled Fishy! The Story of the Fisherman & His Wife As Told by the Wife. Gunderson, Jessica. 2018. (Other Side of the Story Ser.). (ENG.). (J). pap. 41.70 ***(978-1-5158-2327-8(X)***, 27518); 24p. (gr. -1-3). lib. bdg. 27.99 *(978-1-5158-2298-1(2)*, 137007) Capstone. (Picture Window Bks.).
Guerlais, Gérald & Bernardini, Cristian. Trust Me, Jack's Beanstalk Stinks! The Story of Jack & the Beanstalk as Told by the Giant. Loewen, Nancy & Braun, Eric. 2013. (Other Side of the Story Ser.). (ENG.). 24p. (J). (gr. -1-3). 9.95 *(978-1-4795-1942-2(1)*, Picture Window Bks.) Capstone.
Guerlais, Gérald & Cox, Russ. For Real, I Paraded in My Underpants! The Story of the Emperor's New Clothes As Told by the Emperor. Loewen, Nancy. 2018. (Other Side of the Story Ser.). (ENG.). 24p. (J). (gr. -1-3). lib. bdg. 27.99 *(978-1-5158-2294-3(X)*, 137004, Picture Window Bks.) Capstone.
Guerlais, Gérald, jt. illus. see Bernardini, Cristian.
Guerlais, Gerald Claude. De Veras, ¡Cenicienta Es Bien Pesada! El Cuento de Cenicienta Contado Por la Madrastra Malvada. Speed Shaskan, Trisha Sue. (Otro Lado Del Cuento Ser.).Tr. of Seriously, Cinderella Is SO Annoying!. (SPA.). 24p. (J). (gr. -1-3). 2020. pap. 6.95 *(978-1-5158-6090-7(6)*, 142366); 2019. lib. bdg. 27.99 *(978-1-5158-4652-9(0)*, 141254) Capstone. (Picture Window Bks.).
—Honestamente, ¡Caperucita Roja Era Muy Vanidosa! El Cuento de Caperucita Roja Contado Por el Lobo. Speed Shaskan, Trisha Sue. (Otro Lado Del Cuento Ser.).Tr. of Honestly, Red Riding Hood Was Rotten!. (SPA.). 24p. (J). (gr. -1-3). 2020. pap. 6.95 *(978-1-5158-6087-7(6)*, 142364); 2019. lib. bdg. 27.99 *(978-1-5158-4651-2(2)*, 141252) Capstone. (Picture Window Bks.).
Guerra, Joycelyne. Meeting My Anxiety. Rader, Elisa Silverglade. Keen, Tammi Croteau, ed. 2018. (ENG.). 36p. (J). pap. 14.95 *(978-1-9853-0078-1(8))* CreateSpace Independent Publishing Platform.
—Meeting My Anxiety - a Companion Book. Rader, Elisa Silverglade. Keen, Tammi Croteau, ed. 2018. (ENG.). 48p. (J). pap. 14.95 *(978-1-9853-0082-8(6))* CreateSpace Independent Publishing Platform.
Guerrero, Andres. Los Cazadores de Monstruos. Vallejo-Nagera, Alejandra.Tr. of Monsters Hunters. (SPA.). 31p. (J). (gr. k-1). 8.95 *(978-1-58986-549-5(9))* Santillana USA Publishing Co., Inc.
—Cuando Llegara Mi Cumpleanos? Vallejo-Nagera, Alejandra. (SPA.). 29p. (J). (gr. k-1). 8.95 *(978-1-58986-548-8(0))* Santillana USA Publishing Co., Inc.
—Cuanto me Quieren! Vallejo-Nagera, Alejandra. 2003. (SPA.). 23p. (J). (gr. k-1). 8.95 *(978-84-204-4951-7(2))* Santillana USA Publishing Co., Inc.
Guerrero, Andrés. Los Bigotes de Chocolate. Vallejo-Nágera, Alejandra. 2008. (Serie Verde / Colección Ricardetes -Ricardetes Collection). (SPA.). 27p. (J). (gr. k-1). pap. 9.99 *(978-1-63113-949-9(5))* Santillana USA Publishing Co., Inc.
Guerrero, Andres. Mira Como He Crecido. Vallejo-Nagera, Alejandra. (SPA.). 31p. (J). (gr. k-1). 8.95 *(978-1-58986-547-1(2))* Santillana USA Publishing Co., Inc.
—No Tengo Sueno! Vallejo-Nagera, Alejandra. (SPA.). 31p. (J). (gr. k-1). 8.95 *(978-1-58986-546-4(4))* Santillana USA Publishing Co., Inc.
Guerrero, Andres. La Noche. Guerrero, Andres. 2003. (SPA.). 28p. (J). (gr. k-3). 7.95 *(978-84-204-4321-8(2))* Santillana USA Publishing Co., Inc.
Guesné, Maude & Guesné, Maude. Once upon a Fairy Tale. 2016. (Coloring Studio Ser.: 1). (ENG.). 32p. (J). (gr. 1-17). pap. 7.99 *(978-0-316-39292-1(8))* Little, Brown Bks. for Young Readers.
Guesné, Maude, jt. illus. see Guesné, Maude.
Guest, Leigh H. Fred the Tree. Guest, Leigh H. 2019. (ENG.). 36p. (J). 19.99 ***(978-0-578-58627-4(4))*** Guest, Leigh.
Guest, Peggy. J. Milton Turner, an American Hero. Barile, Mary Collins. 2013. 52p. 24.95 *(978-0-9889643-0-3(9))* MathisJones Communications, LLC.
Guettier, Bénédicte. Dinosaurs. Guettier, Bénédicte. 2005. (ENG.). 14p. (J). (gr. -1-k). 11.95 *(978-1-929132-86-7(7))* Kane Miller.

Guevara, Alejandra. Ale / Ale (Buenas Noches) 2017. (Buenas Noches Ser.). (ENG & SPA.). (J). (gr. -1-2). pap. *(978-958-776-538-0(9))* Norma Ediciones, S.A.

Guevara, Dennis Villanueva. Pepitina. Iturrondo, Angeles Molina. 2004. (Green Ser.). 24p. (J). *(978-1-57581-435-3(8))* Ediciones Santillana, Inc.

Guevara, Susan. Chato & the Party Animals. Soto, Gary. (Chato Ser.). 25.95 incl. audio *(978-1-59112-460-3(3))*; 28.95 incl. audio compact disk *(978-1-59112-920-2(6))*; pap. 37.95 incl. audio *(978-1-59112-461-0(1))*; pap. 39.95 incl. audio compact disk *(978-1-59112-921-9(4))* Live Oak Media.

—Chato & the Party Animals. Soto, Gary. 2004. 32p. (J). (gr. -1-3). reprint ed. pap. 7.99 *(978-0-14-240032-6(7),* Puffin Books) Penguin Young Readers Group.

—Chato & the Party Animals. Soto, Gary. 2004. (Chato Ser.). (gr. -1-3). 17.00 *(978-0-7569-2921-3(0))* Perfection Learning Corp.

—Chato & the Party Animals/Chato y Los Amigos Pachangueros (Bilingual Set) Soto, Gary. 2006. (Chato Ser.). (ENG.). (J). pap. 39.95 incl. audio compact disk *(978-1-59519-671-2(4))* Live Oak Media.

—Chato Goes Cruisin' Soto, Gary. 2008. (Chato Ser.). (J). 25.95 incl. audio *(978-1-59519-906-5(3))*; pap. 16.95 *(978-1-59519-905-8(5))* Live Oak Media.

—Chato Goes Cruisin' Soto, Gary. 2007. (Chato Ser.). (J). (gr. -1-3). 14.65 *(978-0-7569-8147-1(6))* Perfection Learning Corp.

—Chato y los Amigos Pachangueros. Soto, Gary. 2004.Tr. of Chato & the Party Animals. 32p. (J). (gr. -1-3). reprint ed. pap. 8.99 *(978-0-14-240033-3(5),* Puffin Books) Penguin Young Readers Group.

—Chato's Kitchen. Soto, Gary. 2003. (Chato Ser.). (J). (gr. -1-2). pap. 39.95 *(978-1-59112-527-3(8))* Live Oak Media.

—Isabel's House of Butterflies. Johnston, Tony. 2005. 32p. pap. 6.95 *(978-1-58685-844-5(0))* Gibbs Smith, Publisher.

—Little Roja Riding Hood. Elya, Susan Middleton. 2014. (ENG.). 32p. (J). (gr. k-3). 17.99 *(978-0-399-24767-5(X),* G.P. Putnam's Sons Books for Young Readers) Penguin Young Readers Group.

—Not One Damsel in Distress: Heroic Girls from World Folklore. Yolen, Jane. 2018. (ENG.). 144p. (J). (gr. 3-7). 15.99 *(978-1-328-90020-3(7),* 1700057, HMH Books For Young Readers) Houghton Mifflin Harcourt Publishing Co.

Gueyfier, Judith. Chandra's Magic Light. Heine, Theresa & Barefoot Books Staff. 2013. (J). 16.99 *(978-1-84686-493-3(3))* Barefoot Bks., Inc.

—Songs in the Shade of the Cashew & Coconut Trees: Lullabies & Nursery Rhymes from West Africa & the Caribbean. Soussana, Nathalie. 2019. (ENG.). 52p. (J). (gr. k-1). 16.95 *(978-2-924774-53-5(5))* La Montagne Secrete CAN. Dist: Independent Pubs. Group.

Guggenheim, Jaenet, photos by. Triassic Hall: Building the Triassic Exhibit from the Ground Up. Guggenheim, Jaenet. Lucas, Spencer G. Lucas, Spencer G., ed. 2011. (ENG., 130p. 25.00 *(978-1-929115-21-1(0))* Azro Pr., Inc.

Gugliotti, Chris, jt. illus. see Corona, Jorge.

Gugu, Abdul M. Juma & Little Sungura. Burgess, Lisa Maria. 2013. 32p. 19.95 *(978-1-939604-06-4(0))*; pap. 9.99 *(978-1-939604-02-6(8))* Barranca Pr.

—Juma Cooks Chapati. Burgess, Lisa Maria. 2013. 32p. 19.95 *(978-1-939604-08-8(7))*; pap. 9.99 *(978-1-939604-04-0(4))* Barranca Pr.

—Juma on Safari. Burgess, Lisa Maria. 2013. 32p. 19.95 *(978-1-939604-07-1(9))*; pap. 9.99 *(978-1-939604-03-3(6))* Barranca Pr.

—Juma's Dhow Race. Burgess, Lisa Maria. 2013. 32p. 19.95 *(978-1-939604-09-5(5))*; pap. 9.99 *(978-1-939604-05-7(2))* Barranca Pr.

Guiberson, Brenda Z. Disasters: Natural & Man-Made Catastrophes Through the Centuries. Guiberson, Brenda Z. 2014. (ENG.). 256p. (J). (gr. 5-9). pap. 13.99 *(978-1-250-05066-3(9),* 900134136) Square Fish.

Guibord, Charity. Plug into the Power. Liebenow, Todd et al. 2003. 28p. (YA). spiral bd. 18.00 *(978-1-58302-231-3(7))* Creative Ministry Solutions.

Guicciardini, Desideria. But What If? Graves, Sue. 2013. (Our Emotions & Behavior Ser.). (ENG.). 28p. (J). (gr. -1-3). 12.99 *(978-1-57542-444-6(4))* Free Spirit Publishing, Inc.

—Crabby Gabby. Graves, Sue. 2008. (Tadpoles Ser.). (ENG.). 24p. (J). (gr. -1-3). pap. *(978-0-7787-3883-1(3))* Crabtree Publishing Co.

—I Hate Everything! Graves, Sue. 2013. (Our Emotions & Behavior Ser.). (ENG.). 28p. (J). (gr. -1-3). 12.99 *(978-1-57542-443-9(6))* Free Spirit Publishing, Inc.

—Max & Millie Start School. Brooks, Felicity. 2013. (Toddler Bks.). (ENG.). 23p. (gr. -1). 7.99 *(978-0-7945-3302-1(7),* Usborne) EDC Publishing.

—Rumpelstiltskin. 2007. (Young Reading Series 1 Gift Bks.). 47p. (J). (gr. -1-3). 8.99 *(978-0-7945-1446-4(4),* Usborne) EDC Publishing.

—Take a Deep Breath. Graves, Sue. 2013. (Our Emotions & Behavior Ser.). (ENG.). 28p. (J). (gr. -1-3). 12.99 *(978-1-57542-446-0(0))* Free Spirit Publishing, Inc.

Guicciardini, Desideria & McNicholas, Shelagh. Hop, Skip & Jump. 2008. (Usborne Baby Board Bks.). 8p. (J). (gr. -1). bds. 15.99 incl. audio compact disk *(978-0-7945-1914-8(8),* Usborne) EDC Publishing.

Guicciardini, Desideria, jt. illus. see Carletti, Emanuela.

Guice, Butch. Black Panther & the Crew: We Are the Streets, Vol. 1. 2017. (ENG.). 136p. (YA). (gr. 8-17). pap. 17.99 *(978-1-302-90832-4(4))* Marvel Worldwide, Inc.

Guice, Butch, et al. Criminal Intent, Vol. 3. Beatty, Scott. (Ruse Traveler Ser.: Vol. 3). 160p. 2004. (YA). pap. 9.95 *(978-1-59314-060-1(6))*; 2003. (gr. 7-18). pap. 15.95 *(978-1-931484-74-9(0))* CrossGeneration Comics, Inc.

—Iron Man Epic Collection: Return of the Ghost. 2019. (ENG.). 480p. (YA). (gr. 8-17). pap. 39.99 *(978-1-302-91629-9(7))* Marvel Worldwide, Inc.

—Murder in Mind, Vol. 4. Beatty, Scott. 2004. (Ruse Ser.: Vol. 4). 160p. (YA). pap. 15.95 *(978-1-59314-047-2(9))* CrossGeneration Comics, Inc.

—The Silent Partner, Vol. 2. Waid, Mark & Beatty, Scott. 2003. (Ruse Ser.: Vol. 2). 160p. (YA). (gr. 7-18). 15.95 *(978-1-931484-48-0(1))* CrossGeneration Comics, Inc.

Guice, Butch & Perkins, Mike. Enter the Detective. Waid, Mark. 2003. (Ruse Traveler Ser.: Vol. 1). 192p. (YA). (gr. 7-18). pap. 9.95 *(978-1-59314-012-0(6))* CrossGeneration Comics, Inc.

Guice, Butch, jt. illus. see Magno, Carlos.

Guice, Jackson. Albion. Busiek, Kurt et al. 2006. (ENG.). 144p. (YA). pap. 19.99 *(978-1-4012-0994-0(7))* DC Comics.

Guice, Jackson, et al. Captain America: The Complete Collection. 2013. 568p. (YA). (gr. 8-17). pap. 39.99 *(978-0-7851-8379-2(5))* Marvel Worldwide, Inc.

Guida, Liisa & Klein, Nancy. Wee Sing Mother Goose, 1 vol. Beall, Pamela Conn & Nipp, Susan Hagen. 2006. (Wee Sing Ser.). (ENG.). 64p. (J). (gr. -1-2). 10.99 *(978-0-8431-0485-1(6),* Price Stern Sloan) Penguin Young Readers Group.

Guida, Liisa C. Stars. Tomecek, Steve. 2003. (Jump into Science Ser.). (J). 16.95 *(978-0-7922-8203-7(5))* CENGAGE Learning.

Guida, Liisa Chauncy & Klein, Nancy. Wee Sing & Move. Beall, Pamela Conn & Nipp, Susan Hagen. 2009. (Wee Sing Ser.). 64p. (J). (gr. -1-2). 10.99 *(978-0-8431-8959-9(2),* Price Stern Sloan) Penguin Young Readers Group.

Guidera, Daniel. The Deep Dish on Pizza! Krensky, Stephen. 2014. (History of Fun Stuff Ser.). (ENG.). 48p. (J). (gr. 1-3). pap. 4.99 *(978-1-4814-2055-6(0),* Simon Spotlight) Simon Spotlight.

—The Explosive Story of Fireworks! Einhorn, Kama. 2015. (History of Fun Stuff Ser.). (ENG.). 48p. (J). (gr. 1-3). 16.99 *(978-1-4814-3848-3(4))* Simon & Schuster Children's Publishing.

Guidi, Guido. Iron Man: I Am Iron Man! Rao, Lisa. 2008. (I Can Read Bks.). 32p. (J). (gr. -1-2). pap. 3.99 *(978-0-06-082193-7(0),* Harper Trophy) HarperCollins Pubs.

Guidotti, Barbara S. The Bumbleseed Tree. Guidotti, Barbara Swift. 2017. (Wallaboos Ser.: Vol. 6). (ENG.). (J). 14.99 *(978-0-9983526-6-4(7))* Sagaponack Bks.

Guidotti, Barbara Swift. The Baby Wallosaurus. Guidotti, Barbara Swift. 2018. (Wallaboos Ser.: Vol. 11). (ENG.). 32p. (J). 14.99 *(978-0-9997045-1-6(6))* Sagaponack Bks.

Guidotti, Barbara Swift. The Great Ballawoo. Guidotti, Barbara Swift. 2019. (ENG.). (J). 36p. 15.99 ***(978-1-7339651-3-2(0))***; (Wallaboos Ser.: Vol. 17). 48p. pap. 9.95 ***(978-1-7339651-2-5(2))*** Sagaponack Bks.

Guidotti, Barbara Swift. The Humming Bubble. Guidotti, Barbara Swift. 2018. (ENG.). 32p. (J). 14.99 *(978-0-9997045-4-7(0))* Sagaponack Bks.

Guidry, Cassie M. How the Animals Found Out. Rector, Roger B. 2015. (ENG.). 68p. (J). pap. 15.00 *(978-1-7234-3502-7(3))* CreateSpace Independent Publishing Platform.

Guignard, Monica. Turtle Day. Scavone, Jordan J. 2019. (ENG.). 40p. (J). pap. 10.00 ***(978-1-7117-9182-1(2))*** Independently Published.

Guile, Gill. Bear Picks a Pumpkin, 1 vol. 2018. (ENG.). 24p. (J). bds. 8.99 *(978-0-310-76621-6(4))* Zonderkidz.

—Huff & Puff. Rabe, Tish. 2014. (My First I Can Read Ser.). (ENG.). 24p. (J). (gr. -1-3). 16.99 *(978-0-06-230502-2(6))* HarperCollins Pubs.

—Huff & Puff. Rabe, Tish. 2014. (My First I Can Read Ser.). (ENG.). 24p. (J). (gr. -1-3). pap. 4.99 *(978-0-06-230501-5(8),* HarperCollins) HarperCollins Pubs. Ltd. GBR. Dist: HarperCollins Pubs.

—Huff & Puff & the New Train. Rabe, Tish. 2014. (My First I Can Read Ser.). (ENG.). 24p. (J). (gr. -1-3). pap. 4.99 *(978-0-06-230503-9(4))* HarperCollins Pubs.

—Huff & Puff Have Too Much Stuff! Rabe, Tish. 2014. (My First I Can Read Ser.). (ENG.). 24p. (J). (gr. -1-3). pap. 4.99 *(978-0-06-230505-3(0))* HarperCollins Pubs.

—In My Garden. 20p. (J). *(978-1-932209-38-9(7))* Bendon, Inc.

—My Nursery Rhyme Pop-up Book. 20p. (J). *(978-1-59394-119-2(6))* Bendon, Inc.

—My Nursery Rhyme Pop-up Book. Davies, Gill. 2005. 20p. (J). (gr. k-4). reprint ed. 20.00 *(978-0-7567-8704-2(1))* DIANE Publishing Co.

—My Very Own Kitten. Hubbard, Ben. 2014. (ENG.). 12p. (J). (gr. -1). *(978-1-78244-602-6(8))* Top That! Publishing PLC.

—My Very Own Puppy. Hubbard, Ben. 2014. (ENG.). 12p. (gr. -1). *(978-1-78244-603-3(6))* Top That! Publishing PLC.

—Pumpkin Party! Powell-Tuck, Maudie. 2015. (ENG.). 22p. (J). (gr. -1-k). bds. 8.99 *(978-1-58925-206-6(3))* Tiger Tales.

—Silly Tilly Witch: And Other Stories. Jordan, Jennifer. 2004. (Early Learning Ser.). 18p. (J). bds. 2.99 *(978-1-85854-825-8(X))* Brimax Books Ltd. GBR. Dist: Byeway Bks.

—The Story of Creation. Davidson, Alice Joyce. 2016. (ENG.). (J). 9.95 *(978-0-87029-708-3(2))* Abbey Pr.

—The Story of Noah. Davidson, Alice Joyce. 2016. (ENG.). (J). 9.95 *(978-0-87029-706-9(6))* Abbey Pr.

—Ten in a Bed: A Pop-up Counting Book. Davies, Gill. 20p. (J). *(978-1-59394-120-8(X))* Bendon, Inc.

—Ten in the Bed. Tiger Tales. 2017. (ENG.). 22p. (J). (gr. -1-k). bds. 8.99 *(978-1-68010-518-6(3))* Tiger Tales.

—Twinkle Twinkle Little Star. 2016. (ENG.). (J). 8.95 *(978-1-58925-504-3(6))* Tiger Tales.

—Unstoppable Me, 1 vol. Dirks, Adam. 2018. (ENG.). 26p. (J). bds. 9.99 *(978-0-310-76497-7(1))* Zonderkidz.

—A Very Merry Christmas. Powell-Tuck, Maudie. 2014. (ENG.). 22p. (J). (gr. -1-k). bds. 8.99 *(978-1-58925-560-9(7))* Tiger Tales.

Guilfoy, Paul. Hi! I'm Your School Counselor! Perkins, Nathan. 2019. (ENG.). 26p. (J). pap. 14.99 *(978-1-5390-7339-0(4))* CreateSpace Independent Publishing Platform.

Guilhaumond, Gregory, jt. illus. see Futaki, Attila.

Guillain, Charlotte & Chatterton, Chris. Christmas Gremlins. Guillain, Adam. 2019. (ENG.). 18p. (J). (gr. -1-k). pap. 12.99 *(978-1-4052-8506-3(0))* Egmont Bks., Ltd. GBR. Dist: Independent Pubs. Group.

Guillain, Charlotte & Wildish, Lee. Marshmallows for Martians. Guillain, Adam. 2nd ed. 2014. (George's Amazing Adventures Ser.). (ENG.). 32p. (J). (-k). pap. 10.99 *(978-1-4052-6681-9(3))* Egmont Bks., Ltd. GBR. Dist: Independent Pubs. Group.

Guille, Rosanne & Mayer, Uwe. Caterpillars & Butterflies. Turnbull, Stephanie. 2007. (Usborne Beginners Ser.). 32p. (J). (gr. -1-3). 4.99 *(978-0-7945-1337-5(9),* Usborne) EDC Publishing.

Guillet, Francois. La Puce Cosmique et le Rayon Bleuge. Guillet, Jean-Pierre. 2004. (Des 9 Ans. Ser.). (FRE.). 120p. (J). *(978-2-922565-98-0(X))* Editions de la Paix CAN. Dist: World of Reading, Ltd.

Guillon, Eric. Minions: Sleepy Kittens. Paul, Cinco & Daurio, Ken. 2010. (Despicable Me Ser.). (ENG.). 10p. (J). (gr. -1 — 1). bds. 8.99 *(978-0-316-08381-2(X))* Hachette Bk. Group.

Guillope, Antoine. White Fang. London, Jack. 2013. 40p. (J). (gr. 2). 14.95 *(978-2-7338-2145-9(8))* Auzou, Philippe Editions FRA. Dist: Consortium Bk. Sales & Distribution.

Guilloppe, Antoine. Mephisto. Villiot, Bernard. 2019. (ENG.). 32p. (J). (gr. k-2). 17.99 *(978-988-8341-86-3(3),* Minedition) Neugebauer, Michael (Publishing) Limited HKG. Dist: Penguin Random Hse. LLC.

Guillory, Mike. Daniela's Big Book of Poppin' Poetry. Arnold, Daniela. 2017. (J). *(978-1-942945-55-0(8))* Night Heron Media.

Guimbellot, Hannabill. My Adventures on a Jungle Safari. Hester, Joe. 2017. (ENG.). (J). 23.95 *(978-1-64003-348-1(3))*; pap. 12.95 *(978-1-64003-347-4(5))* Covenant Bks.

Guinaldo, Andres, jt. illus. see Izaakse, Sean.

Guinard, Geraldine. Dreamstone. Smith, Helene. 2005. 80p. (YA). pap. 13.50 *(978-1-920731-63-2(6))* Fremantle Pr. AUS. Dist: Independent Pubs. Group.

Guion, Melissa. Baby Penguins Everywhere! Guion, Melissa. 2013. 30p. (J). (gr. -1-k). bds. 6.99 *(978-0-399-16516-0(9),* Philomel Bks.) Penguin Young Readers Group.

Guion, Tamara. Hello, Grand Mamoon! Steinmann, Donna. 2005. 32p. (J). 16.95 *(978-0-9663286-4-6(7))* EarthTime Pubns.

Guitian, Cristina. Climate Change. Jackson, Tom. 2020. (What's the Issue? Ser.). (ENG.). 96p. (J). (gr. 4-7). pap. 16.95 ***(978-0-7112-5030-7(8))*** QEB Publishing Inc.

—Fake News: Censorship - Hows - Whys - Secret Agendas - Wrongs - Rights - Conspiracy Theories - the Media vs Politicians - Wiki Leaks. Jackson, Tom. 2020. (What's the Issue? Ser.). (ENG.). 96p. (J). (gr. 4-7). pap. 16.95 ***(978-0-7112-5034-5(0))*** QEB Publishing Inc.

Guiza, Vic. Bat in the Bunk: Summer Camp Stories Seires. 2015. (ENG.). 32p. (J). (gr. 1-18). 19.99 *(978-0-9863743-0-2(X))* Summer Camp Stories LLC.

Guiza, Victor. Counselor Dynamite: Twas the Day Before Christmas Break. Burgess, Starr. 2012. 28p. (J). 16.95 *(978-1-60131-118-4(4),* Castlebridge Bks.) Big Tent Bks.

—Counselor Dynamite Befuddles the Bullyville Crew. Burgess, Starr. 2013. 52p. (J). 19.95 *(978-1-60131-156-6(7),* Castlebridge Bks.) Big Tent Bks.

—Ms. Irene Is so Demanding. Barret, Marie. 2012. 26p. (J). 14.95 *(978-1-60131-110-8(9))* Big Tent Bks.

—Potato Pie Pirate. Purtle, Louise. 2009. 24p. (J). 15.99 *(978-0-9818145-0-6(6))* Biggaloo Bks.

—Recorder Karate. Shammas, Anna. 2012. 32p. pap. 8.95 *(978-0-9843869-2-5(0),* Castlebridge Bks.) Big Tent Bks.

—The Safety Pin: Summer Camp Stories. Sloyer, Elliot. 2014. (ENG.). 32p. (J). 16.95 *(978-1-60131-182-5(6),* Castlebridge Bks.) Big Tent Bks.

—Treasure Kai & the Lost Gold of Shark Island: Library Version (no chests or Toys) Robertson, Karen. 2008. (ENG.). 28p. (J). *(978-0-9804614-1-1(3))* Treasure Bound Books.

—Treasure Kai & the Lost Gold of Shark Island: Treasure chest & toys Version. Robertson, Karen. 2008. (ENG.). 28p. (J). *(978-0-9804614-0-4(5))* Treasure Bound Books.

—The X-Tails in a Merry Monster Trucking Christmas. Fielding, L. A. 2017. (X-Tails Ser.). (ENG.). (J). *(978-1-928199-14-4(3))*; pap. *(978-1-928199-13-7(5))* X-tails Enterprises, The.

Gula, Ettore. Toy Story. Ferrari, Alessandro. 2020. (Disney & Pixar Movies Ser.). (ENG.). 52p. (J). (gr. 2-6). lib. bdg. 28.50 ***(978-1-5321-4554-4(3),*** 35201, Graphic Novels) Spotlight.

Gulacy, Paul. Shang-Chi - Master of Kung Fu Vol. 1: The Hellfire Apocalypse. Moench, Doug. 2003. (Master of Kung Fu Ser.). 144p. pap. 14.99 *(978-0-7851-1124-5(7))* Marvel Worldwide, Inc.

Gulbis, Stephen. A Mom in a Million. Lewis, Jill. 2005. 32p. (J). *(978-1-84458-368-3(6),* Pavilion Children's Books) Pavilion Bks.

—Old MacDonald Had a Barn. 2003. 22p. (YA). *(978-1-85602-453-2(9),* Pavilion Children's Books) Pavilion Bks.

—Sleep Little Angel. Brown, Margaret Wise. 2019. (Margaret Wise Brown Classics Ser.). (ENG.). 32p. (J). (gr. -1-k). 12.99 *(978-1-68412-754-2(8),* Silver Dolphin Bks.) Printers Row Publishing Group.

—The Wheels on the Bus. 2003. 22p. (YA). *(978-1-85602-454-9(7),* Pavilion Children's Books) Pavilion Bks.

Gulemetova, Maria, et al. Enjoying Our Differences Book Set Of 4. Gulemetova, Maria et al. 2020. (Social & Emotional Learning Sets Ser.). (ENG.). 144p. (J). pap., pap., pap. ***(978-1-78628-538-6(X))*** Child's Play International Ltd.

Gulemetova, Maria. Beyond the Fence. Gulemetova, Maria. 2018. (Child's Play Library). 36p. (J). *(978-1-84643-931-5(0))*; pap. *(978-1-84643-930-8(2))* Child's Play International Ltd.

Guler, Greg & Ulene, Nancy. Learn to Draw Plus Disney Phineas & Ferb. Peterson, Scott. 2012. (J). *(978-1-936309-71-9(8))* Quarto Publishing Group USA.

Gullens, Lee M. Off I Go! Cochran, Jean M. 2008. (ENG.). 32p. (J). (gr. -1-k). 16.95 *(978-0-9792035-1-0(1))* Pleasant St. Pr.

—Your Tummy's Talking! Cochran, Jean M. 2008. (ENG.). 32p. (J). (gr. -1-k). 16.95 *(978-0-9792035-3-4(8))* Pleasant St. Pr.

Gulley, Hardrick M. Buger the Butterfly & the Lion Kitties' First Adventure. Garrett, Diane Marie. 2008. 16p. pap. 24.95 *(978-1-60672-237-4(9))* America Star Bks.

Gulley, Martha. Champlain & the Silent One. Messner, Kate. 2008. (J). *(978-1-59531-050-7(9))* North Country Bks., Inc.

—New York Patriots. Blackman, Dorothy L. 2007. v, 122p. (J). *(978-1-59531-020-0(7))* North Country Bks., Inc.

Gulley SR, Wayne A. Michelangelo Tangelo - a Bully No More. Gulley Sr, Wayne A. Gulley, Robin, ed. 2012. 40p. pap. 13.99 *(978-0-9843505-5-1(1))* Gulley, Wayne.

Gulley Sr, Wayne A. Nick Gets Moving. Prevedel, Brenda. Gulley, Robin R., ed. 2013. 32p. pap. 9.99 *(978-0-9886117-1-9(6))* Gulley, Wayne.

—Punky the Penguin's Special Day. Munoz, Dennis. Gulley, Robin a, ed. 2015. (ENG.). 18p. (J). (gr. k-4). pap. 6.99 *(978-0-578-46382-7(2))* Munoz, Dennis.

Gulliver, Amanda. The Big Mud Puddle, 1 vol. Dale, Jay. 2012. (Engage Literacy Yellow Ser.). (ENG.). 32p. (gr. k-2). pap. 5.99 *(978-1-4296-8956-4(0),* Capstone Pr.) Capstone.

—Colors. 2011. (Baby Rattle Bks.). 12p. (J). (gr. -1 — 1). 5.99 *(978-0-7641-6391-3(4),* B.E.S. Publishing) Peterson's.

—I Am Big, 1 vol. Dale, Jay. 2012. (Engage Literacy Magenta Ser.). (ENG.). 32p. (gr. k-2). pap. 5.99 *(978-1-4296-8874-1(2),* Capstone Pr.) Capstone.

—I Can See It Too!, 1 vol. Dale, Jay. 2012. (Wonder Words Ser.). (ENG.). 32p. (gr. k-2). pap. 5.99 *(978-1-4296-8896-3(3),* Capstone Pr.) Capstone.

—I Go Up, 1 vol. Dale, Jay. 2012. (Engage Literacy Magenta Ser.). (ENG.). 32p. (gr. k-2). pap. 5.99 *(978-1-4296-8832-1(7),* Capstone Pr.) Capstone.

—Lea Is Hungry, 1 vol. Dale, Jay. 2012. (Engage Literacy Red Ser.). (ENG.). 32p. (gr. k-2). pap. 5.99 *(978-1-4296-8833-8(5),* Capstone Pr.) Capstone.

—Lea's Birthday, 1 vol. Dale, Jay. 2012. (Engage Literacy Yellow Ser.). (ENG.). 32p. (gr. k-2). pap. 5.99 *(978-1-4296-8964-9(1),* Capstone Pr.) Capstone.

—Mine! A Counting Book about Sharing, Vol. Rivadeneira, Caryn. 2018. (ENG.). 28p. (J). 7.99 *(978-1-5064-4679-0(5),* Beaming Books) Augsburg Fortress, Pubs.

—No Difference Between Us: Teach Children about Gender Equality, Respectful Relationships, Feelings, Choice, Self-Esteem, Empathy, Tolerance. Sanders, Jayneen. 2017. (ENG.). 32p. (J). (gr. k-3). *(978-1-925089-17-2(7),* Educate2Empower Publishing) UpLoad Publishing Pty, Ltd.

—Pets. 2011. (Baby Rattle Bks.). 12p. (J). (gr. -1 — 1). 6.99 *(978-0-7641-6392-0(2),* B.E.S. Publishing) Peterson's.

—Zoo. 2011. (Baby Rattle Bks.). 12p. (J). (gr. -1-k). 6.99 *(978-0-7641-6394-4(9),* B.E.S. Publishing) Peterson's.

Gullotti, Pat. Pig Kissing. LaSala, Paige. 2010. 24p. pap. 12.99 *(978-1-4520-2849-1(4))* AuthorHouse.

Gully, Mario. Death in the Forest, 1 vol., Vol. 4. Thomas, Roy & Stevenson, Robert Louis. 2010. (Kidnapped! Ser.). (ENG.). 24p. (J). (gr. 6-12). 27.07 *(978-1-59961-784-8(6),* 10964) ABDO Publishing Co.

—The End of the Quest, 1 vol., Vol. 5. Thomas, Roy & Stevenson, Robert Louis. 2010. (Kidnapped! Ser.). (ENG.). 24p. (J). (gr. 6-12). 27.07 *(978-1-59961-785-5(4),* 10965) ABDO Publishing Co.

—I Go to Sea, 1 vol., Vol. 2. Thomas, Roy & Stevenson, Robert Louis. 2010. (Kidnapped! Ser.). (ENG.). 24p. (J). (gr. 6-12). 27.07 *(978-1-59961-782-4(X),* 10962) ABDO Publishing Co.

—The Loss of the Brig, 1 vol., Vol. 3. Thomas, Roy & Stevenson, Robert Louis. 2010. (Kidnapped! Ser.). (ENG.). 24p. (J). (gr. 6-12). 27.07 *(978-1-59961-783-1(8),* 10963) ABDO Publishing Co.

Gully, Mario & Davidson, Pat. Embassy - And Attack. Stevenson, Robert Louis & Thomas, Roy. 2009. (Treasure Island Ser.: Vol. 4). (ENG.). 24p. (J). (gr. 6-12). 27.07 *(978-1-59961-604-9(1),* 14898) ABDO Publishing Co.

—Mutiny on the Hispaniola. Stevenson, Robert Louis & Thomas, Roy. 2009. (Treasure Island Ser.: Vol. 3). (ENG.). 24p. (J). (gr. 6-12). 27.07 *(978-1-59961-603-2(3),* 14897) ABDO Publishing Co.

—Treasure Island. Stevenson, Robert Louis & Thomas, Roy. 2009. (Treasure Island Ser.). (ENG.). 24p. (J). (gr. 6-12). 27.07 *(978-1-59961-601-8(7),* 14895);Pt. 2. 27.07 *(978-1-59961-602-5(5),* 14896) ABDO Publishing Co.

Gultepe, Evin. Ninemden Tekerlemeler. 2020. (TUR.). 28p. (J). pap. 11.99 ***(978-1-7345359-0-7(3))*** Gultepe, Evin.

Gulzeth, Ray. Warren Is Wonderful. Becklund, Annette L. 2009. 52p. pap. 12.95 *(978-1-4401-2042-8(0))* iUniverse, Inc.

Gunawardhana, Udari. The Hunger in the Forest Fuuuurrrrr N'Bum: In English & Portuguese. Brandao, Rosaalda. 2019. (ENG.). 48p. (J). *(978-1-78623-535-0(8))*; pap. *(978-1-78623-534-3(X))* Grosvenor Hse. Publishing Ltd.

Gundert, Marjorie. D. Q. & the SOOYOO, 1 vol. Gundert, Margaret. 2010. 20p. 24.95 *(978-1-4512-1226-6(7))* PublishAmerica, Inc.

Gunnell, Beth. I Heart Drawing. Gunnell, Beth. 2017. (I Heart Ser.). (ENG.). 128p. (J). (gr. 2). pap. 8.99 *(978-1-78055-414-3(1))* O'Mara, Michael Bks., Ltd. GBR. Dist: Independent Pubs. Group.

Gunnell, Beth, jt. illus. see Davies, Hannah.

Gunson, Dave. Dinosaurs. Martin, Justin McCory. 2008. 32p. *(978-0-545-08456-7(3))* Scholastic, Inc.

Gunther, Richard. The Day the World Went Wacky. Suter, Janine. 2009. 32p. (J). 10.99 *(978-0-89051-575-4(1),* Master Books) New Leaf Publishing Group.

—Noah's Floating Animal Park. Suter, Janine. 2009. 32p. (J). 10.99 *(978-0-89051-576-1(X),* Master Books) New Leaf Publishing Group.

Gunto, El. Escape Game Adventure: the Mad Hacker: The Mad Hacker, 4 vols. Prieu, Remi & Vives, Melanie. 2020. (Escape Game Adventure Ser.: 1). (ENG.). 48p. (gr. 3-6). pap. 9.99 *(978-0-7643-5896-8(0)*, 17502) Schiffer Publishing, Ltd.

Guo, Beidi. Kunkush: The True Story of a Refugee Cat. Ventura, Marne. 2017. (Encounter: Narrative Nonfiction Picture Bks.). (ENG.). 32p. (J). (gr. 3-6). lib. bdg. 29.32 *(978-1-5157-7319-1(1)*, 135665, Capstone Pr.) Capstone.

Guojing. The Only Child. Guojing. 2015. (ENG.). 112p. (J). (gr. k-4). 22.99 *(978-0-553-49705-2(7)*, Schwartz & Wade Bks.) Random Hse. Children's Bks.

Gupta, Garima. The Mustache Man. Ramanathan, Priya. 2013. (ENG.). 32p. (J). (gr. -1). pap. 9.95 *(978-81-8190-186-6(X))* Karadi Tales Co. Pvt, Ltd. IND. Dist: Consortium Bk. Sales & Distribution.

Gupta, Priyankar, jt. illus. see Sen Gupta, Subhadra.

Gupton, Gary Neil. Time to Meet Max: Adventures in Guatemala with Anna & Cole. Gupton, Gary Neil. 2017. (Time to Meet Max Ser.: Vol. 2). (ENG.). (J). (gr. 2-4). 16.99 *(978-0-692-97766-8(X))* Gupton, Gary Neil.

—Time to Meet Max: Adventures in Guatemala with Anna & Cole. Gupton, Gary Neil. 2nd ed. 2017. (Time to Meet Max Ser.: Vol. 2). (ENG.). (J). (gr. 2-4). pap. 8.99 *(978-0-692-95396-9(5))* Gupton, Gary Neil.

Guridi. Parco. Nogués, Alex. 2019. (SPA.). 40p. (J). (gr. 2-4). pap. 17.95 *(978-84-17440-21-3(6))* Akiara Bks. ESP. Dist: Independent Pubs. Group.

Guridi, Raúl. The Flock. Del Mazo, Margarita. 2019. (ENG.). 36p. (J). (gr. -1-k). 17.95 *(978-84-16566-83-9(6))* Ediciones La Fragatina ESP. Dist: Independent Pubs. Group.

Guridi, Raúl Nieto. A Drop of the Sea. Chabbert, Ingrid. 2018. (ENG.). 36p. (J). (gr. -1-2). 16.99 *(978-1-5253-0124-7(1))* Kids Can Pr., Ltd. CAN. Dist: Hachette Bk. Group.

Gurihiru. Avatar: the Last Airbender - Smoke & Shadow Part One, Pt. 1. Yang, Gene Luen. 2015. (Avatar: the Last Airbender Ser.). (ENG.). 80p. pap. 12.99 *(978-1-61655-761-4(3)*, Dark Horse Books) Dark Horse Comics.

—Avatar: the Last Airbender - the Lost Adventures. Koneitzko, Bryan. 2011. (Avatar: the Last Airbender Ser.). (ENG.). 240p. pap. 17.99 *(978-1-59582-748-7(X)*, Dark Horse Books) Dark Horse Comics.

—Avatar: the Last Airbender - the Rift Part 1, Pt. 1. Yang, Gene Luen. 2014. (Avatar: the Last Airbender Ser.). (ENG.). 80p. pap. 12.99 *(978-1-61655-295-4(6)*, Dark Horse Books) Dark Horse Comics.

—Avatar: the Last Airbender - the Search Part 1, Pt. 1. Yang, Gene Luen & Koneitzko, Bryan. 2013. (Avatar: the Last Airbender Ser.). (ENG.). 80p. pap. 12.99 *(978-1-61655-054-7(6)*, Dark Horse Books) Dark Horse Comics.

—Incredibles 2: Sweet Dreams, Jack-Jack. Rusu, Meredith. 2018. (ENG.). 40p. (J). (gr. -1-k). 16.99 *(978-1-368-01193-8(4))* Disney Pr.

—Spider-Man & Venom: Double Trouble. 2020. 112p. (J). (gr. 4-7). pap. 12.99 *(978-1-302-92039-5(1))* Marvel Worldwide, Inc.

—The Unstoppable Wasp: Unlimited Vol. 1: Fix Everything. 2019. 112p. (YA). pap. 15.99 *(978-1-302-91426-4(X))* Marvel Worldwide, Inc.

Gurihiru & Gurihiru. Avatar: the Last Airbender: the Promise Library Edition. Yang, Gene Luen & Koneitzko, Bryan. 2013. (ENG.). 242p. 39.99 *(978-1-61655-074-5(0)*, Dark Horse Books) Dark Horse Comics.

Gurihiru, jt. illus. see Gurihiru.

Gurihiru, jt. illus. see Konietzko, Bryan.

Gurihiru, jt. illus. see Random House Disney Staff.

Gurihiru Staff. Big Trouble at the Big Top! Sumerak, Marc. 2006. (X-Men Power Pack - 4 Titles Ser.). 24p. lib. bdg. 22.78 *(978-1-59961-219-5(4))* Spotlight.

—Costumes On! Sumerak, Marc. 2006. (X-Men Power Pack - 4 Titles Ser.). 24p. lib. bdg. 22.78 *(978-1-59961-220-1(8))* Spotlight.

—Mind over Matter. Sumerak, Marc. 2006. (X-Men Power Pack - 4 Titles Ser.). 24p. lib. bdg. 22.78 *(978-1-59961-222-5(4))* Spotlight.

Gurihiru Staff, jt. illus. see Random House Disney Staff.

Gurin, Lara. Ella the Baby Elephant: A Baby Elephant's Story. Duey, Kathleen. 2008. (My Animal Family Ser.). (ENG.). 32p. (J). (gr. -1-3). 12.99 *(978-0-8249-5584-7(6)*, Ideal Pubns.) Worthy Publishing.

—Father & Son Read-Aloud Old Testament Stories. Gould, Robert. 2010. (Father & Son Read-Aloud Stories Ser.). (ENG.). 60p. (J). (gr. -1-k). 14.95 *(978-1-929945-73-3(6))* Big Guy Bks., Inc.

—Father & Son Read-Aloud Stories. Gould, Robert. 2006. (ENG.). 56p. (J). (gr. -1-k). 12.95 *(978-1-929945-67-2(1))* Big Guy Bks., Inc.

—Korow: A Baby Chimpanzee's Story. Duey, Kathleen. 2008. (My Animal Family Ser.). (ENG.). 32p. (J). (gr. -1-3). 12.99 *(978-0-8249-1816-3(9)*, Ideal Pubns.) Worthy Publishing.

—Leo: A Baby Lion's Story. Duey, Kathleen. 2008. (My Animal Family Ser.). 32p. (J). (gr. -1-3). 12.99 *(978-0-8249-1817-0(7)*, Ideal Pubns.) Worthy Publishing.

—Nanuq: A Baby Polar Bear's Story. Duey, Kathleen. 2008. (ENG.). 32p. (J). (gr. -1-3). 12.99 *(978-0-8249-1818-7(5)*, Ideal Pubns.) Worthy Publishing.

—Tahi: A Baby Dolphin's Story. Duey, Kathleen. 2009. (ENG.). 32p. 12.99 *(978-0-8249-1434-9(1)*, Ideal Pubns.) Worthy Publishing.

Gurin, Laura. Leo the Lion - Book & Dvd. Duey, Kathleen. 2007. 32p. 14.99 *(978-0-8249-6724-6(0)*, Ideal Pubns.) Worthy Publishing.

Guritz, Linda F. The Giving Gnome. Button, Kevin. 2010. 28p. pap. 12.95 *(978-1-936343-22-5(3))* Peppertree Pr., The.

Gurney, James. Dinotopia: The World Beneath. Gurney, James. 2003. (Dinotopia Ser.). (ENG.). 160p. (J). pap. 19.99 *(978-0-06-053065-5(0))* HarperCollins Pubs.

Gurney, James & Gurney, James. A Land Apart from Time. Gurney, James & Gurney, James. 2003. (Dinotopia Ser.). (ENG.). 160p. (J). (gr. 3-7). pap. 21.99 *(978-0-06-053064-8(2))* HarperCollins Pubs.

Gurney, James, jt. illus. see Gurney, James.

Gurney, John S. The Adventures of Yogasaurus: The First Three Books. Duncan, Kenneth E. Light, Susan Betsy, ed. 2015. (ENG.). 108p. (J). pap. 18.95 *(978-0-9831418-7-7(8))* Yogasaurus.

Gurney, John Steven. A to Z Mysteries Super Edition #10: Colossal Fossil. Roy, Ron. 2018. (to Z Mysteries Ser.: 10). (ENG.). 144p. (J). (gr. 1-4). lib. bdg. 12.99 *(978-0-399-55199-4(9)*, Random Hse. Bks. for Young Readers) Random Hse. Children's Bks.

—The Absent Author. Roy, Ron. unabr. ed. 2004. (A to Z Mysteries Ser.: No. 1). 86p. (J). (gr. k-3). pap. 17.00 incl. audio *(978-0-8072-1703-0(4)*, S FTR 269 SP, Listening Library) Random Hse. Audio Publishing Group.

—The Bald Bandit. Roy, Ron. unabr. ed. 2004. (A to Z Mysteries Ser.: No. 2). 80p. (J). (gr. k-3). pap. 17.00 incl. audio *(978-0-8072-1704-7(2)*, S FTR 270 SP, Listening Library) Random Hse. Audio Publishing Group.

—Bub, Snow, & the Burly Bear Scare. Wallace, Carol & Wallace, Bill. 2003. (ENG.). 128p. (J). (gr. 3-7). pap. 7.99 *(978-0-7434-0640-6(0)*, Aladdin) Simon & Schuster Children's Publishing.

—Calendar Mysteries #10: October Ogre. Roy, Ron. 2013. (Calendar Mysteries Ser.: 10). 80p. (J). (gr. 1-4). 5.99 *(978-0-375-86888-7(7)*, Random Hse. Bks. for Young Readers) Random Hse. Children's Bks.

—Calendar Mysteries #11: November Night. Roy, Ron. 2014. (Calendar Mysteries Ser.: 11). 80p. (J). (gr. 1-4). 5.99 *(978-0-385-37165-0(9)*, Random Hse. Bks. for Young Readers) Random Hse. Children's Bks.

—Calendar Mysteries #12: December Dog. Roy, Ron. 2014. (Calendar Mysteries Ser.: 12). 80p. (J). (gr. 1-4). 5.99 *(978-0-385-37168-1(3)*, Random Hse. Bks. for Young Readers) Random Hse. Children's Bks.

—Calendar Mysteries #2: February Friend. Roy, Ron. 2009. (Calendar Mysteries Ser.: 2). 80p. (J). (gr. 1-4). 5.99 *(978-0-375-85662-4(5)*, Random Hse. Bks. for Young Readers) Random Hse. Children's Bks.

—Calendar Mysteries #4: April Adventure. Roy, Ron. 2010. (Calendar Mysteries Ser.: 4). 80p. (J). (gr. 1-4). 5.99 *(978-0-375-86116-1(5)*, Random Hse. Bks. for Young Readers) Random Hse. Children's Bks.

—Calendar Mysteries #5: May Magic. Roy, Ron. 2011. (Calendar Mysteries Ser.: 5). 80p. (J). (gr. 1-4). 5.99 *(978-0-375-86111-6(4)*, Random Hse. Bks. for Young Readers) Random Hse. Children's Bks.

—Calendar Mysteries #6: June Jam. Roy, Ron. 2011. (Calendar Mysteries Ser.: 6). 80p. (J). (gr. 1-4). 5.99 *(978-0-375-86112-3(2)*, Random Hse. Bks. for Young Readers) Random Hse. Children's Bks.

—Calendar Mysteries #8: August Acrobat. Roy, Ron. 2012. (Calendar Mysteries Ser.: 8). 80p. (J). (gr. 1-4). 5.99 *(978-0-375-86886-3(0)*, Random Hse. Bks. for Young Readers) Random Hse. Children's Bks.

—Calendar Mysteries #9: September Sneakers. Roy, Ron. 2013. (Calendar Mysteries Ser.: 9). 80p. (J). (gr. 1-4). 5.99 *(978-0-375-86887-0(9)*, Random Hse. Bks. for Young Readers) Random Hse. Children's Bks.

—The Canary Caper. Roy, Ron. unabr. ed. 2004. (A to Z Mysteries Ser.: No. 3). 80p. (J). (gr. k-3). pap. 17.00 incl. audio *(978-0-8072-1705-4(0)*, S FTR 271 SP, Listening Library) Random Hse. Audio Publishing Group.

—Chatterbox: The Bird Who Wore Glasses. Uslan, Michael E. 2006. 34p. (J). 17.99 *(978-0-9753843-2-9(5))* ee publishing & productions, inc.

—Grand Canyon Grab. Roy, Ron. 2019. (to Z Mysteries Ser.: 11). 144p. (J). (gr. 1-4). 5.99 *(978-0-525-57886-4(2)*, Random Hse. Bks. for Young Readers) Random Hse. Children's Bks.

—January Joker. Roy, Ron. 2009. (Calendar Mysteries Ser.: 1). 96p. (J). (gr. 1-4). 5.99 *(978-0-375-85661-7(7)*, Random Hse. Bks. for Young Readers) Random Hse. Children's Bks.

—July Jitters: Calendar Mysteries #7. Roy, Ron. 2012. (Calendar Mysteries Ser.: 7). 80p. (J). (gr. 1-4). 5.99 *(978-0-375-86882-5(8)*, Random Hse. Bks. for Young Readers) Random Hse. Children's Bks.

—June Jam, 6. Roy, Ron. 2011. (Calendar Mysteries Ser.). (ENG.). 80p. (J). (gr. 1-4). lib. bdg. 18.69 *(978-0-375-96112-0(7))* Random House Publishing Group.

—March Mischief: Calendar Mysteries #3. Roy, Ron. 2010. (Calendar Mysteries Ser.: 3). 80p. (J). (gr. 1-4). 5.99 *(978-0-375-85663-1(3)*, Random Hse. Bks. for Young Readers) Random Hse. Children's Bks.

—Mayflower Treasure Hunt. Roy, Ron. ed. 2007. (to Z Mysteries Ser.: 28). 114p. (gr. 4-7). lib. bdg. 16.00 *(978-1-4177-9141-5(1))* Turtleback.

—The Meanest Hound Around. Wallace, Carol & Wallace, Bill. 2004. 149p. (J). (gr. 2-5). 12.65 *(978-0-7569-3960-1(7))* Perfection Learning Corp.

—The Meanest Hound Around. Wallace, Carol & Wallace, Bill. 2004. (ENG.). 160p. (J). (gr. 2-5). pap. 6.99 *(978-0-7434-3786-8(1)*, Aladdin) Simon & Schuster Children's Publishing.

—New Year's Eve Thieves. Roy, Ronald. 2014. (Calendar Mysteries Ser.: 13). 80p. (J). (gr. 1-4). 4.99 *(978-0-385-37171-1(3)*, Random Hse. Bks. for Young Readers) Random Hse. Children's Bks.

—On with the Show! Finch, Kate. 2014. 76p. (J). *(978-1-4242-5954-0(1))* Scholastic, Inc.

—Roscoe & the Pony Parade. Earhart, Kristin. 2008. (Little Apple Ser.). 88p. (J). *(978-0-545-08094-1(0))* Scholastic, Inc.

—The School Skeleton. Roy, Ron. ed. 2003. (to Z Mysteries Ser.: 19). (gr. k-3). lib. bdg. 14.75 *(978-0-613-62405-3(X))* Turtleback.

—The Talking T. Rex. Roy, Ron. ed. 2003. (to Z Mysteries Ser.: 20). (gr. 3-6). lib. bdg. 14.75 *(978-0-613-85127-5(7))* Turtleback.

—A to Z Mysteries: Collection #1, No. 1. Roy, Ron. ed. 2010. (to Z Mysteries Ser.: Nos. 1-4). (ENG.). 384p. (J). (gr. 1-4). 9.99 *(978-0-375-85946-5(2)*, Random Hse. Bks. for Young Readers) Random Hse. Children's Bks.

—A to Z Mysteries Super Edition 1: Detective Camp. Roy, Ron. 2006. (to Z Mysteries Ser.: 1). 144p. (J). (gr. 1-4). per. 5.99 *(978-0-375-83534-6(2)*, Random Hse. Bks. for Young Readers) Random Hse. Children's Bks.

—A to Z Mysteries Super Edition #10: Colossal Fossil. Roy, Ron. 2018. (to Z Mysteries Ser.: 10). (ENG.). 144p. (J). (gr. 1-4). 5.99 *(978-0-399-55198-7(0)*, Random Hse. Bks. for Young Readers) Random Hse. Children's Bks.

—A to Z Mysteries Super Edition #12: Space Shuttle Scam. Roy, Ron. 2020. (to Z Mysteries Ser.). 144p. (J). (gr. 1-4). (ENG.). 5.99 *(978-0-525-57889-5(7))*; lib. bdg. 12.99 *(978-0-525-57890-1(0))* Random Hse. Children's Bks. (Random Hse. Bks. for Young Readers).

—A to Z Mysteries Super Edition 2: Mayflower Treasure Hunt. Roy, Ron. 2nd ed. 2007. (to Z Mysteries Ser.: 2). 128p. (J). (gr. 1-4). per. 5.99 *(978-0-375-83937-5(2)*, Random Hse. Bks. for Young Readers) Random Hse. Children's Bks.

—A to Z Mysteries Super Edition 3: White House White-Out. Roy, Ron. 2008. (to Z Mysteries Ser.: 3). 144p. (J). (gr. 1-4). 5.99 *(978-0-375-84721-9(9)*, Random Hse. Bks. for Young Readers) Random Hse. Children's Bks.

—A to Z Mysteries Super Edition #4: Sleepy Hollow Sleepover. Roy, Ron. 4th ed. 2010. (to Z Mysteries Ser.: 4). 144p. (J). (gr. 1-4). pap. 5.99 *(978-0-375-86669-2(8)*, Random Hse. Bks. for Young Readers) Random Hse. Children's Bks.

—A to Z Mysteries Super Edition #5: the New Year Dragon Dilemma. Roy, Ron. 2011. (to Z Mysteries Ser.: 5). 144p. (J). (gr. 1-4). 5.99 *(978-0-375-86880-1(1)*, Random Hse. Bks. for Young Readers) Random Hse. Children's Bks.

—A to Z Mysteries Super Edition #6: the Castle Crime. Roy, Ron. 2014. (to Z Mysteries Ser.: 6). 144p. (J). (gr. 1-4). 5.99 *(978-0-385-37159-9(4)*, Random Hse. Bks. for Young Readers) Random Hse. Children's Bks.

—A to Z Mysteries Super Edition #8: Secret Admirer. Roy, Ron. 2015. (to Z Mysteries Ser.: 8). 144p. (J). (gr. 1-4). 5.99 *(978-0-553-52399-7(6)*, Random Hse. Bks. for Young Readers) Random Hse. Children's Bks.

—A to Z Mysteries Super Edition #9: April Fools' Fiasco. Roy, Ron. 2017. (to Z Mysteries Ser.: 9). (ENG.). 144p. (J). (gr. 1-4). 5.99 *(978-0-399-55195-6(6)*, Random Hse. Bks. for Young Readers) Random Hse. Children's Bks.

—A to Z Mysteries: the School Skeleton. Roy, Ron. 2003. (to Z Mysteries Ser.: 19). 96p. (J). (gr. 1-4). pap. 4.99 *(978-0-375-81368-9(3)*, Random Hse. Bks. for Young Readers) Random Hse. Children's Bks.

—A to Z Mysteries: the Talking T. Rex. Roy, Ron. 2003. (to Z Mysteries Ser.: 20). 96p. (J). (gr. 1-4). pap. 5.99 *(978-0-375-81369-6(1)*, Random Hse. Bks. for Young Readers) Random Hse. Children's Bks.

—A to Z Mysteries: the Unwilling Umpire. Roy, Ron. 2004. (to Z Mysteries Ser.: 21). 96p. (J). (gr. 1-4). 5.99 *(978-0-375-81370-2(5)*, Random Hse. Bks. for Young Readers) Random Hse. Children's Bks.

—A to Z Mysteries: the Vampire's Vacation. Roy, Ron. 2004. (to Z Mysteries Ser.: 22). 96p. (J). (gr. 1-4). pap. 5.99 *(978-0-375-82479-1(0)*, Random Hse. Bks. for Young Readers) Random Hse. Children's Bks.

—A to Z Mysteries: the White Wolf. Roy, Ron. 2004. (to Z Mysteries Ser.: 23). 96p. (J). (gr. 1-4). pap. 5.99 *(978-0-375-82480-7(4)*, Random Hse. Bks. for Young Readers) Random Hse. Children's Bks.

—A to Z Mysteries: the Yellow Yacht. Roy, Ron. 2005. (to Z Mysteries Ser.: 25). 96p. (J). (gr. 1-4). pap. 5.99 *(978-0-375-82482-1(0)*, Random Hse. Bks. for Young Readers) Random Hse. Children's Bks.

—A to Z Mysteries: the Zombie Zone. Roy, Ron. 2005. (to Z Mysteries Ser.: 26). 96p. (J). (gr. 1-4). pap. 5.99 *(978-0-375-82483-8(9)*, Random Hse. Bks. for Young Readers) Random Hse. Children's Bks.

—The Unwilling Umpire. Roy, Ron. ed. 2004. (to Z Mysteries Ser.: 21). (gr. k-3). lib. bdg. 14.75 *(978-0-613-82496-5(2))* Turtleback.

—White House White-Out. Roy, Ron. 2008. (A to Z Mysteries Ser.: No. 3). 124p. (gr. 1-4). 15.00 *(978-0-7569-8799-2(7))* Perfection Learning Corp.

—The X'ed-Out X-Ray. Roy, Ron. 2005. (to Z Mysteries Ser.: 24). 96p. (J). (gr. 1-4). 5.99 *(978-0-375-82481-4(2)*, Random Hse. Bks. for Young Readers) Random Hse. Children's Bks.

Gurney, John Steven & Slonim, David. The Meanest Hound Around & Other Tales. Wallace, Bill & Wallace, Carol. 2014. 149p. (J). *(978-1-4351-5264-9(6)*, Simon & Schuster/Paula Wiseman Bks.) Simon & Schuster/Paula Wiseman Bks.

Gurovich, Natalia. Los Numeros Tragaldabas. Robleda, Margarita. 2004. (SPA.). 24p. (J). 12.95 *(978-970-690-807-0(2))* Planeta Mexicana Editorial S. A. de C. V. MEX. Dist: Lectorum Pubns., Inc.

—Quien Soy? Adivinanzas Animales. Robleda, Margarita. 2003. (SPA.). 32p. (J). 12.95 *(978-970-690-805-6(6))* Planeta Mexicana Editorial S. A. de C. V. MEX. Dist: Lectorum Pubns., Inc.

Gurr, Simon. Darwin: A Graphic Biography. Byrne, Eugene. 2013. (ENG.). 100p. (gr. 7). pap. 9.95 *(978-1-58834-352-9(9)*, Smithsonian Bks.) Smithsonian Institution Scholarly Pr.

Gurrea, Susana. Collins Big Cat Phonics for Letters & Sounds - Sound Walk: Band 00/Lilac. Guille-Marrett, Emily & Raby, Charlotte. 2018. (Collins Big Cat Phonics Ser.). (ENG.). 16p. (J). (— 1). pap. 6.99 *(978-0-00-825127-7(4))* HarperCollins Pubs. Ltd. GBR. Dist: Independent Pubs. Group.

—A Super Scotland Activity Book: Games, Puzzles, Drawing, Stickers & More, 30 vols. 2018. (ENG.). 40p. (J). 9.95 *(978-1-78250-479-5(6)*, Kelpies) Floris Bks. GBR. Dist: Consortium Bk. Sales & Distribution.

—A Super Scotland Sticker Book, 30 vols. 2018. (ENG.). 24p. (J). 9.95 *(978-1-78250-422-1(2)*, Kelpies) Floris Bks. GBR. Dist: Consortium Bk. Sales & Distribution.

Gürth, Per-Henrik. ABC of Toronto. Gürth, Per-Henrik. 2013. (ENG.). 32p. (J). (gr. -1-k). 15.95 *(978-1-77138-037-9(3))* Kids Can Pr., Ltd. CAN. Dist: Hachette Bk. Group.

—Canada All Year. Gürth, Per-Henrik. 2011. (ENG.). 32p. (J). (gr. -1-1). 14.95 *(978-1-55453-709-9(6))* Kids Can Pr., Ltd. CAN. Dist: Hachette Bk. Group.

—Canada in Colours. Gürth, Per-Henrik. 2013. (ENG.). 24p. (J). (gr. -1 — 1). pap. 7.95 *(978-1-55453-760-0(6))* Kids Can Pr., Ltd. CAN. Dist: Hachette Bk. Group.

Gürth, Per-Henrik & Gürth, Per-Henrik. ABC of Canada. Bellefontaine, Kim. (ENG.). (J). (gr. -1 — 1). 2006. 30p. bds. 8.95 *(978-1-55337-979-9(9))*; 2004. 32p. 7.95 *(978-1-55337-685-9(4))* Kids Can Pr., Ltd. CAN. Dist: Hachette Bk. Group.

—Canada 123. Bellefontaine, Kim. (ENG.). 24p. (J). (gr. -1-1). 2011. 7.95 *(978-1-55453-659-7(6))*; 2008. bds. 8.95 *(978-1-55453-235-3(3))* Kids Can Pr., Ltd. CAN. Dist: Hachette Bk. Group.

—Canada 123. Bellefontaine, Kim. 2006. (ENG.). 24p. (J). (gr. -1-1). 15.95 *(978-1-55337-897-6(0))* Kids Can Pr., Ltd. CAN. Dist: Hachette Bk. Group.

—Canada in Colours. Gürth, Per-Henrik & Gürth, Per-Henrik. 2011. (ENG.). 24p. (J). (gr. -1 — 1). bds. 9.99 *(978-1-55453-757-0(6))* Kids Can Pr., Ltd. CAN. Dist: Hachette Bk. Group.

—Canada in Words. Gürth, Per-Henrik & Gürth, Per-Henrik. 2012. (ENG.). 32p. (J). (gr. -1-1). 14.95 *(978-1-55453-710-5(X))* Kids Can Pr., Ltd. CAN. Dist: Hachette Bk. Group.

—Oh, Canada! Gürth, Per-Henrik & Gürth, Per-Henrik. 2009. (ENG.). 32p. (J). (gr. -1-2). 15.99 *(978-1-55453-374-9(0))* Kids Can Pr., Ltd. CAN. Dist: Hachette Bk. Group.

—Snowy Sports: Ready, Set, Play! Gürth, Per-Henrik & Gürth, Per-Henrik. 2009. (ENG.). 24p. (J). (gr. -1-2). 14.95 *(978-1-55337-367-4(7))* Kids Can Pr., Ltd. CAN. Dist: Hachette Bk. Group.

Gürth, Per-Henrik, jt. illus. see Gürth, Per-Henrik.

Guru Animation Studio. True & the Rainbow Kingdom: the Living Sea. 2020. (True & the Rainbow Kingdom Ser.). (ENG.). 24p. (J). (gr. -1-1). 3.99 ***(978-2-89802-223-4(3)***, CrackBoom! Bks.) Chouette Publishing CAN. Dist: Publishers Group West (PGW).

—True & the Rainbow Kingdom: the Super Sticky Rescue. 2020. (True & the Rainbow Kingdom Ser.). (ENG.). 24p. (J). (gr. -1-1). 3.99 ***(978-2-89802-249-4(7)***, CrackBoom! Bks.) Chouette Publishing CAN. Dist: Publishers Group West (PGW).

—True & the Rainbow Kingdom: the Tricky Treat (Halloween Special) Includes a Halloween Mask! 2020. (True & the Rainbow Kingdom Ser.). (ENG.). 24p. (J). (gr. -1-1). 4.99 ***(978-2-89802-116-9(4)***, CrackBoom! Bks.) Chouette Publishing CAN. Dist: Publishers Group West (PGW).

Guru Animation Studio Ltd. Cosmic Feather: With Two-Way Sequins! ed. 2019. (True & the Rainbow Kingdom Ser.). 24p. (J). (gr. -1-k). 9.99 *(978-2-89802-077-3(X)*, CrackBoom! Bks.) Chouette Publishing CAN. Dist: Publishers Group West (PGW).

Guru Animation Studio Ltd. Magical Flower. 2019. 24p. (J). (gr. -1-1). 3.99 *(978-2-89802-034-6(6)*, CrackBoom! Bks.) Chouette Publishing CAN. Dist: Publishers Group West (PGW).

Guru Animation Studio Ltd. My First Sticker Book. 2019. (True & the Rainbow Kingdom Ser.). 64p. (J). (gr. -1). 10.99 *(978-2-89802-038-4(9)*, CrackBoom! Bks.) Chouette Publishing CAN. Dist: Publishers Group West (PGW).

Guru Animation Studio Ltd. Read with True: a Royal Stink (Level 1: Little Star) 2020. (True & the Rainbow Kingdom Ser.). (ENG.). 32p. (J). (gr. -1). 3.99 ***(978-2-89802-268-5(3)***, CrackBoom! Bks.) Chouette Publishing CAN. Dist: Publishers Group West (PGW).

—Read with True: Wishing Heart Hollow (Level 2: Rising Star) 2020. (True & the Rainbow Kingdom Ser.). (ENG.). 32p. (J). (gr. -1-1). 3.99 ***(978-2-89802-269-2(1)***, CrackBoom! Bks.) Chouette Publishing CAN. Dist: Publishers Group West (PGW).

Guru Animation Studio Ltd. True & the Rainbow Kingdom: the Great Rainbow Race. 2019. (True & the Rainbow Kingdom Ser.). (ENG.). 24p. (J). (gr. -1-1). 3.99 *(978-2-89802-033-9(8)*, CrackBoom! Bks.) Chouette Publishing CAN. Dist: Publishers Group West (PGW).

Guru Animation Studio Ltd. True & the Rainbow Kingdom: Welcome to the Rainbow Kingdom (Little Detectives) A Search & Find Book. 2019. 14p. (J). (gr. -1-1). bds. 11.99 *(978-2-89802-040-7(0)*, CrackBoom! Bks.) Chouette Publishing CAN. Dist: Publishers Group West (PGW).

Gurule, Jennifer. Look at Aunt Clare's Hair. Gurule, Jennifer. ed. 2005. (Daddy's Collection). (J). pap. 11.50 *(978-1-59134-033-1(0))* Maval Publishing, Inc.

Guscha, Ekaterina. Colors to Learn: Lift-The-Flap Book. Clever Publishing. 2018. (Clever Flaps Ser.). (ENG.). 16p. (J). (gr. -1 — 1). bds. 12.99 *(978-1-948418-47-8(9))* Clever Media Group.

—Search & Find Colors: Learn Colors. Clever Publishing. 2018. (Clever Things to Learn Ser.). (ENG.). 20p. (J). (gr. -1 — 1). 9.99 *(978-1-948418-39-3(8))* Clever Media Group.

—Search & Find Numbers: Count To 10. Clever Publishing. 2018. (Clever Things to Learn Ser.). (ENG.). 20p. (J). (gr. -1 — 1). 9.99 *(978-1-948418-40-9(1))* Clever Media Group.

Gustafson, Nick. Mira. Dobrowolska, Kate. 2018. (ENG.). 44p. (J). (gr. k-2). pap. *(978-1-78222-632-1(X))* Paragon Publishing, Rothersthorpe.

Gustafson, Samantha. My Mom the Police Officer. Bentrim, William G. 2019. (ENG.). 28p. (J). pap. 10.99 *(978-1-7962-1034-7(X))* Independently Published.

Gustafson, Scott. Cuentos de Hadas Clasicos. 2020. (SPA.). 152p. (J). 26.95 *(978-84-9145-291-1(5)*, Picarona Editorial) Ediciones Obelisco ESP. Dist: Spanish Pubs., LLC.

—Cuentos y Cantos de Navidad. 2004. (ESP & SPA.). 98p. (YA). 12.98 *(978-1-4127-0628-5(9)*, 7137007) Phoenix International Publications, Inc.

Gustafson, Scott. Eddie: The Lost Youth of Edgar Allan Po. Gustafson, Scott. 2012. (ENG.). (J). (gr. 3-7). lib. bdg. 17.60 *(978-1-68065-137-9(4))* Perfection Learning Corp.

—Eddie: The Lost Youth of Edgar Allan Poe. Gustafson, Scott. 2012. (ENG.). 208p. (J). (gr. 3-7). pap. 6.99 *(978-1-4169-9765-8(2)*, Simon & Schuster Bks. For

G

Young Readers) Simon & Schuster Bks. For Young Readers.
—Eddie: The Lost Youth of Edgar Allan Poe. Gustafson, Scott. 2012. (ENG.). 208p. (J). (gr. 4-6). 21.19 *(978-1-4169-9764-1(4))* Simon & Schuster, Inc.
Gustavson, Adam. Better Than You. Ludwig, Trudy. 2011. 32p. (J). (gr. 1-4). 16.99 *(978-1-58246-380-3(8)*, Knopf Bks. for Young Readers) Random Hse. Children's Bks.
—The Blue House Dog, 1 vol. Blumenthal, Deborah. 2010. (ENG.). 32p. (J). (gr. -1-3). 16.95 *(978-1-56145-537-9(7)*, Peachtree Junior) Peachtree Publishing Co. Inc.
—Calico Dorsey: Mail Dog of the Mining Camps. Lendroth, Susan. 2010. (ENG.). 32p. (J). (gr. -1-2). 16.99 *(978-1-58246-318-6(2)*, Tricycle Pr.) Random Hse. Children's Bks.
—Charlie Bumpers vs. His Big Blabby Mouth. Harley, Bill. (Charlie Bumpers Ser.). (ENG.). 160p. (J). (gr. 2-5). 2018. pap. 6.95 *(978-1-68263-064-8(1))*; 2017. 14.95 *(978-1-56145-940-7(2))* Peachtree Publishing Co. Inc.
—Charlie Bumpers vs. the End of the Year, 1 vol. Harley, Bill. (Charlie Bumpers Ser.). (ENG.). 208p. (J). (gr. 2-5). 2020. pap. 7.99 *(978-1-68263-162-1(1))*; 2019. 14.95 *(978-1-68263-042-6(0))* Peachtree Publishing Co. Inc.
—Charlie Bumpers vs. the Perfect Little Turkey, 1 vol. Harley, Bill. (Charlie Bumpers Ser.: 4). (ENG.). 176p. (J). (gr. 2-4). 2016. pap. 6.95 *(978-1-56145-963-6(1))*; 2015. 13.95 *(978-1-56145-835-6(X))* Peachtree Publishing Co. Inc.
—Charlie Bumpers vs. the Puny Pirates, 1 vol. Harley, Bill. (Charlie Bumpers Ser.). (ENG.). (J). (gr. 2-4). 2017. 176p. pap. 6.95 *(978-1-68263-001-3(3))*; 2016. 160p. 14.95 *(978-1-56145-939-1(9))* Peachtree Publishing Co. Inc.
—Charlie Bumpers vs. the Really Nice Gnome, 1 vol. Harley, Bill. (Charlie Bumpers Ser.). (ENG.). 160p. (J). (gr. 2-4). 2015. pap. 6.95 *(978-1-56145-831-8(7))*; 2014. 13.95 *(978-1-56145-740-3(X))* Peachtree Publishing Co. Inc.
—Charlie Bumpers vs. the Squeaking Skull, 1 vol. Harley, Bill. 2015. (Charlie Bumpers Ser.). (ENG.). 176p. (J). (gr. 2-4). pap. 6.95 *(978-1-56145-888-2(0))* Peachtree Publishing Co. Inc.
—Charlie Bumpers vs. the Teacher of the Year, 1 vol. Harley, Bill. (Charlie Bumpers Ser.). (ENG.). 160p. (J). 2014. pap. 6.95 *(978-1-56145-824-0(4))*; 2013. (gr. 2-4). 14.95 *(978-1-56145-732-8(9))* Peachtree Publishing Co. Inc.
—Dirty Rats? Lunde, Darrin. 2015. 32p. (J). (gr. -1-2). 16.95 *(978-1-58089-566-8(2))* Charlesbridge Publishing, Inc.
—Hannah's Way. Glaser, Linda. 2012. (Shabbat Ser.). 32p. (J). (gr. k-3). lib. bdg. 17.95 *(978-0-7613-5137-5(X))*; Vol. (ENG.). pap. 7.95 *(978-0-7613-5138-2(8)*, 9780761351382) Lerner Publishing Group. (Kar-Ben Publishing).
—Hillary Clinton: The Life of a Leader. Corey, Shana. 2016. (Step into Reading Ser.). 48p. (J). (gr. k-3). 3.99 *(978-1-101-93235-3(X)*, Random Hse. Bks. for Young Readers) Random Hse. Children's Bks.
—Jingle Bells: How the Holiday Classic Came to Be, 1 vol. Harris, John. 2011. (ENG.). 32p. (J). 16.95 *(978-1-56145-590-4(3))* Peachtree Publishing Co. Inc.
—The John Hancock Club. Borden, Louise. 2007. (ENG.). 48p. (J). (gr. 2-5). 17.99 *(978-1-4169-1813-4(2)*, McElderry, Margaret K. Bks.) McElderry, Margaret K. Bks.
—Just Kidding. Ludwig, Trudy. 2006. 32p. (J). (gr. 1-4). 16.99 *(978-1-58246-163-2(5)*, Tricycle Pr.) Random Hse. Children's Bks.
—King of the Tightrope: When the Great Blondin Ruled Niagara, 1 vol. Bowman, Donna Janell. 2019. (ENG.). 48p. (J). (gr. 1-5). 17.95 *(978-1-56145-937-7(2))* Peachtree Publishing Co. Inc.
—The Last Day of School. Borden, Louise. 2006. (ENG.). 40p. (J). (gr. 2-5). 19.99 *(978-0-689-86869-6(3)*, McElderry, Margaret K. Bks.) McElderry, Margaret K. Bks.
—The Little Rock Nine Stand up for Their Rights. Lucas, Eileen. 2011. 48p. pap. 9.95 *(978-0-7613-7118-2(4))*; pap. 56.72 *(978-0-7613-7634-7(8))*; (ENG.). (gr. 2-4). lib. bdg. 27.93 *(978-0-7613-5874-9(9)*, Millbrook Pr.) Lerner Publishing Group.
—Long-Armed Ludy & the First Women's Olympics. Patrick, Jean L. S. 2019. 32p. (J). (gr. 1-4). pap. 8.99 *(978-1-62354-168-2(9))* Charlesbridge Publishing, Inc.
—Lost & Found, 1 vol. Harley, Bill. 2012. (ENG.). 32p. (J). 16.95 *(978-1-56145-628-4(4))* Peachtree Publishing Co. Inc.
—The Lost-And-Found Tooth. Borden, Louise. 2008. (ENG.). 40p. (J). (gr. 2-5). 16.99 *(978-1-4169-1814-1(0)*, McElderry, Margaret K. Bks.) McElderry, Margaret K. Bks.
—Mind Your Manners, Alice Roosevelt!, 1 vol. Kimmelman, Leslie. 2009. (ENG.). 32p. (J). (gr. -1-3). 16.95 *(978-1-56145-492-1(3))* Peachtree Publishing Co. Inc.
—Rock & Roll Highway: The Robbie Robertson Story. Robertson, Sebastian. 2014. (ENG.). 40p. (J). (gr. 1-4). 17.99 *(978-0-8050-9473-2(3)*, 900079390, Holt, Henry & Co. Bks. For Young Readers) Holt, Henry & Co.
—Snow Day!, 1 vol. Laminack, Lester L. (ENG.). 32p. (J). 2010. (gr. -1-3). 19.95 *(978-1-56145-554-6(7))*; 2010. (gr. -1-3). pap. 7.95 *(978-1-56145-553-9(9))*; 2007. (gr. k-2). 16.95 *(978-1-56145-418-1(4))* Peachtree Publishing Co. Inc.
—Stand up & Sing! Pete Seeger, Folk Music, & the Path to Justice. Reich, Susanna. 2017. 48p. (J). 17.99 *(978-0-8027-3812-7(5)*, 900141410, Bloomsbury USA Childrens) Bloomsbury Publishing USA.
—The Trouble with May Amelia. Holm, Jennifer L. 2012. (ENG.). 224p. (J). (gr. 3-7). pap. 5.99 *(978-1-4169-1374-0(2))*;2. (gr. 4-6). 18.69 *(978-1-4169-1373-3(4))* Simon & Schuster Children's Publishing. (Atheneum Bks. for Young Readers).
—A Very Improbable Story. Einhorn, Edward. 2008. (Charlesbridge Math Adventures Ser.). 32p. (J). (gr. 2-5). pap. 7.95 *(978-1-57091-872-8(4))* Charlesbridge Publishing, Inc.
Gustavson, Adam. The A+ Custodian. Gustavson, Adam, tr. Borden, Louise. 2004. (ENG.). 40p. (J). (gr. 2-5). 19.99 *(978-0-689-84995-4(8)*, McElderry, Margaret K. Bks.) McElderry, Margaret K. Bks.
Gusterson, Leigh. Hey Bossie, You're a Spokescow! de Rham, Mickey. 2004. 24p. (J). 9.95 *(978-0-9755216-0-1(8))* Plaidswede Publishing.
Gusti. Los Disfraces de Tento. Alcántara, Ricardo. 2011. (Perrito Tento Ser.). (SPA.). (J). (gr. -1). bds. *(978-84-263-7665-7(7))* Vives, Luis Editorial (Edelvives).
—The Grey Boy. Farre, Lluis. Willis, Judith, tr. from CAT. 2007. (ENG.). 44p. (J). (gr. k-2). 12.95 *(978-1-905341-08-5(3))* WingedChariot Pr. GBR. Dist: Independent Pubs. Group.
—I Love My Colorful Nails. Acosta, Alicia & Amavisca, Luis. 2019. (ENG.). 36p. (J). 15.95 *(978-84-17123-59-8(8))* NubeOcho Ediciones ESP. Dist: Consortium Bk. Sales & Distribution.
—Quién es Tento? Alcántara, Ricardo. 2011. (SPA.). (J). (gr. -1). bds. *(978-84-263-7663-3(0))* Vives, Luis Editorial (Edelvives).
—Tento Busca su Osito. Alcántara, Ricardo. 2010. (SPA.). (J). (gr. -1). bds. *(978-84-263-7664-0(9))* Vives, Luis Editorial (Edelvives).
—Tento y el Color del Mar. Alcántara, Ricardo. 2011. (SPA.). (J). (gr. -1). bds. *(978-84-263-7666-4(5))* Vives, Luis Editorial (Edelvives).
—Tento y el Diente. Alcántara, Ricardo. (SPA.). 28p. (J). *(978-84-263-4140-2(3))* Vives, Luis Editorial (Edelvives) ESP. Dist: Lectorum Pubns., Inc.
—Tento y el Perro Granduilon. Alcántara, Ricardo. (SPA.). 28p. (J). *(978-84-263-4141-9(1))* Vives, Luis Editorial (Edelvives) ESP. Dist: Lectorum Pubns., Inc.
—Tento y la Tormenta. Alcántara, Ricardo. (SPA.). 28p. (J). *(978-84-263-4144-0(6))* Vives, Luis Editorial (Edelvives) ESP. Dist: Lectorum Pubns., Inc.
—Tento y Su Amigo, Tento and His Friend. Alcántara, Ricardo. 2nd ed. (SPA.). 28p. (J). *(978-84-263-4139-6(X))* Vives, Luis Editorial (Edelvives) ESP. Dist: Lectorum Pubns., Inc.
—Valentin Se Parece A... Montes, Graciela & Montes, Graciela. 7th ed. (SPA.). 64p. (J). (gr. 2-3). *(978-84-348-3847-5(8))* SM Ediciones.
—Vivan Las Uñas de Colores! Acosta, Alicia & Amavisca, Luis. 2019. (SPA.). 36p. (J). 15.95 *(978-84-17123-58-1(X))* NubeOcho Ediciones ESP. Dist: Consortium Bk. Sales & Distribution.
Gusti. ¡Esta Caca Es Mía! Gusti. 2020. (SPA.). 40p. (J). 15.95 ***(978-84-17673-87-1(3))*** NubeOcho Ediciones ESP. Dist: Consortium Bk. Sales & Distribution.
—This Poop Is Mine! Gusti. 2020. (ENG.). 40p. (J). 15.95 ***(978-84-17673-88-8(1))*** NubeOcho Ediciones ESP. Dist: Consortium Bk. Sales & Distribution.
Gustiawan, Gustiawan. The Adventures of Mrs. Picklebottom: Four Terrific Train Tales for Tots & Tykes. Connelly, Ben & Connelly, Charlotte. 2019. (Mrs. Picklebottom Ser.: Vol. 1). (ENG.). 42p. (J). pap. 11.99 ***(978-1-6501-1799-7(X))*** Independently Published.
Gustovich, Michael, et al. Heroes Unlimited. Siembieda, Kevin. Marciniszyn, Alex, ed. 2nd rev. ed. 2006. 248p. (YA). (gr. 8-18). pap. 26.95 *(978-1-57457-006-9(4)*, 500) Palladium Bks., Inc.
Guthridge, Bettina. Making Sense of Asperger's: A Story for Children. Ende, Debra. 2011. 24p. pap. 36.95 *(978-0-86431-847-3(2))* ACER Pr. AUS. Dist: Independent Pubs. Group.
—My Mom Tarzan. Shanahan, Lisa. 2008. (ENG.). 32p. (J). (gr. -1-3). *(978-1-59692-239-6(7))* MacAdam/Cage Publishing, Inc.
Guthrie, Anna Marie. Mrs. Smudge. 2018. (Around the Pond Ser.: Vol. 4). (ENG.). 38p. (J). pap. 9.99 *(978-1-7329953-4-5(6))* Scott, Sue Ann.
Guthrie, Lewis. Leah Bug & Her Flying Friends. Satterfield, April. 2011. 20p. pap. 24.95 *(978-1-4560-8422-6(4))* America Star Bks.
Gutierez, Francisco & Renteria, Justin. As I Look in Your Eyes. Dupont, Matthew. 2003. 20p. (YA). pap. 5.99 *(978-0-9728134-0-2(3))* A & E Children's Pr.
Gutierrez, Akemi. Ella's Trip to Israel, Vol. Newman, Vivian Bonnie. 2011. (ENG.). 24p. (J). (gr. -1 — 1). pap. 8.95 *(978-0-7613-6029-2(8)*, 9780761360292, Kar-Ben Publishing) Lerner Publishing Group.
—I'M a New Big Sister. Gaydos, Nora. 2010. (ENG.). 30p. (J). (gr. -1-17). 6.99 *(978-1-60169-009-8(6))* Innovative Kids.
—I'm Just Like My Mom; I'm Just Like My Dad/Me Parezco Tanto a Mi Mama; Me Parez: Bilingual Spanish-English Chilkdren's Book. Ramos, Jorge. 2008.Tr. of Me Parezco Tanto a mi Papá. (ENG.). 40p. (J). (gr. -1-3). 16.99 *(978-0-06-123968-7(2))* HarperCollins Español.
—Lotsa Matzah. Vol. Balsley, Tilda. 2013. (ENG.). 12p. (J). (gr. -1-1). bds. 5.99 *(978-0-7613-6629-4(6)*, 9780761366294, Kar-Ben Publishing) Lerner Publishing Group.
—Now I'm Growing! - A Visit to the Doctor. Gaydos, Nora. 2011. (ENG.). 30p. (J). (gr. -1-17). 8.99 *(978-1-60169-153-8(X))* Innovative Kids.
—Now I'm Growing! - First Day of School. Gaydos, Nora. 2011. (ENG.). 30p. (J). (gr. -1-17). 8.99 *(978-1-60169-152-1(1))* Innovative Kids.
—Now I'm Growing! Hands Are Not for Hurting. Gaydos, Nora. 2012. (ENG.). 30p. (J). (gr. -1-17). 8.99 *(978-1-60169-222-1(6))* Innovative Kids.
—Now I'm Growing! Prince of the Potty - Little Steps for Big Kids! Gaydos, Nora. 2011. (ENG.). 30p. (J). (gr. -1-17). 8.99 *(978-1-60169-077-7(0))* Innovative Kids.
—Princess of the Potty - Little Steps for Big Kids! Gaydos, Nora. 2011. (ENG.). 30p. (J). (gr. -1-17). 8.99 *(978-1-60169-076-0(2))* Innovative Kids.
—Three Little Bears Play All Day. Martin, David. 2010. (Brand New Readers Ser.). 48p. (J). (gr. -1-3). pap. 5.99 *(978-0-7636-4230-3(4))* Candlewick Pr.
Gutierrez, Chris. Jesus, It's Me Nicholas! Sanchez, Elizabeth. 2005. 12p. (J). per. 9.99 *(978-1-59879-062-7(5))* Lifevest Publishing, Inc.
Gutierrez, Elisa. A Duck in a Sock: Four Phonics Stories. Rae, Elspeth & Rae, Rowena. 2017. (Meg & Greg Ser.). (ENG.). (J). (gr. 1-4). pap. *(978-0-9952933-0-4(9))* 44 Sounds Publishing.
Gutierrez, Elisa. Meg & Greg: a Duck in a Sock. Rae, Elspeth & Rae, Rowena. 2020. (Orca Two Read Ser.: 1). (ENG.). 168p. (J). (gr. 1-3). pap. 14.95 ***(978-1-4598-2490-4(3))*** Orca Bk. Pubs. USA.
Gutiérrez, Elisa. Meg & Greg: Frank & the Skunk. Rae, Elspeth & Rae, Rowena. 2020. (Orca Two Read Ser.: 2). (ENG.). 160p. (J). (gr. 1-3). pap. 14.95 ***(978-1-4598-2493-5(8))*** Orca Bk. Pubs. USA.
Gutierrez, Jorge. Día de Los Muertos. Eliot, Hannah. 2018. (Celebrate the World Ser.). (ENG.). 24p. (J). (gr. -1 — 1). bds. 8.99 *(978-1-5344-1515-7(7)*, Little Simon) Little Simon.
Gutiérrez, Lorena. Ópatas, Tarahumaras, Yaquis y Seris. Ocegueda, Aleida. 2019. (Historias de Verdad Ser.). (SPA.). 88p. (J). (gr. 4-7). pap. 12.00 *(978-607-8469-56-7(8))* Nostra Ediciones MEX. Dist: Independent Pubs. Group.
Gutierrez, Lucia Doblas, jt. illus. see Cortes, Laura Gutierrez.
Gutierrez, Manuel. Everything's Bigger in Texas #2. Fortsch, Samuel P. 2020. (Pawtriot Dogs Ser.: 2). 96p. (J). (gr. 2-4). 5.99 ***(978-0-593-22234-8(2)***, Grosset & Dunlap) Penguin Young Readers Group.
Gutierrez, Manuel, et al. Marvel Knights Punisher by Peyer & Gutierrez: Taxi Wars. 2019. (ENG.). 192p. (gr. 10-17). pap. 24.99 *(978-1-302-91633-6(5))* Marvel Worldwide, Inc.
Gutierrez, Manuel. Save the Sanctuary #1. Fortsch, Samuel P. 2020. (Pawtriot Dogs Ser.: 1). 96p. (J). (gr. 2-4). 5.99 ***(978-0-593-22233-1(4)***, Grosset & Dunlap) Penguin Young Readers Group.
Gutierrez, Manuel. Where Is the Serengeti? Medina, Nico & Who HQ. 2019. (Where Is? Ser.). 112p. (J). (gr. 3-7). 5.99 *(978-1-5247-9256-5(X))*; 15.99 *(978-1-5247-9257-2(8))* Penguin Young Readers Group. (Penguin Workshop).
Gutierrez, Manuel. Who Is Greta Thunberg? Who HQ & Leonard, Jill. 2020. (Who HQ NOW Ser.). 56p. (J). (gr. 3-7). 4.99 ***(978-0-593-22567-7(8))***; 12.99 ***(978-0-593-22568-4(6))*** Penguin Young Readers Group. (Penguin Workshop).
Gutierrez, Manuel, IV & Gutierrez, Manuel. Who Was Richard Nixon? Stine, Megan & Who HQ. 2020. (Who Was? Ser.). 112p. (J). 1p. (J). (gr. 3-7). 5.99 *(978-1-5247-8980-0(1))*; 15.99 *(978-1-5247-8981-7(X))* Penguin Young Readers Group. (Penguin Workshop).
Gutierrez, Manuel, jt. illus. see Gutierrez, Manuel, IV.
Gutierrez, Monica. Barnyard Bubbe's Hanukkah. Klein-Higger, Joni & Sharf, Barbara. 2019. (ENG.). 12p. (J). (gr. -1 — 1). bds. 5.99 *(978-1-5415-2215-2(X)*, Kar-Ben Publishing) Lerner Publishing Group.
Gutiérrez, Mónica. Little Red Rosie, Vol. Kimmel, Eric A. 2016. (ENG.). (J). *(978-1-68115-518-0(4))* Behrman Hse., Inc.
Gutierrez, Regina. Wind Smith: The Fall of Broken Hearts. Fernandez Mendez, Maria. 2018. (Wind Smith Ser.: Vol. 1). (ENG.). 134p. (J). pap. 9.99 *(978-1-5449-7912-0(6))* CreateSpace Independent Publishing Platform.
Gutierrez, Rudy. Carlos Santana: Sound of the Heart, Song of the World. Golio, Gary. 2018. (ENG.). 40p. (J). 18.99 *(978-1-62779-512-8(X)*, 900153244, Holt, Henry & Co. Bks. For Young Readers) Holt, Henry & Co.
—Double Bass Blues. Loney, Andrea J. 2019. 32p. (J). (gr. -1-3). 17.99 *(978-1-5247-1852-7(1)*, Knopf Bks. for Young Readers) Random Hse. Children's Bks.
—Jazz Owls: A Novel of the Zoot Suit Riots. Engle, Margarita. 2018. (ENG.). 192p. (YA). (gr. 7). 17.99 *(978-1-5344-0943-9(2))* Simon & Schuster Children's Publishing.
—Mama & Me. Dorros, Arthur. 2011. (ENG.). 32p. (J). (gr. -1-3). 16.99 *(978-0-06-058160-2(3)*, Rayo) HarperCollins Pubs.
—Papa & Me. Dorros, Arthur. 2008. (ENG.). 32p. (J). (gr. -1-3). 16.99 *(978-0-06-058156-5(5)*, Rayo) HarperCollins Pubs.
—Pele, King of Soccer/Pele, el Rey Del Futbol: Bilingual Spanish-English Children's Book. Brown, Monica. 2008. (ENG.). 40p. (J). (gr. -1-3). 17.99 *(978-0-06-122779-0(X))* HarperCollins Español.
—Pele, King of Soccer/Pele, el Rey Del Futbol: Bilingual Spanish-English Children's Book. Brown, Monica. 2017. (ENG.). 40p. (J). (gr. -1-3). pap. 6.99 *(978-0-06-122780-6(3)*, Rayo) HarperCollins Pubs.
—When I Get Older: The Story Behind Wavin' Flag. Sol & K'naan. 2012. (ENG.). 1p. (J). (gr. 1-4). 17.95 *(978-1-77049-302-5(6)*, Tundra Bks.) Tundra Bks. CAN. Dist: Penguin Random Hse. LLC.
Gutierrez, Santy. The Great Pumpkin Smash. Dixon, Franklin W. 2019. (Hardy Boys Clue Book Ser.: 10). (ENG.). 96p. (J). (gr. 1-4). pap. 5.99 *(978-1-5344-3123-2(3)*, Simon & Schuster/Paula Wiseman Bks.) Simon & Schuster/Paula Wiseman Bks.
—The Pirate Ghost. Dixon, Franklin W. 2018. (Hardy Boys Clue Book Ser.: 7). (ENG.). 96p. (J). (gr. 1-4). 16.99 *(978-1-4814-8873-0(2))*; pap. 5.99 *(978-1-4814-8872-3(4))* Simon & Schuster Children's Publishing. (Aladdin).
Gutierrez, Santy. Sea Life Secrets. Dixon, Franklin W. 2020. (Hardy Boys Clue Book Ser.: 12). (ENG.). 96p. (J). (gr. 1-4). 17.99 ***(978-1-5344-4259-7(6))***; pap. 5.99 ***(978-1-5344-4258-0(8))*** Simon & Schuster Children's Publishing. (Aladdin).
Gutierrez, Santy. The Time Warp Wonder. Dixon, Franklin W. 2018. (Hardy Boys Clue Book Ser.: 8). (ENG.). 96p. (J). (gr. 1-4). 16.99 *(978-1-5344-1392-4(8))*; pap. 5.99 *(978-1-5344-1391-7(X))* Simon & Schuster Children's Publishing. (Aladdin).
—Who Let the Frogs Out? Dixon, Franklin W. 2019. (Hardy Boys Clue Book Ser.: 9). (ENG.). 96p. (J). (gr. 1-4). pap. 5.99 *(978-1-5344-1485-3(1)*, Simon & Schuster/Paula Wiseman Bks.) Simon & Schuster/Paula Wiseman Bks.
Gutkovskiy, Katherine. Mister: Nature, Nurture & Teenage Trouble. Chennamchetty, Elizabeth. 2019. (ENG.). 36p. (J). (gr. k-4). 17.99 *(978-0-9983615-9-8(3))*; pap. 9.99 *(978-0-9983615-8-1(5))* EC Pr. Bks.
Gutkovskiy, Kathrine. Bunny & Bear Work It Out. Anderson, Jason. 2019. (ENG.). 64p. (J). pap. 12.99 *(978-1-5439-7833-9(9))* BookBaby.
Gutkovskiy, Kathrine. The Tent Mouse & the RV Mouse. Sponsler, Loretta. 2019. (ENG.). 34p. (J). (gr. k-3). 17.99 ***(978-1-951633-01-1(6))*** Kids Camping Bks.
Gutosky, Jennifer. Bella's Magic Brush. Gutosky, Jennifer. 2018. (ENG.). 32p. (J). pap. 11.49 *(978-1-7262-5770-1(3))* CreateSpace Independent Publishing Platform.
Guttiere, Benedicte. When Christmas Comes - Welsh Edition. Guttiere, Benedicte. 2011. (Funny Faces Ser.). 14p. bds. *(978-1-84089-711-1(2))* Zero to Ten, Ltd.
Guttormsen, Trygve Lund. The Most Beautiful Dawn. Vars, Elle Márjá. Janda, Laura A., tr. 2013. 80p. (J). pap. 17.99 *(978-0-9772714-6-7(3))* Nordic Studies Pr.
Gutwein, Gwendolyn. Dee Diddly Dragon Is Not a Wimp. Molnar, Cheri Eplin. 2004. 32p. (J). per. 17.95 *(978-0-9746330-3-9(8))* Anton Berkshire Publishing.
—More Than You'll Ever Know. Mustaine Hettinger, Cynthia. 2004. 32p. (J). per. 19.95 *(978-0-9746330-7-7(0))* Anton Berkshire Publishing.
Guy, Robert. Maile. Gilchrist, Reona. 2004. (J). 19.95 *(978-0-9747990-0-1(9))* Gilchrist & Guy Publishing.
Guy, Sue. Four Wheels West: A Wyoming Number Book. Gagliano, Eugene M. 2006. (Count Your Way Across the U. S. A. Ser.). (ENG.). 40p. (J). (gr. -1-3). 17.95 *(978-1-58536-210-3(7))* Sleeping Bear Pr.
Guy, Sue & Guy, Susan. B Is for Buckaroo: A Cowboy Alphabet. Whitney, Gleaves & Whitney, Louise Doak. rev. ed. 2003. (Sports Ser.). (ENG.). 40p. (J). (gr. 1-4). 17.95 *(978-1-58536-139-7(9)*, 202000) Sleeping Bear Pr.
Guy, Susan. B Is for Buckaroo: A Cowboy Alphabet. Whitney, Gleaves & Whitney, Louise Doak. 2006. (Sleeping Bear Alphabets Ser.). (ENG.). 40p. (J). (gr. -1-3). pap. 7.95 *(978-1-58536-336-0(7))* Sleeping Bear Pr.
—C Is for Cowboy: A Wyoming Alphabet. Gagliano, Eugene. 2003. (Discover America State by State Ser.). (ENG.). 40p. (J). 17.95 *(978-1-58536-097-0(X))* Sleeping Bear Pr.
Guy, Susan, jt. illus. see Guy, Sue.
Guy, Will. Romeo the Rhino's Rocky Romance: A Cautionary Tale about Differences. Ulick, Michael Ackerman. 32p. (J). 15.95 *(978-0-9679813-0-7(1))* Footprints Pr.
Guyard, Romain. 45 Games... Out & About! 2018. (ENG.). 52p. (J). 6.99 *(978-2-7338-5623-9(5))* Auzou, Philippe Editions FRA. Dist: Consortium Bk. Sales & Distribution.
Guymon, Jennette King. Daily Discoveries for August. Midgley, Elizabeth Cole. Mitchell, Judith, ed. 2005. 192p. (J). pap. 12.95 *(978-1-57310-452-4(3))* Teaching & Learning Co.
—Daily Discoveries for October. Midgley, Elizabeth Cole. Mitchell, Judith, ed. 2005. 192p. (J). pap. 12.95 *(978-1-57310-454-8(X))* Teaching & Learning Co.
—Daily Discoveries for September. Midgley, Elizabeth Cole. Mitchess, Judith, ed. 2005. 192p. (J). pap. 12.95 *(978-1-57310-453-1(1))* Teaching & Learning Co.
Guymon-King, Jennette. Primary Partners Singing Fun. Ross, Mary H. 2004. *(978-1-59156-793-6(9))* Covenant Communications.
Guze, Tessa. Harry Goes Rowing. Tetlow, Karin. 2013. 32p. pap. 11.95 *(978-0-615-75585-4(2))* Juping Horse Pr.
—Harry the Carousel Horse. Tetlow, Karin. 2012. 32p. pap. 15.96 *(978-0-615-55671-0(X))* Juping Horse Pr.
Guzek, Greta. The Airplane Ride. White, Howard. unabr. ed. 2006. (ENG.). 32p. (J). 16.95 *(978-0-88971-224-9(7))* Nightwood Editions CAN. Dist: Harbour Publishing Co., Ltd.
—Down at the Seaweed Cafe. Perry, Robert. unabr. ed. 2010. (ENG.). 32p. (J). pap. 9.95 *(978-0-88971-246-1(8))* Nightwood Editions CAN. Dist: Harbour Publishing Co., Ltd.
—The Ferryboat Ride. Perry, Robert. 2017. (ENG.). 20p. (J). bds. 9.95 *(978-0-88971-340-6(5))* Nightwood Editions CAN. Dist: Harbour Publishing Co., Ltd.
—My Vancouver Sketchbook. Perry, Robert. unabr. ed. 2010. (ENG.). 32p. (J). pap. 9.95 *(978-0-88971-248-5(4))* Nightwood Editions CAN. Dist: Publishers Group West (PGW).
Guzman, Gabriel, et al. Star Wars Legends Epic Collection: the Empire Vol. 4. 2018. 496p. (J). (gr. 4-17). pap. 39.99 *(978-1-302-91208-6(9))* Marvel Worldwide, Inc.
Guzman, Jacob. The Adventures of Eliseo & Stefano: My Daddy Can Fly! Guzman, Raquel. 2006. 28p. (J). 16.95 *(978-0-9788332-0-6(1))* Images & Pages.
Guzman, Lula. Sophie Wonders about Marriage. Bradley, Debby. 2013. (Sophie Wonders about the Sacraments Ser.). (ENG.). 31p. (J). pap. 4.99 *(978-0-7648-2351-0(5))* Liguori Pubns.
Guzman, Minerva. The Punctuation Pals Go Snow Skiing. Olker, Constance. 2005. 22p. (J). (gr. -1-3). per. 18.95 *(978-1-933449-14-2(4))* Nightengale Pr.
—The Punctuation Pals Go to the Baseball Park. Olker, Constance. 2005. (Punctuation Pals Ser.). 44p. (J). per. 18.95 *(978-1-933449-15-9(2))* Nightengale Pr.
—The Punctuation Pals Go to the Beach. Olker, Constance. 2005. (Punctuation Pals Ser.). 36p. (J). per. 18.95 *(978-1-933449-12-8(8))* Nightengale Pr.
—The Punctuation Pals Meet at School. Olker, Constance. 2004. (Punctuation Pals Ser.). 24p. (J). (gr. 1-18). 19.95 *(978-0-9743348-6-8(3))* Nightengale Pr.
Guzzo, Andra. The Little Woods Runner. Barksdale, Colleen. 2016. (ENG.). (J). pap. 19.99 *(978-1-4984-8864-8(1))* Salem Author Services.
Gwangjo & Park, Jung-a. Dancing Bear. Subramaniam, Manasi. 2013. (ENG.). 32p. (J). (gr. k). pap. 9.95 *(978-81-8190-200-9(9))* Karadi Tales Co. Pvt, Ltd. IND. Dist: Consortium Bk. Sales & Distribution.
Gwé. My First Fairy Tales: the Three Little Pigs. 2019. (My First Fairy Tales Ser.). (ENG.). 10p. (J). bds. 10.99 *(978-2-7338-6150-9(6))* Auzou, Philippe Editions FRA. Dist: Consortium Bk. Sales & Distribution.
Gwinner, Patricia. Sailor the Cat. Hooker, Adele. 2011. 24p. pap. 24.95 *(978-1-4560-8026-6(1))* America Star Bks.
Gwynne, Fred. The Battle of the Frogs & the Mice: A Homeric Fable. Martin, George. 2013. (ENG.). 64p. (gr. k-12). pap. 18.95 *(978-0-399-16285-5(2)*, TarcherPerigee) Penguin Publishing Group.
Gyatso, Lobsang. Pola's Flower. Nadeau, Diana Lynne. 2017. (ENG.). (J). 37p. *(978-1-945432-16-3(0))*; pap. *(978-1-945432-18-7(7))* Aurora Production AG.

Gynux. Digger the Dinosaur. Dotlich, Rebecca. 2013. (My First I Can Read Ser.). (ENG.). 24p. (J). (gr. -1-3). 16.99 *(978-0-06-222222-0(8))* HarperCollins Pubs.
—Digger the Dinosaur. Dotlich, Rebecca. 2013. (My First I Can Read Ser.). (ENG.). 24p. (J). (gr. -1-3). pap. 4.99 *(978-0-06-222221-3(X)*, HarperCollins) HarperCollins Pubs. Ltd. GBR. Dist: HarperCollins Pubs.
—Digger the Dinosaur & the Cake Mistake. Dotlich, Rebecca. 2013. (My First I Can Read Ser.). (ENG.). 24p. (J). (gr. -1-3). 16.99 *(978-0-06-222224-4(4))*; pap. 4.99 *(978-0-06-222223-7(6))* HarperCollins Pubs.
—Jesus Loves Me, 1 vol. 2017. (Sing-Along Book Ser.). (ENG.). 20p. (J). bds. 8.99 *(978-0-310-75894-5(7))* Zonderkidz.
—Storm Song, 0 vols. Viau, Nancy. 2013. 24p. (gr. k-3). (ENG.). (J). 12.99 *(978-1-4778-1646-2(1)*, 9781477816462, Two Lions); pap. 12.99 *(978-1-4778-6646-7(9))* Amazon Publishing.

H

H. J. Ford. The Orange Fairy Book. Andrew Lang, ed. 2010. 260p. pap. 6.89 *(978-1-60386-308-7(7)*, Merchant Bks.) Rough Draft Printing.
—The Pink Fairy Book. Andrew Lang, ed. 2010. 276p. pap. 6.89 *(978-1-60386-291-2(9)*, Merchant Bks.) Rough Draft Printing.
H-P. Carnet Blanc Projection Cinema. 2016. (Bnf Affiches Ser.). (FRE.). (J). pap. *(978-2-01-116975-4(5))* Hachette Groupe Livre.
—Carnet Ligne Projection Cinema. 2016. (Bnf Affiches Ser.). (FRE.). (J). pap. *(978-2-01-116950-1(X))* Hachette Groupe Livre.
Ha, Robin. Almost American Girl: An Illustrated Memoir. Ha, Robin. 2020. (ENG.). 240p. (J). (gr. 8). 22.99 *(978-0-06-268510-0(4))*; pap. 12.99 *(978-0-06-268509-4(0))* HarperCollins Pubs. (Balzer & Bray).
Ha, Vinh. The Adventures of Charlie Chipmunk. Rubel, Michael J. 2019. (ENG.). 160p. (J). *(978-1-5255-4087-5(4))*; pap. *(978-1-5255-4088-2(2))* FriesenPress.
Ha, Ying-Hwa, jt. illus. see Van Wright, Cornelius.
Haag, Bob. A Guide to Cottage Architecture As Seen in Lakeside, Ohio. Haag, Ruth. 2004. 13p. 6.00 *(978-0-9710260-8-7(4))* Haag Pr.
Haan, Linda de & Nijland, Stern. King & King. Haan, Linda de & Nijland, Stern. 2003. (ENG.). 32p. (J). (gr. k-3). 16.99 *(978-1-58246-061-1(2)*, Tricycle Pr.) Random Hse. Children's Bks.
Haas, Cornelia. Mein Allersch&#65533;nster Traum - Мой самый прекрасный сон (Deutsch - Russisch) Zweisprachiges Kinderbuch, Mit H&#65533;rbuch Zum Herunterladen. Renz, Ulrich. Baden, Valeria, tr. 2020. (Sefa Bilinguale Bilderb&#65533;cher Ser.). (GER.). 42p. (J). pap. *(978-3-7399-6416-4(2))* Boedeker, Kirsten. Sefa Verlag.
—Mein Allersch&#65533;nster Traum - わたしの とびっきり すてきな ゆめ (Deutsch - Japanisch) Zweisprachiges Kinderbuch, Mit H&#65533;rbuch Zum Herunterladen. Renz, Ulrich. Saito, Yumiko, tr. 2020. (Sefa Bilinguale Bilderb&#65533;cher Ser.). (GER.). 42p. (J). pap. *(978-3-7399-6387-7(5))* Boedeker, Kirsten. Sefa Verlag.
—Mein Allersch&#65533;nster Traum - قشنگترین رویایمن (Deutsch - Persisch, Farsi, Dari) Zweisprachiges Kinderbuch, Mit H&#65533;rbuch Zum Herunterladen. Renz, Ulrich. Bahar, Talai, tr. 2020. (Sefa Bilinguale Bilderb&#65533;cher Ser.). (GER.). 42p. (J). pap. *(978-3-7399-6418-8(9))* Boedeker, Kirsten. Sefa Verlag.
—Mein Allersch&#65533;nster Traum - আমার সবচেয়ে সুন্দর স্বপ্ন (Deutsch - Bengalisch) Zweisprachiges Kinderbuch, Mit H&#65533;rbuch Zum Herunterladen. Renz, Ulrich. Dutta, Kuheli, tr. 2020. (Sefa Bilinguale Bilderb&#65533;cher Ser.). (GER.). 42p. (J). pap. *(978-3-7399-6423-2(5))* Boedeker, Kirsten. Sefa Verlag.
—Mi Sue&#65533;o M&#65533;s Bonito - Мой самый прекрасный сон (espa&#65533;ol - Ruso) Libro Infantil Biling&#65533;e, con Audiolibro Descargable. Renz, Ulrich. Deev, Oleg, tr. 2020. (Sefa Libros Ilustrados en DOS Idiomas Ser.). (SPA.). 42p. (J). pap. *(978-3-7399-6404-1(9))* Boedeker, Kirsten. Sefa Verlag.
—Mi Sue&#65533;o M&#65533;s Bonito - わたしの とびっきり すてきな ゆめ (espa&#65533;ol - Japon&#65533;s) Libro Infantil Biling&#65533;e, con Audiolibro Descargable. Renz, Ulrich. Saito, Yumiko, tr. 2020. (Sefa Libros Ilustrados en DOS Idiomas Ser.). (SPA.). 42p. (J). pap. *(978-3-7399-6401-0(4))* Boedeker, Kirsten. Sefa Verlag.
—Mi Sue&#65533;o M&#65533;s Bonito - قشنگترین رویایمن (espa&#65533;ol - Persa) Libro Infantil Biling&#65533;e, con Audiolibro Descargable. Renz, Ulrich. Talai, Bahar, tr. 2020. (Sefa Libros Ilustrados en DOS Idiomas Ser.). (SPA.). 42p. (J). pap. *(978-3-7399-6372-3(7))* Boedeker, Kirsten. Sefa Verlag.
—Mi Sue&#65533;o M&#65533;s Bonito - 我最美的梦乡 (espa&#65533;ol - Chino) Libro Infantil Biling&#65533;e. Renz, Ulrich. Wang, Yanxing, tr. 2020. (Sefa Libros Ilustrados en DOS Idiomas Ser.). (SPA.). 42p. (J). pap. *(978-3-7399-6399-0(9))* Boedeker, Kirsten. Sefa Verlag.
—Mi Sue&#65533;o M&#65533;s Bonito - il Mio Pi&#65533; Bel Sogno (espa&#65533;ol - Italiano) Libro Infantil Biling&#65533;e, con Audiolibro Descargable. Renz, Ulrich. Catala, Raquel, tr. 2020. (Sefa Libros Ilustrados en DOS Idiomas Ser.). (SPA.). 42p. (J). pap. *(978-3-7399-6385-3(9))* Boedeker, Kirsten. Sefa Verlag.
—Mi Sue&#65533;o M&#65533;s Bonito - Mein Allersch&#65533;nster Traum (espa&#65533;ol - Alem&#65533;n) Libro Infantil Biling&#65533;e, con Audiolibro Descargable. Renz, Ulrich & Catala, Raquel. 2020. (Sefa Libros Ilustrados en DOS Idiomas Ser.). (SPA.). 42p. (J). pap. *(978-3-7399-6367-9(0))* Boedeker, Kirsten. Sefa Verlag.
—Mi Sue&#65533;o M&#65533;s Bonito - Min Allra Vackraste Dr&#65533;m (espa&#65533;ol - Sueco) Libro Infantil Biling&#65533;e, con Audiolibro Descargable. Renz, Ulrich. Thordsen, Narona, tr. 2020. (Sefa Libros Ilustrados en DOS Idiomas Ser.). (SPA.). 42p. (J). pap. *(978-3-7399-6403-4(0))* Boedeker, Kirsten. Sefa Verlag.
—Mi Sue&#65533;o M&#65533;s Bonito - Moj Najljepsi San (espa&#65533;ol - Croata) Libro Infantil Biling&#65533;e, con Audiolibro Descargable. Renz, Ulrich. Fedeli, Karmen, tr. 2020. (Sefa Libros Ilustrados en DOS Idiomas Ser.). (SPA.). 42p. (J). pap. *(978-3-7399-6400-3(6))* Boedeker, Kirsten. Sefa Verlag.
—Mi Sue&#65533;o M&#65533;s Bonito - Mon Plus Beau R&#65533;ve (espa&#65533;ol - Franc&#65533;s) Libro Infantil Biling&#65533;e, con Audiolibro Descargable. Renz, Ulrich. Andler, Martin, tr. 2020. (Sefa Libros Ilustrados en DOS Idiomas Ser.). (SPA.). 42p. (J). pap. *(978-3-7399-6366-2(2))* Boedeker, Kirsten. Sefa Verlag.
—Mi Sue&#65533;o M&#65533;s Bonito - My Most Beautiful Dream (espa&#65533;ol - Ingl&#65533;s) Libro Infantil Biling&#65533;e, con Audiolibro Descargable. Renz, Ulrich. Agnew, Sefa, tr. 2020. (Sefa Libros Ilustrados en DOS Idiomas Ser.). (SPA.). 42p. (J). pap. *(978-3-7399-6365-5(4))* Boedeker, Kirsten. Sefa Verlag.
—Mi Sue&#65533;o M&#65533;s Bonito - Ndoto Yangu Nzuri Sana Kuliko Zote (espa&#65533;ol - Suajili) Libro Infantil Biling&#65533;e. Renz, Ulrich. Machenje, Levina, tr. 2020. (Sefa Libros Ilustrados en DOS Idiomas Ser.). (SPA.). 42p. (J). pap. *(978-3-7399-6390-7(5))* Boedeker, Kirsten. Sefa Verlag.
—Min Aller Fineste Dr&#65533;m - Mein Allersch&#65533;nster Traum (norsk - Tysk) Tospr&#65533;klig Barnebok, Med Nedlastbar Lydbok. Renz, Ulrich. Skalla, Werner, tr. 2020. (Sefa Bildeb&#65533;ker P&#65533; to Spr&#65533;k Ser.). (NOR.). 42p. (J). pap. *(978-3-7399-6395-2(6))* Boedeker, Kirsten. Sefa Verlag.
—Min Aller Fineste Dr&#65533;m - My Most Beautiful Dream (norsk - Engelsk) Tospr&#65533;klig Barnebok, Med Nedlastbar Lydbok. Renz, Ulrich. Skalla, Werner, tr. 2020. (Sefa Bildeb&#65533;ker P&#65533; to Spr&#65533;k Ser.). (NOR.). 42p. (J). pap. *(978-3-7399-6394-5(8))* Boedeker, Kirsten. Sefa Verlag.
—Min Allra Vackraste Dr&#65533;m - il Mio Pi&#65533; Bel Sogno (svenska - Italienska) Tv&#65533;spr&#65533;kig Barnbok, Med Ljudbok Som Nedladdning. Renz, Ulrich. Thordsen, Narona, tr. 2020. (Sefa Bilderb&#65533;cker P&#65533; Tv&#65533; Spr&#65533;k Ser.). (SWE.). 42p. (J). pap. *(978-3-7399-6386-0(7))* Boedeker, Kirsten. Sefa Verlag.
—Minun Kaikista Kaunein Uneni - Мой самый прекрасный сон (suomi - Ven&#65533;j&#65533;) Kaksikielinen Lastenkirja, Mukana &#65533;&#65533;nikirja Ladattavaksi. Renz, Ulrich. Deev, Oleg, tr. 2020. (Sefa Kuvakirjoja Kahdella Kielell&#65533; Ser.). (FIN.). 42p. (J). pap. *(978-3-7399-6445-4(6))* Boedeker, Kirsten. Sefa Verlag.
—Minun Kaikista Kaunein Uneni - わたしの とびっきり すてきな ゆめ (suomi - Japani) Kaksikielinen Lastenkirja, Mukana &#65533;&#65533;nikirja Ladattavaksi. Renz, Ulrich. Saito, Yumiko, tr. 2020. (Sefa Kuvakirjoja Kahdella Kielell&#65533; Ser.). (FIN.). 42p. (J). pap. *(978-3-7399-6443-0(X))* Boedeker, Kirsten. Sefa Verlag.
—Minun Kaikista Kaunein Uneni - قشنگترین رویایمن (suomi - Persia) Kaksikielinen Lastenkirja, Mukana &#65533;&#65533;nikirja Ladattavaksi. Renz, Ulrich. Talai, Bahar, tr. 2020. (Sefa Kuvakirjoja Kahdella Kielell&#65533; Ser.). (FIN.). 42p. (J). pap. *(978-3-7399-6444-7(8))* Boedeker, Kirsten. Sefa Verlag.
—Minun Kaikista Kaunein Uneni - 我最美的梦乡 (suomi - Kiina) Kaksikielinen Lastenkirja, Mukana &#65533;&#65533;nikirja Ladattavaksi. Renz, Ulrich. Wang, Yanxing, tr. 2020. (Sefa Kuvakirjoja Kahdella Kielell&#65533; Ser.). (FIN.). 42p. (J). pap. *(978-3-7399-6442-3(1))* Boedeker, Kirsten. Sefa Verlag.
—Minun Kaikista Kaunein Uneni - il Mio Pi&#65533; Bel Sogno (suomi - Italia) Kaksikielinen Lastenkirja, Mukana &#65533;&#65533;nikirja Ladattavaksi. Renz, Ulrich. Galeati, Clara, tr. 2020. (Sefa Kuvakirjoja Kahdella Kielell&#65533; Ser.). (FIN.). 42p. (J). pap. *(978-3-7399-6446-1(4))* Boedeker, Kirsten. Sefa Verlag.
—Minun Kaikista Kaunein Uneni - Mein Allersch&#65533;nster Traum (suomi - Saksa) Kaksikielinen Lastenkirja, Mukana &#65533;&#65533;nikirja Ladattavaksi. Renz, Ulrich. Konttinen, Janika Tuulia, tr. 2020. (Sefa Kuvakirjoja Kahdella Kielell&#65533; Ser.). (FIN.). 42p. (J). pap. *(978-3-7399-6449-2(9))* Boedeker, Kirsten. Sefa Verlag.
—Minun Kaikista Kaunein Uneni - Mi Sue&#65533;o M&#65533;s Bonito (suomi - Espanja) Kaksikielinen Lastenkirja, Mukana &#65533;&#65533;nikirja Ladattavaksi. Renz, Ulrich. Catala, Raquel, tr. 2020. (Sefa Kuvakirjoja Kahdella Kielell&#65533; Ser.). (FIN.). 42p. (J). pap. *(978-3-7399-6447-8(2))* Boedeker, Kirsten. Sefa Verlag.
—Minun Kaikista Kaunein Uneni - Min Aller Fineste Dr&#65533;m (suomi - Norja) Kaksikielinen Lastenkirja, Mukana &#65533;&#65533;nikirja Ladattavaksi. Renz, Ulrich. Konttinen, Janika Tuulia, tr. 2020. (Sefa Kuvakirjoja Kahdella Kielell&#65533; Ser.). (FIN.). 42p. (J). pap. *(978-3-7399-6441-6(3))* Boedeker, Kirsten. Sefa Verlag.
—Minun Kaikista Kaunein Uneni - Min Allra Vackraste Dr&#65533;m (suomi - Ruotsi) Kaksikielinen Lastenkirja, Mukana &#65533;&#65533;nikirja Ladattavaksi. Renz, Ulrich. Konttinen, Janika Tuulia, tr. 2020. (FIN.). 42p. (J). pap. *(978-3-7399-6422-5(7))* Boedeker, Kirsten. Sefa Verlag.
—Minun Kaikista Kaunein Uneni - Mon Plus Beau R&#65533;ve (suomi - Ranska) Kaksikielinen Lastenkirja, Mukana &#65533;&#65533;nikirja Ladattavaksi. Renz, Ulrich. Andler, Martin, tr. 2020. (Sefa Kuvakirjoja Kahdella Kielell&#65533; Ser.). (FIN.). 42p. (J). pap. *(978-3-7399-6448-5(0))* Boedeker, Kirsten. Sefa Verlag.
—Minun Kaikista Kaunein Uneni - My Most Beautiful Dream (suomi - Englanti) Kaksikielinen Lastenkirja, Mukana &#65533;&#65533;nikirja Ladattavaksi. Renz, Ulrich. Konttinen, Janika Tuulia, tr. 2020. (FIN.). 42p. (J). pap. *(978-3-7399-6421-8(9))* Boedeker, Kirsten. Sefa Verlag.
—Il Mio Pi&#65533; Bel Sogno - 我最美的梦乡 (italiano - Cinese) Libro per Bambini Bilingue, con Audiolibro Da Scaricare. Renz, Ulrich. Wang, Yanxing, tr. 2020. (Sefa Bilinguale Bilderb&#65533;cher Ser.). (ITA.). 42p. (J). pap. *(978-3-7399-6398-3(0))* Boedeker, Kirsten. Sefa Verlag.
—Il Mio Pi&#65533; Bel Sogno - Mein Allersch&#65533;nster Traum (italiano - Tedesco) Libro per Bambini Bilingue, con Audiolibro Da Scaricare. Renz, Ulrich. Galeati, Clara, tr. 2020. (Sefa Bilinguale Bilderb&#65533;cher Ser.). (ITA.). 42p. (J). pap. *(978-3-7399-6382-2(4))* Boedeker, Kirsten. Sefa Verlag.
—Il Mio Pi&#65533; Bel Sogno - Mi Sue&#65533;o M&#65533;s Bonito (italiano - Spagnolo) Libro per Bambini Bilingue, con Audiolibro Da Scaricare. Renz, Ulrich. Catala, Raquel, tr. 2020. (Sefa Bilinguale Bilderb&#65533;cher Ser.). (ITA.). 42p. (J). pap. *(978-3-7399-6384-6(0))* Boedeker, Kirsten. Sefa Verlag.
—Il Mio Pi&#65533; Bel Sogno - My Most Beautiful Dream (italiano - Inglese) Libro per Bambini Bilingue, con Audiolibro Da Scaricare. Renz, Ulrich. Galeati, Clara, tr. 2020. (Sefa Bilinguale Bilderb&#65533;cher Ser.). (ITA.). 42p. (J). pap. *(978-3-7399-6381-5(6))* Boedeker, Kirsten. Sefa Verlag.
—Il Mio Pi&#65533; Bel Sogno - Visul Meu Cel Mai Frumos (italiano - Rumeno) Libro per Bambini Bilingue, con Audiolibro Da Scaricare. Renz, Ulrich. Roiban, Bianca, tr. 2020. (Sefa Bilinguale Bilderb&#65533;cher Ser.). (ITA.). 42p. (J). pap. *(978-3-7399-6383-9(2))* Boedeker, Kirsten. Sefa Verlag.
—Moj Najljepsi San - il Mio Pi&#65533; Bel Sogno (hrvatski - Talijanski) Dvojezična Knjiga Za Decu, Sa Audioknjigom Za Preuzimanje. Renz, Ulrich. Fedeli, Karmen, tr. 2020. (Sefa Picture Books in Two Languages Ser.). (HRV.). 42p. (J). pap. *(978-3-7399-6466-9(9))* Boedeker, Kirsten. Sefa Verlag.
—Moj Najljepsi San - Mein Allersch&#65533;nster Traum (hrvatski - Njemački) Dvojezična Knjiga Za Decu, Sa Audioknjigom Za Preuzimanje. Renz, Ulrich. Fedeli, Karmen, tr. 2020. (Sefa Picture Books in Two Languages Ser.). (HRV.). 42p. (J). pap. *(978-3-7399-6474-4(X))* Boedeker, Kirsten. Sefa Verlag.
—Moj Najljepsi San - My Most Beautiful Dream (hrvatski - Engleski) Dvojezična Knjiga Za Decu, Sa Audioknjigom Za Preuzimanje. Renz, Ulrich. Fedeli, Karmen, tr. 2020. (Sefa Picture Books in Two Languages Ser.). (HRV.). 42p. (J). pap. *(978-3-7399-6362-4(X))* Boedeker, Kirsten. Sefa Verlag.
—Mon Plus Beau R&#65533;ve - Мой самый прекрасный сон (fran&#65533;ais - Russe) Livre Bilingue Pour Enfants, Avec Livre Audio &#65533; T&#65533;l&#65533;charger. Renz, Ulrich. Deev, Oleg, tr. 2020. (Sefa Albums Illustr&#65533;s en Deux Langues Ser.). (FRE.). 42p. (J). pap. *(978-3-7399-6376-1(X))* Boedeker, Kirsten. Sefa Verlag.
—Mon Plus Beau R&#65533;ve - わたしの とびっきり すてきな ゆめ (fran&#65533;ais - Japonais) Livre Bilingue Pour Enfants, Avec Livre Audio &#65533; T&#65533;l&#65533;charger. Renz, Ulrich. Saito, Yumiko, tr. 2020. (Sefa Albums Illustr&#65533;s en Deux Langues Ser.). (FRE.). 42p. (J). pap. *(978-3-7399-6402-7(2))* Boedeker, Kirsten. Sefa Verlag.
—Mon Plus Beau R&#65533;ve - قشنگترین رویایمن Fran&#65533;ais - Persan (farsi, Dari): Livre Bilingue Pour Enfants, Avec Livre Audio &#65533; T&#65533;l&#65533;charger. Renz, Ulrich. Bahrami, Sadegh, tr. 2020. (Sefa Albums Illustr&#65533;s en Deux Langues Ser.). (FRE.). 42p. (J). pap. *(978-3-7399-6419-5(7))* Boedeker, Kirsten. Sefa Verlag.
—Mon Plus Beau R&#65533;ve - il Mio Pi&#65533; Bel Sogno (fran&#65533;ais - Italien) Livre Bilingue Pour Enfants, Avec Livre Audio &#65533; T&#65533;l&#65533;charger. Renz, Ulrich. Galeati, Clara, tr. 2020. (Sefa Albums Illustr&#65533;s en Deux Langues Ser.). (FRE.). 42p. (J). pap. *(978-3-7399-6379-2(4))* Boedeker, Kirsten. Sefa Verlag.
—Mon Plus Beau R&#65533;ve - Mein Allersch&#65533;nster Traum (fran&#65533;ais - Allemand) Livre Bilingue Pour Enfants, Avec Livre Audio &#65533; T&#65533;l&#65533;charger. Renz, Ulrich. Andler, Martin, tr. 2020. (Sefa Albums Illustr&#65533;s en Deux Langues Ser.). (FRE.). 42p. (J). pap. *(978-3-7399-6407-2(3))* Boedeker, Kirsten. Sefa Verlag.
—Mon Plus Beau R&#65533;ve - Min Aller Fineste Dr&#65533;m (fran&#65533;ais - Norv&#65533;gien) Livre Bilingue Pour Enfants, Avec Livre Audio &#65533; T&#65533;l&#65533;charger. Renz, Ulrich. Skalla, Werner, tr. 2020. (Sefa Albums Illustr&#65533;s en Deux Langues Ser.). (FRE.). 42p. (J). pap. *(978-3-7399-6396-9(4))* Boedeker, Kirsten. Sefa Verlag.
—Mon Plus Beau R&#65533;ve - Min Allra Vackraste Dr&#65533;m (fran&#65533;ais - Su&#65533;dois) Livre Bilingue Pour Enfants, Avec Livre Audio &#65533; T&#65533;l&#65533;charger. Renz, Ulrich. Thordsen, Narona, tr. 2020. (Sefa Albums Illustr&#65533;s en Deux Langues Ser.). (FRE.). 42p. (J). pap. *(978-3-7399-6412-6(X))* Boedeker, Kirsten. Sefa Verlag.
—Mon Plus Beau R&#65533;ve - Moj Najljepsi San (fran&#65533;ais - Croate) Livre Bilingue Pour Enfants, Avec Livre Audio &#65533; T&#65533;l&#65533;charger. Renz, Ulrich. Fedeli, Karmen, tr. 2020. (Sefa Albums Illustr&#65533;s en Deux Langues Ser.). (FRE.). 42p. (J). pap. *(978-3-7399-6411-9(1))* Boedeker, Kirsten. Sefa Verlag.
—Mon Plus Beau R&#65533;ve - My Most Beautiful Dream (fran&#65533;ais - Anglais) Livre Bilingue Pour Enfants, Avec Livre Audio &#65533; T&#65533;l&#65533;charger. Renz, Ulrich. Andler, Martin, tr. 2020. (Sefa Albums Illustr&#65533;s en Deux Langues Ser.). (FRE.). 42p. (J). pap. *(978-3-7399-6406-5(5))* Boedeker, Kirsten. Sefa Verlag.
—Mon Plus Beau R&#65533;ve - Ndoto Yangu Nzuri Sana Kuliko Zote (fran&#65533;ais - Swahili) Livre Bilingue Pour Enfants, Avec Livre Audio &#65533; T&#65533;l&#65533;charger. Renz, Ulrich. Machenje, Levina, tr. 2020. (Sefa Albums Illustr&#65533;s en Deux Langues Ser.). (FRE.). 42p. (J). pap. *(978-3-7399-6391-4(3))* Boedeker, Kirsten. Sefa Verlag.
—Mon Plus Beau R&#65533;ve - Visul Meu Cel Mai Frumos (fran&#65533;ais - Roumain) Livre Bilingue Pour Enfants, Avec Livre Audio &#65533; T&#65533;l&#65533;charger. Renz, Ulrich. Roiban, Bianca, tr. 2020. (Sefa Albums Illustr&#65533;s en Deux Langues Ser.). (FRE.). 42p. (J). pap. *(978-3-7399-6413-3(8))* Boedeker, Kirsten. Sefa Verlag.
—My Most Beautiful Dream - Мой самый прекрасный сон (English - Russian) Bilingual Children's Picture Book, with Audiobook for Download. Renz, Ulrich. Baden, Valeria, tr. 2020. (Sefa Picture Books in Two Languages Ser.). (ENG.). 42p. (J). pap. *(978-3-7399-6417-1(0))* Boedeker, Kirsten. Sefa Verlag.
—My Most Beautiful Dream - わたしの とびっきり すてきな ゆめ (English - Japanese) Bilingual Children's Picture Book, with Audiobook for Download. Renz, Ulrich. Saito, Yumiko, tr. 2020. (Sefa Picture Books in Two Languages Ser.). (ENG.). 42p. (J). pap. *(978-3-7399-6388-4(3))* Boedeker, Kirsten. Sefa Verlag.
—My Most Beautiful Dream - قشنگترین رویایمن (English - Persian, Farsi, Dari) Bilingual Children's Picture Book, with Audiobook for Download. Renz, Ulrich. Bahrami, Sadegh, tr. 2020. (Sefa Picture Books in Two Languages Ser.). (ENG.). 42p. (J). pap. *(978-3-7399-6420-1(0))* Boedeker, Kirsten. Sefa Verlag.
—My Most Beautiful Dream - আমার সবচেয়ে সুন্দর স্বপ্ন (English - Bengali) Bilingual Children's Picture Book, with Audiobook for Download. Renz, Ulrich. Dutta, Kuheli, tr. 2020. (Sefa Picture Books in Two Languages Ser.). (ENG.). 42p. (J). pap. *(978-3-7399-6424-9(3))* Boedeker, Kirsten. Sefa Verlag.
—My Most Beautiful Dream - 我最美的梦乡 (English - Mandarin Chinese) Bilingual Children's Picture Book, with Audiobook for Download. Renz, Ulrich. Wang, Yanxing, tr. 2020. (Sefa Picture Books in Two Languages Ser.). (ENG.). 42p. (J). pap. *(978-3-7399-6452-2(9))* Boedeker, Kirsten. Sefa Verlag.
—My Most Beautiful Dream - il Mio Pi&#65533; Bel Sogno (English - Italian) Bilingual Children's Picture Book, with Audiobook for Download. Renz, Ulrich. Agnew, Sefa, tr. 2020. (Sefa Picture Books in Two Languages Ser.). (ENG.). 42p. (J). pap. *(978-3-7399-6378-5(6))* Boedeker, Kirsten. Sefa Verlag.
—My Most Beautiful Dream - M&#65533;j Najpiękniejszy Sen (English - Polish) Bilingual Children's Picture Book, with Audiobook for Download. Renz, Ulrich. Wallmann, Joanna Barbara, tr. 2020. (Sefa Picture Books in Two Languages Ser.). (ENG.). 42p. (J). pap. *(978-3-7399-6435-5(9))* Boedeker, Kirsten. Sefa Verlag.

H

—My Most Beautiful Dream - Mein Allersch�nster Traum (English - German) Bilingual Children's Picture Book, with Audiobook for Download. Renz, Ulrich. Agnew, Sefa, tr. 2020. (Sefa Picture Books in Two Languages Ser.). (ENG.). 42p. (J). pap. ***(978-3-7399-6361-7(1))*** Boedeker, Kirsten. Sefa Verlag.

—My Most Beautiful Dream - Mi Sue�o M�s Bonito (English - Spanish) Bilingual Children's Picture Book, with Audiobook for Download. Renz, Ulrich. Catala, Raquel, tr. 2020. (Sefa Picture Books in Two Languages Ser.). (ENG.). 42p. (J). pap. ***(978-3-7399-6368-6(9))*** Boedeker, Kirsten. Sefa Verlag.

—My Most Beautiful Dream - Min Aller Fineste Dr�m (English - Norwegian) Bilingual Children's Picture Book, with Audiobook for Download. Renz, Ulrich. Skalla, Werner, tr. 2020. (Sefa Picture Books in Two Languages Ser.). (ENG.). 42p. (J). pap. ***(978-3-7399-6455-3(3))*** Boedeker, Kirsten. Sefa Verlag.

—My Most Beautiful Dream - Min Allra Vackraste Dr�m (English - Swedish) Renz, Ulrich. Thordsen, Narona, tr. 2020. (Sefa Picture Books in Two Languages Ser.). (ENG.). 42p. (J). pap. ***(978-3-7399-6364-8(6))*** Boedeker, Kirsten. Sefa Verlag.

—My Most Beautiful Dream - Minun Kaikista Kaunein Uneni (English - Finnish) Bilingual Children's Picture Book, with Audiobook for Download. Renz, Ulrich. Konttinen, Janika, tr. 2020. (Sefa Picture Books in Two Languages Ser.). (ENG.). 42p. (J). pap. ***(978-3-7399-6440-9(5))*** Boedeker, Kirsten. Sefa Verlag.

—My Most Beautiful Dream - Moj Najljepsi San (English - Croatian) Bilingual Children's Picture Book, with Audiobook for Download. Renz, Ulrich. Agnew, Sefa, tr. 2020. (Sefa Picture Books in Two Languages Ser.). (ENG.). 42p. (J). pap. ***(978-3-7399-6410-2(3))*** Boedeker, Kirsten. Sefa Verlag.

—My Most Beautiful Dream - Mon Plus Beau R�ve (English - French) Bilingual Children's Picture Book, with Audiobook for Download. Renz, Ulrich. Agnew, Sefa, tr. 2020. (Sefa Picture Books in Two Languages Ser.). (ENG.). 42p. (J). pap. ***(978-3-7399-6389-1(1))*** Boedeker, Kirsten. Sefa Verlag.

—My Most Beautiful Dream - Ndoto Yangu Nzuri Sana Kuliko Zote (English - Swahili) Bilingual Children's Picture Book, with Audiobook for Download. Renz, Ulrich. Saito, Yumiko, tr. 2020. (Sefa Picture Books in Two Languages Ser.). (ENG.). 42p. (J). pap. ***(978-3-7399-6392-1(1))*** Boedeker, Kirsten. Sefa Verlag.

—My Most Beautiful Dream - Visul Meu Cel Mai Frumos (English - Romanian) Bilingual Children's Picture Book, with Audiobook for Download. Renz, Ulrich. Roiban, Bianca, tr. 2020. (Sefa Picture Books in Two Languages Ser.). (ENG.). 42p. (J). pap. ***(978-3-7399-6414-0(6))*** Boedeker, Kirsten. Sefa Verlag.

—Мой самый прекрасный сон - Mein Allersch�nster Traum (русский - нем Двуязычная книга для детей;, с аудиокнигой Renz, Ulrich. Deev, Oleg, tr. 2020. (Sefa Picture Books in Two Languages Ser.). (RUS.). 42p. (J). pap. ***(978-3-7399-6373-0(5))*** Boedeker, Kirsten. Sefa Verlag.

—Мой самый прекрасный сон - Mi Sue�o M�s Bonito (русский - испа&# Двуязычная книга для детей;, с аудиокнигой Renz, Ulrich. Baden, Valeria, tr. 2020. (Sefa Picture Books in Two Languages Ser.). (RUS.). 42p. (J). pap. ***(978-3-7399-6375-4(1))*** Boedeker, Kirsten. Sefa Verlag.

—Мой самый прекрасный сон - Mon Plus Beau R�ve (русский - фран Двуязычная книга для детей;, с аудиокнигой Renz, Ulrich. Baden, Valeria, tr. 2020. (Sefa Picture Books in Two Languages Ser.). (RUS.). 42p. (J). pap. ***(978-3-7399-6374-7(3))*** Boedeker, Kirsten. Sefa Verlag.

—Мой самый прекрасный сон - My Most Beautiful Dream (русский - Aнгл Двуязычная книга для детей;, с аудиокнигой Renz, Ulrich. Baden, Valeria, tr. 2020. (Sefa Picture Books in Two Languages Ser.). (RUS.). 42p. (J). pap. ***(978-3-7399-6426-3(X))*** Boedeker, Kirsten. Sefa Verlag.

—قشنگ]ترین رویایمن - (فارسی - آلمانی;) کتاب کودکان دوزبانه;, با کتاب صوتی Renz, Ulrich. Bahrami, Sadegh, tr. 2020. (Sefa Picture Books in Two Languages Ser.). (PER.). 42p. (J). pap. ***(978-3-7399-6427-0(8))*** Boedeker, Kirsten. Sefa Verlag.

—قشنگ]ترین رویایمن (فارسی - انگلیسی;) کتاب کودکان دوزبانه;, با کتاب صوتی Renz, Ulrich. Bahrami, Sadegh, tr. 2020. (Sefa Picture Books in Two Languages Ser.). (PER.). 42p. (J). pap. ***(978-3-7399-6371-6(9))*** Boedeker, Kirsten. Sefa Verlag.

Haas, Deborah. Native American Rhymes: The People of the Far North, 9 vols. Rhodes, Sam. Howard, Kimberley, ed. 2003. 92p. (J). (gr. 3-5). mass mkt. 7.50 *(978-0-9743214-0-0(0))* Rhodes Educational Pubns.

Haas, Esti. Smile with Avigayil #1: Avigayil & the Little Student. Fuks, Menuhah & Tager, Gavriella. 2006. 64p. (J). 12.95 *(978-1-932443-60-8(6))* Judaica Pr., Inc., The.

—Smile with Avigayil #2: Avigayil & the Black Cat. Fuks, Menuhah & Tager, Gavriella. 2006. (ENG.). 64p. (J). 12.95 *(978-1-932443-58-5(4))* Judaica Pr., Inc., The.

Haas, Irene. Bess & Bella. Haas, Irene. 2006. (ENG.). 32p. (J). (gr. -1-2). 17.99 *(978-1-4169-0013-9(6)*, McElderry, Margaret K. Bks.) McElderry, Margaret K. Bks.

Haas, Shelly O. Northern Lights: A Hanukkah Story. Conway, Diana Cohen. 2004. (J). 16.95 *(978-0-929371-79-5(8)*, Kar-Ben Publishing) Lerner Publishing Group.

—The Schoolchildren's Blizzard. Figley, Marty Rhodes. 2004. (On My Own History Ser.). (ENG.). 48p. (J). (gr. 2-4). pap. 7.99 *(978-1-57505-619-7(4)*, First Avenue Editions) Lerner Publishing Group.

—Thank You, God! A Jewish Child's Book of Prayers, Vol. Groner, Judyth & Wikler, Madeline. 2003. (ENG.). 32p. (J). (gr. -1-2). pap. 8.99 *(978-1-58013-101-8(8)*, Kar-Ben Publishing) Lerner Publishing Group.

—Where Do People Go When They Die?, Vol. Portnoy, Mindy Avra. 2004. (Carolrhoda Picture Books Ser.). (ENG.). 24p. (J). (gr. -1-3). 15.95 *(978-1-58013-081-3(X)*, Kar-Ben Publishing) Lerner Publishing Group.

Habbas, Frank. Mark Twain at Work! Goldsmith, Howard. ed. 2005. 32p. (J). lib. bdg. 15.00 *(978-1-59054-951-3(1))* Fitzgerald Bks.

—Mark Twain at Work! Goldsmith, Howard. 2003. (Ready-To-read COFA Ser.). (ENG.). 32p. (J). (gr. k-2). pap. 4.99 *(978-0-689-85399-9(8)*, Simon Spotlight) Simon Spotlight.

Habbley, Kathleen. What Is Your Dog Doing? Singer, Marilyn. 2011. (ENG.). 32p. (J). (gr. -1-2). 12.99 *(978-1-4169-7931-9(X)*, Atheneum Bks. for Young Readers) Simon & Schuster Children's Publishing.

Habel, Helen. Puppy Scents: The Kids' Guide to Puppy Care. Kaleta, Don. 2010. (ENG.). 72p. (J). pap. 17.95 *(978-0-615-39881-5(2))* Kaleta Publishing, LLC.

Haberstroh, Anne. Ant King, 1 vol. Hanson, Anders. 2006. (Critter Chronicles Ser.). (ENG.). 24p. (J). (gr. k-3). lib. bdg. 27.07 *(978-1-59928-430-9(8)*, 4962, SandCastle) ABDO Publishing Co.

—Cow Licks. Scheunemann, Pam. 2006. (Fact & Fiction Ser.). 24p. (J). pap. 48.42 *(978-1-59679-930-1(7))*; (ENG.). lib. bdg. 27.07 *(978-1-59679-929-5(3)*, 2725, SandCastle) ABDO Publishing Co.

—Crab Cakes, 1 vol. Doudna, Kelly. 2006. (Critter Chronicles Ser.). (ENG.). 24p. (J). (gr. k-3). lib. bdg. 27.07 *(978-1-59928-434-7(0)*, 4966, SandCastle) ABDO Publishing Co.

—Doggie Pants. Doudna, Kelly. 2006. (Fact & Fiction Ser.). 24p. (J). pap. 48.42 *(978-1-59679-932-5(3))*; (ENG.). lib. bdg. 27.07 *(978-1-59679-931-8(5)*, 2727, SandCastle) ABDO Publishing Co.

—Duck Bills. Kompelien, Tracy. 2006. (Fact & Fiction Ser.). 24p. (J). pap. 48.42 *(978-1-59679-934-9(X))*; (ENG.). lib. bdg. 27.07 *(978-1-59679-933-2(1)*, 2729, SandCastle) ABDO Publishing Co.

—Fly Paper, 1 vol. Kompelien, Tracy. 2006. (Critter Chronicles Ser.). (ENG.). 24p. (J). (gr. k-3). lib. bdg. 27.07 *(978-1-59928-438-5(3)*, 4970, SandCastle) ABDO Publishing Co.

Haberstroh, Anne, et al. The Funny Farm: Jokes about Dogs, Cats, Ducks, Snakes, Bears, & Other Animals, 1 vol. Ziegler, Mark & Dahl, Michael. 2010. (Michael Dahl Presents Super Funny Joke Bks.). (ENG.). 80p. (J). (gr. 1-3). 25.32 *(978-1-4048-5772-8(9)*, Picture Window Bks.) Capstone.

Haberstroh, Anne. Goat Cheese. Doudna, Kelly. 2006. (Fact & Fiction Ser.). 24p. (J). pap. 48.42 *(978-1-59679-938-7(2))*; (ENG.). lib. bdg. 27.07 *(978-1-59679-937-0(4)*, 2733, SandCastle) ABDO Publishing Co.

—Goose Down. Doudna, Kelly. 2006. (Fact & Fiction Ser.). 24p. (J). pap. 48.42 *(978-1-59679-942-4(0))*; (ENG.). lib. bdg. 27.07 *(978-1-59679-941-7(2)*, 2737, SandCastle) ABDO Publishing Co.

—Leap Frog. Kompelien, Tracy. 2006. (Fact & Fiction Ser.). 24p. (J). 48.42 *(978-1-59928-449-1(9))*; (ENG.). lib. bdg. 27.07 *(978-1-59928-448-4(0)*, 4980, SandCastle) ABDO Publishing Co.

—Lion Manes, 1 vol. Kompelien, Tracy. 2006. (Animal Tales Ser.). (ENG.). 24p. (J). (gr. k-3). lib. bdg. 27.07 *(978-1-59679-949-3(8)*, 2745, SandCastle) ABDO Publishing Co.

—Lone Shark, 1 vol. Hanson, Anders. 2006. (Critter Chronicles Ser.). (ENG.). 24p. (J). (gr. k-3). lib. bdg. 27.07 *(978-1-59928-452-1(9)*, 4984, SandCastle) ABDO Publishing Co.

Haberstroh, Anne, et al. Michael Dahl's Big Book of Jokes. Dahl, Michael et al. 2019. (ENG.). 224p. (J). (gr. 1-3). pap. 9.95 *(978-1-4965-8551-6(8)*, 141305, Stone Arch Bks.) Capstone.

Haberstroh, Anne. Night Owl. Hanson, Anders. 2006. (Fact & Fiction Ser.). 24p. (J). pap. 48.42 *(978-1-59679-954-7(4))*; (ENG.). lib. bdg. 27.07 *(978-1-59679-953-0(6)*, 2749, SandCastle) ABDO Publishing Co.

—Parrot Crackers, 1 vol. Doudna, Kelly. 2006. (Critter Chronicles Ser.). (ENG.). 24p. (J). (gr. k-3). lib. bdg. 27.07 *(978-1-59928-458-3(8)*, 4990, SandCastle) ABDO Publishing Co.

—El Peinado Del Gallo. Doudna, Kelly. 2006. (Cuentos de Animales Ser.).Tr. of Rooster Combs. (SPA.). 24p. (J). (gr. k-3). lib. bdg. 27.07 *(978-1-59928-663-1(7)*, 5022, SandCastle) ABDO Publishing Co.

—Robin Hoods, 1 vol. Salzmann, Mary Elizabeth. 2006. (Critter Chronicles Ser.). (ENG.). 24p. (J). (gr. k-3). lib. bdg. 27.07 *(978-1-59928-466-8(9)*, 4998, SandCastle) ABDO Publishing Co.

—Rooster Combs. Doudna, Kelly. 2006. (Fact & Fiction Ser.). 24p. (J). pap. 48.42 *(978-1-59679-966-0(8))*; (ENG.). lib. bdg. 27.07 *(978-1-59679-965-3(X)*, 2761, SandCastle) ABDO Publishing Co.

—Spider Web, 1 vol. Kompelien, Tracy. 2006. (Critter Chronicles Ser.). (ENG.). 24p. (J). (gr. k-3). lib. bdg. 27.07 *(978-1-59928-474-3(X)*, 5006, SandCastle) ABDO Publishing Co.

Haberstroh, Anne & Reibeling, Brandon. Screaming with Laughter: Jokes about Ghosts, Ghouls, Zombies, Dinosaurs, Bugs, & Other Scary Creatures, 1 vol. Dahl, Michael & Moore, Mark. 2010. (Michael Dahl Presents Super Funny Joke Bks.). (ENG.). 80p. (J). (gr. 1-3). 25.32 *(978-1-4048-6101-5(7)*, Picture Window Bks.) Capstone.

Habinger, Renate. El Viejo John. Härtling, Peter. 2003.Tr. of Old John. (SPA.). 144p. (YA). (gr. 5-8). 12.95 *(978-84-204-4816-9(8))* Ediciones Alfaguara ESP. Dist: Santillana USA Publishing Co., Inc.

—El viejo John. Härtling, Peter. (SPA.). 144p. (J). (gr. 5-8). pap. 9.95 *(978-968-19-0720-4(5))* Santillana USA Publishing Co., Inc.

Hachler, Bruno. The Teddy Bears' Christmas Surprise. Hachler, Bruno. 2019. (ENG.). 32p. (J). (gr. k-2). 17.99 *(978-988-8341-63-4(4)*, Minedition) Neugebauer, Michael (Publishing) Limited HKG. Dist: Penguin Random Hse. LLC.

Hacikyan, Talleen. Aesop's Fables, 1 vol. Rosen, Michael. 2013. (ENG.). 32p. (J). (gr. 1-3). 16.95 *(978-1-896580-81-4(5))* Tradewind Bks. CAN. Dist: Orca Bk. Pubs. USA.

Hack, Robert. Chilling Adventures of Sabrina. Aguirre-Sacasa, Roberto. 2016. (Chilling Adventures of Sabrina Ser.). (ENG.). 176p. pap. 17.99 *(978-1-62738-987-7(3))* Archie Comic Pubns., Inc.

Hack, Robert, et al. Diary of a Stinky Dead Kid, 5. Gerrold, David et al. 2009. (Tales from the Crypt Ser.: 8). (ENG.). 96p. (J). (gr. 5-12). 22.44 *(978-1-59707-164-2(1)*, 900063017) Papercutz.

Hacker, Charlie. Baryonyx: My Dinosaur Friend. Enbashi, Dejana. 2019. (ENG.). 36p. (J). pap. 14.99 ***(978-1-64550-316-3(X))*** BookPatch LLC, The.

Hacker, Randy. The Puppy Who Found a Boy, 1 vol. Dean, Sara. 2009. 13p. pap. 24.95 *(978-1-61546-278-0(3))* America Star Bks.

Hackett, Michael. Jesus Returns to Heaven. Baden, Robert. rev. ed. 2004. (ENG.). 16p. (J). 1.99 *(978-0-7586-0407-1(6))* Concordia Publishing Hse.

Hackett, Tamara. Holiday Mindful Memory Keeper: The First Five Years - Kids Edition. Hackett, Tamara. 2019. (Mindful Memory Keeper Ser.: Vol. 1). (ENG.). 28p. (J). pap. ***(978-1-7753443-3-9(9))*** Sweet Clover Studios.

—Little Star, I See You: A Mindful Memory Keeper for You & Your Toddler. Hackett, Tamara. 2019. (Mindful Memory Keepers Ser.: Vol. 2). (ENG.). 30p. (J). pap. ***(978-1-7753443-2-2(0))*** Sweet Clover Studios.

Hackett, Tamara. Welcome Little Star: A Memory Keeper of Mindful Moments. Hackett, Tamara. 2018. (ENG.). 32p. (J). pap. *(978-0-9948875-9-7(0))* Sweet Clover Studios.

Hackings, Chip. Learn to Spell, Read & Say ABC's with the Backyard Buddis. Owens, John & Davis, Cedric Levonne. 2019. (ENG.). 54p. (J). pap. 5.99 ***(978-1-0925-0782-0(5))*** Independently Published.

Hackman, Evelyn. Dan & God's Gifts. Hege, Lynnita Rae. 2016. (ENG.). 110p. (J). 6.25 *(978-0-7399-2520-1(2))* Rod & Staff Pubs., Inc.

—The Rooster's Fate: And Other Stories. Martin, Elaine S. Bowman. 2014. 184p. (J). *(978-0-7399-2481-5(8))* Rod & Staff Pubs., Inc.

Hackmann, Bethany. It Doesn't Have to be Pink. Baliko, Janelle. 2007. 32p. (J). 14.95 *(978-0-9799012-0-1(0))* Baliko, Janelle A.

Hadad, Sasha. Al-Fusul Al-Arbah. Qays, Nabiah Khudur. 2018. (ARA.). 27p. (J). *(978-9953-37-293-8(4))* Academia.

Hadadi, Hoda. Deep in the Sahara. Cunnane, Kelly. 40p. (J). (gr. -1-3). 2018. 7.99 *(978-0-525-64566-5(7))*; 2013. 17.99 *(978-0-375-87034-7(2))* Random Hse. Children's Bks. (Schwartz & Wade Bks.).

Haddad-Hamwi, Louise. A Shoulder for Oscar. Craig, Joni. 2013. 40p. pap. 11.95 *(978-0-9887836-6-9(5))* Taylor and Seale Publishing.

Haddon, George. My Book about Brains, Change & Dementia: What Dementia Is & What Does It Do? Moore, Lynda. 2018. (ENG.). 48p. (J). 16.95 *(978-1-78592-511-5(3)*, 696712) Kingsley, Jessica Pubs. GBR. Dist: Hachette UK Distribution.

Hadilaksono, Caroline. The Lotterys More or Less. Donoghue, Emma. 2018. (ENG.). 304p. (J). (gr. 3-7). 17.99 *(978-1-338-20753-8(9)*, Levine, Arthur A. Bks.) Scholastic, Inc.

—The Lotterys Plus One. Donoghue, Emma. (ENG.). (J). (gr. 3-7). 2018. 336p. pap. 7.99 *(978-0-545-92584-6(3))*; 2017. 320p. 17.99 *(978-0-545-92581-5(9))* Scholastic, Inc.

Haefele, Steve. Bangs & Twangs: Science Fun with Sound. Cobb, Vicki. 2007. (Science Fun with Vicki Cobb Ser.). 48p. (J). (gr. 4-7). per. 7.95 *(978-0-8225-7022-6(X)*, First Avenue Editions) Lerner Publishing Group.

—Beach Day. Lee, Quinlan B. 2006. (J). *(978-0-439-81618-2(1))* Scholastic, Inc.

—Clifford's Best School Day. Lee, Quinlan B. & Bridwell, Norman. 2007. (J). *(978-0-545-02844-8(2))* Scholastic, Inc.

—Happy St. Patrick's Day, Clifford! Lee, Quinlan B. & Bridwell, Norman. 2010. (Clifford the Big Red Dog Ser.). (J). *(978-0-545-23401-6(8))* Scholastic, Inc.

—Merry Ham-Ham Christmas. Field, Ellen. 2003. (Hamtaro Ser.). (ENG.). 32p. (J). pap. 3.99 *(978-0-439-54249-4(9)*, Scholastic Paperbacks) Scholastic, Inc.

—Polar Bear Patrol. Stamper, Judith B. 2003. (Magic School Bus Science Chapter Bks.). 91p. (J). (gr. 2-5). 12.65 *(978-0-7569-1577-3(5))* Perfection Learning Corp.

—Polar Bear Patrol. Stamper, Judith. 2010. (Magic School Bus Science Chapter Bks.). (KOR.). 106p. (J). *(978-89-491-5321-6(1))* Biryongso Publishing Co.

—Santa's Big Red Helper. Aboff, Marcie. 2005. (Clifford Ser.). (ENG.). 80p. (J). (gr. k — 1). 2.99 *(978-0-439-79150-2(2))* Scholastic, Inc.

—The Snow Champion. Pugiano-Martin, Carol & Bridwell, Norman. 2006. (Big Red Reader Ser.). (J). *(978-0-439-80845-3(6))* Scholastic, Inc.

—The Snow Dog. Marsoli, Lisa Ann & Bridwell, Norman. 2004. (Big Red Reader Ser.). (J). pap. *(978-0-439-58559-0(7))* Scholastic, Inc.

—Sources of Forces: Science Fun with Force Fields. Cobb, Vicki. 2007. (Science Fun with Vicki Cobb Ser.). 48p. (J). (gr. 4-7). per. 7.95 *(978-0-8225-7023-3(8)*, First Avenue Editions) Lerner Publishing Group.

—Squirts & Spurts: Science Fun with Water. Cobb, Vicki. 2007. (Science Fun with Vicki Cobb Ser.). 48p. (J). (gr. 4-7). per. 7.95 *(978-0-8225-7024-0(6)*, First Avenue Editions) Lerner Publishing Group.

—Valentine Surprise. Lee, Quinlan B. 2008. (Clifford the Big Red Dog Ser.). (J). *(978-0-545-02845-5(0))* Scholastic, Inc.

—Where Can That Silly Monkey Be? Your Turn, My Turn Reader. Shepherd, Jodie. 2010. (Playskool Ser.). (ENG.). 24p. (J). (gr. -1-k). pap. 3.99 *(978-1-4169-9047-5(X)*, Simon Spotlight) Simon Spotlight.

—Whirlers & Twirlers: Science Fun with Spinning. Cobb, Vicki. 2007. (Science Fun with Vicki Cobb Ser.). (J). (gr. 4-7). per. 7.95 *(978-0-8225-7025-7(4)*, First Avenue Editions) Lerner Publishing Group.

Haezer, Jane. Christopher the Choo Choo Train. Kropik, Linda Kristine. 2011. 24p. pap. 11.50 *(978-1-60911-522-7(8)*, Strategic Bk. Publishing) Strategic Book Publishing & Rights Agency (SBPRA).

Hafner, Marylin. Germs Make Me Sick! Berger, Melvin. 2015. (Let's-Read-And-Find-Out Science 2 Ser.). (ENG.). 32p. (J). (gr. -1-3). pap. 6.99 *(978-0-06-238187-3(3))* HarperCollins Pubs.

—Hanukkah! Schotter, Roni. 2014. (ENG.). 32p. (J). (gr. -1-3). pap. 7.99 *(978-0-316-37028-8(2))* Little, Brown Bks. for Young Readers.

—It's Christmas! Prelutsky, Jack. 2012. (I Can Read Level 3 Ser.). (ENG.). 48p. (J). (gr. k-3). pap. 4.99 *(978-0-06-053708-1(6)*, Greenwillow Bks.) HarperCollins Pubs.

—It's Thanksgiving! Prelutsky, Jack. 2008. (I Can Read Level 3 Ser.). (ENG.). 48p. (J). (gr. k-3). pap. 4.99 *(978-0-06-053711-1(6))* HarperCollins Pubs.

—It's Valentine's Day. Prelutsky, Jack. 2013. (I Can Read Level 3 Ser.). (ENG.). 48p. (J). (gr. -1-3). pap. 4.99 *(978-0-06-053714-2(0)*, Greenwillow Bks.) HarperCollins Pubs.

—Passover Magic, 0 vols. Schotter, Roni. 2011. (ENG.). 34p. (J). (gr. -1-3). pap. 7.99 *(978-0-7614-5842-5(5)*, 9780761458425, Two Lions) Amazon Publishing.

—The Pepins & Their Problems, 1 vol. Horvath, Polly. (ENG.). 192p. pap. 13.95 *(978-0-88899-633-6(0))* Groundwood Bks. CAN. Dist: Publishers Group West (PGW).

—The Pepins & Their Problems. Horvath, Polly. 2008. (ENG.). 208p. (J). (gr. 3-7). per. 9.99 *(978-0-312-37751-9(7)*, 900049141) Square Fish.

—Purim Play, 0 vols. Schotter, Roni. 2010. (ENG.). 34p. (J). (gr. -1-2). pap. 6.99 *(978-0-7614-5800-5(X)*, 9780761458005, Two Lions) Amazon Publishing.

Hagan, Donell. These Hands. George, Mindy Lee. 2013. 30p. pap. *(978-0-9878208-4-6(2))* Catching Rainbows.

Hagan, Julie Henderson. One Thing after Another: An Aunt Sue's Barn Book. Newhouse, Sue. Basoco, Kathleen P., ed. 2019. (Aunt Sue's Barn Ser.: Vol. 1). (ENG.). 66p. (J). pap. 8.99 *(978-1-9814-0828-3(2))* CreateSpace Independent Publishing Platform.

Hagan, Stacy. Kumi the Bear. Toh, Irene. 2008. (ENG.). 24p. pap. 12.75 *(978-1-4389-1368-1(0))* AuthorHouse.

Hagedorn, Kara, photos by. Hawk Mother: The Story of a Red-Tailed Hawk Who Hatched Chickens. Hagedorn, Kara. 2017. (ENG., 32p. (J). (gr. k-4). 16.95 *(978-0-9883303-7-5(7))* Web of Life Children's Bks.

Hagel, Brooke. All or Nothing. Gurevich, Margaret. 2016. (Chloe by Design Ser.). (ENG.). 96p. (J). (gr. 5-8). lib. bdg. 25.32 *(978-1-4965-3263-3(5)*, Stone Arch Bks.) Capstone.

—Back to Basics. Gurevich, Margaret. 2016. (Chloe by Design Ser.). (ENG.). 96p. (J). (gr. 5-8). lib. bdg. 25.32 *(978-1-4965-3261-9(9)*, Stone Arch Bks.) Capstone.

—Balancing ACT. Gurevich, Margaret. 2015. (Chloe by Design Ser.). (ENG.). 384p. (J). (gr. 4-8). 14.95 *(978-1-62370-258-8(5)*, Capstone Young Readers) Capstone.

—Chloe by Design: Making the Cut, 1 vol. Gurevich, Margaret. 2014. (Chloe by Design Ser.). (ENG.). 384p. (J). (gr. 4-8). 14.95 *(978-1-62370-112-3(0),* Capstone Young Readers) Capstone.

—Chloe by Design: Measuring Up. Gurevich, Margaret. 2016. (Chloe by Design Ser.). (ENG.). 384p. (J). (gr. 4-8). 14.95 *(978-1-62370-727-9(7),* Capstone Young Readers) Capstone.

—Design Destiny, 1 vol. Gurevich, Margaret. 2014. (Chloe by Design Ser.). (ENG.). 96p. (J). (gr. 5-8). 25.32 *(978-1-4342-9180-6(4),* Stone Arch Bks.) Capstone.

—Design Disaster. Gurevich, Margaret. 2015. (Chloe by Design Ser.). (ENG.). 96p. (J). (gr. 5-8). 25.32 *(978-1-4965-0505-7(0),* Stone Arch Bks.) Capstone.

—Design Diva, 1 vol. Gurevich, Margaret. 2014. (Chloe by Design Ser.). (ENG.). 96p. (J). (gr. 5-8). 25.32 *(978-1-4342-9177-6(4),* Stone Arch Bks.) Capstone.

Hagel, Brooke, et al. Fashion Drawing Studio: A Guide to Sketching Stylish Fashions, 1 vol. Bolte, Marissa. 2013. (Craft It Yourself Ser.). (ENG.). 144p. (J). (gr. 3-9). pap. 14.95 *(978-1-62370-005-8(1),* Capstone Young Readers) Capstone.

Hagel, Brooke. Fashion Week Finale. Gurevich, Margaret. 2015. (Chloe by Design Ser.). (ENG.). 96p. (J). (gr. 5-8). 25.32 *(978-1-4965-0507-1(7),* Stone Arch Bks.) Capstone.

—The Final Cut. Gurevich, Margaret. 2016. (Chloe by Design Ser.). (ENG.). 96p. (J). (gr. 5-8). lib. bdg. 25.32 *(978-1-4965-3264-0(3),* Stone Arch Bks.) Capstone.

—The First Cut, 1 vol. Gurevich, Margaret. 2014. (Chloe by Design Ser.). (ENG.). 96p. (J). (gr. 5-8). 25.32 *(978-1-4342-9178-3(2),* Stone Arch Bks.) Capstone.

—Girly Girl Style: Fun Fashions You Can Sketch, 1 vol. Bolte, Mari. 2013. (Drawing Fun Fashions Ser.). (ENG.). 32p. (J). (gr. 3-9). lib. bdg. 28.65 *(978-1-62065-035-6(5))* Capstone.

—Harajuku Style: Fun Fashions You Can Sketch, 1 vol. Bolte, Mari. 2013. (Drawing Fun Fashions Ser.). (ENG.). 32p. (J). (gr. 3-9). lib. bdg. 28.65 *(978-1-62065-034-9(7))* Capstone.

—Intern Ambition. Gurevich, Margaret. 2015. (Chloe by Design Ser.). (ENG.). 96p. (J). (gr. 5-8). 25.32 *(978-1-4965-0504-0(2),* Stone Arch Bks.) Capstone.

—Made to Measure. Gurevich, Margaret. 2016. (Chloe by Design Ser.). (ENG.). 96p. (J). (gr. 5-8). lib. bdg. 25.32 *(978-1-4965-3262-6(7),* Stone Arch Bks.) Capstone.

—Rosie Wants to Be a Fireman. Klein, Marissa. 2013. 30p. (J). 19.95 *(978-0-9894933-3-8(4))* Rissylyn.

—Runway Rundown. Gurevich, Margaret. 2015. (Chloe by Design Ser.). (ENG.). 96p. (J). (gr. 5-8). 25.32 *(978-1-4965-0506-4(9),* Stone Arch Bks.) Capstone.

—Unraveling, 1 vol. Gurevich, Margaret. 2014. (Chloe by Design Ser.). (ENG.). 96p. (J). (gr. 5-8). 25.32 *(978-1-4342-9179-0(0),* Stone Arch Bks.) Capstone.

Hagel, Megan. Libby's Adventures: To the Creek. Golz, Lindsay. 2016. (ENG.). (J). (gr. -1-3). 17.00 *(978-1-59298-727-6(3))* Beaver's Pond Pr., Inc.

Hageman, Erik. Kokopelli & the Island of Change. Sterns, Michael. 2nd ed. 2005. 64p. (J). 17.95 net. *(978-0-615-12724-8(X))* Grasshopper Dream Productions.

Hager, Christian & Schroeder, Binette. The Frog Prince: Or Iron Henry. Grimm, J. & W. & Grimm, J. 2013. 32p. (J). (gr. -1-3). 17.95 *(978-0-7358-4140-6(3))* North-South Bks., Inc.

Hagerman, Jennifer. Say it with Music: A Story about Irving Berlin. Streissguth, Tom. 64p. (J). (gr. 3-6). 16.95 *(978-1-58013-206-0(5),* Kar-Ben Publishing) Lerner Publishing Group.

Hagerman, Jessica. Even Odder: More Stories to Chill the Heart. Burt, Steve. 2003. 144p. pap. 14.95 *(978-0-9741407-0-4(8))* Burt, Steven E.

—Oddest Yet: Even More Stories to Chill the Heart. Burt, Steve. 2004. 144p. (gr. 5-18). pap. 14.95 *(978-0-9741407-1-1(6))* Burt, Steven E.

—Wicked Odd: Still More Stories to Chill the Heart. Burt, Steve. 2006. 144p. (gr. 5-18). pap. 14.95 *(978-0-9741407-2-8(4))* Burt, Steven E.

Hagerty, Jillian Jo. A Fable about Miss Able: Based on the Survival of the First Monkey into Outer Space. McGrath, Kim Pollock. 2019. (ENG.). 48p. (J). pap. 11.00 ***(978-1-0964-7193-6(0))*** Independently Published.

Hagerty, Kim. Rosemary Potatoes & Her Three Bears. Hagerty, Terry. 2018. (ENG.). 58p. (J). pap. 12.99 *(978-1-941015-40-7(9))* Red Sky Presents.

Hägg, Elinor. Gusto & Gecko Travel to China. Han, Longy. 2018. (ENG.). 36p. (J). (gr. k-2). 16.95 *(978-0-9943413-2-7(6))* Pandasaurus, LLC.

Haggerty, Kyle. Some Kind of Special. Haggerty, Tiffany. 2018. (ENG.). 42p. (J). 23.95 *(978-1-64300-672-7(X));* pap. 14.95 *(978-1-64300-671-0(1))* Covenant Bks.

Haggerty, Tim. Being a Good Citizen: A Kids' Guide to Community Involvement. Kreisman, Rachelle. ed. 2015. (Start Smart (tm) — Community Ser.). (ENG.). 32p. (J). (gr. 1-3). E-Book 39.99 *(978-1-937529-50-5(9))* Red Chair Pr.

—People Who Help: A Kids' Guide to Community Heroes. Kreisman, Rachelle. ed. 2015. (Start Smart (tm) — Community Ser.). (ENG.). 32p. (J). (gr. 1-3). E-Book 39.99 *(978-1-937529-35-2(5))* Red Chair Pr.

—Places We Go: A Kids' Guide to Community Sites. Kreisman, Rachelle. ed. 2015. (Start Smart (tm) — Community Ser.). (ENG.). 32p. (J). (gr. 1-3). E-Book 39.99 *(978-1-937529-36-9(3))* Red Chair Pr.

—Things We Do: A Kids' Guide to Community Activity. Kreisman, Rachelle. ed. 2015. (Start Smart (tm) — Community Ser.). (ENG.). 32p. (J). (gr. 1-3). E-Book 39.99 *(978-1-937529-51-2(7))* Red Chair Pr.

—Wacky Football Facts to Kick Around. Sweeny, Sheila. Safro, Jill, ed. Date not set. 32p. (Orig.). (J). (gr. k-3). pap. 2.95 *(978-1-886749-17-7(5))* Sports Illustrated For Kids.

—Why Do We Eat? Turnbull, Stephanie. 2006. (Beginners Science: Level 2 Ser.). 32p. (J). (gr. 1-3). 4.99 *(978-0-7945-1333-7(6));* (gr. 4-7). lib. bdg. 12.99 *(978-1-58086-933-1(5))* EDC Publishing. (Usborne).

Haggerty, Tim, jt. illus. see Donaera, Patrizia.

Haggerty, Tim, jt. illus. see Gaudenzi, Giacinto.

Haggerty, Tim, jt. illus. see Pastor, Terry.

Haggerty, Tim, jt. illus. see Tudor, Andy.

Haggman-Sund, Hedvig. Little Leo. Esnaashari, Farnaz. 2020. (ENG.). 40p. (J). (gr. -1-3). 17.99 ***(978-1-5344-4610-6(9),*** Aladdin) Simon & Schuster Children's Publishing.

Häggman-Sund, Hedvig, jt. illus. see Schank, Amanda.

Hagin, Sally. A Book of Pacific Lullabies. Duder, Tessa, ed. 2003. 32p. (J). pap. *(978-1-86950-393-2(7))* HarperCollins Pubs. New Zealand.

—Milet Flashwords English. Turhan, Sedat. 2005. (Milet Flashwords Ser.). (ENG.). 60p. (J). (gr. 4-7). 8.95 *(978-1-84059-455-3(1))* Milet Publishing.

Hagin, Sally. Milet Picture Dictionary. Hagin, Sally. Turhan, Sedat. 18th ed. 2003. (Milet Picture Dictionary Ser.). (ENG.). 48p. (J). (gr. -1). 13.95 *(978-1-84059-346-4(6))* Milet Publishing.

Hagon, Amilee. Princess Sterling: Escape from the Manticore. Myradon, Aaron E. 2016. (ENG.). 34p. (J). pap. *(978-0-9953015-0-4(6))* Myradon.

Hague, Michael. The Tale of Peter Rabbit. Potter, Beatrix. 2003. 29p. (J). (gr. 2-5). reprint ed. 16.00 *(978-0-7567-6968-0(X))* DIANE Publishing Co.

—The Velveteen Rabbit. Williams, Margery. 2008. (ENG.). 48p. (J). (gr. -1-2). per. 7.99 *(978-0-312-37750-2(9),* 900049139) Square Fish.

—White Christmas. Berlin, Irving. 2010. (ENG.). 32p. (J). 16.99 *(978-0-06-029123-5(0))* HarperCollins Pubs.

Hague, Michael. The Book of Fairies. Hague, Michael. 2006. (ENG.). 128p. (J). (gr. 2-7). pap., pap. 9.99 *(978-0-06-089187-9(4),* Harper Trophy) HarperCollins Pubs.

—A Child's Book of Prayers. Hague, Michael. 2018. (ENG.). 20p. (J). bds. 9.99 *(978-1-250-16089-8(8),* 9781250160898, Holt, Henry & Co. Bks. For Young Readers) Holt, Henry & Co.

—Michael Hague's Magical World of Unicorns. Hague, Michael. 2012. (ENG.). 36p. (J). (gr. -1-3). pap. 17.99 *(978-1-4424-6041-6(5),* Simon & Schuster Bks. For Young Readers) Simon & Schuster Bks. For Young Readers.

—Michael Hague's Read-To-Me Book of Fairy Tales. Hague, Michael. 2013. (ENG.). 128p. (J). (gr. -1-3). 19.99 *(978-0-688-14010-6(6))* HarperCollins Pubs.

Hahessy, Roisin. All I Want for Christmas. McLean, Danielle. 2019. (ENG.). 12p. (J). (gr. 2-k). bds. 8.99 *(978-1-68010-580-3(9))* Tiger Tales.

—Five Spooky Pumpkins. McLean, Danielle. 2019. (ENG.). 12p. (J). (gr. 2-k). bds. 8.99 *(978-1-68010-581-0(7))* Tiger Tales.

Hahn, Beverly. Twenty Acres of Love: Irrigation Time. Hahn, Beverly. 2003. v, 65p. (J). (gr. -1-6). spiral bd. 12.95 *(978-0-9722494-0-9(0))* Hahn, Beverly.

Hahn, Beverly & Silva, Tom. Twenty Acres of Love: Little Bit, 8 vols. Hahn, Beverly. 2003. (J). (gr. k-6). 12.95 *(978-0-9722494-1-6(9))* Hahn, Beverly.

Hahn, Daniel & Hahn, David. Girls Who Rocked the World. McCann, Michelle Roehm & Welden, Amelie. 2012. (ENG.). (J). (gr. 3-7). lib. bdg. 21.60 *(978-1-62765-647-4(2))* Perfection Learning Corp.

—Girls Who Rocked the World: Heroines from Joan of Arc to Mother Teresa. McCann, Michelle Roehm & Welden, Amelie. 2012. (ENG.). 256p. (J). (gr. 3-7). 21.99 *(978-1-58270-361-9(2))* Aladdin/Beyond Words.

Hahn, David. Boys Who Rocked the World: Heroes from King Tut to Bruce Lee. McCann, Michelle Roehm. 2012. (ENG.). 256p. (J). (gr. 3-7). pap. 11.99 *(978-1-58270-331-2(0))* Aladdin/Beyond Words.

—Boys Who Rocked the World: Heroes from King Tut to Bruce Lee. McCann, Michelle Roehm. 2012. (ENG.). 256p. (J). (gr. 5-7). 28.69 *(978-1-58270-362-6(0))* Simon & Schuster, Inc.

—Girls Who Rocked the World: Heroines from Joan of Arc to Mother Teresa. McCann, Michelle Roehm & Welden, Amelie. 2012. (ENG.). 256p. (J). (gr. 3-7). pap. 11.99 *(978-1-58270-302-2(7))* Aladdin/Beyond Words.

—More Girls Who Rocked the World: Heroines from Ada Lovelace to Misty Copeland. McCann, Michelle Roehm. 2017. (ENG.). 320p. (J). (gr. 3-7). 21.99 *(978-1-58270-640-5(9));* pap. 11.99 *(978-1-58270-641-2(7))* Aladdin/Beyond Words.

—The Rocked the World Collection: Boys Who Rocked the World; Girls Who Rocked the World; More Girls Who Rocked the World. McCann, Michelle Roehm & Welden, Amelie. ed. 2018. (ENG.). 832p. (J). (gr. 3-7). pap. 34.99 *(978-1-58270-679-5(4))* Aladdin/Beyond Words.

Hahn, David, jt. illus. see Hahn, Daniel.

Hahn, Marika. Things to Wear. (Picture Bks.: No. S8817-4). 28p. (J). (gr. -1). pap. 3.95 *(978-0-7214-5143-5(8),* Dutton Juvenile) Penguin Publishing Group.

Hahn, Michael T., photos by. Dad's Deer Tactics 1000: Tom Hahn's Hunting Secrets Revealed by His Son. Hahn, Michael T. unabr. ed. 2003. 295p. (YA). pap. 19.95 *(978-0-9721716-0-1(6),* 1) In Cider Pr.

Hahner, Chris. Eloise Dresses Up. Cheshire, Marc. 2005. (Eloise Ser.). (ENG.). 12p. (J). (gr. -1-1). pap. 7.99 *(978-0-689-87455-0(3),* Little Simon) Little Simon.

Hahnl, Olivia. Pocket & Toast, 1 vol. Hahnl, John. 2010. 40p. 24.95 *(978-1-4489-8425-1(4))* PublishAmerica, Inc.

Haider Ali, Nabigal-Nayagam. All the Way to the Top: How One Girl's Fight for Americans with Disabilities Changed Everything. Bay Pimentel, Annette. 2020. (ENG.). 32p. (J). (-4). 17.99 *(978-1-4926-8897-6(5))* Sourcebooks, Inc.

Haidle, David. Journey to the Cross & Victory: The Complete Easter Story of Jesus' Death & Resurrection. Haidle, Helen. 2008. (ENG.). (J). cd-rom 19.99 *(978-1-60101-024-7(9))* Seed Faith Bks.

Haidle, David, jt. illus. see Haidle, Helen.

Haidle, Elizabeth. The Girl Who Named Pluto: The Story of Venetia Burney. McGinty, Alice B. 2019. 40p. (J). (gr. -1-3). 17.99 *(978-1-5247-6831-7(6));* (ENG.). lib. bdg. 20.99 *(978-1-5247-6832-4(4))* Random Hse. Children's Bks. (Schwartz & Wade Bks.).

Haidle, Helen & Haidle, David. Creation Story for Children. Haidle, Helen & Haidle, David. Bladholm, Cheri. 2009. 40p. (J). 14.99 *(978-0-89051-565-5(4),* Master Books) New Leaf Publishing Group.

Haight, Joelle. The Journals of Aiden Hunter: The Marakata Shard. Albright, David Edward. 2012. 262p. 24.99 *(978-0-9858325-0-6(9))* Storm Leaf.

Haile, Carol J. Christmas Cows. Haile, Carol J. 2012. (ENG.). 40p. (J). 19.95 *(978-0-9711236-5-6(9))* Firenze Pr.

—Elephant Overboard! Haile, Carol J. 2007. (J). lib. bdg. 19.95 *(978-0-9711236-3-2(2))* Firenze Pr.

Hailwood, David. Deadwood Hall: 'a Thrilling Magical Fantasy Adventure for Children Aged 7-10' Jones, Linda. 2018. (Oozing Magic Ser.: Vol. 1). (ENG.). 94p. (J). pap. *(978-1-9993248-0-3(3))* Bavoom Publishing.

Hailwood, David. Blank Comic Book for Creative Kids: Includes a Variety of Templates, Comic Making Tips, & a Dozen Fun Characters to Draw. Hailwood, David. 2020. (Blank Comic Ser.: Vol. 2). (ENG.). 110p. (J). pap. 6.99 ***(978-1-6586-0206-8(4))*** Independently Published.

Haimura, Kiyotaka. A Certain Magical Index, Vol. 1 (light Novel), Vol. 1. Kamachi, Kazuma. 2014. (Certain Magical Index Ser.: 1). (ENG.). 224p. (gr. 8-17). 14.00 *(978-0-316-33912-4(1),* Yen Pr.) Orbit.

—A Certain Magical Index, Vol. 12 (light Novel) Kamachi, Kazuma. 2017. (Certain Magical Index Ser.: 12). (ENG.). 260p. (gr. 8-17). pap. 14.00 *(978-0-316-36002-9(3),* Yen Pr.) Orbit.

—A Certain Magical Index, Vol. 13 (light Novel) Kamachi, Kazuma. 2017. (Certain Magical Index Ser.: 13). (ENG.). 260p. (gr. 8-17). pap. 14.00 *(978-0-316-44267-1(4),* Yen Pr.) Orbit.

—A Certain Magical Index, Vol. 14 (light Novel) Kamachi, Kazuma. 2018. (Certain Magical Index Ser.: 14). (ENG.). 260p. (gr. 8-17). pap. 14.00 *(978-0-316-44270-1(4),* Yen Pr.) Orbit.

—A Certain Magical Index, Vol. 15 (light Novel) Kamachi, Kazuma. 2018. (Certain Magical Index Ser.: 15). (ENG.). 260p. (gr. 8-17). pap. 14.00 *(978-0-316-44272-5(0),* Yen Pr.) Orbit.

—A Certain Magical Index, Vol. 4 (light Novel), Vol. 4. Kamachi, Kazuma. 2015. (Certain Magical Index Ser.: 4). (ENG.). 240p. (gr. 8-17). pap. 14.00 *(978-0-316-34056-4(1),* Yen Pr.) Orbit.

Haines, Emma. Busy Bee's Garden! Small World Creations, Small World. 2018. (Bath Bugs Bath Bks.). (ENG.). 8p. (J). (gr. -1 — 1). 6.99 *(978-1-4380-7905-9(2),* B.E.S. Publishing) Peterson's.

—God Made the World, 1 vol. Rivers-Moore, Debbie. 2017. 4p. 11.99 *(978-0-8254-4520-0(5))* Kregel Pubns.

Haines, Genny. Five Little Ducks: A Move-Along Counting Book. 2016. (ENG.). 10p. (J). (gr. -1 — 1). bds. 8.99 *(978-1-4998-0217-7(X))* Little Bee Books Inc.

—Five Little Puppies. Wang, Margaret. 2006. (ENG.). 12p. (J). (gr. -1-k). 9.95 *(978-1-58117-487-8(X),* Intervisual/Piggy Toes) Bendon, Inc.

Haines, Geri Berger. The Little Lost Lamb. Haines, Geri Berger. 2009. 40p. (J). (gr. -1-k). 8.95 *(978-0-8198-4528-3(0))* Pauline Bks. & Media.

Hairs, Joya, photos by. Un Barrilete: Para el Día de los Muertos, 1 vol. Amado, Elisa. 2012. (ENG., 32p. (J). (gr. k-4). pap. 9.95 *(978-1-55498-112-0(3))* Groundwood Bks. CAN. Dist: Publishers Group West (PGW).

Haisch, Joshua. Just the Way He Wanted Me to Be. Soske, Becky. 2007. 32p. (J). (gr. -1-3). per. 11.99 *(978-1-59879-339-0(X))* Lifevest Publishing, Inc.

Hajdyla, Ken. Men Who Changed the World Vol. I: The Henry Ford Story. Arrathoon, Leigh A. Davio, John, ed. 56p. (J). (gr. 5-6). pap. 5.95 *(978-0-9648564-5-5(X))* Archus Pr., LLC.

—Men Who Changed the World Vol. II: The First Birdmen: Wilbur & Orville Wright. Arrathoon, Leigh A. Davio, John, ed. 56p. (J). (gr. 5-6). pap. 5.95 *(978-0-9648564-6-2(8))* Archus Pr., LLC.

Hajek, Olaf. Flower Power: The Magic of Nature's Healers. Paxmann, Christine. 2020. (ENG.). 40p. (J). (gr. 3-7). 19.95 *(978-3-7913-7399-7(4))* Prestel Verlag GmbH & Co KG. DEU. Dist: Penguin Random Hse. LLC.

Hajny, Chris. The Life Heroic: How to Unleash Your Most Amazing Self. Svoboda, Elizabeth. 2019. (ENG.). 144p. (J). (gr. 4-8). pap. 16.99 *(978-1-942186-25-0(8));* lib. bdg. 37.32 *(978-1-5415-7860-9(0))* Lerner Publishing Group. (Zest Bks.).

Hakkarainen, Anna-Liisa. Grateful: A Song of Giving Thanks. Bucchino, John. (Julie Andrews Collection). 40p. (J). (gr. -1-3). 2006. pap. 6.99 *(978-0-06-051635-2(6),* Julie Andrews Collection); 2003. (ENG.). 17.99 *(978-0-06-051633-8(X))* HarperCollins Pubs.

Halasz, Andras, jt. illus. see Horen, Michael.

Halbleib, Michael. Promise Comics - Issue 1. MacKenzie, Erin. Nummela, Pam, ed. 2017. (ENG.). (J). pap. 1.49 *(978-0-7586-5742-8(0))* Concordia Publishing Hse.

Halbower, Susan J. The Boar's Head Festival: A Christmas Celebration. Lehman, LaLonnie. 2015. (ENG.). 32p. 22.95 *(978-0-87565-626-7(9))* Texas Christian Univ. Pr.

—Log Cabin Kitty. Rubin, Donna. 2012. (ENG.). 56p. pap. 20.00 *(978-0-87565-503-1(3))* Texas Christian Univ. Pr.

—Smurglets Are Everywhere. Birkelbach, Alan. 2010. (ENG.). 48p. (J). (gr. -1-6). 19.95 *(978-0-87565-415-7(0))* Texas Christian Univ. Pr.

Halder, Sayantan. The Little Ninja Sparrows. Lal, Ranjit. 2017. (ENG.). 168p. (YA). (gr. 8-12). pap. *(978-93-87164-46-8(2))* Speaking Tiger Publishing.

Hale, Bruce. Fuzzy Freaks Out. Hale, Bruce. 2018. (Class Pets Ser.: 3). (ENG.). 192p. (J). (gr. 3-7). pap. 5.99 *(978-1-338-14524-3(X),* Scholastic Paperbacks); lib. bdg. 16.99 *(978-1-338-14525-0(8),* Scholastic Pr.) Scholastic, Inc.

—Fuzzy Takes Charge. Hale, Bruce. 2018. (Class Pets Ser.: 2). (ENG.). 192p. (J). (gr. 3-7). pap. 5.99 *(978-1-338-14521-2(5),* Scholastic Paperbacks) Scholastic, Inc.

—Fuzzy's Great Escape. Hale, Bruce. 2018. (Class Pets Ser.: 1). (ENG.). 192p. (J). (gr. 3-7). pap. 5.99 *(978-1-338-14518-2(5));* lib. bdg. 16.99 *(978-1-338-14519-9(3))* Scholastic, Inc. (Scholastic Paperbacks).

—Key Lardo: A Chet Gecko Mystery. Hale, Bruce. 2007. (Chet Gecko Ser.: 12). (ENG.). 128p. (J). (gr. 3-7). pap. 5.99 *(978-0-15-205235-5(6),* 1195772) Houghton Mifflin Harcourt Publishing Co.

—The Mystery of Mr. Nice. Hale, Bruce. 2008. (Chet Gecko Ser.: 2). (ENG.). 128p. (J). (gr. 3-7). pap. 6.99 *(978-0-15-202515-1(4),* 1193021) Houghton Mifflin Harcourt Publishing Co.

—The Possum Always Rings Twice. Hale, Bruce. 2007. (Chet Gecko Ser.: 11). (ENG.). 128p. (J). (gr. 3-7). pap. 6.99 *(978-0-15-205233-1(X),* 1195769) Houghton Mifflin Harcourt Publishing Co.

Hale, Christy. Ansty Ansel: Ansel Adams, a Life in Nature. Jenson-Elliott, Cindy. 2016. (ENG.). 32p. (J). 18.99 *(978-1-62779-082-6(9),* 900134303, Holt, Henry & Co. Bks. For Young Readers) Holt, Henry & Co.

—Cambodian Dancer: Sophany's Gift of Hope. Reicherter, Daryn. Penh, Bophal, tr. ed. 2018. 32p. (J). (gr. k-3). 7.99 *(978-0-8048-5036-0(4))* Tuttle Publishing.

—La Escuela de Elizabeti. Stuve-Bodeen, Stephanie. Sarfatti, Esther, tr. from ENG. 2007. (SPA.). 32p. (J). (gr. -1-2). pap. 10.95 *(978-1-60060-235-1(5))* Lee & Low Bks., Inc.

—Guess Again! Riddle Poems. Morrison, Lillian. 2006. (ENG.). 48p. (J). (gr. 1-4). 16.95 *(978-0-87483-730-8(8))* August Hse. Pubs., Inc.

—La Muneca de Elizabeti. Stuve-Bodeen, Stephanie. Sarfatti, Esther, tr. braille ed. 2004. (SPA.). (J). (gr. k-3). spiral bd. *(978-0-616-08966-8(X))* Canadian National Institute for the Blind/Institut National Canadien pour les Aveugles.

—La Muneca de Elizabeti, 1 vol. Stuve-Bodeen, Stephanie. Sarfatti, Esther, tr. 2009. (Elizabeti Ser.). (SPA.). 32p. (J). (gr. -1-2). pap. 8.95 *(978-1-58430-001-4(9),* a51362ac-116e-4433-af07-b27db24c394d) Lee & Low Bks., Inc.

—Our School Garden! Swann, Rick. 2018. (ENG.). 32p. (J). (gr. 1-4). pap. 9.95 *(978-0-9984366-3-0(1))* READERS to EATERS.

—Sky Dancers, 1 vol. Kirk, Connie Ann. 2013. (ENG.). 32p. (J). (gr. 2-4). pap. 10.95 *(978-1-62014-147-2(7),* 0acaa542-222a-4edc-86c3-055986d5dad5) Lee & Low Bks., Inc.

Hale, Christy. The East-West House: Noguchi's Childhood in Japan. Hale, Christy. 2012. (ENG.). 32p. (J). (gr. 2-7). 17.95 *(978-1-60060-363-1(7))* Lee & Low Bks., Inc.

—Todos Iguales / All Equal: Un Corrido de Lemon Grove/a Ballad of Lemon Grove, 1 vol. Hale, Christy. ed. 2019. (ENG & SPA.). 40p. (J). (gr. 3-7). 19.95 *(978-0-89239-427-2(7),* bc03a9d0-2149-440c-9571-3bf2c39c6cd6, Children's Book Press) Lee & Low Bks., Inc.

—Water Land: Land & Water Forms Around the World. Hale, Christy. 2018. (ENG.). 32p. (J). 17.99 *(978-1-250-15244-2(5),* 900183618) Roaring Brook Pr.

Hale, Christy. It Rained All Day That Night: Autograph Album Verses & Inscriptions. Hale, Christy, tr. 2005. (ENG.). 80p. (J). (gr. 3-7). pap. 9.95 *(978-0-87483-726-1(X))* August Hse. Pubs., Inc.

Hale, Christy, jt. illus. see Soentpiet, Chris K.

Hale, Christy, jt. illus. see Soentpiet, Chris.

Hale, Cole. Everyone Has Hope. Lynch, Jason. 2011. (J). *(978-0-938467-09-0(3))* Headline Bks., Inc.

Hale, Cynthia G. The Tree Monkeys. Marshall, Wynne. 2019. (Tree Monkeys Trilogy Ser.: Vol. 1). (ENG.). 38p. (J). pap. 9.13 ***(978-1-950361-02-1(0))*** High Bar Bks.

Hale, Cynthia G. The Tree Monkeys. Marshall, Wynne. 2nd ed. 2019. (Tree Monkeys Trilogy Ser.). (ENG.). 38p. (J). (gr. 2-4). 21.99 *(978-1-950361-00-7(4))* High Bar Bks.

Hale, J. P. Dontay's Alphabet Book of Color. Hall, Eve D. 2004. 46p. (J). per. 13.00 *(978-0-9758899-1-6(5))* Imagine Publishing.

Hale, James Graham. From Seed to Pumpkin. Pfeffer, Wendy. (Let's-Read-And-Find-Out Science 1 Ser.). (ENG.). 40p. (J). (gr. -1-3). 2015. pap. 6.99 *(978-0-06-238185-9(7));* 2004. 15.99 *(978-0-06-028038-3(7))* HarperCollins Pubs.

—From Seed to Pumpkin. Pfeffer, Wendy. 2015. (Let's-Read-And-Find-Out Science 1 Ser.). (ENG.). (J). (gr. -1-3). lib. bdg. 17.60 *(978-1-68065-161-4(7))* Perfection Learning Corp.

—How Mountains Are Made. Zoehfeld, Kathleen Weidner. 2015. (Let's-Read-And-Find-Out Science 2 Ser.). (ENG.). 32p. (J). (gr. -1-3). pap. 6.99 *(978-0-06-238203-0(9))* HarperCollins Pubs.

Hale, Jason. Historic Savannah, GA Coloring Book. Lynn, Richard & Nova Blue. Claughton, Dena, ed. 2003. 32p. *(978-0-9725584-0-2(3))* Nova Blue, Inc.

Hale, Jennifer, photos by. Baby See, Baby Do. Rogge, Robie. 2018. (ENG., 20p. (J). (gr. -1 — 1). bds. 9.99 *(978-1-4521-6890-6(3))* Chronicle Bks. LLC.

Hale, Jenny. The Big Book of Animals & Bugs. Novick, Mary. (Double Delights Ser.). (ENG.). 32p. (J). pap. *(978-1-877003-38-7(7))* Little Hare Bks. AUS. Dist: HarperCollins Pubs. Australia.

—The Big Book of Nursery Rhymes & Songs. Novick, Mary. 2004. 32p. *(978-1-877003-39-4(5))* Little Hare Bks. AUS. Dist: HarperCollins Pubs. Australia.

—Bugs. Novick, Mary. 2003. 16p. (Orig.). pap. *(978-1-877003-32-5(8))* Little Hare Bks. AUS. Dist: HarperCollins Pubs. Australia.

—Nursery Songs. Novick, Mary. 2003. (ENG.). 16p. (Orig.). pap. *(978-1-877003-33-2(6))* Little Hare Bks. AUS. Dist: HarperCollins Pubs. Australia.

Hale-Jones, Stevie. Maddie Makes Money. Garrett, Sonia. 2019. (ENG.). 128p. (J). (gr. 3-5). pap. *(978-1-7750106-2-3(7))* Garrett, Sonia.

Hale, Kendall. Crypt Quest/Space Battles: A Play-Your-Way Book. Soria, Gabe. 2019. (Midnight Arcade Ser.: 1). 256p. (J). (gr. 5). pap. 8.99 *(978-0-593-09365-8(8),* Penguin Workshop) Penguin Young Readers Group.

—Excellent Ernesto Cousins 3/Wrestlevania: A Play-Your-Way Adventure. Soria, Gabe. 2019. (Midnight Arcade Ser.: 2). (ENG.). 288p. (J). (gr. 5). pap. 8.99

H

(978-0-593-09366-5(6), Penguin Workshop) Penguin Young Readers Group.
—Fantastic Fist/MowTown. Soria, Gabe. 2019. (Midnight Arcade Ser.: 3). 256p. (J). (gr. 5). 8.99 *(978-1-5247-8433-1(8)*, Penguin Workshop) Penguin Young Readers Group.
—Magician's Gambit/Wild Goose Chase! A Play-Your-Way Adventure. Soria, Gabe. 2019. (Midnight Arcade Ser.: 4). 240p. (J). (gr. 5). pap. 8.99 *(978-1-5247-8435-5(4)*, Penguin Workshop) Penguin Young Readers Group.
Hale, Kendall, jt. illus. see Robles, Nick.
Hale, Nathan. Calamity Jack. Hale, Shannon & Hale, Dean. 2010. 144p. (YA). (gr. 6-18). pap. 16.99 *(978-1-59990-373-6(3)*, 900060616, Bloomsbury USA Childrens) Bloomsbury Publishing USA.
—The Dinosaurs' Night Before Christmas. Muecke, Anne. 2008. (ENG.). 36p. (J). (gr. -1-3). 18.99 *(978-0-8118-6322-3(0))* Chronicle Bks. LLC.
—Frankenstein: A Monstrous Parody. Walton, Rick. 2012. (ENG.). 48p. (J). (gr. -1-3). 14.99 *(978-0-312-55366-1(8)*, 900077344) Feiwel & Friends.
—Ghost Mysteries: Unraveling the World's Most Mysterious Hauntings. Zoehfeld, Kathleen Weidner. 2009. (ENG.). 128p. (J). (gr. 4-8). pap. 5.99 *(978-1-4169-6448-3(7)*, Aladdin) Simon & Schuster Children's Publishing.
—Panic in Pompeii. Peacock, L. A. 2011. 92p. (J). pap. *(978-0-545-34062-5(4))* Scholastic, Inc.
—Rapunzel's Revenge. Hale, Shannon & Hale, Dean. 2008. (ENG.). 144p. (YA). (gr. 5-8). pap. 16.99 *(978-1-59990-288-3(5)*, 900053426, Bloomsbury USA Childrens) Bloomsbury Publishing USA.
—Terror at Troy. Peacock, L. A. 2012. 90p. (J). *(978-0-545-34063-2(2))* Scholastic, Inc.
Hale, Pattie. Nathan's Thread. Grabowski, Leo. 2009. 32p. (J). pap. 14.95 *(978-0-9822375-1-9(0))* Relevant Graces Productions.
Hale, Randy. The Sun & the Wind. Ritz, Lee F. 2013. 62p. 23.99 *(978-1-940840-00-0(7))* Ritz, Lee Pubns.
Hale, Sally. Fixin' Buddy's Little Red Wagon. McGougan, Kathy. 2009. (ENG.). 24p. pap. 9.95 *(978-1-4251-8975-4(X))* Trafford Publishing.
Hales, J. Rulon. When Grandfather Was a Boy. Driggs, Howard R. 2011. 88p. 38.95 *(978-1-258-07716-7(7))* Literary Licensing, LLC.
Hales, Liz. Jimmie Bean. Forsythe, Piercy & Forsythe, Kay. 2020. (ENG.). 30p. (J). pap. 14.95 ***(978-1-6901-5379-5(2))*** Independently Published.
Hales, Tanya. Barnabas & Bird Run Away from the Circus. Baird, Jeri. 2018. (Barnabas Ser.: Vol. 1). (ENG.). 214p. (J). (gr. 2-6). pap. 11.99 ***(978-0-692-07599-9(2))*** Baird, Jeri.
Haley, Amanda. The Blossoms & the Green Phantom. Byars, Betsy. 2008. (Blossom Family Ser.: 3). (ENG.). 176p. (J). (gr. 4-6). 21.19 *(978-0-8234-2146-6(5))* Holiday Hse., Inc.
—If You're Happy & You Know It, 1 vol. Zondervan Staff. 2008. (I Can Read! / Song Ser.). (ENG.). 32p. (J). (gr. -1-3). pap. 4.99 *(978-0-310-71621-1(7))* Zonderkidz.
—The New Baby. Packard, Mary. 2004. (My First Reader Ser.). (ENG.). 32p. (J). (gr. k-1). pap. 3.95 *(978-0-516-25506-4(1)*, Children's Pr.) Scholastic Library Publishing.
—The Secret Chicken Society. Cox, Judy. 2013. (ENG.). 96p. (J). (gr. 2-5). pap. 5.99 *(978-0-8234-2765-9(X))* Holiday Hse., Inc.
—Snowzilla, 0 vols. Lawler, Janet. 2012. (ENG.). 32p. (J). (gr. -1-3). 16.99 *(978-0-7614-6188-3(4)*, 9780761461883, Two Lions) Amazon Publishing.
—Wanted... Mud Blossom. Byars, Betsy. 5th ed. 2008. (Blossom Family Book Ser.: Bk. 5). (ENG.). 192p. (J). (gr. 3-7). pap. 9.99 *(978-0-8234-2148-0(1))* Holiday Hse., Inc.
Haley, Gail E. Isabella Propeller & the Magic Beanie. Graves, Jonathan. 2011. (J). 15.95 *(978-1-933251-74-5(3))* Parkway Pubs., Inc.
Haley, MacKenzie. Funny Little Ghost. VonFeder, Rosa. Cottage Door Press, ed. 2020. (ENG.). 10p. (J). (gr. -1-k). bds. 4.99 ***(978-1-68052-928-9(5)***, 1005700) Cottage Door Pr.
Haley, MacKenzie. Laugh-Out-Loud Back-To-School Jokes: Lift-the-Flap. Elliott, Rob. 2020. (Laugh-Out-Loud Jokes for Kids Ser.). 28p. (J). (gr. -1-3). 6.99 *(978-0-06-299078-5(0)*, HarperCollins) HarperCollins Pubs. Ltd. GBR. Dist: HarperCollins Pubs.
Halfen, Veronica. From My Eyes. Halfen, Veronica. 2019. (ENG.). 20p. (J). (gr. 3-6). pap. 9.99 *(978-0-578-46950-8(2))* SDH Studio, LLC.
Halford, Katy. My Friends & Me: A Celebration of Different Kinds of Families. Stansbie, Stephanie. 2019. (ENG.). 32p. (J). (gr. -1-2). 17.99 *(978-1-68010-154-6(4))* Tiger Tales.
Halford, Katy. Around the World in 80 Ways. Halford, Katy. 2018. (ENG.). 48p. (J). (gr. -1-3). 14.99 *(978-1-4654-7572-5(9)*, DK Children) Dorling Kindersley Publishing, Inc.
—Celebrations Around the World. Halford, Katy. 2019. (ENG.). 48p. (J). (gr. -1-1). 14.99 *(978-1-4654-8390-4(X)*, DK Children) Dorling Kindersley Publishing, Inc.
Hall, Abi. City. 2020. (Making Tracks 2 Ser.: 4). (ENG.). 12p. (J). bds. ***(978-1-78628-414-3(6))*** Child's Play International Ltd.
—Desert. 2020. (Making Tracks 2 Ser.: 4). (ENG.). 12p. (J). bds. ***(978-1-78628-412-9(X))*** Child's Play International Ltd.
—Jungle. 2020. (Making Tracks 2 Ser.: 4). (ENG.). 12p. (J). bds. ***(978-1-78628-413-6(8))*** Child's Play International Ltd.
—Mountain. 2020. (Making Tracks 2 Ser.: 4). (ENG.). 12p. (J). bds. ***(978-1-78628-415-0(4))*** Child's Play International Ltd.
Hall, Aiden. The Three Little Pork Chops & Other Food Fables. Cano, Katelyn. 2018. (ENG.). 74p. (J). pap. 14.99 *(978-1-9734-7516-3(2))* Independently Published.
Hall, Amanda. Animal Tales. 8p. (J). 19.99 *(978-1-84148-977-3(8))* Barefoot Bks., Inc.
—Animal Tales: From Around the World. Adler, Naomi. 2018. (ENG.). 80p. (J). (gr. k-2). pap. 16.99 *(978-1-78285-396-1(0))* Barefoot Bks., Inc.
—Babushka: A Christmas Tale. Casey, Dawn. 2016. (ENG.). 32p. (J). (gr. -1-3). 16.99 *(978-1-68099-188-8(4)*, Good Bks.) Skyhorse Publishing Co., Inc.
—The Barefoot Book of Animal Tales. Adler, Naomi. 2004. 80p. (J). 9.99 *(978-1-84148-547-8(0))* Barefoot Bks., Inc.
—The Barefoot Book of Jewish Tales. Gelfand, Shoshana Boyd. 2017. (ENG.). 96p. (J). (gr. 1-4). pap. 16.99 *(978-1-78285-354-1(5))* Barefoot Bks., Inc.
—Brother Giovanni's Little Reward. Smucker, Anna Egan. 2015. (ENG.). 34p. (J). 17.00 *(978-0-8028-5420-9(6)*, Eerdmans Bks For Young Readers) Eerdmans, William B. Publishing Co.
—The Fantastic Jungles of Henri Rousseau. Markel, Michelle. 2019. (J). *(978-0-8028-5523-7(7)*, Eerdmans Bks For Young Readers) Eerdmans, William B. Publishing Co.
—The Fantastic Jungles of Henri Rousseau. Markel, Michelle & Rousseau, Henri. 2012. 34p. (J). 17.00 *(978-0-8028-5364-6(1)*, Eerdmans Bks For Young Readers) Eerdmans, William B. Publishing Co.
—The Hard to Swallow Tale of Jonah & the Whale, 1 vol. Denham, Joyce. ed. 2015. (ENG.). 32p. (J). (gr. -1-3). pap. 8.99 *(978-0-7459-6584-0(9))* Lion Hudson PLC GBR. Dist: Independent Pubs. Group.
—In Andal's House. 2013. (Tales of the World Ser.). (ENG.). 40p. (J). (gr. 2-5). 17.95 *(978-1-58536-603-3(X)*, 202358) Sleeping Bear Pr.
—Jewish Tales. Gelfand, Shoshana Boyd. 2013. 80p. (J). (gr. 4-6). 19.99 *(978-1-84686-884-9(X))* Barefoot Bks., Inc.
—The Lion Book of Day-by-Day Prayers. Joslin, Mary. 2010. 159p. (J). (gr. k-4). 16.99 *(978-0-8254-7948-9(7))* Kregel Pubns.
—The Lion Classic Aesop's Fables. McAllister, Margaret. 11th ed. 2011. (ENG.). 128p. (J). (gr. 2-4). 16.99 *(978-0-7459-6200-9(9))* Lion Hudson PLC GBR. Dist: Independent Pubs. Group.
—The Lion Day-by-Day Bible. Joslin, Mary. 2008. (ENG.). 384p. (J). (gr. 2-4). 19.95 *(978-0-7459-6132-3(0))* Lion Hudson PLC GBR. Dist: Independent Pubs. Group.
—The Loyola Treasury of Saints: From the Time of Jesus to the Present Day. Self, David. 2003. (ENG.). 224p. (J). (gr. 2-7). 28.95 *(978-0-8294-1785-2(0))* Loyola Pr.
—Out of This World: The Surreal Art of Leonora Carrington. Markel, Michelle. 2019. (ENG.). 40p. (J). (gr. -1-3). 17.99 *(978-0-06-244109-6(4)*, Balzer & Bray) HarperCollins Pubs.
—Tales from India. Gavin, Jamila. 2011. (ENG.). 96p. (J). (gr. 4-7). 19.99 *(978-0-7636-5564-8(3)*, Templar) Candlewick Pr.
Hall, Amanda. The Stolen Sun. Hall, Amanda. 2004. 32p. (J). (gr. 10-18). 17.00 *(978-0-8028-5225-0(4))* Eerdmans, William B. Publishing Co.
Hall, Amanda. Giant Tales. Hall, Amanda, tr. 2003. 96p. (YA). *(978-1-84365-017-1(7)*, Pavilion Children's Books) Pavilion Bks.
Hall, Arthur & Terrazzini, Daniela Jaglenka. Adventures of Robin Hood. Green, Roger Lancelyn & Green, Richard. 2010. (Puffin Classics Ser.). (ENG.). 320p. (J). (gr. 5-7). 16.99 *(978-0-14-133489-9(4)*, Puffin Books) Penguin Young Readers Group.
Hall, August. Keeper. Appelt, Kathi. (ENG.). (J). (gr. 3-7). 2012. 432p. pap. 9.99 *(978-1-4169-5061-5(3))*; 2010. 416p. 17.99 *(978-1-4169-5060-8(5))* Simon & Schuster Children's Publishing. (Atheneum Bks. for Young Readers).
Hall, Becca. Our Animal Neighbors: Compassion for Every Furry, Slimy, Prickly Creature on Earth. Ricard, Matthieu & Gruhl, Jason. 2020. 32p. (gr. -1-3). 17.95 *(978-1-61180-723-3(9)*, Bala Kids) Shambhala Pubns., Inc.
Hall, Beverly H. Take Your Students on a Cruise: Paul's Journeys Lesson Guide. Fisher, Nancy. Witte, Carol, ed. 2004. 40p. (gr. 4-8). wbk. ed. 9.95 *(978-1-890947-00-2(8)*, 308X) Rose Publishing.
Hall, Carey. Lines & Triangles & Squares, Oh My! Burke, Zoe. 2017. 24p. (J). bds. 10.95 *(978-0-7649-7864-7(0)*, POMEGRANATE KIDS) Pomegranate Communications, Inc.
Hall, David, photos by. Partners in the Sea. Hall, David. Rhodes, Mary Jo. 2006. (Undersea Encounters Ser.). (ENG., 48p. (J). (gr. 3-7). per. 6.95 *(978-0-516-25492-0(8)*, Children's Pr.) Scholastic Library Publishing.
—Predators of the Sea. Hall, David. Rhodes, Mary Jo. 2007. (Undersea Encounters Ser.). (ENG., 48p. (J). (gr. 3-7). pap. 6.95 *(978-0-516-25465-4(0)*, Children's Pr.) Scholastic Library Publishing.
—Seahorses & Sea Dragons. Hall, David. Rhodes, Mary Jo. 2005. (Undersea Encounters Ser.). (ENG., 48p. (J). (gr. 3-7). lib. bdg. 27.00 *(978-0-516-24393-1(4)*, Children's Pr.) Scholastic Library Publishing.
Hall, Dee & Hesselbein, Kent. Can You Imagine? Hall, Dee. 2013. 64p. pap. 8.95 *(978-1-935786-59-7(8))* St. Clair Pubns.
Hall, Dorothy Louise. Forever Friends. Cohen, Barbara S. 2015. (ENG.). 100p. (J). reprint ed. pap. 9.95 *(978-1-931290-54-8(7))* Tallfellow Pr.
Hall Dsm, Richard J., jt. illus. see Hall, Elspeth Grace.
Hall, Elspeth Grace & Hall Dsm, Richard J. The Final Adventures of Puss-Puss: Puss-Puss, the Red, the Selki, the Tunneling Hump, Happy Hibernation, Sprung & the Final Adventure. Hall, Elspeth Grace. 2016. (ENG.). (J). pap. 11.00 *(978-1-910853-16-0(X))* Lioness Publishing.
Hall, Francois. The Emperor's New Clothes. 2007. (First Fairy Tales Ser.). 32p. (J). (gr. -1-3). lib. bdg. 28.50 *(978-1-59771-071-8(7)*, 1262700) Sea-To-Sea Pubns.
Hall, Gladys. Red Riding Hood. 2007. (Shape Bks.). (ENG.). (J). (gr. -1-3). pap. 9.95 *(978-1-59583-133-0(9)*, 9781595831330, Green Tiger Pr.) Laughing Elephant.
Hall, Janine. Maya's Story: An Adoption Fairytale. Christie, Romie. 2019. (ENG.). 42p. (J). pap. ***(978-1-988993-25-6(3))*** Yildiz Ilkin.
Hall, Jennifer. Miguel & Michelle Visit Spaceport America. Hall, Loretta. 2017. (ENG.). (J). (gr. 1-5). pap. 16.95 *(978-1-943681-17-4(1))* Nuevo Bks.
Hall, Joan. Alotta the Girl Who Walks with Dragons. Hall, Joan. 2017. (Enchanted Ser.: Vol. 1). (ENG.). 234p. (J). pap. 11.99 *(978-0-9819815-8-1(5))* Hall, Joan.
Hall, Jon. Coding Projects. Woodcock, Jon. 2017. 95p. (J). *(978-1-4654-7418-6(8))* Dorling Kindersley Publishing, Inc.
Hall, Lowell. Can Checkers Come Too? Hall, Christina. 2011. 36p. pap. 24.95 *(978-1-4560-7753-2(8))* America Star Bks.
Hall, Marcellus. Because I Am Your Daddy. North, Sherry. 2010. (ENG.). 32p. (J). (gr. -1-1). 16.95 *(978-0-8109-8392-2(3)*, Abrams Bks. for Young Readers) Abrams, Inc.
—The Cow Loves Cookies. Wilson, Karma. 2010. (ENG.). 40p. (J). (gr. -1-3). 18.99 *(978-1-4169-4206-1(8)*, McElderry, Margaret K. Bks.) McElderry, Margaret K. Bks.
—Duddle Puck: The Puddle Duck. Wilson, Karma. 2015. (ENG.). 40p. (J). (gr. -1-3). 17.99 *(978-1-4424-4927-5(6)*, McElderry, Margaret K. Bks.) McElderry, Margaret K. Bks.
Hall, Marion. Let's Go! Animal Tracks in the Snow! Polley, Diane. 2018. (ENG.). 40p. (J). (gr. k-2). 17.99 *(978-1-7320580-0-2(8))*; pap. 12.99 *(978-1-7320580-1-9(6))* Polley Publishing.
Hall, Mary. Bubbe's Got the Beat. Vol. Press, Judy. 2017. (ENG.). 12p. (J). (gr. -1 — 1). bds. 5.99 *(978-1-5124-4763-7(3)*, Kar-Ben Publishing) Lerner Publishing Group.
—A Peek-a-Boo Christmas! Oakes, Loretta. 2010. 16p. (J). (gr. -1). pap. 9.95 *(978-0-8091-6754-8(9)*, Ambassador Bks.) Paulist Pr.
—Peek-a-Boo Jesus! Oakes, Loretta. 2010. 16p. (J). (gr. -1). pap. 9.95 *(978-0-8091-6755-5(7)*, Ambassador Bks.) Paulist Pr.
—Spell Sisters: Amelia the Silver Sister. Castle, Amber. 2012. (ENG.). 160p. (J). (gr. 2-4). pap. 7.99 *(978-0-85707-250-4(1)*, Simon & Schuster Children's) Simon & Schuster, Ltd. GBR. Dist: Simon & Schuster, Inc.
—Spell Sisters: Chloe the Storm Sister. Castle, Amber. 2013. (ENG.). 160p. (J). (gr. 2-4). pap. 7.99 *(978-0-85707-254-2(4)*, Simon & Schuster Children's) Simon & Schuster, Ltd. GBR. Dist: Simon & Schuster, Inc.
—Spell Sisters: Evie the Swan Sister. Castle, Amber. 2012. (ENG.). 160p. (J). (gr. 2-4). pap. 7.99 *(978-0-85707-252-8(8)*, Simon & Schuster Children's) Simon & Schuster, Ltd. GBR. Dist: Simon & Schuster, Inc.
—Spell Sisters: Grace the Sea Sister. Castle, Amber. 2012. (ENG.). 160p. (J). (gr. 2-4). pap. 5.99 *(978-0-85707-251-1(X)*, Simon & Schuster Children's) Simon & Schuster, Ltd. GBR. Dist: Simon & Schuster, Inc.
—Spell Sisters: Isabella the Butterfly Sister. Castle, Amber. 2012. (ENG.). 160p. (J). (gr. 2-4). pap. 7.99 *(978-0-85707-249-8(8)*, Simon & Schuster Children's) Simon & Schuster, Ltd. GBR. Dist: Simon & Schuster, Inc.
—Spell Sisters: Olivia the Otter Sister. Castle, Amber. 2013. (ENG.). 160p. (J). (gr. 2-4). pap. 7.99 *(978-0-85707-253-5(6)*, Simon & Schuster Children's) Simon & Schuster, Ltd. GBR. Dist: Simon & Schuster, Inc.
—Spell Sisters: Sophia the Flame Sister. Castle, Amber. 2012. (ENG.). 160p. (J). (gr. 2-4). pap. 7.99 *(978-0-85707-247-4(1)*, Simon & Schuster Children's) Simon & Schuster, Ltd. GBR. Dist: Simon & Schuster, Inc.
Hall, Melanie. Born on Christmas Morn. Busch, Melinda Kay. 2003. (Arch Bks.). (ENG.). 16p. (J). (gr. k-4). 1.99 *(978-0-570-07584-4(X))* Concordia Publishing Hse.
—Every Second Something Happens: Poems for the Mind & Senses. 2009. (ENG.). 48p. (J). (gr. k-2). 17.99 *(978-1-59078-622-2(X)*, Wordsong) Boyds Mills Pr.
—Goodnight Sh'ma, Vol. Jules, Jacqueline. 2008. (Very First Board Bks.). (ENG.). 12p. (J). (gr. -1 — 1). bds. 5.99 *(978-0-8225-8945-7(1)*, Kar-Ben Publishing) Lerner Publishing Group.
—Hanukkah Lights: Holiday Poetry. Hopkins, Lee Bennett. 2004. (I Can Read Bks.). (J). (gr. k-3). 15.99 *(978-0-06-008051-8(5))*; 32p. lib. bdg. 16.89 *(978-0-06-008052-5(3))* HarperCollins Pubs.
—How Did the Animals Help God? Swartz, Nancy Sohn. 2004. (ENG.). 24p. (J). bds. 8.99 *(978-1-59473-044-3(X)*, fca3eb2d-b92c-4f00-bab7-e96f8e02db05, Skylight Paths Publishing) LongHill Partners, Inc.
—In Our Image: God's First Creatures. Swartz, Nancy Sohn. 2011. (ENG.). 32p. (J). pap. 9.95 *(978-1-68336-652-2(2)*, Jewish Lights Publishing) LongHill Partners, Inc.
—The Littlest Mountain. Rosenstock, Barb. 2011. (ENG.). 24p. (J). (gr. -1-2). 17.95 *(978-0-7613-4495-7(0)*, 9780761344957); Vol. pap. 7.95 *(978-0-7613-4497-1(7)*, 9780761344971) Lerner Publishing Group. (Kar-Ben Publishing).
—The Magic Pomegranate. Schram, Peninnah. 2007. (On My Own Folklore Ser.). 48p. (J). lib. bdg. 17.95 *(978-0-8225-8856-6(0)*, Kar-Ben Publishing) Lerner Publishing Group.
—The Magic Pomegranate: [a Jewish Folktale], Vol. Schram, Peninnah. 2008. (On My Own Folklore Ser.). (ENG.). 48p. (J). (gr. 2-4). pap. 7.99 *(978-0-8225-6746-2(6)*, First Avenue Editions) Lerner Publishing Group.
—On Sukkot & Simchat Torah, Vol. Fishman, Cathy Goldberg. 2006. (ENG.). 32p. (J). (gr. -1-4). lib. bdg. 17.95 *(978-1-58013-165-0(4)*, Kar-Ben Publishing) Lerner Publishing Group.
—Savior of the Nations-Mini BK. Busch, Melinda Kay. 2009. 16p. pap. 2.29 *(978-0-7586-1756-9(9))* Concordia Publishing Hse.
—The Seventh Day. Cohen, Deborah Bodin. 2005. (ENG.). 24p. (J). (gr. -1-2). 16.95 *(978-0-929371-24-5(0)*, Kar-Ben Publishing) Lerner Publishing Group.
Hall, Melanie W. Christmas Presents: Holiday Poetry. Hopkins, Lee Bennett. 2004. (I Can Read Bks.). 32p. (J). (gr. k-3). 15.99 *(978-0-06-008054-9(X))*; lib. bdg. 16.89 *(978-0-06-008055-6(8))* HarperCollins Pubs.
—On Hanukkah. Fishman, Cathy Goldberg. 2005. 27p. (J). (gr. k-4). reprint ed. 16.00 *(978-0-7567-9289-3(4))* DIANE Publishing Co.
—Passover Haggadah. Berger, Barry W. 2004. 36p. *(978-0-9674319-3-2(X))* Messianic Perspectives.
Hall, Michael. Cat Tale. Hall, Michael. 2012. (ENG.). 40p. (J). (gr. -1-k). 16.99 *(978-0-06-191516-1(5)*, Greenwillow Bks.) HarperCollins Pubs.
—Frankencrayon. Hall, Michael. 2016. (ENG.). 40p. (J). (gr. -1-3). 17.99 *(978-0-06-225211-1(9))*; lib. bdg. 18.89 *(978-0-06-225212-8(7))* HarperCollins Pubs. (Greenwillow Bks.).
—It's an Orange Aardvark! Hall, Michael. 2014. (ENG.). 40p. (J). (gr. -1-3). 17.99 *(978-0-06-225206-7(2)*, Greenwillow Bks.) HarperCollins Pubs.
—Little I. Hall, Michael. 2017. (ENG.). 48p. (J). (gr. -1-3). 17.99 *(978-0-06-238300-6(0)*, Greenwillow Bks.) HarperCollins Pubs.
—Monkey Time. Hall, Michael. 2019. (ENG.). 48p. (J). (gr. -1-3). 17.99 *(978-0-06-238302-0(7)*, Greenwillow Bks.) HarperCollins Pubs.
—My Heart Is Like a Zoo. Hall, Michael. 2009. (ENG.). 32p. (J). (gr. -1-3). 16.99 *(978-0-06-191510-9(6)*, Greenwillow Bks.) HarperCollins Pubs.
—My Heart Is Like a Zoo Board Book. Hall, Michael. 2013. (ENG.). 34p. (J). (gr. -1-k). bds. 7.99 *(978-0-06-191512-3(2)*, Greenwillow Bks.) HarperCollins Pubs.
—Perfect Square. Hall, Michael. 2011. (ENG.). 40p. (J). (gr. -1-k). 17.99 *(978-0-06-191513-0(0)*, Greenwillow Bks.) HarperCollins Pubs.
—Red: A Crayon's Story. Hall, Michael. 2015. (ENG.). 40p. (J). (gr. -1-3). 17.99 *(978-0-06-225207-4(0)*, Greenwillow Bks.) HarperCollins Pubs.
—Swing. Hall, Michael. 2020. 40p. (J). (gr. -1-3). 17.99 *(978-0-06-286617-2(6)*, Greenwillow Bks.) HarperCollins Pubs.
—Wonderfall. Hall, Michael. 2016. (ENG.). 40p. (J). (gr. -1-3). 17.99 *(978-0-06-238298-6(5)*, Greenwillow Bks.) HarperCollins Pubs.
Hall, Milton. Human Body, Grades 4 - 6: Fun Activities, Experiments, Investigations, & Observations! Carothers, Sue & Henke, Elizabeth. 2003. (Skills for Success Ser.). (ENG.). 128p. (gr. 4-6). pap. 16.99 *(978-0-88724-954-9(X)*, 4329) Carson-Dellosa Publishing, LLC.
Hall, Nancy R. My Grandparents Live in an RV. Hall, Nancy R. l.t. ed. 2005. 32p. (J). 16.95 *(978-0-9761759-0-2(8))* Jasnans Publishing Co.
Hall, Norris. The All Animal Band. Moore, Jim. l.t. ed. 2004. 36p. (J). 16.00 *(978-0-9752619-0-3(8))* Animal Band Productions, Inc., The.
—The Silliest Bug & Insect Book Ever. Hensley, Terri Anne. 2007. 28p. per. 6.99 *(978-0-9789057-4-7(6))* Huntington Ludlow Media Group.
—Tobias Andrew Bartholomew. Hensley, Terri Anne. 2007. 32p. per. 8.99 *(978-0-9789057-6-7(8))* Huntington Ludlow Media Group.
Hall, Pat. The Musubi Baby. Takayama, Sandi. 2007. 32p. (J). (gr. -1-3). 10.95 *(978-1-57306-272-5(3))* Bess Pr., Inc.
Hall, Peter. Snugs the Snow Bear. Davies, Suzy. 2016. (ENG.). (J). 18.50 *(978-1-944361-43-3(X))*; pap. 10.00 *(978-1-944361-42-6(1))* Snow Leopard Publishing.
Hall-Pinner, Alexandra. Everybody Loves Bernie: A Book of Bedtime Stories from a Legendary Grandpa. Kerschhofer, Rachel. 2017. (ENG.). 62p. (J). 19.99 *(978-0-692-04504-6(X))* Bedbug Bks.
Hall, Ron. Dancing with the Cranes, 1 vol. Armstrong, Jeannette C. 2nd rev. ed. 2017. (ENG.). 24p. (J). (gr. 1-3). pap. 10.95 *(978-1-894778-70-1(7))* Theytus Bks., Ltd. CAN. Dist: Orca Bk. Pubs. USA.
Hall, Shikia. Jack the Dog & Mr. Frog. Griffith, Tara. 2016. (ENG.). (J). pap. 8.00 *(978-0-692-83481-7(8))* Griffith, Tara.
Hall, Showyuh. Chinese Zodiac Bedtime Stories: (Color) Hall, Michael R. 2019. (ENG.). 124p. (J). pap. 23.95 *(978-1-7210-9392-2(3))* CreateSpace Independent Publishing Platform.
Hall, Showyuh S. Chinese Zodiac Bedtime Stories: (Black & White) Hall, Michael R. 2019. (ENG.). 124p. (J). pap. 11.95 *(978-1-0992-5666-0(6))* Independently Published.
Hall, Susan. The Big Birthday Surprise. Finnegan, Delphine. 2017. (Step into Reading Ser.). (ENG.). 24p. (J). (gr. -1-1). pap. 4.99 *(978-1-5247-1688-2(X))*; lib. bdg. 12.99 *(978-1-5247-1689-9(8))* Random Hse. Children's Bks. (Random Hse. Bks. for Young Readers).
—The Big Birthday Surprise! Finnegan, Delphine. 2017. 24p. (J). *(978-1-5182-5213-6(3))* Random Hse., Inc.
—Buenas Noches, Dora! Cuento Para Levantar la Tapita. Ricci, Christine. 2004. (Dora the Explorer Ser.).Tr. of Good Night, Dora!. (SPA.). 16p. (J). pap. 5.99 *(978-0-689-86648-7(8)*, Libros Para Ninos) Libros Para Ninos.
—Busy Bunny (Sunny Day) Huntley, Tex. 2020. (Step into Reading Ser.). (ENG.). 24p. (J). (gr. -1-1). 5.99 *(978-0-593-12806-0(0))*; 12.99 *(978-0-593-12807-7(9))* Random Hse. Children's Bks. (Random Hse. Bks. for Young Readers).
—Dora & the Winter Games (Dora the Explorer) Ottersley, Martha T. 2013. (Pictureback(R) Ser.). (ENG.). 24p. (J). (gr. -1-2). 3.99 *(978-0-385-37930-4(7)*, Random Hse. Bks. for Young Readers) Random Hse. Children's Bks.
—Dora's Book of Manners. Ricci, Christine. ed. 2005. (Dora the Explorer Ser.: No. 7). 22p. (J). lib. bdg. 15.00 *(978-1-59054-793-9(4))* Fitzgerald Bks.
—Dora's Cousin Diego. 2011. (Dora & Diego Ser.). (ENG.). 24p. (J). pap. 3.99 *(978-1-4424-1399-3(9)*, Simon Spotlight/Nickelodeon) Simon Spotlight/Nickelodeon.
—Dora's Picnic. Ricci, Christine. 2003. (Ready-to-Read Ser.: Vol. 1). (ENG.). 24p. (J). pap. 3.99 *(978-0-689-85238-1(X)*, Simon Spotlight/Nickelodeon) Simon Spotlight/Nickelodeon.
—Fisher-Price Little People: Easter Is Here! 2020. (Fisher Price Lift-The-Flap Ser.). (ENG.). 10p. (J). (gr. -1-k). bds. 9.99 *(978-0-7944-4361-0(3)*, Studio Fun International) Printers Row Publishing Group.
—Follow Those Feet! Ricci, Christine. 2003. (Dora the Explorer Ser.: Vol. 2). (ENG.). 24p. (J). pap. 3.99

(978-0-689-85239-8(8), Simon Spotlight/Nickelodeon) Simon Spotlight/Nickelodeon.

—Good Night, Dora! (Dora the Explorer) Random House Staff. 2013. (Pictureback(R) Ser.). (ENG.). 16p. (J). (gr. -1-2). 4.99 *(978-0-449-81781-0(4)*, Random Hse. Bks. for Young Readers) Random Hse. Children's Bks.

—Helping Hands. Ricci, Christine. 2007. (J). pap. *(978-1-4127-8921-9(4))* Publications International, Ltd.

—Meet Diego! Valdes, Leslie. ed. 2005. (Dora the Explorer Ser.: No. 4). 22p. (J). lib. bdg. 15.00 *(978-1-59054-799-1(3))* Fitzgerald Bks.

—Pancake Party! (Sunny Day) Sisler, Celeste. 2019. (Step into Reading Ser.). (ENG.). 24p. (J). (gr. -1-1). 5.99 *(978-1-9848-4805-5(4))*; 12.99 *(978-1-9848-4806-2(2))* Random Hse. Children's Bks. (Random Hse. Bks. for Young Readers).

—Rain, Rain, Go Away. 2010. (Backyardigans Ser.). (ENG.). 24p. (J). (gr. -1-1). 16.19 *(978-1-4169-8509-9(3))* Simon & Schuster, Inc.

—Robot Repairman to the Rescue! 2009. (Backyardigans Ser.). (ENG.). 24p. (J). (gr. -1-2). pap. 3.99 *(978-1-4169-9012-3(7)*, Simon Spotlight/Nickelodeon) Simon Spotlight/Nickelodeon.

—Rock Stars! 2018. 24p. (J). *(978-1-5444-0161-4(2))* Random Hse., Inc.

—Rock Stars! (Sunny Day) Carbone, Courtney. 2018. (Step into Reading Ser.). (ENG.). 24p. (J). (gr. -1-1). pap. 4.99 *(978-1-5247-6862-1(6))*; lib. bdg. 12.99 *(978-1-5247-6863-8(4))* Random Hse. Children's Bks. (Random Hse. Bks. for Young Readers).

Hall, Susan & Hall, Susan. Diego Saves the Tree Frogs. 2006. (Go, Diego, Go! Ser.). (ENG.). 24p. (J). (gr. -1-1). pap. 3.99 *(978-1-4169-1574-4(5)*, Simon Spotlight/Nickelodeon) Simon Spotlight/Nickelodeon.

—Dora Explora los Colores. Beinstein, Phoebe. 2007. (Dora la Exploradora Ser.).Tr. of Dora Explores Colors. (SPA & ENG.). 14p. (J). (gr. -1). bds. 4.99 *(978-1-4169-4726-4(4)*, Libros Para Ninos) Libros Para Ninos.

—Hooray for School! Going to School with Nick Jr. Lindner, Brooke. 2008. (ENG.). 16p. (J). (gr. -1-2). pap. 6.99 *(978-1-4169-5861-1(4)*, Simon Spotlight/Nickelodeon) Simon Spotlight/Nickelodeon.

—Surf That Wave! 2006. (Backyardigans Ser.). (ENG.). 24p. (J). (gr. -1-3). pap. 3.99 *(978-1-4169-1482-2(X)*, Simon Spotlight/Nickelodeon) Simon Spotlight/Nickelodeon.

Hall, Susan & Roper, Robert. The Super Soccer Game. Ricci, Christine. 2007. (J). pap. *(978-1-4127-8926-4(5))* Publications International, Ltd.

Hall, Susan, jt. illus. see Hall, Susan.

Hall, Susan, jt. illus. see Random House.

Hall, Susan T. Presentamos a Diego! 2005. (Dora the Explorer Ser.). Orig. Title: Meet Diego!. (SPA.). 24p. (J). pap. 3.99 *(978-0-689-87749-0(8)*, Libros Para Ninos) Libros Para Ninos.

Hall, Terri L. & Babeaux, Dennis, photos by. Denny & Denise: A Story of Two Ducks: Introducing Pretty Boy & Fella, 1 vol. Hall, Terri L. 2009. 42p. pap. 24.95 *(978-1-60749-609-0(7))* America Star Bks.

Hall, Tracy. Washington Irving. Irving, Washington. 2004. (Great American Short Stories Ser.). 80p. (gr. 4-7). lib. bdg. 24.00 *(978-0-8368-4253-1(7)*, Gareth Stevens Learning Library) Stevens, Gareth Publishing LLLP.

Hall, Wendell E. Buried Treasures of California. Jameson, W. C. 2006. (Buried Treasure Ser.). (ENG.). 175p. (Orig.). (J). (gr. 4-17). pap. 14.95 *(978-0-87483-406-2(6))* August Hse. Pubs., Inc.

—Curing the Cross-Eyed Mule: Appalachian Mountain Humor. Jones, Loyal & Wheeler, Billy Edd. 2005. (ENG.). 212p. (Orig.). (J). (gr. -1-12). pap. 12.95 *(978-0-87483-083-5(4))* August Hse. Pubs., Inc.

—More Laughter in Appalachia: Southern Mountain Humor. Jones, Loyal & Wheeler, Billy Edd. 2005. (American Storytelling Ser.). (ENG.). 218p. (J). (gr. -1-12). pap. 12.95 *(978-0-87483-411-6(2))* August Hse. Pubs., Inc.

—Queen of the Cold-Blooded Tales. Brown, Roberta Simpson. 2005. (American Storytelling Ser.). (ENG.). 175p. (J). (gr. 5-17). pap. 9.95 *(978-0-87483-408-6(2))* August Hse. Pubs., Inc.

—The Stable Boy. Taylor, Shirley A. 2012. (ENG.). 40p. (J). (gr. 2-17). 17.95 *(978-1-935166-79-5(4))* Parkhurst Brothers, Inc., Pubs.

Hallam, Colleen and Peggy. The Adventures of Donny the Doorknob. Ross, Marlene. 2009. 32p. pap. 24.95 *(978-1-61546-539-2(1))* America Star Bks.

Hallam, Steve. Hippo in the Stable. Trodd, Mark. 2019. (ENG.). 38p. (J). pap. ***(978-1-922355-40-9(2))*** Tablo Publishing.

Hallatt, Alexandra. Fab (Friends Against Bullying) Club. Hallatt, Alexandra. 2016. (ENG.). (J). (gr. 4-6). pap. *(978-0-9955482-0-6(X))* Moontoon Publishing.

Hallensleben, Georg. And If the Moon Could Talk. Banks, Kate. 2005. (ENG.). 40p. (J). (gr. -1-1). reprint ed. per. 7.99 *(978-0-374-43558-5(8)*, 900030432, Farrar, Straus & Giroux (BYR)) Farrar, Straus & Giroux.

—The Cat Who Walked Across France. Banks, Kate. 2004. (ENG.). 40p. (J). (gr. -1-2). 19.99 *(978-0-374-39968-9(9)*, 900021865, Farrar, Straus & Giroux (BYR)) Farrar, Straus & Giroux.

—Close Your Eyes. Banks, Kate. 2015. (ENG.). 36p. (J). (gr. -1-1). bds. 7.99 *(978-0-374-30101-9(8)*, 9780374301019, Farrar, Straus & Giroux (BYR)) Farrar, Straus & Giroux.

—Gaspard & Lisa's Christmas Surprise. Gutman, Anne. 2012. (ENG.). 32p. (J). (gr. k-3). pap. 6.99 *(978-0-449-81013-2(5)*, Dragonfly Bks.) Random Hse. Children's Bks.

—Gaspard & Lisa's Christmas Surprise. Gutman, Anne. ed. 2012. lib. bdg. 17.20 *(978-0-606-26782-3(4))* Turtleback.

—Gaspard et Lisa - Brioche. Gutman, Anne. 2008. (Gaspard et Lisa Ser.: Vol. 2259745). (FRE.). (J). (gr. -1-2). *(978-2-01-225974-4(X))* Hachette Jeunesse.

—Lisa's Baby Sister. Gutman, Anne. 2012. (ENG.). 32p. (J). (gr. k-3). pap. 6.99 *(978-0-449-81012-5(7)*, Dragonfly Bks.) Random Hse. Children's Bks.

—The Night Worker. Banks, Kate. 2007. (ENG.). 40p. (J). (gr. -1-1). 8.99 *(978-0-374-40000-2(8)*, 900038843) Square Fish.

Hallensleben, Georg. Baños. Hallensleben, Georg. Gutman, Anne & Gutmann-Hellensleben. 2003. (Coleccion Mira Mira Look Look Ser.). (SPA.). 16p. (J). (gr. -1-k). 9.99 *(978-84-261-3322-9(3))* Juventud, Editorial ESP. Dist: Lectorum Pubns., Inc.

Haller, Reese. Giving & Receiving. Haller, Reese. 2007. (Fred the Mouse Ser.). 104p. (J). (gr. 4-7). per. 4.97 *(978-0-9772321-5-4(8))* Personal Power Pr.

Haller, Thomas. Rescuing Freedom. Haller, Reese. 3rd ed. 2006. (Fred the Mouse Ser.). 112p. (J). (gr. k-4). per. 4.97 *(978-0-9772321-3-0(1))* Personal Power Pr.

Hallett, Joy Davies. Kelly Bear Earth. Davies, Leah. Davies, Leah, ed. 2008. 32p. (J). pap. 5.95 *(978-0-9621054-3-2(0))* Kelly Bear Pr., Inc.

Hallett, Mark. Wild Horses: Galloping Through Time. Halls, Kelly Milner. 2008. (Darby Creek Exceptional Titles Ser.). 72p. (J). (gr. 1-7). 18.95 *(978-1-58196-065-5(4)*, Darby Creek) Lerner Publishing Group.

Halligan, Kelly C., et al. The Smart Princess: And Other Deaf Tales, 1 vol. Carey, Keelin et al. 2007. (ENG.). 148p. (J). (gr. 4-7). per. 9.95 *(978-1-896764-90-0(8))* Second Story Pr. CAN. Dist: Orca Bk. Pubs. USA.

Hallinan, Susan. Sassy the Seahag. Canfield, Andrea. 2003. Orig. Title: Sassy the Seahag. (J). per. *(978-0-9721327-3-2(2))* Bad Choices Media.

Hallman, Lizzy. Star Wishes. Cox, Marjean. 2019. (ENG.). 26p. (J). (gr. -1-2). pap. 9.99 ***(978-1-61254-402-1(9))*** Brown Books Publishing Group.

Hallmark, Darla. More Dragons: Coloring Book by Darla Hallmark. 2007. 20p. (YA). 10.00 *(978-0-9795206-8-6(1))* Unseen Gallery.

Halloween Books, Ernest. Halloween Coloring Book for Kids: Funny & Cute Coloring Pages for Kids - Halloween Drawing Book - Halloween Children's Activity Books - Halloween Gifts for Girls. Designs, Ernest Creative. 2019. (ENG.). 70p. (J). pap. 7.99 ***(978-1-6932-2337-2(6))*** Independently Published.

—Halloween Coloring Book for Kids: Funny & Cute Coloring Pages for Kids - Halloween Sketchbook - Halloween Children's Activity Books - Halloween Gifts for Girls. Designs, Ernest Creative. 2019. (ENG.). 70p. (J). pap. 6.99 ***(978-1-6933-7932-1(5))*** Independently Published.

—My Halloween Journal: Halloween Lined Journal Notebook - Halloween Gifts - Journal to Write in for Kids & Adults. Designs, Ernest Creative. 2019. (ENG.). 100p. (J). pap. 5.99 ***(978-1-6936-7928-5(0))*** Independently Published.

Halperin, Wendy Anderson. Cobble Street Cousins Complete Collection: In Aunt Lucy's Kitchen; a Little Shopping; Special Gifts; Some Good News; Summer Party; Wedding Flowers. Rylant, Cynthia. ed. 2018. (Cobble Street Cousins Ser.). (ENG.). 400p. (J). (gr. 2-5). pap. 34.99 *(978-1-5344-1633-8(1)*, Aladdin) Simon & Schuster Children's Publishing.

—Let's Go Home: The Wonderful Things about a House. Rylant, Cynthia. 2005. (ENG.). 32p. (J). (gr. -1-3). 8.99 *(978-1-4169-0839-5(0)*, Simon & Schuster Bks. For Young Readers) Simon & Schuster Bks. For Young Readers.

—Love Is ... King James Bible Staff. 2004. (ENG.). 32p. (J). 11.99 *(978-0-689-86675-3(5)*, Simon & Schuster/Paula Wiseman Bks.) Simon & Schuster/Paula Wiseman Bks.

—Peace. 2013. (ENG.). 40p. (J). (gr. -1-3). 18.99 *(978-0-689-82552-1(8)*, Atheneum Bks. for Young Readers) Simon & Schuster Children's Publishing.

—Planting the Wild Garden, 1 vol. Galbraith, Kathryn O. (ENG.). 32p. (J). 2015. (gr. 1-3). pap. 7.95 *(978-1-56145-791-5(4))*; 2011. (gr. -1-3). 15.95 *(978-1-56145-563-8(6))* Peachtree Publishing Co. Inc.

—The Racketty-Packetty House. Burnett, Frances Hodgson. 100th anniv. ed. 2006. (ENG.). 96p. (J). (gr. 4-7). 21.99 *(978-0-689-86974-7(6)*, Simon & Schuster Bks. For Young Readers) Simon & Schuster Bks. For Young Readers.

—Strawberry Hill. Hoberman, Mary Ann. 2009. (ENG.). 240p. (J). (gr. 4-6). 21.19 *(978-0-316-04136-2(X))* Little Brown & Co.

—Wedding Flowers. Rylant, Cynthia. 2003. (Cobble Street Cousins Ser.). 72p. (gr. 2-5). 15.00 *(978-0-7569-1476-9(0))* Perfection Learning Corp.

—Wedding Flowers. Rylant, Cynthia. 2003. (Cobble Street Cousins Ser.: 6). (ENG.). 80p. (J). (gr. 2-5). pap. 5.99 *(978-0-689-83418-9(7)*, Aladdin) Simon & Schuster Children's Publishing.

Halpern, Chaiky. The Hamentash That Ran Away. (J). (gr. -1-4). 2.95 *(978-0-87306-250-3(7))* Feldheim Pubs.

Halpern, Shari. I Love Bugs! Sturges, Philemon. 2005. (ENG.). 32p. (J). (gr. -1-3). 17.99 *(978-0-06-056168-0(8))* HarperCollins Pubs.

—I Love Cranes! Sturges, Philemon. Date not set. 32p. (J). (gr. -1-1). 5.99 *(978-0-06-443666-3(7))* HarperCollins Pubs.

—I Love Planes! Sturges, Philemon. 2003. (ENG.). 32p. (J). (gr. -1-1). 16.99 *(978-0-06-028898-3(1))* HarperCollins Pubs.

—I Love School! Sturges, Philemon. 2014. 32p. pap. 7.00 *(978-1-61003-329-9(9))* Center for the Collaborative Classroom.

—I Love School! Sturges, Philemon. 32p. (J). (gr. -1-1). 2004. lib. bdg. 14.89 *(978-0-06-009285-6(8))*; 2006. (ENG.). reprint ed. pap. 7.99 *(978-0-06-009286-3(6))* HarperCollins Pubs.

—I Love Tools! Sturges, Philemon. 2006. 24p. (J). (gr. -1-1). 14.89 *(978-0-06-009288-7(2))* HarperCollins Pubs.

—I Love Trains. Sturges, Philemon. 2003. (ENG.). 32p. (J). (gr. -1-1). pap. 7.99 *(978-0-06-443667-0(5))* HarperCollins Pubs.

—I Love Trains! Board Book. Sturges, Philemon. 2006. (ENG.). 28p. (J). (gr. -1-1). bds. 6.99 *(978-0-06-083774-7(8)*, HarperFestival) HarperCollins Pubs.

—I Love Trucks! Board Book. Sturges, Philemon. 2003. (ENG.). 34p. (J). (gr. -1-3). bds. 7.99 *(978-0-06-052666-5(1)*, HarperFestival) HarperCollins Pubs.

—There Once Was a Puffin. Jacques, Florence Page. 2016. (ENG.). 32p. (J). 15.95 *(978-0-7358-4245-8(0))* North-South Bks., Inc.

Halpern, Shari. Dinosaur Parade. Halpern, Shari. 2018. (ENG.). 24p. (J). bds. 7.99 *(978-1-250-15524-5(X)*, 900184596, Holt, Henry & Co. Bks. For Young Readers) Holt, Henry & Co.

Halperni, Wendy Anderson. Planting the Wild Garden. Galbraith, Kathryn O. 2015. (ENG.). (J). (gr. 1-4). lib. bdg. 18.55 *(978-1-62765-752-5(5))* Perfection Learning Corp.

Halpin, Abigail. Anne Arrives: Inspired by Anne of Green Gables. George, Kallie. 2018. (Anne Chapter Book Ser.: 1). (ENG.). 72p. (J). (gr. 1-3). 12.99 *(978-1-77049-930-0(X)*, Tundra Bks.) Tundra Bks. CAN. Dist: Penguin Random Hse. LLC.

Halpin, Abigail. Anne's Kindred Spirits. George, Kallie. 2020. (Anne Chapter Book Ser.: 2). 64p. (J). (gr. 1-3). pap. 8.99 ***(978-0-7352-6694-0(8)***, Tundra Bks.) Tundra Bks. CAN. Dist: Penguin Random Hse. LLC.

Halpin, Abigail. Anne's Kindred Spirits: Inspired by Anne of Green Gables. George, Kallie. 2019. (Anne Chapter Book Ser.: 2). (ENG.). 64p. (J). (gr. 1-3). 12.99 *(978-1-77049-932-4(6)*, Tundra Bks.) Tundra Bks. CAN. Dist: Penguin Random Hse. LLC.

—Finding Wild. Wagner Lloyd, Megan. 2016. 32p. (J). (gr. -1-2). 16.99 *(978-1-101-93281-0(3)*, Knopf Bks. for Young Readers) Random Hse. Children's Bks.

—Fort-Building Time. Lloyd, Megan Wagner. 2017. 32p. (J). (gr. -1-2). 17.99 *(978-0-399-55655-5(9)*, Knopf Bks. for Young Readers) Random Hse. Children's Bks.

—The Grand Plan to Fix Everything. Krishnaswami, Uma. 2013. (ENG.). 288p. (J). (gr. 3-7). pap. 8.99 *(978-1-4169-9590-6(0)*, Atheneum Bks. for Young Readers) Simon & Schuster Children's Publishing.

—Itzhak: A Boy Who Loved the Violin. Newman, Tracy. 2020. (ENG.). 40p. (J). (gr. -1-3). 18.99 *(978-1-4197-4110-4(1)*, Abrams Bks. for Young Readers) Abrams, Inc.

Halpin, Abigail. Itzhak (PJ Library Edition) A Boy Who Loved the Violin. Newman, Tracy. 2020. (ENG.). (J). (gr. -1-3). pap. 18.99 ***(978-1-4197-4989-6(7))*** Abrams, Inc.

Halpin, Abigail. Mama's Belly. Hosford, Kate. 2018. (ENG.). 32p. (J). (gr. -1-k). 16.99 *(978-1-4197-2841-9(5)*, Abrams Bks. for Young Readers) Abrams, Inc.

—Maybe Yes, Maybe No, Maybe Maybe. Patron, Susan. 2009. (ENG.). (J). (gr. 3-5). lib. bdg. 16.60 *(978-1-61383-707-8(0))* Perfection Learning Corp.

—Maybe Yes, Maybe No, Maybe Maybe. Patron, Susan. 2009. (ENG.). 128p. (J). (gr. 3-5). pap. 5.99 *(978-1-4169-6176-5(3)*, Atheneum Bks. for Young Readers) Simon & Schuster Children's Publishing.

—The Melancholic Mermaid. George, Kallie. 2011. (ENG.). 64p. (J). (gr. k-4). 16.95 *(978-1-897476-53-6(1))* Simply Read Bks. CAN. Dist: Ingram Publisher Services.

—Penny Dreadful. Snyder, Laurel. 320p. (J). 2012. (ENG.). (gr. 4-6). lib. bdg. 22.44 *(978-0-375-96199-1(2))*; 2011. (gr. 3-7). 8.99 *(978-0-375-86169-7(6))* Random Hse. Children's Bks. (Yearling).

—The Problem with Being Slightly Heroic. Krishnaswami, Uma. (ENG.). 288p. (J). (gr. 3-7). 2014. pap. 7.99 *(978-1-4424-2329-9(3)*, Atheneum Bks. for Young Readers); 2013. 16.99 *(978-1-4424-2328-2(5))* Simon & Schuster Children's Publishing.

—The Year of the Book. Cheng, Andrea. (Anna Wang Novel Ser.: 1). (ENG.). 160p. (J). (gr. 1-4). 2013. pap. 6.99 *(978-0-544-02263-8(7)*, 1528485); 2012. 16.99 *(978-0-547-68463-5(0)*, 1476526) Houghton Mifflin Harcourt Publishing Co.

Halpin, D. Thomas & Richards, Virginia Helen. Saint Paul. Halpin, D. Thomas & Richards, Virginia Helen. 2008. (COMIColor Saints Ser.: 1). (J). 2.95 *(978-0-8198-7109-1(5))* Pauline Bks. & Media.

Halpin, D. Thomas, jt. illus. see Richards, Virginia Helen.

Halsey, Megan. Four Seasons Make a Year. Rockwell, Anne. 2004. (ENG.). 32p. (J). (gr. k-3). 17.99 *(978-0-8027-8883-2(1)*, 900032718, Bloomsbury USA Childrens) Bloomsbury Publishing USA.

—Trucks: Whizz! Zoom! Rumble!, 0 vols. Hubbell, Patricia. 2006. (ENG.). 32p. (J). (gr. -1-1). per. 9.99 *(978-0-7614-5328-4(8)*, 9780761453284, Two Lions) Amazon Publishing.

Halsey, Megan & Addy, Sean. Akira to Zoltan: Twenty-Six Men Who Changed the World. Chin-Lee, Cynthia. 2006. 32p. (J). (gr. 3-7). lib. bdg. 15.95 *(978-1-57091-579-6(2))* Charlesbridge Publishing, Inc.

—Amelia to Zora: Twenty-Six Women Who Changed the World. Chin-Lee, Cynthia. 2008. (ENG.). 32p. (J). (gr. 3-7). pap. 7.95 *(978-1-57091-523-9(7))* Charlesbridge Publishing, Inc.

—Boats: Speeding! Sailing! Cruising!, 0 vols. Hubbell, Patricia. 2009. (ENG.). 32p. (J). (gr. -1-1). 17.99 *(978-0-7614-5524-0(8)*, 9780761455240, Two Lions) Amazon Publishing.

—Cars: Rushing! Honking! Zooming!, 0 vols. Hubbell, Patricia. 2010. (ENG.). 32p. (J). (gr. -1-1). pap. 7.99 *(978-0-7614-5616-2(3)*, 9780761456162, Two Lions) Amazon Publishing.

—Trains: Steaming! Pulling! Huffing!, 0 vols. Hubbell, Patricia. 2009. (ENG.). 34p. (J). (gr. -1-1). pap. 9.99 *(978-0-7614-5593-6(0)*, 9780761455936, Two Lions) Amazon Publishing.

—Valentine Be Mine. Farmer, Jacqueline. 2013. 32p. (J). (gr. k-3). pap. 7.95 *(978-1-58089-390-9(2))* Charlesbridge Publishing, Inc.

Halsey, Megan, jt. illus. see Addy, Sean.

Halter, Paige. Read Me I'm a Good Book. Luv, Christian. 2019. (ENG.). 50p. (J). (gr. k-4). pap. 13.49 *(978-1-5456-6416-2(1))* Salem Author Services.

Haltermon, Becky. A Rabbit Hash Christmas. Clare, Caitlen. 2012. 36p. (J). 10.00 *(978-0-9816123-9-3(3))* Merlot Group, LLC, The.

Halverson, Lydia. Baby Looney Tunes Visit a Haunted House. Ritchie, Joseph R. 2005. (Baby Looney Tunes Ser.). 14p. (J). (gr. -1-3). bds. 9.95 *(978-0-8249-6609-6(0)*, Ideal Pubns.) Worthy Publishing.

—Frosty the Snowman. Rollins, Jack & Nelson, Steve. 2005. 18p. (J). (gr. -1-k). bds. 9.95 *(978-0-8249-6595-2(7)*, Ideal Pubns.) Worthy Publishing.

—Nursery Rhymes. 2004. (Elements of Reading: Phonics Ser.). 24p. pap. 40.00 *(978-0-7398-9014-1(X))* Houghton Mifflin Harcourt Supplemental Pubs.

—Peter Cottontail's Easter Surprise. Ritchie, Joseph R. 2006. (ENG.). 18p. (J). (gr. -1-k). bds. 9.95 *(978-0-8249-6627-0(9)*, Ideal Pubns.) Worthy Publishing.

—The Red Door Detective Club Mysteries, 4 bks., Set. Riehecky, Janet. (J). (gr. 3-6). lib. bdg. 51.80 *(978-1-56674-900-8(X))* Forest Hse. Publishing Co., Inc.

—Where's Santa? Ritchie, Joseph R. 2006. (ENG.). 14p. (J). (gr. -1-k). bds. 7.95 *(978-0-8249-6673-7(2)*, Ideal Pubns.) Worthy Publishing.

Halverson, Lydia, jt. illus. see Cowdrey, Richard.

Halverson, Randal. Rainbows for Rosa. Byers, Arlene. 2016. (ENG.). 172p. 9.50 *(978-0-7399-2521-8(0))* Rod & Staff Pubs., Inc.

Halverson, Tom. The Incredible Rescues. Dunlop, Ed. 2003. 166p. (J). (gr. 4-7). 7.49 *(978-1-59166-012-5(2))* BJU Pr.

—The Search for the Silver Eagle. Dunlop, Ed. 2003. 159p. (J). (gr. 4-7). 7.49 *(978-1-59166-014-9(9))* BJU Pr.

Halvorson, Adeline. La Primera: The Story of Wild Mustangs. Tyson, Ian. 2009. 32p. (J). (gr. 2-4). 20.95 *(978-0-88776-863-7(6)*, Tundra Bks.) Tundra Bks. CAN. Dist: Penguin Random Hse. LLC.

Hama, Larry & Dixon, Chuck. Punisher: Suicide Run. 2017. (ENG.). 344p. (J). (gr. 4-17). pap. 34.99 *(978-1-302-90697-9(6))* Marvel Worldwide, Inc.

Hamaker, Steve. The Mystery of the Moon Tower. Sedita, Francesco & Seraydarian, Prescott. 2020. (Pathfinders Society Ser.). 176p. (J). (gr. 3-7). 18.99 *(978-0-425-29186-3(3))*; pap. 12.99 *(978-0-425-29187-0(1))* Penguin Young Readers Group. (Viking Books for Young Readers).

Hamaker, Steve, jt. illus. see Smith, Jeff.

Hamanaka, Sheila. Class Clown. Hurwitz, Johanna. 2011. (ENG.). 112p. (J). (gr. 1-4). 16.19 *(978-0-590-41821-8(1))* Scholastic, Inc.

Hamanaka, Sheila. Grandparents Song. Hamanaka, Sheila. 2003. 32p. (J). 15.99 *(978-0-688-17852-9(9))* HarperCollins Pubs.

Hambleton, Laura. American English with Abby & Zak. Traynor, Tracy. 2007. (Abby & Zak Ser.). (ENG.). 48p. (J). (gr. k-2). pap. 16.95 *(978-1-84059-491-1(8))* Milet Publishing.

—Ece Ve Efe Ile Türkçe. Erdogan, Fatih. 2007. (Abby & Zak Ser.). (ENG.). 48p. (J). (gr. k-2). pap. 16.95 *(978-1-84059-493-5(4))* Milet Publishing.

Hambleton, Laura. Pat-A-Cake: Llamas. Editors of Silver Dolphin Books. 2020. (Pat-A-Cake Ser.). (ENG.). 10p. (J). (— 1). bds. 7.99 ***(978-1-64517-016-7(0)***, Silver Dolphin Bks.) Printers Row Publishing Group.

Hambleton, Laura. Spanish with Abby & Zak. Traynor, Tracy & Pérez, María. 2008. (Abby & Zak Ser.). (SPA & ENG.). 48p. (J). (gr. k-2). pap. 16.95 *(978-1-84059-515-4(9))* Milet Publishing.

Hambleton, Laura. Collins Big Cat Phonics for Letters & Sounds - Fantastic Yak: Band 02A/Red A, Bd. 2. Hambleton, Laura. 2018. (Collins Big Cat Phonics Ser.). (ENG.). 16p. (J). (gr. -1-k). pap. 6.99 *(978-0-00-825141-3(X))* HarperCollins Pubs. Ltd. GBR. Dist: Independent Pubs. Group.

—Collins Big Cat Phonics for Letters & Sounds - Pink Boat, Pink Car: Band 02B/Red B, Bd. 2B. Hambleton, Laura. 2018. (Collins Big Cat Phonics Ser.). (ENG.). 16p. (J). (gr. -1-k). pap. 6.99 *(978-0-00-825147-5(9))* HarperCollins Pubs. Ltd. GBR. Dist: Independent Pubs. Group.

—Telling Tails: Fun with Homonyms. Hambleton, Laura. Turhan, Sedat. 2007. (Milet Wordwise Ser.). (ENG.). 28p. (J). (gr. k-2). pap. 6.95 *(978-1-84059-498-0(5))* Milet Publishing.

Hamblin, George. Nathan & Nicole Learn about Nouns. Malaspina, Ann. 2014. (Language Builders Ser.). (ENG.). 32p. (J). (gr. 2-4). pap. 11.94 *(978-1-60357-701-4(7))*; lib. bdg. 25.27 *(978-1-59953-666-8(8))* Norwood Hse. Pr.

—Teachers' Favorites Fun Activities for Fall! Fort, Holli et al. 2010. 96p. (J). *(978-1-4508-2765-2(9))* Publications International, Ltd.

Hamburger, Carole. The Zippity-Do-Dot: The Dot Who Dared to Pick Her Knows. Hamburger, Carole. 2008. 40p. (J). 16.95 *(978-0-9764921-1-5(3))* Cherry Street Pr.

Hamdan, Noah. Riding on a Beam of Light: Albert Einstein. Dean, Ramsey. 2013. 48p. pap. 10.48 *(978-0-9893372-1-2(9))* Ramsey Dean, Inc.

Hameister, Ann. Enter the Earth. Welles, Lee. (Gaia Girls Ser.: 1). (ENG.). 336p. (YA). (gr. 4-7). 2007. pap. 24.95 *(978-1-933609-01-0(X))*; 2006. 18.95 *(978-1-933609-00-3(1))* Chelsea Green Publishing.

Hamel, Caroline. How to Become a Perfect Knight in Five Days. Dube, Pierrette. 2009. (Rainy Day Readers Ser.). 32p. (J). (gr. -1-3). 25.60 *(978-1-60754-373-2(7))*; pap. 10.55 *(978-1-60754-374-9(5))* Windmill Bks.

—Lucy & the Dragonfly. Papineau, Lucie. 2018. 40p. (J). (gr. k-3). 16.95 *(978-2-7338-5620-8(0))* Auzou, Philippe Editions FRA. Dist: Consortium Bk. Sales & Distribution.

Hamelin, Marie-Micheline. Eat, Run & Live Healthy. Olson, Karen. 2nd rev. ed. 2009. (Caring for Me Ser.). (ENG.). 20p. (J). (gr. -1-k). pap. 10.95 *(978-1-894778-50-3(2))* Theytus Bks., Ltd. CAN. Dist: Orca Bk. Pubs. USA.

—Healthy Choices, Healthy Lives. Olson, Karen W. (ENG.). 20p. 2005. (J). pap. 10.95 *(978-1-894778-31-2(6))*; 2009. pap. 9.95 *(978-1-894778-53-4(7))* Theytus Bks., Ltd. CAN. Dist: Univ. of Toronto Pr.

—Living Safe, Playing Safe. Olson, Karen W. 2005. (Caring for Me Ser.). (ENG.). 20p. (J). pap. 10.95 *(978-1-894778-33-6(2))* Theytus Bks., Ltd. CAN. Dist: Univ. of Toronto Pr.

—Looking after Me. Lecoy, Denise. 2nd rev. ed. 2009. (Caring for Me Ser.). (ENG.). 20p. (J). (gr. -1-k). pap. 9.95

(978-1-894778-54-1(5)) Theytus Bks., Ltd. CAN. Dist: Orca Bk. Pubs. USA.
—Taking Care of Mother Earth. Kruger, Leanne Flett. 2005. (ENG.). 20p. (J). pap. 10.95 *(978-1-894778-30-5(8))* Theytus Bks., Ltd. CAN. Dist: Univ. of Toronto Pr.
—Taking Care of Mother Earth. Kruger, Leanne Flett. ed. 2009. (Caring for Me Ser.). (ENG.). 20p. pap. 9.95 *(978-1-894778-55-8(3))* Theytus Bks., Ltd. CAN. Dist: Univ. of Toronto Pr.
Hamer, Arthur. Captain Valiant & Me. Britten, Adam. 2014. (Captain Valiant Ser.). (ENG.). 160p. (J). (gr. k-3). pap. 9.99 *(978-1-84812-353-3(1))* Bonnier Publishing GBR. Dist: Independent Pubs. Group.
—Captain Valiant & Me: Revenge of the Black Phantom. Britten, Adam. 2013. (Captain Valiant Ser.). (ENG.). 160p. (J). (gr. k-3). pap. 9.99 *(978-1-84812-311-3(6))* Bonnier Publishing GBR. Dist: Independent Pubs. Group.
Hames, Cassandra. A New Baby Is Love: Padded Board Book. Bunting, Rose. Cottage Door Press, ed. 2019. (Love You Always Ser.). (ENG.). 18p. (J). (gr. -1-1). bds. 9.99 *(978-1-68052-243-3(4),* 1002290) Cottage Door Pr.
Hames, Holland. Teddy No Stuff. Hayes, Mj. 2016. (ENG.). (J). pap. 9.99 *(978-0-9819634-0-2(4))* St. Augustine Pr.
Hamill, Dion. Amazeing Ruins: Journey Through Lost Civilisations. Hamill, Dion. 2004. (ENG.). 32p. (Orig.). pap., act. bk. ed. *(978-1-877003-69-1(7))* Little Hare Bks. AUS. Dist: HarperCollins Pubs. Australia.
Hamilton, Allen, jt. illus. see Stojic, Manya.
Hamilton, Andrew. Robots. Punter, Russell. 2004. 48p. (J). (gr. 2-18). pap. 5.95 *(978-0-7945-0760-2(3),* Usborne) EDC Publishing.
Hamilton, Dorothy. Magic Snow Bird: And Other Stories. Blyton, Enid. 2013. (ENG.). 192p. (J). 9.95 *(978-1-84135-420-0(1))* Award Pubns. Ltd. GBR. Dist: Parkwest Pubns., Inc.
Hamilton, Helen S. The Happy Hollisters. West, Jerry. 2019. (Happy Hollisters Ser.: Vol. 1). (ENG.). 190p. (J). (gr. 1-6). pap. 11.98 *(978-1-949436-34-1(9))* Svenson Group, Inc., The.
—The Happy Hollisters & the Castle Rock Mystery. West, Jerry. 2019. (Happy Hollisters Ser.: Vol. 23). (ENG.). 172p. (J). (gr. 1-6). pap. 11.98 *(978-1-949436-56-3(X))* Svenson Group, Inc., The.
Hamilton, Helen S. The Happy Hollisters & the Cowboy Mystery. West, Jerry. 2020. (Happy Hollisters Ser.: Vol. 20). (ENG.). 180p. (J). (gr. 1-6). pap. 11.98 ***(978-1-949436-53-2(5))*** Svenson Group, Inc., The.
Hamilton, Helen S. The Happy Hollisters & the Cuckoo Clock Mystery. West, Jerry. (ENG.). 180p. (J). 2019. (Happy Hollisters Ser.: Vol. 24). (gr. 1-6). pap. 11.98 *(978-1-949436-57-0(8));* 2018. pap. 9.95 *(978-1-949436-24-2(1))* Svenson Group, Inc., The.
—The Happy Hollisters & the Ghost Horse Mystery. West, Jerry. 2019. (Happy Hollisters Ser.: Vol. 29). (ENG.). 184p. (J). (gr. 1-6). pap. 11.98 *(978-1-949436-62-4(4))* Svenson Group, Inc., The.
—The Happy Hollisters & the Ghost Horse Mystery: (volume 29) West, Jerry. 2019. (Happy Hollisters Ser.: Vol. 29). (ENG.). 184p. (J). pap. 11.95 *(978-1-949436-29-7(2))* Svenson Group, Inc., The.
Hamilton, Helen S. The Happy Hollisters & the Ice Carnival Mystery. West, Jerry. 2020. (Happy Hollisters Ser.: Vol. 16). (ENG.). 170p. (J). (gr. 1-6). pap. 11.98 ***(978-1-949436-49-5(7))*** Svenson Group, Inc., The.
—The Happy Hollisters & the Indian Treasure. West, Jerry. 2020. (Happy Hollisters Ser.: Vol. 4). (ENG.). 190p. (J). (gr. 1-6). pap. 11.98 ***(978-1-949436-37-2(3))*** Svenson Group, Inc., The.
—The Happy Hollisters & the Merry-Go-Round Mystery. West, Jerry. 2020. (Happy Hollisters Ser.: Vol. 10). (SPA.). 180p. (J). (gr. 1-6). pap. 11.98 ***(978-1-949436-43-3(8))*** Svenson Group, Inc., The.
Hamilton, Helen S. The Happy Hollisters & the Monster Mystery. West, Jerry. 2019. (Happy Hollisters Ser.: Vol. 32). (ENG.). 174p. (J). (gr. 1-6). pap. 11.95 *(978-1-949436-65-5(9))* Svenson Group, Inc., The.
Hamilton, Helen S. The Happy Hollisters & the Mystery at Missile Town. West, Jerry. 2020. (Happy Hollisters Ser.: Vol. 19). (ENG.). 176p. (J). (gr. 1-6). pap. 11.98 ***(978-1-949436-52-5(7))*** Svenson Group, Inc., The.
—The Happy Hollisters & the Mystery in Skyscraper City. West, Jerry. 2020. (Happy Hollisters Ser.: Vol. 17). (ENG.). 184p. (J). (gr. 1-6). pap. 11.98 ***(978-1-949436-50-1(0))*** Svenson Group, Inc., The.
Hamilton, Helen S. The Happy Hollisters & the Mystery of the Golden Witch. West, Jerry. 2019. (Happy Hollisters Ser.: Vol. 30). (ENG.). 184p. (J). (gr. 1-6). pap. 11.95 *(978-1-949436-63-1(2))* Svenson Group, Inc., The.
—The Happy Hollisters & the Mystery of the Golden Witch: (Volume 30) West, Jerry. 2019. (Happy Hollisters Ser.: Vol. 30). (ENG.). 184p. (J). pap. 11.95 *(978-1-949436-30-3(6))* Svenson Group, Inc., The.
Hamilton, Helen S. The Happy Hollisters & the Mystery of the Little Mermaid. West, Jerry. 2020. (Happy Hollisters Ser.: Vol. 18). (ENG.). 176p. (J). (gr. 1-6). pap. 11.98 ***(978-1-949436-51-8(9))*** Svenson Group, Inc., The.
Hamilton, Helen S. The Happy Hollisters & the Mystery of the Mexican Idol. West, Jerry. 2019. (Happy Hollisters Ser.: Vol. 31). (ENG.). 182p. (J). (gr. 1-6). pap. 11.98 *(978-1-949436-64-8(0))* Svenson Group, Inc., The.
Hamilton, Helen S. The Happy Hollisters & the Mystery of the Midnight Trolls. West, Jerry. 2019. (Happy Hollisters Ser.: Vol. 33). (ENG.). 174p. (J). (gr. 1-6). pap. 11.95 ***(978-1-949436-66-2(7))*** Svenson Group, Inc., The.
—The Happy Hollisters & the Mystery of the Totem Faces. West, Jerry. 2020. (Happy Hollisters Ser.: Vol. 15). (ENG.). 168p. (J). (gr. 1-6). pap. 11.98 ***(978-1-949436-48-8(9))*** Svenson Group, Inc., The.
—The Happy Hollisters & the Old Clipper Ship. West, Jerry. 2020. (Happy Hollisters Ser.: Vol. 12). (ENG.). 180p. (J). (gr. 1-6). pap. 11.98 ***(978-1-949436-45-7(4))*** Svenson Group, Inc., The.
Hamilton, Helen S. The Happy Hollisters & the Punch & Judy Mystery. West, Jerry. 2019. (Happy Hollisters Ser.: Vol. 27). (ENG.). 186p. (J). (gr. 1-6). pap. 11.98 *(978-1-949436-60-0(8))* Svenson Group, Inc., The.
—The Happy Hollisters & the Punch & Judy Mystery: (volume 27) West, Jerry. 2018. (Happy Hollisters Ser.: Vol. 27). (ENG.). 186p. (J). pap. 9.95 *(978-1-949436-27-3(6))* Svenson Group, Inc., The.
Hamilton, Helen S. The Happy Hollisters & the Scarecrow Mystery. West, Jerry. 2020. (Happy Hollisters Ser.: Vol. 14). (ENG.). 174p. (J). (gr. 1-6). pap. 11.98 ***(978-1-949436-47-1(0))*** Svenson Group, Inc., The.
Hamilton, Helen S. The Happy Hollisters & the Sea Turtle Mystery. West, Jerry. 2019. (Happy Hollisters Ser.: Vol. 26). (ENG.). 174p. (J). (gr. 1-6). pap. 11.98 *(978-1-949436-59-4(4))* Svenson Group, Inc., The.
—The Happy Hollisters & the Sea Turtle Mystery: (volume 26) West, Jerry. 2018. (Happy Hollisters Ser.: Vol. 26). (ENG.). 174p. (J). pap. 9.95 *(978-1-949436-26-6(8))* Svenson Group, Inc., The.
Hamilton, Helen S. The Happy Hollisters & the Secret Fort. West, Jerry. 2020. (Happy Hollisters Ser.: Vol. 9). (ENG.). 178p. (J). (gr. 1-6). pap. 11.98 ***(978-1-949436-42-6(X))*** Svenson Group, Inc., The.
—The Happy Hollisters & the Secret of the Lucky Coins. West, Jerry. 2020. (Happy Hollisters Ser.: Vol. 22). (ENG.). 170p. (J). (gr. 1-6). pap. 11.98 ***(978-1-949436-55-6(1))*** Svenson Group, Inc., The.
Hamilton, Helen S. The Happy Hollisters & the Swiss Echo Mystery: (volume 25) West, Jerry. 2018. (Happy Hollisters Ser.: Vol. 25). (ENG.). 174p. (J). pap. 9.95 *(978-1-949436-25-9(X))* Svenson Group, Inc., The.
Hamilton, Helen S. The Happy Hollisters & the Trading Post Mystery. West, Jerry. 2020. (Happy Hollisters Ser.: Vol. 7). (ENG.). 190p. (J). (gr. 1-6). pap. 11.98 ***(978-1-949436-40-2(3))*** Svenson Group, Inc., The.
Hamilton, Helen S. The Happy Hollisters & the Whistle-Pig Mystery. West, Jerry. 2019. (Happy Hollisters Ser.: Vol. 28). (ENG.). 184p. (J). (gr. 1-6). pap. 11.98 *(978-1-949436-61-7(6))* Svenson Group, Inc., The.
—The Happy Hollisters & the Whistle-Pig Mystery: (volume 28) West, Jerry. 2019. (ENG.). 184p. (J). pap. 9.95 *(978-1-949436-28-0(4))* Svenson Group, Inc., The.
Hamilton, Helen S. The Happy Hollisters at Circus Island. West, Jerry. 2020. (Happy Hollisters Ser.: Vol. 8). (ENG.). 188p. (J). (gr. 1-6). pap. 11.98 ***(978-1-949436-41-9(1))*** Svenson Group, Inc., The.
—The Happy Hollisters at Lizard Cove. West, Jerry. 2020. (Happy Hollisters Ser.: Vol. 13). (ENG.). 170p. (J). (gr. 1-6). pap. 11.98 ***(978-1-949436-46-4(2))*** Svenson Group, Inc., The.
—The Happy Hollisters at Mystery Mountain. West, Jerry. 2019. (Happy Hollisters Ser.: Vol. 5). (ENG.). 188p. (J). (gr. 1-6). pap. 11.98 ***(978-1-949436-38-9(1))*** Svenson Group, Inc., The.
—The Happy Hollisters at Sea Gull Beach. West, Jerry. 2019. (Happy Hollisters Ser.: Vol. 3). (ENG.). 190p. (J). (gr. 1-6). pap. 11.98 ***(978-1-949436-36-5(5))*** Svenson Group, Inc., The.
—The Happy Hollisters at Snowflake Camp. West, Jerry. 2019. (Happy Hollisters Ser.: Vol. 6). (ENG.). 190p. (J). (gr. 1-6). pap. 11.98 ***(978-1-949436-39-6(X))*** Svenson Group, Inc., The.
—The Happy Hollisters Coloring & Activity Book. 2020. (ENG.). 96p. (J). (gr. k-6). pap. 11.98 ***(978-1-949436-77-8(2))*** Svenson Group, Inc., The.
—The Happy Hollisters on a River Trip. West, Jerry. 2019. (Happy Hollisters Ser.: Vol. 2). (ENG.). 190p. (J). (gr. 1-6). pap. 11.95 ***(978-1-949436-35-8(7))*** Svenson Group, Inc., The.
Hamilton, James. The Ire of Iron Claw. Hamilton, Kersten. 2016. (Gadgets & Gears Ser.: 2). (ENG.). 192p. (J). (gr. 3-7). pap. 6.99 *(978-0-544-66854-6(5),* 1625480, HMH Books For Young Readers) Houghton Mifflin Harcourt Publishing Co.
—The Mesmer Menace. Hamilton, Kersten. 2015. (Gadgets & Gears Ser.: 1). (ENG.). 160p. (J). (gr. 3-7). pap. 6.99 *(978-0-544-43934-4(1),* 1596833, HMH Books For Young Readers) Houghton Mifflin Harcourt Publishing Co.
—The Tick-Tock Man: Gadgets & Gears, Book 3. Hamilton, Kersten. 2017. (Gadgets & Gears Ser.: 3). (ENG.). 144p. (J). (gr. 3-7). pap. 6.99 *(978-0-544-93715-4(5),* 1658349, HMH Books For Young Readers) Houghton Mifflin Harcourt Publishing Co.
Hamilton, Jan. Mr. How Do You Do Learns to Pray: Teaching Children the Joy & Simplicity of Prayer (Spanish Edition) Johnson, Kelly. Scruggs, Kathy, tr. 2016. (Mr. How Do You Do Ser.: Vol. 1). (SPA.). (J). (gr. k-6). pap. 15.95 *(978-1-61314-341-4(9))* Innovo Publishing, LLC.
Hamilton, John. The Girl Who Really Really Really Loves Dinosaurs. 2018. (ENG.). 28p. (J). (gr. -1-k). pap. 10.99 *(978-0-565-09459-1(9))* Natural History Museum Pubns. GBR. Dist: Independent Pubs. Group.
Hamilton, John C., photos by. Lewis & Clark: An Illustrated Journey. Hamilton, John C. 2003. 192p. (J). 28.00 *(978-0-9719304-2-1(2))* Sparrow Media Group, Inc.
Hamilton, Julie, jt. illus. see Lionni, Leo.
Hamilton, Meredith. A Child's Introduction to Art: The World's Greatest Paintings & Sculptures. Alexander, Heather. 2014. (Child's Introduction Ser.). 96p. (J). (gr. -1-17). 19.99 *(978-1-57912-956-9(0),* 81956, Black Dog & Leventhal Pubs. Inc.) Hachette Bks.
—A Child's Introduction to Greek Mythology: The Stories of the Gods, Goddesses, Heroes, Monsters, & Other Mythical Creatures. Alexander, Heather. 2011. (Child's Introduction Ser.). 96p. (J). (gr. 3-7). 19.99 *(978-1-57912-867-8(X),* 81867, Black Dog & Leventhal Pubs. Inc.) Hachette Bks.
—A Child's Introduction to Natural History: The Story of Our Living Earth-From Amazing Animals & Plants to Fascinating Fossils & Gems. Alexander, Heather. 2016. (Child's Introduction Ser.). 96p. (J). (gr. 3-7). 19.99 *(978-0-316-31136-6(7),* Black Dog & Leventhal Pubs. Inc.) Hachette Bks.
—A Child's Introduction to Norse Mythology: Odin, Thor, Loki, & Other Viking Gods, Goddesses, Giants, & Monsters. Alexander, Heather. 2018. (Child's Introduction Ser.). 96p. (J). (gr. 3-7). 19.99 *(978-0-316-48215-8(3),* Black Dog & Leventhal Pubs. Inc.) Hachette Bks.
—A Child's Introduction to the Orchestra (Revised & Updated) Listen to 37 Selections While You Learn about the Instruments, the Music, & the Composers Who Wrote the Music! Levine, Robert. rev. ed. 2019. (Child's Introduction Ser.). 96p. (J). (gr. 3-7). 19.99 *(978-0-7624-9547-4(2),* Black Dog & Leventhal Pubs. Inc.) Running Pr.
—A Child's Introduction to the World: Geography, Cultures, & People — From the Grand Canyon to the Great Wall of China. Alexander, Heather. 2010. (Child's Introduction Ser.). 96p. (J). (gr. -1-17). 19.99 *(978-1-57912-832-6(7),* 81832, Black Dog & Leventhal Pubs. Inc.) Hachette Bks.
—They're Poets & They Know It! A Collection of 30 Timeless Poems. 2007. 31p. (J). pap. *(978-0-545-03017-5(X))* Scholastic, Inc.
Hamilton, Michael. Hands-on English. Hamilton, Fran Santoro. 2nd l.t. ed. 2004. 192p. per. 14.95 *(978-0-9664867-5-9(7))* Portico Bks.
Hamilton, Pamela. Phonics Comics: Pony Tales - Level 1. Gaydos, Nora. 2007. (ENG.). 24p. (J). (gr. 1-17). per. 3.99 *(978-1-58476-553-0(4))* Innovative Kids.
Hamilton, Piky, jt. illus. see Lavina, Zulema Scotto.
Hamilton, Prissy. A Rainbow Within: An Introduction to the Emotional Energies for Children. Hamilton, Prissy. Hamilton, Prissy, ed. 2005. (J). pap. 14.00 *(978-0-9655933-1-1(2))* IGMI Publishing.
Hamilton, S. D. Wanted Letters PH: Fun with Phonics - How Ironic! Hamilton, S. D. 2017. (ENG.). (J). pap. *(978-0-9916747-3-2(1))* Sanham Works.
Hamilton, William. What I Love about My Pet: You Fill in the Blanks. Hamilton, Sommer. 2020. (ENG.). 58p. (J). pap. 12.28 ***(978-1-9782-5700-9(7))*** CreateSpace Independent Publishing Platform.
Hamlin, Janet. Blasts of Gas: The Secrets of Breathing, Burping, & Farting. Stewart, Melissa. 2010. (Gross & Goofy Body Ser.). 48p. (gr. 3-3). 30.93 *(978-0-7614-4155-7(7))* Cavendish Square Publishing LLC.
—The Eyes Have It: The Secrets of Eyes & Seeing. Stewart, Melissa. 2010. (Gross & Goofy Body Ser.). 48p. (gr. 3-3). 30.93 *(978-0-7614-4167-0(0))* Cavendish Square Publishing LLC.
—Give Me a Hand: The Secrets of Hands, Feet, Arms, & Legs. Stewart, Melissa. 2011. (Gross & Goofy Body Ser.). 48p. (gr. 3-3). lib. bdg. 30.93 *(978-0-7614-4158-8(1))* Cavendish Square Publishing LLC.
—Here We Grow: The Secrets of Hair & Nails. Stewart, Melissa. 2011. (Gross & Goofy Body Ser.). 48p. (gr. 3-3). 30.93 *(978-0-7614-4172-4(7))* Cavendish Square Publishing LLC.
—It's Spit-Acular! The Secrets of Saliva. Stewart, Melissa. 2010. (Gross & Goofy Body Ser.). 48p. (gr. 3-3). 30.93 *(978-0-7614-4163-2(8))* Cavendish Square Publishing LLC.
—The Kids' Yoga Book of Feelings, 1 vol. Frost, Michael, photos by. Humphrey, Mary. 2008. (ENG.). 40p. (J). (gr. 3-7). 15.99 *(978-0-7614-5424-3(1))* Marshall Cavendish Corp.
—Moving & Grooving: The Secrets of Muscles & Bones. Stewart, Melissa. 2011. (Gross & Goofy Body Ser.). 48p. (gr. 3-3). 30.93 *(978-0-7614-4166-3(2))* Cavendish Square Publishing LLC.
—Musical Genius: A Story about Wolfgang Amadeus Mozart. Allman, Barbara. 2004. (Creative Minds Biographies Ser.). (ENG.). 64p. (gr. 4-8). (J). per. 9.99 *(978-1-57505-637-1(2));* 22.60 *(978-1-57505-604-3(6))* Lerner Publishing Group.
—Now Hear This! The Secrets of Ears & Hearing. Stewart, Melissa. 2010. (Gross & Goofy Body Ser.). 48p. (gr. 3-3). 30.93 *(978-0-7614-4161-8(1))* Cavendish Square Publishing LLC.
—Pump It Up! The Secrets of the Heart & Blood. Stewart, Melissa. 2010. (Gross & Goofy Body Ser.). 48p. (gr. 3-3). 30.93 *(978-0-7614-4164-9(6))* Cavendish Square Publishing LLC.
—The Skin You're In: The Secrets of Skin. Stewart, Melissa. 2011. (Gross & Goofy Body Ser.). 48p. (gr. 3-3). 30.93 *(978-0-7614-4169-4(7))* Cavendish Square Publishing LLC.
—Up Your Nose! The Secrets of Schnozes & Snouts. Stewart, Melissa. 2010. (Gross & Goofy Body Ser.). 48p. (gr. 3-3). 30.93 *(978-0-7614-4170-0(0))* Cavendish Square Publishing LLC.
—You've Got Nerve! The Secrets of the Brain & Nerves. Stewart, Melissa. 2011. (Gross & Goofy Body Ser.). 48p. (gr. 3-3). 30.93 *(978-0-7614-4157-1(3))* Cavendish Square Publishing LLC.
Hamlin, Janet L. Germ Wars! The Secrets of the Immune System. Stewart, Melissa. 2011. (Gross & Goofy Body Ser.). 48p. (gr. 3-3). 30.93 *(978-0-7614-4165-6(4))* Cavendish Square Publishing LLC.
Hamm, Jolie. My Name Is Squirt. Tobin, Sharon. 2016. (ENG.). (J). pap. *(978-0-9950013-0-5(8))* SHAMIK FARM PUBLISHING.
—My Name Is Squirt Coloring Book Pages. Tobin, Sharon. 2016. (ENG.). (J). pap. *(978-0-9950013-3-6(2))* SHAMIK FARM PUBLISHING.
Hammack, Debi. Eerey Tocsin in the Cryptoid Zoo. Olson, Kevin Noel. 2006. (ENG.). 176p. (YA). per. 15.95 *(978-1-887560-17-7(3),* Cornerstone Bk. Publishers) Cornerstone Bk. Pubs.
Hammack, Sandra. A Walk with Papa. Zemanick, Patty. 2006. pap. 14.95 *(978-0-9788289-0-5(9))* Dragonfly Ministries.
Hammah, Aisha. A Family Secret. Green, Judith. 2013. 32p. pap. *(978-0-9810759-7-6(5))* WTL International.
Hammah, Aisha. The Image Game. Hammah, Aisha. Stubblefield, Linda, ed. 2013. 192p. pap. *(978-0-9810759-8-3(3));* pap. *(978-0-9810759-3-8(2))* WTL International.
Hammer, Susie. All Kids Are Good Kids. Carey Nevin, Judy. 2019. (ENG.). 26p. (J). (gr. -1 — 1). bds. 7.99 *(978-1-5344-3204-8(3),* Little Simon) Little Simon.
Hammer, Susie. All Kinds of Kindness. Carey Nevin, Judy. 2020. (ENG.). 26p. (J). (gr. -1 — 1). bds. 7.99 ***(978-1-5344-3206-2(X),*** Little Simon) Little Simon.
Hammer, Susie. Construction Zoo. Thorne, Jenn Marie & Thorne, Jennifer. 2018. (ENG.). 32p. (J). (gr. -1-3). 16.99 *(978-0-8075-1282-1(6),* 807512826) Whitman, Albert & Co.
—Happy Heart. Eliot, Hannah. 2019. (ENG.). 14p. (J). (gr. -1-k). bds. 7.99 *(978-1-5344-3202-4(7),* Little Simon) Little Simon.
Hammer, Susie. Happy Rainbow. Eliot, Hannah. 2020. (ENG.). 14p. (J). (gr. -1-k). bds. 7.99 ***(978-1-5344-3203-1(5),*** Little Simon) Little Simon.
Hammerquist, Theresa. My Daddy Makes the Best Motorcycles in the Whole Wide World, the Harley-Davidson. Davidson, Jean. 2004. (J). 16.95 *(978-1-930596-26-9(X))* Amherst Pr.
Hammersley, Karen. Sparkles Meets the Easter Bunny: The Adventures of Sparkles. Wellings, Chris R. 2011. 48p. pap. 24.95 *(978-1-4560-7063-2(0))* America Star Bks.
Hammerstrom, Kent. The Adventures of Sunny & the Chocolate Dog: Sunny & the Chocolate Dog Go to the Beach. Neimark, Susie. 2003. per. *(978-0-9725945-1-6(5))* Sunny & The Chocolate Dog, LLC.
—The Adventures of Sunny & the Chocolate Dog: Sunny & the Chocolate Dog Go to the Doctor. Neimark, Susie. 2003. per. *(978-0-9725945-2-3(3))* Sunny & The Chocolate Dog, LLC.
—The Adventures of Sunny & the Chocolate Dog: Sunny Meets Her Baby Sister. Neimark, Susie. 2003. per. *(978-0-9725945-0-9(7))* Sunny & The Chocolate Dog, LLC.
Hammes, Karalee. Rosie & Me. Shepherd, Joy. 2019. (Book Ser.: Vol. 3). (ENG.). 26p. (J). pap. 11.99 *(978-1-7942-4253-1(8))* Independently Published.
Hammond, Andy. Alf Saves the Day. Peet, Mal. 2004. (ENG.). 24p. (J). lib. bdg. 23.65 *(978-1-59646-692-0(8))* Dingles & Co.
—A Day Out: Band 02A/Red a (Collins Big Cat) Owen, Anna. 2005. (Collins Big Cat Ser.). (ENG.). 16p. (J). (gr. -1-k). pap. 6.99 *(978-0-00-718555-9(3))* HarperCollins Pubs. Ltd. GBR. Dist: Independent Pubs. Group.
—Fourth-Grade Fuss. Hurwitz, Johanna. 2004. 144p. (J). lib. bdg. 16.89 *(978-0-06-052344-2(1));* (ENG.). (gr. 3-7). 16.99 *(978-0-06-052343-5(3))* HarperCollins Pubs.
—The Muffin Man. Blane, Francisco. 2010. (Rising Readers Ser.). (J). 3.49 *(978-1-60719-691-4(3))* Newmark Learning LLC.
Hammond, Barbara. The Duffy Chronicles. Hammond, Barbara, . 2007. 60p. pap. 11.99 *(978-0-9800675-4-5(5))* Mirror Publishing.
Hammond, Julie. Birds in the Flower Basket. Kelso, Mary Jean. 2012. 26p. 19.95 *(978-1-61633-343-0(X))* Guardian Angel Publishing, Inc.
—Hockey Agony. McDine, Donna M. 2013. 20p. pap. 9.95 *(978-1-61633-360-7(X))* Guardian Angel Publishing, Inc.
—Riley's Heart MacHine. Jones, Lori M. 2012. 16p. pap. 9.95 *(978-1-61633-312-6(X))* Guardian Angel Publishing, Inc.
Hammond, Nancy Robinson. A Snug Little Island, Mara, Sarah Robinson. 2005. 60p. (J). 18.50 *(978-0-9766737-0-5(3))* Pink Granite Pr.
Hammond, Paul. Gary the Seagull, 1 vol. Johnston, Christian. 2020. (ENG.). 32p. (J). 9.95 ***(978-1-77108-836-7(2),*** e45906b0-7c7b-4585-b6a0-69141809ebed) Nimbus Publishing, Ltd. CAN. Dist: Baker & Taylor Publisher Services (BTPS).
Hammond, Steven. Ribbett the Frog. Latham, Jon. 2019. (ENG.). 48p. (J). pap. 11.95 ***(978-1-7322763-3-8(1))*** Latham, Jon Bks.
Hammond, Ted. What Is LEGO? Who HQ & O'Connor, Jim. 2020. (What Was? Ser.). 112p. (J). (gr. 3-7). (ENG.). 5.99 *(978-0-593-09294-1(5));* 15.99 *(978-0-593-09295-8(3))* Penguin Young Readers Group. (Penguin Workshop).
—What Is NASA? Fabiny, Sarah & Who HQ. 2019. (What Was? Ser.). 112p. (J). (gr. 3-7). (ENG.). 5.99 *(978-1-5247-8603-8(9));* 15.99 *(978-1-5247-8605-2(5))* Penguin Young Readers Group. (Penguin Workshop).
—What Was the San Francisco Earthquake? Hoobler, Dorothy et al. 2016. (What Was? Ser.). 112p. (J). (gr. 3-7). 5.99 *(978-0-399-54159-9(4),* Penguin Workshop) Penguin Young Readers Group.
—What Was the San Francisco Earthquake? Hoobler, Dorothy & Hoobler, Thomas. ed. 2016. (What Was... Ser.). (ENG.). 112p. (J). (gr. 3-7). 16.00 *(978-0-606-39329-4(3))* Turtleback.
—What Were the Twin Towers? Who HQ & O'Connor, Jim. 2016. (What Was? Ser.). 112p. (J). (gr. 3-7). lib. bdg. 15.99 *(978-0-399-54231-2(0),* Penguin Workshop) Penguin Young Readers Group.
—Where Is Our Solar System? Sabol, Stephanie & Who HQ. 2018. (Where Is? Ser.). (ENG.). 112p. (J). (gr. 3-7). 5.99 *(978-0-515-15818-2(6));* lib. bdg. 15.99 *(978-0-515-15820-5(8))* Penguin Young Readers Group. (Penguin Workshop).
—Where Is the Mississippi River? Anastasio, Dina & Who HQ. 2017. (Where Is? Ser.). 112p. (J). (gr. 3-7). 5.99 *(978-0-515-15824-3(0));* lib. bdg. 15.99 *(978-0-515-15826-7(7))* Penguin Young Readers Group. (Penguin Workshop).
—Who Is Bill Gates? Demuth, Patricia Brennan & Who HQ. 2013. (Who Was? Ser.). 112p. (J). (gr. 3-7). pap. 5.99 *(978-0-448-46332-2(6),* Penguin Workshop) Penguin Young Readers Group.
—Who Is George Lucas? Belviso, Meg et al. 2014. (Who Was? Ser.). 112p. (J). (gr. 3-7). 5.99 *(978-0-448-47947-7(8),* Penguin Workshop) Penguin Young Readers Group.
—Who Is Judy Blume? Anderson, Kirsten & Who HQ. 2018. (Who Was? Ser.). 112p. (J). (gr. 3-7). 5.99 *(978-0-448-48849-3(3));* (ENG.). lib. bdg. 15.99

(978-1-5247-8852-0(X)) Penguin Young Readers Group. (Penguin Workshop).
—Who Is Richard Branson? Burgan, Michael & Who HQ. 2015. (Who Was? Ser.). 112p. (J). (gr. 3-7). 5.99 (978-0-448-48315-3(7), Penguin Workshop) Penguin Young Readers Group.
—Who Is Richard Branson? Burgan, Michael. 2015. (Who Was-? Chapters Ser.). (ENG.). 112p. (J). (gr. 4-6). 18.69 (978-1-4844-6180-8(0)) Penguin Young Readers Group.
—Who Is Wayne Gretzky? Herman, Gail & Who HQ. 2015. (Who Was? Ser.). 112p. (J). (gr. 3-7). 5.99 (978-0-448-48321-4(1), Penguin Workshop) Penguin Young Readers Group.
—Who Was Babe Ruth? Holub, Joan & Who HQ. 2012. (Who Was? Ser.). 112p. (J). (gr. 3-7). pap. 5.99 (978-0-448-45586-0(2), Penguin Workshop) Penguin Young Readers Group.
—Who Was Cesar Chavez? Rau, Dana Meachen & Who HQ. 2017. (Who Was? Ser.). 112p. (J). (gr. 3-7). lib. bdg. 15.99 (978-0-451-53362-3(3), Penguin Workshop) Penguin Young Readers Group.
—Who Was Fidel Castro? Fabiny, Sarah & Who HQ. 2017. (Who Was? Ser.). 112p. (J). (gr. 3-7). 5.99 (978-0-451-53333-3(X)); lib. bdg. 15.99 (978-0-451-53335-7(6)) Penguin Young Readers Group. (Penguin Workshop).
—Who Was Henry Ford? Burgan, Michael. 2014. (Who Was-? Chapters Ser.). (ENG.). 112p. (J). (gr. 4-6). lib. bdg. 18.69 (978-1-4844-3671-4(7)) Penguin Young Readers Group.
—Who Was Henry Ford? Burgan, Michael & Who HQ. 2014. (Who Was? Ser.). 112p. (J). (gr. 3-7). 5.99 (978-0-448-47957-6(5), Penguin Workshop) Penguin Young Readers Group.
—Who Was Ida B. Wells? Fabiny, Sarah & Who HQ. 2020. (Who Was? Ser.). 112p. (J). (gr. 3-7). 5.99 (978-0-593-09335-1(6)); 15.99 (978-0-593-09336-8(4)) Penguin Young Readers Group. (Penguin Workshop).
—Who Was Marie Curie? Stine, Megan & Who HQ. 2014. (Who Was? Ser.). (ENG.). 112p. (J). (gr. 3-7). 5.99 (978-0-448-47896-8(X), Penguin Workshop) Penguin Young Readers Group.
—Who Was Milton Hershey? Buckley, James, Jr. et al. 2013. (Who Was? Ser.). (ENG.). 112p. (J). (gr. 3-7). 5.99 (978-0-448-47936-1(2), Penguin Workshop) Penguin Young Readers Group.
—Who Was Roberto Clemente? Buckley, James, Jr. et al. 2014. (Who Was? Ser.). 112p. (J). (gr. 3-7). 5.99 (978-0-448-47961-3(3), Penguin Workshop) Penguin Young Readers Group.
—Who Was Sally Ride? Stine, Megan & Who HQ. 2013. (Who Was? Ser.). 112p. (J). (gr. 3-7). pap. 5.99 (978-0-448-46687-3(2), Penguin Workshop) Penguin Young Readers Group.
—Who Was Sally Ride? Stine, Megan. 2013. (Who Was... ? Ser.). (ENG.). (J). (gr. 3-7). lib. bdg. 16.60 (978-1-68065-151-5(X)) Perfection Learning Corp.
—Who Was Sam Walton? Buckley, James, Jr. et al. 2019. (Who Was? Ser.). 112p. (J). (gr. 3-7). (ENG.). 5.99 (978-1-5247-9270-1(5)); 15.99 (978-1-5247-9271-8(3)) Penguin Young Readers Group. (Penguin Workshop).
—Who Were the Three Stooges? Pollack, Pam et al. 2016. (Who Was? Ser.). (ENG.). 112p. (J). (gr. 3-7). 5.99 (978-0-448-48866-0(3), Penguin Workshop) Penguin Young Readers Group.

Hammond, Ted & Carbajal, Richard. The Baseball Adventure of Jackie Mitchell, Girl Pitcher vs. Babe Ruth. Patrick, Jean L. S. 2011. (History's Kid Heroes Ser.). 32p. pap. 51.02 (978-0-7613-7635-4(6)); (ENG.). (J). (gr. 3-5). pap. 8.99 (978-0-7613-7072-7(2), 9780761370727) Lerner Publishing Group. (Graphic Universe™).
—The Horse-Riding Adventure of Sybil Ludington, Revolutionary War Messenger. Amstel, Marsha. 2011. (History's Kid Heroes Ser.). (ENG.). 32p. (J). (gr. 3-5). pap. 8.99 (978-0-7613-7073-4(0), 9780761370734, Graphic Universe™) Lerner Publishing Group.
—The Prairie Adventure of Sarah & Annie, Blizzard Survivors. Figley, Marty Rhodes. 2011. (History's Kid Heroes Ser.). (ENG.). 32p. (J). (gr. 3-5). pap. 8.99 (978-0-7613-7808-2(1), 9780761378082, Graphic Universe™) Lerner Publishing Group.
—The Prison-Ship Adventure of James Forten, Revolutionary War Captive. Figley, Marty Rhodes. 2011. (History's Kid Heroes Ser.). 32p. pap. 51.02 (978-0-7613-7637-8(2)); (ENG.). (J). (gr. 3-5). pap. 8.99 (978-0-7613-7075-8(7), 9780761370758) Lerner Publishing Group. (Graphic Universe™).
—The Rescue Adventure of Stenny Green, Hindenburg Crash Eyewitness. Ransom, Candice. 2011. (History's Kid Heroes Ser.). 32p. pap. 51.02 (978-0-7613-7638-5(0), Graphic Universe™) Lerner Publishing Group.
—The Rooftop Adventure of Minnie & Tessa, Factory Fire Survivors. Littlefield, Holly. 2011. (History's Kid Heroes Ser.). 32p. pap. 51.02 (978-0-7613-7639-2(9), Graphic Universe™) Lerner Publishing Group.

Hammond, Ted & Carbajal, Richard Pimentel. The Horse-Riding Adventure of Sybil Ludington, Revolutionary War Messenger. Amstel, Marsha. 2011. (History's Kid Heroes Set III Ser.). pap. 51.02 (978-0-7613-7636-1(4), Graphic Universe™) Lerner Publishing Group.
—The Prairie Adventure of Sarah & Annie, Blizzard Survivors. Figley, Marty Rhodes. 2011. (History's Kid Heroes Set III Ser.). pap. 51.02 (978-0-7613-8621-6(1), Graphic Universe™) Lerner Publishing Group.
—The Underground Adventure of Arly Dunbar, Cave Explorer. Ransom, Candice. 2011. (History's Kid Heroes Set III Ser.). pap. 51.02 (978-0-7613-7640-8(2), Graphic Universe™) Lerner Publishing Group.
—The Underground Railroad Adventure of Allen Jay, Antislavery Activist. Brill, Marlene Targ. 2011. (History's Kid Heroes Set III Ser.). pap. 51.02 (978-0-7613-8622-3(X), Graphic Universe™) Lerner Publishing Group.

Hammond, The Boy Fitz. A Mumbelievable Challenge. Lowe, Dave. 2017. (Incredible Dadventure Ser.: 2). (ENG.). 192p. (J). (gr. 2-4). pap. 8.99 (978-1-84812-589-6(5)) Bonnier Publishing GBR. Dist: Independent Pubs. Group.
—The Spring Break Prank War. Hernandez, Christopher. 2015. 32p. (J). (978-0-545-83030-0(3)) Scholastic, Inc.

Hammons, Barbara. Alphabetland the Beginning. McAtee, Rick. 2005. 48p. (J). 12.95 (978-0-9762030-0-1(6)) Turning a New Page.
—Alphabetland the Story of R. McAtee, Rick. ed. 2005. (J). 14.95 (978-0-9762030-1-8(4), 1000) Turning a New Page.

Hammons, Mark. My Grandma Calls Me Lovey. Hartman, Colleen Kelley. 2011. pap. 19.95 (978-1-934333-26-6(3)) Eagle Bk. Bindery.

Hamp, Georgia. Lady Lucy's Ghost Quest. Gross, Karen. 2019. (ENG.). 56p. (J). (gr. k-6). pap. 18.00 **(978-1-60571-509-4(3)**, Shires Press) Northshire Pr.

Hample, Stoo, jt. illus. see Hample, Stuart E.

Hample, Stuart E. & Hample, Stoo. The Silly Book. Hample, Stuart E. & Hample, Stoo. 2010. 32p. (J). (gr. -1-3). 16.99 (978-0-7636-4124-5(3)) Candlewick Pr.

Hampton, Chasity. Dream Sweet Baby. Tuck, Kioka C. 2019. (ENG.). 26p. (J). pap. 12.16 **(978-1-0803-8873-8(7))** Independently Published.

Hampton, David. Living in India. Thomson, Ruth. 2006. (Living In- Ser.). 32p. (J). (gr. 4-7). lib. bdg. 27.10 (978-1-59771-046-6(6)) Sea-To-Sea Pubns.

Hampton, David, photos by. Living in Kenya. Thomson, Ruth. 2006. (Living In- Ser.). 32p. (J). (gr. 4-7). lib. bdg. 27.10 (978-1-59771-044-2(X)) Sea-To-Sea Pubns.
—Living in Spain. Kent, Su. 2006. (Living In- Ser.). 32p. (J). (gr. 4-7). lib. bdg. 27.10 (978-1-59771-048-0(2)) Sea-To-Sea Pubns.

Hampton, David, photos by. Living in Australia. Hampton, David. 2006. (Living In- Ser.). 32p. (J). (gr. 4-7). lib. bdg. 27.10 (978-1-59771-041-1(5), 1268834) Sea-To-Sea Pubns.

Hampton, John. Gene Autry & the Golden Stallion. Fannin, Cole. 2011. 284p. 48.95 (978-1-258-02563-2(9)) Literary Licensing, LLC.

Hampton, John W. Gene Autry & Arapaho War Drums. Patten, Lewis B. 2011. 280p. 47.95 (978-1-258-04495-4(1)) Literary Licensing, LLC.

Hampton, Lin. Bo & the Missing Dogs, 1 vol. Simmons, Lynn Sheffield. 2003. (Bo Ser.). (ENG.). 128p. (J). (gr. 3-6). 8.95 (978-1-58980-219-3(5), Pelican Publishing) Arcadia Publishing.
—Bo, the Famous Retriever, 1 vol. Simmons, Lynn Sheffield. 2003. (Bo Ser.). (ENG.). 128p. (J). (gr. 3-6). 10.95 (978-1-58980-217-9(9), Pelican Publishing) Arcadia Publishing.

Hampton, Patricia A. E. A Witchful Friend: An Amazing Tale of a Pumpkin. Hampton, Patricia A. E. 2020. (ENG.). 36p. (J). pap. 12.99 **(978-1-7294-4367-5(2))** Independently Published.

Hampton, Scott. Sky Horizon. Brin, David. 2007. (Colony High Ser.: Bk. 1). 120p. (YA). (gr. 6-18). 35.00 (978-1-59606-109-5(X)) Subterranean Pr.

Hamscher, Cory. Breaking up Is Venomous to Do! Van Lente, Fred. Paniccia, Mark, ed. 2007. (Spider-Man Ser.: No. 3). (ENG.). 24p. (J). (gr. 2-6). lib. bdg. 27.07 (978-1-59961-393-2(X), 13631, Marvel Age) Spotlight.
—Dust-up in Aisle Seven! Van Lente, Fred. Paniccia, Mark, ed. 2007. (Spider-Man Ser.: No. 3). (ENG.). 24p. (J). (gr. 2-6). lib. bdg. 27.07 (978-1-59961-394-9(8), 13632, Marvel Age) Spotlight.
—The Sinister Six. David, Erica. 2007. (Spider-Man Ser.: No. 2). (ENG.). 24p. (J). (gr. 2-6). lib. bdg. 27.07 (978-1-59961-216-4(X), 13628, Marvel Age) Spotlight.
—Vulture Hunt! McKeever, Sean. 2007. (Spider-Man Ser.: No. 2). (ENG.). 24p. (J). (gr. 2-6). lib. bdg. 27.07 (978-1-59961-217-1(8), 13629, Marvel Age) Spotlight.
—World War G. Van Lente, Fred. Paniccia, Mark, ed. 2007. (Spider-Man Ser.: No. 3). (ENG.). 24p. (J). (gr. 2-6). lib. bdg. 27.07 (978-1-59961-396-3(4), 13634, Marvel Age) Spotlight.

Hamzah, Layla. Man Labisa Thiyab Sanjub? Ataallah, Salma. 2017. (ARA.). 24p. (J). (978-9953-37-287-7(X)) Academia.

Han, Heung-gi. Let's Visit Korea. Han, Suzanne C. rev. ed. 2006. (ENG.). 34p. (J). 18.50 (978-1-56591-010-2(9)) Hollym International Corp.

Han, Joon-ho. Pinocchio. Collodi, Carlo. Cowley, Joy, ed. 2015. (World Classics Ser.). (ENG.). 32p. (gr. k-4). 26.65 (978-1-925246-17-9(5)); 7.99 (978-1-925246-69-8(8)); 26.65 (978-1-925246-43-8(4)) ChoiceMaker Pty. Ltd., The AUS. (Big and SMALL). Dist: Lerner Publishing Group.

Han, Joy. Little Guy Haiku: Life with Bailey, a Maltese. Han, John J. 2009. 48p. pap. 24.95 (978-1-61546-044-1(6)) America Star Bks.

Han, Kyung Eun. Hard Work, but It's Worth It: The Life of Jimmy Carter. Hegedus, Bethany. 2020. (ENG.). 40p. (J). (gr. -1-3). 18.99 (978-0-06-264378-0(9), Balzer & Bray) HarperCollins Pubs.

Han, Kyung Eun. Moonbeams: A Lullaby of the Phases of the Moon. Bausum, Ann. 2020. (ENG.). 40p. (J). (gr. -1-3). 17.99 **(978-1-4998-1033-2(4))** Little Bee Books Inc.

Han, Mylene. The Things I See & the Things I Do. Settel, Jim. 2013. 52p. pap. 19.95 (978-1-4787-0879-7(4)) Outskirts Pr., Inc.

Han, Oki S. Basho & Fox, 1 vol. Myers, Tim. 2005. (ENG.). 32p. (J). pap. 5.95 (978-0-7614-5190-7(0)) Marshall Cavendish Corp.
—Basho & the River Stones, 0 vols. Myers, Tim J. 2013. (ENG.). 34p. (J). (gr. 1-4). pap. 9.99 (978-1-4778-1682-0(8), 9781477816820, Two Lions) Amazon Publishing.
—K Is for Kabuki: A Japan Alphabet. Whelan, Gloria & Nolan, Jenny. 2009. (Discover the World Ser.). (ENG.). 40p. (J). (gr. 1-3). 17.95 (978-1-58536-444-2(4), 202169) Sleeping Bear Pr.

Han, Sadie. 12 Little Elves Visit California. Madson, Trish. 2017. (12 Little Elves Ser.: 3). (ENG.). 32p. (J). 16.99 (978-1-945547-11-9(1), 554711) Familius LLC.
—12 Little Elves Visit Oregon. Madson, Trish. 2017. (12 Little Elves Ser.: 4). (ENG.). 32p. (J). 16.99 (978-1-945547-10-2(3), 554710) Familius LLC.

Han, Soma. Land of Morning Calm: Korean Culture Then & Now. Stickler, John. 2003. (Land of Morning Calm Ser.). 32p. (J). (gr. 4-7). 16.95 (978-1-885008-22-0(8), Shen's Bks.) Lee & Low Bks., Inc.
—Land of Morning Calm: Korean Culture Then & Now. Stickler, John. 2014. (ENG.). 32p. (J). pap. 8.95 (978-1-885008-47-3(3), Shen's Bks.) Lee & Low Bks., Inc.

Han, Soma. Maya & the Turtle: A Korean Fairy Tale. Han, Soma. Stickler, John C. 2012. (ENG.). 32p. (J). (gr. -1-3). 14.95 (978-0-8048-4277-8(9)) Tuttle Publishing.

Han, SooJin. Nicknames. Kim, Cecil. 2014. (MySELF Bookshelf Ser.). (ENG.). 32p. (J). (gr. k-2). pap. 11.94 (978-1-60357-699-4(1)); lib. bdg. 25.27 (978-1-59953-664-4(1)) Norwood Hse. Pr.

Han, Than T. Media Ethics: Ethics, Law & Accountability in the Australian Media. Hendtlass, Jane & Nichols, Alan. 2003. (Ethics in Daily Life Ser.: 3). (ENG.). 80p. (Orig.). (C). pap. (978-0-908284-45-0(4)) Acorn Press, Ltd.

Han, Xuemei. Brave Little Mongolian Sisters. Han, Xuemei. 2007. (J). pap. 12.99 (978-0-9763168-7-9(0)) DigitalKu.
—The Radish & the Girl with Long Hair. Han, Xuemei. 2008. (J). per. (978-0-9763168-6-2(2)) DigitalKu.

Han, Yu-Mei. The Brave Servant: A Tale from China. Barchers, Suzanne. 2013. (Tales of Honor Ser.). (ENG.). 32p. (J). (gr. 1-3). pap. 8.99 (978-1-937529-57-4(6)); E-Book 39.99 (978-1-936163-89-2(6)) Red Chair Pr.
—Neil & Nan Build Narrative Nonfiction. Pelleschi, Andrea. 2014. (Writing Builders Ser.). (ENG.). 32p. (J). (gr. 2-4). pap. 11.94 (978-1-60357-560-7(X)); lib. bdg. 25.27 (978-1-59953-586-9(6)) Norwood Hse. Pr.
—Pulgarcito. Hillert, Margaret. 2018. (BeginningtoRead Ser.).Tr. of Tom Thumb. (SPA.). 32p. (J). (gr. -1-2). pap. 11.94 (978-1-68404-244-9(5)) Norwood Hse. Pr.

Han, Yu-Mei. Pulgarcito. Han, Yu-Mei. Hillert, Margaret & Del Risco, Eida. 2018. (BeginningtoRead Ser.).Tr. of Tom Thumb. (SPA.). 32p. (J). (gr. -1-2). lib. bdg. 22.60 (978-1-59953-960-7(8)) Norwood Hse. Pr.

Han, Yu-Mei, jt. illus. see Beam, Burgandy.

Han, Yu-Mei, jt. illus. see Jack Pullan.

Hanakata, Felia. Blue Ribbon Pup. Kim, Carol. 2019. (Doggie Daycare (Set Of 4) Ser.). (ENG.). 48p. (J). pap. 6.99 (978-1-63163-328-7(7), 1631633287); lib. bdg. 24.27 (978-1-63163-327-0(9), 1631633279) North Star Editions. (Jolly Fish Pr.).
—Dog Sled Star. Kim, Carol. 2019. (Doggie Daycare (Set Of 4) Ser.). (ENG.). 48p. (J). pap. 6.99 (978-1-63163-332-4(5), 1631633325); lib. bdg. 24.27 (978-1-63163-331-7(7), 1631633317) North Star Editions. (Jolly Fish Pr.).
—Doggie Daycare (Set Of 4) Kim, Carol. 2019. (Doggie Daycare (Set Of 4) Ser.). (ENG.). 192p. (J). pap. 27.96 (978-1-63163-324-9(4), 1631633244); lib. bdg. 97.08 (978-1-63163-323-2(6), 1631633236) North Star Editions. (Jolly Fish Pr.).
—Library Buddy. Kim, Carol. 2019. (Doggie Daycare (Set Of 4) Ser.). (ENG.). 48p. (J). pap. 6.99 (978-1-63163-336-2(8), 1631633368); lib. bdg. 24.27 (978-1-63163-335-5(X), 163163335X) North Star Editions. (Jolly Fish Pr.).
—A Little Colt. Wren, Rosalee. Cottage Door Press, ed. 2019. (ENG.). 10p. (J). (gr. -1-k). bds. 4.99 (978-1-68052-777-3(0), 1005000) Cottage Door Pr.
—Most Valuable Puppy. Kim, Carol. 2019. (Doggie Daycare (Set Of 4) Ser.). (ENG.). 48p. (J). pap. 6.99 (978-1-63163-340-9(6), 1631633406); lib. bdg. 24.27 (978-1-63163-339-3(2), 1631633392) North Star Editions. (Jolly Fish Pr.).

Hanako Momohara, Emily. In Summer/en Verano. Madinabeitia Manso, Susana. 2018. (Seasons/Estaciones Ser.). (ENG.). 14p. (J). (— 1). bds. 7.99 (978-1-936669-64-6(1)) Blue Manatee Press.

Hanan, Yaakov. Di Geshikhte Fun Kriyes Yam Suf: Mitgelebt Loyt Di Hayntige Velt. Safra, M. 2017. (YID.). 64p. (J). (978-1-68091-170-1(8)) Kinder Shpiel USA, Inc.

Hanawalt, Josh. Grammy's Curtain Calls, 1 vol. Dierenfeldt, Jane. 2010. 22p. 24.95 (978-1-4512-1051-4(5)) PublishAmerica, Inc.
—A Time for Everything. Dierenfeldt, Jane. 2012. 36p. 24.95 (978-1-4626-6146-6(7)) America Star Bks.

Hanawalt, Lisa. Benny's Brigade. Bradford, Arthur. 2012. 48p. (J). 19.95 (978-1-936365-61-6(8), 467ba46e-e7ae-4872-9075-07a7d3f30dd7) McSweeney's Publishing.

Hancher, Adam. The Little Pioneer. Hancher, Adam. 2018. (ENG.). 32p. (J). (gr. -1-3). 17.99 (978-1-5247-1792-6(4), Doubleday Bks. for Young Readers) Random Hse. Children's Bks.

Hancock, Anna. Bananas in My Tummy, 1 vol. Dale, Jay. 2012. (Engage Literacy Yellow Ser.). (ENG.). 32p. (gr. k-2). pap. 5.99 (978-1-4296-8835-2(1), Capstone Pr.) Capstone.
—Big Green Crocodile, 1 vol. Dale, Jay. 2012. (Engage Literacy Blue Ser.). (ENG.). 32p. (gr. k-2). pap. 5.99 (978-1-4296-8984-7(6), Capstone Pr.) Capstone.
—In the Water, 1 vol. Giulieri, Anne. 2012. (Engage Literacy Magenta Ser.). (ENG.). 32p. (gr. k-2). pap. 5.99 (978-1-4296-8854-3(8), Capstone Pr.) Capstone.
—Min Monkey, 1 vol. Dale, Jay. 2012. (Engage Literacy Red Ser.). (ENG.). 32p. (gr. k-2). pap. 5.99 (978-1-4296-8944-1(7), Capstone Pr.) Capstone.
—My Body! What I Say Goes! Teach Children about Body Safety, Safe & Unsafe Touch, Private Parts, Consent, Respect, Secrets & Surprises. Sanders, Jayneen. 2017. (ENG.). 40p. (J). (gr. k-5). (978-1-925089-16-5(9), Educate2Empower Publishing) UpLoad Publishing Pty, Ltd.
—Up Here, 1 vol. Dale, Jay. 2012. (Engage Literacy Magenta Ser.). (ENG.). 32p. (gr. k-2). pap. 5.99 (978-1-4296-8862-8(9), Capstone Pr.) Capstone.

Hancock, David. First Encyclopedia of Dinosaurs - Internet Linked. Taplin, Sam. 2004. (First Encyclopedias Ser.). (ENG.). 64p. (J). (gr. 3-18). pap. 9.99 (978-0-7945-0696-4(8), Usborne) EDC Publishing.
—First Encyclopedia of Dinosaurs & Prehistoric Life: Internet-Linked. Taplin, Sam. 2004. (Usborne First Encyclopedia Library). 64p. (J). (gr. 2-18). lib. bdg. 17.95 (978-1-58086-657-6(3), Usborne) EDC Publishing.
—First Encyclopedia of the Human Body - Internet Linked. Chandler, Fiona. 2004. (First Encyclopedias Ser.). (ENG.). 64p. (J). (gr. 3-18). pap. 9.99 (978-0-7945-0695-7(X), Usborne) EDC Publishing.
—The Great World Search. Khanduri, Kamini. 2007. (Great Searches (EDC Hardcover) Ser.). 48p. (J). (gr. 3). lib. bdg. 16.99 (978-1-58086-966-9(1), Usborne) EDC Publishing.
—See Inside Ancient Egypt. Lloyd Jones, Rob. 2008. (Usborne Flap Book Ser.). 14p. (J). (gr. -1-3). bds. 12.99 (978-0-7945-2037-3(5), Usborne) EDC Publishing.
—See Inside Ancient Rome. Daynes, Katie. 2006. (See Inside Board Bks.). 16p. (J). (gr. 2-5). bds. 12.99 (978-0-7945-1321-4(2), Usborne) EDC Publishing.
—See inside Castles. Daynes, Katie. 2005. 16p. (J). 12.95 (978-0-7945-1022-0(1), Usborne) EDC Publishing.
—The Usborne First Encyclopedia of History. Chandler, Fiona et al. 2005. 64p. (J). (978-0-439-78717-8(3)) Scholastic, Inc.
—The Usborne Little Encyclopedia of Science: Internet-Linked. Firth, Rachel. 2006. 64p. (J). 6.99 (978-0-7945-1095-4(7), Usborne) EDC Publishing.
—Usborne the Great World Search. Khanduri, Kamini. rev. ed. 2005. (Great Searches (EDC Paperback) Ser.). 48p. (J). (gr. -1). pap. 8.99 (978-0-7945-1030-5(2), Usborne) EDC Publishing.

Hancock, David & Woodcock, John. First Encyclopedia of the Human Body: Internet-Linked. Chandler, Fiona. 2004. (Usborne First Encyclopedia Library). 64p. (J). (gr. 3-18). lib. bdg. 17.95 (978-1-58086-653-8(0), Usborne) EDC Publishing.
—The Usborne Little Encyclopedia of the Human Body: Internet-Linked. Chandler, Fiona. 2006. 64p. (J). (gr. 4-7). 6.99 (978-0-7945-1094-7(9), Usborne) EDC Publishing.

Hancock, David, jt. illus. see Bines, Gary.

Hancock House Publishers Staff. Wildlife Coloring Book. 2004. (Act Ser.). (ENG.). 24p. (J). pap. 4.95 (978-0-88839-599-3(X)) Hancock Hse. Pubs.

Hancock, Imojen Faith. Miss Lionheart & the Laboratory of Death. Ponder, A. J. 2019. (ENG.). 242p. (J). pap. 9.99 **(978-1-7001-6295-3(0))** Independently Published.

Hancock, James Gulliver. Airports, 1 vol. Lonely Planet Kids. 2020. (How Things Work Ser.). (ENG.). 26p. (J). (gr. -1 — 1). bds. 8.99 (978-1-83869-055-7(7), Lonely Planet Kids) Lonely Planet Global Ltd. IRL. Dist: Hachette Bk. Group.
—Cities, 1 vol. Lonely Planet Kids. 2020. (How Things Work Ser.). (ENG.). 26p. (J). (gr. -1 — 1). bds. 8.99 (978-1-83869-053-3(0), Lonely Planet Kids) Lonely Planet Global Ltd. IRL. Dist: Hachette Bk. Group.
—Engineered! Engineering Design at Work. Hunt, Shannon. 2017. (ENG.). 48p. (J). (gr. 3-7). 17.99 (978-1-77138-560-2(X)) Kids Can Pr., Ltd. CAN. Dist: Hachette Bk. Group.
—How Airports Work, 1 vol. Gifford, Clive et al. 2018. (How Things Work Ser.). (ENG.). 24p. (J). (gr. 1-3). 18.99 (978-1-78701-293-6(X), 5719) Lonely Planet Global Ltd. IRL. Dist: Hachette Bk. Group.
—How Airports Work Activity Book, 1 vol. Lonely Planet Kids. 2020. (How Things Work Ser.). (ENG.). 48p. (J). (gr. 1-3). 8.99 (978-1-83869-106-6(5), Lonely Planet Kids) Lonely Planet Global Ltd. IRL. Dist: Hachette Bk. Group.
—How Cities Work, 1 vol. Feroze, Jen & Lonely Planet Kids. 2016. (How Things Work Ser.). (ENG.). 24p. (J). (gr. 1-3). 18.99 (978-1-78657-022-2(X), 5192) Lonely Planet Global Ltd. IRL. Dist: Hachette Bk. Group.
—How Cities Work Activity Book, 1 vol. Lonely Planet Kids. 2020. (How Things Work Ser.). (ENG.). 48p. (J). (gr. 1-3). 8.99 (978-1-83869-104-2(9), Lonely Planet Kids) Lonely Planet Global Ltd. IRL. Dist: Hachette Bk. Group.

Hancock, James Gulliver. How Ships Work. Lonely Planet Kids & Gifford, Clive. 2020. (How Things Work Ser.). (ENG.). 24p. (J). (gr. 1-3). 18.99 **(978-1-83869-059-5(X)**, Lonely Planet Kids) Lonely Planet Global Ltd. IRL. Dist: Hachette Bk. Group.

Hancock, James Gulliver. How Trains Work, 1 vol. Lonely Planet Kids & Gifford, Clive. 2019. (How Things Work Ser.). (ENG.). 24p. (J). (gr. 1-3). 18.99 (978-1-78868-328-9(5)) Lonely Planet Global Ltd. IRL. Dist: Hachette Bk. Group.
—Meet Banjo Paterson. Weidenbach, Kristin. (J). 2016. 36p. (gr. k-2). 15.99 (978-0-85798-009-0(2)); 2015. (Meet... Ser.: Bk. 7). (ENG.). 32p. (gr. -1-k). 21.99 (978-0-85798-008-3(4)) Random Hse. Australia AUS. Dist: Independent Pubs. Group.
—Trains, 1 vol. Lonely Planet Kids. 2020. (How Things Work Ser.). (ENG.). 26p. (J). (gr. -1 — 1). bds. 8.99 (978-1-83869-057-1(3), Lonely Planet Kids) Lonely Planet Global Ltd. IRL. Dist: Hachette Bk. Group.
—Underworld: Exploring the Secret World Beneath Your Feet, 0 vols. Price, Jane. 2014. (ENG.). 96p. (J). (gr. 3-7). 18.95 (978-1-894786-89-8(0)) Kids Can Pr., Ltd. CAN. Dist: Hachette Bk. Group.

Hancock, Stefanie. Indian Legends of the Great Dismal Swamp. Traylor, Waverley. Traylor, Margaret, ed. 2004. 72p. (gr. 8-18). pap. 9.95 (978-0-9715068-3-1(3)) Traylor, Waverley Publishing.

Hancock, Uyen. Goodnight on the Farm. Hancock, Dennis. 2012. 28p. pap. 24.95 (978-1-4626-7233-2(7)) America Star Bks.
—The Tree House on the Bluff. Hancock, Dennis & Uyen. 2012. 36p. pap. 24.95 (978-1-4626-7318-6(X)) America Star Bks.
—What If There Are No Colors. Hancock, Dennis & Hancock, Shawn. 2012. 36p. pap. 24.95 (978-1-4626-7203-5(5)) America Star Bks.

H

Hancock, W. Allan. Amazing Animals: The Remarkable Things That Creatures Do. Ruurs, Margriet. 2011. (ENG.). 34p. (J). (gr. 1-4). 17.95 (978-0-88776-973-3(X), Tundra Bks.) Tundra Bks. CAN. Dist: Penguin Random Hse. LLC.

Hancocks, Helen. Penguin in Peril. Hancocks, Helen. 2014. (ENG.). 32p. (J). (gr. -1-2). 16.99 (978-0-7636-7159-4(2), Templar) Candlewick Pr.

Hand, Jason, jt. illus. see Golden Books Staff.

Handelman, Dorothy. The Pet Vet. Handelman, Dorothy, photos by. Leonard, Marcia, photos by. Leonard, Marcia. 2005. (ENG & SPA.). 32p. (J). (gr. -1-1). pap. 4.99 (978-0-8225-3299-6(9)) Lerner Publishing Group.

Handelman, Dorothy, photos by. Canciones de Monstruos. Eaton, Deborah. Translations.com Staff, tr. from ENG. 2007. (Lecturas para niños de verdad - Nivel 2 (Real Kids Readers - Level 2) Ser.).Tr. of Monster Songs. (SPA., 32p. (gr. k-3). per. 5.95 (978-0-8225-7803-1(4)) Lerner Publishing Group.

—Charley Waters Goes to Gettysburg. Sinnott, Susan. 2003. 48p. (J). (gr. 4-7). pap. 8.95 (978-0-7613-1887-3(9), Millbrook Pr.) Lerner Publishing Group.

—El Hombre de Hojalata. Leonard, Marcia. 2005. (ENG & SPA., 32p. (J). (gr. -1-1). pap. 4.99 (978-0-8225-3310-8(3)) Lerner Publishing Group.

—El Hombre de Hojalata: Nivel 1. Leonard, Marcia. 2005. (Lecturas para Niños de Verdad (Real Kids Readers) Ser.).Tr. of Tin Can Man. (SPA., 32p. (gr. 3-k). per. 5.95 (978-0-8225-3309-2(X), Ediciones Lerner) Lerner Publishing Group.

—Lo Haré Después. Tidd, Louise Vitellaro. Translations.com Staff, tr. from ENG. 2007. (Lecturas para niños de verdad - Nivel 2 (Real Kids Readers - Level 2) Ser.).Tr. of I'll Do It Later. (SPA., 32p. (gr. k-3). per. 5.95 (978-0-8225-7805-5(0)) Lerner Publishing Group.

—Lodo! Simon, Charnan. 2005.Tr. of Mud!. (ENG & SPA., 32p. (J). (gr. -1-1). pap. 4.99 (978-0-8225-3295-8(6)) Lerner Publishing Group.

—Lodo! Nivel 1. Simon, Charnan. 2005. (Lecturas para Niños de Verdad (Real Kids Readers) Ser.).Tr. of Mud!. (SPA., 32p. (J). (gr. 1-1). per. 5.95 (978-0-8225-3294-1(8), Ediciones Lerner) Lerner Publishing Group.

—Me Gusta el Desorden. Leonard, Marcia. Translations.com Staff, tr. from ENG. 2007. (Lecturas para niños de Verdad - Nivel 1 (Real Kids Readers - Level 1) Ser.).Tr. of I Like Mess. (SPA., 32p. (gr. k-2). per. 5.95 (978-0-8225-7800-0(X), Ediciones Lerner) Lerner Publishing Group.

—Me Gusta Ganar! Simon, Charnan. Translations.com Staff, tr. from ENG. 2007. (Lecturas para niños de Verdad - Nivel 1 (Real Kids Readers - Level 1) Ser.).Tr. of I Like to Win!. (SPA., 32p. (gr. k-2). per. 5.95 (978-0-8225-7801-7(8), Ediciones Lerner) Lerner Publishing Group.

—La Mejor Mascota. Tidd, Louise Vitellaro. 2007. (Lecturas para niños de verdad - Nivel 2 (Real Kids Readers - Level 2) Ser.).Tr. of Best Pet Yet. (SPA., 32p. (J). (gr. -1-3). per. 5.95 (978-0-8225-7804-8(2), Ediciones Lerner) Lerner Publishing Group.

—Mejores Amigas. Leonard, Marcia. 2005. (ENG & SPA., 32p. (J). (gr. -1-1). pap. 4.99 (978-0-8225-3291-0(3)) Lerner Publishing Group.

—Mejores Amigas: Nivel 1. Leonard, Marcia. 2005. (Lecturas para Niños de Verdad (Real Kids Readers) Ser.).Tr. of Best Friends. (SPA., 32p. (J). (gr. 1-1). per. 5.95 (978-0-8225-3290-3(5), Ediciones Lerner) Lerner Publishing Group.

—Mi Dia de Campamento. Leonard, Marcia. Translations.com Staff, tr. from ENG. 2007. (Lecturas para niños de Verdad - Nivel 1 (Real Kids Readers - Level 1) Ser.).Tr. of My Camp-Out. (SPA., 32p. (gr. k-2). per. 5.95 (978-0-8225-7798-0(4), Ediciones Lerner) Lerner Publishing Group.

—Pantalones Nuevos, No! Leonard, Marcia. 2005.Tr. of No New Pants!. 32p. (J). (ENG & SPA., (gr. -1-1). pap. 4.99 (978-0-8225-3297-2(2)); (SPA., (gr. 1-1). per. 5.95 (978-0-8225-3296-5(4), Ediciones Lerner) Lerner Publishing Group.

—Saltar, Brincar, Correr (Hop, Skip, Run) Leonard, Marcia. 2007. (Lecturas para niños de Verdad — Nivel 1 (Real Kids Readers — Level 1) Ser.). (SPA., 32p. (J). (gr. k-2). per. 5.95 (978-0-8225-7799-7(2), Ediciones Lerner) Lerner Publishing Group.

—Trae la Pelota, Tito. Leonard, Marcia. 2005.Tr. of Get the Ball, Slim. 32p. (J). (ENG & SPA., (gr. -1-1). pap. 4.99 (978-0-8225-3293-4(X)); (SPA., (gr. 1-1). per. 5.95 (978-0-8225-3292-7(1), Ediciones Lerner) Lerner Publishing Group.

—El Veterinario: Nivel 1. Leonard, Marcia. 2005. (Lecturas para Niños de Verdad (Real Kids Readers) Ser.).Tr. of Pet Vet. (SPA., 32p. (J). (gr. 1-1). per. 5.95 (978-0-8225-3298-9(0), Ediciones Lerner) Lerner Publishing Group.

—Ya Te Enteraste? Tidd, Louise Vitellaro. 2007. (Lecturas para niños de verdad - Nivel 2 (Real Kids Readers - Level 2) Ser.).Tr. of Did You Hear About Jake?. (SPA., 32p. (J). (gr. -1-3). per. 5.95 (978-0-8225-7802-4(6), Ediciones Lerner) Lerner Publishing Group.

Handford, Martin. Exciting Expeditions! Play! Search! Create Your Own Stories! Handford, Martin. 2019. (Where's Waldo? Ser.). (ENG.). 72p. (J). (gr. k-4). pap. 12.99 (978-1-5362-0670-8(9)) Candlewick Pr.

—Where's Waldo? Handford, Martin. (Where's Waldo? Ser.). (ENG.). (J). (gr. k-4). 2019. 36p. 8.99 (978-1-5362-1065-1(X)); 2011. 64p. pap. 9.99 (978-0-7636-5416-0(7)); 2nd ed. 2007. 32p. pap. 7.99 (978-0-7636-3498-8(0)); 30th anniv. ed. 2017. 36p. 7.99 (978-0-7636-9579-8(3)) Candlewick Pr.

—Where's Waldo? Deluxe Edition. Handford, Martin. 25th anniv. deluxe ed. 2012. (Where's Waldo? Ser.). (ENG.). 32p. (J). (gr. k-4). 16.99 (978-0-7636-4525-0(7)) Candlewick Pr.

—Where's Waldo? Destination: Everywhere! 12 Classic Scenes As You've Never Seen Them Before! Handford, Martin. 2017. (Where's Waldo? Ser.). (ENG.). 32p. (J). (gr. k-4). 19.99 (978-0-7636-9726-6(5)) Candlewick Pr.

—Where's Waldo? Double Trouble at the Museum: the Ultimate Spot-The-Difference Book. Handford, Martin. 2019. (Where's Waldo? Ser.). (ENG.). 32p. (J). (gr. k-4). 18.99 (978-1-5362-0139-0(1)) Candlewick Pr.

—Where's Waldo? Games on the Go! Puzzles, Activities, & Searches. Handford, Martin. 2018. (Where's Waldo? Ser.). (ENG.). 64p. (J). (gr. k-4). pap. 12.99 (978-1-5362-0155-0(3)) Candlewick Pr.

—Where's Waldo? in Hollywood. Handford, Martin. (Where's Waldo? Ser.). (ENG.). 32p. (J). (gr. k-4). 2020. 8.99 (978-1-5362-1306-5(3)); 2007. pap. 7.99 (978-0-7636-3501-5(4)); 2013. 16.99 (978-0-7636-4527-4(3)) Candlewick Pr.

—Where's Waldo? Paper Pandemonium. Handford, Martin. 2020. (Where's Waldo? Ser.). (ENG.). 96p. (J). (gr. k-12). pap. 12.99 (978-1-5362-1157-3(5)) Candlewick Pr.

Handford, Martin. Where's Waldo? Spooky Spotlight Search. Handford, Martin. 2020. (Where's Waldo? Ser.). (ENG.). 16p. (J). (gr. k-4). 18.99 **(978-1-5362-1158-0(3))** Candlewick Pr.

Handford, Martin. Where's Waldo? the Boredom Buster Book: 5-Minute Challenges. Handford, Martin. 2020. (Where's Waldo? Ser.). (ENG.). 220p. (J). (gr. k-4). 12.99 (978-1-5362-1145-0(1)) Candlewick Pr.

—Where's Waldo? the Coloring Collection. Handford, Martin. 2017. (Where's Waldo? Ser.). (ENG.). 80p. (J). (gr. k-12). pap. 12.99 (978-0-7636-9577-4(7)) Candlewick Pr.

—Where's Waldo? the Fantastic Journey. Handford, Martin. (Where's Waldo? Ser.). (ENG.). (J). (gr. k-4). 2019. 36p. 8.99 (978-1-5362-1097-2(8)); 2007. 32p. pap. 7.99 (978-0-7636-3500-8(6)) Candlewick Pr.

—Where's Waldo? the Fantastic Journey: Deluxe Edition. Handford, Martin. deluxe ed. 2013. (Where's Waldo? Ser.). (ENG.). 32p. (J). (gr. k-12). 16.99 (978-0-7636-4528-1(1)) Candlewick Pr.

—Where's Waldo? the Great Picture Hunt. Handford, Martin. (Where's Waldo? Ser.). (ENG.). 24p. (J). (gr. k-4). 2010. pap. 7.99 (978-0-7636-4215-0(0)); 2006. 15.99 (978-0-7636-3043-0(8)) Candlewick Pr.

—Where's Waldo? the Great Picture Hunt! Handford, Martin. 2020. (Where's Waldo? Ser.). (ENG.). 24p. (J). (gr. k-4). 8.99 (978-1-5362-1307-2(1)) Candlewick Pr.

—Where's Waldo? the Incredible Paper Chase. Handford, Martin. (Where's Waldo? Ser.). (ENG.). 24p. (J). (gr. k-4). 2011. pap. 7.99 (978-0-7636-4725-4(X)); 2009. 15.99 (978-0-7636-4689-9(X)) Candlewick Pr.

—Where's Waldo? the Magnificent Mini Boxed Set. Handford, Martin. 2013. (Where's Waldo? Ser.). (ENG.). 40p. (J). (gr. k-4). 19.99 (978-0-7636-4873-2(6)) Candlewick Pr.

—Where's Waldo? the Search for the Lost Things. Handford, Martin. 2012. (Where's Waldo? Ser.). (ENG.). 104p. (J). (gr. 2-5). pap. 12.99 (978-0-7636-5832-8(4)) Candlewick Pr.

—Where's Waldo? the Spectacular Spotlight Search. Handford, Martin. 2018. (Where's Waldo? Ser.). (ENG.). 16p. (J). (gr. k-4). 18.99 (978-1-5362-0176-5(6)) Candlewick Pr.

—Where's Waldo? the Sticker Book! Handford, Martin. 2015. (Where's Waldo? Ser.). (ENG.). 96p. (J). (gr. k-4). pap. 12.99 (978-0-7636-8128-9(8)) Candlewick Pr.

—Where's Waldo? the Totally Essential Travel Collection. Handford, Martin. 2017. (Where's Waldo? Ser.). (ENG.). 172p. (J). (gr. k-12). pap. 14.99 (978-0-7636-9580-4(7)) Candlewick Pr.

—Where's Waldo? the Treasure Hunt Activity Book. Handford, Martin. 2016. (Where's Waldo? Ser.). (ENG.). 96p. (J). (gr. 2-5). pap. 12.99 (978-0-7636-8811-0(8)) Candlewick Pr.

—Where's Waldo? the Wonder Book. Handford, Martin. 2020. (Where's Waldo? Ser.). (ENG.). 32p. (J). (gr. k-4). 8.99 (978-1-5362-1308-9(X)) Candlewick Pr.

—Where's Waldo? the Wonder Book: Deluxe Edition. Handford, Martin. 2014. (Where's Waldo? Ser.). (ENG.). 32p. (J). (gr. k-12). 16.99 (978-0-7636-4530-4(3)) Candlewick Pr.

—Where's Waldo? the Wow Collection: Six Amazing Books & a Puzzle. Handford, Martin. 2012. (Where's Waldo? Ser.). (ENG.). (J). (gr. k-4). 49.99 (978-0-7636-6179-3(1)) Candlewick Pr.

—Where's Waldo Now? Handford, Martin. (Where's Waldo? Ser.). (ENG.). 32p. (J). (gr. k-4). 2019. 8.99 (978-1-5362-1066-8(8)); 2007. pap. 7.99 (978-0-7636-3499-5(9)) Candlewick Pr.

—Where's Waldo Now? Deluxe Edition. Handford, Martin. 25th anniv. deluxe ed. 2012. (Where's Waldo? Ser.). (ENG.). 32p. (J). (gr. k-4). 16.99 (978-0-7636-4526-7(5)) Candlewick Pr.

Handley, David, photos by. I Love Gymnastics: School. Bray-Moffatt, Naia & Howard, Blanche. 2005. (DK Favorite Sports & Activities Ser.). (ENG., 48p. (J). (gr. k-3). 31.19 (978-0-7566-1011-1(7)) Dorling Kindersley Publishing, Inc.

Handy, Stephone. The Story of Jacob. Blair, Pamela. 2012. (ENG.). 34p. (J). pap. 9.99 **(978-0-9848104-4-4(7))** Fifth Ribb Publishing.

Hanes, Don, jt. illus. see Kopervas, Gary.

Hanke, Karen. Jazz Fly 2: The Jungle Pachanga. Gollub, Matthew. 2010. (J). (gr. k-2). (ENG.). 32p. 18.95 (978-1-889910-44-4(9)); (978-1-889910-45-1(7)) Tortuga Pr.

—Jazz Fly 3: The Caribbean Sea. Gollub, Matthew. 2020. (Jazz Fly Ser.: 3). (ENG.). 40p. (J). (gr. 2-4). 18.95 (978-1-889910-54-3(6)) Tortuga Pr.

—Monkey in the Story Tree. Williams, Rozanne Lanczak. 2006. (Learn to Write Ser.). 8p. (J). (gr. k-2). pap. 3.49 (978-1-59198-282-1(0), 6176) Creative Teaching Pr., Inc.

—Monkey in the Story Tree. Williams, Rozanne Lanczak. Maio, Barbara & Faulkner, Stacey, eds. 2006. (J). per. 6.99 (978-1-59198-333-0(9)) Creative Teaching Pr., Inc.

—Rhyme Time. Scelsa, Greg. Faulkner, Stacey, ed. 2006. (J). pap. 2.99 (978-1-59198-323-1(1)) Creative Teaching Pr., Inc.

Hankey, Ger. Lil' Lukie. Brennan, Christopher. 2017. (ENG.). 30p. (J). pap. (978-1-911596-69-1(1)) Spiderwize.

Hankinson, Kim. Cool Circuits & Wicked Wires: Special, Sparky Experiments! Martineau, Susan & Bushell, Nick. 2020. (Next Steps in STEM Ser.). (ENG.). 48p. (J). (gr. 2-6). pap. 9.99 (978-1-911509-95-0(0)) B Small Publishing GBR. Dist: Independent Pubs. Group.

—Slimy Science & Awesome Experiments: Amazing Tests & Tricks! Martineau, Susan. 2020. (Next Steps in STEM Ser.). (ENG.). 24p. (J). (gr. 2-7). pap. 9.99 (978-1-911509-94-3(2)) B Small Publishing GBR. Dist: Independent Pubs. Group.

Hankley, Patrick. Horace. Butler, Roberta. 2019. (ENG.). 24p. (J). 24.95 **(978-1-0980-1957-0(1))** Christian Faith Publishing.

Hanks, Carol. Emma & Allie. Slaughter, Kristi. 2009. 28p. pap. 12.49 (978-1-4389-9812-1(0)) AuthorHouse.

Hanley, John. W Is for Wrigley: A Friendly Confines Alphabet. Herzog, Brad. 2013. (ENG.). (J). (978-1-58536-816-7(4)) Sleeping Bear Pr.

Hanley, Sinéad & Hanley, Sinéad. Chooky-Doodle-Doo. Whiten, Jan. 2015. (ENG.). 32p. (J). (-k). 12.99 (978-0-7636-7327-7(7)) Candlewick Pr.

Hanley, Sinéad, jt. illus. see Hanley, Sinéad.

Hanley, Zachary. Ernie the Eagle Goes to Maine. Tata, Cb. 2012. 42p. 24.95 (978-1-4626-4545-9(3)) America Star Bks.

—Ernie the Eagle Goes to Texas. Tata, Cb. 2012. 44p. 24.95 (978-1-4626-5374-4(X)) America Star Bks.

Hanlon, Leslie. Traveling with Aunt Patty: Aunt Patty Visits London. Brundige, Patricia. Wright, Cindy, ed. Date not set. (J). (gr. 1-4). 12.95 (978-0-9659668-0-1(1)) Aunt Patty's Travels-London.

Hanmer, Clayton. Not Your Typical Book about the Environment. Kelsey, Elin. 2010. (ENG.). 64p. (J). (gr. 4-7). pap. 14.95 (978-1-897349-84-7(X), Owlkids) Owlkids Bks. Inc. CAN. Dist: Publishers Group West (PGW).

Hanna, Cheryl. Donavan's Word Jar. DeGross, Monalisa. 2018. (Trophy Chapter Bks.). (ENG.). 80p. (J). (gr. 1-5). pap. 4.99 (978-0-06-442089-1(2), Amistad) HarperCollins Pubs.

Hanna, Dan. Be Thankful, Pout-Pout Fish. Diesen, Deborah. 2019. (Pout-Pout Fish Mini Adventure Ser.: 10). (ENG.). 12p. (J). bds. 5.99 (978-0-374-30913-8(2), 900189661, Farrar, Straus & Giroux (BYR)) Farrar, Straus & Giroux.

—Happy Easter, Pout-Pout Fish. Diesen, Deborah. 2017. (Pout-Pout Fish Mini Adventure Ser.: 8). (ENG.). 12p. (J). bds. 5.99 (978-0-374-30400-3(9), 900158630, Farrar, Straus & Giroux (BYR)) Farrar, Straus & Giroux.

Hanna, Dan. Happy Hanukkah, Pout-Pout Fish. Diesen, Deborah. 2020. (Pout-Pout Fish Mini Adventure Ser.: 11). (ENG.). 12p. (J). bds. 5.99 **(978-0-374-30936-7(1),** 900189999, Farrar, Straus & Giroux (BYR)) Farrar, Straus & Giroux.

Hanna, Dan. Kiss, Kiss, Pout-Pout Fish. Diesen, Deborah. 2015. (Pout-Pout Fish Mini Adventure Ser.: 6). (ENG.). 14p. (J). (gr. -1 — 1). bds. 5.99 (978-0-374-30190-3(5), 900141730, Farrar, Straus & Giroux (BYR)) Farrar, Straus & Giroux.

—Lift-The-Flap Tab: Hide-and-Seek, Pout-Pout Fish. Diesen, Deborah. 2015. (Pout-Pout Fish Novelty Ser.). (ENG.). 18p. (J). (gr. -1 — 1). bds. 8.99 (978-1-250-06011-2(7), 900140949) Square Fish.

—The Not Very Merry Pout-Pout Fish. Diesen, Deborah. (Pout-Pout Fish Adventure Ser.). (ENG.). (J). 2017. 34p. bds. 7.99 (978-0-374-30459-1(9), 900159459); 2015. 32p. (gr. -1-1). 16.99 (978-0-374-35549-4(5), 900122565) Farrar, Straus & Giroux. (Farrar, Straus & Giroux (BYR)).

—The Pout-Pout Fish. Diesen, Deborah. (Pout-Pout Fish Adventure Ser.: 1). (ENG.). (J). (gr. -1 — 1). 2013. 34p. bds. 7.99 (978-0-374-36097-9(9), 900075215); 2008. 32p. 17.99 (978-0-374-36096-2(0), 900031428) Farrar, Straus & Giroux. (Farrar, Straus & Giroux (BYR)).

—The Pout-Pout Fish & the Bully-Bully Shark. Diesen, Deborah. (Pout-Pout Fish Adventure Ser.). (ENG.). 32p. (J). 2019. bds. 7.99 (978-0-374-31222-0(2), 900200299); 2017. 17.99 (978-0-374-30402-7(5), 900158632) Farrar, Straus & Giroux. (Farrar, Straus & Giroux (BYR)).

Hanna, Dan. The Pout-Pout Fish & the Can't-Sleep Blues. Diesen, Deborah. (Pout-Pout Fish Adventure Ser.). (ENG.). 32p. (J). 2020. bds. 8.99 **(978-0-374-31231-2(1),** 900200300); 2018. 17.99 (978-0-374-30403-4(3), 900158633) Farrar, Straus & Giroux. (Farrar, Straus & Giroux (BYR)).

Hanna, Dan. Pout-Pout Fish: Back to School. Diesen, Deborah. 2019. (Pout-Pout Fish Paperback Adventure Ser.). (ENG.). 24p. (J). 5.99 (978-0-374-31047-9(5), 900193159, Farrar, Straus & Giroux (BYR)) Farrar, Straus & Giroux.

—Pout-Pout Fish: Christmas Spirit. Diesen, Deborah. 2019. (Pout-Pout Fish Paperback Adventure Ser.). (ENG.). 24p. (J). 5.99 (978-0-374-31048-6(3), 900193160, Farrar, Straus & Giroux (BYR)) Farrar, Straus & Giroux.

—The Pout-Pout Fish Cleans up the Ocean. Diesen, Deborah. 2019. (Pout-Pout Fish Adventure Ser.: 4). (ENG.). 32p. (J). 17.99 (978-0-374-30934-3(5), 900189997, Farrar, Straus & Giroux (BYR)) Farrar, Straus & Giroux.

—Pout-Pout Fish: Easter Surprise. Diesen, Deborah. 2018. (Pout-Pout Fish Paperback Adventure Ser.). (ENG.). 24p. (J). 5.99 (978-0-374-31051-6(3), 900193163, Farrar, Straus & Giroux (BYR)) Farrar, Straus & Giroux.

—The Pout-Pout Fish, Far, Far from Home. Diesen, Deborah. (Pout-Pout Fish Adventure Ser.). (ENG.). 32p. (J). 2019. bds. 7.99 (978-0-374-31078-3(5), 900194752); 2017. 16.99 (978-0-374-30194-1(8), 900141733) Farrar, Straus & Giroux. (Farrar, Straus & Giroux (BYR)).

—The Pout-Pout Fish Giant Sticker Book: Over 1000 Stickers. Diesen, Deborah. 2016. (Pout-Pout Fish Novelty Ser.). (ENG.). 128p. (J). pap. 12.99 (978-1-250-06394-6(9), 900143401, Farrar, Straus & Giroux (BYR)) Farrar, Straus & Giroux.

—The Pout-Pout Fish Goes to School. Diesen, Deborah. (Pout-Pout Fish Adventure Ser.). (ENG.). (J). 2018. 34p. bds. 7.99 (978-0-374-30852-0(7), 900187130); 2014. 32p. (gr. -1-k). 17.99 (978-0-374-36095-5(2), 900085614) Farrar, Straus & Giroux. (Farrar, Straus & Giroux (BYR)).

—Pout-Pout Fish: Goes to the Dentist. Diesen, Deborah. 2020. (Pout-Pout Fish Paperback Adventure Ser.). (ENG.). 24p. (J). 5.99 (978-0-374-31049-3(1), 900193161, Farrar, Straus & Giroux (BYR)) Farrar, Straus & Giroux.

—Pout-Pout Fish: Goes to the Doctor. Diesen, Deborah. 2020. (Pout-Pout Fish Paperback Adventure Ser.). (ENG.). 24p. (J). 5.99 (978-0-374-31050-9(5), 900193162, Farrar, Straus & Giroux (BYR)) Farrar, Straus & Giroux.

—Pout-Pout Fish: Haunted House. Diesen, Deborah. 2019. (Pout-Pout Fish Paperback Adventure Ser.). (ENG.). 24p. (J). 5.99 (978-0-374-31052-3(1), 900193164, Farrar, Straus & Giroux (BYR)) Farrar, Straus & Giroux.

—The Pout-Pout Fish in the Big-Big Dark. Diesen, Deborah. (Pout-Pout Fish Adventure Ser.: 2). (ENG.). (J). (gr. -1-1). 2015. 34p. 7.99 (978-0-374-30189-7(1), 900141680); 2010. 32p. 17.99 (978-0-374-30798-1(9), 900064075) Farrar, Straus & Giroux. (Farrar, Straus & Giroux (BYR)).

—Pout-Pout Fish: Lucky Leprechaun. Diesen, Deborah. 2019. (Pout-Pout Fish Paperback Adventure Ser.). (ENG.). 24p. (J). 5.99 (978-0-374-31054-7(8), 900193165, Farrar, Straus & Giroux (BYR)) Farrar, Straus & Giroux.

—Pout-Pout Fish: Special Valentine. Diesen, Deborah. 2019. (Pout-Pout Fish Paperback Adventure Ser.). (ENG.). 24p. (J). 5.99 (978-0-374-31055-4(6), 900193166, Farrar, Straus & Giroux (BYR)) Farrar, Straus & Giroux.

—The Pout-Pout Fish Undersea Alphabet: Touch & Feel. Diesen, Deborah. 2016. (Pout-Pout Fish Novelty Ser.). (ENG.). 20p. (J). bds. 12.99 (978-1-250-06392-2(2), 900143400, Farrar, Straus & Giroux (BYR)) Farrar, Straus & Giroux.

—Pout-Pout Fish Wipe Clean Dot to Dot. Diesen, Deborah. 2017. (Pout-Pout Fish Novelty Ser.). (ENG.). 56p. (J). pap. 12.99 (978-0-374-30445-4(9), 900159360, Farrar, Straus & Giroux (BYR)) Farrar, Straus & Giroux.

—Smile, Pout-Pout Fish. Diesen, Deborah. 2014. (Pout-Pout Fish Mini Adventure Ser.: 1). (ENG.). 12p. (J). (gr. -1 — 1). bds. 5.99 (978-0-374-37084-8(2), 900122559, Farrar, Straus & Giroux (BYR)) Farrar, Straus & Giroux.

—Trick or Treat, Pout-Pout Fish. Diesen, Deborah. 2016. (Pout-Pout Fish Mini Adventure Ser.: 7). (ENG.). 12p. (J). 5.99 (978-0-374-30191-0(3), 900141731, Farrar, Straus & Giroux (BYR)) Farrar, Straus & Giroux.

—You Can Be Kind, Pout-Pout Fish! Diesen, Deborah. 2020. (Pout-Pout Fish Reader Ser.: 3). (ENG.). 24p. (J). 16.99 (978-0-374-31292-3(3), 900206792); pap. 4.99 (978-0-374-31293-0(1), 900206793) Farrar, Straus & Giroux. (Farrar, Straus & Giroux (BYR)).

—You Can Read, Pout-Pout Fish! Diesen, Deborah. 2020. (Pout-Pout Fish Reader Ser.: 4). (ENG.). 24p. (J). 16.99 (978-0-374-31288-6(5), 900206790); pap. 4.99 (978-0-374-31290-9(7), 900206791) Farrar, Straus & Giroux. (Farrar, Straus & Giroux (BYR)).

Hanna, Dan. 5-Minute Pout-Pout Fish Stories. Diesen, Deborah. 2020. (Pout-Pout Fish Mini Adventure Ser.: 12). (ENG.). 192p. (J). 12.99 **(978-0-374-31400-2(4),** 900223498, Farrar, Straus & Giroux (BYR)) Farrar, Straus & Giroux.

Hanna, Gary. Burrow. Spilsbury, Richard. 2013. (Look Inside Ser.). (ENG.). 32p. (J). (gr. 1-3). pap. 8.29 (978-1-4329-7200-4(6), Heinemann) Capstone.

—Cave. Spilsbury, Richard. 2013. (Look Inside Ser.). (ENG.). 32p. (J). (gr. 1-3). 27.99 (978-1-4329-7194-6(8)); pap. 8.29 (978-1-4329-7201-1(4)) Capstone. (Heinemann).

—Elephant. Costain, Meredith. 2016. (Wild World Ser.). 00032p. (J). (gr. 1-2). pap. 10.00 (978-1-4994-8206-5(X), Windmill Bks.) Rosen Publishing Group, Inc., The.

—Garbage Can. Spilsbury, Louise. 2013. (Look Inside Ser.). (ENG.). 32p. (J). (gr. 1-3). 27.99 (978-1-4329-7195-3(6)); pap. 8.29 (978-1-4329-7202-8(2)) Capstone. (Heinemann).

—Otter. Costain, Meredith. 2016. (Wild World Ser.). 00032p. (J). (gr. 1-2). pap. 10.00 (978-1-4994-8218-8(3), Windmill Bks.) Rosen Publishing Group, Inc., The.

—Penguin. Costain, Meredith. 2016. (Wild World Ser.). 00032p. (J). (gr. 1-2). pap. 10.00 (978-1-4994-8223-2(X), Windmill Bks.) Rosen Publishing Group, Inc., The.

—Pond. Spilsbury, Louise. 2013. (Look Inside Ser.). (ENG.). 32p. (J). (gr. 1-3). 27.99 (978-1-4329-7196-0(4)); pap. 8.29 (978-1-4329-7203-5(0)) Capstone. (Heinemann).

—Tide Pool. Spilsbury, Louise. 2013. (Look Inside Ser.). (ENG.). 32p. (J). (gr. 1-3). 27.99 (978-1-4329-7197-7(2)); pap. 8.29 (978-1-4329-7204-2(9)) Capstone. (Heinemann).

—Tree. Spilsbury, Richard. 2013. (Look Inside Ser.). (ENG.). 32p. (J). (gr. 1-3). 27.99 (978-1-4329-7198-4(0)); pap. 8.29 (978-1-4329-7205-9(7)) Capstone. (Heinemann).

Hannaford, Sharon. Adeline's Not-So-Boring Weekend. Hannaman, Norah S. 2019. (Adeline Ser.: Vol. 1). (ENG.). 88p. (J). pap. 8.50 **(978-1-7130-1587-1(0))** Independently Published.

Hannah, Byford. The Magical Shoe Tree. Mullett, Mary and Phil. 2016. (ENG.). (J). (978-1-78623-044-7(5)) Grosvenor Hse. Publishing Ltd.

Hannah Lane. A Frog Named Dude. 2007. 16p. (J). (978-0-9800870-0-0(7)) Robillard, Kristy.

Hannan, Peter. Freddy! Deep-Space Food Fighter. Hannan, Peter. 2011. (Freddy! Ser.: 2). (ENG.). 144p. (J). (gr. 2-6). pap. 5.99 (978-0-06-128468-7(8)) HarperCollins Pubs.

—Freddy! King of Flurb. Hannan, Peter. 2011. (Freddy! Ser.: 1). (ENG.). 160p. (J). (gr. 2-6). pap. 5.99 (978-0-06-128466-3(1)) HarperCollins Pubs.

—Freddy! Locked in Space, 2. Hannan, Peter. 2011. (Freddy! Ser.: 3). (ENG.). 160p. (J). (gr. 2-6). pap. 5.99 (978-0-06-128470-0(X)) HarperCollins Pubs.

—The Greatest Snowman in the World! Hannan, Peter. 2010. (ENG.). 32p. (J). (gr. -1-3). 16.99 (978-0-06-128480-9(7)) HarperCollins Pubs.

—Petlandia. Hannan, Peter. 2015. (ENG.). 144p. (J). (gr. 2-5). 8.99 (978-0-545-16211-1(4), Scholastic Pr.) Scholastic, Inc.

Hanner, Albert. Animales del Mar. Brewster, Joy. ed. 2011. (SPA.). 32p. (J). pap. 49.00 net. *(978-1-4108-2337-3(7),* A23377) Benchmark Education Co.
—From Caves to Canvas & de las cuevas a los Lienzos: 6 English, 6 Spanish Adaptations, 122 vols. Prigioniero, Lily. ed. 2011. (SPA.). (J). instr.'s gde. ed. 89.00 net. *(978-1-4108-2227-7(3),* 22273) Benchmark Education Co.
—Grandes inventos y cómo Surgieron. Glassman, Jackie. ed. 2011. (SPA.). (J). pap. 45.00 net. *(978-1-4108-2206-2(0),* 22060) Benchmark Education Co.
—Great Inventions & Where They Came from & Grandes inventos y cómo Surgieron: 6 English, 6 Spanish Adaptations, 122 vols. Glassman, Jackie. ed. 2011. (J). instr.'s gde. ed. 89.00 net. *(978-1-4108-2228-4(1),* 22281) Benchmark Education Co.
—Human Emotions & Las emociones Humanas: 6 English, 6 Spanish Adaptations, 122 vols., Vol. 2. Smith, Carrie. ed. 2011. (SPA.). (J). instr.'s gde. ed. 97.00 net. *(978-1-4108-2405-9(5),* 24055) Benchmark Education Co.
—Las emociones Humanas. Smith, Carrie. ed. 2011. (SPA.). 32p. (J). pap. 49.00 net. *(978-1-4108-2345-8(8),* A23458) Benchmark Education Co.
—Matemáticas en el Jardín. McCay, William. ed. 2011. (SPA.). (J). pap. 45.00 net. *(978-1-4108-2207-9(9),* 22079) Benchmark Education Co.
—Matemáticas en la Luna. Sullilvan, Erin. ed. 2011. (SPA.). (J). pap. 45.00 net. *(978-1-4108-2199-7(4),* 21994) Benchmark Education Co.
—Math in the Garden & Matemáticas en el Jardín: 6 English, 6 Spanish Adaptations, 122 vols. McCay, William. ed. 2011. (SPA.). (J). instr.'s gde. ed. 89.00 net. *(978-1-4108-2229-1(X),* 2229X) Benchmark Education Co.
—Math on the Moon & Matemáticas en la Luna: 6 English, 6 Spanish Adaptations, 122 vols., Vol. 2. Sullivan, Erin. ed. 2011. (SPA.). (J). instr.'s gde. ed. 89.00 net. *(978-1-4108-2221-5(4),* 22214) Benchmark Education Co.
—El mundo bajo las Olas. Brewster, Joy. ed. 2011. (SPA.). 32p. (J). pap. 49.00 net. *(978-1-4108-2339-7(3),* A23393) Benchmark Education Co.
—Stormy Weather And ¡Tormentas! 6 English, 6 Spanish Adaptations, 122 vols. Lunis, Natalie. ed. 2011. (SPA.). (J). instr.'s gde. ed. 89.00 net. *(978-1-4108-2224-6(9),* 22249) Benchmark Education Co.
—¡Tormentas! Lunis, Natalie. ed. 2011. (SPA.). (J). pap. 45.00 net. *(978-1-4108-2202-4(8),* 22028) Benchmark Education Co.
Hanner, Albert & Hortens, Mike. La genética de las Plantas. Cameron, Ken. ed. 2011. (SPA.). 32p. (J). pap. 49.00 net. *(978-1-4108-2341-0(5),* A23415) Benchmark Education Co.
Hannigan, Ed, et al. Cloak & Dagger Omnibus. 2020. (ENG.). 880p. (YA). (gr. 8-17). 100.00 ***(978-1-302-92466-9(4))*** Marvel Worldwide, Inc.
Hannigan, Katherine. Dirt + Water = Mud. Hannigan, Katherine. 2016. (ENG.). 40p. (J). (gr. -1-3). 17.99 *(978-0-06-234517-2(6),* Greenwillow Bks.) HarperCollins Pubs.
—Emmaline & the Bunny. Hannigan, Katherine. 2009. (ENG.). 112p. (J). (gr. 2-7). 16.99 *(978-0-06-162654-8(6),* Greenwillow Bks.) HarperCollins Pubs.
—Gwendolyn Grace. Hannigan, Katherine. 2015. (ENG.). 32p. (J). (gr. -1-3). 17.99 *(978-0-06-234519-6(2),* Greenwillow Bks.) HarperCollins Pubs.
Hannigan, Pauline, et al. International Primary Science Student's Book 1, Bk. 1. Baxter, Tracey et al. Miller, Jonathan & Pilling, Anne, eds. Robinson, Pete, tr. 2014. (Collins International Primary Science Ser.). (ENG.). 96p. (J). (gr. -1-k). pap., stu. ed. 12.95 *(978-0-00-758609-7(4))* HarperCollins Pubs. Ltd. GBR. Dist: Independent Pubs. Group.
—International Primary Science Student's Book 3. MacGregor, Fiona et al. Miller, Jonathan & Pilling, Anne, eds. Robinson, Pete, tr. 2015. (Collins International Primary Science Ser.). (ENG.). 96p. (J). (gr. 2). pap. 12.95 *(978-0-00-758616-5(7))* HarperCollins Pubs. Ltd. GBR. Dist: Independent Pubs. Group.
—International Primary Science Student's Book 5. Paizee, Daphne et al. Miller, Jonathan & Pilling, Anne, eds. Robinson, Pete, tr. 2015. (Collins International Primary Science Ser.). (ENG.). 96p. (gr. 4). pap., stu. ed. 12.95 *(978-0-00-758623-3(X))* HarperCollins Pubs. Ltd. GBR. Dist: Independent Pubs. Group.
Hannon, Holly. The Littlest Candlesticks. Rouss, Sylvia A. 2005. (Littlest Ser.). 32p. (J). 14.95 *(978-1-930143-48-7(6));* pap. 9.95 *(978-1-930143-49-4(4))* Simcha Media Group. (Devora Publishing).
—The Littlest Frog. Rouss, Sylvia A. 2005. 32p. (J). pap. 9.95 *(978-1-930143-13-5(3));* (gr. -1-1). 14.95 *(978-1-930143-12-8(5))* Simcha Media Group. (Devora Publishing).
—The Littlest Pair. Rouss, Sylvia A. 2005. 32p. (J). (gr. -1-1). 14.95 *(978-1-930143-17-3(6),* Devora Publishing) Simcha Media Group.
—The Littlest Pair. Rouss, Sylvia. 2005. 32p. (J). pap. 9.95 *(978-1-930143-18-0(4),* Devora Publishing) Simcha Media Group.
—The Littlest Pair, Vol. Rouss, Sylviaa01. 2015. (ENG.). 32p. (J). pap. 9.99 *(978-1-68115-505-0(2),* Apples & Honey Pr.) Behrman Hse., Inc.
—Sweet Pea: Escape in the Garden. Meachen Rau, Dana. 2006. (J). *(978-1-58987-200-4(2))* Kindermusik International.
Hannon, Kenneth, photos by. Without a Home. Grantner, Anne M. & Haggart, Gary. 2003. 35p. (YA). (gr. 5-18). pap. 12.95 *(978-0-9740929-0-4(8))* Shelter of Flint, Inc.
Hannon, Tara. Santa Claus Was Once a Kid Too / German Edition: Babl Children's Books in German & English. Scharper, Philip. l.t. ed. 2016. (ENG.). (J). 14.99 *(978-1-68304-199-3(2))* Babl Books, Incorporated.
Hannon, Tara J. Planes USA! Parker, Jo. 2020. 24p. (J). (— 1). bds. 9.99 ***(978-0-593-22369-7(1),*** Grosset & Dunlap) Penguin Young Readers Group.
Hans, Rhian & Ingo. The Flizkins Take Off: The Wooliest Aliens in the Universe. Hans, Rhian & Hans, Ingo. 2018. (ENG.). 106p. (J). (gr. 1-6). ***(978-1-9999506-1-3(5))*** Sebold's originals.
Hans, Stephanie. Loki: Where Mischief Lies. Lee, Mackenzi. 2019. (ENG.). 416p. (YA). (gr. 7-12). 17.99 *(978-1-368-02226-2(X),* Marvel Pr.) Disney Publishing Worldwide.
—The Magnificent Lizzie Brown & the Ghost Ship. Lockwood, Vicki. 2015. (Magnificent Lizzie Brown Ser.). (ENG.). 200p. (J). (gr. 5-9). lib. bdg. 26.65 *(978-1-4342-9806-5(X),* Stone Arch Bks.) Capstone.
—The Magnificent Lizzie Brown & the Mysterious Phantom, 1 vol. Lockwood, Vicki. 2014. (Magnificent Lizzie Brown Ser.). (ENG.). 200p. (J). (gr. 5-9). pap. 7.95 *(978-1-4342-7942-2(1),* Stone Arch Bks.) Capstone.
—The Outlaw of Sherwood Forest, 1 vol. Seven, John. 2014. (Time-Tripping Faradays Ser.). (ENG.). 192p. (J). (gr. 4-8). lib. bdg. 26.65 *(978-1-4342-9174-5(X),* Stone Arch Bks.) Capstone.
—The Terror of the Tengu, 1 vol. Seven, John. 2014. (Time-Tripping Faradays Ser.). (ENG.). 192p. (J). (gr. 4-8). 26.65 *(978-1-4342-9173-8(1),* Stone Arch Bks.) Capstone.
Hansell, Louis. Moody Mona Tells Scary Christmas Stories! Bradley, Kelly. 2020. (ENG.). 38p. (J). pap. 13.99 ***(978-1-7347046-1-7(6))*** New Montgomery Pr.
Hansell, Louis. Witch Rabbit. Bradley, Kelly Marie. 2016. (ENG.). (J). pap. 13.99 *(978-0-692-77662-9(1))* New Montgomery Pr.
Hansell, Louis. Zombie Spiders from Outer Space! Bradley, Kelly Marie. 2020. (ENG.). (J). pap. 13.99 ***(978-0-578-64136-2(4))*** New Montgomery Pr.
Hansen, Amelia. Are You Ready for Me? Buchwald, Claire. (Sit! Stay! Read! Ser.). (ENG.). 24p. (J). (gr. k-1). 2009. pap. 7.95 *(978-0-940719-08-8(8));* 2007. 15.95 *(978-0-940719-04-0(5))* Gryphon Pr., The.
—At the Dog Park with Sam & Lucy. Bix, Daisy. 2006. (Sit! Stay! Read! Ser.). (ENG.). 24p. (J). (gr. k-2). 15.95 *(978-0-940719-00-2(2))* Gryphon Pr., The.
—It's Raining Cats & Cats! Prevost, Jeanne. 2008. (ENG.). 24p. (J). (gr. k-2). 16.95 *(978-0-940719-06-4(1))* Gryphon Pr., The.
—It's Raining Pups & Dogs! 2013. (Sit! Stay! Read! Ser.). (ENG.). 24p. (J). (gr. k). 16.95 *(978-0-940719-16-3(9))* Gryphon Pr., The.
Hansen, Angela. Lovely Lily. Holzer, Angela. 2009. (ENG.). 36p. (J). lib. bdg. 8.99 *(978-0-9821563-2-2(4))* Good Sound Publishing.
Hansen, Bjarne. Light Brigade. Tomasi, Peter J. rev. ed. 2005. 200p. pap. 19.99 *(978-1-4012-0795-3(2))* DC Comics.
Hansen, Brenna. Good Night Long Island. Gamble, Adam & Jasper, Mark. 2020. (Good Night Our World Ser.). 20p. (J). (— 1). bds. 9.95 *(978-1-60219-849-4(7))* Good Night Bks.
Hansen, Christine. Watch Me Swim, 6 pack. Holden, Pam. 2009. (Red Rocket Readers Ser.). 16p. (gr. -1-1). pap. *(978-1-877363-31-3(6),* Red Rocket Readers) Flying Start Bks.
Hansen, Christine. Mira Como Nado. Hansen, Christine. Holden, Pam & Elias, Annette Torres. 2012.Tr. of Watch Me Swim. (SPA.). 16p. (gr. -1-1). pap. *(978-1-877506-90-1(7),* Red Rocket Readers) Flying Start Bks.
Hansen, Clint. The Christmas Flower. Ellis, Gwen. 2005. 32p. (J). (gr. -1-3). 9.99 *(978-1-59185-728-0(7))* Charisma Media.
—Dear Mr. Leprechaun: Letters from My First Friendship. Tanner, Dean, photos by. Burton, Martin Nelson. 2003. (ENG.). 32p. (J). 17.00 *(978-0-9666490-0-0(1))* London Town Pr.
—La Flor de Pascua. Ellis, Gwen. 2005. 32p. (J). (gr. -1-3). 8.99 *(978-1-59185-827-0(5),* Charisma Kids) Charisma Media.
—Fooling the Tooth Fairy. Tanner, Dean, photos by. Burton, Martin Nelson. 2005. (ENG.). 32p. (J). 17.00 *(978-0-9666490-2-4(8))* London Town Pr.
—Fooling the Tooth Fairy. Burton, Martin Nelson. 2005. (J). pap. *(978-0-9666490-3-1(6))* London Town Pr.
Hansen, Craig. This Is Lucy. Hansen, Craig. 2020. (ENG.). 42p. (J). (gr. k-4). pap. 16.00 ***(978-1-0878-6870-7(X))*** Hansen, Craig.
Hansen, Doug. The Sierra Adventure Coloring Book: Featuring Yosemite National Park. 2013. (ENG.). 24p. (J). (gr. -1-2). pap. 4.95 *(978-1-930238-39-8(8))* Yosemite Conservancy.
—The Super Silly Yosemite Sticker & Activity Book: Puzzles, Games, Mazes & More! Brumage, Katherine. 2011. (ENG.). 24p. (J). (gr. -1-5). 8.99 *(978-1-930238-80-0(0))* Yosemite Conservancy.
Hansen, Dustin. Microsaurs: Adventure Awaits. Hansen, Dustin. 2017. (Microsaurs Ser.: 1). (ENG.). 224p. (J). 13.99 *(978-1-250-09021-8(0),* 9781250090218) Feiwel & Friends.
—Microsaurs: Tiny-Raptor Pack Attack. Hansen, Dustin. 2017. (Microsaurs Ser.: 2). (ENG.). 240p. (J). 13.99 *(978-1-250-09025-6(3),* 9781250090256) Feiwel & Friends.
—Microsaurs: Beware the Tiny-Spino. Hansen, Dustin. 2019. (Microsaurs Ser.: 5). (ENG.). 224p. (J). 14.99 *(978-1-250-09035-5(0),* 900158987) Feiwel & Friends.
—Microsaurs: That's MY Tiny-Saurus Rex. Hansen, Dustin. 2018. (Microsaurs Ser.: 3). (ENG.). 224p. (J). 13.99 *(978-1-250-09029-4(6),* 9781250090294) Feiwel & Friends.
—Microsaurs: Tiny-Tricera Troubles. Hansen, Dustin. 2019. (Microsaurs Ser.: 6). (ENG.). 224p. (J). 14.99 *(978-1-250-09038-6(5),* 900158993) Feiwel & Friends.
—My Video Game Ate My Homework. Hansen, Dustin. 2020. (ENG.). 160p. (J). (gr. 3-7). pap. 9.99 *(978-1-4012-9326-0(3))* DC Comics.
—Tiny-Stego Stampede. Hansen, Dustin. 2018. (Microsaurs Ser.: 4). (ENG.). 224p. (J). 13.99 *(978-1-250-09032-4(6),* 900158984) Feiwel & Friends.
Hansen, Ernest. The Eagle's Gift: Alaska Eskimo Tales. Rasmussen, Knud. Hutchinson, Isabel, tr. 2011. 258p. 47.95 *(978-1-258-10170-1(X))* Literary Licensing, LLC.
Hansen, Gaby. Are You Ready for Bed? Johnson, Jane. (J). 2017. (ENG.). 28p. (gr. -1-k). bds. 7.99 *(978-1-68010-513-1(2));* 2010. (ENG.). 22p. (-k). bds. 8.95 *(978-1-58925-806-8(1));* 2004. 32p. tchr. ed. 14.95 *(978-1-58925-017-8(6))* Tiger Tales.
—Big Bears Can! Bedford, David. 2007. (Storytime Board Bks.). 16p. (J). (gr. -1-k). bds. 6.95 *(978-1-58925-826-6(6))* Tiger Tales.
—Little Bear's Special Wish. Lobel, Gill. (Storytime Board Bks.). (J). 2005. 16p. (gr. -1-k). bds. 6.95 *(978-1-58925-769-6(3));* 2004. 32p. tchr. ed. 16.95 *(978-1-58925-034-5(6))* Tiger Tales.
—Little Bunny's Bedtime. Johnson, Jane. 2006. Orig. Title: Are You Ready for Bed?. 16p. (J). bds. 6.95 *(978-1-58925-773-3(1))* Tiger Tales.
—Molly & the Storm. Leeson, Christine. 2003. 32p. (J). (gr. k-2). tchr. ed. 15.95 *(978-1-58925-027-7(3))* Tiger Tales.
—Oops-a-Daisy! Freedman, Claire. 32p. (J). 2004. tchr. ed. 15.95 *(978-1-58925-037-6(0));* 2006. reprint ed. 6.95 *(978-1-58925-398-8(1))* Tiger Tales.
—The Very Worried Sparrow. Doney, Meryl. 2008. (J). (gr. -1-3). 12.95 *(978-0-8198-8038-3(8))* Pauline Bks. & Media.
Hansen, Grant. Moon 514: Blaze & the White Griffon. Briney, Drew. 2018. (ENG.). 366p. (J). pap. 13.25 *(978-1-61463-992-3(2))* On The Fly Pubns.
Hansen, Jimmy. Wallace & Gromit: A Pier Too Far. Abnett, Dan. 2005. (Wallace & Gromit Ser.). (ENG.). 48p. 12.95 *(978-1-84023-953-9(0),* Titan Bks.) Titan Bks. Ltd. GBR. Dist: Penguin Random Hse. LLC.
—The Whippet Vanishes. Rimmer, Ian. 2004. (Wallace & Gromit Ser.). (ENG.). 48p. 12.95 *(978-1-84023-497-8(0),* Titan Bks.) Titan Bks. Ltd. GBR. Dist: Penguin Random Hse. LLC.
—Whippet Vanishes. Rimmer, Ian. 2004. (Wallace & Gromit Ser.). (ENG.). 48p. pap. 8.95 *(978-1-84023-498-5(9),* Titan Bks.) Titan Bks. Ltd. GBR. Dist: Penguin Random Hse. LLC.
Hansen, Jimmy & Williamson, Brian. Wallace & Gromit: The Bootiful Game. Rimmer, Ian. 2005. (Wallace & Gromit Ser.). (ENG.). 48p. pap. 8.95 *(978-1-84023-948-5(4),* Titan Bks.) Titan Bks. Ltd. GBR. Dist: Penguin Random Hse. LLC.
Hansen, Laurie. A Puppy for the White House. Smith, Kathleen. 2009. 32p. (J). 16.99 *(978-0-615-30165-5(7))* Lollipop Publishing, LLC.
Hansen, Lorie. Can I Have Some Money Please? Prindle, Twyla D. 2004. (ENG & SPA.). 20p. (J). (gr. k-4). 7.95 *(978-0-9759527-2-6(2))* Prindle Hse. Publishing Co.
Hansen, Lorie Miller. Can I Have Some Money Please? Prindle, Twyla. 2005. (J). (gr. -1-3). 14.95 *(978-0-9759527-3-3(0),* Prindle House Publishing Co.) Prindle Hse. Publishing Co.
Hansen, Melissa. Butterflies & Magic Dreams. Henderson, Tim. l.t. ed. 2003. 28p. (J). *(978-0-9728691-0-2(7))* Logan Bks.
Hansen, Neil, et al. Punisher Epic Collection: Jigsaw Puzzle. 2020. (ENG.). 496p. (YA). (gr. 8-17). pap. 39.99 *(978-1-302-92275-7(0))* Marvel Worldwide, Inc.
Hansen, Paisley. The Popcorn Tree. French, Joyce. 2012. 22p. 15.95 *(978-1-60414-639-4(7))* Fideli Publishing, Inc.
—Tar Bread. Chapman, Payge. 2016. (ENG.). (J). (gr. k-3). 15.95 *(978-1-60414-941-8(8))* Fidell Publishing, Inc.
Hansen, Red. The Princess Twins & the Puppy, 1 vol. Hodgson, Mona Gansberg. 2011. (I Can Read! / Princess Twins Ser.). (ENG.). 32p. (J). pap. 4.99 *(978-0-310-72709-5(X))* Zonderkidz.
Hansen Rolli, Jennifer. How to Trick the Tooth Fairy. Russell, Erin Danielle. 2018. (ENG.). 40p. (J). (gr. -1-3). 17.99 *(978-1-4814-6732-2(8),* Aladdin) Simon & Schuster Children's Publishing.
Hansen, Tevin. Kids Count. Hansen, Nichole. 2015. 44p. (J). pap. 9.49 *(978-1-941429-18-1(1))* Handersen Publishing.
—When I Was a Grown-Up. Hansen, Nichole. 2015. (ENG.). 28p. (YA). pap. 9.49 *(978-1-941429-13-6(0))* Handersen Publishing.
Hansen, Tevin. Alexia Versus the Birthday Bear. Hansen, Tevin. 2016. (J). pap. 5.99 *(978-1-941429-37-2(8))* Handersen Publishing.
—Rhomby the Skater Zombie. Hansen, Tevin. 2016. (ENG.). 134p. (J). pap. 7.99 *(978-1-941429-32-7(7))* Handersen Publishing.
—Rhomby the Skater Zombie & Me. Hansen, Tevin. 2nd ed. 2018. (J). pap. 8.99 *(978-1-947854-19-2(4))* Handersen Publishing.
—The Thumb Book. Hansen, Tevin. Hansen, Nichole. 2015. (ENG.). 48p. pap. 9.99 *(978-1-941429-21-1(1))* Handersen Publishing.
Hansen, Thore. The Little Paintbrush. Rørvik, Bjø F. 2014. (ENG.). 32p. (J). (gr. -1-k). 12.95 *(978-1-62087-996-2(4),* 620996, Sky Pony Pr.) Skyhorse Publishing Co., Inc.
—Ruffen: The Escape to Loch Ness. Bringsvaerd, Tor Age. 2009. (Ruffen Ser.). 72p. (J). (gr. 1-4). 16.95 *(978-0-9815761-2-1(5))* Mackenzie Smiles, LLC.
—Ruffen: The Sea Serpent Who Couldn't Swim. Bringsvaerd, Tor Age. 2008. (Ruffen Ser.). 64p. (J). (gr. -1-3). 16.95 *(978-0-9790347-9-4(5))* Mackenzie Smiles, LLC.
Hansman, Bob and Jovan. Traveling the Blue Road: Poems of the Sea. Bennett Hopkins, Lee, ed. 2017. (ENG.). 32p. (J). (gr. 3-7). 17.95 *(978-1-63322-276-2(4),* Seagrass) Quarto Publishing Group USA.
Hanson, Dana. Terror in the Tetons. Ahlman, Larry. Larsen, Chuck, ed. 2005. (YA). (gr. 9-12). pap. 9.95 *(978-0-9712906-2-4(8))* Ahlman Publishing.
Hanson, Eric Wolfe & Newell, Luke. This Book Is Haunted!: a Halloween Joke & Activity Book. Fischer, Maggie. 2019. (ENG.). 64p. (J). (gr. 1-3). pap. 5.99 *(978-1-68412-715-3(7),* Silver Dolphin Bks.) Printers Row Publishing Group.
Hanson, Faye. Cinderella's Secret Diary. Hanson, Faye. ed. 2013. (ENG.). 20p. (J). (gr. 1-3). 19.99 *(978-0-230-74204-8(1))* Pan Macmillan GBR. Dist: Independent Pubs. Group.
—The Wonder. Hanson, Faye. 2015. (ENG.). 40p. (J). (gr. -1-2). 16.99 *(978-0-7636-7957-6(7),* Templar) Candlewick Pr.
Hanson, Joan. Can You Match This? Jokes about Unlikely Pairs. Walton, Rick & Walton, Ann. (Make Me Laugh! Joke Bks.). 36p. (J). reprint ed. pap. 2.95 *(978-0-8225-9565-6(6),* Lerner Pubns.) Lerner Publishing Group.
—Kiss a Frog! Jokes about Fairy Tales, Knights, & Dragons. Walton, Rick & Walton, Ann. 40p. (J). (gr. 1-4). reprint ed. pap. 2.95 *(978-0-8225-9566-3(4),* Lerner Pubns.) Lerner Publishing Group.
Hanson, Joan. Still More Homonyms: Night & Knight & Other Words That Sound the Same but Look As Different As Ball & Bawl. Hanson, Joan. (Joan Hanson Word Bks.). (J). (gr. -1-3). lib. bdg. 4.95 *(978-0-8225-1107-6(X),* Lerner Pubns.) Lerner Publishing Group.
Hanson, Julie. Coralie the Cotton Candy Angel: Learning about Trusting Strangers. Hanson, Julie. 2018. (ENG.). 34p. (J). pap. 9.99 *(978-1-7326633-1-2(9));* 17.99 *(978-1-7326633-0-5(0))* Candlelight Bay Publishing.
Hanson, Julie. Molly Mcbean Clutterbug Queen. Hanson, Julie. 2019. (ENG.). 34p. (J). (gr. k-3). 17.95 ***(978-1-7326633-2-9(7));*** pap. 9.99 ***(978-1-7326633-3-6(5))*** Candlelight Bay Publishing.
Hanson, Lori. Bubblegum Princess. Gribble, Julie. 2013. 32p. (J). 16.99 *(978-0-9890914-0-4(6))* NY Media Works, LLC.
Hanson, Peter E. Botones Para el General Washington. Roop, Peter & Roop, Connie. 2006. (Yo Solo - Historia (on My Own - History) Ser.).Tr. of Buttons for General Washington. (SPA.). 48p. (gr. 2-4). lib. bdg. 25.26 *(978-0-8225-6261-0(8))* Lerner Publishing Group.
—Buttons for General Washington, 4 bks., Set. Roop, Peter & Roop, Connie. unabr. ed. 2007. (Readalongs for Beginning Readers Ser.). (J). (gr. 2-3). pap. 39.95 incl. audio compact disk *(978-1-59519-935-5(7))* Live Oak Media.
—Keep the Lights Burning, Abbie. Roop, Connie & Roop, Peter. 2016. (On My Own History Ser.). (ENG.). 40p. (J). (gr. 2-4). 38.65 *(978-1-5124-1862-0(5),* Millbrook Pr.) Lerner Publishing Group.
—Manten Las Luces Encendidas, Abbie. Roop, Peter & Roop, Connie. 2005. (Yo Solo Biografías Ser.). (SPA.). (gr. 2-5). 40p. (J). per. 6.95 *(978-0-8225-3099-2(6));* 48p. lib. bdg. 25.26 *(978-0-8225-3098-5(8))* Lerner Publishing Group.
Hanson-Roberts, Mary. Cinderella: A Tale of Kindness. 2006. (J). 6.99 *(978-1-59939-001-7(9))* Cornerstone Pr.
Hanson, Sandy & Delage, Kristi. A Camel's Story: A Search for the Messiah. Hanson, Sandy. 2005. 53p. (J). lib. bdg. 21.95 *(978-0-9763271-0-3(4))* MK Publishing.
Hanson, Susan Jo. Ivar, the Short, but Brave Viking. Jacobsen, Annie. 2007. (J). lib. bdg. 16.95 *(978-0-9778276-1-9(5))* Pickled Herring Pr.
—The Terrible Troll Cat. Jacobsen, Annie. (J). 2012. 32p. 9.98 *(978-0-9778276-4-0(X));* 2006. 16.95 *(978-0-9778276-0-2(7))* Pickled Herring Pr.
Hanson, Sydney. Construction Cat. Odanaka, Barbara. 2018. (ENG.). 40p. (J). (gr. -1-1). 17.99 *(978-1-4814-9094-8(X),* McElderry, Margaret K. Bks.) McElderry, Margaret K. Bks.
—Cuddle up, Cows!, 1 vol. 2020. (Bedtime Barn Ser.). (ENG.). 20p. (J). bds. 8.99 *(978-1-4002-1208-8(1))* Nelson, Thomas Inc.
—Drawing Puppies, Chicks, & Other Baby Animals: 4D an Augmented Reading Drawing Experience. Cella, Clara. 2018. (Drawing With 4D Ser.). (ENG.). 32p. (J). (gr. 3-9). lib. bdg. 31.99 *(978-1-5435-3189-3(X),* 138815, Capstone Pr.) Capstone.
—Escargot. Slater, Dashka. 2017. (Escargot Ser.). (ENG.). 40p. (J). 16.99 *(978-0-374-30281-8(2),* 900151640, Farrar, Straus & Giroux (BYR)) Farrar, Straus & Giroux.
—Five Fuzzy Chicks. Murray, Diana. 2020. (ENG.). 32p. (J). 16.99 *(978-1-250-30122-2(X),* 900196678) Imprint IND. Dist: Macmillan.
—His Royal Whiskers. Gayton, Sam. (ENG.). (J). (gr. 3-7). 2018. 336p. pap. 8.99 *(978-1-4814-9091-7(5));* 2017. 320p. 16.99 *(978-1-4814-9090-0(7))* McElderry, Margaret K. Bks. (McElderry, Margaret K. Bks.).
—How Do You Go to Sleep? McMullan, Kate. 2019. 32p. (J). (gr. -1-3). 17.99 *(978-0-525-57944-1(3),* Knopf Bks. for Young Readers) Random Hse. Children's Bks.
—How Do You Take a Bath? McMullan, Kate. 2018. (ENG.). 32p. (J). (gr. -1-3). lib. bdg. 20.99 *(978-1-5247-6518-7(X),* Knopf Bks. for Young Readers) Random Hse. Children's Bks.
—I Love You Like No Otter. Rossner, Rose. 2020. (Punderland Ser.). 24p. (J). bds. 8.99 *(978-1-7282-1374-3(6))* Sourcebooks, Inc.
—The Little Elephant Who Wants to Fall Asleep: A New Way of Getting Children to Sleep. Ehrlin, Carl-Johan Forssén. 2016. (ENG.). 40p. (J). (gr. -1-2). 16.99 *(978-0-399-55423-0(8),* Crown Books For Young Readers) Random Hse. Children's Bks.
—A Little Hedgehog. Wren, Rosalee. Cottage Door Press, ed. 2019. (ENG.). 10p. (J). (gr. -1-k). bds. 4.99 *(978-1-68052-632-5(4),* 1004251) Cottage Door Pr.
—A Little Otter. Wren, Rosalee. Cottage Door Press, ed. 2019. (ENG.). 10p. (J). (gr. -1-k). bds. 4.99 *(978-1-68052-778-0(9),* 1005010) Cottage Door Pr.
—Love You, Little 'Potamus: Early Bird Sound. Rose, Robin. Cottage Door Press, ed. 2018. (ENG.). 12p. (J). (gr. -1-k). bds. 9.99 *(978-1-68052-381-2(3),* 1003460) Cottage Door Pr.
—Mommy & Me. Hall, Tiya. Cottage Door Press, ed. 2018. (ENG.). 20p. (J). (gr. -1-1). bds. 9.99 *(978-1-68052-453-6(4),* 2000520) Cottage Door Pr.
—New Little Puppy: Sound Book Wood Module with Handle. Rose, Robin. Cottage Door Press, ed. 2017. (Early Bird Sound Bks.). (ENG.). 10p. (J). (gr. -1-k). bds. 9.99 *(978-1-68052-159-7(4),* 1001570) Cottage Door Pr.

H

—Next to You: A Book of Adorableness. Houran, Lori Haskins. (ENG.). (J). (gr. -1 — 1). 2019. 28p. bds. 7.99 *(978-0-8075-5599-6(1)*, 0807555991); 2016. 32p. 16.99 *(978-0-8075-5600-9(9)*, 807556009) Whitman, Albert & Co.

—Panda Pants. Davies, Jacqueline. 2016. 32p. (J). (gr. -1-2). 17.99 *(978-0-553-53576-1(5)*, Knopf Bks. for Young Readers) Random Hse. Children's Bks.

—Psst! I Love You. Parker, Marjorie Blain. (Snuggle Time Stories Ser.: 7). (J). 2018. 22p. (— 1). bds. 8.95 *(978-1-4549-2705-1(4))*; 2017. 32p. (gr. -1-k). 9.95 *(978-1-4549-1721-2(0))* Sterling Publishing Co., Inc.

—Put on Your PJs, Piggies!, 1 vol. Neutzling, Laura. 2019. (Bedtime Barn Ser.). (ENG.). 20p. (J). bds. 8.99 *(978-1-4002-1200-2(6))* Nelson, Thomas Inc.

—Teddy Bear of the Year. VanSickle, Vikki. 2020. (ENG.). 40p. (J). (gr. -1-2). 17.99 *(978-0-7352-6392-5(2)*, Tundra Bks.) Tundra Bks. CAN. Dist: Penguin Random Hse. LLC.

—The Tractor Who Wants to Fall Asleep: A New Way of Getting Children to Sleep. Forssen Ehrlin, Carl. 2017. (ENG.). (J). (gr. -1-2). pap. *(978-91-88375-15-5(3))* Ehrlin Publishing AB.

—The Tractor Who Wants to Fall Asleep: A New Way of Getting Children to Sleep. Forssen Ehrlin, Carl-Johan. 2017. (ENG.). (J). (gr. -1-2). pap. *(978-91-88375-24-7(2))* Ehrlin Publishing AB.

—Unicorn Princesses 1: Sunbeam's Shine. Bliss, Emily. 2017. (Unicorn Princesses Ser.: 1). (ENG.). 128p. (J). 15.99 *(978-1-68119-325-0(6)*, 900170033, Bloomsbury USA Childrens) Bloomsbury Publishing USA.

Hanson, Sydney. Unicorn Princesses 10: the Wing Spell. Bliss, Emily. 2020. (Unicorn Princesses Ser.: 10). (ENG.). 128p. (J). 16.99 ***(978-1-5476-0489-0(1)***, 900225265); pap. 5.99 ***(978-1-5476-0488-3(3)***, 900225269) Bloomsbury Publishing USA. (Bloomsbury Children's Bks.).

Hanson, Sydney. Unicorn Princesses 2: Flash's Dash. Bliss, Emily. 2017. (Unicorn Princesses Ser.: 2). (ENG.). 128p. (J). 15.99 *(978-1-68119-329-8(9)*, 900170030, Bloomsbury USA Childrens) Bloomsbury Publishing USA.

—Unicorn Princesses 3: Bloom's Ball. Bliss, Emily. 2017. (Unicorn Princesses Ser.: 3). 128p. (J). pap. 5.99 *(978-1-68119-334-2(5)*, 900170042, Bloomsbury USA Childrens) Bloomsbury Publishing USA.

—Unicorn Princesses 4: Prism's Paint. Bliss, Emily. 2017. (Unicorn Princesses Ser.: 4). 128p. (J). 15.99 *(978-1-68119-337-3(X)*, 900170038); pap. 5.99 *(978-1-68119-338-0(8)*, 900170045) Bloomsbury Publishing USA. (Bloomsbury USA Childrens).

—Unicorn Princesses 5: Breeze's Blast. Bliss, Emily. 2018. (Unicorn Princesses Ser.: 5). 128p. (J). 16.99 *(978-1-68119-650-3(6)*, 900179833); (ENG.). pap. 5.99 *(978-1-68119-649-7(2)*, 900179849) Bloomsbury Publishing USA. (Bloomsbury USA Childrens).

—Unicorn Princesses 6: Moon's Dance. Bliss, Emily. 2018. (Unicorn Princesses Ser.: 6). 128p. (J). 16.99 *(978-1-68119-653-4(0)*, 900179852); pap. 5.99 *(978-1-68119-652-7(2)*, 900179844) Bloomsbury Publishing USA. (Bloomsbury USA Childrens).

—Unicorn Princesses 7: Firefly's Glow. Bliss, Emily. 2018. (Unicorn Princesses Ser.: 7). 128p. (J). 16.99 *(978-1-68119-927-6(0)*, 900192376); pap. 5.99 *(978-1-68119-926-9(2)*, 900192401) Bloomsbury Publishing USA. (Bloomsbury Children's Bks.).

—Unicorn Princesses 8: Feather's Flight. Bliss, Emily. 2018. (Unicorn Princesses Ser.: 8). 128p. (J). 16.99 *(978-1-68119-930-6(0)*, 900192387); pap. 5.99 *(978-1-68119-929-0(7)*, 900192375) Bloomsbury Publishing USA. (Bloomsbury Children's Bks.).

Hanson, Sydney. Unicorn Princesses 9: the Moonbeams. Bliss, Emily. 2020. (Unicorn Princesses Ser.: 9). (ENG.). 128p. (J). 16.99 ***(978-1-5476-0484-5(0)***, 900225268); pap. 5.99 ***(978-1-5476-0483-8(2)***, 900225261) Bloomsbury Publishing USA. (Bloomsbury Children's Bks.).

Hanson, Sydney. Unicorn Princesses Bind-Up Books 1-3: Sunbeam's Shine, Flash's Dash, & Bloom's Ball. Bliss, Emily. 2017. (Unicorn Princesses Ser.). (ENG.). 368p. (J). 10.99 *(978-1-68119-935-1(1)*, 900193212, Bloomsbury USA Childrens) Bloomsbury Publishing USA.

—Unicorn Princesses Bind-Up Books 4-6: Prism's Paint, Breeze's Blast, & Moon's Dance. Bliss, Emily. 2018. (Unicorn Princesses Ser.). (ENG.). 368p. (J). 10.99 *(978-1-5476-0234-6(1)*, 900206736, Bloomsbury Children's Bks.) Bloomsbury Publishing USA.

Hanson, Sydney. Unicorn Princesses Bind-Up Books 7-9: Firefly's Glow, Feather's Flight, & the Moonbeams. Bliss, Emily. 2020. (Unicorn Princesses Ser.). (ENG.). 368p. (J). 10.99 ***(978-1-5476-0522-4(7)***, 900226573, Bloomsbury Children's Bks.) Bloomsbury Publishing USA.

Hanson, Sydney. Warts & All: A Book of Unconditional Love. Houran, Lori Haskins. 2017. (ENG.). 32p. (J). (gr. -1-3). 15.99 *(978-0-8075-8658-7(7)*, 807586587) Whitman, Albert & Co.

—We Both Read - Little Chipper. McKay, Sindy. 2017. (ENG.). 41p. (J). 9.95 *(978-1-60115-295-4(7))* Treasure Bay, Inc.

—Why a Daughter Needs a Dad. Lang, Gregory & Hill, Susanna Leonard. 2019. 32p. (J). (-3). 10.99 *(978-1-4926-6783-4(8)*, Sourcebooks Jabberwocky) Sourcebooks, Inc.

—Why a Daughter Needs a Mom. Lang, Gregory & Hill, Susanna Leonard. 2019. (ENG.). 32p. (J). (-3). 10.99 *(978-1-4926-6781-0(1)*, Sourcebooks Jabberwocky) Sourcebooks, Inc.

Hanson, Tippi. Rainbow Weaver. Hanson, Tippi. Russell, Lyndsey. 2007. (ENG.). 48p. (J). (gr. k-2). 13.99 *(978-1-84243-229-7(X))* Oldcastle Bks., Ltd. GBR. Dist: Independent Pubs. Group.

Hanson, Warren. Tell Me What We Did Today. Kupchella, Rick. (ENG.). 32p. (J). 15.95 *(978-0-9726504-0-3(7))* TRISTAN Publishing, Inc.

Hanson, Warren. Kiki's Hats: Our Gifts Live on & On. Hanson, Warren. 2007. (ENG.). 36p. (J). (gr. -1-3). 16.95 *(978-0-931674-94-5(8)*, Waldman House Pr.) TRISTAN Publishing, Inc.

Hanson, Warren, jt. illus. see Hegg, Tom.

Hanstick, Kevin. My Trip to Washington, D. C., 1 vol. Polley, JoAnn. 3rd rev. ed. 2009. (My Trip Ser.). (ENG.). 80p. (J). (gr. 3-7). spiral bd. 16.99 *(978-1-58980-671-9(9)*, Pelican Publishing) Arcadia Publishing.

Hanstick, Kevin R. My Trip to Gettysburg, 1 vol. Polley, J. Patrick & Polley, JoAnn. Shekerow, Mark D., ed. 2007. (My Trip Ser.). (ENG.). 80p. (J). (gr. 4-6). spiral bd. 14.95 *(978-1-58980-456-2(2)*, Pelican Publishing) Arcadia Publishing.

Hantel, Johanna. Como Yo. Neasi, Barbara J. 2003. (Rookie Reader Español Ser.).Tr. of Just Like Me. (SPA.). 32p. (J). (gr. k-2). pap. 4.95 *(978-0-516-27795-0(2)*, Children's Pr.) Scholastic Library Publishing.

—I Am Sick. Jensen, Patricia. (My First Reader Ser.). (ENG.). 32p. (J). (gr. k-1). 2006. per. 3.95 *(978-0-516-24970-4(3))*; 2005. lib. bdg. 18.50 *(978-0-516-24878-3(2))* Scholastic Library Publishing. (Children's Pr.).

—I Hate Reading: How to Get Through 20 Minutes of Reading a Day Without Really Reading. Bacon, Arthur & Bacon, Henry. 2008. 20p. (J). (gr. -1-3). 17.95 *(978-1-60213-025-8(6)*, Upstart Bks.) Highsmith Inc.

—Just Like Me. Neasi, Barbara J. 2003. (Rookie Readers: Level B (Pb) Ser.). (ENG.). (J). (gr. 1-1). lib. bdg. 15.55 *(978-0-7569-1328-1(4))* Perfection Learning Corp.

—Just Like Me. Neasi, Barbara J. 2011. (Rookie Ready to Learn — All about Me! Ser.). 40p. (J). (gr. -1-k). lib. bdg. 25.00 *(978-0-531-26371-6(1))*; (ENG.). pap. 5.95 *(978-0-531-26676-2(1))* Scholastic Library Publishing. (Children's Pr.).

Hantel, Johanna, jt. illus. see Clar, David Austin.

Hanton, Sophie. Hugs: Tuck Each Baby into a Loving Hug. 2010. (ENG.). 12p. (J). (gr. -1 — 1). 9.99 *(978-1-60169-020-3(7))* Innovative Kids.

—Noah & the Animals, 1 vol. Williamson, Karen. ed. 2014. (Candle Tiny Tots Ser.). (ENG.). 16p. (J). 11.99 *(978-1-78128-110-9(6)*, Candle Bks.) Lion Hudson PLC GBR. Dist: Kregel Pubns.

Hantula, Timothy James. The Flower Girl / the Ring Bear. Sharp, N. L. 2009. 40p. (J). 19.95 *(978-0-9759829-3-8(1))* Prairieland Pr.

Hao, Katrina Mae, jt. illus. see Cucca, Vincenzo.

Hao, Mae, jt. illus. see Franscisco, Tina.

Happel, Sally. Eve. Golden, Robert Charles. 2012. 32p. 24.95 *(978-1-4626-7621-7(9))* America Star Bks.

Haq, Matto. ABC: Robots of the Alphabet Planet. Ngwala, Xander. Ngwala, Nakia, ed. 2017. (ENG.). (J). 19.99 *(978-0-9846663-5-5(4))* Genet Pr. LLC.

—123: Robots of the Numeric Planet. Ngwala, Xander. Ngwala, Nakia, ed. 2018. (ENG.). 26p. (J). 19.99 *(978-0-9846663-7-9(0))* Genet Pr. LLC.

haRA, EddiE. I Is for Indonesia. Rush, Elizabeth. 2013. (Alphabetical World Ser.). (ENG.). 48p. (gr. k-4). 12.95 *(978-1-934159-41-5(7))* ThingsAsian Pr.

Hara, Josh. Some People Do. Lowe, Frank. 2019. (Some People Children's Ser.). (ENG.). 54p. (J). (gr. k-2). 18.95 *(978-1-945448-30-0(X)*, BQB Publishing) Boutique of Quality Books Publishing Co., Inc.

Harasimowicz, Ellen. Beetle Busters: A Rogue Insect & the People Who Track It. Griffin Burns, Loree. 2018. (Scientists in the Field Ser.). (ENG.). 64p. (J). (gr. 5-7). pap. 9.99 *(978-1-328-89572-1(6)*, 1699517, HMH Books For Young Readers) Houghton Mifflin Harcourt Publishing Co.

—Handle with Care: An Unusual Butterfly Journey. Burns, Loree Griffin. 2014. (ENG.). 32p. (J). (gr. 1-4). lib. bdg. 26.65 *(978-0-7613-9342-9(0)*, Millbrook Pr.) Lerner Publishing Group.

—The Hive Detectives: Chronicle of a Honey Bee Catastrophe. Burns, Loree Griffin. (Scientists in the Field Ser.). (ENG.). 80p. (J). (gr. 5-7). 2013. pap. 9.99 *(978-0-544-00326-2(8)*, 1526368); 2010. 18.99 *(978-0-547-15231-8(0)*, 1051949) Houghton Mifflin Harcourt Publishing Co.

—You're Invited to a Moth Ball: A Nighttime Insect Celebration. Burns, Loree. 2020. 40p. (J). (gr. k-3). lib. bdg. 16.99 *(978-1-58089-686-3(3))* Charlesbridge Publishing, Inc.

Harasimowicz, Ellen. Beetle Busters: A Rogue Insect & the People Who Track It. Harasimowicz, Ellen, photos by. Burns, Loree Griffin. 2014. (Scientists in the Field Ser.). (ENG.). 64p. (J). (gr. 5-7). 18.99 *(978-0-547-79267-5(0)*, 1493179, HMH Books For Young Readers) Houghton Mifflin Harcourt Publishing Co.

Harasimowicz, Ellen, photos by. Citizen Scientists: Be a Part of Scientific Discovery from Your Own Backyard. Burns, Loree Griffin. 2012. (ENG., 80p. (J). (gr. 3-7). pap. 14.99 *(978-0-8050-9517-3(9)*, 900081493) Square Fish.

Harasymowicz, Sawa. The Life & Art of Vincent Van Gogh. Roddam, George. 2016. (Lives of Great Artists Ser.). 00080p. (J). (gr. 8-8). 35.75 *(978-1-4994-6583-9(1))* Rosen Publishing Group, Inc., The.

Harasymowicz, Slawa. The Life & Art of Paul Gauguin. Roddam, George. 2016. (Lives of Great Artists Ser.). 00080p. (J). (gr. 8-8). 35.75 *(978-1-4994-6581-5(5)*, Rosen Young Adult) Rosen Publishing Group, Inc., The.

Harber, Hulya. Simon the Policeman on Safari - Claude the Camel. Harber, Chris. 2013. 24p. pap. *(978-0-7552-1552-2(4)*, Bright Pen) Authors OnLine, Ltd.

—Simon the Policeman on the Number Planet. Harber, Chris. 2013. 28p. pap. *(978-0-7552-1560-7(5)*, Bright Pen) Authors OnLine, Ltd.

Harbin, Rhonda. Rescue the Night: The Sandman & the Darkest Nights Series. Stuhl, John. 2018. (Sandman & the Darkest Night Ser.: Vol. 1). (ENG.). 94p. (YA). (gr. 7-12). pap. 12.00 *(978-0-692-99808-3(X))* Stuhl, John.

Harbinson, Karen. Pony Palace Camp. Burgess, Pauline. 2014. (Pony Friends Forever Ser.). (ENG.). 96p. (J). pap. 12.00 *(978-0-85640-923-3(5))* Blackstaff Pr., Ltd. GBR. Dist: Casemate Pubs. & Bk. Distributors, LLC.

Harbo, Gary. The Northern Woods Adventure: Advanced Reader, 6 vols. Harbo, Gary. l.t. ed. 2004. (If You Want to Succeed, You Need to Read! Ser.: 6). (ENG.). 33p. (J). 10.95 *(978-1-884149-15-3(4))* Kutie Kari Bks., Inc.

—The Northern Woods Adventure: Early Reader. Harbo, Gary. l.t. ed. 2004. (If You Want to Succeed, You Need to Read! Ser.: 6). (ENG.). 33p. (J). 10.95 *(978-1-884149-16-0(2))* Kutie Kari Bks., Inc.

—Where Is My Sister? Harbo, Gary. 2008. (ENG.). 33p. (J). lib. bdg. 12.95 *(978-1-884149-40-5(5))* Kutie Kari Bks., Inc.

Harchy, Atelier Philippe. Chicken Little: A Tale about Common Sense. 2006. (J). 6.99 *(978-1-59939-019-2(1))* Cornerstone Pr.

—Friends for a Princess (Disney Princess) Lagonegro, Melissa. 2016. (Step into Reading Ser.). (ENG.). 24p. (J). (gr. -1-1). pap. 4.99 *(978-0-7364-3670-0(7)*, RH/Disney) Random Hse. Children's Bks.

—Just Keep Swimming. Lagonegro, Melissa & RH Disney Staff. 2005. (Step into Reading Ser.). (ENG.). 32p. (J). (gr. k-3). pap. 4.99 *(978-0-7364-2319-9(2)*, RH/Disney) Random Hse. Children's Bks.

—A Surprise Garden, 15 vols. Parent, Nancy. 2003. (It's Fun to Learn Ser.). 32p. (J). (gr. -1-3). 3.99 *(978-1-57973-126-7(0))* Advance Pubs. LLC.

—A Tiggeriffic Band, 15 vols. Marsoli, Lisa Ann. 2003. (It's Fun to Learn Ser.). 32p. (J). (gr. -1-3). *(978-1-57973-128-1(7))* Advance Pubs. LLC.

—A Tree for Me, 15 vols. Parent, Nancy. 2003. (It's Fun to Learn Ser.). 32p. (J). (gr. -1-3). 3.99 *(978-1-57973-138-0(4))* Advance Pubs. LLC.

—What Is a Princess? (Disney Princess) Liberts, Jennifer. 2016. (Step into Reading Ser.). (ENG.). 24p. (J). (gr. -1-1). pap. 4.99 *(978-0-7364-3666-3(9)*, RH/Disney) Random Hse. Children's Bks.

Harchy, Atelier Philippe, jt. illus. see Harding, Niall.

Harcus, Britt. Cook, Pot, Cook! Bedford, David. 2014. (Traditional Tales Ser.). (ENG.). 16p. (J). (gr. k-1). pap. 6.95 *(978-1-62521-548-2(7)*, Capstone Classroom) Capstone.

Hardaker, Heidy. Slimy Grimy Odd Cod. Hardaker, Heidy. 2018. (Heidy's Story Rhymies Ser.: Vol. 1). (ENG.). 28p. (J). pap. 9.50 *(978-1-7928-5354-8(8))* Independently Published.

Hardcastle, Nick. Day of Deliverance. O'Brien, Johnny. 2010. (Jack Christie Adventure Ser.: 2). (ENG.). 192p. (J). (gr. 4-7). 15.99 *(978-0-7636-5075-9(7)*, Templar) Candlewick Pr.

—Day of the Assassins. O'Brien, Johnny. 2010. (Jack Christie Adventure Ser.: 1). (ENG.). 224p. (J). (gr. 4-7). pap. 6.99 *(978-0-7636-4995-1(3)*, Templar) Candlewick Pr.

—Day of the Assassins: A Jack Christie Novel, 1. O'Brien, Johnny. 2010. (Jack Christie Adventure Ser.: 1). (ENG.). 224p. (J). (gr. 4-6). 21.19 *(978-0-7636-4595-3(8))* Candlewick Pr.

—Unstoppable: How Jim Thorpe & the Carlisle Indian School Defeated the Army. Coulson, Art. 2018. (Encounter: Narrative Nonfiction Picture Bks.). (ENG.). 40p. (J). (gr. 1-5). 15.95 *(978-1-5435-0406-4(X)*, 137233, Capstone Editions) Capstone.

Hardcastle, Nick, jt. illus. see Wallis, Diz.

Harden, Laurie. The Day of the Black Blizzard. Ransom, Candice. (On My Own History Ser.). 48p. (J). 2016. (ENG.). (gr. 2-4). pap. 7.99 *(978-1-5124-1152-2(3))*; 2011. pap. 6.95 *(978-0-7613-3938-0(8))* Lerner Publishing Group. (First Avenue Editions).

—Living with the Senecas: A Story about Mary Jemison. Aller, Susan Bivin. 2007. (Creative Minds Biographies Ser.). 64p. (J). (gr. 3-7). lib. bdg. 22.60 *(978-0-8225-5989-4(7))* Lerner Publishing Group.

—Nick's Secret. Blatchford, Claire H. 2003. (Lerner Mysteries Ser.). 168p. (J). (gr. 4-7). 14.95 *(978-0-8225-0743-7(9)*, Lerner Pubns.) Lerner Publishing Group.

Harder, Miki. Bears Don't Ski. Mapel, Tiffany. 2018. (J). *(978-0-692-96831-4(8))* Rock Wren Pr.

Harder, Rolf. It's Tough to Nap on a Turtle. Harder, Christopher. 2008. (ENG.). 11p. (J). (gr. -1). bds. 5.95 *(978-0-9726614-9-2(2))* Shenanigan Bks.

Hardie, Chris. Bobby & Mandee's Good Touch/Bad Touch: Children's Safety Book. Kahn, Robert. 2011. (ENG.). 25p. (J). pap. 6.95 *(978-1-935274-54-4(6))* Future Horizons, Inc.

Hardiman, Eleanor. The Sleepy Pebble & Other Stories: Calming Tales to Read at Bedtime. Gregory, Alice & Kirkpatrick, Christy. 2019. 96p. (gr. k-2). 17.95 *(978-1-911171-81-2(X))* Flying Eye Bks. GBR. Dist: Penguin Random Hse. LLC.

Hardin, Teresa. The Tooth Fairy's Quest. Medders, James. 2008. 32p. pap. 24.95 *(978-1-60672-549-8(1))* America Star Bks.

Harding, Emma & Gosney, Joy. Singing Languages - Singing Spanish (Book + CD): 22 Photocopiable Songs & Chants for Learning Spanish, 1 vol. MacGregor, Helen & Chadwick, Stephen. 2008. (Singing Languages Ser.). 64p. (J). (gr. 2-6). audio compact disk 32.95 *(978-0-7136-8880-1(7))* HarperCollins Pubs. Ltd. GBR. Dist: Independent Pubs. Group.

Harding, Emma, jt. illus. see Gosney, Joy.

Harding, Niall. Ballerina Princess (Disney Princess) RH Disney. 2007. (Step into Reading Ser.). (ENG.). 32p. (J). (gr. k-3). pap. 4.99 *(978-0-7364-2428-8(8)*, RH/Disney) Random Hse. Children's Bks.

—Ten Gifts from Santa Claus: A Counting Book. Bak, Jenny. 2011. (ENG.). 22p. (J). (gr. -1-k). 14.99 *(978-1-4052-5127-3(1))* Egmont Bks., Ltd. GBR. Dist: Independent Pubs. Group.

Harding, Niall & Harchy, Atelier Philippe. Polite as a Princess. Arps, Melissa & Lagonegro, Melissa. 2006. (Pictureback(R) Ser.). (ENG.). 24p. (J). (gr. -1-2). pap. 3.99 *(978-0-7364-2367-0(2)*, RH/Disney) Random Hse. Children's Bks.

Hardison, Brian. ABCs of Character for People Around the World. Mitchell-Tulloss, Delores. 2007. 32p. (J). pap. *(978-0-9670712-6-8(7))* zReyomi Publishing.

Hardiyono. The Tiny Boy & Other Tales from Indonesia, 1 vol. Bunanta, Murti. 2013. (ENG.). 80p. (J). (gr. 3). 24.95 *(978-1-55498-193-9(X))* Groundwood Bks. CAN. Dist: Publishers Group West (PGW).

Hardwick, Holly. Maine: A Wicked Good Book of Verse: the Way Wildlife Should Be. Pottle, Robert. 2005. 64p. (J). per. 8.95 *(978-0-9709569-3-4(2))* Blue Lobster Pr.

Hardwick, Patricia. Music of the Butterfly: A Story of Hope. Klein, Gail & Leis, Ann. 2018. (ENG.). 40p. (J). 19.95 *(978-1-942945-56-7(6)*, 9781942945567) Night Heron Media.

Hardy, Candace J. August Nights. Hardy, Candace. l.t. ed. 2017. (ENG.). (J). (gr. 3-5). pap. 10.95 *(978-1-61633-896-1(2))* Guardian Angel Publishing, Inc.

—Cody Knows. Wiesner, Karen Sue. 2012. 16p. pap. 9.95 *(978-1-61633-260-0(3))* Guardian Angel Publishing, Inc.

Hardy, Chris. Miss Tilly's Marching Band. Thompson, Yvonne. 2004. (J). per. 12.95 *(978-0-9749561-1-4(2))* My Sunshine Bks.

Hardy, E. Stuart. The Pigeon Tale. Bennett, Virginia. 2007. 48p. per. *(978-1-4065-4810-5(3))* Dodo Pr.

Hardy, Frank. Ernest's Gift. Windham, Kathryn Tucker. 2004. (ENG.). 20p. (J). 16.95 *(978-1-58838-149-1(8)*, NewSouth Bks.) NewSouth, Inc.

Hardy, Lara. Mommy's Having a Homebirth. Johanik, Natalie. 2019. (ENG.). 34p. (J). pap. 14.95 ***(978-1-7037-4717-1(8))*** Independently Published.

—Mummy's Having a Homebirth. Johanik, Natalie. 2019. (ENG.). 34p. (J). pap. 15.12 ***(978-1-6865-1502-6(2))*** Independently Published.

Hardy, Paul. Little Peter (Illustrated) A Christmas Morality for Children of Any Age. Malet, Lucas. Barry, ed. 2019. (Christmas Stories Ser.: Vol. 1). (ENG.). 116p. (J). pap. 19.95 ***(978-1-7054-1758-4(2))*** Independently Published.

Hardy, Pris. Austin & Harlow's First Adventure. Jeanne Taylor Thomas Illustrator. Pr. 2011. 28p. pap. 24.95 *(978-1-4560-8383-0(X))* America Star Bks.

Hardy, Samara. Arlo & the Great Big Cover-Up. Howard, Betsy Childs. 2020. (Gospel Coalition Ser.). (ENG.). 40p. 12.99 *(978-1-4335-6852-7(7))* Crossway.

—Don't Wake the Dragon: An Interactive Bedtime Story! Schulze, Bianca & Clever Publishing. 2020. (Clever Storytime Ser.). (ENG.). 32p. (J). (gr. -1-17). 10.99 *(978-1-949998-64-1(9))* Clever Media Group.

Hardy, Sarah Frances. Paint Me! Hardy, Sarah Frances. 2014. 32p. (J). (-k). 14.95 *(978-1-62873-813-1(8)*, Sky Pony Pr.) Skyhorse Publishing Co., Inc.

Hardy, Vincent. Brown Bear, White Bear. Petrovic, Svetlana. 2009. 28p. (J). (gr. -1-3). 17.00 *(978-0-8028-5353-0(6)*, Eerdmans Bks For Young Readers) Eerdmans, William B. Publishing Co.

Hardyman, Nathan. 10 Little Monsters Visit New York City. Smiley, Jess Smart. 2016. (10 Little Monsters Ser.: 5). (ENG.). 32p. (J). 16.95 *(978-1-942934-67-7(X)*, 553467) Familius LLC.

—10 Little Monsters Visit Texas. Madson, Trish. 2017. (10 Little Monsters Ser.: 5). (ENG.). 32p. (J). 14.99 *(978-1-945547-08-9(1)*, 554708) Familius LLC.

Hare, John. Great Walker: Ioway Leader. Olson, Greg. 2014. (ENG.). 48p. (J). lib. bdg. 24.00 *(978-1-61248-112-8(4))* Truman State Univ. Pr.

—Helen Stephens: The Fulton Flash. Offutt, Jason. 2014. (ENG.). 48p. (J). lib. bdg. 24.00 *(978-1-61248-114-2(0))* Truman State Univ. Pr.

—Joseph Kinney: Steamboat Captain. McVicker, Maryellen. 2014. (ENG.). 48p. (J). lib. bdg. 24.00 *(978-1-61248-116-6(7))* Truman State Univ. Pr.

—Olive Boone: Frontier Woman. Russell, Greta. 2014. (Notable Missourians Ser.). (ENG.). 48p. (J). lib. bdg. 24.00 *(978-1-61248-118-0(3))* Truman State Univ. Pr.

—This Is Kansas City. Kmeck, Angela. 2015. (ENG.). 20p. (J). bds. 11.99 *(978-0-9962289-4-7(2))* Possum Trot Productions LLC.

Hare, Mary Alyce. Cindy's Story, 1 vol. Crosby, Sarah. 2009. 47p. pap. 24.95 *(978-1-60749-608-3(9))* America Star Bks.

Harets, Mykyta. Surviving Christmas: An Adventure Story for Kids 8-12. Burke, Joy A. Stowe, Lisa, ed. 2017. (Keegan Rees Ser.: Vol. 1). (ENG.). 74p. (J). pap. 9.99 *(978-1-946380-02-9(4))* Crooked Tail Pr.

Hargens, Charles. Silver Spurs for Cowboy Boots. Garst, Shannon. 2011. 194p. 42.95 *(978-1-258-08454-7(6))* Literary Licensing, LLC.

Hargis, Wes. Agatha Parrot & the Heart of Mud. Poskitt, Kjartan. (Agatha Parrot Ser.). (ENG.). 160p. (J). (gr. 3-7). 2017. pap. 7.99 *(978-1-328-74212-4(1)*, 1677332, HMH Books For Young Readers); 2016. 16.99 *(978-0-544-50876-7(9)*, 1605253) Houghton Mifflin Harcourt Publishing Co.

—Agatha Parrot & the Odd Street School Ghost. Poskitt, Kjartan. (Agatha Parrot Ser.). (ENG.). 160p. (J). (gr. 3-7). 2017. pap. 6.99 *(978-0-544-93530-3(6)*, 1658369, HMH Books For Young Readers); 2016. 16.99 *(978-0-544-50672-5(3)*, 1605230) Houghton Mifflin Harcourt Publishing Co.

—I Need My Own Country! Walton, Rick. 2012. (ENG.). 40p. (J). (gr. -1-3). 17.89 *(978-1-59990-560-0(4)*, 9781599905600, Bloomsbury USA Childrens) Bloomsbury Publishing USA.

—I Need My Own Country! Walton, Rick & Kraus, Franz. 2012. (ENG.). 40p. (J). (gr. -1-8). 17.99 *(978-1-59990-559-4(0)*, 9781599905594, Bloomsbury USA Childrens) Bloomsbury Publishing USA.

—Let's Investigate with Nate #1: the Water Cycle. Ball, Nate. 2017. (Let's Investigate with Nate Ser.: 1). (ENG.). 40p. (J). (gr. -1-3). pap. 7.99 *(978-0-06-235739-7(5))* HarperCollins Pubs.

—Let's Investigate with Nate #2: the Solar System. Ball, Nate. 2017. (Let's Investigate with Nate Ser.: 2). (ENG.). 40p. (J). (gr. -1-3). pap. 6.99 *(978-0-06-235742-7(5))* HarperCollins Pubs.

—Let's Investigate with Nate #3: Dinosaurs. Ball, Nate. 2018. (Let's Investigate with Nate Ser.: 3). (ENG.). 40p. (J). (gr. -1-3). 17.99 *(978-0-06-235746-5(8))*; pap. 6.99 *(978-0-06-235745-8(X))* HarperCollins Pubs.

—Let's Investigate with Nate #4: the Life Cycle. Ball, Nate. 2018. (Let's Investigate with Nate Ser.: 4). (ENG.). 32p. (J). (gr. -1-3). 17.99 *(978-0-06-235749-6(2))*; pap. 6.99 *(978-0-06-235748-9(4))* HarperCollins Pubs.

—My New Teacher & Me! Yankovic, Al. 2013. (ENG.). 40p. (J). (gr. -1-3). 17.99 *(978-0-06-219203-5(5))* HarperCollins Pubs.

—When I Grow Up. Yankovic, Al. 2011. (ENG.). 32p. (J). (gr. -1-3). 17.99 *(978-0-06-192691-4(4))* HarperCollins Pubs.

Hargraves, Caitlin Rae & Tyree, Mark. The Adventures of Guitar Gary: How Gary Got His Name. Holbrook, Sandy D. 2019. (ENG.). 26p. (J). pap. 14.00 *(978-1-7296-9529-6(9))* CreateSpace Independent Publishing Platform.

Hargreaves, Adam. Little Miss Splendid & the Princess. Hargreaves, Roger. 2007. (Mr. Men & Little Miss Ser.). (ENG.). 32p. (J). (gr. -1-2). mass mkt. 4.99 *(978-0-8431-2489-7(X),* Grosset & Dunlap) Penguin Young Readers Group.

—Mr. Nobody. Hargreaves, Roger. 2011. (Mr. Men & Little Miss Ser.). (ENG.). 32p. (J). (gr. -1-2). mass mkt. 4.99 *(978-0-8431-9876-8(1),* Price Stern Sloan) Penguin Young Readers Group.

Hargreaves, Adam. Dr. Fifth. Hargreaves, Adam. 2018. (Doctor Who / Roger Hargreaves Ser.). (ENG.). 32p. (J). (gr. -1-2). pap. 5.99 *(978-1-5247-8494-2(X),* Penguin Young Readers Licenses) Penguin Young Readers Group.

—Dr. First. Hargreaves, Adam. Price Stern Sloan. 2017. (Doctor Who / Roger Hargreaves Ser.). (ENG.). 32p. (J). (gr. -1-2). pap. 5.99 *(978-0-515-15846-5(1),* Penguin Young Readers Licenses) Penguin Young Readers Group.

—Dr. Sixth. Hargreaves, Adam. 2018. (Doctor Who / Roger Hargreaves Ser.). (ENG.). 32p. (J). (gr. -1-2). pap. 5.99 *(978-1-5247-8496-6(6),* Penguin Young Readers Licenses) Penguin Young Readers Group.

—Dr. Tenth. Hargreaves, Adam. 2018. (Doctor Who / Roger Hargreaves Ser.). (ENG.). 32p. (J). (gr. -1-2). pap. 5.99 *(978-1-5247-8495-9(8),* Penguin Young Readers Licenses) Penguin Young Readers Group.

—Dr. Third. Hargreaves, Adam. 2018. (Doctor Who / Roger Hargreaves Ser.). (ENG.). 32p. (J). (gr. -1-2). pap. 5.99 *(978-1-5247-8493-5(1),* Penguin Young Readers Licenses) Penguin Young Readers Group.

—Dr. Thirteenth. Hargreaves, Adam. 2019. (Doctor Who / Roger Hargreaves Ser.). (ENG.). 32p. (J). (gr. -1-2). pap. 5.99 *(978-1-5247-8860-5(0),* Penguin Young Readers Licenses) Penguin Young Readers Group.

—Dr. Twelfth. Hargreaves, Adam. Price Stern Sloan. 2017. (Doctor Who / Roger Hargreaves Ser.). (ENG.). 32p. (J). (gr. -1-2). pap. 5.99 *(978-0-515-15849-6(6),* Penguin Young Readers Licenses) Penguin Young Readers Group.

—Little Miss Hug. Hargreaves, Adam. 2014. (Mr. Men & Little Miss Ser.). (ENG.). 32p. (J). (gr. -1-2). 4.99 *(978-0-8431-8059-6(5),* Grosset & Dunlap) Penguin Young Readers Group.

—Little Miss Naughty & the Good Fairy. Hargreaves, Adam. Hargreaves, Roger. 2007. (Mr. Men & Little Miss Ser.). (ENG.). 32p. (J). (gr. -1-2). mass mkt. 4.99 *(978-0-8431-2122-3(X),* Price Stern Sloan) Penguin Young Readers Group.

—Little Miss Trouble & the Mermaid. Hargreaves, Adam. Hargreaves, Roger. 2008. (Mr. Men & Little Miss Ser.). (ENG.). 32p. (J). (gr. -1-2). mass mkt. 4.99 *(978-0-8431-3277-9(9),* Grosset & Dunlap) Penguin Young Readers Group.

—Little Miss Valentine. Hargreaves, Adam. 2019. (Mr. Men & Little Miss Ser.). (ENG.). 32p. (J). (-k). 16.99 *(978-1-5247-9360-9(4),* Grosset & Dunlap) Penguin Young Readers Group.

—Mr. Birthday. Hargreaves, Adam. Hargreaves, Roger. 2007. (Mr. Men & Little Miss Ser.). (ENG.). 32p. (J). (gr. -1-2). mass mkt. 4.99 *(978-0-8431-2130-8(0),* Grosset & Dunlap) Penguin Young Readers Group.

—Mr. Moustache. Hargreaves, Adam. 2014. (Mr. Men & Little Miss Ser.). (ENG.). 32p. (J). (gr. -1-2). 4.99 *(978-0-8431-8081-7(1),* Grosset & Dunlap) Penguin Young Readers Group.

—Mr. Noisy & the Silent Night. Hargreaves, Adam. 2016. (Mr. Men & Little Miss Ser.). (ENG.). 32p. (J). (gr. -1-2). pap. 4.99 *(978-0-399-54149-0(7),* Price Stern Sloan) Penguin Young Readers Group.

Hargreaves, Adam. Little Miss Princess. Hargreaves, Adam, creator. 2011. (Mr. Men & Little Miss Ser.). (ENG.). 32p. (J). (gr. -1-2). mass mkt. 4.99 *(978-0-8431-9834-8(6),* Grosset & Dunlap) Penguin Young Readers Group.

Hargreaves, Greg. Stone Fox. Gardiner, John Reynolds. 30th anniv. ed. 2010. (Trophy Bk.). (ENG.). 96p. (J). (gr. 2-6). pap. 6.99 *(978-0-06-440132-6(4),* HarperCollins) HarperCollins Pubs. Ltd. GBR. Dist: HarperCollins Pubs.

Hargrove, Kayla. Raina & the Lazy Snowflakes. Diogene, Sophia. 2019. (ENG.). 34p. (J). pap. 12.95 ***(978-1-5346-6301-5(0))*** CreateSpace Independent Publishing Platform.

Haring, Dan. The Star Shepherd. Connolly, MarcyKate. 2019. 320p. (J). (gr. 3-9). 17.99 *(978-1-4926-5820-7(0),* Sourcebooks Jabberwocky) Sourcebooks, Inc.

Haring, Keith. Nina's Book of Little Things. Haring, Keith. 2013. (ENG.). 80p. (J). (gr. 1-4). pap. 19.99 *(978-0-7636-6893-8(1),* Big Picture Press) Candlewick Pr.

Haring, Mary. The Scales of the Silver Fish. Krohn, Gretchen & Johnson, John Norton. 2011. 238p. 46.95 *(978-1-258-08176-8(8))* Literary Licensing, LLC.

Hariton, Anca. A Fruit Is a Suitcase for Seeds. Richards, Jean. 2006. (ENG.). 32p. (J). (gr. -1-3). pap. 8.99 *(978-0-8225-5991-7(9),* First Avenue Editions) Lerner Publishing Group.

Harker, George A. Stories of the Ancient Greeks. Shaw, Charles D. 2008. 332p. pap. 13.95 *(978-1-59915-269-1(X))* Yesterday's Classics.

Harker, Kay. Why Do We Have to Be So Quiet in Church? And 12 Other Questions Kids Have. Simpson, Clare. 2019. (ENG.). 32p. (J). (gr. -1-3). pap. 12.99 *(978-1-64060-451-3(0))* Paraclete Pr., Inc.

Harker, Lesley. Down to Earth. Hooper, Mary. 2008. (Two Naughty Angels Ser.). 96p. (J). (gr. 2-4). pap. 11.95 *(978-0-7475-9061-3(3))* Bloomsbury Publishing Plc GBR. Dist: Independent Pubs. Group.

—Everyone Matters: A First Look at Respect for Others. Thomas, Pat. 2010. (First Look At... Ser.). (ENG.). 32p. (J). (gr. k-2). pap. 8.99 *(978-0-7641-4517-9(7),* B.E.S. Publishing) Peterson's.

—The Ghoul at School. Hooper, Mary. 2008. (Two Naughty Angels Ser.). 96p. (J). (gr. 2-4). pap. 11.95 *(978-0-7475-9060-6(5))* Bloomsbury Publishing Plc GBR. Dist: Independent Pubs. Group.

—I Can Be Safe: A First Look at Safety. Thomas, Pat. 2003. (First Look At... Ser.). (ENG.). 32p. (J). (gr. -1-2). pap. 7.99 *(978-0-7641-2460-0(9),* B.E.S. Publishing) Peterson's.

—I Miss My Pet: A First Look at When a Pet Dies. Thomas, Pat. 2012. (First Look At... Ser.). (ENG.). 32p. (J). (gr. k-2). pap. 7.99 *(978-1-4380-0188-3(6),* B.E.S. Publishing) Peterson's.

—Round the Rainbow. Hooper, Mary. 2008. (Two Naughty Angels Ser.). 96p. (J). (gr. 2-4). pap. 11.95 *(978-0-7475-9062-0(1))* Bloomsbury Publishing Plc GBR. Dist: Independent Pubs. Group.

—The Skin I'm In: A First Look at Racism. Thomas, Pat. 2003. (First Look At... Ser.). (ENG.). 32p. (J). (gr. -1-2). pap. 8.99 *(978-0-7641-2459-4(5),* B.E.S. Publishing) Peterson's.

—This Is My Family: A First Look at Same-Sex Parents. Thomas, Pat. 2012. (First Look At... Ser.). (ENG.). 32p. (J). (gr. k-2). pap. 7.99 *(978-1-4380-0187-6(8),* B.E.S. Publishing) Peterson's.

Harker, Leslie. Why Is It So Hard to Breathe? Thomas, Pat. 2008. (First Look At... Book Ser.). (ENG.). 29p. (J). (gr. k-3). 21.19 *(978-0-7641-3898-0(7),* B.E.S. Publishing) Peterson's.

Harkins, Nathan. Miss Lyla's Banana Pancakes to the Rescue! Rossman, Alicia. 2012. 26p. (J). (-18). 19.95 *(978-1-61863-342-2(2))* Bookstand Publishing.

Harland, Jackie. Ding! Dong! Fairley, Melissa. 2011. (ENG.). 12p. (J). (gr. -1-k). 15.95 *(978-1-84898-362-5(X),* TickTock Books) Octopus Publishing Group GBR. Dist: Independent Pubs. Group.

Harley, Avis. The Monarch's Progress: Poems with Wings. Harley, Avis. 2008. (ENG.). 32p. (J). (gr. 2-k). 16.95 *(978-1-59078-558-4(4),* Wordsong) Boyds Mills Pr.

Harlin, Greg. We the People: The Story of Our Constitution. Cheney, Lynne. (ENG.). 40p. (J). (gr. k-4). 2012. 9.99 *(978-1-4424-4422-5(3));* 2008. 19.99 *(978-1-4169-5418-7(X))* Simon & Schuster/Paula Wiseman Bks. (Simon & Schuster/Paula Wiseman Bks.).

Harlin, Sybel. The Big Book of Alphabet & Numbers. Novick, Mary. (Double Delights Ser.). (ENG.). 32p. (J). *(978-1-877003-11-0(5))* Little Hare Bks. AUS. Dist: HarperCollins Pubs. Australia.

—Numbers. Novick, Mary & Hale, Jenny. 2010. (Double Delight Ser.). (ENG.). 24p. (J). (gr. -1 — 1). pap. 8.99 *(978-1-877003-57-8(3))* Little Hare Bks. AUS. Dist: Independent Pubs. Group.

Harlow, Janet. Can You Find Jesus? Introducing Your Child to the Gospels. Gallery, Philip D. 2003. (Search & Learn Book Ser.). 40p. (J). *(978-2-89088-782-4(0))* Novalis Publishing.

Harlow, Janet L. Can You Find Saints? Introducing Your Child to Holy Men & Women. Harlow, Janet L., tr. Gallery, Philip D. 2003. (J). (ENG.). 41p. (gr. 2-4). 18.99 *(978-0-86716-487-9(5),* B16487); 40p. *(978-2-89507-437-3(2))* Franciscan Media.

Harman, Dominic. Secrets & Shadows. Ferguson, R. L. 2019. (School of Alyxa Ser.). (ENG.). 304p. (J). (gr. 4-8). pap. 7.99 *(978-1-78958-194-2(X))* Willow Tree Bks. GBR. Dist: Independent Pubs. Group.

Harman, Micah. The Blue Baboon. Dwyer, Kevin & Dwyer, Shawnae. 2007. 40p. per. 13.95 *(978-1-59800-247-8(3))* Outskirts Pr., Inc.

Harmer, Sharon. The Cholent Brigade. Herman, Michael. 2017. (ENG.). 24p. (J). (gr. -1-2). 17.99 *(978-1-5124-0844-7(1),* 9781512408447, Kar-Ben Publishing) Lerner Publishing Group.

—If I Were a Major League Baseball Player. Braun, Eric. 2009. (Dream Big! Ser.). (ENG.). 24p. (J). (gr. k-3). lib. bdg. 27.32 *(978-1-4048-5536-6(X),* Picture Window Bks.) Capstone.

—If I Were an Astronaut, 1 vol. Braun, Eric. 2009. (Dream Big! Ser.). (ENG.). 24p. (J). (gr. k-3). pap. 8.95 *(978-1-4048-5710-0(9),* Picture Window Bks.) Capstone.

Harmon, Gedge. Saint Maria Goretti. Windeatt, Mary F. 2009. (ENG.). 32p. (J). (gr. k-2). reprint ed. pap., stu. ed. 4.50 *(978-0-89555-374-4(0))* TAN Bks.

—Saint Teresa of Avila. Windeatt, Mary F. 2009. (ENG.). 32p. (J). (gr. k-2). reprint ed. pap., stu. ed. 4.50 *(978-0-89555-372-0(4))* TAN Bks.

Harmon, Glenn. Always the Elf. Jensen, Kimberly. 2007. 38p. (J). (gr. -1-3). 15.99 *(978-1-59955-086-2(5))* Cedar Fort, Inc./CFI Distribution.

—I Am a Child of God. Setzer, Lee Ann. 2007. (Tiny Talks Ser.). 74p. (J). per. 7.99 *(978-1-59955-076-3(8))* Cedar Fort, Inc./CFI Distribution.

—My Wedding Day. Rowley, Deborah Pace. 2007. 24p. (J). (gr. -1-3). 15.99 *(978-1-59955-016-9(4))* Cedar Fort, Inc./CFI Distribution.

—Tiny Talks 2009: My Eternal Family. Setzer, LeeAnn. 2008. 114p. (J). pap. 8.99 *(978-1-59955-210-1(8))* Cedar Fort, Inc./CFI Distribution.

—The Wisemen of Bountiful. Potter, George. 2005. per. 11.99 *(978-1-55517-814-7(6))* Cedar Fort, Inc./CFI Distribution.

Harmon, Mark. Where in Cuba Is Mr. Roosevelt? 2018. (Adventures of Little David & the Magic Coin Ser.: Vol. 8). (ENG.). 148p. (J). pap. 8.99 *(978-1-7208-8649-5(0))* CreateSpace Independent Publishing Platform.

Harmon, Steve. Papa's New Home. Curtis, Jessica Lynn. 2012. (ENG.). 40p. (J). *(978-0-931674-64-8(6),* Waldman House Pr.) TRISTAN Publishing, Inc.

Harms, Jeanine. Boss Mouse Coloring Book & Theme Song. 2006. (J). 4.00 *(978-1-4276-0118-6(6))* Aardvark Global Publishing.

Harms, Quinten. Joy's Journey: Grapes on Toast. Brown, Susan. 2019. (ENG.). 46p. (J). *(978-0-2288-1481-8(2));* pap. *(978-0-2288-1480-1(4))* Tellwell Talent.

Harness, Cheryl. M Is for Mount Rushmore: A South Dakota Alphabet. Anderson, William. 2005. (Discover America State by State Ser.). (ENG.). 40p. (J). 17.95 *(978-1-58536-141-0(0))* Sleeping Bear Pr.

—Shovelful of Sunshine. Hutton, Stacie Vaughn. 2012. (ENG.). 32p. (J). 16.95 *(978-0-938467-39-7(5))* Headline Bks., Inc.

—Women Explorers. Cummins, Julie. 2015. 48p. (J). (gr. 2-5). 8.99 *(978-0-14-751736-4(2),* Puffin Books) Penguin Young Readers Group.

Harness, Cheryl. Ghosts of the Civil War. Harness, Cheryl. 2004. (ENG.). 48p. (J). (gr. 2-5). 8.99 *(978-0-689-86992-1(4),* Simon & Schuster Bks. For Young Readers) Simon & Schuster Bks. For Young Readers.

—Ghosts of the Nile. Harness, Cheryl. 2010. (ENG.). 32p. (J). (gr. 2-5). 13.99 *(978-1-4424-2200-1(9),* Simon & Schuster Bks. For Young Readers) Simon & Schuster Bks. For Young Readers.

—Remember the Ladies: 100 Great American Women. Harness, Cheryl. 2003. (ENG.). 64p. (J). (gr. 3-18). pap. 8.99 *(978-0-06-443869-8(4))* HarperCollins Pubs.

Harnett, Katie. Franklin & Luna Go to the Moon. Campbell, Jen. 2018. (Franklin & Luna Ser.: 0). (ENG.). 32p. (J). (gr. -1-1). 17.95 *(978-0-500-65146-9(9),* 565146) Thames & Hudson.

—Franklin's Flying Bookshop. Campbell, Jen. 2017. (Franklin & Luna Ser.: 0). (ENG.). 32p. (J). (gr. -1-3). 17.95 *(978-0-500-65109-4(4),* 565109) Thames & Hudson.

—The Language of Spells. Weyr, Garret. 2018. (ENG.). 256p. (J). (gr. 5-9). 16.99 *(978-1-4521-5958-4(0))* Chronicle Bks. LLC.

—Little Bits of Sky. Durrant, S. E. 2017. (ENG.). 208p. (J). (gr. 3-7). 16.95 *(978-0-8234-3839-6(2))* Holiday Hse., Inc.

Harney, Jenn. Hazy Bloom & the Mystery Next Door. Hamburg, Jennifer. 2019. (Hazy Bloom Ser.: 3). (ENG.). 176p. (J). 15.99 *(978-0-374-30501-7(3),* 900162032, Farrar, Straus & Giroux (BYR)) Farrar, Straus & Giroux.

—Hazy Bloom & the Mystery Next Door. Hamburg, Jennifer. 2020. (Hazy Bloom Ser.: 3). (ENG.). 176p. (J). pap. 6.99 *(978-1-250-23327-1(5),* 900162033) Square Fish.

—Hazy Bloom & the Pet Project. Hamburg, Jennifer. 2019. (Hazy Bloom Ser.: 2). (ENG.). 208p. (J). pap. 6.99 *(978-1-250-29411-1(8),* 900162030) Square Fish.

—Hazy Bloom & the Tomorrow Power. Hamburg, Jennifer. 2018. (Hazy Bloom Ser.: 1). (ENG.). 192p. (J). pap. 9.99 *(978-1-250-14355-6(1),* 900162027) Square Fish.

—Never Trumpet with a Crumpet. Gibson, Amy. 2019. 32p. (J). (gr. -1-2). 17.95 *(978-1-62979-304-7(3))* Boyds Mills Pr.

Harney, Jenn. Wanda Seasongood & the Mostly True Secret. Lurie, Susan. 2020. (Wanda Seasongood Ser.: 1). 224p. (J). (gr. 3-7). 15.99 ***(978-1-368-04315-1(1))*** Little, Brown Bks. for Young Readers.

Harney, Jennifer. How to Become a Knight (in Ten Easy Lessons) Tarpley, Todd. 2018. (ENG.). 32p. (J). (gr. -1). 16.95 *(978-1-4549-2330-5(X))* Sterling Publishing Co., Inc.

Harnish, Alexander. The Duck Who Drove a Boat. Harnish, Jeannette. 2008. 31p. pap. 24.95 *(978-1-60610-665-5(1))* America Star Bks.

Harold, Elsie Louise. Stop Bullying: An ABC Guide for Children & the Adults Who Interact with Them. Harold, Elsie Louise. 2004. (J). spiral bd. 14.99 *(978-0-9764644-0-2(3))* Harold, Elsie L.

Harper, Betty. Color My World Vol. 1: Early Elvis (Coloring Book) Harper, Betty. 2004. 32p. (J). 4.95 *(978-0-932117-42-7(2))* Osborne Enterprises Publishing.

Harper, Charise Mericle. Chocolate: A Sweet History. Markle, Sandra. 2005. (Smart about History Ser.). (ENG.). 32p. (J). (gr. 3-6). 21.19 *(978-0-448-43566-4(7))* Penguin Young Readers Group.

—Smart about Chocolate: Smart about History. Markle, Sandra. 2004. (Smart about History Ser.). 32p. (J). (gr. k-4). mass mkt. 6.99 *(978-0-448-43480-3(6),* Grosset & Dunlap) Penguin Young Readers Group.

Harper, Charise Mericle. Cupcake. Harper, Charise Mericle. 2010. 32p. (J). (gr. -1-3). 14.99 *(978-1-4231-1897-8(9))* Hyperion Pr.

Harper, Charise Mericle, jt. illus. see Willems, Mo.

Harper, Charley. Charley Harper's Animal Alphabet. Burke, Zoe. 2015. (ENG.). 24p. (J). bds. *(978-0-7649-7233-1(2))* Pomegranate Communications, Inc.

—Charley Harper's Birds. 2013. (ENG.). (J). 7.95 *(978-0-7649-6513-5(1))* Pomegranate Communications, Inc.

—Charley Harper's Book of Colors. Burke, Zoe. 2015. (ENG.). 24p. (J). bds. 10.95 *(978-0-7649-7261-4(8),* POMEGRANATE KIDS) Pomegranate Communications, Inc.

—Charley Harper's Count the Birds. Burke, Zoe. 2015. (ENG.). 24p. (J). bds. 10.95 *(978-0-7649-7246-1(4),* POMEGRANATE KIDS) Pomegranate Communications, Inc.

—Charley Harper's Sticky Birds: An Animal Sticker Kit. 2013. (ENG.). (J). 19.95 *(978-0-7649-6467-1(4))* Pomegranate Communications, Inc.

—Charley Harper's Tree of Life. 2013. (ENG.). (J). 7.95 *(978-0-7649-6514-2(X))* Pomegranate Communications, Inc.

—Charley Harper's What's in the Rain Forest? A Nature Discovery Book. Burke, Zoe. 2013. 34p. (J). 14.95 *(978-0-7649-6584-5(0))* Pomegranate Communications, Inc.

—Charley Harper's What's in the Woods? A Nature Discovery Book. Burke, Zoe. 2013. (ENG.). 32p. (J). 14.95 *(978-0-7649-6453-4(4))* Pomegranate Communications, Inc.

Harper, Charley. ABC's. Harper, Charley. Fowler, Gloria, ed. 2008. (ENG.). 20p. (J). (gr. -1-3). bds. 9.95 *(978-1-934429-21-1(X))* AMMO Bks., LLC.

—123's. Harper, Charley. 2008. (ENG.). 20p. (J). (gr. -1-3). bds. 9.95 *(978-1-934429-22-8(8))* AMMO Bks., LLC.

Harper, Chris. The Dogges of Barkshire - the Grand Kennel. Harper, Chris. 2013. 26p. (J). pap. *(978-1-78222-086-2(0))* Paragon Publishing, Rothersthorpe.

Harper, Clifford. A Little History of the World. Gombrich, E. H. Mustill, Caroline, tr. 2008. (Little Histories Ser.). (ENG.). 304p. pap. 15.00 *(978-0-300-14332-4(X))* Yale Univ. Pr.

—A Little History of the World. Gombrich, E. H. Mustill, Caroline, tr. 2005. (Little Histories Ser.). (ENG.). 320p. 25.00 *(978-0-300-10883-5(4))* Yale Univ. Pr.

Harper, Diane. Jace's Adventure at Children's Hospital. Harper, D. W. 2018. (Jace Adventure Ser.: Vol. 3). (ENG.). 116p. (J). (gr. 1-5). pap. 7.99 *(978-0-9848736-2-3(7))* HayMarBks., LLC.

Harper, Jamie. EllRay Jakes Is a Rock Star, 2 vols. Warner, Sally. 2012. (EllRay Jakes Ser.: 2). (ENG.). 128p. (J). (gr. 1-3). 5.99 *(978-0-14-241989-2(3),* Puffin Books) Penguin Young Readers Group.

—EllRay Jakes Is Not a Chicken, 1 vol. Warner, Sally. 2012. (EllRay Jakes Ser.: 1). (ENG.). 128p. (J). (gr. 1-3). 5.99 *(978-0-14-241988-5(5),* Puffin Books) Penguin Young Readers Group.

—Excellent Emma. Warner, Sally. 2010. (Emma Ser.: 5). (ENG.). 144p. (J). (gr. 3-7). 6.99 *(978-0-14-241569-6(3),* Puffin Books) Penguin Young Readers Group.

—Only Emma. Warner, Sally. 2006. (Emma Ser.: 1). (ENG.). 144p. (J). (gr. 3-7). 6.99 *(978-0-14-240711-0(9),* Puffin Books) Penguin Young Readers Group.

—Super Emma. Warner, Sally. 2008. (Emma Ser.: 3). (ENG.). 112p. (J). (gr. 3-7). 5.99 *(978-0-14-241088-2(8),* Puffin Books) Penguin Young Readers Group.

—Walks the Plank! Warner, Sally. 2013. (EllRay Jakes Ser.: 3). (ENG.). 128p. (J). (gr. 1-3). pap. 5.99 *(978-0-14-242409-4(9),* Puffin Books) Penguin Young Readers Group.

Harper, Jamie. Miles to Go. Harper, Jamie. 2010. (ENG.). 32p. (J). (gr. -1-2). 12.99 *(978-0-7636-3598-5(7))* Candlewick Pr.

—Miss Mingo & the Fire Drill. Harper, Jamie. 2012. (Miss Mingo Ser.). 40p. (J). (gr. -1-3). pap. 6.99 *(978-0-7636-6086-4(8))* Candlewick Pr.

—Miss Mingo & the First Day of School. Harper, Jamie. 2009. (Miss Mingo Ser.). 32p. (J). (gr. -1-3). pap. 6.99 *(978-0-7636-4134-4(0))* Candlewick Pr.

—Miss Mingo Weathers the Storm. Harper, Jamie. (Miss Mingo Ser.). 40p. (J). (gr. -1-3). 2017. 6.99 *(978-0-7636-9514-9(9));* 2012. (ENG.). 15.99 *(978-0-7636-4931-9(7))* Candlewick Pr.

—Splish Splash, Baby Bundt: A Recipe for Bath Time. Harper, Jamie. 2007. 24p. (J). (— 1). bds. 6.99 *(978-0-7636-3240-3(6))* Candlewick Pr.

Harper, Lee. Ready or Not, Woolbur Goes to School! Helakoski, Leslie. 2018. (ENG.). 32p. (J). (gr. -1-3). 17.99 *(978-0-06-136657-4(9))* HarperCollins Pubs.

—Turkey Claus, 0 vols. Silvano, Wendi J. 2012. (Turkey Trouble Ser.: 2). (ENG.). 40p. (J). (gr. -1-3). 16.99 *(978-0-7614-6239-2(2),* 9780761462392, Two Lions) Amazon Publishing.

—Woolbur. Helakoski, Leslie. 2008. (ENG.). 32p. (J). (gr. -1-3). 17.89 *(978-0-06-084727-2(1));* 17.99 *(978-0-06-084726-5(3))* HarperCollins Pubs.

Harper, Lee. Snow! Snow! Snow! Harper, Lee. 2009. (ENG.). 40p. (J). (gr. -1-3). 17.99 *(978-1-4169-8454-2(2),* Simon & Schuster/Paula Wiseman Bks.) Simon & Schuster/Paula Wiseman Bks.

Harper, Lee & Lee, Harper. Looking for the Easy Life. Myers, Walter Dean. 2011. (Looking at Other Countries Ser.). (ENG.). 40p. (J). (gr. -1-3). 16.99 *(978-0-06-054375-4(2))* HarperCollins Pubs.

Harper, Piers. The Young Learner's Bible Storybook: 52 Stories with Activities for Family Fun & Learning. Simon, Mary Manz. 2006. (First Virtues for Toddlers Ser.). 336p. (J). (gr. -1-2). 17.99 *(978-0-7847-1277-1(8),* 04010) Standard Publishing.

Harper, Ruth. Un Beso en Mi Mano (the Kissing Hand) Penn, Audrey. 2006. (ENG.). 32p. (J). (gr. -1-3). 16.95 *(978-1-933718-01-9(3))* Tanglewood Pr.

Harper, Ruth. The Kissing Hand. Penn, Audrey. 2007. (ENG.). 32p. (J). 12.99 ***(978-1-939100-53-5(4));*** (gr. -1-3). 28.95 *(978-1-933718-07-1(2))* Tanglewood Pr.

Harper, Ruth. The Kissing Hand (with CD) Penn, Audrey. unabr. ed. 2007. (ENG.). 32p. (J). (gr. -1-3). pap. 12.99 incl. audio compact disk *(978-1-933718-10-1(2))* Tanglewood Pr.

—Sassafras. Penn, Audrey. 2006. (ENG.). 32p. (J). (gr. -1-3). 16.95 *(978-1-933718-03-3(X))* Tanglewood Pr.

Harper, Ruth E. Mamis Felices. Pelley, Kathleen T. 2016. (SPA.). (J). 14.95 *(978-1-58760-161-3(3),* CWLA Pr.) Child Welfare League of America, Inc.

Harper, Suzanne. The Real Spy's Guide to Becoming a Spy. Ernest, Peter. 2009. (ENG.). 144p. (J). (gr. -1-3). 19.95 *(978-0-8109-8329-8(X),* Abrams Bks. for Young Readers) Abrams, Inc.

Harpster, Steve. Ack's New Pet, 1 vol. Hoena, Blake A. 2014. (Eek & Ack Early Chapter Bks.). (ENG.). 32p. (J). (gr. k-2). lib. bdg. 22.65 *(978-1-4342-6406-0(8),* Stone Arch Bks.) Capstone.

—Arnold Gets Angry: An Emotional Literacy Book. 2004. (Emotional Literacy Ser.). 45p. (J). (gr. 2-18). 14.95 *(978-0-9747789-0-7(7),* 67312) CTC Publishing.

—The Beach Bandit, 1 vol. Yasuda, Anita. 2013. (Dino Detectives Ser.). (ENG.). 32p. (J). (gr. 1-2). pap. 5.95 *(978-1-4342-4830-5(5));* lib. bdg. 22.65 *(978-1-4342-4154-2(8))* Capstone. (Stone Arch Bks.).

—Betty Stops the Bully: An Emotional Literacy Book. 2004. (Emotional Literacy Ser.). 44p. (J). (gr. 2-18). 14.95 *(978-0-9747789-1-4(5),* 67313) CTC Publishing.

—Beyond the Black Hole. Hoena, Blake A. 2008. (Graphic Sparks Ser.). (ENG.). 40p. (J). (gr. 2-5). pap. 5.95 *(978-1-4342-0855-2(9),* Stone Arch Bks.) Capstone.

—Big City Sights, 1 vol. Yasuda, Anita. 2011. (My First Graphic Novel Ser.). (ENG.). 32p. (J). (gr. k-2). pap. 6.25 *(978-1-4342-3060-7(0));* lib. bdg. 24.65 *(978-1-4342-2515-3(1))* Capstone. (Stone Arch Bks.).

—The Big Mistake, 1 vol. Hoena, Blake A. 2014. (Eek & Ack Early Chapter Bks.). (ENG.). 32p. (J). (gr. k-2). lib. bdg. 22.65 *(978-1-4342-6408-4(4),* Stone Arch Bks.) Capstone.

H

—The Black Hole Report, 1 vol. Hoena, Blake A. 2014. (Eek & Ack Early Chapter Bks.). (ENG.). 32p. (J). (gr. k-2). lib. bdg. 22.65 *(978-1-4342-6409-1(2)*, Stone Arch Bks.) Capstone.

—Blast to the Past. Nickel, Scott. 2006. (Graphic Sparks Ser.). (ENG.). 40p. (J). (gr. 2-5). 5.95 *(978-1-59889-167-6(7)*, Stone Arch Bks.) Capstone.

—The Boy Who Burped Too Much, 1 vol. Nickel, Scott. 2006. (Graphic Sparks Ser.). (ENG.). 40p. (J). (gr. 2-5). 23.99 *(978-1-59889-037-2(9)*, Stone Arch Bks.) Capstone.

—The Brave Puffer Fish, 1 vol. Meister, Cari. 2011. (Ocean Tales Ser.). (ENG.). 32p. (J). (gr. 2-3). pap. 6.25 *(978-1-4342-3389-9(8)*, Stone Arch Bks.) Capstone.

—Catherine Finds Her Courage: An Emotional Literacy Book. 2004. (Emotional Literacy Ser.). 44p. (J). (gr. 2-18). 14.95 *(978-0-9747789-2-1(3)*, 67314) CTC Publishing.

—Chicken Little: Classic Tales Series. Smith, Carrie. 2011. (Classic Tales Ser.). (J). *(978-1-936258-74-1(9))* Benchmark Education Co.

—Chicken Little - 6 Pack: Set of 6 with Common Core Teacher Materials. 2015. (Classic Tales Ser.). (J). (gr. k-1). 39.00 *(978-1-5125-8329-8(4))* Benchmark Education Co.

—Christmas Eve. Torres, J. 2006. (Scribble & Sing Ser.). (ENG.). 80p. (J). 4.99 *(978-1-4169-2731-0(X)*, Simon Scribbles) Simon Scribbles.

—The Clever Dolphin, 1 vol. Meister, Cari. 2012. (Ocean Tales Ser.). (ENG.). 32p. (J). (gr. 2-3). pap. 6.25 *(978-1-4342-4229-7(3)*, Stone Arch Bks.) Capstone.

—The Crazy Clues, 1 vol. Yasuda, Anita. 2013. (Dino Detectives Ser.). (ENG.). 32p. (J). (gr. 1-2). lib. bdg. 22.65 *(978-1-4342-5971-4(4)*, Stone Arch Bks.) Capstone.

—Crazy Clues. Yasuda, Anita. 2013. (Dino Detectives Ser.). (ENG.). 32p. (J). (gr. 1-2). pap. 5.95 *(978-1-4342-6200-4(6)*, Stone Arch Bks.) Capstone.

—Curse of the Red Scorpion, 1 vol. Nickel, Scott. 2006. (Graphic Sparks Ser.). (ENG.). 40p. (J). (gr. 2-5). per. 5.95 *(978-1-59889-169-0(3))*; 23.99 *(978-1-59889-034-1(4))* Capstone. (Stone Arch Bks.).

—Debra Doesn't Take the Dare: An Emotional Literacy Book. 2004. 54p. (J). 14.95 *(978-0-9747789-3-8(1)*, 20705) CTC Publishing.

—Dino Detectives. Yasuda, Anita. 2013. (Dino Detectives Ser.). (ENG.). 32p. (J). (gr. 1-3). pap., pap., pap. 31.60 *(978-1-4342-6221-9(9))*; lib. bdg., lib. bdg., lib. bdg. 158.55 *(978-1-4342-6059-8(3))* Capstone. (Stone Arch Bks.).

—Dognapped! Jimmy Sniffles. Nickel, Scott. 2006. (Graphic Sparks Ser.). (ENG.). 40p. (J). (gr. 2-5). per. 5.95 *(978-1-59889-226-0(6)*, Stone Arch Bks.) Capstone.

—Double Trouble. Nickel, Scott. 2007. (Graphic Sparks Ser.). (ENG.). 40p. (J). (gr. 2-5). per. 5.95 *(978-1-59889-411-0(0)*, Stone Arch Bks.) Capstone.

—Down on the Farm, 1 vol. Houts, Amy. 2011. (My First Graphic Novel Ser.). (ENG.). 32p. (J). (gr. k-2). pap. 6.25 *(978-1-4342-3063-8(5))*; lib. bdg. 24.65 *(978-1-4342-2516-0(X))* Capstone. (Stone Arch Bks.).

—Eek & Ack vs the Wolfman, 1 vol. Hoena, Blake A. 2009. (Eek & Ack Ser.). (ENG.). 40p. (J). (gr. 2-5). lib. bdg. 23.99 *(978-1-4342-1189-7(4)*, Stone Arch Bks.) Capstone.

—Eek Discovers Earth, 1 vol. Hoena, Blake A. 2014. (Eek & Ack Early Chapter Bks.). (ENG.). 32p. (J). (gr. k-2). lib. bdg. 22.65 *(978-1-4342-6407-7(6)*, Stone Arch Bks.) Capstone.

—Ethan Has Too Much Energy: An Emotional Literacy Book. Shapiro, Lawrence. 2005. (Emotional Literacy Ser.). 42p. (J). 14.95 *(978-0-9747789-4-5(X)*, 36027) CTC Publishing.

—The Fancy Octopus, 1 vol. Meister, Cari. 2011. (Ocean Tales Ser.). (ENG.). 32p. (J). (gr. 2-3). pap. 6.25 *(978-1-4342-3392-9(8))*; lib. bdg. 22.65 *(978-1-4342-3201-4(8))* Capstone. (Stone Arch Bks.).

—First Base Blues, 1 vol. Yasuda, Anita. 2012. (My First Graphic Novel Ser.). (ENG.). 32p. (J). (gr. k-2). pap. 6.25 *(978-1-4342-3863-4(6)*, Stone Arch Bks.) Capstone.

—First Word Search: Easy First Words. 2011. (First Word Search Ser.). 64p. (J). (gr. -1-1). pap. 4.95 *(978-1-4027-7808-7(2))* Sterling Publishing Co., Inc.

—First Word Search: Fun First Words. 2011. (First Word Search Ser.). 64p. (J). pap. 4.95 *(978-1-4027-7807-0(4))* Sterling Publishing Co., Inc.

—The Forest Surprise, 1 vol. Mooney, Carla. 2011. (My First Graphic Novel Ser.). (ENG.). 32p. (J). (gr. k-2). pap. 6.25 *(978-1-4342-3064-5(3))*; lib. bdg. 24.65 *(978-1-4342-2520-7(8))* Capstone. (Stone Arch Bks.).

—Freddy Fights Fat: An Emotional Literacy Book. Shapiro, Lawrence E. 2004. (Emotional Literacy Ser.). 54p. (J). (gr. 2-18). 14.95 *(978-0-9747789-5-2(8)*, 67873) CTC Publishing.

—Ghost Sounds, 1 vol. Yasuda, Anita. 2013. (Dino Detectives Ser.). (ENG.). 32p. (J). (gr. 1-2). pap. 5.95 *(978-1-4342-4831-2(3))*; lib. bdg. 22.65 *(978-1-4342-4152-8(1))* Capstone. (Stone Arch Bks.).

—Growing up Happy: Arnold Gets Angry, Betty Stops the Bully & Catherine Finds Her Courage: the Emotional Literacy Series, 3, 3 vols., Set. 2004. (Emotional Literacy Ser.). 135p. (J). lib. bdg. 52.00 *(978-0-9747789-9-0(0))* CTC Publishing.

—The Grumpy Lobster, 1 vol. Meister, Cari. 2012. (Ocean Tales Ser.). (ENG.). 32p. (J). (gr. 2-3). pap. 6.25 *(978-1-4342-4230-3(7))*; lib. bdg. 22.65 *(978-1-4342-4025-5(8))* Capstone. (Stone Arch Bks.).

—Haunted House. Yasuda, Anita. 2013. (Dino Detectives Ser.). (ENG.). 32p. (J). (gr. 1-2). pap. 5.95 *(978-1-4342-6199-1(9)*, Stone Arch Bks.) Capstone.

—The Hiding Eel, 1 vol. Meister, Cari. 2011. (Ocean Tales Ser.). (ENG.). 32p. (J). (gr. 2-3). pap. 6.25 *(978-1-4342-3390-5(1))*; lib. bdg. 22.65 *(978-1-4342-3199-4(2))* Capstone. (Stone Arch Bks.).

—The Jumping Monkeys. Smith, Carrie. 2009. (Reader's Theater Nursery Rhymes & Songs Set B Ser.). 48p. (J). pap. *(978-1-60859-155-8(7))* Benchmark Education Co.

—The Lucky Manatee, 1 vol. Meister, Cari. 2012. (Ocean Tales Ser.). (ENG.). 32p. (J). (gr. 2-3). pap. 6.25 *(978-1-4342-4231-0(5))*; lib. bdg. 22.65 *(978-1-4342-4028-6(2))* Capstone. (Stone Arch Bks.).

—The Missing Trumpet, 1 vol. Yasuda, Anita. 2013. (Dino Detectives Ser.). (ENG.). 32p. (J). (gr. 1-2). pap. 5.95 *(978-1-4342-4832-9(1))*; lib. bdg. 22.65 *(978-1-4342-4155-9(6))* Capstone. (Stone Arch Bks.).

—Mr. Potato Head Upside down Joke World. Charney, Steve. 2008. (Jokes & Riddles Ser.). (ENG.). 96p. (J). (gr. k-3). 17.44 *(978-1-4027-5361-9(6))* Sterling Publishing Co., Inc.

—The Mystery Coins, 1 vol. Yasuda, Anita. 2013. (Dino Detectives Ser.). (ENG.). 32p. (J). (gr. 1-2). lib. bdg. 22.65 *(978-1-4342-5972-1(2)*, Stone Arch Bks.) Capstone.

—Mystery Coins. Yasuda, Anita. 2013. (Dino Detectives Ser.). (ENG.). 32p. (J). (gr. 1-2). pap. 5.95 *(978-1-4342-6201-1(4)*, Stone Arch Bks.) Capstone.

—A Nose for Danger. Temple, Bob. 2006. (Graphic Sparks Ser.). (ENG.). 40p. (J). (gr. 2-5). per. 5.95 *(978-1-59889-171-3(5))*; lib. bdg. 23.99 *(978-1-59889-036-5(0))* Capstone. (Stone Arch Bks.).

—Ocean Tales. Meister, Cari. 2013. (Ocean Tales Ser.). (ENG.). 32p. (J). (gr. -1-3). lib. bdg., lib. bdg., lib. bdg. 158.55 *(978-1-4342-8844-8(7)*, Stone Arch Bks.) Capstone.

—Ooze Slingers from Outer Space. Hoena, Blake A. 2007. (Graphic Sparks Ser.). (ENG.). 40p. (J). (gr. 2-5). per. 5.95 *(978-1-59889-410-3(2)*, Stone Arch Bks.) Capstone.

—The Princess & the Pea: Classic Tales Edition. Smith, Carrie. 2011. (Classic Tales Ser.). (J). *(978-1-936258-76-5(5))* Benchmark Education Co.

—The Princess & the Pea - 6 Pack: Set of 6 with Common Core Teacher Materials. 2015. (Classic Tales Ser.). (J). (gr. k-1). 39.00 *(978-1-5125-8361-8(8))* Benchmark Education Co.

—The Puzzling Pluto Plot: Eek & Ack, 1 vol. Hoena, Blake A. 2008. (Graphic Sparks Ser.). (ENG.). 40p. (J). (gr. 2-5). pap. 5.95 *(978-1-4342-0502-5(9)*, Stone Arch Bks.) Capstone.

—The Quick Quarterback, 1 vol. Lord, Michelle. 2012. (My First Graphic Novel Ser.). (ENG.). 32p. (J). (gr. k-2). pap. 6.25 *(978-1-4342-3861-0(X)*, Stone Arch Bks.) Capstone.

—Race on the River, 1 vol. Nickel, Scott. 2011. (My First Graphic Novel Ser.). (ENG.). 32p. (J). (gr. k-2). pap. 6.25 *(978-1-4342-3061-4(9))*; lib. bdg. 24.65 *(978-1-4342-2521-4(6))* Capstone. (Stone Arch Bks.).

—The Scary Slopes, 1 vol. Pattison, Darcy. 2011. (My First Graphic Novel Ser.). (ENG.). 32p. (J). (gr. k-2). lib. bdg. 24.65 *(978-1-4342-2534-4(8)*, Stone Arch Bks.) Capstone.

—The Shivery Shark, 1 vol. Meister, Cari. 2011. (Ocean Tales Ser.). (ENG.). 32p. (J). (gr. 2-3). pap. 6.25 *(978-1-4342-3391-2(X))*; lib. bdg. 22.65 *(978-1-4342-3200-7(X))* Capstone. (Stone Arch Bks.).

—The Slime Attack, 1 vol. Yasuda, Anita. 2013. (Dino Detectives Ser.). (ENG.). 32p. (J). (gr. 1-2). pap. 5.95 *(978-1-4342-4833-6(X))*; lib. bdg. 22.65 *(978-1-4342-4153-5(X))* Capstone. (Stone Arch Bks.).

—The Stranded Orca, 1 vol. Meister, Cari. 2012. (Ocean Tales Ser.). (ENG.). 32p. (J). (gr. 2-3). pap. 6.25 *(978-1-4342-4232-7(3))*; lib. bdg. 22.65 *(978-1-4342-4026-2(6))* Capstone. (Stone Arch Bks.).

—Super Knock-Knocks. Keller, Charles. 2003. (Giggle Fit Ser.). (ENG.). 48p. (J). (gr. k-3). 16.19 *(978-1-4027-0863-3(7))* Sterling Publishing Co., Inc.

—The Super-Powered Sneeze. Nickel, Scott. 2007. (Graphic Sparks Ser.). (ENG.). 40p. (J). (gr. 2-5). per. 5.95 *(978-1-59889-409-7(9)*, Stone Arch Bks.) Capstone.

—The Surprise Prize, 1 vol. Yasuda, Anita. 2013. (Dino Detectives Ser.). (ENG.). 32p. (J). (gr. 1-2). lib. bdg. 22.65 *(978-1-4342-5969-1(2)*, Stone Arch Bks.) Capstone.

—Surprise Prize. Yasuda, Anita. 2013. (Dino Detectives Ser.). (ENG.). 32p. (J). (gr. 1-2). pap. 5.95 *(978-1-4342-6198-4(0)*, Stone Arch Bks.) Capstone.

—The Swim Race, 1 vol. Yasuda, Anita. 2012. (My First Graphic Novel Ser.). (ENG.). 32p. (J). (gr. k-2). pap. 6.25 *(978-1-4342-3864-1(4))*; lib. bdg. 24.65 *(978-1-4342-3280-9(8))* Capstone. (Stone Arch Bks.).

—The Three Billy Goats Gruff: Classic Tales Edition. Adams, Alison. 2011. (Classic Tales Ser.). (J). *(978-1-936258-62-8(5))* Benchmark Education Co.

—Tide Pool Trouble, 1 vol. Lord, Michelle. 2011. (My First Graphic Novel Ser.). (ENG.). 32p. (J). (gr. k-2). pap. 6.25 *(978-1-4342-3059-1(7))*; lib. bdg. 24.65 *(978-1-4342-2517-7(8))* Capstone. (Stone Arch Bks.).

—Too Short for the Court, 1 vol. Lemke, Amy J. 2012. (My First Graphic Novel Ser.). (ENG.). 32p. (J). (gr. k-2). pap. 6.25 *(978-1-4342-3862-7(8))*; lib. bdg. 24.65 *(978-1-4342-3282-3(4))* Capstone. (Stone Arch Bks.).

—Wonderful Weather. Levine, Shar & Johnstone, Leslie. 2005. (First Science Experiments Ser.). (ENG.). 48p. (J). (gr. 2-4). 17.44 *(978-0-8069-7249-7(1))* Sterling Publishing Co., Inc.

Harr, Alexandra. Make a Stand: When Life Gives You Lemons, Change the World! 2014. (ENG.). (J). (gr. -1-3). 18.99 *(978-0-9911314-0-2(1))* Chocolate Sauce.

Harr, Lynn. The Ice Angel. Spoon, Cynthia. 2006. 24p. (J). (gr. -1-3). per. 8.50 *(978-1-60002-280-7(4)*, 4233) Mountain Valley Publishing, LLC.

Harrad, Matthew. Composting: Nature's Recyclers, 1 vol. Koontz, Robin Michal. 2006. (Amazing Science Ser.). (ENG.). 24p. (J). (gr. k-4). per. 8.95 *(978-1-4048-2200-9(3)*, Picture Window Bks.) Capstone.

—Erosion: Changing Earth's Surface, 1 vol. Koontz, Robin Michal. 2006. (Amazing Science Ser.). (ENG.). 24p. (J). (gr. k-4). per. 8.95 *(978-1-4048-2201-6(1)*, Picture Window Bks.) Capstone.

Harrald-Pilz, Marilee. Buttercup Hill. Berry, Eileen M. 2006. 39p. (J). (gr. -1-3). pap. *(978-1-59166-667-7(8))* BJU Pr.

—Five Spooky Ghosts Playing Tricks at School. Metzger, Steve. 2005. (J). *(978-0-439-80381-6(0))* Scholastic, Inc.

—Just the Right Home. Schmauss, Judy Kentor. 2006. (Reader's Clubhouse Level 2 Reader Ser.). (ENG.). 24p. (J). (gr. k-1). pap. 3.99 *(978-0-7641-3299-5(7)*, B.E.S. Publishing) Peterson's.

Harrel, Tina. My Blended Family. Picone, Emma Lee. 2012. 32p. pap. 12.95 *(978-0-9829803-9-2(6))* Joshua Tree Publishing.

Harrell, Kim. Perry's Baltimore Adventure: A Bird's-Eye View of Charm City. Dans, Peter E. 2007. (ENG.). 32p. (J). (gr. -1-1). 14.95 *(978-1-933822-08-2(2))* Camino Bks., Inc.

—Perry's Baltimore Adventure: A Bird's-Eye View of Charm City. Dans, Peter E. 2003. 30p. (J). 11.95 *(978-0-87033-540-2(5)*, Cornell Maritime Pr./Tidewater Pubs.) Schiffer Publishing, Ltd.

—While a Tree Grew: The Story of Maryland's Wye Oak. Bachmann, Elaine Rice. 2009. (ENG.). 30p. (gr. -1-3). 10.50 *(978-0-87033-577-8(4)*, 9780870335778, Cornell Maritime Pr./Tidewater Pubs.) Schiffer Publishing, Ltd.

Harrell, Maurice. The Boy Who Loved to Be Like Michael Jackson. Yolanda And Reese. 2012. 32p. 24.95 *(978-1-4560-8506-3(9))* America Star Bks.

Harrell, Michael. Busy Bumble Bee Rides the Waves. Moore, Carol Hair. 2009. (I Wish You Ice Cream & Cake Ser.: 2). (ENG.). 32p. (J). lib. bdg. 15.95 *(978-1-935083-06-1(6))* CyPress Pubns.

—Marvin the Magnificent Nubian Goat. Moore, Carol Hair. 2009. (I Wish You Ice Cream & Cake Ser.). 28p. (J). lib. bdg. 15.95 *(978-1-935083-03-0(1))* CyPress Pubns.

Harrell, Micheal. Marvin the Magnificent Nubian Goat. Moore, Carol H. 2006. (J). 20.00 *(978-0-9792019-0-5(X))* iwishyouicecreamandcake.

Harrell, Symear. On Christmas Day. Londa And Pop-Pop. 2011. 16p. pap. 24.95 *(978-1-4560-7078-6(9))* America Star Bks.

Harren, Kayla. A Boy Like You. Murphy, Frank. 2019. (ENG.). 32p. (J). (gr. -1-2). 16.99 *(978-1-5341-1046-5(1)*, 204756) Sleeping Bear Pr.

—The Boy Who Grew a Forest: The True Story of Jadav Payeng. Gohlz, Sophia. 2019. (ENG.). 32p. (J). (gr. k-3). 16.99 *(978-1-5341-1024-3(0)*, 204656) Sleeping Bear Pr.

Harren, Kayla. Fiery Night: A Boy, His Goat, & the Great Chicago Fire. Walker, Sally M. 2020. (ENG.). 40p. (J). (gr. 3-5). lib. bdg. 18.99 ***(978-1-68446-086-1(7)***, 140987, Capstone Editions) Capstone.

Harren, Kayla. Hannah's Tall Order: An a to Z Sandwich. Heyden, Linda Vander. 2018. (ENG.). 32p. (J). (gr. k-2). 16.99 *(978-1-58536-382-7(0)*, 204587) Sleeping Bear Pr.

—Helping Brother Rhinoceros. Bond, Monica L. 2018. (ENG.). 34p. (J). pap. 12.00 *(978-1-7323234-1-4(0))* Wild Nature Institute.

—Juma the Giraffe. Bond, Monica L. 2018. (ENG.). 34p. (J). pap. 12.00 *(978-0-9898182-9-2(2))* Wild Nature Institute.

—Our Elephant Neighbours. Bond, Monica L. 2018. (ENG.). 34p. (J). pap. 12.00 *(978-1-7323234-0-7(2))* Wild Nature Institute.

—Who Sang the First Song? Holcomb, Ellie. 2018. (ENG.). 24p. (J). (— 1). bds. 12.99 *(978-1-4627-9445-4(9)*, 005801949, B&H Kids) B&H Publishing Group.

Harricks, Tannya. Dingo. Saxby, Claire. 2018. (ENG.). 32p. (J). (gr. k-4). 16.99 *(978-0-7636-9886-7(5))* Candlewick Pr.

Harrigan, Dayna & Pomeroy, Shan. Come on We Goes: Around the What? & the Great Foggy Day. Silver, Karen. 2018. (ENG.). 64p. (J). *(978-1-5255-2537-7(9))*; pap. *(978-1-5255-2538-4(7))* FriesenPress.

Harrigan, Mike. Shadow Fox: Sons of Liberty. Hardman, Ron & Hardman, Jessica. Barnecut, Suzanne, ed. 2010. (Shadow Fox Ser.). 186p. (J). (gr. 4-8). 22.99 *(978-0-9819607-1-5(5))* Fox Run Pr., LLC.

—Shadow Fox: Sons of Liberty. Hardman, Ron & Hardman, Jessica. Barnecut, Suzanne, ed. 2010. (Shadow Fox Ser.). 186p. (J). (gr. 4-8). pap. 11.99 *(978-0-9819607-0-8(7))* Fox Run Pr., LLC.

—Shadow Fox: Sons of Liberty Teacher's Edition. Hardman, Ron & Hardman, Jessica. Barnecutt, Suzanne, ed. 2010. (Shadow Fox Ser.: 1). 186p. (J). 34.99 *(978-0-9819607-2-2(3))* Fox Run Pr., LLC.

Harrill, Cory. One Dream & Collected Stories. Pecora, Bet Shoshannah. 2003. 128p. (J). pap. 10.00 *(978-1-882190-60-7(2))* Polar Bear & Co.

Harriman, Marinell & Harriman, Robert. A Myriad of Minstrels. Harriman, Marinell & Harriman, Robert. 32p. (Orig.). (J). (gr. 5-7). pap. 3.50 *(978-0-940920-00-2(X))* Drollery Pr.

Harriman, Robert, jt. illus. see Harriman, Marinell.

Harrington, Chris. Cellphone Call of the Wild. Blohm, Katherine. 2016. (ENG.). (J). pap. 9.99 *(978-0-9861143-1-6(0))* Pentland Pr., Inc.

Harrington, David. The Ant Farm Escape!, 1 vol. Macht, Heather. 2019. (ENG.). 32p. (J). (gr. -1-3). 16.99 *(978-1-4556-2429-4(2)*, Pelican Publishing) Arcadia Publishing.

—Chachalaca Chiquita, 1 vol. Chrismer, Melanie. 2012. (ENG.). 32p. (J). (gr. k-3). 16.99 *(978-1-4556-1704-3(0)*, Pelican Publishing) Arcadia Publishing.

—Charlie's Magical Night. Thomasian, Sara. 2007. (J). per. 11.99 *(978-1-59879-381-9(0))* Lifevest Publishing, Inc.

—Friends with God Story Bible: Why God Loves People Like Me. White, Jeff. 2017. (ENG.). 352p. (J). (gr. -1 — 1). 19.99 *(978-1-4707-4861-6(4))* Group Publishing, Inc.

—From Head to Toe, God Made Me. Keefer, Mikal. 2017. (Best of Li'l Buddies Ser.). (ENG.). 16p. (J). bds. 6.99 *(978-1-4707-4858-6(4))* Group Publishing, Inc.

—Griego el Magnifico y la Gotita Verde Golosa Pegajos. Alfaro, Manuel. 2007. (SPA.). 36p. per. 15.50 *(978-1-59858-337-3(9))* Dog Ear Publishing, LLC.

—Maccabee! The Story of Hanukkah, Vol. Balsley, Tilda. 2010. (ENG.). 32p. (J). (gr. -1-2). pap. 7.95 *(978-0-7613-4508-4(6)*, 9780761345084, Kar-Ben Publishing) Lerner Publishing Group.

—Mary, Mary, Quite Contrary. Grudzina, Rebecca. 2010. (Rising Readers Ser.). (J). 3.49 *(978-1-60719-704-1(9))* Newmark Learning LLC.

—Olé! Cinco de Mayo!, 1 vol. McManis, Margaret. 2013. (ENG.). 32p. (J). (gr. k-3). 16.99 *(978-1-4556-1754-8(7)*, Pelican Publishing) Arcadia Publishing.

—Pease Porridge, Please! Grudzina, Rebecca. 2009. (Reader's Theater Nursery Rhymes & Songs Set B Ser.). 48p. (J). pap. *(978-1-60859-163-3(8))* Benchmark Education Co.

—Pecos Bill Invents the Ten-Gallon Hat, 1 vol. Strauss, Kevin. 2012. (ENG.). 32p. (J). (gr. k-3). 16.99 *(978-1-4556-1502-5(1)*, Pelican Publishing) Arcadia Publishing.

—Since We're Friends: An Autism Picture Book. Shally, Celeste. 2007. 32p. (J). (gr. -1-3). per. 8.99 *(978-0-9794713-0-8(3))* Awaken Specialty Pr.

—Since We're Friends: An Autism Picture Book. Shally, Celeste. 2012. 32p. (J). (gr. -1-3). 12.95 *(978-1-61608-656-5(4)*, 608656, Sky Pony Pr.) Skyhorse Publishing Co., Inc.

—Spaghetti Smiles, 1 vol. Sorenson, Margo. 2014. (ENG.). 32p. (J). (gr. k-3). 16.99 *(978-1-4556-1922-1(1)*, Pelican Publishing) Arcadia Publishing.

—Super Griego the Great & the Secret Mission to the Moon. Alfaro, Manuel. 2009. 40p. pap. 15.95 *(978-1-60844-028-3(1))* Dog Ear Publishing, LLC.

—Twinkle, Twinkle, Little Star. Harris, Brooke. 2010. (Rising Readers Ser.). (J). 3.49 *(978-1-60719-697-6(2))* Newmark Learning LLC.

—The Twinkling Stars. Harris, Brooke. 2009. (Reader's Theater Nursery Rhymes & Songs Set B Ser.). 48p. (J). pap. *(978-1-60859-170-1(0))* Benchmark Education Co.

—Uh-Oh! I Did It Again! White, Jeff. 2017. (Best of Buddies Ser.). (ENG.). 32p. (J). 12.99 *(978-1-4707-4854-8(1))* Group Publishing, Inc.

—When Pigs Fly: A Bible Memory Buddy Book. Nappa, Mike. 2012. (ENG.). 32p. (J). (-3). 9.99 *(978-0-7644-8189-5(4))* Group Publishing, Inc.

—Where Has My Dog Gone? Harris, Brooke. 2010. (Rising Readers Ser.). (J). 3.49 *(978-1-60719-693-8(X))* Newmark Learning LLC.

—Whistling Willie from Amarillo, Texas, 1 vol. Harper, Jo & Harper, Josephine. 2015. (ENG.). 32p. (J). (gr. k-3). 16.99 *(978-1-4556-2056-2(4)*, Pelican Publishing) Arcadia Publishing.

Harrington, David. The Boy Who Wouldn't Read, 1 vol. Harrington, David. McConduit, Denise. 2013. (ENG.). 32p. (J). (gr. k-3). 16.99 *(978-1-4556-1829-3(2)*, Pelican Publishing) Arcadia Publishing.

Harrington, Glenn. William Shakespeare. Kasten, David Scott & Kastan, Marina, eds. 2008. (Poetry for Young People Ser.: 10). 48p. (J). (gr. 3). pap. 6.95 *(978-1-4027-5478-4(7))* Sterling Publishing Co., Inc.

Harrington, jOHN. Meet Mindy: A Native Girl from the Southwest. Harrington, jOHN, photos by. Secakuku, Susan, photos by. 2013. 48p. (J). *(978-1-933565-20-0(9))* Smithsonian National Museum of the American Indian.

Harrington, jOHN, photos by. Meet Lydia: A Native Girl from Southeast Alaska. Belarde-Lewis, Miranda. 2004. (My World: Young Native Americans Today Ser.). (ENG., 48p. (J). 15.95 *(978-1-57178-147-5(1))* Council Oak Bks.

—Meet Mindy: A Native Girl from the Southwest. Secakuku, Susan. 2006. (ENG., 48p. (J). 15.95 *(978-1-57178-148-2(X))* Council Oak Bks.

—Meet Naiche: A Native Boy from the Chesapeake Bay Area. Tayac, Gabrielle. 2007. (My World: Young Native Americans Today Ser.). (ENG., 48p. (J). (gr. 4-7). 15.95 *(978-1-57178-146-8(3))* Council Oak Bks.

Harrington, Leslie. Conrad Saves Pinger Park. Winans, Carvin. 2010. 32p. (J). (gr. -1-3). 8.95 *(978-1-60349-024-5(8)*, Marimba Bks.) Just Us Bks., Inc.

—The Remarkable Ronald Reagan: Cowboy & Commander in Chief. Allen, Susan. 2013. (ENG.). 36p. (J). (gr. 1). 16.99 *(978-1-62157-038-7(X))* Regnery Publishing, Inc., An Eagle Publishing Co.

Harrington, Linda. The Voyage of Billy Buckins, 1 vol. Arrington, R. Region. 2009. 73p. pap. 19.95 *(978-1-4489-2083-9(3))* America Star Bks.

Harrington, Rich. The Almost Invisible Cases. Alfonsi, Alice. 2007. 96p. (J). *(978-0-545-01585-1(5))* Scholastic, Inc.

—The Audio Files. West, Tracey. 2006. 96p. (J). pap. *(978-0-439-90719-4(5))* Scholastic, Inc.

—The Clothing Capers. West, Tracey. 2007. 96p. (J). pap. *(978-0-439-91452-9(3))* Scholastic, Inc.

—The Code Red Cases. Alfonsi, Alice. 2006. 96p. (J). *(978-0-439-91447-5(7))* Scholastic, Inc.

—The Fingerprint Files. West, Tracey. 2007. 96p. (J). *(978-0-439-91451-2(5))* Scholastic, Inc.

—The Playing Card Cases. Alfonsi, Alice. 2007. 96p. (J). *(978-0-545-01087-0(X))* Scholastic, Inc.

—The Secret Cipher Cases. West, Tracey. 2006. 96p. (J). *(978-0-439-91448-2(5))* Scholastic, Inc.

—The Teeny Tiny Cases. West, Tracey. 2007. 96p. (J). *(978-0-439-91450-5(7))* Scholastic, Inc.

Harrington, Shomari. Q Saves the Sun. Perry, Isaac. 2016. (ENG.). (J). pap. 9.99 *(978-0-9905895-2-5(8))* Tiger Stripe Publishing.

Harrington, Tim. Nose to Toes, You Are Yummy! Harrington, Tim. 2015. (ENG.). 32p. (J). (gr. -1-3). 17.99 *(978-0-06-232816-8(6))* HarperCollins Pubs.

—This Little Piggy. Harrington, Tim. 2013. (ENG.). 32p. (J). (gr. -1-3). 15.99 *(978-0-06-221808-7(5))* HarperCollins Pubs.

Harris, - Crystal. My Friend Michael: A Short Story about Autism - A Pedro Collection. Saleem-Muhammad, Rasheedah. 2011. 30p. 19.95 *(978-1-4575-0295-8(X))*; pap. 14.95 *(978-1-4575-0037-4(X))* Dog Ear Publishing, LLC.

Harris, Alleanna. The Day Abuelo Got Lost: Memory Loss of a Loved Grandfather. de Anda, Diane. 2019. (ENG.). 32p. (J). (gr. -1-3). 16.99 *(978-0-8075-1492-4(6)*, 807514926) Whitman, Albert & Co.

—The Journey of York: The Unsung Hero of the Lewis & Clark Expedition. Davis, Hasan. 2019. (ENG.). 40p. (J). (gr. 3-4). lib. bdg. 17.95 *(978-1-5435-1282-3(8)*, 137748, Capstone Editions) Capstone.

—Making Their Voices Heard: The Inspiring Friendship of Ella Fitzgerald & Marilyn Monroe. Kirkfield, Vivian. 2020. (ENG.). 40p. (J). (gr. -1-3). 17.99 *(978-1-4998-0915-2(8))* Little Bee Books Inc.

—Patricia's Vision: The Doctor Who Saved Sight. Lord, Michelle. 2020. (People Who Shaped Our World Ser.: 7). 48p. (J). (gr. k). 16.95 *(978-1-4549-3137-9(X))* Sterling Publishing Co., Inc.

—Secret Friends. Laird, Elizabeth. 2020. (ENG.). 160p. (J). (gr. 4-6). 10.99 *(978-1-5290-1540-9(5)*, Macmillan

Children's Bks.) Pan Macmillan GBR. Dist: Independent Pubs. Group.

Harris, Andrew. Your Body Battles a Broken Bone. Cobb, Vicki. 2009. (Body Battles Ser.). (ENG.). 32p. (gr. 2-5). 25.26 *(978-0-8225-7468-2(3))* Lerner Publishing Group.
—Your Body Battles a Cavity. Kunkel, Dennis, photos by. Cobb, Vicki. 2009. (Body Battles Ser.). (ENG.). 32p. (gr. 2-5). 25.26 *(978-0-8225-7469-9(1))* Lerner Publishing Group.
—Your Body Battles a Cold. Kunkel, Dennis, photos by. Cobb, Vicki. 2009. (Body Battles Ser.). (ENG.). 32p. (gr. 2-5). lib. bdg. 25.26 *(978-0-8225-6813-1(6))* Lerner Publishing Group.
—Your Body Battles a Skinned Knee. Kunkel, Dennis, photos by. Cobb, Vicki. 2009. (Body Battles Ser.). (ENG.). 32p. (gr. 2-5). lib. bdg. 25.26 *(978-0-8225-6814-8(4))* Lerner Publishing Group.
—Your Body Battles a Stomachache. Kunkel, Dennis, photos by. Cobb, Vicki. 2009. (Body Battles Ser.). (ENG.). 32p. (gr. 2-5). lib. bdg. 25.26 *(978-0-8225-7166-7(8))* Lerner Publishing Group.
—Your Body Battles an Earache. Kunkel, Dennis, photos by. Cobb, Vicki. 2009. (Body Battles Ser.). (ENG.). 32p. (gr. 2-5). 25.26 *(978-0-8225-6812-4(8))* Lerner Publishing Group.

Harris, Aubrianna. The Mighty Dandelion. Morris, Scott. 2019. (ENG.). 28p. (J). pap. 9.99 *(978-1-0962-1950-7(6))* Independently Published.

Harris, Brandy. Freckles from Heaven. Harris, Mary. 2007. 28p. per. 24.95 *(978-1-4241-8647-1(1))* America Star Bks.

Harris, Brian. Up We Grow! A Year in the Life of a Small Local Farm. Hodge, Deborah. 2010. (ENG.). 32p. (J). (gr. -1-2). 16.95 *(978-1-55453-561-3(1))* Kids Can Pr., Ltd. CAN. Dist: Hachette Bk. Group.

Harris, Cherise. Nia & the Kingdoms of Celebration. Robinson, Philip. 2017. (ENG.). (J). pap. *(978-1-9998923-0-2(5))*; 2nd ed. 50p. (gr. 2-4). pap. *(978-1-9998923-1-9(3))* Kingdoms of Celebration Publishing.

Harris, Doreen & Jennings, Ann. The Waterfall House: An Australian Fairy Story. Harris, Doreen. 2020. (ENG.). 44p. (J). pap. 10.00 ***(978-1-4841-0463-7(3))*** CreateSpace Independent Publishing Platform.

Harris, Dylan. Max's Tea Party: Major Max & Friends. Haun, Charles G. 2018. (ENG.). 26p. (J). pap. 6.99 *(978-1-5375-1290-7(0))* CreateSpace Independent Publishing Platform.

Harris, Eelonqa K. Eagle Woman's Bones. Harris, Eelonqa K. Kenney, Lisa, ed. 2019. (ENG.). 40p. (J). pap. *(978-1-989388-03-7(5))* TaleFeather Publishing.

Harris, Eelonqa K. Eagle Womans Knochen. Harris, Eelonqa K. 2019. (GER.). 40p. (J). pap. ***(978-1-989388-05-1(1))*** TaleFeather Publishing.
—Katiktaak & Kaviksaak. Harris, Eelonqa K. 2019. (ENG.). 52p. (J). pap. ***(978-1-7752783-6-8(0))*** TaleFeather Publishing.
—Katiktaak und Kaviksaak. Harris, Eelonqa K. 2019. (GER.). 52p. (J). pap. ***(978-1-7752783-8-2(7))*** TaleFeather Publishing.

Harris, Jack. Packed with Poison! Deadly Animal Defenses. Souza, D. M. 2006. (On My Own Science Ser.). 48p. (J). (gr. -1-3). per. 6.95 *(978-0-8225-6448-5(3)*, First Avenue Editions); (ENG.). (gr. 2-4). lib. bdg. 25.26 *(978-1-57505-877-1(4)*, Millbrook Pr.) Lerner Publishing Group.

Harris, Jennifer Beck. Creepy, Crawly Bugs. Williams, Rozanne Lanczak. 2005. (Reading for Fluency Ser.). 8p. (J). pap. 3.49 *(978-1-59198-149-7(2)*, 4249) Creative Teaching Pr., Inc.
—Hog & Dog. Landolf, Diane Wright. 2005. (Step into Reading Ser.: Vol. 1). 32p. (J). (gr. -1-1). per. 4.99 *(978-0-375-83165-2(7)*, Random Hse. Bks. for Young Readers) Random Hse. Children's Bks.

Harris, Jenny B. Tess Builds a Snowman. Williams, Rozanne Lanczak. 2006. (Learn to Write Ser.). 8p. (J). (gr. k-2). pap. 3.49 *(978-1-59198-286-9(3)*, 6180) Creative Teaching Pr., Inc.
—Tess Builds a Snowman. Williams, Rozanne Lanczak. Maio, Barbara & Faulkner, Stacey, eds. 2006. (J). per. 6.99 *(978-1-59198-337-8(1))* Creative Teaching Pr., Inc.

Harris, Jim. The Boy & the Dragon, 1 vol. Ode, Eric. 2013. (ENG.). 32p. (J). (gr. k-3). 16.99 *(978-1-4556-1813-2(6)*, Pelican Publishing) Arcadia Publishing.
—Librarian's Night Before Christmas, 1 vol. Davis, David. 2007. (Night Before Christmas Ser.). (ENG.). 32p. (J). (gr. k-3). 16.99 *(978-1-58980-336-7(1)*, Pelican Publishing) Arcadia Publishing.
—Petite Rouge. Artell, Mike. 2003. 32p. (J). (gr. k-3). 7.99 *(978-0-14-250070-5(4)*, Puffin Books) Penguin Young Readers Group.
—Ten Little Dinosaurs. Schnetzler, Pattie. 2013. (ENG.). 26p. (J). 12.99 *(978-1-4494-4160-9(2))* Andrews McMeel Publishing.
—Ten Little Kittens. Harris, Marian. 2010. (ENG.). 28p. (J). (gr. k). 15.99 *(978-0-7407-9197-0(4))* Andrews McMeel Publishing.
—Ten Little Puppies. Harris, Marian. 2009. (ENG.). 26p. (J). (gr. -1-3). 16.99 *(978-0-7407-8481-1(1))* Andrews McMeel Publishing.
—Three Little Cajun Pigs. Artell, Mike. 2006. 32p. (J). (gr. k-3). 17.99 *(978-0-8037-2815-8(8)*, Dial Bks) Penguin Young Readers Group.
—The Tortoise & the Jackrabbit: La Tortuga y la Liebre. Lowell, Susan. 2004. (New Bilingual Picture Book Ser.). (ENG, MUL & SPA.). 32p. (J). (gr. -1-3). pap. 7.95 *(978-0-87358-869-0(X))* Cooper Square Publishing Llc.
—Los Tres Pequenos Jabalies: The Three Little Javelinas. Lowell, Susan. 2004. (ENG, MUL & SPA.). 32p. (J). (gr. -1-3). 15.95 *(978-0-87358-661-0(1)*, NP611) Rowman & Littlefield Publishers, Inc.
—A Very Hairy Christmas. Lowell, Susan. 2012. (J). *(978-1-933855-80-6(0))* Rio Nuevo Pubs.
—When You're a Pirate Dog & Other Pirate Poems, 1 vol. Ode, Eric. 2012. (ENG.). 40p. (gr. k-3). 17.99 *(978-1-4556-1493-6(9)*, Pelican Publishing) Arcadia Publishing.

Harris, Jim. Dinosaur's Night Before Christmas, 1 vol. Harris, Jim. 2010. (Night Before Christmas Ser.). (ENG.). 40p. (J). (gr. k-3). 16.99 *(978-1-58980-850-8(9)*, Pelican Publishing) Arcadia Publishing.

Harris-Jones, Kirsteen. Lizzy the Lioness, 1 vol. Bevere, Lisa. 2017. (ENG.). 32p. (J). 17.99 *(978-0-7180-9658-8(4))* Nelson, Thomas Inc.
—No Such Thing As Nessie!, 30 vols. McBain, Chani. 2013. (ENG.). 32p. (J). pap. 11.95 *(978-0-86315-953-4(2)*, Kelpies) Floris Bks. GBR. Dist: Consortium Bk. Sales & Distribution.
—Willow the Wildcat, 48 vols. Rickards, Lynne. 2020. (ENG.). 28p. (J). 11.95 *(978-1-78250-630-0(6)*, Kelpies) Floris Bks. GBR. Dist: Consortium Bk. Sales & Distribution.

Harris Jr, Alvin. Demarcus Jones & the Solar Calendar V. Ragsdale, Quineka. 2019. (Demarcus Jones & the Solar Calendar Ser.: Vol. 5). (ENG.). 158p. (J). pap. 10.00 *(978-0-9889100-7-2(1))* CJK Publishing.

Harris, La Verne Abe. Little Drop & the Healing Place. Carr, Sheryl. 2006. (J). 10.00 *(978-0-9791383-0-0(2))* Reliant Energy.

Harris, Lorrayne R. Poodles Tigers Monsters & You. Lewis, L. W. 2004. 64p. kivar 12.95 *(978-0-9711572-1-7(9))* Red Pumpkin Pr.

Harris, Mike, et al. Punisher Invades The 'Nam. 2018. (ENG.). 352p. (YA). (gr. 8-17). pap. 34.99 *(978-1-302-91177-5(5))* Marvel Worldwide, Inc.

Harris, Miki. Tales of the Monkey King. Jones, Teresa Chin. 2008. (J). *(978-1-881896-30-2(7))* Pacific View Pr.

Harris, Nick. Dragon Quest. Dixon, Andy. Brooks, Felicity, ed. rev. ed. 2005. (Usborne Fantasy Puzzle Bks.). 32p. (J). (gr. 3-7). per. 7.99 *(978-0-7945-1098-5(1)*, Usborne) EDC Publishing.
—Star Quest. Dixon, Andy. Brooks, Felicity, ed. 2006. (Usborne Fantasy Puzzle Bks.). 32p. (YA). (gr. 7). lib. bdg. 15.99 *(978-1-58086-906-5(8))*; pap. 7.99 *(978-0-7945-1099-2(X))* EDC Publishing. (Usborne).
—The Wooden Horse of Troy, 1 vol. 2011. (Greek Myths Ser.). (ENG.). 32p. (J). (gr. 3-5). lib. bdg. 29.32 *(978-1-4048-6670-6(1)*, Picture Window Bks.) Capstone.

Harris, Patrick O'Neil. Country Hands. Welch, Michelle Rose. 2013. 24p. pap. 24.95 *(978-1-63000-898-7(2))* America Star Bks.

Harris, Phyllis. The Artsy Fartsy Auction: Book 8, 1 vol. Mullarkey, Lisa. 2012. (Katharine the Almost Great Ser.). (ENG.). 80p. (J). (gr. 2-5). 29.93 *(978-1-61641-829-8(X)*, 10922, Calico Chapter Bks.) ABDO Publishing Co.
—Bent Out of Shape, 1 vol. Mullarkey, Lisa. 2009. (Katharine the Almost Great Ser.: No. 1). (ENG.). 80p. (J). (gr. 2-5). 28.50 *(978-1-60270-582-1(8)*, 10912, Calico Chapter Bks.) ABDO Publishing Co.
—The Biggest Star by Far, 1 vol. Mullarkey, Lisa. 2009. (Katharine the Almost Great Ser.: No. 1). (ENG.). 80p. (J). (gr. 2-5). 29.93 *(978-1-60270-581-4(X)*, 10910, Calico Chapter Bks.) ABDO Publishing Co.
—Can't Keep Trackula of Jackula, 1 vol. Mullarkey, Lisa. 2009. (Katharine the Almost Great Ser.: No. 1). (ENG.). 80p. (J). (gr. 2-5). 28.50 *(978-1-60270-584-5(4)*, 10916, Calico Chapter Bks.) ABDO Publishing Co.
—The Ding Dong Ditch-a-Roo. Mullarkey, Lisa. 2012. (Katharine the Almost Great Ser.). (ENG.). 80p. (J). (gr. 2-5). 29.93 *(978-1-61641-830-4(3)*, 10924, Calico Chapter Bks.) ABDO Publishing Co.
—Hair's Looking at You: Book 12, 1 vol. Mullarkey, Lisa. 2012. (Katharine the Almost Great Ser.). (ENG.). 80p. (J). (gr. 2-5). 29.93 *(978-1-61641-833-5(8)*, 10930, Calico Chapter Bks.) ABDO Publishing Co.
—Major Mama Drama, 1 vol. Mullarkey, Lisa. 2009. (Katharine the Almost Great Ser.: No. 1). (ENG.). 80p. (J). (gr. 2-5). 29.93 *(978-1-60270-580-7(1)*, 10908, Calico Chapter Bks.) ABDO Publishing Co.
—Maverick & Me. Schwarzenegger, Katherine. 2017. 32p. (J). 16.99 *(978-0-8249-5687-5(7))* Worthy Publishing.
—On Christmas Day. Brown, Margaret. 2011. (J). 12.99 *(978-1-882077-10-6(5))* WaterMark, Inc.
—On Christmas Day. Brown, Margaret Wise. 2019. 26p. (J). (gr. -1 — 1). bds. 7.99 *(978-1-5460-1456-0(X)*, Worthy Kids/Ideals) Worthy Publishing.
—The Purr-Fect-O Present: Book 10, 1 vol. Mullarkey, Lisa. 2012. (Katharine the Almost Great Ser.). (ENG.). 80p. (J). (gr. 2-5). 29.93 *(978-1-61641-831-1(1)*, 10926, Calico Chapter Bks.) ABDO Publishing Co.
—Swim, Swam, Swum. Marsaw, Roy. 2007. 32p. (J). pap. 14.95 *(978-0-9744446-8-0(5))* All About Kids Publishing.
—Swimming with the Sharks: Book 11, 1 vol. Mullarkey, Lisa. 2012. (Katharine the Almost Great Ser.). (ENG.). 80p. (J). (gr. 2-5). 29.93 *(978-1-61641-832-8(X)*, 10928, Calico Chapter Bks.) ABDO Publishing Co.
—Uses Her Common Cents, 1 vol. Mullarkey, Lisa. 2009. (Katharine the Almost Great Ser.: No. 1). (ENG.). 80p. (J). (gr. 2-5). 29.93 *(978-1-60270-579-1(8)*, 10906, Calico Chapter Bks.) ABDO Publishing Co.
—The Write Stuff: Book 7, 1 vol. Mullarkey, Lisa. 2012. (Katharine the Almost Great Ser.). 80p. (J). (gr. 2-5). 28.50 *(978-1-61641-828-1(1)*, 10920, Calico Chapter Bks.) ABDO Publishing Co.

Harris, Phyllis & Clearwater, Linda. Koala Does His Best. Simon, Mary Manz. 2006. (First Virtuestm for Toddlers Ser.). 20p. (J). 5.99 *(978-0-7847-1578-9(5)*, 04072) Standard Publishing.
—Lamb Is Joyful. Simon, Mary Manz. 2006. (First Virtuestm for Toddlers Ser.). 20p. (J). 5.99 *(978-0-7847-1575-8(0)*, 04069) Standard Publishing.
—Lion Can Share. Simon, Mary Manz. 2006. (First Virtuestm for Toddlers Ser.). 20p. (J). 5.99 *(978-0-7847-1576-5(9)*, 04070) Standard Publishing.

Harris, R. Craig. I'm Walking, I'm Running, I'm Jumping, I'm Hopping. Harris, Richard. 2005. (ENG.). 32p. 16.95 *(978-0-9704504-1-8(9))* Hampton Roads Publishing Co., Inc.

Harris, Shawn. Everyone's Awake: (Read-Aloud Bedtime Book, Goodnight Book for Kids) Meloy, Colin. 2020. (ENG.). 48p. (J). (gr. k-3). 17.99 *(978-1-4521-7805-9(4))* Chronicle Bks. LLC.
—What Can a Citizen Do? Eggers, Dave. 2018. (ENG.). 52p. (J). (gr. -1-k). 17.99 *(978-1-4521-7313-9(3))* Chronicle Bks. LLC.

Harris, Steve J. Turtle's Way: Loggy, Greeny & Leather. Hixon, Mara Uman. 2004. 25p. (J). (gr. -1-3). 16.00 *(978-1-887774-20-8(3)*, Wynden) Canmore Pr.

Harris, Steven, et al. Deadpool Classic - Volume 4. 2011. (ENG.). 296p. (YA). (gr. 8-17). pap. 29.99 *(978-0-7851-5302-3(0))* Marvel Worldwide, Inc.

Harris, Tiffany. Freddie the Frog & the Bass Clef Monster. Burch, Sharon. 2010. (ENG.). 44p. (gr. -1-4). 24.99 incl. audio compact disk *(978-0-9747454-8-0(0)*, 09971501) Mystic Publishing.

Harris, Todd. The Hero's Guide to Being an Outlaw. Healy, Christopher. 2014. (Hero's Guide Ser.: 3). (ENG.). 528p. (J). (gr. 3-7). 16.99 *(978-0-06-211848-6(X)*, Waldon Pond Pr.) HarperCollins Pubs.
—The Hero's Guide to Saving Your Kingdom. Healy, Christopher. (Hero's Guide Ser.: 1). (ENG.). (J). (gr. 3-7). 2013. 480p. pap. 7.99 *(978-0-06-211745-8(9))*; 2012. 448p. 16.99 *(978-0-06-211743-4(2))* HarperCollins Pubs. (Waldon Pond Pr.).

Harris, Wayne. DragonQuest. Baillie, Allan. 2013. (ENG.). 40p. (J). (gr. k-4). 16.99 *(978-0-7636-6617-0(3))* Candlewick Pr.

Harrison, Amina & Harrison, Shoshannah. Beamer the Cat: Discovers He Has Diabetes. Harrison, Shoshannah. 2018. (ENG.). 32p. (J). pap. 9.95 *(978-1-7307-6603-9(X))* Independently Published.

Harrison, April. What Is Given from the Heart. McKissack, Patricia C. 2019. 40p. (J). (gr. -1-3). 17.99 *(978-0-375-83615-2(2))*; (ENG.). lib. bdg. 20.99 *(978-0-375-93615-9(7))* Random Hse. Children's Bks. (Schwartz & Wade Bks.).

Harrison, Casey. From the Universe to You. Harrison, Casey. 2018. (ENG.). 28p. (J). 16.99 *(978-0-9600441-0-8(8))* Brewer Bear Bks.

Harrison, Charles a. Harrison the Husky: The Little Dog That Could. Harrison, Charles J. 2019. (ENG.). 40p. (J). pap. 6.00 ***(978-1-0707-9838-7(X))*** Independently Published.

Harrison, Chris. Casketball Capers, 1. Bently, Peter. 2011. (Vampire School Ser.: 1). (ENG.). 96p. (J). (gr. 1-4). 17.44 *(978-0-8075-8462-0(2))* Whitman, Albert & Co.

Harrison, Easweh. Seasonal Flaws. Jacobs, Jaydah. Harris, LaTanya, ed. 2019. (ENG.). 208p. (J). pap. 9.99 ***(978-1-6862-0153-0(2))*** Independently Published.

Harrison, Erica. Box of Fairies. 2005. 6p. (J). 11.95 *(978-0-7945-1125-8(2)*, Usborne) EDC Publishing.
—Cowboy Things to Make & Do. Bone, Emily. 2008. (Activity Bks). 34p. (J). (gr. 1). pap. 6.99 *(978-0-7945-2077-9(4)*, Usborne) EDC Publishing.
—Little Traveler Board Book Set. Mudpuppy. 2019. (ENG.). (J). (gr. -1-k). bds. 14.99 *(978-0-7353-6105-8(3)*, Mudpuppy) Galison.

Harrison, Erica, et al. Monster Things to Make & Do. Allman, Howard, photos by. Gilpin, Rebecca. 2006. (Usborne Activities Ser.). 32p. (J). (gr. -1-3). pap. 6.99 *(978-0-7945-1354-2(9)*, Usborne) EDC Publishing.

Harrison, Erica. The Usborne Book of Drawing, Doodling & Coloring for Christmas. Watt, Fiona. 2010. 96p. (J). (gr. -1-3). pap. 13.99 *(978-0-7945-2918-5(6))* EDC Publishing.
—The Usborne Color by Numbers Book. Watt, Fiona. 2014. (ENG.). (J). pap. 5.99 *(978-0-7945-3251-2(9)*, Usborne) EDC Publishing.

Harrison, Erica, et al. The Usborne Little Boys' Activity Book. MacLaine, James & Bowman, Lucy. Watt, Fiona, ed. 2014. (ENG.). 64p. (J). pap. 9.99 *(978-0-7945-2888-1(0)*, Usborne) EDC Publishing.
—The Usborne Little Children's Travel Activity Book. MacLaine, James. Watt, Fiona, ed. 2013. (Activity Books for Little Children Ser.). (ENG.). 63p. (J). pap. 9.99 *(978-0-7945-3127-0(X)*, Usborne) EDC Publishing.
—The Usborne Little Girls' Activity Book. Bowman, Lucy & MacLaine, James. Watt, Fiona, ed. 2014. (ENG.). 64p. (J). pap. 9.99 *(978-0-7945-2790-7(6)*, Usborne) EDC Publishing.

Harrison, Erica. Wizard, Pirate & Princess Things to Make & Do. Gilpin, Rebecca & Brocklehurst, Ruth. 2006. 96p. (J). (gr. 1-4). 14.99 *(978-0-7945-1415-0(4)*, Usborne) EDC Publishing.
—365 Things to Make & Do. Watt, Fiona. 2008. (Usborne Activities Ser.). 127p. (J). (gr. 1). 24.99 *(978-0-7945-1954-4(7)*, Usborne) EDC Publishing.

Harrison, Erica. Monster Snap. Harrison, Erica. 2007. (Card Games Ser.). 52p. (J). 8.99 *(978-0-7945-1449-5(9)*, Usborne) EDC Publishing.

Harrison, Erica & Lovell, Katie. The Usborne Book of Drawing, Doodling & Coloring Book. Watt, Fiona. 2010. 126p. (J). pap. 13.99 *(978-0-7945-2788-4(4))* EDC Publishing.

Harrison, Freya. The Owner's Manual for Driving Your Adolescent Brain. Deak, JoAnn & Deak, Terrence. 2013. (ENG.). 80p. (J). (gr. 4-9). pap. 16.99 *(978-1-939775-02-3(7)*, 9781939775023, Little Pickle Pr.) Sourcebooks, Inc.

Harrison, Harry. A Dirty Story. Brennan, Sarah. 2012. (ENG.). 24p. (J). 21.95 *(978-1-937160-26-5(2))* Eliassen Creative.
—An Even Dirtier Story. Brennan, Sarah. 2012. (ENG.). 24p. (J). 21.95 *(978-1-937160-27-2(0))* Eliassen Creative.
—Rock Tales. Fletcher, Chris. 2012. (ENG.). 72p. (J). pap., pap. 13.95 *(978-1-84771-380-3(7))* Y Lolfa GBR. Dist: Casemate Pubs. & Bk. Distributors, LLC.
—The Tale of Chester Choi. Brennan, Sarah. 2013. (ENG.). 32p. (J). 24.95 *(978-1-937160-16-6(5))* Eliassen Creative.
—The Tale of Oswald Ox. Brennan, Sarah. 2012. (J). (ENG.). 32p. *(978-1-937160-24-1(6))*; 36p. pap. *(978-988-18882-8-0(X))* Auspicious Times.
—The Tale of Pin Yin Panda. Brennan, Sarah. 2012. (ENG.). 32p. (J). 24.95 *(978-1-937160-15-9(7))* Eliassen Creative.
—The Tale of Rhonda Rabbit. Brennan, Sarah. 2012. (ENG.). 32p. (J). 24.95 *(978-1-937160-22-7(X))* Eliassen Creative.
—The Tale of Rodney Ram. Brennan, Sarah. 2014. (J). *(978-1-937160-60-9(2))* Eliassen Creative.
—The Tale of Run Run Rat. Brennan, Sarah. 2012. (ENG.). 32p. (J). 24.95 *(978-1-937160-25-8(4))* Eliassen Creative.
—The Tale of Sybil Snake. Brennan, Sarah. 2012. (ENG.). 32p. (J). *(978-1-937160-53-1(X))* Auspicious Times.
—The Tale of Temujin. Brennan, Sarah. 2012. (ENG.). 32p. (J). *(978-1-937160-23-4(8))* Auspicious Times.

Harrison, J. J. Llama Llama & Friends. Dewdney, Anna. 2017. (Llama Llama Ser.). 32p. (J). (gr. -1-1). 16.99 *(978-1-5247-8392-1(7)*, Penguin Young Readers Licenses) Penguin Young Readers Group.

Harrison, J. J. & Clester, Shane. I Am He-Man! (He-Man) Berrios, Frank. 2019. (Little Golden Book Ser.). (ENG.). 24p. (J). (-k). 4.99 *(978-1-9848-5033-1(4)*, Golden Bks.) Random Hse. Children's Bks.

Harrison, John. Fergal Onions. Harrison, John. 2004. 36p. *(978-0-7022-3448-4(6))* Univ. of Queensland Pr.

Harrison, John, photos by. Buzz, Ruby, & Their City Chicks: A True Red-Tailed Hawk Story. Drexler, Wendy & Kaplan, Joan Fleiss. 2016. (ENG.). (J). pap. 12.95 *(978-0-9963747-4-3(4))* Ziggy Owl Pr.

Harrison, Jon. ¿Por Qué el Agua Vale la Pena? Harrison, Lori & Water Environment Federation. 2019. (SPA.). 42p. (gr. k-4). pap. 12.95 *(978-1-57278-363-8(X))* Water Environment Federation.

Harrison, Jon. ¿Por qué el agua vale la pena? Harrison, Lori & Water Environment Federation. 2019. (SPA.). 42p. (gr. k-5). 16.95 ***(978-1-57278-364-5(8))*** Water Environment Federation.
—Pourquoi l'eau en Vaut la Peine. Harrison, Lori & Water Environment Federation. 2019. (FRE.). 42p. (gr. k-5). 16.95 ***(978-1-57278-366-9(4))*** Water Environment Federation.

Harrison, Jon. Why Water's Worth It. Harrison, Lori & Water Environment Federation. 2019. (ENG.). 42p. (gr. k-4). 16.95 *(978-1-57278-362-1(1))*; (gr. -1-3). pap. 12.99 *(978-1-57278-354-6(0))* Water Environment Federation.

Harrison, Kathryn. I Smile for Grandpa: A Loving Story about Dementia Disease for Young Children. Guenette, Jaclyn. 2018. (ENG.). 34p. (J). (gr. k-3). pap. *(978-0-9949467-6-8(7))* Fliptum Publishing.

Harrison, Kelly P. The First Ostrich to Fly. Steidl, Erik. 2019. (ENG.). 32p. (J). pap. 9.99 ***(978-1-6896-0491-8(3))*** Independently Published.

Harrison, Kenny. Hide & Seek Harry at the Playground. Harrison, Kenny. 2015. 20p. (J). (-k). bds. 6.99 *(978-0-7636-7347-5(1))* Candlewick Pr.
—Hide & Seek Harry on the Farm. Harrison, Kenny. 2015. 20p. (J). (-k). bds. 6.99 *(978-0-7636-7370-3(6))* Candlewick Pr.

Harrison, Laura. Sir Cook, the Knight? Mortensen, Erik. 2008. *(978-0-9782026-5-1(1))* Crackjaw Publishing.

Harrison, Lee. Wee Wurri: The Woolly Hat of Power. Harrison, Lee. 2018. (ENG.). 46p. (J). pap. *(978-1-9164428-0-1(3))* Brave Little Bks.
—Wee Wurri & the Woolly Hat of Power: The Hide Monster. Harrison, Lee. 2018. (ENG.). 48p. (J). pap. *(978-1-9164428-1-8(1))* Brave Little Bks.
—Wee Wurri & the Woolly Hat of Power: The Shadow Monster. Harrison, Lee. 2018. (ENG.). 46p. (J). pap. *(978-1-9164428-2-5(X))* Brave Little Bks.

Harrison-Lever, Brian. In Flanders Fields. Jorgensen, Norman. 2003. (ENG.). 32p. (J). (gr. -1-3). 16.95 *(978-1-894965-01-9(9))* Simply Read Bks. CAN. Dist: Ingram Publisher Services.
—In Flanders Fields. Jorgenson, Norman. 2010. (ENG.). 32p. (J). (gr. -1-3). pap. 9.95 *(978-1-894965-83-5(3))* Simply Read Bks. CAN. Dist: Ingram Publisher Services.

Harrison, Nancy. The Land of Counterpane. Stevenson, Robert Louis. 2011. (Poetry for Children Ser.). (ENG.). 24p. (J). (gr. k-3). 27.07 *(978-1-60973-152-6(2)*, 201183) Child's World, Inc., The.
—Who Is (Your Name Here)? The Story of My Life. Manzanero, Paula K. & Who HQ. 2015. (Who Was? Ser.). 112p. (J). (gr. 3-7). 9.99 *(978-0-448-48715-1(2)*, Penguin Workshop) Penguin Young Readers Group.
—Who Was Anne Frank? Abramson, Ann & Who HQ. 2007. (Who Was? Ser.). (ENG.). 112p. (J). (gr. 3-7). pap. 5.99 *(978-0-448-44482-6(8)*, Penguin Workshop) Penguin Young Readers Group.
—Who Was Anne Frank? Abramson, Ann. 2007. (Who Was... ? Ser.). 103p. (gr. 2-6). 15.00 *(978-0-7569-8166-2(2))* Perfection Learning Corp.
—Who Was Anne Frank? Abramson, Ann. ed. 2007. (Who Was... ? Ser.). 103p. (J). (gr. 4-7). 16.00 *(978-1-4177-6854-7(1))* Turtleback.
—Who Was Charles Darwin? Hopkinson, Deborah & Who HQ. 2005. (Who Was? Ser.). 112p. (J). (gr. 3-7). pap. 5.99 *(978-0-448-43764-4(3)*, Penguin Workshop) Penguin Young Readers Group.
—Who Was Christopher Columbus? Bader, Bonnie & Who HQ. 2013. (Who Was? Ser.). 112p. (J). (gr. 3-7). pap. 5.99 *(978-0-448-46333-9(4)*, Penguin Workshop) Penguin Young Readers Group.
—Who Was Christopher Columbus? Bader, Bonnie. 2013. (Who Was... ? Ser.). (ENG.). (J). (gr. 3-7). lib. bdg. 16.60 *(978-1-68065-149-2(8))* Perfection Learning Corp.
—Who Was Dr. Seuss? Pascal, Janet B. & Who HQ. 2011. (Who Was? Ser.). 112p. (J). (gr. 3-7). pap. 5.99 *(978-0-448-45585-3(4)*, Penguin Workshop) Penguin Young Readers Group.
—Who Was Harriet Tubman? McDonough, Yona Zeldis & Who HQ. 2019. (Who Was? Ser.). (ENG.). 112p. (J). (gr. 3-7). 5.99 *(978-0-593-09722-9(X))*; 15.99 *(978-0-593-09723-6(8))* Penguin Young Readers Group. (Penguin Workshop).
—Who Was Harriet Tubman? McDonough, Yona Zeldis. 2003. (Who Was... ? Ser.). 106p. (gr. 4-7). 15.00 *(978-0-7569-1590-2(2))* Perfection Learning Corp.
—Who Was Helen Keller? O'Brien, John A. 2003. (Who Was... ? Ser.). 107p. (J). (gr. 3-7). 12.65 *(978-0-7569-1596-4(1))* Perfection Learning Corp.
—Who Was Helen Keller? Thompson, Gare & Who HQ. 2003. (Who Was? Ser.). (ENG.). 112p. (J). (gr. 3-7). pap.

H

5.99 (978-0-448-43144-4(0), Penguin Workshop) Penguin Young Readers Group.

—Who Was Helen Keller? O'Brien, John A. & Thompson, Gare. ed. 2003. (Who Was... ? Ser.). 107p. (J). (gr. 3-7). 16.00 (978-0-613-63485-4(3)) Turtleback.

—Who Was Jim Henson? Holub, Joan & Who HQ. 2010. (Who Was? Ser.). 112p. (J). (gr. 3-7). pap. 5.99 (978-0-448-45406-1(8), Penguin Workshop) Penguin Young Readers Group.

—Who Was Queen Elizabeth? Eding, June & Who HQ. 2008. (Who Was? Ser.). 112p. (J). (gr. 3-7). pap. 5.99 (978-0-448-44839-8(4), Penguin Workshop) Penguin Young Readers Group.

—Who Was Walt Disney? Stewart, Whitney & Who HQ. 2009. (Who Was? Ser.). (ENG.). 112p. (J). (gr. 3-7). pap. 5.99 (978-0-448-45052-0(6), Penguin Workshop) Penguin Young Readers Group.

Harrison, Nancy & Putra, Dede. Who Was Julia Child? Edgers, Geoff & Hempel, Carlene. 2015. (Who Was? Ser.). 112p. (J). (gr. 3-7). 5.99 (978-0-448-48297-2(5), Penguin Workshop) Penguin Young Readers Group.

Harrison, Nancy, jt. illus. see Burroughs, Scott.

Harrison, Nancy, jt. illus. see Moore, Jonathan.

Harrison, Nicholas. Grandma Asks: Were You Good at School Today? Harris, Patrice. 2013. 26p. pap. 10.00 (978-0-9892358-5-3(8)) CLF Publishing.

Harrison, Shizue. Grey the Dog: A Tail of a Dream. Hall, S. D. 2019. (ENG.). 32p. (J). 19.95 **(978-1-4808-8601-8(7))**; pap. 16.95 **(978-1-4808-8599-8(1))** Archway Publishing.

Harrison, Shoshannah, jt. illus. see Harrison, Amina.

Harrison, Stephen. Bubbles: The Fabubbulous Story of Angelique's Nursery School. Howard, Malcolm. 2017. (ENG.). (J). pap. (978-1-911525-13-4(1)) Clink Street Publishing.

Harrison, Steve. The Lion Graphic Bible: The Whole Story from Genesis to Revelation. Maddox, Mike & Anderson, Jeff. ed. 2004. (ENG.). 256p. (J). (gr. 7-12). pap. 12.95 (978-0-7459-4923-9(1)) Lion Hudson PLC GBR. Dist: Independent Pubs. Group.

Harrison, T. Latin: A Fresh Approach, Vol. Seigel, Mike. 2003. 174p. pap. 19.95 (978-1-898855-27-9(7), 1898855277) Anthem Pr. GBR. Dist: Books International, Inc.

Harrison, Vashti. Cece Loves Science. Derting, Kimberly. 2020. (Cece Loves Science Ser.: 1). 40p. (J). (gr. -1-3). pap. 7.99 (978-0-06-249961-5(0), Greenwillow Bks.) HarperCollins Pubs.

—Cece Loves Science. Derting, Kimberly & Johannes, Shelli R. 2018. (Cece Loves Science Ser.: 1). (ENG.). 40p. (J). (gr. -1-3). 17.99 (978-0-06-249960-8(2), Greenwillow Bks.) HarperCollins Pubs.

—Cece Loves Science & Adventure. Derting, Kimberly & Johannes, Shelli R. 2019. (Cece Loves Science Ser.: 2). (ENG.). 40p. (J). (gr. -1-3). 17.99 (978-0-06-249962-2(9), Harper Design) HarperCollins Pubs.

—Cece Loves Science: Push & Pull. Derting, Kimberly & Johannes, Shelli R. 2020. (I Can Read Level 3 Ser.). (ENG.). 40p. (J). (gr. -1-3). 16.99 (978-0-06-294609-6(9)); pap. 4.99 (978-0-06-294608-9(0)) HarperCollins Pubs. (Greenwillow Bks.).

—Festival of Colors. Sehgal, Surishtha & Sehgal, Kabir. 2018. (ENG.). 32p. (J). (gr. -1-3). 17.99 (978-1-4814-2049-5(6), Beach Lane Bks.) Beach Lane Bks.

—Hair Love. Cherry, Matthew A. 2019. (ENG.). 32p. (J). (gr. -1-3). 17.99 (978-0-525-55336-6(3), Kokila) Penguin Young Readers Group.

—Sulwe. Nyong'o, Lupita. 2019. (ENG.). 48p. (J). (gr. -1-3). 17.99 (978-1-5344-2536-1(5), Simon & Schuster Bks. For Young Readers) Simon & Schuster Bks. For Young Readers.

Harrold, Brian. Catchin' Cooties Consuelo. Thompson, Tolya L. 2004. (Smarties Ser.: 3). (SPA.). (J). 16.00 (978-0-9708296-3-4(9)) Savor Publishing Hse., Inc.

Harry, Rebecca. By the Light of the Moon. Shaw, Stephanie. 2016. (ENG.). 22p. (J). (gr. -1-k). bds. 8.99 (978-1-58925-221-9(7)) Tiger Tales.

—Foxes in the Snow, 11. Emmett, Jonathan. 3rd ed. 2012. (ENG.). 32p. (J). (gr. -1-k). pap. 9.99 (978-0-230-71229-4(0)) Pan Macmillan GBR. Dist: Independent Pubs. Group.

—Lullaby Farm. Shaw, Stephanie. 2017. (ENG.). 22p. (J). (gr. -1-k). bds. 8.99 (978-1-68010-512-4(4)) Tiger Tales.

—My First Farm Stories. Sweeney, Samantha et al. 2018. (ENG.). 44p. (J). (gr. -1-k). bds. 9.99 (978-1-68010-544-5(2)) Tiger Tales.

—This Way, Ruby! Emmett, Jonathan. 2010. (Scholastic Bookshelf Ser.). (ENG.). 32p. (J). (gr. -1-3). pap. 6.99 (978-0-545-16910-3(0), Scholastic Paperbacks) Scholastic, Inc.

—Under the Sleepy Stars. Shaw, Stephanie. 2015. (ENG.). 22p. (J). (gr. -1-k). bds. 8.99 (978-1-58925-204-2(7)) Tiger Tales.

—The Winter Fox. Knapman, Timothy. 2017. (ENG.). 24p. (J). (gr. -1-2). 14.99 (978-0-7636-9631-3(5), Nosy Crow) Candlewick Pr.

Harston, David. If the Earth Is Round... Fleishman, Brett. 2017. (ENG.). (J). (gr. k-2). pap. 13.99 (978-0-9991507-7-1(4)) Mindstir Media.

—Michigan Coloring Book. 2005. 24p. (J). pap. (978-1-893624-32-0(3)) Penrod/Hiawatha Co.

—Missy Moo, Where Are You off to? Surfing Adventure. Mindes, Erin. 2011. (J). 14.95 (978-0-9841558-8-0(0)) Tasty Minstrel Games.

—Twist & Shout! (Intermediate: Vol 1) Fleishman, Brett. 2017. (ENG.). (J). (gr. 3-5). pap. 16.99 (978-0-9993872-0-7(0)) Mindstir Media.

Harston, Jerry. Believe & You're There When Ammon Was a Missionary. Johnson, Alice W. & Warner, Allison H. 2010. (J). (978-1-60641-247-3(7)) Deseret Bk. Co.

—Believe & You're There When Lehi Left Jerusalem. Johnson, Alice W. & Warner, Allison H. 2010. (J). (978-1-60641-246-6(9)) Deseret Bk. Co.

—Believe & You're There When the Night Was Bright As Day. Johnson, Alice W. & Warner, Allison H. 2010. viii, 81p. (J). (978-1-60641-249-7(3)) Deseret Bk. Co.

—Believe & You're There When the Prince of Peace Was Born. Johnson, Alice W. & Warner, Allison H. 2009. 74p. (J). (978-1-60641-200-8(0)) Deseret Bk. Co.

—A Child's Collection of Parables. Wach, Randy-Lynne. 2007. 13.95 (978-1-59038-724-5(4)) Deseret Bk. Co.

—How to Make Snack Mix: Math B. Oppenlander, Meredith. l.t. ed. 2003. (ENG.). 16p. (gr. k-1). pap. 7.95 (978-1-57874-004-8(5), Kaeden Bks.) Kaeden Corp.

—More of My First Book of Mormon Stories. 2005. 32p. (J). 13.99 (978-1-59038-402-2(4)) Deseret Bk. Co.

—My First Scripture Stories. Buck, Deanna Draper;. 2014. (J). pap. 14.99 (978-1-60907-948-2(5)) Deseret Bk. Co.

—My First Story of the First Christmas. Buck, Deanna Draper;. (J). 2016. bds. 6.99 (978-1-62972-240-5(5)); 2006. 24p. 13.95 (978-1-59038-635-4(3)) Deseret Bk. Co.

—My Magic Bike. Worthington, Lisa & Moon, Susan. 2006. (ENG.). 16p. (gr. k-2). pap. 7.95 (978-1-57874-039-0(8), Kaeden Bks.) Kaeden Corp.

—Sleepy Polar Bear. Hiris, Monica. l.t. ed. 2006. (ENG.). 24p. (gr. k-2). pap. 8.95 (978-1-57874-072-7(X), Kaeden Bks.) Kaeden Corp.

—Sneezles & Wheezles. Passey, Marion. 2006. 32p. (J). (gr. -1-3). 15.99 (978-1-55517-912-0(6)) Cedar Fort, Inc./CFI Distribution.

Hart, Cheryl N. The Dewey Hotel. Robbins, Lisa. 2019. (ENG.). 26p. (J). pap. 11.99 **(978-1-945620-66-9(8))** Hear My Heart Publishing.

Hart, Curt, photos by. Birds: Discovering North American Species. Raines, Shirley. 2017. (My Wonderful World Ser.). (ENG., 32p. (J). (gr. k-2). 12.99 (978-1-4867-1320-2(3), a39fe304-b7c6-4111-b118-98ea78a058fc); pap. 9.99 (978-1-4867-1372-1(6), b43708f0-b0a5-4c00-9abf-be9329a726c7) Flowerpot Pr.

—Butterflies: Exploring the Life Cycle. Raines, Shirley. 2017. (My Wonderful World Ser.). (ENG., 32p. (J). (gr. k-2). 12.99 (978-1-4867-1321-9(1), 894b20c0-7d06-4785-a53c-c600100811c4); pap. 9.99 (978-1-4867-1371-4(8), df961aff-00cd-451e-9cc5-3978c7cb9e98) Flowerpot Pr.

Hart, Edna F. Hans Christian Andersen's Fairy Tales: The Ugly Duckling, Thumbelina, & Other Stories. Andersen, Hans Christian. ed. 2017. (First Avenue Classics (tm) Ser.). (ENG.). 422p. (J). (gr. 3-8). E-Book 19.99 (978-1-5124-2611-3(3)); E-Book 19.99 (978-1-5124-6655-3(7), 9781512466553) Lerner Publishing Group. (First Avenue Editions).

Hart, James. Big Stink: D-Bot Squad 4. Park, Mac. 2018. (D-Bot Squad Ser.: 4). (ENG.). 80p. (J). (gr. k-2). pap. 8.99 (978-1-76029-600-1(7)) Allen & Unwin AUS. Dist: Independent Pubs. Group.

—D-Bot Squad Complete Collection (slipcase) Park, Mac. 2019. (ENG.). 640p. (J). (gr. k-2). 24.99 (978-1-76052-860-7(9)) Allen & Unwin AUS. Dist: Independent Pubs. Group.

—Deep Dive: D-Bot Squad 6. Park, Mac. 2018. (D-Bot Squad Ser.: 6). (ENG.). 80p. (J). (gr. k-2). pap. 8.99 (978-1-76029-602-5(3)) Allen & Unwin AUS. Dist: Independent Pubs. Group.

—Dino Corp: D-Bot Squad 8. Park, Mac. 2019. (D-Bot Squad Ser.: 8). (ENG.). 80p. (J). (gr. k-2). pap. 8.99 (978-1-76029-604-9(X)) Allen & Unwin AUS. Dist: Independent Pubs. Group.

—Dino Hunter: D-Bot Squad 1. Park, Mac. 2018. (D-Bot Squad Ser.: 1). (ENG.). 80p. (J). (gr. k-2). pap. 7.99 (978-1-76029-597-4(3)) Allen & Unwin AUS. Dist: Independent Pubs. Group.

—Double Trouble: D-Bot Squad 3. Park, Mac. 2018. (D-Bot Squad Ser.: 3). (ENG.). 80p. (J). (gr. k-2). pap. 8.99 (978-1-76029-599-8(X)) Allen & Unwin AUS. Dist: Independent Pubs. Group.

Hart, James, III. How to Save the Whole Stinkin' Planet: A Garbological Adventure. Constable, Lee. 2019. (ENG.). 256p. (J). (gr. 2-4). 18.99 **(978-1-76089-026-1(X)**, Puffin) Penguin Random Hse. AUS. Dist: Independent Pubs. Group.

Hart, James. Mega Hatch: D-Bot Squad 7. Park, Mac. 2019. (D-Bot Squad Ser.: 7). (ENG.). 80p. (J). (gr. k-2). pap. 8.99 (978-1-76029-603-2(1)) Allen & Unwin AUS. Dist: Independent Pubs. Group.

—Sky High: D-Bot Squad 2. Park, Mac. 2018. (D-Bot Squad Ser.: 2). (ENG.). 80p. (J). (gr. k-2). pap. 7.99 (978-1-76029-598-1(1)) Allen & Unwin AUS. Dist: Independent Pubs. Group.

—Stack Attack: D-Bot Squad 5. Park, Mac. 2018. (D-Bot Squad Ser.: 5). (ENG.). 80p. (J). (gr. k-2). pap. 8.99 (978-1-76029-601-8(5)) Allen & Unwin AUS. Dist: Independent Pubs. Group.

—State Showdown. Loughlin, Patrick. 2015. (Glenn Maxwell Ser.: 3). 192p. (J). (gr. 4-7). pap. 12.99 (978-0-85798-611-5(2)) Random Hse. Australia AUS. Dist: Independent Pubs. Group.

—Super Sports Stories for Kids. Loughlin, Patrick. 2016. 208p. (J). (gr. 1-3). pap. 11.99 (978-0-85798-966-6(9)) Random Hse. Australia AUS. Dist: Independent Pubs. Group.

—World Domination. Loughlin, Patrick. 2015. (Glenn Maxwell Ser.: 4). 192p. (J). (gr. 4-7). pap. 12.99 (978-0-85798-613-9(9)) Random Hse. Australia AUS. Dist: Independent Pubs. Group.

Hart, Jason. Good Night Utah. Jasper, Mark. 2012. (Good Night Our World Ser.). (ENG.). 20p. (J). (gr. k — 1). bds. 9.95 (978-1-60219-059-7(3)) Good Night Bks.

Hart, Jennifer. Baxter Returns to Imagination Land: Coloring & Activity Book. Hart, Jennifer. 2018. (ENG.). 50p. (J). pap. 6.99 (978-1-7321588-0-1(0)) Baxter The Dog Bks.

Hart, Lorena Mary. The Monster Who Had a Kind Face. Clark, Lyn Wells. 2019. (ENG.). 22p. (J). (gr. k-2). 18.95 **(978-0-9994409-4-0(2))** Blue-Eyed Star Creations, LLC.

Hart, Lorena Mary. The Unlikely Adventure of a Turtle, a Mouse & a Shark. Clark, Lyn Wells. 2017. (ENG.). 36p. (J). (gr. k-2). pap. 12.99 (978-0-9994409-2-6(6)) Blue-Eyed Star Creations, LLC.

Hart, Natalie Rose. Riley's Reveille: New Beginnings. Nunes, Cheryl & Spector, David, eds. 2019. (ENG.). 178p. (J). pap. 9.99 **(978-1-7296-0563-9(X))** CreateSpace Independent Publishing Platform.

Hart, Paul. Quien Es?/Who's That? Larsson Perfect, Maria. 2017. (SPA.). (J). (gr. k-4). pap. 12.99 (978-1-943331-44-4(8)) Orange Hat Publishing.

Hart, Sam. Messenger: the Legend of Joan of Arc. Lee, Tony. 2015. (ENG.). 112p. (J). (gr. 5). 21.99 (978-0-7636-7613-1(6)) Candlewick Pr.

—Pirate Queen: the Legend of Grace O'Malley. Lee, Tony. (ENG.). 128p. (J). (gr. 5). 2020. pap. 12.99 **(978-1-5362-0020-1(4))**; 2019. 19.99 (978-1-5362-0019-5(0)) Candlewick Pr.

Hart, Sam & Fujita, Artur. Outlaw: The Legend of Robin Hood. Lee, Tony. 2009. (ENG.). 160p. (J). (gr. 5). pap. 12.99 (978-0-7636-4400-0(5)) Candlewick Pr.

Hartas, Freya. Frankie Frog & the Throaty Croakers. 2019. (ENG.). 32p. (J). (gr. -1-k). 16.99 (978-0-8075-2543-2(X), 080752543X) Whitman, Albert & Co.

—Isle of Misfits 1: First Class. Mae, Jamie. 2019. (Isle of Misfits Ser.: 1). (ENG.). 112p. (J). (gr. k-3). 16.99 (978-1-4998-0822-3(4)); pap. 5.99 (978-1-4998-0821-6(6)) Little Bee Books Inc.

—Isle of Misfits 2: the Missing Pot of Gold. Mae, Jamie. 2019. (Isle of Misfits Ser.: 2). (ENG.). 112p. (J). (gr. k-3). 16.99 (978-1-4998-0825-4(9)); pap. 5.99 (978-1-4998-0824-7(0)) Little Bee Books Inc.

—Isle of Misfits 3: Prank Wars! Mae, Jamie. 2019. (Isle of Misfits Ser.: 3). (ENG.). 112p. (J). (gr. k-3). 16.99 (978-1-4998-0853-7(4)); pap. 5.99 (978-1-4998-0852-0(6)) Little Bee Books Inc.

—Isle of Misfits: 4 Books In 1! Mae, Jamie. 2019. (Isle of Misfits Ser.: 1). (ENG.). 416p. (J). (gr. k-3). 14.99 (978-1-4998-0999-2(9)) Little Bee Books Inc.

—Isle of Misfits 4: the Candy Cane Culprit. Mae, Jamie. 2019. (Isle of Misfits Ser.: 4). (ENG.). 112p. (J). (gr. k-3). 16.99 (978-1-4998-0856-8(9)); pap. 5.99 (978-1-4998-0855-1(0)) Little Bee Books Inc.

Hartas, Freya. Slow Down: 50 Mindful Moments in Nature. Williams, Rachel. 2020. (ENG.). 128p. (J). (gr. 3-7). 24.99 **(978-1-4197-4838-7(6)**, 1708801) Magic Cat GBR. Dist: Hachette Bk. Group.

Hartas, Leo, et al. Greek Myths. 2014. 46p. (J). (978-1-4351-5823-8(7)) Barnes & Noble, Inc.

Hartas, Leo. Mindfulness for Vikings: Inspirational Quotes & Pictures Encouraging a Happy Stress Free Life for Adults & Kids. Boulter, Amanda. 2017. (ENG.). (J). (gr. -1-3). pap. (978-1-9999011-0-3(X)) Hartas, Leo.

Hartberg, Flu. Chess: Be the King! Reppen, Ellisiv. 2016. 176p. (J). (gr. 6-6). pap. 14.99 (978-1-63450-160-6(8), Sky Pony Pr.) Skyhorse Publishing Co., Inc.

Harter, Debbie. Bear about Town / Ours en Ville. Blackstone, Stella. rev. ed. 2017. (ENG & FRE.). 24p. (J). (gr. -1-1). pap. 6.99 (978-1-78285-329-9(4)) Barefoot Bks., Inc.

—Bear about Town Gift Wrap. (J). 4.99 (978-1-84148-622-2(1)) Barefoot Bks., Inc.

—Bear about Town (Oso en las Ciudad) Blackstone, Stella. 2010. 24p. (J). (gr. -1-1). pap. 6.99 (978-1-84686-377-6(5)) Barefoot Bks., Inc.

—Bear at Home (Oso en Casa) Blackstone, Stella. 2010. 24p. (J). (gr. -1-1). pap. 7.99 (978-1-84686-422-3(4)) Barefoot Bks., Inc.

—Bear at Work. Blackstone, Stella. 2011. (ENG & SPA.). 24p. (J). (gr. -1-k). pap. 6.99 (978-1-84686-554-1(9)) Barefoot Bks., Inc.

—Bear in a Square. Books, Barefoot. 2018. (ENG.). (J). (gr. -1-2). 19.99 (978-1-78285-429-6(0)) Barefoot Bks., Inc.

—Bear in a Square / Ours Dans un Carré. Blackstone, Stella. rev. ed. 2017. (ENG & FRE.). 24p. (J). (gr. -1-1). pap. 6.99 (978-1-78285-330-5(8)) Barefoot Bks., Inc.

—Bear in Sunshine / Ours Au Soleil. Blackstone, Stella. rev. ed. 2017. (ENG & FRE.). 24p. (J). (gr. -1-1). pap. 6.99 (978-1-78285-331-2(6)) Barefoot Bks., Inc.

—Bear on a Bike / Ours À Vélo. Blackstone, Stella. 2017. (ENG & FRE.). 32p. (J). (gr. -1-1). pap. 6.99 (978-1-78285-328-2(6)) Barefoot Bks., Inc.

—Bear on a Bike (Oso en Bicicleta) Blackstone, Stella & Barefoot Books. 2014. 32p. (J). (gr. -1-1). pap. 6.99 (978-1-78285-079-3(1)) Barefoot Bks., Inc.

—Bear Takes a Trip (Oso Se Va de Viaje) Blackstone, Stella. 2014. (ENG & SPA.). 32p. (J). (gr. k-1). pap. 7.99 (978-1-84686-945-7(5)) Barefoot Bks., Inc.

—Bear's Birthday. Blackstone, Stella. 2011.Tr. of El Cumpleanos de Oso. 24p. (J). (gr. -1-1). pap. 6.99 (978-1-84686-515-2(8)); bds. 7.99 (978-1-84686-516-9(6)) Barefoot Bks., Inc.

—Bear's Birthday (L'Anniversaire de l'Ours) Blackstone, Stella. 2013. 24p. (J). (gr. k-1). pap. 6.99 (978-1-84686-944-0(7)) Barefoot Bks., Inc.

—Bear's Birthday/El Cumpleanos de Oso. Blackstone, Stella. 2013. (ENG & SPA.). 24p. (J). (gr. k-1). 6.99 (978-1-84686-943-3(9)) Barefoot Bks., Inc.

—Bear's Busy Year. 12p. (J). 12.99 (978-1-84148-689-5(2)) Barefoot Bks., Inc.

—Bear's School Day. Blackstone, Stella & Barefoot Books Staff. 2014. 24p. (J). (gr. -1-1). pap. 6.99 (978-1-78285-085-4(6)) Barefoot Bks., Inc.

—Busy Bear Count & Sort. Barefoot Books Staff. 2018. (ENG.). (J). (gr. -1-2). 12.99 (978-1-78285-430-2(4)) Barefoot Bks., Inc.

—Creepy Crawly Calypso. Langham, Tony. (ENG.). 32p. (J). 2007. pap. 6.99 (978-1-84686-133-8(0)); 2004. 16.99 (978-1-84148-699-4(X)) Barefoot Bks., Inc.

—Creepy Crawly Calypso. Sherab, Chodzin & Langham, Tony. 2012. 32p. (J). (gr. -1-2). 9.99 (978-1-84686-828-3(9)) Barefoot Bks., Inc.

—Dancing Dinos Dominoes. Barefoot Books Staff. 2018. (ENG.). (J). (gr. -1-2). 12.99 (978-1-78285-431-9(2)) Barefoot Bks., Inc.

—Dinosaur Rap. Foster, John. 2016. (ENG.). 32p. (J). (gr. -1-1). 16.99 (978-1-78285-301-5(4)) Barefoot Bks., Inc.

—A Dragon on the Doorstep. Blackstone, Stella. 32p. (J). 2012. (gr. -1-2). 9.99 (978-1-84686-826-9(2)); 2006. (ENG.). pap. 9.99 (978-1-905236-66-4(2)); 2006. (ENG.). (gr. -1-k). pap. 6.99 (978-1-84686-032-4(6)); 2005. (ENG.). (gr. -1-1). 15.99 (978-1-84148-227-9(7)) Barefoot Bks., Inc.

—La Familia Activa de Oso. Blackstone, Stella. Sarfatti, Esther, tr. 2003. (Bear Ser.). (SPA.). 24p. (J). pap. 6.99 (978-1-84148-777-9(5)) Barefoot Bks., Inc.

—Florian, le Dragon Végétarien. Bass, Jules. 2017. (FRE.). 32p. (J). (gr. k-5). pap. 8.99 (978-1-78285-326-8(X)) Barefoot Bks., Inc.

—Herb, the Vegetarian Dragon. Bass, Jules. 2005. 32p. (J). (gr. k-3). pap. 8.99 (978-1-905236-47-3(6)); (gr. 1-5). reprint ed. pap. 6.99 (978-1-84148-127-2(0)) Barefoot Bks., Inc.

—Herb, the Vegetarian Dragon: Book & Bendo Gift Set. Bass, Jules. 2005. 32p. (J). 14.99 (978-1-905236-43-5(3)) Barefoot Bks., Inc.

—Herb's Vegetable Patch. (Bear Series Gift Wrap Ser.). (J). 50.00 (978-1-84148-506-5(3)) Barefoot Bks., Inc.

—L'Ours Fait un Voyage. Blackstone, Stella & Parker, Elizabeth. 2013.Tr. of Bear Takes a Trip. (FRE & ENG.). 24p. (J). (gr. k-1). pap. 6.99 (978-1-84686-946-4(3)) Barefoot Bks., Inc.

—Oso Bajo el Sol. Blackstone, Stella & Meza-Riedewald, Leticia. 2009. 24p. (J). (gr. -1-1). pap. 6.99 (978-1-84686-389-9(9)) Barefoot Bks., Inc.

—Oso Bajo el Sol. Blackstone, Stella. Sarfatti, Esther, tr. 2003. (Bear Ser.). (SPA.). 24p. (J). pap. 6.99 (978-1-84148-778-6(3)) Barefoot Bks., Inc.

—Oso en Bicicleta. Blackstone, Stella. Sarfatti, Esther, tr. 2003. (Bear Ser.). (SPA.). 32p. (J). pap. 6.99 (978-1-84148-775-5(9)) Barefoot Bks., Inc.

—Oso en Casa. Blackstone, Stella. Sarfatti, Esther, tr. 2003. (Bear Ser.). (SPA.). 24p. (J). pap. 6.99 (978-1-84148-779-3(1)) Barefoot Bks., Inc.

—Oso en la Ciudad. Blackstone, Stella. Sarfatti, Esther, tr. 2003. (Bear Ser.). (SPA.). 24p. (J). pap. 6.99 (978-1-84148-776-2(7)) Barefoot Bks., Inc.

—Oso en un Cuadrado. Blackstone, Stella. Sarfatti, Esther, tr. 2003. (Bear Ser.). (SPA.). 24p. (J). pap. 6.99 (978-1-84148-774-8(0)) Barefoot Bks., Inc.

—Oso en un Cuadrado. Blackstone, Stella & Meza-Riedewald, Leticia. ed. 2009. 24p. (J). (gr. -1-k). pap. 6.99 (978-1-84686-387-5(2)) Barefoot Bks., Inc.

—Port Side Pirates! Seaworthy, Oscar & Collins, Mark. 2011. 32p. (J). (gr. -1-2). 9.99 (978-1-84686-667-8(7)) Barefoot Bks., Inc.

—Port Side Pirates Puzzle. Seaworthy, Oscar. 2011. n/ap. (J). 14.99 (978-1-84686-666-1(9)) Barefoot Bks., Inc.

—Snow Bear Gift Wrap. (J). 4.99 (978-1-84148-987-2(5)) Barefoot Bks., Inc.

—Thesaurus Rex. Steinberg, Laya. 24p. (J). 2005. (gr. -1-2). pap. 6.99 (978-1-84148-180-7(7)); 2003. (ENG.). 15.99 (978-1-84148-042-8(8)) Barefoot Bks., Inc.

—Thesaurus Rex Finds a Friend. Steinberg, Laya. 2006. (J). (978-1-905236-48-0(4)) Barefoot Bks., Inc.

—Walking Through the Jungle. Blackstone, Stella. 2004. (ENG.). 32p. (J). (gr. -1-k). pap. 6.99 (978-1-84148-548-5(9)) Barefoot Bks., Inc.

—Walking Through the Jungle. 2004. 30p. (J). (978-1-85269-807-2(1)); (978-1-85269-811-9(X)); (978-1-85269-826-3(8)); (978-1-85269-831-7(4)); (GUJ.). (978-1-85269-841-6(1)); (978-1-85269-846-1(2)); (978-1-85269-856-0(X)); (978-1-85269-861-4(6)); (978-1-85269-866-9(7)); (ENG & SPA.). (978-1-85269-871-3(3)); (978-1-85269-876-8(4)); (978-1-85269-881-2(0)); (978-1-85269-886-7(1)) Mantra Lingua.

—Walking Through the Jungle. Blackstone, Stella & Penner, Fred. 2011. 32p. (J). (gr. -1-2). 9.99 (978-1-84686-660-9(X)) Barefoot Bks., Inc.

—Walking Through the Jungle. Blackstone, Stella. 32p. (J). 2006. (ENG.). 9.99 (978-1-905236-99-2(9)); 2004. 9.99 (978-1-84148-182-1(3)) Barefoot Bks., Inc.

—Where's the Cat? Blackstone, Stella. 2003. (ENG.). 24p. (J). (gr. k-2). bds. 6.99 (978-1-84148-607-9(8)) Barefoot Bks., Inc.

Harter, Debbie. The Animal Boogie. Harter, Debbie. 32p. pap. 6.99 (978-1-84148-996-4(4)); 2005. (ENG.). (J). (gr. -1-2). 6.99 (978-1-905236-60-2(3)) Barefoot Bks., Inc.

—The Animal Boogie Fun Activities. Harter, Debbie. Barefoot College Staff. 2009. 16p. (J). pap. 5.99 (978-1-84686-285-4(X)) Barefoot Bks., Inc.

—The Animal Boogie W/ CD. Harter, Debbie. 2011. (ENG.). (J). (gr. -1-2). lib. bdg. 20.60 (978-1-62765-870-6(X)) Perfection Learning Corp.

—Bear at Work. Harter, Debbie. Blackstone, Stella. 2008. (Bear Ser.). 24p. (J). (gr. -1-1). pap. 6.99 (978-1-84686-110-9(1)) Barefoot Bks., Inc.

—Bear at Work: Fun Activities. Harter, Debbie. Blackstone, Stella. 2010. 16p. (J). (gr. -1-3). pap. 5.99 (978-1-84686-444-5(5)) Barefoot Bks., Inc.

—Cha-Cha-Cha en la Selva. Harter, Debbie. Canetti, Yanitzia, tr. 2003.Tr. of Animal Boogie. (SPA.). 32p. (J). pap. 6.99 (978-1-84148-265-1(X)) Barefoot Bks., Inc.

—Cha-Cha-Cha en la Selva. Harter, Debbie. 2003. 32p. (J). (gr. -1-1). 9.99 (978-1-84148-913-1(1)) Barefoot Bks., Inc.

—De Paseo Por la Selva. Harter, Debbie. Ugalde, Raquel, tr. 2003. (SPA.). 32p. (J). pap. 6.99 (978-1-84148-995-7(6)) Barefoot Bks., Inc.

—Mira Quien Toca Calipso! Harter, Debbie. Langham, Tony. 2009. 32p. (J). (gr. -1-2). pap. 7.99 (978-1-84686-281-6(7)) Barefoot Bks., Inc.

—Walking Through the Jungle. Harter, Debbie. 2004. (ENG & PAN.). 32p. (J). pap. (978-1-85269-851-5(9)) Mantra Lingua.

—Who Are You? Harter, Debbie. Blackstone, Stella. 2003. 24p. (J). (gr. k-2). bds. 6.99 (978-1-84148-609-3(4)) Barefoot Bks., Inc.

Harter, Debbie. Walking Through the Jungle: Duke Ecur Neper Xhungel. Harter, Debbie, tr. 2004. 30p. (J). (978-1-85269-806-5(3)) Mantra Lingua.

—Walking Through the Jungle: Marchant a Travers la Jungle. Harter, Debbie, tr. 2004. (ENG & FRE.). 32p. (J). pap. (978-1-85269-836-2(5)) Mantra Lingua.

Harter, Debbie & Beaton, Clare. A to Z. (Bear Series Gift Wrap Ser.). (J). 4.99 *(978-1-84148-508-9(X))* Barefoot Bks., Inc.

—1 To 20. (Bear Series Gift Wrap Ser.). (J). 4.99 *(978-1-84148-507-2(1))* Barefoot Bks., Inc.

Harter, Debbie & Penner, Fred. Animal Boogie. Books, Barefoot. 2011. 32p. (J). (gr. -1-2). 9.99 *(978-1-84686-620-3(0))* Barefoot Bks., Inc.

Hartigan, Gladys. Tiny the Turtle: A Story about Bullying. Hartigan, Tina. 2017. (ENG.). 20p. (J). pap. 12.95 *(978-1-64003-538-6(9))* Covenant Bks.

Hartland, Jessie. Ada Lovelace, Poet of Science: The First Computer Programmer. Stanley, Diane. 2016. (ENG.). 40p. (J). (gr. -1-3). 18.99 *(978-1-4814-5249-6(5),* Simon & Schuster Bks. For Young Readers) Simon & Schuster Bks. For Young Readers.

—Harlem Grown: How One Big Idea Transformed a Neighborhood. Hillery, Tony. 2020. (ENG.). 40p. (J). (gr. -1-3). 17.99 *(978-1-5344-0231-7(4))* Simon & Schuster, Inc.

—Lexie the Word Wrangler. Van Slyke, Rebecca. 2017. 40p. (J). (gr. k-3). 17.99 *(978-0-399-16957-1(1),* Nancy Paulsen Books) Penguin Young Readers Group.

—Messing Around on the Monkey Bars: And Other School Poems for Two Voices. Franco, Betsy. 2009. 48p. (J). (gr. 3-7). 18.99 *(978-0-7636-3174-1(4))* Candlewick Pr.

Hartland, Jessie. Bon Appétit! The Delicious Life of Julia Child. Hartland, Jessie. 2012. 48p. (J). (gr. k-12). 17.99 *(978-0-375-86944-0(1),* Schwartz & Wade Bks.) Random Hse. Children's Bks.

—My Tiny Pet. Hartland, Jessie. 2019. 32p. (J). (gr. -1-3). 17.99 *(978-1-5247-3753-5(4),* Nancy Paulsen Books) Penguin Young Readers Group.

—Our Flag Was Still There: The True Story of Mary Pickersgill & the Star-Spangled Banner. Hartland, Jessie. 2019. (ENG.). 48p. (J). (gr. -1-3). 17.99 *(978-1-5344-0233-1(0),* Simon & Schuster Bks. For Young Readers) Simon & Schuster Bks. For Young Readers.

—Steve Jobs: Insanely Great. Hartland, Jessie. 2015. (ENG.). 240p. (YA). (gr. 7). 22.95 *(978-0-307-98295-7(5),* Schwartz & Wade Bks.) Random Hse. Children's Bks.

Hartley, Brian. Countdown to Christmas, Vol. Simon, Mary Manz. 2019. (ENG.). 52p. (J). (gr. -1-k). 14.99 *(978-1-5064-4854-1(2),* Beaming Books) Augsburg Fortress, Pubs.

—Fall Colors. Gates, Margo. 2019. (Seasons All Around Me (Pull Ahead Readers — Fiction) Ser.). (ENG.). 16p. (J). (gr. -1-1). 22.65 *(978-1-5415-5874-8(X),* 9781541558748, Lerner Pubns.) Lerner Publishing Group.

—Maya Likes the Beach. Gates, Margo. 2019. (Seasons All Around Me (Pull Ahead Readers — Fiction) Ser.). (ENG.). 16p. (J). (gr. -1-1). 22.65 *(978-1-5415-5873-1(1),* 4705caf0-312b-46da-aee0-b295a2cdb1ea, Lerner Pubns.) Lerner Publishing Group.

—Thanksgiving Day. Morey, Allan. 2017. (Holidays in Rhythm & Rhyme Ser.). (ENG.). 24p. (J). (gr. -1-3). lib. bdg. 33.99 incl. audio compact disk *(978-1-68410-055-2(0),* 31521) Cantata Learning.

—Turtles in the Sun. Gates, Margo. 2019. (Let's Look at Weather (Pull Ahead Readers — Fiction) Ser.). (ENG.). 16p. (J). (gr. -1-1). 22.65 *(978-1-5415-5842-7(1),* 9781541558427, Lerner Pubns.) Lerner Publishing Group.

Hartley, Joshua. For the Love of My Pet. The Guide Dog, Thelma. 2012. (ENG.). 26p. (gr. k-5). pap. 14.95 *(978-1-61448-338-0(8))* Morgan James Publishing.

Hartley, Stephanie Olga. Between Hither & Yon Where Good Things Go On! Hartley, Stephanie Olga. 2004. (J). bds. *(978-0-9676717-5-8(2))* Freet Publishing.

Hartman, Adrienne. The Children's Travel Journal. Banks, Ann. 2nd ed. 2004. 48p. (gr. 1-11). 19.95 *(978-0-9641262-0-6(6),* Little Bookroom) New York Review of Bks., Inc., The.

Hartman, Carrie. The Clock Struck One: A Time-Telling Tale. Harris, Trudy. 2009. (Math Is Fun! Ser.). (ENG.). 32p. (J). (gr. k-2). 19.99 *(978-0-8225-9067-5(0),* 9780822590675, Millbrook Pr.) Lerner Publishing Group.

—Feelings to Share. Snow, Todd. 2007. (ENG.). 24p. (J). bds. 7.99 *(978-1-934277-01-0(0))* Marn Green Publishing, Inc.

—Feelings to Share from a to Z. Snow, Todd & Snow, Peggy. 2007. (ENG.). 32p. (J). pap. 9.99 *(978-1-934277-00-3(2))* Marn Green Publishing, Inc.

—It's Hard to Be a Verb! Cook, Julia. 2008. (ENG.). 32p. (J). (gr. 4-7). pap. 9.95 *(978-1-931636-84-1(2))* National Ctr. For Youth Issues.

—Manners Are Important. Snow, Todd. 2007. (ENG.). 24p. (J). (gr. -1-3). bds. 7.99 *(978-1-934277-05-8(3))* Marn Green Publishing, Inc.

—Manners Are Important for You & Me. Snow, Todd. 2007. (ENG.). 32p. (J). pap. 10.99 *(978-1-934277-04-1(5))* Marn Green Publishing, Inc.

—The Mischievous Mom at the Art Gallery. Eckler, Rebecca & Ehm, Erica. 2010. (ENG.). 32p. (J). (gr. -1). *(978-1-55470-267-1(4))* Me to We.

—My Mouth Is a Volcano! Cook, Julia. 2008. 32p. (J). (gr. -1-3). pap. 9.95 *(978-1-931636-85-8(0))* National Ctr. For Youth Issues.

—Personal Space Camp. Cook, Julia. 32p. (J). 2009. 15.95 *(978-1-931636-89-6(3));* 2008. (gr. -1-3). pap. 9.95 *(978-1-931636-87-2(7))* National Ctr. For Youth Issues.

—Where Are All the Minnesotans? Coleman, Karlyn. 2017. (ENG.). 32p. (J). 16.95 *(978-1-68134-040-1(2))* Minnesota Historical Society Pr.

Hartman, Dan. When the Wolves Returned: Restoring Nature's Balance in Yellowstone. Hartman, Dan, photos by. Hartman, Cassie, photos by. Patent, Dorothy Hinshaw. 2008. (ENG.). 40p. (J). (gr. 1-4). 19.99 *(978-0-8027-9686-8(9),* 900045639, Bloomsbury USA Childrens) Bloomsbury Publishing USA.

Hartman, John, jt. illus. see Feldmeier Sims, Julie.

Hartman, Kurt. Life One. Rifkin, L. 2007. (Nine Lives of Romeo Crumb Ser.). (ENG.). 311p. (J). (gr. 6-8). per. 8.95 *(978-0-9743221-3-1(X))* Stratford Road Pr., Ltd.

—Mystery at Manzanar: A WWII Internment Camp Story, 1 vol. Fein, Eric. 2008. (Historical Fiction Ser.). (ENG.). 56p. (J). (gr. 3-6). pap. 6.25 *(978-1-4342-0847-7(8),* Stone Arch Bks.) Capstone.

—The Nine Lives of Romeo Crumb: Life 6. Rifkin, L. 2010. (ENG.). 246p. (YA). pap. 8.95 *(978-0-9743221-8-6(0))* Stratford Road Pr., Ltd.

—The Nine Lives of Romeo Crumb: Life Five. Rifkin, L. (Lauren). 2009. (ENG.). 169p. (YA). pap. 8.95 *(978-0-9743221-7-9(2))* Stratford Road Pr., Ltd.

Hartman, Nancy Lee. I See Without My Eyes. Hayward, Mark Brauner. 2009. 32p. pap. 12.99 *(978-1-4343-3823-5(1))* AuthorHouse.

Hartman, Scott. ABC Dinosaurs. American Museum of Natural History Staff. 2011. (AMNH ABC Board Bks.). 18p. (J). (gr. -1-k). bds. 9.95 *(978-1-4027-7715-8(9))* Sterling Publishing Co., Inc.

Hartmann, April. The Alpha Building Crew. Leman, Nora. 2005. (J). *(978-1-58987-110-6(3))* Kindermusik International.

Hartmann, Dario. A Gallery Girls Collection: Mermaid. 2005. (Gallery Girls Collection). 64p. (YA). per. 9.95 *(978-0-86562-113-8(6))* Diamond Bk. Distributors.

Hartono, Natalia. Tara Shine. Berment, Rhonda. 2019. (ENG.). 40p. (J). pap. 12.00 *(978-1-7990-1837-7(7))* Independently Published.

Hartter, Sean. A Calling of Quarrels: Ebook. Shannon, Jason. 2008. (J). per. 12.95 *(978-0-9790889-5-7(X))* CatsCurious Pr.

—Three Things about Animals... And Only One of Them's True! Shannon, Jason. 2nd rev. ed. 2008. (J). per. 12.95 *(978-0-9790889-4-0(1))* CatsCurious Pr.

Hartung, Susan Kathleen. Follow Me, Mittens. Schaefer, Lola M. (My First I Can Read Ser.). 32p. (J). (gr. -1 — 1). 2008. (ENG.). pap. 4.99 *(978-0-06-054667-0(0));* 2007. (ENG.). 15.99 *(978-0-06-054665-6(4));* 2007. lib. bdg. 16.89 *(978-0-06-054666-3(2))* HarperCollins Pubs.

—Happy Halloween, Mittens. Schaefer, Lola M. 2010. (My First I Can Read Ser.). (ENG.). 32p. (J). (gr. -1-3). 16.99 *(978-0-06-170222-8(6));* pap. 4.99 *(978-0-06-170221-1(8))* HarperCollins Pubs.

—Little David Sings for the King, 1 vol. Bowman, Crystal. 2010. (I Can Read! / Little David Ser.). (ENG.). 32p. (J). pap. 4.99 *(978-0-310-71711-9(6))* Zonderkidz.

—Mittens. Schaefer, Lola M. 2007. (My First I Can Read Ser.). (ENG.). 32p. (J). (gr. -1-3). pap. 4.99 *(978-0-06-054661-8(1),* HarperCollins) HarperCollins Pubs. Ltd. GBR. Dist: HarperCollins Pubs.

—Mittens. Schaefer, Lola M. 2007. (I Can Read Bks.). 25p. (gr. -1-k). 14.00 *(978-0-7569-8104-4(2))* Perfection Learning Corp.

—Mittens at School. Schaefer, Lola M. 2012. (My First I Can Read Ser.). (ENG.). 32p. (J). (gr. -1-3). 16.99 *(978-0-06-170224-2(2));* pap. 4.99 *(978-0-06-170223-5(4))* HarperCollins Pubs.

—Mittens, Where Is Max? Schaefer, Lola M. 2011. (My First I Can Read Ser.). (ENG.). 32p. (J). (gr. -1 — 1). 16.99 *(978-0-06-170227-3(7));* pap. 4.99 *(978-0-06-170226-6(9))* HarperCollins Pubs.

—One Leaf Rides the Wind. Mannis, Celeste Davidson. 2005. (ENG.). 32p. (J). (gr. k-3). pap. 7.99 *(978-0-14-240195-8(1),* Puffin Books) Penguin Young Readers Group.

—One Leaf Rides the Wind. Mannis, Celeste Davidson. 2005. (gr. -1-3). 17.00 *(978-0-7569-5213-6(1))* Perfection Learning Corp.

—Three Scoops & a Fig, 1 vol. Akin, Sara Laux. 2010. (ENG.). 32p. (J). (gr. -1-3). 15.95 *(978-1-56145-522-5(9))* Peachtree Publishing Co. Inc.

—What's That, Mittens? Schaefer, Lola M. 2009. (My First I Can Read Ser.). (ENG.). 32p. (J). (gr. -1 — 1). pap. 4.99 *(978-0-06-054664-9(6))* HarperCollins Pubs.

—Where's the Poop? Markes, Julie. 2020. (ENG.). 20p. (J). (gr. -1 — 1). pap. 10.99 *(978-0-06-053089-1(8),* HarperFestival) HarperCollins Pubs.

—Your Own Big Bed. Bergstein, Rita M. 2008. 36p. (J). (gr. -1-k). 16.99 *(978-0-670-06079-5(8),* Viking Books for Young Readers) Penguin Young Readers Group.

Hartung, Susan Kathleen & Endersby, Frank. Little David's Big Heart, 1 vol. Bowman, Crystal. 2010. (I Can Read! Ser.). (ENG.). 32p. (J). pap. 4.99 *(978-0-310-71708-9(6))* Zonderkidz.

Hartung, Susan Kathleen & Endersly, Frank. Little David & His Best Friend, 1 vol. Bowman, Crystal. 2010. (I Can Read! / Little David Ser.). (ENG.). 32p. (J). pap. 4.99 *(978-0-310-71710-2(8))* Zonderkidz.

—Little David's Brave Day, 1 vol. Bowman, Crystal. 2010. (I Can Read! / Little David Ser.). (ENG.). 32p. (J). pap. 4.99 *(978-0-310-71709-6(4))* Zonderkidz.

Hartzler, Maria. Good Morning Baby! Zimmerman, Mary Joyce. 2013. 48p. (J). pap. 7.99 *(978-0-7399-2458-7(3))* Rod & Staff Pubs., Inc.

Harvancik, Monica. The Little Brown Horse. Revere, John J. 2011. 34p. 17.95 *(978-1-4327-8146-0(4))* Outskirts Pr., Inc.

Harvey, Amanda. Snowed in with Grandmother Silk. Fenner, Carol. 2005. (ENG.). (J). (gr. 2-5). lib. bdg. 17.60 *(978-1-62765-248-3(5))* Perfection Learning Corp.

Harvey, Bob. The Hound of the Baskervilles. Doyle, Arthur Conan, ed. 2004. (Paperback Classics Ser.). 158p. (J). (gr. 5). lib. bdg. 12.95 *(978-1-58086-605-7(0))* EDC Publishing.

—Jane Eyre: From the Story by Charlotte Bronte. Brontë, Charlotte. rev. ed. 2007. (Usborne Classics Retold Ser.). 176p. (J). (gr. 4). per. 4.99 *(978-0-7945-1870-7(2),* Usborne) EDC Publishing.

—Kidnapped. Stevenson, Robert Louis. 2004. (Paperback Classics Ser.). 144p. (J). pap. 4.95 *(978-0-7945-0659-9(3),* Usborne) EDC Publishing.

Harvey, Gil. Encyclopedia of Planet Earth: Internet-Linked. Punter, Russell. 2009. (Geography Ser.). 160p. (YA). (gr. 4-18). 9.99 *(978-0-7945-2469-2(9),* Usborne) EDC Publishing.

Harvey II, Alvin. Bryce & the Blood Ninjas. Weber, Erec-Michael Ollier. 2013. 38p. pap. 20.00 *(978-0-9716481-9-7(0))* Kila Springs Pr.

Harvey, Jasmine. Hicc'up. Gordon, Robert. 2017. (ENG.). 24p. (J). pap. *(978-0-646-97925-0(6))* Gordon, Robert.

Harvey, Jeff. Timmy's Monster Diary: Screen Time Stress (but I Tame It, Big Time) Meimed, Raun & Sexton, Annette. 2017. (Monster Diaries: 2). (ENG.). 116p. (J). pap. 12.99 *(978-1-945547-19-5(7),* 554719) Familius LLC.

Harvey, Julianna. Friends Count: Dudley & Friends. Brown, Lori. Tabor, Sierra, ed. 2020. (Dudley & Friends Ser.). (ENG.). 32p. (J). (gr. k-2). pap. 16.95 ***(978-1-949711-27-1(7))*** Bluewater Pubns.

—Nouns: Dudley & Friends. Brown, Lori. Tabor, Sierra, ed. 2020. (Dudley & Friends Ser.: Vol. 2). (ENG.). 28p. (J). pap. 16.95 ***(978-1-949711-28-8(5))*** Bluewater Pubns.

Harvey, Kathleen. Bubble. Dannenbring-Eichstadt, Lana. 2004. 24p. (J). *(978-1-57579-282-8(6))* Pine Hill Pr.

Harvey, Lisa. Freedom Seeker: A Story about William Penn. Swain, Gwenyth. 2003. (Creative Minds Biographies Ser.). 64p. (J). 22.60 *(978-1-57505-176-5(1),* Carolrhoda Bks.) Lerner Publishing Group.

Harvey, Martin, photos by. Busy Elephants. Schindel, John. 2011. (Busy Book Ser.). 20p. (J). (— 1). 6.99 *(978-1-58246-383-4(2),* Tricycle Pr.) Random Hse. Children's Bks.

Harvey, Michael C. Bread Garden. Ketchum, Sally. 2008. 164p. pap. 12.95 *(978-0-595-52862-2(7))* iUniverse, Inc.

Harvey, Robin. Exploring Idaho from A to Z. Taylor, Gwen. 2003. (J). pap. *(978-1-930043-35-0(X))* Scott Publishing Co.

Harvey, Roland. At the Beach: Postcards from Crabby Spit. Harvey, Roland. 2007. (ENG.). 32p. (J). (gr. -1-k). pap. 13.99 *(978-1-74114-704-9(2))* Allen & Unwin AUS. Dist: Independent Pubs. Group.

—In the Bush: Our Holiday at Wombat Flat. Harvey, Roland. 2008. (ENG.). 32p. (J). (gr. k-2). pap. 14.99 *(978-1-74175-084-3(9))* Allen & Unwin AUS. Dist: Independent Pubs. Group.

—In the City: Our Scrapbook of Souvenirs. Harvey, Roland. 2010. (ENG.). 32p. (J). (gr. 1-4). pap. 11.99 *(978-1-74175-662-3(6))* Allen & Unwin AUS. Dist: Independent Pubs. Group.

Harvey, Ronald. The Wombats Go on Camp. Harvey, Ronald. 2013. (ENG.). 32p. (J). 22.99 *(978-1-74331-504-0(X))* Allen & Unwin AUS. Dist: Independent Pubs. Group.

Harvey, Shannara. Bee Is for Bernie. Kurjan, Sally. 2019. (Bernie the One-Eyed Puppy Ser.: Vol. 3). (ENG.). 32p. (J). (gr. k-6). pap. 11.99 *(978-0-578-52747-5(2))* Kurjan, Sally.

—Bernie & the Beast. Kurjan, Sally. 2019. (Bernie the One-Eyed Puppy Ser.: Vol. 2). (ENG.). 40p. (J). (gr. k-6). pap. 11.99 *(978-0-578-44656-1(1))* Kurjan, Sally.

—Bernie the One-Eyed Puppy. Kurjan, Sally. 2018. (Bernie the One-Eyed Puppy Ser.: Vol. 1). (ENG.). 32p. (J). (gr. -1-1). pap. 11.99 *(978-0-692-13852-6(8))* Kurjan, Sally.

Harwood, Jerry. Jokes for Kids about Their School Days: Calendar Series Volume 3. Harwood, Jerry. 2019. (Calendar Ser.: Vol. 3). (ENG.). 28p. (J). (gr. 1-6). pap. 9.95 ***(978-1-63498-864-3(7))*** Bookstand Publishing.

Harwood, Jerry. Jokes for Kids for All Their Days: Calendar Series Volume 1. Harwood, Jerry. 2017. (Calendar Ser.: Vol. 1). (ENG.). (J). (gr. k-6). pap. 9.95 *(978-1-63498-460-7(9))* Bookstand Publishing.

Has, M. Di Zeksling Hagodeh. 2017. (HEB & YID.). 85p. (J). *(978-1-68091-246-3(1))* Kinder Shpiel USA, Inc.

Hasanah, Julian. The Wary Scary Magic Tree & Me. Gill, Andrea L. 2019. (ENG.). 30p. (J). *(978-0-6485505-4-9(0));* pap. *(978-0-6485197-4-4(0))* Australian EBk. Pub.

Hascamp, Steve. Eight Silly Monkeys. 2006. (ENG.). 18p. (J). 9.95 *(978-1-58117-186-0(2),* Intervisual/Piggy Toes) Bendon, Inc.

Hasegawa, Naomi. The Saffron Collectors: A World Where Transformation Is Contagious. Dennis, Kingsley L. 2018. (ENG.). 270p. (YA). (gr. 8-11). pap. *(978-1-9999053-2-3(6))* Beautiful Traitor Bks.

Hasegawa, Shihoko. My Grandma's Hands. Dua, Makiko. 2019. (ENG.). 40p. (J). pap. 9.95 ***(978-1-7021-4523-7(9))*** Independently Published.

Haseloff, Ulrike. Cinderella: A Grimm's Fairy Tale, 40 vols. Grimm, Jacob and Wilhelm. 2013. Orig. Title: Aschenputtel. (ENG.). 32p. (J). 17.95 *(978-0-86315-948-0(6))* Floris Bks. GBR. Dist: Consortium Bk. Sales & Distribution.

Hasford, Elaine Collins. Lifted: A Story of Flight & Friendship. Hasford, Elaine Collins. 2017. (ENG.). 38p. (J). pap. 10.99 *(978-0-9996666-0-9(6))* Extreme Explorers LLC.

Hashey, Kim, photos by. I'm A Big Sister. Hashey, Heather. 2010. 16p. 8.49 *(978-1-4520-6293-8(5))* AuthorHouse.

Hashimoto, Molly. Molly Hashimoto's Birds! Season by Season. Burke, Zoe. 2018. 24p. (J). bds. 10.95 *(978-0-7649-8217-0(6),* POMEGRANATE KIDS) Pomegranate Communications, Inc.

Hashimoto, Satoshi, jt. illus. see RH Disney Staff.

Haskamp, Steve. Este Cerdito. 2005.Tr. of This Little Piggy. (SPA & ENG.). 22p. (J). 9.95 *(978-1-58117-328-4(8),* Intervisual/Piggy Toes) Bendon, Inc.

—Five Silly Monkeys. 2006. (ENG.). 12p. (J). bds. 14.95 *(978-1-58117-264-5(8),* Intervisual/Piggy Toes) Bendon, Inc.

—Ocho Monitos. 2005.Tr. of Eight Silly Monkeys. (SPA & ENG.). 18p. (J). 9.95 *(978-1-58117-334-5(2),* Intervisual/Piggy Toes) Bendon, Inc.

—Over, under, in, & Ouch! Harris, Trudy. 2003. (Silly Millies Ser.). (ENG.). 32p. (gr. k-3). lib. bdg. 17.44 *(978-0-7613-2912-1(9),* Lerner Pubns.) Lerner Publishing Group.

—This Little Piggy. Imperato, Teresa. 2006. (ENG.). 22p. (J). 9.95 *(978-1-58117-281-2(8),* Intervisual/Piggy Toes) Bendon, Inc.

Haskamp, Steven. Eight Silly Monkeys. 2007. (ENG.). 18p. (J). (gr. -1-3). bds. 15.95 *(978-1-58117-577-6(9),* Intervisual/Piggy Toes) Bendon, Inc.

—Five Silly Monkeys. 2006. (ENG.). 12p. (J). (gr. -1-k). 12.95 *(978-1-58117-460-1(8),* Intervisual/Piggy Toes) Bendon, Inc.

Haskett, Dan & Goddard-Laurence, Brenda. My Heart Is Bright! (Nella the Princess Knight) Tillworth, Mary. 2017. (Little Golden Book Ser.). (ENG.). 24p. (J). (-k). 4.99 *(978-1-5247-6887-4(1),* Golden Bks.) Random Hse. Children's Bks.

Haskett, Dan, jt. illus. see Goddard, Brenda.

Haskett, Dan, jt. illus. see Goddard-Laurence, Brenda.

Haskins, Phillipa. My Cat Thinks She's a Dog: A Scottish Fold Story. Fawcett, Amber. 2019. (ENG.). 30p. (J). pap. 9.99 ***(978-1-6948-5414-8(0))*** Independently Published.

Haskins, Phillipa. My Dog Toots: A French Bulldog Story. Fawcett, Amber. 2019. (ENG.). 28p. (J). pap. 9.99 *(978-1-0966-8553-1(1))* Independently Published.

Haslam, John. Good Manners at School, 1 vol. Marsico, Katie. 2009. (Good Manners Matter! Ser.). (ENG.). 32p. (J). (gr. k-3). 28.50 *(978-1-60270-608-8(5),* 8946, Looking Glass Library) Magic Wagon.

—Good Manners in Public, 1 vol. Marsico, Katie. 2009. (Good Manners Matter! Ser.). (ENG.). 32p. (J). (gr. k-3). 28.50 *(978-1-60270-610-1(7),* 8950, Looking Glass Library) Magic Wagon.

—Good Manners on the Phone, 1 vol. Marsico, Katie. 2009. (Good Manners Matter! Ser.). (ENG.). 32p. (J). (gr. k-3). 28.50 *(978-1-60270-611-8(5),* 8952, Looking Glass Library) Magic Wagon.

—Good Manners on the Playground, 1 vol. Marsico, Katie. 2009. (Good Manners Matter! Ser.). (ENG.). 32p. (J). (gr. k-3). 28.50 *(978-1-60270-612-5(3),* 8954, Looking Glass Library) Magic Wagon.

—A Journey Through Transport. Oxlade, Chris. 2017. (Journey Through Ser.). (ENG.). 48p. (J). (gr. k-3). 16.95 *(978-1-68297-152-9(X))* QEB Publishing Inc.

—Tom the Whistling Wonder. Rosselson, Leon. 2005. (ENG.). 24p. (J). lib. bdg. 23.65 *(978-1-59646-758-3(4))* Dingles & Co.

Haspiel, Dean. Cyclops. Black, Lee. 2011. (X-Men: First Class Ser.: No. 2). (ENG.). 24p. (J). (gr. 2-6). 27.07 *(978-1-59961-947-7(4),* 15634, Marvel Age) Spotlight.

—Mo & Jo: Fighting Together Forever. Lynch, Jay. (ENG.). 40p. (J). (gr. -1-3). 2013. pap. 6.99 *(978-1-935179-37-5(3));* 2008. 12.95 *(978-0-9799238-5-2(9))* TOON Books / RAW Junior, LLC.

Haspiel, Dean, et al. Scary Summer. Stine, R. L. 2007. (Goosebumps Graphix Ser.: 3). (ENG.). 144p. (J). (gr. 3-7). pap. 9.99 *(978-0-439-85782-6(1))* Scholastic, Inc.

Haspiel, Dean. The Fox - Freak Magnet. Haspiel, Dean. Waid, Mark. 2014. (Fox Ser.). (ENG.). 144p. pap. 14.99 *(978-1-936975-93-8(9),* Dark Circle Comics) Archie Comic Pubns., Inc.

Haspiel, Dean & Doe, Juan. X-Men: First Class: Class Portraits. 2011. (ENG.). 144p. (J). (gr. 4-17). pap., pap. 14.99 *(978-0-7851-5559-1(7))* Marvel Worldwide, Inc.

Hass, Estie. Menucha V'Simcha Series #11: All Aboard! Fuchs, Menucha. 2008. (Menucha V'Simcha Ser.). 20p. (J). 8.95 *(978-1-932443-82-0(7),* PSHH) Judaica Pr., Inc., The.

Hassall, John. Popular Nursery Stories - Illustrated by John Hassall. 2016. (ENG.). (J). *(978-1-4733-3514-1(0))* Read Bks.

Hassan, Nafeeza. My Yoga Workbook: Mindful Bedtime Habits. Hocheiser, Lara. 2019. (ENG.). 70p. (J). (gr. k-6). pap. 24.95 *(978-1-68418-145-2(3))* Primedia eLaunch LLC.

Hassan, Wala. The Birthday Sleepover. Noel, Cheryl E. 2016. (ENG.). (J). pap. 9.99 *(978-1-4984-8648-4(7))* Salem Author Services.

Hassani, Kwess. Where Did My Half-Brother Come From? Hancock-Johnson, Dionna. 2018. (ENG.). 28p. (J). (gr. k-3). pap. 20.00 *(978-0-9913988-0-5(7))* Dr. Dionna Hancock Johnson International Corp.

Hasselberth, Joyce. Child's Book of Animal Poems & Blessings. 2010. (ENG.). 32p. (J). 12.00 *(978-1-55896-558-4(0),* Skinner Hse. Bks.) Unitarian Universalist Assn.

Hasselfeldt, Lori. The under the Ocean Alphabet Book. Hasselfeldt, Lori. 2013. 32p. 24.95 *(978-1-61493-155-3(0));* pap. 14.95 *(978-1-61493-154-6(2))* Peppertree Pr., The.

Hasselriis, Malthe. Tales of a Chinese Grandmother: 30 Traditional Tales from China. Carpenter, Frances. 2019. (ENG.). 304p. (J). (gr. 4-7). pap. 8.99 *(978-0-8048-5161-9(1))* Tuttle Publishing.

Hassett, John. Bob's Rock. Hassett, Ann. 2017. (ENG.). 32p. (J). (gr. -1-3). 16.99 *(978-0-8075-0672-1(9),* 807506729) Whitman, Albert & Co.

—Goodnight Bob. Hassett, Ann. 2016. (ENG.). 32p. (J). (gr. -1-3). 16.99 *(978-0-8075-3003-0(4),* 807530034) Whitman, Albert & Co.

Hastings, Howard L. Hot Dog Partners. Heyliger, William. 2011. 216p. 44.95 *(978-1-258-08024-2(9))* Literary Licensing, LLC.

—Sunny Boy in the Far West. White, Ramy Allison. 2011. 216p. 44.95 *(978-1-258-09942-8(X))* Literary Licensing, LLC.

Hastings, Ken. Danny the Dump Truck. Creed, Julie. 2003. per. *(978-0-9728181-0-0(3))* Creed, Julie.

Hastings, Levi. Mayor Pete: The Story of Pete Buttigieg. Sanders, Rob. 2020. (Who Did It First? Ser.: 4). (ENG.). 32p. (J). 19.99 *(978-1-250-26757-3(9),* 900222539, Holt, Henry & Co. Bks. For Young Readers) Holt, Henry & Co.

—The Spirit of Springer: The Real-Life Rescue of an Orphaned Orca. Abler, Amanda. 2020. 48p. (J). (gr. 2-5). 18.99 *(978-1-63217-212-9(7),* Little Bigfoot) Sasquatch Bks.

Hata, Kenjiro. Hayate the Combat Butler, Vol. 1. Hata, Kenjiro. Hata, Kenjiro & Giambruno, Mark. 2006. (ENG.). 208p. (gr. 11). pap. 9.99 *(978-1-4215-0851-1(6))* Viz Media.

—Hayate the Combat Butler, Vol. 2. Hata, Kenjiro. Giambruno, Mark & Hata, Kenjiro. 2007. (ENG.). 200p. pap. 9.99 *(978-1-4215-0852-8(4))* Viz Media.

—Hayate the Combat Butler, Vol. 3. Hata, Kenjiro. Giambruno, Mark. 2007. (ENG.). 208p. (gr. 11). pap. 9.99 *(978-1-4215-0853-5(2))* Viz Media.

H

Hata, Kowshiro. On the Seesaw Bridge. Kimura, Yuichi. 2011. (ENG.). 36p. (J). (gr. -1-3). 14.95 *(978-1-935654-18-6(7)*, Vertical) Kodansha America, Inc.

Hatakeyama, Hiroshi. Goodnight, I Wish You Goodnight, Vol. 1. Hood, Karen Jean Matsko. Whispering Pine Press International, Inc. Staff, ed. 2014. (Hood Picture Book Ser.). (ENG.). 44p. (J). 24.95 *(978-1-930948-97-6(2))* Whispering Pine Pr. International, Inc.

—Goodnight, I Wish You Goodnight, Bilingual English & Icelandic, Vol. 1. Hood, Karen Jean Matsko. Whispering Pine Press International, ed. ed. 2015. (Hood Picture Book Ser.). (ENG & ICE.). 60p. (J). 94.99 *(978-1-930948-83-9(2))*; 34.95 *(978-1-59649-920-1(6))*; pap. 29.95 *(978-1-59649-919-5(2))* Whispering Pine Pr. International, Inc.

Hatakeyama, Hiroshi. Adventure Travel Activity & Coloring Book. Hatakeyama, Hiroshi, tr. Hood, Karen Jean Matsko. Whispering Pine Press International, ed. ed. 2014. (Hood Activity & Coloring Book Ser.). (ENG & JPN.). 160p. (J). spiral bd. 19.95 *(978-1-59649-334-6(8))*; per. 19.95 *(978-1-59210-590-8(4))* Whispering Pine Pr. International, Inc.

Hatala, Dan. Daisy on the Farm. O'Donnell, Liam. 2005. (Pet Tales Ser.). (ENG.). 32p. (J). (gr. -1-2). 2.95 *(978-1-59249-451-4(X)*, 1B036) Soundprints.

—Daisy the Farm Pony. O'Donnell, Liam. 2005. (Pet Tales Ser.). (ENG.). 32p. (J). (gr. -1 — 1). 4.95 *(978-1-59249-450-7(1)*, 1B035) Soundprints.

—Patches Finds a Home. Giancamilli, Vanessa. 2006. (Pet Tales Ser.). (ENG.). 32p. (J). (gr. -1-3). 4.95 *(978-1-59249-639-6(3))*; pap. 2.95 *(978-1-59249-640-2(7))* Soundprints.

—Winston in the City. O'Donnell, Liam. 2005. (Pet Tales Ser.). (ENG.). 32p. (J). (gr. -1-2). pap. 2.95 *(978-1-59249-448-4(X)*, 1B032) Soundprints.

—Winston in the City. O'Donnell, Liam. 2005. (Pet Tales Ser.). (ENG.). 32p. (J). (gr. -1 — 1). 4.95 *(978-1-59249-447-7(1)*, 1B031) Soundprints.

Hatam, Holly. The Acadia Files: Book Four, Spring Science, 1 vol. Coppens, Katie. 2020. (ENG.). 88p. (J). (gr. 3-7). 13.95 *(978-0-88448-610-7(9)*, 884610) Tilbury Hse. Pubs.

—The Acadia Files: Book Two, Autumn Science, 1 vol. Coppens, Katie. 2018. (ENG.). 88p. (J). (gr. 4-7). 13.95 *(978-0-88448-604-6(4)*, 884604) Tilbury Hse. Pubs.

—Cinderella Rex (Once Before Time Book 1) Webster, Christy. 2019. (Once Before Time Ser.: 1). (ENG.). 32p. (J). bds. 8.99 *(978-1-5248-5516-1(2))* Andrews McMeel Publishing.

Hatam, Holly. Dear Baby, A Love Letter to Little Ones. Rosenthal, Paris. 2020. (ENG.). 40p. (J). (gr. -1-3). 18.99 ***(978-0-06-301272-1(3)***, HarperCollins) HarperCollins Pubs. Ltd. GBR. Dist: HarperCollins Pubs.

Hatam, Holly. Dear Boy, A Celebration of Cool, Clever, Compassionate You! Rosenthal, Paris & Rosenthal, Jason B. 2019. (ENG.). 40p. (J). (gr. -1-3). 17.99 *(978-0-06-242251-4(0)*, HarperCollins) HarperCollins Pubs. Ltd. GBR. Dist: HarperCollins Pubs.

—Dear Girl, A Celebration of Wonderful, Smart, Beautiful You! Rosenthal, Amy Krouse & Rosenthal, Paris. 2017. (ENG.). 40p. (J). (gr. -1-3). 17.99 *(978-0-06-242250-7(2)*, HarperCollins) HarperCollins Pubs. Ltd. GBR. Dist: HarperCollins Pubs.

—Happy Right Now. Berry, Julie. 2019. (ENG.). 32p. (J). 17.95 *(978-1-68364-352-4(6)*, 900214691) Sounds True, Inc.

—Jack (Not Jackie) Silverman, Erica. 2018. (ENG.). 40p. (J). (gr. -1-3). 17.99 *(978-1-4998-0731-8(7))* Little Bee Books Inc.

—Made by Maxine. Spiro, Ruth. 2018. 32p. (J). (gr. -1-3). 16.99 *(978-0-399-18629-5(8)*, Dial Bks) Penguin Young Readers Group.

—Tree Song. Stone, Tiffany. 2018. (ENG.). 32p. (J). (gr. k-2). 18.95 *(978-1-77321-001-8(7))* Annick Pr., Ltd. CAN. Dist: Publishers Group West (PGW).

Hatam, Holly. What Matters. Hughes, Alison. 2020. (ENG.). 32p. (J). (gr. -1-k). 12.95 ***(978-1-4598-2641-0(8))*** Orca Bk. Pubs. USA.

Hatam, Holly. Winter Science, 1 vol., Bk. 3. Coppens, Katie. 2019. (ENG.). 88p. (J). (gr. 3-7). 13.95 *(978-0-88448-607-7(9)*, 884607) Tilbury Hse. Pubs.

Hatam, Samer. Clever Crow. Holden, Pam & Aesop, Aesop. 26p. (gr. 3-3). pap. *(978-1-927197-34-9(1)*, Red Rocket Readers) Flying Start Bks.

—Dinner with Fox. Holden, Pam. 2015. 16p. (-1). pap. *(978-1-77654-129-4(4)*, Red Rocket Readers) Flying Start Bks.

—Don't Cry Wolf. Holden, Pam. 2015. 16p. (-1). pap. *(978-1-77654-130-0(8)*, Red Rocket Readers) Flying Start Bks.

—Fire in the Jungle, 6 pack. Holden, Pam. 2009. (Red Rocket Readers Ser.). 17p. (gr. 2-2). pap. *(978-1-877363-73-3(1))* Flying Start Bks.

—The Gentle Giant, 6 pack. Holden, Pam. 2009. (Red Rocket Readers Ser.). 19p. (gr. 2-2). pap. *(978-1-877363-81-8(2))* Flying Start Bks.

—Jungle Fire. Holden, Pam. 2015. 16p. (-1). pap. *(978-1-77654-132-4(4)*, Red Rocket Readers) Flying Start Bks.

—Seal on the Loose. Holden, Pam. 2015. 16p. (-1). pap. *(978-1-77654-134-8(0)*, Red Rocket Readers) Flying Start Bks.

—Too Big & Heavy, 6 pack. Holden, Pam. 2009. (Red Rocket Readers Ser.). 22p. (gr. 2-2). pap. *(978-1-877363-70-2(7))* Flying Start Bks.

Hatanaka, Kellen. Maggie's Treasure, 1 vol. Lappano, Jon-Erik. 2020. (ENG.). 32p. (J). (gr. -1-2). 18.95 ***(978-1-77306-237-2(9))*** Groundwood Bks. CAN. Dist: Publishers Group West (PGW).

Hatanaka, Kellen. Tokyo Digs a Garden, 1 vol. Lappano, Jon-Erik. 2016. (ENG.). 32p. (J). (gr. -1-2). 18.95 *(978-1-55498-798-6(9))* Groundwood Bks. CAN. Dist: Publishers Group West (PGW).

Hatfield, Cynthia. Mosquito Get in Trouble Too. Lewis-Brown, Alscess. 2009. (J). *(978-1-934370-09-4(6))* Editorial Campana.

Hatfield, Richard. Ocean Deep. Baker, Sue. 2011. (Information Bks.). 14p. (J). (gr. -1-3). spiral bd. *(978-0-85953-929-6(6))* Child's Play International Ltd.

Hatfield, Tommy. Josiah's School Fun Day. Carrier, Therese & Carrier, Stephen. 2007. 29p. (J). 16.95 *(978-0-9797648-0-6(7))* Carrier, Therese.

Hatfield, Tyrel. Fix Your Eyes on Jesus. Hatfield, Tyrel. Hatfield, Justin. Hatfield, Lisa & Hatfield, Kari, eds. 2006. (J). cd-rom 99.00 *(978-0-9766703-1-5(3))* Little Acorn LLC.

—The Mystery of Christ. Hatfield, Tyrel. Hatfield, Justin. Hatfield, Lisa & Hatfield, Kari, eds. 2006. (J). cd-rom 99.00 *(978-0-9766703-2-2(1))* Little Acorn LLC.

—Righteous Roundup: Wanted: Righteous children of God. Hatfield, Tyrel. Hatfield, Justin. 2008. (J). cd-rom 99.00 *(978-0-9766703-6-0(4))* Little Acorn LLC.

Hatfield, Tyrel S. Fix your eyes on Jesus. Hatfield, Tyrel S. Hatfield, Justin R. 2005. 108p. (J). spiral bd. 150.00 *(978-0-9766703-0-8(5))* Little Acorn LLC.

Hathaway, Karen. Eelfish, a Rock & Roll King. Salton, Liz. 2004. 38p. pap. 24.95 *(978-1-4137-1847-8(7))* PublishAmerica, Inc.

Hathi, Garva, jt. illus. see DiCicco, Sue.

Hatke, Ben. Angel in the Waters. Doman, Regina. (J). (gr. -1-3). 2004. 48p. pap. 6.95 *(978-1-928832-81-2(4))*; 10th ed. 2014. (ENG.). 11.95 *(978-1-62282-208-9(0))* Sophia Institute Pr.

—Around the Year Once upon a Time Saints. Pochocki, Ethel. 2009. (ENG.). 211p. (J). (gr. 4-6). pap. 14.95 *(978-1-932350-26-5(8))* Ignatius Pr.

—Can God See Me in the Dark? Lozano, Neal. 2007. (ENG.). 32p. (J). 16.95 *(978-1-883551-45-2(5)*, Maple Corners Press) Attic Studio Publishing Hse.

—Mi Angelito en Las Aguas. Doman, Regina. 2006. (SPA.). 40p. (J). (gr. -1-3). pap. 6.95 *(978-1-933184-22-7(1))* Sophia Institute Pr.

—Missy Piggle-Wiggle & the Sticky-Fingers Cure. Martin, Ann M. & Parnell, Annie. 2018. (Missy Piggle-Wiggle Ser.: 3). (ENG.). 240p. (J). 16.99 *(978-1-250-13229-1(0)*, 900176807) Feiwel & Friends.

—Missy Piggle-Wiggle & the Sticky-Fingers Cure. Martin, Ann M. & Parnell, Annie. 2019. (Missy Piggle-Wiggle Ser.: 3). (ENG.). 240p. (J). pap. 7.99 *(978-1-250-21139-2(5)*, 900176808) Square Fish.

—Missy Piggle-Wiggle & the Whatever Cure. Martin, Ann M. & Parnell, Annie. 2016. (Missy Piggle-Wiggle Ser.: 1). (ENG.). 256p. (J). 16.99 *(978-1-250-07169-9(0)*, 900149727) Feiwel & Friends.

—Missy Piggle-Wiggle & the Whatever Cure. Martin, Ann M. & Parnell, Annie. 2017. (Missy Piggle-Wiggle Ser.: 1). (ENG.). 272p. (J). pap. 8.99 *(978-1-250-12953-6(2)*, 900176094) Square Fish.

—Missy Piggle-Wiggle & the Won't-Walk-The-Dog Cure. Martin, Ann M. & Parnell, Annie. 2017. (Missy Piggle-Wiggle Ser.: 2). (ENG.). 240p. (J). 16.99 *(978-1-250-07170-5(4)*, 900149729) Feiwel & Friends.

—Missy Piggle-Wiggle & the Won't-Walk-The-Dog Cure. Martin, Ann M. & Parnell, Annie. 2018. (Missy Piggle-Wiggle Ser.: 2). (ENG.). 256p. (J). pap. 7.99 *(978-1-250-17903-6(3)*, 900189918) Square Fish.

—Saint John Vianney: A Priest for All People. DeDomenico, Elizabeth Marie. 2008. (Encounter the Saints Ser.). 122p. (J). (gr. 4-7). pap. 7.95 *(978-0-8198-7115-2(X))* Pauline Bks. & Media.

—The Story of Job. 2018. (ENG.). 55p. (J). (gr. 1-4). pap. 16.95 *(978-1-5051-1175-0(7)*, 2742) TAN Bks.

—Will You Bless Me? Lozano, Neal. 2009. 32p. (J). lib. bdg. 16.95 *(978-1-883551-32-2(3)*, MCP-323, Maple Corners Press) Attic Studio Publishing Hse.

—The Worm Whisperer. Hicks, Betty. 2017. (ENG.). 192p. (J). pap. 7.99 *(978-1-250-14820-9(0)*, 900181893) Square Fish.

Hatke, Ben. Julia's House for Lost Creatures. Hatke, Ben. 2014. (Julia's House Ser.). (ENG.). 40p. (J). (gr. k-3). 18.99 *(978-1-59643-866-8(5)*, 900099011, First Second Bks.) Roaring Brook Pr.

Hatke, Ben. Julia's House Moves On. Hatke, Ben. 2020. (Julia's House Ser.). (ENG.). 40p. (J). 18.99 ***(978-1-250-19137-3(8)***, 900192707, First Second Bks.) Roaring Brook Pr.

Hatke, Ben. Legends of Zita the Spacegirl. Hatke, Ben. 2012. (Zita the Spacegirl Ser.: 2). (ENG.). 224p. (J). (gr. 3-7). pap. 12.99 *(978-1-59643-447-9(3)*, 900054804, First Second Bks.) Roaring Brook Pr.

—Zita the Spacegirl. Hatke, Ben. 2011. (Zita the Spacegirl Ser.: 1). (ENG.). 192p. (J). (gr. 3-7). 19.99 *(978-1-59643-695-4(6)*, 900073109); pap. 12.99 *(978-1-59643-446-2(5)*, 900054803) Roaring Brook Pr. (First Second Bks.).

Hattenhauer, Ina. Dollhouse Sticker Book. ed. 2012. (Sticker Activity Book Ser.). 24p. (J). pap. 8.99 *(978-0-7945-2944-4(5)*, Usborne) EDC Publishing.

Hatton, Libby. Pete Puffin's Wild Ride Cruising Alaska's Currents. Hatton, Libby. 2008. (J). pap. 16.95 *(978-0-930931-92-6(0))* Alaska Geographic Assn.

Hau, Joseph. I Can Live To 100! Secrets Just for Kids. Hau, Stephanie. 2005. 60p. (J). per. 9.95 *(978-0-9767324-0-2(8)*, Kids Can) Proactive Publishing.

Hauck, Christie. Things I See When I Open My Eyes. Culver, Kathy. 2007. 32p. per. 13.95 *(978-1-59858-306-9(9))* Dog Ear Publishing, LLC.

Hauer, Leigh. Papa & Gigi's Day Off. Koziel, Mary & Koziel, Richard. 2020. (ENG.). 48p. (J). ***(978-1-5255-7275-3(X))***; pap. ***(978-1-5255-7276-0(8))*** FriesenPress.

Hauge, Carl & Hauge, Mary. Thornton Burgess Bedtime Stories: Includes Downloadable MP3s. Burgess, Thornton W. 2013. (Dover Read & Listen Ser.). (ENG.). 112p. (J). (gr. 1). pap. 14.99 *(978-0-486-49189-9(7)*, 491897) Dover Pubns., Inc.

Hauge, Mary, jt. illus. see Hauge, Carl.

Haugen, Ryan, et al. Chuckle Squad: Jokes about Classrooms, Sports, Food, Teachers, & Other School Subjects, 1 vol. Donahue, Jill L. et al. 2010. (Michael Dahl Presents Super Funny Joke Bks.). (ENG.). 80p. (J). (gr. 1-3). 25.32 *(978-1-4048-5773-5(7)*, Picture Window Bks.) Capstone.

Haugen, Ryan. El Cuadro de Mary, 1 vol. Blackaby, Susan & Jones, Christianne C. Ruiz, Carlos, tr. 2006. (Read-It! Readers en Español: Story Collection).Tr. of Mary's Art. (SPA.). 32p. (J). (gr. -1-3). 21.32 *(978-1-4048-1649-7(6)*, Picture Window Bks.) Capstone.

—Moving Day, 1 vol. Blackaby, Susan. 2005. (Read-It! Readers Ser.). (ENG.). 24p. (J). (gr. -1-3). 21.32 *(978-1-4048-1006-8(4)*, Picture Window Bks.) Capstone.

—There Are Millions of Millionaires: And Other Freaky Facts About Earning, Saving, & Spending. Seuling, Barbara. 2010. (Freaky Facts Ser.). 40p. pap. 0.35 *(978-1-4048-6550-1(0)*, Picture Window Bks.) Capstone.

Haugen, Ryan, et al. Wise Crackers: Riddles & Jokes about Numbers, Names, Letters, & Silly Words, 1 vol. Dahl, Michael et al. 2010. (Michael Dahl Presents Super Funny Joke Bks.). (ENG.). 80p. (J). (gr. 1-3). 25.32 *(978-1-4048-6102-2(5)*, Picture Window Bks.) Capstone.

Haugen, Ryan & Jensen, Brian. Knock Your Socks Off: A Book of Knock-Knock Jokes, 1 vol. Dahl, Michael. 2010. (Michael Dahl Presents Super Funny Joke Bks.). (ENG.). 80p. (J). (gr. 1-3). 25.32 *(978-1-4048-5774-2(5)*, Picture Window Bks.) Capstone.

—Laughs for a Living: Jokes about Doctors, Teachers, Firefighters, & Other People Who Work, 1 vol. Dahl, Michael & Ziegler, Mark. 2010. (Michael Dahl Presents Super Funny Joke Bks.). (ENG.). 80p. (J). (gr. 1-3). 25.32 *(978-1-4048-5771-1(0)*, Picture Window Bks.) Capstone.

Haughom, Lisa. People, Places & Things. 2010. (J). *(978-1-58865-541-7(5))* Kidsbooks, LLC.

—Things That Go! 2010. 16p. (J). *(978-1-58865-542-4(3))* Kidsbooks, LLC.

Haughton, Chris. Don't Worry, Little Crab. Haughton, Chris. 2020. (ENG.). 48p. (J). (-k). 17.99 *(978-1-5362-1119-1(2))* Candlewick Pr.

—Goodnight Everyone. Haughton, Chris. 2016. (ENG.). 32p. (J). (-k). 15.99 *(978-0-7636-9079-3(1))* Candlewick Pr.

—Little Owl Lost. Haughton, Chris. (ENG.). (J). 2013. 30p. (-k). bds. 7.99 *(978-0-7636-6750-4(1))*; 2010. 32p. (gr. -1-k). 14.99 *(978-0-7636-5022-3(6))* Candlewick Pr.

—No Tengas Miedo Cangrejito. Haughton, Chris. 2019. (SPA.). 52p. (J). 16.95 *(978-84-17673-19-2(9))* NubeOcho Ediciones ESP. Dist: Consortium Bk. Sales & Distribution.

—Oh No, George! Haughton, Chris. (ENG.). 32p. (J). 2015. (-k). bds. 7.99 *(978-0-7636-7652-0(7))*; 2012. (gr. -1-k). 16.99 *(978-0-7636-5546-4(5))* Candlewick Pr.

—Un Poco Perdido. Haughton, Chris. 2019. (ENG.). 40p. (J). 16.95 *(978-84-17673-13-0(X))* NubeOcho Ediciones ESP. Dist: Consortium Bk. Sales & Distribution.

—Shh! A Chris Haughton Boxed Set. Haughton, Chris. 2017. (ENG.). 102p. (J). (-k). bds. 24.97 *(978-0-7636-9538-5(6))* Candlewick Pr.

—Shh! We Have a Plan. Haughton, Chris. (ENG.). 40p. (J). 2015. (-k). bds. 8.99 *(978-0-7636-7977-4(1))*; 2014. (gr. -1-2). 17.99 *(978-0-7636-7293-5(9))* Candlewick Pr.

—¡Shhh! Tenemos un Plan. Haughton, Chris. 2019. (SPA.). 48p. (J). 16.95 *(978-84-17673-21-5(0))* NubeOcho Ediciones ESP. Dist: Consortium Bk. Sales & Distribution.

Hauman, Doris, jt. illus. see Hauman, George and Doris.

Hauman, Doris, jt. illus. see Hauman, George.

Hauman, George & Hauman, Doris. The Little Engine That Could. Piper, Watty. deluxe ed. 2009. (Little Engine That Could Ser.). (ENG.). 48p. (J). (gr. -1-2). 17.99 *(978-0-448-45257-9(X)*, Grosset & Dunlap) Penguin Young Readers Group.

Hauman, George and Doris. The Little Engine That Could. Piper, Watty. 2020. (Little Engine That Could Ser.). (ENG.). 40p. (J). (gr. -1-2). pap. 5.99 *(978-0-593-09600-0(2)*, Grosset & Dunlap) Penguin Young Readers Group.

Hauman, George and Doris. The Little Engine That Could: Read Together Edition. Piper, Watty. 2020. (Read Together, Be Together Ser.). (ENG.). 48p. (J). (gr. -1-2). 9.99 ***(978-0-593-22423-6(X)***, Grosset & Dunlap) Penguin Young Readers Group.

Hauman, George and Doris & Hauman, Doris. The Little Engine That Could. Piper, Watty & dePaola, Tomie. 2015. (Little Engine That Could Ser.). 26p. (J). (gr. -1 — 1). bds. 11.99 *(978-0-448-48731-1(4)*, Grosset & Dunlap) Penguin Young Readers Group.

Haus, Estudio. Ancient Myths. 2015. (Ancient Myths Ser.). (ENG.). 32p. (J). (gr. 3-9). lib. bdg., lib. bdg., lib. bdg. 187.92 *(978-1-4914-2522-0(9)*, Capstone Pr.) Capstone.

—Cailyn & Chloe Learn about Conjunctions. Atwood, Megan. 2014. (Language Builders Ser.). (ENG.). 32p. (J). (gr. 2-4). pap. 11.94 *(978-1-60357-706-9(8))* Norwood Hse. Pr.

—Ghosts & Atoms, 1 vol. Wheeler-Toppen, Jodi. 2011. (Monster Science Ser.). (ENG.). 32p. (gr. 3-9). (J). pap. 8.10 *(978-1-4296-7329-7(X))*; pap. 47.70 *(978-1-4296-7330-3(3))* Capstone. (Capstone Pr.).

Haus Grandpre, Karen. Misty's Twilight. Henry, Marguerite. 2016. (ENG.). 144p. (J). (gr. 3-7). 19.99 *(978-1-4814-5221-2(5)*, Aladdin) Simon & Schuster Children's Publishing.

Hause, C. L. The Best Native American Stories for Children. Mullins, G. W. 2016. (Native American Storytelling Ser.: Vol. 1). (ENG.). (J). (gr. 2-6). 24.99 *(978-1-68418-540-5(8))*; pap. 14.99 *(978-1-68418-532-0(7))* Primedia eLaunch LLC.

—The Native American Story Book Volume Five Stories of the American Indians for Children. Mullins, G. W. (Native American Story Book Ser.: Vol. 5). (ENG.). (J). 2016. (gr. 1-6). 25.99 *(978-1-68418-527-6(0))*; 2nd ed. 2019. 198p. (gr. 3-6). pap. 14.99 ***(978-1-64713-307-8(6))*** Primedia eLaunch LLC.

—The Native American Story Book Volume Four Stories of the American Indians for Children. Mullins, G. W. (Native American Story Book Ser.: Vol. 4). (ENG.). (J). 2016. (gr. 1-6). 25.99 *(978-1-68418-531-3(9))*; 2nd ed. 2019. 196p. (gr. 3-6). pap. 14.99 ***(978-1-64713-331-3(9))*** Primedia eLaunch LLC.

Hause, C. L. The Native American Story Book Volume Three Stories of the American Indians for Children. Mullins, G. W. 2nd ed. 2019. (Native American Story Ser.: Vol. 3). (ENG.). 178p. (J). (gr. 2-6). pap. 13.99 ***(978-1-64713-305-4(X))*** Primedia eLaunch LLC.

Hausen, Julie. We All Love: A Book for Compassionate Little Vegans & Vegetarians. Hausen, Julie. 2017. (ENG.). 32p. (J). pap. 12.95 *(978-0-692-98786-5(X))* Hausen, Julie.

Hauser, Bill. Four Secrets. Willey, Margaret. (ENG.). 288p. (YA). (gr. 7-12). 2014. pap. 9.95 *(978-1-4677-1626-0(X)*, 9781467716260); 2012. 17.95 *(978-0-7613-8535-6(5)*, 9780761385356) Lerner Publishing Group. (Carolrhoda Lab™).

—Mousetraps. Schmatz, Pat. 2008. (ENG.). 192p. (YA). (gr. 7-12). 17.95 *(978-0-8225-8657-9(6)*, Carolrhoda Bks.) Lerner Publishing Group.

Hauser, Jessica. Taffy & Troy. Davidchuk, Wendy & Grovum, Marilyn. 2020. (Taffy & Troy Ser.). (ENG.). 40p. (J). ***(978-1-5255-5436-0(0))***; pap. ***(978-1-5255-5437-7(9))*** FriesenPress.

Hauser, Salvan. Kindergarten Success. Hauser, Jill Frankel. 2005. (Little Hands! Ser.). 128p. (J). (gr. k-18). pap. 12.95 *(978-0-8249-6751-2(8)*, Ideal Pubns.) Worthy Publishing.

Hauser, Sheri, photos by. Crosscurrents. Tolpen, Stanley. 2008. (ENG.). 82p. (J). ring bd. 14.95 *(978-1-60789-013-3(5))* Glorybound Publishing.

Hauser, Solaire. Chieftains' Summit. Hauser, Tamina & Patel, Tiara, eds. 2019. (Famir Chronicles Ser.: Vol. 2). (ENG.). 436p. (J). pap. 15.99 ***(978-1-7927-2722-1(4))*** Independently Published.

Hausman, Sid. Cactus Critter Bash. Hausman, Sid. 2006. (ENG.). 32p. (J). 21.95 *(978-1-929115-15-0(6))* Azro Pr., Inc.

Hausmann, Rex. The Apastron Reports: Quest for Life, 1 vol. Senneff, John A. 2005. 317p. (YA). 22.95 *(978-0-9671107-7-6(7))* Quality Pubs.

Hautman, Pete. Invisible. Hautman, Pete. 2006. (ENG.). 160p. (YA). (gr. 7-12). reprint ed. pap. 10.99 *(978-0-689-86903-7(7)*, Simon & Schuster Bks. For Young Readers) Simon & Schuster Bks. For Young Readers.

Hauvette, Marion. A Puzzling Picnic. Knight, Deborah Janet. 2010. 32p. pap. 13.00 *(978-1-60860-963-5(4)*, Eloquent Bks.) Strategic Book Publishing & Rights Agency (SBPRA).

Hauviller, Gastón. Conoce a Miguel de Cervantes. Iturralde, Edna. 2012. (Personajes Del Mundo Hispánico Ser.). (SPA.). 32p. (J). (gr. 3-8). pap. 13.95 *(978-1-63113-929-1(0))* Santillana USA Publishing Co., Inc.

Haverfield, Mary. Johnny Appleseed. Kurtz, Jane. 2004. (Ready-To-Reads Ser.). (ENG.). 32p. (J). (gr. -1-1). pap. 4.99 *(978-0-689-85958-8(9)*, Simon Spotlight) Simon Spotlight.

—Mister Bones: Dinosaur Hunter. Kurtz, Jane. 2004. (Ready-To-Reads Ser.). (ENG.). 32p. (J). (gr. -1-1). pap. 4.99 *(978-0-689-85960-1(0)*, Simon Spotlight) Simon Spotlight.

—Mister Bones Dinosaur Hunter. Kurtz, Jane. ed. 2005. (Ready-to-Read Ser.). 32p. (J). lib. bdg. 15.00 *(978-1-59054-929-2(5))* Fitzgerald Bks.

—Sometimes It's Grandmas & Grandpas: Not Mommies & Daddies. Byrne, Gayle. 2009. (ENG.). 32p. (J). (gr. -1-3). 17.95 *(978-0-7892-1028-9(2)*, 791028, Abbeville Kids) Abbeville Pr., Inc.

Havice, Susan. Who Needs Friends? Taylor-Butler, Christine. 2006. (Rookie Readers Ser.). (ENG.). 32p. (J). (gr. k-2). pap. 4.95 *(978-0-516-24997-1(5)*, Children's Pr.) Scholastic Library Publishing.

Haw, Brenda. L' Ile Fantastique: Fantastic Island. Leigh, Susannah. Gemmell, Kathy & Irving, Nicole, eds. (FRE.). 25p. (J). (gr. 2-3). reprint ed. 17.00 *(978-0-7881-9300-2(7))* DIANE Publishing Co.

—The Incredible Dinosaur Expedition. Dolby, Karen. 2004. (Puzzle Adventures Ser.). 48p. (J). pap. 4.95 *(978-0-7945-0022-1(6)*, Usborne) EDC Publishing.

—Puzzle Car Race. Heywood, Rosie. 2004. (Young Puzzles Ser.). 32p. (J). pap. 6.95 *(978-0-7945-0689-6(5)*, Usborne) EDC Publishing.

—Puzzle Castle. Leigh, Susannah. Waters, Gaby, ed. 2004. (Usborne Young Puzzles Ser.). 32p. (J). (gr. 1). lib. bdg. 14.95 *(978-1-58086-674-3(3))*; pap. 6.95 *(978-0-7945-0433-5(7))* EDC Publishing. (Usborne).

—Puzzle Dinosaurs. Leigh, Susannah. Tyler, Jenny, ed. 2007. (Young Puzzles Ser.). 32p. (J). pap. 6.99 *(978-0-7945-1778-6(1)*, Usborne) EDC Publishing.

—Puzzle Dungeon. Leigh, Susannah. 2004. (Young Puzzles Ser.). 32p. (J). (gr. 1). lib. bdg. 14.95 *(978-1-58086-599-9(2))* EDC Publishing.

—Puzzle Farm. Leigh, Susannah. Waters, Gaby, ed. 2004. (Young Puzzles Ser.). 32p. (J). (gr. 1). lib. bdg. 14.95 *(978-1-58086-627-9(1)*, Usborne) EDC Publishing.

—Puzzle Mountain. Leigh, Susannah. Waters, Gaby, ed. 2005. (Usborne Young Puzzles Ser.). 32p. (J). (gr. 1). lib. bdg. 14.95 *(978-1-58086-694-1(8)*, Usborne) EDC Publishing.

—Puzzle Mountain. Leigh, Susannah. 2003. 32p. (J). pap. 6.95 *(978-0-7945-0713-8(1)*, Usborne) EDC Publishing.

—Puzzle Ocean. Leigh, Susannah. 2006. (Young Puzzles Ser.). 32p. (J). (gr. 1). lib. bdg. 14.95 *(978-1-58086-535-7(6))* EDC Publishing.

—Puzzle Palace. Leigh, Susannah. Tyler, Jenny, ed. 2005. (Usborne Young Puzzles Ser.). 32p. (J). (gr. -1-3). per. 6.95 *(978-0-7945-1120-3(1)*, Usborne) EDC Publishing.

—Puzzle Pirates. Leigh, Susannah. 2006. (Usborne Young Puzzles Ser.). 32p. (J). (gr. 1). lib. bdg. 14.99 *(978-1-58086-973-7(4)*, Usborne) EDC Publishing.

—Puzzle Pirates. Leigh, Susannah. Tyler, Jenny, ed. 2006. (Usborne Young Puzzles Ser.). 32p. (J). (gr. 1-4). pap. 6.99 *(978-0-7945-1359-7(X)*, Usborne) EDC Publishing.

—Puzzle Planet. Leigh, Susannah. Waters, Gaby, ed. 2006. (Young Puzzles Ser.). 32p. (J). (gr. 1). lib. bdg. 14.95 *(978-1-58086-536-4(4))* EDC Publishing.

—Puzzle Pyramid. Leigh, Susannah. 2004. 32p. (J). pap. 6.95 *(978-0-7945-0791-6(3)*, Usborne) EDC Publishing.
—Puzzle School. Leigh, Susannah. 2004. (Young Puzzles Ser.). 32p. (Orig.). (J). (gr. 1). lib. bdg. 14.95 *(978-1-58086-600-2(X))* EDC Publishing.
—Puzzle Town. Leigh, Susannah. Waters, Gaby, ed. 2006. (Young Puzzles Ser.). 32p. (J). (gr. 1). lib. bdg. 14.95 *(978-1-58086-537-1(2)*, Usborne) EDC Publishing.
—Puzzle Train. Leigh, Susannah. 2004. (Young Puzzles Ser.). 32p. (J). (gr. 1). lib. bdg. 14.95 *(978-1-58086-633-0(6)*, Usborne) EDC Publishing.
—Puzzle Train. Leigh, Susannah. Waters, Gaby, ed. 2003. (Young Puzzles Ser.). 32p. (J). pap. 6.95 *(978-0-7945-0683-4(6)*, Usborne) EDC Publishing.
—Puzzle World: Combined Volume. Leigh, Susannah. Waters, Gaby, ed. 2004. (Young Puzzles Ser.). 96p. (J). pap. 13.95 *(978-0-7945-0688-9(7)*, Usborne) EDC Publishing.
—Travel Puzzles Sticker Book. Heywood, Rosie, ed. rev. ed. 2005. (Travel Puzzles Sticker Book Ser.). 24p. (J). (gr. 1). pap. 6.95 *(978-0-7945-0729-9(8)*, Usborne) EDC Publishing.
Haw, Brenda & Dawes, Will. Uncle Pete's Pirate Adventure. Leigh, Susannah. Stowell, Louie, ed. rev. ed. 2007. (Young Puzzle Adventures Ser.). 32p. (J). (gr. -1-3). pap. 4.99 *(978-0-7945-1848-6(6)*, Usborne) EDC Publishing.
Hawcock, David. 0-20. Hawcock, David. 2015. (ENG.). 52p. (J). (gr. -1-k). 14.99 *(978-1-85707-898-5(5))* Tango Bks. GBR. Dist: Independent Pubs. Group.
Hawcock, David, jt. illus. see Elzbieta.
Hawke, Jessamy. Inventors: Incredible Stories of the World's Most Ingenious Inventions. Winston, Robert. 2020. (ENG.). 144p. (J). (gr. 2-4). 21.99 ***(978-1-4654-9228-9(3)***, DK Children) Dorling Kindersley Publishing, Inc.
Hawke, Richard, jt. illus. see Bouttell, Robin.
Hawkes, Kevin. And to Think That We Thought That We'd Never Be Friends. Hoberman, Mary Ann. 2003. (ENG.). 40p. (J). (gr. -1-2). pap. 7.99 *(978-0-440-41776-7(7)*, Dragonfly Bks.) Random Hse. Children's Bks.
—Brunolandia. Fleischman, Paul. 2003. (SPA.). 16p. (J). *(978-84-348-6640-9(4)*, SM30969) SM Ediciones ESP. Dist: Lectorum Pubns., Inc.
—By the Light of the Halloween Moon, 0 vols. Stutson, Caroline. 2012. (ENG.). 32p. (J). (gr. k-3). pap. 7.99 *(978-0-7614-6244-6(9)*, 9780761462446, Two Lions) Amazon Publishing.
—Chicken Cheeks. Black, Michael Ian. 2009. (ENG.). 40p. (J). (gr. -1-3). 18.99 *(978-1-4169-4864-3(3)*, Simon & Schuster Bks. For Young Readers) Simon & Schuster Bks. For Young Readers.
—Dial-a-Ghost. Ibbotson, Eva. 2003. (ENG.). 224p. (J). (gr. 3-7). pap. 6.99 *(978-0-14-250018-7(6)*, Puffin Books) Penguin Young Readers Group.
—Dogosaurus Rex. Staniszewski, Anna. 2017. (ENG.). 40p. (J). 18.99 *(978-0-8050-9706-1(6)*, 900096793, Holt, Henry & Co. Bks. For Young Readers) Holt, Henry & Co.
—The Great Ghost Rescue. Ibbotson, Eva. 2003. (ENG.). 192p. (J). (gr. 3-7). pap. 6.99 *(978-0-14-250087-3(9)*, Puffin Books) Penguin Young Readers Group.
—Handel, Who Knew What He Liked. Anderson, M. T. 2013. (Candlewick Biographies Ser.). 48p. (J). (gr. 3-7). (ENG.). 14.99 *(978-0-7636-6599-9(1))*; pap. 4.99 *(978-0-7636-6600-2(9))* Candlewick Pr.
—The Hanukkah Magic of Nate Gadol. Levine, Arthur A. 2020. (ENG.). 40p. (J). (gr. k-3). 19.99 *(978-0-7636-9741-9(9))* Candlewick Pr.
—The Haunting of Granite Falls. Ibbotson, Eva. 2005. (ENG.). 224p. (J). (gr. 3-7). 6.99 *(978-0-14-240371-6(7)*, Puffin Books) Penguin Young Readers Group.
—Have a Look, Says Book. Jackson, Richard. 2016. (ENG.). 48p. (J). (gr. -1-2). 17.99 *(978-1-4814-2105-8(0))* Simon & Schuster Children's Publishing.
—Journey to the River Sea. Ibbotson, Eva. 2003. 298p. (gr. 3-7). 18.00 *(978-0-7569-1552-0(X))* Perfection Learning Corp.
—Journey to the River Sea. Ibbotson, Eva. 2003. (ENG.). 304p. (J). (gr. 3-7). pap. 8.99 *(978-0-14-250184-9(0)*, Puffin Books) Penguin Young Readers Group.
—Library Lion. Knudsen, Michelle. 2006. 48p. (J). (gr. -1-3). 17.99 *(978-0-7636-2262-6(1))* Candlewick Pr.
—Library Lion. Knudsen, Michelle. 2009. (ENG.). 48p. (J). (gr. -1-3). pap. 7.99 *(978-0-7636-3784-2(X))* Candlewick Pr.
—A Little Bitty Man & Other Poems for the Very Young. Rasmussen, Halfdan Wedel et al. 2011. 32p. (J). (gr. k-12). 15.99 *(978-0-7636-2379-1(2))* Candlewick Pr.
—Me, All Alone, at the End of the World. Anderson, M. T. 2017. 48p. (J). (gr. 1-4). 14.99 *(978-0-7636-8902-5(5))* Candlewick Pr.
—Meanwhile, Back at the Ranch. Isaacs, Anne. 2014. 56p. (J). (gr. k-4). 17.99 *(978-0-375-86745-3(7)*, Schwartz & Wade Bks.) Random Hse. Children's Bks.
—Mountain Manor Mystery. Trumbauer, Lisa. 2006. 96p. (J). pap. *(978-1-59034-810-9(9))* Mondo Publishing.
—My Little Sister Ate One Hare. Grossman, Bill. 2014. 32p. pap. 7.00 *(978-1-61003-374-9(4))* Center for the Collaborative Classroom.
—My Little Sister Hugged an Ape. Grossman, Bill. 2008. (ENG.). (J). (gr. -1-2). lib. bdg. 17.60 *(978-1-61383-748-1(8))* Perfection Learning Corp.
—My Little Sister Hugged an Ape. Grossman, Bill. 2008. (ENG.). 40p. (J). (gr. -1-2). pap. 7.99 *(978-0-385-73660-2(6)*, Dragonfly Bks.) Random Hse. Children's Bks.
—A Necklace of Raindrops & Other Stories. Aiken, Joan. 2003. 84p. (J). (gr. 1-5). 13.15 *(978-0-7569-5686-8(2))* Perfection Learning Corp.
—Newton's Rainbow: The Miraculous Discoveries of a Young Scientist. Lasky, Kathryn. 2017. (ENG.). 48p. (J). 17.99 *(978-0-374-35513-5(4)*, 9780374355135, Farrar, Straus & Giroux (BYR)) Farrar, Straus & Giroux.
—Not Just a Witch. Ibbotson, Eva. 2004. (ENG.). 192p. (J). (gr. 3-7). pap. 5.99 *(978-0-14-240232-0(X)*, Puffin Books) Penguin Young Readers Group.
—A Pig Parade Is a Terrible Idea. Black, Michael Ian. 2010. (ENG.). 40p. (J). (gr. -1-3). 18.99 *(978-1-4169-7922-7(0)*, Simon & Schuster Bks. For Young Readers) Simon & Schuster Bks. For Young Readers.
—The Road to Oz: Twists, Turns, Bumps, & Triumphs in the Life of L. Frank Baum. Krull, Kathleen. 2008. (ENG.). 48p. (J). (gr. -1-2). 19.99 *(978-0-375-83216-1(5)*, Knopf Bks. for Young Readers) Random Hse. Children's Bks.
—Santa from Cincinnati. Barrett, Judi. 2012. (ENG.). 48p. (J). (gr. -1-3). 16.99 *(978-1-4424-2993-2(3)*, Atheneum Bks. for Young Readers) Simon & Schuster Children's Publishing.
—Sidewalk Circus. Fleischman, Paul. 2007. (ENG.). 32p. (J). (gr. k-4). 7.99 *(978-0-7636-2795-9(X))* Candlewick Pr.
—Sidewalk Circus. Fleischman, Paul. 2007. (gr. k-4). 18.00 *(978-0-7569-8182-2(4))* Perfection Learning Corp.
—There's a Dinosaur on the 13th Floor. Bradford, Wade. 2018. (ENG.). 40p. (J). (gr. -1-3). 16.99 *(978-0-7636-8665-9(4))* Candlewick Pr.
—The Three Mouths of Little Tom Drum. Willard, Nancy. 2015. 48p. (J). (gr. -1-3). 16.99 *(978-0-7636-5476-4(0))* Candlewick Pr.
—Velma Gratch & the Way Cool Butterfly. Madison, Alan. 2007. (ENG.). 40p. (J). (gr. -1-3). 17.99 *(978-0-375-83597-1(0)*, Schwartz & Wade Bks.) Random Hse. Children's Bks.
—Velma Gratch & the Way Cool Butterfly. Madison, Alan. 2012. 40p. (J). (gr. -1-3). pap. 7.99 *(978-0-307-97804-2(4)*, Schwartz & Wade Bks.) Random Hse. Children's Bks.
—Weslandia. Fleischman, Paul. 2006. (gr. -1-3). 17.00 *(978-0-7569-6566-2(7))* Perfection Learning Corp.
—The Worry Week. Lindbergh, Anne M. 2010. (ENG.). 128p. (J). reprint ed. pap. 12.95 *(978-1-56792-239-4(2))* Godine, David R. Pub.
Hawkes, Spencer. Beagles in My Bed Coloring Book. 2005. 50p. (J). 5.95 *(978-0-9774563-1-4(5))* Ladd, David Pr.
Hawkins, Aaron. The Year Money Grew on Trees. Hawkins, Aaron. 2011. (ENG.). (J). (gr. 5-7). lib. bdg. 17.60 *(978-1-61383-363-6(6))* Perfection Learning Corp.
Hawkins, Alison. The Noisy Classroom. Shanté, Angela. 2020. 32p. (J). (gr. 1-3). 16.99 *(978-1-5132-6292-5(0)*, West Margin Pr.) West Margin Pr.
Hawkins, Brett. A Triune Tale of Diminutive Swine. 2012. pap. 15.00 *(978-0-9854699-0-0(0))* Rockshow Comedy, Inc.
Hawkins, Colin, et al. Madcap Book of Laughs. Brandreth, Gyles. 288p. (J). pap. 6.95 *(978-0-233-99569-4(2))* Andre Deutsch GBR. Dist: Trafalgar Square Publishing.
—Pirate Ship: A Pop-up Adventure. Hawkins, Colin. 2006. 28p. (J). (gr. 4-8). reprint ed. 20.00 *(978-0-7567-9827-7(2))* DIANE Publishing Co.
Hawkins, Klara. Race to the North Pole. Roth, Megan. 2017. (ENG.). 12p. (J). (gr. -1 — 1). bds. 9.99 *(978-1-62686-770-3(4)*, Silver Dolphin Bks.) Printers Row Publishing Group.
Hawkins, Kristen. Rollie Pollie Review. Holley, Kim. 2013. 16p. pap. 10.00 *(978-1-939054-22-7(2))* Rowe Publishing.
Hawkins, Linda. The Happy Girl. Heyde, Christiane. 2003. 48p. 14.95 *(978-0-87516-618-6(0)*, Devorss Pubns.) DeVorss & Co.
Hawkins, Patrick. Tommy Turner's Battle for Yorintown. Seegar, Ali. Garnsworthy, Mario, ed. 2019. (Tommy Turner's Travels Ser.: Vol. 2). (ENG.). 200p. (J). (gr. 3-6). pap. *(978-99959-965-5-0(3))* Kingsbury, A.K.
Hawksley, Gerald. Danny Dog's Car: Press Out Parts Make a Car Carrying Danny Dog!, 1 vol. 2009. (Toddler Make & Play Ser.). (ENG.). 10p. (J). 6.95 *(978-1-59496-184-7(0))* Teora USA LLC.
—Patty Cow's Tractor: Press Out Parts Make a Tractor Carrying Patty Cow, 1 vol. 2009. (Toddler Make & Play Ser.). (ENG.). 10p. 6.95 *(978-1-59496-182-3(4))* Teora USA LLC.
—Quacky Duck's Plane: Press Out Parts Make an Airplane Carrying Quacky Duck!, 1 vol. 2009. (Toddler Make & Play Ser.). (ENG.). 10p. 6.95 *(978-1-59496-185-4(9))* Teora USA LLC.
—Splashy Dolphin's Boat: Press Out Parts Make a Boat Carrying Splashy Dolphin, 1 vol. 2009. (Toddler Make & Play Ser.). (ENG.). 10p. 6.95 *(978-1-59496-183-0(2))* Teora USA LLC.
Hawksley, Gerald. My Big Book of the World. Hawksley, Gerald. Royston, Angela. 2017. 40p. (J). (gr. k-6). 12.99 *(978-1-84322-893-6(9)*, Armadillo) Anness Publishing GBR. Dist: National Bk. Network.
Hawksworth, Jess. Blue Teaches a Lesson. Malone, Jae. 2020. (ENG.). 18p. (J). (gr. k-3). pap. ***(978-1-80031-994-3(0))*** Authors OnLine, Ltd.
Hawksworth, Jess. Lorna & the Loch Ness Monster. Malone, Jae. 2019. (ENG.). 20p. (J). (gr. k-3). pap. *(978-1-78955-470-0(5))* Authors OnLine, Ltd.
Hawksworth, Jess. Mrs Pringles Needs a Nurse. Malone, Jae. 2020. (ENG.). 18p. (J). (gr. k-3). pap. ***(978-1-80031-954-7(1))*** Authors OnLine, Ltd.
Hawley, Kelvin. Are You Hungry?, 6 pack. Holden, Pam. 2009. (Red Rocket Readers Ser.). 16p. (gr. -1-1). pap. *(978-1-877363-23-8(5)*, Red Rocket Readers) Flying Start Bks.
—The Big Bad Wolf, 6 pack. Holden, Pam. 2009. (Red Rocket Readers Ser.). 20p. (gr. 2-2). pap. *(978-1-877363-56-6(1)*, Red Rocket Readers) Flying Start Bks.
—Charlie to the Rescue. Holden, Pam. 2015. 16p. (-1). pap. *(978-1-77654-128-7(6)*, Red Rocket Readers) Flying Start Bks.
—Crumpet, the Cat: 3-in-1 Package. Eggleton, Jill. (Sails Literacy Ser.). 24p. (gr. 1-18). 57.00 *(978-0-7578-8619-5(1))* Rigby Education.
—Crumpet, the Cat: Big Book Only. Eggleton, Jill. (Sails Literacy Ser.). 24p. (gr. 1-18). 27.00 *(978-0-7578-6203-8(9))* Rigby Education.
—Farm Friends, 6 pack. Holden, Pam. 2009. (Red Rocket Readers Ser.). 16p. (gr. -1-1). pap. *(978-1-877363-14-6(6)*, Red Rocket Readers) Flying Start Bks.
—The Giant's Ice Cream: 3-in-1 Package. Eggleton, Jill. (Sails Literacy Ser.). 24p. (gr. k-18). 57.00 *(978-0-7578-3195-9(8))* Rigby Education.
—The Giant's Ice Cream: Big Book Only. Eggleton, Jill. (Sails Literacy Ser.). 24p. (gr. k-18). 27.00 *(978-0-7635-6986-0(0))* Rigby Education.
—Going Up, 6 pack. Holden, Pam. 2009. (Red Rocket Readers Ser.). 16p. (gr. -1-1). pap. *(978-1-877363-18-4(9)*, Red Rocket Readers) Flying Start Bks.
—Happy Birthday, 6 pack. Holden, Pam. 2009. (Red Rocket Readers Ser.). 16p. (gr. -1-1). pap. *(978-1-877363-03-0(0)*, Red Rocket Readers) Flying Start Bks.
—Magic Stone Soup - BIG BOOK. Holden, Pam. 2016. 16p. (-1). *(978-1-77654-164-5(2)*, Red Rocket Readers) Flying Start Bks.
—My Hands, 6 pack. Holden, Pam. 2009. (Red Rocket Readers Ser.). 16p. (gr. -1-1). pap. *(978-1-877363-25-2(1)*, Red Rocket Readers) Flying Start Bks.
—My Things, 6 Packs. (Sails Literacy Ser.). 16p. (gr. k-18). 27.00 *(978-0-7635-4395-2(0))* Rigby Education.
—The Paper Trail, 6 pack. Holden, Pam. 2009. (Red Rocket Readers Ser.). 21p. (gr. 2-2). pap. *(978-1-877363-69-6(3))* Flying Start Bks.
—Pass It On, 6 pack. Holden, Pam. 2009. (Red Rocket Readers Ser.). 20p. (gr. 2-2). pap. *(978-1-877363-66-5(9)*, Red Rocket Readers) Flying Start Bks.
—Pin the Tail on the Donkey, 6 pack. Holden, Pam. 2009. (Red Rocket Readers Ser.). 21p. pap. *(978-1-877363-78-8(2))* Flying Start Bks.
—Presents for Grace, 6 pack. Holden, Pam. 2009. (Red Rocket Readers Ser.). 18p. (gr. 2-2). pap. *(978-1-877363-61-0(8)*, Red Rocket Readers) Flying Start Bks.
—Red Riding Hood, 6 pack. Holden, Pam. 2009. (Red Rocket Readers Ser.). 16p. (gr. -1-1). pap. *(978-1-877363-09-2(X)*, Red Rocket Readers) Flying Start Bks.
—Shark & Crab Big Book Edition. Ellis, Julie. 2014. 16p. (gr. 1-1). *(978-1-77654-094-5(8)*, Red Rocket Readers) Flying Start Bks.
—Stone Soup, 6 pack. Holden, Pam. 2009. (Red Rocket Readers Ser.). 18p. (gr. 2-2). pap. *(978-1-877363-84-9(7))* Flying Start Bks.
—Three Billy Goats Gruff, 6 pack. Holden, Pam. 2009. (Red Rocket Readers Ser.). 16p. (gr. -1-1). pap. *(978-1-877363-10-8(3)*, Red Rocket Readers) Flying Start Bks.
—Tin Lizzy, 6 pack. Holden, Pam. 2009. (Red Rocket Readers Ser.). 22p. (gr. 2-2). pap. *(978-1-877363-86-3(3))* Flying Start Bks.
—Tony's Dad. Eggleton, Jill. 2003. (Rigby Sails Sailing Solo Ser.). (ENG.). 24p. (gr. 1-2). pap. 9.05 *(978-0-7578-3975-7(4))* Rigby Education.
—Trip, Trap!, 6 pack. Holden, Pam. 2009. (Red Rocket Readers Ser.). 22p. (gr. 2-2). pap. *(978-1-877363-62-7(6)*, Red Rocket Readers) Flying Start Bks.
—The Ugly Troll. Holden, Pam. 2017. 16p. (J). pap. *(978-1-77654-191-1(X)*, Red Rocket Readers) Flying Start Bks.
—The Vacation: Individual Title Six-Packs. (Sails Literacy Ser.). 16p. (gr. k-18). 27.00 *(978-0-7635-4434-8(5))* Rigby Education.
Hawley, Kelvin, jt. illus. see Storey, Jim.
Hawley, R. Spencer. There's a Monster in My Nose. Hawley, Richard And Elizabeth. 2009. 36p. pap. 24.95 *(978-1-61546-177-6(9))* America Star Bks.
Haworth, Hennie. ArtCards: Accessorize. Broom, Jenny. 2013. (ENG.). 72p. (J). (gr. 1-4). pap. 17.99 *(978-0-7636-6892-1(3)*, Big Picture Press) Candlewick Pr.
—Artcards: Fashion. Broom, Jenny. 2014. (ENG.). 72p. (J). (gr. 1-4). pap. 17.99 *(978-0-7636-7519-6(9)*, Big Picture Press) Candlewick Pr.
—Rebel Women: Discover History Through Fashion. Bruzzone, Catherine. 2019. (Fashion Paper Dolls Ser.). (ENG.). 24p. (J). (gr. 2-4). pap. 9.99 *(978-1-911509-22-6(5))* B Small Publishing GBR. Dist: Independent Pubs. Group.
Haworth, Margaret, photos by. Jarry, Garry Palas: Cat Tail Stories. Haworth, Margaret. I.t. ed. 2003. (Books That Help Ser.: Vol. 3). 34p. (J). (gr. 1-6). pap. 9.95 *(978-0-9740313-5-4(6))* Haworth, Margaret.
—Oh Holly Dallig: Cat Tail Stories. Haworth, Margaret. I.t. ed. 2003. (Books That Help Ser.: Vol. 3). 34p. (J). (gr. 1-6). pap. 9.95 *(978-0-9740313-4-7(8))* Haworth, Margaret.
Hawthorn, Hennie. Dress-Up Jane Austen: Discover History Through Fashion. Bruzzone, Catherine. 2018. (Fashion Paper Dolls Ser.). (ENG.). 24p. (J). (gr. 2-4). pap. 9.99 *(978-1-911509-13-4(6))* B Small Publishing GBR. Dist: Independent Pubs. Group.
—Dress-Up Russian Revolution. Bruzzone, Catherine. 2018. (Fashion Paper Dolls Ser.). (ENG.). 24p. (J). (gr. 2-4). pap. 9.99 *(978-1-911509-14-1(4))* B Small Publishing GBR. Dist: Independent Pubs. Group.
Hawthorn, Paul & Hopkins, Simon. Gammy. Helliwell, Sheila. 2nd ed. 2013. 70p. pap. *(978-0-9560331-4-7(8))* Children' Story Pubs.
Hawthorne, Lara. 12 Days of Christmas. ed. 2020. (Christmas Choir Ser.). (ENG.). 32p. (J). (gr. -1-k). 16.99 ***(978-0-7112-4540-2(1)***, Frances Lincoln Children's Bks.) Quarto Publishing Group UK GBR. Dist: Hachette Bk. Group.
Hawthorne, Lara. Alba & the Ocean Cleanup. Hawthorne, Lara. 2020. (ENG.). 32p. (J). (gr. -1-2). 16.99 *(978-1-5362-1044-6(7)*, Big Picture Press) Candlewick Pr.
—The Night Flower: the Blooming of the Saguaro Cactus. Hawthorne, Lara. 2019. (ENG.). 32p. (J). (gr. -1-2). 16.99 *(978-1-5362-0616-6(4)*, Big Picture Press) Candlewick Pr.
Hawthorne, Mike, et al. The End. 2020. 200p. (YA). (gr. 8-17). pap. 24.99 ***(978-1-302-92499-7(0))*** Marvel Worldwide, Inc.
Hawyard, Charlie O. Sidecar Scooter. Caldwell, Bruce. 2008. 32p. (J). pap. 9.95 *(978-0-9792612-9-9(5))* Blue Gate Bks.
Haxton-Johns, Rebecca. Grandpa Goes to College. Haxton, Charles. 2004. 14p. (J). 4.95 *(978-1-59466-017-7(4)*, Little Ones) Port Town Publishing.
Hay DeSimone, Corkey. Air & Space Activity & Coloring Book: An Early Introduction to the History of Flight. Hay DeSimone, Corkey. 2006. (J). 7.95 *(978-0-9747921-4-9(4))* Gentle Giraffe Pr.
—Dinosaur Explore Activity & Coloring Book: Dinosaurs designed for their littlest Fans. Hay DeSimone, Corkey. 2006. (J). 4.95 *(978-0-9777394-0-0(6))* Gentle Giraffe Pr.
—Future Sports Legend Board Book: An Early Introduction to Sports in Maryland. Hay DeSimone, Corkey. 2006. (J). bds. 4.99 *(978-0-9747921-5-6(2))* Gentle Giraffe Pr.
—Mammal Animal Board Book 2nd Edition. Hay DeSimone, Corkey. 2007. 24p. (J). 7.95 *(978-0-9777394-2-4(2))* Gentle Giraffe Pr.
—Panda Promise Activity & Coloring Book. Hay DeSimone, Corkey. 2006. (J). 4.95 *(978-0-9747921-9-4(5))* Gentle Giraffe Pr.
Hay, Peter. Lesson of the White Eagle. Hay, Barbara. 2012. (ENG.). 144p. (YA). pap. 11.99 *(978-1-937054-01-4(2))* RoadRunner Pr.
Haya, Erwin. Bible Freaks & Geeks, 1 vol. Strauss, Ed. 2007. (2:52 Ser.). (ENG.). 128p. (J). (gr. 3-7). pap. 7.99 *(978-0-310-71309-8(9))* Zonderkidz.
—Grammar Girl Presents the Ultimate Writing Guide for Students. Fogarty, Mignon. 2019. (Quick & Dirty Tips Ser.). (ENG.). 304p. (YA). pap. 16.99 *(978-1-250-21751-6(2)*, 900206991, St. Martin's Griffin) St. Martin's Pr.
—Picture a Home Run: A Baseball Drawing Book, 1 vol. Wacholtz, Anthony. 2013. (Drawing with Sports Illustrated Kids Ser.). (ENG.). 64p. (J). (gr. 5-9). 34.65 *(978-1-4765-3106-9(4))* Capstone.
—Picture a Slam Dunk: A Basketball Drawing Book, 1 vol. Wacholtz, Anthony. 2013. (Drawing with Sports Illustrated Kids Ser.). (ENG.). 64p. (J). (gr. 5-9). 34.65 *(978-1-4765-3107-6(2))* Capstone.
—Seriously Sick Bible Stuff, 1 vol. Strauss, Ed. 2007. (2:52 Ser.). (ENG.). 128p. (J). (gr. 3-7). pap. 7.99 *(978-0-310-71310-4(2))* Zonderkidz.
—Ultimate Writing Guide for Students. Fogarty, Mignon. 2011. (Quick & Dirty Tips Ser.). (ENG.). (YA). (gr. 7). lib. bdg. 25.60 *(978-1-68065-205-5(2))* Perfection Learning Corp.
Haya, Erwin & Ray, Mike. Drawing with Sports Illustrated Kids, 1 vol. Wacholtz, Anthony. 2013. (Drawing with Sports Illustrated Kids Ser.). (ENG.). 144p. (J). (gr. 5-9). pap. 14.95 *(978-1-4765-3581-4(7)*, Capstone Pr.) Capstone.
Haya, Erwin, jt. illus. see Jenkins, Ward.
Haya, Erwin, jt. illus. see Ray, Mike.
Hayashi, Kenzo. Squiggle! Doodle over 200 One-Line Animals! 2017. (ENG.). 176p. (gr. k). pap. 12.95 *(978-1-5235-0109-0(X)*, 100109) Workman Publishing Co., Inc.
Hayashi, Nancy. Camp K-9, 1 vol. Rodman, Mary Ann. 2011. (ENG.). 32p. (J). (gr. -1-3). 15.95 *(978-1-56145-561-4(X))* Peachtree Publishing Co. Inc.
—I Can Do It Myself!, 1 vol. Adams, Diane. (ENG.). 32p. (J). (gr. -1-1). 2013. 7.95 *(978-1-56145-725-0(6))*; 2009. 15.95 *(978-1-56145-471-6(0))* Peachtree Publishing Co. Inc.
—I Know It's Autumn. Spinelli, Eileen. 2004. (ENG.). 32p. (J). (gr. -1-2). 16.99 *(978-0-06-029422-9(1))* HarperCollins Pubs.
—I Want to Help!, 1 vol. Adams, Diane. 2012. (ENG.). 32p. (J). 15.95 *(978-1-56145-630-7(6))* Peachtree Publishing Co. Inc.
—Raymond & Nelda, 1 vol. Bottner, Barbara. 2007. (ENG.). 32p. (J). (gr. k-3). 15.95 *(978-1-56145-394-8(3))* Peachtree Publishing Co. Inc.
Hayashi, Nancy. I Know It's Autumn. Hayashi, Nancy, tr. Spinelli, Eileen. 2004. 32p. (J). (gr. -1-2). lib. bdg. 17.89 *(978-0-06-029423-6(X))* HarperCollins Pubs.
Hayashi, Yoshio. Folktales from Japan: Fables, Myths & Fairy Tales for Children. Sakade, Florence. 2020. 80p. (J). (gr. k-5). 14.99 ***(978-4-8053-1472-2(9))*** Tuttle Publishing.
Hayashi, Yoshio. Kintaro's Adventures & Other Japanese Children's Stories. Sakade, Florence. rev. ed. 2018. 48p. (J). (gr. -1-3). 9.99 *(978-0-8048-5056-8(9))* Tuttle Publishing.
—More Japanese Children's Favorite Stories. Sakade, Florence. anniv. ed. 2014. 96p. (J). (gr. 3-8). 17.95 *(978-4-8053-1265-0(3))* Tuttle Publishing.
—Urashima Taro & Other Japanese Children's Favorite Stories. Sakade, Florence. 2018. 48p. (J). (gr. -1-3). 9.99 *(978-0-8048-5072-8(0))* Tuttle Publishing.
Haycraft, Marilynn J. The Cowbears of Texas: The Hero. Edgell, Ernest. 2004. 25p. pap. 24.95 *(978-1-4137-3507-9(X))* PublishAmerica, Inc.
Hayden, Christine. Everybody Has a Hat. Hayden, Christine. 2016. (ENG.). (J). pap. *(978-0-9937447-4-7(5))* Hayden, Helen Christine.
Hayden, Jennifer. Liberty Cafe Is Open. Trimble, Marcia. ed. 2006. (J). pap. 895.00 *(978-1-891577-91-8(3))*; 32p. lib. bdg. 15.95 *(978-1-891577-90-1(5))* Images Pr.
Hayden, Jennifer H. Marsby & the Martian Detectives. Trimble, Marcia J. 2004. 56p. (J). per. 9.95 *(978-1-891577-52-9(2)*, SAN299-4844) Images Pr.
Hayden, Sean. The Three Musketeers. Ladybird Books Staff & Dumas, Alexandre. 2016. (Ladybird Classics Ser.). 72p. (J). (gr. 3-7). 10.99 *(978-1-4093-1355-7(7))* Penguin Bks., Ltd. GBR. Dist: Independent Pubs. Group.
Hayden, Seito & Chandler, Alton. Beginning Conversations with God: A Prayer & Spiritual Journal for Children. Banks, Calvin J. (J). (gr. -1-3). pap. 14.95 *(978-1-877804-14-4(2))* Chandler/White Publishing Co.
Hayden, Seitu. A Biography of Malcolm X. Gunderson, Jessica. 2010. (American Graphic Ser.). (ENG.). 32p. (J). (gr. 3-9). lib. bdg. 31.32 *(978-1-4296-5471-5(6)*, Capstone Pr.) Capstone.
—Come to Galapagos at Sea to See. Fogerty, Ramona. 2004. (SPA.). (J). pap. 22.95 *(978-0-9759889-1-6(3))* Potenial Psychotherapy Counseling & Remedial Service.
—Obama: The Historic Election of America's 44th President, 1 vol. Biskup, Agnieszka. 2011. (American Graphic Ser.).

H

(ENG.). 32p. (gr. 3-9). (J). pap. 8.10 *(978-1-4296-7339-6(7))*; pap. 47.70 *(978-1-4296-7340-2(0)*, Capstone Pr.) Capstone.

—Olivia's Potty Adventures: Potty Training Adventures. Clarke, Terreece M. 2018. (ENG.). 26p. (J). (gr. -1-k). 14.95 *(978-1-941958-40-7(0))* Cedar Grove Bks.

—X: A Biography of Malcolm X. Gunderson, Jessica. 2011. (American Graphic Ser.). (ENG.). 32p. (gr. 3-9). (J). pap. 8.10 *(978-1-4296-6267-3(0))*; pap. 47.70 *(978-1-4296-6438-7(X))* Capstone. (Capstone Pr.).

Hayden, Seitu, jt. illus. see Still, Wayne A.

Hayden, Wendy. El Dolor de Barriga de Dash: Un Libro para ni�os Que No Pueden o No Quieren Hacer Popo. Hayden, Wendy. 2020. (SPA.). 34p. (J). pap. 9.99 ***(978-1-7106-9476-5(9))*** Independently Published.

Hayes, Betsy. Cozy Clozy: From Fibers to Fabrics. Alford, Douglas. 2004. (J). 6.96 net. *(978-0-9762208-0-0(6))* Mfg Application Konsulting Engineering.

Hayes, Dan. Jamie the Germ Slayer in a Place Called Little While. DeWitt Hall, Suzanne. 2020. (ENG.). 40p. (J). pap. 9.99 ***(978-1-7347427-0-1(4))*** DH Strategies.

Hayes, Dan. The Thanksgiving. 24p. (J). pap., act. bk. ed. 7.95 *(978-0-8249-5324-9(X)*, Ideal Pubns.) Worthy Publishing.

Hayes, David, jt. illus. see Hayes, Kathy.

Hayes, Don. The Easter. 24p. (Orig.). (J). pap., act. bk. ed. 4.95 *(978-0-8249-5368-3(1)*, Ideal Pubns.) Worthy Publishing.

Hayes, Geoffrey. Patrick Eats His Peas & Other Stories. 2013. (Patrick Bear Ser.). (ENG.). 32p. (J). (gr. -1-3). 12.95 *(978-1-935179-34-4(9))* TOON Books / RAW Junior, LLC.

—Patrick in a Teddy Bear's Picnic & Other Stories. 2011. (Patrick Bear Ser.). (ENG.). 32p. (J). (gr. -1-3). 12.95 *(978-1-935179-09-2(8))* TOON Books / RAW Junior, LLC.

Hayes, Geoffrey. Benny & Penny in Just Pretend, 1 vol. Hayes, Geoffrey. 2013. (Toon Bks.). (ENG.). 36p. (J). (gr. 1-2). lib. bdg. 29.93 *(978-1-61479-148-5(1)*, 14840) Spotlight.

—Benny & Penny in Just Pretend. Hayes, Geoffrey. 2008. (Benny & Penny Ser.). (ENG.). 32p. (J). (gr. -1-3). 12.95 *(978-0-9799238-0-7(8))* TOON Books / RAW Junior, LLC.

—Benny & Penny in the Big No-No! Hayes, Geoffrey. Mouly, Françoise, ed. 2009. (Benny & Penny Ser.). (ENG.). 32p. (J). (gr. -1-3). 12.95 *(978-0-9799238-9-0(1))* TOON Books / RAW Junior, LLC.

—Benny & Penny in the Toy Breaker, 1 vol. Hayes, Geoffrey. 2013. (Toon Bks.). (ENG.). 36p. (J). (gr. 1-2). lib. bdg. 29.93 *(978-1-61479-149-2(X)*, 14841) Spotlight.

—A Night-Light for Bunny. Hayes, Geoffrey. 2004. 32p. (J). (gr. -1-3). 14.99 *(978-0-06-029163-1(X))* HarperCollins Pubs.

Hayes, Karel. Little Loon. Hodgkins, Fran. 2015. (ENG.). 32p. (J). (gr. -1-3). 16.95 *(978-1-60893-372-3(5))* Down East Bks.

—Time for the Fair. Train, Mary. ed. 2005. (ENG.). 28p. (J). (gr. k-17). 15.95 *(978-0-89272-694-3(6))* Down East Bks.

—The Witches: A Winnipesaukee Adventure. Opel, Andy. 2011. (ENG.). 32p. (J). 19.95 *(978-0-9828236-6-8(5)*, Jetty Hse.) Randall, Peter E. Pub.

Hayes, Karel. The Summer Visitors, 10 vols. Hayes, Karel. ed. 2011. (ENG.). 32p. (gr. -1-3). 17.95 *(978-0-89272-918-0(X))* Down East Bks.

Hayes, Karel & Gorey, John. The Bobhouse: A Winnipesaukee Christmas. Opel, Andrew. 2017. (ENG.). 32p. (J). 19.95 *(978-1-937721-45-9(0)*, Jetty Hse.) Randall, Peter E. Pub.

Hayes, Kathy & Hayes, David. The Camp Caper: A Shubin Cousins Adventure. Shubin, Masha. 2013. 88p. pap. 6.95 *(978-0-9792145-1-6(3))* Anno Domini.

Hayes, Noah. The Avant-Guards Vol. 1. Usdin, Carly. 2019. (Avant-Guards Ser.). (ENG.). 112p. (J). pap. 14.99 *(978-1-68415-367-1(0))* Boom! Studios.

—The Avant-Guards Vol. 2. Usdin, Carly. 2020. (Avant-Guards Ser.: 2). (ENG.). 112p. (J). pap. 14.99 *(978-1-68415-568-2(1))* Boom! Studios.

Hayes, Steve. Let's Eat! Maji Teaches Mongo What It Means to Eat Clean! Norton, J. Renae. 2013. (Maji & Mongo Ser.: 2). (ENG.). 40p. (J). (gr. 1-7). 17.95 *(978-1-934759-61-5(9))* Reed, Robert D. Pubs.

Hayes, Steve & Cole, Amy. How Maji Gets Mongo off the Couch! Norton, J. Renae. Reed, Cleone, ed. ed. 2012. (Maji & Mongo Bks.: 0). (ENG.). 32p. (J). (gr. k-3). 17.95 *(978-1-934759-60-8(0))* Reed, Robert D. Pubs.

Hayn, Walter. Slovenly Betsy: the American Struwwelpeter: From the Struwwelpeter Library. Hoffmann, Heinrich. 2013. (Dover Children's Classics Ser.). (ENG.). 96p. (J). (gr. 3-8). pap. 12.99 *(978-0-486-49828-7(X))* Dover Pubns., Inc.

Hayne, Mark. The Young Captives: A Story of Judah & Babylon. Jones, Erasmus W. 2007. 200p. per. *(978-1-4065-2718-6(1))* Dodo Pr.

Haynes, Gibby. Me & Mr. Cigar. Haynes, Gibby. 2020. (ENG.). 256p. (YA). (gr. 9). 18.99 *(978-1-61695-812-1(X)*, Soho Teen) Soho Pr., Inc.

Haynes, Jason & Oke, Rachel. Rudy the Red Pig. Guess, Catherine Ritch. 2006. (ENG.). 32p. (J). 13.95 *(978-1-933341-13-2(0))* CRM.

Haynes, Joyce. The Diary of Marie Landry, Acadian Exile, 1 vol. Allbritton, Stacy Demoran. 2012. (ENG.). 160p. (J). (gr. 3-7). pap. 14.95 *(978-1-58980-865-2(7)*, Pelican Publishing) Arcadia Publishing.

—Good Soup Attracts Chairs, 1 vol. Osseo-Asare, Fran. 2006. (ENG.). 160p. (J). (gr. 5-8). pap. 12.95 *(978-1-56554-918-0(X)*, Pelican Publishing) Arcadia Publishing.

—Jane Wilkinson Long: Texas Pioneer, 1 vol. Petrick, Neila Skinner. 2004. (ENG.). 32p. (J). (gr. k-3). 16.99 *(978-1-58980-147-9(4)*, Pelican Publishing) Arcadia Publishing.

—Lipstick Like Lindsay's & Other Christmas Stories, 1 vol. Toner, Gerald R. 2005. (ENG.). 112p. per. 14.95 *(978-1-58980-357-2(4)*, Pelican Publishing) Arcadia Publishing.

Haynes, Penny. Maisie the Animal Minder: Maisie & Ben. Littlefield, Eireann. 2012. 34p. pap. *(978-1-908128-35-5(6))* Spiderwize.

Haynes, Rob & Ross, Dave. Marvel Knights by Joe Quesada Omnibus. 2018. (Marvel Knights Ser.: 1). (ENG.). 720p. (YA). (gr. 8-17). 100.00 *(978-1-302-91406-6(5))* Marvel Worldwide, Inc.

—Marvel Knights Daredevil by Mack & Quesada: Parts of a Hole. 2018. (Marvel Knights Daredevil by Mack & Quesada: Parts of a Hole Ser.: 1). (ENG.). 176p. (YA). (gr. 8-17). pap. 17.99 *(978-1-302-91473-8(1))* Marvel Worldwide, Inc.

Hays, Anna Jane, et al. Smarty Sara. 2008. (Step into Reading Ser.). 48p. (J). (gr. -1-1). pap. 4.99 *(978-0-375-83512-4(1)*, Random Hse. Bks. for Young Readers) Random Hse. Children's Bks.

Hays, Ethel. The Town Mouse & the Country Mouse. 2007. (Shape Bks.). (ENG.). 14p. (J). (gr. -1-3). pap. 9.95 *(978-1-59583-192-7(4)*, 9781595831927, Green Tiger Pr.) Laughing Elephant.

Hays, Michael. Abiyoyo Returns. Seeger, Pete & Jacobs, Paul DuBois. 2004. (ENG.). 40p. (J). (gr. -1-3). 8.99 *(978-0-689-87054-5(X)*, Aladdin) Simon & Schuster Children's Publishing.

—W Is for Windy City: A Chicago City Alphabet. Layne, Steven et al. 2010. (Sleeping Bear City Alphabet Ser.). (ENG.). 40p. (J). 17.95 *(978-1-58536-420-6(7))* Sleeping Bear Pr.

Hays, Shannon. Magic Mermaids. Make Believe Ideas Ltd & Greening, Rosie. 2020. (ENG.). 12p. (J). bds. ***(978-1-78947-743-6(3))*** Make Believe Ideas.

—Magical Unicorns. Make Believe Ideas Ltd & Greening, Rosie. 2020. (ENG.). 12p. (J). bds. ***(978-1-78947-370-4(5))*** Make Believe Ideas.

—Never Feed a Bear. Make Believe Ideas Ltd & Greening, Rosie. 2020. (Felt Teeth Ser.). (ENG.). 12p. (J). bds. ***(978-1-78947-574-6(0))*** Make Believe Ideas.

—Never Touch Never Touch a Crocodile. Make Believe Ideas Ltd. 2020. (Never Touch A Ser.). (ENG.). 12p. (J). bds. ***(978-1-78947-956-0(8))*** Make Believe Ideas.

Hays, Shannon. U Is for Unicorn. Make Believe Ideas Ltd. 2019. (ENG.). 12p. (J). (gr. -1-k). bds. *(978-1-78843-826-1(4))* Make Believe Ideas.

—Wish upon a Rainbow. Make Believe Ideas Ltd. 2019. (ENG.). 12p. (J). bds. *(978-1-78947-002-4(1))* Make Believe Ideas.

Haysom, John. The First Christmas. Frank, Penny & Allsopp, Sophie. 2nd rev. ed. (ENG.). 24p. pap. 2.99 *(978-0-7459-4115-8(X)*, Lion Books) Lion Hudson PLC GBR. Dist: Trafalgar Square Publishing.

—The First Easter. Frank, Penny & Allsopp, Sophie. 2nd rev. ed. (ENG.). 24p. pap. 2.99 *(978-0-7459-4123-3(0)*, Lion Books) Lion Hudson PLC GBR. Dist: Trafalgar Square Publishing.

—Good News for Everyone. Frank, Penny. 2nd rev. ed. (ENG.). 24p. pap. 2.99 *(978-0-7459-4124-0(9)*, Lion Books) Lion Hudson PLC GBR. Dist: Trafalgar Square Publishing.

—Jesus on Trial. Frank, Penny. 2nd rev. ed. (ENG.). 24p. pap. 2.99 *(978-0-7459-4122-6(2)*, Lion Books) Lion Hudson PLC GBR. Dist: Trafalgar Square Publishing.

—Jesus the Teacher. Frank, Penny. 2nd rev. ed. (ENG.). 24p. pap. 2.99 *(978-0-7459-4117-2(6)*, Lion Books) Lion Hudson PLC GBR. Dist: Trafalgar Square Publishing.

—The Story of Easter. Doyle, Christopher. (J). (gr. k-3). 2008. 29p. pap. 7.49 *(978-0-7586-1495-7(0))*; 2005. 32p. 13.49 *(978-0-7586-0837-6(3))* Concordia Publishing Hse.

Hayward, Annie. Baba Didi & the Godwits Fly, 1 vol. Muir, Nicola. 2013. 32p. (J). (gr. k-4). 8.95 *(978-1-78026-130-0(6))* New Internationalist Pubns., Ltd. GBR. Dist: Consortium Bk. Sales & Distribution.

Hayward, Heather. H Is for Holy: An Orthodox Christian Alphabet. Boyd, Nika & Boyd, Nika. 2015. 32p. (J). 18.95 *(978-1-936270-19-4(6))* Ancient Faith Publishing.

Hayward, Roy. The Christmas Elf. Scott, D. P. 2013. 86p. pap. *(978-0-9880635-2-5(2))* Scott, Daren.

Haywood, Ian Benfold. Always by My Side, 1 vol. Kerner, Susan. 2013. (ENG.). 32p. (J). 16.99 *(978-1-59572-336-9(6))*; pap. 6.99 *(978-1-59572-337-6(4))* Star Bright Bks., Inc.

—Tim & the Iceberg, 1 vol. Coates, Paul. 2011. (ENG.). 32p. (J). (gr. k-3). 16.95 *(978-1-59572-205-8(X))*; pap. 6.95 *(978-1-59572-206-5(8))* Star Bright Bks., Inc.

Hayworth, Lola. On the African Safari. Gumunyu, Victoria. 2018. (ENG.). 28p. (J). pap. 9.13 *(978-1-9735-4186-8(6))* Independently Published.

Hazan, Maurice. Les Animaux et les Verbes. Travis, Joelle & Figueras, Ligaya, eds. 2003. (FRE.). (J). per. 20.00 *(978-1-932770-18-6(6)*, FWLB1) Symtalk, Inc.

—Chiffres, Couleurs, Verbes et Phrases. Travis, Joelle & Figueras, Ligaya, eds. 2003. (FRE.). 114p. (J). per. 20.00 *(978-1-932770-19-3(4)*, FWLB2) Symtalk, Inc.

—En Plena Vista Level 1. Figueras, Ligaya, ed. 5th ed. 2003. (SPA.). 140p. per. 22.00 *(978-1-932770-98-8(4)*, SHB-SM) Symtalk, Inc.

—Le Français en Images, Livre 3. Travis, Joelle & Figueras, Ligaya, eds. 5th ed. 2003. (FRE.). 160p. spiral bd. 22.00 *(978-1-932770-14-8(3)*, FB3-SM-0.5) Symtalk, Inc.

—Le Francais en Images, Vol. 3. Travis, Joelle & Figueras, Ligaya, eds. 5th ed. 2003. (FRE.). 160p. tchr. ed., spiral bd. 30.00 *(978-1-932770-15-5(1)*, FB3-TG-0.5) Symtalk, Inc.

—French, Bk. 1. 2004. (FRE.). (J). 140.00 *(978-1-932770-30-8(5)*, FC-FB1) Symtalk, Inc.

—French Gerard et Ses Copains, Bk. 1. Travis, Joelle & Figueras, Ligaya, eds. 7th ed. 2004. (FRE.). 120p. tchr. ed., spiral bd. 30.00 *(978-1-932770-11-7(9)*, FB1-TG) Symtalk, Inc.

—French Gérard et ses Copains. Travis, Joelle & Figueras, Ligaya, eds. (FRE.). Bk. 1. 7th l.t. ed. 2004. 111p. per. 20.00 *(978-1-932770-10-0(0)*, FB1-SM); Bk. 2. 6th ed. 2003. 163p. tchr. ed., spiral bd. 30.00 *(978-1-932770-13-1(5)*, FB2-TG) Symtalk, Inc.

—French Gérard et ses Copains, Bk. 2. Travis, Joelle & Figueras, Ligaya, eds. 6th ed. 2003. (FRE.). 163p. spiral bd. 20.00 *(978-1-932770-12-4(7)*, FB2-SM) Symtalk, Inc.

—French Junior Book Gérard et ses Copains. Travis, Joelle & Figueras, Ligaya, eds. 5th l.t. ed. 2003. (FRE.). 84p. per. 20.00 *(978-1-932770-08-7(9)*, FJRB-SM) Symtalk, Inc.

—French Junior Book Gérard et ses Copains Teacher's Guide. Travis, Joelle & Figueras, Ligaya, eds. 5th ed. 2003. (FRE.). 110p. tchr. ed., spiral bd. 30.00 *(978-1-932770-09-4(7)*, FJRB-TG) Symtalk, Inc.

—French Level 1 Assessment with Stickers. Travis, Joelle, ed. 2003. (FRE.). (J). 30.00 *(978-1-932770-23-0(2)*, FR LEVEL 1) Symtalk, Inc.

—Los Animales y los Verbos. Travis, Joelle & Figueras, Ligaya, eds. 2003. (SPA.). 89p. (J). per. 20.00 *(978-1-932770-16-2(X)*, SWLB1) Symtalk, Inc.

—Numeros, Colores, Verbos y Frases. Travis, Joelle & Figueras, Ligaya, eds. 2003. (SPA.). 112p. (J). per. 20.00 *(978-1-932770-17-9(8)*, SWLB2) Symtalk, Inc.

—Spanish Espanol en Imagenes, Vol. 3. Travis, Joelle & Figueras, Ligaya, eds. 6th ed. 2003. (SPA.). 252p. tchr. ed., spiral bd. 30.00 *(978-1-932770-07-0(0)*, SB3-TG); 179p. spiral bd. 22.00 *(978-1-932770-06-3(2)*, SB3-SM) Symtalk, Inc.

—Spanish Junior Book Pablo y sus Amigos. Travis, Joelle & Figueras, Ligaya, eds. 5th l.t. ed. 2003. (SPA.). 87p. per. 20.00 *(978-1-932770-00-1(3)*, SJRB-SM) Symtalk, Inc.

—Spanish Junior Book Pablo y sus amigos Teacher's Guide. Travis, Joelle & Figueras, Ligaya, eds. 5th ed. 2003. (SPA.). 118p. tchr. ed., spiral bd. 30.00 *(978-1-932770-01-8(1)*, SJRB-TG) Symtalk, Inc.

—Spanish Level 1 Assessment. Travis, Joelle & Figueras, Ligaya, eds. 2003. (SPA.). (J). 30.00 *(978-1-932770-21-6(6)*, SP LEVEL 1) Symtalk, Inc.

—Spanish Pablo y sus amigos, Bk. 1. Travis, Joelle & Figueras, Ligaya, eds. 7th ed. 2004. (SPA.). 156p. tchr. ed., spiral bd. 30.00 *(978-1-932770-03-2(8)*, SB1-TG) Symtalk, Inc.

—Spanish Pablo y sus Amigos. Travis, Joelle & Figueras, Ligaya, eds. (SPA.). Bk. 1. 7th l.t. ed. 2004. 111p. per. 20.00 *(978-1-932770-02-5(X)*, SB1-SM); Bk. 2. 5th ed. 2003. 131p. per. 20.00 *(978-1-932770-04-9(6)*, SB2-SM) Symtalk, Inc.

—Spanish Pablo y sus amigos, Bk. 2. Travis, Joelle & Figueras, Ligaya, eds. 5th ed. 2003. (SPA.). 148p. tchr. ed., spiral bd. 30.00 *(978-1-932770-05-6(4)*, SB2-TG) Symtalk, Inc.

Hazan, Maurice. Les Animaux et les verbes flash card Set. Hazan, Maurice, creator. 2003. (FRE.). (J). 95.00 *(978-1-932770-38-4(0)*, FC-FWLB1) Symtalk, Inc.

—Chiffres, couleurs, verbes et phrases flash card Set. Hazan, Maurice, creator. 2003. (FRE.). (J). 115.00 *(978-1-932770-39-1(9)*, FC-FWLB2) Symtalk, Inc.

—French. Hazan, Maurice, creator. 2004. (FRE.). Bk. 2. (J). 175.00 *(978-1-932770-32-2(1)*, FC-FB2); Bk. 3. 199.00 *(978-1-932770-34-6(8)*, FC-FB3) Symtalk, Inc.

Hazard, Andrea. Zack Attack! Perez, Angela J. 2007. 36p. (J). 17.95 *(978-0-9778328-9-7(9))* His Work Christian Publishing.

Hazel, Andrew. Seeing Red: Story Seeds Vol 1. Hamilton, George. 2008. 20p. pap. 13.99 *(978-1-4343-8004-3(1))* AuthorHouse.

Hazel, Law. The Little Silver Fox. Bryson, Pope R. 2018. (ENG.). 28p. (J). 14.99 *(978-0-692-10683-9(9))* Pope, Bryson.

Hazelaar, Cor. The Man Who Lived in a Hollow Tree. Shelby, Anne. 2009. (ENG.). 40p. (J). (gr. -1-2). 19.99 *(978-0-689-86169-7(9)*, Atheneum/Richard Jackson Bks.) Simon & Schuster Children's Publishing.

Hazelgrove, Cary, photos by. Weekends for Two in the Southwest: 50 Romantic Getaways. Gleeson, Bill. 2nd rev. ed. 2005. (ENG., 124p. (gr. 8-17). pap. 18.95 *(978-0-8118-4624-0(5))* Chronicle Bks. LLC.

Hazelton, Jack W. Charlie Duck. Hazelton, Jack W. l.t. ed. 2003. 24p. (J). 12.95 *(978-1-928907-54-1(7))* Jack's Bookshelf, Inc.

Hazouri, Aaron. Ser Agradable. Glover, Larry. Benton, Kimberly, ed. 2020.Tr. of Be Nice. (SPA.). 25p. (gr. -1-3). pap. 9.99 ***(978-1-7348268-6-9(X))*** Child Like Faith Children's Bks. LLC.

Head, Mat. Warduff & the Corncob Caper. Head, Mat. 2011. (ENG.). 32p. (J). (gr. -1-3). 16.95 *(978-0-7613-8095-5(7)*, 9780761380955) Lerner Publishing Group.

Head, Murray. Will You Be My Friend? Lurie, Susan. 2016. (ENG.). 32p. (J). 16.99 *(978-1-250-04643-7(2)*, 900131546) Feiwel & Friends.

Head, Murray, photos by. I Can Run. 2017. (I Like to Read Ser.). (ENG., 32p. (J). (gr. -1-3). 7.99 *(978-0-8234-3846-4(5))*; 14.95 *(978-0-8234-3831-0(7))* Holiday Hse., Inc.

Head, Pat. Hood River Home. Marlow, Herb. 2005. 162p. (YA). per. 18.95 *(978-1-893595-47-7(1))*; lib. bdg. 28.95 *(978-1-893595-13-2(7))* Four Seasons Bks., Inc.

—The Lost Kitten. Marlow, Herb. 2003. 16p. (J). 19.95 *(978-1-893595-34-7(X))* Four Seasons Bks., Inc.

—The Tiger's Den. Marlow, Herb. 2003. 22p. (J). 19.95 *(978-1-893595-37-8(4))* Four Seasons Bks., Inc.

Head-Weston, Alex, et al. Know How Know Why Dinosaurs. Matthews, Rupert. 2004. (Know How Know Why Ser.). 48p. (J). (gr. 3-7). pap. *(978-1-84510-031-5(X))* Top That! Publishing PLC.

Headley, Aaron. Evangel Meets Orsen Whale. Gray, Rick & Gray, Coral. 2007. (ENG.). 32p. (J). (gr. -1-3). 14.95 *(978-0-9790210-1-5(4))* Evening Star Enterprise, Inc.

—Evangel Meets Orsen Whale. Gray, Rick & Gray, Coral. 2018. (Evangel the Smallest Angel Ser.: Vol. 2). (ENG.). 32p. (J). (gr. -1-3). pap. 12.95 *(978-1-7177-4053-3(7))* Independently Published.

Headley, Nathan. The Wise King: A Fairytale. Headley, Judy. 2017. (ENG.). (J). pap. *(978-1-5255-1134-9(3))* FriesenPress.

Healy, Jack. Rachael's Dilemma & the Missing Whirly Spinner: A Girl with Special Needs Learns How to Overcome Her Shyness. Miller, Shelly. 2018. (ENG.). 32p. (J). pap. 8.99 *(978-1-7259-4170-0(8))* CreateSpace Independent Publishing Platform.

Healy, Jeane. Exploring Art: Create It - Display It. Wilmes, Liz & Wilmes, Dick. 2004. 256p. (J). pap. 19.95 *(978-0-943452-05-0(8)*, 20160) Building Blocks, LLC.

Healy, Maggie. A Coming of Winter in the Adirondacks. Heinz, Brian J. 2011. 32p. (J). 19.95 *(978-1-59531-038-5(X))* North Country Bks., Inc.

Heaney Dunn, John. The Little Red House with No Doors & No Windows & A Star Inside. 2011. 25p. (J). pap. 15.95 *(978-1-58909-915-9(X))* Bookstand Publishing.

Heap, Jonathon. Othello. Mulherin, Jennifer & Frost, Abigail. 31p. pap. *(978-1-84234-034-9(4))* Cherrytree Bks.

Heap, Sue. How to Be a Baby ... by Me, the Big Sister. Lloyd-Jones, Sally. (ENG.). 40p. (J). (gr. -1-3). 2011. pap. 7.99 *(978-0-375-87388-1(0))*; 2007. 16.99 *(978-0-375-83843-9(0))* Random Hse. Children's Bks. (Schwartz & Wade Bks.).

—How to Be a Baby... by Me, the Big Sister. Lloyd-Jones, Sally. 2011. (How to Ser.). (ENG.). 40p. (J). (gr. -1-1). 21.19 *(978-0-375-93843-6(5)*, Dragonfly Bks.) Random Hse. Children's Bks.

—Polly's Pink Pajamas. French, Vivian. 2010. (ENG.). 32p. (J). (gr. -1-2). 14.99 *(978-0-7636-4807-7(8))* Candlewick Pr.

—Very Little Cinderella. Heapy, Teresa. 2015. (Very Little Ser.). (ENG.). 32p. (J). (gr. -1-3). 16.99 *(978-0-544-28223-0(X)*, 1570976, HMH Books For Young Readers) Houghton Mifflin Harcourt Publishing Co.

—Very Little Red Riding Hood. Heapy, Teresa. 2014. (Very Little Ser.). (ENG.). 32p. (J). (gr. -1-3). 16.99 *(978-0-544-28000-7(8)*, 1570487, HMH Books For Young Readers) Houghton Mifflin Harcourt Publishing Co.

—Very Little Sleeping Beauty. Heapy, Teresa. 2016. (Very Little Ser.). (ENG.). 32p. (J). (gr. -1-3). 16.99 *(978-0-544-28279-7(5)*, 1570975, HMH Books For Young Readers) Houghton Mifflin Harcourt Publishing Co.

Heap, Sue. Danny's Drawing Book. Heap, Sue. 2008. (ENG.). 32p. (J). (gr. -1-3). 9.99 *(978-0-7636-3654-8(1))* Candlewick Pr.

—Mine! Heap, Sue. 2014. (ENG.). 32p. (J). (-k). 15.99 *(978-0-7636-6888-4(5))* Candlewick Pr.

Heaphy, Paula. Dare!, Bk. 2. Frankel, Erin. 2013. (Weird! Ser.). (ENG.). 48p. (J). (gr. k-4). pap. 9.99 *(978-1-57542-439-2(8))* Free Spirit Publishing, Inc.

—Tough!, Bk. 3. Frankel, Erin. 2013. (Weird! Ser.). (ENG.). 48p. (J). (gr. k-4). pap. 9.99 *(978-1-57542-438-5(X))* Free Spirit Publishing, Inc.

—Weird! Frankel, Erin. 2013. (Weird! Ser.). (ENG.). 48p. (J). (gr. k-4). pap. 9.99 *(978-1-57542-437-8(1))* Free Spirit Publishing, Inc.

—Weird! Frankel, Erin. 2013. (Weird (Free Spirit) Ser.: Vol. 1). (ENG.). (J). (gr. k-4). lib. bdg. 20.60 *(978-1-62765-392-3(9))* Perfection Learning Corp.

Heard, Brendan. A Is for Aboriginal. MacLean, Joseph. 2014. (ENG.). 96p. (J). (gr. k). 19.95 *(978-0-9918589-0-3(5))* Interactive Publishing Corporation CAN. Dist: Independent Pubs. Group.

Heard, Tom. Ankylosaurus: The Clumsy Club, 1 vol. Bromage, Fran. 2019. (Dinosaur Adventures Ser.). (ENG.). 24p. (J). (gr. 1-2). 24.60 *(978-1-7253-9509-1(6))*; pap. 8.25 *(978-1-7253-9507-7(X))* Rosen Publishing Group, Inc., The. (Windmill Bks.).

—School Success: Telling the Time: Wipe-Clean Book with Pen. Woolley, Katie. 2018. (School Success Ser.). 16p. (J). (gr. -1-3). pap. 7.99 *(978-1-5263-8086-9(2)*, Pat-a-Cake) Hachette Children's Group GBR. Dist: Hachette Bk. Group.

Hearld, Mark. Outside Your Window: A First Book of Nature. Davies, Nicola. 2012. (ENG.). 108p. (J). (gr. -1-2). 22.00 *(978-0-7636-5549-5(X))* Candlewick Pr.

Hearn, Diane Dawson. George Washington's First Victory. Krensky, Stephen. 2005. (Ready-To-read COFA Ser.). (ENG.). 32p. (J). (gr. k-2). pap. 4.99 *(978-0-689-85942-7(2)*, Simon Spotlight) Simon Spotlight.

Hearn, Marilyn. My Dear Child, I Have Gone to Heaven Let's Talk: A Child's Recovery Plan, 1 vol. Carson, Shonette. 2010. 36p. 24.95 *(978-1-4489-6341-6(9))* PublishAmerica, Inc.

Hearn, Sam. Ordinary Oscar. Adkins, Laura. 2010. (ENG.). 32p. (J). (gr. -1-2). 15.95 *(978-1-58925-085-7(0))*; (gr. k-2). pap. 7.95 *(978-1-58925-418-3(X))* Tiger Tales.

Hearn, Sam. Beep! Beep! Hearn, Sam. 2016. (ENG.). 12p. (J). (gr. -1-k). 10.99 *(978-0-545-79958-4(9)*, Cartwheel Bks.) Scholastic, Inc.

Hearne, James. Lucy Joue Au Basketball, 1 vol. Bowes, Lisa. 2019. (Lucy Tries Sports Ser.: 5). (FRE.). 32p. (J). (gr. 1-3). 12.95 *(978-1-4598-2338-9(9))* Orca Bk. Pubs. USA.

—Lucy Tries Basketball, 1 vol. Bowes, Lisa. 2019. (Lucy Tries Sports Ser.: 5). (ENG.). 32p. (J). (gr. 1-3). 12.95 *(978-1-4598-1697-8(8))* Orca Bk. Pubs. USA.

—Lucy Tries Luge, 1 vol. Bowes, Lisa. 2015. (Lucy Tries Sports Ser.: 1). (ENG.). 32p. (J). (gr. 1-3). pap. 12.95 *(978-1-4598-1019-8(8))* Orca Bk. Pubs. USA.

—Lucy Tries Short Track, 1 vol. Bowes, Lisa. 2016. (Lucy Tries Sports Ser.: 2). (ENG.). 32p. (J). (gr. 1-3). pap. 12.95 *(978-1-4598-1025-9(2))* Orca Bk. Pubs. USA.

Hearne, James. Lucy Tries Sports High-Five Pack. Bowes, Lisa. 2020. (Lucy Tries Sports Ser.). (ENG.). 160p. (J). (gr. 1-3). pap., pap., pap. 49.95 ***(978-1-4598-0262-9(4))*** Orca Bk. Pubs. USA.

Hearson, Ruth. Leo Can Swim. McQuinn, Anna. 2016. (ENG.). 24p. (J). (— 1). lib. bdg. 9.95 *(978-1-58089-725-9(8))* Charlesbridge Publishing, Inc.

—Leo Gets a Checkup. McQuinn, Anna. 2018. (ENG.). 24p. (J). (— 1). lib. bdg. 9.99 *(978-1-58089-891-1(2))* Charlesbridge Publishing, Inc.

—Leo Loves Baby Time. McQuinn, Anna. 2014. (ENG.). 24p. (J). (— 1). lib. bdg. 9.95 *(978-1-58089-665-8(0))* Charlesbridge Publishing, Inc.

Hearson, Ruth. Wonderful Baby. Hartman, Bob. ed. 2020. (ENG.). 10p. (J). (— 1). bds. 7.99 ***(978-0-7459-7791-1(X)***, Lion Children's) Lion Hudson PLC GBR. Dist: Independent Pubs. Group.

Hearson, Ruth. A Leo le Gusta Bebelandia. Hearson, Ruth. McQuinn, Anna & Mlawer, Teresa. 2015. (SPA & ENG.). 24p. (J). (— 1). lib. bdg. 9.95 *(978-1-58089-704-4(5))* Charlesbridge Publishing, Inc.
Heasley, Brock. Paper Bag Mask. Heasley, Brock. 2018. (ENG.). 330p. (YA). pap. 15.99 *(978-1-941541-40-1(2))* Pen Name Publishing.
Heaston, Rebecca J. Before You Were Born. Nixon, Joan Lowery. 2nd sensormatic ed. 2006. 31p. pap. 10.95 *(978-1-59276-219-4(0))* Our Sunday Visitor, Publishing Div.
Heath. Aussie's Adventures. Miller, Sophia. 2nd rev. ed. 2016. (ENG.). (J). (gr. -1-4). 9.99 *(978-1-945033-07-0(X)*, Atlas Publishing) Atlas Publishing LLC.
Heath, Jim. Gertrude & Toby's Friday Adventure, bks. 3. Tharp, Shari. l.t. ed. 2016. (ENG.). (J). (gr. -1-3). bk. 3. 48p. 16.99 *(978-0-9969679-0-7(7))*; Bk.1. 46p. pap. 7.99 *(978-0-9969679-1-4(5))* Atlas Publishing LLC. (Atlas Publishing).
Heath McKenzie. A Banana Is a Banana. Clarke, Justine & Pyke, Josh. 2019. (ENG.). 24p. (J). (— 1). 19.99 ***(978-1-76089-166-4(5)***, Puffin) Penguin Random Hse. AUS. Dist: Independent Pubs. Group.
—Nit Boy. Bancks, Tristan. 2020. 288p. (J). (gr. 2-4). 14.99 ***(978-1-76089-630-0(6)***, Puffin) Penguin Random Hse. AUS. Dist: Independent Pubs. Group.
Heath, Paul Reaves. My Dad Wears Striped Pajamas. DeStout, Carole. 2003. (Children's Outreach Ser.). 38p. (J). pap. 5.00 *(978-1-880994-83-2(6))* Mount Olive College Pr.
Heath, Willow. Lasting Love. Wright, Caroline. 2019. 40p. (J). (gr. -1-2). 17.99 *(978-1-9848-5014-0(8))*; (ENG.). lib. bdg. 20.99 *(978-1-9848-5015-7(6))* Random Hse. Children's Bks. (Rodale Kids).
Heatley, David. Otis Dooda: Downright Dangerous. Potter, Ellen. 2014. (Otis Dooda Ser.: 2). (ENG.). 240p. (J). (gr. 2-5). 13.99 *(978-1-250-01177-0(9)*, 900085244) Feiwel & Friends.
Heaton, Jr. I Just Love You So Much. Hulslander, Dyan. 2009. 28p. pap. 14.49 *(978-1-4490-0454-5(7))* AuthorHouse.
Heaton, Layce. The Weeping Willow Tree. Page, Lawana. Amaya, Laura, tr. 2006. (SPA.). 32p. 10.95 *(978-0-9761128-2-2(5))* KB Bks. & More.
Heaton, Layce D. The Many Tracks of Lap'n Tap, 1. Heaton, Layce D. 2006. 32p. (J). lib. bdg. 18.95 *(978-0-9761128-3-9(3))* KB Bks. & More.
Heavner, Jodi. The Three Wives of Hero the Second. Randall, Marilyn Mae. 2004. (J). per. 14.99 *(978-0-9713589-7-3(4))* Ubavie's Gifts.
Hebb, Matt & Dalton, Alex. Home Collection, Vol. 1. Davison, Max. 2016. (Home Ser.: 1). 112p. (J). (gr. 3-7). pap. 12.99 *(978-1-78276-698-8(7))* Titan Bks. Ltd. GBR. Dist: Penguin Random Hse. LLC.
Hebert, Hannah, et al. Anger Mountain. Hebert, Bryna. 2005. (ENG.). 24p. pap. 11.00 *(978-1-4120-5066-1(9))* Trafford Publishing.
Hechtenkopf, Omar. Feel the Power (Blaze & the Monster Machines) Random House. 2016. (Touch-And-Feel Ser.). (ENG.). 10p. (J). (— 1). bds. 12.99 *(978-0-399-55372-1(X)*, Random Hse. Bks. for Young Readers) Random Hse. Children's Bks.
—Pop the Hood! (Blaze & the Monster Machines) Random House. 2016. (Lift-The-Flap Ser.). (ENG.). 12p. (J). (gr. -1 — 1). bds. 6.99 *(978-0-553-53893-9(4)*, Random Hse. Bks. for Young Readers) Random Hse. Children's Bks.
—Stuntmania! (Blaze & the Monster Machines) Tillworth, Mary. 2016. (Pictureback(R) Ser.). (ENG.). 16p. (J). (gr. -1-2). 4.99 *(978-1-101-93868-3(4)*, Random Hse. Bks. for Young Readers) Random Hse. Children's Bks.
—To the Limit! (Blaze & the Monster Machines) Golden Books. 2015. (ENG.). 128p. (J). (gr. -1-2). pap. 7.99 *(978-0-553-52459-8(3)*, Golden Bks.) Random Hse. Children's Bks.
Hechter, Janice. Avi's Choice: A Story about Bikur Cholim-Visiting the Sick. Simhaee, Rebeka. 2014. 35p. (J). *(978-0-8266-0043-1(3))* Merkos L'Inyonei Chinuch.
—The Great Elephant Escape, 1 vol. Townsend, Una Belle. 2012. (ENG.). 32p. (J). (gr. k-3). 16.99 *(978-1-4556-1582-7(X)*, Pelican Publishing) Arcadia Publishing.
—The Little Esrog. Kochin, Rochelle. 2016. (ENG.). (J). 14.95 *(978-0-8266-0044-8(1))* Merkos L'Inyonei Chinuch.
Hechtkopf, H. Chatzkel, Mendel & Me: An adventure Story. Fuchs, Menucha. Daykin, Rachmiel, tr. from HEB. 2005. Orig. Title: Mah Shekarah Ba'Ayarah. 192p. (J). 15.95 *(978-1-932443-39-4(8)*, CHMH) Judaica Pr., Inc., The.
Heck, Don, et al. Adventures of the X-Men: Tooth & Claw. 2020. (ENG.). 128p. (J). (gr. 3-7). pap. 9.99 *(978-1-302-92312-9(9))* Marvel Worldwide, Inc.
Heck, Don, et al. Iron Man Epic Collection: the Fury of the Firebrand. 2020. (ENG.). 472p. (J). (gr. 4-17). pap. 39.99 ***(978-1-302-92207-8(6))*** Marvel Worldwide, Inc.
Heck, Ed. Teensy Meensy Mice. Merritt, Donna Marie. 2018. (ENG.). 34p. (J). (gr. k-6). 19.99 *(978-1-365-86085-0(X))*; pap. 15.99 *(978-1-365-86084-3(1))* Lulu Pr., Inc.
—Teensy Meensy Mice Dyslexic Edition: Dyslexic Font. Merritt, Donna Marie. ed. 2018. (ENG.). 34p. (J). (gr. k-6). pap. 15.99 *(978-1-64372-065-4(1))* Lulu Pr., Inc.
—Teensy Meensy Mice Dyslexic Font. Merritt, Donna Marie. ed. 2018. (ENG.). 34p. (J). (gr. k-6). 19.99 *(978-1-64372-064-7(3))* Lulu Pr., Inc.
Hecker, Vera. Fancy the Beautiful Little Dragon: Book Number Two Little One's Series. Banta, Sandra F. l.t. ed. 2006. 45p. per. 11.99 *(978-1-59879-157-0(5))* Lifevest Publishing, Inc.
—A Home for Rainbow. 2007. 32p. (J). *(978-0-9799729-0-4(6))* Banta, Sandra.
—Muffy the Dragon. Banta, Sandra F. l.t. ed. 2005. 19p. (J). per. 9.99 *(978-1-59879-060-3(9))* Lifevest Publishing, Inc.
Hecker, Vera. Mystic World Coloring Book. Hecker, Vera. 2007. (YA). per. *(978-0-9799729-1-1(4))* Banta, Sandra.
Heckman, Mark. Sooper Yooper: Environmental Defender. Newman, Mark. 2010. 48p. (J). 17.95 *(978-1-933272-26-9(0))* Thunder Bay Pr.
Hector, Julian. C. R. Mudgeon. Muir, Leslie. 2012. (ENG.). 32p. (J). (gr. -1-3). 15.99 *(978-1-4169-7906-7(9)*, Atheneum Bks. for Young Readers) Simon & Schuster Children's Publishing.
—Monday Is One Day. Levine, Arthur A. 2015. (ENG.). 32p. (J). (gr. -1-k). 6.99 *(978-0-439-78925-7(7))* Scholastic, Inc.
Hector, Julian. This Is the Construction Worker. Godwin, Laura. 2019. 24p. (J). bds. 6.99 ***(978-1-368-04693-0(2))*** Little, Brown Bks. for Young Readers.
Hector, Julian. The Gentleman Bug. Hector, Julian. 2010. (ENG.). 40p. (J). (gr. -1-k). 16.99 *(978-1-4169-9467-1(X)*, Atheneum Bks. for Young Readers) Simon & Schuster Children's Publishing.
Hed, Ben. Paper Towel. Byrd, Lucas & Byrd, Bransen. 2019. (ENG.). 26p. (J). pap. 16.95 ***(978-1-9736-6760-5(6)***, WestBow Pr.) Author Solutions, Inc.
Hedderich, Tom. Father Like a Tree. Field, Matthew S. 2005. (ENG.). (J). 19.95 *(978-0-9761528-0-4(0))* Matting Leah Publishing Co.
—The Three Pigs, Business School, & Wolf Hash Stew. Field, Matthew S. 2006. (ENG.). (J). 19.95 *(978-0-9761528-1-1(9))* Matting Leah Publishing Co.
Hedderwick, Mairi. The Adventures of Hamish & Mirren: Magical Scotish Stories for Children, 50 vols. Miller, Moira. 2015. (ENG.). 224p. (J). 9.95 *(978-1-78250-211-1(4)*, Kelpies) Floris Bks. GBR. Dist: Consortium Bk. Sales & Distribution.
—The Old Woman Who Lived in a Vinegar Bottle, 40 vols. Godden, Rumer. 2018. (Traditional Scottish Tales Ser.). (ENG.). 32p. (J). pap. 11.95 *(978-1-78250-510-5(5)*, Kelpies) Floris Bks. GBR. Dist: Consortium Bk. Sales & Distribution.
Hedderwick, Mairi. Katie Morag & the Big Boy Cousins. Hedderwick, Mairi. 2010. (Katie Morag Ser.: 5). 32p. (J). (gr. k-2). pap. 12.99 *(978-1-84941-089-2(5)*, Red Fox) Random House Children's Books GBR. Dist: Independent Pubs. Group.
—Katie Morag & the Birthdays. Hedderwick, Mairi. 2005. (Katie Morag Ser.). 48p. (J). (gr. k-4). per. 14.99 *(978-0-09-946426-6(8)*, Red Fox) Random House Children's Books GBR. Dist: Independent Pubs. Group.
—Katie Morag & the Grand Concert. Hedderwick, Mairi. ed. 2010. (Katie Morag Ser.: 6). 32p. (J). (gr. k-2). pap. 12.99 *(978-1-84941-087-8(9)*, Red Fox) Random House Children's Books GBR. Dist: Independent Pubs. Group.
—Katie Morag & the Riddles. Hedderwick, Mairi. ed. 2010. (Katie Morag Ser.: 10). 32p. (J). (gr. k-2). pap. 12.99 *(978-1-84941-092-2(5)*, Red Fox) Random House Children's Books GBR. Dist: Independent Pubs. Group.
—Katie Morag & the Two Grandmothers. Hedderwick, Mairi. 2010. (Katie Morag Ser.: 2). 32p. (J). (gr. k-2). pap. 12.99 *(978-1-84941-086-1(0)*, Red Fox) Random House Children's Books GBR. Dist: Independent Pubs. Group.
—Katie Morag Delivers the Mail. Hedderwick, Mairi. ed. 2010. (Katie Morag Ser.: 1). (ENG.). 32p. (J). (gr. k-2). pap. 12.99 *(978-1-84941-091-5(7)*, Red Fox) Random House Children's Books GBR. Dist: Independent Pubs. Group.
—The New Pier. Hedderwick, Mairi. 3rd ed. 2013. (Katie Morag Ser.: 3). (ENG.). 32p. (J). (gr. k-2). pap. 13.99 *(978-1-86230-938-8(8)*, Red Fox) Random House Children's Books GBR. Dist: Independent Pubs. Group.
Heddings, Anthony. Zombies Ate My Homework: Redstone Junior High #1. Stevens, Cara. 2017. (Redstone Junior High Ser.). (ENG.). (J). (gr. 3-7). 11.99 *(978-1-5107-2857-8(0)*, Sky Pony Pr.) Skyhorse Publishing Co., Inc.
Heddington, Richard. Henry the Hedgenome & the Birthday Socks. Heddington, Richard. 2016. (Hedgenomes Ser.: Vol. 2). (ENG.). (J). pap. *(978-0-9934827-2-4(4))* Hedsite Pr.
—Henry the Hedgenome & the Forgetful Fairy. Heddington, Richard. 2019. (Hedgenomes Ser.: Vol. 6). (ENG.). 32p. (J). pap. *(978-0-9934827-8-6(3))* Hedsite Pr.
—Henry the Hedgenome the Unfunny Clown. Heddington, Richard. 2017. (Hedgenomes Ser.: Vol. 4). (ENG.). (J). pap. *(978-0-9934827-6-2(7))* Hedsite Pr.
Heder, Thyra. The School Show. Gianferrari, Maria. 2015. (Penny & Jelly Ser.). (ENG.). 32p. (J). (gr. -1-3). 16.99 *(978-0-544-23014-9(0)*, 1563785, HMH Books For Young Readers) Houghton Mifflin Harcourt Publishing Co.
—Slumber under the Stars. Gianferrari, Maria. 2016. (Penny & Jelly Ser.). (ENG.). 32p. (J). (gr. -1-3). 16.99 *(978-0-544-28005-2(9)*, 1570631, HMH Books For Young Readers) Houghton Mifflin Harcourt Publishing Co.
Hedgecock, Lucie. Peek-A-Boooo Who? A Lift-the-Flap & Sound Book. DePrisco, Dorothea. 2009. 12p. 8.95 *(978-1-58117-952-1(9)*, Intervisual/Piggy Toes) Bendon, Inc.
Hedgecock, Sean. God's Incredible Creatures: The Gift of Sharing. Soleim, Heather. Greisen, Steve, ed. ed. 2005. 24p. (J). bds. 14.95 *(978-0-9707422-9-2(0))* Reel Productions, LLC.
Hedicker, Lisa. Buzz with the Bees, 1 vol. Kenney, Karen Latchana. 2010. (Bug's World Ser.). (ENG.). 32p. (J). (gr. k-4). 28.50 *(978-1-60270-784-9(7)*, 3705, Looking Glass Library) Magic Wagon.
Hedison, Debby & Dachamont Earth, Kaewket. The Mad Dash - Bite My Dust. Kiernan, Tom. 2016. (Mad Dash Ser.: Vol. 1). (ENG.). (J). (gr. 4-6). 19.99 *(978-0-9975965-2-6(X))* Mad Dash Co., The.
Hedrick, Mandy. Dylan's Tale. Porter, Harry. 2011. 52p. pap. 10.99 *(978-0-9828346-1-9(6))* 4RV Pub.
Hedstrom, Joel. A Wolf at the Gate. Van Steenwyk, Mark. 2016. (Reach & Teach Ser.). (ENG.). 70p. (YA). (gr. 7). pap. 14.95 *(978-1-62963-150-9(7))* PM Pr.
Hedstrom, Leigh. Becoming God's Friend. Watson, Rhonda. 2006. (J). pap. incl. cd-rom *(978-1-920935-85-6(1))* Anglican Youthworks.
Hee-Joon, Son. PhD Vol. 1: Phantasy Degree. Hee-Joon, Son. 2005. 192p. pap. 9.99 *(978-1-59532-319-4(8))* TOKYOPOP, Inc.
Hee-Joon, Son. PHD: Phantasy Degree, Vol. 2. Hee-Joon, Son, creator. rev. ed. 2005. 192p. (YA). pap. 9.99 *(978-1-59532-320-0(1))* TOKYOPOP, Inc.
—PhD Vol. 1: Phantasy Degree. Hee-Joon, Son, creator. rev. ed. 2005. 184p. pap. 9.99 *(978-1-59532-321-7(X))* TOKYOPOP, Inc.
Hee-Ju, Kim. Saint Clare of Assisi: Runaway Rich Girl. Hee-Ju, Kim. 2017. (ENG.). (J). (gr. 4-7). pap. *(978-0-8198-9087-0(1))* Pauline Bks. & Media Ctr.
Hee, Liana. Backyard Ballet (Shimmer & Shine) Tillworth, Mary. 2016. (Little Golden Book Ser.). (ENG.). 24p. (J). (gr. -1-2). 4.99 *(978-0-553-52202-0(7)*, Golden Bks.) Random Hse. Children's Bks.
—Wish upon a Sleepover (Shimmer & Shine) Tillworth, Mary. 2016. (Little Golden Book Ser.). (ENG.). 24p. (J). (gr. -1-2). 4.99 *(978-1-101-93672-6(X)*, Golden Bks.) Random Hse. Children's Bks.
Heebner, Mary D. A Sacred Geography: Sonnets of the Himalaya & Tibet. Craig, Sienna R. 100th collector's ed. 2005. 24p. bds. 85.00 *(978-0-9766811-0-6(2))* Simplemente Maria Pr.
Heeley, Ted. Anxiety: Deal with It Before It Ties You up in Knots. Mandel, Joey. 2014. (Lorimer Deal with It Ser.). (ENG.). 32p. (YA). (gr. 4-6). pap. 12.95 *(978-1-4594-0709-1(1)*, 0709) James Lorimer & Co. Ltd., Pubs. CAN. Dist: Formac Lorimer Bks. Ltd.
—Hockey Talk: The Language of Hockey from A-Z, 1 vol. Goldner, John. 2009. (ENG.). 96p. (J). (gr. 4-6). pap. 9.95 *(978-1-55455-092-0(0)*, c1d22d23-2551-4f75-ac2e-e21549442975) éditeur, Annika Parance CAN. Dist: Firefly Bks., Ltd.
Heers, Matt & Heers, Nate. South Dakota: A Journey Through Time Student Workbook. Turnipseed, Susan. 2003. 28p. (J). pap. *(978-1-57579-268-2(0))* Pine Hill Pr.
—South Dakota: A Journey Through Time Student Workbook Answer Key. Turnipseed, Susan. 2003. 28p. (J). pap. *(978-1-57579-269-9(9))* Pine Hill Pr.
Heers, Nate, jt. illus. see Heers, Matt.
Hefferan, Rob. The Bridge Is Up! Hajdusiewicz, Babs Bell. 2006. (J). pap. 7.99 *(978-0-15-365089-5(3))* Houghton Mifflin Harcourt School Pubs.
—Henry's Turn. Fontes, Justine. 2004. (J). *(978-1-59336-004-7(5))*; pap. *(978-1-59336-005-4(3))* Mondo Publishing.
—Little Monster Becomes an Author. Williams, Rozanne Lanczak. 2006. (Learn to Write Ser.). 16p. (J). (gr. k-2). pap. 3.49 *(978-1-59198-300-2(2)*, 6192) Creative Teaching Pr., Inc.
—Little Monster Becomes an Author. Williams, Rozanne Lanczak. Maio, Barbara, ed. 2006. (J). per. 8.99 *(978-1-59198-349-1(5))* Creative Teaching Pr., Inc.
—My Pop-up Nursery Rhymes. 2006. (ENG.). 10p. (J). (gr. -1-3). 4.95 *(978-1-58117-439-7(X)*, Intervisual/Piggy Toes) Bendon, Inc.
—My Sparkling Nursery Rhymes. 2005. (ENG.). 10p. (J). 8.95 *(978-1-58117-295-9(8)*, Intervisual/Piggy Toes) Bendon, Inc.
—Toy Trouble. Fontes, Justine. 2003. 24p. (J). pap. *(978-1-59034-447-7(2))*; 14.95 *(978-1-59034-446-0(4))* Mondo Publishing.
Hefflin, Toby. The Tortoise & the Hairpiece. Winn, Don M. 2009. 20p. pap. 7.99 *(978-0-88144-452-0(9))* Yorkshire Publishing Group.
Hefke, Debbie. BB Gets Braces. Lucas-Serluco, Kristin. 2019. (ENG.). 34p. (J). pap. 10.99 ***(978-1-6906-1642-9(3))*** Independently Published.
Hefke, Debbie J. The Adventures of Jake & the Talking Christmas Tree. Sobel, Ron. 2019. (ENG.). 34p. (J). pap. 10.99 ***(978-1-6923-5342-1(X))*** Independently Published.
Hefke, Debbie J. Alejandro & the Bacon Breakfast. Diaz, Claudia & Diaz, Chris. 2019. (ENG.). 36p. (J). (gr. k-4). 17.99 *(978-0-578-47320-8(8))* Diaz, Claudia.
Heflin, Jenifer, jt. illus. see Thrall, Gordon.
Hegan, Robin. Birds of a Feather. Oelschlager, Vanita. 2011. (ENG.). 32p. (J). (gr. -1-3). pap. 8.95 *(978-0-9826366-1-9(X))* VanitaBooks.
—Birds of a Feather: A Book of Idioms & Silly Pictures. Oelschlager, Vanita. 2009. (ENG.). 32p. (J). (gr. -1-3). 17.95 *(978-0-9800162-8-4(2))* VanitaBooks.
—Mother Goose/Other Goose. Oelschlager, Vanita. 2008. (ENG.). 32p. (J). (gr. -1-3). 17.95 *(978-0-9800162-6-0(6))* VanitaBooks.
—Out of the Blue: A book of color idioms & silly Pictures. Oelschlager, Vanita. 2012. (Idioms by Vanita Ser.). (ENG.). 40p. (J). (gr. k-2). 24.94 *(978-0-9832904-2-1(3))*; (gr. -1-3). pap. 8.95 *(978-0-9832904-1-4(5))* VanitaBooks.
Hegan, Robin & Blackwood, Kristin. My Grampy Can't Walk. Oelschlager, Vanita. 2008. (ENG.). 36p. (J). (gr. -1-3). 9.95 *(978-0-9800162-0-8(7))* VanitaBooks.
Hegbrook, Thomas. The Earth Book: A World of Exploration & Wonder. Litton, Jonathan. 2017. (ENG.). 64p. (J). (gr. 2-12). 29.99 *(978-1-944530-06-8(1)*, 360 Degrees) Tiger Tales.
Hegbrook, Thomas. StoryWorlds: a Moment in Time: A Perpetual Picture Atlas. Hegbrook, Thomas. 2017. (ENG.). 80p. (J). (gr. 1-4). 24.99 *(978-1-944530-07-5(X)*, 360 Degrees) Tiger Tales.
—StoryWorlds: Nature. Hegbrook, Thomas. 2016. (ENG.). 64p. (J). (gr. 2-12). 24.99 *(978-1-944530-01-3(0)*, 360 Degrees) Tiger Tales.
Hegeman, Mark S. Mind Your Manners: A Social Skills Guide for Children. Hegeman, Kathryn T. 2003. (ENG.). x, 185p. pap. 19.95 *(978-0-9725218-0-2(1)*, 9780972521802) Aesop Pubs., LLC.
Hegerhorst, Bethany Brady. The Littlest Snowflake. Brady, S. Lamar. 2013. 36p. pap. 24.95 *(978-1-63000-850-5(8))* America Star Bks.
Hegg, Tom & Hanson, Warren. Peef & the Baby Sister. Hegg, Tom & Hanson, Warren. 2006. (ENG.). 36p. (J). (gr. -1-3). 16.95 *(978-0-931674-67-9(0)*, Waldman House Pr.) TRISTAN Publishing, Inc.
Hehenberger, Shelly. The Moment You Were Born: A NICU Story for You & Your Preemie. Lane, Sandra & Miles, Brenda. 2015. 32p. (J). *(978-1-4338-1964-3(3)*, Magination Pr.) American Psychological Assn.
—Sanji's Seed: A Story about Honesty. Beinhard, B. J. l.t. ed. 2003. 32p. (J). reprint ed. 13.99 *(978-0-9670843-2-9(6)*, Abiding Life Pr.) Abiding Life Ministries International.
—Visiting Feelings. Rubenstein, Laurence Z. 2013. 32p. (J). 14.95 *(978-1-4338-1339-9(4))* American Psychological Assn.
—Visiting Feelings. Rubenstein, Lauren. 2014. (J). pap. *(978-1-4338-1340-5(8)*, Magination Pr.) American Psychological Assn.
Heid, Karen. Katie's Cabbage. Stagliano, Katie. 2014. (Young Palmetto Bks.). (ENG.). 40p. 19.99 *(978-1-61117-504-2(6))* Univ. of South Carolina Pr.
Heide, Christiane. Ponga Visits Her Orangutan Family. Larue-Baker, Lisa. 2019. (ENG.). 26p. (J). pap. 10.95 ***(978-1-6877-1975-1(6))*** Independently Published.
Heidi-Kate, Greef. Little Santa: The Prophecy. Nashreen, Seepersad. 2017. (Little Santa Ser.: Vol. 3). (ENG.). 22p. (J). (gr. 3-6). pap. *(978-0-620-78491-7(1))* Seepersad, Nashreen.
Heidi, Kim Linh B. All Sizes Cry: A Book of Self Love. Igou, Asia H. 2016. (ENG.). (J). (gr. k-3). 15.00 *(978-0-692-67491-8(8))* igou, asia.
Heidschötter, Uwe. Box (Book One) Wirbeleit, Patrick. 2019. 72p. (J). (gr. k-4). pap. 9.99 *(978-1-60309-449-8(0))* Top Shelf Productions.
Heiduczek, Martina. The Boy & the Egg. DeLange, Ellen. 2019. (ENG.). 32p. (J). 17.95 *(978-1-60537-460-4(1))*; 9.95 *(978-1-60537-477-2(6))* Clavis Publishing.
Heigh, Stephen. Mr. George & the Red Hat. Heigh, Stephen. Burton, Kevin, ed. 2004. 32p. (J). 18.95 *(978-0-9745715-2-0(0))* KRBY Creations, LLC.
—The Snowman in the Moon. Heigh, Stephen. Burton, Kevin, ed. 2005. 28p. (J). (gr. -1-3). 16.95 *(978-0-9745715-5-3(5))* KRBY Creations, LLC.
Heighway-Bury, Robin. Who Built the Pyramid? Hooper, Meredith. 2014. (ENG.). 40p. (J). (gr. 2-5). pap. 7.99 *(978-0-7636-7380-2(3))* Candlewick Pr.
Heighway, Richard. The Fables of Aesop. Aesop. 2013. (ENG.). 252p. pap. 17.95 *(978-1-4290-9807-6(4))* New-York Historical Society.
Heikkilä, Cecilia. Badger's Journey. Heikkilä, Cecilia. 2020. (ENG.). 32p. (J). 18.95 ***(978-1-62371-951-7(8)***, Crocodile Bks.) Interlink Publishing Group, Inc.
—A Christmas Sweater for Nina. Heikkilä, Cecilia. 2020. (ENG.). 32p. (J). pap. 8.95 ***(978-1-62371-948-7(8)***, Crocodile Bks.) Interlink Publishing Group, Inc.
Heimann, Rolf. Brain Busting Bonanza. Heimann, Rolf. 2003. (ENG.). 64p. (Orig.). pap., act. bk. ed. *(978-1-877003-21-9(2))* Little Hare Bks. AUS. Dist: HarperCollins Pubs. Australia.
—Life's Like a Crocodile. Heimann, Rolf. 2004. 108p. *(978-1-877003-55-4(7))* Little Hare Bks. AUS. Dist: HarperCollins Pubs. Australia.
—Puzzle Mazia. Heimann, Rolf. 2004. (ENG.). 32p. pap., act. bk. ed. *(978-1-877003-64-6(6))* Little Hare Bks. AUS. Dist: HarperCollins Pubs. Australia.
Heimerl, Caitlin. Monet Paints a Day. Danneberg, Julie & Monet, Claude. 2012. (J). pap. 15.95 *(978-1-58089-241-4(8))* Charlesbridge Publishing, Inc.
—Monet Paints a Day. Danneberg, Julie. 2012. 32p. (J). (gr. 1-4). 16.99 *(978-1-58089-240-7(X))* Charlesbridge Publishing, Inc.
Hein, Joy Fisher. Miss Lady Bird's Wildflowers: How a First Lady Changed America. Appelt, Kathi. 2005. 40p. (J). lib. bdg. 17.89 *(978-0-06-001108-6(4))* HarperCollins Pubs.
—Miss Lady Bird's Wildflowers: How a First Lady Changed America. Appelt, Kathi. 2005. (ENG.). 40p. (J). (gr. -1-3). 17.99 *(978-0-06-001107-9(6)*, HarperCollins) HarperCollins Pubs. Ltd. GBR. Dist: HarperCollins Pubs.
Hein, Madeline. Dan the Man. Martinez-Mangold, C. 2019. (ENG.). 26p. (J). pap. 14.95 ***(978-1-7023-7629-7(X))*** Independently Published.
Heine, Helme. Ricardo. Heine, Helme. 2003. (la Orilla Del Viento Ser.). (SPA.). 40p. (J). (gr. -1-7). per. 7.50 *(978-968-16-6422-0(1)*, 152) Fondo de Cultura Economica USA.
Heinen, Sandy. Melissa & the Little Red Book. Sanford, Agnes. (J). (gr. 1-6). pap. 3.95 *(978-0-910924-81-8(3))* Macalester Park Publishing Co., Inc.
Heinlen, Marieka. Bedtime. Verdick, Elizabeth. 2010. (Toddler Tools® Ser.). (ENG.). 24p. (J). (gr. -1). bds. 8.99 *(978-1-57542-315-9(4)*, 23159) Free Spirit Publishing, Inc.
—Bye-Bye Time. Verdick, Elizabeth. 2008. (Toddler Tools® Ser.). (ENG.). 24p. (J). (gr. k — 1). bds. 8.99 *(978-1-57542-299-2(9))* Free Spirit Publishing, Inc.
—Bye-Bye Time/Momento de la Despedida. Verdick, Elizabeth. 2017. (Toddler Tools Ser.). (SPA.). 24p. (J). bds. 8.99 *(978-1-63198-151-7(X))* Free Spirit Publishing, Inc.
—Calm-Down Time. Verdick, Elizabeth. 2010. (Toddler Tools® Ser.). (ENG.). 24p. (J). (gr. -1). bds. 8.99 *(978-1-57542-316-6(2)*, 23166) Free Spirit Publishing, Inc.
—Calm-Down Time/Momento para Calmarse. Verdick, Elizabeth. 2016. (Toddler Tools® Ser.). (SPA & ENG.). 24p. (J). bds. 8.99 *(978-1-63198-093-0(9))* Free Spirit Publishing, Inc.
—Clean-Up Time. Verdick, Elizabeth. 2008. (Toddler Tools® Ser.). (ENG.). 24p. (J). (gr. k — 1). bds. 8.99 *(978-1-57542-298-5(0))* Free Spirit Publishing, Inc.
—Clean-Up Time/Momento de Arreglar. Verdick, Elizabeth. 2017. (Toddler Tools® Ser.). (SPA.). 24p. (J). bds. 7.95 *(978-1-63198-154-8(4))* Free Spirit Publishing, Inc.
—Diapers Are Not Forever. Verdick, Elizabeth. (Best Behavior® Board Book Ser.). 24p. (J). 2014. (SPA.). bds. 8.99 *(978-1-57542-429-3(0))*; 2008. (ENG.). bds. 8.99 *(978-1-57542-296-1(4)*, 22961) Free Spirit Publishing, Inc.
—Feet Are Not for Kicking. Verdick, Elizabeth. 2004. (Best Behavior® Board Book Ser.). (ENG.). 24p. (J). bds. 8.99 *(978-1-57542-158-2(5)*, 896) Free Spirit Publishing, Inc.
—Feet Are Not for Kicking / los Pies No Son para Patear. Verdick, Elizabeth. 2017. (Best Behavior® Board Book Ser.). (SPA.). 24p. (J). (— 1). bds. 8.99 *(978-1-63198-197-5(8)*, 81975) Free Spirit Publishing, Inc.
—Germs Are Not for Sharing. Verdick, Elizabeth. 2006. (Best Behavior® Paperback Ser.).Tr. of Germenes No Son para Compartir. (ENG.). (J). (gr. -1-2). 40p. pap. 11.95 *(978-1-57542-197-1(6)*, 1018); 24p. bds. 8.99 *(978-1-57542-196-4(8)*, 1017) Free Spirit Publishing, Inc.

H

—Hands Are Not for Hitting. Agassi, Martine. rev. ed. 2009. (Best Behavior® Paperback Ser.). (ENG.). 40p. (J). (gr. -1-2). pap. 11.95 (978-1-57542-308-1(1), 23081) Free Spirit Publishing, Inc.

—Listening Time. Verdick, Elizabeth. 2008. (Toddler Tools® Ser.). (ENG.). 24p. (J). (gr. k — 1). bds. 8.99 (978-1-57542-301-2(4)) Free Spirit Publishing, Inc.

—Manners Time. Verdick, Elizabeth. 2009. (Toddler Tools® Ser.). (ENG.). 24p. (J). (gr. -1). bds. 8.99 (978-1-57542-313-5(8), 1301012) Free Spirit Publishing, Inc.

—Manners Time / Los Buenos Modales. Verdick, Elizabeth. 2016. (Toddler Tools® Ser.). (SPA.). 24p. (J). bds. 8.99 (978-1-63198-120-3(X)) Free Spirit Publishing, Inc.

—Las Manos No Son para Pegar. Agassi, Martine. 2009. (Best Behavior® Board Book Ser.).Tr. of Hands Are Not for Hitting. (SPA & ENG.). (J). (gr. -1 — 1). 24p. bds. 8.99 (978-1-57542-309-8(X), 23098); 40p. pap. 11.95 (978-1-57542-310-4(3), 23104) Free Spirit Publishing, Inc.

—Mealtime. Verdick, Elizabeth. 2011. (Toddler Tools Ser.). (ENG.). 24p. (J). (gr. k — 1). bds. 8.99 (978-1-57542-366-1(9), 1322977) Free Spirit Publishing, Inc.

—Naptime. Verdick, Elizabeth. 2008. (Toddler Tools® Ser.). (ENG.). 24p. (J). (gr. k — 1). bds. 8.99 (978-1-57542-300-5(6), 1285965) Free Spirit Publishing, Inc.

—Noses Are Not for Picking. Verdick, Elizabeth. 2014. (Best Behavior® Board Book Ser.). (ENG.). 24p. (J). bds. 8.99 (978-1-57542-471-2(1)) Free Spirit Publishing, Inc.

—On-the-Go Time. Verdick, Elizabeth. 2011. (Toddler Tools® Ser.). (ENG.). 24p. (J). bds. 8.99 (978-1-57542-379-1(0), 23791) Free Spirit Publishing, Inc.

—Pacifiers Are Not Forever. Verdick, Elizabeth. 2007. (Best Behavior® Board Book Ser.). (ENG.). 24p. (J). (gr. -1-k). bds. 8.99 (978-1-57542-257-2(3), 1232) Free Spirit Publishing, Inc.

—Sharing Time. Verdick, Elizabeth. 2009. (Toddler Tools® Ser.). (ENG.). 24p. (J). (gr. -1). bds. 8.99 (978-1-57542-314-2(6), 23142) Free Spirit Publishing, Inc.

—Sharing Time/Tiempo para Compartir. Verdick, Elizabeth. 2016. (Toddler Tools Ser.). (SPA.). 24p. (J). bds. 8.99 (978-1-63198-096-1(3)) Free Spirit Publishing, Inc.

—Tails Are Not for Pulling. Verdick, Elizabeth. 2005. (ENG.). (J). (Best Behavior® Paperback Ser.). 40p. (gr. 4-7). pap. 11.95 (978-1-57542-181-0(X), 990); (Best Behavior® Board Book Ser.: Bk. 3). 24p. (gr. 3-7). bds. 8.99 (978-1-57542-180-3(1), 989) Free Spirit Publishing, Inc.

—Teeth Are Not for Biting. Verdick, Elizabeth. 2003. (Best Behavior® Board Book Ser.). (ENG.). 24p. (J). bds. 8.99 (978-1-57542-128-5(3), 794) Free Spirit Publishing, Inc.

—Teeth Are Not for Biting/Los Dientes No Son para Morder. Verdick, Elizabeth. 2017. (Best Behavior® Board Book Ser.). (SPA.). 24p. (J). bds. 8.99 (978-1-63198-157-9(9), 81579) Free Spirit Publishing, Inc.

—Voices Are Not for Yelling. Verdick, Elizabeth. 2015. (Best Behavior® Paperback Ser.). (ENG.). 40p. (J). (gr. -1-2). pap. 11.95 (978-1-57542-501-6(7)) Free Spirit Publishing, Inc.

—Voices Are Not for Yelling / la Voz No Es para Gritar. Verdick, Elizabeth. 2017. (Best Behavior® Board Book Ser.). (SPA.). (J). 24p. bds. 8.99 (978-1-63198-194-4(3), 81944); 40p. (gr. -1-2). pap. 11.95 (978-1-63198-191-3(9), 81913) Free Spirit Publishing, Inc.

—Waiting Is Not Forever. Verdick, Elizabeth. 2019. (Best Behavior® Board Book Ser.). (ENG.). 24p. (J). bds. 8.99 (978-1-63198-466-2(7), 84662) Free Spirit Publishing, Inc.

—Words Are Not for Hurting. Verdick, Elizabeth. (Best Behavior® Paperback Ser.). (J). 2009. (SPA.). 40p. (gr. -1-2). pap. 11.95 (978-1-57542-312-8(X), 23128); 2004. (ENG.). 40p. (gr. k-3). pap. 11.95 (978-1-57542-156-8(9), 854); 2004. (ENG.). 24p. bds. 8.99 (978-1-57542-155-1(0), 840) Free Spirit Publishing, Inc.

—Words Are Not for Hurting (Las Palabras No Son para Lastimar) Verdick, Elizabeth. 2009. (Best Behavior® Board Book Ser.). (SPA.). 24p. (J). (gr. -1). bds. 8.99 (978-1-57542-311-1(1), 23111) Free Spirit Publishing, Inc.

—Worries Are Not Forever. Verdick, Elizabeth. 2018. (Best Behavior® Paperback Ser.). (ENG.). (J). 40p. (gr. -1-2). pap. 11.95 (978-1-63198-314-6(8), 83146); 24p. (-k). bds. 8.99 (978-1-63198-316-0(4), 83160) Free Spirit Publishing, Inc.

Heinlen, Marieka. Worries Are Not Forever / Las Preocupaciones No Duran para Siempre. Verdick, Elizabeth. 2020. (Best Behavior® Board Book Ser.). (SPA.). 24p. (J). (gr. -1 — 1). bds. 8.99 **(978-1-63198-474-7(8)**, 84747) Free Spirit Publishing, Inc.

Heinrich, Sally. Diary of a Tennis Prodigy. Flint, Shamini. 2016. (Diary of A... Ser.). (ENG.). 112p. (J). (gr. 2-6). 8.99 (978-1-76029-088-7(2)) Allen & Unwin AUS. Dist: Independent Pubs. Group.

—Game Changer! the Susie K Files 2. Flint, Shamini. 2018. (Susie K Files Ser.: 2). (ENG.). 112p. (J). (gr. 2-7). pap. 8.99 (978-1-76029-669-8(4)) Allen & Unwin AUS. Dist: Independent Pubs. Group.

—Life of the Party! the Susie K Files 1. Flint, Shamini. 2018. (Susie K Files Ser.: 1). (ENG.). 96p. (J). (gr. 2-6). pap. 8.99 (978-1-76029-668-1(6)) Allen & Unwin AUS. Dist: Independent Pubs. Group.

Heinrichs, Jane. How I Learn: A Kid's Guide to Learning Disability. Miles, Brenda & Patterson, Colleen A. 2014. 32p. (J). (978-1-4338-1660-4(1)); pap. (978-1-4338-1661-1(X)) American Psychological Assn.

—On Our Nature Walk: Our First Talk about Our Impact on the Environment. Roberts, Jillian. 2020. (World Around Us Ser.: 6). (ENG.). 32p. (J). (gr. 1-3). 19.95 (978-1-4598-2100-2(9)) Orca Bk. Pubs. USA.

—On Our Street: Our First Talk about Poverty, 1 vol. Roberts, Jillian & Casap, Jaime. 2018. (World Around Us Ser.: 1). (ENG.). 32p. (J). (gr. 1-3). 19.95 (978-1-4598-1617-6(X)) Orca Bk. Pubs. USA.

—On the Internet: Our First Talk about Online Safety, 1 vol. Roberts, Jillian. 2019. (World Around Us Ser.: 3). (ENG.). 32p. (J). (gr. 1-3). 19.95 (978-1-4598-2094-4(0)) Orca Bk. Pubs. USA.

—On the News: Our First Talk about Tragedy, 1 vol. Roberts, Jillian. 2018. (World Around Us Ser.: 2). (ENG.). 32p. (J). (gr. 1-3). 19.95 (978-1-4598-1784-5(2)) Orca Bk. Pubs. USA.

—On the Playground: Our First Talk about Prejudice, 1 vol. Roberts, Jillian. 2019. (World Around Us Ser.: 4). (ENG.). 32p. (J). (gr. 1-3). 19.95 (978-1-4598-2091-3(6)) Orca Bk. Pubs. USA.

—Princess Angelica: Camp Catastrophe. Polak, Monique. 2018. (Orca Echoes Ser.). (ENG.). 108p. (J). (gr. 2-4). 21.19 (978-1-5364-3162-9(1)) Orca Bk. Pubs. USA.

—Princess Angelica, Camp Catastrophe, 1 vol. Polak, Monique. 2018. (Orca Echoes Ser.). (ENG.). 104p. (J). (gr. 1-3). pap. 6.95 (978-1-4598-1538-4(6)) Orca Bk. Pubs. USA.

—Princess Angelica, Junior Reporter. Polak, Monique. 2020. (Orca Echoes Ser.). (ENG.). 112p. (J). (gr. 1-3). pap. 7.95 (978-1-4598-2358-7(3)) Orca Bk. Pubs. USA.

—Princess Angelica, Part-Time Lion Trainer, 1 vol. Polak, Monique. 2019. (Orca Echoes Ser.). (ENG.). 96p. (J). (gr. 1-3). pap. 6.95 (978-1-4598-1547-6(5)) Orca Bk. Pubs. USA.

—Under Our Clothes: Our First Talk about Our Bodies, 1 vol. Roberts, Jillian. 2019. (World Around Us Ser.: 5). (ENG.). 32p. (J). (gr. 1-3). 19.95 (978-1-4598-2097-5(5)) Orca Bk. Pubs. USA.

Heins, Tanya & Gallenson, Ann. Digital Narrative Project for Macromedia Flash MX 2004: Communicating Information & Ideas in Science & Other Disciplines. Dharkar, Anuja & Tapley, Scott. Aho, Kirsti & McCain, Malinda, eds. 2003. 52p. spiral bd. 10.00 (978-0-9742273-7-5(4), Macromedia Education) Macromedia, Inc.

Heinsz, Joshua. Buzzing Breath. Kenney, Karen Latchana. 2019. (Physics of Music Ser.). (ENG.). 24p. (J). (gr. k-2). lib. bdg. 33.99 (978-1-68410-342-3(8), 140262) Cantata Learning.

—Except When They Don't. Gehl, Laura. 2019. (ENG.). 32p. (J). (gr. -1-3). 16.99 (978-1-4998-0804-9(6)) Little Bee Books Inc.

—Frog Boots. Esbaum, Jill. 2020. 32p. (J). (gr. -1-2). 16.95 (978-1-4549-3297-0(X)) Sterling Publishing Co., Inc.

—Happy Little School: Chunky Lift a Flap Board Book. Swift, Ginger. Cottage Door Press, ed. 2017. (Chunky Lift-A-Flap Board Book Ser.). (ENG.). 12p. (J). (gr. -1-k). bds. 7.99 (978-1-68052-187-0(X), 1001850) Cottage Door Pr.

—A Paintbrush for Paco. Kyle, Tracey. 2018. (ENG.). 40p. (J). (gr. -1-3). 17.99 (978-1-4998-0544-4(6)) Little Bee Books Inc.

—Striking Sounds. Kenney, Karen Latchana. 2019. (Physics of Music Ser.). (ENG.). 24p. (J). (gr. k-2). lib. bdg. 33.99 (978-1-68410-343-0(6), 140263) Cantata Learning.

—Swaying Strings. Kenney, Karen Latchana. 2019. (Physics of Music Ser.). (ENG.). 24p. (J). (gr. k-2). lib. bdg. 33.99 (978-1-68410-344-7(4), 140264) Cantata Learning.

—Tuneful Tubes. Kenney, Karen Latchana. 2019. (Physics of Music Ser.). (ENG.). 24p. (J). (gr. k-2). lib. bdg. 33.99 (978-1-68410-345-4(2), 140265) Cantata Learning.

Heinsz, Joshua & Lebrun, Maxime. Rainbow Rangers: the Quest for the Confetti Crystal. Greene, Summer. 2019. (Rainbow Rangers Ser.). (ENG.). 32p. (J). 17.99 (978-1-250-19033-8(9), 900192455) Imprint IND. Dist: Macmillan.

Heinzen, Kory S., jt. illus. see Lorbiecki, Marybeth.

Heiser, Aline. Gotta Have God 2: Ages 10-12. Brewer, Michael. 2005. (Gotta Have God Ser.). 238p. (J). spiral bd. 12.99 (978-1-58411-059-0(7), Legacy Pr.) Rainbow Pubs. & Legacy Pr.

—Gotta Have God 2: Ages 2-5, 3. Klammer, Lynn. 2005. (Gotta Have God Ser.). 238p. (J). spiral bd. 12.99 (978-1-58411-057-6(0), Legacy Pr.) Rainbow Pubs. & Legacy Pr.

—Gotta Have God 2: Ages 6-9. Cory, Diane. 2005. (Gotta Have God Ser.). 238p. (J). spiral bd. 12.99 (978-1-58411-058-3(9), Legacy Pr.) Rainbow Pubs. & Legacy Pr.

Heiser, Aline & DuFalla, Anita. The Christian Girl's Guide to Money. Totilo, Rebecca Park. 2005. 192p. (J). pap. 9.99 (978-1-58411-067-5(8)) Rainbow Pubs. & Legacy Pr.

Heiser, Aline L. Willie Wonders Why. Patrick, Patsy S. l.t. ed. 2003. 32p. (J). (gr. -1-6). 14.95 (978-0-9726832-0-3(8)) Lu, Melissa Productions.

Heisler, Camille. Exploring Soils: A Hidden World Underground. Grover, Samantha. 2017. 32p. (J). (gr. 9-13). 18.95 (978-1-4863-0500-1(8)) CSIRO Publishing AUS. Dist: Stylus Publishing, LLC.

Heitger, Ellen Bencsics. The Dime Store Nativity. Puckett, Kathleen. 2019. (ENG.). 34p. (J). pap. 13.99 (978-1-9853-2116-8(5)) CreateSpace Independent Publishing Platform.

Heitz, Tim. Balancing Act. Cooper, Brigitte Henry. 2017. (Game Face Ser.). (ENG.). 112p. (J). (gr. 2-5). lib. bdg. 29.93 (978-1-5321-3043-4(0), 27045, Calico Chapter Bks.) ABDO Publishing Co.

—Between the Sticks, 1 vol. Wallace, Rich. 2015. (Game Face Ser.). (ENG.). 112p. (J). (gr. 2-5). 29.93 (978-1-62402-132-9(8), 19192, Calico Chapter Bks.) ABDO Publishing Co.

—Chasing the Baton, 1 vol. Wallace, Rich. 2015. (Game Face Ser.). (ENG.). 112p. (J). (gr. 2-5). 29.93 (978-1-62402-133-6(6), 19194, Calico Chapter Bks.) ABDO Publishing Co.

—Missing Pieces. West, Carly Anne. 2018. (Hello Neighbor Ser.: 1). 208p. (J). (gr. 5-5). pap. 7.99 (978-1-338-28007-4(4)) Scholastic, Inc.

—No Relief, 1 vol. Wallace, Rich. 2015. (Game Face Ser.). (ENG.). 112p. (J). (gr. 2-5). 29.93 (978-1-62402-134-3(4), 19196, Calico Chapter Bks.) ABDO Publishing Co.

—Pressure Point, 1 vol. Wallace, Rich. 2015. (Game Face Ser.). (ENG.). 112p. (J). (gr. 2-5). 29.93 (978-1-62402-135-0(2), 19198, Calico Chapter Bks.) ABDO Publishing Co.

—Softball Surprise. Cooper, Brigitte Henry. 2017. (Game Face Ser.). (ENG.). 112p. (J). (gr. 2-5). lib. bdg. 29.93 (978-1-5321-3044-1(9), 27046, Calico Chapter Bks.) ABDO Publishing Co.

—Sports Report. Cooper, Brigitte Henry. 2017. (Game Face Ser.). (ENG.). 112p. (J). (gr. 2-5). lib. bdg. 29.93 (978-1-5321-3045-8(7), 27047, Calico Chapter Bks.) ABDO Publishing Co.

—Steam & Ice. Cooper, Brigitte Henry. 2017. (Game Face Ser.). (ENG.). 112p. (J). (gr. 2-5). lib. bdg. 29.93 (978-1-5321-3046-5(5), 27048, Calico Chapter Bks.) ABDO Publishing Co.

—Waking Nightmare. West, Carly Anne. 2018. (Hello Neighbor Ser.: 2). 208p. (J). (gr. 7-7). pap. 7.99 (978-1-338-28909-1(8)) Scholastic, Inc.

—Wayside School Beneath the Cloud of Doom. Sachar, Louis. 2020. (Wayside School Ser.: 4). (ENG.). 192p. (J). (gr. 3-7). 17.99 (978-0-06-296538-7(7)); 18.89 (978-0-06-296540-0(9)) HarperCollins Pubs. Ltd. GBR. (HarperCollins). Dist: HarperCollins Pubs.

Heket, Richard. Peter Pepper Minted Mints of Peppermint. Heket, Richard. 2019. (ENG.). 46p. (J). pap. 9.85 **(978-1-9776-0599-3(0))** CreateSpace Independent Publishing Platform.

Held, Jean, photos by. Phased: Poems, Etc. Held, George. 2008. (ENG., 34p. pap. 12.00 (978-0-9817678-0-2(X)) Poets Wear Prada.

Helen, Rushworth. Billy Has a Birthday: Bullying. Minter, James. 2016. (Billy Growing Up Ser.: Vol. 1). (ENG.). (J). (gr. 3-6). (978-1-910727-07-2(5)) Minter Publishing Ltd.

Helena, Crevel. Kateri o'Leary & the Computer Mouse. Martin, Shirley. 2019. (ENG.). 156p. (J). (gr. 3-6). pap. **(978-0-9920615-2-4(0))** Martin, Shirley.

Helenschmidt, Devon. The Littlest Turtle. Lawson, R. J. 2004. (ENG.). 50p. (YA). pap. 23.75 (978-1-4120-2376-4(9)) Trafford Publishing.

Heler, Moti. Di Vunderlikhe Ertseylung Fun Motl. Valder, Hayim. 2017. (YID.). 57p. (J). (978-1-68091-169-5(4)) Kinder Shpiel USA, Inc.

Heler, Shraga. Dragonlions & the Spacemen. Halevy, Hanita H. 2012. (ENG.). 140p. (J). pap. 13.00 (978-965-550-085-1(3)) Contento De Semrik ISR. Dist: Baker & Taylor Publisher Services (BTPS).

Heliadore. Butterflies. Jeunesse, Gallimard & Delafosse, Claude. 2007. (First Discovery Book Ser.). (ENG.). 24p. (J). (gr. -1-k). 5.99 (978-0-439-91087-3(0)) Scholastic, Inc.

Heliadore. Animals at Night. Heliadore. Delafosse, Claude. Best, Clare, tr. 2013. (ENG.). 36p. (J). (gr. -1-k). spiral bd. 13.99 (978-1-85103-413-0(7)) Moonlight Publishing, Ltd. GBR. Dist: Independent Pubs. Group.

—The Butterfly. Heliadore. Delafosse, Claude. Best, Clare, tr. from FRE. 2012. (ENG.). 36p. (J). (gr. -1-k). spiral bd. 14.99 (978-1-85103-404-8(8)) Moonlight Publishing, Ltd. GBR. Dist: Independent Pubs. Group.

Heliot, Eric. Piano, Piano. Cali, Davide. Rivers, Randi, tr. from FRE. 2007. 28p. (J). (gr. 4-7). 15.95 (978-1-58089-191-2(8)) Charlesbridge Publishing, Inc.

Hellard, Sue. Princesses Are Not Just Pretty. Lum, Kate. 2014. (ENG.). 32p. (J). (gr. -1-1). 16.99 (978-1-59990-778-9(X), 9781599907789, Bloomsbury USA Childrens) Bloomsbury Publishing USA.

Hellard, Susan. Anne of Green Gables. Montgomery, L. M. 2017. (Alma Junior Classics Ser.). (ENG.). 256p. (J). pap. 10.99 (978-1-84749-639-3(3), 351545) Alma Classics GBR. Dist: Bloomsbury Publishing Plc.

—Blossom & Beany. Dale, Jenny. 2004. 60p. (J). (978-0-439-66991-7(X)) Scholastic, Inc.

—Bubble & Squeak. Dale, Jenny. 2005. 60p. (J). (978-0-439-79122-9(7)) Scholastic, Inc.

—Dilly & the Birthday Treat. Bradman, Tony. 2016. (Reading Ladder Ser.). (ENG.). 48p. (J). (gr. k-2). 7.99 (978-1-4052-8210-9(X)) Egmont Bks., Ltd. GBR. Dist: Independent Pubs. Group.

—Dilly the Dinosaur: 30th Anniversary Edition. Bradman, Tony. 2nd ed. 2016. (ENG.). 64p. (J). (gr. 1-4). pap. 7.99 (978-1-4052-8466-0(8)) Egmont Bks., Ltd. GBR. Dist: Independent Pubs. Group.

—Heidi: Her Early Lessons & Travels. Spyri, Johanna. Bowman, Peter James, tr. 2017. (Alma Junior Classics Ser.). 288p. (J). pap. 11.00 (978-1-84749-665-2(2), 367214) Alma Classics GBR. Dist: Bloomsbury Publishing Plc.

—Poetry & Potatoes. Harrison, Troon. 2003. 32p. (YA). (978-1-84365-020-1(7), Pavilion Children's Books) Pavilion Bks.

—Snowy the Surprise Puppy. Dale, Jenny. 2005. 60p. (J). pap. (978-0-439-79124-3(3)) Scholastic, Inc.

—Who Loves Mr. Tubs? Bel, Mooney & Mooney, Bel. 2016. (Reading Ladder Ser.). (ENG.). 48p. (J). (gr. k-2). pap. 7.99 (978-1-4052-8205-5(3)) Egmont Bks., Ltd. GBR. Dist: Independent Pubs. Group.

Hellberg, Kristian & Hellberg, Madalyn. The Alv. Hellberg, Joanne S. 2010. 68p. pap. 23.49 (978-1-4490-6868-4(5)) AuthorHouse.

Hellberg, Madalyn, jt. illus. see Hellberg, Kristian.

Helle, Lucy. We Are the Monsters! Williams, Rozanne Lanczak. Hamaguchi, Carla, ed. l.t. ed. 2003. (Sight Word Readers Ser.). (J). (gr. k-2). pap. 3.49 (978-1-57471-966-6(1), 3588) Creative Teaching Pr., Inc.

Hellegouarch, Natasha. Brick Building 101: LEGO Activities to Teach Kids about STEAM. Sanchez, Courtney & Wright, Jessica. 2019. (Little Engineers Ser.). (ENG.). 32p. (J). (gr. -1-2). 26.65 (978-1-942875-79-6(7), Walter Foster Jr) Quarto Publishing Group USA.

—Brick Building Basics: LEGO Activities to Teach Kids about STEAM. Sanchez, Courtney & Wright, Jessica. 2019. (Little Engineers Ser.). (ENG.). 32p. (J). (gr. -1-2). 26.65 (978-1-942875-78-9(9), Walter Foster Jr) Quarto Publishing Group USA.

Helleman, Anneke. How Easy Company Became a Band of Brothers. Langlois, Chris. 2018. (ENG.). 62p. (YA). (gr. 8-12). pap. 20.00 (978-0-692-06979-0(8)) Doc Roe Publishing.

Hellen, Nancy. A Visit to the Farm: Pop-up. Hellen, Nancy. 2004. 16p. (J). (gr. k-2). reprint ed. 7.00 (978-0-7567-7063-1(7)) DIANE Publishing Co.

Heller, Julek. The Last Apprentice: the Spook's Bestiary: The Guide to Creatures of the Dark. Delaney, Joseph. (Last Apprentice Short Fiction Ser.: 3). (ENG.). 240p. (YA). (gr. 8). 2014. pap. 8.99 (978-0-06-208115-5(2)); 2011. 16.99 (978-0-06-208114-8(4)) HarperCollins Pubs. (Greenwillow Bks.).

Heller, Ruth. King Solomon & the Bee. Renberg, Dalia Hardof. 2010. (ENG.). 32p. (J). (gr. -1-3). pap. 9.95 (978-1-56656-815-9(3)) Interlink Publishing Group, Inc.

—Merriam-Webster's First Dictionary. Merriam-Webster, Inc. Staff. rev. ed. 2011. (ENG.). 448p. (gr. k-2). 16.95 (978-0-87779-274-1(7)) Merriam-Webster, Inc.

Heller, Ruth. Galapagos Means Tortoises. Heller, Ruth. ed. 2003. (ENG.). 48p. (J). (gr. k-4). reprint ed. pap. 7.95 (978-1-57805-101-4(0)) Gibbs Smith, Publisher.

—A Sea within a Sea: Secrets of the Sargasso. Heller, Ruth. 2006. 29p. (J). (gr. 4-8). reprint ed. 17.00 (978-1-4223-5731-6(7)) DIANE Publishing Co.

Heller, Susan. Rabbits & Rats, Birds & Seeds, Cactus & Trees: Plants & Animals at Work in the Sonoran Desert. Dayton, Paul. 2019. (ENG.). 34p. (J). 16.99 (978-1-7325265-7-0(5)) Dayton Publishing.

Hellier, Scott. Can I Tell You about Epilepsy? A Guide for Friends, Family & Professionals. Lambert, Kate. 2012. (Can I Tell You About... ? Ser.). (ENG.). 48p. (J). pap. 13.95 (978-1-84905-309-9(X), 694417) Kingsley, Jessica Pubs. GBR. Dist: Hachette UK Distribution.

Hello!Lucky, jt. illus. see Moyle, Eunice.

Helm, Zebedee. Kit & Willy's Guide to Art. 2017. (ENG.). (J). (gr. 1-4). 16.95 (978-1-58423-678-8(7), 25814f46-bc08-40c6-ac9f-607eded48a33) Gingko Pr., Inc.

Helmer, Der-shing. The Great Space Case: A Mystery about Astronomy. Beauregard, Lynda. 2013. (Summer Camp Science Mysteries Ser.: 7). (ENG.). 48p. (J). (gr. 3-6). pap. 6.95 (978-1-4677-0735-0(X), 9781467707350, Graphic Universe™) Lerner Publishing Group.

—In Search of the Fog Zombie: A Mystery about Matter. Beauregard, Lynda. 2012. (Summer Camp Science Mysteries Ser.: 1). (ENG.). 48p. (gr. 3-6). pap. 39.62 (978-0-7613-9268-2(8), Graphic Universe™) Lerner Publishing Group.

—In Search of the Fog Zombie No. 1: A Mystery about Matter. Beauregard, Lynda. 2012. (Summer Camp Science Mysteries Ser.: 1). (ENG.). 48p. (J). (gr. 3-6). pap. 6.95 (978-0-7613-8544-8(4), 9780761385448, Graphic Universe™) Lerner Publishing Group.

—The Kung Fu Puzzle No. 4: A Mystery with Time & Temperature. Thielbar, Melinda. 2010. (Manga Math Mysteries Ser.: 4). (ENG.). 48p. (J). (gr. 3-5). pap. 6.95 (978-0-7613-5246-4(5), 9780761352464, Graphic Universe™) Lerner Publishing Group.

—The Missing Cuckoo Clock No. 5: A Mystery about Gravity. Beauregard, Lynda. 2013. (Summer Camp Science Mysteries Ser.: 5). (ENG.). 48p. (J). (gr. 3-6). lib. bdg. 29.32 (978-1-4677-0167-9(X), 9781467701679, Graphic Universe™) Lerner Publishing Group.

—The Missing Cuckoo Clock No. 8: A Mystery about Gravity. Beauregard, Lynda. 2013. (Summer Camp Science Mysteries Ser.: 5). (ENG.). 48p. (J). (gr. 3-6). pap. 6.95 (978-1-4677-0733-6(3), 9781467707336, Graphic Universe™) Lerner Publishing Group.

—The Nighttime Cabin Thief: A Mystery about Light. Beauregard, Lynda. 2012. (Summer Camp Science Mysteries Ser.: 2). (ENG.). 48p. (gr. 3-6). pap. 39.62 (978-0-7613-9269-9(6), Graphic Universe™) Lerner Publishing Group.

—The Nighttime Cabin Thief No. 2: A Mystery about Light. Beauregard, Lynda. 2012. (Summer Camp Science Mysteries Ser.: 2). (ENG.). 48p. (J). (gr. 3-6). pap. 6.95 (978-0-7613-8543-1(6), 9780761385431, Graphic Universe™) Lerner Publishing Group.

—Summer Camp Science Mysteries. Beauregard, Lynda. 2012. (Summer Camp Science Mysteries Ser.). (ENG.). 48p. (gr. 3-6). pap. 52.82 (978-0-7613-9272-9(6));Pack, Set. pap. 316.92 (978-0-7613-9273-6(4)) Lerner Publishing Group. (Graphic Universe™).

—Summer Camp Science Mysteries: Spring 2012 New Releases. Beauregard, Lynda. 2012. (Summer Camp Science Mysteries Ser.). 48p. (J). (gr. 3-6). lib. bdg. 117.08 (978-0-7613-5688-2(6), Graphic Universe™) Lerner Publishing Group.

Helmer, Der-shing, jt. illus. see Ota, Yuko.

Helmer, Grace. The Van Gogh Activity Book. Helmer, Grace. 2019. (Modern Art Activity Book Ser.). (ENG.). 64p. (J). (gr. 3). pap. 16.95 (978-1-910552-85-8(2)) O'Mara, Michael Bks., Ltd. GBR. Dist: Independent Pubs. Group.

Helms, Dana. Future Hope. Bowlby, Linda S. 2008. 298p. (J). (gr. -1-3). pap. 9.95 (978-0-9779993-6-1(X)) Red Earth Publishing.

—How Amazon Got Her Name. Bowlby, Linda S. 2008. 30p. (J). pap. 9.95 (978-0-9779993-7-8(8)) Red Earth Publishing.

—Is That So. Bowlby, Linda S. 2008. 29p. (J). pap. 9.95 (978-0-9779993-5-4(1)) Red Earth Publishing.

—Nasaria's Family/la Familia de Nasaria. Bowlby, Linda S. 2008. 45p. (J). (gr. -1-3). pap. 10.95 (978-0-9779993-9-2(4)) Red Earth Publishing.

—Nentuck's New Family. Bowlby, Linda S. 2008. 30p. (J). (gr. -1-3). pap. 9.95 (978-0-9779993-8-5(6)) Red Earth Publishing.

—The Rock Garden. Bowlby, Linda S. 2008. 29p. (J). (gr. -1-3). pap. 9.95 (978-0-9779993-4-7(3)) Red Earth Publishing.

Helquist, Brett. The Austere Academy. Snicket, Lemony. 2008. (Series of Unfortunate Events Ser.: Bk. 5). (ENG.). 240p. (J). (gr. 5-18). pap. 6.99 (978-0-06-114634-3(X), Harper Trophy) HarperCollins Pubs.

—Bear's Big Breakfast. Reed, Lynn Rowe. 2016. (ENG.). 32p. (J). (gr. -1-3). 17.99 (978-0-06-226455-8(9)) HarperCollins Pubs.

—Bud Barkin, Private Eye. Howe, James. 2004. (Tales from the House of Bunnicula Ser.: 5). (ENG.). 112p. (J). (gr. 2-5). pap. 6.99 (978-0-689-86989-1(4), Atheneum Bks.

for Young Readers) Simon & Schuster Children's Publishing.
—The Calder Game. Balliett, Blue. 2010. 416p. (J). (gr. 3-7). 7.99 *(978-0-439-85208-1(0))* Scholastic, Inc.
—Chasing Vermeer. Balliett, Blue. 2005. (ENG.). 304p. (J). (gr. 4-7). reprint ed. pap. 7.99 *(978-0-439-37297-8(6))* Scholastic, Inc.
—A Christmas Carol. Dickens, Charles. 2009. (ENG.). 40p. (Orig.). (J). (gr. k). 17.99 *(978-0-06-165099-4(4)*, Balzer & Bray) HarperCollins Pubs.
—The Crooked Sixpence. Bell, Jennifer. 2017. (Uncommoners Ser.: 1). (ENG.). 320p. (J). (gr. 3-7). 16.99 *(978-0-553-49843-1(6)*, Crown Books For Young Readers) Random Hse. Children's Bks.
—The Doll People Set Sail. Martin, Ann M. & Godwin, Laura. (Doll People Ser.: 4). 304p. (J). (gr. 3-7). 2016. pap. 7.99 *(978-1-4231-3998-0(4))*; 2014. (ENG.). 17.99 *(978-1-4231-3683-5(7))* Hyperion Bks. for Children.
—The End. Snicket, Lemony. 2006. (Series of Unfortunate Events Ser.: Bk. 13). 368p. (J). lib. bdg. 15.89 *(978-0-06-029644-5(5))* HarperCollins Pubs.
—The Fort That Jack Built. Ashburn, Boni. 2013. (ENG.). 32p. (J). (gr. -1-3). 18.95 *(978-1-4197-0795-7(7)*, Abrams Bks. for Young Readers) Abrams, Inc.
—The Grim Grotto. Snicket, Lemony. 2004. (Series of Unfortunate Events Ser.: Bk. 11). 352p. (J). (gr. 3-6). lib. bdg. 15.89 *(978-0-06-029642-1(9))* HarperCollins Pubs.
—Groundhog's Day Off. Pearlman, Robb. 2015. 40p. (J). (gr. -1-1). 16.99 *(978-1-61963-289-9(6)*, 900131859, Bloomsbury USA Childrens) Bloomsbury Publishing USA.
—Guitar Genius: How les Paul Engineered the Solid-Body Electric Guitar & Rocked the World (Children's Music Books, Picture Books, Guitar Books, Music Books for Kids) Tomsic, Kim. 2019. (ENG.). 56p. (J). (gr. k-3). 17.99 *(978-1-4521-5919-5(X))* Chronicle Bks. LLC.
—Guys Read: Thriller. Scieszka, Jon. 2011. (Guys Read Ser.: 2). (ENG.). 288p. (J). (gr. 3-7). 16.99 *(978-0-06-196376-6(3))*; pap. 7.99 *(978-0-06-196375-9(5))* HarperCollins Pubs. (Waldon Pond Pr.).
—Historias de Miedo para Contar en la Oscuridad 1. Schwartz, Alvin. 2017. (Historias de Miedo para Contar en la Osc Ser.). (SPA.). 152p. (J). (gr. 4-7). pap. 11.95 *(978-607-527-126-2(0))* Editorial Oceano de Mexico MEX. Dist: Independent Pubs. Group.
—Historias de Miedo para Contar en la Oscuridad 3. Schwartz, Alvin. 2018. (Historias de Miedo para Contar en la Osc Ser.). (SPA.). 152p. (J). (gr. 4-7). pap. 11.95 *(978-607-527-140-8(6))* Editorial Oceano de Mexico MEX. Dist: Independent Pubs. Group.
—Howie Monroe & the Doghouse of Doom. Howe, James. 2003. (Tales from the House of Bunnicula Ser.: 3). (ENG.). 112p. (J). (gr. 2-4). pap. 6.99 *(978-0-689-83952-8(9)*, Atheneum Bks. for Young Readers) Simon & Schuster Children's Publishing.
—Invasion of the Mind Swappers from Asteroid 6! Howe, James. 2003. (Tales from the House of Bunnicula Ser.). 89p. (J). (gr. 2-5). 11.65 *(978-0-7569-2814-8(1))* Perfection Learning Corp.
—Invasion of the Mind Swappers from Asteroid 6! Howe, James. 2003. (Tales from the House of Bunnicula Ser.: 2). (ENG.). 112p. (J). (gr. 2-5). pap. 5.99 *(978-0-689-83950-4(2)*, Simon & Schuster/Paula Wiseman Bks.) Simon & Schuster/Paula Wiseman Bks.
—It Came from Beneath the Bed! Howe, James. 2003. (Tales from the House of Bunnicula Ser.: 1). (ENG.). 112p. (J). (gr. 2-4). pap. 6.99 *(978-0-689-83948-1(0)*, Atheneum Bks. for Young Readers) Simon & Schuster Children's Publishing.
—The League of Seven. Gratz, Alan. 2015. (League of Seven Ser.: 1). (ENG.). 352p. (J). (gr. 5-9). pap. 9.99 *(978-0-7653-3825-9(4)*, 900126212, Starscape) Doherty, Tom Assocs., LLC.
—The Loathsome Library, Bks. 1-6. Snicket, Lemony. 2005. (Series of Unfortunate Events Ser.: Bks. 1-6). (J). (gr. 5). 65.00 *(978-0-06-083353-4(X))* HarperCollins Pubs.
—The Lump of Coal. Snicket, Lemony. 2008. 40p. (J). (gr. -1). lib. bdg. 14.89 *(978-0-06-157425-2(2))*; (ENG.). 12.99 *(978-0-06-157428-3(7))* HarperCollins Pubs.
—Martina & Chrissie: The Greatest Rivalry in the History of Sports. Bildner, Phil. 40p. (J). (gr. 2-5). 2019. 7.99 *(978-1-5362-0564-0(8))*; 2017. 16.99 *(978-0-7636-7308-6(0))* Candlewick Pr.
—Más Historias de Miedo para Contar en la Oscuridad. Schwartz, Alvin. 2018. (Historias de Miedo para Contar en la Osc Ser.). (SPA.). 156p. (J). (gr. 4-7). pap. 11.95 *(978-607-527-131-6(7))* Editorial Oceano de Mexico MEX. Dist: Independent Pubs. Group.
—Milly & the Macy's Parade. Corey, Shana. 2006. 38p. (J). (gr. 4-8). reprint ed. 17.00 *(978-1-4223-5174-1(2))* DIANE Publishing Co.
—The Miserable Mill, 13 vols. Snicket, Lemony. 2008. (Series of Unfortunate Events Ser.: Bk. 4). (ENG.). 208p. (J). (gr. 5-18). pap. 6.99 *(978-0-06-114632-9(3)*, Harper Trophy) HarperCollins Pubs.
—More Scary Stories to Tell in the Dark. Schwartz, Alvin. 2010. (Scary Stories Ser.). (ENG.). 128p. (J). (gr. 4-18). 16.99 *(978-0-06-083521-7(4))* HarperCollins Pubs.
—More Scary Stories to Tell in the Dark. Schwartz, Alvin. 2010. (Scary Stories Ser.). (ENG.). 128p. (J). (gr. 4-18). pap. 7.99 *(978-0-06-083522-4(2)*, HarperCollins) HarperCollins Pubs. Ltd. GBR. Dist: HarperCollins Pubs.
—More Scary Stories to Tell in the Dark. Schwartz, Alvin. 2010. (Scary Stories Ser.). (ENG.). 111p. (gr. 5-8). 16.00 *(978-1-60686-868-3(3))* Perfection Learning Corp.
—Nadya Skylung & the Cloudship Rescue. Seymour, Jeff. 2018. 288p. (J). (gr. 3-7). 16.99 *(978-1-5247-3865-5(4)*, G.P. Putnam's Sons Books for Young Readers) Penguin Young Readers Group.
Helquist, Brett. The Nutcracker Mice. Kladstrup, Kristin. (ENG.). 336p. (J). (gr. 2-5). 2020. pap. 8.99 ***(978-1-5362-1576-2(7))***; 2017. 17.99 *(978-0-7636-8519-5(4))* Candlewick Pr.
Helquist, Brett. Odd & the Frost Giants. Gaiman, Neil. 2008. 128p. (J). lib. bdg. 15.89 *(978-0-06-167175-3(4))* HarperCollins Pubs.
—Odd & the Frost Giants. Gaiman, Neil. 2009. (ENG.). 128p. (J). (gr. 3-18). 14.99 *(978-0-06-167173-9(8)*, HarperCollins) HarperCollins Pubs. Ltd. GBR. Dist: HarperCollins Pubs.
—The Odorous Adventures of Stinky Dog. Howe, James. 2003. (Tales from the House of Bunnicula Ser.: 6). (ENG.). 112p. (J). (gr. 2-5). 13.99 *(978-0-689-85633-4(4)*, Atheneum Bks. for Young Readers) Simon & Schuster Children's Publishing.
—The Odorous Adventures of Stinky Dog. Howe, James. 2004. (Tales from the House of Bunnicula Ser.: 6). (ENG.). 112p. (J). (gr. 2-5). pap. 4.99 *(978-0-689-87412-3(X)*, Simon & Schuster/Paula Wiseman Bks.) Simon & Schuster/Paula Wiseman Bks.
—The Rise & Fall of Mount Majestic. Trafton, Jennifer. 2011. (ENG.). 352p. (J). (gr. 3-7). 6.99 *(978-0-14-241934-2(6)*, Puffin Books) Penguin Young Readers Group.
—Scary Stories 3: More Tales to Chill Your Bones. Schwartz, Alvin. 2011. (Scary Stories Ser.). (ENG.). 128p. (J). (gr. 4-18). 16.99 *(978-0-06-083523-1(0))* HarperCollins Pubs.
—Scary Stories 3: More Tales to Chill Your Bones. Schwartz, Alvin. 2011. (Scary Stories Ser.). (ENG.). 128p. (J). (gr. 4-18). pap. 7.99 *(978-0-06-083524-8(9)*, HarperCollins) HarperCollins Pubs. Ltd. GBR. Dist: HarperCollins Pubs.
—Scary Stories 3: More Tales to Chill Your Bones. 2011. 109p. (J). pap. *(978-0-545-38507-7(5))* Scholastic, Inc.
—Scary Stories 3: More Tales to Chill Your Bones. Schwartz, Alvin. 2011. (Scary Stories Ser.). (ENG.). (J). (gr. 4). lib. bdg. 16.60 *(978-1-61383-284-4(2))* Perfection Learning Corp.
—Scary Stories Box Set: Complete Collection with Brett Helquist Art, 3 vols. Schwartz, Alvin. 2011. (Scary Stories Ser.). (ENG.). 128p. (J). (gr. 4). pap. 23.97 *(978-0-06-198093-0(5))* HarperCollins Pubs.
—Scary Stories to Tell in the Dark. Schwartz, Alvin. 2010. (Scary Stories Ser.). (ENG.). 128p. (J). (gr. 4-18). 16.99 *(978-0-06-083519-4(2))*; pap. 7.99 *(978-0-06-083520-0(6))* HarperCollins Pubs.
—Screaming Mummies of the Pharaoh's Tomb II. Howe, James. 2004. (Tales from the House of Bunnicula Ser.: 4). (ENG.). 112p. (J). (gr. 2-5). pap. 6.99 *(978-0-689-83954-2(5)*, Atheneum Bks. for Young Readers) Simon & Schuster Children's Publishing.
—Screaming Mummies of the Pharaoh's Tomb II, 4. Howe, James. 2004. (Tales from the House of Bunnicula Ser.: 4). (ENG.). 112p. (J). (gr. 4-6). 18.69 *(978-0-689-83953-5(7))* Simon & Schuster, Inc.
—A Series of Unfortunate Events: The Bad Beginning; The Reptile Room; The Wide Window. Snicket, Lemony. 2004. (Series of Unfortunate Events Ser.: Bks. 1-3). (ENG.). 624p. (J). 24.99 *(978-0-06-055621-1(8))* HarperCollins Pubs.
—A Series of Unfortunate Events #1-4 Netflix Tie-In Box Set. Snicket, Lemony. 2017. (Series of Unfortunate Events Ser.). (ENG.). 832p. (J). (gr. 3-7). 55.96 *(978-0-06-279614-1(3))* HarperCollins Pubs.
—A Series of Unfortunate Events #1: the Bad Beginning. Snicket, Lemony. 2007. (Series of Unfortunate Events Ser.: 1). (ENG.). 176p. (J). (gr. 5-9). pap. 7.99 *(978-0-06-114630-5(7)*, HarperCollins) HarperCollins Pubs. Ltd. GBR. Dist: HarperCollins Pubs.
—A Series of Unfortunate Events #1: the Bad Beginning Netflix Tie-In. Snicket, Lemony. 2017. (Series of Unfortunate Events Ser.: 1). (ENG.). 192p. (J). (gr. 3-7). 13.99 *(978-0-06-279602-8(X))* HarperCollins Pubs.
—A Series of Unfortunate Events #5-9 Netflix Tie-In Box Set. Snicket, Lemony. 2018. (Series of Unfortunate Events Ser.). (ENG.). 1056p. (J). (gr. 3-7). 60.00 *(978-0-06-279619-6(4))* HarperCollins Pubs.
—A Series of Unfortunate Events Box: the Complete Wreck (Books 1-13), Bks. 1-13. Snicket, Lemony. 2006. (Series of Unfortunate Events Ser.: Bks. 1-13). (ENG.). (J). (gr. 5). 180.00 *(978-0-06-111906-4(7))* HarperCollins Pubs.
—A Series of Unfortunate Events Box: the Dilemma Deepens (Books 7-9), 3 vols. Snicket, Lemony. 2003. (Series of Unfortunate Events Ser.: Bks. 7-9). (ENG.). (J). (gr. 5-6). 41.99 *(978-0-06-055620-4(X))* HarperCollins Pubs.
—A Series of Unfortunate Events Box: the Gloom Looms (Books 10-12), Bks. 10-12. Snicket, Lemony. 2005. (Series of Unfortunate Events Ser.: Bks. 10-12). (ENG.). (J). (gr. 5). 41.99 *(978-0-06-083909-3(0))* HarperCollins Pubs.
—A Series of Unfortunate Events: the Beatrice Letters. Snicket, Lemony. 2006. (Series of Unfortunate Events Ser.). (ENG.). 72p. (J). (gr. 5-7). 22.99 *(978-0-06-058658-4(3))* HarperCollins Pubs.
—The Shadowhand Covenant. Farrey, Brian. (Vengekeep Prophecies Ser.: 2). (ENG.). (J). (gr. 3-7). 2014. 400p. pap. 7.99 *(978-0-06-204932-2(1))*; 2013. 384p. 16.99 *(978-0-06-204931-5(3))* HarperCollins Pubs.
—The Slippery Slope. Snicket, Lemony. 2003. (Series of Unfortunate Events Ser.: Bk. 10). (YA). (gr. 5-18). 197.82 *(978-0-06-057743-8(6))*; 352p. (J). (gr. 3-6). lib. bdg. 15.89 *(978-0-06-029641-4(0))* HarperCollins Pubs.
—The Storm Makers. Smith, Jennifer E. 2013. (ENG.). 384p. (J). (gr. 3-7). pap. 19.99 *(978-0-316-17959-1(0))* Little, Brown Bks. for Young Readers.
—The Trouble Begins. Snicket, Lemony. movie tie-in ed. 2004. (Series of Unfortunate Events Ser.: Bks. 1-3). (J). 35.99 *(978-0-06-075773-1(6))* HarperCollins Pubs.
—The Vengekeep Prophecies. Farrey, Brian. 2013. (Vengekeep Prophecies Ser.: 1). (ENG.). 416p. (J). (gr. 3-7). pap. 7.99 *(978-0-06-204929-2(1))* HarperCollins Pubs.
—The Wright 3. Balliett, Blue. 2008. 318p. (gr. 4-7). 18.00 *(978-0-7569-8942-2(6))* Perfection Learning Corp.
—The Wright 3. Balliett, Blue. 2007. (ENG.). 352p. (J). (gr. 4-7). pap. 7.99 *(978-0-439-69368-4(3)*, Scholastic Paperbacks) Scholastic, Inc.
Helquist, Brett. Grumpy Goat. Helquist, Brett. 2013. (ENG.). 40p. (J). (gr. -1-3). 18.99 *(978-0-06-113953-6(X))* HarperCollins Pubs.
—Roger: The Jolly Pirate. Helquist, Brett. 2004. (ENG.). 40p. (J). (gr. -1-3). 16.99 *(978-0-06-623805-0(6))* HarperCollins Pubs.
—Roger, the Jolly Pirate. Helquist, Brett. 40p. (J). (gr. -1-2). 2007. (ENG.). pap. 7.99 *(978-0-06-443851-3(1))*; 2004. lib. bdg. 17.89 *(978-0-06-623806-7(4))* HarperCollins Pubs.
Helquist, Brett & Kupperman, Michael. A Series of Unfortunate Events #10: the Slippery Slope. Snicket, Lemony. 2003. (Series of Unfortunate Events Ser.: 10). (ENG.). 352p. (J). (gr. 5-6). 13.99 *(978-0-06-441013-7(7))* HarperCollins Pubs.
—A Series of Unfortunate Events #10: the Slippery Slope Netflix Tie-In. Snicket, Lemony. ed. 2018. (Series of Unfortunate Events Ser.: 10). (ENG.). 352p. (J). (gr. 3-7). 13.99 *(978-0-06-286512-0(9))* HarperCollins Pubs.
—A Series of Unfortunate Events #11: the Grim Grotto. Snicket, Lemony. 2004. (Series of Unfortunate Events Ser.: 11). (ENG.). 352p. (J). (gr. 5-6). 13.99 *(978-0-06-441014-4(5))* HarperCollins Pubs.
—A Series of Unfortunate Events #11: the Grim Grotto Netflix Tie-In. Snicket, Lemony. ed. 2018. (Series of Unfortunate Events Ser.: 11). (ENG.). 352p. (J). (gr. 3-7). 13.99 *(978-0-06-286513-7(7))* HarperCollins Pubs.
—A Series of Unfortunate Events #12: the Penultimate Peril. Snicket, Lemony. 2005. (Series of Unfortunate Events Ser.: 12). (ENG.). 368p. (J). (gr. 5). 13.99 *(978-0-06-441015-1(3))* HarperCollins Pubs.
—A Series of Unfortunate Events #12: the Penultimate Peril Netflix Tie-In. Snicket, Lemony. ed. 2018. (Series of Unfortunate Events Ser.: 12). (ENG.). 368p. (J). (gr. 3-7). 13.99 *(978-0-06-286514-4(5))* HarperCollins Pubs.
—A Series of Unfortunate Events #13: the End. Snicket, Lemony. 2006. (Series of Unfortunate Events Ser.: 13). (ENG.). 368p. (J). (gr. 5-18). 13.99 *(978-0-06-441016-8(1))* HarperCollins Pubs.
—A Series of Unfortunate Events #13: the End Netflix Tie-In. Snicket, Lemony. movie tie-in ed. 2018. (Series of Unfortunate Events Ser.: 13). (ENG.). 368p. (J). (gr. 3-7). 13.99 *(978-0-06-286515-1(3))* HarperCollins Pubs.
—A Series of Unfortunate Events #2: the Reptile Room. Snicket, Lemony. 2007. (Series of Unfortunate Events Ser.: 2). (ENG.). 192p. (J). (gr. 5-9). pap. 7.99 *(978-0-06-114631-2(5)*, HarperCollins) HarperCollins Pubs. Ltd. GBR. Dist: HarperCollins Pubs.
—A Series of Unfortunate Events #2: the Reptile Room Netflix Tie-In. Snicket, Lemony. ed. 2017. (Series of Unfortunate Events Ser.: 2). (ENG.). 208p. (J). (gr. 3-7). 13.99 *(978-0-06-279603-5(8))* HarperCollins Pubs.
—A Series of Unfortunate Events #3: the Wide Window. Snicket, Lemony. 2007. (Series of Unfortunate Events Ser.: 3). (ENG.). 208p. (J). (gr. 5). pap. 7.99 *(978-0-06-114633-6(1))* HarperCollins Pubs.
—A Series of Unfortunate Events #3: the Wide Window Netflix Tie-In. Snicket, Lemony. ed. 2017. (Series of Unfortunate Events Ser.: 3). (ENG.). 224p. (J). (gr. 3-7). 13.99 *(978-0-06-279604-2(6))* HarperCollins Pubs.
—A Series of Unfortunate Events #4: the Miserable Mill Netflix Tie-In. Snicket, Lemony. ed. 2017. (Series of Unfortunate Events Ser.: 4). (ENG.). 208p. (J). (gr. 3-7). 13.99 *(978-0-06-279605-9(4))* HarperCollins Pubs.
—A Series of Unfortunate Events #5: the Austere Academy Netflix Tie-In. Snicket, Lemony. 5th ed. 2018. (Series of Unfortunate Events Ser.: 5). (ENG.). 240p. (J). (gr. 3-7). 13.99 *(978-0-06-279615-8(1))* HarperCollins Pubs.
—A Series of Unfortunate Events #6: the Ersatz Elevator Netflix Tie-In. Snicket, Lemony. ed. 2018. (Series of Unfortunate Events Ser.: 6). (ENG.). 272p. (J). (gr. 3-7). 13.99 *(978-0-06-279616-5(X))* HarperCollins Pubs.
—A Series of Unfortunate Events #7: the Vile Village Netflix Tie-In. Snicket, Lemony. ed. 2018. (Series of Unfortunate Events Ser.: 7). (ENG.). 272p. (J). (gr. 3-7). 13.99 *(978-0-06-279617-2(8))* HarperCollins Pubs.
—A Series of Unfortunate Events #8: the Hostile Hospital Netflix Tie-In. Snicket, Lemony. ed. 2018. (Series of Unfortunate Events Ser.: 8). (ENG.). 272p. (J). (gr. 3-7). 13.99 *(978-0-06-279618-9(6))* HarperCollins Pubs.
—A Series of Unfortunate Events #9: the Carnivorous Carnival Netflix Tie-In. Snicket, Lemony. ed. 2018. (Series of Unfortunate Events Ser.: 9). (ENG.). 304p. (J). (gr. 3-7). 13.99 *(978-0-06-286511-3(0))* HarperCollins Pubs.
Helsom, Geoff. Ella's Joy: Signs of Joy. Dykema, Marjorie. 2009. (ENG.). 32p. (J). 16.95 *(978-0-615-31066-4(4))* One Coin Publishing, LLC.
Helson, Rachel Annette. Philanthropy: A Big Word for Big Hearted People. Helson, Rachel Annette. Helson, Jan. 2010. 32p. (J). (gr. 3-5). 16.99 *(978-1-935497-20-2(0))* Butler Bks.
Helsten, Hayley. The Adventures of Tallulah Froom un-Book One. Madden, Sara. 2020. (ENG.). 156p. (J). pap. 33.99 ***(978-1-5462-4810-1(2))*** AuthorHouse.
Helvey, Rebecca. Greta's Purpose. Helvey, Rebecca. 2008. 68p. (J). pap. 14.95 *(978-0-9774754-7-6(6))* Spiritbuilding Pubs.
Helweg, Hans & Crawford, Mel. Roy Rogers & the New Cowboy. Bedford, Annie North. 2011. 30p. 35.95 *(978-1-258-03516-7(2))* Literary Licensing, LLC.
Hemby, Margaret. How Much Do I Love You? Shaw, Wendy M. 2006. (J). 14.95 *(978-0-9788398-1-9(1))* Jostens Bks.
Hemenway, David. Amazing Ants! McCuen, Renee. 2011. (ENG.). (J). (gr. 1-2). 9.95 *(978-0-9833667-0-6(5))* Danny & Ester's Fortunate Adventures.
—Lost in the Wild. Jacobson, Ryan. 2008. (Choose Your Path Ser.). (ENG.). 152p. (J). (gr. 3-8). pap. 11.95 *(978-1-59193-090-7(1)*, Adventure Pubns.) AdventureKEEN.
—Slimy Salamanders! McCuen, Renee. 2012. (ENG.). (J). (gr. 1-2). 9.95 *(978-0-9833667-2-0(1))* Danny & Ester's Fortunate Adventures.
Heming, Leah-Ellen. Humpty Dumpty's Great Fall. Durant, Alan. 2012. (ENG.). 32p. (J). *(978-0-7787-8028-1(7))*; pap. *(978-0-7787-8039-7(2))* Crabtree Publishing Co.
—Little Bo-Peep's Missing Sheep. Durant, Alan. 2012. (ENG.). 32p. (J). *(978-0-7787-8029-8(5))*; pap. *(978-0-7787-8040-3(6))* Crabtree Publishing Co.
—Little Miss Muffet's Big Scare. Durant, Alan. 2012. (ENG.). 32p. (J). *(978-0-7787-8030-4(9))*; pap. *(978-0-7787-8041-0(4))* Crabtree Publishing Co.
—Old Mother Hubbard's Stolen Bone. Durant, Alan. 2012. (ENG.). 32p. (J). *(978-0-7787-8031-1(7))*; pap. *(978-0-7787-8042-7(2))* Crabtree Publishing Co.
Hemingway, Edward. My Miserable Life. Block, F. L. 2016. (ENG.). 192p. (J). 13.99 *(978-0-8050-9628-6(0)*, 9780805096286, Holt, Henry & Co. Bks. For Young Readers) Holt, Henry & Co.
—Tiny Pie. Bailey, Mark & Oatman, Michael. 2013. 32p. (J). (gr. -1-1). 15.95 *(978-0-7624-4482-3(7)*, Running Pr. Kids) Running Pr.
Hemingway, Edward. Bad Apple: A Tale of Friendship. Hemingway, Edward. 2015. 32p. (J). (gr. -1-k). 8.99 *(978-0-14-751748-7(6)*, Puffin Books) Penguin Young Readers Group.
—Tough Cookie: A Christmas Story. Hemingway, Edward. 2018. (ENG.). 40p. (J). 17.99 *(978-1-62779-441-1(7)*, 900150610, Holt, Henry & Co. Bks. For Young Readers) Holt, Henry & Co.
Hemman, Karen. I'm Not a Chihuahua! Cappuccino. Hemman, Karen. 2020. (Cappuccino Ser.: Vol. 1). (ENG.). 28p. (J). pap. 12.00 ***(978-1-6613-7808-0(0))*** Independently Published.
Hemmingson, Nancy S. Lazy Hero Cat of Egypt. Crow, Stanford. 2013. 24p. 24.00 *(978-1-940021-01-0(4))* Bliss Group.
Hemphill, Rick. The Adventures of Kirra & Rincon: Li'l Kids, Big Waves. 2005. 32p. (J). 17.99 *(978-0-9766408-0-6(5))* Kerr, Justin & Shelley.
Henaff, Carole. The Arabian Nights. Tarnowska, Wafa'. 2010. (ENG.). 128p. (J). (gr. 3-18). 24.99 *(978-1-84686-122-2(5))* Barefoot Bks., Inc.
Hénaff, Carole. The Arabian Nights Chapter. Tarnowska, Wafa'. 2011. (ENG.). 160p. (J). (gr. 4-6). pap. 12.99 *(978-1-84686-568-8(9))* Barefoot Bks., Inc.
—The Blue Bird's Palace. Lallemand, Orianne & Strickland, Tessa. 2016. (J). *(978-1-78285-308-4(1))* Barefoot Bks., Inc.
Henaff, Carole. Conte des Mille et une Nuits. Tarnowska. 2010. (Recueil Ser.: Vol. 3932936). (FRE.). (J). pap. *(978-2-01-393293-6(6))* Gautier-Languereau.
Hénaff, Carole. Demeter & Persephone, 1. Lupton, Hugh. 2013. (Greek Myths Ser.: 1). 40p. (J). (gr. 3-6). pap. 22.44 *(978-1-84686-834-4(3))* Barefoot Bks., Ltd. GBR. Dist: Children's Plus, Inc.
Henaff, Carole. Greek Myths: Three Heroic Tales. Lupton, Hugh & Morton, Daniel. 2017. (ENG.). 136p. (J). (gr. 1-4). pap. 12.99 *(978-1-78285-349-7(9))* Barefoot Bks., Inc.
Hénaff, Carole. Orpheus & Eurydice. Lupton, Hugh. 2013. (Greek Myths Ser.: 3). 40p. (J). (gr. 3-6). pap. 8.99 *(978-1-84686-784-2(3))* Barefoot Bks., Inc.
—Theseus & the Minotaur, 2. Lupton, Hugh. 2013. (Greek Myths Ser.: 2). 40p. (J). (gr. 3-6). pap. 24.94 *(978-1-84686-782-8(7))* Barefoot Bks., Ltd. GBR. Dist: Children's Plus, Inc.
Henaff, Carole. The Adventures of Achilles. Henaff, Carole. Lupton, Hugh & Morden, Daniel. 2012. (Advanced Readers: Classics Ser.). (J). 128p. (gr. 3-6). pap. 12.99 *(978-1-84686-800-9(9))*; 96p. (gr. 6-9). 23.99 *(978-1-84686-420-9(8))* Barefoot Bks., Inc.
Henderson, Cecil. Zoo 1000 Miles. Alexander, Carmen. 2005. 42p. (J). (gr. -1-5). pap. 9.99 *(978-1-886383-57-9(X))* Blue Forge Pr.
Henderson, Dana. Isabelle's Dream: A Story & Activity Book for a Child's Grief Journey. Arenella, Betsy Bottino. 2007. 64p. (gr. -1-3). per. 7.95 *(978-0-9675532-9-0(6))* Quality of Life Publishing Co.
Henderson, Dave. A Story of Three Trees: And the miracle of Prayer. 2005. (ENG.). 12p. (J). bds. 5.99 *(978-1-4037-1197-7(6)*, Spirit Pr.) Bendon, Inc.
Henderson, Erica. The Unbeatable Squirrel Girl: Powers of a Squirrel. 2019. (ENG.). 184p. (J). (gr. 4-7). pap. 12.99 *(978-1-302-92045-6(6))* Marvel Worldwide, Inc.
—The Unbeatable Squirrel Girl Vol. 6: Who Run the World? Squirrels, Vol. 6. 2017. 136p. (J). (gr. 4-17). pap. 15.99 *(978-1-302-90664-1(X))* Marvel Worldwide, Inc.
—The Unbeatable Squirrel Girl Vol. 7: I've Been Waiting for a Squirrel Like You. 2018. (ENG.). 128p. (J). (gr. 4-17). pap. 17.99 *(978-1-302-90665-8(8))* Marvel Worldwide, Inc.
Henderson, Erica & Gorman, Zac. The Unbeatable Squirrel Girl Vol. 3. 2018. (ENG.). 256p. (J). (gr. 4-17). 34.99 *(978-1-302-90844-7(8))* Marvel Worldwide, Inc.
Henderson, Erica & Oum, Siya. The Unbeatable Squirrel Girl Vol. 4. 2019. (Unbeatable Squirrel Girl HC - 2015 Ser.: 4). (ENG.). 272p. (J). (gr. 4-17). 34.99 *(978-1-302-91544-5(4))* Marvel Worldwide, Inc.
Henderson, Erica & Quinones, Joe. The Unbeatable Squirrel Girl: Big Squirrels Don't Cry. 2020. 288p. (J). (gr. 5-9). pap. 12.99 *(978-1-302-92116-3(9))* Marvel Worldwide, Inc.
Henderson, James. Our Dog Benji. Carter, Pete. 2017. (ENG.). 32p. (J). (gr. -1-3). 17.99 *(978-1-925335-33-0(X)*, 317119, EK Bks.) Exisle Publishing Pty Ltd. AUS. Dist: Hachette UK Distribution.
Henderson, Kathy. And the Good Brown Earth. Henderson, Kathy. 2008. (ENG.). 40p. (J). (gr. -1-2). per. 6.99 *(978-0-7636-3841-2(2))* Candlewick Pr.
Henderson, Ken. Once upon a Family: A Son's Journey of Love, Loss, & Hope. Adams, Pamela L. l.t. ed. 2003. 116p. per. *(978-1-891029-35-6(5))* Henderson Publishing.
Henderson, Liz. Bible Folks Shape Books. Gray, Charlotte. 2003. (J). spiral bd. 14.99 *(978-0-89098-267-9(8))* Twentieth Century Christian Bks.
—My Bible Box in Color. Gray, Charlotte. 2003. (J). spiral bd. 24.99 *(978-0-89098-266-2(X))* Twentieth Century Christian Bks.
—Traveling Through the Bible with Bible Folks. Gray, Charlotte. (J). spiral bd. 14.99 *(978-0-89098-265-5(1))* Twentieth Century Christian Bks.
Henderson, McDavid. The Jacket. Clements, Andrew. 2003. (ENG.). 96p. (J). (gr. 3-7). pap. 6.99 *(978-0-689-86010-2(2)*, Atheneum Bks. for Young Readers) Simon & Schuster Children's Publishing.

H

Henderson, Meryl. Andrew Jackson: Young Patriot. Stanley, George E. 2003. (Childhood of Famous Americans Ser.). (ENG.). 192p. (J). (gr. 3-7). pap. 9.99 *(978-0-689-85744-7(6)*, Simon & Schuster/Paula Wiseman Bks.) Simon & Schuster/Paula Wiseman Bks.

—Arthur Ashe: Young Tennis Champion. Mantell, Paul. 2006. (Childhood of Famous Americans Ser.). 213p. (J). 13.65 *(978-0-7569-6387-3(7))* Perfection Learning Corp.

—Arthur Ashe: Young Tennis Champion. Mantell, Paul. 2006. (Childhood of Famous Americans Ser.). (ENG.). 224p. (J). (gr. 3-7). pap. 7.99 *(978-0-689-87346-1(8)*, Simon & Schuster/Paula Wiseman Bks.) Simon & Schuster/Paula Wiseman Bks.

—Bats! Strange & Wonderful. Pringle, Laurence. (Strange & Wonderful Ser.). (ENG.). 32p. (J). 2009. (gr. 3-5). pap. 9.99 *(978-1-59078-781-6(1))*; 2003. (gr. 2-5). 24.94 *(978-1-56397-327-7(8))* Boyds Mills Pr.

—Christopher Reeve: Young Actor. Kudlinski, Kathleen V. & Kudlinski, Kathleen. 2007. (Childhood of Famous Americans Ser.). (ENG.). 200p. (J). (gr. 4-6). 18.69 *(978-1-4169-1544-7(3))* Simon & Schuster, Inc.

—Coretta Scott King: First Lady of Civil Rights. Stanley, George E. 2008. (Childhood of Famous Americans Ser.). (ENG.). 224p. (J). (gr. 3-7). pap. 7.99 *(978-1-4169-6800-9(8)*, Simon & Schuster/Paula Wiseman Bks.) Simon & Schuster/Paula Wiseman Bks.

—Crazy Horse: Young War Chief. Stanley, George E. 2005. (Childhood of Famous Americans Ser.). (ENG.). 208p. (J). (gr. 3-7). pap. 7.99 *(978-0-689-85746-1(2)*, Aladdin) Simon & Schuster Children's Publishing.

—Dale Earnhardt: Young Race Car Driver. Mantell, Paul. 2006. 216p. (J). lib. bdg. 18.46 *(978-1-4242-2205-6(2))* Fitzgerald Bks.

—Dolphins! Pringle, Laurence. 2019. (Strange & Wonderful Ser.). 32p. (J). (gr. 3-5). 17.95 *(978-1-62979-680-2(8))* Boyds Mills Pr.

—Dr. Seuss: Young Author & Artist. Kudlinski, Kathleen. 2005. 184p. (J). lib. bdg. 18.46 *(978-1-4242-2201-8(X))* Fitzgerald Bks.

—Dr. Seuss: Young Author & Artist. Kudlinski, Kathleen. 2005. (Childhood of Famous Americans Ser.). (ENG.). 192p. (J). (gr. 3-7). pap. 7.99 *(978-0-689-87347-8(6)*, Simon & Schuster/Paula Wiseman Bks.) Simon & Schuster/Paula Wiseman Bks.

—Franklin Delano Roosevelt: Champion of Freedom. Kudlinski, Kathleen. 2003. (Childhood of Famous Americans Ser.). (ENG.). 192p. (J). (gr. 3-7). pap. 6.99 *(978-0-689-85745-4(4)*, Simon & Schuster/Paula Wiseman Bks.) Simon & Schuster/Paula Wiseman Bks.

—Frederick Douglass: Abolitionist Hero. Stanley, George E. 2008. (Childhood of Famous Americans Ser.). (ENG.). 208p. (J). (gr. 3-7). pap. 7.99 *(978-1-4169-5547-4(X)*, Aladdin) Simon & Schuster Children's Publishing.

—Frogs! Strange & Wonderful. Pringle, Laurence. 2012. (Strange & Wonderful Ser.). (ENG.). 32p. (J). (gr. 2-4). 17.99 *(978-1-59078-371-9(9))* Boyds Mills Pr.

—George S. Patton: War Hero. Stanley, George E. 2007. (Childhood of Famous Americans Ser.). (ENG.). 192p. (J). (gr. 3-7). pap. 6.99 *(978-1-4169-1547-8(8)*, Simon & Schuster/Paula Wiseman Bks.) Simon & Schuster/Paula Wiseman Bks.

—Harry S. Truman: Thirty-Third President of the United States. Stanley, George E. 2004. (Childhood of Famous Americans Ser.). (ENG.). 256p. (J). (gr. 3-7). pap. 7.99 *(978-0-689-86247-2(4)*, Aladdin) Simon & Schuster Children's Publishing.

—Jesse Owens: Young Record Breaker. Eboch, M. M. 2008. (Childhood of Famous Americans Ser.). (ENG.). 208p. (J). (gr. 3-7). pap. 7.99 *(978-1-4169-3922-1(9)*, Aladdin) Simon & Schuster Children's Publishing.

—Mickey Mantle: All-Star Athlete. Jackson, Max. 2009. (Childhood of Famous Americans Ser.). (ENG.). 224p. (J). pap. 5.99 *(978-1-4169-7472-7(5)*, Simon & Schuster/Paula Wiseman Bks.) Simon & Schuster/Paula Wiseman Bks.

—Milton Hershey: Young Chocolatier. Eboch, M. M. 2008. (Childhood of Famous Americans Ser.). (ENG.). 224p. (J). (gr. 3-7). pap. 6.99 *(978-1-4169-5569-6(0)*, Simon & Schuster/Paula Wiseman Bks.) Simon & Schuster/Paula Wiseman Bks.

—Mr. Rogers: Young Friend & Neighbor. Stanley, George E. 2004. (Childhood of Famous Americans Ser.). (ENG.). 208p. (J). (gr. 3-7). mass mkt. 7.99 *(978-0-689-87186-3(4)*, Simon & Schuster/Paula Wiseman Bks.) Simon & Schuster/Paula Wiseman Bks.

—Ray Charles: Young Musician. Sloate, Susan. 2007. (Childhood of Famous Americans Ser.). (ENG.). 176p. (J). (gr. 3-7). pap. 6.99 *(978-1-4169-1437-2(4)*, Simon & Schuster/Paula Wiseman Bks.) Simon & Schuster/Paula Wiseman Bks.

—Snakes! Strange & Wonderful. Pringle, Laurence. 2004. (Strange & Wonderful Ser.). (ENG.). 32p. (gr. 2-k). 15.95 *(978-1-59078-003-9(5))* Boyds Mills Pr.

—Things to Play With. (Picture Bks.: No. S8817-5). 28p. (J). (gr. -1). pap. 3.95 *(978-0-7214-5144-2(6)*, Dutton Juvenile) Penguin Publishing Group.

—Whales! Strange & Wonderful. Pringle, Laurence. 2003. (Strange & Wonderful Ser.). (ENG.). 32p. (gr. 2-k). 16.95 *(978-1-56397-439-7(8))* Boyds Mills Pr.

—Wilma Rudolph: Olympic Runner. Harper, Jo. 2004. (Childhood of Famous Americans Ser.). (ENG.). 192p. (J). (gr. 3-7). pap. 7.99 *(978-0-689-85873-4(6)*, Simon & Schuster/Paula Wiseman Bks.) Simon & Schuster/Paula Wiseman Bks.

Henderson, Meryl Learnihan. Cicadas! Strange & Wonderful. Pringle, Laurence. unabr. ed. 2010. (Strange & Wonderful Ser.). (ENG.). 32p. (J). (gr. 2-4). 16.95 *(978-1-59078-673-4(4))* Boyds Mills Pr.

—Octopuses! Strange & Wonderful. Pringle, Laurence. 2015. (Strange & Wonderful Ser.). (ENG.). 32p. (J). (gr. 3-7). 17.99 *(978-1-59078-928-5(8))* Boyds Mills Pr.

—Owls! Strange & Wonderful. Pringle, Laurence. 2016. (Strange & Wonderful Ser.). (ENG.). 32p. (J). (gr. 3-4). 16.95 *(978-1-62091-651-3(7))* Boyds Mills Pr.

—Penguins! Strange & Wonderful. Pringle, Laurence. 2013. (Strange & Wonderful Ser.). (ENG.). 32p. (J). (gr. 3-7). pap. 9.95 *(978-1-62091-591-2(X))* Boyds Mills Pr.

—Scorpions! Strange & Wonderful. Pringle, Laurence. 2013. (Strange & Wonderful Ser.). (ENG.). 32p. (J). (gr. 3-7). 16.95 *(978-1-59078-473-0(1))* Boyds Mills Pr.

—Sharks! Strange & Wonderful. Pringle, Laurence. 2008. (Strange & Wonderful Ser.). (ENG.). 32p. (J). (gr. 2-k). pap. 9.95 *(978-1-59078-571-3(1))* Boyds Mills Pr.

—Snakes! Strange & Wonderful. Pringle, Laurence. 2009. (Strange & Wonderful Ser.). (ENG.). 32p. (J). (gr. 2-k). pap. 9.95 *(978-1-59078-744-1(7))* Boyds Mills Pr.

—Spiders! Strange & Wonderful. Pringle, Laurence. 2017. (Strange & Wonderful Ser.). (ENG.). 32p. (J). (gr. 2-5). 17.95 *(978-1-62979-321-4(3))* Boyds Mills Pr.

—Whales! Strange & Wonderful. Pringle, Laurence. 2012. (Strange & Wonderful Ser.). (ENG.). 32p. (J). (gr. 2-4). pap. 9.95 *(978-1-59078-917-9(2))* Boyds Mills Pr.

Henderson, Mike. Daredevil: Back in Black Vol. 7: Mayor Murdock. 2018. (Daredevil: Back in Black Ser.: 7). (ENG.). 112p. (YA). (gr. 8-17). pap. 15.99 *(978-1-302-91063-1(9))* Marvel Worldwide, Inc.

Henderson, Sara & Zenz, Aaron. Howie Goes Shopping(Fido Va de Compras), 1 vol. Henderson, Sara & Zenz, Aaron. ed. 2009. (I Can Read! / Howie Series / ¡Yo Sé Leer! / Serie: Fido Ser.). (ENG.). 32p. (J). pap. 3.99 *(978-0-310-71874-1(0))* Zonderkidz.

—Howie Wants to Play, 1 vol. Henderson, Sara & Zenz, Aaron. ed. 2009. (I Can Read! / Howie Series / ¡Yo Sé Leer! / Serie: Fido Ser.). (ENG.). 32p. (J). pap. 4.99 *(978-0-310-71875-8(9))* Vida Pubs.

Henderson, Scott B. The Ballad of Nancy April: Shawnadithit. Robertson, David A. 2014. (Tales from Big Spirit Ser.: 6). (ENG.). 30p. (J). (gr. 4-6). pap. *(978-1-55379-477-6(X)*, 7a5bbbca-e620-446e-8c13-29bf73a0b984, HighWater Pr.) Portage & Main Pr.

—Betty: The Helen Betty Osborne Story, 1 vol. Robertson, David A. 2016. (ENG.). 30p. (YA). (gr. 8-12). pap. 16.00 *(978-1-55379-544-5(X)*, 155379544X, HighWater Pr.) Portage & Main Pr. CAN. Dist: Orca Bk. Pubs. USA.

—Ends/Begins. Robertson, David A. 2010. (7 Generations Ser.: 3). (ENG.). 30p. (YA). (gr. 9-12). pap. *(978-1-55379-262-8(9)*, 72bc3568-4f12-4574-9f82-146597fa1b3a, HighWater Pr.) Portage & Main Pr.

—The Pact. Robertson, David A. 2011. (7 Generations Ser.: 4). (ENG.). 30p. (YA). (gr. 9-12). pap. *(978-1-55379-230-7(0)*, 9781553792307, HighWater Pr.) Portage & Main Pr.

—The Poet: Pauline Johnson. Robertson, David A. 2014. (Tales from Big Spirit Ser.: 6). (ENG.). 30p. (J). (gr. 4-6). pap. *(978-1-55379-481-3(8)*, ab04cc8e-58f6-479c-9f04-879c4a722ff3, HighWater Pr.) Portage & Main Pr.

—Scars. Robertson, David A. 2010. (7 Generations Ser.: 2). (ENG.). 30p. (YA). (gr. 9-12). pap. *(978-1-55379-228-4(9)*, 4ae83eb9-baca-4c13-a381-ea5771ba95b7, HighWater Pr.) Portage & Main Pr.

—The Scout: Tommy Prince. Robertson, David A. 2014. (Tales from Big Spirit Ser.: 6). (ENG.). 30p. (J). (gr. 4-6). pap. *(978-1-55379-478-3(8)*, 78912685-2d85-4153-9f88-b7d8feb31ffe, HighWater Pr.) Portage & Main Pr.

—Stone. Robertson, David A. 2010. (7 Generations Ser.: 1). (ENG.). 30p. (YA). (gr. 9-12). pap. *(978-1-55379-227-7(0)*, 4ae83eb9-baca-4c13-a381-ea5771ba95b7, HighWater Pr.) Portage & Main Pr.

—Sugar Falls: A Residential School Story. Robertson, David A. 2012. (ENG.). 40p. (YA). (gr. 9-12). pap. *(978-1-55379-334-2(X)*, 9781553793342, HighWater Pr.) Portage & Main Pr.

—7 Generations: A Plains Cree Saga, 1 vol. Robertson, David A. 2016. (7 Generations Ser.). (ENG.). 130p. (YA). (gr. 8-12). pap. 34.00 *(978-1-55379-355-7(2)*, 9781553793557, HighWater Pr.) Portage & Main Pr. CAN. Dist: Orca Bk. Pubs. USA.

Henderson, Scott B. & Yaciuk, Donovan. Northwest Resistance. Vermette, Katherena. 2020. (Girl Called Echo Ser.: 3). (ENG.). 48p. (YA). (gr. 8-12). 18.95 *(978-1-55379-831-6(7)*, HighWater Pr.) Portage & Main Pr. CAN. Dist: Orca Bk. Pubs. USA.

—Pemmican Wars, 1 vol. Vermette, Katherena. 2018. (Girl Called Echo Ser.: 1). (ENG.). 47p. (YA). (gr. 8-12). pap. 18.95 *(978-1-55379-678-7(0)*, HighWater Pr.) Portage & Main Pr. CAN. Dist: Orca Bk. Pubs. USA.

—Red River Resistance, 1 vol. Vermette, Katherena. 2018. (Girl Called Echo Ser.: 2). (ENG.). 47p. (YA). (gr. 8-12). pap. 18.95 *(978-1-55379-747-0(7)*, HighWater Pr.) Portage & Main Pr. CAN. Dist: Orca Bk. Pubs. USA.

Hendley, Tess. Stump. Hendley, Jeff. 2007. (J). pap. *(978-0-9762014-7-2(X))* L'Edge Pr.

Hendra, Sue. Dragon Jelly. Freedman, Claire. 2015. (ENG.). 32p. (J). (gr. k-3). 14.99 *(978-1-61963-682-8(4)*, 900145471, Bloomsbury USA Childrens) Bloomsbury Publishing USA.

—Monsters Don't Eat Broccoli. Hicks, Barbara Jean. 40p. (J). (gr. -1-2). 2014. 7.99 *(978-0-385-75521-4(X)*, Dragonfly Bks.); 2009. 16.99 *(978-0-375-85686-0(2)*, Knopf Bks. for Young Readers) Random Hse. Children's Bks.

—Quiet as a Mouse: A Moving Picture Storybook. Powell, Richard. 2003. 16p. (J). 7.95 *(978-1-58925-678-1(6))* Tiger Tales.

—Sight Words, Set. Kertell, Lynn Maslen. 2010. (Bob Bks.). (ENG.). 48p. (J). (gr. -1-k). 16.99 *(978-0-545-01923-1(0)*, Cartwheel Bks.) Scholastic, Inc.

—Sight Words, First Grade, Set. Kertell, Lynn Maslen. 2010. (Bob Bks.). (ENG.). 48p. (J). (gr. -1-1). 17.99 *(978-0-545-01924-8(9)*, Cartwheel Bks.) Scholastic, Inc.

—Spider Sandwiches. Freedman, Claire. 2014. (ENG.). 32p. (J). (gr. k-3). 14.99 *(978-1-61963-364-3(7)*, 900134246, Bloomsbury USA Childrens) Bloomsbury Publishing USA.

—Under the Sea. Mayfield, Sue. 2nd ed. 2016. (Reading Ladder Ser.). (ENG.). 48p. (J). (gr. k-2). 7.99 *(978-1-4052-8230-7(4))* Egmont Bks., Ltd. GBR. Dist: Independent Pubs. Group.

Hendra, Sue. Cake. Hendra, Sue. Linnet, Paul. 2019. (ENG.). 32p. (J). (gr. -1-3). 17.99 *(978-1-5344-2550-7(0)*, Aladdin) Simon & Schuster Children's Publishing.

—I Need to Wee! Hendra, Sue. Linnet, Paul. 2019. (ENG.). 32p. (J). (gr. -1-3). 17.99 *(978-1-4814-9039-9(7)*, Aladdin) Simon & Schuster Children's Publishing.

—Keith the Cat with the Magic Hat. Hendra, Sue. 2018. (ENG.). 32p. (J). (gr. -1-3). 14.99 *(978-1-4814-9035-1(4)*, Aladdin) Simon & Schuster Children's Publishing.

—Norman the Slug with the Silly Shell. Hendra, Sue. Linnet, Paul. 2017. (ENG.). 32p. (J). (gr. -1-3). 14.99 *(978-1-4814-9032-0(X)*, Aladdin) Simon & Schuster Children's Publishing.

Hendra, Sue & Linnet, Paul. Supertato. Hendra, Sue & Linnet, Paul. 2020. (ENG.). 32p. (J). (gr. -1-3). 17.99 ***(978-1-4814-9037-5(0)**, Aladdin)* Simon & Schuster Children's Publishing.

Hendra, Sue & Maslen, John R. Pre-Reading Skills. Kertell, Lynn Maslen. 2008. (Bob Bks.). (ENG.). 48p. (J). (gr. -1-k). 16.99 *(978-0-545-01922-4(2)*, Cartwheel Bks.) Scholastic, Inc.

Hendra, Sue, jt. illus. see Maslen, John R.

Hendrick, Betty Acey. No Half, No Step, Just a Whole. Furcron, Bertha Phillips. 2003. Orig. Title: Yes. 32p. (J). (gr. 1-3). lib. bdg. 15.95 *(978-1-884242-55-7(3))*; pap. 7.95 *(978-1-884242-57-1(X))* Multicultural Pubns.

Hendricks, Brenda K. The German Girl. Lickel, Lisa J. 2013. 38p. pap. 5.95 *(978-0-9856215-4-4(0))* Fox Ridge Pubns.

—The Potawatomi Boy. Lickel, Lisa J. 2013. 34p. pap. 5.95 *(978-0-9856215-2-0(4))* Fox Ridge Pubns.

Hendricks, Brenda K. Much More to Christmas. Hendricks, Brenda K. 2013. 30p. pap. 9.99 *(978-0-9826582-5-3(7))* Two Small Fish Pubns.

—What's Better Than That, Seren Dippity? Hendricks, Brenda K. 2013. 32p. pap. 9.99 *(978-0-9826582-4-6(9))* Two Small Fish Pubns.

—What's the Buzz, Bumbly Bee? Hendricks, Brenda K. 2013. 30p. pap. 9.99 *(978-0-9826582-3-9(0))* Two Small Fish Pubns.

Hendricks, Sandy. T-Bear the Most Special Bear. Mason, Bonita. 2008. 26p. (J). 19.95 *(978-0-9798718-0-1(8))* Encore Pubns.

Hendricks, Tracey. Wake up & Recognize: Life of a Stepdaughter. Robbins-Turner, Darlene. Date not set. (YA). 16.95 *(978-1-889506-09-8(5))* Kendar Publishing, Inc.

Hendrickson, Chelsea. Boom Dee Loom Annie's Adventure: Annie's Adventure. Dansereau, Karla. 2016. (ENG.). (J). pap. 14.99 *(978-0-9890340-0-5(3))* Unicorn Castle Bks.

Hendrickson, Linda. Abe's Bear Adventure. Martin, Kathleen. 2019. (ENG.). 36p. (J). pap. 9.99 ***(978-1-6956-3950-8(2))*** Independently Published.

Hendrix, Bryan. 100 Monsters in My School. Bader, Bonnie. 2003. (All Aboard Math Reader Ser.). 48p. (gr. -1-3). 14.00 *(978-0-7569-1648-0(8))* Perfection Learning Corp.

Hendrix, John. Abe Lincoln Crosses a Creek: A Tall, Thin Tale (Introducing His Forgotten Frontier Friend) Hopkinson, Deborah. 2016. 40p. (J). (gr. -1-3). 7.99 *(978-1-5247-0158-1(0)*, Dragonfly Bks.) Random Hse. Children's Bks.

—The Giant Rat of Sumatra. Fleischman, Sid. 2005. 208p. (J). (gr. 5-18). 15.99 *(978-0-06-074238-6(0))* HarperCollins Pubs.

—The Giant Rat of Sumatra: Or Pirates Galore. Fleischman, Sid. 2006. (ENG.). 208p. (J). (gr. 5-9). reprint ed. pap. 6.99 *(978-0-06-074240-9(2)*, Greenwillow Bks.) HarperCollins Pubs.

—Hook's Revenge. Schulz, Heidi. 2014. (Hook's Revenge Ser.: 1). 304p. (J). (gr. 3-7). 16.99 *(978-1-4231-9867-3(0))* Hyperion Bks. for Children.

—Hook's Revenge, Book 2: the Pirate Code. Schulz, Heidi. ed. 2016. (Hook's Revenge Ser.: 2). (ENG.). (J). (gr. 3-7). lib. bdg. 18.40 *(978-0-606-39169-6(X))* Turtleback.

—Ice Whale. George, Jean Craighead. 2015. (ENG.). 224p. (J). (gr. 4-7). 7.99 *(978-0-14-242741-5(1)*, Puffin Books) Penguin Young Readers Group.

—Like a River Glorious. Carson, Rae. (Gold Seer Trilogy Ser.: 2). (ENG.). (YA). (gr. 8). 2017. 432p. pap. 9.99 *(978-0-06-224295-2(4))*; 2016. 416p. 17.99 *(978-0-06-224294-5(6))* HarperCollins Pubs. (Greenwillow Bks.).

—McToad Mows Tiny Island. Angleberger, Tom. 2015. (ENG.). 40p. (J). (gr. -1-3). 16.95 *(978-1-4197-1650-8(6)*, Abrams Bks. for Young Readers) Abrams, Inc.

—Nurse, Soldier, Spy: The Story of Sarah Edmonds, a Civil War Hero. Moss, Marissa. 2011. (ENG.). 48p. (J). (gr. 3-7). 19.95 *(978-0-8109-9735-6(5)*, Abrams Bks. for Young Readers) Abrams, Inc.

—Ronan Boyle & the Bridge of Riddles. Lennon, Thomas. (Ronan Boyle Ser.). (ENG.). (J). 2020. 336p. (gr. 5-9). pap. 8.99 *(978-1-4197-4093-0(8))*; 2019. 304p. (gr. 5-9). 17.99 *(978-1-4197-3491-5(1))*; 2019. 304p. pap. *(978-1-4197-3905-7(0))* Abrams, Inc. (Amulet Bks.).

—Ronan Boyle & the Swamp of Certain Death (Ronan Boyle #2) Lennon, Thomas. 2020. (ENG.). 304p. (J). (gr. 3-7). 17.99 *(978-1-4197-4113-5(6)*, 1267001, Amulet Bks.) Abrams, Inc.

—Rutherford B., Who Was He? Poems about Our Presidents. Singer, Marilyn. 2013. 56p. (J). (gr. -1-3). 17.99 *(978-1-4231-7100-3(4))* Hyperion Pr.

—Shooting at the Stars. 2014. (ENG.). 40p. (J). (gr. 3-7). 18.95 *(978-1-4197-1175-6(X)*, Abrams Bks. for Young Readers) Abrams, Inc.

Hendry, Linda. Benny Bensky & the Parrot-Napper. Borsky, Mary. 2008. 128p. (J). (gr. 4-7). pap. 9.95 *(978-0-88776-840-8(7)*, Tundra Bks.) Tundra Bks. CAN. Dist: Penguin Random Hse. LLC.

—How to Make Super Pop-Ups. Irvine, Joan. 2008. (Dover Origami Papercraft Ser.). (ENG.). 96p. (gr. 3-7). per. 8.95 *(978-0-486-46589-0(6))* Dover Pubns., Inc.

—Jocelyn & the Ballerina, 1 vol. Hartry, Nancy. 2nd ed. 2003. (ENG.). 32p. (J). (gr. k-3). pap. 8.95 *(978-1-55041-803-3(3)*, 642af142-ad0d-4a49-bf32-ff2b002a892d) éditeur, Annika Parance CAN. Dist: Firefly Bks., Ltd.

—The Kids Can Press French & English Phrase Book. Kenny, Chantal Lacourcière. 2004. 40p. (J). 7.95 *(978-1-55337-650-7(1))* Kids Can Pr., Ltd. CAN. Dist: Hachette Bk. Group.

—No Frogs for Dinner, 1 vol. Wishinsky, Frieda. 2012. (ENG.). 32p. (J). (gr. k-1). pap. 6.95 *(978-1-55455-189-7(7)*, 227e000a-9bdf-497e-98a8-e88fa5d29738) Trifolium Bks., Inc. CAN. Dist: Firefly Bks., Ltd.

—Pup & Hound. Hood, Susan. 2004. (Kids Can Read Ser.). 32p. (J). (gr. k-1). (ENG.). 11.99 *(978-1-55337-673-6(0))*; 14.95 *(978-1-55337-572-2(6))* Kids Can Pr., Ltd. CAN. Dist: Hachette Bk. Group.

—Pup & Hound at Sea. Hood, Susan. 2006. (Kids Can Read Ser.). (ENG.). 32p. (J). (gr. k-1). 11.99 *(978-1-55337-805-1(9))* Kids Can Pr., Ltd. CAN. Dist: Hachette Bk. Group.

—Pup & Hound Hatch an Egg. Hood, Susan. 2007. (Kids Can Read Ser.). (ENG.). 32p. (J). (gr. k-1). 3.95 *(978-1-55337-975-1(6))* Kids Can Pr., Ltd. CAN. Dist: Hachette Bk. Group.

—Pup & Hound in Trouble. Hood, Susan. 2005. (Kids Can Read Ser.). (ENG.). 32p. (J). (gr. k-1). 11.99 *(978-1-55337-677-4(3))* Kids Can Pr., Ltd. CAN. Dist: Hachette Bk. Group.

—Pup & Hound Lost & Found. Hood, Susan. 2006. (Kids Can Read Ser.). (ENG.). 32p. (J). (gr. k-1). 11.99 *(978-1-55337-807-5(5))* Kids Can Pr., Ltd. CAN. Dist: Hachette Bk. Group.

—Pup & Hound Move In. Hood, Susan. 2004. (Kids Can Read Ser.). (ENG.). 32p. (J). (gr. k-1). 11.99 *(978-1-55337-675-0(7))* Kids Can Pr., Ltd. CAN. Dist: Hachette Bk. Group.

—Pup & Hound Scare a Ghost. Hood, Susan. 2007. (Kids Can Read Ser.). (ENG.). 32p. (J). (gr. k-1). 11.99 *(978-1-55453-143-1(8))* Kids Can Pr., Ltd. CAN. Dist: Hachette Bk. Group.

—Pup & Hound Stay up Late. Hood, Susan. 2005. (Kids Can Read Ser.). 32p. (J). (gr. k-1). (ENG.). 11.99 *(978-1-55337-679-8(X))*; 14.95 *(978-1-55337-678-1(1))* Kids Can Pr., Ltd. CAN. Dist: Hachette Bk. Group.

—Room 207. Tokio, Marnelle. 2006. 120p. (J). (gr. 4-7). pap. 8.95 *(978-0-88776-695-4(1)*, Tundra Bks.) Tundra Bks. CAN. Dist: Penguin Random Hse. LLC.

Hendry, Linda. Outside the Box! Creative Activities for Ecology-Minded Kids. Hendry, Linda. Irvine, Joan. 2009. (Dover Children's Activity Bks.). (ENG.). 96p. (J). (gr. 2-5). pap. 8.99 *(978-0-486-47000-9(8))* Dover Pubns., Inc.

Heney, Clare, jt. illus. see Hunter, Carl.

Heng Jing. Guan Yin: La Virgen de Esperanza: Un Cuento Relatado Del Sutra de Loto. Jin Rou & Hsüan Hua. 2018. (SPA.). (J). *(978-1-64217-023-8(2))* Buddhist Text Translation Society.

—Guan Yin: The Buddha's Helper. Jin Rou et al. 2018. (J). *(978-1-64217-021-4(6))* Buddhist Text Translation Society.

Henke, Amanda. Pocketful of Dreams - Spanish Edition: Teacher's Edition. Long, George. 2016. (SPA.). (J). pap. 10.99 *(978-0-9844946-8-2(5))* Long, George Children's Books.

Henkel, D. B., VIII. Painted Treasures or the Original 288 Tree Gnomes. Henkel, Donald G. 2006. (J). mass mkt. 20.50 *(978-0-9673504-1-7(7))* Quillpen.

Henkel, Vern. Faith Volume 02: Old Testament Volume 2 Genesis Part 2. Piepgrass, Arlene. 2014. 36p. (J). pap. *(978-1-932381-67-2(8)*, 2002) Bible Visuals International, Inc.

Henkel, Vernon. Election Chosen by God Vol. 06: Old Testament Volume 6 Exodus Part 1. Piepgrass, Arlene. 2013. 36p. (J). pap. *(978-1-932381-32-0(5)*, 2006) Bible Visuals International, Inc.

Henkel, Vernon, et al. Eternity Vol. 45: New Testament, Revelation Part 4: the Lord Reigns Forever. Greiner, Ruth B. et al. 2005. 36p. (J). pap. *(978-1-932381-31-3(7)*, 1045) Bible Visuals International, Inc.

—Fellowship, Enjoying God Vol. 41: New Testament Volume 41: 1, 2 & 3 John & Jude. Kiefer, Velma et al. 2004. (ENG.). 36p. (J). pap. *(978-1-932381-00-9(7)*, 1041) Bible Visuals International, Inc.

Henkel, Vernon. In the Beginning Volume 01: Creation & Man's Fall Old Testament Volume 1 Genesis Part 1. Piepgrass, Arlene. 2013. 36p. (J). pap. *(978-1-932381-66-5(X)*, 2001) Bible Visuals International, Inc.

—Joseph, a Picture of the Lord Jesus Christ Part 1 Pt. 1, Vol. 4: Old Testament Volume 04 Genesis Part 4. Piepgrass, Arlene. 2015. 36p. (J). pap. *(978-1-932381-69-6(4)*, 2004) Bible Visuals International, Inc.

—Joseph, a Picture of the Lord Jesus Christ, Part 2 Pt. 2, Vol. 5: Old Testament Volume 05 Genesis Part 5. Piepgrass, Arlene. 2015. 36p. (J). pap. *(978-1-932381-70-2(8)*, 2005) Bible Visuals International, Inc.

—Nature of Man: Old Testament Volume 03 Genesis Part 3. Piepgrass, Arlene. 2014. 36p. (J). pap. *(978-1-932381-68-9(6)*, 2003) Bible Visuals International, Inc.

—Redemption Set Free from Sin Vol. 07: Old Testament Volume 07 Exodus Part 2. Piepgrass, Arlene. 2012. 40p. (J). pap. *(978-1-932381-33-7(3)*, 2007) Bible Visuals International, Inc.

Henkel, Vernon & Hertzler, Frances H.. God, the Trinity, Worthy of Worship Vol. 43: New Testament Volume 43 Revelation Part 2. Greiner, Ruth B. 2013. 40p. (J). pap. *(978-1-932381-65-8(1)*, 1043) Bible Visuals International, Inc.

Henkel, Vernon & Tweed, Sean. Esther Vol. 28: Old Testament Volume 28: Esther. 2003. (ENG.). 30p. (J). pap. *(978-1-932381-01-6(5)*, 2028) Bible Visuals International, Inc.

Henkes, Kevin. All Alone. Henkes, Kevin. 2003. (ENG.). 40p. (J). (gr. -1-3). 16.99 *(978-0-06-054115-6(6)*, Greenwillow Bks.) HarperCollins Pubs.

—A Box Full of Lilly. Henkes, Kevin. 2006. (ENG.). (J). (gr. -1-4). 27.99 *(978-0-06-112852-3(X)*, Greenwillow Bks.) HarperCollins Pubs.

—A Box of Treats: Five Little Picture Books about Lilly & Her Friends. Henkes, Kevin. 2004. (ENG.). 120p. (J). (gr.

-1-k). pap. 14.99 *(978-0-06-073211-0(3)*, Greenwillow Bks.) HarperCollins Pubs.

—Chrysanthemum. Henkes, Kevin. 2020. (ENG.). 32p. (J). (gr. -1-3). pap. 8.99 *(978-0-06-298337-4(7)*, Greenwillow Bks.) HarperCollins Pubs.

—Chrysanthemum Big Book. Henkes, Kevin. 2007. (ENG.). 32p. (J). (gr. -1-3). pap. 24.99 *(978-0-06-111974-3(1)*, Greenwillow Bks.) HarperCollins Pubs.

—Egg. Henkes, Kevin. 2017. (ENG.). 40p. (J). (gr. -1-3). 17.99 *(978-0-06-240872-3(0)*, Greenwillow Bks.) HarperCollins Pubs.

—Egg Board Book. Henkes, Kevin. 2019. (ENG.). 32p. (J). (gr. -1 — 1). bds. 7.99 *(978-0-06-240874-7(7)*, Greenwillow Bks.) HarperCollins Pubs.

—A Good Day. Henkes, Kevin. 2007. (ENG.). 32p. (J). (gr. -1-3). 16.99 *(978-0-06-114018-1(X)*, Greenwillow Bks.) HarperCollins Pubs.

—A Good Day Board Book. Henkes, Kevin. 2010. (ENG.). 28p. (J). (gr. -1 — 1). bds. 7.99 *(978-0-06-185778-2(5)*, Greenwillow Bks.) HarperCollins Pubs.

—El Gran día de Lily: Lily's Big Day (Spanish Edition), 1 vol. Henkes, Kevin. 2008. (SPA.). 40p. (J). (gr. -1-3). 17.99 *(978-0-06-136316-0(2)*, HarperCollins Español) HarperCollins Christian Publishing.

—Julius, the Baby of the World. Henkes, Kevin. 2003. (J). 25.95 incl. audio *(978-1-59112-250-0(3))*; 28.95 incl. audio compact disk *(978-1-59112-518-1(9))*; pap. 33.95 incl. audio *(978-1-59112-251-7(1))*; pap. 35.95 incl. audio compact disk *(978-1-59112-523-5(5))* Live Oak Media.

—Julius's Candy Corn. Henkes, Kevin. 2003. (ENG.). 24p. (J). (gr. -1-k). bds. 6.99 *(978-0-06-053789-0(2)*, Greenwillow Bks.) HarperCollins Pubs.

—Junonia. Henkes, Kevin. (ENG.). 192p. (J). (gr. 3-7). 2012. pap. 6.99 *(978-0-06-196419-0(0))*; 2011. 15.99 *(978-0-06-196417-6(4))* HarperCollins Pubs. (Greenwillow Bks.).

—Kitten's First Full Moon. Henkes, Kevin. 2004. (ENG.). 40p. (J). (gr. -1-3). 17.99 *(978-0-06-058828-1(4)*, Greenwillow Bks.) HarperCollins Pubs.

—Kitten's First Full Moon Board Book. Henkes, Kevin. 2015. (ENG.). 34p. (J). (gr. -1 — 1). bds. 8.99 *(978-0-06-241710-7(X)*, Greenwillow Bks.) HarperCollins Pubs.

Henkes, Kevin. Lilly & Friends: A Picture Book Treasury. Henkes, Kevin. 2020. (ENG.). 312p. (J). (gr. -1-3). 24.99 ***(978-0-06-299551-3(0)***, Greenwillow Bks.) HarperCollins Pubs.

Henkes, Kevin. Lilly's Big Day. Henkes, Kevin. (ENG.). 40p. (J). (gr. -1-3). 2014. pap. 7.99 *(978-0-06-231358-4(4))*; 2006. 17.99 *(978-0-06-074236-2(4))*; 2006. lib. bdg. 18.89 *(978-0-06-074237-9(2))* HarperCollins Pubs. (Greenwillow Bks.).

—Lilly's Chocolate Heart. Henkes, Kevin. 2003. (ENG.). 24p. (J). (gr. -1-k). bds. 6.99 *(978-0-06-056066-9(5)*, Greenwillow Bks.) HarperCollins Pubs.

—Lilly's Purple Plastic Purse. Henkes, Kevin. 10th anniv. ed. 2006. (ENG.). 40p. (J). (gr. -1-4). 17.99 *(978-0-688-12897-5(1)*, Greenwillow Bks.) HarperCollins Pubs.

—Lilly's Purple Plastic Purse. Henkes, Kevin. pap. 16.95 incl. audio *(978-0-87499-686-9(4))*; pap. incl. audio *(978-0-87499-688-3(0))*; pap. 18.95 incl. audio compact disk *(978-1-59112-347-7(X))*; pap. incl. audio compact disk *(978-1-59112-557-0(X))* Live Oak Media.

—Lilly's Purple Plastic Purse 20th Anniversary Edition. Henkes, Kevin. 20th ed. 2016. (ENG.). 40p. (J). (gr. -1-3). 17.99 *(978-0-06-242419-8(X)*, Greenwillow Bks.) HarperCollins Pubs.

—Little White Rabbit. Henkes, Kevin. 2011. (ENG.). 40p. (J). (gr. -1-3). 16.99 *(978-0-06-200642-4(8)*, Greenwillow Bks.) HarperCollins Pubs.

—Little White Rabbit Board Book. Henkes, Kevin. 2014. (ENG.). 34p. (J). (gr. -1-3). bds. 7.99 *(978-0-06-231409-3(2)*, Greenwillow Bks.) HarperCollins Pubs.

—My Garden. Henkes, Kevin. 2010. (ENG.). 40p. (J). (gr. -1-2). 17.99 *(978-0-06-171517-4(4))*; lib. bdg. 18.89 *(978-0-06-171518-1(2))* HarperCollins Pubs. (Greenwillow Bks.).

—Old Bear. Henkes, Kevin. 2008. (ENG.). 32p. (J). (gr. -1-5). 17.99 *(978-0-06-155205-2(4))*; lib. bdg. 18.89 *(978-0-06-155206-9(2))* HarperCollins Pubs. (Greenwillow Bks.).

—Old Bear Board Book. Henkes, Kevin. 2011. (ENG.). 28p. (J). (gr. -1 — 1). bds. 7.99 *(978-0-06-208963-2(3)*, Greenwillow Bks.) HarperCollins Pubs.

—A Parade of Elephants. Henkes, Kevin. 2018. (ENG.). 40p. (J). (gr. -1-3). 18.99 *(978-0-06-266827-1(7))*; lib. bdg. 19.89 *(978-0-06-266828-8(5))* HarperCollins Pubs. (Greenwillow Bks.).

—A Parade of Elephants Board Book. Henkes, Kevin. 2020. (ENG.). 36p. (J). (gr. -1-3). bds. 7.99 *(978-0-06-266829-5(3)*, Greenwillow Bks.) HarperCollins Pubs.

—Penny & Her Doll. Henkes, Kevin. 2012. (ENG.). 32p. (J). (gr. -1-3). 14.99 *(978-0-06-208199-5(3))*; lib. bdg. 15.89 *(978-0-06-208200-8(0))* HarperCollins Pubs. (Greenwillow Bks.).

—Penny & Her Marble. Henkes, Kevin. 2013. (I Can Read Level 1 Ser.). (ENG.). 48p. (J). (gr. -1-3). pap. 4.99 *(978-0-06-208205-3(1))*; 12.99 *(978-0-06-208203-9(5))*; 14.89 *(978-0-06-208204-6(3))* HarperCollins Pubs. (Greenwillow Bks.).

—Penny & Her Sled. Henkes, Kevin. 2019. (ENG.). 56p. (J). (gr. -1-3). 14.99 *(978-0-06-293453-6(8))*; lib. bdg. 15.89 *(978-0-06-293454-3(6))* HarperCollins Pubs. (Greenwillow Bks.).

—Penny & Her Song. Henkes, Kevin. 2012. (I Can Read Level 1 Ser.). (ENG.). 32p. (J). (gr. -1-3). pap. 4.99 *(978-0-06-208197-1(7))*; 12.99 *(978-0-06-208195-7(0))*; lib. bdg. 14.89 *(978-0-06-208196-4(9))* HarperCollins Pubs. (Greenwillow Bks.).

—La Primera Luna Llena de Gatita: Kitten's First Full Moon (Spanish Edition), 1 vol. Henkes, Kevin. 2006. Orig. Title: Kitten's First Full Moon. (SPA.). 40p. (J). (gr. -1-3). 17.99 *(978-0-06-087223-6(3))* HarperCollins Español.

—Sheila Rae, the Brave. Henkes, Kevin. 9.95 *(978-1-59112-865-6(X))* Live Oak Media.

—Two under Par. Henkes, Kevin. 2005. (ENG.). 128p. (J). (gr. 3-7). pap. 5.99 *(978-0-06-075695-6(0)*, Greenwillow Bks.) HarperCollins Pubs.

—Waiting. Henkes, Kevin. 2015. (ENG.). 32p. (J). (gr. -1-3). 17.99 *(978-0-06-236843-0(5))*; lib. bdg. 18.89 *(978-0-06-236844-7(3))* HarperCollins Pubs. (Greenwillow Bks.).

—Wemberly Worried. Henkes, Kevin. 2010. (ENG.). 32p. (J). (gr. -1-4). pap. 7.99 *(978-0-06-185776-8(9)*, Greenwillow Bks.) HarperCollins Pubs.

—Wemberly Worried. Henkes, Kevin. pap. 16.95 incl. audio *(978-0-87499-806-1(9))*; pap. incl. audio *(978-0-87499-808-5(5))*; pap. 18.95 incl. audio compact disk *(978-1-59112-359-0(3))*; pap. 39.95 incl. audio compact disk *(978-1-59112-561-7(8))* Live Oak Media.

—Wemberly's Ice-Cream Star. Henkes, Kevin. 2003. (ENG.). 24p. (J). (gr. -1-k). bds. 6.99 *(978-0-06-050405-2(6)*, Greenwillow Bks.) HarperCollins Pubs.

—The Year of Billy Miller. Henkes, Kevin. 2013. (ENG.). 240p. (J). (gr. 3-7). 16.99 *(978-0-06-226812-9(0))*; lib. bdg. 17.89 *(978-0-06-226813-6(9))* HarperCollins Pubs. (Greenwillow Bks.).

—The Year of Billy Miller. Henkes, Kevin. 2015. (ENG.). (J). (gr. 3-7). lib. bdg. 17.60 *(978-1-62765-762-4(2))* Perfection Learning Corp.

Henley, Claire. In My Little Blue Bed. Top That Publishing Staff, ed. 2007. 11p. (J). (gr. -1-k). bds. *(978-1-84666-280-5(X)*, Tide Mill Pr.) Top That! Publishing PLC.

—In My Little Pink Bed: A Counting Book. Top That Publishing Staff, ed. 2007. (In My Bed Book Ser.). 11p. (J). (gr. -1-k). bds. *(978-1-84666-285-0(0)*, Tide Mill Pr.) Top That! Publishing PLC.

Henn, Judy Hanks. Hanukkah Cat. Burstein, Chaya M. 2003. 32p. (J). (gr. -1-3). pap. 6.95 *(978-1-58013-029-5(1)*, Kar-Ben Publishing) Lerner Publishing Group.

Henn, Sophy. Edie Is Ever So Helpful. Henn, Sophy. 2018. (ENG.). 32p. (J). (gr. -1-2). 16.99 *(978-0-399-54806-2(8)*, Philomel Bks.) Penguin Young Readers Group.

—Lifesize. Henn, Sophy. 2019. (J). 14.99 *(978-1-61067-731-8(5))* Kane Miller.

—Pass It On. Henn, Sophy. 2017. (ENG.). 32p. (J). (gr. -1-2). 17.99 *(978-0-399-54775-1(4)*, Philomel Bks.) Penguin Young Readers Group.

Henneberger, Robert. The Lucky Baseball Bat. Christopher, Matt. ed. 2019. 128p. (J). pap. 6.99 *(978-0-316-53132-0(4))* Little, Brown Bks. for Young Readers.

—The Lucky Baseball Bat. Christopher, Matt. 2005. 123p. (gr. -1-3). 16.00 *(978-0-7569-4890-0(8))* Perfection Learning Corp.

Henninger, Michelle. Block Party Surprise. Nolen, Jerdine. 2015. 41p. (J). *(978-1-4806-8574-1(7))* Harcourt.

—Bradford Street Buddies: Backyard Camp-Out. Nolen, Jerdine et al. 2015. (Green Light Readers Level 3 Ser.). (ENG.). 48p. (J). (gr. 1-4). pap. 4.99 *(978-0-544-36844-6(4)*, 1590919, HMH Books For Young Readers) Houghton Mifflin Harcourt Publishing Co.

—Bradford Street Buddies: Block Party Surprise. Nolen, Jerdine. 2015. (Green Light Readers Level 3 Ser.). (ENG.). 48p. (J). (gr. 1-4). pap. 4.99 *(978-0-544-35863-8(5)*, 1587297, HMH Books For Young Readers) Houghton Mifflin Harcourt Publishing Co.

—Bradford Street Buddies: Springtime Blossoms. Nolen, Jerdine. 2017. (Green Light Readers Level 3 Ser.). (ENG.). 48p. (J). (gr. 1-4). pap. 4.99 *(978-0-544-87390-2(4)*, 1649393, HMH Books For Young Readers) Houghton Mifflin Harcourt Publishing Co.

—Princess & the Frog: A Readers' Theater Script & Guide. Wallace, Nancy K. 2013. (Readers' Theater: How to Put on a Production Ser.). (ENG.). 32p. (J). (gr. 2-6). lib. bdg. 28.50 *(978-1-61641-989-9(X)*, 551, Looking Glass Library) Magic Wagon.

Hennon, Carrie. Baby Sharks LOVE Pop Music! Lily, Amber. 2019. (Lift the Flap Storymaker Ser.). (ENG.). 10p. (J). (gr. -1-k). bds. 7.99 *(978-1-78958-238-3(5))* Top That! Publishing PLC GBR. Dist: Independent Pubs. Group.

—Can You Count the Love? Wren, Georgina. 2020. (Glow-In-the-Dark Bedtime Book Ser.). (ENG.). 10p. (J). (gr. -1-k). bds. 8.99 *(978-1-78958-425-7(6))* Top That! Publishing PLC GBR. Dist: Independent Pubs. Group.

—Can You Count the Stars? Wren, Georgina. 2020. (Glow-In-the-Dark Bedtime Book Ser.). (ENG.). 10p. (J). (gr. -1-k). bds. 8.99 *(978-1-78958-426-4(4))* Top That! Publishing PLC GBR. Dist: Independent Pubs. Group.

—Dinosaur Dash Maze Book. Isaacs, Connie. 2020. (Pull-The-Tab Wipe Clean Bks.). (ENG.). 12p. (J). 9.99 *(978-1-78958-472-1(8))* Top That! Publishing PLC GBR. Dist: Independent Pubs. Group.

—Dinosaurs LOVE Stinky Socks! Copper, Jenny. 2019. (Lift the Flap Storymaker Ser.). (ENG.). 10p. (J). (gr. -1-k). bds. 7.99 *(978-1-78958-236-9(9))*; bds. 7.99 *(978-1-78700-986-8(6))* Top That! Publishing PLC GBR. Dist: Independent Pubs. Group.

Hennon, Carrie. Dragons Love Ice Cream. Wren, Georgina. 2020. (Lift the Flap Storymaker Ser.). (ENG.). 10p. (J). (-k). bds. 7.99 ***(978-1-78958-631-2(3))*** Top That! Publishing PLC GBR. Dist: Independent Pubs. Group.

Hennon, Carrie. Five Little Monkeys. Copper, Jenny. 2019. (Finger Puppet Bks.). (ENG.). 14p. (J). 8.99 *(978-1-78700-753-6(7))* Top That! Publishing PLC GBR. Dist: Independent Pubs. Group.

—Heart Full of Love. Cooper, Jenny. 2020. (Shake, Shimmer & Sparkle Bks.). (ENG.). 10p. (J). bds. 9.99 *(978-1-78958-325-0(X))* Top That! Publishing PLC GBR. Dist: Independent Pubs. Group.

—Itsy Bitsy Spider. Copper, Jenny. 2019. (Finger Puppet Bks.). (ENG.). 14p. (J). 8.99 *(978-1-78700-754-3(5))* Top That! Publishing PLC GBR. Dist: Independent Pubs. Group.

—My Little Star. Cooper, Jenny. 2020. (Shake, Shimmer & Sparkle Bks.). (ENG.). 10p. (J). bds. 9.99 *(978-1-78958-326-7(8))* Top That! Publishing PLC GBR. Dist: Independent Pubs. Group.

—Old MacDonald Had a Farm. Copper, Jenny. 2019. (Finger Puppet Bks.). (ENG.). 14p. (J). (— 1). 8.99 *(978-1-78958-046-4(3))* Top That! Publishing PLC GBR. Dist: Independent Pubs. Group.

Hennon, Carrie. Over the Rainbow. Wren, Georgina. 2020. (Shake, Shimmer & Sparkle Bks.). (ENG.). 10p. (J). (— 1). bds. 9.99 ***(978-1-78958-570-4(8))*** Top That! Publishing PLC GBR. Dist: Independent Pubs. Group.

Hennon, Carrie. Reach for the Moon. Copper, Jenny. 2020. (Shake, Shimmer & Sparkle Bks.). (ENG.). 10p. (J). (-k). bds. 9.99 *(978-1-78958-327-4(6))* Top That! Publishing PLC GBR. Dist: Independent Pubs. Group.

—Shh Shh Shark! Copper, Jenny. 2020. (Wobbly-Eye Zipper Bks.). (ENG.). 10p. (J). (-k). bds. 9.99 *(978-1-78958-317-5(9))* Top That! Publishing PLC GBR. Dist: Independent Pubs. Group.

—Squishy Squashy Lion. Copper, Jenny. 2019. (Squishy Squashy Bks.). (ENG.). 12p. (J). (— 1). bds. 8.99 *(978-1-78958-146-1(X))* Top That! Publishing PLC GBR. Dist: Independent Pubs. Group.

—Squishy Squashy Panda. Copper, Jenny. 2019. (Squishy Squashy Bks.). (ENG.). 12p. (J). (— 1). bds. 8.99 *(978-1-78958-147-8(8))* Top That! Publishing PLC GBR. Dist: Independent Pubs. Group.

—Squishy Squashy Pumpkin. Wren, Georgina. 2020. (Squishy Squashy Bks.). (ENG.). 10p. (J). (gr. -1-2). bds. 9.99 *(978-1-78958-341-0(1))* Top That! Publishing PLC GBR. Dist: Independent Pubs. Group.

—Squishy Squashy Puppy. Copper, Jenny. 2019. (Squishy Squashy Bks.). (ENG.). 12p. (J). (— 1). bds. 8.99 *(978-1-78958-148-5(6))* Top That! Publishing PLC GBR. Dist: Independent Pubs. Group.

—Squishy Squashy Santa. Wren, Georgina. 2020. (Squishy Squashy Bks.). (ENG.). 10p. (J). (gr. -1-2). bds. 9.99 *(978-1-78958-212-3(1))* Top That! Publishing PLC GBR. Dist: Independent Pubs. Group.

—Squishy Squashy Whale. Copper, Jenny. 2019. (Squishy Squashy Bks.). (ENG.). 12p. (J). (— 1). bds. 8.99 *(978-1-78958-149-2(4))* Top That! Publishing PLC GBR. Dist: Independent Pubs. Group.

—Too Many Monsters, Pirates & Dinosaurs. Copper, Jenny. 2019. (Flip, Flap & Find Ser.). (ENG.). 10p. (J). (gr. k-4). bds. 8.99 *(978-1-78700-990-5(4))* Top That! Publishing PLC GBR. Dist: Independent Pubs. Group.

—Too Many Unicorns, Fairies & Mermaids. Copper, Jenny. 2019. (Flip, Flap & Find Ser.). (ENG.). 10p. (J). (gr. k-4). bds. 8.99 *(978-1-78700-991-2(2))* Top That! Publishing PLC GBR. Dist: Independent Pubs. Group.

—Twinkle, Twinkle Little Star. Copper, Jenny. 2019. (Finger Puppet Bks.). (ENG.). 14p. (J). 8.99 *(978-1-78700-992-9(0))* Top That! Publishing PLC GBR. Dist: Independent Pubs. Group.

—Unicorn Dance Maze Book. Isaacs, Connie. 2020. (Pull-The-Tab Wipe Clean Bks.). (ENG.). 12p. (J). 9.99 *(978-1-78958-473-8(6))* Top That! Publishing PLC GBR. Dist: Independent Pubs. Group.

—Unicorns LOVE Rainbow Underpants! Copper, Jenny. 2019. (Lift the Flap Storymaker Ser.). (ENG.). 10p. (J). (gr. -1-k). bds. 7.99 *(978-1-78958-237-6(7))*; bds. 7.99 *(978-1-78700-987-5(4))* Top That! Publishing PLC GBR. Dist: Independent Pubs. Group.

Henny, Rose. Teddy Finds His Way: A Teddy Tale. Henny, Rose. l.t. ed. 2005. 22p. (J). per. 17.95 *(978-0-9705458-7-9(8))* Royalty Bks. International, Inc.

Henrichon, Niko. Doctor Strange by Donny Cates Vol. 2: City of Sin. 2018. (Doctor Strange (2015) Ser.: 7). (ENG.). 112p. (YA). (gr. 8-17). pap. 15.99 *(978-1-302-91065-5(5))* Marvel Worldwide, Inc.

—Meet the Skrulls. 2019. (ENG.). 112p. (YA). (gr. 8-17). pap. 15.99 *(978-1-302-91713-5(7))* Marvel Worldwide, Inc.

Henriksen, Rebecca. With Butterfly Eyes. Harrold, Yvette. 2009. 36p. pap. 15.49 *(978-1-4490-0946-5(8))* AuthorHouse.

Henrique, Eriberto. Al�m Do Horizonte Em Contos. Leite, Elisabete. 2019. (POR.). 74p. (J). pap. 6.99 ***(978-1-7005-1610-7(8))*** Independently Published.

Henrique, Paulo. Break-Up!, 2. Conway, Gerry. 2011. (Hardy Boys: New Case Files Graphic Novel Ser.: 2). (ENG.). 64p. (J). (gr. 5-8). 21.19 *(978-1-59707-243-4(5)*, 900073812) Papercutz.

—Dude Ranch O' Death!, 12. Lobdell, Scott. 12th ed. 2008. (Hardy Boys Undercover Brothers Graphic Novels Ser.: 12). (ENG.). 112p. (J). (gr. 4-7). 22.44 *(978-1-59707-089-8(0)*, 9781597070898) Papercutz.

—Hardy Boys #19: Chaos at 30,000 Feet!, 19. Lobdell, Scott. 2009. (Hardy Boys Undercover Brothers Graphic Novels Ser.: 19). (ENG.). 96p. (J). (gr. 4-7). 22.44 *(978-1-59707-170-3(6))* Papercutz.

—The Hyde & Shriek, 6. Lobdell, Scott & Lima, Sidney. 6th rev. ed. 2006. (Hardy Boys Undercover Brothers Graphic Novels Ser.: 6). (ENG.). 96p. (J). (gr. 4-7). 22.44 *(978-1-59707-029-4(7)*, 9781597070294) Papercutz.

—Shhhhhh!, 16. Lobdell, Scott. 16th ed. 2009. (Hardy Boys Undercover Brothers Graphic Novels Ser.: 16). (ENG.). 96p. (J). (gr. 4-7). 16.19 *(978-1-59707-139-0(0)*, 9781597071390) Papercutz.

—Terrible Toys, 2. Petrucha, Stefan. 2013. (Papercutz Slices Ser.: 2). (ENG.). 64p. (J). (gr. 6-8). 21.19 *(978-1-59707-339-4(3))* Papercutz.

—Word Up!, 17. Lobdell, Scott. 2009. (Hardy Boys Undercover Brothers Graphic Novels Ser.: 17). (ENG.). 96p. (J). (gr. 4-7). 22.44 *(978-1-59707-148-2(X)*, 9781597071482) Papercutz.

Henrique, Paulo & Lima, Sidney. The Opposite Numbers, 7. Lobdell, Scott. 7th rev. ed. 2006. (Hardy Boys Undercover Brothers Graphic Novels Ser.: 7). (ENG.). 96p. (J). (gr. 4-7). 22.44 *(978-1-59707-035-5(1)*, 9781597070355) Papercutz.

Henriquez, Cesar. Jonathan's Colorful Campus Tour - University of Connecticut A-Z. 2004. (J). 9.99 *(978-1-933069-06-7(6))* Odd Duck Ink, Inc.

—Sebastian's Colorful Campus Tour - University of Miami A-Z. 2004. (J). 9.99 *(978-1-933069-05-0(8))* Odd Duck Ink, Inc.

Henriquez, Emile. The Battle of New Orleans: The Drummer's Story, 1 vol. Williams Evans, Freddi & Evans, Freddi Williams. 2005. (ENG.). 32p. (J). (gr. k-3). 16.99 *(978-1-58980-300-8(0)*, Pelican Publishing) Arcadia Publishing.

—Mr. Okra Sells Fresh Fruits & Vegetables, 1 vol. Daley, Lashon. 2016. (ENG.). 32p. (J). (gr. k-3). 16.99 *(978-1-4556-2112-5(9)*, Pelican Publishing) Arcadia Publishing.

—My Grandmother Lives in a Shotgun House, 1 vol. Harrison, Daisy. 2018. (ENG.). 32p. (J). (gr. -1-3). 16.99 *(978-1-4556-2302-0(4)*, Pelican Publishing) Arcadia Publishing.

—The Oklahoma Land Run, 1 vol. Townsend, Una Belle. 2008. (ENG.). 32p. (J). (gr. k-3). 16.99 *(978-1-58980-566-8(6)*, Pelican Publishing) Arcadia Publishing.

—Toby Belfer Learns about Heroes & Martyrs, 1 vol. Pushker, Gloria Teles & Tarman, Mel. 2009. (Toby Belfer Ser.). (ENG.). 128p. (J). (gr. 3-7). 14.95 *(978-1-58980-647-4(6)*, Pelican Publishing) Arcadia Publishing.

Henriquez, Emile F. D. J. & the Debutante Ball, 1 vol. McConduit, Denise Walter. 2004. (D. J. Ser.). (ENG.). 32p. (J). (gr. k-3). 16.99 *(978-1-58980-173-8(3)*, Pelican Publishing) Arcadia Publishing.

Henry, Adam. Bibby, a Bunny's Jouney. Henry, Adam. 2018. (ENG.). 42p. (J). pap. 11.95 *(978-1-7268-8902-5(5))* Independently Published.

Henry, Blake. Chronal Engine. Smith, Greg Leitich. ed. 2013. (ENG.). 192p. (J). (gr. 5-7). pap. 6.99 *(978-0-544-02277-5(7)*, 1528498) Houghton Mifflin Harcourt Publishing Co.

Henry, Clayton. Citadel. Van Lente, Fred. 2009. (Wolverine: First Class Ser.). (ENG.). 24p. (J). (gr. 2-6). lib. bdg. 27.07 *(978-1-59961-670-4(X)*, 15318, Marvel Age) Spotlight.

Henry, Clayton, jt. illus. see Espin, Salvador.

Henry, Heather French. Claire's Magic Sades. Henry, Heather French. 2004. (Claire's Everyday Adventures Ser.). 32p. (J). (gr. k-4). pap. 8.95 *(978-0-9706341-7-7(X)*, 1231609) Cubbie Blue Publishing.

—Claire's Magic Shoes. Henry, Heather French. 2004. (Claire's Everyday Adventures Ser.). (ENG.). 32p. (J). (gr. k-4). 15.95 *(978-0-9706341-3-9(7)*, 1231609) Cubbie Blue Publishing.

—Flying Away. Henry, Heather French. 2004. (Claire's Everyday Adventures Ser.). 32p. (J). (gr. k-4). pap. 8.95 *(978-0-9706341-8-4(8)*, 1231610); (ENG.). 15.95 *(978-0-9706341-4-6(5)*, 1231610) Cubbie Blue Publishing.

—Pepper's Purple Heart: A Veteran's Day Story. Henry, Heather French. 2004. (Claire's Holiday Adventures Ser.: Vol. 1). 32p. (J). (gr. k-4). pap. 8.95 *(978-0-9706341-1-5(0))* Cubbie Blue Publishing.

—What Freedom Means to Me: A Flag Day Story. Henry, Heather French. 2004. (Claire's Holiday Adventures Ser.). 32p. (J). (gr. k-4). (ENG.). 15.95 *(978-0-9706341-2-2(9)*, 1231611); pap. 8.95 *(978-0-9706341-9-1(6))* Cubbie Blue Publishing.

Henry, Henther French. Life, Liberty & the Pursuit of Jellybeans: A Fourth of July Story. Henry, Henther French. 2004. (Claire's Holiday Adventures Ser.). (ENG.). 32p. (J). (gr. k-4). 15.95 *(978-0-9706341-6-0(1))* Cubbie Blue Publishing.

—Life, Liberty & the Pursuit of Jellybeans: An Independence Day Story. Henry, Henther French. 2004. (Claire's Holiday Adventures Ser.). (ENG.). 32p. (J). (gr. k-4). 16.95 *(978-0-9706341-5-3(3))* Cubbie Blue Publishing.

Henry, Jalisa. Alpha-Mania Adventures: Captain Ray & the Rhyming Pirates: a Rhyming Book. Makwana, Jennifer. 2016. (Pirates Ser.: Vol. 1). (ENG.). (J). pap. *(978-0-9947637-4-7(3))* Ruth Rumack's Learning Space.

—Alpha-Mania Adventures: Slomo's Secret Treasure: a Blending Book. Makwana, Jennifer. 2016. (Pirates Ser.: Vol. 2). (ENG.). (J). pap. *(978-0-9947637-5-4(1))* Ruth Rumack's Learning Space.

—Alpha-Mania Adventures: The Complete Set. Makwana, Jennifer. 2017. (ENG.). 188p. (J). (gr. k-3). pap. *(978-0-9959587-5-3(0))* Ruth Rumack's Learning Space.

—Alpha-Mania Adventures: The Fantastic Floating Feast: an Alliteration Book. Van Bakel, Danielle. 2016. (Pirates Ser.: Vol. 3). (ENG.). (J). pap. *(978-0-9947637-6-1(X))* Ruth Rumack's Learning Space.

—Alpha-Mania Adventures: The Great Riddle Race: a Sound Manipulation Book. Makwana, Jennifer. 2016. (Pirates Ser.: Vol. 5). (ENG.). (J). pap. *(978-0-9947637-8-5(6))* Ruth Rumack's Learning Space.

—Alpha-Mania Adventures: The Splitter Critter & the Greedy Pirates: a Segmenting Book. Makwana, Jennifer. 2016. (Pirates Ser.: Vol. 4). (ENG.). (J). pap. *(978-0-9947637-7-8(8))* Ruth Rumack's Learning Space.

—The Yak Pack: Comics & Phonics: Book 1: Learn to Read Decodable Short Vowel Words. Makwana, Jennifer. 2017. (Yak Pack: Comics & Phonics Ser.: Vol. 1). (ENG.). (J). (gr. k-6). pap. *(978-0-9947637-9-2(4))* Ruth Rumack's Learning Space.

—The Yak Pack: Comics & Phonics: Book 3: Learn to Read Decodable Blend Words. Muscovitch, Susan. 2017. (Yak Pack: Comics & Phonics Ser.: Vol. 3). (ENG.). (J). (gr. k-6). pap. *(978-0-9959587-4-6(2))* Ruth Rumack's Learning Space.

—The Yak Pack: Comics & Phonics: Book 4: Learn to Read Decodable Bossy e Words. Muscovitch, Susan. 2017. (Yak Pack: Comics & Phonics Ser.: Vol. 4). (ENG.). (J). (gr. k-6). pap. *(978-0-9959587-6-0(9))* Ruth Rumack's Learning Space.

—The Yak Pack: Sight Word Comics: Book 1: Comic Books to Practice Reading Dolch Sight Words (1-20) Muscovitch, Susan. 2017. (Yak Pack: Sight Word Comics Ser.: Vol. 1). (ENG.). (J). (gr. k-6). pap. *(978-0-9959587-0-8(X))* Ruth Rumack's Learning Space.

—The Yak Pack: Sight Word Comics: Book 2: Comic Books to Practice Reading Dolch Sight Words (21-40) Muscovitch, Susan. 2017. (Yak Pack: Sight Word Comics Ser.: Vol. 2).

(ENG.). (J). (gr. k-6). pap. *(978-0-9959587-1-5(8))* Ruth Rumack's Learning Space.

—The Yak Pack: Sight Word Comics: Book 3: Comic Books to Practice Reading Dolch Sight Words (41-60) Muscovitch, Susan. 2017. (Yak Pack: Sight Word Comics Ser.: Vol. 3). (ENG.). (J). (gr. k-6). pap. *(978-0-9959587-2-2(6))* Ruth Rumack's Learning Space.

—The Yak Pack: Sight Word Comics: Book 4: Comic Books to Practice Reading Dolch Sight Words (61-80) Muscovitch, Susan. 2017. (Yak Pack: Sight Word Comics Ser.: Vol. 4). (ENG.). (J). (gr. k-6). pap. *(978-0-9959587-7-7(7))* Ruth Rumack's Learning Space.

—The Yak Pack: Sight Word Comics: Book 5: Comic Books to Practice Reading Dolch Sight Words (81-100) Muscovitch, Susan. 2017. (Yak Pack: Sight Word Comics Ser.: Vol. 5). (ENG.). (J). (gr. k-6). pap. *(978-0-9959587-8-4(5))* Ruth Rumack's Learning Space.

Henry, Jed. Friends of a Feather. Myracle, Lauren. 2015. (Life of Ty Ser.: 3). (ENG.). 144p. (J). (gr. 1-4). 7.99 *(978-0-14-242320-2(3)*, Puffin Books); 12.99 *(978-0-525-42288-4(9)*, Dutton Books for Young Readers) Penguin Young Readers Group.

—I Love You near & Far. Parker, Marjorie Blain. 2015. (Snuggle Time Stories Ser.: 4). 24p. (J). (gr. -1-1). 9.95 *(978-1-4549-0507-3(7))* Sterling Publishing Co., Inc.

—Just Say Boo! Hood, Susan. 2012. (ENG.). 32p. (J). (gr. -1-3). 12.99 *(978-0-06-201029-2(8))* HarperCollins Pubs.

—The Life of Ty - Non-Random Acts of Kindness. Myracle, Lauren. 2015. (Life of Ty Ser.: 2). (ENG.). 128p. (J). (gr. 1-4). 5.99 *(978-0-14-242319-6(X)*, Puffin Books) Penguin Young Readers Group.

—My Dream Playground. Becker, Kate M. 2013. 32p. (J). (gr. -1-3). 15.99 *(978-0-7636-5531-0(7))* Candlewick Pr.

—El Perro con Sombrero: A Bilingual Doggy Tale. Taylor Kent, Derek. ed. 2015. (SPA.). 40p. (J). (gr. -1-2). 18.99 *(978-0-8050-9989-8(1)*, 900129320, Holt, Henry & Co. Bks. For Young Readers) Holt, Henry & Co.

—Pick a Pup. Chall, Marsha Wilson. 2011. (ENG.). 32p. (J). (gr. -1-k). 16.99 *(978-1-4169-7961-6(1)*, McElderry, Margaret K. Bks.) McElderry, Margaret K. Bks.

—Time for Cranberries. Detlefsen, Lisl H. 2015. (ENG.). 32p. (J). (gr. -1-2). 17.99 *(978-1-62672-098-5(3)*, 900136033) Roaring Brook Pr.

Henry Jr, Nelson K. Judah Bear's Beary Scary Night. Henry Jr, Nelson K. 2018. (ENG.). 48p. (J). 20.00 *(978-0-578-43221-2(8))* Henry, Nelson K. Jr.

Henry, Maggie. Adirondack Lullaby. Heinz, Brian J. 2016. (J). *(978-1-59531-053-8(3))* North Country Bks., Inc.

—Forest Green: A Walk Through the Adirondack Seasons. Mahoney, Liana. 2014. (J). *(978-1-59531-047-7(9))* North Country Bks., Inc.

Henry, Marilyn. Marilyn Monroe Paper Dolls. Henry, Marilyn. 2007. (ENG.). 16p. pap. 12.00 *(978-0-9790668-8-7(3))* Paper Studio Pr.

Henry, Mike. Cuzzies Find the Rainbow's End. Kapai, Tommy. 2006. (ENG.). 32p. (gr. -1-3). pap. 9.00 *(978-0-9582517-0-9(3)*, 2990) Huia Pubs. NZL. Dist: Univ. of Hawaii Pr.

—Cuzzies Meet the Motuhoa Shark. Kapai, Tommy. 2006. (Cuzzies Adventures Ser.). (MAO & ENG.). 32p. (J). (gr. -1-3). pap. 9.00 *(978-1-86969-100-4(8))* Huia Pubs. NZL. Dist: Univ. of Hawaii Pr.

Henry, Reginald. The Backyard Adventures of Dutchess & Domino. Henry, Cathy. 2017. (ENG.). 26p. (J). pap. 12.95 *(978-1-64003-136-4(7))* Covenant Bks.

Henry, Robert M. When I Get Scared. Johnson, Diana Lynne. 2018. (ENG.). 30p. (J). pap. 11.11 *(978-1-7903-0511-7(X))* Independently Published.

Henry, Steve. Here Is Big Bunny. Henry, Steve. 2016. (ENG.). 32p. (J). (gr. -1-3). 15.95 *(978-0-8234-3458-9(3))* Holiday Hse., Inc.

Henry, Steven. All Kinds of Kisses. Swain, Heather. 2017. (ENG.). 32p. (J). bds. 7.99 *(978-1-250-11375-7(X)*, 9781250113757) Feiwel & Friends.

—Goodnight, Sleepyville. Hellman, Blake Liliane. 2020. (ENG.). 40p. (J). 18.99 *(978-1-68119-876-7(2)*, 900190993, Bloomsbury Children's Bks.) Bloomsbury Publishing USA.

—Herbert's First Halloween. Rylant, Cynthia. 2017. (ENG.). 36p. (J). (gr. -1 — 1). 15.99 *(978-1-4521-2533-6(3))* Chronicle Bks. LLC.

—How Many Hugs? Swain, Heather. 2018. (ENG.). 28p. (J). bds. 7.99 *(978-1-250-17500-7(3)*, 900189288) Feiwel & Friends.

—It's Raining Bats & Frogs. Colby, Rebecca. 2015. (ENG.). 40p. (J). (gr. -1-k). 16.99 *(978-1-250-04992-6(X)*, 9781250049926) Feiwel & Friends.

—A Lucky Author Has a Dog. Ray, Mary Lyn. 2015. (ENG.). 40p. (J). (gr. -1-3). 16.99 *(978-0-545-51876-5(8))* Scholastic, Inc.

—Something Smells! Hellman, Blake Liliane. 2018. (ENG.). 48p. (J). (gr. -1-3). 17.99 *(978-1-4814-8864-8(3)*, Atheneum Bks. for Young Readers) Simon & Schuster Children's Publishing.

—Welcome to Morningtown. Hellman, Blake Liliane. 2019. (ENG.). 40p. (J). 17.99 *(978-1-68119-873-6(8)*, 900190996, Bloomsbury Children's Bks.) Bloomsbury Publishing USA.

Henry, Thomas. Just Jimmy Again. Crompton, Richmal. 2003. (ENG.). 256p. (J). 16.95 *(978-0-333-71231-3(5))* Macmillan Pubs., Ltd. GBR. Dist: Trafalgar Square Publishing.

—Just William: Book 1. Crompton, Richmal. 2018. (Macmillan Classics Ser.). (ENG.). 288p. (J). (gr. 2-6). 14.99 *(978-1-4472-8101-6(2))* Pan Macmillan GBR. Dist: Independent Pubs. Group.

—More William. Crompton, Richmal. 2008. 196p. pap. *(978-1-4099-4227-6(9))* Dodo Pr.

Henry, Thomas & Monks, Lydia. William the Fourth. Crompton, Richmal. 2015. (Just William Ser.). (ENG.). 304p. (J). (gr. 4-6). pap. 12.99 *(978-1-4472-8561-8(1))* Pan Macmillan GBR. Dist: Independent Pubs. Group.

Henry, Thomas & Ogilvie, Sara. William the Outlaw. Crompton, Richmal. 2016. (Just William Ser.). (ENG.). 352p. (J). (gr. 4-6). pap. 10.99 *(978-1-4472-8555-7(7))* Pan Macmillan GBR. Dist: Independent Pubs. Group.

Henry, Thomas & Pichon, Liz. William the Good. Crompton, Richmal. 2016. (Just William Ser.: 9). (ENG.). 336p. (J). (gr. 4-7). pap. 11.99 *(978-1-5098-0520-4(6))* Pan Macmillan GBR. Dist: Independent Pubs. Group.

Henry, Thomas & Roberts, David. Just William at Christmas. Crompton, Richmal. 2015. (Just William Ser.). (ENG.). 256p. (J). (gr. 4-6). pap. 10.99 *(978-1-4472-8535-9(2))* Pan Macmillan GBR. Dist: Independent Pubs. Group.

Henry, Thomas & Stower, Adam. William Again. Crompton, Richmal. 2015. (Just William Ser.). (ENG.). 224p. (J). (gr. 4-6). pap. 10.99 *(978-1-4472-8560-1(3))* Pan Macmillan GBR. Dist: Independent Pubs. Group.

Hensley, Dimitrios. Clowning Around: With Red Skelton. Zimmerman, Nancy. 2018. (Young Artist Ser.: Vol. 7). (ENG.). 36p. (J). pap. 10.00 *(978-1-7186-7649-7(2))* CreateSpace Independent Publishing Platform.

Hensley, Kendra. Mousy Mouse & Kitty Tales: Modern Day Parables & Bible Stories. McEwen, Elvina. 2019. (ENG.). 86p. (J). pap. 18.00 *(978-1-7273-4538-4(X))* CreateSpace Independent Publishing Platform.

Henson, Allah El. Black Invention Rap. Stewart, Ajamu T. 2019. (ENG.). 32p. (J). pap. 9.95 ***(978-1-6986-7780-4(4))*** Independently Published.

Henson, Brooke. Counting in the Crazy Garden. Burnette, Margarette. 2008. (Chipper Kids Ser.). 30p. (J). (gr. -1-2). 15.95 *(978-0-9653791-3-7(2))* JenPrint Pubns., LLC.

Henson, Gaby. We Love Animals on the Farm. Baxter, Nicola. 2013. 12p. (J). (gr. -1-12). 9.99 *(978-1-84322-693-2(6)*, Armadillo) Anness Publishing GBR. Dist: National Bk. Network.

Henson, Mike. Level 2: A Step-By-Step Guide to Computer Coding. Wainewright, Max. 2017. (How to Code: a Step by Step Guide to Computer Coding Ser.). (ENG.). 32p. (J). (gr. 2-4). pap. 8.99 *(978-1-68297-077-5(9))* QEB Publishing Inc.

—Level 3. Wainewright, Max. 2017. (How to Code: a Step by Step Guide to Computer Coding Ser.). (ENG.). 32p. (J). (gr. 2-4). pap. 8.99 *(978-1-68297-078-2(7))* QEB Publishing Inc.

—What Is a Rainbow? Blackford, Harriet. 2019. (TechTots(tm) Ser.). (ENG.). 32p. (J). (gr. -1-k). 12.95 *(978-1-912757-06-0(0))* Boxer Bks., Ltd. GBR. Dist: Sterling Publishing Co., Inc.

—Where Does the Sun Go? Blackford, Harriet. 2019. (TechTots(tm) Ser.). (ENG.). 32p. (J). (gr. -1-k). 12.95 *(978-1-912757-02-2(8))* Boxer Bks., Ltd. GBR. Dist: Sterling Publishing Co., Inc.

—Why Do Things Fall Down? Blackford, Harriet. 2019. (TechTots(tm) Ser.). (ENG.). 32p. (J). (gr. -1-k). 12.95 *(978-1-912757-08-4(7))* Boxer Bks., Ltd. GBR. Dist: Sterling Publishing Co., Inc.

—Why Do We Poop? Blackford, Harriet. 2019. (TechTots(tm) Ser.). (ENG.). 32p. (J). (gr. -1-k). 12.95 *(978-1-912757-04-6(4))* Boxer Bks., Ltd. GBR. Dist: Sterling Publishing Co., Inc.

Henson, Mike. Surprise! Henson, Mike. 2017. (ENG.). 32p. (J). (gr. -1-1). 17.95 *(978-1-910277-41-6(X)*, Words & Pictures) Quarto Publishing Group UK GBR. Dist: Hachette Bk. Group.

Henterly, Jamichael. Forest Bright, Forest Night. Ward, Jennifer. 2005. (Sharing Nature with Children Book Ser.). 32p. (J). (gr. k-3). 16.95 *(978-1-58469-066-5(6))* Dawn Pubns.

—Forest Bright, Forest Night. Ward, Jennifer. 2005. (ENG.). (J). 26p. (gr. -1 — 1). bds. 7.95 *(978-1-58469-089-4(5))*; 32p. (gr. k-3). pap. 8.95 *(978-1-58469-067-2(4))* Sourcebooks, Inc. (Dawn Pubns.).

Hentzell, Brittany. Annie & Arnie's Arduous Afternoon. 2005. spiral bd. 12.95 *(978-0-9773550-0-6(4))* Smartypants Bks.

Heo, Yumi. Pirican Pic & Pirican Mor. Lupton, Hugh. 2003. (ENG.). 40p. (J). (gr. 1-3). 16.99 *(978-1-84148-070-1(3))* Barefoot Bks., Inc.

—Sometimes I'm Bombaloo. Vail, Rachel. 2005. (Scholastic Bookshelf Ser.). (ENG.). 32p. (J). (gr. -1-3). pap. 6.99 *(978-0-439-66941-2(3))* Scholastic, Inc.

—Uncle Peter's Amazing Chinese Wedding. Look, Lenore. 2006. (ENG.). 40p. (J). (gr. -1-3). 18.99 *(978-0-689-84458-4(1)*, Atheneum Bks. for Young Readers) Simon & Schuster Children's Publishing.

Hepburn, C J. Reading & Language Arts: Level J. 2003. (Test Best for Success Ser.). 63p. (gr. 9-12). per. *(978-0-7398-6714-3(8))* Steck-Vaughn.

Hepburn, Scott. The Clone Wars: In Service of the Republic Vol. 3: Blood & Snow, 1 vol. Gilroy, Henry. 2011. (Star Wars: Clone Wars Ser.: No. 2). (ENG.). 24p. (J). (gr. 6-12). 27.07 *(978-1-59961-840-1(0)*, 13800, Graphic Novels) Spotlight.

—The Clone Wars - Slaves of the Republic: A Slave Now, a Slave Forever. Gilroy, Henry. 2010. (Star Wars: Clone Wars Ser.: No. 1). (ENG.). 24p. (J). (gr. 6-12). 27.07 *(978-1-59961-714-5(5)*, 13795, Graphic Novels) Spotlight.

—The Clone Wars - Slaves of the Republic Vol. 3: The Depths of Zygerria. Gilroy, Henry. 2010. (Star Wars: Clone Wars Ser.: No. 1). (ENG.). 24p. (J). (gr. 6-12). 27.07 *(978-1-59961-712-1(9)*, 13793, Graphic Novels) Spotlight.

—The Clone Wars - Slaves of the Republic Vol. 4: Auction of a Million Souls. Gilroy, Henry. 2010. (Star Wars: Clone Wars Ser.: No. 1). (ENG.). 24p. (J). (gr. 6-12). 27.07 *(978-1-59961-713-8(7)*, 13794, Graphic Novels) Spotlight.

—The Clone Wars - Slaves of the Republic Vol. 6: Escape from Kadavo. Gilroy, Henry. 2010. (Star Wars: Clone Wars Ser.: No. 1). (ENG.). 24p. (J). (gr. 6-12). 27.07 *(978-1-59961-715-2(3)*, 13796, Graphic Novels) Spotlight.

—Frozen Doom! In Service of the Republic, 2. Gilroy, Henry. 2011. (Star Wars: Clone Wars Ser.: No. 2). (ENG.). 24p. (J). (gr. 6-12). 27.07 *(978-1-59961-839-5(7)*, 13799, Graphic Novels) Spotlight.

—In Service of the Republic, Vol. 1. Gilroy, Henry. 2011. (Star Wars: Clone Wars Ser.: No. 2). (ENG.). 24p. (J). (gr. 6-12). 27.07 *(978-1-59961-838-8(9)*, 13798, Graphic Novels) Spotlight.

—The Mystery of Kiros. Gilroy, Henry. 2010. (Star Wars: Clone Wars Ser.: No. 1). (ENG.). 24p. (J). (gr. 6-12). 27.07 *(978-1-59961-710-7(2)*, 13791, Graphic Novels) Spotlight.

Hepburn, Scott, et al. Spider-Man/Deadpool Vol. 8: Road Trip. 2019. (ENG.). 136p. (YA). (gr. 8-17). pap. 15.99 *(978-1-302-91112-6(0))* Marvel Worldwide, Inc.

Heran, Michelle, jt. illus. see Rogers, Melissa.

Heras, Ruth. The Chronicles of Pillowcase. Simpson, Lupe. 2017. (ENG.). (J). 27.49 *(978-1-5456-1277-4(3))*; pap. 16.49 *(978-1-5456-1276-7(5))* Salem Author Services.

Herba, Gosia. The Ancient World in 100 Words: Start Conversations & Spark Inspiration. Gifford, Clive. 2019. (In a Nutshell Ser.). (ENG.). 112p. (J). (gr. 2-6). 19.95 ***(978-0-7112-4466-5(9)***, Words & Pictures) Quarto Publishing Group UK GBR. Dist: Hachette Bk. Group.

Herbert, Frances. Fran's Van & the Magic Box. Herbert, Frances. 2013. 24p. pap. *(978-1-78222-085-5(2))* Paragon Publishing, Rothersthorpe.

—Fran's Van & the Naughty Terrier. Herbert, Frances. 2013. 32p. pap. *(978-1-78222-164-7(6))* Paragon Publishing, Rothersthorpe.

Herbert, Jennifer. What Am I? Granfield, Linda. 2007. 32p. (J). (gr. k-k). 15.95 *(978-0-88776-812-5(1)*, Tundra Bks.) Tundra Bks. CAN. Dist: Penguin Random Hse. LLC.

—What Will We Do with the Baby-O? Heras, Theo. 2004. 32p. (J). (gr. k-k). 12.95 *(978-0-88776-689-3(7)*, Tundra Bks.) Tundra Bks. CAN. Dist: Penguin Random Hse. LLC.

Herbert-Liew, Maria. Children's Dictionary: Illustrated Dictionary for Ages 7+ (Collins Children's Dictionaries) Collins Dictionaries & Collins Dictionaries (Children's Dictionaries Store), Collins Dictionaries. 2018. (ENG.). 472p. (J). (gr. 4). 18.99 *(978-0-00-827117-6(8))* HarperCollins Pubs. Ltd. GBR. Dist: Independent Pubs. Group.

—Children's Thesaurus: Illustrated Thesaurus for Ages 7+ (Collins Children's Dictionaries) Collins Dictionaries & Collins Dictionaries (Children's Dictionaries Store), Collins Dictionaries. 2018. (ENG.). 388p. (YA). (gr. 7-9). 21.99 *(978-0-00-827118-3(6))* HarperCollins Pubs. Ltd. GBR. Dist: Independent Pubs. Group.

—First French Dictionary: 500 First Words for Ages 5+ (Collins First Dictionaries) Collins Dictionaries & Collins Dictionaries (Children's Dictionaries Store), Collins Dictionaries. 3rd rev. ed. 2020. (ENG.). 80p. (J). (gr. k-2). pap. 10.99 *(978-0-00-831271-8(0))* HarperCollins Pubs. Ltd. GBR. Dist: Independent Pubs. Group.

—First School Dictionary: Illustrated Dictionary for Ages 5+ (Collins First Dictionaries) Collins Dictionaries & Collins Dictionaries (Children's Dictionaries Store), Collins Dictionaries. 2017. (Collins Primary Dictionaries Ser.). (ENG.). 176p. (J). (gr. 3-6). pap. 16.99 *(978-0-00-820676-5(7))* HarperCollins Pubs. Ltd. GBR. Dist: Independent Pubs. Group.

—First Spanish Dictionary: 500 First Words for Ages 5+ (Collins First Dictionaries) Collins Dictionaries & Collins Dictionaries (Children's Dictionaries Store), Collins Dictionaries. 3rd rev. ed. 2020. (ENG.). 80p. (J). (gr. k-k). pap. 10.99 *(978-0-00-831272-5(9))* HarperCollins Pubs. Ltd. GBR. Dist: Independent Pubs. Group.

—Maths Dictionary: Illustrated Dictionary for Ages 7+ (Collins Primary Dictionaries) Broadbent, Paul et al. 2017. (ENG.). 144p. (J). (gr. k-6). pap. 15.99 *(978-0-00-821237-7(6))* HarperCollins Pubs. Ltd. GBR. Dist: Independent Pubs. Group.

—Primary Dictionary: Illustrated Dictionary for Ages 7+ (Collins Primary Dictionaries) Collins Dictionaries & Collins Dictionaries (Children's Dictionaries Store), Collins Dictionaries. 3rd ed. 2018. (Collins Primary Dictionaries Ser.). (ENG.). 472p. (J). (gr. 2). pap. 16.99 *(978-0-00-820678-9(3))* HarperCollins Pubs. Ltd. GBR. Dist: Independent Pubs. Group.

—Primary French Dictionary: Illustrated Dictionary for Ages 7+ (Collins Primary Dictionaries) Collins Dictionaries & Collins Dictionaries (Children's Dictionaries Store), Collins Dictionaries. 2nd rev. ed. 2020. (Collins Primary Dictionaries Ser.). (ENG.). 592p. (J). (gr. 2-4). 16.99 *(978-0-00-831270-1(2))* HarperCollins Pubs. Ltd. GBR. Dist: Independent Pubs. Group.

—Primary Spanish Dictionary: Illustrated Dictionary for Ages 7+ (Collins Primary Dictionaries) Collins Dictionaries & Collins Dictionaries (Children's Dictionaries Store), Collins Dictionaries. 2nd rev. ed. 2019. (Collins Primary Dictionaries Ser.). (ENG.). 624p. (gr. 2-6). 16.95 *(978-0-00-831269-5(9))* HarperCollins Pubs. Ltd. GBR. Dist: Independent Pubs. Group.

Herbert Yee, Wong. Hammy & Gerbee: Mummies at the Museum. Herbert Yee, Wong. 2018. (ENG.). 112p. (J). pap. 12.99 *(978-1-62779-462-6(X)*, 900151451, Holt, Henry & Co. Bks. For Young Readers) Holt, Henry & Co.

Herbstritt, T. J. God Loves You More Than Rainbows & Butterflies! Herbstritt, Rj. 2011. 40p. pap. 24.95 *(978-1-4560-6735-9(4))* America Star Bks.

Hercka, Roch. The Path to Jordan. Knight, Ruthi & Stantus, Megan, eds. 2019. (ENG.). 48p. (J). pap. 14.44 *(978-1-7974-1868-1(8))* Independently Published.

Herford, Oliver. Aaron in the Wildwoods (Illustrated Edition) Harris, Joel Chandler. 2016. (ENG.). (J). pap. *(978-1-4068-7987-2(8))* Echo Library.

Herford, Oliver. The Peter Pan Alphabet. Herford, Oliver. 2015. (ENG.). 62p. pap. 5.99 *(978-1-61242-874-1(6)*, Serenity Pubs.) Arc Manor.

Hergenroeder, Ernie. Daddy Got His Orders. Mitchell, Kathy. 2004. 16p. (J). pap. 14.95 *(978-0-9760811-0-4(5))* T.J. Publishing.

—The Hamburger Tree. Pacheco, Maria & Garcia-Martinez, Julia. 2006. 24p. (J). *(978-0-9776835-0-5(8))* Run With Me Publishing.

—Little Drop of Water. 2007. 24p. (J). 15.00 *(978-0-9724272-4-1(4))* Katydid Publishing LLC.

Hergenroeder, Ernie (HERGIE). WHO Did It? WHO Created Earth & Heaven? Chatfield Ma, Cricket. 2019. (ENG.). 34p. (J). 22.95 *(978-1-64300-839-4(0))*; pap. 13.95 *(978-1-64300-838-7(2))* Covenant Bks.

Hergenrother, Max. Tomorrow Is the First Day of School. MacDowell, Maureen. 2007. 32p. (J). 15.95 *(978-0-9791463-0-5(5))* Wading River Bks., LLC.

—Who Is Gloria Steinem? Fabiny, Sarah & Who HQ. 2014. (Who Was? Ser.). 112p. (J). (gr. 3-7). 5.99 *(978-0-448-48238-5(X)*, Penguin Workshop) Penguin Young Readers Group.

—Who Was Ernest Shackleton? Buckley, James, Jr. et al. 2013. (Who Was? Ser.). (ENG.). 112p. (J). (gr. 3-7). 5.99 *(978-0-448-47931-6(1)*, Penguin Workshop) Penguin Young Readers Group.

—Who Was Ernest Shackleton? Buckley, James, Jr. 2013. (Who Was... ? Ser.). (ENG.). (J). (gr. 3-7). lib. bdg. 16.60 *(978-1-68065-150-8(1))* Perfection Learning Corp.

—Who Was Queen Victoria? Gigliotti, Jim & Who HQ. 2014. (Who Was? Ser.). 112p. (J). (gr. 3-7). 5.99 *(978-0-448-48182-1(0)*, Penguin Workshop) Penguin Young Readers Group.

Herges, Connie. Grandma Lucy Feeds the Birds, 1 vol. Simonson, Lona Marie. 2009. 44p. pap. 24.95 *(978-1-60836-732-0(0))* America Star Bks.

—Noodles by Mcnoodle. Simonson, Lona. 2008. 28p. pap. 24.95 *(978-1-60441-644-2(0))* America Star Bks.

Herkert, Barbara. Birds in Your Backyard. 2004. (Sharing Nature with Children Book Ser.). 36p. (J). pap. 8.95 *(978-1-58469-025-2(9))*; 17.95 *(978-1-58469-026-9(7))* Dawn Pubns.

Herman, Scott. Wisdom for Young Hearts Volume 1 Wisdom's Foundation. Delea, Pattie. DeLea, Ray and Daniella, ed. 2011. 114p. pap. 20.00 *(978-1-61286-030-5(3))* Avid Readers Publishing Group.

Hermans, Delphine. Green Almonds: Letters from Palestine. Hermans, Anaële. 2018. (ENG.). 152p. pap. 19.99 *(978-1-941302-89-7(0)*, e52a0679-4e39-4931-bcbf-705889d77a50, Lion Forge) Oni Pr., Inc.

Hermanson, Kyle. Chicken Little, 1 vol. Jones, Christianne C. 2011. (My First Classic Story Ser.). (ENG.). 32p. (J). (gr. k-3). pap. 7.10 *(978-1-4048-7355-1(4)*, Picture Window Bks.) Capstone.

—Pollita Pequenita, 1 vol. Jones, Christianne C. Abello, Patricia, tr. 2006. (Read-It! Readers en Español: Cuentos Folclóricos Ser.).Tr. of Chicken Little. (SPA.). 32p. (J). (gr. k-3). 21.32 *(978-1-4048-1646-6(1)*, Picture Window Bks.) Capstone.

Hermelin, Aviva. Summer Vacation with the Grizzbears: Book 5 in the Animals Build Character Series. Hermelin, Aviva. Mazo, Chaim, ed. l.t. ed. 2017. (Animals Build Character Ser.: Vol. 5). (ENG.). (J). pap. 9.95 *(978-1-946124-06-7(0))* Mazo Pubs.

Hermes, Mary Sue. The 'Fridge Games. Harvey, Ken. 2003. (Life in the 'Fridge Ser.). (J). *(978-1-930093-20-1(9))* Brookfield Reader, Inc., The.

—The Leftovers. Harvey, Ken. 2003. (Life in the 'Fridge Ser.). (J). *(978-1-930093-21-8(7))* Brookfield Reader, Inc., The.

Herms, Matt, jt. illus. see Prasetya, Hendry.

Herms, Matt, jt. illus. see Stanley, Evan.

Hernandez, Adua. Dear Queens. Roach, Nastashia. 2018. (ENG.). (J). 12.45 *(978-1-62676-792-8(0)*, Melanin Origins, LLC) Grivante Pr.

Hernandez, Beatriz Gutierrez. Dreams from Many Rivers: A Hispanic History of the United States Told in Poems. Engle, Margarita. 2019. (ENG.). 208p. (J). 18.99 *(978-1-62779-531-9(6)*, 900153936, Holt, Henry & Co. Bks. For Young Readers) Holt, Henry & Co.

Hernandez, Bibi. Mary's Gift. Shaw, Sandra Anne. Rosales, Mary, tr. 2011. 12p. (J). (gr. k-3). pap. 1.00 *(978-0-946889-14-3(7))*; (gr. 1-6). mass mkt. 2.50 *(978-0-9668891-4-7(2))* Teach My Children Pubns.

Hernandez, Gabriel, et al. Creepy Creatures. Stine, R. L. 2006. (Goosebumps Graphic Novels Ser.: 1). (ENG.). 144p. (J). (gr. 4-7). pap. 9.99 *(978-0-439-84125-2(9)*, Graphix) Scholastic, Inc.

Hernandez, Gilbert & Mazzucchelli, David. Fairy Tale Comics: Classic Tales Told by Extraordinary Cartoonists. Various Authors. Duffy, Chris, ed. 2013. (ENG.). 128p. (J). (gr. 1-7). 22.99 *(978-1-59643-823-1(1)*, 900087403, First Second Bks.) Roaring Brook Pr.

Hernandez Gonzalez, Ana M. José, un Joven Como Tú. Hernandez Gonzalez, Ana M. Ortiz Bello, Frank J., ed. 2019. (SPA.). 42p. (J). pap. 15.00 *(978-1-881741-90-9(7))* Ediciones Eleos.

Hernandez, Jennifer & Breckel, Heather. Fallout Part 3. Flynn, Ian. 2019. (Sonic the Hedgehog Ser.). (ENG.). 24p. (J). (gr. 2-8). lib. bdg. 27.07 *(978-1-5321-4435-6(0)*, 33840, Graphic Novels) Spotlight.

Hernandez, Lea. Teen Titans GO! Vol. 3: Mumbo Jumble, Vol. 3. Fisch, Sholly. 2017. (ENG.). 128p. (J). (gr. 1-3). pap. 12.99 *(978-1-4012-6765-0(3))* DC Comics.

Hernandez, Lea & Austen, Chuck. Marvel Mangaverse: the Complete Collection. 2018. (ENG.). 392p. (YA). (gr. 8-17). pap. 34.99 *(978-1-302-90765-5(4))* Marvel Worldwide, Inc.

Hernandez, Lea & Corona, Jorge. Idol Hands & Cold Blooded. Fisch, Sholly & Hagan, Merrill. 2019. (DC Teen Titans Go! Ser.). (ENG.). 32p. (J). (gr. 2-6). lib. bdg. 21.93 *(978-1-4965-7994-2(1)*, 139825, Stone Arch Bks.) Capstone.

Hernandez, Lea, jt. illus. see Brizuela, Dario.

Hernandez, Lea, jt. illus. see Corona, Jorge.

Hernandez, Leeza. Bored Bella Learns about Fiction & Nonfiction, 1 vol. Donovan, Sandy. 2010. (In the Library). (ENG.). 24p. (J). (gr. k-4). lib. bdg. 27.32 *(978-1-4048-5758-2(3)*, Picture Window Bks.) Capstone.

—Did You Burp? How to Ask Questions (or Not!) Sayre, April Pulley. 2019. 32p. (J). (gr. -1-3). lib. bdg. 17.99 *(978-1-58089-737-2(1))* Charlesbridge Publishing, Inc.

—Eat Your Math Homework: Recipes for Hungry Minds. McCallum, Ann. 2011. (Eat Your Homework Ser.: 1). (ENG.). 48p. (J). (gr. 2-5). pap. 8.99 *(978-1-57091-780-6(9))* Charlesbridge Publishing, Inc.

—Eat Your Science Homework: Recipes for Inquiring Minds. McCallum, Ann. 2014. (Eat Your Homework Ser.: 2). 48p. (J). (gr. 2-5). 16.95 *(978-1-57091-298-6(X))* Charlesbridge Publishing, Inc.

—Eat Your U. S. History Homework: Recipes for Revolutionary Minds. McCallum, Ann. 2015. (Eat Your Homework Ser.: 3). 48p. (J). (gr. 2-5). lib. bdg. 15.95 *(978-1-57091-923-7(2))* Charlesbridge Publishing, Inc.

Hernandez, Leeza. Mia Mayhem & the Super Family Field Day. West, Kara. 2020. (Mia Mayhem Ser.: 9). (ENG.). 128p. (J). (gr. k-4). 17.99 ***(978-1-5344-7721-6(7))***; pap. 5.99 ***(978-1-5344-7720-9(9))*** Little Simon. (Little Simon).

Hernandez, Leeza. Mia Mayhem Breaks down Walls. West, Kara. 2019. (Mia Mayhem Ser.: 4). (ENG.). 128p. (J). (gr. k-4). 16.99 *(978-1-5344-4477-5(7))*; pap. 5.99 *(978-1-5344-4476-8(9))* Little Simon. (Little Simon).

—The Mia Mayhem Collection: Mia Mayhem Is a Superhero!; Mia Mayhem Learns to Fly!; Mia Mayhem vs. the Super Bully; Mia Mayhem Breaks down Walls. West, Kara. ed. 2019. (Mia Mayhem Ser.). (ENG.). 512p. (J). (gr. k-4). pap. 23.99 *(978-1-5344-4640-3(0)*, Little Simon) Little Simon.

Hernandez, Leeza. The Mia Mayhem Collection #2: Mia Mayhem Stops Time!; Mia Mayhem vs. the Mighty Robot; Mia Mayhem Gets X-Ray Specs; Mia Mayhem Steals the Show! West, Kara. ed. 2020. (Mia Mayhem Ser.). (ENG.). 512p. (J). (gr. k-4). pap. 23.99 ***(978-1-5344-6536-7(7)***, Little Simon) Little Simon.

Hernandez, Leeza. Mia Mayhem Gets X-Ray Specs. West, Kara. 2020. (Mia Mayhem Ser.: 7). (ENG.). 128p. (J). (gr. k-4). 16.99 *(978-1-5344-6101-7(9))*; pap. 5.99 *(978-1-5344-6100-0(0))* Little Simon. (Little Simon).

—Mia Mayhem Is a Superhero! West, Kara. 2018. (Mia Mayhem Ser.: 1). (ENG.). 128p. (J). (gr. k-4). 16.99 *(978-1-5344-3270-3(1))*; pap. 5.99 *(978-1-5344-3269-7(8))* Little Simon. (Little Simon).

—Mia Mayhem Learns to Fly! West, Kara. 2018. (Mia Mayhem Ser.: 2). (ENG.). 128p. (J). (gr. k-4). 16.99 *(978-1-5344-3273-4(6))*; pap. 5.99 *(978-1-5344-3272-7(8))* Little Simon. (Little Simon).

Hernandez, Leeza. Mia Mayhem Steals the Show! West, Kara. 2020. (Mia Mayhem Ser.: 8). (ENG.). 128p. (J). (gr. k-4). 17.99 ***(978-1-5344-6724-8(6))***; pap. 5.99 ***(978-1-5344-6723-1(8))*** Little Simon. (Little Simon).

Hernandez, Leeza. Mia Mayhem Stops Time! West, Kara. 2019. (Mia Mayhem Ser.: 5). (ENG.). 128p. (J). (gr. k-4). 16.99 *(978-1-5344-4943-5(4))*; pap. 5.99 *(978-1-5344-4942-8(6))* Little Simon. (Little Simon).

—Mia Mayhem vs. the Mighty Robot. West, Kara. 2019. (Mia Mayhem Ser.: 6). (ENG.). 128p. (J). (gr. k-4). 16.99 *(978-1-5344-4946-6(9))*; pap. 5.99 *(978-1-5344-4945-9(0))* Little Simon. (Little Simon).

—Mia Mayhem vs. the Super Bully. West, Kara. 2019. (Mia Mayhem Ser.: 3). (ENG.). 128p. (J). (gr. k-4). 16.99 *(978-1-5344-4474-4(2))*; pap. 5.99 *(978-1-5344-4473-7(4))* Little Simon. (Little Simon).

—Never Play Music Right Next to the Zoo. Lithgow, John. 2013. (ENG.). 40p. (J). (gr. -1-1). 19.99 *(978-1-4424-6743-9(6)*, Simon & Schuster Bks. For Young Readers) Simon & Schuster Bks. For Young Readers.

—This Is the Day! Parker, Amy. 2018. (ENG.). 32p. (J). (gr. -1-3). 16.99 *(978-1-338-04703-5(5)*, Orchard Bks.) Scholastic, Inc.

—This Is the Day! / ¡Este Es el Día! Parker, Amy. 2018. (SPA & ENG.). 32p. (J). (gr. -1-3). 16.99 *(978-1-338-05038-7(9)*, Scholastic en Espanol) Scholastic, Inc.

Hernandez, Macario. The Legend of Sassafras House. Stafford, Anita. King-Morgan, Kristi, ed. 2018. (ENG.). 116p. (J). pap. 8.00 *(978-1-947381-08-7(3))* Dreaming Big Pubns.

Hernández, Mar. Once upon a Star. Carter, James. 2018. (ENG.). 32p. (J). (gr. -1-2). 17.99 *(978-0-525-57933-5(8)*, Doubleday Bks. for Young Readers) Random Hse. Children's Bks.

Hernandez, Purificacion. Bamboo for Me, Bamboo for You! Manushkin, Fran. 2017. (ENG.). 32p. (J). (gr. -1-3). 17.99 *(978-1-4814-5063-8(8)*, Aladdin) Simon & Schuster Children's Publishing.

Hernández, René Mario. Vidas Desesperadas. Mederos, Miriam. 2004. (SPA.). 106p. (YA). pap. 15.00 *(978-1-931481-39-7(3))* LiArt-Literature & Art.

Hernandez, Rick & Rhino, Black. Dinosaur - Coloring & Activity Book - Volume 3: A Coloring Book for Kids & Adults. Zoo, Abc. 2019. (Volume Ser.: Vol. 3). (ENG.). 114p. (J). pap. 6.97 ***(978-1-6862-0521-7(X))*** Independently Published.

Hernandez, Sarah, jt. illus. see RH Disney Staff.

Hernandez, Stacy. Welcome to Humming Meadow Ranch. Hernandez, Elaine. 2005. 28p. (J). lib. bdg. 16.95 *(978-0-9766431-0-4(3))* Humming Meadow Ranch.

Hernandez, Stephanie. The Turtle & the Universe, Vol. Whitt, Stephen. 2008. (ENG.). 86p. (gr. 3-7). pap. 14.99 *(978-1-59102-626-6(1))* Prometheus Bks., Pubs.

Hernandez, Steven. City Dancin' Dancin' at Peppy's. Berton, Judy. 2004. 36p. (J). per. 16.95 *(978-0-9761051-0-7(1))* Kidrich Corp.

Hernandez, Tino Santanach. Uncle Scrooge #355. Korhonen, Kari et al. Clark, John, ed. 2006. (ENG.). 64p. pap. 6.95 *(978-1-888472-24-0(3)*, 9781888472240) Gemstone Publishing, Inc.

Hernandez, Wanda Y. The Lost Pumpkin's Halloween Adventure: Adapted from the Lost Son Parable from the Gospel of Luke. Hernandez, Wanda Y. 2018. (ENG.). 38p. (J). pap. 15.00 *(978-0-692-16936-0(9))* W&D Parables.

Hernando, Saeta. Juan Silbador en la Copa de un Pino. 2018. (SPA.). 48p. (J). (gr. 2-4). pap. 11.00 *(978-607-8469-43-7(6))* Nostra Ediciones MEX. Dist: Independent Pubs. Group.

Hernden, Anjonette. School Wasn't Always Awesome. Treisch, Justin. 2019. (ENG.). 38p. (J). pap. 20.99 ***(978-1-7283-3897-2(2))*** AuthorHouse.

Herold, Lee Adam. Thunderous Applause. Greene, Thomas. 2020. (ENG.). 24p. (J). pap. 12.95 ***(978-1-4808-9014-5(6))*** Archway Publishing.

Heroldt, Richard. He's Risen! He's Alive! Bader, Joanne. 2003. (Arch Bks.). (ENG.). 16p. (J). 1.99 *(978-0-570-07583-7(1))* Concordia Publishing Hse.

Herpin, K. K. Katrina & the Rinky-Dink Sewing Machine. Riebel, Jessica Mire. 2008. 32p. pap. 24.95 *(978-1-60813-545-5(4))* America Star Bks.

Herr, Tad. Germs. Oetting, Judy. (Rookie Ready to Learn: First Science — Me & My World Ser.). (ENG.). (J). 2011. 40p. (gr. -1-1). lib. bdg. 18.69 *(978-0-531-26500-0(5)*, Children's Pr.); 2011. 40p. (gr. -1-k). pap. 5.95 *(978-0-531-26732-5(6)*, Children's Pr.); 2006. 32p. (gr. k-2). pap. 4.95 *(978-0-516-24995-7(9))* Scholastic Library Publishing.

Herrenberger, Marcus. Little Rabbit Has Friends. Herrenberger, Marcus. 2018. (ENG.). 32p. (J). (gr. k-2). 17.99 *(978-988-8341-09-2(X)*, Minedition) Neugebauer, Michael (Publishing) Limited HKG. Dist: Penguin Random Hse. LLC.

Herrera, Aaron. Brown Girl, Brown Girl, Hasn't Anyone? Jeanmarie, Michele. 2020. (ENG.). 38p. (J). pap. ***(978-1-78830-526-6(4))*** Olympia Publishers.

Herrera, Aaron Jeremiah, jt. illus. see McGhee, Katie Mariah.

Herrera, Ben, et al. Adventures of the X-Men: Clear & Present Dangers. 2019. (ENG.). 176p. (J). (gr. 1-3). pap. 12.99 *(978-1-302-91796-8(X))* Marvel Worldwide, Inc.

Herrera, Danko. Hockey Wars 4: Championships. Lawrence, Sam & Jackson, Ben. 2019. (Hockey Wars Ser.: Vol. 4). (ENG.). (J). 168p. 21.99 ***(978-1-988656-35-9(4))***; 136p. pap. 10.99 ***(978-1-988656-34-2(6))*** Indie Publishing Group.

—Hockey Wars 5: Lacrosse Wars. Lawrence, Sam & Jackson, Ben. 2020. (ENG.). 134p. (J). 21.99 ***(978-1-988656-37-3(0))***; (Hockey Wars Ser.: Vol. 5). pap. 10.99 ***(978-1-988656-36-6(2))*** Indie Publishing Group.

Herrera, Diego - Yayo. The Mysterious Stones. Pérez Díaz, Enrique. Ruiz, Alina, tr. 2020. (ENG.). 32p. (J). 17.95 ***(978-1-62371-869-5(4)***, Crocodile Bks.) Interlink Publishing Group, Inc.

Herrera, Juan Felipe. Jabberwalking. Herrera, Juan Felipe. 2018. 144p. (J). (gr. 5). 22.99 *(978-1-5362-0140-6(5))*; pap. 14.99 *(978-0-7636-9264-3(6))* Candlewick Pr.

Herrera, Juan Felipe & Cuevas, Ernesto. Featherless, 1 vol. ed. 2013.Tr. of Desplumado. (ENG & SPA.). 32p. (J). (gr. k-3). pap. 10.95 *(978-0-89239-303-9(3)*, 050f9da4-f798-4483-a4a9-3923bfd1bb2f) Lee & Low Bks., Inc.

Herrera, Velino. In My Mother's House. Clark, Ann Nolan. 2004. 56p. (J). (gr. k-3). reprint ed. pap. 14.00 *(978-0-7567-7104-1(8))* DIANE Publishing Co.

Herrerias, Alex. When Cesar Chavez Climbed the Umbrella Tree. Hanel, Rachael. 2019. (Leaders Doing Headstands Ser.). (ENG.). 32p. (J). (gr. 1-4). lib. bdg. 28.65 *(978-1-5158-3042-9(X)*, 138682, Picture Window Bks.) Capstone.

Herrero, Oscar. Socal So Cool: Travel Book. Rector, Ryan Ashley & Rector, Clarence A. 2017. (ENG.). (J). (gr. k-6). 17.99 *(978-0-9969085-5-9(2))* Rector Tales.

Herrick, Cynthia Ramirez. How Grace Became Amazing. Reckert-Reusing, Sandy. 2017. (ENG.). (J). 15.95 *(978-1-63505-574-0(1))* Salem Author Services.

Herrick, Mark. Buck Wilder's Animal Wisdom. Smith, Tim. 2006. 32p. (J). (gr. 3-7). *(978-1-934133-02-6(7)*, 1269518, Mackinac Island Press, Inc.) Charlesbridge Publishing, Inc.

Herrick, Mark J. Core Democratic Values with Rock U. S. A. Stephens, Edna Cucksey. 2004. (Connect-It Ser.). 62p. (J). (gr. -1-3). pap. 24.95 *(978-0-9749412-0-2(4))* EDCO Publishing, Inc.

—Lost in the Woods: A Photographic Fantasy. Sams, Carl R., II & Stoick, Jean. 2005. (Connect-It Ser.). 68p. (J). (gr. -1-3). pap. 24.95 *(978-0-9749412-2-6(0))* EDCO Publishing, Inc.

—Rock U. S. A. & the American Way! A Freedom Handbook. Stephens, Edna Cucksey. 2004. (Connect-It Ser.). 124p. (J). (gr. -1-3). pap. 29.95 *(978-0-9749412-1-9(2))* EDCO Publishing, Inc.

Herridge, Debbie. Milly's Magic Play House: The Hospital, 1 vol. Wakem, Samantha. 2010. 20p. 24.95 *(978-1-4489-5114-7(3))* PublishAmerica, Inc.

Herring, Aimée & Herring, Aimée, photos by. Holiday Crafting & Baking with Kids: Gifts, Sweets, & Treats for the Whole Family. Strand, Jessica. 2011. (ENG., 128p. (gr. 13-17). pap. 19.95 *(978-1-4521-0109-5(4))* Chronicle Bks. LLC.

Herring, Aimée, jt. photos by see Herring, Aimée.

Herring, Carol. Duck Sees the Rain. Gates, Margo. 2019. (Let's Look at Weather (Pull Ahead Readers — Fiction) Ser.). (ENG.). 16p. (J). (gr. -1-1). 22.65 *(978-1-5415-5839-7(1)*, 9781541558397, Lerner Pubns.) Lerner Publishing Group.

—A Good Nut. Gates, Margo. 2019. (Let's Look at Animal Habitats (Pull Ahead Readers — Fiction) Ser.). (ENG.). 16p. (J). (gr. -1-1). 22.65 *(978-1-5415-5865-6(0)*, 9781541558656, Lerner Pubns.) Lerner Publishing Group.

Herring, Carol. If It's Christmas & You Know It. Eliot, Hannah. 2020. (ENG.). 16p. (J). (gr. -1). bds. 6.99 ***(978-1-5344-7578-6(8)***, Little Simon) Little Simon.

Herring, Carol. Mia Can See Patterns. Gates, Margo. 2019. (Science All Around Me (Pull Ahead Readers — Fiction) Ser.). (ENG.). 16p. (J). (gr. -1-1). pap. 6.99 *(978-1-5415-7334-5(X)*, 9781541573345, Lerner Pubns.) Lerner Publishing Group.

—Writing a Biography. Minden, Cecilia. 2020. (Write It Right Ser.). (ENG.). 24p. (J). (gr. 1-4). pap. 12.79 *(978-1-5341-6129-0(5)*, 214516); lib. bdg. 28.50 *(978-1-5341-5899-3(5)*, 214515) Cherry Lake Publishing.

—Writing a Blog. Minden, Cecilia. 2019. (Write It Right Ser.). (ENG.). 24p. (J). (gr. 1-4). pap. 12.79 *(978-1-5341-5004-1(8)*, 213323); lib. bdg. 28.50 *(978-1-5341-4718-8(7)*, 213322) Cherry Lake Publishing.

—Writing a Business Letter. Minden, Cecilia. 2020. (Write It Right Ser.). (ENG.). 24p. (J). (gr. 1-4). pap. 12.79 *(978-1-5341-6130-6(9)*, 214520); lib. bdg. 28.50 *(978-1-5341-5900-6(2)*, 214519) Cherry Lake Publishing.

—Writing a Comic Book. Minden, Cecilia. 2019. (Write It Right Ser.). (ENG.). 24p. (J). (gr. 1-4). pap. 12.79 *(978-1-5341-5007-2(2)*, 213335); lib. bdg. 28.50 *(978-1-5341-4721-8(7)*, 213334) Cherry Lake Publishing.

—Writing a Fairy Tale. Minden, Cecilia. 2020. (Write It Right Ser.). (ENG.). 24p. (J). (gr. 1-4). pap. 12.79 *(978-1-5341-6131-3(7)*, 214524); lib. bdg. 28.50 *(978-1-5341-5901-3(0)*, 214523) Cherry Lake Publishing.

—Writing a Fractured Fairy Tale. Minden, Cecilia. 2020. (Write It Right Ser.). (ENG.). 24p. (J). (gr. 1-4). pap. 12.79 *(978-1-5341-6132-0(5)*, 214528); lib. bdg. 28.50 *(978-1-5341-5902-0(9)*, 214527) Cherry Lake Publishing.

—Writing a Journal. Minden, Cecilia. 2019. (Write It Right Ser.). (ENG.). 24p. (J). (gr. 1-4). pap. 12.79 *(978-1-5341-5003-4(X)*, 213319); lib. bdg. 28.50 *(978-1-5341-4717-1(9)*, 213318) Cherry Lake Publishing.

—Writing a Lab Report. Minden, Cecilia. 2020. (Write It Right Ser.). (ENG.). 24p. (J). (gr. 1-4). pap. 12.79 *(978-1-5341-6133-7(3)*, 214532); lib. bdg. 28.50 *(978-1-5341-5903-7(7)*, 214531) Cherry Lake Publishing.

—Writing a Letter. Minden, Cecilia. 2019. (Write It Right Ser.). (ENG.). 24p. (J). (gr. 1-4). pap. 12.79 *(978-1-5341-5001-0(3)*, 213311); lib. bdg. 28.50 *(978-1-5341-4715-7(2)*, 213310) Cherry Lake Publishing.

—Writing a Memoir. Minden, Cecilia. 2020. (Write It Right Ser.). (ENG.). 24p. (J). (gr. 1-4). pap. 12.79 *(978-1-5341-6134-4(1)*, 214536); lib. bdg. 28.50 *(978-1-5341-5904-4(5)*, 214535) Cherry Lake Publishing.

—Writing a Mystery. Minden, Cecilia. 2020. (Write It Right Ser.). (ENG.). 24p. (J). (gr. 1-4). pap. 12.79 *(978-1-5341-6135-1(X)*, 214540); lib. bdg. 28.50 *(978-1-5341-5905-1(3)*, 214539) Cherry Lake Publishing.

—Writing a News Article. Minden, Cecilia. 2019. (Write It Right Ser.). (ENG.). 24p. (J). (gr. 1-4). pap. 12.79 *(978-1-5341-5008-9(0)*, 213339); lib. bdg. 28.50 *(978-1-5341-4722-5(5)*, 213338) Cherry Lake Publishing.

—Writing a Review. Minden, Cecilia. 2020. (Write It Right Ser.). (ENG.). 24p. (J). (gr. 1-4). pap. 12.79 *(978-1-5341-6136-8(8)*, 214544); lib. bdg. 28.50 *(978-1-5341-5906-8(1)*, 214543) Cherry Lake Publishing.

—Writing a Thank-You Letter. Minden, Cecilia. 2019. (Write It Right Ser.). (ENG.). 24p. (J). (gr. 1-4). pap. 12.79 *(978-1-5341-5006-5(4)*, 213331); lib. bdg. 28.50 *(978-1-5341-4720-1(9)*, 213330) Cherry Lake Publishing.

—Writing an Essay. Minden, Cecilia. 2019. (Write It Right Ser.). (ENG.). 24p. (J). (gr. 1-4). pap. 12.79 *(978-1-5341-5005-8(6)*, 213327); lib. bdg. 28.50 *(978-1-5341-4719-5(5)*, 213326) Cherry Lake Publishing.

—Writing an Interview. Minden, Cecilia. 2019. (Write It Right Ser.). (ENG.). 24p. (J). (gr. 1-4). pap. 12.79 *(978-1-5341-5002-7(1)*, 213315); lib. bdg. 28.50 *(978-1-5341-4716-4(0)*, 213314) Cherry Lake Publishing.

Herring, M. L. Ellie's Log: Exploring the Forest Where the Great Tree Fell. Li, Judith L. 2013. (ENG.). 112p. (J). (gr. 3-6). pap. 17.95 *(978-0-87071-696-6(4))* Oregon State Univ. Pr.

Herrington, Taylor. The Fox Went Out on a Chilly Night. Feierabend, John. 2020. (First Steps in Music Ser.). (ENG.). 32p. (J). (gr. -1-k). 17.95 ***(978-1-62277-435-7(3))*** G I A Pubns., Inc.

Herrod, Mike. Why Did the Farmer Cross the Road? James, Brooke Herter. 2017. (ENG.). 32p. (J). (gr. k-2). 16.99 *(978-1-58536-963-8(2)*, 204224) Sleeping Bear Pr.

Herron, Carolivia, photos by. Little Georgia & the Apples: A Retelling of Aunt Georgia's First Catalpa Tale. Herron, Carolivia, told to. I.t. ed. 2004. 33p. (J). 10.00 *(978-0-9760222-0-6(6)*, Catalpa01) Epicenter Literary Software.

Herron, D. J. The Fox Wife. Deer, Beatrice. 2019. (ENG.). 40p. (J). 16.95 *(978-1-77227-212-3(4))* Inhabit Media Inc. CAN. Dist: Consortium Bk. Sales & Distribution.

Herron, Dorothy. The Butterfly Adventure. Lorraine, Nancy. 2nd ed. 2013. 50p. 22.50 *(978-0-9886194-9-4(0))* ProsePress.

—Tatty, the Lonely Monarch. Lorraine, Nancy. 2013. 48p. pap. 17.50 *(978-0-9893063-8-6(0))* ProsePress.

Herron, Mark. Balancing the Energy Equation: One Step at a Time! Lombardo, Michelle. 2003. (J). lib. bdg. 17.95 *(978-1-931212-51-9(1))* OrganWise Guys Inc., The.

—The OrganWise Guys Pepto's Place Activity Book. Lombardo, Michelle. 2003. (J). pap., act. bk. ed. 4.95 *(978-1-931212-52-6(X))* OrganWise Guys Inc., The.

—Pepto's Place: Where Every Portion Size Is OrganWise! Lombardo, Michelle. 2003. 32p. (J). lib. bdg. 17.95 *(978-1-931212-50-2(3))* OrganWise Guys Inc., The.

Hersey, Bob. Birds of Prey. Legg, Gerald. 2004. (Scary Creatures Ser.). (ENG.). 32p. (J). (gr. 2-4). pap. 6.95 *(978-0-531-16747-2(X)*, Watts, Franklin) Scholastic Library Publishing.

—Little Red Riding Hood. Skevington, Andrea. 2003. 48p. (J). *(978-0-439-57189-0(8))* Scholastic, Inc.

—Norman Rockwell: A Pop-Up Art Experience. 2004. 6p. (J). (gr. k-4). reprint ed. 19.00 *(978-0-7567-7642-8(2))* DIANE Publishing Co.

—Wolves. Clarke, Penny. 2004. (Scary Creatures Ser.). (ENG.). 32p. (J). (gr. 2-4). pap. 6.95 *(978-0-531-16749-6(6)*, Watts, Franklin) Scholastic Library Publishing.

Hersey, John. Amazing Space. Prinja, Raman. 2019. (ENG.). 48p. (J). (gr. 2-4). 19.99 *(978-1-78312-393-3(1))* Carlton Bks., Ltd. GBR. Dist: Two Rivers Distribution.

Hershey, Allison. Adventures with Zap: 107 Creative Prompts for Beginning Writers — For Earthlings Ages 4 & Up. Landy, Diane. 2018. (ENG.). 128p. (gr. -1-3). pap. 10.95 *(978-1-61519-441-4(X)*, 779441) Experiment LLC, The.

Hershey, Kurt. Can I. Nagra, Jessie. 2020. (ENG.). 36p. (J). ***(978-1-5255-6337-9(8))***; pap. ***(978-1-5255-6338-6(6))*** FriesenPress.

—Sprinkles. Stempel, Kate. 2019. (ENG.). 56p. (J). (gr. 2-6). ***(978-1-5255-3554-3(4))***; pap. ***(978-1-5255-3555-0(2))*** FriesenPress.

Hertling, Heiner. A Pirate's Quest: For His Family Heirloom Peg Leg. Sams, Laura & Sams, Robert. 2008. 48p. (J). 19.95 *(978-0-9770108-7-5(2))* Sams, II, Carl R. Photography, Inc.

Hertzler, Frances, et al. No Darkness at All: An Adaptation of Patricia St. John's Star of Light. St. John, Patricia et al. 2005. 56p. (J). pap. *(978-1-933206-14-1(4)*, 5340) Bible Visuals International, Inc.

Hertzler, Frances & Olson, Ed. The Inspiration of the Scriptures: New Testament Volume 33: 1 & 2 Timothy, Titus, Philemon. Lyster, R. Iona et al. 2004. 34p. (J). pap. *(978-1-932381-05-4(8)*, 1033) Bible Visuals International, Inc.

Hertzler, Frances B. & Ober, Jonathan. The Eternal God Vol. 1: New Testament. 2004. 36p. (J). pap. *(978-1-932381-03-0(1)*, 1001) Bible Visuals International, Inc.

Hertzler, Frances H.. Christian Joy: New Testament Volume 30. Habecker, Marilyn P. 2014. 36p. (J). pap. *(978-1-932381-27-6(9)*, 1030) Bible Visuals International, Inc.

—Doming the Popsicle Boy: A Story of the Philippines. Carvin, Rose-Mae. 2010. (ENG.). 68p. (J). spiral bd. *(978-1-932381-11-5(2)*, 5100) Bible Visuals International, Inc.

Hertzler, Frances H.., et al. Faith Volume 5: New Testament. Greiner, Ruth B. 2004. 36p. (J). pap. *(978-1-932381-36-8(8))* Bible Visuals International, Inc.

Hertzler, Frances H.. The Resurrection of Christ Vol. 14: Death Conquered! NT Volume 13 Life of Christ Part 13. Greiner, Ruth B. 2012. 36p. (J). pap. *(978-1-932381-43-6(0)*, 1013) Bible Visuals International, Inc.

Hertzler, Frances H.., et al. The Saviour Vol. 3: New Testament Volume 3: the Life of Christ Part 3: Everybody Needs Jesus. Greiner, Ruth B. 2004. (ENG.). 36p. (J). pap. *(978-1-932381-02-3(3)*, 1003) Bible Visuals International, Inc.

—Sin Vol. 4: New Testament Volume 4, Life of Christ, Part 4. Greiner, Ruth B. et al. 2005. 36p. (J). pap. *(978-1-932381-23-8(6)*, 1004) Bible Visuals International, Inc.

Hertzler, Frances H.. & Olson, Ed. GOD His Son, His Book, His Home: New Testament Introductory Volume. Greiner, Ruth B. et al. 2004. 32p. (J). pap. *(978-1-932381-35-1(X)*, 1000) Bible Visuals International, Inc.

Hertzler, Frances H.., jt. illus. see Henkel, Vernon.

Herzlich, Valori. I Have a Grandma Who ... Zibart, Rosemary. 2014. (J). *(978-1-929115-25-9(3))* Azro Pr., Inc.

Herzner, Alisha. Unsere Welt und Ihre Sprachen: Alisha Herzner. Herzner, Alisha. 2018. (GER.). 26p. (J). pap. 6.33 *(978-1-7228-1189-1(7))* CreateSpace Independent Publishing Platform.

Herzog, Inge. Animal Island. Shue, Jenna. 2005. 27p. (J). (gr. -1-3). per. 14.95 *(978-1-4259-0039-7(9))* AuthorHouse.

Herzog, Jonathan. Ninja Birds! McFadden, Sheree. 2019. (ENG.). 26p. (J). (gr. 1-6). pap. 9.99 ***(978-0-578-57784-5(4))*** McFadden, Sheree.

Heschke, Elena. Hair Care Tips & Tricks. Hunt, Sara R. & Kenney, Karen Latchana. 2015. (Style Secrets Ser.). (ENG.). 32p. (J). (gr. 4-8). lib. bdg. 26.65 *(978-1-4677-5218-3(5)*, 9781467752183, Lerner Pubns.) Lerner Publishing Group.

—Hair Care Tips & Tricks. Kenney, Karen Latchana. ed. 2015. (Style Secrets Ser.). (ENG.). 32p. (J). (gr. 4-8). E-Book 39.99 *(978-1-4677-8653-9(5)*, Lerner Pubns.) Lerner Publishing Group.

—Jewelry Tips & Tricks. Berne, Emma Carlson. 2015. (Style Secrets Ser.). (ENG.). 32p. (J). (gr. 4-8). lib. bdg. 26.65 *(978-1-4677-5220-6(7)*, 9781467752206, Lerner Pubns.) Lerner Publishing Group.

—Jewelry Tips & Tricks. Carlson-Berne, Emma. ed. 2015. (Style Secrets Ser.). (ENG.). 32p. (J). (gr. 4-8). E-Book 39.99 *(978-1-4677-8654-6(3)*, Lerner Pubns.) Lerner Publishing Group.

—Nail Care Tips & Tricks. Berne, Emma Carlson. 2015. (Style Secrets Ser.). (ENG.). 32p. (J). (gr. 4-8). lib. bdg. 26.65 *(978-1-4677-5221-3(5)*, 9781467752213, Lerner Pubns.) Lerner Publishing Group.

—Nail Care Tips & Tricks. Carlson-Berne, Emma. ed. 2015. (Style Secrets Ser.). (ENG.). 32p. (J). (gr. 4-8). E-Book 39.99 *(978-1-4677-8655-3(1)*, Lerner Pubns.) Lerner Publishing Group.

—Skin Care & Makeup Tips & Tricks. Kenney, Karen Latchana. ed. 2015. (Style Secrets Ser.). (ENG.). 32p. (J). (gr. 4-8). E-Book 39.99 *(978-1-4677-8656-0(X)*, Lerner Pubns.) Lerner Publishing Group.

Heshka, Ryan. Welcome to Monster Town. Heshka, Ryan. 2012. (ENG.). 32p. (J). (gr. -1-1). 18.69 *(978-1-250-00405-5(5))* Square Fish.

Hess, Ann. The Silly Adventures of Petunia & Herman the Worm. Baker, Sam. 2018. (ENG.). 108p. (J). (gr. 1-6). pap. 21.00 *(978-0-9996603-4-8(9))* Happy Publishing.

Hess, Erwin L. Convoy Patrol: A Thrilling Story of the U. S. Navy. Winterbotham, R. R. 2011. 426p. 56.95 *(978-1-258-01444-5(0))* Literary Licensing, LLC.

—Roy Rogers: Robin Hood of the Range. Gruskin, Edward I. 2011. 420p. 54.95 *(978-1-258-04369-8(6))* Literary Licensing, LLC.

Hess, Ingrid. The Family Song. Peifer, Jane Hoober. 2008. 64p. (J). (gr. -1-3). pap. 18.99 incl. audio compact disk *(978-0-8361-9414-2(4))* Herald Pr.

—Knitting Knights: Beyond the Sounds of ABC. Eide, Denise. 2017. (J). *(978-1-942154-14-3(3))* Logic of English, Inc.

—Praying with Our Feet. Weaver, Lisa D. 2005. 40p. (J). pap. 12.99 *(978-0-8361-9306-0(7))* Herald Pr.

—Whistling Whales: Beyond the Sounds of ABC. Eide, Denise. 2017. (J). *(978-1-942154-13-6(5))* Logic of English, Inc.

Hess, Justin. Chip's Stories of Imagination & Adventure Volume 5: Chip Is a Six Year Old Boy with Too Much Imagination. Wartell, Jules. Pearlman, Judith, ed. 2019. (Chip's Stories of Imagination & Adventure Ser.: Vol. 5). (ENG.). 30p. (J). pap. 9.95 *(978-1-7278-9398-4(0))* CreateSpace Independent Publishing Platform.

Hess, Mark. When Mr. Jefferson Came to Philadelphia: What I Learned of Freedom 1776. Turner, Ann Warren. 2004. 32p. (J). (gr. -1-3). 15.99 *(978-0-06-027579-2(0))* HarperCollins Pubs.

H

Hess, Paul. Amethyst. Lisle, Rebecca. 2007. (ENG.). 176p. (J). (gr. 4-7). per. 8.99 *(978-1-84270-541-4(5))* Andersen Pr. GBR. Dist: Independent Pubs. Group.

—The Ghosts Who Danced: And Other Spooky Stories. Pirotta, Saviour. 2015. (ENG.). 64p. (J). (gr. 1-5). 22.99 *(978-1-84780-435-8(7)*, Frances Lincoln Children's Bks.) Quarto Publishing Group UK GBR. Dist: Hachette Bk. Group.

—The King with Horse's Ears. Maddern, Eric. 2003. (ENG.). 36p. (J). *(978-0-7112-1957-1(5))* ReiseArt Buchhandlung GmbH.

—The Pig in a Wig. MacDonald, Alan. 2003. 32p. (J). (gr. k-3). pap. 6.95 *(978-1-56145-299-6(8)*, Q32523) Peachtree Publishing Co. Inc.

—Rainforest Animals. 2003. (Animals Ser.). 24p. (J). pap. *(978-1-84089-172-0(6))* Zero to Ten, Ltd.

Hess, Paul. Farmyard Animals. Hess, Paul. 2009. (Animal Verse Ser.). (ENG.). 24p. (J). (gr. -1-k). pap. *(978-1-84089-559-9(4))* Zero to Ten, Ltd.

—Polar Animals. Hess, Paul. 2009. (Animal Verse Ser.). (ENG.). 24p. (J). (gr. -1-k). pap. *(978-1-84089-561-2(6))* Zero to Ten, Ltd.

—Rainforest Animals. Hess, Paul. 2009. (Animal Verse Ser.). (ENG.). 24p. (J). (gr. -1-k). pap. *(978-1-84089-560-5(8))* Zero to Ten, Ltd.

—Safari Animals. Hess, Paul. 2009. (Animal Verse Ser.). (ENG.). 24p. (J). (gr. -1-k). pap. *(978-1-84089-562-9(4))* Zero to Ten, Ltd.

Hesselbein, Kent, jt. illus. see Hall, Dee.

Hesselbein, Kent, jt. illus. see Warren, David Michael.

Hesselberth, Joyce. Mapping Sam. Hesselberth, Joyce. 2018. (ENG.). 40p. (J). (gr. -1-3). 17.99 *(978-0-06-274122-6(5)*, Greenwillow Bks.) HarperCollins Pubs.

—Pitter Pattern. Hesselberth, Joyce. 2020. (ENG.). 40p. (J). (gr. -1-3). 17.99 *(978-0-06-274123-3(3)*, Greenwillow Bks.) HarperCollins Pubs.

—Shape Shift. Hesselberth, Joyce. 2016. (ENG.). 32p. (J). 16.99 *(978-1-62779-057-4(8)*, 900132836, Holt, Henry & Co. Bks. For Young Readers) Holt, Henry & Co.

Heston, Charles. The True Book of Indians. Martini, Teri. 2011. 48p. 35.95 *(978-1-258-05468-7(X))* Literary Licensing, LLC.

Hetherington, Jan. Where's Pa? Hetherington, Sally. 2013. 28p. pap. 15.97 *(978-1-62516-299-1(5)*, Strategic Bk. Publishing) Strategic Book Publishing & Rights Agency (SBPRA).

Hetland, Beth. Mapping & Navigation: Explore the History & Science of Finding Your Way with 20 Projects. Brown, Cynthia Light & McGinty, Patrick. 2013. (Build It Yourself Ser.). 128p. (J). (gr. 3-7). 21.95 *(978-1-61930-194-8(6)*, ede54b80-cd85-4d9f-af0e-381fafe63114); pap. 16.95 *(978-1-61930-198-6(9)*, 36b79fb3-ad85-45e5-8784-fc6ed44cb32a) Nomad Pr.

—Native Americans: Discover the History & Cultures of the First Americans with 15 Projects. Kavin, Kim. 2013. (Build It Yourself Ser.). 128p. (J). (gr. 3-7). 21.95 *(978-1-61930-175-7(X)*, 77ad7416-030b-4eb9-9c4a-9fd3d43cb229); pap. 16.95 *(978-1-61930-170-2(9)*, 32e90524-639f-4e84-8430-215ed1772dba) Nomad Pr.

Hetmerová, Alexandra. How Things Are Made. Ruzicka, Oldrich. 2016. (ENG.). 36p. (J). (gr. 1-5). 16.95 *(978-1-4549-2085-4(8))* Sterling Publishing Co., Inc.

Heuer, Christoph. Lola & Fred & Tom. 2007. (Lola & Fred Ser.). (ENG.). 48p. (J). (gr. -1-3). 15.95 *(978-0-9741319-9-3(7))* 4N Publishing LLC.

Heuninck, Ronald. Rain or Shine, 1 vol. Heuninck, Ronald. Orig. Title: Buiten Spelen. (ENG.). 12p. (J). 5.50 *(978-0-86315-089-0(6)*, 20269) Floris Bks. GBR. Dist: Gryphon Hse., Inc.

Heuvel, Eric. A Family Secret. Heuvel, Eric. Miller, Lorraine T. Miller, Lorraine T., tr. 2009. (ENG.). 64p. (J). (gr. 5-8). 26.19 *(978-0-374-42265-3(6)*, 900057558, Farrar, Straus & Giroux) Farrar, Straus & Giroux.

—The Search. Heuvel, Eric. van der Rol, Ruud et al. Miller, Lorraine T., tr. from ENG. 2009. (ENG.). 64p. (J). (gr. 4-8). pap. 17.99 *(978-0-374-46455-4(3)*, 900057560, Farrar, Straus & Giroux (BYR)) Farrar, Straus & Giroux.

Hevron, Amy. Moon Babies. Jameson, Karen. 2019. 32p. (J). (-k). 16.99 *(978-0-525-51481-7(3)*, G.P. Putnam's Sons Books for Young Readers) Penguin Young Readers Group.

—Trevor. Averbeck, Jim. 2018. (ENG.). 40p. (J). 17.99 *(978-1-250-14828-5(6)*, 900181911) Roaring Brook Pr.

Hewetson, N. J. Planes, Rockets — And Other — Flying Machines. Graham, Ian & Salariya, David. 2014. (Time Shift Speed Ser.). 32p. (gr. 3-6). 31.35 *(978-1-908973-95-5(1))* Book Hse. GBR. Dist: Black Rabbit Bks.

—Super Bikes. Graham, Ian & Salariya, David. 2014. (Time Shift Speed Ser.). 32p. (gr. 3-6). 31.35 *(978-1-908973-96-2(X))* Book Hse. GBR. Dist: Black Rabbit Bks.

Hewetson, N. J., jt. illus. see Bergin, Mark.

Hewetson, Nicholas J. The Usborne Book of World Religions. Meredith, Susan. Evans, Cheryl, ed. 2006. (World Religions (Usborne) Ser.). 64p. (J). (gr. 5). lib. bdg. 17.99 *(978-1-58086-908-9(4)*, Usborne) EDC Publishing.

Hewetson, Nicholas J. & Gower, Jeremy. The Usborne Book of World Religions. Meredith, Susan. Evans, Cheryl, ed. rev. ed. 2006. (World Cultures Ser.). 64p. (J). (gr. 5). pap. 9.99 *(978-0-7945-1027-5(2))* EDC Publishing.

Hewetson, Nick. Dinosaurs. Stewart, David. 2013. (World of Wonder Ser.). (ENG.). 32p. (gr. 1-3). lib. bdg. 31.35 *(978-1-908973-98-6(6))* Book Hse. GBR. Dist: Black Rabbit Bks.

—Dinosaurs. Stewart, David. 2008. (World of Wonder Ser.). (ENG.). 32p. (J). (gr. 1-4). 29.00 *(978-0-531-20450-4(2)*, Children's Pr.) Scholastic Library Publishing.

Hewett, Angela, et al. Animals: Touch & Trace Early Learning Fun! Award, Anna. 2014. (ENG.). 26p. (J). bds. 13.50 *(978-1-84135-944-1(0))* Award Pubns. Ltd. GBR. Dist: Parkwest Pubns., Inc.

—A B C: Touch & Trace Early Learning Fun! Award, Anna. 2014. (ENG.). 26p. (J). bds. 13.50 *(978-1-84135-942-7(4))* Award Pubns. Ltd. GBR. Dist: Parkwest Pubns., Inc.

Hewett, Angela. Bedtime. Picthall, Chez. 2015. 10p. (J). bds. 11.99 *(978-1-909763-43-2(8))* Award Pubns. Ltd. GBR. Dist: Parkwest Pubns., Inc.

—Bumper Junior Art: Colour by Numbers. 2013. (ENG.). 64p. (J). (gr. -1-3). pap. 8.50 *(978-1-84135-998-4(X))* Parkwest Pubns., Inc.

Hewett, Angela, jt. illus. see Peters, Andy.

Hewett, Richard. A Giraffe Calf Grows Up. Hewett, Richard, photos by. Hewett, Joan, photos by. 2004. (Baby Animals Ser.). 32p. (J). (gr. -1-2). pap. 6.95 *(978-1-57505-630-2(5))*; (gr. k-3). lib. bdg. 21.27 *(978-1-57505-197-0(4))* Lerner Publishing Group.

—A Koala Joey Grows Up. Hewett, Richard, photos by. Hewett, Joan, photos by. 2004. (Baby Animals Ser.). 32p. (J). (gr. k-3). lib. bdg. 21.27 *(978-1-57505-198-7(2))* Lerner Publishing Group.

—A Monkey Baby Grows Up. Hewett, Richard, photos by. Hewett, Joan, photos by. 2004. (Baby Animals Ser.). 32p. (J). (gr. k-3). lib. bdg. 21.27 *(978-1-57505-199-4(0))* Lerner Publishing Group.

—A Penguin Chick Grows Up. Hewett, Richard, photos by. Hewett, Joan, photos by. 2004. (Baby Animals Ser.). 32p. (J). (gr. k-3). lib. bdg. 21.27 *(978-1-57505-200-7(8))* Lerner Publishing Group.

Hewett, Richard, photos by. A Flamingo Chick Grows Up. Hewett, Joan. (Baby Animals Ser.). 32p. 2005. (gr. k-3). lib. bdg. 21.27 *(978-1-57505-164-2(8))*; 2003. (J). (gr. -1-2). pap. 6.95 *(978-0-8225-0090-2(6)*, Lerner Pubns.) Lerner Publishing Group.

—A Kangaroo Joey Grows Up. Hewett, Joan. 2005. (Baby Animals Ser.). 32p. (J). (gr. k-3). lib. bdg. 21.27 *(978-1-57505-165-9(6))* Lerner Publishing Group.

Hewins, Shirley. No Bulley Destroy's Chloe's Hairdo. Hawkins-Rodgers, Donzella. 2003. 32p. (J). (gr. 3-18). lib. bdg. 16.95 *(978-1-884242-56-4(1))* Multicultural Pubns.

—Rainy Brown & the Seven Midgets. l.t. ed. 2006. (J). (gr. k-3). pap. 11.95 *(978-1-884242-24-3(3)*, RB1STED); 44p. lib. bdg. 19.95 *(978-1-884242-25-0(1)*, RB1STED) Multicultural Pubns.

Hewitt, Dylan. The Kingdom of Nothing. Wohlman, Ronald. 2020. (ENG.). 52p. (J). (gr. -1-k). 18.99 *(978-0-7112-4526-6(6)*, 327907, Frances Lincoln Children's Bks.) Quarto Publishing Group UK GBR. Dist: Hachette UK Distribution.

Hewitt, Elizabeth. How Full Is Sophia's Backpack? Jacobs, Karen & Miller, Leah. 2012. 40p. pap. 11.95 *(978-0-9850440-0-8(4))* Jacobs, Karen.

Hewitt, Kathryn. Flower Garden. Bunting, Eve. 2004. 28p. (gr. -1-2). 17.00 *(978-0-7569-4113-0(X))* Perfection Learning Corp.

—Jamaica Tag-Along. Bunting, Eve. 2015. 32p. pap. 7.00 *(978-1-61003-504-0(6))* Center for the Collaborative Classroom.

—Lives of the Artists: Masterpieces, Messes (and What the Neighbors Thought) Krull, Kathleen. 2014. (Lives Of ... Ser.). (ENG.). 96p. (J). (gr. 5-7). pap. 8.99 *(978-0-544-25223-3(3)*, 1566543, HMH Books For Young Readers) Houghton Mifflin Harcourt Publishing Co.

—Lives of the Athletes: Thrills, Spills (and What the Neighbors Thought) Krull, Kathleen. 2013. (Lives Of ... Ser.). (ENG.). 96p. (J). (gr. 5-7). pap. 8.99 *(978-0-544-24760-4(4)*, 1566172) Houghton Mifflin Harcourt Publishing Co.

—Lives of the Explorers: Discoveries, Disasters (and What the Neighbors Thought) Krull, Kathleen. (Lives Of ... Ser.). (ENG.). 96p. (J). (gr. 5-7). 2018. pap. 8.99 *(978-1-328-74091-5(9)*, 1677133); 2014. 20.99 *(978-0-15-205910-1(5)*, 1197746) Houghton Mifflin Harcourt Publishing Co. (HMH Books For Young Readers).

—Lives of the Musicians: Good Times, Bad Times (and What the Neighbors Thought) Krull, Kathleen. 2013. (Lives Of ... Ser.). (ENG.). 96p. (J). (gr. 5-7). pap. 8.99 *(978-0-544-23806-0(0)*, 1564791) Houghton Mifflin Harcourt Publishing Co.

—Lives of the Pirates: Swashbucklers, Scoundrels (Neighbors Beware!) Krull, Kathleen. 2013. (Lives Of ... Ser.). (ENG.). 96p. (J). (gr. 5-7). pap. 8.99 *(978-0-544-10495-2(1)*, 1540801) Houghton Mifflin Harcourt Publishing Co.

—Lives of the Presidents: Fame, Shame (And What the Neighbors Thought) Krull, Kathleen. 2011. (Lives Of ... Ser.). (ENG.). 104p. (J). (gr. 5-7). 21.00 *(978-0-547-49809-6(8)*, 1442014) Houghton Mifflin Harcourt Publishing Co.

—Lives of the Scientists: Experiments, Explosions (and What the Neighbors Thought) Krull, Kathleen. 2016. (Lives Of ... Ser.). (ENG.). 96p. (J). (gr. 5-7). 8.99 *(978-0-544-81087-7(2)*, 1641669, HMH Books For Young Readers) Houghton Mifflin Harcourt Publishing Co.

—Lives of the Scientists: Experiments, Explosions (And What the Neighbors Thought) Krull, Kathleen. 2013. (Lives Of ... Ser.). (ENG.). 96p. (J). (gr. 5-7). 20.99 *(978-0-15-205909-5(1)*, 1197743) Houghton Mifflin Harcourt Publishing Co.

—Uncle Sam's America. Hewitt, David. 2011. (ENG.). 40p. (J). (gr. 2-5). pap. 19.99 *(978-1-4424-3092-1(3))* Simon & Schuster Children's Publishing.

Heyer. Alanna: The First Adventure, 1. Pierce, Tamora. 2011. (Song of the Lioness Ser.: Bk. 1). (ENG.). 240p. (J). (gr. 7-12). 26.19 *(978-0-689-85323-4(8))* Simon & Schuster, Inc.

Heyer, Brianna. The Other Side of That Way. Panek, Bob. 2019. (ENG.). 28p. (J). pap. 9.95 *(978-1-7289-2715-2(3))* Independently Published.

Heyer, Carol. The Christmas Story. (J). 6.95 *(978-0-8249-5347-8(9)*, Ideal Pubns.) Worthy Publishing.

—The Crow & the Pitcher: A Tale about Problem Solving. Aesop, Aesop. 2006. (J). *(978-1-59939-096-3(5)*, Reader's Digest Young Families, Inc.) Studio Fun International.

—Let's Read About — George W. Bush. Fry, Sonali. 2003. (Scholastic First Biographies Ser.). (J). pap. *(978-0-439-45953-2(2))* Scholastic, Inc.

—Mother Earth's Lullaby: A Song for Endangered Animals, 1 vol. Pierce, Terry. 2018. (Tilbury House Nature Book Ser.: 0). (ENG.). 36p. (J). (gr. -1-2). 17.95 *(978-0-88448-557-5(9)*, 884557) Tilbury Hse. Pubs.

Heyer, Carol, et al. Once upon a Cool Motorcycle Dude. O'Malley, Kevin. 2005. (ENG.). 32p. (J). (gr. 1-5). 17.99 *(978-0-8027-8947-1(1)*, 900034867, Bloomsbury USA Childrens) Bloomsbury Publishing USA.

—Once upon a Royal Superbaby. O'Malley, Kevin. 2010. (ENG.). 40p. (J). (gr. k-3). 17.99 *(978-0-8027-2164-8(8)*, 900067940, Bloomsbury USA Childrens) Bloomsbury Publishing USA.

Heyer, Carol. The Easter Story. Heyer, Carol, retold by. 32p. (J). 12.95 *(978-0-8249-5363-8(0)*, Ideal Pubns.) Worthy Publishing.

—Excalibur. Heyer, Carol, retold by. *(978-1-59093-022-9(3)*, Eager Minds Pr.) Warehousing & Fulfillment Specialists, LLC (WFS, LLC).

Heyer, Carol & White, Charlotte L. Tommy Wilson, Junior Veterinarian: The Case of the Orphaned Bobcat. Smith, Maggie Caldwell. 2006. (J). per. 7.95 *(978-0-9788391-1-6(0))* Magpie Pr., Pine Mountain Club, CA.

Heyes, Jane. Candle Day by Day Bible, 1 vol. David, Juliet. ed. 2016. (ENG.). 368p. (J). spiral bd. 16.99 *(978-1-78128-281-6(1)*, Candle Bks.) Lion Hudson PLC GBR. Dist: Independent Pubs. Group.

—Candle Day by Day Bible & Prayers Gift Set, 1 vol. David, Juliet. 2017. (ENG.). 560p. (J). bds. 29.99 *(978-1-78128-346-2(X)*, Candle Bks.) Lion Hudson PLC GBR. Dist: Independent Pubs. Group.

—Candle Day by Day Prayers: Children's Prayers for Every Day, 1 vol. David, Juliet. ed. 2016. (ENG.). 160p. (J). 12.99 *(978-1-78128-265-6(X)*, Candle Bks.) Lion Hudson PLC GBR. Dist: Kregel Pubns.

—Candle Day by Day Walk with Jesus: The Story of Jesus Retold in 40 Days, 1 vol. David, Juliet. ed. 2016. (ENG.). 48p. (J). 9.99 *(978-1-78128-291-5(9)*, Candle Bks.) Lion Hudson PLC GBR. Dist: Kregel Pubns.

Heyman, Eric. The Battle of the Blighty Bling. Quayle, Ruth. 2018. 224p. (J). (gr. 3). pap. 14.99 ***(978-1-78344-692-6(7))*** Andersen Pr. GBR. Dist: Independent Pubs. Group.

—Princesses Don't Fart. Bently, Peter. 2020. (ENG.). 32p. (J). 18.00 ***(978-1-4711-8341-6(6)***, Simon & Schuster Children's) Simon & Schuster, Ltd. GBR. Dist: Simon & Schuster, Inc.

Heyman, Ken, photos by. On the Go. Morris, Ann. 2015. 32p. pap. 7.00 *(978-1-61003-611-5(5))* Center for the Collaborative Classroom.

—Tools. Morris, Ann. 2015. 32p. pap. 7.00 *(978-1-61003-622-1(0))* Center for the Collaborative Classroom.

Heymans, Mau. Mickey Mouse: the Fire Eye of Atlantis. Castellan, Andrea et al. 2019. (Mickey Mouse Ser.). (ENG.). 96p. (J). (gr. 4-7). pap. 12.99 *(978-1-68405-405-3(2))* Idea & Design Works, LLC.

Heymans, Mau & Branca, Daniel. Donald & Mickey: Quest for the Faceplant. Van Horn, William & McGreal, Pat. 2017. (Walt Disney's Comics & Stories Ser.). (ENG.). 116p. (J). (gr. 4-7). pap. 12.99 *(978-1-63140-956-1(5))* Idea & Design Works, LLC.

Heymans, Mau & Hubbard, Al. Donald Duck: Shellfish Motives. Kinney, Dick et al. 2015. (Donald Duck Ser.). 148p. (J). (gr. 4-7). pap. 12.99 *(978-1-63140-403-0(2)*, 9781631404030) Idea & Design Works, LLC.

Heywood, Alex. Making Dreams. Orenshein, Jesse. 2019. (ENG.). 36p. (J). pap. 9.99 ***(978-1-6981-4424-5(5))*** Independently Published.

Heyworth, Heather. Dress-Up Day, 1 vol. Dale, Jay. 2012. (Engage Literacy Green Ser.). (ENG.). 32p. (gr. k-2). pap. 5.99 *(978-1-4296-9003-4(8)*, Capstone Pr.) Capstone.

—If I Were the President [Scholastic]. Troupe, Thomas Kingsley. 2010. (Dream Big! Ser.). 24p. pap. 0.62 *(978-1-4048-6196-1(3)*, Picture Window Bks.) Capstone.

—My Princesses Learn to Be Brave. Rische, Stephanie. 2014. (ENG.). 24p. (J). 6.99 *(978-1-4143-9661-3(9)*, 4608651) Tyndale Hse. Pubs.

—My Princesses Learn to Share. Carlson, Amie. 2014. (ENG.). 24p. (J). 6.99 *(978-1-4143-9662-0(7)*, 4608652) Tyndale Hse. Pubs.

Hezlep, Amber. It Could Happen... on the Bus. Higbee, Heidi. 2012. 32p. (J). pap. 16.95 *(978-0-9882940-0-4(1))* Bryson Taylor Publishing.

Hiam, Alex. Silent Lee: And the Adventure of the Side Door Key. Hiam, Alex. 2017. (ENG.). 136p. (gr. 5-10). pap. 6.99 *(978-1-63558-000-6(5))* Webster Pr. LLC.

Hiatt, Rebekah Lund. A Book of Bible Opposites. Coburn, Maggie. 2019. (ENG.). 22p. (J). (gr. -1-k). bds. 12.99 *(978-1-4621-2300-1(7))* Cedar Fort, Inc./CFI Distribution.

Hibbert, Hollie. Echo's Lucky Charm. Hapka, Catherine. 2016. (Dolphin School Ser.: 2). (ENG.). 112p. (J). (gr. 2-5). pap. 4.99 *(978-0-545-75025-7(3))* Scholastic, Inc.

—Pearl's Ocean Magic. Hapka, Catherine. 2016. (Dolphin School Ser.: 1). (ENG.). 112p. (J). (gr. 2-5). pap. 4.99 *(978-0-545-75024-0(5))* Scholastic, Inc.

Hibbert, Hollie. Trouble on the Wild West Express. 2020. (Boxcar Children Interactive Mysteries Ser.). (ENG.). 144p. (J). (gr. 1-5). 6.99 ***(978-0-8075-2862-4(5)***, 0807528625) Whitman, Albert & Co.

Hibbert, Rhonda. Share Day, 1 vol. Hibbert, Dee. 2009. 31p. pap. 24.95 *(978-1-60813-294-2(3))* America Star Bks.

Hibbs, Gillian. Errol's Garden. Hibbs, Gillian. 2018. (Child's Play Library). (ENG.). 32p. (J). pap. *(978-1-78628-084-8(1))*; *(978-1-78628-085-5(X))* Child's Play International Ltd.

—Tilly's Staycation. Hibbs, Gillian. 2014. (Child's Play Library). (ENG.). 32p. (J). *(978-1-84643-601-7(X))* Child's Play International Ltd.

Hibbs, Gillian & Dicmas, Courtney. Never Giving up Hope Book Set Of 4. Alborozo & Hibbs, Gillian. Dicmas, Courtney. 2020. (Social & Emotional Learning Sets Ser.). (ENG.). 144p. (J). pap., pap., pap. ***(978-1-78628-537-9(1))*** Child's Play International Ltd.

Hibon, Ben. Shadow Magic. Khan, Joshua. (Shadow Magic Novel Ser.). (ENG.). (J). (gr. 3-7). 2017. 352p. pap. 6.99 *(978-1-4847-3788-0(1))*; 2016. 336p. 16.99 *(978-1-4847-3272-4(3))* Hyperion Bks. for Children.

Hickerson, Joel. ImagineLand's Bubble Gum Trouble, Vol. 1. l.t. ed. 2004. 32p. (J). *(978-0-9765038-0-4(8))* Imagineland, Ltd.

Hickey, Brenda. Applejack, 1 vol. Curnow, Bobby. 2015. (My Little Pony Ser.). (ENG.). 24p. (J). (gr. 1-8). 27.07 *(978-1-61479-331-1(X)*, 17153, Graphic Novels) Spotlight.

Hickey, Brenda, et al. Applejack & Mayor Mare. Curnow, Bobby. 2018. (My Little Pony: Friends Forever Ser.). (ENG.). 24p. (J). (gr. 1-8). lib. bdg. 27.07 *(978-1-5321-4234-5(X)*, 28562, Graphic Novels) Spotlight.

—My Little Pony Art Is Magic! 2015. (MLP Art Is Magic Ser.: 1). 148p. pap. 19.99 *(978-1-63140-467-2(9)*, 9781631404672) Idea & Design Works, LLC.

—My Little Pony: Friendship Is Magic: Vol. 13. Nuhfer, Heather. 2018. (My Little Pony: Friendship Is Magic Ser.). (ENG.). 24p. (J). (gr. 2-8). lib. bdg. 27.07 *(978-1-5321-4229-1(3)*, 31106, Graphic Novels) Spotlight.

—My Little Pony: Friendship Is Magic: Vol. 14. Nuhfer, Heather. 2018. (My Little Pony: Friendship Is Magic Ser.). (ENG.). 24p. (J). (gr. 2-8). lib. bdg. 27.07 *(978-1-5321-4230-7(7)*, 31107, Graphic Novels) Spotlight.

Hickey, Brenda. My Little Pony: Legends of Magic, Vol. 1. Whitley, Jeremy. 2017. (MLP Legends of Magic Ser.: 1). 124p. (J). (gr. 4-7). pap. 19.99 *(978-1-68405-059-8(6))* Idea & Design Works, LLC.

—My Little Pony: Spirit of the Forest. Anderson, Ted. 2019. 80p. (J). (gr. 4-7). pap. 9.99 *(978-1-68405-609-5(8))* Idea & Design Works, LLC.

Hickey, Brenda, et al. Pinkie Pie & Twilight Sparkle. Kesel, Barbara Randall. 2018. (My Little Pony: Friends Forever Ser.). (ENG.). 24p. (J). (gr. 1-8). lib. bdg. 27.07 *(978-1-5321-4238-3(2)*, 28566, Graphic Novels) Spotlight.

Hickey, Brenda. Ward's Valley. Curnow, Bobby. 2018. 128p. (YA). (gr. 7). pap. 19.99 *(978-1-60309-424-5(5))* Top Shelf Productions.

Hickey, Brenda & Fleecs, Tony. My Little Pony: Legends of Magic Omnibus. Whitley, Jeremy. 2020. (MLP Legends of Magic Ser.). 296p. (J). (gr. 4-7). pap. 24.99 *(978-1-68405-566-1(0))* Idea & Design Works, LLC.

Hickey, Brenda & Mebberson, Amy. My Little Pony: Friendship Is Magic Volume 4, Vol. 4. Nuhfer, Heather. 2014. (My Little Pony Ser.: 4). 104p. (J). (gr. 4-7). pap. 17.99 *(978-1-61377-960-6(7)*, 9781613779606) Idea & Design Works, LLC.

Hickey, Brenda, jt. illus. see Garbowska, Agnes.

Hickey, Josh. Betsy Beansprout Camping Guide. Elmore, Amber. 2013. 50p. pap. 13.99 *(978-1-937331-37-5(7))* ShadeTree Publishing, LLC.

Hickey, Katie. Christmas Is Coming! an Advent Book: Crafts, Games, Recipes, Stories, & More! (Christmas Calendar, Advent Calendar for Families, Family Craft & Holiday Activity Book) Chronicle Books. 2019. (ENG.). 72p. (J). (gr. k-5). 17.99 *(978-1-4521-7407-5(5))* Chronicle Bks. LLC.

—Lumber Jills: The Unsung Heroines of World War II. Davis, Alexandra. 2019. (ENG.). 32p. (J). (gr. -1-k). 16.99 *(978-0-8075-4795-3(6)*, 807547956) Whitman, Albert & Co.

Hickey, Katie. Ocean Speaks: How Marie Tharp Revealed the Ocean's Biggest Secret. Keating, Jess. 2020. 34p. (J). (gr. -1-3). 17.99 ***(978-0-7352-6508-0(9)***, Tundra Bks.) Tundra Bks. CAN. Dist: Penguin Random Hse. LLC.

—Plant & Grow. Redwing, Jack. Cottage Door Press, ed. 2020. (John Deere Lift-A-Flap Board Book Ser.). (ENG.). 12p. (J). (gr. -1-k). bds. 7.99 ***(978-1-68052-815-2(7)***, 1005280) Cottage Door Pr.

Hickman, Jen. Bezkamp. Sattin, Samuel. 2019. (ENG.). 256p. (YA). pap. 14.99 *(978-1-5493-0404-0(6)*, df5c6401-1840-458c-aeb9-e1915c392b23, Lion Forge) Oni Pr., Inc.

Hickman, Jessica. Little Jackie Lantern. Waltz, Tom. 2019. 12p. (J). (-k). bds. 7.99 *(978-1-68405-540-1(7))* Idea & Design Works, LLC.

Hickman, Paula. Tiberius Meets Sneaky Cat. Harvey, Keith. 2010. (Tiberius Tales Ser.). 24p. (J). (gr. -1-2). pap. 8.15 *(978-1-60754-835-5(6))*; lib. bdg. 25.60 *(978-1-60754-831-7(3))* Windmill Bks.

Hickman, Paula, jt. illus. see Brown, Kate.

Hicks, Alan and Aaron. Twin Hicks Noah's Ark. Richardson, Robert. 2008. 36p. pap. 16.95 *(978-1-4389-1809-9(7))* AuthorHouse.

Hicks, Angela, jt. illus. see Burton, Terry.

Hicks, Angie. Alien. 2012. (ENG.). 24p. (J). 4.95 *(978-1-84135-585-6(2))* Award Pubns. Ltd. GBR. Dist: Parkwest Pubns., Inc.

—Butterfly. 2012. (ENG.). 24p. (J). 4.95 *(978-1-84135-582-5(8))* Award Pubns. Ltd. GBR. Dist: Parkwest Pubns., Inc.

—Colour by Numbers. 2012. (ENG.). 16p. (J). 3.25 *(978-1-84135-860-4(6))* Award Pubns. Ltd. GBR. Dist: Parkwest Pubns., Inc.

—Fish. 2012. (ENG.). 24p. (J). 4.95 *(978-1-84135-584-9(4))* Award Pubns. Ltd. GBR. Dist: Parkwest Pubns., Inc.

—Junior Art Colour By Numbers: Lion. 2012. (ENG.). 16p. (J). 3.25 *(978-1-84135-857-4(6))* Award Pubns. Ltd. GBR. Dist: Parkwest Pubns., Inc.

—The Little Fairy Horse. 2012. (ENG.). 24p. (J). 9.95 *(978-1-84135-834-5(7))* Award Pubns. Ltd. GBR. Dist: Parkwest Pubns., Inc.

—Mermaid. 2012. (ENG.). 16p. (J). 3.25 *(978-1-84135-859-8(2))* Award Pubns. Ltd. GBR. Dist: Parkwest Pubns., Inc.

—Moonlight & the Mermaid. 2012. (ENG.). 24p. (J). 9.95 *(978-1-84135-833-8(9))* Award Pubns. Ltd. GBR. Dist: Parkwest Pubns., Inc.

—Pirate. 2012. (ENG.). 24p. (J). 4.95 *(978-1-84135-583-2(6))* Award Pubns. Ltd. GBR. Dist: Parkwest Pubns., Inc.
—Shark. 2012. (ENG.). 16p. (J). 3.25 *(978-1-84135-858-1(4))* Award Pubns. Ltd. GBR. Dist: Parkwest Pubns., Inc.
—Sparkle the Seahorse. King, Karen. 2012. (ENG.). 24p. (J). 9.95 *(978-1-84135-879-6(7))* Award Pubns. Ltd. GBR. Dist: Parkwest Pubns., Inc.
—Unicorn Magic. King, Karen. 2012. (ENG.). 24p. 9.95 *(978-1-84135-832-1(0))* Award Pubns. Ltd. GBR. Dist: Parkwest Pubns., Inc.
Hicks, Astred. How to Feel Awesome Every Day. Awesome, Elly. 2018. (ENG.). 192p. (J). (gr. 8-12). pap. 16.00 *(978-1-4926-7008-7(1))* Sourcebooks, Inc.
Hicks, Bob. Cornelius, the Little Dragon Book. Hicks, Bob. 2004. (J). ring bd. incl. audio compact disk *(978-0-9722036-5-4(6))* T. E. Publishing, Inc.
Hicks, Faith. Nellie in the News. Kelly, Claire. 2007. 48p. (J). lib. bdg. 23.08 *(978-1-4242-1631-4(1))* Fitzgerald Bks.
Hicks, Faith Erin. Nothing Can Possibly Go Wrong. Shen, Prudence. 2013. (Nothing Can Possibly Go Wrong Ser.). (ENG.). 288p. (YA). (gr. 7). pap. 18.99 *(978-1-59643-659-6(X),* 900069585, First Second Bks.) Roaring Brook Pr.
—Pumpkinheads. Rowell, Rainbow. 2019. (ENG.). 224p. (YA). 24.99 *(978-1-250-31285-3(X),* 900199288); pap. 17.99 *(978-1-62672-162-3(9),* 900140620) Roaring Brook Pr. (First Second Bks.).
—The Sound of Thunder. Torres, J. 2014. (Bigfoot Boy Ser.). (ENG.). 100p. (J). (gr. 2-5). pap. 9.95 *(978-1-894786-59-1(9))* Kids Can Pr., Ltd. CAN. Dist: Hachette Bk. Group.
Hicks, Faith Erin. The Last of Us: American Dreams. Hicks, Faith Erin. Druckmann, Neil. Wright, Brendan, ed. 2013. (Last of Us Ser.). (ENG.). 96p. pap. 19.99 *(978-1-61655-212-1(3),* Dark Horse Books) Dark Horse Comics.
Hicks, Kaylee. I'm So Cute, You Can't Be Mad. Bruton, Seth. 2012. 24p. pap. 13.97 *(978-1-61204-897-0(8),* Strategic Bk. Publishing) Strategic Book Publishing & Rights Agency (SBPRA).
Hicks, Mark A. Coyote Claus. Hansen, Cory Copper. 2019. (ENG.). 32p. (J). (gr. -1-2). pap. 9.95 *(978-1-941384-53-4(6))* Sunbelt Pubns., Inc.
Hicks, Rebecca. Little Vampires. Hicks, Rebecca. 2007. 56p. per. 8.95 *(978-0-9799290-0-7(8))* Lunasea Studios.
Hicks, Zehra. The Problem with Problems. Rooney, Rachel. import ed. 2020. (ENG.). 32p. (J). (gr. -1-2). 17.99 ***(978-0-593-17317-6(1),*** Rodale Kids) Random Hse. Children's Bks.
Hidayat, Elaine. Matts Fantastiska Vecka. Lundqvist, Martin. 2019. (SWE.). 42p. (J). pap. 6.00 ***(978-1-0897-8208-7(X))*** Independently Published.
Hié, Vanessa. The Mermaid & the Parakeet: A Children's Book Inspired by Henri Matisse. Massenot, Véronique. 2016. (Children's Books Inspired by Famous Artworks Ser.). (ENG.). 32p. (J). (gr. -1-3). 14.95 *(978-3-7913-7265-5(3))* Prestel Verlag GmbH & Co KG. DEU. Dist: Penguin Random Hse. LLC.
Hief, Gina. The Garden Adventures: The Mishaps of Martha & Matilda. Rothchild, Erik. 2013. 44p. *(978-0-9883568-5-6(6))* Inkwell Books LLC.
Hiemstra, Femke. The Timid Cabbage. Krafft, Charles. 2013. (ENG.). 48p. (J). 39.99 *(978-0-578-12457-5(2))* Sympathetic Pr.
Hierlmaier, Joy. Green Yellow Go! Nat Knows Bananas. Hierlmaier Nelson, Christine M. 2004. 26p. (J). spiral bd. 14.95 *(978-0-9759362-0-7(4))* Expressive Ink.
Hiers, Christopher. Rush Revere & the American Revolution. Limbaugh, Rush H., III & Limbaugh, Kathryn Adams. 2014. 244p. (J). pap. *(978-1-4767-8989-7(4),* Threshold Editions) Threshold Editions.
Hierstein, Judith. The American Revolution from A to Z, 1 vol. Crawford, Laura. 2009. (ABC Ser.). (ENG.). 32p. (J). (gr. k-3). 16.99 *(978-1-58980-515-6(1),* Pelican Publishing) Arcadia Publishing.
—Benjamin Franklin from A to Z, 1 vol. Crawford, Laura. 2013. (ABC Ser.). (ENG.). 32p. (J). (gr. k-3). 16.99 *(978-1-4556-1713-5(X),* Pelican Publishing) Arcadia Publishing.
—Nathan's Hanukkah Bargain, 1 vol. Greene, Jacqueline. 2008. (ENG.). 32p. (J). (gr. 1-3). 16.99 *(978-1-58980-454-8(6),* Pelican Publishing) Arcadia Publishing.
—The Pilgrims' Thanksgiving from A to Z, 1 vol. Crawford, Laura. 2005. (ABC Ser.). (ENG.). 32p. (J). (gr. k-3). per. 8.99 *(978-1-58980-238-4(1),* Pelican Publishing) Arcadia Publishing.
—Toby Belfer Visits Ellis Island, 1 vol. Pushker, Gloria Teles. 2003. (Toby Belfer Ser.). (ENG.). 32p. (J). (gr. k-3). 16.99 *(978-1-58980-117-2(2),* Pelican Publishing) Arcadia Publishing.
—Two Sides to Every Story. Lipson, Greta Barclay. 2004. 128p. (J). pap. 14.95 *(978-1-57310-439-5(6))* Teaching & Learning Co.
—Voices of Gettysburg, 1 vol. Garland, Sherry. 2010. (Voices of History Ser.). (ENG.). 40p. (J). (gr. 3-3). 17.99 *(978-1-58980-653-5(0),* Pelican Publishing) Arcadia Publishing.
—Voices of the Dust Bowl, 1 vol. Garland, Sherry. 2012. (Voices of History Ser.). (ENG.). 40p. (J). (gr. 3-3). 17.99 *(978-1-58980-964-2(5),* Pelican Publishing) Arcadia Publishing.
Hierstein, Judith, jt. illus. see Kerr, Thomas.
Hierstein, Judy & Boyer, Lyn. The Ultimate Book of Second Grade Skills: Grade 2. Fetty, Margaret, ed. 2009. (Ultimate Book of Skills Ser.). 224p. pap. 16.99 *(978-1-4190-9953-3(1))* Steck-Vaughn.
Higashi, Sandra, jt. illus. see Glaser, Byron.
Higashi, Satoko. Bailey Bandicoot Finds Treasure. Davis, K. S. 2019. (ENG.). 50p. (J). pap. 10.99 ***(978-1-7014-0519-6(9))*** Independently Published.
Higashi, Satoko. Bailey Bandicoot's Treasure Hunt. Davis, K. S. 2019. (ENG.). 50p. (J). pap. 10.99 *(978-1-0925-4374-3(0))* Independently Published.
Higgie, Will K., jt. illus. see Vincent, Andrew M.
Higginbotham, Jeremy. De la Silla de lv�n, Sali�... Un Misterio. Beckstrand, Karl. 2019. (Misterios para Los Menores Ser.: Vol. 5). (SPA.). 38p. (J). pap. 9.85 ***(978-1-0760-0651-6(5))*** Independently Published.
—De la Silla de lv�n, Sali�... Un Misterio. Beckstrand, Karl. l.t. ed. 2019. (Misterios para Los Menores Ser.: Vol. 5). (SPA.). 38p. (J). (gr. k-2). 26.55 ***(978-1-7320696-5-7(4))*** Premio Publishing & Gozo Bks., LLC.
—It Came from under the High Chair - Salió de Debajo de la Silla para Comer: A Mystery (in English & Spanish) Beckstrand, Karl. 2019. (Mini-Mysteries for Minors Ser.: Vol. 5). (ENG.). 38p. (J). pap. 9.85 ***(978-0-692-22099-3(2))*** Premio Publishing & Gozo Bks., LLC.
Higgins, Anne Keenan. Blowout, 1. Morris, Taylor. 2011. (Hello, Gorgeous! Ser.: 1). (ENG.). 224p. (J). (gr. 6-8). 18.69 *(978-0-448-45526-6(9),* Grosset & Dunlap) Penguin Publishing Group.
—Do's & Don'ts, 5 vols., 5. Morris, Taylor. 2012. (Hello, Gorgeous! Ser.: 5). (ENG.). 224p. (J). (gr. 6-8). 21.19 *(978-0-448-45861-8(6))* Penguin Young Readers Group.
Higgins, Beatrice. The Rangers of the Forest. Henninger, Robert. 2003. (ENG.). 82p. pap. 12.95 ***(978-1-4120-0368-1(7))*** Trafford Publishing.
Higgins, Clark L. We've Seen Sant. Higgins, Tiffany A. 2011. 26p. pap. 12.27 *(978-1-61204-267-1(8),* Eloquent Bks.) Strategic Book Publishing & Rights Agency (SBPRA).
Higgins, Dusty. Attack of the Alien Horde. Venditti, Robert. 2015. (Miles Taylor & the Golden Cape Ser.: 1). (ENG.). 304p. (J). (gr. 4-7). 16.99 *(978-1-4814-0542-3(X))* Simon & Schuster, Inc.
—Rise of the Robot Army. Venditti, Robert. 2016. (Miles Taylor & the Golden Cape Ser.: 2). (ENG.). 304p. (J). (gr. 4-7). 16.99 *(978-1-4814-0557-7(8),* Simon & Schuster Bks. For Young Readers) Simon & Schuster Bks. For Young Readers.
Higgins, John, et al. Death's Head: Freelance Peacekeeping Agent. 2020. (ENG.). 408p. (YA). (gr. 8-17). pap. 39.99 *(978-1-302-92336-5(6))* Marvel Worldwide, Inc.
Higgins, Kayla. The True Tails of Togo the Sled Dog! Hayes, Jonathan Nathaniel. 2018. (ENG.). 68p. (J). pap. 15.95 ***(978-1-0992-5671-4(2))*** Independently Published.
Higgins, Krystal. Hello Smokey! Aryal, Aimee. 2004. 22p. (J). 19.95 *(978-1-932888-09-6(8))* Mascot Bks., Inc.
Higgins, Quentin R. Hippity Has a Hot Idea. Higgins, Quentin R. 2003. 30p. (J). *(978-1-929204-11-3(6))* Dryden Publishing.
Higgins, Ryan. Wilfred. Higgins, Ryan. 2013. 40p. (J). (gr. -1-k). 17.99 *(978-0-8037-3732-7(7),* Dial Bks) Penguin Young Readers Group.
Higgins, Ryan T. Be Quiet! Higgins, Ryan T. 2017. 40p. (J). (gr. -1-k). 17.99 *(978-1-4847-3162-8(X))* Hyperion Bks. for Children.
—Bruce's Big Fun Day. Higgins, Ryan T. 2019. (World of Reading Ser.). 32p. (J). (gr. -1-k). 14.99 *(978-1-368-01577-6(8))* Disney Pr.
—Bruce's Big Fun Day. Higgins, Ryan T. 2019. (World of Reading Ser.). 32p. (J). (gr. -1-k). pap. 4.99 *(978-1-368-02281-1(2))* Hyperion Bks. for Children.
—Bruce's Big Move (a Mother Bruce Book) Higgins, Ryan T. 2017. (Mother Bruce Ser.: 4). 48p. (J). (gr. -1-k). 17.99 *(978-1-368-00354-4(0))* Hyperion Bks. for Children.
—Bruce's Big Storm. Higgins, Ryan T. 2019. (Mother Bruce Ser.). (ENG.). 48p. (J). (gr. -1-k). 17.99 *(978-1-368-02622-2(2))* Hyperion Bks. for Children.
—Hotel Bruce (Mother Bruce Series, Book 2) Higgins, Ryan T. 2016. (Mother Bruce Ser.: 2). 48p. (J). (gr. -1-k). 17.99 *(978-1-4847-4362-1(8))* Hyperion Bks. for Children.
—Mother Bruce (Mother Bruce, Book 1) Higgins, Ryan T. 2015. (Mother Bruce Ser.: 1). 48p. (J). (gr. -1-k). 17.99 *(978-1-4847-3088-1(7))* Disney Pr.
—Peek-A-Bruce. Higgins, Ryan T. 2019. (Mother Bruce Ser.). (ENG.). 24p. (J). (gr. -1 — 1). bds. 7.99 *(978-1-368-02857-8(8))* Hyperion Bks. for Children.
—Santa Bruce (a Mother Bruce Book) Higgins, Ryan T. 2018. (Mother Bruce Ser.: 4). (ENG.). 48p. (J). (gr. -1-k). pap. 17.99 *(978-1-4847-8290-3(9))* Hyperion Bks. for Children.
—We Don't Eat Our Classmates. Higgins, Ryan T. 2018. 48p. (J). (gr. -1-k). 17.99 *(978-1-368-00355-1(9))* Hyperion Bks. for Children.
—1 Grumpy Bruce (a Mother Bruce Book) A Counting Board Book. Higgins, Ryan T. 2018. (Mother Bruce Ser.). (ENG.). 24p. (J). (gr. -1 — 1). bds. 7.99 *(978-1-368-02363-4(0))* Hyperion Bks. for Children.
Higgins, Tabitha & Shirk, Linda. Moses, the Meekest Man. Miller, Mary R. 2016. (ENG.). 32p. (J). (gr. -1-3). 3.25 *(978-0-7399-2536-2(9))* Rod & Staff Pubs., Inc.
Highfield, Whitney. Everybody Has a Body. Behrens, Janice. 2018. (Rookie Toddler Ser.). (ENG.). 12p. (J). (gr. -1 — 1). bds. 6.95 *(978-0-531-12705-6(2),* Children's Pr.) Scholastic Library Publishing.
—I See Animal Colors. Falk, Laine. 2018. (Rookie Toddler Ser.). (ENG.). 12p. (J). (gr. -1 — 1). bds. 6.95 *(978-0-531-22892-0(4),* Children's Pr.) Scholastic Library Publishing.
—Wave Hello, Wave Bye-Bye. Chanko, Pamela. 2018. (Rookie Toddler Ser.). (ENG.). 12p. (J). (gr. -1 — 1). bds. 6.95 *(978-0-531-22890-6(8),* Children's Pr.) Scholastic Library Publishing.
Hight, Lloyd R. 44 Animals of the Bible. Johnson, Nancy Pelander. 2014. (ENG.). 44p. (J). (gr. -1-3). 9.99 *(978-0-89051-843-4(2),* Master Books) New Leaf Publishing Group.
Hight, Michael. Flamingo Bendalingo: Poems from the Zoo. Green, Paula. 2006. (ENG.). 100p. (gr. 4-7). 24.95 *(978-1-86940-353-9(3))* Auckland Univ. Pr. NZL. Dist: Independent Pubs. Group.
Higman, Valisa. My Coyote Nose & Ptarmigan Toes: An Almost-True Alaskan Adventure. McKittrick, Erin. 2016. (Paws IV Ser.). 32p. (J). (gr. -1-2). 17.99 *(978-1-63217-052-1(3));* pap. 10.99 *(978-1-63217-031-6(0))* Sasquatch Bks. (Little Bigfoot).
Hikadova, Katerina, et al. World Atlas. Dusek, Jiri et al. 2014. (ENG.). 42p. (J). (gr. 3-5). 16.95 *(978-1-4549-1235-4(9))* Sterling Publishing Co., Inc.
Hilb, Nora. Animachines. Pearson, Deborah. 2016. (ENG.). 16p. (J). (— 1). bds. 7.99 *(978-1-55451-831-9(8))* Annick Pr., Ltd. CAN. Dist: Publishers Group West (PGW).
—The Dreadful Doings of Jelly Belly. Lee, Dennis. rev. ed. 2009. (ENG.). 16p. (J). (gr. k-k). bds. *(978-1-55263-767-8(0))* Me to We.
—Itsy Bitsy Spider. (Classic Books with Holes 8x8 with CD Ser.). (J). 2017. (ENG.). 16p. pap. incl. audio compact disk *(978-1-78628-079-4(5));* 2017. (ENG.). 16p. pap. *(978-1-84643-974-2(4));* 2014. 16p. spiral bd. *(978-1-84643-666-6(4));* 2012. 14p. spiral bd. *(978-1-84643-509-6(9));* 2012. 16p. pap. *(978-1-84643-498-3(X))* Child's Play International Ltd.
—The Kitty Ran up the Tree. Lee, Dennis. rev. ed. 2009. (ENG.). 16p. (J). (gr. k-k). bds. *(978-1-55263-813-2(8))* Me to We.
—Leo's Tree. Pearson, Debora. 2nd ed. 2004. (ENG.). 24p. (J). (gr. -1-1). 19.95 *(978-1-55037-845-0(7),* 9781550378450) Annick Pr., Ltd. CAN. Dist: Publishers Group West (PGW).
—Little Chick & Mommy Cat. Zafrilla, Marta. Brokenbrow, Jon, tr. 2012. 32p. (J). (gr. k-2). 14.95 *(978-84-15241-96-6(8))* Cuento de Luz SL ESP. Dist: Publishers Group West (PGW).
—The Magic Ball of Wool. Isern, Susanna. Brokenbrow, Jon, tr. (ENG.). 32p. (J). (gr. -1-k). 2019. 11.95 *(978-84-16733-66-8(X));* 2013. 16.95 *(978-84-15619-89-5(8))* Cuento de Luz SL ESP. Dist: Publishers Group West (PGW).
—Una Montana para Pancho. Maine, Margarita. (SPA.). 32p. (J). *(978-84-236-4740-8(4))* Edebé ESP. Dist: Lectorum Pubns., Inc.
—Nora's Ark, 1 vol. Spinelli, Eileen. 2018. (ENG.). 24p. (J). bds. 8.99 *(978-0-310-76144-0(1))* Zonderkidz.
—Silverly/Good Night, Good Night. Lee, Dennis. rev. ed. 2008. (ENG.). 16p. (J). (gr. k-k). bds. *(978-1-55263-769-2(7))* Me to We.
—Skyscraper. Lee, Dennis. rev. ed. 2009. (ENG.). 16p. (J). (gr. k-k). bds. *(978-1-55263-811-8(1))* Me to We.
—Willoughby Wallaby Woo. Lee, Dennis. rev. ed. 2008. (ENG.). 16p. (J). (gr. k-k). bds. *(978-1-55263-676-3(3))* Me to We.
Hilb, Nora, jt. illus. see Newfeld, Frank.
HildaRose & Rose, Hilda. Baby's Lullaby, 1 vol. Barber, Jill. ed. 2010. (ENG.). 16p. (J). (gr. -1 — 1). bds. 8.95 *(978-1-55109-795-4(8),* 696021f2-4598-47df-9789-32a6ddbcdcc2) Nimbus Publishing, Ltd. CAN. Dist: Baker & Taylor Publisher Services (BTPS).
Hildebrandt, Lowell. Salma & the Christmas Star. Torres, Christopher S. 2010. 24p. 12.99 *(978-1-4490-8981-8(X))* AuthorHouse.
Hilder, Rowland. The Midnight Folk. Masefield, John. 2008. (Kay Harker Ser.). (ENG.). 256p. (J). (gr. 4-7). 17.95 *(978-1-59017-290-2(6),* NYR Children's Collection) New York Review of Bks., Inc., The.
Hiley, F. E. The Little Betty Wilkinson. Smith, Evelyn. 2016. (ENG.). 151p. (J). pap. *(978-1-909423-70-1(X))* Bks. to Treasure.
Hiley, Francis E. Terry's Best Term. Smith, Evelyn. 2019. (ENG.). 152p. (J). pap. *(978-1-909423-46-6(7))* Bks. to Treasure.
Hilgemann, Judy. The Great Grizzlies Go Home. Hilgemann, Judy. 2020. (ENG.). 32p. (J). 23.95 *(978-1-55017-907-1(1))* Harbour Publishing Co., Ltd. CAN. Dist: Publishers Group West (PGW).
Hilinski, Clint. Ali Baba: Fooling the Forty Thieves [an Arabian Tale]. Croall, Marie P. 2009. (Graphic Myths & Legends Ser.). (ENG.). 48p. (J). (gr. 4-8). pap. 9.99 *(978-1-58013-887-1(X),* Graphic Universe™) Lerner Publishing Group.
—Sinbad: Sailing into Peril [an Arabian Tale]. Croall, Marie P. 2008. (Graphic Myths & Legends Ser.). (ENG.). 48p. (J). (gr. 4-8). pap. 9.99 *(978-0-8225-8516-9(2),* Graphic Universe™) Lerner Publishing Group.
—The Treasure of Mount Fate. Limke, Jeff. 2007. (Twisted Journeys ® Ser.: 4). (ENG.). (J). (gr. 4-7). pap. 45.32 *(978-0-8225-9468-0(4))* Lerner Publishing Group.
Hill, Armond. The Adventures of Coach & Little Dell: My First Tie. Eskridge, Tanae Denean & Frame, Brandon M. 2019. (ENG.). 48p. (J). *(978-1-78324-109-5(8));* pap. *(978-1-78324-108-8(X))* Wordzworth Publishing.
Hill, Beth. Pup & Pokey. Kantner, Seth. 2014. (ENG.). 48p. pap. 14.95 *(978-1-60223-241-9(5))* Univ. of Alaska Pr.
Hill, Bethanne. Why the Oyster Has the Pearl, 1 vol. Downing, Johnette. 2011. (ENG.). 32p. (J). (gr. k-3). 16.99 *(978-1-4556-1460-8(2),* Pelican Publishing) Arcadia Publishing.
Hill, Bodhi. The ABC's of Going Green. Dunn, Jill. 2012. 64p. (J). 21.99 *(978-0-9852146-2-3(7))* AM Ink Publishing.
Hill, Chris. What Does It Mean to Be Global? Little Pickle Press & DiOrio, Rana. ed. 2009. (What Does It Mean to Be... ? Ser.: 0). 32p. (J). (gr. -1-3). 17.95 *(978-0-9840806-0-1(0),* Little Pickle Pr.) Sourcebooks, Inc.
Hill, Dave. Calvin Graham's World War II Story. Marsico, Katie. 2018. (Narrative Nonfiction: Kids in War Ser.). (ENG.). 32p. (J). (gr. 2-4). lib. bdg. 27.99 *(978-1-5124-5681-3(0),* Lerner Pubns.) Lerner Publishing Group.
—Jesus' Beach Breakfast - Arch Books. 2017. (Arch Books Ser.). (ENG.). (J). pap. 2.99 *(978-0-7586-5737-4(4))* Concordia Publishing Hse.
—The Pentecost Story. Jaeger, Elizabeth. 2014. (Arch Bks.). (ENG.). 16p. (J). pap. 2.49 *(978-0-7586-4604-0(6))* Concordia Publishing Hse.
—Princess Polly & the Pony. Davidson, Susanna. 2007. (First Reading Level 4 Ser.). 48p. (J). 8.99 *(978-0-7945-1756-4(0),* Usborne) EDC Publishing.
—There's a Mouse in the House. Sanna, Charles A. 2006. (J). 10.00 *(978-0-9762839-1-1(3))* Elizabooks.
—What Happened to Merry Christmas? Baker, Robert C. 2007. 32p. (J). (gr. -1-3). 13.49 *(978-0-7586-1346-2(6))* Concordia Publishing Hse.
—The Wonder of Christmas. Mackall, Dandi Daley. 2008. 32p. (J). (gr. -1-3). 13.49 *(978-0-7586-1499-5(3))* Concordia Publishing Hse.
Hill, David. Hildegard's Gift. Hoyt, Megan. 2014. (ENG.). 32p. (J). (gr. -1-5). pap. 15.99 *(978-1-61261-358-1(6),* 3581) Paraclete Pr., Inc.
—Kristoph & the First Christmas Tree: A Legend of St. Boniface. McAdam, Claudia Cangilla. 2015. (ENG.). 32p. (J). (gr. -1). 16.99 *(978-1-61261-630-8(5),* 6308) Paraclete Pr., Inc.
—Sharing God's Love: The Jesus Creed for Children. McKnight, Scot & McKnight Barringer, Laura. 2014. (ENG.). 32p. (J). pap. 15.99 *(978-1-61261-581-3(3),* 5813) Paraclete Pr., Inc.
—The Teacher Who Became a Spy: The Story of Dietrich Bonhoeffer. Wilmington, Molly Frye. 2019. (J). *(978-1-64060-005-8(1))* Paraclete Pr., Inc.
Hill, Eric. Find Spot at the Library. Hill, Eric. 2019. (Spot Ser.). (ENG.). 16p. (J). (-k). bds. 9.99 *(978-0-241-38796-2(5),* Warne) Penguin Young Readers Group.
—Find Spot at the Stadium. Hill, Eric. 2020. (Spot Ser.). (ENG.). 16p. (J). (-k). bds. 9.99 *(978-0-241-42621-0(9),* Warne) Penguin Young Readers Group.
—Good Night, Spot. Hill, Eric. 2004. (Spot Ser.). (ENG.). 16p. (J). (gr. -1 — 1). bds. 4.99 *(978-0-399-24319-6(4),* Warne) Penguin Young Readers Group.
—Night-Night, Spot. Hill, Eric. 2005. (Spot Ser.). (ENG.). 32p. (J). (gr. -1-k). pap. 4.99 *(978-0-448-43810-8(0),* Warne) Penguin Young Readers Group.
—Spot Bakes a Cake. Hill, Eric. 2003. (ENG.). 22p. (J). (gr. -1-1). bds. 7.99 *(978-0-399-24013-3(6))* Penguin Publishing Group.
—Spot Bakes a Cake. Hill, Eric. 2005. (Spot Ser.). (ENG.). 20p. (J). (gr. k — 1). 6.99 *(978-0-14-240329-7(6),* Warne) Penguin Young Readers Group.
—Spot Can Count. Hill, Eric. 2005. (ENG.). 22p. (J). (gr. -1-1). bds. 7.99 *(978-0-399-24361-5(5))* Penguin Publishing Group.
—Spot Can Count (Color) First Edition. Hill, Eric. 2003. (Spot Ser.). (ENG.). 24p. (J). (gr. -1-k). 6.99 *(978-0-14-250121-4(2),* Warne) Penguin Young Readers Group.
—Spot Goes Shopping. Hill, Eric. 2014. (Spot Ser.). (ENG.). 14p. (J). (gr. -1-k). bds. 5.99 *(978-0-7232-8997-5(2),* Warne) Penguin Young Readers Group.
—Spot Goes to School. Hill, Eric. 2004. (Spot Ser.). (ENG.). 24p. (J). (gr. -1-k). 6.99 *(978-0-14-240167-5(6),* Warne) Penguin Young Readers Group.
—Spot Goes to the Beach. Hill, Eric. 2019. (Spot Ser.). (ENG.). 12p. (J). (-k). bds. 6.99 *(978-0-241-35182-6(0),* Warne) Penguin Young Readers Group.
—Spot Goes to the Farm (color) Hill, Eric. 2003. (Spot Ser.). (ENG.). 24p. (J). (gr. -1-k). 7.99 *(978-0-14-250123-8(9),* Warne) Penguin Young Readers Group.
—Spot Goes to the Park. Hill, Eric. 2005. (Spot Ser.). (ENG.). 24p. (J). (gr. -1 — 1). bds. 9.99 *(978-0-399-24363-9(1),* Warne) Penguin Young Readers Group.
—Spot Loves His Daddy. Hill, Eric. 2005. (Spot Ser.). (ENG.). 14p. (J). (gr. -1 — 1). bds. 6.99 *(978-0-399-24351-6(8),* Warne) Penguin Young Readers Group.
—Spot Loves His Mommy. Hill, Eric. 2006. (Spot Ser.). (ENG.). 14p. (J). (gr. -1 — 1). bds. 6.99 *(978-0-399-24511-4(1),* Warne) Penguin Young Readers Group.
—Spot Loves School. Hill, Eric. 2015. (Spot Ser.). 10p. (J). (gr. -1-k). bds. 5.99 *(978-0-14-135654-9(5),* Warne) Penguin Publishing Group.
—Spot Says Please. Hill, Eric. 2013. (Spot Ser.). (ENG.). 14p. (J). (gr. -1-k). bds. 6.99 *(978-0-7232-7832-0(6),* Warne) Penguin Young Readers Group.
—Spot's Baby Sister. Hill, Eric. 2004. (Spot Ser.). (ENG.). 24p. (J). (gr. -1-k). 7.99 *(978-0-14-240169-9(2),* Warne) Penguin Young Readers Group.
—Spot's Birthday Party. Hill, Eric. 2007. (Spot Ser.). (ENG.). 24p. (J). (gr. -1 — 1). bds. 9.99 *(978-0-399-24770-5(X),* Warne) Penguin Young Readers Group.
—Spot's Christmas. Hill, Eric. 2004. (Spot Ser.). (ENG.). 12p. (J). (gr. -1 — 1). bds. 6.99 *(978-0-399-24320-2(8),* Warne) Penguin Young Readers Group.
—Spot's Christmas Plush Doll. Hill, Eric. 2005. (J). 11.00 *(978-0-399-24472-8(7),* Putnam Juvenile) Penguin Publishing Group.
—Spot's Easter Surprise. Hill, Eric. 2020. (Spot Ser.). (ENG.). 10p. (J). (gr. -1-k). bds. 5.99 *(978-0-399-24743-9(2),* Warne) Penguin Young Readers Group.
—Spot's First Christmas (color) Hill, Eric. 2004. (Spot Ser.). (ENG.). 20p. (J). (gr. -1-k). 7.99 *(978-0-14-240202-3(8),* Warne) Penguin Young Readers Group.
—Spot's First Walk. Hill, Eric. (Spot Ser.). (ENG.). 24p. (J). (gr. -1 — 1). 2005. bds. 9.99 *(978-0-399-24482-7(4));* 2004. 7.99 *(978-0-14-240085-2(8))* Penguin Young Readers Group. (Warne).
—Spot's Halloween. Hill, Eric. 2003. (Spot Ser.). (ENG.). 14p. (J). (gr. -1 — 1). bds. 5.99 *(978-0-399-24185-7(X),* Warne) Penguin Young Readers Group.
—Spot's Peekaboo. Hill, Eric. 2015. (Spot Ser.). (ENG.). 12p. (J). (-k). bds. 9.99 *(978-0-14-136170-3(0),* Warne) Penguin Young Readers Group.
—Spot's Thanksgiving. Hill, Eric. 2016. (Spot Ser.). 10p. (J). (gr. -1-k). bds. 6.99 *(978-0-399-24186-4(8),* Warne) Penguin Young Readers Group.
—Where's Spot? Hill, Eric. 2003. (Spot Ser.). (ENG.). 22p. (J). (gr. -1 — 1). bds. 7.99 *(978-0-399-24046-1(2),* 53517281, Warne) Penguin Young Readers Group.
—Where's Spot? Hill, Eric. 2007. (Spot Ser.). (ENG.). 18.00 *(978-0-7569-7965-2(X))* Perfection Learning Corp.
—Where's Spot (color) Hill, Eric. 2003. (Spot Ser.). (ENG.). 24p. (J). (gr. -1-k). 7.99 *(978-0-14-250126-9(3),* Warne) Penguin Young Readers Group.
Hill, Heather C. & Roush, April. Picture Me Christmas Princess. Hapka, Cathy. 2003. (Picture Me Holiday Ser.). 10p. (J). (gr. -1-18). bds. 6.99 *(978-1-57151-571-1(2))* Playhouse Publishing.

H

Hill, Isabel, photos by. Urban Animals of Washington, D. C. Hill, Isabel. 2013. (ENG., (J). 17.99 (978-1-59572-658-2(6)) Star Bright Bks., Inc.

Hill, Isabel T., photos by. Urban Animals, 1 vol. Hill, Isabel T. 2009. (ENG., 32p. (J). (gr. 2-7). 17.95 (978-1-59572-209-6(2)); pap. 7.95 (978-1-59572-210-2(6)) Star Bright Bks., Inc.

Hill, Jen. Be Kind. Zietlow Miller, Pat. 2018. (Be Kind Ser.: 1). (ENG.). 32p. (J). 17.99 (978-1-62672-321-4(4), 900152054) Roaring Brook Pr.

—Diana's White House Garden. Carbone, Elisa & Wells, Rosemary. 2016. 44p. (J). (gr. k-3). bds. 17.99 (978-0-670-01649-5(7), Viking Books for Young Readers) Penguin Young Readers Group.

—Doing Her Bit: A Story about the Women's Land Army of America. Hagar, Erin. 2016. 32p. (J). (gr. 1-4). lib. bdg. 16.95 (978-1-58089-646-7(4)) Charlesbridge Publishing, Inc.

—Flight of the Bluebird (the Unintentional Adventures of the Bland Sisters Book 3) LaReau, Kara. (Unintentional Adventures of the Bland Sisters Ser.). (ENG.). (J). (gr. 3-7). 2020. 176p. pap. 7.99 (978-1-4197-4349-8(X), 1139503); 2019. 224p. 14.99 (978-1-4197-3144-0(0)) Abrams, Inc. (Amulet Bks.).

—The Jolly Regina (the Unintentional Adventures of the Bland Sisters Book 1) LaReau, Kara. 2018. (ENG.). 184p. (J). (gr. 3-7). pap. 7.99 (978-1-4197-2605-7(6), Amulet Bks.) Abrams, Inc.

—Spring for Sophie. Werber, Yael. 2017. (ENG.). 32p. (J). (gr. -1-3). 17.99 (978-1-4814-5134-5(0), Simon & Schuster Bks. For Young Readers) Simon & Schuster Bks. For Young Readers.

—The Uncanny Express (the Unintentional Adventures of the Bland Sisters Book 2) LaReau, Kara. 2018. (Unintentional Adventures of the Bland Sisters Ser.). (ENG.). (J). (gr. 3-7). 184p. pap. 7.99 (978-1-4197-3204-1(8)); 176p. 14.99 (978-1-4197-2568-5(8)) Abrams, Inc. (Amulet Bks.).

—Unintentional Adventures of the Bland Sisters: The Jolly Regina. LaReau, Kara. 2017. (ENG.). 176p. (J). (gr. 3-7). 14.95 (978-1-4197-2136-6(4), Amulet Bks.) Abrams, Inc.

Hill, Jessie. No Ordinary Princess. Johnson, Rachel N. 2012. 32p. pap. 16.97 (978-1-61204-993-9(1), Strategic Bk. Publishing) Strategic Book Publishing & Rights Agency (SBPRA).

Hill, Jodi. Zack Gives Back. Lewis, Vena. 2019. (ENG.). 32p. (J). pap. 9.99 **(978-1-7192-7143-1(7))** CreateSpace Independent Publishing Platform.

Hill, Jonathan. Americus. Reed, M. K. 2011. (ENG.). 224p. (YA). (gr. 7). pap. 16.99 (978-1-59643-601-5(8), 900065623, First Second Bks.) Roaring Brook Pr.

—Science Comics: Wild Weather: Storms, Meteorology, & Climate. Reed, M. K. 2019. (Science Comics Ser.). (ENG.). 128p. (J). 19.99 (978-1-62672-789-2(9), 900173602); pap. 12.99 (978-1-62672-790-8(2), 900173603) Roaring Brook Pr. (First Second Bks.).

Hill, Kelly. Anne's Colors. 2018. (Anne of Green Gables Ser.). (ENG.). 20p. (J). (— 1). bds. 7.99 (978-0-7352-6284-3(5), Tundra Bks.) Tundra Bks. CAN. Dist: Penguin Random Hse. LLC.

—Anne's Numbers. 2018. (Anne of Green Gables Ser.). (ENG.). 22p. (J). (— 1). bds. 7.99 (978-0-7352-6285-0(3), Tundra Bks.) Tundra Bks. CAN. Dist: Penguin Random Hse. LLC.

Hill, Kevin. Me & My Big Career, , Byrd-Hill, Ida. Hill, Karen, ed. 2010. (ENG.). 24p. (J). 14.95 (978-0-9829610-0-1(6)) Upheaval Media, Inc.

Hill, Laila. Dinosaur Shapes. Rainstorm Publishing, ed. 2018. (Early Learning Rhymes Ser.). (ENG.). 20p. (J). bds. 7.99 **(978-1-989219-64-5(0))** Rainstorm Pr.

Hill, Lynn. Old Woman's Garbage. Pyatt, A. K. 2003. (978-0-9718431-3-4(9)) M.O.T.H.E.R. Publishing Co., Inc., The.

Hill, Malissa. A Ladybug's Defense: Part One of the Fascinating Bug's Series. Healan, Tammy. 2011. 24p. pap. 24.95 (978-1-4626-4459-9(7)) America Star Bks.

Hill-Peterson, Jodi. Cartwheeling. Given, Cate. 2006. (J). (978-0-9790057-1-8(X)) Paws In the Sand Publishing.

—The Great Pogo Stick. Given, Cate. 2006. (J). (978-0-9790057-0-1(1)) Paws In the Sand Publishing.

—Moosu Goes to the Dentist. Vincent-Layton, Kimberly. 2006. (ENG.). 24p. pap. 10.99 (978-1-4120-7791-0(5)) Trafford Publishing.

Hill, Prescott. Lalaloopsy: Cinder Slippers & the Grand Ball. Cecil, Lauren. 2013. (Lalaloopsy Ser.). (ENG.). 24p. (J). (gr. -1-3). pap. 3.99 (978-0-545-47769-7(7)) Scholastic, Inc.

—Lalaloopsy: Easter Eggs-Travaganza. Simon, Jenne. 2014. (ENG.). 24p. (J). (gr. -1-3). pap. 4.99 (978-0-545-60802-2(3)) Scholastic, Inc.

—Lalaloopsy: Here Come the Little Sisters! Cecil, Lauren. 2013. (Lalaloopsy Ser.). (ENG.). 5p. (J). (gr. -1-k). bds. 9.99 (978-0-545-44266-4(4)) Scholastic, Inc.

—Lalaloopsy: School Day! Simon, Jenne. 2012. (Lalaloopsy Ser.). (ENG.). 32p. (J). (gr. -1-3). pap. 3.99 (978-0-545-40321-4(9)) Scholastic, Inc.

—Lalaloopsy: the Ballet Recital. Simon, Jenne. 2012. (Lalaloopsy Ser.). (ENG.). 32p. (J). (gr. -1-3). pap. 3.99 (978-0-545-39216-7(0)) Scholastic, Inc.

—Let's Pick Apples. Simon, Jenne. 2013. (Lalaloopsy Ser.). (ENG.). 32p. (J). (gr. -1-3). pap. 3.99 (978-0-545-53182-5(9)) Scholastic, Inc.

—Party Time! Cecil, Lauren. 2011. (Lalaloopsy Ser.: 2). (ENG.). 24p. (J). (gr. -1-3). pap. 3.99 (978-0-545-37998-4(9)) Scholastic, Inc.

—Snow Day!, Level 2. Simon, Jenne. 2013. (Lalaloopsy Ser.). (ENG.). 32p. (J). (gr. -1-3). pap. 3.99 (978-0-545-58123-3(0)) Scholastic, Inc.

Hill, Ros. Shamooo: A Whale of a Cow. Hill, Ros. 2005. 32p. (J). 15.95 (978-0-689-04634-6(0), Milk & Cookies) ibooks, Inc.

Hill, Scott. Lulu, Are You Going to Sleep All Day? Monday. Miller, L. S. 2018. (ENG.). 32p. (J). (gr. k-4). (978-1-989049-02-0(8)) Twin Kids Media Inc.

Hill, Shannon. Sammie the Lil' Dog on the Porch. Owens, Wanda. 2011. 20p. pap. 24.95 (978-1-4560-5736-7(7)) America Star Bks.

Hill, Stephanie. God Deserves Your Best. Hill, Clarissa. 2005. (ENG.). 20p. (J). pap. 11.00 (978-0-9785539-0-6(X)) Hill, Stephanie & Clarissa.

Hill, Steve. The Bear Man. Scott, Keith. 2010. (ENG.). 32p. (J). pap. 5.95 (978-0-88839-655-6(4)) Hancock Hse. Pubs.

Hill, Stuart. The Atlas of Monsters: Mythical Creatures from Around the World. Lawrence, Sandra. 2019. (ENG.). 64p. (J). (gr. 2-7). 19.99 (978-0-7624-9484-2(0), Running Pr. Kids) Running Pr.

Hill, T. J. Stuart the Donkey: A Tale of His Tail. Hipp, Diane. 2010. 52p. pap. 21.99 (978-1-4520-3420-1(6)) AuthorHouse.

Hill, Tracy. Cosmo's Cosmic Adventure. Carpenter, Patti. 2020. (ENG.). 32p. (J). (gr. k-4). 18.99 **(978-1-0878-5886-9(0))** Indy Pub.

Hill, Trish. Lulu. Zail, Suzy. 2004. iv, 36p. (J). pap. (978-0-7608-6741-9(0)) Sundance/Newbridge Educational Publishing.

Hill, Vicki Trego & Pennypacker, Mona. La Llorona - The Weeping Woman: An Hispanic Legend Told in Spanish & English. Hayes, Joe. 2006. (SPA.). 32p. (J). (gr. 4-6). pap. 7.95 (978-0-938317-39-5(3)) Cinco Puntos Pr.

Hillam, Corbin. Ancient China. Sylvester, Diane. 2006. (Museum Ser.). 64p. (J). (gr. 5-8). per. 13.99 (978-0-88160-389-7(9), LW444, Learning Works, The) Creative Teaching Pr., Inc.

—Ancient Rome. Sylvester, Diane. 2006. (Museum Ser.). 64p. (J). (gr. 5-8). pap. 13.99 (978-0-88160-390-3(2), LW445, Learning Works, The) Creative Teaching Pr., Inc.

—The Complete Book of Multiplication & Division: Grades 2-3. Kim, Hy. Applebaum, Teri L. & Rous, Sheri, eds. 2004. 144p. per. 16.99 (978-1-59198-034-6(8), CTP 2571) Creative Teaching Pr., Inc.

—I Have, Who Has? Language Arts, Grades 3-4: 38 Interactive Card Games, Vol. 2206. Callella, Trisha. Hamaguchi, Carla, ed. 2006. (I Have, Who Has? Ser.). 204p. (J). (gr. 3-4). per. 19.99 (978-1-59198-228-9(6), 2206) Creative Teaching Pr., Inc.

—I Have, Who Has? Language Arts, Grades 5-6: 38 Interactive Card Games. Callella, Trisha. Hamaguchi, Carla, ed. 2006. (I Have, Who Has? Ser.). 204p. (J). (gr. 5-6). per. 19.99 (978-1-59198-229-6(4)) Creative Teaching Pr., Inc.

—I Have, Who Has? Math, Grades 3-4: 38 Interactive Card Games. Callella, Trisha. Hamaguchi, Carla, ed. 2006. (I Have, Who Has? Ser.). 204p. (J). (gr. 3-4). per. 19.99 (978-1-59198-230-2(8), 2208) Creative Teaching Pr., Inc.

—More Greek & Latin Roots: Teaching Vocabulary to Improve Reading Comprehension. Callella, Trisha. Faulkner, Stacey, ed. 2006. (J). pap. 18.99 (978-1-59198-326-6(2)) Creative Teaching Pr., Inc.

—Passport to Genre: A Literature Enrichment Guide. Connolly, Debbie & Danley, Laurie. Mitchell, Judy, ed. 2006. 64p. (J). pap. 9.95 (978-1-57310-488-3(4)) Teaching & Learning Co.

Hillam, Corbin & Ciccarelli, Gary. Ancient Greece. Sylvester, Diane. VanBlaricum, Pam, ed. 2006. (Museum Ser.). 64p. pap. 13.99 (978-0-88160-387-3(2), LW441, Learning Works, The) Creative Teaching Pr., Inc.

Hillam, Corbin & Grayson, Rick. Electing Our President: The Process to Elect the Nation's Leader. Jennett, Pamela & Marchant, Sherry. Jennett, Pamela, ed. 2004. 48p. pap. 8.99 (978-0-88160-379-8(1), LW-436) Creative Teaching Pr., Inc.

Hillam, Corbin & Vangsgard, Amy. American History Reader's Theater Vol. 2244: Develop Reading Fluency & Text Comprehension Skills. Hults, Alaska, ed. 2004. 96p. (J). pap. 14.99 (978-1-59198-039-1(9), 2244) Creative Teaching Pr., Inc.

—Ancient Civilizations Reader's Theater Vol. 2246: Develop Reading Fluency & Text Comprehension Skills. Ellermeyer, Deborah & Rowell, Judy. Hults, Alaska, ed. 2004. 96p. (J). pap. 12.99 (978-1-59198-041-4(0), 2246) Creative Teaching Pr., Inc.

—Fables & Folklore Reader's Theater: Develop Reading Fluency & Text Comprehension Skills. Allen, Margaret. Hults, Alaska, ed. 2004. 96p. (J). (gr. 1-2). pap. 14.99 (978-1-59198-037-7(2), 2242) Creative Teaching Pr., Inc.

—Fairy Tales Reader's Theater: Develop Reading Fluency & Text Comprehension Skills. Allen, Margaret. Hults, Alaska, ed. 2004. 96p. (J). pap. 14.99 (978-1-59198-036-0(4)) Creative Teaching Pr., Inc.

—Philosophers to Astronauts Reader's Theater Vol. 2243: Develop Reading Fluency & Text Comprehension Skills. Hults, Alaska, ed. 2004. 96p. (J). pap. 12.99 (978-1-59198-038-4(0), 2243) Creative Teaching Pr., Inc.

Hillard Good, Karen. A Snowman Named Just Bob. Moulton, Mark Kimball. 2006. (ENG.). 16p. (J). (gr. k-3). 14.95 (978-0-8249-1707-4(3), Ideal Pubns.) Worthy Publishing.

Hillenbrand, Will. Andy & Tamika. Adler, David A. 2005. (Andy Russell Ser.: 2). (ENG.). 144p. (J). (gr. 1-4). pap. 7.99 (978-0-15-205446-5(4), 1196390) Houghton Mifflin Harcourt Publishing Co.

—Andy & Tamika. Adler, David A. 2005. (Andy Russell Ser.: Bk. 2). 129p. 16.00 (978-0-7569-4898-6(3)) Perfection Learning Corp.

—Bear & Bunny. Pinkwater, Daniel M. 2015. 40p. (J). 15.99 (978-0-7636-7153-2(3)) Candlewick Pr.

—Bear in Love. Pinkwater, Daniel M. 2012. (ENG.). 40p. (J). (gr. k-k). 15.99 (978-0-7636-4569-4(9)) Candlewick Pr.

—Down on the Farm. Kutner, Merrily. (ENG.). (J). (gr. -1 — 1). 2016. 24p. bds. 7.99 (978-0-8234-2177-0(5)); 2005. 32p. pap. 8.99 (978-0-8234-1985-2(1)) Holiday Hse., Inc.

—I'm a Duck. Bunting, Eve. 2018. 32p. (J). (gr. -1-2). 15.99 (978-0-7636-8032-9(X)) Candlewick Pr.

—The Journey of the One & Only Declaration of Independence. St. George, Judith. 2014. 48p. (J). (gr. 2-5). 8.99 (978-0-14-751164-5(X), Puffin Books) Penguin Young Readers Group.

—The Journey of the One & Only Declaration of Independence. St. George, Judith. 2011. (J). (gr. 1-7). 29.95 (978-0-439-02760-1(8), WHCD806) Weston Woods Studios, Inc.

—Journey of the One & Only Declaration of Independence. St George, Judith. 2014. (ENG.). 48p. (J). (gr. 2-5). 19.80 (978-1-5311-8647-0(5)) Perfection Learning Corp.

—The Many Troubles of Andy Russell. Adler, David A. 2005. (Andy Russell Ser.: 1). (ENG.). 144p. (J). (gr. 1-4). pap. 7.99 (978-0-15-205440-3(5), 1196371) Houghton Mifflin Harcourt Publishing Co.

—Mighty Reader & the Big Freeze. 2019. (J). (978-0-8234-4733-6(2)) Holiday Hse., Inc.

—Please Say Please! Penguin's Guide to Manners. Cuyler, Margery. 2005. (J). (978-0-439-67874-2(9)) Scholastic, Inc.

—School Trouble for Andy Russell. Adler, David A. 2005. (Andy Russell Ser.: Bk. 3). (ENG.). 128p. (J). (gr. 1-4). pap. 9.95 (978-0-15-205428-1(6), 1196335) Houghton Mifflin Harcourt Publishing Co.

—School Trouble for Andy Russell. Adler, David A. 2007. (Andy Russell Ser.: Bk. 3). 118p. pap. 6.60 (978-1-4189-5227-3(3)) Houghton Mifflin Harcourt Supplemental Pubs.

—School Trouble for Andy Russell. Adler, David A. 2008. (Andy Russell Ser.: Bk. 3). (J). (gr. 2-5). pap. 28.95 incl. audio compact disk (978-1-4301-0484-1(8)); pap. 24.95 incl. audio (978-1-4301-0483-4(X)) Live Oak Media.

—Sleep, Big Bear, Sleep!, 0 vols. Wright, Maureen. 2009. (ENG.). 32p. (J). (gr. -1-3). 16.99 (978-0-7614-5560-8(4), 9780761455608, Two Lions) Amazon Publishing.

—Smash! Mash! Crash! There Goes the Trash! Odanaka, Barbara. 2006. (ENG.). 32p. (J). (gr. -1-3). 19.99 (978-0-689-85160-5(X), McElderry, Margaret K. Bks.) McElderry, Margaret K. Bks.

—Sneeze, Big Bear, Sneeze!, 0 vols. Wright, Maureen. 2011. (ENG.). 32p. (J). (gr. -1-3). 16.99 (978-0-7614-5959-0(6), 9780761459590, Two Lions) Amazon Publishing.

—What a Treasure! Hillenbrand, Jane. (I Like to Read Ser.). (ENG.). (J). (gr. -1-3). 2018. 32p. 7.99 (978-0-8234-3987-4(9)); 2017. 24p. bds. 7.99 (978-0-8234-3763-4(9)) Holiday Hse., Inc.

—Whopper Cake. Wilson, Karma. 2007. (ENG.). 32p. (J). (gr. -1-3). 19.99 (978-0-689-83844-6(1), McElderry, Margaret K. Bks.) McElderry, Margaret K. Bks.

Hillenbrand, Will. Kite Day: A Bear & Mole Story. Hillenbrand, Will. 2012. (Bear & Mole Ser.: 2). (ENG.). 32p. (J). (-k). 16.95 (978-0-8234-1603-5(8)) Holiday Hse., Inc.

—Mother Goose Picture Puzzles, 0 vols. Hillenbrand, Will. 2011. (ENG.). 40p. (J). (gr. k-3). 17.99 (978-0-7614-5808-1(5), 9780761458081, Two Lions) Amazon Publishing.

—Off We Go! A Bear & Mole Story. Hillenbrand, Will. 2014. (Bear & Mole Ser.: 3). (ENG.). 32p. (J). (gr. -1-k). pap. 7.99 (978-0-8234-3172-4(X)) Holiday Hse., Inc.

—Spring Is Here. Hillenbrand, Will. 2012. (Bear & Mole Ser.: 1). (ENG.). 32p. (J). (-k). pap. 7.99 (978-0-8234-2431-3(6)) Holiday Hse., Inc.

Hilley, Thomas. Billy Black Ant's Exciting Adventures. Danley, Jerry J. 2012. 56p. pap. 12.99 (978-0-9885180-5-6(8)) Mindstir Media.

Hilliam, Corbin & Ellithorpe, Chris. Math Graphic Organizers 1-2: Simple & Effective Strategies for Solving Math Word Problems. Harding, Davilla. Hults, Alaska, ed. 2003. (Math Graphic Organizers Ser.). 112p. (J). pap. 13.99 (978-1-57471-979-6(3), 2573) Creative Teaching Pr., Inc.

—Math Graphic Organizers 3-5: Simple & Effective Strategies for Solving Math Word Problems. Harding, Davilla. Hults, Alaska, ed. 2003. (Math Graphic Organizers Ser.). 112p. (J). (gr. 2-7). pap. 13.99 (978-1-57471-980-2(7), 2574) Creative Teaching Pr., Inc.

Hilliam, Corbin & Vangsgard, Amy. Discoverers & Inventors Reader's Theater Vol. 2245: Develop Reading Fluency & Test Comprehension Skills. Jennett, Pamela. Hults, Alaska, ed. 2004. 96p. (J). pap. 12.99 (978-1-59198-040-7(2), 2245) Creative Teaching Pr., Inc.

Hilliard, Beverly. Seven Magical Tooth Fairies. Johnson, Margaret. 2007. (ENG.). 84p. per. 9.95 (978-0-595-37420-5(4)) iUniverse, Inc.

Hilliard, Carol. I Like Dogs. Cheehy, Debra/Ilene. 2009. 52p. (J). 16.95 (978-0-9820817-0-9(7)) Four Foot Pr. LLC.

Hilliard, Richard. Mammoth Bones & Broken Stones: The Mystery of North America's First People. Harrison, David L. 2010. (ENG.). 48p. (J). (gr. 4-7). 18.95 (978-1-59078-561-4(4)) Boyds Mills Pr.

Hillier, Angela. Bird. Gerloch, Malcolm. 2019. (ENG.). 40p. (YA). (gr. 7-12). pap. **(978-1-912021-47-5(1)**, Nightingale Books) Pegasus Elliot Mackenzie Pubs.

—Flea. Gerloch, Malcolm. 2020. (ENG.). 36p. (YA). (gr. 7-12). pap. **(978-1-912021-30-7(7)**, Nightingale Books) Pegasus Elliot Mackenzie Pubs.

Hilliker, Phillip. I Dare You! Brezenoff, Steve. 2008. (Vortex Bks.). (ENG.). 112p. (J). (gr. 5-9). 26.65 (978-1-4342-0798-2(6), Stone Arch Bks.) Capstone.

—The Runaway Skeleton. Muldoon, Kathleen M. 2008. (Vortex Bks.). (ENG.). 112p. (J). (gr. 5-9). 26.65 (978-1-4342-0800-2(1), Stone Arch Bks.) Capstone.

Hillman, Shane. Fat Cat of Underwhere. Hale, Bruce. 2009. (Underwhere Ser.). 176p. (J). pap. 5.99 (978-0-06-085135-4(X)) HarperCollins Pubs.

—Mole Men of Underwhere. Hale, Bruce. 2009. (Underwhere Ser.). 160p. (J). 15.99 (978-0-06-085136-1(8)) HarperCollins Pubs.

—Pirates of Underwhere. Hale, Bruce. (Underwhere Ser.). (J). (gr. 3-7). 2008. 164p. lib. bdg. 16.89 (978-0-06-085128-6(7)); 2. 2009. (ENG.). 176p. pap. 6.99 (978-0-06-085129-3(5)) HarperCollins Pubs.

—Prince of Underwhere. Hale, Bruce. 2009. (Underwhere Ser.: 1). (ENG.). 176p. (J). (gr. 3-7). pap. 5.99 (978-0-06-085126-2(0)) HarperCollins Pubs.

Hillmann, Joe & Cox, Chad. Snort, Wheeze, Rattle & Grunt. Reich, J. J. 2006. (J). 8.99 (978-0-9762971-1-6(6)) Outdoor Originals LLC.

Hills, Jodi. Believe. Hills, Jodi. 2003. (ENG.). 48p. (J). 39.95 (978-0-931674-52-5(2), Waldman House Pr.) TRISTAN Publishing, Inc.

Hills, Laila. Alphabet. Rainstorm Publishing, ed. 2019. (Love to Learn Ser.). (ENG.). 20p. (J). bds. 8.99 **(978-1-926444-61-1(2))** Rainstorm Pr.

Hills, Laila. Animal Friends. 2017. (J). (978-1-62885-342-1(5)) Kidsbooks, LLC.

Hills, Laila. Animals. Rainstorm Publishing, ed. 2019. (Love to Learn Ser.). (ENG.). 20p. (J). bds. 8.99 **(978-1-926444-63-5(9))** Rainstorm Pr.

—Colors. Rainstorm Publishing, ed. 2019. (Love to Learn Ser.). (ENG.). 20p. (J). bds. 8.99 **(978-1-926444-62-8(0))** Rainstorm Pr.

—Farmyard ABC. Rainstorm Publishing, ed. 2018. (Early Learning Rhymes Ser.). (ENG.). 20p. (J). bds. 7.99 **(978-1-989219-62-1(4))** Rainstorm Pr.

—Jungle 123. Rainstorm Publishing, ed. 2019. (Early Learning Rhymes Ser.). (ENG.). 20p. (J). bds. 7.99 **(978-1-989219-61-4(6))** Rainstorm Pr.

—Monster Colors. Rainstorm Publishing, ed. 2019. (Early Learning Rhymes Ser.). (ENG.). 20p. (J). bds. 7.99 **(978-1-989219-63-8(2))** Rainstorm Pr.

—Numbers. Rainstorm Publishing, ed. 2019. (Love to Learn Ser.). (ENG.). 20p. (J). bds. 8.99 **(978-1-926444-65-9(5))** Rainstorm Pr.

—Peek-A-Boo Animals. Rainstorm Publishing, ed. 2018. (ENG.). 20p. (J). bds. 7.99 **(978-1-989219-93-5(4))** Rainstorm Pr.

—Peek-A-Boo Colors. Rainstorm Publishing, ed. 2018. (ENG.). 20p. (J). bds. 7.99 **(978-1-989219-91-1(8))** Rainstorm Pr.

—Peek-A-Boo Numbers. Rainstorm Publishing, ed. 2018. (ENG.). 20p. (J). bds. 7.99 **(978-1-989219-92-8(6))** Rainstorm Pr.

—Peek-A-Boo Words. Rainstorm Publishing, ed. 2018. (ENG.). 20p. (J). bds. 7.99 **(978-1-989219-90-4(X))** Rainstorm Pr.

Hills, Laila. Sword to Words. Su, Tami. 2010. 36p. pap. 14.99 (978-1-60844-524-0(0)) Dog Ear Publishing, LLC.

Hills, Laila. Vehicles. Rainstorm Publishing, ed. 2019. (Love to Learn Ser.). (ENG.). 20p. (J). bds. 8.99 **(978-1-926444-64-2(7))** Rainstorm Pr.

—Words. Rainstorm Publishing, ed. 2019. (Love to Learn Ser.). (ENG.). 20p. (J). bds. 8.99 **(978-1-926444-66-6(3))** Rainstorm Pr.

Hills, Tad. Rocket's Very Fine Day. 2019. (Step into Reading Ser.). (ENG.). 32p. (J). (gr. k-1). 14.96 **(978-0-87617-768-6(2))** Penworthy Co., LLC, The.

Hills, Tad. Drop It, Rocket! Hills, Tad. 2014. (Rocket Ser.). (ENG.). 32p. (J). (gr. -1-1). 12.99 (978-0-385-37247-3(7), Schwartz & Wade Bks.) Random Hse. Children's Bks.

—Duck & Goose. Hills, Tad. 2006. (Duck & Goose Ser.). (ENG.). 40p. (J). (gr. -1-2). 17.99 (978-0-375-83611-4(X), Schwartz & Wade Bks.) Random Hse. Children's Bks.

—Duck & Goose, 1, 2, 3. Hills, Tad. 2008. (Duck & Goose Ser.). (ENG.). 22p. (J). (gr. k — 1). bds. 7.99 (978-0-375-85621-1(8), Schwartz & Wade Bks.) Random Hse. Children's Bks.

—Duck & Goose Colors. Hills, Tad. 2015. (Duck & Goose Ser.). (ENG.). 22p. (J). (— 1). bds. 7.99 (978-0-553-50806-2(7), Schwartz & Wade Bks.) Random Hse. Children's Bks.

—Duck & Goose, Find a Pumpkin. Hills, Tad. 2009. (Duck & Goose Ser.). (ENG.). 22p. (J). (gr. k — 1). bds. 7.99 (978-0-375-85813-0(X), Schwartz & Wade Bks.) Random Hse. Children's Bks.

—Duck & Goose, Find a Pumpkin (Oversized Board Book) Hills, Tad. 2012. (Duck & Goose Ser.). (ENG.). 22p. (J). (gr. k-k). bds. 10.99 (978-0-307-98155-4(X), Schwartz & Wade Bks.) Random Hse. Children's Bks.

—Duck & Goose Go to the Beach. Hills, Tad. 2014. (Duck & Goose Ser.). (ENG.). 40p. (J). (gr. -1-2). 17.99 (978-0-385-37235-0(3), Schwartz & Wade Bks.) Random Hse. Children's Bks.

—Duck & Goose, Goose Needs a Hug. Hills, Tad. 2012. (Duck & Goose Ser.). (ENG.). 22p. (J). (-k). bds. 7.99 (978-0-307-98293-3(9), Schwartz & Wade Bks.) Random Hse. Children's Bks.

—Duck & Goose, Here Comes the Easter Bunny! Hills, Tad. 2012. (Duck & Goose Ser.). (ENG.). 22p. (J). (gr. k-k). bds. 7.99 (978-0-375-87280-8(9), Schwartz & Wade Bks.) Random Hse. Children's Bks.

—Duck & Goose, How Are You Feeling? Hills, Tad. 2009. (Duck & Goose Ser.). (ENG.). 22p. (J). (gr. -1 — 1). bds. 7.99 (978-0-375-84629-8(8), Schwartz & Wade Bks.) Random Hse. Children's Bks.

—Duck & Goose, It's Time for Christmas! Hills, Tad. 2010. (Duck & Goose Ser.). 22p. (J). (gr. k — 1). bds. 7.99 (978-0-375-86484-1(9), Schwartz & Wade Bks.) Random Hse. Children's Bks.

—Duck & Goose, It's Time for Christmas! (Oversized Board Book) Hills, Tad. 2011. (Duck & Goose Ser.). (ENG.). 22p. (J). (gr. -1 — 1). bds. 10.99 (978-0-375-87112-2(8), Schwartz & Wade Bks.) Random Hse. Children's Bks.

—Duck & Goose, Let's Dance! (with an Original Song) Hills, Tad. Savage, Lauren. 2016. (Duck & Goose Ser.). (ENG.). 26p. (J). (gr. -1-2). bds. 8.99 (978-0-385-37245-9(0), Schwartz & Wade Bks.) Random Hse. Children's Bks.

—Duck, Duck, Goose. Hills, Tad. (Duck & Goose Ser.). (ENG.). (J). (gr. -1-2). 2018. 36p. bds. 8.99 (978-1-5247-6615-3(1)); 2007. 40p. 17.99 (978-0-375-84068-5(0)) Random Hse. Children's Bks. (Schwartz & Wade Bks.).

—How Rocket Learned to Read. Hills, Tad. 2010. (Rocket Ser.). (ENG.). 40p. (J). (gr. -1-2). 17.99 (978-0-375-85899-4(7), Schwartz & Wade Bks.) Random Hse. Children's Bks.

—R Is for Rocket: an ABC Book. Hills, Tad. 2015. (Rocket Ser.). (ENG.). 32p. (J). (gr. -1-2). 17.99 (978-0-553-52228-0(0), Schwartz & Wade Bks.) Random Hse. Children's Bks.

—Rocket Writes a Story. Hills, Tad. 2012. (Rocket Ser.). (ENG.). 40p. (J). (gr. -1-3). 17.99 (978-0-375-87086-6(5), Schwartz & Wade Bks.) Random Hse. Children's Bks.

—Rocket's Learning Box, 2 vols. Hills, Tad. 2012. (ENG.). 40p. (J). (gr. -1-3). 35.98 *(978-0-307-98235-3(1),* Schwartz & Wade Bks.) Random Hse. Children's Bks.

—Rocket's Mighty Words. Hills, Tad. 2015. (Rocket Ser.). (ENG.). 22p. (J). (-k). bds. 7.99 *(978-0-553-53866-3(7),* Schwartz & Wade Bks.) Random Hse. Children's Bks.

—Rocket's Mighty Words (Oversized Board Book) Hills, Tad. 2013. (Rocket Ser.). (ENG.). 22p. (J). (-k). bds. 10.99 *(978-0-385-37233-6(7),* Schwartz & Wade Bks.) Random Hse. Children's Bks.

—What's up, Duck? A Book of Opposites. Hills, Tad. 2008. (Duck & Goose Ser.). (ENG.). 22p. (J). (gr. k — 1). bds. 7.99 *(978-0-375-84738-7(3),* Schwartz & Wade Bks.) Random Hse. Children's Bks.

Hillyard, T. K., jt. illus. see Kaye, Justin.

Hilpuesch, Jutta. An ABC of Flowers. Hilpuesch, Jutta. (J). (— 1). 2020. 30p. bds. 8.99 *(978-0-593-11410-0(8));* 2019. (ENG.). 32p. 16.99 *(978-0-525-51785-6(5))* Penguin Young Readers Group. (Philomel Bks.).

Hilsgen, Melissa. Don't Eat the Soap! Hilland, April. 2017. (ENG.). (J). pap. *(978-1-5255-1430-2(X))* FriesenPress.

Hilton, Kyle & Marlin, Lissy. The Magic Misfits: the Second Story. Harris, Neil Patrick. 2018. (Magic Misfits Ser.: 2). (ENG.). (J). (gr. 3-7). 336p. 16.99 *(978-0-316-39185-6(9));* 400p. 18.99 *(978-0-316-41986-4(9))* Little, Brown Bks. for Young Readers.

Hilton, Kyle, jt. illus. see Marlin, Lissy.

Hilts, The Brothers. Seaver the Weaver. Czajak, Paul. 2015. (ENG.). 32p. (J). (-k). 15.95 *(978-1-938063-57-2(0),* Mighty Media Kids) Mighty Media Pr.

Himekawa, Akira. The Legend of Zelda: Hyrule Historia. Himekawa, Akira. Miyamoto, Shigeru & Aonuma, Eiji. Thorpe, Patrick, ed. 2013. (ENG.). 276p. 39.99 *(978-1-61655-041-7(4))* Dark Horse Comics.

—The Legend of Zelda, Vol. 10: Phantom Hourglass. Himekawa, Akira. 2010. (Legend of Zelda Ser.: 10). (ENG.). 200p. (J). (gr. 2-5). pap. 9.99 *(978-1-4215-3724-5(9))* Viz Media.

—The Legend of Zelda, Vol. 2. Himekawa, Akira. 2008. (Legend of Zelda Ser.: 2). (ENG.). 200p. (J). (gr. 1). pap. 9.99 *(978-1-4215-2328-6(0))* Viz Media.

—The Legend of Zelda, Vol. 3: Majora's Mask. Himekawa, Akira. 2009. (Legend of Zelda Ser.: 3). (ENG.). 216p. (J). pap. 9.99 *(978-1-4215-2329-3(9))* Viz Media.

—The Legend of Zelda, Vol. 5: Oracle of Ages. Himekawa, Akira. 2009. (Legend of Zelda Ser.: 5). (ENG.). 200p. (J). pap. 9.99 *(978-1-4215-2331-6(0))* Viz Media.

—The Legend of Zelda, Vol. 6: Four Swords - Part 1. Himekawa, Akira. 2009. (Legend of Zelda Ser.: 6). (ENG.). 200p. (J). pap. 9.99 *(978-1-4215-2332-3(9))* Viz Media.

—The Legend of Zelda, Vol. 7: Four Swords - Part 2. Himekawa, Akira. 2009. (Legend of Zelda Ser.: 7). (ENG.). 176p. (J). pap. 9.99 *(978-1-4215-2333-0(7))* Viz Media.

—The Legend of Zelda, Vol. 8: The Minish Cap. Himekawa, Akira. 2009. (Legend of Zelda Ser.: 8). (ENG.). 192p. (J). pap. 9.99 *(978-1-4215-2334-7(5))* Viz Media.

—The Legend of Zelda, Vol. 9: A Link to the Past. Himekawa, Akira. 2010. (Legend of Zelda Ser.: 9). (ENG.). 192p. (YA). pap. 9.99 *(978-1-4215-2335-4(3))* Viz Media.

Himes, Rachel. Princess & the Peas. Himes, Rachel. 2017. 32p. (J). (gr. k-3). 16.99 *(978-1-58089-718-1(5))* Charlesbridge Publishing, Inc.

himesuz. The Magic in This Other World Is Too Far Behind! Volume 1. Hitsuji, Gamei. Hikoki, tr. 2019. (Magic in This Other World Is Too Far Behind! (light Novel) Ser.: 1). (ENG.). 288p. pap. 14.99 *(978-1-7183-5400-5(2))* J-Novel Club.

—The Magic in This Other World Is Too Far Behind! Volume 2. Hitsuji, Gamei. Hikoki, tr. 2019. (Magic in This Other World Is Too Far Behind! (light Novel) Ser.: 2). (ENG.). 328p. pap. 14.99 *(978-1-7183-5401-2(0))* J-Novel Club.

—The Magic in This Other World Is Too Far Behind! Volume 3. Hitsuji, Gamei. Hikoki, tr. 2019. (Magic in This Other World Is Too Far Behind! (light Novel) Ser.: 3). (ENG.). 308p. pap. 14.99 *(978-1-7183-5402-9(9))* J-Novel Club.

—The Magic in This Other World Is Too Far Behind! Volume 4. Hitsuji, Gamei. Hikoki, tr. 2019. (Magic in This Other World Is Too Far Behind! (light Novel) Ser.: 4). (ENG.). 300p. pap. 14.99 *(978-1-7183-5403-6(7))* J-Novel Club.

—The Magic in This Other World Is Too Far Behind! Volume 5. Hitsuji, Gamei. Hikoki, tr. 2019. (Magic in This Other World Is Too Far Behind! (light Novel) Ser.: 5). (ENG.). 300p. pap. 14.99 *(978-1-7183-5404-3(5))* J-Novel Club.

Himler, Ron. Dream Big: A True Story of Courage & Determination. McGillivray, Dave & Feehrer, Nancy. 2018. (ENG.). 32p. (J). 16.95 *(978-1-61930-618-9(2),* 9781619306189) Nomad Pr.

Himler, Ronald. Always with You. Vander Zee, Ruth. 2008. (ENG.). 32p. (J). (gr. -1-3). 17.00 *(978-0-8028-5295-3(5),* Eerdmans Bks For Young Readers) Eerdmans, William B. Publishing Co.

—Anna & Natalie, 1 vol. Cole, Barbara. 2007. (ENG.). 32p. (J). 16.95 *(978-1-59572-105-1(3))* Star Bright Bks., Inc.

—Anna & Natalie, 1 vol. Cole, Barbara H. 2010. (ENG.). 32p. (J). pap. 6.95 *(978-1-59572-211-9(4))* Star Bright Bks., Inc.

—Bee My Valentine!, 1 vol. Cohen, Miriam. 2008. (ENG.). 32p. (J). (gr. k-3). 15.95 *(978-1-59572-085-6(5))* Star Bright Bks., Inc.

—The Best Cat in the World. Newman, Lesléa. 2004. 32p. (J). (gr. 1-4). 16.00 *(978-0-8028-5252-6(1));* (gr. -1-3). 8.00 *(978-0-8028-5294-6(7),* Eerdmans Bks For Young Readers) Eerdmans, William B. Publishing Co.

—The Buffalo Soldier, 1 vol. Garland, Sherry. 2006. (ENG.). 32p. (J). (gr. k-3). 16.99 *(978-1-58980-391-6(4),* Pelican Publishing) Arcadia Publishing.

—First Grade Takes a Test, 1 vol. Cohen, Miriam. 2006. (ENG.). 32p. (J). (gr. -1-3). 15.95 *(978-1-59572-054-2(5));* (gr. k-3). pap. 5.95 *(978-1-59572-055-9(3))* Star Bright Bks., Inc.

—First Grade Takes a Test (Spanish/English), 1 vol. Cohen, Miriam. 2008. (ENG & SPA.). 32p. (J). (gr. k-3). 15.95 *(978-1-59572-150-1(9));* pap. 5.95 *(978-1-59572-151-8(7))* Star Bright Bks., Inc.

—I Wonder As I Wander. Swain, Gwenyth. 2004. 32p. (J). (gr. 2-5). 16.00 *(978-0-8028-5214-4(9))* Eerdmans, William B. Publishing Co.

—I Wonder as I Wander. Swain, Gwenyth. 2005. 32p. (J). (gr. k-3). pap. 8.00 *(978-0-8028-5298-4(X),* Eerdmans Bks For Young Readers) Eerdmans, William B. Publishing Co.

—Janey. Zolotow, Charlotte. Date not set. 32p. (J). (gr. -1-3). 15.89 *(978-0-06-027872-4(2))* HarperCollins Pubs.

—Jim's Dog Muffins, 1 vol. Cohen, Miriam. 2008. 32p. (J). (ENG.). 15.95 *(978-1-59572-099-3(5));* (gr. -1-3). pap. 5.95 *(978-1-59572-100-6(2))* Star Bright Bks., Inc.

—Layla's Head Scarf, 1 vol. Cohen, Miriam. 2009. (ENG.). 32p. (J). (gr. -1-3). 15.95 *(978-1-59572-177-8(0));* pap. 5.95 *(978-1-59572-178-5(9))* Star Bright Bks., Inc.

—Liar, Liar, Pants on Fire!, 1 vol. Cohen, Miriam. 2008. (ENG.). 32p. (J). (gr. -1-3). 15.95 *(978-1-59572-077-1(4));* pap. 5.95 *(978-1-59572-078-8(2))* Star Bright Bks., Inc.

—The Log Cabin Wedding. Howard, Ellen. 2006. (ENG.). 64p. (J). (gr. -1-3). 15.95 *(978-0-8234-1989-0(4))* Holiday Hse., Inc.

—My Big Brother, 1 vol. Cohen, Miriam. 2005. (ENG.). 32p. (J). 15.95 *(978-1-59572-007-8(3));* pap. 6.95 *(978-1-59572-158-7(4))* Star Bright Bks., Inc.

—My Big Brother (Spanish/English), 1 vol. Cohen, Miriam. 2008. (ABK, SPA & ENG.). 32p. (J). (gr. -1-3). pap. 5.95 *(978-1-59572-037-5(5))* Star Bright Bks., Inc.

—A Picture Book of Lewis & Clark. Adler, David A. 2003. (Picture Book Biography Ser.). (ENG.). 32p. (J). (gr. -1-3). 7.99 *(978-0-8234-1795-7(6))* Holiday Hse., Inc.

—Prairie Christmas. Van Steenwyk, Elizabeth. 2006. 32p. (J). (gr. k). 17.00 *(978-0-8028-5280-9(7),* Eerdmans Bks For Young Readers) Eerdmans, William B. Publishing Co.

—Redcoats & Petticoats. Kirkpatrick, Katherine. 2018. (ENG.). 34p. (J). (gr. 2-4). pap. 9.99 *(978-1-7180-8921-1(X))* Independently Published.

—The Roses in My Carpets, 1 vol. Khan, Rukhsana. 2004. (ENG.). 32p. (J). (gr. 1-3). pap. 9.95 *(978-1-55005-069-1(9),* 2950eb86-8b63-45cd-a73a-8abcacacb8b1) Fitzhenry & Whiteside, Ltd. CAN. Dist: Firefly Bks., Ltd.

—Rudi's Pond. Bunting, Eve. 2004. (ENG.). 32p. (J). (gr. -1-3). pap. 7.99 *(978-0-618-48604-5(6),* 100392) Houghton Mifflin Harcourt Publishing Co.

—Sadako & the Thousand Paper Cranes (Puffin Modern Classics) Coerr, Eleanor. 2004. (Puffin Modern Classics Ser.). (ENG.). 80p. (J). (gr. 3-7). pap. 6.99 *(978-0-14-240113-2(7),* Puffin Books) Penguin Young Readers Group.

—Someday a Tree. Bunting, Eve. 2004. (ENG.). 32p. (gr. -1-3). pap. 7.99 *(978-0-395-76478-7(5),* 111821) Perfection Learning Corp.

—Tough Jim, 1 vol. Cohen, Miriam. (ENG.). 32p. (J). (gr. -1-3). 2008. 15.95 *(978-1-59572-071-9(5));* 2007. pap. 5.95 *(978-1-59572-072-6(3))* Star Bright Bks., Inc.

—Train to Somewhere. Bunting, Eve. 2004. 32p. (gr. -1-3). 18.00 *(978-0-7569-4260-1(8))* Perfection Learning Corp.

—Voices of the Alamo, 1 vol. Garland, Sherry. 2017. (Voices of History Ser.). (ENG.). 40p. (J). (gr. 3-3). 17.99 *(978-1-58980-222-3(5),* Pelican Publishing) Arcadia Publishing.

—Wash Day, 1 vol. Cole, Barbara H. 2004. (ENG.). 32p. (J). 15.95 *(978-1-932065-36-7(9),* 7187849112) Star Bright Bks., Inc.

—Why Did Daddy Have to Leave? 2018. (J). 17.95 *(978-0-9885295-9-5(9))* Blue Marlin Pubns.

—Will I Have a Friend?, 1 vol. Cohen, Miriam. 2008. (ENG.). 32p. (J). (gr. k-3). 15.95 *(978-1-59572-069-6(3))* Star Bright Bks., Inc.

Himler, Ronald. Dancing Boy, 1 vol. Himler, Ronald. 2005. (ENG.). 32p. (J). (gr. -1-k). 15.95 *(978-1-59572-020-7(0))* Star Bright Bks., Inc.

—El examen de primer Grado, 1 vol. Himler, Ronald. Cohen, Miriam. 2006.Tr. of First Grade Takes a Test. (SPA.). 32p. (J). (gr. k-3). 15.95 *(978-1-59572-153-2(3));* pap. 5.95 *(978-1-59572-152-5(5))* Star Bright Bks., Inc.

—The Girl on the Yellow Giraffe, 1 vol. Himler, Ronald. 2004. (ENG.). 32p. (J). 15.95 *(978-1-932065-93-0(8))* Star Bright Bks., Inc.

Himmelman, Jeff. The Giant from the Fire Sea. Himmelman, John. 2019. (ENG.). 256p. (J). 16.99 *(978-1-250-19650-7(7),* 900194120, Holt, Henry & Co. Bks. For Young Readers) Holt, Henry & Co.

—The Giant from the Fire Sea. Himmelman, John. 2020. (ENG.). 40p. (J). pap. 7.99 *(978-1-250-25045-2(5),* 900194121) Square Fish.

Himmelman, John. A Daddy Longlegs Isn't a Spider. Stewart, Melissa. 2009. 32p. (J). (gr. 1-7). pap. 8.95 *(978-0-89317-069-1(0),* Windward Publishing) Finney Co., Inc.

Himmelman, John. Albert Hopper, Science Hero. Himmelman, John. 2020. (Albert Hopper, Science Hero Ser.: 1). (ENG.). 160p. (J). 13.99 *(978-1-250-23016-4(0),* 900209343, Holt, Henry & Co. Bks. For Young Readers) Holt, Henry & Co.

—Bunjitsu Bunny Jumps to the Moon. Himmelman, John. 2016. (Bunjitsu Bunny Ser.: 3). (ENG.). 128p. (J). 13.99 *(978-1-62779-732-0(7),* 9781627797320, Holt, Henry & Co. Bks. For Young Readers) Holt, Henry & Co.

—Bunjitsu Bunny Jumps to the Moon. Himmelman, John. 2017. (Bunjitsu Bunny Ser.: 3). (ENG.). 144p. (J). pap. 6.99 *(978-1-250-12940-6(0),* 900158780) Square Fish.

—Bunjitsu Bunny vs. Bunjitsu Bunny. Himmelman, John. 2017. (Bunjitsu Bunny Ser.: 4). (ENG.). 128p. (J). 13.99 *(978-1-62779-733-7(5),* 9781627797337, Holt, Henry & Co. Bks. For Young Readers) Holt, Henry & Co.

—Bunjitsu Bunny vs. Bunjitsu Bunny. Himmelman, John. 2018. (Bunjitsu Bunny Ser.: 4). (ENG.). 128p. (J). pap. 7.99 *(978-1-250-17720-9(0),* 900158783) Square Fish.

—Bunjitsu Bunny's Best Move. Himmelman, John. 2015. (Bunjitsu Bunny Ser.: 2). (ENG.). 128p. (J). (gr. 1-3). 13.99 *(978-0-8050-9971-3(9),* 9780805099713, Holt, Henry & Co. Bks. For Young Readers) Holt, Henry & Co.

—Bunjitsu Bunny's Best Move. Himmelman, John. ed. 2016. (Bunjitsu Bunny Ser.: 2). (ENG.). 128p. (J). (gr. 1-3). 16.00 *(978-0-606-39298-3(X))* Turtleback.

—Chickens to the Rescue. Himmelman, John. 2006. (Barnyard Rescue Ser.). (ENG.). 32p. (J). (gr. -1-3). 18.99 *(978-0-8050-7951-7(3),* 900031912, Holt, Henry & Co. Bks. For Young Readers) Holt, Henry & Co.

—The Cow Said Meow. Himmelman, John. 2016. (ENG.). 32p. (J). 16.99 *(978-1-62779-378-0(X),* 9781627793780, Holt, Henry & Co. Bks. For Young Readers) Holt, Henry & Co.

—Floaty. Himmelman, John. 2018. (ENG.). 32p. (J). 17.99 *(978-1-250-12805-8(6),* 9781250128058, Holt, Henry & Co. Bks. For Young Readers) Holt, Henry & Co.

—Frog in a Bog. Himmelman, John. 2004. 32p. (J). (gr. -1-2). pap. 7.95 *(978-1-57091-518-5(0))* Charlesbridge Publishing, Inc.

—Noisy Bird Sing-Along, 1 vol. Himmelman, John. 2015. (ENG.). 32p. (J). (gr. -1-4). pap. 16.95 *(978-1-58469-514-1(5),* Dawn Pubns.) Sourcebooks, Inc.

—Noisy Bug Sing-Along, 1 vol. Himmelman, John. 2013. (ENG.). 32p. (J). (gr. -1-4). 16.95 *(978-1-58469-191-4(3))* Dawn Pubns.

—Noisy Bug Sing-Along, 1 vol. Himmelman, John. 2013. (ENG.). 32p. (J). (gr. -1-4). pap. 8.95 *(978-1-58469-192-1(1),* Dawn Pubns.) Sourcebooks, Inc.

—Noisy Frog Sing-Along. Himmelman, John. 2013. (ENG.). 32p. (J). (gr. -1-4). 16.95 *(978-1-58469-339-0(8));* pap. 8.95 *(978-1-58469-340-6(1))* Sourcebooks, Inc. (Dawn Pubns.).

—Pigs to the Rescue: A Picture Book. Himmelman, John. 2010. (Barnyard Rescue Ser.). (ENG.). 32p. (J). (gr. -1-3). 18.99 *(978-0-8050-8683-6(8),* 900045788, Holt, Henry & Co. Bks. For Young Readers) Holt, Henry & Co.

—Tales of Bunjitsu Bunny. Himmelman, John. 2014. (Bunjitsu Bunny Ser.: 1). (ENG.). 128p. (J). (gr. 1-3). 13.99 *(978-0-8050-9970-6(0),* 900128463, Holt, Henry & Co. Bks. For Young Readers) Holt, Henry & Co.

—There's a Bug on My Book!, 1 vol. Himmelman, John. 2017. (ENG.). 32p. (J). (gr. -1-3). 16.95 *(978-1-58469-587-5(0),* Dawn Pubns.) Sourcebooks, Inc.

—Tudley Didn't Know, 1 vol. Himmelman, John. 2006. (ENG.). 32p. (J). (gr. -1-3). 15.95 *(978-0-9764943-6-2(1));* pap. 8.95 *(978-1-934359-04-4(1))* Arbordale Publishing.

Himmler, Ronald. Bee My Valentine, 1 vol. Cohen, Miriam. 2009. (ENG.). 32p. (J). (gr. k-3). pap. 5.95 *(978-1-59572-086-3(3))* Star Bright Bks., Inc.

Hinch, Ali. Kamik Takes the Lead. Baker, Darryl. 2020. (Kamik Ser.). (ENG.). 32p. (J). 10.95 *(978-1-77227-266-6(3))* Inhabit Media Inc. CAN. Dist: Consortium Bk. Sales & Distribution.

Hinch, Ali. Saila & Betty (English) Rooney, Christina. ed. 2020. (Nunavummi Ser.). (ENG.). 24p. (J). (gr. 1-1). pap. 8.95 ***(978-1-77450-183-2(X))*** Inhabit Education CAN. Dist: Consortium Bk. Sales & Distribution.

Hinch, Ali. Simonie & the Dance Contest. Matthews, Gail. 2019. (ENG.). 36p. (J). pap. 10.95 *(978-1-77227-224-6(8))* Inhabit Media Inc. CAN. Dist: Consortium Bk. Sales & Distribution.

Hinch, Ali. Tuktu's Birthday (Inuktitut/English) Rupke, Rachel. ed. 2020. (Arvaaq Bks.). (ENG.). 40p. (J). pap. 10.95 ***(978-0-2287-0360-0(3),*** Arvaaq Books) Inhabit Education CAN. Dist: Consortium Bk. Sales & Distribution.

—Uqi's New Parka (Inuktitut/English) Wilman, Jennifer. ed. 2020. (ENG.). 40p. (J). pap. 10.95 ***(978-0-2287-0494-2(4))*** Inhabit Education CAN. Dist: Consortium Bk. Sales & Distribution.

—Viivi's New Kamiks (English) Mike, Nadia. ed. 2020. (Nunavummi Ser.). (ENG.). 28p. (J). (gr. 2-2). pap. 8.95 ***(978-1-77450-176-4(7))*** Inhabit Education CAN. Dist: Consortium Bk. Sales & Distribution.

Hinch, Ali. Nanuq & Nuka: Cleaning up the Campsite (Inuktitut/English) Hinch, Ali. ed. 2020. (Arvaaq Bks.). (ENG.). 32p. (J). pap. 10.95 ***(978-0-2287-0489-8(8),*** Arvaaq Books) Inhabit Education CAN. Dist: Consortium Bk. Sales & Distribution.

—Nanuq & Nuka: Get Up! (Inuktitut/English) Hinch, Ali. ed. 2020. (Arvaaq Bks.). (ENG.). 32p. (J). pap. 10.95 ***(978-0-2287-0487-4(1),*** Arvaaq Books) Inhabit Education CAN. Dist: Consortium Bk. Sales & Distribution.

—Nanuq & Nuka: Try Again, Nuka! (Inuktitut/English) Hinch, Ali. ed. 2020. (Arvaaq Bks.). (ENG.). 28p. (J). pap. 10.95 ***(978-0-2287-0488-1(X),*** Arvaaq Books) Inhabit Education CAN. Dist: Consortium Bk. Sales & Distribution.

Hinckley, Greg. An Ancient Tale of Rags & Riches. Cahn, Yehudah. 126p. (J). (gr. 5-8). 12.95 *(978-1-56062-073-0(0),* CJR119H); pap. 9.95 *(978-1-56062-074-7(9),* CJR119S) C I S Communications, Inc.

Hinde, Deborah. Moo & Moo & Can You Guess Who? Millton, Jane. 2017. (ENG.). 32p. (J). (-3). pap. 13.99 *(978-1-76063-161-1(2))* Allen & Unwin AUS. Dist: Independent Pubs. Group.

—Moo & Moo & the Little Calf Too. Millton, Jane. 2017. (ENG.). 32p. (J). (-3). pap. 14.99 *(978-1-877505-92-8(7))* Allen & Unwin AUS. Dist: Independent Pubs. Group.

Hinder, Carine. A Little Fox. Wren, Rosalee. Cottage Door Press, ed. 2019. (ENG.). 10p. (J). (gr. -1-k). bds. 4.99 *(978-1-68052-630-1(8),* 1004231) Cottage Door Pr.

Hinder, Sarah Jane. Breathe with Me: Using Breath to Feel Strong, Calm, & Happy. Gates, Mariam. 2019. (ENG.). 32p. (J). 17.95 *(978-1-68364-030-1(6),* 900220846) Sounds True, Inc.

Hinder, Sarah Jane. Good Morning Yoga: A Pose-By-Pose Wake up Story. Gates, Mariam. (Good Night Yoga Ser.: 5). (ENG.). (J). 2020. 22p. bds. 9.99 ***(978-1-68364-573-3(1),*** 900223841); 2016. 36p. 17.95 *(978-1-62203-602-8(6),* 900220700) Sounds True, Inc.

Hinder, Sarah Jane. Good Night Yoga: A Pose-By-Pose Bedtime Story. Gates, Mariam. (Good Night Yoga Ser.: 4). (ENG.). (J). 2018. 22p. bds. 9.95 *(978-1-68364-107-0(8),* 900220873); 2015. 36p. 17.95 *(978-1-62203-466-6(X),* 900220589) Sounds True, Inc.

—Yoga Friends: A Pose-By-Pose Partner Adventure for Kids. Gates, Mariam & Gates, Rolf. 2018. (Good Night Yoga Ser.: 3). (ENG.). 32p. (J). 17.95 *(978-1-62203-816-9(9),* 900220772) Sounds True, Inc.

—Zen & Bodhi's Snowy Day. Brown, Gina Bates. 2014. (ENG.). 24p. (J). 15.95 *(978-1-61429-165-7(9))* Wisdom Pubns.

Hinder, Sarah Jane. Hello, Sun! A Yoga Sun Salutation to Start Your Day. Hinder, Sarah Jane. 2019. (Hello, Sun! Ser.). (ENG.). 32p. (J). 17.95 *(978-1-68364-283-1(X),* 900214679) Sounds True, Inc.

—Yoga Bug: Simple Poses for Little Ones. Hinder, Sarah Jane. 2017. (Yoga Bug Board Book Ser.: 1). (ENG.). 24p. (J). bds. 9.99 *(978-1-62203-979-1(3),* 900220837) Sounds True, Inc.

Hinder, Sarah Jane. Yoga Kids & Animal Friends Boxed Set: Simple Poses for Little Ones. Hinder, Sarah Jane. 2020. (ENG.). (J). 39.99 ***(978-1-68364-811-6(0),*** 900237580) Sounds True, Inc.

Hinderliter, John. What Is Climate Change? Herman, Gail & Who HQ. 2018. (What Was? Ser.). 112p. (J). (gr. 3-7). (ENG.). 5.99 *(978-1-5247-8615-1(2));* lib. bdg. 15.99 *(978-1-5247-8617-5(9))* Penguin Young Readers Group. (Penguin Workshop).

—What Is the Statue of Liberty? Holub, Joan & Who HQ. 2014. (What Was? Ser.). (ENG.). 112p. (J). (gr. 3-7). 5.99 *(978-0-448-47917-0(6),* Penguin Workshop) Penguin Young Readers Group.

—What Is the Story of Looney Tunes? Who HQ & Korte, Steve. 2020. (What Is the Story Of? Ser.). 112p. (J). (gr. 3-7). 6.99 *(978-1-5247-8836-0(8));* 15.99 *(978-1-5247-8837-7(6))* Penguin Young Readers Group. (Penguin Workshop).

—What Was Hurricane Katrina? Koontz, Robin & Who HQ. 2015. (What Was? Ser.). 112p. (J). (gr. 3-7). 5.99 *(978-0-448-48662-8(8),* Penguin Workshop) Penguin Young Readers Group.

—What Was Pompeii? Who HQ & O'Connor, Jim. 2014. (What Was? Ser.). 112p. (J). (gr. 3-7). 5.99 *(978-0-448-47907-1(9),* Penguin Workshop) Penguin Young Readers Group.

—Where Are the Galapagos Islands? Stine, Megan & Who HQ. 2017. (Where Is? Ser.). (ENG.). 112p. (J). (gr. 3-7). pap. 5.99 *(978-0-451-53387-6(9),* Penguin Workshop) Penguin Young Readers Group.

—Where Is Broadway? Yacka, Douglas et al. 2019. (Where Is? Ser.). 112p. (J). (gr. 3-7). 5.99 *(978-1-5247-8650-2(0));* 15.99 *(978-1-5247-8651-9(9))* Penguin Young Readers Group. (Penguin Workshop).

—Where Is Easter Island? Stine, Megan & Who HQ. 2017. (Where Is? Ser.). 112p. (J). (gr. 3-7). (ENG.). 5.99 *(978-0-515-15948-6(4));* lib. bdg. 15.99 *(978-0-515-15950-9(6))* Penguin Young Readers Group. (Penguin Workshop).

—Where Is Mount Everest? Medina, Nico & Who HQ. 2015. (Where Is? Ser.). 112p. (J). (gr. 3-7). 5.99 *(978-0-448-48408-2(0),* Penguin Workshop) Penguin Young Readers Group.

—Where Is Mount Rushmore? Kelley, True & Who HQ. 2015. (Where Is? Ser.). (ENG.). 112p. (J). (gr. 3-7). 5.99 *(978-0-448-48356-6(4),* Penguin Workshop) Penguin Young Readers Group.

—Where Is Stonehenge? Kelley, True & Who HQ. 2016. (Where Is? Ser.). (ENG.). 112p. (J). (gr. 3-7). pap. 5.99 *(978-0-448-48693-2(8),* Penguin Workshop) Penguin Young Readers Group.

—Where Is the Brooklyn Bridge? Stine, Megan & Who HQ. 2016. (Where Is? Ser.). 112p. (J). (gr. 3-7). 5.99 *(978-0-448-48424-2(2),* Penguin Workshop) Penguin Young Readers Group.

—Where Is the Great Barrier Reef? Medina, Nico & Who HQ. 2016. (Where Is? Ser.). 112p. (J). (gr. 3-7). (ENG.). pap. 5.99 *(978-0-448-48699-4(7));* lib. bdg. 15.99 *(978-0-399-54239-8(6))* Penguin Young Readers Group. (Penguin Workshop).

—Where Is the Great Barrier Reef? Medina, Nico. 2016. (Where Is-? Chapters Ser.). (ENG.). 112p. (J). (gr. 4-6). lib. bdg. 18.69 *(978-1-4844-9197-3(1))* Penguin Young Readers Group.

—Where Is the Great Barrier Reef? Medina, Nico. ed. 2016. (Where Is... ? Ser.). (ENG.). 112p. (J). (gr. 3-7). 16.00 *(978-0-606-39316-4(1))* Turtleback.

—Where Is the Parthenon? Edwards, Roberta & Who HQ. 2016. (Where Is? Ser.). 112p. (J). (gr. 3-7). 5.99 *(978-0-448-48889-9(2),* Penguin Workshop) Penguin Young Readers Group.

—Where Is the Taj Mahal? Hoobler, Dorothy et al. 2017. (Where Is? Ser.). 112p. (J). (gr. 3-7). 5.99 *(978-0-399-54214-5(0),* Penguin Workshop) Penguin Young Readers Group.

Hinderliter, John. Who Is David Beckham? Labrecque, Ellen & Who HQ. 2020. (Who Was? Ser.). 112p. (J). (gr. 3-7). 5.99 ***(978-0-399-54404-0(6));*** 15.99 ***(978-0-399-54406-4(2))*** Penguin Young Readers Group. (Penguin Workshop).

Hinderliter, John. Who Is Jeff Kinney? Kinney, Patrick & Who HQ. 2015. (Who Was? Ser.). 112p. (J). (gr. 3-7). 5.99 *(978-0-448-48677-2(6),* Penguin Workshop) Penguin Young Readers Group.

—Who Was Bruce Lee? Gigliotti, Jim & Who HQ. 2014. (Who Was? Ser.). (ENG.). 112p. (J). (gr. 3-7). 5.99 *(978-0-448-47949-1(4),* Penguin Workshop) Penguin Young Readers Group.

—Who Was Chuck Jones? Gigliotti, Jim & Who HQ. 2017. (Who Was? Ser.). 112p. (J). (gr. 3-7). 5.99 *(978-0-448-48857-8(4));* lib. bdg. 15.99 *(978-0-515-15917-2(4))* Penguin Young Readers Group. (Penguin Workshop).

—Who Was Nikola Tesla? Gigliotti, Jim & Who HQ. 2018. (Who Was? Ser.). 112p. (J). (gr. 3-7). (ENG.). 5.99 *(978-0-448-48859-2(0));* lib. bdg. 15.99 *(978-1-5247-8854-4(6))* Penguin Young Readers Group. (Penguin Workshop).

—Who Was Stan Lee? Edgers, Geoff & Who HQ. 2014. (Who Was? Ser.). (ENG.). 112p. (J). (gr. 3-7). pap. 5.99 *(978-0-448-48236-1(3),* Penguin Workshop) Penguin Young Readers Group.

Hinderliter, John & Groff, David. Where Is Stonehenge? Kelley, True. ed. 2016. (Where Is... ? Ser.). (ENG.). 112p. (J). (gr. 3-7). 16.00 *(978-0-606-39317-1(X))* Turtleback.

Hindle, James K. Mothman's Curse. Hayes, Christine. 2015. (ENG.). 320p. (J). (gr. 3-7). 15.99 *(978-1-62672-027-5(4),* 900131845) Roaring Brook Pr.

Hindley, Kate. Don't Call Me Choochie Pooh! Taylor, Sean. 2016. (ENG.). 32p. (J). (gr. -1-2). 16.99 *(978-0-7636-8119-7(9))* Candlewick Pr.

—Escape from the Palace. Montefiore, Santa & Montefiore, Simon Sebag. (Royal Rabbits Ser.: 2). (ENG.). 224p. (J). (gr. 3-7). 2020. pap. 7.99 *(978-1-4814-9864-7(9));* 2019. 16.99 *(978-1-4814-9863-0(0))* Simon & Schuster Children's Publishing. (Aladdin).

—How to Wash a Woolly Mammoth. Robinson, Michelle. 2014. (ENG.). 32p. (J). (gr. -1-3). 18.99 *(978-0-8050-9966-9(2),* 900128169, Holt, Henry & Co. Bks. For Young Readers) Holt, Henry & Co.

—The Knight Who Said No! Rowland, Lucy. 2019. (ENG.). 32p. (J). (-k). 16.99 *(978-1-5362-0813-9(2),* Nosy Crow) Candlewick Pr.

—Pollyanna. Porter, Eleanor H. 2017. 288p. (J). pap. 10.99 *(978-1-84749-640-9(7),* 900184120, Alma Classics) Bloomsbury Publishing USA.

—The Royal Rabbits of London. Montefiore, Santa & Montefiore, Simon Sebag. 2018. (Royal Rabbits Ser.: 1). (ENG.). 208p. (J). (gr. 3-7). 16.99 *(978-1-4814-9860-9(6),* Aladdin) Simon & Schuster Children's Publishing.

—The Royal Rabbits of London. Montefiore, Santa & Montefiore, Simon Sebag. 2019. (Royal Rabbits Ser.: 1). (ENG.). 224p. (J). (gr. 3-7). pap. 7.99 *(978-1-4814-9861-6(4),* Aladdin) Simon & Schuster Children's Publishing.

—The Same but Different Too. Newson, Karl. 2020. (ENG.). 32p. (J). (-k). 16.99 *(978-1-5362-1201-3(6),* Nosy Crow) Candlewick Pr.

—Smashie Mcperter & the Mystery of Room 11. Griffin, N. 2015. (Smashie Mcperter Investigates Ser.: 1). 256p. (J). (gr. 2-5). 15.99 *(978-0-7636-6145-8(7))* Candlewick Pr.

—Smashie Mcperter & the Mystery of the Missing Goop. Griffin, N. (Smashie Mcperter Investigates Ser.: 2). 304p. (J). (gr. 2-5). 2017. pap. 5.99 *(978-0-7636-9795-2(8));* 2016. 15.99 *(978-0-7636-8535-5(6))* Candlewick Pr.

—Worst in Show. Bee, William. 2015. (ENG.). 40p. (J). (gr. -1-2). 15.99 *(978-0-7636-7318-5(8))* Candlewick Pr.

—You Must Bring a Hat! Philip, Simon. 2017. (ENG.). 40p. (J). (gr. -1). 16.95 *(978-1-4549-2688-7(0))* Sterling Publishing Co., Inc.

Hinds, Gareth. Gifts from the Gods: Ancient Words & Wisdom from Greek & Roman Mythology. Lunge-Larsen, Lise. 2011. (ENG.). 96p. (J). (gr. 5-7). 18.99 *(978-0-547-15229-5(9),* 1051948) Houghton Mifflin Harcourt Publishing Co.

—Samurai Rising: The Epic Life of Minamoto Yoshitsune. Turner, Pamela S. 256p. (gr. 7). 2018. (J). pap. 9.99 *(978-1-58089-585-9(9));* 2016. (YA). 16.95 *(978-1-58089-584-2(0))* Charlesbridge Publishing, Inc.

Hinds, Gareth. Beowulf. Hinds, Gareth, adapted by. 2007. (ENG.). 128p. (J). (gr. 5-12). pap. 14.99 *(978-0-7636-3023-2(3))* Candlewick Pr.

Hinds, Gareth. The Iliad. Hinds, Gareth. 2019. 272p. (J). (gr. 7). 27.99 *(978-0-7636-8113-5(X));* pap. 16.99 *(978-0-7636-9663-4(3))* Candlewick Pr.

—Macbeth. Hinds, Gareth. 2015. (ENG.). 152p. (YA). (gr. 7). 21.99 *(978-0-7636-6943-0(1))* Candlewick Pr.

—The Merchant of Venice. Hinds, Gareth. 2008. (ENG.). 80p. (YA). (gr. 7-12). pap. 14.99 *(978-0-7636-3025-6(X))* Candlewick Pr.

—The Merchant of Venice. Hinds, Gareth. Shakespeare, William. 2008. (ENG.). 80p. (YA). (gr. 7-12). 21.99 *(978-0-7636-3024-9(1))* Candlewick Pr.

—The Odyssey. Hinds, Gareth. 2010. 256p. (YA). (gr. 7-18). (ENG.). 24.99 *(978-0-7636-4266-2(5));* pap. 16.99 *(978-0-7636-4268-6(1))* Candlewick Pr.

—Poe: Stories & Poems: A Graphic Novel Adaptation by Gareth Hinds. Hinds, Gareth. 2017. 120p. (J). (gr. 7). 22.00 *(978-0-7636-8112-8(1))* Candlewick Pr.

—Romeo & Juliet. Hinds, Gareth. 2013. (ENG.). 144p. (gr. 7). (J). 21.99 *(978-0-7636-5948-6(7));* (YA). pap. 14.99 *(978-0-7636-6807-5(9))* Candlewick Pr.

Hine, Eileen. Desert Opposites. 2005. (ENG.). 12p. (J). (gr. -1 — 1). bds. 5.95 *(978-0-87358-890-4(8))* Cooper Square Publishing Llc.

Hines, Anna Grossnickle. Curious George & the Firefighters, 1 vol. Rey, H. A. & Rey, Margret. 2008. (Curious George Ser.). (ENG.). 24p. (J). (gr. k-3). lib. bdg. 27.07 *(978-1-59961-411-3(1),* 5052, Picture Bk.) Spotlight.

—Curious George at the Baseball Game. Driscoll, Laura & Rey, H. A. 2006. (Curious George Ser.). (ENG.). 24p. (J). (gr. -1-3). pap. 4.99 *(978-0-618-66375-0(4),* 461984) Houghton Mifflin Harcourt Publishing Co.

—Curious George's Dinosaur Discovery. Hapka, Catherine & Rey, H. A. 2006. (Curious George Ser.). (ENG.). 24p. (J). (gr. -1-3). pap. 4.99 *(978-0-618-66377-4(0),* 446458) Houghton Mifflin Harcourt Publishing Co.

—Curious George's First Day of School. Rey, Margret & Rey, H. A. 2005. (Curious George Ser.). (ENG.). 24p. (J). (gr. -1-3). 14.99 *(978-0-618-60563-7(0),* 548941); pap. 4.99 *(978-0-618-60564-4(9),* 448941) Houghton Mifflin Harcourt Publishing Co.

—Dinosaur Discovery. Hapka, Catherine et al. 2006. (Curious George Ser.). (ENG.). 24p. (J). (gr. -1-3). 10.99 *(978-0-618-68945-3(1),* 426461) Houghton Mifflin Harcourt Publishing Co.

—Learns to Count from 1 to 100: Counting, Grouping, Mapping, & More! Rey, H. A. 2005. (Curious George Ser.). (ENG.). 64p. (J). (gr. -1-3). 16.99 *(978-0-618-47602-2(4),* 594465) Houghton Mifflin Harcourt Publishing Co.

—Whistling. 2003. 40p. (J). 16.89 *(978-0-06-050236-2(3))* HarperCollins Pubs.

Hines, Anna Grossnickle. Gramma's Walk. Hines, Anna Grossnickle. 2016. (ENG.). (J). (gr. -1-3). 18.95 *(978-1-930900-66-0(X))* Purple Hse. Pr.

—I Am a Tyrannosaurus. Hines, Anna Grossnickle. 2011. (ENG.). 40p. (J). (gr. -1-2). 12.99 *(978-1-58246-413-8(8),* Tricycle Pr.) Random Hse. Children's Bks.

—Peaceful Pieces: Poems & Quilts about Peace. Hines, Anna Grossnickle. 2011. (ENG.). 32p. (J). (gr. -1-3). 18.99 *(978-0-8050-8996-7(9),* 900058871, Holt, Henry & Co. Bks. For Young Readers) Holt, Henry & Co.

—Pieces: A Year in Poems & Quilts. Hines, Anna Grossnickle. 2003. (ENG.). 32p. (J). (gr. k-5). pap. 6.99 *(978-0-06-055960-1(8),* Greenwillow Bks.) HarperCollins Pubs.

—Winter Lights: A Season in Poems & Quilts. Hines, Anna Grossnickle. 2005. 32p. (J). lib. bdg. 17.89 *(978-0-06-000818-5(0))* HarperCollins Pubs.

Hines, Anna Grossnickle, jt. illus. see Rey, H. A.

Hines, Irene. Baa. Arnold, Shauna. 2004. 19p. (J). (gr. -1-3). 12.00 *(978-0-9743669-0-6(0))* Trinity Bks.

Hines, Ken. Searching for an Oasis: Featuring Barrel Bob & Cousin Fishhook. 2019. (J). pap. *(978-1-63293-248-8(2))* Sunstone Pr.

Hines, Laura Freeman. L Is for Liberty. Lewison, Wendy Cheyette. 2003. 24p. (J). (gr. -1-3). mass mkt. 4.99 *(978-0-448-43228-1(5),* Grosset & Dunlap) Penguin Young Readers Group.

Hines, Marcel. Santana's Harrowing Halloween. Dunagan, Jennifer. 2012. 26p. pap. 12.95 *(978-1-60911-977-5(0),* Strategic Bk. Publishing) Strategic Book Publishing & Rights Agency (SBPRA).

Hines, Thomas. The Bubble Machine. l.t. ed. 2003. 26p. (J). per. *(978-1-887636-02-5(1))* Creative Writing & Publishing Co.

Hinlicky, Gregg. Moving Again Mom! Sportelli-Rehak, Angela. (J). 2004. (Uncle Sam's Kids Ser.: Bk. 2). 40p. (gr. -1-7). pap. 7.95 *(978-0-9714515-0-6(8));* 2003. (gr. k-7). pap. *(978-0-9714515-3-7(2))* Abidenme Bks.

—Uncle Sam's Kids: Moving Again Mom. Sportelli-Rehak, Angela. 2004. (Uncle Sam's Kids Ser.: Bk. 2). 40p. (gr. k-6). 16.95 *(978-0-9714515-2-0(4))* Abidenme Bks.

—Uncle Sam's Kids: When Duty Calls. Sportelli-Rehak, Angela. 2004. (Uncle Sam's Kids Ser.: Bk. 1). 40p. (gr. k-6). 15.95 *(978-0-9714515-1-3(6))* Abidenme Bks.

Hino, Hideshi. The Bug Boy No. 2: Hino Horror: A Graphic Novel. Hino, Hideshi. 2005. 204p. (YA). (gr. 4-9). reprint ed. pap. 10.00 *(978-0-7567-9709-6(8))* DIANE Publishing Co.

Hino, Sachiho. Hello Kitty: Garden Party. Woodhouse, Emma. 2015. 22p. (J). *(978-0-545-73447-9(9))* Scholastic, Inc.

—Tell the Time! Simon, Jenne. 2015. (J). *(978-0-545-74720-2(1))* Scholastic, Inc.

Hinojosa, Ana. Plastic Probs. Bartek, Cara. 2019. (Serafina Loves Science! Ser.: Vol. 3). (ENG.). 156p. (J). (gr. 3-7). pap. 7.99 ***(978-1-7018-3242-8(9))*** Independently Published.

Hinojosa, Felix, jt. illus. see Cosmo, A. J.

Hinojosa, Francisco. Yanka, Yanka. Hinojosa, Francisco. 2003. (SPA.). 44p. (J). (gr. k-3). pap. 10.95 *(978-968-19-0440-1(0))* Santillana USA Publishing Co., Inc.

Hinojosa, Jennifer. Blood Wielders. Jeanjcques, Andre. 2018. (ENG.). 114p. (J). pap. 6.00 *(978-1-7908-0053-7(6))* Independently Published.

Hinrichsen, Natalie. Something to Do. Walton, Ann. 2010. (ENG.). 24p. (J). (gr. k-2). pap. 6.00 *(978-1-77009-706-3(6))* Jacana Media ZAF. Dist: Independent Pubs. Group.

—The Ugly Duckling. Magona, Sindiwe. 2011. (Best Loved Tales for Africa Ser.). (ENG.). 32p. (J). (gr. k-2). pap. 10.95 *(978-1-77009-823-7(2))* Jacana Media ZAF. Dist: Independent Pubs. Group.

Hinrichsen, Tamsin. Illustrated Treasury of Christmas Stories. Kelly, Richard, ed. 2017. 384p. (J). 39.95 *(978-1-78209-988-8(3))* Miles Kelly Publishing, Ltd. GBR. Dist: Parkwest Pubns., Inc.

—Refilwe: Best Loved Tales for Africa. Wanner, Zukiswa. 2015. (ENG.). 32p. (J). (gr. -1-k). pap. 9.95 *(978-1-4314-0098-0(X))* Jacana Media ZAF. Dist: Independent Pubs. Group.

—The Tale of Sun & Moon. Walton, Ann. 2010. (ENG.). 32p. (J). (gr. k-2). 11.95 *(978-1-77009-705-6(8))* Jacana Media ZAF. Dist: Independent Pubs. Group.

Hinson, Billy & Hinson, Megan. Farmer Joe & Snake: A Tale of Unlikely Friends. Hinson, Billy. 2018. (Farmer Joe Ser.: Vol. 1). (ENG.). 30p. (J). pap. 10.99 *(978-1-7274-4517-6(1))* CreateSpace Independent Publishing Platform.

—Farmer Joe & Spider: Another Tale of Unlikely Friends. Hinson, Billy. 2019. (ENG.). 30p. (J). pap. 10.99 *(978-1-7940-5372-4(7))* Independently Published.

Hinson, Megan, jt. illus. see Hinson, Billy.

Hinton, David W. I Wonder If George Washington Owned a Pooper Scooper? Walkington, Jen. 2019. (ENG.). 28p. (J). (gr. 2-4). 19.99 ***(978-1-64538-004-7(1))*** Orange Hat Publishing.

Hinton, Steph. Christmas. Morey, Allan. 2018. (Holidays in Rhythm & Rhyme Ser.). (ENG.). 24p. (J). (gr. -1-3). lib. bdg. 33.99 *(978-1-68410-380-5(0),* 140353) Cantata Learning.

—Sticker Dress-Up Dolls Playful Mermaids: 200 Reusable Stickers! Over, Arthur. 2019. (Dover Children's Activity Bks.). (ENG.). 24p. (J). (gr. -1-2). pap. 8.99 *(978-0-486-83796-3(3))* Dover Pubns., Inc.

—Sticker Dress-Up Dolls Pretty Princesses: 200 Reusable Stickers! Isaacs, Connie. 2019. (Dover Children's Activity Bks.). (ENG.). 24p. (J). (gr. -1-2). pap. 8.99 *(978-0-486-83795-6(5))* Dover Pubns., Inc.

Hinton, Stephanie. At the Carnival! Reid, Hunter. 2017. (Fluorescent Pop! Ser.). (ENG.). 14p. (J). (gr. -1-k). bds. 5.99 *(978-1-4998-0242-9(0))* Little Bee Books Inc.

—Beach Day! Reid, Hunter. 2016. (Fluorescent Pop! Ser.). (ENG.). 14p. (J). (gr. -1-k). bds. 5.99 *(978-1-4998-0219-1(6))* Little Bee Books Inc.

—Beep! Honk! Zoom! Wooden Slider Book with Sound. Byrd, Ruby. Cottage Door Press, ed. 2017. (Slide & Sound Ser.). (ENG.). 16p. (J). (gr. -1-1). bds. 19.99 *(978-1-68052-185-6(3),* 1001831) Cottage Door Pr.

—Bright Lights, Bright City. Reid, Hunter. 2017. (Fluorescent Pop! Ser.). (ENG.). 14p. (J). (gr. -1-k). bds. 5.99 *(978-1-4998-0243-6(9))* Little Bee Books Inc.

—Busy Book for Boys: 550 Things to Find. 2014. (J). *(978-1-4351-5358-5(8))* Barnes & Noble, Inc.

—Busy Book for Girls: 550 Things to Find. 2014. (J). *(978-1-4351-5359-2(6))* Barnes & Noble, Inc.

—A Day on the Farm: A Pull-The-Tab Book. Hopgood, Sally. 2014. (J). *(978-1-4351-5688-3(9))* Barnes & Noble, Inc.

—In the Forest: A Pull-The-Tab Book. Hopgood, Sally. 2014. (J). *(978-1-4351-5689-0(7))* Barnes & Noble, Inc.

—Let's Have a Picnic! Reid, Hunter. 2016. (Fluorescent Pop! Ser.). (ENG.). 14p. (J). (gr. -1-k). bds. 5.99 *(978-1-4998-0220-7(X))* Little Bee Books Inc.

—Muddle & Match: Adventure. 2014. 16p. (J). bds. 8.99 *(978-1-61067-288-7(7))* Kane Miller.

—Muddle & Match: Imagine. 2014. 16p. (J). bds. 8.99 *(978-1-61067-289-4(5))* Kane Miller.

—Muddle & Match Fairy Tales. Campling, Hannah. 2018. (ENG.). 16p. (J). 8.99 *(978-1-61067-631-1(9))* Kane Miller.

—Muddle & Match Farm Animals. 2018. (ENG.). 16p. (J). bds. 8.99 *(978-1-61067-687-8(4))* Kane Miller.

—Muddle & Match Jobs. Jones, Frankie. 2016. 16p. (J). bds. 8.99 *(978-1-61067-491-1(X))* Kane Miller.

—Muddle & Match Jungle Animals. 2015. (ENG.). 16p. (J). bds. 8.00 *(978-1-61067-401-0(4))* Kane Miller.

—Muddle & Match Monsters. 2015. (ENG.). 16p. (J). bds. *(978-1-61067-423-2(5))* Kane Miller.

—Muddle & Match Sports. Jones, Frankie. 2016. 16p. (J). bds. 8.99 *(978-1-61067-493-5(6))* Kane Miller.

—The Sweetest Treats. Reid, Hunter. 2016. (Fluorescent Pop! Ser.). (ENG.). 14p. (J). (gr. -1-k). bds. 5.99 *(978-1-4998-0222-1(6))* Little Bee Books Inc.

—A Trip to Busy Town: A Pull-The-Tab Book. Hopgood, Sally. 2014. (J). *(978-1-4351-5690-6(0))* Barnes & Noble, Inc.

Hintz, Amy. Once upon a Time: An Adoption Story. Bigler, Ashley Hansen. 2010. (J). pap. 12.99 *(978-1-59955-310-8(4))* Cedar Fort, Inc./CFI Distribution.

Hintze, Amy. I'm So Glad When Daddy Comes Home. 2006. 16p. (J). 5.99 *(978-1-59156-562-8(6))* Covenant Communications, Inc.

Hiotis, Andrea. Kitty Kapers: Lily Kat. 2019. (Kitty Kapers Ser.: Vol. 1). (ENG.). 42p. (J). pap. 5.99 ***(978-1-7234-7362-3(6))*** CreateSpace Independent Publishing Platform.

Hipp, Ryan, jt. illus. see Kammeraad, Kevin.

Hippen, Seth. If the Shoe Fits, 1 vol. Guarino, Deborah. 2019. (ENG.). 32p. pap. 9.99 *(978-0-7643-5882-1(0),* 20593) Schiffer Publishing, Ltd.

Hirao, Amiko. How the Fisherman Tricked the Genie. Sunami, Christopher. 2007. (ENG.). 40p. (J). (gr. k-3). 14.99 *(978-1-4169-6137-6(2),* Simon & Schuster/Paula Wiseman Bks.) Simon & Schuster/Paula Wiseman Bks.

—Take Me Out to the Ball Game. Norworth, Jack. 2016. 24p. (J). (— 1). bds. 7.95 *(978-1-62354-071-5(2))* Charlesbridge Publishing, Inc.

—Take Me Out to the Ball Game. 2011. (ENG.). 26p. (J). (gr. k-4). 17.95 *(978-1-936140-26-8(8))* Charlesbridge Publishing, Inc.

—Write to Me: Letters from Japanese American Children to the Librarian They Left Behind. Grady, Cynthia. 2018. 32p. (J). (gr. -1-3). 16.99 *(978-1-58089-688-7(X))* Charlesbridge Publishing, Inc.

Hirashima, Jean. A Home for Little Fish. Ferrier, Charlotte. 2005. (J). *(978-1-890647-16-2(0))* TOMY International, Inc.

Hires, Josh. A Stone in the Soup. Gilmore, Dorina Lazo. 2006. 39p. per. 15.00 *(978-0-938911-29-6(5))* Individualized Education Systems/Poppy Lane Publishing.

Hires, Josh, photos by. Children of the San Joaquin Valley. Lazo, Dorina. 2005. 35p. (YA). (gr. 7-12). pap. 15.00 *(978-0-938911-28-9(7))* Individualized Education Systems/Poppy Lane Publishing.

Hirose, George, photos by. I Catch My Moment: Art & Writing by Children on the Life of Play. 2008. (ENG., 56p. (J). (gr. -1-3). pap. 10.00 *(978-1-929299-06-5(0))* Touchstone Ctr. Pubns.

Hirsch, Andy. Dogs: From Predator to Protector. 2017. 119p. (J). *(978-0-605-99390-7(4),* First Second Bks.) Roaring Brook Pr.

Hirsch, Andy. Science Comics: Trees: Kings of the Forest. Hirsch, Andy. 2018. (Science Comics Ser.). (ENG.). 128p. (J). 19.99 *(978-1-250-14311-2(X),* 900180428); pap. 12.99 *(978-1-250-14310-5(1),* 900180429) Roaring Brook Pr. (First Second Bks.).

Hirsch, Charmaine. Walter's Discovery. Magers, Ramona Hirsch. 2008. 26p. pap. 24.95 *(978-1-60563-623-8(1))* America Star Bks.

Hirsch, Kerry. Whiskers. Silk, Max V. 2004. (J). pap. 12.00 *(978-0-9748524-6-1(5))* Biblio Bks. International.

Hirschmann, Kris & Langdo, Bryan. We're Going on a Ghost Hunt. 2011. (J). *(978-0-545-34173-8(6))* Scholastic, Inc.

Hirsh, Alice. The Wonder of Light: A Picture Story of How & Why We See. Ruchlis, Hyman. 2011. 160p. 41.95 *(978-1-258-09816-2(4))* Literary Licensing, LLC.

Hirsheimer, Christopher, photos by. The New Irish Table: 70 Contemporary Recipes. Johnson, Margaret M. 2003. (ENG., 168p. (gr. 8-17). pap. 24.95 *(978-0-8118-3387-5(9))* Chronicle Bks. LLC.

—The San Francisco Ferry Plaza Farmers' Market Cookbook: A Comprehensive Guide to Impeccable Produce Plus 130 Seasonal Recipes. Knickerbocker, Peggy. 2006. (ENG., 288p. (gr. 8-17). pap. 22.95 *(978-0-8118-4462-8(5))* Chronicle Bks. LLC.

Hirst, Daisy. Alphonse, That Is Not OK to Do! Hirst, Daisy. 2016. (ENG.). 40p. (J). (-k). 15.99 *(978-0-7636-8103-6(2))* Candlewick Pr.

—Alphonse, There's Mud on the Ceiling! Hirst, Daisy. 2020. (ENG.). 32p. (J). (-k). 16.99 *(978-1-5362-1117-7(6))* Candlewick Pr.

—The Girl with the Parrot on Her Head. Hirst, Daisy. 2016. (ENG.). 40p. (J). (-k). 16.99 *(978-0-7636-7829-6(5))* Candlewick Pr.

Hirst, Daisy. Hamish Takes the Train. Hirst, Daisy. 2020. (ENG.). 40p. (J). (gr. -1-2). 16.99 ***(978-1-5362-1659-2(3))*** Candlewick Pr.

Hirst, Daisy. Hilda & the Runaway Baby. Hirst, Daisy. 2017. (ENG.). 32p. (J). (-k). 16.99 *(978-0-7636-9490-6(8))* Candlewick Pr.

—I Do Not Like Books Anymore! Hirst, Daisy. 2018. (ENG.). 40p. (J). (gr. -1-2). 15.99 *(978-1-5362-0334-9(3))* Candlewick Pr.

Hirst, Damien. Don't Be So... Fryer, Paul. 2004. 168p. 39.95 *(978-0-9542079-1-5(2))* Trolley GBR. Dist: D.A.P./Distributed Art Pubs.

Hische, Jessica. Five Children & It. Nesbit, E. 2013. (Penguin Drop Caps Ser.). (ENG.). 256p. (gr. 12). 27.00 *(978-0-14-312466-5(8),* Penguin Bks.) Penguin Publishing Group.

Hische, Jessica. Tomorrow I'll Be Brave. Hische, Jessica. (ENG.). (J). (gr. -1-2). 2019. 32p. bds. 9.99 *(978-1-5247-8702-8(7));* 2018. 40p. 17.99 *(978-1-5247-8701-1(9))* Penguin Young Readers Group. (Penguin Workshop).

—Tomorrow I'll Be Kind. Hische, Jessica. 2020. (ENG.). 40p. (J). (gr. -1-2). 17.99 *(978-1-5247-8704-2(3),* Penguin Workshop) Penguin Young Readers Group.

Hiscock, Bruce. Turtle Tide: The Ways of Sea Turtles. swinburne, stephen r. 2010. (ENG.). 32p. (J). (gr. 2-4). pap. 11.99 *(978-1-59078-827-1(3))* Boyds Mills Pr.

Hiscock, Bruce. Armadillo Trail: The Northward Journey of the Armadillo. Hiscock, Bruce. Swinburne, Stephen R. 2009. (ENG.). 32p. (J). (gr. 2-k). 16.95 *(978-1-59078-463-1(4))* Boyds Mills Pr.

Hit Entertainment Staff. Friends from Sodor (Thomas & Friends) Golden Books Staff. 2008. (ENG.). 128p. (J). (gr. -1-2). pap. 7.99 *(978-0-375-84292-4(6),* Golden Bks.) Random Hse. Children's Bks.

Hitch, Bryan, et al. Avengers by Brian Michael Bendis: the Complete Collection Vol. 2. 2017. (ENG.). 480p. (YA). (gr. 8-17). pap. 39.99 *(978-1-302-90774-7(3))* Marvel Worldwide, Inc.

Hitch, Bryan. Ultimates - Volume 1: Super-Human, Vol. 1. 2006. (ENG.). 160p. (gr. 10-17). pap. 12.99 *(978-0-7851-0960-0(9))* Marvel Worldwide, Inc.

—Ultimates 2 - Volume 1: Gods & Monsters, Vol. 1. 2006. (ENG.). 152p. (gr. 10-17). 15.99 *(978-0-7851-1093-4(3))* Marvel Worldwide, Inc.

Hitch, David. I Love You, Grandma! Rabe, Tish. 2016. (Little Golden Book Ser.). (J). (-k). 24p. 4.99 *(978-1-101-93455-5(7));* *(978-1-5182-1618-3(8))* Random Hse. Children's Bks. (Golden Bks.).

—One of a Kind. Winter, Ariel S. 2012. (ENG.). 32p. (J). (gr. -1-2). 15.99 *(978-1-4424-2016-8(2),* Aladdin) Simon & Schuster Children's Publishing.

Hitchman, Heather R. Wee Beasties: Pretend Time. Smith, Andi. 2019. (ENG.). 46p. (J). pap. 20.00 *(978-1-0820-9557-3(5))* Independently Published.

Hites, Kati. Winnie & Waldorf. Hites, Kati. 2015. (ENG.). 40p. (J). (gr. -1-3). 17.99 *(978-0-06-231161-0(1))* HarperCollins Pubs.

Hiti, Sam. The Chinese: Life in China's Golden Age. Doeden, Matt. 2009. (Life in Ancient Civilizations Ser.). (ENG.). 48p. (gr. 3-6). lib. bdg. 29.27 *(978-0-8225-8681-4(9),* Millbrook Pr.) Lerner Publishing Group.

Hiti, Samuel. Addition. Midthun, Joseph. 2013. (Building Blocks of Mathematics Ser.). 32p. (J). pap. 169.00 *(978-0-7166-1432-6(4))* World Bk., Inc.

—Animal Behavior. Midthun, Joseph. 2016. (Building Blocks of Life Science 2/Soft Cover Ser.: Vol. 1). (ENG.). 34p. (J). pap. *(978-0-7166-7884-7(5))* World Bk.-Childcraft International.

—The Aztecs: Life in Tenochtitlan. Doeden, Matt. 2009. (Life in Ancient Civilizations Ser.). (ENG.). 48p. (gr. 3-6). lib. bdg. 29.27 *(978-0-8225-8684-5(3),* Millbrook Pr.) Lerner Publishing Group.

—Cells to Organ Systems. Midthun, Joseph. 2016. (Building Blocks of Life Science 1/Soft Cover Ser.: Vol. 1). (ENG.). 34p. (J). (gr. 3-7). pap. *(978-0-7166-7868-7(3))* World Bk.-Childcraft International.

—The Circulatory System. Midthun, Joseph. 2016. (Building Blocks of Life Science 1/Hardcover Ser.: Vol. 2). (ENG.). 34p. (J). *(978-0-7166-7861-8(6))* World Bk.-Childcraft International.

—The Digestive & Urinary Systems. Midthun, Joseph. 2016. (Building Blocks of Life Science 1/Soft Cover Ser.: Vol. 3). (ENG.). 34p. (J). (gr. 3-7). pap. *(978-0-7166-7870-0(5))* World Bk.-Childcraft International.

—Division. Midthun, Joseph. 2013. (Building Blocks of Mathematics Ser.). 32p. pap. 169.00 *(978-0-7166-1433-3(2))* World Bk., Inc.

—Division. Midthun, Joseph. 2016. (Building Blocks of Math/Hardcover Ser.: Vol. 2). (ENG.). 34p. (J). *(978-0-7166-7893-9(4))* World Bk.-Childcraft International.

—Electricity. Midthun, Joseph. 2016. (Building Blocks of Physical Science/Hardcover Ser.: Vol. 1). (ENG.). 34p. (J). *(978-0-7166-7850-2(0))* World Bk.-Childcraft International.

—Energy. Midthun, Joseph. (Building Blocks of Physical Science/Hardcover Ser.: Vol. 2). (ENG.). 34p. (J). 2016. *(978-0-7166-7851-9(9));* 2012. pap. *(978-0-7166-1464-7(2))* World Bk.-Childcraft International.

—Fighting Sickness. Midthun, Joseph. 2016. (Building Blocks of Life Science 1/Soft Cover Ser.: Vol. 5). (ENG.). 34p. (J). pap. *(978-0-7166-7872-4(1))* World Bk.-Childcraft International.

—Fractions. Midthun, Joseph. 2013. (Building Blocks of Mathematics Ser.). 32p. (J). pap. 169.00 *(978-0-7166-1435-7(9))* World Bk., Inc.

—The Greeks: Life in Ancient Greece. Levine, Michelle. 2009. (Life in Ancient Civilizations Ser.). (ENG.). 48p. (J). (gr. 3-6). lib. bdg. 29.27 *(978-0-8225-8680-7(0),* Lerner Pubns.) Lerner Publishing Group.

—Light. Midthun, Joseph. 2012. (Building Blocks of Physical Science/Soft Cover Ser.: Vol. 6). (ENG.). 34p. (J). (gr.

3-7). pap. *(978-0-7166-1468-5(5))* World Bk.-Childcraft International.

—Magnetism. Midthun, Joseph. 2016. (Building Blocks of Physical Science/Hardcover Ser.: Vol. 7). (ENG.). 34p. (J). *(978-0-7166-7856-4(X))* World Bk.-Childcraft International.

—Matter & How It Changes. Midthun, Joseph. 2012. (Building Blocks of Physical Science/Soft Cover Ser.: Vol. 8). (ENG.). 34p. (J). (gr. 3-7). pap. *(978-0-7166-1470-8(7))* World Bk.-Childcraft International.

—Matter & Its Properties. Midthun, Joseph. 2012. (Building Blocks of Physical Science/Soft Cover Ser.: Vol. 9). (ENG.). 34p. (J). pap. *(978-0-7166-1471-5(5))* World Bk.-Childcraft International.

—Multiplication. Midthun, Joseph. 2013. (Building Blocks of Mathematics Ser.). 32p. (J). pap. 169.00 *(978-0-7166-1437-1(5))* World Bk., Inc.

—Plant Life Cycles. Midthun, Joseph. 2016. (Building Blocks of Life Science 2/Hardcover Ser.: Vol. 6). (ENG.). 34p. (J). *(978-0-7166-7881-6(0))* World Bk.-Childcraft International.

—Plant Structure & Classification. Midthun, Joseph. 2016. (Building Blocks of Life Science 2/Hardcover Ser.: Vol. 7). (ENG.). 34p. (J). *(978-0-7166-7882-3(9))*; pap. *(978-0-7166-7890-8(X))* World Bk.-Childcraft International.

—The Respiratory System. Midthun, Joseph. 2016. (Building Blocks of Life Science 1/Hardcover Ser.: Vol. 7). (ENG.). 34p. (J). *(978-0-7166-7866-3(7))*; pap. *(978-0-7166-7874-8(8))* World Bk.-Childcraft International.

—The Romans: Life in Ancient Rome. Sonnebom, Liz. 2009. (Life in Ancient Civilizations Ser.). (ENG.). 48p. (gr. 3-6). lib. bdg. 29.27 *(978-0-8225-8679-1(7)*, Millbrook Pr.) Lerner Publishing Group.

—Traits & Heredity. Midthun, Joseph. 2016. (Building Blocks of Life Science 2/Soft Cover Ser.: Vol. 8). (ENG.). 34p. (J). pap. *(978-0-7166-7891-5(8))* World Bk.-Childcraft International.

Hitori De, Nicola. Yu & the Great Flood Gold Band. Bradman, Tony. 2016. (Cambridge Reading Adventures Ser.). (ENG.). 24p. pap. 8.08 *(978-1-107-56225-7(2))* Cambridge Univ. Pr.

Hitschler, Cynthia. Gleb... the Terrible! 2004. 36p. pap. *(978-0-9761041-1-7(3)*, 1239008) Celstumo Publishing.

—The Perils of Pink Cat. 2004. 36p. (J). pap. *(978-0-9761041-2-4(1)*, 1239009) Celstumo Publishing.

—The World of Jacky Blue & Other Cats. 2004. 40p. (J). pap. *(978-0-9761041-0-0(5)*, 1239007) Celstumo Publishing.

Hix, Todd. Traveling down an Irish Road. Ireland, Daniel. 2013. (ENG.). 32p. (J). pap. 9.75 *(978-0-9845866-5-3(2))* Three Leaf Pr.

Hixson, Bryce. Dig It! DeWitt, Lockwood. 2003. (J). per. 14.95 *(978-1-931801-02-7(9))* Loose In The Lab.

Hixson, Bryce. Anatomy Academy. Hixson, Bryce. 2003. (J). per. 14.95 *(978-1-931801-03-4(7))* Loose In The Lab.

—Digits, Midgets, & Degrees Kelvin. Hixson, Bryce. 2003. (J). per. 9.95 *(978-1-931801-04-1(5))* Loose In The Lab.

—Galactic Cookie Dough. Hixson, Bryce. 2003. (J). per. 14.95 *(978-1-931801-06-5(1))* Loose In The Lab.

—Get Your Poop in a Group. Hixson, Bryce. 2003. (J). per. 9.95 *(978-1-931801-01-0(0))* Loose In The Lab.

—Great Graphs in Ten Days. Hixson, Bryce. 2003. (J). 6.95 *(978-1-931801-18-8(5))* Loose In The Lab.

—Newton Take 3. Hixson, Bryce. 2003. (J). per. 14.95 *(978-0-9660965-3-8(3))* Loose In The Lab.

—The Original World Wide Web. Hixson, Bryce. 2003. (J). per. 12.95 *(978-1-931801-07-2(X))* Loose In The Lab.

—Plant Stigmas & Other Botanical Concerns. Hixson, Bryce. 2003. (J). per. 12.95 *(978-1-931801-09-6(6))* Loose In The Lab.

—What's Up? Hixson, Bryce. 2003. (J). per. 14.95 *(978-1-931801-05-8(3))* Loose In The Lab.

HL Studios, H. L. Shhh! Listen!: Hearing Sounds, 1 vol. Spilsbury, Louise & Spilsbury, Richard. 2014. (Exploring Sound Ser.). (ENG.). 32p. (J). (gr. 2-4). lib. bdg. 31.32 *(978-1-4109-6002-3(1)*, Raintree) Capstone.

HL Studios Staff. Caves. Claybourne, Anna. 2013. (Explorer Travel Guides). (ENG.). 48p. (J). (gr. 3-6). pap. 8.95 *(978-1-4109-5435-0(8)*, Raintree) Capstone.

—Deserts: An Explorer Travel Guide, 1 vol. Hunter, Nick. 2013. (Explorer Travel Guides). (ENG.). 48p. (J). (gr. 3-6). 30.65 *(978-1-4109-5429-9(3))*; pap. 8.95 *(978-1-4109-5436-7(6))* Capstone. (Raintree).

—John F. Kennedy, 1 vol. Burgan, Michael. 2013. (ENG.). 56p. (J). (gr. 4-8). 33.99 *(978-1-4329-8096-2(3))*; pap. 10.95 *(978-1-4329-8097-9(1))* Capstone. (Heinemann).

—Polar Scientist: The Coolest Jobs on the Planet, 1 vol. Shuckburgh, Emily & Chambers, Catherine. 2014. (Coolest Jobs on the Planet Ser.). (ENG.). 48p. (J). (gr. 5-8). pap. 8.99 *(978-1-4109-6648-3(8)*, Raintree) Capstone.

—Turn It up!; Turn It down!: Volume, 1 vol. Spilsbury, Louise & Spilsbury, Richard. 2014. (Exploring Sound Ser.). (ENG.). 32p. (J). (gr. 2-4). lib. bdg. 31.32 *(978-1-4109-6001-6(3)*, Raintree) Capstone.

—Volcanologist: The Coolest Jobs on the Planet, 1 vol. Tuffen, Hugh & Waldron, Melanie. 2014. (Coolest Jobs on the Planet Ser.). (ENG.). 48p. (J). (gr. 5-8). 33.32 *(978-1-4109-6643-8(7))*; pap. 8.99 *(978-1-4109-6649-0(6))* Capstone. (Raintree).

—Who Journeyed on the Mayflower?, 1 vol. Barber, Nicola. 2014. (Primary Source Detectives Ser.). (ENG.). 64p. (J). (gr. 6-11). lib. bdg. 36.65 *(978-1-4329-9602-4(9)*, Heinemann) Capstone.

—Who Marched for Civil Rights?, 1 vol. Spilsbury, Richard. 2014. (Primary Source Detectives Ser.). (ENG.). 64p. (J). (gr. 6-11). lib. bdg. 36.65 *(978-1-4329-9604-8(5)*, Heinemann) Capstone.

Hnatiuk, Charlie. A Hero's Worth. Ouellet, Debbie. 120p. *(978-1-897039-47-2(6))* High Interest Publishing (HIP).

Hnatov, Catherine. Valentino Finds a Home, 1 vol. Whiteside, Andy. 2012. (ENG.). (J). 32p. 15.95 *(978-1-59572-284-3(X))*; 24p. pap. 5.95 *(978-1-59572-286-7(6))* Star Bright Bks., Inc.

Hnatov, Catherine. Up & Down, 1 vol. Hnatov, Catherine. 2014. (ENG.). 32p. (J). bds. 5.99 *(978-1-59572-340-6(4))* Star Bright Bks., Inc.

—Up & Down (Spanish/English), 1 vol. Hnatov, Catherine. 2014. (ENG & SPA.). 32p. (J). bds. 5.99 *(978-1-59572-341-3(2))* Star Bright Bks., Inc.

Ho, Annie. Dream Girls Portrait & Coloring Book 2. Kong, Rowena. 2019. (Dream Girls Ser.: Vol. 2). (ENG.). 42p. (J). pap. 9.17 ***(978-1-6701-1714-4(6))*** Independently Published.

—Dream Girls Portrait & Minako's Endearing Adventure 1. Kong, Rowena. 2020. (Dream Girls Collection: Vol. 4). (ENG.). 48p. (J). pap. 10.39 ***(978-1-6608-9886-2(2))*** Independently Published.

—Dream Girls Portrait & Quote Book 1. Kong, Rowena. 2020. (Dream Girls Collection: Vol. 1). (ENG.). 34p. (J). pap. 9.17 ***(978-1-6558-1654-3(3))*** Independently Published.

—Rolleen Rabbit & Her Mommy's Birthday on Christmas. Kong, Rowena. 2019. (Rolleen Rabbit Collection of Stories Ser.: Vol. 8). (ENG.). 24p. (J). pap. 9.19 ***(978-1-6524-4576-0(5))*** Independently Published.

—Rolleen Rabbit, Mommy & Friends Picture & Coloring Book 3. Kong, Rowena. 2019. (ENG.). 50p. (J). pap. 10.80 ***(978-1-6725-8251-3(2))*** Independently Published.

Ho, David. Dragon Games. Catanese, P. W. (Books of Umber Ser.: 2). (ENG.). (J). (gr. 3-7). 2011. 400p. pap. 7.99 *(978-1-4169-5383-8(3))*; 2010. 384p. 17.99 *(978-1-4169-7521-2(7))* Simon & Schuster Children's Publishing. (Aladdin).

—The End of Time. Catanese, P. W. 2012. (Books of Umber Ser.: 3). (ENG.). 432p. (J). (gr. 3-7). pap. 8.99 *(978-1-4169-5384-5(1)*, Aladdin) Simon & Schuster Children's Publishing.

—The End of Time. Catanese, P. W. 2011. (Books of Umber Ser.: 3). (ENG.). 432p. (J). (gr. 3-7). 16.99 *(978-1-4169-7520-5(9)*, Simon & Schuster/Paula Wiseman Bks.) Simon & Schuster/Paula Wiseman Bks.

Ho, Dung. Mindy Kim & the Birthday Puppy. Lee, Lyla. 2020. (Mindy Kim Ser.: 3). (ENG.). 96p. (J). (gr. 1-4). 17.99 ***(978-1-5344-4014-2(3))***; pap. 5.99 ***(978-1-5344-4013-5(5))*** Simon & Schuster Children's Publishing. (Aladdin).

Ho, Dung. Mindy Kim & the Lunar New Year Parade. Lee, Lyla. 2020. (Mindy Kim Ser.: 2). (ENG.). 96p. (J). (gr. 1-4). 16.99 *(978-1-5344-4011-1(9))*; pap. 5.99 *(978-1-5344-4010-4(0))* Simon & Schuster Children's Publishing. (Aladdin).

—Mindy Kim & the Yummy Seaweed Business. Lee, Lyla. 2020. (Mindy Kim Ser.: 1). (ENG.). 96p. (J). (gr. 1-4). 16.99 *(978-1-5344-4009-8(7))*; pap. 5.99 *(978-1-5344-4007-4(0))* Simon & Schuster Children's Publishing. (Aladdin).

Ho, Dung. Mindy Kim, Class President. Lee, Lyla. 2020. (Mindy Kim Ser.: 4). (ENG.). 96p. (J). (gr. 1-4). 17.99 ***(978-1-5344-4017-3(8))***; pap. 5.99 ***(978-1-5344-4016-6(X))*** Simon & Schuster Children's Publishing. (Aladdin).

Ho, Hanh Dung. He's Got the Whole World in His Hands. Tiger Tales. 2020. (ENG.). 16p. (J). (-k). bds. 9.99 *(978-1-68010-587-2(6))* Tiger Tales.

Ho, Jannie. The Chicks in the Barn. Fronis, Aly. 2018. (ENG.). 16p. (J). (gr. -1-k). bds. 5.99 *(978-1-4998-0483-6(0))* Little Bee Books Inc.

—Christmas ABC. Nosy Crow. 2018. (ENG.). 26p. (J). (— 1). bds. 6.99 *(978-1-5362-0249-6(5)*, Nosy Crow) Candlewick Pr.

—Cutie Pie Looks for the Easter Bunny: A Tiny Tab Book. Nosy Crow. 2015. (Tiny Tab Ser.). (ENG.). 8p. (J). (— 1). bds. 7.99 *(978-0-7636-7599-8(7)*, Nosy Crow) Candlewick Pr.

—The Great Matzoh Hunt, Vol. 2010. (ENG.). 12p. (J). (gr. -1-k). bds. 6.99 *(978-0-8431-8969-8(X)*, Price Stern Sloan) Penguin Young Readers Group.

—The Great Reindeer Rebellion. Trumbauer, Lisa. 2014. 32p. (J). (gr. -1). pap. 6.95 *(978-1-4549-1356-6(8))* Sterling Publishing Co., Inc.

—Halloween ABC. Nosy Crow. 2017. (ENG.). 26p. (J). (— 1). bds. 6.99 *(978-0-7636-9527-9(0)*, Nosy Crow) Candlewick Pr.

—Halloween Howlers: Frightfully Funny Knock-Knock Jokes. Teitelbaum, Michael. 2011. (ENG.). 16p. (J). (gr. k-3). 6.99 *(978-0-06-180891-3(1)*, HarperFestival) HarperCollins Pubs.

—If You're Spooky & You Know It. Fronis, Aly. 2016. (ENG.). 16p. (J). (gr. -1-k). bds. 5.99 *(978-1-4998-0165-1(3))* Little Bee Books Inc.

—Light the Menorah. 2009. (ENG.). 12p. (J). (gr. -1-k). 7.99 *(978-0-8431-8954-4(1)*, Price Stem Sloan) Penguin Young Readers Group.

—Lily's Lucky Leotard, 1 vol. Meister, Cari. 2009. (My First Graphic Novel Ser.). (ENG.). 32p. (J). (gr. k-2). pap. 6.25 *(978-1-4342-1411-9(7))*; lib. bdg. 24.65 *(978-1-4342-1296-2(3))* Capstone. (Stone Arch Bks.).

—Little Bubba Looks for His Elephant. Nosy Crow Staff. 2014. (Tiny Tab Ser.). (ENG.). 8p. (J). (— 1). bds. 7.99 *(978-0-7636-7401-4(X)*, Nosy Crow) Candlewick Pr.

—The Little Engine's Easter Egg Hunt. Piper, Watty. 2020. (Little Engine That Could Ser.). 32p. (J). (gr. k-3). 15.99 *(978-0-593-09435-8(2))*; pap. 4.99 *(978-0-593-09434-1(4))* Penguin Young Readers Group. (Penguin Young Readers).

—The Magic Garden: A Step-By-step Drawing & Story Book. Chagollan, Samantha. 2019. (Watch Me Read & Draw Ser.). (ENG.). 32p. (J). (gr. -1-2). lib. bdg. 26.65 *(978-1-60058-796-2(8)*, Walter Foster Jr) Quarto Publishing Group USA.

—The Mixed-Up Alphabet. Metzger, Steve. 2007. (J). *(978-0-545-00098-7(X))* Scholastic, Inc.

—Muddle Zoo. 2013. (Muddle Bks.). (ENG.). 8p. (J). (gr. -1 — 1). 10.99 *(978-0-7641-6623-5(9)*, B.E.S. Publishing) Peterson's.

—Ocean Friends: A Step-By-step Drawing & Story Book. Chagollan, Samantha. 2019. (Watch Me Read & Draw Ser.). (ENG.). 32p. (J). (gr. -1-2). lib. bdg. 26.65 *(978-1-60058-799-3(2)*, Walter Foster Jr) Quarto Publishing Group USA.

—Pookie Pop Plays Hide-And-Seek: A Tiny Tab Book. Nosy Crow Staff. 2015. (Tiny Tab Ser.). (ENG.). 8p. (J). (— 1). bds. 7.99 *(978-0-7636-7600-1(4)*, Nosy Crow) Candlewick Pr.

—Roly Poly Looks for Santa Claus: A Tiny Tab Book. Nosy Crow Staff. 2016. (Tiny Tab Ser.). (ENG.). 8p. (J). (— 1). bds. 7.99 *(978-0-7636-8938-4(6)*, Nosy Crow) Candlewick Pr.

—Snuggly Puppy Looks for the Perfect Hug: A Tiny Tab Book. Nosy Crow Staff. 2016. (Tiny Tab Ser.). (ENG.). 8p. (J). (— 1). bds. 7.99 *(978-0-7636-8937-7(8)*, Nosy Crow) Candlewick Pr.

—T-Ball Trouble, 1 vol. Meister, Cari. 2009. (My First Graphic Novel Ser.). (ENG.). 32p. (J). (gr. k-2). pap. 6.25 *(978-1-4342-1413-3(3))*; lib. bdg. 24.65 *(978-1-4342-1300-6(5))* Capstone. (Stone Arch Bks.).

—Teeny Weeny Looks for His Mommy: A Tiny Tab Book. Crow, Nosy. 2014. (Tiny Tab Ser.). (ENG.). 8p. (J). (— 1). bds. 7.99 *(978-0-7636-7273-7(4)*, Nosy Crow) Candlewick Pr.

—Violet Rose & the Little School. Nosy Crow Staff. 2016. (Violet Rose Ser.). (ENG.). 52p. (J). (gr. -1-3). 8.99 *(978-0-7636-9002-1(3)*, Nosy Crow) Candlewick Pr.

—Violet Rose & the Summer Campout. Nosy Crow Staff. 2017. (Violet Rose Ser.). (ENG.). 52p. (J). (gr. -1-3). 8.99 *(978-0-7636-9333-6(2)*, Nosy Crow) Candlewick Pr.

—Violet Rose & the Surprise Party. Nosy Crow Staff. 2016. (Violet Rose Ser.). (ENG.). (J). (gr. -1-3). 8.99 *(978-0-7636-8917-9(3)*, Nosy Crow) Candlewick Pr.

—Violet Rose & the Very Snowy Christmas. Crow, Nosy. 2016. (Violet Rose Ser.). (ENG.). 52p. (J). (gr. -1-3). 8.99 *(978-0-7636-9003-8(1)*, Nosy Crow) Candlewick Pr.

—Watch Me Read & Draw: Noah's Ark: A Step-By-step Drawing & Story Book. Walter Foster Jr. Creative Team. 2019. (Watch Me Read & Draw Ser.). (ENG.). 36p. (J). (gr. -1-3). pap. 8.95 *(978-1-63322-764-4(2)*, 325975, Walter Foster Jr) Quarto Publishing Group USA.

—Watch Me Read & Draw: on the Farm: A Step-By-step Drawing & Story Book - Includes Flip-out Drawing Pad & More Than 30 Stickers. Chagollan, Samantha. 2019. (Watch Me Read & Draw Ser.). (ENG.). 36p. (J). (gr. -1-3). pap. 8.95 *(978-1-63322-719-4(7)*, 307819, Walter Foster Jr) Quarto Publishing Group USA.

—Watch Me Read & Draw: Things Girls Love: A Step-By-step Drawing & Story Book. Chagollan, Samantha. 2018. (Watch Me Read & Draw Ser.). (ENG.). 36p. (J). (gr. -1-3). pap. 8.95 *(978-1-63322-535-0(6)*, Walter Foster Jr) Quarto Publishing Group USA.

—Wheels on the Bus: Board Book with Handle. Wing, Scarlett. Cottage Door Press, ed. 2015. (Sing & Smile Stories Ser.). (ENG.). 10p. (J). (gr. -1-k). bds. 8.99 *(978-1-68052-004-0(0)*, 1000050) Cottage Door Pr.

—Wickle Woo Has a Halloween Party. Nosy Crow Staff. 2014. (Tiny Tab Ser.). (ENG.). 8p. (J). (— 1). bds. 7.99 *(978-0-7636-7400-7(1)*, Nosy Crow) Candlewick Pr.

—Zoom Zoom Point N Match: Hardcover Board Book. Winget, Rosie. 2015. (Look Look Baby Ser.). (ENG.). 14p. (J). (gr. -1-k). bds. 8.99 *(978-1-68052-014-9(8)*, 1000150) Cottage Door Pr.

Ho, Jannie. Guess Who? Ho, Jannie. 2013. (ENG.). 8p. (J). (gr. -1 — 1). bds. 7.99 *(978-0-545-49331-4(5)*, Cartwheel Bks.) Scholastic, Inc.

—You Can Draw Zoo Animals, 1 vol. Ho, Jannie. Bruning, Matt. 2010. (You Can Draw Ser.). (ENG.). 24p. (J). (gr. k-3). lib. bdg. 27.32 *(978-1-4048-6275-3(7)*, Picture Window Bks.) Capstone.

Ho, Jannie & Fisher, Diana. Watch Me Read & Draw: On the Farm. Chagollan, Samantha. 2019. (J). *(978-1-942875-81-9(9))* Quarto Publishing Group USA.

Ho, Jannie & McClurkan, Rob. Sing & Smile: Wheels on the Bus & Itsy Bitsy Spider: Board Book with Handle 2 Pack. Wing, Scarlett. Cottage Door Press, ed. 2016. (Sing & Smile Stories Ser.). (ENG.). 10p. (J). (gr. -1-k). bds., bds., bds. 17.98 *(978-1-68052-246-4(9)*, 9000800) Cottage Door Pr.

Ho, Jason. Frankenstein, 1 vol. Shelley, Mary. 2007. (Graphic Horror Ser.). (ENG.). 32p. (J). (gr. 3-6). 29.93 *(978-1-60270-059-8(1)*, 9072, Graphic Planet - Fiction) Magic Wagon.

Ho, Jonathan & Ho, Yumi. Cookie Book: Financial Concepts for Kids - Saving. Ho, Jonathan. 2018. (Financial Concepts for Kids Ser.: Vol. 1). (ENG.). 30p. (J). pap. *(978-1-7752178-0-0(9))* Ho, Jonathan.

Ho, Louise. I Love You More Each Day. Lewis, Gill. 2017. (ENG.). 20p. (J). (gr. -1 — 1). bds. 6.99 *(978-1-68412-042-0(X)*, Silver Dolphin Bks.) Printers Row Publishing Group.

Ho, Y. Monthly Journal-Ing with Rolleen, the Pink Rabbit. Kong, Rowena. 2019. (ENG.). 30p. (J). pap. 9.17 ***(978-1-0864-9935-3(2))*** Independently Published.

Ho, Y. Rolleen & Her Special Flower Delivery. Kong, Rowena. 2019. (Rolleen Rabbit Collection of Stories Ser.: Vol. 4). (ENG.). 30p. (J). pap. 9.27 *(978-1-0804-3190-8(X))* Independently Published.

Ho, Y. Rolleen Rabbit & Her Pretty Forget-Me-Nots for Mommy. Kong, Rowena. 2019. (Rolleen Rabbit Collection of Stories Ser.: Vol. 6). (ENG.). 26p. (J). pap. 9.17 ***(978-1-6915-1037-5(8))*** Independently Published.

—Rolleen Rabbit Short Stories 1. Kong, Rowena. 2019. (ENG.). 48p. (J). pap. 10.22 ***(978-1-0887-4345-4(5))*** Independently Published.

Ho, Y. M. Little Rolleen Rabbit & Her Week with Mommy: Reading & Picture Book. Kong, Rowena. 2019. (Rolleen Rabbit Collection of Stories Ser.: Vol. 4). (ENG.). 28p. (J). pap. 9.19 *(978-1-0734-4857-9(6))* Independently Published.

—Little Rolleen's Monday with Mommy. Kong, Rowena. 2019. (Rolleen Rabbit Collection of Stories Ser.: Vol. 3). (ENG.). 26p. (J). pap. 9.29 *(978-1-0965-9965-4(1))* Independently Published.

—Rolleen & a Lost Football. Kong, Rowena. 2019. (ENG.). 24p. (J). pap. 9.13 *(978-1-0759-8815-8(2))* Independently Published.

Ho, Y. M. Rolleen Rabbit: My Mommy Is Back. Kong, Rowena. 2019. (Rolleen Rabbit Collection of Stories Ser.: Vol. 5). (ENG.). 26p. (J). pap. 9.17 ***(978-1-0862-2254-8(7))*** Independently Published.

—Rolleen Rabbit & Her Day 2. Kong, Rowena. 2019. (ENG.). 24p. (J). pap. 9.15 ***(978-1-7106-5804-0(5))*** Independently Published.

Ho, Y. M. Rolleen Rabbit & Her Day Reading & Picture Book. Kong, Rowena. 2019. (Rolleen Rabbit Reading & Picture Book Ser.: Vol. 1). (ENG.). 28p. (J). pap. 9.19 *(978-1-0708-7289-6(X))* Independently Published.

Ho, Y. M. Rolleen Rabbit & Her First Train Trip with Mommy & Friends. Kong, Rowena. 2019. (Rolleen Rabbit Collection of Stories Ser.: Vol. 7). (ENG.). 28p. (J). pap. 9.19 ***(978-1-7023-8799-6(2))*** Independently Published.

Ho, Y. M. Rolleen Rabbit, Mommy & Friends Picture & Coloring Book 1. Kong, Rowena. 2019. (Rolleen Rabbit Picture & Coloring Book Ser.: Vol. 1). (ENG.). 44p. (J). pap. 9.69 *(978-1-0753-2897-8(7))* Independently Published.

—Rolleen, the Rabbit, & Friends Coloring Book 3. Kong, Rowena. 2019. (Rolleen Rabbit & Friends Coloring Book Ser.: Vol. 3). (ENG.). (J). 46p. pap. 9.89 *(978-1-0724-1890-0(8))*; 42p. pap. 9.25 *(978-1-0996-4997-4(8))* Independently Published.

Ho, Yumi, jt. illus. see Ho, Jonathan.

Hoagland, Craig. Don't Wash My Hair! Mozee, Tara F. 2017. (ENG.). (J). (gr. k-2). 21.99 *(978-0-9976846-7-4(4))*; pap. 17.99 *(978-0-9976846-4-3(X))* Sevenhorns Publishing.

Hoang, Hannah. Sangeeta's House of Too Much Hair. Clark, Izabella a. 2018. (ENG.). 38p. (J). (gr. -1-3). 15.00 *(978-0-692-08981-1(0))* PaperMaze Media.

Hoang, Zara Gonzalez. Thread of Love. Sehgal, Kabir & Sehgal, Surishtha. 2018. (ENG.). 40p. (J). (gr. -1-3). 17.99 *(978-1-5344-0473-1(2)*, Beach Lane Bks.) Beach Lane Bks.

Hoang, Zara Gonzalez. A New Kind of Wild. Hoang, Zara Gonzalez. 2020. 32p. (J). (gr. -1-3). 17.99 *(978-0-525-55389-2(4)*, Dial Bks) Penguin Young Readers Group.

Hoar, Gail. Grandmother's Guest: The Blue Lady of Wilton. Schoen, Robin. 2013. 32p. 16.95 *(978-0-615-89154-5(3))* Hobby Horse Publishing, LLC.

Hoard, Angela. Did the Aardvarks Say "No Ark"? Coburn, Claudia. 2004. 32p. (J). *(978-0-9759343-1-9(7))* Purfect Promises.

Hoare, Jerry. George Ferris, What a Wheel! Lowell, Barbara. 2014. (Penguin Core Concepts Ser.). 32p. (J). (gr. -1-k). 4.99 *(978-0-448-47925-5(7)*, Grosset & Dunlap) Penguin Young Readers Group.

—What Is the Declaration of Independence? Harris, Michael C. & Who HQ. 2016. (What Was? Ser.). 112p. (J). (gr. 3-7). lib. bdg. 15.99 *(978-0-399-54230-5(2)*, Penguin Workshop) Penguin Young Readers Group.

—What Was the Holocaust? Herman, Gail & Who HQ. 2018. (What Was? Ser.). 112p. (J). (gr. 3-7). (ENG.). 5.99 *(978-0-451-53390-6(9))*; lib. bdg. 15.99 *(978-0-451-53392-0(5))* Penguin Young Readers Group. (Penguin Workshop).

—Where Are the Great Pyramids? Hoobler, Dorothy et al. 2015. (Where Is? Ser.). 112p. (J). (gr. 3-7). 5.99 *(978-0-448-48409-9(9)*, Penguin Workshop) Penguin Young Readers Group.

—Where Is Antarctica? Fabiny, Sarah & Who HQ. 2019. (Where Is? Ser.). 112p. (J). (gr. 3-7). (ENG.). 5.99 *(978-1-5247-8759-2(0))*; lib. bdg. 15.99 *(978-1-5247-8760-8(4))* Penguin Young Readers Group. (Penguin Workshop).

—Where Is the Great Wall? Demuth, Patricia Brennan & Who HQ. 2015. (Where Is? Ser.). 112p. (J). (gr. 3-7). 5.99 *(978-0-448-48358-0(0)*, Penguin Workshop) Penguin Young Readers Group.

—Who Was Che Guevara? Labrecque, Ellen & Who HQ. 2019. (Who Was? Ser.). 112p. (J). (gr. 3-7). 5.99 *(978-0-399-54401-9(1))*; 15.99 *(978-0-399-54403-3(8))* Penguin Young Readers Group. (Penguin Workshop).

—Who Was Frida Kahlo? Fabiny, Sarah & Who HQ. 2013. (Who Was? Ser.). 112p. (J). (gr. 3-7). 5.99 *(978-0-448-47938-5(9)*, Penguin Workshop) Penguin Young Readers Group.

—Who Was Gandhi? Rau, Dana Meachen & Who HQ. 2014. (Who Was? Ser.). (ENG.). 112p. (J). (gr. 3-7). pap. 5.99 *(978-0-448-48235-4(5)*, Penguin Workshop) Penguin Young Readers Group.

—Who Was Jane Austen? Fabiny, Sarah & Who HQ. 2017. (Who Was? Ser.). 112p. (J). (gr. 3-7). 5.99 *(978-0-448-48863-9(9)*, Penguin Workshop) Penguin Young Readers Group.

—Who Was Princess Diana? Labrecque, Ellen & Who HQ. 2017. (Who Was? Ser.). 112p. (J). (gr. 3-7). 5.99 *(978-0-448-48855-4(8)*, Penguin Workshop) Penguin Young Readers Group.

—Who Was Theodore Roosevelt? Burgan, Michael & Who HQ. 2014. (Who Was? Ser.). (ENG.). 112p. (J). (gr. 3-7). 5.99 *(978-0-448-47945-3(1)*, Penguin Workshop) Penguin Young Readers Group.

—Who Was Winston Churchill? Labrecque, Ellen & Who HQ. 2015. (Who Was? Ser.). 112p. (J). (gr. 3-7). 5.99 *(978-0-448-48300-9(9)*, Penguin Workshop) Penguin Young Readers Group.

Hobai, Ioana. Before You Sleep: A Bedtime Book of Gratitude. Romano, Ann Marie. 2018. (ENG.). 40p. (J). 17.99 *(978-1-62414-578-0(7)*, 900192299) Page Street Publishing Co.

—Just in Case. Krensky, Stephen. 2017. (J). *(978-0-7680-8422-1(9))* SAE Intl.

—My Home Is Better Than Yours! Krensky, Stephen. 2017. (J). *(978-0-7680-8415-3(6))* SAE Intl.

—My Pet Tree, Albert. Krensky, Stephen. 2016. (J). *(978-0-7680-8372-9(9))* SAE Intl.

Hoban, Lillian. A Baby Sister for Frances. Hoban, Russell. 2011. (I Can Read Level 2 Ser.). (ENG.). 48p. (J). (gr. k-3). 16.99 *(978-0-06-083804-1(3))*; pap. 4.99 *(978-0-06-083806-5(X))* HarperCollins Pubs.

—A Bargain for Frances. Hoban, Russell. l.t. ed. 2003. (I Can Read Level 2 Ser.). (ENG.). 64p. (J). (gr. k-3). pap. 4.99 *(978-0-06-444001-1(X),* HarperCollins) HarperCollins Pubs. Ltd. GBR. Dist: HarperCollins Pubs.

—Best Friends for Frances. Hoban, Russell. (J). 2016. (ENG.). 32p. (gr. -1-3). pap. 5.99 *(978-0-06-239244-2(1),* HarperFestival); 2009. 48p. (gr. -1-3). 16.99 *(978-0-06-083801-0(9));* 2009. (ENG.). 48p. (gr. k-3). pap. 4.99 *(978-0-06-083803-4(5))* HarperCollins Pubs.

—A Birthday for Frances. Hoban, Russell. 2012. (I Can Read Level 2 Ser.). (ENG.). 48p. (J). (gr. k-3). 16.99 *(978-0-06-083795-2(0));* pap. 4.99 *(978-0-06-083797-6(7))* HarperCollins Pubs.

—Bread & Jam for Frances. Hoban, Russell. (ENG.). (J). 2015. 32p. (gr. -1-3). pap. 5.99 *(978-0-06-239237-4(9),* HarperFestival); 2008. 48p. (gr. k-3). 16.99 *(978-0-06-083798-3(5));* 2008. 48p. (gr. k-3). pap. 4.99 *(978-0-06-083800-3(0))* HarperCollins Pubs.

—Charlie the Tramp. Hoban, Russell. 2016. (ENG.). 48p. 16.00 *(978-0-87486-780-0(0))* Plough Publishing Hse.

—Emmet Otter's Jug-Band Christmas. Hoban, Russell. 2017. (ENG.). 48p. (J). (gr. -1-2). 14.99 *(978-1-5247-1457-4(7),* Doubleday Bks. for Young Readers) Random Hse. Children's Bks.

—Harvey's Hideout. Hoban, Russell. 2018. 42p. (gr. -1-3). 16.00 *(978-0-87486-138-9(1))* Plough Publishing Hse.

—The Little Brute Family. Hoban, Russell. (My Readers: Level 2 Ser.). (ENG.). 40p. (J). (gr. k-2). 2012. 17.44 *(978-0-312-62138-4(8));* 2011. pap. 4.99 *(978-0-312-56373-8(6),* 900074764) Square Fish.

—The Sorely Trying Day. Hoban, Russell. 2010. (ENG.). 48p. (J). (gr. -1-3). 14.95 *(978-1-59017-343-5(0),* NYR Children's Collection) New York Review of Bks., Inc., The.

Hoban, Tana. Black & White Board Book. Hoban, Tana. 2007. (ENG.). 16p. (J). (gr. -1 — 1). bds. 7.99 *(978-0-06-117211-3(1),* Greenwillow Bks.) HarperCollins Pubs.

—Black White. Hoban, Tana. 2017. (ENG.). 36p. (J). (gr. -1 — 1). bds. 8.99 *(978-0-06-265690-2(2),* Greenwillow Bks.) HarperCollins Pubs.

—Over, under & Through. Hoban, Tana. 2008. (ENG.). 32p. (J). (gr. -1-2). 8.99 *(978-1-4169-7541-0(1),* Simon & Schuster/Paula Wiseman Bks.) Simon & Schuster/Paula Wiseman Bks.

Hobbie, Jocelyn. Priscilla & the Pixie Princess. Hobbie, Nathaniel. 2011. 32p. (J). (gr. -1-3). pap. 6.99 *(978-0-316-08349-2(6))* Little, Brown Bks. for Young Readers.

Hobbs, Dan, jt. illus. see Eastman, Dianne.

Hobbs, Guy. Little Otter Learns to Swim. Knapp, Artie. 2018. (ENG.). 32p. (J). 15.95 *(978-0-8214-2340-0(1))* Ohio Univ. Pr.

Hobbs, Leigh. Bad Buster: Being Bad Is Not Just for the Dogs! Laguna, Sofie. 2019. (Puffin Nibbles Ser.). 80p. (J). (gr. 2-4). pap. 9.99 *(978-0-14-330033-5(4),* Puffin) Penguin Random Hse. AUS. Dist: Independent Pubs. Group.

Hobbs, Leigh. Hooray for Horrible Harriet. Hobbs, Leigh. 2013. (Horrible Harriet Ser.). (ENG.). 32p. (J). (gr. k-2). mass mkt. 11.99 *(978-1-74114-703-2(4))* Allen & Unwin AUS. Dist: Independent Pubs. Group.

—Horrible Harriet. Hobbs, Leigh. 2013. (Horrible Harriet Ser.). (ENG.). 32p. (J). (gr. k-2). mass mkt. 11.99 *(978-1-86508-440-4(9))* Allen & Unwin AUS. Dist: Independent Pubs. Group.

—Mr Badger & the Magic Mirror. Hobbs, Leigh. 2013. (Mr Badger Ser.: 4). (ENG.). 80p. (J). (gr. 2-4). 10.99 *(978-1-74237-420-8(4))* Allen & Unwin AUS. Dist: Independent Pubs. Group.

—Old Tom Man of Mystery. Hobbs, Leigh. 2017. (Old Tom Ser.). (ENG.). 32p. (J). (gr. -1-k). 10.99 *(978-1-877003-53-0(0))* Little Hare Bks. AUS. Dist: Independent Pubs. Group.

Hoberg, Rick. Icarus. Mishkin, Dan. 2008. (Short Tales Greek Myths Ser.). (ENG.). 32p. (J). (gr. 3-6). 27.07 *(978-1-60270-136-6(9),* 13437, Short Tales) Magic Wagon.

Hobson, Charles. The Wolf Who Ate the Sky. Hobson, Mary Daniel & Rauh, Anna Isabel. 2015. (ENG.). 32p. (J). 16.00 *(978-1-59714-298-4(0))* Heyday.

Hobson, Ryan & Beach, Joshua. Uncover an Egyptian Mummy. Hopping, Lorraine Jean. 2020. (Uncover Ser.). (ENG.). 16p. (J). (gr. 3-7). 22.99 *(978-1-68412-295-0(3),* Silver Dolphin Bks.) Printers Row Publishing Group.

Hoch, Doug. Beaser the Bear's Rocky Mountain Christmas. Derrick Patricia. 2007. 32p. (J). (gr. -1-3). 18.95 incl. audio compact disk *(978-1-933818-09-2(3))* Animalations.

Hoch, Kevin. The Squirrel Who Was Afraid to Climb Trees. Simpson, Richard. 2003. 55p. (J). pap. 9.95 *(978-0-7414-1825-8(8))* Infinity Publishing.

Hochain, Serge. Building Liberty: A Statue Is Born. Hochain, Serge. 2006. 46p. (J). (gr. 4-8). reprint ed. 25.00 *(978-1-4223-5181-9(5))* DIANE Publishing Co.

Hochstatter, Daniel J. Italian. 2003. (Just Look 'n Learn Picture Dictionary Ser.). (ITA & ENG.). 96p. (J). (gr. 4-7). pap. 11.95 *(978-0-8442-8057-8(7),* 80577) McGraw-Hill Trade.

Hochstrasser, Karin. The Whole Armor of God. Buck, Deanna Draper;. 2019. (J). 12.99 *(978-1-62972-577-2(3))* Deseret Bk. Co.

Hock, Dan. The Birthday Bash 2 vols. An Iggy & Igor Mystery (#2) Hock, Dan. l.t. ed. 2004. 51p. (J). per. 4.99 *(978-0-9754046-1-4(X))* Anticipation Pr.

Hockensmith, Laura & Vandenheede, Ruben. Kiba Saves Christmas. Hockensmith, Laura. 2018. (Kiba Tales Ser.: Vol. 2). (ENG.). 44p. (J). pap. *(978-90-828545-3-4(8))* Smith & Heath.

—Kiba's Fun in the Sky. Hockensmith, Laura. 2018. (ENG.). 44p. (J). pap. *(978-90-828545-0-3(3))* Smith & Heath.

Hocker, Katherine. The Singer in the Stream: A Story of American Dippers. Willson, Mary. 2015. (ENG.). 32p. (J). (gr. k-3). 14.95 *(978-1-930238-56-5(8))* Yosemite Conservancy.

Hockerman, Dennis. The Big Hungry Bear. Williams, Rozanne Lanczak. 2005. (Reading for Fluency Ser.). 8p. (J). pap. 3.49 *(978-1-59198-146-6(8),* 4246) Creative Teaching Pr., Inc.

—The Country Mouse & the City Mouse: A Tale of Tolerance. 2006. (J). 6.99 *(978-1-59939-003-1(5))* Cornerstone Pr.

Hockerman, Dennis, et al. Folktales from Ecosystems Around the World. 2009. (Steck-Vaughn Pair-It Books Proficiency Stage 6 Ser.). (ENG.). 48p. (gr. 5-5). pap. 9.65 *(978-0-7398-6171-4(9))* Houghton Mifflin Harcourt Publishing Co.

Hockerman, Dennis. Good Night, Little Kitten. Christensen-Hall, Nancy. 2004. (My First Reader Ser.). (ENG.). 32p. (J). (gr. k-1). pap. 3.95 *(978-0-516-24628-4(3),* Children's Pr.) Scholastic Library Publishing.

—The Grasshopper & the Ant: A Tale about Planning. Aesop, Aesop. 2006. (J). *(978-1-59939-082-6(5),* Reader's Digest Young Families, Inc.) Studio Fun International.

—Lights! Action! California! Wilsdon, Christina. 2006. 26p. (J). 7.99 *(978-1-59939-009-3(4))* Cornerstone Pr.

—The Lion & the Mouse: A Tale about Being Helpful. 2006. (J). 6.99 *(978-1-59939-007-9(8))* Cornerstone Pr.

—The Little Seed: A Tale about Integrity. 2006. (J). *(978-1-59939-094-9(9),* Reader's Digest Young Families, Inc.) Studio Fun International.

—A New York Sailing Adventure. Wilsdon, Christina. 2006. 26p. (J). 7.99 *(978-1-59939-014-7(0))* Cornerstone Pr.

Hocking, Deborah. Build, Beaver, Build! Life at the Longest Beaver Dam. Markle, Sandra. 2016. (ENG.). 32p. (J). (gr. k-3). 26.65 *(978-1-4677-4900-8(1),* 9781467749008); E-Book 39.99 *(978-1-4677-9725-2(1))* Lerner Publishing Group. (Millbrook Pr.).

—Max Explains Everything: Grocery Store Expert. McAnulty, Stacy. 2018. 32p. (J). (gr. -1-2). 16.99 *(978-1-101-99644-7(7),* G.P. Putnam's Sons Books for Young Readers) Penguin Young Readers Group.

—Max Explains Everything: Puppy Expert. McAnulty, Stacy. 2020. 32p. (J). (gr. -1-2). 16.99 *(978-0-399-54502-3(6),* G.P. Putnam's Sons Books for Young Readers) Penguin Young Readers Group.

—Max Explains Everything: Soccer Expert. McAnulty, Stacy. 2019. 32p. (J). (gr. -1-2). 16.99 *(978-1-101-99640-9(4),* G.P. Putnam's Sons Books for Young Readers) Penguin Young Readers Group.

Hocking, Geoff. Jamie Wins Again. Marwood, Lorraine. 2004. iv, 36p. (J). pap. *(978-0-7608-6743-3(7))* Sundance/Newbridge Educational Publishing.

Hoda, Rubina. Diwali: A Cultural Adventure. Sood, Sana Hoda. 2013. (ENG.). (J). (gr. -1-3). 14.95 *(978-1-62086-396-1(0))* Mascot Bks., Inc.

Hoddy, Matt. How I Survived: Four Nights on the Ice. Ittusardjuat, Serapio. 2020. (ENG.). 48p. (YA). 18.95 *(978-1-77227-272-7(8))* Inhabit Media Inc. CAN. Dist: Consortium Bk. Sales & Distribution.

Hodes, Loren. Who Would Have Guessed? It's All for the Best! Hodes, Loren. 2006. 32p. (J). (gr. -1-3). 13.95 *(978-1-932443-48-6(7))* Judaica Pr., Inc., The.

Hodge, Chelsea. I Am a Duck. Perry, Susan J. 2019. (ENG.). 36p. (J). pap. 9.95 ***(978-1-6990-3620-4(9))*** Independently Published.

Hodgen, Leigh Norridge. Hilmy the Hippo Learns to Share. Norridge, Rae. 2007. (ENG.). 32p. 7.95 *(978-0-86037-585-2(4))* Kube Publishing Ltd. GBR. Dist: Consortium Bk. Sales & Distribution.

Hodges, Benjamin. Wandihnu & the Old Dugong. Wymarra, Elizabeth & Wymarra, Wandihnu. 2007. 28p. (J). (gr. k-7). pap. 13.95 *(978-1-921248-18-4(1))* Magabala Bks. AUS. Dist: Independent Pubs. Group.

Hodges, C. Walter. The Eagle of the Ninth. Sutcliff, Rosemary. 2015. (Everyman's Library Children's Classics Ser.). (ENG.). 256p. 20.00 *(978-1-101-90769-6(X),* Everyman's Library) Knopf Doubleday Publishing Group.

—The Eagle of the Ninth. Sutcliff, Rosemary. 2015. 304p. (J). *(978-1-85715-520-4(3))* Knopf, Alfred A. Inc.

Hodges, Demetria. Princess Pfeiffer & the Knight. Owens, Belinda K. 2019. (ENG.). 32p. (J). pap. 9.50 ***(978-1-7103-4511-7(X))*** Independently Published.

Hodges, Jared. Peach Fuzz, 1 vol., Vol. 1. Cibos, Lindsay. 2008. (Tokyopop Ser.). (ENG.). 160p. (J). (gr. 2-6). 28.50 *(978-1-59961-571-4(1),* 14812, Graphic Novels) Spotlight.

—Peach Fuzz Vol. 2: Show & Tell, 1 vol. Cibos, Lindsay. 2008. (Tokyopop Ser.). (ENG.). 176p. (J). (gr. 2-6). 28.50 *(978-1-59961-572-1(X),* 14813, Graphic Novels) Spotlight.

—Peach Fuzz Vol. 3: Prince Edwin, 1 vol. Cibos, Lindsay. 2008. (Tokyopop Ser.). (ENG.). 176p. (J). (gr. 2-6). 28.50 *(978-1-59961-573-8(8),* 14814, Graphic Novels) Spotlight.

Hodgkins, James, et al. Devil in the Gateway. Carey, Mike et al. Bond, Shelly & Kwitney, Alisa, eds. rev. ed. 2006. (Lucifer Ser.: Bk. 1). (ENG.). 160p. (YA). pap. 14.99 *(978-1-56389-733-7(4),* Vertigo) DC Comics.

Hodgkinson, Jo. A Big Day for Migs. Hodgkinson, Jo. 2014. (ENG.). 32p. (J). (gr. -1-3). 16.95 *(978-1-4677-5014-1(X),* 9781467750141) Lerner Publishing Group.

Hodgkinson, Leigh. Magical Mix-Ups: Birthdays & Bridesmaids. Edwards, Marnie. 2012. (Magical Mix-Ups Ser.: 1). (ENG.). 96p. (J). (gr. 2-5). pap. 6.99 *(978-0-7636-6272-1(0),* Nosy Crow) Candlewick Pr.

—Magical Mix-Ups: Spells & Surprises. Edwards, Marnie. 2014. (Magical Mix-Ups Ser.: 4). (ENG.). (J). (gr. 2-5). pap. 6.99 *(978-0-7636-6610-1(6),* Nosy Crow) Candlewick Pr.

—Pets & Parties. Edwards, Marnie. 2013. (Magical Mix-Ups Ser.: 3). (ENG.). 96p. (J). (gr. 2-5). pap. 6.99 *(978-0-7636-6371-1(9),* Nosy Crow) Candlewick Pr.

Hodgkinson, Leigh. The Big Monster Snorey Book. Hodgkinson, Leigh. 2016. (ENG.). (J). (gr. -1-2). 16.99 *(978-0-7636-8660-4(3),* Nosy Crow) Candlewick Pr.

—Boris & the Snoozebox. Hodgkinson, Leigh. 2008. (Tiger Tales Ser.). 40p. (J). (gr. -1-3). 15.95 *(978-1-58925-071-0(0))* Tiger Tales.

—Boris & the Wrong Shadow. Hodgkinson, Leigh. 2009. 32p. (J). (gr. -1-2). 15.95 *(978-1-58925-082-6(6))* Tiger Tales.

—Goldilocks & Just One Bear. Hodgkinson, Leigh. 2012. (ENG.). 32p. (J). (gr. -1-2). 16.99 *(978-0-7636-6172-4(4),* Nosy Crow) Candlewick Pr.

—Goldilocks & the Just Right Potty. Hodgkinson, Leigh. 2017. (ENG.). 32p. (J). (-k). 16.99 *(978-0-7636-9799-0(0),* Nosy Crow) Candlewick Pr.

—Limelight Larry. Hodgkinson, Leigh. 2011. (ENG.). 32p. (J). *(978-1-58925-102-1(4))* Tiger Tales.

—Troll Swap. Hodgkinson, Leigh. 2014. (ENG.). 32p. (J). (gr. -1-2). 15.99 *(978-0-7636-7101-3(0),* Nosy Crow) Candlewick Pr.

Hodgman, Ann, photos by. How to Die of Embarrassment Every Day. Hodgman, Ann. 2011. (ENG., 224p. (J). (gr. 3-7). 25.99 *(978-0-8050-8705-5(2),* 900048466, Holt, Henry & Co. Bks. For Young Readers) Holt, Henry & Co.

Hodgson, Rob. A Good Day for a Hat. Fuller, T. Nat. 2017. (ENG.). 32p. (J). (gr. -1-k). 15.95 *(978-1-4197-2300-1(6),* Abrams Appleseed) Abrams, Inc.

—Scary Bingo: Fun with Monsters & Crazy Creatures. 2017. (ENG.). (J). (gr. -1-k). 19.99 *(978-1-78627-008-5(0),* King, Laurence Publishing) Orion Publishing Group, Ltd. GBR. Dist: Hachette Bk. Group.

Hodnefjeld, Hilde. Elephant Man. Di Fiore, Mariangela. Hedger, Rosie, tr. 2015. (ENG.). 52p. (J). (gr. 3-6). 19.95 *(978-1-55451-778-7(8),* 9781554517787) Annick Pr., Ltd. CAN. Dist: Publishers Group West (PGW).

Hodson, Ben. Captain Jake, 1 vol. Stewart, Shannon. 2008. (Orca Echoes Ser.). (ENG.). 64p. (J). (gr. 1-3). pap. 6.95 *(978-1-55143-896-2(8))* Orca Bk. Pubs. USA.

—Fun with Ed & Fred: Teaches 50+ Sight Words! Bolger, Kevin. 2016. (ENG.). 40p. (J). (gr. -1-3). 7.99 *(978-0-06-228600-0(5))* HarperCollins Pubs.

—Gran on a Fan: Silly Short Vowels. Bolger, Kevin. 2015. (ENG.). 40p. (J). (gr. -1-3). 7.99 *(978-0-06-228596-6(3))* HarperCollins Pubs.

Hodson, Ben. Hey Little Rockabye: A Lullaby for Pet Adoption. Sainte-Marie, Buffy. 2020. (ENG.). 32p. (J). (gr. -1-2). 16.95 ***(978-1-77164-482-2(6),*** Greystone Bks.) Greystone Books Ltd. CAN. Dist: Publishers Group West (PGW).

Hodson, Ben. How the Moon Regained Her Shape, 1 vol. Heller, Janet Ruth. 2006. (ENG.). 32p. (J). (gr. 1-5). 15.95 *(978-0-9764943-4-8(5))* Arbordale Publishing.

—I Love Yoga: A Source Book for Teens. Schwartz, Ellen. 2003. (ENG.). 128p. (J). (gr. 5-18). pap. 9.95 *(978-0-88776-598-8(X),* Tundra Bks.) Tundra Bks. CAN. Dist: Penguin Random Hse. LLC.

—In Arctic Waters, 1 vol. Crawford, Laura. 2007. (ENG.). 32p. (J). (gr. -1-2). 15.95 *(978-0-9768823-4-3(5))* Arbordale Publishing.

—Jeffrey & Sloth, 1 vol. Winters, Kari-Lynn. 2008. (ENG.). 32p. (J). (gr. -1-k). per. 9.95 *(978-1-55143-974-7(3))* Orca Bk. Pubs. USA.

—Lazy Bear, Crazy Bear: Loony Long Vowels. Bolger, Kevin. 2015. (ENG.). 40p. (J). (gr. -1-3). 7.99 *(978-0-06-228598-0(X))* HarperCollins Pubs.

—Richard Was a Picker, 1 vol. Beck, Carolyn. 2010. (ENG.). 32p. (J). (gr. -1-k). 19.95 *(978-1-55469-088-6(9))* Orca Bk. Pubs. USA.

—See Fred Run: Teaches 50+ Sight Words! Bolger, Kevin. 2017. (ENG.). 40p. (J). (gr. -1-3). 7.99 *(978-0-06-228602-4(1))* HarperCollins Pubs.

—'Twas the Day Before Zoo Day, 1 vol. Ipcizade, Catherine. 2008. (Basic Math Operations Ser.). (ENG.). 32p. (J). (gr. -1-2). 17.95 *(978-1-60718-585-7(7))* Arbordale Publishing.

Hodson, Jewel. White Dresses: A Baptism Keepsake for Girls. Rowley, Deborah Pace. 2006. 32p. (J). 16.99 *(978-1-59038-632-3(9))* Deseret Bk. Co.

Hodzic, Ena. Charlotte's New York Adventure: A Girl Takes the Lead. Dunton, Lese. 2018. (ENG.). 28p. (J). pap. 11.99 *(978-0-578-40647-3(0))* Dunton Publishing.

Hoedl, Lee, photos by. Jesse the Wait of the Wood. Hoedl, Lee. 2006. 30p. (J). per. 12.95 *(978-1-59879-139-6(7))* Lifevest Publishing, Inc.

Hoeffner, Deb. Andi's Choice. Messer, Celeste M. 2004. 82-92p. 4.95 *(978-0-9702171-6-5(1))* AshleyAlan Enterprises.

—The Boy Who Cried Wolf. Messer, Celeste M. 2004. 82-92p. 4.95 *(978-0-9702171-9-6(6))* AshleyAlan Enterprises.

—The Broken Wing: The Adventures of Andi O'Malley. Messer, Celeste M. 2004. (Adventures of Andi O'Malley Ser.). 82-92p. (J). (gr. 4-7). 4.95 *(978-0-9702171-1-0(0))* AshleyAlan Enterprises.

—Forever & Always. Messer, Celeste M. 2004. 82-92p. 4.95 *(978-0-9710145-0-3(7))* AshleyAlan Enterprises.

—Forever Home: Tales of Four Lucky Dogs. Whitman, Lynn. 2012. 32p. (J). 14.95 *(978-0-9860222-0-3(9))* Becklyns, LLC.

—The Ghost of Piper's Landing. Messer, Celeste M. 2004. 82-92p. 4.95 *(978-0-9702171-7-2(X))* AshleyAlan Enterprises.

—A Message from Teddy. Messer, Celeste M. 2004. 82-92p. 4.95 *(978-0-9702171-5-8(3))* AshleyAlan Enterprises.

—Silent Swoop: An Owl, an Egg, & a Warm Shirt Pocket. Houts, Michelle. 2019. (ENG.). 32p. (J). (gr. -1-3). 16.95 *(978-1-58469-646-9(X),* Dawn Pubns.) Sourcebooks, Inc.

—When Eagles Fly. Messer, Celeste M. 2004. 82-92p. 4.95 *(978-0-9702171-8-9(8))* AshleyAlan Enterprises.

Høegh, Aka. A Journey to the Mother of the Sea. Vebæk, Måliâraq. 2019. (ENG.). 32p. (J). 16.95 *(978-1-77227-251-2(5))* Inhabit Media Inc. CAN. Dist: Consortium Bk. Sales & Distribution.

Hofer, Ernst & Hofer, Nelly. The Wild Swans. 2003. (ENG.). 40p. (J). (gr. 2-5). 17.95 *(978-0-88776-615-2(3),* Tundra Bks.) Tundra Bks. CAN. Dist: Penguin Random Hse. LLC.

Hofer, Nelly, jt. illus. see Hofer, Ernst.

Hoff, Syd. Chester. Hoff, Syd. 2004. (I Can Read Level 1 Ser.). (ENG.). 64p. (gr. k-3). 4.99 *(978-0-06-444095-0(8))* Perfection Learning Corp.

—Danny & the Dinosaur. Hoff, Syd. 2017. (I Can Read Level 1 Ser.). (ENG.). 72p. (J). (gr. -1-3). 9.99 *(978-0-06-257277-6(6))* HarperCollins Pubs.

—Danny & the Dinosaur. Hoff, Syd. 50th anniv. ed. 2008. (I Can Read Level 1 Ser.). (ENG.). 64p. (J). (gr. -1-3). pap. 4.99 *(978-0-06-444002-8(8),* HarperCollins) HarperCollins Pubs. Ltd. GBR. Dist: HarperCollins Pubs.

—Danny & the Dinosaur 3-Book Box Set: Danny & the Dinosaur; Happy Birthday, Danny & the Dinosaur!; Danny & the Dinosaur Go to Camp, Set. Hoff, Syd. 50th anniv. ed. 2008. (I Can Read Level 1 Ser.). (ENG.). 32p. (J). (gr. k-3). pap. 11.99 *(978-0-06-143083-1(8))* HarperCollins Pubs.

—Danny & the Dinosaur & the Big Storm. Hoff, Syd. 2017. (ENG.). 24p. (J). (gr. -1-3). pap. 4.99 *(978-0-06-241045-0(8),* HarperFestival) HarperCollins Pubs.

—Danny & the Dinosaur & the Girl Next Door. Hoff, Syd. 2017. (I Can Read Level 1 Ser.). (ENG.). 32p. (J). (gr. -1-3). pap. 4.99 *(978-0-06-228158-6(5))* HarperCollins Pubs.

—Danny & the Dinosaur & the New Puppy. Hoff, Syd. 2015. (I Can Read Level 1 Ser.). (ENG.). 32p. (J). (gr. -1-3). pap. 4.99 *(978-0-06-228152-4(6))* HarperCollins Pubs.

—Danny & the Dinosaur & the Sand Castle Contest, No. 5. Hoff, Syd. 2018. (I Can Read Level 1 Ser.). (ENG.). 32p. (J). (gr. -1-3). 16.99 *(978-0-06-241049-8(0));* pap. 4.99 *(978-0-06-241048-1(2))* HarperCollins Pubs.

—Danny & the Dinosaur: Big Reading Collection: 5 Books Featuring Danny & His Friend the Dinosaur! Hoff, Syd. 2017. (I Can Read Level 1 Ser.). (ENG.). 190p. (J). (gr. -1-3). pap. 19.99 *(978-0-06-241047-4(4))* HarperCollins Pubs.

—Danny & the Dinosaur: Eggs, Eggs, Eggs! Hoff, Syd. 2018. (ENG.). 24p. (J). (gr. -1-3). pap. 6.99 *(978-0-06-241051-1(2),* HarperFestival) HarperCollins Pubs.

—Danny & the Dinosaur: First Valentine's Day. Hoff, Syd. 2016. (ENG.). 24p. (J). (gr. -1-3). pap. 6.99 *(978-0-06-241044-3(X),* HarperFestival) HarperCollins Pubs.

—Danny & the Dinosaur: Happy Halloween. Hoff, Syd. 2016. (ENG.). 24p. (J). (gr. -1-3). pap. 6.99 *(978-0-06-241043-6(1),* HarperFestival) HarperCollins Pubs.

—Danny & the Dinosaur in the Big City. Hoff, Syd. 2019. (I Can Read Level 1 Ser.). (ENG.). 32p. (J). (gr. -1-3). 16.99 *(978-0-06-241060-3(1));* pap. 4.99 *(978-0-06-241059-7(8))* HarperCollins Pubs.

—Danny & the Dinosaur Mind Their Manners. Hoff, Syd. 2019. (I Can Read Level 1 Ser.). (ENG.). 32p. (J). (gr. -1-3). 16.99 *(978-0-06-241057-3(1));* pap. 4.99 *(978-0-06-241056-6(3))* HarperCollins Pubs.

—Danny & the Dinosaur Ride a Bike. Hoff, Syd. 2020. (I Can Read Level 1 Ser.). (ENG.). 32p. (J). (gr. -1-3). 16.99 *(978-0-06-285761-3(4));* pap. 4.99 *(978-0-06-241055-9(5))* HarperCollins Pubs.

—Danny & the Dinosaur: School Days. Hoff, Syd. 2017. (I Can Read Level 1 Ser.). (ENG.). 32p. (J). (gr. -1-3). pap. 4.99 *(978-0-06-228161-6(5))* HarperCollins Pubs.

—The Danny & the Dinosaur Storybook Collection. Hoff, Syd. 2016. (I Can Read Level 1 Ser.). 192p. (J). (gr. -1-3). 11.99 *(978-0-06-247070-6(1))* HarperCollins Pubs.

—Danny & the Dinosaur Storybook Favorites: Includes 5 Stories Plus Stickers! Hoff, Syd. 2019. (I Can Read Level 1 Ser.). (ENG.). 192p. (J). (gr. -1-3). 13.99 *(978-0-06-288311-7(9))* HarperCollins Pubs.

—Danny & the Dinosaur: the Big Sneeze. Hoff, Syd. 2018. (I Can Read Level 1 Ser.). (ENG.). 32p. (J). (gr. -1-3). 16.99 *(978-0-06-241053-5(9));* pap. 4.99 *(978-0-06-241052-8(0))* HarperCollins Pubs.

—Danny & the Dinosaur: Too Tall. Hoff, Syd. 2015. (I Can Read Level 1 Ser.). (ENG.). 32p. (J). (gr. -1-3). pap. 4.99 *(978-0-06-228155-5(0))* HarperCollins Pubs.

—The Littlest Leaguer. Hoff, Syd. 2008. (I Can Read Level 1 Ser.). (ENG.). 48p. (J). (gr. -1-3). pap. 4.99 *(978-0-06-053774-6(4))* HarperCollins Pubs.

—Sammy the Seal. Hoff, Syd. 2017. (I Can Read Level 1 Ser.). (ENG.). 72p. (J). (gr. -1-3). 9.99 *(978-0-06-257274-5(1))* HarperCollins Pubs.

—Santa's Moose. Hoff, Syd. 2017. (I Can Read Level 1 Ser.). (ENG.). 32p. (J). (gr. -1-3). 16.99 *(978-0-06-264308-7(8));* pap. 4.99 *(978-0-06-264307-0(X))* HarperCollins Pubs.

Hoff, Syd & Cutting, David. Danny & the Dinosaur: First Valentine's Day. Hale, Bruce. 2016. (J). *(978-1-4844-9973-3(5),* HarperFestival) HarperCollins Pubs.

—Danny & the Dinosaur: a Very Dino Christmas. Hoff, Syd. 2017. (ENG.). 24p. (J). (gr. -1-3). pap. 6.99 *(978-0-06-241046-7(6),* HarperFestival) HarperCollins Pubs.

Hoffbauer, Wyng, jt. illus. see Eakins, Bonny Mae.

Hoffman, Amalia. Dreidel Day, Vol. Hoffman, Amalia. 2018. (ENG.). 18p. (J). (gr. -1 — 1). bds. 5.99 *(978-1-5415-0245-1(0),* Kar-Ben Publishing) Lerner Publishing Group.

Hoffman, H. Lawrence. Father Kino: Priest to the Pimas. Clark, Ann Nolan. 2019. (ENG.). 184p. (J). pap. 12.95 *(978-1-64051-085-2(0))* St. Augustine Academy Pr.

Hoffman, Isobel. It's Not Easy Being a Pelican. Dabritz, Evelyn. 2012. 32p. (J). *(978-1-930401-87-7(6))* Central Coast Bks./Pr.

Hoffman, Mary Hramiec. Lolek the Boy Who Became Pope John Paul II. Hoffman, Mary Hramiec. 2008. 56p. (J). 18.95 *(978-0-9746901-1-7(2))* Hramiec Hoffman Publishing.

Hoffman, Paul G. Tales with a Texas Twist: Original Stories & Enduring Folklore from the Lone Star State. Ingham, Donna. 2005. (ENG.). 160p. (gr. -1-7). per. 12.95 *(978-0-7627-3899-1(5))* Globe Pequot Pr., The.

Hoffman, Robin. Shirley Link & the Safe Case. Graham, Ben. 2019. (Shirley Link Ser.: Vol. 1). (ENG.). 102p. (J). pap. 6.99 ***(978-1-7055-7379-2(7))*** Independently Published.

Hoffman, Roger. Casting Call: The Saltwater Twins Book II. Hoffman, Nancy. 2019. (Saltwater Kids Ser.: Vol. 2). (ENG.). 140p. (J). (gr. 4-6). pap. 5.95 *(978-1-7323345-1-9(X))* Reader Publishing Group.

Hoffman, Sanford. Joke & Riddle Bonanza. Pellowski, Michael J. 96p. (J). 2017. (gr. k-8). pap. 6.95 *(978-1-4549-2247-6(8));* 2012. (gr. 3-6). pap. 17.44 *(978-1-4027-8837-6(1))* Sterling Publishing Co., Inc.

Hoffman, Steve. 'Twas the Night Before Christ. Roberts, Tom. 2003rd ed. 2004. (J). per. *(978-0-9723868-1-4(5))* T & T Roberts Publishing.

Hoffmann, Felix. Hans in Luck: Seven Stories by the Brothers Grimm. Brothers Grimm. 2017. (ENG.). 256p. (J). (gr. -1-3). 30.00 *(978-0-7358-4281-6(7))* North-South Bks., Inc.

Hoffmann, Mark. Explosion at the Poem Factory, 1 vol. Lukoff, Kyle. 2020. 44p. (J). (gr. 1-4). 18.95 *(978-1-77306-132-0(1))* Groundwood Bks. CAN. Dist: Publishers Group West (PGW).

—Hawks Kettle, Puffins Wheel: And Other Poems of Birds in Flight. Vande Griek, Susan. 2019. (ENG.). 36p. (J). (gr. 1-4). 16.99 *(978-1-77138-995-2(8))* Kids Can Pr., Ltd. CAN. Dist: Hachette Bk. Group.

Hoffmire, A. B. The Ogre Bully. Hoffmire, A. B., as told by. 2007. (Story Cove Ser.). (ENG.). 32p. (J). (gr. -1-3). 3.95 *(978-0-87483-803-9(7))* August Hse. Pubs., Inc.

Hoffmire, Baird. Anansi & the Pot of Beans. Norfolk, Bobby & Norfolk, Sherry. 2006. (Story Cove Ser.). (ENG.). 32p. (J). (gr. -1-3). 4.95 *(978-0-87483-811-4(8))* August Hse. Pubs., Inc.

—Anansi & the Sky Kingdom. Norfolk, Bobby & Norfolk, Sherry. 2008. (Story Cove Ser.). (ENG.). 32p. (J). (gr. -1-3). pap. 4.95 *(978-0-87483-881-7(9))* August Hse. Pubs., Inc.

—Anansi & the Tug O' War. 2007. (Story Cove Ser.). (ENG.). 32p. (J). (gr. -1-3). pap. 4.95 *(978-0-87483-825-1(8))* August Hse. Pubs., Inc.

—Anansi & Turtle Go to Dinner. Norfolk, Bobby & Norfolk, Sherry. 2007. (Story Cove Ser.). (ENG.). 32p. (J). (gr. -1-3). pap. 4.95 *(978-0-87483-856-5(8))* August Hse. Pubs., Inc.

—Anansi Goes to Lunch. Norfolk, Bobby & Norfolk, Sherry. 2007. (Story Cove Ser.). (ENG.). 32p. (J). (gr. -1-3). pap. 4.95 *(978-0-87483-852-7(5))* August Hse. Pubs., Inc.

—The Archer & the Sun: A Tale from China. Cleveland, Rob. 2007. (Story Cove Ser.). (ENG.). 24p. (J). (gr. -1-3). pap. 3.95 *(978-0-87483-878-7(9))* August Hse. Pubs., Inc.

—The Bear, the Bat & the Dove: Three Stories from Aesop. Cleveland, Rob. 2006. (Story Cove Ser.). (ENG.). 32p. (J). (gr. -1-3). pap. 3.95 *(978-0-87483-810-7(X))* August Hse. Pubs., Inc.

—The Big Wide-Mouth Frog. 2009. (J). pap. *(978-0-87483-890-9(8)*, August House Story Cove) August Hse. Pubs., Inc.

—Billy Brown & the Belly Button Beastie. Norfolk, Bobby & Norfolk, Sherry. 2007. (Buried Treasure Ser.). (ENG.). 32p. (J). (gr. -1-3). 16.95 *(978-0-87483-831-2(2))* August Hse. Pubs., Inc.

—The Clever Monkey: A Folktale from West Africa. Cleveland, Rob. 2006. (Story Cove Ser.). (ENG.). 32p. (J). (gr. -1-3). pap. 4.95 *(978-0-87483-801-5(0))* August Hse. Pubs., Inc.

—How Tiger Got His Stripes: A Folktale from Vietnam. 2006. (Story Cove Ser.). (ENG.). 32p. (J). (gr. -1-3). pap. 4.95 *(978-0-87483-799-5(5))* August Hse. Pubs., Inc.

—The Magic Apple: A Middle Eastern Folktale. Cleveland, Rob. 2006. (Story Cove Ser.). (ENG.). 32p. (J). (gr. -1-3). pap. 4.95 *(978-0-87483-800-8(2))* August Hse. Pubs., Inc.

—Rooster's Night Out. Weiss, Mitch & Hamilton, Martha. 2007. (Story Cove Ser.). (ENG.). 32p. (J). (gr. -1-3). pap. 3.95 *(978-0-87483-826-8(6))* August Hse. Pubs., Inc.

Hofher, Cathy. Take a Deep Breath: Little Lessons from Flowers for a Happier World. Stoutland, Allison. l.t. ed. 2003. 32p. 14.95 *(978-0-9670941-2-0(7))* Inch By Inch Pubns., LLC.

—What Day Is Today? Parker, Sandy. l.t. ed. 2003. 24p. (gr. k-1). 13.95 *(978-0-9643462-3-9(0)*, 10, Just Think Bks.) Canary Connect Pubns.

—What Month Is It? Parker, Sandy. l.t. ed. 2004. 32p. 15.95 *(978-0-9643462-5-3(7)*, Just Think Bks.) Canary Connect Pubns.

Hofmann, Ginnie. Who Wants an Old Teddy Bear?, 5 vols. Hofmann, Ginnie. 2003. 32p. (J). pap. 5.95 *(978-1-932485-00-4(7))* Reverie Publishing Co.

Hofmann, Ginnie, jt. illus. see Bart, Kathleen.

Hofmann-Maniyar, Ariane, et al. How Can I Make New Friends? Book Set Of 4. Hofmann-Maniyar, Ariane et al. 2020. (Social & Emotional Learning Sets Ser.). (ENG.). 144p. (J). pap., pap. ***(978-1-78628-540-9(1))*** Child's Play International Ltd.

Hofmann-Maniyar, Ariane. Ice in the Jungle. Hofmann-Maniyar, Ariane. (Child's Play Library). 32p. (J). 2016. pap. *(978-1-84643-730-4(X))*; 2015. (ENG.). *(978-1-84643-731-1(8))* Child's Play International Ltd.

—Max & Xam. Hofmann-Maniyar, Ariane. 2020. (Child's Play Library). 32p. (J). pap. *(978-1-78628-086-2(8))*; ***(978-1-78628-087-9(6))*** Child's Play International Ltd.

—That's NOT How You Do It! Hofmann-Maniyar, Ariane. 2017. (Child's Play Library). 32p. (J). (ENG.). *(978-1-84643-929-2(9))*; pap. *(978-1-84643-928-5(0))* Child's Play International Ltd.

Hofmeister, Michael. The Cactus. Hofmeister, Michael. 2019. (ENG.). 28p. (J). pap. 10.00 *(978-1-0935-0978-6(3))* Independently Published.

Hofmeister, Michael. The Cloud. Hofmeister, Michael. 2019. (ENG.). 40p. (J). pap. 10.00 ***(978-1-7034-0218-6(9))*** Independently Published.

Hofner, Cathy. What Can I Do Today? To Make This World a Happier Place. Stoutland, Allison. 2005. 32p. (J). (gr. -1-3). 16.95 *(978-0-9670941-3-7(5))* Inch By Inch Pubns., LLC.

Hogan, Eric. Tea Parties with Grandm. McNair, Barbara. 2009. 48p. pap. 24.95 *(978-1-60749-617-5(8))* America Star Bks.

Hogan, Jamie. Here Come the Humpbacks! Sayre, April Pulley. 2013. 40p. (J). (gr. -1-3). pap. 7.95 *(978-1-58089-406-7(2))*; lib. bdg. 17.95 *(978-1-58089-405-0(4))* Charlesbridge Publishing, Inc.

—John Muir Wrestles a Waterfall. Danneberg, Julie. 2015. 32p. (J). (gr. -1-3). lib. bdg. 16.95 *(978-1-58089-586-6(7))* Charlesbridge Publishing, Inc.

—Nest, Nook & Cranny. Blackaby, Susan. 2010. 60p. (J). (gr. 4-7). 15.95 *(978-1-58089-350-3(3))* Charlesbridge Publishing, Inc.

—Rickshaw Girl. Perkins, Mitali. 96p. (J). (gr. 2-5). 2008. (ENG.). pap. 6.95 *(978-1-58089-309-1(0))*; 2007. 14.95 *(978-1-58089-308-4(2))* Charlesbridge Publishing, Inc.

—Tiger Boy. Perkins, Mitali. 2015. 96p. (J). (gr. 2-5). lib. bdg. 14.95 *(978-1-58089-660-3(X))* Charlesbridge Publishing, Inc.

—A Warmer World. Arnold, Caroline. 2012. 32p. (J). (gr. 2-5). pap. 7.95 *(978-1-58089-267-4(1))* Charlesbridge Publishing, Inc.

Hogan, Jamie. Seven Days of Daisy, 1 vol. Hogan, Jamie. ed. 2011. (ENG.). 32p. (gr. -1-3). 14.95 *(978-0-89272-919-7(8))* Down East Bks.

Hogan, Martina. Alphabetter. Ragsdale, Linda. 2017. (Peace Dragon Tales Ser.). (ENG.). 32p. (J). (gr. 3-6). 16.99 *(978-1-4867-1210-6(X)*, 9bcb726d-c766-413d-bb6f-1ca334082415) Flowerpot Pr.

—Animals: 5 Flaps to Flip! Ackland, Nick & Clever Publishing. 2020. (Peek-A-Boo Ser.). (ENG.). 10p. (J). (gr. -1 — 1). bds. 5.99 *(978-1-949998-49-8(5))* Clever Media Group.

—Babies Love Animales. Wing, Scarlett. Cottage Door Press, ed. 2019. (Babies Love Ser.). (SPA.). 12p. (J). (gr. -1-k). bds. 7.99 *(978-1-68052-618-9(9)*, 1000110-SLA) Cottage Door Pr.

—Babies Love Animals, First Words, Things That Go, & Opposities 4 Pack: Chunky Lift a Flap Board Book 4 Pack. Wing, Scarlett. Cottage Door Press, ed. 2015. (Babies Love Ser.). (ENG.). 48p. (J). (gr. -1-k). bds. 31.96 *(978-1-68052-108-5(X)*, 9000220) Cottage Door Pr.

—Babies Love Opposites: Chunky Lift a Flap Board Book. Wing, Scarlett. Cottage Door Press, ed. 2015. (Babies Love Ser.). (ENG.). 12p. (J). (gr. -1-k). bds. 7.99 *(978-1-68052-028-6(8)*, 1000291) Cottage Door Pr.

—Babies Love Opuestos. Wing, Scarlett. Cottage Door Press, ed. 2019. (Babies Love Ser.). (SPA.). 12p. (J). (gr. -1-k). bds. 7.99 *(978-1-68052-620-2(0)*, 1000290-SLA) Cottage Door Pr.

—Babies Love Primeras Palabras. Wing, Scarlett. Cottage Door Press, ed. 2019. (Babies Love Ser.). (SPA.). 12p. (J). (gr. -1-k). bds. 7.99 *(978-1-68052-617-2(0)*, 1000100-SLA) Cottage Door Pr.

—Babies Love Valentines: Chunky Lift a Flap Board Book. Berry Byrd, Holly. Cottage Door Press, ed. 2016. (Chunky Lift-A-Flap Board Book Ser.). (ENG.). 12p. (J). (gr. -1-k). bds. 7.99 *(978-1-68052-149-8(7)*, 1001430) Cottage Door Pr.

—Babies Love Vehículos. Wing, Scarlett. Cottage Door Press, ed. 2019. (Babies Love Ser.). (SPA.). 12p. (J). (gr. -1-k). bds. 7.99 *(978-1-68052-619-6(7)*, 1000120-SLA) Cottage Door Pr.

—First Words: 5 Flaps to Flip! Ackland, Nick & Clever Publishing. 2020. (Peek-A-Boo Ser.). (ENG.). 10p. (J). (gr. -1 — 1). bds. 5.99 *(978-1-949998-51-1(7))* Clever Media Group.

—First Words & Animals 2 Pack: Chunky Lift a Flap Board Book 2 Pack. Wing, Scarlett. Cottage Door Press, ed. 2015. (Babies Love Ser.). (ENG.). 12p. (J). (gr. -1-k). bds. 15.98 *(978-1-68052-098-9(9)*, 9000150) Cottage Door Pr.

—Roar! Shh! A Sounds Board Book. 2016. (Early Birds Ser.). (ENG.). 12p. (J). (gr. -1 — 1). bds. 6.99 *(978-1-4998-0183-5(1))* Little Bee Books Inc.

—Vehicles: 5 Flaps to Flip! Ackland, Nick & Clever Publishing. 2020. (Peek-A-Boo Ser.). (ENG.). 10p. (J). (gr. -1 — 1). bds. 5.99 *(978-1-949998-50-4(9))* Clever Media Group.

Hogan, Martina, jt. illus. see Galloway, Fhiona.

Hogan, Mike. Talk about the Monster. Christopher, Mistofer. 2019. (ENG.). 36p. (J). 19.99 *(978-1-7321266-1-9(5))* Hse. of Mistofer Christopher.

Hogan, Sophie. Where's Mom's Hair? A Family's Journey Through Cancer, 1 vol. Watters, Debbie et al. 2005. (ENG.). 32p. (J). (gr. 1-3). per. 14.95 *(978-1-896764-94-8(0))* Second Story Pr. CAN. Dist: Orca Bk. Pubs. USA.

Hogan, Tom, jt. illus. see Hogan, Wes.

Hogan, Wes & Hogan, Tom. Balloons. Hogan, Wes. 2008. 24p. pap. 13.99 *(978-1-4389-0206-7(9))* AuthorHouse.

Hoglund, Anna. Can You Whistle, Johanna? A Boy's Search for a Grandfather. Stark, Ulf. Segerberg, Ebba, tr. from SWE. 2004. 48p. (J). (gr. 2-5). 16.95 *(978-1-57143-057-1(1))* RDR Bks.

Höglund, Anna. The Stone Giant. Höglund, Anna. 2020. (ENG.). 44p. (J). (gr. k-3). 17.99 *(978-1-77657-273-1(4))* Gecko Pr. NZL. Dist: Lerner Publishing Group.

Hogner, Nils. Our American Horse. Hogner, Dorothy Childs. 2015. (Dover Children's Science Bks.). (ENG.). 128p. (J). (gr. 3-12). pap. 5.99 *(978-0-486-78441-0(X))* Dover Pubns., Inc.

Hogrogian, Nonny. Come Back, Moon. Kherdian, David. 2013. (ENG.). 32p. (J). (gr. -1-3). 17.99 *(978-1-4424-5887-1(9)*, Beach Lane Bks.) Beach Lane Bks.

Hogrogian, Nonny. One Fine Day. Hogrogian, Nonny. 2nd ed. 2005. (Stories to Go! Ser.). (ENG.). 32p. (J). 4.99 *(978-1-4169-0312-3(7)*, Simon & Schuster/Paula Wiseman Bks.) Simon & Schuster/Paula Wiseman Bks.

Hogue, Ann. How the Rabbit Became the Easter Bunny. Bohlken, Bob. 2016. (ENG.). 32p. (J). pap. 10.95 *(978-0-930643-36-2(4)*, Snaptail Pr.) Images Unlimited Publishing.

Hohn, David. Addie, the Playful Pekingese. Howell, Trisha Adelena. 2005. 128p. (YA). pap. 11.95 *(978-1-931210-27-0(6))* Howell Canyon Pr.

—God Gave Us Christmas. Bergren, Lisa Tawn. 2019. (ENG.). 30p. (J). (— 1). bds. 6.99 *(978-0-525-65349-3(X)*, WaterBrook Pr.) Crown Publishing Group, The.

—God Gave Us Family: A Picture Book. Bergren, Lisa Tawn. 2017. (ENG.). 40p. (J). (gr. -1-2). 10.99 *(978-1-60142-876-9(6)*, WaterBrook Pr.) Crown Publishing Group, The.

—God Gave Us Thankful Hearts. Bergren, Lisa Tawn. 2016. (ENG.). 40p. (J). (gr. -1-2). 10.99 *(978-1-60142-874-5(X)*, WaterBrook Pr.) Crown Publishing Group, The.

—God Gave Us the Bible: Forty-Five Favorite Stories for Little Ones. Bergren, Lisa Tawn. 2019. (ENG.). 160p. (J). (gr. -1-2). 17.99 *(978-0-7352-9190-4(X)*, WaterBrook Pr.) Crown Publishing Group, The.

—Just Like Beverly: A Biography of Beverly Cleary. Conrad, Vicki. 2019. (Growing to Greatness Ser.). 48p. (J). (gr. k-4). 18.99 *(978-1-63217-222-8(4)*, Little Bigfoot) Sasquatch Bks.

—La Navidad Es un Regalo de Dios/God Gave Us Christmas. Bergren, Lisa Tawn. 2018. (SPA.). 40p. (J). (gr. -1-2). 9.95 *(978-1-947783-05-8(X))* Penguin Random House Grupo Editorial ESP. Dist: Penguin Random Hse. LLC.

—Talia & the Great Sapphire of Knowledge. Howell, Trisha Adelena. 2005. 128p. (J). pap. 11.95 *(978-1-931210-11-9(X))* Howell Canyon Pr.

Hohn, David & Clark, David. Shape Transformer - Zachary Zormer. Reisberg, Joanne. 2006. (Charlesbridge Math Adventures Ser.). 32p. (J). (gr. 2-5). per. 7.95 *(978-1-57091-876-6(7))* Charlesbridge Publishing, Inc.

Hohn, Tracy. Héroes Necesitar Práctica, ¡También! Una Historia de Mike y Su Abuelo. Durden, Angela K. 2019. (SPA.). 30p. (J). pap. 10.00 *(978-1-950729-00-5(1)*, Blue Room Bks.) WRITER for HIRE!.

—Heroes Need Practice, Too! Durden, Angela K. 2006. (J). 11.95 *(978-0-9701356-1-2(0))* WRITER for HIRE!.

—Héros Avoir Besoin Pratique, Aussi! Un Histoire de Mike et Gran-Père. Durden, Angela K. 2019. (FRE.). 30p. (J). pap. 10.00 *(978-1-950729-01-2(X)*, Blue Room Bks.) WRITER for HIRE!.

Hohnstadt, Cedric. Big Shark's Valentine Surprise. Metzger, Steve. 2007. (J). pap. *(978-0-439-92251-7(8))* Scholastic, Inc.

—Day of the Field Trip Zombies. Nickel, Scott. 2007. (Graphic Sparks Ser.). (ENG.). 40p. (J). (gr. 2-5). per. 5.95 *(978-1-59889-890-3(6)*, 1271403, Stone Arch Bks.) Capstone.

—The Purple Cow. Harris, Brooke. 2009. (Reader's Theater Nursery Rhymes & Songs Set B Ser.). 48p. (J). pap. *(978-1-60859-166-4(2))* Benchmark Education Co.

—Scratch & Sniff. Comfort, Ray. 2007. (Creation for Kids Ser.). 24p. (gr. -1-5). 14.99 *(978-0-88270-328-2(5))* Bridge-Logos, Inc.

—What Your Nose Shows. Comfort, Ray. 2007. (Creation for Kids Ser.). 24p. (gr. -1-5). bds. 14.99 *(978-0-88270-326-8(9))* Bridge-Logos, Inc.

Hoit, Richard. Katie Did It. McDaniel, Becky Bring. rev. ed. 2003. (Rookie Reader Ser.). (ENG.). 32p. (J). (gr. k-2). pap. 4.95 *(978-0-516-27832-2(0)*, Children's Pr.) Scholastic Library Publishing.

—Knock, Knock!, 6 pack. Holden, Pam. 2009. (Red Rocket Readers Ser.). 18p. (gr. 2-2). pap. *(978-1-877363-60-3(X)*, Red Rocket Readers) Flying Start Bks.

—Naughty Goldilocks, 6 pack. Holden, Pam. 2009. (Red Rocket Readers Ser.). 16p. (gr. -1-1). pap. *(978-1-877363-08-5(1)*, Red Rocket Readers) Flying Start Bks.

—Saturday Morning Soccer. Smith, Annette. 2009. 16p. pap. 10.67 *(978-1-4190-5503-4(8))* Rigby Education.

—The Surprise Visitor, 6 pack. Holden, Pam. 2009. (Red Rocket Readers Ser.). 21p. (gr. 2-2). pap. *(978-1-877363-85-6(5))* Flying Start Bks.

—The Tallest Truck Gets Stuck. Chapman, Patricia. 2018. 32p. (J). (gr. -1-k). pap. 9.99 *(978-1-927262-40-5(2))* Upstart Pr. NZL. Dist: Independent Pubs. Group.

Hoke, Jason. Sam Loses His Sneaker. Dara Cicciarelli. 2011. 20p. pap. 24.95 *(978-1-4560-9178-1(6))* America Star Bks.

Hoke, Jeenhyun. My Lemonade Stand Can't Stand Me. Thomas, Mark Lawton. 114p. 2013. pap. 9.99 *(978-1-935711-23-0(7))*; 2012. (ENG.). (J). pap. 9.99 *(978-1-935711-22-3(9))* Peak City Publishing, LLC.

Hokie. The Life & Adventures of Santa Claus (Yesterday's Classics) Houghton, Amelia C. 2006. (J). per. 8.95 *(978-1-59915-191-5(X))* Yesterday's Classics.

Holbert, Raymond. The Barber's Cutting Edge. Battle-Lavert, Gwendolyn. 2004. (ENG.). 32p. (J). pap. 7.95 *(978-0-89239-196-7(0))* Lee & Low Bks., Inc.

Holbrook, Jef, jt. illus. see Scott, Stephen K.

Holbrough, Brooklin. Rinny & Oko. Hennigar, Hunter R. 2017. (ENG.). 48p. (J). (gr. k-2). pap. *(978-1-7752255-0-8(X))* Hennigar, Hunter R.

Holcomb, Michele. What Would You Be? MacMillan, Lesley. 2006. 21p. (J). (gr. -1-3). per. 12.99 *(978-1-59879-228-7(8))* Lifevest Publishing, Inc.

Holcomb, Nicholas. One Bright Monster. Sisler, Stephanie. 2012. 36p. pap. 12.95 *(978-1-61493-124-9(0))* Peppertree Pr., The.

Holcomb, Sue A. Tex R Masaur: Down in the Dump. Holcomb, Sue A. Holcomb, J. Paul. (Tex R Masaur, Dinodillo Bks.). 32p. (Orig.). (J). (gr. k-3). pap. 3.95 *(978-0-9636122-2-9(0))* Post Oak Hill.

Holcroft, John. The Story of Flight: Panorama Pops. Candlewick Press Staff. 2015. (Panorama Pops Ser.). (ENG.). 30p. (J). (gr. k-4). 8.99 *(978-0-7636-7700-8(0))* Candlewick Pr.

Holcroft, John. Space Exploration: Panorama Pops. Holcroft, John. Candlewick Press Staff. 2015. (Panorama Pops Ser.). (ENG.). 30p. (J). (gr. k-4). 8.99 *(978-0-7636-7699-5(3))* Candlewick Pr.

Holdeen, Bonnie, jt. illus. see Boynton, Jeannette.

Holden, Anthony. The Pirate Who's Afraid of Everything. Bondor-Stone, Annabeth & White, Connor. 2015. (Shivers! Ser.: 1). (ENG.). 192p. (J). (gr. 3-7). 12.99 *(978-0-06-231387-4(8))* HarperCollins Pubs.

—The Pirate Who's Back in Bunny Slippers. Bondor-Stone, Annabeth & White, Connor. 2016. (Shivers! Ser.: 2). (ENG.). 208p. (J). (gr. 3-7). 12.99 *(978-0-06-231389-8(4))* HarperCollins Pubs.

—Shivers!: the Pirate Book You've Been Looking For. Bondor-Stone, Annabeth & White, Connor. 2018. (Shivers! Ser.: 3). (ENG.). 208p. (J). (gr. 3-7). 12.99 *(978-0-06-231391-1(6))* HarperCollins Pubs.

—Shivers!: the Pirate Who's More Terrified Than Ever. Bondor-Stone, Annabeth & White, Connor. 2020. (Shivers! Ser.: 4). (ENG.). 208p. (J). (gr. 3-7). 12.99 *(978-0-06-231393-5(2)*, HarperCollins) HarperCollins Pubs. Ltd. GBR. Dist: HarperCollins Pubs.

Holden, Chanler. On the Flippy Side. Mese, John R. & Kelsey, Dawn M. 2009. 30p. (J). 10.95 *(978-0-9725853-1-6(1))* Mosscovered Gumbo Barn.

Holden, Olivia. The Barefoot King: A Story about Feeling Frustrated. Nance, Andrew Jordan. 2020. (ENG.). 32p. (J). (gr. -1-3). 16.95 *(978-1-61180-748-6(4)*, Bala Kids) Shambhala Pubns., Inc.

—Grow. Platt, Cynthia. 2018. 32p. (J). (gr. 1-3). 17.99 *(978-1-68152-239-5(X))* Amicus.

Holder, Jimmy. Fake Out, 2. Wallace, Rich. 2011. (Kickers Ser.: Bk. 2). (ENG.). 128p. (J). (gr. 2-5). lib. bdg. 18.69 *(978-0-375-95755-0(3)*, Knopf Bks. for Young Readers) Random Hse. Children's Bks.

—Good Night Fairies. Gamble, Adam & Jasper, Mark. 2018. (Good Night Our World Ser.). 20p. (J). (— 1). bds. 9.95 *(978-1-60219-433-5(5))* Good Night Bks.

—Isle Be Seeing You. Beech, Sandy. 2005. (Castaways Ser.: 3). (ENG.). 192p. (J). (gr. 3-7). mass mkt. 9.99 *(978-0-689-87598-4(3)*, Aladdin) Simon & Schuster Children's Publishing.

—Kickers #1: the Ball Hogs, Bk. 1. Wallace, Rich. 2011. (Kickers Ser.: 1). 128p. (J). (gr. 1-4). 5.99 *(978-0-375-85092-9(9)*, Yearling) Random Hse. Children's Bks.

—Kickers #2: Fake Out. Wallace, Rich. 2011. (Kickers Ser.: 2). 128p. (J). (gr. 1-4). 6.99 *(978-0-375-85093-6(7)*, Yearling) Random Hse. Children's Bks.

—Kickers #3: Benched. Wallace, Rich. 2011. (Kickers Ser.: 3). 128p. (J). (gr. 1-4). 5.99 *(978-0-375-85094-3(5)*, Yearling) Random Hse. Children's Bks.

—Kickers #4: Game-Day Jitters. Wallace, Rich. 2012. (Kickers Ser.: 4). 128p. (J). (gr. 2-5). 5.99 *(978-0-375-85095-0(3)*, Yearling) Random Hse. Children's Bks.

—Pig Pigger Piggest. Walton, Rick. ed. 2003. (ENG.). 32p. (J). (gr. 1). reprint ed. pap. 6.99 *(978-1-58685-318-1(X))* Gibbs Smith, Publisher.

—Soccer 'Cats: the Captain Contest. Christopher, Matt. 2018. (Matt Christopher Sports Readers Ser.). (ENG.). 32p. (J). (gr. 1-4). lib. bdg. 27.07 *(978-1-5321-4258-1(7)*, 31058) Spotlight.

—Weather's Here, Wish You Were Great, 2. Beech, Sandy. 2005. (Castaways Ser.). (ENG.). 185p. (J). (gr. 3-6). 17.44 *(978-0-689-87597-7(5))* Simon & Schuster, Inc.

—Worst Class Trip Ever. Beech, Sandy. 2005. (Castaways Ser.: 1). (ENG.). 176p. (J). (gr. 3-7). pap. 9.99 *(978-0-689-87596-0(7)*, Aladdin) Simon & Schuster Children's Publishing.

Holder, Jimmy & Kelly, Cooper. Good Night Sea Shore. Gamble, Adam & Jasper, Mark. 2019. (Good Night Our World Ser.). 20p. (J). (— 1). bds. 9.95 *(978-1-60219-665-0(6))* Good Night Bks.

Holder, Jimmy & Veno, Joe. Good Night Phoenix. Gamble, Adam & Jasper, Mark. 2018. (Good Night Our World Ser.). 20p. (J). (— 1). bds. 9.95 *(978-1-60219-676-6(1))* Good Night Bks.

Holder, John, jt. illus. see Fricker, Steve.

Holderness, Grizelda. The Story of Queen Esther. Koralek, Jenny. 2009. (ENG.). 28p. (J). (gr. -1-3). 17.50 *(978-0-8028-5348-6(X)*, Eerdmans Bks For Young Readers) Eerdmans, William B. Publishing Co.

Holdredge, Jon, jt. illus. see Calafiore, Jim.

Holdren, Maria K. Pack Your Bags... . Go U. S. A. Weaver, Kimberley & Murphy, Allyson. 2005. (J). 15.99 *(978-0-9767351-0-6(5))* Sorella Bks.

Holdsworth, Henry, photos by. Moose Family Close Up. Krauskopf, Sharma. 2007. 28p. per. *(978-0-9543367-4-5(7))* Scottish Radiance Pubns.

Hole, Stian. Night Guard. Lea, Synne. 2016. (ENG.). 82p. (J). (-13). 17.00 *(978-0-8028-5458-2(3)*, Eerdmans Bks For Young Readers) Eerdmans, William B. Publishing Co.

Hole, Stian. Garmann's Secret. Hole, Stian. 2011. (ENG.). 56p. (J). 17.00 *(978-0-8028-5400-1(1)*, Eerdmans Bks For Young Readers) Eerdmans, William B. Publishing Co.

—Garmann's Summer. Hole, Stian. Bartlett, Don, tr. 2008. (ENG.). 42p. (J). (gr. k-3). 17.50 *(978-0-8028-5339-4(0)*, Eerdmans Bks For Young Readers) Eerdmans, William B. Publishing Co.

Holgate, Doug. The Adventures of Commander Zack Proton & the Red Giant. Anderson, Brian. 2006. (Adventures of Commander Zack Proton Ser.: 1). (ENG.). 128p. (J). (gr. 2-5). pap. 5.99 *(978-1-4169-1364-1(5)*, Simon & Schuster/Paula Wiseman Bks.) Simon & Schuster/Paula Wiseman Bks.

—The Adventures of Commander Zack Proton & the Warlords of Nibblecheese. Anderson, Brian. 2006. (Adventures of Commander Zack Proton Ser.: 2). (ENG.). 112p. (J). (gr. 2-5). pap. 5.99 *(978-1-4169-1365-8(3)*, Aladdin) Simon & Schuster Children's Publishing.

—The Adventures of Commander Zack Proton & the Wrong Planet. Anderson, Brian. 2007. (Adventures of Commander Zack Proton Ser.: 3). (ENG.). 112p. (J). (gr. 2-5). pap. 6.99 *(978-1-4169-1366-5(1)*, Simon & Schuster/Paula Wiseman Bks.) Simon & Schuster/Paula Wiseman Bks.

—Case File 13 #2: Making the Team. Savage, J. Scott. (Case File 13 Ser.: 2). (ENG.). (J). (gr. 3-7). 2015. 288p. pap. 6.99 *(978-0-06-213335-9(7))*; 2013. 272p. 14.99 *(978-0-06-213331-1(4))* HarperCollins Pubs.

—Case File 13 #3: Evil Twins. Savage, J. Scott. (Case File 13 Ser.: 3). (ENG.). (J). (gr. 3-7). 2015. 288p. pap. 7.99 *(978-0-06-213338-0(1))*; 2014. 272p. 14.99 *(978-0-06-213337-3(3))* HarperCollins Pubs.

—Case File 13 #4: Curse of the Mummy's Uncle. Savage, J. Scott. 2016. (Case File 13 Ser.: 4). (ENG.). 272p. (J). (gr. 3-7). pap. 7.99 *(978-0-06-232407-8(1))* HarperCollins Pubs.

—Case File 13: Zombie Kid. Savage, J. Scott. (Case File 13 Ser.: 1). (ENG.). (J). (gr. 3-7). 2013. 304p. pap. 7.99 *(978-0-06-213327-4(6))*; 2012. 288p. 14.99 *(978-0-06-213325-0(X))* HarperCollins Pubs.

—Planet Tad. Carvell, Tim. (Planet Tad Ser.: 1). (ENG.). 256p. (J). (gr. 3-7). 2014. pap. 6.99 *(978-0-06-193438-4(0))*; 2012. 12.99 *(978-0-06-193436-0(4))*; 2012. lib. bdg. 14.89 *(978-0-06-193437-7(2))* HarperCollins Pubs.

H

—Return to Planet Tad. Carvell, Tim. 2014. (Planet Tad Ser.: 2). (ENG.). 240p. (J). (gr. 3-7). 12.99 *(978-0-06-226625-5(X))* HarperCollins Pubs.
—Super-Dragon, 0 vols. Kroll, Steven. 2011. (ENG.). 32p. (J). (gr. -1-2). 16.99 *(978-0-7614-5819-7(0)*, 9780761458197, Two Lions) Amazon Publishing.
Holgate, Douglas. Cheesie Mack Is Running Like Crazy! Cotler, Steve. (Cheesie Mack Ser.: 3). (J). (gr. 3-7). 2014. 256p. pap. 7.99 *(978-0-307-97716-8(1)*, Yearling); 2013. 240p. 15.99 *(978-0-307-97713-7(7)*, Random Hse. Bks. for Young Readers) Random Hse. Children's Bks.
—Cheesie Mack Is Sort of Freaked Out. Cotler, Steve. 2014. (Cheesie Mack Ser.: 5). 240p. (J). (gr. 3-7). 15.99 *(978-0-385-36988-6(3)*, Random Hse. Bks. for Young Readers) Random Hse. Children's Bks.
—Clem Hetherington & the Ironwood Race. Breach, Jen. 2018. (Clem Hetherington Ser.: 1). 208p. (J). (gr. 3-7). pap. 14.99 *(978-0-545-81446-1(4)*, Graphix) Scholastic, Inc.
—Coldfinger, 1 vol. Lemke, Donald B. 2009. (Graphic Sparks Ser.). (ENG.). 40p. (J). (gr. 2-5). lib. bdg. 23.99 *(978-1-4342-1586-4(5)*, Stone Arch Bks.) Capstone.
—Coldfinger: Zinc Alloy. Lemke, Donald. 2010. (Graphic Sparks Ser.). (ENG.). 40p. (J). (gr. 2-5). pap. 5.95 *(978-1-4342-2314-2(0)*, Stone Arch Bks.) Capstone.
—Laff-O-Tronic Joke Books. Dahl, Michael & Collins, Daryll. 2013. (Laff-O-Tronic Joke Books! Ser.). (ENG.). 96p. (J). (gr. 1-3). lib. bdg., lib. bdg., lib. bdg. 101.28 *(978-1-4342-6325-4(8)*, Stone Arch Bks.) Capstone.
—The Last Kids on Earth. Brallier, Max. 2015. (Last Kids on Earth Ser.: 1). (ENG.). 240p. (J). (gr. 3-7). 13.99 *(978-0-670-01661-7(6)*, Viking Books for Young Readers) Penguin Young Readers Group.
—The Last Kids on Earth & the Cosmic Beyond. Brallier, Max. 2017. 257p. (J). pap. *(978-0-425-28872-6(2)*, Viking Books for Young Readers) Penguin Young Readers Group.
—The Last Kids on Earth & the Nightmare King. Brallier, Max. 2017. (Last Kids on Earth Ser.: 3). (ENG.). 272p. (J). (gr. 3-7). 13.99 *(978-0-425-28871-9(4)*, Viking Books for Young Readers) Penguin Young Readers Group.
Holgate, Douglas. The Last Kids on Earth & the Skeleton Road. Brallier, Max. 2020. (Last Kids on Earth Ser.: 6). (ENG.). 320p. (J). (gr. 3-7). 13.99 ***(978-1-9848-3534-5(3)***, Viking Books for Young Readers) Penguin Young Readers Group.
Holgate, Douglas. The Last Kids on Earth & the Zombie Parade. Brallier, Max. 2016. (Last Kids on Earth Ser.: 2). (ENG.). 304p. (J). (gr. 3-7). 13.99 *(978-0-670-01662-4(4)*, Viking Books for Young Readers) Penguin Young Readers Group.
Holgate, Douglas. The Last Kids on Earth: June's Wild Flight. Brallier, Max. 2020. (Last Kids on Earth Ser.). (ENG.). 272p. (J). (gr. 3-7). 13.99 ***(978-0-593-11718-7(2)***, Viking Books for Young Readers) Penguin Young Readers Group.
—The Last Kids on Earth: Next Level Monster Box (books 4-6), 3 vols. Brallier, Max. 2020. (ENG.). (J). (gr. 3-7). 41.97 ***(978-0-593-34968-7(7)***, Viking Books for Young Readers) Penguin Young Readers Group.
Holgate, Douglas. The Last Kids on Earth: the Monster Box (books 1-3), 3 vols., Set. Brallier, Max. 2018. (ENG.). 816p. (J). (gr. 3-7). 41.97 *(978-0-451-48108-5(9)*, Viking Books for Young Readers) Penguin Young Readers Group.
—Revealed!, 1 vol. Lemke, Donald. 2008. (Graphic Sparks Ser.). (ENG.). 40p. (J). (gr. 2-5). 23.99 *(978-1-4342-0763-0(3)*, Stone Arch Bks.) Capstone.
—Revealed! Zinc Alloy, 1 vol. Lemke, Donald. 2008. (Graphic Sparks Ser.). (ENG.). 40p. (J). (gr. 2-5). pap. 5.95 *(978-1-4342-0859-0(1)*, Stone Arch Bks.) Capstone.
—Spokes on the Water, 1 vol. Lemke, Donald B. 2011. (Bike Rider Ser.). (ENG.). 40p. (J). (gr. 2-5). lib. bdg. 23.99 *(978-1-4342-2537-5(2)*, Stone Arch Bks.) Capstone.
—Super Zero, 1 vol. Lemke, Donald. 2008. (Graphic Sparks Ser.). (ENG.). 40p. (J). (gr. 2-5). 23.99 *(978-1-4342-0762-3(5))*; pap. 5.95 *(978-1-4342-0858-3(3))* Capstone. (Stone Arch Bks.).
—There's a Worm on My Eyeball: The Alien Zoo of Germs, Worms & Lurgies That Could Be Living Inside You. Taor, Adam. 2009. (ENG.). 192p. (J). (gr. 4-7). pap. 7.99 *(978-1-74166-213-9(3))* Random Hse. Australia AUS. Dist: Independent Pubs. Group.
—Wheelies of Justice, 1 vol. Lemke, Donald B. 2010. (Bike Rider Ser.). (ENG.). 40p. (J). (gr. 2-5). lib. bdg. 23.99 *(978-1-4342-1892-6(9)*, Stone Arch Bks.) Capstone.
—Wires & Nerve. Meyer, Marissa. 2017. (Wires & Nerve Ser.: 1). (ENG.). 240p. (YA). 21.99 *(978-1-250-07826-1(1)*, 900153572) Feiwel & Friends.
—Wires & Nerve: Volume 1. Meyer, Marissa. 2019. (Wires & Nerve Ser.: 1). (ENG.). 240p. (YA). pap. 17.99 *(978-1-250-07827-8(X)*, 900153573) Square Fish.
—Zinc Alloy vs Frankenstein, 1 vol. Lemke, Donald B. (Graphic Sparks Ser.). (ENG.). 40p. (J). (gr. 2-5). 2010. pap. 5.95 *(978-1-4342-1391-4(9))*; 2009. lib. bdg. 23.99 *(978-1-4342-1188-0(6))* Capstone. (Stone Arch Bks.).
Holgate, Douglas & Collins, Daryll. Laff-O-Tronic Animal Jokes! Dahl, Michael. 2013. (Laff-O-Tronic Joke Books! Ser.). (ENG.). 96p. (gr. k-3). pap. 29.70 *(978-1-4342-6238-7(3)*, Stone Arch Bks.) Capstone.
—Laff-O-Tronic School Jokes! Dahl, Michael. 2013. (Laff-O-Tronic Joke Books! Ser.). (ENG.). 96p. (gr. k-3). pap. 29.70 *(978-1-4342-6240-0(5)*, Stone Arch Bks.) Capstone.
—Laff-O-Tronic Sports Jokes! Dahl, Michael. 2013. (Laff-O-Tronic Joke Books! Ser.). (ENG.). 96p. (gr. k-3). pap. 29.70 *(978-1-4342-6241-7(3)*, Stone Arch Bks.) Capstone.
Holgate, Douglas, jt. illus. see Collins, Daryll.
Holgate, Douglas Anthony. Zinc Alloy: The Complete Comics Collection. Lemke, Donald. ed. 2020. (Stone Arch Graphic Novels Ser.). (ENG.). 144p. (J). (gr. 3-6). pap. 8.95 *(978-1-4965-9322-1(7)*, 142352); lib. bdg. 27.99 *(978-1-4965-8733-6(2)*, 141611) Capstone. (Stone Arch Bks.).
Holgren, Anna C. Where's My Face? A Simon-the-Cat Tale. Collins, C. B. 2008. 36p. pap. 24.95 *(978-1-60441-009-9(4))* America Star Bks.
Holidarling, Franki. The Great Stirring: The Way of the Gentle Giant Book One. Mazzitelli, Donna. 2017. (The Way of the Gentle Giant Ser.: 1). (ENG.). (J). 17.95 *(978-1-939919-55-7(X))* Merry Dissonance Pr.
Holiday, Henry, jt. illus. see Tenniel, John.
Holiday, J. D. Janoose the Goose. Holiday, J. D. 2008. 24p. (J). pap. 10.00 *(978-0-9818614-0-1(7))* Bk. Garden Publishing.
Holiday, Jd. The Great Snowball Escapade. Holiday, Jd. 2019. (ENG.). 90p. (J). pap. 5.99 *(978-1-0936-1605-7(9))* Independently Published.
Holifield, Vicky. Hiking the Benton MacKaye Trail, 1 vol. Homan, Tim. 2004. (ENG.). 272p. pap. 15.95 *(978-1-56145-311-5(0))* Peachtree Publishing Co. Inc.
Holinaty, Josh. A Beginner's Guide to Immortality: from Alchemy to Avatars. Birmingham, Maria. 2015. (ENG.). 48p. (J). (gr. 3-7). 16.95 *(978-1-77147-045-2(3)*, Owlkids) Owlkids Bks. Inc. CAN. Dist: Publishers Group West (PGW).
Holinaty, Josh. In the Dark: The Science of What Happens at Night. Deresti Betik, Lisa. 2020. (ENG.). 48p. (J). (gr. 3-7). 18.99 ***(978-1-5253-0109-4(8))*** Kids Can Pr., Ltd. CAN. Dist: Hachette Bk. Group.
Holinaty, Josh. Ira Crumb Makes a Pretty Good Friend. Hrab, Naseem. 2017. (Ira Crumb Ser.: 1). (ENG.). 32p. (J). (gr. 1-4). 17.95 *(978-1-77147-171-8(9))* Owlkids Bks. Inc. CAN. Dist: Publishers Group West (PGW).
—It's Catching: The Infectious World of Germs & Microbes. Gardy, Jennifer. 2014. (ENG.). 64p. (J). (gr. 3-7). pap. 13.95 *(978-1-77147-053-7(4)*, Owlkids) Owlkids Bks. Inc. CAN. Dist: Publishers Group West (PGW).
—Liam Takes a Stand. Wilson, Troy. 2017. (ENG.). 32p. (J). (gr. k-4). 16.95 *(978-1-77147-161-9(1))* Owlkids Bks. Inc. CAN. Dist: Publishers Group West (PGW).
—The Space Adventurer's Guide: Your Passport to the Coolest Things to See & Do in the Universe. McMahon, Peter. 2018. (ENG.). 100p. (J). (gr. 3-7). pap. 17.99 *(978-1-77138-032-4(2))* Kids Can Pr., Ltd. CAN. Dist: Hachette Bk. Group.
Holladay, Ashtin. Switch. Klein, K. C. 2018. (ENG.). 134p. (J). pap. 7.99 *(978-1-7308-4354-9(9))* Independently Published.
Holladay, Jason. Why Do I Have to Make My Bed? Perry, Winona. 2018. (ENG.). 26p. (J). pap. 9.99 *(978-1-7249-0652-6(6))* CreateSpace Independent Publishing Platform.
Holladay, Reggie. The Little Red Hen (La Gallinita Roja), Grades Pk - 3. Ottolenghi, Carol. ed. 2007. (Keepsake Stories Ser.). (ENG.). 32p. (gr. -1-3). pap. 3.99 *(978-0-7696-5417-1(7)*, 0769654177, Brighter Child) Carson-Dellosa Publishing, LLC.
Hollan, Ana. The Old One. Roberts, Rebecca. 2016. (ENG.). (J). pap. 11.99 *(978-0-9862331-7-3(X))* Hear My Heart Publishing.
Holland, Gay W. Brilliant Bees. Glaser, Linda. 2003. 32p. lib. bdg. 22.90 *(978-0-7613-2670-0(7)*, Millbrook Pr.) Lerner Publishing Group.
—Dream Catcher. Kavasch, E. Barrie. 2003. (Books for Young Learners). (ENG.). 16p. (J). 5.75 net. *(978-1-57274-257-4(7)*, 2733, Bks. for Young Learners) Owen, Richard C. Pubs., Inc.
—An Introduction to Bug-Watching. 2003. (Look Closer Ser.: 4). 32p. lib. bdg. 22.90 *(978-0-7613-2664-9(2)*, Millbrook Pr.) Lerner Publishing Group.
Holland, Janice. The Blue Cat of Castle Town. Coblentz, Catherine Cate. 2017. (ENG.). 128p. pap. 5.95 *(978-0-486-81527-5(7)*, 815277) Dover Pubns., Inc.
Holland, Joe. Monsoon Murder: Forensic Meteorology, 12 vols. McIntosh, Kenneth. 2007. (Crime Scene Club Ser.). 144p. (YA). (gr. 9-12). lib. bdg. 24.95 *(978-1-4222-0258-6(5))* Mason Crest.
Holland, Kathy. Sam Snake Says. Dunlap, Jim. 2008. 35p. pap. 24.95 *(978-1-60672-709-6(5))* America Star Bks.
Holland, Lee. Bedtime on Noah's Ark. Eastman, Brock & Eastman, Declan. 2020. (ENG.). 20p. (J). (— 1). bds. 12.99 ***(978-0-7369-7954-2(9)***, 6979542) Harvest Hse. Pubs.
Holland, Lee. A Birthday Party for Jesus. Jones, Susan. 2017. (Forest of Faith Bks.). (ENG.). 32p. (J). (gr. -1-1). 12.99 *(978-1-68099-319-6(4)*, Good Bks.) Skyhorse Publishing Co., Inc.
—Counting Blessings, 1 vol. Spinelli, Eileen. 2016. (ENG.). 20p. (J). bds. 9.99 *(978-0-310-75072-7(5))* Zonderkidz.
—An Easter Egg Hunt for Jesus. Jones, Susan. 2019. (Forest of Faith Bks.). (ENG.). 32p. (J). (gr. -1-1). 12.99 *(978-1-68099-437-7(9)*, Good Bks.) Skyhorse Publishing Co., Inc.
—Easter Gift from Jesus: His Love Lifts Us Up. Jones, Susan. 2020. (Forest of Faith Bks.). 32p. (J). (-1). 12.99 *(978-1-68099-569-5(3)*, Good Bks.) Skyhorse Publishing Co., Inc.
—Everyone Is Invited to Christmas. Jones, Susan. 2018. (Forest of Faith Bks.). (ENG.). 32p. (J). 12.99 *(978-1-68099-410-0(7)*, Good Bks.) Skyhorse Publishing Co., Inc.
—God's Love Is a Warm Cookie: Sharing with Others Is Sweet As Can Be. Jones, Susan. 2020. (Forest of Faith Bks.). 32p. (J). (-1). 12.99 *(978-1-68099-570-1(7)*, Good Bks.) Skyhorse Publishing Co., Inc.
—Grandma's Promise. Jones, Susan. 2019. (ENG.). 32p. (J). (gr. -1 — 1). 9.99 *(978-1-5107-4269-7(7)*, Sky Pony Pr.) Skyhorse Publishing Co., Inc.
—Grandpa's Promise. Jones, Susan. 2019. (ENG.). 32p. (J). (gr. -1 — 1). 9.99 *(978-1-5107-4818-7(0)*, Sky Pony Pr.) Skyhorse Publishing Co., Inc.
—Just You & Me. King, Alice. 2015. (ENG.). 26p. (J). bds. 8.95 *(978-1-78440-394-2(6))* Igloo Bks. GBR. Dist: Simon & Schuster, Inc.
Holland, Lisa Tomms. Baxter & the Sidewalk Alligator. Engram, Teta. 2009. 32p. pap. 12.99 *(978-1-4389-9367-6(6))* AuthorHouse.
Holland, Mary, photos by. The Beavers' Busy Year, 1 vol. Holland, Mary. 2014. (ENG., 32p. (J). (gr. 1-4). pap. 9.95 *(978-1-62855-213-3(1))* Arbordale Publishing.
—Milkweed Visitors. Holland, Mary. 2006. 32p. (J). per. 10.95 *(978-0-9657472-4-0(7))* Bas Relief, LLC.
Holland, Richard. Ali Baba & the Forty Thieves. Clynes, Kate et al. 2005. (ENG & BEN.). 32p. (J). pap. *(978-1-84444-402-1(3))*; pap. *(978-1-84444-411-3(2))*; pap. *(978-1-84444-414-4(7))*; pap. *(978-1-84444-415-1(5))*; pap. *(978-1-84444-424-3(4))* Mantra Lingua.
—Ali Baba & the Forty Thieves. Attard, Enebor. 32p. (J). 2005. (GRE & ENG.). pap. *(978-1-84444-526-4(7))*; 2004. (CHI & ENG.). bds. *(978-1-84444-530-1(5))* Mantra Lingua.
—Happy Harry's Cafe. Rosen, Michael. 2012. (ENG.). 32p. (J). (gr. -1-2). 16.99 *(978-0-7636-6239-4(9))* Candlewick Pr.
—The Museum Book. Mark, Jan. 2014. (ENG.). (J). (gr. 2-5). lib. bdg. 19.60 *(978-1-62765-767-9(3))* Perfection Learning Corp.
—The Museum Book: A Guide to Strange & Wonderful Collections. Mark, Jan. (ENG.). 56p. (J). 2014. (gr. 2-5). 8.99 *(978-0-7636-7500-4(8))*; 2007. (gr. 3-7). 18.99 *(978-0-7636-3370-7(4))* Candlewick Pr.
Holland, Ruth. The Night of the Round Stable. Wrench, Peter. 2012. 174p. pap. *(978-1-908895-49-3(7))* FeedARead.com.
Hollander, Sarah. I Paint a Rainbow. Plummer, David & Archambault, John. 2007. (J). *(978-1-58669-228-5(3))*; *(978-1-58669-227-8(5))* Childcraft Education Corp.
—The Twelve Days of Christmas in Washington, D. C. Ransom, Candice. (Twelve Days of Christmas in America Ser.). (J). (-k). 2018. 22p. bds. 7.95 *(978-1-4549-2966-6(9))*; 2010. 40p. 12.95 *(978-1-4027-6394-6(8))* Sterling Publishing Co., Inc.
—Two Birds SAT upon a Stone. Archambault, John & Plummer, David. 2006. (J). pap. *(978-1-58669-187-5(2))* Childcraft Education Corp.
Höllbacher, Franziska. All about Me: A Fill-In-and-Keep Activity Book. Hutchinson, Sam & Morton, Lone. 2018. (First Record Bks.). (ENG.). 32p. (J). (gr. 2-4). pap. 8.99 *(978-1-911509-15-8(2))* B Small Publishing GBR. Dist: Independent Pubs. Group.
—Mindful Bea & the Worry Tree. Silver, Gail. 2019. 32p. (J). *(978-1-4338-2954-3(1)*, Magination Pr.) American Psychological Assn.
Hollenbach, Dave. Tykes on Bikes: A Tale of Two Races. Hollenbach, Dave. Hollenbach Ross, Lorri. 2018. (ENG.). 26p. (J). (gr. k-3). 17.99 *(978-0-578-41371-6(X))* Hollenbach, David A.
Hollenbach, David. Ella No Quiere Los Gusanos: Un Misterio (with Pronunciation Guide in English) Beckstrand, Karl. 2019. (Misterios para Los Menores Ser.: Vol. 3). (SPA.). 26p. (J). (gr. -1-3). 26.55 ***(978-1-7320696-4-0(6))*** Premio Publishing & Gozo Bks., LLC.
Hollenbach, David. She Doesn't Want the Worms: A Mystery - with Online Secrets. Beckstrand, Karl. l.t. ed. 2011. (Mini-Mysteries for Minors Ser.: 3).Tr. of Ella No Quiere Los Gusanos. (ENG.). 24p. (gr. -1-2). pap. 9.18 *(978-0-615-49278-0(9))* Premio Publishing & Gozo Bks., LLC.
—She Doesn't Want the Worms - Ella No Quiere Los Gusanos: A Mystery in English & Spanish. Beckstrand, Karl. ed. 2017. (Mini-Mysteries for Minors Ser.: 3).Tr. of Ella No Quiere Los Gusanos. (SPA & ENG.). (J). (gr. -1-3). 26.95 *(978-0-9853988-2-8(5))* Premio Publishing & Gozo Bks., LLC.
Hollenbach, David & Jones, Channing. 4 Spanish-English Books for Kids. Beckstrand, Karl. ed. 2017. (ENG & SPA.). 100p. (J). 36.95 *(978-0-9853988-9-7(2))* Premio Publishing & Gozo Bks., LLC.
Holley, Mark. The Adventures of Billy the Bean: Introducing Billy the Bean. Gregory, Des. 2020. (Adventures of Billy the Bean Ser.: Vol. 1). (ENG.). 26p. (J). pap. 10.00 ***(978-1-0776-1766-7(6))*** Independently Published.
Holley, Vanessa. My Shoelaces Are Hard to Tie! Scholastic, Inc. Staff & Roberson, Karla. 2004. (Just for You Ser.). (ENG.). 32p. pap. 3.99 *(978-0-439-56869-2(2)*, Teaching Resources) Scholastic, Inc.
Holley, Vanessa. Ohene Goes to the Library. Cornelius, Ohene Kwadwo Opoku & Cornelius Jr, Robert Banks. 2020. (ENG.). 26p. (J). pap. 12.95 ***(978-1-6724-2555-1(7))*** Independently Published.
Hollick, Johnny. The Shooing Cave. Lee, Ingrid. 2019. (ENG.). 40p. (J). (gr. k-2). 17.95 *(978-1-943431-51-9(5))* Tumblehome Learning.
Holliday, Carole. Fish Out of Water. Holliday, Carole. 2017. (ENG.). (J). (gr. k-6). 17.99 *(978-0-692-95833-9(9))* Happy Holliday Bks.
Holliday, Holly. Ellie's Big Day. Keithley, Laura Lee. 2008. 40p. pap. 24.95 *(978-1-60672-474-3(6))* America Star Bks.
Holliday, Jeremy Tinson & Sasiain, Leire. Ralph the Robot Monkey. Newton, Jay. 2018. (ENG.). 40p. (J). pap. *(978-1-9997232-8-6(7))* Dark Paradigm Publishing.
Holliday, Reggie. Test Prep with a Twist Grade 2, 3 vols., 2253. Jacks, Cyndie & Lewis, Dawn. Rous, Sheri, ed. 2003. 64p. pap. 9.99 *(978-1-57471-974-1(2))* Creative Teaching Pr., Inc.
Hollinger, Deanne. They Led the Way: 14 American Women. Johnston, Johanna. 2004. 128p. (J). (gr. 3-7). 5.99 *(978-0-14-240057-9(2)*, Puffin Books) Penguin Young Readers Group.
Hollinger, Valerie Bunch. Gift/ Book Combo. O'Connor, Crystal Ball. 2005. (J). 25.00 *(978-0-9774038-0-6(7))* Monarch Pubs.
—Jake & the Migration of the Monarch. O'Connor, Crystal Ball. 2005. 32p. (J). 17.95 *(978-0-615-12659-3(6))* Monarch Pubs.
—Jake & the Migration of the Monarch with CD. O'Connor, Crystal Ball. 2005. (J). audio compact disk 18.95 *(978-0-9774038-3-7(1))* Monarch Pubs.
—Jake y la Migraci'on de la Monarca. O'Connor, Crystal Ball. Brenes-Sotela, Guillermo J. & Quave, Gloria Martinez, trs. from ENG. 2005. (SPA.). (J). 17.95 *(978-0-9774038-2-0(3))* Monarch Pubs.
Hollinrake, Chriss. Jasmin & the Nature Fairies. Apted, Violet. 2012. 16p. pap. 10.00 *(978-1-61897-806-6(3)*, Strategic Bk. Publishing) Strategic Book Publishing & Rights Agency (SBPRA).
Hollis, Michael. You'll See, Little Tree. Trembley, Skip & Ochs, Susan A. 2003. (J). pap. 7.95 *(978-0-9643452-2-5(6))* Graphics North.
Hollis, Tyler. The Blossoms of Floraland. Hollis, Tyler, ed. Khan, Miranda. 2019. (ENG.). 36p. (J). pap. 12.95 ***(978-1-6940-6764-7(5))*** Independently Published.
Hollman, Jeremie, jt. photos by see Glastetter, KC.
Holly, Davison. Jack's Cap: More Short Vowel Stories. Sylvia, Davison. 2003. 96p. (gr. 1-18). spiral bd. 17.00 *(978-0-9726479-4-6(5))* Foundations for Learning, LLC.
—Noses & Roses: More Long Vowel Stories. Sylvia, Davison. 2003. 64p. (gr. 1-18). spiral bd. 12.00 *(978-0-9726479-5-3(3))* Foundations for Learning, LLC.
Holly, Julia. Mrs Winkler's Cure. Holly, Julia. 2010. 214p. pap. 19.99 *(978-1-883376-45-1(9))* Stellium Pr.
Holm, Jennifer L. & Holm, Matthew. Babymouse #14: Mad Scientist. Holm, Jennifer L. & Holm, Matthew. 2011. (Babymouse Ser.: 14). (ENG.). 96p. (J). (gr. 2-5). lib. bdg. 12.99 *(978-0-375-96574-6(2)*, Random Hse. Bks. for Young Readers) Random Hse. Children's Bks.
—Babymouse #15: a Very Babymouse Christmas. Holm, Jennifer L. & Holm, Matthew. 2011. (Babymouse Ser.: 15). (ENG.). 96p. (J). (gr. 2-5). 12.99 *(978-0-375-96779-5(6))*; pap. 6.99 *(978-0-375-86779-8(1))* Random Hse. Children's Bks. (Random Hse. Bks. for Young Readers).
—Babymouse #20: Babymouse Goes for the Gold. Holm, Jennifer L. & Holm, Matthew. 2016. (Babymouse Ser.: 20). (ENG.). 96p. (J). (gr. 2-5). pap. 6.99 *(978-0-307-93163-4(3)*, Random Hse. Bks. for Young Readers) Random Hse. Children's Bks.
—Babymouse #9: Monster Mash. Holm, Jennifer L. & Holm, Matthew. 2008. (Babymouse Ser.: 9). (ENG.). 96p. (J). (gr. 2-5). pap. 6.99 *(978-0-375-84387-7(6)*, Random Hse. Bks. for Young Readers) Random Hse. Children's Bks.
—Babymouse for President. Holm, Jennifer L. & Holm, Matthew. 2012. (Babymouse Ser.: 16). (ENG.). 96p. (J). (gr. 2-5). 12.99 *(978-0-375-96780-1(X))*; pap. 6.99 *(978-0-375-86780-4(5))* Random Hse. Children's Bks. (Random Hse. Bks. for Young Readers).
—Bad Babysitter. Holm, Jennifer L. & Holm, Matthew. 2015. (Babymouse Ser.: 19). (ENG.). 96p. (J). (gr. 2-5). pap. 6.99 *(978-0-307-93162-7(5)*, Random Hse. Bks. for Young Readers) Random Hse. Children's Bks.
—Burns Rubber. Holm, Jennifer L. & Holm, Matthew. 2010. (Babymouse Ser.: 12). (ENG.). 96p. (J). (gr. 2-5). pap. 6.99 *(978-0-375-85713-3(3))*; lib. bdg. 12.99 *(978-0-375-95713-0(8))* Random Hse. Children's Bks. (Random Hse. Bks. for Young Readers).
—Captain Disaster. Holm, Jennifer L. & Holm, Matthew. 2012. (Squish Ser.: 4). (ENG.). 96p. (J). (gr. 2-5). lib. bdg. 12.99 *(978-0-375-93786-6(2)*, Random Hse. Bks. for Young Readers) Random Hse. Children's Bks.
—Cupcake Tycoon. Holm, Jennifer L. & Holm, Matthew. 2010. (Babymouse Ser.: 13). (ENG.). 96p. (J). (gr. 2-5). pap. 6.99 *(978-0-375-86573-2(X))*; lib. bdg. 12.99 *(978-0-375-96573-9(4))* Random Hse. Children's Bks. (Random Hse. Bks. for Young Readers).
—Deadly Disease of Doom. Holm, Jennifer L. & Holm, Matthew. 2015. (Squish Ser.). (ENG.). 96p. (J). (gr. 2-5). lib. bdg. 12.99 *(978-0-307-98306-0(4)*, Random Hse. Bks. for Young Readers) Random Hse. Children's Bks.
—Dragonslayer. Holm, Jennifer L. & Holm, Matthew. 2009. (Babymouse Ser.: 11). (ENG.). 96p. (J). (gr. 2-5). pap. 6.99 *(978-0-375-85712-6(5))*; lib. bdg. 12.99 *(978-0-375-95712-3(X))* Random Hse. Children's Bks. (Random Hse. Bks. for Young Readers).
—Extreme Babymouse. Holm, Jennifer L. & Holm, Matthew. 2013. (Babymouse Ser.: 17). (ENG.). 96p. (J). (gr. 2-5). pap. 6.99 *(978-0-307-93160-3(9))*; lib. bdg. 12.99 *(978-0-375-97096-2(7))* Random Hse. Children's Bks. (Random Hse. Bks. for Young Readers).
—Fear the Amoeba. Holm, Jennifer L. & Holm, Matthew. 2014. (Squish Ser.: 6). (ENG.). 96p. (J). (gr. 2-5). 12.99 *(978-0-307-98303-9(X)*, Random Hse. Bks. for Young Readers) Random Hse. Children's Bks.
—Happy Birthday, Babymouse! Holm, Jennifer L. & Holm, Matthew. 2014. (Babymouse Ser.: 18). (ENG.). 96p. (J). (gr. 2-5). 12.99 *(978-0-375-97097-9(5)*, Random Hse. Bks. for Young Readers) Random Hse. Children's Bks.
—Happy Birthday, Babymouse. Holm, Jennifer L. & Holm, Matthew. 2014. (Babymouse Ser.: 18). (ENG.). 96p. (J). (gr. 2-5). pap. 6.99 *(978-0-307-93161-0(7)*, Random Hse. Bks. for Young Readers) Random Hse. Children's Bks.
—Mad Scientist. Holm, Jennifer L. & Holm, Matthew. 2011. (Babymouse Ser.: 14). (ENG.). 96p. (J). (gr. 2-5). pap. 6.99 *(978-0-375-86574-9(8)*, Random Hse. Bks. for Young Readers) Random Hse. Children's Bks.
—Monster Mash. Holm, Jennifer L. & Holm, Matthew. 2008. (Babymouse Ser.: 9). (ENG.). 96p. (J). (gr. 2-5). lib. bdg. 12.99 *(978-0-375-93789-7(7)*, Random Hse. Bks. for Young Readers) Random Hse. Children's Bks.
—The Musical. Holm, Jennifer L. & Holm, Matthew. 2009. (Babymouse Ser.: 10). (ENG.). 96p. (J). (gr. 2-5). pap. 6.99 *(978-0-375-84388-4(4))*; lib. bdg. 12.99 *(978-0-375-93791-0(9))* Random Hse. Children's Bks. (Random Hse. Bks. for Young Readers).
—Squish #1: Super Amoeba. Holm, Jennifer L. & Holm, Matthew. 2011. (Squish Ser.: 1). (ENG.). 96p. (J). (gr. 3-7). pap. 6.99 *(978-0-375-84389-1(2))*; lib. bdg. 12.99 *(978-0-375-93783-5(8))* Random Hse. Children's Bks. (Random Hse. Bks. for Young Readers).
—Squish #2: Brave New Pond. Holm, Jennifer L. & Holm, Matthew. 2011. (Squish Ser.: 2). (ENG.). 96p. (J). (gr. 3-7). 12.99 *(978-0-375-93784-2(6))*; pap. 6.99 *(978-0-375-84390-7(6))* Random Hse. Children's Bks. (Random Hse. Bks. for Young Readers).
—Squish #3: the Power of the Parasite. Holm, Jennifer L. & Holm, Matthew. 2012. (Squish Ser.: 3). (ENG.). 96p. (J).

(gr. 2-5). pap. 6.99 *(978-0-375-84391-4(4)*, Random Hse. Bks. for Young Readers) Random Hse. Children's Bks.

—Squish #4: Captain Disaster. Holm, Jennifer L. & Holm, Matthew. 2012. (Squish Ser.: 4). (ENG.). 96p. (J). (gr. 2-5). pap. 6.99 *(978-0-375-84392-1(2)*, Random Hse. Bks. for Young Readers) Random Hse. Children's Bks.

—Squish #5: Game On!, No. 5. Holm, Jennifer L. & Holm, Matthew. 2013. (Squish Ser.: 5). (ENG.). 96p. (J). (gr. 2-5). pap. 6.99 *(978-0-307-98299-5(8)*, Random Hse. Bks. for Young Readers) Random Hse. Children's Bks.

—Squish #6: Fear the Amoeba, No. 6. Holm, Jennifer L. & Holm, Matthew. 2014. (Squish Ser.: 6). (ENG.). 96p. (J). (gr. 2-5). pap. 6.99 *(978-0-307-98302-2(1)*, Random Hse. Bks. for Young Readers) Random Hse. Children's Bks.

—Squish #8: Pod vs. Pod. Holm, Jennifer L. & Holm, Matthew. 2016. (Squish Ser.: 8). (ENG.). 96p. (J). (gr. 2-5). pap. 6.99 *(978-0-307-98308-4(0))*; lib. bdg. 12.99 *(978-0-307-98309-1(9))* Random Hse. Children's Bks. (Random Hse. Bks. for Young Readers).

Holm, Liselotte. Pions Hemlighet. Holm, Liselotte. 2018. (SWE.). 286p. (YA). (gr. 7-12). pap. *(978-91-978383-5-1(7))* Solibris Pubs.

Holm, Matthew. The Evil Princess vs. the Brave Knight. Holm, Jennifer L. 2019. (ENG.). 40p. (J). (gr. -1-2). 17.99 *(978-1-5247-7134-8(1))*; lib. bdg. 20.99 *(978-1-5247-7135-5(X))* Random Hse. Children's Bks. (Random Hse. Bks. for Young Readers).

Holm, Matthew. The Evil Princess vs. the Brave Knight: Take Turns. Holm, Jennifer L. 2020. (Step into Reading Ser.). (ENG.). 32p. (J). (gr. -1-1). pap. 4.99 ***(978-1-5247-7137-9(6))***; lib. bdg. 14.99 ***(978-1-5247-7138-6(4))*** Random Hse. Children's Bks. (Random Hse. Bks. for Young Readers).

Holm, Matthew. I'm Grumpy (My First Comics) Holm, Jennifer L. 2016. (My First Comics Ser.). 24p. (J). (— 1). bds. 7.99 *(978-0-553-53344-6(4)*, Random Hse. Bks. for Young Readers) Random Hse. Children's Bks.

—I'm Scared (My First Comics) Holm, Jennifer L. 2017. (My First Comics Ser.). (ENG.). 22p. (J). (— 1). bds. 7.99 *(978-0-553-53350-7(9)*, Random Hse. Bks. for Young Readers) Random Hse. Children's Bks.

—I'm Sunny! (My First Comics) Holm, Jennifer L. 2016. (My First Comics Ser.). (ENG.). 22p. (J). (— 1). bds. 7.99 *(978-0-553-53346-0(0)*, Random Hse. Bks. for Young Readers) Random Hse. Children's Bks.

—Little Babymouse & the Christmas Cupcakes. Holm, Jennifer L. 2016. (ENG.). 40p. (J). (gr. -1-2). 17.99 *(978-1-101-93743-3(2)*, Random Hse. Bks. for Young Readers) Random Hse. Children's Bks.

—Miss Communication. Holm, Jennifer L. 2018. (Babymouse Tales from the Locker Ser.: 2). (ENG.). 208p. (J). (gr. 3-7). 13.99 *(978-0-399-55441-4(6)*, Random Hse. Bks. for Young Readers) Random Hse. Children's Bks.

—School-Tripped. Holm, Jennifer L. 2019. (Babymouse Tales from the Locker Ser.: 3). (ENG.). 208p. (J). (gr. 3-7). 13.99 *(978-0-399-55444-5(0))*; lib. bdg. 16.99 *(978-0-399-55445-2(9))* Random Hse. Children's Bks. (Random Hse. Bks. for Young Readers).

—Sunny Rolls the Dice. Holm, Jennifer L. 2019. (Sunny Ser.). (ENG.). 224p. (J). (gr. 3-7). pap. 12.99 *(978-1-338-23314-8(9)*, Graphix) Scholastic, Inc.

—Sunny Side Up. Holm, Jennifer L. 2015. (ENG.). 224p. (J). (gr. 3-7). 24.99 *(978-0-545-74165-1(3))*; pap. 12.99 *(978-0-545-74166-8(1))* Scholastic, Inc. (Graphix).

—Sunny Side up & Swing It, Sunny, Set. Holm, Jennifer L. 2018. (ENG.). (J). (gr. 3-7). 25.98 *(978-1-338-28595-6(5)*, Graphix) Scholastic, Inc.

—Swing It, Sunny. Holm, Jennifer L. 2017. (Sunny Ser.: 2). (ENG.). 224p. (J). (gr. 3-7). 24.99 *(978-0-545-74170-5(X))*; pap. 12.99 *(978-0-545-74172-9(6))* Scholastic, Inc. (Graphix).

Holm, Matthew, jt. illus. see Holm, Jennifer L.

Holm, Sharon. All Week at School. Williams, Rozanne Lanczak. Hamaguchi, Carla, ed. 2003. (Sight Word Readers Ser.). 16p. (J). (gr. k-2). pap. 3.49 *(978-1-57471-962-8(9)*, 3584) Creative Teaching Pr., Inc.

—Balancing Bears: Comparing Numbers, 1 vol. Atwood, Megan. 2012. (Count the Critters Ser.). (ENG.). 24p. (J). (gr. k-3). 27.07 *(978-1-61641-851-9(6)*, 4826, Looking Glass Library) Magic Wagon.

—Busy Beavers: Counting By 5s, 1 vol. Atwood, Megan. 2012. (Count the Critters Ser.). (ENG.). 24p. (J). (gr. k-3). 27.07 *(978-1-61641-852-6(4)*, 4828, Looking Glass Library) Magic Wagon.

—Cuddly Kittens: Discovering Fractions, 1 vol. Atwood, Megan. 2012. (Count the Critters Ser.). (ENG.). 24p. (J). (gr. k-3). 27.07 *(978-1-61641-853-3(2)*, 4830, Looking Glass Library) Magic Wagon.

—Monarch Migration: Counting by 10s, 1 vol. Atwood, Megan. 2012. (Count the Critters Ser.). (ENG.). 24p. (J). (gr. k-3). 27.07 *(978-1-61641-854-0(0)*, 4832, Looking Glass Library) Magic Wagon.

—Ovals, 1 vol. Vogel, Julia. 2007. (Shapes Ser.). (ENG.). 24p. (J). (gr. -1-2). 27.07 *(978-1-60270-045-1(1)*, 13316, Looking Glass Library) Magic Wagon.

—Piglets Playing: Counting from 11 To 20, 1 vol. Atwood, Megan. 2012. (Count the Critters Ser.). (ENG.). 24p. (J). (gr. k-3). 27.07 *(978-1-61641-855-7(9)*, 4834, Looking Glass Library) Magic Wagon.

—101 Questions about Reproduction: Or How 1 + 1 = 3 or 4 or More. Brynie, Faith Hickman. 2005. (101 Questions... Ser.). (ENG.). 176p. (gr. 7-12). 30.60 *(978-0-7613-2311-2(2))* Lerner Publishing Group.

—101 Questions about Sex & Sexuality: With Answers for the Curious, Cautious, & Confused. Brynie, Faith Hickman. 2003. (101 Questions... Ser.). (ENG.). 176p. (gr. 7-12). lib. bdg. 30.60 *(978-0-7613-2310-5(4)*, Twenty-First Century Bks.) Lerner Publishing Group.

—101 Questions about Sleep & Dreams: That Kept You Awake Nights... until Now. Brynie, Faith Hickman. 2006. (101 Questions... Ser.). (ENG.). 176p. (gr. 7-12). lib. bdg. 30.60 *(978-0-7613-2312-9(0))* Lerner Publishing Group.

Holm, Sharon, jt. illus. see Leonard, Barbara.

Holm, Sharon Lane. All New Crafts for Earth Day. Ross, Kathy. 2006. (All New Holiday Crafts for Kids Ser.). (ENG.). 48p. (gr. k-3). lib. bdg. 25.26 *(978-0-7613-3400-2(9)*, Millbrook Pr.); per. 7.95 *(978-0-8225-5976-4(5)*, First Avenue Editions) Lerner Publishing Group.

—All New Crafts for Kwanzaa. Ross, Kathy. 2006. (All New Holiday Crafts for Kids Ser.). 48p. (J). (gr. -1-3). per. 7.95 *(978-0-8225-3435-8(5)*, First Avenue Editions) Lerner Publishing Group.

—All New Crafts for Mother's Day & Father's Day. Ross, Kathy. 2007. (All New Holiday Crafts for Kids Ser.). (ENG.). 48p. (gr. k-3). per. 7.95 *(978-0-8225-6368-6(1)*, First Avenue Editions) Lerner Publishing Group.

—All New Crafts for Thanksgiving. Ross, Kathy. 2005. 48p. (J). (gr. k-2). per. 7.95 *(978-0-7613-2394-5(5)*, First Avenue Editions); (ENG.). lib. bdg. 25.26 *(978-0-7613-2922-0(6)*, Millbrook Pr.) Lerner Publishing Group.

—All New Holiday Crafts for Mother's & Father's Day. Ross, Kathy. 2007. (All New Holiday Crafts for Kids Ser.). (ENG.). 48p. (gr. k-3). lib. bdg. 25.26 *(978-0-8225-6367-9(3)*, Millbrook Pr.) Lerner Publishing Group.

—B-I-n-g-o. Bell, Lucy. 2017. (ENG.). 20p. (J). (gr. -1-1). bds. *(978-1-4867-1249-6(5))* Flowerpot Children's Pr. Inc.

—Buzzing Bees: Discovering Odd Numbers, 1 vol. Tourville, Amanda Doering. 2008. (Count the Critters Ser.). (ENG.). 24p. (J). (gr. k-3). 27.07 *(978-1-60270-262-2(4)*, 4812, Looking Glass Library) Magic Wagon.

—Hiding Hippos: Counting from 1 To 10, 1 vol. Tourville, Amanda Doering. 2008. (Count the Critters Ser.). (ENG.). 24p. (J). (gr. k-3). 27.07 *(978-1-60270-263-9(2)*, 4814, Looking Glass Library) Magic Wagon.

—More of the Best Holiday Crafts Ever! Ross, Kathy. 2005. 160p. (J). (gr. k-4). bds. 19.95 *(978-0-7613-2345-7(7))* Lerner Publishing Group.

—Penguin Pairs: Counting By 2s, 1 vol. Tourville, Amanda Doering. 2008. (Count the Critters Ser.). (ENG.). 24p. (J). (gr. k-3). 27.07 *(978-1-60270-265-3(9)*, 4818, Looking Glass Library) Magic Wagon.

—Prairie Dogs Perching: Counting By 3s, 1 vol. Tourville, Amanda Doering. 2008. (Count the Critters Ser.). (ENG.). 24p. (J). (gr. k-3). 27.07 *(978-1-60270-266-0(7)*, 4820, Looking Glass Library) Magic Wagon.

—Sunning Sea Lions: Discovering Even Numbers, 1 vol. Tourville, Amanda Doering. 2008. (Count the Critters Ser.). (ENG.). 24p. (J). (gr. k-3). 27.07 *(978-1-60270-267-7(5)*, 4822, Looking Glass Library) Magic Wagon.

—The Wheels on the Bus. Thompson, Kim Mitzo. 2010. (Padded Board Book W/CD Ser.). 8p. (J). (gr. k-2). bds. 10.99 incl. audio compact disk *(978-1-59922-580-7(8))* Twin Sisters IP, LLC.

—Where, Oh Where Has My Little Dog Gone. Everett, Melissa. 2017. (ENG.). 20p. (J). (gr. -1-1). bds. *(978-1-4867-1248-9(7))* Flowerpot Children's Pr. Inc.

—5 Steps to Drawing Crawlers & Fliers. Kesselring, Susan. 2018. (5 Steps to Drawing Ser.). (ENG.). 32p. (J). (gr. k-3). 29.93 *(978-1-5038-2476-8(4)*, 212236) Child's World, Inc., The.

—5 Steps to Drawing Farm Animals. Hall, Pamela. 2018. (5 Steps to Drawing Ser.). (ENG.). 32p. (J). (gr. k-3). 29.93 *(978-1-5038-2481-2(0)*, 212240) Child's World, Inc., The.

Holm, Sharon Lane. All New Crafts for Easter. Holm, Sharon Lane, tr. Ross, Kathy. 2005. (All New Holiday Crafts for Kids Ser.). (ENG.). 48p. (gr. k-3). pap. 7.95 *(978-0-7613-2392-1(9))*; lib. bdg. 25.26 *(978-0-7613-2921-3(8))* Lerner Publishing Group. (Millbrook Pr.).

Holman, Delaina. Sleepy Land: Everyone Goes There. Morris, Larresa. 2020. (ENG.). 30p. (J). 23.00 ***(978-1-64610-588-5(5))*** Dorrance Publishing Co., Inc.

Holman, Karen Busch. Minn from Minnesota. Wargin, Kathy-jo. 2006. (Mitt Midwest Ser.: 2). 144p. (J). (gr. k-7). 14.95 *(978-1-58726-304-0(1)*, Mitten Pr.) Ann Arbor Editions LLC.

—Mitt & Minn at the Wisconsin Cheese Jamboree. Wargin, Kathy-jo. 2007. (Mitt Midwest Ser.: 3). 144p. (J). (gr. k-7). 14.95 *(978-1-58726-305-7(X)*, Mitten Pr.) Ann Arbor Editions LLC.

—Mitt & Minn's Illinois Adventure. Wargin, Kathy-jo. 2007. (Mitt Midwest Ser.: 4). 144p. (J). (gr. k-7). 14.95 *(978-1-58726-306-4(8)*, Mitten Pr.) Ann Arbor Editions LLC.

—Mitt, the Michigan Mouse. Wargin, Kathy-jo. 2015. (Mitt Midwest Ser.: 1). 160p. (J). (gr. k-7). pap. 8.95 *(978-1-938170-65-2(2)*, Mitten Pr.) Ann Arbor Editions LLC.

—Nicholas: A New Hampshire Tale. Arenstam, Peter. 2009. (Nicholas Northeastern Ser.: 3). 144p. (J). (gr. k-7). 14.95 *(978-1-58726-521-1(4)*, Mitten Pr.) Ann Arbor Editions LLC.

—Nicholas: A Vermont Tale. Arenstam, Peter. 2010. (Nicholas Northeastern Ser.: 4). (ENG.). 144p. (J). (gr. k-7). 14.95 *(978-1-58726-522-8(2)*, Mitten Pr.) Ann Arbor Editions LLC.

—Nicholas, a Maine Tale. Arenstam, Peter. 2015. (Nicholas Northeastern Ser.: 2). 166p. (J). (gr. k-7). pap. 8.95 *(978-1-938170-67-6(9)*, Mitten Pr.) Ann Arbor Editions LLC.

—Nicholas, a Massachusetts Tale. Arenstam, Peter. 2015. (Nicholas Northeastern Ser.: 1). 152p. (J). (gr. k-7). pap. 8.95 *(978-1-938170-66-9(0)*, Mitten Pr.) Ann Arbor Editions LLC.

—Nicholas, a New Hampshire Tale. Arenstam, Peter. 2015. (Nicholas Northeastern Ser.: 3). 158p. (J). (gr. k-7). pap. 8.95 *(978-1-938170-68-3(7)*, Mitten Pr.) Ann Arbor Editions LLC.

—Nicholas, a Vermont Tale. Arenstam, Peter. 2015. (Nicholas Northeastern Ser.: 4). 156p. (J). (gr. k-7). pap. 8.95 *(978-1-938170-69-0(5)*, Mitten Pr.) Ann Arbor Editions LLC.

—Primary Numbers: A New Hampshire Numbers Book. Harris, Marie. 2004. (Count Your Way Across the U. S. A. Ser.). (ENG.). 40p. (J). 16.95 *(978-1-58536-192-2(5))* Sleeping Bear Pr.

Holmberg, Ansgar & Connelly, Gwen. Days of Faith: Assignment Book & Student Planner/Intermediate Grades 2005-2006. Fischer, Carl. 2005. 108p. (J). spiral bd. 4.99 *(978-1-933178-03-5(5)*, 9807) Pflaum Publishing Group.

Holmberg, Ansgar, jt. illus. see Connelly, Gwen.

Holme, Sharon. Meg Sale a Pasear, 1 vol. Blackaby, Susan. Ruiz, Carlos, tr. 2006. (Read-It! Readers en Español: Story Collection).Tr. of Meg Takes a Walk. (SPA.). 24p. (J). (gr. -1-3). 21.32 *(978-1-4048-1685-5(2)*, Picture Window Bks.) Capstone.

Holmer, Anders. Rain. 2018. (ENG.). 32p. (J). 17.00 *(978-0-8028-5507-7(5)*, Eerdmans Bks For Young Readers) Eerdmans, William B. Publishing Co.

Holmes, Denise. If I Wrote a Book about You. Aulenback, Stephany. 2014. (ENG.). 32p. (J). (gr. -1-3). 16.95 *(978-1-927018-46-0(3)*, 9781927018460) Simply Read Bks. CAN. Dist: Ingram Publisher Services.

—Where Are the Words? McKay, Jodi. 2016. (ENG.). 32p. (J). (gr. -1-3). 16.99 *(978-0-8075-8733-1(8)*, 807587338) Whitman, Albert & Co.

—The Yoga Game by the Sea. Beliveau, Kathy. 2015. (Yoga Game Ser.: 1). 32p. (J). 16.95 *(978-1-927018-49-1(8))* Simply Read Bks. CAN. Dist: Ingram Publisher Services.

Holmes, Denise. The Yoga Game in the Garden. Beliveau, Kathy. 2016. (Yoga Game Ser.: 2). 32p. (J). (gr. -1-3). 16.95 ***(978-1-927018-71-2(4))*** Simply Read Bks. CAN. Dist: Ingram Publisher Services.

Holmes, Ekua. Black Is a Rainbow Color. Joy, Angela. 2020. (ENG.). 40p. (J). 17.99 *(978-1-62672-631-4(0)*, 900163693) Roaring Brook Pr.

—Out of Wonder: Poems Celebrating Poets. Alexander, Kwame et al. 2017. 56p. (J). (gr. 3-7). 16.99 *(978-0-7636-8094-7(X))* Candlewick Pr.

—The Stuff of Stars. Bauer, Marion Dane. 2018. 40p. (J). (gr. -1-3). 17.99 *(978-0-7636-7883-8(X))* Candlewick Pr.

—Voice of Freedom: Fannie Lou Hamer: The Spirit of the Civil Rights Movement. Weatherford, Carole Boston. 56p. (J). 2018. (gr. 5). pap. 10.99 *(978-1-5362-0325-7(4))*; 2015. (ENG.). (gr. 4-7). 17.99 *(978-0-7636-6531-9(2))* Candlewick Pr.

—What Do You Do with a Voice Like That? The Story of Extraordinary Congresswoman Barbara Jordan. Barton, Chris. 2018. (ENG.). 48p. (J). (gr. -1-3). 18.99 *(978-1-4814-6561-8(9)*, Beach Lane Bks.) Beach Lane Bks.

Holmes, Fay. The Happy Little Ghost: A Halloween Tale. Holmes, Fay. 2003. 20p. (J). (gr. 1-3). pap. 5.00 *(978-0-9674241-4-9(3))* IZA Publishing Co.

Holmes, Gerald L. The Big Question. Erickson, John. 2012. 128p. (J). pap. *(978-1-59188-160-5(9))* Maverick Bks.

—The Big Question. Erickson, John. 2012. (Hank the Cowdog Ser.: Vol. 60). (ENG.). 128p. (J). (gr. 3-6). 15.99 *(978-1-59188-260-2(5))* Maverick Bks., Inc.

—The Case of the Black-Hooded Hangmans. Erickson, John. 2011. (Hank the Cowdog Ser.). (ENG.). 113p. (J). (gr. 3-6). pap. 5.99 *(978-1-59188-124-7(2))* Maverick Bks., Inc.

—The Case of the Black-Hooded Hangmans. Erickson, John R. 2017. (Hank the Cowdog Ser.: Vol. 24). (ENG.). 113p. (J). (gr. 3-6). 15.99 *(978-1-59188-224-4(9))* Maverick Bks., Inc.

—The Case of the Blazing Sky. Erickson, John. 2011. (Hank the Cowdog Ser.). (ENG.). 129p. (J). (gr. 3-6). pap. 5.99 *(978-1-59188-151-3(X))* Maverick Bks., Inc.

—The Case of the Blazing Sky. Erickson, John R. 2017. (Hank the Cowdog Ser.: Vol. 51). (ENG.). 129p. (J). (gr. 3-6). 15.99 *(978-1-59188-251-0(6))* Maverick Bks., Inc.

—The Case of the Booby-Trapped Pickup. Erickson, John. 2011. (Hank the Cowdog Ser.). (ENG.). 129p. (J). (gr. 3-6). pap. 5.99 *(978-1-59188-149-0(8))* Maverick Bks., Inc.

—The Case of the Booby-Trapped Pickup. Erickson, John R. 2017. (Hank the Cowdog Ser.: Vol. 49). (ENG.). 129p. (J). (gr. 3-6). 15.99 *(978-1-59188-249-7(4))* Maverick Bks., Inc.

—The Case of the Buried Deer. Erickson, John R. 2019. (Hank the Cowdog Ser.: Vol. 73). (ENG.). 129p. (J). (gr. 3-7). 15.99 *(978-1-59188-273-2(7))*; pap. 5.99 *(978-1-59188-173-5(0))* Maverick Bks., Inc.

—The Case of the Burrowing Robot. Erickson, John. 2011. (Hank the Cowdog Ser.). (ENG.). 125p. (J). (gr. 3-6). pap. 5.99 *(978-1-59188-142-1(0))* Maverick Bks., Inc.

—The Case of the Burrowing Robot. Erickson, John R. 2017. (Hank the Cowdog Ser.: Vol. 42). (ENG.). 125p. (J). (gr. 3-6). 15.99 *(978-1-59188-242-8(7))* Maverick Bks., Inc.

—The Case of the Car-Barkaholic Dog. Erickson, John. 2011. (Hank the Cowdog Ser.). (ENG.). 115p. (J). (gr. 3-6). pap. 5.99 *(978-1-59188-117-9(X))* Maverick Bks., Inc.

—The Case of the Car-Barkaholic Dog. Erickson, John R. 2017. (Hank the Cowdog Ser.: Vol. 17). (ENG.). 115p. (J). (gr. 3-6). 15.99 *(978-1-59188-217-6(6))* Maverick Bks., Inc.

—The Case of the Coyote Invasion. Erickson, John. 2011. (Hank the Cowdog Ser.: No. 56). (ENG.). 132p. (J). (gr. 3-6). pap. 5.99 *(978-1-59188-156-8(0))* Maverick Bks., Inc.

—The Case of the Coyote Invasion. Erickson, John R. 2017. (Hank the Cowdog Ser.: Vol. 56). (ENG.). 132p. (J). (gr. 3-6). 15.99 *(978-1-59188-256-5(7))* Maverick Bks., Inc.

—The Case of the Deadly Ha-Ha Game. Erickson, John. 2011. (Hank the Cowdog Ser.). (ENG.). 128p. (J). (gr. 3-6). pap. 5.99 *(978-1-59188-137-7(4))* Maverick Bks., Inc.

—The Case of the Deadly Ha-Ha Game. Erickson, John R. 2017. (Hank the Cowdog Ser.: Vol. 37). (ENG.). 128p. (J). (gr. 3-6). 15.99 *(978-1-59188-237-4(0))* Maverick Bks., Inc.

—The Case of the Dinosaur Birds. Erickson, John. 2011. (Hank the Cowdog Ser.). (ENG.). 125p. (J). (gr. 3-6). pap. 5.99 *(978-1-59188-154-4(4))* Maverick Bks., Inc.

—The Case of the Dinosaur Birds. Erickson, John R. 2017. (Hank the Cowdog Ser.: Vol. 54). (ENG.). 125p. (J). (gr. 3-6). 15.99 *(978-1-59188-254-1(0))* Maverick Bks., Inc.

—The Case of the Double Bumblebee Sting. Erickson, John. 2011. (Hank the Cowdog Ser.: No. 22). (ENG.). 114p. (J). (gr. 3-6). pap. 5.99 *(978-1-59188-122-3(6))* Maverick Bks., Inc.

—The Case of the Double Bumblebee Sting. Erickson, John R. 2017. (Hank the Cowdog Ser.: Vol. 22). (ENG.). 114p. (J). (gr. 3-6). 15.99 *(978-1-59188-222-0(2))* Maverick Bks., Inc.

—The Case of the Falling Sky. Erickson, John. 2011. (Hank the Cowdog Ser.: No. 45). (ENG.). 129p. (J). (gr. 3-6). pap. 5.99 *(978-1-59188-145-2(5))* Maverick Bks., Inc.

—The Case of the Falling Sky. Erickson, John R. 2017. (Hank the Cowdog Ser.: Vol. 45). (ENG.). 129p. (J). (gr. 3-6). 15.99 *(978-1-59188-245-9(1))* Maverick Bks., Inc.

—The Case of the Fiddle-Playing Fox. Erickson, John. 2011. (Hank the Cowdog Ser.: No. 12). (ENG.). 118p. (J). (gr. 3-6). pap. 5.99 *(978-1-59188-112-4(9))* Maverick Bks., Inc.

—The Case of the Fiddle-Playing Fox. Erickson, John R. 2017. (Hank the Cowdog Ser.: Vol. 12). (ENG.). 113p. (J). (gr. 3-6). 15.99 *(978-1-59188-212-1(5))* Maverick Bks., Inc.

—The Case of the Halloween Ghost. Erickson, John. 2011. (Hank the Cowdog Ser.). (ENG.). 123p. (J). (gr. 3-6). pap. 5.99 *(978-1-59188-109-4(9))* Maverick Bks., Inc.

—The Case of the Halloween Ghost. Erickson, John R. 2017. (Hank the Cowdog Ser.: Vol. 9). (ENG.). 123p. (J). (gr. 3-6). 15.99 *(978-1-59188-209-1(5))* Maverick Bks., Inc.

—The Case of the Haystack Kitties. Erickson, John. 2011. (Hank the Cowdog Ser.). (ENG.). 123p. (J). (gr. 3-6). pap. 5.99 *(978-1-59188-130-8(7))* Maverick Bks., Inc.

—The Case of the Haystack Kitties. Erickson, John R. 2017. (Hank the Cowdog Ser.: Vol. 30). (ENG.). 123p. (J). (gr. 3-6). 15.99 *(978-1-59188-230-5(3))* Maverick Bks., Inc.

—The Case of the Hooking Bull. Erickson, John. 2011. (Hank the Cowdog Ser.). (ENG.). 119p. (J). (gr. 3-6). pap. 5.99 *(978-1-59188-118-6(8))* Maverick Bks., Inc.

—The Case of the Hooking Bull. Erickson, John R. 2017. (Hank the Cowdog Ser.: Vol. 18). (ENG.). 119p. (J). (gr. 3-6). 15.99 *(978-1-59188-218-3(4))* Maverick Bks., Inc.

—The Case of the Kidnapped Collie. Erickson, John. 2011. (Hank the Cowdog Ser.). (ENG.). 113p. (J). (gr. 3-6). pap. 5.99 *(978-1-59188-126-1(9))* Maverick Bks., Inc.

—The Case of the Kidnapped Collie. Erickson, John R. 2017. (Hank the Cowdog Ser.: Vol. 26). (ENG.). 113p. (J). (gr. 3-6). 15.99 *(978-1-59188-226-8(5))* Maverick Bks., Inc.

—The Case of the Measled Cowboy. Erickson, John. 2011. (Hank the Cowdog Ser.: No. 33). (ENG.). 126p. (J). (gr. 3-6). pap. 5.99 *(978-1-59188-133-9(1))* Maverick Bks., Inc.

—The Case of the Measled Cowboy. Erickson, John R. 2017. (Hank the Cowdog Ser.: Vol. 33). (ENG.). 126p. (J). (gr. 3-6). 15.99 *(978-1-59188-233-6(8))* Maverick Bks., Inc.

—The Case of the Midnight Rustler. Erickson, John. 2011. (Hank the Cowdog Ser.: No. 19). (ENG.). 113p. (J). (gr. 3-6). pap. 5.99 *(978-1-59188-119-3(6))* Maverick Bks., Inc.

—The Case of the Midnight Rustler. Erickson, John R. 2017. (Hank the Cowdog Ser.: Vol. 19). (ENG.). 113p. (J). (gr. 3-6). 15.99 *(978-1-59188-219-0(2))* Maverick Bks., Inc.

—The Case of the Missing Bird Dog. Erickson, John. 2011. (Hank the Cowdog Ser.: No. 40). (ENG.). 126p. (J). (gr. 3-6). pap. 5.99 *(978-1-59188-140-7(4))* Maverick Bks., Inc.

—The Case of the Missing Bird Dog. Erickson, John R. 2017. (Hank the Cowdog Ser.: Vol. 40). (ENG.). 126p. (J). (gr. 3-6). 15.99 *(978-1-59188-240-4(0))* Maverick Bks., Inc.

—The Case of the Missing Cat. Erickson, John. 2011. (Hank the Cowdog Ser.: No. 15). (ENG.). 114p. (J). (gr. 3-6). pap. 5.99 *(978-1-59188-115-5(3))* Maverick Bks., Inc.

—The Case of the Missing Cat. Erickson, John R. 2017. (Hank the Cowdog Ser.: Vol. 15). (ENG.). 114p. (J). (gr. 3-6). 15.99 *(978-1-59188-215-2(X))* Maverick Bks., Inc.

—The Case of the Monkey Burglar. Erickson, John. 2011. (Hank the Cowdog Ser.: No. 48). (ENG.). 129p. (J). (gr. 3-6). pap. 5.99 *(978-1-59188-148-3(X))* Maverick Bks., Inc.

—The Case of the Monkey Burglar. Erickson, John R. 2017. (Hank the Cowdog Ser.: Vol. 48). (ENG.). 129p. (J). (gr. 3-6). 15.99 *(978-1-59188-248-0(6))* Maverick Bks., Inc.

—The Case of the Monster Fire. Erickson, John R. 2018. (Hank the Cowdog Ser.: Vol. 71). (ENG.). 115p. (J). (gr. 3-7). 15.99 *(978-1-59188-271-8(0))*; pap. 5.99 *(978-1-59188-171-1(4))* Maverick Bks., Inc.

—The Case of the Most Ancient Bone. Erickson, John. 2011. (Hank the Cowdog Ser.). (ENG.). 239p. (J). (gr. 3-6). pap. 5.99 *(978-1-59188-150-6(1))* Maverick Bks., Inc.

—The Case of the Most Ancient Bone. Erickson, John R. 2017. (Hank the Cowdog Ser.: Vol. 50). (ENG.). 239p. (J). (gr. 3-6). 16.99 *(978-1-59188-250-3(8))* Maverick Bks., Inc.

—The Case of the Mysterious Voice. Erickson, John. 2012. (Hank the Cowdog (Quality) Ser.: Vol. 58). (ENG.). 123p. (J). (gr. 3-6). pap. 5.99 *(978-1-59188-158-2(7))* Maverick Bks., Inc.

—The Case of the Mysterious Voice. Erickson, John R. 2017. (Hank the Cowdog Ser.: Vol. 58). (ENG.). 123p. (J). (gr. 3-6). 15.99 *(978-1-59188-258-9(3))* Maverick Bks., Inc.

—The Case of the Night-Stalking Bone Monster. Erickson, John. 2011. (Hank the Cowdog Ser.). (ENG.). 115p. (J). (gr. 3-6). pap. 5.99 *(978-1-59188-127-8(7))* Maverick Bks., Inc.

—The Case of the Night-Stalking Bone Monster. Erickson, John R. 2017. (Hank the Cowdog Ser.: Vol. 27). (ENG.). 115p. (J). (gr. 3-6). 15.99 *(978-1-59188-227-5(3))* Maverick Bks., Inc.

—The Case of the One-Eyed Killer Stud Horse. Erickson, John. 2011. (Hank the Cowdog Ser.: No. 8). (ENG.). 120p. (J). (gr. 3-6). pap. 5.99 *(978-1-59188-108-7(0))* Maverick Bks., Inc.

—The Case of the One-Eyed Killer Stud Horse. Erickson, John R. 2017. (Hank the Cowdog Ser.: Vol. 8). (ENG.).

H

120p. (J). (gr. 3-6). 15.99 *(978-1-59188-208-4(7))* Maverick Bks., Inc.
—The Case of the Perfect Dog. Erickson, John. 2012. 127p. (J). *(978-1-59188-259-6(1))* Maverick Bks.
—The Case of the Perfect Dog. Erickson, John. 2012. (Hank the Cowdog (Quality) Ser.). (ENG.). 127p. (J). (gr. 3-6). pap. 5.99 *(978-1-59188-159-9(5))* Maverick Bks., Inc.
—The Case of the Raging Rottweiler. Erickson, John. 2011. (Hank the Cowdog Ser.). (ENG.). 131p. (J). (gr. 3-6). pap. 5.99 *(978-1-59188-136-0(6))* Maverick Bks., Inc.
—The Case of the Raging Rottweiler. Erickson, John R. 2017. (Hank the Cowdog Ser.: Vol. 36). (ENG.). 131p. (J). (gr. 3-6). 15.99 *(978-1-59188-236-7(2))* Maverick Bks., Inc.
—The Case of the Saddle House Robbery. Erickson, John. 2011. (Hank the Cowdog Ser.: No. 35). (ENG.). 125p. (J). (gr. 3-6). pap. 5.99 *(978-1-59188-135-3(8))* Maverick Bks., Inc.
—The Case of the Saddle House Robbery. Erickson, John R. 2017. (Hank the Cowdog Ser.: Vol. 35). (ENG.). 125p. (J). (gr. 3-6). 15.99 *(978-1-59188-235-0(4))* Maverick Bks., Inc.
—The Case of the Secret Weapon. Erickson, John. 2011. (Hank the Cowdog Ser.). (ENG.). 125p. (J). (gr. 3-6). pap. 5.99 *(978-1-59188-155-1(2))* Maverick Bks., Inc.
—The Case of the Secret Weapon. Erickson, John R. 2017. (Hank the Cowdog Ser.: Vol. 55). (ENG.). 125p. (J). (gr. 3-6). 15.99 *(978-1-59188-255-8(9))* Maverick Bks., Inc.
—The Case of the Shipwrecked Tree. Erickson, John. 2011. (Hank the Cowdog Ser.: No. 41). (ENG.). 119p. (J). (gr. 3-6). pap. 5.99 *(978-1-59188-141-4(2))* Maverick Bks., Inc.
—The Case of the Shipwrecked Tree. Erickson, John R. 2017. (Hank the Cowdog Ser.: Vol. 41). (ENG.). 119p. (J). (gr. 3-6). 15.99 *(978-1-59188-241-1(9))* Maverick Bks., Inc.
—The Case of the Swirling Killer Tornado. Erickson, John. 2011. (Hank the Cowdog Ser.). (ENG.). 112p. (J). (gr. 3-6). pap. 5.99 *(978-1-59188-125-4(0))* Maverick Bks., Inc.
—The Case of the Swirling Killer Tornado. Erickson, John R. 2017. (Hank the Cowdog Ser.: Vol. 25). (ENG.). 112p. (J). (gr. 3-6). 15.99 *(978-1-59188-225-1(7))* Maverick Bks., Inc.
—The Case of the Tender Cheeping Chickies. Erickson, John. 2011. (Hank the Cowdog Ser.). (ENG.). 129p. (J). (gr. 3-6). pap. 5.99 *(978-1-59188-147-6(1))* Maverick Bks., Inc.
—The Case of the Tender Cheeping Chickies. Erickson, John R. 2017. (Hank the Cowdog Ser.: Vol. 47). (ENG.). 129p. (J). (gr. 3-6). 15.99 *(978-1-59188-247-3(8))* Maverick Bks., Inc.
—The Case of the Three Rings. Erickson, John. 2014. 124p. (J). pap. *(978-1-59188-164-3(1))* Maverick Bks., Inc.
—The Case of the Three-Toed Sloth. Erickson, John R. 2018. (Hank the Cowdog Ser.: Vol. 72). (ENG.). 119p. (J). (gr. 3-7). 15.99 *(978-1-59188-272-5(9))*; pap. 5.99 *(978-1-59188-172-8(2))* Maverick Bks., Inc.
—The Case of the Tricky Trap. Erickson, John. 2011. (Hank the Cowdog Ser.). (ENG.). 126p. (J). (gr. 3-6). pap. 5.99 *(978-1-59188-146-9(3))* Maverick Bks., Inc.
—The Case of the Tricky Trap. Erickson, John R. 2017. (Hank the Cowdog Ser.: Vol. 46). (ENG.). 126p. (J). (gr. 3-6). 15.99 *(978-1-59188-246-6(X))* Maverick Bks., Inc.
—The Case of the Twisted Kitty. Erickson, John. 2004. (Hank the Cowdog Ser.: No. 43). 131p. (J). lib. bdg. 17.00 *(978-1-4242-1600-0(1))* Fitzgerald Bks.
—The Case of the Twisted Kitty. Erickson, John. 2011. (Hank the Cowdog Ser.). (ENG.). 131p. (J). (gr. 3-6). pap. 5.99 *(978-1-59188-143-8(9))* Maverick Bks., Inc.
—The Case of the Twisted Kitty. Erickson, John R. 2017. (Hank the Cowdog Ser.: Vol. 43). (ENG.). 131p. (J). (gr. 3-6). 15.99 *(978-1-59188-243-5(5))* Maverick Bks., Inc.
—The Case of the Vampire Cat. Erickson, John. 2011. (Hank the Cowdog Ser.). (ENG.). 115p. (J). (gr. 3-6). pap. 5.99 *(978-1-59188-121-6(8))* Maverick Bks., Inc.
—The Case of the Vampire Cat. Erickson, John R. 2017. (Hank the Cowdog Ser.: Vol. 21). (ENG.). 115p. (J). (gr. 3-6). 15.99 *(978-1-59188-221-3(4))* Maverick Bks., Inc.
—The Case of the Vampire Vacuum Sweeper. Erickson, John. 2011. (Hank the Cowdog Ser.). (ENG.). 119p. (J). (gr. 3-6). pap. 5.99 *(978-1-59188-129-2(3))* Maverick Bks., Inc.
—The Case of the Vampire Vacuum Sweeper. Erickson, John R. 2017. (Hank the Cowdog Ser.: Vol. 29). (ENG.). 119p. (J). (gr. 3-6). 15.99 *(978-1-59188-229-9(X))* Maverick Bks., Inc.
—The Case of the Vanishing Fishhook. Erickson, John. 2011. (Hank the Cowdog Ser.: No. 31). (ENG.). 124p. (J). (gr. 3-6). pap. 5.99 *(978-1-59188-131-5(5))* Maverick Bks., Inc.
—The Case of the Vanishing Fishhook. Erickson, John R. 2017. (Hank the Cowdog Ser.: Vol. 31). (ENG.). 124p. (J). (gr. 3-6). 15.99 *(978-1-59188-231-2(1))* Maverick Bks., Inc.
—Cowboys & Horses. Erickson, John R. 2017. 74p. (J). *(978-1-5444-0370-0(4))* Maverick Bks., Inc.
—The Curse of the Incredible Preiceless Corncob. Erickson, John R. 2017. (Hank the Cowdog Ser.: Vol. 7). (ENG.). 127p. (J). (gr. 3-6). 15.99 *(978-1-59188-207-7(9))* Maverick Bks., Inc.
—The Curse of the Incredible Priceless Corncob. Erickson, John. 2011. (Hank the Cowdog Ser.: No. 7). (ENG.). 127p. (J). (gr. 3-6). pap. 5.99 *(978-1-59188-107-0(2))* Maverick Bks., Inc.
—The Disappearance of Drover. Erickson, John. 2011. (Hank the Cowdog Ser.). (ENG.). 122p. (J). (gr. 3-6). pap. 5.99 *(978-1-59188-157-5(9))* Maverick Bks., Inc.
—The Disappearance of Drover. Erickson, John R. 2017. (Hank the Cowdog Ser.: Vol. 57). (ENG.). 122p. (J). (gr. 3-6). 15.99 *(978-1-59188-257-2(5))* Maverick Bks., Inc.
—Drover's Secret Life. Erickson, John. 2011. (Hank the Cowdog Ser.). (ENG.). 118p. (J). (gr. 3-6). pap. 5.99 *(978-1-59188-153-7(6))* Maverick Bks., Inc.
—Drover's Secret Life. Erickson, John R. 2017. (Hank the Cowdog Ser.: Vol. 53). (ENG.). 118p. (J). (gr. 3-6). 15.99 *(978-1-59188-253-4(2))* Maverick Bks., Inc.
—The Dungeon of Doom. Erickson, John. 2004. (Hank the Cowdog Ser.: No. 44). 122p. (J). lib. bdg. 17.00 *(978-1-4242-1601-7(X))* Fitzgerald Bks.
—The Dungeon of Doom. Erickson, John. 2011. (Hank the Cowdog Ser.). (ENG.). 122p. (J). (gr. 3-6). pap. 5.99 *(978-1-59188-144-5(7))* Maverick Bks., Inc.
—The Dungeon of Doom. Erickson, John R. 2017. (Hank the Cowdog Ser.: Vol. 44). (ENG.). 122p. (J). (gr. 3-6). 15.99 *(978-1-59188-244-2(3))* Maverick Bks., Inc.
—Every Dog Has His Day. Erickson, John. 2011. (Hank the Cowdog Ser.). (ENG.). 118p. (J). (gr. 3-6). pap. 5.99 *(978-1-59188-110-0(2))* Maverick Bks., Inc.
—Every Dog Has His Day. Erickson, John R. 2017. (Hank the Cowdog Ser.: Vol. 10). (ENG.). 118p. (J). (gr. 3-6). 15.99 *(978-1-59188-210-7(9))* Maverick Bks., Inc.
—Faded Love. Erickson, John. 2011. (Hank the Cowdog Ser.: No. 5). (ENG.). 125p. (J). (gr. 3-6). pap. 5.99 *(978-1-59188-105-6(6))* Maverick Bks., Inc.
—Faded Love. Erickson, John R. 2017. (Hank the Cowdog Ser.: Vol. 5). (ENG.). (J). (gr. 3-6). 15.99 *(978-1-59188-205-3(2))* Maverick Bks., Inc.
—The Fling. Erickson, John. 2011. (Hank the Cowdog Ser.). (ENG.). 126p. (J). (gr. 3-6). pap. 5.99 *(978-1-59188-138-4(2))* Maverick Bks., Inc.
—The Fling. Erickson, John R. 2017. (Hank the Cowdog Ser.: Vol. 38). (ENG.). 126p. (J). (gr. 3-6). 15.99 *(978-1-59188-238-1(9))* Maverick Bks., Inc.
—The Further Adventures of Hank the Cowdog. Erickson, John R. 2017. (Hank the Cowdog Ser.: Vol. 2). (ENG.). 127p. (J). (gr. 3-6). 15.99 *(978-1-59188-202-2(8))* Maverick Bks., Inc.
—The Garbage Monster from Outer Space. Erickson, John. 2011. (Hank the Cowdog Ser.). (ENG.). 126p. (J). (gr. 3-6). pap. 5.99 *(978-1-59188-132-2(3))* Maverick Bks., Inc.
—The Garbage Monster from Outer Space. Erickson, John R. 2017. (Hank the Cowdog Ser.: Vol. 32). (ENG.). 126p. (J). (gr. 3-6). 15.99 *(978-1-59188-232-9(X))* Maverick Bks., Inc.
—The Ghost of Rabbits Past. Erickson, John. 2013. 128p. (J). pap. *(978-1-59188-162-9(5))* Maverick Bks., Inc.
—Hank Cowdog 50. Erickson, John. 2007. 256p. 16.99 *(978-0-670-62249-8(4)*, Viking Adult) Penguin Publishing Group.
—Hank the Cowdog & Monkey Business. Erickson, John. 2011. (Hank the Cowdog Ser.). (ENG.). 110p. (J). (gr. 3-6). pap. 5.99 *(978-1-59188-114-8(5))* Maverick Bks., Inc.
—Hank the Cowdog & Monkey Business. Erickson, John R. 2017. (Hank the Cowdog Ser.: Vol. 14). (ENG.). 110p. (J). (gr. 3-6). 15.99 *(978-1-59188-214-5(1))* Maverick Bks., Inc.
—It's a Dog's Life. Erickson, John. (Hank the Cowdog Ser.: No. 3). (J). 100p. (gr. 2-5). 9.95 *(978-0-916941-04-8(3))*; 2011. (ENG.). 127p. (gr. 3-6). pap. 5.99 *(978-1-59188-103-2(X))* Maverick Bks., Inc.
—It's a Dog's Life. Erickson, John R. 2017. (Hank the Cowdog Ser.: Vol. 3). (ENG.). 120p. (J). (gr. 3-6). 15.99 *(978-1-59188-203-9(6))* Maverick Bks., Inc.
—Las Verdaderas Aventuras de Hank, el Perro Vaquero. Erickson, John R. 2018. (Hank the Cowdog Ser.: Vol. 1). (SPA.). (J). (gr. 3-6). pap. 6.99 *(978-1-59188-351-7(2))* Maverick Bks., Inc.
—Let Sleeping Dogs Lie. Erickson, John. 2011. (Hank the Cowdog Ser.: No. 6). (ENG.). 129p. (J). (gr. 3-6). pap. 5.99 *(978-1-59188-106-3(4))* Maverick Bks., Inc.
—Let Sleeping Dogs Lie. Erickson, John R. 2017. (Hank the Cowdog Ser.: Vol. 6). (ENG.). 129p. (J). (gr. 3-6). 15.99 *(978-1-59188-206-0(0))* Maverick Bks., Inc.
—Lost in the Blinded Blizzard. Erickson, John. 2011. (Hank the Cowdog Ser.). (ENG.). 115p. (J). (gr. 3-6). pap. 5.99 *(978-1-59188-116-2(1))* Maverick Bks., Inc.
—Lost in the Blinded Blizzard. Erickson, John R. 2017. (Hank the Cowdog Ser.: Vol. 16). (ENG.). 115p. (J). (gr. 3-6). 15.99 *(978-1-59188-216-9(8))* Maverick Bks., Inc.
—Lost in the Dark Unchanted Forest. Erickson, John. 2011. (Hank the Cowdog Ser.). (ENG.). 124p. (J). (gr. 3-6). pap. 5.99 *(978-1-59188-111-7(0))* Maverick Bks., Inc.
—Lost in the Dark Unchanted Forest. Erickson, John R. 2017. (Hank the Cowdog Ser.: Vol. 11). (ENG.). 124p. (J). (gr. 3-6). 15.99 *(978-1-59188-211-4(7))* Maverick Bks., Inc.
—Moonlight Madness. Erickson, John. 2011. (Hank the Cowdog Ser.: No. 23). (ENG.). 114p. (J). (gr. 3-6). pap. 5.99 *(978-1-59188-123-0(4))* Maverick Bks., Inc.
—Moonlight Madness. Erickson, John R. 2017. (Hank the Cowdog Ser.: Vol. 23). (ENG.). 114p. (J). (gr. 3-6). 15.99 *(978-1-59188-223-7(0))* Maverick Bks., Inc.
—The Mopwater Files. Erickson, John. 2011. (Hank the Cowdog Ser.). (ENG.). 111p. (J). (gr. 3-6). pap. 5.99 *(978-1-59188-128-5(5))* Maverick Bks., Inc.
—The Mopwater Files. Erickson, John R. 2017. (Hank the Cowdog Ser.: Vol. 28). (ENG.). 111p. (J). (gr. 3-6). 15.99 *(978-1-59188-228-2(1))* Maverick Bks., Inc.
—Murder in the Middle Pasture. Erickson, John. 2011. (Hank the Cowdog Ser.). (ENG.). 120p. (J). (gr. 3-6). pap. 5.99 *(978-1-59188-104-9(8))* Maverick Bks., Inc.
—Murder in the Middle Pasture. Erickson, John R. 2017. (Hank the Cowdog Ser.: Vol. 4). (ENG.). (J). (gr. 3-6). 15.99 *(978-1-59188-204-6(4))* Maverick Bks., Inc.
—The Original Adventures of Hank the Cowdog. Erickson, John. (ENG.). 127p. (J). (gr. 3-6). 2012. (Hank the Cowdog Ser.: Vol. 1). 15.99 *(978-1-59188-201-5(X))*; 2011. (Hank the Cowdog Ser.: No. 1). pap. 5.99 *(978-1-59188-101-8(3))* Maverick Bks., Inc.
—The Phantom in the Mirror. Erickson, John. 2011. (Hank the Cowdog Ser.: No. 20). (ENG.). 114p. (J). (gr. 3-6). pap. 5.99 *(978-1-59188-120-9(X))* Maverick Bks., Inc.
—The Phantom in the Mirror. Erickson, John R. 2017. (Hank the Cowdog Ser.: Vol. 20). (ENG.). 114p. (J). (gr. 3-6). 15.99 *(978-1-59188-220-6(6))* Maverick Bks., Inc.
—The Quest for the Great White Quail. Erickson, John. 2011. (Hank the Cowdog Ser.). (ENG.). 123p. (J). (gr. 3-6). pap. 5.99 *(978-1-59188-152-0(8))* Maverick Bks., Inc.
—The Quest for the Great White Quail. Erickson, John R. 2017. (Hank the Cowdog Ser.: Vol. 52). (ENG.). 123p. (J). (gr. 3-6). 15.99 *(978-1-59188-252-7(4))* Maverick Bks., Inc.
—Ranch Life: Ranch Wildlife: Hank's Ranch Life #3. Erickson, John R. 2018. (Hank's Ranch Life Ser.: Vol. 3). (ENG.). 111p. (J). (gr. 3-7). pap. 6.99 *(978-1-59188-993-9(6))* Maverick Bks., Inc.
—The Return of the Charlie Monsters. Erickson, John. 2014. 128p. (J). pap. *(978-1-59188-163-6(3))* Maverick Bks., Inc.
—The Secret Laundry Monster Files. Erickson, John. 2011. (Hank the Cowdog Ser.). (ENG.). 128p. (J). (gr. 3-6). pap. 5.99 *(978-1-59188-139-1(0))* Maverick Bks., Inc.
—The Secret Laundry Monster Files. Erickson, John R. 2017. (Hank the Cowdog Ser.: Vol. 39). (ENG.). 128p. (J). (gr. 3-6). 15.99 *(978-1-59188-239-8(7))* Maverick Bks., Inc.
—The Secret Pledge. Erickson, John. 2016. 117p. (J). (Hank the Cowdog Ser.: Vol. 68). (ENG.). (gr. 3-6). 15.99 *(978-1-59188-268-8(0))*; (Hank the Cowdog Ser.: Vol. 68). (ENG.). (gr. 3-6). pap. 5.99 *(978-1-59188-168-1(4))*; *(978-1-5182-4067-6(4))* Maverick Bks., Inc.
—Slim's Good-Bye. Erickson, John. 2011. (Hank the Cowdog Ser.). (ENG.). 132p. (J). (gr. 3-6). pap. 5.99 *(978-1-59188-134-6(X))* Maverick Bks., Inc.
—Slim's Good-Bye. Erickson, John R. 2017. (Hank the Cowdog Ser.: Vol. 34). (ENG.). 132p. (J). (gr. 3-6). 15.99 *(978-1-59188-234-3(6))* Maverick Bks., Inc.
—The Wounded Buzzard on Christmas Eve. Erickson, John. 2011. (Hank the Cowdog Ser.: No. 13). (ENG.). 112p. (J). (gr. 3-6). pap. 5.99 *(978-1-59188-113-1(7))* Maverick Bks., Inc.
—The Wounded Buzzard on Christmas Eve. Erickson, John R. 2017. (Hank the Cowdog Ser.: Vol. 13). (ENG.). 112p. (J). (gr. 3-6). 15.99 *(978-1-59188-213-8(3))* Maverick Bks., Inc.

Holmes, Gerald L., jt. illus. see Erickson, John.

Holmes, Jeremy. The Emperor of Mars. Samphire, Patrick. 2017. (Secrets of the Dragon Tomb Ser.: 2). (ENG.). 368p. (J). 34.99 *(978-0-8050-9908-9(5)*, 900125300, Holt, Henry & Co. Bks. For Young Readers) Holt, Henry & Co.
—The Eye That Never Sleeps: How Detective Pinkerton Saved President Lincoln. Moss, Marissa. 2018. (ENG.). 48p. (J). (gr. 1-4). 17.99 *(978-1-4197-3064-1(9)*, Abrams Bks. for Young Readers) Abrams, Inc.
—Great Ball of Light. Kuhlman, Evan. 2015. (ENG.). 304p. (J). (gr. 5-9). 16.99 *(978-1-4169-6461-2(4))* Simon & Schuster Children's Publishing.
—Poem-Mobiles: Crazy Car Poems. Lewis, J. Patrick & Florian, Douglas. (ENG.). 40p. (J). (gr. -1-3). 2020. 7.99 *(978-1-9848-9447-2(1))*; 2014. 17.99 *(978-0-375-86690-6(6))* Random Hse. Children's Bks. (Schwartz & Wade Bks.).
—The Templeton Twins Have an Idea: Book. Weiner, Ellis. 2013. (Templeton Twins Ser.: Vol. 1). (ENG.). (J). (gr. 3-7). lib. bdg. 17.60 *(978-1-68065-132-4(3))* Perfection Learning Corp.
—The Templeton Twins Have an Idea: Book 1. Weiner, Ellis. 2013. (Templeton Twins Ser.: 1). (ENG.). 240p. (J). (gr. 3-7). pap. 6.99 *(978-1-4521-2704-0(2))* Chronicle Bks. LLC.
—The Templeton Twins Have an Idea: Book One. Weiner, Ellis. 2012. (ENG.). 232p. (J). (gr. 4-7). 16.99 *(978-0-8118-6679-8(3))* Chronicle Bks. LLC.

Holmes, Joshua D. The Raindrop. Firely, G. M. 2004. 21p. pap. 24.95 *(978-1-4137-3388-4(3))* PublishAmerica, Inc.

Holmes, Matthew. Pizza Counting. Dobson, Christina. 2003. 32p. (J). (gr. 1-4). pap. 7.95 *(978-0-88106-339-4(8))* Charlesbridge Publishing, Inc.

Holmes, Mike. The Dragonet Prophecy. Sutherland, Tui T. 2018. (Wings of Fire Graphic Novel Ser.: 1). 224p. (J). (gr. 3-7). (ENG.). 24.99 *(978-0-545-94216-4(0))*; pap. 12.99 *(978-0-545-94215-7(2))* Scholastic, Inc. (Graphix).
—The Lost Heir, Bk. 2. Sutherland, Tui T. 2019. (Wings of Fire Graphic Novel Ser.: 2). 224p. (J). (gr. 3-7). (ENG.). 24.99 *(978-0-545-94221-8(7))*; pap. 12.99 *(978-0-545-94220-1(9))* Scholastic, Inc. (Graphix).
—Secret Coders. Yang, Gene Luen. 2015. (Secret Coders Ser.: 1). (ENG.). 96p. (J). (gr. 3-7). pap. 10.99 *(978-1-62672-075-6(4)*, 900134876, First Second Bks.) Roaring Brook Pr.
—Secret Coders: Monsters & Modules. Luen Yang, Gene. 2018. (Secret Coders Ser.: 6). (ENG.). 112p. (J). 18.99 *(978-1-62672-609-3(4)*, 900162985, First Second Bks.) Roaring Brook Pr.
—Secret Coders: Monsters & Modules. Yang, Gene Luen. 2018. (Secret Coders Ser.: 6). (ENG.). 112p. (J). pap. 10.99 *(978-1-62672-610-9(8)*, 900162986, First Second Bks.) Roaring Brook Pr.
—Secret Coders: Paths & Portals. Yang, Gene Luen. 2016. (Secret Coders Ser.: 2). (ENG.). 96p. (J). pap. 10.99 *(978-1-62672-076-3(2)*, 900134877, First Second Bks.) Roaring Brook Pr.
—Secret Coders: Potions & Parameters. Luen Yang, Gene. 2018. (Secret Coders Ser.: 5). (ENG.). 112p. (J). 18.99 *(978-1-62672-608-6(6)*, 900162981, First Second Bks.) Roaring Brook Pr.
—Secret Coders: Potions & Parameters. Yang, Gene Luen. 2018. (Secret Coders Ser.: 5). (ENG.). 112p. (J). pap. 10.99 *(978-1-62672-607-9(8)*, 900162982, First Second Bks.) Roaring Brook Pr.
—Secret Coders: Robots & Repeats. Yang, Gene Luen. 2017. (Secret Coders Ser.: 4). (ENG.). 96p. (J). pap. 10.99 *(978-1-62672-606-2(X)*, 900162979, First Second Bks.) Roaring Brook Pr.
—Secret Coders: Secrets & Sequences. Yang, Gene Luen. 2017. (Secret Coders Ser.: 3). (ENG.). 112p. (J). pap. 10.99 *(978-1-62672-077-0(0)*, 900134878, First Second Bks.) Roaring Brook Pr.

Holmes, Mike. Bravest Warriors, Vol. 2. Holmes, Mike. Comeau, Joey. 2014. (Bravest Warriors Ser.: 2). (ENG.). 128p. (J). (gr. 4). pap. 14.99 *(978-1-60886-352-5(2))* Boom! Studios.

Holmes, Phyllis. Big-Hearted Charlie Learns How to Make Friends. Keating-Joseph, Krista. 2018. (Big-Hearted Charlie Ser.: Vol. 3). (ENG.). 44p. (J). (gr. k-3). pap. 13.95 *(978-1-7322135-0-0(X))* Legacies & Memories.
—Big-Hearted Charlie Never Gives Up: Fun Adventures. Keating-Joseph, Krista. 2017. (Big-Hearted Charlie Ser.: Vol. 2). (ENG.). (J). (gr. 1-3). pap. 13.95 *(978-0-9972523-9-2(1))* Legacies & Memories.
—Big-Hearted Charlie's Coloring Book: The Story of a Dog Named Turtle & a Turtle Named Dog. Keating-Joseph, Krista. 2019. (Big-Hearted Charlie Ser.: Vol. 4). (ENG.). 50p. (J). (gr. k-2). 10.95 *(978-1-7322135-4-8(2))* Legacies & Memories.

Holmes, Rebecca. Little Shoko & the Crocodile. Sithole, Thelma. 2007. 36p. per. 12.00 *(978-1-59858-330-4(1))* Dog Ear Publishing, LLC.

Holmes, Sally. Little Red Riding Hood & Other Fairy Tales from Charles Perrault: Eleven Classic Stories Including Cinderella, the Sleeping Beauty & Puss-In-Boots. 2020. 160p. (J). (gr. -1-12). 16.00 *(978-1-86147-868-9(2)*, Armadillo) Anness Publishing GBR. Dist: National Bk. Network.
—The Snow Queen: A Story in Seven Parts. Andersen, Hans. 2019. 64p. (J). (gr. -1-12). 13.00 *(978-1-86147-856-6(9)*, Armadillo) Anness Publishing GBR. Dist: National Bk. Network.

Holmes, Stephen, jt. illus. see Faulkner, Keith.

Holmes, Steve. Animales Marinos: Mezcla y Diviertete. 2005. (Mezcla y Diviertete Ser.). (SPA.). 5p. (J). (gr. -1-7). *(978-970-718-291-2(1)*, Silver Dolphin en Español) Advanced Marketing, S. de R. L. de C. V.
—Nature's Neighborhoods. Hilton, Samantha. 2004. (Interfact Ladders Ser.). (ENG.). 48p. (J). (gr. -1-2). 14.95 incl. cd-rom *(978-1-58728-420-5(0))* Cooper Square Publishing Llc.
—Rain Forest Animals. Wilkes, Angela et al. rev. ed. 2004. (Ladders Ser.). 32p. (J). (gr. -1-3). 12.95 *(978-1-58728-606-3(8)*, Two-Can Publishing) T&N Children's Publishing.
—World of Insects. Hilton, Samantha. 2004. (Interfact Ladders Ser.). (ENG.). 48p. (J). (gr. -1-2). 14.95 incl. cd-rom *(978-1-58728-419-9(7))* Cooper Square Publishing Llc.

Holmes, Tom. ABCs of the Web. Vanden-Heuvel, John C., Sr. & Ostrovsky, Andrey. 2016. (ENG.). 28p. (J). (gr. -1-3). bds. 8.99 *(978-1-4998-0312-9(5))* Little Bee Books Inc.

Holmes, Wednesday. Pride 1 2 3. Joosten, Michael. 2020. (ENG.). 22p. (J). (gr. -1-k). bds. 7.99 ***(978-1-5344-6499-5(9)***, Little Simon) Little Simon.

Holmlund, Heather D. As Long As the Rivers Flow, 1 vol. Loyie, Larry & Brissenden, Constance. 2005. (ENG.). 48p. (J). (gr. 4-7). pap. 9.95 *(978-0-88899-696-1(9))* Groundwood Bks. CAN. Dist: Publishers Group West (PGW).

Holmlund, Jenny. Consciously Barefoot- about Earthing & Healing Inflammations: Consciously Barefoot. Alterskjaer, Lilian. 2019. (ENG.). 156p. (J). pap. 17.65 ***(978-1-6925-4184-2(6))*** Independently Published.

Holoska, Jiri, photos by. Kirigami Greeting Cards: The Art of Paper Cutting & Folding. Krcmár, Karol. Simekova, Jela, ed. Chorvathova, Michaela, tr. 2005. (Kirigami Craft Books Ser.). 80p. (J). pap. 14.95 *(978-0-9715411-7-7(5))* Kotzig Publishing, Inc.
—Kirigami Paper Kingdom: The Art of Paper Cutting & Folding. Krcmár, Karol. Simekova, Jela, ed. Kovac, Stefan Patrik, tr. 2005. (Kirigami Craft Books Ser.). 112p. (J). pap. 14.95 *(978-0-9715411-6-0(7))* Kotzig Publishing, Inc.

Holroyd, Geraldine. Caught in the Net. Pavese, Candace. 2013. 84p. pap. 9.95 *(978-1-937449-19-3(X))* YAV.

Holsather, Bill. Henry of York: The Secret of Juan de Vega. Holsather, Kent. 2003. 176p. (YA). (gr. 5-18). 22.95 *(978-0-9729101-0-1(7))*; 2nd ed. per. 12.95 *(978-0-9729101-1-8(5))* Lonejack Mountain Pr.

Holsinger, Carol. Abadaba Alphabet: Learning Letter Sounds. Moore, Sheila. 2006. 31p. (gr. -1-3). 19.95 *(978-0-9789473-0-9(4))* Abadaba Reading LLC.

Holstad, Kathy, photos by. Tillamook Cheese Cookbook: Celebrating 100 Years of Excellence. Holstad, Kathy. Tillamook County Creamery Association. 2008. (ENG., 196p. 24.95 *(978-0-9801942-4-1(5))* ACS, LLC Amica Creative Services.

Holt Ayriss, Linda. E Is for Evergreen: A Washington State Alphabet. Smith, Roland & Smith, Marie. 2004. (State Ser.). (ENG.). 40p. (J). 17.95 *(978-1-58536-143-4(7))* Sleeping Bear Pr.

Holt, Lindsey. Harold's Adventures. Love, Makada H. 2008. 92p. pap. 10.99 *(978-1-4343-6875-1(0))* AuthorHouse.

Holt, Steven. Busy Piggies. Holt, Steven, photos by. Schindel, John. 2006. (Busy Book Ser.). 20p. (J). (gr. k — 1). bds. 7.99 *(978-1-58246-169-4(4)*, Tricycle Pr.) Random Hse. Children's Bks.

Holt, Steven, photos by. Busy Barnyard. Schindel, John. 2006. (Busy Book Ser.). (ENG., 20p. (J). (— 1). bds. 7.99 *(978-1-58246-168-7(6)*, Tricycle Pr.) Random Hse. Children's Bks.
—Busy Birdies. Schindel, John. 2010. (Busy Book Ser.). (ENG., 20p. (J). (gr. -1 — 1). bds. 7.99 *(978-1-58246-317-9(4)*, Tricycle Pr.) Random Hse. Children's Bks.
—Busy Bunnies. Schindel, John. 2008. (Busy Book Ser.). 20p. (J). (— 1). bds. 6.99 *(978-1-58246-242-4(9)*, Knopf Bks. for Young Readers) Random Hse. Children's Bks.

Holt, Steven, photos by. Busy Chickens. Holt, Steven. Schindel, John. 2009. (Busy Book Ser.). 20p. (J). (gr. -1 — 1). bds. 6.99 *(978-1-58246-275-2(5)*, Knopf Bks. for Young Readers) Random Hse. Children's Bks.

Holt, Terry L. Little Miss Talk to the Trees. Anderson, Gertrude Richmond. 2016. (ENG.). (J). pap. 9.75 *(978-1-945344-02-2(4))* M.O.R.E. Pubs.

Holtfreter, Nastja. Push Puzzles: in the Woods. 2016. (ENG.). 10p. (J). (gr. -1 — 1). bds. 7.99 *(978-1-4998-0349-5(4))* Little Bee Books Inc.
—Push Puzzles: on the Farm. 2016. (ENG.). 10p. (J). (gr. -1 — 1). bds. 7.99 *(978-1-4998-0348-8(6))* Little Bee Books Inc.

Holtfreter, Nastja. Colorful World: Farm. Holtfreter, Nastja. 2017. (ENG.). 14p. (J). bds. 5.99 *(978-1-61067-578-9(9))* Kane Miller.
—Colorful World: Forest. Holtfreter, Nastja. 2017. (ENG.). 14p. (J). bds. 5.99 *(978-1-61067-577-2(0))* Kane Miller.

—Colorful World: Mountain. Holtfreter, Nastja. 2017. (ENG.). 14p. (J). bds. 5.99 *(978-1-61067-579-6(7))* Kane Miller.
—Colorful World: Sea. Holtfreter, Nastja. 2017. (ENG.). 14p. (J). bds. 5.99 *(978-1-61067-576-5(2))* Kane Miller.
Holtsberg, Sarah. Dagah: The Great Fish. McCarty, Victoria. 2016. (ENG.). (J). pap. 12.95 *(978-1-61244-491-8(1))* Halo Publishing International.
Holtsclaw, Josh. Jurassic Park. Crichton, Michael & Koepp, David. 2018. (J). *(978-1-5444-0887-3(0)*, Golden Bks.) Random Hse. Children's Bks.
—Jurassic Park Little Golden Book (Jurassic Park) Kaplan, Arie. 2018. (Little Golden Book Ser.). (ENG.). 24p. (J). (-k). 4.99 *(978-0-525-58068-3(9)*, Golden Bks.) Random Hse. Children's Bks.
Holtsclaw, Josh, jt. illus. see RH Disney Staff.
Holub, Joan. All about You with Inspector McQ. Mullins, Patty Rutland. 2004. (Treasure Tree Ser.). 32p. (J). *(978-0-7166-1646-7(7))* World Bk., Inc.
—Hot Cha-Cha!, Nobisso, Josephine. 2009. (ENG.). 32p. (J). (gr. k-2). 16.95 *(978-0-940112-18-6(3))* Gingerbread Hse.
—I'm Not Scared. Hall, Kirsten. 2003. (My First Reader Ser.). (ENG.). 32p. (J). 18.50 *(978-0-516-22929-4(X)*, Children's Pr.) Scholastic Library Publishing.
Holub, Joan. My First Book of Sign Language. Holub, Joan. 2004. (ENG.). 32p. (J). (gr. -1-3). pap. 4.99 *(978-0-439-63582-0(9))* Scholastic, Inc.
Holub, Joan & Fisher, Cynthia. Deena y Su Centavo de la Suerte (Deena's Lucky Penny) Money. deRubertis, Barbara. 2007. (Math Matters en Español Ser.). (SPA.). 32p. (J). (gr. k-2). pap. 5.95 *(978-1-57565-249-8(8))* Astra Publishing Hse.
—Deena's Lucky Penny: Money. deRubertis, Barbara. 2006. (Math Matters ® Ser.). (ENG.). 32p. (J). (gr. k-2). pap. 5.95 *(978-1-57565-091-3(6))* Astra Publishing Hse.
Holyfield, John. Belle, the Last Mule at Gee's Bend: A Civil Rights Story. Stroud, Bettye & Ramsey, Calvin Alexander. 2016. 32p. (J). (gr. k-3). 7.99 *(978-0-7636-8769-4(3))* Candlewick Pr.
—The Hallelujah Flight. Bildner, Phil. 2010. (ENG.). 32p. (J). (gr. k-3). 17.99 *(978-0-399-24789-7(0)*, G.P. Putnam's Sons Books for Young Readers) Penguin Young Readers Group.
—Hard-Times Jar. Smothers, Ethel Footman & Smothers, Ethel F. 2003. (ENG.). 32p. (J). (gr. k-3). 18.99 *(978-0-374-32852-8(8)*, 900021204, Farrar, Straus & Giroux (BYR)) Farrar, Straus & Giroux.
—Mahalia Jackson: Walking with Kings & Queens. Nolan, Nina. 2015. (ENG.). 32p. (J). (gr. -1-3). 17.99 *(978-0-06-087944-0(0))* HarperCollins Pubs.
—Meet Miss Fancy. Latham, Irene. 2019. 32p. (J). (gr. k-3). 17.99 *(978-0-399-54668-6(5)*, G.P. Putnam's Sons Books for Young Readers) Penguin Young Readers Group.
Holyoake, Corrina. A Flamboyance of Flamingos. King, Sally. 2019. (Reading in Rhyme Ser.: Vol. 2). (ENG.). 40p. (J). *(978-1-78623-455-1(6))* Grosvenor Hse. Publishing Ltd.
Holzmann, Angela. The First Good Shepherd: Psalm 23 for Children. Steinkühler, Martina. 2015. (ENG.). 28p. (J). 12.95 *(978-0-8091-6774-6(3))* Paulist Pr.
Holzwarth, Devon. Papa, Daddy, & Riley. Kirst, Seamus. 2020. (J). ***(978-1-4338-3239-0(9)***, Magination Pr.) American Psychological Assn.
Hom, John. Diego & Papi to the Rescue. Wax, Wendy. 2007. (Go, Diego, Go! Ser.: 3). (ENG.). 24p. (J). pap. 3.99 *(978-1-4169-2781-5(6)*, Simon Spotlight/Nickelodeon) Simon Spotlight/Nickelodeon.
—Diego y Papi al Rescate. Wax, Wendy. Ziegler, Argentina Palacios, tr. 2008. (Go, Diego, Go! Ser.).Tr. of Diego & Papi to the Rescue. (SPA.). 24p. (J). (gr. -1-2). pap. 3.99 *(978-1-4169-5044-8(3)*, Libros Para Ninos) Libros Para Ninos.
Hom, Nancy. Nine-In-One:Grr! Grr! Spagnoli, Cathy. 2013. (ENG.). 32p. (J). (gr. -1-5). pap. 9.95 *(978-0-89239-048-9(4))* Lee & Low Bks., Inc.
Homberg, Ansgar. Days of Faith Assignment Book & Student Planner. Fischer, Carl. 2003. 108p. (J). spiral bd. 4.99 *(978-0-89837-232-8(1)*, 9804) Pflaum Publishing Group.
Hombs, Alexandra. Sassie's New Home: A Coloring Book. Albright, Erin. 2020. (ENG.). 22p. (J). (gr. k-5). pap. 11.95 ***(978-0-578-68069-9(6))*** Albright Creative, LLC.
Homfray, Nick. The Adventures of Eric Seagull. Greenham, Caz. 2013. 40p. pap. *(978-1-78132-093-8(4))* SilverWood Bks.
—The Adventures of Eric Seagull 'Story-Teller' Book 2 a Fairy's Wish. Greenham, Caz. 2013. 48p. pap. *(978-1-78132-110-2(8))* SilverWood Bks.
Honasan, Violeta. The Boy That Wanted Clean Teeth. Banks, Glenn. Haltar, Batsuuri, tr. 2017. (MON.). (J). pap. 9.98 *(978-1-943417-23-0(7))* B-Bright publishing.
—The Boy That Wanted Clean Teeth. Banks, Glenn. Tayyab, Abdullah, tr. 2017. (URD.). (J). pap. 9.98 *(978-1-943417-24-7(5))* B-Bright publishing.
Hondel, Gary. Pudgee Woodchuck. Hondel, Gary. 2007. 36p. per. 14.95 *(978-1-59858-323-6(9))* Dog Ear Publishing, LLC.
Hondru, Ovi. Robert Louis Stevenson's Treasure Island: My Sea Adventure Israel Hands. Fuerst, Jeffrey B. & Benchmark Education Co., LLC. 2014. (Text Connections Ser.). (J). (gr. 3). *(978-1-4509-9652-5(3))* Benchmark Education Co.
—Robert Louis Stevenson's Treasure Lsland - My Sea Adventure - Israel Hands: Set Of 6. Fuerst, Jeffrey B. 2014. (Text Connections Ser.). (J). (gr. 3). 49.00 net. *(978-1-4900-0128-9(X))* Benchmark Education Co.
Honesta, Kathrin. One Good Thing about America. Freeman, Ruth. 2017. (ENG.). 160p. (J). (gr. 3-7). 16.95 *(978-0-8234-3695-8(0))* Holiday Hse., Inc.
—She Spoke: 14 Women Who Raised Their Voices & Changed the World. Bernardi, Manuela & MacMillan, Kathy. 2019. (ENG.). 32p. (gr. k-3). 24.99 *(978-1-64170-131-0(5)*, 550131) Familius LLC.
Honey, Elizabeth. Asmir No Quiere Pistolas. Mattingley, Christobel. Balseiro, Maria Luisa, tr.Tr. of No Gun for Asmir. (SPA.). 129p. (J). (gr. 5-8). pap. 9.95 *(978-84-204-4891-6(5))* Santillana USA Publishing Co., Inc.
Honey, Elizabeth. That's Not a Daffodil! Honey, Elizabeth. 2011. (ENG.). 32p. (J). (gr. -1-k). 19.99 *(978-1-74237-248-8(1))* Allen & Unwin AUS. Dist: Independent Pubs. Group.
—To the Boy in Berlin. Honey, Elizabeth. Brandt, Heike. 2007. (ENG.). 288p. (J). (gr. 5-9). 12.99 *(978-1-74175-004-1(0))* Allen & Unwin AUS. Dist: Independent Pubs. Group.
Honey, Elizabeth & Johnson, Sue. I'm Still Awake, Still! Honey, Elizabeth. 2009. (ENG.). 32p. (J). (gr. k-1). 19.99 *(978-1-74175-321-9(X))* Allen & Unwin AUS. Dist: Independent Pubs. Group.
Honeycutt, Pam. Pj's Ponies. Honeycutt, Pam. 2018. (ENG.). 110p. (J). (gr. k-6). 24.95 *(978-1-946540-28-7(5))*; pap. 14.95 *(978-1-946540-29-4(3))* Strategic Book Publishing & Rights Agency (SBPRA).
Hong, Chan-joo. What Are Shadows? Shadow. Kim, Seong-Eun. 2020. (Science Storybooks Ser.). (ENG.). 32p. (J). (gr. k-4). lib. bdg. 27.99 *(978-1-925235-53-1(X)*, Big and SMALL) ChoiceMaker Pty. Ltd., The AUS. Dist: Lerner Publishing Group.
—What Are Shadows? Shadow. Kim, Seong-Eun. 2020. (Science Storybooks Ser.). (ENG.). 32p. (J). (gr. k-4). pap. 8.99 *(978-1-925235-49-4(1)*, Big and SMALL) ChoiceMaker Pty. Ltd., The AUS. Dist: Lerner Publishing Group.
Hong, Denise, jt. illus. see Lopez, Paul.
Hong, Gyeong-Ju. Tomemos en Cuenta Los Sentidos. Kim, Hyeong-Suk. 2018. (Click Click: Ciencia B�sica / Basic Science Ser.). (SPA.). 32p. (J). pap. 17.99 ***(978-1-64101-218-8(8))*** Santillana USA Publishing Co., Inc.
Hong, Jess. From Maybe to Forever: An Adoption Story. Gold, M. L. & Fong, N. V. 2020. (ENG.). 32p. (J). (gr. -1-2). 18.99 ***(978-1-939547-75-0(X))*** Creston Bks.
Hong, Lily T. El Senor Sol y el Senor Mar, Level 3. Butler, Andrea. Flor Ada, Alma, tr. 2003. (Dejame Leer Ser.). (SPA.). 16p. (J). (gr. -1-3). 6.50 *(978-0-673-36302-2(3)*, Good Year Bks.) Celebration Pr.
Hong, Lily Toy. Two of Everything. Hong, Lily Toy. 2017. (ENG.). 32p. (J). (gr. -1-3). pap. 7.99 *(978-0-8075-8158-2(5)*, 807581585) Whitman, Albert & Co.
Hong, Lily Toy. Two of Everything. Hong, Lily Toy, retold by. 2012. (J). *(978-1-61913-138-5(2))* Weigl Pubs., Inc.
Hong, Nari. Days with Dad. 2017. (ENG.). 40p. (J). (gr. -1-3). 16.95 *(978-1-59270-233-6(3))* Enchanted Lion Bks., LLC.
Hong, Nicholas. Meddy Teddy: A Mindful Journey. Jordan, Apple. 2018. 32p. (J). (gr. -1-3). 17.99 *(978-1-63565-046-4(1)*, 9781635650464, Rodale Kids) Random Hse. Children's Bks.
Hong, Richard. The Book of Bad Habits for Young (and Not So Young!) Men & Women: How to Chuck the Worst & Turn the Rest to Your Advantage. Hawkins, Frank C. & Laube, Greta L. B. 2010. (ENG.). 148p. (J). (gr. 7). pap. 12.95 *(978-0-9793219-3-1(X))* Big Book Pr., LLC.
Hong, Sung. Sean Awesome: A Mission at Night. Hwang, Jiwon. 2018. (Sean Awesome Ser.: 1). (ENG.). 40p. (J). (gr. -1-2). 15.95 *(978-1-77229-029-5(7))* Simply Read Bks. CAN. Dist: Ingram Publisher Services.
Honor Roberts, Ley. My Bike Ride: Band 02A/Red a (Collins Big Cat) Kelly, Maoliosa. 2006. (Collins Big Cat Ser.). (ENG.). 16p. (J). (gr. -1-k). pap. 6.99 *(978-0-00-718661-7(4))* HarperCollins Pubs. Ltd. GBR. Dist: Independent Pubs. Group.
—My First Train Trip. Rickards, Lynne. 2016. (Cambridge Reading Adventures Ser.). (ENG.). 16p. pap. 7.37 *(978-1-107-57594-3(X))* Cambridge Univ. Pr.
Honore, Paul. Tales from Silver Lands. Finger, Charles J. 2017. (ENG.). 256p. pap. 9.99 *(978-0-486-82093-4(9)*, 820939) Dover Pubns., Inc.
Honsinger, Alise. Leonard Lou: Beautiful, Brave, Strong, & True. Honsinger, Linda. 2012. 38p. 24.95 *(978-1-4626-6872-4(0))* America Star Bks.
Hoobler, David. Zonk & the Secret Lagoon: The Further Adventures of Zonk the Dreaming Tortoise. Hoobler, David. l.t. ed. 2005. 32p. (J). lib. bdg. 18.95 *(978-0-9706537-1-0(9))* Zonk Galleries and Pubns.
Hood, George W. The Chinese Fairy Book. Wilhelm, Richard, ed. Martens, Frederick H., tr. 2008. (Dover Children's Classics Ser.). (ENG.). 224p. (J). (gr. 4-7). pap. 10.95 *(978-0-486-45435-1(5))* Dover Pubns., Inc.
—The Swedish Fairy Book: [Illustrated Edition]. Stroebe, Clara, ed. 2019. (ENG.). 206p. (J). (gr. k-5). pap. *(978-605-7876-88-1(1))* Uhrayoglu, Murat E Kitap Projesi.
Hood, George W. The Swedish Fairy Book: [Illustrated Edition]. Stroebe, Clara, ed. 2019. (ENG.). 206p. (J). (gr. k-5). ***(978-605-7748-86-7(7))*** Uhrayoglu, Murat E Kitap Projesi.
Hood, Jack B. The Legend of Holly Boy. rev. ed. 38p. (J). (gr. -1-12). pap. 3.95 *(978-0-9640474-2-6(X))* Latino, Frank Publishing Co.
Hood, Jacomb, jt. illus. see Crane, Walter.
Hood, Joyce. Lightning Bugs. Ketch, Ann. 2003. (ENG.). 12p. (gr. k-1). pap. 7.95 *(978-1-57874-038-3(X)*, Kaeden Bks.) Kaeden Corp.
Hood, Morag. Aalfred & Aalbert. Hood, Morag. 2019. (ENG.). 32p. (J). (gr. -1-3). 16.95 *(978-1-68263-121-8(4))* Peachtree Publishing Co. Inc.
Hood, Philip. Supercroc Found. Walker, Sally M. 2005. (On My Own Science Ser.). 48p. (J). (gr. 3-7). lib. bdg. 25.26 *(978-1-57505-760-6(3))* Lerner Publishing Group.
—SuperCroc Found. Walker, Sally M. 2006. (On My Own Science Ser.). 48p. (J). (gr. 3-7). per. 6.95 *(978-1-57505-852-8(9)*, First Avenue Editions) Lerner Publishing Group.
Hood, Philip, jt. illus. see Rane, Walter.
Hood, Shayne. Bear's Lullaby. Hauenstein, Katie. 2019. (ENG.). 24p. (J). pap. 9.50 *(978-1-0932-7956-6(7))* Independently Published.
Hooff Andreozzi, Maremi. I. M. Green. Hooff, Gudren. 2011. 32p. (J). pap. 12.00 *(978-0-9825922-6-7(4))* Commonwealth Books of Virginia, LLC.
Hoofnagle, Therese. Bug, Bug, Where's the Bug? Dawson, J. M. 2008. 26p. pap. 24.95 *(978-1-60474-365-4(4))* America Star Bks.
Hooge, J. R. Leafensong: First Telling. Hooge, J. R. 2019. (Leafensong Ser.: Vol. 1). (ENG.). 332p. (YA). (gr. 7-12). pap. 14.99 ***(978-1-947927-02-5(7))*** Sautrelle Publishing Co.
Hoogstad, Alice. How Much Does the Gray in an Elephant Weigh? Van Os, Erik & Van Lieshout, Elle. 2013. (ENG.). 32p. (J). (gr. -1). 17.95 *(978-1-935954-27-9(X)*, 9781935954279) Lemniscaat USA.
Hook, Christa. British Infantryman in South Africa 1877-81. Castle, Ian. 2003. (Warrior Ser.: 83). 64p. pap. 20.00 *(978-1-84176-555-6(4)*, 900167841, Osprey) Bloomsbury Publishing USA.
Hook, Frances, jt. illus. see Hook, Richard.
Hook, Katie Jo. Momma Loves You. Hook, Katie Jo. 2015. (ENG.). 32p. pap. 9.99 *(978-1-63047-495-9(9))* Morgan James Publishing.
Hook, Richard. Martin Luther: Hero of Faith. Nohl, Frederick. 2003. 160p. (YA). pap. 9.99 *(978-0-7586-0592-4(7))* Concordia Publishing Hse.
Hook, Richard & Hook, Frances. Jesus the Friend of Children. 6th ed. 2006. (David C Cook Read to Me Bible Stories Ser.). 112p. (J). (gr. 3-7). 14.99 *(978-0-7814-4390-6(3))* Cook, David C.
Hooper, Ashley Kay. Hungry, Hungry Baby. Knox, Arron. 2020. (ENG.). 30p. (J). pap. 10.99 ***(978-1-6534-8159-0(5))*** Independently Published.
Hooper, Ashley Kay. Maisie. -Berggren, Monique Moore. 2019. (ENG.). 36p. (J). pap. 10.00 *(978-1-0776-8066-1(X))* Independently Published.
Hooper, Hadley. Around America to Win the Vote: Two Suffragists, a Kitten, & 10,000 Miles. Rockliff, Mara. 40p. (J). (gr. k-3). 2019. 7.99 *(978-1-5362-0836-8(1))*; 2016. 16.99 *(978-0-7636-7893-7(7))* Candlewick Pr.
—Here Come the Girl Scouts! Corey, Shana. 2012. (ENG.). 40p. (J). (gr. -1-3). 17.99 *(978-0-545-34278-0(3)*, Scholastic Pr.) Scholastic, Inc.
—How I Discovered Poetry. Nelson, Marilyn. 2014. (ENG.). 112p. (YA). (gr. 7). 17.99 *(978-0-8037-3304-6(6)*, Dial Bks) Penguin Young Readers Group.
—The Iridescence of Birds. MacLachlan, Patricia. 2014. (ENG.). 40p. (J). (gr. -1-3). 18.99 *(978-1-59643-948-1(3)*, 900123811) Roaring Brook Pr.
—Mabel & Sam at Home. Urban, Linda. 2018. (ENG.). 60p. (J). (gr. k-3). 17.99 *(978-1-4521-3996-8(2))* Chronicle Bks. LLC.
—A Small Thing ... but Big. Johnston, Tony. 2016. (ENG.). 40p. (J). 17.99 *(978-1-62672-256-9(0)*, 900147871) Roaring Brook Pr.
—Two Brothers, Four Hands. Greenberg, Jan & Jordan, Sandra. 2019. 64p. (J). (gr. 2-5). 21.99 *(978-0-8234-4170-9(9)*, Neal Porter Bks) Holiday Hse., Inc.
Hooper, Hadley & Stryk, Suzanne. Sow What? Person, Naomi et al. 2009. 94p. (YA). pap. *(978-0-88441-735-4(2))* Girl Scouts of the USA.
Hoopes, Natalie. Alice's Magic Garden: Before the Rabbit Hole ... Herz, Henry. 2018. (ENG.). 32p. 16.99 *(978-1-64170-032-0(7)*, 550032) Familius LLC.
—Book. Miles, David W. 2015. (ENG.). 32p. (J). 16.95 *(978-1-939629-65-4(9)*, 552965) Familius LLC.
Hooson, Neil. Snazzy Cat Capers. Kent, Deanna. 2018. (Snazzy Cat Capers Ser.: 1). (ENG.). 224p. (J). 13.99 *(978-1-250-14343-3(8)*, 900180506) Imprint IND. Dist: Macmillan.
—Snazzy Cat Capers. Kent, Deanna. 2020. (Snazzy Cat Capers Ser.: 1). (ENG.). 240p. (J). pap. 6.99 *(978-1-250-21114-9(X)*, 900180507) Square Fish.
Hooson, Neil. Snazzy Cat Capers: Meow or Never. Kent, Deanna. 2020. (Snazzy Cat Capers Ser.: 3). (ENG.). 224p. (J). 13.99 ***(978-1-250-14349-5(7)***, 900180517) Imprint IND. Dist: Macmillan.
Hooson, Neil. Snazzy Cat Capers: the Fast & the Furriest. Kent, Deanna. 2019. (Snazzy Cat Capers Ser.: 2). (ENG.). 224p. (J). 13.99 *(978-1-250-14347-1(0)*, 900180514) Imprint IND. Dist: Macmillan.
Hooson, Neil. Snazzy Cat Capers: the Fast & the Furriest. Kent, Deanna. 2020. (Snazzy Cat Capers Ser.: 2). (ENG.). 240p. (J). pap. 6.99 ***(978-1-250-61866-5(5)***, 900180515) Square Fish.
Hoover, Charity. Days with Mary. Martin, Mabel. 2015. (ENG.). 159p. (J). (gr. -1). 9.25 *(978-0-7399-2515-7(6))* Rod & Staff Pubs., Inc.
—Grandma's Goose. Martin, Mary. 2012. 188p. *(978-0-7399-2452-5(4))* Rod & Staff Pubs., Inc.
—Olive & Her Lost Friend. Boll, Darlene. 2013. 176p. (J). *(978-0-7399-2463-1(X))* Rod & Staff Pubs., Inc.
—Olive & Macy. Boll, Darlene. 2015. (ENG.). 182p. (J). (gr. -1). 9.50 *(978-0-7399-2506-5(7))* Rod & Staff Pubs., Inc.
Hoover, Dave, et al. Levi Strauss & Blue Jeans, 1 vol. Olson, Nathan. 2006. (Inventions & Discovery Ser.). (ENG.). 32p. (J). (gr. 3-9). 31.32 *(978-0-7368-6484-8(9)*, Capstone Pr.) Capstone.
Hoover, Dave & Anderson, Bill. Harriet Tubman & the Underground Railroad, 1 vol. Martin, Michael J. 2005. (Graphic History Ser.). (ENG.). 32p. (J). (gr. 3-9). per. 8.10 *(978-0-7368-5245-6(X)*, Capstone Pr.) Capstone.
Hoover, Dave & Raimondi, Pablo. Uncanny Origins: Mutants & Monsters. 2019. (ENG.). 256p. (J). (gr. 3-7). pap. 12.99 *(978-1-302-91983-2(0))* Marvel Worldwide, Inc.
Hoover, Dave, jt. illus. see Barnett, Charles, III.
Hoover, Rowena. The Joy of Forgiveness. Fitzsimmons, Karen. 2017. (ENG.). 46p. (J). 17.00 *(978-0-9994887-1-3(6))* Write Place, The.
Hoover, Sandra J. Bailey's Path. Javor, Ronald S. 2019. (ENG.). 46p. (J). pap. 10.95 *(978-1-0729-6697-5(2))* Independently Published.
Hoover, William. The Contagious Yawn: A Journey Around the World. Barmettler, Timothy. 2017. (J). pap. *(978-1-63293-189-4(3))* Sunstone Pr.
Hop, Nguyen Thi, jt. illus. see Ames, Philippe.
Hope, Adrian. The Old Pincushion (Illustrated Edition) Molesworth. 2018. (ENG.). 104p. (J). pap. *(978-1-4068-8749-5(8))* Echo Library.
Hope, Bill. Buzzbomb: Adventures in the Forbidden Zone. Matheson, Jason. 2013. 80p. (J). pap. *(978-1-925011-26-5(7))* Australian Self Publishing Group/ Inspiring Pubs.
Hope, Lorraine. Greta. Roberts, Adele A. 2018. (ENG.). 26p. (J). pap. 10.00 *(978-1-7276-2851-7(9))* CreateSpace Independent Publishing Platform.
Hope, Marie, jt. illus. see Garrett, De'coriyanna.
Hope, Michelle. When Bees Win. Galjanic, Lisa. 2007. (J). 9.95 *(978-1-933532-04-2(1))* LSG Pubns.
—When Caterpillars Grow Up. Galjanic, Lisa. 2007. (J). 9.95 *(978-1-933532-03-5(3))* LSG Pubns.
—When Fish Are Mean. Galjanic, Lisa. 2007. (J). 9.95 *(978-1-933532-01-1(7))* LSG Pubns.
—When Flowers Dance. Galjanic, Lisa. 2007. (J). 9.95 *(978-1-933532-05-9(X))* LSG Pubns.
—When Leaves Die. Galjanic, Lisa. 2007. (J). 9.95 *(978-1-933532-00-4(9))* LSG Pubns.
—When Squirrels Try. Galjanic, Lisa. 2007. (J). 9.95 *(978-1-933532-02-8(5))* LSG Pubns.
Hope, Mister. Uncle Birthday. Hope, Rachael. 2016. (ENG.). (J). pap. *(978-1-78222-492-1(0))* Paragon Publishing, Rothersthorpe.
Hopgood, Andrew. Let's Grow a Garden. Reynolds, Alison. 2009. (Save Our Planet! Ser.). 12p. (J). (gr. -1-3). bds. 11.40 *(978-1-60754-412-8(1))* Windmill Bks.
—Let's Save Water. Reynolds, Alison. 2009. (Save Our Planet! Ser.). 12p. (J). (gr. -1-3). bds. 11.40 *(978-1-60754-413-5(X))* Windmill Bks.
—Let's Turn It Off. Reynolds, Alison. 2009. (Save Our Planet! Ser.). 12p. (J). (gr. -1-3). bds. 11.40 *(978-1-60754-414-2(8))* Windmill Bks.
—Let's Use It Again. Reynolds, Alison. 2009. (Save Our Planet! Ser.). 12p. (J). (gr. -1-3). bds. 11.40 *(978-1-60754-415-9(6))* Windmill Bks.
—Water. Walker, Kate. 2012. (Investigating Earth Ser.). 32p. (gr. 2-2). 29.50 *(978-1-60870-562-7(5))* Cavendish Square Publishing LLC.
Hopgood, Kevin. The Shocking Story of Electricity. Claybourne, Anna. 2006. (Young Reading Series 2 Ser.). 63p. (J). (gr. 2-5). pap. 5.99 *(978-0-7945-1248-4(8)*, Usborne) EDC Publishing.
Hopgood, Tim. Fabulous Frogs. Jenkins, Martin. (Read & Wonder Ser.). (ENG.). 32p. (J). (gr. k-3). 2018. 7.99 *(978-0-7636-9970-3(5))*; 2016. 16.99 *(978-0-7636-8100-5(8))* Candlewick Pr.
—Moon River. Williams, Andy. 2018. (ENG.). 32p. (J). 17.99 *(978-1-250-15900-7(8)*, 900185546, Holt, Henry & Co. Bks. For Young Readers) Holt, Henry & Co.
—Singing in the Rain. 2017. (ENG.). 32p. (J). 17.99 *(978-1-250-12770-9(X)*, 900175515, Holt, Henry & Co. Bks. For Young Readers) Holt, Henry & Co.
—Walking in a Winter Wonderland. Smith, Richard B. & Bernard, Felix. 2016. (ENG.). 32p. (J). 17.99 *(978-1-62779-304-9(6)*, 900146038, Holt, Henry & Co. Bks. For Young Readers) Holt, Henry & Co.
—Walking in a Winter Wonderland: Based on the Song by Felix Bernard & Richard B. Smith. Smith, Richard B. & Bernard, Felix. 2016. (J). *(978-0-19-275988-7(4))* Holt, Henry & Co.
—What a Wonderful World. Thiele, Bob & Weiss, George David. 2014. (ENG.). 32p. (J). (gr. -1-k). 17.99 *(978-1-62779-254-7(6)*, 900144000, Holt, Henry & Co. Bks. For Young Readers) Holt, Henry & Co.
Hopgood, Tim. Wonderful World ABC. Hopgood, Tim. 2020. (ENG.). 26p. (J). bds. 9.99 *(978-1-250-23881-8(1)*, 900211036, Holt, Henry & Co. Bks. For Young Readers) Holt, Henry & Co.
—Wow! Said the Owl: A Book about Colors. Hopgood, Tim. 2009. (ENG.). 32p. (J). (gr. -1-k). 17.99 *(978-0-374-38518-7(1)*, 900061586, Farrar, Straus & Giroux (BYR)) Farrar, Straus & Giroux.
Hopkins, Colby. There's a Bully in the White House. Hopkins, Colby. 2018. (ENG.). 36p. (J). (gr. 5-6). 13.99 *(978-0-9891086-2-1(7))* Humanness Project Pr., The.
Hopkins, Emily. Alphabear. Willeford, Tammy Jean. 2013. 32p. pap. 8.00 *(978-1-62080-998-3(2))* Hopkins Publishing.
Hopkins, Jeff. I Like Things. Hillert, Margaret. 2016. (BeginningtoRead Ser.). (ENG.). 32p. (J). (gr. 1-2). 22.60 *(978-1-59953-817-4(2))* Norwood Hse. Pr.
Hopkins, Joseph. Luna Lucy. Van Der Wielen, Lisa. 2018. (Luna Lucy Ser.: Vol. 1). (ENG.). 26p. (J). (gr. k-4). pap. *(978-1-5272-2863-4(0))* Van Der Wielen, Lisa.
—Morris the Stealing Magpie. Parkhouse, Nicola. 2017. (ENG.). 28p. (J). pap. 10.49 *(978-1-9998868-0-6(1))* Ormond, Jennifer.
—The Rat & the Cat, Well, Fancy That! Parkhouse, Nicola. 2018. (ENG.). 36p. (J). pap. *(978-1-9998868-1-3(X))* Parkhouse, Nicola.
—Where Is Maggie's Moo? Parkhouse, Nicola. 2019. (Tumbledown Farm Collection: Vol. 2). (ENG.). 30p. (J). pap. *(978-1-9998868-4-4(4))* Lane, Betty.
Hopkins, Simon, jt. illus. see Farrelly, Linda.
Hopkins, Simon, jt. illus. see Hawthorn, Paul.
Hopman, Philip. Mikis & the Donkey. Tak, Bibi Dumon. 2014. (ENG.). 89p. (J). 13.00 *(978-0-8028-5430-8(3)*, Eerdmans Bks For Young Readers) Eerdmans, William B. Publishing Co.
—Soldier Bear. Tak, Bibi Dumon & Dumon Tak, Bibi. 2011. (ENG.). 158p. (J). 13.00 *(978-0-8028-5375-2(7)*, Eerdmans Bks For Young Readers) Eerdmans, William B. Publishing Co.
—Soldier Bear. Tak, Bibi Dumon. Watkinson, Laura, tr. 2013. (ENG.). (J). (gr. 4-7). lib. bdg. 19.10 *(978-1-62765-455-5(0))* Perfection Learning Corp.
—Spider Mcdrew & the Egyptians: Band 12/Copper (Collins Big Cat), Bd. 12. Durant, Alan. 2007. (Collins Big Cat Ser.). (ENG.). 32p. (J). (gr. 2-3). pap., pap. 10.99 *(978-0-00-723076-1(1))* HarperCollins Pubs. Ltd. GBR. Dist: Independent Pubs. Group.
—Spider's Big Match: Band 13/Topaz (Collins Big Cat) Durant, Alan. 2007. (Collins Big Cat Ser.). (ENG.). 32p. (J). (gr. 2-4). pap. 9.99 *(978-0-00-723081-5(8))* HarperCollins Pubs. Ltd. GBR. Dist: Independent Pubs. Group.

H

—Tom the Tamer. Veldkamp, Tjibbe. 2011. (ENG.). 32p. (J). (gr. -1). 16.95 *(978-1-935954-05-7(9),* 9781935954057) Lemniscaat USA.

—The Usborne First Book of Art. Dickins, Rosie. 2008. (Usborne First Book Ser.). 62p. (J). (gr. -1-3). 18.99 *(978-0-7945-2035-9(9),* Usborne) EDC Publishing.

Hoppe, Paul. Good Vibrations: A Children's Picture Book. Love, Mike & Wilson, Brian. 2020. (LyricPop Ser.). 32p. (J). 16.95 *(978-1-61775-787-7(X))* Akashic Bks.

—Last-But-Not-Least Lola & a Knot the Size of Texas. Pakkala, Christine. (Last-But-Not-Least Lola Ser.). (J). (gr. 2-5). 2018. 168p. pap. 9.99 *(978-1-62979-890-5(8));* 2016. (ENG.). 169p. 16.95 *(978-1-62979-324-5(8))* Boyds Mills Pr.

—Last-But-Not-Least Lola & the Cupcake Queens. Pakkala, Christine. 2015. (Last-But-Not-Least Lola Ser.). (ENG.). 168p. (J). (gr. 2-5). 16.95 *(978-1-62091-596-7(0),* 1396889) Boyds Mills Pr.

—Last-But-Not-Least Lola & the Wild Chicken. Pakkala, Christine. (Last-But-Not-Least Lola Ser.). (ENG.). 216p. (J). (gr. 2-5). 2015. pap. 7.95 *(978-1-62979-404-4(X));* 2014. 15.95 *(978-1-59078-983-4(0))* Boyds Mills Pr.

—Last-But-Not-Least Lola Going Green. Pakkala, Christine. (Last-But-Not-Least Lola Ser.). (ENG.). 192p. (J). (gr. 2-5). 2014. pap. 9.99 *(978-1-62979-113-5(X));* 2013. 15.95 *(978-1-59078-935-3(0))* Boyds Mills Pr.

—Metal Man. Reynolds, Aaron. 2010. (ENG.). 32p. (J). (gr. k-3). pap. 7.95 *(978-1-58089-151-6(9))* Charlesbridge Publishing, Inc.

—Neymar: a Soccer Dream Come True. Javaherbin, Mina. 2018. (ENG.). 32p. (J). 16.99 *(978-0-374-31066-0(1),* 900193748, Farrar, Straus & Giroux (BYR)) Farrar, Straus & Giroux.

Hopper, Andy Lee. Bleep the Purple Bear. Hopper, Bobby E. 2009. 36p. pap. 18.99 *(978-1-4389-1908-9(5))* AuthorHouse.

Hopper, Billy. The Dynamic Dinosaur of Faith's History Vol. I: From Christ to 1000 AD. Bertch, David P. & Bertch, Barbara A. Martin, Terry & Martin, Dyna, eds. (Roots of the Past Ser.: Bk. 1). 150p. (J). (gr. 6). stu. ed. 9.95 *(978-0-9634472-4-1(6))* Good Works Pr.

Hopper, Pegge. Clever Dog. Finney, Jefferson. 2007. 32p. (J). pap. 15.95 *(978-1-56647-845-8(6))* Mutual Publishing LLC.

Hopson, Keenan. The Blocks Come Out at Night. Garay, Javier. 2019. (ENG.). 34p. (J). (gr. k-3). pap. 9.99 ***(978-1-7335441-1-5(9));*** (Blocks Bks.: Vol. 1). 18.99 *(978-1-7335441-0-8(0))* Gil Harp Bks.

—The Blocks Get Lost in India. Garay, Javier. 2020. (Blocks Bks.: Vol. 2). (ENG.). 34p. (J). 18.99 ***(978-1-7335441-6-0(X))*** Gil Harp Bks.

—Los Bloques Salen de Noche/the Blocks Come Out at Night (Spanish) Garay, Javier. 2019. (Los Bloques / the Blocks Bks.: Vol. 1). (SPA.). 34p. (J). (gr. k-3). 18.99 ***(978-1-7335441-3-9(5));*** pap. 9.99 ***(978-1-7335441-4-6(3))*** Gil Harp Bks.

Hopson, Keenan. Racing Days. Crockett, Amanda. 2018. (ENG.). 32p. (J). pap. 15.97 *(978-1-7307-5101-1(6))* Independently Published.

Horacek, Judy. Bonnie & Ben Rhyme Again. Fox, Mem. 2020. (ENG.). 32p. (J). (-3). 17.99 *(978-1-5344-5352-4(0),* Beach Lane Bks.) Beach Lane Bks.

—Ducks Away! Fox, Mem. 2018. (ENG.). 32p. (J). (gr. -1-k). 16.99 *(978-1-338-18566-9(7),* Scholastic Pr.) Scholastic, Inc.

—Good Night, Sleep Tight. Fox, Mem. 2013. (ENG.). 32p. (J). (gr. -1-k). 16.99 *(978-0-545-53370-6(8),* Orchard Bks.) Scholastic, Inc.

—This & That. Fox, Mem. 2017. (ENG.). 32p. (J). (gr. -1-k). 17.99 *(978-1-338-03780-7(3),* Scholastic Pr.) Scholastic, Inc.

—Where Is the Green Sheep? Fox, Mem. 2019. (ENG.). 32p. (J). (— 1). bds. 8.99 *(978-1-328-48266-2(9),* 1715797, HMH Books For Young Readers) Houghton Mifflin Harcourt Publishing Co.

Horacek, Judy. Where Is the Green Sheep? (¿Dónde Está la Oveja Verde?) Horacek, Judy. Fox, Mem. 2010. (SPA.). 32p. (J). (gr. k — 1). bds. 4.99 *(978-0-547-39694-1(5),* 1427473) Houghton Mifflin Harcourt Publishing Co.

—Yellow Is My Color Star. Horacek, Judy. 2014. (ENG.). 32p. (J). (gr. -1-3). 16.99 *(978-1-4424-9299-8(6),* Beach Lane Bks.) Beach Lane Bks.

Horácek, Petr. Grumpy Duck. Dunbar, Joyce. 2019. (ENG.). 32p. (J). (gr. -1-2). 16.99 *(978-1-5362-0424-7(2))* Candlewick Pr.

—Little Moon's Christmas: Imagination - Objects. Kim, Cecil. Cowley, Joy, ed. 2015. (Step up - Creative Thinking Ser.). (ENG.). 32p. (gr. -1-2). 26.65 *(978-1-925246-11-7(6));* 7.99 *(978-1-925246-63-6(9));* 26.65 *(978-1-925246-37-7(X));* (J). 10.00 *(978-1-925186-39-0(3))* ChoiceMaker Pty. Ltd., The AUS. (Big and SMALL). Dist: Lerner Publishing Group.

—Song of the Wild: A First Book of Animals. Davies, Nicola. 2017. (ENG.). 108p. (J). (gr. -1-2). 22.00 *(978-0-7636-9160-8(7))* Candlewick Pr.

Horácek, Petr. Animal Opposites. Horácek, Petr. 2013. (ENG.). 20p. (J). (gr. -1-2). 15.99 *(978-0-7636-6776-4(5))* Candlewick Pr.

—Beep Beep. Horácek, Petr. 2008. (ENG.). 16p. (J). (gr. k-k). bds. 6.99 *(978-0-7636-3482-7(4))* Candlewick Pr.

—Beep Beep / Pip Pip. Horácek, Petr. 2019. 16p. (J). (-k). bds. 6.99 *(978-1-5362-0350-9(5))* Candlewick Pr.

—Blue Penguin. Horácek, Petr. 2016. (ENG.). 32p. (J). (gr. -1-2). 15.99 *(978-0-7636-9251-3(4))* Candlewick Pr.

—Butterfly Butterfly: A Book of Colors. Horácek, Petr. 2007. (ENG.). 16p. (J). (gr. -1-2). 15.99 *(978-0-7636-3343-1(7))* Candlewick Pr.

—Choo Choo. Horácek, Petr. 2008. (ENG.). 16p. (J). (gr. k-k). bds. 5.99 *(978-0-7636-3477-3(8))* Candlewick Pr.

—Choo Choo / Chuu Chuu. Horácek, Petr. 2019. 16p. (J). (-k). bds. 6.99 *(978-1-5362-0351-6(3))* Candlewick Pr.

—The Fly. Horácek, Petr. 2015. (ENG.). 32p. (J). (gr. -1-2). 14.99 *(978-0-7636-7480-9(X))* Candlewick Pr.

—The Greedy Goat. Horácek, Petr. 2018. (ENG.). 32p. (J). (-k). 15.99 *(978-0-7636-9497-5(5))* Candlewick Pr.

—Honk, Honk! Baa, Baa! Horácek, Petr. 2014. (ENG.). 16p. (J). (— 1). bds. 7.99 *(978-0-7636-6780-1(3))* Candlewick Pr.

—Las Fresas Son Rojas. Horácek, Petr. 2014. 16p. (J). (-k). bds. 5.99 *(978-0-7636-7393-2(5))* Candlewick Pr.

Horacek, Petr. The Mouse Who Ate the Moon. Horacek, Petr. 2014. (ENG.). 32p. (J). (gr. -1-2). 15.99 *(978-0-7636-7059-7(6))* Candlewick Pr.

Horácek, Petr. The Mouse Who Reached the Sky. Horácek, Petr. 2016. (ENG.). 32p. (J). (-k). 16.99 *(978-0-7636-7916-3(X))* Candlewick Pr.

Horacek, Petr. Puffin Peter. Horacek, Petr. 2013. (ENG.). 40p. (J). (gr. -1-2). 16.99 *(978-0-7636-6572-2(X))* Candlewick Pr.

Horácek, Petr. A Surprise for Tiny Mouse. Horácek, Petr. 2015. (ENG.). 16p. (J). (— 1). bds. 8.99 *(978-0-7636-7967-5(4))* Candlewick Pr.

—Suzy Goose & the Christmas Star: Midi Edition. Horácek, Petr. 2010. (ENG.). 32p. (J). (gr. -1-2). 7.99 *(978-0-7636-5000-1(5))* Candlewick Pr.

—Time for Bed. Horácek, Petr. 2014. (ENG.). 16p. (J). (— 1). bds. 7.99 *(978-0-7636-6779-5(X))* Candlewick Pr.

—Who Is Sleeping? Horácek, Petr. 2019. (ENG.). 16p. (J). (— 1). bds. 8.99 *(978-1-5362-0172-7(3))* Candlewick Pr.

—Who Is the Biggest? Horácek, Petr. 2019. (ENG.). 16p. (J). (— 1). bds. 8.99 *(978-1-5362-0171-0(5))* Candlewick Pr.

Horak, Mila. Fearless John: The Legend of John Beargrease. Rauzi, Kelly Emerling. 2006. 32p. 19.95 *(978-0-9774831-3-6(4))* Singing River Pubns.

Horelyk, Mariia. Jesus, Mein Held. Rittgarn, Georg J., tr. 2019. (GER.). 26p. (J). pap. 9.13 *(978-1-0968-8883-3(1))* Independently Published.

Horen, Michael. My Blessings for Food. 2003. (ArtScroll Ser.). (ENG, ARC & HEB.). (J). 49.99 *(978-0-89906-702-5(6),* TCH3) Mesorah Pubns., Ltd.

Horen, Michael & Halasz, Andras. Pirkei Avos, Vol. 2. Gold, Avie. (J). pap. 12.99 *(978-0-89906-199-3(0),* PIYP) Mesorah Pubns., Ltd.

Horensen, Henri. Christmas in the Trenches, 1 vol. McCutcheon, John. 2006. (ENG.). 32p. (J). (gr. 1-5). 19.95 *(978-1-56145-374-0(9))* Peachtree Publishing Co. Inc.

Hori, Hatsuki. A Snowflake Fell: Poems about Winter. Whipple, Laura. 2003. 40p. (J). 16.99 *(978-1-84148-033-6(9))* Barefoot Bks., Inc.

Horiuchi, Risa. Malty the Blue Tiger (Maddie la Tigresse Bleue) A Dual Language Children's Book in English & French. Kloss, K. Pebay-Maes, Eliette, tr. 2019. (ENG.). 42p. (J). pap. 11.95 *(978-0-578-48064-0(6))* Rincon Point, LLC.

—Malty the Blue Tiger (Marita la Tigresita Azul) Kloss, K. 2018. (ENG.). 42p. (J). (gr. k-2). pap. 11.95 *(978-0-692-97467-4(9))* Rincon Point, LLC.

Hornbacher, Jd. Keep on Keepin' On: Helping Kids to Never Give Up! Layton, Dian. 2020. (ENG.). 32p. (J). (gr. k-3). 24.99 ***(978-0-7684-5246-4(5))*** Destiny Image Pubs.

Hornbacher, Jd. Ooky Pooky Spooky Fear: Telling Fear to Go Away! Layton, Dian. 2018. (ENG.). 34p. (J). 14.99 *(978-0-7684-5021-7(7))* Destiny Image Pubs.

Horne, Adrienne. Semer des Graines a Recolter: Le Guide des Enfants Pour L'entreprenariat. White, Jeffrey. Cherry, Veronique, tr. 2019. (FRE.). 26p. (J). pap. 11.06 ***(978-1-7004-0018-5(5))*** Independently Published.

Horne, Diantha W. Mildred's Inheritance, Just Her Way & Ann's Own Way. Johnston, Annie Fellows. 2007. 48p. per. *(978-1-4065-3515-0(X))* Dodo Pr.

—The Sandman: His Sea Stories (Yesterday's Classics) Hopkins, William J. 2009. 188p. pap. 9.95 *(978-1-59915-303-2(3))* Yesterday's Classics.

—The Sandman: His Ship Stories (Yesterday's Classics) Hopkins, William J. 2009. 174p. pap. 9.95 *(978-1-59915-302-5(5))* Yesterday's Classics.

Horne, Doug. Big Bad Bible Bullies. Hagan, Scott. 2005. 24p. (J). (gr. -1-3). 9.99 *(978-1-59185-604-7(3))* Charisma Media.

—Los Buscapleitos de la Biblia. Hagan, Scott. 2005. 22p. (J). (gr. 1-3). 8.99 *(978-1-59185-482-1(2),* Charisma Kids) Charisma Media.

Horne, Grace. Greedy Pigeon the Hungry Porcupine & Friends. Rossitter, Derek. 2004. 60p. pap. *(978-0-7552-0142-6(6))* Authors OnLine, Ltd.

Horne, J. My Pretty Pink School Purse. Bugbird, T. 2010. 16p. (J). 12.99 *(978-1-84879-379-8(0))* Make Believe Ideas GBR. Dist: Nelson, Thomas Inc.

Horne, Nathan. Poppy. Booth, Sara. 2012. 28p. pap. 12.50 *(978-1-61897-666-6(4),* Strategic Bk. Publishing) Strategic Book Publishing & Rights Agency (SBPRA).

Horne, Philip & Loter, John. Fish School. Mackerel, Seymour & RH Disney Staff. 2003. (Pictureback(R) Ser.). (ENG.). 24p. (J). (gr. -1-2). pap. 3.99 *(978-0-7364-2127-0(0),* RH/Disney) Random Hse. Children's Bks.

Horne, Sarah. Animal Survivors. Gifford, Clive. 2017. (Reading Ladder Ser.). (ENG.). 32p. (J). (gr. 1-3). pap. 6.99 *(978-1-4052-8492-9(7))* Egmont Bks., Ltd. GBR. Dist: Independent Pubs. Group.

—Cat Detective. Greenfield, A. B. 2018. (Ra the Mighty Ser.: 1). (ENG.). 224p. (J). (gr. 2-5). 16.99 *(978-0-8234-4027-6(3))* Holiday Hse., Inc.

—The Dessert That Wouldn't Wobble. Mitchell, Angela. 2019. (Early Bird Readers — Purple (Early Bird Stories (tm)) Ser.). (ENG.). 32p. (J). (gr. k-3). 27.99 *(978-1-5415-4232-7(0),* 9781541542327); pap. 7.99 *(978-1-5415-7417-5(6),* 9781541574175) Lerner Publishing Group. (Lerner Pubns.).

—Fizzlebert Stump: The Boy Who Cried Fish. Harrold, A. F. 2014. (Fizzlebert Stump Ser.: 3). 224p. (J). (gr. 2-4). pap. *(978-1-4088-4246-1(7),* 230937, Bloomsbury Children's Bks.) Bloomsbury Publishing Plc.

—Fizzlebert Stump: The Boy Who Did P. E. in His Pants. Harrold, A. F. 2016. (Fizzlebert Stump Ser.: 5). 320p. (J). pap. *(978-1-4088-5339-9(6),* 253994, Bloomsbury Children's Bks.) Bloomsbury Publishing Plc.

—Fizzlebert Stump: The Boy Who Ran Away from the Circus (And Joined the Library) Harrold, A. F. 2012. (Fizzlebert Stump Ser.: 1). 256p. (J). (gr. 3-6). pap. *(978-1-4088-3003-1(5),* 149177, Bloomsbury Children's Bks.) Bloomsbury Publishing Plc.

—Fizzlebert Stump & the Bearded Boy. Harrold, A. F. 2013. (Fizzlebert Stump Ser.: 2). 256p. (J). (gr. 3-6). pap. *(978-1-4088-3521-0(5),* 160362, Bloomsbury Children's Bks.) Bloomsbury Publishing Plc.

—Fizzlebert Stump & the Great Supermarket Showdown. Harrold, A. F. 2016. (Fizzlebert Stump Ser.: 6). 304p. (J). pap. *(978-1-4088-6945-1(4),* 291154, Bloomsbury Children's Bks.) Bloomsbury Publishing Plc.

—I Am Here, Where Are You? Jones, Anita. 2019. 32p. (J). (gr. k-2). pap. 10.99 *(978-1-4451-5162-5(6),* Franklin Watts) Hachette Children's Group GBR. Dist: Hachette Bk. Group.

—I Got a Chicken for My Birthday. Gehl, Laura. 2018. (ENG.). 32p. (J). (gr. -1-2). 17.99 *(978-1-5124-3130-8(3),* 9781512431308, Carolrhoda Bks.) Lerner Publishing Group.

Horne, Sarah. Las Cosas Son Como Son. Gassman, Julie. 2020. (Pasito a Pasito Ser.).Tr. of You Get What You Get. (SPA.). 32p. (J). (gr. -1-1). 9.95 ***(978-1-5158-7333-4(1),*** 201744); lib. bdg. 23.99 ***(978-1-5158-7192-7(4),*** 200640) Capstone. (Picture Window Bks.).

Horne, Sarah. Llamas Go Large: Llama United Book 2: A World Cup Story. Allen, Scott. 2018. (ENG.). 304p. (J). (gr. 2-4). 9.99 *(978-1-5098-4092-2(3))* Pan Macmillan GBR. Dist: Independent Pubs. Group.

—The Long-Lost Secret Diary of the World's Worst Knight. Collins, Tim. 2018. (Long-Lost Secret Diary Ser.). (ENG.). 216p. (J). lib. bdg. 28.50 *(978-1-63163-136-8(5),* 1631631365, Jolly Fish Pr.) North Star Editions.

—The Long-Lost Secret Diary of the World's Worst Pirate. Collins, Tim. 2018. (Long-Lost Secret Diary Ser.). (ENG.). 216p. (J). lib. bdg. 28.50 *(978-1-63163-140-5(3),* 1631631403, Jolly Fish Pr.) North Star Editions.

—Mission 1: Flying Solo. Coburn, Ann. 2006. (Dream Team Ser.: Vol. 1). 80p. (J). pap. *(978-1-84428-118-3(3))* Walker & Co.

—Murphy & the Great Surf Rescue. Lewis, Gill. 2017. (Puppy Academy Ser.). (ENG.). 128p. (J). 16.99 *(978-1-62779-800-6(5),* 9781627798006, Holt, Henry & Co. Bks. For Young Readers) Holt, Henry & Co.

—Nana Cracks the Case! Lane, Kathleen et al. 2009. (ENG.). 112p. (J). (gr. -1-7). 14.99 *(978-0-8118-6258-5(5))* Chronicle Bks. LLC.

—Old Woman Who Swallowed a Fly. Davies, Kate, ed. 2009. (First Reading Level 3 Ser.). 48p. (J). (gr. 2). 6.99 *(978-0-7945-2267-4(X),* Usborne) EDC Publishing.

—Pip & the Paw of Friendship. Lewis, Gill. 2017. (Puppy Academy Ser.). (ENG.). 128p. (J). pap. 5.99 *(978-1-250-09285-4(X),* 9781250092854, Holt, Henry & Co. Bks. For Young Readers) Holt, Henry & Co.

—Puppy Academy Bindup Books 1-4: Scout & the Sausage Thief, Star on Stormy Mountain, Pip & the Paw of Friendship, Murphy & the Great Surf Rescue. Lewis, Gill. 2019. (Puppy Academy Ser.). (ENG.). 496p. (J). 13.99 *(978-1-250-21761-5(X),* 900207017, Holt, Henry & Co. Bks. For Young Readers) Holt, Henry & Co.

—Ra the Mighty: Cat Detective. Greenfield, A. B. 2019. (Ra the Mighty Ser.: 1). (ENG.). 240p. (J). (gr. 2-5). pap. 7.99 *(978-0-8234-4438-0(4))* Holiday Hse., Inc.

—Ra the Mighty: the Great Tomb Robbery. Greenfield, A. B. 2019. (Ra the Mighty Ser.: 2). (ENG.). 256p. (J). (gr. 2-5). 16.99 *(978-0-8234-4240-9(3))* Holiday Hse., Inc.

—Showtime. Coburn, Ann. 2006. (Dream Team Mission Ser.: Vol. 2). 80p. (J). pap. *(978-1-84428-071-1(3))* Walker Bks., Ltd.

—There's a Dragon in My Backpack! Nicoll, Tom. 2019. (There's a Dragon Ser.). (ENG.). 160p. (J). (gr. 1-4). 5.99 *(978-1-68010-445-5(4));* lib. bdg. 21.99 *(978-1-68010-167-6(6))* Tiger Tales.

—There's a Dragon in My Boot. Nicoll, Tom. 2020. (There's a Dragon Ser.). (ENG.). 160p. (J). (gr. 1-4). 22.99 *(978-1-68010-180-5(3));* pap. 6.99 *(978-1-68010-454-7(3))* Tiger Tales.

—There's a Dragon in My Dinner! Nicoll, Tom. 2019. (There's a Dragon Ser.). (ENG.). 160p. (J). (gr. 1-4). 5.99 *(978-1-68010-444-8(6));* lib. bdg. 21.99 *(978-1-68010-166-9(8))* Tiger Tales.

—There's a Dragon in My Toilet. Nicoll, Tom. 2020. (There's a Dragon Ser.). (ENG.). 160p. (J). (gr. 1-4). 22.99 *(978-1-68010-181-2(1));* pap. 6.99 *(978-1-68010-455-4(1))* Tiger Tales.

—Thirty Days Has September: Cool Ways to Remember Stuff. Scholastic, Inc. Staff & Stevens, Chris. 2008. (Best at Everything Ser.). (ENG.). 128p. (J). (gr. 3-7). 14.99 *(978-0-545-10740-2(7),* Scholastic Nonfiction) Scholastic, Inc.

—Thumbelina: The Graphic Novel, 1 vol. Andersen, Hans & Sandoval, Gerardo. 2009. (Graphic Spin Ser.). (ENG.). 40p. (J). (gr. 3-6). pap. 5.95 *(978-1-4342-1741-7(8),* Stone Arch Bks.) Capstone.

—The Ultimate Animal Criminals. Gifford, Clive. 2016. (ENG.). 48p. (J). (gr. 2-4). 14.99 *(978-1-4052-7381-7(X))* Egmont Bks., Ltd. GBR. Dist: Independent Pubs. Group.

—Vile: A Cautionary Tale for Little Monsters. Robinson, Mark. 2011. (ENG.). 32p. (J). (gr. k-2). 14.99 *(978-0-7459-6254-2(8))* Lion Hudson PLC GBR. Dist: Independent Pubs. Group.

—Where Do I Find Jesus? Walsh, Sheila. 2017. (ENG.). 32p. (J). (gr. -1-3). 14.99 *(978-1-4336-8806-5(9),* 005750223, B&H Kids) B&H Publishing Group.

—World's Worst Knight. Collins, Tim. 2017. (Long-Lost Secret Diary Ser.). (ENG.). 216p. (J). pap. 9.99 *(978-1-63163-137-5(3),* 1631631373, Jolly Fish Pr.) North Star Editions.

—World's Worst Pirate. Collins, Tim. 2017. (Long-Lost Secret Diary Ser.). (ENG.). 216p. (J). pap. 9.99 *(978-1-63163-141-2(1),* 1631631411, Jolly Fish Pr.) North Star Editions.

—You Get What You Get, 1 vol. Gassman, Julie A. (Little Boost Ser.). (ENG.). 32p. (J). (gr. -1-1). 2013. 14.95 *(978-1-4795-2157-9(4));* 2012. lib. bdg. 23.99 *(978-1-4048-6794-9(5))* Capstone. (Picture Window Bks.).

Horne, Sarah & Barker, Vicky. The Usborne Animal Alphabet Activity Book. MacKinnon, Mairi. 2014. (ENG.). (J). pap. 9.99 *(978-0-7945-3274-1(8),* Usborne) EDC Publishing.

Horneman, Lars. Zenobia. Durr, Morten. 2018. (ENG.). 96p. (J). (gr. 5). 19.95 *(978-1-60980-873-0(8),* Triangle Square) Seven Stories Pr.

Horner, Doogie. Kid Artists: True Tales of Childhood from Creative Legends. Stabler, David. 2016. (Kid Legends Ser.: 3). 208p. (J). (gr. 4-7). 13.95 *(978-1-59474-896-7(9))* Quirk Bks.

—Kid Athletes: True Tales of Childhood from Sports Legends. Stabler, David. 2015. (Kid Legends Ser.: 2). (ENG.). 208p. (J). (gr. 4-7). 13.95 *(978-1-59474-802-8(0))* Quirk Bks.

—Kid Authors: True Tales of Childhood from Famous Writers. Stabler, David. 2017. (Kid Legends Ser.: 4). (ENG.). 200p. (J). (gr. 4-7). 13.95 *(978-1-59474-987-2(6))* Quirk Bks.

—Kid Presidents: True Tales of Childhood from America's Presidents. Stabler, David. 2014. (Kid Legends Ser.: 1). 224p. (J). (gr. 4-7). 13.95 *(978-1-59474-731-1(8))* Quirk Bks.

Horner, Maree. A Windy Day Walk. Dixon, Pamela. 2016. (ENG.). 32p. (J). (gr. 1-4). *(978-0-473-34486-3(6))* Lizzy Web Bks.

Hornsby, Lindsay. The Computer Code Mystery. Taylor, Justin. 2016. (Celia Science & Anna Art Ser.: Vol. 1). (ENG.). (J). (gr. 4-5). pap. *(978-1-911079-17-0(4))* Acorn Independent Pr.

Hornung, Phyllis. Bubbe Isabella & the Sukkot Cake. Terwilliger, Kelly. 2005. 24p. (J). (gr. -1-3). 15.95 *(978-1-58013-187-2(5));* (gr. 3-8). per. 6.95 *(978-1-58013-128-5(X))* Lerner Publishing Group. (Kar-Ben Publishing).

—A Place for Zero. LoPresti, Angeline Sparagna. alt. ed. 2003. (Charlesbridge Math Adventures Ser.). (ENG.). 32p. (J). (gr. 1-4). pap. 7.95 *(978-1-57091-196-5(7))* Charlesbridge Publishing, Inc.

—What's Your Angle, Pythagoras? Ellis, Julie. 2004. (Charlesbridge Math Adventures Ser.). 32p. (J). (gr. 2-5). pap. 7.95 *(978-1-57091-150-7(9))* Charlesbridge Publishing, Inc.

Hornung, Phyllis. Simon Can't Say Hippopotamus. Hornung, Phyllis, tr. Taylor, Bonnie Highsmith. 2003. 24p. (J). 14.95 *(978-1-59336-017-7(7));* pap. *(978-1-59336-018-4(5))* Mondo Publishing.

Horowitz, Alena Netia & De La Fuente, Mary. The Tlytiettlym Tree. Horowitz, Alena Netia. l.t. ed. 2003. 64p. (J). per. 12.95 *(978-0-923550-42-4(9))* Tetrahedron Publishing LLC.

Horowitz, Dave. Five Little Gefiltes. Horowitz, Dave. 2007. (ENG.). 32p. (J). (gr. -1-3). 15.99 *(978-0-399-24608-1(8),* G.P. Putnam's Sons Books for Young Readers) Penguin Young Readers Group.

—Humpty Dumpty Climbs Again. Horowitz, Dave. 2011. (ENG.). 32p. (J). (gr. -1-k). pap. 6.99 *(978-0-14-241932-8(X),* Puffin Books) Penguin Young Readers Group.

—A Monkey among Us. Horowitz, Dave. 2004. 40p. (J). (gr. -1-1). 14.99 *(978-0-06-054335-8(3),* HarperFestival) HarperCollins Pubs.

—The Ugly Pumpkin. Horowitz, Dave. (ENG.). (J). 2017. 32p. (-k). bds. 7.99 *(978-1-5247-4084-9(5),* Nancy Paulsen Books); 2008. 40p. (gr. -1-k). pap. 7.99 *(978-0-14-241145-2(0),* Puffin Books) Penguin Young Readers Group.

Horrell, Charles. Etheldreda the Ready. Vaizey, George de Horne. 2007. 200p. per. *(978-1-4065-4688-0(7))* Dodo Pr.

Horrocks, Steve. Gulliver's Travels: Band 11 Lime/Band 17 Diamond (Collins Big Cat Progress) Matthews, Andrew. 2014. (Collins Big Cat Progress Ser.). (ENG.). 32p. (J). (gr. 5-6). pap. 9.99 *(978-0-00-751937-8(0))* HarperCollins Pubs. Ltd. GBR. Dist: Independent Pubs. Group.

Horse, Harry. The Last Castaways. Horse, Harry. 2009. (ENG.). 128p. (J). (gr. 1-5). 12.95 *(978-1-56145-439-6(7))* Peachtree Publishing Co. Inc.

—The Last Cowboys. Horse, Harry. 2008. (ENG.). 128p. (J). (gr. 1-5). 12.95 *(978-1-56145-451-8(6),* Peachtree Junior) Peachtree Publishing Co. Inc.

—The Last Gold Diggers. Horse, Harry. 2008. (ENG.). 128p. (J). (gr. 1-5). 12.95 *(978-1-56145-435-8(4))* Peachtree Publishing Co. Inc.

—Little Rabbit Goes to School, 1 vol. Horse, Harry. (Little Rabbit Ser.). (ENG.). 32p. (J). 2011. (gr. -1-1). pap. 7.95 *(978-1-56145-574-4(1));* 2004. (gr. k-1). 15.95 *(978-1-56145-320-7(X))* Peachtree Publishing Co. Inc.

—Little Rabbit Lost. Horse, Harry. (Little Rabbit Ser.). (ENG.). 32p. (J). 2019. (gr. -1-1). pap. 7.95 *(978-1-68263-107-2(9));* 2005. (gr. k-1). bds. 9.95 *(978-1-56145-345-0(5))* Peachtree Publishing Co. Inc.

—Little Rabbit Runaway, 1 vol. Horse, Harry. 2005. (Little Rabbit Ser.). (ENG.). 32p. (J). (gr. k-1). 15.95 *(978-1-56145-343-6(9))* Peachtree Publishing Co. Inc.

—Little Rabbit's Christmas. Horse, Harry. (Little Rabbit Ser.). (ENG.). 32p. (J). 2010. (gr. -1-1). pap. 7.95 *(978-1-56145-557-7(1));* 2007. (gr. k-3). 15.95 *(978-1-56145-419-8(2))* Peachtree Publishing Co. Inc.

—Little Rabbit's New Baby, 1 vol. Horse, Harry. (Little Rabbit Ser.). (ENG.). 32p. (J). 2016. (gr. -1-k). pap. 7.95 *(978-1-56145-915-5(1));* 2008. (gr. k-1). 16.95 *(978-1-56145-431-0(1))* Peachtree Publishing Co. Inc.

Horsepool, Adam. King Arthur. 2017. (10 Minute Classics Ser.). (ENG.). 32p. (J). (gr. 1-5). 16.99 *(978-1-4867-1222-9(3),* 9c0ab110-33c7-47e1-b5fb-0df6482e1dc5) Flowerpot Pr.

—Moby Dick. 2017. (10 Minute Classics Ser.). (ENG.). 32p. (J). (gr. 1-5). 16.99 *(978-1-4867-1200-7(2),* ab2a03b1-a930-41a4-85d2-2b2c545197a9) Flowerpot Pr.

—Robin Hood. 2017. (10 Minute Classics Ser.). (ENG.). 32p. (J). (gr. 1-4). 16.99 *(978-1-4867-1310-3(6),* 7dfdcce0-b575-4205-9d1b-ea86f4f20f07) Flowerpot Pr.

—The Three Musketeers. 2019. (10 Minute Classics Ser.). (ENG.). 32p. (J). (gr. 1-5). 16.99 *(978-1-4867-1311-0(4),* 2e3e5f7a-0305-4d86-95df-4355be40bbfe) Flowerpot Pr.

Horsfall, Robert Bruce. The Lay of the Land (Yesterday's Classics) Sharp, Dallas Lore. 2018. (ENG.). 176p. (YA). (gr. 7-12). pap. 10.95 *(978-1-59915-463-3(3))* Yesterday's Classics.

—Summer (Yesterday's Classics) Sharp, Dallas Lore. 2019. (ENG.). 130p. (J). (gr. 4-6). pap. 10.95 *(978-1-59915-498-5(6))* Yesterday's Classics.

Horsley, Sandy. Selfie. Horsley, Sandy. 2020. (ENG.). 32p. (J). (gr. k-2). 17.99 ***(978-1-68446-145-5(6)***, 141996, Capstone Editions) Capstone.

Horst, Melisa. The Daudyhouse. Bowman, Silas. 2012. 51p. (J). *(978-0-7399-2450-1(8))* Rod & Staff Pubs., Inc.

Horst, Melissa, jt. illus. see Reinford, Luanne.

Horsted, Paul, photos by. Custer State Park: From the Mountains to the Plains. Horsted, Paul. 2004. 96p. 19.95 *(978-0-9718053-2-3(6))* Golden Valley Pr.

Horstman, Lisa. One Baby Mountain Goat. Ketel, Debbie M. 2005. (J). bds. 6.99 *(978-0-9752617-3-6(8))* Mount Rushmore Bookstores.

Horstman, Lisa. Smoky Mountain Wee Ones. Horstman, Lisa. Kemp, Steve, ed. 2003. 16p. (J). bds. 6.99 *(978-0-937207-41-3(1))* Great Smoky Mountains Assn.

Hortens, Mike, jt. illus. see Hanner, Albert.

Horton, Laura. Babies in the Wild: Chunky Lift a Flap Board Book. Swift, Ginger. Cottage Door Press, ed. 2017. (Lift a Flap Ser.). (ENG.). 12p. (J). (gr. -1-k). bds. 7.99 *(978-1-68052-233-4(7)*, 1002190) Cottage Door Pr.

—Can't Wait to Show You: Belly Book. Boyle, Jacqueline & Lupone Stonis, Susan. 2018. (Belly Book Ser.). (ENG.). 16p. (J). (gr. -1-k). bds. 9.99 *(978-1-68052-331-7(7)*, 1003070) Cottage Door Pr.

—Never Too Young! 50 Unstoppable Kids Who Made a Difference. Weintraub, Aileen. 2018. 112p. (J). (gr. 3-7). 14.95 *(978-1-4549-2917-8(0))* Sterling Publishing Co., Inc.

—Winicker & the American Boy. Lute, Renee Beauregard. 2017. (Winicker Wallace Ser.). (ENG.). 112p. (J). (gr. 3-7). lib. bdg. 29.93 *(978-1-5321-3048-9(1)*, 27055, Calico Chapter Bks.) ABDO Publishing Co.

—Winicker & the Baby Wait. Lute, Renee Beauregard. 2017. (Winicker Wallace Ser.). (ENG.). 112p. (J). (gr. 3-7). lib. bdg. 29.93 *(978-1-5321-3049-6(X)*, 27056, Calico Chapter Bks.) ABDO Publishing Co.

—Winicker & the Christmas Visit. Lute, Renee Beauregard. 2017. (Winicker Wallace Ser.). (ENG.). 112p. (J). (gr. 3-7). lib. bdg. 29.93 *(978-1-5321-3050-2(3)*, 27057, Calico Chapter Bks.) ABDO Publishing Co.

—Winicker Hates Paris. Lute, Renee Beauregard. 2017. (Winicker Wallace Ser.). (ENG.). 112p. (J). (gr. 3-7). lib. bdg. 29.93 *(978-1-5321-3051-9(1)*, 27058, Calico Chapter Bks.) ABDO Publishing Co.

Horton, Laura K. The Fairies of Honeysuckle Hollow. Frampton, Robyn. 2020. (ENG.). 32p. (J). 17.99 *(978-1-250-12264-3(3)*, 900173914) Imprint IND. Dist: Macmillan.

—The Gift of Ramadan. Lumbard, Rabiah York. 2019. (ENG.). 32p. (J). (gr. -1-3). 16.99 *(978-0-8075-2906-5(0)*, 807529060) Whitman, Albert & Co.

Horton, Lori. Whose Hat Is That? Opheim, Sandra. 2004. (J). 5.95 *(978-0-9758958-0-1(X))* Better Than One Publishing.

Horvath, Anna. Have I Ever Told You? King, Shani. 2017. (ENG.). 32p. (J). (gr. -1-3). 16.95 *(978-1-59298-694-1(3))* Beaver's Pond Pr., Inc.

Horváth, Anna. Have I Ever Told You?, 1 vol. King, Shani. 2019. (ENG.). 32p. (J). (gr. -1-5). 14.95 *(978-0-88448-719-7(9)*, 884719) Tilbury Hse. Pubs.

Horvath, Ferdinand H. Golden Tusk. Slaughter, Charles E. 2011. 180p. 42.95 *(978-1-258-09834-6(2))* Literary Licensing, LLC.

Horvath, James. Talkin' Baseball. Buckley, James. 2020. (Talkin' Sports Ser.). (ENG.). 24p. (J). (gr. 2-5). lib. bdg. 28.50 *(978-1-5038-3571-9(5)*, 213421) Child's World, Inc., The.

—Talkin' Basketball. Buckley, James. 2020. (Talkin' Sports Ser.). (ENG.). 24p. (J). (gr. 2-5). lib. bdg. 28.50 *(978-1-5038-3574-0(X)*, 213422) Child's World, Inc., The.

—Talkin' Football. Gigliotti, Jim. 2020. (Talkin' Sports Ser.). (ENG.). 24p. (J). (gr. 2-5). lib. bdg. 28.50 *(978-1-5038-3572-6(3)*, 213423) Child's World, Inc., The.

—Talkin' Golf & Tennis. Gigliotti, Jim. 2020. (Talkin' Sports Ser.). (ENG.). 24p. (J). (gr. 2-5). lib. bdg. 28.50 *(978-1-5038-3578-8(2)*, 213424) Child's World, Inc., The.

—Talkin' Hockey. Gigliotti, Jim. 2020. (Talkin' Sports Ser.). (ENG.). 24p. (J). (gr. 2-5). lib. bdg. 28.50 *(978-1-5038-3575-7(8)*, 213425) Child's World, Inc., The.

—Talkin' Lacrosse. Buckley, James. 2020. (Talkin' Sports Ser.). (ENG.). 24p. (J). (gr. 2-5). lib. bdg. 28.50 *(978-1-5038-3576-4(6)*, 213426) Child's World, Inc., The.

—Talkin' Motor Sports. Buckley, James. 2020. (Talkin' Sports Ser.). (ENG.). 24p. (J). (gr. 2-5). lib. bdg. 28.50 *(978-1-5038-3577-1(4)*, 213427) Child's World, Inc., The.

—Talkin' Soccer. Buckley, James. 2020. (Talkin' Sports Ser.). (ENG.). 24p. (J). (gr. 2-5). lib. bdg. 28.50 *(978-1-5038-3573-3(1)*, 213428) Child's World, Inc., The.

Horvath, James. Build, Dogs, Build: A Tall Tail. Horvath, James. 2016. (I Can Read Level 1 Ser.). (ENG.). 32p. (J). (gr. -1-3). pap. 4.99 *(978-0-06-235705-2(0))* HarperCollins Pubs.

—Build, Dogs, Build: A Tall Tail. Horvath, James. 2013. (ENG.). 40p. (J). (gr. -1-3). 16.99 *(978-0-06-218967-7(0)*, HarperCollins) HarperCollins Pubs. Ltd. GBR. Dist: HarperCollins Pubs.

—Dig, Dogs, Dig: A Construction Tail. Horvath, James. (I Can Read Level 1 Ser.). (ENG.). (J). (gr. -1-3). 2016. 32p. pap. 4.99 *(978-0-06-235702-1(6))*; 2013. 40p. 15.99 *(978-0-06-218964-6(6))* HarperCollins Pubs.

—Work, Dogs, Work: A Highway Tail. Horvath, James. (I Can Read Level 1 Ser.). (ENG.). (J). (gr. -1-3). 2017. 32p. pap. 4.99 *(978-0-06-235708-3(5))*; 2014. 40p. 15.99 *(978-0-06-218970-7(0))* HarperCollins Pubs.

Horvath, Marie-Noëlle. Farm. 2018. (My First Touch & Find Ser.). (ENG.). 12p. (J). (— 1). bds. 8.95 *(978-1-4549-2946-8(4))* Sterling Publishing Co., Inc.

—Park. 2018. (My First Touch & Find Ser.). (ENG.). 12p. (J). (— 1). bds. 8.95 *(978-1-4549-2944-4(8))* Sterling Publishing Co., Inc.

Horvath, Michelle. Down the Drain. Horvath, Michelle. 2019. (ENG.). 76p. (J). pap. 16.50 *(978-1-0769-2426-1(3))* Independently Published.

Horwitz, Suzanne. Bella's 3-Day Adventure. Bone, Rose. 2017. (ENG.). (J). pap. 10.95 *(978-1-946753-25-0(4))* Avant-garde Bks.

Horwitz, Suzanne. The Cardinal. Hardy, Felicia Carmelita. 2019. (ENG.). 24p. (J). pap. 12.95 ***(978-1-946753-43-4(2))*** Avant-garde Bks.

Horwitz, Suzanne. Jamal Loves Numbers. Hardy, C. Cherie. 2019. (ENG.). 32p. (J). pap. 10.95 *(978-1-946753-37-3(8))* Avant-garde Bks.

—My Lost Shoe: A Story about Staying Safe. Ferguson, Rhonda S. Books, Avant-Garde, ed. 2018. (ENG.). 36p. (J). pap. 12.95 *(978-1-946753-34-2(3))* Avant-garde Bks.

—The Orange Zebra & the Kind Giraffe. Hardy, C. Cherie. 2016. (ENG.). (J). pap. 10.95 *(978-0-9977566-4-7(0))* Avant-garde Bks.

—Princess Felicia: The Bully Warrior. Hardy, C. Cherie. 2018. (ENG.). 26p. (J). pap. 10.95 *(978-1-946753-36-6(X))* Avant-garde Bks.

—Princess Valerie: A Story about Generosity & Service. Hardy, C. Cherie. 2017. (ENG.). (J). pap. 10.95 *(978-1-946753-21-2(1))* Avant-garde Bks.

—This Beautiful Skin of Mine. Hardy, C. Cherie. 2017. (ENG.). (J). pap. 12.95 *(978-1-946753-12-0(2))* Avant-garde Bks.

Horwitz, Suzanne. Visions of My Future: A Book about Careers. Hardy, C. Cherie. 2019. (ENG.). 36p. (J). pap. 12.95 ***(978-1-946753-39-7(4))*** Avant-garde Bks.

Horwitz, Suzanne. Zoe's Bun. Butler, E. Danielle. 2017. (ENG.). (J). pap. 10.95 *(978-1-946753-00-7(9))* Avant-garde Bks.

Horwitz, Suzanne, jt. illus. see Billups, Takarais.

Hosack, Leona. Jamila Does Not Want a Bat in Her House. Ring, Phyllis Edgerly. 2016. 30p. (J). *(978-0-87743-718-5(1))* Baha'i Publishing Trust, U.S.

Hosam, Basma. The World of Little Muslims. Can, Huvaida. 2019. (ENG.). 108p. (J). (gr. -1-k). pap. 14.95 ***(978-1-59784-938-8(3)***, Tughra Bks.) Blue Dome, Inc.

Hose, Ryan. Bobby & Buddy Friends for Life. Edward, J. P. 2011. 16p. pap. 24.95 *(978-1-4560-7520-0(9))* America Star Bks.

Hoseley, Rantz. Rich Dad's Escape from the Rat Race: How to Become a Rich Kid by Following Rich Dad's Advice. Kiyosaki, Robert T. & Lechter, Sharon L. 2005. (ENG.). 64p. (J). (gr. 3-7). pap. 9.99 *(978-0-316-00047-5(7))* Little, Brown Bks. for Young Readers.

Hosemann, Theodor. Slovenly Kate & Other Stories: From the Struwwelpeter Library. Hoffmann, Heinrich. 2012. (Dover Children's Classics Ser.). (ENG.). 96p. (J). (gr. 3-5). pap. 12.99 *(978-0-486-49032-8(7))* Dover Pubns., Inc.

Hosford, Eric. The Princess Fables. Clark, Marc. 2013. 114p. pap. 5.99 *(978-0-9910345-0-5(3))* Seven C's Productions, Inc.

Hosford, William. ABalloonC. Hosford, William. 2007. 32p. (J). per. 10.00 *(978-0-9776562-1-9(7))* WGH Arts LLC.

Hosford, William G. Geo the Geode. Hosford, William G. 2006. 32p. (J). lib. bdg. 19.95 *(978-0-9776562-0-2(9)*, CN0601) WGH Arts LLC.

Hoshine, Ken. Macbeth. SparkNotes Staff. 2008. (No Fear Shakespeare Illustrated Ser.: 2). 208p. (gr. 5-7). per. 9.95 *(978-1-4114-9871-6(2)*, Spark Notes) Sterling Publishing Co., Inc.

Hoshino, Felicia. Four-Handed Piano. Conway, Diana C. 2020. (ENG.). 22p. (J). pap. ***(978-1-922331-99-1(6))*** Library For All Limited.

Hoshino, Felicia. Juna's Jar. Bahk, Jane. 2015. (ENG.). 32p. (J). 17.95 *(978-1-60060-853-7(1)*, 9781600000000) Lee & Low Bks., Inc.

—A Place Where Sunflowers Grow, 1 vol. Lee-Tai, Amy. 32p. (J). 2015. (ENG & JPN.). (gr. 2-5). pap. 10.95 *(978-0-89239-274-2(6)*, 8a3aa636-567d-49c5-9127-645b4bb81841, Children's Book Press); 2006. (JPN & ENG.). (gr. k-3). 17.95 *(978-0-89239-215-5(0))* Lee & Low Bks., Inc.

Hosler, Danamarie. The Different Dragon. Bryan, Jennifer Liu. 2006. (J). pap. 12.95 *(978-0-9674468-6-8(4))* Two Lives Publishing.

—El Dragón Diferente. Bryan, Jennifer. 2nd ed. 2015.Tr. of Different Dragon. (SPA.). 36p. (Orig.). (J). pap. 12.95 *(978-0-9674468-9-9(9))* Two Lives Publishing.

Hosoe, Eikoh, photos by. Taka-Chan & I: A Dog's Journey to Japan by Runcible. Lifton, Betty Jean. 2012. 64p. (J). (gr. k-4). 16.95 *(978-1-59017-502-6(6)*, NYR Children's Collection) New York Review of Bks., Inc., The.

Hosoya, Toko. The Secret Garden. 2017. (10 Minute Classics Ser.). (ENG.). 32p. (J). (gr. 1-4). 16.99 *(978-1-4867-1199-4(5)*, 83df95b6-8cdb-4fa5-a7d0-7eb0c97ba935) Flowerpot Pr.

Hosselkus, Devin. The Apple Tree's Secret, 1 vol. Gates, Pat. 2009. 47p. pap. 24.95 *(978-1-60836-637-8(5))* America Star Bks.

Hosta, Dar. I Love the Night. Hosta, Dar. l.t. ed. 2003. 32p. (J). (gr. k-3). 16.95 *(978-0-9721967-0-3(6))* Brown Dog Bks.

Hoston, Jim. Shop Talk. Scholastic, Inc. Staff & Ford, Juwanda G. 2004. (Just for You Ser.). (ENG.). 32p. (gr. k-3). pap. 3.99 *(978-0-439-56873-9(0)*, Teaching Resources) Scholastic, Inc.

—Shop Talk. Ford, Juwanda G. 2004. 32p. (J). lib. bdg. 15.00 *(978-1-4242-0236-2(1))* Fitzgerald Bks.

Hotchkiss, Conrad & Graham, Heather. I Have Been in Danger, 1 vol. Foggo, Cheryl. 2005. (In the Same Boat Ser.: No. 3). (ENG.). 184p. (J). (gr. 4-6). pap. 7.95 *(978-1-55050-185-8(2))* Coteau Bks. CAN. Dist: Fitzhenry & Whiteside, Ltd.

Houbre, Gilbert. Light. Houbre, Gilbert. Verdet, Jean-Pierre. Matthews, Sarah, tr. 2012. (ENG.). 36p. (J). (gr. -1-k). spiral bd. 14.99 *(978-1-85103-405-5(6))* Moonlight Publishing, Ltd. GBR. Dist: Independent Pubs. Group.

—Vegetables. Houbre, Gilbert. 2012. (ENG.). 36p. (J). (gr. -1-k). spiral bd. 13.99 *(978-1-85103-402-4(1))* Moonlight Publishing, Ltd. GBR. Dist: Independent Pubs. Group.

Houdeshell, Jennifer T. Ebeneezer's Cousin. Zajac, Kristen J. 2010. 20p. pap. 10.95 *(978-1-61633-045-3(7))* Guardian Angel Publishing, Inc.

Houdeshell, Jennifer Thomas. Ebeneezer's Cousin. Zajac, Kristen K. 2013. 24p. 19.95 *(978-1-61633-440-6(1))* Guardian Angel Publishing, Inc.

—El Primo de Ebeneezer. Zajac, Kristen K. 2011. 20p. pap. 10.95 *(978-1-61633-164-1(X))* Guardian Angel Publishing, Inc.

—That's a Lot of Love. Reed, Jennifer Bond. 2011. 16p. pap. 9.95 *(978-1-61633-172-6(0))* Guardian Angel Publishing, Inc.

Hough, Hannah Bliss. See with Me. Lewis, Joan Lane. 2011. 32p. pap. 24.95 *(978-1-4626-2347-1(6))* America Star Bks.

Houghton, Chris & Morrison, Jeff. Jeff Gordon. Carney, Larry. PC Treasures Staff, ed. 2009. (Nascar Drivers Coloring/Sticker Book Ser.). (ENG.). 96p. (J). pap. 6.95 *(978-1-60072-162-5(1))* PC Treasures, Inc.

Houghton, Diane R. Helpin' Bugs. Lonborg, Rosemary. 2006. 32p. (J). (gr. -1-3). reprint ed. pap. 7.00 *(978-1-4223-5405-6(9))* DIANE Publishing Co.

—My Little Friend Goes to a Baseball Game. Finnegan, Evelyn M. 2006. 32p. (J). (gr. -1-3). reprint ed. pap. 7.00 *(978-1-4223-5403-2(2))* DIANE Publishing Co.

—My Little Friend Goes to the Dentist. Finnegan, Evelyn M. 2006. 32p. (J). (gr. -1-3). reprint ed. pap. 7.00 *(978-1-4223-5404-9(0))* DIANE Publishing Co.

Houghton, Jane Moore. Gracie Brave. Krikke, Pamela & Eldean Ma, Mft Kate. 2017. (ENG.). 38p. (J). 16.99 *(978-0-9996085-2-4(5))* Mindstir Media.

Houghton, Roswitha. City Zoo Blizzard Revue. Crispin, Barbara. 2003. 40p. 14.95 *(978-0-9716346-1-9(0))* Dancing Words Pr., Inc.

Houlette, Yutaka. Fred Korematsu Speaks Up. Atkins, Laura & Yogi, Stan. 2017. (Fighting for Justice Ser.: 1). (ENG.). 112p. (J). 18.00 *(978-1-59714-368-4(5))* Heyday.

Houpt, Beverly. The Adventures of Rhemmie & Squeak: How It All Began. Black, Shelley. 2019. (ENG.). 32p. (J). 23.95 ***(978-1-64670-120-9(8))***; pap. 13.95 ***(978-1-64670-119-3(4))*** Covenant Bks.

House, Charles. Alcatraz Believe It or Not. Bakker, T. C. 2016. 110p. *(978-1-932519-36-5(X))* Golden Gate National Parks Conservancy.

Housley, Cathren. The Christmas Cats, 1 vol. Wallace, Nancy K. 2011. (ENG.). 32p. (J). (gr. k-3). 16.99 *(978-1-58980-979-6(3)*, Pelican Publishing) Arcadia Publishing.

Housman, Clemence. Moonshine & Clover. Housman, Laurence, ed. 2013. 236p. (J). pap. *(978-1-909302-25-9(2))* Abela Publishing.

Houston, Bronwyn. Loongie, the Greedy Crocodile. Dann, Lucy & Dann, Kiefer. 2010. 24p. (J). (gr. k-2). pap. 12.95 *(978-1-921248-54-2(8))* Magabala Bks. AUS. Dist: Independent Pubs. Group.

Houston, Lauren, jt. illus. see Disney Storybook Art Team.

Houston, Melissa. Is the Moon God's? Jordan, Stephanie. 2005. (J). bds. 9.99 *(978-1-4183-0062-3(4))* Christ Inspired, Inc.

Houx, Emily Marie Cornell du. The Adventures of Sir Goblin, the Feline Knight. Moss, Barbara E. 2009. 336p. pap. 15.95 *(978-1-882190-03-4(3))* Polar Bear & Co.

Hovda, Lily & Fieger, Grace. Tom, the Listening Tree. Hovda, Ruby. 2019. (ENG.). 24p. (J). pap. 15.99 ***(978-1-7960-6254-0(5))*** Xlibris Corp.

Hovell, John. Jenny Found a Penny. Harris, Trudy. 2007. (Math Is Fun! Ser.). (ENG.). 32p. (gr. k-3). lib. bdg. 23.93 *(978-0-8225-6725-7(3)*, Millbrook Pr.) Lerner Publishing Group.

Hovemann, Anisa Claire. Earth Heroes, Champions of the Wilderness, 1 vol. Malnor, Bruce & Malnor, Carol. 2011. (ENG.). 143p. (J). (gr. 5-8). pap. 12.95 *(978-1-58469-116-7(6)*, Dawn Pubns.) Sourcebooks, Inc.

—Earth Heroes, Champions of Wild Animals, 1 vol. Malnor, Carol L. & Malnor, Bruce. 2011. (ENG.). 144p. (J). (gr. 5-8). pap. 12.95 *(978-1-58469-123-5(9)*, Dawn Pubns.) Sourcebooks, Inc.

—Eliza & the Dragonfly. Rinehart, Susie Caldwell. 2004. (Sharing Nature with Children Book Ser.). 32p. (J). 16.95 *(978-1-58469-060-3(7))* Dawn Pubns.

—Eliza & the Dragonfly. Rinehart, Susie Caldwell. 2012. (ENG.). 32p. (J). (-4). pap. 8.95 *(978-1-58469-059-7(3)*, Dawn Pubns.) Sourcebooks, Inc.

—If You Give a T-Rex a Bone. Myers, Tim. 2007. (Sharing Nature with Children Book Ser.). 32p. (J). (gr. -1-5). 16.95 *(978-1-58469-097-9(6))* Dawn Pubns.

—If You Give a T-Rex a Bone, 1 vol. Myers, Tim. 2013. (ENG.). 32p. (J). (gr. -1-4). 8.95 *(978-1-58469-098-6(4)*, Dawn Pubns.) Sourcebooks, Inc.

Hovemann, Anisa Claire, jt. illus. see Canyon, Christopher.

Hovhannisyan, Nune. A Bike of Bees. Velikanje, Kathryn. 2013. 58p. (J). pap. 12.28 *(978-1-939896-03-2(7))* Levity Pr.

—Zebras Paint Themselves Rainbow. Velikanje, Kathryn. 2013. 58p. pap. 12.28 *(978-1-939896-02-5(9))* Levity Pr.

Hovland, Gary. The Goldfish in the Chandelier. Kesterson, Casie. 2012. (ENG.). 32p. 17.95 *(978-1-60606-094-0(5)*, J. Paul Getty Museum) Getty Pubns.

—If the Walls Could Talk: Family Life at the White House. O'Connor, Jane. 2004. (ENG.). 48p. (J). (gr. 1-4). 19.99 *(978-0-689-86863-4(4)*, Simon & Schuster/Paula Wiseman Bks.) Simon & Schuster/Paula Wiseman Bks.

Hovland, Øivind. Time Trails: Dinosaurs. Gogerly, Liz & Hunt, Rob. 2020. (Time Trails Ser.). (ENG.). 32p. (J). (gr. 4-6). pap. 12.99 *(978-1-4451-5856-3(6)*, Franklin Watts) Hachette Children's Group GBR. Dist: Hachette Bk. Group.

—Time Trails: Rainforest. Gogerly, Liz & Hunt, Rob. 2020. (Time Trails Ser.). (ENG.). 32p. (J). (gr. 4-6). pap. 12.99 *(978-1-4451-5852-5(3)*, Franklin Watts) Hachette Children's Group GBR. Dist: Hachette Bk. Group.

Hovland, Oivind. Time Trails: Rainforest. Gogerly, Liz & Hunt, Rob. ed. 2019. (Time Trails Ser.). 32p. (J). (gr. 2-17). 16.99 *(978-1-4451-5851-8(5)*, Franklin Watts) Hachette Children's Group GBR. Dist: Hachette Bk. Group.

—Vampires. Orme, David. 2010. (Fact to Fiction Grafx Ser.). 36p. pap. 7.45 *(978-0-7891-7999-9(7))* Perfection Learning Corp.

Howard, Arthur. Bubba & Beau, Best Friends. Appelt, Kathi. 2006. (Bubba & Beau Ser.). (ENG.). 32p. (J). (gr. -1-3). pap. 6.99 *(978-0-15-205580-6(0)*, 1196783) Houghton Mifflin Harcourt Publishing Co.

—Bullies Never Win. Cuyler, Margery. 2009. (ENG.). 32p. (J). (gr. k-3). 18.99 *(978-0-689-86187-1(7)*, Simon & Schuster Bks. For Young Readers) Simon & Schuster Bks. For Young Readers.

—Friendship Stories You Can Share. Lobel, Arnold & Rylant, Cynthia. 2004. 64p. (J). (gr. 1-4). reprint ed. 15.00 *(978-0-7567-7149-2(8))* DIANE Publishing Co.

—Goatilocks & the Three Bears. Perl, Erica S. 2014. (ENG.). 40p. (J). (gr. -1-3). 17.99 *(978-1-4424-0168-6(0)*, Beach Lane Bks.) Beach Lane Bks.

—Gooseberry Park. Rylant, Cynthia. 2007. (ENG.). 144p. (J). (gr. 3-7). pap. 7.99 *(978-0-15-206159-3(2)*, 1198490) Houghton Mifflin Harcourt Publishing Co.

—Gooseberry Park & the Master Plan. Rylant, Cynthia. 2015. (ENG.). 128p. (J). (gr. 3-7). 16.99 *(978-1-4814-0449-5(0)*, Beach Lane Bks.) Beach Lane Bks.

—Hooray for Reading Day! Cuyler, Margery. 2008. (Jessica Worries Ser.). (ENG.). 32p. (J). (gr. k-3). 17.99 *(978-0-689-86188-8(5)*, Simon & Schuster Bks. For Young Readers) Simon & Schuster Bks. For Young Readers.

—Hooray for Reading Day! Cuyler, Margery. 2008. (J). (gr. k-1). 27.95 incl. audio *(978-0-8045-6969-9(X))*; 29.95 incl. audio compact disk *(978-0-8045-4194-7(9))* Spoken Arts, Inc.

—I Repeat, Don't Cheat! Cuyler, Margery. 2010. (ENG.). 32p. (J). (gr. k-3). 19.99 *(978-1-4169-7167-2(X)*, Simon & Schuster Bks. For Young Readers) Simon & Schuster Bks. For Young Readers.

—Life As We Knew It. Pfeffer, Susan Beth. 2006. (Life As We Knew It Ser.: 1). (ENG.). 352p. (YA). (gr. 7-12). 17.99 *(978-0-15-205826-5(5)*, 1197505) Houghton Mifflin Harcourt Publishing Co.

—Motor Mouse. Rylant, Cynthia. 2019. (Motor Mouse Bks.). (ENG.). 64p. (J). (gr. -1-3). 17.99 *(978-1-4814-9126-6(1)*, Beach Lane Bks.) Beach Lane Bks.

—Motor Mouse Delivers. Rylant, Cynthia. 2020. (Motor Mouse Bks.). (ENG.). 72p. (J). (gr. -1-3). 18.99 *(978-1-4814-9128-0(8)*, Beach Lane Bks.) Beach Lane Bks.

—Mr. Putter & Tabby Catch the Cold. Rylant, Cynthia. 2007. (Mr. Putter & Tabby Ser.). pap. 7.93 *(978-1-4189-5220-4(6))* Houghton Mifflin Harcourt Trade & Reference Pubs.

—Mr. Putter & Tabby Catch the Cold. Rylant, Cynthia. 2003. (Mr. Putter & Tabby Ser.). (gr. 1-4). 16.00 *(978-0-7569-1514-8(7))* Perfection Learning Corp.

—Mr. Putter & Tabby Clear the Decks. Rylant, Cynthia. alt. ed. 2011. (Mr. Putter & Tabby Ser.). (ENG.). 44p. (J). (gr. 1-4). pap. 5.99 *(978-0-547-57695-4(1)*, 1458450) Houghton Mifflin Harcourt Publishing Co.

—Mr. Putter & Tabby Drop the Ball. Rylant, Cynthia. (Mr. Putter & Tabby Ser.). (ENG.). 44p. (J). (gr. 1-4). 2014. pap. 5.99 *(978-0-544-34115-9(5)*, 1584856, HMH Books For Young Readers); 2013. 14.99 *(978-0-15-205072-6(8)*, 1195319) Houghton Mifflin Harcourt Publishing Co.

—Mr. Putter & Tabby Drop the Ball. Rylant, Cynthia. 2014. (Mr. Putter & Tabby Ser.). (ENG.). (J). (gr. 1-4). lib. bdg. 16.60 *(978-1-62765-745-7(2))* Perfection Learning Corp.

—Mr. Putter & Tabby Feed the Fish. Rylant, Cynthia. 2007. (Mr. Putter & Tabby Ser.). pap. 7.93 *(978-1-4189-5238-9(9))* Houghton Mifflin Harcourt Supplemental Pubs.

—Mr. Putter & Tabby Hit the Slope. Rylant, Cynthia. (Mr. Putter & Tabby Ser.). (ENG.). 40p. (J). (gr. 1-4). 2017. pap. 5.99 *(978-1-328-74060-1(9)*, 1677037); 2016. 14.99 *(978-0-15-206427-3(3)*, 1199224) Houghton Mifflin Harcourt Publishing Co. (HMH Books For Young Readers).

—Mr. Putter & Tabby Make a Wish. Rylant, Cynthia. 2006. (Mr. Putter & Tabby Ser.). (ENG.). 44p. (J). (gr. -1-3). pap. 5.99 *(978-0-15-205443-4(X)*, 1196381) Houghton Mifflin Harcourt Publishing Co.

—Mr. Putter & Tabby Make a Wish. Rylant, Cynthia. 2006. (Mr. Putter & Tabby Ser.). (gr. 1-4). 16.00 *(978-0-7569-6892-2(5))* Perfection Learning Corp.

—Mr. Putter & Tabby Ring the Bell. Rylant, Cynthia. 2012. (Mr. Putter & Tabby Ser.). (ENG.). 44p. (J). (gr. 1-4). pap. 5.99 *(978-0-547-85075-7(1)*, 1501053) Houghton Mifflin Harcourt Publishing Co.

—Mr. Putter & Tabby Ring the Bell. Rylant, Cynthia. ed. 2012. (Mr. Putter & Tabby Ser.). lib. bdg. 16.00 *(978-0-606-26614-7(3))* Turtleback.

—Mr. Putter & Tabby Run the Race. Rylant, Cynthia. 2010. (Mr. Putter & Tabby Ser.). (ENG.). 44p. (J). (gr. 1-4). pap. 5.99 *(978-0-547-24824-0(5)*, 1100731) Houghton Mifflin Harcourt Publishing Co.

—Mr. Putter & Tabby See the Stars. Rylant, Cynthia. 2008. (Mr. Putter & Tabby Ser.). (ENG.). 44p. (J). (gr. 1-4). pap. 5.99 *(978-0-15-206366-5(8)*, 1199066) Houghton Mifflin Harcourt Publishing Co.

—Mr. Putter & Tabby Smell the Roses. Rylant, Cynthia. (Mr. Putter & Tabby Ser.: 24). (ENG.). 40p. (J). (gr. 1-4). 2016. pap. 5.99 *(978-0-544-80907-9(6)*, 1641356); 2015. 14.99 *(978-0-15-206081-7(2)*, 1198266) Houghton Mifflin Harcourt Publishing Co. (HMH Books For Young Readers).

—Mr. Putter & Tabby Spill the Beans. Rylant, Cynthia. 2010. (Mr. Putter & Tabby Ser.). (ENG.). 44p. (J). (gr. 1-4). pap. 5.99 *(978-0-547-41433-1(1)*, 1429464) Houghton Mifflin Harcourt Publishing Co.

—Mr. Putter & Tabby Spin the Yarn. Rylant, Cynthia. 2007. (Mr. Putter & Tabby Ser.). (ENG.). 44p. (J). (gr. 1-4). pap. 5.99 *(978-0-15-206095-4(2)*, 1198308) Houghton Mifflin Harcourt Publishing Co.

—Mr. Putter & Tabby Spin the Yarn. Rylant, Cynthia. 2007. (Mr. Putter & Tabby Ser.). (gr. 1-4). lib. bdg. 16.00 *(978-0-7569-8062-7(3))* Perfection Learning Corp.

H

—Mr. Putter & Tabby Stir the Soup. Rylant, Cynthia. 2004. (Mr. Putter & Tabby Ser.). (ENG.). 44p. (J). (gr. 1-4). pap. 5.99 *(978-0-15-205058-0(2)*, 1195275) Houghton Mifflin Harcourt Publishing Co.

—Mr. Putter & Tabby Stir the Soup. Rylant, Cynthia. 2004. (Mr. Putter & Tabby Ser.). (gr. 1-4). 16.00 *(978-0-7569-3915-1(1))* Perfection Learning Corp.

—Mr. Putter & Tabby Turn the Page. Rylant, Cynthia. (Mr. Putter & Tabby Ser.). (ENG.). 40p. (J). (gr. 1-4). 2015. pap. 5.99 *(978-0-544-58232-3(2)*, 1613542); 2014. 14.99 *(978-0-15-206063-3(4)*, 1198212) Houghton Mifflin Harcourt Publishing Co. (HMH Books For Young Readers).

—Mr. Putter & Tabby Walk the Dog. Rylant, Cynthia. 2007. (Mr. Putter & Tabby Ser.). pap. 7.93 *(978-1-4189-5209-9(5))* Houghton Mifflin Harcourt Trade & Reference Pubs.

—Mr. Putter & Tabby Write the Book. Rylant, Cynthia. ed. 2005. (Mr. Putter & Tabby Ser.). (ENG.). 44p. (J). (gr. 1-4). pap. 5.99 *(978-0-15-200242-8(1)*, 1186259) Houghton Mifflin Harcourt Publishing Co.

—Mr. Putter & Tabby Write the Book. Rylant, Cynthia. 2005. (Mr. Putter & Tabby Ser.). 36p. (J). (gr. 1-4). 13.60 *(978-0-7569-5446-8(0))* Perfection Learning Corp.

—Noodle & Lou. Scanlon, Liz Garton. 2011. (ENG.). 32p. (J). (gr. -1-1). 15.99 *(978-1-4424-0288-1(1)*, Beach Lane Bks.) Beach Lane Bks.

—Quiet Wyatt. Sauer, Tammi. 2018. (ENG.). 32p. (J). (gr. -1-3). 17.99 *(978-0-544-11330-5(6)*, 1541760, Clarion Bks.) Houghton Mifflin Harcourt Trade & Reference Pubs.

—Stop Drop & Roll. Cuyler, Margery. 25.95 incl. audio *(978-1-59112-976-9(1))*; 28.95 incl. audio compact disk *(978-1-59112-980-6(X))*; pap. 16.95 incl. audio *(978-1-59112-975-2(3))*; pap. incl. audio *(978-1-59112-977-6(X))*; pap. 18.95 incl. audio compact disk *(978-1-59112-979-0(6))*; pap. incl. audio compact disk *(978-1-59112-981-3(8))* Live Oak Media.

—100th Day Worries. Cuyler, Margery. 2006. (ENG.). 32p. (J). (gr. k-3). reprint ed. 7.99 *(978-1-4169-0789-3(0)*, Simon & Schuster Bks. For Young Readers) Simon & Schuster Bks. For Young Readers.

Howard, Arthur. Mr. Putter & Tabby Catch the Cold. Howard, Arthur. Rylant, Cynthia. 2003. (Mr. Putter & Tabby Ser.). (ENG.). 44p. (J). (gr. 1-4). pap. 5.99 *(978-0-15-204760-3(3)*, 1194359) Houghton Mifflin Harcourt Publishing Co.

—Mr. Putter & Tabby Dance the Dance. Howard, Arthur. Rylant, Cynthia. 2013. (Mr. Putter & Tabby Ser.). (ENG.). 40p. (J). (gr. 1-4). pap. 5.99 *(978-0-544-10496-9(X)*, 1540802) Houghton Mifflin Harcourt Publishing Co.

—My Dream Dog. Howard, Arthur. 2016. (ENG.). 32p. (J). (gr. -1-3). 17.99 *(978-1-4814-5838-2(8)*, Beach Lane Bks.) Beach Lane Bks.

Howard, Becky L. Harrison Goes Camping. Howard, Becky L. Pine, Margherita N., ed. 2nd ed. 2012. 26p. (-18). pap. 11.98 *(978-0-9848782-1-5(1))* Palmetto Street Publishing.

Howard, Bob. Rainbow Zoo: A Book of Poems (Mostly) for Children. Greene, Rick. 2019. (ENG.). 56p. (J). pap. 10.50 *(978-1-5393-0003-8(X))* CreateSpace Independent Publishing Platform.

Howard, Colin. Drawing Fascinating Animals. Colich, Abby. 2015. (Drawing Amazing Animals Ser.). (ENG.). 32p. (J). (gr. 3-9). 28.65 *(978-1-4914-2133-8(9)*, Capstone Pr.) Capstone.

Howard, Colin, et al. How to Draw Griffins, Unicorns, & Other Mythical Beasts. Sautter, A. J. 2016. (Drawing Fantasy Creatures Ser.). (ENG.). 32p. (J). (gr. 3-9). lib. bdg. 28.65 *(978-1-4914-8025-0(4)*, Capstone Pr.) Capstone.

Howard, Colin. The Ultimate Girls' Guide to Drawing: Puppies, Polar Bears, & Other Adorable Animals. Colich, Abby. 2015. (ENG.). 144p. (J). (gr. 3-9). pap. 14.95 *(978-1-62370-229-8(1)*, Capstone Young Readers) Capstone.

—Wolves. Black, Robyn Hood. 2008. (ENG.). 24p. (J). (gr. 3-18). 19.95 *(978-1-58117-817-3(4)*, Intervisual/Piggy Toes) Bendon, Inc.

Howard, Colin, jt. illus. see Calle, Juan.

Howard, Dave. Lady's Day to Play. Howard, Dave. 2011. (ENG.). 32p. (J). (gr. -1-3). pap. 14.95 *(978-0-938467-25-0(5))* Headline Bks., Inc.

Howard, Devon, photos by. Surfboards: From Start to Finish. Smith, Ryan A. 2006. (Made in the U. S. A. Ser.). (ENG., 32p. (J). (gr. 3-7). lib. bdg. 25.65 *(978-1-4103-0728-6(X)*, Blackbirch Pr., Inc.) Cengage Gale.

Howard, Ellie Nothaus. Daddies Don't Get Snow Days. Ball, S. N. 2013. (ENG.). 28p. (J). pap. 13.95 *(978-1-4787-1188-9(4))* Outskirts Pr., Inc.

Howard, Josh. Dead@17: Blood of Saints. Howard, Josh. 2004. 112p. (YA). per. 14.95 *(978-0-9754193-1-1(5))* Viper Comics.

—Dead@17: The Complete First Series. Howard, Josh. 2004. (YA). per. 14.95 *(978-0-9754193-0-4(7))* Viper Comics.

Howard, Juliet. My Very Own Dreidel: A Pop-up Hanakkah Celebration! Kollin, Dani. 2007. (ENG.). 12p. 10.95 *(978-1-58117-592-9(2)*, Intervisual/Piggy Toes) Bendon, Inc.

Howard, Kate. On Our Way to First Grade. 2015. 32p. (J). *(978-0-545-82340-1(4))* Scholastic, Inc.

Howard, Linda & Dockray, Tracy Arah. Mi Gran Libro de Palabras Play-Doh. 2006. (SPA.). 10p. (J). (gr. -1-4). reprint ed. 10.00 *(978-1-4223-5586-2(1))* DIANE Publishing Co.

Howard, Megz. Fiona Faintly: A Goats Tale. Bristol, P. L. & Branda, Barnabus. 2011. 32p. pap. 24.95 *(978-1-4626-3362-3(5))* America Star Bks.

Howard, Molly. Henry Benett & the Hidden Book of Magic: Part 2 - More Magical Secrets. Howard, K. J. 2016. (ENG.). (J). pap. *(978-0-9946205-6-9(X))* Lilly Pilly Publishing.

Howard, Monique. The Moon Creeper (Simplified Chinese & English) Howard, Monique. Li, Helen, tr. 2010. (CHI & ENG.). 40p. (YA). pap. 7.95 *(978-1-935706-24-3(1))* Wiggles Pr.

Howard, Norma. Walking the Choctaw Road: Stories from Red People Memory. Tingle, Tim. 2003. (ENG.). 128p. (J). (gr. 7-9). 16.95 *(978-0-938317-74-6(1))* Cinco Puntos Pr.

Howard, Pam. Alex & the Amazing Lemonade Stand. Scott, Liz et al. 2005. 32p. (gr. -1-5). 15.95 *(978-0-9753200-0-6(9))* PAJE Publishing Co.

Howard, Patricia. Live! From the Classroom! It's Mythology! Five Read-Aloud Plays Based on Hero Myths from Around the World. Thurston, Cheryl Miller & Etzel, Laurie Hopkins. 2003. (ENG.). 82p. per. 16.95 *(978-1-877673-59-7(5)*, MYTH-BWK03) Cottonwood Pr., Inc.

Howard, Paul. The Cat Who Wanted to Go Home. Tomlinson, Jill. 2014. (ENG.). 96p. (J). (gr. -1-2). pap. 10.99 *(978-1-4052-7196-7(5))* Egmont Bks., Ltd. GBR. Dist: Independent Pubs. Group.

—Classic Poetry: Candlewick Illustrated Classic. Rosen, Michael, ed. 2009. (Candlewick Illustrated Classics Ser.). (ENG.). 160p. (J). (gr. 5-7). pap. 12.99 *(978-0-7636-4210-5(X))* Candlewick Pr.

—Full, Full, Full of Love. Cooke, Trish. 2008. (ENG.). 32p. (J). (gr. -1-k). pap. 5.99 *(978-0-7636-3883-2(8))* Candlewick Pr.

—The Gorilla Who Wanted to Grow Up. Tomlinson, Jill. 2014. (ENG.). 112p. (J). (gr. -1-2). pap. 9.99 *(978-1-4052-7195-0(7))* Egmont Bks., Ltd. GBR. Dist: Independent Pubs. Group.

—The Otter Who Wanted to Know. Tomlinson, Jill. 2014. (ENG.). 96p. (J). (gr. -1-2). pap. 8.99 *(978-1-4052-7194-3(9))* Egmont Bks., Ltd. GBR. Dist: Independent Pubs. Group.

—The Owl Who Was Afraid of the Dark. Tomlinson, Jill. 2014. (ENG.). 112p. (J). (gr. -1-2). pap. 9.99 *(978-1-4052-7197-4(3))* Egmont Bks., Ltd. GBR. Dist: Independent Pubs. Group.

—Owl Who Was Afraid of the Dark. Tomlinson, Jill. ed. 2008. (ENG.). 32p. (J). (gr. k-2). pap. 10.99 *(978-1-4052-0177-3(0))* Egmont Bks., Ltd. GBR. Dist: Independent Pubs. Group.

—The Penguin Who Wanted to Find Out. Tomlinson, Jill. 2014. (ENG.). 96p. (J). (gr. -1-2). pap. 10.99 *(978-1-4052-7191-2(4))* Egmont Bks., Ltd. GBR. Dist: Independent Pubs. Group.

Howard, Pauline Rodriguez. Icy Watermelon/Sandia Fria: CD & Book Set. 2008. (ENG & SPA.). 32p. (J). 23.95 *(978-0-9815686-0-7(2))* Lorito Bks., Inc.

Howard, Pauline Rodriguez, jt. illus. see Rodriguez Howard, Pauline.

Howard, Philip & Miller, Josh. Mystery at Blackbeard's Cove. Penn, Audrey. 2004. (ENG.). 200p. (J). (gr. 3-7). 14.95 *(978-0-9749303-1-2(8))* Tanglewood Pr.

Howard, Rebecca. Flagtastic Flags. 2006. (ENG.). 32p. (J). (gr. -1-3). 14.95 *(978-0-7145-3305-6(X))* Boyars, Marion Pubs., Ltd. GBR. Dist: Consortium Bk. Sales & Distribution.

Howard, Rushton. Sebastian Reckless. Howard, Rushton. 2005. 263p. (J). per. 8.99 *(978-0-9768088-0-0(3))* Abdiel Productions.

Howard, Russell. Bernard Jones Is Going Places: Book One. Bernard, Teko. 2018. (ENG.). 108p. (J). (gr. 2-5). pap. 9.99 *(978-0-9860593-4-6(X))* Elmdale Park Books.

Howard, Tait. The Sunken Tower. Howard, Tait. 2020. (Sunken Tower Ser.). (ENG.). 136p. (J). 17.99 *(978-1-62010-687-7(6)*, Lion Forge) Oni Pr., Inc.

Howard, Uncle Dave. Flutter Flutter, Hop Hop. Silassy, Malisa. 2018. (ENG.). 26p. (J). pap. 10.00 *(978-1-7905-9549-5(5))* Independently Published.

Howard, Virginia. Timothy Hubble & the King Cake Party, 1 vol. Prieto, Anita C. 2008. (ENG.). 32p. (J). (gr. k-3). 16.99 *(978-1-58980-584-2(4)*, Pelican Publishing) Arcadia Publishing.

Howard, Zachariah. The Shroud of A'Ranka. Sniegoski, Thomas E. 2008. (Brimstone Network Ser.: 2). (ENG.). 288p. (J). (gr. 4-8). pap. 5.99 *(978-1-4169-5105-6(9)*, Simon & Schuster/Paula Wiseman Bks.) Simon & Schuster/Paula Wiseman Bks.

Howarth, Craig. Bess Takes a Ride. Kilgus, Walter C. 2008. (ENG.). 36p. pap. 17.49 *(978-1-4257-8807-0(6))* Xlibris Corp.

—Dear Joey. Kruse, Donald W. 3rd ed. 2019. (ENG.). 60p. (J). (gr. 3-6). pap. 15.95 *(978-0-9994571-8-4(7))* Zaccheus Entertainment Co.

—Dirkle Smat Inside Mount Flatbottom. Garthwaite, Lynn D. 2006. 48p. (J). pap. 9.95 *(978-1-59663-512-8(6)*, Castle Keep Pr.) Rock, James A. & Co. Pubs.

—Emma & the Wild Boar. Kilgus, Walter C. 2006. (ENG.). 46p. per. 17.99 *(978-1-4257-1088-0(3))* Xlibris Corp.

Howarth, Craig. The Game. Karlberg, Michael. 2020. (ENG.). 50p. (J). ***(978-1-876322-52-6(7))*** Baha'i Pubns. Australia.

Howarth, Craig. The Ghost of Wolverine Forest. Kruse, Donald W. 2nd ed. 2019. (Ghost of Wolverine Forest Trilogy Ser.: Vol. 1). (ENG.). 84p. (YA). (gr. 7-12). pap. 7.99 *(978-0-9994571-5-3(2))* Zaccheus Entertainment Co.

—The Ghost of Wolverine Forest, Part 2: Son of Cytok. Kruse, Donald W. 2nd ed. 2019. (Ghost of Wolverine Forest Ser.: Vol. 2). (ENG.). 84p. (YA). (gr. 7-12). pap. 7.99 *(978-0-9994571-6-0(0))* Zaccheus Entertainment Co.

—Michael's Safari. Francis, JennaKay. 2013. 12p. pap. 8.95 *(978-1-61633-411-6(8))* Guardian Angel Publishing, Inc.

—Moose Pee & Tea! Kruse, Donald W. 2018. (ENG.). 40p. (J). (gr. k-5). pap. 14.95 *(978-0-9985191-3-5(8))* Zaccheus Entertainment Co.

—Spinosaur Island. Kruse, Donald W. 2nd ed. 2018. (ENG.). 164p. (YA). (gr. 7-12). pap. 9.99 *(978-0-9994571-2-2(8))* Zaccheus Entertainment Co.

—That's Not A Pickle! Kruse, Donald W. 2008. (ENG.). 40p. (J). pap. 12.95 *(978-1-59663-560-9(6)*, Castle Keep Pr.) Rock, James A. & Co. Pubs.

—That's Not a Pickle! Kruse, Donald W. 2018. (That's Not a Pickle! Ser.: Vol. 1). (ENG.). 40p. (J). (gr. k-5). pap. 12.95 *(978-0-9985191-5-9(4))* Zaccheus Entertainment Co.

—That's Not a Pickle! Part 2. Kruse, Donald W. 2018. (That's Not a Pickle! Ser.: Vol. 2). (ENG.). 48p. (J). (gr. k-5). pap. 14.95 *(978-0-9985191-6-6(2))* Zaccheus Entertainment Co.

—That's Not a Pickle! Part 2 Pt. 2. Kruse, Donald W. 2010. 44p. (J). pap. 12.95 *(978-1-59663-686-6(6)*, Castle Keep Pr.) Rock, James A. & Co. Pubs.

—That's Not a Pickle! Part 3. Kruse, Donald W. 2018. (That's Not a Pickle! Ser.: Vol. 3). (ENG.). 44p. (J). (gr. k-5). pap. 14.95 *(978-0-9985191-7-3(0))* Zaccheus Entertainment Co.

—That's Not a Pickle! Part 4. Kruse, Donald W. 2018. (That's Not a Pickle! Ser.: Vol. 4). (ENG.). 48p. (J). (gr. k-5). pap. 14.95 *(978-0-9985191-8-0(9))* Zaccheus Entertainment Co.

—That's Not a Pickle! Part 6. Kruse, Donald W. 2018. (ENG.). 48p. (J). (gr. k-5). pap. 14.95 *(978-0-9994571-0-8(1))* Zaccheus Entertainment Co.

—Whiskers. Kruse, Donald W. 2nd ed. 2019. (ENG.). 192p. (YA). (gr. 7-12). pap. 9.99 *(978-0-9994571-4-6(4))* Zaccheus Entertainment Co.

Howarth, Daniel. Good Night Little Moo. Cabral, Jeane. 2007. (Night Light Book Ser.). 10p. (gr. -1-k). *(978-1-84666-128-0(5)*, Tide Mill Pr.) Top That! Publishing PLC.

—Good Night Little Piggy. Williams, Becky. 2007. (Night Light Book Ser.). 10p. (gr. -1-k). bds. *(978-1-84666-129-7(3)*, Tide Mill Pr.) Top That! Publishing PLC.

—The Goose That Laid the Golden Eggs. 2006. (First Reading Level 3 Ser.). 48p. (J). (gr. 1-4). 8.99 *(978-0-7945-1378-8(6)*, Usborne) EDC Publishing.

—The Hare & the Tortoise. MacKinnon, Mairi, ed. 2007. (First Reading Level 4 Ser.). 48p. (J). (gr. -1-3). 8.99 *(978-0-7945-1612-3(2)*, Usborne) EDC Publishing.

—Home Is Where My Heart Lives. Howarth, Heidi. 2018. (ENG.). 35p. (J). 10.95 *(978-0-8091-6787-6(5))* Paulist Pr.

—I Am a Mole, & I Live in a Hole. Conchie, Kathryn. Top That Publishing Staff, ed. 2008. (Story Book Ser.). 12p. (J). (gr. -1). *(978-1-84666-575-2(2)*, Tide Mill Pr.) Top That! Publishing PLC.

—Land of the lost Teddies. Fischel, Emma. rev. ed. 2003. 32p. (J). (gr. 2-18). pap. 4.95 *(978-0-7945-0402-1(7)*, Usborne) EDC Publishing.

—My Bedtime Story Bible for Little Ones, 1 vol. Syswerda, Jean E. 2016. (ENG.). 32p. (J). bds. 9.99 *(978-0-310-75330-8(9))* Zonderkidz.

—The Otter Who Loved to Hold Hands. Howarth, Heidi. 2014. (J). *(978-1-4351-5537-4(8))* Barnes & Noble, Inc.

—Owl's Winter Rescue. Loughrey, Anita. 2016. (J). *(978-1-4351-6415-4(6))* Barnes & Noble, Inc.

—Paddywack. Spinner, Stephanie. 2010. (Step into Reading Ser.). 48p. (J). (gr. k-3). pap. 4.99 *(978-0-375-86186-4(6)*, Random Hse. Bks. for Young Readers) Random Hse. Children's Bks.

—Polar Bears: Internet-Referenced. Mason, Conrad. 2009. (First Reading Level 4 Ser.). 48p. (J). 6.99 *(978-0-7945-2457-9(5)*, Usborne) EDC Publishing.

—Scaredy Cat! Joyce, Melanie. 2018. (ENG.). 26p. (J). bds. 8.99 *(978-1-4998-8011-3(1))* Igloo Bks. GBR. Dist: Simon & Schuster, Inc.

—Scaredy Cat! A Roaringly Good Tale. Joyce, Melanie. 2015. (ENG.). 24p. (J). 9.95 *(978-1-78343-439-8(2))* Igloo Bks. GBR. Dist: Simon & Schuster, Inc.

—The Teddy Bears' Picnic. Baxter, Nicola. 2015. (ENG.). 24p. pap. 6.99 *(978-1-86147-654-8(X)*, Armadillo) Anness Publishing GBR. Dist: National Bk. Network.

—Voting with a Porpoise. Glass, Russell & Callahan, Sean. 2018. (ENG.). 32p. (J). 24.99 *(978-1-7327454-0-7(4))*; pap. 14.99 *(978-1-7327454-1-4(2))* Bks. with a Porpoise, LLC.

—Who's Been Eating My Porridge? Butler, M. Christina. 2004. 32p. (J). (gr. -1). tchr. ed. 15.95 *(978-1-58925-040-6(0))* Tiger Tales.

—Why I Love My Daddy. 2013. (ENG.). 32p. (J). pap. 6.99 *(978-0-00-750866-2(2)*, HarperCollins Children's Bks.) HarperCollins Pubs. Ltd. GBR. Dist: HarperCollins Pubs.

—Will You Still Love Me? Roth, Carol. 2013. (AV2 Fiction Readalong Ser.: Vol. 75). (ENG.). (J). (gr. -1 — 1). 32.71 *(978-1-62127-911-2(1)*, AV2 by Weigl) Weigl Pubs., Inc.

Howarth, Jill. The ABCs of Christmas. 2016. 26p. (J). (gr. -1 — 1). 7.95 *(978-0-7624-6125-7(X)*, Running Pr. Kids) Running Pr.

—The Colors of Christmas. 2019. 22p. (J). (gr. -1 — 1). bds. 9.99 *(978-0-7624-6610-8(3)*, Running Pr. Kids) Running Pr.

—GOA Kids - Goats of Anarchy: Angel & Her Wonderful Wheels: A True Story of a Little Goat Who Walked with Wheels. Lauricella, Leanne. 2018. (GOA Kids - Goats of Anarchy Ser.: 4). (ENG.). 32p. (J). (gr. -1-1). 17.95 *(978-1-63322-674-6(3)*, Walter Foster Jr) Quarto Publishing Group USA.

—GOA Kids - Goats of Anarchy: Polly & Her Duck Costume: + the True Story of a Little Blind Rescue Goat. Lauricella, Leanne. 2017. (GOA Kids - Goats of Anarchy Ser.: 1). (ENG.). 32p. (J). (gr. -1-1). 17.95 *(978-1-63322-418-6(X)*, Walter Foster Jr) Quarto Publishing Group USA.

—Good Night, Little Engine. Piper, Watty & Lawler, Janet. 2020. (Little Engine That Could Ser.). 32p. (J). (-k). 14.99 *(978-0-593-09457-0(3)*, Grosset & Dunlap) Penguin Young Readers Group.

—Jingle Bells. 2015. 8p. (J). (gr. -1 — 1). 10.95 *(978-0-7624-5842-4(9)*, Running Pr. Kids) Running Pr.

—Love from the Little Engine That Could. Piper, Watty. 2019. (Little Engine That Could Ser.). 32p. (J). (gr. k-3). 9.99 *(978-0-593-09433-4(6)*, Grosset & Dunlap) Penguin Young Readers Group.

—Peek-A-Bright Christmas: Tall Tiered Board Book. Berry Byrd, Holly. Cottage Door Press, ed. 2018. (ENG.). 10p. (J). (gr. -1-k). bds. 9.99 *(978-1-68052-343-0(0)*, 1003150) Cottage Door Pr.

—You Can! Words of Wisdom from the Little Engine That Could. Piper, Watty & Hart, Charlie. 2018. (Little Engine That Could Ser.). (ENG.). 80p. (J). (gr. 5-12). 12.99 *(978-1-5247-8468-3(0)*, Grosset & Dunlap) Penguin Young Readers Group.

—The 12 Days of Christmas. 2018. 26p. (J). (gr. -1 — 1). 7.99 *(978-0-7624-9142-1(6)*, Running Pr. Kids) Running Pr.

Howarth, Naomi. What's That Noise? Howarth, Naomi. 2020. (ENG.). 32p. (J). (gr. -1-2). 16.99 *(978-1-5362-1352-2(7))* Candlewick Pr.

Howcroft, Jay. Thumper's Hospital Adventure. Vandrilla, Katie. 2018. (ENG.). 38p. (J). pap. 11.99 *(978-1-7297-4454-3(0))* CreateSpace Independent Publishing Platform.

Howe, Cindy T. From Bullies to Friends. Nikolet, C. T. 2008. 25p. pap. 24.95 *(978-1-60610-121-6(8))* America Star Bks.

Howe, John. Literary Lessons from The Lord of the Rings. Harper, Amelia. 2004. 622p. (YA). (gr. 7-12). stu. ed., spiral bd. 50.00 *(978-0-9754934-1-0(8)*, Literary Lessons) HomeScholar Bks.

Howe, Kim. American Life Series: Family, Teacher, Friend, 3 books. 2006. 80p. 19.95 *(978-1-59971-554-4(6))* Aardvark Global Publishing.

Howe, Norma. Crocodile Tours. Tye, Peter. 2012. 80p. pap. *(978-1-78176-536-4(7))* FeedARead.com.

Howe, Philip. Kailey. Koss, Amy Goldman. 2003. (American Girl of Today Ser.). (ENG.). 160p. (J). pap. 6.95 *(978-1-58485-591-0(6))* American Girl Publishing, Inc.

Howe, Tina Field. Snailsworth, a slow little Story. Howe, Tina Field. 2007. 24p. (J). per. 12.95 *(978-0-9768585-3-9(3))* Howe, Tina Field.

Howell, Corin & Pitre-Durocher, Sara. Transformers: Windblade - Distant Stars. Scott, Mairghread. 2016. (Transformers Ser.). (ENG.). 120p. pap. 19.99 *(978-1-63140-600-3(0)*, 9781631406003) Idea & Design Works, LLC.

Howell, Jason W. Remember Me Always: A Remembrance Scrapbook. Crain, Suzanne L. 2004. 52p. spiral bd. *(978-0-9763254-0-6(3))* Crain, Suzanne.

Howell, Karen. Mackinac Passage: A Summer Adventure. Lytle, Robert A. 2020. (ENG.). 176p. (J). (gr. 4-7). pap. 12.95 *(978-1-882376-11-7(0))* Thunder Bay Pr.

Howell, Laura. Regular Show Original Graphic Novel Vol. 5: the Meatening: The Meatening. Andelfinger, Nicole. 2018. (Regular Show Ser.). (ENG.). 144p. (J). (gr. 4-7). pap. 14.99 *(978-1-68415-198-1(8))* Boom! Studios.

—Regular Show Vol. 10. Rupert, Mad. 2018. (Regular Show Ser.: 10). (ENG.). 112p. (J). (gr. 4-7). pap. 14.99 *(978-1-68415-061-8(2))* Boom! Studios.

—Regular Show Vol. 9. Freitas, Erick & Farinas, Ulises. 2017. (Regular Show Ser.: 9). (ENG.). 112p. (J). (gr. 4-7). pap. 14.99 *(978-1-68415-018-2(3))* Boom! Studios.

Howell, Troy. First Prayers: A Celebration of Faith & Love. 2012. 32p. (J). 12.95 *(978-1-4027-6454-7(5))* Sterling Publishing Co., Inc.

—Goliath: Hero of the Great Baltimore Fire. Friddell, Claudia. 2010. (True Stories Ser.). (ENG.). 32p. (J). (gr. 1-4). 17.95 *(978-1-58536-455-8(X)*, 202179) Sleeping Bear Pr.

—The Last of the Mohicans. Cooper, James Fenimore. 2008. (Classic Starts® Ser.). 160p. (J). (gr. 2-4). 6.95 *(978-1-4027-4577-5(X))* Sterling Publishing Co., Inc.

—The Man in the Iron Mask. Dumas, Alexandre. 2008. (Classic Starts® Ser.). 160p. (J). (gr. 2-4). 6.95 *(978-1-4027-4579-9(6))* Sterling Publishing Co., Inc.

—O Is for Old Dominion: A Virginia Alphabet. Edwards, Pamela Duncan. 2005. (State Ser.). (ENG.). 40p. (J). (gr. -1-3). 17.95 *(978-1-58536-161-8(5))* Sleeping Bear Pr.

—The Phantom of the Opera. Leroux, Gaston. 2008. (Classic Starts® Ser.). 160p. (J). (gr. 2-4). 6.95 *(978-1-4027-4580-5(X))* Sterling Publishing Co., Inc.

—The Time Machine. Wells, H. G. 2008. (Classic Starts® Ser.). 160p. (J). (gr. 2-4). 6.95 *(978-1-4027-4582-9(6))* Sterling Publishing Co., Inc.

Howells, Graham. Children's Stories from Myths & Legends: Classic Tales from Around the World. Randall, Ronne. 2017. 128p. (J). (gr. 3-12). 16.99 *(978-1-86147-852-8(6)*, Armadillo) Anness Publishing GBR. Dist: National Bk. Network.

—Creu Brawddegau. Meek, Elin. ed. 2005. (Helpwch Eich Plentyn / Help Your Child Ser.).Tr. of Forming Sentences. (WEL.). 48p. pap. 4.99 *(978-1-84323-354-1(1))* Gomer Pr. GBR. Dist: Gomer Pr.

—Power of the Fire Dragon. West, Tracey. 2015. (Dragon Masters Ser.: 4). (ENG.). 96p. (J). (gr. 1-3). pap. 4.99 *(978-0-545-64631-4(6))* Scholastic, Inc.

—Rise of the Earth Dragon. West, Tracey. 2014. (Dragon Masters Ser.: 1). (ENG.). 96p. (J). (gr. 1-3). 15.99 *(978-0-545-64624-6(3))*; pap. 4.99 *(978-0-545-64623-9(5))* Scholastic, Inc.

Howells, Graham & Jones, Damien. Saving the Sun Dragon. West, Tracey. 2014. (Dragon Masters Ser.: 2). (ENG.). 96p. (J). (gr. 1-3). 15.99 *(978-0-545-64626-0(X))*; pap. 4.99 *(978-0-545-64625-3(1))* Scholastic, Inc.

—Secret of the Water Dragon. West, Tracey. 2015. (Dragon Masters Ser.: 3). (ENG.). 96p. (J). (gr. 1-3). pap. 5.99 *(978-0-545-64628-4(6))* Scholastic, Inc.

Howells, Tania. Willow Finds a Way. Button, Lana. 2020. (Willow Ser.). (ENG.). 32p. (J). (gr. -1-2). 15.99 ***(978-1-5253-0650-1(2))*** Kids Can Pr., Ltd. CAN. Dist: Hachette Bk. Group.

Howells, Tania. Willow's Whispers, 0 vols. Button, Lana. (Willow Ser.). 32p. (J). (gr. -1-2). 2014. (ENG.). pap. 15.99 *(978-1-55453-744-0(4))*; 2010. 16.95 *(978-1-55453-280-3(9))* Kids Can Pr., Ltd. CAN. Dist: Hachette Bk. Group.

Howells, Tania. Starring Shapes! Howells, Tania. 2015. (ENG.). 24p. (J). (gr. -1-2). 15.95 *(978-1-55453-743-3(6))* Kids Can Pr., Ltd. CAN. Dist: Hachette Bk. Group.

Hower, Rebekah. The Adventures of Natalie the Dolphin Girl & Annie the Mermaid: Pictures by Rebekah Hower. Shorkey, Kevin & Shorkey, Natalie Rodriguez and Kevin. 2019. (Cousins Bks.: Vol. 1). (ENG.). 102p. (J). pap. 5.99 ***(978-1-0862-6445-6(2))*** Independently Published.

Howes, Bryan Arthur. The Purple Scarf. Coughlin, Jennie Rose. 2008. 20p. per. 24.95 *(978-1-60441-733-3(1))* America Star Bks.

Howitt, Mary. The Emperor's New Clothes. Andersen, Hans Christian. Paull, Susannah Mary, tr. 2019. (ENG.). 26p. (J). pap. 6.00 ***(978-1-0868-9328-1(X))*** Independently Published.

Howl, Kathryn. My Groundhogs. Blaker, Louise. 2018. (ENG.). 28p. (J). pap. 10.00 *(978-1-7901-9369-1(9))* Independently Published.

Howland, Naomi. The Nutcracker. Dewhurst, Carin. 2006. 24p. (J). (gr. 4-8). reprint ed. 20.00 *(978-1-4223-5524-4(1))* DIANE Publishing Co.

Howland, Naomi. The Mystery Bear: A Purim Story. Howland, Naomi, tr. Adelson, Leone. 2004. 32p. (J). (gr. -1-2). 15.00 *(978-0-618-33727-9(X)*, Clarion Bks.) Houghton Mifflin Harcourt Trade & Reference Pubs.

Hox, Joe. Buster's Ears Trip Him Up: When You Fail. Welch, Edward. 2018. (ENG.). 32p. (J). 15.99 *(978-1-948130-25-7(4))* New Growth Pr.

—Jax's Tail Twitches: When You Are Angry. Powlison, David. 2018. 32p. (J). 15.99 *(978-1-948130-24-0(6))* New Growth Pr.

Hoy, Molly. Coloring Book Kathryn the Grape Affirmation Series Seven-Book Special Edition. Cloward, Kathryn. 2019. (ENG.). (J). pap. 24.99 ***(978-1-970163-23-0(2))*** Kandon UnLtd., Inc.

Hoy Schmidt, Mary. The Most Love Ever! Hoy Schmidt, Mary. 2018. (Love Series, by Infinity Times Eternity Ser.: Vol. 1). (ENG.). 32p. (J). (gr. k-3). *(978-1-7752565-4-0(5))*; *(978-1-7752565-3-3(7))* Rising Intent.

Hoyes, Kerry. What You Eat It's up to You. Yanisko, Thomas. 2012. 36p. pap. 9.99 *(978-1-937260-26-2(7))* Sleepytown Pr.

Hoyle, Leighanna. My Day with the Dalai Lama: A Coloring Book for All Ages. Hellstrom, Travis. 2017. (ENG.). 48p. (J). (gr. -1-2). pap. 5.99 *(978-1-57826-639-5(4)*, Hatherleigh Pr.) Hatherleigh Co., Ltd., The.

Hoyle, Norma. The Keeper of the Shell. Bell, Eileen. 2019. (ENG.). 68p. (J). (gr. 3-6). *(978-1-989092-18-7(7))* Celticfrog Publishing.

Hoyt, Ard. Alice from Dallas. Sadler, Marilyn. 2014. (ENG.). 40p. (J). (gr. -1-3). 16.95 *(978-1-4197-0790-2(6)*, Abrams Bks. for Young Readers) Abrams, Inc.

—Bingo Did It! Harris, Amber. 2016. (Wisteria Jane Book Ser.). (ENG.). 32p. (J). (gr. -1-3). 16.95 *(978-1-60554-491-5(4))* Redleaf Pr.

—Chasing George Washington. Kennedy Center, The. 2011. (ENG.). 80p. (J). (gr. 2-5). pap. 5.99 *(978-1-4169-4861-2(9)*, Simon & Schuster Bks. For Young Readers) Simon & Schuster Bks. For Young Readers.

—Chasing George Washington. Kidd, Ronald et al. 2009. (ENG.). 80p. (J). (gr. 2-5). 12.99 *(978-1-4169-4858-2(9)*, Simon & Schuster Bks. For Young Readers) Simon & Schuster Bks. For Young Readers.

—The Hair of Zoe Fleefenbacher Goes to School. Halse Anderson, Laurie. 2009. (ENG.). 32p. (J). (gr. 1-5). 17.99 *(978-0-689-85809-3(4)*, Simon & Schuster Bks. For Young Readers) Simon & Schuster Bks. For Young Readers.

—The Hair of Zoe Fleefenbacher Goes to School. Anderson, Laurie Halse. 2019. (ENG.). 32p. (J). (gr. -1-3). 7.99 *(978-1-5344-5226-8(5)*, Atheneum Bks. for Young Readers) Simon & Schuster Children's Publishing.

—I'M a Manatee. Lithgow, John. 2003. (ENG.). 32p. (J). (gr. -1-3). 19.99 *(978-0-689-85427-9(7)*, Simon & Schuster Bks. For Young Readers) Simon & Schuster Bks. For Young Readers.

—I'm a Manatee: (Book & CD) Lithgow, John. 2007. (ENG.). 32p. (J). (gr. -1-3). pap. 9.99 *(978-0-689-85452-1(8)*, Little Simon) Little Simon.

—Love the Baby, 1 vol. Layne, Steven L. 2007. (ENG.). 32p. (J). (gr. k-k). 16.99 *(978-1-58980-392-3(2)*, Pelican Publishing) Arcadia Publishing.

—One-Dog Canoe. Casanova, Mary. 2009. (ENG.). 32p. (J). (gr. -1-1). pap. 7.99 *(978-0-312-56118-5(0)*, 900058848) Square Fish.

—One-Dog Sleigh: A Picture Book. Casanova, Mary. 2013. (ENG.). 32p. (J). (gr. k-3). 16.99 *(978-0-374-35639-2(4)*, 900080525, Farrar, Straus & Giroux (BYR)) Farrar, Straus & Giroux.

—Piggies in Pajamas. Meadows, Michelle. 2013. (ENG.). 32p. (J). (gr. -1-2). 15.99 *(978-1-4169-4982-4(8)*, Simon & Schuster Bks. For Young Readers) Simon & Schuster Bks. For Young Readers.

—Piggies in the Kitchen. Meadows, Michelle. 2011. (ENG.). 32p. (J). (gr. -1-2). 14.99 *(978-1-4169-3787-6(0)*, Simon & Schuster Bks. For Young Readers) Simon & Schuster Bks. For Young Readers.

—Play with Puppy, 1 vol. Layne, Steven. 2018. (ENG.). 32p. (J). (gr. -1-3). 16.99 *(978-1-4556-2374-7(1)*, Pelican Publishing) Arcadia Publishing.

—Saying Goodbye to Lulu. Demas, Corinne. 2009. (ENG.). 32p. (J). (gr. -1-3). 8.99 *(978-0-316-04749-4(X))* Little Brown & Co.

—Share with Brother, 1 vol. Layne, Steven L. 2010. (ENG.). 32p. (J). (gr. k-3). 16.99 *(978-1-58980-860-7(6)*, Pelican Publishing) Arcadia Publishing.

—Some Cat! Casanova, Mary. 2012. (ENG.). 40p. (J). (gr. -1-k). 17.99 *(978-0-374-37123-4(7)*, 900068629, Farrar, Straus & Giroux (BYR)) Farrar, Straus & Giroux.

—Stay with Sister, 1 vol. Layne, Steven L. 2012. (ENG.). 32p. (J). (gr. k-3). 16.99 *(978-1-4556-1523-0(4)*, Pelican Publishing) Arcadia Publishing.

—Teddy Roosevelt & the Treasure of Ursa Major. Kennedy Center, The. 2011. (ENG.). 128p. (J). (gr. 2-5). pap. 7.99 *(978-1-4169-4860-5(0)*, Simon & Schuster Bks. For Young Readers) Simon & Schuster Bks. For Young Readers.

—Tilly the Trickster. Shannon, Molly. 2011. (ENG.). 32p. (J). (gr. -1-3). 16.95 *(978-1-4197-0030-9(8)*, Abrams Bks. for Young Readers) Abrams, Inc.

—Unleashed: The Lives of White House Pets. Kennedy Center, The. 2011. (ENG.). 112p. (J). (gr. 2-5). pap. 5.99 *(978-1-4169-4862-9(7)*, Simon & Schuster Bks. For Young Readers) Simon & Schuster Bks. For Young Readers.

—Utterly Otterly Day. Casanova, Mary. 2008. (ENG.). 40p. (J). (gr. -1-3). 18.99 *(978-1-4169-0868-5(4)*, Simon & Schuster Bks. For Young Readers) Simon & Schuster Bks. For Young Readers.

—Utterly Otterly Night. Casanova, Mary. 2011. (ENG.). 40p. (J). (gr. -1-1). 16.99 *(978-1-4169-7562-5(4)*, Simon & Schuster Bks. For Young Readers) Simon & Schuster Bks. For Young Readers.

—When the Cows Got Loose. Weis, Carol. 2006. (ENG.). 40p. (J). (gr. -1-1). 17.99 *(978-0-689-85166-7(9)*, Simon & Schuster Bks. For Young Readers) Simon & Schuster Bks. For Young Readers.

—Wisteria Jane. Harris, Amber. 2015. (Wisteria Jane Book Ser.). (ENG.). 32p. (J). (gr. -1-3). 16.95 *(978-1-60554-411-3(6))* Redleaf Pr.

Hoyt, Christopher. A Giant Man from a Tiny Town: A Story of Angus MacAskill, 1 vol. Ryan, Tom. 2018. (ENG.). 32p. (J). (gr. -1-k). 22.95 *(978-1-77108-654-7(8)*, 0f143481-12eb-48d4-a34c-58d41e5afc8c) Nimbus Publishing, Ltd. CAN. Dist: Baker & Taylor Publisher Services (BTPS).

Hoyt, Richard, photos by. Living with a Star: From Sunscreen to Space Weather. Glaser, David et al. 2004. (Great Explorations in Math & Science Ser.). 176p. (YA). (gr. 6-8). pap. 28.00 incl. cd-rom *(978-0-924886-73-7(0)*, GEMS) Univ. of California, Berkeley, Lawrence Hall of Science.

Hrabe, Melodie. Anansi & the Apple Tree. Lockwood-Bean, Simon. 2019. (ENG.). 32p. (J). (gr. k-3). 18.95 *(978-1-7333606-1-6(1))*; pap. 9.99 *(978-0-578-47162-4(0))* Bennett Day Schl., Inc.

Hranilovich, Barbara. Pretty Little Lilly & the Land of Sweet Dreams (Hard Bound) Hornsby, Ashley Brooke. 2007. (J). 15.95 *(978-0-9777241-2-3(3))* Cepia LLC.

—Pretty Little Lilly & the Land of Sweet Dreams (Paperback) Hornsby, Ashley Brooke. 2007. (J). *(978-0-9777241-3-0(1))* Cepia LLC.

—Skimper-Scamper. Newell, Jeff. 2005. (Green Light Readers Level 2 Ser.). (J). (gr. k-2). 11.60 *(978-0-7569-5244-0(1))* Perfection Learning Corp.

Hrytskova, Polina. The Dolphin's Secret: A Meditational Journey for Children. Lowell, Meryl B. 2019. (ENG.). 34p. (J). (gr. k-2). pap. 9.95 *(978-0-578-21442-9(3))* Lowell, Meryl.

—Reach for the Stars. Albanese, Michael. 2018. (ENG.). 28p. (J). pap. 9.99 *(978-1-7328987-0-7(7))* Weight of Ink, The.

Hryvtsova, Anastasiia. Scrabble Sam. Aspinall, Susan. 2018. (ENG.). 26p. (J). pap. 9.99 *(978-1-7904-1954-8(9))* Independently Published.

Hsieh, Fiona. Wings of Olympus. George, Kallie. 2019. (Wings of Olympus Ser.: 1). (ENG.). 224p. (J). (gr. 3-7). 16.99 *(978-0-06-274152-3(7))* HarperCollins Pubs.

—Wings of Olympus. George, Kallie. 2020. (Wings of Olympus Ser.: 1). (ENG.). 240p. (J). (gr. 3-7). pap. 7.99 *(978-0-06-274151-6(9)*, HarperCollins) HarperCollins Pubs. Ltd. GBR. Dist: HarperCollins Pubs.

Hsieh, Nadia. Ida Lewis Guards the Shore: Courageous Kid of the Atlantic. Gunderson, Jessica. 2020. (Courageous Kids Ser.). (ENG.). 32p. (J). (gr. 3-5). pap. 7.95 ***(978-1-4966-8806-4(6)***, 201691); lib. bdg. 31.32 ***(978-1-4966-8505-6(9)***, 200561) Capstone. (Capstone Pr.).

Hsinping, Pan. Big Words for Little Geniuses. Patterson, Sue & Patterson, James. 2017. (J). pap. *(978-0-316-48708-5(2)*, Jimmy Patterson) Little Brown & Co.

Hsu, Chris. The Boo-Boos That Changed the World: A True Story about an Accidental Invention (Really!) Wittenstein, Barry. 2018. 32p. (J). (gr. -1-3). lib. bdg. 16.99 *(978-1-58089-745-7(2))* Charlesbridge Publishing, Inc.

Hsu, Florence. Perfect Solution. Keay, Ben. 2009. (YA). *(978-1-933791-09-8(8))* Finial Publishing.

Hsu, Ginnie. The Farm That Feeds Us: A Year in the Life of an Organic Farm. Castaldo, Nancy. 2020. (ENG.). 80p. (J). (gr. 2-6). 18.95 ***(978-0-7112-4253-1(4)***, Words & Pictures) Quarto Publishing Group UK GBR. Dist: Hachette Bk. Group.

Hsu, Jack. Poppie's Adventures: Serpents in Paradise. Yeh, Julie. 2003. 48p. (J). per. *(978-0-9742386-0-9(0))* Way Out Comics.

Hsu, Timothy, jt. photos by see Shebs, Stan.

Hu, Caroline. The Elephant Dancer: A Story of Ancient India, 1 vol. Gunderson, Jessica. 2009. (Read-It! Chapter Books: Historical Tales Ser.). (ENG.). 64p. (J). (gr. 2-4). 22.65 *(978-1-4048-5219-8(0)*, Picture Window Bks.) Capstone.

—The Horse on the Hill: A Story of Ancient India, 1 vol. Gunderson, Jessica. 2009. (Read-It! Chapter Books: Historical Tales Ser.). (ENG.). 64p. (J). (gr. 2-4). 22.65 *(978-1-4048-5222-8(0)*, Picture Window Bks.) Capstone.

—The King's Warrior: A Story of Ancient India, 1 vol. Gunderson, Jessica. 2009. (Read-It! Chapter Books: Historical Tales Ser.). (ENG.). 64p. (J). (gr. 2-4). 22.65 *(978-1-4048-5228-0(X)*, Picture Window Bks.) Capstone.

—Olivia & Oscar Build an Opinion Piece. Pelleschi, Andrea. 2014. (Writing Builders Ser.). (ENG.). 32p. (J). (gr. 2-4). pap. 11.94 *(978-1-60357-556-0(1))*; lib. bdg. 25.27 *(978-1-59953-582-1(3))* Norwood Hse. Pr.

—Phillip & Penny Learn about Pronouns. Robinson, Joanna Jarc. 2014. (Language Builders Ser.). (ENG.). 32p. (J). (gr. 2-4). pap. 11.94 *(978-1-60357-705-2(X))*; lib. bdg. 25.27 *(978-1-59953-670-5(6))* Norwood Hse. Pr.

—The Servant & the Water Princess: A Story of Ancient India, 1 vol. Gunderson, Jessica. 2009. (Read-It! Chapter Books: Historical Tales Ser.). (ENG.). 64p. (J). (gr. 2-4). 22.65 *(978-1-4048-5225-9(5)*, Picture Window Bks.) Capstone.

Hu, Tiger. My Neighbors Are All Cats: Collecting Stars. Onlyanose & Kelly, Charlene. 2020. (ENG.). 28p. (J). 25.99 ***(978-1-4808-9118-0(5))***; pap. 13.95 ***(978-1-4808-9119-7(3))*** Archway Publishing.

Hu, Ying-Hwa. Red Socks, bks. 7, bk. 2. Mayer, Ellen. 2015. (ENG.). 18p. (J). pap. 6.99 *(978-1-59572-706-0(X))* Star Bright Bks., Inc.

—The Three Billy Goats Gruff, 1 vol. Wright, Rebecca Hu-Van & Asbjørnsen, Peter Christen. 2014. (ENG.). 32p. (J). *(978-1-59572-666-7(7))*; pap. 6.99 *(978-1-59572-667-4(5))* Star Bright Bks., Inc.

Hu, Ying-Hwa & Van Wright, Cornelius. Alicia's Happy Day, 1 vol. Starr, Meg. 2003. (ENG.). 32p. (J). (gr. -1-3). 15.95 *(978-1-887734-85-1(6))* Star Bright Bks., Inc.

—Jumping the Broom. Scholastic, Inc. Staff & Black, Sonia. 2004. (Just for You Ser.). (ENG.). 32p. (J). (gr. k-3). pap. 3.99 *(978-0-439-56878-4(1))* Scholastic, Inc.

—Singing for Dr. King. Medearis, Angela Shelf. 2004. 32p. (J). lib. bdg. 15.00 *(978-1-4242-0237-9(X))* Fitzgerald Bks.

Hu, Ying-Hwa & Wright, Cornelius Van. American Slave, American Hero: York of the Lewis & Clark Expedition. Pringle, Laurence. 2006. (ENG.). 40p. (J). (gr. 4-7). 19.95 *(978-1-59078-282-8(8)*, Calkins Creek) Boyds Mills Pr.

—Snow in Jerusalem. Costa, Deborah Da. 2008. (ENG.). 32p. (J). (gr. -1-3). 6.99 *(978-0-8075-7525-3(9)*, 807575259) Whitman, Albert & Co.

Hu, Ying-Hwa, jt. illus. see Van Wright, Cornelius.

Hu, Ying-Hwa, jt. illus. see Wright, Cornelius Van.

Huadi. Leyendas, Mitos, Cuentos y Otros Relatos de las Praderas Norteamericanas. Sugobono, Nahuel. 2003. (SPA.). 96p. pap. 11.95 *(978-987-550-278-9(2))* Longseller S.A. ARG. Dist: Bilingual Pubns. Co., The.

—Leyendas, Mitos, Cuentos y Otros Relatos Tobas. Sugobono, Nahuel. 2003. (SPA.). 86p. pap. 11.95 *(978-987-550-296-3(0))* Longseller S.A. ARG. Dist: Bilingual Pubns. Co., The.

—Tinke Tinke. Bornemann, Elsa. 2015. 152p. (J). (gr. 4-8). pap. 10.95 *(978-968-19-1518-6(6))* Aguilar, Altea, Taurus, Alfaguara, S.A. de C.V MEX. Dist: Santillana USA Publishing Co., Inc.

Huang, Benrei. Dragon Dance: A Chinese New Year Lift-The-Flap Book. Holub, Joan. 2003. (Puffin Lift-The-Flap Ser.). 16p. (J). (gr. -1-k). 7.99 *(978-0-14-240000-5(9)*, Puffin Books) Penguin Young Readers Group.

—Fiona's Fairy Magic. Imperato, Teresa. 2005. 14p. (J). 10.95 *(978-1-58117-322-2(9)*, Intervisual/Piggy Toes) Bendon, Inc.

—Las Gallinas de la Senora Sato, Level 1. Min, Laura. Flor Ada, Alma, tr. 2003. (Dejame Leer Ser.). (SPA.). 8p. (J). (gr. -1-3). 6.50 *(978-0-673-36298-8(1)*, Good Year Bks.) Celebration Pr.

—Hunting the Daddyosaurus. Bateman, Teresa. 2004. 29p. (J). (gr. k-4). reprint ed. 16.00 *(978-0-7567-7796-8(8))* DIANE Publishing Co.

—The Kite. Packard, Mary. 2003. (My First Reader Ser.). (ENG.). 32p. (J). 18.50 *(978-0-516-22930-0(3)*, Children's Pr.) Scholastic Library Publishing.

—Luna the Wake-Up Cat. Simon, Charnan. 2011. (Rookie Ready to Learn — Animals Ser.). 40p. (J). (gr. -1-k). lib. bdg. 25.00 *(978-0-531-26414-0(9))*; (ENG.). pap. 5.95 *(978-0-531-26695-3(8))* Scholastic Library Publishing. (Children's Pr.).

—Oh, Come, Little Children. Stohs, Anita Reith. 2006. 22p. (J). (gr. -1-3). 14.99 *(978-0-7586-1215-1(X))* Concordia Publishing Hse.

—The Quiet Way Home. Becker, Bonny. 2019. (ENG.). 28p. (J). (gr. -1-3). 18.95 *(978-1-948959-02-5(X))* Purple Hse. Pr.

—Surprise! Packard, Mary. 2003. (My First Reader Ser.). (ENG.). 32p. (J). 18.50 *(978-0-516-22937-9(0)*, Children's Pr.) Scholastic Library Publishing.

Huang, Helen. Caitlin in Charge. Hutton, Clare. 2018. (American Girl: Like Sisters Ser.: 4). (ENG.). 176p. (J). (gr. 3-7). pap. 6.99 *(978-1-338-11506-2(5)*, Scholastic Paperbacks) Scholastic, Inc.

—Emma Moves In. Hutton, Clare. 2017. (American Girl: Like Sisters Ser.: 1). (ENG.). 192p. (J). (gr. 3-7). pap. 6.99 *(978-1-338-11499-7(9)*, Scholastic Pr.) Scholastic, Inc.

—Natalia Takes the Lead (American Girl: Like Sisters #2) Hutton, Clare. 2017. (American Girl: Like Sisters Ser.: 2). (ENG.). 192p. (J). (gr. 3-7). pap. 6.99 *(978-1-338-11502-4(2)*, Scholastic Pr.) Scholastic, Inc.

—Zoe Is on the Air. Hutton, Clare. 2018. (American Girl: Like Sisters Ser.: 3). (ENG.). 176p. (J). (gr. 3-7). pap. 6.99 *(978-1-338-11504-8(9)*, Scholastic Pr.) Scholastic, Inc.

Huang, Linda & Carroll, Jackie. Kingdom of the Silver Cat. Carroll, Thomas M. 2019. (Sapphire Fruit Chronicles Ser.). (ENG.). 408p. (J). (gr. 2-6). pap. 14.95 ***(978-1-7330917-0-1(X))*** Author Pubns.

Huang, Rebecca. Queen of Physics: How Wu Chien Shiung Helped Unlock the Secrets of the Atom. Robeson, Teresa. 2019. (People Who Shaped Our World Ser.: 6). 48p. (J). (gr. k). 16.95 *(978-1-4549-3220-8(1))* Sterling Publishing Co., Inc.

Huang, Yu-Hsuan. Baby Animals. 2018. (My First Interactive Board Book Ser.). (ENG.). 10p. (J). bds. 9.99 *(978-2-7338-5915-5(3))* Auzou, Philippe Editions FRA. Dist: Consortium Bk. Sales & Distribution.

—Baby Bear: Finger Puppet Book: (Finger Puppet Book for Toddlers & Babies, Baby Books for First Year, Animal Finger Puppets) Chronicle Books. 2016. (ENG.). 12p. (J). (gr. -1 — 1). 6.99 *(978-1-4521-4235-7(1))* Chronicle Bks. LLC.

—Baby Bunny: Finger Puppet Book. Chronicle Books Staff. 2017. (ENG.). 12p. (J). bds. 7.99 *(978-1-4521-5609-5(3))* Chronicle Bks. LLC.

—Baby Chipmunk. Chronicle Books Staff. 2017. (ENG.). 12p. (J). (gr. -1 — 1). bds. 7.99 *(978-1-4521-5612-5(3))* Chronicle Bks. LLC.

—Baby Duck: Finger Puppet Book. Chronicle Books Staff. 2018. (ENG.). 12p. (J). (gr. -1 — 1). bds. 7.99 *(978-1-4521-6373-4(1))* Chronicle Bks. LLC.

—Baby Elephant. 2016. (ENG.). 12p. (J). (gr. -1 — 1). bds. 7.99 *(978-1-4521-4237-1(8))* Chronicle Bks. LLC.

—Baby Fish. Chronicle Books Staff. 2017. (ENG.). 12p. (J). bds. 6.99 *(978-1-4521-5610-1(7))* Chronicle Bks. LLC.

Huang, Yu-Hsuan. Baby Fox: Finger Puppet Book. Chronicle Books. 2020. (ENG.). 12p. (J). (gr. -1 — 1). bds. 7.99 ***(978-1-4521-8173-8(X))*** Chronicle Bks. LLC.

Huang, Yu-Hsuan. Baby Giraffe: Finger Puppet Book. Chronicle Books. 2017. (ENG.). 12p. (J). (gr. -1 — 1). bds. 7.99 *(978-1-4521-5611-8(5))* Chronicle Bks. LLC.

—Baby Goat: Finger Puppet Book. Chronicle Books. 2020. (ENG.). 12p. (J). (gr. -1 — 1). bds. 7.99 *(978-1-4521-8171-4(3))* Chronicle Bks. LLC.

—Baby Hedgehog. Chronicle Books Editors. 2018. (ENG.). 12p. (J). (gr. -1 — 1). bds. 6.99 *(978-1-4521-6376-5(6))* Chronicle Bks. LLC.

—Baby Kitten: Finger Puppet Book: (Board Book with Plush Baby Cat, Best Baby Book for Newborns) Chronicle Books. 2020. (ENG.). 12p. (J). (gr. -1 — 1). bds. 7.99 *(978-1-4521-8172-1(1))* Chronicle Bks. LLC.

—Baby Koala: Finger Puppet Book. Chronicle Books. 2018. (ENG.). 12p. (J). (gr. -1 — 1). bds. 7.99 *(978-1-4521-6374-1(X))* Chronicle Bks. LLC.

—Baby Llama: Finger Puppet Book. Chronicle Books. 2019. (ENG.). 12p. (J). (gr. -1 — 1). bds. 7.99 *(978-1-4521-7081-7(9))* Chronicle Bks. LLC.

—Baby Orca: Finger Puppet Book. 2019. (ENG.). 12p. (J). (gr. -1 — 1). bds. 6.99 *(978-1-4521-7079-4(7))* Chronicle Bks. LLC.

—Baby Penguin: Finger Puppet Book. Chronicle Books. 2018. (ENG.). 12p. (J). (gr. -1 — 1). bds. 7.99 *(978-1-4521-6375-8(8))* Chronicle Bks. LLC.

—Baby Piglet: Finger Puppet Book (Pig Puppet Book, Piggy Book for Babies, Tiny Finger Puppet Books) Chronicle Books. 2019. (ENG.). 12p. (J). (gr. -1 — 1). bds. 6.99 *(978-1-4521-7078-7(9))* Chronicle Bks. LLC.

Huang, Yu-Hsuan. Baby Raccoon: Finger Puppet Book. Chronicle Books. 2020. (ENG.). 12p. (J). (gr. -1 — 1). 7.99 ***(978-1-4521-7080-0(0))*** Chronicle Bks. LLC.

Huang, Yu-Hsuan. Baby Reindeer. Chronicle Books Staff. 2016. (ENG.). 12p. (J). (gr. -1 — 1). bds. 6.99 *(978-1-4521-4661-4(6))* Chronicle Bks. LLC.

—Baby Sloth: Finger Puppet Book: (Finger Puppet Book for Toddlers & Babies, Baby Books for First Year, Animal Finger Puppets) Chronicle Books. 2019. (ENG.). 12p. (J). (gr. -1 — 1). bds. 7.99 *(978-1-4521-8029-8(6))* Chronicle Bks. LLC.

—Baby Tiger. Chronicle Books Staff. 2016. (ENG.). 12p. (J). (gr. -1 — 1). bds. 6.99 *(978-1-4521-4236-4(X))* Chronicle Bks. LLC.

—Enchanted Castle. 2020. (Pop-Up Carousel Ser.). (ENG.). 10p. (J). (gr. -1-k). 24.99 *(978-1-5098-7935-9(8)*, Campbell Bks.) Pan Macmillan GBR. Dist: Independent Pubs. Group.

—Happy Birthday. Nosy Crow Staff. 2017. (Sing along with Me! Ser.). (ENG.). 10p. (J). (-k). bds. 8.99 *(978-0-7636-9505-7(X)*, Nosy Crow) Candlewick Pr.

—Hey Diddle Diddle: Sing along with Me! Nosy Crow Staff. 2017. (Sing along with Me! Ser.). (ENG.). 10p. (J). (-k). bds. 8.99 *(978-0-7636-9320-6(0)*, Nosy Crow) Candlewick Pr.

—The Itsy Bitsy Spider: Sing along with Me! Nosy Crow Staff. 2017. (Sing along with Me! Ser.). (ENG.). 10p. (J). (-k). bds. 8.99 *(978-0-7636-9581-1(5)*, Nosy Crow) Candlewick Pr.

—Let's Play Fairy Homes. 2016. (Let's Play Ser.). (ENG.). 12p. (J). (gr. -1-k). bds. 16.99 *(978-1-4472-7723-1(6)*, Campbell Bks.) Pan Macmillan GBR. Dist: Independent Pubs. Group.

—Old MacDonald Had a Farm: Sing along with Me! Nosy Crow Staff. 2016. (Sing along with Me! Ser.). (ENG.). 10p. (J). (-k). bds. 8.99 *(978-0-7636-8652-9(2)*, Nosy Crow) Candlewick Pr.

—Old MacDonald Had a Farm: Sing along with Me! Nosy Crow. 2020. (Sing along with Me! Ser.). (ENG.). 8p. (J). (-k). bds. 8.99 *(978-1-5362-1218-1(0)*, Nosy Crow) Candlewick Pr.

—Peekaboo! Stroller Cards: on the Farm. Rogge, Robie. 2017. (ENG.). 10p. (J). 9.99 *(978-1-4521-5385-8(X))* Chronicle Bks. LLC.

—Row, Row, Row Your Boat: Sing along with Me! Nosy Crow Staff. 2017. (Sing along with Me! Ser.). (ENG.). 10p. (J). (-k). bds. 8.99 *(978-0-7636-9240-7(9)*, Nosy Crow) Candlewick Pr.

Huang, Yu-Hsuan. Row, Row, Row Your Boat: Sing along with Me! Nosy Crow. 2020. (Sing along with Me! Ser.). (ENG.). 8p. (J). (-k). bds. 8.99 ***(978-1-5362-1484-0(1)***, Nosy Crow) Candlewick Pr.

Huang, Yu-Hsuan. This Is the Way We Go to School: Sing along with Me! Nosy Crow. 2020. (Sing along with Me! Ser.). (ENG.). 8p. (J). (-k). bds. 8.99 *(978-1-5362-0832-0(9)*, Nosy Crow) Candlewick Pr.

—Twinkle, Twinkle, Little Star: Sing along with Me! Nosy Crow Staff. 2017. (Sing along with Me! Ser.). (ENG.). 10p. (J). (-k). bds. 8.99 *(978-0-7636-9241-4(7)*, Nosy Crow) Candlewick Pr.

—We Wish You a Merry Christmas: Sing along with Me! Nosy Crow Staff. 2017. (Sing along with Me! Ser.). (ENG.). 10p. (J). (-k). bds. 8.99 *(978-0-7636-9612-2(9)*, Nosy Crow) Candlewick Pr.

Huang, Yu-Hsuan. We Wish You a Merry Christmas: Sing along with Me! Nosy Crow. 2020. (Sing along with Me! Ser.). (ENG.). 8p. (J). (-k). bds. 8.99 ***(978-1-5362-1645-5(3)***, Nosy Crow) Candlewick Pr.

Huang, Yu-Hsuan. The Wheels on the Bus: Sing along with Me! Nosy Crow Staff. 2016. (Sing along with Me! Ser.). (ENG.). 10p. (J). (-k). bds. 8.99 *(978-0-7636-8648-2(4)*, Nosy Crow) Candlewick Pr.

Huang, Yu-Hsuan. The Wheels on the Bus: Sing along with Me! Nosy Crow. 2020. (Sing along with Me! Ser.). (ENG.). 8p. (J). (-k). bds. 8.99 ***(978-1-5362-1483-3(3)***, Nosy Crow) Candlewick Pr.

Huang, Yu-Hsuan. Let's Play Aliens in Space. Huang, Yu-Hsuan. 2016. (Let's Play Ser.). (ENG.). 10p. (J). (gr. -1-k). bds. 16.99 *(978-1-4472-8653-0(7)*, Campbell Bks.) Pan Macmillan GBR. Dist: Independent Pubs. Group.

—Peek-A-Boo Little Chick. Huang, Yu-Hsuan. 2020. (ENG.). 10p. (J). (— 1). bds. 7.99 *(978-1-5344-5177-3(3)*, Little Simon) Little Simon.

Huang, Yu-Hsuan. Peek-A-Boo Little Dinosaur. Huang, Yu-Hsuan. 2020. (ENG.). 10p. (J). (— 1). bds. 7.99 ***(978-1-5344-5179-7(X)***, Little Simon) Little Simon.

—Peek-A-Boo Little Reindeer. Huang, Yu-Hsuan. 2020. (ENG.). 10p. (J). (— 1). bds. 7.99 ***(978-1-5344-5181-0(1)***, Little Simon) Little Simon.

Huat, Tan Eng & Pham, Khoi. Legion: Son of X Vol. 4: For We Are Many. 2018. (ENG.). 136p. (YA). (gr. 8-17). pap. 15.99 *(978-1-302-91083-9(3))* Marvel Worldwide, Inc.

H

Hubbard, Al, jt. illus. see Heymans, Mau.
Hubbard, Suzanna. The Lady Who Lived in a Car. Hubbard, Suzanna. 2007. (ENG.). 32p. (J). (gr. k-2). pap. 6.99 *(978-1-84458-055-2(5))* Pavilion Bks. GBR. Dist: Independent Pubs. Group.
Hubbell, Will. Apples Here! 2015. 32p. (J). *(978-1-4896-3846-5(6))* Weigl Pubs., Inc.
Hubbell, Will. Pumpkin Jack. Hubbell, Will. 2013. (AV2 Fiction Readalong Ser.). (ENG.). (J). (gr. -1-3). 34.28 *(978-1-62127-914-3(6),* AV2 by Weigl) Weigl Pubs., Inc.
Hubbs, Erin. Scrumptious Sweet Treats: 25 Easy Baking Recipes for Kids. Long, Lidan. 2016. (ENG.). (J). pap. 15.00 *(978-1-938812-83-5(2))* Full Court Pr.
Hubenthal, Dayna. The Last Goose Concert. Fey, Jaki. 2012. 126p. pap. 12.99 *(978-1-938282-02-7(7))* Koho Pono, LLC.
Huber, Becca & Pope, Lauren. Erin & Katrina. Sugg, Nan. 2007. 32p. (J). 19.90 *(978-0-9788889-0-9(1))* Acorn Hill Pr.
Huber, Jim. Beamer Visits the Emergency Room. Chambers, Cindy & Demme, Tina. 2012. 32p. pap. 14.95 *(978-1-4575-1289-6(0))* Dog Ear Publishing, LLC.
Huber, Joyce. Porridge Poetry. Lofting, Hugh. 2nd collector's rev. l.t. ed. 2005. (ENG.). 54p. (J). lib. bdg. 7.95 *(978-0-9643844-8-4(5),* sku PP1, Doctor Dolittle's Library) PhotoGraphics Publishing.
Huber, Philip. A Crossing of Zebras: Animal Packs in Poetry. Maddox, Marjorie. 2019. (ENG.). 34p. (J). (gr. -1-1). pap. 16.00 ***(978-1-5326-9731-9(7))*** Resource Pubns., Inc.
—I'm Feeling Blue, Too! Maddox, Marjorie. 2020. (ENG.). 34p. (J). pap. 16.00 ***(978-1-7252-5309-4(7))*** Resource Pubns., Inc.
Hubert, Marie-Luce & Klein, Jean-Louis, photos by. Face-to-Face with the Dog: Loyal Companion. Tracqui, Valérie. Laird, Lisa, tr. from FRE. 2004. (Face-to-Face Ser.). 28p. (J). (gr. 2-4). 9.95 *(978-1-57091-452-2(4))* Charlesbridge Publishing, Inc.
Hubert, Marie-Luce, jt. illus. see Klein, Jean-Louis.
Hubesch, Nicolas. Bruno: Some of the More Interesting Days in My Life So Far. Valckx, Catharina. 2017. (ENG.). 96p. (J). (gr. k-4). 19.99 *(978-1-77657-124-6(X))* Gecko Pr. NZL. Dist: Lerner Publishing Group.
Huche, Magali Le. With Dad, It's Like That. Brun-Cosme, Nadine. 2016. (ENG.). 24p. (J). (gr. -1-3). 16.99 *(978-0-8075-8731-7(1),* 807587311) Whitman, Albert & Co.
Huckin, J. J., photos by. Inspire. Huckin, J. J. 2005. 164p. (YA). per. 39.99 net. *(978-0-9765700-1-1(7))* WayaMedia.
Huddle, Ryan. The Adventures of Riley, the Museum Dog, Vol. First, Devra. 2019. (ENG.). 37p. (J). (gr. -1-12). 16.95 *(978-1-63076-360-2(8))* Muddy Boots Pr.
Huddleston, Courtney. Decoy TPB II: Storm of the Century. Scalera, Buddy. 2003. 160p. pap. 17.95 *(978-0-9719012-0-9(1))* Penny-Farthing Productions, Inc.
—Fitness Fiasco. Weaver, Verity. 2020. (What Happened? Set 2 Ser.). (ENG.). 120p. (J). pap. 7.99 *(978-1-63163-412-3(7),* 1631634127); lib. bdg. 27.13 *(978-1-63163-411-6(9),* 1631634119) North Star Editions. (Jolly Fish Pr.).
—Horror in Space. Young, J. E. 2011. (Twisted Journeys Ser.: 18). (ENG.). 112p. (J). (gr. 4-7). pap. 45.32 *(978-0-7613-7614-9(3));* lib. bdg. 27.99 *(978-0-8225-9265-5(7))* Lerner Publishing Group. (Graphic Universe™).
—Jam-Bo, Litta-Girl, & the Bullies. Ford, Adam B. 2013. 44p. pap. 12.95 *(978-0-9794104-9-9(5))* H Bar Pr.
—Lab Mice Heist. Weaver, Verity. 2019. (What Happened? (Set Of 4) Ser.). (ENG.). 120p. (J). pap. 7.99 *(978-1-63163-308-9(2),* 1631633082); lib. bdg. 27.13 *(978-1-63163-307-2(4),* 1631633074) North Star Editions. (Jolly Fish Pr.).
—Math Test Mischief. Weaver, Verity. 2019. (What Happened? (Set Of 4) Ser.). (ENG.). 120p. (J). pap. 7.99 *(978-1-63163-312-6(0),* 1631633120); lib. bdg. 27.13 *(978-1-63163-311-9(2),* 1631633112) North Star Editions. (Jolly Fish Pr.).
—Sandwich Shenanigans. Weaver, Verity. 2019. (What Happened? (Set Of 4) Ser.). (ENG.). 120p. (J). pap. 7.99 *(978-1-63163-316-4(3),* 1631633163); lib. bdg. 27.13 *(978-1-63163-315-7(5),* 1631633155) North Star Editions. (Jolly Fish Pr.).
—Showtime Sabotage. Weaver, Verity. 2020. (What Happened? Set 2 Ser.). (ENG.). 120p. (J). pap. 7.99 *(978-1-63163-416-1(X),* 163163416X); lib. bdg. 27.13 *(978-1-63163-415-4(1),* 1631634151) North Star Editions. (Jolly Fish Pr.).
—Stage Two Hullabaloo. Weaver, Verity. 2019. (What Happened? (Set Of 4) Ser.). (ENG.). 120p. (J). pap. 7.99 *(978-1-63163-320-1(1),* 1631633201); lib. bdg. 27.13 *(978-1-63163-319-5(8),* 1631633198) North Star Editions. (Jolly Fish Pr.).
—Switchback Switcheroo. Weaver, Verity. 2020. (What Happened? Set 2 Ser.). (ENG.). 120p. (J). pap. 7.99 *(978-1-63163-420-8(8),* 1631634208); lib. bdg. 27.13 *(978-1-63163-419-2(4),* 1631634194) North Star Editions. (Jolly Fish Pr.).
—Tricky Spider Tales. Schweizer, Chris. 2011. (Tricky Journeys Ser.: 5). (ENG.). (J). (gr. 2-4). pap. 39.62 *(978-0-7613-8629-2(7))* Lerner Publishing Group.
—Trojan Horse Trouble. Weaver, Verity. 2020. (What Happened? Set 2 Ser.). (ENG.). 120p. (J). pap. 7.99 *(978-1-63163-424-6(0),* 1631634240); lib. bdg. 27.13 *(978-1-63163-423-9(2),* 1631634232) North Star Editions. (Jolly Fish Pr.).
—What Happened? Set 2 (Set Of 4) Weaver, Verity. 2020. (What Happened? Set 2 Ser.). (ENG.). 480p. (J). pap. 31.96 *(978-1-63163-408-6(9),* 1631634089); lib. bdg. 108.52 *(978-1-63163-407-9(0),* 1631634070) North Star Editions. (Jolly Fish Pr.).
—What Happened? (Set Of 4) Weaver, Verity. 2019. (What Happened? (Set Of 4) Ser.). (ENG.). 480p. (J). pap. 31.96 *(978-1-63163-304-1(X),* 163163304X); lib. bdg. 108.52 *(978-1-63163-303-4(1),* 1631633031) North Star Editions. (Jolly Fish Pr.).
Huddleston, Courtney. A Bit Haywire. Huddleston, Courtney. Zirkel, Scott. 2006. 112p. per. 11.95 *(978-0-9777883-5-4(0))* Viper Comics.
Huddleston, Mike, et al. Cable: Soldier X. 2018. (Cable: Soldier X Ser.: 1). (ENG.). 584p. (YA). (gr. 8-17). 75.00 *(978-1-302-91398-4(0))* Marvel Worldwide, Inc.
Huddleston, Terry. Tiamat: Grace Flynn Chronicles: Book 2. Cathalson. 2019. (ENG.). 200p. 29.99 *(978-0-9822656-9-7(7),* Cathal Entertainment) Cathal Entertainment.
Hudecki, Peter. City Dogs, 1 vol. Goertzen, Glenda. 2007. (ENG.). 133p. (J). (gr. 4-7). pap. *(978-1-55455-005-0(X))* Fitzhenry & Whiteside, Ltd.
Hudgens, Melica. Flim Flam & Other Such Gobbledygook. 2015. (J). 14.99 *(978-1-4621-1684-3(1))* Cedar Fort, Inc./CFI Distribution.
Hudgins, Tim. The Town of Nowhere, 1 vol. Hudgins, Mary Jane. 2009. 17p. pap. 24.95 *(978-1-60672-544-3(0))* America Star Bks.
Hudnall, Ken, photos by. Spirits of the Border: The History & Mystery of Fort Bliss, 2 vols. Hudnall, Ken. 2003. (Spirits of the Border Ser.: 2). 208p. per. 16.95 *(978-0-9626087-4-2(2))* Omega Pr.
Hudon-Verrelli, Jacqueline. Charlie's Dirt Day, 1 vol. Larsen, Andrew. 2014. (Tell Me More Storybook Ser.). (ENG.). 32p. (J). (gr. k-3). 17.95 *(978-1-55455-334-1(2),* 607e7573-2b58-4544-8217-d40214317f7b) Fitzhenry & Whiteside, Ltd. CAN. Dist: Firefly Bks., Ltd.
Hudrisier, Cecile. We Both Read-the Horse Lover's Book. Ledu, Stephanie. 2009. 44p. (J). 9.95 *(978-1-60115-019-6(9))* Treasure Bay, Inc.
—We Both Read-The Horse Lover's Book. Ledu, Stéphanie. 2009. 44p. (J). pap. 4.99 *(978-1-60115-020-2(2))* Treasure Bay, Inc.
Hudson, Andrea. The Ringtail Cat & the Doodle Alley Tap. Kerr, Donny. 2019. (ENG.). 60p. (J). pap. 12.45 ***(978-1-6882-1412-5(7))*** Independently Published.
Hudson, Annabel. Bible Stories. Goodings, Christina. ed. 2008. (ENG.). 24p. (J). (gr. -1-k). 8.99 *(978-0-7459-6091-3(X))* Lion Hudson PLC GBR. Dist: Independent Pubs. Group.
—Lift-the-Flap Christmas Stories. Goodings, Christina. 2010. (ENG.). 16p. (J). (gr. -1-k). 12.99 *(978-0-7459-6203-0(3))* Lion Hudson PLC GBR. Dist: Independent Pubs. Group.
—My Look & Point Bible. Goodings, Christina. ed. 2011. (ENG.). 224p. (J). (gr. -1-k). 16.99 *(978-0-7459-6206-1(8))* Lion Hudson PLC GBR. Dist: Independent Pubs. Group.
—My Look & Point First Easter, 1 vol. Goodings, Christina. ed. 2014. (ENG.). 16p. (J). (gr. -1-k). 6.99 *(978-0-7459-6453-9(2))* Lion Hudson PLC GBR. Dist: Independent Pubs. Group.
—My Look & Point in the Beginning Stick-A-Story Book. Goodings, Christina. ed. 2015. (ENG.). 16p. (J). (gr. -1-k). 6.99 *(978-0-7459-6540-6(7))* Lion Hudson PLC GBR. Dist: Independent Pubs. Group.
—My Look & Point Jonah & the Whale. Goodings, Christina. ed. 2014. (ENG.). 16p. (J). (gr. -1-k). 6.99 *(978-0-7459-6454-6(0))* Lion Hudson PLC GBR. Dist: Independent Pubs. Group.
—My Look & Point Story of Jesus Stick-A-Story Book. Goodings, Christina. ed. 2015. (ENG.). 16p. (J). (gr. -1-k). 6.99 *(978-0-7459-6539-0(3))* Lion Hudson PLC GBR. Dist: Independent Pubs. Group.
—Thinking of Heaven: Prayers for Sad Goodbyes, 1 vol. Piper, Sophie. 2009. 48p. (J). 7.95 *(978-0-8254-7856-7(1),* Lion Children's) Lion Hudson PLC GBR. Dist: Kregel Pubns.
Hudson, Annabel. Brown Bear Gets in Shape. Hudson, Annabel. Durant, Alan. 2004. (I Am Reading Ser.). (ENG.). (J). (gr. 1-1). lib. bdg. 14.55 *(978-0-7569-5450-5(9))* Perfection Learning Corp.
Hudson, Brett. Cave Discovery: When Did We Start Asking Questions? Golding, Julia et al. ed. 2018. (Curious Science Ser.). (ENG.). 128p. (J). (gr. 4-7). pap. 7.99 *(978-0-7459-7744-7(8))* Lion Hudson PLC GBR. Dist: Independent Pubs. Group.
—Copy Cat. George, Olivia. 2004. (My First Reader Ser.). (J). 18.50 *(978-0-516-24679-6(8),* Children's Pr.) Scholastic Library Publishing.
—Greek Adventure: Who Were the First Scientists? Briggs, Andrew et al. ed. 2018. (Curious Science Ser.). (ENG.). 128p. (J). (gr. 4-6). pap. 7.99 *(978-0-7459-7745-4(6))* Lion Hudson PLC GBR. Dist: Independent Pubs. Group.
—Hunt with Newton: What Are the Secrets of the Universe? Golding, Julia et al. ed. 2018. (Curious Science Ser.). (ENG.). 112p. (J). (gr. 4-7). pap. 7.99 *(978-0-7459-7753-9(7))* Lion Hudson PLC GBR. Dist: Independent Pubs. Group.
—Modern Flights: Where Next? Golding, Julia et al. ed. 2019. (Curious Science Ser.). (ENG.). 128p. (J). (gr. 4-7). pap. 7.99 *(978-0-7459-7755-3(3))* Lion Hudson PLC GBR. Dist: Independent Pubs. Group.
—The Noisy Stable & Other Christmas Stories. Hartman, Bob. ed. 2004. (Storyteller Tales Ser.). (ENG.). 64p. (J). (gr. k-4). pap. 6.99 *(978-0-7459-4824-9(3))* Lion Hudson PLC GBR. Dist: Independent Pubs. Group.
—Rocky Road to Galileo: What Is Our Place in the Solar System. Golding, Julia et al. ed. 2018. (Curious Science Ser.). (ENG.). 112p. (J). (gr. 4-7). pap. 7.99 *(978-0-7459-7752-2(9))* Lion Hudson PLC GBR. Dist: Independent Pubs. Group.
—Victorian Voyages: Where Did We Come From? Golding, Julia et al. ed. 2019. (Curious Science Ser.). (ENG.). 128p. (J). (gr. 4-7). pap. 7.99 *(978-0-7459-7754-6(5))* Lion Hudson PLC GBR. Dist: Independent Pubs. Group.
Hudson, Cullan. Strange State: Mysteries & legends of Oklahoma. Centennial edition, expanded & Revised, 1. Hudson, Cullan. rev. exp. ed. 2007. (ENG.). 222p. (YA). per. 24.00 *(978-0-9778850-8-4(9),* 20071, WhorlBooks Thumbprints) Whorl Bks.
Hudson, David W., photos by. A Spiritual Trilogy. Ume, Anne. 2003. (ENG., 352p. (YA). pap. 21.00 *(978-0-9727967-0-5(3),* 77707) Bois Pubns.
Hudson, Don. Activist: A Story of the Marjory Stoneman Douglas Shooting. Hogg, Lauren Elizabeth. 2019. (Zuiker Teen Topics Ser.). (ENG.). 96p. (YA). (gr. 6). 12.99 *(978-1-947378-21-6(X))* Zuiker Pr.
—Goodbye: a Story of Suicide. Lamberth, Hailee Joy. 2020. (Zuiker Teen Topics Ser.). (ENG.). 88p. (J). (gr. 6). 12.99 *(978-1-947378-27-8(9))* Zuiker Pr.
—Warriors: Tigerstar & Sasha #1: into the Woods. Hunter, Erin. 2008. (Warriors Graphic Novel Ser.: 1). (ENG.). 112p. (J). (gr. 3-7). pap. 7.99 *(978-0-06-154792-8(1))* HarperCollins Pubs.
—Warriors: Tigerstar & Sasha #2: Escape from the Forest. Hunter, Erin. 2008. (Warriors Graphic Novel Ser.: 2). (ENG.). 112p. (J). (gr. 3-7). pap. 7.99 *(978-0-06-154793-5(X))* HarperCollins Pubs.
—Warriors: Tigerstar & Sasha #3: Return to the Clans. Hunter, Erin. 2009. (Warriors Graphic Novel Ser.: 3). (ENG.). 112p. (J). (gr. 3-7). pap. 7.99 *(978-0-06-154794-2(8))* HarperCollins Pubs.
Hudson, Elizabeth. Gloria's Dream. Pernetz, Adriana. 2018. (ENG.). 42p. (J). pap. 14.95 *(978-1-64299-478-0(2))* Christian Faith Publishing.
Hudson, Katy. All Things Bright & Beautiful. Alexander, Cecil Frances. 2017. (ENG.). 20p. (J). (gr. -1-k). bds. 9.99 *(978-0-8249-1654-1(9))* Worthy Publishing.
—A Long Time That I've Loved You. Brown, Margaret Wise. 2019. (Margaret Wise Brown Classics Ser.). (ENG.). 32p. (J). (gr. -1-k). 12.99 *(978-1-68412-766-5(1),* Silver Dolphin Bks.) Printers Row Publishing Group.
Hudson, Katy. Bear & Duck. Hudson, Katy. 2015. (ENG.). 32p. (J). (gr. -1-3). 17.99 *(978-0-06-232051-3(3),* HarperCollins) HarperCollins Pubs. Ltd. GBR. Dist: HarperCollins Pubs.
—A Loud Winter's Nap. Hudson, Katy. 2017. (ENG.). 32p. (gr. -1-1). 15.95 *(978-1-62370-869-6(9),* 135087, Capstone Young Readers) Capstone.
—The Perfect Birthday Recipe. Hudson, Katy. 2020. (ENG.). 32p. (J). (gr. -1-1). 17.95 *(978-1-68446-037-3(9),* 139811, Capstone Editions) Capstone.
Hudson, Neesha. Annie & the Swiss Cheese Scarf. Dakos, Alana. 2012. (ENG.). 32p. (J). (gr. k-2). 18.95 *(978-0-9883249-0-9(3))* Never Not Knitting.
Hudson, Stephan, photos by. Langston's Legacy: 101 Ways to Celebrate the Life & Work of Langston Hughes. Hudson, Katura J. & Hudson, Cheryl Willis. 2004. 48p. (J). (gr. 4-18). pap. 7.95 *(978-0-940975-99-6(8),* Sankofa Bks.) Just Us Bks., Inc.
Hudson, Stephen J. Poetry from the Masters: The Pioneers. Hudson, Wade. 2003. (Poetry from the Masters Ser.). (ENG.). 88p. (J). pap. 9.95 *(978-0-940975-96-5(3),* Sankofa Bks.) Just Us Bks., Inc.
Hudson, Takhesha. B. J. the Frog. Hudson, Roberta y. 2019. (ENG.). 32p. (J). pap. 14.99 ***(978-1-7028-1038-8(0))*** Independently Published.
Hudson, Takhesha. Able Hutch Goes to the Zoo. Hudson, Takhesha. 2019. (Able Hutch Ser.: Vol. 2). (ENG.). 30p. (J). pap. 10.99 ***(978-1-7014-0162-4(2))*** Independently Published.
Hudson, Takhesha. Briella's Thanksgiving Song. Hudson, Takhesha. 2019. (ENG.). 28p. (J). pap. 9.99 *(978-1-0818-9053-7(3))* Independently Published.
—The Flookwukals. Hudson, Takhesha. 2019. (ENG.). 32p. (J). pap. 11.99 *(978-1-0957-3383-7(4))* Independently Published.
—The Padoinedoink Forest 2. Hudson, Takhesha. 2019. (Padoinedoink Ser.: Vol. 2). (ENG.). 44p. (J). pap. 11.99 *(978-1-0922-0435-4(0))* Independently Published.
Hudson, Takhesha. The Wish Witch. Hudson, Takhesha. 2019. (ENG.). 32p. (J). pap. 13.99 ***(978-1-7038-4419-1(X))*** Independently Published.
Hudspith, Peter. The Giant from Nowhere. Dickens, Frances. 2018. (ENG.). 56p. 19.95 *(978-1-78592-535-1(0),* 696800) Kingsley, Jessica Pubs. GBR. Dist: Hachette UK Distribution.
Huerta, Catherine. Hoppy Goes to School. Bentley, Dawn. 2006. (ENG.). 32p. (J). pap. 9.95 *(978-1-59249-559-7(1));* (gr. -1-3). 4.95 *(978-1-59249-556-6(7))* Soundprints.
—Hoppy Goes to School. Bentley, Catherine & Bentley, Dawn. 2006. (Pet Tales Ser.). (ENG.). 32p. (J). 2.95 *(978-1-59249-558-0(3))* Soundprints.
—Me, Minerva & the Flying Flora. Emmer, E. R. 2nd rev. ed. 2003. (Going to Ser.). Orig. Title: Me, Minera & the Flying Car. (ENG.). 133p. (J). (gr. 4-8). pap. 6.95 *(978-1-893577-10-7(4))* Four Corners Publishing Co., Inc.
—Princess: A Lucky Kitten. Schwaeber, Barbie Heit. 2007. (Pet Tales Ser.). (ENG.). 32p. (J). 4.95 *(978-1-59249-675-4(X))* Soundprints.
—Princess: A Lucky Kitten. Schwaeber, Barbie H. 2007. (Pet Tales Ser.). (ENG.). 32p. (J). per. 2.95 *(978-1-59249-676-1(8))* Soundprints.
—Princess a Lucky Kitten. Schwaeber, Barbie Heit. 2007. (ENG.). 32p. (J). 9.95 *(978-1-59249-677-8(6))* Soundprints.
—Scout Hits the Trail. O'Donnell, Liam. 2007. (ENG.). 32p. (J). 2.95 *(978-1-59249-741-6(1))* Soundprints.
—Scout Hits the Trail. O'Donnel, Liam. (Pet Tales Ser.). (ENG.). 32p. (J). (gr. -1-3). 2008. 4.95 *(978-1-59249-740-9(3));* 2007. 9.95 *(978-1-59249-742-3(X))* Soundprints.
—Speechless in New York. Dreyer, Ellen. 2nd rev. ed. 2003. (Going to Ser.). (ENG.). 129p. (J). (gr. 4-8). pap. 6.95 *(978-1-893577-09-1(0))* Four Corners Publishing Co., Inc.
Huff, Ariella. Tanny's Meow. Ferro, Ursula. 2005. 51p. (J). pap. 12.95 *(978-0-9766006-0-2(9))* Marti Bks.
Huff, Jeane. Amy Armadillo: Mind Your Mama, 15 vols. Sargent, Dave & Sargent, Pat. 2003. (Animal Pride Ser.: 15). 42p. (J). pap. 6.95 *(978-1-56763-788-5(4));* lib. bdg. 20.95 *(978-1-56763-787-8(6))* Ozark Publishing.
—Bandit: I Help Others, 56 vols., Vol. 14. Sargent, Dave & Sargent, Pat. 2003. (Animal Pride Ser.: 14). 42p. (J). lib. bdg. 20.95 *(978-1-56763-785-4(X));* 2nd rev. ed. pap. 10.95 *(978-1-56763-786-1(8))* Ozark Publishing.
—Big Jake: I'm Very Curious, 56 vols., Vol. 12. Sargent, Dave & Sargent, Pat. 2nd rev. ed. 2003. (Animal Pride Ser.: 12). 42p. (J). lib. bdg. 20.95 *(978-1-56763-781-6(7))* Ozark Publishing.
—Billy Beaver: A New Beginning, 15 vols., Vol. 2. Sargent, Dave & Sargent, Pat. 2nd rev. ed. 2003. (Animal Pride Ser.: 2). 42p. (J). pap. 6.95 *(978-1-56763-762-5(0));* lib. bdg. 20.95 *(978-1-56763-761-8(2))* Ozark Publishing.
—Bobby Bobcat: Be a Friend, 15 vols., Vol. 10. Sargent, Dave & Sargent, Pat. 2nd rev. ed. 2003. (Animal Pride Ser.: No. 10). 42p. (J). pap. 6.95 *(978-1-56763-778-6(7));* lib. bdg. 20.95 *(978-1-56763-777-9(9))* Ozark Publishing.
—Brutus the Bear: Show Respect, 15 vols., Vol. 4. Sargent, Dave & Sargent, Pat. 2nd rev. ed. 2003. (Animal Pride Ser.: 4). 42p. (J). pap. 6.95 *(978-1-56763-766-3(3));* lib. bdg. 20.95 *(978-1-56763-765-6(5))* Ozark Publishing.
—Buddy Badger: I'm a Little Bully, 15 vols., Vol. 17. Sargent, Dave & Sargent, Pat. 2nd rev. ed. 2003. (Animal Pride Ser.: 17). 42p. (J). pap. 10.95 *(978-1-56763-792-2(2));* lib. bdg. 20.95 *(978-1-56763-791-5(4))* Ozark Publishing.
—Chrissy Cottontail: Mind Your Mama, 15 bks. Sargent, Dave & Sargent, Pat. 2nd rev. ed. 2003. (Animal Pride Ser.: 7). 42p. (J). 7. pap. 6.95 *(978-1-56763-772-4(8));* Vol. 7. lib. bdg. 20.95 *(978-1-56763-771-7(X))* Ozark Publishing.
—Dawn the Deer: Family & Friends, 56 vols., Vol. 8. Sargent, Dave & Sargent, Pat. 2nd rev. ed. 2003. (Animal Pride Ser.: Vol. 8). 42p. (J). lib. bdg. 20.95 *(978-1-56763-773-1(6))* Ozark Publishing.
—Dike the Wolf: Teamwork, 56 vols., Vol. 5. Sargent, Dave & Sargent, Pat. 2nd rev. ed. 2003. (Animal Pride Ser.: Vol. 15). 42p. (J). lib. bdg. 20.95 *(978-1-56763-767-0(1))* Ozark Publishing.
—Emma! Sargent, David M. 2004. (Doggie Tails Ser.). (J). *(978-1-56763-851-6(1));* pap. *(978-1-56763-852-3(X))* Ozark Publishing.
—Greta Groundhog: I'm Special!, 20 vols., Vol. 20. Sargent, Dave & Sargent, Pat. 2nd rev. ed. 2003. (Animal Pride Ser.: 20). 42p. (J). pap. 10.95 *(978-1-56763-798-4(1));* lib. bdg. 20.95 *(978-1-56763-797-7(3))* Ozark Publishing.
—Mad Jack: I Throw Fits, 15 vols., Vol. 16. Sargent, Dave & Sargent, Pat. 2nd rev. ed. 2003. (Animal Pride Ser.: 16). 42p. (J). pap. 10.95 *(978-1-56763-790-8(6));* lib. bdg. 20.95 *(978-1-56763-789-2(2))* Ozark Publishing.
—Molly's Journey: I'm Getting Older, 15 vols., Vol. 19. Sargent, Dave & Sargent, Pat. 2nd rev. ed. 2003. (Animal Pride Ser.: 19). 42p. (J). pap. 10.95 *(978-1-56763-796-0(5));* lib. bdg. 20.95 *(978-1-56763-795-3(7))* Ozark Publishing.
—Peggy Porcupine: Don't Wander Off, 15 vols., Vol. 13. Sargent, Dave & Sargent, Pat. 2nd rev. ed. 2003. (Animal Pride Ser.: 13). 42p. (J). (AFA.). pap. 10.95 *(978-1-56763-784-7(1));* lib. bdg. 20.95 *(978-1-56763-783-0(3))* Ozark Publishing.
—Pokey Opossum: I'm Kinda Slow, 15 vols., Vol. 18. Sargent, Dave & Sargent, Pat. 2nd rev. ed. 2003. (Animal Pride Ser.: 18). 42p. (J). pap. 10.95 *(978-1-56763-794-6(9));* lib. bdg. 20.95 *(978-1-56763-793-9(0))* Ozark Publishing.
—Redi Fox: Friendship, 15 vols., Vol. 3. Sargent, Dave & Sargent, Pat. 2nd rev. ed. 2003. (Animal Pride Ser.: 3). 42p. (J). pap. 10.95 *(978-1-56763-764-9(7));* lib. bdg. 20.95 *(978-1-56763-763-2(9))* Ozark Publishing.
—Roy Raccoon: I Love Adventure, 15 vols., Vol. 1. Sargent, Dave & Sargent, Pat. 2nd rev. ed. 2003. (Animal Pride Ser.: 1). 42p. (J). pap. 10.95 *(978-1-56763-760-1(4));* lib. bdg. 20.95 *(978-1-56763-759-5(0))* Ozark Publishing.
—Sammy Skunk: I'm a Little Stinker, 56 vols., Vol. 9. Sargent, Dave & Sargent, Pat. 2nd rev. ed. 2003. (Animal Pride Ser.: 9). 42p. (J). lib. bdg. 20.95 *(978-1-56763-775-5(2))* Ozark Publishing.
—Tunnel King: I Work Hard, 15 vols., Vol. 11. Sargent, Dave & Sargent, Pat. 2nd rev. ed. 2003. (Animal Pride Ser.: No. 11). 42p. (J). pap. 10.95 *(978-1-56763-780-9(9));* lib. bdg. 20.95 *(978-1-56763-779-3(5))* Ozark Publishing.
—White Thunder: I'm a Leader, 56 vols., Vol. 6. Sargent, Dave & Sargent, Pat. 2nd rev. ed. 2003. (Animal Pride Ser.: 6). 42p. (J). lib. bdg. 20.95 *(978-1-56763-769-4(8))* Ozark Publishing.
Huff, Jeane Lirley. Autumn's Emergency. Sargent, David M., Jr. 2003. (Doggie Tails Ser.). 32p. (J). pap. 10.95 *(978-1-56763-846-2(5));* lib. bdg. 19.95 *(978-1-56763-845-5(7))* Ozark Publishing.
—Buffy's Revenge. Sargent, David M., Jr. 2003. (Doggie Tails Ser.). 32p. (J). pap. 10.95 *(978-1-56763-844-8(9));* lib. bdg. 20.95 *(978-1-56763-843-1(0))* Ozark Publishing.
—Guard Dog Mary, 9 vols. Sargent, David M., Jr. 2003. (Doggie Tails Ser.). 32p. (J). pap. 10.95 *(978-1-56763-850-9(3))* Ozark Publishing.
—Portia's Prank, 9 vols. Sargent, David M., Jr. 2003. (Doggie Tails Ser.). 32p. (J). pap. 10.95 *(978-1-56763-848-6(1));* lib. bdg. 20.95 *(978-1-56763-847-9(3))* Ozark Publishing.
—Vicious Vera, 9 vols. Sargent, Dave M., Jr. 2004. (Doggie Tails Ser.: 9). (J). pap. 10.95 *(978-1-56763-854-7(6))* Ozark Publishing.
Huff Jr, Steven. Is It Time Yet? Appleby, Chrissie. 2019. (ENG.). 26p. (J). pap. 12.49 *(978-1-5456-6645-6(8))* Salem Author Services.
Huff, Morgan. The Arctic Fox's Journey. Pfeffer, Wendy. 2019. (Let's-Read-And-Find-Out Science 1 Ser.). (ENG.). 40p. (J). (gr. -1-3). 17.99 *(978-0-06-249083-4(4));* pap. 6.99 *(978-0-06-249082-7(6))* HarperCollins Pubs.
—Bedtime Bear. Hegarty, Patricia. 2019. (ENG.). 10p. (J). (gr. 2-k). bds. 7.99 *(978-1-68010-591-9(4))* Tiger Tales.
—First Christmas: Lift a Flap Pop up Board Book. Berry Byrd, Holly. Cottage Door Press, ed. 2017. (Lift a Pop Ser.). (ENG.). 12p. (J). (gr. -1-2). bds. 8.99 *(978-1-68052-231-0(0),* 1002170) Cottage Door Pr.
—How Much Is a Little Girl Worth? Denhollander, Rachael. 2019. (ENG.). 32p. (J). 14.99 *(978-1-4964-4168-3(0),* 20_33524, Tyndale Kids) Tyndale Hse. Pubs.
—Lulu the Llamacorn. Mirabella, Rosina. 2020. (ENG.). 24p. (J). (gr. -1-3). 9.99 *(978-0-06-297866-0(7),* HarperCollins) HarperCollins Pubs. Ltd. GBR. Dist: HarperCollins Pubs.
—My Dad Knows How! Skwish, Emily. 2019. (ENG.). 12p. (J). *(978-1-5037-4531-5(7),* 65a8ea76-beaa-4aae-8e88-ac8e1cf4e80a, p i kids) Phoenix International Publications, Inc.

—The Purpose Driven Life 100 Devotions for Children, 1 vol. Warren, Rick. 2019. (Purpose Driven Life Ser.). (ENG.). 208p. (J). 16.99 *(978-0-310-76674-2(5))* Zonderkidz.

Huff, Tim. The Cardboard Shack Beneath the Bridge. 2007. 31p. *(978-1-897186-09-1(6))* Castle Quay Bks. Canada.

—It's Hard Not to Stare: Helping Children Understand Disabilities. Fukumoto, Jan. 2013. 38p. pap. *(978-1-927355-28-2(1))* BayRidge Bks.

Huff, Tim. Am I Safe? Exploring Fear & Anxiety with Children. Huff, Tim. Snair, Iona. 2018. (Compassion Ser.). (ENG.). 44p. (J). pap. *(978-1-988928-07-4(9))* BayRidge Bks.

Huffman, Jared & Rampley, Leigh. The Lost Piece. Huffman, Jared. 2011. 36p. pap. 24.95 *(978-1-4626-1784-5(0))* America Star Bks.

Huffman, Joe. Santa's Magic Ring. McVay, Jared. Burr, Jerri, ed. 2017. (ENG.). (J). (gr. k). 19.99 *(978-0-692-94096-9(0))* Creative Texts Pubs., LLC.

Huffman, Tom. The Dove Dove: Funny Homograph Riddles. Terban, Marvin. 2008. (ENG.). 64p. (J). (gr. 5-7). pap. 6.95 *(978-0-547-03186-6(6)*, 1033405) Houghton Mifflin Harcourt Publishing Co.

Huffmaster, Elizabeth. Chelsea's Healthy Secrets. Schiavi, Sherry. 2004. (J). per. 14.95 *(978-0-9746378-0-8(7))* Celltrition.

Hufford, Stephanie. The Care & Feeding of Stuffed Ducks: 2nd Edition. Blaha, Margaret. 2015. (ENG.). 62p. (J). pap. 13.00 *(978-1-7933-2611-9(8))* Independently Published.

Huffy, Joe. Mrs. Frost. Goble, Sara Grace. 2018. (ENG.). 38p. (J). (gr. -1-3). 14.95 *(978-1-68401-585-6(5))* Mascot Bks., Inc.

Huggens, Karin. School Is Cool. Rainey. 2004. (J). *(978-0-9666199-9-7(4))* DreamDog Pr.

Huggins, Carl. The Lion & the Man: A Fable. Baron, Lindamichelle. 2009. 72p. pap. 15.95 *(978-0-940938-25-0(1))* Harlin Jacque Pubns.

Hughes, Adam. Dark Horse Heroes, Vol. 1. Richardson, Mike. Dark Horse Comics Staff & Warner, Christopher S., eds. 2008. (ENG.). 488p. pap. 24.95 *(978-1-59307-734-1(3))* Dark Horse Comics.

Hughes, Arthur. The Princess & the Goblin. MacDonald, George. 2003. 136p. pap. 12.99 *(978-1-57646-633-9(7))* Quiet Vision Publishing.

Hughes, Arthur, jt. illus. see Kirk, Maria L.

Hughes, Beth. The Fox & the Grapes. Hoena, Blake. 2018. (Classic Fables in Rhythm & Rhyme Ser.). (ENG.). 24p. (C). (gr. k-2). lib. bdg. 33.99 *(978-1-68410-384-3(3)*, 140363) Cantata Learning.

—I Love Me! Middlemiss, LaRonda Gardner. 2020. (ENG.). 32p. (J). (gr. -1-k). 17.99 *(978-1-5064-5554-9(9)*, Beaming Books) Augsburg Fortress, Pubs.

—Locomotion! March, Hop, Skip, Gallop, Run. Dahl, Michael. 2018. (Creative Movement Ser.). (ENG.). 24p. (J). (gr. -1-2). lib. bdg. 33.99 *(978-1-68410-243-3(X)*, 138433) Cantata Learning.

—Swim Bark Run. Boyle, Brian & Boyle, Pamela. 2018. (ENG.). 32p. (J). (gr. -1-1). 16.99 *(978-1-5107-2696-3(9)*, Sky Pony Pr.) Skyhorse Publishing Co., Inc.

—The Three Little Pigs (Tales to Grow By) A Story about Patience. 2020. (Tales to Grow By Ser.). (ENG.). 32p. (J). (gr. k-1). pap. 6.95 *(978-0-531-24623-8(X))*; lib. bdg. 26.00 *(978-0-531-23189-0(5))* Scholastic Library Publishing. (Children's Pr.).

Hughes, Brooke Boynton. Brave Molly. 2019. (ENG.). 48p. (J). (gr. k-3). 16.99 *(978-1-4521-6100-6(3))* Chronicle Bks. LLC.

Hughes, Brooke Boynton. Henry Wants More! Ashman, Linda. 2020. 32p. (J). (gr. -1-2). pap. 7.99 ***(978-0-593-17441-8(0)**,* Dragonfly Bks.) Random Hse. Children's Bks.

Hughes, Brooke Boynton. Where's My Turtle? Bottner, Barbara. 2020. (ENG.). 40p. (J). (gr. -1-2). 17.99 *(978-1-5247-1805-3(X))*; lib. bdg. 20.99 *(978-1-5247-1806-0(8))* Random Hse. Children's Bks. (Random Hse. Bks. for Young Readers).

Hughes, Cathy. Little Bunny's Easter. Goodings, Christina. ed. 2014. (My Carry-Along Ser.). (ENG.). 32p. (J). (gr. -1-k). pap. 7.99 *(978-0-7459-6440-9(0))* Lion Hudson PLC GBR. Dist: Independent Pubs. Group.

—My Carry-Along Nativity: Activity Book with Stickers. Goodings, Christina. ed. 2015. (My Carry-Along Ser.). (ENG.). 32p. (J). (gr. -1-2). pap. 7.99 *(978-0-7459-6511-6(3))* Lion Hudson PLC GBR. Dist: Independent Pubs. Group.

Hughes, D. L. The Adventures of Reddy Redbeet. O, Danny. 2018. (ENG.). 30p. (J). pap. 15.95 *(978-1-64003-607-9(5))* Covenant Bks.

Hughes, Denise. Snuggle Tight, Kiss Goodnight. McLean, Danielle. 2020. (ENG.). 12p. (J). (-k). bds. 9.99 *(978-1-68010-601-5(5))* Tiger Tales.

Hughes, Emily. A Brave Bear. Taylor, Sean. 2016. (ENG.). 32p. (J). (-k). 16.99 *(978-0-7636-8224-8(1))* Candlewick Pr.

—Brilliant. Doyle, Roddy. 2015. (ENG.). 192p. (J). (gr. 3-7). 16.95 *(978-1-4197-1479-5(1)*, Amulet Bks.) Abrams, Inc.

—Charlie & Mouse. Snyder, Laurel. (Charlie & Mouse Ser.: 1). (ENG.). (J). 2019. 60p. (gr. 1-4). pap. 6.99 *(978-1-4521-7263-7(3))*; 2017. 48p. 14.99 *(978-1-4521-3153-5(8))* Chronicle Bks. LLC.

—Charlie & Mouse & Grumpy. Snyder, Laurel. (ENG.). (J). (gr. 1-4). 2019. 60p. pap. 6.99 *(978-1-4521-7264-4(1))*; 2017. (Charlie & Mouse Ser.: 2). 48p. 14.99 *(978-1-4521-3748-3(X))* Chronicle Bks. LLC.

—Charlie & Mouse Even Better, Bk. 3. Snyder, Laurel. 2019. (Charlie & Mouse Ser.: 3). (ENG.). 40p. (J). (gr. 1-4). 14.99 *(978-1-4521-7065-7(7))* Chronicle Bks. LLC.

Hughes, Emily. Charlie & Mouse Even Better: Book 3. Snyder, Laurel. 2020. (ENG.). 60p. (J). (gr. 1-4). pap. 7.99 ***(978-1-4521-8342-8(2))*** Chronicle Bks. LLC.

Hughes, Emily. Charlie & Mouse Outdoors: Book 4 (Classic Children's Book, Beginning Chapter Book, Illustrated Books for Children), Bk. 4. Snyder, Laurel. 2020. (ENG.). 48p. (J). (gr. 1-4). 14.99 *(978-1-4521-7066-4(5))* Chronicle Bks. LLC.

—Everything You Need for a Treehouse. Higgins, Carter. 2018. (ENG.). 40p. (J). (gr. -1-k). 17.99 *(978-1-4521-4255-5(6))* Chronicle Bks. LLC.

—The Little Gardener. 2015. 40p. (J). (gr. -1-2). 17.95 *(978-1-909263-43-7(5))* Flying Eye Bks. GBR. Dist: Penguin Random Hse. LLC.

Hughes, Evan. The Quest for Comfort: The Story of the Heidelberg Catechism. Boekestein, William. 2011. 32p. (J). pap. 10.00 *(978-1-60178-152-9(0))* Reformation Heritage Bks.

Hughes, Faryn. Bubba Heard You Like to Color: (All Ages Coloring Book) Dad, Bubba's. 2019. (ENG.). 82p. (J). pap. 11.95 *(978-1-0720-1212-2(X))* Independently Published.

Hughes, Fox Carlton. Rainbow Rhino. Hughes, Fox Carlton. 2007. (ENG.). 36p. (J). (gr. -1-3). 16.95 *(978-0-9790275-3-6(5))* Ovation Bks.

Hughes, George. Help! I'm a Prisoner in the Library. Clifford, Eth. 2004. (Jo-Beth & Mary Rose Mystery Ser.). (ENG.). 112p. (J). (gr. 3-7). pap. 7.99 *(978-0-618-49482-8(0)*, 483926) Houghton Mifflin Harcourt Publishing Co.

Hughes, Greg. The Shapes & Colors Bible. Hughes, Greg. 2004. 80p. (J). 7.99 *(978-0-9741091-3-8(4)*, 7002) smart Life Ministries, Inc., The.

Hughes, Jack. Brandon's So Bossy! Heneghan, Judith. 2016. (Dragon School Ser.). (ENG.). 32p. (J). (gr. -1-k). pap. *(978-0-7502-8357-1(2)*, Wayland) Hachette Children's Group GBR. Dist: Hachette Bk. Group.

Hughes, Janet. The Life Story of TV Star Herman the Worm. Sroda, George. 199p. (Orig.). (J). (gr. 3-18). 10.95 *(978-0-9604486-2-3(4))* Sroda, George.

Hughes, Jon. Allosaurus & Its Relatives: The Need-To-Know Facts. Peterson, Megan Cooley. 2016. (Dinosaur Fact Dig Ser.). (ENG.). 32p. (J). (gr. -1-2). lib. bdg. 27.99 *(978-1-5157-2697-5(5)*, Capstone Pr.) Capstone.

—Ankylosaurus & Other Armored Dinosaurs: The Need-To-Know Facts. Clay, Kathryn & Vonne, Mira. 2016. (Dinosaur Fact Dig Ser.). (ENG.). 32p. (J). (gr. -1-2). lib. bdg. 27.99 *(978-1-4914-9646-6(0)*, Capstone Pr.) Capstone.

—Brachiosaurus & Other Big Long-Necked Dinosaurs: The Need-To-Know Facts. Rissman, Rebecca. 2016. (Dinosaur Fact Dig Ser.). (ENG.). 32p. (J). (gr. -1-2). lib. bdg. 27.99 *(978-1-4914-9647-3(9)*, Capstone Pr.) Capstone.

—Carnotaurus & Other Odd Meat-Eaters: The Need-To-Know Facts. Riehecky, Janet. 2016. (Dinosaur Fact Dig Ser.). (ENG.). 32p. (J). (gr. -1-2). lib. bdg. 27.99 *(978-1-5157-2695-1(9)*, Capstone Pr.) Capstone.

—Dinosaur Atlas. Malam, John et al. 2006. (ENG.). 96p. (J). (gr. 5-12). 21.99 *(978-0-7566-2235-0(2)*, DK Children) Dorling Kindersley Publishing, Inc.

—Edmontosaurus & Other Duck-Billed Dinosaurs: The Need-to-Know Facts. Rissman, Rebecca. 2016. (Dinosaur Fact Dig Ser.). (ENG.). 32p. (J). (gr. -1-2). lib. bdg. 27.99 *(978-1-5157-2698-2(3)*, Capstone Pr.) Capstone.

—Iguanodon & Other Bird-Footed Dinosaurs: The Need-To-Know Facts. Riehecky, Janet. 2016. (Dinosaur Fact Dig Ser.). (ENG.). 32p. (J). (gr. -1-2). lib. bdg. 27.99 *(978-1-5157-2696-8(7)*, Capstone Pr.) Capstone.

—Megalodon, 1 vol. Riehecky, Janet. Saunders-Smith, Gail, ed. 2006. (Dinosaurs & Prehistoric Animals Ser.). (ENG.). 24p. (J). (gr. -1-2). 27.32 *(978-0-7368-5354-5(5)*, Capstone Pr.) Capstone.

—Sabertooth Cat [Scholastic]. Frost, Helen. 2009. (Dinosaurs & Prehistoric Animals Ser.). 24p. (gr. k-1). pap. 1.00 *(978-1-4296-4249-1(1)*, Capstone Pr.) Capstone.

—Stegosaurus & Other Plated Dinosaurs: The Need-To-Know Facts. Clay, Kathryn & Vonne, Mira. 2016. (Dinosaur Fact Dig Ser.). (ENG.). 32p. (J). (gr. -1-2). lib. bdg. 27.99 *(978-1-4914-9648-0(7)*, Capstone Pr.) Capstone.

—Triceratops & Other Horned Dinosaurs: The Need-To-Know Facts. Clay, Kathryn & Vonne, Mira. 2016. (Dinosaur Fact Dig Ser.). (ENG.). 32p. (J). (gr. -1-2). lib. bdg. 27.99 *(978-1-4914-9649-7(5)*, Capstone Pr.) Capstone.

—Tyrannosaurus Rex & Its Relatives: The Need-To-Know Facts. Cooley Peterson, Megan. 2016. (Dinosaur Fact Dig Ser.). (ENG.). 32p. (J). (gr. -1-2). lib. bdg. 27.99 *(978-1-4914-9650-3(9)*, Capstone Pr.) Capstone.

—Velociraptor & Other Raptors: The Need-To-Know Facts. Rissman, Rebecca. 2016. (Dinosaur Fact Dig Ser.). (ENG.). 32p. (J). (gr. -1-2). lib. bdg. 27.99 *(978-1-4914-9651-0(7)*, Capstone Pr.) Capstone.

—Velociraptor [Scholastic]. Lindeen, Carol K. 2009. (Dinosaurs & Prehistoric Animals Ser.). 24p. (gr. k-1). pap. 1.00 *(978-1-4296-4247-7(5)*, Capstone Pr.) Capstone.

—Woolly Mammoth [Scholastic]. Frost, Helen. 2009. (Dinosaurs & Prehistoric Animals Ser.). 24p. (gr. k-1). pap. 1.00 *(978-1-4296-4250-7(5)*, Capstone Pr.) Capstone.

Hughes, Jon. What Happened to the Dinosaurs?: Band 13/Topaz (Collins Big Cat) Hughes, Jon. 2007. (Collins Big Cat Ser.). (ENG.). 32p. (J). (gr. 2-4). pap. 9.99 *(978-0-00-723084-6(2))* HarperCollins Pubs. Ltd. GBR. Dist: Independent Pubs. Group.

Hughes, Laura. Chocolate Monster. Jones, Pip. 2019. (Ruby Roo Ser.: 2). (ENG.). 32p. pap. 9.95 *(978-0-571-32751-5(6)*, Faber & Faber Children's Bks.) Faber & Faber, Inc.

—The Eighth Menorah. Wohl, Lauren L. 2014. (AV2 Fiction Readalong Ser.: Vol. 115). (ENG.). (J). (gr. -1-3). lib. bdg. 34.28 *(978-1-4896-2320-1(5)*, AV2 by Weigl) Weigl Pubs., Inc.

—The Eighth Menorah. Wohl, Lauren L. 2013. (ENG.). 32p. (J). (gr. -1-3). 16.99 *(978-0-8075-1892-2(1)*, 807518921) Whitman, Albert & Co.

—Hop Little Bunnies. Mumford, Martha. 2020. (ENG.). 24p. (J). 17.99 *(978-1-5476-0268-1(6)*, 900209360, Bloomsbury Children's Bks.) Bloomsbury Publishing USA.

—On the First Day of Kindergarten. Rabe, Tish. 2016. (ENG.). 32p. (J). (gr. -1-3). 9.99 *(978-0-06-234834-0(5))* HarperCollins Pubs.

—Quick, Barney, RUN! Jones, Pip. 2018. (Ruby Roo Ser.: 3). (ENG.). 32p. pap. 9.95 *(978-0-571-32752-2(4)*, Faber & Faber Children's Bks.) Faber & Faber, Inc.

—Rabbit on the Run. Lane, Alex. 2014. (Traditional Tales Ser.). (ENG.). 16p. (J). (gr. -1-k). pap. 6.95 *(978-1-62521-594-9(0)*, Capstone Classroom) Capstone.

—River Rose & the Magical Lullaby. Clarkson, Kelly. 2016. (ENG.). 32p. (J). (gr. -1-3). 18.99 *(978-0-06-242756-4(3))* HarperCollins Pubs.

—River Rose & the Magical Lullaby Board Book. Clarkson, Kelly. 2018. (ENG.). 32p. (J). (gr. -1 — 1). bds. 7.99 *(978-0-06-242757-1(1)*, HarperFestival) HarperCollins Pubs.

—Terrible Tim! Haworth, Katie. 2016. (ENG.). 32p. (J). (gr. -1-3). 16.99 *(978-1-4998-0137-8(8))* Little Bee Books Inc.

—There's a Pig up My Nose! Dougherty, John. 2017. (ENG.). 32p. (J). (gr. -1-k). pap. 9.99 *(978-1-4052-7716-7(5))* Egmont Bks., Ltd. GBR. Dist: Independent Pubs. Group.

—We're Going on an Egg Hunt. (ENG.). (J). 2018. 22p. bds. 7.99 *(978-1-68119-838-5(X)*, 900188675); 2017. 24p. 17.99 *(978-1-68119-314-4(0)*, 900165670) Bloomsbury Publishing USA. (Bloomsbury USA Childrens).

Hughes, Lynn. The Crystal Caves. Sherman, Candace L. 2018. (ENG.). 164p. (J). pap. 9.95 *(978-0-9972284-9-6(0)*, Crystal Bks.) Words In The Works, LLC.

Hughes, Madison. Witch's Brew. Graves, Callie. 2019. (ENG.). 26p. (J). pap. 14.95 ***(978-1-6959-0124-7(X))*** Independently Published.

Hughes-Odgers, Kyle. Ten Tiny Things. McKinlay, Meg. 2012. 36p. (J). (gr. -1-k). 18.00 *(978-1-921888-94-6(6))* Fremantle Pr. AUS. Dist: Independent Pubs. Group.

Hughes-Odgers, Kyle. Can a Skeleton Have an X-Ray? Hughes-Odgers, Kyle. 2016. 32p. (J). (gr. -1-k). 16.99 *(978-1-925162-69-1(9))* Fremantle Pr. AUS. Dist: Independent Pubs. Group.

Hughes, R. J. The Saint Nicholas Day Snow. Riggle, Charlotte. 2017. (ENG.). (J). (gr. 2-4). 24.99 *(978-0-9846124-5-1(9))*; pap. 9.99 *(978-0-9846124-6-8(7))* Phoenix Flair Pr.

Hughes, Sarah Anne. Butterflies. Pyle, Robert Michael & Peterson, Roger Tory. Peterson, Roger Tory, ed. 2nd ed. 2013. (Peterson Field Guide Color-In Bks.). (ENG.). 64p. (J). 8.95 *(978-0-544-03339-9(6)*, 1529317) Houghton Mifflin Harcourt Publishing Co.

Hughes, Sarah Anne. Reptiles & Amphibians. Hughes, Sarah Anne. Peterson, Roger Tory, ed. 2nd ed. 2013. (Peterson Field Guide Color-In Bks.). (ENG.). 64p. (J). 10.99 *(978-0-544-02695-7(0)*, 1529290) Houghton Mifflin Harcourt Publishing Co.

Hughes, Shirley. The Bell Family. Streatfeild, Noel. 2015. (Vintage Children's Classics Ser.). 368p. (J). (gr. 4-6). 12.99 *(978-0-09-958336-3(4))* Penguin Random Hse. GBR. Dist: Independent Pubs. Group.

—My Naughty Little Sister. Edwards, Dorothy. (My Naughty Little Sister Ser.). (ENG.). 2018. 160p. (J). (gr. 2-4). 17.99 *(978-1-4052-8449-3(8))*; 2nd ed. 2010. 192p. (gr. -1-2). pap. 9.99 *(978-1-4052-5334-5(7))* Egmont Bks., Ltd. GBR. Dist: Independent Pubs. Group.

—My Naughty Little Sister's Friends. Edwards, Dorothy. 2nd ed. 2010. (My Naughty Little Sister Ser.). (ENG.). 160p. (J). (gr. -1-2). pap. 10.99 *(978-1-4052-5335-2(5))* Egmont Bks., Ltd. GBR. Dist: Independent Pubs. Group.

Hughes, Shirley. Alfie & Dad. Hughes, Shirley. 2017. (Alfie Ser.). 32p. (J). (gr. -1-k). 22.99 *(978-1-78230-066-3(X))* Penguin Random Hse. GBR. Dist: Independent Pubs. Group.

—Alfie & the Big Boys. Hughes, Shirley. 2009. (Alfie Ser.). (ENG.). 32p. (J). (gr. -1-k). pap. 13.99 *(978-0-09-948844-6(2)*, Red Fox) Random House Children's Books GBR. Dist: Independent Pubs. Group.

—Alfie at Nursery School. Hughes, Shirley. 2018. 32p. (J). (-k). 19.99 *(978-1-78230-071-7(6))* Penguin Random Hse. GBR. Dist: Independent Pubs. Group.

—Alfie Gets in First. Hughes, Shirley. ed. 2009. (Alfie Ser.). 32p. (J). (gr. -1-k). pap. 14.99 *(978-1-86230-783-4(0)*, Red Fox) Random House Children's Books GBR. Dist: Independent Pubs. Group.

—Alfie Gives a Hand. Hughes, Shirley. ed. 2009. (Alfie Ser.). 32p. (J). (gr. -1-k). pap. 13.99 *(978-1-86230-785-8(7)*, Red Fox) Random House Children's Books GBR. Dist: Independent Pubs. Group.

—Alfie Weather. Hughes, Shirley. 2007. (Alfie Ser.). 48p. (J). (gr. -1-k). pap. 15.99 *(978-0-09-940425-5(7)*, Red Fox) Random House Children's Books GBR. Dist: Independent Pubs. Group.

—Alfie Wins a Prize. Hughes, Shirley. rev. ed. 2010. (Alfie Ser.). 32p. (J). (gr. k-k). pap. 12.99 *(978-1-86230-788-9(1)*, Red Fox) Random House Children's Books GBR. Dist: Independent Pubs. Group.

—Alfie's Feet. Hughes, Shirley. ed. 2009. (Alfie Ser.). (ENG.). 32p. (J). (gr. -1-k). pap. 9.99 *(978-1-86230-784-1(9)*, Red Fox) Random House Children's Books GBR. Dist: Independent Pubs. Group.

—The Big Alfie & Annie Rose Storybook. Hughes, Shirley. 2007. (Alfie Ser.). 64p. (J). (gr. -1-k). pap. 14.99 *(978-0-09-975030-7(9)*, Red Fox) Random House Children's Books GBR. Dist: Independent Pubs. Group.

—The Big Alfie Out of Doors Storybook. Hughes, Shirley. 2007. (Alfie Ser.). (ENG.). 64p. (J). (gr. -1-k). 15.95 *(978-0-09-925891-9(9)*, Red Fox) Random House Children's Books GBR. Dist: Independent Pubs. Group.

—Bobbo Goes to School. Hughes, Shirley. 2013. (ENG.). 32p. (J). (gr. -1-2). 16.99 *(978-0-7636-6524-1(X))* Candlewick Pr.

—The Christmas Eve Ghost. Hughes, Shirley. 2010. (ENG.). 32p. (J). (gr. -1-3). 15.99 *(978-0-7636-4472-7(2))* Candlewick Pr.

—Daisy Saves the Day. Hughes, Shirley. 2015. (ENG.). 32p. (J). (gr. k-4). 16.99 *(978-0-7636-7323-9(4))* Candlewick Pr.

—Don't Want to Go! Hughes, Shirley. 2010. (ENG.). 32p. (J). (gr. -1-2). 16.99 *(978-0-7636-5091-9(9))* Candlewick Pr.

—An Evening at Alfie's. Hughes, Shirley. ed. 2009. (Alfie Ser.). (ENG.). 32p. (J). (gr. k-k). pap. 12.99 *(978-1-86230-786-5(5)*, Red Fox) Random House Children's Books GBR. Dist: Independent Pubs. Group.

—From A to Z. Hughes, Shirley. 2018. (Lucy & Tom Ser.). 32p. (J). (-k). pap. 11.99 *(978-1-78295-725-6(1)*, Red Fox) Random House Children's Books GBR. Dist: Independent Pubs. Group.

—Jonadab & Rita. Hughes, Shirley. 2010. (Alfie Ser.). 32p. (J). (gr. -1-k). pap. 11.99 *(978-1-86230-313-3(4)*, Red Fox) Random House Children's Books GBR. Dist: Independent Pubs. Group.

—My First ABC. Hughes, Shirley. 2019. (ENG.). 32p. (J). (-k). 16.99 *(978-0-7636-9729-7(X))* Candlewick Pr.

—Out & About: A First Book of Poems. Hughes, Shirley. 2015. (ENG.). 56p. (J). (-k). 16.99 *(978-0-7636-7644-5(6))* Candlewick Pr.

—Ruby in the Ruins. Hughes, Shirley. 2018. (ENG.). 32p. (J). (gr. k-4). 15.99 *(978-0-7636-9237-7(9))* Candlewick Pr.

Hughes, Steven. Tru Detective, 1 vol. McClintock, Norah. 2015. (ENG.). 128p. (YA). (gr. 8-12). pap. 19.95 *(978-1-4598-0379-4(5))* Orca Bk. Pubs. USA.

Hughes, Steven P. Tales from Beyond the Brain, 1 vol. Szpirglas, Jeff. 2019. (ENG.). 192p. (J). (gr. 4-7). pap. 12.95 *(978-1-4598-2079-1(7))* Orca Bk. Pubs. USA.

Hughes, Steven P. Tales from the Fringes of Fear. Szpirglas, Jeff. 2020. (ENG.). 192p. (J). (gr. 4-7). pap. 12.95 ***(978-1-4598-2458-4(X))*** Orca Bk. Pubs. USA.

Hughey, Sue C. Herby's Secret Formula. Hughey, Sue C. 2013. 232p. pap. 11.95 *(978-0-9840358-1-6(8))* Associated Arts Pub.

Hugo, Pierre de. Let's Look at the Hedge. Allaire, Caroline & Krawczyk, Sabine. 2012. (ENG.). 38p. (J). (gr. 1-4). spiral bd. 11.99 *(978-1-85103-339-3(4))* Moonlight Publishing, Ltd. GBR. Dist: Independent Pubs. Group.

—The Seashore. 2012. (My First Discoveries Ser.: 13). (ENG.). 38p. (J). (gr. -1-k). spiral bd. 13.99 *(978-1-85103-394-2(7))* Moonlight Publishing, Ltd. GBR. Dist: Independent Pubs. Group.

Hui-Jin, Park. Chronicles of Cursed Sword, Vol. 10. Beop-Ryong, Yeo. rev. ed. 2005. 192p. (YA). pap. 9.99 *(978-1-59532-387-3(2))* TOKYOPOP, Inc.

—Chronicles of the Cursed Sword, 10 vols. Beop-Ryong, Yuy. 2004. 176p. Vol. 4. rev. ed. pap. 9.99 *(978-1-59182-421-3(4))*; Vol. 5. 5th rev. ed. pap. 9.99 *(978-1-59182-422-0(2))* TOKYOPOP, Inc.

—Chronicles of the Cursed Sword, 12 vols. Yeo, Beop-Ryong. 2004. Vol. 8. 8th rev. ed. 168p. pap. 9.99 *(978-1-59182-425-1(7))*; Vol. 9. 9th rev. ed. 176p. pap. 9.99 *(978-1-59182-426-8(5))* TOKYOPOP, Inc.

—Chronicles of the Cursed Sword, Vol. 11. rev. ed. 2005. 192p. pap. 9.99 *(978-1-59532-388-0(0))* TOKYOPOP, Inc.

—Chronicles of the Cursed Sword. Beop-Ryong, Yeo. (Chronicles of the Cursed Sword Ser.). 192p. Vol. 12. rev. ed. 2005. pap. 9.99 *(978-1-59532-389-7(9))*; Vol. 13. 13th rev. ed. 2005. per. 9.99 *(978-1-59532-645-4(6))*; Vol. 14. rev. ed. 2006. per. 9.99 *(978-1-59532-646-1(4))* TOKYOPOP, Inc.

Huie, Wing Young, photos by. Dads. Coy, John. 2020. (ENG., 32p. (J). (gr. -1-2). 19.99 *(978-1-5415-7839-5(2)*, Carolrhoda Bks.) Lerner Publishing Group.

—Their Great Gift: Courage, Sacrifice, & Hope in a New Land. Coy, John. 2016. (ENG., 32p. (J). (gr. k-3). 19.99 *(978-1-4677-8054-4(5)*, 9781467780544); E-Book 30.65 *(978-1-4677-9756-6(1))* Lerner Publishing Group. (Carolrhoda Bks.).

Huiett, William, jt. illus. see Denman, Michael.

Huiett, William J., jt. illus. see Denman, Michael L.

Huiett, William J., jt. illus. see Denman, Michael.

Huismann, Duane. Nobody's Lion. Fisher, Barbara. 2004. (J). per. 16.95 *(978-1-59571-049-9(3))* Word Association Pubs.

Huizar, Ignacio Zárate. El Castigo de Lucas. Hinojosa, Francisco. 2014. (SPA.). 88p. (J). (gr. 2-4). pap. 7.95 *(978-607-8237-39-5(X))* Nostra Ediciones MEX. Dist: Independent Pubs. Group.

Huling, Phil. Cactus Soup, 0 vols. Kimmel, Eric A. 2011. (ENG.). 34p. (J). (gr. -1-3). pap. 9.99 *(978-0-7614-5832-6(8)*, 9780761458326, Two Lions) Amazon Publishing.

—Puss in Cowboy Boots. Huling, Jan. 2007. (ENG.). 40p. (J). (gr. 1-4). 11.99 *(978-1-4169-6749-1(4)*, Simon & Schuster/Paula Wiseman Bks.) Simon & Schuster/Paula Wiseman Bks.

Huliska-Beith, Laura. Bubble Gum, Bubble Gum. Wheeler, Lisa. 2019. (ENG.). 32p. (J). 18.95 ***(978-1-948959-09-4(7))*** Purple Hse. Pr.

Huliska-Beith, Laura. Cinco Pequenas Mariquitas. 2005.Tr. of Five Little Ladybugs. (SPA & ENG.). 12p. (J). 4.95 *(978-1-58117-333-8(4)*, Intervisual/Piggy Toes) Bendon, Inc.

—Diez Pequeñas Mariquitas. Gerth, Melanie. 2005. Orig. Title: Ten Little Ladybugs. (SPA & ENG.). 22p. (J). (gr. -1). 10.95 *(978-1-58117-006-1(8)*, Intervisual/Piggy Toes) Bendon, Inc.

Huliska-Beith, Laura, et al. Dream-Along Nursery Rhymes. Scholastic Inc., Staff. 2016. (Rookie Nursery Rhymes Ser.). (ENG.). 32p. (J). (gr. -1-k). 25.00 *(978-0-531-22877-7(0)*, Children's Pr.) Scholastic Library Publishing.

Huliska-Beith, Laura. A Farmer's Life for Me. Dobbins, Jan. 2013. 24p. (J). (gr. -1-2). 9.99 *(978-1-84686-791-0(6))*; (gr. k-3). 16.99 *(978-1-84686-790-3(8))*; (gr. k-3). pap. 6.99 *(978-1-84686-939-6(0))* Barefoot Bks., Inc.

—Five Little Ladybugs. Gerth, Melanie. 2006. 12p. (J). bds. 14.95 *(978-1-58117-218-8(4)*, Intervisual/Piggy Toes) Bendon, Inc.

—The Goodnight Train. Sobel, June. (Goodnight Train Ser.). (ENG.). 32p. (J). (gr. -1-3). 2017. pap. 7.99 *(978-1-328-74002-1(1)*, 1677042, HMH Books For Young Readers); 2006. 17.99 *(978-0-15-205436-6(7)*, 1196359) Houghton Mifflin Harcourt Publishing Co.

—The Goodnight Train (lap Board Book) Sobel, June. 2017. (Goodnight Train Ser.). (ENG.). 30p. (J). (— 1). bds. 12.99 *(978-1-328-76438-6(9)*, 1681068, HMH Books For Young Readers) Houghton Mifflin Harcourt Publishing Co.

—The Goodnight Train Rolls On! Sobel, June. 2018. (Goodnight Train Ser.). (ENG.). 32p. (J). (gr. -1-3). 17.99 *(978-1-328-50019-9(5)*, 1717900, HMH Books For Young Readers) Houghton Mifflin Harcourt Publishing Co.

H

—Little Red Hot, 0 vols. Kimmel, Eric A. 2013. (ENG.). 32p. (J). (gr. -1-3). 17.99 *(978-1-4778-1638-7(0),* 9781477816387, Two Lions) Amazon Publishing.

Huliska-Beith, Laura, et al. Move-Along Nursery Rhymes. (Rookie Read-Aloud Ser.). (ENG.). 32p. (J). (gr. -1-k). 2017. pap. 12.00 *(978-0-531-23047-3(3));* 2016. 25.00 *(978-0-531-22878-4(9))* Scholastic Library Publishing. (Children's Pr.).

Huliska-Beith, Laura. Santa & the Goodnight Train. Sobel, June. (Goodnight Train Ser.). (ENG.). (J). 2020. 28p. (— 1). bds. 8.99 ***(978-0-358-36266-1(0),*** 1784603); 2019. 32p. (gr. -1-3). 17.99 *(978-1-328-61840-5(4),* 1733753) Houghton Mifflin Harcourt Publishing Co. (HMH Books For Young Readers).

Huliska-Beith, Laura. Ten Little Ladybugs. Gerth, Melanie. 2007. (ENG.). 22p. (J). (gr. -1-3). bds. 15.95 *(978-1-58117-578-3(7),* Intervisual/Piggy Toes) Bendon, Inc.

—The Twelve Days of Christmas in Missouri. Ingalls, Ann. (Twelve Days of Christmas in America Ser.). (J). (-k). 2018. 22p. bds. 7.95 *(978-1-4549-3032-7(2));* 2017. 40p. 12.95 *(978-1-4549-2075-5(0))* Sterling Publishing Co., Inc.

—Violet's Music. Johnson, Angela. 2004. 32p. (J). (gr. -1-3). 17.99 *(978-0-8037-2740-3(2),* Dial Bks) Penguin Young Readers Group.

—Vivamos la Granja! Dobbins, Jan & Bernal, Natalia. 2013. 24p. (J). (gr. -1-1). 9.99 *(978-1-84686-860-3(2))* Barefoot Bks., Inc.

—The Wild, Wild Inside: A View from Mommy's Tummy! Feiffer, Kate. 2010. (ENG.). 32p. (J). (gr. -1-3). 15.99 *(978-1-4169-4099-9(5),* Simon & Schuster/Paula Wiseman Bks.) Simon & Schuster/Paula Wiseman Bks.

Hull, Biz. Starlight Surprise. Chapman, Linda. 2003. (My Secret Unicorn Ser.). 130p. (J). *(978-0-439-65275-9(8))* Scholastic, Inc.

Hull, Biz & Farley, Andrew. Flying High. Chapman, Linda. 2004. (My Secret Unicorn Ser.). 118p. (J). *(978-0-439-65273-5(1))* Scholastic, Inc.

Hull, Jim. Casey at the Bat. Thayer, Ernest L. & Gardner, Martin. 2012. (Dover Children's Classics Ser.). (ENG.). 72p. (J). (gr. 2-5). pap. 6.99 *(978-0-486-48510-2(2),* 485102) Dover Pubns., Inc.

Hull, Pamela Hubbard. Hello My Name Is Jenny: I Have Alopecia. West, Jennifer Thomas. 2019. (ENG.). 30p. (J). pap. 12.99 *(978-1-0727-9125-6(0))* Independently Published.

Hull, Pamela Hubbard. Hello My Name Is Thomas: I Have Tourette Syndrome. West, Jennifer Thomas. 2019. (ENG.). 34p. (J). pap. 12.99 ***(978-1-7016-5135-7(1))*** Independently Published.

Hullah, Gwen. The Bear Who Used up All His Growls. Bonah, Zizzi. 2017. (ENG.). 64p. (J). pap. *(978-0-9957479-8-2(9))* She & the Cat's Mother.

Hullenbaugh, Arnie. Hockey with My Hero: A Jimmy Sprinkles Adventure. Rowsick, Scott. 2016. (ENG.). (J). pap. 10.99 *(978-0-692-77305-5(3))* Pastime Pubns., LLC.

Hullinger, C. D. The Weather. Rosa-Mendoza, Gladys. Cifuentes, Carolina, ed. 2004. (English-Spanish Foundations Ser.: Vol. 6). Orig. Title: El Tiempo. (ENG & SPA.). 20p. (J). (gr. -1-4). bds. 6.95 *(978-0-9679748-5-9(2))* Me+Mi Publishing.

—The Weather. Cifuentes, Carolina. 2010. (My World Ser.). Orig. Title: El Tiempo. (ENG.). 24p. (J). (gr. -1-1). lib. bdg. 25.60 *(978-1-60754-955-0(7))* Windmill Bks.

—The Weather. Cifuentes, Carolina, ed. 2010. (My World Ser.). Orig. Title: El Tiempo. (ENG.). 24p. (J). (gr. -1-1). pap. 8.15 *(978-1-61533-043-0(7))* Windmill Bks.

Hulse, Gillian. Rainforest. Morris, Ting & Morris, Neil. 2006. (Sticky Fingers Ser.). 32p. (J). lib. bdg. 28.50 *(978-1-59771-028-2(8))* Sea-To-Sea Pubns.

Hulse, Kris. A Cowhand Christmas. Hulse, Kris. 2006. 32p. (J). lib. bdg. 21.95 *(978-0-9761128-6-0(8))* KB Bks. & More.

Hulst, W. G. van de & Hulst, Willem G. van de. Annie & the Goat. 2014. 48p. (J). *(978-1-928136-06-4(0))* Inheritance Pubns.

—The Basket. 2014. (J). *(978-1-928136-04-0(4))* Inheritance Pubns.

—The Black Kitten. 2014. (J). *(978-1-928136-07-1(9))* Inheritance Pubns.

—Bruno the Bear. 2014. (J). *(978-1-928136-03-3(6))* Inheritance Pubns.

—Footprints in the Snow. 2014. (J). *(978-1-928136-13-2(3))* Inheritance Pubns.

—Herbie, the Runaway Duck. 2014. (J). *(978-1-928136-19-4(2))* Inheritance Pubns.

—Kittens, Kittens Everywhere. 2014. (J). *(978-1-928136-20-0(6))* Inheritance Pubns.

—The Little Wooden Shoe. 2014. (J). *(978-1-928136-01-9(X))* Inheritance Pubns.

—The Pig under the Pew. 2014. (J). *(978-1-928136-10-1(9))* Inheritance Pubns.

—The Rockity Rowboat. 2014. (J). *(978-1-928136-18-7(4))* Inheritance Pubns.

—The Search for Christmas. 2014. (J). *(978-1-928136-12-5(5))* Inheritance Pubns.

—The Secret Hiding Place. 2014. (J). *(978-1-928136-16-3(8))* Inheritance Pubns.

—The Secret in the Box. 2014. (J). *(978-1-928136-17-0(6))* Inheritance Pubns.

—Three Foolish Sisters. 2014. (J). *(978-1-928136-15-6(X))* Inheritance Pubns.

—Through the Thunderstorm. 2014. (J). *(978-1-928136-02-6(8))* Inheritance Pubns.

—The Woods Beyond the Wall. 2017. (J). *(978-1-928136-08-8(7))* Inheritance Pubns.

Hulst, Willem G. van de, jt. illus. see Hulst, W. G. van de.

Human, Becca. Maiden & Princess. Haack, Daniel & Galupo, Isabel. 2019. (ENG.). 40p. (J). (gr. -1-3). 17.99 *(978-1-4998-0776-9(7))* Little Bee Books Inc.

Hume, Jeff. The Shining Thing, 1 vol. Ballard, John. 2009. 35p. pap. 19.95 *(978-1-61546-655-9(X))* PublishAmerica, Inc.

Hume, John. My Florida Alphabet, Vol. Johnson, Annie P. & Johnson, Russell. 2014. (ENG.). 66p. (J). (gr. -1-12). pap. 15.95 *(978-1-56164-729-3(2))* Pineapple Pr., Inc.

Hume, John E. Henney Hen & the Zookeeper. Noles, Cynthia. 2019. (ENG.). (J). 44p. 24.95 ***(978-1-950434-17-6(6));*** 48p. pap. 14.95 ***(978-1-950434-16-9(8))*** Janneck Bks.

Hume, Jr John E. Bee, Flea, & Me. Noles, Cynthia. 2019. (ENG.). 44p. (J). (gr. k-3). 24.95 *(978-1-7329687-0-7(5))* Janneck Bks.

—Minch Moogan. Noles, Cynthia. 2018. (ENG.). 48p. (J). pap. 14.95 *(978-1-7322236-3-9(7))* Janneck Bks.

Humiston, Erin, et al. Calla Cthulhu. Dorkin, Evan & Dyer, Sarah. 2017. (ENG.). 136p. (gr. 5-9). pap. 12.99 *(978-1-5067-0293-3(7))* Dark Horse Comics.

Huml Durda, Lois. Summer in Jane's Garden. Huml, Jane. 2016. (ENG.). (J). pap. 11.95 *(978-1-63525-372-6(1))* Christian Faith Publishing.

Hummel, Benjamin. Lights On! Ike Hoover Electrifies the White House. Becker, Cynthia Simmelink. 2017. (ENG.). 40p. (J). 19.95 *(978-0-86541-244-6(8))* Filter Pr., LLC.

Hummingbird, Jesse T. Native American Night Before Christmas. Robinson, Gary. 2007. 40p. (J). *(978-1-57416-093-2(1))* Clear Light Pubs.

—Native American Twelve Days of Christmas. Robinson, Gary. 2011. (ENG.). 32p. (J). 19.95 *(978-1-57416-105-2(9))* Clear Light Pubs.

Humphrey, Bobby, photos by. Rules of the Game. Nixon, James. 2011. (Soccer File Ser.). 32p. (gr. 4-7). lib. bdg. 31.35 *(978-1-59920-529-8(7))* Black Rabbit Bks.

Humphrey Williams, Ann. The Journey Through Middle School Math. Crews, Elizabeth, photos by. Mayfield-Ingram, Karen. 2005. (Equals Ser.). 140p. pap. 18.95 *(978-0-912511-31-3(1),* EQUALS) Univ. of California, Berkeley, Lawrence Hall of Science.

—El Viaje—Por la matematica de la escuela Secundaria. Ramirez, Alma. 2005. (Equals Ser.). (SPA.). (J). pap. 18.95 *(978-0-912511-32-0(X),* EQUALS) Univ. of California, Berkeley, Lawrence Hall of Science.

Humphreys, Dolores. The Adventures of J. G. & Echo: The Land of All Creatures & the Swamp Creature, 1. 2003. 81p. (J). per. 16.00 *(978-0-9727415-2-1(6))* Cuccia, Louis.

Humphreys, Graham. Jason & the Argonauts. Brooks, Felicity. 2005. 144p. (J). pap. 4.95 *(978-0-7945-0275-1(X),* Usborne) EDC Publishing.

Humphries, Tudor. Are You a Bee? Allen, Judy. 2004. (Backyard Bks.). (ENG.). 32p. (J). (gr. k-3). pap. 7.99 *(978-0-7534-5804-4(7),* 900052580, Kingfisher) Roaring Brook Pr.

—Are You a Butterfly? Allen, Judy. 2003. (Backyard Bks.). (ENG.). 28p. (J). (gr. k-3). pap. 7.99 *(978-0-7534-5608-8(7),* 900052553, Kingfisher) Roaring Brook Pr.

—Are You a Dragonfly? Allen, Judy. 2004. (Backyard Bks.). (ENG.). 32p. (J). (gr. k-3). pap. 7.99 *(978-0-7534-5805-1(5),* 900052581, Kingfisher) Roaring Brook Pr.

—Are You a Grasshopper? Allen, Judy. 2004. (Backyard Bks.). (ENG.). 32p. (J). (gr. k-3). pap. 7.99 *(978-0-7534-5806-8(3),* 900052582, Kingfisher) Roaring Brook Pr.

—Are You a Ladybug? Allen, Judy. 2003. (Backyard Bks.). (ENG.). 31p. (J). (gr. k-3). pap. 7.99 *(978-0-7534-5603-3(6),* 900052551, Kingfisher) Roaring Brook Pr.

—Are You a Snail? Allen, Judy. 2003. (Backyard Bks.). (ENG.). 31p. (J). (gr. k-3). pap. 7.99 *(978-0-7534-5604-0(4),* 9780753456040, Kingfisher) Roaring Brook Pr.

—Are You a Spider? Allen, Judy. 2003. (Backyard Bks.). (ENG.). 31p. (J). (gr. k-3). pap. 7.99 *(978-0-7534-5609-5(5),* 900052554, Kingfisher) Roaring Brook Pr.

—Are You an Ant? Allen, Judy. 2004. (Backyard Bks.). (ENG.). 32p. (J). (gr. k-3). pap. 7.99 *(978-0-7534-5803-7(9),* 900052579, Kingfisher) Roaring Brook Pr.

—Flip the Flaps: Dinosaurs. Allen, Judy. 2011. (Flip the Flaps Ser.). (ENG.). 32p. (J). (gr. -1-1). pap. 7.99 *(978-0-7534-6496-0(9),* 9780753464960, Kingfisher) Roaring Brook Pr.

—The Giant Surprise: A Narnia Story. Oram, Hiawyn. 2005. (Step into Narnia Ser.). 40p. (J). (gr. -1-2). lib. bdg. 16.89 *(978-0-06-001360-8(5))* HarperCollins Pubs.

—The Lion, the Witch & the Wardrobe. Lewis, C. S. 2004. (Chronicles of Narnia Ser.). 48p. (J). (gr. -1-2). lib. bdg. 17.89 *(978-0-06-055651-8(X))* HarperCollins Pubs.

—The Lion, the Witch & the Wardrobe: Picture Book Edition. Lewis, C. S. 2004. (Chronicles of Narnia Ser.). (ENG.). 48p. (J). (gr. -1-2). 17.99 *(978-0-06-055650-1(1),* HarperCollins) HarperCollins Pubs. Ltd. GBR. Dist: HarperCollins Pubs.

Humphrys-Bajaj, Holly. Tails of Sweetbrier. Humphrys-Dunne, Deanie. 2013. 82p. pap. 9.95 *(978-1-61286-182-1(2))* Avid Readers Publishing Group.

Huna Smith, Ryan. The Three Little Sheep/Dibe Yazhi Taa'go Baa Hane' Yazzie, Seraphine G. Thomas, Peter A., tr. 2006. (ENG & NAV.). 32p. (J). (gr. 4-7). 12.95 *(978-1-893354-09-8(1))* Salina Bookshelf Inc.

Hund, Marjolein. Pirates. Boshouwers, Suzan. 2012. (Want to Know Ser.). (ENG.). 30p. (J). (gr. k-2). 16.95 *(978-1-60537-135-1(1))* Clavis Publishing.

Hundley, Sam. Our Fantasy Island: An Interactive Book. Suhay, Lisa. 2006. 30p. (J). pap. 8.00 *(978-0-9766628-0-8(9))* Fantasy Island Pr.

Hundley, Sterling. O Captain, My Captain: Walt Whitman, Abraham Lincoln, & the Civil War. Burleigh, Robert. 2019. (ENG.). 64p. (J). (gr. 5-17). 19.99 *(978-1-4197-3358-1(3),* Abrams Bks. for Young Readers) Abrams, Inc.

Huneke, Rebekah. Carrie Mouse & the Giant Garage. Huneke, Morgan Elizabeth. 2018. (ENG.). 30p. (J). pap. 12.99 *(978-1-7246-2774-2(0))* CreateSpace Independent Publishing Platform.

Hunerdosse, Katie L. The Monster Dog: A Small Dog with a Big Heart Learns about Alzheimer's Disease. Tribbett, Carmen R. 2019. (Monster Dog Ser.: Vol. 2). (ENG.). 34p. (J). (gr. 2-6). 19.95 ***(978-0-578-57118-8(8))*** KHallBks.

Hunkel, Cary. Discovering Wolves. Field, Nancy & Karasov, Corliss. 2011. (Discovering Nature Library). (ENG.). 40p. (J). (gr. 3-8). pap. 6.95 *(978-0-941042-39-0(1))* Dog-Eared Pubns.

Hunner, Trina L. Green Bean! Green Bean! Thomas, Patricia. 2016. (ENG.). 32p. (J). (gr. k-4). 16.95 *(978-1-58469-543-1(9),* Dawn Pubns.) Sourcebooks, Inc.

—On Kiki's Reef, 1 vol. Malnor, Carol L. 2014. (ENG.). 32p. (J). (gr. k-4). 16.95 *(978-1-58469-476-2(9),* Dawn Pubns.) Sourcebooks, Inc.

Hunner, Trina L. Molly's Organic Farm. Hunner, Trina L. Malnor, Carol L. 2012. (ENG.). 32p. (J). (gr. k-4). 16.95 *(978-1-58469-166-2(2))* Dawn Pubns.

—Molly's Organic Farm, 1 vol. Hunner, Trina L. Malnor, Carol L. 2012. (ENG.). 32p. (J). (gr. k-4). pap. 8.95 *(978-1-58469-167-9(0),* Dawn Pubns.) Sourcebooks, Inc.

Hunt, Brad. Ten Little Unicorns. Linn, Susie. 2018. (Counting to Ten Bks.). (ENG.). 20p. (J). (gr. -1-1). 9.99 *(978-1-78700-376-7(0))* Top That! Publishing PLC GBR. Dist: Independent Pubs. Group.

Hunt, Craig J. S. The Dinosaur Who Loved to Bake & Eat Cakes. Hunt, Debbie Colleen. 2012. 32p. 24.95 *(978-1-4626-3213-8(0))* America Star Bks.

Hunt, E. Marlene. Every Apple. Hunt, E. Marlene. I.t. ed. 2003. 12p. pap. 10.00 *(978-1-893555-45-7(3))* Grace Publishing.

Hunt, Jane. There's Something in My Sandwich. Ayers, Linda. 50p. (J). 2006. 13.95 *(978-0-9760505-7-5(9));* 2005. per. 6.95 *(978-0-9760505-5-1(2))* Blue Thistle Pr.

—Tiger Does the Write Thing. Ayers, Linda. I.t. ed. 2005. 35p. (J). per. 7.95 *(978-0-9760505-4-4(4))* Blue Thistle Pr.

—Tiger Goes Collecting. Ayers, Linda. I.t. ed. 2004. 55p. (J). per. 7.95 *(978-0-9760505-2-0(8))* Blue Thistle Pr.

Hunt, Jim. Baby Kong. Stroud, Scott. 2006. (J). 8.95 *(978-1-60131-001-9(3),* Castlebridge Bks.) Big Tent Bks.

—Boomer Explores Annapolis, 1 vol. Clarke, Angelique. 2012. (ENG.). 32p. (J). (gr. -1-3). 12.99 *(978-0-7643-4008-6(5),* 9780764340086) Schiffer Publishing, Ltd.

—Grumpy Mr. Grady. Stroud, Scott. 2007. 24p. (J). 8.95 *(978-1-60131-008-8(0),* Castlebridge Bks.) Big Tent Bks.

—My Loveable Little Monster. Lara, Sahai. 2011. 22p. (J). pap. 5.99 *(978-0-615-48221-7(X))* SNL Publishing.

Hunt, John, jt. illus. see Barry, James L.

Hunt, Judith. Animals under Our Feet. McKay, Sindy. 2007. 40p. (J). *(978-1-891327-97-1(6));* pap. *(978-1-891327-98-8(4))* Treasure Bay, Inc.

—Half & Half-Earthquake! Hodgkins, Fran. 2011. (ENG.). 52p. (J). 9.95 *(978-1-60115-217-6(5));* pap. 4.99 *(978-1-60115-218-3(3))* Treasure Bay, Inc.

—Prunes & Rupe. Griffin, Lydia. 2007. 32p. (J). 16.00 *(978-0-86541-086-2(0))* Filter Pr., LLC.

—We Both Read-Animals under Our Feet. McKay, Sindy. 2007. (We Both Read Ser.). 40p. (J). (gr. -1-3). pap. 4.99 *(978-1-60115-004-2(0))* Treasure Bay, Inc.

Hunt, Judith & Smith, Wendy. We Both Read Bilingual Edition-Sharks!/Tiburones. McKay, Sindy. ed. 2015.Tr. of Tiburones. (ENG & SPA.). 44p. (J). (gr. 1-2). pap. 4.99 *(978-1-60115-068-4(7))* Treasure Bay, Inc.

—We Both Read-Sharks! McKay, Sindy. 2012. 44p. (J). 9.95 *(978-1-60115-261-9(2));* pap. 4.99 *(978-1-60115-262-6(0))* Treasure Bay, Inc.

Hunt, Judith A. The Bald Eagle, 1 vol. Kenney, Karen Latchana. 2011. (Our Nation's Pride Ser.). (ENG.). 32p. (J). (gr. k-4). 28.50 *(978-1-61641-149-7(X),* 11980, Looking Glass Library) Magic Wagon.

—Ellis Island, 1 vol. Kenney, Karen Latchana. 2011. (Our Nation's Pride Ser.). (ENG.). 32p. (J). (gr. k-4). 28.50 *(978-1-61641-150-3(3),* 11982, Looking Glass Library) Magic Wagon.

—The Lincoln Memorial, 1 vol. Kenney, Karen Latchana. 2011. (Our Nation's Pride Ser.). (ENG.). 32p. (J). (gr. k-4). 28.50 *(978-1-61641-151-0(1),* 11984, Looking Glass Library) Magic Wagon.

—Memorial Day, 1 vol. Kenney, Karen Latchana. 2011. (Our Nation's Pride Ser.). (ENG.). 32p. (J). (gr. k-4). 28.50 *(978-1-61641-152-7(X),* 11986, Looking Glass Library) Magic Wagon.

—Mount Rushmore, 1 vol. Kenney, Karen Latchana. 2011. (Our Nation's Pride Ser.). (ENG.). 32p. (J). (gr. k-4). 28.50 *(978-1-61641-153-4(8),* 11988, Looking Glass Library) Magic Wagon.

—The White House, 1 vol. Kenney, Karen Latchana. 2011. (Our Nation's Pride Ser.). (ENG.). 32p. (J). (gr. k-4). 28.50 *(978-1-61641-154-1(6),* 11990, Looking Glass Library) Magic Wagon.

Hunt, Kathy. Chronicles of the Steam Alliance: Book 4 Desolation of the Ghost Train. Hunt, Kathy. Hunt, Tim. 2019. (Chronicles of the Steam Alliance Ser.: Vol. 4). (ENG.). 168p. (J). pap. 8.99 *(978-1-7310-3949-1(2))* Independently Published.

Hunt, Lisa. Bean Soup. Gates, Margo. 2020. (Plant Life Cycles (Pull Ahead Readers — Fiction) Ser.). (ENG.). 16p. (J). (gr. -1-1). pap. 6.99 ***(978-1-7284-0306-9(5));*** lib. bdg. 22.65 ***(978-1-5415-9030-4(9))*** Lerner Publishing Group. (Lerner Pubns.).

—Dandelions to Eat. Gates, Margo. 2020. (Plant Life Cycles (Pull Ahead Readers — Fiction) Ser.). (ENG.). 16p. (J). (gr. -1-1). pap. 6.99 ***(978-1-7284-0307-6(3));*** lib. bdg. 22.65 ***(978-1-5415-9031-1(7))*** Lerner Publishing Group. (Lerner Pubns.).

Hunt, Lisa. The Egg. Gates, Margo. 2019. (Seasons All Around Me (Pull Ahead Readers — Fiction) Ser.). (ENG.). 16p. (J). (gr. -1-1). 22.65 *(978-1-5415-5876-2(6),* 9781541558762, Lerner Pubns.) Lerner Publishing Group.

—In the Garden. Gates, Margo. 2019. (Science All Around Me (Pull Ahead Readers — Fiction) Ser.). (ENG.). 16p. (J). (gr. -1-1). 22.65 *(978-1-5415-5854-0(5),* 9781541558540, Lerner Pubns.) Lerner Publishing Group.

—Mabel Beecher: Future Teacher. Best, Cari. 2018. (ENG.). 32p. (J). (gr. -1 — 1). 16.99 *(978-1-5107-2071-8(5),* Sky Pony Pr.) Skyhorse Publishing Co., Inc.

—Manners Matter in the Classroom. Mortensen, Lori. (First Graphics: Manners Matter Ser.). (ENG.). 24p. (gr. 1-2). 2011. pap. 35.70 *(978-1-4296-6392-6(2));* 2010. (J). lib. bdg. 24.65 *(978-1-4296-5333-6(7))* Capstone.

—Manners Matter in the Library. Mortensen, Lori. (First Graphics: Manners Matter Ser.). (ENG.). 24p. (gr. 1-2). 2011. pap. 35.70 *(978-1-4296-6393-9(6));* 2010. (J). lib. bdg. 24.65 *(978-1-4296-5330-5(2))* Capstone.

—Manners Matter on a Field Trip. Mortensen, Lori. (First Graphics: Manners Matter Ser.). (ENG.). 24p. (gr. 1-2). 2011. pap. 35.70 *(978-1-4296-6394-6(4));* 2010. (J). lib. bdg. 24.65 *(978-1-4296-5331-2(0))* Capstone.

—Manners Matter on the Playground. Mortensen, Lori. (First Graphics: Manners Matter Ser.). (ENG.). 24p. (gr. 1-2). 2011. pap. 35.70 *(978-1-4296-6395-3(2));* 2010. (J). lib. bdg. 24.65 *(978-1-4296-5332-9(9))* Capstone.

—Snow Clothes. Gates, Margo. 2019. (Seasons All Around Me (Pull Ahead Readers — Fiction) Ser.). (ENG.). 16p. (J). (gr. -1-1). pap. 6.99 *(978-1-5415-7342-0(0),* 9781541573420, Lerner Pubns.) Lerner Publishing Group.

Hunt, Lou D. Gnubie to Eagle Scout: Adventures along the Eagle Scout Trail. Hunt, Kevin V. 2019. (ENG.). 218p. (J). pap. 16.95 *(978-1-7930-3462-5(1))* Independently Published.

Hunt, Matt. Her Royal Slyness. Hinuss, Roy L. 2018. 136p. (J). *(978-1-5490-5505-8(4))* ETT Imprint.

—How about a Night Out? Williams, Sam. 2019. (ENG.). 32p. (J). (gr. -1-1). 17.95 *(978-1-912757-14-5(1))* Boxer Bks., Ltd. GBR. Dist: Sterling Publishing Co., Inc.

—Lady Liberty's Holiday. Arena, Jen. 2016. 40p. (J). (gr. k-3). 17.99 *(978-0-553-52067-5(9),* Knopf Bks. for Young Readers) Random Hse. Children's Bks.

—Once upon a Prank. Hinuss, Roy L. 2018. 120p. (J). *(978-1-5490-5506-5(2))* ETT Imprint.

Hunt, Matt. The Pirates Are Coming! Condon, John. 2020. (ENG.). 32p. (J). (gr. -1-2). 16.99 ***(978-1-5362-1216-7(4),*** Nosy Crow) Candlewick Pr.

Hunt, Matt. Prince Not-So Charming: Happily Ever Laughter. Hinuss, Roy L. 2018. (Prince Not-So Charming Ser.: 4). (ENG.). 128p. (J). pap. 5.99 *(978-1-250-14244-3(X),* 900180223) Imprint IND. Dist: Macmillan.

—Prince Not-So Charming: Her Royal Slyness. Hinuss, Roy L. 2018. (Prince Not-So Charming Ser.: 2). (ENG.). 144p. (J). pap. 5.99 *(978-1-250-14240-5(7),* 900180219) Imprint IND. Dist: Macmillan.

—Prince Not-So Charming: Once upon a Prank. Hinuss, Roy L. 2018. (Prince Not-So Charming Ser.: 1). (ENG.). 144p. (J). pap. 6.99 *(978-1-250-14238-2(5),* 900180194) Imprint IND. Dist: Macmillan.

—Prince Not-So Charming: the Dork Knight. Hinuss, Roy L. 2018. (Prince Not-So Charming Ser.: 3). (ENG.). 128p. (J). pap. 5.99 *(978-1-250-14242-9(3),* 900180221) Imprint IND. Dist: Macmillan.

Hunt, Matt. Stephen Hawking. Sanchez Vegara, Maria Isabel. ed. 2019. (Little People, Big Dreams Ser.: Vol. 27). (ENG.). 32p. (J). (gr. -1-2). ***(978-1-78603-333-8(X))*** Frances Lincoln Childrens Bks.

Hunt, Matt. Walrus in the Bathtub. Underwood, Deborah. 2018. 40p. (J). (gr. -1-3). 17.99 *(978-0-8037-4101-0(4),* Dial Bks) Penguin Young Readers Group.

—Worm Weather. Taft, Jean. 2015. 32p. (J). (-k). bds. 4.99 *(978-0-448-48740-3(3),* Grosset & Dunlap) Penguin Young Readers Group.

—Would You Dare... ? A Lift-The-flap Adventure. Flyte, Min. 2017. (ENG.). 24p. (J). (gr. -1-2). 14.99 *(978-0-7636-9619-1(6),* Nosy Crow) Candlewick Pr.

Hunt, Meg. Bunk 9's Guide to Growing Up: Secrets, Tips, & Expert Advice on the Good, the Bad, & the Awkward. Nuchi, Adah. 2017. (ENG.). 192p. (J). (gr. 3-8). pap. 12.95 *(978-0-7611-9359-3(6),* 19359) Workman Publishing Co., Inc.

—Yoshi the Stonecutter. Heddle, Becca. 2014. (Traditional Tales Ser.). (ENG.). 24p. (J). (gr. 1-2). pap. 6.95 *(978-1-62521-610-6(6),* Capstone Classroom) Capstone.

Hunt, Miguel, photos by. Berlin. Garner, Simon. 2007. (Global Cities Ser.). 61p. (gr. 5-8). lib. bdg. 30.00 *(978-0-7910-8846-3(4),* Chelsea Hse.) Facts On File, Inc.

Hunt, Paul. Rodeo Rocky. Oldfield, Jenny. 2009. (J). Non-ISBN Publisher.

—Wild Horses. Oldfield, Jenny. 2009. (J). Non-ISBN Publisher.

Hunt, Robert. Julie Story Collection. Mcdonald, Megan. 2007. 472p. pap. 29.95 *(978-1-59369-450-0(4))* American Girl Publishing, Inc.

—Rebecca Story Collection. Greene, Jacqueline. Hirsch, Jennifer, ed. 2009. (ENG.). 456p. (YA). (gr. 3-18). 29.95 *(978-1-59369-626-9(4))* American Girl Publishing, Inc.

—Swiss Family Robinson. Wyss, Johann David. 2006. (Stepping Stone Book(TM) Ser.). 112p. (J). (gr. 1-4). per. 4.99 *(978-0-375-87525-0(5),* Random Hse. Bks. for Young Readers) Random Hse. Children's Bks.

—What Was America's Deadliest War? And Other Questions about the Civil War. Sandler, Martin W. 2014. (Good Question! Ser.). (ENG.). 32p. (J). pap. 6.95 *(978-1-4027-9046-1(5))* Sterling Publishing Co., Inc.

Hunt, Robert, jt. illus. see Elliott, Mark.

Hunt, Robert, jt. illus. see McAliley, Susan.

Hunt, Sally K., photos by. The Make a Face Exercise Book: E. B. Willis Children's Exercise Book. Willis, E. B. 2016. (ENG., (J). pap. 9.99 *(978-0-9976634-2-6(1))* Willis, E.B. Bks.

Hunt, Scott. Becoming Joe Dimaggio. Testa, Maria. 2005. (ENG.). 64p. (J). (gr. 5-9). reprint ed. pap. 6.99 *(978-0-7636-2444-6(6))* Candlewick Pr.

—Becoming Joe Dimaggio. Testa, Maria. 2006. 51p. (gr. 5-9). 17.00 *(978-0-7569-6576-1(4))* Perfection Learning Corp.

Hunt, Suzanne. Dragon Kingdom & the Wishing Stone. Eirich, Stacie. 2019. (Dream Chronicles Ser.: Vol. 3). (ENG.). 292p. (J). pap. 10.99 *(978-1-7312-3923-5(8))* Independently Published.

Hunter, Anne. The Nest That Wren Built. Sonenshine, Randi. 2020. 32p. (J). (gr. -1-3). 16.99 *(978-1-5362-0153-6(7))* Candlewick Pr.
—Who Would Like a Christmas Tree? A Tree for Each Season, 1 vol. Obed, Ellen. 2019. (ENG.). 32p. (J). pap. 12.95 *(978-1-944762-83-4(3),* c1f190c4-8508-47e0-abee-d153ea09009d) Islandport Pr., Inc.
Hunter, Carl & Heney, Clare. The Unforgotten Coat. Hunter, Carl & Heney, Clare, photos by. Boyce, Frank Cottrell. 2011. (ENG.). 112p. (J). (gr. 3-7). 16.99 *(978-0-7636-5729-1(8))* Candlewick Pr.
Hunter, Charlene. See You in Heaven. Stripling, Joe. Carroll, Joan, ed. Date not set. (Sunday School Two Thousand Ser.). 38p. (J). pap. 12.95 *(978-1-881223-07-8(8))* Zulema Enterprises LLC.
Hunter, Erin E. A Day in the Deep, 1 vol. Kurtz, Kevin. 2013. (Day in the Habitat Ser.). (ENG.). 32p. (J). (gr. 1-4). 17.95 *(978-1-60718-617-5(9))*; pap. 9.95 *(978-1-60718-629-8(2))* Arbordale Publishing.
—A Day on the Mountain, 1 vol. Kurtz, Kevin. 2010. (Day in the Habitat Ser.). (ENG.). 32p. (J). (gr. -1-4). 16.95 *(978-1-60718-073-9(1))* Arbordale Publishing.
—Un Día en la Profundidad, 1 vol. Kurtz, Kevin. 2013. (SPA.). 32p. (J). (gr. 1-4). 17.95 *(978-1-60718-715-8(9))* Arbordale Publishing.
—The Great Divide, 1 vol. Slade, Suzanne. 2012. (Basic Math Operations Ser.). (ENG.). 32p. (J). (gr. -1-4). 17.95 *(978-1-60718-521-5(0))*; pap. 9.95 *(978-1-60718-530-7(X))* Arbordale Publishing.
—Multiply on the Fly, 1 vol. Slade, Suzanne. 2011. (ENG.). 32p. (J). (gr. -1-4). 16.95 *(978-1-60718-128-6(2))*; pap. 8.95 *(978-1-60718-138-5(X),* 9781607181385) Arbordale Publishing.
Hunter, Gerald. Miss B's First Cookbook: Twenty Family-Sized Recipes for for the Youngest Cook. Hoffmann, Peggy. 2011. 48p. pap. 35.95 *(978-1-258-08433-2(3))* Literary Licensing, LLC.
Hunter, Helen D. Crabby Crab. Howard, Ruth I. 2004. (ENG.). 24p. (YA). pap. 9.00 *(978-1-4120-1432-8(8))* Trafford Publishing.
Hunter, Linzie. Astrid Lindgren. Sanchez Vegara, Maria Isabel. 2020. (Little People, Big Dreams Ser.: Vol. 35). (ENG.). 32p. (J). (gr. -1-2). ***(978-0-7112-5217-2(3))*** Frances Lincoln Childrens Bks.
Hunter, Linzie. If You Had a Jetpack. Detlefsen, Lisl H. 2018. 40p. (J). (gr. -1-3). 17.99 *(978-0-399-55329-5(0),* Knopf Bks. for Young Readers) Random Hse. Children's Bks.
Hunter, Llyn. A Little Book of Magical Beings. Hunter, Llyn. 2008. 32p. (J). 7.95 *(978-0-9776419-1-8(0))* Bobcat Publishing.
—A Little Book of Monsters. Hunter, Llyn. 2007. 32p. (J). 7.95 *(978-0-9776419-0-1(2),* 0-9776419-0-2) Bobcat Publishing.
Hunter, Rob. Sounds of Nature: World of Oceans: Press Each Note to Hear Animal Sounds. Grace, Claire. ed. 2019. (Sounds of Nature Ser.). (ENG.). 24p. (J). (gr. k-2). 22.99 *(978-1-78603-793-0(9),* Wide Eyed Editions) Quarto Publishing Group UK GBR. Dist: Hachette Bk. Group.
Hunter, Robbie Chase. The Adventures of Pillow Head: The Fallen Star. Ruzycki, Dan Dan. 2012. 26p. (J). 13.95 *(978-0-9834315-5-8(8))* Dan Dan Fantasy.
Hunter, Robert Frank. Sounds of Nature: World of Forests: Press Each Note to Hear Animal Sounds. 2019. (Sounds of Nature Ser.). (ENG.). 24p. (J). (gr. k-2). 22.99 *(978-1-78603-327-7(5),* Wide Eyed Editions) Quarto Publishing Group UK GBR. Dist: Hachette Bk. Group.
Hunting, Erin. Catkwondo. Detlefsen, Lisl H. 2020. (ENG.). 32p. (J). (gr. k-2). 17.99 ***(978-1-68446-100-4(6),*** 141335, Capstone Editions) Capstone.
Hunting, Erin. The Tooth Fairy vs. Santa. Deenihan, Jamie L. B. 2019. 32p. (J). (gr. -1-2). 12.99 *(978-1-5247-9080-6(X),* Penguin Workshop) Penguin Young Readers Group.
—The Tooth Fairy vs. the Easter Bunny. Deenihan, Jamie L. B. 2020. 32p. (J). (gr. -1-2). 12.99 *(978-0-593-09405-1(0),* Penguin Workshop) Penguin Young Readers Group.
Huntington, Amy. Adding with Sebastian Pig & Friends at the Circus. Anderson, Jill. 2009. (Math Fun with Sebastian Pig & Friends! Ser.). 32p. (gr. k-2). lib. bdg. 24.94 *(978-0-7660-3360-3(0))* Enslow Publishing, LLC.
—Finding Shapes with Sebastian Pig & Friends at the Museum. Anderson, Jill. 2009. (Math Fun with Sebastian Pig & Friends! Ser.). 32p. (gr. k-2). lib. bdg. 24.94 *(978-0-7660-3363-4(5))* Enslow Publishing, LLC.
—Fresh-Picked Poetry: A Day at the Farmers' Market. Schaub, Michelle. 32p. (J). (gr. -1-3). 2020. pap. 7.99 *(978-1-62354-170-5(0))*; 2017. lib. bdg. 16.99 *(978-1-58089-547-7(6))* Charlesbridge Publishing, Inc.
—Grandma Drove the Garbage Truck. Clark, Katie. 2006. (ENG.). 32p. (J). (gr. -1-17). 15.95 *(978-0-89272-698-1(9))* Down East Bks.
—Grandma Drove the Lobsterboat, 1 vol. Clark, Katie. 2012. (ENG.). 32p. (J). (gr. -1-1). 16.95 *(978-1-60893-004-3(1))* Down East Bks.
—Matthew & Tall Rabbit Go Camping. Meyer, Susan. ed. 2008. (ENG.). 32p. (J). (gr. -1-3). 15.95 *(978-0-89272-769-8(1))* Down East Bks.
—Measuring with Sebastian Pig & Friends on a Road Trip. Anderson, Jill. 2009. (Math Fun with Sebastian Pig & Friends! Ser.). 32p. (gr. k-2). lib. bdg. 24.94 *(978-0-7660-3362-7(7))* Enslow Publishing, LLC.
—Money Math with Sebastian Pig & Friends at the Farmer's Market. Anderson, Jill. 2009. (Math Fun with Sebastian Pig & Friends! Ser.). 32p. (gr. k-2). lib. bdg. 24.94 *(978-0-7660-3364-1(3))* Enslow Publishing, LLC.
—Penelope & Pip Build a Prose Poem. Heiden, Pete. 2011. (Poetry Builders Ser.). 32p. (J). (gr. 2-4). lib. bdg. 25.27 *(978-1-59953-438-1(X))* Norwood Hse. Pr.
—Seagull Sam. Clark, Katherine. ed. 2007. (ENG.). 32p. (J). (gr. -1-3). 15.95 *(978-0-89272-715-5(2))* Down East Bks.
—Subtracting with Sebastian Pig & Friends on a Camping Trip. Anderson, Jill. 2009. (Math Fun with Sebastian Pig & Friends! Ser.). 32p. (gr. k-2). lib. bdg. 24.94 *(978-0-7660-3361-0(9))* Enslow Publishing, LLC.
Huntley, Doris. I'm Da Muva, Said Miss Bossy. Dowell, Vivian "Vee". 2008. 32p. pap. 24.95 *(978-1-60610-045-5(9))* America Star Bks.
Hupf, Zetta. Detective Buddy & the Case of the Missing Football, 1 vol. Hupf, Zetta. Hupf, Mitchellx. 2009. 23p. pap. 19.95 *(978-1-61582-312-3(3))* PublishAmerica, Inc.
—Henry Goes to the Park, 1 vol. Hupf, Zetta. Hupf, Mitchell. 2009. 33p. pap. 24.95 *(978-1-61546-279-7(1))* America Star Bks.
Huras, Lynne. Ned: The Story of Bear Six Nine Three, 1 vol. Pavelka, Joe. 2007. (ENG.). 32p. (J). (gr. -1-1). *(978-1-894765-95-4(8))* RMB Rocky Mountain Bks.
Hurd, Angie. You Can Be Anything, Major. Harris, Chris B. 2020. (ENG.). 24p. (J). pap. 10.86 ***(978-1-0983-2413-1(7))*** BookBaby.
Hurd, Clement. A Baby's Gift: Goodnight Moon & the Runaway Bunny, 2 vols. Brown, Margaret Wise. 2014. (ENG.). 70p. (J). (gr. -1 — 1). pap. 15.99 *(978-0-694-01638-9(1),* HarperFestival) HarperCollins Pubs.
—Buenas Noches, Luna: Goodnight Moon (Spanish Edition), 1 vol. Brown, Margaret Wise. 2006.Tr. of Goodnight Moon. (SPA.). 32p. (J). (gr. -1-3). 17.99 *(978-0-06-026214-3(1),* HC0528); pap. 8.99 *(978-0-06-443416-4(8),* HC0527) HarperCollins Pubs. Ltd. GBR. (HarperCollins). Dist: HarperCollins Pubs.
—El Conejito Andarín: The Runaway Bunny (Spanish Edition), 1 vol. Brown, Margaret Wise. 2006. (SPA.). 48p. (J). (gr. -1-3). pap. 7.99 *(978-0-06-077694-7(3),* HarperCollins Español) HarperCollins Christian Publishing.
Hurd, Clement. From the World of Goodnight Moon: 100 First Words. Brown, Margaret Wise. 2020. 16p. (J). (gr. -1 — 1). bds. 12.99 ***(978-0-06-299367-0(4),*** HarperCollins) HarperCollins Pubs. Ltd. GBR. Dist: HarperCollins Pubs.
Hurd, Clement. Goodnight Moon. Brown, Margaret Wise. 2005. (ENG.). 32p. (J). (gr. -1-3). lib. bdg. 18.89 *(978-0-06-077586-5(6))* HarperCollins Pubs.
—Goodnight Moon. Brown, Margaret Wise. 60th anniv. ed. 2007. (ENG.). 32p. (J). (gr. -1-3). 18.99 *(978-0-06-077585-8(8))*; pap. 8.99 *(978-0-06-443017-3(0))* HarperCollins Pubs. Ltd. GBR. (HarperCollins). Dist: HarperCollins Pubs.
—Goodnight Moon. Brown, Margaret Wise. (J). pap. 32.75 incl. audio. (gr. -1-3). 24.95 incl. audio Weston Woods Studios, Inc.
—Goodnight Moon 123: A Counting Book. Brown, Margaret Wise. 2007. (J). (ENG.). 32p. (gr. -1-k). 16.99 *(978-0-06-112593-5(8))*; 32p. (gr. -1-k). lib. bdg. 17.89 *(978-0-06-112594-2(6))*; *(978-1-4287-4853-8(9))* HarperCollins Pubs.
—Goodnight Moon 123 Board Book: A Counting Book. Brown, Margaret Wise. 2008. (ENG.). 30p. (J). (gr. -1-k). bds. 8.99 *(978-0-06-112597-3(0),* HarperFestival) HarperCollins Pubs.
—Goodnight Moon 123 Lap Edition. Brown, Margaret Wise. 2008. (ENG.). 30p. (J). (gr. -1 — 1). bds. 12.99 *(978-0-06-166755-8(2),* HarperFestival) HarperCollins Pubs.
—Goodnight Moon 123 Padded Board Book: A Counting Book. Brown, Margaret Wise. 2013. (ENG.). 30p. (J). (gr. -1-k). bds. 9.99 *(978-0-06-224405-5(1),* HarperFestival) HarperCollins Pubs.
—Goodnight Moon 123/Buenas Noches, Luna 123: A Counting Book/un Libro para Contar. Brown, Margaret Wise. 2007. (ENG & SPA.). 32p. (J). (gr. -1-k). 16.99 *(978-0-06-117325-7(8),* Rayo) HarperCollins Pubs.
—Goodnight Moon 123/Buenas Noches, Luna 123: Bilingual Spanish-English Children's Book. Brown, Margaret Wise. 2020. (ENG.). 32p. (J). (gr. -1 — 1). 17.99 *(978-0-06-297123-4(9))* HarperCollins Pubs.
—Goodnight Moon 123/Buenas Noches, Luna 123 Board Book: Bilingual Spanish-English Children's Book. Brown, Margaret Wise. 2020. (ENG.). 30p. (J). (gr. -1 — 1). bds. 8.99 *(978-0-06-297124-1(7),* HarperFestival) HarperCollins Pubs.
—Goodnight Moon ABC: An Alphabet Book. Brown, Margaret Wise. 2010. (ENG.). 32p. (J). (gr. -1-k). 16.99 *(978-0-06-189484-8(2))* HarperCollins Pubs.
—Goodnight Moon ABC Board Book: An Alphabet Book. Brown, Margaret Wise. 2010. (ENG.). 30p. (J). (gr. -1-k). bds. 8.99 *(978-0-06-189490-9(7),* HarperFestival) HarperCollins Pubs.
—Goodnight Moon ABC Padded Board Book: An Alphabet Book. Brown, Margaret Wise. 2013. (ENG.). 30p. (J). (gr. -1-k). bds. 9.99 *(978-0-06-224404-8(3),* HarperFestival) HarperCollins Pubs.
—Goodnight Moon Big Book. Brown, Margaret Wise. 2007. (ENG.). 32p. (J). (gr. -1-3). pap. 24.99 *(978-0-06-111977-4(6),* HarperCollins) HarperCollins Pubs. Ltd. GBR. Dist: HarperCollins Pubs.
—Goodnight Moon Board Book. Brown, Margaret Wise. 60th anniv. ed. 2007. (ENG.). 34p. (J). (gr. -1 — 1). bds. 8.99 *(978-0-694-00361-7(1),* HarperFestival) HarperCollins Pubs.
—Goodnight Moon Board Book & Bunny. Brown, Margaret Wise. 2005. (ENG.). 34p. (J). (gr. -1 — 1). bds. 16.99 *(978-0-06-076027-4(3),* HarperFestival) HarperCollins Pubs.
—Goodnight Moon Classic Library: Contains Goodnight Moon, the Runaway Bunny, & My World. Brown, Margaret Wise. 2011. (ENG.). 32p. (J). (gr. -1-1). 17.99 *(978-0-06-199823-2(0))* HarperCollins Pubs.
—Goodnight Moon Cloth Book. Brown, Margaret Wise. 2012. (ENG.). 8p. (J). (gr. -1 — 1). pap. 14.99 *(978-0-06-076224-7(1),* HarperFestival) HarperCollins Pubs.
—Goodnight Moon Cloth Book Box. Brown, Margaret Wise. 2012. (ENG.). 8p. (J). (gr. -1 — 1). pap. 14.99 *(978-0-06-223589-3(3),* HarperFestival) HarperCollins Pubs.
—Goodnight Moon Padded Board Book. Brown, Margaret Wise. 2017. (ENG.). 34p. (J). (gr. -1 — 1). bds. 10.99 *(978-0-06-257309-4(8),* HarperFestival) HarperCollins Pubs.
—Goodnight Moon/Buenas Noches, Luna: Bilingual Spanish-English Children's Book. Brown, Margaret Wise. 2014. (ENG.). 34p. (J). (gr. -1-3). bds. 8.99 *(978-0-06-236791-4(9),* HarperFestival) HarperCollins Pubs.
—My World: A Companion to Goodnight Moon. Brown, Margaret Wise. 2004. (ENG.). 32p. (J). (gr. -1 — 1). pap. 7.99 *(978-0-694-01660-0(8))* HarperCollins Pubs.
—My World Board Book: A Companion to Goodnight Moon. Brown, Margaret Wise. 2003. (ENG.). 36p. (J). (gr. -1 — 1). bds. 9.99 *(978-0-694-00862-9(1),* HarperFestival) HarperCollins Pubs.
—Over the Moon: a Collection of First Books: Goodnight Moon, the Runaway Bunny, & My World. Brown, Margaret Wise. 2006. (ENG.). 108p. (J). (gr. -1-1). 19.99 *(978-0-06-076162-2(8))* HarperCollins Pubs.
—The Runaway Bunny. Brown, Margaret Wise. 2005. (ENG.). 48p. (J). (gr. -1 — 1). lib. bdg. 18.89 *(978-0-06-077583-4(1))* HarperCollins Pubs.
—The Runaway Bunny. Brown, Margaret Wise. 2017. (ENG.). 48p. (J). (gr. -1-3). 17.99 *(978-0-06-077582-7(3))*; pap. 8.99 *(978-0-06-443018-0(9))* HarperCollins Pubs. Ltd. GBR. (HarperCollins). Dist: HarperCollins Pubs.
—The Runaway Bunny: a 75th Anniversary Retrospective. Brown, Margaret Wise & Marcus, Leonard S. 2017. (ENG.). 64p. (J). (gr. -1-3). 19.99 *(978-0-06-248994-4(1))* HarperCollins Pubs.
—The Runaway Bunny Board Book. Brown, Margaret Wise. 2017. (ENG.). 34p. (J). (gr. -1 — 1). bds. 8.99 *(978-0-06-107429-5(2),* HarperFestival) HarperCollins Pubs.
—The Runaway Bunny Lap Edition. Brown, Margaret Wise. 2017. (ENG.). 36p. (J). (gr. -1 — 1). bds. 12.99 *(978-0-694-01671-6(3),* HarperFestival) HarperCollins Pubs.
—The Runaway Bunny Padded Board Book. Brown, Margaret Wise. 2017. (ENG.). 36p. (J). (gr. -1 — 1). bds. 9.99 *(978-0-06-245959-6(7),* HarperFestival) HarperCollins Pubs.
Hurd, Clement & Long, Loren. Buen día, Buenas Noches, 1 vol. Brown, Margaret Wise. 2017. (SPA.). 40p. (J). (gr. -1-3). 17.99 *(978-1-4185-9890-7(9),* HarperCollins Español) HarperCollins Christian Publishing.
Hurd, Thacher. Art Dog. Hurd, Thacher. 2004. (ENG.). 32p. (J). (gr. -1-3). 18.99 *(978-0-06-024424-8(0),* HarperCollins) HarperCollins Pubs. Ltd. GBR. Dist: HarperCollins Pubs.
—Bad Frogs. Hurd, Thacher. 2009. (ENG.). 40p. (J). (gr. -1-2). 15.99 *(978-0-7636-3253-3(8))* Candlewick Pr.
—Mama Don't Allow 25th Anniversary Edition. Hurd, Thacher. 25th anniv. ed. 2008. (Trophy Picture Bks.). (ENG.). 40p. (J). (gr. -1-3). pap. 7.99 *(978-0-06-443078-4(2),* HarperCollins) HarperCollins Pubs. Ltd. GBR. Dist: HarperCollins Pubs.
—Mystery on the Docks 25th Anniversary Edition. Hurd, Thacher. 25th anniv. ed. 2008. (Trophy Picture Bks.). (ENG.). 32p. (J). (gr. -1-3). pap. 8.99 *(978-0-06-443058-6(8),* HarperCollins) HarperCollins Pubs. Ltd. GBR. Dist: HarperCollins Pubs.
—The Pea Patch Jig. Hurd, Thacher. rev. ed. 2015. (ENG.). 40p. (J). (gr. k-3). 16.95 *(978-1-939547-21-7(0))* Creston Bks.
Hurley, Anna. A Little Zodiac Book: Baby Aquarius. Harper, Daria. 2020. (ENG.). 12p. (J). (gr. -1 — 1). bds. 7.99 ***(978-1-7972-0237-2(5))*** Chronicle Bks. LLC.
—A Little Zodiac Book: Baby Aries. Harper, Daria. 2020. (ENG.). 12p. (J). (gr. -1 — 1). bds. 7.99 ***(978-1-7972-0227-3(8))*** Chronicle Bks. LLC.
—A Little Zodiac Book: Baby Cancer. Harper, Daria. 2020. (ENG.). 12p. (J). (gr. -1 — 1). bds. 7.99 ***(978-1-7972-0230-3(8))*** Chronicle Bks. LLC.
—A Little Zodiac Book: Baby Capricorn. Harper, Daria. 2020. (ENG.). 12p. (J). (gr. -1 — 1). bds. 7.99 ***(978-1-7972-0236-5(7))*** Chronicle Bks. LLC.
—A Little Zodiac Book: Baby Gemini. Harper, Daria. 2020. (ENG.). 12p. (J). (gr. -1 — 1). bds. 7.99 ***(978-1-7972-0229-7(4))*** Chronicle Bks. LLC.
—A Little Zodiac Book: Baby Leo. Harper, Daria. 2020. (ENG.). 12p. (J). (gr. -1 — 1). bds. 7.99 ***(978-1-7972-0231-0(6))*** Chronicle Bks. LLC.
—A Little Zodiac Book: Baby Libra. Harper, Daria. 2020. (ENG.). 12p. (J). (gr. -1 — 1). bds. 7.99 ***(978-1-7972-0233-4(2))*** Chronicle Bks. LLC.
—A Little Zodiac Book: Baby Pisces. Harper, Daria. 2020. (ENG.). 12p. (J). (gr. -1 — 1). bds. 7.99 ***(978-1-7972-0238-9(3))*** Chronicle Bks. LLC.
—A Little Zodiac Book: Baby Sagittarius. Harper, Daria. 2020. (ENG.). 12p. (J). (gr. -1 — 1). bds. 7.99 ***(978-1-7972-0235-8(9))*** Chronicle Bks. LLC.
—A Little Zodiac Book: Baby Scorpio. Harper, Daria. 2020. (ENG.). 12p. (J). (gr. -1 — 1). bds. 7.99 ***(978-1-7972-0234-1(0))*** Chronicle Bks. LLC.
—A Little Zodiac Book: Baby Taurus. Harper, Daria. 2020. (ENG.). 12p. (J). (gr. -1 — 1). bds. 7.99 ***(978-1-7972-0228-0(6))*** Chronicle Bks. LLC.
—Little Zodiac Book: Baby Virgo. Harper, Daria. 2020. (ENG.). 12p. (J). (gr. -1 — 1). bds. 7.99 ***(978-1-7972-0232-7(4))*** Chronicle Bks. LLC.
Hurley, Jorey. Beehive. Hurley, Jorey. 2020. (ENG.). 40p. (J). (gr. -1-2). 17.99 *(978-1-4814-7003-2(5),* Simon & Schuster Bks. For Young Readers) Simon & Schuster Bks. For Young Readers.
—Every Color Soup. Hurley, Jorey. 2018. (ENG.). 40p. (J). (gr. -1-2). 17.99 *(978-1-4814-6999-9(1),* Simon & Schuster/Paula Wiseman Bks.) Simon & Schuster/Paula Wiseman Bks.
—Fetch. Hurley, Jorey. 2015. (ENG.). 40p. (J). (gr. -1-2). 17.99 *(978-1-4424-8969-1(3),* Simon & Schuster Bks. For Young Readers) Simon & Schuster Bks. For Young Readers.
—Hop. Hurley, Jorey. 2019. (Classic Board Bks.). (ENG.). 34p. (J). (gr. -1 — 1). bds. 7.99 *(978-1-5344-2988-8(3),* Little Simon) Little Simon.
—Hop. Hurley, Jorey. 2016. (ENG.). 40p. (J). (gr. -1-2). 17.99 *(978-1-4814-3272-6(9),* Simon & Schuster/Paula Wiseman Bks.) Simon & Schuster/Paula Wiseman Bks.
—Nest. Hurley, Jorey. 2015. (Classic Board Bks.). (ENG.). 34p. (J). (gr. -1 — 1). bds. 8.99 *(978-1-4814-5210-6(X),* Little Simon) Little Simon.
—Nest. Hurley, Jorey. 2014. (ENG.). 40p. (J). (gr. -1-2). 17.99 *(978-1-4424-8971-4(5),* Simon & Schuster/Paula Wiseman Bks.) Simon & Schuster/Paula Wiseman Bks.
—Ribbit. Hurley, Jorey. 2017. (ENG.). 40p. (J). (gr. -1-3). 17.99 *(978-1-4814-3274-0(5),* Simon & Schuster/Paula Wiseman Bks.) Simon & Schuster/Paula Wiseman Bks.
—Skyscraper. Hurley, Jorey. 2019. (ENG.). 40p. (J). (gr. -1-2). 17.99 *(978-1-4814-7001-8(9),* Simon & Schuster/Paula Wiseman Bks.) Simon & Schuster/Paula Wiseman Bks.
Hurry, Helen. Peepo! Boo! Who Are You? 2014. (ENG.). 12p. (J). 17.00 *(978-0-85707-679-3(5),* Simon & Schuster Children's) Simon & Schuster, Ltd. GBR. Dist: Simon & Schuster, Inc.
Hurst, Debbie. About Gossip: What Would Jesus Do, 1 vol. Gould, M. & Gould, R. 2009. 28p. pap. 24.95 *(978-1-60749-680-9(1))* America Star Bks.
—The Bleeks: The Bleek Family's First Christmas, 1 vol. Gould, M&R. 2010. 30p. pap. 24.95 *(978-1-4489-2770-8(6))* PublishAmerica, Inc.
Hurst, Elise. Girl on Wire. Estela, Lucy. 2018. 32p. (J). (gr. 1). 23.99 ***(978-0-14-378716-7(0),*** Viking Adult) Penguin Publishing Group.
Hurst, Elise. The Twin Competition. Trussell-Cullen, Alan. 2009. (Rigby PM Stars Bridge Bks.). (ENG.). 16p. (gr. 2-3). pap. 8.25 *(978-1-4190-5510-2(0))* Rigby Education.
Hurst, Margaret. The First Days of the Dinosaurs: Text Edition. Gabriele, Joseph. 32p. (Orig.). (J). (gr. 1-3). pap. 1.95 *(978-0-911211-55-9(1))* Penny Lane Pubns., Inc.
Hurst, Oliver. Finn at Clee Point. Knight, Richard et al. 2012. 128p. (J). pap. 12.99 *(978-1-84686-401-8(1))* Barefoot Bks., Inc.
Hurt, William, jt. illus. see Johnson, David.
Hurtado, Maria. Hey, I'm a Story! Leask, Amy. 2018. (ENG.). 42p. (J). pap. *(978-1-927425-21-3(2))* Enable Training and Consulting Inc.
Hurtado, Vanessa. Sophie's Pony Tales. Van Oort, Glenn. 2019. (ENG.). 52p. (J). (gr. k-5). pap. 14.99 ***(978-0-578-59850-5(7))*** Glenn N. Van Oort.
Husar, Lisa & Husar, Mike, photos by. Bobcat Babies. 2013. 26p. (J). 8.95 *(978-1-56037-133-5(1))* Farcountry Pr.
—Busy Bear Cubs. Schindel, John. 2009. (Busy Book Ser.). 20p. (J). (gr. k — 1). bds. 6.99 *(978-1-58246-302-5(6),* Tricycle Pr.) Random Hse. Children's Bks.
—Busy Pandas. Schindel, John. 2008. (Busy Book Ser.). 20p. (J). (gr. k — 1). bds. 6.99 *(978-1-58246-259-2(3),* Knopf Bks. for Young Readers) Random Hse. Children's Bks.
Husar, Mike, jt. photos by see Husar, Lisa.
Husband, Amy. Emergency Vehicles Sticker Book. Channing, Margot. ed. 2018. (Scribblers Fun Activity Ser.). 32p. (J). (gr. k-2). pap. 5.95 *(978-1-912537-18-1(4),* Scribblers) Book Hse. GBR. Dist: Sterling Publishing Co., Inc.
—Hanukkah Delight! Newman, Lesléa & Newman, Lesléa. ed. 2016. (ENG.). 12p. (J). (gr. -1 — 1). E-Book 23.99 *(978-1-5124-0937-6(5),* Kar-Ben Publishing) Lerner Publishing Group.
—L Is for Love (and Lion!) Rathjen, Melinda Lee. 2019. 20p. (J). (gr. -1 — 1). bds. 7.99 *(978-1-5460-1432-4(2),* Worthy Kids/Ideals) Worthy Publishing.
Husband, Amy. S Is for Sharing (and Shark!) Chidlow-Irvin, Georgina & Rathjen, Melinda Lee. 2020. (ENG.). 20p. (J). (gr. -1 — 1). 7.99 ***(978-1-5460-3376-9(9),*** Worthy Kids/Ideals) Worthy Publishing.
—The Story of Inventions. Barr, Catherine. ed. 2020. (Story Of... Ser.). (ENG.). 40p. (J). (gr. k-3). 19.99 ***(978-0-7112-4536-5(3),*** 326185, Frances Lincoln Children's Bks.) Quarto Publishing Group UK GBR. Dist: Hachette UK Distribution.
Husband, Amy. The Story of Life: A First Book about Evolution. Barr, Catherine & Williams, Steve. 2015. (Story Of... Ser.). (ENG.). 40p. (J). (gr. k-3). 19.99 *(978-1-84780-485-3(3),* 314915, Frances Lincoln Children's Bks.) Quarto Publishing Group UK GBR. Dist: Hachette UK Distribution.
Husband, Amy. The Story of People: A First Book about Humankind. Barr, Catherine & Williams, Steve. 2019. (Story Of... Ser.). (ENG.). 40p. (J). (gr. 1-4). 18.99 ***(978-0-7112-4172-5(4),*** Frances Lincoln Children's Bks.) Quarto Publishing Group UK GBR. Dist: Hachette Bk. Group.
Husband, Amy. The Story of Space: A First Book about Our Universe. Barr, Catherine & Williams, Steve. 2017. (ENG.). 40p. (J). (gr. k-3). 18.99 *(978-1-78603-003-0(9),* Frances Lincoln Children's Bks.) Quarto Publishing Group UK GBR. Dist: Hachette Bk. Group.
—T Is for Thanks (and Turkey!) Rathjen, Melinda Lee. 2019. 20p. (J). (gr. -1 — 1). bds. 7.99 *(978-1-5460-1457-7(8),* Worthy Kids/Ideals) Worthy Publishing.
Husband, Ron. Steamboat School. Hopkinson, Deborah. 2016. 40p. (J). (gr. -1-k). 17.99 *(978-1-4231-2196-1(1))* Disney Pr.
Husberg, Rob. Better Than a Lemonade Stand! Small Business Ideas for Kids. Bernstein, Daryl. 2012. (ENG.). 224p. (J). (gr. 4-9). pap. 13.99 *(978-1-58270-330-5(2))* Aladdin/Beyond Words.
Huseman, Ryan. Peter's Purpose. Oramas, Jennifer. 2012. 34p. 24.95 *(978-1-4626-6585-3(3))* America Star Bks.
Huskins, Suzanne Hallier. No Matter What! 2004. (J). *(978-1-887905-93-0(6))* Parkway Pubs., Inc.
—Sunbeam. Wyont, Wanda. 2006. 32p. (J). 12.50 *(978-1-933251-07-3(7))* Parkway Pubs., Inc.
Huskmitnavn. The Family Fun Coloring Book. 2018. (ENG.). 64p. pap. 14.95 *(978-1-58423-674-0(4),* cd8e9611-5eda-45ef-97e3-47fff20a34e8, Gingko Pr.) Gingko Pr., Inc.
HuskMitNavn. The Wrong Book. 2018. (ENG.). 14p. (J). bds. 12.95 *(978-1-58423-673-3(6),* 2a00f5cc-f841-4c71-bc2d-b1df524a6413, Gingko Pr.) Gingko Pr., Inc.

H

Huss, Sally. Lara Takes Charge: For Kids with Diabetes, Their Friends, & Siblings, 2 bks, Book 1. Lang, Rocky. 2nd ed. 2012. 28p. (J). 12.95 *(978-1-934980-05-7(6))* Cable Publishing.

Hussain, Nelupa, jt. illus. see Fearn, Katrina.

Hussain, Raazia. Let's Learn about Jealousy. 2017. (ENG.). (J). pap. 8.25 *(978-1-366-15599-3(8))* Blurb, Inc.

Hussain, Zara. Cones & Electricity. Madeley, Chris. 2016. (Cones Ser.: Vol. 4). (ENG.). (J). pap. *(978-1-910406-54-0(6))* Fisher King Publishing.

—Nose Nibbling Monster. Skivington, Peter. 2016. (ENG.). (J). pap. *(978-1-910406-24-3(4))* Fisher King Publishing.

Hussey, Lorna. The Little Christmas Tree, 1 vol. Skevington, Andrea. 2015. 32p. (J). (gr. -1-k). 16.99 *(978-0-7459-6579-6(2))* Lion Hudson PLC GBR. Dist: Kregel Pubns.

—Little Christmas Tree. Skevington, Andrea. ed. 2015. (ENG.). 32p. (J). pap. 8.99 *(978-0-7459-6550-5(4))* Lion Hudson PLC GBR. Dist: Independent Pubs. Group.

—The Nonsense Verse of Lewis Caroll. Carroll, Lewis. 2004. 32p. (J). (gr. 4). pap. 12.99 *(978-0-7475-5019-8(0))* Bloomsbury Publishing Plc GBR. Dist: Independent Pubs. Group.

—Owls: Internet-Referenced. Courtauld, Sarah. 2009. (First Reading Level 3 Ser.). 48p. (J). (gr. 2). 6.99 *(978-0-7945-2502-6(4),* Usborne) EDC Publishing.

—Pigloo. Pace, Anne Marie. 2016. (ENG.). 32p. (J). 16.99 *(978-1-62779-202-8(3),* 900140747, Holt, Henry & Co. Bks. For Young Readers) Holt, Henry & Co.

—The Star in the Christmas Play, Vol. Marie, Lynne. 2018. (ENG.). 32p. (J). 16.99 *(978-1-5064-3813-9(X),* Beaming Books) Augsburg Fortress, Pubs.

Hustace, Billy, photos by. My Pet Dog. Berman, Ruth. 2005. (All about Pets Ser.). 64p. (gr. 2-6). lib. bdg. 22.60 *(978-0-8225-2259-1(4))* Lerner Publishing Group.

Hustache, Timothy. My Dad Is a Builder Pink B Band. Rickards, Lynne. 2016. (Cambridge Reading Adventures Ser.). (ENG.). 16p. pap. 7.37 *(978-1-107-54973-9(6))* Cambridge Univ. Pr.

Husted, Marty. We Share One World. Hoffelt, Jane. 2004. 32p. (J). per. 15.95 *(978-0-9701907-8-9(6))* Illumination Arts Publishing Co., Inc.

Hustins, Shelley. No Room: A Read-Aloud Story of Christmas. Riddle, Peter H. 2009. 40p. (J). pap. *(978-1-926585-43-7(7),* CCB Publishing) CCB Publishing.

Huston, Anne. Lemkus & Ledo. Huston, Baxter. 2018. (ENG.). 26p. (J). pap. 5.58 *(978-1-7291-8906-1(7))* Independently Published.

Huston, Kyle, jt. illus. see Leon, Loni.

Huszar, Susan. My Pet. Bailey, Debbie. 3rd ed. 2003. (Talk-About-Bks.: 18). (ENG.). 16p. (J). (gr. -1 — 1). bds. 6.95 *(978-1-55037-816-0(3),* 9781550378160) Annick Pr., Ltd. CAN. Dist: Publishers Group West (PGW).

Huszar, Susan, photos by. Mi Animalito. Bailey, Debbie. 2003. (Hablemos Ser.).Tr. of My Pet. (SPA., 16p. (J). (gr. -1 — 1). bds. 5.95 *(978-1-55037-826-9(0),* 9781550378269) Annick Pr., Ltd. CAN. Dist: Publishers Group West (PGW).

—Mis Amigos. Bailey, Debbie. 2003. (Hablemos Ser.).Tr. of My Friends. (SPA., 16p. (J). (gr. -1 — 1). bds. 5.95 *(978-1-55037-827-6(9),* 9781550378276) Annick Pr., Ltd. CAN. Dist: Publishers Group West (PGW).

—My Friends. Bailey, Debbie. 6th ed. 2003. (Talk-About-Bks.: 17). (ENG., 16p. (J). (gr. -1 — 1). bds. 6.95 *(978-1-55037-817-7(1),* 9781550378177) Annick Pr., Ltd. CAN. Dist: Publishers Group West (PGW).

—Talk-About Family Set. Bailey, Debbie. 2018. (Talk-About Bks.). (ENG., 16p. (J). 41.70 *(978-1-77321-121-3(8))* Annick Pr., Ltd. CAN. Dist: Publishers Group West (PGW).

Huszar, Tekla. Kitten & Boy. Gittle, Aviva. 2018. (ENG.). 44p. (J). pap. 12.99 *(978-1-7926-6653-7(5))* Independently Published.

Hutch Matthews, Kristina. The Cat Flap: A Tale of Harmony & Balance. Hutch Matthews, Kristina. 2014. 44p. (J). 18.95 *(978-0-9914513-1-9(7))* BrightShadow Publishing.

Hutchcraft, Steve, photos by. B Is for Bufflehead: Flying Through the ABC's with Fun Feathered Friends. Hutchcraft, Steve. 2009. 80p. (J). (gr. -1-4). 19.95 *(978-0-9824925-0-5(2))* PhotoHutch.

Hutcheon, Nathan. The Long Ride Home. Lawrence, Susan. 2017. 139p. (J). *(978-1-62856-445-7(8))* BJU Pr.

Hutcherson, Darren. Papa Golley's Journey Home. Norton, George. Date not set. 14.95 *(978-1-889506-06-7(0))* Kendar Publishing, Inc.

—Ten Buttermilk Pancakes. Norton, George. Date not set. (J). 9.95 *(978-1-889506-10-4(9))* Kendar Publishing, Inc.

Hutcherson, Morgan. Herbs a to Z. The St. Louis Herb Society. Fathman, Liz, ed. 2018. (ENG.). 100p. (J). pap. 12.00 *(978-0-9884551-5-3(3))* Missouri Botanical Garden Pr.

Hutcheson, James. Here Come the Trolls! Butlin, Ron. 2015. 32p. (J). (gr. -1-2). pap. 10.99 *(978-1-78027-295-5(2),* 1780272952, Birlinn) Birlinn, Ltd. GBR. Dist: Casemate Pubs. & Bk. Distributors, LLC.

Hutchings, Ben. The Invisible War: A World War I Tale on Two Scales. Wild, Aisla et al. 2019. (ENG.). 80p. (YA). (gr. 8-12). 29.32 *(978-1-5415-4155-9(3),* Graphic Universe™) Lerner Publishing Group.

Hutchings, Tony. A Day on the Farm. 2016. (J). *(978-1-4351-6337-9(0))* Barnes & Noble, Inc.

—Okomi & the Tickling Game, Vol. 2. Dorman, Helen & Dorman, Clive. 2004. (Sharing Nature with Children Book Ser.: 2). 24p. (J). pap. 4.95 *(978-1-58469-046-7(1))* Dawn Pubns.

—Okomi Climbs a Tree, Vol. 4. Dorman, Helen & Dorman, Clive. 2004. (Sharing Nature with Children Book Ser.: 4). 24p. (J). pap. 4.95 *(978-1-58469-045-0(3))* Dawn Pubns.

—Okomi Enjoys His Outings, Vol. 5. Dorman, Clive & Dorman, Helen. 2004. (Okomi Stories Ser.). 24p. (J). pap. 4.95 *(978-1-58469-055-9(0))* Dawn Pubns.

—Okomi Goes Fishing, Vol. 7. Dorman, Clive & Dorman, Helen. 2004. (Okomi Stories Ser.). 24p. (J). pap. 4.95 *(978-1-58469-057-3(7))* Dawn Pubns.

—Okomi Plays in the Leaves, Vol. 3. Dorman, Helen & Dorman, Clive. 2004. (Sharing Nature with Children Book Ser.: 3). 24p. (J). pap. 4.95 *(978-1-58469-047-4(X))* Dawn Pubns.

—Okomi, the New Baby. Dorman, Helen & Dorman, Clive. 2004. (Sharing Nature with Children Book Ser.: 1). 24p. (J). pap. 4.95 *(978-1-58469-044-3(5))* Dawn Pubns.

—Okomi Wakes up Early, Vol. 6. Dorman, Clive & Dorman, Helen. 2004. (Sharing Nature with Children Book Ser.). 24p. (J). pap. 4.95 *(978-1-58469-056-6(9))* Dawn Pubns.

—Okomi Wanders Too Far, Vol. 8. Dorman, Clive & Dorman, Helen. 2004. (Sharing Nature with Children Book Ser.). 24p. (J). pap. 4.95 *(978-1-58469-058-0(5))* Dawn Pubns.

—A Week at the Seaside. 2014. (J). *(978-1-4351-5464-3(9))* Barnes & Noble, Inc.

Hutchins, Annie H. Barnyard Buddies II. Brown, Pamela. 2004. 90p. (J). pap. 16.00 *(978-1-928589-21-1(9))* Gival Pr., LLC.

Hutchins, Melanie. Look Twice. Garzon, M. 2019. (Blaze of Glory Ser.: Vol. 2). (ENG.). 306p. (YA). ***(978-1-988844-07-7(X))*** Petal Pr.

Hutchins, Pat. Good-Night, Owl! Hutchins, Pat. 2015. (Classic Board Bks.). (ENG.). 34p. (J). (gr. -1 — 1). bds. 7.99 *(978-1-4814-4424-8(7),* Little Simon) Little Simon.

Hutchinson, David. Macbeth, 1 vol. Dunn, Joeming. 2008. (Graphic Shakespeare Ser.). (ENG.). 48p. (J). (gr. 5-10). 31.35 *(978-1-60270-190-8(3),* 9142, Graphic Planet - Fiction) Magic Wagon.

Hutchinson, Joy. Gifts for a King. Aston, Al. 2005. 16p. pap. 2.00 *(978-1-84427-179-5(X))* Scripture Union GBR. Dist: Send The Light Distribution LLC.

—A Message for Mary. Aston, Al. 2005. 16p. 2.00 *(978-1-84427-176-4(5))* Scripture Union GBR. Dist: Send The Light Distribution LLC.

—The Shepherds' Surprise. Aston, Al. 2005. 16p. pap., pap. 2.00 *(978-1-84427-178-8(1))* Scripture Union GBR. Dist: Send The Light Distribution LLC.

Hutchinson, Michelle. Malcolm Dooswaddles Good Day. Ten Hagen, Evelyn. 2013. 82p. pap. 12.95 *(978-1-59930-415-1(5))* TAG Publishing, LLC.

Hutchinson, Tim. Alien Adventure: Peek Inside the Pop-Up Windows! Taylor, Dereen. 2015. (ENG.). 12p. 16.99 *(978-1-86147-487-2(3),* Armadillo) Anness Publishing GBR. Dist: National Bk. Network.

—A Cool Kid's Field Guide to Weather. Regan, Lisa. 2009. (Cool Kid's Field Guide Ser.). 26p. (J). (gr. 1-3). spiral bd. 6.99 *(978-0-8416-7147-8(8))* Hammond World Atlas Corp.

—The Dragon's Magic Wish. Taylor, Dereen. 2012. 12p. (J). (gr. 1-6). 16.99 *(978-1-84322-856-1(4))* Anness Publishing GBR. Dist: National Bk. Network.

—Find Out about China: Learn Chinese Words & Phrases & about Life in China. Qing, Zheng. 2006. (Find Out about Bks.). (ENG.). 64p. (J). (gr. 3-7). 14.99 *(978-0-7641-5952-7(6),* B.E.S. Publishing) Peterson's.

—How Animals Build, 1 vol. Lonely Planet Kids & Butterfield, Moira. 2017. (How Things Work Ser.). (ENG.). 24p. (J). (gr. 1-3). 18.99 *(978-1-78657-663-7(5),* 5633) Lonely Planet Global Ltd. IRL. Dist: Hachette Bk. Group.

—The Lost Treasure of the Jungle Temple: Peek Inside the 3D Windows! Taylor, Dereen. 2013. (ENG.). 12p. (J). (gr. 1-8). 16.99 *(978-1-84322-822-6(X),* Armadillo) Anness Publishing GBR. Dist: National Bk. Network.

—Paulo & the Football Thieves: Peek Inside the Pop-Up Windows! Taylor, Dereen. 2014. 12p. 16.99 *(978-1-86147-409-4(1),* Armadillo) Anness Publishing GBR. Dist: National Bk. Network.

—Robo-Pup to the Rescue! Taylor, Dereen. 2013. (ENG.). 12p. (J). (gr. 1-8). 16.99 *(978-1-84322-821-9(1),* Armadillo) Anness Publishing GBR. Dist: National Bk. Network.

—Stuff You Need to Know about the Human Body. Farndon, John. 2017. (ENG.). 80p. (J). (gr. 4-12). pap. 14.95 *(978-1-77085-981-4(0),* 08fd2653-e95e-4f3d-9313-64e8e447ffbf) Firefly Bks., Ltd.

Hutchinson, William. The Tinker's Armor: The Story of John Bunyan. Barr, Gladys H. 2011. 176p. 42.95 *(978-1-258-05498-4(1))* Literary Licensing, LLC.

Hutchison, D. C. The Eyes of the Woods: A Story of the Ancient Wilderness. Altsheler, Joseph A. 2008. (Young Trailers Ser.: Vol. 4). 256p. (J). reprint ed. pap. *(978-1-4065-4512-8(0))* Dodo Pr.

Hutchison, David, jt. illus. see Espinosa, Rod.

Hutto, Victoria. Hello, Bunny! Hirschmann, Kris. 2010. (Paint Me Pals Ser.). (ENG.). 24p. (J). 9.99 *(978-1-4169-7903-6(4),* Simon Scribbles) Simon Scribbles.

—The Twelve Days of Christmas in Oklahoma. Sauer, Tammi. (Twelve Days of Christmas in America Ser.). (J). (-k). 2018. 22p. bds. 7.95 *(978-1-4549-2965-9(0));* 2012. 40p. 12.95 *(978-1-4027-9224-3(7))* Sterling Publishing Co., Inc.

Hutton, Eleanor A. Dasher & the Sleigh-Train. Shelley, E. Dorinda. 2019. (ENG.). 30p. (J). pap. 12.95 *(978-1-0799-3060-3(4))* Independently Published.

Hutton, Jason. A Piffleduck Christmas. Lessard, Charles S. 2017. (ENG.). (J). pap. 13.99 *(978-0-9985781-0-1(X))* Mindstir Media.

Huxley, Oliver. My Brother. Huxley, Dee & Huxley, Tiffany. 2019. 32p. pap. 6.99 *(978-1-921504-95-2(1),* Working Title Pr.) HarperCollins Pubs. Australia AUS. Dist: HarperCollins Pubs.

Huxley, Sam & Huxley, Torrey. Max's Best Day Ever! Gray, Jan. 2019. (ENG.). 40p. (J). ***(978-1-5255-5583-1(9));*** pap. ***(978-1-5255-5584-8(7))*** FriesenPress.

Huxley, Torrey, jt. illus. see Huxley, Sam.

Huxtable, John. Giddy-Up, Guppies! (Bubble Guppies) Nagaraj, Josephine. 2014. (Step into Reading Ser.). (ENG.). 32p. (J). (gr. -1-1). 3.99 *(978-0-385-36974-9(3),* Random Hse. Bks. for Young Readers) Random Hse. Children's Bks.

Huxtable, John, jt. illus. see Huxtable, Tonja.

Huxtable, Tonja & Huxtable, John. Rapunzel. Bryant, Megan E. 2007. (Berry Fairy Tales Ser.). (J). *(978-1-4287-4159-1(3),* Grosset & Dunlap) Penguin Publishing Group.

Huyck, David. If Kids Ruled the World. Bailey, Linda. 2014. (ENG.). 32p. (J). (gr. -1-2). 16.95 *(978-1-55453-591-0(3))* Kids Can Pr., Ltd. CAN. Dist: Hachette Bk. Group.

—Manners Are Not for Monkeys. Tekavec, Heather. 2016. (ENG.). 32p. (J). (gr. -1-2). 16.95 *(978-1-77138-051-5(9))* Kids Can Pr., Ltd. CAN. Dist: Hachette Bk. Group.

—Nine Words Max. Bar-El, Dan. 2014. (ENG.). 32p. (J). (gr. k-4). 17.99 *(978-1-77049-562-3(2),* Tundra Bks.) Tundra Bks. CAN. Dist: Penguin Random Hse. LLC.

—That One Spooky Night. Bar-el, Dan. 2012. (ENG.). 80p. (J). (gr. 2-5). 8.95 *(978-1-55453-752-5(5));* 16.95 *(978-1-55453-751-8(7))* Kids Can Pr., Ltd. CAN. Dist: Hachette Bk. Group.

Huynh, Jessica. Phases. Buckner, Caitlynn. 2019. (ENG.). 44p. (J). pap. 11.00 *(978-1-7231-8774-2(7))* CreateSpace Independent Publishing Platform.

Hvass&Hannibal. Wild World. McAllister, Angela. 2018. (ENG.). 32p. (J). (gr. -1-2). 16.99 *(978-1-84780-966-7(9),* Wide Eyed Editions) Quarto Publishing Group UK GBR. Dist: Hachette Bk. Group.

Hviding, Heather C. Sofas Only Come Out at Night. Lane, W. David. 2018. (ENG.). 38p. (J). (gr. k-3). 19.50 *(978-1-7328112-3-2(7))* Bear's Place Publishing.

Hwan, Diandra. How Popo Got His Name. Reich, Tina. 2019. (ENG.). 34p. (J). pap. 9.99 ***(978-1-7343186-0-9(0))*** Reich, Tina.

Hwang, Seong-hye. Getting Rid of the Worms: A Soil Story. Lee, Hye-Ok. 2020. (Green Earth Tales Ser.). (ENG.). 32p. (J). (gr. k-4). pap. 8.99 ***(978-1-925235-60-9(2));*** lib. bdg. 27.99 ***(978-1-925235-64-7(5))*** ChoiceMaker Pty. Ltd., The AUS. (Big and SMALL). Dist: Lerner Publishing Group.

Hwang, YoSeob. The Wise Boy. Kim, JiYu. 2014. (MySELF Bookshelf Ser.). (ENG.). 32p. (J). (gr. k-2). pap. 11.94 *(978-1-60357-690-1(8));* lib. bdg. 25.27 *(978-1-59953-655-2(2))* Norwood Hse. Pr.

Hyatt, Joe. Buddy Unchained. Bix, Daisy. 2006. (Sit! Stay! Read! Ser.). (ENG.). 24p. (J). (gr. k-2). 17.95 *(978-0-940719-01-9(0))* Gryphon Pr., The.

Hyatt, Sean. Naja Plays Hide-Go-Seek, 1 vol. White. 2010. 28p. pap. 24.95 *(978-1-4489-8842-6(X))* America Star Bks.

Hyatt, Sean & McGrath, Michael. Naja Learns to Ride. White. 2011. 32p. pap. 24.95 *(978-1-4489-8369-8(X))* America Star Bks.

Hyde, Catherine Ryan. The Princess's Blankets. Duffy, Carol Ann. 2009. (ENG.). 40p. (J). (gr. k-3). 18.99 *(978-0-7636-4547-2(8),* Templar) Candlewick Pr.

Hyde, Maureen. Francis Woke up Early. Nobisso, Josephine. 2011. (ENG.). 32p. (J). (gr. k-2). 17.95 *(978-0-940112-20-9(5));* pap. 9.95 *(978-0-940112-22-3(1))* Gingerbread Hse.

Hyde, Michelle Hazelwood. Night Night, Birmingham. 2011. (J). *(978-1-59421-074-7(8))* Seacoast Publishing, Inc.

Hyde, Robert. Granny Butterfly. French, Jean. 2017. (ENG.). 12p. (J). pap. *(978-1-78623-833-7(0))* Grosvenor Hse. Publishing Ltd.

Hyde, Shaney. Arabella & the Magic Pencil. Ward, Stephanie. (ENG.). 32p. (J). (gr. -1-2). 2019. 17.99 *(978-1-925820-01-0(7));* 2nd ed. 2020. pap. 15.99 ***(978-1-925820-55-3(6),*** 337886) Exisle Publishing Pty Ltd. AUS. (EK Bks.). Dist: Hachette UK Distribution.

Hyder, Brittany. Even in the Night. Hyder, Brittany. 2018. (ENG.). 32p. (J). pap. 10.95 *(978-0-692-18822-4(3))* Wilkinson, Brittany.

Hyland, Greg, jt. illus. see Wang, Sean.

Hylkema, Noah. Noah's Story. Kim, Grace. 2018. (ENG.). 34p. (J). *(978-0-6484525-5-3(7))* Serenity Press.

Hyman, Miles & Alibert, Eric. Half & Half-Giants of the Ocean: Great Story & Cool Facts. Craipeau, Jean-Lou & Dutrieux, Julien. 2009. 56p. (J). 9.95 *(978-1-60115-211-4(6))* Treasure Bay, Inc.

—Half & Half-Giants of the Ocean: Great Story & Cool Facts. Craipeau, Jean-Lou & Dutrieux, Brigitte. 2009. 56p. (J). pap. 4.99 *(978-1-60115-212-1(4))* Treasure Bay, Inc.

Hyman, Trina Schart. The Adventures of Hershel of Ostropol. Kimmel, Eric A. 2019. (ENG.). 64p. (J). (gr. 3-7). pap. 8.99 *(978-0-8234-4244-7(6))* Holiday Hse., Inc.

—Children of the Dragon: Selected Tales from Vietnam, 1 vol. Garland, Sherry. 2012. (ENG.). 32p. (J). (gr. 3-7). 16.99 *(978-1-4556-1709-8(1),* Pelican Publishing) Arcadia Publishing.

—A Child's Calendar, 4 bks. Updike, John. 2004. (J). (gr. k-4). pap. 37.95 incl. audio *(978-1-59112-473-3(5));* 25.95 incl. audio *(978-1-59112-472-6(7))* Live Oak Media.

—A Child's Calendar (20th Anniversary Edition) Updike, John. (ENG.). 32p. (J). (gr. -1-3). 2020. pap. 8.99 *(978-0-8234-4534-9(8));* 20th ed. 2019. 18.99 *(978-0-8234-3956-0(9))* Holiday Hse., Inc.

—A Child's Christmas in Wales: Gift Edition. Thomas, Dylan. ed. 2017. (ENG.). 48p. (J). (gr. 3-7). 14.95 *(978-0-8234-3870-9(8))* Holiday Hse., Inc.

—The Ghost Next Door. St. John, Wylly Folk. 2019. 184p. (J). pap. *(978-1-948959-08-7(9))* Purple Hse. Pr.

—Hershel & the Hanukkah Goblins: 25th Anniversary Edition. Kimmel, Eric A. 25th anniv. ed. 2014. (ENG.). 32p. (J). (gr. -1-3). 7.99 *(978-0-8234-3194-6(0));* 17.99 *(978-0-8234-3164-9(9))* Holiday Hse., Inc.

—The Kitchen Knight: A Tale of King Arthur. 2007. (ENG.). 32p. (J). (gr. 1-4). 8.99 *(978-0-8234-1063-7(3))* Holiday Hse., Inc.

—Let's Steal the Moon: Jewish Tales, Ancient & Recent. Serwer-Bernstein, Blanche. 2005. 96p. 14.95 *(978-1-56171-896-2(3))* SPI Bks.

—Rapunzel. Rogasky, Barbara. 2019. 32p. (J). (gr. -1-3). 18.99 *(978-0-8234-4280-5(2))* Holiday Hse., Inc.

—Star Mother's Youngest Child. Moeri, Louise. 30th ed. 2005. (ENG.). 48p. (J). (gr. -1-3). 8.95 *(978-0-618-61509-4(1),* 428090) Houghton Mifflin Harcourt Publishing Co.

—Will You Sign Here, John Hancock? Fritz, Jean. 2005. (J). (gr. 2-7). 29.95 *(978-0-439-76750-7(4),* WHCD480) Weston Woods Studios, Inc.

Hyman, Trina Schart, jt. illus. see Updike, John.

Hymas, Anna. The Boy Who Harnessed the Wind: Young Readers Edition. Kamkwamba, William & Mealer, Bryan. 304p. (J). (gr. 5). 2016. (ENG.). 8.99 *(978-0-14-751042-6(2),* Puffin Books); 2015. 18.99 *(978-0-8037-4080-8(8),* Dial Bks) Penguin Young Readers Group.

—The Boy Who Harnessed the Wind (Movie Tie-In Edition) Young Readers Edition. Kamkwamba, William & Mealer, Bryan. ed. 2019. (ENG.). 304p. (J). (gr. 5). 8.99 *(978-1-9848-1612-2(8),* Puffin Books) Penguin Young Readers Group.

Hymper, W. & Stacey, W. S. Cassy. Stretton, Hesba. 2006. (Golden Inheritance Ser.: Vol. 9). 117p. (J). pap. *(978-0-921100-94-2(9))* Inheritance Pubns.

Hyndman, Kerry. Coming Home. Morpurgo, Michael. 2018. (ENG.). 32p. (J). (gr. -1-2). 17.99 *(978-1-5362-0042-3(5))* Candlewick Pr.

—Heroes: Inspiring True Stories of Courageous Animals. Long, David. 2018. (ENG.). 192p. 22.95 *(978-0-571-34210-5(8),* Faber & Faber Children's Bks.) Faber & Faber, Inc.

—Survivors. Long, David. 2017. (ENG.). 192p. 19.95 *(978-0-571-31601-4(8),* Faber & Faber Children's Bks.) Faber & Faber, Inc.

Hynes, Robert. Animal Families, Animal Friends. Woelfle, Gretchen. 2005. (ENG.). 32p. (J). (gr. k-3). 15.95 *(978-1-55971-901-8(X))* Cooper Square Publishing Llc.

—Baxter Needs a Home. O'Donnell, Liam. 2005. (Pet Tales Ser.). (ENG.). 32p. (J). (gr. -1-2). 2.95 *(978-1-59249-298-5(3),* 1B015); 9.95 *(978-1-59249-320-3(3),* 1B016) Soundprints.

—Baxter Needs a Home. O'Donnell, Liam. 2004. (ENG.). 32p. (J). (gr. -1-2). 4.95 *(978-1-59249-297-8(5),* 1B013) Soundprints.

—Duncan: A Brave Rescue. O'Donnell, Liam & O'Donnell, Laura. 2004. (Pet Tales Ser.). (ENG.). 32p. (J). (gr. -1-3). 4.95 *(978-1-59249-291-6(6),* 1B001) Soundprints.

—Duncan: A Brave Rescue. O'Donnell, Liam & O'Donnell, Laura. 2005. (Pet Tales Ser.). (ENG.). 32p. (J). (gr. -1-2). 2.95 *(978-1-59249-292-3(4),* 1B003) Soundprints.

—Duncan: A Brave Rescue. O'Donnell, Liam. 2004. (ENG.). 32p. (J). (gr. -1-2). 9.95 *(978-1-59249-317-3(3),* 1B004) Soundprints.

—Gray Wolf Pup's Adventure. Smith, Stephanie & Smith, Stephanie A. 2nd ed. 2003. (ENG.). 32p. (J). (gr. 1-3). 12.95 *(978-1-931465-43-4(6),* PS2077) Soundprints.

—Hedgehog Haven: The Story of an English Hedgerow Community. Dennard, Deborah. 2005. (ENG.). (J). (gr. 1-4). 32p. 19.95 *(978-1-56899-989-0(5),* BC7020); 36p. 15.95 *(978-1-56899-987-6(9),* B7020); 36p. pap. 6.95 *(978-1-56899-988-3(7),* S7020) Soundprints.

—Hurry up, Hedgehog! Dennard, Deborah. 2003. (Soundprints' Read-and-Discover Ser.). (ENG.). 32p. (gr. -1-1). 12.95 *(978-1-59249-150-6(2),* PS2012) Soundprints.

—Hurry up, Hedgehog! Dennard, Deborah. 2003. (Amazing Animal Adventures Ser.). (ENG.). 32p. (J). (gr. -1-3). per. 3.95 *(978-1-59249-149-0(9),* S2012) Soundprints.

—Lucy & the Busy Boat. O'Donnell, Liam. (Pet Tales Ser.). (ENG.). 32p. (J). (gr. -1-2). 2005. 2.95 *(978-1-59249-296-1(7),* 1B021); 2004. 4.95 *(978-1-59249-295-4(9),* 1B019); 2004. 9.95 *(978-1-59249-319-7(X),* 1B022) Soundprints.

—Snowshoe Hare's Family. Smith, Stephanie. 2nd ed. 2007. (Soundprints' Read-and-Discover Ser.). (ENG.). (J). (gr. 1-3). 32p. 12.95 *(978-1-931465-44-1(4),* PS2053); 48p. pap. 3.95 *(978-1-931465-15-1(0),* S2003) Soundprints.

—Tracker on the Job. O'Donnell, Liam. (Pet Tales Ser.). (ENG.). 32p. (J). (gr. -1-2). 2005. 2.95 *(978-1-59249-294-7(0),* 1B009); 2004. 9.95 *(978-1-59249-318-0(1),* 1B010) Soundprints.

—Tracker on the Job. O'Donnell, Liam. 2004. (Pet Tales Ser.). (ENG.). 32p. (J). (gr. -1-2). 4.95 *(978-1-59249-293-0(2),* 1B007) Soundprints.

Hyoun-Ju, Lee. The Legend of St. Christopher: Quest for a King. Hyoun-Ju, Lee. 2017. (ENG.). (J). (gr. 4-7). pap. *(978-0-8198-4588-7(4))* Pauline Bks. & Media Ctr.

Hyson, Elliot F. The Halloween Dragon & Ghost & Wizard. Hyson, Sarah M. 2019. (Halloween Dragon Ser.: Vol. 3). (ENG.). 34p. (J). pap. 9.49 ***(978-1-7117-7523-4(1))*** Independently Published.

Hyun, Jinsun. Doodle Bug: Digging to Reach the Top. Cordell, Greg. 2004. (J). *(978-0-9759699-0-8(0))* Greenville Family Partnership.

Hyun, Kim. Best Friends. Gooly, Gooly et al. 2015. (Chat About Ser.). (ENG.). 22p. (J). (— 1). bds. 9.99 *(978-1-4472-7730-9(9))* Pan Macmillan GBR. Dist: Independent Pubs. Group.

Hyun, You. Faeries' Landing. Hyun, You. rev. ed. 2006. (Faeries' Landing Ser.: Vol. 12). 192p. per. 9.99 *(978-1-59532-400-9(3));* Vol. 13. pap. 9.99 *(978-1-59532-401-6(1))* TOKYOPOP, Inc.

Hyun, You. Faeries' Landing, Vol. 8. Hyun, You, creator. rev. ed. 2005. 192p. pap. 9.99 *(978-1-59532-396-5(1))* TOKYOPOP, Inc.

Hyung Kim, Tae. Planet Blood, Vol. 2. Hyung Kim, Tae, creator. rev. ed. 2005. 200p. (J). pap. 9.99 *(978-1-59532-538-9(7))* TOKYOPOP, Inc.

Hyung, Min-Woo. Justice N Mercy, Vol. 1. 2005. 120p. pap. 39.99 *(978-1-59532-980-6(3))* TOKYOPOP, Inc.

Hyung, Min-Woo. Priest, 9 vols., Vol. 4. Hyung, Min-Woo. Kim, Jessica, tr. from JPN. rev. ed. 2003. 208p. (gr. 11-18). pap. 9.99 *(978-1-59182-088-8(X))* TOKYOPOP, Inc.

—Priest, 9 vols. Hyung, Min-Woo. Vol. 8. rev. ed. 2003. 192p. (YA). pap. 9.99 *(978-1-59182-204-2(1));* Vol. 9. 9th rev. ed. 2003. 176p. pap. 9.99 *(978-1-59182-205-9(X));* Vol. 10. rev. ed. 2004. 192p. pap. 9.99 *(978-1-59182-511-1(3))* TOKYOPOP, Inc.

I

Iacolina, Mark. Frances Dances. Iacolina, Mark. Bader, Bonnie. 2015. (Penguin Young Readers, Level 2 Ser.). 32p. (J). (gr. 1-2). 3.99 *(978-0-448-47929-3(X)*, Penguin Young Readers) Penguin Young Readers Group.

Iacopo, Bruno & Bruno, Iacopo. The Soprano's Last Song, 1 vol. Adler, Irene. 2014. (Sherlock, Lupin, & Me Ser.). (ENG.). 240p. (J). (gr. 4-8). lib. bdg. 26.65 *(978-1-4342-6522-7(6)*, Stone Arch Bks.) Capstone.

Iacuzzi, Pat. Is Santa Real? Duncan, Lillian. 2018. (ENG.). 32p. (J). pap. 9.99 *(978-1-7292-0428-3(7))* Independently Published.

Iadonisi, Carmin & Word, Amanda. Whiny Whiny Rhino. Iadonisi, Carmin & Word, Amanda. 2014. (ENG.). 32p. (J). 16.99 *(978-0-9903623-0-2(2))* Blue Blanket Publishing.

Ian, Crowe. Clouds. Nietzsche, Friedrich. Ian, Johnston, tr. 2009. 145p. (gr. 8-17). pap. 9.95 *(978-0-9797571-3-6(4))* Richer Resources Pubns.

Ian, Johnstone D. The Wildlife Rescue Fairy. Bryant, Tracey. 2019. (ENG.). 72p. (J). (gr. 4-6). pap. *(978-1-9997989-2-5(9))* Bryant, Tracey.

Ian, Shickle. The Other Side of the Window. Cameron, Kristy. 2013. 28p. pap. *(978-0-9859790-2-7(X))* LP Publishing.

Iannaco, Nick. Vax-Force. Rowe, Kelsey. 2019. (ENG.). 44p. (J). ***(978-1-5255-5120-8(5))***; pap. ***(978-1-5255-5121-5(3))*** FriesenPress.

Iantorno, Danlyn. Books for Children of the World: The Story of Jella Lepman, 1 vol. Pearl, Sydelle. 2007. (ENG.). 32p. (J). (gr. k-3). 16.99 *(978-1-58980-438-8(4)*, Pelican Publishing) Arcadia Publishing.

Ibanez, Victor. Jean Grey Vol. 1: Nightmare Fuel. 2017. (ENG.). 136p. (YA). (gr. 8-17). pap. 17.99 *(978-1-302-90877-5(4))* Marvel Worldwide, Inc.

—Jean Grey Vol. 2: Final Fight. 2018. (ENG.). 136p. (YA). (gr. 8-17). pap. 15.99 *(978-1-302-90878-2(2))* Marvel Worldwide, Inc.

Ibarra, Rosa. Soledad Sigh-Sighs. Gonzalez, Rigoberto & González, Rigoberto. 2014.Tr. of Soledad Suspiros. (ENG & SPA.). 32p. (J). pap. 8.95 *(978-0-89239-309-1(2)*, Children's Book Press) Lee & Low Bks., Inc.

Ibatoulline, Bagram. The Animal Hedge. Fleischman, Paul. 2008. 48p. (J). (gr. 1-4). pap. 8.99 *(978-0-7636-3842-9(0))* Candlewick Pr.

—Bella at Midnight. Stanley, Diane. 2007. (ENG.). 304p. (J). (gr. 3-7). pap. 7.99 *(978-0-06-077575-9(0))* HarperCollins Pubs.

—Boom Boom Go Away! Geringer, Laura. 2010. (ENG.). 40p. (J). (gr. -1-1). 15.99 *(978-0-689-85093-6(X)*, Atheneum Bks. for Young Readers) Simon & Schuster Children's Publishing.

—Crow Call. Lois, Lowry. 2009. 32p. (J). (gr. 3-7). 19.99 *(978-0-545-03035-9(8)*, Scholastic Pr.) Scholastic, Inc.

—The Granddaughter Necklace. Wyeth, Sharon Dennis. (J). 2013. (ENG.). 32p. (gr. -1-3). 18.99 *(978-0-545-08125-2(4))*; 2012. pap. *(978-0-545-23983-7(4))* Scholastic, Inc. (Levine, Arthur A. Bks.).

—Graven Images. Fleischman, Paul. 2005. (ENG.). 128p. (YA). (gr. 5-9). per. 8.99 *(978-0-7636-2984-7(7))* Candlewick Pr.

—Great Joy. Dicamillo, Kate. 2010. 32p. (J). (gr. -1-3). 8.99 *(978-0-7636-4996-8(1))* Candlewick Pr.

—Great Joy. DiCamillo, Kate. 2007. 32p. (J). (gr. -1-3). 17.99 *(978-0-7636-2920-5(0))* Candlewick Pr.

—The Hawk of the Castle: A Story of Medieval Falconry. Smith, Danna. 2017. (ENG.). 40p. (J). (gr. -1-3). 17.99 *(978-0-7636-7992-7(5))* Candlewick Pr.

—A Little Women Christmas. Frederick, Heather Vogel. 2014. (ENG.). 32p. (J). (gr. -1-3). 17.99 *(978-1-4424-1359-7(X)*, Simon & Schuster Bks. For Young Readers) Simon & Schuster Bks. For Young Readers.

—The Matchbox Diary. Fleischman, Paul. 40p. (J). (gr. 1-4). 2016. (ENG.). 7.99 *(978-0-7636-7638-4(1))*; 2013. 16.99 *(978-0-7636-4601-1(6))* Candlewick Pr.

—The Matchbox Diary. Fleischman, Paul. ed. 2016. (ENG.). 40p. (J). (gr. 1-4). 18.40 *(978-0-606-39097-2(9))* Turtleback.

—The Miraculous Journey of Edward Tulane. Dicamillo, Kate. 228p. (J). 2009. (gr. 2-5). pap. 11.99 *(978-0-7636-4783-4(7))*; 2006. (ENG.). (gr. 1-4). 19.99 *(978-0-7636-2589-4(2))* Candlewick Pr.

—The Miraculous Journey of Edward Tulane. DiCamillo, Kate. 2015. 240p. (J). (gr. 2-5). pap. 7.99 *(978-0-7636-8090-9(7))* Candlewick Pr.

—The Miraculous Journey of Edward Tulane. Dicamillo, Kate. ed. 2009. 198p. (gr. 8-12). 23.30 *(978-1-4178-0763-5(6))* Turtleback.

—On the Blue Comet. Wells, Rosemary. 336p. (J). (gr. 5). 2012. pap. 9.99 *(978-0-7636-5815-1(4))*; 2010. 16.99 *(978-0-7636-3722-4(X))* Candlewick Pr.

—The Scarecrow's Dance. Yolen, Jane. 2009. (ENG.). 32p. (J). (gr. -1-3). 19.99 *(978-1-4169-3770-8(6)*, Simon & Schuster Bks. For Young Readers) Simon & Schuster Bks. For Young Readers.

—Sea Glass Summer. Houts, Michelle. 2019. 32p. (J). (gr. -1-3). 16.99 *(978-0-7636-8443-3(0))* Candlewick Pr.

—The Snow Queen, Vol. Andersen, Hans Christian. 2013. (ENG.). 40p. (J). (gr. -1-3). 17.99 *(978-0-06-220950-4(7))* HarperCollins Pubs.

—Stand There! She Shouted: The Invincible Photographer Julia Margaret Cameron. Rubin, Susan Goldman. 2014. 80p. (J). (gr. 3-7). 18.99 *(978-0-7636-5753-6(0))* Candlewick Pr.

—The Third Gift. Park, Linda Sue. 2011. (ENG.). 32p. (J). (gr. 1-4). 17.99 *(978-0-547-20195-5(8)*, 1058916) Houghton Mifflin Harcourt Publishing Co.

Ibelings, Anne. From Mud Huts to Skyscrapers. Paxmann, Christine. 2012. (ENG.). 64p. (J). (gr. 3-7). 19.95 *(978-3-7913-7113-9(4))* Prestel Verlag GmbH & Co KG. DEU. Dist: Penguin Random Hse. LLC.

Ibrahim, Mina. The Bubble Princess. Ibrahim, Mina. 2017. (ENG.). 34p. (J). (gr. 1-6). *(978-1-7750745-3-3(6))* Average Joe Comics.

Ibsen, Henrik. The Wild Duck. Landes, William-Alan, ed. 2003. 85p. (YA). (gr. 8-12). pap. 8.00 *(978-0-88734-747-4(9))* Players Pr., Inc.

Ice, Corinna. With Love, from Me to You, 1 vol. Simon, Mary Manz. 2017. (ENG.). 18p. (J). bds. 8.99 *(978-0-310-75815-0(7))* Zonderkidz.

Ice, D. C. Acrylics, 1 vol. Bolte, Mari. 2013. (Paint It Ser.). (ENG.). 32p. (J). (gr. 3-9). 28.65 *(978-1-4765-3109-0(9))* Capstone.

—Casey's Great Escape. Shaw, Nancy Jo. 2016. (ENG.). (J). 18.95 *(978-1-59298-774-0(5))* Beaver's Pond Pr., Inc.

—The Legend of the Loch Ness Monster, 1 vol. Troupe, Thomas Kingsley. 2011. (Legend Has It Ser.). (ENG.). 32p. (J). (gr. 2-4). lib. bdg. 27.99 *(978-1-4048-6659-1(0)*, Picture Window Bks.) Capstone.

—The Legend of the Werewolf, 1 vol. Troupe, Thomas Kingsley. 2010. (Legend Has It Ser.). (ENG.). 32p. (J). (gr. 2-4). lib. bdg. 27.99 *(978-1-4048-6033-9(9)*, Picture Window Bks.) Capstone.

—Paint It: The Art of Acrylics, Oils, Pastels, & Watercolors, 1 vol. Bolte, Mari. 2013. (Craft It Yourself Ser.). (ENG.). 144p. (J). (gr. 3-9). pap. 14.95 *(978-1-62370-009-6(4)*, Capstone Young Readers) Capstone.

—Watercolors, 1 vol. Bolte, Mari. 2013. (Paint It Ser.). (ENG.). 32p. (J). (gr. 3-9). 28.65 *(978-1-4765-3108-3(0)*, Capstone Pr.) Capstone.

Ichikawa, Santomi. Grandpa's Soup. Kadono, Eiko. 2009. (ENG.). 40p. (J). (gr. -1-3). pap. 9.00 *(978-0-8028-5347-9(1)*, Eerdmans Bks For Young Readers) Eerdmans, William B. Publishing Co.

Ichikawa, Satomi. You Are My I Love You. Cusimano Love, Maryann. 2018. (ENG.). 28p. (J). (— 1). bds. 12.99 *(978-1-9848-1257-5(2)*, Philomel Bks.) Penguin Young Readers Group.

—You Are My I Love You. Cusimano Love, Maryann. 2012. (ENG.). 28p. (J). (gr. -1 — 1). bds. 6.99 *(978-0-399-24396-7(8)*, Philomel Bks.) Penguin Young Readers Group.

—You Are My I Love You: Board Book. Cusimano Love, Maryann. 2010. (ENG.). 30p. (J). (gr. -1 — 1). bds. 6.99 *(978-0-399-24395-0(X)*, Philomel Bks.) Penguin Young Readers Group.

—You Are My Miracle. Love, Maryann Cusimano. 2012. 28p. (J). (gr. -1 — 1). bds. 6.99 *(978-0-399-25791-9(8)*, Philomel Bks.) Penguin Young Readers Group.

—You Are My Wish. Love, Maryann Cusimano. 2010. (ENG.). 32p. (J). (gr. -1-k). 17.99 *(978-0-399-24752-1(1)*, Philomel Bks.) Penguin Young Readers Group.

Idle, Molly. He's Got the Whole World in His Hands, 1 vol. Zondervan Staff. 2008. (I Can Read! / Song Ser.). (ENG.). 32p. (J). (gr. -1-3). pap. 4.99 *(978-0-310-71622-8(5))* Zonderkidz.

—My Shadow. Stevenson, Robert Louis. 2011. (Poetry for Children Ser.). (ENG.). 24p. (J). (gr. k-3). 27.07 *(978-1-60973-154-0(9)*, 201181) Child's World, Inc., The.

—People Don't Bite People. Wheeler, Lisa. 2018. (People Bks.). (ENG.). 40p. (J). (gr. -1-3). 17.99 *(978-1-4814-9082-5(6)*, Atheneum Bks. for Young Readers) Simon & Schuster Children's Publishing.

—People Share with People. Wheeler, Lisa. 2019. (People Bks.). (ENG.). 40p. (J). (gr. -1-3). 17.99 *(978-1-5344-2559-0(4)*, Atheneum Bks. for Young Readers) Simon & Schuster Children's Publishing.

—Santa's Workshop: A Mini Animotion Book. Accord Publishing Staff. 2011. (ENG.). 12p. (J). 9.99 *(978-1-4494-0834-3(6))* Andrews McMeel Publishing.

—Zombelina: School Days. Crow, Kristyn. 2013. (ENG.). 32p. (J). (gr. -1-3). 16.99 *(978-0-8027-2803-6(0)*, 9780802728036, Bloomsbury USA Childrens) Bloomsbury Publishing USA.

—Zombelina Dances the Nutcracker. Crow, Kristyn. 2015. 40p. (J). (gr. -1-3). 16.99 *(978-1-61963-640-8(9)*, 900143827, Bloomsbury USA Childrens) Bloomsbury Publishing USA.

—Zombelina School Days. Crow, Kristyn. 2017. 32p. (J). 16.99 *(978-1-61963-641-5(7)*, 900143822, Bloomsbury USA Childrens) Bloomsbury Publishing USA.

Idle, Molly. Camp Rex. Idle, Molly. 2014. 40p. (J). (gr. -1-k). 16.99 *(978-0-670-78573-5(3)*, Viking Books for Young Readers) Penguin Young Readers Group.

—Sea Rex. Idle, Molly. 2015. 34p. (J). (-k). 17.99 *(978-0-670-78574-2(1)*, Viking Books for Young Readers) Penguin Young Readers Group.

Idumi, Rei. Hack//Ai Buster, 2 vols. Hamazaki, Tatsuya & Tatsuya, Hamazaki. 2006. (Hack//AI Buster Ser.: Vol. 2). 192p. pap. 7.99 *(978-1-59816-407-7(4))* TOKYOPOP, Inc.

Igle, Jamal, jt. illus. see Robinson, Roger.

Iglesias, Álvaro. Sgt. Reckless - The War Horse: Korean War Hero. Higgins, Melissa. 2014. (Animal Heroes Ser.). (ENG.). 32p. (J). (gr. k-2). 29.32 *(978-1-4795-5462-1(6)*, Picture Window Bks.) Capstone.

Iglesias, Amanda. Johnny Winters. Davis, Brittney. 2019. (ENG.). 30p. (J). (gr. 2-6). pap. 19.99 *(978-0-578-47171-6(X))* Davis, Brittney.

IglooBooks, Paula. Noah's Ark. 2015. (ENG.). 26p. (J). (-k). bds. 8.99 *(978-1-78343-472-5(4))* Igloo Bks. GBR. Dist: Simon & Schuster, Inc.

Ignaczak, Alicja. OMG... I Did It Again?! Aikens-Nuñez, Talia. 2016. (Omg... Ser.: 2). (ENG.). 96p. (J). (gr. 2-4). 8.95 *(978-1-77168-034-9(2))* Central Avenue Publishing CAN. Dist: Independent Pubs. Group.

Ignaczak, Alicja & Gil, Alicja. OMG... Is He Also a Witch?! Aikens-Nunez, Talia. 2017. (Omg... Ser.). (ENG.). 96p. (J). (gr. 2-4). pap. 8.95 *(978-1-77168-114-8(4))* Central Avenue Publishing CAN. Dist: Independent Pubs. Group.

Ihara, Shigekatsu. Pokémon: Diamond & Pearl Adventure!, Vol. 1. Ihara, Shigekatsu. 2008. (Pokemon Ser.: 1). (ENG.). 208p. (J). (gr. k). pap. 9.99 *(978-1-4215-2286-9(1))* Viz Media.

—Pokémon: Diamond & Pearl Adventure!, Vol. 3. Ihara, Shigekatsu. 2009. (Pokemon Ser.: 3). (ENG.). 200p. (J). pap. 9.99 *(978-1-4215-2574-7(7))* Viz Media.

—Pokémon: Diamond & Pearl Adventure!, Vol. 4, Vol. 4. Ihara, Shigekatsu. 2009. (Pokemon Ser.: 4). (ENG.). 192p. (J). pap. 9.99 *(978-1-4215-2674-4(3))* Viz Media.

—Pokémon: Diamond & Pearl Adventure!, Vol. 5. Ihara, Shigekatsu. 2009. (Pokemon Ser.: 5). (ENG.). 200p. (J). pap. 9.99 *(978-1-4215-2923-3(8))* Viz Media.

—Pokémon: Diamond & Pearl Adventure!, Vol. 6. Ihara, Shigekatsu. 2010. (Pokemon Ser.: 6). (ENG.). 192p. (J). pap. 9.99 *(978-1-4215-3170-0(4))* Viz Media.

—Pokémon: Diamond & Pearl Adventure!, Vol. 7. Ihara, Shigekatsu. 2010. (Pokemon Ser.: 7). (ENG.). 192p. (J). pap. 9.99 *(978-1-4215-3491-6(6))* Viz Media.

—Pokémon: Diamond & Pearl Adventure!, Vol. 8 Vol. 8. Ihara, Shigekatsu. 2010. (Pokemon Ser.: 8). (ENG.). 192p. (J). pap. 9.99 *(978-1-4215-3671-2(4))* Viz Media.

Iida, Haruko. Crescent Moon, Vol. 5. Iida, Haruko, creator. rev. ed. 2005. 176p. pap. 9.99 *(978-1-59182-952-2(6)*, Tokyopop Adult) TOKYOPOP, Inc.

Iida, Toshitsugu. Wolf's Rain. Nobumoto, Keiko. (YA). 14.95 *(978-1-59116-791-4(4))* Viz Media.

III, Maxwell Eaton. The Truth about Hawks. III, Maxwell Eaton. 2019. (Truth about Your Favorite Animals Ser.). (ENG.). 32p. (J). 16.99 *(978-1-250-19845-7(3)*, 900194596) Roaring Brook Pr.

—The Truth about Hippos. III, Maxwell Eaton. 2018. (Truth about Your Favorite Animals Ser.). (ENG.). 32p. (J). 15.99 *(978-1-62672-667-3(1)*, 900169984) Roaring Brook Pr.

III, Theodore Taylor. Woke Baby. Browne, Mahogany L. 2018. (ENG.). 32p. (J). 16.99 *(978-1-62672-295-8(1)*, 900150273) Roaring Brook Pr.

Ikaia Aten, Dayle Marc, jt. illus. see Castulo Aten, Vicky Talaro.

Ike, Edson. Soccerverse: Poems about Soccer. Steinglass, Elizabeth. 2019. (ENG.). 32p. (J). (gr. 1-4). 17.99 *(978-1-62979-249-1(7)*, Wordsong) Boyds Mills Pr.

Ikegami, Aiko. Why Worry? Kimmel, Eric A. 2019. (ENG.). 32p. (J). (gr. k-3). 16.99 *(978-1-5132-6200-0(9)*, West Margin Pr.) West Margin Pr.

Ikegami, Aiko. Friends. Ikegami, Aiko. 2016. (ENG.). 32p. (J). (gr. -1-3). 16.99 *(978-0-8075-2550-0(2)*, 807525502) Whitman, Albert & Co.

—Hello. Ikegami, Aiko. 2019. (ENG.). 34p. (J). (gr. -1-2). 17.99 *(978-1-939547-58-3(X))* Creston Bks.

—Seed Man. Ikegami, Aiko. 2018. (ENG.). 32p. (J). (gr. k-3). 16.99 *(978-1-58536-379-7(0)*, 204403) Sleeping Bear Pr.

Ikemoto, Mikio. Boruto: Naruto Next Generations, Vol. 1. Kodachi, Ukyo. 2017. (Boruto: Naruto Next Generations Ser.: 1). (ENG.). 208p. pap. 9.99 *(978-1-4215-9211-4(8))* Viz Media.

Ikhwan, M. The Courageous Millie Rose. Swain, D. C. 2017. (ENG.). 26p. (J). (gr. k-2). pap. *(978-0-473-39296-3(8))* Cambridge Town Pr.

Ikumi, Mia. Tokyo Mew Mew a la Mode, 2 vols., Vol. 1. Kodansha. 2005. (Tokyo Mew-Mew a la Mode Ser.). 192p. (J). pap. 14.99 *(978-1-59532-789-5(4)*, Tokyopop Kids) TOKYOPOP, Inc.

Ilchuck, Nadia. Le R�ve de Khalil et Autres Histoires: Histoires Pour Gar�ons et Fi Lles. Michaud Aubrey, Danielle. 2019. (Walk in the Wind Ser.: Vol. 3). (FRE.). 126p. (J). (gr. 1-6). ***(978-1-989048-45-0(5))*** Petra Bks.

Ilchuk, Nadia. Catching Memories on the Lake: A Father & Son Fishing Tail. Skoubye, Nathan L. 2019. (ENG.). 28p. (J). pap. 9.99 *(978-1-0935-4249-3(7))* Independently Published.

Ilchuk, Nadia. Khalil's Dream & Other Stories: Stories for Boys & Girls. Michaud Aubrey, Danielle. 2019. (Walk in the Wind Ser.: Vol. 3). (ENG.). 118p. (J). (gr. 1-6). ***(978-1-989048-26-9(9))*** Petra Bks.

—L'�cureuil Feignant et Autres Histoires: Histoires Pour Gar�ons et Filles. Michaud Aubrey, Danielle. 2019. (Promenade Dans le Vent Ser.: Vol. 1). (FRE.). 120p. (J). (gr. 1-4). ***(978-1-989048-43-6(9))*** Petra Bks.

—Le Pacte et Autres Histoires: Histoires Pour Gar�ons et Filles. Michaud Aubrey, Danielle. 2nd ed. 2019. (Promenade Dans le Vent Ser.: Vol. 2). (FRE.). 106p. (J). (gr. 1-4). ***(978-1-989048-44-3(7))*** Petra Bks.

Ilic, Nikolas. Mr. Dog & the Rabbit Habit (Mr. Dog) Fogle, Ben & Cole, Steve. 2020. (Mr. Dog Ser.). (ENG.). 144p. (J). 4.99 *(978-0-00-838446-3(0)*, HarperCollins Children's Bks.) HarperCollins Pubs. Ltd. GBR. Dist: HarperCollins Pubs.

Ilic, Nikolas & West, Eddie. The Amazing Planet Earth. Emmons, Scott. 2017. 31p. (J). *(978-1-5182-5200-6(1))* Random Hse., Inc.

—Tyrannosaurus Rex. Emmons, Scott. 2017. 31p. (J). *(978-1-5182-5197-9(8))* Random Hse., Inc.

Ilievski, Goce. The Strongest Boy. Irving Lee, Renee. 2019. (ENG.). 34p. (J). pap. *(978-0-6484672-1-2(X))*; *(978-0-6484672-0-5(1))* Irving Lee, Renee.

Ilina, Anna. Oh, Mari! Cordero, Cynthia. 2018. (ENG.). 32p. (J). pap. 12.00 *(978-0-9998853-0-7(8))* CC Conglomerate LLC.

Ilincic, Nataea. The Treasure of the Loch Ness Monster, 30 vols. Don, Lari. 2018. (Traditional Scottish Tales Ser.). (ENG.). 32p. (J). (gr. -1-2). 17.95 *(978-1-78250-485-6(0)*, Kelpies) Floris Bks. GBR. Dist: Consortium Bk. Sales & Distribution.

Ilka, Benjamin Alexander. A Boy & His Shadow. Ilka, Benjamin Alexander. (YA). Pt. 1. 2005. per. 4.95 net. *(978-0-9779504-0-9(9))*; Pt. 2. 2006. 3.95 net. *(978-0-9779504-1-6(7))* Hogan Publishing LLC.

Ill, Noel. Teo in Palo Verde/Teo en Palo Verde. Del Rio, Adam. 2008. (ENG & SPA.). (J). (gr. k-3). 28p. 15.95 *(978-1-60448-000-9(9))*; 32p. pap. 8.95 *(978-1-60448-001-6(7))* Lectura Bks.

Illingworth, Jamie. Harold the Bionic Hamster. Watson, Philip. 2017. (ENG.). (J). pap. *(978-0-9927162-8-8(4))* Watson, Philip.

Illingworth, Sasha, photos by. First Love. Patterson, James & Raymond, Emily. 2015. (ENG., 336p. (YA). (gr. 10-17). pap. 9.99 *(978-0-316-20703-4(9)*, Jimmy Patterson) Little Brown & Co.

Illustrated by: Charles Duke. Nosey Rosey. Carr, Suzanna & Crutchfield, Tylicia. 2011. 44p. pap. 24.95 *(978-1-4560-7939-0(5))* America Star Bks.

Illustration, Kadysha. The Adventures of Bizzi Bee - the Queen's Birthday. Dennington, Katie. 2018. (ENG.). 30p. (J). pap. 10.99 *(978-1-7271-3794-1(9))* CreateSpace Independent Publishing Platform.

Illustrations, Blueberry. An Amazing Miracle. Williams, Adrienne a. 2019. (ENG.). 26p. (J). pap. 12.99 ***(978-1-6965-0314-3(0))*** Independently Published.

—Carrie Scores a Win. Swain, Brenda. 2019. (ENG.). 28p. (J). pap. 11.99 ***(978-1-6913-3488-9(X))*** Independently Published.

Illustrations, Blueberry. Caz & the Lucky Necklace. Stewart, Kitria. 2017. (ENG.). (J). pap. 12.00 *(978-0-692-82924-0(5))* Read More! Run More!.

—Charlie... the Merry Christmoose. Sherwood, John. 2018. (Children's Christmas Book Ser.). (ENG.). 36p. (J). (gr. k-3). 17.99 *(978-0-578-42731-7(1))* Charlie Co.

Illustrations, Blueberry. Color My World. Casella, Karen. 2019. (ENG.). 28p. (J). pap. 11.99 ***(978-1-6931-3426-5(8))*** Independently Published.

Illustrations, Blueberry. ¿cómo Voy a Hablar con Abuela? Publisher, La Luz Books & Reyes, Maria de la Luz. 2018. (SPA.). 36p. (J). (gr. 1-6). 20.00 *(978-0-9972790-1-6(X))* REYES, MARIA DE LA LUZ.

Illustrations, Blueberry. Free to Be Me. Zarriello, Nancy. 2019. (ENG.). 32p. (J). (gr. 1-6). 19.99 ***(978-0-578-53204-2(2))*** Zarriello, Nancy.

Illustrations, Blueberry. Frog & the ... Chewy, Wiggly, Quacky, Jumpy Day. Singletery, Mildred F. 2018. (ENG.). 30p. (J). pap. 9.99 *(978-1-7308-9956-0(0))* Independently Published.

Illustrations, Blueberry. A Girl & Her Cows. Goodman, Peggy. 2020. (ENG.). 38p. (J). (gr. k-6). 14.95 ***(978-0-9990606-6-7(X))*** goodman, peggy.

Illustrations, Blueberry. Grandma Mable, Are You Able? Wright, Willie Etta. 2018. (ENG.). 64p. (J). (gr. 3-4). 21.99 *(978-0-9703551-5-7(7))* Wright, Willie Etta.

—In His Absence I Can Still Feel His Presence: (English with a Spanish Version Inside) Smith, Jalisa Rose. 2019. (ENG.). 54p. (J). (gr. 1-6). 20.00 *(978-0-578-50956-3(3))* Author Pubns.

—The Incredible Microbiome. Davies, Sean Fnp-C & Davies, Tori. 2018. (ENG.). 38p. (J). (gr. k-6). 18.00 *(978-0-692-96866-6(0))* Davies, Sean.

—Jose the Reindeer: Jose el Venadito. Olivarez, Ernest. 2019. (ENG.). 62p. (J). (gr. k-6). 29.99 *(978-1-7328080-0-3(7))* Ernest Michael Olivarez Publishing LLC.

Illustrations, Blueberry. The Legend of Scarlett & Ryman. Davis, Kristalin & Davis, Kate. 2019. (ENG.). 36p. (J). (gr. k-6). 22.95 ***(978-0-578-59675-4(X))*** Davis, Kristalin.

Illustrations, Blueberry. Lilian's First Playdate. Saint-Fleur, Julie M. 2019. (ENG.). 40p. (J). pap. 14.99 *(978-1-0986-7849-4(4))* Independently Published.

—My Little Sister. Gay, Benita. 2019. (ENG.). 26p. (J). pap. 12.99 *(978-1-0760-7948-0(2))* Independently Published.

—Nicholas & the Magic Greek Coin. Kelly, Valerie. 2019. (ENG.). 34p. (J). pap. 10.99 *(978-1-9746-3150-6(8))* CreateSpace Independent Publishing Platform.

—Rainbow Falls. Reiersen, Ron. 2018. (Callie & Ivan Ser.: Vol. 7). (ENG.). 46p. (J). pap. 12.99 *(978-1-7278-0727-1(8))* CreateSpace Independent Publishing Platform.

—Sadie & Claire: The Fire Horses. Pattarozzi, Michael. 2018. (ENG.). 48p. (J). (gr. k-6). 19.95 *(978-0-692-16621-5(1))* Singing Magpies.

Illustrations, Blueberry. The Secret Life of Sam the Soccer Ball. Goodman, Peggy. 2020. (ENG.). 38p. (J). (gr. k-6). 14.95 ***(978-0-9990606-7-4(8))*** goodman, peggy.

Illustrations, Blueberry. Three Princesses: (powers & Gifts Revealed) Holcomb, Marlena Brown. 2018. (ENG.). 26p. (J). (gr. k-6). 16.99 *(978-0-578-41006-7(0))* Marlena Brown-Holcomb.

—Trees Please. Wildes, Cynthia. 2018. (ENG.). 76p. (J). (gr. k-6). 25.00 *(978-0-692-96767-6(2))* Cynthia Harvest Moon Intuitive Psychic Medium.

—The Unfriendly Bee. Hayton, Pauline. 2018. (ENG.). 48p. (J). (gr. 1-3). pap. 12.99 *(978-0-9835863-8-8(1))* PH Publishing.

—What's So Special about Grandparents? Guralnick, Sara. 2019. (ENG.). 56p. (J). pap. 12.95 *(978-1-7259-9667-0(7))* CreateSpace Independent Publishing Platform.

Illustrations byVoigt, Karen S. Spike the Sewer Cat. Hansen, Kate. 2008. 27p. pap. 24.95 *(978-1-60474-094-3(9))* America Star Bks.

Illustrations, Maa. The Treebobs & the Dizzy Broomsticks. Harney, Declan. 2017. (Treebob Ser.: Vol. 1). (ENG.). 34p. (J). (gr. k-3). *(978-0-9955971-1-2(1))*; pap. *(978-0-9955971-0-5(3))* Tales4all.

Illustrations, rks. Yes You Can. Williams, Nana & Wiltz, Kaley. 2019. (ENG.). 50p. (J). (gr. k-6). 21.99 *(978-1-7336818-0-3(9))* Amazon Creations.

Illustrator, West Yorkshire, jt. illus. see Machell, Dawn.

Iluzada, Nicholas. In the Deep Blue Sea: Jack & the Geniuses Book #2. Nye, Bill & Mone, Gregory. 2018. (Jack & the Geniuses Ser.). (ENG.). 336p. (J). (gr. 3-7). pap. 7.99 *(978-1-4197-3342-0(7)*, 1158003, Amulet Bks.) Abrams, Inc.

—Jack & the Geniuses: At the Bottom of the World. Nye, Bill & Mone, Gregory. (ENG.). (J). (gr. 3-7). 2018. 272p. pap. 7.99 *(978-1-4197-3288-1(9)*, 1152603); 2017. 256p. 13.95 *(978-1-4197-2303-2(0)*, 1152601) Abrams, Inc. (Amulet Bks.).

—Lost in the Jungle: Jack & the Geniuses Book #3. Nye, Bill & Mone, Gregory. (Jack & the Geniuses Ser.). (ENG.). 288p. (J). (gr. 3-7). 2019. pap. 7.99 *(978-1-4197-3485-4(7)*, 1158103); 2018. 13.99 *(978-1-4197-2867-9(9)*, 1158101) Abrams, Inc. (Amulet Bks.).

Ilyas, Taymoor. The Visitor. Solberg, Kristian. 2019. (ENG.). 68p. (J). pap. 13.90 (978-1-0816-7382-6(6)) Independently Published.

Imagineers, The. The Imagineering Field Guide to Disneyland. Wright, Alex. 2008. (Imagineering Field Guide Ser.). (ENG.). 128p. (J). (gr. 5-9). pap., instr.'s gde. ed. 9.99 (978-1-4231-0975-4(9), Disney Editions) Disney Pr.

Imaginism Studio, jt. illus. see Disney Storybook Art Team.

Imaginism Studios, Imaginism. Disney Junior Fancy Nancy: Meet Fancy Nancy. Parent, Nancy. 2018. (Disney Junior Fancy Nancy Ser.). (ENG.). 18p. (J). (gr. -1 — 1). bds. 8.99 (978-0-06-284398-2(2)) HarperCollins Pubs.

Imaginism Studios, Inc., jt. illus. see Disney Storybook Art Team.

Imaginism Studios Staff, jt. illus. see Disney Storybook Art Team.

Imai, Ayano. Forest Dream. Imai, Ayano. 2018. (ENG.). 32p. (J). (gr. k-2). 17.99 (978-988-8341-64-1(2), Minedition) Neugebauer, Michael (Publishing) Limited HKG. Dist: Penguin Random Hse. LLC.

—The 108th Sheep. Imai, Ayano. 2007. (ENG.). 32p. (gr. -1-1). 22.44 (978-1-58925-063-5(X)) Tiger Tales.

Imai, Yasue. B. B. Explosion. Imai, Yasue. 2004. (B. B. Explosion Ser.: 3). (ENG.). 192p. Vol. 3. pap. 9.95 (978-1-59116-386-2(2)); Vol. 4. pap. 9.95 (978-1-59116-387-9(0)) Viz Media.

—B.B. Explosion, Vol. 5. Imai, Yasue. Anzai, Nobuyuki. 2005. (ENG.). 192p. pap. 9.95 (978-1-59116-388-6(9)) Viz Media.

Imai, Yasue & Imai, Yasue. B.B. Explosion, Vol. 1. Imai, Yasue. 2004. (ENG.). 192p. pap. 9.95 (978-1-59116-384-8(6)) Viz Media.

Imai, Yasue, jt. illus. see Imai, Yasue.

Imamura, Yas. Winged Wonders: Solving the Monarch Migration Mystery. Pincus, Meeg. 2020. (ENG.). 40p. (J). (gr. 2-5). 17.99 (978-1-5341-1040-3(2), 204849) Sleeping Bear Pr.

Imamura, Yasmin. The Very Oldest Pear Tree. Sanders, Nancy I. 2020. (ENG.). 32p. (J). (gr. -1-3). 16.99 **(978-0-8075-6681-7(0)**, 807566810) Whitman, Albert & Co.

Immelman, Sarita. African Dream. Wyss, Tyan. 2006. 48p. (J). pap. 15.95 (978-1-58939-915-0(3)) Virtualbookworm.com Publishing, Inc.

—Night Flyer. Wyss, Tyan. 2006. 40p. (J). per. 14.95 (978-1-58939-916-7(1)) Virtualbookworm.com Publishing, Inc.

Immonen, Stuart, et al. Amazing Spider-Man: Red Goblin. 2019. (ENG.). 264p. (YA). (gr. 8-17). pap. 24.99 (978-1-302-92042-5(1)) Marvel Worldwide, Inc.

Immonen, Stuart. Amazing Spider-Man: Worldwide Vol. 6. 2017. (ENG.). 160p. (J). (gr. 4-17). pap. 19.99 (978-1-302-90293-3(8)) Marvel Worldwide, Inc.

Immonen, Stuart, et al. Captain America: Sam Wilson - the Complete Collection Vol. 1. 2020. (ENG.). 488p. (YA). (gr. 8-17). pap. 39.99 (978-1-302-92325-9(0)) Marvel Worldwide, Inc.

—New Avengers by Brian Michael Bendis: the Complete Collection Vol. 6. 2017. (ENG.). 392p. (YA). (gr. 8-17). pap. 34.99 (978-1-302-90867-6(7)) Marvel Worldwide, Inc.

—Showdown on the Smuggler's Moon: Volume 2. Aaron, Jason. 2016. (Star Wars: Showdown on the Smuggler's Moon Ser.). (ENG.). 24p. (J). (gr. 6-12). lib. bdg. 27.07 (978-1-61479-555-1(X), 24389, Graphic Novels) Spotlight.

—Showdown on the Smuggler's Moon: Volume 3. Aaron, Jason. 2016. (Star Wars: Showdown on the Smuggler's Moon Ser.). (ENG.). 24p. (J). (gr. 6-12). lib. bdg. 27.07 (978-1-61479-556-8(8), 24390, Graphic Novels) Spotlight.

—Showdown on the Smuggler's Moon: Volume 4. Aaron, Jason. 2016. (Star Wars: Showdown on the Smuggler's Moon Ser.). (ENG.). 24p. (J). (gr. 6-12). lib. bdg. 27.07 (978-1-61479-557-5(6), 24391, Graphic Novels) Spotlight.

—Showdown on the Smuggler's Moon: Volume 5. Aaron, Jason. 2016. (Star Wars: Showdown on the Smuggler's Moon Ser.). (ENG.). 24p. (J). (gr. 6-12). lib. bdg. 27.07 (978-1-61479-558-2(4), 24392, Graphic Novels) Spotlight.

—Showdown on the Smuggler's Moon: Volume 6. Aaron, Jason. 2016. (Star Wars: Showdown on the Smuggler's Moon Ser.). (ENG.). 24p. (J). (gr. 6-12). lib. bdg. 27.07 (978-1-61479-559-9(2), 24393, Graphic Novels) Spotlight.

Immonen, Stuart, jt. illus. see Larroca, Salvador.

Imodraj. Baa, Baa, Black Sheep. Everett, Melissa. 2013. (ENG.). 20p. (J). (gr. -1-3). bds. 8.99 (978-1-77093-537-2(1)) Flowerpot Children's Pr. Inc. CAN. Dist: Cardinal Pubs. Group.

—Baa, Baa, Black Sheep. Everett, Melissa. 2017. (ENG.). 24p. (J). (gr. -1-3). (978-1-4867-1259-5(2)) Flowerpot Children's Pr. Inc.

—The Brave Little Tailor. Austin, Patrick. 2014. (ENG.). 16p. (J). (gr. -1-3). 7.99 (978-1-4867-0016-5(0)) Flowerpot Children's Pr. Inc. CAN. Dist: Cardinal Pubs. Group.

—Diddle Diddle Dumpling. Everett, Melissa. 2013. (ENG.). 20p. (J). (gr. -1-1). bds. 8.99 (978-1-77093-522-8(3)) Flowerpot Children's Pr. Inc. CAN. Dist: Cardinal Pubs. Group.

—Jack & Jill. Everett, Melissa. Paiva, Johannah Gilman, ed. 2014. (ENG.). 20p. (J). (gr. -1-1). 8.99 (978-1-77093-843-4(5)) Flowerpot Children's Pr. Inc. CAN. Dist: Cardinal Pubs. Group.

Impey, Martin. Hetty's New Hat. Nash, Margaret. 2005. (Reading Corner Ser.). 24p. (J). (gr. k-3). lib. bdg. 22.80 (978-1-59771-007-7(5)) Sea-To-Sea Pubns.

—Rapunzel. 2006. (First Fairy Tales Ser.). 31p. (J). (gr. -1-3). lib. bdg. 28.50 (978-1-59771-076-3(8)) Sea-To-Sea Pubns.

Imports Dragon Studio Staff. Squeezamals: Adorable Sticker & Activity Book: More Than 100 Stickers. 2019. (Squeezamals Ser.). (ENG.). 32p. (J). (gr. -1). 5.99 (978-2-89802-069-8(9), CrackBoom! Bks.) Chouette Publishing CAN. Dist: Publishers Group West (PGW).

Imports Dragon Studios. Squeezamals: Wonderland (Little Detectives) A Look-And-Find Book. 2020. (Squeezamals Ser.). 14p. (J). (gr. -1-1). bds. 9.99 (978-2-89802-166-4(0), CrackBoom! Bks.) Chouette Publishing CAN. Dist: Publishers Group West (PGW).

Imports Dragon Studios Staff. Sunny Bunnies: Welcome to Earth (Little Detectives) A Look-And-Find Book. 2019. (Sunny Bunnies Ser.). 14p. (J). (gr. -1-1). bds. 11.99 (978-2-89802-068-1(0), CrackBoom! Bks.) Chouette Publishing CAN. Dist: Publishers Group West (PGW).

Imre Geis, Alissa. Our Friendship Rules, 1 vol. Moss, Peggy. 2nd ed. 2017. (ENG.). 36p. (J). (gr. 2-6). pap. 8.95 (978-0-88448-596-4(X), 884596) Tilbury Hse. Pubs.

Imtiaz, Hina. C Jumped over Three Pots & a Pan & Landed Smack in the Garbage Can, 1 vol. Jane, Pamela. 2019. (ENG.). 40p. (J). 14.99 (978-0-7643-5795-4(6), 16293) Schiffer Publishing, Ltd.

In Den Bosch, Nicole. Beautiful Beads. Ross, Kathy. 2009. (Girl Crafts Ser.). 48p. (J). (gr. 2-6). pap. 7.95 (978-1-58013-884-0(5), First Avenue Editions) Lerner Publishing Group.

—Creative Kitchen Crafts. Ross, Kathy. 2010. (Girl Crafts Ser.). (ENG.). 48p. (gr. 2-5). pap. 7.95 (978-1-58013-886-4(1), First Avenue Editions) Lerner Publishing Group.

—Fairy World Crafts. Ross, Kathy. 2008. (Girl Crafts Ser.). (ENG.). 48p. (gr. 2-5). per. 7.95 (978-0-8225-9024-8(7), First Avenue Editions) Lerner Publishing Group.

—Girlfriends' Get-Together Craft Book. Ross, Kathy. 2007. (Girl Crafts Ser.). (ENG.). 48p. (gr. 2-5). lib. bdg. 26.60 (978-0-7613-3408-8(4), Millbrook Pr.) Lerner Publishing Group.

in den Bosch, Nicole. The Mouse in the Matzah Factory, Vol. Medoff, Francine. 2003. (ENG.). 32p. (J). (gr. -1-3). pap. 6.95 (978-1-58013-048-6(8), Kar-Ben Publishing) Lerner Publishing Group.

In-Soo, Ra. King of Hell, 6 vols., Vol. 6. Jae-Hwan, Kim. Na, Lauren, tr. from KOR. rev. ed. 2004. 192p. pap. 9.99 (978-1-59182-484-8(2)) TOKYOPOP, Inc.

Inc, Learning Dodo. Alphabet Book of Uppercase Letters (Workbook) Inc, Learning Dodo. 2019. (Education Series, Reading Ser.: Vol. 1). (ENG.). 58p. (J). pap. (978-1-9994773-5-6(9)) Learning Dodo.

Inc., Loter. Mickey Mouse Clubhouse: 8-Book Set. Brooke, Susan Rich. 2019. (ENG.). 192p. (J). (978-1-5037-4990-0(8), 504393b4-7a9a-47cd-ad8d-ab1b433becad, p i kids) Phoenix International Publications, Inc.

Inc., Loter & Storybook Art Team, Disney. Mickey Mouse Clubhouse: Portable Keyboard & 8-Book Library. Keast, Jennifer H. (Play-A-Song Ser.). (ENG.). 192p. (J). 2019. (978-1-5037-4995-5(9), b86a9c6a-6667-4605-89ae-f732c7e07397); 2014. (978-1-4508-8189-0(0), 66a84663-1cc0-4af3-95da-5c5c4e4199a5) Phoenix International Publications, Inc. (p i kids).

Incrocci, Rick. Bible Stories for Tiny Tots. Larsen, Carolyn. 2008. 35p. (J). bds. (978-1-86920-241-5(4)) Christian Art Pubs.

—Little Angels Bible Storybook. Larsen, Carolyn. 2012. (ENG.). 432p. (J). 16.99 (978-1-4143-7022-4(9), 4606012) Tyndale Hse. Pubs.

—Psalms for Toddlers. 2012. 32p. (J). pap. 12.00 (978-1-935014-43-0(9)) Hutchings, John Pubs.

—See It/Say It Bible Storybook. Adams, Anne. 2006. 191p. 12.99 (978-0-7814-4403-3(9)) Cook, David C.

—Stories about Jesus for Little Ones. Larsen, Carolyn. 2008. 35p. (gr. -1-k). bds. (978-1-86920-173-9(6)) Christian Art Pubs.

—What Does the Bible Say about That? Larsen, Carolyn. 2009. (ENG.). 352p. (J). (gr. 3-7). pap. 19.99 (978-1-4335-0213-2(5)) Crossway.

Indigo, Bre. Meg, Jo, Beth, & Amy: a Graphic Novel: A Modern Retelling of Little Women. Terciero, Rey. 2019. 240p. (J). (gr. 3-7). pap. 12.99 (978-0-316-52288-5(0)) Little, Brown Bks. for Young Readers.

Infante, Charli. More Spooky Kine Tales of Supernatural Hawaii. Brown, Christian. 2018. (ENG.). 60p. (J). pap. 6.99 (978-1-7202-7612-8(9)) Independently Published.

Infante, Francesc. El Pastorcito Mentiroso. Bailer, Darice et al. 2007. (SPA & ENG.). 28p. (J). (978-0-545-02960-5(0)) Scholastic, Inc.

Infante, Sara. Bodies of Water. Higgins, Nadia. 2017. (Water All Around Us Ser.). (ENG.). 24p. (J). (gr. 1-3). lib. bdg. 33.99 incl. audio compact disk (978-1-68410-011-8(9), 31529) Cantata Learning.

—Get Me Out of This Book: Rules & Tools for Being Brave. Dakos, Kalli & Cholette, Deborah. 2019. 32p. (J). (gr. -1-3). 17.99 (978-0-8234-3862-4(7)) Holiday Hse., Inc.

—Hop on the Water Cycle. Higgins, Nadia. 2017. (Water All Around Us Ser.). (ENG.). 24p. (J). (gr. 1-3). lib. bdg. 33.99 incl. audio compact disk (978-1-68410-035-4(6), 31530) Cantata Learning.

—Types of Precipitation. Higgins, Nadia. 2017. (Water All Around Us Ser.). (ENG.). 24p. (J). (gr. 1-3). lib. bdg. 33.99 incl. audio compact disk (978-1-68410-057-6(7), 31531) Cantata Learning.

—What Kind of Clouds? Higgins, Nadia. 2017. (Water All Around Us Ser.). (ENG.). 24p. (J). (gr. 1-3). lib. bdg. 33.99 incl. audio compact disk (978-1-68410-061-3(5), 31532) Cantata Learning.

Infantino, Carmine & Giella, Joe. The Flash. Kanigher, Robert & Broome, John. rev. ed. 2007. (Showcase Presents Ser.). (ENG.). 552p. (YA). (gr. 11-18). pap. 16.99 (978-1-4012-1327-5(8)) DC Comics.

Infantino, Carmine & Vosburg, Mike. Star Wars Legends Epic Collection: the Original Marvel Years Vol. 2. 2017. (ENG.). 448p. (J). (gr. 4-17). pap. 39.99 (978-1-302-90680-1(1)) Marvel Worldwide, Inc.

Infomon, Catherine. Thumbelina: A Favorite Story in Rhythm & Rhyme. Peale, Jonathan. 2018. (Fairy Tale Tunes Ser.). (ENG.). 24p. (J). (gr. -1-3). lib. bdg. 33.99 (978-1-68410-382-9(7), 140350) Cantata Learning.

Ingham, Julie. Sweet Treats. Eliot, Hannah. 2014. (Dream Doodle Draw! Ser.). (ENG.). 96p. (J). (gr. -1-2). pap. 7.99 (978-1-4814-0452-5(0), Little Simon) Little Simon.

Inglese, Judith. I See the Sun in Afghanistan. King, Dedie. Vahidi, Mohd, tr. 2011. (I See the Sun in ... Ser.: 3). (PER.). 40p. (J). (gr. k). pap. 12.95 (978-0-9818720-8-7(5)) Satya Hse. Pubns.

—I See the Sun in India. King, Dedie. ed. 2019. (I See the Sun In ... Ser.: 9). (ENG.). 40p. (J). (gr. k-4). pap. 12.95 (978-1-935874-35-5(7)) Satya Hse. Pubns.

—I See the Sun in Mexico, 1 vol. King, Dedie. ed. 2012. (I See the Sun Ser.: 5). (ENG.). 40p. (J). (gr. 1-7). pap. 12.95 (978-1-935874-14-0(4)) Satya Hse. Pubns.

—I See the Sun in Russia. King, Dedie. Ossipova, Irina, tr. ed. 2012. (I See the Sun Ser.: 4). (RUS.). 40p. (J). (gr. 1-7). 12.95 (978-1-935874-08-9(X)) Satya Hse. Pubns.

—I See the Sun in the USA. King, Dedie. 2018. (I See the Sun In ... Ser.: 8). (ENG.). 40p. (J). (gr. k-4). pap. 12.95 (978-1-935874-36-2(5)) Satya Hse. Pubns.

—I See the Sun in Turkey. King, Dedie. Sen, Hilal, tr. ed. 2017. (I See the Sun In ... Ser.: 7). (TUR.). 44p. (J). (gr. k-10). 12.95 (978-1-935874-34-8(9)) Satya Hse. Pubns.

Inglese, Judith. I Have a Friend. Inglese, Judith. ed. 2014. (ENG.). 40p. (J). 17.95 (978-1-935874-22-5(5)) Satya Hse. Pubns.

Inglish, Nick. Bamibee, la Abejita Asombrosa. Short, J. Rodney. 2018. (SPA.). 28p. (J). (gr. 1-6). pap. 9.95 (978-1-7320129-3-6(8)) JRSK Bks.

Ingman, Bruce. Double Pink. Feiffer, Kate. 2013. (ENG.). 32p. (J). (gr. -1-1). 21.19 (978-0-689-87190-0(2)) Simon & Schuster, Inc.

—Double Pink. Feiffer, Kate. 2013. (ENG.). 32p. (J). (gr. -1-1). 8.99 (978-1-4424-6033-1(4), Simon & Schuster/Paula Wiseman Bks.) Simon & Schuster/Paula Wiseman Bks.

—Everybody Was a Baby Once: And Other Poems. Ahlberg, Allan. 2010. (ENG.). 64p. (J). (gr. -1-k). 15.99 (978-0-7636-4682-0(2)) Candlewick Pr.

—The Hole Story. Bright, Paul. 2017. (Andersen Press Picture Bks.). (ENG.). 32p. (gr. -1-3). 35.99 (978-1-5124-3972-4(X)) Lerner Publishing Group.

—The Pencil. Ahlberg, Allan. 2012. (ENG.). 48p. (J). (gr. -1-3). pap. 6.99 (978-0-7636-6088-8(4)) Candlewick Pr.

—The Pencil. Ahlberg, Allan. ed. 2012. lib. bdg. 17.20 (978-0-606-26942-1(8)) Turtleback.

—Previously. Ahlberg, Allan. 2011. (ENG.). 32p. (J). (gr. -1-3). pap. 6.99 (978-0-7636-5304-0(7)) Candlewick Pr.

—The Runaway Dinner. Ahlberg, Allan. 2006. (ENG.). 40p. (J). (gr. -1-1). 21.19 (978-0-7636-3142-0(6)) Candlewick Pr.

Ingpen, Robert. The Adventures of Tom Sawyer. Twain, Mark. 2020. (ENG.). 208p. (J). (gr. 2-4). 24.99 (978-1-78675-055-6(4)) Palazzo Editions, Ltd. GBR. Dist: Independent Pubs. Group.

—Alice's Adventures in Wonderland: Abridged Edition for Younger Readers. Carroll, Lewis. 2018. (Palazzo Abridged Classics Ser.). (ENG.). 64p. (J). (gr. k-2). 16.99 (978-1-78675-045-7(7)) Palazzo Editions, Ltd. GBR. Dist: Independent Pubs. Group.

—Around the World in Eighty Days. Verne, Jules. 2020.Tr. of Tour du Monde en Quatre-Vingts Jours. (ENG.). 224p. (J). (gr. 2-4). 24.99 (978-1-78675-056-3(2)) Palazzo Editions, Ltd. GBR. Dist: Independent Pubs. Group.

—A Christmas Carol. Dickens, Charles. 2018. (Palazzo Abridged Classics Ser.). (ENG.). 64p. (Orig.). (J). (gr. k-2). 16.99 (978-1-78675-050-1(3)) Palazzo Editions, Ltd. GBR. Dist: Independent Pubs. Group.

—The Jungle Book: Mowgli's Story. Kipling, Rudyard. abr. ed. 2018. (Palazzo Abridged Classics Ser.). (ENG.). 64p. (J). (gr. k-2). 16.99 (978-1-78675-044-0(9)) Palazzo Editions, Ltd. GBR. Dist: Independent Pubs. Group.

—Just So Stories. Kipling, Rudyard. 2nd ed. 2018. (ENG.). 192p. (J). (gr. k-2). 24.99 (978-1-78675-051-8(1)) Palazzo Editions, Ltd. GBR. Dist: Independent Pubs. Group.

—Pinocchio. Collodi, Carlo. 2020. (ENG.). 208p. (J). (gr. 2-4). 24.99 (978-1-78675-036-5(8)) Palazzo Editions, Ltd. GBR. Dist: Independent Pubs. Group.

—Treasure Island. Stevenson, R. L. 2018. (Palazzo Abridged Classics Ser.). (ENG.). 64p. (J). (gr. k-2). 16.99 (978-1-78675-047-1(3)) Palazzo Editions, Ltd. GBR. Dist: Independent Pubs. Group.

Ingpen, Robert. The Dream Keeper. Ingpen, Robert. 2019. (Minedition Classic Ser.). 32p. (J). (gr. k-4). 12.00 (978-988-8341-93-1(6), Minedition) Neugebauer, Michael (Publishing) Limited HKG. Dist: Penguin Random Hse. LLC.

Ingpen, Robert R. Alice's Adventures in Wonderland. Carroll, Lewis. 2009. (Sterling Illustrated Classics Ser.). (ENG.). 192p. (J). (gr. 5-18). 19.95 (978-1-4027-6835-4(4)) Sterling Publishing Co., Inc.

—Broken Beaks. Lachenmeyer, Nathaniel. 2005. 32p. (J). 15.95 (978-0-85572-335-4(1)) Warwick Publishing CAN. Dist: Two Rivers Distribution.

—Dickens: His Work & His World. Rosen, Michael. 2005. (ENG.). 96p. (YA). (gr. 7-11). 19.99 (978-0-7636-2752-2(6)) Candlewick Pr.

—The Jungle Book. Kipling, Rudyard. 2012. (Sterling Illustrated Classics Ser.). (ENG.). 192p. (J). (gr. 5-8). 19.95 (978-1-4027-8284-8(5)) Sterling Publishing Co., Inc.

—Lifetimes: The Beautiful Way to Explain Death to Children. Mellonie, Bryan. 2006. (ENG.). 40p. (gr. 2-18). 15.00 (978-0-553-34402-8(1)) Perfection Learning Corp.

—Peter Pan & Wendy: Centenary Edition. Barrie, J. M. 2004. (ENG.). 216p. (J). (978-1-897035-12-2(8), Blue Heron Bks.) Raincoast Bk. Distribution.

—Scott y Amundsen: La Conquista del Polo Sur. Hao, K. T. & Fulla, Monserrat. 2006.Tr. of Scott & Amundsen, The Conquest of the South Pole. (SPA.). (J). (gr. 6-8). 9.60 (978-84-316-7172-3(6), W32815) Vicens-Vives, Editorial, S.A. ESP. Dist: Lectorum Pubns., Inc.

—Shakespeare: His Work & His World. Rosen, Michael. 2006. 96p. (J). (gr. 7-11). pap. 10.99 (978-0-7636-3201-4(5)) Candlewick Pr.

—Storm Boy. Thiele, Colin. 40th anniv. ed. 2006. 60p. (J). (gr. -1-3). pap. 7.95 (978-1-86436-804-8(7)) New Holland Pubs. Pty. Ltd. AUS. Dist: Tuttle Publishing.

—Treasure Island. Stevenson, Robert Louis. 2006. (ENG.). 192p. (J). (978-1-897035-30-6(6), Blue Heron Bks.) Raincoast Bk. Distribution.

—The Wind in the Willows. Grahame, Kenneth. 2012. (Sterling Illustrated Classics Ser.). (ENG.). 224p. (J). (gr. 2-8). 24.95 (978-1-4027-8283-1(7)) Sterling Publishing Co., Inc.

Ingram, Anne. A Visit to Hawaii. Holm, Barbara. 2005. 32p. (J). pap. 5.95 (978-0-9772200-0-7(1)) Visit to Hawaii, A.

Ingram, Charles. Seven Spectral: The Orange World Outlaw. Wicks, Valerie. Lang, Leslie, ed. 2013. 342p. pap. 12.99 (978-0-9912594-0-3(8)) Wicks, Valerie.

Ingram, Chris. Superhighway. Oldman, James. 2012. 184p. pap. (978-1-78176-206-6(6)) FeedARead.com.

Ingram, Glenda Brown. Uga Hunkers down in Athens Town. Weaver, Jack. 2004. (J). (978-0-9773370-0-2(6)) Weaver, Jack R. Company.

Ingram, Jan. Purple Frogs & Pumpkin Seeds. Lovvorn, Ann R. 2008. 44p. per. 24.95 (978-1-4241-8734-8(6)) America Star Bks.

Ingram, Mark. Squirrelly Sally. Ingram, Doreen. 2019. (ENG.). 62p. (J). (gr. k-6). 15.95 **(978-0-9915252-7-0(2)**, Susanna Lagoon Bks.) J. K. Eckert & Co., Inc.

Ingram, Rella. In the Hills of Arkansas. Stamps, Sarah. Stamps, Rich, ed. 2016. (ENG.). (J). pap. 24.95 (978-1-68394-328-0(7)) America Star Bks.

Ingram, Syria. The Day of the Ravens. Ingram, Bradford. 2020. (ENG.). 60p. (J). 38.99 **(978-1-63050-506-6(4))**; pap. 28.99 **(978-1-63050-505-9(6))** Salem Author Services.

Ingram, Zoe. The Last Message Received. Trunko, Emily. 2017. (ENG.). 176p. (YA). (gr. 9). 14.99 (978-0-399-55776-7(8), Crown Books For Young Readers) Random Hse. Children's Bks.

—Press Out & Color: Birds. Nosy Crow. 2017. (ENG.). 20p. (J). (gr. 2-5). 15.99 (978-0-7636-9532-3(7), Nosy Crow) Candlewick Pr.

—Press Out & Color: Butterflies. Nosy Crow. 2017. (ENG.). 20p. (J). (gr. 5). 15.99 (978-0-7636-9506-4(8), Nosy Crow) Candlewick Pr.

Ingram, Zoe. America the Beautiful to Color: Road Trip Adventures to Color. Ingram, Zoe. 2017. (ENG.). 96p. (J). (gr. -1). pap. 15.99 (978-0-06-256990-5(2)) HarperCollins Pubs.

—Wise Words to Color: Inspiration to Live & Color By. Ingram, Zoe. 2016. (ENG.). 96p. (J). (gr. -1). pap. 15.99 (978-0-06-248192-4(4)) HarperCollins Pubs.

Inherited, Art. The Day Before Tomorrow: Hush Now, It's Time to Take Your Nap. Stevens, Dannie Jean. 2019. (ENG.). 30p. (J). pap. 16.99 **(978-1-7283-3214-7(1))** AuthorHouse.

Ink, Breadcrumbs. The Dragon Grammar Book: Grammar for Kids, Dragons, & the Whole Kingdom. Robinson, Diane Mae. 2017. (ENG.). 140p. (J). pap. (978-1-988714-01-1(X)) Robinson, Diane Mae.

Ink, Bruce. Party Pups: The Game of Prepositional Fun! Webber, Sharon et al. 2011. (J). 39.95 net. (978-1-60723-002-1(X)) Super Duper Pubns.

Ink, Bruce & Golliher, Bill. Webber HearBuilder Following Directions Fun Sheets: Hbbk55. Holland, Beth. 2011. 216p. (J). spiral bd. 34.95 net. (978-1-58650-992-7(6)) Super Duper Pubns.

Ink, Bruce & Schwartz, Marty. Early Articulation Roundup! Bk305. Foster, Beverly & Foster, Stacy Lynn. 2003. (J). per. 34.95 (978-1-58650-284-3(0)) Super Duper Pubns.

Ink, Lancman. El Baúl de los Oficios: Un Libro Sobre Las Vocales. Chaktoura, Julia. 2008. (Baúl / Treasure Chest Collection). (SPA.). 16p. (J). (gr. -1-1). pap. 6.99 (978-1-63113-905-5(3)) Santillana USA Publishing Co., Inc.

—Chaucha y Palito. Walsh, Maria Elena. 2003. (SPA.). 134p. (J). (gr. 5-8). pap. 11.95 (978-950-511-615-7(2)) Santillana USA Publishing Co., Inc.

—Hotel Pioho's Palace. 2003. (SPA.). 164p. (J). (gr. 5-8). pap. 12.95 (978-950-511-781-9(7)) Santillana USA Publishing Co., Inc.

Inklink Staff. Uncover Nature. Brookes, Olivia. 2009. (Hide-and-Seek Visual Adventures Ser.). 24p. (J). (gr. 2-5). lib. bdg. 25.60 (978-1-60754-655-9(8)) Windmill Bks.

Inklink, Studio. The Human Body in Action. Gallavotti, Barbara. Shapiro, Brett, tr. from ITA. 2004. 123p. (J). (gr. 4-8). reprint ed. pap. 9.00 (978-0-7567-8334-1(8)) DIANE Publishing Co.

Inkpen, Chloe. I Love You, Fred. Inkpen, Mick. 2019. (ENG.). 32p. (J). (gr. -1-1). 17.99 (978-1-5344-1475-4(4), Aladdin) Simon & Schuster Children's Publishing.

—I Will Love You Anyway. Inkpen, Mick. 2016. (ENG.). 32p. (J). (gr. -1-1). 17.99 (978-1-4814-7099-5(X), Aladdin) Simon & Schuster Children's Publishing.

Inkpen, Mick. Bible Stories & Tales Green Collection. Butterworth, Nick. ed. 2016. (ENG.). 168p. (J). (gr. k-2). 12.99 (978-1-78128-290-8(0)) Lion Hudson PLC GBR. Dist: Independent Pubs. Group.

—The House on the Rock. Butterworth, Nick. ed. 2008. (ENG.). 32p. pap. (978-1-85985-749-6(3), Candle Bks.) Lion Hudson PLC.

—Lost Sheep. Butterworth, Nick. ed. 2008. (ENG.). 32p. (J). (gr. k-2). pap. 5.99 (978-1-85985-746-5(9)) Lion Hudson PLC GBR. Dist: Independent Pubs. Group.

Inkpen, Mick, jt. illus. see Butterworth, Nick.

Innerebner, Jessika von. A Bad Day at Pirate School. Gohmann, Johanna. 2017. (Pirate Kids Ser.). (ENG.). 32p. (J). (gr. -1-3). lib. bdg. 28.50 (978-1-5321-3038-0(4), 27040, Calico Chapter Bks) Magic Wagon.

—The Great Treasure Hunt. Gohmann, Johanna. 2017. (Pirate Kids Ser.). (ENG.). 32p. (J). (gr. -1-3). lib. bdg. 28.50 (978-1-5321-3039-7(2), 27041, Calico Chapter Bks) Magic Wagon.

—A Spooky Day at Sea. Gohmann, Johanna. 2017. (Pirate Kids Ser.). (ENG.). 32p. (J). (gr. -1-3). lib. bdg. 28.50 (978-1-5321-3040-3(6), 27042, Calico Chapter Bks) Magic Wagon.

—The Very Quiet Parrot. Gohmann, Johanna. 2017. (Pirate Kids Ser.). (ENG.). 32p. (J). (gr. -1-3). lib. bdg. 28.50 *(978-1-5321-3041-0(4)*, 27043, Calico Chapter Bks) Magic Wagon.

—El Viene Conmigo. Schmauss, Judy Kentor. 2016. (Early Rising Readers Ser.). (SPA.). 16p. (J). (gr. 1-1). 6.67 *(978-1-4788-3761-9(6))* Newmark Learning LLC.

Innerst, Stacy. The Beatles Were Fab (and They Were Funny) Krull, Kathleen & Brewer, Paul. 2013. (ENG.). 40p. (J). (gr. 1-4). lib. bdg. 16.99 *(978-0-547-50991-4(X)*, 1443649) Houghton Mifflin Harcourt Publishing Co.

—The Book Rescuer: How a Mensch from Massachusetts Saved Yiddish Literature for Generations to Come. Macy, Sue. 2019. (ENG.). 48p. (J). (gr. k-3). 17.99 *(978-1-4814-7220-3(8))* Simon & Schuster.

—Levi Strauss Gets a Bright Idea: A Fairly Fabricated Story of a Pair of Pants. Johnston, Tony. 2011. (ENG.). 32p. (J). (gr. -1-3). 17.99 *(978-0-15-206145-6(2)*, 1198451) Houghton Mifflin Harcourt Publishing Co.

—Lincoln Tells a Joke: How Laughter Saved the President (and the Country) Krull, Kathleen & Brewer, Paul. 2010. (ENG.). 40p. (J). (gr. 1-4). 17.99 *(978-0-15-206639-0(X)*, 1199695) Houghton Mifflin Harcourt Publishing Co.

—M Is for Music. Krull, Kathleen. 2009. (ENG.). 48p. (J). (gr. -1-3). pap. 7.99 *(978-0-15-206479-2(6)*, 1099014) Houghton Mifflin Harcourt Publishing Co.

—Ruth Bader Ginsburg: The Case of R. B. G. vs. Inequality. Winter, Jonah. 2017. (ENG.). 48p. (J). (gr. 1-4). 18.95 *(978-1-4197-2559-3(9)*, Abrams Bks. for Young Readers) Abrams, Inc.

Innerst, Stacy. Saving Lady Liberty: Joseph Pulitzer's Fight for the Statue of Liberty. Friddell, Claudia. 2020. (ENG.). 48p. (J). (gr. 2-5). 18.99 ***(978-1-68437-130-3(9)***, Calkins Creek) Boyds Mills Pr.

Innerst, Stacy. Thomas Jefferson Grows a Nation. Thomas, Peggy. 2015. (ENG.). 48p. (J). (gr. 4-7). 16.95 *(978-1-62091-628-5(2)*, Calkins Creek) Boyds Mills Pr.

Innes, Calvin. Mini Mysteries & Kooky Spookies. Nass, Marcia & Campisi, Stephanie. 2007. 176p. per. 6.99 *(978-0-9795364-2-7(1))* Chowder Bay Bks.

Innocente, Agnese, et al. Disney Mulan's Adventure Journal: the Palace of Secrets. Cleary, Rhona. 2020. (ENG.). 96p. (J). (gr. 3-7). pap. 10.99 *(978-1-5067-1653-4(9)*, Dark Horse Books) Dark Horse Comics.

Innocenti, Roberto. The Adventures of Pinocchio. Collodi, Carlo. rev. ed. 2004. (ENG.). 192p. (J). (gr. 1-3). 35.00 *(978-1-56846-190-8(9))* Creative Co., The.

—Christmas Carol. Dickens, Charles. 2005. 152p. (J). (gr. 4-6). 35.00 *(978-1-56846-182-3(8))* Creative Co., The.

—Cinderella. Perrault, Charles. 2013. (ENG.). 32p. (J). (gr. 1-17). pap. 7.99 *(978-0-89812-828-4(5)*, Creative Paperbacks) Creative Co., The.

—Erika's Story. Vander Zee, Ruth. (ENG.). 24p. (J). (gr. 1-3). 2013. pap. 10.99 *(978-0-89812-891-8(9)*, Creative Paperbacks); 2003. 19.99 *(978-1-56846-176-2(3))* Creative Co., The.

—The House. Lewis, J. Patrick. 2009. (ENG.). 64p. (J). (gr. 4-7). 19.95 *(978-1-56846-201-1(8)*, 1300178, Creative Editions) Creative Co., The.

—The Last Resort. Lewis, J. Patrick. 2003. (ENG.). 48p. (J). (gr. 1-3). 24.99 *(978-1-56846-172-4(0)*, Creative Editions) Creative Co., The.

—The Nutcracker. Hoffmann, E. T. A. 2017. (ENG.). 136p. (J). (gr. 3-5). 29.99 *(978-1-56846-313-1(8)*, Creative Editions) Creative Co., The.

—Rose Blanche. Gallaz, Christophe. 2011. (ENG.). 32p. (J). (gr. 5-17). pap. 10.99 *(978-0-89812-385-2(2))* Creative Co., The.

Inoue, Kazurou. Midori Days. Inoue, Kazurou. 2006. (Midori Days Ser.). (ENG.). 208p. Vol. 4. pap. 9.99 *(978-1-4215-0254-0(2))*; Vol. 5. pap. 9.99 *(978-1-4215-0287-8(9))*; Vol. 6. pap. 9.99 *(978-1-4215-0495-7(2))*; Vol. 7. pap. 9.99 *(978-1-4215-0496-4(0))* Viz Media.

Inoue, Kazurou & Inoue, Kazurou. Midori Days, Vol. 1. Inoue, Kazurou. 2005. (Midori Days Ser.). (ENG.). 200p. pap. 9.99 *(978-1-59116-905-5(4))* Viz Media.

Inoue, Kazurou, jt. illus. see Inoue, Kazurou.

Inoue, Takehiko. Vagabond Vol. 14: The Letter. Inoue, Takehiko. 2004. (Vagabond Ser.: 14). (ENG.). 200p. pap. 9.95 *(978-1-59116-452-4(4))* Viz Media.

—Vagabond, Vol. 6, Vol. 6. Inoue, Takehiko. 2003. (Vagabond Ser.: 6). (ENG.). 216p. pap. 9.95 *(978-1-56931-894-2(8))* Viz Media.

Inoue, Takehiko, jt. illus. see Yoshikawa, Eiji.

Inouye, Carol. Anthony Best: A Picture Book about Asperger's. Fahy, Davene. 2020. (ENG.). 32p. (J). (gr. -1-2). pap. 9.99 ***(978-1-5107-5815-5(1)***, Sky Pony Pr.) Skyhorse Publishing Co., Inc.

Inouye, Carol. Anthony Best: A Picture Book about Asperger's. Fahy, Davene & Mueller, Dagmar H. 2013. 32p. (J). (gr. -1-3). 16.95 *(978-1-61608-961-0(X)*, 608961, Sky Pony Pr.) Skyhorse Publishing Co., Inc.

—Charlie, Who Couldn't Say His Name. Fahy, Davene. 2004. 32p. (J). per. 12.95 *(978-0-9746589-0-2(1))* Limerock Bks.

—Kids Cooking Without a Stove: A Cookbook for Young Children. Paul, Aileen. rev. ed. 2005. 64p. (J). pap. 10.95 *(978-0-86534-060-2(9))* Sunstone Pr.

Instructors from Clark College Economic & Bradley, Katie. Work: Everyday Ethiopian Life in Amharic & English. Ready Set Go Books. 2020. (ENG.). 36p. (J). pap. 9.99 ***(978-1-6541-4990-1(X))*** Independently Published.

Interactive, Vipah. Curious George & the Dump Truck, 1 vol. Rey, H. A. & Rey, Margret. 2008. (Curious George Ser.). (ENG.). 24p. (J). (gr. k-3). lib. bdg. 27.07 *(978-1-59961-410-6(3)*, 5051, Picture Bk.) Spotlight.

—Curious George Goes Camping, 1 vol. Rey, Margret & Rey, H. A. 2008. (Curious George Ser.). (ENG.). 24p. (J). (gr. k-3). lib. bdg. 27.07 *(978-1-59961-414-4(6)*, 5055, Picture Bk.) Spotlight.

—Curious George Goes to a Movie, 1 vol. Rey, H. A. & Rey, Margret. 2008. (Curious George Ser.). (ENG.). 24p. (J). (gr. k-3). lib. bdg. 27.07 *(978-1-59961-415-1(4)*, 5056, Picture Bk.) Spotlight.

Internicola, Annie Dwyer. Hay un Perro Sobre la Mesa Del Comedor. Maginnis, Elizabeth. 2018. (Xist Kids Spanish Bks.). (SPA.). 32p. (J). (gr. -1-3). pap. 9.99 *(978-1-5324-0715-4(7))* Xist Publishing.

—If a Dog Could Wear a Hat. Maginnis, Elizabeth. 2018. (ENG.). 32p. (J). (gr. -1-3). pap. 9.99 *(978-1-5324-0758-1(0))* Xist Publishing.

—There's a Dog on the Dining Room Table / Hay un Perro Sobre la Mesa Del Comedor. Maginnis, Elizabeth. 2018. (Xist Kids Bilingual Spanish English Ser.). (ENG & SPA.). 32p. (J). (gr. -1-3). pap. 9.99 *(978-1-5324-0689-8(4))* Xist Publishing.

Intessimone, Bridgette J. Cracking the Mystery of Money. Potts, Thomas W. 2018. (ENG.). 200p. (YA). 26.99 *(978-1-5320-3633-0(7))*; pap. 13.99 *(978-1-5320-3631-6(0))* iUniverse, Inc.

Intrater, Roberta Grobel, photos by. Peek-a-Boo, You! Intrater, Roberta Grobel. 2nd rev. l.t. ed. 2005. 14p. (J). 14.99 *(978-0-9764985-0-6(2))* 1212 Pr.

Intriago, Patricia. Dot. Intriago, Patricia. 2011. (ENG.). 40p. (J). (gr. -1-1). 17.99 *(978-0-374-31835-2(2)*, 900071516, Farrar, Straus & Giroux (BYR)) Farrar, Straus & Giroux.

Inui, Sekihiko. Comic Party, Vol. 4. Inui, Sekihiko, creator. rev. ed. 2004. 192p. pap. 14.99 *(978-1-59532-584-6(0)*, Tokyopop Adult) TOKYOPOP, Inc.

Inuit artists and printmakers of Kinngait Studios. Owls & Loons. Burke, Zoe. 2016. 24p. (J). bds. 10.95 *(978-0-7649-7542-4(0)*, POMEGRANATE KIDS) Pomegranate Communications, Inc.

Inzerillo, Joe. Jesus My Friend. Inzerillo, Kristina. 2019. (ENG.). 28p. (J). ***(978-1-7340735-1-5(9))***; pap. ***(978-1-7340735-0-8(0))*** Tellwell Talent.

Iosa, Ann. I Need a Little Help. Schulz, Kathy. 2011. (Rookie Ready to Learn — All about Me! Ser.). 32p. (J). (gr. -1-k). lib. bdg. 25.00 *(978-0-531-26526-0(9)*, Children's Pr.) Scholastic Library Publishing.

—Jobs Around My Neighborhood/Oficios en Mi Vecindario. Rosa-Mendoza, Gladys. 2007. (English Spanish Foundations Ser.). 20p. (gr. -1-k). pap. 19.95 *(978-1-931398-81-7(X))* Me+Mi Publishing.

—Jobs in My Neighborhood. 2010. (My World Ser.). (ENG.). 24p. (J). (gr. -1-1). pap. 8.15 *(978-1-61533-037-9(2))*; lib. bdg. 22.60 *(978-1-60754-952-9(2))* Windmill Bks.

—Necesito una Ayudita. Schulz, Kathy. 2011. (Rookie Ready to Learn Español Ser.). (SPA.). 32p. (J). pap. 5.95 *(978-0-531-26782-0(2))*; (gr. -1-1). lib. bdg. 23.00 *(978-0-531-26114-9(X))* Scholastic Library Publishing. (Children's Pr.).

—The Open Road. Grahame, Kenneth. 2003. 32p. (J). *(978-0-7607-3215-1(9))* Barnes & Noble, Inc.

—Reading Fluency: Using Modeled Reading, Phrasing, & Repeated Oral Reading. Callella, Trisha. Hults, Alaska, ed. 2004. (J). Vol. 2232. 96p. (gr. 5-18). pap. 12.99 *(978-1-59198-065-0(8)*, 2232); Vol. 2233. (gr. 6-8). pap. 12.99 *(978-1-59198-066-7(6)*, 2233) Creative Teaching Pr., Inc.

—Restless Rat, No. 6. Grahame, Kenneth. 2010. (Easy Reader Classics Ser.). (ENG.). 32p. (J). (gr. k-3). 16.19 *(978-1-4027-6730-2(7))* Sterling Publishing Co., Inc.

—A Watermelon in the Sukkah. Rouss, Sylvia A. & Rouss, Shannan. ed. 2013. (ENG.). 24p. (J). (gr. -1-2). E-Book 23.99 *(978-1-4677-1642-0(1)*, Kar-Ben Publishing) Lerner Publishing Group.

—The Wind in the Willows. Grahame, Kenneth. 2003. 32p. (J). *(978-0-7607-3214-4(0))* Barnes & Noble, Inc.

Iosa, Ann, jt. illus. see Grayson, Rick.

Iosa, Ann W. Developing Reading Fluency, Grade 2: Using Modeled Reading, Phrasing, & Repeated Oral Reading. Callella, Trisha. Fisch, Teri L., ed. 2003. (Developing Reading Fluency Ser.). 96p. (J). (gr. 2-3). pap. 14.99 *(978-1-57471-995-6(5)*, 2248) Creative Teaching Pr., Inc.

—Developing Reading Fluency, Grade 4: Using Modeled Reading, Phrasing, & Repeated Oral Reading. Callella, Trisha. Fisch, Teri L., ed. 2003. (Developing Reading Fluency Ser.). 96p. (J). (gr. 4-5). pap. 14.99 *(978-1-57471-997-0(1)*, 2250) Creative Teaching Pr., Inc.

Iosa, Ann W. & Grayson, Rick. Math Tub Topics: Math Instruction Through Discovery. Morton, Debra & Stover, Elizabeth. Jennett, Pamela, ed. 2003. 128p. (J). (gr. k-3). pap. 13.99 *(978-1-57471-954-3(8)*, 2812) Creative Teaching Pr., Inc.

Iossa, Federica. Dinosaurs Magic Painting Book. 2018. (Magic Painting Bks.). (ENG.). 16p. pap. 9.99 *(978-0-7945-4126-2(7)*, Usborne) EDC Publishing.

—Peekaboo Teddy. 2016. (Peekaboo Bks.). (ENG.). 8p. (J). (gr. -1 — 1). bds. 7.99 *(978-0-7641-6862-8(2)*, B.E.S. Publishing) Peterson's.

Ipcar, Dahlov. Black & White. 2015. (ENG.). 40p. (J). (gr. -1-2). 17.95 *(978-1-909263-44-4(3))* Flying Eye Bks. GBR. Dist: Penguin Random Hse. LLC.

—I Like Animals. 2014. 40p. (J). (gr. -1-2). 17.95 *(978-1-909263-25-3(7))* Flying Eye Bks. GBR. Dist: Penguin Random Hse. LLC.

—The Little Fisherman, 1 vol. Brown, Margaret Wise. 2017. (ENG.). 40p. (J). pap. 12.95 *(978-1-944762-15-5(9)*, 9781944762155) Islandport Pr., Inc.

—The Wonderful Egg. 2014. (Dahlov Ipcar Collection). 48p. (J). (gr. -1-2). 19.95 *(978-1-909263-28-4(1))* Flying Eye Bks. GBR. Dist: Penguin Random Hse. LLC.

Ipcar, Dahlov. One Horse Farm, 1 vol. Ipcar, Dahlov. ed. 2011. (ENG.). 36p. (J). 17.95 *(978-1-934031-39-1(9)*, 9c1cb594-de8e-4edf-b155-de5e1e50fbce) Islandport Pr., Inc.

Ippolito, Eva Marie. The Donkey's Tale. Ippolito, Eva Marie. 2003. Ill, 15p. (J). (gr. -1-3). pap. 1.95 *(978-0-9705350-3-0(1))* Ippolito, Eva Marie.

—Hear, O Lord. Ippolito, Eva Marie. l.t. ed. 2009. 72p. (YA). (gr. 7-12). pap. 13.69 *(978-1-4389-2422-9(4))* AuthorHouse.

Iput. I Say Alhamdulillah. Dee, Noor H. 2019. (I Say Board Bks.). (ENG.). 20p. (J). bds. 9.95 *(978-0-86037-638-5(9))* Kube Publishing Ltd. GBR. Dist: Consortium Bk. Sales & Distribution.

—I Say As-Salamu 'Alaykum. Dee, Noor H. 2020. (Good Little Deeds Ser.). (ENG.). 20p. (J). bds. 9.95 *(978-0-86037-648-4(6))* Kube Publishing Ltd. GBR. Dist: Consortium Bk. Sales & Distribution.

—I Say Bismillah. Dee, Noor H. 2019. (I Say Board Bks.). (ENG.). 20p. (J). bds. 9.95 *(978-0-86037-633-0(8))* Kube Publishing Ltd. GBR. Dist: Consortium Bk. Sales & Distribution.

—I Say Mashallah. Dee, Noor H. 2020. (Good Little Deeds Ser.). (ENG.). 20p. (J). bds. 9.95 *(978-0-86037-643-9(5))* Kube Publishing Ltd. GBR. Dist: Consortium Bk. Sales & Distribution.

Irala, Daniel. The Fat Cat in the Red Hat Runs for Office. John, Barron. 2018. (Fat Cat in the Red Hat Ser.: Vol. 1). (ENG.). 30p. (J). pap. 11.99 *(978-1-948747-12-7(X))* J2B Publishing LLC.

Iredale, Julia. Myths & Legends of the World, 1 vol. Lonely Planet Kids & Brydon, Alli. 2019. (ENG.). 192p. (J). (gr. 4-7). 19.99 *(978-1-78868-308-1(0))* Lonely Planet Global Ltd. IRL. Dist: Hachette Bk. Group.

Irfan, Saib. Woolly the Wandering Sheep. Navarro, Maximo. 2019. (ENG.). 40p. (J). pap. 13.35 ***(978-1-6928-5417-1(8))*** Independently Published.

Iriarte, Carmen. Inquisitive Quincie: Getting Ready for Halloween. Iriarte, Carmen. 2019. (ENG.). 28p. (J). pap. 12.89 ***(978-1-6986-2115-9(9))*** Independently Published.

—Inquisitive Quincie (Full Color) A Day Learning about Teeth. Iriarte, Carmen. Roman, Regina, ed. 2020. (ENG.). 34p. (J). pap. 12.89 ***(978-1-5028-3339-6(5))*** CreateSpace Independent Publishing Platform.

Irish, Leigh Ann. I Love You, Baby Deer. Gilleland, Linda. 2012. 56p. 19.99 *(978-1-61254-025-2(2))* Brown Books Publishing Group.

Irish, Martin. Flip-Flap Math: Flip the Flpas to Check Your Answers! Faulkner, Keith. 2005. 12 p.p. (J). *(978-0-439-78578-5(2))* Scholastic, Inc.

Irvin, Sioux. Rusty, the Rainbow Trout: Moving Day. Irvin, David. 2007. 24p. per. 24.95 *(978-1-4241-8455-2(X))* America Star Bks.

Irvine, Wil. Butterflies Don't Crawl. Grateful Steps Publishing & Tipton, Angela. 2009. 32p. (J). 16.95 *(978-1-935130-14-7(5))* Grateful Steps.

Irving, Frazer, et al. Doctor Strange Vol. 4: Mr. Misery. 2018. 136p. (YA). (gr. 8-17). pap. 19.99 *(978-1-302-90587-3(2))* Marvel Worldwide, Inc.

Irving, Frazer. Frankenstein. Shelley, Mary. 2005. 176p. (gr. 3-7). 21.00 *(978-0-7569-5809-1(1))* Perfection Learning Corp.

Irving, George S. Historias de Miedo. Schwartz, Alvin & Alvin, Schwartz. 2003. (Historias de Miedo Scary Stories to Tell in the Dark Ser.). (SPA.). 120p. (YA). (gr. 5-8). pap. 11.99 *(978-84-241-8662-3(1))* Everest Editora ESP. Dist: Lectorum Pubns., Inc.

—Historias de Miedo 2: Relatos Espeluznantes para No Dejarte Dormir. Schwartz, Alvin & Alvin, Schwartz. 2003. (Historias de Miedo Scary Stories to Tell in the Dark Ser.).Tr. of More Scary Stories to Tell in the Dark. (SPA.). 112p. (YA). (gr. 5-8). pap. 11.99 *(978-84-241-8663-0(X))* Everest Editora ESP. Dist: Lectorum Pubns., Inc.

—Historias de Miedo 3: Relatos Aterradores para Helarte la Sangre. Schwartz, Alvin & Alvin, Schwartz. 2003. (Historias de Miedo Scary Stories to Tell in the Dark Ser.).Tr. of Scary Stories 3: More Tales to Chill Your Bones. (SPA.). 128p. (YA). (gr. 5-8). pap. 11.99 *(978-84-241-8664-7(8))* Everest Editora ESP. Dist: Lectorum Pubns., Inc.

Irwin, April. Daisy. Clark, Danell. 2008. 28p. pap. 11.95 *(978-1-59858-642-8(4))* Dog Ear Publishing, LLC.

Irwin, Dana. Grandpa & the Truck Book One. Mellor, Colleen Kelly. 2012. 34p. pap. 9.99 *(978-0-9856770-0-8(7))* truckerkidzPr.

Irwin, Dana M. Grandpa & the Truck Book 2. Mellor, Colleen Kelly. 2012. 34p. pap. 9.99 *(978-0-9856770-2-2(3))* truckerkidzPr.

Irwin, Kendra. Catching Fireflies: Family Night Devotional Fun. Lyttle, Marcy. 2007. 273p. 12.99 *(978-1-932307-77-1(X)*, Ambassador International) Emerald Hse. Group, Inc.

Irwin, Will. The Christmas Story: Mary & Joseph in Bethlehem. Jillions, John A. 2020. (ENG.). 28p. (J). (gr. -1-3). 12.99 ***(978-1-5324-1567-8(2))***; pap. 12.99 ***(978-1-5324-1566-1(4))*** Xist Publishing.

Isaac, Andy. Antarctic Attack. Bott, Adrian C. 2017. 137p. (J). *(978-1-61067-704-2(8))* Kane Miller.

—Antarctic Attack: Axel & Beast. Bott, Adrian C. 2018. (ENG.). 144p. (J). pap. 5.99 *(978-1-61067-634-2(3))* Kane Miller.

—Castle of Cyborgs: Axel & Beast. Bott, Adrian C. 2019. (ENG.). 144p. (J). pap. 5.99 *(978-1-61067-851-3(6))* Kane Miller.

—The Grabbem Getaway. Bott, Adrian C. 2017. 134p. (J). *(978-1-61067-703-5(X))* Kane Miller.

—The Grabbem Getaway: Axel & Beast. Bott, Adrian C. 2018. (ENG.). 144p. (J). pap. 5.99 *(978-1-61067-633-5(5))* Kane Miller.

—The Omega Operation: Axel & Beast. Bott, Adrian C. 2019. (ENG.). 144p. (J). pap. *(978-1-61067-850-6(8))* Kane Miller.

—Robotic Rumble. Bott, Adrian C. 2017. 121p. (J). *(978-1-61067-706-6(4))* Kane Miller.

—Robotic Rumble: Axel & Beast. Bott, Adrian C. 2018. (ENG.). 144p. (J). pap. 5.99 *(978-1-61067-636-6(X))* Kane Miller.

—Tropical Tangle. Bott, Adrian C. 2017. 119p. (J). *(978-1-61067-705-9(6))* Kane Miller.

—Tropical Tangle: Axel & Beast. Bott, Adrian C. 2018. (ENG.). 144p. (J). pap. 5.99 *(978-1-61067-635-9(1))* Kane Miller.

Isaac-Samuel, Sarah. A Claus of Many Colors: Skinny Claus. Maleski, Michael. 2019. (ENG.). 36p. (J). pap. 12.49 *(978-1-5456-7084-2(6))*; 22.99 ***(978-1-5456-7085-9(4))*** Salem Author Services.

Isaac, W. Smiley. If Daddy Can, I Can. Arceneaux, Kitty. 2012. 24p. 24.95 *(978-1-4626-4945-7(9))*; pap. 12.99 *(978-1-4626-7852-5(1))* America Star Bks.

Isaacs, Rebekah, et al. Captain Marvel: Carol Danvers - the Ms. Marvel Years Vol. 3. 2018. (Captain Marvel: Carol Danvers - the Ms. Marvel Years Ser.: 3). (ENG.). 448p. (YA). (gr. 8-17). pap. 34.99 *(978-1-302-91563-6(0))* Marvel Worldwide, Inc.

Isaacs, Rebekah & Timmons, Jonathan. Los Hermanos Wright. Mayo, Gretchen Will & O'Hern, Kerri. 2007. (Biografías Gráficas (Graphic Biographies) Ser.). (SPA.). 32p. (gr. 5-8). lib. bdg. 28.00 *(978-0-8368-7883-7(3))* Stevens, Gareth Publishing LLLP.

Isabel, Michelle & Thomas, Franselica. Murtle the Sea Turtle. Isabel, Michelle. 2011. 24p. pap. 24.95 *(978-1-4626-0114-1(6))* America Star Bks.

Isabelle, Decenciere. It's Me! Drachman, Eric. 2005. (ENG.). 32p. (J). (gr. -1-2). 18.95 incl. audio compact disk *(978-0-9703809-2-0(5))* Kidwick Bks.

Isadora, Rachel. In the Small, Small Night. Kurtz, Jane. 2005. (Amistad Ser.). (ENG.). 32p. (J). (gr. k-5). 17.99 *(978-0-06-623814-2(5)*, Greenwillow Bks.) HarperCollins Pubs.

Isadora, Rachel. Bea at Ballet. Isadora, Rachel. 2014. (ENG.). 32p. (J). (gr. -1 — 1). bds. 7.99 *(978-0-399-16844-4(3)*, Nancy Paulsen Books) Penguin Young Readers Group.

—Bea in the Nutcracker. Isadora, Rachel. 2015. (ENG.). 32p. (J). (gr. -1-k). 16.99 *(978-0-399-25231-0(2)*, Nancy Paulsen Books) Penguin Young Readers Group.

—Do I Have to Wear a Coat? Isadora, Rachel. 2020. 32p. (J). (-k). 17.99 *(978-0-525-51660-6(3)*, Nancy Paulsen Books) Penguin Young Readers Group.

—The Fisherman & His Wife. Isadora, Rachel. 2008. (ENG.). 32p. (J). (gr. -1-3). 17.99 *(978-0-399-24771-2(8)*, G.P. Putnam's Sons Books for Young Readers) Penguin Young Readers Group.

—Hansel & Gretel. Isadora, Rachel. 2009. 32p. (J). (gr. 1-3). 17.99 *(978-0-399-25028-6(X)*, G.P. Putnam's Sons Books for Young Readers) Penguin Young Readers Group.

—I Hear a Pickle: And Smell, See, Touch, & Taste It, Too! Isadora, Rachel. 2017. 30p. (J). (-k). bds. 7.99 *(978-1-5247-3958-4(8)*, Nancy Paulsen Books) Penguin Young Readers Group.

—I Hear a Pickle: And Smell, See, Touch, & Taste It, Too! Isadora, Rachel. 2016. (ENG.). 32p. (J). (-k). 16.99 *(978-0-399-16049-3(3)*, Nancy Paulsen Books) Penguin Young Readers Group.

—I Just Want to Say Good Night. Isadora, Rachel. 2017. (ENG.). 32p. (J). (-k). 17.99 *(978-0-399-17384-4(6)*, Nancy Paulsen Books) Penguin Young Readers Group.

—Lili at Ballet. Isadora, Rachel. 2013. (ENG.). 32p. (J). (gr. k-2). 21.19 *(978-0-698-11408-1(6))* Penguin Young Readers Group.

—My Dog Laughs. Isadora, Rachel. 2018. 32p. (J). (-k). 17.99 *(978-0-399-17385-1(4)*, Nancy Paulsen Books) Penguin Young Readers Group.

—Old Mikamba Had a Farm. Isadora, Rachel. 2013. (ENG.). 40p. (J). (gr. -1-k). 17.99 *(978-0-399-25740-7(3)*, Nancy Paulsen Books) Penguin Young Readers Group.

—Peekaboo Morning. Isadora, Rachel. 2008. (ENG.). 24p. (J). (gr. -1 — 1). bds. 7.99 *(978-0-399-25153-5(7)*, G.P. Putnam's Sons Books for Young Readers) Penguin Young Readers Group.

—Say Hello! Isadora, Rachel. (ENG.). (J). 2017. 30p. (-k). bds. 7.99 *(978-0-399-25632-5(6)*, Nancy Paulsen Books); 2010. 32p. (gr. -1-k). 17.99 *(978-0-399-25230-3(4)*, G.P. Putnam's Sons Books for Young Readers) Penguin Young Readers Group.

—The Twelve Dancing Princesses. Isadora, Rachel. 2009. (ENG.). 32p. (J). (gr. k-3). pap. 7.99 *(978-0-14-241450-7(6)*, Puffin Books) Penguin Young Readers Group.

Isaksen, Lisa A. Nazi Zombies. Bozanich, Tony L. & Wight, Joe. Isaksen, Patricia, ed. 2013. (ENG.). 112p. (gr. -1-4). pap. 14.95 *(978-0-930655-00-6(1)*, 6ebd62cf-d17f-47de-86dc-6e9b7d70845f) Antarctic Pr., Inc.

Isanove, Richard, et al. Amazing Spider-Man: Edge of Spider-Verse. 2015. (ENG.). 112p. (YA). (gr. 8-17). pap. 15.99 *(978-0-7851-9728-7(1))* Marvel Worldwide, Inc.

—Guardians of the Galaxy: New Guard Vol. 3: Civil War II. 2017. (ENG.). 136p. (J). (gr. 4-17). pap. 19.99 *(978-1-302-90302-2(0))* Marvel Worldwide, Inc.

Isaza, Juanita. Conjuros y Sortilegios. Vasco, Irene. 2004. (SPA.). 29p. (J). (gr. -1-7). pap. *(978-958-30-0522-0(3))* Panamericana Editorial.

—Historias Inmorales. Quiroga, Horacio. 2004. (Cajon de Cuentos Ser.). (SPA.). 246p. (J). (gr. 8-12). *(978-958-30-0457-5(X))* Panamericana Editorial.

—El Quinto Viaje y Otras Historias del Nuevo Mundo. Nino, Jairo Anibal. 2004. (Literatura Juvenil (Panamericana Editorial) Ser.). (SPA.). 153p. (J). (gr. 4-7). pap. *(978-958-30-0573-2(8)*, PV4381) Centro de Informacion y Desarrollo de la Comunicacion y la Literatura MEX. Dist: Lectorum Pubns., Inc.

Isbell, Toby. Silly Rules: Jokes for Kids. Campbell, Anna. 2008. (ENG.). 100p. (J). pap. 4.99 *(978-0-9801861-3-0(7))* Summerhill Pr.

Ische, Bryan. On Your Own: A College Readiness Guide for Teens with ADHD/LD. Quinn, Patricia O. & Maitland, Theresa E. Laurie. 2011. 128p. (YA). (gr. 9-18). 14.95 *(978-1-4338-0955-2(9)*, Magination Pr.) American Psychological Assn.

Isely, Chad. The Power of a Positive No: Willie Bohanon & Friends Learn the Power of Resisting Peer Pressure. Jones, Kip. 2016. (Urban Character Education Ser.: 1). (ENG.). 32p. (J). (gr. 2-6). pap. 10.95 *(978-1-944862-06-8(5))* Boys Town Pr.

—The Power of an Attitude of Gratitude: Willie Bohanon & Friends Learn the Power of Showing Appreciation. Jones, Kip. 2016. (Urban Character Education Ser.: Vol. 3). (ENG.). 40p. (J). pap. 10.95 *(978-1-934490-92-1(X))* Boys Town Pr.

Iseminger, Jonathan, jt. illus. see Sjostrom, Nicole.

Iseminger, Jonathon, jt. illus. see Sjostrom, Nicole.

Iserles, Inbali. The Taken. 2015. 252p. (J). pap. *(978-0-545-91869-5(3)*, Scholastic Pr.) Scholastic, Inc.

Ishe, Bryan. Type 1 Teens: A Guide to Managing Your Diabetes. Hood, Korey K. 2010. 150p. (YA). (gr. 7-18). pap. 14.95 *(978-1-4338-0788-6(2)*, Magination Pr.) American Psychological Assn.

I

Isherwood, Matthew & Artful Doodlers, Artful. Baby Animals Sticker Activities. Litton, Jonathan. 2014. (My First Ser.). (ENG.). 96p. (J). (gr. -1-2). pap. 9.99 *(978-1-58925-302-5(7))* Tiger Tales.

Ishibash, Toshiharu, jt. illus. see Mizuno, Junko.

Ishida, Jui. Goodnight Little One: Bedtime Around the World. Matsuda, Christine. 2008. (J). 15.95 *(978-0-87358-925-3(4)*, Rising Moon Bks. for Young Readers) Northland Publishing.

—Sail Away, Little Boat. Buell, Janet. 2006. 32p. (J). 15.95 *(978-1-57505-821-4(9)*, Carolrhoda Bks.) Lerner Publishing Group.

—The Silver Moon: Lullabies & Cradle Songs. Prelutsky, Jack. 2013. (ENG.). 48p. (J). (gr. -1-3). 17.99 *(978-0-06-201467-2(6)*, Greenwillow Bks.) HarperCollins Pubs.

—Who Says Baa? A Touch & Feel Board Book. 2005. (Board Books). 16p. (J). bds. 6.95 *(978-1-58117-177-8(3)*, Intervisual/Piggy Toes) Bendon, Inc.

—Who Says Moo? A Touch & Feel Board Book. 2005. 16p. (J). bds. 6.95 *(978-1-58117-178-5(1)*, Intervisual/Piggy Toes) Bendon, Inc.

Ishihara, Meg. Hound Won't Go. Rogers, Lisa. 2020. (ENG.). 32p. (J). (gr. -1-3). 16.99 ***(978-0-8075-3408-3(0)***, 807534080) Whitman, Albert & Co.

Ishii, Minako, photos by. Girls' Day/Boys' Day. Ishii, Minako. 2007. 64p. (J). (gr. 4-7). 16.95 *(978-1-57306-274-9(X))* Bess Pr., Inc.

Ishimaru, Hiroko. Let Rhinoceros Be. Miller, Kerry S. 2020. (ENG.). 54p. (J). pap. 12.99 ***(978-1-0987-7455-4(8))*** Independently Published.

Isik, Semur. Australia. Ganeri, Anita. 2015. (Country Guides, with Benjamin Blog & His Inquisitive Dog Ser.). (ENG.). 32p. (J). (gr. 3-5). 30.65 *(978-1-4109-6846-3(4)*, Raintree) Capstone.

—Brazil: A Benjamin Blog & His Inquisitive Dog Guide, 1 vol. Ganeri, Anita. 2014. (Country Guides, with Benjamin Blog & His Inquisitive Dog Ser.). (ENG.). 32p. (J). (gr. 3-5). pap. 7.99 *(978-1-4109-6674-2(7)*, Raintree) Capstone.

—Canada. Ganeri, Anita. 2015. (Country Guides, with Benjamin Blog & His Inquisitive Dog Ser.). (ENG.). 32p. (J). (gr. 3-5). 30.65 *(978-1-4109-6847-0(2)*, Raintree) Capstone.

—China: A Benjamin Blog & His Inquisitive Dog Guide, 1 vol. Ganeri, Anita. 2014. (Country Guides, with Benjamin Blog & His Inquisitive Dog Ser.). (ENG.). 32p. (J). (gr. 3-5). pap. 7.99 *(978-1-4109-6670-4(4)*, Raintree) Capstone.

—Country Guides, with Benjamin Blog & His Inquisitive Dog, 1 vol. Ganeri, Anita. 2014. (Country Guides, with Benjamin Blog & His Inquisitive Dog Ser.). (ENG.). 32p. (gr. 1-3). 245.20 *(978-1-4109-6669-8(0)*, Raintree) Capstone.

—Dream Birthday, 1 vol. Phillips, Ruby Ann. 2014. (Krystal Ball Ser.). (ENG.). 112p. (J). (gr. 1-3). 25.32 *(978-1-4795-2178-4(7)*, Picture Window Bks.) Capstone.

—Egypt: A Benjamin Blog & His Inquisitive Dog Guide, 1 vol. Ganeri, Anita. 2014. (Country Guides, with Benjamin Blog & His Inquisitive Dog Ser.). (ENG.). 32p. (J). (gr. 3-5). pap. 7.99 *(978-1-4109-6672-8(0)*, Raintree) Capstone.

—England. Ganeri, Anita. 2015. (Country Guides, with Benjamin Blog & His Inquisitive Dog Ser.). (ENG.). 32p. (J). (gr. 3-5). 30.65 *(978-1-4109-6848-7(0)*, Raintree) Capstone.

—Fortune Cookie Fiasco. Phillips, Ruby Ann. 2015. (Krystal Ball Ser.). (ENG.). 112p. (J). (gr. 1-3). lib. bdg. 25.32 *(978-1-4795-5874-2(5)*, Picture Window Bks.) Capstone.

—France: A Benjamin Blog & His Inquisitive Dog Guide, 1 vol. Ganeri, Anita. 2014. (Country Guides, with Benjamin Blog & His Inquisitive Dog Ser.). (ENG.). 32p. (J). (gr. 3-5). pap. 7.99 *(978-1-4109-6676-6(3)*, Raintree) Capstone.

—Germany. Ganeri, Anita. 2015. (Country Guides, with Benjamin Blog & His Inquisitive Dog Ser.). (ENG.). 32p. (J). (gr. 3-5). 30.65 *(978-1-4109-7994-0(6)*, Raintree) Capstone.

—The Great & Powerful, 1 vol. Phillips, Ruby Ann. 2014. (Krystal Ball Ser.). (ENG.). 112p. (J). (gr. 1-3). 25.32 *(978-1-4795-2179-1(5)*, Picture Window Bks.) Capstone.

—India: A Benjamin Blog & His Inquisitive Dog Guide, 1 vol. Ganeri, Anita. 2014. (Country Guides, with Benjamin Blog & His Inquisitive Dog Ser.). (ENG.). 32p. (J). (gr. 3-5). pap. 7.99 *(978-1-4109-6671-1(2)*, Raintree) Capstone.

—Italy. Ganeri, Anita. 2015. (Country Guides, with Benjamin Blog & His Inquisitive Dog Ser.). (ENG.). 32p. (J). (gr. 3-5). 30.65 *(978-1-4109-7995-7(4)*, Raintree) Capstone.

—Japan: A Benjamin Blog & His Inquisitive Dog Guide, 1 vol. Ganeri, Anita. 2014. (Country Guides, with Benjamin Blog & His Inquisitive Dog Ser.). (ENG.). 32p. (J). (gr. 3-5). 30.65 *(978-1-4109-6666-7(6)*, Raintree) Capstone.

—Mexico: A Benjamin Blog & His Inquisitive Dog Guide, 1 vol. Ganeri, Anita. 2014. (Country Guides, with Benjamin Blog & His Inquisitive Dog Ser.). (ENG.). 32p. (J). (gr. 3-5). 30.65 *(978-1-4109-6664-3(X)*, Raintree) Capstone.

—Pet Psychic. Phillips, Ruby Ann. 2015. (Krystal Ball Ser.). (ENG.). 112p. (J). (gr. 1-3). lib. bdg. 25.32 *(978-1-4795-5875-9(3)*, Picture Window Bks.) Capstone.

—The Prehistoric Masters of Art Volume 2: Discover Art History with a Prehistoric Twist! Wallace, Elise. 2018. (Jurassic Classics Ser.). (ENG.). 32p. (J). (gr. 4-7). lib. bdg. 26.65 *(978-1-942875-54-3(1)*, Walter Foster Jr) Quarto Publishing Group USA.

—The Prehistoric Masters of Literature Volume 1: Discover Literary History with a Prehistoric Twist! Lacey, Saskia & Wallace, Elise. 2018. (Jurassic Classics Ser.). (ENG.). 32p. (J). (gr. 4-7). lib. bdg. 26.65 *(978-1-942875-55-0(X)*, Walter Foster Jr) Quarto Publishing Group USA.

—The Prehistoric Masters of Literature Volume 2: Discover Literary History with a Prehistoric Twist! Lacey, Saskia & Wallace, Elise. 2018. (Jurassic Classics Ser.). (ENG.). 32p. (J). (gr. 4-7). lib. bdg. 26.65 *(978-1-942875-56-7(8)*, Walter Foster Jr) Quarto Publishing Group USA.

—The Presidential Masters of Prehistory Volume 1: Discover America's Prehistoric Forefathers. Lacey, Saskia & Wallace, Elise. 2018. (Jurassic Classics Ser.). (ENG.). 32p. (J). (gr. 4-7). lib. bdg. 26.65 *(978-1-942875-51-2(7)*, Walter Foster Jr) Quarto Publishing Group USA.

—The Presidential Masters of Prehistory Volume 2: Discover America's Prehistoric Forefathers. Lacey, Saskia & Wallace, Elise. 2018. (Jurassic Classics Ser.). (ENG.). 32p. (J). (gr. 4-7). lib. bdg. 26.65 *(978-1-942875-52-9(5)*, Walter Foster Jr) Quarto Publishing Group USA.

—Republic of Ireland. Ganeri, Anita. 2015. (Country Guides, with Benjamin Blog & His Inquisitive Dog Ser.). (ENG.). 32p. (J). (gr. 3-5). 30.65 *(978-1-4109-6849-4(9)*, Raintree) Capstone.

—Russia. Ganeri, Anita. 2015. (Country Guides, with Benjamin Blog & His Inquisitive Dog Ser.). (ENG.). 32p. (J). (gr. 3-5). 30.65 *(978-1-4109-7997-1(0)*, Raintree) Capstone.

—Scotland. Ganeri, Anita. 2015. (Country Guides, with Benjamin Blog & His Inquisitive Dog Ser.). (ENG.). 32p. (J). (gr. 3-5). 30.65 *(978-1-4109-6850-0(2)*, Raintree) Capstone.

—South Africa: A Benjamin Blog & His Inquisitive Dog Guide, 1 vol. Ganeri, Anita. 2014. (Country Guides, with Benjamin Blog & His Inquisitive Dog Ser.). (ENG.). 32p. (J). (gr. 3-5). 30.65 *(978-1-4109-6668-1(2))*; pap. 7.99 *(978-1-4109-6677-3(1))* Capstone. (Raintree).

—Spain - Jouney Through. Ganeri, Anita. 2015. (Country Guides, with Benjamin Blog & His Inquisitive Dog Ser.). (ENG.). 32p. (J). (gr. 3-5). 30.65 *(978-1-4109-7996-4(2)*, Raintree) Capstone.

—United States of America. Ganeri, Anita. 2015. (Country Guides, with Benjamin Blog & His Inquisitive Dog Ser.). (ENG.). 32p. (J). (gr. 3-5). 30.65 *(978-1-4109-6851-7(0)*, Raintree) Capstone.

Isings, J. H. Bible Stories for Our Little Ones. Hulst, W. G. van de. 2004. 262p. *(978-1-894666-69-5(0))* Inheritance Pubns.

Isisi, Isisi. El Rey Cachivache. Felsen, Jorge Ricardo. 2019. (SPA.). 28p. (J). pap. 5.99 ***(978-1-6784-5774-7(4))*** Independently Published.

Iskander, Kazimir Lee. Epic Athletes: Tom Brady. Wetzel, Dan. 2019. (Epic Athletes Ser.: 4). (ENG.). 176p. (J). 16.99 *(978-1-250-29579-8(3)*, 900195492, Holt, Henry & Co. Bks. For Young Readers) Holt, Henry & Co.

—Epic Athletes: Tom Brady. Wetzel, Dan. 2020. (Epic Athletes Ser.: 4). (ENG.). 176p. (J). pap. 7.99 *(978-1-250-25061-2(7)*, 900198024) Square Fish.

Iskowitz, Joel. Rebekkah's Journey: A World War II Refugee Story. Burg, Ann E. 2006. (Tales of Young Americans Ser.). (ENG.). 32p. (J). (gr. 1-4). 17.95 *(978-1-58536-275-2(1)*, 202086) Sleeping Bear Pr.

Islam, Maira. Cocoa Goes to School. Robaina, Khadijah Y. 2020. (Adventures of Kevin & Cocoa Ser.: Vol. 1). (ENG.). 32p. (J). pap. 9.95 ***(978-1-9820-9781-3(7))*** CreateSpace Independent Publishing Platform.

Isley, Chad. The Power of Bystanders: Willie Bohanon & Friends Learn to Handle Bullying Like a Boss. Jones, Kip. 2015. (ENG.). 32p. (J). pap. 10.95 *(978-1-934490-79-2(2))* Boys Town Pr.

Ismail, Yasmeen. Love by Sophia. Averbeck, Jim. 2020. (Sophia Bks.). (ENG.). 40p. (J). (gr. -1-3). 17.99 ***(978-1-4814-7790-1(0)***, McElderry, Margaret K. Bks.) McElderry, Margaret K. Bks.

Ismail, Yasmeen. Nuts! Peacock, Lou. 2019. (ENG.). 32p. (J). (-k). 15.99 *(978-1-5362-0824-5(8)*, Nosy Crow) Candlewick Pr.

—One Word from Sophia. Averbeck, Jim. 2015. (Sophia Bks.). (ENG.). 40p. (J). (gr. -1-3). 17.99 *(978-1-4814-0514-0(4))* Simon & Schuster Children's Publishing.

—Two Problems for Sophia. Averbeck, Jim. 2018. (Sophia Bks.). (ENG.). 40p. (J). (gr. -1-3). 17.99 *(978-1-4814-7788-8(9)*, McElderry, Margaret K. Bks.) McElderry, Margaret K. Bks.

Ismail, Yasmeen. Christmas for Greta & Gracie. Ismail, Yasmeen. 2016. (ENG.). 32p. (J). (gr. -1-2). 15.99 *(978-0-7636-8943-8(2)*, Nosy Crow) Candlewick Pr.

Isol. Daytime Visions: An Alphabet. 2016. 56p. (J). (-2). 17.95 *(978-1-59270-195-7(7))* Enchanted Lion Bks., LLC.

—Doggy Slippers, 1 vol. Luján, Jorge. Amado, Elisa, tr. 2010. (ENG.). 32p. (J). (gr. k-k). 18.95 *(978-0-88899-983-2(6))* Groundwood Bks. CAN. Dist: Publishers Group West (PGW).

—Habia una Vez una Llave. Montes, Graciela. 2005. (Pictocuentos Ser.). (SPA.). 24p. (J). 8.95 *(978-1-59820-213-7(8)*, Alfaguara) Santillana USA Publishing Co., Inc.

Isol. Regalo Sorpresa. Isol. 2nd ed. 2007. (la Orilla del Viento Ser.). (SPA.). 33p. (J). (gr. 1-2). pap. *(978-968-16-6151-9(6)*, FC33641) Fondo de Cultura Economica.

Isol Staff. Numeralia, 1 vol. Luján, Jorge. Ouriou, Susan, tr. 2014. (ENG.). 32p. (J). (gr. -1). 18.95 *(978-1-55498-444-2(0))* Groundwood Bks. CAN. Dist: Publishers Group West (PGW).

Israel, Benjamin. The Past Repeated: Not Everything Is What It Seems ... Israel, Madeline. 2018. (ENG.). 132p. (YA). pap. 19.99 *(978-1-9845-1698-5(1))* Xlibris Corp.

Israel, David, et al, photos by. Offerings of the Spirit: Tributes to Brother Thomas. Gressler, Jeanne, ed. 2003. 88p. 35.00 *(978-1-879985-09-4(8)*, Pucker Art Pubns.) Pucker Gallery.

Israeli, Ann. Please Explain Terrorism to Me: A Story for Children, PEARLS of Wisdom for Their Parents. Zelinger, Laurie E. 2016. 73p. (J). pap. *(978-1-61599-291-1(X))* Loving Healing Pr., Inc.

Issa, Valeria. Go, Nan, Go! & on the Log. Jones, Cath. 2020. (Early Bird Readers — Pink (Early Bird Stories (tm)) Ser.). (ENG.). 32p. (J). (gr. -1-2). pap. 7.99 *(978-1-5415-8725-0(1)*, Lerner Pubns.) Lerner Publishing Group.

Ito, Akihiro. Geobreeders 1, Vol. 1. Ito, Akihiro. 2004. 224p. pap. 9.99 *(978-1-58664-929-6(9)*, CMX 61501MM, CPM Comics) Central Park Media Corp.

Ito, Hazel. P Is for Poppadoms! An Indian Alphabet Book. Sehgal, Kabir & Sehgal, Surishtha. 2019. (ENG.). 32p. (J). (gr. -1-3). 17.99 *(978-1-5344-2172-1(6)*, Beach Lane Bks.) Beach Lane Bks.

Ito, Willie. A Boy of Heart Mountain. Bazaldua, Barbara. 2010. (YA). pap. *(978-0-578-05342-4(X))* Yabitoon Bks.

Itoïz, Mayana & Cauuet, Paul. The Wolf in Underpants Freezes His Buns Off. Lupano, Wilfrid. 2020. (Wolf in Underpants Ser.). 40p. (J). (gr. 2-5). (ENG.). pap. 8.99 *(978-1-5415-8694-9(8))*; lib. bdg. 26.65 *(978-1-5415-2819-2(0))* Lerner Publishing Group. (Graphic Universe™).

Itoïz, Mayana & Cuuet, Paul. The Wolf in Underpants. Lupano, Wilfrid. Sacks, Nathan, tr. 2019. (Wolf in Underpants Ser.). 40p. (J). (gr. 2-5). 26.65 *(978-1-5415-2818-5(2)*, Graphic Universe™) Lerner Publishing Group.

Iuga, Denisa Mihaela. Le Avventure Della Piccola Farfett: Fiaba. Iuga, Denisa Mihaela. 2014. (ITA.). 26p. (J). pap. *(978-606-716-035-2(8))* ePubs.

—Little Farfett's Adventures: A Children's Story. Iuga, Denisa Mihaela. 2014. (ENG.). 26p. (J). pap. *(978-606-716-036-9(6))* ePubs.

Ivanke. Sparkling Easter Eggs: A Glittery Counting Book. 2008. (ENG.). 10p. (J). bds. 7.95 *(978-1-58117-685-8(6)*, Intervisual/Piggy Toes) Bendon, Inc.

Ivanke, jt. illus. see Lola.

Ivanov, A. & Ivanov, O. Adventures of MIA. Farley, Robin. 2013. 158p. (J). *(978-1-4351-5061-4(9))* Barnes & Noble, Inc.

Ivanov, A., jt. illus. see Ivanov, O.

Ivanov, Aleksey. Boomer to the Rescue. Parente, Peter. l.t. ed. 2005. 28p. 15.95 *(978-0-9745052-3-7(4)*, Peeper & Friends) Tree Of Life Publishing.

Ivanov, Aleksey & Ivanov, Olga. Dios es Bueno Todo el Tiempo. McCombs, Margi. 2012. (SPA.). 20p. (J). (gr. -1-k). bds. 9.99 *(978-0-545-45618-0(5)*, Scholastic en Espanol) Scholastic, Inc.

—Flappy & Scrappy. Yorinks, Arthur. 2010. (I Can Read Level 2 Ser.). (ENG.). 48p. (J). (gr. k-3). pap. 4.99 *(978-0-06-205913-0(0)*, HarperCollins) HarperCollins Pubs. Ltd. GBR. Dist: HarperCollins Pubs.

—Mia & the Tiny Toe Shoes. Farley, Robin. 2012. (My First I Can Read Ser.). (ENG.). 32p. (J). (gr. -1-3). 16.99 *(978-0-06-208683-9(9))*; pap. 4.99 *(978-0-06-208682-2(0))* HarperCollins Pubs.

—Mia & the Too Big Tutu. Farley, Robin. 2010. (My First I Can Read Ser.). (ENG.). 32p. (J). (gr. -1-3). 16.99 *(978-0-06-173302-4(4))*; pap. 4.99 *(978-0-06-173301-7(6))* HarperCollins Pubs. Ltd. GBR. (HarperCollins). Dist: HarperCollins Pubs.

—Mia: the Sweetest Valentine. Farley, Robin. 2012. (Mia Ser.). (ENG.). 24p. (J). (gr. -1-3). 4.99 *(978-0-06-210012-2(2)*, HarperFestival) HarperCollins Pubs.

—Mountain Dog. Engle, Margarita. 2014. (ENG.). 240p. (J). (gr. 3-7). pap. 7.99 *(978-1-250-04424-2(3)*, 9781250044242) Square Fish.

—Revenge of Superstition Mountain. Broach, Elise. 2014. (Superstition Mountain Mysteries Ser.: 3). (ENG.). 304p. (J). (gr. 3-7). 16.99 *(978-0-8050-8909-7(8)*, 9780805089097, Holt, Henry & Co. Bks. For Young Readers) Holt, Henry & Co.

—The Tall Book of Mother Goose. Public Domain, Public. 2006. (Harper Tall Book Ser.). (ENG.). 80p. (J). (gr. -1-2). 6.99 *(978-0-06-054373-0(6))* HarperCollins Pubs.

Ivanov, Aleksey, jt. illus. see Ivanov, Olga.

Ivanov, Aleksey & Olga. Because of Shoe & Other Dog Stories. Martin, Ann M., ed. 2013. (ENG.). 288p. (J). (gr. 3-7). pap. 7.99 *(978-1-250-02728-3(4)*, 900098300) Square Fish.

—Lassie Come-Home: An Adaptation of Eric Knight's Classic Story. Hill, Susan. 75th ed. 2015. (ENG.). 32p. (J). (gr. -1-3). 17.99 *(978-1-62779-294-3(5)*, 900145461, Holt, Henry & Co. Bks. For Young Readers) Holt, Henry & Co.

—Revenge of Superstition Mountain. Broach, Elise. 2015. (Superstition Mountain Mysteries Ser.: 3). (ENG.). 320p. (J). (gr. 3-7). pap. 12.99 *(978-1-250-05686-3(1)*, 900139059) Square Fish.

Ivanov, Alex, photos by. The Complete Visual Dictionary. Reynolds, David West et al. 2006. (ENG., 272p. (J). (gr. 5-12). 40.00 *(978-0-7566-2238-1(7)*, DK Children) Dorling Kindersley Publishing, Inc.

Ivanov, Alexey & Ivanov, Olga. Live Brave: Devotions, Recipes, Experiments, & Projects for Every Brave Girl, 1 vol. Fortner, Tama. 2020. (Brave Girls Ser.). 160p. (J). pap. 16.99 ***(978-1-4002-1959-9(0))*** Nelson, Thomas Inc.

Ivanov, Alexsey & Ivanov, Olga. Cake: Love, Chickens, & a Taste of Peculiar, 1 vol. Magnin, Joyce. 2013. (ENG.). 224p. (J). 14.99 *(978-0-310-73333-1(2))* Zonderkidz.

Ivanov, Evgueni. Bursunsul & Paskualina. Tavadze, Olesya. 2007. (POL & ENG.). 32p. (J). pap. 16.95 *(978-1-60195-095-6(0))* International Step by Step Assn.

Ivanov, O. & Ivanov, A. Walt Disney's Magic. Klimo, Kate. 2017. (J). pap. *(978-0-399-55534-3(X))* Random Hse., Inc.

Ivanov, O., jt. illus. see Ivanov, A.

Ivanov, Olga & Ivanov, Aleksey. Flappy & Scrappy. Yorinks, Arthur. 2010. (I Can Read Level 2 Ser.). (ENG.). 48p. (J). (gr. k-3). 16.99 *(978-0-06-205117-2(2))* HarperCollins Pubs.

—Mia & the Big Sister Ballet. Farley, Robin. 2012. (My First I Can Read Ser.). (ENG.). 32p. (J). (gr. -1-3). pap. 4.99 *(978-0-06-173307-9(5))* HarperCollins Pubs.

—Mia & the Daisy Dance. Farley, Robin. 2012. (My First I Can Read Ser.). (ENG.). 32p. (J). (gr. -1-3). pap. 4.99 *(978-0-06-173305-5(9))* HarperCollins Pubs.

—Mia & the Dance for Two. Farley, Robin. 2011. (My First I Can Read Ser.). (ENG.). 32p. (J). (gr. -1-3). 16.99 *(978-0-06-173304-8(0))*; pap. 4.99 *(978-0-06-173303-1(2))* HarperCollins Pubs.

—Mia & the Girl with a Twirl. Farley, Robin. 2013. (My First I Can Read Ser.). (ENG.). 32p. (J). (gr. -1-3). 16.99 *(978-0-06-208689-1(8))*; pap. 4.99 *(978-0-06-208688-4(X))* HarperCollins Pubs.

—Mia Dances Back to School! Farley, Robin. 2013. (Mia Ser.). (ENG.). 24p. (J). (gr. -1-3). 4.99 *(978-0-06-210014-6(9)*, HarperFestival) HarperCollins Pubs.

—Mia Jazzes It Up! Farley, Robin. 2013. (My First I Can Read Ser.). (ENG.). 32p. (J). (gr. -1-3). 16.99 *(978-0-06-208692-1(8))*; pap. 4.99 *(978-0-06-208691-4(X))* HarperCollins Pubs.

—Mia Sets the Stage. Farley, Robin. 2013. (My First I Can Read Ser.). (ENG.). 32p. (J). (gr. -1-3). pap. 4.99 *(978-0-06-208685-3(5))* HarperCollins Pubs.

—Mia: the Snow Day Ballet. Farley, Robin. 2014. (Mia Ser.). (ENG.). 24p. (J). (gr. -1-k). pap. 4.99 *(978-0-06-210015-3(7)*, HarperFestival) HarperCollins Pubs.

—Mia: Time to Trick or Treat! Farley, Robin. 2012. (Mia Ser.). (ENG.). 24p. (J). (gr. -1-3). pap. 4.99 *(978-0-06-210011-5(4)*, HarperFestival) HarperCollins Pubs.

—Mia's Nutcracker Ballet. Farley, Robin. 2013. (Mia Ser.). (ENG.). 32p. (J). (gr. -1-3). 9.99 *(978-0-06-223830-6(2))* HarperCollins Pubs.

Ivanov, Olga, jt. illus. see Glasser, Robin Preiss.

Ivanov, Olga, jt. illus. see Ivanov, Aleksey.

Ivanov, Olga, jt. illus. see Ivanov, Alexey.

Ivanov, Olga, jt. illus. see Ivanov, Alexsey.

Ivanov, Olga and Aleksey. I Am Brave: Devotions, Questions, & Quizzes for Brave Girls, 1 vol. Thomas Nelson Publishing Staff. 2019. (Brave Girls Ser.). (ENG.). 208p. (J). 16.99 *(978-1-4002-1192-0(1))* Nelson, Thomas Inc.

—Tommy Nelson's Brave Girls Confidential: Stories & Secrets about Faith & Friendship, 1 vol. Thrasher, Travis. 2017. (Brave Girls Ser.). (ENG.). 224p. (J). 16.99 *(978-0-7180-9725-7(4))* Nelson, Thomas Inc.

Iverson, Diane. The DesertAlphabet Encyclopedia. Allred, Sylvester. 2006. 50p. (YA). pap. 7.95 *(978-0-88045-168-0(8)*, NaturEncyclopedia) Stemmer Hse. Pubs.

—The ForestAlphabet: Encyclopedia. Allred, Sylvester. unabr. ed. 2005. (Naturencyclopedia Ser.). 48p. (J). (gr. k-3). pap. 24.95 *(978-0-88045-155-0(6))* Stemmer Hse. Pubs.

—The Freshwater Alphabet. Allred, Sylvester. 2009. 48p. (J). (gr. 4-7). pap. 8.95 *(978-0-916144-48-7(8))* Stemmer Hse. Pubs.

—Jabber the Steller's Jay. Allred, Sylvester. 2017. (ENG.). 32p. (J). (gr. k-3). 16.99 *(978-1-943328-89-5(7)*, West Winds Pr.) West Margin Pr.

—Ready to Wean: The Return of the Dangling Red Earrings. April, Elyse. 2012. (Family & World Health / We Like To Ser.). (ENG.). 32p. (J). pap. 9.95 *(978-1-935387-30-5(8))* Hohm Pr.

—We Like to Help Cook: Nos Gusta Ayudar a Cocinar. Allsop, Marcus. (We Like To Ser.). (ENG.). 32p. 2011. (J). pap. 10.95 *(978-1-935826-00-2(X))*; 2007. (gr. -1-1). pap. 9.95 *(978-1-890772-70-3(4))*; 2011th alt. ed. 2012. (J). pap. 9.95 *(978-1-935826-05-7(0))* Kalindi Pr.

Iverson, Diane. Nos Gusta Ayudar a Cocinar: We Like to Help Cook. Iverson, Diane. Allsop, Marcus. 2009. (SPA & ENG.). (J). pap. *(978-1-890772-97-0(6))* Hohm Pr.

—Nos Gusta Movernos: El Ejercicio Es Divertido = We Like to Move: Exercise Is Fun. Iverson, Diane. April, Elyse & Ryan, Regina Sara. 2009. (SPA & ENG.). (J). pap. *(978-1-890772-95-6(X))* Hohm Pr.

Ives, Penny. Five Little Ducks. (Classic Books with Holes 8x8 with CD Ser.). (ENG.). 16p. (J). 2007. audio compact disk *(978-1-84643-137-1(9))*; 2005. pap. *(978-0-85953-447-5(2))*; 2004. bds. *(978-0-85953-204-4(6))* Child's Play International Ltd.

—I'll Always Love You. Lewis, Paeony. (J). 2013. (ENG.). 32p. (gr. -1-2). pap. 3.99 *(978-1-58925-441-1(4))*; 2008. 12p. (gr. -1-3). bds. 7.95 *(978-1-58925-833-4(9))*; 2004. 32p. pap. 5.95 *(978-1-58925-360-5(4))* Tiger Tales.

Ives, Penny. Rabbit Pie. Ives, Penny. (Child's Play Library). (J). (gr. 1-1). 2012. 22p. spiral bd. *(978-1-84643-513-3(7))*; 2010. 32p. pap. *(978-1-84643-353-5(3))* Child's Play International Ltd.

Ives, Rob. Make Your Own Optical Illusions: 50 Hands-On Models & Experiment to Make & Do. Gifford, Clive. 2019. (ENG.). 64p. (J). (gr. 2-4). 19.95 ***(978-1-78603-862-3(5))*** QEB Publishing Inc.

Ives, Sarah Noble. Mother Stories. Lindsay, Maud. 2008. 160p. pap. 9.95 *(978-1-59915-167-0(7))* Yesterday's Classics.

Ivinson, Yvonne. Fox & the Box. Ivinson, Yvonne. 2019. (ENG.). 40p. (J). (gr. -1-3). 17.99 *(978-0-06-284287-9(0)*, Greenwillow Bks.) HarperCollins Pubs.

Ivy, Elena T. Learn About... Texas Birds. Lockwood, Mark W. 2007. (ENG.). 52p. (J). (gr. 1-7). pap. 10.95 *(978-0-292-71685-8(0))* Univ. of Texas Pr.

—Texas Indians. Zappler, Georg. 2007. (ENG.). 48p. (J). (gr. 1-7). pap. 10.95 *(978-0-292-71684-1(2))* Univ. of Texas Pr.

Ivy, Maggie. Beware the Bell Witch. 2018. (Haunted States of America Ser.). (ENG.). 136p. (J). lib. bdg. 27.13 *(978-1-63163-203-7(5)*, 1631632035, Jolly Fish Pr.) North Star Editions.

—Beware the Bell Witch. 2018. (Haunted States of America Ser.). (ENG.). 136p. (J). pap. 7.99 *(978-1-63163-204-4(3)*, 1631632043, Jolly Fish Pr.) North Star Editions.

—Curse of the Dead-Eyed Doll. Kingsley Troupe, Thomas. 2019. (Haunted States of America Set 2 (Set Of 4) Ser.). (ENG.). 136p. (J). pap. 7.99 *(978-1-63163-348-5(1)*, 1631633481); lib. bdg. 27.13 *(978-1-63163-347-8(3)*, 1631633473) North Star Editions. (Jolly Fish Pr.).

—Ghostly Reunion. Kingsley Troupe, Thomas. 2018. (Haunted States of America Ser.). (ENG.). 136p. (J). pap. 7.99 *(978-1-63163-208-2(6)*, 1631632086, Jolly Fish Pr.) North Star Editions.

—Ghostly Reunion. 2018. (Haunted States of America Ser.). (ENG.). 136p. (J). lib. bdg. 27.13 *(978-1-63163-207-5(8)*, 1631632078, Jolly Fish Pr.) North Star Editions.

—Haunted States of America Set 2 (Set Of 4) Kingsley Troupe, Thomas. 2019. (Haunted States of America Set 2 (Set Of 4) Ser.). (ENG.). 544p. (J). pap. 31.96 *(978-1-63163-344-7(9)*, 1631633449); lib. bdg. 108.52 *(978-1-63163-343-0(0)*, 1631633430) North Star Editions. (Jolly Fish Pr.).

—Haunted States of America (set Of 4) Kingsley Troupe, Thomas. 2018. (Haunted States of America Ser.). (ENG.). 544p. (J). pap. 31.96 *(978-1-63163-200-6(0)*,

1631632000); lib. bdg. 108.52 *(978-1-63163-199-3(3)*, 1631631993) North Star Editions. (Jolly Fish Pr.).

—Phantom of the Tracks. Kingsley Troupe, Thomas. 2019. (Haunted States of America Set 2 (Set Of 4) Ser.). (ENG.). 136p. (J). pap. 7.99 *(978-1-63163-352-2(X)*, 163163352X); lib. bdg. 27.13 *(978-1-63163-351-5(1)*, 1631633511) North Star Editions. (Jolly Fish Pr.).

—Spirits of the Storm. 2018. (Haunted States of America Ser.). (ENG.). 136p. (J). lib. bdg. 27.13 *(978-1-63163-211-2(6)*, 1631632116, Jolly Fish Pr.) North Star Editions.

—Spirits of the Storm. 2018. (Haunted States of America Ser.). (ENG.). 136p. (J). pap. 7.99 *(978-1-63163-212-9(4)*, 1631632124, Jolly Fish Pr.) North Star Editions.

—A Starlet's Shadow. Kingsley Troupe, Thomas. 2019. (Haunted States of America Set 2 (Set Of 4) Ser.). (ENG.). 136p. (J). pap. 7.99 *(978-1-63163-360-7(0)*, 1631633600); lib. bdg. 27.13 *(978-1-63163-359-1(7)*, 1631633597) North Star Editions. (Jolly Fish Pr.).

—Swamp of Lost Souls. Kingsley Troupe, Thomas. 2019. (Haunted States of America Set 2 (Set Of 4) Ser.). (ENG.). 136p. (J). pap. 7.99 *(978-1-63163-356-0(2)*, 1631633562); lib. bdg. 27.13 *(978-1-63163-355-3(4)*, 1631633554) North Star Editions. (Jolly Fish Pr.).

—Trapped in Room 217. Kingsley Troupe, Thomas. 2018. (Haunted States of America Ser.). (ENG.). 136p. (J). pap. 7.99 *(978-1-63163-216-7(7)*, 1631632167); lib. bdg. 27.13 *(978-1-63163-215-0(9)*, 1631632159) North Star Editions. (Jolly Fish Pr.).

Iwai, Melissa. B Is for Bulldozer: A Construction ABC. Sobel, June. 2006. 28p. (gr. -1-k). 17.00 *(978-0-7569-7037-6(7))* Perfection Learning Corp.

—B Is for Bulldozer: A Construction ABC. Sobel, June. 2006. (ENG.). 32p. (J). (gr. -1-3). pap. 7.99 *(978-0-15-205774-9(9)*, 1197355) Houghton Mifflin Harcourt Publishing Co.

—B Is for Bulldozer (lap Board Book) A Construction ABC. Sobel, June. 2018. (ENG.). 32p. (J). (— 1). bds. 12.99 *(978-1-328-77052-3(4)*, 1681071, HMH Books For Young Readers) Houghton Mifflin Harcourt Publishing Co.

—Bim & Bom, 2nd Edition: A Shabbat Tale, Vol. Swartz, Daniel. 2nd rev. ed. 2011. (ENG.). 24p. (J). (gr. -1-1). pap. 8.95 *(978-0-7613-6717-8(9)*, 9780761367178, Kar-Ben Publishing) Lerner Publishing Group.

—Chanukah Lights Everywhere. Rosen, Michael J. 2006. (ENG.). 32p. (J). (gr. -1-3). pap. 7.99 *(978-0-15-205675-9(0)*, 1197061) Houghton Mifflin Harcourt Publishing Co.

—Corn Aplenty. Rau, Dana Meachen. 2009. (Step into Reading Ser.). 32p. (J). (gr. -1-1). 3.99 *(978-0-375-85575-7(0)*, Random Hse. Bks. for Young Readers) Random Hse. Children's Bks.

—Eight Chanukah Lights. Auerbach, Annie. 2005. (ENG.). 18p. (J). 10.95 *(978-1-58117-326-0(1)*, Intervisual/Piggy Toes) Bendon, Inc.

—Hush, Little Monster. Markell, Denis. 2012. (ENG.). 32p. (J). (gr. -1-1). 9.99 *(978-1-4424-4195-8(X)*, Little Simon) Little Simon.

—I'll Hug You More. Duksta, Laura. 2017. (J). 22p. bds. 8.99 *(978-1-4926-4187-2(1)*, 9781492641872); (ENG.). 32p. 16.99 *(978-1-4926-2618-3(X)*, 9781492626183) Sourcebooks, Inc. (Sourcebooks Jabberwocky).

—Just Because I Am: A Child's Book of Affirmation. Payne, Lauren Murphy. 2nd rev. ed. 2015. (ENG.). 36p. (J). (gr. -1-2). 14.99 *(978-1-63198-051-0(3))* Free Spirit Publishing, Inc.

—Just Because I Am / Solo Porque Soy Yo: A Child's Book of Affirmation / un Libro de Afirmaciones para Niños. Payne, Lauren Murphy. 2018. (SPA.). 42p. (J). (gr. -1-3). pap. 12.45 *(978-1-63198-335-1(0))* Free Spirit Publishing, Inc.

—My Easter Egg: a Sparkly Peek-Through Story. Bryant, Megan E. 2017. 10p. (J). (gr. -1 — 1). 7.99 *(978-0-545-92180-0(5)*, Cartwheel Bks.) Scholastic, Inc.

—My Snow Globe: a Sparkly Peek-Through Story. Bryant, Megan E. 2016. (ENG.). 10p. (J). 7.99 *(978-0-545-92176-3(7)*, Cartwheel Bks.) Scholastic, Inc.

—One Is Enough. Cook, Julie Kidd. 2005. (Rookie Reader Skill Set Ser.). (ENG.). 24p. (J). (gr. 1-2). per. 4.95 *(978-0-516-25283-4(6)*, Children's Pr.) Scholastic Library Publishing.

—So Big! Yosemite. 2017. (ENG.). 15p. bds. 7.99 *(978-1-930238-77-0(0))* Yosemite Conservancy.

—So Small! Yosemite. 2018. (ENG.). 15p. (J). bds. 7.99 *(978-1-930238-86-2(X))* Yosemite Conservancy.

Iwai, Melissa. The Stray & the Strangers, 1 vol. Heighton, Steven. 2020. (ENG.). 112p. (J). (gr. 1-4). 14.95 ***(978-1-77306-381-2(2))*** Groundwood Bks. CAN. Dist: Publishers Group West (PGW).

Iwai, Melissa. Thirty Minutes over Oregon: A Japanese Pilot's World War II Story. Nobleman, Marc Tyler. 2018. (ENG.). 40p. (J). (gr. 1-4). 17.99 *(978-0-544-43076-1(X)*, 1595751, Clarion Bks.) Houghton Mifflin Harcourt Trade & Reference Pubs.

—We Can Get Along: A Child's Book of Choices. Payne, Lauren Murphy. 2nd rev. ed. 2015. (ENG.). 40p. (Orig.). (J). (gr. -1-2). pap. 11.99 *(978-1-63198-027-5(0))* Free Spirit Publishing, Inc.

—We Can Get along / Podemos Llevarnos Bien: A Child's Book of Choices / un Libro de Alternativas para Niños. Payne, Lauren Murphy. 2018. (SPA.). 48p. (J). (gr. -1-3). pap. 12.45 *(978-1-63198-338-2(5))* Free Spirit Publishing, Inc.

Iwai, Melissa. B Is for Bulldozer: A Construction ABC. Iwai, Melissa. Sobel, June. 2013. (ENG.). 32p. (J). (— 1). bds. 7.99 *(978-0-544-10808-0(6)*, 1540731) Houghton Mifflin Harcourt Publishing Co.

—Soup Day: a Board Book. Iwai, Melissa. 2017. (ENG.). 32p. (J). bds. 8.99 *(978-1-250-12772-3(6)*, 900175517, Holt, Henry & Co. Bks. For Young Readers) Holt, Henry & Co.

—Soup Day: a Picture Book. Iwai, Melissa. 2010. (ENG.). 40p. (J). (gr. -1-k). 17.99 *(978-0-8050-9004-8(5)*, 900058965, Holt, Henry & Co. Bks. For Young Readers) Holt, Henry & Co.

Iwanaga, Kent. The Girl & Her Cat. Squadrito, Vanessa. 2011. 24p. 12.56 *(978-1-4269-5531-0(6))* Trafford Publishing.

Iwasaki, Glen. Nikkei Donburi: A Japanese American Cultural Survival Guide. Aihara, Chris. 2004. 124p. (J). (gr. 1-4). pap. 18.95 *(978-1-879965-18-8(6))* Polychrome Publishing Corp.

Iwasaki, Masakazu. Popo Can, Vol. 3. Iwasaki, Masakazu. 2005. (Po Po Tan Ser.: Vol. 3). 208p. (YA). per. 9.95 *(978-1-59697-113-4(4))* Infinity Studios LLC.

Iwata, Nat. Steampunk Alphabet. 2013. (ENG.). 56p. (J). (gr. -1-1). 14.95 *(978-1-937359-40-9(9)*, Cameron Books) Cameron + Co.

—The Transatlantic Conspiracy. Falksen, G. D. 240p. (YA). 2017. (ENG.). (gr. 9). pap. 10.99 *(978-1-61695-814-5(6))*; 2016. (gr. 7). 18.99 *(978-1-61695-417-8(5))* Soho Pr., Inc. (Soho Teen).

Iwicki, Lizzie. The Happiest Herder: The Discovery of Coffee, in Amharic & English. 2020. (ENG.). 36p. (J). pap. 11.99 ***(978-1-6587-1254-5(4))*** Independently Published.

Iwicki, Lizzie & Students from Christa McAuliffe Elementa. The Happiest Herder: In English & Tigrinya. Ready Set Go Books. 2019. (ENG.). 34p. (J). pap. 11.99 ***(978-1-6897-8003-2(7))*** Independently Published.

Iwohn, Sebastien & Mansfield, Andy. First Words - English, 1 vol. Lonely Planet Kids. 2017. (First Words Ser.). (ENG.). 208p. (J). (gr. 1-3). pap. 12.99 *(978-1-78701-279-0(4)*, 5716) Lonely Planet Global Ltd. IRL. Dist: Hachette Bk. Group.

—First Words - Italian: 100 Italian Words to Learn, 1 vol. Lonely Planet Kids. 2018. (First Words Ser.). (ENG.). 208p. (J). (gr. 1-3). pap. 12.99 *(978-1-78701-268-4(9)*, 5709) Lonely Planet Global Ltd. IRL. Dist: Hachette Bk. Group.

—First Words - Japanese: 100 Japanese Words to Learn, 1 vol. Lonely Planet Kids. 2018. (First Words Ser.). (ENG.). 208p. (J). (gr. 1-3). pap. 12.99 *(978-1-78701-270-7(0)*, 5711) Lonely Planet Global Ltd. IRL. Dist: Hachette Bk. Group.

—First Words - Mandarin: 100 Mandarin Words to Learn, 1 vol. Lonely Planet Kids. 2018. (First Words Ser.). (ENG.). 208p. (J). (gr. 1-3). pap. 12.99 *(978-1-78701-272-1(7)*, 5713) Lonely Planet Global Ltd. IRL. Dist: Hachette Bk. Group.

—First Words - Spanish, 1 vol. Lonely Planet Kids. 2017. (First Words Ser.). (ENG.). 208p. (J). (gr. 1-3). pap. 12.99 *(978-1-78657-317-9(2)*, 5403) Lonely Planet Global Ltd. IRL. Dist: Hachette Bk. Group.

Iyad de Luna, Vivas and. Let's Be Thoughtful: Thinking of Others! Noble, Loren. 2019. (ENG.). 28p. (J). pap. 9.49 ***(978-1-9812-5801-7(9))*** CreateSpace Independent Publishing Platform.

Iybish, Shirin. Tariq Faris Al-Arab. Iybish, Shirin. 2017. (ARA.). 21p. (J). *(978-9953-37-274-7(8))* Academia.

Iyengar, Malathi. Dance & Devotion: A Hand Book on 'Bharatanatyam' Dance & Traditional Prayers for Students Pursuing Indian Classical Dance. Iyengar, Malathi, compiled by. 2004. (SAN, ENG & HIN.). 184p. 20.00 *(978-0-9753912-0-4(8))* Iyengar, Malathi.

Iyengar, Uma. The Shoshan. Iyengar, Uma. 2005. (ESP.). 228p. (YA). *(978-0-9771184-0-3(1))* Infobus, Inc.

Izaakse, Sean. Champions Vol. 4: Northern Lights. 2018. (Champions (2016) Ser.: 4). (ENG.). 112p. (YA). (gr. 8-17). pap. 15.99 *(978-1-302-90982-6(7))* Marvel Worldwide, Inc.

—Fantastic Four by Dan Slott Vol. 4: Thing vs. Immortal Hulk. 2020. (Fantastic Four by Dan Slott Ser.: 4). (ENG.). 120p. (YA). (gr. 4-17). pap. 15.99 *(978-1-302-91725-8(0))* Marvel Worldwide, Inc.

Izaakse, Sean, et al. Monsters Unleashed: Battleground. 2017. (ENG.). 264p. (YA). (gr. 8-17). pap. 29.99 *(978-1-302-90719-8(0))* Marvel Worldwide, Inc.

Izaakse, Sean & Guinaldo, Andres. Captain America: Secret Empire. 2017. (ENG.). 136p. (YA). (gr. 8-17). pap. 17.99 *(978-1-302-90849-2(9))* Marvel Worldwide, Inc.

Izaakse, Sean & Libranda, Kevin. Champions Vol. 5: Weird War One. 2019. (Champions (2016) Ser.: 5). (ENG.). 176p. (J). (gr. 4-17). pap. 19.99 *(978-1-302-91505-6(3))* Marvel Worldwide, Inc.

Izaakse, Sean, jt. illus. see Malin, Jon.

Izaakse, Sean, jt. illus. see Medina, Paco.

Izenwata, Chinwendu. Why, Oh Why, Why Must I Be So Shy!?!, 1 vol. Ajiri, Ijeoma. 2010. 16p. 24.95 *(978-1-4512-0928-0(2))* PublishAmerica, Inc.

Izgarevic, Radomir. Kingdom Adventures: Meet the Giant. Donahue, Michael Scott. 2019. (Kingdom Adventures Ser.: Vol. 1). (ENG.). 26p. (J). pap. 10.99 ***(978-1-7100-8718-5(8))*** Independently Published.

Izu, Kenro, photos by. Passage to Angkor. 2nd ed. 2006. (ENG., 116p. pap. 59.95 *(978-0-9653574-7-0(3))* Friends Without a Border.

Izumi, Kaneyoshi. Doubt!! Izumi, Kaneyoshi. Kokubo, Naomi, tr. from JPN. 2005. (Doubt Ser.: 3). (ENG.). 200p. pap. 9.99 *(978-1-59116-910-9(0))* Viz Media.

—Doubt!!, Vol. 2. Izumi, Kaneyoshi. 2005. (Doubt Ser.: 2). (ENG.). 184p. pap. 9.99 *(978-1-59116-909-3(7))* Viz Media.

—Doubt!!, Vol. 1. Izumi, Kaneyoshi. 2005. (ENG.). 192p. pap. 9.99 *(978-1-59116-908-6(9))* Viz Media.

Izumi, Rei. .Hack: //Legend of the Twilight, 3 vols. Hamazaki, Tatsuya. Kokubo, Naomi, tr. from JPN. 2003. 192p. (YA). (gr. 4-12). pap. 9.99 *(978-1-59182-414-5(1))* TOKYOPOP, Inc.

—. hack //Legend of the Twilight, Volume 1: Kaplan SAT/ACT Vocabulary-Building Manga. Hamazaki, Tatsuya. 2007. (Kaplan SAT/ACT Score-Raising Manga Ser.). 192p. pap. 9.99 *(978-1-4277-5497-4(7))* Kaplan Publishing.

—. Hack//Ai Buster. 2005. 192p. pap. 7.99 *(978-1-59532-869-4(6))* TOKYOPOP, Inc.

—Legend of the Twilight Bracelet, 3 vols. Hamazaki, Tatsuya. rev. ed. 192p. Vol. 2. 2003. pap. 9.99 *(978-1-59182-415-2(X))*; Vol. 3. 2004. (YA). pap. 9.99 *(978-1-59532-369-9(4))* TOKYOPOP, Inc.

J

J, Vuttipat. Lilly & Her Unicorn Doll: Book 5: Forgiveness & Compassion. Chandler, Aaron. 2019. (Magic of My Unicorn Doll Ser.: Vol. 5). (ENG.). 34p. (J). pap. 9.99 *(978-1-0969-4088-3(4))* Independently Published.

J, Vuttipat. Lilly & Her Unicorn Doll: Vol. 6: the Importance of Learning. Chandler, Aaron. 2019. (Magic of My Unicorn Doll Ser.: Vol. 6). (ENG.). 30p. (J). pap. 9.95 ***(978-1-7098-7614-1(X))*** Independently Published.

Jabar, Cynthia. One Frog Sang. Parenteau, Shirley. 2007. (ENG.). 32p. (J). (gr. -1-1). 21.19 *(978-0-7636-2394-4(6))* Candlewick Pr.

—The Scrubbly-Bubbly Car Wash. O'Garden, Irene. 2003. (ENG.). 32p. (J). (gr. -1-1). 15.99 *(978-0-694-00871-1(0))* HarperCollins Pubs.

—Tally O'Malley. Murphy, Stuart J. 2004. (MathStart Ser.). 40p. (J). (gr. 1-18). 15.99 *(978-0-06-053162-1(2))*; (ENG.). pap. 5.99 *(978-0-06-053164-5(9))* HarperCollins Pubs.

Jacana Agency, photos by. The Wolf: Night Howler. Havard, Christian. 2006. (Animal Close-Ups Ser.). 28p. (Orig.). (J). (gr. -1-3). pap. 6.95 *(978-1-57091-630-4(6))* Charlesbridge Publishing, Inc.

Jacinto, K. I. M., jt. illus. see Cassara, J.

Jacinto, K. I. M., jt. illus. see Pacheco, Carlos.

Jack, Colin. The Blunders: a Counting Catastrophe! Soontornvat, Christina. 2020. 32p. (J). (gr. -1-2). 16.99 *(978-1-5362-0109-3(X))* Candlewick Pr.

—Dragons from Mars. Aronson, Deborah. 2016. (ENG.). 32p. (J). (gr. -1-3). 17.99 *(978-0-06-236850-8(8))* HarperCollins Pubs.

—Dragons from Mars Go to School. Aronson, Deborah. 2019. (ENG.). 32p. (J). (gr. -1-3). 17.99 *(978-0-06-236851-5(6))* HarperCollins Pubs.

—Drake Makes a Splash! O'Ryan, Ray. 2014. (Galaxy Zack Ser.: 8). (ENG.). 128p. (J). (gr. k-2). pap. 5.99 *(978-1-4424-9360-5(7)*, Little Simon) Little Simon.

—Eureka! Lachenmeyer, Nathaniel. 2013. (J). *(978-0-8037-3514-9(6)*, Dial) Penguin Publishing Group.

—A Galactic Easter! O'Ryan, Ray. 2014. (Galaxy Zack Ser.: 7). (ENG.). 128p. (J). (gr. k-4). pap. 5.99 *(978-1-4424-9357-5(7)*, Little Simon) Little Simon.

—Galaxy Zack 3 Books In 1! Hello, Nebulon!; Journey to Juno; the Prehistoric Planet. O'Ryan, Ray. 2015. (Galaxy Zack Ser.). (ENG.). 384p. (J). (gr. k-4). pap. 8.99 *(978-1-4814-5641-8(5)*, Little Simon) Little Simon.

—Gnome-A-geddon. Holt, K. A. (ENG.). 304p. (J). (gr. 3-7). 2018. pap. 7.99 *(978-1-4814-7846-5(X))*; 2017. 16.99 *(978-1-4814-7845-8(1))* McElderry, Margaret K. Bks. (McElderry, Margaret K. Bks.).

—Go to School. Falatko, Julie. 2018. (Two Dogs in a Trench Coat Ser.: 1). (ENG.). 192p. (J). (gr. 3-7). 9.99 *(978-1-338-18951-3(4))* Scholastic, Inc.

—A Green Christmas! O'Ryan, Ray. 2013. (Galaxy Zack Ser.: 6). (ENG.). 128p. (J). (gr. k-2). 16.99 *(978-1-4424-8225-8(7))*; pap. 5.99 *(978-1-4424-8224-1(9))* Little Simon. (Little Simon).

—Hello, Nebulon! O'Ryan, Ray. 2013. (Galaxy Zack Ser.: 1). (ENG.). 128p. (J). (gr. k-2). 16.99 *(978-1-4424-5387-6(7))*; pap. 5.99 *(978-1-4424-5386-9(9))* Little Simon. (Little Simon).

—Hello, Nebulon! O'Ryan, Ray. ed. 2015. (Galaxy Zack Ser.). (ENG.). 128p. (J). (gr. 2-5). 27.07 *(978-1-61479-367-0(0)*, 18202, Chapter Bks.) Spotlight.

—If You Happen to Have a Dinosaur. Bailey, Linda. (ENG.). (J). 2017. 30p. (— 1). bds. 8.99 *(978-1-101-91891-3(8))*; 2014. 40p. (gr. -1-2). 17.99 *(978-1-77049-568-5(1))* Tundra Bks. CAN. (Tundra Bks.). Dist: Penguin Random Hse. LLC.

—Jack & Jill Flip-Side Rhymes. Harbo, Christopher L. 2015. (Flip-Side Nursery Rhymes Ser.). (ENG.). 24p. (J). (gr. -1-2). lib. bdg. 27.99 *(978-1-4795-5988-6(1)*, Picture Window Bks.) Capstone.

—Journey to Juno. O'Ryan, Ray. 2013. (Galaxy Zack Ser.: 2). (ENG.). 128p. (J). (gr. k-4). 17.99 *(978-1-4424-5391-3(5))*; pap. 5.99 *(978-1-4424-5390-6(7))* Little Simon. (Little Simon).

—Little Miss Muffet Flip-Side Rhymes. Harbo, Christopher L. 2015. (Flip-Side Nursery Rhymes Ser.). (ENG.). 24p. (J). (gr. -1-2). lib. bdg. 27.99 *(978-1-4795-5987-9(3)*, Picture Window Bks.) Capstone.

—Monsters in Space! O'Ryan, Ray. 2013. (Galaxy Zack Ser.: 4). (ENG.). 128p. (J). (gr. k-2). 16.99 *(978-1-4424-6721-7(5))*; pap. 5.99 *(978-1-4424-6718-7(5))* Little Simon. (Little Simon).

—Noah Noasaurus. Kearns, Elaine Kiely. 2019. (ENG.). 32p. (J). (gr. -1-k). 16.99 *(978-0-8075-5703-7(X)*, 080755703X) Whitman, Albert & Co.

—Plans Gone Wrong. Griffin, Molly Beth. 2019. (ENG.). 32p. (J). pap. *(978-1-4747-7178-8(5)*, Picture Window Bks.) Capstone.

—The Prehistoric Planet. O'Ryan, Ray. 2013. (Galaxy Zack Ser.: 3). (ENG.). 128p. (J). (gr. k-4). 16.99 *(978-1-4424-6716-3(9)*, Little Simon) Little Simon.

—The Prehistoric Planet. O'Ryan, Ray. 2013. (Galaxy Zack Ser.: 3). (ENG.). 128p. (J). (gr. k-4). pap. 5.99 *(978-1-4424-6715-6(0)*, Little Simon) Little Simon.

—The Prizewinners of Piedmont Place. Doyle, Bill. 2016. (Prizewinners of Piedmont Place Ser.: 1). 192p. (J). (gr. 3-7). 15.99 *(978-0-553-52177-1(2)*, Random Hse. Bks. for Young Readers) Random Hse. Children's Bks.

—The Quirks & the Freaky Field Trip. Soderberg, Erin. 2015. (Quirks Ser.). 208p. (YA). (gr. 3-6). 13.99 *(978-1-61963-668-2(9)*, 9781619636682, Bloomsbury USA Childrens) Bloomsbury Publishing USA.

—Three's a Crowd! O'Ryan, Ray. 2013. (Galaxy Zack Ser.: 5). (ENG.). 128p. (J). (gr. k-4). 17.99 *(978-1-4424-8222-7(2)*, Little Simon) Little Simon.

—Three's a Crowd! O'Ryan, Ray. 2013. (Galaxy Zack Ser.: 5). (ENG.). 128p. (J). (gr. k-4). pap. 5.99 *(978-1-4424-8221-0(4)*, Little Simon) Little Simon.

—Toads on Toast. Bailey, Linda. 2012. (ENG.). 32p. (J). (gr. -1-2). 16.95 *(978-1-55453-662-7(6))* Kids Can Pr., Ltd. CAN. Dist: Hachette Bk. Group.

—Two Dogs in a Trench Coat Start a Club by Accident. Falatko, Julie. 2019. (Two Dogs in a Trench Coat Ser.: 2). (ENG.). 208p. (J). (gr. 3-7). 9.99 *(978-1-338-18953-7(0))* Scholastic, Inc.

—1 Zany Zoo. Degman, Lori. 2010. (ENG.). 32p. (J). (gr. -1-2). 19.99 *(978-1-4169-8990-5(0)*, Simon & Schuster Bks. For Young Readers) Simon & Schuster Bks. For Young Readers.

—7 Days of Awesome: A Creation Tale, 1 vol. Byous, Shawn. 2016. (ENG.). 40p. (J). 16.99 *(978-0-310-74349-1(4))* Zonderkidz.

Jack, Colin & Chatzikonstantinou, Danny. Flip-Side Nursery Rhymes. Harbo, Christopher. 2015. (Flip-Side Nursery Rhymes Ser.). (ENG.). 24p. (J). (gr. -1-2). lib. bdg., lib. bdg. 111.96 *(978-1-4795-6022-6(7)*, Picture Window Bks.) Capstone.

Jack, Colin, jt. illus. see Chatzikonstantinou, Danny.

Jack Pullan & Banks, Timothy. Los Tres Chivos. Hillert, Margaret. 2017. (BeginningtoRead Ser.).Tr. of Three Goats. (ENG & SPA.). 32p. (J). (-2). 22.60 *(978-1-59953-851-8(2))*; pap. 11.94 *(978-1-68404-050-6(7))* Norwood Hse. Pr.

Jack Pullan & Barnum-Newman, Winifred. Caperucita Roja. Hillert, Margaret. 2017. (BeginningtoRead Ser.).Tr. of Little Red Riding Hood. (ENG & SPA.). 32p. (J). (-2). 22.60 *(978-1-59953-846-4(6))*; pap. 11.94 *(978-1-68404-045-2(0))* Norwood Hse. Pr.

Jack Pullan & Caminador, Juan. Cenicienta en el Baile. Hillert, Margaret. 2017. (BeginningtoRead Ser.).Tr. of Cinderella at the Ball. (ENG & SPA.). 32p. (J). (-2). 22.60 *(978-1-59953-841-9(5))*; pap. 11.94 *(978-1-68404-040-7(X))* Norwood Hse. Pr.

Jack Pullan & Collier-Morales, Roberta. Cuatro Buenos Amigos. Hillert, Margaret. 2017. (BeginningtoRead Ser.).Tr. of Four Good Friends. (ENG & SPA.). 32p. (J). (-2). 22.60 *(978-1-59953-843-3(1))*; pap. 11.94 *(978-1-68404-042-1(6))* Norwood Hse. Pr.

Jack Pullan & Dodson, Bert. Yo No, Yo No. Hillert, Margaret. 2017. (BeginningtoRead Ser.).Tr. of Not I, Not I. (ENG & SPA.). 32p. (J). (-2). 22.60 *(978-1-59953-848-8(2))*; pap. 11.94 *(978-1-68404-047-6(7))* Norwood Hse. Pr.

Jack Pullan & Dorenkamp, Michelle. Los Tres Cerditos. Hillert, Margaret. 2017. (BeginningtoRead Ser.).Tr. of Three Little Pigs. (ENG & SPA.). 32p. (J). (-2). 22.60 *(978-1-59953-852-5(0))*; pap. 11.94 *(978-1-68404-051-3(5))* Norwood Hse. Pr.

Jack Pullan & Han, Yu-Mei. Pulgarcito. Hillert, Margaret. 2017. (BeginningtoRead Ser.).Tr. of Tom Thumb. (ENG & SPA.). 32p. (J). (-2). 22.60 *(978-1-59953-853-2(9))*; pap. 11.94 *(978-1-68404-052-0(3))* Norwood Hse. Pr.

Jack Pullan & Petruccio, Steven James. La Galletita. Hillert, Margaret. 2017. (BeginningtoRead Ser.).Tr. of Little Cookie. (ENG & SPA.). 32p. (J). (-2). 22.60 *(978-1-59953-845-7(8))*; pap. 11.94 *(978-1-68404-044-5(2))* Norwood Hse. Pr.

Jack Pullan & Regan, Dana. Pinocho. Hillert, Margaret. 2017. (BeginningtoRead Ser.).Tr. of Pinocchio. (ENG & SPA.). 32p. (J). (-2). 22.60 *(978-1-59953-849-5(0))*; pap. 11.94 *(978-1-68404-048-3(5))* Norwood Hse. Pr.

Jack Pullan & Szulyovszky, Sarolta. El Niño y los Chivos. Hillert, Margaret. 2017. (BeginningtoRead Ser.).Tr. of Boy & the Goats. (ENG & SPA.). 32p. (J). (-2). 22.60 *(978-1-59953-840-2(7))*; pap. 11.94 *(978-1-68404-039-1(6))* Norwood Hse. Pr.

Jack Pullan & Undercuffler, Gary. Los Tres Osos. Hillert, Margaret. 2017. (BeginningtoRead Ser.).Tr. of Three Bears. (ENG & SPA.). 32p. (J). (-2). 22.60 *(978-1-59953-850-1(4))*; pap. 11.94 *(978-1-68404-049-0(3))* Norwood Hse. Pr.

Jack Pullan & Utomo, Gabhor. La Casa de Galletitas. Hillert, Margaret. 2017. (BeginningtoRead Ser.).Tr. of Cookie House. (ENG & SPA.). 32p. (J). (-2). 22.60 *(978-1-59953-842-6(3))*; pap. 11.94 *(978-1-68404-041-4(8))* Norwood Hse. Pr.

Jack Pullan & Wendland, Paula. El Bebé Raro. Hillert, Margaret. 2017. (BeginningtoRead Ser.).Tr. of Funny Baby. (ENG & SPA.). 32p. (J). (-2). 22.60 *(978-1-59953-844-0(X))*; pap. 11.94 *(978-1-68404-043-8(4))* Norwood Hse. Pr.

Jack Pullan & Zaman, Farida. Los Frijoles Mágicos. Hillert, Margaret. 2017. (BeginningtoRead Ser.).Tr. of Magic Beans. (ENG & SPA.). 32p. (J). (-2). 22.60 *(978-1-59953-847-1(4))*; pap. 11.94 *(978-1-68404-046-9(9))* Norwood Hse. Pr.

Jack, Ryann. Aunt Fab the Fabulous. Saar, Maureen. 2019. (ENG.). 32p. (J). pap. 10.00 ***(978-1-7087-3446-6(5))*** Independently Published.

Jack, Sari. The Bean Family Sprouts: Growing Stronger Through New Experiences. Shahine, Lora. 2019. (ENG.). 28p. (J). pap. 11.99 ***(978-0-9987146-6-0(6))*** Shahine, Lora.

Jackman, Tierra N. The Sky Is Falling. Joseph, Phara. 2nd ed. 2019. (ENG.). 28p. (J). 20.00 ***(978-0-692-92795-3(6))*** Penned By Fafa, LLC.

Jackowski, Amélie. The Day Everything Went Wrong. Petz, Moritz. 2015. 32p. (J). 17.95 *(978-0-7358-4209-0(4))* North-South Bks., Inc.

—Doctor Mouse. Kempter, Christa. 2020. (ENG.). 32p. (J). (gr. -1-2). 17.95 *(978-0-7358-4410-0(0))* North-South Bks., Inc.

Jackowski, Amélie. The Bad Mood. Jackowski, Amélie. Petz, Moritz. 2019. (ENG.). 24p. (J). (-k). bds. 8.95 *(978-0-7358-4387-5(2))* North-South Bks., Inc.

Jackson, Anthony B. Oliver Vance Pull up Your Pants! McBride, Maurice & Wallace, Jessica K. 2011. 32p. (J). 13.95 *(978-1-935802-06-8(2))* Father & Son Publishing.

Jackson, April Eley & DeShazo, Sharon B. Carpentry & Woodworking Tools of Hope Plantation. Jones, Alice Eley. 2004. 100p. (YA). (gr. 4-18). pap. 20.00 *(978-0-9727480-4-9(0))* Minnie Troy Pubs.

J

Jackson, Barry E. Bedtime for Little Bulldozer. Broach, Elise. 2019. (ENG.). 40p. (J). 17.99 *(978-1-250-10928-6(0),* 900165515, Holt, Henry & Co. Bks. For Young Readers) Holt, Henry & Co.

Jackson, Barry E. Danny Diamondback. Jackson, Barry E. 2008. 40p. (J). (gr. k-2). lib. bdg. 17.89 *(978-0-06-113185-1(7))* HarperCollins Pubs.

Jackson, Bert. The Adventures of Robin Hood: An English Legend. 2004. (ENG.). 24p. (J). (gr. 3-3). pap. 6.47 net. *(978-0-7685-2125-2(4),* Dominie Elementary) Savvas Learning Co.

Jackson, Brittany. Parker Looks Up: An Extraordinary Moment. Curry, Parker & Curry, Jessica. 2019. (ENG.). 40p. (J). (gr. -1-3). 17.99 *(978-1-5344-5186-5(2),* Aladdin) Simon & Schuster Children's Publishing.

Jackson, Brittany. Saving Eli's Library. Horowitz, Ruth. 2020. (ENG.). 32p. (J). (gr. -1-3). 16.99 ***(978-0-8075-1971-4(5),*** 0807519715) Whitman, Albert & Co.

Jackson, Brittany Janay. Tim the Cat. Hansen, Roland. 2008. (ARA.). 28p. per. 8.85 *(978-0-9814650-0-5(5))* G Publishing LLC.

Jackson-Carter, Stuart. Gorilla. Costain, Meredith. 2016. (Wild World Ser.). 00032p. (J). (gr. 1-2). pap. 10.00 *(978-1-4994-8209-6(4),* Windmill Bks.) Rosen Publishing Group, Inc., The.

—Kangaroo. Costain, Meredith. 2016. (Wild World Ser.). 00032p. (J). (gr. 1-2). pap. 10.00 *(978-1-4994-8212-6(4),* Windmill Bks.) Rosen Publishing Group, Inc., The.

—Lemur. Costain, Meredith. 2016. (Wild World Ser.). 00032p. (J). (gr. 1-2). pap. 10.00 *(978-1-4994-8215-7(9),* Windmill Bks.) Rosen Publishing Group, Inc., The.

—Panda. Costain, Meredith. 2016. (Wild World Ser.). 00032p. (J). (gr. 1-2). 27.25 *(978-1-4994-8221-8(3),* Windmill Bks.) Rosen Publishing Group, Inc., The.

Jackson, Dan. Angel & Faith Volume 3: Family Reunion. Gage, Christos. Allie, Scott & Hahn, Sierra, eds. 2013. (Angel Ser.). (ENG.). 136p. pap. 17.99 *(978-1-61655-079-0(1))* Dark Horse Comics.

—Troublemaker. Evanovich, Alex & Evanovich, Janet. 2011. (ENG.). 112p. pap. 16.99 *(978-1-59582-722-7(6))* Dark Horse Comics.

Jackson, Faye. Dinkville. Moncrieff, Celia. 2019. (Zest Ser.: Vol. 3). (ENG.). 48p. (J). (gr. k-6). *(978-0-6483559-1-5(8));* pap. *(978-0-6483559-2-2(6))* Bobbin Bks.

—Our Funny Dunny. Moncrieff, Celia. 2018. (ENG.). 34p. (J). (gr. k-6). *(978-0-6483558-0-9(2))* Bobbin Bks.

—The Town of Killsnackary. Moncrieff, Celia. 2019. (Zest Ser.: Vol. 1). (ENG.). 50p. (J). (gr. k-6). *(978-0-6483558-7-8(X));* pap. *(978-0-6483558-8-5(8))* Bobbin Bks.

—The Town of Wen. Moncrieff, Celia. 2019. (Zest Ser.: Vol. 2). (ENG.). 50p. (J). (gr. k-6). pap. *(978-0-6483559-0-8(X));* *(978-0-6483558-9-2(6))* Bobbin Bks.

—Twimble & Twomble. Moncrieff, Celia. 2019. (Zest Ser.: Vol. 4). (ENG.). 48p. (J). (gr. k-6). *(978-0-6483559-6-0(9))* Bobbin Bks.

—Wendy the Wyandotte. Moncrieff, Celia. 2018. (ENG.). 36p. (J). (gr. k-6). *(978-0-6483558-3-0(7));* pap. *(978-0-6483558-4-7(5))* Bobbin Bks.

Jackson, Helston & Anderson, Betheny. Pepere's Little Girl. Jackson, Penny. 2008. 27p. pap. 24.95 *(978-1-60441-881-1(8))* America Star Bks.

Jackson, I. L. Colour the Holidays Activity Book. Newton, Bev. 2019. (ENG.). 120p. (J). pap. *(978-1-989322-12-3(3))* Pine Lake Bks.

—The Girl & the Toad:; or the Toad Prince. Henderson, Lynn. 2017. (ENG.). (J). pap. *(978-1-926898-93-3(1))* Pine Lake Bks.

—Tommy's Bike. Henderson, Lynn. 2019. (ENG.). 32p. (J). pap. *(978-1-989322-13-0(1))* Pine Lake Bks.

Jackson, I. L. & Simpson, L. M. Tessy the Teapot That Couldn't Drip. Daulby, Joan. 2019. (ENG.). 32p. (J). pap. *(978-1-989322-04-8(2))* Pine Lake Bks.

Jackson, Ian. Baby Animals. Parker, Steve. 2010. (I Love Animals Ser.). (ENG.). 24p. (J). (gr. 1-5). pap. 8.15 *(978-1-61533-231-1(6));* lib. bdg. 25.60 *(978-1-61533-225-0(1))* Windmill Bks.

—Big Bug Search. Young, Caroline. rev. ed. 2005. 32p. (J). pap. 7.99 *(978-0-7945-1045-9(0),* Usborne) EDC Publishing.

—Big Cats. Parker, Steve. 2010. (I Love Animals Ser.). (ENG.). 24p. (J). (gr. 1-5). pap. 8.15 *(978-1-61533-251-9(0));* lib. bdg. 25.60 *(978-1-61533-245-8(6))* Windmill Bks.

—The Great Animal Search. Young, Caroline. 2006. (Great Searches New Format Ser.). 48p. (J). (gr. 3). lib. bdg. 15.99 *(978-1-58086-965-2(3));* (gr. -1-3). pap. 8.99 *(978-0-7945-1028-2(0),* Usborne) EDC Publishing.

—Great Planet Earth Search. Helbrough, Emma. Milbourne, Anna, ed. 2005. (Great Searches Ser.). 32p. (J). (gr. 3). lib. bdg. 15.95 *(978-1-58086-827-3(4))* EDC Publishing.

—Great Planet Earth Search. Helbrough, Emma. 2006. 32p. (J). *(978-0-439-83402-5(3))* Scholastic, Inc.

—Great Prehistoric Search. Bingham, Jane. 2004. (Great Searches Ser.). 32p. (J). pap. 8.95 *(978-0-7945-0663-6(1),* Usborne) EDC Publishing.

—Great Wildlife Search: Big Bug Search, Great Animal Search & Great Undersea Search. Young, Caroline & Needham, Kate. 2004. (Great Searches Ser.). 112p. (J). pap. 15.99 *(978-0-7945-0892-0(8),* Usborne) EDC Publishing.

—Greeks. Peach, Susan & Millard, Anne. 2004. (Illustrated World History Ser.). 96p. (J). (gr. 6). lib. bdg. 20.95 *(978-1-58086-631-6(X),* Usborne) EDC Publishing.

—Horses. Regan, Lisa. 2010. (I Love Animals Ser.). (ENG.). 24p. (J). (gr. 1-5). pap. 8.15 *(978-1-61533-234-2(0));* lib. bdg. 25.60 *(978-1-61533-228-1(6))* Windmill Bks.

—Usborne the Great Undersea Search. Needham, Kate. Brooks, Felicity, ed. rev. ed. 2006. (Great Searches Ser.). 32p. (J). (gr. -1-3). per. 7.99 *(978-0-7945-1228-6(3),* Usborne) EDC Publishing.

—The Young Naturalist. Mitchell, Andrew. Jacquemier, Sue & Bramwell, Martyn, eds. 2008. (Hobby Guides Ser.). 32p. (J). (gr. 5-9). pap. 6.99 *(978-0-7945-2219-3(X),* Usborne) EDC Publishing.

—10 Things You Should Know about Big Cats. Parker, Steve. Borton, Paula, ed. 2004. (Things You Should Know about Ser.). 24p. (J). 6.99 *(978-1-84236-119-1(8))* Miles Kelly Publishing, Ltd. GBR. Dist: Independent Pubs. Group.

—50 Horses & Ponies to Spot. Kahn, Sarah, ed. 2009. (Spotter's Cards Ser.). 52p. (J). 9.99 *(978-0-7945-2171-4(1),* Usborne) EDC Publishing.

Jackson, Ian & Suttie, Alan. Rocks & Fossils. Bramwell, Martyn. Bramwell, Martyn, ed. rev. ed. 2007. (Hobby Guides). 31p. (J). pap. 6.99 *(978-0-7945-1526-3(6),* Usborne) EDC Publishing.

Jackson, Ian & Wood, Gerald. Romans. Marks, Anthony & Tingay, Graham. 2005. (Illustrated World History Ser.). 96p. (J). (gr. 6-12). lib. bdg. 20.95 *(978-1-58086-782-5(0),* Usborne) EDC Publishing.

Jackson, Ian, jt. illus. see McGregor, Malcolm.

Jackson, Ian, jt. illus. see Montgomery, Lee.

Jackson, Jack. New Texas History Movies. Jackson, Jack. Magruder, Jana. 2007. (ENG.). 66p. pap. 19.95 *(978-0-87611-231-1(9))* Texas State Historical Assn.

Jackson, James. Dancing with David. Date not set. 24p. (J). *(978-1-887399-02-9(X))* Colbert Hse., LLC, The.

Jackson, Jeannie. Squizzy the Black Squirrel: A Fabulous Fable of Friendship. Jackson, Jeannie, tr. Stone, Chuck. 2003. 30p. (J). 16.95 *(978-0-940880-71-9(7))* Open Hand Publishing, LLC.

Jackson, Jeff. Le Jeune Coq Stupide: French-Arabic Edition. Shah, Idries. 2018. (Hoopoe Teaching-Stories Ser.). (FRE.). 40p. (J). (gr. k-2). pap. 9.99 ***(978-1-949358-51-3(8),*** Hoopoe Bks.) I S H K.

—Le Lion Qui Se Vit Dans L'eau: French-Arabic Edition. Shah, Idries. 2018. (Hoopoe Teaching-Stories Ser.). (FRE.). 40p. (J). (gr. k-4). pap. 9.99 ***(978-1-949358-46-9(1),*** Hoopoe Bks.) I S H K.

Jackson, Jeff. Me & My Feelings: What Emotions Are & How We Can Manage Them. Guarino, Robert. 2010. 168p. (YA). (gr. 7-18). pap. 15.99 *(978-1-933779-71-3(3),* Hoopoe Bks.) I S H K.

—The Silly Chicken. Shah, Idries. 2005. 32p. (J). pap., pap. 6.99 *(978-1-883536-50-3(2),* Hoopoe Bks.) I S H K.

—The Silly Chicken: English-Dari Edition. Shah, Idries. 2017. (Hoopoe Teaching-Stories Ser.). (ENG.). (J). (gr. k-6). pap. 9.99 *(978-1-946270-18-4(0),* Hoopoe Bks.) I S H K.

—The Silly Chicken: English-Pashto Edition. Shah, Idries. 2017. (Hoopoe Teaching-Stories Ser.). (ENG & PUS.). (J). (gr. 1-6). pap. 9.99 *(978-1-944493-63-9(8),* Hoopoe Bks.) I S H K.

—The Silly Chicken: English-Urdu Edition. Shah, Idries. 2016. (URD & ENG.). (J). (gr. k-6). pap. 9.99 *(978-1-942698-79-1(8),* Hoopoe Bks.) I S H K.

—The Silly Chicken/el Pollo Bobo. Shah, Idries. Wirkala, Rita, tr. 2005. 32p. (J). (gr. -1-3). 18.00 *(978-1-883536-37-4(5),* Hoopoe Bks.) I S H K.

—What's the Catch: How to Avoid Getting Hooked & Manipulated. Sobel, David S. 2010. 144p. (YA). (gr. 7-18). pap. 15.99 *(978-1-933779-78-2(0),* Hoopoe Bks.) I S H K.

Jackson, Joel. Penny & Friends. McGhee, Jamil. 2019. (ENG.). 24p. (J). (gr. k-3). pap. 10.95 ***(978-1-62787-770-1(3))*** Wheatmark, Inc.

Jackson, Josh. Tickle Mites Adventures of R. A. R. Rocky, AJ, & Ramello. Outlaw, Rebecca a. 2019. (Tickle Mites Ser.: Vol. 1). (ENG.). 156p. (J). (gr. 1-6). pap. 26.00 ***(978-1-7980-7240-0(8))*** Independently Published.

Jackson, Katy. Beauty & the Beast. Hay, Sam. 2017. (3D Colouring & Activity Ser.). (ENG.). 24p. (J). (gr. 1-4). pap. 11.99 *(978-1-4052-8160-7(X))* Egmont Bks., Ltd. GBR. Dist: Independent Pubs. Group.

Jackson, Katy, et al. Girls' Gorgeous World: Doodling & Colouring. Gunnell, Beth et al. 2015. (ENG.). 128p. (J). (gr. 2). pap. 12.99 *(978-1-78055-151-7(7))* O'Mara, Michael Bks., Ltd. GBR. Dist: Independent Pubs. Group.

Jackson, Katy. Little Sam, 1 vol. Dale, Jay. 2012. (Wonder Words Ser.). (ENG.). 32p. (gr. k-2). pap. 5.99 *(978-1-4296-8900-7(5),* Capstone Pr.) Capstone.

—Melinda Manners. Frances, Celia. 2018. (ENG.). 24p. (J). (gr. k-3). 15.99 *(978-0-692-13655-3(X))* Frances, Celia.

—Pretty Fashions: Beautiful Fashions to Color! 2014. (ENG.). 96p. (J). (gr. -1-2). 7.99 *(978-1-4424-8386-6(5),* Little Simon) Little Simon.

—Shopping for Socks, 1 vol. Dale, Jay. 2012. (Engage Literacy Red Ser.). (ENG.). 32p. (gr. k-2). pap. 5.99 *(978-1-4296-8942-7(0),* Capstone Pr.) Capstone.

—Where Is Molly's Teddy?, 1 vol. Dale, Jay. 2012. (Wonder Words Ser.). (ENG.). 32p. (gr. k-2). pap. 5.99 *(978-1-4296-8914-4(5),* Capstone Pr.) Capstone.

Jackson, Kay. Shag Finds a Home. Whisler, Barbara. 2008. 24p. pap. 24.95 *(978-1-60703-730-9(0))* America Star Bks.

Jackson, Kay Whytock. Adventures with Mama Scottie & the Kids. Scott, Elizabeth M. 2008. 60p. pap. 8.95 *(978-0-595-51760-2(9))* iUniverse, Inc.

Jackson, Kendall "Mavis". The Wishing Stone: #1 Mary's Miracle. Hoopes, Lorana. 2018. (ENG.). 44p. (J). pap. 12.99 *(978-1-7917-7110-2(6));* (Wishing Stone Inspirations Ser.: Vol. 1). pap. 7.99 *(978-1-7917-6998-7(5))* Independently Published.

Jackson, Laurence. How Are You Feeling Today Baby Bear? Exploring Big Feelings after Living in a Stormy Home. Evans, Jane. 2014. (ENG.). 32p. (C). 16.95 *(978-1-84905-424-9(X),* 694274) Kingsley, Jessica Pubs. GBR. Dist: Hachette UK Distribution.

Jackson, Lena S. Why Do I Have to Be a Duck? Jackson, Jesse a. 2020. (ENG.). 34p. (J). pap. 9.15 ***(978-1-5002-7911-0(0))*** CreateSpace Independent Publishing Platform.

Jackson, Liana Haley. The Day My Imagination Went Berserk. Ciampa, Clare. 2019. (ENG.). 48p. (J). 24.95 ***(978-1-64559-410-9(6));*** pap. 14.95 ***(978-1-64559-409-3(2))*** Covenant Bks.

Jackson, Lisa. Best-Loved Irish Legends. Massey, Eithne. 2018. (ENG.). 64p. pap. 21.00 *(978-1-78849-030-6(4))* O'Brien Pr., Ltd., The IRL. Dist: Casemate Pubs. & Bk. Distributors, LLC.

—Best-Loved Irish Legends: Mini Edition. Massey, Eithne. 2011. (ENG.). 64p. (J). 8.95 *(978-1-84717-237-2(7))* O'Brien Pr., Ltd., The IRL. Dist: Casemate Pubs. & Bk. Distributors, LLC.

—Irish Legends: Newgrange, Tara & the Boyne Valley. Massey, Eithne. 2016. (ENG.). 64p. (J). 20.00 *(978-1-84717-683-7(6))* O'Brien Pr., Ltd., The IRL. Dist: Casemate Pubs. & Bk. Distributors, LLC.

Jackson, Mark. Bilby: Secrets of an Australian Marsupial. Wignell, Edel. 2015. (ENG.). 32p. (J). (gr. k-4). 16.99 *(978-0-7636-6759-7(5))* Candlewick Pr.

—Platypus. Whiting, Sue. 2016. (ENG.). 32p. (J). (gr. k-4). 16.99 *(978-0-7636-8098-5(2))* Candlewick Pr.

—Python. Cheng, Christopher. 2016. (Read & Wonder Ser.). (ENG.). 32p. (J). (gr. k-3). 7.99 *(978-0-7636-8773-1(1))* Candlewick Pr.

—The Snow Wombat. Chambers, Susannah. 2016. (ENG.). 32p. (J). (gr. -1-1). 16.99 *(978-1-76011-381-0(6))* Allen & Unwin AUS. Dist: Independent Pubs. Group.

—The Snow Wombat. Chambers, Susannah. 2019. (ENG.). 32p. (J). (gr. -1-k). bds. 9.99 *(978-1-76063-293-9(7))* Allen & Unwin AUS. Dist: Independent Pubs. Group.

Jackson, Max, jt. illus. see Clucas, Jack.

Jackson, Meredith. A Dog's Adventure: The Story of How One Dog Transforms His Day, with His Imagination. Chambers, R. K. 2019. (ENG.). 26p. (J). pap. 12.99 ***(978-1-6884-2625-2(6))*** Independently Published.

Jackson, Mike. Baby Shark! Golden Books. 2019. (Little Golden Book Ser.). (ENG.). 24p. (J). (-k). 4.99 *(978-0-593-12509-0(6),* Golden Bks.) Random Hse. Children's Bks.

—The Big Magic Show! (Bubble Guppies) Nagaraj, Josephine. 2015. (Step into Reading Ser.). (ENG.). 24p. (J). (gr. -1-1). 4.99 *(978-0-385-38457-5(2),* Random Hse. Bks. for Young Readers) Random Hse. Children's Bks.

—Big Truck Show! Random House Staff. 2013. (Step into Reading Ser.). (ENG.). 32p. (J). (gr. -1-1). 3.99 *(978-0-449-81896-1(9),* Random Hse. Bks. for Young Readers) Random Hse. Children's Bks.

—Bubble Power! (Bubble Guppies) Man-Kong, Mary. 2016. (Step into Reading Ser.). (ENG.). 24p. (J). (gr. -1-2). 4.99 *(978-0-553-52091-0(1),* Random Hse. Bks. for Young Readers) Random Hse. Children's Bks.

—Chase's Space Case (Paw Patrol) Depken, Kristen L. 2016. (Step into Reading Ser.). (ENG.). 24p. (J). (gr. -1-1). 4.99 *(978-0-553-53886-1(1),* Random Hse. Bks. for Young Readers) Random Hse. Children's Bks.

—Disney Muppet Babies: Fly South. Fischer, Maggie. 2019. (Googly Eyes Ser.). (ENG.). 12p. (J). (gr. -1-k). bds. 9.99 *(978-0-7944-4297-2(8),* Studio Fun International) Printers Row Publishing Group.

—Disney the Lion King: Roar of the Pride Lands. Fischer, Maggie. 2019. (Sliding Tab Ser.). (ENG.). 12p. (J). (gr. -1-k). bds. 10.99 *(978-0-7944-4279-8(X),* Studio Fun International) Printers Row Publishing Group.

—A Fairytale Adventure (Dora the Explorer) Tillworth, Mary. 2014. (Pictureback(R) Ser.). (ENG.). 24p. (J). (gr. -1-2). 3.99 *(978-0-385-37443-9(7),* Random Hse. Bks. for Young Readers) Random Hse. Children's Bks.

—Happy Holidays, Bubble Guppies! (Bubble Guppies) Tillworth, Mary. 2013. (Pictureback(R) Ser.). (ENG.). 16p. (J). (gr. -1-2). 4.99 *(978-0-449-81779-7(2),* Random Hse. Bks. for Young Readers) Random Hse. Children's Bks.

—Ice Team (Paw Patrol) Random House. 2015. (Glitter Picturebook Ser.). (ENG.). 16p. (J). (gr. -1-2). 5.99 *(978-0-553-52281-5(7),* Random Hse. Bks. for Young Readers) Random Hse. Children's Bks.

—King for a Day! (PAW Patrol) Tillworth, Mary. 2016. (Step into Reading Ser.). (ENG.). 24p. (J). (gr. -1-1). 4.99 *(978-1-101-93684-9(3),* Random Hse. Bks. for Young Readers) Random Hse. Children's Bks.

—Lend a Helping Paw (PAW Patrol) Random House. 2016. (Touch-And-Feel Ser.). (ENG.). 10p. (J). (— 1). 12.99 *(978-1-101-94027-3(1),* Random Hse. Bks. for Young Readers) Random Hse. Children's Bks.

—Let's Find Adventure! (Paw Patrol) Random House. 2015. (ENG.). 12p. (J). (-k). bds. 5.99 *(978-0-553-51027-0(4),* Random Hse. Bks. for Young Readers) Random Hse. Children's Bks.

—Nickelodeon Butterbean's Café: Sweet As Pie. Acampora, Courtney. 2020. (ENG.). 10p. (J). (gr. -1-k). bds. 9.99 *(978-0-7944-4464-8(4),* Studio Fun International) Printers Row Publishing Group.

—Nickelodeon PAW Patrol: a Day at the Farm. 2018. (ENG.). 10p. (J). (gr. -1-k). bds. 8.99 *(978-0-7944-4113-5(0),* Reader's Digest Children's Bks.) Studio Fun International.

—Nickelodeon PAW Patrol: Group Hug! Stevens, Cara. 2017. (Hugs Book Ser.). (ENG.). 12p. (J). (gr. -1-k). bds. 10.99 *(978-0-7944-4068-8(1),* Reader's Digest Children's Bks.) Studio Fun International.

—Nickelodeon PAW Patrol: Happy Tails! Fischer, Maggie. 2019. (ENG.). 12p. (J). (gr. -1-k). bds. 10.99 *(978-0-7944-4309-2(5),* Studio Fun International) Printers Row Publishing Group.

Jackson, Mike. Nickelodeon PAW Patrol Mighty Pups: Charged Up! Fischer, Maggie. 2020. (Lift & Slide Ser.). (ENG.). 10p. (J). (gr. -1-k). bds. 11.99 ***(978-0-7944-4533-1(0),*** Studio Fun International) Printers Row Publishing Group.

Jackson, Mike. Nickelodeon PAW Patrol: Mission: Crown. 2018. (ENG.). 10p. (J). (gr. -1-k). bds. 11.99 *(978-0-7944-4213-2(7),* Studio Fun International) Printers Row Publishing Group.

—Nickelodeon PAW Patrol: Pups on Patrol. Fischer, Maggie. 2018. (Deluxe Guess Who? Ser.). (ENG.). 12p. (J). (gr. -1-k). bds. 10.99 *(978-0-7944-4241-5(2),* Studio Fun International) Printers Row Publishing Group.

—Nickelodeon PAW Patrol: Super Star Pups. 2018. (Magnetic Hardcover Ser.). (ENG.). 10p. (J). (gr. -1-k). 12.99 *(978-0-7944-4045-9(2),* Reader's Digest Children's Bks.) Studio Fun International.

—On the Farm (Bubble Guppies) Golden Books. 2012. (ENG.). 96p. (J). (gr. -1-2). pap. 3.99 *(978-0-307-93096-5(3),* Golden Bks.) Random Hse. Children's Bks.

—Pit Crew Pups (Paw Patrol) Depken, Kristen L. 2015. (Step into Reading Ser.). (ENG.). 24p. (J). (gr. -1-1). 4.99 *(978-0-553-50853-6(9),* Random Hse. Bks. for Young Readers) Random Hse. Children's Bks.

—The Pups Save Friendship Day! (PAW Patrol) Golden Books. 2016. (Big Golden Book Ser.). (ENG.). 32p. (J). (gr. -1-2). 9.99 *(978-1-5247-1388-1(0),* Golden Bks.) Random Hse. Children's Bks.

—The Pups Save the Bunnies (Paw Patrol) Random House. 2016. (Pictureback(R) Ser.). (ENG.). 16p. (J). (gr. -1-1). 4.99 *(978-1-101-93168-4(X),* Random Hse. Bks. for Young Readers) Random Hse. Children's Bks.

—Rubble to the Rescue! (Paw Patrol) Depken, Kristen L. 2015. (Step into Reading Ser.). (ENG.). 24p. (J). (gr. -1-1). 4.99 *(978-0-553-52290-7(6),* Random Hse. Bks. for Young Readers) Random Hse. Children's Bks.

—We Totally Rock! (Bubble Guppies) Golden Books. 2012. (Hologramatic Sticker Book Ser.). (ENG.). 48p. (J). (gr. -1-2). pap. 3.99 *(978-0-307-93095-8(5),* Golden Bks.) Random Hse. Children's Bks.

—Wild Winter Adventure! (Rusty Rivets) Behling, Steve. 2017. (Big Golden Book Ser.). (ENG.). 48p. (J). (gr. -1-2). 10.99 *(978-1-5247-2067-4(4),* Golden Bks.) Random Hse. Children's Bks.

Jackson, Mike & MJ Illustrations Staff. Break the Ice! Carbone, Courtney. 2017. (Step into Reading Ser.). (ENG.). 48p. (J). (gr. -1-1). pap. 5.99 *(978-1-5247-6400-5(0));* lib. bdg. 12.99 *(978-1-5247-6401-2(9))* Random Hse. Children's Bks. (Random Hse. Bks. for Young Readers).

Jackson, Mike, jt. illus. see Golden Books.

Jackson, Nicholas. Chuck's Completely Credible Contingencies. Nast, Andrew. 2019. (ENG.). 54p. (J). pap. 11.99 ***(978-1-5078-4768-8(8))*** CreateSpace Independent Publishing Platform.

Jackson, Nicholas. Hall of the Bulls: Band 10 White/Band 12 Copper (Collins Big Cat Progress) Bradman, Tom. 2014. (Collins Big Cat Progress Ser.). (ENG.). 32p. (J). (gr. 2-3). pap. 9.99 *(978-0-00-751927-9(3))* HarperCollins Pubs. Ltd. GBR. Dist: Independent Pubs. Group.

Jackson, Obol Andrew. A Gift for the Giver: The Power of Christmas. Eyvari, Leila. 2018. (ENG.). 24p. (J). *(978-1-5255-3221-4(9));* pap. *(978-1-5255-3222-1(7))* FriesenPress.

—Longger-Jo Takes on the Bully. Dorival, Sharon. 2018. (ENG.). 64p. (J). pap. *(978-1-5255-0912-4(8))* FriesenPress.

Jackson, Shelley. The Chicken-Chasing Queen of Lamar County. Harrington, Janice N. 2007. (ENG.). 40p. (J). (gr. -1-3). 18.99 *(978-0-374-31251-0(6),* 900028253, Farrar, Straus & Giroux (BYR)) Farrar, Straus & Giroux.

Jackson, Shelley & Crosby, Jeff. Ten Texas Babies, 1 vol. Davis, David. 2014. (ENG.). 32p. (J). (gr. k-3). 16.99 *(978-1-4556-1874-3(8),* Pelican Publishing) Arcadia Publishing.

Jackson, Shelley Ann, jt. illus. see Crosby, Jeff.

Jackson, Tim. Big Papa's Good Deed. Cobb, Robert. 2016. (ENG.). (J). pap. 11.50 *(978-1-68197-755-3(9))* Christian Faith Publishing.

Jackson, Trey. Polie Peter Memoirs: A Collection of Shorts & Poems. John-Rose, Jade. David, Winnie, ed. 2018. (ENG.). 144p. (J). pap. 14.99 *(978-1-7177-0273-9(2))* Independently Published.

Jackson, Vicky. Poepal's Purpose. l.t. ed. 2005. 20p. (J). 7.95 *(978-0-9718741-0-7(7))* Tawa Productions.

Jacob, Murv. The Boy Who Lived with the Bears: And Other Iroquois Stories. Bruchac, Joseph. 2003. (Storytime Ser.). 63p. (J). (gr. k-5). pap. 11.95 *(978-0-930407-61-2(X))* Parabola Bks.

—How Rabbit Tricked Otter: And Other Cherokee Trickster Stories. Ross, Gayle. 2003. (Storytime Ser.). 78p. (J). (gr. k-6). per. 12.95 *(978-0-930407-60-5(1))* Parabola Bks.

—Rabbit & the Fingerbone Necklace. Duvall, Deborah L. 2009. (ENG.). 32p. (J). (gr. 1). 19.95 *(978-0-8263-4723-7(1))* Univ. of New Mexico Pr.

—Rabbit & the Wolves. Duvall, Deborah L. 2005. (Grandmother Stories Ser.). (ENG.). 32p. (J). (gr. 3-7). 16.95 *(978-0-8263-3563-0(2))* Univ. of New Mexico Pr.

—Rabbit Goes Duck Hunting: A Traditional Cherokee Legend. Duvall, Deborah L. 2004. (Grandmother Stories, 5 Ser.). (ENG.). 32p. (J). 16.95 *(978-0-8263-3336-0(2))* Univ. of New Mexico Pr.

—Rabbit Goes to Kansas. Duvall, Deborah L. 2007. (ENG.). 32p. (J). (gr. 1-18). 16.95 *(978-0-8263-4181-5(0))* Univ. of New Mexico Pr.

—Rabbit Plants the Forest. Duvall, Deborah L. 2006. (ENG.). 32p. (J). (gr. 3-7). 18.95 *(978-0-8263-3691-0(4))* Univ. of New Mexico Pr.

Jacobs, Brittany. Big Breath: A Guided Meditation for Kids. Meyer, William. 2019. (ENG.). 32p. (J). (gr. -1-5). 16.95 *(978-1-60868-633-9(7))* New World Library.

Jacobs, D. K. Jinja of the Munjyburr. Thomas, Kerrie Annette. 2011. 34p. pap. 13.50 *(978-1-61204-421-7(2),* Eloquent Bks.) Strategic Book Publishing & Rights Agency (SBPRA).

Jacobs, Joyce M. Moxie. Connelly, Claire K. 2010. 84p. pap. 10.49 *(978-1-4520-7634-8(0))* AuthorHouse.

Jacobs, Kim. Princess Rosie's Rainbows, Vol. Killion, Bette. 2015. 36p. (J). (gr. k-3). 16.95 *(978-1-937786-44-1(7),* Wisdom Tales) World Wisdom, Inc.

Jacobs, Kim. Princess Sophie & the Six Swans: A Tale from the Brothers Grimm. Jacobs, Kim, retold by. 2017. 40p. (J). (gr. k-3). 16.95 *(978-1-937786-67-0(6),* Wisdom Tales) World Wisdom, Inc.

Jacobs, Nadine. Un Bebe Caido del Cielo. Jacobs, Nadine. Hellings, Collete. 2003. (SPA.). 32p. (J). (gr. k-1). 16.95 *(978-84-95150-10-3(7),* COR4033) Corimbo, Editorial S.L. ESP. Dist: Distribooks, Inc.

—Zefir, la Cebrita en Peligro. Jacobs, Nadine. Vicens, Paula, tr. 2004. (SPA.). 32p. (J). 15.99 *(978-84-8470-108-8(5))* Corimbo, Editorial S.L. ESP. Dist: Lectorum Pubns., Inc.

Jacobsen, Amie. Spenser Goes to el Paso. Brooks, Melanie & Spenser and Mom Staff. 2010. (ENG.). 32p. (J). 14.95 *(978-0-9817598-3-8(1),* cbc0cc91-0341-4e1a-a28e-405962e8c495) Simple Fish Bk. Co., LLC.

—Spenser Goes to Portland. Spenser & Mom. 2008. (ENG.). 32p. (J). 14.95 *(978-0-9817598-0-7(7)*, cf47a802-b05d-4aa8-9dd0-abec385a8af9) Simple Fish Bk. Co., LLC.

—Spenser Via a el Paso. Spenser & Brooks, Melanie. 2010. (ENG.). 32p. (J). 14.95 *(978-0-9817598-5-2(8)*, e87219c4-b810-49f7-81c2-eb35fd1a4e0b) Simple Fish Bk. Co., LLC.

Jacobsen, Laura. The Best Eid Ever. Mobin-Uddin, Asma. 2007. (ENG.). 32p. (J). (gr. 2-k). 16.95 *(978-1-59078-431-0(6))* Boyds Mills Pr.

—Exploring the West: Tales of Courage on the Lewis & Clark Expedition. Mead, Maggie. 2015. (Setting the Stage for Fluency Ser.). (ENG.). 40p. (J). (gr. 3-5). lib. bdg. 27.99 *(978-1-939656-65-0(6))* Red Chair Pr.

—My Muslim Friend: A Young Catholic Learns about Islam. Kemmetmueller, Donna Jean. 2006. 47p. (J). 15.95 *(978-0-8198-4844-4(1))* Pauline Bks. & Media.

—A Party in Ramadan. Mobin-Uddin, Asma. 2009. (ENG.). 34p. (J). (gr. 2-k). 16.95 *(978-1-59078-604-8(1))* Boyds Mills Pr.

—A Party in Ramadan. Mobin-Uddin, Asma. 2017. (ENG.). 32p. (J). (gr. 2-4). pap. 7.95 *(978-1-62979-847-9(9))* Boyds Mills Pr.

Jacobsen, Mike. The Daredevil's Guide to Dangerous Places, 1 vol. Brett, Anna & Lonely Planet Kids. 2018. (Daredevil's Guide Ser.). (ENG.). 80p. (J). (gr. 4-7). pap. 12.99 *(978-1-78701-695-8(1)*, 5869) Lonely Planet Global Ltd. IRL. Dist: Hachette Bk. Group.

Jacobsen, Terry. The Littlest Cowboy's Christmas, 2 vols. Chandler, Michael. 2006. (ENG.). 32p. (J). (gr. k-3). 17.95 *(978-1-58980-381-7(7)*, Pelican Publishing) Arcadia Publishing.

Jacobson, James. A Special Present from Puddles! A St. Patrick's Day Story! McMahon, Maryann. 2020. (ENG.). 32p. (J). (gr. k-3). pap. 10.99 ***(978-1-7320725-7-2(4))*** Maryann.

Jacobson, Judith. El Vuelo de los Colibries. Flor Ada, Alma. 32p. (J). (gr. 3-6). pap. 9.95 *(978-1-56492-211-3(1))* Laredo Publishing Co., Inc.

Jacobson, Rick & Fernandez, Laura. The Mona Lisa Caper. Jacobson, Rick. 2005. 24p. (J). (gr. k-3). 16.99 *(978-0-88776-726-5(5)*, Tundra Bks.) Tundra Bks. CAN. Dist: Penguin Random Hse. LLC.

—Picasso: Soul on Fire. Jacobson, Rick. (ENG.). 32p. (J). (gr. 5-18). 2011. pap. 8.95 *(978-1-77049-263-9(1))*; 2004. 15.95 *(978-0-88776-599-5(8))* Tundra Bks. CAN. (Tundra Bks.). Dist: Penguin Random Hse. LLC.

Jacobson, Rick, jt. illus. see Fernandez, Laura.

Jacobus, Tim. The Search for Truth. Kingsley, Kaza. (Erec Rex Ser.: 3). (ENG.). (J). (gr. 5-9). 2010. 464p. pap. 9.99 *(978-1-4169-7989-0(1))*; 2009. 448p. 17.99 *(978-1-4169-7988-3(3))* Simon & Schuster Bks. For Young Readers. (Simon & Schuster Bks. For Young Readers).

Jacoby, Nickolina Dye. Little Miss Neat-As-A-Pin. Eberhard, Phyllis Lunde Brees. 2007. (J). *(978-0-9722741-7-3(0))* Publishing Factory, The.

Jacoby, Sarah. The Important Thing about Margaret Wise Brown. Barnett, Mac. 2019. (ENG.). 48p. (J). (gr. -1-3). 17.99 *(978-0-06-239344-9(8)*, Balzer & Bray) HarperCollins Pubs.

—The Road Home. Cotton, Katie. 2017. (ENG.). 32p. (J). (gr. k-2). 15.95 *(978-1-4197-2374-2(X)*, Abrams Bks. for Young Readers) Abrams, Inc.

Jácome, Mauricio. Cuando Callaron Las Armas. Iturralde, Edna. 2015. (Serie Roja Ser.). (SPA.). 120p. (J). (gr. 9-12). pap. 15.95 *(978-9942-19-306-3(5)*, Loqueleo) Santillana USA Publishing Co., Inc.

Jacome, Mauricio. El Pais de Los Juguetes. Garcia, Edgar Allan. 2015. 24p. (J). (gr. -1-2). pap. 12.95 *(978-9942-05-066-3(3)*, Alfaguara Infantil) Santillana Ecuador ECU. Dist: Santillana USA Publishing Co., Inc.

Jacome, Nelson. Albert Einstein. Lazaro, Flores. Diaz Ycaza, Rafael, ed. 2017. (SPA.). 110p. (J). pap. *(978-9978-18-443-1(0))* Radmandi Editorial, Compania Ltd.

Jacome, Nelson. Alexander Fleming. Lazaro, Flores. 2017. (Ariel Juvenil Ilustrada Ser.: Vol. 41). (SPA.). 128p. (J). pap. ***(978-9978-18-448-6(1))*** Radmandi Editorial, Compania Ltd.

Jacome, Nelson. Alfredo Nobel. Lazaro, Flores. Diaz Ycaza, Rafael, ed. 2017. (SPA.). 128p. (J). pap. *(978-9978-18-445-5(7))* Radmandi Editorial, Compania Ltd.

—Cristóbal Colón: Ilustrado. Rodriguez, Armonia. 2019. (Ariel Juvenil Ilustrada Ser.: Vol. 43). (SPA.). 116p. (J). pap. *(978-9978-18-496-7(1))* Radmandi Editorial, Compania Ltd.

—Cuentos de Edgar Allan Poe: Los Crímenes de la Calle Morgue, el Barril de Amontillado y el Escarabajo de Oro. Allan Poe, Edgar. 2017. (SPA.). 110p. (J). pap. *(978-9978-18-447-9(3))* Radmandi Editorial, Compania Ltd.

—Cyrano de Bergerac (Ilustrado) 2019. (Ariel Juvenil Ilustrada Ser.: Vol. 21). (SPA.). 128p. (J). pap. *(978-9978-18-514-8(3))* Radmandi Editorial, Compania Ltd.

—El Extraño Caso Del Dr. Jekyll y Mr. Hyde. Stevenson, Robert Louis. 2017.Tr. of Strange Case of Dr. Jekyll & Mr. Hyde. (SPA.). 128p. (J). pap. *(978-9978-18-451-6(1))* Radmandi Editorial, Compania Ltd.

—Napoleón Bonaparte. Diaz Ycaza, Rafael, ed. 2017. (Ariel Juvenil Ilustrada Ser.: Vol. 35). (SPA.). 126p. (J). pap. *(978-9978-18-444-8(9))* Radmandi Editorial, Compania Ltd.

—El Retrato: Ilustrado. Bergholtz, Ana. 2019. (Ariel Juvenil Ilustrada Ser.: Vol. 58). (SPA.). 110p. (J). pap. *(978-9978-18-517-9(8))* Radmandi Editorial, Compania Ltd.

Jacome, Nelson, jt. illus. see Palacios, William.

Jacquemain, Patti. Journey of the Great Bear: Through California's Golden Past. Jacquemain, Patti. 2006. (J). *(978-0-929702-10-0(7))* Mission Creek Studios.

Jacques, Benoit. Sagesses et Malices des Dieux Grecs. Mistral, Laure. 2004. (A. M. Sag Malice Ser.). (FRE.). 156p. (J). *(978-2-226-14337-2(8))* Albin-Michel, Editions.

Jacques, Christophe. Green Machine: The Slightly Gross Truth about Turning Your Food Scraps into Green Energy. Donnelly, Rebecca. 2020. (ENG.). 32p. (J). 17.99 *(978-1-250-30406-3(7)*, 900197214, Holt, Henry & Co. Bks. For Young Readers) Holt, Henry & Co.

Jacques, Faith. Charlie y el Gran Ascensor de Cristal. Dahl, Roald. 2003.Tr. of Charlie & the Great Glass Elevator. (SPA.). 164p. (J). (gr. 5-8). pap. 12.95 *(978-968-19-0988-8(7))* Santillana USA Publishing Co., Inc.

—Charlie y la Fabrica de Chocolate. Dahl, Roald. 2003.Tr. of Charlie & the Chocolate Factory. (FRE & SPA.). 176p. (J). (gr. 4-7). *(978-84-204-4771-1(4)*, AF0153) Ediciones Alfaguara.

Jacques Huiswood. Nandi & Masani. Mineuittie, Abike. 2011. 40p. pap. 24.95 *(978-1-4560-2700-1(X))* America Star Bks.

Jacques, Laura. Baby Owl's Rescue, 1 vol. Curtis, Jennifer Keats. 2009. (ENG.). 32p. (J). (gr. -1-3). 16.95 *(978-1-934359-95-2(5)*, 9781934359952) Arbordale Publishing.

—El Domador de Tornados, 1 vol. Fields, Terri. 2016. (SPA.). 32p. (J). (gr. k-3). pap. 9.95 *(978-1-62855-747-3(8))* Arbordale Publishing.

—For the Birds: The Life of Roger Tory Peterson. Thomas, Peggy. 2011. (ENG.). 40p. (J). (gr. 3-7). 16.95 *(978-1-59078-764-9(1)*, Calkins Creek) Boyds Mills Pr.

—Los Más Peligrosos, 1 vol. Fields, Terri. 2012. (SPA.). 32p. (J). (gr. -1-3). pap. 11.95 *(978-1-62855-424-3(X))* Arbordale Publishing.

—Los Más Peligrosos, 1 vol. Fields, Terri. 2012. (SPA.). 32p. (J). (gr. -1-3). 17.95 *(978-1-60718-677-9(2))* Arbordale Publishing.

—The Most Dangerous, 1 vol. Fields, Terri. 2012. (ENG.). 32p. (J). (gr. -1-3). 17.95 *(978-1-60718-526-0(1))* Arbordale Publishing.

—Os Mais Perigosos (the Most Dangerous in Portuguese) Fields, Terri. Sacciotto, Adriana & Wiedemann, Tatiana, trs. 2019. (POR.). 32p. (J). (gr. k-3). pap. 11.95 *(978-1-64351-413-0(X))* Arbordale Publishing.

—Tornado Tamer, 1 vol. Fields, Terri. 2016. (ENG & SPA.). 32p. (J). (gr. k-3). 17.95 *(978-1-62855-733-6(8))*; pap. 9.95 *(978-1-62855-740-4(0))* Arbordale Publishing.

—Whistling Wings, 1 vol. Goering, Laura. 2008. (ENG.). 32p. (J). (gr. -1-3). 16.95 *(978-1-934359-12-9(2))*; pap. 8.95 *(978-1-934359-30-3(0)*, 9781934359303) Arbordale Publishing.

Jacqui, Smith. African Leaders of the World Coloring & Activity Book. Galloway, Erica. 2018. (ENG.). 20p. (J). pap. 12.99 *(978-0-578-42665-5(X))* Kelly Cochran Publishing.

Jae-Hwan, Kim. Dragon Hunt: World of Warcraft, Vol. 1. 2005. (Sunwell Trilogy: Vol. 1). 176p. (YA). pap. 9.99 *(978-1-59532-712-3(6))* TOKYOPOP, Inc.

—King of Hell, 13 vols. In-Soo, Ra & Ra, In-Soo. 12th rev. ed. 2006. (King of Hell Ser.: Vol. 12). 192p. (gr. 8-12). pap. 9.99 *(978-1-59816-060-4(5))* TOKYOPOP, Inc.

—King of Hell, Vol. 2. Na, In-Soo. rev. ed. 2003.Tr. of Ma-Je. 216p. (YA). (gr. 8-18). pap. 9.99 *(978-1-59182-188-5(6))* TOKYOPOP, Inc.

—King of Hell, 5 vols., Vol. 4. In-Soo, Na. rev. ed. 2004. 192p. pap. 9.99 *(978-1-59182-482-4(6))* TOKYOPOP, Inc.

—King of Hell, 8 vols., Vol. 7. Ra, In-Soo. 7th rev. ed. 2004. 200p. pap. 9.99 *(978-1-59182-867-9(8))* TOKYOPOP, Inc.

—King of Hell, 8 vols. In-Soo, Ra. rev. ed. 2005. Vol. 8. 200p. pap. 9.99 *(978-1-59182-914-0(3))*; Vol. 9. 192p. pap. 9.99 *(978-1-59532-597-6(2))* TOKYOPOP, Inc.

—King of Hell, Vol. 10. rev. ed. 2005. 192p. (YA). pap. 9.99 *(978-1-59532-598-3(0))* TOKYOPOP, Inc.

—King of Hell, Vol. 11. In-Soo, Ra. 11th rev. ed. 2005. (King of Hell Ser.). 192p. per. 9.99 *(978-1-59816-059-8(1))* TOKYOPOP, Inc.

Jae-Hwan, Na. King of Hell, 3 vols., Vol. 3. In-Soo, Na. rev. ed. 2003. 192p. (YA). pap. 9.99 *(978-1-59182-189-2(4))* TOKYOPOP, Inc.

Jaeggi, Yoshiko. I Am Tama, Lucky Cat: A Japanese Legend, 1 vol. Henrichs, Wendy. (ENG.). 32p. (J). (gr. k-3). 2016. pap. 7.99 *(978-1-56145-916-2(X))*; 2011. 16.95 *(978-1-56145-589-8(X)*, Peachtree Junior) Peachtree Publishing Co. Inc.

—Monsoon Afternoon, 1 vol. Sheth, Kashmira. (ENG.). 32p. (J). (gr. k-3). 2008. 16.95 *(978-1-56145-455-6(9)*, Peachtree Junior); 2018. pap. 7.95 *(978-1-68263-061-7(7))* Peachtree Publishing Co. Inc.

—My Dadima Wears a Sari, 1 vol. Sheth, Kashmira. 2007. (ENG.). 32p. (J). (gr. k-3). 16.95 *(978-1-56145-392-4(7))* Peachtree Publishing Co. Inc.

—Sona & the Wedding Game, 1 vol. Sheth, Kashmira. 2015. (ENG.). 32p. (J). (gr. 1-3). 16.95 *(978-1-56145-735-9(3))* Peachtree Publishing Co. Inc.

Jaekel, Susan. Marie Curie: Prize-Winning Scientist, 1 vol. Mortensen, Lori. 2008. (Biographies Ser.). (ENG.). 24p. (J). (gr. k-3). lib. bdg. 27.32 *(978-1-4048-3731-7(0)*, Picture Window Bks.) Capstone.

—The Tortoise & the Hare: A Tale about Determination. 2006. (J). 6.99 *(978-1-59939-015-4(9))* Cornerstone Pr.

—A Wild Ride in Texas. Wilsdon, Christina. 2006. 26p. (J). 7.99 *(978-1-59939-011-6(6))* Cornerstone Pr.

Jaekel, Susan M. The Gift of the Magi: A Story about Giving. Henry, O. 2006. (J). *(978-1-59939-084-0(1)*, Reader's Digest Young Families, Inc.) Studio Fun International.

—Stone Soup: A Tale about Sharing. 2006. (J). *(978-1-59939-080-2(9)*, Reader's Digest Young Families, Inc.) Studio Fun International.

—Tug of War: A Tale about Being Resourceful. 2006. (J). *(978-1-59939-091-8(4)*, Reader's Digest Young Families, Inc.) Studio Fun International.

Jael, jt. illus. see Gribbon, Sean.

Jael, jt. illus. see Griffin, Georgene.

Jaenicke, Birgit. Marie und Lu: Das Geheimnis der Weihnachtskapelle. Rehberger, Jo. 2018. (Marie und Lu Ser.: Vol. 1). (GER.). 112p. (J). pap. 8.31 *(978-1-7294-4096-4(7))* Independently Published.

Jager, Korin Elizabeth. Introducing Myself. Jager, Phyllis. 2005. (J). 9.95 *(978-1-59571-080-2(9))* Word Association Pubs.

Jago. Ali Baba & the Forty Thieves. 2004. (ITA, ENG & KUR.). 31p. (J). *(978-1-84444-543-1(7))* Mantra Lingua.

—Ali Baba & the Forty Thieves. Gregory, Manju. 2004. (J). *(978-1-84444-544-8(5))* Mantra Lingua.

—Always Remember. Meng, Cece. 2016. 32p. (J). (gr. -1-2). 17.99 *(978-0-399-16809-3(5)*, Philomel Bks.) Penguin Young Readers Group.

—Found: Psalm 23, 1 vol. Lloyd-Jones, Sally. 2017. (Jesus Storybook Bible Ser.). (ENG.). 20p. (J). bds. 9.99 *(978-0-310-75750-4(9))* Zonderkidz.

—The Jesus Storybook Bible: Every Story Whispers His Name, 1 vol. Lloyd-Jones, Sally. (Jesus Storybook Bible Ser.). (ENG.). 352p. (J). (gr. -1-3). 2007. 18.99 *(978-0-310-70825-4(7))*; 2009. 24.99 *(978-0-310-71878-9(3))* Zonderkidz.

—The Jesus Storybook Bible Coloring Book: Every Story Whispers His Name, 1 vol. Lloyd-Jones, Sally. 2020. (Jesus Storybook Bible Ser.). (ENG.). 64p. (J). pap. 9.99 *(978-0-310-76930-9(2))* Zonderkidz.

—Little Red Hen & the Grains of Wheat. Johnson, Richard & Barkow, Henriette. 2005. 32p. (J). (KOR & ENG.). pap. *(978-1-84444-210-2(1))*; (ENG & BEN.). pap. *(978-1-84444-200-3(4))*; (ENG & CHI.). pap. *(978-1-84444-201-0(2))*; (FRE & ENG.). pap. *(978-1-84444-205-8(5))*; (ENG & HIN.). pap. *(978-1-84444-208-9(X))*; (PAN & ENG.). pap. *(978-1-84444-211-9(X))*; (ENG & POR.). pap. *(978-1-84444-212-6(8))*; (ENG & URD.). pap. *(978-1-84444-217-1(9))*; (POL & ENG.). pap. *(978-1-84444-394-9(9))*; (ENG & TGL.). pap. *(978-1-84444-395-6(7))*; (ENG & RUS.). pap. *(978-1-84444-398-7(1))* Mantra Lingua.

—The Story of God's Love for You, 1 vol. Lloyd-Jones, Sally. 2015. (ENG.). 208p. (YA). 14.99 *(978-0-310-73602-8(1))* Zondervan.

—Thank You, God. Wigger, J. Bradley. 2014. (ENG.). 26p. (J). 16.00 *(978-0-8028-5424-7(9)*, Eerdmans Bks For Young Readers) Eerdmans, William B. Publishing Co.

Jago & Moxley, Sheila. Grandpa's Garden. Fry, Stella. 2012. (ENG.). 40p. (J). 16.99 *(978-1-84686-053-9(9))* Barefoot Bks., Inc.

Jagodits, Carolyn Lee. Angel of the Poor: A Story of Mother Emmelie Gamelin. Ernest, Brother. 2011. 96p. 38.95 *(978-1-258-06652-9(1))* Literary Licensing, LLC.

—Don't Push! a Story of Cesar Franck. Roberto, Brother. 2011. 94p. 38.95 *(978-1-258-07305-3(6))* Literary Licensing, LLC.

—A Dream Come True: A Story of St. Isaac Jogues. Pelous, Donald. 2011. 94p. 38.95 *(978-1-258-06266-8(6))* Literary Licensing, LLC.

—Father of the American Cavalry: A Story of Brigadier General Casimir Pulaski. Flavius, Brother. 2011. 96p. 38.95 *(978-1-258-07161-5(4))* Literary Licensing, LLC.

—Music for Millions: A Story of Ignace Paderewski. Roberto, Brother. 2011. 94p. 38.95 *(978-1-258-09336-5(7))* Literary Licensing, LLC.

Jagucki, Marek. Any Fin Is Possible: My Big Fat Zombie Goldfish. O'Hara, Mo. 2016. (My Big Fat Zombie Goldfish Ser.: 4). (ENG.). 224p. (J). (gr. 3-5). 12.99 *(978-1-250-06353-3(1)*, 900142805) Feiwel & Friends.

—Cats in the Crater: My FANGtastically Evil Vampire Pet. O'Hara, Mo. 2020. (My FANGtastically Evil Vampire Pet Ser.: 3). (ENG.). 192p. (J). 13.99 *(978-1-250-12815-7(3)*, 900175682) Feiwel & Friends.

—The Election: North America Edition. Levenson, Eleanor. 2018. (ENG.). 34p. (J). (gr. k-5). pap. *(978-0-9930773-6-4(6))* Fisherton Pr. Ltd.

—The Fin-Tastic Fish-Sitter. O'Hara, Mo. 2016. (My Big Fat Zombie Goldfish Ser.). (ENG.). 40p. (J). (gr. -1-2). 16.99 *(978-1-250-06523-0(2)*, 9781250065230) Feiwel & Friends.

—Fins of Fury: My Big Fat Zombie Goldfish. O'Hara, Mo. 2015. (My Big Fat Zombie Goldfish Ser.: 3). (ENG.). 224p. (J). (gr. 2-5). 12.99 *(978-1-250-02921-8(X)*, 900118407) Feiwel & Friends.

—Jurassic Carp: My Big Fat Zombie Goldfish. O'Hara, Mo. 2017. (My Big Fat Zombie Goldfish Ser.: 6). (ENG.). 224p. (J). 12.99 *(978-1-250-06357-1(4)*, 900142809) Feiwel & Friends.

—Jurassic Carp: My Big Fat Zombie Goldfish. O'Hara, Mo. 2017. (My Big Fat Zombie Goldfish Ser.: 6). (ENG.). 224p. (J). pap. 6.99 *(978-1-250-10260-7(X)*, 900163247) Square Fish.

—Language on the Loose, 4 vols. Meister, Cari & Loewen, Nancy. 2015. (Language on the Loose Ser.). (ENG.). 24p. (gr. 2-4). 114.60 *(978-1-4795-8021-7(X)*, Picture Window Bks.) Capstone.

—My Big Fat Zombie Fun Book. West, Dillon James & O'Hara, Mo. 2018. (My Big Fat Zombie Goldfish Ser.: 7). (ENG.). 192p. (J). 12.99 *(978-1-250-12250-6(3)*, 900173649) Feiwel & Friends.

—My Big Fat Zombie Goldfish. O'Hara, Mo. 2013. (My Big Fat Zombie Goldfish Ser.: 1). (ENG.). 192p. (J). (gr. 2-5). 13.99 *(978-1-250-02919-5(8)*, 900118405) Feiwel & Friends.

—My Big Fat Zombie Goldfish. O'Hara, Mo. 2014. (My Big Fat Zombie Goldfish Ser.: 1). (ENG.). 208p. (J). (gr. 2-5). pap. 6.99 *(978-1-250-05215-5(7)*, 900135657) Square Fish.

—My FANGtastically Evil Vampire Pet. O'Hara, Mo. 2018. (My FANGtastically Evil Vampire Pet Ser.: 1). (ENG.). 208p. (J). 12.99 *(978-1-250-12811-9(0)*, 900175671) Feiwel & Friends.

—My FANGtastically Evil Vampire Pet. O'Hara, Mo. 2019. (My FANGtastically Evil Vampire Pet Ser.: 1). (ENG.). 224p. (J). pap. 7.99 *(978-1-250-29412-8(6)*, 900175672) Square Fish.

—The SeaQuel: My Big Fat Zombie Goldfish. O'Hara, Mo. 2014. (My Big Fat Zombie Goldfish Ser.: 2). (ENG.). 208p. (J). (gr. 2-5). 13.99 *(978-1-250-02920-1(1)*, 900118406) Feiwel & Friends.

—Space Cat-Astrophe: My FANGtastically Evil Vampire Pet. O'Hara, Mo. 2020. (My FANGtastically Evil Vampire Pet Ser.: 2). (ENG.). 208p. (J). pap. 7.99 *(978-1-250-23319-6(4)*, 900175677) Square Fish.

—Space Cat-Astrophe: My FANGtastically Evil Vampire Pet. O'Hara, Mo. 2019. (My FANGtastically Evil Vampire Pet Ser.: 2). (ENG.). 192p. (J). 13.99 *(978-1-250-12813-3(7)*, 900175676) Feiwel & Friends.

—Spy Penguins. Hay, Sam. 2020. (Spy Penguins Ser.: 1). (ENG.). 256p. (J). pap. 6.99 *(978-1-250-21104-0(2)*, 900192085) Square Fish.

—Spy Penguins. Hay, Sam. 2018. (Spy Penguins Ser.: 1). (ENG.). 240p. (J). 13.99 *(978-1-250-18838-0(5)*, 900192084) Feiwel & Friends.

Jagucki, Marek. Spy Penguins: Golden Egg. Hay, Sam. 2020. (Spy Penguins Ser.: 3). (ENG.). 240p. (J). 13.99 ***(978-1-250-18863-2(6)***, 900192120) Feiwel & Friends.

Jagucki, Marek. Spy Penguins: the Spy Who Loved Ice Cream. Hay, Sam. 2019. (Spy Penguins Ser.: 2). (ENG.). 240p. (J). 13.99 *(978-1-250-18858-8(X)*, 900192114) Feiwel & Friends.

Jagucki, Marek. Spy Penguins: the Spy Who Loved Ice Cream. Hay, Sam. 2020. (Spy Penguins Ser.: 2). (ENG.). 256p. (J). pap. 6.99 ***(978-1-250-61863-4(0)***, 900192115) Square Fish.

—We Love the NHS. Levenson, Eleanor. 2020. (ENG.). 36p. (J). pap. ***(978-0-9930773-9-5(0))*** Fisherton Pr. Ltd.

Jagucki, Marek. When & Why Did the Horse Fly? Knowing & Using Question Words, 1 vol. Meister, Cari. 2013. (Language on the Loose Ser.). (ENG.). 24p. (J). (gr. 2-4). pap. 7.95 *(978-1-4795-1918-7(9))*; lib. bdg. 28.65 *(978-1-4048-8319-2(3))* Capstone. (Picture Window Bks.).

Jahier, Milena. The Best Breakfast, 1 vol. Bowman, Crystal & Hodgson, Mona. 2008. (I Can Read! Ser.). (ENG.). 32p. (J). pap. 4.99 *(978-0-310-71740-9(X))* Zonderkidz.

—Thank You God for Rain, 1 vol. Hodgson, Mona. 2008. (I Can Read Book: Level 1 Ser.). (ENG.). 32p. (J). (gr. -1-1). 16.19 *(978-0-310-71741-6(8))* Zonderkidz.

Jahn, Alix. Mining Trucks. Mold, Gary. 2019. (ENG.). 32p. (J). pap. 10.00 ***(978-1-6536-6726-0(5))*** Independently Published.

Jaime, Daniel, jt. illus. see Torres, Nora Estela.

Jaime Diaz Studios. Disney Mickey & Friends. p i kids. 2018. (Look & Find Ser.). (ENG.). 24p. (J). *(978-1-5037-3968-0(6)*, a8d1bfd5-5727-40ce-9acc-b1bbffd3bf7b, p i kids) Phoenix International Publications, Inc.

—The Lion King: Look & Find Activity Book. 2019. (Look & Find Ser.). (ENG.). 24p. (J). *(978-0-7853-9532-4(6)*, 9e02fe67-62b7-47b7-98f1-4616d81e3679, p i kids) Phoenix International Publications, Inc.

Jain, Pallavi. The Mountains of Mumbai. Ghosh, Labanya. 2020. (ENG.). 40p. (J). 15.95 ***(978-81-936542-9-3(3))*** Karadi Tales Co. Pvt, Ltd. IND. Dist: Consortium Bk. Sales & Distribution.

Jain, Priti. Christmas in Bermuda: The Purple Grumblies. Marsh, Mike. 2016. (Purple Grumblies Ser.: Vol. 15). (ENG.). (J). (gr. k-1). pap. *(978-1-927506-46-2(8))* Yellow Toadstool Pr.

—The Efelant Hunters Part One: Shipwreck! Marsh, Mike. 2013. 28p. pap. *(978-1-927506-21-9(2))* Yellow Toadstool Pr.

—The Grumblies Set a Trap. Marsh, Mike. 2012. 24p. pap. *(978-0-9878019-2-0(9))* Yellow Toadstool Pr.

—The Skyrats Capture the Grumblies! Marsh, Mike. 2012. 28p. pap. *(978-1-927506-01-1(8))* Yellow Toadstool Pr.

Jainschigg, Nicholas. Ethan of Athos. Bujold, Lois McMaster. Lewis, Suford, ed. 2003. (Vorkosigan Ser.). 23.00 *(978-1-886778-39-9(6))* New England Science Fiction Assn., Inc.

Jakesevic, Nenad. Walk Across the Sea. Fletcher, Susan. 2003. (ENG.). 224p. (J). (gr. 4-8). pap. 11.95 *(978-0-689-85707-2(1)*, Atheneum Bks. for Young Readers) Simon & Schuster Children's Publishing.

Jakobsen, Kathy. This Land Is Your Land. Guthrie, Woody. ed. 2020. (ENG.). 42p. (J). (gr. -1-3). 18.99 *(978-0-316-45805-4(8))* Little, Brown Bks. for Young Readers.

Jakobsen, Kathy. My New York. Jakobsen, Kathy. anniv. rev. ed. 2005. 54p. (J). (gr. k-4). 19.00 *(978-0-7567-8588-8(X))* DIANE Publishing Co.

Jakobsen, Lars. The Mysterious Manuscript. Jakobsen, Lars. 2012. (Mortensen's Escapades Ser.: 1). 48p. (gr. 6-12). pap. 6.95 *(978-0-8225-9409-3(9)*, Graphic Universe™) Lerner Publishing Group.

—The Santa Fe Jail. Jakobsen, Lars. 2012. (Mortensen's Escapades Ser.: 2). 48p. (gr. 6-12). pap. 6.95 *(978-0-8225-9421-5(8)*, Graphic Universe™) Lerner Publishing Group.

Jakosalem, Lyle John. Tail of a Rat, Pink Turtle & a Cat. Finney, Melvin. 2019. (ENG.). 70p. (J). pap. 14.99 ***(978-1-948581-41-7(8))*** Lincross Publishing.

Jakson, Helen. Ben & the Big Balloon. Graves, Sue. 2008. (Tadpoles Ser.). (ENG.). 24p. (J). (gr. -1-3). pap. *(978-0-7787-3891-6(4))* Crabtree Publishing Co.

Jaleel, Aaliya. Muslim Girls Rise: Inspirational Champions of Our Time. Mir, Saira. 2019. (ENG.). 48p. (J). (gr. 1). 18.99 *(978-1-5344-1888-2(1))* Simon & Schuster, Inc.

—Under My Hijab, 1 vol. Khan, Hena. 2019. (ENG.). 32p. (J). (gr. -1-3). 18.95 *(978-1-62014-792-4(0)*, 23c8225f-7985-4830-a964-efdfff441271) Lee & Low Bks., Inc.

Jam Media. Becca's Bunch: B Is for Becca: An ABC Book. Jam Media. 2020. (Becca's Bunch Ser.). (ENG.). 26p. (J). (-k). bds. 7.99 *(978-0-7636-9086-1(4)*, Candlewick Entertainment) Candlewick Pr.

—Becca's Bunch: Becca's Big Decision. Jam Media. 2020. (Becca's Bunch Ser.). (ENG.). 32p. (J). (-k). 12.99 *(978-0-7636-9247-6(6)*, Candlewick Entertainment) Candlewick Pr.

Jamaldinian, Joe. Bob Winging It. Jamaldinian, Joe. 2005. 32p. (J). 14.00 *(978-0-9766657-0-0(0))* Jamaldinian, Yousef.

Jamana, Pharida. Los Frijoles Magicos. Hillert, Margaret & Del Risco, Elda. 2018. (BeginningtoRead Ser.). (SPA.). 32p. (J). (gr. -1-2). lib. bdg. 22.60 *(978-1-59953-955-3(1))* Norwood Hse. Pr.

Jamana, Pharida & Zaman, Farida. The Magic Beans. Hillert, Margaret. 2016. (BeginningtoRead Ser.). (ENG.). 32p. (J). (-2). lib. bdg. 22.60 *(978-1-59953-784-9(2))* Norwood Hse. Pr.

James, Ann. Audrey Goes to Town. Harris, Christine. 2014. (Audrey Ser.: 2). (ENG.). 176p. (J). (gr. 2-4). pap. 8.99 *(978-1-74297-796-6(0))* Little Hare Bks. AUS. Dist: Independent Pubs. Group.

—Audrey of the Outback. Harris, Christine. 2015. (Audrey Ser.: 1). (ENG.). 192p. (J). (gr. 2-4). pap. 8.99 *(978-1-74297-795-9(2))* Little Hare Bks. AUS. Dist: Independent Pubs. Group.

—A Coat of Cats. Kroll, Jeri. 32p. pap. *(978-0-7344-0118-2(3)*, Lothian Children's Bks.) Hachette Australia.

—Go Baby Go! Rippin, Sally. 2009. (ENG.). 12p. (J). (gr. k—1). bds. 7.99 *(978-1-74175-388-2(0))* Allen & Unwin AUS. Dist: Independent Pubs. Group.

—It's a Miroocool! Harris, Christine. 2012. (ENG.). 32p. (J). (gr. -1). 22.99 *(978-1-921541-01-8(6))* Little Hare Bks. AUS. Dist: Independent Pubs. Group.

—Sadie & Ratz. Hartnett, Sonya. (ENG.). 64p. (J). (gr. k-3). 2013. pap. 6.99 *(978-0-7636-6461-9(8))*; 2012. 14.99 *(978-0-7636-5315-6(2))* Candlewick Pr.

James, Annie. The Adventures of Elbert & Leopoldina. Kubik, Dorothy. 2006. 104p. (J). per. 15.00 *(978-0-9790775-1-7(6))* Touchstone Communications.

James, Ashleigh. Wilma's Magic Hat. Rae, Philippa. 2020. (ENG.). 42p. (J). pap. ***(978-1-910542-53-8(9))*** Chapeltown.

James, Ben. Los Tres Reyes Magos, the Three Wise Men. 2006. (J). bds. *(978-0-9786863-2-1(2))* ITRON Publishing.

James, Cate. The Dragon's Hoard: Stories from the Viking Sagas. Don, Lari. 2016. (ENG.). 64p. (J). (gr. 3-6). 22.99 *(978-1-84780-681-9(3)*, Frances Lincoln Children's Bks.) Quarto Publishing Group UK GBR. Dist: Hachette Bk. Group.

James, Claire. Zebedee's Bedtime: Dinosaurs, Colours Child Bedtime Magic Bed Seagull Mermaid Pyjamas Beach Sand Water Dolphin Travel Picture Book Rhyming Children Rock Pool Seaweed. Crofts, Maureen. 2018. (ENG.). 32p. (J). pap. *(978-1-9995862-0-1(4))* Crofts, Maureen.

James Crawford Publishing. Der Kleine Schutzengel. Muller, Stefanie Claudia. 2018. (GER.). 84p. (J). pap. 19.00 *(978-1-7902-2212-4(5))* Independently Published.

James, Diane. Watch It Cook, Vol. Bulloch, Ivan. 2004. (I Can Do It Ser.). (ENG.). 32p. (J). (gr. 2-5). 12.95 *(978-1-58728-510-3(X)*, Two-Can Publishing) T&N Children's Publishing.

James, Emma J. A Surprise for Santa. James, Emma J. 32p. (Orig.). (J). (gr. -1-3). pap. *(978-1-885935-02-1(1))* Appalachian Log Publishing Co., The.

James, Eric. Celebrate My Hopi Name. Poleahla, Anita. 2013. (CAI & ENG.). (J). *(978-1-893354-65-4(2))* Salina Bookshelf Inc.

James, Estes. Octavus Octopus, Vol. Rose, Williams. 2008. (ENG.). 20p. (J). pap. 10.00 *(978-0-86516-698-1(6))* Bolchazy-Carducci Pubs.

—Rena Rhinoceros, Vol. Rose, Williams. 2008. (ENG.). 20p. (J). pap. 10.00 *(978-0-86516-699-8(4))* Bolchazy-Carducci Pubs.

—Taurus Rex, Vol. Rose, Williams. 2008. (ENG.). 20p. (J). pap. 10.00 *(978-0-86516-700-1(1))* Bolchazy-Carducci Pubs.

—Ursus et Porcus, Vol. Rose, Williams. 2008. (ENG.). 20p. (J). pap. 10.00 *(978-0-86516-701-8(X))* Bolchazy-Carducci Pubs.

James Foley. Toffle Towers 2: the Great River Race. Harris, Tim. 2020. (Toffle Towers Ser.: 2). (ENG.). 272p. (J). (gr. 3-5). 14.99 ***(978-0-14-379543-8(0)**, Puffin)* Penguin Random Hse. AUS. Dist: Independent Pubs. Group.

James, Gordon C. Abby Takes a Stand. McKissack, Patricia C. 2007. 104p. (J). *(978-0-439-02797-7(7))* Scholastic, Inc.

—Abby Takes a Stand. McKissack, Patricia. 2006. (Scraps of Time Ser.). (ENG.). 128p. (J). (gr. 3-7). 6.99 *(978-0-14-240687-8(2)*, Puffin Books) Penguin Young Readers Group.

—Away West. McKissack, Patricia. 2006. (Scraps of Time Ser.). (ENG.). 144p. (J). (gr. 3-7). 7.99 *(978-0-14-240688-5(0)*, Puffin Books) Penguin Young Readers Group.

—Crown: An Ode to the Fresh Cut. Barnes, Derrick. 2017. 32p. (J). (gr. -1-3). 18.95 *(978-1-57284-224-3(5))* Agate Publishing, Inc.

James, Gordon C. I Am Every Good Thing. Barnes, Derrick. 2020. (ENG.). 32p. (J). (gr. -1-2). 17.99 ***(978-0-525-51877-8(0)**,* Nancy Paulsen Books) Penguin Young Readers Group.

James, Gordon C. Let 'Er Buck! George Fletcher, the People's Champion. Nelson, Vaunda Micheaux. 2019. (ENG.). 40p. (J). (gr. 3-6). 18.99 *(978-1-5124-9808-0(4)*, Carolrhoda Bks.) Lerner Publishing Group.

James, Helen. Fall. Butterworth Moira. 2005. (Seasons (Smart Apple Media) Ser.). 32p. (YA). (gr. 2-4). lib. bdg. 27.10 *(978-1-58340-616-8(6))* Black Rabbit Bks.

—Spring. Butterfield, Moira. 2005. (Seasons (Smart Apple Media) Ser.). 32p. (YA). (gr. 2-4). lib. bdg. 27.10 *(978-1-58340-614-4(X))* Black Rabbit Bks.

—Summer. Butterworth Moira. 2005. (Seasons (Smart Apple Media) Ser.). 32p. (YA). (gr. 2-4). lib. bdg. 27.10 *(978-1-58340-615-1(8))* Black Rabbit Bks.

—Winter. Butterworth Moira. 2005. (Seasons (Smart Apple Media) Ser.). 32p. (YA). (gr. 2-4). lib. bdg. 27.10 *(978-1-58340-617-5(4))* Black Rabbit Bks.

James, J. America's Flag Story, 1 vol. Robbins, Karen S. 2020. (ENG.). 32p. (J). (gr. -1-3). 16.99 *(978-0-7643-5921-7(5)*, 16218) Schiffer Publishing, Ltd.

James, Janice. The Mysterious Adventures of Maggie Mcgee Collection: All Five Mysteries in One Place. Ellis, Eren. Latta, Megan, ed. 2018. (ENG.). 246p. (J). pap. 15.00 *(978-1-7916-1518-5(X))* Independently Published.

James, John, et al. Inside Ancient Rome. Stewart, David. 2005. (Inside... Ser.). 48p. (J). (gr. 5). lib. bdg. 19.95 *(978-1-59270-045-5(4))* Enchanted Lion Bks., LLC.

James, John. Inside the Tomb of Tutankhamun. Morley, Jacqueline. 2005. (ENG.). 48p. (J). (gr. 3-7). 19.95 *(978-1-59270-042-4(X))* Enchanted Lion Bks., LLC.

—Real Pirates. Hibbert, Clare. 2009. (Real Adventurers Ser.). (ENG.). 48p. (gr. 3-3). 23.79 *(978-1-59270-018-9(7))* Cavendish Square Publishing LLC.

James, Josie. Marie's Ocean: Marie Tharp Maps the Mountains under the Sea. James, Josie. 2020. (ENG.). 48p. (J). 19.99 ***(978-1-250-21473-7(4)**,* 900204216, Holt, Henry & Co. Bks. For Young Readers) Holt, Henry & Co.

James, Katie. This Little Dragon. Rutherford, Robynn. 2013. (ENG.). 24p. (J). pap. *(978-0-9920222-0-4(7))* Robynn's Nest Publishing.

James, Kelly E. Alejandro: The Story of a Racehorse. Minor-Smith, Michelle. 2019. (ENG.). 40p. (J). 25.95 ***(978-1-64471-967-1(3))***; pap. 15.95 ***(978-1-64471-966-4(5))*** Covenant Bks.

James, Kennon. Abraham Lincoln: Will You Ever Give Up?, 1bk. Uglow, Loyd. 2003. (Another Great Achiever Ser.). (J). lib. bdg. 23.95 incl. audio *(978-1-57537-790-2(X))*; 48p. (YA). 16.95 incl. audio compact disk *(978-1-57537-540-3(0))*; (ENG.). 48p. (YA). lib. bdg. 23.95 incl. audio compact disk *(978-1-57537-740-7(3))* Advance Publishing, Inc.

—George Washington Carver: What Do You See?, 1bk. Benge, Janet. 2003. (Another Great Achiever Ser.). (J). lib. bdg. 23.95 incl. audio *(978-1-57537-792-6(6))* Advance Publishing, Inc.

—Helen Keller: Facing Her Challenges - Challenging the World, 1 bk. Benge, Janet. 2003. (Another Great Achiever Ser.). (J). lib. bdg. 23.95 incl. audio *(978-1-57537-793-3(4))* Advance Publishing, Inc.

—If Only I Were. . . Sommer, Carl. 2003. (Another Sommer-Time Story Ser.). (ENG.). 48p. (J). 16.95 incl. audio compact disk *(978-1-57537-502-1(8))* Advance Publishing, Inc.

—If Only I Were... Sommer, Carl. 2003. (Another Sommer-Time Story Ser.). (ENG.). 48p. (J). (gr. k-4). lib. bdg. 23.95 incl. audio compact disk *(978-1-57537-702-5(0))* Advance Publishing, Inc.

—If Only I Were- Sommer, Carl. 2014. (J). pap. *(978-1-57537-954-8(6))* Advance Publishing, Inc.

—If Only I Were...(Si Yo Fuese...) Sommer, Carl. ed. 2009. (Another Sommer-Time Story Bilingual Ser.). (SPA & ENG.). 48p. (J). lib. bdg. 16.95 *(978-1-57537-154-2(5))* Advance Publishing, Inc.

—Light Your Candle. Sommer, Carl. (J). 2014. pap. *(978-1-57537-957-9(0))*; 2003. (ENG.). 48p. 16.95 incl. audio compact disk *(978-1-57537-518-2(4))*; 2003. 48p. lib. bdg. 23.95 incl. audio compact disk *(978-1-57537-718-6(7))* Advance Publishing, Inc.

—Light Your Candle(Enciende Tu Vela) Sommer, Carl. ed. 2009. (Another Sommer-Time Story Bilingual Ser.). (SPA & ENG.). 48p. (J). lib. bdg. 16.95 *(978-1-57537-157-3(X))* Advance Publishing, Inc.

—The Little Red Train. Sommer, Carl. (J). 2014. pap. *(978-1-57537-958-6(9))*; 2003. (ENG.). 48p. 16.95 incl. audio compact disk *(978-1-57537-014-9(X))*; 2003. (ENG.). 48p. lib. bdg. 23.95 incl. audio compact disk *(978-1-57537-714-8(4))* Advance Publishing, Inc.

—The Little Red Train(El Trenecito Rojo) Sommer, Carl. ed. 2009. (Another Sommer-Time Story Bilingual Ser.). (SPA & ENG.). 48p. (J). lib. bdg. 16.95 *(978-1-57537-158-0(8))* Advance Publishing, Inc.

—No Longer a Dilly Dally. Sommer, Carl. (J). 2014. pap. *(978-1-57537-961-6(9))*; 2003. (ENG.). 48p. (gr. 1-4). 16.95 incl. audio compact disk *(978-1-57537-501-4(X))* Advance Publishing, Inc.

—No Longer a Dilly Dally Read-Along. Sommer, Carl. 2003. (Another Sommer-Time Story Ser.). (ENG.). 48p. (J). lib. bdg. 23.95 incl. audio compact disk *(978-1-57537-701-8(2))* Advance Publishing, Inc.

—No Longer a Dilly Dally(Nunca Mas a Troche y Moche) Sommer, Carl. ed. 2009. (Another Sommer-Time Story Bilingual Ser.). (SPA & ENG.). 48p. (J). lib. bdg. 16.95 *(978-1-57537-162-7(6))* Advance Publishing, Inc.

—Noise! Noise! Noise! Sommer, Carl. (J). 2014. pap. *(978-1-57537-963-0(5))*; 2003. (ENG.). 48p. 9.95 *(978-1-57537-020-0(4))*; 2003. (ENG.). 48p. lib. bdg. 16.95 *(978-1-57537-069-9(7))*; 2003. (ENG.). 48p. lib. bdg. 23.95 incl. audio compact disk *(978-1-57537-719-3(5))*; 2003. (ENG.). 48p. (gr. 1-4). 16.95 incl. audio compact disk *(978-1-57537-519-9(2))* Advance Publishing, Inc.

—Noise! Noise! Noise!(Ruido! Ruido! Ruido!) Sommer, Carl. ed. 2009. (Another Sommer-Time Story Bilingual Ser.). (SPA & ENG.). 48p. (J). lib. bdg. 16.95 *(978-1-57537-161-0(8))* Advance Publishing, Inc.

—The Sly Fox & the Chicks. Sommer, Carl. (J). 2014. pap. *(978-1-57537-966-1(X))*; 2003. (ENG.). 48p. 16.95 incl. audio compact disk *(978-1-57537-504-5(4))* Advance Publishing, Inc.

—The Sly Fox & the Chicks Read-along. Sommer, Carl. 2003. (Another Sommer-Time Story Ser.). (ENG.). 48p. (J). lib. bdg. 23.95 incl. audio compact disk *(978-1-57537-704-9(7))* Advance Publishing, Inc.

—The Sly Fox & the Chicks(El Zorro Astuto y los Pollitos) Sommer, Carl. ed. 2009. (Another Sommer-Time Story Bilingual Ser.). (SPA & ENG.). 48p. (J). lib. bdg. 16.95 *(978-1-57537-166-5(9))* Advance Publishing, Inc.

—You Move You Lose. Sommer, Carl. (J). 2014. pap. *(978-1-57537-972-2(4))*; 2003. (ENG.). 48p. lib. bdg. 23.95 incl. audio compact disk *(978-1-57537-705-6(5))*; 2003. (ENG.). 48p. (gr. 1-4). 16.95 incl. audio compact disk *(978-1-57537-505-2(2))* Advance Publishing, Inc.

—You Move You Lose(El Que Se Mueva, Pierde) Sommer, Carl. ed. 2009. (Another Sommer-Time Story Bilingual Ser.). (SPA & ENG.). 48p. (J). lib. bdg. 16.95 *(978-1-57537-172-6(3))* Advance Publishing, Inc.

—Your Job Is Easy. Sommer, Carl. (J). 2014. pap. *(978-1-57537-973-9(2))*; 2003. (ENG.). 48p. (gr. -1-4). 9.95 *(978-1-57537-018-7(2))*; 2003. (ENG.). 48p. (gr. 1-4). 16.95 incl. audio compact disk *(978-1-57537-517-5(6))*; 2003. (ENG.). 48p. (gr. 2-4). lib. bdg. 16.95 *(978-1-57537-067-5(0))* Advance Publishing, Inc.

—Your Job Is Easy Read-along. Sommer, Carl. 2003. (Another Sommer-Time Story Ser.). (ENG.). 48p. (J). lib. bdg. 23.95 incl. audio compact disk *(978-1-57537-717-9(9))* Advance Publishing, Inc.

—Your Job Is Easy(Tu Trabajo Es Facil) Sommer, Carl. ed. 2009. (Another Sommer-Time Story Bilingual Ser.). (SPA & ENG.). 48p. (J). lib. bdg. 16.95 *(978-1-57537-173-3(1))* Advance Publishing, Inc.

James, Larry W. & Freshman, Floris R. Captain Petey: An Adventure at Sea. James, Larry W. Ramos, Violet M., ed. 2003. 28p. pap. 6.99 *(978-0-9742154-0-2(6))* Cross Pointe Printing.

James, Laura. Anna Carries Water, 1 vol. Senior, Olive. 2014. (ENG.). 40p. (J). (gr. -1-k). 18.95 *(978-1-896580-60-9(2))* Tradewind Bks. CAN. Dist: Orca Bk. Pubs. USA.

—Boonoonoonous Hair, 1 vol. Senior, Olive. 2019. (ENG.). 32p. (J). (gr. 1-3). 17.95 *(978-1-926890-07-4(8))* Tradewind Bks. CAN. Dist: Orca Bk. Pubs. USA.

James, Margaret Ray. Thank You, God. Lundy, Charlotte. Waldrep, Evelyn L., ed. 2004. 32p. (J). (gr. k-3). 15.95 *(978-0-9670280-9-5(4))* Bay Light Publishing.

James, Martin, et al. How to Draw the Craziest, Creepiest Characters, 1 vol. Singh, Asavari. 2011. (Drawing Ser.). (ENG.). 48p. (J). (gr. 5-9). lib. bdg. 32.65 *(978-1-4296-6595-7(5))* Capstone.

—How to Draw the Fastest, Coolest Cars, 1 vol. Singh, Asavari. 2011. (Drawing Ser.). (ENG.). 48p. (J). (gr. 5-9). lib. bdg. 32.65 *(978-1-4296-6596-4(3))* Capstone.

—How to Draw the Most Exciting, Awesome Manga, 1 vol. Singh, Asavari. 2011. (Drawing Ser.). (ENG.). 48p. (J). (gr. 5-9). lib. bdg. 32.65 *(978-1-4296-6593-3(9))* Capstone.

James, Martin, jt. illus. see Ahmad, Aadil.

James, Matt. From There to Here, 1 vol. Croza, Laurel. 2014. (ENG.). 36p. (J). (gr. -1-2). 18.95 *(978-1-55498-365-0(7))* Groundwood Bks. CAN. Dist: Publishers Group West (PGW).

—Northwest Passage, 1 vol. Rogers, Stan. 2013. (ENG.). 56p. (J). (gr. k). 24.95 *(978-1-55498-153-3(0))* Groundwood Bks. CAN. Dist: Publishers Group West (PGW).

—The Stone Thrower: A Daughter's Lessons, a Father's Life, 1 vol. Richardson, Jael Ealey. 2016. (ENG.). 32p. (J). (gr. k). 18.95 *(978-1-55498-752-8(0))* Groundwood Bks. CAN. Dist: Publishers Group West (PGW).

—Yellow Moon, Apple Moon, 1 vol. Porter, Pamela. 2008. (ENG.). 32p. (J). (gr. k — 1). 17.95 *(978-0-88899-809-5(0))* Groundwood Bks. CAN. Dist: Publishers Group West (PGW).

James, Matteson. The Funeral, 1 vol. 2018. (ENG.). 40p. (J). 18.95 *(978-1-55498-908-9(6))* Groundwood Bks. CAN. Dist: Publishers Group West (PGW).

James, McKelvy Walker. My Way: The Memoirs of Coach Larry Folloni. Folloni, Larry. Michael, Folloni, ed. 2003. per. 19.95 *(978-0-9740480-0-0(3))* Light Energy Bks.

James, Melody. The Ivory Lace Shawl. Ballard, George Anne. l.t. ed. 2016. (Ballard Family Ser.: Vol. 1). (ENG.). (J). (gr. k-1). pap. 10.00 *(978-1-68418-336-4(7))* Primedia eLaunch LLC.

James, Melody. Walk along with Me. Ballard, George Anne. Bolton, Helen, ed. l.t. ed. 2019. (ENG.). 28p. (J). pap. 10.00 ***(978-1-64786-996-0(X))*** Primedia eLaunch LLC.

James, Melody. White Fire, the Indian Boy. Ballard, George Anne. 2012. 24p. pap. 12.00 *(978-0-9855312-3-2(1))* Bolton Publishing LLC.

James, Melody A. & Arelys, Aguilar. Read to Me! Ballard, George Anne. 2013. 60p. pap. 10.00 *(978-0-9855312-8-7(2))* Bolton Publishing LLC.

James, Nolan Karras. Black Sheep, White Crow & Other Windmill Tales: Stories from Navajo Country. Kristofic, Jim. 2017. (ENG.). 120p. (J). pap. 19.95 *(978-0-8263-5819-6(5))* Univ. of New Mexico Pr.

James, Rhian Nest. Owl Ninja. Fussell, Sandy. 2011. (Samurai Kids Ser.: 2). (ENG.). 272p. (J). (gr. 4-7). 15.99 *(978-0-7636-5003-2(X))* Candlewick Pr.

—Samurai Kids #4: Monkey Fist. Fussell, Sandy. 2012. (Samurai Kids Ser.: 4). (ENG.). 272p. (J). (gr. 4-7). pap. 6.99 *(978-0-7636-5827-4(8))* Candlewick Pr.

—Shaolin Tiger. Fussell, Sandy. 2011. (Samurai Kids Ser.: 3). (ENG.). 272p. (J). (gr. 4-7). pap. 6.99 *(978-0-7636-5702-4(6))* Candlewick Pr.

—Toppling. Murphy, Sally. 2012. (ENG.). 128p. (J). (gr. 3-7). 15.99 *(978-0-7636-5921-9(5))* Candlewick Pr.

—White Crane. Fussell, Sandy. 2010. (Samurai Kids Ser.: 1). (ENG.). 256p. (J). (gr. 4-7). 15.99 *(978-0-7636-4503-8(6))* Candlewick Pr.

James, Robin. Alaska's Dog Heroes: True Stories of Remarkable Canines. Gill, Shelley. 2014. (Paws IV Ser.). 32p. (J). (gr. 1-4). pap. 10.99 *(978-1-57061-909-0(3)*, Little Bigfoot) Sasquatch Bks.

—Buttermilk. Cosgrove, Stephen. 2013. (Serendipity Ser.: 2). (ENG.). 32p. (J). (gr. k-4). pap. 7.95 *(978-1-939011-52-7(3))* Heritage Builders, LLC.

—Creole. Cosgrove, Stephen. 2013. (Serendipity Ser.: 3). (ENG.). 32p. (J). (gr. k-4). pap. 7.95 *(978-1-939011-53-4(1))* Heritage Builders, LLC.

—Fanny. Cosgrove, Stephen. 2013. (Serendipity Ser.: 4). (ENG.). 32p. (J). (gr. k-4). pap. 7.95 *(978-1-939011-54-1(X))* Heritage Builders, LLC.

—Flutterby. Cosgrove, Stephen. 2013. (Serendipity Ser.: 5). (ENG.). 32p. (J). (gr. k-4). pap. 7.95 *(978-1-939011-55-8(8))* Heritage Builders, LLC.

—Gnome from Nome. Cosgrove, Stephen. 2012. (Paws IV Ser.). 32p. (J). (gr. -1-2). pap. 10.99 *(978-1-57061-777-5(5)*, Little Bigfoot) Sasquatch Bks.

—Good Night, Wheedle. Cosgrove, Stephen. 2016. 20p. (J). (— 1). bds. 9.99 *(978-1-63217-075-0(2)*, Little Bigfoot) Sasquatch Bks.

—The Grumpling. Cosgrove, Stephen. 2003. (Serendipity Bks.). (Orig.). (J). (gr. k-4). 12.65 *(978-0-7569-5259-4(X))* Perfection Learning Corp.

—Jalopy. Cosgrove, Stephen. 2016. (Serendipity Ser.: 21). (ENG.). 32p. (Orig.). (J). (gr. k-4). pap. 7.95 *(978-1-941437-32-2(X))* Heritage Builders, LLC.

James, Robin. Journey: Based on the True Story of OR7, the Most Famous Wolf in the West. Smith, Emma Bland. (ENG.). 32p. (J). (gr. k-4). 2020. pap. 10.99 ***(978-1-63217-337-9(9))***; 2016. 17.99 *(978-1-63217-065-1(5))* Sasquatch Bks. (Little Bigfoot).

James, Robin. Leo the Lop. Cosgrove, Stephen. 2013. (Serendipity Ser.: 6). (ENG.). 32p. (J). (gr. k-4). pap. 7.95 *(978-1-939011-56-5(6))* Heritage Builders, LLC.

—Morgan & Me. Cosgrove, Stephen. 2013. (Serendipity Ser.: 7). (ENG.). 32p. (J). (gr. k-4). pap. 7.95 *(978-1-939011-57-2(4))* Heritage Builders, LLC.

—The Muffin Dragon. Cosgrove, Stephen. 2013. (Serendipity Ser.: 8). (ENG.). 32p. (J). (gr. k-4). pap. 7.95 *(978-1-939011-59-6(0))* Heritage Builders, LLC.

—Nitter Pitter. Cosgrove, Stephen. 2015. (Serendipity Ser.: 20). (ENG.). 32p. (J). (gr. k-4). pap. 7.95 *(978-1-941437-38-4(9))* Heritage Builders, LLC.

—Paddle Pines. Cosgrove, Stephen. 2016. (Serendipity Ser.: 24). (ENG.). 32p. (J). (gr. k-4). pap. 7.95 *(978-1-941437-28-5(1))* Heritage Builders, LLC.

—Persnickety. Cosgrove, Stephen. 2016. (Serendipity Ser.: 23). 32p. (J). (gr. k-4). pap. 7.95 *(978-1-941437-40-7(0))* Heritage Builders, LLC.

—Pickles & the P-Flock Bullies. Cosgrove, Stephen. 2014. 32p. (J). (gr. k-3). 16.99 *(978-1-57061-887-1(9)*, Little Bigfoot) Sasquatch Bks.

—Saveopotomas. Cosgrove, Stephen. 2015. (Serendipity Ser.: 23). (ENG.). 32p. (J). (gr. k-4). pap. 7.95 *(978-1-941437-42-1(7))* Heritage Builders, LLC.

—Sniffles. Cosgrove, Stephen. 2013. (Serendipity Ser.: 1). (ENG.). 32p. (J). (gr. k-4). pap. 7.95 *(978-1-939011-58-9(2))* Heritage Builders, LLC.

—Sooty-Foot. Cosgrove, Stephen. 2015. (Serendipity Ser.: 21). (ENG.). 32p. (J). (gr. k-4). pap. 7.95 *(978-1-941437-30-8(3))* Heritage Builders, LLC.

—Tee-Tee. Cosgrove, Stephen. 2015. (Serendipity Ser.: 17). (ENG.). 32p. (J). (gr. k-4). pap. 7.95 *(978-1-941437-36-0(2))* Heritage Builders, LLC.

—Tickle's Tale. Cosgrove, Stephen. 2016. (Serendipity Ser.: 22). (ENG.). 32p. (Orig.). (J). (gr. k-4). pap. 7.95 *(978-1-941437-34-6(6))* Heritage Builders, LLC.

—Wheedle & the Noodle. Cosgrove, Stephen. 2011. 32p. (J). (gr. -1-2). 17.99 *(978-1-57061-730-0(9)*, Little Bigfoot) Sasquatch Bks.

—Wheedle on the Needle. Cosgrove, Stephen. 2009. 32p. (J). (gr. -1-2). 17.99 *(978-1-57061-628-0(0)*, Little Bigfoot) Sasquatch Bks.

James, Sandra. Mark of Seneca Basin. Langdale, Hazel Raybold. 2019. (ENG.). 218p. (J). (gr. 1-6). pap. 12.99 ***(978-1-4794-4485-4(5))*** Wildside Pr., LLC.

James, Shelly. The Carefree Tumbleweed. McGrath, Kim Pollock. 2019. (ENG.). 44p. (J). pap. 10.00 *(978-1-7906-7045-1(4))* Independently Published.

James, Simon. Baby Brains. James, Simon. 2016. (ENG.). 32p. (J). (gr. -1-3). 9.99 *(978-0-7636-8177-7(6))* Candlewick Pr.

—The Boy from Mars. James, Simon. 2018. (ENG.). 32p. (J). (gr. -1-2). 16.99 *(978-0-7636-9598-9(X))* Candlewick Pr.

—Frog & Beaver. James, Simon. 2018. (ENG.). 32p. (J). (gr. -1-2). 16.99 *(978-0-7636-9819-5(9))* Candlewick Pr.

—Leon & Bob. James, Simon. 2016. (ENG.). 32p. (J). (gr. -1-3). 7.99 *(978-0-7636-8175-3(X))* Candlewick Pr.

—Little One Step. James, Simon. (ENG.). (J). (-k). 2016. 32p. 7.99 *(978-0-7636-8176-0(8))*; 2007. 24p. bds. 6.99 *(978-0-7636-3520-6(0))* Candlewick Pr.

—Mr. Scruff. James, Simon. 2019. (ENG.). 32p. (J). (gr. -1-2). 16.99 *(978-1-5362-0935-8(X))* Candlewick Pr.

—Rex. James, Simon. 2016. (ENG.). 40p. (J). (-k). 16.99 *(978-0-7636-7294-2(7))* Candlewick Pr.

—The Smartest Baby in the Whole World. James, Simon. 2004. (Baby Brains Ser.). (ENG.). 32p. (J). (gr. -1-1). 21.19 *(978-0-7636-2507-8(8))* Candlewick Pr.

James, Simon. Days Like This: A Collection of Small Poems. James, Simon, compiled by. 2005. 48p. (J). (gr. 1-4). reprint ed. pap. 6.99 *(978-0-7636-2314-2(8))* Candlewick Pr.

James, Steve. Heart on Fire: Susan B. Anthony Votes for President. Malaspina, Ann. 2014. (AV2 Fiction Readalong Ser.: Vol. 139). (ENG.). (J). (gr. 1-4). lib. bdg. 34.28 *(978-1-4896-2335-5(3)*, AV2 by Weigl) Weigl Pubs., Inc.

—Monster Trucks. Downy, Rufus. Cottage Door Press, ed. 2019. (Colorforms Activity Bks.). (ENG.). 12p. (J). (gr. -1-2). bds. 9.99 *(978-1-68052-741-4(X)*, 1004620) Cottage Door Pr.

—More Lunch Lines: Tear-Out Riddles for Lunchtime Giggles (Lunch Jokes for Kids, Notes for Kids' Lunch Boxes with Silly Kid Jokes) Signer, Dan. 2020. (ENG.). 408p. (J). (gr. k-3). 9.99 *(978-1-4521-7442-6(3))* Chronicle Bks. LLC.

—Staying a Hive, 3. Colleen, Marcie. 2017. (Super Happy Party Bears Ser.). (ENG.). 144p. (J). (gr. 1-3). 18.69 *(978-1-5364-0566-8(3))* Macmillan.

—Super Happy Party Bears: Cruising for a Snoozing. Colleen, Marcie. 2018. (Super Happy Party Bears Ser.: 8). (ENG.). 144p. (J). pap. 5.99 *(978-1-250-12416-6(6)*, 900174360) Imprint IND. Dist: Macmillan.

—Super Happy Party Bears: Going Nuts. Colleen, Marcie. 2017. (Super Happy Party Bears Ser.: 4). (ENG.). 144p. (J). pap. 5.99 *(978-1-250-10049-8(6)*, 900162461) Imprint IND. Dist: Macmillan.

—The Walnut Cup. Carman, Patrick. 2009. (Elliot's Park Ser.: Bk. 3). 80p. (J). (gr. 1-5). 8.99 *(978-0-545-01932-3(X)*, Orchard Bks.) Scholastic, Inc.

James, Steven. Heart on Fire: Susan B. Anthony Votes for President. Malaspina, Ann. 2012. (ENG.). 32p. (J). (gr. 1-3). 16.99 *(978-0-8075-3188-4(X)*, 080753188X) Whitman, Albert & Co.

James, Will. The Dark Horse, Vol. 1. James, Will. rev. ed. 288p. (J). (gr. 4). pap. *(978-0-87842-486-3(5)*, 817) Mountain Pr. Publishing Co., Inc.

Jameson, Caitlyn. Cora Lynn: A Butterfly's Secret Tale. Caceres-Davis, Jessica. 2016. (ENG.). 24p. pap. 14.99 *(978-0-87565-655-7(2))* Texas Christian Univ. Pr.

Jamie, Meckel. Noodles for Baby. BeachHouse Publishing. 2011. (ENG.). 16p. (J). (gr. -1-1). bds. 7.95 *(978-1-933067-40-7(3))* Beachhouse Publishing, LLC.

Jamieson, Eden, jt. illus. see Levy, Shaun.

Jamieson, Sandy. Adam Cox Meets the CrackleCrunch for Lunch. Benesch, Walter. 2004. 32p. (J). 24.95 *(978-1-932053-09-8(3))* Nonetheless Pr.

Jamieson, Victoria. The Gollywhopper Games. Feldman, Jody. 2013. (Gollywhopper Games Ser.: 1). (ENG.). 336p. (J). (gr. 3-7). pap. 7.99 *(978-0-06-121452-3(3)*, Greenwillow Bks.) HarperCollins Pubs.

—The Gollywhopper Games: Friend or Foe. Feldman, Jody. (Gollywhopper Games Ser.: 3). (ENG.). 432p. (J). (gr. 3-7). 2016. pap. 6.99 *(978-0-06-221129-3(3))*; 2015. 16.99 *(978-0-06-221128-6(5))* HarperCollins Pubs. (Greenwillow Bks.).

—The Gollywhopper Games: the New Champion. Feldman, Jody. (Gollywhopper Games Ser.: 2). (ENG.). 400p. (J). (gr. 3-7). 2015. pap. 6.99 *(978-0-06-221126-2(9))*; 2014. 16.99 *(978-0-06-221125-5(0))* HarperCollins Pubs. (Greenwillow Bks.).

—Grandpa, What's That Sound in the Middle of the Night? Singlehurst, Naomi. Ellen Koski, Rachel, ed. 2008. (ENG.). 32p. (J). (gr. k-2). 14.95 *(978-1-930650-24-4(8))* mTrellis Publishing, Inc.

—The Lightning Catcher. Cameron, Anne. 2013. (Lightning Catcher Ser.: 1). (ENG.). 432p. (J). (gr. 3-7). 16.99 *(978-0-06-211276-7(7)*, Greenwillow Bks.) HarperCollins Pubs.

—The Storm Tower Thief. Cameron, Anne. 2014. (Lightning Catcher Ser.: 2). (ENG.). 432p. (J). (gr. 3-7). 16.99 *(978-0-06-211279-8(1)*, Greenwillow Bks.) HarperCollins Pubs.

—The Tiny Hero of Ferny Creek Library. Bailey, Linda. 2017. (ENG.). 336p. (J). (gr. 3-7). 16.99 *(978-0-06-244093-8(4)*, Greenwillow Bks.) HarperCollins Pubs.

Jamieson, Victoria. The Great Art Caper. Jamieson, Victoria. 2017. (Pets on the Loose! Ser.). (ENG.). 64p. (J). 15.99 *(978-1-62779-118-2(3)*, 9781627791182, Holt, Henry & Co. Bks. For Young Readers) Holt, Henry & Co.

—The Great Pet Escape. Jamieson, Victoria. 2016. (Pets on the Loose! Ser.). (ENG.). 64p. (J). 15.99 *(978-1-62779-105-2(1)*, 9781627791052, Holt, Henry & Co. Bks. For Young Readers) Holt, Henry & Co.

Jamieson, Victoria & Geddy, Iman. When Stars Are Scattered. Jamieson, Victoria & Mohamed, Omar. 2020. (ENG.). 264p. (J). (gr. 4-7). 20.99 *(978-0-525-55391-5(6))*; pap. 12.99 *(978-0-525-55390-8(8))* Penguin Young Readers Group. (Dial Bks).

Jamiol, Paul. Banger the Sausage Dog - Lost in London. McMullan, David. Habib, Linda, ed. 2019. (ENG.). 40p. (J). pap. 14.95 ***(978-1-64237-752-1(X))*** Gatekeeper Pr.

Jamison, Sharon. Farmyard Coloring Book. Goril, Cindy. 2016. (ENG.). 96p. (J). (gr. k-4). pap. 13.95 *(978-1-935188-80-3(1))* Star Publish LLC.

—Lacey's Legacy: Stretch's Story. Goril, Cindy. 2013. 28p. (J). pap. 12.95 *(978-1-935188-56-8(9))* Star Publish LLC.

Jampole, Ryan. Geeky Fab 5 Vol. 1: It's Not Rocket Science. Lareau, Liz & Lareau, Lucy. 2019. (Geeky Fab Five Ser.: 1). (ENG.). 64p. (J). pap. 7.99 *(978-1-5458-0123-9(1)*, 900191091) Papercutz.

—Geeky Fab 5 Vol. 2: Mystery of the Missing Monarchs. Lareau, Liz & Lareau, Lucy. 2019. (Geeky Fab Five Ser.). (ENG.). 64p. (J). pap. 7.99 *(978-1-5458-0365-3(X)*, 900210349) Papercutz.

—Geeky Fab 5 Vol. 3: DOGgone CATastrophe. Lareau, Lucy & Lareau, Liz. 2019. (Geeky Fab Five Ser.). (ENG.). 64p. (J). 12.99 *(978-1-5458-0323-3(4)*, 900207216); pap. 7.99 *(978-1-5458-0361-5(7)*, 900210341) Papercutz.

—Geeky Fab 5 Vol. 4: Food Fight for Fiona. Lareau, Liz & Lareau, Lucy. 2020. (Geeky Fab Five Ser.). (ENG.). 64p. (J). 12.99 *(978-1-5458-0346-2(3)*, 900209663); Vol. 4. pap. 7.99 *(978-1-5458-0364-6(1)*, 900210348) Papercutz.

—Melowy Vol. 1: The Test of Magic. Powell, Cortney Faye. 2019. (Melowy Ser.: 1). (ENG.). 64p. (J). pap. 7.99 *(978-1-5458-0003-4(0)*, 900191125) Papercutz.

—Melowy Vol. 2: The Fashion Club of Colors. Powell, Cortney Faye. 2020. (Melowy Ser.: 2). (ENG.). 64p. (J). pap. 7.99 *(978-1-5458-0363-9(3)*, 900210344) Papercutz.

—Melowy Vol. 3: Time to Fly. Powell, Cortney Faye. 2019. (Melowy Ser.: 3). (ENG.). 64p. (J). 12.99 *(978-1-5458-0309-7(9)*, 900206552); pap. 7.99 *(978-1-5458-0359-2(5)*, 900210337) Papercutz.

—Melowy Vol. 4: Frozen in Time. Star, Danielle & Powell, Cortney Faye. 2020. (Melowy Ser.: 4). (ENG.). 64p. (J). 12.99 *(978-1-5458-0350-9(1)*, 900209662); pap. 7.99 *(978-1-5458-0362-2(5)*, 900210342) Papercutz.

—Thea Stilton Graphic Novels #8: The Thea Sisters & the Secret Treasure Hunt. Stilton, Thea. Cooper-McGuinness, Nanette, tr. 2017. (Thea Stilton Graphic Novels Ser.: 8). (ENG.). 56p. (J). 9.99 *(978-1-62991-836-5(9)*, 900181005) Papercutz.

Jan, R. R. Piko the Penguinaut. Abraham, M. K. 2012. 112p. (J). 12.95 *(978-1-937489-00-7(0))* StoryRobin Co.

Janco, Tania. El Tejon de la Barca: Y Otras Historias. Howker, Janni. Tovar Cross, Juan Elias, tr. 2003. (la Orilla del Viento Ser.). (SPA.). 160p. (J). per. *(978-968-16-6282-0(2))* Fondo de Cultura Economica.

Jandran, James. A Dog, a Cat, & a Bama Hat. Jandran, Audrey. 2018. (ENG.). 26p. (J). pap. 9.45 *(978-1-7202-2007-7(7))* Independently Published.

Jane, Emily. The Caffeinated Squirrel. Page, Gwyneth Jane. 2020. (ENG.). 30p. (J). ***(978-1-989302-07-1(6))***; pap. ***(978-1-989302-06-4(8))*** Gwyneth Jane Page.

—The Caffeinated Squirrel - Colouring Book. Page, Gwyneth Jane. 2020. (ENG.). 30p. (J). pap. ***(978-1-989302-05-7(X))*** Gwyneth Jane Page.

Jane, Fred T. Tsar Wars Episode One: Angel of the Revolution. Griffith, George. Rowland, Marcus L., ed. 2003. Orig. Title: The Angel of the Revolution. 275p. per. 14.95 *(978-1-930658-16-5(8)*, HEL 5816) Heliograph, Inc.

—Tsar Wars Episode Two: Syren of the Skies. Griffith, George. Rowland, Marcus L., ed. 2003. Orig. Title: Olga Romanoff or Syren of the Skies. 274p. per. 14.95 *(978-1-930658-17-2(6)*, HEL 5817) Heliograph, Inc.

Jane, Nance'. If I Had a Daddy. Sullivan, Mary M. 2008. 28p. pap. 24.95 *(978-1-60610-555-9(8))* America Star Bks.

Jane, Ramsey. Madam President: Women Who Paved the Way. Gutgold, Nichola D. & Kennedy, Abigail. 2019. (ENG.). 38p. (J). pap. 9.99 ***(978-1-63233-227-1(2))*** Eifrig Publishing.

Janelle, Dimmed. Harry the Christmas Mouse: (Hardback) Gk, N. 2016. (ENG.). (J). (gr. k-3). *(978-0-9933670-3-8(8))* ngk media.

Janes, Andy. Blast to the Past, 6. Howard, Martin. 2017. (Shaun the Sheep: Tales from Mossy Bottom Farm Ser.). (ENG.). 112p. (J). (gr. 1-3). 17.44 *(978-1-5364-1044-0(6))* Candlewick Pr.

—Shaun the Sheep: Blast to the Past. Howard, Martin. 2017. (Tales from Mossy Bottom Farm Ser.: 6). (ENG.). 112p. (J). (gr. k-3). pap. 4.99 *(978-0-7636-9093-9(7)*, Candlewick Entertainment) Candlewick Pr.

—Shaun the Sheep: Flock to the Seaside. Howard, Martin. 2015. (Tales from Mossy Bottom Farm Ser.: 3). (ENG.). 112p. (J). (gr. k-3). pap. 4.99 *(978-0-7636-8058-9(3)*, Candlewick Entertainment) Candlewick Pr.

—Shaun the Sheep: on the Ball. Howard, Martin. 2015. (Tales from Mossy Bottom Farm Ser.: 4). (ENG.). 112p. (J). (gr. k-3). pap. 4.99 *(978-0-7636-8059-6(1)*, Candlewick Entertainment) Candlewick Pr.

—Shaun the Sheep: Pranks a Lot! Howard, Martin. 2016. (Tales from Mossy Bottom Farm Ser.: 5). (ENG.). 96p. (J). (gr. k-3). pap. 4.99 *(978-0-7636-8742-7(1)*, Candlewick Entertainment) Candlewick Pr.

—Shaun the Sheep: the Beast of Soggy Moor. Howard, Martin. 2015. (Tales from Mossy Bottom Farm Ser.: 2). (ENG.). 91p. (J). (gr. k-3). pap. 4.99 *(978-0-7636-7586-8(5)*, Candlewick Entertainment) Candlewick Pr.

—Shaun the Sheep: the Flock Factor. Howard, Martin. 2014. (Tales from Mossy Bottom Farm Ser.: 1). (ENG.). 96p. (J). (gr. k-3). pap. 4.99 *(978-0-7636-7535-6(0)*, Candlewick Entertainment) Candlewick Pr.

Janev, Svetlana. Bridget Knotterfield & the Hiccup Fantasy Trees. Blum, Ingo. 2018. (ENG.). 268p. (YA). (gr. 7-11). pap. *(978-3-947410-46-0(8))* Blum, Ingo Planet-Oh Concepts.

Jang, Dong-Il. The Quiet Observer: The Art of Degas. Kim, Miae. 2017. (Stories of Art Ser.). (ENG.). 36p. (J). (gr. 3-5). lib. bdg. 10.00 *(978-1-925235-28-9(9)*, Big and SMALL) ChoiceMaker Pty. Ltd., The AUS. Dist: Lerner Publishing Group.

Jang, Erin, jt. illus. see The Indigo Bunting.

Jang, EunJoo. The Chirping Band. Lee, WonKyeong. 2014. (MySELF Bookshelf Ser.). (ENG.). 32p. (J). (gr. k-2). pap. 11.94 *(978-1-60357-698-7(3))*; lib. bdg. 25.27 *(978-1-59953-663-7(3))* Norwood Hse. Pr.

Jang, Yeong-seon. Peter Pan. Barrie, J. M. Cowley, Joy, ed. 2015. (World Classics Ser.). (ENG.). 32p. (gr. k-4). (J). 10.00 *(978-1-925186-71-0(7))*; 26.65 *(978-1-925246-19-3(1))*; 7.99 *(978-1-925246-71-1(X))*; 26.65 *(978-1-925246-45-2(0))* ChoiceMaker Pty. Ltd., The AUS. (Big and SMALL). Dist: Lerner Publishing Group.

—Peter Pan. Barrie, J. M. 2015. (World Classics Ser.). (ENG.). 32p. (J). (gr. k-4). pap. 5.00 *(978-1-925186-65-9(2)*, Big and SMALL) ChoiceMaker Pty. Ltd., The AUS. Dist: Lerner Publishing Group.

Jangid, Bhumika. My Vision Quest: The Power of Dreaming Big. Jones, Eevi. 2020. (Braving the World Ser.: Vol. 5). (ENG.). 40p. (J). 16.00 ***(978-1-952517-94-5(X))*** LHC Publishing.

Janguay, Patricia. There's A Giant in the Garden. Stuefloten, Helen. I.t. ed. 2006. 35p. (J). per. 11.99 *(978-1-59879-161-7(3))* Lifevest Publishing, Inc.

Janicke, Gregory. The Conquerors, 1 vol. Janicke, Gregory. 2008. (Outcasts Ser.: Bk. 4). (ENG.). 328p. (YA). (gr. 5-18). pap. 7.99 *(978-0-7614-5442-7(X))* Marshall Cavendish Corp.

—The Shadow Beasts, 1 vol. Janicke, Gregory. 2007. (Outcasts Ser.: Bk. 1). (ENG.). 276p. (YA). (gr. 8-12). pap. 6.99 *(978-0-7614-5364-2(4))* Marshall Cavendish Corp.

Jankowski, Dan. Up Close & Gross. Hall, Kirsten. 2009. 64p. (J). *(978-0-545-13583-2(4))* Scholastic, Inc.

—What's a Jaybird to Do? Sauer, Cat. I.t. ed. 2003. (Brown Bag Bedtime Bks.: 1). 31p. (YA). spiral bd. 16.95 *(978-0-9704460-8-4(X))* Writer's Ink. Studios, Inc.

Jankowski, Daniel. Dinosaur Bites. Dakota, Heather. 2015. 48p. (J). *(978-0-545-82098-1(7)*, Tangerine Pr.) Scholastic, Inc.

—Flip Flop & Hoot. Sauer, Cat. I.t. ed. 2006. (Brown Bag Bedtime Bks.: 1). 35p. (J). (gr. -1-2). 16.95 incl. audio compact disk *(978-0-9704460-6-0(3))* Writer's Ink. Studios, Inc.

—Gwendolyn the Ghost. Sauer, Cat. I.t. ed. 2006. (Brown Bag Bedtime Bks.: 1). 29p. (J). (gr. -1-2). 16.95 incl. audio compact disk *(978-0-9704460-9-1(8))* Writer's Ink. Studios, Inc.

—A Possum in the Roses. Sauer, Cat. I.t. ed. 2006. (Brown Bag Bedtime Bks.: 1). 27p. (J). (gr. -1-2). 16.95 incl. audio compact disk *(978-0-9704460-7-7(1))* Writer's Ink. Studios, Inc.

—Rocks, Minerals, & Gemstones. Salzano, Tammi J. 2009. 24p. (J). pap. *(978-0-545-19868-4(2))* Scholastic, Inc.

—Shark Bites. Dakota, Heather. 2016. 48p. (J). pap. *(978-1-338-13718-7(2))* Scholastic, Inc.

Janos, Orban. Medieval Knights: Europe's Fearsome Armored Soldiers. Hoena, Blake. 2019. (Graphic History: Warriors Ser.). (ENG.). 32p. (J). (gr. 3-9). pap. 7.95 *(978-1-5435-5928-6(X)*, 139906); lib. bdg. 31.32 *(978-1-5435-5501-1(2)*, 139374) Capstone.

—Samurai: Japan's Noble Servant-Warriors. Hoena, Blake. 2019. (Graphic History: Warriors Ser.). (ENG.). 32p. (J). (gr. 3-9). pap. 7.95 *(978-1-5435-5930-9(1)*, 139908); lib. bdg. 31.32 *(978-1-5435-5504-2(7)*, 139376) Capstone.

Janosch. Yo Te Curare, Dijo el Pequeno Oso. Janosch. 2003. (SPA.). 48p. (J). (gr. k-3). pap. 8.95 *(978-958-24-0110-8(9))* Santillana USA Publishing Co., Inc.

—Zampano y Su Oso. Janosch. (Coleccion el Faro Azul). (SPA.). (J). 8.95 *(978-84-348-1571-1(0)*, SM004) SM Ediciones ESP. Dist: Continental Bk. Co., Inc.

Janovitz, Marilyn. Airplane Adventure, 1 vol. Meister, Cari. 2010. (My First Graphic Novel Ser.). 32p. (gr. k-2). (ENG.). (J). pap. 6.25 *(978-1-4342-2286-2(1))*; pap. 4.95 *(978-1-4342-3602-9(1))* Capstone. (Stone Arch Bks.).

—Innovative Kids Readers: Milly's Silly Suitcase - Level 1. Rabe, Tish. 2006. (J). (gr. -1-1). 6.99 *(978-1-58476-493-9(7))* Innovative Kids.

—Pirate Pickle & the White Balloon. Burg, Ann E. 2007. (Rookie Reader Skill Set Ser.). (ENG.). 32p. (J). (gr. -1-3). pap. 4.95 *(978-0-531-17778-5(5)*, Children's Pr.) Scholastic Library Publishing.

—Pirate Pickle & the White Balloon. Burg, Ann. 2007. (Rookie Reader: Opposites Ser.). (ENG.). 32p. (J). (gr. k-2). 17.44 *(978-0-531-17544-6(8))* Scholastic Library Publishing.

—Train Trip, 1 vol. Meister, Cari & Stone Arch Books Staff. 2010. (My First Graphic Novel Ser.). (ENG.). 32p. (J). (gr. k-2). pap. 6.25 *(978-1-4342-2289-3(6)*, Stone Arch Bks.) Capstone.

—Train Trip, 1 vol. Meister, Cari. 2009. (My First Graphic Novel Ser.). (ENG.). 32p. (J). (gr. k-2). 24.65 *(978-1-4342-1616-8(0)*, Stone Arch Bks.) Capstone.

Janovitz, Marilyn. I Will Try. Janovitz, Marilyn. 2012. (I Like to Read Ser.). (ENG.). 24p. (J). (gr. -1-3). 14.95 *(978-0-8234-2399-6(9))* Holiday Hse., Inc.

—We Love School (¡Nos Encanta la Escuela!) Janovitz, Marilyn. 2009. (SPA.). 32p. (J). (gr. -1-k). 7.95 *(978-0-7358-2246-7(8))* North-South Bks., Inc.

Janry. Adventure down Under, Vol. 1. Tome. Saincantin, Jerome, tr. 2010. (Spirou Ser.: 1). (ENG.). 48p. (J). (gr. 4-7). pap. 11.95 *(978-1-84918-011-5(3))* CineBook GBR. Dist: National Bk. Network.

—Spirou & Fantasio - Valley of the Exiles. 2013. (Spirou & Fantasio Ser.: 4). Orig. Title: Vol. 4. (ENG.). 48p. pap. 11.95 *(978-1-84918-157-0(8))* CineBook GBR. Dist: National Bk. Network.

—Spirou & Fantasio in New York. Tome. 2011. (Spirou & Fantasio Ser.: 2). (ENG.). 48p. (J). (gr. 3-17). pap. 11.95 *(978-1-84918-054-2(7))* CineBook GBR. Dist: National Bk. Network.

—Spirou & Fantasio Vol. 14: The Clockmaker & the Comet. 2018. (Spirou & Fantasio Ser.: 14). (ENG.). 48p. pap. 11.95 *(978-1-84918-404-5(6))* CineBook GBR. Dist: National Bk. Network.

Janry, Tome. Spirou & Fantasio in Moscow, Vol. 6. 2014. (Spirou & Fantasio Ser.: 6). (ENG.). 48p. pap. 11.95 *(978-1-84918-193-8(4))* CineBook GBR. Dist: National Bk. Network.

Jansen, Anna Katharina. Baby Loves Calm: An ABC of Mindfulness. Eckford, Jennifer. ed. 2020. (Baby Loves Ser.). (ENG.). 30p. (J). (gr. -1 — 1). bds. 12.99 ***(978-0-7112-5315-5(3)***, 334938, Frances Lincoln Children's Bks.) Quarto Publishing Group UK GBR. Dist: Hachette UK Distribution.

—Jesse Owens. Sanchez Vegara, Maria Isabel. 2020. (Little People, Big Dreams Ser.: Vol. 42). (ENG.). 32p. (J). (gr. -1-2). ***(978-0-7112-4583-9(5))*** Frances Lincoln Childrens Bks.

—Jesse Owens. ed. 2020. (Little People, BIG DREAMS Ser.: 42). (ENG.). 32p. (J). (gr. -1-2). 14.99 ***(978-0-7112-4582-2(7)***, 329404, Frances Lincoln Children's Bks.) Quarto Publishing Group UK GBR. Dist: Hachette UK Distribution.

Jansen, Paula. Mammoths: Ice-Age Giants. Jansen, Paula, photos by. Nelson, Lisa W. & Agenbroad, Larry D. 2005. (Discovery! Ser.). 120p. (gr. 5-12). lib. bdg. 27.93 *(978-0-8225-2862-3(2))* Lerner Publishing Group.

Jansson, Alexander. The Cabinet of Curiosities: 36 Tales Brief & Sinister. Bachmann, Stefan et al. 2014. (ENG.). 496p. (J). (gr. 3-7). 16.99 *(978-0-06-233105-2(1))*; pap. 6.99 *(978-0-06-231314-0(2))* HarperCollins Pubs. (Greenwillow Bks.).

Jansson, Tove. Comet in Moominland. Jansson, Tove. Portch, Elizabeth, tr. 2010. (Moomins Ser.: 2). (ENG.). 192p. (J). (gr. 4-7). pap. 7.99 *(978-0-312-60888-0(8)*, 900065183) Square Fish.

—Finn Family Moomintroll. Jansson, Tove. Portch, Elizabeth, tr. 2010. (Moomins Ser.: 3). (ENG.). 176p. (J). (gr. 4-7). pap. 8.99 *(978-0-312-60889-7(6)*, 900065184) Square Fish.

—Moomin & the Birthday Button. Jansson, Tove. 2011. (Moomins Ser.). (ENG.). 32p. (J). (gr. -1-1). 13.99 *(978-0-374-35050-5(7)*, 900070720, Farrar, Straus & Giroux (BYR)) Farrar, Straus & Giroux.

—Moominland Midwinter. Jansson, Tove. Warburton, Thomas, tr. 2010. (Moomins Ser.: 6). (ENG.). 160p. (J). (gr. 4-7). pap. 8.99 *(978-0-312-62541-2(3)*, 900066518) Square Fish.

—Moominpappa at Sea. Jansson, Tove. Hart, Kingsley, tr. 2010. (Moomins Ser.: 8). (ENG.). 240p. (J). (gr. 4-7). pap. 8.99 *(978-0-312-60892-7(6)*, 900065186) Square Fish.

—Moominpappa's Memoirs. Jansson, Tove. Warburton, Thomas, tr. 2010. (Moomins Ser.: 4). (ENG.). 192p. (J). (gr. 4-7). pap. 8.99 *(978-0-312-62543-6(X)*, 900066521) Square Fish.

—Moominsummer Madness. Jansson, Tove. Warburton, Thomas, tr. 2010. (Moomins Ser.: 5). (ENG.). 176p. (J). (gr. 4-7). pap. 7.99 *(978-0-312-60891-0(8)*, 900065185) Square Fish.

—Moominvalley in November. Jansson, Tove. Hart, Kingsley, tr. 2010. (Moomins Ser.: 9). (ENG.). 208p. (J). (gr. 4-7). pap. 7.99 *(978-0-312-62544-3(8)*, 900066522) Square Fish.

—Tales from Moominvalley. Jansson, Tove. Warburton, Thomas, tr. 2010. (Moomins Ser.: 7).Tr. of Osynliga Barnet. (ENG.). 192p. (J). (gr. 4-7). pap. 8.99 *(978-0-312-62542-9(1)*, 900066520) Square Fish.

Jantner, Janos. Drawing Fantasy Monsters. 2013. (How to Draw Monsters Ser.). (ENG.). 32p. (J). (gr. 3-6). pap. 11.75 *(978-1-4777-0344-1(6))*; lib. bdg. 28.50 *(978-1-4777-0311-3(X))* Rosen Publishing Group, Inc., The. (PowerKids Pr.).

—Drawing Horror-Movie Monsters. 2013. (How to Draw Monsters Ser.). (ENG.). 32p. (J). (gr. 3-6). 28.50 *(978-1-4777-0308-3(X))*; pap. 11.75 *(978-1-4777-0338-0(1))* Rosen Publishing Group, Inc., The. (PowerKids Pr.).

—Drawing Monsters from Great Books. 2013. (How to Draw Monsters Ser.). (ENG.). 32p. (J). (gr. 3-6). pap. 11.75 *(978-1-4777-0348-9(9))*; lib. bdg. 28.50 *(978-1-4777-0313-7(6))* Rosen Publishing Group, Inc., The. (PowerKids Pr.).

—Drawing Mythological Monsters. 2013. (How to Draw Monsters Ser.). (ENG.). 32p. (J). (gr. 3-6). pap. 11.75 *(978-1-4777-0340-3(3))*; lib. bdg. 28.50 *(978-1-4777-0309-0(8))* Rosen Publishing Group, Inc., The. (PowerKids Pr.).

—Drawing Science-Fiction Monsters. 2013. (How to Draw Monsters Ser.). (ENG.). 32p. (J). (gr. 3-6). pap. 11.75 *(978-1-4777-0342-7(X))*; lib. bdg. 28.50 *(978-1-4777-0310-6(1))* Rosen Publishing Group, Inc., The. (PowerKids Pr.).

—Drawing Unexplained-Mystery Monsters. 2013. (How to Draw Monsters Ser.). (ENG.). 32p. (J). (gr. 3-6). pap. 11.75 *(978-1-4777-0346-5(2))*; lib. bdg. 28.50 *(978-1-4777-0312-0(8))* Rosen Publishing Group, Inc., The. (PowerKids Pr.).

Jaques, Laura. The Most Dangerous, 1 vol. Fields, Terri. 2012. (ENG.). 32p. (J). (gr. -1-3). pap. 9.95 *(978-1-60718-535-2(0))* Arbordale Publishing.

Jaquet, Gertie. Macie's Mirror. Ciccio, Adam. 2020. 32p. (J). (gr. k). (ENG.). 17.95 *(978-1-60537-513-7(6))*; 9.95 *(978-1-60537-537-3(3))* Clavis Publishing.

Jara, José. The Stranger & the Red Rooster / el Forastero y el Gallo Rojo. Villaseñor, Victor. 2019. (ENG & SPA.). 32p. (J). (gr. 1-3). pap. 7.95 *(978-1-55885-470-3(3))* Arte Publico Pr.

Jaraiz, David. Storytime with Paige. Friden, Chris & Rodriguez Braojos, Alberto. 2008. (J). *(978-0-9758785-8-3(1))*; *(978-0-9801849-4-5(0))* Haydenburn Lane.

Jaramillo, Carlos. Two Hearts of Gold. Drumheller, Joseph. 2019. (ENG.). 32p. (J). pap. 12.99 *(978-1-0996-7320-7(8))* Independently Published.

Jaramillo, Raquel. The Handiest Things in the World. Clements, Andrew. 2010. (ENG.). 48p. (J). (gr. -1-3). 18.99 *(978-1-4169-6166-6(6)*, Atheneum Bks. for Young Readers) Simon & Schuster Children's Publishing.

Jaramillo, Raquel. Peter Pan: The Original Tale of Neverland. Jaramillo, Raquel, photos by. Barrie, J. M. unabr. ed. 2003. 135p. (YA). (gr. 5-8). reprint ed. 25.00 *(978-0-7567-6883-6(7))* DIANE Publishing Co.

Jardine, David. There's a Cow under My Bed, 1 vol. Sherrard, Valerie. 2008. (ENG.). 32p. (J). (gr. 1-8). *(978-1-897174-34-0(9))* Breakwater Bks., Ltd.

—There's a Goldfish in My Shoe!, 1 vol. Sherrard, Valerie. 2009. (ENG.). 32p. (J). (gr. 1-7). *(978-1-897174-47-0(0))* Breakwater Bks., Ltd.

Jarkins, Sheila. Adv Marco Flamingo Under Sea. Jarkins, Sheila. 2010. (ENG.). 32p. (J). (gr. -1-12). pap. 7.95 *(978-1-934960-69-1(1)*, Raven Tree Pr.,Csi) Continental Sales, Inc.

—The Adventures of Marco Flamingo in the Jungle. Jarkins, Sheila. 2012. 32p. (J). 1.99 *(978-1-936299-31-7(3)*, Raven Tree Pr.) Delta Systems Company, Inc.

—Marco Flamenco. Jarkins, Sheila. de la Vega, Eida, tr. 2008. (SPA & ENG.). 32p. (J). (gr. -1-3). 16.95 *(978-0-9794462-7-6(9)*, Raven Tree Pr.,Csi) Continental Sales, Inc.

Jarman, Brandy S. The Halloween Chase. Hooley, Rachelle B. & Butler, Mackay M. 2012. 36p. 24.95 *(978-1-4626-7160-1(8))* America Star Bks.

Jaro, Jose & Shelfer, Michael. Incidentals Vol. 3: City of Demons. Easton, Brandon & Govea, Ramón Slamet. 2019. (ENG.). 144p. (YA). pap. 14.99 *(978-1-5493-0273-2(6)*, 4b2f36bd-b218-4d0a-9ac1-583a6c474d82, Lion Forge) Oni Pr., Inc.

Jaroszko, Mike. Away in a Manger. 2008. 32p. (J). (gr. -1). 13.49 *(978-0-7586-1496-4(9))* Concordia Publishing Hse.

—Away in a Manger Devotional. 2008. pap. 2.29 *(978-0-7586-1449-0(7))* Concordia Publishing Hse.

Jarret, Judy. Every Day & Sunday, Too. Ramshaw, Gail. 2004. 44p. 15.99 *(978-0-8066-2334-4(9)*, 10-23349, Augsburg Bks.) Augsburg Fortress, Pubs.

Jarrett, Michael. Adding. Jarrett, Michael, photos by. Williams, Rozanne Lanczak. 2004. (I Can Do Math Ser.). 24p. (gr. k-3). lib. bdg. 23.00 *(978-0-8368-4108-4(5)*, Gareth Stevens Learning Library) Stevens, Gareth Publishing LLLP.

—Crayola Counting. Jarrett, Michael, photos by. Williams, Rozanne Lanczak. 2004. (I Can Do Math Ser.). 24p. (gr. k-3). lib. bdg. 23.00 *(978-0-8368-4109-1(3)*, Gareth Stevens Learning Library) Stevens, Gareth Publishing LLLP.

Jarrett, Michael, photos by. I Can Share with Others. Burch, Regina G. & Donovan Guntly, Jenette. 2004. (Doing the Right Thing Ser.). 16p. (gr. -1-2). lib. bdg. 21.00 *(978-0-8368-4246-3(4)*, Gareth Stevens Learning Library) Stevens, Gareth Publishing LLLP.

—I Can Show I Care. Burch, Regina G. & Donovan Guntly, Jenette. 2004. (Doing the Right Thing Ser.). 16p. (gr. -1-2). lib. bdg. 21.00 *(978-0-8368-4247-0(2)*, Gareth Stevens Learning Library) Stevens, Gareth Publishing LLLP.

—Learning about Coins. Williams, Rozanne Lanczak. 2004. (I Can Do Math Ser.). 24p. (gr. k-3). lib. bdg. 22.00 *(978-0-8368-4110-7(7)*, Gareth Stevens Learning Library) Stevens, Gareth Publishing LLLP.

—My Favorites, Your Favorites. Williams, Rozanne Lanczak. Hamaguchi, Carla, ed. 2003. (Sight Word Readers Ser.). 16p. (J). (gr. k-2). pap. 3.49 *(978-1-57471-964-2(5)*, 3586) Creative Teaching Pr., Inc.

—Subtracting. Williams, Rozanne Lanczak. 2004. (I Can Do Math Ser.). 24p. (gr. k-3). lib. bdg. 23.00 *(978-0-8368-4113-8(1)*, Gareth Stevens Learning Library) Stevens, Gareth Publishing LLLP.

J

Jarrett, Sandra. Who Is He in Yonder Stall? Neal, Sharon, ed. 2008. (ENG.). 24p. (J). pap. *(978-1-932381-21-4(X)*, 6500) Bible Visuals International, Inc.

Jarrett, Tom. Handball! Arena, Felice. 6th ed. 2017. (Sporty Kids Ser.). 80p. (J). (gr. 1-3). 8.99 *(978-0-14-330890-4(4))* Random Hse. Australia AUS. Dist: Independent Pubs. Group.

Jarrie, Martin. Abejas, Hormigas, Termitas Insectos Que Viven en Familia / Bees, Ants, Termites: Insects That Live in Families. Saint-Dizier, Marie. 2018. (SPA.). 32p. (J). (gr. 2-5). pap. 10.99 *(978-1-947783-81-2(5)*, Altea) Penguin Random House Grupo Editorial ESP. Dist: Penguin Random Hse. LLC.

Jarvinen, Kirk, et al. Avengers Epic Collection: Fear the Reaper. 2019. (ENG.). 480p. (J). (gr. 4-17). pap. 39.99 *(978-1-302-91616-9(5))* Marvel Worldwide, Inc.

Jarvis. I'm in Charge! Willis, Jeanne. 2018. (ENG.). 32p. (J). (-k). 16.99 *(978-1-5362-0259-5(2)*, Nosy Crow) Candlewick Pr.

—Pick a Pine Tree. Toht, Patricia. 2017. (ENG.). 40p. (J). (gr. -1-2). 16.99 *(978-0-7636-9571-2(8))* Candlewick Pr.

—Pick a Pumpkin. Toht, Patricia. 2019. (ENG.). 40p. (J). (gr. -1-2). 16.99 *(978-1-5362-0764-4(0))* Candlewick Pr.

—Pig & Pug. Marchesani, Laura & Medina, Zenaides A., Jr. 2015. (Penguin Young Readers, Level 2 Ser.). 32p. (J). (gr. 1-2). pap. 4.99 *(978-0-448-48342-9(4)*, Penguin Young Readers) Penguin Young Readers Group.

—Poles Apart. Willis, Jeanne. 2016. (ENG.). 32p. (J). (gr. -1-2). 15.99 *(978-0-7636-8944-5(0)*, Nosy Crow) Candlewick Pr.

—Ready, Set, Build! Fleming, Meg. (ENG.). (J). (gr. -1-k). 2019. 26p. bds. 7.99 *(978-1-4998-0802-5(X))*; 2017. 32p. 16.99 *(978-1-4998-0175-0(0))* Little Bee Books Inc.

Jarvis. Alan's Big, Scary Teeth. Jarvis. (ENG.). 32p. (J). (-k). 2020. 7.99 ***(978-1-5362-1590-8(2))***; 2016. 16.99 *(978-0-7636-8120-3(2))* Candlewick Pr.

Jarvis. Follow Me, Flo! Jarvis. 2020. (ENG.). 32p. (J). (gr. -1-2). 16.99 *(978-1-5362-1270-9(9))* Candlewick Pr.

—Fred Forgets. Jarvis. 2016. (ENG.). 32p. (J). (gr. -1-3). 17.99 *(978-0-06-234916-3(3))* HarperCollins Pubs.

—Lazy Dave. Jarvis. 2015. (ENG.). 32p. (J). (gr. -1-3). 17.99 *(978-0-06-235598-0(8))* HarperCollins Pubs.

—Mary Had a Little Lamb: a Colors Book. Jarvis. 2019. (ENG.). 22p. (J). (— 1). bds. 8.99 *(978-1-5362-1111-5(7))* Candlewick Pr.

—Mrs Mole, I'm Home! Jarvis. 2018. (ENG.). 32p. (J). (-k). 15.99 *(978-0-7636-9495-1(9))* Candlewick Pr.

—This Little Piggy. Jarvis. 2019. (ENG.). 22p. (J). (— 1). bds. 8.99 *(978-1-5362-1110-8(9))* Candlewick Pr.

—Tropical Terry. Jarvis. 2019. (ENG.). 32p. (J). (-k). 16.99 *(978-1-5362-0546-6(X))* Candlewick Pr.

Jarvis, Nathan Y. ABCs at the Beach. Walters, Jennifer Marino. 2020. (ABC Adventures Ser.). (ENG.). 32p. (J). (gr. -1-2). lib. bdg. 17.99 *(978-1-63440-881-3(0))* Red Chair Pr.

—ABCs at the Haunted House. Walters, Jennifer Marino. 2019. (ABC Adventures Ser.). (ENG.). 32p. (J). (gr. -1-2). 17.99 *(978-1-63440-876-9(4))* Red Chair Pr.

—ABCs in the Forest. Walters, Jennifer Marino. 2020. (ABC Adventures Ser.). (ENG.). 32p. (J). (gr. -1-2). lib. bdg. 17.99 *(978-1-63440-891-2(8))* Red Chair Pr.

—ABCs on Skis. Walters, Jennifer Marino. 2020. (ABC Adventures Ser.). (ENG.). 32p. (J). (gr. -1-2). lib. bdg. 17.99 *(978-1-63440-886-8(1))* Red Chair Pr.

Jarvis, Peter. Piggypine. Morris, Richard T. 2017. (J). *(978-0-525-43000-1(8)*, Dial Bks) Penguin Young Readers Group.

Jarzabek, Ela. Animal Colors. Rainstorm Publishing, ed. 2019. (ENG.). 20p. (J). bds. 7.99 ***(978-1-989219-98-0(5))*** Rainstorm Pr.

—Animal Numbers. Rainstorm Publishing, ed. 2019. (ENG.). 20p. (J). bds. 7.99 ***(978-1-989219-97-3(7))*** Rainstorm Pr.

Jarzabek, Ela. Guess Who Noah's Boat, 1 vol. Mitter, Matt. 2014. 10p. (J). 11.99 *(978-0-8254-4205-6(2))* Kregel Pubns.

Jarzabek, Ela & Wood, Hannah. The Baby Animals. Jarzabek, Ela & Wood, Hannah. 2017. (ENG.). 64p. (J). (gr. -1-3). pap. 6.99 *(978-1-78055-306-1(4))* O'Mara, Michael Bks., Ltd. GBR. Dist: Independent Pubs. Group.

Jasinski, Aaron. Fall Leaves. Curry, Don L. (Rookie Reader Ser.). (J). (gr. k-2). 2005. (ENG.). 24p. pap. 4.95 *(978-0-516-26831-6(7))*; 2004. 23p. 19.50 *(978-0-516-25904-8(0))* Scholastic Library Publishing. (Children's Pr.).

—The Golem's Latkes, 0 vols. Kimmel, Eric A. 2011. (ENG.). 40p. (J). (gr. k-3). 17.99 *(978-0-7614-5904-0(9)*, 9780761459040, Two Lions) Amazon Publishing.

Jaskiel, Stan. Battle for the Knotty List, 1 vol. Lewis, Micahel G. 2016. (ENG.). 32p. (J). (gr. k-8). 16.99 *(978-1-4556-2133-0(1)*, Pelican Publishing) Arcadia Publishing.

—Dinomorphosis, 1 vol. Many, Paul. 2018. (ENG.). 32p. (J). (gr. k-3). 16.99 *(978-1-4556-2304-4(0)*, Pelican Publishing) Arcadia Publishing.

—Dumplings Are Delicious. Capone, Deb. 2006. 24p. (J). (gr. -1-3). 14.95 *(978-0-9728666-4-4(7))* As Simple As That Publishing.

—The Great Pirate Christmas Battle, 1 vol. Lewis, Michael G. 2014. (ENG.). 32p. (J). (gr. k-3). 16.99 *(978-1-4556-1934-4(5)*, Pelican Publishing) Arcadia Publishing.

—The Great Thanksgiving Food Fight, 1 vol. Lewis, Michael. 2017. (ENG.). 32p. (J). (gr. -1-3). 16.99 *(978-1-4556-2285-6(0)*, Pelican Publishing) Arcadia Publishing.

—An Orangutan's Night Before Christmas, 1 vol. Bolden-Fournier, Laura. 2016. (Night Before Christmas Ser.). (ENG.). 32p. (J). (gr. k-3). 16.99 *(978-1-4556-2154-5(4)*, Pelican Publishing) Arcadia Publishing.

—Super Color Rangers. Cameron Licsw, Dorie & Felty, Rick. 2018. (ENG.). 52p. (J). pap. 14.95 *(978-0-9899128-7-7(6))* Dreamschooner Pr.

Jaskina, Valentina. A Big Birthday Hug. Kurani, Jennifer. 2017. (ENG.). 32p. (J). (gr. -1-k). 14.99 *(978-1-5107-3636-8(0)*, Sky Pony Pr.) Skyhorse Publishing Co., Inc.

—We Like to Grow Our Food. Incao, Denise A. 2019. (Family & World Health Ser.). (ENG.). 32p. (J). pap. 9.95 *(978-1-935826-49-1(2))* Kalindi Pr.

Jasmine, Mills. A Message from God: A Book Journal for Children to Connect, Write, & Release. Olivia, Asha. 2019. (ENG.). 34p. (J). (gr. k-3). 22.95 ***(978-0-578-48466-2(8))*** Message to God, for God Inc, A.

Jasnoch, Dorothy. The Adventures of Oskar: Oskar's New School. Saldivar, Jose A. Nilsson, Janet Busbey, ed. 2013. 32p. pap. 13.99 *(978-1-937752-14-9(3))*; (ENG.). pap. 13.99 *(978-1-937752-07-1(0))* Owl About Bks. Pubs.

Jasnoch, Dorothy. Adventure of Little Mouse Maggie. Jasnoch, Dorothy. Kern, Kimberly, ed. 2012. (ENG.). 36p. (J). pap. 14.99 *(978-1-937752-06-4(2))* Owl About Bks. Pubs.

—The Adventures of Oskar: Oskar's New School. Jasnoch, Dorothy. Korzeniowski, Samson O., ed. 2013. 32p. 18.99 *(978-1-937752-27-9(5))* Owl About Bks. Pubs.

—Frankie the Bunny: Helping the Birds. Jasnoch, Dorothy. Korzeniowski, Samson O., ed. 2013. 28p. 17.99 *(978-1-937752-20-0(8))* Owl About Bks. Pubs.

—Frankie the Bunny: Mystery in the Forest. Jasnoch, Dorothy. Korzeniowski, Samson O., ed. 2013. 32p. 17.99 *(978-1-937752-16-3(X))* Owl About Bks. Pubs.

—Frankie the Bunny: Newfound Friends. Jasnoch, Dorothy. Korzeniowski, Samson O., ed. 2013. 28p. 17.99 *(978-1-937752-15-6(1))* Owl About Bks. Pubs.

—Frankie the Bunny: The Fall Scramble Begins. Jasnoch, Dorothy. Korzeniowski, Samson O., ed. 2013. 28p. 17.99 *(978-1-937752-19-4(4))* Owl About Bks. Pubs.

—Frankie the Bunny: Wheels of Fortune. Jasnoch, Dorothy. Korzeniowski, Samson O., ed. 2013. 28p. 17.99 *(978-1-937752-17-0(8))* Owl About Bks. Pubs.

—Frankie the Bunny: Woodland Warning. Jasnoch, Dorothy. Korzeniowski, Samson O., ed. 2013. 28p. 17.99 *(978-1-937752-18-7(6))* Owl About Bks. Pubs.

—Frankie the Bunny: Woodland Warning. Jasnoch, Dorothy. Korzeniowski, Samson, ed. 2012. 28p. pap. 12.99 *(978-1-937752-03-3(8))* Owl About Bks. Pubs.

—Frankie the Bunny Helping the Birds. Jasnoch, Dorothy. Korzeniowski, Samson, ed. 2012. (ENG.). 28p. pap. 12.99 *(978-1-937752-05-7(4))* Owl About Bks. Pubs.

—Frankie the Bunny the Fall Scramble Begins. Jasnoch, Dorothy. Korzeniowski, Samson, ed. 2012. 28p. pap. 12.99 *(978-1-937752-04-0(6))* Owl About Bks. Pubs.

Jason, Albert, jt. illus. see Phillips, Rebekah.

Jasper, Mark. Good Night Christmas. Gamble, Adam. 2015. (Good Night Our World Ser.). (ENG.). 20p. (J). (— 1). bds. 9.95 *(978-1-60219-197-6(2))* Good Night Bks.

—Good Night North Pole. Gamble, Adam. 2012. (Good Night Our World Ser.). (ENG.). 20p. (J). (gr. k — 1). bds. 9.95 *(978-1-60219-071-9(2)*, 1350772) Good Night Bks.

—Good Night Ohio. Gamble, Adam. 2013. (Good Night Our World Ser.). (ENG.). 20p. (J). (— 1). bds. 9.95 *(978-1-60219-076-4(3))* Good Night Bks.

Jasper, Mark, jt. illus. see Rosen, Anne.

Jasper, Mark, jt. illus. see Veno, Joe.

Jaspersen, Jason. A Mighty Fortress Is Our God. Luther, Martin. 2017. (ENG.). 32p. (J). 11.99 *(978-1-933737-02-7(6))* Kloria Publishing LLC.

Jasperson, Ann. The Elephant & the King - Rebrand. Medina, Sylvia M. Hill, Krista, ed. 2019. (ENG.). 36p. (J). pap. 10.75 *(978-1-939871-80-0(8))* Green Kids Club, Inc.

Jastrzebski, Brandy. Brayden & Ryan's Summer Vacation. Reimiller, Diane. 2012. 24p. pap. 24.95 *(978-1-4626-7792-4(4))* America Star Bks.

—A Duck Named Quackers, 1 vol. Reimiller, Diane L. 2009. 12p. pap. 24.95 *(978-1-60836-771-9(1))* America Star Bks.

—Ike & Jamie. Reimiller, Diane L. 2008. 32p. pap. 24.95 *(978-1-60610-227-5(3))* America Star Bks.

Jasuna, Aija. The Bee in Bonnie Bondelle's Bow. Sauers, Charlotte. 2008. (J). 16.95 *(978-1-60131-014-9(5))* Big Tent Bks.

—Casey & Bella Go to New York. Lovascio, Jane. 2008. 24p. (J). 14.95 *(978-1-60131-007-1(2))* Big Tent Bks.

—Clean Clara. Oltchick, Peter. 2012. 34p. (J). (-18). 16.95 *(978-1-60131-127-6(3)*, Castlebridge Bks.) Big Tent Bks.

—One Step at a Time. Sax, Anita. 2013. 24p. (J). 17.95 *(978-1-60131-152-8(4)*, Castlebridge Bks.) Big Tent Bks.

—Oscar & the Zoo. Sax, Anita. 2013. 32p. (J). 14.95 *(978-1-60131-174-0(5))* Big Tent Bks.

—The River of Glass. Corwin, Katherine. 2009. 24p. (J). 14.95 *(978-1-60131-002-6(1)*, Castlebridge Bks.) Big Tent Bks.

Jatkowska, Ag. The Alphabet Parade. Ghigna, Charles. 2014. 24p. (J). pap. *(978-1-4795-1930-9(8)*, Picture Window Bks.) Capstone.

—Alphabet Parade. Ghigna, Charles. 2013. (Learning Parade Ser.). (ENG.). 24p. (J). (gr. -1-2). 22.65 *(978-1-4048-8310-9(X)*, Picture Window Bks.) Capstone.

—A Christmas Gift for Santa: A Bedtime Book, 1 vol. Elkins, John T. 2019. (ENG.). 32p. (J). 17.99 *(978-0-310-72961-7(0))* Zonderkidz.

—Dad Can Do Anything. Thomas, Martin. 2018. (ENG.). 18p. (gr. -1 — 1). bds. 8.99 *(978-1-5107-3617-7(4)*, Sky Pony Pr.) Skyhorse Publishing Co., Inc.

—Fairy Forest. 2020. (Pop-Up Carousel Ser.: 2). (ENG.). 1p. (J). (gr. -1-k). 24.99 *(978-1-5098-7933-5(1)*, Campbell Bks.) Pan Macmillan GBR. Dist: Independent Pubs. Group.

—Good Night Hugs, 1 vol. 2019. (ENG.). 20p. (J). bds. 8.99 *(978-1-4002-1239-2(1))* Nelson, Thomas Inc.

—I Love You ... Bigger Than the Sky. Adams, Michelle Medlock. 2020. 20p. (J). (gr. -1 — 1). bds. 10.99 *(978-1-5460-1543-7(4)*, Worthy Kids/Ideals) Worthy Publishing.

—I Love You Too. Marley, Ziggy. 2014. (ENG.). 48p. (J). (-2). 15.95 *(978-1-61775-310-7(6))* Akashic Bks.

—I See Fall, 1 vol. Ghigna, Charles. 2011. (I See Ser.). (ENG.). 24p. (J). (gr. -1 — 1). pap. 6.10 *(978-1-4048-6851-9(8)*, Picture Window Bks.) Capstone.

—I See Spring, 1 vol. Ghigna, Charles. 2011. (I See Ser.). (ENG.). 24p. (J). (gr. -1 — 1). pap. 6.10 *(978-1-4048-6849-6(6)*, Picture Window Bks.) Capstone.

—I See Summer, 1 vol. Ghigna, Charles. 2011. (I See Ser.). (ENG.). 24p. (J). (gr. -1 — 1). pap. 6.10 *(978-1-4048-6852-6(6)*, Picture Window Bks.) Capstone.

—I See Winter, 1 vol. Ghigna, Charles. 2011. (I See Ser.). (ENG.). 24p. (J). (gr. -1 — 1). pap. 6.10 *(978-1-4048-6850-2(X)*, Picture Window Bks.) Capstone.

—Inch & Roly & the Sunny Day Scare. Wiley, Melissa. 2014. (Inch & Roly Ser.). (ENG.). 24p. (J). (gr. -1-1). 16.99 *(978-1-4424-9072-7(1)*, Simon Spotlight) Simon Spotlight.

—Inch & Roly & the Very Small Hiding Place. Wiley, Melissa. 2013. (Inch & Roly Ser.). (ENG.). 24p. (J). (gr. -1-1). 16.99 *(978-1-4424-5281-7(1))*; pap. 3.99 *(978-1-4424-5279-4(X))* Simon Spotlight. (Simon Spotlight).

—Inch & Roly Make a Wish. Wiley, Melissa. 2012. (Inch & Roly Ser.). (ENG.). 24p. (J). (gr. -1-1). 15.99 *(978-1-4424-5277-0(3))*; pap. 3.99 *(978-1-4424-5276-3(5))* Simon Spotlight. (Simon Spotlight).

—The Lion Book of Fairy Tales. Stone, Julia. ed. 2015. (ENG.). 128p. (J). (gr. -1-k). 12.99 *(978-0-7459-6468-3(0))* Lion Hudson PLC GBR. Dist: Independent Pubs. Group.

—Little Seeds, 1 vol. Ghigna, Charles. 2012. (My Little Planet Ser.). (ENG.). 24p. (J). (gr. -1 — 1). 6.95 *(978-1-4048-7226-4(4)*, Picture Window Bks.) Capstone.

—The Littlest Dragon. Quinn, Susan. 2016. (J). *(978-1-4351-6573-1(X))* Barnes & Noble, Inc.

—Mermaid Kingdom: Carousel. 2018. (Little Worlds Ser.). (ENG.). 10p. (J). (gr. -1-2). 21.99 *(978-1-5098-4435-7(X))* Pan Macmillan GBR. Dist: Independent Pubs. Group.

—My Mom Is There. Thomas, Martin. 2018. (ENG.). 18p. (gr. -1 — 1). bds. 8.99 *(978-1-5107-3616-0(6)*, Sky Pony Pr.) Skyhorse Publishing Co., Inc.

—My Name Is Aviva. Newman, Lesléa. 2015. (ENG.). 32p. (J). (gr. -1-2). lib. bdg. 17.99 *(978-1-4677-2654-2(0)*, 9781467726542, Kar-Ben Publishing) Lerner Publishing Group.

—My Name Is Aviva, Vol. Newman, Lesléa. 2015. (ENG.). 32p. (J). (gr. -1-2). pap. 7.99 *(978-1-4677-2656-6(7)*, 9781467726566, Kar-Ben Publishing) Lerner Publishing Group.

—Palabras Que Hablan de Amor, 1 vol. Warren, Rick. 2019. (SPA.). 32p. (J). 12.99 *(978-0-8297-6976-0(5))* Vida Pubs.

—Pick up the Park, 1 vol. Ghigna, Charles. 2012. (My Little Planet Ser.). (ENG.). 24p. (J). (gr. -1 — 1). 6.95 *(978-1-4048-7228-8(0)*, Picture Window Bks.) Capstone.

—Recycling Is Fun, 1 vol. Ghigna, Charles. 2012. (My Little Planet Ser.). (ENG.). 24p. (J). (gr. -1 — 1). 6.95 *(978-1-4048-7229-5(9)*, Picture Window Bks.) Capstone.

—Shalom Bayit. Marshall, Linda Elovitz. 2020. (ENG.). 12p. (J). (gr. -1 — 1). bds. 6.99 *(978-1-5415-4247-1(9)*, Kar-Ben Publishing) Lerner Publishing Group.

—Shapes Are Everywhere! Ghigna, Charles. 2013. 24p. (J). pap. *(978-1-4795-1929-3(4)*, Picture Window Bks.) Capstone.

—Star Bright, Christmas Night. Hall, Hannah C. 2017. (ENG.). 20p. (J). (gr. -1-k). bds. 7.99 *(978-0-8249-1658-9(1))* Worthy Publishing.

—Sunrise, Easter Surprise! Hall, Hannah C. 2018. (ENG.). 20p. (J). (gr. -1-k). bds. 6.99 *(978-0-8249-1659-6(X))* Worthy Publishing.

—Three Little Pigs. Tiger Tales. 2016. (My First Fairy Tales Ser.). (ENG.). 32p. (J). (gr. -1-2). pap. 7.99 *(978-1-58925-479-4(1))* Tiger Tales.

—Wonders of the Color Wheel. Ghigna, Charles. 2013. (My Little School House Ser.). (ENG.). 24p. (J). (gr. -1-2). 22.65 *(978-1-4048-8307-9(X)*, Picture Window Bks.) Capstone.

—The Wonders of the Color Wheel. Ghigna, Charles. 2014. 24p. (J). pap. *(978-1-4795-1927-9(8)*, Picture Window Bks.) Capstone.

—Words to Love By, 1 vol. Warren, Rick. 2018. (ENG.). 32p. (J). 17.99 *(978-0-310-75282-0(5))* Zonderkidz.

—Words to Love by for Little Ones, 1 vol. Warren, Rick. 2019. (ENG.). 20p. (J). bds. 8.99 *(978-0-310-75357-5(0))* Zonderkidz.

Jauregui, Julian J. If I Could Be an Animal. Jauregui, Julian J. 2018. (ENG.). 20p. (J). (gr. 1-3). pap. 11.99 *(978-0-578-43568-8(3))* Jauregui, Julian.

Jauss, Anne Marie. The Living Year (Yesterday's Classics) Headstrom, Richard. 2018. (ENG.). 308p. (J). (gr. 1-6). pap. 13.95 *(978-1-63334-043-5(0))* Yesterday's Classics.

—The Storks of Lillegaard. Frisch, Wilhelmine. 2011. 230p. 46.95 *(978-1-258-08105-8(9))* Literary Licensing, LLC.

—Turn Here for Strawberry Roam. Myers, Byrona. 2011. 134p. 40.95 *(978-1-258-08195-9(4))* Literary Licensing, LLC.

—Yo Ho for Strawberry Roam! Myers, Byrona. 2011. 154p. 41.95 *(978-1-258-08204-8(7))* Literary Licensing, LLC.

Javier, Duarte. Chester the Chipmunk: A Chesapeake Bay Adventure. Freland, Cindy. 2016. (ENG.). (J). (gr. k-1). 18.00 *(978-1-941927-85-4(8))*; pap. 12.00 *(978-1-941927-84-7(X))* Maryland Secretarial Services, Inc.

Jawa, Sadhvi. An Elephant in My Backyard. Viswanath, Shobha. 2013. (ENG.). 28p. (J). (gr. -1). 11.95 *(978-81-8190-240-5(8))* Karadi Tales Co. Pvt, Ltd. IND. Dist: Consortium Bk. Sales & Distribution.

Jawhari, Lamaa. Baba, What Does My Name Mean? A Journey to Palestine. Ebeid, Rifk. 2020. (ENG.). 32p. (J). ***(978-1-922381-01-9(2))***; pap. ***(978-1-922381-00-2(4))*** Tablo Publishing.

Jax, T. L. Fraidy-Frieda's Light Show. Jax, T. L. I.t. ed. 2004. 30p. (J). 9.95 *(978-0-9743890-2-8(1))* Flaxenfluff Pr., LLC.

Jay, Alison. Bee & Me. 2017. (J). *(978-0-605-97081-6(5))* Candlewick Pr.

—I Took the Moon for a Walk. Curtis, Carolyn. 32p. (J). 2012. (gr. -1-2). pap. 8.99 *(978-1-84148-803-5(8))*; 2004. (ENG.). 16.99 *(978-1-84148-611-6(6))* Barefoot Bks., Inc.

—I Took the Moon for a Walk. Curtis, Carolyn. 2008. 32p. (J). (gr. -1-2). bds. 14.99 *(978-1-84686-200-7(0))* Barefoot Bks., Inc.

—If Kisses Were Colors Board Book. Lawler, Janet. 2010. (ENG.). 22p. (J). (gr. -1 — 1). bds. 7.99 *(978-0-8037-3530-9(8)*, Dial Bks) Penguin Young Readers Group.

—A Lady Has the Floor: Belva Lockwood Speaks Out for Women's Rights. Hannigan, Kate. 2018. 32p. (J). (gr. 2-5). 17.95 *(978-1-62979-453-2(8)*, Calkins Creek) Boyds Mills Pr.

—Listen, Listen. Gershator, Phillis. 2007. (ENG.). 32p. (J). (gr. -1-3). 16.99 *(978-1-84686-084-3(9))* Barefoot Bks., Inc.

—Listen, Listen. Gershator, Phillis. 2008. 32p. (J). (gr. -1-k). bds. 14.99 *(978-1-84686-201-4(9))* Barefoot Bks., Inc.

—My Bed Is an Air Balloon. Copus, Julia. 2018. (ENG.). 32p. 15.95 *(978-0-571-33484-1(9)*, Faber & Faber Children's Bks.) Faber & Faber, Inc.

—The Nutcracker. Harris, Annmarie. 2010. (ENG.). 40p. (J). (gr. -1-k). 16.99 *(978-0-8037-3285-8(6)*, Dial Bks) Penguin Young Readers Group.

—On That Christmas Night. Rock, Lois. ed. (ENG.). 32p. (J). (gr. k-3). 2018. pap. 8.99 *(978-0-7459-6509-3(1))*; 2015. 16.99 *(978-0-7459-6588-8(1))* Lion Hudson PLC GBR. Dist: Independent Pubs. Group.

—Prayers & Verses for Your First Holy Communion. Rock, Lois. ed. 2016. (ENG.). 64p. (J). (gr. k-2). 12.99 *(978-0-7459-7634-1(4))* Lion Hudson PLC GBR. Dist: Independent Pubs. Group.

—Song of the Stars, 1 vol. Lloyd-Jones, Sally. 2015. (ENG.). 32p. (J). bds. 7.99 *(978-0-310-73630-1(7))* Zonderkidz.

Jay, Alison. The Tiny Baker. Barrett, Hayley. 2020. (ENG.). 32p. (J). ***(978-1-64686-070-8(5))*** Barefoot Bks., Inc.

Jay, Alison. ABC: A Child's First Alphabet Book. Jay, Alison. 2005. (ENG.). 32p. (J). (gr. -1 — 1). bds. 10.99 *(978-0-525-47524-8(9)*, Dutton Books for Young Readers) Penguin Young Readers Group.

—Bee & Me. Jay, Alison. 2017. (Old Barn Bks.). (ENG.). 32p. (J). (-k). 15.99 *(978-0-7636-9010-6(4))* Candlewick Pr.

—Lleve a la Luna a Pasear. Jay, Alison. Curtis, Carolyn & Barefoot Books. 2014. 32p. (J). (gr. -1-2). pap. 8.99 *(978-1-78285-084-7(8))* Barefoot Bks., Inc.

—Looking for Yesterday. Jay, Alison. 2019. (ENG.). 32p. (J). (gr. -1-k). 16.99 *(978-1-5362-0421-6(8))* Candlewick Pr.

Jay, Alison, jt. illus. see Alison, Jay.

Jay, Daniel. Clarissa's Disappointment: And Resources for Families, Teachers & Counselors of Children of Incarcerated Parents. Sullivan, Megan. 2017. (ENG.). (J). (gr. 4-6). pap. 14.00 *(978-0-9861597-5-6(1)*, Shining Hall) Twelve Winters Pr.

Jay, James Robert. I Love My Humans: Where Is Madison? Ewington, Linda Jay. 2020. (ENG.). 34p. (J). pap. 12.60 ***(978-1-951932-40-4(4))*** Legaia Bks. USA.

Jay, Leisten, jt. illus. see Land, Greg.

Jay, Missi. Jesus Shows Me: Knowing My God Series. Grant, Callie. 2013. (Knowing My God Ser.). (ENG.). 18p. (J). bds. 8.99 *(978-0-9854090-3-6(7))* Blanchard, Graham.

—Your Newborn Promise Project Wings: An Enriching Activity & Coloring Book. 2017. (ENG.). 32p. (J). pap. 6.99 *(978-0-692-85033-6(3))* Blanchard, Graham.

Jaye, Jessica. A Tree for Me. Jaye, Jessica. 2019. (ENG.). 50p. (J). pap. *(978-0-9957323-7-7(X))* SRL Publishing Ltd.

Jayne, Emma. My Little Golden Book about Bugs. Bader, Bonnie. 2020. (Little Golden Book Ser.). 24p. (J). (-k). 4.99 ***(978-0-593-12388-1(3)***, Golden Bks.) Random Hse. Children's Bks.

Jaynes, Christin. Thank God There Is Christmas. Snell, Theresa Marie. 2019. (ENG.). 40p. (J). pap. 10.00 ***(978-1-7015-2681-5(6))*** Independently Published.

Jazvic, Beryl. After the Storm. Hall, Rose. 2005. (J). bds. 19.95 *(978-0-9770503-0-7(0))* Institute For Behavior Change Incorporated The.

Jean, Cassandra & Jennings, Kathleen. City of Bones: 10th Anniversary Edition. Clare, Cassandra. 10th anniv. ed. 2017. (Mortal Instruments Ser.: 1). (ENG.). 528p. (YA). (gr. 9). 24.99 *(978-1-5344-0625-4(5)*, McElderry, Margaret K. Bks.) McElderry, Margaret K. Bks.

Jean, David. Rainbow Crow, 1 vol. Bouchard, David. 2012. (ENG.). 32p. (J). (gr. 2-4). 24.95 *(978-0-88995-458-8(5)*, 9e24d24e-71d7-4868-b85b-0d154e06060f) Trifolium Bks., Inc. CAN. Dist: Firefly Bks., Ltd.

Jean-P, Tibbles. Spy on the Home Front. Alison, Hart. 2005. (American Girls Collection). (ENG.). 176p. (J). 10.95 *(978-1-58485-996-3(2)*, American Girl) American Girl Publishing, Inc.

Jean, Texier. Alfie Green & the Magical Gift. Joe, O'Brien. 2007. (Alfie Green Ser.: 1). (ENG.). 80p. (J). pap. 13.00 *(978-1-84717-041-5(2))* O'Brien Pr., Ltd., The IRL. Dist: Casemate Pubs. & Bk. Distributors, LLC.

Jeanes, Janet. Jemma's Journey. Peters, Janet. 2013. 26p. pap. *(978-0-473-26839-8(6))* Wakkajak Pubs.

Jeanette, Canyon. Over in the Jungle: A Rainforest Rhyme. Marianne, Berkes. 2008. 26p. (J). (gr. -1). bds. 7.95 *(978-1-58469-108-2(5))* Dawn Pubns.

Jeanine-Jonee. The Barnyard Buddies Meet a Newcomer. Penshorn, Julie D. 2020. (ENG.). 34p. (J). (gr. k-3). 19.95 ***(978-0-9988691-7-9(1))*** Growing Communities for Peace.

Jeanne, Arnold. Carlos Digs to China Carlos Excava Hasta la China. Jan, Romero Stevens. 2004. (Carlos Digs to China / Carlos Excava Hasta la China Ser.). (SPA, MUL & ENG.). 32p. (J). (gr. k-3). pap. 7.95 *(978-0-87358-870-6(3))* Cooper Square Publishing Llc.

Jeanne, Miss. The Wise Mullet of Cook Bayou. Weeks, Timothy. rev. ed. 2006. 48p. (J). per. 14.99 *(978-0-9779928-0-5(2))* Foolosophy Media.

Jeannotte, Lawrence. The Black Cherry Forest: Storybook 1. Utsler, Elaine. Wendle, Stan, ed. 2nd ed. 2003. 48p. (J). per. 6.95 *(978-0-9727787-1-8(3)*, BCF1B) EV Publishing Corp.

Jeanty, Georges. Age of X-Man: X-Tremists. 2019. (ENG.). 112p. (YA). (gr. 8-17). pap. 15.99 *(978-1-302-91578-0(9))* Marvel Worldwide, Inc.

Jeanty, Georges, et al. No Future for You, 8 vols., Vol. 2. Goddard, Drew & Jeanty, Georges. Vaughan, Brian K. 2008. (Buffy the Vampire Slayer Ser.). (ENG.). 320p. pap. 15.99 *(978-1-59307-963-5(X))* Dark Horse Comics.

Jeanty, Georges. Weapon X: The Underground, Vol. 2. Tieri, Frank. Youngquist, Jeff, ed. 2004. (X-Men Ser.). 184p. pap. 19.99 *(978-0-7851-1253-2(7))* Marvel Worldwide, Inc.

Jeanty, Georges & Leon, John Paul. Weapon X: Defection, Vol. 3. Tieri, Frank. Youngquist, Jeff, ed. 2004. (X-Men Ser.). 120p. pap. 13.99 *(978-0-7851-1407-9(6))* Marvel Worldwide, Inc.

Jeanty, Georges & Robinson, Roger. Gambit: Thieves' World. 2019. (ENG.). 296p. (YA). (gr. 8-17). pap. 29.99 *(978-1-302-91605-3(X))* Marvel Worldwide, Inc.

Jeaurond, Paul. Ava & the Mermaid. Green, Stella. 2016. (ENG.). (J). pap. *(978-0-9937118-0-0(4))* Green, Stella Mary.

Jeaurond, Paul, jt. illus. see Woodyard, Benjamin.

Jecan, Gavriel, photos by. Alaska Animal Babies. Vanasse, Deb. 2005. (Paws IV Ser.). 32p. (J). (gr. -1-2). pap. 10.99 *(978-1-57061-433-0(4)*, Little Bigfoot) Sasquatch Bks.

—Southwest Colors. Helman, Andrea. 2011. 24p. (J). 12.95 *(978-1-933855-64-6(9))* Rio Nuevo Pubs.

Jedda Robaard. I'm Ready for Easter. Jedda Robaard. 2020. (ENG.). 14p. (J). (gr. -1-k). bds. 12.99 ***(978-1-76089-159-6(2)***, Puffin) Penguin Random Hse. AUS. Dist: Independent Pubs. Group.

—I'm Ready for the New Baby. Jedda Robaard. 2020. (ENG.). 14p. (J). (gr. -1-k). bds. 12.99 ***(978-1-76089-162-6(2)***, Puffin) Penguin Random Hse. AUS. Dist: Independent Pubs. Group.

Jedele, Christie. Andrea's Fiddle. Klippenstein, Blaine. 2008. (J). incl. audio compact disk *(978-1-896201-82-5(2))* Loon Bks. Pub.

Jedor, Cyril. Franny & POM POM & the Painted Leaves. Smith, Kristi & Jackson, Nena. 2017. (ENG.). (J). pap. 10.95 *(978-1-947303-02-7(3))* Relevant Pages Pr.

—Franny & POM POM Get Boots for Christmas. Smith, Kristi & Jackson, Nena. 2017. (ENG.). (J). pap. 10.95 *(978-1-947303-05-8(8))* Relevant Pages Pr.

Jeevan, Dhamindra. Mars Colony. Cutting, Robert. 2007. 48p. (J). lib. bdg. 23.08 *(978-1-4242-1630-7(3))* Fitzgerald Bks.

Jeff Albrecht Studios, Jeff Albrecht. Presidential Pets: The Weird, Wacky, Little, Big, Scary, Strange Animals That Have Lived in the White House. Moberg, Julia. 2016. 96p. (J). (gr. 3-7). pap. 9.95 *(978-1-62354-086-9(0))* Charlesbridge Publishing, Inc.

Jeff Albrecht Studios Staff. Historical Animals. Moberg, Julia. 2015. 96p. (J). (gr. 3-7). 15.95 *(978-1-62354-048-7(8))* Charlesbridge Publishing, Inc.

Jeff, Marsh & Povenmire, Dan. Phineas & Ferb: Lights, Camera, Perry? O'Ryan, Ellie. 2014. (World of Reading Level 3 Ser.). (ENG.). 48p. (J). (gr. 1-4). lib. bdg. 27.07 *(978-1-61479-268-0(2)*, 1754) Spotlight.

Jeffers, Oliver. The Boy in the Striped Pajamas (Deluxe Illustrated Edition) Boyne, John. 2016. (ENG.). 352p. (YA). (gr. 7). 21.99 *(978-0-399-55931-0(0)*, Knopf Bks. for Young Readers) Random Hse. Children's Bks.

—The Boy Who Swam with Piranhas. Almond, David. (ENG.). 256p. (J). (gr. 4-7). 2015. pap. 7.99 *(978-0-7636-7680-3(2))*; 2013. 15.99 *(978-0-7636-6169-4(4))* Candlewick Pr.

—The Crayons: a Set of Books & Finger Puppets. Daywalt, Drew. 2018. (ENG.). 36p. (J). (-k). 19.99 *(978-1-5247-9141-4(5)*, Grosset & Dunlap) Penguin Young Readers Group.

—The Crayons' Book of Numbers. Daywalt, Drew. 2016. (ENG.). 18p. (J). (-k). bds. 8.99 *(978-0-451-53405-7(0)*, Grosset & Dunlap) Penguin Young Readers Group.

—The Crayons' Christmas. Daywalt, Drew. 2019. (ENG.). 52p. (J). (gr. -1-2). 19.99 *(978-0-525-51574-6(7)*, Penguin Workshop) Penguin Young Readers Group.

—The Day the Crayons Came Home. Daywalt, Drew. 2015. 48p. (J). (gr. k-3). 18.99 *(978-0-399-17275-5(0)*, Philomel Bks.) Penguin Publishing Group.

—The Day the Crayons Quit, 2 vols. Daywalt, Drew. (ENG.). (J). (gr. -1-2). 2016. 88p. 40.00 *(978-0-399-54892-5(0))*; 2013. 40p. 17.99 *(978-0-399-25537-3(0))* Penguin Young Readers Group. (Philomel Bks.).

—Imaginary Fred. Colfer, Eoin. 2015. (ENG.). 48p. (J). (gr. -1-3). 18.99 *(978-0-06-237955-9(0))* HarperCollins Pubs.

—Love from the Crayons. Daywalt, Drew. 2019. (ENG.). 32p. (J). (gr. k-3). 9.99 *(978-1-5247-9268-8(3)*, Penguin Workshop) Penguin Young Readers Group.

—Una Nina Hecha de Libros. Winston, Sam. 2017. (Especiales de a la Orilla Del Viento Ser.). (SPA.). 40p. (J). 17.99 *(978-607-16-4746-7(0))* Fondo de Cultura Economica USA.

—Noah Barleywater Runs Away. Boyne, John. 2012. (ENG.). 240p. (J). (gr. 3-7). 7.99 *(978-0-385-75264-0(4)*, Yearling) Random Hse. Children's Bks.

—Stay Where You Are & Then Leave. Boyne, John. 2014. (ENG.). 256p. (J). (gr. 4-7). 16.99 *(978-1-62779-031-4(4)*, 900131928, Holt, Henry & Co. Bks. For Young Readers) Holt, Henry & Co.

—The Terrible Thing That Happened to Barnaby Brocket. Boyne, John. 2014. (ENG.). 288p. (J). (gr. 3-7). 7.99 *(978-0-307-97765-6(X)*, Yearling) Random Hse. Children's Bks.

Jeffers, Oliver. Cómo Atrapar una Estrella. Jeffers, Oliver. Lujan, Jorge, tr. 2005. (Los Especiales de A la Orilla del Viento Ser.). (SPA.). 32p. (J). (gr. -1-3). *(978-968-16-7758-9(7))* Fondo de Cultura Economica.

—The Great Paper Caper. Jeffers, Oliver. 2009. (ENG.). 40p. (J). (gr. -1-k). 18.99 *(978-0-399-25097-2(2)*, Philomel Bks.) Penguin Young Readers Group.

—The Heart & the Bottle. Jeffers, Oliver. 2010. (ENG.). 32p. (J). (gr. -1-3). 18.99 *(978-0-399-25452-9(8)*, Philomel Bks.) Penguin Young Readers Group.

—Here We Are: Notes for Living on Planet Earth. Jeffers, Oliver. 2017. (ENG.). 48p. (J). (gr. -1-2). 19.99 *(978-0-399-16789-8(7)*, Philomel Bks.) Penguin Young Readers Group.

—How to Catch a Star. Jeffers, Oliver. 2004. (ENG.). 32p. (J). (gr. -1-2). 18.99 *(978-0-399-24286-1(4)*, Philomel Bks.) Penguin Young Readers Group.

—The Hueys in It Wasn't Me. Jeffers, Oliver. 2014. (Hueys Ser.: 2). (ENG.). 32p. (J). (gr. -1-k). 17.99 *(978-0-399-25768-1(3)*, Philomel Bks.) Penguin Young Readers Group.

—The Hueys in the New Sweater. Jeffers, Oliver. 2015. (Hueys Ser.: 1). (ENG.). 24p. (J). (gr. -1-k). bds. 6.99 *(978-0-399-17391-2(9)*, Philomel Bks.) Penguin Young Readers Group.

—The Incredible Book Eating Boy. Jeffers, Oliver. (ENG.). 32p. pap. *(978-0-00-718231-2(7)*, HarperCollins Children's Bks.) HarperCollins Pubs. Ltd.

—The Incredible Book Eating Boy. Jeffers, Oliver. 2007. (ENG.). 32p. (J). (gr. -1-3). 18.99 *(978-0-399-24749-1(1)*, Philomel Bks.) Penguin Young Readers Group.

—Lost & Found. Jeffers, Oliver. 2005. (ENG.). 32p. (J). (gr. -1-2). 18.99 *(978-0-399-24503-9(0)*, Philomel Bks.) Penguin Young Readers Group.

—Once upon an Alphabet: Short Stories for All the Letters. Jeffers, Oliver. 2014. 112p. (J). (gr. -1-k). 26.99 *(978-0-399-16791-1(9)*, Philomel Bks.) Penguin Publishing Group.

—Once upon an Alphabet: Short Stories for All the Letters. Jeffers, Oliver. 2017. (ENG.). 26p. (J). (— 1). bds. 8.99 *(978-0-399-54542-9(5)*, Philomel Bks.) Penguin Young Readers Group.

—Stuck. Jeffers, Oliver. 2011. (ENG.). 32p. (J). (gr. -1-2). 18.99 *(978-0-399-25737-7(3)*, Philomel Bks.) Penguin Young Readers Group.

—This Moose Belongs to Me. Jeffers, Oliver. 2012. (ENG.). 32p. (J). (gr. -1-2). 18.99 *(978-0-399-16103-2(1)*, Philomel Bks.) Penguin Young Readers Group.

—Up & Down. Jeffers, Oliver. 2010. (ENG.). 40p. (J). (gr. -1-2). 19.99 *(978-0-399-25545-8(1)*, Philomel Bks.) Penguin Young Readers Group.

—The Way Back Home. Jeffers, Oliver. 2008. (ENG.). 32p. (J). (gr. -1-3). 18.99 *(978-0-399-25074-3(3)*, Philomel Bks.) Penguin Young Readers Group.

Jeffers, Oliver & Winston, Sam. A Child of Books. Jeffers, Oliver & Winston, Sam. 2016. 40p. (J). (gr. k-12). 17.99 *(978-0-7636-9077-9(5))* Candlewick Pr.

Jeffers, Susan. McDuff Comes Home. Wells, Rosemary. 2007. 24p. (J). pap. 4.99 *(978-0-7868-1192-2(7))* Hyperion Paperbacks for Children.

—McDuff Comes Home. Wells, Rosemary. rev. ed. 2006. (ENG.). 32p. (J). (gr. -1-k). 9.99 *(978-0-7868-3833-2(7))* Hyperion Pr.

—McDuff Moves In. Wells, Rosemary. 2019. (ENG.). 25p. (J). 17.95 *(978-0-940719-42-2(8))* Gryphon Pr., The.

—Stopping by Woods on a Snowy Evening. Frost, Robert. 2004. 27p. (J). (gr. k-4). 16.00 *(978-0-7567-7973-3(1))* DIANE Publishing Co.

—The Twelve Days of Christmas. 2013. (J). *(978-0-06-206616-9(1))* Harper & Row Ltd.

Jeffers, Susan. Jingle Bells. Jeffers, Susan. 2017. (ENG.). 40p. (J). (gr. -1-3). 17.99 *(978-0-06-236020-5(5))* HarperCollins Pubs.

—My Pony. Jeffers, Susan. 2008. 32p. (J). (gr. -1-k). 6.99 *(978-1-4231-1295-2(4))* Hyperion Pr.

—The Nutcracker. Jeffers, Susan. 2007. 40p. (J). (gr. -1-3). 17.89 *(978-0-06-074387-1(5))*; (ENG.). 17.99 *(978-0-06-074386-4(7))* HarperCollins Pubs.

—The Twelve Days of Christmas, Vol. Jeffers, Susan. 2013. (ENG.). 40p. (J). (gr. -1-3). 17.99 *(978-0-06-206615-2(3))* HarperCollins Pubs.

Jefferson, Daniel E. The Luck of the Dragonfly. Jefferson, Barbara. 2008. 31p. pap. 24.95 *(978-1-60672-283-1(2))* America Star Bks.

Jefferson Elementary Art Club. Domino. 2007. 32p. (J). 15.00 *(978-0-9767244-2-1(1))* SkyMacSyd Publishing.

Jefferson, Graham. Would You Like to Know Jesus?, 1 vol. Reeves, Eira. ed. 2014. (Would You Like to Know? Ser.). (ENG.). 28p. (J). (gr. -1-k). 2.99 *(978-1-78128-103-1(3)*, Candle Bks.) Lion Hudson PLC GBR. Dist: Independent Pubs. Group.

Jefferson, Patti Brassard. How Long Will You Love Me? Jefferson, Patti Brassard. 2013. 28p. pap. 12.95 *(978-1-61244-178-8(5))* Halo Publishing International.

Jefferson, Robert Louis. Road Map to Wholeness. Cretan, Gladys Yessayan. 145.00 *(978-0-687-02526-8(5))* Abingdon Pr.

Jeffery, Megan E., jt. illus. see Barr, Marilynn G.

Jefferys, Charles W. Old Man Savarin Stories (Illustrated Edition) Thomson, Edward William. 2017. (ENG.). (J). pap. *(978-1-4068-8635-1(1))* Echo Library.

Jefferys, Rhys. Let's Explore the Dinosaur World: Includes a Slot-Together 3-D Model! Regan, Lisa. 2020. (ENG.). 8p. (J). bds. 9.99 *(978-1-78950-857-4(6)*, 3ef84fee-9afa-40a9-ab40-2f7982d20ce2) Arcturus Publishing GBR. Dist: Baker & Taylor Publisher Services (BTPS).

—Mind-Blowing Math. Regan, Lisa. 2019. (ENG.). 128p. (J). pap. 12.99 *(978-1-78888-309-2(8)*, f16d08d7-9101-404c-9215-e095af23caf7) Arcturus Publishing GBR. Dist: Baker & Taylor Publisher Services (BTPS).

—Motorcycle Road Trip! Strickland, Stanley. 2018. (Take the Wheel! Ser.). (ENG.). 14p. (J). (gr. -1-k). bds. 8.99 *(978-1-4998-0626-7(4))* Little Bee Books Inc.

—Police Car Patrol! Strickland, Stanley. 2018. (Take the Wheel! Ser.). (ENG.). 14p. (J). (gr. -1-k). bds. 8.99 *(978-1-4998-0719-6(8))* Little Bee Books Inc.

—Race Car Rally! Copeland, Alan. 2018. (Take the Wheel! Ser.). (ENG.). 14p. (J). (gr. -1-k). bds. 8.99 *(978-1-4998-0718-9(X))* Little Bee Books Inc.

—Speedboat Splash! Copeland, Alan. 2018. (Take the Wheel! Ser.). (ENG.). 14p. (J). (gr. -1-k). bds. 8.99 *(978-1-4998-0627-4(2))* Little Bee Books Inc.

—Supercharged Science. Regan, Lisa. 2019. (ENG.). 128p. (J). pap. 12.99 *(978-1-78888-128-9(1)*, 2a3be0cb-b02a-4732-b4f7-21e27e56ee62) Arcturus Publishing GBR. Dist: Baker & Taylor Publisher Services (BTPS).

Jefferys, Rhys. Let's Explore the Solar System: Includes a Slot-Together 3-D Model. Jefferys, Rhys. 2020. (ENG.). 8p. (J). bds. 9.99 *(978-1-78950-606-8(9)*, 35cdd6e6-c523-4cc2-90ff-c1df1b7df379) Arcturus Publishing GBR. Dist: Baker & Taylor Publisher Services (BTPS).

Jeffirs, Matt. Sharks. Kasso, Martin. 2008. (ENG.). 24p. (J). (gr. 3-18). 19.95 *(978-1-58117-797-8(6)*, Intervisual/Piggy Toes) Bendon, Inc.

Jeffrey, Gary. Defying Death in the Desert. 2010. (Graphic Survival Stories Ser.). 48p. (YA). (gr. 5-8). lib. bdg. 35.45 *(978-1-4358-3528-3(X)*, Rosen Reference) Rosen Publishing Group, Inc., The.

—Defying Death in the Jungle. 2010. (Graphic Survival Stories Ser.). 48p. (YA). (gr. 5-8). lib. bdg. 35.45 *(978-1-4358-3529-0(8))* Rosen Publishing Group, Inc., The.

—Tsunamis & Floods. 2007. (Graphic Natural Disasters Ser.). (ENG.). 48p. (J). (gr. 5-9). lib. bdg. 35.45 *(978-1-4042-1990-8(0))* Rosen Publishing Group, Inc., The.

Jeffrey, Gary & Riley, Terry. The Cuban Missile Crisis. 2013. (ENG.). 48p. (J). *(978-0-7787-1233-6(8))*; pap. *(978-0-7787-1237-4(0))* Crabtree Publishing Co.

—The Korean War. 2013. (ENG.). 48p. (J). *(978-0-7787-1234-3(6))*; pap. *(978-0-7787-1238-1(9))* Crabtree Publishing Co.

Jeffrey, Gary & Spender, Nik. The Vietnam War. 2013. (ENG.). 48p. (J). *(978-0-7787-1236-7(2))*; pap. *(978-0-7787-1240-4(0))* Crabtree Publishing Co.

Jeffrey, Sean, et al. Franklin Stays Up. Jennings, Sharon. 2003. 32p. (J). pap. *(978-0-439-41815-7(1))* Scholastic, Inc.

—Franklin's Trading Cards. Jennings, Sharon & Bourgeois, Paulette. 2004. (Franklin Ser.). 32p. (gr. 1-2). 13.95 *(978-0-7569-4402-5(3))* Perfection Learning Corp.

—Franklin's Trading Cards. Jennings, Sharon. 2003. 32p. (J). *(978-0-439-41816-4(X))* Scholastic, Inc.

Jelen, Oldrich. The Keeper of the Crock of Gold: Irish Leprechaun Tales. McCarthy, Bairbre. ed. 2017. (ENG.). 96p. (J). 16.99 *(978-1-85635-564-3(0))* Mercier Pr., Ltd., The IRL. Dist: Casemate Pubs. & Bk. Distributors, LLC.

Jellett, Tom. Blast Off! Clark, Margaret. 2019. (Puffin Nibbles Ser.). 80p. (Orig.). (J). (gr. 2-4). pap. 9.99 *(978-0-14-330185-1(3)*, Puffin) Penguin Random Hse. AUS. Dist: Independent Pubs. Group.

—Cricket. Arena, Felice. 2017. (Sporty Kids Ser.). 80p. (J). (gr. 1-3). 8.99 *(978-0-14-330909-3(0))* Random Hse. Australia AUS. Dist: Independent Pubs. Group.

—Freddy Tangles - Champ or Chicken? Brand, Jack. 2017. (Freddy Tangles Ser.: 2). (ENG.). 128p. (J). (gr. 2-5). 7.99 *(978-1-76011-035-2(3))* Allen & Unwin AUS. Dist: Independent Pubs. Group.

—Freddy Tangles - Legend or Loser? Brand, Jack. 2017. (Freddy Tangles Ser.: 1). (ENG.). 128p. (J). (gr. 2-5). 7.99 *(978-1-76011-034-5(5))* Allen & Unwin AUS. Dist: Independent Pubs. Group.

—Gobbledygook Is Eating a Book. Clarke, Justine & Baysting, Arthur. 2016. 32p. (J). (gr. -1-2). 13.99 *(978-0-14-350693-5(5))* Random Hse. Australia AUS. Dist: Independent Pubs. Group.

Jellett, Tom. Grandpa's Space Adventure. Newman, Paul. 2018. (ENG.). 32p. (J). (-k). 18.99 ***(978-0-14-378556-9(7)***, Picture Puffin) Penguin Random Hse. AUS. Dist: Independent Pubs. Group.

Jellett, Tom. Little Athletics! Arena, Felice. 2018. (Sporty Kids Ser.). 80p. (J). (gr. 1-3). 8.99 *(978-0-14-378318-3(1))* Random Hse. Australia AUS. Dist: Independent Pubs. Group.

—The Littlest Pirate. Clark, Sherryl. 2019. (Puffin Nibbles Ser.). 80p. (J). (gr. k-2). pap. 9.99 *(978-0-14-131338-2(2)*, Puffin) Penguin Random Hse. AUS. Dist: Independent Pubs. Group.

—My Amazing Dad. Kwaymullina, Ezekiel. 2016. (ENG.). 24p. (J). (gr. -1-k). 16.99 *(978-1-5107-0584-5(8)*, Sky Pony Pr.) Skyhorse Publishing Co., Inc.

—My Dad Thinks He's Funny. Germein, Katrina. 2013. (ENG.). 32p. (J). (gr. k-3). 14.99 *(978-0-7636-6522-7(3))* Candlewick Pr.

—Netball. Arena, Felice. 2017. (Sporty Kids Ser.). 80p. (J). (gr. 1-3). 7.99 *(978-0-14-330908-6(0))* Random Hse. Australia AUS. Dist: Independent Pubs. Group.

—Quiz Champs. Halliday, Susan. l.t. ed. 2014. 44p. pap. *(978-1-4596-7622-0(X))* ReadHowYouWant.com, Ltd.

—Rabby the Brave. Guest, Patrick. 2018. (ENG.). 24p. (J). (— 1). 19.99 *(978-1-76012-753-4(1))* Little Hare Bks. AUS. Dist: Independent Pubs. Group.

—Santa's Secret. Dumbleton, Mike. 2014. 32p. (J). (gr. -1-k). 9.99 *(978-1-74275-240-2(3))* Random Hse. Australia AUS. Dist: Independent Pubs. Group.

—Seadog. Saxby, Claire. 2014. 32p. (J). (gr. -1-k). 11.99 *(978-1-74275-651-6(4))* Random Hse. Australia AUS. Dist: Independent Pubs. Group.

—Sporty Kids: Basketball! Arena, Felice. 5th ed. 2017. (Sporty Kids Ser.). 80p. (J). (gr. 1-3). 8.99 *(978-0-14-330889-8(0))* Random Hse. Australia AUS. Dist: Independent Pubs. Group.

—Stories for Eight Year Olds. Knight, Linsay, ed. 2015. 208p. (Orig.). (J). (gr. 2-4). 9.99 *(978-0-85798-475-3(6))* Random Hse. Australia AUS. Dist: Independent Pubs. Group.

—Stories for Nine Year Olds. Knight, Linsay, ed. 2015. 208p. (Orig.). (J). (gr. 3-5). 9.99 *(978-0-85798-477-7(2))* Random Hse. Australia AUS. Dist: Independent Pubs. Group.

—Stories for Seven Year Olds. Knight, Linsay, ed. 2015. 208p. (Orig.). (J). (gr. 1-3). 9.99 *(978-0-85798-479-1(9))* Random Hse. Australia AUS. Dist: Independent Pubs. Group.

—Stories for Six Year Olds. Knight, Linsay, ed. 2015. 208p. (Orig.). (J). (gr. k-2). 9.99 *(978-0-85798-481-4(0))* Random Hse. Australia AUS. Dist: Independent Pubs. Group.

—A Whale in the Bathtub. Westaway, Kylie. 2016. (ENG.). 40p. (J). (gr. -1-3). 16.99 *(978-0-544-53535-0(9)*, 1608120) Houghton Mifflin Harcourt Publishing Co.

—Why Can't I Be a Dinosaur? Westaway, Kylie. 2017. (ENG.). 32p. (J). (gr. -1-k). 19.99 *(978-1-76029-472-4(1)*, A&U Children's) Allen & Unwin AUS. Dist: Independent Pubs. Group.

—Why I Love Footy. Wagner, Michael. 2018. 32p. (J). (gr. -1-2). 13.99 *(978-0-14-350600-3(5)*, Puffin) Penguin Random Hse. AUS. Dist: Independent Pubs. Group.

Jellett, Tom. Why I Love Summer. Wagner, Michael. 2018. (ENG.). 32p. (J). (-k). 18.99 ***(978-0-14-378374-9(2)***, Viking Adult) Penguin Publishing Group.

Jelliman, Lindy. Tinker Tailor's Toolbox: For Mending Broken Hearts. Jelliman, Lindy. Davy, Denise, ed. 2020. (ENG.). 34p. (J). pap. ***(978-0-6487357-0-0(2))*** Shine Bright Pr.

Jen, Kallin, photos by. He's My God!-(Book 2) Knowing God Through His Names - a Childrens' Devotional. Joanna, Harris. 2012. 48p. (J). 7.99 *(978-1-930547-78-0(1))* Deeper Roots Pubns. & Media.

Jen, Pei. The Lonely Cloud. Heschel, Marcey Louise. 2020. (ENG.). 32p. (J). ***(978-1-5255-7197-8(4))***; pap. ***(978-1-5255-7198-5(2))*** FriesenPress.

Jendrysik, Barbara L. Winnie's Farm. Schaberg, Jan Eberle. 2018. (ENG.). 40p. (J). (gr. k-4). 26.95 *(978-1-61493-614-5(5))* Peppertree Pr., The.

Jenkins, C. S. The Bears & the Baby. McLean, P. J. 2012. 44p. pap. 17.44 *(978-1-4669-1335-6(5))* Trafford Publishing.

Jenkins, Debra Reid. Glory. Carlstrom, Nancy White. 2004. 32p. (J). (gr. -1-3). 17.00 *(978-0-8028-5143-7(6))* Eerdmans, William B. Publishing Co.

—I See the Moon. Appelt, Kathi. 2004. 24p. (J). (gr. -1-2). 15.00 *(978-0-8028-5118-5(5))* Eerdmans, William B. Publishing Co.

—I Wanted to Know All about God. Kroll, Virginia. 2010. (ENG.). 12p. (J). (gr. -1). bds. 8.00 *(978-0-8028-5380-6(3))* Eerdmans, William B. Publishing Co.

—My Freedom Trip: A Child's Escape from North Korea. Park, Frances & Park, Ginger. 2010. (ENG.). 32p. (gr. k-2). 29.94 *(978-1-56397-468-7(1))* Boyds Mills Pr.

Jenkins, Delores. Preep II: More Tales of Early Texas. Jackson, Sarah. 2007. 48p. (J). 19.95 *(978-1-931823-52-4(9))* Halcyon Pr., Ltd.

—Preep of Old Washington Square: A Collection of East Texas Tales. Jackson, Sarah. l.t. ed. 2005. 48p. (J). 16.95 *(978-1-931823-25-8(1))* Halcyon Pr., Ltd.

Jenkins, Ellie. Goldilocks Sticker Book. Channing, Margot. ed. 2019. (Scribblers Fun Activity Ser.). 32p. (J). (gr. -1). pap. 5.95 *(978-1-912904-50-1(0)*, Scribblers) Book Hse. GBR. Dist: Sterling Publishing Co., Inc.

—Poems for the Seasons. 2017. (Poems Just for Me Ser.). 32p. (gr. 7-8). 27.25 *(978-1-4994-8387-1(2)*, Windmill Bks.) Rosen Publishing Group, Inc., The.

Jenkins, Ellie & Battuz, Christine. Goldilocks & the Three Bears. Channing, Margot. ed. 2017. (Scribblers Look & Say Ser.). (ENG.). 18p. (J). (gr. -1-1). bds. 9.95 *(978-1-912006-24-3(3)*, Scribblers) Book Hse. GBR. Dist: Sterling Publishing Co., Inc.

Jenkins, Emily. That New Animal. Jenkins, Emily. 2006. (J). (gr. -1-4). 29.95 *(978-0-439-84925-8(X)*, WHCD687) Weston Woods Studios, Inc.

Jenkins, Harvey. Merkel Sings the Blues. Jenkins, Harvey. 2018. (Adventures of Vargas & Merkel Ser.: Vol. 5). (ENG.). 52p. (J). pap. 19.99 *(978-1-7310-5121-9(2))* Independently Published.

Jenkins, Jackie. The Beekeeper & the Turtle. Heimsoth, Kathie. 2019. (ENG.). 30p. (J). (gr. -1-3). pap. 12.49 ***(978-1-5456-8098-8(1))*** Salem Author Services.

Jenkins, Jacqueline. Faith's Star. Kauffman, Christopher G. 2011. 32p. pap. 24.95 *(978-1-4560-9584-0(6))* America Star Bks.

Jenkins, Laura. The Crystal Fountain. Williams, David Morgan. 2017. (ENG.). 48p. (J). 11.00 *(978-1-78461-348-8(7))* Y Lolfa GBR. Dist: Casemate Pubs. & Bk. Distributors, LLC.

Jenkins, Leonard. I've Already Forgotten Your Name, Philip Hall! Greene, Bette. 2004. 176p. (J). (gr. 5-18). 15.99 *(978-0-06-051835-6(9))* HarperCollins Pubs.

—I've Seen the Promised Land: The Life of Dr. Martin Luther King, Jr. Myers, Walter Dean. (ENG.). 40p. (J). (gr. -1-3). 2012. pap. 7.99 *(978-0-06-225002-5(7))*; 2003. 17.99 *(978-0-06-027703-1(3))* HarperCollins Pubs. (Amistad).

—Malcolm X: A Fire Burning Brightly. Myers, Walter Dean. 2003. (ENG.). 40p. (J). (gr. k-3). pap. 7.99 *(978-0-06-056201-4(3)*, Amistad) HarperCollins Pubs.

—Motorcycle Song. Siebert, Diane. Date not set. 32p. (J). (gr. -1-3). 5.99 *(978-0-06-443632-8(2))* HarperCollins Pubs.

—Sweet Land of Liberty, 1 vol. Hopkinson, Deborah. 2019. (ENG.). 32p. (J). (gr. 1-5). pap. 7.95 *(978-1-68263-124-9(9))* Peachtree Publishing Co. Inc.

Jenkins, Reid Debra. I See the Moon. Appelt, Kathi. 2009. (ENG.). 12p. (J). (gr. -1). bds. 8.00 *(978-0-8028-5358-5(7)*, Eerdmans Bks For Young Readers) Eerdmans, William B. Publishing Co.

Jenkins, Sandra. When Father Christmas Resigned. Jenkins, Peter. 2012. 36p. pap. *(978-1-908775-94-8(7))* Legend Pr.

Jenkins, Sharon I. Remember the Ten Commandments with Jam & Jean Jellybean. Jenkins, Sharon I. l.t. ed. 2006. 32p. (J). (gr. -1-3). per. 10.99 *(978-1-59879-240-9(7))* Lifevest Publishing, Inc.

Jenkins, Simon. Being Confirmed. Aiken, Nick. 2004. 160p. pap. *(978-0-281-05631-6(5))* SPCK Publishing.

Jenkins, Steve. Animal Poems. Worth, Valerie. 2007. (ENG.). 48p. (J). (gr. -1-3). 18.99 *(978-0-374-38057-1(0)*, 9780374380571, Farrar, Straus & Giroux (BYR)) Farrar, Straus & Giroux.

—Bees, Snails, & Peacock Tails: Patterns & Shapes ... Naturally. Franco, Betsy. 2008. (ENG.). 40p. (J). (gr. -1-3). 19.99 *(978-1-4169-0386-4(0)*, McElderry, Margaret K. Bks.) McElderry, Margaret K. Bks.

—Billions of Years, Amazing Changes: The Story of Evolution. Pringle, Laurence. 2011. (ENG.). 112p. (J). (gr. 3-7). 17.95 *(978-1-59078-723-6(4))* Boyds Mills Pr.

J

—Birdsongs. Franco, Betsy. 2007. (ENG.). 40p. (J). (gr. -1-3). 19.99 *(978-0-689-87777-3(3)*, McElderry, Margaret K. Bks.) McElderry, Margaret K. Bks.

—Bugs Are Insects. Rockwell, Anne. 2015. (Let's-Read-And-Find-Out Science 1 Ser.). (ENG.). 40p. (J). (gr. -1-3). pap. 6.99 *(978-0-06-238182-8(2))* HarperCollins Pubs.

—Can an Aardvark Bark? Stewart, Melissa. 2017. (ENG.). 32p. (J). (gr. -1-3). 17.99 *(978-1-4814-5852-8(3)*, Beach Lane Bks.) Beach Lane Bks.

—Eat Like a Bear. Sayre, April Pulley. 2013. (ENG.). 32p. (J). (gr. -1-3). 17.99 *(978-0-8050-9039-0(8)*, 900059366, Holt, Henry & Co. Bks. For Young Readers) Holt, Henry & Co.

—Hello Baby! Fox, Mem. 2009. (ENG.). 32p. (J). (gr. -1-k). 17.99 *(978-1-4169-8513-6(1)*, Beach Lane Bks.) Beach Lane Bks.

—Life in a Coral Reef. Pfeffer, Wendy. 2009. (Let's-Read-And-Find-Out Science 2 Ser.). (ENG.). 40p. (J). (gr. 1-4). pap. 5.99 *(978-0-06-445222-9(0))* HarperCollins Pubs.

—Mama Built a Little Nest. Ward, Jennifer. 2014. (ENG.). 40p. (J). (gr. -1-3). 18.99 *(978-1-4424-2116-5(9)*, Beach Lane Bks.) Beach Lane Bks.

—Mama Dug a Little Den. Ward, Jennifer. 2018. (ENG.). 32p. (J). (gr. -1-3). 17.99 *(978-1-4814-8037-6(5)*, Beach Lane Bks.) Beach Lane Bks.

—Move! Page, Robin. 2006. (ENG.). 32p. (J). (gr. -1-3). 17.99 *(978-0-618-64637-1(X)*, 595918) Houghton Mifflin Harcourt Publishing Co.

—Move! Page, Robin. 2018. (ENG.). 32p. (J). (gr. -1-3). pap. 7.99 *(978-1-328-89573-8(4)*, 1699519, HMH Books For Young Readers) Houghton Mifflin Harcourt Publishing Co.

—Pug: And Other Animal Poems. Worth, Valerie. 2013. (ENG.). 40p. (J). (gr. -1-1). 16.99 *(978-0-374-35024-6(8)*, 900069184, Farrar, Straus & Giroux (BYR)) Farrar, Straus & Giroux.

—Squirrels Leap, Squirrels Sleep. Sayre, April Pulley. 2016. (ENG.). 40p. (J). 17.99 *(978-0-8050-9251-6(X)*, 900068146, Holt, Henry & Co. Bks. For Young Readers) Holt, Henry & Co.

—What Do You Do with a Tail Like This? Page, Robin. 2011. (J). (gr. -1-3). 29.95 *(978-0-545-10698-6(2))* Weston Woods Studios, Inc.

—Wiggling Worms at Work. Pfeffer, Wendy. 2003. (Let's-Read-And-Find-Out Science 2 Ser.). (ENG.). 40p. (J). (gr. k-4). 16.99 *(978-0-06-028448-0(X)*, Collins); pap. 5.99 *(978-0-06-445199-4(2))* HarperCollins Pubs.

—Wiggling Worms at Work. Pfeffer, Wendy. 2004. (Let's-Read-and-Find-Out Science Ser.). 31p. (gr. -1-3). 16.00 *(978-0-7569-3095-0(2))* Perfection Learning Corp.

—Woodpecker Wham! Sayre, April Pulley. 2015. (ENG.). 40p. (J). (gr. -1-3). 17.99 *(978-0-8050-8842-7(3)*, 900051901, Holt, Henry & Co. Bks. For Young Readers) Holt, Henry & Co.

Jenkins, Steve. Almost Gone: The World's Rarest Animals. Jenkins, Steve. 2006. (Let's-Read-And-Find-Out Science 2 Ser.). (ENG.). 40p. (J). (gr. k-4). pap. 5.99 *(978-0-06-053600-8(4))* HarperCollins Pubs.

—The Animal Book: A Collection of the Fastest, Fiercest, Toughest, Cleverest, Shyest - And Most Surprising - Animals on Earth. Jenkins, Steve. 2013. (ENG.). 208p. (J). (gr. 1-4). 24.99 *(978-0-547-55799-1(X)*, 1453456) Houghton Mifflin Harcourt Publishing Co.

—Animals in Flight. Jenkins, Steve. Page, Robin. 2005. (ENG.). 32p. (J). (gr. -1-3). pap. 7.99 *(978-0-618-54882-8(3)*, 410221) Houghton Mifflin Harcourt Publishing Co.

—Animals Upside Down: A Pull, Pop, Lift & Learn Book! Jenkins, Steve. Page, Robin. 2013. (ENG.). 24p. (J). (gr. -1-3). 24.99 *(978-0-547-34127-9(X)*, 1418857) Houghton Mifflin Harcourt Publishing Co.

—The Beetle Book. Jenkins, Steve. 2012. (ENG.). 40p. (J). (gr. -1-3). 17.99 *(978-0-547-68084-2(8)*, 1475449) Houghton Mifflin Harcourt Publishing Co.

—Bones: Skeletons & How They Work. Jenkins, Steve. 2010. (ENG.). 48p. (J). (gr. 2-5). 23.99 *(978-0-545-04651-0(3)*, Scholastic Reference) Scholastic, Inc.

—Creature Features: Twenty-Five Animals Explain Why They Look the Way They Do. Jenkins, Steve. Page, Robin. 2014. (ENG.). 32p. (J). (gr. -1-3). 17.99 *(978-0-544-23351-5(4)*, 1563485, HMH Books For Young Readers) Houghton Mifflin Harcourt Publishing Co.

—Down, Down, Down: A Journey to the Bottom of the Sea. Jenkins, Steve. 2009. (ENG.). 40p. (J). (gr. -1-3). 17.99 *(978-0-618-96636-3(6)*, 1023024) Houghton Mifflin Harcourt Publishing Co.

—How to Clean a Hippopotamus: A Look at Unusual Animal Partnerships. Jenkins, Steve. Page, Robin. (ENG.). 32p. (J). (gr. 1-4). 2013. pap. 7.99 *(978-0-547-99484-0(2)*, 1525239); 2010. 17.99 *(978-0-547-24515-7(7)*, 1100006) Houghton Mifflin Harcourt Publishing Co.

—How to Swallow a Pig: Step-By-Step Advice from the Animal Kingdom. Jenkins, Steve. Page, Robin. 2015. (ENG.). 32p. (J). (gr. 1-4). 17.99 *(978-0-544-31365-1(8)*, 1581805, HMH Books For Young Readers) Houghton Mifflin Harcourt Publishing Co.

—My First Day: What Animals Do on Day One. Jenkins, Steve. Page, Robin. 2013. (ENG.). 32p. (J). (gr. -1-3). 17.99 *(978-0-547-73851-2(X)*, 1485226) Houghton Mifflin Harcourt Publishing Co.

—Never Smile at a Monkey: And 17 Other Important Things to Remember. Jenkins, Steve. 2009. (ENG.). 32p. (J). (gr. -1-3). 17.99 *(978-0-618-96620-2(X)*, 1023023) Houghton Mifflin Harcourt Publishing Co.

—Time for a Bath. Jenkins, Steve. Page, Robin. 2011. (ENG.). 24p. (J). (gr. -1-3). 12.99 *(978-0-547-25037-3(1)*, 1101406) Houghton Mifflin Harcourt Publishing Co.

—Time to Eat. Jenkins, Steve. Page, Robin. 2011. (ENG.). 24p. (J). (gr. -1-3). 14.99 *(978-0-547-25032-8(0)*, 1101404) Houghton Mifflin Harcourt Publishing Co.

—Time to Sleep. Jenkins, Steve. Page, Robin. 2011. (ENG.). 24p. (J). (gr. -1-3). 12.99 *(978-0-547-25040-3(1)*, 1101409) Houghton Mifflin Harcourt Publishing Co.

Jenkins, Steve & Rodriguez, Edel. The Mystery of Darwin's Frog. Crump, Marty. 2013. (ENG.). 40p. (J). (gr. 2-5). 16.95 *(978-1-59078-864-6(8))* Boyds Mills Pr.

Jenkins, Ward. Chicks Run Wild. Bardhan-Quallen, Sudipta. 2011. (ENG.). 32p. (J). (gr. -1-1). 19.99 *(978-1-4424-0673-5(9)*, Simon & Schuster Bks. For Young Readers) Simon & Schuster Bks. For Young Readers.

—Dog Gone! Amato, Mary. 2014. (Good Crooks Ser.). (ENG.). 128p. (J). (gr. 2-4). 14.99 *(978-1-60684-397-0(4)*, 9781606843970); 6.99 *(978-1-60684-510-3(1)*, 9781606845103) Lerner Publishing Group. (Darby Creek).

—How to Train with a T. Rex & Win 8 Gold Medals. Phelps, Michael & Abrahamson, Alan. 2009. (ENG.). 32p. (J). (gr. -1-3). 19.99 *(978-1-4169-8669-0(3)*, Simon & Schuster Bks. For Young Readers) Simon & Schuster Bks. For Young Readers.

—Missing Monkey! Amato, Mary. 2014. (Good Crooks Ser.: Bk. 1). (ENG.). 128p. (J). (gr. 2-4). 6.99 *(978-1-60684-509-7(8)*, 9781606845097, Darby Creek) Lerner Publishing Group.

—New York, Baby! Chronicle Books Staff. 2012. (ENG.). 24p. (J). (gr. -1 — 1). 12.99 *(978-1-4521-0619-9(3))* Chronicle Bks. LLC.

—Rocket Shoes. Skinner, Sharon. 2017. 40p. (J). (gr. k-4). 16.95 *(978-1-4549-2152-3(8))* Sterling Publishing Co., Inc.

—Salam Alaikum: A Message of Peace. J, Harris. 2017. (ENG.). 40p. (J). (gr. -1-3). 17.99 *(978-1-4814-8938-6(0)*, Salaam Reads) Simon & Schuster Bks. For Young Readers.

—San Francisco, Baby! Chronicle Books Staff. 2012. (ENG.). 24p. (J). (gr. -1 — 1). 12.99 *(978-1-4521-0620-5(7))* Chronicle Bks. LLC.

—Sniff a Skunk! Amato, Mary. ed. 2015. (Good Crooks Ser.: 3). (ENG.). 128p. (J). (gr. 2-4). E-Book 22.65 *(978-1-5124-0169-1(2))*;Bk. 3. pap. 6.99 *(978-1-60684-599-8(3)*, 9781606845998) Lerner Publishing Group. (Darby Creek).

Jenkins, Ward & Haya, Erwin. Not Your Parents' Money Book: Making, Saving, & Spending Your Own Money. Chatzky, Jean. 2010. (ENG.). 176p. (J). (gr. 5-9). pap. 12.99 *(978-1-4169-9472-5(6)*, Simon & Schuster Bks. For Young Readers) Simon & Schuster Bks. For Young Readers.

Jenks, D., jt. illus. see S, Agnes.

Jenneman, Mike. Scooter the Mischievous Elf. Dworkin, James B. 2019. (ENG.). 44p. (J). pap. 9.99 ***(978-1-6936-3604-2(2))*** Independently Published.

Jennenga, John. The Attack of Mr. Crohn's. Albers, Megan & Albers, Christine. Albers, Randy, ed. 2008. 71p. (YA). pap. 8.00 *(978-0-615-19666-4(7))* Albers, Christine.

Jenner, Lorelai. Castlecliff & the Fossil Princess. Pulford, Elizabeth. 2007. (ENG.). 144p. pap. *(978-1-921150-11-1(4))* Walker Bks. Australia Pty, Ltd.

Jennewein, Daniel. Chick-O-Saurus Rex. Jennewein, Lenore. 2013. (ENG.). 32p. (J). (gr. -1-3). 16.99 *(978-1-4424-5186-5(6)*, Simon & Schuster Bks. For Young Readers) Simon & Schuster Bks. For Young Readers.

—Fakespeare: Something Stinks in Hamlet. Castle, M. E. 2017. 261p. (J). pap. *(978-1-250-10157-0(3))* St. Martin's Pr.

—Fakespeare: Starcrossed in Romeo & Juliet. Castle, M. E. 2017. 295p. (J). pap. *(978-1-250-10160-0(3))* St. Martin's Pr.

—Is Your Buffalo Ready for Kindergarten? Vernick, Audrey. 2010. (ENG.). 32p. (J). (gr. -1-3). 16.99 *(978-0-06-176275-8(X)*, Balzer & Bray) HarperCollins Pubs.

—Teach Your Buffalo to Play Drums. Vernick, Audrey. 2011. (ENG.). 32p. (J). (gr. -1-3). 16.99 *(978-0-06-176253-6(9)*, Balzer & Bray) HarperCollins Pubs.

Jennifer, Tipton Cappoen. Tenino's Adventure Through Italy. Robbins, Cathy. Lynn, Berner Coble, ed. 2019. (ENG.). 34p. (J). (gr. 2-5). pap. 13.99 ***(978-1-946198-18-1(8))*** Paws and Claws Publishing, LLC.

Jennings, Ann, jt. illus. see Harris, Doreen.

Jennings, C. S. The Dozer Strikes! Dahl, Michael & Nickel, Scott. 2010. (Incredible Rockhead Ser.). (ENG.). 40p. (J). (gr. 2-5). lib. bdg. 23.99 *(978-1-4342-1894-0(5)*, Stone Arch Bks.) Capstone.

—From an Idea to Disney: How Branding Made Disney a Household Name. Sichol, Lowey Bundy. 2019. (From an Idea To Ser.). (ENG.). 112p. (J). (gr. 5-7). 16.99 *(978-1-328-45360-0(X)*, 1711801); pap. 6.99 *(978-1-328-45361-7(8)*, 1711803) Houghton Mifflin Harcourt Publishing Co. (HMH Books For Young Readers).

—From an Idea to Nike: How Marketing Made Nike a Global Success. Sichol, Lowey Bundy. 2019. (From an Idea To Ser.). (ENG.). 128p. (J). (gr. 5-7). pap. 6.99 *(978-1-328-45363-1(4)*, 1711807, HMH Books For Young Readers) Houghton Mifflin Harcourt Publishing Co.

—Goldilocks & the Three Vampires: A Graphic Novel. Sutton, Laurie S. 2016. (Far Out Fairy Tales Ser.). (ENG.). 40p. (J). (gr. 3-6). lib. bdg. 25.32 *(978-1-4965-3783-6(1)*, Stone Arch Bks.) Capstone.

—The Incredible Rockhead, 1 vol. Nickel, Scott. 2009. (Incredible Rockhead Ser.). (ENG.). 40p. (J). (gr. 2-5). lib. bdg. 23.99 *(978-1-4342-1591-8(1)*, Stone Arch Bks.) Capstone.

—The Incredible Rockhead & the Spectacular Scissorlegz, 1 vol. Nickel, Scott et al. 2010. (Incredible Rockhead Ser.). (ENG.). 40p. (J). (gr. 2-5). 23.99 *(978-1-4342-2127-8(X)*, Stone Arch Bks.) Capstone.

—The Incredible Rockhead vs Papercut!, 1 vol. Nickel, Scott. 2010. (Incredible Rockhead Ser.). (ENG.). 40p. (J). (gr. 2-5). 23.99 *(978-1-4342-1976-3(3)*, Stone Arch Bks.) Capstone.

—Rock, Paper, Scissorlegz. Nickel, Scott. 2012. (Incredible Rockhead Ser.). (ENG.). 128p. (J). (gr. 2-5). pap. 8.95 *(978-1-4342-4596-0(9)*, Stone Arch Bks.) Capstone.

—A Serious Case of the Sillies. Hirschmann, Kris. 2013. 32p. (J). pap. *(978-0-545-56765-7(3))* Scholastic, Inc.

—Teeny Genie. Katschke, Judy. 2009. (ENG.). 24p. (J). (gr. 1-17). pap. 3.99 *(978-1-58476-813-5(4))* Innovative Kids.

Jennings, C. S. & López, Àlex. Far Out Fairy Tales. Sutton, Laurie S. & Peters, Stephanie True. 2016. (Far Out Fairy Tales Ser.). (ENG.). 40p. (J). (gr. 3-6). lib. bdg., lib. bdg., lib. bdg. 202.56 *(978-1-4965-3793-5(9)*, Stone Arch Bks.) Capstone.

Jennings, Christopher S. The Incredible Rockhead: The Complete Comics Collection. Lemke, Donald et al. ed. 2020. (Stone Arch Graphic Novels Ser.). (ENG.). 144p. (J). (gr. 3-6). pap. 8.95 *(978-1-4965-9321-4(9)*, 142351); lib. bdg. 27.99 *(978-1-4965-8732-9(4)*, 141610) Capstone. (Stone Arch Bks.).

Jennings, Christopher S., et al. More Far Out Fairy Tales: Five Full-Color Graphic Novels. Bowen, Carl et al. ed. 2020. (Far Out Fairy Tales Ser.). (ENG.). 176p. (J). (gr. 3-6). pap. 12.95 *(978-1-4965-9342-9(1)*, 142369, Stone Arch Bks.) Capstone.

Jennings, John, jt. illus. see Robinson, Stacey.

Jennings, Kathleen, jt. illus. see Jean, Cassandra.

Jennings, R. W. The Burksfield Bike Club, Book 2: Lost & Found. Finkelstein, Chaim. 2007. 224p. (J). 15.95 *(978-1-932443-69-1(X)*, BBC1H) Judaica Pr., Inc., The.

Jennings, Randy. Don't You Wish Your Momma Could Cook Like Mine? Blake, Colleen H. Robley. 2012. 40p. pap. 16.97 *(978-1-61204-876-5(5)*, Strategic Bk. Publishing) Strategic Book Publishing & Rights Agency (SBPRA).

—Maggiemoosetracks: Making Friends. Campbell, Mari. Katsumoto, Sayaka, tr. 2013. 108p. pap. 21.99 *(978-0-9895205-6-0(0))* MaggieMooseTracks.

—Maggiemoosetracks: Making Friends. Campbell, Mari. 2013. 84p. pap. 21.00 *(978-0-9895205-0-8(1))* MaggieMooseTracks.

—Maggiemoosetracks: Wolf Pack. Campbell, Mari. 2013. 106p. pap. 21.00 *(978-0-9895205-5-3(2))* MaggieMooseTracks.

—"What Are Parents?" Fox-Lee, Susan & Fox-Lee, Kyme. 2005. 32p. (J). 15.95 *(978-0-9753699-0-6(3))* StoryTyme Publishing.

—What Are Parents? Fox-Lee, Kyme & Fox-Lee, Susan. 2007. 32p. (J). 15.95 *(978-0-9753699-1-3(1))* StoryTyme Publishing.

—Where Is My Money? Prindle, Twyla. 2007. (ENG & SPA.). (J). bds. 14.95 *(978-0-9759527-8-8(1)*, 1000, Prindle House Publishing Co.) Prindle Hse. Publishing Co.

—Who Stole Pop Pop's Underwear? Greenberg, Carmel. 2009. (ENG.). 46p. 16.99 *(978-0-615-20924-1(6)*, d1f87490-1e8c-4369-845e-33a85fc9fd96) Kicks and Giggles Today.

Jennings, Sarah. Collins Big Cat Phonics for Letters & Sounds - Noisy Neesha: Band 06/Orange, Bd. 6. Rickards, Lynne. 2018. (Collins Big Cat Phonics Ser.). (ENG.). 24p. (J). (gr. 1-2). pap. 6.99 *(978-0-00-825174-1(6))* HarperCollins Pubs. Ltd. GBR. Dist: Independent Pubs. Group.

—Crayon, Paper, Scissors. Lindeen, Mary. 2015. (Early Rising Readers Ser.). (J). (gr. -1-k). 5.83 *(978-1-4788-1680-5(5))* Newmark Learning LLC.

—Crayones, Papel y Tijeras. Lindeen, Mary. 2016. (Early Rising Readers Ser.). (SPA.). (J). (gr. -1). 6.67 *(978-1-4788-3710-7(1))* Newmark Learning LLC.

Jennings, Sarah. Face Your Fears. Hasson, Gill. 2020. (Kids Can Cope Ser.). (ENG.). 32p. (J). (gr. 1-5). 13.99 ***(978-1-63198-529-4(9)***, 85294) Free Spirit Publishing, Inc.

Jennings, Sarah. Ho-Ho-Hopeless Santa. Gerlings, Rebecca. 2016. (ENG.). 32p. (J). 8.99 *(978-1-4711-4600-8(6)*, Simon & Schuster Children's) Simon & Schuster, Ltd. GBR. Dist: Simon & Schuster, Inc.

—Know about Storms - Paul Takes a Walk - City Lights: BuildUp Unit 10 Lap Book. Ochoa, Louisa et al. 2015. (Build up Core Phonics Ser.). (J). (gr. 1). *(978-1-4900-2609-1(6))* Benchmark Education Co.

—Lavado de Carros. Koons, Linda. 2016. (Early Rising Readers Ser.). (SPA.). 16p. (J). (gr. 1-1). 6.67 *(978-1-4788-3729-9(2))* Newmark Learning LLC.

—Milo & the Ball. Gates, Margo. 2019. (Science All Around Me (Pull Ahead Readers — Fiction) Ser.). (ENG.). 16p. (J). (gr. -1-1). 22.65 *(978-1-5415-5853-3(7)*, 9781541558533, Lerner Pubns.) Lerner Publishing Group.

—My Baby Elephant. Gates, Margo. 2019. (Let's Look at Animal Habitats (Pull Ahead Readers — Fiction) Ser.). (ENG.). 16p. (J). (gr. -1-1). 22.65 *(978-1-5415-5864-9(2)*, 9781541558649, Lerner Pubns.) Lerner Publishing Group.

—My Feelings. 2017. (ENG.). 14p. (J). bds. 9.99 *(978-1-68119-539-1(9)*, 900176716, Bloomsbury Activity Bks.) Bloomsbury Publishing USA.

—No Hugs! Prischmann, Deirdre. 2019. (ENG.). 32p. (J). (gr. k-3). 16.99 *(978-1-68152-415-3(5))* Amicus.

—On the First Day of First Grade. Rabe, Tish. 2018. (ENG.). 32p. (J). (gr. -1-3). 9.99 *(978-0-06-266851-6(X))* HarperCollins Pubs.

—On the First Day of Summer Vacation. Rabe, Tish. 2019. (ENG.). 32p. (J). (gr. -1-3). 9.99 *(978-0-06-266852-3(8))* HarperCollins Pubs.

—Packing My Bag Pink a Band. Hawes, Alison. 2016. (Cambridge Reading Adventures Ser.). (ENG.). 16p. pap. 7.37 *(978-1-316-60082-5(3))* Cambridge Univ. Pr.

—Pony on the Twelfth Floor. Faber, Polly. 2020. (ENG.). 256p. (J). (gr. 3-7). 16.99 *(978-1-5362-0930-3(9))* Candlewick Pr.

—Put Your Worries Away. Hasson, Gill. 2019. (Kids Can Cope Ser.). (ENG.). 32p. (J). 13.99 *(978-1-63198-431-0(4))* Free Spirit Publishing, Inc.

Jennings, Sarah. Que Sucede Dentro de Mi Cabeza? Potter, Molly. 2020. (SPA.). 40p. (J). (gr. -1-2). 15.95 ***(978-84-9145-299-7(0)***, Picarona Editorial) Ediciones Obelisco ESP. Dist: Spanish Pubs., LLC.

Jennings, Sarah. Rules Are Cool. Parkes, Brenda. 2015. (Shared Reading Contemporary Tales Ser.). (J). (gr. k-1). *(978-1-4900-2119-5(1))* Benchmark Education Co.

—Rules Are Cool: Big Book Edition. Parkes, Brenda. 2015. (Shared Reading Contemporary Tales Ser.). (J). (gr. k-1). *(978-1-4900-2114-0(0))* Benchmark Education Co.

Jennings, Sarah. Sharing Berries. Gates, Margo. 2020. (Plant Life Cycles (Pull Ahead Readers — Fiction) Ser.). (ENG.). 16p. (J). (gr. -1-1). pap. 6.99 ***(978-1-7284-0309-0(X))***; lib. bdg. 22.65 ***(978-1-5415-9029-8(5))*** Lerner Publishing Group. (Lerner Pubns.).

Jennings, Sarah. Take Charge of Anger. Hasson, Gill. 2019. (Kids Can Cope Ser.). (ENG.). 32p. (J). 13.99 *(978-1-63198-457-0(8)*, 84570) Free Spirit Publishing, Inc.

—A Teacher Is the Greatest Gift. Cobbler, E. B. 2020. (ENG.). 32p. (J). (gr. -1-3). 10.99 *(978-0-06-302000-9(9)*, HarperFestival) HarperCollins Pubs.

—Three Waggy Tales. Goodhart, Pippa. 2018. (Reading Ladder Ser.). (ENG.). 48p. (J). (gr. k-2). pap. 7.99 *(978-1-4052-8643-5(1))* Egmont Bks., Ltd. GBR. Dist: Independent Pubs. Group.

Jennings, Sarah. Turn Away from Teasing. Hasson, Gill. 2020. (Kids Can Cope Ser.). (ENG.). 32p. (J). (gr. 1-5). 13.99 ***(978-1-63198-528-7(0)***, 85287) Free Spirit Publishing, Inc.

Jennings, Sarah. Twinkle, Twinkle, Little Lamb. Heos, Bridget. 2018. 32p. (J). (gr. k-3). 17.99 *(978-1-68152-405-4(8))* Amicus.

Jennings, Sarah. What's Worrying You? Potter, Molly. 2018. 32p. (J). ***(978-1-4729-4980-6(3)***, 361185, Featherstone) Bloomsbury Publishing Plc.

Jennings, Sarah. A Windy Day. Gates, Margo. 2019. (Let's Look at Weather (Pull Ahead Readers — Fiction) Ser.). (ENG.). 16p. (J). (gr. -1-1). 22.65 *(978-1-5415-5843-4(X)*, 9781541558434, Lerner Pubns.) Lerner Publishing Group.

Jenny, Lindley, jt. photos by see Reuben, Borgen.

Jenny, Pivor. Gideon's Deep. Sharpe, Diane. 2016. (ENG.). (J). (gr. 4-6). pap. 24.99 *(978-1-945756-06-1(3))* Merrimack Media.

Jenny Press Staff. Sleeping Beauty. 2016. 24p. pap. 7.99 *(978-1-86147-816-0(X)*, Armadillo) Anness Publishing GBR. Dist: National Bk. Network.

Jensema, Marissa. ASL Songs for Kids - 1: With Songs in American Sign Language. 2003. (J). cd-rom 29.95 *(978-0-9752933-1-7(1))* Institute for Disabilities Research & Training, Inc.

Jensen, Astrid & Teo, Ali. Oh Hogwash, Sweet Pea! Gabel, Ngareta. Rainforth, Hannah, tr. 2007.Tr. of Tekiteora, Kei Hea o Hu?. 32p. (J). (gr. 4-8). pap. 12.00 *(978-1-877283-96-3(7))* Huia Pubs. NZL. Dist: Univ. of Hawaii Pr.

Jensen, Brian, jt. illus. see Dahl, Michael.

Jensen, Brian, jt. illus. see Fitzpatrick, Brad.

Jensen, Brian, jt. illus. see Haugen, Ryan.

Jensen, Chase. Monster Cake, 1 vol. Knowlton, Laurie. 2018. (ENG.). 32p. (J). (gr. -1-3). 16.99 *(978-1-4556-2377-8(6)*, Pelican Publishing) Arcadia Publishing.

—The Sacrament Is for Me. Ellingson, Jessica B. 2016. (ENG.). (J). (gr. k-3). 14.99 *(978-1-4621-1880-9(1))* Cedar Fort, Inc./CFI Distribution.

—The Ten Leopards. Harris, Nina. 2019. (ENG.). 32p. (J). 15.99 *(978-1-4621-3587-5(0))* Cedar Fort, Inc./CFI Distribution.

Jensen, Cynthia. The Tiniest Little Star: A Children's Book about Love & Acceptance. Jensen, Cynthia. 2019. (Tiniest Little Star Ser.: Vol. 1). (ENG.). 30p. (J). pap. 12.95 ***(978-1-7118-2881-7(5))*** Independently Published.

Jensen, Hans. Rescue Vehicles. Somerville, Louisa. (J). mass mkt. 8.99 *(978-0-590-24557-9(0))* Scholastic, Inc.

Jensen, Jakob Hjort. The Mystery Hat. Bennicke, Rune Brandt. 2014. 32p. (J). (gr. -1-k). 16.95 *(978-1-62914-621-8(8)*, Sky Pony Pr.) Skyhorse Publishing Co., Inc.

Jensen, Josh, jt. illus. see Morales, Jethro.

Jensen, Justin. The Bread That Satisfies. Lippert, Jonah. 2018. (ENG.). 32p. (J). (gr. 1-3). pap. 11.95 *(978-0-578-42147-6(X))* J. M. Jensen.

Jensen, Leyah. My First Ballet Class: A Book with Foldout Pages. Jensen, Leyah, photos by. Capucilli, Alyssa Satin. 2011. (My First Ser.). (ENG.). 14p. (J). (gr. -1-k). 9.99 *(978-1-4424-0895-1(2)*, Little Simon) Little Simon.

Jensen, Leyah, photos by. My First Karate Class: A Book with Foldout Pages. Capucilli, Alyssa Satin. 2012. (My First Ser.). (ENG., 14p. (J). (gr. -1-k). 9.99 *(978-1-4424-2748-8(5)*, Little Simon) Little Simon.

—My First Soccer Game. Capucilli, Alyssa Satin. 2016. (My First Ser.). (ENG., 32p. (J). (gr. -1-k). pap. 4.99 *(978-1-4814-6185-6(0)*, Simon Spotlight) Simon Spotlight.

—My First Soccer Game: A Book with Foldout Pages. Capucilli, Alyssa Satin. 2011. (My First Ser.). (ENG., 14p. (J). (gr. -1-k). 9.99 *(978-1-4424-2747-1(7)*, Little Simon) Little Simon.

Jensen, Lisa. If My Hair Were Like Spagetti. Jensen, Lisa. Date not set. (J). (gr. -1-3). mass mkt. 15.95 *(978-0-9666973-0-8(8))* Jensen, Lissa.

Jensen, Nate. My Adventures in Alphabetland: How I Learned the Letters of the Alphabet - I Met Every One of Them. Jensen, Nathaniel. 2018. (ENG.). 34p. (J). (gr. k-1). 19.99 *(978-1-7327161-2-4(9))* Creative Avenues Media.

Jensen, Nate P. Into the Oblivion: Animal Tales of Peril & Perseverance for Young Readers by Young Writers. Wierth, David a. 2016. (ENG.). (J). pap. 16.99 *(978-1-945687-01-3(0))* Idle Winter Pr.

—Pablo & Koji Best Friends Forever. Tran, Melinda M. 2019. (ENG.). 34p. (J). (gr. k-3). 17.99 *(978-1-7327484-1-5(1))* Banana Tree Publishing.

Jensen, Nathaniel P. Desert Night Shift: A Pack Rat Story. Storad, Conrad J. 2006. 48p. (J). (gr. -1-3). 15.95 *(978-1-891795-16-9(3))* RGU Group, The.

—Don't Ever Cross That Road! An Armadillo Story. Storad, Conrad J. 2006. (Sonoran Desert Tails Ser.). 32p. (J). (gr. k-4). 15.95 *(978-1-891795-08-4(2))* RGU Group, The.

—Large Sitting Armadillo Character. Storad, Conrad J. (J). 10.95 *(978-1-891795-12-1(0)*, 652910 177077) RGU Group, The.

—Rattlesnake Rules. Storad, Conrad J. 2012. (ENG.). 40p. (J). (gr. 1-4). pap. 8.95 *(978-1-58985-211-2(7),* Story Monsters Pr.) Story Monsters LLC.

—Small Standing Armadillo Character. Storad, Conrad J. (J). 3.95 *(978-1-891795-13-8(9),* 652910 176070) RGU Group, The.

Jensen, Rebecca Ridges. My Heavenly Father Loves Me. 2015. (J). 10.99 *(978-1-4621-1564-8(0),* Horizon Pubs.) Cedar Fort, Inc./CFI Distribution.

Jentsch, Joyce Harp. Froggy & Friends Go to the Creek, 1 vol. Jentsch, R. D. 2009. 41p. pap. 24.95 *(978-1-60836-966-9(8))* America Star Bks.

Jeong, HaJin. Friendship Quilt. Kim, Cecil. rev. ed. 2014. (MySELF Bookshelf Ser.). (ENG.). 32p. (J). (gr. k-2). pap. 11.94 *(978-1-60357-659-8(2));* lib. bdg. 25.27 *(978-1-59953-650-7(1))* Norwood Hse. Pr.

Jeong, Se-Yeon. Joining the Dots: The Art of Seurat. Kim, In-Sook. 2017. (Stories of Art Ser.). (ENG.). 36p. (J). (gr. 3-5). lib. bdg. 10.00 *(978-1-925235-29-6(7),* Big and SMALL) ChoiceMaker Pty. Ltd., The AUS. Dist: Lerner Publishing Group.

Jeong, Soo. Playing Games, 4. Wayans, Kim & Knotts, Kevin. 2008. (Amy Hodgepodge Ser.: 4). (ENG.). 105p. (J). (gr. k-3). 17.44 *(978-0-448-44898-5(X))* Penguin Young Readers Group.

Jeong, Su-bi. The Warli People. Shin, Hye-eun & Cowley, Joy. 2017. (J). 10.00 *(978-0-8028-5476-6(1),* Eerdmans Bks For Young Readers) Eerdmans, William B. Publishing Co.

Jeong, Sung-Hwa. S�lidos, l�quidos y Gases. Gwak, Yeong-Jik. 2018. (Click Click: Ciencia B�sica / Basic Science Ser.). (SPA.). 32p. (J). pap. 17.99 ***(978-1-64101-217-1(X))*** Santillana USA Publishing Co., Inc.

Jeppesen, Ryan. Bible Ites: An Illustrated Guide to the People in the Holy Bible. Butler, David. 2015. 107p. (J). 19.99 *(978-1-62972-108-8(5))* Deseret Bk. Co.

—Celebrating a Christ-Centered Christmas: Children's Edition. Freeman, Emily Belle & Butler, David. 2017. (ENG.). 32p. (J). (gr. k-3). 17.99 *(978-1-62972-357-0(6),* Ensign Peak) Shadow Mountain Publishing.

—Celebrating a Christ-Centered Easter: Children's Edition. Freeman, Emily Belle & Butler, David. 2018. (ENG.). 32p. (J). (gr. k-3). 17.99 *(978-1-62972-418-8(1),* Ensign Peak) Shadow Mountain Publishing.

Jepson, Beth. The Tooth Fairy's Guide to Lost Teeth: A Fortune for Every Day a Tooth Is Lost. Caldwell, J. Lynn. 2005. (J). per. 11.95 *(978-0-9774463-0-8(1))* Caldwell, Judy.

Jeralds, Scott. Be Kind, Be Brave, Be You! Schulz, Charles M. & Barton, Elizabeth Dennis. 2018. (Peanuts Ser.). (ENG.). 26p. (J). (gr. -1). bds. 7.99 *(978-1-5344-1251-4(4),* Simon Spotlight) Simon Spotlight.

Jeralds, Scott. Be Thankful, Be Giving. Schulz, Charles M. 2020. (Peanuts Ser.). (ENG.). 14p. (J). (gr. -1-1). bds. 6.99 ***(978-1-5344-6905-1(2),*** Simon Spotlight) Simon Spotlight.

Jeralds, Scott. A Charlie Brown Thanksgiving. Schulz, Charles M. 2016. (Peanuts Ser.). (ENG.). 32p. (J). (gr. -1). 7.99 *(978-1-4814-6805-3(7),* Simon Spotlight) Simon Spotlight.

—Creepy Cowboy Caper. Steele, Michael Anthony. 2017. (Scooby-Doo! Beginner Mysteries Ser.). (ENG.). 112p. (J). (gr. 1-3). lib. bdg. 22.65 *(978-1-4965-4768-2(3),* 135305, Stone Arch Bks.) Capstone.

—Gobble up, Snoopy! Schulz, Charles M. 2019. (Peanuts Ser.). (ENG.). 32p. (J). (gr. k-2). 17.99 *(978-1-5344-4861-2(6));* pap. 4.99 *(978-1-5344-4860-5(8))* Simon Spotlight. (Simon Spotlight).

—Happy Thanksgiving, Snoopy! Schulz, Charles M. 2018. (Peanuts Ser.). (ENG.). 24p. (J). (gr. -1-2). pap. 4.99 *(978-1-5344-2528-6(4),* Simon Spotlight) Simon Spotlight.

—Happy Valentine's Day, Charlie Brown! Schulz, Charles M. 2017. (Peanuts Ser.). (ENG.). 32p. (J). (gr. k-2). pap. 4.99 *(978-1-5344-0502-8(X),* Simon Spotlight) Simon Spotlight.

—It's Hockey Time, Franklin! Schulz, Charles M. 2017. (Peanuts Ser.). (ENG.). 24p. (J). (gr. -1-2). pap. 4.99 *(978-1-4814-8011-6(1),* Simon Spotlight) Simon Spotlight.

—Monster Mutt Madness. Steele, Michael Anthony. 2017. (Scooby-Doo! Beginner Mysteries Ser.). (ENG.). 112p. (J). (gr. 1-3). lib. bdg. 22.65 *(978-1-4965-4767-5(5),* 135304, Stone Arch Bks.) Capstone.

—No Rest for the Easter Beagle. Schulz, Charles M. 2020. (Peanuts Ser.). (ENG.). 32p. (J). (gr. k-2). 17.99 *(978-1-5344-5480-4(2));* pap. 4.99 *(978-1-5344-5479-8(9))* Simon Spotlight. (Simon Spotlight).

—Scooby-Doo & the Night of the Undead!, 1 vol. Kupperberg, Paul. 2013. (Scooby-Doo Graphic Novels Ser.). (ENG.). 24p. (J). (gr. 2-6). lib. bdg. 27.07 *(978-1-61479-050-1(7),* 583, Graphic Novels) Spotlight.

—Scooby-Doo Animal Jokes. Dahl, Michael. 2015. (Scooby-Doo Joke Bks.). (ENG.). 64p. (J). (gr. 2-6). lib. bdg. 22.65 *(978-1-4342-9683-2(0),* Stone Arch Bks.) Capstone.

—Scooby-Doo! Food Jokes! Dahl, Michael. 2015. (Scooby-Doo Joke Bks.). (ENG.). 64p. (J). (gr. 2-6). lib. bdg. 22.65 *(978-1-4342-9682-5(2),* Stone Arch Bks.) Capstone.

—Scooby Doo Joke Books. Dahl, Michael. 2015. (Scooby-Doo Joke Bks.). (ENG.). 64p. (J). (gr. 2-6). lib. bdg., lib. bdg., lib. bdg. 67.95 *(978-1-4965-0300-8(7),* Stone Arch Bks.) Capstone.

—Scooby-Doo on the Go Jokes. Dahl, Michael. 2015. (Scooby-Doo Joke Bks.). (ENG.). 64p. (J). (gr. 2-6). lib. bdg. 22.65 *(978-1-4342-9684-9(9),* Stone Arch Bks.) Capstone.

—Scooby-Doo's Laugh-Out-Loud Jokes! Dahl, Michael. 2015. (Scooby-Doo Joke Bks.). (ENG.). 224p. (J). (gr. 2-6). pap. 9.95 *(978-1-62370-182-6(1),* Capstone Young Readers) Capstone.

—Skeleton Crew Showdown. Steele, Michael Anthony. 2017. (Scooby-Doo! Beginner Mysteries Ser.). (ENG.). 112p. (J). (gr. 1-3). lib. bdg. 22.65 *(978-1-4965-4769-9(1),* 135306, Stone Arch Bks.) Capstone.

—A Valentine for Linus! Schulz, Charles M. 2018. (Peanuts Ser.). (ENG.). 16p. (J). (gr. -1-2). 5.99 *(978-1-5344-2043-4(6),* Simon Spotlight) Simon Spotlight.

—Vampire Zoo Hullabaloo. Steele, Michael Anthony. 2017. (Scooby-Doo! Beginner Mysteries Ser.). (ENG.). 112p. (J). (gr. 1-3). lib. bdg. 22.65 *(978-1-4965-4770-5(5),* 135307, Stone Arch Bks.) Capstone.

Jeralds, Scott. Woodstock's First Flight! Schulz, Charles M. 2020. (Peanuts Ser.). (ENG.). 16p. (J). (gr. -1-2). pap. 6.99 ***(978-1-5344-6432-2(8),*** Simon Spotlight) Simon Spotlight.

Jeralds, Scott. You're a Big Brother, Charlie Brown! Schulz, Charles M. 2018. (Peanuts Ser.). (ENG.). 24p. (J). (gr. -1-2). pap. 4.99 *(978-1-5344-0961-3(0),* Simon Spotlight) Simon Spotlight.

Jeram, Anita. All Pigs Are Beautiful. King-Smith, Dick. 2008. (Read, Listen, & Wonder Ser.). (ENG.). 32p. (J). (gr. -1-3). pap. 8.99 *(978-0-7636-3866-5(8))* Candlewick Pr.

—Un Beso de Buenas Noches. Hest, Amy. Rubio, Esther, tr. (SPA.). (J). 16.00 *(978-1-930332-04-1(1),* LC3294) Lectorum Pubns., Inc.

—Colors Everywhere: a Guess How Much I Love You Storybook. McBratney, Sam. 2007. (Guess How Much I Love You Ser.). (ENG.). 24p. (J). (-k). bds. 7.99 *(978-0-7636-3545-9(6))* Candlewick Pr.

—Don't You Feel Well, Sam? Hest, Amy. 2007. (Sam Bks.). (ENG.). 32p. (J). (gr. -1-k). 4.99 *(978-0-7636-2408-8(X))* Candlewick Pr.

—Guess How Much I Love You. McBratney, Sam. 2005. 34p. (J). bds. 19.95 *(978-0-9769313-1-7(1))* BrailleInk.

—Guess How Much I Love You. McBratney, Sam. (Guess How Much I Love You Ser.). (J). 2019. (ENG.). 24p. (— 1). bds. 8.99 *(978-1-5362-1063-7(3));* 2014. (ENG.). 40p. (gr. k-12). 16.99 *(978-0-7636-7448-9(6));* 2011. (gr. -1-k). bds. 9.99 *(978-0-7636-4976-0(7));* 2006. 32p. (gr. -1-3). 15.99 *(978-0-7636-3503-9(0))* Candlewick Pr.

—Guess How Much I Love You. McBratney, Sam. 2008. (Guess How Much I Love You Ser.). (ENG.). 24p. (J). (— 1). bds. 7.99 *(978-0-7636-4264-8(9))* Candlewick Pr.

—Guess How Much I Love You: a Book of Valentines. McBratney, Sam. 2017. (Guess How Much I Love You Ser.). (ENG.). 18p. (J). (gr. -1-3). pap. 9.99 *(978-0-7636-9801-0(6))* Candlewick Pr.

—Guess How Much I Love You All Year Round. McBratney, Sam. 2010. (Guess How Much I Love You Ser.). (ENG.). 72p. (J). (gr. -1-2). 16.99 *(978-0-7636-4654-7(7))* Candlewick Pr.

—Guess How Much I Love You: Baby Book. McBratney, Sam. 2014. (Guess How Much I Love You Ser.). (ENG.). 64p. (J). (gr. k-12). 14.99 *(978-0-7636-7023-8(5))* Candlewick Pr.

—Guess How Much I Love You: Baby Milestone Moments: Board Book & Cards Gift Set. McBratney, Sam. 2018. (Guess How Much I Love You Ser.). (ENG.). 22p. (J). (— 1). bds. 17.99 *(978-1-5362-0149-9(9))* Candlewick Pr.

—Guess How Much I Love You Coloring Book. McBratney, Sam. 2017. (Guess How Much I Love You Ser.). (ENG.). 96p. (J). (gr. k-12). pap. 7.99 *(978-0-7636-9467-8(3))* Candlewick Pr.

—Guess How Much I Love You: Colors. McBratney, Sam. 2013. (Guess How Much I Love You Ser.). (ENG.). 14p. (J). (— 1). bds. 4.99 *(978-0-7636-6476-3(6))* Candlewick Pr.

—Guess How Much I Love You in the Winter: Deluxe Cut Paper Edition. McBratney, Sam. 2016. (Guess How Much I Love You Ser.). (ENG.). 12p. (J). (-k). 18.99 *(978-0-7636-9057-1(0))* Candlewick Pr.

—Guess How Much I Love You Lap-Size Board Book. McBratney, Sam. 2013. (Guess How Much I Love You Ser.). (ENG.). 24p. (J). (— 1). bds. 14.99 *(978-0-7636-7006-1(5))* Candlewick Pr.

—Guess How Much I Love You: Look What I Can Do: A First Concepts Book. McBratney, Sam. 2014. (Guess How Much I Love You Ser.). (ENG.). 16p. (J). (— 1). bds. 9.99 *(978-0-7636-7064-1(2))* Candlewick Pr.

—Guess How Much I Love You: One More Tickle! A Puppet Book. McBratney, Sam. 2016. (Guess How Much I Love You Ser.). (ENG.). (J). (gr. k-k). bds. 17.99 *(978-0-7636-8819-6(3))* Candlewick Pr.

—Guess How Much I Love You Padded Board Book. McBratney, Sam. 2019. (Guess How Much I Love You Ser.). (ENG.). 30p. (J). (— 1). bds. 10.99 *(978-1-5362-1062-0(5))* Candlewick Pr.

—Guess How Much I Love You: Panorama Pops. McBratney, Sam. 2014. (Guess How Much I Love You Ser.). (ENG.). 30p. (J). (gr. k-4). 9.99 *(978-0-7636-7446-5(X))* Candlewick Pr.

—Guess How Much I Love You: Pop-Up. McBratney, Sam. 2011. (Guess How Much I Love You Ser.). (ENG.). 16p. (J). (gr. -1-2). 19.99 *(978-0-7636-5378-1(0))* Candlewick Pr.

—Guess How Much I Love You Sweetheart Gift Edition. McBratney, Sam. 2016. (Guess How Much I Love You Ser.). (ENG.). 32p. (J). (gr. k-12). 12.00 *(978-0-7636-9058-8(9))* Candlewick Pr.

—Here I Am!: a Finger Puppet Book: A Guess How Much I Love You Book. McBratney, Sam. 2018. (Guess How Much I Love You Ser.). (ENG.). 16p. (J). (— 1). bds. 12.99 *(978-1-5362-0389-9(0))* Candlewick Pr.

—Kiss Good Night. Hest, Amy. (ENG.). (J). (— 1). 2019. 30p. bds. 9.99 *(978-1-5362-0674-6(1));* 2006. 32p. pap. 5.99 *(978-0-7636-2114-8(5));* 2004. 30p. bds. 6.99 *(978-0-7636-2094-3(7))* Candlewick Pr.

—Kiss Good Night: Book & Toy Gift Set. Hest, Amy. gif. ed. 2004. (Sam Bks.). (ENG.). 30p. (J). (gr. k-12). bds. 15.99 *(978-0-7636-2524-5(8))* Candlewick Pr.

—Kiss Good Night Lap-Size Board Book. Hest, Amy. 2014. (Sam Bks.). (ENG.). 32p. (J). (— 1). bds. 12.99 *(978-0-7636-4748-3(9))* Candlewick Pr.

—Little Chick. Hest, Amy. 2009. (ENG.). 56p. (J). (gr. -1-k). 17.99 *(978-0-7636-2890-1(5))* Candlewick Pr.

—A Nutbrown Hare Storybook Pair Boxed Set. McBratney, Sam. 2008. (Guess How Much I Love You Ser.). (ENG.). 48p. (J). (gr. k-k). bds. 14.99 *(978-0-7636-4265-5(7))* Candlewick Pr.

—Skip to the Loo! a Potty Book. Lloyd-Jones, Sally. 2018. (ENG.). 30p. (J). (-k). bds. 8.99 *(978-0-7636-9977-2(2))* Candlewick Pr.

—Skip to the Loo, My Darling! a Potty Book. Lloyd-Jones, Sally. 2016. (ENG.). 32p. (J). (-k). 11.99 *(978-0-7636-7234-8(3))* Candlewick Pr.

—A Surprise for the Nutbrown Hares. McBratney, Sam. 2009. (J). *(978-0-7636-4903-6(1))* Candlewick Pr.

—Todos Son Mis Favoritos. McBratney, Sam. 2004.Tr. of You're All My Favorites. (SPA.). 32p. (J). 16.99 *(978-84-88342-67-6(5))* S.A. Kokinos ESP. Dist: Lectorum Pubns., Inc.

—Tomhais Méid Mo Ghrá Duit (Guess How Much I Love You in Irish) McBratney, Sam. 2013. (Guess How Much I Love You Ser.). (GLE.). 32p. (J). (gr. -1-2). 9.99 *(978-0-7636-6570-8(3))* Candlewick Pr.

—Tu Puedes Hacerlo, Sam. Hest, Amy. 2004.Tr. of You Can Do It, Sam. (SPA.). (J). 16.00 *(978-1-930332-53-9(X))* Lectorum Pubns., Inc.

—You Can Do It, Sam. Hest, Amy. 2007. (Sam Bks.). 32p. (J). (gr. -1-k). pap. 4.99 *(978-0-7636-3688-3(6))* Candlewick Pr.

—You're All My Favorites. McBratney, Sam. 2008. (ENG.). 32p. (J). (gr. k-k). bds. 7.99 *(978-0-7636-4297-6(5))* Candlewick Pr.

Jeram, Anita. I Love My Little Storybook. Jeram, Anita. 2010. (ENG.). 32p. (J). (-k). 7.99 *(978-0-7636-4806-0(X))* Candlewick Pr.

Jeras, Maja Bertole. King of the Night. McGhee, Tate. 2017. (ENG.). (J). pap. 9.99 *(978-0-692-84306-2(X))* Skyway Pictures LLC.

Jerde, Susan. Inuit Tales: Read Well Level K Unit 10 Storybook. Gunn, Barbara. 2003. (Read Well Level K Ser.). 20p. (J). *(978-1-57035-681-0(5))* Cambium Education, Inc.

—Rhyming Fun: Read Well Level K Unit 6 Storybook. Sprick, Marilyn et al. 2003. (Read Well Level K Ser.). 20p. (J). *(978-1-57035-678-0(5))* Cambium Education, Inc.

—Shells on the Shore: Read Well Level K Unit 14 Storybook. Jones, Shelley V. & Gunn, Barbara. 2003. (Read Well Level K Ser.). 20p. (J). *(978-1-57035-685-8(8),* 55546) Cambium Education, Inc.

Jeremiah. Tanner's Turtle. Labadie, Sally. 2012. 32p. pap. 12.95 *(978-1-61244-085-9(1))* Halo Publishing International.

Jeria, Ximena. The Magic of Unicorns: Magic. Grandi, Gina. 2018. (ENG.). 48p. (J). (gr. k-3). 17.99 *(978-1-941367-61-2(5))* Downtown Bookworks.

Jermann, David. The Secret of the Lost Kingdom. Bolton, Michael. 2004. 36p. (J). (gr. k-4). reprint ed. *(978-0-7567-7849-1(2))* DIANE Publishing Co.

—El Secreto del Reino Perdido. Bolton, Michael. (Buenas Noches Ser.). (SPA.). (J). (gr. 3). pap. 7.16 *(978-958-04-4904-1(X))* Norma S.A. COL. Dist: Lectorum Pubns., Inc.

Jerome, Barb. Solomon & Lily. Schield, Allie Schield. 2003. 34p. (J). per. 11.99 *(978-0-9743948-0-0(7))* One Little Miracle.

Jerome, Elaine. Sundays on Fourth Street/Los Domingos en la Calle Cuatro. Costales, Amy. 2009. (SPA & ENG.). 32p. (J). (gr. -1-3). 16.95 *(978-1-55885-520-5(3))* Arte Publico Pr.

—The Woodcutter's Gift/el Regalo del Lenador. Ruiz-Flores, Lupe. Ventura, Gabriela Baeza, tr. from ENG. 2007. (SPA & ENG.). 32p. (J). (gr. -1-2). 16.95 *(978-1-55885-489-5(4),* Piñata Books) Arte Publico Pr.

Jerome, Karen A. If Nathan Were Here. Bahr, Mary. 2004. 32p. (J). (gr. 1-7). 16.00 *(978-0-8028-5187-1(8))* Eerdmans, William B. Publishing Co.

—Sometimes Smart Is Good/A Veces Es Bueno Ser Listo. Luchsinger, Dena. 2007. (SPA & ENG.). 32p. (J). (gr. -1). 16.00 *(978-0-8028-5215-1(7),* Eerdmans Bks For Young Readers) Eerdmans, William B. Publishing Co.

Jeschke, Stefanie. I Wish I Were A... Holzwarth, Werner. 2013. 40p. (J). (gr. -1-k). 16.95 *(978-1-62087-993-1(X),* 620993, Sky Pony Pr.) Skyhorse Publishing Co., Inc.

Jesner, Alois. 101 Life Skills Games for Children: Learning, Growing, Getting Along (Ages 6-12) Badegruber, Bernie. 2005. (SmartFun Activity Bks.). (ENG.). 160p. spiral bd. 19.95 *(978-0-89793-442-8(3),* 1251580); per. 15.99 *(978-0-89793-441-1(5),* 1251580) Turner Publishing Co. (Hunter Hse.).

Jess Racklyeft. The First Christmas. Anonymous. 2019. (ENG.). 32p. (J). (— 1). 24.99 ***(978-0-14-379690-9(9),*** Puffin) Penguin Random Hse. AUS. Dist: Independent Pubs. Group.

Jessa, Azra. Ramadhan & Eid-Ul-Fitr. 2008. (ENG.). 16p. (J). (gr. -1). 12.95 *(978-1-879402-23-2(8))* Tahrike Tarsile Quran, Inc.

Jesse, Brady. Trapped in a Video Game (Book 1) Brady, Dustin. 2018. (Trapped in a Video Game Ser.: 1). (ENG.). 144p. (J). 13.99 *(978-1-4494-9608-1(3))* Andrews McMeel Publishing.

Jessee, Diana. Lawyer Will: The Story of an Appalachian Lawyer. Cooper, Ann Goode & Bowlin, William Harrison. 2004. 36p. (J). 12.95 *(978-1-887905-90-9(1))* Parkway Pubs., Inc.

—Zebordee Goes to the Races. Cooper, Ann Goode. 2005. 32p. (J). (gr. -1-3). *(978-1-933251-01-1(8))* Parkway Pubs., Inc.

Jessell, Tim. Babe Ruth & the Baseball Curse. Kelly, David A. 2009. (Totally True Adventures Ser.). (ENG.). 112p. (J). (gr. 2-5). 5.99 *(978-0-375-85603-7(X),* Random Hse. Bks. for Young Readers) Random Hse. Children's Bks.

—Barry. Klimo, Kate. 2013. (Dog Diaries: 3). 160p. (J). (gr. 2-5). pap. 7.99 *(978-0-449-81280-8(4),* Random Hse. Bks. for Young Readers) Random Hse. Children's Bks.

—The Boxcar Children, Set. 2013. (Boxcar Children Mysteries Ser.). (ENG.). 538p. (J). (gr. 1-5). 45.00 *(978-0-8075-0864-0(0),* 807508640) Whitman, Albert & Co.

—The Boxcar Children Beginning. Maclachlan, Patricia. (Boxcar Children Mysteries Ser.). (ENG.). 144p. (J). (gr. 1-5). 2013. 6.99 *(978-0-8075-6617-6(9),* 807566179); 2012. 16.99 *(978-0-8075-6616-9(0),* 807566160) Whitman, Albert & Co.

—City in the Clouds. Abbott, Tony. 2004. (Secrets of Droon Ser.: No. 4). 88p. 15.00 *(978-0-7569-3930-4(5))* Perfection Learning Corp.

—Dog Diaries. Ingle, Annie & Klimo, Kate. 2013. (Dog Diaries: 2). 160p. (J). (gr. 2-5). pap. 7.99 *(978-0-307-97904-9(0),* Random Hse. Bks. for Young Readers) Random Hse. Children's Bks.

—Dog Diaries #11: Tiny Tim (Dog Diaries Special Edition) Klimo, Kate. 2017. (Dog Diaries: 11). 176p. (J). (gr. 2-5). pap. 7.99 *(978-0-399-55131-4(X),* Random Hse. Bks. for Young Readers) Random Hse. Children's Bks.

—Dog Diaries #12: Susan. Klimo, Kate. 2018. (Dog Diaries: 12). (ENG.). 160p. (J). (gr. 2-5). lib. bdg. 12.99 *(978-1-5247-1965-4(X),* Random Hse. Bks. for Young Readers) Random Hse. Children's Bks.

—Dog Diaries #14: Sunny. Klimo, Kate. 2019. (Dog Diaries: 14). 160p. (J). (gr. 2-5). pap. 7.99 *(978-0-525-64823-9(2),* Random Hse. Bks. for Young Readers) Random Hse. Children's Bks.

—Dog Diaries #4: Togo No. 4. Klimo, Kate. 2014. (Dog Diaries: 4). 176p. (J). (gr. 2-5). pap. 7.99 *(978-0-385-37335-7(X),* Random Hse. Bks. for Young Readers) Random Hse. Children's Bks.

—Dog Diaries #5: Dash, Bk. 5. Klimo, Kate. 2014. (Dog Diaries: 5). 160p. (J). (gr. 2-5). pap. 7.99 *(978-0-385-37338-8(4),* Random Hse. Bks. for Young Readers) Random Hse. Children's Bks.

—Dog Diaries #8: Fala. Klimo, Kate. 2016. (Dog Diaries: 8). (ENG.). 160p. (J). (gr. 2-5). lib. bdg. 12.99 *(978-0-553-53491-7(2),* Random Hse. Bks. for Young Readers) Random Hse. Children's Bks.

—Double Team. Stoudemire, Amar'e. ed. 2012. (STAT: Standing Tall & Talented Ser.: 2). lib. bdg. 16.00 *(978-0-606-26762-5(X))* Turtleback.

—Fala. Klimo, Kate. 2016. (Dog Diaries: 8). 160p. (J). (gr. 2-5). pap. 7.99 *(978-0-553-53490-0(4),* Random Hse. Bks. for Young Readers) Random Hse. Children's Bks.

—Flight of the Genie. Abbott, Tony. 2004. (Secrets of Droon Ser.: No. 21). 122p. (J). lib. bdg. 15.38 *(978-1-4242-0314-7(7))* Fitzgerald Bks.

—Ginger. Worth, Bonnie & Klimo, Kate. 2013. (Dog Diaries: 1). 160p. (J). (gr. 2-5). pap. 7.99 *(978-0-307-97899-8(0),* Random Hse. Bks. for Young Readers) Random Hse. Children's Bks.

—The Hidden Stairs & the Magic Carpet. Abbott, Tony. 2004. (Secrets of Droon Ser.: No. 1). 80p. (gr. 2-5). 15.00 *(978-0-7569-3939-7(9))* Perfection Learning Corp.

—Home Court. Stoudemire, Amar'e. 2012. (STAT: Standing Tall & Talented Ser.: 1). (ENG.). 144p. (J). (gr. 3-7). pap. 5.99 *(978-0-545-38759-0(0),* Scholastic Pr.) Scholastic, Inc.

—The Hunter. Wahl, Jan. 2018. (ENG.). 32p. (J). (gr. 1-3). 18.99 *(978-1-56846-297-4(2),* Creative Editions) Creative Co., The.

—Looking for Marco Polo. Armstrong, Alan W. 2011. (ENG.). 304p. (J). (gr. 4-6). lib. bdg. 21.19 *(978-0-375-93321-9(2),* Yearling) Random Hse. Children's Bks.

—The Magic Escapes. Abbott, Tony. 2004. (Secrets of Droon Ser.: No. 1). 161p. (gr. 2-5). 16.00 *(978-0-7569-3944-1(5))* Perfection Learning Corp.

—The Moon Scroll. Abbott, Tony. 2004. (Secrets of Droon Ser.: No. 15). 129p. (gr. 2-5). 15.00 *(978-0-7569-3946-5(1))* Perfection Learning Corp.

—Mystery of the Fallen Treasure. 2013. (Boxcar Children Mysteries Ser.: 132). (ENG.). 128p. (J). (gr. 1-5). 5.99 *(978-0-8075-5506-4(1),* 807555061); 15.99 *(978-0-8075-5508-8(8),* 807555088) Whitman, Albert & Co.

—Raleigh's Page. Armstrong, Alan W. 2007. (ENG.). 336p. (J). (gr. 6-8). lib. bdg. 21.19 *(978-0-375-93319-6(0))* Random House Publishing Group.

—Raleigh's Page. Armstrong, Alan. 2009. (ENG.). 336p. (J). (gr. 3-7). 7.99 *(978-0-375-83320-5(X),* Yearling) Random Hse. Children's Bks.

—The Return of the Graveyard Ghost. 2013. (Boxcar Children Mysteries Ser.: 133). (ENG.). 128p. (J). (gr. 1-5). 15.99 *(978-0-8075-6935-1(6),* 807569356); 5.99 *(978-0-8075-6936-8(4),* 807569364) Whitman, Albert & Co.

—Rolf: Dog Diaries #10. Klimo, Kate. 2017. (Dog Diaries: 10). 160p. (J). (gr. 2-5). pap. 7.99 *(978-0-399-55128-4(X),* Random Hse. Bks. for Young Readers) Random Hse. Children's Bks.

—Slam Dunk: Standing Tall & Talented, 3. Stoudemire, Amar'e. 2013. (Stat Ser.: 3). (ENG.). 144p. (J). (gr. 3-7). pap. 5.99 *(978-0-545-38761-3(2))* Scholastic, Inc.

—Sparky. Klimo, Kate. 2016. (Dog Diaries: 9). 160p. (J). (gr. 2-5). pap. 7.99 *(978-0-553-53493-1(9),* Random Hse. Bks. for Young Readers) Random Hse. Children's Bks.

—Stan Lee's Superhero Christmas. Lee, Stan. 2nd ed. 2016. (ENG.). 32p. (gr. k-2). pap. 27.95 *(978-1-59687-526-5(7),* ipicturebooks) ibooks, Inc.

—Standing Tall & Talented - Most Valuable. Stoudemire, Amar'e. 2014. (ENG.). 144p. (J). (gr. 3-7). pap. 5.99 *(978-0-545-60613-4(6),* Scholastic Paperbacks) Scholastic, Inc.

—STAT #4: Schooled. Stoudemire, Amar'e. 2013. (ENG.). 144p. (J). (gr. 3-7). pap. 5.99 *(978-0-545-60607-3(1),* Scholastic Paperbacks) Scholastic, Inc.

—Stubby. Klimo, Kate. 2015. (Dog Diaries: 7). (ENG.). 160p. (J). (gr. 2-5). lib. bdg. 12.99 *(978-0-385-39244-0(3),* Random Hse. Bks. for Young Readers) Random Hse. Children's Bks.

—Superhero Christmas. Lee, Stan. 2004. 32p. (J). (gr. -1-2). 16.89 *(978-0-06-056560-2(8))* HarperCollins Pubs.

—Susan. Klimo, Kate. 2018. (Dog Diaries: 12). 160p. (J). (gr. 2-5). pap. 7.99 *(978-1-5247-1964-7(1),* Random Hse. Bks. for Young Readers) Random Hse. Children's Bks.

—Sweetie. Klimo, Kate. 2015. (Dog Diaries: 6). 160p. (J). (gr. 2-5). pap. 7.99 *(978-0-385-39240-2(0),* Random Hse. Bks. for Young Readers) Random Hse. Children's Bks.

J

—This Side of Wild: Mutts, Mares, & Laughing Dinosaurs. Paulsen, Gary. (ENG.). (J). (gr. 5). 2016. 160p. pap. 7.99 *(978-1-4814-5151-2(0))*; 2015. 144p. 16.99 *(978-1-4814-5150-5(2))* Simon & Schuster Bks. For Young Readers. (Simon & Schuster Bks. For Young Readers).

—Tiny Tim. Klimo, Kate. 2017. (Dog Diaries: 11). (ENG.). 176p. (J). (gr. 2-5). lib. bdg. 12.99 *(978-0-399-55132-1(8)*, Random Hse. Bks. for Young Readers) Random Hse. Children's Bks.

—Two Hot Dogs with Everything. Haven, Paul. 2007. (ENG.). 320p. (J). (gr. 3-7). per. 7.99 *(978-0-375-83349-6(8)*, Yearling) Random Hse. Children's Bks.

Jessell, Tim & Fitzgerald, Royce. The Lost Empire of Koomba, 35. Abbott, Tony. 2009. (Secrets of Droon Ser.: 35). (ENG.). 128p. (J). (gr. 2-4). 17.44 *(978-0-545-09883-0(1))* Scholastic, Inc.

Jessell, Tim, jt. illus. see Adams, Gil.

Jessell, Tim, jt. illus. see Dunn, Robert.

Jessell, Tim, jt. illus. see Fitzgerald, Royce.

Jessell, Tim, jt. illus. see Merrell, David.

Jesset, Aurore & Korthues, Barbara. Loopy. Jesset, Aurore. 2009. 32p. (J). (gr. -1-3). 7.95 *(978-0-7358-2261-0(1))* North-South Bks., Inc.

JessT, Grant, jt. illus. see Scott, Peter.

Jevons, Chris. Can't Scare Me! Archer, Mandy. 2019. (ENG.). 12p. (J). (gr. -1-k). bds. 8.99 *(978-1-68412-798-6(X)*, Silver Dolphin Bks.) Printers Row Publishing Group.

—Hansel & Gretel & the Green Witch. North, Laura. 2015. (Tadpoles: Fairytale Twists Ser.). (ENG.). 32p. (J). (gr. 1-2). *(978-0-7787-1928-1(6))* Crabtree Publishing Co.

—Max's Amazing Models. Chapman, Linda. 2017. (Reading Ladder Ser.). (ENG.). 48p. (J). (gr. k-2). pap. 7.99 *(978-1-4052-7823-2(4))* Egmont Bks., Ltd. GBR. Dist: Independent Pubs. Group.

—My Best Friend Is a Goldfish. Lee, Mark. 2018. (ENG.). 24p. (J). (gr. -1-2). 17.99 *(978-1-5124-2601-4(6)*, 9781512426014, Carolrhoda Bks.) Lerner Publishing Group.

—A Pirate Alphabet: The ABCs of Piracy! Butzer, Anna. 2016. (Alphabet Connection Ser.). (ENG.). 32p. (J). (gr. -1-2). lib. bdg. 27.99 *(978-1-4795-6886-4(4)*, Picture Window Bks.) Capstone.

—T. Rex: The Big Scare, 1 vol. Bromage, Fran. 2019. (Dinosaur Adventures Ser.). (ENG.). 24p. (J). (gr. 1-2). 24.60 *(978-1-7253-9517-6(7))*; pap. 8.25 *(978-1-7253-9515-2(0))* Rosen Publishing Group, Inc., The. (Windmill Bks.).

Jevons, Chris, jt. illus. see Loram, James.

Jevtic, Vladimir. World's Biggest Reptiles. Jackson, Tom. 2018. (Extreme Reptiles Ser.). (ENG.). 32p. (J). (gr. 3-6). lib. bdg. 27.99 *(978-1-5415-0091-4(1)*, Hungry Tomato ®) Lerner Publishing Group.

—World's Deadliest Reptiles. Jackson, Tom. 2018. (Extreme Reptiles Ser.). (ENG.). 32p. (J). (gr. 3-6). lib. bdg. 27.99 *(978-1-5415-0090-7(3)*, Hungry Tomato ®) Lerner Publishing Group.

—World's Sneakiest Reptiles. Jackson, Tom. 2018. (Extreme Reptiles Ser.). (ENG.). 32p. (J). (gr. 3-6). lib. bdg. 27.99 *(978-1-5415-0092-1(X)*, Hungry Tomato ®) Lerner Publishing Group.

Jewett, Anne. The Warmest Place of All. Rando, Licia. 2009. (ENG.). 32p. (J). (gr. -1-k). 16.95 *(978-0-9792035-8-9(9))* Pleasant St. Pr.

Jeyakkumar, Melanie. Kosmic & Raven. Jeyakkumar, Melanie. 2018. (Kosmic & Raven Ser.: Vol. 1). (ENG.). 52p. (J). (gr. 2-6). pap. 11.99 *(978-1-68160-553-1(8))* Crimson Cloak Publishing.

Jeyaveeran, Ruth. El árbol Más Feliz: Un Cuento Sobre Yoga. Krishnaswami, Uma. 2008.Tr. of Happiest Tree: a Yoga Story. (SPA.). 32p. (J). pap. 10.95 *(978-1-62014-149-6(3))* Lee & Low Bks., Inc.

—A Dog Named Haku: A Holiday Story from Nepal. Engle, Margarita et al. 2018. (ENG.). 32p. (J). (gr. k-3). 19.99 *(978-1-5124-3205-3(9)*, Millbrook Pr.) Lerner Publishing Group.

Jeyaveeran, Ruth & Akib, Jamel. Bringing Asha Home, 1 vol. Krishnaswami, Uma. 2006. (ENG.). 32p. (J). (gr. -1-3). 16.95 *(978-1-58430-259-9(3))* Lee & Low Bks., Inc.

Ji-won, Lee. Jumong: Founder of Goguryeo. Seong-eun, Kim. Park, Christian J. & Park, Christian J., trs. 2011. (ENG.). 40p. 14.00 *(978-89-91913-49-3(0)*, 1619) Seoul Selection KOR. Dist: Univ. of Hawaii Pr.

Jiale, Kuang, jt. illus. see Vallejo, Monse.

Jian, Li. Prince & His Porcelain Cup: A Tale of the Famous Chicken Cup, Retold in English & Chinese. ed. 2018. 42p. (J). (gr. k-4). 16.95 *(978-1-60220-451-5(9))* Shanghai Translation Publishing Hse. CHN. Dist: Publishers Group West (PGW).

Jian, Li. The Little Monkey King's Journey: Retold in English & Chinese. Jian, Li. Wert, Yijin, tr. ed. 2012. (Stories of the Chinese Zodiac Ser.). 48p. (J). (gr. -1-3). 16.95 *(978-1-60220-981-7(2))* Shanghai Translation Publishing Hse. CHN. Dist: Publishers Group West (PGW).

—The Little Rat & the Golden Seed: A Story Told in English & Chinese (Stories of the Chinese Zodiac) Jian, Li. Wert, Yijin, tr. 2019. (Stories of the Chinese Zodiac Ser.). 42p. (J). (gr. -1-3). 16.95 *(978-1-60220-459-1(4))* Shanghai Translation Publishing Hse. CHN. Dist: Publishers Group West (PGW).

—The Snake Goddess Colors the World: A Chinese Tale Told in English & Chinese. Jian, Li. ed. 2013. (Stories of the Chinese Zodiac Ser.). (ENG.). 42p. (J). (gr. -1-3). 16.95 *(978-1-60220-982-4(0))* Shanghai Translation Publishing Hse. CHN. Dist: Publishers Group West (PGW).

Jiao, Bingzhen. A Picture Book of Agricultural Cultivation in Ancient China. Jiang, Junjing. 2017. *(978-1-62246-042-7(1))* Homa & Sekey Bks.

—A Picture Book of Silk Weaving in Ancient China. Jiang, Junjing. 2017. *(978-1-62246-043-4(X))* Homa & Sekey Bks.

JibJab Bros Studios. Cars Are Cool! (StoryBots) Storybots. 2017. (ENG.). 24p. (J). (— 1). bds. 7.99 *(978-1-5247-1823-7(8)*, Random Hse. Bks. for Young Readers) Random Hse. Children's Bks.

Jim Connelly. The Mouse Who Lived in Fenway Park. Bradford James Nolan. 2009. 36p. pap. 19.99 *(978-1-4389-4491-3(8))* AuthorHouse.

Jimena Pinto-Krowjiline. Quirky Kids Zoo. Brannon, Pat. 2011. 32p. pap. 11.99 *(978-1-933300-83-2(3))* Wandering Sage Pubns., LLC.

Jimenez, Leticia Serrano. DOS Casos de Casas y Algunas Otras Cosas. Avila, Juan Casas. rev. ed. 2006. (Castillo de la Lectura Verde Ser.). (SPA & ENG.). 72p. (J). (gr. 2-4). pap. 7.95 *(978-970-20-0175-1(7))* Castillo, Ediciones, S. A. de C. V. MEX. Dist: Macmillan.

Jimenez, Martin Rodriguez. La Pulga Que Grunchen Sanchen Grunchen. Jimenez Valdeita, Marta. 2019. (SPA.). 26p. (J). pap. 10.00 ***(978-1-6887-6722-5(3))*** Independently Published.

Jimenez, Resu. Amigos en el Bosque. Lopez, Minia. 2006. (SPA.). (J). 8.00 *(978-0-9773531-3-2(3))* Charming Pubns.

—Friends in the Forest. Lopez, Minia. 2006. (J). 8.00 *(978-0-9773531-4-9(1))* Charming Pubns.

Jimenez, Rey J. StarZOOOM: The Fastest Starfish in the Sea. Jimenez, Noelle a. 2018. (Starzooom Ser.: Vol. 1). (ENG.). 40p. (J). pap. 12.50 *(978-1-0743-8755-6(4))* Independently Published.

Jimenz, Jim & Calero, Dennis. The Fall of the House of Usher, 1 vol. Manning, Matthew K. & Poe, Edgar Allen. 2013. (Edgar Allan Poe Graphic Novels Ser.). (ENG.). 72p. (J). (gr. 5-9). pap. 6.10 *(978-1-4342-4258-7(7)*, Stone Arch Bks.) Capstone.

Jimerson, Rose, jt. illus. see Tran, Danh.

Jimison, Erin. Ants in the Plants. Thomas, Michael. 2019. (ENG.). 26p. (J). pap. 9.95 ***(978-1-6883-4863-9(8))*** Independently Published.

Jin-Ho, Jung. Look Up! Jin-Ho, Jung. Kim, Mi Hyun, tr. from KOR. 2016. (ENG.). 32p. (J). (gr. -1-3). 16.95 *(978-0-8234-3652-1(7))* Holiday Hse., Inc.

Jin, Katherine. Sam & Nate. Collins, P. J. Sarah. 2005. 60p. (J). lib. bdg. 20.00 *(978-1-4242-1261-3(8))* Fitzgerald Bks.

—Sam & Nate, 1 vol. Collins, P. J. Sarah. 2005. (Orca Echoes Ser.). (ENG.). 64p. (J). (gr. 1-3). per. 6.95 *(978-1-55143-334-9(6))* Orca Bk. Pubs. USA.

Jin Song, Keum. Rice from Heaven: The Secret Mission to Feed North Koreans. Cho, Tina. 2018. (ENG.). 40p. (J). (gr. -1-3). 17.99 *(978-1-4998-0682-3(5))* Little Bee Books Inc.

Jin, Susie Lee. Mine! Jin, Susie Lee. 2016. (ENG.). 40p. (J). (gr. -1-3). 16.99 *(978-1-4814-2772-2(5)*, Simon & Schuster Bks. For Young Readers) Simon & Schuster Bks. For Young Readers.

Jinshan Painting Academy. We See the Moon. Kitze, Carrie A. l.t. ed. 2003. 32p. (J). (gr. -1-3). 16.95 *(978-0-9726244-0-4(6))* EMK Pr.

Jippes, Daan. Mickey Mouse: Darkenblot. Gray, Jonathan et al. 2017. (Mickey Mouse Ser.). 124p. (J). (gr. 4-7). pap. 12.99 *(978-1-63140-932-5(8))* Idea & Design Works, LLC.

Jirak, Tracey. Our Cool School Zoo Revue. Berthiaume, Donna M. 2008. 36p. pap. 24.95 *(978-1-60672-672-3(2))* America Star Bks.

Jirankova-Limbrick, Martina. Name That Dinosaur. Edwards, Amelia. 2009. (ENG.). 40p. (J). (gr. -1-3). 17.99 *(978-0-7636-3473-5(5))* Candlewick Pr.

JiSeung, Kook. Ouch! It Stings! JiSeung, Kook. rev. ed. 2014. (MySELF Bookshelf Ser.). (ENG.). 32p. (J). (gr. k-2). pap. 11.94 *(978-1-60357-653-6(3))*; lib. bdg. 25.27 *(978-1-59953-644-6(7))* Norwood Hse. Pr.

Jjmarkatt. If Our World Was White... Jjmarkatt. 2016. (If... Ser.: Vol. 1). (ENG.). (J). 17.99 *(978-0-9977181-0-2(2))*; pap. 9.99 *(978-0-9977181-7-1(X))* MonkeyMantra.

Jo, Eun-hwa. What Does the Bee See? Observation - Parts & Whole. Kim, Soo-hyeon. Cowley, Joy, ed. 2015. (Step up - Creative Thinking Ser.). (ENG.). 32p. (gr. -1-2). 26.65 *(978-1-925246-08-7(6))*; 26.65 *(978-1-925246-34-6(5))*; 7.99 *(978-1-925246-60-5(4))* ChoiceMaker Pty. Ltd., The AUS. (Big and SMALL). Dist: Lerner Publishing Group.

—What Does the Bee See? Observation - Parts & Whole. Kim, Soo-hyeon. 2015. (Step up — Creative Thinking Ser.). (ENG.). 32p. (J). (gr. -1-2). 5.00 *(978-1-925186-54-3(7)*, Big and SMALL) ChoiceMaker Pty. Ltd., The AUS. Dist: Lerner Publishing Group.

—What Does the Bee See? Observation - Parts & Whole. Kim, Soo-hyeon. Cowley, Joy, ed. 2015. (Step up — Creative Thinking Ser.). (ENG.). 32p. (J). (gr. -1-2). 10.00 *(978-1-925186-36-9(9)*, Big and SMALL) ChoiceMaker Pty. Ltd., The AUS. Dist: Lerner Publishing Group.

Jo, Hyeon-suk. Hansel & Gretel. Brothers Grimm. 2015. (World Classics Ser.). (ENG.). 32p. (J). (gr. k-4). pap. 5.00 *(978-1-925186-60-4(1)*, Big and SMALL) ChoiceMaker Pty. Ltd., The AUS. Dist: Lerner Publishing Group.

—Hansel & Gretel. Brothers Grimm. Cowley, Joy, ed. 2015. (World Classics Ser.). (ENG.). 32p. (gr. k-4). (J). 10.00 *(978-1-925186-66-6(0))*; 26.65 *(978-1-925246-14-8(0))*; 7.99 *(978-1-925246-66-7(3))*; 26.65 *(978-1-925246-40-7(X))* ChoiceMaker Pty. Ltd., The AUS. (Big and SMALL). Dist: Lerner Publishing Group.

Jo, Sinae. Song of the Mekong River: Vietnam. Choi, Na-mi. 2015. (Global Kids Storybooks Ser.). (ENG.). 32p. (J). (gr. 1-4). pap. 8.99 *(978-1-925233-44-5(8)*, Big and SMALL) ChoiceMaker Pty. Ltd., The AUS. Dist: Lerner Publishing Group.

—Song of the Mekong River: Vietnam. Choi, Na-mi. Cowley, Joy, ed. 2015. (Global Kids Storybooks Ser.). (ENG.). 32p. (gr. 1-4). 26.65 *(978-1-925246-01-8(9))*; 26.65 *(978-1-925246-27-8(2))*; 7.99 *(978-1-925246-53-7(1))* ChoiceMaker Pty. Ltd., The AUS. (Big and SMALL). Dist: Lerner Publishing Group.

Jo, Soo-Jin. What Can Tails Do? Tails. Ahn, Mi-yeon. 2017. (Science Storybooks Ser.). (ENG.). 32p. (J). (gr. k-4). lib. bdg. 27.99 *(978-1-925235-18-0(1)*, Big and SMALL) ChoiceMaker Pty. Ltd., The AUS. Dist: Lerner Publishing Group.

Joan, Dominique. Princess to the Rescue. Caldwell, Carol. 2nd ed. 2019. (Princess Claire Ser.: Vol. 1). (ENG.). 36p. (J). (gr. k-4). pap. 12.00 ***(978-0-578-57048-8(3))*** Touch of Color.

Joan, Pere. The Three Little Pigs/Los Tres Cerditos. Escardó i Bas, Mercè. 2006. (Bilingual Fairy Tales Ser.: BILI). (ENG.). 32p. (J). (gr. -1-7). pap. 6.99 *(978-0-8118-5064-3(1))* Chronicle Bks. LLC.

—Los Tres Cerditos. Escardo Bas, Mercè. 2003. (SPA.). 24p. *(978-84-246-1939-8(0)*, GL30510) La Galera, S.A. Editorial ESP. Dist: Lectorum Pubns., Inc.

Joane', E'nea. Momzilla, 1 vol. Keonna-E'nea. 2009. 18p. pap. 24.95 *(978-1-60749-607-6(0))* America Star Bks.

Joanna, Gniady. Mikolay & Julia: In the Attic. Magda, Olchawska. 2016. (Mikolay & Julia Adventures Ser.: Vol. 2). (ENG.). (J). (gr. 1-3). pap. *(978-83-946520-0-5(X))* Olchawska, Magdalena.

Joanna, Pasek. Halloween with Snowman Paul. Lapid, Yossi. 2018. (Snowman Paul Ser.: Vol. 6). (ENG.). 40p. (J). (gr. k-2). 24.99 *(978-1-949091-08-3(2))* Lapid, Yosef.

Joaquin, Javier. The Great Pasta Escape. Paul, Miranda. 2017. (ENG.). 40p. (J). (gr. -1-3). 17.99 *(978-1-4998-0480-5(6))* Little Bee Books Inc.

Jobe, Wesley J. Laughter Is a Child. Krupich, Leila. 2019. (ENG.). 82p. (J). pap. 8.99 ***(978-1-9822-2770-8(2)***, Balboa Pr.) Author Solutions, Inc.

Jobling, Curtis. The Skeleton in the Closet. Schertle, Alice. 2003. (ENG.). 32p. (J). (gr. 1-18). 15.99 *(978-0-688-17738-6(7))* HarperCollins Pubs.

Jobling, Curtis. My Daddy. Jobling, Curtis. 2007. (ENG.). 32p. (J). (gr. -1-k). 9.99 *(978-0-00-722164-6(9)*, HarperCollins Children's Bks.) HarperCollins Pubs. Ltd. GBR. Dist: Independent Pubs. Group.

Jocelyn, Drozda. Candy for Breakfast. Jocelyn, Drozda. 2018. (ENG.). 52p. (J). (gr. k-4). pap. *(978-1-988001-38-8(2))* Ahelia Publishing, Inc.

Jocelyn, Marthe. One Patch of Blue, 1 vol. 2019. (ENG.). 24p. (J). (gr. -1 — 1). bds. 9.95 *(978-1-4598-2073-9(8))* Orca Bk. Pubs. USA.

—One Yellow Ribbon, 1 vol. 2019. (ENG.). 24p. (J). (gr. -1 — 1). bds. 9.95 *(978-1-4598-2076-0(2))* Orca Bk. Pubs. USA.

—Time Is When. Gleick, Beth. 2008. 32p. (J). (gr. -1-2). 15.95 *(978-0-88776-870-5(9)*, Tundra Bks.) Tundra Bks. CAN. Dist: Penguin Random Hse. LLC.

Jocelyn, Marthe. A Day with Nellie. Jocelyn, Marthe. 2008. 16p. (J). (gr. k-k). 7.95 *(978-0-88776-869-9(5)*, Tundra Bks.) Tundra Bks. CAN. Dist: Penguin Random Hse. LLC.

—Sneaky Art: Crafty Surprises to Hide in Plain Sight. Jocelyn, Marthe. 2013. 64p. (J). (gr. 3-7). 12.99 *(978-0-7636-5648-5(8))* Candlewick Pr.

Jodie, Dias & Wendy, Watson. Lexi & Hippocrates: Find Trouble at the Olympics. Keen, Marian. 2014. (ENG.). 92p. pap. *(978-1-77141-026-7(4)*, Influence Publishing) Lean Marketing Pr.

Joe Kent. The Beginning of People's Chicken. Delena Deatherage. 2009. 40p. pap. 18.95 *(978-1-4208-9094-5(8))* AuthorHouse.

Joe, Michael. Duck & Rabbit - Superhero. Joe, Michael. 2019. (ENG.). 60p. (J). pap. 12.99 *(978-1-0990-8614-4(0))* Independently Published.

Joe, Staton, et al. Crossovers, Vol. 2. 2004. (Crossovers Ser.). 160p. (YA). pap. 9.95 *(978-1-59314-051-9(7))* CrossGeneration Comics, Inc.

Joelle Avelino, Joelle. The Power Book: What Is It, Who Has It & Why? Saunders, Claire et al. 2019. (ENG.). 64p. (J). (gr. 2-6). 19.99 ***(978-1-78240-927-4(0)***, Ivy Kids) Ivy Group, The GBR. Dist: Hachette Bk. Group.

Joey, Alfie. The Ghost Who Couldn't Scare. Wraith, Steve. 2018. (ENG.). 18p. (J). pap. *(978-1-910565-73-5(3))* Britain's Next Bestseller.

Joglekar, Devika. Cómo Se Hacen Las Almas: Mystical Journey of the Soul from the Land of Love. Sood, Roma Chadha. Gomez, Irene, tr. 2019. (How Souls Are Made Ser.: Vol. 2). (SPA.). 34p. (J). pap. 11.99 *(978-1-7989-9060-5(1))* Independently Published.

—A Dragon Princess Is Hatched. Farhad, Asad S. 2019. (Wonderful Adventures of Sheena, Shawn & Lili the Magical D Ser.: Vol. 1). (ENG.). 44p. (J). pap. 9.99 *(978-1-7969-2611-8(6))* Independently Published.

—Exploring Afghanistan: A Land Destroyed by Violence & Evil. Farhad, Asad S. 2019. (Wonderful Adventures of Sheena, Shawn & Lili the Magical D Ser.: Vol. 3). (ENG.). 62p. (J). pap. 13.00 *(978-1-7969-9552-7(5))* Independently Published.

—Herat, Afghanistan: The Land of Poetry, Literature & Antiquity. Farhad, Asad S. 2019. (Wonderful Adventures of Sheena, Shawn & Lili the Magical D Ser.: Vol. 4). (ENG.). 62p. (J). pap. 13.50 *(978-1-7969-9773-6(0))* Independently Published.

—Mazari-Sharif, Afghanistan: The Fountainhead of Wisdom. Farhad, Asad S. 2019. (Wonderful Adventures of Sheena, Shawn & Lili the Magical D Ser.: Vol. 6). (ENG.). 68p. (J). pap. 14.25 *(978-1-7974-0330-4(3))* Independently Published.

—Polly Pearl, Pirate Girl. McKinnis, Sara Conover. 2019. (ENG.). 36p. (J). pap. 12.00 *(978-0-578-51508-3(3))* Mot de Mere Publishing.

Joglekar, Devika. Until There Was You. Siebenaler, Sarina. 2019. (ENG.). 36p. (J). (gr. k-3). pap. 12.99 ***(978-0-578-60610-1(0))*** Siebenaler, Sarina.

Joglekar, Devika. Lilu Makes Diyas. Joglekar, Devika. 2019. (Lilu Ser.: Vol. 4). (ENG.). 50p. (J). pap. 12.99 ***(978-1-7014-1943-8(2))*** Independently Published.

Joglekar, Devika. Lilu's Rangoli. Joglekar, Devika. 2018. (Lilu Ser.: Vol. 3). (ENG.). 46p. (J). pap. 12.99 *(978-1-7292-9907-4(5))* Independently Published.

Joglekar, Devika. Mimi & Soni Discover Dussehra Legends. Joglekar, Devika. 2019. (Mimi & Soni Ser.: Vol. 3). (ENG.). 32p. (J). pap. 12.99 ***(978-1-6926-3052-2(0))*** Independently Published.

Joglekar, Mihir. Coming Round the Mountain: In the Year of Independence. Bond, Ruskin. 2019. (ENG.). 128p. (J). 9.99 ***(978-0-14-333356-2(9)***, Puffin) Penguin Bks. India PVT, Ltd IND. Dist: Independent Pubs. Group.

—Till the Clouds Roll By. Bond, Ruskin. 2017. (ENG.). 184p. (J). pap. 9.99 ***(978-0-14-344212-7(0)***, Puffin) Penguin Bks. India PVT, Ltd IND. Dist: Independent Pubs. Group.

Johannes, Holly. Kitty Cat Kind of Love. Johannes, Holly. 2020. (ENG.). 30p. (J). 16.99 ***(978-1-64538-111-2(0))***; pap. 10.99 ***(978-1-64538-110-5(2))*** Orange Hat Publishing.

Johannes, Shelley. Feelings Only I Know: Mom & Dad Are Getting Divorced. McKenna, Susan. 2007. 24p. (J). 14.95 *(978-0-9789965-0-5(X))* Wayfarer Pr., LLC.

—More Feelings Only I Know: Divorce & Fighting Are Hurting My Heart. McKenna, Susan. 2007. 24p. (J). 14.95 *(978-0-9789965-1-2(8))* Wayfarer Pr., LLC.

—Sleep Sweet, My Little One, 1 vol. Clairmont, Patsy. 2014. (ENG.). 24p. (J). bds. 12.99 *(978-1-4003-2401-9(7))* Nelson, Thomas Inc.

—Super Luke Faces His Bully: GiggleHeart Adventures #2. Cogswell, Jackie Chirco. 2011. 224p. (J). 14.99 *(978-0-9820490-2-0(1))*; pap. 9.99 *(978-0-9820490-1-3(3))* Divine Inspiration Publishing, LLC.

Johannes, Shelley. Beatrice Zinker, Upside down Thinker. Johannes, Shelley. 2017. (Beatrice Zinker, Upside down Thinker Ser.: 1). (ENG.). 160p. (J). (gr. 2-5). 14.99 *(978-1-4847-6738-2(1))* Hyperion Bks. for Children.

—Beatrice Zinker Upside down Thinker. Johannes, Shelley. 2018. (Beatrice Zinker, Upside down Thinker Ser.: 1). (ENG.). 160p. (J). (gr. 2-5). pap. 5.99 *(978-1-4847-6814-3(0))* Hyperion Bks. for Children.

—Incognito. Johannes, Shelley. 2018. (Beatrice Zinker, Upside down Thinker Ser.: 2). (ENG.). 224p. (J). (gr. 1-5). 14.99 *(978-1-4847-6739-9(X))*; (gr. 2-5). pap. 5.99 *(978-1-4847-6815-0(9))* Hyperion Bks. for Children.

—Sabotage. Johannes, Shelley. 2020. (Beatrice Zinker, Upside down Thinker Ser.: 3). (ENG.). 224p. (J). (gr. 1-5). 14.99 *(978-1-4847-6740-5(3))*; pap. 5.99 *(978-1-4847-6816-7(7))* Hyperion Bks. for Children.

Johannot, Tony, jt. illus. see Gavarni.

Johansen Newman, Barbara. Bones & the Apple Pie Mystery. Adler, David A. 2014. (Bones Ser.: 10). (ENG.). 32p. (J). (gr. 1-3). pap. 4.99 *(978-0-448-48231-6(2)*, Penguin Young Readers) Penguin Young Readers Group.

—Bones & the Big Yellow Mystery, No. 1. Adler, David A. 2008. (Bones Ser.: 1). (ENG.). 32p. (J). (gr. 1-3). mass mkt. 4.99 *(978-0-14-241042-4(X)*, Penguin Young Readers) Penguin Young Readers Group.

—Bones & the Clown Mix-Up Mystery, No. 8. Adler, David A. 2011. (Bones Ser.: 8). (ENG.). 32p. (J). (gr. 1-3). 4.99 *(978-0-14-241825-3(0)*, Penguin Young Readers) Penguin Young Readers Group.

—The Night Before the Tooth Fairy. Wing, Natasha. 2003. (Night Before Ser.). 32p. (J). (gr. -1-3). pap. 4.99 *(978-0-448-43252-6(8)*, Grosset & Dunlap) Penguin Young Readers Group.

Johansen, Tesia, jt. illus. see Johnson, Gary.

Johanson, Anna. There's a Frog Trapped in the Bathroom. Snyder, Susan. 2005. 23p. (J). (gr. 1-3). 9.95 *(978-0-9715411-0-8(8))* Kotzig Publishing, Inc.

—The Very Stubborn Centipede. Snyder, Susan. 2005. 24p. (J). (gr. 2-4). 9.95 *(978-0-9767163-0-3(5))* Kotzig Publishing, Inc.

Johansson, Anna. The Peaceable Forest: India's Tale of Kindness to Animals. Ely, Kosa. 2012. (ENG.). 32p. (gr. k). 16.99 *(978-1-60887-115-5(0))* Mandala Publishing.

Johansson, Cecilia. The Haunted Shipwreck. McKain, Kelly. 2004. (Mermaid Rock Ser.). 48p. (J). *(978-0-439-62647-7(1))* Scholastic, Inc.

—Just Like Mommy. 2006. (ENG.). 16p. (J). (gr. -1 — 1). bds. 7.99 *(978-1-4169-1218-7(5)*, Little Simon) Little Simon.

—Zoo (First Sticker Book) Taplin, Sam. ed. 2011. (First Sticker Book Ser.). 24p. (J). pap. 6.99 *(978-0-7945-2927-7(5)*, Usborne) EDC Publishing.

Johari, Sandeep. Karna: The Greatest Archer in the World. Sperling, Vatsala. 2007. (ENG.). 32p. (J). (gr. -1-6). 15.95 *(978-1-59143-073-5(9)*, Bear Cub Bks.) Bear & Co.

John & Wendy. Free the Worms! Krulik, Nancy. 2008. (Katie Kazoo, Switcheroo Ser.). 78p. (J). 11.65 *(978-0-7569-8807-4(1))* Perfection Learning Corp.

—Something's Fishy. Krulik, Nancy. 2008. (Katie Kazoo, Switcheroo Ser.). 76p. 14.00 *(978-0-7569-8348-2(7))* Perfection Learning Corp.

John and Gus art, John and. Collins Big Cat Phonics for Letters & Sounds - in the Fish Tank: Band 02A/Red A, Bd. 2A. Hawes, Alison. 2018. (Collins Big Cat Phonics Ser.). (ENG.). 16p. (J). (gr. -1-k). pap. 6.99 *(978-0-00-825142-0(8))* HarperCollins Pubs. Ltd. GBR. Dist: Independent Pubs. Group.

John and Wendy. Be Nice to Mice #20, No. 20. Krulik, Nancy. 2006. (Katie Kazoo, Switcheroo Ser.: 20). (ENG.). 80p. (J). (gr. 2-4). pap. 4.99 *(978-0-448-44132-0(2)*, Grosset & Dunlap) Penguin Young Readers Group.

—Cat Days. Andrews, Alexa. 2012. (Penguin Young Readers, Level 1 Ser.). (ENG.). 32p. (J). (gr. k-1). pap. 4.99 *(978-0-448-46305-6(9)*, Penguin Young Readers) Penguin Young Readers Group.

—A Collection of Katie: Books 1-4. Krulik, Nancy. 2012. (Katie Kazoo, Switcheroo Ser.). 320p. (J). (gr. 2-4). pap. 8.99 *(978-0-448-46304-9(0)*, Grosset & Dunlap) Penguin Young Readers Group.

—Girls Don't Have Cooties #4. Krulik, Nancy. 4th ed. 2005. (Katie Kazoo, Switcheroo Ser.: 4). (ENG.). 80p. (J). (gr. 2-4). mass mkt. 5.99 *(978-0-448-42705-8(2)*, Grosset & Dunlap) Penguin Young Readers Group.

—A Katie Kazoo Christmas: Super Super Special. Krulik, Nancy. 2005. (Katie Kazoo, Switcheroo Ser.). (ENG.). 240p. (J). (gr. 2-4). pap. 6.99 *(978-0-448-43970-9(0)*, Grosset & Dunlap) Penguin Young Readers Group.

—Love Stinks! #15. Krulik, Nancy. 2004. (Katie Kazoo, Switcheroo Ser.: 15). (ENG.). 80p. (J). (gr. 2-4). pap. 4.99 *(978-0-448-43640-1(X)*, Grosset & Dunlap) Penguin Young Readers Group.

—Something's Fishy #26, No. 26. Krulik, Nancy. 2007. (Katie Kazoo, Switcheroo Ser.: 26). (ENG.). 80p. (J). (gr. 2-4). 4.99 *(978-0-448-44442-0(9)*, Grosset & Dunlap) Penguin Young Readers Group.

—Who's Afraid of Fourth Grade? Super Special. Krulik, Nancy. 2004. (Katie Kazoo, Switcheroo Ser.: No. 1). (ENG.).

160p. (J). (gr. 2-4). mass mkt. 4.99 *(978-0-448-43555-8(1)*, Grosset & Dunlap) Penguin Young Readers Group.
—Witch Switch: Super Special. Krulik, Nancy. 2006. (Katie Kazoo, Switcheroo Ser.: No. 4). 160p. (J). (gr. 2-4). pap. 4.99 *(978-0-448-44330-0(9)*, Grosset & Dunlap) Penguin Young Readers Group.
John and Wendy Staff. Any Way You Slice It. Krulik, Nancy. 9th ed. 2003. (Katie Kazoo, Switcheroo Ser.: 9). 80p. (J). (gr. 2-4). pap. 4.99 *(978-0-448-43204-5(8)*, Grosset & Dunlap) Penguin Young Readers Group.
—Bad Rap. Krulik, Nancy. 2005. (Katie Kazoo, Switcheroo Ser.: 16). 80p. (J). (gr. 2-4). 16.19 *(978-0-448-43741-5(4))* Penguin Young Readers Group.
—Camp Rules! Krulik, Nancy. 2007. (Katie Kazoo, Switcheroo Ser.: No. 5). 160p. (J). (gr. 2-4). pap. 5.99 *(978-0-448-44542-7(5)*, Grosset & Dunlap) Penguin Young Readers Group.
—Doggone It! Krulik, Nancy. 8th ed. 2003. (Katie Kazoo, Switcheroo Ser.: 8). (ENG.). 76p. (J). (gr. 2-4). 16.19 *(978-0-448-43172-7(6))* Penguin Young Readers Group.
—Don't Be Such a Turkey! Krulik, Nancy. 2010. (Katie Kazoo, Switcheroo Ser.). 160p. (J). (gr. 2-4). pap. 5.99 *(978-0-448-45448-1(3)*, Grosset & Dunlap) Penguin Young Readers Group.
—Flower Power. Krulik, Nancy. 2008. (Katie Kazoo, Switcheroo Ser.: 27). 80p. (J). (gr. 2-4). pap. 4.99 *(978-0-448-44674-5(X)*, Grosset & Dunlap) Penguin Young Readers Group.
—Flower Power. Krulik, Nancy. 2008. (Katie Kazoo, Switcheroo Ser.). 78p. (gr. 2-5). 14.00 *(978-0-7569-8806-7(3))* Perfection Learning Corp.
—Friends for Never, 14 vols., 14. Krulik, Nancy. 2004. (Katie Kazoo, Switcheroo Ser.: 14). 80p. (J). (gr. 2-4). 16.19 *(978-0-448-43606-7(X))* Penguin Young Readers Group.
—Get Lost!, 6 vols. Krulik, Nancy. 6th ed. 2011. (Katie Kazoo, Switcheroo Ser.: 6). 80p. (J). (gr. 2-4). 16.19 *(978-0-448-43101-7(7))* Penguin Young Readers Group.
—Going Batty. Krulik, Nancy. 2009. (Katie Kazoo, Switcheroo Ser.: 32). 80p. (J). (gr. 2-4). pap. 4.99 *(978-0-448-45042-1(9)*, Grosset & Dunlap) Penguin Young Readers Group.
—Going Overboard! Krulik, Nancy. 2012. (Katie Kazoo, Switcheroo Ser.: No. 9). 144p. (J). (gr. 2-4). pap. 5.99 *(978-0-448-45681-2(8)*, Grosset & Dunlap) Penguin Young Readers Group.
—Gotcha! Gotcha Back! Krulik, Nancy. 2006. (Katie Kazoo, Switcheroo Ser.: 19). 80p. (J). (gr. 2-4). pap. 4.99 *(978-0-448-43768-2(6)*, Grosset & Dunlap) Penguin Young Readers Group.
—Hair Today, Gone Tomorrow!, 34 vols., No. 34. Krulik, Nancy. 2010. (Katie Kazoo, Switcheroo Ser.: 34). 80p. (J). (gr. 2-4). 16.19 *(978-0-448-45231-9(6))* Penguin Young Readers Group.
—Horsing Around. Krulik, Nancy. 2009. (Katie Kazoo, Switcheroo Ser.: 30). 80p. (J). (gr. 2-4). pap. 3.99 *(978-0-448-44677-6(4)*, Grosset & Dunlap) Penguin Young Readers Group.
—I Hate Rules! Krulik, Nancy. 5th ed. 2006. (Katie Kazoo, Switcheroo Ser.: 5). 80p. (J). (gr. 2-4). pap. 4.99 *(978-0-448-43100-0(9)*, Grosset & Dunlap) Penguin Young Readers Group.
—I'm Game!, No. 21. Krulik, Nancy. 2006. (Katie Kazoo, Switcheroo Ser.: 21). 80p. (J). (gr. 2-4). pap. 3.99 *(978-0-448-44133-7(0)*, Grosset & Dunlap) Penguin Young Readers Group.
—Major League Mess-Up. Krulik, Nancy. 2008. (Katie Kazoo, Switcheroo Ser.: 29). 80p. (J). (gr. 2-4). pap. 4.99 *(978-0-448-44676-9(6)*, Grosset & Dunlap) Penguin Young Readers Group.
—No Biz Like Show Biz. Krulik, Nancy. 2007. (Katie Kazoo, Switcheroo Ser.: 24). 80p. (J). (gr. 2-4). pap. 4.99 *(978-0-448-44440-6(2)*, Grosset & Dunlap) Penguin Young Readers Group.
—No Bones about It. Krulik, Nancy. 12th ed. 2004. (Katie Kazoo, Switcheroo Ser.: 12). 80p. (J). (gr. 2-4). pap. 3.99 *(978-0-448-43358-5(3)*, Grosset & Dunlap) Penguin Young Readers Group.
—Oh, Baby!, 3 vols., No. 3. Krulik, Nancy. 3rd ed. 2005. (Katie Kazoo, Switcheroo Ser.: 3). 80p. (J). (gr. 2-4). pap. 4.99 *(978-0-448-42704-1(4)*, Grosset & Dunlap) Penguin Young Readers Group.
—Quiet on the Set! Krulik, Nancy. 10th ed. 2003. (Katie Kazoo, Switcheroo Ser.: 10). 80p. (J). (gr. 2-4). pap. 4.99 *(978-0-448-43214-4(5)*, Grosset & Dunlap) Penguin Young Readers Group.
—Three Cheers For... Who? Krulik, Nancy. 2011. (Katie Kazoo, Switcheroo Ser.: 35). 80p. (J). (gr. 2-4). pap. 3.99 *(978-0-448-45449-8(1)*, Grosset & Dunlap) Penguin Young Readers Group.
—Tip-Top Tappin' Mom!, 31 vols. Krulik, Nancy. 2009. (Katie Kazoo, Switcheroo Ser.: 31). 80p. (J). (gr. 2-4). 17.44 *(978-0-448-45041-4(0))* Penguin Young Readers Group.
—A Whirlwind Vacation. Krulik, Nancy. 2005. (Katie Kazoo, Switcheroo Ser.: No. 2). 160p. (J). (gr. 2-4). mass mkt. 5.99 *(978-0-448-43748-4(1)*, Grosset & Dunlap) Penguin Young Readers Group.
—Write On! Krulik, Nancy. 2005. (Katie Kazoo, Switcheroo Ser.: 17). 80p. (J). (gr. 2-4). pap. 4.99 *(978-0-448-43742-2(2)*, Grosset & Dunlap) Penguin Young Readers Group.
John Bajet, John. Planting Seeds of Kindness: Padded Board Book. Bunting, Rose. 2018. (Love You Always Ser.). (ENG.). 18p. (J). (gr. -1-k). bds. 9.99 *(978-1-68052-180-1(2)*, 1001780) Cottage Door Pr.
John, Cathryn, jt. illus. see Welch, Jazmin.
John, Matthew. Las Rocas: Duras, Blandas, Lisas y Ásperas. Rosinsky, Natalie M. & Picture Window Books Staff. Robledo, Sol, tr. 2007. (Ciencia Asombrosa Ser.). (SPA.). 24p. (J). (gr. k-4). 27.32 *(978-1-4048-3225-1(4)*, Picture Window Bks.) Capstone.
—El Sonido: Fuerte, Suave, Alto y Bajo, 1 vol. Rosinsky, Natalie M. & Picture Window Books Staff. Robledo, Sol, tr. 2007. (Ciencia Asombrosa Ser.). (SPA.). 24p. (J). (gr. k-4). 27.32 *(978-1-4048-3229-9(7)*, Picture Window Bks.) Capstone.
—El Sonido: Fuerte, Suave, Alto y Bajo, 1 vol. Rosinsky, Natalie M. Robledo, Sol, tr. 2007. (Ciencia Asombrosa Ser.). (SPA.). 24p. (J). (gr. k-4). per. 8.19 *(978-1-4048-2493-5(6)*, Picture Window Bks.) Capstone.
John R Neill. Glinda of Oz. Baum, L. Frank. 2010. 144p. pap. 5.88 *(978-1-60386-310-0(9)*, Merchant Bks.) Rough Draft Printing.
John, Tom H. A Duck's Tail. Nigro, Rose. 2015. 48p. (J). 26.95 *(978-0-9860833-0-3(5))* Reeves Bay Press.
Johnathan, Kuehl. Deer Dad: Kampp Tales Outdoor Adventures. Reich, J. J. 2006. (BAT.). 32p. (J). *(978-0-9762971-0-9(8))* Outdoor Originals LLC.
—Snort, Wheeze, Rattle & Grunt: Kampp Tales Outdoor Adventures. Reich, J. J. 2006. 64p. (J). *(978-0-9762971-2-3(4))* Outdoor Originals LLC.
Johns, Dick. Sammy Squirrel & the Sunflower Seeds. Mayer, Marvin S. 2008. 73p. pap. 19.95 *(978-1-60672-193-3(3))* America Star Bks.
Johns, Melissa. Tabitha & the Raincloud. Sillett, Devon. 2020. (ENG.). 24p. (J). (gr. -1-3). 18.99 *(978-1-925820-13-3(0)*, 332025, EK Bks.) Exisle Publishing Pty Ltd. AUS. Dist: Hachette Bk. Group.
Johnson, Aaron C. Momma I Hate My Hair. Braxton, Theresa S. 2017. (ENG.). (J). (gr. k-3). 18.99 *(978-0-692-95780-6(4))* Braxton, Theresa.
Johnson, Adrian. There's a Wardrobe in My Monster! Geoghegan, Adrienne. 2003. (Picture Bks.). 32p. (J). (gr. -1-3). 15.95 *(978-1-57505-414-8(0)*, Carolrhoda Bks.) Lerner Publishing Group.
Johnson, Amber W. Sam the Walrus: A Grumpy Day to Play. Adams, Tonya. 2008. 28p. pap. 24.95 *(978-1-60672-861-1(X))* America Star Bks.
Johnson, Amy Koch. Little Big Wheels. Bradford, Elizabeth. 2018. (ENG.). 32p. (J). pap. 7.99 *(978-0-692-18388-5(4))* Bradford, Elizabeth.
Johnson, Amy Koch. Travel the Seven Continents of the World with Ollie & Mollie. Oliver, Betty. 2017. (ENG.). 44p. (J). pap. 10.00 ***(978-1-7199-6254-4(5))*** Independently Published.
—Travel to Egypt with Ollie & Mollie. Oliver, Betty. 2019. (ENG.). 42p. (J). pap. 12.00 ***(978-1-6877-9732-2(3))*** Independently Published.
Johnson, Andi. Ali in Egypt. Popper, Garry. 2004. 36p. (gr. -1-7). 4.00 *(978-1-84161-078-8(X))* Ravette Publishing, Ltd. GBR. Dist: Parkwest Pubns., Inc.
—Big World. Popper, Garry. 2004. 36p. (gr. -1-7). 4.00 *(978-1-84161-052-8(6))* Ravette Publishing, Ltd. GBR. Dist: Parkwest Pubns., Inc.
—Big World Activity Sticker Book. Popper, Garry & Volke, Gordon. 2004. 16p. 6.00 *(978-1-84161-082-5(8))* Ravette Publishing, Ltd. GBR. Dist: Parkwest Pubns., Inc.
—Billy Joe in the U. S. A. Popper, Garry. 2004. 36p. (gr. -1-7). 4.00 *(978-1-84161-053-5(4))* Ravette Publishing, Ltd. GBR. Dist: Parkwest Pubns., Inc.
—James & Jemma in Great Britain. Popper, Garry. 2004. 36p. (gr. -1-7). 4.00 *(978-1-84161-054-2(2))* Ravette Publishing, Ltd. GBR. Dist: Parkwest Pubns., Inc.
—Keito in Japan. Popper, Garry. 2004. 36p. (gr. -1-7). 4.00 *(978-1-84161-058-0(5))* Ravette Publishing, Ltd. GBR. Dist: Parkwest Pubns., Inc.
—Kez in Australia. Popper, Garry. 2004. 36p. (gr. -1-7). 4.00 *(978-1-84161-055-9(0))* Ravette Publishing, Ltd. GBR. Dist: Parkwest Pubns., Inc.
—Lena & Peter in Germany. Popper, Garry. 2004. 36p. (gr. -1-7). 4.00 *(978-1-84161-060-3(7))* Ravette Publishing, Ltd. GBR. Dist: Parkwest Pubns., Inc.
—Li & Lilly May in China. Popper, Garry. 2004. 36p. (gr. -1-7). 4.00 *(978-1-84161-057-3(7))* Ravette Publishing, Ltd. GBR. Dist: Parkwest Pubns., Inc.
—Mario in Italy. Popper, Garry. 2004. 36p. (gr. -1-7). 4.00 *(978-1-84161-059-7(3))* Ravette Publishing, Ltd. GBR. Dist: Parkwest Pubns., Inc.
—Mina in India. Popper, Garry. 2004. 36p. (gr. -1-7). 4.00 *(978-1-84161-079-5(8))* Ravette Publishing, Ltd. GBR. Dist: Parkwest Pubns., Inc.
—Paul in France. Popper, Garry. 2004. 36p. (gr. -1-7). 4.00 *(978-1-84161-056-6(9))* Ravette Publishing, Ltd. GBR. Dist: Parkwest Pubns., Inc.
—Winston in the Caribbean. Popper, Garry. 2004. 36p. (gr. -1-7). 4.00 *(978-1-84161-061-0(5))* Ravette Publishing, Ltd. GBR. Dist: Parkwest Pubns., Inc.
Johnson, Andrew. Alice in Verse the Lost Rhymes of Wonderland: The Lost Rhymes of Wonderland. Holden, J. T. 2011. (ENG.). 112p. (J). 14.99 *(978-0-9825089-9-2(9))* Candleshoe Bks.
Johnson, Anne M. My Name Is Sugar. Snyder, Stacy T. 2018. (My Name Is Sugar Ser.: Vol. 1). (ENG.). 32p. (J). 17.99 *(978-0-9600041-0-2(6))* Snyder, Stacy.
Johnson, Anne M. The Sugar Shack. Snyder, Stacy T. 2020. (ENG.). 36p. (J). (gr. k-4). 19.75 ***(978-0-9600041-3-3(0))*** Snyder, Stacy.
Johnson, Arden. Wherever Bears Be. Alderson, Sue Ann. 2003. 32p. (J). (gr. -1-3). 14.95 *(978-1-883672-77-5(5)*, Tricycle Pr.) Ten Speed Pr.
Johnson, Becca. Kindness in a Scary World. Hubbard, Rebecca. 2017. (ENG.). 50p. (J). (gr. 3-8). 14.95 *(978-0-9969426-9-0(6))* Titletown Publishing, LLC.
Johnson, Bee. En la Estación Espacial: Shine-A-light. Brown, Carron. 2019.Tr. of On the Space Station. (SPA.). (J). 12.99 *(978-1-61067-913-8(X))* Kane Miller.
—Space Station. Brown, Carron. 2016. (ENG.). 36p. (J). 12.99 *(978-1-61067-411-9(1))* Kane Miller.
Johnson, Beverly. Max Einstein: The Genius Experiment. Patterson, James & Grabenstein, Chris. 2018. 338p. (J). ***(978-0-316-45219-9(X)***, Jimmy Patterson) Little Brown & Co.
Johnson, Beverly. Max Einstein: Rebels with a Cause. Patterson, James & Grabenstein, Chris. 2019. (Max Einstein Ser.: 2). (ENG.). 320p. (J). (gr. 3-9). 14.99 *(978-0-316-48816-7(X)*, Jimmy Patterson) Little Brown & Co.
Johnson, Beverly. Max Einstein: Saves the Future. Patterson, James & Grabenstein, Chris. 2020. (Max Einstein Ser.: 3). (ENG.). 352p. (J). (gr. 3-9). 14.99 ***(978-0-316-48821-1(6)***, Jimmy Patterson) Little Brown & Co.
Johnson, Beverly. Max Einstein: the Genius Experiment. Patterson, James & Grabenstein, Chris. (Max Einstein Ser.: 1). (ENG.). (J). 2019. 368p. pap. 8.99 *(978-0-316-52397-4(6))*; 2018. 352p. (gr. 3-9). 14.99 *(978-0-316-52396-7(8))* Little Brown & Co. (Jimmy Patterson).
Johnson, Bill. Monster Cheese. Wolfson, Steve. 2013. 34p. pap. 10.95 *(978-0-9798324-3-7(8))* Argami Productions, LLC.
Johnson, Bob. The Lost Mine of the Mechanical Spider. Johnson, Bob. 2006. (Squatland Chronicles Ser.). 53p. (J). (gr. -1-3). per. 11.00 *(978-1-60002-185-5(9)*, 3977) Mountain Valley Publishing, LLC.
Johnson, Brandon. Life on Peavine Creek: Sam's Story. Bonner, Gayle. 2008. 33p. pap. 24.95 *(978-1-60610-624-2(4))* America Star Bks.
Johnson, Britt. Legend of the Blue Unicorn: Return of the Dragons, 3 vols. Johnson, Britt. Durant, Sybrina & Johnson, Sandi. I.t. ed. 2003. (ENG.). 25p. (J). (gr. k-5). spiral bd. 8.99 *(978-1-929063-93-2(8)*, 331) Moons & Stars Publishing For Children.
Johnson, Bruce. Hey Latrell, 1 vol. Benson, Linda Sue. 2009. 48p. pap. 16.95 *(978-1-60813-961-3(1))* America Star Bks.
Johnson, Bruce & Johnson, Meredith. A Day at the Zoo. 2012. 27p. (J). *(978-1-60115-595-5(6))* Treasure Bay, Inc.
—Zoo Day: Día Del Zoológico. McKay, Sindy & Canetti, Yanitzia. 2016. (SPA & ENG.). 41p. (J). *(978-1-4844-8058-8(9))* Treasure Bay, Inc.
Johnson, Bryant. Bone Wars: The Game of Ruthless Paleontology. 2005. (YA). 19.95 *(978-0-9770419-0-9(5))* Zygote Games LLC.
Johnson-Cadwell, Warwick. No 1 Car Spotter & the Firebird. Atinuke. ed. 2012. (Fiction Ser.). (ENG.). 112p. (J). pap. 4.99 *(978-1-61067-052-4(3))* Kane Miller.
Johnson, Carol Ann. The Heirloom. Folz, Alexandra. 2016. (ENG.). (J). (gr. 3-6). 24.95 *(978-0-9982769-1-5(X))*; pap. 15.95 *(978-0-9982769-0-8(1))* Feather Insight Pr.
—The Magic Shark Learns to Cook. Laird, Donivee Martin. 2004. 48p. (J). 9.95 *(978-1-57306-233-6(2))* Bess Pr., Inc.
Johnson, Catherine LeAnn. The Bus Trip, 1 vol. DeMico, Judy. 2010. 26p. pap. 24.95 *(978-1-4489-2767-8(6))* PublishAmerica, Inc.
Johnson, Cathy Ann. The Girls in the Circle. Scholastic, Inc. Staff & Giovanni, Nikki. 2004. (Just for You Ser.). (ENG.). 32p. pap. 3.99 *(978-0-439-56861-6(7)*, Teaching Resources) Scholastic, Inc.
—My Nana & Me. Smalls, Irene. 2012. (ENG.). 32p. (J). (gr. -1-2). pap. 9.99 *(978-1-62395-584-7(X))* Xist Publishing.
Johnson, Cathy Ann. What Is Light? Sheppard, Markette. 2020. (ENG.). 32p. (J). (gr. -1-3). 17.99 ***(978-1-5344-7651-6(2))*** Simon & Schuster, Inc.
Johnson, Celeste. T Is for Tortilla: A Southwestern Alphabet Book. Alpers, Jody. 2006. (J). (gr. -1-3). *(978-1-929115-14-3(8))* Azro Pr., Inc.
Johnson, Charles. The Adventures of Emery Jones, Boy Science Wonder: Bending Time. Johnson, Charles. Johnson, Elisheba. 2013. 110p. pap. 9.99 *(978-1-62015-181-5(2)*, Booktrope Editions) Booktrope.
Johnson, Charles Howard. Baron Trump's Marvellous Underground Journey. Lockwood, Ingersoll. Seale, Stephen E., ed. 2019. (ENG.). 208p. (J). pap. 8.99 *(978-1-0922-9134-7(2))* Independently Published.
—Baron Trump's Marvellous Underground Journey. Lockwood, Ingersoll. 2019. (ENG.). 260p. (J). pap. 13.00 *(978-1-7969-0624-0(7))* Independently Published.
—Baron Trump's Marvellous Underground Journey: Illustrated Facsimile of 1892 Edition. Lockwood, Ingersoll. 2019. (ENG.). 254p. (J). pap. 6.95 *(978-1-68422-343-5(1))* Martino Fine Bks.
—Baron Trump's Marvellous Underground Journey (Illustrated Edition) Lockwood, Ingersoll. 2018. (ENG.). 176p. (J). pap. *(978-1-4068-1858-1(5))* Echo Library.
Johnson, Chelsea. A House for Wally & Me. Stelten, Gene. 2009. 32p. (J). 13.95 *(978-1-935130-13-0(7))* Grateful Steps.
Johnson, Christy M. If I Ever Go to the Moon ... Kruse, Donald. 2018. (ENG.). 52p. (J). (gr. k-5). pap. 14.95 *(978-0-9985191-4-2(6))* Zaccheus Entertainment Co.
Johnson, Craig. Harry the Woodpecker's Search for a Home. Johnson, Joy. 2013. 28p. (J). pap. 9.95 *(978-0-9785191-7-9(5))* Orange Spot Publishing.
Johnson, Crockett. The Carrot Seed. Krauss, Ruth. 60th anniv. ed. 2004. (ENG.). 32p. (J). (gr. -1-3). lib. bdg. 17.89 *(978-0-06-023351-8(6)*, HarperCollins) HarperCollins Pubs. Ltd. GBR. Dist: HarperCollins Pubs.
—The Carrot Seed: 75th Anniversary. Krauss, Ruth. 60th anniv. ed. 2020. (ENG.). 32p. (J). (gr. -1-3). 16.99 *(978-0-06-023350-1(8))*; pap. 7.99 *(978-0-06-443210-8(6))* HarperCollins Pubs. Ltd. GBR. (HarperCollins). Dist: HarperCollins Pubs.
—The Carrot Seed Board Book: 75th Anniversary. Krauss, Ruth. 2020. (ENG.). 26p. (J). (gr. -1 — 1). bds. 6.99 *(978-0-694-00492-8(8)*, HarperFestival) HarperCollins Pubs.
—The Happy Egg. Krauss, Ruth. (ENG.). (J). (gr. -1-3). 2016. 40p. 14.99 *(978-0-06-243031-1(9))*; 2005. 32p. 12.99 *(978-0-06-076005-2(2))* HarperCollins Pubs.
—The Little Fish That Got Away. Cook, Bernadine. 64p. (J). (gr. -1-3). 2019. (ENG.). 16.99 *(978-0-06-243180-6(3))*; 2005. lib. bdg. 15.89 *(978-0-06-055714-0(1))* HarperCollins Pubs.
Johnson, Crockett. Harold & the Purple Crayon. Johnson, Crockett. 50th anniv. ed. 2015. (ENG.). 64p. (J). (gr. -1-3). pap. 7.99 *(978-0-06-443022-7(7))*; 17.99 *(978-0-06-022935-1(7))* HarperCollins Pubs. Ltd. GBR. (HarperCollins). Dist: HarperCollins Pubs.
—Harold & the Purple Crayon Board Book. Johnson, Crockett. 60th ed. 2015. (ENG.). 34p. (J). (gr. -1-3). bds. 7.99 *(978-0-06-208652-5(9)*, HarperFestival) HarperCollins Pubs.
—Harold & the Purple Crayon Lap Edition. Johnson, Crockett. 2016. (ENG.). 34p. (J). (gr. -1 — 1). pap. 12.99 *(978-0-06-242730-4(X)*, HarperFestival) HarperCollins Pubs.
—Harold at the North Pole. Johnson, Crockett. 2015. (ENG.). 48p. (J). (gr. -1-3). 16.99 *(978-0-06-242861-5(6))* HarperCollins Pubs.
—Harold at the North Pole Board Book. Johnson, Crockett. 2018. (ENG.). 34p. (J). (gr. -1 — 1). bds. 7.99 *(978-0-06-279697-4(6)*, HarperFestival) HarperCollins Pubs.
—Harold's ABC Board Book. Johnson, Crockett. 2015. (ENG.). 34p. (J). (gr. -1 — 1). bds. 7.99 *(978-0-06-242731-1(8)*, HarperFestival) HarperCollins Pubs.
—Harold's Imagination: 3 Adventures with the Purple Crayon. Johnson, Crockett. 2018. (ENG.). 208p. (J). (gr. -1-3). 19.99 *(978-0-06-283945-9(4))* HarperCollins Pubs.
—Harold's Treasure Hunt. Johnson, Crockett. 2020. 64p. (J). (gr. -1-3). 16.99 *(978-0-06-265531-8(0)*, HarperCollins) HarperCollins Pubs. Ltd. GBR. Dist: HarperCollins Pubs.
—Time for Spring. Johnson, Crockett. 2016. (ENG.). 40p. (J). (gr. -1-3). 14.99 *(978-0-06-243033-5(5))* HarperCollins Pubs.
—Will Spring Be Early? or Will Spring Be Late? Johnson, Crockett. 2016. (ENG.). 48p. (J). (gr. -1-3). 14.99 *(978-0-06-243037-3(8))* HarperCollins Pubs.
Johnson, Curtis, photos by. BrainerdBound: Landmarks to the Lakes. Rustad, Mark & Utter, Mark. 2004. 224p. (YA). 27.95 *(978-0-9726738-0-8(6))* Landmark Publishing Inc.
Johnson, D. B. Four Legs Bad, Two Legs Good! 2007. (J). *(978-1-4287-6423-1(2))* Houghton Mifflin Harcourt Publishing Co.
Johnson, D. B. Henry Hikes to Fitchburg. Johnson, D. B. 2006. (gr. -1-3). 16.95 *(978-0-7569-6798-7(8))* Perfection Learning Corp.
—Magritte's Marvelous Hat. Johnson, D. B. 2012. (ENG.). 32p. (J). (gr. -1-3). 17.99 *(978-0-547-55864-6(3)*, 1453619) Houghton Mifflin Harcourt Publishing Co.
Johnson, D. C. & Johnson, Darnell. Let's Be Friends. Johnson, D. C. & Turner, Sandra. 2007. (J). per. 9.95 *(978-1-933556-66-6(8))* Publishers' Graphics, L.L.C.
Johnson, Daniel. Monstrocities 2: Dream Factory. Somerville, Ethan. 2020. (Monstrocities Ser.: Vol. 2). (ENG.). 202p. (J). pap. 12.99 ***(978-1-6543-8783-9(5))*** Independently Published.
Johnson, Darnell, jt. illus. see Johnson, D. C.
Johnson, David. Call Me Marianne. Bryant, Jen. 2006. 32p. (J). (gr. 1-4). 16.00 *(978-0-8028-5242-7(4)*, Eerdmans Bks For Young Readers) Eerdmans, William B. Publishing Co.
—When No One Is Watching. Spinelli, Eileen. 2013. (ENG.). 26p. (J). 16.00 *(978-0-8028-5303-5(X)*, Eerdmans Bks For Young Readers) Eerdmans, William B. Publishing Co.
Johnson, David & Hurt, William. The Boy Who Drew Cats, 1 vol. Johnson, David. 2007. (Rabbit Ears-A Classic Tale Ser.). (ENG.). 36p. (J). (gr. 2-6). 28.50 *(978-1-59961-305-5(0)*, 12958, Picture Bk.) Spotlight.
Johnson, David A. Attack of the Turtle. Carlson, Drew. 2008. (ENG.). 157p. (YA). (gr. 4-6). pap. 22.44 *(978-0-8028-5338-7(2)*, Eerdmans Bks For Young Readers) Eerdmans, William B. Publishing Co.
Johnson, Deborah. Everyone Reads - BIG BOOK. Holden, Pam. 2016. 16p. (-1). *(978-1-77654-162-1(6)*, Red Rocket Readers) Flying Start Bks.
Johnson, Deborah C. Boo's Bad Day. Lockwood, Penny. 2013. 32p. pap. 11.99 *(978-0-9852661-5-8(5))* 4RV Pub.
—My Cat. Lopresti, Tony. 2012. 24p. pap. 13.99 *(978-0-9838018-6-3(X))* 4RV Pub.
Johnson, Dell. Rite of Passage. Peterson, Brandon. 2003. (Mystic Traveler Ser.: Vol. 1). 160p. (YA). (gr. 7-18). pap. 9.95 *(978-1-59314-015-1(0))* CrossGeneration Comics, Inc.
Johnson, Dirk. Purdue University Coloring & Activity Adventure Book. 2007. 52p. (J). pap. *(978-0-9790923-0-5(2))* DirkDesigns, LLC.
Johnson, Dolores. Entrepreneurial Kids' Books: Books That Inspire, Teach & Entertain, 4 vols. Linderman, Dianne. 128p. (J). 24.00 *(978-0-9704876-6-7(5))* First Mom's Club, The.
—My Cookie Business. Linderman, Dianne. 2005. 32p. (J). 8.95 *(978-0-9704876-0-5(6))* First Mom's Club, The.
—My Fishing Business. Linderman, Dianne. 2005. 32p. (J). 8.95 *(978-0-9704876-2-9(2))* First Mom's Club, The.
—My Pony Ride Business. Linderman, Dianne. 2005. 32p. (J). 8.95 *(978-0-9704876-1-2(4))* First Mom's Club, The.
Johnson, Dolores Uselman. Animal Adventures at the Farm. Rosie, Maura & Gavlik, Sherry. 32p. (J). 8.95 *(978-0-9764557-0-7(6))* First Mom's Club, The.
—Great American Pony Ride. Boyer, Melody. 32p. (J). 2.00 *(978-0-9704876-3-6(0))* First Mom's Club, The.
Johnson, Donna T. What God Has Made! Gibbons, Joyce. 2004. 36p. 24.95 *(978-1-4137-3566-6(5))* PublishAmerica, Inc.
Johnson, Drew. Infinities: A\New Hope, 1. Warner, Chris. 2011. (Star Wars: Infinites Ser.). (ENG.). 24p. (J). (gr. 6-12). 27.07 *(978-1-59961-845-6(1)*, 13811, Graphic Novels) Spotlight.
—A New Hope. Warner, Chris. 2011. (Star Wars: Infinites Ser.). (ENG.). 24p. (J). (gr. 6-12). Vol. 2. 27.07 *(978-1-59961-846-3(X)*, 13812); Vol. 3. 27.07 *(978-1-59961-847-0(8)*, 13813); Vol. 4. 27.07 *(978-1-59961-848-7(6)*, 13814) Spotlight. (Graphic Novels).
Johnson, Ds. Realms of Edenocht: Descendants & Heirs. Johnson, Ds. 2019. (Terroan Belt Ser.: Vol. 2). (ENG.). 430p. (YA). (gr. 7-12). pap. 15.99 *(978-1-7339333-0-8(1))* Horn, Jonathan.
Johnson, E. Harper. Clara Barton: Soldier of Mercy. Rose, Mary Catherine. 2011. 80p. 37.95 *(978-1-258-07364-0(1))* Literary Licensing, LLC.
Johnson, Earl L., photos by. The Best of the West, Vol. 6. Johnson, Earl L. Hawkins, Grace M., ed. 2005. (World's Greatest Working Trucks Ser.). 104p. (YA). (gr. 8-12). pap. 19.95 *(978-0-9649645-2-5(X))* Johnson, Earl Photography.

J

Johnson, Elijah. Little Edward Pumpernickel. Jordan, Pasquel. 2007. (J). *(978-0-9795586-0-3(3))* Journique Publishing Group, Inc.

Johnson, Elisha. The Gathering. Champion-Hamptom, Tamika. 2017. (Kamden Faith Journey Ser.: Vol. 2). (ENG.). (J). pap. 12.99 *(978-1-63199-470-8(0))* Energion Pubns.

Johnson, Elizabeth Crispina & Wanert, Amandine. In the Candle's Glow. Johnson, Elizabeth Crispina. l.t. ed. 2017. (ENG.). 32p. (J). 19.95 *(978-1-944967-09-3(5))* Ancient Faith Publishing.

Johnson, Emily. The Story of the Little Red Leaf. Johnson, Donna. l.t. ed. 2006. (ENG.). 22p. (J). 25.00 *(978-0-9778774-0-9(X))* Choice Point Editions.

Johnson, Eric. Phoebe's Sweater. Johnson, Joanna. 2010. (ENG.). 38p. (J). 18.95 *(978-0-578-04697-6(0))* Slate Falls Pr., LLC.

Johnson, Eyen. Tex the Explorer: Journey Around the Earth. Smith, Ellie. 2019. (Tex the Explorer Ser.: Vol. 2). (ENG.). 44p. (J). pap. 9.95 ***(978-1-7230-3414-5(2))*** CreateSpace Independent Publishing Platform.

Johnson, Fiona. Illustrated Dictionary of Chemistry. Wertheim, Jane et al. Rogers, Kirsteen, ed. 2008. (Illustrated Dictionaries Ser.). 128p. (YA). (gr. 7). pap. 12.99 *(978-0-7945-1560-7(6),* Usborne) EDC Publishing.

—Illustrated Dictionary of Physics. Stockley, Corinne et al. 2007. (Illustrated Dictionaries Ser.). 128p. (J). (gr. 4-7). pap. 12.99 *(978-0-7945-1561-4(4),* Usborne) EDC Publishing.

Johnson, Gary & Johansen, Tesia. The Christmas Secret. Johansen, Tesia. 2011. 28p. pap. 24.95 *(978-1-4626-3242-8(4))* America Star Bks.

Johnson, Gary M. The Adventures of MolarMan: Oral Health Bilingual (English/Spanish) Coloring Workbook. 2006. (ENG & SPA.). (J). *(978-0-9791794-1-9(6))* Johnson, Gary.

Johnson, Gary R. Deep in Alaska. Johnson, Christine. 2013. (ENG.). 42p. pap. 12.95 *(978-1-60223-215-0(6))* Univ. of Alaska Pr.

Johnson, Gee. Bald Eagles. Fleischer, Jayson. 2010. (2G Predator Animals Ser.). (ENG.). 32p. (J). (gr. k-2). pap. 8.00 *(978-1-61541-492-5(4))* American Reading Co.

Johnson, Gee. The Octopus. Johnson, Gee. 2010. (2G Marine Life Ser.). (ENG.). 20p. (J). (gr. k-2). pap. 9.60 *(978-1-61541-221-1(2))* American Reading Co.

—Polar Bears. Johnson, Gee. 2010. (1-3Y Marine Life Exploration Ser.). (ENG.). 16p. (J). (gr. k-2). pap. 8.00 *(978-1-61541-481-9(9))* American Reading Co.

Johnson, George Ann. Portraits of the Music Masters. Persons, Marjorie Kiel. l.t. ed. 2005. 102p. (J). per. 11.95 *(978-0-9675997-7-9(6))* Classical Magic, Inc.

Johnson, George Ann, jt. illus. see Nellis, Philip.

Johnson, Gillian. Bun Bun's Birthday. Scrimger, Richard. 2003. (ENG.). 24p. (J). (gr. -1-2). pap. 6.95 *(978-0-88776-637-4(4),* Tundra Bks.) Tundra Bks. CAN. Dist: Penguin Random Hse. LLC.

—The Cat & the Wizard. Lee, Dennis. 2013. (ENG.). 32p. (J). 15.99 *(978-1-4434-1175-2(2))* HarperCollins Pubs.

—Eugene's Story. Scrimger, Richard. 2003. 24p. (J). (gr. -1-2). 15.95 *(978-0-88776-544-5(0),* Tundra Bks.) Tundra Bks. CAN. Dist: Penguin Random Hse. LLC.

—James the Dancing Dog. Maybarduk, Linda. 2004. 24p. (J). (gr. -1-2). 15.95 *(978-0-88776-619-0(6),* Tundra Bks.) Tundra Bks. CAN. Dist: Penguin Random Hse. LLC.

—Melonhead. Kelly, Katy. (Melonhead Ser.: 1). (J). 2010. 240p. (gr. 3-7). 7.99 *(978-0-440-42187-0(X),* Yearling); 1. 2009. (ENG.). 224p. (gr. 4-6). lib. bdg. 22.44 *(978-0-385-90426-1(6),* Delacorte Pr.) Random Hse. Children's Bks.

—Melonhead & the Undercover Operation. Kelly, Katy. 2012. (Melonhead Ser.: 3). 256p. (J). (gr. 3-7). 7.99 *(978-0-375-84528-4(3),* Yearling) Random Hse. Children's Bks.

—Melonhead & the We-Fix-It Company. Kelly, Katy. 2014. (Melonhead Ser.: 5). 240p. (J). (gr. 3-7). 7.99 *(978-0-307-92970-9(1),* Yearling) Random Hse. Children's Bks.

Johnson, Gillian. Thora. Johnson, Gillian. 2003. 128p. *(978-0-207-19815-1(2))* HarperCollins Pubs. Australia.

—Thora & the Green Sea-Unicorn. Johnson, Gillian. 2005. 272p. *(978-0-207-20016-8(5))* HarperCollins Pubs. Australia.

Johnson, Gretchen. Gracie, the Glass Tree Frog. Sandusky, Thomas & Hill, Kathy. 2008. 24p. pap. 12.95 *(978-0-9820479-2-7(4))* Peppertree Pr., The.

—Peter the Poison Dart Frog, Stories of the Rainforest. Sandusky, Thomas & Hill, Kathy. 2011. 24p. pap. 12.95 *(978-1-936343-85-0(1))* Peppertree Pr., The.

—Spidy the Spider Monkey. Sandusky, Thomas & Hill, Kathy. 2009. 32p. pap. 12.95 *(978-0-9823002-5-1(5))* Peppertree Pr., The.

Johnson, Gwen. Diggin' the Big'un. Johnson, Gwen. Johnson, Carl. 2007. 16p. (YA). 14.95 *(978-0-9795860-1-9(1))* Fish Tales Publishing.

—Dreamland Friends. Johnson, Gwen. Johnson, Carl. 2007.Tr. of Amigos del Tierra del Sue#324;os. (ENG & SPA.). 18p. (J). 5.95 *(978-0-9795860-7-1(0))* Fish Tales Publishing.

Johnson, Hezekiah. Maya y Su Terapeuta Conductual. Thompkins, A. D. 2018. (SPA.). 48p. (J). pap. 11.00 *(978-0-692-13368-2(2))* Soothing Waterfalls Bks.

Johnson-Isaacs, Cally. Along Came a Fox. Deutsch, Georgiana. 2020. (ENG.). 32p. (J). (gr. -1-2). 17.99 ***(978-1-68010-226-0(5))*** Tiger Tales.

Johnson-Isaacs, Cally. Elephantantrum! Shields, Gillian. 2013. (ENG.). 32p. (J). (gr. -1-3). 14.99 *(978-1-58925-126-7(1))* Tiger Tales.

—Rabbits Don't Lay Eggs! Metcalf, Paula. 2016. (ENG.). 24p. (J). (gr. -1-k). bds. 9.99 *(978-1-4472-8277-8(9))* Pan Macmillan GBR. Dist: Independent Pubs. Group.

—With My Mummy. Brown, James. 2017. (ENG.). 32p. (J). (gr. -1-k). 19.99 *(978-1-5098-3439-6(7),* Macmillan Children's Bks.) Pan Macmillan GBR. Dist: Independent Pubs. Group.

Johnson, Jade. Someday Is Now: Clara Luper & the 1958 Oklahoma City Sit-Ins. Rhuday-Perkovich, Olugbemisola. 2018. (ENG.). 36p. (J). (gr. 1-4). 17.95 *(978-1-63322-498-8(8),* 301516, Seagrass) Quarto Publishing Group USA.

Johnson, Jake. Gingerbread Land. Grim, Katie. 2007. (ENG.). 24p. (J). (gr. 1-18). 19.95 *(978-1-58117-635-3(X),* Intervisual/Piggy Toes) Bendon, Inc.

Johnson, Jane. La Princesa y el Pintor. Johnson, Jane. 2003.Tr. of Princess & the Painter. (SPA.). 32p. (J). (gr. -1-3). pap. 14.95 *(978-1-56014-618-6(4),* SAN6184) Santillana USA Publishing Co., Inc.

Johnson, Jared. One Day at the North Pole. Hurst, Joshua. 2008. 44p. pap. 24.95 *(978-1-60703-327-1(5))* America Star Bks.

Johnson, Jay. Graduation Day. Denega, Danielle. 2007. (J). pap. *(978-0-439-90900-6(7))* Scholastic, Inc.

—My Santa Claus. Karr, Lily. 2012. (ENG.). 12p. (J). (gr. -1-k). bds. 4.99 *(978-0-545-43649-6(4))* Scholastic, Inc.

—Ten Little Pumpkins. 2012. (J). *(978-0-545-46862-6(0))* Scholastic, Inc.

—Ten Lucky Leprechauns. Heling, Kathryn & Hembrook, Deborah. 2013. (ENG.). 24p. (J). (gr. -1-k). pap. 3.99 *(978-0-545-43648-9(6),* Cartwheel Bks.) Scholastic, Inc.

Johnson, Jay B. Lots of Love. Fisch, Sarah & Bridwell, Norman. 2008. (J). *(978-0-545-02843-1(4))* Scholastic, Inc.

—My Easter Bunny! Karr, Lily. 2012. (ENG.). 12p. (J). (gr. -1-k). bds. 4.99 *(978-0-545-37117-9(1),* Cartwheel Bks.) Scholastic, Inc.

Johnson, Jeff, et al. The Dragon's Wake, Vol. 2. Dixon, Chuck. 2003. (Way of the Rat Ser.: Vol. 2). 160p. (YA). (gr. 7-18). pap. 15.95 *(978-1-931484-77-0(5))* CrossGeneration Comics, Inc.

—Haunted Zhumar, Vol. 3. Dixon, Chuck. 2004. (Way of the Rat Ser.: Vol. 3). 160p. (YA). pap. 15.95 *(978-1-59314-042-7(8))* CrossGeneration Comics, Inc.

—The Walls of Zhumar. Dixon, Chuck. 2003. (Way of the Rat Ser.: Vol. 1). 160p. (YA). (gr. 7-18). pap. 9.95 *(978-1-931484-51-0(1))* CrossGeneration Comics, Inc.

Johnson, Jerome A. The Mouse That Went to Find Christmas. Mitchell, Gloria. (J). pap. *(978-0-9706186-0-3(3))* Fourth Generation Pubs.

Johnson, Jill. Ben & Allie's Bible Adventures: New Testament. Ruff, Jerry & Saint Mary's Press Staff. 2017. (Ben & Allie's Bible Adventures Ser.). (ENG.). 18p. (J). (gr. -1 — 1). bds. 24.95 *(978-1-59982-900-5(2))* Saint Mary's Press of Minnesota.

—Ben & Allie's Bible Adventures: Old Testament Set. Ruff, Jerry & Saint Mary's Press Staff. 2017. (Ben & Allie's Bible Adventures Ser.). (ENG.). 18p. (J). (gr. -1 — 1). bds. 24.95 *(978-1-59982-899-2(5))* Saint Mary's Press of Minnesota.

Johnson, Jim. 4 - Dorp the Scottish Dragon Bk. 4: New York Christmas. Johnson, Sandi. Durant, Sybrina, ed. 2014. (Little Choo-Choo Bks.). 46p. (J). (gr. -1-6). pap. 14.99 *(978-1-929063-03-1(2),* 104) Moons & Stars Publishing For Children.

Johnson, Jim & Brundige, Britt. Book 4 - Dorp the Scottish Dragon. Durant, Sybrina, ed. 2019. (Dorp the Scottish Dragon Ser.: Vol. 4). (ENG.). 48p. (J). pap. 12.99 ***(978-1-6720-5994-7(1))*** Independently Published.

Johnson, Jim & Vignolo, Enrique. Whistle the Whale. McCarter, Robert. 2019. (ENG.). 30p. (J). pap. 12.99 ***(978-1-7109-7338-9(2))*** Independently Published.

Johnson, Jim, jt. illus. see Krittendon, Kim.

Johnson, Jim, jt. illus. see Trevino, Juan.

Johnson, John. Blue Wise. Douglas, Babette. 2006. (Kiss a Me Teacher Creature Stories Ser.). 62p. (J). (gr. -1-3). *(978-1-890343-07-1(2))* Kiss A Me Productions, Inc.

—Falcon Eddie. Douglas, Babette. 2006. (Kiss a Me Teacher Creature Stories Ser.). (J). (gr. -1-3). 9.99 *(978-1-890343-21-7(8))* Kiss A Me Productions, Inc.

—Larkspur: And His Wooden Nose. Douglas, Babette. 2006. (Kiss a Me Teacher Creature Stories Ser.). (J). (gr. -1-3). 9.99 *(978-1-890343-23-1(4))* Kiss A Me Productions, Inc.

—The Lyon Bear. Douglas, Babette. 2006. (Kiss a Me Teacher Creature Stories Ser.). (J). (gr. -1-3). 9.99 *(978-1-890343-18-7(8))* Kiss A Me Productions, Inc.

—Miss Evonne: And the Mice of Nice! Douglas, Babette. 2006. (Kiss a Me Teacher Creature Stories Ser.). (J). (gr. -1-3). 9.99 *(978-1-890343-19-4(6))* Kiss A Me Productions, Inc.

—Noreen: The Real King of the Jungle. Douglas, Babette. 2006. (Kiss a Me Teacher Creature Stories Ser.). 20p. (J). (gr. -1-3). 9.99 *(978-1-890343-25-5(0))* Kiss A Me Productions, Inc.

Johnson, Julius I. Tabby Gets Her Feelings Out. Johnson, Tabitha M. 2019. (ENG.). 30p. (J). pap. 9.99 ***(978-1-6701-9124-3(9))*** Independently Published.

Johnson, Karen. 52 Great Family Films. Gordon, Lynn. 2003. (52 Ser.: 52SE). (ENG.). 52p. (gr. 8-17). 6.95 *(978-0-8118-3630-2(4))* Chronicle Bks. LLC.

Johnson, Karen & Synarski, Susan. 52 Fun Things to Do in the Car. Gordon, Lynn. rev. ed. 2009. (ENG.). 54p. (J). (gr. -1-17). 6.95 *(978-0-8118-6371-1(9))* Chronicle Bks. LLC.

—52 Fun Things to Do on the Plane. Gordon, Lynn. rev. ed. 2009. (ENG.). 54p. (J). (gr. -1-17). 6.95 *(978-0-8118-6372-8(7))* Chronicle Bks. LLC.

Johnson, Karen, jt. illus. see Synarski, Susan.

Johnson, Katherine. The Adventures of Abuelito. Tait, Jackie. 2016. (ENG.). (J). pap. 12.99 *(978-0-9978612-9-7(0))* Mindstir Media.

Johnson, Kenny Ray. Charly's Adventure, 1 vol. Hughes, Donna L. 2009. 14p. pap. 24.95 *(978-1-4489-1822-5(7))* America Star Bks.

Johnson, Kim. Prom! The Complete Guide to a Truly Spectacular Night. Krulik, Nancy. 2003. 96p. (YA). 8.00 *(978-0-7567-9038-7(7))* DIANE Publishing Co.

Johnson, Kimberli Anne. My Grandma Mary. Webster, Raelyn & Rasmussen, Kenneth L. 2013. 38p. 22.95 *(978-1-940379-00-5(8))* Telling Family Tales.

Johnson, Kofi. Kleopatra. Muhammad, Joshua Leonard. 2018. (ENG.). 26p. (J). pap. 12.00 *(978-1-7917-6653-5(6))* Independently Published.

—Z-Man & the Right Choice Kids: Obey Your Parents. Smith, Delbert. 2018. (ENG.). 24p. (J). pap. 12.00 *(978-1-7240-2761-0(1))* Independently Published.

Johnson, Kris, photos by. Childsplay: A Collection of Scenes & Monologues for Children, 1 vol. Muir, Kerry. 2004. (Limelight Ser.). (ENG., 286p. (Orig.). (gr. -1-18). pap. 16.99 *(978-0-87910-188-6(1),* 0879101881, Limelight Editions) Leonard, Hal Corp.

Johnson, Larry. Alec's Primer. Walter, Mildred Pitts. 2005. (ENG.). 32p. (J). (gr. -1-3). 15.95 *(978-0-916718-20-6(4))* Vermont Folklife Ctr.

—Heinrich Melchior Muhlenberg. Hovland, Stephenie M. 2012. (Hero of Faith Ser.). (ENG.). 58p. (J). pap. 7.99 *(978-0-7586-3076-6(X))* Concordia Publishing Hse.

—Wilma Rudolph. Sherrow, Victoria. 2006. (Yo Solo Biografías Ser.). (ENG & SPA.). 48p. (J). (gr. 2-3). lib. bdg. 23.93 *(978-0-8225-6260-3(X),* Ediciones Lerner) Lerner Publishing Group.

—Wilma Rudolph. Sherrow, Victoria. Translations.com Staff, tr. 2006. (Yo Solo: Biografías (on My Own Biographies) Ser.). (SPA.). 48p. (gr. 2-4). pap. 6.95 *(978-0-8225-6623-6(0),* Ediciones Lerner) Lerner Publishing Group.

Johnson, Larry. The Reader. Johnson, Larry, ed. Ogletree, Chanelle. 2018. (ENG.). 42p. (J). (gr. 1-6). pap. 19.95 *(978-0-9961916-7-8(4))* Against All Oddz Publishing.

Johnson, Lauren. The Raggedy Beggar. Goyer, Deb. 2008. 19p. pap. 24.95 *(978-1-60703-698-2(3))* America Star Bks.

Johnson, Layne. Damon, Pythias, & the Test of Friendship. Bateman, Teresa. 2013. (AV2 Fiction Readalong Ser.: Vol. 62). (ENG.). (J). (gr. 3-7). 34.28 *(978-1-62127-874-0(3),* AV2 by Weigl) Weigl Pubs., Inc.

—The Declaration of Independence from A to Z, 1 vol. Osornio, Catherine L. 2010. (ABC Ser.). (ENG.). 32p. (J). (gr. 1-7). 16.99 *(978-1-58980-676-4(X),* Pelican Publishing) Arcadia Publishing.

—Farmer George Plants a Nation. Thomas, Peggy. (ENG.). 40p. (J). (gr. 4-7). 2013. pap. 8.95 *(978-1-62091-029-0(2));* 2008. 17.95 *(978-1-59078-460-0(X))* Boyds Mills Pr. (Calkins Creek).

—The Poppy Lady: Moina Belle Michael & Her Tribute to Veterans. Walsh, Barbara E. 2012. (ENG.). 40p. (J). (gr. 2-k). 17.99 *(978-1-59078-754-0(4),* Calkins Creek) Boyds Mills Pr.

—Voices of Pearl Harbor, 1 vol. Garland, Sherry. 2013. (Voices of History Ser.). (ENG.). 40p. (J). (gr. 3-3). 17.99 *(978-1-4556-1609-1(5),* Pelican Publishing) Arcadia Publishing.

Johnson, Maddie, photos by. How Tickles Saved Pickles: A True Story. Johnson, Maddie. 2018. (ENG., 40p. (J). (gr. -1-3). 17.99 *(978-1-5344-3662-6(6),* McElderry, Margaret K. Bks.) McElderry, Margaret K. Bks.

Johnson, Marcella. Kingdom's Reign, 4 bks. Black, Chuck. Black, Andrea & Black, Brittney, eds. 2004. 160p. (YA). per. 9.95 *(978-0-9679240-3-8(0))* Perfect Praise Publishing.

Johnson, Meredith. The Christmas Star. Raum, Elizabeth. 2005. (ENG.). 28p. (J). (gr. -1-k). bds. 7.95 *(978-0-8249-6620-1(1),* Ideal Pubns.) Worthy Publishing.

—Do Not Wake Jake. Willson, Sarah. 2006. (Step-By-Step Readers Ser.). (J). *(978-1-59939-059-8(0),* Reader's Digest Young Families, Inc.) Studio Fun International.

—Genevieve & the Moon. Ryan, Karlene Kay. 2013. 34p. pap. 9.99 *(978-0-9888843-3-5(X))* Ryan, Karlene Kay Author.

—Genevieve Goes to School. Ryan, Karlene Kay. 2013. 34p. pap. 9.99 *(978-0-9888843-2-8(1))* Ryan, Karlene Kay Author.

—Gigi, God's Little Princess, 1 vol. Walsh, Sheila. 2005. (Gigi, God's Little Princess Ser.: 1). (ENG.). 32p. 14.99 *(978-1-4003-0529-2(2))* Nelson, Thomas Inc.

—God's Little Princess Treasury, 1 vol. Walsh, Sheila. 2009. (ENG.). 128p. (gr. -1-2). 19.99 *(978-1-4003-1472-0(0))* Nelson, Thomas Inc.

—Ha! Ha! Halloween. Adams, Michelle Medlock. 2005. 30p. (J). (gr. 3-7). 12.95 *(978-0-8249-5508-3(0),* Ideal Pubns.) Worthy Publishing.

—The Hut in the Forest: A Tale about Being Kind to Animals. Lang, Andrew. 2006. (J). *(978-1-59939-083-3(3),* Reader's Digest Young Families, Inc.) Studio Fun International.

—Know & Follow Rules. Meiners, Cheri J. 2015. (Learning to Get Along® Ser.). (SPA.). 48p. (J). (gr. -1-3). pap. 12.45 *(978-1-57542-498-9(3))* Free Spirit Publishing, Inc.

—Los dos leemos-Fiebre de Beisbol: Nivel 1-2. McKay, Sindy. 2006. (We Both Read Ser.). (SPA.). 48p. (J). (gr. k-4). 7.99 *(978-1-891327-83-4(6))* Treasure Bay, Inc.

—Los dos leemos-Mi Dia. McKay, Sindy. Canetti, Yanitzia James, tr. 2006. (We Both Read Ser.). (SPA.). 48p. (J). (gr. -1-2). pap. 3.99 *(978-1-891327-76-6(3))* Treasure Bay, Inc.

—Los dos leemos-Mi Dia: Nivel K. McKay, Sindy. 2006. (We Both Read Ser.). (SPA.). 48p. (J). (gr. -1-2). 7.99 *(978-1-891327-75-9(5))* Treasure Bay, Inc.

—Meet Robert E. Lee. Pingry, Patricia A. 2004. (J). 9.95 *(978-0-8249-5465-9(3),* Ideal Pubns.) Worthy Publishing.

—Merrilee Mannerly & Her Magnificent Manners. Cashman, Mary & Whipple, Cynthia. 2010. (J). 16.99 *(978-0-615-36448-3(9))* Pink&Brown Publishing, LLP.

—The Missing Christmas Treasure. Sears, Gale. 2012. (J). *(978-1-60861-283-3(X))* Covenant Communications, Inc.

—On Easter Sunday. Pingry, Patricia A. 2007. (ENG.). 26p. (J). (gr. -1-3). bds. 6.99 *(978-0-8249-6692-8(9),* Ideal Pubns.) Worthy Publishing.

—We Both Read-A Pony Named Peanut. McKay, Sindy. 2008. (We Both Read Ser.). 44p. (J). (gr. 1-4). pap. 4.99 *(978-1-60115-016-5(4))* Treasure Bay, Inc.

—We Both Read Bilingual Edition-Museum Day/Dia Del Museo. McKay, Sindy. ed. 2015.Tr. of Dia Del Museo. (ENG & SPA.). 44p. (J). (gr. k-1). pap. 4.99 *(978-1-60115-064-6(4))* Treasure Bay, Inc.

—We Both Read Bilingual Edition-Too Many Cats/Demasiados Gatos. McKay, Sindy. ed. 2011. (ENG & SPA.). 44p. (J). pap. 4.99 *(978-1-60115-040-0(7))* Treasure Bay, Inc.

—We Both Read-My Car Trip. McKay, Sindy. 2005. (We Both Read Ser.). 48p. (J). (gr. -1-2). lib. bdg. 7.99 *(978-1-891327-63-6(1));* per. 4.99 *(978-1-891327-64-3(X))* Treasure Bay, Inc.

—We Both Read-My Town. McKay, Sindy. 2007. (We Both Read Ser.). 44p. (J). (gr. -1-2). 9.95 *(978-1-60115-001-1(6));* pap. 4.99 *(978-1-60115-002-8(4))* Treasure Bay, Inc.

—We Both Read-Oh No! We're Doing a Show! Ross, Dev. 2011. 44p. (J). 9.95 *(978-1-60115-255-8(8));* pap. 4.99 *(978-1-60115-256-5(6))* Treasure Bay, Inc.

—We Both Read-The Ruby Rose Show. McKay, Sindy. 2010. (We Both Read Ser.). 44p. (J). (gr. k-3). pap. 4.99 *(978-1-60115-246-6(9))* Treasure Bay, Inc.

—We Both Read-Too Many Cats. McKay, Sindy. (We Both Read Ser.). 44p. (J). (gr. k-3). 2005. (ENG.). 17.44 *(978-1-891327-49-0(6));* 2003. pap. 4.99 *(978-1-891327-50-6(X))* Treasure Bay, Inc.

—We Both Read-Zoo Day. Johnson, Bruce & McKay, Sindy. 2015. (We Both Read - Level 1 (Quality) Ser.). (ENG.). 44p. (J). (gr. k-2). pap. 4.99 *(978-1-60115-274-9(4))* Treasure Bay, Inc.

—We Read Phonics-A Day at the Zoo. Johnson, Bruce. 2012. 32p. (J). 9.95 *(978-1-60115-349-4(X));* pap. 4.99 *(978-1-60115-350-0(3))* Treasure Bay, Inc.

—We Read Phonics-If I Had a Snake. McGuire, Leslie. 2010. (We Read Phonics Ser.). 32p. (J). (gr. 1-5). 9.95 *(978-1-60115-333-3(3));* pap. 4.99 *(978-1-60115-334-0(1))* Treasure Bay, Inc.

—We Read Phonics-Magic Tricks. McKay, Sindy. 2011. (We Read Phonics Ser.). 32p. (J). (gr. 1-3). 9.95 *(978-1-60115-337-1(6));* pap. 4.99 *(978-1-60115-338-8(4))* Treasure Bay, Inc.

—We Read Phonics-Pat, Cat, & Rat. McKay, Sindy. 2010. 32p. (J). 9.95 *(978-1-60115-311-1(2));* pap. 4.99 *(978-1-60115-312-8(0))* Treasure Bay, Inc.

—We Read Phonics-the Garden Crew. McKay, Sindy. 2011. 32p. (J). 9.95 *(978-1-60115-345-6(7));* pap. 4.99 *(978-1-60115-346-3(5))* Treasure Bay, Inc.

—When Daddy Needs a Timeout. Pearce, Valarie. 2012. 28p. pap. 10.99 *(978-0-9843111-4-9(9))* ImaRa Publishing.

—When Mommy Needs a Timeout. Pearce, Valarie. 2012. 26p. pap. 10.99 *(978-0-9843111-5-6(7))* ImaRa Publishing.

—Will, God's Mighty Warrior, 1 vol. Walsh, Sheila. 2006. (Will, God's Mighty Warrior Ser.: 1). (ENG.). 32p. (gr. -1-3). 14.99 *(978-1-4003-0805-7(4))* Nelson, Thomas Inc.

—Zoo Day/Dia Del Zoologico: Spanish/English Bilingual Edition (We Both Read - Level 1) Johnson, Bruce & McKay, Sindy. 2016. (We Both Read - Level 1 Ser.). (ENG & SPA.). 41p. (J). pap. 4.99 *(978-1-60115-078-3(4))* Treasure Bay, Inc.

Johnson, Meredith. Meet Thomas Jefferson. Johnson, Meredith, ed. Pingry, Patricia A. 2003. 32p. (J). 9.95 *(978-0-8249-5459-8(9),* Ideal Pubns.) Worthy Publishing.

—Milo & the Flapjack Fiasco! Johnson, Meredith, ed. Jane, Pamela. 2004. 32p. (J). 13.95 *(978-1-59336-113-6(0));* pap. *(978-1-59336-114-3(9))* Mondo Publishing.

Johnson, Meredith, jt. illus. see Johnson, Bruce.

Johnson, Meredith, jt. illus. see McKay, Sindy.

Johnson, Michael. Workaholism: Getting a Life in the Killing Fields of Work. Johnson, Michael. Thorne, Paul. 2005. 138p. (YA). reprint ed. pap. 18.00 *(978-0-7567-9220-6(7))* DIANE Publishing Co.

Johnson, Michael J. Can I Play If I Have Fabry? Laney MS, Cgc Dawn Jacob. 2019. (ENG.). 44p. (J). pap. 13.59 ***(978-1-9779-3664-6(4))*** CreateSpace Independent Publishing Platform.

Johnson, Michael J. My Mom Has Pompe. Do You? Laney MS, Cg Dawn & Long MS, Cg Val. 2019. (ENG.). 28p. (J). pap. 13.99 *(978-1-0958-9651-8(2))* Independently Published.

Johnson, Michaela. Whispers of a Dragonfly. Walter, Lilly & Kunze, Candace Renee. 2018. (Ms. Ackermanes Teaching Ser.: Vol. 1). (ENG.). 38p. (J). pap. 19.99 *(978-1-9793-1249-3(4))* CreateSpace Independent Publishing Platform.

Johnson, Mike, et al. Kindergarten: Ages 5-6. Carder, Ken & LaRoy, Sue. 2005. 95p. (J). (gr. -1-3). pap. 12.99 incl. audio compact disk *(978-1-57583-818-2(4))* Twin Sisters IP, LLC.

Johnson, Milton. Little Fishes. Haugaard, Erik Christian. 2008. (J). (gr. 4-7). 23.00 *(978-0-8446-6245-9(3))* Smith, Peter Pub., Inc.

Johnson, Nancy Jo, photos by. Our Journey from Tibet. Dolphin, Laurie. 2006. 40p. (J). (gr. k-4). 16.00 *(978-0-7567-9812-3(4))* DIANE Publishing Co.

Johnson, Nick. Homophobia: Deal with It & Turn Prejudice into Pride, 1 vol. Solomon, Steven. (Lorimer Deal with It Ser.). (ENG.). 32p. (J). (gr. 4-9). 2016. 24.95 *(978-1-4594-0441-0(6),* d03723f6-4323-40c7-a06c-3d25b77b8668); 2013. pap. 12.95 *(978-1-4594-0442-7(4),* 0442) James Lorimer & Co. Ltd., Pubs. CAN. Dist: Lerner Publishing Group.

—Transphobia: Deal with It & Be a Gender Transcender. Skelton, J. Wallace. 2017. (Lorimer Deal with It Ser.). (ENG.). 32p. (J). (gr. 4-9). 22.65 *(978-1-4594-0766-4(0),* de500e8b-62c3-4a67-968e-14a9b05e2714) James Lorimer & Co. Ltd., Pubs. CAN. Dist: Lerner Publishing Group.

Johnson, Nikki. Agate: What Good Is a Moose? Dey, Joy M. 2007. 32p. (J). (gr. -1-3). 17.95 *(978-0-942235-73-9(8))* Lake Superior Publishing LLC.

—Nightlight. Anderson, Jeannine. 2004. 32p. (J). pap. 7.95 *(978-0-89317-057-8(7),* WW-0577); lib. bdg. 16.95 *(978-0-89317-056-1(9),* WW-0569) Finney Co., Inc. (Windward Publishing).

Johnson, Pamela. David & Goliath. 2015. (ENG.). 24p. pap. 6.50 *(978-1-84135-949-6(1))* Award Pubns. Ltd. GBR. Dist: Parkwest Pubns., Inc.

—Dinosaur Eggs. Dussling, Jennifer. 2012. (Penguin Young Readers: Level 3 Ser.). 48p. (J). (gr. 1-3). 16.19 *(978-0-448-42093-6(7))* Penguin Young Readers Group.

—Giant Squid: Mystery of the Deep. Dussling, Jennifer. 2004. (American Museum of Natural History Ser.). 48p. (gr. 1-3). 14.00 *(978-0-7569-1981-8(9))* Perfection Learning Corp.
—If You Lived When There Was Slavery in America. Kamma, Anne. 2004. (If You Lived Ser.). 63p. (J). 14.65 *(978-0-7569-3016-5(2))* Perfection Learning Corp.
—If You Lived When There Was Slavery in America. Kamma, Anne. 2004. (If You... Ser.). (ENG.). 64p. (J). (gr. 2-5). pap. 6.99 *(978-0-439-56706-0(8))* Scholastic, Inc.
—Jonah & the Whale. 2015. (ENG.). 24p. pap. 6.50 *(978-1-84135-950-2(5))* Award Pubns. Ltd. GBR. Dist: Parkwest Pubns., Inc.
—Joseph & His Brothers. 2015. (ENG.). 24p. pap. 6.50 *(978-1-84135-952-6(1))* Award Pubns. Ltd. GBR. Dist: Parkwest Pubns., Inc.
—Kenya's Song. Trice, Linda. 2013. 32p. (J). (gr. -1-3). pap. 7.95 *(978-1-57091-847-6(3))*; lib. bdg. 17.95 *(978-1-57091-846-9(5))* Charlesbridge Publishing, Inc.
—Polar Bears: In Danger. Edwards, Roberta. 2008. (All Aboard Science Reader Station Stop 2 Ser.). 48p. (J). (gr. 1-3). 16.19 *(978-0-448-44924-1(2))* Penguin Young Readers Group.
Johnson, Pamela & Squier, Robert. The Good Samaritan. Berendes, Mary. 2011. (Parables Ser.). (ENG.). 24p. (J). (gr. k-3). lib. bdg. 14.21 *(978-1-60954-391-4(2)*, 201186) Child's World, Inc., The.
Johnson, Pamela Ford. If You Lived at the Time of Squanto. Kamma, Anne. 2006. 63p. (J). pap. *(978-0-439-87628-5(1))* Scholastic, Inc.
Johnson, Pamela G. Outside My Window. Rappoport, Bernice. 2004. (Treasure Tree Ser.). 32p. (J). *(978-0-7166-1622-1(X))* World Bk., Inc.
Johnson, Patrick Henry. Feeling Great with Jasper State: Eat Your Green Things Every Day. Johnson, Judith Margaret. 2011. 32p. 14.95 *(978-0-9820228-5-6(9))* Jasper State Brand, Inc.
Johnson, Paul. Bible Story Hidden Pictures: Coloring & Activity Book. Fogle, Robin. 2006. 16p. (J). (gr. 1-5). 1.79 *(978-1-59317-160-5(9))* Warner Pr., Inc.
Johnson, Paul Brett. Jack Outwits the Giants. Johnson, Paul Brett, adapted by. 2008. (ENG.). 36p. (J). (gr. -1-3). 11.99 *(978-1-4169-7861-9(5)*, Simon & Schuster/Paula Wiseman Bks.) Simon & Schuster/Paula Wiseman Bks.
Johnson, Paul Brett. Fearless Jack. Johnson, Paul Brett. 2007. (ENG.). 32p. (J). (gr. -1-3). 10.99 *(978-1-4169-6833-7(4)*, Simon & Schuster/Paula Wiseman Bks.) Simon & Schuster/Paula Wiseman Bks.
Johnson, Penny. Here Comes Santa! 2016. (J). *(978-1-4351-6387-4(7))* Barnes & Noble, Inc.
Johnson, Regan. Kichi in Jungle Jeopardy. Guzman, Lila. (J). 2007. (ENG.). 135p. (gr. 2-7). pap. 8.95 *(978-0-9769417-2-9(4))*; 2006. 144p. 13.95 *(978-0-9769417-1-2(6))* Blooming Tree Pr.
Johnson, Regan. Hold on to Your Tail: Letters from Camp Lizard. Johnson, Regan. 2008. (Letters From Camp Lizard Ser.). (ENG.). 112p. (J). (gr. 1-5). pap. 7.95 *(978-1-933831-04-6(9))* Blooming Tree Pr.
—Little Bunny Kung Fu. Johnson, Regan. 2005. (ENG.). 32p. (J). (gr. -1 — 1). 14.95 *(978-0-9769417-8-1(3))* Blooming Tree Pr.
Johnson, Richard. A Is for Acadia: Mount Desert Island from A to Z. Grierson, Ruth. 2007. (ENG.). 32p. (J). 15.95 *(978-1-934031-03-2(8)*, ad5a2bed-0585-4a33-8918-dbcbc7cdedb1) Islandport Pr., Inc.
—Aesop's Fables. Pirotta, Saviour. 2020. (ENG.). 80p. (J). 19.99 *(978-0-7534-7640-6(1)*, 900226437, Kingfisher) Roaring Brook Pr.
—Don't Cry, Sly! 2004. 32p. (J). (SPA & ENG.). pap. *(978-1-85269-662-7(1))*; (ENG & POR.). pap. *(978-1-85269-659-7(1))*; (ENG & PER.). pap. *(978-1-85269-653-5(2))*; (ENG, ARA & BEN.). pap. *(978-1-85269-649-8(4))* Mantra Lingua.
—Don't Cry, Sly! Barkow, Henriette. 2004. 32p. (J). (ENG & CZE.). pap. *(978-1-85269-652-8(4))*; (ENG & CHI.). pap. *(978-1-85269-651-1(6))*; (GER & ENG.). pap. *(978-1-85269-655-9(9))*; (ENG & GUJ.). pap. *(978-1-85269-656-6(7))*; (ENG & ITA.). pap. *(978-1-85269-657-3(5))*; (ENG & PAN.). pap. *(978-1-85269-658-0(3))*; (ENG & BEN.). pap. *(978-1-85269-650-4(8))*; (ENG.). pap. *(978-1-85269-660-3(5))*; (ENG & SOM.). pap. *(978-1-85269-661-0(3))*; (ENG & TAM.). pap. *(978-1-85269-663-4(X))*; (ENG & TUR.). pap. *(978-1-85269-670-2(2))*; (ENG & URD.). pap. *(978-1-85269-671-9(0))*; (ENG & VIE.). pap. *(978-1-85269-672-6(9))*; (ENG & POL.). pap. *(978-1-85269-813-3(6))* Mantra Lingua.
—Don't Cry Sly: Big Book English Only. Barkaw, Henriette. 2004. (J). *(978-1-85269-999-4(X))* Mantra Lingua.
—Don't Cry, Sly! Ne Pleure Pas Sly! Barkow, Henriette. 2004. (ENG & FRE.). 32p. (J). pap. *(978-1-85269-654-2(0))* Mantra Lingua.
—Easter Egg Hunt. Wang, Margaret. 2005. (ENG.). 10p. (J). bds. 9.95 *(978-1-58117-375-8(X)*, Intervisual/Piggy Toes) Bendon, Inc.
—The Fourth Wise Man. Joslin, Mary. 2007. 28p. (J). (gr. -1-2). 14.99 *(978-0-7814-4545-0(0))* Cook, David C.
—The Giant Turnip. 2004. (J). 24p. *(978-1-85269-789-1(X))*; 24p. *(978-1-85269-749-5(0))*; 24p. *(978-1-85269-748-8(2))*; 24p. *(978-1-85269-747-1(4))*; 24p. *(978-1-85269-746-4(6))*; 24p. *(978-1-85269-745-7(8))*; 24p. *(978-1-85269-741-9(5))*; 24p. *(978-1-85269-740-2(7))*; 24p. *(978-1-85269-739-6(3))*; 24p. *(978-1-85269-736-5(9))*; 24p. *(978-1-85269-735-8(0))*; 24p. *(978-1-85269-733-4(4))*; (ENG & RUS.). 32p. pap. *(978-1-85269-788-4(1))* Mantra Lingua.
—The Giant Turnip. Barkow, Henriette. 2004. 32p. (J). (ENG & PAN.). pap. *(978-1-85269-742-6(3))*; (POL & ENG.). pap. *(978-1-85269-743-3(1))*; (ENG & POR.). pap. *(978-1-85269-744-0(X))*; (ENG & BEN.). pap. *(978-1-85269-734-1(2))*; (ENG & URD.). pap. *(978-1-85269-750-1(4))* Mantra Lingua.
—Giant Turnip. 2004. (J). E-Book incl. cd-rom *(978-1-84444-459-5(7))* Mantra Lingua.
—The Giant Turnip. 2nd ed. 2004. (PER.). 24p. (J). *(978-1-85269-737-2(7))* Mantra Lingua.
—The Giant Turnip: Le Navet Geant. Barkow, Henriette. 2004. (ENG & FRE.). 32p. (J). pap. *(978-1-85269-738-9(5))* Mantra Lingua.
—Giant Turnip - Big Book. Barkow, Henriette. 2004. (ENG & MAY.). 23p. (J). *(978-1-85269-896-6(9))* Mantra Lingua.
—It's Tu B'Shevat!, Vol. Zolkower, Edie Stoltz. 2005. (ENG.). 12p. (J). (gr. -1 — 1). bds. 5.95 *(978-1-58013-127-8(1)*, Kar-Ben Publishing) Lerner Publishing Group.
—Solar System. Shealy, Dennis R. 2018. (Little Golden Book Ser.). 24p. (J). (-k). 4.99 *(978-1-5247-6684-9(4)*, Golden Bks.) Random Hse. Children's Bks.
—Three Billy Goats Gruff. Barkow, Henriette. 2004. (J). (SER & ENG.). 24p. *(978-1-85269-620-7(6))*; (ENG & ALB.). 32p. pap. *(978-1-85269-611-5(7))*; (ARA & ENG.). 32p. pap. *(978-1-85269-612-2(5))*; (ENG & PER.). 32p. pap. *(978-1-85269-615-3(X))*; (FRE & ENG.). 32p. pap. *(978-1-85269-616-0(8))*; (ENG & GUJ.). 32p. pap. *(978-1-85269-617-7(6))*; (ENG & PAN.). 32p. pap. *(978-1-85269-618-4(4))*; (ENG & POR.). 32p. pap. *(978-1-85269-619-1(2))*; (ENG & SOM.). 32p. pap. *(978-1-85269-621-4(4))*; (ENG & SPA.). 32p. pap. *(978-1-85269-622-1(2))*; (ENG & TAM.). 32p. pap. *(978-1-85269-623-8(0))*; (ENG & TUR.). 32p. pap. *(978-1-85269-624-5(9))*; (ENG & URD.). 32p. pap. *(978-1-85269-625-2(7))*; (ENG & CZE.). 32p. pap. *(978-1-85269-627-6(3))*; (GER & ENG.). 32p. pap. *(978-1-85269-785-3(7))*; (ITA & ENG.). 32p. pap. *(978-1-85269-786-0(5))* Mantra Lingua.
—Three Billy Goats Gruff: English Big Book. Barkow, Henriette. 2004. (ENG.). 32p. (J). pap. *(978-1-85269-784-6(9))* Mantra Lingua.
—Three Little Pigs. (Flip-Up Fairy Tales Ser.). 24p. (J). 2007. (gr. -1-2). *(978-1-84643-087-9(9))*; 2005. pap. *(978-1-904550-21-1(5))* Child's Play International Ltd.
—Winter Shadow. Knight, Richard John & Walker, Richard. 2009. 80p. (J). (gr. 3-9). 16.99 *(978-1-84686-116-1(0))* Barefoot Bks., Inc.
—Winter Shadow. Knight, Richard. 2011. 80p. (J). (gr. 1-5). pap. 9.99 *(978-1-84686-624-1(3))* Barefoot Bks., Inc.
Johnson, Richard. Jack & the Beanstalk. Johnson, Richard, tr. 2004. 31p. (J). *(978-1-84444-108-2(3))* Mantra Lingua.
Johnson, Richard, jt. illus. see Barkow, Henriette.
Johnson, Robyn. The Enchanted Dolls' House Wedding. Johnson, Robyn. 2006. 28p. *(978-1-74178-090-1(X))* Five Mile Australia.
Johnson, Shane. Ninja Dad! (Teenage Mutant Ninja Turtles) Random House. 2016. (Step into Reading Ser.). (ENG.). 24p. (J). (gr. -1-1). 4.99 *(978-0-553-53937-0(X)*, Random Hse. Bks. for Young Readers) Random Hse. Children's Bks.
Johnson, Shane L. Cutetitos Sleepover Party! A Sticker & Activity Book. Reynolds, Daphne. 2020. (Cutetitos Ser.). 16p. (J). (gr. -1-1). pap. 7.99 ***(978-0-593-09631-4(2)***, Penguin Young Readers Licenses) Penguin Young Readers Group.
Johnson, Shane L. Fashion Face-off. Black, Allyson. 2011. (Scarlett & Crimson Ser.). (ENG.). 112p. (J). (gr. 3-7). pap. 6.99 *(978-1-4169-5937-3(8)*, Simon Spotlight) Simon Spotlight.
—Fingerlings: Let the Games Begin! a Sticker & Activity Book. Vitale, Brooke. 2019. (Fingerlings Ser.). 16p. (J). (gr. -1-1). pap. 7.99 *(978-1-5247-9215-2(2)*, Penguin Young Readers Licenses) Penguin Young Readers Group.
—The Lost Scrolls: Air. Mason, Tom & Danko, Dan. 2007. (Avatar, the Last Airbender: Lost Scrolls Ser.). (ENG.). 64p. (J). (gr. 2-4). 17.44 *(978-1-4169-1879-0(5))* Simon & Schuster, Inc.
—Meet the New Dragons. Testa, Maggie. ed. 2019. (How to Train Your Dragon: Hidden World Ser.). (ENG.). 16p. (J). (gr. -1-2). pap. 6.99 *(978-1-5344-3811-8(4)*, Simon Spotlight) Simon Spotlight.
—The Night Fury & the Light Fury. ed. 2019. (How to Train Your Dragon: Hidden World Ser.). (ENG.). 32p. (J). (gr. k-2). 17.99 *(978-1-5344-3835-4(1))*; pap. 4.99 *(978-1-5344-3834-7(3))* Simon Spotlight. (Simon Spotlight).
Johnson, Shane L., jt. illus. see Osterhold, Jared.
Johnson, Sharon. Spinman, Katydid & Bump: A Spider Vane Collection. Nash, Myrna Lee. 2003. 48p. (YA). (gr. 4-10). 11.95 *(978-0-9724549-0-2(X))* Chapter & Verse Pr.
Johnson, Staz. Dracula. Stoker, Bram. 2012. (ENG.). 144p. (gr. 6). pap. 16.95 *(978-1-906332-68-6(1))*; pap. 16.95 *(978-1-906332-67-9(3)*, Classical Comics, Ltd.) Classical Comics GBR. Dist: Publishers Group West (PGW).
—Special Forces. Brook, Henry. Frith, Alex, ed. 2014. (ENG.). 80p. (J). pap. 8.99 *(978-0-7945-3337-3(X)*, Usborne) EDC Publishing.
Johnson, Staz & Roots, Adrian. Spying. Brook, Henry. Frith, Alex, ed. 2014. (ENG.). 80p. (J). (gr. 4-7). pap. 8.99 *(978-0-7945-2809-6(0)*, Usborne) EDC Publishing.
Johnson, Ste. Wow! Look What Birds Can Do. de la Bedoyere, Camilla. 2020. (Wow! Ser.). (ENG.). 32p. (J). 15.99 *(978-0-7534-7566-9(9)*, 900219367); pap. 8.99 *(978-0-7534-7567-6(7)*, 900219368) Roaring Brook Pr. (Kingfisher).
—Wow! Look What Bugs Can Do! de la Bedoyere, Camilla. 2019. (Wow! Ser.). (ENG.). 32p. (J). 15.99 *(978-0-7534-7515-7(4)*, 900207579); pap. 8.99 *(978-0-7534-7516-4(2)*, 900207580) Roaring Brook Pr. (Kingfisher).
—Wow! Look What Dinosaurs Could Do! McCann, Jacqueline. 2019. (Wow! Ser.). (ENG.). 32p. (J). 15.99 *(978-0-7534-7453-2(0)*, 900191859); pap. 8.99 *(978-0-7534-7454-9(9)*, 900191860) Roaring Brook Pr. (Kingfisher).
—Wow! Look What Vehicles Can Do! McCann, Jacqueline. 2019. (Wow! Ser.). (ENG.). 32p. (J). 15.99 *(978-0-7534-7451-8(4)*, 900191854); pap. 8.99 *(978-0-7534-7452-5(2)*, 900191855) Roaring Brook Pr. (Kingfisher).
—Wow! Look What's in Space! Stott, Carole. 2020. (Wow! Ser.). (ENG.). 32p. (J). 15.99 *(978-0-7534-7549-2(9)*, 900211455); pap. 8.99 *(978-0-7534-7550-8(2)*, 900211456) Roaring Brook Pr. (Kingfisher).
—Wow! Look What's in the Oceans. de la Bedoyere, Camilla. 2019. (Wow! Ser.). (ENG.). 32p. (J). 15.99 *(978-0-7534-7517-1(0)*, 900207581); pap. 8.99 *(978-0-7534-7518-8(9)*, 900207582) Roaring Brook Pr. (Kingfisher).
Johnson, Stephen T. Alphabet School. Johnson, Stephen T. 2015. (ENG.). 32p. (J). (gr. -1-3). 17.99 *(978-1-4169-2521-7(X)*, Simon & Schuster Bks. For Young Readers) Simon & Schuster Bks. For Young Readers.
—City by Numbers. Johnson, Stephen T. Johnson, Stephen. 2003. (ENG.). 32p. (J). (gr. k-3). 7.99 *(978-0-14-056636-9(8)*, Puffin Books) Penguin Young Readers Group.
—My Little Blue Robot. Johnson, Stephen T. 2012. (ENG.). 16p. (J). (gr. -1-3). 19.99 *(978-1-4424-5416-3(4)*, Simon & Schuster/Paula Wiseman Bks.) Simon & Schuster/Paula Wiseman Bks.
—My Little Pink Princess Purse. Johnson, Stephen T. 2010. (ENG.). 16p. (J). (gr. -1-3). 19.99 *(978-1-4169-7979-1(4)*, Simon & Schuster/Paula Wiseman Bks.) Simon & Schuster/Paula Wiseman Bks.
—My Little Red Fire Truck. Johnson, Stephen T. 2009. (ENG.). 16p. (J). (gr. -1-2). 29.99 *(978-1-4169-2522-4(8)*, Simon & Schuster/Paula Wiseman Bks.) Simon & Schuster/Paula Wiseman Bks.
Johnson, Steve. The Frog Prince. Scieszka, Jon. 2014. 32p. pap. 7.00 *(978-1-61003-314-5(0))* Center for the Collaborative Classroom.
—The Frog Prince, Continued. Scieszka, Jon. 2003. pap. 39.95 incl. audio compact disk *(978-1-59112-522-8(7))* Live Oak Media.
Johnson, Steve & Fancher, Lou. Amazing Peace: A Christmas Poem, 1 vol. Angelou, Maya. 2008. (ENG.). 40p. (J). (gr. -1-3). 18.99 *(978-0-375-84150-7(4)*, Schwartz & Wade Bks.) Random Hse. Children's Bks.
—A Boy Named FDR: How Franklin D. Roosevelt Grew up to Change America. Krull, Kathleen. 48p. (J). (gr. 1-4). 2016. 7.99 *(978-1-101-93251-3(1)*, Dragonfly Bks.); 2010. 17.99 *(978-0-375-85716-4(8)*, Knopf Bks. for Young Readers) Random Hse. Children's Bks.
—The Boy on Fairfield Street: How Ted Geisel Grew up to Become Dr. Seuss. Krull, Kathleen. 2010. 48p. (J). (gr. k-4). pap. 7.99 *(978-0-375-85550-4(5)*, Dragonfly Bks.) Random Hse. Children's Bks.
—Bugtown Boogie. Hanson, Warren. 2008. 32p. (J). (gr. -1-3). 17.89 *(978-0-06-059938-6(3)*, Geringer, Laura Book) HarperCollins Pubs.
—Casey Back at Bat. Gutman, Dan. 2009. (ENG.). 32p. (J). (gr. -1-3). pap. 7.99 *(978-0-06-056027-0(4))* HarperCollins Pubs.
—The Cheese. Palatini, Margie. 2007. (ENG.). 32p. (J). (gr. -1-2). 17.99 *(978-0-06-052630-6(0)*, Tegen, Katherine Bks) HarperCollins Pubs.
—Dr. Seuss: The Great Doodler. Klimo, Kate. 2016. (Step into Reading Ser.). 48p. (J). (gr. k-3). 12.99 *(978-1-101-93551-4(0)*, Random Hse. Bks. for Young Readers) Random Hse. Children's Bks.
—Good Morning, Snowplow! Bruss, Deborah. 2018. (ENG.). 32p. (J). (gr. -1 — 1). 17.99 *(978-1-338-08949-3(8)*, Levine, Arthur A. Bks.) Scholastic, Inc.
—It's Milking Time. Alsdurf, Phyllis. 2019. (ENG.). 32p. (J). 16.95 *(978-1-68134-139-2(5))* Minnesota Historical Society Pr.
—The King's Taster. Oppel, Kenneth. 2009. (ENG.). 32p. (J). (gr. -1-1). 17.99 *(978-0-06-075372-6(2))* HarperCollins Pubs.
—New York's Bravest. Osborne, Mary Pope & National Geographic Learning Staff. 2006. (ENG.). 32p. (J). (gr. -1-2). 7.99 *(978-0-375-83841-5(4)*, Dragonfly Bks.) Random Hse. Children's Bks.
—No Star Nights. Smucker, Anna. 2012. 40p. (J). pap. 8.95 *(978-1-891852-82-4(5))* Quarrier Pr.
—A Poem for Peter: The Story of Ezra Jack Keats & the Creation of the Snowy Day. Pinkney, Andrea Davis & Wells, Rosemary. 2016. 60p. (J). (gr. 2-5). bds. 18.99 *(978-0-425-28768-2(8)*, Viking Books for Young Readers) Penguin Young Readers Group.
—Shh! Bears Sleeping. Martin, David. 2017. 28p. (J). (-k). bds. 8.99 *(978-0-425-29179-5(0)*, Viking Books for Young Readers) Penguin Young Readers Group.
—A Special Gift for Grammy. George, Jean Craighead. 2013. (ENG.). 32p. (J). (gr. -1-3). 17.99 *(978-0-06-053176-8(2))* HarperCollins Pubs.
Johnson, Steve, jt. illus. see Fancher, Lou.
Johnson, Steven. Chuckles & Boomerang. Massey, Stephen. 2018. (Chuckles & Boomerang Ser.: Vol. 1). (ENG.). 58p. (J). pap. *(978-1-7752964-0-9(7))* Massey, Stephen.
—Miss Gorilla Lost Her Keys. Taylor, Miya. 2018. (Miss Gorilla & Friends Ser.: Vol. 1). (ENG.). 38p. (J). pap. *(978-1-7752963-0-0(X))* Taylor, Miya.
Johnson, Sue, jt. illus. see Honey, Elizabeth.
Johnson, Tamaris. Seaweed, the Purrfect Cat. Williams, Lee. 2013. 36p. (J). 9.99 *(978-1-937493-47-9(4))* Dancing Moon Pr.
—Twin Dragons. Williams, Lee. 2012. 32p. (J). 8.99 *(978-1-937493-18-9(0))* Dancing Moon Pr.
Johnson, Taryn. TinkerActive Workbooks: Kindergarten Science. Butler, Megan Hewes & Odd Dot. 2019. (TinkerActive Workbooks Ser.: 4). (ENG.). 128p. (J). pap. 12.99 *(978-1-250-30724-8(4)*, 900197987, Odd Dot) St. Martin's Pr.
Johnson, Tucker. All Hallows' Eve: The Story of the Halloween Fairy. Johnson, Lisa. l.t. ed. 2005. 32p. (J). 12.95 *(978-0-9773096-0-3(6))* Positive Spin Pr.
Johnson, Vickie. Time for Bed - The Secret of Shadows: Shadow Theater Inside. Allen, Lisa & Sharp, Julis. 26p. (J). (gr. -1-2). pap. *(978-1-56021-355-0(8)*, 206) W.J. Fantasy, Inc.
—The Troll of MacKinac. Thome, K. C. 2010. 32p. pap. 13.00 *(978-1-60911-178-6(8)*, Eloquent Bks.) Strategic Book Publishing & Rights Agency (SBPRA).
Johnson, Virginia. Don't, 1 vol. 2014. (ENG.). 24p. (J). (— 1). bds. 9.95 *(978-1-55498-355-1(X))* Groundwood Bks. CAN. Dist: Publishers Group West (PGW).
—This New Baby, 1 vol. Jam, Teddy. 2011. (ENG.). 22p. (J). (gr. k — 1). bds. 8.95 *(978-1-55498-088-8(7))* Groundwood Bks. CAN. Dist: Publishers Group West (PGW).
Johnston, Claire. Everyone Is Special. Anderson, Cori. 2018. (ENG.). 28p. (J). pap. 12.95 *(978-1-7297-6704-7(4))* CreateSpace Independent Publishing Platform.
Johnston, Jenna. Pick a Pup. O'Neill, Juliana. 2020. (Reading Stars Ser.). (ENG.). 24p. (J). (gr. k-2). 12.99 *(978-1-5324-1561-6(3))*; pap. 12.99 *(978-1-5324-1560-9(5))* Xist Publishing.
Johnston, Jillian S. In That Land There Are Giants. Powell, Gary Allison. 2011. 38p. pap. 14.50 *(978-1-60860-891-1(3)*, Eloquent Bks.) Strategic Book Publishing & Rights Agency (SBPRA).
Johnston, Joe. Snag & Me - Christmas Miracle in Blanchard Forks. Johnston, Joe. 2004. (YA). per. 10.00 *(978-1-932496-15-4(7))* Penman Publishing, Inc.
Johnston, Lisa Harp. Mason's Mashed Potato Tree. Waszak, Madonna. 2011. 34p. pap. 14.95 *(978-1-4575-0159-3(7))* Dog Ear Publishing, LLC.
Johnston, Nicky. At the End of Holyrood Lane. Powell, Dimity. (ENG.). 32p. (J). (gr. -1-3). 2018. 17.99 *(978-1-925335-76-7(3)*, 321861); 2nd ed. 2020. pap. 15.99 *(978-1-925820-45-4(9))* Exisle Publishing Pty Ltd. AUS. (EK Bks.). Dist: Hachette UK Distribution, Hachette Bk. Group.
—The Fix-It Man. Powell, Dimity. 2017. (ENG.). 32p. (J). (gr. -1-3). 17.99 *(978-1-925335-34-7(8)*, EK Bks.) Exisle Publishing Pty Ltd. AUS. Dist: Hachette Bk. Group.
—Grandma Forgets. Russell, Paul. 2017. (ENG.). 24p. (J). (gr. -1-3). 17.99 *(978-1-925335-47-7(X)*, EK Bks.) Exisle Publishing Pty Ltd. AUS. Dist: Hachette Bk. Group.
—Saying Goodbye to Barkley. Sillett, Devon. 2nd ed. 2020. (ENG.). 32p. (J). (gr. -1-3). pap. 14.99 *(978-1-925820-44-7(0)*, EK Bks.) Exisle Publishing Pty Ltd. AUS. Dist: Hachette Bk. Group.
Johnston, Phillip. Nathan Meets His Monsters. Kropp, Joseph P. 2012. 34p. 16.95 *(978-1-890905-59-0(3))*; pap. 9.95 *(978-1-890905-58-3(5))* Day to Day Enterprises.
Johnstone, Anna. Regular Show: 25 Years Later. Hastings, Christopher. 2019. (Regular Show Ser.). (ENG.). 160p. (J). pap. 19.99 *(978-1-68415-375-6(1))* Boom! Studios.
Johnstone, Anne Grahame. The Water Babies. Kingsley, Charles. 2012. (ENG.). 32p. 9.95 *(978-1-84135-236-7(5))* Award Pubns. Ltd. GBR. Dist: Parkwest Pubns., Inc.
Johnstone, Matt. Curious Constructions: A Peculiar Portfolio of Fifty Fascinating Structures. Hearst, Michael. 2017. (ENG.). 112p. (J). 19.99 *(978-1-4521-4484-9(2))* Chronicle Bks. LLC.
Johri, Shaan Mohammad. The Snackman & His Son, 1 vol. Johri, Subia Ali. 2010. 28p. 24.95 *(978-1-4512-0978-5(9))* America Star Bks.
Joiner, D. Wayne, Sr. Dudley Gloworm & the Saving Light. Joiner, D. Wayne, Sr. 2006. (J). 25.00 *(978-0-9785103-0-5(5))* Willy Waw wees, LLC.
Jok. Vampires & Cells. Biskup, Agnieszka. 2011. (Monster Science Ser.). (ENG.). 32p. (gr. 3-4). pap. 47.70 *(978-1-4296-7332-7(X)*, Capstone Pr.) Capstone.
—Zombies & Electricity, 6 vols. Weakland, Mark. 2013. (Monster Science Ser.). (ENG.). 32p. (gr. 3-4). 47.70 *(978-1-62065-823-9(2)*, Capstone Pr.) Capstone.
Jok, Diego. Vampires & Cells, 1 vol. Biskup, Agnieszka. 2011. (Monster Science Ser.). (ENG.). 32p. (J). (gr. 3-9). pap. 8.10 *(978-1-4296-7331-0(1))*; lib. bdg. 31.32 *(978-1-4296-6582-7(3))* Capstone. (Capstone Pr.).
—Zombies & Electricity, 1 vol. Weakland, Mark. 2013. (Monster Science Ser.). (ENG.). 32p. (J). (gr. 3-9). pap. 8.10 *(978-1-62065-822-2(4))*; lib. bdg. 31.32 *(978-1-4296-9929-7(9))* Capstone. (Capstone Pr.).
Jolby. Monsters under Bridges. Coddington, Rachel Roellke & ANZ014 Staff. 2013. 32p. (J). (gr. -1-3). 16.99 *(978-1-57061-856-7(9)*, Little Bigfoot) Sasquatch Bks.
Jolet, Stefan. Cinderellaphant, 1 vol. de Las Casas, Dianne. 2014. (ENG.). 32p. (J). (gr. k-3). 16.99 *(978-1-4556-1900-9(0)*, Pelican Publishing) Arcadia Publishing.
Jolivet, Joëlle. Moby-Dick: A Pop-Up Book from the Novel by Herman Melville. 2019. (ENG.). 16p. 40.00 *(978-1-4521-7384-9(2))* Chronicle Bks. LLC.
Jolivet, Joëlle. Almost Everything. Jolivet, Joëlle. Siegel, Alexis, tr. 2005. (ENG.). 40p. (J). (gr. -1-3). 32.99 *(978-1-59643-090-7(7)*, 900031451) Roaring Brook Pr.
—Zoo - Ology. Jolivet, Joëlle. rev. ed. 2003. (ENG.). 40p. (J). (gr. -1-3). 32.99 *(978-0-7613-1894-1(1)*, 9780761318941) Roaring Brook Pr.
Jolivet, Joëlle & Jolivet, Joëlle. Bonesville. Fromental, Jean-Luc. 2016. (ENG.). 48p. (J). (gr. k-2). 18.95 *(978-1-4197-2277-6(8)*, Abrams Bks. for Young Readers) Abrams, Inc.
—Oops! Fromental, Jean-Luc. 2010. (ENG.). 42p. (J). (gr. -1-3). 17.95 *(978-0-8109-8749-4(X))* Abrams, Inc.
—Rapido's Next Stop. Fromental, Jean-Luc. 2012. (ENG.). 20p. (J). (gr. -1-3). 17.95 *(978-1-4197-0195-5(9)*, Abrams Bks. for Young Readers) Abrams, Inc.
—365 Penguins (Reissue) Fromental, Jean-Luc. ed. 2017. (ENG.). 48p. (J). (gr. k-2). 17.99 *(978-1-4197-2917-1(9)*, Abrams Bks. for Young Readers) Abrams, Inc.
Jolivet, Joëlle, jt. illus. see Jolivet, Joëlle.
Jolley, Mack. I Can't Go to Church. Brown, Toni Sorenson. 2005. (J). *(978-1-59156-270-2(8))* Covenant Communications.
Jollife, Angela. Fun with Action Rhymes & Poems. Williams, Brenda. 2004. 108p. pap. *(978-1-903853-50-4(8))* Brilliant Pubns.
Jolliffe, Angela. Noah. Clayden, Julie. 2005. (First Word Heroes Ser.). (ENG.). 12p. (J). (gr. 3-5). bds. 7.99 *(978-1-904637-11-0(6)*, 1904637116) Authentic Media GBR. Dist: EMI CMG Distribution.

J

Jomepour Bell, Rahele. Playdate. Macdonald, Maryann. 2019. (ENG.). 24p. (J). (gr. -1-3). 15.99 (978-0-8075-6552-0(0), 807565520) Whitman, Albert & Co.

Jonas, Ann. Stars Beneath Your Bed: The Surprising Story of Dust. Sayre, April Pulley. 2005. 32p. (J). lib. bdg. 17.89 (978-0-06-057189-4(6)); (ENG.). 17.99 (978-0-06-057188-7(8), Greenwillow Bks.) HarperCollins Pubs.

Jonason, Dave. Midge & Max's Scavenger Hunt. Ellis, Libby. 2005. 12p. (J). (gr. -1-3). act. bk. ed. 14.95 (978-1-58117-109-9(9), Intervisual/Piggy Toes) Bendon, Inc.

Jonathan Siruno. Moxie Day the Prankster: Another Laugh & Learn Book of Poetry. Pottle, Robert. 2004. 64p. (J). per. 8.95 (978-0-9709569-2-7(4), MDTP) Blue Lobster Pr.

Jonatronix. Making a Car. Llewellyn, Claire. 2016. (Cambridge Reading Adventures Ser.). (ENG.). 16p. pap. 7.37 (978-1-107-57597-4(4)) Cambridge Univ. Pr.

—The Weather Today Red Band. Llewellyn, Claire. 2016. (Cambridge Reading Adventures Ser.). (ENG.). 16p. pap. 7.37 (978-1-107-57676-6(8)) Cambridge Univ. Pr.

Jonea, Annalisa. Time to Write Letters & Facts (6-9 Years) Time to Read & Write Series. Jones, Sally & Jones, Amanda. 2018. (Time to Read & Write Ser.: Vol. 3). (ENG.). 77p. (J). (gr. k-4). pap. (978-1-910824-02-3(X)) Guinea Pig Education.

Jonee, Jeanine. The Barnyard Buddies Meet a Newcomer. Penshorn, Julie. 2020. (ENG.). 34p. (J). pap. 9.99 (978-0-9988691-9-3(8)) Growing Communities for Peace.

Jones., Amber. Ollie & Grampa Go to the Zoo: How the Polar Bear Got to the Zoo. Ken Lindstrom To Ken Lindstrom. 2011. 28p. pap. 12.49 (978-1-4520-1529-3(5)) AuthorHouse.

Jones, Andrew Lloyd. Mary Slessor: Servant to the Slave. MacKenzie, Catherine. 2010. (Trail Blazers Ser.). (ENG.). 192p. (J). per. 8.99 (978-1-85792-348-3(0), b0e5b557-7536-4a53-ae75-2d67c059d5e1) Christian Focus Pubns. GBR. Dist: Baker & Taylor Publisher Services (BTPS).

Jones, Ann. Granny's Clan: A Tale of Wild Orcas. Hodson, Sally. 2012. (ENG.). 32p. (J). (gr. 1-4). 24.94 (978-1-58469-171-6(9)) Dawn Pubns.

—Granny's Clan: A Tale of Wild Orcas. Hodson, Sally. 2012. (ENG.). 32p. (J). (gr. k-4). pap. 8.95 (978-1-58469-172-3(7), Dawn Pubns.) Sourcebooks, Inc.

Jones, Anna. Dame un Beso (Kiss Me) 2016. (SPA.). 26p. (J). bds. 8.99 (978-1-78670-434-4(X)) Igloo Bks. GBR. Dist: Simon & Schuster, Inc.

—Dinosaur Disasters. Agnew, Kate. (Reading Ladder Ser.). (ENG.). 48p. (J). (gr. k-2). 2016. 7.99 (978-1-4052-8228-4(2)); 2010. pap. 5.99 (978-1-4052-4778-8(9)) Egmont Bks., Ltd. GBR. Dist: Independent Pubs. Group.

—Hello, Bunny. Cottage Door Press & Parragon Books, eds. 2019. (Peek-A-Boo Board Bks.). (ENG.). 10p. (J). (gr. -1 — 1). bds. 5.99 (978-1-68052-697-4(9), 2002940, Parragon Books) Cottage Door Pr.

—Hello, Puppy. Cottage Door Press & Parragon Books, eds. ed. 2019. (Peek-A-Boo Bks.). (ENG.). 10p. (J). (gr. -1 — 1). bds. 5.99 (978-1-68052-536-6(0), 2000970, Parragon Books) Cottage Door Pr.

—Kiss Me. 2014. (ENG.). 26p. (J). bds. 8.95 (978-1-78440-559-5(0)) Igloo Bks. GBR. Dist: Simon & Schuster, Inc.

—My Blessings for You. 2018. (Special Delivery Bks.). (ENG.). 8p. (J). (— 1). bds. 6.49 (978-1-68412-275-2(9), Silver Dolphin Bks.) Printers Row Publishing Group.

—My First Bedtime Prayers. Tiger Tales. 2017. (ENG.). 38p. (J). (gr. -1-k). bds. 9.99 (978-1-68010-520-9(5)) Tiger Tales.

—My First Bible Stories. 2016. (ENG.). 38p. (J). (gr. -1-k). bds. 9.99 (978-1-58925-222-6(5)) Tiger Tales.

—My Little Book of Bedtime Prayers. Tiger Tales. 2016. (ENG.). 32p. (J). (gr. -1-k). mass mkt. 3.99 (978-1-58925-486-2(4)) Tiger Tales.

—Peek-A-Boo Dinosaur. Cottage Door Press & Parragon Books, eds. ed. 2019. (Peek-A-Boo Board Bks.). (ENG.). 10p. (J). (gr. -1 — 1). bds. 5.99 (978-1-68052-533-5(6), 2000940, Parragon Books) Cottage Door Pr.

—Scrub-a-Dub Froggy: Bath Mitt & Book Set. 2013. (Scrub-A-Dub Bath Mitt & Book Sets Ser.). (ENG.). 8p. (J). (gr. -1 — 1). 9.99 (978-1-4380-7439-9(5), B.E.S. Publishing) Peterson's.

Jones, Annalisa. Let's Imagine & Write a Story (6-9 Years) Time to Read & Write Series. Jones, Sally & Jones, Amanda. 2018. (Time to Read & Write Ser.: Vol. 1). (ENG.). 76p. (J). (gr. k-3). pap. (978-1-910824-03-0(8)) Guinea Pig Education.

—Let's Practise Our Reading Comprehension (Ages 6-9 Years) Time to Read & Write Series. Jones, Sally & Jones, Amanda. 2018. (Time to Read & Write Ser.: Vol. 2). (ENG.). 77p. (J). (gr. k-4). pap. (978-1-910824-05-4(4)) Guinea Pig Education.

—Time to Write a Diary (6-9 Years) Time to Read & Write Series. Jones, Sally & Jones, Amanda. 2018. (Time to Read & Write Ser.: Vol. 4). (ENG.). 45p. (J). (gr. k-4). pap. (978-1-910824-01-6(1)) Guinea Pig Education.

—What We Do (7-13 Years) Get Going with Creative Writing (and Other Forms of Writing) Jones, Sally & Jones, Amanda. 2018. (Get Going with Creative Writing Ser.: Vol. 5). (ENG.). 91p. (J). (gr. 2-6). pap. (978-1-907733-17-8(5)) Guinea Pig Education.

—Zoggy's Christmas. Jones, Sally & Jones, Amanda. 2015. (ENG.). (J). pap. (978-1-910824-23-8(2)) Guinea Pig Education.

Jones, Aria. The Adventures of Tutu & Tula Christmas. Gray, John H. 2019. (Tutu & Tula Ser.: Vol. 2). (ENG.). 36p. (J). (gr. k). pap. (978-0-9952387-8-7(2)) Gray, John H.

—The Adventures of Tutu & Tula. Christmas. Gray, John H. 2019. (Tutu & Tula Ser.: Vol. 1). (ENG.). 36p. (J). (gr. k). (978-1-9992344-1-6(3)) Gray, John H.

—The Adventures of Tutu & Tula. Lost. Gray, John H. 2019. (Tutu & Tula Ser.: Vol. 1). (ENG.). 30p. (J). (gr. k-1). (978-1-9992344-0-9(5)); pap. (978-0-9952387-6-3(6)) Gray, John H.

—The Adventures of Tutu & Tula. Rescue. Gray, John. 2019. (Adventures of Tutu & Tula Ser.: Vol. 3). (ENG.). 52p. (J). (gr. k-4). pap. (978-1-9992344-2-3(1)) Gray, John H.

—Les Aventures de Toutou et Toula Perdu. Gray, John H. 2019. (Tyhe Aventures de Toutou et Toula Ser.). (FRE.). 30p. (J). pap. (978-0-9952387-7-0(4)) Gray, John H.

—Les Aventures Toutu et Toula: Noel. Gray, John H. Thibert, Francine, tr. 2019. (Toutu et Toula Ser.: Vol. 2). (FRE.). 36p. (J). (gr. k-1). pap. (978-0-9952387-9-4(0)) Gray, John H.

—Brianna Bounces. George, Tracilyn. 2020. (ENG.). 26p. (J). pap. 11.99 (978-1-6601-6789-0(2)) Independently Published.

Jones, Ayanna. Friends Will Be There Forever. Walter-Goodspeed, Dee Dee. 2012. 26p. (J). (-18). pap. 15.99 (978-1-933846-36-1(4)) Fairwood Pr.

Jones, Barbara. Kacey's Question: Who Will I Marry? Consolver, Peggy Miracle. 2018. (ENG.). 32p. (J). 15.99 (978-1-945507-57-1(8)) Clovercroft Publishing.

Jones, Barry. Dracula. Stoker, Bram. 2004. (Paperback Classics Ser.). 144p. (J). pap. 4.95 (978-0-7945-0089-4(7), Usborne) EDC Publishing.

—Frankenstein. Shelley, Mary & Shelley, Mary. 2004. (Paperback Classics Ser.). 144p. (J). pap. 4.95 (978-0-7945-0090-0(0), Usborne) EDC Publishing.

—Tales of Mystery & Imagination. Poe, Edgar Allen. 2004. (Paperback Classics Ser.). 144p. (J). pap. 4.95 (978-0-7945-0186-0(9), Usborne) EDC Publishing.

Jones, Bob. Pinuccio. Diroma, Joseph. 2009. 24p. pap. 14.99 (978-1-60844-036-8(2)) Dog Ear Publishing, LLC.

Jones, Branson & Mikle, Toby. Alphabet Anatomy: Meet the Capital Letters. Jones, Linda. 2012. 32p. pap. (978-1-4602-0047-6(0)) FriesenPress.

Jones, Brenda. Born: A Foal, Five Kittens & Confederation, 1 vol. Kessler, Deirdre. 2014. (ENG.). 48p. (J). (gr. 1-3). pap. 12.95 (978-1-927502-33-4(0), fb759eed-8cbd-4dbc-b88e-afb2471a97a1) Acorn Pr., The CAN. Dist: Baker & Taylor Publisher Services (BTPS).

—Bubba Begonia, You'll Be Sorry. O'Brien, Gerry. ed. 2006. (ENG.). 80p. (J). per. 6.95 (978-1-894838-23-8(8)) Acorn Pr., The CAN. Dist: Univ. of Toronto Pr.

—Hockey Night Tonight, 1 vol. Connors, Stompin' Tom. ed. 2009. (ENG.). 24p. (J). (gr. -1 — 1). bds. 12.95 (978-1-55109-733-6(8), 1575ee55-ef3d-4ef0-a09a-978916e6eaf1) Nimbus Publishing, Ltd. CAN. Dist: Baker & Taylor Publisher Services (BTPS).

—I Is for Island: A Prince Edward Island Alphabet. MacDonald, Hugh. 2012. (ENG.). 40p. (J). (gr. 1-5). 16.95 (978-1-58536-367-4(7)) Sleeping Bear Pr.

—Lobster Fishing on the Sea, 1 vol. Hull, Maureen. ed. 2010. (ENG.). 32p. (J). (gr. 1-3). pap. 9.95 (978-1-55109-754-1(0), 6f786d89-f6be-463e-a8be-9421274ca3fb) Nimbus Publishing, Ltd. CAN. Dist: Baker & Taylor Publisher Services (BTPS).

—Lobster in My Pocket, 1 vol. Kessler, Deirdre. 2nd ed. 2010. (ENG.). 32p. (J). (gr. 1-3). pap. 9.95 (978-1-55109-767-1(2), bbb59ab1-82e7-4a51-b736-63e482bedbb6) Nimbus Publishing, Ltd. CAN. Dist: Baker & Taylor Publisher Services (BTPS).

—Sid the Kid & the Dryer, 1 vol. Choyce, Lesley. 2019. (ENG.). 32p. (J). pap. 9.95 (978-1-77108-775-9(7), 6cc7a61a-ca26-4183-b851-210c0c6ca7d8) Nimbus Publishing, Ltd. CAN. Dist: Baker & Taylor Publisher Services (BTPS).

—Simon & Catapult Man's Perilous Playground Adventure, 1 vol. Smiley, Norene. ed. 2009. (ENG.). 32p. (J). (gr. -1-k). pap. 8.95 (978-1-55109-714-5(1), 74fb930e-b3af-4f9d-9a07-f73e1677553f) Nimbus Publishing, Ltd. CAN. Dist: Baker & Taylor Publisher Services (BTPS).

—Skunks for Breakfast, 1 vol. Choyce, Lesley. 2nd ed. 2019. (ENG.). 32p. (J). pap. 8.95 (978-1-77108-785-8(4), 415739d8-23ba-41d6-b300-fd733cfbddb2) Nimbus Publishing, Ltd. CAN. Dist: Baker & Taylor Publisher Services (BTPS).

Jones, Brian T. You Can't Milk a Dancing Cow. Dunsmuir, Tom. 2005. (ENG.). 24p. (J). (gr. -1-3). 14.95 (978-0-9749303-3-6(4)) Tanglewood Pr.

Jones, Bruce Patrick. Action Stars Paper Dolls. Jones, Bruce Patrick. 2010. (Dover Celebrity Paper Dolls Ser.). (ENG.). 32p. (J). (gr. 3-5). 9.99 (978-0-486-47606-3(5)) Dover Pubns., Inc.

Jones, Buck. The Great Treasure Quest. McDowell, Josh & Johnson, Kevin. 2006. 103p. (J). (gr. 3-7). per. 10.99 (978-1-932587-85-2(3)) Practical Christianity Foundation.

—Greatest Goofiest Jokes. Pierce, Terry. 2010. (Jokes & Riddles Ser.). (ENG.). 96p. (J). (gr. k-3). 17.44 (978-1-4027-7847-6(3)) Sterling Publishing Co., Inc.

—Kids' Silliest Jokes. Horsfall, Jacqueline. 2003. 96p. (J). pap. 4.95 (978-1-4027-0598-4(0)) Sterling Publishing Co., Inc.

—Ridiculous Tongue Twisters. Tait, Chris. 2010. (Jokes & Riddles Ser.). (ENG.). 96p. (J). (gr. k-3). 17.44 (978-1-4027-7854-4(6)) Sterling Publishing Co., Inc.

—Simple Solutions Obesity: With Weight Loss Tips. Moore, Arden. 2005. (Simple Solutions Ser.). (ENG.). 64p. per. 6.95 (978-1-931993-62-3(9), 623S, CompanionHouse Bks.) Fox Chapel Publishing Co., Inc.

—Ten-Second Tongue Twisters. Artell, Mike. 2010. 96p. (J). pap. 4.95 (978-1-4027-7858-2(9)) Sterling Publishing Co., Inc.

Jones, C. Denise West & Darby, Stephania Pierce. Koko & Friends: Born to Play-Destined to Win! Jones, C. Denise West & Darby, Stephania Pierce. (J). (978-1-892313-00-3(6)) D. W. Ink.

Jones, Cameron. Nite-Nite Tales: The Adventures of Bubbles & the Seeds of Joy. Williams, Iris M., ed. 2019. (Nite-Nite Tales Ser.: Vol. 1). (ENG.). 36p. (J). pap. 15.95 (978-1-947656-28-4(7)) Butterfly Typeface, The.

Jones, Carly. Aydin the Alien: Aydin & Zak Meet Granny Pat. Moccia, Antonio. 2016. (ENG.). (J). pap. (978-1-911113-89-8(5)) Spiderwize.

Jones, Chamira. Where Do Crickets Go When Winter Comes? Russell-Gilmer, Phyllis A. 2009. 32p. (J). 16.95 (978-1-934363-10-2(3)) Zoe Life Publishing.

Jones, Channing. Ruidos en la Casa: Un Misterio. Beckstrand, Karl. I.t. ed. 2019. (Misterios para Los Menores Ser.: Vol. 1).Tr. of Sounds in the House. (SPA.). 26p. (J). 26.55 (978-1-951599-00-3(4)) Premio Publishing & Gozo Bks., LLC.

Jones, Channing. Sounds in the House! A Mystery. Beckstrand, Karl. 2004.Tr. of Sonidos en la Casa. (ENG.). 24p. (J). per. 4.00 (978-0-9672012-5-2(X)) Premio Publishing & Gozo Bks., LLC.

Jones, Channing. Sounds in the House: A Mystery. Beckstrand, Karl. 2020. (Mini-Mysteries for Minors Ser.: Vol. 1). (ENG.). 26p. (J). pap. 9.95 (978-1-951599-05-8(5)) Premio Publishing & Gozo Bks., LLC.

Jones, Channing. Sounds in the House - Sonidos en la Casa: A Mystery in English & Spanish. Beckstrand, Karl. ed. 2017. (Mini-Mysteries for Minors Ser.: 1).Tr. of Ruidos en la Casa. (ENG & SPA.). 24p. (J). (gr. -1-8). 26.95 (978-0-9853988-7-3(6)) Premio Publishing & Gozo Bks., LLC.

Jones, Channing, jt. illus. see Hollenbach, David.

Jones, Chris. Jim Nasium Is a Strikeout King. McKnight, Marty. 2016. (Jim Nasium Ser.). (ENG.). 88p. (J). (gr. 2-3). lib. bdg. 25.32 (978-1-4965-3025-7(X), Stone Arch Bks.) Capstone.

—Jim Nasium Is a Tennis Mismatch. McKnight, Marty. 2016. (Jim Nasium Ser.). (ENG.). 88p. (J). (gr. 2-3). lib. bdg. 25.32 (978-1-4965-3026-4(8), Stone Arch Bks.) Capstone.

Jones, Chris B. First Graphics: Body Systems. Kolpin, Molly et al. 2012. (First Graphics: Body Systems Ser.). (ENG.). 24p. (gr. 1-2). pap. 178.50 (978-1-4296-9333-2(9)) Capstone.

—Jim Nasium Is a Basket Case. McKnight, Marty. 2015. (Jim Nasium Ser.). (ENG.). 88p. (J). (gr. 2-3). pap. 5.95 (978-1-4965-0526-2(3), Stone Arch Bks.) Capstone.

—Jim Nasium Is a Football Fumbler. McKnight, Marty. 2015. (Jim Nasium Ser.). (ENG.). 88p. (J). (gr. 2-3). lib. bdg. 25.32 (978-1-4965-0522-4(0), Stone Arch Bks.) Capstone.

—Jim Nasium Is a Hockey Hazard. McKnight, Marty. 2015. (Jim Nasium Ser.). (ENG.). 88p. (J). (gr. 2-3). pap. 5.95 (978-1-4965-0524-8(7), Stone Arch Bks.) Capstone.

—Jim Nasium Is a Soccer Goofball. McKnight, Marty. 2015. (Jim Nasium Ser.). (ENG.). 88p. (J). (gr. 2-3). pap. 5.95 (978-1-4965-0525-5(5), Stone Arch Bks.) Capstone.

—A Tour of Your Circulatory System, 1 vol. Ballen, Karen. 2012. (First Graphics: Body Systems Ser.). (ENG.). 24p. (J). (gr. k-3). pap. 6.29 (978-1-4296-9322-6(3)); (gr. 1-2). pap. 35.70 (978-1-4296-9323-3(1)) Capstone.

—A Tour of Your Digestive System, 1 vol. Kolpin, Molly Erin. 2012. (First Graphics: Body Systems Ser.). (ENG.). 24p. (J). (gr. k-3). pap. 6.29 (978-1-4296-9324-0(X)) Capstone.

—A Tour of Your Digestive System. Kolpin, Molly. 2012. (First Graphics: Body Systems Ser.). (ENG.). 24p. (gr. 1-2). pap. 35.70 (978-1-4296-9325-7(8)) Capstone.

—A Tour of Your Muscular & Skeletal Systems. Clark, Katie. 2012. (First Graphics: Body Systems Ser.). (ENG.). 24p. (gr. 1-2). pap. 35.70 (978-1-4296-9327-1(4)) Capstone.

—A Tour of Your Nervous System. Kolpin, Molly. 2012. (First Graphics: Body Systems Ser.). (ENG.). 24p. (J). (gr. k-3). lib. bdg. 24.65 (978-1-4296-8739-3(8)); (gr. 1-2). pap. 35.70 (978-1-4296-9329-5(0)) Capstone.

—A Tour of Your Respiratory System, 1 vol. Reina, Mary. 2012. (First Graphics: Body Systems Ser.). (ENG.). 24p. (J). (gr. k-3). pap. 6.29 (978-1-4296-9330-1(4)); (gr. 1-2). pap. 35.70 (978-1-4296-9331-8(2)) Capstone.

Jones, Christina. This Is Not a Fairytale. Altman, Courteney. 2019. (ENG.). 116p. (J). pap. 10.00 (978-1-6970-0112-9(2)) Independently Published.

Jones, Christina B. Run, Run, Run. Jackson, Alonzo. 2019. (ENG.). 26p. (J). pap. 15.99 (978-1-68314-443-4(0), Reliant Publishing) Redemption Pr.

Jones, Christopher. Fears, 1 vol. Baltazar, Art et al. 2013. (Young Justice Ser.). (ENG.). 32p. (J). (gr. 3-6). 22.60 (978-1-4342-6038-3(0), Stone Arch Bks.) Capstone.

—Marvel Action: Spider-Man: Spider-Chase (Book Two) Burnham, Erik. 2019. (Marvel Action: Spider-Man Ser.: 2). (ENG.). 72p. (J). (gr. 4-7). pap. 9.99 (978-1-68405-521-0(0)) Idea & Design Works, LLC.

Jones, Chuck. The White Seal. Kipling, Rudyard. 2006. (ENG.). 32p. (J). (gr. -1-3). 8.95 (978-0-8249-6598-3(1), Ideal Pubns.) Worthy Publishing.

Jones, Cory. Are We Still Friends? Goodgame, Randall. 2019. (Slugs & Bugs Ser.). (ENG.). 64p. (J). (gr. -1-3). 9.99 (978-1-5359-3971-3(0), 005811095, B&H Kids) B&H Publishing Group.

—The Donkey & Jesus. Schmidt, Troy. 2015. (Their Side of the Story Ser.). (ENG.). 32p. (J). (gr. -1-3). pap. 3.99 (978-1-4336-8719-8(4), 005742021, B&H Kids) B&H Publishing Group.

—The Donkey Tells His Side of the Story: Hey God, I'm Sorry to Be Stubborn, but I Just Don't Like Anyone Riding on My Back! Schmidt, Troy. 2014. (ENG.). 32p. (gr. -1-3). 9.99 (978-1-4336-8309-1(1), 005613349, B&H Kids) B&H Publishing Group.

—The Frog & the Plagues. Schmidt, Troy. 2015. (Their Side of the Story Ser.). (ENG.). 32p. (J). (gr. -1-3). pap. 3.99 (978-1-4336-8720-4(8), 005742022, B&H Kids) B&H Publishing Group.

—The Lion & Daniel. Schmidt, Troy. 2015. (Their Side of the Story Ser.). (ENG.). 32p. (J). (gr. -1-3). pap. 3.99 (978-1-4336-8721-1(6), 005742023, B&H Kids) B&H Publishing Group.

—The Lion Tells His Side of the Story: Hey God, I'm Starving in This Den So Why Won't You Let Me Eat This Guy Named Daniel?! Schmidt, Troy. 2014. (ENG.). 32p. (gr. -1-3). 9.99 (978-1-4336-8310-7(5), 005613350, B&H Kids) B&H Publishing Group.

—The Raven & Noah's Ark. Schmidt, Troy. 2015. (Their Side of the Story Ser.). (ENG.). 32p. (J). (gr. -1-3). pap. 3.99 (978-1-4336-8722-8(4), 005742024, B&H Kids) B&H Publishing Group.

—VeggieTales SuperComics: Vol 1. Big Idea Entertainment, LLC. 2015. (VeggieTales Super Comics Ser.: 1). (ENG.). 104p. (J). (gr. -1-3). pap. 12.99 (978-1-4336-8534-7(5), 005700962, B&H Kids) B&H Publishing Group.

—The Whale & Jonah. Schmidt, Troy. 2015. (Their Side of the Story Ser.). (ENG.). 32p. (J). (gr. -1-3). pap. 3.99 (978-1-4336-8723-5(2), 005742025, B&H Kids) B&H Publishing Group.

—Where's God When I'm S-Scared? Big Idea Entertainment, LLC. 2016. (VeggieTales Ser.). (ENG.). 32p. (J). (gr. -1-3). pap. 3.99 (978-1-4336-4353-8(7), 005786226, B&H Kids) B&H Publishing Group.

—Who Will Play with Me? Goodgame, Randall. 2019. (Slugs & Bugs Ser.). (ENG.). 64p. (J). (gr. -1-3). 9.99 (978-1-5359-3972-0(9), 005811096, B&H Kids) B&H Publishing Group.

Jones, Damien. Derek Jeter's Ultimate Baseball Guide 2015. Dobrow, Larry. 2015. (Jeter Publishing Ser.). (ENG.). 96p. (J). (gr. 3-5). pap. 9.99 (978-1-4814-2318-2(5), Little Simon) Little Simon.

—Flight of the Moon Dragon. West, Tracey. 2016. (Dragon Masters Ser.: 6). (ENG.). 96p. (J). (gr. 1-3). pap. 4.99 (978-0-545-91392-8(6)) Scholastic, Inc.

—Flight of the Moon Dragon. West, Tracey. ed. 2016. (Dragon Masters Ser.: bk.6). (ENG.). 96p. (J). (gr. 1-3). 14.75 (978-0-606-39155-9(X)) Turtleback.

—Roar of the Thunder Dragon. West, Tracey. 2017. (Dragon Masters Ser.: 8). (ENG.). 96p. (J). (gr. 1-3). pap. 4.99 (978-1-338-04292-4(0)); lib. bdg. 15.99 (978-1-338-04293-1(9)) Scholastic, Inc.

—Search for the Lightning Dragon. West, Tracey. 2017. (Dragon Masters Ser.: 7). (ENG.). 96p. (J). (gr. 1-3). pap. 4.99 (978-1-338-04288-7(2)); lib. bdg. 24.99 (978-1-338-04289-4(0)) Scholastic, Inc.

—Song of the Poison Dragon. West, Tracey. 2016. (Dragon Masters Ser.: 5). (ENG.). 96p. (J). (gr. 1-3). 15.99 (978-0-545-91388-1(8)) Scholastic, Inc.

—Song of the Poison Dragon. West, Tracey. 2016. (Dragon Masters Ser.: 5). (ENG.). 96p. (J). (gr. 1-3). pap. 4.99 (978-0-545-91387-4(X)) Scholastic, Inc.

—Waking the Rainbow Dragon. West, Tracey. 2018. (Dragon Masters Ser.: 10). (ENG.). 96p. (J). (gr. 1-3). pap. 4.99 (978-1-338-16989-8(0)); lib. bdg. 24.99 (978-1-338-16990-4(4)) Scholastic, Inc.

Jones, Damien, jt. illus. see Howells, Graham.

Jones, Damien, jt. illus. see Patton, Julia.

Jones, Dani. The One-Eyed People Eater: The Story of Cyclops. Holub, Joan. 2014. (Ready-To-Reads Ser.). (ENG.). 48p. (J). (gr. 1-3). pap. 3.99 (978-1-4424-8500-6(0), Simon Spotlight) Simon Spotlight.

—PopularMMOs Presents a Hole New Activity Book: Mazes, Puzzles, Games, & More! PopularMMOs. 2019. (ENG.). 128p. (J). (gr. 3-7). pap. 10.99 (978-0-06-291662-4(9)) HarperCollins Pubs.

—PopularMMOs Presents a Hole New World. PopularMMOs. 2020. (ENG.). 208p. (J). (gr. 3-7). pap. 11.99 (978-0-06-279088-0(9)) HarperCollins Pubs.

—PopularMMOs Presents a Hole New World. PopularMMOs. 2018. (ENG.). 208p. (J). (gr. 3-7). 19.99 (978-0-06-279087-3(0)) HarperCollins Pubs.

—PopularMMOs Presents Enter the Mine. PopularMMOs. 2020. 208p. (J). (gr. 3-7). pap. 11.99 (978-0-06-289429-8(3)) HarperCollins Pubs.

—PopularMMOs Presents Enter the Mine. PopularMMOs. 2019. (ENG.). 208p. (J). (gr. 3-7). 19.99 (978-0-06-289428-1(5)) HarperCollins Pubs.

—Surprise, Trojans! The Story of the Trojan Horse. Holub, Joan. 2014. (Ready-To-Reads Ser.). (ENG.). 32p. (J). (gr. k-2). 16.99 (978-1-4814-2087-7(9)); pap. 3.99 (978-1-4814-2086-0(0)) Simon Spotlight. (Simon Spotlight).

—What If You Get Lost?, 1 vol. Guard, Anara. 2011. (Danger Zone Ser.). (ENG.). 24p. (J). (gr. k-2). lib. bdg. 26.65 (978-1-4048-6684-3(1), Picture Window Bks.) Capstone.

Jones, Davy. In a Dark, Dark House. Dussling, Jennifer. Date not set. (All Aboard Reading Ser.). 32p. (J). (gr. -1-k). pap. (978-0-448-40974-0(7), Grosset & Dunlap) Penguin Publishing Group.

Jones, Davy. Ruedas! Jones, Davy. Cobb, Annie. 2003. (Road to Reading Ser.). (J). lib. bdg. 11.99 (978-0-375-91500-0(1), Golden Bks.) Random Hse. Children's Bks.

Jones, Deborah. The Starlight Ballerina. Baxter, Nicola. 2025. 14p. (J). bds. (978-1-84322-885-1(8)) Anness Publishing.

Jones, Denise & Jones, Miranda, photos by. The Green in the Grass: A Book of Colors. Jones, Denise & Jones, Miranda. 2016. 32p. (J). (978-0-9969574-3-4(X)) Kids At Heart Publishing, LLC.

Jones, Denise West & Darby, Stephania Pierce. Koko & Friends: Friends? Oh, Really!!! Jones, Denise West & Darby, Stephania Pierce. (J). (978-1-892313-01-0(4)) D. W. Ink.

Jones, Dennis. Adam & Eve, God's First People, 1 vol. Zondervan Staff. 2010. (I Can Read! / Dennis Jones Ser.). (ENG.). 32p. (J). (gr. -1-2). pap. 4.99 (978-0-310-71883-3(X)) Zonderkidz.

—Daniel God's Faithful Follower, 1 vol. Zondervan Staff. 2010. (I Can Read! / Dennis Jones Ser.). (ENG.). 32p. (J). (gr. -1-2). pap. 4.99 (978-0-310-71834-5(1)) Zonderkidz.

—David & God's Giant Victory: Biblical Values, 1 vol. Zondervan Staff. 2010. (I Can Read! / Dennis Jones Ser.). (ENG.). 32p. (J). (gr. -1-2). pap. 4.99 (978-0-310-71879-6(1)) Zonderkidz.

—The First Christmas Ever, 1 vol. Zondervan, A. 2014. (ENG.). 32p. (J). pap. 1.99 (978-0-310-74083-4(5)) Zonderkidz.

—Jesus God's Only Son, 1 vol. Zondervan Staff. 2010. (I Can Read! / Dennis Jones Ser.). (ENG.). 32p. (J). (gr. -1-2). pap. 4.99 (978-0-310-71880-2(5)) Zonderkidz.

—Jonah, God's Messenger, 1 vol. Zondervan Bibles Staff. 2011. (I Can Read! / Dennis Jones Ser.). (ENG.). 32p. (J). pap. 4.99 *(978-0-310-71835-2(X))* Zonderkidz.

—Noah & God's Great Promise, 1 vol. Zondervan Staff. 2010. (I Can Read! / Dennis Jones Ser.). (ENG.). 32p. (J). (gr. -1-2). pap. 4.99 *(978-0-310-71884-0(8))* Zonderkidz.

—Paul's Journey - One in Christ Bible Story Book. Kolbrek, Loyal. 2011. (ENG.). 24p. (J). pap. 2.99 *(978-0-7586-2812-1(9))* Concordia Publishing Hse.

—Read with Me Bible for Little Ones, 1 vol. 2016. (ENG.). 32p. (J). bds. 9.99 *(978-0-310-75386-5(4))* Zonderkidz.

Jones, Dennis G. Jesus God's Great Gift, 1 vol. Zondervan Staff. 2010. (I Can Read! / Dennis Jones Ser.). (ENG.). 32p. (J). (gr. -1-2). pap. 4.99 *(978-0-310-71881-9(3))* Zonderkidz.

—Moses, God's Brave Servant, 1 vol. Zondervan Staff. 2010. (I Can Read! / Dennis Jones Ser.). (ENG.). 32p. (J). (gr. -1-2). pap. 4.99 *(978-0-310-71882-6(1))* Zonderkidz.

Jones, Don. What You Can See, You Can Be! Anderson, David A. 2003. 48p. (gr. 3-8). 13.95 *(978-0-87516-603-2(2)*, Devorss Pubns.) DeVorss & Co.

Jones, Donald M., photos by. Buffalo Country: America's National Bison Range. 2005. (ENG., 72p. per. 14.95 *(978-1-931832-56-4(0)*, 8667872363) Riverbend Publishing.

Jones, Doug. Crazy Buildings. Rosen, Michael J. & Kassoy, Ben. 2013. (No Way! Ser.). (ENG.). 32p. (gr. 3-5). lib. bdg. 26.60 *(978-0-7613-8986-6(5))*; (J). E-Book 39.99 *(978-1-4677-1705-2(3))* Lerner Publishing Group. (Millbrook Pr.).

—The Itchy-Scratchy Caterpillar. Tomblin, Mark. 2010. 16p. (J). *(978-0-545-24822-8(1))* Scholastic, Inc.

—Three Bouncing Balls. Charlesworth, Liza. 2005. (ENG.). 16p. (J). (gr. -1-1). pap. 2.99 *(978-0-439-68999-1(6))* Scholastic, Inc.

—Totally Lent! A Teen's Journey to Easter 2004. Broslavick, Chris & Pichler, Tony. Cannizzo, Karen, ed. 2003. 64p. (J). 5.95 *(978-0-89837-233-5(X)*, 3564) Pflaum Publishing Group.

—Totally Lent! A Teen's Journey to Lent 2005. Broslavick, Chris & Pichler, Tony. Cannizzo, Karen, ed. 2004. 64p. (YA). 5.95 *(978-0-89837-247-2(X)*, 3565) Pflaum Publishing Group.

—Two Bunny Slippers. Charlesworth, Liza. 2005. (ENG.). 16p. (J). (gr. -1-1). pap. 2.99 *(978-0-439-68998-4(8))* Scholastic, Inc.

—Zero Spots. Charlesworth, Liza. 2005. (ENG.). 16p. (J). (gr. -1-1). pap. 2.99 *(978-0-439-69022-5(6))* Scholastic, Inc.

Jones, Douglas B. Madam President: The Extraordinary, True (and Evolving) Story of Women in Politics. Thimmesh, Catherine. 2008. (ENG.). 80p. (J). (gr. 1-4). pap. 8.95 *(978-0-618-97143-5(2)*, 1023070) Houghton Mifflin Harcourt Publishing Co.

—The Milkman. Cordsen, Carol Foskett. 2007. (gr. -1-3). 17.00 *(978-0-7569-8148-8(4))* Perfection Learning Corp.

Jones, Elizabeth Orton. The Peddler's Clock. Hunt, Mabel Leigh. 2011. 30p. 35.95 *(978-1-258-09998-5(5))* Literary Licensing, LLC.

—Prayer for a Child. Field, Rachel. 2005. (ENG.). 32p. (J). (gr. -1-k). bds. 7.99 *(978-0-689-87886-2(9)*, Little Simon) Little Simon.

—Prayer for a Child: Diamond Anniversary Edition. Field, Rachel. 100th anniv. ed. 2004. (ENG.). 32p. (J). (gr. -1-3). 13.99 *(978-0-689-87356-0(5)*, Simon & Schuster Bks. For Young Readers) Simon & Schuster Bks. For Young Readers.

—Prayer for a Child: Lap Edition. Field, Rachel. 2013. (ENG.). 32p. (J). (gr. -1-2). bds. 12.99 *(978-1-4424-7659-2(1)*, Little Simon) Little Simon.

Jones, Emily. Face 2 Face. Ster, Caroline Rose. 2011. 110p. (J). pap. 16.95 *(978-1-61660-002-0(0))* GFC Pr.

—Ted on the Bed. Allen, Suzanne. 2019. (ENG.). 28p. (J). pap. 9.13 *(978-1-7943-0135-1(6))* Independently Published.

Jones, Eric. Evil in a Skirt! #5, 1 vol. Walker, Landry Q. & Mason, Joey. 2013. (Supergirl: Cosmic Adventures in the 8th Grade Ser.). (ENG.). 32p. (J). (gr. 3-6). 22.60 *(978-1-4342-6045-1(3)*, Stone Arch Bks.) Capstone.

—Her First Extra-Ordinary Adventure! #1, 1 vol. Walker, Landry Q. & Mason, Joey. 2013. (Supergirl: Cosmic Adventures in the 8th Grade Ser.). (ENG.). 32p. (J). (gr. 3-6). 22.60 *(978-1-4342-4717-9(1)*, Stone Arch Bks.) Capstone.

—My Own Best Frenemy: #2, 1 vol. Walker, Landry Q. & Mason, Joey. 2013. (Supergirl: Cosmic Adventures in the 8th Grade Ser.). (ENG.). 32p. (J). (gr. 3-6). 22.60 *(978-1-4342-4718-6(X)*, Stone Arch Bks.) Capstone.

—Off to Save the Day..., No. 6. Walker, Landry Q. & Mason, Joey. 2013. (Supergirl: Cosmic Adventures in the 8th Grade Ser.). (ENG.). 32p. (J). (gr. 3-6). 22.60 *(978-1-4342-6046-8(1)*, Stone Arch Bks.) Capstone.

—Secret Entity! #4, 1 vol. Walker, Landry Q. 2013. (Supergirl: Cosmic Adventures in the 8th Grade Ser.). (ENG.). 32p. (J). (gr. 3-6). 22.60 *(978-1-4342-4720-9(1)*, Stone Arch Bks.) Capstone.

Jones, Eric, et al. Star Wars Adventures #3: Pest Control. Walker, Landry Q. et al. 2018. (Star Wars Adventures Ser.). (ENG.). 24p. (J). (gr. 4-9). lib. bdg. 27.07 *(978-1-5321-4287-1(0)*, 31113, Graphic Novels) Spotlight.

—Star Wars Adventures #4: the Trouble at Tibrin, Part 1. Walker, Landry Q. et al. 2018. (Star Wars Adventures Ser.). (ENG.). 24p. (J). (gr. 4-9). lib. bdg. 27.07 *(978-1-5321-4288-8(9)*, 31114, Graphic Novels) Spotlight.

—Star Wars Adventures #5: the Trouble at Tibrin, Part 2. Walker, Landry Q. & Dawson, Delilah S. 2018. (Star Wars Adventures Ser.). (ENG.). 24p. (J). (gr. 4-9). lib. bdg. 27.07 *(978-1-5321-4289-5(7)*, 31115, Graphic Novels) Spotlight.

Jones, Eric. Super Hero School: #3, 1 vol. Walker, Landry Q. 2013. (Supergirl: Cosmic Adventures in the 8th Grade Ser.). (ENG.). 32p. (J). (gr. 3-6). 22.60 *(978-1-4342-4719-3(8)*, Stone Arch Bks.) Capstone.

—Supergirl: Cosmic Adventures in the 8th Grade. Walker, Landry Q. 2013. (Supergirl: Cosmic Adventures in the 8th Grade Ser.). (ENG.). 32p. (J). (gr. 3-6). lib. bdg., lib. bdg., lib. bdg. 135.60 *(978-1-4342-8830-1(7)*, Stone Arch Bks.) Capstone.

Jones, Erik. God Is in the Refrigerator. 2006. 38p. (J). 18.95 *(978-0-9771936-4-6(0))* InterWeave Corp.

—God Is in the Window. King, Kimberly. 2007. 37p. (J). 18.95 *(978-0-9771936-6-0(7))* InterWeave Corp.

Jones, Ernest. The Great Mix Up. 2005. (ENG.). 42p. (J). 17.99 *(978-0-9772282-0-1(7))* B. T. Brooks.

Jones, Gregory Burgess. Brady Needs a Nightlight. Barlics, Brian. 2013. (ENG.). 32p. (J). pap. 18.95 *(978-1-61296-195-8(9))* Black Rose Writing.

Jones, Gwynneth. The Chalk Rainbow. Kelly, Deborah. 2017. (ENG.). 32p. (J). (gr. -1-3). 17.99 *(978-1-925335-45-3(3)*, EK Bks.) Exisle Publishing Pty Ltd. AUS. Dist: Hachette Bk. Group.

—Dance with Me. Harrison, Penny. 2016. (ENG.). 32p. (J). (gr. -1-3). 17.99 *(978-1-925335-23-1(2)*, 1093974, EK Bks.) Exisle Publishing Pty Ltd. AUS. Dist: Hachette Bk. Group.

—Don't Think about Purple Elephants. Merritt, Susanne. 2017. (ENG.). 32p. (J). (gr. -1-3). 13.99 *(978-1-925335-48-4(8)*, 317169) Exisle Publishing Pty Ltd. AUS. Dist: Hachette Bk. Group.

—Finding Granny: We Never Really Lose the People We Love ... Simpson, Kate. 2018. (ENG.). 32p. (J). (gr. -1-3). 17.99 *(978-1-925335-69-9(0)*, 321550, EK Bks.) Exisle Publishing Pty Ltd. AUS. Dist: Hachette Bk. Group.

—The Great Sock Secret. Merritt, Susanne. 2016. (ENG.). 32p. (J). (gr. -1-3). 17.99 *(978-1-925335-24-8(0)*, 1093975, EK Bks.) Exisle Publishing Pty Ltd. AUS. Dist: Hachette Bk. Group.

—Patch & Ruby. Jones, Anouska. 2016. (ENG.). 32p. (J). (gr. -1-3). 17.99 *(978-1-925335-22-4(4)*, 1093973, EK Bks.) Exisle Publishing Pty Ltd. AUS. Dist: Hachette UK Distribution.

Jones Halpern, Krickett. Bounce Back Like a Ball. Jones Halpern, Krickett. 2019. (ENG.). 42p. (J). (gr. k-3). 15.99 ***(978-1-7333567-0-1(3))*** Krickett Enterprises.

Jones, Henrietta. Amish Moving Day. Seyfert, Ella Maie. 2011. 132p. 40.95 *(978-1-258-01315-8(0))* Literary Licensing, LLC.

Jones, J. G. Journey to Star Wars: the Last Jedi the Legends of Luke Skywalker. Liu, Ken. 2017. (ENG.). 432p. (J). (gr. 3-7). 14.99 *(978-1-4847-8077-0(9)*, Disney Lucasfilm Press) Disney Publishing Worldwide.

—Marvel Knights Marvel Boy by Morrison & Jones. 2018. (Marvel Knights Ser.: 1). (ENG.). 1p. (YA). (gr. 8-17). pap. 17.99 *(978-1-302-91425-7(1))* Marvel Worldwide, Inc.

Jones, Jac. In Chatter Wood. Jones, Jac. 2004. (ENG.). 40p. pap. 13.95 *(978-1-84323-290-2(1))* Beekman Bks., Inc.

Jones, Jan. The Secret of the Dragonfly: A Story of Hope & Promise. Cramer, Gayle Shaw. 2006. (YA). pap. 19.95 *(978-0-9729346-7-1(7))* Ambrosia Press LLC.

Jones, Jan Naimo. The Apple Bandit. Keene, Carolyn. 2005. (Nancy Drew Notebooks). 74p. (J). (gr. 1-4). 11.65 *(978-0-7569-6505-1(5))* Perfection Learning Corp.

—The Apple Bandit. Keene, Carolyn. 68th ed. 2005. (Nancy Drew Notebooks Ser.: 68). (ENG.). 80p. (J). (gr. 1-4). pap. 5.99 *(978-1-4169-0829-6(3))* Simon & Schuster, Inc.

—The Bunny-Hop Hoax. Keene, Carolyn. 2005. (Nancy Drew Notebooks). 70p. (J). (gr. 1-4). 11.65 *(978-0-7569-5884-8(9))* Perfection Learning Corp.

—The Bunny-Hop Hoax. Keene, Carolyn. 64th ed. 2005. (Nancy Drew Notebooks Ser.: 64). (ENG.). 80p. (J). (gr. 1-4). pap. 3.99 *(978-0-689-87754-4(4)*, Simon & Schuster/Paula Wiseman Bks.) Simon & Schuster/Paula Wiseman Bks.

—Candy Is Dandy. Keene, Carolyn. 2004. (Nancy Drew Notebooks). 74p. (gr. 2-4). 17.00 *(978-0-7569-3437-8(0))* Perfection Learning Corp.

—The Dollhouse Mystery. Keene, Carolyn. 2004. (Nancy Drew Notebooks). 68p. (J). (gr. 1-4). 12.65 *(978-0-7569-5524-3(6))* Perfection Learning Corp.

—The Dollhouse Mystery. Keene, Carolyn. 58th ed. 2004. (Nancy Drew Notebooks Ser.: 58). (ENG.). 80p. (J). (gr. 1-4). pap. 5.99 *(978-0-689-86534-3(1)*, Aladdin) Simon & Schuster Children's Publishing.

—Farmland Innovator: A Story about Cyrus Mccormick. Welch, Catherine A. 2007. (Creative Minds Biographies Ser.). (ENG.). 64p. (gr. 4-8). lib. bdg. 22.60 *(978-0-8225-5988-7(9))* Lerner Publishing Group.

—The Kitten Caper. Keene, Carolyn. 69th ed. 2005. (Nancy Drew Notebooks Ser.: 69). (ENG.). 80p. (J). (gr. 1-4). pap. 5.99 *(978-1-4169-0830-2(7)*, Simon & Schuster/Paula Wiseman Bks.) Simon & Schuster/Paula Wiseman Bks.

—The Singing Suspects. Keene, Carolyn. 2005. (Nancy Drew Notebooks). 69p. (J). (gr. 1-4). 11.65 *(978-0-7569-5952-4(7))* Perfection Learning Corp.

—The Singing Suspects. Keene, Carolyn. 67th ed. 2005. (Nancy Drew Notebooks Ser.: 67). (ENG.). 80p. (J). (gr. 1-4). pap. 4.99 *(978-1-4169-0087-0(X)*, Simon & Schuster/Paula Wiseman Bks.) Simon & Schuster/Paula Wiseman Bks.

Jones, Jan Naimo. Maker of Machines: A Story about Eli Whitney. Jones, Jan Naimo, tr. Mitchell, Barbara. 2004. (Creative Minds Biographies Ser.). (ENG.). 64p. (gr. 4-8). 22.60 *(978-1-57505-603-6(8)*, Carolrhoda Bks.) Lerner Publishing Group.

Jones, Janet M. I Like the SUN. Vitacco, Deborah a. 2019. (Fun Poetry for Young Children Ser.: Vol. 1). (ENG.). 26p. (J). pap. 12.95 *(978-1-9869-0460-5(1))* CreateSpace Independent Publishing Platform.

—One Day at the Seashore: Poetry for Young Children. Vitacco, Deborah a. 2019. (ENG.). 32p. (J). pap. 12.99 *(978-1-0741-7526-9(3))* Independently Published.

Jones, Jennie. Surgeon - Craftsman: Laurence Knight Groves, M. D. 1922-2007. Jones, Jennie, . 2008. (ENG.). 78p. (YA). pap. 35.00 net. *(978-0-9617637-8-7(7))* Cleveland Stock Images.

Jones, Joelle. Supergirl: Being Super. Tamaki, Mariko. 2020. 208p. (YA). (gr. 8-12). pap. 16.99 ***(978-1-77950-319-0(9))*** DC Comics.

Jones, Joëlle & Jones, Joëlle. The Girl Who Owned a City: The Graphic Novel. Nelson, O. T. (Terry). 2012. (ENG.). 128p. (YA). (gr. 5-12). pap. 9.99 *(978-0-7613-5634-9(7)*, 9780761356349, Graphic Universe™) Lerner Publishing Group.

Jones, Joëlle, jt. illus. see Jones, Joëlle.

Jones, Joff. Hit Em' with Words, 1 vol. Nettles Jr, J. H. 2010. 22p. 24.95 *(978-1-4489-4102-5(4))* PublishAmerica, Inc.

Jones, John R. Dinosaur Hunters. McMullan, Kate. 2005. (Step into Reading Ser.: No. 5). 48p. (J). (gr. 2-4). per. 4.99 *(978-0-375-82450-0(2)*, Random Hse. Bks. for Young Readers) Random Hse. Children's Bks.

Jones, John Randolph. Dinosaur Hunters. McMullan, Kate. 2005. (Step into Reading: Step 5 Ser.). (ENG.). 48p. (J). (gr. 2-4). lib. bdg. 16.19 *(978-0-375-92450-7(7))* Random House Publishing Group.

Jones, Juan Luis. A La Rueda, Rueda: Traditional Latin American Folk Songs for Children. Cabrera, Mirna Y. et al, eds. 2010. (LAT & ENG.). 64p. pap. 29.99 incl. audio compact disk *(978-1-4234-7797-6(9)*, 1423477979) Leonard, Hal Corp.

Jones, Julie. The Problem at Pepperpine Zoo. Jones, Julie. l.t. ed. 2004. 24p. (J). pap. 7.95 *(978-0-9745553-0-0(4))* Greenwood Street Publishing. GSP.

Jones, Julienne. Makimba's Animal World. Jackson, Bobby L. 2nd rev. l.t. ed. 2004. 32p. (J). (gr. k-4). 19.95 *(978-1-884242-00-7(6)*, MAW2NED); pap. 11.95 *(978-1-884242-01-4(4)*, MAW2NED) Multicultural Pubns.

Jones, K. L. Space Race. Welsh, C. E. L. 2011. (Campfire Graphic Novels Ser.). (ENG.). 68p. (YA). (gr. 5-12). pap. 9.99 *(978-93-80028-62-0(8)*, Campfire) Steerforth Pr.

Jones, K. L. & Manikandan. Abraham Lincoln: From the Log Cabin to the White House - Campfire Heroes Line. Helfand, Lewis. 2013. (Campfire Graphic Novels: Biography Ser.). (ENG.). 108p. (YA). (gr. 6-9). pap. 31.19 *(978-93-80741-21-5(9))* Random House Publishing Group.

Jones, Karen. Locura de Medianoche en el Zoológico, 1 vol. Craig, Sherryn. 2016.Tr. of Midnight Madness at the Zoo. (SPA.). 32p. (J). (gr. k-3). pap. 11.95 *(978-1-62855-744-2(3))* Arbordale Publishing.

—Midnight Madness at the Zoo, 1 vol. Craig, Sherryn. 2016. (ENG & SPA.). 32p. (J). (gr. k-3). 17.95 *(978-1-62855-730-5(3))* Arbordale Publishing.

Jones, Katie. Not Far to Go Now. Jones, Jet. 2018. (ENG.). 28p. (J). pap. *(978-0-6482549-0-4(9))* KB7 Publishing.

Jones, Kelley. Tales from the Haunted Mansion: Volume I: The Fearsome Foursome. Arcane, Amicus. 2016. (Tales from the Haunted Mansion Ser.: 1). (ENG.). 240p. (J). (gr. 3-7). 14.99 *(978-1-4847-1329-7(X))* Disney Pr.

—Tales from the Haunted Mansion: Volume II: Midnight at Madame Leota's. Arcane, Amicus. 2017. (Tales from the Haunted Mansion Ser.: 2). (ENG.). 208p. (J). (gr. 3-7). 14.99 *(978-1-4847-1471-3(7))* Disney Pr.

—Tales from the Haunted Mansion, Volume III: Grim Grinning Ghosts. Arcane, Amicus. 2018. (Tales from the Haunted Mansion Ser.: 3). (ENG.). 240p. (J). (gr. 3-7). 14.99 *(978-1-4847-1472-0(5))* Disney Pr.

—Tales from the Haunted Mansion, Volume IV: Memento Mori. Arcane, Amicus. 2019. (Tales from the Haunted Mansion Ser.: 4). (ENG.). 240p. (J). (gr. 3-7). 14.99 *(978-1-4847-1473-7(3))* Disney Pr.

Jones, Kevin. Stepper the Dream Horse: The True Story of a Girl, Her Dream, & Her Horse. Swift-Floyd, Laurel. 2019. (ENG.). 48p. (J). (gr. k-6). pap. 21.95 ***(978-1-4796-1020-4(8))*** TEACH Services, Inc.

Jones, Kirk. Lisa the Ministering Mole: Meet the Mole. Jones, Kirk. 2004. 24p. (J). bds. 5.00 net. *(978-0-9759688-0-2(7))* Jones, Kirk.

Jones, Kirsteen H. Tag! Bryant, Ann. 2009. (Tadpoles Ser.). (ENG.). (J). (gr. k-k). lib. bdg. 17.55 *(978-1-61383-947-8(2))* Perfection Learning Corp.

Jones, Koa. School of Awake: A Fun Girl's Guide to Expression & Heart Wisdom. Jones, Kidada. 2017. (ENG.). 168p. (YA). (gr. 9-13). pap. 18.95 *(978-1-60868-458-8(X))* New World Library.

Jones, Lara. Poppy Cat's Garden. ed. 2008. (ENG.). 8p. (J). (gr. 3-6). bds. 16.95 *(978-0-230-01715-3(0)*, Macmillan) Pan Macmillan GBR. Dist: Trans-Atlantic Pubns., Inc.

Jones, Lilah, jt. illus. see Jones, Sarah & Rew.

Jones, Lisa & Underwood, Edward. Baby's First Cloth Book: Christmas. Nosy Crow. 2018. (ENG.). 8p. (J). (— 1). 18.00 *(978-1-5362-0275-5(4)*, Nosy Crow) Candlewick Pr.

—Baby's First Cloth Book: Farm. Nosy Crow. 2018. (ENG.). 8p. (J). (— 1). 18.00 *(978-1-5362-0177-2(4)*, Nosy Crow) Candlewick Pr.

—Baby's First Cloth Book: Park. Nosy Crow. 2018. (ENG.). 8p. (J). (— 1). 18.00 *(978-0-7636-9910-9(1)*, Nosy Crow) Candlewick Pr.

—Baby's First Cloth Book: Zoo. Nosy Crow. 2018. (ENG.). 8p. (J). (— 1). 18.00 *(978-0-7636-9911-6(X)*, Nosy Crow) Candlewick Pr.

Jones, Lloyd. Pearla & Her Unpredictably Perfect Day: How Life's Bumps & Twists Can Turn Out OK! Lieberman, Rochel. 2016. (ENG.). 40p. (J). 16.95 *(978-1-78592-734-8(5)*, 696274) Kingsley, Jessica Pubs. GBR. Dist: Hachette UK Distribution.

Jones, Lloyd. The Princess & the Fog: A Story for Children with Depression. Jones, Lloyd. 2015. (ENG.). 48p. (J). 17.95 *(978-1-84905-655-7(2)*, 693825) Kingsley, Jessica Pubs. GBR. Dist: Hachette UK Distribution.

Jones, Margaret. King Arthur. Thomas, Gwyn. 2006. (ENG.). 144p. (J). pap. 21.95 *(978-0-86243-798-5(9))* Y Lolfa GBR. Dist: Casemate Pubs. & Bk. Distributors, LLC.

—Story of Dafydd AP Gwilym. Thomas, Gwyn. 2004. (ENG.). 108p. (J). pap. 13.95 *(978-0-86243-712-1(1))* Y Lolfa GBR. Dist: Casemate Pubs. & Bk. Distributors, LLC.

Jones, Margot Elain. Beneath the Dragonwood Trees: In the Beginning. Jones, Margot Elaine. 2018. (ENG.). 88p. (J). (gr. 1-6). pap. 19.95 *(978-1-7328166-1-9(1))* Lord & Dooney Pr.

Jones, Mark. Janjak & Freda Go to the Iron Market. Turnbull, Elizabeth J. Turnbull, Wally R., tr. 2013. 36p. pap. 12.95 *(978-1-61153-062-9(8))* Light Messages Publishing.

—Janjak & Freda Go to the Iron Market. Turnbull, Elizabeth. Turnbull, Wally, tr. 2013. 36p. 18.95 *(978-1-61153-072-8(5))* Light Messages Publishing.

—Snuggle Time Devotions That End with a Hug! Elkins, Stephen. 2015. (Share-A-Hug! Ser.). (ENG.). 168p. (J). 14.99 *(978-1-4143-9948-5(0)*, 4608938) Tyndale Hse. Pubs.

Jones, Mary Noble. Itsy Rabbit & Friends: Itsy's First Adventure. Jones, Mary Noble. 2007. 28p. (J). per. 15.00 *(978-0-9796209-8-0(8))* Righter Publishing Co., Inc.

Jones, Matt. Oliver Twist. Dickens, Charles. 2018. (ENG.). 416p. (J). (gr. 5). 16.99 *(978-0-241-33126-2(9))* Penguin Bks., Ltd. GBR. Dist: Independent Pubs. Group.

Jones, Maurice I. MAX the Dog Who Thought He Was a GOAT! McFarland, Ta'lor, ed. 2019. (ENG.). 82p. (J). pap. 14.99 ***(978-1-0860-4299-3(9))*** Independently Published.

Jones, Miranda, jt. photos by see Jones, Denise.

Jones, Nathan. Gotta See Nathan! Gray, Susannah. 2012. 20p. pap. 15.00 *(978-1-4575-1315-2(3))* Dog Ear Publishing, LLC.

Jones, Noah. Here Comes Trouble! Demas, Corinne. 2013. (J). *(978-0-545-55449-7(7)*, Scholastic Pr.) Scholastic, Inc.

—Poem Runs: Baseball Poems & Paintings. Florian, Douglas. 2012. (ENG.). 32p. (J). (gr. 1-4). 16.99 *(978-0-547-68838-1(5)*, 1477607) Houghton Mifflin Harcourt Publishing Co.

—Those Shoes. Boelts, Maribeth. 2007. (J). *(978-1-4287-6554-2(9))* Candlewick Pr.

Jones, Noah Z. Una Bicicleta Como la de Sergio. Boelts, Maribeth. 2019. 40p. (J). (gr. k-3). 6.99 *(978-1-5362-0565-7(6))* Candlewick Pr.

—A Bike Like Sergio's. Boelts, Maribeth. 40p. (J). (gr. k-3). 2018. 6.99 *(978-1-5362-0295-3(9))*; 2016. 15.99 *(978-0-7636-6649-1(1))* Candlewick Pr.

Jones, Noah Z. Duck, Duck, Moose! Bardhan-Quallen, Sudipta. 2020. 32p. (J). 7.99 ***(978-1-368-05485-0(4))*** Little, Brown Bks. for Young Readers.

Jones, Noah Z. Esos Zapatos. Boelts, Maribeth. 2018. (SPA.). 40p. (J). (gr. k-3). 15.99 *(978-1-5362-0392-9(0))*; 7.99 *(978-0-7636-9979-6(9))* Candlewick Pr.

—Little Sweet Potato. Bloom, Amy Beth. 2012. (ENG.). 32p. (J). (gr. -1-2). 16.99 *(978-0-06-180439-7(8)*, Tegen, Katherine Bks) HarperCollins Pubs.

—Magic at the Bed & Biscuit. Carris, Joan. 2012. 112p. (J). (gr. 1-4). pap. 5.99 *(978-0-7636-5849-6(9))* Candlewick Pr.

—The Monster in the Backpack. Moser, Lisa. 2013. (Candlewick Sparks Ser.). 40p. (J). (gr. k-4). pap. 4.99 *(978-0-7636-6643-9(2))* Candlewick Pr.

—No a Norman: La Historia de un Pececito Dorado. Bennett, Kelly. 2016. 32p. (J). (gr. -1-3). 6.99 *(978-0-7636-8906-3(8))* Candlewick Pr.

Jones, Noah Z. Norman: One Amazing Goldfish! Bennett, Kelly. 2020. (ENG.). 32p. (J). (gr. -1-3). 16.99 ***(978-1-5362-0671-5(7))*** Candlewick Pr.

Jones, Noah Z. Not Norman: A Goldfish Story. Bennett, Kelly. 2008. (ENG.). 32p. (J). (gr. -1-3). pap. 6.99 *(978-0-7636-2763-8(1))* Candlewick Pr.

—Stuff. Palatini, Margie. 2011. (ENG.). 32p. (J). (gr. -1-2). 16.99 *(978-0-06-171921-9(8)*, Tegen, Katherine Bks) HarperCollins Pubs.

—Those Shoes. Boelts, Maribeth. 2009. (ENG.). 40p. (J). (gr. k-3). pap. 7.99 *(978-0-7636-4284-6(3))* Candlewick Pr.

—Welcome to the Bed & Biscuit. Carris, Joan. 2009. (Bed & Biscuit Ser.). (ENG.). 128p. (J). (gr. 2-4). 18.69 *(978-0-7636-2151-3(X))* Candlewick Pr.

—Wild Times at the Bed & Biscuit. Carris, Joan. 2011. (Bed & Biscuit Ser.). 128p. (J). (gr. 2-4). 18.69 *(978-0-7636-3705-7(X))* Candlewick Pr.

Jones, Noah Z. Little Red Quacking Hood. Jones, Noah Z. 2014. (Princess Pink & the Land of Fake-Believe Ser.: 2). (ENG.). 80p. (J). (gr. k-2). pap. 4.99 *(978-0-545-63841-8(0))* Scholastic, Inc.

—Moldylocks & the Three Beards. Jones, Noah Z. 2014. (Princess Pink & the Land of Fake-Believe Ser.: 1). (ENG.). 80p. (J). (gr. k-2). pap. 4.99 *(978-0-545-63839-5(9))* Scholastic, Inc.

—The Three Little Pugs. Jones, Noah Z. 2015. (ENG.). 80p. (J). (gr. k-2). pap. 4.99 *(978-0-545-84857-2(1))* Scholastic, Inc.

Jones, Noah Z., jt. illus. see Meserve, Jessica.

Jones, Paul, jt. illus. see Takhar, Jodi.

Jones, Penny & Norris, Aaron. Bangu the Flying Fox: A Dreamtime Story of the Yuin People of Wallaga Lake. 2nd ed. 2011. 22p. (J). (gr. -1-k). pap. 17.95 *(978-0-85575-700-7(0))* Aboriginal Studies Pr. AUS. Dist: Independent Pubs. Group.

Jones, Phil. Airport Mouse. Clark, Ruth E. 2008. (ENG.). 32p. (J). (gr. -1-3). 15.95 *(978-0-9792963-2-1(3))* Hibiscus Publishing.

—Airport Mouse Activity Fun Book 1. Clark, Ruth E. 2010. 16p. (J). pap. 5.99 *(978-0-9792963-6-9(6))* Hibiscus Publishing.

—Airport Mouse Becomes a VIP/VIM World Traveler. Clark, Ruth E. 2009. 32p. (J). 15.95 *(978-0-9792963-5-2(8))* Hibiscus Publishing.

—Airport Mouse Becomes a VIP/VIM World Traveler Activity Fun Book 4. Clark, Ruth E. 2010. 16p. (J). pap. 5.99 *(978-0-9792963-9-0(0))* Hibiscus Publishing.

—Airport Mouse Explores on Opening Day Activity Fun Book 3. Clark, Ruth E. 2010. 16p. (J). pap. 5.99 *(978-0-9792963-8-3(2))* Hibiscus Publishing.

—Airport Mouse Works the Night Shift Activity Fun Book 2. Clark, Ruth E. 2010. 16p. (J). pap. 5.99 *(978-0-9792963-7-6(4))* Hibiscus Publishing.

Jones, Randy. Places in Time: A New Atlas of American History. Leacock, Elspeth & Buckley, Susan. 2006. 48p. (J). (gr. 4-8). reprint ed. 15.00 *(978-1-4223-5555-8(1))* DIANE Publishing Co.

—Places in Time: A New Atlas of American History. Leacock, Elspeth & Buckley, Susan Washburn. 2003. (ENG.). 48p. (J). (gr. 5-7). pap. 6.99 *(978-0-618-31113-2(0)*, 410073) Houghton Mifflin Harcourt Publishing Co.

Jones Ray, Christie. Lula Kate Meets Eliza. Jones Ray, Christie. 2018. (ENG.). 38p. (J). (gr. 2-5). 18.95 *(978-0-9961393-5-9(4))* Rose Water Cottage Pr.

Jones, Rebecca. The Coloring Book of Cards & Envelopes: a Year of Celebrations. Nosy Crow Staff. 2017. (ENG.). 74p. (J). (gr. k-12). pap. 15.99 *(978-0-7636-9529-3(7)*, Nosy Crow) Candlewick Pr.

—The Coloring Book of Cards & Envelopes: Christmas. Crow, Nosy. 2016. (ENG.). 74p. (J). (gr. k-12). pap. 10.99 *(978-0-7636-9242-1(5)*, Nosy Crow) Candlewick Pr.

—The Coloring Book of Cards & Envelopes: Flowers & Butterflies. Nosy Crow Staff. 2016. (ENG.). 74p. (J). (gr. k-12). pap. 10.99 *(978-0-7636-9244-5(1)*, Nosy Crow) Candlewick Pr.

—The Coloring Book of Cards & Envelopes: Nature. Nosy Crow Staff. 2016. (ENG.). 74p. (J). (gr. k-12). pap. 10.99 *(978-0-7636-9245-2(X)*, Nosy Crow) Candlewick Pr.

—The Coloring Book of Cards & Envelopes: Summertime. Nosy Crow Staff. 2017. (ENG.). 74p. (J). (gr. k-12). pap. 10.99 *(978-0-7636-9340-4(5)*, Nosy Crow) Candlewick Pr.

—My Body. 2018. (First Explorers Ser.). (ENG.). 10p. (J). (— 1). bds. 8.95 *(978-1-4549-2942-0(1))* Sterling Publishing Co., Inc.

Jones, Rhonda R. Sir Wishal Dot the Birthday Dragon. Jones, Rhonda R. Reynolds, George E., ed. 2019. (ENG.). 46p. (J). pap. 10.00 *(978-1-0939-7559-8(8))* Independently Published.

Jones, Richard. Bird Builds a Nest: A First Science Storybook. Jenkins, Martin. (ENG.). 32p. (J). (gr. -1-1). 2020. pap. 7.99 *(978-1-5362-1056-9(0))*; 2018. 16.99 *(978-0-7636-9346-6(4))* Candlewick Pr.

—Chrissa, Bk. 1. Casanova, Mary. England, Tamara, ed. 2009. (American Girl: Chrissa Ser.). (ENG.). 130p. (YA). (gr. 2-4). pap. 21.19 *(978-1-59369-566-8(7))* American Girl Publishing, Inc.

—Our Planet: the One Place We All Call Home. Whyman, Matt. 2019. (ENG.). 96p. (J). 24.99 *(978-0-00-837831-8(2)*, HarperCollins Children's Bks.) HarperCollins Pubs. Ltd. GBR. Dist: HarperCollins Pubs.

—Paper Planes. Helmore, Jim. 2020. (ENG.). 32p. (J). (gr. -1-3). 17.99 *(978-1-68263-161-4(3))* Peachtree Publishing Co. Inc.

—The Proper Way to Meet a Hedgehog & Other How-To Poems. Janeczko, Paul B. 2019. (ENG.). 48p. (J). (gr. 1-4). 17.99 *(978-0-7636-8168-5(7))* Candlewick Pr.

—The Snow Lion. Helmore, Jim. rev. ed. 2018. (ENG.). 32p. (J). (gr. -1-3). 17.95 *(978-1-68263-048-8(X))* Peachtree Publishing Co. Inc.

—The Squirrels' Busy Year: A First Science Storybook. Jenkins, Martin. 2018. (Science Storybooks Ser.). (ENG.). 32p. (J). (gr. -1-1). 16.99 *(978-0-7636-9600-9(5))* Candlewick Pr.

—Whale in a Fishbowl. Howell, Troy. 2018. 40p. (J). (gr. -1-3). 17.99 *(978-1-5247-1518-2(2)*, Schwartz & Wade Bks.) Random Hse. Children's Bks.

—Winter Dance. Bauer, Marion Dane. 2017. (ENG.). 40p. (J). (gr. -1-3). 16.99 *(978-0-544-31334-7(8)*, 1581571, HMH Books For Young Readers) Houghton Mifflin Harcourt Publishing Co.

—Winter Dance (board Book) Bauer, Marion Dane. 2018. (ENG.). 30p. (J). (— 1). bds. 8.99 *(978-1-328-52534-5(1)*, 1721228, HMH Books For Young Readers) Houghton Mifflin Harcourt Publishing Co.

Jones, Rob. Burly & Grum & the Birthday Surprise. Tenbeth, Kate. 2012. 108p. pap. *(978-0-9572119-9-5(6))* Magic Toy Bks.

—Burly & Grum & the Secret City. Tenbeth, Kate. 2012. 108p. pap. *(978-0-9572119-5-7(3))* Magic Toy Bks.

—Burly & Grum & the Tiger's Tale. Tenbeth, Kate. 2013. 36p. pap. *(978-0-9572119-7-1(X))* Magic Toy Bks.

Jones, Robert. One & One & One. Untermeyer, Louis. 2016. (ENG.). 64p. (J). (gr. k-3). pap. 9.99 *(978-0-486-81065-2(8))* Dover Pubns., Inc.

Jones, Russell. Snout about Town: A Tale for Precocious Canines & Their Personal Assistants. Mitchum, Petrine Day. 2017. (ENG.). (J). (gr. -1-3). 24.95 *(978-0-692-94429-5(X))* Petrine Day Mitchum.

Jones, Ryan. Too Much Picnic. Honigsberg, Peter John. 2006. 32p. (J). 16.95 *(978-1-57143-154-7(3))* RDR Bks.

Jones, Sandy. A New Baby for Jayden. Jones, Sandy. 2019. (ENG.). 26p. (J). pap. 10.00 *(978-1-0707-2329-7(0))* Independently Published.

Jones, Sarah. Ears, Nose, Eyes... Surprise! Jones, Sarah. 2018. (ROYGBaby Ser.). (ENG.). 14p. (J). (— 1). bds. 7.99 *(978-1-936669-62-2(5))* Blue Manatee Press.

Jones, Sarah & Rew & Jones, Lilah. Evalina's Egg. Jones, Sarah & Rew. 2019. (ENG.). 36p. (J). pap. 9.89 ***(978-1-7113-5875-8(4))*** Independently Published.

Jones, Seth. The Man in the Clouds, 1 vol. Stamey, Marsha. 2009. 21p. pap. 24.95 *(978-1-60836-730-6(4))* PublishAmerica, Inc.

Jones, Sherilyn. Can't Keep up with the Joneses: Created to Be. Jones, Sherilyn. 2015. (ENG.). (J). pap. 9.99 *(978-0-9864191-0-2(9))* Concept Media Group, LLC, The.

Jones, Sophie. Animals in a Mess. Dobrowolska, Kate. 2018. (ENG.). 46p. (J). (gr. k-1). pap. *(978-1-78222-625-3(7))* Paragon Publishing, Rothersthorpe.

Jones, Stephanie. Bedtime. 2007. (Luxury Look & Say Board Bks.). 12p. (J). (gr. -1-k). bds. 12.99 *(978-0-7945-1461-7(8)*, Usborne) EDC Publishing.

—123. Allman, Howard & MMStudios, photos by. Litchfield, Jo & Sanchez Gallego, Maria Isabel. 2007. (Dime lo Que Ves Ser.). 22p. (J). bds. 14.99 *(978-0-7460-8354-3(8)*, Usborne) EDC Publishing.

Jones, Stephanie, jt. illus. see Durber, Matt.

Jones, Stephanie, jt. illus. see Litchfield, Jo.

Jones, Steven E., Jr. The Ballad of Blue Eagle. Jones, Steven E. 2011. (Blue Eagle Ser.). (ENG.). 48p. (J). (gr. -1-2). 18.95 *(978-0-9794655-1-2(6))* Blue Eagle Bks., Inc.

—Blue Eagle Meets Double Trouble. Jones, Steven E. 2008. (Blue Eagle Ser.). (ENG.). 40p. (J). (gr. -1-2). 15.95 *(978-0-9794655-0-5(8))* Blue Eagle Bks., Inc.

Jones, Terry, jt. illus. see Fairgray, Richard.

Jones, Tim. En Busca de Freda. Murphy, Stuart J. Mlawer, Teresa, tr. 2012. (I See I Learn Ser.: 23). 32p. (J). (-k). 14.95 *(978-1-58089-494-4(1))* Charlesbridge Publishing, Inc.

—Freda Says Please. Murphy, Stuart J. 2013. (I See I Learn Ser.: 15). 32p. (J). (-k). pap. 6.95 *(978-1-58089-475-3(5))* Charlesbridge Publishing, Inc.

—Freda Stops a Bully. Murphy, Stuart J. 2012. (I See I Learn Ser.: 11). 32p. (J). (-k). 14.95 *(978-1-58089-466-1(6))*; pap. 6.95 *(978-1-58089-467-8(4))* Charlesbridge Publishing, Inc.

—Percy Gets Upset: Percy Se Enoja. Murphy, Stuart J. 2017. (SPA & ENG.). (J). pap. *(978-1-63289-029-0(1))* Charlesbridge Publishing, Inc.

—Scrubba Dub, Carlos. Murphy, Stuart J. 2013. (I See I Learn Ser.: 16). 32p. (J). (-k). pap. 6.95 *(978-1-58089-479-1(8))* Charlesbridge Publishing, Inc.

—Write on, Carlos! Murphy, Stuart J. 2011. (I See I Learn Ser.). 32p. (J). (-k). pap. 6.95 *(978-1-58089-465-4(8))* Charlesbridge Publishing, Inc.

—Write on, Carlos! ¡Carlos Escribe Su Nombre! Murphy, Stuart J. 2017. (J). pap. *(978-1-63289-030-6(5))* Charlesbridge Publishing, Inc.

Jones, Tina C. & Balogh, Jared. Mothballs, Mothballs All in the Hall: Memories of a Great World War II Hero. Jones, Tina C. 2012. 48p. pap. 24.95 *(978-1-4560-7483-8(0))* America Star Bks.

Jones, Val. Who Wants Broccoli? Jones, Val. 2015. (ENG.). 40p. (J). (gr. -1-3). 17.99 *(978-0-06-230351-6(1))* HarperCollins Pubs.

Jones, Veronica V. Contando Los Cangrejos Herradura a la Luz de la Luna. Bathala, Neeti & Curtis, Jennifer Keats. 2017. (SPA.). 32p. (J). (gr. k-3). pap. 9.95 *(978-1-62855-932-3(2))* Arbordale Publishing.

—L' Adoption de Bebe Ours. Curtis, Jennifer Keats. Troff, Sophie, tr. 2019. (FRE.). 32p. (J). 11.95 *(978-1-64351-585-4(3))* Arbordale Publishing.

—Moonlight Crab Count. Bathala, Neeti & Curtis, Jennifer Keats. 2017. (ENG & SPA.). 32p. (J). (gr. k-3). 17.95 *(978-1-62855-930-9(6))* Arbordale Publishing.

Jones, Wilfred. The Island of the Mighty. Colum, Padraic. 2019. (ENG.). 240p. (J). (gr. 5-9). 18.99 *(978-1-5344-4561-1(7))*; pap. 9.99 *(978-1-5344-4560-4(9))* Simon & Schuster Children's Publishing. (Aladdin).

Jones, Zach. Alligators Coming! Gray, Susannah. 2012. 20p. pap. 15.00 *(978-1-4575-1316-9(1))* Dog Ear Publishing, LLC.

Jonke, Tim. The Tale of Three Trees. Hunt, Angela E. 25th ed. 2014. (ENG.). 32p. (J). 13.99 *(978-0-7459-6512-3(1))* Lion Hudson PLC GBR. Dist: Independent Pubs. Group.

—Los Tres Árboles / The Tale of Three Trees (bilingual) Cento Tradicional. Hunt, Angela Elwell. ed. 2010. Orig. Title: The Tale of Three Trees - A Traditional Folktale. 32p. (J). 5.99 *(978-1-4143-3737-1(X)*, 4602727) Tyndale Hse. Pubs.

Jonsdottir, Aslaug. The Story of the Blue Planet. Magnason, Andri Snaer. D'Arcy, Julian Meldon, tr. 2013. 136p. (J). (gr. 2-5). pap. 9.95 *(978-1-60980-506-7(2)*, Triangle Square) Seven Stories Pr.

Joo, Soon-kyo. Dad's Favorite Cookie: Japan. Jeong, Gu-mi. 2015. (Global Kids Storybooks Ser.). (ENG.). 32p. (J). (gr. 1-4). pap. 8.99 *(978-1-925233-42-1(1)*, Big and SMALL) ChoiceMaker Pty. Ltd., The AUS. Dist: Lerner Publishing Group.

—Dad's Favorite Cookie: Japan. Jeong, Gu-mi. Cowley, Joy, ed. 2015. (Global Kids Storybooks Ser.). (ENG.). 32p. (gr. 1-4). 26.65 *(978-1-925246-00-1(0))*; 26.65 *(978-1-925246-26-1(4))*; 7.99 *(978-1-925246-52-0(3))* ChoiceMaker Pty. Ltd., The AUS. (Big and SMALL). Dist: Lerner Publishing Group.

Joost, Trudy. Cassandra's Angel, Set. Otto, Gina. 2003. 32p. (J). 34.99 *(978-0-9740454-3-6(8))* Gina's Ink.

Jordan, Apple, et al. Merida Is Our Babysitter. 2016. *(978-1-5182-2107-1(6)*, Golden Bks.) Random Hse. Children's Bks.

Jordan, Carol. I Know You Won't Forget. Truly Blessed Ink. 2007. (ENG.). 40p. (J). 16.95 *(978-0-9789066-1-0(6))* Square Circle Pr. LLC.

Jordan, Carrie. America the Beautiful: A Pop-up Book about the Famous Song by Katharine Lee Bates. Lee Bates, Katharine & Gamwell, Calvert. 2006. 16p. (J). (gr. 4-8). reprint ed. 17.00 *(978-1-4223-5447-6(4))* DIANE Publishing Co.

Jordan, Cecil Lee. My Grandma Is a Unicorn. Danson, Christian Ivilla. 2019. (ENG.). 26p. (J). (gr. 1-6). 15.00 ***(978-0-578-58872-8(2))*** Wall, Christian.

Jordan, Charles. Daniel el Descortes: Rude Ralph. Fontes, Justine. 2005. (Rookie Reader Español Ser.). 32p. (gr. k-2). 19.50 *(978-0-516-24444-0(2)*, Children's Pr.) Scholastic Library Publishing.

—Rude Ralph: A Rookie Reader. Fontes, Justine. 2011. (Rookie Ready to Learn Ser.). 40p. (J). pap. 5.95 *(978-0-531-26711-0(3))*; (ENG.). (gr. -1-1). lib. bdg. 23.00 *(978-0-531-26529-1(3))* Scholastic Library Publishing. (Children's Pr.).

Jordan, Charles. Daniel el Descortés. Jordan, Charles. Fontes, Justine. 2011. (Rookie Ready to Learn Español Ser.). (SPA.). 40p. (J). pap. 5.95 *(978-0-531-26790-5(3))*; (gr. -1-1). lib. bdg. 23.00 *(978-0-531-26122-4(0))* Scholastic Library Publishing. (Children's Pr.).

Jordan, Jenae. My Diary: My First Journal (Primary Composition Notebook with Picture Box) Creations, Custom Book. 2018. (My First Creative Books: Rainbow Teddy Bear Ser.: Vol. 2). (ENG.). 102p. (J). pap. 7.87 *(978-1-949301-01-4(X))* Rhythm & Reasoning Pubns.

—My Journal: My First Journal (Primary Composition Notebook with Picture Box) Creations, Custom Book. 2018. (My First Creative Books: Primary Colors Teddy Bear Ser.: Vol. 2). (ENG.). 102p. (J). pap. 7.87 *(978-1-949301-05-2(2))* Rhythm & Reasoning Pubns.

—My Picture Book: My First Story Book (Primary Composition Notebook with Picture Box) Creations, Custom Book. 2018. (My First Creative Books: Rainbow Teddy Bear Ser.: Vol. 3). (ENG.). 102p. (J). pap. 7.87 *(978-1-949301-03-8(6))*; pap. 7.87 *(978-1-949301-06-9(0))* Rhythm & Reasoning Pubns.

—My Sketchbook: My First Sketch Book (Drawing Notebook with Picture Box) Creations, Custom Book. 2018. (My First Creative Books: Primary Colors Teddy Bear Ser.: Vol. 1). (ENG.). 102p. (J). pap. 7.87 *(978-1-949301-04-5(4))*; pap. 7.87 *(978-1-949301-02-1(8))* Rhythm & Reasoning Pubns.

Jordan, John. Lopsided. Ferguson, Sherry Ann. 2019. (ENG.). 88p. (J). pap. 9.95 ***(978-1-9736-7345-3(2)***, WestBow Pr.) Author Solutions, Inc.

Jordan, Yasmine. Apollo: A Light in Shining Armor. Heredia, Denise. 2018. (ENG.). 52p. (J). (gr. k-4). pap. 10.99 *(978-0-692-10461-3(5))* Heredia, Denise.

Jordon, Zoe. Timmy's Small Mind. Runnels, Alyson. 2019. (ENG.). 26p. (J). pap. 13.99 *(978-1-7277-0859-2(8))* CreateSpace Independent Publishing Platform.

—Words That Soar. Alexander, John. 2018. (ENG.). 34p. (J). 19.95 *(978-0-578-40682-4(9))* Alexander, John.

Jorge, Gutiérrez Sahagún. Dicionario Inicial Everest. Equipo Staff. (SPA.). 336p. *(978-84-241-1013-0(7))* Everest Editora ESP. Dist: Lectorum Pubns., Inc.

Jorge Sarrio, Silvia. Jeremies, el Ratolí de Biblioteca. Gomez Parrado, Catalina. 2018. (CAT.). 46p. (J). pap. 10.99 *(978-1-7315-8618-6(3))* Independently Published.

Jorgensen, David. The Steadfast Tin Soldier. Andersen, Hans. 2005. (Rabbit Ears-A Classic Tale Ser.).Tr. of Standhaftige Tinsoldat. (ENG.). 42p. (J). (gr. 2-6). 28.50 *(978-1-59679-346-0(5)*, 12947, Picture Bk.) Spotlight.

—The Tailor of Gloucester, 1 vol. Potter, Beatrix. 2007. (Rabbit Ears-A Classic Tale Ser.). (ENG.). 44p. (J). (gr. 2-6). 28.50 *(978-1-59961-312-3(3)*, 12965, Picture Bk.) Spotlight.

—The Tale of Mr. Jeremy Fisher, 1 vol. Potter, Beatrix. 2005. (Rabbit Ears-A Classic Tale Ser.). (ENG.). 28p. (J). (gr. 2-6). 28.50 *(978-1-59197-753-7(3)*, 12955, Picture Bk.) Spotlight.

—The Three Billy Goats Gruff, 1 vol. Roberts, Tom & Asbjørnsen, Peter Christen. 2005. (Rabbit Ears-A Classic Tale Ser.). (ENG.). 28p. (J). (gr. 2-6). 28.50 *(978-1-59197-754-4(1)*, 12939, Picture Bk.) Spotlight.

—The Velveteen Rabbit. Williams, Margery. 2005. (Rabbit Ears-A Classic Tale Ser.). (ENG.). 42p. (J). (gr. 2-6). 28.50 *(978-1-59197-757-5(6)*, 12956, Picture Bk.) Spotlight.

Jorisch, Stéphane. Betty Bunny Didn't Do It. Kaplan, Michael B. 2013. (Betty Bunny Ser.). 32p. (J). (gr. -1-k). 17.99 *(978-0-8037-3858-4(7)*, Dial Bks) Penguin Young Readers Group.

—Betty Bunny Loves Chocolate Cake. Kaplan, Michael. 2011. (Betty Bunny Ser.). 32p. (J). (gr. -1-k). 17.99 *(978-0-8037-3407-4(7)*, Dial Bks) Penguin Young Readers Group.

—Betty Bunny Loves Chocolate Cake (1 Paperback/1 CD) Kaplan, Michael B. 2012. (Betty Bunny Ser.). (ENG.). (J). (gr. -1-k). 19.95 *(978-1-4301-1131-3(3))* Live Oak Media.

—Betty Bunny Loves Chocolate Cake (4 Paperback/1 CD) Kaplan, Michael B. 2012. (Betty Bunny Ser.). (ENG.). (J). (gr. -1-k). 48.95 *(978-1-4301-1133-7(X))* Live Oak Media.

—Betty Bunny Loves Easter. Kaplan, Michael B. 2015. (Betty Bunny Ser.). 32p. (J). (gr. -1-k). 16.99 *(978-0-8037-4061-7(1)*, Dial Bks) Penguin Young Readers Group.

—Betty Bunny Wants a Goal. Kaplan, Michael B. 2014. (Betty Bunny Ser.). 32p. (J). (gr. -1-k). 17.99 *(978-0-8037-3859-1(5)*, Dial Bks) Penguin Young Readers Group.

—Betty Bunny Wants Everything. Kaplan, Michael B. 2012. (Betty Bunny Ser.). 32p. (J). (gr. -1-k). 17.99 *(978-0-8037-3408-1(5)*, Dial Bks) Penguin Young Readers Group.

—La Boite a Bonheur. Gingras, Charlotte. 2004. (Mon Roman Ser.). (FRE.). 64p. (J). (gr. 2). pap. *(978-2-89021-668-6(3))* Diffusion du livre Mirabel (DLM).

—Un Cadeau Pour Sophie: Conte et Chansons. Vigneault, Gilles. 2013. (FRE & ENG.). 40p. (J). (gr. k-2). 16.95 *(978-2-923163-38-3(9))* La Montagne Secrete CAN. Dist: Independent Pubs. Group.

—Footwork: The Story of Fred & Adele Astaire. Orgill, Roxane. (Candlewick Biographies Ser.). 48p. (J). 2013. (gr. 3-7). pap. 4.99 *(978-0-7636-6215-8(1))*; 2007. (gr. 4-6). 17.44 *(978-0-7636-2121-6(8))* Candlewick Pr.

—Footwork: The Story of Fred & Adele Astaire. Orgill, Roxane. 2013. (Candlewick Biographies Ser.). 48p. (J). (gr. 3-7). 14.99 *(978-0-7636-6460-2(X))* Candlewick Pr.

—Le Gardien du Sommeil. Tibo, Gilles. 2004. (Mon Roman Ser.). (FRE.). 64p. (J). (gr. 2). pap. *(978-2-89021-691-4(8))* Diffusion du livre Mirabel (DLM).

—A Gift for Sophie. Vigneault, Gilles. 2013. (ENG.). 44p. (J). (gr. k-2). 16.95 *(978-2-923163-98-7(2))* La Montagne Secrete CAN. Dist: Independent Pubs. Group.

—My Father Knows the Names of Things. Yolen, Jane. 2010. (ENG.). 32p. (J). (gr. -1-3). 19.99 *(978-1-4169-4895-7(3)*, Simon & Schuster Bks. For Young Readers) Simon & Schuster Bks. For Young Readers.

—My Name Is Chicken Joe. Trout Fishing in America Staff et al. 2009. (ENG.). 50p. (J). (gr. -1-2). 16.95 *(978-2-923163-49-9(4))* La Montagne Secrete CAN. Dist: Independent Pubs. Group.

—New Year at the Pier: A Rosh Hashanah Story. Wayland, April Halprin. 2009. 352p. (J). *(978-0-8037-3110-3(8)*, Dial) Penguin Publishing Group.

—El Principe y el Mendigo. Bourgeois, Paulette & Paulette, Bourgeois. 2003.Tr. of Oma's Quilt. (SPA.). 32p. (J). (gr. k-2). 14.99 *(978-84-241-8644-9(3))* Everest Editora ESP. Dist: Lectorum Pubns., Inc.

—The Real Story of Stone Soup. Compestine, Ying Chang. 2007. 32p. (J). (gr. k-3). 16.99 *(978-0-525-47493-7(5)*, Dutton Books for Young Readers) Penguin Young Readers Group.

—The Riddlemaster, 1 vol. Crossley-Holland, Kevin. 2016. (ENG.). 32p. (J). (gr. 1-3). 16.95 *(978-1-926890-11-1(6))* Tradewind Bks. CAN. Dist: Orca Bk. Pubs. USA.

—Suki's Kimono. Uegaki, Chieri. 2005. (ENG.). 32p. (J). (gr. -1-3). pap. 8.95 *(978-1-55337-752-8(4))* Kids Can Pr., Ltd. CAN. Dist: Hachette Bk. Group.

—Les Tenebres Piegees, Vol. RJ 65. Gauthier, Bertrand. 2003. (Roman Jeunesse Ser.). (FRE.). 96p. (YA). (gr. 4-7). pap. *(978-2-89021-292-3(0))* Diffusion du livre Mirabel (DLM).

—A Treasure in My Garden. Vigneault, Gilles. 2007. (ENG & FRE.). 36p. (J). (gr. -1-2). 16.95 *(978-2-923163-14-7(1))* La Montagne Secrete CAN. Dist: Independent Pubs. Group.

Jorisch, Stephane. What Does It Mean to Be Kind? DiOrio, Rana. 2015. (What Does It Mean to Be... ? Ser.: 0). 36p. (J). (gr. -1-3). 17.95 *(978-1-939775-09-2(4)*, Little Pickle Pr.) Sourcebooks, Inc.

Jorisch, Stéphane. What Does It Mean to Be Kind? DiOrio, Rana. 2020. (What Does It Mean to Be... ? Ser.). 32p. (J). (-3). 8.99 ***(978-1-7282-2305-6(9)***, Little Pickle Pr.) Sourcebooks, Inc.

Jorisch, Stéphane, jt. illus. see Trout Fishing in America Staff.

Jory, John. The Terrible Two's Last Laugh. Barnett, Mac. 2018. (Terrible Two Ser.). (ENG.). 224p. (J). (gr. 3-7). 13.99 *(978-1-4197-2565-4(3)*, 1093901, Amulet Bks.) Abrams, Inc.

Jos, Luis Telleria. Mis Primeros Relatos de Miedo. Mañeru, Maria et al. 2004. 312p. (J). *(978-968-13-3782-7(4))* Editorial Diana, S.A. MEX. Dist: Lectorum Pubns., Inc.

Jose, Gladys. The Elephants' Guide to Hide-And-Seek. Hayes, Kjersten. 2020. 32p. (J). (-3). 17.99 *(978-1-4926-7846-5(5)*, Sourcebooks Jabberwocky) Sourcebooks, Inc.

—Fresh Princess. Millner, Denene. 2019. (ENG.). 32p. (J). (gr. -1-3). 18.99 *(978-0-06-288457-2(3)*, HarperCollins) HarperCollins Pubs. Ltd. GBR. Dist: HarperCollins Pubs.

—Fresh Princess: Style Rules! Millner, Denene. 2020. (ENG.). 32p. (J). (gr. -1-3). 18.99 *(978-0-06-288458-9(1)*, HarperCollins) HarperCollins Pubs. Ltd. GBR. Dist: HarperCollins Pubs.

Jose, Gladys. Pterapunzel (Once Before Time Book 3) Webster, Christy. 2020. (Once Before Time Ser.). (ENG.). 32p. (J). bds. 8.99 ***(978-1-5248-5823-0(4))*** Andrews McMeel Publishing.

Jose, Gladys. Sleeping Bronty (Once Before Time Book 2) Webster, Christy. 2020. (Once Before Time Ser.). (ENG.). 32p. (J). bds. 8.99 *(978-1-5248-5571-0(5))* Andrews McMeel Publishing.

Joseph, Albert. The Magic Log. Mesibere, Ellen. Naime, Sophie, ed. 2012. 24p. pap. *(978-9980-945-68-6(0))* Univ. of Papua New Guinea Pr.

Joseph, Andrew. The Giant Robot Dinosaur. Joseph, Andrew. Chung, Katrina, ed. 2018. (Orange Ninja Versus Ser.: Vol. 1). (ENG.). 28p. (J). pap. 9.15 *(978-1-7907-6070-1(4))* Independently Published.

Joseph, Audeav. Lila Plays Soccer / Lila Ap Jwe Boul. Doret, Christina. 2019. (ENG.). 26p. (J). pap. 12.95 ***(978-1-951446-02-4(X)***, Nabu Pr.) Creative Media Partners, LLC.

Joseph, Audeva. Princess Maniya / Prenses Maniya. Jean Baptiste, Saonha Lyrvole. Lamour, Wynnie, tr. 2019. (ENG.). 20p. (J). pap. 12.95 ***(978-1-951446-01-7(1)***, Nabu Pr.) Creative Media Partners, LLC.

Joseph, Chris. Anxious Little Pishy. Joseph, Brittany. Murillo, Jess, ed. 2018. (ENG.). 42p. (J). (gr. k-3). 19.99 *(978-0-9998328-1-3(6))* Mischief Productions.

Joseph, John. Brother Lorenzo's Pretzels: Prayer & the Holy Trinity. Bilinsky, Cornelia Mary. 2019. (ENG.). 40p. (J). pap. 12.95 ***(978-0-8198-1242-1(0))*** Pauline Bks. & Media.

Joseph, John. Dear Santa: Let Me Explain... Hill, Susanna Leonard. 2019. 40p. (J). (-3). 17.99 *(978-1-4926-9474-8(6)*, Sourcebooks Jabberwocky) Sourcebooks, Inc.

—Rain, Rain, Go Away, the Dinosaurs All Want to Play. Fitzpatrick, Joe. 2019. (Dino Rhymes Ser.). (ENG.). 20p. (J). (gr. -1-1). bds. 7.99 *(978-1-4867-1558-9(3)*, 3779f89e-7eb3-4e72-8fe4-38a1c721bf2d) Flowerpot Pr.

—Star Light, Star Bright, Even Dinosaurs Say Good Night. Fitzpatrick, Joe. 2019. (Dino Rhymes Ser.). (ENG.). 20p. (J). (gr. -1-1). bds. 7.99 *(978-1-4867-1557-2(5)*, 3f7e9ecd-3f04-4cf7-93b7-b5eb726b4a7f) Flowerpot Pr.

—When Eleanor Roosevelt Learned to Jump a Horse. Weakland, Mark. 2019. (Leaders Doing Headstands Ser.). (ENG.). 32p. (J). (gr. 1-4). pap. 7.95 *(978-1-5158-3050-4(0)*, 138685, Picture Window Bks.) Capstone.

Joseph, John, jt. illus. see Newman Gray, James.

Joseph, Patricia. Daddy's Number One Little Girl. Cooper, Glenessa. 2008. 10p. pap. 24.95 *(978-1-60563-983-3(4))* America Star Bks.

Joseph, Robin & Campbell, Scott. Zombie in Love. DiPucchio, Kelly. 2011. (ENG.). 32p. (J). (gr. -1-3). 15.99 *(978-1-4424-0270-6(9)*, Atheneum Bks. for Young Readers) Simon & Schuster Children's Publishing.

Josephine, Wall. Scented Adventures of the Bouquet Sisters in Fairyland. Hall, Susan Liberty. 2011. 85p. (YA). pap. 21.50 *(978-0-9833247-6-8(X))* Inkwell Books LLC.

Josephs, Alison. Custard & Mustard: Carlos in Coney Island. Sullivan, Maureen. 2009. 32p. 17.95 *(978-0-9820381-1-6(9))* MoJo InkWorks.

Josephs, Alison. Ankle Soup: A Thanksgiving Story. Josephs, Alison. Sullivan, Maureen. 2008. 32p. 17.95 *(978-0-9820381-0-9(0))* MoJo InkWorks.

Josey, Clarke, jt. illus. see Redd, Zai.

Josh Green. My Sanctuary: A Place I Call Home - Keepers of the Wild. Ingram, Doreen. 2013. 54p. pap. 17.50 *(978-1-62516-273-1(1)*, Strategic Bk. Publishing) Strategic Book Publishing & Rights Agency (SBPRA).

Joshi, Dileep. The Blue Jackal. Viswanath, Shobha. 2016. (ENG.). 34p. (J). 15.00 *(978-0-8028-5466-7(4)*, Eerdmans Bks For Young Readers) Eerdmans, William B. Publishing Co.

Joshi, Jagdish. The Ramayana in Pictures. Dayal, Mala. 2006. 64p. (J). *(978-81-291-0896-8(8))* Rupa & Co.

Joshua, Aaron. There Was a Man & He Was Mad. 2008. (First Steps in Music Ser.). (ENG.). 24p. (J). (gr. -1-k). 17.95 *(978-1-57999-681-9(7))* G I A Pubns., Inc.

Joshua, Benson Benson Joshua. Who Were the Magi. Benson, Lyn. 2007. 56p. pap. 23.99 *(978-0-615-13524-3(2))* Benson, Lyn.

Josie, Melinda. Powwow Counting in Cree. Thomas, Penny M. 2013. (ENG.). 24p. (J). (gr. k-3). *(978-1-55379-392-2(7)*, 9781553793922, HighWater Pr.) Portage & Main Pr.

Joslin, Irene. Never Too Big for Monkey Hugs. Neely, Judith. 2009. 16p. pap. 8.49 *(978-1-4389-7289-3(X))* AuthorHouse.

—What If Marshmallows Fell from the Sky. Becker, Michele Joy. 2009. 32p. pap. 12.99 *(978-1-4389-0152-7(6))* AuthorHouse.

—When I Grow Up. Eisenberg, Kristy. 2009. 28p. pap. 12.49 *(978-1-4389-0183-1(6))* AuthorHouse.

Josse, Annabelle. Noah's Garden: When Someone You Love Is in the Hospital. Johnson, Mo. 2010. (ENG.). 32p. (J). (gr. -1-2). 15.99 *(978-0-7636-4782-7(9))* Candlewick Pr.

Jossem, Carol. Ula Li'i & the Magic Shark. Laird, Donivee M. 2003. 49p. (J). (gr. k-3). 9.95 *(978-0-940350-23-6(8))* Barnaby Bks., Inc.

—Will Wai Kula & the Three Mongooses. Laird, Donivee M. 2003. 41p. (J). (gr. k-3). 9.95 *(978-0-940350-24-3(6))* Barnaby Bks., Inc.

Jotave, Jazmin Velasco. Confidencias de un Superhéroe. Sandoval, Jaime Alfonso et al. rev. ed. 2004. (Castillo de la Lectura Roja Ser.). (SPA & ENG.). 232p. (J). pap. 8.95 *(978-970-20-0180-5(3))* Castillo, Ediciones, S. A. de C. V. MEX. Dist: Macmillan.

Joubert, Tamara. Where Are You Going? Pink B Band. Franklin, Glen & Bodman, Sue. 2017. (Cambridge Reading Adventures Ser.). (ENG.). 16p. (J). pap. 5.62 *(978-1-108-43967-1(5))* Cambridge Univ. Pr.

Jougla, Karina. Tricked on Halloween: Rina & Jax's Stories. Jougla, Frederic. l.t. ed. 2004. 36p. (J). bds. 14.99 *(978-0-9754287-0-2(5))* Imagery Pr.

Jourdan, Diego & Galligher, John. Haunted Hijinks. Check, S. A. et al. 2019. (ENG.). 128p. (J). pap. 19.99 *(978-1-945205-17-0(2),* f812e2dd-3798-4f3b-a937-d4eba6ba49ba) American Mythology Productions.

Jourdenais-Martin, Norma Jean. Make Your Own Puppets & Puppet Theaters. Carreiro, Carolyn. 2005. (ENG.). 64p. (YA). 10.95 *(978-0-8249-6776-5(3),* 1249275); per. 10.95 *(978-0-8249-6770-3(4),* 1249275) Worthy Publishing. (Ideal Pubns.).

Jovanovic, Luka. Amazing Dreams: A Good Morning Story. Sandusky, Mark. 2019. (ENG.). 26p. (J). pap. 9.99 ***(978-1-0737-4327-8(6))*** Independently Published.

—The Purpose of a Porpoise: A Rhyming Underwater Tale of Self-Discovery. Sandusky, Mark. 2019. (ENG.). 26p. (J). pap. 9.99 ***(978-1-0737-5938-5(5))*** Independently Published.

Jovanovic, Vanja Vuleta. I Am Violet. Stehlik, Tania Duprey. 2020. (ENG.). 18p. (J). (gr. -1-k). bds. 10.95 ***(978-1-77260-131-2(4))*** Second Story Pr. CAN. Dist: Orca Bk. Pubs. USA.

Jovanovic, Vanja Vuleta & Second Story Press Staff. Violet, 1 vol. Stehlik, Tania Duprey. 2009. (ENG.). 32p. (J). (gr. 1-3). 15.95 *(978-1-897187-60-9(2))* Second Story Pr. CAN. Dist: Orca Bk. Pubs. USA.

Joven, John. Bulldozer Dreams. Chriscoe, Sharon. 2017. 32p. (J). (gr. -1-3). 16.99 *(978-0-7624-5966-7(2),* Running Pr. Kids) Running Pr.

—Charlie Takes His Shot: How Charlie Sifford Broke the Color Barrier in Golf. Churnin, Nancy. 2018. (ENG.). 32p. (J). (gr. -1-3). 16.99 *(978-0-8075-1128-2(5),* 807511285) Whitman, Albert & Co.

—Christmas Activity Book. Jones, Karl. 2019. 16p. (J). (gr. 3-7). pap. 9.99 *(978-0-593-09458-7(1),* Penguin Workshop) Penguin Young Readers Group.

—Digging for Dinosaurs: Deluxe Multi Activity Book. Garnett, Jaye. 2017. (Smithsonian Kids Ser.). (ENG.). 12p. (J). (gr. -1-2). bds. 12.99 *(978-1-68052-234-1(5),* 1002200) Cottage Door Pr.

—Hillel Takes a Bath. Weber, Vicki L. 2019. (J). *(978-1-68115-546-3(X),* Apples & Honey Pr.) Behrman Hse., Inc.

—Plan para Desenmascarar Brujas. Dávila, Valeria. 2014. (SPA.). 96p. (J). (gr. 2-4). pap. 7.95 *(978-607-8237-29-6(2))* Nostra Ediciones MEX. Dist: Independent Pubs. Group.

—Preschool, Here I Come! Steinberg, D. J. (Here I Come! Ser.). (J). (-k). 2020. 26p. bds. 9.99 *(978-1-5247-9054-7(0));* 2019. (ENG.). 32p. 9.99 *(978-1-5247-9052-3(4));* 2019. (ENG.). 32p. pap. 5.99 *(978-1-5247-9051-6(6))* Penguin Young Readers Group. (Grosset & Dunlap).

Joy, Delgado. Zooprise Party / Fiesta Zoorpresa Activity Book / Actividades. Joy, Delgado. 2008. (ENG & SPA.). 20p. (J). 4.95 *(978-0-9755454-2-3(6),* Laughing Zebra - Bks. for Children) J.O.Y. Publishing.

Joy, Tara. The Inner Sense of Trees. Joy, Tara. 2016. (ENG.). (J). (gr. 2-6). pap. *(978-0-9956110-1-6(7))* Art of Joy Pubns.The.

Joyce, John. Black John the Bogus Pirate - Cartoon Workbook of Marine Beasts. Joyce, John. 2012. (ENG.). 20p. (J). *(978-0-9557637-8-6(9))* Sprindrift Pr.

Joyce, Mark. Mythical Irish Beasts. 2018. (ENG.). viii, 128p. 46.99 *(978-1-78218-905-3(X))* Currach Pr. IRL. Dist: Casemate Pubs. & Bk. Distributors, LLC.

Joyce, Peter. The Once upon a Time Map Book: Take a Tour of Six Enchanted Lands. Hennessy, Barbara G. 2013. 16p. (J). (gr. 1-4). 24.99 *(978-0-7636-6475-6(8))* Candlewick Pr.

—The Once upon a Time Map Book: Take a Tour of Six Enchanted Lands. Hennessy, B. G. 2010. (ENG.). 16p. (J). (gr. 1-4). pap. 9.99 *(978-0-7636-2682-2(1))* Candlewick Pr.

Joyce, Sophie. The Glowworm Who Lost Her Glow. Bedford, William. 2005. (Blue Go Bananas Ser.). (ENG.). 48p. (J). (gr. 1-2). *(978-0-7787-2652-4(5));* lib. bdg. *(978-0-7787-2630-2(4))* Crabtree Publishing Co.

Joyce, William. Bently & Egg. Joyce, William. 2017. (World of William Joyce Ser.). (ENG.). 32p. (J). (gr. -1-3). 17.99 *(978-1-4814-8949-2(6),* Atheneum/Caitlyn Dlouhy Books) Simon & Schuster Children's Publishing.

—Big Time Olie. Joyce, William. 2018. (World of William Joyce Ser.). (ENG.). 40p. (J). (gr. -1-2). 17.99 *(978-1-4814-8969-0(0),* Atheneum Bks. for Young Readers) Simon & Schuster Children's Publishing.

—Billy's Booger. Joyce, William. Moonbot. 2015. (ENG.). 40p. (J). (gr. -1-3). 19.99 *(978-1-4424-7351-5(7))* Simon & Schuster Children's Publishing.

—Buddy: Based on the True Story of Gertrude Lintz. Joyce, William. 2018. (World of William Joyce Ser.). (ENG.). 48p. (J). (gr. k-4). 17.99 *(978-1-4814-8961-4(5))* Simon & Schuster Children's Publishing.

—A Day with Wilbur Robinson. Joyce, William. 2006. (ENG.). 40p. (J). (gr. -1-3). 16.99 *(978-0-06-089098-8(3))* HarperCollins Pubs.

—A Day with Wilbur Robinson. Joyce, William. 2017. (World of William Joyce Ser.). (ENG.). 40p. (J). (gr. -1-3). 17.99 *(978-1-4814-8951-5(8),* Atheneum/Caitlyn Dlouhy Books) Simon & Schuster Children's Publishing.

—Dinosaur Bob & His Adventures with the Family Lazardo. Joyce, William. 2017. (World of William Joyce Ser.). (ENG.). 48p. (J). (gr. -1-3). 18.99 *(978-1-4814-8947-8(X),* Atheneum/Caitlyn Dlouhy Books) Simon & Schuster Children's Publishing.

—E. Aster Bunnymund & the Warrior Eggs at the Earth's Core! Joyce, William. (Guardians Ser.: 2). (ENG.). (J). (gr. 2-6). 2018. 288p. pap. 7.99 *(978-1-4424-3051-8(6));* Bk. 2. 2012. 272p. 17.99 *(978-1-4424-3050-1(8))* Simon & Schuster Children's Publishing. (Atheneum Bks. for Young Readers).

—George Shrinks. Joyce, William. 2017. (World of William Joyce Ser.). (ENG.). 40p. (J). (gr. -1-3). 17.99 *(978-1-4814-8953-9(4),* Atheneum/Caitlyn Dlouhy Books) Simon & Schuster Children's Publishing.

—The Guardians Collection: Nicholas St. North & the Battle of the Nightmare King; E. Aster Bunnymund & the Warrior Eggs at the Earth's Core!; Toothiana, Queen of the Tooth Fairy Armies; the Sandman & the War of Dreams; Jack Frost. Joyce, William. ed. 2018. (Guardians Ser.). (ENG.). 1376p. (J). (gr. 2-6). 89.99 *(978-1-5344-4001-2(1),* Atheneum/Caitlyn Dlouhy Books) Simon & Schuster Children's Publishing.

—Jack Frost. Joyce, William. 2015. (Guardians of Childhood Ser.). (ENG.). 48p. (J). (gr. -1-3). 19.99 *(978-1-4424-3043-3(5),* Atheneum Bks. for Young Readers) Simon & Schuster Children's Publishing.

—Jack Frost: The End Becomes the Beginning. Joyce, William. 2020. (Guardians Ser.: 5). (ENG.). 400p. (J). (gr. 2-6). pap. 8.99 *(978-1-4424-3057-0(5),* Atheneum Bks. for Young Readers) Simon & Schuster Children's Publishing.

—The Leaf Men: And the Brave Good Bugs. Joyce, William. 2017. (World of William Joyce Ser.). (ENG.). 40p. (J). (gr. -1-3). 17.99 *(978-1-4814-8955-3(0),* Atheneum/Caitlyn Dlouhy Books) Simon & Schuster Children's Publishing.

—The Man in the Moon. Joyce, William. 2011. (Guardians of Childhood Ser.). (ENG.). 56p. (J). (gr. -1-3). 17.99 *(978-1-4424-3041-9(9),* Atheneum Bks. for Young Readers) Simon & Schuster Children's Publishing.

—The Man in the Moon (Limited Edition) Joyce, William. ltd. ed. 2011. (Guardians of Childhood Ser.). (ENG.). 56p. (J). (gr. -1-3). 200.00 *(978-1-4424-4357-0(X),* Atheneum Bks. for Young Readers) Simon & Schuster Children's Publishing.

—The Mischievians. Joyce, William. 2013. (ENG.). 56p. (J). (gr. k-3). 17.99 *(978-1-4424-7347-8(9),* Atheneum Bks. for Young Readers) Simon & Schuster Children's Publishing.

—Nicholas St. North & the Battle of the Nightmare King. Joyce, William. Geringer, Laura. 2018. (Guardians Ser.: 1). (ENG.). 256p. (J). (gr. 2-6). pap. 7.99 *(978-1-4424-3049-5(4),* Atheneum Bks. for Young Readers) Simon & Schuster Children's Publishing.

—Nicholas St. North & the Battle of the Nightmare King, Bk. 1. Joyce, William. Geringer, Laura. 2011. (Guardians Ser.: 1). (ENG.). 240p. (J). (gr. 2-6). 17.99 *(978-1-4424-3048-8(6),* Atheneum Bks. for Young Readers) Simon & Schuster Children's Publishing.

—Ollie's Odyssey. Joyce, William. 2017. (ENG.). 304p. (J). (gr. 2-6). pap. 12.99 *(978-1-4424-7356-0(8))* Simon & Schuster, Inc.

—Rolie Polie Olie. Joyce, William. 2017. (World of William Joyce Ser.). (ENG.). 48p. (J). (gr. -1-2). 17.99 *(978-1-4814-8957-7(7),* Atheneum Bks. for Young Readers) Simon & Schuster Children's Publishing.

—The Sandman: The Story of Sanderson Mansnoozie. Joyce, William. 2012. (Guardians of Childhood Ser.). (ENG.). 48p. (J). (gr. -1-3). 19.99 *(978-1-4424-3042-6(7),* Atheneum Bks. for Young Readers) Simon & Schuster Children's Publishing.

—The Sandman & the War of Dreams. Joyce, William. (Guardians Ser.: 4). (ENG.). (J). (gr. 2-6). 2018. 256p. pap. 7.99 *(978-1-4424-3055-6(9));* 2013. 240p. 18.99 *(978-1-4424-3054-9(0))* Simon & Schuster Children's Publishing. (Atheneum Bks. for Young Readers).

—Santa Calls. Joyce, William. 2017. (World of William Joyce Ser.). (ENG.). 40p. (J). (gr. -1). 18.99 *(978-1-4814-8959-1(3),* Atheneum Bks. for Young Readers) Simon & Schuster Children's Publishing.

—Sleepy Time Olie. Joyce, William. 2018. (World of William Joyce Ser.). (ENG.). 40p. (J). (gr. -1-2). 17.99 *(978-1-4814-8963-8(1))* Simon & Schuster Children's Publishing.

—Snowie Rolie. Joyce, William. 2017. (World of William Joyce Ser.). (ENG.). 40p. (J). (gr. -1-2). 17.99 *(978-1-4814-8967-6(4),* Atheneum Bks. for Young Readers) Simon & Schuster Children's Publishing.

—Toothiana, Queen of the Tooth Fairy Armies. Joyce, William. 2018. (Guardians Ser.: 3). (ENG.). 256p. (J). (gr. 2-6). pap. 7.99 *(978-1-4424-3053-2(2),* Atheneum Bks. for Young Readers) Simon & Schuster Children's Publishing.

—Toothiana, Queen of the Tooth Fairy Armies Bk. 3. Joyce, William. 2012. (Guardians Ser.: 3). (ENG.). 240p. (J). (gr. 2-6). 17.99 *(978-1-4424-3052-5(4),* Atheneum Bks. for Young Readers) Simon & Schuster Children's Publishing.

Joyce, William & Bluhm, Joe. The Fantastic Flying Books of Mr. Morris Lessmore. Joyce, William. 2012. (ENG.). 56p. (J). (gr. -1-3). 19.99 *(978-1-4424-5702-7(3),* Atheneum Bks. for Young Readers) Simon & Schuster Children's Publishing.

Joyce, William & Callicutt, Kenny. A Bean, a Stalk & a Boy Named Jack. Joyce, William. 2014. (ENG.). 56p. (J). (gr. -1-3). 18.99 *(978-1-4424-7349-2(5),* Atheneum Bks. for Young Readers) Simon & Schuster Children's Publishing.

Joyce, William & Ellis, Christina. The Numberlys. Joyce, William. 2014. (ENG.). 56p. (J). (gr. -1-2). 17.99 *(978-1-4424-7343-0(6),* Atheneum Bks. for Young Readers) Simon & Schuster Children's Publishing.

Joyner, Andrew. The Baby Swap. Ormerod, Jan. 2015. (ENG.). 32p. (J). (gr. -1-1). 16.99 *(978-1-4814-1914-7(5),* Little Simon) Little Simon.

—Bear Make Den. Godwin, Jane & Wagner, Michael. 2017. (ENG.). 40p. (J). (gr. -1-3). 16.99 *(978-0-7636-9061-8(9))* Candlewick Pr.

—Brindabella. Dubosarsky, Ursula. 2019. (ENG.). 208p. (J). (gr. 3-5). pap. 13.99 *(978-1-76011-204-2(6),* A&U Children's) Allen & Unwin AUS. Dist: Independent Pubs. Group.

—Dr. Seuss's Horse Museum. Seuss. 2019. (Classic Seuss Ser.). (ENG.). 80p. (J). (gr. 2). 18.99 *(978-0-399-55912-9(4));* lib. bdg. 21.99 *(978-0-399-55913-6(2))* Random Hse. Children's Bks. (Random Hse. Bks. for Young Readers).

—Duck & Hippo in the Rainstorm. London, Jonathan. 2017. (Duck & Hippo Ser.: 1). (ENG.). 32p. (J). (gr. -1-2). 17.99 *(978-1-5039-3723-9(2),* 9781503937239, Two Lions) Amazon Publishing.

—Duck & Hippo the Secret Valentine. London, Jonathan. 2018. (Duck & Hippo Ser.: 4). 32p. (J). (gr. -1-2). 17.99 *(978-1-5039-0035-6(5),* 9781503900356, Two Lions) Amazon Publishing.

—The Hair Book. TETHER, Graham. 2019. (Bright & Early Books(R) Ser.). (ENG.). 36p. (J). (-k). 9.99 *(978-1-5247-7340-3(9),* Random Hse. Bks. for Young Readers) Random Hse. Children's Bks.

—The Legend of King Arthur-A-tops. O'Hara, Mo. 2020. (ENG.). 40p. (J). (gr. -1-3). 17.99 *(978-0-06-265275-1(3),* HarperCollins) HarperCollins Pubs. Ltd. GBR. Dist: HarperCollins Pubs.

Joyner, Andrew. The Man with Small Hair. Jolly, Jane. 2020. (ENG.). 32p. (J). (gr. -1-k). 18.99 ***(978-1-74297-758-4(8))*** Little Hare Bks. AUS. Dist: Independent Pubs. Group.

—Nana Says I Will Be Famous One Day. Stott, Ann. 2020. (ENG.). 32p. (J). (gr. -1-2). 16.99 ***(978-0-7636-9560-6(2))*** Candlewick Pr.

Joyner, Andrew. One Little Goat. Dubosarsky, Ursula. 2019. (ENG.). 32p. (J). (— 1). pap. 11.99 *(978-1-76050-375-8(4))* Little Hare Bks. AUS. Dist: Independent Pubs. Group.

—Romeosaurus & Juliet Rex. O'Hara, Mo. 2018. (ENG.). 40p. (J). (gr. -1-3). 17.99 *(978-0-06-265274-4(5))* HarperCollins Pubs.

—Too Many Elephants in This House. Dubosarsky, Ursula. 2017. 32p. (J). (gr. -1-k). 10.99 *(978-0-14-378539-2(7))* Random Hse. Australia AUS. Dist: Independent Pubs. Group.

—Unstoppable Me. Verde, Susan. 2019. (ENG.). 32p. (J). 17.99 *(978-0-374-30738-7(5),* 900179771, Farrar, Straus & Giroux (BYR)) Farrar, Straus & Giroux.

—What's the Matter, Aunty May? Friend, Peter. 2019. (ENG.). 24p. (J). (gr. -1-k). pap. 9.99 *(978-1-76050-340-6(1))* Little Hare Bks. AUS. Dist: Independent Pubs. Group.

Joyner, Andrew. Boris for the Win. Joyner, Andrew. 2013. (Boris Ser.: 3). (ENG.). 80p. (J). (gr. k-2). pap. 4.99 *(978-0-545-48449-7(9))* Scholastic, Inc.

—Boris on the Move, Bk. 1. Joyner, Andrew. 2013. (Boris Ser.: 1). (ENG.). 80p. (J). (gr. k-2). pap. 4.99 *(978-0-545-48443-5(X))* Scholastic, Inc.

—Boris Sees the Light. Joyner, Andrew. 2013. (Boris Ser.: 4). (ENG.). 80p. (J). (gr. k-2). pap. 5.99 *(978-0-545-48454-1(5))* Scholastic, Inc.

Joyner, Andrew, jt. illus. see Freya Blackwood.

Joyo, Oscar. Petra's Pier Picnic. Wezeman, Phyllis Vos. 2019. (ENG.). 19.95 *(978-0-87946-670-1(7))* ACTA Pubns.

JoySoul Corporation. God Is for Every Day® - Horse Dreams: Teach-A-Child Companion Book with VCD, 2 vols., Vol. 2. Monson, Lois, photos by. Monson, Lois. 2006. 24p. (J). spiral bd. 14.95 *(978-0-9727786-9-5(1))* JoySoul Corp.

Ju-Yeon, Rhim. President Dad. Ju-Yeon, Rhim. (President Dad Ser.). Vol. 4. 4th rev. ed. 2005. 192p. per. 9.99 *(978-1-59532-237-1(X));* Vol. 5. 5th rev. ed. 2006. 208p. per. 9.99 *(978-1-59532-238-8(8))* TOKYOPOP, Inc.

Ju-Young Im, Joy & Da-Young Im, Linda. Mr Otagiri's Promise. Roberts, Deborah. 2012. 40p. pap. *(978-1-77067-719-7(4))* FriesenPress.

Juan, Ana. The Boy Who Lost Fairyland. Valente, Catherynne M. 2015. (Fairyland Ser.: 4). (ENG.). 240p. (YA). (gr. 5-9). 16.99 *(978-1-250-02349-0(1),* 9781250023490) Feiwel & Friends.

—Elena's Serenade. Geeslin, Campbell. 2004. (ENG.). 40p. (J). (gr. -1-2). 19.99 *(978-0-689-84908-4(7),* Atheneum Bks. for Young Readers) Simon & Schuster Children's Publishing.

—For You Are a Kenyan Child. Cunnane, Kelly. 2006. (ENG.). 40p. (J). (gr. -1-3). 17.99 *(978-0-689-86194-9(X),* Atheneum Bks. for Young Readers) Simon & Schuster Children's Publishing.

—The Girl Who Circumnavigated Fairyland in a Ship of Her Own Making. Valente, Catherynne M. 2011. (Fairyland Ser.: 1). (ENG.). 256p. (YA). (gr. 5-9). 16.99 *(978-0-312-64961-6(4),* 900069129) Feiwel & Friends.

—The Girl Who Circumnavigated Fairyland in a Ship of Her Own Making. Valente, Catherynne M. 2012. (Fairyland Ser.: 1). (ENG.). 288p. (YA). (gr. 5-9). pap. 7.99 *(978-1-250-01019-3(5),* 900084756) Square Fish.

—The Girl Who Fell Beneath Fairyland & Led the Revels There. Valente, Catherynne M. 2013. (Fairyland Ser.: 2). (ENG.). 304p. (YA). (gr. 5-9). pap. 8.99 *(978-1-250-03412-0(4),* 900120582) Square Fish.

—The Girl Who Soared over Fairyland & Cut the Moon in Two. Valente, Catherynne M. 2013. (Fairyland Ser.: 3). (ENG.). 256p. (YA). (gr. 5-9). 16.99 *(978-1-250-02350-6(5),* 9781250023506) Feiwel & Friends.

—Pablo & Birdy. McGhee, Alison. 2017. (ENG.). 304p. (J). (gr. 3-7). 17.99 *(978-1-4814-7026-1(4),* Atheneum/Caitlyn Dlouhy Books) Simon & Schuster Children's Publishing.

Juan, Mel Joy San. Dance Team Double Trouble. Maddox, Jake. 2020. (Jake Maddox Graphic Novels Ser.). (ENG.). 72p. (J). (gr. 3-6). pap. 6.95 ***(978-1-4965-9923-0(3),*** 201334); lib. bdg. 26.65 ***(978-1-4965-9713-7(3),*** 199336) Capstone. (Stone Arch Bks.).

Juan, Mel Joy San. Soccer Superstar. Maddox, Jake. 2020. (Jake Maddox Graphic Novels Ser.). (ENG.). 72p. (J). (gr. 3-8). pap. 6.95 *(978-1-4965-8457-1(0),* 140982); lib. bdg. 26.65 *(978-1-4965-8378-9(7),* 140677) Capstone. (Stone Arch Bks.).

Juan Oliver, Juan Batista. Sail with Me: Set Of 6. Bostrom, Kathleen & Bostrom, Christopher R. 2014. (Shared Reading Foundations Ser.). (J). (gr. 1). 36.00 net. *(978-1-4900-0051-0(8))* Benchmark Education Co.

—Sail with Me Book Set. Bostrom, Kathleen & Bostrom, Christopher R. 2014. (Shared Reading Foundations Ser.). (J). (gr. 1). 72.00 net. *(978-1-4900-0021-3(6))* Benchmark Education Co.

Juanita, Kaylani. Ta-Da! Davis, Kathy Ellen. 2018. (ENG.). 40p. (J). (gr. -1-k). 16.99 *(978-1-4521-4513-6(X))* Chronicle Bks. LLC.

—When Aidan Became a Brother, 1 vol. Lukoff, Kyle. 2019. (ENG.). 32p. (J). (gr. -1-3). 18.95 *(978-1-62014-837-2(4),* 50901cdd-6c37-4b76-814f-ab706e634d5a) Lee & Low Bks., Inc.

Juarez, Adriana & Puglisi, Adriana. The Doggone Dog, 1 vol. Gallagher, Diana G. 2013. (Pet Friends Forever Ser.). (ENG.). 88p. (J). (gr. 2-3). pap. 5.95 *(978-1-4795-1865-4(4));* lib. bdg. 25.32 *(978-1-4048-7502-9(6))* Capstone. (Picture Window Bks.).

—The Great Kitten Challenge, 1 vol. Gallagher, Diana G. 2013. (Pet Friends Forever Ser.). (ENG.). 88p. (J). (gr. 1-3). pap. 5.95 *(978-1-4795-1864-7(6));* lib. bdg. 25.32 *(978-1-4048-7501-2(8))* Capstone. (Picture Window Bks.).

—Mice Capades, 1 vol. Gallagher, Diana G. 2013. (Pet Friends Forever Ser.). (ENG.). 88p. (J). (gr. 1-3). pap. 5.95 *(978-1-4795-1863-0(8));* lib. bdg. 25.32 *(978-1-4048-7500-5(X))* Capstone. (Picture Window Bks.).

—A No-Sneeze Pet, 1 vol. Gallagher, Diana G. 2013. (Pet Friends Forever Ser.). (ENG.). 88p. (J). (gr. 1-3). pap. 5.95 *(978-1-4795-1862-3(X));* lib. bdg. 25.32 *(978-1-4048-7499-2(2))* Capstone. (Picture Window Bks.).

Juarez, Fernando. Phonics Comics: Twisted Tales - Level 3, Level 3. Richards, Kitty. 2006. (ENG.). 24p. (J). (gr. 1-17). per. 3.99 *(978-1-58476-514-1(3),* IKIDS) Innovative Kids.

—The Spirit of God Illustrated Bible: Over 40 Stories of God's Power & Presence, 1 vol. Rikkers, Doris Wynbeek. 2018. (ENG.). 312p. (J). 17.99 *(978-0-310-74973-8(5))* Zonderkidz.

Jubb, Kendahl Jan. Flashy Fantastic Rain Forest Frogs. Patent, Dorothy Hinshaw. 2015. 32p. pap. 8.00 *(978-1-61003-544-6(5))* Center for the Collaborative Classroom.

Judah, Nathan. Mrs. Kisses. Fanning, Meghan. 2013. 28p. pap. 9.99 *(978-1-61225-227-8(3))* Mirror Publishing.

Judah, Susan. Anansi & the Alligator Eggs y Los Huevos Del Caimán. Sherlock, Philip. Rickham, Elethia, tr. 2nd ed. 2013. 42p. pap. 15.00 *(978-976-95510-6-0(6))* Minna Pr.

Judal. Vampire Game, Vol. 11. Coffman, Patrick, tr. from JPN. rev. ed. 2005. 192p. pap. 9.99 *(978-1-59532-441-2(0))* TOKYOPOP, Inc.

Judal, et al. Vampire Game, Vol. 12. Judal & Judal. 12th rev. ed. 2005. (Vampire Game Ser.). 192p. per. 9.99 *(978-1-59532-442-9(9))* TOKYOPOP, Inc.

Judal. Vampire Game. Judal. Judal. 14th rev. ed. 2006. (Vampire Game Ser.: Vol. 14). 192p. per. 9.99 *(978-1-59532-444-3(5))* TOKYOPOP, Inc.

—Vampire Game, Vol. 10. Judal. Coffman, Patrick, tr. from JPN. rev. ed. 2005. 192p. (YA). pap. 9.99 *(978-1-59532-440-5(2))* TOKYOPOP, Inc.

Judal & Judal. Vampire Game. Judal & Judal. 13th rev. ed. 2005. (Vampire Game Ser.: Vol. 13). 192p. per. 9.99 *(978-1-59532-443-6(7))* TOKYOPOP, Inc.

Judal, jt. illus. see Judal.

Jude, Conny. Acting & Theatre. Putsman, Helen, photos by. Evans, Cheryl & Smith, Lucy. Evans, Cheryl, ed. 2008. (Acting & Theatre Ser.). 64p. (J). pap. 8.99 *(978-0-7945-2216-2(5),* Usborne) EDC Publishing.

Judge, Chris. Awesome Achievers in Science: Super & Strange Facts about 12 Almost Famous History Makers. Katz, Alan. 2019. (Awesome Achievers Ser.: 2). 112p. (J). (gr. 3-7). pap. 11.99 *(978-0-7624-6338-1(4),* Running Pr. Kids) Running Pr.

—Awesome Achievers in Technology: Super & Strange Facts about 12 Almost Famous History Makers. Katz, Alan. 2019. (Awesome Achievers Ser.). 112p. (J). (gr. 3-7). pap. 11.99 *(978-0-7624-6336-7(8),* Running Pr. Kids) Running Pr.

—Danger Is Everywhere: A Handbook for Avoiding Danger. O'Doherty, David. 2017. (Danger Is Everywhere Ser.: 1). (ENG.). 272p. (J). (gr. 3-7). pap. 6.99 *(978-0-316-50183-5(2))* Little, Brown Bks. for Young Readers.

—Danger Is Still Everywhere: Beware of the Dog! O'Doherty, David. (Danger Is Everywhere Ser.: 2). (ENG.). (J). (gr. 3-7). 2018. 256p. pap. 7.99 *(978-0-316-50185-9(9));* 2015. 224p. 12.99 *(978-0-316-29934-3(0))* Little, Brown Bks. for Young Readers.

—The First Christmas Sweater & the Sheep Who Changed Everything. Tubridy, Ryan. 2019. (ENG.). 144p. (J). (gr. 2-5). 14.99 *(978-1-5362-1132-0(X))* Candlewick Pr.

—Ogres Do Disco. McKay, Kirsty. 2016. 160p. (J). (gr. 2-4). 9.99 *(978-1-78344-296-6(4))* Andersen Pr. GBR. Dist: Independent Pubs. Group.

J

—Rover & the Big Fat Baby. Doyle, Roddy. 2018. (ENG.). 112p. (J). (gr. 1-4). 10.99 *(978-1-5098-3686-4(1))* Pan Macmillan GBR. Dist: Independent Pubs. Group.

Judge, Chris. The Baby Beast. Judge, Chris. 2019. (ENG.). 32p. (J). (gr. -1-3). 17.99 *(978-1-5415-5512-9(0))* Lerner Publishing Group.

—The Lonely Beast. Judge, Chris. 2011. (ENG.). 32p. (J). (gr. -1-3). 16.95 *(978-0-7613-8097-9(3),* 9780761380979) Lerner Publishing Group.

—The Snow Beast. Judge, Chris. 2015. (ENG.). 32p. (J). (gr. -1-3). 17.99 *(978-1-4677-9313-1(2),* 9781467793131) Lerner Publishing Group.

—Tin. Judge, Chris. 2014. (ENG.). 32p. (J). (gr. -1-3). 16.95 *(978-1-4677-5013-4(1),* 9781467750134) Lerner Publishing Group.

Judge, Kathleen. Growing up in Slavery: Stories of Young Slaves as Told by Themselves. Taylor, Yuval, ed. 2007. (ENG.). 256p. (J). (gr. 9). pap. 14.99 *(978-1-55652-635-0(0))* Chicago Review Pr., Inc.

Judge, Lita. Quick, Little Monkey! Thomson, Sarah L. 2016. (ENG.). 32p. (J). (gr. -1-2). 16.95 *(978-1-62979-100-5(8))* Boyds Mills Pr.

—S Is for S'mores: A Camping Alphabet. James, Helen Foster. rev. ed. 2007. (ENG.). 40p. (J). (gr. k-6). 17.95 *(978-1-58536-302-5(2))* Sleeping Bear Pr.

Judge, Lita. Bird Talk: What Birds Are Saying & Why. Judge, Lita. 2012. (ENG.). 48p. (J). (gr. 1-4). 18.99 *(978-1-59643-646-6(8),* 900068986) Roaring Brook Pr.

—Born in the Wild: Baby Animals & Their Parents. Judge, Lita. 2019. (In the Wild Ser.). (ENG.). 24p. (J). bds. 7.99 *(978-1-250-18990-5(X),* 900192328) Roaring Brook Pr.

—Born in the Wild: Baby Mammals & Their Parents. Judge, Lita. 2014. (In the Wild Ser.). (ENG.). 48p. (J). (gr. k-3). 18.99 *(978-1-59643-925-2(4),* 900121828) Roaring Brook Pr.

—D Is for Dinosaur: A Prehistoric Alphabet. Judge, Lita. Chapman, Todd. 2007. (Science Alphabet Ser.). (ENG.). 48p. (J). (gr. 1-4). 19.99 *(978-1-58536-242-4(5),* 202065) Sleeping Bear Pr.

—Flight School. Judge, Lita. 2019. (Flight School Ser.). (ENG.). 36p. (J). (gr. -1-k). bds. 7.99 *(978-1-5344-4481-2(5),* Little Simon) Little Simon.

—Flight School. Judge, Lita. 2014. (Flight School Ser.). (ENG.). 40p. (J). (gr. -1-3). 17.99 *(978-1-4424-8177-0(3),* Atheneum Bks. for Young Readers) Simon & Schuster Children's Publishing.

—Good Morning to Me! Judge, Lita. 2015. (ENG.). 40p. (J). (gr. -1-3). 17.99 *(978-1-4814-0369-6(9))* Simon & Schuster Children's Publishing.

—Homes in the Wild: Where Baby Animals & Their Parents Live. Judge, Lita. 2019. (In the Wild Ser.). (ENG.). 48p. (J). 18.99 *(978-1-62672-724-3(4),* 900171760) Roaring Brook Pr.

—How Big Were Dinosaurs? Judge, Lita. 2013. (ENG.). 40p. (J). (gr. 1-4). 18.99 *(978-1-59643-719-7(7),* 900075230) Roaring Brook Pr.

—Penguin Flies Home. Judge, Lita. 2019. (Flight School Ser.). (ENG.). 40p. (J). (gr. -1-3). 17.99 *(978-1-5344-1441-9(X),* Atheneum Bks. for Young Readers) Simon & Schuster Children's Publishing.

—Red Hat. Judge, Lita. 2013. (ENG.). 40p. (J). (gr. -1-k). 16.99 *(978-1-4424-4232-0(8),* Atheneum Bks. for Young Readers) Simon & Schuster Children's Publishing.

—Red Sled. Judge, Lita. 2019. (Classic Board Bks.). (ENG.). 38p. (J). (gr. -1-k). bds. 7.99 *(978-1-5344-4638-0(9),* Little Simon) Little Simon.

—Red Sled. Judge, Lita. 2011. (ENG.). 40p. (J). (gr. -1-3). 18.99 *(978-1-4424-2007-6(3),* Atheneum Bks. for Young Readers) Simon & Schuster Children's Publishing.

—When You Need Wings. Judge, Lita. 2020. (ENG.). 40p. (J). (gr. -1-3). 17.99 *(978-1-5344-3755-5(X),* Atheneum Bks. for Young Readers) Simon & Schuster Children's Publishing.

Judowitz, Chani. The Adventures of PJ Pepperjay. Backenroth, Yehudis. 2014. 95p. (J). *(978-1-4226-1535-5(9))* Mesorah Pubns., Ltd.

—Baruch & His Disappearing Yarmulke. Gerstenblit, Rivke. 2014. 32p. (J). *(978-1-4226-1530-0(8))* Mesorah Pubns., Ltd.

Judowitz, Chani. Baruch's Magical Bedtime, 1 vol. Gerstenblit, Rivke. 2016. (ENG.). 32p. (J). ***(978-1-4226-1672-7(X))*** Mesorah Pubns., Ltd.

Judowitz, Chani. More Adventures of PJ Pepperjay, 1 vol. Backenroth, Yehudis. 2016. (ENG.). 96p. (J). *(978-1-4226-1688-8(6),* ArtScroll Series) Mesorah Pubns., Ltd.

—My Very Own Letter. Hecht, Zalmy. 2016. (ENG.). 20p. (J). 10.95 *(978-1-929628-89-6(7))* Hachai Publishing.

Judowitz, Yoel. Middos Man Book & CD. Ornstein, Esther. 2013. 33p. 19.95 *(978-1-60091-257-3(5))* Israel Bookshop Pubns.

Judson, Gemini. To the Stars. Hurley, Suzanne M. Josephsen, Laura, ed. 2016. (ENG.). 242p. (J). pap. 16.99 *(978-1-61160-891-5(0),* Whiskey Creek Pr.) Whiskey Creek Pr., LLC.

Juhani, Teemu. The Dog & the Bone. Berne, Emma Carlson. 2019. (Classic Fables in Rhythm & Rhyme Ser.). (ENG.). 24p. (J). (gr. -1-2). lib. bdg. 33.99 *(978-1-68410-331-7(2),* 140251) Cantata Learning.

Juhasz, Brenda. Posey & Mosey Go Camping. Juhasz, Mike. 2008. 16p. pap. 24.95 *(978-1-60610-258-9(3))* America Star Bks.

Juhasz, George. Henry Chow & Other Stories, 1 vol. Miles, Victoria et al. 2010. (ENG.). 120p. (YA). (gr. 8-12). pap. 12.95 *(978-1-896580-33-5(5))* Tradewind Bks. CAN. Dist: Orca Bk. Pubs. USA.

—Pacific Tree Frogs, 1 vol. Owen, Leslie E. 2003. (ENG.). 32p. (J). (gr. 1-3). pap. 7.95 *(978-1-896580-42-5(4))* Tradewind Bks. CAN. Dist: Orca Bk. Pubs. USA.

—Rescuing Einstein's Compass. Oppenheim, Shulamith. 2003. (ENG.). 32p. (J). (gr. k-3). 15.95 *(978-1-56656-507-3(3),* Interlink Bks.) Interlink Publishing Group, Inc.

Juhasz, Victor. D Is for Democracy: A Citizen's Alphabet. Grodin, Elissa. (ENG.). 40p. (J). (gr. 1-4). 2006. per. 7.95 *(978-1-58536-328-5(6),* 203807); 2004. 16.95 *(978-1-58536-234-9(4),* 202059) Sleeping Bear Pr.

—Everyone Counts: A Citizens' Number Book. Elissa Grodin. rev. ed. 2006. (Count Your Way Across the U. S. A. Ser.). (ENG.). 40p. (J). (gr. -1-3). 17.95 *(978-1-58536-295-0(6))* Sleeping Bear Pr.

—G Is for Gladiators: An Ancient Rome Alphabet. Shoulders, Debbie & Shoulders, Michael. 2010. (Sleeping Bear Alphabets Ser.). (ENG.). 40p. (J). (gr. 1-4). 19.99 *(978-1-58536-457-2(6),* 202180) Sleeping Bear Pr.

—H Is for Honor: A Military Family Alphabet. Scillian, Devin. 2006. (ENG.). 40p. (J). (gr. k-6). 17.95 *(978-1-58536-292-9(1))* Sleeping Bear Pr.

—R Is for Rhyme: A Poetry Alphabet. Young, Judy & A12. 2010. (ENG.). 48p. (J). pap. 7.95 *(978-1-58536-519-7(X))* Sleeping Bear Pr.

—R Is for Rhyme: A Poetry Alphabet. Young, Judy. rev. ed. 2006. (Art & Culture Ser.). (ENG.). 40p. (J). (gr. -1-3). 17.95 *(978-1-58536-240-0(9))* Sleeping Bear Pr.

—Z Is for Zeus: A Greek Mythology Alphabet. Wilbur, Helen L. rev. ed. 2008. (Art & Culture Ser.). (ENG.). 40p. (J). (gr. 1-7). 17.95 *(978-1-58536-341-4(3))* Sleeping Bear Pr.

Juillard, André. The Sarcophagi of the Sixth Coninent, Pt. 1, Vol. 9. Sente, Yves. 2011. (Blake & Mortimer Ser.: 9). (ENG.). 64p. (gr. 5-17). pap. 15.95 *(978-1-84918-067-2(9))* CineBook GBR. Dist: National Bk. Network.

Jul Saavedra, Jescae. A Day in the Life of Dexter: Dexter Goes to the Zoo. Urban, Kerri. 2018. (ENG.). 30p. (J). pap. 12.95 *(978-1-64079-017-9(9))* Christian Faith Publishing.

Jules, Prud'homme, jt. illus. see Prud'homme, Jules.

Julia, Hessler, jt. illus. see Trinity, Shaya.

Julia, Marina. Adventure Time: Beginning of the End. Anderson, Ted. 2018. (ENG.). 112p. (J). (gr. 4-7). pap. 14.99 *(978-1-68415-246-9(1))* Boom! Studios.

—Adventure Time Season 11. Liew, Sonny & Anderson, Ted. 2019. (Adventure Time Season 11 Ser.: 1). (ENG.). 112p. (J). pap. 19.99 *(978-1-68415-365-7(4))* Boom! Studios.

Julian, Alison. The Nutcracker. Hoffmann, E. T. A. 2005. (J). *(978-0-7607-6690-3(8))* Barnes & Noble, Inc.

—The 12 Days of Christmas. 2005. (J). *(978-1-74157-281-0(9))* Hinkler Bks. Pty, Ltd.

Julian, Russell. The Magic Footprints. Balfour, Melissa. 2005. (Green Bananas Ser.). (ENG.). 48p. (J). lib. bdg. *(978-0-7787-1023-3(8))* Crabtree Publishing Co.

—The Monster of the Woods! Freedman, Claire. 2013. (ENG.). 32p. (J). pap. *(978-0-545-51571-9(8),* Cartwheel Bks.) Scholastic, Inc.

—The Monster of the Woods!/By Claire Freedman & Russell Julian. Freedman, Claire. 2013. (J). *(978-0-545-56837-1(4),* Cartwheel Bks.) Scholastic, Inc.

—Splitting the Herd: A Corral of Odds & Evens. Harris, Trudy. 2008. (Math Is Fun! Ser.). (ENG.). 32p. (gr. k-2). 16.95 *(978-0-8225-7466-8(7),* Millbrook Pr.) Lerner Publishing Group.

—Ten Little Bluebirds. Ford, Emily. 2016. (ENG.). 22p. (J). (gr. -1-k). 10.99 *(978-0-545-79441-1(2),* Cartwheel Bks.) Scholastic, Inc.

—Ten Playful Penguins. Ford, Emily. 2015. (ENG.). 22p. (J). (gr. -1-k). 12.99 *(978-0-545-79439-8(0),* Cartwheel Bks.) Scholastic, Inc.

—Ten Twinkly Stars. 2017. (J). *(978-1-84857-579-0(3))* Little Tiger Pr. Group.

—Ten Twinkly Stars. Tiger Tales. 2016. (ENG.). 28p. (J). (gr. -1-k). mass mkt. 3.99 *(978-1-58925-475-6(9))* Tiger Tales.

Julian, Sean. Bear Can't Sleep! McGee, Marni. 2015. (ENG.). 32p. (J). (gr. -1-2). 16.99 *(978-1-58925-189-2(X))* Tiger Tales.

—Five Little Ducklings Go to Bed. Roth, Carol. 2014. 32p. (J). (gr. k-3). 17.95 *(978-0-7358-4128-4(4))* North-South Bks., Inc.

—Five Little Ducklings Go to School. Roth, Carol. 32p. (J). (gr. -1-2). 2019. (ENG.). pap. 8.95 *(978-0-7358-4346-2(5));* 2015. 17.95 *(978-0-7358-4132-1(2))* North-South Bks., Inc.

—A Friend Like You. Rottgen, Barbara & Schomburg, Andrea. 2016. (ENG.). 32p. (J). (gr. -1-2). 16.99 *(978-1-68010-031-0(9))* Tiger Tales.

—I Love You Brighter Than the Stars. Hart, Owen. 2019. (ENG.). 32p. (J). (gr. -1-2). 17.99 *(978-1-68010-151-5(X))* Tiger Tales.

—I Love You, Funny Bunny, 1 vol. 2019. (ENG.). 32p. (J). 17.99 *(978-0-310-76541-7(2))* Zonderkidz.

—I'll Love You Forever. Hart, Owen. 2017. (ENG.). 32p. (J). (gr. -1-2). 16.99 *(978-1-68010-070-9(X))* Tiger Tales.

—I'm Sorry! Timms, Barry. 2020. (ENG.). 32p. (J). (gr. -1-2). 17.99 *(978-1-68010-190-4(0))* Tiger Tales.

—Muffin. Rooney, Anne. 2009. (Go! Readers Ser.). 48p. (J). (gr. 2-5). pap. 12.85 *(978-1-60754-270-4(6));* lib. bdg. 32.25 *(978-1-60754-269-8(2))* Windmill Bks.

—Ten Sparkly Snowflakes. Tiger Tales. 2017. (ENG.). 26p. (J). (gr. -1-k). mass mkt. 4.99 *(978-1-68010-413-4(6))* Tiger Tales.

—Where's My Mommy? Roth, Carol. 2012. (ENG.). 32p. (J). 17.95 *(978-0-7358-4032-4(6))* North-South Bks., Inc.

—The Worry Box. Chiew, Suzanne. 2018. (ENG.). 32p. (J). (gr. -1-2). 16.99 *(978-1-68010-083-9(1))* Tiger Tales.

Juliano, Dana. Brisko: A True Tale of Holocaust Survival. Winkelstein, Steven Paul. 2014. 104p. (J). *(978-0-9824498-6-8(0))* Winkelstein Studios.

Juliano, Phil. Desert Life of the Southwest Activity Book. Krebbs, Karen. 2017. (Color & Learn Ser.). (ENG.). 64p. (J). (gr. k-5). pap. 6.95 *(978-1-59193-655-8(1),* Adventure Pubns.) AdventureKEEN.

—Outer Space Activity Book. Ortler, Brett. 2017. (Color & Learn Ser.). (ENG.). 64p. (J). (gr. k-5). pap. 6.95 *(978-1-59193-708-1(6),* Adventure Pubns.) AdventureKEEN.

Julich, Jenniffer. Bows, Does & Bucks! An Introduction to Archery Deer Hunting. DiLorenzo, Michael A. 2010. 88p. (J). 19.95 *(978-0-9777210-2-3(7))* Running Moose Publications.

—Cole Family Christmas. Bryan, Jennifer Liu & Kendle, Hazel Cole. 2008. 74p. (J). (gr. 4-7). 17.95 *(978-0-9816265-0-5(5))* Next Chapter Pr.

—Encounter at Ogre Island. Greene, John McBride. 2006. 96p. pap. 9.50 *(978-0-9772809-0-2(X))* Comprecom.

—Nonnie, What's God? Lile, Linda L. 2008. 16p. (J). 13.95 *(978-0-9817092-0-8(6))* A-Lu Publishing.

—The Player Piano Mouse. Dachman, Adam. 2008. 32p. (J). 14.99 *(978-0-9797794-0-4(5))* Player Piano Mouse Productions (PPMP).

—Walter's Pond: The True Story of Three Brothers Who Went Fishing for Trouble. Farrell, Bill. 2008. 16p. 8.95 *(978-0-9797790-0-8(6))* Lower Lane Publishing LLC.

—Yolandababy: A Pooch Finds Her Purpose! an Adventure in Self-Esteem. Bennett-Boltinghouse, Jo Ann. 2007. (YolandaBaby Ser.). 28p. (J). (gr. -1-3). 16.00 *(978-0-9785151-0-2(2))* Ginger Pr., The.

Julie, jt. illus. see Fil.

Julie, Mme Ferrand. Abecedaire et Petits Poemes Caledoniens. Celine, Mme Fuentes. 2016. (FRE.). (J). pap. *(978-2-9556904-9-9(X))* Julie, Ferrand.

Julie, Pegan. Brave Enough to Fly. Jenny, Hoskins. 2018. (ENG.). 42p. (J). (gr. 1-4). 19.99 *(978-1-7324318-0-5(9))* Hoskins, Jenny.

Julien, Terry. Abraham Trusts God. Holder, Jennifer. 2015. (Faith That Sticks Bks.). (ENG.). 24p. (J). pap. 3.99 *(978-1-4964-0320-9(7),* 4611995) Tyndale Hse. Pubs.

—Away in a Manger. Luther, Martin. 2015. (Faith That Sticks Bks.). (ENG.). 24p. (J). pap. 3.99 *(978-1-4964-0318-6(5),* 4611993) Tyndale Hse. Pubs.

—Brave & Beautiful Queen Esther. Holder, Jennifer. 2015. (Faith That Sticks Bks.). (ENG.). 24p. (J). pap. 3.99 *(978-1-4964-0314-8(2),* 4611989) Tyndale Hse. Pubs.

—Go, Jonah, Go! Holder, Jennifer. 2014. (Happy Day Ser.). (ENG.). 16p. (J). pap. 2.49 *(978-1-4143-9526-5(4),* 4608516) Tyndale Hse. Pubs.

—Jesus Blesses the Children. Cooley, Karen. 2015. (Faith That Sticks Bks.). (ENG.). 24p. (J). pap. 3.99 *(978-1-4964-0316-2(9),* 4611991) Tyndale Hse. Pubs.

Julien, Terry & Carter, Nancy. Jesus Loves Me. 2015. (Faith That Sticks Bks.). (ENG.). 24p. (J). pap. 3.99 *(978-1-4964-0315-5(0),* 4611990) Tyndale Hse. Pubs.

Julien, Terry, jt. illus. see Marlin, Kathryn.

Julieta, Irla. Entre Suenos. Garza, Ben. rev. ed. 2007. (Castillo de la Lectura Roja Ser.). (SPA & ENG.). 108p. (YA). (gr. 7). pap. 8.95 *(978-970-20-0199-7(4))* Castillo, Ediciones, S. A. de C. V. MEX. Dist: Macmillan.

Julilustrador. All about Sloths/Sloth Sees the World. Brooke, Susan Rich. 2019. (ENG.). 24p. (J). bds. *(978-1-5037-4821-7(9),* 02d2f6e1-a54b-45ea-82f2-ac4a53c0928f, p i kids) Phoenix International Publications, Inc.

Julings, Emma, jt. photos by see Freeman, Mike.

Jullien, Jean. Bruno, the Standing Cat. Robert, Nadine. 2019. (ENG.). 48p. (J). (gr. -1-2). 17.99 *(978-0-525-64714-0(7));* lib. bdg. 20.99 *(978-0-525-64715-7(5))* Random Hse. Children's Bks. (Random Hse. Bks. for Young Readers).

—Hoot Owl, Master of Disguise. Taylor, Sean. 2015. (ENG.). 48p. (J). (gr. -1-2). 15.99 *(978-0-7636-7578-3(4))* Candlewick Pr.

—I Want to Be in a Scary Story. Taylor, Sean. 2017. (ENG.). 32p. (J). (-k). 15.99 *(978-0-7636-8953-7(X))* Candlewick Pr.

—Imagine. Lennon, John. 2017. (ENG.). 32p. (J). (gr. -1-3). 18.99 *(978-1-328-80865-3(3),* 1688259, Clarion Bks.) Houghton Mifflin Harcourt Trade & Reference Pubs.

Jun, Tan. Father's Road novel. Jang, Ji-yun. 2016. (J). 10.00 *(978-0-8028-5472-8(9),* Eerdmans Bks For Young Readers) Eerdmans, William B. Publishing Co.

June, Cathy. We Eat Food That's Fresh. Russ-Ayon, Angela. 2009. 32p. (J). (gr. -1-2). 11.99 *(978-1-934214-09-1(4))* OurRainbow Pr., LLC.

Jung, Anna-Maria. The Most Dangerous Book: an Illustrated Introduction to Archery: An Illustrated Introduction to Archery. Nayeri, Daniel. 2017. (ENG.). 88p. (J). (gr. 3-7). 22.95 *(978-1-5235-0119-9(7),* 100119) Workman Publishing Co., Inc.

Jung, Minkyu. Ms. Marvel by Saladin Ahmed Vol. 1: Destined. 2019. (Ms. Marvel by Saladin Ahmed Ser.: 1). (ENG.). 136p. (YA). (gr. 8-17). pap. 17.99 *(978-1-302-91829-3(X))* Marvel Worldwide, Inc.

Jung, Sebastian J. H. A Bird & the Voice Coloring Book. Jung, Sebastian J. H. 2019. (ENG.). 60p. (J). pap. 5.99 ***(978-1-7118-4685-9(6))*** Independently Published.

—Toward the Ocean Coloring Book. Jung, Sebastian J. H. 2019. (ENG.). 60p. (J). pap. 5.88 ***(978-1-7103-7684-5(8))*** Independently Published.

Jung, Shirley. Ten Spunky Monkeys. Phillips, Clifton. 2007. 32p. (J). 8.99 *(978-0-9797106-4-3(2))* Avid Readers Publishing Group.

Jung Woo, Nam. El Pato Que Voló Al Cielo. Sang-Kwen, Lee. 2016. (SPA.). 128p. (J). (gr. 4-7). pap. 7.95 *(978-607-8469-15-4(0))* Nostra Ediciones MEX. Dist: Independent Pubs. Group.

Jung, Wook Jin. Robot, Go Bot! Rau, Dana Meachen. 2013. (Step into Reading Ser.). 32p. (J). (gr. -1-1). 4.99 *(978-0-375-87083-5(0),* Random Hse. Bks. for Young Readers) Random Hse. Children's Bks.

—Robot, Go Bot! (Step into Reading Comic Reader) Read & Listen Edition. Rau, Dana M. ed. 2013. (Step into Reading Ser.). (ENG.). 32p. (J). (gr. -1-1). E-Book *(978-0-449-81429-1(7),* Random Hse. Bks. for Young Readers) Random Hse. Children's Bks.

Junghans, Olivia. Freddy the Furious. Ott Lcsw, Melody. 2019. (ENG.). 24p. (J). pap. 12.99 ***(978-1-7960-5115-5(2))*** Xlibris Corp.

Junghans, Olivia, jt. illus. see Kehl, Bob.

Jupin, David Perez. Love. 2013. 20p. pap. 11.95 *(978-1-937504-67-0(0))* Worthy Shorts.

Jurado, Carlos. Krissy's Amazing Gift. Rhodeman II, Paul. 2019. (ENG.). 28p. (J). (gr. k-6). 19.99 ***(978-0-578-44805-3(X))*** II, Paul Duane Rhodeman.

Jurek, Kathy. The Tale of Noel: The Holiday Horse Angel. Halverson, Kristen. 2017. (ENG.). (J). (gr. k-4). 24.99 *(978-0-692-94230-7(0))* The Tale of Noel: The Holiday Horse Angel, The.

Jurevicius, Luke. Apples & Ants. Pike, Katy. 2006. (Funny Photo Alphabet Ser.). (J). pap. 3.95 *(978-0-8225-6267-2(7),* Lerner Pubns.) Lerner Publishing Group.

—Big Bad Bears. Pike, Katy. 2006. (Funny Photo Alphabet Ser.). 11p. (J). pap. 3.95 *(978-0-8225-6268-9(5),* Lerner Pubns.) Lerner Publishing Group.

—Candles on a Cake. Pike, Katy. 2006. (Funny Photo Alphabet Ser.). 11p. (J). pap. 3.95 *(978-0-8225-6269-6(3),* Lerner Pubns.) Lerner Publishing Group.

—Dancing Dog. Pike, Katy. 2006. (Funny Photo Alphabet Ser.). 11p. (J). pap. 3.95 *(978-0-8225-6270-2(7),* Lerner Pubns.) Lerner Publishing Group.

—Eggs & Elephants. Pike, Katy. 2006. (Funny Photo Alphabet Ser.). 11p. (J). pap. 3.95 *(978-0-8225-6271-9(5),* Lerner Pubns.) Lerner Publishing Group.

—Funny Fish. Pike, Katy. 2006. (Funny Photo Alphabet Ser.). 11p. (J). pap. 3.95 *(978-0-8225-6272-6(3),* Lerner Pubns.) Lerner Publishing Group.

—Giggly Goat. Pike, Katy. 2006. (Funny Photo Alphabet Ser.). 11p. (J). pap. 3.95 *(978-0-8225-6273-3(1),* Lerner Pubns.) Lerner Publishing Group.

—Happy Horse. Pike, Katy. 2006. (Funny Photo Alphabet Ser.). 11p. (J). pap. 3.95 *(978-0-8225-6274-0(X),* Lerner Pubns.) Lerner Publishing Group.

—Icky Insects. Pike, Katy. 2006. (Funny Photo Alphabet Ser.). 11p. (J). pap. 3.95 *(978-0-8225-6275-7(8),* Lerner Pubns.) Lerner Publishing Group.

—Jolly Jellybeans. Pike, Katy. 2006. (Funny Photo Alphabet Ser.). 11p. (J). pap. 3.95 *(978-0-8225-6276-4(6),* Lerner Pubns.) Lerner Publishing Group.

—Lots of Lizards. Pike, Katy. 2006. (Funny Photo Alphabet Ser.). 11p. (J). pap. 3.95 *(978-0-8225-6278-8(2),* Lerner Pubns.) Lerner Publishing Group.

—Mini Mouse. Pike, Katy. 2006. (Funny Photo Alphabet Ser.). 11p. (J). pap. 3.95 *(978-0-8225-6279-5(0),* Lerner Pubns.) Lerner Publishing Group.

—New Beds, 6 vols. Chifney, Katrina. 2005. (ENG.). (J). (gr. 1). pap., pap. 54.80 *(978-1-4189-1986-3(1))* Rigby Education.

—Nine Nuts. Pike, Katy. 2006. (Funny Photo Alphabet Ser.). 11p. (J). pap. 3.95 *(978-0-8225-6280-1(4),* Lerner Pubns.) Lerner Publishing Group.

—Orange Octopus. Pike, Katy. 2006. (Funny Photo Alphabet Ser.). 11p. (J). (gr. k-k). pap. 3.95 *(978-0-8225-6281-8(2),* Lerner Pubns.) Lerner Publishing Group.

—Our Sand Castle, 7 vols. Haydon, Julie. 2005. (ENG.). (J). (gr. 1). pap. 54.80 *(978-1-4189-1337-3(5))* Houghton Mifflin Harcourt Supplemental Pubs.

—Penguin Pond. Pike, Katy. 2006. (Funny Photo Alphabet Ser.). 11p. (J). pap. 3.95 *(978-0-8225-6282-5(0),* Lerner Pubns.) Lerner Publishing Group.

—The Queen's Question. Pike, Katy. 2006. (Funny Photo Alphabet Ser.). 11p. (J). pap. 3.95 *(978-0-8225-6283-2(9),* Lerner Pubns.) Lerner Publishing Group.

—Rabbit on a Raft. Pike, Katy. 2006. (Funny Photo Alphabet Ser.). 11p. (J). pap. 3.95 *(978-0-8225-6284-9(7),* Lerner Pubns.) Lerner Publishing Group.

—Silly Seagulls. Pike, Katy. 2006. (Funny Photo Alphabet Ser.). 11p. (J). pap. 3.95 *(978-0-8225-6285-6(5),* Lerner Pubns.) Lerner Publishing Group.

—Talking Tigers. Pike, Katy. 2006. (Funny Photo Alphabet Ser.). 11p. (J). pap. 3.95 *(978-0-8225-6286-3(3),* Lerner Pubns.) Lerner Publishing Group.

—Under Umbrellas. Pike, Katy. 2006. (Funny Photo Alphabet Ser.). 11p. (J). pap. 3.95 *(978-0-8225-6287-0(1),* Lerner Pubns.) Lerner Publishing Group.

—Vegetables in a Van. Pike, Katy. 2006. (Funny Photo Alphabet Ser.). 11p. (J). pap. 3.95 *(978-0-8225-6288-7(X),* Lerner Pubns.) Lerner Publishing Group.

—Wet Whales. Pike, Katy. 2006. (Funny Photo Alphabet Ser.). 11p. (J). pap. 3.95 *(978-0-8225-6289-4(8),* Lerner Pubns.) Lerner Publishing Group.

—X As in Fox. Pike, Katy. 2006. (Funny Photo Alphabet Ser.). 11p. (J). pap. 3.95 *(978-0-8225-6290-0(1),* Lerner Pubns.) Lerner Publishing Group.

—Yellow Yo-Yo. Pike, Katy. 2006. (Funny Photo Alphabet Ser.). (J). pap. 3.95 *(978-0-8225-6291-7(X),* Lerner Pubns.) Lerner Publishing Group.

—Zebras in a Zoo. Pike, Katy. 2006. (Funny Photo Alphabet Ser.). (J). pap. 3.95 *(978-0-8225-6292-4(8),* Lerner Pubns.) Lerner Publishing Group.

Jurevicius, Luke, photos by. Funny Photo Alphabet. Pike, Katy. 2006. (Funny Photo Alphabet Ser.). 32p. (J). lib. bdg. 26.95 *(978-0-8225-6076-0(3),* Lerner Pubns.) Lerner Publishing Group.

Jurgens, Dan, et al. Heroes Reborn: the Return Omnibus. 2020. (ENG.). 1136p. (J). (gr. 4-17). 125.00 ***(978-1-302-92517-8(2))*** Marvel Worldwide, Inc.

Jurinich, Anna. Where Do the Balloons Go? Davis, Elena. 2006. (ENG.). 32p. (J). (gr. -1-3). 16.95 *(978-0-9714372-3-4(8))* Red Rock Pr., Inc.

Jury, Santi. Zombies Just Love People. Sorensen, Joshua P. 2018. (ENG.). 32p. (J). pap. 7.99 *(978-1-7323662-0-6(9))* War Monkey Pubns., LLC.

Just, John. The Amazing Tale of Archie the Alligator. Kick, J. D. 2nd ed. 2003. (J). per. 12.95 *(978-1-929424-14-6(0),* Owl Creek Farm Bks.) Owl Tree Pr.

—A Goose Tale — Downside up. Kick, J. D. 2nd l.t. ed. 2003. 80p. (J). per. 16.95 *(978-1-929424-13-9(2),* Owl Creek Farm Bks.) Owl Tree Pr.

Justice, B. Martin, jt. illus. see Gruger, F. R.

Justin McGovern. Be Kind to the Earth: A Little Kid's Guide to Reducing your Carbon Footprint. Kelly McGovern Lu. 2009. 28p. pap. 14.99 *(978-1-4389-7356-2(X))* AuthorHouse.

Justine, Torode, jt. illus. see Scott, Peter.

Justinen, Kim. Shoebox Kids Bible Stories, Vol. 5. Thomas, Jerry D. 2003. 128p. (J). 7.99 *(978-0-8163-1971-8(5))* Pacific Pr. Publishing Assn.

Juta, Jason. Drawing Wild Animals. Colich, Abby. 2015. (Drawing Amazing Animals Ser.). (ENG.). 32p. (J). (gr. 3-9). 28.65 *(978-1-4914-2132-1(0),* Capstone Pr.) Capstone.

—A Field Guide to Griffins, Unicorns, & Other Mythical Beasts, 1 vol. Sautter, A. J. 2014. (Fantasy Field Guides). (ENG.). 32p. (J). (gr. 3-9). lib. bdg. 28.65 *(978-1-4914-0690-8(9),* Capstone Pr.) Capstone.

Juta, Jason, jt. illus. see McGrath, Tom.

K

K, A. Alices Adventures in Wonderland: Dream Edition with Illustrations. K, A., ed. Carroll, Lewis. 2019. (ENG.). 130p. (J). pap. 25.00 *(978-1-0730-8839-3(1))* Independently Published.

—Through the Looking-Glass: Mirror Dream Edition, with Colourful Illustrations Inkluding the Forgotten Chapter a Wasp in a Wig. K, A., ed. Carroll, Lewis. 2019. (ENG.). 162p. (J). pap. 30.25 *(978-1-0747-8209-2(7))* Independently Published.

Kaa Illustration, jt. illus. see Myers, Christopher.

Kaadan, Nadine. The Jasmine Sneeze. Kaadan, Nadine. 2018. (ENG.). 32p. (J). (gr. -1-2). 17.99 *(978-1-911373-27-8(7))* Lantana Publishing GBR. Dist: Lerner Publishing Group.

—Tomorrow. Kaadan, Nadine. 2018. 32p. (J). (gr. k-2). 17.99 *(978-1-911373-43-8(9))* Lantana Publishing GBR. Dist: Lerner Publishing Group.

Kaban, Eda. Arctic Freeze. Earhart, Kristin. 2015. 121p. (J). *(978-1-5182-0297-1(7))* Scholastic, Inc.

—Captain Marvel What Makes a Hero. Bobowicz, Pamela. 2019. (ENG.). 32p. (J). (gr. 1-3). 12.99 *(978-1-368-04807-1(2),* Marvel Pr.) Disney Publishing Worldwide.

—Even Superheroes Have Bad Days. Becker, Shelly. 2016. 40p. (J). (gr. -1-4). 14.95 *(978-1-4549-1394-8(0))* Sterling Publishing Co., Inc.

—Even Superheroes Make Mistakes. Becker, Shelly. 2018. 40p. (J). (gr. -1-4). 16.95 *(978-1-4549-2703-7(8))* Sterling Publishing Co., Inc.

—The Magnificent Mya Tibbs: Spirit Week Showdown. Allen, Crystal. (Magnificent Mya Tibbs Ser.: 1). (ENG.). (J). (gr. 3-7). 2017. 256p. pap. 6.99 *(978-0-06-234234-8(7));* 2016. 240p. 16.99 *(978-0-06-234233-1(9))* HarperCollins Pubs.

—The Magnificent Mya Tibbs: the Wall of Fame Game. Allen, Crystal. (ENG.). 272p. (J). (gr. 3-7). 2018. pap. 7.99 *(978-0-06-234237-9(1),* Balzer & Bray); 2017. 16.99 *(978-0-06-234236-2(3))* HarperCollins Pubs.

—Old MacDonald Had a Boat. Goetz, Steve. 2018. (ENG.). 44p. (J). (gr. -1-k). 16.99 *(978-1-4521-6505-9(X))* Chronicle Bks. LLC.

—Old MacDonald Had a Truck. Goetz, Steve. 2019. (ENG.). 30p. (J). (gr. -1-k). bds. 8.99 *(978-1-4521-8176-9(4))* Chronicle Bks. LLC.

—Old MacDonald Had a Truck: (Preschool Read Aloud Books, Books for Kids, Kids Construction Books) Goetz, Steve. 2016. (ENG.). 40p. (J). (gr. -1-k). 16.99 *(978-1-4521-3260-0(7))* Chronicle Bks. LLC.

—Pink Is for Boys. Pearlman, Robb. 2018. 40p. (J). (gr. -1-3). 17.99 *(978-0-7624-6247-6(7),* Running Pr. Kids) Running Pr.

—Pirates Don't Go to Kindergarten! Robinson, Lisa. 2019. 32p. (J). (gr. -1-2). 17.99 *(978-1-5420-9275-3(2),* 9781542092753, Two Lions) Amazon Publishing.

Kaban, Eda. Princess Power. Davis, Natalie. 2020. (ENG.). 40p. (J). (gr. -1-k). 16.99 ***(978-1-368-02594-2(3))*** Hyperion Bks. for Children.

Kaban, Eda. Star Wars: the Rise of Skywalker the Galaxy Needs You. Kennedy, Caitlin. 2019. (ENG.). 48p. (J). (gr. k-3). 17.99 *(978-1-368-05182-8(0),* Disney Lucasfilm Press) Disney Publishing Worldwide.

Kabita Studio. Billy Beetle Bug & His Beetle Bug Board. Fyhrie, Sumi. 2nd ed. 2019. (ENG.). 32p. (J). (gr. k-6). 19.95 ***(978-1-944072-07-0(1),*** White Parrot Pr.) First Steps Publishing.

Kacer, Stephen. The Harry Bear Story. Painter, Grace. 2011. 28p. pap. 24.95 *(978-1-4626-3327-2(7))* America Star Bks.

Kachmar, Maryana. Julian & the Magical Treehouse. Douros, Danielle Robyn. 2016. (ENG.). (J). pap. 10.99 *(978-1-68160-183-0(4))* Crimson Cloak Publishing.

Kachmar, Maryana. Pinky Swear. Forti, Diane Wright. 2020. (ENG.). 32p. (J). (gr. k-5). 22.95 ***(978-1-951565-35-0(5));*** pap. 13.95 ***(978-1-951565-36-7(3))*** Brandylane Pubs., Inc. (Belle Isle Bks.).

—Who Knows Jordan? Manor, Yael. 2017. (ENG.). 34p. (J). pap. 10.55 ***(978-1-64204-635-9(3))*** Primedia eLaunch LLC.

Kadair, Deborah. Today Is Monday in Kentucky, 1 vol. 2012. (Today Is Monday Ser.). (ENG.). 32p. (J). (gr. k-k). 16.99 *(978-1-4556-1533-9(1),* Pelican Publishing) Arcadia Publishing.

—Today Is Monday in New York, 1 vol. 2011. (Today Is Monday Ser.). (ENG.). 32p. (J). (gr. k-k). 16.99 *(978-1-58980-886-7(X),* Pelican Publishing) Arcadia Publishing.

Kadair, Deborah. I Spy in the Louisiana Sky, 1 vol. Kadair, Deborah. 2011. (I Spy Ser.). (ENG.). 32p. (J). (gr. k-3). 16.99 *(978-1-58980-885-0(1),* Pelican Publishing) Arcadia Publishing.

Kadair, Deborah Ousley. Down in Louisiana, 1 vol. Downing, Johnette. 2007. (ENG.). 32p. (J). (gr. k-3). 16.99 *(978-1-58980-451-7(1),* Pelican Publishing) Arcadia Publishing.

—There Was a Tall Texan Who Swallowed a Flea, 1 vol. Kralovansky, Susan Holt. 2013. (ENG.). 32p. (J). (gr. -1-k). 16.99 *(978-1-4556-1717-3(2),* Pelican Publishing) Arcadia Publishing.

—Today Is Monday in Louisiana, 1 vol. Downing, Johnette. 2006. (ENG.). 32p. (J). (gr. k-k). 16.99 *(978-1-58980-406-7(6),* Pelican Publishing) Arcadia Publishing.

—Today Is Monday in Texas, 1 vol. 2010. (Today Is Monday Ser.). (ENG.). 32p. (J). (gr. k-k). 16.99 *(978-1-58980-701-3(4),* Pelican Publishing) Arcadia Publishing.

Kadair, Deborah Ousley. Grandma's Gumbo, 1 vol. Kadair, Deborah Ousley. 2003. (ENG.). 32p. (J). (gr. k-3). 16.99 *(978-1-58980-133-2(4),* Pelican Publishing) Arcadia Publishing.

Kadlecik, Sebastian. Adventures in the Circulatory System. Lowe, Alexander. 2020. (Norwood Discovery Graphics: the Bod Squad Ser.). (ENG.). 32p. (J). (gr. 2-3). 29.27 ***(978-1-68450-862-4(2));*** pap. 13.26 ***(978-1-68404-580-8(0))*** Norwood Hse. Pr.

—Adventures in the Digestive System. Lowe, Alexander. 2020. (Norwood Discovery Graphics: the Bod Squad Ser.). (ENG.). 32p. (J). (gr. 2-3). 29.27 ***(978-1-68450-861-7(4));*** pap. 13.26 ***(978-1-68404-581-5(9))*** Norwood Hse. Pr.

—Adventures in the Muscular System. Lowe, Alexander. 2020. (Norwood Discovery Graphics: the Bod Squad Ser.). (ENG.). 32p. (J). (gr. 2-3). 29.27 ***(978-1-68450-859-4(2));*** pap. 13.26 ***(978-1-68404-583-9(5))*** Norwood Hse. Pr.

—Adventures in the Nervous System. Lowe, Alexander. 2020. (Norwood Discovery Graphics: the Bod Squad Ser.). (ENG.). 32p. (J). (gr. 2-3). 29.27 ***(978-1-68450-863-1(0));*** pap. 13.26 ***(978-1-68404-579-2(7))*** Norwood Hse. Pr.

—Adventures in the Respiratory System. Lowe, Alexander. 2020. (Norwood Discovery Graphics: the Bod Squad Ser.). (ENG.). 32p. (J). (gr. 2-3). 29.27 ***(978-1-68450-860-0(6));*** pap. 13.26 ***(978-1-68404-582-2(7))*** Norwood Hse. Pr.

—Drought Daze. Lowe, Alexander. 2020. (Norwood Discovery Graphics: Weather Warriors Ser.). (ENG.). 32p. (J). (gr. 2-3). 29.27 ***(978-1-68450-856-3(8));*** pap. 13.26 ***(978-1-68404-591-4(6))*** Norwood Hse. Pr.

—Eye of the Hurricane. Lowe, Alexander. 2020. (Norwood Discovery Graphics: Weather Warriors Ser.). (ENG.). 32p. (J). (gr. 2-3). 29.27 ***(978-1-68450-857-0(6));*** pap. 13.26 ***(978-1-68404-590-7(8))*** Norwood Hse. Pr.

—Hail Alley. Lowe, Alexander. 2020. (Norwood Discovery Graphics: Weather Warriors Ser.). (ENG.). 32p. (J). (gr. 2-3). 29.27 ***(978-1-68450-854-9(1));*** pap. 13.26 ***(978-1-68404-593-8(2))*** Norwood Hse. Pr.

—Inside the Tornado. Lowe, Alexander. 2020. (Norwood Discovery Graphics: Weather Warriors Ser.). (ENG.). 32p. (J). (gr. 2-3). 29.27 ***(978-1-68450-858-7(4));*** pap. 13.26 ***(978-1-68404-589-1(4))*** Norwood Hse. Pr.

—Whiteout. Lowe, Alexander. 2020. (Norwood Discovery Graphics: Weather Warriors Ser.). (ENG.). 32p. (J). (gr. 2-3). 29.27 ***(978-1-68450-855-6(X));*** pap. 13.26 ***(978-1-68404-592-1(4))*** Norwood Hse. Pr.

Kadmon, Cristina. The Best Father of All. Horn, Peter. James, J. Alison, tr. 2005. (ENG.). 32p. (J). (gr. -1). pap. 6.95 *(978-0-7358-1977-1(7))* North-South Bks., Inc.

—When I Grow Up... Horn, Peter. 2014. 32p. pap. 8.00 *(978-1-61003-370-1(1))* Center for the Collaborative Classroom.

Kaergel, Julia. Luisa Quiere Ser Princesa. Dorrie, Doris & Dörrie, Doris. 2005. (SPA.). (J). (gr. 1-3). 16.80 *(978-84-89804-70-8(2),* LG32983) Lóguez Ediciones ESP. Dist: Lectorum Pubns., Inc.

Kaeser, Gigi, photos by. Nothing to Hide: Mental Illness in the Family. Beard, Jean J. & Gillespie, Peggy, eds. 2005. 296p. (YA). reprint ed. pap. 30.00 *(978-0-7567-9382-1(3))* DIANE Publishing Co.

Kafer, Jenny. I Love You When You Feel. Grace, Stephy. 2020. (ENG.). 40p. (J). pap. 17.45 ***(978-1-9736-8323-0(7),*** WestBow Pr.) Author Solutions, Inc.

Kahn, Katherine. A Holiday for Ari Ant, Vol. Rouss, Sylvia A. 2016. (ENG.). (J). pap. *(978-1-68115-507-4(9))* Behrman Hse., Inc.

—Sammy Spider's New Friend. Rouss, Sylvia A. 2012. (Kar-Ben Favorites Ser.). (ENG.). 32p. (J). (gr. -1-2). lib. bdg. 17.95 *(978-0-7613-6663-8(6),* Kar-Ben Publishing) Lerner Publishing Group.

Kahn, Katherine Janus. A Family Haggadah II, Vol. 2. Silberman, Shoshana. I.t. ed. 2003. 64p. (J). pap. 6.95 *(978-1-58013-014-1(3),* Kar-Ben Publishing) Lerner Publishing Group.

—Noah & the Ziz, Vol. Jules, Jacqueline & Hechtkopf, Jacqueline. 2005. (ENG.). 32p. (J). (gr. -1-2). 9.95 *(978-0-929371-01-6(1),* Kar-Ben Publishing) Lerner Publishing Group.

—The Princess & the Ziz. Jules, Jacqueline. 2008. 32p. (J). (gr. -1-3). lib. bdg. 17.95 *(978-0-8225-7377-7(6),* Kar-Ben Publishing) Lerner Publishing Group.

—Sammy Spider Series, 11 vols., Set. Rouss, Sylvia A. 2003. (J). (gr. -1-3). 70.61 *(978-1-58013-046-2(1),* Kar-Ben Publishing) Lerner Publishing Group.

—Sammy Spider Sets. Rouss, Sylvia A. (J). (gr. -1-3). 28.62 *(978-1-58013-217-6(0),* Kar-Ben Publishing) Lerner Publishing Group.

—Sammy Spider's First Bar Mitzvah. Rouss, Sylvia A. 2016. (ENG.). 32p. (J). (gr. -1-3). 17.99 *(978-1-4677-8931-8(3),* 9781467789318, Kar-Ben Publishing) Lerner Publishing Group.

—Sammy Spider's First Book of Jewish Holidays, Vol. Rouss, Sylvia A. 2013. (Very First Board Bks.). (ENG.). 12p. (J). (gr. -1 — 1). bds. 6.99 *(978-1-4677-1916-2(1),* 9781467719162, Kar-Ben Publishing) Lerner Publishing Group.

—Sammy Spider's First Day of School. Rouss, Sylvia A. 2009. (Kar-Ben Favorites Ser.). (ENG.). 32p. (J). (gr. -1-2). 16.95 *(978-0-8225-8583-1(9));* Vol. pap. 7.99 *(978-0-8225-8584-8(7),* 9780822585848) Lerner Publishing Group. (Kar-Ben Publishing).

—Sammy Spider's First Haggadah, Vol. Rouss, Sylvia A. 2007. (ENG.). 32p. (J). (gr. -1-3). per. 6.99 *(978-1-58013-230-5(8),* Kar-Ben Publishing) Lerner Publishing Group.

—Sammy Spider's First Mitzvah. Rouss, Sylvia A. 2014. (ENG.). 24p. (J). (gr. -1-3). 17.95 *(978-1-4677-1947-6(1),* 9781467719476, Kar-Ben Publishing) Lerner Publishing Group.

—Sammy Spider's First Shavuot. Rouss, Sylvia A. 2008. (ENG.). 32p. (J). (gr. -1-3). lib. bdg. 15.95 *(978-0-8225-7224-4(9));* Vol. per. 7.95 *(978-0-8225-7225-1(7))* Lerner Publishing Group. (Kar-Ben Publishing).

—Sammy Spider's First Simchat Torah, Vol. Rouss, Sylvia A. 2010. (ENG.). 32p. (J). (gr. -1-2). pap. 7.99 *(978-0-7613-3966-3(3),* 9780761339663, Kar-Ben Publishing) Lerner Publishing Group.

—Sammy Spider's First Sukkot. Rouss, Sylvia A. 2004. (ENG.). 32p. (J). (gr. -1-3). 17.95 *(978-1-58013-142-1(5));* Vol. pap. 7.95 *(978-1-58013-083-7(6),* 9781580130837) Lerner Publishing Group. (Kar-Ben Publishing).

—Sammy Spider's First Taste of Hanukkah: A Cookbook. Rouss, Sylvia A. & Turndorf, Genene Levy. 2015. (ENG.). 32p. (J). (gr. -1-3). 16.99 *(978-1-4677-5237-4(1),* 9781467752374); E-Book 27.99 *(978-1-4677-8842-7(2));* Vol. pap. 7.99 *(978-1-4677-5243-5(6),* 9781467752435) Lerner Publishing Group. (Kar-Ben Publishing).

—Sammy Spider's First Wedding. Rouss, Sylvia A. 2019. (ENG.). 32p. (J). (gr. -1-3). 17.99 *(978-1-5124-8366-6(4),* Kar-Ben Publishing) Lerner Publishing Group.

—Sammy Spider's First Yom Kippur. Rouss, Sylvia A. ed. 2013. (ENG.). 32p. (J). (gr. -1-3). E-Book 27.99 *(978-1-4677-1639-0(1));* Vol. 7.99 *(978-0-7613-9196-8(7),* 9780761391968); Vol. lib. bdg. 16.95 *(978-0-7613-9195-1(9),* 9780761391951) Lerner Publishing Group. (Kar-Ben Publishing).

—Sammy Spider's Hanukkah Colors, Vol. Rouss, Sylvia A. 2017. (ENG.). 12p. (J). (gr. -1 — 1). bds. 5.99 *(978-1-4677-5238-1(X),* 9781467752381, Kar-Ben Publishing) Lerner Publishing Group.

—Sammy Spider's New Friend, Vol. Rouss, Sylvia A. 2012. (ENG.). 32p. (J). (gr. -1-3). 7.95 *(978-0-7613-6664-5(4),* 9780761366645, Kar-Ben Publishing) Lerner Publishing Group.

—Sammy Spider's Passover Shapes. Rouss, Sylvia A. ed. 2017. (ENG.). 12p. (J). (gr. -1 — 1). E-Book 23.99 *(978-1-5124-2727-1(6),* 9781512427271); Vol. bds. 5.99 *(978-1-4677-7970-8(9),* 9781467779708) Lerner Publishing Group. (Kar-Ben Publishing).

—Sammy Spider's Shabbat Fun Book, Vol. Rouss, Sylvia A. 2006. (ENG.). 24p. (J). (gr. -1-3). pap. 4.95 *(978-1-58013-147-6(6),* Kar-Ben Publishing) Lerner Publishing Group.

—Tamar's Sukkah. Gellman, Ellie B. ed. 2015. (ENG.). 32p. (J). (gr. -1-2). E-Book 23.99 *(978-1-4677-8845-8(7));* lib. bdg. 9.99 *(978-1-4677-5636-5(9),* 9781467756365) Lerner Publishing Group. (Kar-Ben Publishing).

—The Ziz & the Hanukkah Miracle. Jules, Jacqueline. 2006. (ENG.). 32p. (J). (gr. -1-2). lib. bdg. 17.95 *(978-1-58013-160-5(3),* Kar-Ben Publishing) Lerner Publishing Group.

Kahn, M. The Charlie & Molly Coloring & Word Search Book for Kids: Dog Coloring Book for Ages 5 & up. (Us Version) Selbherr, C. 2018. (ENG.). 68p. (J). pap. *(978-3-947677-08-5(1))* Selbherr. , Charlotte Harlescott Bks.

—Charlie Makes a Friend: Join in Charlie's Adventures As He Searches for a Playmate. Book 2 from 'the Charlie & Molly Book Collection'. Bedtime Story, Rhyming Books, Picture Books, Dog Books. Selbherr, C. 2018. (ENG.). 34p. (J). pap. *(978-3-947677-03-0(0))* Selbherr. , Charlotte Harlescott Bks.

—Coloring & Word Search Book for Kids: Book 1 - Coloring Book for Ages 5 & up. (Us Version) Selbherr, C. 2019. (Coloring & Word Search Book for Kids Ser.: Vol. 1). (ENG.). 68p. (J). pap. *(978-3-947677-11-5(1))* Selbherr. , Charlotte Harlescott Bks.

—My Mate Molly & My Chum Charlie: Children's Book Introducing Two Dog Friends & Their Family, Bedtime Story, Rhyming Books, Picture Books, Book 1. Selbherr, C. 2018. (ENG.). 32p. (J). pap. *(978-3-947677-05-4(7));* pap. *(978-3-947677-00-9(6))* Selbherr. , Charlotte Harlescott Bks.

Kahn, Patty. Seeds, Leaves, Fruits, & Roots. Henrikson, Jerilynn. 2016. (ENG.). (J). (gr. k-2). 20.00 *(978-1-939054-79-1(6))* Rowe Publishing.

Kahn, Sara & Palacios, Sara. The Three Lucys, 1 vol. Charara, Hayan & Brown, Monica. 2016. (ENG.). 40p. (J). 18.95 *(978-1-60060-998-5(8))* Lee & Low Bks., Inc.

Kai. Peter Wanted a Pet. Summers, Terry. 2012. 26p. 24.95 *(978-1-4626-6120-6(3))* America Star Bks.

Kai, Hanane. Global Conflict. Spilsbury, Louise. 2018. (Children in Our World Ser.). (ENG.). 32p. (J). (gr. 1-5). 9.99 *(978-1-4380-5021-8(6),* B.E.S. Publishing) Peterson's.

—Racism & Intolerance. Spilsbury, Louise. 2018. (Children in Our World Ser.). (ENG.). 32p. (J). (gr. 1-2). 9.99 *(978-1-4380-5022-5(4),* B.E.S. Publishing) Peterson's.

—Refugees & Migrants. Roberts, Ceri. 2017. (Children in Our World Ser.). (ENG.). 32p. (J). (gr. 1-4). 9.99 *(978-1-4380-5020-1(8),* B.E.S. Publishing) Peterson's.

Kaichi, Keiko. Old Lion & the Little Rabbit. Kaichi, Keiko. 2017. (ENG.). 32p. (J). (gr. -1-k). 17.99 *(978-988-8341-24-5(3),* Minedition) Neugebauer, Michael (Publishing) Limited HKG. Dist: Penguin Random Hse. LLC.

Kaida, Garrett. Fire Truck! Ulz, Ivan. 2013. 36p. 19.00 *(978-0-9896231-0-0(6))* Temple Street Pr.

Kailuweit, Conny. Die Kleine Hexe Laurin und Ihr Kleiner Rabe Rudolf. Hiller, Marion. 2019. (GER.). 60p. (J). pap. 7.50 ***(978-1-6710-4431-9(2))*** Independently Published.

Kain, Bob. Joking Around with Chirp. Chirp Magazine, The Editors of. 2013. (ENG.). 96p. (J). (gr. -1-3). pap. 11.95 *(978-1-926973-65-4(8))* Owlkids Bks. Inc. CAN. Dist: Publishers Group West (PGW).

Kaino, Kim, jt. illus. see Youso, Justin.

Kaiser, Lisa. A Little Story, about the Biggest thing that Ever Happened. Dalton, William. 2006. per. *(978-0-9764395-0-9(6))* Dalton, William.

Kaiser, Lori. Florence Flamingo Gets the Flu. Kaiser, Lori. 2012. 30p. pap. *(978-0-9836651-5-1(X))* Roxby Media Ltd.

—George Washington. Kaiser, Lori. 2012. 26p. pap. *(978-0-9836651-7-5(6))* Roxby Media Ltd.

—Gigi the Greedy Giraffe. Kaiser, Lori. 2012. 28p. pap. *(978-0-9836651-8-2(4))* Roxby Media Ltd.

—Megan the Moody Moose. Kaiser, Lori. 2013. 26p. pap. *(978-0-9883770-5-9(5))* Roxby Media Ltd.

Kako, Franco. Encountering Ghosts: Eyewitness Accounts, 1 vol. Bolte, Mari. 2014. (Eyewitness to the Unexplained Ser.). (ENG.). 32p. (J). (gr. 3-9). 31.32 *(978-1-4914-0245-0(8),* Capstone Pr.) Capstone.

Kako, Satoshi. Where Is Little Toko? Matsuoka, Kyoko. 2006. 32p. (J). 11.95 *(978-1-74126-022-9(1))* R.I.C. Pubns. AUS. Dist: SCB Distributors.

Kala, Sabah. Momma's Song. El Khatiri, Basma. 2016. (Stories & Fables from Around the World Ser.). (ENG.). 24p. (J). (gr. 2-1). lib. bdg. 24.60 *(978-1-4777-5694-2(9),* Windmill Bks.) Rosen Publishing Group, Inc., The.

—My Beautiful Hair. Abassi, Ines. 2016. (Stories & Fables from Around the World Ser.). (ENG.). 24p. (J). (gr. 2-1). lib. bdg. 24.60 *(978-1-4777-5695-9(7),* Windmill Bks.) Rosen Publishing Group, Inc., The.

Kalafatis, John, jt. illus. see Smith, Jacquelyn.

Kalahele, Imaikalani. Breaking the Blood. Eyre, David. 2008. 40p. 14.95 *(978-0-87336-162-0(8))* Kamehameha Publishing.

—Lumpy Poi & Twisting Eels. Eyre, David. 2007. 32p. 14.95 *(978-0-87336-154-5(7))* Kamehameha Publishing.

—Sacred Awa Piercing Spears. Eyre, David. 2009. 31p. 14.95 *(978-0-87336-217-7(9))* Kamehameha Publishing.

Kalal, Dan. Rosa Parks & the Montgomery Bus Boycott, 1 vol. Miller, Connie Colwell. 2006. (Graphic History Ser.). (ENG.). 32p. (J). (gr. 3-9). per. 8.10 *(978-0-7368-9658-0(9))* Capstone.

Kalar, Steve. Finding Joy. Poelking, Jordyn. 2019. (ENG.). 76p. (J). pap. 19.95 *(978-1-7904-9043-1(X))* Independently Published.

Kalasea. What Might I Find in a Geyser. Declus, Jennifer. 2004. (J). *(978-0-9743690-0-6(4))* Britt Allcroft Productions.

—What Might I Find in a Rainforest. Declus, Jennifer. 2004. (ENG.). (J). *(978-0-9743690-1-3(2))* Britt Allcroft Productions.

—What Might I Find in a Swamp. Declus, Jennifer. 2004. (J). *(978-0-9743690-3-7(9))* Britt Allcroft Productions.

—What Might I Find in a Tidepool. Declus, Jennifer. 2004. (J). *(978-0-9743690-4-4(7))* Britt Allcroft Productions.

—What Might I Find on a Pond. Declus, Jennifer. 2004. (J). *(978-0-9743690-2-0(0))* Britt Allcroft Productions.

Kalb, Chris. Rachael Ray's 30-Minute Meals for Kids: Cooking Rocks! Ray, Rachael. 2004. (ENG.). 192p. (J). (gr. -1-12). spiral bd. 16.95 *(978-1-891105-15-9(9))* Lake Isle Pr., Inc.

Kalbacher, Karen. Giraffes in Outer Space. Melaas, Christine. 2019. (Giraffes in Outer Space Ser.: Vol. 1). (ENG.). 58p. (J). pap. 13.99 *(978-1-0711-5557-8(1))* Independently Published.

Kalbandi, Sunil. The Fortress. Carlisle, Faye. 2017. (Kodo Ser.: Vol. 1). (ENG.). (J). (gr. k-4). pap. *(978-0-9957101-0-8(4))* Keen Zebra.

—The Magma Chambers. Carlisle, Faye. 2017. (ENG.). 140p. (J). pap. *(978-0-9957101-2-2(0))* Keen Zebra.

Kalbandi, Sunil. The Pyramid. Carlisle, Faye. 2019. (Kodo Ser.: Vol. 3). (ENG.). 128p. (J). pap. ***(978-0-9957101-3-9(9))*** Keen Zebra.

Kalda, Sam. When Darwin Sailed the Sea: Uncover How Darwin's Revolutionary Ideas Helped Change the World. Long, David. 2020. (ENG.). 80p. (J). (gr. 3-5). ***(978-0-7112-4968-4(7),*** Wide Eyed Editions) Quarto Publishing Group UK.

Kale, Ann Stephanian. Artie - The Ugly Frog. Kale, Ann Stephanian. 2004. 20p. (J). pap. 10.00 *(978-0-9704131-6-1(5))* Abril BookStore & Publishing.

—Marco & Princess Gina. Kale, Ann Stephanian. 2003. 24p. (J). (gr. k-3). pap. 10.00 *(978-0-9704131-5-4(7))* Abril BookStore & Publishing.

Kale, Kavita Singh. Good Night Delhi. Khemka, Nitya & Gamble, Adam. 2017. (Good Night Our World Ser.). 20p. (J). (— 1). bds. 9.95 *(978-1-60219-481-6(5))* Good Night Bks.

—Good Night India. Khemka, Nitya. 2017. (Good Night Our World Ser.). 20p. (J). (— 1). bds. 9.95 *(978-1-60219-477-9(7))* Good Night Bks.

—Good Night Mumbai. Khemka, Nitya. 2017. (Good Night Our World Ser.). 20p. (J). (— 1). bds. 9.95 *(978-1-60219-483-0(1))* Good Night Bks.

—Good Night Rajasthan. Khemka, Nitya. 2017. (Good Night Our World Ser.). 20p. (J). (— 1). bds. 9.95 *(978-1-60219-479-3(3))* Good Night Bks.

Kalender, Oznur. Animal Wonders of the Sky. Kaplan, Osman. 2009. (Amazing Animals Ser.). 56p. (J). (gr. 2-4). 9.95 *(978-1-59784-201-3(X),* Tughra Bks.) Blue Dome, Inc.

—Animal Wonders of the Water. Kaplan, Osman. 2009. (Amazing Animals Ser.). 56p. (J). (gr. 2-4). 9.95 *(978-1-59784-200-6(1),* Tughra Bks.) Blue Dome, Inc.

—Giants of the World. Kaplan, Osman. 2008. (Amazing Animals Ser.). 56p. (J). (gr. 2-4). 9.95 *(978-1-59784-139-9(0),* Tughra Bks.) Blue Dome, Inc.

—Wonders of the Land. Kaplan, Osman. 2008. (Amazing Animals Ser.). 56p. (J). (gr. -1-3). 9.95 *(978-1-59784-145-0(5),* Tughra Bks.) Blue Dome, Inc.

Kaliaha, Volha. B Is for Boston. Farley, Christin & Miles, Stephanie. 2018. (ABC Regional Board Bks.). (ENG.). 20p. (J). bds. 12.99 *(978-1-945547-89-8(8),* 554789) Familius LLC.

—C Is for Colorado. Farley, Christin & Miles, Stephanie. 2018. (ABC Regional Board Bks.). (ENG.). 20p. (J). bds. 12.99 *(978-1-945547-86-7(3),* 554786) Familius LLC.

—Let's Count Colorado: Numbers & Colors in the Centennial State. Farley, Christin & Miles, Stephanie. 2018. (Let's Count Regional Board Bks.). (ENG.). 20p. (J). bds. 12.99 *(978-1-945547-85-0(5),* 554785) Familius LLC.

K

—Little Lacers: 123: Lace & Learn Your First Numbers! Hinckley, Peter. 2019. (Little Lacers Ser.). (ENG.). 14p. (J). bds. 16.99 (978-1-64170-008-5(4), 550008) Familius LLC.

—M Is for Montana. Farley, Christin & Miles, Stephanie. 2018. (ABC Regional Board Bks.). (ENG.). 20p. (J). bds. 12.99 (978-1-945547-88-1(X), 554788) Familius LLC.

Kalimeris, Constantina. I Found My Dreidel. Abelson, Joel Samuel. 2016. (ENG.). (J). pap. 12.95 (978-0-9830421-4-3(4)) Abelson Pr.

Kalina, Lacey & Norris, Cameron. Buck Finds a Buck. Phillips, Scott. 2019. (Buck Finds a Buck Ser.: Vol. 1). (ENG.). 24p. (J). pap. 9.99 (978-1-6910-2219-9(5)) Independently Published.

Kalinichenko, Solomea. God Always Hears. Grettler, Kelly. 2019. (ENG.). 36p. (J). (gr. k-6). 19.99 (978-0-578-57187-4(0)) Grettler, Kelly.

Kalinina, Viktoriia. A Bear, a Moose & a Princess. Stein, Bob. 2018. (ENG.). 24p. (J). pap. 12.95 (978-1-64458-580-1(4)) Christian Faith Publishing.

Kalis, Jennifer. The BFF Journal, 1 vol. Wood, Anita. 2011. (ENG.). 144p. (J). (gr. 1). spiral bd. 12.99 (978-1-4236-1814-0(9)) Gibbs Smith, Publisher.

—The Big Book of Girl Stuff, 1 vol. King, Bart. 2014. (ENG.). 320p. (J). pap. 19.99 (978-1-4236-3762-2(3)) Gibbs Smith, Publisher.

—Campfire Mallory. Friedman, Laurie. (Mallory Ser.: 9). (ENG.). 176p. (J). (gr. 2-5). 2009. pap. 6.99 (978-1-58013-841-3(1)); 2008. lib. bdg. 15.95 (978-0-8225-7657-0(0)) Lerner Publishing Group. (Darby Creek).

—Change Is in the Air, Mallory. Friedman, Laurie. ed. 2015. (Mallory Ser.: 24). (ENG.). 160p. (J). (gr. 2-5). E-Book 23.99 (978-1-4677-8822-9(8));No. 24. 15.95 (978-1-4677-0924-8(7), 9781467709248) Lerner Publishing Group. (Darby Creek).

—Doodle Your Day, 1 vol. Wood, Anita. 2013. (ENG.). 224p. (J). pap. 16.99 (978-1-4236-2368-7(1)) Gibbs Smith, Publisher.

—Fairy Doodles, 1 vol. Wood, Anita. 2014. 240p. (J). pap. 9.99 (978-1-4236-3606-9(6)) Gibbs Smith, Publisher.

—Fashion Doodles, 1 vol. Wood, Anita. 2014. 240p. (J). pap. 16.99 (978-1-4236-3607-6(4)) Gibbs Smith, Publisher.

—Game Time, Mallory! Friedman, Laurie. ed. 2015. (Mallory Ser.). (ENG.). 160p. (J). (gr. 2-5). E-Book 23.99 (978-1-4677-6188-8(5), Darby Creek) Lerner Publishing Group.

—Game Time, Mallory!, No. 23. Friedman, Laurie. 2015. (Mallory Ser.: 23). (ENG.). 160p. (J). (gr. 2-5). 15.95 (978-1-4677-0923-1(9), 9781467709231, Darby Creek) Lerner Publishing Group.

—Happy New Year, Mallory! Friedman, Laurie. (Mallory Ser.: 12). (ENG.). 176p. (J). (gr. 2-5). 2010. pap. 6.99 (978-0-7613-3947-2(7)); 2009. 15.95 (978-0-8225-8883-2(8)) Lerner Publishing Group. (Darby Creek).

—High Five, Mallory! Friedman, Laurie. ed. (Mallory Ser.: 26). (ENG.). 160p. (J). (gr. 2-5). 2016. E-Book 23.99 (978-1-5124-0898-0(0), 9781512408980); No. 26. 2017. pap. 6.99 (978-1-5124-5867-1(8), 9781512458671) Lerner Publishing Group. (Darby Creek).

—High Five, Mallory!, No. 26. Friedman, Laurie. 2016. (Mallory Ser.: 26). (ENG.). 160p. (J). (gr. 2-5). 15.95 (978-1-4677-5030-1(1), 9781467750301, Darby Creek) Lerner Publishing Group.

—Made with Love for Mom. Ikids Staff. 2008. (ENG.). 24p. (J). (gr. 1-17). 7.99 (978-1-58476-660-5(3), IKIDS) Innovative Kids.

—Mallory & Mary Ann Take New York, No. 19. Friedman, Laurie. (Mallory Ser.: 19). (ENG.). 160p. (J). (gr. 2-5). 2014. pap. 6.99 (978-1-4677-0935-4(2), 9781467709354); 2013. 15.95 (978-0-7613-6074-2(3), 9780761360742) Lerner Publishing Group. (Darby Creek).

—Mallory Goes Green! Friedman, Laurie. (Mallory Ser.). 160p. (J). 2011. pap. 33.92 (978-0-7613-7606-4(2), Darby Creek); 2011. (ENG.). (gr. 2-5). pap. 6.99 (978-0-7613-3949-6(3), Darby Creek); 2010. (ENG.). (gr. 2-5). 15.95 (978-0-8225-8885-6(4), Carolrhoda Bks.) Lerner Publishing Group.

—Mallory in the Spotlight. Friedman, Laurie. (Mallory Ser.). 2011. pap. 33.92 (978-0-7613-8359-8(X)); 2011. (ENG.). 160p. (J). (gr. 2-5). pap. 6.99 (978-0-7613-3948-9(5)); 2010. (ENG.). 160p. (J). (gr. 2-5). 15.95 (978-0-8225-8884-9(6)) Lerner Publishing Group. (Darby Creek).

—Mallory Makes a Difference. Friedman, Laurie. (Mallory Ser.). (ENG.). 152p. (J). (gr. 2-5). 2018. pap. 6.99 (978-1-5415-2816-1(6)); No. 28. 2017. 15.95 (978-1-4677-5032-5(8), 9781467750325) Lerner Publishing Group. (Darby Creek).

—Mallory Mcdonald, Baby Expert, Bk. 22. Friedman, Laurie. (Mallory Ser.: Vol. 22). (ENG.). 152p. (J). (gr. 2-5). 2015. pap. 6.99 (978-1-4677-0938-5(7), 9781467709385); 2014. 15.95 (978-1-4677-0922-4(0), 9781467709224) Lerner Publishing Group. (Darby Creek).

—Mallory Mcdonald, Super Sitter. Friedman, Laurie. ed. (Mallory Ser.: 27). (ENG.). 160p. (J). (gr. 2-5). 2017. E-Book 23.99 (978-1-5124-2696-0(2)); Bk. 27. 2018. pap. 6.99 (978-1-5415-0110-2(1), 9781541501102); Bk. 27. 2017. 15.95 (978-1-4677-5031-8(X), 9781467750318) Lerner Publishing Group. (Darby Creek).

—Mallory Mcdonald, Super Snoop. Friedman, Laurie. (Mallory Ser.: 18). (ENG.). 152p. (J). (gr. 2-5). 2013. pap. 6.99 (978-1-4677-0929-3(8), 9781467709293); 2012. 15.95 (978-0-7613-6073-5(5), 9780761360735) Lerner Publishing Group. (Darby Creek).

—Mallory's Guide to Boys, Brothers, Dads, & Dogs. Friedman, Laurie. 2012. (Mallory Ser.). 160p. (J). (gr. 2-5). pap. 33.92 (978-0-7613-9206-4(8)); (ENG.). pap. 6.99 (978-0-7613-5250-1(3)) Lerner Publishing Group. (Darby Creek).

—Mallory's Super Sleepover. Friedman, Laurie. (Mallory Ser.: 16). (ENG.). 160p. (J). (gr. 2-5). 2012. pap. 6.99 (978-1-4677-0209-6(9)); No. 16. 2011. 15.95 (978-0-8225-8887-0(0)) Lerner Publishing Group. (Darby Creek).

—Mama's Many Hats. Erhard, Lorie. 2014. (ENG.). 32p. (J). 18.99 (978-0-9914701-4-3(1)) Bumble Bee Bks.

—Mary Cassatt: Family Pictures. O'Connor, Jane. 2003. (Smart about Art Ser.). (ENG.). 32p. (J). (gr. k-4). mass mkt. 6.99 (978-0-448-43152-9(1), Grosset & Dunlap) Penguin Young Readers Group.

—Oh Boy, Mallory, No. 17. Friedman, Laurie. 2013. (Mallory Ser.: 17). (ENG.). 160p. (J). (gr. 2-5). pap. 6.99 (978-1-4677-0863-0(1), 9781467708630, Darby Creek) Lerner Publishing Group.

—On the Road with Mallory. Friedman, Laurie. ed. 2016. (Mallory Ser.: 25). (ENG.). 160p. (J). (gr. 2-5). E-Book 23.99 (978-1-4677-9567-8(4));No. 25. 15.95 (978-1-4677-5029-5(8), 9781467750295) Lerner Publishing Group. (Darby Creek).

—Play It Again, Mallory, No. 20. Friedman, Laurie. (Mallory Ser.: 20). (ENG.). 160p. (J). (gr. 2-5). 2014. pap. 6.99 (978-1-4677-0936-1(0), 9781467709361); 2013. 15.95 (978-0-7613-6075-9(1), 9780761360759) Lerner Publishing Group. (Darby Creek).

—Pocketdoodles for Girls, 1 vol. Wood, Anita. 2010. 272p. (J). (gr. 1). pap. 9.99 (978-1-4236-0755-7(4)) Gibbs Smith, Publisher.

—Pocketdoodles for Princesses, 1 vol. Wood, Anita. 2011. 272p. (J). (gr. 3). pap. 9.99 (978-1-4236-1877-5(7)) Gibbs Smith, Publisher.

—Red, White & True Blue Mallory. Friedman, Laurie. (Mallory Ser.: 11). (ENG.). 184p. (J). (gr. 2-5). 2010. pap. 6.99 (978-0-7613-3946-5(9)); 2009. 15.95 (978-0-8225-8882-5(X)) Lerner Publishing Group. (Darby Creek).

—Step Fourth, Mallory! Friedman, Laurie. (Mallory Ser.: 10). (ENG.). 176p. (J). (gr. 2-5). 2009. pap. 6.99 (978-1-58013-842-0(X), Darby Creek); 2008. 15.95 (978-0-8225-8881-8(1), Carolrhoda Bks.) Lerner Publishing Group.

—Three's Company, Mallory!, No. 21. Friedman, Laurie. 2014. (Mallory Ser.: 21). (ENG.). 160p. (J). (gr. 2-5). 15.95 (978-1-4677-0921-7(2), 9781467709217, Darby Creek) Lerner Publishing Group.

—Welcome to the Daisy Flower Garden. Tuchman, Laura. 2008. 88p. (J). (978-0-88441-709-5(3)) Girl Scouts of the USA.

Kaliszewski, Justin. The Adventures of Babu: From There to Here. Kaliszewski, Justin. 2016. (ENG.). (J). (gr. k-6). 19.95 (978-1-939919-44-1(4)) Merry Dissonance Pr.

Kaliwo, Vanessa. The Adventures of Dr. Brain & Mr. Strong. Hall, Lashandra Monique. 2019. (ENG.). 30p. (J). pap. 19.99 (978-1-7908-6674-8(X)) Elnoir Jane Publishing.

Kalla, Siski. You Are a Superhero, Too! Blackburn, Brittnie. 2020. (ENG.). 30p. (J). pap. 13.95 (978-1-9736-9644-5(4), WestBow Pr.) Author Solutions, Inc.

Kallai, Kriszta Nagy. Silent Night. Howie, Vicki. 2009. 32p. (J). (gr. -1). pap. 13.49 (978-0-7586-1779-8(8)) Concordia Publishing Hse.

Kallai Nagy, Krisztina. Animal Lullabies. Ross, Mandy. (Poems for the Young Ser.). 32p. (J). 2007. audio compact disk (978-1-84643-052-7(6)); 2005. (ENG.). audio compact disk (978-1-904550-93-8(2)); 2003. (gr. 2-3). (978-0-85953-116-0(3)) Child's Play International Ltd.

Kallai Nagy, Krisztina. The Lion Storyteller Family Bible. Hartman, Bob. ed. 2020. (ENG.). 160p. (J). (gr. 1). 18.99 (978-0-7459-7842-0(8), Lion Children's) Lion Hudson PLC GBR. Dist: Independent Pubs. Group.

Kallick, Ingrid. Sophia's Quest. Ellertson, Wendy. 2018. (ENG.). 156p. (J). pap. 12.99 (978-1-7212-6958-7(4)) CreateSpace Independent Publishing Platform.

Kallis, Samantha. Beware! Shadows in the Night #3. Oliver, Lin. (Fantastic Frame Ser.: 3). (ENG.). 128p. (J). (gr. 2-4). 2019. 7.99 (978-0-448-48090-9(5), Penguin Workshop); 2016. 11.99 (978-0-448-48091-6(3), Grosset & Dunlap) Penguin Young Readers Group.

—Danger! Tiger Crossing #1. Oliver, Lin. 2018. (Fantastic Frame Ser.: 1). (ENG.). 128p. (J). (gr. 2-4). pap. 7.99 (978-0-448-48086-2(7), Penguin Workshop) Penguin Young Readers Group.

—Look Out! Ghost Mountain Below #4. Oliver, Lin. (Fantastic Frame Ser.: 4). (ENG.). 128p. (J). (gr. 2-4). 2019. 7.99 (978-0-448-48092-3(1), Penguin Workshop); 2017. 11.99 (978-0-448-48093-0(X), Grosset & Dunlap) Penguin Young Readers Group.

—Splat! Another Messy Sunday #2. Oliver, Lin. 2018. (Fantastic Frame Ser.: 2). 128p. (J). (gr. 2-4). 7.99 (978-0-448-48088-6(3), Penguin Workshop) Penguin Young Readers Group.

Kallis, Samantha, jt. illus. see Kimbell, Emily.

Kalman, Bobbie, photos by. Les Bébés Lapins. 2012. (FRE., 24p. (J). pap. 9.95 (978-2-89579-441-7(3)) Bayard Canada CAN. Dist: Crabtree Publishing Co.

—La Gymnastique. Crossingham, John. 2011. (FRE., 32p. (J). pap. 9.95 (978-2-89579-414-1(6)) Bayard Canada CAN. Dist: Crabtree Publishing Co.

Kalman, Lola. Bullies to Buddies - How to Turn Your Enemies into Friends! How to Turn Your Enemies into Friends! Kalman, Izzy C. 2005. (ENG.). 128p. (YA). per. 15.00 (978-0-9706482-1-1(9)) The Wisdom Pages, Inc.

Kalman, Maira. Bold & Brave: Ten Heroes Who Won Women the Right to Vote. Gillibrand, Kirsten. (ENG.). 40p. (J). (gr. 1-4). 2020. pap. 7.99 (978-0-593-30266-8(4), Dragonfly Bks.); 2018. 18.99 (978-0-525-57901-4(X), Knopf Bks. for Young Readers); 2018. lib. bdg. 21.99 (978-0-525-57902-1(8), Knopf Bks. for Young Readers) Random Hse. Children's Bks.

Kalman, Maira. Girls Standing on the Lawn. Handler, Daniel. 2014. (ENG.). 64p. (J). (gr. 3-7). 14.95 (978-0-87070-908-1(9)) Museum of Modern Art.

—Why We Broke Up. Handler, Daniel. 2013. (ENG.). 368p. (YA). (gr. 10-17). pap. 18.99 (978-0-316-12726-4(4)) Little, Brown Bks. for Young Readers.

—13 Words. Snicket, Lemony. 2010. (ENG.). 40p. (J). (gr. -1-3). 16.99 (978-0-06-166465-6(0)) HarperCollins Pubs.

—13 Words. Snicket, Lemony. 2014. (ENG.). 40p. (J). (gr. -1-3). pap. 7.99 (978-0-06-166467-0(7), HarperCollins) HarperCollins Pubs. Ltd. GBR. Dist: HarperCollins Pubs.

Kalman, Maira. Fireboat: The Heroic Adventures of the John J. Harvey. Kalman, Maira. 2005. (ENG.). 48p. (J). (gr. -1-3). reprint ed. pap. 7.99 (978-0-14-240362-4(8), Puffin Books) Penguin Young Readers Group.

—Looking at Lincoln. Kalman, Maira. (ENG.). (J). (gr. k-3). 2017. 48p. pap. 8.99 (978-0-14-751798-2(2), Puffin Books); 2012. 32p. 17.99 (978-0-399-24039-3(X), Nancy Paulsen Books) Penguin Young Readers Group.

—Thomas Jefferson: Life, Liberty & the Pursuit of Everything. Kalman, Maira. 2014. (ENG.). 40p. (J). (gr. k-3). 17.99 (978-0-399-24040-9(3), Nancy Paulsen Books) Penguin Young Readers Group.

Kalmenoff, Matthew. Charles John Seghers: Pioneer in Alaska. Bosco, Antoinette. 2011. 194p. 42.95 (978-1-258-01868-9(3)) Literary Licensing, LLC.

—In the Steps of the Great American Herpetologist. Wright, A. Gilbert. 2014. (ENG.). 128p. (J). (gr. 2-6). pap. 11.95 (978-1-59077-360-4(8)) Evans, M. & Co., Inc.

Kalorkoti, Eleni. Garbage Dog. Wilkinson, Robbie. Little Gestalten, Little, ed. 2019. (ENG.). 32p. (J). 19.95 (978-3-89955-832-6(4)) Die Gestalten Verlag DEU. Dist: Ingram Publisher Services.

Kalpart. An Adventurous Cub Meets Nessssss. Dunne, R. N. 2017. (ENG.). (J). (gr. k-6). pap. 10.95 (978-1-68181-438-4(2)) Strategic Book Publishing & Rights Agency (SBPRA).

—The Amazing Apple Tree. Brooks, Donna B. 2017. (ENG.). 52p. (J). (gr. k-6). 15.50 (978-1-941739-78-5(4)) Enchanted Pages Publishing LLC.

—Boogie Bigelow's Big Day. Dolmo, M. Ed Psy D. Norma a. 2019. (ENG.). 38p. (J). (gr. k-6). pap. 13.00 (978-1-62212-481-7(2)) Strategic Book Publishing & Rights Agency (SBPRA).

—Daisy & Friends Outside Our Window. Meredith, Barbara J. 2018. (ENG.). 24p. (J). (gr. k-6). pap. 11.50 (978-1-63135-386-4(1)) Strategic Book Publishing & Rights Agency (SBPRA).

—DOS Historias Cortas para Dormir: La Historia de la Rana Amelia y el Gran Pirata Malaquias. Quinonez, Lina. 2017. (SPA.). 58p. (J). (gr. k-6). pap. 12.99 (978-1-946540-40-9(4)) Strategic Book Publishing & Rights Agency (SBPRA).

—The Fabulous Fanshaws. Rosenberg, Michael. 2016. (ENG.). (YA). (gr. 7-12). pap. 9.95 (978-1-68181-719-4(5)) Strategic Book Publishing & Rights Agency (SBPRA).

—The Fabulous Fanshaws Book Two: The Return to Lendorth. Rosenberg, Michael. 2019. (ENG.). 44p. (YA). pap. 8.95 (978-1-946540-88-1(9)) Strategic Book Publishing & Rights Agency (SBPRA).

—Gem's Gift. Cazes, Christine Conrad. 2018. (ENG.). 34p. (J). (gr. k-6). 20.95 (978-1-948260-31-2(X)); (gr. 6). pap. 11.50 (978-1-948260-30-5(1)) Strategic Book Publishing & Rights Agency (SBPRA).

—Know You're Not Alone. Casaluci, Stacy. 2019. (ENG.). 42p. (J). (gr. k-6). pap. 15.00 (978-1-68181-242-7(8)) Strategic Book Publishing & Rights Agency (SBPRA).

—Know You're Not Alone. Casaluci, Stacy Manning. 2019. (ENG.). 42p. (J). (gr. k-6). 25.50 (978-1-68181-243-4(6)) Strategic Book Publishing & Rights Agency (SBPRA).

—Paddy's Recess Adventures at Hilltop School. Rooney, Sean. 2018. (ENG.). 30p. (J). (gr. k-6). pap. 12.50 (978-1-68181-986-0(4)) Strategic Book Publishing & Rights Agency (SBPRA).

—Punkin. Cazes, Christine Conrad. 2017. (ENG.). (J). (gr. k-6). 20.50 (978-1-946540-50-8(1)); (gr. -1-3). 10.95 (978-1-946540-23-2(4)) Strategic Book Publishing & Rights Agency (SBPRA).

—Quack-A-Nack: The Duck That Couldn't Quack. Jones, Finis T. 2018. (ENG.). 32p. (J). (gr. k-6). pap. 13.95 (978-1-946539-39-7(2)) Strategic Book Publishing & Rights Agency (SBPRA).

—Remy's First Day of School. Davis, Melissa. 2013. 20p. pap. 10.95 (978-1-62212-480-0(4), Strategic Bk. Publishing) Strategic Book Publishing & Rights Agency (SBPRA).

—Santa's Team. Old Nana. 2016. (ENG.). (J). (gr. k-6). pap. 13.00 (978-1-68181-646-3(6)) Strategic Book Publishing & Rights Agency (SBPRA).

—Sea Shoes. Mayhew, Vicki Dean. 2016. (ENG.). (J). (gr. k-6). pap. 19.50 (978-1-63135-014-6(5)) Strategic Book Publishing & Rights Agency (SBPRA).

—Seven Cats & the Big Gray Fence. Risselada, Melissa. 2013. 28p. pap. 12.50 (978-1-62516-777-4(6), Strategic Bk. Publishing) Strategic Book Publishing & Rights Agency (SBPRA).

—Someone You Love Has Cancer: A Child's Guide to Understanding. Duttmann, Robin Martin. 2017. (ENG.). (J). (gr. -1-2). pap. 12.97 (978-1-68181-949-5(X)) Strategic Book Publishing & Rights Agency (SBPRA).

—The Tiny Tomato & His Terrific Manners. Prignano, Barbara. 2013. 32p. pap. 12.95 (978-1-62857-080-9(6), Strategic Bk. Publishing) Strategic Book Publishing & Rights Agency (SBPRA).

—What Shall I Do? Sighed Emily. Smith, Faith P. 2017. (ENG.). (J). (gr. k-6). pap. 8.95 (978-1-63135-099-3(4)) Strategic Book Publishing & Rights Agency (SBPRA).

Kalpart Designs. The Big Squeal: A True Story about a Homeless Pig's Search for Life, Liberty & the Pursuit of Happiness. Alexander, Carol. 2012. (ENG.). 24p. (J). 24.00 (978-1-61009-036-0(5), Acorn) Oak Tree Publishing.

Kaltenborn, Karl. Ikky Dikky Dak: Magical Adventures with Googler! Book Two. McGee, Helen. 2011. pap. 21.95 (978-1-60494-573-7(7)) Wheatmark, Inc.

Kalthoff, Robert. Viking Life. 2005. spiral bd. 20.00 net. (978-0-9762042-4-4(X)) Hubbell, Gerald.

Kalvoda, LeAnn. Lost & Found Teaching Unit. Holmes, Wayne & Pelletier, Christine. rev. ed. 2003. 96p. (J). ring bd. 35.00 (978-1-58302-232-0(5)) Creative Ministry Solutions.

Kam, Kathleen. The Legend of Kuamo'o Mo'okini & Hamumu the Great Whale. Lum, Leimomi o. Kamahae Kuamoo Mookini. 2004. 24p. (J). 12.95 (978-1-58178-036-9(2)) Bishop Museum Pr.

Kamerer, Justin & Bascle, Brian. The Salem Witch Trials, 1 vol. Martin, Michael & Martin, Michael J. 2005. (Graphic History Ser.). (ENG.). 32p. (J). (gr. 3-9). 31.32 (978-0-7368-3847-4(3), Capstone Pr.) Capstone.

Kamerl, Dazze. Astronomy for Young & Old: A Beginner's Guide to the Visible Sky, 10 vols. Kraul, Walter. Maclean, Christian, tr. 2014. Orig. Title: Erscheinungen Am Sternenhimmel: Die Bewegungen der Gestirne Beobachten und Verstehen. (ENG.). 168p. pap. 24.95 (978-1-78250-046-9(4)) Floris Bks. GBR. Dist: Consortium Bk. Sales & Distribution.

Kami, Y. Z. The Sun, the Moon, & the Gardener's Son. Bronn, Charles Heil. 2006. 30p. (J). (gr. 4-12). reprint ed. 16.00 (978-1-4223-5222-9(6)) DIANE Publishing Co.

Kamijyo, Akimine. Samurai Deeper Kyo, 18 vols. Kamijyo, Akimine. rev. ed. (YA). Vol. 4. 2003. 192p. pap. 14.99 (978-1-59182-249-3(1)); Vol. 11. 2005. 200p. pap. 14.99 (978-1-59532-451-1(8)) TOKYOPOP, Inc. (Tokyopop Adult).

Kamijyo, Akimine. Samurai Deeper Kyo, Vol. 10. Kamijyo, Akimine, creator. rev. ed. 2004. 208p. (YA). pap. 14.99 (978-1-59532-450-4(X), Tokyopop Adult) TOKYOPOP, Inc.

Kaminska, Marina. Mr. Badger: Book 1. Ivy, Olive. 2018. (Currantberry Tales Ser.: Vol. 1). (ENG.). 106p. (J). pap. 9.99 (978-1-7171-6358-5(0)) CreateSpace Independent Publishing Platform.

Kaminski, Karol. Every Body Is a Gift: God Made Us to Love. Ashour, Monica. 2015. (J). 12.95 (978-0-8198-2376-2(7)) Pauline Bks. & Media.

—Every Body Is Smart: God Helps Me Listen & Choose. Ashour, Monica. 2015. (J). 12.95 (978-0-8198-2372-4(4)) Pauline Bks. & Media.

—Everybody Has a Body: God Made Boys & Girls. Ashour, Monica. 2015. (J). 12.95 (978-0-8198-2368-7(6)) Pauline Bks. & Media.

—God Made Wonderful Me! Monchamp, Genny. 2008. 14p. (J). (gr. -1). 8.95 (978-0-8198-3108-8(5)) Pauline Bks. & Media.

—Shine: Choices to Make God Smile. Monchamp, Genny. 2011. (J). 10.95 (978-0-8198-7149-7(4)) Pauline Bks. & Media.

Kaminski, Karol, jt. illus. see Williams, Ted.

Kaminsky, Jef. Dear Santasaurus. McAnulty, Stacy. 2013. (ENG.). 32p. (J). (gr. k-3). 15.95 (978-1-59078-876-9(1)) Boyds Mills Pr.

Kamio, Yoko. Boys over Flowers. Kamio, Yoko. (Boys over Flowers Ser.). (ENG.). Vol. 14. 2005. 192p. pap. 9.99 (978-1-4215-0018-3(9)); Vol. 18. 2006. 208p. pap. 9.99 (978-1-4215-0532-9(0)) Viz Media.

—Boys over Flowers, Vol. 11. Kamio, Yoko. 2005. (ENG.). 184p. (YA). pap. 9.99 (978-1-59116-747-1(7)) Viz Media.

—Hana Yori Dango. Kamio, Yoko. 2004. (Boys over Flowers Ser.). (ENG.). 200p. Vol. 7. pap. 9.95 (978-1-59116-370-1(6)); Vol. 8. pap. 9.95 (978-1-59116-371-8(4)) Viz Media.

Kammeraad, Kevin & Hipp, Ryan. A Curious Glimpse of Michigan. Kammeraad, Kevin & Kammeraad, Stephanie. 32p. (J). 2006. (gr. 4-7). pap. 9.95 (978-0-9749412-9-5(8)); 2004. (gr. 3-7). 19.95 (978-0-9712692-9-3(7)) EDCO Publishing, Inc.

Kampe, Rosi. Spider-Gwen: Ghost-Spider Vol. 1, Vol. 1. 2019. (ENG.). 112p. (YA). pap. 15.99 (978-1-302-91476-9(6)) Marvel Worldwide, Inc.

Kamrath, Michelle. Irving, the Grateful Toad. Archer, Mary. 2019. (ENG.). 34p. (J). pap. 10.00 (978-1-6906-0435-8(2)) Independently Published.

Kanae, Billy. Hanauma Bay. Markrich, Mike & Bourke, Bob. (J). pap. 5.95 (978-0-9643421-0-1(3)) Ecology Comics.

Kanagy, Audrey Ann Zimmerman, jt. illus. see Zimmerman, Edith Fay Martin.

Kanako & Yuzuru. Eagle Strike: an Alex Rider Graphic Novel. Horowitz, Anthony & Johnston, Antony. 2017. (Alex Rider Ser.). (ENG.). 176p. (J). (gr. 4-7). pap. 14.99 (978-0-7636-9256-8(5)) Candlewick Pr.

—Skeleton Key: the Graphic Novel. Horowitz, Anthony. 2009. (Alex Rider Ser.: Bk. 3). (ENG.). 176p. (J). (gr. 5-18). pap. 16.99 (978-0-399-25418-5(8), Philomel Bks.) Penguin Young Readers Group.

Kanako, jt. illus. see Yuzuru.

Kanaley, Mary Pat. Grandpa Is My Elevator. Mannion, Kathleen a. 2019. (ENG.). 26p. (J). pap. 9.99 (978-1-0986-2640-2(0)) Independently Published.

Kanarek, Michael. I Wanna Be Purr-Fect! ShowCat. Corrado, Diane. 2006. 48p. (J). 14.95 incl. audio compact disk (978-0-9795049-2-1(9)) Kidz Entertainment, Inc.

Kane, Brenden. Abby's Adventures: Abby the Pirate. Hartley, Susan. 2005. 37p. pap. 24.95 (978-1-4137-4491-0(5)) PublishAmerica, Inc.

Kane, Gil, et al. Man-Wolf: the Complete Collection. 2019. (ENG.). 408p. (YA). (gr. 4-17). pap. 39.99 (978-1-302-92000-5(6)) Marvel Worldwide, Inc.

—Marvel Masterworks: Daredevil Vol. 14. 2020. 320p. (YA). (gr. 4-17). 75.00 (978-1-302-92163-7(0)) Marvel Worldwide, Inc.

Kane, Gil, et al. Morbius the Living Vampire Omnibus. 2020. 864p. (gr. 10-17). 100.00 (978-1-302-92240-5(8)) Marvel Worldwide, Inc.

Kane, Gil. Star Hawks, Vol. 2: 1978-1979, Vol. 2. Goulart, Ron & Goodwin, Archie. 2017. (Star Hawks Ser.: 2). (ENG.). 328p. 39.99 (978-1-68405-016-1(2)) Idea & Design Works, LLC.

Kane, Gil, jt. illus. see Windsor-Smith, Barry.

Kane, Herb K., jt. illus. see Feher, Joseph.

Kane, John. You're Going to Be an Aunt. Kane, Louise. 2019. (You're Going to Be ... Ser.). (ENG.). 12p. (J). (gr. k-2). bds. (978-1-909857-15-5(7)) Pooter Publishing Ltd.

Kane, John, photos by. The Human Alphabet: Pilobolus. Pilobolus. 2003. 40p. (J). (978-1-58717-225-0(9)); lib. bdg. (978-1-58717-226-7(7)) Chronicle Bks. LLC. (SeaStar Bks.).

Kane, Kata. Ghost Friends Forever #1. Gallagher, Monica. 2017. (Ghost Friends Forever Ser.: 1). (ENG.). 96p. (J). 14.99 *(978-1-62991-803-7(2),* 900181024) Papercutz.
Kane, Sharon. Little Mommy. Kane, Sharon. 2008. (Little Golden Book Ser.). 32p. (J). (gr. -1-2). 4.99 *(978-0-375-84820-9(7),* Golden Bks.) Random Hse. Children's Bks.
Kaneda, Mario. Girls Bravo, Vol. 2. Kaneda, Mario. 2nd rev. ed. 2005. (Girls Bravo Ser.). 192p. pap. 9.99 *(978-1-59816-041-3(9),* Tokyopop Adult) TOKYOPOP, Inc.
Kaneko, Shinya. Culdcept, Vol. 4. Kaneko, Shinya. rev. ed. 2005. 234p. pap. 14.99 *(978-1-59532-447-4(X),* Tokyopop Adult) TOKYOPOP, Inc.
Kanekuni, Daniel. Okazu at the Zoo. Ide, Laurie Shimizu. 2006. (J). *(978-1-56647-776-5(X))* Mutual Publishing LLC.
Kanemoto, Dan. Happy Easter, Sprinkles! Silverhardt, Lauryn. 2008. (Blue's Clues Ser.). (ENG.). 12p. (J). (gr. -1-k). bds. 5.99 *(978-1-4169-4775-2(2),* Simon Spotlight/Nickelodeon) Simon Spotlight/Nickelodeon.
Kanemoto, Dan & Oxley, Jennifer. A Blue's Clues Chanukah, 14. Lissy, Jessica. 2003. (Blue's Clues Ser.: Vol. 14). (ENG.). 24p. (J). (gr. -1-3). 16.19 *(978-0-689-85840-6(X))* Simon & Schuster, Inc.
Kanesata, Yukio. Kamikaze Girls. Takemoto, Novala. 2006. (Kamikaza Girls Ser.). (ENG.). 208p. (YA). pap. 8.99 *(978-1-4215-0268-7(2))* Viz Media.
Kaneshiro, Scott. Limu: The Blue Turtle & His Hawaiian Garden. Armitage, Kimo. 2004. 28p. (J). 11.95 *(978-0-931548-64-2(0))* Island Heritage Publishing.
Kaneyoshi, Izumi. Doubt!! Kaneyoshi, Izumi. 2005. (Doubt Ser.: 4). (ENG.). 192p. Vol. 4. pap. 9.99 *(978-1-59116-984-0(4));* Vol. 5. pap. 9.99 *(978-1-4215-0055-3(8))* Viz Media.
Kang, A. N. Celebrate You! Rinker, Sherri Duskey. 2019. (ENG.). 40p. (J). (gr. -1-3). 17.99 *(978-0-06-256402-3(1),* Balzer & Bray) HarperCollins Pubs.
—Squirrel's Family Tree. Ferry, Beth. 2019. (ENG.). 40p. (J). (gr. -1-k). 17.99 *(978-1-338-18736-6(8),* Orchard Bks.) Scholastic, Inc.
Kang, A. N. My Big Bad Monster. Kang, A. N. 2019. (ENG.). 40p. (J). (gr. -1-3). 16.99 *(978-1-4847-2882-6(3))* Disney Pr.
Kang, A. N. Papillon Goes to the Vet. Kang, A. N. 2017. (Papillon Ser.: 2). (ENG.). 40p. (J). (gr. -1-3). 16.99 ***(978-1-4847-2881-9(5))*** Little, Brown Bks. for Young Readers.
—The Very Fluffy Kitty. Kang, A. N. 2016. (Papillon Ser.: 1). (ENG.). 40p. (J). 16.99 ***(978-1-4847-1798-1(8))*** Little, Brown Bks. for Young Readers.
—The Very Fluffy Kitty, Papillon. Kang, A. N. 2018. (Papillon Ser.: 1). (ENG.). 32p. (J). (gr. -1 — 1). bds. 7.99 ***(978-1-4847-8845-5(1))*** Little, Brown Bks. for Young Readers.
Kang, Andrea. Beach: Baby Unplugged. Hutton, John. 2012. (Baby Unplugged Ser.). (ENG.). 14p. (J). (— 1). bds. 7.99 *(978-1-936669-07-3(2))* Blue Manatee Press.
—Blanket: Baby Unplugged. Hutton, John. 2011. (Baby Unplugged Ser.). (ENG.). 14p. (J). (— 1). bds. 7.99 *(978-1-936669-00-4(5))* Blue Manatee Press.
—Blocks: Baby Unplugged. Hutton, John. Hutton, John, ed. 2013. (Baby Unplugged Ser.). (ENG.). 14p. (J). (— 1). bds. 7.99 *(978-1-936669-13-4(7))* Blue Manatee Press.
—Book: Baby Unplugged. Hutton, John. Hutton, John, ed. 2012. (Baby Unplugged Ser.). (ENG.). 14p. (J). (— 1). bds. 7.99 *(978-1-936669-06-6(4))* Blue Manatee Press.
—Box: Baby Unplugged. Hutton, John. 2012. (Baby Unplugged Ser.). (ENG.). 14p. (J). (— 1). bds. 7.99 *(978-1-936669-08-0(0))* Blue Manatee Press.
—Pets: Baby Unplugged. Hutton, John. 2011. (Baby Unplugged Ser.). (ENG.). 14p. (J). (— 1). bds. 7.99 *(978-1-936669-02-8(1))* Blue Manatee Press.
—Yard: Baby Unplugged. Hutton, John. 2011. (Baby Unplugged Ser.). (ENG.). 14p. (J). (— 1). bds. 7.99 *(978-1-936669-01-1(3))* Blue Manatee Press.
Kang, Mi-Sun. The Lazy Man/the Spring of Youth. 2008. (Korean Folk Tales for Children Ser.: Vol. 3). (ENG.). 44p. (J). (gr. 2-5). lib. bdg. 14.50 *(978-0-930878-73-3(6))* Hollym International Corp.
—The Snail Lady/the Magic Vase. 2008. (Korean Folk Tales for Children Ser.: Vol. 6). (ENG.). 44p. (J). (gr. 2-5). lib. bdg. 14.50 *(978-0-930878-89-4(2))* Hollym International Corp.
Kang, Mi-Sun & Kim, Yon-Kyong. Brave Hong Gil-Dong/the Man Who Bought the Shade of a Tree. 2008. (Korean Folk Tales for Children Ser.: Vol. 8). (ENG.). 44p. (J). (gr. 2-5). lib. bdg. 14.50 *(978-0-930878-91-7(4))* Hollym International Corp.
—The Faithful Daughter Sim Cheong/the Little Frog Who Never Listened. 2008. (Korean Folk Tales for Children Ser.: Vol. 9). (ENG.). 44p. (J). (gr. 2-5). lib. bdg. 14.50 *(978-0-930878-92-4(2))* Hollym International Corp.
Kang, Mi-Sun, jt. illus. see Kim, Yon-Kyong.
Kang Won, Kim. The Queen's Knight, 15 vols. Kang Won, Kim. 5th rev. ed. 2006. (Queen's Knight Ser.: Vol. 5). 192p. per. 9.99 *(978-1-59532-261-6(2))* TOKYOPOP, Inc.
Kang Won, Kim. The Queen's Knight. Kang Won, Kim, creator. 2005. Vol. 3. 3rd rev. ed. 208p. pap. 9.99 *(978-1-59532-259-3(0));* Vol. 4. rev. ed. 192p. pap. 9.99 *(978-1-59532-260-9(4))* TOKYOPOP, Inc.
Kang, Yong Ling. Tanna's Owl. Qitsualik-Tinsley, Rachel & Qitsualik-Tinsley, Sean. 2020. (ENG.). 32p. (J). 16.95 *(978-1-77227-250-5(7))* Inhabit Media Inc. CAN. Dist: Consortium Bk. Sales & Distribution.
—William's Getaway. Dunklee, Annika. 2020. (ENG.). 32p. (J). (gr. -1-3). 16.95 *(978-1-77147-337-8(1))* Owlkids Bks. Inc. CAN. Dist: Publishers Group West (PGW).
Kangas, Juli. Good Night, Baddies. Underwood, Deborah. 2016. (ENG.). 32p. (J). (gr. -1-3). 17.99 *(978-1-4814-0984-1(0),* Beach Lane Bks.) Beach Lane Bks.
Kanhai, Kai. The Red Jellybean. Hogue, Stephen. 2019. (ENG.). 34p. (J). pap. 9.99 *(978-1-0903-4816-6(9))* Independently Published.
Kania, Matt. Alabama. Heinrichs, Ann. 2017. (U. S. A. Travel Guides). (ENG.). 40p. (J). (gr. 2-5). lib. bdg. 28.50 *(978-1-5038-1941-2(8),* 211578) Child's World, Inc., The.
—Alaska. Heinrichs, Ann. 2017. (U. S. A. Travel Guides). (ENG.). 40p. (J). (gr. 2-5). lib. bdg. 28.50 *(978-1-5038-1942-9(6),* 211579) Child's World, Inc., The.
—Arizona. Heinrichs, Ann. 2017. (U. S. A. Travel Guides). (ENG.). 40p. (J). (gr. 2-5). lib. bdg. 28.50 *(978-1-5038-1943-6(4),* 211580) Child's World, Inc., The.
—Arkansas. Heinrichs, Ann. 2017. (U. S. A. Travel Guides). (ENG.). 40p. (J). (gr. 2-5). lib. bdg. 28.50 *(978-1-5038-1944-3(2),* 211581) Child's World, Inc., The.
—California. Heinrichs, Ann. 2017. (U. S. A. Travel Guides). (ENG.). 40p. (J). (gr. 2-5). lib. bdg. 28.50 *(978-1-5038-1945-0(0),* 211582) Child's World, Inc., The.
—Colorado. Heinrichs, Ann. 2017. (U. S. A. Travel Guides). (ENG.). 40p. (J). (gr. 2-5). lib. bdg. 28.50 *(978-1-5038-1946-7(9),* 211583) Child's World, Inc., The.
—Connecticut. Heinrichs, Ann. 2017. (U. S. A. Travel Guides). (ENG.). 40p. (J). (gr. 2-5). lib. bdg. 28.50 *(978-1-5038-1947-4(7),* 211584) Child's World, Inc., The.
—Delaware. Heinrichs, Ann. 2017. (U. S. A. Travel Guides). (ENG.). 40p. (J). (gr. 2-5). lib. bdg. 28.50 *(978-1-5038-1948-1(5),* 211585) Child's World, Inc., The.
—Florida. Heinrichs, Ann. 2017. (U. S. A. Travel Guides). (ENG.). 40p. (J). (gr. 2-5). lib. bdg. 28.50 *(978-1-5038-1949-8(3),* 211586) Child's World, Inc., The.
—Georgia. Heinrichs, Ann. 2017. (U. S. A. Travel Guides). (ENG.). 40p. (J). (gr. 2-5). lib. bdg. 28.50 *(978-1-5038-1950-4(7),* 211587) Child's World, Inc., The.
—Hawai'i. Heinrichs, Ann. 2017. (U. S. A. Travel Guides). (ENG.). 40p. (J). (gr. 2-5). lib. bdg. 28.50 *(978-1-5038-1951-1(5),* 211588) Child's World, Inc., The.
—Idaho. Heinrichs, Ann. 2017. (U. S. A. Travel Guides). (ENG.). 40p. (J). (gr. 2-5). lib. bdg. 28.50 *(978-1-5038-1952-8(3),* 211589) Child's World, Inc., The.
—Illinois. Heinrichs, Ann. 2017. (U. S. A. Travel Guides). (ENG.). 40p. (J). (gr. 2-5). lib. bdg. 28.50 *(978-1-5038-1953-5(1),* 211590) Child's World, Inc., The.
—Indiana. Heinrichs, Ann. 2017. (U. S. A. Travel Guides). (ENG.). 40p. (J). (gr. 2-5). lib. bdg. 28.50 *(978-1-5038-1954-2(X),* 211591) Child's World, Inc., The.
—Iowa. Heinrichs, Ann. 2017. (U. S. A. Travel Guides). (ENG.). 40p. (J). (gr. 2-5). lib. bdg. 28.50 *(978-1-5038-1955-9(8),* 211592) Child's World, Inc., The.
—Kansas. Heinrichs, Ann. 2017. (U. S. A. Travel Guides). (ENG.). 40p. (J). (gr. 2-5). lib. bdg. 28.50 *(978-1-5038-1956-6(6),* 211593) Child's World, Inc., The.
—Kentucky. Heinrichs, Ann. 2017. (U. S. A. Travel Guides). (ENG.). 40p. (J). (gr. 2-5). lib. bdg. 28.50 *(978-1-5038-1957-3(4),* 211594) Child's World, Inc., The.
—Louisiana. Heinrichs, Ann. 2017. (U. S. A. Travel Guides). (ENG.). 40p. (J). (gr. 2-5). lib. bdg. 28.50 *(978-1-5038-1958-0(2),* 211595) Child's World, Inc., The.
—Maine. Heinrichs, Ann. 2017. (U. S. A. Travel Guides). (ENG.). 40p. (J). (gr. 2-5). lib. bdg. 28.50 *(978-1-5038-1959-7(0),* 211596) Child's World, Inc., The.
—Maryland. Heinrichs, Ann. 2017. (U. S. A. Travel Guides). (ENG.). 40p. (J). (gr. 2-5). lib. bdg. 28.50 *(978-1-5038-1960-3(4),* 211597) Child's World, Inc., The.
—Massachusetts. Heinrichs, Ann. 2017. (U. S. A. Travel Guides). (ENG.). 40p. (J). (gr. 2-5). lib. bdg. 28.50 *(978-1-5038-1961-0(2),* 211598) Child's World, Inc., The.
—Michigan. Heinrichs, Ann. 2017. (U. S. A. Travel Guides). (ENG.). 40p. (J). (gr. 2-5). lib. bdg. 28.50 *(978-1-5038-1962-7(0),* 211599) Child's World, Inc., The.
—Minnesota. Heinrichs, Ann. 2017. (U. S. A. Travel Guides). (ENG.). 40p. (J). (gr. 2-5). lib. bdg. 28.50 *(978-1-5038-1963-4(9),* 211600) Child's World, Inc., The.
—Mississippi. Heinrichs, Ann. 2017. (U. S. A. Travel Guides). (ENG.). 40p. (J). (gr. 2-5). lib. bdg. 28.50 *(978-1-5038-1964-1(7),* 211601) Child's World, Inc., The.
—Missouri. Heinrichs, Ann. 2017. (U. S. A. Travel Guides). (ENG.). 40p. (J). (gr. 2-5). lib. bdg. 28.50 *(978-1-5038-1965-8(5),* 211602) Child's World, Inc., The.
—Montana. Heinrichs, Ann. 2017. (U. S. A. Travel Guides). (ENG.). 40p. (J). (gr. 2-5). lib. bdg. 28.50 *(978-1-5038-1966-5(3),* 211603) Child's World, Inc., The.
—Nebraska. Heinrichs, Ann. 2017. (U. S. A. Travel Guides). (ENG.). 40p. (J). (gr. 2-5). lib. bdg. 28.50 *(978-1-5038-1967-2(1),* 211604) Child's World, Inc., The.
—Nevada. Heinrichs, Ann. 2017. (U. S. A. Travel Guides). (ENG.). 40p. (J). (gr. 2-5). lib. bdg. 28.50 *(978-1-5038-1968-9(X),* 211605) Child's World, Inc., The.
—New Hampshire. Heinrichs, Ann. 2017. (U. S. A. Travel Guides). (ENG.). 40p. (J). (gr. 2-5). lib. bdg. 28.50 *(978-1-5038-1969-6(8),* 211606) Child's World, Inc., The.
—New Jersey. Heinrichs, Ann. 2017. (U. S. A. Travel Guides). (ENG.). 40p. (J). (gr. 2-5). lib. bdg. 28.50 *(978-1-5038-1970-2(1),* 211607) Child's World, Inc., The.
—New Mexico. Heinrichs, Ann. 2017. (U. S. A. Travel Guides). (ENG.). 40p. (J). (gr. 2-5). lib. bdg. 28.50 *(978-1-5038-1971-9(X),* 211608) Child's World, Inc., The.
—New York. Heinrichs, Ann. 2017. (U. S. A. Travel Guides). (ENG.). 40p. (J). (gr. 2-5). lib. bdg. 28.50 *(978-1-5038-1972-6(8),* 211577) Child's World, Inc., The.
—North Carolina. Heinrichs, Ann. 2017. (U. S. A. Travel Guides). (ENG.). 40p. (J). (gr. 2-5). lib. bdg. 28.50 *(978-1-5038-1973-3(6),* 211609) Child's World, Inc., The.
—North Dakota. Heinrichs, Ann. 2017. (U. S. A. Travel Guides). (ENG.). 40p. (J). (gr. 2-5). lib. bdg. 28.50 *(978-1-5038-1974-0(4),* 211610) Child's World, Inc., The.
—Ohio. Heinrichs, Ann. 2017. (U. S. A. Travel Guides). (ENG.). 40p. (J). (gr. 2-5). lib. bdg. 28.50 *(978-1-5038-1975-7(2),* 211611) Child's World, Inc., The.
—Oklahoma. Heinrichs, Ann. 2017. (U. S. A. Travel Guides). (ENG.). 40p. (J). (gr. 2-5). lib. bdg. 28.50 *(978-1-5038-1976-4(0),* 211612) Child's World, Inc., The.
—Oregon. Heinrichs, Ann. 2017. (U. S. A. Travel Guides). (ENG.). 40p. (J). (gr. 2-5). lib. bdg. 28.50 *(978-1-5038-1977-1(9),* 211613) Child's World, Inc., The.
—Pennsylvania. Heinrichs, Ann. 2017. (U. S. A. Travel Guides). (ENG.). 40p. (J). (gr. 2-5). lib. bdg. 28.50 *(978-1-5038-1978-8(7),* 211614) Child's World, Inc., The.
—Puerto Rico. Heinrichs, Ann. 2017. (U. S. A. Travel Guides). (ENG.). 40p. (J). (gr. 2-5). lib. bdg. 28.50 *(978-1-5038-1992-4(2),* 211615) Child's World, Inc., The.
—Rhode Island. Heinrichs, Ann. 2017. (U. S. A. Travel Guides). (ENG.). 40p. (J). (gr. 2-5). lib. bdg. 28.50 *(978-1-5038-1979-5(5),* 211616) Child's World, Inc., The.
—South Carolina. Heinrichs, Ann. 2017. (U. S. A. Travel Guides). (ENG.). 40p. (J). (gr. 2-5). lib. bdg. 28.50 *(978-1-5038-1980-1(9),* 211617) Child's World, Inc., The.
—South Dakota. Heinrichs, Ann. 2017. (U. S. A. Travel Guides). (ENG.). 40p. (J). (gr. 2-5). lib. bdg. 28.50 *(978-1-5038-1981-8(7),* 211618) Child's World, Inc., The.
—Tennessee. Heinrichs, Ann. 2017. (U. S. A. Travel Guides). (ENG.). 40p. (J). (gr. 2-5). lib. bdg. 28.50 *(978-1-5038-1982-5(5),* 211619) Child's World, Inc., The.
—Texas. Heinrichs, Ann. 2017. (U. S. A. Travel Guides). (ENG.). 40p. (J). (gr. 2-5). lib. bdg. 28.50 *(978-1-5038-1983-2(3),* 211620) Child's World, Inc., The.
—Texas. Peterson, Sheryl. 2009. (This Land Called America Ser.). 32p. (YA). (gr. 3-6). 19.95 *(978-1-58341-796-6(6))* Creative Co., The.
—Utah. Heinrichs, Ann. 2017. (U. S. A. Travel Guides). (ENG.). 40p. (J). (gr. 2-5). lib. bdg. 28.50 *(978-1-5038-1984-9(1),* 211621) Child's World, Inc., The.
—Vermont. Heinrichs, Ann. 2017. (U. S. A. Travel Guides). (ENG.). 40p. (J). (gr. 2-5). lib. bdg. 28.50 *(978-1-5038-1985-6(X),* 211622) Child's World, Inc., The.
—Virginia. Heinrichs, Ann. 2017. (U. S. A. Travel Guides). (ENG.). 40p. (J). (gr. 2-5). lib. bdg. 28.50 *(978-1-5038-1986-3(8),* 211623) Child's World, Inc., The.
—Washington. Heinrichs, Ann. 2017. (U. S. A. Travel Guides). (ENG.). 40p. (J). (gr. 2-5). lib. bdg. 28.50 *(978-1-5038-1987-0(6),* 211624) Child's World, Inc., The.
—Washington, DC. Heinrichs, Ann. 2017. (U. S. A. Travel Guides). (ENG.). 40p. (J). (gr. 2-5). lib. bdg. 28.50 *(978-1-5038-1991-7(4),* 211625) Child's World, Inc., The.
—West Virginia. Heinrichs, Ann. 2017. (U. S. A. Travel Guides). (ENG.). 40p. (J). (gr. 2-5). lib. bdg. 28.50 *(978-1-5038-1988-7(4),* 211626) Child's World, Inc., The.
—Wisconsin. Heinrichs, Ann. 2017. (U. S. A. Travel Guides). (ENG.). 40p. (J). (gr. 2-5). lib. bdg. 28.50 *(978-1-5038-1989-4(2),* 211627) Child's World, Inc., The.
—Wyoming. Heinrichs, Ann. 2017. (U. S. A. Travel Guides). (ENG.). 40p. (J). (gr. 2-5). lib. bdg. 28.50 *(978-1-5038-1990-0(6),* 211628) Child's World, Inc., The.
Kanitsch, Christine. Harry the Hopetown Hermit Crab. Williams, Jonnie. Date not set. (Abaco Ser.). (J). (gr. -1-3). pap. 5.97 *(978-0-9657849-1-7(6))* Island Ink.
Kann, Victoria. Pinkalicious & the Sick Day. 2015. 30p. (J). *(978-1-4806-8664-9(6))* Harper & Row Ltd.
—Pinkalicious at the Fair. 2018. 32p. (J). *(978-1-5182-5372-0(5))* Harper & Row Ltd.
Kann, Victoria. Apples, Apples, Apples! Kann, Victoria. ed. 2016. (Pinkalicious Ser.). (ENG.). 24p. (J). (gr. -1-3). 14.75 *(978-0-606-39267-9(X))* Turtleback.
—Aqualicious. Kann, Victoria. 2015. (ENG.). 40p. (J). (gr. -1-3). 17.99 *(978-0-06-233016-1(0))* HarperCollins Pubs.
—Emeraldalicious. Kann, Victoria. 2013. (Pinkalicious Ser.). (ENG.). 40p. (J). (gr. -1-3). 17.99 *(978-0-06-178126-1(6),* HarperCollins) HarperCollins Pubs.
—Emeraldalicious. Kann, Victoria. 2013. (ENG.). 40p. (J). (gr. -1-3). lib. bdg. 18.89 *(978-0-06-178127-8(4),* HarperCollins) HarperCollins Pubs. Ltd. GBR. Dist: HarperCollins Pubs.
—Fashion Fun. Kann, Victoria. ed. 2016. (Pinkalicious I Can Read Ser.). (ENG.). 32p. (J). (gr. -1-3). 13.55 *(978-0-606-39265-5(3))* Turtleback.
—Goldilicious. Kann, Victoria. 2009. (ENG.). 40p. (J). (gr. k-3). 17.99 *(978-0-06-124408-7(2));* lib. bdg. 18.89 *(978-0-06-124409-4(0))* HarperCollins Pubs.
—Peterrific. Kann, Victoria. 2017. (Pinkalicious Ser.). (ENG.). 40p. (J). (gr. -1-3). 17.99 *(978-0-06-256356-9(4),* HarperCollins) HarperCollins Pubs. Ltd. GBR. Dist: HarperCollins Pubs.
—Pinkalicious. Kann, Victoria. Kann, Elizabeth. (Pinkalicious Ser.). (ENG.). 40p. (J). (gr. -1-3). 2016. 17.99 *(978-0-06-077639-8(0),* HarperCollins); 2006. lib. bdg. 17.89 *(978-0-06-077640-4(4))* HarperCollins Pubs.
—Pinkalicious: Pinkalicious (Spanish Edition), 1 vol. Kann, Victoria. Kann, Elizabeth. 2011. (Pinkalicious Ser.). (SPA.). 40p. (J). (gr. -1-3). 17.99 *(978-0-06-179959-4(9),* HarperCollins Español) HarperCollins Christian Publishing.
—Pinkalicious 123: A Counting Book. Kann, Victoria. 2016. (Pinkalicious Ser.). (ENG.). 32p. (J). (gr. -1 — 1). bds. 7.99 *(978-0-06-243757-0(7),* HarperFestival) HarperCollins Pubs.
—Pinkalicious: 5-Minute Pinkalicious Stories: Includes 12 Pinkatastic Stories! Kann, Victoria. 2017. (Pinkalicious Ser.). (ENG.). 192p. (J). (gr. -1-3). 12.99 *(978-0-06-256697-3(0))* HarperCollins Pubs.
—Pinkalicious ABC: An Alphabet Book. Kann, Victoria. 2016. (Pinkalicious Ser.). (ENG.). 32p. (J). (gr. -1 — 1). bds. 7.99 *(978-0-06-243755-6(0),* HarperFestival) HarperCollins Pubs.
—Pinkalicious & Aqua, the Mini-Mermaid. Kann, Victoria. 2016. (Pinkalicious Ser.). (ENG.). 24p. (J). (gr. -1-3). pap. 4.99 *(978-0-06-241075-7(X),* HarperFestival) HarperCollins Pubs.
—Pinkalicious & Planet Pink. Kann, Victoria. 2016. (I Can Read Level 1 Ser.). (ENG.). 32p. (J). (gr. -1-3). pap. 4.99 *(978-0-06-241068-9(7))* HarperCollins Pubs.
—Pinkalicious & the Amazing Sled Run. Kann, Victoria. 2018. (I Can Read Level 1 Ser.). (ENG.). 32p. (J). (gr. -1-3). 16.99 *(978-0-06-267565-1(6));* pap. 4.99 *(978-0-06-256696-6(2))* HarperCollins Pubs.
—Pinkalicious & the Babysitter. Kann, Victoria. 2017. (I Can Read Level 1 Ser.). (ENG.). 32p. (J). (gr. -1-3). 16.99 *(978-0-06-256689-8(X));* pap. 4.99 *(978-0-06-256688-1(1))* HarperCollins Pubs.
—Pinkalicious & the Cupcake Calamity. Kann, Victoria. 2013. (I Can Read Level 1 Ser.). (ENG.). 32p. (J). (gr. -1-3). 16.99 *(978-0-06-218777-2(5));* pap. 4.99 *(978-0-06-218776-5(7))* HarperCollins Pubs.
—Pinkalicious & the Flower Fairy. Kann, Victoria. 2018. (I Can Read Level 1 Ser.). (ENG.). 32p. (J). (gr. -1-3). 16.99 *(978-0-06-267567-5(2));* pap. 4.99 *(978-0-06-256701-7(2))* HarperCollins Pubs.
—Pinkalicious & the Little Butterfly. Kann, Victoria. 2016. (Pinkalicious Ser.). (ENG.). 24p. (J). (gr. -1-3). pap. 4.99 *(978-0-06-241071-9(7),* HarperFestival) HarperCollins Pubs.
—Pinkalicious & the Merminnies. Kann, Victoria. 2020. (I Can Read Level 1 Ser.). (ENG.). 32p. (J). (gr. -1-3). 16.99 *(978-0-06-284045-5(2));* pap. 4.99 *(978-0-06-284044-8(4))* HarperCollins Pubs. Ltd. GBR. (HarperCollins). Dist: HarperCollins Pubs.
—Pinkalicious & the New Teacher. Kann, Victoria. 2014. (Pinkalicious Ser.). (ENG.). 24p. (J). (gr. -1-3). pap. 6.99 *(978-0-06-218913-4(1),* HarperFestival) HarperCollins Pubs.
—Pinkalicious & the Perfect Present. Kann, Victoria. 2014. (I Can Read Level 1 Ser.). (ENG.). 32p. (J). (gr. -1-3). 16.99 *(978-0-06-218789-5(9));* pap. 4.99 *(978-0-06-218788-8(0))* HarperCollins Pubs.
—Pinkalicious & the Pink Drink. Kann, Victoria. 2010. (Pinkalicious Ser.). (ENG.). 24p. (J). (gr. -1-3). pap. 3.99 *(978-0-06-192732-4(5),* HarperFestival) HarperCollins Pubs.
—Pinkalicious & the Pink Hat Parade. Kann, Victoria. 2012. (Pinkalicious Ser.). (ENG.). 24p. (J). (gr. -1-2). pap. 7.99 *(978-0-06-198960-5(6),* HarperFestival) HarperCollins Pubs.
—Pinkalicious & the Pink Parakeet. Kann, Victoria. 2015. (I Can Read Level 1 Ser.). (ENG.). 32p. (J). (gr. -1-3). 16.99 *(978-0-06-224596-0(1))* HarperCollins Pubs.
—Pinkalicious & the Pink Pumpkin. Kann, Victoria. 2011. (Pinkalicious Ser.). (ENG.). 16p. (J). (gr. -1-2). pap. 6.99 *(978-0-06-198961-2(4),* HarperFestival) HarperCollins Pubs.
—Pinkalicious & the Pinkadorable Pony. Kann, Victoria. 2020. (I Can Read Level 1 Ser.). (ENG.). 32p. (J). (gr. -1-3). pap. 4.99 *(978-0-06-284047-9(9),* HarperCollins) HarperCollins Pubs. Ltd. GBR. Dist: HarperCollins Pubs.
—Pinkalicious & the Pinkatastic Zoo Day. Kann, Victoria. 2012. (I Can Read Level 1 Ser.). (ENG.). 32p. (J). (gr. -1-3). 16.99 *(978-0-06-218780-2(5));* pap. 4.99 *(978-0-06-218779-6(1))* HarperCollins Pubs.
Kann, Victoria. Pinkalicious & the Pinkettes. Kann, Victoria. 2020. (I Can Read Level 1 Ser.). (ENG.). 32p. (J). (gr. -1-3). 16.99 ***(978-0-06-284051-6(7));*** pap. 4.99 ***(978-0-06-284050-9(9))*** HarperCollins Pubs. Ltd. GBR. (HarperCollins). Dist: HarperCollins Pubs.
Kann, Victoria. Pinkalicious & the Pirates. Kann, Victoria. 2018. (I Can Read Level 1 Ser.). (ENG.). 32p. (J). (gr. -1-3). 16.99 *(978-0-06-256699-7(7));* pap. 4.99 *(978-0-06-256698-0(9))* HarperCollins Pubs.
—Pinkalicious & the Sick Day. Kann, Victoria. 2015. (I Can Read Level 1 Ser.). (ENG.). 32p. (J). (gr. -1-3). 16.99 *(978-0-06-224599-1(6))* HarperCollins Pubs.
—Pinkalicious & the Snow Globe. Kann, Victoria. 2015. (Pinkalicious Ser.). (ENG.). 24p. (J). (gr. -1-3). pap. 4.99 *(978-0-06-224588-5(0),* HarperFestival) HarperCollins Pubs.
—Pinkalicious: Apples, Apples, Apples! Kann, Victoria. 2016. (Pinkalicious Ser.). (ENG.). 24p. (J). (gr. -1-3). pap. 4.99 *(978-0-06-241079-5(2),* HarperFestival) HarperCollins Pubs.
—Pinkalicious at the Fair. Kann, Victoria. 2018. (I Can Read Level 1 Ser.). (ENG.). 32p. (J). (gr. -1-3). pap. 4.99 *(978-0-06-256691-1(1))* HarperCollins Pubs.
—Pinkalicious at the Fair. Kann, Victoria. 2018. (I Can Read Level 1 Ser.). (ENG.). 32p. (J). (gr. -1-3). 16.99 *(978-0-06-256694-2(6),* HarperCollins) HarperCollins Pubs. Ltd. GBR. Dist: HarperCollins Pubs.
—Pinkalicious: Cherry Blossom. Kann, Victoria. 2015. (I Can Read Level 1 Ser.). (ENG.). 32p. (J). (gr. -1-3). 16.99 *(978-0-06-224593-9(7));* pap. 4.99 *(978-0-06-224594-6(5))* HarperCollins Pubs.
—Pinkalicious: Crazy Hair Day. Kann, Victoria. 2014. (Pinkalicious Ser.). (ENG.). 24p. (J). (gr. -1-3). pap. 3.99 *(978-0-06-218768-0(6),* HarperFestival) HarperCollins Pubs.
—Pinkalicious Cupcake Cookbook. Kann, Victoria. 2013. (Pinkalicious Ser.). (ENG.). 64p. (J). (gr. 1-5). 14.99 *(978-0-06-202357-5(8))* HarperCollins Pubs.
—Pinkalicious: Dragon to the Rescue. Kann, Victoria. 2019. (I Can Read Level 1 Ser.). (ENG.). 32p. (J). (gr. -1-3). 16.99 *(978-0-06-284042-4(8))* HarperCollins Pubs.
—Pinkalicious: Dragon to the Rescue. Kann, Victoria. 2019. (I Can Read Level 1 Ser.). (ENG.). 32p. (J). (gr. -1-3). pap. 4.99 *(978-0-06-284041-7(X),* HarperCollins) HarperCollins Pubs. Ltd. GBR. Dist: HarperCollins Pubs.
—Pinkalicious: Eggstraordinary Easter. Kann, Victoria. 2014. (Pinkalicious Ser.). (ENG.). 24p. (J). (gr. -1-3). pap. 4.99 *(978-0-06-218772-7(4),* HarperFestival) HarperCollins Pubs.
—Pinkalicious: Fairy House. Kann, Victoria. 2013. (I Can Read Level 1 Ser.). (ENG.). 32p. (J). (gr. -1-3). 16.99 *(978-0-06-218783-3(X))* HarperCollins Pubs.
—Pinkalicious: Fashion Fun. Kann, Victoria. 2016. (I Can Read Level 1 Ser.). (ENG.). 32p. (J). (gr. -1-3). pap. 4.99 *(978-0-06-241076-4(8))* HarperCollins Pubs.
—Pinkalicious: Fishtastic! Kann, Victoria. 2019. (I Can Read Level 1 Ser.). (ENG.). 32p. (J). (gr. -1-3). 16.99 *(978-0-06-284039-4(8))* HarperCollins Pubs.
—Pinkalicious: Fishtastic! Kann, Victoria. 2019. (I Can Read Level 1 Ser.). (ENG.). 32p. (J). (gr. -1-3). pap. 4.99 *(978-0-06-284038-7(X),* HarperCollins) HarperCollins Pubs. Ltd. GBR. Dist: HarperCollins Pubs.
—Pinkalicious: Flower Girl. Kann, Victoria. 2013. (Pinkalicious Ser.). (ENG.). 24p. (J). (gr. -1-3). pap. 3.99 *(978-0-06-218766-6(X),* HarperFestival) HarperCollins Pubs.
—Pinkalicious: Goldidoodles. Kann, Victoria. 2013. (Pinkalicious Ser.). (ENG.). 128p. (J). (gr. -1-3). pap. 12.99 *(978-0-06-223334-9(3),* HarperFestival) HarperCollins Pubs.

K

—Pinkalicious: Love, Pinkalicious Reusable Sticker Book. Kann, Victoria. 2009. (Pinkalicious Ser.). (ENG.). 12p. (J). (gr. -1-2). 6.99 *(978-0-06-192731-7(7)*, HarperFestival) HarperCollins Pubs.

—Pinkalicious: Merry Pinkmas! Kann, Victoria. 2013. (Pinkalicious Ser.). (ENG.). 24p. (J). (gr. -1-3). 6.99 *(978-0-06-218912-7(3)*, HarperFestival) HarperCollins Pubs.

—Pinkalicious: Mother's Day Surprise. Kann, Victoria. 2015. (Pinkalicious Ser.). (ENG.). 24p. (J). (gr. -1-3). pap. 6.99 *(978-0-06-224587-8(2)*, HarperFestival) HarperCollins Pubs.

—Pinkalicious: Pink-A-rama. Kann, Victoria. 2012. (I Can Read Level 1 Ser.). (ENG.). 96p. (J). (gr. k-3). pap. 19.99 *(978-0-06-198966-7(5))* HarperCollins Pubs.

—Pinkalicious: Pink Around the Rink. Kann, Victoria. 2010. (I Can Read Level 1 Ser.). (ENG.). 32p. (J). (gr. -1-3). 16.99 *(978-0-06-192880-2(1))*; pap. 4.99 *(978-0-06-192879-6(8))* HarperCollins Pubs.

—Pinkalicious: Pink of Hearts. Kann, Victoria. 2011. (Pinkalicious Ser.). (ENG.). 24p. (J). (gr. -1-2). pap. 6.99 *(978-0-06-198923-0(1)*, HarperFestival) HarperCollins Pubs.

—Pinkalicious: Pink or Treat! Kann, Victoria. 2013. (Pinkalicious Ser.). (ENG.). 24p. (J). (gr. -1-3). pap. 4.99 *(978-0-06-218770-3(8)*, HarperFestival) HarperCollins Pubs.

—Pinkalicious: Pinkadoodles. Kann, Victoria. 2011. (Pinkalicious Ser.). (ENG.). 128p. (J). (gr. -1-7). pap. 12.99 *(978-0-06-202265-3(2)*, HarperFestival) HarperCollins Pubs.

—Pinkalicious: Pinkafy Your World: a Reusable Sticker Book. Kann, Victoria. 2013. (Pinkalicious Ser.). (ENG.). 12p. (J). (gr. -1-3). 6.99 *(978-0-06-223333-2(5)*, HarperFestival) HarperCollins Pubs.

—Pinkalicious: Pinkamazing Storybook Favorites: Includes 6 Stories Plus Stickers! Kann, Victoria. 2019. (Pinkalicious Ser.). (ENG.). 192p. (J). (gr. -1-3). 13.99 *(978-0-06-289860-9(4))* HarperCollins Pubs.

—Pinkalicious: Pinkie Promise. Kann, Victoria. 2011. (I Can Read Level 1 Ser.). (ENG.). 32p. (J). (gr. -1-3). 16.99 *(978-0-06-192888-8(7))*; pap. 4.99 *(978-0-06-192887-1(9))* HarperCollins Pubs.

—Pinkalicious: Puptastic! Kann, Victoria. 2013. (I Can Read Level 1 Ser.). (ENG.). 32p. (J). (gr. -1-3). 16.99 *(978-0-06-218786-4(4))*; pap. 4.99 *(978-0-06-218785-7(6))* HarperCollins Pubs.

—Pinkalicious: Purpledoodles. Kann, Victoria. 2012. (Pinkalicious Ser.). (ENG.). 128p. (J). (gr. -1-7). pap. 12.99 *(978-0-06-208586-3(7)*, HarperFestival) HarperCollins Pubs.

—Pinkalicious: School Lunch. Kann, Victoria. 2015. (Pinkalicious Ser.). (ENG.). 24p. (J). (gr. -1-3). pap. 4.99 *(978-0-06-224590-8(2)*, HarperFestival) HarperCollins Pubs.

—Pinkalicious: School Rules! Kann, Victoria. 2010. (I Can Read Level 1 Ser.). (ENG.). 32p. (J). (gr. -1-3). 16.99 *(978-0-06-192886-4(0))*; pap. 4.99 *(978-0-06-192885-7(2))* HarperCollins Pubs.

—Pinkalicious: Schooltastic Storybook Favorites. Kann, Victoria. 2020. (Pinkalicious Ser.). 192p. (J). (gr. -1-3). 13.99 *(978-0-06-300390-3(2)*, HarperCollins) HarperCollins Pubs. Ltd. GBR. Dist: HarperCollins Pubs.

—Pinkalicious: Soccer Star. Kann, Victoria. 2012. (I Can Read Level 1 Ser.). (ENG.). 32p. (J). (gr. -1-3). 16.99 *(978-0-06-198965-0(7))*; pap. 4.99 *(978-0-06-198964-3(9))* HarperCollins Pubs.

—Pinkalicious: Story Time. Kann, Victoria. 2016. (I Can Read Level 1 Ser.). (ENG.). 32p. (J). (gr. -1-3). pap. 4.99 *(978-0-06-241072-6(5))* HarperCollins Pubs.

—The Pinkalicious Take-Along Storybook Set: Tickled Pink, Pinkalicious & the Pink Drink, Flower Girl, Crazy Hair Day, Pinkalicious & the New Teacher. Kann, Victoria. 2015. (Pinkalicious Ser.). (ENG.). 120p. (J). (gr. -1-3). pap. 11.99 *(978-0-06-241080-1(6)*, HarperFestival) HarperCollins Pubs.

—Pinkalicious: Thanksgiving Helper. Kann, Victoria. 2014. (Pinkalicious Ser.). (ENG.). 24p. (J). (gr. -1-3). pap. 6.99 *(978-0-06-218774-1(0)*, HarperFestival) HarperCollins Pubs.

—Pinkalicious: the Perfectly Pink Collection. Kann, Victoria. 2010. (Pinkalicious Ser.). (ENG.). 100p. (J). (gr. k-3). 15.99 *(978-0-06-199048-9(5)*, HarperFestival) HarperCollins Pubs.

—Pinkalicious: the Pinkamazing Storybook Collection. Kann, Victoria. 2013. (Pinkalicious Ser.). (ENG.). 192p. (J). (gr. -1-3). 11.99 *(978-0-06-218800-7(3))* HarperCollins Pubs.

—Pinkalicious: the Pinkatastic Giant Sticker Book. Kann, Victoria. 2011. (Pinkalicious Ser.). (ENG.). 100p. (J). (gr. -1-2). 12.99 *(978-0-06-192889-5(5)*, HarperFestival) HarperCollins Pubs.

—Pinkalicious: the Pinkerrific Playdate. Kann, Victoria. 2011. (I Can Read Level 1 Ser.). (ENG.). 32p. (J). (gr. -1-3). 16.99 *(978-0-06-192884-0(4))*; pap. 4.99 *(978-0-06-192883-3(6))* HarperCollins Pubs.

—Pinkalicious: the Princess of Pink Slumber Party. Kann, Victoria. 2012. (I Can Read Level 1 Ser.). (ENG.). 32p. (J). (gr. -1-3). 16.99 *(978-0-06-198963-6(0))*; pap. 4.99 *(978-0-06-198962-9(2))* HarperCollins Pubs.

—Pinkalicious: the Princess of Pink Treasury. Kann, Victoria. 2011. (Pinkalicious Ser.). (ENG.). 208p. (J). (gr. -1-3). 19.99 *(978-0-06-210236-2(2)*, HarperFestival) HarperCollins Pubs.

—Pinkalicious: the Royal Tea Party. Kann, Victoria. 2014. (I Can Read Level 1 Ser.). (ENG.). 32p. (J). (gr. -1-3). pap. 4.99 *(978-0-06-218791-8(0))* HarperCollins Pubs.

—Pinkalicious: Tickled Pink. Kann, Victoria. 2010. (Pinkalicious Ser.). (ENG.). 24p. (J). (gr. -1-3). pap. 3.99 *(978-0-06-192877-2(1)*, HarperFestival) HarperCollins Pubs.

—Pinkalicious: Tutu-Rrific. Kann, Victoria. (I Can Read Level 1 Ser.). (ENG.). (J). (gr. -1-3). 2017. 40p. 9.99 *(978-0-06-257278-3(4))*; 2014. 32p. pap. 4.99 *(978-0-06-218795-6(3))* HarperCollins Pubs.

—Purplicious. Kann, Victoria. Kann, Elizabeth. 2007. (ENG.). 40p. (J). (gr. k-3). 17.99 *(978-0-06-124405-6(8))*; lib. bdg. 17.89 *(978-0-06-124406-3(6))* HarperCollins Pubs.

—Silverlicious. Kann, Victoria. 2011. (ENG.). 40p. (J). (gr. k-3). 17.99 *(978-0-06-178123-0(1))*; lib. bdg. 18.89 *(978-0-06-178124-7(X))* HarperCollins Pubs.

—Tickled Pink. Kann, Victoria. ed. 2010. (Pinkalicious Ser.). (J). lib. bdg. 13.55 *(978-0-606-14869-6(8))* Turtleback.

Kano, Shiuko. Yakuza in Love, 3 vols., Vol. 3. Kano, Shiuko. Weber, Adrienne & Behrens, H. Ryland. 2008. 224p. pap. 12.95 *(978-1-934496-31-2(6))* Aurora Publishing, Inc.

Kano, Yasuhiro. Pretty Face, Vol. 2. Kano, Yasuhiro. 2007. (ENG.). 200p. pap. 7.99 *(978-1-4215-1369-0(2))* Viz Media.

Kantar, Fran Keleher. The Extraordinary Capers of Lochlin de Carlo. Villanueva Jr, David. 2018. (ENG.). 160p. (J). (gr. 5-6). pap. 11.99 *(978-1-942922-45-2(0))* Wee Creek Pr. LLC.

Kantjas, Linda. Surfer Dude: The Legendary Stallion of Chincoteague, 1 vol. Szymanski, Lois. 2017. (ENG.). 40p. (J). (gr. -1-3). 14.99 *(978-0-7643-5366-6(7)*, 7632) Schiffer Publishing, Ltd.

—Wild Colt, 1 vol. Szymanski, Lois. 2012. (ENG.). 40p. (J). 16.99 *(978-0-7643-3975-2(3)*, 9780764339752) Schiffer Publishing, Ltd.

Kantor, Frantz. Stargazer. McDonell, Prue. 2020. (ENG.). 50p. (J). pap. 23.95 ***(978-1-5043-2037-5(9)**, Balboa Pr.)* Author Solutions, Inc.

Kantorovitz, Sylvie. The Very Tiny Baby. Kantorovitz, Sylvie. 2014. 240p. (J). (gr. -1-2). lib. bdg. 14.95 *(978-1-58089-445-6(3))* Charlesbridge Publishing, Inc.

Kantrowitz, David. Mission to California. Pillsbury, Samuel H. 2003. (Planet Wampetter Adventure Ser.). 140p. (J). pap. 8.95 *(978-1-930085-03-9(6))* Perspective Publishing, Inc.

Kantz, Bill. Miss Molly's Adventure at the Beach: Another Great Adventure Brought to You by Miss Molly & Her Dog Reyburn, 10 vols. Tompkins, Robyn Lee. 2004. (J). per. *(978-0-9741647-5-5(5))* NRG Pubns.

Kantz, John. Chibi. Acosta, Robert. 2005. (ENG.). 144p. (YA). pap. 19.95 *(978-1-932453-88-1(1)*, ac24e871-4b8b-4ec3-a067-1bb98e233a08) Antarctic Pr., Inc.

Kanzler, John. Animal Talk. Lofting, Hugh. 2007. (Easy Reader Classics Ser.). (ENG.). 32p. (J). (gr. k-3). lib. bdg. 27.07 *(978-1-59961-338-3(7)*, 6215) Spotlight.

—Battle in a Bottle. Asch, Frank. 2014. (Class Pets Ser.). (ENG.). 96p. (J). (gr. 2-6). pap. 13.99 *(978-1-4814-3625-0(2)*, Simon & Schuster/Paula Wiseman Bks.) Simon & Schuster/Paula Wiseman Bks.

—The Christmas Pups. Bateman, Teresa. 2012. (J). *(978-1-61913-112-5(9))* Weigl Pubs., Inc.

—The Ghost of P. S. 42. Asch, Frank. 2014. (Class Pets Ser.). (ENG.). 96p. (J). (gr. 2-5). pap. 13.99 *(978-1-4814-3624-3(4)*, Simon & Schuster/Paula Wiseman Bks.) Simon & Schuster/Paula Wiseman Bks.

—Hush Little One: A Lullaby for God's Children. Stohs, Anita Reith. 2006. 20p. (J). (gr. -1). bds. 5.49 *(978-0-7586-0861-1(6))* Concordia Publishing Hse.

—Little Lucy. Cooper, Ilene. 2011. (Step into Reading Ser.). 48p. (J). (gr. k-3). pap. 4.99 *(978-0-375-86760-6(0)*, Random Hse. Bks. for Young Readers) Random Hse. Children's Bks.

—Paul Bunyan: My Story. Harrison, David L. 2008. (Step into Reading Ser.). 48p. (J). (gr. k-3). 4.99 *(978-0-375-84688-5(3)*, Random Hse. Bks. for Young Readers) Random Hse. Children's Bks.

—Priceless Gifts: A Tale from Italy. Hamilton, Martha & Weiss, Mitch. 2006. (ENG.). 32p. (J). (gr. k-3). 16.95 *(978-0-87483-788-9(X))* August Hse. Pubs., Inc.

Kanzler, John. Rock-a -Bye Baby. Kanzler, John. Tiger Tales Staff, ed. 2011. (ENG.). 24p. (J). (gr. -1-k). bds. 8.95 *(978-1-58925-853-2(3))* Tiger Tales.

Kanzler, John. The Big Rock Candy Mountain. Kanzler, John, tr. 2004. 24p. (J). 15.95 *(978-1-59336-062-7(2))*; pap. *(978-1-59336-063-4(0))* Mondo Publishing.

—Hush, Little One: A Lullaby for God's Children. Kanzler, John, tr. Stohs, Anita Reith. 2004. 32p. (J). 12.99 *(978-0-570-07144-0(5))* Concordia Publishing Hse.

—Whose Feet? Kanzler, John, tr. Hess, Nina. 2004. (Step into Reading Ser.). 32p. (J). (gr. -1-1). pap. 4.99 *(978-0-375-82623-8(8)*, Random Hse. Bks. for Young Readers) Random Hse. Children's Bks.

Kao, Sleepless. Monchan's Bag. 2010. (ENG.). 36p. (J). (gr. -1-3). 16.95 *(978-1-897476-32-1(9))* Simply Read Bks. CAN. Dist: Ingram Publisher Services.

Kaopuiki, Stacey. The Eye of the Lion: The Story of My First Hurricane. Jeffers, Mark. 2012. (ENG.). 42p. (J). pap. 14.95 *(978-0-9742224-6-2(1))* Storybook Theatre of Hawaii.

Kapart. It's Turtle Time. Howard, Cheryl L. 2011. 28p. pap. 24.95 *(978-1-4560-6676-5(5))* America Star Bks.

Kapatos, Elizabeth. The Adventures of Exokid & the Teachings of Money. Outram, Richard. 2009. 36p. pap. 12.95 *(978-1-59858-898-9(2))* Dog Ear Publishing, LLC.

Kaplan, Bruce Eric. Cousin Irv from Mars. Kaplan, Bruce Eric. 2013. (ENG.). 40p. (J). (gr. -1-3). 19.99 *(978-1-4424-4923-7(3)*, Simon & Schuster Bks. For Young Readers) Simon & Schuster Bks. For Young Readers.

—Meaniehead. Kaplan, Bruce Eric. 2014. (ENG.). 40p. (J). (gr. -1-3). 17.99 *(978-1-4424-8542-6(6)*, Simon & Schuster Bks. For Young Readers) Simon & Schuster Bks. For Young Readers.

—Monsters Eat Whiny Children. Kaplan, Bruce Eric. 2010. (ENG.). 40p. (J). (gr. -1-3). 18.99 *(978-1-4169-8689-8(8)*, Simon & Schuster Bks. For Young Readers) Simon & Schuster Bks. For Young Readers.

—Someone Farted. Kaplan, Bruce Eric. 2018. (ENG.). 48p. (J). (gr. -1-3). 15.99 *(978-1-4814-9063-4(X)*, Simon & Schuster Bks. For Young Readers) Simon & Schuster Bks. For Young Readers.

Kappus, Martha, et al. Melissa in the Caribbean. 2019. (Melissa in the Caribbean Ser.: Vol. 3). (ENG.). 108p. (J). pap. 9.40 ***(978-1-0779-7287-2(3))*** Independently Published.

Kara, György. Demon Diary. Hyong, Lee Chi. 2003. 192p. (gr. 8-18). pap. 9.99 *(978-1-59182-154-0(1))* TOKYOPOP, Inc.

—Demon Diary, Vol. 3. Hee, Lee Yun. Na, Lauren, tr. from KOR. rev. ed. 2003. 192p. pap. 9.99 *(978-1-59182-156-4(8))* TOKYOPOP, Inc.

Karabach, Alena. The Blustery Day. Thornton, Caroline L. 2018. (ENG.). 32p. (J). (gr. k-3). *(978-1-78926-437-1(5))*; pap. *(978-1-78926-165-3(1))* Independent Publishing Network.

Karabatzia, Villie. Gingerbread Man: A Favorite Story in Rhythm & Rhyme. Walker, Susan Sandvig. 2018. (Fairy Tale Tunes Ser.). (ENG.). 24p. (J). (gr. -1-3). lib. bdg. 33.99 *(978-1-68410-392-8(4)*, 140348) Cantata Learning.

—Jack & the Beanstalk: A Favorite Story in Rhythm & Rhyme. Peale, Jonathan. 2020. (Fairy Tale Tunes Ser.). (ENG.). 20p. (J). (gr. -1-3). bds. 7.99 *(978-1-5158-6096-9(5)*, 142376) Cantata Learning.

—Not Without My Whale. Coughlan, Billy. 2019. (Early Bird Readers — Green (Early Bird Stories (tm)) Ser.). (ENG.). 32p. (J). (gr. k-3). 27.99 *(978-1-5415-4204-4(5)*, 9781541542044); pap. 7.99 *(978-1-5415-7409-0(5)*, 9781541574090) Lerner Publishing Group. (Lerner Pubns.).

—Rapunzel: A Favorite Story in Rhythm & Rhyme. Peale, Jonathan. 2020. (Fairy Tale Tunes Ser.). (ENG.). 20p. (J). (gr. -1-3). bds. 7.99 *(978-1-5158-6098-3(1)*, 142378) Cantata Learning.

—Toddler's World: 123. 2018. (Toddler's World Ser.). (ENG.). 14p. (J). (— 1). bds. 7.99 *(978-1-68412-301-8(1)*, Silver Dolphin Bks.) Printers Row Publishing Group.

—Toddler's World: ABC. 2018. (Toddler's World Ser.). (ENG.). 14p. (J). (— 1). bds. 7.99 *(978-1-68412-302-5(X)*, Silver Dolphin Bks.) Printers Row Publishing Group.

Karacan, Tugrul. The Angry Birds Movie: Big Trouble on Bird Island. Stephens, Sarah. 2016. (Angry Birds Ser.). (ENG.). 24p. (J). (gr. -1-3). pap. 3.99 *(978-0-06-245340-2(8)*, HarperFestival) HarperCollins Pubs.

—The Angry Birds Movie: Seeing Red. Stephens, Sarah. 2016. (Angry Birds Ser.). (ENG.). 24p. (J). (gr. -1-3). pap. 3.99 *(978-0-06-245338-9(6)*, HarperFestival) HarperCollins Pubs.

Karactaz. Dr. Neal's Squeaky Wheels. Pulford, Elizabeth. 2010. (ENG.). 24p. (gr. k-2). pap. 8.95 *(978-1-61181-057-8(4)*, Kaeden Bks.) Kaeden Corp.

—Farmer Mcfuddy's Garden. Mills, Tania. 2010. (ENG.). 20p. (gr. 1-3). pap. 8.95 *(978-1-61181-077-6(9)*, Kaeden Bks.) Kaeden Corp.

—Firefighter Fred's Busy Day. Haley, Patty. 2010. (ENG.). 24p. (gr. 1-2). pap. 8.95 *(978-1-61181-071-4(X)*, Kaeden Bks.) Kaeden Corp.

Karaivanova, Mona. Brain Vacation: A Guide to Meditation. Zelas, Cara. 2018. (Big World of Little Dude Ser.: Vol. 2). (ENG.). 32p. (J). pap. 9.95 ***(978-0-9967943-8-1(7))*** Kindness Learning Co. LLC, The.

Karanja, Geoffrey Gacheru. My Sister's Wedding: A Story of Kenya. Mbuthia, Waithira. 2005. (Make Friends Around the World Ser.). (ENG.). 32p. (J). (gr. k-3). 19.95 *(978-1-56899-898-5(8)*, BC8006); 15.95 *(978-1-56899-896-1(1)*, B8006) Soundprints.

Karas, G. Brian. Almost Time. Schmidt, Gary D. & Stickney, Elizabeth. 2020. (ENG.). 32p. (J). (gr. -1-3). 17.99 *(978-0-544-78581-6(9)*, 1638579, Clarion Bks.) Houghton Mifflin Harcourt Trade & Reference Pubs.

—Ant & Honey Bee: A Pair of Friends at Halloween. Mcdonald, Megan. 2nd ed. 2010. (Candlewick Sparks: Ant & Honey Bee Ser.). (ENG.). 44p. (J). (gr. k-3). 17.44 *(978-0-7636-4662-2(8))* Candlewick Pr.

—Ant & Honey Bee: A Pair of Friends in Winter. Mcdonald, Megan. (Candlewick Sparks Ser.). 64p. (J). (gr. k-4). 2014. pap. 3.99 *(978-0-7636-6862-4(1))*; 2013. 14.99 *(978-0-7636-5712-3(3))* Candlewick Pr.

—Anywhere Farm. Root, Phyllis. (ENG.). 32p. (J). (-k). 2020. 7.99 *(978-1-5362-1055-2(2))*; 2017. 16.99 *(978-0-7636-7499-1(0))* Candlewick Pr.

—The Apple Orchard Riddle (Mr. Tiffin's Classroom Series) McNamara, Margaret. 2013. (Mr. Tiffin's Classroom Ser.). 40p. (J). (gr. -1-3). 17.99 *(978-0-375-84744-8(8)*, Schwartz & Wade Bks.) Random Hse. Children's Bks.

Karas, G. Brian. El Ascensor Mágico: Elevator Magic (Spanish Edition) Murphy, Stuart J. 2020. (MathStart 2 Ser.). (ENG.). 40p. (J). (gr. -1-3). pap. 5.99 ***(978-0-06-298330-5(X)**, HarperCollins)* HarperCollins Pubs. Ltd. GBR. Dist: HarperCollins Pubs.

Karas, G. Brian. Best Friends. Michaels, Anna. 2004. 24p. (J). lib. bdg. 10.00 *(978-1-4242-0217-1(5))* Fitzgerald Bks.

—Best Friends. Michaels, Anna. 2004. (Green Light Readers Level 1 Ser.). (ENG.). 32p. (J). (gr. -1-3). pap. 4.99 *(978-0-15-205133-4(3)*, 1195497) Houghton Mifflin Harcourt Publishing Co.

—Best Friends. Michaels, Anna. 2004. (Green Light Readers Level 1 Ser.). (gr. -1-1). 13.95 *(978-0-7569-4282-3(9))* Perfection Learning Corp.

—Big Bad Bunny. Billingsley, Franny. 2008. (ENG.). 40p. (J). (gr. k-3). 17.99 *(978-1-4169-0601-8(0)*, Atheneum/Richard Jackson Bks.) Simon & Schuster Children's Publishing.

—The Case of the Climbing Cat. Rylant, Cynthia. 2003. (High-Rise Private Eyes Ser.: No. 2). (J). (gr. -1-3). 25.96 incl. audio *(978-1-59112-190-9(6))*; (gr. -1-3). pap. 29.95 incl. audio *(978-1-59112-191-6(4))*; (gr. k-3). 28.95 incl. audio compact disk *(978-1-59112-611-9(8))* Live Oak Media.

—The Case of the Desperate Duck. Rylant, Cynthia. 2005. (High-Rise Private Eyes Ser.: No. 8). 48p. (J). (gr. k-3). 14.99 *(978-0-06-053451-6(6))*; lib. bdg. 15.89 *(978-0-06-053452-3(4))* HarperCollins Pubs.

—The Case of the Desperate Duck. Rylant, Cynthia. 2006. (High-Rise Private Eyes Ser.). 48p. (gr. -1-3). 14.00 *(978-0-7569-6958-5(1))* Perfection Learning Corp.

—The Case of the Fidgety Fox. Rylant, Cynthia. unabr. ed. 2005. (High-Rise Private Eyes Ser.: No. 6). (J). (gr. k-4). 25.95 incl. audio *(978-1-59519-405-3(3))*;Set. pap. 29.95 incl. audio *(978-1-59519-406-0(1))*;Set. pap. 31.95 incl. audio compact disk *(978-1-59519-410-7(X))* Live Oak Media.

—The Case of the Fidgety Fox. Rylant, Cynthia. 2004. (High-Rise Private Eyes Ser.). 58p. (J). (gr. 1-3). 11.65 *(978-0-7569-3210-7(6))* Perfection Learning Corp.

—The Case of the Missing Monkey. Rylant, Cynthia. 2003. (High-Rise Private Eyes Ser.: No. 1). 28.95 incl. audio compact disk *(978-1-59112-615-7(0))*; (J). 25.95 incl. audio *(978-1-59112-194-7(9))*; (J). pap. 29.95 incl. audio *(978-1-59112-195-4(7))* Live Oak Media.

—The Case of the Missing Monkey. 2004. (High-Rise Private Eyes Ser.: No. 1). (J). (gr. -1-2). pap. 31.95 incl. audio compact disk *(978-1-59112-616-4(9))* Live Oak Media.

—The Case of the Missing Monkey. Rylant, Cynthia. ed. 2003. (High-Rise Private Eyes Ser.: 1). 46p. (J). (gr. 1-17). 14.75 *(978-0-613-44194-0(X))* Turtleback.

—The Case of the Puzzling Possum. Rylant, Cynthia. 2003. (High-Rise Private Eyes Ser.: No. 3). (J). (gr. -1-3). 25.95 incl. audio *(978-1-59112-198-5(1))*; (gr. k-3). 28.95 incl. audio compact disk *(978-1-59112-619-5(3))*; (gr. k-3). pap. 29.95 incl. audio *(978-1-59112-199-2(X))* Live Oak Media.

—The Case of the Puzzling Possum. 2004. (High-Rise Private Eyes Ser.: No. 3). (J). (gr. -1-2). pap. 31.95 incl. audio compact disk *(978-1-59112-620-1(7))* Live Oak Media.

—The Case of the Sleepy Sloth. Rylant, Cynthia. unabr. ed. 2005. (High-Rise Private Eyes Ser.: No. 5). (J). (gr. k-4). 29.95 incl. audio *(978-1-59519-413-8(4))*; 28.95 incl. audio compact disk *(978-1-59519-417-6(7))*;Set. pap. 29.95 incl. audio *(978-1-59519-414-5(2))*;Set. pap. 31.95 incl. audio compact disk *(978-1-59519-418-3(5))* Live Oak Media.

—Clever Jack Takes the Cake. Fleming, Candace. 2010. 40p. (J). (gr. -1-3). 17.99 *(978-0-375-84979-4(3)*, Schwartz & Wade Bks.) Random Hse. Children's Bks.

—Daniel y Su Mascota. Flor Ada, Alma. 2008. (Green Light Readers Level 1 Ser.).Tr. of Daniel's Pet. (ENG.). 28p. (J). (gr. -1-3). pap. 4.99 *(978-0-15-206243-9(2)*, 1198722) Houghton Mifflin Harcourt Publishing Co.

—Daniel's Mystery Egg. Flor Ada, Alma. 2003. (Green Light Readers Level 2 Ser.). (ENG.). 24p. (J). (gr. -1-3). pap. 4.99 *(978-0-15-204845-7(6)*, 1194630) Houghton Mifflin Harcourt Publishing Co.

—Daniel's Pet. Flor Ada, Alma. 2003. (Green Light Readers Level 1 Ser.). (ENG.). 24p. (J). (gr. -1-3). pap. 4.99 *(978-0-15-204865-5(0)*, 1194691) Houghton Mifflin Harcourt Publishing Co.

—Daniel's Pet. Flor Ada, Alma. 2003. (Green Light Readers: Level 1 Ser.). (ENG.). (J). (gr. -1-3). lib. bdg. 14.55 *(978-0-7569-1243-7(1))* Perfection Learning Corp.

—The Dinosaur Expert. McNamara, Margaret. 2018. (Mr. Tiffin's Classroom Ser.). 40p. (J). (gr. -1-3). 17.99 *(978-0-553-51143-7(2)*, Schwartz & Wade Bks.) Random Hse. Children's Bks.

—A Hat for Mrs. Goldman: A Story about Knitting & Love. Edwards, Michelle. 2016. 40p. (J). (gr. -1-3). 17.99 *(978-0-553-49710-6(3)*, Schwartz & Wade Bks.) Random Hse. Children's Bks.

—The High-Rise Private Eye: The Case of the Troublesome Turtle. Rylant, Cynthia. 2003. (High-Rise Private Eyes Ser.: No. 4). (J). (gr. k-3). 25.95 incl. audio *(978-1-59112-202-9(3))*; 28.95 incl. audio compact disk *(978-1-59112-623-2(1))*; pap. 29.95 incl. audio *(978-1-59112-203-6(1))*; pap. 31.95 incl. audio compact disk *(978-1-59112-624-9(X))* Live Oak Media.

—The High-Rise Private Eyes #1: the Case of the Missing Monkey. Rylant, Cynthia. 2003. (I Can Read Level 2 Ser.: No. 1). (ENG.). 48p. (J). (gr. k-3). pap. 4.99 *(978-0-06-444306-7(X)*, Greenwillow Bks.) HarperCollins Pubs.

—The High-Rise Private Eyes #7: the Case of the Baffled Bear. Rylant, Cynthia. 2006. (I Can Read Level 2 Ser.: No. 7). (ENG.). 48p. (J). (gr. k-3). per. 4.99 *(978-0-06-053450-9(8)*, Greenwillow Bks.) HarperCollins Pubs.

—The High-Rise Private Eyes #8: the Case of the Desperate Duck. Rylant, Cynthia. 2006. (I Can Read Level 2 Ser.: No. 8). (ENG.). 48p. (J). (gr. k-3). pap. 4.99 *(978-0-06-053453-0(2)*, Greenwillow Bks.) HarperCollins Pubs.

—The High-Rise Private Eyes Series. Rylant, Cynthia. 2003. pap. 61.95 incl. audio *(978-1-59112-430-6(1))*; pap. 68.95 incl. audio compact disk *(978-1-59112-858-8(7))* Live Oak Media.

—How Many Seeds in a Pumpkin? (Mr. Tiffin's Classroom Series) McNamara, Margaret. 2007. (Mr. Tiffin's Classroom Ser.). (ENG.). 40p. (J). (gr. -1-2). 17.99 *(978-0-375-84014-2(1)*, Schwartz & Wade Bks.) Random Hse. Children's Bks.

—If It Weren't for You. Zolotow, Charlotte. 2006. 32p. (J). (gr. -1-3). 16.89 *(978-0-06-027876-2(5))* HarperCollins Pubs.

—Incredible Me! Appelt, Kathi. 2003. 32p. (J). (gr. -1-1). lib. bdg. 16.89 *(978-0-06-028623-1(7))*; (ENG.). 16.99 *(978-0-06-028622-4(9))* HarperCollins Pubs.

Karas, G. Brian. Ivan: a Gorilla's True Story. Applegate, Katherine. 2020. (ENG.). 40p. (J). (gr. -1-3). 10.99 ***(978-0-358-41746-0(5)**,* 1791037, Clarion Bks.) Houghton Mifflin Harcourt Trade & Reference Pubs.

Karas, G. Brian. Ivan: the Remarkable True Story of the Shopping Mall Gorilla. Applegate, Katherine. 2014. (ENG.). 40p. (J). (gr. -1-3). 18.99 *(978-0-544-25230-1(6)*, 1566586, Clarion Bks.) Houghton Mifflin Harcourt Publishing Co.

—Lemonade in Winter: A Book about Two Kids Counting Money. Jenkins, Emily. 2012. 40p. (J). (gr. -1-2). 16.99 *(978-0-375-85883-3(0)*, Schwartz & Wade Bks.) Random Hse. Children's Bks.

—Make Way for Readers. Sierra, Judy. 2016. (ENG.). 32p. (J). (gr. -1-3). 17.99 *(978-1-4814-1851-5(3)*, Simon & Schuster Bks. For Young Readers) Simon & Schuster Bks. For Young Readers.

—El Misterioso Huevo de Daniel. Flor Ada, Alma. Flor Ada, Alma, tr. 2007. (Green Light Readers Level 2 Ser.).Tr. of Daniel's Mystery Egg. (ENG.). 28p. (J). (gr. 1-4). pap. 4.99 *(978-0-15-205971-2(7)*, 1197932) Houghton Mifflin Harcourt Publishing Co.

—More-Igami. Kleber, Dori. 40p. (J). (gr. -1-3). 2019. 6.99 *(978-1-5362-0971-6(6))*; 2016. 15.99 *(978-0-7636-6819-8(2))* Candlewick Pr.
—Muncha! Muncha! Muncha! Fleming, Candace. pap. 16.95 incl. audio *(978-1-59112-463-4(8))*; pap. incl. audio *(978-1-59112-465-8(4))*; pap. 18.95 incl. audio compact disk *(978-1-59112-923-3(0))*; pap. incl. audio compact disk *(978-1-59112-925-7(7))* Live Oak Media.
—My Wild Woolly. Eaton, Deborah J. 2005. (Green Light Readers Level 2 Ser.). (ENG.). 24p. (J). (gr. -1-3). pap. 4.99 *(978-0-15-205147-1(3)*, 1195533) Houghton Mifflin Harcourt Publishing Co.
—My Wild Woolly. Eaton, Deborah J. 2005. (Green Light Readers Level 2 Ser.). (gr. k-2). 13.95 *(978-0-7569-5445-1(2))* Perfection Learning Corp.
—Nam! Nam! Nam! Fleming, Candace. Schmidt, Alejandra, tr. from ENG. 2007. (SPA.). 32p. (J). (gr. -1-2). 15.95 *(978-1-933032-35-1(9))* Lectorum Pubns., Inc.
—Neville. Juster, Norton. 2011. 32p. (J). (gr. -1-3). 17.99 *(978-0-375-86765-1(1)*, Schwartz & Wade Bks.) Random Hse. Children's Bks.
—Night Job. Hesse, Karen. 2018. (ENG.). 32p. (J). (gr. -1-2). 16.99 *(978-0-7636-6238-7(0))* Candlewick Pr.
—Oh No, Gotta Go! Elya, Susan Middleton. 2005. 29p. (J). (gr. k-4). reprint ed. 15.00 *(978-0-7567-8946-6(X))* DIANE Publishing Co.
—Oh No, Gotta Go! Elya, Susan Middleton. 2003. (ENG.). 32p. (J). (gr. -1-2). 16.99 *(978-0-399-23493-4(4)*, G.P. Putnam's Sons Books for Young Readers) Penguin Young Readers Group.
—A Place Called Kindergarten. Harper, Jessica. 2008. (ENG.). 32p. (J). (gr. -1-k). pap. 6.99 *(978-0-14-241174-2(4)*, Puffin Books) Penguin Young Readers Group.
—A Poem in Your Pocket (Mr. Tiffin's Classroom Series) McNamara, Margaret. 2015. (Mr. Tiffin's Classroom Ser.). 40p. (J). (gr. -1-3). 16.99 *(978-0-307-97947-6(4)*, Schwartz & Wade Bks.) Random Hse. Children's Bks.
—Raising Sweetness, 4 bks. Stanley, Diane. 2004. (J). pap. 39.95 incl. audio compact disk *(978-1-59112-524-2(3))* Live Oak Media.
—The Seals on the Bus. Hort, Lenny. 2008. (ENG.). 32p. (J). (gr. -1-k). pap. 27.99 *(978-0-8050-8678-2(1)*, 900045720, Holt, Henry & Co. Bks. For Young Readers) Holt, Henry & Co.
—The Seals on the Bus. Hort, Lenny. rev. ed. 2003. (ENG.). 32p. (J). (gr. -1-k). pap. 7.99 *(978-0-8050-7263-1(2)*, 900018971) Square Fish.
—Sweetness Series. Stanley, Diane. 2003. pap. 30.95 incl. audio *(978-1-59112-847-2(1))*; pap. 34.95 incl. audio compact disk *(978-1-59112-860-1(9))* Live Oak Media.
—Switching on the Moon: A Very First Book of Bedtime Poems. 2010. 96p. (J). (gr. k-12). 21.99 *(978-0-7636-4249-5(5))* Candlewick Pr.
—Tap Tap Boom Boom. Bluemle, Elizabeth. 2014. 32p. (J). (gr. -1-2). 16.99 *(978-0-7636-5696-6(8))* Candlewick Pr.
—Throw Your Tooth on the Roof. Beeler, Selby B. 2015. 32p. pap. 7.00 *(978-1-61003-501-9(1))* Center for the Collaborative Classroom.
—Tippy-Tippy-Tippy, Splash! Fleming, Candace. 2014. (ENG.). 40p. (J). (gr. -1-3). 16.99 *(978-1-4169-5403-3(1)*, Atheneum Bks. for Young Readers) Simon & Schuster Children's Publishing.
—The Village Blacksmith. Longfellow, Henry Wadsworth. 2020. 32p. (J). (gr. 1-4). 16.99 *(978-1-5362-0443-8(9))* Candlewick Pr.
—Whale Trails, Before & Now. Cline-Ransome, Lesa. 2015. (ENG.). 40p. (J). (gr. k-4). 17.99 *(978-0-8050-9642-2(6)*, 900086974, Holt, Henry & Co. Bks. For Young Readers) Holt, Henry & Co.
—Young Zeus. 2010. (ENG.). 48p. (J). (gr. -1-3). 17.99 *(978-0-439-72806-5(1)*, Scholastic Pr.) Scholastic, Inc.
—7 X 9 = Trouble! Mills, Claudia. 2004. 103p. (J). (gr. 2-5). 13.60 *(978-0-7569-3397-5(8))* Perfection Learning Corp.
—7 X 9 = Trouble! Mills, Claudia. 2004. (ENG.). 112p. (J). (gr. 2-5). pap. 7.99 *(978-0-374-46452-3(9)*, 900024513) Square Fish.
Karas, G. Brian. As an Oak Tree Grows. Karas, G. Brian. 2014. 32p. (J). (gr. k-3). 19.99 *(978-0-399-25233-4(9)*, Nancy Paulsen Books) Penguin Young Readers Group.
—Atlantic. Karas, G. Brian. 2004. (ENG.). 32p. (J). (gr. -1-3). reprint ed. pap. 7.99 *(978-0-14-240027-2(0)*, Puffin Books) Penguin Young Readers Group.
—On Earth. Karas, G. Brian. 2008. 32p. (J). (gr. k-3). pap. 8.99 *(978-0-14-241063-9(2)*, Puffin Books) Penguin Young Readers Group.
—On Earth. Karas, G. Brian. 2008. (gr. k-3). 18.00 *(978-0-7569-8926-2(4))* Perfection Learning Corp.
Karas, Greg. Hospital Coloring Book: 12 Pictures to Color for Kids in the Hospital. Karas, Greg. 2019. (ENG.). 26p. (J). pap. 7.00 *(978-1-7957-3040-2(4))* Independently Published.
Karas, Roma. Mural on Second Avenue & Other City Poems. Moore, Lilian. 32p. (J). (gr. k-4). 2013. pap. 6.99 *(978-0-7636-6349-0(2))*; 2005. (ENG.). 16.99 *(978-0-7636-1987-9(6))* Candlewick Pr.
—Mural on Second Avenue & Other City Poems. Moore, Lilian. 2013. (ENG.). (J). (gr. k-4). lib. bdg. 17.60 *(978-1-62765-430-2(5))* Perfection Learning Corp.
Karash, Igor. Sir Drakon. Karash, Igor. collector's ltd. num. ed. 2018. (ENG.). 72p. (J). pap. 19.95 *(978-1-62804-123-1(4))* Liberty Publishing Hse., Inc.
Karasz, Ilonka. The Heavenly Tenants. Maxwell, William. 2017. (ENG.). 64p. pap. 16.95 *(978-0-486-81529-9(3))* Dover Pubns., Inc.
Karcz, Katherine. Paddle, the Extraordinary Duck. Craig, Deborah Anne. Glueck, Michael Wells, ed. 2011. 42p. pap. 19.95 *(978-1-4583-6916-1(1))* Lulu Pr., Inc.
—Weighty Words, Too. Levitt, Paul M. et al. 2009. (ENG.). 96p. (J). (gr. 4-18). 21.95 *(978-0-8263-4558-5(1))* Univ. of New Mexico Pr.
Kardos, Stéphane, jt. illus. see McClements, George.
Karen Blair. Aussie Kids: Meet Eve in the Outback. Caisley, Raewyn. 2020. (Aussie Kids Ser.). (ENG.). 64p. (J). (gr. 1-3). 12.99 ***(978-1-76089-410-8(9)**, Puffin) Penguin Random Hse. AUS. Dist: Independent Pubs. Group.
—Hello from Nowhere. Caisley, Raewyn. 2020. (ENG.). 32p. (J). (gr. k-2). 14.99 ***(978-1-76089-773-4(6)**, Puffin) Penguin Random Hse. AUS. Dist: Independent Pubs. Group.
Karen, Nolan. A Handful of Eggs. Belinda, Mellor. 2017. (Fire Lizards Ser.). (ENG.). 32p. (J). (gr. k-1). *(978-0-473-43252-2(8))* Intrepid Sparks.
Karensac. Aster & the Accidental Magic. Pico, Thom. 2020. (Aster Ser.). (ENG.). 224p. (J). (gr. 3-7). 20.99 *(978-0-593-12417-8(0))* Penguin Random Hse. LLC.
Karetak, Charlotte. Am I Really Inuk? Noah, Noah. Allurut, Ida, tr. 2020. (ENG.). 24p. (J). pap. ***(978-1-5255-1432-6(6))*** FriesenPress.
Karibo, Princess. All Hair Is Good Hair. Taylor, Annagjid Kee. 2019. (ENG.). 36p. 29.99 ***(978-1-7283-3192-8(7))***; pap. 16.99 ***(978-1-7283-3190-4(0))*** AuthorHouse.
Karim, Joseph & Karim, Silvana. What Does Happy Look Like? Karim, Joseph & Karim, Silvana. 2009. 47p. (J). pap. 18.95 *(978-1-934575-54-3(2))* Autism Asperger Publishing Co.
Karim, Silvana, jt. illus. see Karim, Joseph.
Karimbeik, Yasamin. The Big Bad Pig & the Three Little Wolves: Children's Story Written by a Child Author. Karimbeik, Yasamin. 2019. (ENG.). 30p. (J). pap. 9.99 *(978-1-0806-1113-3(4))* Independently Published.
Karipidou, Maria. Angry Cookie. Dockrill, Laura. 2019. (ENG.). 40p. (J). (gr. -1-2). 16.99 *(978-1-5362-0544-2(3))* Candlewick Pr.
Karipidou, Maria. Shut the Door! Lopshire, Robert. 2020. (Beginner Books(R) Ser.). 48p. (J). (gr. -1-2). 9.99 ***(978-0-525-58033-1(6))***; (ENG.). lib. bdg. 12.99 ***(978-0-525-58036-2(0))*** Random Hse. Children's Bks. (Random Hse. Bks. for Young Readers).
Karkavelas, Spiros. Denali Storm: A 4D Book. Spradlin, Michael P. 2018. (Pararescue Corps Ser.). (ENG.). 128p. (J). (gr. 4-8). lib. bdg. 26.65 *(978-1-4965-5203-7(2)*, 136213, Stone Arch Bks.) Capstone.
—Nile Chaos: A 4D Book. Spradlin, Michael P. 2018. (Pararescue Corps Ser.). (ENG.). 128p. (J). (gr. 4-8). lib. bdg. 26.65 *(978-1-4965-5201-3(6)*, 136212, Stone Arch Bks.) Capstone.
—Pararescue Corps. Spradlin, Michael P. ed. 2019. (Pararescue Corps Ser.). (ENG.). 240p. (J). (gr. 4-8). pap. 9.95 *(978-1-4965-8105-1(9)*, 140248, Stone Arch Bks.) Capstone.
—Sandstorm Blast: A 4D Book. Spradlin, Michael P. 2018. (Pararescue Corps Ser.). (ENG.). 128p. (J). (gr. 4-8). lib. bdg. 26.65 *(978-1-4965-5159-7(1)*, 136172, Stone Arch Bks.) Capstone.
—Viper Strike: A 4D Book. Spradlin, Michael P. 2018. (Pararescue Corps Ser.). (ENG.). 128p. (J). (gr. 4-8). lib. bdg. 26.65 *(978-1-4965-5202-0(4)*, 136214, Stone Arch Bks.) Capstone.
Karl, Linda. Cabbage Patch Kids: We Are All Best Friends. Masino, Brian. 2006. (J). pap. *(978-0-439-76820-7(9))* Scholastic, Inc.
—Easter Stencil Fun! (Peter Cottontail) Man-Kong, Mary. 2014. (Color Plus Stencil Ser.). (ENG.). 64p. (J). (gr. -1-2). pap. 5.99 *(978-0-385-37442-2(9)*, Golden Bks.) Random Hse. Children's Bks.
—Hoppy Easter! (Peter Cottontail) Man-Kong, Mary. 2013. (ENG.). 32p. (J). (gr. -1-2). pap. 3.99 *(978-0-307-98230-8(0)*, Golden Bks.) Random Hse. Children's Bks.
—Rudolph the Red-Nosed Reindeer. Depken, Kristen L. 2014. (My Readers Ser.). (ENG.). 32p. (J). (gr. k-2). 15.99 *(978-1-250-05044-1(8)*, 900134031) Square Fish.
Karl, Therese. A Buddy in Winter: Lost & Found. Karl, Mary Eileen. 2010. 44p. pap. 15.50 *(978-1-60911-424-4(8)*, Eloquent Bks.) Strategic Book Publishing & Rights Agency (SBPRA).
Karla, Nicolee. Rossi & Lucy Go to the Beach. Bonacci, Ross. 2013. 38p. pap. *(978-0-9873831-2-9(4))* Bonacci Publishing.
Karmaga, Ramanda. Psy-Comm, Vol. 2. Henderson, Jason & Salvaggio, Tony. 2007. (Psy-Comm Ser.). 192p. per. 9.99 *(978-1-59816-270-7(5))* TOKYOPOP, Inc.
Karman, Bijou. Born to Fly: The First Women's Air Race Across America. Sheinkin, Steve. 2019. (ENG.). 288p. (J). 19.99 *(978-1-62672-130-2(0)*, 900139632) Roaring Brook Pr.
—Girls Who Run the World: 31 CEOs Who Mean Business. Kapp, Diana. 2019. 320p. (YA). (gr. k-12). 19.99 *(978-1-9848-9305-5(X))*; (ENG.). lib. bdg. 22.99 *(978-0-593-11907-5(X))* Random Hse. Children's Bks. (Delacorte Bks. for Young Readers).
Karn, Mike. Lighten up Lenny. Snyder, Vicki & West, Lois. 2005. (J). *(978-0-9773187-0-4(2))* Snyder, Vicki.
Karp, Cindy. Sharing Our Homeland: Palestinian & Jewish Children at Summer Peace Camp, 1 vol. Marx, Trish. 2010. (ENG.). 48p. (J). (gr. 1-6). 19.95 *(978-1-58430-260-5(7))* Lee & Low Bks., Inc.
Karp, Cindy. Everglades Forever: Restoring America's Great Wetland, 1 vol. Karp, Cindy, photos by. Marx, Trish. 2004. (ENG.). 40p. (J). 17.95 *(978-1-58430-164-6(3))* Lee & Low Bks., Inc.
Karp, Ken. Will You Wear a Blue Hat? 2009. (Rookie Toddler Ser.). (ENG.). 12p. (J). (gr. -1 — 1). bds. 6.95 *(978-0-531-24549-1(7)*, Children's Pr.) Scholastic Library Publishing.
Karp, Ken, photos by. Petting Farm. Set. Ackerman, Jill & Bryan, Beth. 2007. (Little Scholastic Ser.). (ENG., 12p. (J). (gr. k — 1). 12.99 *(978-0-439-88558-4(2)*, Cartwheel Bks.) Scholastic, Inc.
Karsky, A. K. Dreams of the Super Bowl. Wojciechowska, Maia. (Dreams of...Ser.). 80p. (J). 14.50 *(978-1-883740-20-7(7))* Pebble Beach Pr., Ltd.
Kary. Caillou: I Can Do It Myself! L'Heureux, Christine. 2019. (Caillou's Essentials Ser.). (ENG.). 24p. (J). (gr. -1-k). bds. 7.99 *(978-2-89718-488-9(4))* Caillouet, Gerry.
Kary & Dupuis, Karina. Baby Caillou: Christmas Hide-And-Seek: A Lift-The-Flap Book. 2018. (Baby Caillou Ser.). (ENG.). 10p. (J). bds. 7.99 *(978-2-89718-492-6(2))* Caillouet, Gerry.
—Good Morning Hide-and-Seek. 2018. (Baby Caillou Ser.). (ENG.). 10p. (J). (gr. -1-1). bds. 6.99 *(978-2-89718-465-0(5))* Caillouet, Gerry.
Kary & Legdani, Sanaa. Baby Caillou, Bedtime Hide & Seek: A Lift-the-Flap Book. Anne Paradis, Anne. Chouette Publishing Staff, ed. 2016. (Baby Caillou Ser.). (ENG.). 10p. (J). (— 1). bds. 6.99 *(978-2-89718-351-6(9))* Caillouet, Gerry.
—Caillou: My First Words: A Carry along Book. 2017. (ENG.). 24p. (J). (gr. -1-1). bds. 7.99 *(978-2-89718-443-8(4))* Caillouet, Gerry.
Kasha, Manka. Mindful Wonders: A Book about Mindfulness Using the Wonders of Nature. Zivkov, Michelle. 2020. (ENG.). 46p. (J). (gr. k-5). 16.99 ***(978-0-578-67378-3(9))*** Mindful Wonders, LLC.
Kashiwara, Akio. Baby Sees Colors: A Totally Mesmerizing High-Contrast Book for Babies. 2018. (Baby Sees! Ser.). (ENG.). 24p. (J). (gr. -1 — 1). bds. 9.99 *(978-4-05-621040-8(3))* Gakken Plus Co., Ltd. JPN. Dist: Simon & Schuster, Inc.
—Baby Sees First Colors: Black, White & Red: A Totally Mesmerizing High-Contrast Book for Babies. 2019. (Baby Sees! Ser.). (ENG.). 24p. (J). bds. 9.99 *(978-4-05-621054-5(3))* Gakken Plus Co., Ltd. JPN. Dist: Simon & Schuster, Inc.
—Baby Sees Shapes: Circles: A Totally Mesmerizing High-Contrast Book for Babies. 2020. (Baby Sees! Ser.). (ENG.). 24p. (J). bds. 9.99 *(978-4-05-621068-2(3))* Gakken Plus Co., Ltd. JPN. Dist: Simon & Schuster, Inc.
Kasko, John, photos by. Breaking Benjamin: The Road to Platinum. Kasko, John. Fabbri, Freddie. 2005. (YA). 19.95 *(978-0-9767234-0-0(9))* On Tour Publishing.
Kasparavicius, Kestutis. El Viaje de Lisa. Maar, Paul. 2008. (la Orilla del Viento Ser.). (SPA.). 28p. (J). (gr. -1-3). 12.99 *(978-968-16-7452-6(9))* Fondo de Cultura Economica USA.
Kasper, Denisa. Girl's Dream: Accidental Trips of Animals into Space. Kasper, Denisa. Roberts, Eanna, ed. 2019. (ENG.). 26p. (J). pap. 9.99 *(978-1-0927-2310-7(2))* Independently Published.
Kasper, Megan Leigh. The Shulamite's Story. Fellers, Leah. 2019. (ENG.). 36p. (J). 16.99 *(978-1-7339571-9-9(7))* Mindstir Media.
Kassab, Selena. Mommy & Daddy Are Going on a Trip. Asher, Penny & Booker, Ricki. 2006. 32p. (J). 12.95 *(978-0-9755902-1-8(9))* Change Is Strange, Inc.
—My First Day of School. Asher, Penny & Booker, Ricki. 2006. 32p. (J). 12.95 *(978-0-9755902-2-5(7))* Change Is Strange, Inc.
—No More Pacifier. Asher, Penny & Booker, Ricki. 2006. 32p. (J). 12.95 *(978-0-9755902-3-2(5))* Change Is Strange, Inc.
—We're Having a Baby. Asher, Penny & Booker, Ricki. 2006. 32p. 12.95 *(978-0-9755902-0-1(0))* Change Is Strange, Inc.
Kassem, Shadia. The Adventures of Laila & Ahmed in Syria. Alloo, Nushin. 2nd ed. 2019. (1 Ser.: Vol. 1). (ENG.). 62p. (J). pap. 20.00 *(978-0-578-46226-4(5))* Beauty Beneath the Rubble.
Kassian, Olena. What Kind of Seeds Are These? Roemer, Heidi. 2006. (ENG.). 32p. (J). (gr. k-1). 16.95 *(978-1-55971-955-1(9))* Cooper Square Publishing Llc.
Kastan, Bill. Dragon in My Pocket. Coughlin, Denise. 2005. (J). *(978-0-9765905-0-7(6))* Rose Valley Publishing.
Kastelic, Maja. Elsie. Robert, Nadine. 2020. (ENG.). 40p. (J). (gr. -1-3). 16.99 *(978-1-4197-4072-5(5)*, 1303701, Abrams Bks. for Young Readers) Abrams, Inc.
—Far Apart, Close in Heart. Birtha, Becky. 2017. (ENG.). 32p. (J). (gr. -1-3). 16.99 *(978-0-8075-1275-3(3)*, 807512753) Whitman, Albert & Co.
Kastelic, Maja. Hans Christian Andersen: The Journey of His Life. Janisch, Heinz. 2020. (ENG.). 56p. (J). (gr. -1-2). 18.95 ***(978-0-7358-4388-2(0))*** North-South Bks., Inc.
Kasten, Nancy. First Feather. 2003. 70p. (J). pap. 9.99 *(978-0-9744863-0-7(2))* Paulus Publishing.
Kastl, Christine. Cat's Egg. Karthikeyan, Aparna. 2019. (ENG.). 36p. (J). 13.95 *(978-81-936542-2-4(6))* Karadi Tales Co. Pvt. Ltd. IND. Dist: Consortium Bk. Sales & Distribution.
Kastner, Emmy. Nerdy Babies: Ocean. Kastner, Emmy. 2019. (Nerdy Babies Ser.: 1). (ENG.). (J). 32p. 16.99 *(978-1-250-31215-0(9)*, 900199117); 22p. bds. 7.99 *(978-1-250-31216-7(7)*, 900199118) Roaring Brook Pr.
—Nerdy Babies: Rocks. Kastner, Emmy. 2020. (Nerdy Babies Ser.: 3). (ENG.). (J). 32p. 18.99 *(978-1-250-31219-8(1)*, 900199122); 22p. bds. 7.99 *(978-1-250-31224-2(8)*, 900199123) Roaring Brook Pr.
—Nerdy Babies: Space. Kastner, Emmy. 2019. (Nerdy Babies Ser.: 2). (ENG.). (J). 32p. 16.99 *(978-1-250-31204-4(3)*, 900199104); 24p. bds. 7.99 *(978-1-250-31205-1(1)*, 900199105) Roaring Brook Pr.
—Nerdy Babies: Weather. Kastner, Emmy. 2020. (Nerdy Babies Ser.: 4). (ENG.). (J). 32p. 18.99 *(978-1-250-31231-0(0)*, 900199124); 22p. bds. 7.99 *(978-1-250-31232-7(9)*, 900199125) Roaring Brook Pr.
Kastner, Jill. Beardream. Hobbs, Will. 2014. 32p. pap. 8.00 *(978-1-61003-340-4(X))* Center for the Collaborative Classroom.
—In November. Rylant, Cynthia. 2014. 32p. pap. 7.00 *(978-1-61003-180-6(6))* Center for the Collaborative Classroom.
—In November. Rylant, Cynthia. 2008. (ENG.). 32p. (J). (gr. -1-3). pap. 7.99 *(978-0-15-206342-9(0)*, 1198996) Houghton Mifflin Harcourt Publishing Co.
—The Lizard Man of Crabtree County, 1 vol. Nolan, Lucy. 2003. (ENG.). 32p. (J). (gr. 1-4). pap. 5.95 *(978-0-7614-5144-0(7))* Marshall Cavendish Corp.
Kasun, Mike. Charlie Canoe & Other Boats, Too. Tuzee, John & Tuzee, Diane. 2006. (J). *(978-0-9755348-2-3(3))* Kids Life Pr.
Kasun, Mike, jt. illus. see Nunn, Paul E.
Kasy, Frank. Blue: The Luckiest Dog in the World. Liepelt, Juanita. 2008. 48p. 19.95 *(978-0-9791317-0-7(7)*, RealityIs Bks.) RealityIsBooks.com, Inc.
Kasyanchuk, Katya. You Can Do Anything You Want: All Your Dreams Can Come True. Griffin, Oliver. 2019. (ENG.). 26p. (J). pap. 9.15 ***(978-1-6938-6999-0(3))*** Independently Published.
Kasza, Keiko. The Dog Who Cried Wolf. Kasza, Keiko. 2009. 32p. (J). (gr. -1-2). pap. 7.99 *(978-0-14-241305-0(4)*, Puffin Books) Penguin Young Readers Group.
—Finders Keepers. Kasza, Keiko. McPike, Elizabeth. 2015. 32p. (J). (gr. -1-k). bds. 16.99 *(978-0-399-16898-7(2)*, G.P. Putnam's Sons Books for Young Readers) Penguin Young Readers Group.
—My Lucky Day. Kasza, Keiko. 32p. (J). (gr. -1-3). 2005. pap. 6.99 *(978-0-14-240456-0(X)*, Puffin Books); 2003. (ENG.). 17.99 *(978-0-399-23874-1(3)*, G.P. Putnam's Sons Books for Young Readers) Penguin Young Readers Group.
—My Lucky Day. Kasza, Keiko. 2005. (gr. -1-3). lib. bdg. 16.00 *(978-0-7569-5492-5(4))* Perfection Learning Corp.
—Silly Goose's Big Story. Kasza, Keiko. 2012. 32p. (J). (gr. -1-k). 16.99 *(978-0-399-25542-7(7)*, G.P. Putnam's Sons Books for Young Readers) Penguin Young Readers Group.
—When the Elephant Walks. Kasza, Keiko. 2004. (ENG.). 30p. (J). (gr. -1 — 1). bds. 7.99 *(978-0-399-24261-8(9)*, G.P. Putnam's Sons Books for Young Readers) Penguin Young Readers Group.
Kaszonyi, Janet. Racin' Jason, 1 vol. Wagner, Elaine. ed. 2009. (ENG.). 52p. (J). (gr. 1-3). pap. 10.95 *(978-1-894778-73-2(1))* Theytus Bks., Ltd. CAN. Dist: Orca Bk. Pubs. USA.
Kate Greenaway. The Queen of the Pirate Isle. Harte, Bret. 2010. 56p. pap. 3.49 *(978-1-60386-381-0(8)*, Watchmaker Publishing) Wexford College Pr.
Kate, Shostokova. Super Jonny's Tour of Ward Seventeen. Colwill, Simone. 2020. (Super Jonny Ser.: Vol. 2). (ENG.). 34p. (J). (gr. k-6). pap. ***(978-0-473-50240-9(2))*** Sick Mom.
Kate Smith Designs. Who's Playing on the Farm? 2011. (Magic Bath Bks.). (ENG.). 8p. (J). (gr. -1-3). 5.99 *(978-1-4380-7179-4(5)*, B.E.S. Publishing) Peterson's.
—Who's Playing Outdoors? 2011. (Magic Bath Bks.). (ENG.). 8p. (J). (gr. -1-3). 5.99 *(978-1-4380-7178-7(7)*, B.E.S. Publishing) Peterson's.
Kates, Dani. Hanukkah Activity Book: Puzzles, Games, Fun Questions, Coloring & More. Ages 6 & Up. Kates, Dani. 2018. (ENG.). 82p. (J). pap. 10.00 *(978-1-7286-8786-5(1))* Independently Published.
Kath, Katie. Animal Stories. Kertell, Lynn Maslen. 2019. (Bob Bks.). (ENG.). 12p. (J). (gr. -1-k). 16.99 *(978-1-338-31512-7(9))* Scholastic, Inc.
—Are You Ready to Hatch an Unusual Chicken? Jones, Kelly. 320p. (J). (gr. 3-7). 2019. 7.99 *(978-1-5247-6594-1(5)*, Yearling); 2018. 16.99 *(978-1-5247-6591-0(0)*, Knopf Bks. for Young Readers); 2018. (ENG.). lib. bdg. 19.99 *(978-1-5247-6592-7(9)*, Knopf Bks. for Young Readers) Random Hse. Children's Bks.
—Come over to My House. Seuss, Dr. 2016. (Beginner Books(R) Ser.). (ENG.). 64p. (J). (gr. k-4). 9.99 *(978-0-553-53665-2(6)*, Random Hse. Bks. for Young Readers) Random Hse. Children's Bks.
—Home Base: A Mother-Daughter Story. Tate, Nikki. 2020. 32p. (J). (gr. -1-3). 18.99 *(978-0-8234-3663-7(2))* Holiday Hse., Inc.
—Me & the Measure of Things. Sweeney, Joan. 2019. 32p. (J). (gr. -1-2). 12.99 *(978-1-9848-2959-7(9)*, Knopf Bks. for Young Readers) Random Hse. Children's Bks.
—More Than Enough. Wayland, April Halprin. 2016. 40p. (J). (-k). 16.99 *(978-0-8037-4126-3(X)*, Dial Bks) Penguin Young Readers Group.
—My Kicks: A Sneaker Story! Verde, Susan. 2017. (ENG.). 40p. (J). (gr. k-2). 16.95 *(978-1-4197-2309-4(X)*, Abrams Bks. for Young Readers) Abrams, Inc.
—The Nora Notebooks, Book 1: the Trouble with Ants. Mills, Claudia. 2016. (Nora Notebooks Ser.: 1). (ENG.). 176p. (J). (gr. 2-5). 7.99 *(978-0-385-39163-4(3)*, Yearling) Random Hse. Children's Bks.
—Road Trip with Max & His Mom. Urban, Linda. 2018. (ENG.). 160p. (J). (gr. 3-7). 16.99 *(978-0-544-80912-3(2)*, 1641407, HMH Books For Young Readers) Houghton Mifflin Harcourt Publishing Co.
—The Trouble with Ants. Mills, Claudia. 2015. (Nora Notebooks Ser.: 1). (ENG.). 176p. (J). (gr. 2-5). lib. bdg. 17.99 *(978-0-385-39162-7(5)*, Knopf Bks. for Young Readers) Random Hse. Children's Bks.
—The Trouble with Babies: The Nora Notebooks. Mills, Claudia. 2016. (Nora Notebooks Ser.: 2). 192p. (J). (gr. 2-5). 12.99 *(978-0-385-39165-8(X)*, Knopf Bks. for Young Readers) Random Hse. Children's Bks.
—The Trouble with Friends: The Nora Notebooks. Mills, Claudia. 2017. (Nora Notebooks Ser.: 3). 192p. (J). (gr. 2-5). 12.99 *(978-0-385-39169-6(2)*, Knopf Bks. for Young Readers) Random Hse. Children's Bks.
—Unusual Chickens for the Exceptional Poultry Farmer. Jones, Kelly. 2015. 224p. (J). (gr. 3-7). 16.99 *(978-0-385-75552-8(X)*, Knopf Bks. for Young Readers) Random Hse. Children's Bks.
—Ven a Mi Casa (Come over to My House Spanish Edition) Seuss. 2019. (Beginner Books(R) Ser.). (SPA.). 64p. (J). (gr. -1-2). 9.99 *(978-1-9848-3105-7(4))*; lib. bdg. 12.99 *(978-0-593-12148-1(1))* Random Hse. Children's Bks. (Random Hse. Bks. for Young Readers).
—Weekends with Max & His Dad. Urban, Linda. (ENG.). (J). 2018. 176p. (gr. 1-4). pap. 6.99 *(978-1-328-90019-7(3)*, 1700055); 2016. 160p. (gr. 3-7). 16.99 *(978-0-544-59817-1(2)*, 1615821) Houghton Mifflin Harcourt Publishing Co. (HMH Books For Young Readers).
Katherine, Graves. Gifts of the Season- an Indigenous Coloring Book: Life among the Northwest First Peoples. Batdorf, Carol. 2018. (Indigenous Coloring Book Ser.: Vol. 3). (ENG.). 32p. (J). (gr. 2-6). pap. 14.95 *(978-0-88839-180-3(3))* Hancock Hse. Pubs.
Kathie, Gabriel. Grandma's Roses. Hawkesworth, Asha. 2006. (J). per. *(978-0-9738442-9-0(9))* Avatar Pubns., Inc. CAN. Dist: .

K

Kathleen Rietz. The ABCs of Yoga for Kids Softcover. Teresa Anne Power. 2019. (ENG.). 32p. (J). pap. 9.99 ***(978-0-9822587-9-8(8))*** Stafford House.

Kaths, Kathy. The Last Eagle. Hoover, T. A. 2004. 38p. (J). 16.00 *(978-0-9702216-3-6(0))* Sport Story Publishing.

Kathuria, Rohit. Children Ask Kalam. Abdul Kalam, A. P. J. 2006. 109p. (J). *(978-81-7758-245-1(3))* Pearson Education.

Kathy, Newell-Worby. When Horses Could Fly: And Other Fantastic Tales. Sharon, Janusz. 2007. 80p. (J). pap. 19.95 *(978-0-9658533-6-1(5))* Amigo Pubns., Inc.

Katie, Katzenmeyer & Molly, Crouch. Fruit of the Spirit Is Not a Coconut. Jenkins, Bj. 2019. (ENG.). 34p. (J). pap. 9.99 ***(978-1-58169-714-8(7)***, Evergreen Pr.) Genesis Communications, Inc.

Katstaller, Rachel. Ada & the Number-Crunching Machine. Tucker, Zoë. 2019. (ENG.). 32p. (J). (gr. -1-2). 18.95 *(978-0-7358-4317-2(1))* North-South Bks., Inc.

—A Portrait in Poems: The Storied Life of Gertrude Stein & Alice B. Toklas. Robillard, Evie. 2020. (ENG.). 48p. (J). (gr. 1-4). 17.99 *(978-1-5253-0056-1(3))* Kids Can Pr., Ltd. CAN. Dist: Hachette Bk. Group.

Katsura, Masakazu & Oshii, Mamoru. Ghost in the Shell 2: Innocence, 4 vols. Katsura, Masakazu & Oshii, Mamoru. 2005. (Ghost in the Shell 2 Ani-Manga Ser.). (ENG.). 200p. pap. 39.99 *(978-1-59116-829-4(5))* Viz Media.

Katz, Avi. The Adventures of Jeremy & Heddy Levi. Ganz, Yaffa. 2005. 204p. (J). 16.95 *(978-1-930143-50-0(8)*, 3508); pap. 12.95 *(978-1-930143-51-7(6)*, 3516) Simcha Media Group. (Devora Publishing).

—The Best Hanukkah Ever, 0 vols. Goldin, Barbara Diamond. 2013. (ENG.). 34p. (J). (gr. 1-3). pap. 9.99 *(978-1-4778-1055-2(2)*, 9781477810552, Two Lions) Amazon Publishing.

—The Boy from Seville, Vol. Orgad, Dorit. Silverston, Sondra, tr. 2007. (Kar-Ben for Older Readers Ser.). (ENG.). 200p. (J). (gr. 5-7). lib. bdg. 16.95 *(978-1-58013-253-4(7)*, Kar-Ben Publishing) Lerner Publishing Group.

—The Boy in the Invisible Box. Reiss, I. 2007. 24p. per. 9.95 *(978-965-7344-30-9(1))* Mazo Pubs.

—The Burning Light. Ramsay, Elizabeth. 2005. 144p. (J). (gr. 4-9). 14.95 *(978-1-930143-43-2(5))*; pap. 9.95 *(978-1-930143-44-9(3))* Simcha Media Group. (Devora Publishing).

—A Day Full of Mitzvos. Seltzer, Sara Leah. 2009. 26p. (J). *(978-1-4226-0949-1(9))* Mesorah Pubns., Ltd.

—The Little Peninsula. Dran, Ruth. 2011. (ENG.). 264p. (YA). pap. 18.95 *(978-1-936778-87-4(4))* Mazo Pubs.

—Shemot Muzarim. Greenspan, Shari Dash. 2005.Tr. of Strange Names. (HEB.). 32p. 14.00 *(978-965-7108-58-1(6))* Urim Pubns. ISR. Dist: Coronet Bks.

—The Stupendous Adventures of Shragi & Shia. Mermelstein, Yael. 2008. 93p. (J). pap. *(978-1-4226-0865-4(4))* Mesorah Pubns., Ltd.

—Too Far from Home. Shmuel, Naomi. 2020. (ENG.). 96p. (J). (gr. 3-7). 15.99 *(978-1-5415-4671-4(7)*, Kar-Ben Publishing) Lerner Publishing Group.

—A Verseful of Jewish Holidays. Gordon, Ellen. 2008. 24p. pap. 9.95 *(978-965-7344-47-7(6))* Mazo Pubs.

Katz, Avi, jt. illus. see Reilly, Joan.

Katz, David. Electricity & You: Be Smart, Be Safe. Friend, Robyn & Cohen, Judith. l.t. ed. 2012. (ENG.). 40p. (J). pap. 7.00 *(978-1-935999-02-7(8))* Cascade Pass, Inc.

katz, david A. A Clean Planet: The Solar Power Story. friend, robyn C. & cohen, Judith Love. 2009. 48p. (J). pap. 7.00 *(978-1-880599-86-0(4))* Cascade Pass, Inc.

Katz, David A. A Clean Planet: The Solar Power Story. friend, robyn C. & Cohen, Judith Love. 2009. 48p. (J). 13.95 *(978-1-880599-87-7(2))* Cascade Pass, Inc.

—A Clean Sky: The Global Warming Story. Cohen, Judith Love & Friend, Robyn C. 2007. (J). (gr. 4-8). 46p. pap. 7.00 *(978-1-880599-81-5(3))*; 42p. 13.95 *(978-1-880599-82-2(1))* Cascade Pass, Inc.

katz, david A. Future Engineering: The Clean Water Challenge. cohen, judith L. & friend, robyn. 2015. 44p. (J). pap. 7.00 *(978-1-935999-08-9(7))* Cascade Pass, Inc.

Katz, David A. Los Angeles' Clean Energy Future. Cohen, Judith L. & Friend, Robyn. 2015. 40p. (J). pap. 7.00 *(978-1-935999-09-6(5))* Cascade Pass, Inc.

—Los Angeles' Water Future. Cohen, Judith L. & Friend, Robyn. 2015. 40p. (J). pap. 7.00 *(978-1-935999-11-9(7))* Cascade Pass, Inc.

—You Can Be A Chemist. Cohen, Judith Love. l.t. ed. 2005. Orig. Title: You Can Be A Woman Chemist. 40p. (J). per. 7.00 *(978-1-880599-71-6(6))* Cascade Pass, Inc.

—You Can Be A Woman Chemist. Cohen, Judith Love. l.t. ed. 2005. 40p. (J). 13.95 *(978-1-880599-72-3(4))* Cascade Pass, Inc.

Katz, David Arthur. A Cleaner Port; A Brighter Future: The Greening of the Port of Los Angeles. Friend, Robyn C. & Cohen, Judith Love. 2011. 46p. (J). 13.95 *(978-1-935999-01-0(X))*; pap. 7.00 *(978-1-935999-00-3(1))* Cascade Pass, Inc.

—The Women of Apollo. Friend, Robyn C. l.t. ed. 2006. 80p. (J). 17.95 *(978-1-880599-80-8(5))*; pap. 12.95 *(978-1-880599-79-2(1))* Cascade Pass, Inc.

—You Can Be A Woman Astronomer. Ghez, Andrea Mia & Cohen, Judith Love. l.t. ed. 40p. (J). 2006. pap. 12.95 incl. DVD *(978-1-880599-77-8(5))*; 2005. 17.95 incl. DVD *(978-1-880599-78-5(3))* Cascade Pass, Inc.

—You Can Be a Woman Botanist. Bozak, Kristin & Cohen, Judith Love. Date not set. 40p. (J). (gr. 3-6). 13.95 *(978-1-880599-41-9(4))*; pap. 12.95 *(978-1-880599-42-6(2))* Cascade Pass, Inc.

—You Can Be A Woman Oceanographer. Franks, Sharon E. & Cohen, Judith Love. 2004. (J). 40p. 19.95 incl. DVD *(978-1-880599-67-9(8))*; pap. 13.95 incl. DVD *(978-1-880599-66-2(X))* Cascade Pass, Inc.

Katz, Deborah R. La Rareté Est Partout. Katz, Deborah R. 2018. (FRE.). 34p. (J). (gr. k-4). *(978-0-9958261-3-7(7))* Miss Bird Bks.

Katz, Jon, photos by. Lenore Finds a Friend: A True Story from Bedlam Farm. Katz, Jon. 2014. (My Readers Ser.). (ENG., 32p. (J). (gr. -1-3). 15.99 *(978-1-250-03432-8(9)*, 900120607) Square Fish.

Katz, Karen. A Child's Good Morning Book. Brown, Margaret Wise. 2009. 32p. (J). (gr. -1-3). lib. bdg. 18.89 *(978-0-06-128861-6(6))* HarperCollins Pubs.

—A Child's Good Morning Book Board Book. Brown, Margaret Wise. 2016. (ENG.). 32p. (J). (gr. -1 — 1). bds. 7.99 *(978-0-06-233792-4(0)*, HarperFestival) HarperCollins Pubs.

—In Grandma's Arms. Shelton, Jayne C. 2008. (ENG.). 24p. (J). (gr. -1-k). bds. 6.99 *(978-0-545-06868-0(1))* Scholastic, Inc.

—Sleepy ABC. Brown, Margaret Wise. 2009. (ENG.). 40p. (J). (gr. -1-3). 16.99 *(978-0-06-128863-0(2))* HarperCollins Pubs.

—Sleepy ABC Board Book. Brown, Margaret Wise. 2016. (ENG.). 32p. (J). (gr. -1 — 1). bds. 7.99 *(978-0-06-233793-1(9)*, HarperFestival) HarperCollins Pubs.

—Subway. Suen, Anastasia. 2008. 24p. (J). (gr. -1-k). bds. 6.99 *(978-0-670-01109-4(6)*, Viking Books for Young Readers) Penguin Young Readers Group.

—Toes, Ears, & Nose! A Lift-The-Flap Book. Bauer, Marion Dane. 2003. (ENG.). 16p. (J). (gr. -1 — 1). bds. 6.99 *(978-0-689-84712-7(2)*, Little Simon) Little Simon.

Katz, Karen. Auntie & Me: A Karen Katz Lift-The-Flap Book. Katz, Karen. 2018. (ENG.). 14p. (J). (gr. -1-k). bds. 7.99 *(978-1-5344-2923-9(9)*, Little Simon) Little Simon.

—The Babies on the Bus. Katz, Karen. (ENG.). (J). (gr. -1-k). 2013. 28p. bds. 7.99 *(978-0-8050-9779-5(1)*, 9780805097795); 2011. 32p. 15.99 *(978-0-8050-9011-6(8)*, 900059039) Holt, Henry & Co. (Holt, Henry & Co. Bks. For Young Readers).

—Baby at the Farm: A Touch-And-Feel Book. Katz, Karen. 2009. (ENG.). 12p. (J). (gr. -1 — 1). bds. 7.99 *(978-1-4169-8568-6(9)*, Little Simon) Little Simon.

—Baby Loves Fall! A Karen Katz Lift-The-Flap Book. Katz, Karen. 2013. (ENG.). 14p. (J). (gr. -1 — 1). bds. 7.99 *(978-1-4424-5209-1(9)*, Little Simon) Little Simon.

—Baby Loves Spring! A Karen Katz Lift-The-Flap Book. Katz, Karen. 2012. (ENG.). 14p. (J). (gr. -1 — 1). bds. 6.99 *(978-1-4424-2745-7(0)*, Little Simon) Little Simon.

—Baby Loves Summer! A Karen Katz Lift-The-Flap Book. Katz, Karen. 2012. (ENG.). 14p. (J). (gr. -1 — 1). bds. 7.99 *(978-1-4424-2746-4(9)*, Little Simon) Little Simon.

—Baby Loves Winter! A Karen Katz Lift-The-Flap Book. Katz, Karen. 2013. (ENG.). 14p. (J). (gr. -1 — 1). bds. 6.99 *(978-1-4424-5213-8(7)*, Little Simon) Little Simon.

—Baby's Big Busy Book. Katz, Karen. 2017. (ENG.). 12p. (J). (gr. -1 — 1). bds. 14.99 *(978-1-4814-8830-3(9)*, Little Simon) Little Simon.

—Baby's Box of Family Fun! A 4-Book Lift-The-Flap Gift Set: Where Is Baby's Mommy?; Daddy & Me; Grandpa & Me, Grandma & Me, Set. Katz, Karen. gif. ed. 2006. (ENG.). 56p. (J). (gr. -1 — 1). bds. 27.99 *(978-1-4169-2795-2(6)*, Little Simon) Little Simon.

—Baby's Box of Fun: A Karen Katz Lift-The-Flap Gift Set: Where Is Baby's Bellybutton?; Where Is Baby's Mommy?: Toes, Ears, & Nose! Katz, Karen. Bauer, Marion Dane. gif. ed. 2004. (ENG.). 44p. (J). (gr. -1 — 1). bds. 19.99 *(978-0-689-03862-4(3)*, Little Simon) Little Simon.

—Baby's Colors. Katz, Karen. 2010. (ENG.). 14p. (J). (gr. -1 — 1). bds. 7.99 *(978-1-4169-9821-1(7)*, Little Simon) Little Simon.

—Baby's Day: Cloth Book. Katz, Karen. 2007. (ENG.). 10p. (J). (gr. -1 — 1). 17.99 *(978-1-4169-3580-3(0)*, Little Simon) Little Simon.

—Baby's Numbers. Katz, Karen. 2010. (ENG.). 14p. (J). (gr. -1 — 1). bds. 7.99 *(978-1-4424-0827-2(8)*, Little Simon) Little Simon.

—Baby's Shapes. Katz, Karen. 2010. (ENG.). 14p. (J). (gr. -1 — 1). bds. 7.99 *(978-1-4169-9824-2(1)*, Little Simon) Little Simon.

—Beddy-Bye, Baby: A Touch-And-Feel Book. Katz, Karen. 2009. (ENG.). 12p. (J). (gr. -1 — 1). bds. 7.99 *(978-1-4169-8048-3(2)*, Little Simon) Little Simon.

—Buzz, Buzz, Baby! A Karen Katz Lift-The-Flap Book. Katz, Karen. 2014. (ENG.). 14p. (J). (gr. -1 — 1). bds. 6.99 *(978-1-4424-9313-1(5)*, Little Simon) Little Simon.

—Can You Say Peace? Katz, Karen. 2006. (ENG.). 32p. (J). (gr. -1-2). 19.99 *(978-0-8050-7893-0(2)*, 9780805078930, Holt, Henry & Co. Bks. For Young Readers) Holt, Henry & Co.

—Counting Christmas. Katz, Karen. 2007. (Classic Board Bks.). (ENG.). 32p. (J). (gr. -1-1). bds. 7.99 *(978-1-4169-3624-4(6)*, Little Simon) Little Simon.

—Counting Kisses: Counting Kisses. Katz, Karen. 2003. (Classic Board Bks.). (ENG.). 32p. (J). (gr. -1-k). bds., bds. 7.99 *(978-0-689-85658-7(X)*, Little Simon) Little Simon.

—Counting Kisses: Lap Edition. Katz, Karen. 2010. (ENG.). 26p. (J). (gr. -1 — 1). bds. 12.99 *(978-1-4424-0792-3(1)*, Little Simon) Little Simon.

—¡Cu-Cú, Bebé! (Peek-A-Baby) Katz, Karen. 2009. (SPA.). 14p. (J). (gr. -1 — 1). bds. 7.99 *(978-1-4169-7938-8(7)*, Libros Para Ninos) Libros Para Ninos.

—Daddy & Me. Katz, Karen. 2003. (ENG.). 14p. (J). (gr. -1-k). bds. 6.99 *(978-0-689-84906-0(0)*, Little Simon) Little Simon.

—Daddy Hugs. Katz, Karen. 2007. (Classic Board Bks.). (ENG.). 32p. (J). (gr. -1 — 1). bds. 7.99 *(978-1-4169-4120-0(7)*, Little Simon) Little Simon.

—Daddy Hugs 1 2 3. Katz, Karen. 2005. (ENG.). 32p. (J). (gr. -1-1). 18.99 *(978-0-689-87771-1(4)*, McElderry, Margaret K. Bks.) McElderry, Margaret K. Bks.

—¿dónde Está el Ombliguito? (Where Is Baby's Belly Button?) Un Libro para Levantar Ta Tapita Por Karen Katz (a Lift-The-Flap Story) Katz, Karen. Ziegler, Argentina Palacios, tr. 2004. (SPA.). 14p. (J). (gr. -1-1). bds. 7.99 *(978-0-689-86977-8(0)*, Libros Para Ninos) Libros Para Ninos.

—Grandpa & Me: Grandpa & Me. Katz, Karen. 2004. (ENG.). 14p. (J). (gr. -1-k). bds. 6.99 *(978-0-689-86644-9(5)*, Little Simon) Little Simon.

—How Does Baby Feel? A Karen Katz Lift-The-Flap Book. Katz, Karen. 2013. (ENG.). 14p. (J). (gr. -1 — 1). bds. 7.99 *(978-1-4424-5204-6(8)*, Little Simon) Little Simon.

—I Can Share. Katz, Karen. 2004. 14p. (J). (gr. -1-k). 6.99 *(978-0-448-43611-1(6)*, Grosset & Dunlap) Penguin Young Readers Group.

—Kiss Baby's Boo-Boo: A Karen Katz Lift-The-Flap Book. Katz, Karen. 2016. (ENG.). 14p. (J). (gr. -1 — 1). bds. 6.99 *(978-1-4814-4208-4(2)*, Little Simon) Little Simon.

—Mommy Hugs. Katz, Karen. 2007. (Classic Board Bks.). (ENG.). 32p. (J). (gr. -1 — 1). bds. 7.99 *(978-1-4169-4121-7(5)*, Little Simon) Little Simon.

—Mommy Hugs: Lap Edition. Katz, Karen. 2010. (ENG.). 26p. (J). (gr. -1 — 1). bds. 12.99 *(978-1-4424-0791-6(3)*, Little Simon) Little Simon.

—My First Chinese New Year. Katz, Karen. 2012. (My First Holiday Ser.). (ENG.). 32p. (J). (gr. -1-k). 6.99 *(978-1-250-01868-7(4)*, 900087705) Square Fish.

—My First Karen Katz Library: Peek-A-Baby; Where Is Baby's Tummy?; What Does Baby Say?; Kiss Baby's Boo-Boo; Where Is Baby's Puppy?; Where Is Baby's Birthday Cake?; How Does Baby Feel?; What Does Baby Love?; Baby Loves Winter!; Baby Loves Spring!; Baby Loves Summer!; Baby Loves Fall! Katz, Karen. ed. 2017. (ENG.). 170p. (J). (gr. -1 — 1). bds. 83.99 *(978-1-5344-0238-6(1)*, Little Simon) Little Simon.

—My First Kwanzaa. Katz, Karen. 2014. (My First Holiday Ser.). (ENG.). 32p. (J). (gr. -1-k). 7.99 *(978-1-250-05046-5(4)*, 900134033) Square Fish.

—Now I'm Big! Katz, Karen. 2019. (Classic Board Bks.). (ENG.). 32p. (J). (gr. -1 — 1). bds. 7.99 *(978-1-5344-4306-8(1)*, Little Simon) Little Simon.

—Now I'm Big! Katz, Karen. 2013. (ENG.). 32p. (J). (gr. -1-k). 15.99 *(978-1-4169-3547-6(9)*, McElderry, Margaret K. Bks.) McElderry, Margaret K. Bks.

—Peek-A-Baby: A Lift-The-Flap Book. Katz, Karen. 2007. (ENG.). 14p. (J). (gr. -1 — 1). bds. 7.99 *(978-1-4169-3622-0(X)*, Little Simon) Little Simon.

—Peek-A-Baby: A Lift-The-Flap Book/Lap Edition. Katz, Karen. 2010. (ENG.). 14p. (J). (gr. -1 — 1). 11.99 *(978-1-4424-0790-9(5)*, Little Simon) Little Simon.

—A Potty for Me! Katz, Karen. 2005. (ENG.). 26p. (J). (gr. -1-k). tchr. ed. 7.99 *(978-0-689-87423-9(5)*, Little Simon) Little Simon.

—Princess Baby. Katz, Karen. (Princess Baby Ser.). (J). (gr. k-k). 2012. 30p. 7.99 *(978-0-307-93146-7(3))*; 2008. 32p. 14.99 *(978-0-375-84119-4(9))* Random Hse. Children's Bks. (Schwartz & Wade Bks.).

—Princess Baby, Night-Night. Katz, Karen. 2014. (Princess Baby Ser.). (ENG.). 28p. (J). (— 1). bds. 7.99 *(978-0-385-37848-2(3)*, Schwartz & Wade Bks.) Random Hse. Children's Bks.

—Princess Baby on the Go. Katz, Karen. 2010. (Princess Baby Ser.). 14p. (J). (— 1). bds. 7.99 *(978-0-375-85664-8(1)*, Schwartz & Wade Bks.) Random Hse. Children's Bks.

—Roar, Roar, Baby! A Karen Katz Lift-The-Flap Book. Katz, Karen. 2015. (ENG.). 14p. (J). (gr. -1 — 1). bds. 6.99 *(978-1-4814-1788-4(6)*, Little Simon) Little Simon.

—Rosie Goes to Preschool. Katz, Karen. (J). (-k). 2019. (ENG.). 34p. bds. 8.99 *(978-1-9848-3052-4(X))*; 2015. 40p. 16.99 *(978-0-385-37917-5(X))* Random Hse. Children's Bks. (Schwartz & Wade Bks.).

—Shake It up, Baby! Katz, Karen. 2009. (ENG.). 14p. (J). (gr. -1 — 1). bds. 7.99 *(978-1-4169-6737-8(0)*, Little Simon) Little Simon.

—Splish, Splash, Baby! Katz, Karen. 2015. (ENG.). 14p. (J). (gr. -1 — 1). bds. 7.99 *(978-1-4814-1789-1(4)*, Little Simon) Little Simon.

—Ten Tiny Babies. Katz, Karen. 2011. (Classic Board Bks.). (ENG.). 32p. (J). (gr. -1-k). bds. 7.99 *(978-1-4424-1394-8(8)*, Little Simon) Little Simon.

—Ten Tiny Babies. Katz, Karen. 2008. (ENG.). 32p. (J). (gr. -1-3). 17.99 *(978-1-4169-3546-9(0)*, McElderry, Margaret K. Bks.) McElderry, Margaret K. Bks.

—Ten Tiny Tickles. Katz, Karen. 2008. (Classic Board Bks.). (ENG.). 32p. (J). (gr. -1-k). bds. 7.99 *(978-1-4169-5101-8(6)*, Little Simon) Little Simon.

—Ten Tiny Tickles. Katz, Karen. 2005. (ENG.). 32p. (J). (gr. -1-3). 19.99 *(978-0-689-85976-2(7)*, McElderry, Margaret K. Bks.) McElderry, Margaret K. Bks.

—Vroom, Vroom, Trucks! Katz, Karen. 2016. (ENG.). 14p. (J). (gr. -1 — 1). bds. 6.99 *(978-1-4814-4209-1(0)*, Little Simon) Little Simon.

—Welcome, Baby! A Lift-The-flap Book for New Babies. Katz, Karen. 2019. (ENG.). 14p. (J). (gr. -1-k). bds. 6.99 *(978-1-5344-3071-6(7)*, Little Simon) Little Simon.

—What Does Baby Say? A Lift-The-Flap Book. Katz, Karen. 2004. (ENG.). 16p. (J). (gr. -1-k). bds. 6.99 *(978-0-689-86645-6(3)*, Little Simon) Little Simon.

—Where Are Baby's Easter Eggs? A Lift-The-Flap Book. Katz, Karen. 2008. (ENG.). 14p. (J). (gr. -1 — 1). bds. 7.99 *(978-1-4169-4924-4(0)*, Little Simon) Little Simon.

—Where Is Baby's Beach Ball? A Lift-The-Flap Book. Katz, Karen. 2009. (ENG.). 14p. (J). (gr. -1 — 1). bds. 6.99 *(978-1-4169-4962-6(3)*, Little Simon) Little Simon.

—Where Is Baby's Belly Button? Anniversary Edition/Lap Edition. Katz, Karen. anniv. ed. 2009. (ENG.). 14p. (J). (gr. -1 — 1). bds. 12.99 *(978-1-4169-8733-8(9)*, Little Simon) Little Simon.

—Where Is Baby's Birthday Cake? A Lift-The-Flap Book. Katz, Karen. 2008. (ENG.). 14p. (J). (gr. -1 — 1). bds. 7.99 *(978-1-4169-5817-8(7)*, Little Simon) Little Simon.

—Where Is Baby's Christmas Present? A Lift-The-Flap Book. Katz, Karen. 2009. (ENG.). 14p. (J). (gr. -1 — 1). bds. 7.99 *(978-1-4169-7145-0(9)*, Little Simon) Little Simon.

—Where Is Baby's Dreidel? A Lift-The-Flap Book. Katz, Karen. 2007. (ENG.). 14p. (J). (gr. -1 — 1). bds. 7.99 *(978-1-4169-3623-7(8)*, Little Simon) Little Simon.

—Where Is Baby's Home? A Karen Katz Lift-The-Flap Book. Katz, Karen. 2017. (ENG.). 14p. (J). (gr. -1 — 1). bds. 6.99 *(978-1-5344-0088-7(5)*, Little Simon) Little Simon.

—Where Is Baby's Pumpkin? Katz, Karen. 2006. (ENG.). 14p. (J). (gr. -1 — 1). bds. 7.99 *(978-1-4169-0970-5(2)*, Little Simon) Little Simon.

—Where Is Baby's Puppy? A Lift-The-Flap Book. Katz, Karen. 2011. (ENG.). 14p. (J). (gr. -1 — 1). bds. 7.99 *(978-1-4169-8684-3(7)*, Little Simon) Little Simon.

—Where Is Baby's Turkey? A Karen Katz Lift-The-Flap Book. Katz, Karen. 2017. (ENG.). 14p. (J). (gr. -1 — 1). bds. 7.99 *(978-1-5344-0089-4(3)*, Little Simon) Little Simon.

—Where Is Baby's Valentine? A Lift-The-Flap Book. Katz, Karen. 2006. (ENG.). 14p. (J). (gr. -1 — 1). bds. 7.99 *(978-1-4169-0971-2(0)*, Little Simon) Little Simon.

—Where Is Baby's Yummy Tummy? A Karen Katz Lift-The-Flap Book. Katz, Karen. 2011. (ENG.). 14p. (J). (gr. -1 — 1). bds. 6.99 *(978-1-4424-2165-3(7)*, Little Simon) Little Simon.

—Wiggle Your Toes. Katz, Karen. 2006. (ENG.). 14p. (J). (gr. -1-k). bds. 11.99 *(978-1-4169-0365-9(8)*, Little Simon) Little Simon.

—Zoom, Zoom, Baby! A Karen Katz Lift-The-Flap Book. Katz, Karen. 2014. (ENG.). 14p. (J). (gr. -1 — 1). bds. 7.99 *(978-1-4424-9314-8(3)*, Little Simon) Little Simon.

Katz, Keren. The Wizard's Tears. Kumin, Maxine & Sexton, Anne. 2019. 48p. (J). (gr. k-4). 18.95 *(978-1-60980-875-4(4)*, Triangle Square) Seven Stories Pr.

Katz, Michele. I Saw a Friend. Streza, Katrina. 2015. (ENG.). 32p. (J). (gr. -1-3). E-Book 9.99 *(978-1-62395-357-7(X))* Xist Publishing.

Katz, Pete & Skeate, Sarah. Heroes of Discovery: Who Changed the World. 2019. (Graphic Greats Ser.). (ENG.). 128p. (J). (gr. 4-7). pap. 12.99 *(978-1-4380-1199-8(7)*, B.E.S. Publishing) Peterson's.

Katz, Tova. The Adventures of Aliza & Dovid: Holidays at the Farm. Blitz, Shmuel. 2005. (ArtScroll Youth Ser.). 48p. (J). *(978-1-4226-0021-4(1))* Mesorah Pubns., Ltd.

—ArtScroll Children's Book of Berachos: [Sefer Ha-Berakhot Shel]. Blitz, Shmuel. 2011. (ENG & HEB.). 48p. (J). *(978-1-4226-1170-8(1))* Mesorah Pubns., Ltd.

—Every Story Has a Soul. Blitz, Shmuel. 2006. 47p. (J). 15.99 *(978-1-4226-0224-9(9))* Mesorah Pubns., Ltd.

—[ha-Tehilim Ha-Rishon]: ArtScroll Children's Tehillim. Blitz, Shmuel. 2008. (Artscroll Youth Ser.). 96p. (J). *(978-1-4226-0751-0(8))* Mesorah Pubns., Ltd.

—Megilat Ester: The ArtScroll Children's Megillah. Blitz, Shmuel. 2003. (ArtScroll Ser.). (ENG & HEB.). 79p. (J). 16.99 *(978-1-57819-708-8(2)*, MCHH); pap. 10.99 *(978-1-57819-709-5(0)*, MCHP) Mesorah Pubns., Ltd.

—[Megilat Rut]: The Artscroll Children's Book of Ruth. Blitz, Shmuel. 2005. (ArtScroll Youth Ser.). 48p. (J). *(978-1-57819-069-0(X))*; pap. *(978-1-57819-070-6(3))* Mesorah Pubns., Ltd.

—[Sefer Yonah]: The Artscroll Children's Book of Jonah. Blitz, Shmuel. 2006. 48p. (J). *(978-1-4226-0130-3(7))*; pap. *(978-1-4226-0131-0(5))* Mesorah Pubns., Ltd.

—Stories for a Child's Heart. Pruzansky, Binyomin. 2009. 48p. (J). *(978-1-4226-0915-6(4))* Mesorah Pubns., Ltd.

—The Story of Chanukah. Leon, Sarah & Eisikowitz, Michal. 2008. 63p. (J). *(978-1-4226-0875-3(1))* Mesorah Pubns., Ltd.

Katzenstein, Jason Adam. Kitai's Journal. Peymani, Christine. 2013. (ENG.). 144p. (J). (gr. 3-7). pap. 5.99 *(978-0-06-226857-0(0))* HarperCollins Pubs.

Kauenhofen, Jessica. My First A B C Book. Kauenhofen, Jessica. 2007. (Little Jewel Book Ser.). 24p. (J). (gr. 2). pap. 2.70 *(978-0-7399-2385-6(4))* Rod & Staff Pubs., Inc.

Kaufenberg, Matt. How to Grow Happiness: A Jerome the Gnome Adventure. DiPucchio, Kelly. 2018. 32p. (J). (gr. -1-1). 17.99 *(978-1-63565-140-9(9)*, 9781635651409, Rodale Kids) Random Hse. Children's Bks.

—Toy Story 4 Little Golden Book (Disney/Pixar Toy Story 4) Crute, Josh. 2019. (Little Golden Book Ser.). (ENG.). 24p. (J). (-k). 4.99 *(978-0-7364-3978-7(1)*, Golden/Disney) Random Hse. Children's Bks.

Kauffin, Karlynn. Anit: The Chef. Gaskins, Melda. 2011. 24p. pap. 24.95 *(978-1-4626-4485-8(6))* America Star Bks.

Kaufman, Angelika. Piruleta. Nöstlinger, Christine. 2003. (SPA.). 132p. (gr. 3-5). pap. 9.95 *(978-968-19-0983-3(6))* Santillana USA Publishing Co., Inc.

Kaufman, Elliott, photos by. Numbers Everywhere. 2013. (ENG., 32p. (J). (gr. -1-1). 12.95 *(978-0-7892-1157-6(2)*, 791157, Abbeville Kids) Abbeville Pr., Inc.

Kaufman, Mary Bee. The Journey of Perm. Peterson, Sara Budinger. 2004. 96p. pap. 11.95 *(978-0-9665282-3-7(9))* Saranjon Publishing.

Kaufman, Richard. More Magic Tricks, Science Facts. Friedhoffer, Bob. 2019. (ENG.). 114p. (J). (gr. 4-7). pap. 9.99 *(978-1-0722-7049-2(8))* Independently Published.

Kaufman, Suzanne. All Are Welcome. Penfold, Alexandra. 2018. (ENG.). 44p. (J). (gr. -1-3). 17.99 *(978-0-525-57964-9(8)*, Knopf Bks. for Young Readers) Random Hse. Children's Bks.

—Naughty Claudine's Christmas. Jennings, Patrick. 2017. (ENG.). 32p. (J). (gr. -1-2). 16.99 *(978-1-101-93734-1(3))*; lib. bdg. 19.99 *(978-1-101-93735-8(1))* Random Hse. Children's Bks. (Random Hse. Bks. for Young Readers).

—Samanthasaurus Rex. Mandell, B. B. 2016. (ENG.). 32p. (J). (gr. -1-3). 17.99 *(978-0-06-234873-9(6))* HarperCollins Pubs.

—Take Your Pet to School Day. Ashman, Linda. 2019. (ENG.). 40p. (J). (gr. -1-2). 17.99 *(978-1-5247-6559-0(7))*; 20.99 *(978-1-5247-6560-6(0))* Random Hse. Children's Bks. (Random Hse. Bks. for Young Readers).

—100 Bugs! A Counting Book. Narita, Kate. 2018. (ENG.). 40p. (J). 17.99 *(978-0-374-30631-1(1)*, 900175254, Farrar, Straus & Giroux (BYR)) Farrar, Straus & Giroux.

Kaufman, Suzanne. Confiscated! Kaufman, Suzanne. 2017. (ENG.). 32p. (J). (gr. -1-3). 17.99 *(978-0-06-241086-3(5))* HarperCollins Pubs.

Kaufman, Yaki. The Ant & the Wheat Kernel: For Young Readers. Penina, M. 2012. 24p. 19.75 net. *(978-1-60046-090-6(9))* Yofi Bk. Publishing, Inc.

—Dove Builds a Nest: For Young Readers. Penina, M. 2012. 22p. 19.75 net. *(978-1-60046-091-3(7))* Yofi Bk. Publishing, Inc.

Kaufmann, Angelika. Hoppelpopp & the Best Bunny. Lobe, Mira & Kovács, Cécilie. 2015. (ENG.). 32p. (J). (gr. -1-3). 16.95 *(978-0-8234-3287-5(4))* Holiday Hse., Inc.

—Piruleta. Nöstlinger, Christine. 2003. (SPA.). 136p. (J). (gr. 3-5). 9.95 *(978-84-204-4777-3(3))* Ediciones Alfaguara ESP. Dist: Santillana USA Publishing Co., Inc.

Kaulbach, Kathy, jt. illus. see MacDonald, Clarke.

Kaulbach, Kathy R. Healing the Bruises, 1 vol. Morgan, Lori. 2016. (ENG.). 32p. (J). (gr. 1-4). 16.95 *(978-1-4595-0283-3(3),* 7e714df2-bc98-4cb6-b744-5ff14e71992d) James Lorimer & Co. Ltd., Pubs. CAN. Dist: Lerner Publishing Group.

Kaulitzki, Ramona. Badger's Perfect Garden. Arnold, Marsha Diane. 2019. (ENG.). 32p. (J). (gr. k-3). 16.99 *(978-1-5341-1000-7(3),* 204647) Sleeping Bear Pr.

Kaulitzki, Ramona. Fly, Firefly. Keller, Shana. 2020. (ENG.). 32p. (J). (gr. k-2). 9.99 ***(978-1-5341-1109-7(3),*** 205005); 16.99 *(978-1-5341-1033-5(X),* 204846) Sleeping Bear Pr.

Kaulitzki, Ramona. God Is Love. Parker, Amy. 2019. (God Is Ser.). 28p. (J). (gr. -1 — 1). bds. 9.99 *(978-0-7624-6643-6(X),* Running Pr. Kids) Running Pr.

—God Is with Us. Parker, Amy. 2019. (God Is Ser.). 28p. (J). (gr. -1 — 1). bds. 9.99 *(978-0-7624-6652-8(9),* Running Pr. Kids) Running Pr.

—Sisters First. Bush, Barbara Pierce & Bush Hager, Jenna. 2019. 40p. (J). (gr. -1-3). 18.99 *(978-0-316-53478-9(1))* Little, Brown Bks. for Young Readers.

Kaulitzki, Ramona. Wonderful You. Graff, Lisa. 2020. (ENG.). 32p. (J). (gr. -1-2). 17.99 ***(978-1-9848-3738-7(9),*** Philomel Bks.) Penguin Young Readers Group.

Kaulitzki, Ramona. You're the Cheese in My Blintz. Kimmelman, Leslie. 2020. (Very First Board Bks.). (ENG.). 12p. (J). (gr. -1 — 1). bds. 6.99 *(978-1-5415-3467-4(0),* Kar-Ben Publishing) Lerner Publishing Group.

Kaulitzki, Ramona, jt. illus. see White, Teagan.

Kaur, Bal. The Horncastles & the Magnopeus Medicine. Kaur, K. S. 2012. 154p. pap. *(978-1-78148-023-6(0))* Grosvenor Hse. Publishing Ltd.

Kaur, Baljinder. Fauja Singh Keeps Going: The True Story of the Oldest Person to Ever Run a Marathon. Singh, Simran Jeet. 2020. 48p. (J). (gr. -1-3). 17.99 ***(978-0-525-55509-4(9),*** Kokila) Penguin Young Readers Group.

Kavanagh, Peter. Annie to the Rescue. Lindsay, Elizabeth. 2003. 94p. (J). *(978-0-439-56006-1(3))* Scholastic, Inc.

—Beauty & the Beast. Wilson, Jacqueline. 2012. *(978-0-88734-073-4(3))* Players Pr., Inc.

—Journey to the World of the Dinosaurs: Peek Inside the Pop-Up Windows! Taylor, Dereen. 2014. (ENG.). 12p. (J). (gr. 2-7). 16.99 *(978-1-86147-319-6(2),* Armadillo) Anness Publishing GBR. Dist: National Bk. Network.

—The Knight's First Tournament. Taylor, Dereen. 2012. 12p. (J). (gr. 1-6). 16.99 *(978-1-84322-760-1(6))* Anness Publishing GBR. Dist: National Bk. Network.

—The Soft-Hearted Sheepdog. Green, Sylvia. 2003. 144p. (J). *(978-0-439-62569-2(6))* Scholastic, Inc.

Kavelaris, Amy. Good Night, My Darling Dear: Prayers & Blessings for You, 1 vol. Kavelaris, Amy. 2020. (ENG.). 32p. (J). 16.99 *(978-1-4002-1246-0(4))* Nelson, Thomas Inc.

Kawa, Cosei. Feeding the Flying Fanellis: And Other Poems from a Circus Chef. Hosford, Kate. 2015. (ENG.). 32p. (J). (gr. 1-3). lib. bdg. 17.99 *(978-1-4677-3905-4(7),* 9781467739054); E-Book 27.99 *(978-1-4677-7511-3(8))* Lerner Publishing Group. (Carolrhoda Bks.).

—Rifka Takes a Bow, Vol. Perlov, Rebecca Rosenberg. 2013. (ENG.). 32p. (J). (gr. k-3). 7.95 *(978-0-7613-8128-0(7),* 9780761381280, Kar-Ben Publishing) Lerner Publishing Group.

—Tales of Two Dragons: Band 15/Emerald (Collins Big Cat) Casey, Dawn. 2015. (Collins Big Cat Ser.). (ENG.). 48p. (J). (gr. 3-4). pap. 11.99 *(978-0-00-812784-8(0))* HarperCollins Pubs. Ltd. GBR. Dist: Independent Pubs. Group.

—An Unlikely Ballerina. Goddu, Krystyna Poray. 2018. (ENG.). 32p. (J). (gr. k-4). 17.99 *(978-1-5124-8362-8(1),* Kar-Ben Publishing) Lerner Publishing Group.

Kawaayi, Rodney. Adventure Asana the Rainy Day: Yoga Stories & Poses for Kids of All Ages. Medina, Shanti & Lockwood, Kevin. 2018. (Adventure Asana Ser.: Vol. 1). (ENG.). 64p. (J). pap. 16.95 *(978-1-7237-9272-4(1))* Independently Published.

Kawahara, Yumiko. Dolls. Kawahara, Yumiko. (Dolls Ser.: 1). (ENG.). 1. 2004. 200p. pap. 9.99 *(978-1-59116-508-8(3));* Vol. 2. 2005. 216p. pap. 9.99 *(978-1-59116-670-2(5));* Vol. 3. 2005. 200p. pap. 9.99 *(978-1-59116-769-3(8));* Vol. 4. 2005. 224p. pap. 9.99 *(978-1-59116-866-9(X))* Viz Media.

Kawai, Ritsuko. Hamtaro. Kawai, Ritsuko. 2003. (ENG.). 16p. (J). pap. 7.95 *(978-1-56931-815-7(8))* Viz Media.

—Hamtaro Gets Lost & Other Stories. Kawai, Ritsuko. 2003. (Adventures of Hamtaro Ser.: Vol. 2). (ENG.). 92p. (J). (gr. 1-3). 9.95 *(978-1-56931-817-1(4))* Viz Media.

—Hamtaro Pop-Up Playset. Kawai, Ritsuko. 2003. (Hamtaro Ser.). (ENG.). 20p. (J). pap. 16.95 *(978-1-56931-846-1(8))* Viz Media.

—Hamtaro Postcard Book. Kawai, Ritsuko. 2003. (Hamtaro Ser.). (ENG.). 24p. (J). pap. 7.95 *(978-1-56931-845-4(X))* Viz Media.

—Hamtaro, Vol. 1. Kawai, Ritsuko. 2003. (ENG.). 16p. (J). pap. 7.95 *(978-1-56931-814-0(X))* Viz Media.

—Hamtaro, Vol. 3. Kawai, Ritsuko. 2003. (ENG.). 16p. (J). pap. 7.95 *(978-1-56931-816-4(6))* Viz Media.

—Let's Play! Vol. 4: A Playground for Ham-Ham. Kawai, Ritsuko. 2003. (Hamtaro Ser.). (ENG.). 16p. (J). (gr. 1-3). pap. 7.95 *(978-1-56931-821-8(2))* Viz Media.

Kawaiae, Aaron A. Kohala Kuamoo. Kawaiae, Kekaulelenaeole A. 2010. 32p. 16.00 *(978-0-87336-232-0(2))* Kamehameha Publishing.

KAWAII CREATIVE STUDIOS, jt. illus. see Narciso, Massimiliano.

Kawaii Creative Studios, Kawaii Creative. Disney Frozen: Breaking Boundaries (Graphic Novel) Caramagna, Joe. 2019. (ENG.). 80p. (J). (gr. 3-7). pap. 10.99 *(978-1-5067-1051-8(4))* Dark Horse Comics.

—Disney Frozen: the Hero Within (Graphic Novel) Caramagna, Joe. 2019. (ENG.). 72p. (J). (gr. 3-7). pap. 10.99 *(978-1-5067-1269-7(X),* Dark Horse Books) Dark Horse Comics.

Kawaii Creative Studios, Kawaii Creative, et al. Disney Frozen: True Treasure. Caramagna, Joe. 2020. (ENG.). 72p. (J). (gr. 3-7). pap. 10.99 ***(978-1-5067-1705-0(5),*** Dark Horse Books) Dark Horse Comics.

Kawaii Studio, jt. illus. see Pastrovicchio, Alessandro.

Kawamura, Yayo. Where Is Fuzzy Penguin? a Touch, Feel, Look, & Find Book! 2019. (ENG.). 16p. (J). (gr. -1 — 1). 8.99 *(978-1-338-53802-1(0),* Cartwheel Bks.) Scholastic, Inc.

Kawamura, Yayo. A Day with Pepe & Milli. Kawamura, Yayo. 2017. (Pepe & Millie Ser.). (ENG.). 16p. (J). (gr. -1 — 1). bds. 9.99 *(978-0-8075-6481-3(8),* 807564818) Whitman, Albert & Co.

—Good Night, Pepe & Millie. Kawamura, Yayo. 2018. (Pepe & Millie Ser.). (ENG.). 16p. (J). (gr. -1 — 1). bds. 9.99 *(978-0-8075-6483-7(4),* 807564834) Whitman, Albert & Co.

—Pepe & Millie. Kawamura, Yayo. 2017. (Pepe & Millie Ser.). (ENG.). 16p. (J). (gr. -1 — 1). bds. 9.99 *(978-0-8075-6482-0(6),* 807564826) Whitman, Albert & Co.

Kawanishi, Mikio. Creating Stories. Sugamoto, Junichi. 2007. (How to Draw Manga Ser.: Vol. 39). 140p. (YA). per. 19.99 *(978-4-7661-1330-3(6))* Graphic-Sha JPN. Dist: Diamond Bk. Distributors.

Kawasaki, Shauna Mooney. My Family Can Be Forever: Sharing Time Activities. 2003. 62p. (J). pap. *(978-1-59038-232-5(3))* Deseret Bk. Co.

Kay, Catherine. The Dragon Diamond. Nicholson, James Ashley. 2018. (ENG.). 40p. (J). (gr. k-2). pap. *(978-1-911424-37-6(8))* Black Wolf Edition & Publishing Ltd.

Kay, Gertrude. The Boy Who Lived in Pudding Lane: Being a True Account, If Only You Believe It, of the Life & Ways of Santa, Oldest Son of Mr. & Mrs. Claus. Addington, Sarah. 2017. (ENG.). 104p. (J). 22.95 *(978-1-927979-26-6(9),* 9781927979266) Grafton and Scratch Pubs. CAN. Dist: Baker & Taylor Publisher Services (BTPS).

Kay, Jim. Bugs: A Stunning Pop-Up Look at Insects, Spiders, & Other Creepy-Crawlies. McGavin, George. 2013. (ENG.). 12p. (J). (gr. 2-5). 19.99 *(978-0-7636-6762-7(5))* Candlewick Pr.

—The Great War: Stories Inspired by Items from the First World War. 2019. (ENG.). 304p. (J). (gr. 5). pap. 14.99 *(978-1-5362-0886-3(8))* Candlewick Pr.

—The Great War: Stories Inspired by Items from the First World War. Almond, David et al. 2015. (ENG.). 304p. (J). (gr. 5). 19.99 *(978-0-7636-7554-7(7))* Candlewick Pr.

—Harry Potter & the Chamber of Secrets. Rowling, J. K. ed. 2016. (Harry Potter Ser.: 2). (ENG.). 272p. (J). (gr. 3). 39.99 *(978-0-545-79132-8(4));* 275.00 *(978-1-338-11986-2(9))* Scholastic, Inc. (Levine, Arthur A. Bks.).

—Harry Potter & the Prisoner of Azkaban: the Illustrated Edition. Rowling, J. K. 2017. (Harry Potter Ser.: 3). (ENG.). 336p. (J). (gr. 3-3). 39.99 *(978-0-545-79134-2(0),* Levine, Arthur A. Bks.) Scholastic, Inc.

—Harry Potter & the Sorcerer's Stone. Rowling, J. K. ed. 2015. (Harry Potter Ser.: 1). (ENG.). 256p. (J). (gr. 3). 39.99 *(978-0-545-79035-2(2),* Levine, Arthur A. Bks.) Scholastic, Inc.

Kay, Jim. Harry Potter y el Cáliz de Fuego. Edición Ilustrada / Harry Potter & the Goblet of Fire: the Illustrated Edition. Rowling, J. K. 2020. (Harry Potter Ser.: 4). (SPA.). 464p. (J). (gr. 4-7). 59.95 ***(978-84-9838-996-8(8))*** Publicaciones y Ediciones Salamandra, S.A. ESP. Dist: Penguin Random Hse. LLC.

Kay, Jim. A Monster Calls: Inspired by an Idea from Siobhan Dowd. Ness, Patrick. (ENG.). 224p. (YA). (gr. 7). 2013. pap. 12.00 *(978-0-7636-6065-9(5));* 2011. 18.99 *(978-0-7636-5559-4(7))* Candlewick Pr.

Kay, Linda. The Baseball King. Weiss, Max C. 2015. (ENG.). (J). 14.95 *(978-0-692-47520-1(6))* Castadream LLC.

Kay, Liz. Lift-The-Flap Atlas, 1 vol. Lonely Planet Kids & Baker, Kate. 2020. (ENG.). 16p. (J). (gr. 1-3). 18.99 *(978-1-78868-927-4(5),* Lonely Planet Kids) Lonely Planet Global Ltd. IRL. Dist: Hachette Bk. Group.

Kaye, Charlie. Mr. Dewey's Zoo. Clurtle, Doug. 2019. (ENG.). 50p. (J). 21.99 *(978-1-7335506-1-1(5))* Ten Critters Pr.

Kaye, Donna M. Jewish Holiday Adventures. Stein, Ethel. 2010. 52p. 25.00 *(978-1-4349-9618-3(2),* RoseDog Bks.) Dorrance Publishing Co., Inc.

Kaye, Justin & Hillyard, T. K. Lizard's Lagoon: La Laguna de Lagartija. Kaye, Justin. 2018. (ENG.). 26p. (J). pap. 9.15 *(978-1-945383-00-7(3))* CandleHill Publishing Co.

Kaye, Rosalind Charney. Chanukah on the Prairie. Schuman, Burt E. 2004. (gr. k-3). 13.95 *(978-0-8074-0814-8(X),* 381780) URJ Pr.

—Come, Let Us Be Joyful! The Story of Hava Nagila. Manushkin, Fran. 2004. (gr. k-3). 13.95 *(978-0-8074-0731-8(3),* 101073) URJ Pr.

—Hello, Hello, Are You There, God? Cone, Molly. rev. ed. 2004. viii, 55p. (gr. k-3). pap. 13.95 *(978-0-8074-0648-9(1),* 102553) URJ Pr.

—Hello, Hello, Are You There God?, Grades Preschool-3. Cone, Molly. 2004. (gr. k-3). pap., tchr. ed. 14.95 *(978-0-8074-0655-7(4),* 208048) URJ Pr.

—Sophie & the Shofar. Manushkin, Fran. 2004. (J). (gr. k-3). 13.95 *(978-0-8074-0751-6(8),* 101078) URJ Pr.

Kaye, Shena. Mother's Grimm. Brown, Selena & Parsons, Michelle, eds. 2018. (ENG.). 238p. (J). pap. 19.99 *(978-1-7241-4039-5(6))* Independently Published.

Kayganich, Bob. Flight of the Butterflies. Edwards, Roberta. 2010. (Penguin Young Readers, Level 3 Ser.). 48p. (J). (gr. 1-3). pap. 4.99 *(978-0-448-45396-5(7),* Penguin Young Readers) Penguin Young Readers Group.

—Titanic: The Story Lives On! Driscoll, Laura. 2012. (Penguin Young Readers: Level 4 Ser.). 48p. (J). (ENG.). (gr. 2-4). 17.44 *(978-0-448-45902-8(7));* (gr. 3-4). mass mkt. 4.99 *(978-0-448-45757-4(1),* Penguin Young Readers) Penguin Young Readers Group.

Kaylor, Emiko, jt. illus. see Muronaka, Michael.

Kayser, Jason, jt. illus. see Ross, Bob.

Kazaleh, Mike, jt. illus. see Allan, Chris.

Kazemi, Nahid. The Old Woman, 1 vol. Schwartz, Joanne. 2020. (ENG.). 36p. (J). (gr. k-3). 18.95 ***(978-1-77306-211-2(5))*** Groundwood Bks. CAN. Dist: Publishers Group West (PGW).

Kazemi, Nahid. Over the Rooftops, under the Moon. Lawson, JonArno. 2019. 56p. (J). 17.95 *(978-1-59270-262-6(7))* Enchanted Lion Bks., LLC.

Kazui, Kazumi. Yami No Matsuei. Katayama, Kyoichi. 2005. (Socrates in Love Ser.: Vol. 1). (ENG.). 192p. pap. 8.99 *(978-1-4215-0199-4(6))* Viz Media.

Kazuko. What Will the Weather Be Like Today? Rogers, Paul. 2011. (Houghton Mifflin Reading Ser.). 38p. (J). pap. 61.35 *(978-0-618-03420-8(X))* Houghton Mifflin Harcourt Trade & Reference Pubs.

Kazybrid, Mychailo. The Case of the Lost World Heritage. Holmes & Watson, Well Their Pets, Investigate the Disappearing World Heritage Site. Chatelier, Ed. 2014. (ENG.). (J). pap. *(978-0-9569731-7-7(5))* Edge Group.

—The Case of the Water Crisis. Chatelier, Ed. 2016. (ENG.). (J). pap. *(978-0-9569731-8-4(3))* Edge Group.

Kazybrid, Mychailo, et al. The Lion Kids Bible Comic. Chatelier, Ed. ed. 2019. (ENG.). 112p. (J). (gr. 1-4). pap. 12.99 *(978-0-7459-7719-5(7))* Lion Hudson PLC GBR. Dist: Independent Pubs. Group.

Keaggy, Sarah. The Abcs of Making Good Choices. Young, Dawn. 2013. 34p. 17.00 *(978-0-9860244-8-1(1))* O'More Publishing.

—Little Blue, Little Gray. Gentry, Nancy. 2012. 56p. pap. 10.00 *(978-0-9846244-9-2(X))* O'More Publishing.

—Skyler & the Se. Rogers, Lauren. Sexton, Jessa, ed. 2012. 36p. pap. 8.00 *(978-0-9860150-1-4(6))* O'More Publishing.

—The Sneaky Shoe Bug. Robertson, Robbin Davis. Sexton, Jessa R., ed. 2012. 44p. 16.00 *(978-0-9860150-4-5(0))* O'More Publishing.

Kean, Kaylee. School Is Scary Book 3 & 4: Book 3: Second Grade Stinks; Book 4: Third Grade's Terrible Trip. Brown, Katherine. 2018. (School Is Scary Ser.: Vol. 2). (ENG.). 102p. (J). pap. 7.50 *(978-1-7286-3759-4(7))* Independently Published.

Keane, Claire. Love Is: (Illustrated Story Book about Caring for Others, Book about Love for Parents & Children, Rhyming Picture Book) Adams, Diane. 2017. (ENG.). 32p. (J). 15.99 *(978-1-4521-3997-5(0))* Chronicle Bks. LLC.

—Paolo, Emperor of Rome. Barnett, Mac. 2020. (ENG.). 48p. (J). (gr. -1-3). 17.99 *(978-1-4197-4109-8(8),* 1182201, Abrams Bks. for Young Readers) Abrams, Inc.

—Why? Rex, Adam. 2019. (ENG.). 60p. (J). (gr. k-3). 17.99 *(978-1-4521-6863-0(6))* Chronicle Bks. LLC.

Keane, Dave. Monster School: First Day Frights. Keane, Dave. 2012. (I Can Read Level 2 Ser.). (ENG.). 32p. (J). (gr. -1-3). 16.99 *(978-0-06-085476-8(6));* pap. 4.99 *(978-0-06-085475-1(8))* HarperCollins Pubs.

—Monster School: the Spooky Sleepover. Keane, Dave. 2014. (I Can Read Level 2 Ser.). (ENG.). 32p. (J). (gr. -1-3). pap. 4.99 *(978-0-06-085477-5(4))* HarperCollins Pubs.

Keane, Max. Trash Truck. Keane, Max. 2020. (ENG.). 32p. (J). (gr. -1-3). 14.99 ***(978-0-06-300221-0(3),*** HarperCollins) HarperCollins Pubs. Ltd. GBR. Dist: HarperCollins Pubs.

Kear, Katie. Basketball Buddies. Smith, Elliott. 2020. (Kids' Sports Stories Ser.). (ENG.). 32p. (J). (gr. k-2). pap. 5.95 ***(978-1-5158-7283-2(1),*** 201308); lib. bdg. 21.32 ***(978-1-5158-7094-4(4),*** 199189) Capstone. (Picture Window Bks.).

—Ready, Set, Swim! Smith, Elliott. 2020. (Kids' Sports Stories Ser.). (ENG.). 32p. (J). (gr. k-2). pap. 5.95 ***(978-1-5158-7285-6(8),*** 201310); lib. bdg. 21.32 ***(978-1-5158-7097-5(9),*** 199192) Capstone. (Picture Window Bks.).

Kearney, Brendan. The Big Earth Book, 1 vol. Brake, Mark & Lonely Planet Kids. 2017. (ENG.). 256p. (J). (gr. 4-7). 19.99 *(978-1-78701-278-3(6),* 5715) Lonely Planet Global Ltd. IRL. Dist: Hachette Bk. Group.

—Expandable Explorations: Big Builds. Steele, Philip. 2020. (Expandable Explorations Ser.). (ENG.). 10p. (J). (gr. 1-3). 18.99 *(978-1-68412-672-9(X),* Silver Dolphin Bks.) Printers Row Publishing Group.

—Flying Machines. Candlewick Press Staff & Arnold, Nick. 2014. (ENG.). (J). (gr. 3-7). 19.99 *(978-0-7636-7107-5(X))* Candlewick Pr.

—Lady Pancake & Sir French Toast. Funk, Josh. 2015. (Lady Pancake & Sir French Toast Ser.: 1). 40p. (J). (gr. k). 16.95 *(978-1-4549-1404-4(1),* 1394148) Sterling Publishing Co., Inc.

—Let's Draw Dinosaurs & Prehistoric Beasts with Crayola! Allen, Kathy. 2019. (Let's Draw with Crayola ® ! Ser.). (ENG.). 32p. (J). (gr. -1-3). 27.99 *(978-1-5415-1102-6(6),* Lerner Pubns.) Lerner Publishing Group.

—Let's Draw Dinosaurs & Prehistoric Beasts with Crayola ® ! Allen, Kathy. 2019. (Let's Draw with Crayola ® ! Ser.). (ENG.). 32p. (J). (gr. -1-3). pap. 6.99 *(978-1-5415-4608-0(3),* Lerner Pubns.) Lerner Publishing Group.

—Mission Defrostable. Funk, Josh. 2018. (Lady Pancake & Sir French Toast Ser.: 3). (ENG.). 40p. (J). (gr. k-4). 16.95 *(978-1-4549-2811-9(5))* Sterling Publishing Co., Inc.

Kearney, Jennifer. The Sunflower. King, Ken. 2008. 24p. (J). pap. 14.99 *(978-1-4343-8463-8(2))* AuthorHouse.

Kearney, Mary Lowie. One Ravenwood Halloween. Scott, Tay. 2019. (ENG.). 48p. (J). pap. 14.95 ***(978-1-59594-641-6(1),*** Wingspan Pr.) WingSpan Publishing.

Kearney, Mary Lowie. One Ravenwood Winter. Scott, Tay. 2016. (ENG.). 48p. (J). pap. 12.95 *(978-1-59594-600-3(4))* Aquafire Sulis.

—One Ravenwood Winter. Scott, Tay. 2016. (ENG.). (J). 21.95 *(978-1-59594-667-6(5),* Wingspan Pr.) WingSpan Publishing.

Kearny, Brendan. The Case of the Stinky Stench. Funk, Josh. 2017. (Lady Pancake & Sir French Toast Ser.: 2). 40p. (J). (gr. k-3). 16.95 *(978-1-4549-1960-5(4))* Sterling Publishing Co., Inc.

Keates, Colin, photos by. Crystal & Gem: Eyewitness Books. Symes, R. F. & Harding, Robert. 2004. 63p. (J). (gr. 4-8). reprint ed. 19.00 *(978-0-7567-7687-9(2))* DIANE Publishing Co.

Keating, Jess. Bunbun & Bonbon: Fancy Friends. Keating, Jess. 2020. (Bunbun & Bonbon Ser.: 1). (ENG.). 64p. (J). (gr. 2-5). 22.99 ***(978-1-338-64683-2(4));*** pap. 7.99 ***(978-1-338-64682-5(6))*** Scholastic, Inc. (Graphix).

Keating, Nancy. Forget-Me-Not, 1 vol. Trottier, Maxine. 2008. (ENG.). 32p. (J). (gr. 1-8). pap. *(978-1-897174-24-1(1))* Breakwater Bks., Ltd.

—The Land of a Thousand Whales, 1 vol. Chalker Browne, Susan. 2007. (ENG.). 32p. (J). (gr. 3-7). pap. *(978-1-897174-08-1(X))* Breakwater Bks., Ltd.

—A Puppy Story, 1 vol. Pynn, Susan. 2007. (ENG.). 32p. (J). (gr. -1-3). pap. *(978-1-897174-18-0(7))* Breakwater Bks., Ltd.

—Rebecca's Ducks, 1 vol. Moore, Angela. 2007. (ENG.). 32p. (J). (gr. -1-2). pap. *(978-1-897174-00-5(4))* Breakwater Bks., Ltd.

Keaton, Pam. Burton the Sneezing Cow. Hall, Lisa. 2012. 28p. (-18). pap. 9.95 *(978-1-939289-06-3(8),* Little Creek Bks.) Jan-Carol Publishing, INC.

Keats, Ezra Jack. Jennie's Hat. Keats, Ezra Jack. 2003. (ENG.). 40p. (J). (gr. -1-2). pap. 7.99 *(978-0-14-250035-4(6),* Puffin Books) Penguin Young Readers Group.

—Louie. Keats, Ezra Jack. 2004. (ENG.). 40p. (J). (gr. -1-2). pap. 6.99 *(978-0-14-240080-7(7),* Puffin Books) Penguin Young Readers Group.

Keay, Claire. Bea Gives up Her Dummy: The Book That Makes Children Want to Move on from Dummies! Album, Jenny. 2015. (ENG.). 50p. (J). pap. *(978-0-9926167-3-1(5))* Little Boo Publishing.

—Bee Calm: The Buzz on Yoga. Sileo, Frank J. 2019. (J). *(978-1-4338-2957-4(6),* Magination Pr.) American Psychological Assn.

—Bee Heartful: Spreading Loving-Kindness. Sileo, Frank J. 2020. (J). *(978-1-4338-3157-7(0),* Magination Pr.) American Psychological Assn.

—Bee Still: An Invitation to Meditation. Sileo, Frank J. 2018. 32p. (J). *(978-1-4338-2870-6(7),* Magination Pr.) American Psychological Assn.

—Bumblebee Bike. Levins, Sandra. 2014. 32p. (J). *(978-1-4338-1645-1(8));* pap. *(978-1-4338-1646-8(6))* American Psychological Assn. (Magination Pr.).

—I Love You All Year Long. Metzger, Steve. 2009. 20p. (J). (gr. -1-k). 8.95 *(978-1-58925-847-1(9))* Tiger Tales.

—The Littlest Levine, Vol. Lanton, Sandy. 2014. (ENG.). 24p. (J). (gr. -1-2). 7.95 *(978-0-7613-9046-6(4),* 9780761390466, Kar-Ben Publishing) Lerner Publishing Group.

—M Is for Manger. Bowman, Crystal & McKinley, Teri. 2015. (ENG.). 64p. (J). 7.99 *(978-1-4964-0195-3(6),* 4611870) Tyndale Hse. Pubs.

—M Is for Manger. McKinley, Teri & Bowman, Crystal. 2016. (ENG.). 32p. (J). bds. 6.99 *(978-1-4964-2004-6(7),* 20_29070, Tyndale Kids) Tyndale Hse. Pubs.

—Night-Night, Bunny. Kennedy, Pamela. 2017. 16p. (J). (gr. -1-k). bds. 7.99 *(978-0-8249-1660-2(3))* Worthy Publishing.

—No, No, Bunny. Kennedy, Pamela. 2017. 16p. (J). (gr. -1-k). bds. 7.99 *(978-0-8249-1651-0(4))* Worthy Publishing.

Keay, Claire. The Snow Queen, 1 vol. 2020. (Stories of Christmas Ser.). (ENG.). 24p. (J). (gr. 1-2). lib. bdg. 24.60 ***(978-1-4994-8599-8(9));*** pap. 8.25 ***(978-1-4994-8597-4(2))*** Rosen Publishing Group, Inc., The. (Windmill Bks.).

Keay, Claire. Somebody Cares: A Guide for Kids Who Have Experienced Neglect. Straus, Susan Farber. 2016. 32p. (J). *(978-1-4338-2109-7(5),* Magination Pr.) American Psychological Assn.

—This Old Man. (Classic Books with Holes 8x8 Ser.). 16p. (J). 2019. (ENG.). pap. *(978-1-78628-212-5(7));* 2019. bds. *(978-1-78628-217-0(8));* 2018. (ENG.). *(978-1-78628-229-3(1));* 2018. (ENG.). *(978-1-78628-233-0(X));* 2018. pap. *(978-1-78628-176-0(7))* Child's Play International Ltd.

Keay, Claire. The Twelve Days of Christmas, 1 vol. 2020. (Stories of Christmas Ser.). (ENG.). 24p. (J). (gr. 1-2). pap. 8.25 ***(978-1-4994-8601-8(4));*** lib. bdg. 24.60 ***(978-1-4994-8603-2(0))*** Rosen Publishing Group, Inc., The. (Windmill Bks.).

Keay, Claire. Uh-Oh, Bunny. Kennedy, Pamela. 2017. 16p. (J). (gr. -1-k). bds. 7.99 *(978-0-8249-1650-3(6))* Worthy Publishing.

—You Can Do It, Bunny. Kennedy, Pamela. 2018. 18p. (J). (gr. -1-k). bds. 7.99 *(978-0-8249-1669-5(7))* Worthy Publishing.

—1-2-3 a Calmer Me. Patterson, Colleen A. & Miles, Brenda. 2015. 32p. (J). *(978-1-4338-1931-5(7))* American Psychological Assn.

Keba, Jamila. Beautiful Wild Rose Girl. Magnolia, B. Hugel, William K., ed. 2012. 34p. pap. 7.95 *(978-0-9854289-0-7(2))* Mystic World Pr.

Kecskés, Anna. Danny Strikes Out in Americ: A R. E. A. d Book. Judybee. 2013. 32p. pap. *(978-1-78092-335-2(X))* MX Publishing, Ltd.

—Story Time for Kids with Nlp by the English Sisters: The Little Grasshopper & the Big Ball of Dung. Zuggo, Violeta & Zuggo, Jutka. 2013. 24p. pap. *(978-1-78092-493-9(3))* MX Publishing, Ltd.

KecskTs, Anna. Leah - the Fairy of the Lime Tree. Kisson, Nisha. 2008. 36p. pap. *(978-1-904312-39-0(X))* MX Publishing, Ltd.

Keddy, Brian. Emily to the Rescue. Williamson, Liza. 2011. 28p. pap. 24.95 *(978-1-4626-3342-5(0))* America Star Bks.

Keegan, Charles. The Hunt Begins. Jordan, Robert. 2005. (Great Hunt Ser.: Bk. 1). 397p. (gr. 5-9). 16.00 *(978-0-7569-5065-1(1))* Perfection Learning Corp.

Keegan, Jonathan. The Lambkins. Bunting, Eve. 2005. 192p. (J). (gr. 5-18). (ENG.). 15.99 *(978-0-06-059906-5(5));* lib. bdg. 16.89 *(978-0-06-059907-2(3))* HarperCollins Pubs. (Cotler, Joanna Books).

K

Keele, Kevin. Because of You, Dad. Deseret Book Company. 2018. (J). 13.99 *(978-1-62972-561-1(7))* Deseret Bk. Co.

—Good Night Australia. Gamble, Adam & Jasper, Mark. 2020. (Good Night Our World Ser.). (ENG.). 20p. (J). (— 1). bds. 9.95 *(978-1-60219-803-6(9))* Good Night Bks.

—Good Night Halloween. Gamble, Adam & Jasper, Mark. 2019. (Good Night Our World Ser.). (ENG.). 20p. (J). (— 1). bds. 9.95 *(978-1-60219-817-3(9))* Good Night Bks.

—Good Night Hong Kong. Tougias, Kristin. 2020. (Good Night Our World Ser.). 20p. (J). (— 1). bds. 9.95 *(978-1-60219-827-2(6))* Good Night Bks.

—Good Night Redwoods. Gamble, Adam & Jasper, Mark. 2019. (Good Night Our World Ser.). 20p. (J). (— 1). bds. 9.95 *(978-1-60219-779-4(2))* Good Night Bks.

Keeler, Patricia A. Drumbeat in Our Feet, 1 vol. Keeler, Patricia A. Leitão, Júlio T. 2012. (ENG.). 32p. (J). (gr. 1-6). lib. bdg. 16.95 *(978-1-58430-264-3(X))* Lee & Low Bks., Inc.

Keeler, Renee. Seasons. 2006. (Learn to Write Ser.). 8p. (J). (gr. k-2). pap. 3.49 *(978-1-59198-291-3(X)*, 6185) Creative Teaching Pr., Inc.

Keely, Jack. Animal Grossology: The Science of Creatures Gross & Disgusting. Branzei, Sylvia. 2004. (Grossology Ser.). (ENG.). 80p. (J). (gr. 3-7). reprint ed. mass mkt. 9.99 *(978-0-8431-1011-1(2)*, Price Stern Sloan) Penguin Young Readers Group.

—Grossology: The Science of Really Gross Things. Branzei, Sylvia. 2006. (Grossology Ser.). (ENG.). 80p. (gr. 3-7). 10.99 *(978-0-8431-4914-2(0))* Perfection Learning Corp.

—The History of Vampires & Other Real Blood Drinkers. Branzei, Sylvia. 2009. (All Aboard Reading: Station Stop 3 Ser.). (ENG.). 48p. (J). (gr. 2-4). 16.19 *(978-0-448-45032-2(1))* Penguin Young Readers Group.

—Ickstory: Unraveling the Icky History of Mummies. Branzei, Sylvia. 2009. (Penguin Young Readers, Level 4 Ser.). 48p. (J). (gr. 3-4). mass mkt. 4.99 *(978-0-448-45033-9(X)*, Penguin Young Readers) Penguin Young Readers Group.

Keen, Joseph. Sheerluck Versus the Paranormal Volume 1. Wilkinson, Dean. 2018. (Sheerluck Holmes Ser.: Vol. 1). (ENG.). 90p. (YA). (gr. 7-12). pap. *(978-1-78705-352-6(0))* MX Publishing, Ltd.

—Sheerluck Versus the Paranormal Volume 2. Wilkinson, Dean. 2019. (Sheerluck Holmes Ser.: Vol. 2). (ENG.). 96p. (J). (gr. 2-6). pap. *(978-1-78705-364-9(4))* MX Publishing, Ltd.

—Sheerluck Versus the Paranormal Volume 3. Wilkinson, Dean. 2019. (Sheerluck Holmes Ser.: Vol. 3). (ENG.). 100p. (J). (gr. 2-6). pap. *(978-1-78705-457-8(8))* MX Publishing, Ltd.

Keen, Sophie. My Favorite Michael. Heiman, Laura. 2009. (J). (gr. -1-2). 32p. 15.95 *(978-1-58925-086-4(9))*; 24p. pap. 7.95 *(978-1-58925-419-0(8))* Tiger Tales.

—Selkie Child. Howell, Gill. 2005. (ENG.). 24p. (J). lib. bdg. 23.65 *(978-1-59646-750-7(9))* Dingles & Co.

Keenan, Brona. Kangaroo Christmas. Rose, M. E. 2007. (ENG.). 140p. (YA). 10.95 *(978-1-896209-89-0(0))* Bayeux Arts, Inc. CAN. Dist: Chicago Distribution Ctr.

Keenan, Siobhan. Ghosted in L. A. Vol. 1. Grace, Sina. 2020. (Ghosted in La Ser.: 1). (ENG.). 112p. (YA). pap. 14.99 *(978-1-68415-505-7(3))* Boom! Studios.

Keener, Anna & Wald, Christina. A Day in the Desert. Keener, Anna. 2017. (Long Term Ecological Research Ser.). (ENG.). 32p. (J). (gr. -1-12). 15.95 *(978-1-63076-178-3(8))* Muddy Boots Pr.

Keep, Richard. Clatter Bash! A Day of the Dead Celebration, 1 vol. Keep, Richard. 2008. (ENG.). 32p. (J). (gr. k-3). pap. 7.95 *(978-1-56145-461-7(3))* Peachtree Publishing Co. Inc.

—A Thump from Upstairs: Starring Mr. Boo & Max, 1 vol. Keep, Richard. 2005. (ENG.). 36p. (J). (gr. -1-3). 15.95 *(978-1-56145-348-1(X))* Peachtree Publishing Co. Inc.

Keep, Virginia. The April fool Doll. Gates, Josephine Scribner. 2007. 152p. (J). lib. bdg. 59.00 *(978-1-60304-009-9(9))* Dollworks.

—The dolls in Fairyland. Gates, Josephine Scribner. 2007. 136p. (J). lib. bdg. 59.00 *(978-1-60304-013-6(7))* Dollworks.

—Little girl Blue: Lives in the woods till she learns to say Please. Gates, Josephine Scribner. 2007. 54p. (J). lib. bdg. 59.00 *(978-1-60304-012-9(9))* Dollworks.

—Little red white & Blue. Gates, Josephine Scribner. 2007. 118p. (J). lib. bdg. 59.00 *(978-1-60304-006-8(4))* Dollworks.

—The live dolls' busy Days. Gates, Josephine Scribner. 2007. 106p. (J). lib. bdg. 59.00 *(978-1-60304-007-5(2))* Dollworks.

—The live dolls' house Party. Gates, Josephine Scribner. 2007. 104p. (J). lib. bdg. 59.00 *(978-1-60304-005-1(6))* Dollworks.

—The live dolls in Wonderland. Gates, Josephine Scribner. 2007. 150p. (J). lib. bdg. 59.00 *(978-1-60304-015-0(3))* Dollworks.

—The live dolls' play Days. Gates, Josephine Scribner. 2007. 110p. (J). lib. bdg. 59.00 *(978-1-60304-008-2(0))* Dollworks.

—More about live Dolls. Gates, Josephine Scribner. 2007. 106p. (J). lib. bdg. 59.00 *(978-1-60304-002-0(1))* Dollworks.

—The Story of Live Dolls: Being an account by Josephine Scribner Gates of how, on a certian June morning, all of the dolls in the Cloverdale came Alive. Gates, Josephine Scribner. 2007. 102p. (J). lib. bdg. 59.00 *(978-1-60304-001-3(3))* Dollworks.

—The story of the lost Doll. Gates, Josephine Scribner. 2007. 108p. (J). lib. bdg. 59.00 *(978-1-60304-003-7(X))* Dollworks.

—The Story of the three Dolls. Gates, Josephine Scribner. 2007. 148p. (J). lib. bdg. 59.00 *(978-1-60304-004-4(8))* Dollworks.

Keeping, Charles. God Beneath the Sea. Garfield, Leon & Blishen, Edward. 2015. 224p. (J). (gr. 4-6). 22.99 *(978-0-85753-311-1(8))* Transworld Publishers Ltd. GBR. Dist: Independent Pubs. Group.

—The Highwayman. Noyes, Alfred. ed. 2015. (ENG.). 32p. pap. 12.95 *(978-0-19-279442-0(6))* Oxford Univ. Pr., Inc.

Keepness, Mike. Hommage Au Bison: Une légende des Cris des Plaines. Silverthorne, Judith. Noel-Maw, Martine, tr. 2016. (FRE.). 50p. (J). pap. *(978-2-924237-14-4(9))* Les Editions de la nouvelle plume.

Keeshig-Tobias, Polly. Emma & the Trees. Keeshig-Tobias, Lenore. Date not set. 78p. pap. *(978-0-920813-11-9(9))* Sister Vision Pr.

Keessler, Karen. I Love You More. Duksta, Laura. (ENG.). (J). 2009. 24p. bds. 6.99 *(978-1-4022-2460-7(5))*; 2007. 34p. 16.99 *(978-1-4022-1126-3(0))* Sourcebooks, Inc. (Sourcebooks Jabberwocky).

—I Love You More Padded Board Book. Duksta, Laura. 2013. (ENG.). 24p. (J). bds. 8.99 *(978-1-4022-9250-7(3)*, Sourcebooks Jabberwocky) Sourcebooks, Inc.

—Te Quiero Más. Duksta, Laura. 2013. (SPA.). 24p. (J). bds. 7.99 *(978-1-4022-8177-8(3)*, Sourcebooks Jabberwocky) Sourcebooks, Inc.

Keeter, Susan. An Apple for Harriet Tubman. Turner, Glennette Tilley. 2016. (ENG.). 24p. (J). (gr. -1-3). pap. 6.99 *(978-0-8075-0396-6(7)*, 807503967) Whitman, Albert & Co.

—Honey Baby Sugar Child. Duncan, Alice Faye. 2005. (ENG.). 32p. (J). (gr. -1-1). 19.99 *(978-0-689-84678-6(9)*, Simon & Schuster Bks. For Young Readers) Simon & Schuster Bks. For Young Readers.

—El Leon Ruge. Merlo, Maria. 2012. (SPA.). 16p. (J). pap. 54.70 *(978-0-663-62198-9(4))* Silver, Burdett & Ginn, Inc.

—Phillis Sings Out Freedom: The Story of George Washington & Phillis Wheatley. Malaspina, Ann. 2012. (J). 34.28 *(978-1-61913-149-1(8))* Weigl Pubs., Inc.

—Tippy Lemmey. McKissack, Patricia C. 2003. (Ready-for-Chapters Ser.). 59p. (gr. 2-5). lib. bdg. 15.00 *(978-0-7569-1432-5(9))* Perfection Learning Corp.

—Tippy Lemmey. McKissack, Patricia C. 2003. (Ready-For-Chapters Ser.). (ENG.). 64p. (J). (gr. 2-5). pap. 5.99 *(978-0-689-85019-6(0)*, Simon & Schuster/Paula Wiseman Bks.) Simon & Schuster/Paula Wiseman Bks.

Keevy, Karmyn. Reality Jumpers Series (Book 1) ONE BAD SPELL. Jarvis, Andrew. 2019. (Reality Jumpers Ser.: Vol. 1). (ENG.). 116p. (J). pap. 6.25 ***(978-1-6745-6001-4(X))*** Independently Published.

Kehl, Bob & Junghans, Olivia. The Fur Trader. Ferguson, Sam. 2016. (ENG.). (J). pap. 11.99 *(978-1-943183-50-0(3))* Dragon Scale Publishing.

Kehl, Drusilla. Shoshana & the Native Rose. Levinson, Robin K. 2006. 103p. (J). (gr. 3-5). per. 12.00 *(978-0-9773673-2-0(0))* Gali Girls, Inc.

Kehn, Regina. El Largo Camino Hacia Santa Cruz. Ende, Michael & Michael, Ende. (SPA.). 64p. (J). (gr. 3-5). 6.95 *(978-84-241-3354-2(4)*, EV3073) Everest Editora ESP. Dist: Lectorum Pubns., Inc.

—El Largo Camino Hacia Santa Cruz. Ende, Michael & Michael, Ende. 2003.Tr. of Lange Weg nach Santa Cruz. (SPA.). 63p. (gr. 2-3). 14.99 *(978-84-241-3348-1(X)*, EV0114) Everest Editora ESP. Dist: Lectorum Pubns., Inc.

—The Night of Wishes: Or the Satanarchaeolidealcohellish Notion Potion. Ende, Michael. Schwarzbauer, Heike & Takvorian, Rick, trs. 2017. 216p. (J). (gr. 3-7). 16.95 *(978-1-68137-188-7(X)*, NYR Children's Collection) New York Review of Bks., Inc., The.

Kehoe, Lindy. Home on a Giggle. 2004. (J). *(978-0-9752801-0-2(4))* Beres, Nancy.

Kei. If It's for My Daughter, I'd Even Defeat a Demon Lord: Volume 2. CHIROLU. Warner, Matthew, tr. 2019. (If It's for My Daughter, I'd Even Defeat a Demon Lord (light Novel) Ser.). 236p. pap. 14.99 *(978-1-7183-5301-5(4))* J-Novel Club.

—If It's for My Daughter, I'd Even Defeat a Demon Lord: Volume 3. CHIROLU. Warner, Matthew, tr. 2019. (If It's for My Daughter, I'd Even Defeat a Demon Lord (light Novel) Ser.). 228p. pap. 14.99 *(978-1-7183-5302-2(2))* J-Novel Club.

—If It's for My Daughter, I'd Even Defeat a Demon Lord: Volume 4. CHIROLU. Warner, Matthew, tr. 2019. (If It's for My Daughter, I'd Even Defeat a Demon Lord (light Novel) Ser.). 250p. pap. 14.99 *(978-1-7183-5303-9(0))* J-Novel Club.

—If It's for My Daughter, I'd Even Defeat a Demon Lord: Volume 5. CHIROLU. Warner, Matthew, tr. 2019. (If It's for My Daughter, I'd Even Defeat a Demon Lord (light Novel) Ser.). 250p. pap. 14.99 *(978-1-7183-5304-6(9))* J-Novel Club.

Kei, Deanna. The International Fashionista's Lookbook Diary. Lardner, Dana. 2016. (ENG.). (J). (gr. 3-6). pap. 14.99 *(978-1-61984-577-0(6))* Gatekeeper Pr.

Keimig, Candice. At the Beach. Andrews, Alexa. 2013. (Penguin Young Readers, Level 1 Ser.). 32p. (J). (gr. k-1). pap. 4.99 *(978-0-448-46471-8(3)*, Penguin Young Readers) Penguin Young Readers Group.

—Bears Eat & Grow: Level 2. Gunderson, Megan M. 2014. (Magic Readers Ser.). (ENG.). 24p. (J). (gr. k-3). 25.65 *(978-1-62402-058-2(5)*, 1493) Magic Wagon.

—Bears in the Mountains: Level 3. Gunderson, Megan M. 2014. (Magic Readers Ser.). (ENG.). 24p. (J). (gr. k-3). 25.65 *(978-1-62402-059-9(3)*, 1495) Magic Wagon.

—Black Canvas, 1 vol. Aros, Dana. 2016. (Dark Roads Ser.). (ENG.). 216p. (YA). (gr. 6-12). lib. bdg. 28.56 *(978-1-68076-260-0(5)*, 21461, Epic Extreme) EPIC Pr.

—Bloodline, 1 vol. Aros, Dana. 2016. (Dark Roads Ser.). (ENG.). 216p. (YA). (gr. 6-12). lib. bdg. 28.56 *(978-1-68076-261-7(3)*, 21463, Epic Extreme) EPIC Pr.

—Buffaloes: Level 1. Elston, Heidi M. D. 2014. (Magic Readers Ser.). (ENG.). 24p. (J). (gr. k-3). 25.65 *(978-1-62402-060-5(7)*, 1497) Magic Wagon.

—Buffaloes Eat & Grow: Level 2. Elston, Heidi M. D. 2014. (Magic Readers Ser.). (ENG.). 24p. (J). (gr. k-3). 25.65 *(978-1-62402-061-2(5)*, 1499) Magic Wagon.

—Buffaloes on the Prairie: Level 3. Elston, Heidi M. D. 2014. (Magic Readers Ser.). (ENG.). 24p. (J). (gr. k-3). 25.65 *(978-1-62402-062-9(3)*, 1501) Magic Wagon.

—Chasing the Day, 1 vol. Aros, Dana. 2016. (Dark Roads Ser.). (ENG.). 216p. (YA). (gr. 6-12). lib. bdg. 28.56 *(978-1-68076-262-4(1)*, 21465, Epic Extreme) EPIC Pr.

—Dolphins Eat & Grow: Level 2. Baltzer, Rochelle. 2014. (Magic Readers Ser.). (ENG.). 24p. (J). (gr. k-3). 25.65 *(978-1-62402-067-4(4)*, 1511) Magic Wagon.

—Dolphins in the Ocean: Level 3. Baltzer, Rochelle. 2014. (Magic Readers Ser.). (ENG.). 24p. (J). (gr. k-3). 25.65 *(978-1-62402-068-1(2)*, 1513) Magic Wagon.

—Fade to Black, 1 vol. Aros, Dana. 2016. (Dark Roads Ser.). (ENG.). 216p. (YA). (gr. 6-12). lib. bdg. 28.56 *(978-1-68076-263-1(X)*, 21467, Epic Extreme) EPIC Pr.

—In the Forest. Andrews, Alexa. 2013. (Penguin Young Readers, Level 1 Ser.). 32p. (J). (gr. k-1). pap. 4.99 *(978-0-448-46719-1(4)*, Penguin Young Readers) Penguin Young Readers Group.

—Kiss the Chef, 1 vol. Aros, Dana. 2016. (Dark Roads Ser.). (ENG.). 216p. (YA). (gr. 6-12). lib. bdg. 28.56 *(978-1-68076-264-8(8)*, 21469, Epic Extreme) EPIC Pr.

—On a Farm. Andrews, Alexa. 2013. (Penguin Young Readers: Level 1 Ser.). 32p. (J). (ENG.). (gr. -1-1). 16.19 *(978-0-448-46505-0(1))*; (gr. k-1). mass mkt. 4.99 *(978-0-448-46376-6(8)*, Penguin Young Readers) Penguin Young Readers Group.

—Skeleton Princess, 1 vol. Aros, Dana. 2016. (Dark Roads Ser.). (ENG.). 216p. (YA). (gr. 6-12). lib. bdg. 28.56 *(978-1-68076-265-5(6)*, 21471, Epic Extreme) EPIC Pr.

Keimig, Candice & LaViolette, Renee. Deer. O'Brien, Bridget. 2014. (Magic Readers Ser.). (ENG.). 24p. (J). (gr. k-3). 24.21 *(978-1-62402-063-6(1)*, 1503) Magic Wagon.

—Deer Eat & Grow. O'Brien, Bridget. 2014. (Magic Readers Ser.). (ENG.). 24p. (J). (gr. k-3). 25.65 *(978-1-62402-064-3(X)*, 1505) Magic Wagon.

—Deer in the Woods. O'Brien, Bridget. 2014. (Magic Readers Ser.). (ENG.). 24p. (J). (gr. k-3). 25.65 *(978-1-62402-065-0(8)*, 1507) Magic Wagon.

Keino. Homeroom Diaries. Patterson, James & Papademetriou, Lisa. 2014. (ENG.). 272p. (YA). (gr. 7-17). 28.00 *(978-0-316-20762-1(4)*, Jimmy Patterson) Little Brown & Co.

—How Big? Wacky Ways to Compare Size, 1 vol. Gunderson, Jessica. 2013. (Wacky Comparisons Ser.). (ENG.). 24p. (J). (gr. -1-2). 28.65 *(978-1-4048-8325-3(8))*; pap. 8.95 *(978-1-4795-1915-6(4))* Capstone. (Picture Window Bks.).

Keiser, Hugh M. Annie the River Otter: The Adventures of Pelican Pete. Keiser, Frances R. I.t. ed. 2006. (ENG.). 34p. (J). 19.99 *(978-0-9668845-4-8(X))* Sagaponack Bks.

Keiser, Paige. Big Mouth Elizabeth. Vail, Rachel. 2019. (Is for Elizabeth Ser.: 2). (ENG.). 128p. (J). 13.99 *(978-1-250-16217-5(3)*, 900186217) Feiwel & Friends.

—Big Mouth Elizabeth. Vail, Rachel. 2020. (Is for Elizabeth Ser.: 2). (ENG.). 144p. (J). pap. 6.99 *(978-1-250-25025-4(0)*, 900186218) Square Fish.

—Cat Ears on Elizabeth. Vail, Rachel. 2020. (Is for Elizabeth Ser.: 3). (ENG.). 128p. (J). 13.99 *(978-1-250-16220-5(3)*, 900186222) Feiwel & Friends.

—Doodlebug Elizabeth. Vail, Rachel. 2020. (Is for Elizabeth Ser.: 4). (ENG.). 128p. (J). 13.99 *(978-1-250-16222-9(X)*, 900186225) Feiwel & Friends.

—How Much Does God Love You? Adams, Michelle Medlock. 2019. (ENG.). 22p. (J). (gr. -1-1). bds. 6.99 *(978-0-8249-1689-3(1)*, Worthy Kids/Ideals) Worthy Publishing.

—I Love My Hat, 0 vols. Florian, Douglas. 2014. (ENG.). 24p. (J). (gr. -1-2). 16.99 *(978-1-4778-4780-0(4)*, 9781477847800, Two Lions) Amazon Publishing.

—A Is for Elizabeth. Vail, Rachel. 2019. (Is for Elizabeth Ser.: 1). (ENG.). 128p. (J). 13.99 *(978-1-250-16212-0(2)*, 900186212) Feiwel & Friends.

—A Is for Elizabeth. Vail, Rachel. 2020. (Is for Elizabeth Ser.: 1). (ENG.). 144p. (J). pap. 6.99 *(978-1-250-25024-7(2)*, 900186213) Square Fish.

—Little Chef. Weinberg, Elisabeth & Stine, Matt. 2018. (ENG.). 32p. (J). 17.99 *(978-1-250-09169-7(1)*, 900159528) Feiwel & Friends.

—The Little Green Pea. Barber, Alison. 2009. (ENG.). 28p. (J). (gr. k-6). 15.95 *(978-1-58536-448-0(7))* Sleeping Bear Pr.

—Mia Moves Out. Paul, Miranda. 2018. 32p. (J). (gr. -1-2). 16.99 *(978-0-399-55332-5(0)*, Knopf Bks. for Young Readers) Random Hse. Children's Bks.

—Raj the Bookstore Tiger. Pelley, Kathleen T. 2011. 32p. (J). (gr. -1-3). 15.95 *(978-1-58089-230-8(2))* Charlesbridge Publishing, Inc.

Keiser, Paige. A Friend for Bently. Keiser, Paige. 2019. (ENG.). 40p. (J). (gr. -1-3). 17.99 *(978-0-06-264332-2(0))* HarperCollins Pubs.

Keiser, Tammy L. The Perfect Prayer. Rossoff, Donald. 2003. (gr. k-3). 13.95 *(978-0-8074-0853-7(0)*, 164005) URJ Pr.

—The Purim Costume. Schram, Peninnah. 2004. 13.95 *(978-0-8074-0874-2(3)*, 101312) URJ Pr.

—A Year of Jewish Stories: 52 Tales for Children & Their Families. Maisel, Grace Ragues & Shubert, Samantha. (gr. k-3). 29.95 *(978-0-8074-0895-7(6)*, 101071) URJ Pr.

Keister, Douglas, photos by. El Regalo de Fernando. Keister, Douglas. 2004.Tr. of Fernando's Gift. 32p. (J). (gr. 3-3). reprint ed. 16.95 *(978-0-87156-414-6(9))* Sierra Club Bks. for Children.

Keith, Barbara Benson. Mosaic Zoo: An ABC Book. Keith, Barbara Benson. 2008. 32p. (J). per. 8.99 *(978-0-9789688-1-6(6))* Brownian Bee Pr.

Keith, Barbara Benson. The Girls & Boys of Mother Goose. Keith, Barbara Benson, compiled by. 2006. 32p. (J). per. 7.99 *(978-0-9789688-0-9(8))* Brownian Bee Pr.

Keith, Doug. B Is for Baseball: Alphabet Cards. 2011. (ENG.). 26p. (J). 12.95 *(978-1-897476-55-0(8))* Simply Read Bks. CAN. Dist: Ingram Publisher Services.

—The Bored Book. Slater, David Michael. 2017. (ENG.). 32p. (J). (gr. -1-3). 8.99 *(978-1-77229-018-9(1))* Simply Read Bks. CAN. Dist: Ingram Publisher Services.

—Dear Ichiro. Okimoto, Jean Davies. 2006. 29p. (J). (gr. 4-8). reprint ed. 17.00 *(978-1-4223-5803-0(8))* DIANE Publishing Co.

—The Errant Knight. Tompert, Ann. 2003. 32p. 15.95 *(978-0-9701907-6-5(X))* Illumination Arts Publishing Co., Inc.

—Something Special. Cohlene, Terri. 2005. 32p. (J). (gr. -1-k). 15.95 *(978-0-9740190-1-7(1))* Illumination Arts Publishing Co., Inc.

—Wild Waters: The Continuing Adventures of Farley & Breezy. Adler, Kathy. 2008. 64p. (J). pap. 5.99 *(978-0-9768816-2-9(4))* Beachfront Bks.

Keith, Jeanine-Jonee. I Can See Peace. Penshorn, Julie D. 2018. (ENG.). 34p. (J). (YA). (gr. k-3). 19.95 *(978-0-9988691-3-1(9))*; pap. 11.95 *(978-0-9988691-4-8(7))* Growing Communities for Peace.

Keith, Jenny. Day Cat, Night Cat. Owen, Catherine. 2018. (ENG.). 44p. (J). *(978-1-5255-3473-7(4))*; pap. *(978-1-5255-3474-4(2))* FriesenPress.

Keith, Patty J., photos by. I Wish I Was a Mallard but God Made Me a Pekin Instead. Keith, Patty J. 2013. 32p. pap. 12.95 *(978-0-9893303-0-5(3))* Patty's Blooming Words.

—Will You Be My Friend? Even If I Am Different from You. Keith, Patty J. 2013. 36p. pap. 12.95 *(978-0-615-78050-4(4))* Patty's Blooming Words.

Keithline, Brian. A Story from Graandfather Tree. Redwine, Connie. 2005. 25p. (J). (gr. k-2). pap. 7.95 *(978-0-88100-135-8(X))* National Writers Pr., The.

Keitzmueller, Christian, jt. illus. see Bonadonna, Davide.

Keleher, Fran. Game Face. Kantar, Andrew. 2013. 160p. pap. 12.95 *(978-1-61160-566-2(0))* Whiskey Creek Restorations.

Kelleher, Kathie. Away Go the Boats. Hillert, Margaret. 2016. (BeginningtoRead Ser.). (ENG.). 32p. (J). (gr. -1-2). pap. 11.94 *(978-1-60357-933-9(8))*; (gr. 1-2). 22.60 *(978-1-59953-792-4(3))* Norwood Hse. Pr.

—Buon Natale: Learning Songs & Traditions in Italian. Rossi, Sophia. 2007. (Teach Me Ser.). (SPA.). 32p. (J). (gr. -1-3). 19.95 *(978-1-59972-067-8(1))* Teach Me Tapes, Inc.

—Orangutan Houdini. Neme, Laurel. 2014. (ENG.). 32p. (J). (gr. 1-7). 17.95 *(978-1-59373-153-3(1))* Bunker Hill Publishing, Inc.

—Willow's Walkabout: A Children's Guide to Boston. Cunningham, Sheila S. 2012. (ENG.). 32p. (J). (gr. 1-3). 17.95 *(978-1-59373-096-3(9))* Bunker Hill Publishing, Inc.

Kelleher, Michael, jt. illus. see Massey, Mitch.

Kelleher, Terri. How Truman Found His Roar. Fox, Aaron. 2019. (ENG.). 36p. (J). pap. 9.99 ***(978-1-0890-0176-8(2))*** Independently Published.

Kellem-Kellner, Blynda. There Are No Blankets on the Moon. Miller-Gill, Angela. 2004. 32p. (J). 16.00 *(978-0-9716442-2-9(5))* Jackson Publishing.

Keller (Gerald Kelley), E. G. Last Week Tonight with John Oliver Presents a Day in the Life of Marlon Bundo (Better Bundo Book, LGBT Children's Book) Bundo, Marlon. 2018. (ENG.). 40p. (J). (gr. 1-3). 18.99 *(978-1-4521-7380-1(X))* Chronicle Bks. LLC.

Keller, Dick. Santa Visits the Thingumajigs. Keller, Irene. 2005. (ENG.). 28p. (J). (gr. -1-k). bds. 7.95 *(978-0-8249-6619-5(8)*, Ideal Pubns.) Worthy Publishing.

—Thingamajig Book of Manners. Keller, Irene. 2005. (ENG.). 30p. (J). bds. 7.95 *(978-0-8249-6590-7(6)*, Ideal Pubns.) Worthy Publishing.

—Thingamajig Books of Do's & Don'ts. Keller, Irene. 2005. (ENG.). 30p. (J). bds. 7.95 *(978-0-8249-6591-4(4)*, Ideal Pubns.) Worthy Publishing.

Keller, E. G. Everyone Gets a Say. Twiss, Jill. 2020. (ENG.). 32p. (J). (gr. -1-3). 18.99 *(978-0-06-293375-1(2)*, HarperCollins) HarperCollins Pubs. Ltd. GBR. Dist: HarperCollins Pubs.

—The Someone New. Twiss, Jill. 2019. (ENG.). 32p. (J). (gr. -1-3). 18.99 *(978-0-06-293374-4(4))* HarperCollins Pubs.

—To the Moon & Back for You. Serhant, Emilia Bechrakis. 2020. 32p. (J). (gr. -1-3). 17.99 *(978-0-593-17388-6(0))*; (ENG.). lib. bdg. 20.99 *(978-0-593-17389-3(9))* Random Hse. Children's Bks. (Random Hse. Bks. for Young Readers).

Keller, Holly. From Tadpole to Frog. Pfeffer, Wendy. 2015. (Let's-Read-And-Find-Out Science 1 Ser.). (ENG.). 32p. (J). (gr. -1-3). pap. 6.99 *(978-0-06-238186-6(5))* HarperCollins Pubs.

—What's It Like to Be a Fish? Pfeffer, Wendy. 2015. (Let's-Read-And-Find-Out Science 1 Ser.). (ENG.). 32p. (J). (gr. -1-3). pap. 6.99 *(978-0-06-238199-6(7))* HarperCollins Pubs.

—Who Eats What? Food Chains & Food Webs. Lauber, Patricia. 2016. (Let's-Read-And-Find-Out Science 2 Ser.). (ENG.). 32p. (J). (gr. -1-3). pap. 6.99 *(978-0-06-238211-5(X))* HarperCollins Pubs.

Keller, Holly. Farfallina & Marcel. Keller, Holly. 2005. (ENG.). 32p. (J). (gr. -1-4). reprint ed. pap. 7.99 *(978-0-06-443872-8(4)*, Greenwillow Bks.) HarperCollins Pubs.

—Farfallina & Marcel. Keller, Holly. 2005. (gr. -1-3). 17.00 *(978-0-7569-5785-8(0))* Perfection Learning Corp.

—The Hat. Keller, Holly. 2005. (Green Light Readers Level 1 Ser.). (gr. -1-1). 13.95 *(978-0-7569-5241-9(7))* Perfection Learning Corp.

—Help! A Story of Friendship. Keller, Holly. 2007. (ENG.). 40p. (J). (gr. -1-3). 16.99 *(978-0-06-123913-7(5)*, Greenwillow Bks.) HarperCollins Pubs.

—Miranda's Beach Day. Keller, Holly. 2009. 32p. (J). (gr. -1). lib. bdg. 18.89 *(978-0-06-158300-1(6)*, Greenwillow Bks.) HarperCollins Pubs.

—Pearl's New Skates. Keller, Holly. 2005. 24p. (J). lib. bdg. 17.89 *(978-0-06-056281-6(1))* HarperCollins Pubs.

—Sophie's Window. Keller, Holly. 2005. 32p. (J). 16.89 *(978-0-06-056283-0(8))* HarperCollins Pubs.

Keller, Jennifer. The Roaring Twenties: Discover the Era of Prohibition, Flappers, & Jazz. Amidon Lusted, Marcia. 2014. (Inquire & Investigate Ser.). 128p. (J). (gr. 6-10). 22.95 *(978-1-61930-260-0(8)*, 25e5e393-9e69-4daf-b4a5-76dd3d307712) Nomad Pr.

Keller, Jennifer K. Explore Native American Cultures! With 25 Great Projects. Yasuda, Anita. 2013. (Explore Your World Ser.). 96p. (J). (gr. 4-k). pap. 12.95 *(978-1-61930-160-3(1)*, 6722d8bf-7417-46c3-b9e4-bd4b63e9a0f0) Nomad Pr.

Keller, Laurie. Marty Frye, Private Eye: The Case of the Missing Action Figure. Tashjian, Janet. 2018. (Marty Frye, Private Eye Ser.: 1). (ENG.). 112p. (J). pap. 7.99 *(978-1-250-15880-2(X)*, 900185533) Square Fish.
—Marty Frye, Private Eye Bk. 2. Tashjian, Janet. 2017. (Marty Frye, Private Eye Ser.: 1). (ENG.). 96p. (J). 15.99 *(978-1-250-11661-1(9)*, 900172045, Holt, Henry & Co. Bks. For Young Readers) Holt, Henry & Co.
—Marty Frye, Private Eye: the Case of the Busted Video Games. Tashjian, Janet. 2019. (Marty Frye, Private Eye Ser.: 3). (ENG.). 96p. (J). 15.99 *(978-1-62779-461-9(1)*, 900151450, Holt, Henry & Co. Bks. For Young Readers) Holt, Henry & Co.
—Marty Frye, Private Eye: the Case of the Busted Video Games & Other Mysteries. Tashjian, Janet. 2020. (Marty Frye, Private Eye Ser.: 3). (ENG.). 32p. (J). pap. 6.99 *(978-1-250-30848-1(8)*, 900198355) Square Fish.
—Marty Frye, Private Eye: the Case of the Stolen Poodle. Tashjian, Janet. 2018. (Marty Frye, Private Eye Ser.: 2). (ENG.). 112p. (J). pap. 6.99 *(978-1-250-15879-6(6)*, 900185532) Square Fish.
—Marty Frye, Private Eye: the Case of the Stolen Poodle Bk. 2. Tashjian, Janet. 2017. (Marty Frye, Private Eye Ser.: 2). (ENG.). 96p. (J). 15.99 *(978-1-62779-460-2(3)*, 900151449, Holt, Henry & Co. Bks. For Young Readers) Holt, Henry & Co.
—Pluto Gets the Call. Rex, Adam. 2019. (ENG.). 48p. (J). (gr. -1-3). 17.99 *(978-1-5344-1453-2(3)*, Beach Lane Bks.) Beach Lane Bks.
—Toys. Wulffson, Don. 2014. (ENG.). (J). (gr. 3-7). lib. bdg. 20.60 *(978-1-62765-596-5(4))* Perfection Learning Corp.
Keller, Laurie. Arnie the Doughnut. Keller, Laurie. 2005. (J). (gr. k-4). 29.95 *(978-0-439-76641-8(9)*, WHCD649) Weston Woods Studios, Inc.
—Arnie, the Doughnut. Keller, Laurie. rev. ed. 2003. (Adventures of Arnie the Doughnut Ser.: 1). (ENG.). 40p. (J). (gr. -1-3). 19.99 *(978-0-8050-6283-0(1)*, 900018945, Holt, Henry & Co. Bks. For Young Readers) Holt, Henry & Co.
—Do unto Otters: A Book about Manners. Keller, Laurie. 2007. (ENG.). 40p. (J). (gr. k-3). 18.99 *(978-0-8050-7996-8(3)*, 900034600, Holt, Henry & Co. Bks. For Young Readers) Holt, Henry & Co.
—Do unto Otters: A Book about Manners. Keller, Laurie. 2009. (ENG.). 40p. (J). (gr. k-3). pap. 8.99 *(978-0-312-58140-4(8)*, 900061994) Square Fish.
Keller, Laurie. Hello, Arnie! An Arnie the Doughnut Story. Keller, Laurie. 2020. (Adventures of Arnie the Doughnut Ser.: 5). (ENG.). 40p. (J). 18.99 ***(978-1-250-10724-4(5)***, 900164826, Holt, Henry & Co. Bks. For Young Readers) Holt, Henry & Co.
Keller, Laurie. Open Wide: Tooth School Inside. Keller, Laurie. rev. ed. 2003. (ENG.). 40p. (J). (gr. k-3). pap. 8.99 *(978-0-8050-7268-6(3)*, 900018981) Square Fish.
—Open Wide: Tooth School Inside. Keller, Laurie. unabr. ed. 2006. (J). (gr. k-5). 18.95 *(978-0-439-84920-3(9)*, WPCD650); 29.95 *(978-0-439-84918-0(7)*, WHCD650) Weston Woods Studios, Inc.
—Potato Pants! Keller, Laurie. 2018. (ENG.). 40p. (J). 17.99 *(978-1-250-10723-7(7)*, 900164825, Holt, Henry & Co. Bks. For Young Readers) Holt, Henry & Co.
—The Scrambled States of America Talent Show. Keller, Laurie. 2010. (ENG.). 40p. (J). (gr. 2-5). pap. 8.99 *(978-0-312-62824-6(2)*, 900066819) Square Fish.
Keller, Laurie, jt. illus. see Willems, Mo.
Keller, Matt. Matthew's Bible Stories: Esther Is Brave. Burkum, Rachel. 2011. 52p. (J). 10.00 *(978-1-59799-083-7(3))* Deaf Missions.
Keller, Matthew M. The Whirl Story Bible: Lively Bible Stories to Inspire Faith, Vol. Gibbons, Erin, ed. 2015. (ENG.). 416p. (J). (gr. -1-5). 22.99 *(978-1-5064-0000-6(0)*, Sparkhouse Family) Augsburg Fortress, Pubs.
Keller-Miller, LeAnn Marie. When I Grow Up: An A-Z Poem Book for Children & Their Dreams. 2005. *(978-0-9711480-4-8(X))* ICanPublish.
Keller, Nathan J. The Relik. Keller, Nathan J. 2016. (ENG.). (J). pap. *(978-0-9956814-2-2(2))* NJK Creative Services.
Kelley, Angelina Faith. Herb Worm. Kelley, Juliet Davies. 2019. (Roma the Tomato Girl Ser.: Vol. 2). (ENG.). 54p. (J). pap. 6.00 *(978-1-393-51187-8(2))* Draft2Digital.
—Roma the Tomato Girl. Kelley, Juliet Davies. 2019. (Roma the Tomato Girl Ser.: Vol. 1). (ENG.). 44p. (J). pap. 5.99 *(978-1-386-80652-3(8))* Draft2Digital.
Kelley, Beverly. A Donkey's Tale. Gabbert, Elayne. 2018. (ENG.). 54p. (J). pap. 12.99 *(978-1-7292-1609-5(9))* Independently Published.
Kelley, D. G., et al. An Illustrated Guide to Common Rocks & Their Minerals. Allan, David & Brown, Vinson. rev. ed. 2003. 60p. (Orig.). pap. 4.95 *(978-0-87961-054-8(9))* Naturegraph Pubs., Inc.
Kelley, Gary. And the Soldiers Sang. Lewis, J. Patrick. (ENG.). 32p. (J). 2014. (gr. 1-3). pap. 9.99 *(978-0-89812-975-5(3)*, Creative Paperbacks); 2011. (gr. 4-7). 19.99 *(978-1-56846-220-2(4)*, Creative Editions) Creative Co., The.
—Dark Fiddler. Frisch, Aaron. 2008. (ENG.). 32p. (J). (gr. 1-3). 17.95 *(978-1-56846-200-4(X)*, Creative Editions) Creative Co., The.
—Edgar Allan Poe. Frisch, Aaron. 2014. (Voices in Poetry Ser.). 47p. (J). lib. bdg. 35.65 *(978-1-60818-324-1(6)*, Creative Education) Creative Co., The.
—Eleanor, Quiet No More. Rappaport, Doreen. 2009. (Big Words Book Ser.). 48p. (J). (gr. -1-3). 16.99 *(978-0-7868-5141-6(4))* Hyperion Pr.
—Harlem Hellfighters. Lewis, J. Patrick. 2014. (ENG.). 32p. (J). (gr. 4-7). 19.99 *(978-1-56846-246-2(8)*, Creative Editions) Creative Co., The.
—Jacob Riis's Camera: Bringing Light to Tenement Children. O'Neill, Alexis. 2020. (ENG.). 48p. (J). (gr. 2-5). 18.99 *(978-1-62979-866-0(5)*, Calkins Creek) Boyds Mills Pr.
—The Necklace. de Maupassant, Guy. 2004. (ENG.). 48p. (J). (gr. 4-7). 19.95 *(978-1-56846-193-9(3))* Creative Co., The.
—Next Year. Vander Zee, Ruth. 2017. (ENG.). 32p. (J). (gr. 4-7). 18.99 *(978-1-56846-282-0(4)*, Creative Editions) Creative Co., The.
—The Stolen Smile. Lewis, J. Patrick. 2nd ed. 2015. (ENG.). 40p. (J). (gr. 2-4). 16.99 *(978-1-56846-281-3(6)*, Creative Editions) Creative Co., The.
Kelley, Gary. Virginia Was a Spy. Urdahl, Catherine. 2020. (ENG.). 32p. (J). (gr. 3-5). 19.99 ***(978-1-56846-348-3(0)***, Creative Editions) Creative Co., The.
Kelley, Gerald. Amazing Out-of-Body Experiences. Green, Carl R. & Sanford, William R. 2011. (Investigating the Unknown Ser.). 48p. (gr. 5-7). pap. 10.53 *(978-1-59845-307-2(6))*; lib. bdg. 26.27 *(978-0-7660-3822-6(X))* Enslow Publishing, LLC.
—Astonishing Mind Powers. Green, Carl R. & Sanford, William R. 2011. (Investigating the Unknown Ser.). 48p. (gr. 5-7). pap. 10.53 *(978-1-59845-305-8(X))*; lib. bdg. 26.27 *(978-0-7660-3820-2(3))* Enslow Publishing, LLC.
—Boas & Pythons: Cool Pets! Silverstein, Alvin et al. 2012. (Far-Out & Unusual Pets Ser.). 48p. (gr. 3-3). 26.27 *(978-0-7660-3878-3(5)*, Enslow Elementary) Enslow Publishing, LLC.
—Boas & Pythons: Cool Pets! Silverstein, Alvin et al. 2012. (Far-Out & Unusual Pets Ser.). 48p. (gr. 3-3). pap. 10.53 *(978-1-4644-0129-9(2)*, Enslow Elementary) Enslow Publishing, LLC.
—The Boy Who Cried Wolf: Classic Tales Edition. Smith, Carrie. 2011. (Classic Tales Ser.). (J). *(978-1-936258-59-8(5))* Benchmark Education Co.
—Chocolate Ants, Maggot Cheese, & More: The Yucky Food Book. Silverstein, Alvin et al. 2010. (Yucky Science Ser.). 48p. (gr. 5-7). 26.27 *(978-0-7660-3315-3(5))* Enslow Publishing, LLC.
—Creepy, Crawly Jokes about Spiders & Other Bugs: Laugh & Learn about Science. Stewart, Melissa. 2012. (Super Silly Science Jokes Ser.). 48p. (gr. 3-3). 26.27 *(978-0-7660-3966-7(8))*; pap. 10.53 *(978-1-4644-0167-1(5))* Enslow Publishing, LLC. (Enslow Elementary).
—Dino-Mite Jokes about Prehistoric Life: Laugh & Learn about Science. Stewart, Melissa. 2012. (Super Silly Science Jokes Ser.). 48p. (gr. 3-3). 26.27 *(978-0-7660-3968-1(4)*, Enslow Elementary); pap. 10.53 *(978-1-4644-0164-0(0)*, Enslow Elementary); E-Book 26.27 *(978-1-4645-1071-7(7))* Enslow Publishing, LLC.
—Discovering Past Lives. Green, Carl R. & Sanford, William R. 2011. (Investigating the Unknown Ser.). 48p. (gr. 5-7). pap. 10.53 *(978-1-59845-308-9(4))*; lib. bdg. 26.27 *(978-0-7660-3818-9(1))* Enslow Publishing, LLC.
—Don't Let the Barber Pull Your Teeth: Could You Survive Medieval Medicine? Bredeson, Carmen. 2012. (Ye Yucky Middle Ages Ser.). 48p. (gr. 5-7). pap. 10.53 *(978-1-59845-373-7(4))*; lib. bdg. 26.27 *(978-0-7660-3693-2(6))* Enslow Publishing, LLC.
—Dung Beetles, Slugs, Leeches, & More: The Yucky Animal Book. Silverstein, Alvin et al. 2010. (Yucky Science Ser.). 48p. (gr. 5-7). 26.27 *(978-0-7660-3317-7(1))* Enslow Publishing, LLC.
—Ferrets: Cool Pets! Silverstein, Alvin et al. 2011. (Far-Out & Unusual Pets Ser.). 48p. (gr. 3-3). lib. bdg. 26.27 *(978-0-7660-3683-3(9))* Enslow Publishing, LLC.
—Grover Cleveland, Again! A Treasury of American Presidents. Burns, Ken. 2016. 96p. (J). (gr. 5-12). 25.00 *(978-0-385-39209-9(5))*; (ENG.). lib. bdg. 28.00 *(978-0-385-39210-5(9))* Random Hse. Children's Bks. (Knopf Bks. for Young Readers).
—Hairless Cats: Cool Pets! Silverstein, Alvin et al. 2011. (Far-Out & Unusual Pets Ser.). 48p. (gr. 3-3). lib. bdg. 26.27 *(978-0-7660-3688-8(X)*, Enslow Elementary) Enslow Publishing, LLC.
—Hermit Crabs: Cool Pets! Silverstein, Alvin et al. 2011. (Far-Out & Unusual Pets Ser.). 48p. (gr. 3-3). lib. bdg. 26.27 *(978-0-7660-3684-0(7))* Enslow Publishing, LLC.
—Hissing Cockroaches: Cool Pets! Silverstein, Alvin et al. 2011. (Far-Out & Unusual Pets Ser.). 48p. (gr. 3-3). lib. bdg. 26.27 *(978-0-7660-3685-7(5))* Enslow Publishing, LLC.
—Iguanas: Cool Pets! Silverstein, Alvin et al. 2011. (Far-Out & Unusual Pets Ser.). 48p. (gr. 3-3). lib. bdg. 26.27 *(978-0-7660-3686-4(3))* Enslow Publishing, LLC.
—A Is for America: A Patriotic Alphabet Book. Stone, Tanya Lee. 2011. (ENG.). 24p. (J). (gr. -1-k). mass mkt. 5.99 *(978-0-8431-9877-5(X)*, Price Stern Sloan) Penguin Young Readers Group.
—Lazy Mary. Fuerst, Jeffrey B. 2010. (Rising Readers Ser.). (J). 3.49 *(978-1-60719-699-0(9))* Newmark Learning LLC.
—Lazy Mary Gets Up. Fuerst, Jeffrey B. 2009. (Reader's Theater Nursery Rhymes & Songs Set B Ser.). 48p. (J). pap. *(978-1-60859-156-5(5))* Benchmark Education Co.
—The Legend of the Jersey Devil. Noble, Trinka Hakes. 2013. (ENG.). 32p. (J). (gr. 2-5). 16.99 *(978-1-58536-837-2(7)*, 202886) Sleeping Bear Pr.
—The Little Girl with Curl. Blane, Francisco. 2009. (Reader's Theater Nursery Rhymes & Songs Set B Ser.). 48p. (J). pap. *(978-1-60859-157-2(3))* Benchmark Education Co.
—Little Red Riding Hood: Classic Tales Edition. Smith, Carrie. 2011. (Classic Tales Ser.). (J). *(978-1-936258-75-8(7))* Benchmark Education Co.
—Little Red Riding Hood - 6 Pack: Set of 6 with Common Core Teacher Materials. 2015. (Classic Tales Ser.). (J). (gr. k-1). 39.00 *(978-1-5125-8352-6(9))* Benchmark Education Co.
—Miniature Horses: Cool Pets! Silverstein, Alvin et al. 2012. (Far-Out & Unusual Pets Ser.). 48p. (gr. 3-3). 26.27 *(978-0-7660-3880-6(7)*, Enslow Elementary) Enslow Publishing, LLC.
—Miniature Horses: Cool Pets! Silverstein, Alvin et al. 2012. (Far-Out & Unusual Pets Ser.). 48p. (gr. 3-3). pap. 10.53 *(978-1-4644-0125-1(X)*, Enslow Elementary) Enslow Publishing, LLC.
—Mountains of Jokes about Rocks, Minerals, & Soil: Laugh & Learn about Science. Stewart, Melissa. 2012. (Super Silly Science Jokes Ser.). 48p. (gr. 3-3). 26.27 *(978-0-7660-3969-8(2))*; pap. 10.53 *(978-1-4644-0165-7(9))* Enslow Publishing, LLC. (Enslow Elementary).
—The Mysterious Secrets of Dreams. Green, Carl R. & Sanford, William R. 2011. (Investigating the Unknown Ser.). 48p. (gr. 5-7). pap. 10.53 *(978-1-59845-306-5(8))*; lib. bdg. 26.27 *(978-0-7660-3821-9(1))* Enslow Publishing, LLC.
—The Mystery of Fortune-Telling. Green, Carl R. & Sanford, William R. 2011. (Investigating the Unknown Ser.). 48p. (gr. 5-7). pap. 10.53 *(978-1-59845-304-1(1))*; lib. bdg. 26.27 *(978-0-7660-3819-6(X))* Enslow Publishing, LLC.
—Out of This World Jokes about the Solar System: Laugh & Learn about Science. Stewart, Melissa. 2012. (Super Silly Science Jokes Ser.). 48p. (gr. 3-3). 26.27 *(978-0-7660-3970-4(6))*; pap. 10.53 *(978-1-4644-0166-4(7))* Enslow Publishing, LLC. (Enslow Elementary).
—Poison Dart Frogs: Cool Pets! Silverstein, Alvin et al. 2012. (Far-Out & Unusual Pets Ser.). 48p. (gr. 3-3). 26.27 *(978-0-7660-3881-3(5)*, Enslow Elementary) Enslow Publishing, LLC.
—Poison Dart Frogs: Cool Pets! Silverstein, Alvin et al. 2012. (Far-Out & Unusual Pets Ser.). 48p. (gr. 3-3). pap. 10.53 *(978-1-4644-0126-8(8)*, Enslow Elementary) Enslow Publishing, LLC.
—Poop Collectors, Armpit Sniffers, & More: The Yucky Jobs Book. Silverstein, Alvin et al. 2010. (Yucky Science Ser.). 48p. (gr. 5-7). 26.27 *(978-0-7660-3316-0(3))* Enslow Publishing, LLC.
—Potbellied Pigs: Cool Pets! Silverstein, Alvin et al. 2011. (Far-Out & Unusual Pets Ser.). 48p. (gr. 3-3). lib. bdg. 26.27 *(978-0-7660-3687-1(1))* Enslow Publishing, LLC.
—Rats: Cool Pets! Silverstein, Alvin et al. 2012. (Far-Out & Unusual Pets Ser.). 48p. (gr. 3-3). 26.27 *(978-0-7660-3882-0(3)*, Enslow Elementary) Enslow Publishing, LLC.
—Rats: Cool Pets! Silverstein, Alvin et al. 2012. (Far-Out & Unusual Pets Ser.). 48p. (gr. 3-3). pap. 10.53 *(978-1-4644-0127-5(6)*, Enslow Elementary) Enslow Publishing, LLC.
—Row, Row, Row Your Boat. Blane, Francisco. 2010. (Rising Readers Ser.). (J). 3.49 *(978-1-60719-695-2(6))* Newmark Learning LLC.
—Sensing the Unknown. Green, Carl R. & Sanford, William R. 2011. (Investigating the Unknown Ser.). 48p. (gr. 5-7). 26.27 *(978-0-7660-3823-3(8))*; pap. 10.53 *(978-1-59845-303-4(3))* Enslow Publishing, LLC.
—Shockingly Silly Jokes about Electricity & Magnetism: Laugh & Learn about Science. Stewart, Melissa. 2012. (Super Silly Science Jokes Ser.). 48p. (gr. 3-3). 26.27 *(978-0-7660-3967-4(6)*, Enslow Elementary); pap. 10.53 *(978-1-4644-0163-3(2)*, Enslow Elementary); E-Book 26.27 *(978-1-4645-1070-0(9))* Enslow Publishing, LLC.
—Smog, Oil Spills, Sewage, & More: The Yucky Pollution Book. Silverstein, Alvin et al. 2010. (Yucky Science Ser.). 48p. (gr. 5-7). 26.27 *(978-0-7660-3313-9(9))* Enslow Publishing, LLC.
—Snot, Poop, Vomit, & More: The Yucky Body Book. Silverstein, Alvin et al. 2010. (Yucky Science Ser.). 48p. (gr. 5-7). 26.27 *(978-0-7660-3318-4(X))* Enslow Publishing, LLC.
—Sparky & Tidbit. Galbraith, Kathryn O. 2015. (Ready-To-Reads Ser.). (ENG.). 40p. (J). (gr. 1-3). pap. 4.99 *(978-1-4814-0424-2(5)*, Simon Spotlight) Simon Spotlight.
—Sweaty Suits of Armor: Could You Survive Being a Knight? Stiefel, Chana. 2012. (Ye Yucky Middle Ages Ser.). 48p. (gr. 5-7). pap. 10.53 *(978-1-59845-376-8(9))*; lib. bdg. 26.27 *(978-0-7660-3784-7(3))* Enslow Publishing, LLC.
—T Is for Turkey. Stone, Tanya Lee. 2009. (ENG.). 24p. (J). (gr. -1-k). mass mkt. 5.99 *(978-0-8431-2570-2(5)*, Price Stern Sloan) Penguin Young Readers Group.
—Tapeworms, Foot Fungus, Lice, & More: The Yucky Disease Book. Silverstein, Alvin et al. 2010. (Yucky Science Ser.). 48p. (gr. 5-7). 26.27 *(978-0-7660-3314-6(7))* Enslow Publishing, LLC.
—Tarantulas: Cool Pets! Silverstein, Alvin et al. 2012. (Far-Out & Unusual Pets Ser.). 48p. (gr. 3-3). 26.27 *(978-0-7660-3883-7(1)*, Enslow Elementary) Enslow Publishing, LLC.
—Tarantulas: Cool Pets! Silverstein, Alvin et al. 2012. (Far-Out & Unusual Pets Ser.). 48p. (gr. 3-3). pap. 10.53 *(978-1-4644-0128-2(4)*, Enslow Elementary) Enslow Publishing, LLC.
—There's a Rat in My Soup: Could You Survive Medieval Food? Stiefel, Chana. 2012. (Ye Yucky Middle Ages Ser.). 48p. (gr. 5-7). pap. 10.53 *(978-1-59845-375-1(0))*; lib. bdg. 26.27 *(978-0-7660-3785-4(1))* Enslow Publishing, LLC.
—Wacky Weather & Silly Season Jokes: Laugh & Learn about Science. Stewart, Melissa. 2012. (Super Silly Science Jokes Ser.). 48p. (gr. 3-3). 26.27 *(978-0-7660-3971-1(4))*; pap. 10.53 *(978-1-4644-0168-8(3))* Enslow Publishing, LLC. (Enslow Elementary).
—Ye Castle Stinketh: Could You Survive Living in a Castle? Stiefel, Chana. 2012. (Ye Yucky Middle Ages Ser.). 48p. (gr. 5-7). pap. 10.53 *(978-1-59845-374-4(2))*; lib. bdg. 26.27 *(978-0-7660-3786-1(X))* Enslow Publishing, LLC.
Kelley, Gerald. Please Please the Bees. Kelley, Gerald. 2017. (ENG.). 32p. (J). (gr. -1-3). 16.99 *(978-0-8075-5183-7(X)*, 080755183X) Whitman, Albert & Co.
Kelley, Giuliana. I Am a Part of All Nature. Giffone, Lucille. 2018. (ENG.). 28p. (J). 21.95 *(978-1-64003-557-6(2))*; pap. 12.95 *(978-1-64003-511-9(7))* Covenant Bks.
Kelley, Maria Felicia. Buz Words: Discovering Words in Pairs. Kelley, Maria Felicia. 2007. (J). (gr. -1-3). 32p. 14.95 *(978-0-9650918-1-7(3))*; 29p. per. 7.95 *(978-0-9650918-2-4(1))* April Arts Press & Productions.
Kelley, Mark, photos by. Once upon Alaska: A Kid's Photo Book. Jans, Nick. 2013. (ENG., 56p. (J). 15.95 *(978-1-880865-20-0(3))* Kelley, Mark.
Kelley, Marty. Crustacean Vacation, 1 vol. Benoit, Brian. 2012. (ENG.). 36p. (J). 17.95 *(978-1-934031-95-7(X)*, 394525ff-17a5-4ca7-a881-54fe24bbc3ae) Islandport Pr., Inc.
—M Is for Money: An Economics Alphabet. Shoulders, Michael & Shoulders, Debbie. 2015. (Science Alphabet Ser.). (ENG.). 32p. (J). (gr. 3-6). 16.99 *(978-1-58536-817-4(2)*, 203953) Sleeping Bear Pr.
—Missile Toe: A Very Confused Christmas. Scillian, Devin. 2017. (ENG.). 32p. (J). (gr. k-3). 16.99 *(978-1-58536-371-1(5)*, 204328) Sleeping Bear Pr.
—Santa's Underwear. Figley, Marty Rhodes. 2016. (ENG.). 32p. (J). (gr. k-3). 16.99 *(978-1-58536-954-6(3)*, 204109) Sleeping Bear Pr.
—Spring Goes Squish: A Vibrant Volume of Vociferous Vernal Verse. 2008. (J). (gr. k-2). 14.95 *(978-1-55933-315-3(4))* Zino Pr. Children's Bks.
—Winter Woes. 2003. 32p. (J). 12.95 *(978-1-55933-306-1(5))* Zino Pr. Children's Bks.
Kelley, Marty. The Best Friend Bandit. Kelley, Marty. 2017. (Molly Mac Ser.). (ENG.). 56p. (J). (gr. k-2). lib. bdg. 22.65 *(978-1-5158-0836-7(X)*, Picture Window Bks.) Capstone.
—Lucky Break. Kelley, Marty. 2017. (Molly Mac Ser.). (ENG.). 56p. (J). (gr. k-2). lib. bdg. 22.65 *(978-1-5158-0837-4(8)*, Picture Window Bks.) Capstone.
—Molly Mac. Kelley, Marty. 2017. (Molly Mac Ser.). (ENG.). 56p. (J). (gr. k-2). pap., pap., pap. 19.80 *(978-1-5158-0864-0(5)*, 25924, Picture Window Bks.) Capstone.
—Sammy's Great Escape. Kelley, Marty. 2017. (Molly Mac Ser.). (ENG.). 56p. (J). (gr. k-2). lib. bdg. 22.65 *(978-1-5158-0835-0(1)*, Picture Window Bks.) Capstone.
—Three . . . Two . . .one . . . Blastoff! Kelley, Marty. 2018. (Molly Mac Ser.). (ENG.). 56p. (J). (gr. k-2). pap. 4.95 *(978-1-5158-2391-9(1)*, 137206, Picture Window Bks.) Capstone.
—Three ... Two ... One ... Blastoff! Kelley, Marty. 2018. (Molly Mac Ser.). (ENG.). 56p. (J). (gr. k-2). lib. bdg. 22.65 *(978-1-5158-2387-2(3)*, 137202, Picture Window Bks.) Capstone.
—Tooth Fairy Trouble. Kelley, Marty. 2017. (Molly Mac Ser.). (ENG.). 56p. (J). (gr. k-2). lib. bdg. 22.65 *(978-1-5158-0838-1(6)*, Picture Window Bks.) Capstone.
—Top Secret Author Visit. Kelley, Marty. 2018. (Molly Mac Ser.). (ENG.). 56p. (J). (gr. k-2). lib. bdg. 22.65 *(978-1-5158-2386-5(5)*, 137201, Picture Window Bks.) Capstone.
Kelley, Nichole, jt. illus. see Maguire, Rachel.
Kelley, Patrick. And God Blessed the Irish: The Story of Patrick. Driscoll, Christ. 2007. 59p. (J). (gr. 3-7). 14.95 *(978-1-929039-40-1(9))* Ambassador Bks., Inc.
—Dorothy Day: Champion of the Poor. Stone, Elaine Murray. 2004. (ENG.). 128p. (J). pap. 9.95 *(978-0-8091-6719-7(0)*, 6719-0) Paulist Pr.
—Jake's First Word. Luongo, Jane. 2003. (Books for Young Learners). 16p. (J). 5.75 net. *(978-1-57274-258-1(5)*, 2456, Bks. for Young Learners) Owen, Richard C. Pubs., Inc.
Kelley, True. How People Learned to Fly. Hodgkins, Fran. 2007. (Let's-Read-And-Find-Out Science 2 Ser.). (ENG.). 40p. (J). (gr. -1-3). 16.99 *(978-0-06-029558-5(9)*, Collins); pap. 5.99 *(978-0-06-445221-2(2))* HarperCollins Pubs.
—How People Learned to Fly. Hodgkins, Fran. 2007. (Let's-Read-and-Find-Out Science Ser.). 33p. (gr. k-4). 16.00 *(978-0-7569-8101-3(8))* Perfection Learning Corp.
—Ready, Set, Preschool! Stories, Poems & Picture Games with an Educational Guide for Parents. Hays, Anna Jane. 2016. 40p. (J). (gr. -1-2). 7.99 *(978-1-101-94024-2(7)*, Dragonfly Bks.) Random Hse. Children's Bks.
—What Makes a Magnet? Branley, Franklyn M. rev. ed. 2016. (Let's-Read-And-Find-Out Science 2 Ser.). (ENG.). 32p. (J). (gr. -1-3). pap. 6.99 *(978-0-06-233801-3(3))* HarperCollins Pubs.
—Who Was George Washington? Edwards, Roberta & Who HQ. 2009. (Who Was? Ser.). 112p. (J). (gr. 3-7). pap. 5.99 *(978-0-448-44892-3(0)*, Penguin Workshop) Penguin Young Readers Group.
—Who Was Leonardo Da Vinci? Edwards, Roberta & Who HQ. 2005. (Who Was? Ser.). (ENG.). 112p. (J). (gr. 3-7). pap. 5.99 *(978-0-448-44301-0(5)*, Penguin Workshop) Penguin Young Readers Group.
—Who Was Leonardo da Vinci? Edwards, Roberta. 2005. (Who Was... ? Ser.). 106p. (J). (gr. 2-6). 12.65 *(978-0-7569-6971-4(9))* Perfection Learning Corp.
Kelley, True. ¿Quién Fue Pablo Picasso? Kelley, True. Who HQ. 2012. (¿Quién Fue? Ser.). 112p. (J). (gr. 3-7). pap. 7.99 *(978-0-448-46175-5(7)*, Penguin Workshop) Penguin Young Readers Group.
—Who Was Pablo Picasso? Kelley, True. Who HQ. 2009. (Who Was? Ser.). (ENG.). 103p. (J). (gr. 3-7). pap. 5.99 *(978-0-448-44987-6(0)*, Penguin Workshop) Penguin Young Readers Group.
Kellman, Craig. Secret Life of Pets. Golden Books Staff & Shealy, Dennis R. 2016. (Little Golden Book Ser.). 24p. (J). (gr. -1-2). 4.99 *(978-0-399-55481-0(5)*, Golden Bks.) Random Hse. Children's Bks.
Kellman, Craig, jt. illus. see Golden Books Staff.
Kellogg, Steven. The Baby Beebee Bird. Massie, Diane Redfield. 2003. (ENG.). 32p. (J). (gr. -1-1). pap. 7.99 *(978-0-06-051784-7(0))* HarperCollins Pubs.
—Clorinda. Kinerk, Robert. 2007. (ENG.). 40p. (J). (gr. -1-3). 8.99 *(978-1-4169-3964-1(4)*, Simon & Schuster/Paula Wiseman Bks.) Simon & Schuster/Paula Wiseman Bks.
—Clorinda Plays Baseball! Kinerk, Robert. 2012. (ENG.). 40p. (J). (gr. -1-3). 16.99 *(978-0-689-86865-8(0)*, Simon & Schuster/Paula Wiseman Bks.) Simon & Schuster/Paula Wiseman Bks.
—Clorinda Takes Flight. Kinerk, Robert. 2007. (ENG.). 40p. (J). (gr. -1-3). 19.99 *(978-0-689-86864-1(2)*, Simon & Schuster/Paula Wiseman Bks.) Simon & Schuster/Paula Wiseman Bks.
—Come Back, Cat. Nodset, Joan L. 2008. 40p. (J). (gr. -1-3). lib. bdg. 17.89 *(978-0-06-028082-6(4))* HarperCollins Pubs.
—Cuanto Es un Millon? Schwartz, David M. 2003. (SPA.). (J). (gr. k-3). pap. 3.96 net. *(978-0-590-47393-4(X)*, SO30942) Scholastic, Inc.
—Farty Marty. Ward, B. J. 2013. (ENG.). 32p. (J). (gr. -1-3). 16.99 *(978-1-4424-3901-6(7)*, Simon & Schuster Bks. For Young Readers) Simon & Schuster Bks. For Young Readers.

K

—The Green Bath. Mahy, Margaret. 2013. (J). pap. *(978-0-545-20668-6(5)*, Levine, Arthur A. Bks.) Scholastic, Inc.

—How Much Is a Million? Schwartz, David M. 20th anniv. ed. 2004. (Reading Rainbow Bks.). (ENG.). 40p. (J). (gr. -1-3). pap. 7.99 *(978-0-688-09933-6(5)*, Collins) HarperCollins Pubs.

—If You Decide to Go to the Moon. McNulty, Faith. 2005. (ENG.). 48p. (J). (gr. -1-3). 18.99 *(978-0-590-48359-9(5)*, Scholastic Pr.) Scholastic, Inc.

—The Invisible Moose. Haseley, Dennis. 2008. (ENG.). 40p. (J). (gr. -1-3). pap. 7.99 *(978-0-14-241066-0(7)*, Puffin Books) Penguin Young Readers Group.

—Is Your Mama a Llama? Guarino, Deborah. (ENG.). (J). (gr. -1-3). 2006. 18.95 *(978-0-439-87594-3(3))*; 2004. 32p. pap. 7.99 *(978-0-439-59842-2(7)*, Scholastic Paperbacks); 2006. audio compact disk 10.99 *(978-0-439-87588-2(9))* Scholastic, Inc.

—Jimmy's Boa & the Bungee Jump Slam Dunk. Noble, Trinka Hakes. 2005. 28p. (gr. -1-3). 16.00 *(978-0-7569-5765-0(6))* Perfection Learning Corp.

—Millions to Measure. Schwartz, David M. (ENG.). 40p. (J). (gr. k-7). 2003. 17.99 *(978-0-688-12916-3(1))*; 2006. reprint ed. pap. 7.99 *(978-0-06-084806-4(5))* HarperCollins Pubs.

—Santa Claus Is Comin' to Town. Coots, J. Fred. 2004. 40p. (J). (gr. -1-3). 16.89 *(978-0-06-623849-4(8))* HarperCollins Pubs.

—Snowflakes Fall. Maclachlan, Patricia. 2013. 32p. (J). (gr. -1-2). 17.99 *(978-0-385-37693-8(6))* Random Hse. Children's Bks.

—The Word Pirates. Cooper, Susan. 2019. 40p. (J). (gr. -1-3). 18.99 *(978-0-8234-4359-8(0)*, Neal Porter Bks) Holiday Hse., Inc.

Kellogg, Steven. Johnny Appleseed. Kellogg, Steven. 2008. (ENG.). 48p. (J). (gr. -1-3). reprint ed. pap. 7.99 *(978-0-688-14025-0(4))* HarperCollins Pubs.

—The Missing Mitten Mystery. Kellogg, Steven. 2004. (Picture Puffins Ser.). (gr. -1-3). 17.00 *(978-0-7569-2581-9(9))* Perfection Learning Corp.

—The Mysterious Tadpole. Kellogg, Steven. 25th anniv. ed. 2004. (ENG.). 40p. (J). (gr. k-3). reprint ed. pap. 8.99 *(978-0-14-240140-8(4)*, Puffin Books) Penguin Young Readers Group.

—Paul Bunyan. Kellogg, Steven. 20th anniv. ed. 2004. (ENG.). 48p. (J). (gr. -1-3). pap. 7.99 *(978-0-688-05800-5(0)*, HarperCollins) HarperCollins Pubs. Ltd. GBR. Dist: HarperCollins Pubs.

—Pinkerton, Behave! Revised & Reillustrated Edition. Kellogg, Steven. 2019. (ENG.). 32p. (J). (gr. -1-3). pap. 8.99 *(978-0-451-48152-8(6)*, Puffin Books) Penguin Young Readers Group.

Kellogg, Steven. Johnny Appleseed. Kellogg, Steven, retold by. 2008. (ENG.). (J). (gr. -1-3). lib. bdg. 17.60 *(978-1-62765-183-7(7))* Perfection Learning Corp.

Kellogg, Steven. Santa Claus Is Comin' to Town. Kellogg, Steven, tr. Gillespie, Haven & Coots, J. Fred. 2004. (ENG.). 40p. (J). (gr. -1-3). 15.99 *(978-0-688-14938-3(3))* HarperCollins Pubs.

Kelly, Becky. Heavenly Skies & Lullabies: Illustrated Songbook & CD. Fallon, Kathy Reilly & Pellegrino, Frank. 2006. (J). (gr. -1-3). 29.95 incl. audio compact disk *(978-1-933626-06-2(2)*, Llumina Pr.) Aeon Publishing Inc.

Kelly, Bobbi. The Williams Family Saves Moose the Kangaroo Mouse: When Tiny Is Mighty. Williams, Jennifer Foreman de Grassi. 2019. (Williams Family Animal Tale of Tails Ser.: Vol. 11). (ENG.). 48p. (J). pap. 10.69 ***(978-1-7049-1766-5(2))*** Independently Published.

Kelly, Cassie. The Return of Foggitytree. Tamer, Zach. 2019. (Snugglefink & Friends Book 2 Ser.: Vol. 2). (ENG.). 26p. (J). pap. 12.99 ***(978-1-7003-8818-6(5))*** Independently Published.

—The Story of the Snugglefink. Tamer, Zach. 2019. (Snugglefink & Friends Book 1 Ser.: Vol. 1). (ENG.). 26p. (J). pap. 12.99 ***(978-1-6998-0004-1(9))*** Independently Published.

Kelly, Cathy. The Blue Number Counting Book. Gould, Ellen. 13p. (J). (gr. -1-2). pap. 6.00 *(978-0-938017-01-1(2))* Learning Tools Co.

Kelly, Cooper. Buenas Noches, California. Gamble, Adam. 2012. (Buenas Noches Ser.). (ENG.). 24p. (J). (gr. k — 1). bds. 9.95 *(978-1-60219-070-2(4))* Good Night Bks.

—Good Night Alaska. Gamble, Adam & Jasper, Mark. 2015. (Good Night Our World Ser.). (ENG.). 20p. (J). (— 1). bds. 9.95 *(978-1-60219-219-5(7))* Good Night Bks.

—Good Night Beach. Gamble, Adam. 2007. (Good Night Our World Ser.). (ENG.). 28p. (J). (gr. k — 1). bds. 9.95 *(978-1-60219-002-3(X))* Good Night Bks.

—Good Night California. Gamble, Adam. 2008. (Good Night Our World Ser.). (ENG.). 26p. (J). (gr. k — 1). bds. 9.95 *(978-1-60219-021-4(6))* Good Night Bks.

—Good Night Campsite. Gamble, Adam & Jasper, Mark. 2018. (Good Night Our World Ser.). 20p. (J). (— 1). bds. 9.95 *(978-1-60219-514-1(5))* Good Night Bks.

—Good Night Canada. Gamble, Adam & Adams, David J. 2010. (Good Night Our World Ser.). (ENG.). 28p. (J). (gr. k — 1). bds. 9.95 *(978-1-60219-038-2(0))* Good Night Bks.

—Good Night Charleston. Jasper, Mark. 2007. (Good Night Our World Ser.). (ENG.). 20p. (J). (gr. k — 1). bds. 9.95 *(978-1-60219-022-1(4))* Good Night Bks.

—Good Night Christmas Tree. Gamble, Adam & Jasper, Mark. 2017. (Good Night Our World Ser.). 20p. (J). (— 1). bds. 9.95 *(978-1-60219-469-4(6))* Good Night Bks.

—Good Night Coast Guard. Gamble, Adam et al. 2017. (Good Night Our World Ser.). 20p. (J). (gr. -1 — 1). bds. 9.95 *(978-1-60219-425-0(4))* Good Night Bks.

—Good Night Daddy. Gamble, Adam & Jasper, Mark. 2015. (Good Night Our World Ser.). (ENG.). 20p. (J). (— 1). bds. 9.95 *(978-1-60219-229-4(4))* Good Night Bks.

—Good Night Dinosaur. Gamble, Adam & Jasper, Mark. 2013. (Good Night Our World Ser.). (ENG.). 28p. (J). (— 1). bds. 9.95 *(978-1-60219-078-8(X))* Good Night Bks.

—Good Night Dozers. Gamble, Adam & Jasper, Mark. 2018. (Good Night Our World Ser.). 20p. (J). (— 1). bds. 9.95 *(978-1-60219-487-8(4))* Good Night Bks.

—Good Night Dump Truck. Gamble, Adam & Jasper, Mark. 2014. (Good Night Our World Ser.). (ENG.). 26p. (J). (— 1). bds. 9.95 *(978-1-60219-189-1(1))* Good Night Bks.

—Good Night Families. Gamble, Adam & Jasper, Mark. 2017. (Good Night Our World Ser.). 20p. (J). (— 1). bds. 9.95 *(978-1-60219-465-6(3))* Good Night Bks.

—Good Night Galaxy. Jasper, Mark & Gamble, Adam. 2012. (Good Night Our World Ser.). (ENG.). 20p. (J). (gr. k — 1). bds. 9.95 *(978-1-60219-065-8(8))* Good Night Bks.

—Good Night Grand Canyon. Gamble, Adam & Jasper, Mark. 2016. (Good Night Our World Ser.). (ENG.). 20p. (J). (— 1). bds. 9.95 *(978-1-60219-503-5(X))* Good Night Bks.

—Good Night Grandma. Gamble, Adam & Jasper, Mark. 2016. (ENG.). 20p. (J). (— 1). bds. 9.95 *(978-1-60219-409-0(2))* Good Night Bks.

—Good Night Lake. Gamble, Adam. 2008. (Good Night Our World Ser.). (ENG.). 28p. (J). (gr. k — 1). bds. 9.95 *(978-1-60219-028-3(3))* Good Night Bks.

—Good Night Little Brother. Gamble, Adam & Jasper, Mark. 2016. (Good Night Our World Ser.). (ENG.). 20p. (J). (— 1). bds. 9.95 *(978-1-60219-505-9(6))* Good Night Bks.

—Good Night Little Monsters. Gamble, Adam & Jasper, Mark. 2017. (Good Night Our World Ser.). 20p. (J). (gr. -1 — 1). bds. 9.95 *(978-1-60219-489-2(0))* Good Night Bks.

—Good Night Little Sister. Gamble, Adam & Jasper, Mark. 2016. (Good Night Our World Ser.). (ENG.). 20p. (J). (— 1). bds. 9.95 *(978-1-60219-506-6(4))* Good Night Bks.

—Good Night Los Angeles. Gamble, Adam. 2007. (Good Night Our World Ser.). (ENG.). 20p. (J). (gr. k — 1). bds. 9.95 *(978-1-60219-009-2(7))* Good Night Bks.

—Good Night Mommy. Gamble, Adam & Jasper, Mark. 2015. (Good Night Our World Ser.). (ENG.). 20p. (J). (— 1). bds. 9.95 *(978-1-60219-230-0(8))* Good Night Bks.

—Good Night Montreal. Gamble, Adam. 2007. (Good Night Our World Ser.). (ENG.). 20p. (J). (gr. k — 1). bds. 9.95 *(978-1-60219-012-2(7))* Good Night Bks.

—Good Night Museums. Gamble, Adam & Jasper, Mark. 2018. (Good Night Our World Ser.). 20p. (J). (— 1). bds. 9.95 *(978-1-60219-576-9(5))* Good Night Bks.

—Good Night New Orleans. Gamble, Adam & Jasper, Mark. 2012. (Good Night Our World Ser.). (ENG.). 20p. (J). (gr. k — 1). bds. 9.95 *(978-1-60219-061-0(5))* Good Night Bks.

—Good Night Niagara Falls. Gamble, Adam & Jasper, Mark. 2019. (Good Night Our World Ser.). 20p. (J). (— 1). bds. 9.95 *(978-1-60219-600-1(1))* Good Night Bks.

—Good Night Ocean. Jasper, Mark. 2009. (Good Night Our World Ser.). (ENG.). 28p. (J). (gr. k — 1). bds. 9.95 *(978-1-60219-036-8(4))* Good Night Bks.

—Good Night Paris. Gamble, Adam & Jasper, Mark. 2019. (Good Night Our World Ser.). 20p. (J). (— 1). bds. 9.95 *(978-1-60219-584-4(6))* Good Night Bks.

—Good Night Philadelphia. Gamble, Adam. 2006. (Good Night Our World Ser.). (ENG.). 20p. (J). (gr. k — 1). bds. 9.95 *(978-0-9777979-4-3(5))* Good Night Bks.

—Good Night Pirate Ship. Gamble, Adam & Jasper, Mark. 2015. (Good Night Our World Ser.). (ENG.). 26p. (J). (— 1). bds. 9.95 *(978-1-60219-217-1(0))* Good Night Bks.

—Good Night Planes. Gamble, Adam & Jasper, Mark. 2015. (Good Night Our World Ser.). (ENG.). 26p. (J). (— 1). bds. 9.95 *(978-1-60219-218-8(9))* Good Night Bks.

—Good Night San Diego. Gamble, Adam. 2006. (Good Night Our World Ser.). (ENG.). 20p. (J). (gr. k — 1). bds. 9.95 *(978-0-9777979-6-7(1))* Good Night Bks.

—Good Night Sharks. Gamble, Adam & Jasper, Mark. 2019. (Good Night Our World Ser.). 20p. (J). (— 1). bds. 9.95 *(978-1-60219-663-6(X))* Good Night Bks.

—Good Night Statue of Liberty. Gamble, Adam & Jasper, Mark. 2017. (Good Night Our World Ser.). 20p. (J). (gr. -1 — 1). bds. 9.95 *(978-1-60219-429-8(7))* Good Night Bks.

—Good Night Toronto. Gamble, Adam & Jasper, Mark. 2011. (Good Night Our World Ser.). (ENG.). 20p. (J). (gr. k — 1). bds. 9.95 *(978-1-60219-048-1(8))* Good Night Bks.

—Good Night Tractors. Gamble, Adam & Jasper, Mark. 2020. (Good Night Our World Ser.). (ENG.). 20p. (J). (— 1). bds. 9.95 *(978-1-60219-822-7(5))* Good Night Bks.

—Good Night Trucks. Gamble, Adam & Jasper, Mark. 2019. (Good Night Our World Ser.). 20p. (J). (— 1). bds. 9.95 *(978-1-60219-818-0(7))* Good Night Bks.

—Good Night Vermont. Tougias, Michael. 2007. (Good Night Our World Ser.). (ENG.). 20p. (J). (gr. k — 1). bds. 9.95 *(978-1-60219-017-7(8))* Good Night Bks.

—Good Night Washington State. Gamble, Adam & Jasper, Mark. 2012. (Good Night Our World Ser.). (ENG.). 20p. (J). (gr. k — 1). bds. 9.95 *(978-1-60219-072-6(0))* Good Night Bks.

—Good Night Whales. Gamble, Adam & Jasper, Mark. 2016. (Good Night Our World Ser.). (ENG.). 20p. (J). (— 1). bds. 9.95 *(978-1-60219-507-3(2))* Good Night Bks.

—Good Night Wisconsin. Gamble, Adam & Jasper, Mark. 2012. (Good Night Our World Ser.). (ENG.). 20p. (J). (gr. k — 1). bds. 9.95 *(978-1-60219-064-1(X))* Good Night Bks.

—Good Night World. Gamble, Adam. 2009. (Good Night Our World Ser.). (ENG.). 28p. (J). (gr. k — 1). bds. 9.95 *(978-1-60219-030-6(5))* Good Night Bks.

—Good Night Yellowstone. Gamble, Adam & Jasper, Mark. 2013. (Good Night Our World Ser.). (ENG.). 20p. (J). (— 1). bds. 9.95 *(978-1-60219-079-5(8))* Good Night Bks.

—Good Night Zoo. Gamble, Adam. 2007. (Good Night Our World Ser.). (ENG.). 26p. (J). (gr. k — 1). bds. 9.95 *(978-1-60219-018-4(6))* Good Night Bks.

Kelly, Cooper. Good Night Farm. Kelly, Cooper. Gamble, Adam. 2009. (Good Night Our World Ser.). (ENG.). 28p. (J). (gr. k — 1). bds. 9.95 *(978-1-60219-029-0(1))* Good Night Bks.

Kelly, Cooper & Calo, Marcos. Good Night Aruba. Gamble, Adam & Jasper, Mark. 2017. (Good Night Our World Ser.). 20p. (J). (— 1). bds. 9.95 *(978-1-60219-516-5(1))* Good Night Bks.

Kelly, Cooper, jt. illus. see Holder, Jimmy.

Kelly, Cooper, jt. illus. see Veno, Joe.

Kelly, Diana J. My Colour Collection: Green. Tredget, Sue. 2017. (ENG.). (J). pap. *(978-0-6480901-4-4(0))* Causeway Publishing.

—My Colour Collection: Red. Tredget, Sue. 2017. (ENG.). (J). pap. *(978-0-6480901-5-1(9))* Causeway Publishing.

—My Colour Collection: Yellow. Tredget, Sue. 2017. (ENG.). (J). pap. *(978-0-6480901-6-8(7))* Causeway Publishing.

Kelly, Geoff. Tashi & the Wicked Magician: And Other Stories. Fienberg, Anna et al. 2017. (Tashi Ser.). (ENG.). 96p. (J). (gr. k-3). pap. 10.99 *(978-1-76029-050-4(5))* Allen & Unwin AUS. Dist: Independent Pubs. Group.

Kelly, Gerald. The Nine Lives of Jacob Tibbs. Busby, Cylin. 2016. (ENG.). 272p. (J). (gr. 3-7). 16.99 *(978-0-553-51123-9(8)*, Knopf Bks. for Young Readers) Random Hse. Children's Bks.

Kelly, Jim. Hockey: An Introduction to Being a Good Sport. Derr, Aaron. 2017. (Start Smart (tm) — Sports Ser.). (ENG.). 32p. (J). (gr. k-3). lib. bdg. 26.65 *(978-1-63440-131-9(X))*; E-Book 39.99 *(978-1-63440-143-2(3))* Red Chair Pr.

Kelly, Jo'Anne. Som See & the Magic Elephant. Oliviero, Jamie. 2005. 27p. (J). (gr. -1-2). reprint ed. 17.00 *(978-0-7567-8929-9(X))* DIANE Publishing Co.

Kelly, John. Amazing Things for Boys to Make & Do. Tincknell, Cathy. 2013. (Dover Children's Activity Bks.). (ENG.). 32p. (J). (gr. 3-5). 6.99 *(978-0-486-49723-5(2))* Dover Pubns., Inc.

—Amazing Things for Girls to Make & Do. Tincknell, Cathy. 2013. (Dover Children's Activity Bks.). (ENG.). 32p. (J). (gr. 3-5). 6.99 *(978-0-486-49722-8(4))* Dover Pubns., Inc.

—The Germ Lab. Platt, Richard. 2020. (ENG.). 48p. (J). 16.99 *(978-0-7534-7582-9(0)*, 900219383, Kingfisher) Roaring Brook Pr.

—Slow Magic. Goodhart, Pippa. (Basketball Source Ser.). (J). 2015. (ENG.). 32p. (gr. 3-4). *(978-0-7787-1535-1(3))*; 2003. *(978-0-7787-1489-7(6))* Crabtree Publishing Co.

—Slow Magic. Goodhart, Pippa & Goodheart, Pippa. 2003. (Flying Foxes Ser.). (ENG.). 48p. (J). *(978-0-7787-1528-3(0))*; lib. bdg. *(978-0-7787-1482-8(9))* Crabtree Publishing Co.

—Slow Magic. Goodhart, Pippa. 2004. (Flying Foxes Ser.). (ENG.). (J). (gr. 1-1). lib. bdg. 16.05 *(978-0-7569-3047-9(2))* Perfection Learning Corp.

Kelly, John. Sir Scaly Pants the Dragon Knight. Kelly, John. 2015. 32p. (J). (gr. -1-1). 18.99 *(978-1-4088-5602-4(6)*, 900153463, Bloomsbury Children's Bks.) Bloomsbury Publishing USA.

Kelly, Joseph. Blazing Ahead! Kerrin, Jessica Scott. 2006. (Martin Bridge Ser.). (ENG.). 109p. (J). (gr. 2-4). 17.44 *(978-1-55337-961-4(6))* Kids Can Pr., Ltd. CAN. Dist: Children's Plus, Inc.

—Martin Bridge: On the Lookout! Kerrin, Jessica Scott & Kerrin, Jessica. 2012. (Martin Bridge Ser.). (ENG.). 142p. (J). (gr. 2-4). 17.44 *(978-1-55337-689-7(7))* Kids Can Pr., Ltd. CAN. Dist: Children's Plus, Inc.

—Martin Bridge: Ready for Takeoff! Kerrin, Jessica Scott. 2005. (Martin Bridge Ser.). (ENG.). 120p. (J). (gr. 2-5). 6.95 *(978-1-55337-772-6(9))* Kids Can Pr., Ltd. CAN. Dist: Hachette Bk. Group.

—The Sky's the Limit! Kerrin, Jessica Scott. 2008. (Martin Bridge Ser.). (ENG.). 112p. (J). (gr. 2-4). 21.19 *(978-1-55453-158-5(6))* Kids Can Pr., Ltd. CAN. Dist: Children's Plus, Inc.

Kelly, Judy. Rosie Robin: The Bird Who Loved People, 1 vol. Everson, Hobart G. 2010. 22p. 24.95 *(978-1-4489-4095-0(8))* PublishAmerica, Inc.

Kelly, Julia. Corky's Humane Tail Tale. Brenner, Harriett A. 2006. 32p. (J). bds. 16.95 *(978-0-9768667-0-1(6))* M & D Publishing, Inc.

Kelly, Leslie A. Les Kelly. Anderson, William. Date not set. (J). (gr. 3-7). Vol. 1. 9.99 *(978-0-06-440851-6(5))*; Vol. 2. 9.99 *(978-0-06-440850-9(7))* HarperCollins Pubs.

—The Little House Guidebook: New Edition! Anderson, William. 2007. (Little House Nonfiction Ser.). (ENG.). 96p. (J). (gr. 3-7). pap. 9.99 *(978-0-06-125512-0(2)*, Collins) HarperCollins Pubs.

Kelly, Lucas. Shining Scars. Leonard, Krystian. 2013. (ENG.). 31p. (J). 16.95 *(978-0-938467-72-4(7))* Headline Bks., Inc.

Kelly, Maeve. Drochla Gruaige. Doolan, Catherine. 2004. (Sraith Sos Ser.: 9). (GLE.). 64p. (J). pap. 11.00 *(978-0-86278-866-7(8))* O'Brien Pr., Ltd., The IRL. Dist: Casemate Pubs. & Bk. Distributors, LLC.

Kelly, Mary B. For the Love of Strangers. Horsfall, Jacqueline. 2011. 292p. (YA). (gr. 6-9). pap. 14.99 *(978-1-61603-003-2(8))* Leap Bks.

Kelly, McMahon. 1-2-3 Learn Ages 3-4. Guckian, Mara. ed. 2016. (ENG.). 128p. pap. 14.99 *(978-1-4206-8002-7(1))* Teacher Created Resources, Inc.

Kelly, Robert. Does Noah's Kitten Have Autism Too? Boehm, Patricia. 2013. 16p. pap. 24.95 *(978-1-62709-877-9(1))* America Star Bks.

Kelly, Timothy. Timmy & Superkid Blood Draw Adventure. Wylie, Lisa. 2019. (Timmy & Superkid Blood Draw Adventure Ser.: Vol. 1). (ENG.). 32p. (J). pap. 12.99 *(978-1-0906-1816-0(6))* Independently Published.

Kelly, Zac. Canal Pirates. O'Leary, Tony. 2018. (ENG.). 216p. (J). pap. *(978-1-9993063-0-4(9))* Mambi Bks. Ltd.

Kelner, Noa. In the Jerusalem Forest. Busheri, Devora. 2019. (ENG.). 32p. (J). (gr. -1-3). 17.99 *(978-1-5415-3472-8(7)*, Kar-Ben Publishing) Lerner Publishing Group.

Kelsey, Amanda. Berlina's Quest. Hartley, James. Legge, Barbara, ed. 2013. 146p. (J). pap. 17.99 *(978-1-61572-948-7(8))* Damnation Bks.

—Weather. Winter, Isobelle. Odgers, Sally, ed. 2013. 236p. (J). pap. 23.25 *(978-1-61572-946-3(1))* Damnation Bks.

Kelsey, Avonelle. Grandma Says, 4 bks., Set. Kelsey, Avonelle. (Series of Short Stories). 200p. (J). *(978-0-9640610-1-9(5))* Cheval International.

—Iroquois Medicine Woman. Kelsey, Avonelle. 300p. (Orig.). (YA). *(978-0-9640610-5-7(8))* Cheval International.

Kelsey, Heath. Duke & the Dinosaur Family. Kelsey, Heath. Kelsey, Jill, ed. 2019. (ENG.). 44p. (J). pap. 12.99 *(978-1-0705-4359-8(4))* Independently Published.

Kelsey-Livin, Barbara. Big Fish. Kelsey, Linda J. 2012. 28p. pap. 24.95 *(978-1-4626-6887-8(9))* America Star Bks.

Kelson, Ellen & Cecil, Jennifer. Let's Build a Playground. Rosen, Michael J. & Kaboom! Staff. 2013. 32p. (J). (gr. 1-4). 15.99 *(978-0-7636-5532-7(5))* Candlewick Pr.

Kemarskaya, Oksana. The Legend of the Vampire, 1 vol. Troupe, Thomas Kingsley. 2010. (Legend Has It Ser.). (ENG.). 32p. (J). (gr. 2-4). lib. bdg. 27.99 *(978-1-4048-6031-5(2))*, Picture Window Bks.) Capstone.

—The Patchwork Garden. De Anda, Diane. Ventura, Gabriela Baeza, tr. 2013.Tr. of Pedacitos de Huerto. (ENG & SPA.). 32p. (J). 16.95 *(978-1-55885-763-6(X)*, Piñata Books) Arte Publico Pr.

—Play Ball. Hillert, Margaret. 2016. (BeginningtoRead Ser.). (ENG.). 32p. (J). (gr. -1-2). pap. 11.94 *(978-1-60357-981-0(8))*; (gr. k-2). 22.60 *(978-1-59953-819-8(9))* Norwood Hse. Pr.

—The Secret Lives of Plants!, 1 vol. Slingerland, Janet. 2012. (Adventures in Science Ser.). (ENG.). 32p. (gr. 3-9). (J). pap. 8.10 *(978-1-4296-7989-3(1))*; pap. 47.70 *(978-1-4296-8467-5(4)*, Capstone Pr.) Capstone.

Kemble, E. W. Adventures of Huckleberry Finn (Tom Sawyer's Comrade) [Complete & Unabridged. 174 Original Illustrations.]. Twain, Mark. 2020. (ENG.). 340p. (J). pap. ***(978-1-78943-113-1(1))*** Benediction Classics.

Kemble, Mai. I'm So Not Wearing a Dress! Merberg, Julie. 2010. (ENG.). 32p. (J). 11.99 *(978-1-935703-05-1(6))* Downtown Bookworks.

Kemble, Mai S. I Can Speak Bully. Morrison, Kevin. 2009. 32p. (J). 14.95 *(978-0-8091-6744-9(1)*, Ambassador Bks.) Paulist Pr.

—Lou Lou. Guerras Safia. 2013. (ENG.). 24p. (J). pap. 16.95 *(978-1-4787-2359-2(9))* Outskirts Pr., Inc.

—The Moon & the Night Sweeper. 2007. 30p. (J). (gr. -1-2). 15.95 *(978-1-60108-013-4(1))* Red Cygnet Pr.

—Polka-Dot Fixes Kindergarten. Urdahl, Catherine. 2011. 32p. (J). (gr. -1-3). pap. 7.95 *(978-1-57091-738-7(8))*; 22.44 *(978-1-57091-737-0(X))* Charlesbridge Publishing, Inc.

—Taylor's Birthday Party. Khan, Hana. 2008. (J). *(978-1-60108-048-6(4))* Red Cygnet Pr.

Kemble, Mai S. The Moon & the Night Sweeper. Kemble, Mai S. 2008. (J). pap. 6.95 *(978-1-60108-023-3(9))* Red Cygnet Pr.

Kemly, Kathleen. Benjamin Brown & the Great Steamboat Race. Jordan, Shirley. 2011. (History Speaks: Picture Books Plus Reader's Theater Ser.). 48p. pap. 56.72 *(978-0-7613-7630-9(5))*; (ENG.). (gr. 2-4). pap. 9.95 *(978-0-7613-6133-6(2))* Lerner Publishing Group.

—Dios Lo Hizo para Ti! La Historia de la Creacion. Lehmann, Charles. 2009. (SPA.). 32p. (J). (gr. k). pap. 7.99 *(978-0-7586-1751-4(8))* Concordia Publishing Hse.

—A Fishing Surprise. McDonald, Rae A. 2007. (ENG.). 32p. (J). (gr. -1-3). 16.95 *(978-1-55971-977-3(X))* Cooper Square Publishing Llc.

—God Made It for You! The Story of Creation. Lehmann, Charles. 2007. 32p. (J). (gr. -1-3). 14.99 *(978-0-7586-1287-8(7))* Concordia Publishing Hse.

—Golden Delcious: A Cinderella Apple Story. Smucker, Anna Egan. 2013. (AV2 Fiction Readalong Ser.). (ENG.). (J). (gr. 3-7). 34.28 *(978-1-62127-877-1(8)*, AV2 by Weigl) Weigl Pubs., Inc.

—Molly, by Golly! The Legend of Molly Williams, America's First Female Firefighter. Ochiltree, Dianne. 2012. (ENG.). 32p. (J). (gr. 2-k). 17.95 *(978-1-59078-721-2(8)*, Calkins Creek) Boyds Mills Pr.

Kemmerer, Brooke. The Kid's User Guide to a Human Life: Book Two: an Open Heart. Brenner, Rebecca. 2016. (Kid's User Guide Ser.: 2). (ENG.). 56p. (J). pap. 8.95 *(978-1-63047-866-7(0))* Morgan James Publishing.

Kemp, Dory. Dare to Be Different. Rutledge, Clint. 2017. (ENG.). 34p. (J). 19.99 *(978-0-692-99491-7(2))* Rutledge Development.

Kemp Jr, Joseph a. Isabella & Her Enchanted Family: A Fable for People of All Ages. Barto, Susan Ferrara. 2019. (Isabella Stories Ser.: Vol. 1). (ENG.). 50p. (J). pap. 15.00 *(978-1-0908-5939-6(2))* Independently Published.

Kemp, Kathie. Do Beavers Need Blankets?, 1 vol. Tekiela, Stan. 2015. (Wildlife Picture Bks.). (ENG.). 32p. (J). (gr. -1-3). 12.95 *(978-1-59193-467-7(2)*, Adventure Pubns.) AdventureKEEN.

Kemp, Kathy. Boundary Waters ABC, 1 vol. Erwin, Wes. 2014. (ENG.). 64p. (J). (gr. -1-k). 12.95 *(978-1-59193-498-1(2)*, Adventure Pubns.) AdventureKEEN.

Kemp, Moira. Cachorro. Price, Mathew. Goldman, Judy, tr. 2010. (SPA & ENG.). 10p. bds. 5.99 *(978-1-935021-64-3(8))* Price, Mathew Ltd.

—Gatito. Price, Mathew. Goldman, Judy, tr. 2010. (SPA & ENG.). 10p. bds. 5.99 *(978-1-935021-99-5(0))* Price, Mathew Ltd.

—Grandma Chickenlegs. McCaughrean, Geraldine. 2003. (Picture Bks.). 32p. (J). (gr. -1-3). 15.95 *(978-1-57505-415-5(9))*; pap. 6.95 *(978-0-87614-908-9(5)*, Carolrhoda Bks.) Lerner Publishing Group.

—Pollito. Price, Mathew. Goldman, Judy, tr. 2010. (SPA & ENG.). 10p. bds. 5.99 *(978-1-935021-59-9(1))* Price, Mathew Ltd.

Kempeners, Lucie. King Max's Kingdom: Mischief & Magic: Black-And-white Illustrations. Valluy, Tl. 2019. (ENG.). 106p. (J). pap. 6.99 ***(978-1-6862-5776-6(7))*** Independently Published.

—King Max's Kingdom: Mischief & Magic: Color Illustrations. Valluy, Tl. 2019. (ENG.). 106p. (J). pap. 21.00 ***(978-1-0813-2034-8(6))*** Independently Published.

Ken, Akamatsu. Love Hina, 14 vols., Vol. 14. Ken, Akamatsu. Rymer, Nan, tr. from JPN. rev. ed. 2003. 200p. pap. 14.99 *(978-1-59182-120-5(7)*, Tokyopop Adult) TOKYOPOP, Inc.

Kendall, Bradford. El Ataque Del Papiro. Dahl, Michael. 2019. (Biblioteca Maldita Ser.). (SPA.). 40p. (J). (gr. 4-8). lib. bdg. 23.99 *(978-1-4965-8533-2(X)*, 141282, Stone Arch Bks.) Capstone.

—La Biblioteca Maldita. Dahl, Michael. 2020. (Biblioteca Maldita Ser.).Tr. of Library of Doom. (SPA.). (J). (gr. 4-8). pap., pap., pap. 27.80 *(978-1-4965-9339-9(1))*; lib. bdg., lib. bdg., lib. bdg. 239.90 *(978-1-4965-9184-5(4))* Capstone. (Stone Arch Bks.).

—Blood in the Library, 1 vol. Dahl, Michael. 2011. (Return to the Library of Doom Ser.). (ENG.). 72p. (J). (gr. 4-8). lib.

bdg. 23.99 *(978-1-4342-3228-1(X)*, Stone Arch Bks.) Capstone.

—The Book That Ate My Brother, 1 vol. Dahl, Michael. 2010. (Return to the Library of Doom Ser.). (ENG.). 72p. (J). (gr. 4-8). lib. bdg. 23.99 *(978-1-4342-2144-5(X)*, Stone Arch Bks.) Capstone.

—The Book That Dripped Blood: 10th Anniversary Edition. Dahl, Michael. 10th ed. 2017. (Library of Doom Ser.). (ENG.). 48p. (J). (gr. 4-8). pap. 6.25 *(978-1-4965-5535-9(X)*, 136559); lib. bdg. 23.99 *(978-1-4965-5529-8(5)*, 136553) Capstone. (Stone Arch Bks.).

—Cave of the Bookworms, 1 vol. Dahl, Michael. 2008. (Library of Doom Ser.). (ENG.). 40p. (J). (gr. 4-8). pap. 6.25 *(978-1-4342-0549-0(5))*; lib. bdg. 23.99 *(978-1-4342-0489-9(8))* Capstone. (Stone Arch Bks.).

—The Creeping Bookends, 1 vol. Dahl, Michael. 2008. (Library of Doom Ser.). (ENG.). 40p. (J). (gr. 4-8). pap. 6.25 *(978-1-4342-0546-9(0))*; lib. bdg. 23.99 *(978-1-4342-0486-8(3))* Capstone. (Stone Arch Bks.).

—La Cueva de Los Gusanos. Dahl, Michael. 2020. (Biblioteca Maldita Ser.).Tr. of Cave of the Bookworms. (SPA.). 40p. (J). (gr. 4-8). pap. 6.95 *(978-1-4965-9309-2(X)*, 142321); lib. bdg. 23.99 *(978-1-4965-9170-8(4)*, 142083) Capstone. (Stone Arch Bks.).

—Dictionary of 1,000 Rooms, 1 vol. Dahl, Michael. 2011. (Return to the Library of Doom Ser.). (ENG.). 72p. (J). (gr. 4-8). lib. bdg. 23.99 *(978-1-4342-3229-8(8)*, Stone Arch Bks.) Capstone.

—Don't Open It! Dahl, Michael. 2016. (ENG.). 40p. (J). pap. *(978-1-4747-1054-1(9)*, Stone Arch Bks.) Capstone.

—Escape de la Prisión de Papel. Dahl, Michael. 2020. (Biblioteca Maldita Ser.).Tr. of Escape from the Pop-Up Prison. (SPA.). 40p. (J). (gr. 4-8). pap. 6.95 *(978-1-4965-9310-8(3)*, 142322); lib. bdg. 23.99 *(978-1-4965-9171-5(2)*, 142084) Capstone. (Stone Arch Bks.).

—Escape from the Pop-Up Prison. Dahl, Michael. 2008. (Library of Doom Ser.). (ENG.). 40p. (J). (gr. 4-8). pap. 6.25 *(978-1-4342-0550-6(9))*; lib. bdg. 23.99 *(978-1-4342-0490-5(1))* Capstone. (Stone Arch Bks.).

—Ghost Writer, 1 vol. Dahl, Michael. 2011. (Return to the Library of Doom Ser.). (ENG.). 72p. (J). (gr. 4-8). lib. bdg. 23.99 *(978-1-4342-3230-4(1)*, Stone Arch Bks.) Capstone.

—Inkfoot, 1 vol. Dahl, Michael. 2010. (Return to the Library of Doom Ser.). (ENG.). 72p. (J). (gr. 4-8). 23.99 *(978-1-4342-2146-9(6)*, Stone Arch Bks.) Capstone.

—Killer App, 1 vol. Dahl, Michael. 2011. (Return to the Library of Doom Ser.). (ENG.). 72p. (J). (gr. 4-8). lib. bdg. 23.99 *(978-1-4342-3231-1(X)*, Stone Arch Bks.) Capstone.

—The Last Word. Dahl, Michael. 2016. (ENG.). 40p. (J). pap. *(978-1-4747-1055-8(7)*, Stone Arch Bks.) Capstone.

—Library of Doom: the Final Chapters. Dahl, Michael. 2016. (Library of Doom: the Final Chapters Ser.). (ENG.). 40p. (J). (gr. 4-8). lib. bdg., lib. bdg., lib. bdg. 191.92 *(978-1-4965-2574-1(4)*, Stone Arch Bks.) Capstone.

—El Libro Sangrante. Dahl, Michael. 2019. (Biblioteca Maldita Ser.). (SPA.). 40p. (J). (gr. 4-8). lib. bdg. 23.99 *(978-1-4965-8536-3(4)*, 141285, Stone Arch Bks.) Capstone.

—Los Sujetalibros Horripilantes. Dahl, Michael. 2020. (Biblioteca Maldita Ser.).Tr. of Creeping Bookends. (SPA.). 40p. (J). (gr. 4-8). pap. 6.95 *(978-1-4965-9307-8(3)*, 142319); lib. bdg. 23.99 *(978-1-4965-9168-5(2)*, 142081) Capstone. (Stone Arch Bks.).

—Night of the Scrawler. Dahl, Michael. 2016. (ENG.). 40p. (J). pap. *(978-1-4747-1056-5(5)*, Stone Arch Bks.) Capstone.

—Rats on the Page, 1 vol. Dahl, Michael. 2010. (Return to the Library of Doom Ser.). (ENG.). 72p. (J). (gr. 4-8). lib. bdg. 23.99 *(978-1-4342-2147-6(4)*, Stone Arch Bks.) Capstone.

—The Sea of Lost Books, 1 vol. Dahl, Michael. 2010. (Return to the Library of Doom Ser.). (ENG.). 72p. (J). (gr. 4-8). lib. bdg. 23.99 *(978-1-4342-2142-1(3)*, Stone Arch Bks.) Capstone.

—The Smashing Scroll: 10th Anniversary Edition. Dahl, Michael. 10th ed. 2017. (Library of Doom Ser.). (ENG.). 48p. (J). (gr. 4-8). pap. 6.25 *(978-1-4965-5532-8(5)*, 136556); lib. bdg. 23.99 *(978-1-4965-5526-7(0)*, 136550) Capstone. (Stone Arch Bks.).

—Thesaurus Rex. Dahl, Michael. 2016. (ENG.). 40p. (J). pap. *(978-1-4747-1057-2(3)*, Stone Arch Bks.) Capstone.

—The Twister Trap, 1 vol. Dahl, Michael. 2008. (Library of Doom Ser.). (ENG.). 40p. (J). (gr. 4-8). pap. 6.25 *(978-1-4342-0548-3(7))*; lib. bdg. 23.99 *(978-1-4342-0488-2(X))* Capstone. (Stone Arch Bks.).

—The Vampire Chapter, 1 vol. Dahl, Michael. 2010. (Return to the Library of Doom Ser.). (ENG.). 72p. (J). (gr. 4-8). 23.99 *(978-1-4342-2143-8(1)*, Stone Arch Bks.) Capstone.

—The Word Eater, 1 vol. Dahl, Michael. 2008. (Library of Doom Ser.). (ENG.). 40p. (J). (gr. 4-8). lib. bdg. 23.99 *(978-1-4342-0491-2(X))*; per. 6.25 *(978-1-4342-0551-3(7))* Capstone. (Stone Arch Bks.).

—Zombie in the Library, 1 vol. Dahl, Michael. 2010. (Return to the Library of Doom Ser.). (ENG.). 72p. (J). (gr. 4-8). lib. bdg. 23.99 *(978-1-4342-2145-2(8)*, Stone Arch Bks.) Capstone.

Kendall, Bradford, jt. illus. see Evergreen, Nelson.

Kendall, Bryan. The Story of Mitch. Perry, John. 2018. (ENG.). 28p. (J). 22.95 *(978-1-64349-274-2(8))*; pap. 12.95 *(978-1-64349-040-3(0))* Christian Faith Publishing.

Kendall-Davies, Lesley. Sammy & the Bully. Spanhake, Connie. 2018. (ENG.). 36p. (J). pap. 9.50 *(978-1-7294-9449-3(8))* Independently Published.

Kendall, Gideon. Dinosaurs. Ring, Susan. 2008. (ENG.). 10p. (J). (gr. -1-1). 15.99 *(978-1-58476-730-5(8))* Innovative Kids.

—No Bones about It: Discovering Dinosaurs. Prokos, Anna. 2017. (Imagine That! Ser.). (ENG.). 32p. (J). (gr. 2-4). lib. bdg. 26.65 *(978-1-63440-150-0(6))*; E-Book 39.99 *(978-1-63440-162-3(X))* Red Chair Pr.

—Rabbits Rabbits Everywhere: A Fibonacci Tale. McCallum, Ann. 32p. (J). (gr. 1-4). 2008. (ENG.). 16.95 *(978-1-57091-895-7(3))*; 2007. per. 7.95 *(978-1-57091-896-4(1))* Charlesbridge Publishing, Inc.

—Los Seems: Un Segundo Perdido. Hulme, John & Wexler, Michael. Vidal, Jordi, tr. 2009. (SPA.). 306p. (YA). (gr. 5-8). 19.95 *(978-84-666-4122-7(X))* Ediciones B ESP. Dist: Spanish Pubs., LLC.

Kendall, Monica. Hattie, Get a Haircut! Glatzer, Jenna. 2005. (ENG.). 32p. (J). (gr. -1-3). lib. bdg. 19.95 *(978-0-9724853-0-2(9))* Keene Publishing.

Kendall, Peter. A Sausage Went for a Walk. Majid, Ellisha. 2008. 20p. (J). bds. 12.95 *(978-1-921361-38-8(7))* Fremantle Pr. AUS. Dist: Independent Pubs. Group.

Kendall, Russell. A Day in the Life of a Pilgrim Girl. Waters, Kate. 2008. (Scholastic Bookshelf Ser.). (ENG.). 32p. (J). (gr. -1-3). pap. 7.99 *(978-0-439-81220-7(8)*, Scholastic Paperbacks) Scholastic, Inc.

Kendell, Cam. Fart Quest. Reynolds, Aaron. 2020. (Fart Quest Ser.: 1). (ENG.). 288p. (J). 13.99 *(978-1-250-20636-7(7)*, 900201454) Roaring Brook Pr.

Kendree, McLean. Pandora's Vase, 1 vol. 2011. (Greek Myths Ser.). (ENG.). 32p. (J). (gr. 3-5). lib. bdg. 29.32 *(978-1-4048-6668-3(X)*, Picture Window Bks.) Capstone.

—Vampires vs. Werewolves: Battle of the Bloodthirsty Beasts. O'Hearn, Michael. 2011. (Monster Wars Ser.). (ENG.). 32p. (gr. 3-4). pap. 47.70 *(978-1-4296-7266-5(8))*; (J). lib. bdg. 28.65 *(978-1-4296-6521-6(1))* Capstone. (Capstone Pr.).

Kendrick, D. Seymour Simon's Silly Riddles & Jokes Coloring Book. Simon, Seymour. 2013. (Dover Coloring Bks.). (ENG.). 48p. (J). (gr. 2-5). pap. 4.99 *(978-0-486-48045-9(3))* Dover Pubns., Inc.

Kendrick-TaZiyah, Brandi. Little Lily Mays & the Daddy Dilemma. Lollino, Jessica. 2006. (Little Lily Mays Ser.: vol. 1). 32p. (J). per. 20.00 *(978-0-9712383-1-2(6))* Culturatti Ink.

Kenison, Gale. The Magic at Villa Verde. Nemazie, Maryam. 2020. (ENG.). 84p. (J). pap. 31.95 ***(978-1-9822-4617-4(0)***, Balboa Pr.) Author Solutions, Inc.

Kenison, Misti. The Tiny Traveler: Egypt: A Book of Shapes. 2015. (ENG.). (J). (— 1). bds. 5.95 *(978-1-62914-607-2(2)*, Sky Pony Pr.) Skyhorse Publishing Co., Inc.

—The Tiny Traveler: France: A Book of Colors. 2015. (ENG.). 24p. (J). (— 1). bds. 5.95 *(978-1-62914-609-6(9)*, Sky Pony Pr.) Skyhorse Publishing Co., Inc.

—The Tiny Traveler: Italy: A Book of Numbers. 2016. (ENG.). 24p. (J). (— 1). bds. 5.99 *(978-1-5107-0466-4(3)*, Sky Pony Pr.) Skyhorse Publishing Co., Inc.

—The Tiny Traveler: Japan: A Book of Nature. 2016. (ENG.). 24p. (J). (— 1). bds. 5.99 *(978-1-5107-0472-5(8)*, Sky Pony Pr.) Skyhorse Publishing Co., Inc.

Kenna, Diane. A Lucky Dog: Owney, U.S. Rail Mail Mascot. Wales, Dirk. 2003. 32p. (J). 15.95 *(978-0-9632459-0-8(2))* Great Plains Pr.

—Penny House. Wales, Dirk. 2005. 32p. (J). (gr. -1). 16.95 *(978-0-9632459-1-5(0))* Great Plains Pr.

Kenna, Erin. The Forest Sleeps. Lee, Calee M. 2017. (ENG.). 32p. (J). (gr. -1-2). pap. 9.99 *(978-1-5324-0171-8(X))* Xist Publishing.

Kennard, Michaela. What Shall I Paint? Gibson, Ray. Everett, Felicity, ed. 2006. (What Shall I Do Today? Ser.). 32p. (J). (gr. 2). lib. bdg. 15.95 *(978-1-58086-549-4(6))* EDC Publishing.

Kennard, Thomas, jt. illus. see Armour, Steven.

Kennedy, Allan. Inferences for Young Audiences. Milligan, Jean F. 2004. 96p. (J). (gr. 3-7). 14.95 *(978-0-9637825-2-6(5))* Autumn Hse. Publishing.

Kennedy, Anne. Ballerina Girl. Hall, Kirsten. 2004. (My First Reader Ser.). (ENG.). 32p. (J). (gr. k-1). pap. 3.95 *(978-0-516-24623-9(2)*, Children's Pr.) Scholastic Library Publishing.

—Hedgehog Goes to Kindergarten. Marie, Lynne. 2011. (J). pap. *(978-0-545-29874-2(1))* Scholastic, Inc.

—The Hug Book. Fliess, Sue. 2014. (Little Golden Book Ser.). 24p. (J). (-k). 4.99 *(978-0-385-37907-6(2)*, Golden Bks.) Random Hse. Children's Bks.

—I'm Not Sleepy. Holland, Trish. 2017. 24p. (J). *(978-1-5182-2279-5(X))*; 4.99 *(978-0-399-55058-4(5))* Random Hse. Children's Bks. (Golden Bks.).

—Miss Fox's Class Earns a Field Trip. Spinelli, Eileen. 2012. (J). *(978-1-61913-122-4(6))* Weigl Pubs., Inc.

—Miss Fox's Class Earns a Field Trip. Spinelli, Eileen. 2018. (Miss Fox's Class Ser.). (ENG.). 32p. (J). (gr. -1-3). 7.99 *(978-0-8075-5170-7(8)*, 807551708) Whitman, Albert & Co.

—Miss Fox's Class Gets It Wrong. Spinelli, Eileen. 2013. (AV2 Fiction Readalong Ser.). (ENG.). (J). (gr. -1-2). 34.28 *(978-1-62127-883-2(2)*, AV2 by Weigl) Weigl Pubs., Inc.

—Miss Fox's Class Gets It Wrong. Spinelli, Eileen. 2018. (Miss Fox's Class Ser.). (ENG.). 32p. (J). (gr. k-3). 7.99 *(978-0-8075-5173-8(2)*, 807551732) Whitman, Albert & Co.

—Miss Fox's Class Goes Green. Spinelli, Eileen. 2012. (J). 34.28 *(978-1-61913-123-1(4))* Weigl Pubs., Inc.

—Miss Fox's Class Goes Green. Spinelli, Eileen. 2011. (Miss Fox's Class Ser.). (ENG.). 32p. (J). (gr. -1-3). 7.99 *(978-0-8075-5167-7(8)*, 807551678) Whitman, Albert & Co.

—Miss Fox's Class Shapes Up. Spinelli, Eileen. 2013. (AV2 Fiction Readalong Ser.). (ENG.). (J). (gr. k-3). 34.28 *(978-1-62127-884-9(0)*, AV2 by Weigl) Weigl Pubs., Inc.

—Miss Fox's Class Shapes Up. Spinelli, Eileen. 2018. (Miss Fox's Class Ser.). (ENG.). 32p. (J). (gr. -1-3). 7.99 *(978-0-8075-5172-1(4)*, 807551724) Whitman, Albert & Co.

—One Little, Two Little, Three Little Apples. Ringler, Matt. 2005. (J). pap. *(978-0-439-77500-7(0))* Scholastic, Inc.

—Peace Week in Miss Fox's Class. Spinelli, Eileen. 2012. (J). *(978-1-61913-155-2(2))* Weigl Pubs., Inc.

—Peace Week in Miss Fox's Class. Spinelli, Eileen. 2018. (Miss Fox's Class Ser.). (ENG.). 32p. (J). (gr. -1-3). 7.99 *(978-0-8075-6390-8(0)*, 807563900) Whitman, Albert & Co.

—Pony Scouts: at the Show. Hapka, Catherine. 2011. (I Can Read Level 2 Ser.). (ENG.). 32p. (J). (gr. -1-3). pap. 4.99 *(978-0-06-125544-1(0))* HarperCollins Pubs.

—Pony Scouts: Back in the Saddle. Hapka, Catherine. 2011. (I Can Read Level 2 Ser.). (ENG.). 32p. (J). (gr. k-3). 16.99 *(978-0-06-125539-7(4))*; pap. 4.99 *(978-0-06-125541-0(6))* HarperCollins Pubs.

—Pony Scouts: Blue Ribbon Day. Hapka, Catherine. 2013. (I Can Read Level 2 Ser.). (ENG.). 32p. (J). (gr. -1-3). 16.99 *(978-0-06-208677-8(4))*; pap. 4.99 *(978-0-06-208676-1(6))* HarperCollins Pubs.

—Pony Scouts: Pony Crazy. Hapka, Catherine. (I Can Read Level 2 Ser.). (ENG.). 32p. (J). (gr. -1-3). 2010. pap. 4.99 *(978-0-06-125535-9(1))*; 2009. 16.99 *(978-0-06-125533-5(5))* HarperCollins Pubs.

—Pony Scouts: Pony Party. Hapka, Catherine. 2013. (I Can Read Level 2 Ser.). (ENG.). 32p. (J). (gr. -1-3). 16.99 *(978-0-06-208680-8(4))*; pap. 4.99 *(978-0-06-208679-2(0))* HarperCollins Pubs.

—Pony Scouts: Really Riding! Hapka, Catherine. 2010. (I Can Read Level 2 Ser.). (ENG.). 32p. (J). (gr. -1-3). pap. 4.99 *(978-0-06-125538-0(6))* HarperCollins Pubs.

—Pony Scouts: Runaway Ponies! Hapka, Catherine. 2012. (I Can Read Level 2 Ser.). (ENG.). 32p. (J). (gr. -1-3). 16.99 *(978-0-06-208669-3(3))*; pap. 4.99 *(978-0-06-208667-9(7))* HarperCollins Pubs.

—Pony Scouts: the Camping Trip. Hapka, Catherine. 2014. (I Can Read Level 2 Ser.). (ENG.). 32p. (J). (gr. -1-3). 16.99 *(978-0-06-208665-5(0))*; pap. 4.99 *(978-0-06-208663-1(4))* HarperCollins Pubs.

—Pony Scouts: the New Pony. Hapka, Catherine. 2013. (I Can Read Level 2 Ser.). (ENG.). 32p. (J). (gr. -1-3). 16.99 *(978-0-06-208674-7(X))* HarperCollins Pubs.

—Pony Scouts: the Trail Ride. Hapka, Catherine. 2012. (I Can Read Level 2 Ser.). (ENG.). 32p. (J). (gr. -1-3). 16.99 *(978-0-06-208671-6(5))*; pap. 4.99 *(978-0-06-208670-9(7))* HarperCollins Pubs.

—Riff Raff Sails the High Cheese. Schade, Susan. 2014. (I Can Read Level 2 Ser.). (ENG.). 24p. (J). (gr. -1-3). pap. 3.99 *(978-0-06-230509-1(3))* HarperCollins Pubs.

—Riff Raff the Mouse Pirate. Schade, Susan. 2014. (I Can Read Level 2 Ser.). (ENG.). 24p. (J). (gr. -1-3). pap. 3.99 *(978-0-06-230507-7(7))* HarperCollins Pubs.

—Ten Fingers Can! Charlesworth, Liza & Scholastic, Inc. Staff. 2005. (ENG.). 16p. (J). (gr. -1-1). pap. 2.99 *(978-0-439-69021-8(8))* Scholastic, Inc.

—Where Do Giggles Come From? Muldrow, Diane E. 2011. (Little Golden Book Ser.). 32p. (J). (gr. -1-2). 4.99 *(978-0-375-86133-8(5)*, Golden Bks.) Random Hse. Children's Bks.

—The Zoo Is Closed Today! Beilenson, Evelyn. 2014. (ENG.). 32p. (J). 16.99 *(978-1-4413-1526-7(8)*, 9781441315267) Peter Pauper Pr. Inc.

Kennedy, Anne Vittur. The Farmer's Away! Baa! Neigh! Kennedy, Anne Vittur. 2014. (ENG.). 32p. (J). (-k). 15.99 *(978-0-7636-6679-8(3))* Candlewick Pr.

—Go Baby! Go Dog! Kennedy, Anne Vittur. 2018. (ENG.). 20p. (J). (— 1). bds. 7.99 *(978-0-8075-2971-3(0)*, 807529710) Whitman, Albert & Co.

—Ragweed's Farm Dog Handbook. Kennedy, Anne Vittur. 32p. (J). (gr. -1-2). 2018. 6.99 *(978-1-5362-0143-7(X))*; 2015. 15.99 *(978-0-7636-7417-5(6))* Candlewick Pr.

Kennedy, Annie. We All Fall for Apples. Herman, Emmi S. 2003. (Hello Reader Ser.). 32p. (J). pap. *(978-0-439-57396-2(3))* Scholastic, Inc.

Kennedy, Cam. Strange Case of Dr. Jekyll & Mr. Hyde. Stevenson, Robert Louis. 2008. (ENG.). 48p. (YA). (gr. 5). pap. 11.95 *(978-0-88776-882-8(2)*, Tundra Bks.) Tundra Bks. CAN. Dist: Penguin Random Hse. LLC.

Kennedy, Catherine. Swimming Along. Herbertson, Lisa. 2011. 26p. pap. 12.00 *(978-1-60976-293-3(2)*, Eloquent Bks.) Strategic Book Publishing & Rights Agency (SBPRA).

Kennedy, Debi. The Angry Monster Book. Kennedy, Debi. 2005. 30p. (J). 8.99 *(978-0-9769959-0-6(5))* nJoy Bks.

Kennedy, Doug. Six Foolish Fishermen, 1 vol. San Souci, Robert D. 2011. (ENG.). 32p. (J). (gr. k-3). 16.99 *(978-1-4556-1473-8(4)*, Pelican Publishing) Arcadia Publishing.

Kennedy, Doug & Kennedy, Roy D. Pirate Pete. Kennedy, Kim. ed. 2010. (ENG.). 40p. (J). (gr. -1-3). pap. 8.95 *(978-0-8109-8923-8(9))* Abrams, Inc.

Kennedy, Graham. African Myths. Morris, Neil. 2009. (Myths from Many Lands Ser.). 48p. (YA). (gr. 2-6). pap. 12.85 *(978-1-60754-216-2(1))* Windmill Bks.

—Chinese Myths. Bingham, Jane & Sansom, Fiona. 2009. (Myths from Many Lands Ser.). 48p. (YA). (gr. 2-6). pap. 12.85 *(978-1-60754-219-3(6))*; (gr. 4-7). 32.25 *(978-1-60754-218-6(8))* Windmill Bks.

—Moses the Child: Kept by God. Mackenzie, Carine. 2008. (Bible Alive Ser.). (ENG.). 24p. (J). 4.50 *(978-1-84550-330-7(9)*, 1db89f9b-ad7b-4450-b231-8a029d800549) Christian Focus Pubns. GBR. Dist: Baker & Taylor Publisher Services (BTPS).

—Moses the Leader: Used by God. MacKenzie, Carine. 2008. (Bible Alive Ser.). (ENG.). 24p. (J). 4.50 *(978-1-84550-332-1(5)*, 37cca844-6ed5-4636-94d3-7f7403cf877a) Christian Focus Pubns. GBR. Dist: Baker & Taylor Publisher Services (BTPS).

—Moses the Shepherd: Chosen by God. Mackenzie, Carine. 2008. (Bible Alive Ser.). (ENG.). 24p. (J). 4.50 *(978-1-84550-331-4(7)*, da9a24c7-c4d2-42cf-82fe-119c8d9035aa) Christian Focus Pubns. GBR. Dist: Baker & Taylor Publisher Services (BTPS).

—Moses the Traveller: Guided by God. Mackenzie, Carine. 2008. (Bible Alive Ser.). (ENG.). 24p. (J). 4.50 *(978-1-84550-333-8(3)*, f4288eda-0465-4d9d-bb2f-ae0e185960bb) Christian Focus Pubns. GBR. Dist: Baker & Taylor Publisher Services (BTPS).

Kennedy, Graham, jt. illus. see Sansom, Fiona.

Kennedy, Karen J. The Bee's Lullaby. Young, Lynne. 2017. (ENG.). (J). pap. 12.00 *(978-1-946989-04-8(5))* Full Court Pr.

Kennedy, Kelly. Chicken in the City. Fleming, Maria & Charlesworth, Liza. 2004. (Grammar Tales Ser.). (ENG.). 16p. (J). (gr. 3-7). pap. 3.25 *(978-0-439-45816-0(1))* Scholastic, Inc.

—A Dog Named Opposite. Teagarden, Janine. 2010. 16p. (J). *(978-0-545-24821-1(3))* Scholastic, Inc.

—The Emperor's New Uniform. Haselhurst, Maureen. 2015. (Tadpoles: Fairytale Twists Ser.). (ENG.). 32p. (J). (gr. 1-2). *(978-0-7787-1933-5(2))* Crabtree Publishing Co.

—Four Fiddlers. Slater, Teddy. 2005. (ENG.). 16p. (J). (gr. -1-1). pap. 2.99 *(978-0-439-69008-9(0))* Scholastic, Inc.

Kennedy, Kelly. Goodnight Exomoon: An Astronomical Parody. Arcand, Kimberly K. Cottage Door Press, ed. 2020. (Smithsonian Kids Storybook Ser.). (ENG.). 34p. (J). (gr. -1-2). 9.99 ***(978-1-68052-934-0(X)***, 1005760) Cottage Door Pr.

Kennedy, Kelly. How to Master the School Universe: Homework, Teachers, Tests, Bullies, & Other Ways to Survive the Classroom. Whitney, Brooks. 2004. 80p. (J). pap. *(978-0-439-57902-5(3))* Scholastic, Inc.

—If You Were a Kid at the Iditarod. Gregory, Josh. 2018. (If You Were a Kid Ser.). (ENG.). 32p. (J). (gr. 2-4). lib. bdg. 26.00 *(978-0-531-23213-2(1)*, Children's Pr.) Scholastic Library Publishing.

—If You Were a Kid Surviving a Hurricane. Gregory, Josh. 2017. (If You Were a Kid Ser.). (ENG.). 32p. (J). (gr. 2-4). lib. bdg. 26.00 *(978-0-531-23745-8(1)*, Children's Pr.) Scholastic Library Publishing.

—Juliet Saves the Day! 2018. (Sherlock Gnomes Ser.). (ENG.). 32p. (J). (gr. k-2). pap. 3.99 *(978-1-5344-1094-7(5)*, Simon Spotlight) Simon Spotlight.

—Maybe You Should Fly a Jet! Maybe You Should Be a Vet! Seuss, Dr. 2020. (Beginner Books(R) Ser.). (ENG.). 48p. (J). (gr. k-4). lib. bdg. 12.99 *(978-1-9848-9407-6(2)*, Random Hse. Bks. for Young Readers) Random Hse. Children's Bks.

—Maybe You Should Fly a Jet! Maybe You Should Be a Vet! Seuss. 2020. (Beginner Books(R) Ser.). (ENG.). 48p. (J). (gr. k-4). 9.99 *(978-1-9848-9406-9(4)*, Random Hse. Bks. for Young Readers) Random Hse. Children's Bks.

—The Mystery of the Missing Socks. Martin, Justin McCory. 2004. (Grammar Tales Ser.). (ENG.). 16p. (J). (gr. 3-7). pap. 3.25 *(978-0-439-45823-8(4))* Scholastic, Inc.

—One Little Egg. Lucero, Jaime. 2005. (ENG.). 16p. (J). (gr. -1-1). pap. 2.99 *(978-0-439-68997-7(X))* Scholastic, Inc.

—Operation Fowl Play. Menotti, Andrea. 2004. (Spy Five Ser.). 92p. (J). *(978-0-439-70349-9(2))* Scholastic, Inc.

—Operation Master Mole. Menotti, Andrea. 2004. (Spy Five Ser.). 93p. (J). *(978-0-439-70351-2(4))* Scholastic, Inc.

—Science Quiz Whiz. Schwartz, Linda. Larson, Eric, ed. 2003. 128p. (YA). (gr. 5-8). pap. 13.99 *(978-0-88160-342-2(2)*, LW-416) Creative Teaching Pr., Inc.

—Social Studies Quiz Whiz. Schwartz, Linda. Larson, Eric, ed. 2003. 128p. (YA). (gr. 5-8). pap. 13.99 *(978-0-88160-343-9(0)*, LW-417) Creative Teaching Pr., Inc.

—Who's There? 501 Side-Splitting Knock-Knock Jokes from Highlights. 2012. (Jokes & Riddles-Highlights Ser.). (ENG.). 256p. (J). (gr. 4-6). 18.69 *(978-1-59078-918-6(0))* Boyds Mills Pr.

—100 Wacky Wishes. Charlesworth, Liza & Scholastic, Inc. Staff. 2005. (ENG.). 16p. (J). (gr. -1-1). pap. 2.99 *(978-0-439-69030-0(7))* Scholastic, Inc.

Kennedy, Kelly & Downey, Dagney. The Innings & Outs of Baseball. Brown, Jordan D. 2015. (Science of Fun Stuff Ser.). (ENG.). 48p. (J). (gr. 1-3). 16.99 *(978-1-4814-2862-0(4)*, Simon Spotlight) Simon Spotlight.

Kennedy, Lisa. Birrarung Wilam: a Story from Aboriginal Australia. Murphy, Aunty Joy & Kelly, Andrew. 2020. (ENG.). 40p. (J). (gr. 1-4). 17.99 ***(978-1-5362-0942-6(2))*** Candlewick Pr.

Kennedy, Lisa. Welcome to Country: A Traditional Aboriginal Ceremony. Murphy, Aunty Joy. 2018. (ENG.). 32p. (J). (gr. k-4). 16.99 *(978-0-7636-9499-9(1))* Candlewick Pr.

Kennedy, Nick & Lapovich, Melanie. Lost Beast, Found Friend. Trujillo, Josh. 2020. (Lost Beast, Found Friend Ser.). (ENG.). 48p. (J). 16.99 ***(978-1-62010-742-3(2)***, Lion Forge) Oni Pr., Inc.

Kennedy, Richard. The Kingdom of Carbonel. Sleigh, Barbara. 2009. (Carbonel Ser.). (ENG.). 240p. (J). (gr. 4-7). 17.95 *(978-1-59017-315-2(5)*, NYR Children's Collection) New York Review of Bks., Inc., The.

—The Lost Island. Dillon, Eilis. (ENG.). 208p. (J). (gr. 4-7). 2019. pap. 12.99 *(978-1-68137-355-3(6)*, NYRB Kids); 2006. 17.95 *(978-1-59017-205-6(1)*, NYR Children's Collection) New York Review of Bks., Inc., The.

Kennedy, Roy D., jt. illus. see Kennedy, Doug.

Kennedy, Sam, jt. illus. see Le Feyer, Diane.

Kennedy, Seamus, jt. illus. see Martin, Laura.

Kennedy, Victor. Willy the Scrub. McEwan, Jamie. 2004. (Junior Library Guild Selection Ser.). (ENG.). 64p. (J). (gr. 2-5). 11.95 *(978-1-58196-010-5(7)*, Darby Creek) Lerner Publishing Group.

Kennell, Julie. Sparkles Goes Home for the Holidays. Wellings, Chris R. 2011. 40p. pap. 24.95 *(978-1-4560-4120-5(7))* America Star Bks.

Kennett, Chris. Dig World (Pixel Raiders #1) O'Donnell, Steven & Bendixsen, Stephanie. 2018. (Pixel Raiders Ser.: 1). (ENG.). 192p. (J). (gr. 3-7). pap. 6.99 *(978-1-338-16118-2(0)*, Scholastic Paperbacks) Scholastic, Inc.

—Dragon Land. O'Donnell, Steven & Bendixsen, Stephanie. 2018. (ENG.). 192p. (J). (gr. 3-7). pap. 6.99 *(978-1-338-16119-9(9)*, Scholastic Paperbacks) Scholastic, Inc.

—I Am a Droid (Star Wars) Golden Books. 2016. (Little Golden Book Ser.). (ENG.). 24p. (J). (-k). 4.99 *(978-0-7364-3489-8(5)*, Golden Bks.) Random Hse. Children's Bks.

—I Am a Sith (Star Wars) Golden Books. 2016. (Little Golden Book Ser.). (ENG.). 24p. (J). (-k). 4.99

K

(978-0-7364-3607-6(3), Golden Bks.) Random Hse. Children's Bks.

—I Am a Stormtrooper (Star Wars) Golden Books. 2017. (Little Golden Book Ser.). (ENG.). 24p. (J). (-k). 4.99 *(978-0-7364-3576-5(X)*, Golden Bks.) Random Hse. Children's Bks.

Kennett, Chris. The Marvelous Moleon, Volume 3. Weetman, Nova. 2019. (Noah & Blue's Zooniverse Ser.: 3). (ENG.). 96p. (J). (gr. 2-4). pap. 7.99 ***(978-1-76050-401-4(7))*** Hardie Grant Egmont Pty, Ltd. AUS. Dist: Independent Pubs. Group.

—The Speedy Spidersaurus, Volume 1. Weetman, Nova. 2019. (Noah & Blue's Zooniverse Ser.: 1). (ENG.). 96p. (J). (gr. 2-4). pap. 7.99 ***(978-1-76050-399-4(1))*** Hardie Grant Egmont Pty, Ltd. AUS. Dist: Independent Pubs. Group.

Kennett, Chris. Star Wars: the Empire Strikes Back (Star Wars) Smith, Geof. 2015. (Little Golden Book Ser.). (ENG.). 24p. (J). (-k). 4.99 *(978-0-7364-3544-4(1)*, Golden Bks.) Random Hse. Children's Bks.

Kennett, Chris. The Tumbling Tigerdillo, Volume 4. Weetman, Nova. 2019. (Noah & Blue's Zooniverse Ser.: 4). (ENG.). 96p. (J). (gr. 2-4). pap. 7.99 ***(978-1-76050-402-1(5))*** Hardie Grant Egmont Pty, Ltd. AUS. Dist: Independent Pubs. Group.

Kennett, Chris & Batson, Alan. Everything I Need to Know I Learned from a Star Wars Little Golden Book (Star Wars) Smith, Geof. 2016. (Little Golden Book Ser.). (ENG.). 96p. (J). (gr. 7-12). 9.99 *(978-0-7364-3656-4(1)*, Golden Bks.) Random Hse. Children's Bks.

Kennett, Chris, jt. illus. see Golden Books.

Kennett, David. Armistice. Starke, Ruth. 2019. 48p. 17.99 *(978-1-921504-91-4(9)*, Working Title Pr.) HarperCollins Pubs. Australia AUS. Dist: HarperCollins Pubs.

Kenney, Sean. Cool Cars & Trucks. Kenney, Sean. Barrett, John E., photos by. 2009. (Sean Kenney's Cool Creations Ser.). (ENG.). 32p. (J). (gr. -1-3). 14.99 *(978-0-8050-8761-1(3)*, 900049948, Holt, Henry & Co. Bks. For Young Readers) Holt, Henry & Co.

—Cool City. Kenney, Sean. 2011. (Sean Kenney's Cool Creations Ser.). (ENG.). 32p. (J). (gr. -1-3). 12.99 *(978-0-8050-8762-8(1)*, 900049950, Holt, Henry & Co. Bks. For Young Readers) Holt, Henry & Co.

—Cool Robots. Kenney, Sean. 2010. (Sean Kenney's Cool Creations Ser.). (ENG.). 32p. (J). (gr. -1-3). 14.99 *(978-0-8050-8763-5(X)*, 900049951, Holt, Henry & Co. Bks. For Young Readers) Holt, Henry & Co.

Kenny, Gonzalo. Artemis Fowl: Guide to the World of Fairies. Donkin, Andrew. 2020. (ENG.). 192p. (J). (gr. 3-7). 16.99 *(978-1-368-04077-8(2))* Disney Pr.

Kenny, Gonzalo. Disney the One & Only Ivan: Draw Me a Story. Ferry, Beth. 2020. (ENG.). 40p. (J). (gr. -1-k). 17.99 ***(978-1-368-06024-0(2))*** Disney Pr.

Kent, Hannah. Kenny Kola. French, Joyce. 2016. (ENG.). (J). 15.95 *(978-1-60414-937-1(X))* Fideli Publishing, Inc.

Kent, Jack. Q Is for Duck: An Alphabet Guessing Game. Folsom, Michael & Elting, Mary. 2005. (Alphabet Bks.). (ENG.). 64p. (J). (gr. -1-k). 21.19 *(978-0-618-57389-9(5)*, Clarion Bks.) Houghton Mifflin Harcourt Trade & Reference Pubs.

—Q Is for Duck: An Alphabet Guessing Game. Folsom, Michael & Elting, Mary. 2007. 60p. (gr. -1-k). 16.95 *(978-0-7569-7871-6(8))* Perfection Learning Corp.

—There's No Such Thing As a Dragon. 2009. 32p. (J). (gr. -1-2). pap. 7.99 *(978-0-375-85137-7(2)*, Dragonfly Bks.) Random Hse. Children's Bks.

Kent, Jack. The Caterpillar & the Polliwog. Kent, Jack. 2018. (Classic Board Bks.). (ENG.). 34p. (J). (gr. -1-k). bds. 7.99 *(978-1-5344-1377-1(4)*, Little Simon) Little Simon.

Kent, Jack & Kent, June K. Q Is for Duck: An Alphabet Guessing Game. Folsom, Michael & Elting, Mary. 2005. (ENG.). 64p. (J). (gr. -1-3). pap. 7.99 *(978-0-618-57412-4(3)*, 100419) Houghton Mifflin Harcourt Publishing Co.

Kent, June K., jt. illus. see Kent, Jack.

Kent, Lorna. At the Beach. 2004. 8p. (J). bds. 3.99 *(978-1-85854-087-0(9))* Brimax Books Ltd. GBR. Dist: Byeway Bks.

—At the Zoo. 2004. 8p. (J). bds. 3.99 *(978-1-85854-084-9(4))* Brimax Books Ltd. GBR. Dist: Byeway Bks.

—Baby's First ABC Book. 2004. 12p. (J). bds. 7.99 *(978-1-85854-659-9(1))* Brimax Books Ltd. GBR. Dist: Byeway Bks.

—Baby's First Animal Book. 2004. 12p. (J). bds. 7.99 *(978-1-85854-884-5(5))* Brimax Books Ltd. GBR. Dist: Byeway Bks.

—Baby's First Board Books: On the Move; Animals; My Home; Playtime. 2004. (Baby's First Board Books Gift Set Ser.). 12p. (J). bds. 12.99 *(978-1-85854-694-0(X))* Brimax Books Ltd. GBR. Dist: Byeway Bks.

—Baby's First Counting Book. 2004. 12p. (J). bds. 7.99 *(978-1-85854-616-2(8))* Brimax Books Ltd. GBR. Dist: Byeway Bks.

—Baby's First Toys Book. 2004. 10p. (J). bds. 7.99 *(978-1-85854-882-1(9))* Brimax Books Ltd. GBR. Dist: Byeway Bks.

—Baby's First Word Book. 2004. 12p. (J). bds. 7.99 *(978-1-85854-478-6(5))* Brimax Books Ltd. GBR. Dist: Byeway Bks.

—In My House. 2004. 8p. (J). bds. 3.99 *(978-1-85854-086-3(0))* Brimax Books Ltd. GBR. Dist: Byeway Bks.

—In the Garden. 2004. 8p. (J). bds. 3.99 *(978-1-85854-088-7(7))* Brimax Books Ltd. GBR. Dist: Byeway Bks.

—In the Park. 2004. 8p. (J). bds. 3.99 *(978-1-85854-097-9(6))* Brimax Books Ltd. GBR. Dist: Byeway Bks.

—On the Move. 2004. 8p. (J). pap. 3.99 *(978-1-85854-089-4(5))* Brimax Books Ltd. GBR. Dist: Byeway Bks.

—Word Magic: Magnetic Sentence Builder. 8p. (J). bds. *(978-1-58048-382-7(8))* Sandvik Publishing.

Kent, Nicola. The Strongest Mom. Kent, Nicola. 2018. (ENG.). 32p. (J). (gr. -1-k). 17.99 *(978-0-8075-7616-8(6)*, 807576166) Whitman, Albert & Co.

Kent, Peter. Jesus Detective: A Puzzle Search Book, 1 vol. Martin, Peter. ed. 2014. (ENG.). 48p. (J). (gr. 2-4). 11.99 *(978-0-7459-6444-7(3))* Lion Hudson PLC GBR. Dist: Independent Pubs. Group.

—Uncover History. Brookes, Olivia. 2009. (Hide-and-Seek Visual Adventures Ser.). 24p. (J). (gr. 2-5). lib. bdg. 25.60 *(978-1-60754-653-5(1))* Windmill Bks.

—Uncover Technology. Brookes, Olivia. 2009. (Hide-and-Seek Visual Adventures Ser.). 24p. (J). (gr. 2-5). lib. bdg. 25.60 *(978-1-60754-658-0(2))* Windmill Bks.

Kent, Rockwell. Paul Bunyan. Shephard, Esther. 2006. (ENG.). 256p. (J). (gr. 5-7). pap. 15.95 *(978-0-15-205857-9(5)*, 1197592) Houghton Mifflin Harcourt Publishing Co.

Kenyon, David Grayson. What Is the World Series? Herman, Gail. 2015. (What Was-? Chapter Ser.). (ENG.). 112p. (J). (gr. 3-6). 18.69 *(978-1-4844-5712-2(9))* Penguin Publishing Group.

—What Is the World Series? Herman, Gail & Who HQ. 2015. (What Was? Ser.). (ENG.). 112p. (J). (gr. 3-7). 5.99 *(978-0-448-48406-8(4)*, Penguin Workshop) Penguin Young Readers Group.

—What Was D-Day? Demuth, Patricia Brennan & Who HQ. 2015. (What Was? Ser.). 112p. (J). (gr. 3-7). 5.99 *(978-0-448-48407-5(2)*, Penguin Workshop) Penguin Young Readers Group.

Kenyon, Ray. Amanda Kanda & a Panda. Donoho, Sue & Donoho, Rick. 2019. (ENG.). 40p. (J). pap. 12.99 ***(978-1-6920-3141-1(4))*** Independently Published.

Kenyon, Richard J. The Skunk Who Lost His Stink. Sergiacomi, Jessica E. & Covert, Jacquelyn D. 2018. (ENG.). 34p. (J). pap. 14.50 *(978-0-578-41850-6(9))* Covert & Sergiacomi Publishing.

Kenyon, Tony. Floppy Ears. Symes, Ruth Louise. 2005. (ENG.). 32p. (J). *(978-1-84255-264-3(3)*, Orion Children's Bks.) Hachette Children's Group.

Keoghan, Angela. Animal Stories: 40 Stories & Rhymes to Share. Cottage Door Press, ed. 2019. (Treasury to Read Ser.). (ENG.). 192p. (J). (gr. -1-2). 14.99 *(978-1-68052-468-0(2)*, 2000670) Cottage Door Pr.

—Bedtime Stories: 40 Stories & Rhymes to Share. Cottage Door Press, ed. 2019. (Treasury to Share Ser.). (ENG.). 192p. (J). (gr. -1-2). 14.99 *(978-1-68052-469-7(0)*, 2000680) Cottage Door Pr.

Keown, Dale, et al. Legends of Marvel: Avengers. 2020. (ENG.). 128p. (YA). (gr. 8-17). pap. 17.99 *(978-1-302-92195-8(9))* Marvel Worldwide, Inc.

Keramidas, Nicolas. Mickey's Craziest Adventures. Trondheim, Lewis. 2017. 48p. (J). (gr. 4-7). 14.99 *(978-1-63140-694-2(9)*, 9781631406942) Idea & Design Works, LLC.

Kerascoët. The Bug Girl: A True Story. Spencer, Sophia & McNamara, Margaret. 2020. (ENG.). 44p. (J). (gr. -1-3). 17.99 *(978-0-525-64593-1(4)*, Schwartz & Wade Bks.) Random Hse. Children's Bks.

—Malala's Magic Pencil. Yousafzai, Malala. 2017. (ENG.). 48p. (J). (gr. -1-3). 17.99 *(978-0-316-31957-7(0))* Little Brown & Co.

Kerascoet. Paul & Antoinette. 2016. (ENG.). 40p. (J). (gr. -1-3). 17.95 *(978-1-59270-196-4(5))* Enchanted Lion Bks., LLC.

Kerascoët & Kerascoët. Jacky Ha-Ha. Patterson, James & Grabenstein, Chris. (Jacky Ha-Ha Ser.: 1). (ENG.). 384p. (J). (gr. 3-7). 2017. pap. 7.99 *(978-0-316-43253-5(9))*; 2016. 30.00 *(978-0-316-26249-1(8))* Little Brown & Co. (Jimmy Patterson).

—Jacky Ha-Ha: My Life Is a Joke. Patterson, James & Grabenstein, Chris. 2017. (Jacky Ha-Ha Ser.: 2). (ENG.). 352p. (J). (gr. 3-7). 13.99 *(978-0-316-43376-1(4)*, Jimmy Patterson) Little Brown & Co.

Kerascoët, jt. illus. see Kerascoët.

Keraval, Gwen. Puss in Boots. Perrault, Charles. ed. 2017. 24p. (J). (-k). 14.95 *(978-1-912006-84-7(7)*, Scribblers) Book Hse. GBR. Dist: Sterling Publishing Co., Inc.

Kerber, Kathy. The Backpack Bears' Adventure: No Bullies Allowed. Nelson, Sheila K. 2010. 24p. pap. 14.99 *(978-1-4490-9726-4(X))* AuthorHouse.

Kerby, Johanna, photos by. Little Pink Pup. Kerby, Johanna. 2010. (ENG., 32p. (J). (gr. -1-k). 16.99 *(978-0-399-25435-2(8)*, G.P. Putnam's Sons Books for Young Readers) Penguin Young Readers Group.

Kerchner, Janet Hall. 'Cuz That's Just My Way. RAZ. 2005. 32p. (J). bds. 15.95 *(978-0-9712070-4-2(6))* B2Z Publishing, Inc.

Keren Weaver Graphics. Luke & Lori's Musical Journey: Learning the Basic Elements of Music. Price, Melissa. 2003. 48p. (J). spiral bd. *(978-0-9747792-0-1(2))* Luke & Lori Bks.

Kerins, Tony. Before I Go to Sleep. Randall, Ronne. 2010. (Picture Books Ser.). (J). (gr. -1-k). bds. *(978-1-4075-8756-1(0))* Parragon, Inc.

Kern, Adrienne. The Midnight Ghosts. Fischel, Emma. 2005. (Young Reading Ser.: Vol. 2). 64p. (J). (gr. 2-18). lib. bdg. 13.95 *(978-1-58086-777-1(4)*, Usborne) EDC Publishing.

Kern, Corbyn. Picture Prompts for Writing. Schwartz, Linda. Larson, Eric, ed. 2003. 80p. (YA). (gr. 5-8). pap. 10.99 *(978-0-88160-335-4(X)*, LW-409) Creative Teaching Pr., Inc.

Kern, Debb. The Little Red Frog. Williams, Noele. 2012. 54p. pap. 14.99 *(978-1-61807-066-1(5)*, Little Blue Flower Pr.) Grey Gate Media, LLC.

Kern, Donna. Animal Alphabet. Kern, Donna. 60.00 *(978-1-57281-296-3(6)*, DAA12) U.S. Games Systems, Inc.

—Kern Alphabet Card Games. Kern, Donna. 5.00 *(978-1-57281-092-1(0)*, AZ54) U.S. Games Systems, Inc.

Kern, LaSquizzie & Goudeau, Breanna. Finding My Cool. King, Aja Dionna. 2019. (ENG.). 38p. (J). (gr. 1-2). 21.95 ***(978-0-578-48069-5(7))***; pap. 10.95 ***(978-1-7333333-0-6(4))*** Dr. Aja Dionna King.

Kern, Shelly. Laci the Ladybug. Adams, Wayne. 2012. 16p. pap. 24.95 *(978-1-4626-7615-6(4))* America Star Bks.

Kernen, Steven. Cardinal Connection: A Cardinal Is Near. Resh, Jr Mike. 2019. (ENG.). 34p. (J). pap. 16.00 ***(978-1-5326-8870-6(9))*** Resource Pubns., Inc.

—Cardinal Connection: A Cardinal Is Near. Resh, Mike Jr. 2020. (ENG.). 34p. (J). 24.00 ***(978-1-5326-8871-3(7))*** Resource Pubns., Inc.

Kernen, Steven. The Legend of Papa Balloon, 1 vol. McClure, C. R. 2013. (ENG.). 40p. (J). (gr. -1-3). 16.99 *(978-0-7643-4410-7(2)*, 4714) Schiffer Publishing, Ltd.

Kerr, Annie S. Netti-Spaghetti's Dream Factory. Kerr, Annie S. 2018. (Netti-Spaghetti Ser.: Vol. 2). (ENG.). 36p. (J). *(978-0-6484092-1-2(X))* AskArt.

Kerr, Anthony a. The Dragon Riders (Cowboys & Dragons Book 2) Kerr, Anthony a. 2016. (ENG.). (J). pap. 12.99 *(978-0-9968565-2-2(8))* Thunder Mountain Bks., Co.

Kerr, Bethany. A Rose from Heaven. Milliman, Sharon. 2019. (ENG.). 30p. (J). pap. 12.00 ***(978-1-6945-9409-9(2))*** Independently Published.

Kerr, George. Mother West Wind's Children. Burgess, Thornton W. 2013. (Dover Children's Classics Ser.). (ENG.). 144p. (J). (gr. 1-5). pap. 3.00 *(978-0-486-49724-2(0)*, 497240) Dover Pubns., Inc.

—Old Mother West Wind. Burgess, Thornton W. annot. ed. 2011. (Dover Children's Classics Ser.). (ENG.). 336p. (J). (gr. 1-5). 20.00 *(978-0-486-48051-0(8))* Dover Pubns., Inc.

Kerr, George & Stewart, Pat. Mother West Wind's Neighbors. Burgess, Thornton W. 2003. (Dover Children's Thrift Classics Ser.). (ENG.). 96p. (J). (gr. 3-8). pap. 4.00 *(978-0-486-42846-8(X))* Dover Pubns., Inc.

Kerr, George & Stewart, Pat Ronson. Mother West Wind's Animal Friends. Burgess, Thornton W. Kerr, George, tr. 2003. (Dover Children's Thrift Classics Ser.). (ENG.). 80p. (J). (gr. 3-8). pap. 4.00 *(978-0-486-43030-0(8))* Dover Pubns., Inc.

Kerr, Jay. The Adventures of Jamie, Lord of Ledbury: The Fork in the Road. Kerr, Jay. 2018. (ENG.). 40p. (J). pap. *(978-1-7752191-0-1(0))* Korn Bks.

Kerr, Judith. The Curse of the School Rabbit. Kerr, Judith. 2020. (ENG.). 80p. (J). 16.99 *(978-0-00-837756-4(1)*, HarperCollins Children's Bks.) HarperCollins Pubs. Ltd. GBR. Dist: HarperCollins Pubs.

—Goodbye Mog. Kerr, Judith. 2003. (ENG.). 32p. (J). (gr. k-2). pap. 9.99 *(978-0-00-714969-8(7)*, HarperCollins Children's Bks.) HarperCollins Pubs. Ltd. GBR. Dist: HarperCollins Pubs.

—The Great Granny Gang: Band 11/Lime (Collins Big Cat) Kerr, Judith. 2019. (Collins Big Cat Ser.). (ENG.). 36p. (J). (gr. k-2). pap. 9.99 *(978-0-00-832090-4(X))* HarperCollins Pubs. Ltd. GBR. Dist: Independent Pubs. Group.

—Mog & Barnaby. Kerr, Judith. 2020. (ENG.). 24p. (J). pap. 8.99 *(978-0-00-836382-6(X)*, HarperCollins Children's Bks.) HarperCollins Pubs. Ltd. GBR. Dist: HarperCollins Pubs.

—Mog & Bunny. Kerr, Judith. (ENG.). 32p. (J). 2019. pap. 6.99 *(978-0-00-831055-4(6)*, HarperCollins Children's Bks.); 3rd ed. 2005. pap. 10.99 *(978-0-00-717130-9(7))* HarperCollins Pubs. Ltd. GBR. Dist: HarperCollins Pubs., Independent Pubs. Group.

—Mog & the Baby. Kerr, Judith. 3rd ed. 2005. (ENG.). 32p. (J). (gr. k-2). pap. 11.95 *(978-0-00-717132-3(3)*, HarperCollins Children's Bks.) HarperCollins Pubs. Ltd. GBR. Dist: HarperCollins Pubs.

—Mog & the Granny. Kerr, Judith. 2019. (ENG.). 32p. (J). pap. 6.99 *(978-0-00-832651-7(7)*, HarperCollins Children's Bks.) HarperCollins Pubs. Ltd. GBR. Dist: HarperCollins Pubs.

—Mog & the V. E. T. Kerr, Judith. ed. 2005. (ENG.). 32p. (J). (gr. k-2). pap. 9.99 *(978-0-00-717128-6(5)*, HarperCollins Children's Bks.) HarperCollins Pubs. Ltd. GBR. Dist: HarperCollins Pubs.

—Mog in the Dark. Kerr, Judith. ed. 2006. (ENG.). 48p. (J). (gr. k-2). pap. 9.99 *(978-0-00-717133-0(1)*, HarperCollins Children's Bks.) HarperCollins Pubs. Ltd. GBR. Dist: HarperCollins Pubs.

—Mog in the Garden. Kerr, Judith. 2019. (ENG.). 16p. (J). bds. 6.99 *(978-0-00-831056-1(4)*, HarperCollins Children's Bks.) HarperCollins Pubs. Ltd. GBR. Dist: HarperCollins Pubs.

—Mog on Fox Night. Kerr, Judith. ed. 2004. (ENG.). 32p. (J). (gr. k-2). pap. 12.95 *(978-0-00-717136-1(6)*, HarperCollins Children's Bks.) HarperCollins Pubs. Ltd. GBR. Dist: HarperCollins Pubs.

Kerr, Judith. Mog the Forgetful Cat. Kerr, Judith. ed. 2020. (ENG.). (J). 38p. bds. 7.99 ***(978-0-00-838964-2(0))***; 40p. pap. 7.99 *(978-0-00-717134-7(X))* HarperCollins Pubs. Ltd. GBR. (HarperCollins Children's Bks.). Dist: HarperCollins Pubs.

Kerr, Judith. Mog Time Treasury: Six Stories about Mog the Forgetful Cat. Kerr, Judith. 2019. (ENG.). 208p. (J). 24.99 *(978-0-00-833698-1(9)*, HarperCollins Children's Bks.) HarperCollins Pubs. Ltd. GBR. Dist: HarperCollins Pubs.

Kerr, Judith. The Mog Treasury. Kerr, Judith. 2020. (ENG.). 208p. (J). 24.99 ***(978-0-00-840775-9(4)***, HarperCollins Children's Bks.) HarperCollins Pubs. Ltd. GBR. Dist: HarperCollins Pubs.

Kerr, Judith. Mog's ABC. Kerr, Judith. 3rd ed. 2005. (ENG.). 48p. (J). (gr. -1-k). pap., pap. 8.99 *(978-0-00-717131-6(5)*, HarperCollins Children's Bks.) HarperCollins Pubs. Ltd. GBR. Dist: HarperCollins Pubs.

—Mog's Bad Thing. Kerr, Judith. (ENG.). 32p. (J). 2020. pap. 6.99 *(978-0-00-836381-9(1)*, HarperCollins Children's Bks.); 2004. pap. 9.99 *(978-0-00-664755-3(3)*, HarperSport) HarperCollins Pubs. Ltd. GBR. Dist: HarperCollins Pubs., Independent Pubs. Group.

—Mog's Christmas. Kerr, Judith. 2019. (ENG.). 30p. (J). bds. 7.99 *(978-0-00-834764-2(6)*, HarperCollins Children's Bks.) HarperCollins Pubs. Ltd. GBR. Dist: HarperCollins Pubs.

—My First Mog Books. Kerr, Judith. 2019. (ENG.). 40p. (J). bds. 8.99 *(978-0-00-834765-9(4)*, HarperCollins Children's Bks.) HarperCollins Pubs. Ltd. GBR. Dist: HarperCollins Pubs.

—One Night in the Zoo: Band 11/Lime (Collins Big Cat) Kerr, Judith. 2019. (Collins Big Cat Ser.). (ENG.). 32p. (J). (gr. -1-k). pap. 9.99 *(978-0-00-832089-8(6))* HarperCollins Pubs. Ltd. GBR. Dist: Independent Pubs. Group.

—The Tiger Who Came to Tea. Kerr, Judith. 2019. (ENG.). 32p. (J). (gr. -1-2). 8.99 *(978-1-5362-0962-4(7))* Candlewick Pr.

Kerr, Thomas & Hierstein, Judith. Noah & the Eight Trucks of Hanukkah, 1 vol. Rips, Nancy. 2019. (ENG.). 32p. (J). 16.99 *(978-1-4556-2203-0(6)*, Pelican Publishing) Arcadia Publishing.

Kerri, Fleming Hicks. Thank You Lord for Little Feet. Jimenez, Dawn. 2017. (ENG.). 26p. (J). 22.00 *(978-1-945620-37-9(4))* Hear My Heart Publishing.

Kerrigan, Brooke. Bullying: Deal with It Before Push Comes to Shove. Slavens, Elaine. 3rd ed. 2014. (Lorimer Deal with It Ser.). (ENG.). 32p. (J). (gr. 4-6). pap. 12.95 *(978-1-4594-0653-7(2)*, 9781459406537) James Lorimer & Co. Ltd., Pubs. CAN. Dist: Casemate Pubs. & Bk. Distributors, LLC.

—Dog Breath, 1 vol. Beck, Carolyn. 2011. (ENG.). 32p. (J). 18.95 *(978-1-55455-180-4(3)*, 8ad736c3-96a7-4fd4-86a3-f2856e86136f) Fitzhenry & Whiteside, Ltd. CAN. Dist: Firefly Bks., Ltd.

—Fishermen Through & Through, 1 vol. Sydor, Colleen. 2014. (ENG.). 32p. (J). (gr. 1-4). 17.95 *(978-0-88995-517-2(4)*, 2a6ec1fe-85ce-4b33-9ead-390754051e74) Red Deer Pr. CAN. Dist: Firefly Bks., Ltd.

Kerrigan, Brooke. The Girl & the Cat, 1 vol. Brenna, Beverley. 2020. (ENG.). 32p. (J). (gr. 1-3). 19.95 ***(978-0-88995-531-8(X)***, c31fd056-b073-4703-9360-bd54cf9aef66) Red Deer Pr. CAN. Dist: Firefly Bks., Ltd.

Kerrigan, Brooke. Une Idée Pour Papi, 1 vol. Smith, Heather. 2019. (FRE.). 32p. (J). (gr. -1-k). 19.95 *(978-1-4598-2205-4(6))* Orca Bk. Pubs. USA.

—Jammie Day! Snyder, Carrie. 2017. (ENG.). 32p. (J). (gr. -1-3). 16.95 *(978-1-77147-200-5(6))* Owlkids Bks. Inc. CAN. Dist: Publishers Group West (PGW).

—Kiss Me! (I'm a Prince!), 1 vol. McLeod, Heather. 2010. 32p. (J). (gr. -1-2). 18.95 *(978-1-55455-161-3(7)*, fe3554d1-465b-4bdf-a824-4c6160821ebe) Fitzhenry & Whiteside, Ltd. CAN. Dist: Firefly Bks., Ltd.

—Little Boy Who Lived down the Drain, 1 vol. Mills, Carolyn Huizinga. 2017. (ENG.). 32p. (J). (gr. -1-2). 18.95 *(978-1-55455-395-2(4)*, ae5b4efb-107a-4122-9652-61f8d91b7e20) Trifolium Bks., Inc. CAN. Dist: Firefly Bks., Ltd.

—A Plan for Pops, 1 vol. Smith, Heather. 2019. (ENG.). 32p. (J). (gr. -1-k). 19.95 *(978-1-4598-1614-5(5))* Orca Bk. Pubs. USA.

Kerry, Andre. Lou Knows What to Do: Supermarket. Tice, Kimberly & Litvack, Venita. 2017. (Lou Knows What to Do Ser.: 1). (ENG.). 24p. (J). (gr. -1-6). pap. 10.95 *(978-1-944882-14-3(6))* Boys Town Pr.

Kershaw, Hayley. ABC. Make Believe Ideas Ltd. 2019. (Feel & Fit Ser.). (ENG.). 12p. (J). bds. *(978-1-78843-656-4(3))* Make Believe Ideas.

—Emergency! Make Believe Ideas Ltd. 2019. (ENG.). 12p. (J). bds. *(978-1-78843-657-1(1))* Make Believe Ideas.

—Feel & Fit ABC. Make Believe Ideas Ltd. 2019. (Feel & Fit Ser.). (ENG.). 12p. (J). bds. *(978-1-78843-655-7(5))* Make Believe Ideas.

Kershaw, Linda. Alberta Wayside Wildflowers, 1 vol. Kershaw, Linda. rev. ed. 2003. (ENG.). 160p. (gr. 4). pap. 16.95 *(978-1-55105-350-9(0)*, bc1be25e-add9-4ea7-8ef7-84a2db371b22) Lone Pine Publishing USA.

Kershner, Gerry. Lancaster Landmarks Coloring Book. Kershner, Gerry. 2006. 25p. (J). 4.50 *(978-1-60126-010-9(5))* Masthof Pr.

Kershner, Kyle. Amazing Animals Who Changed the World. Poelman, Heidi. 2019. (ENG.). 20p. (J). (gr. -1-5). bds. 9.99 *(978-1-64170-110-5(2)*, 550110) Familius LLC.

—Courageous People Who Changed the World. Poelman, Heidi. 2018. (ENG.). 16p. (J). bds. 9.99 *(978-1-945547-75-1(8)*, 554775) Familius LLC.

—Inventors Who Changed the World. Poelman, Heidi. 2018. (ENG.). 20p. (J). (gr. -1-5). bds. 9.99 *(978-1-64170-035-1(1)*, 550035) Familius LLC.

—100 First Words for Little Geeks. Jorden, Brooke. 2018. (100 First Words Ser.). (ENG.). 20p. (J). bds. 9.99 *(978-1-945547-95-9(2)*, 554795) Familius LLC.

—100 First Words for Little Geniuses. Jorden, Tyler. 2018. (100 First Words Ser.: 2). (ENG.). 20p. (J). (gr. k-8). bds. 9.99 *(978-1-64170-034-4(3)*, 550034) Familius LLC.

Keshavarz, Mehrafarin. Noel: An Unforgettable Night! Dumont, Claire. 2017. (ENG.). 32p. (J). 14.95 *(978-0-8091-6780-7(8))* Paulist Pr.

Kesinger, Brian. Groot #1. Loveness, Jeff. 2017. (Guardians of the Galaxy: Groot Ser.). (ENG.). 24p. (J). (gr. 4-8). lib. bdg. 27.07 *(978-1-5321-4077-8(0)*, 25482, Marvel Age) Spotlight.

—Groot #2. Loveness, Jeff. 2017. (Guardians of the Galaxy: Groot Ser.). (ENG.). 24p. (J). (gr. 4-8). lib. bdg. 27.07 *(978-1-5321-4078-5(9)*, 25483, Marvel Age) Spotlight.

—Groot #4. Loveness, Jeff. 2017. (Guardians of the Galaxy: Groot Ser.). (ENG.). 24p. (J). (gr. 4-8). lib. bdg. 27.07 *(978-1-5321-4080-8(0)*, 25485, Marvel Age) Spotlight.

—Groot #6. Loveness, Jeff. 2017. (Guardians of the Galaxy: Groot Ser.). (ENG.). 24p. (J). (gr. 4-8). lib. bdg. 27.07 *(978-1-5321-4082-2(7)*, 25487, Marvel Age) Spotlight.

—Star Wars C-3PO Does NOT Like Sand! (a Droid Tales Book) Kennedy, Caitlin. 2019. (Droid Tales Book Ser.). (ENG.). 64p. (J). (gr. 1-3). 10.99 *(978-1-368-04346-5(1)*, Disney Lucasfilm Press) Disney Publishing Worldwide.

—Star Wars R2-D2 Is LOST! Kennedy, Caitlin. 2020. (Droid Tales Book Ser.). (ENG.). 64p. (J). (gr. k-3). 10.99 *(978-1-368-05328-0(9)*, Disney Lucasfilm Press) Disney Publishing Worldwide.

Kesinger, Brian & Gandini, Vero. Groot #3. Loveness, Jeff. 2017. (Guardians of the Galaxy: Groot Ser.). (ENG.). 24p. (J). (gr. 4-8). lib. bdg. 27.07 *(978-1-5321-4079-2(7)*, 25484, Marvel Age) Spotlight.

—Groot #5. Loveness, Jeff. 2017. (Guardians of the Galaxy: Groot Ser.). (ENG.). 24p. (J). (gr. 4-8). lib. bdg. 27.07 *(978-1-5321-4081-5(9)*, 25486, Marvel Age) Spotlight.

Kesler, Matt. The Night Before Christmas. Moore, Clement C. 2012. 16p. (J). 29.95 *(978-1-59530-407-0(X))* Hallmark Card, Inc.

Kessel, Margaret May. Mama Is A Mammal. Kessel, Quinta Cattell. 2005. 80p. (J). 16.95 *(978-0-9725027-3-3(4))* Vernissage Pr., LLC.

Kessler, Leonard P. That's Not Santa! Kessler, Leonard. 2018. (ENG.). 32p. (J). (gr. -1-2). pap. 8.99 *(978-1-948959-01-8(1))* Purple Hse. Pr.

Kessler, Leonard P. Mr. Pine's Purple House. Kessler, Leonard P. 40th anniv. ed. 2005. 64p. (J). 16.00 *(978-1-930900-32-5(5))* Purple Hse. Pr.

—Mrs. Pine Takes a Trip. Kessler, Leonard P. 2005. (J). 16.00 *(978-1-930900-25-7(2))* Purple Hse. Pr.

Kessler, Mario. Moaning Morris. Hubner, Franz. 2004. 32p. (J). pap. *(978-81-87649-93-9(3))* Katha.

Kessler, Siglint. El Verano de los Animales. Fiedler, Christamaria. 2003. (SPA.). 155p. (J). (gr. 5-8). 9.95 *(978-968-19-0706-8(X))* Aguilar, Altea, Taurus, Alfaguara, S.A. de C.V MEX. Dist: Santillana USA Publishing Co., Inc.

Kest, Kristin. Alphabet of Animals. Galvin, Laura Gates. (Alphabet Bks.). (ENG.). 40p. 2011. (J). (gr. -1-3). 9.95 *(978-1-60727-443-8(4))*; 2009. 9.95 *(978-1-59249-991-5(0))*; 2006. (J). (gr. -1-k). 15.95 *(978-1-59249-655-6(5))* Soundprints.

—Animals A to Z. Galvin, Laura Gates & Soundprints Editorial Staff. Schwaeber, Barbie H. & Williams, Tracee, eds. 2008. (ENG.). 36p. (J). (gr. 3-7). 12.99 *(978-1-59069-672-9(7))* Studio Mouse LLC.

—Badger at Sandy Ridge Road. Diaz, Katacha. 2005. (Smithsonian's Backyard Ser.). (ENG.). 32p. (J). (gr. -1-2). 15.95 *(978-1-59249-420-0(X)*, B5028); 4.95 *(978-1-59249-421-7(8)*, B5078); pap. 6.95 *(978-1-59249-422-4(6)*, S5028) Soundprints.

—Badger at Sandy Ridge Road. Diaz, Katacha. 2005. (Smith Sonian's Backyard Ser.). (ENG.). 32p. (J). (gr. 2-2). 19.95 *(978-1-59249-424-8(2)*, BC5028); (gr. 2-2). 8.95 *(978-1-59249-423-1(4)*, SC5028); (gr. -1-2). 9.95 *(978-1-59249-425-5(0)*, PB5078) Soundprints.

—Bullfrog at Magnolia Circle. Dennard, Deborah. 2005. (Smithsonian's Backyard Ser.). (ENG.). 32p. (J). (gr. -1-2). 9.95 *(978-1-931465-09-0(6)*, PB5072); pap. 6.95 *(978-1-931465-39-7(8)*, S5022); 15.95 *(978-1-931465-04-5(5)*, B5022) Soundprints.

—Bumblebee at Apple Tree Lane. Galvin, Laura Gates. 2005. (Smithsonian's Backyard Ser.). (ENG.). 32p. (J). (gr. -1-2). pap. 6.95 *(978-1-931465-41-0(X)*, S5019) Soundprints.

—Bumblee at Apple Tree Lane. Galvin, Laura Gates. 2005. (Smithsonian's Backyard Ser.: Vol. 19). (ENG.). 32p. (J). (gr. -1-2). 15.95 *(978-1-56899-820-6(1)*, B5019) Soundprints.

—Gecko Gathering. Giancamilli, Vanessa. 2005. (Amazing Animal Adventures Ser.). (ENG.). (J). (gr. -1-2). 36p. 2.95 *(978-1-59249-289-3(4)*, S7157); 32p. 9.95 *(978-1-59249-323-4(8)*, PS7157); 36p. 15.95 *(978-1-59249-288-6(6)*, B7107); 36p. pap. 6.95 *(978-1-59249-290-9(8)*, S7107); 32p. 19.95 *(978-1-59249-321-0(1)*, BC7107) Soundprints.

—How Do You Sleep?, 0 vols. Bonnett-Rampersaud, Louise. 2013. (ENG.). 32p. (J). (gr. -1-1). pap. 9.99 *(978-1-4778-1669-1(0)*, 9781477816691, Two Lions) Amazon Publishing.

—How Do You Sleep?, 1 vol. Bonnett-Rampersaud, Louise. 2008. (ENG.). 34p. (J). (gr. -1). 6.99 *(978-0-7614-5449-6(7))* Marshall Cavendish Corp.

—Lemur Landing: A Story of a Madagascan Dry Tropical Forest. Dennard, Deborah. 2005. (Wild Habitats Ser.). (ENG.). 32p. (J). (gr. 1-4). 19.95 *(978-1-56899-980-7(1))* Soundprints.

—The Peregrine's Journey: A Story of Migration. Dunphy, Madeleine. 2008. (ENG.). 32p. (J). (gr. k-4). 16.95 *(978-0-9777539-3-2(X))*; per. 9.95 *(978-0-9777539-2-5(1))* Web of Life Children's Bks.

—500 Palabras Nuevas para Ti (500 Words to Grow on Spanish Edition) Random House. 2005. (Pictureback(R) Ser.). (SPA.). 32p. (J). (gr. -1-2). pap. 3.99 *(978-0-375-83308-3(0)*, Random House Para Ninos) Random Hse. Children's Bks.

—500 Words to Grow On. Random House. 2005. (Pictureback(R) Ser.). 32p. (J). (gr. -1-k). pap. 3.99 *(978-0-375-83307-6(2)*, Random Hse. Bks. for Young Readers) Random Hse. Children's Bks.

Kestere, Ulrika. Otto Goes North. Kestere, Ulrika. 2019. (ENG.). 32p. (J). (gr. k-2). 17.99 *(978-1-77657-241-0(6))* Gecko Pr. NZL. Dist: Lerner Publishing Group.

Ketchum, Ron. Rochestrivia: 2,000 Amazing questions & answers all about Rochester NY, it's people & surrounding Towns. I.t. ed. 2005. 250p. per. 19.95 *(978-0-930249-01-4(1))* Big Kids Productions (Publishing).

Keto, Alexandre. Num Tronco de Iroko Vi a Iúna Cantar. Balbino, Erika. 2014. (POR.). 75p. (J). *(978-85-7596-329-6(5))* Fundacao Peiropolis Ltda.

Kewley, Ken. Mama. Jones, Kelly. 2004. 32p. (J). *(978-0-9745930-0-5(1))* Stunt Publishing.

Key, Pamela. The Cat Who Slept All Day: What Happens While the Cat Sleeps. Coniglio, John. 2006. 24p. (J). per. 2.99 *(978-1-59958-004-3(7))* Journey Stone Creations, LLC.

—The Plight of the Queen Bee. Fairchild, Simone. 2006. 34p. (J). per. 17.95 *(978-0-9767732-3-8(6))* W & B Pubs.

Key, Pamela Marie. Queen Bee's Midnight Caper, 3 vols. Fairchild, Simone. 2006. 33p. (J). (gr. -1-3). per. 17.95 *(978-0-9771971-4-9(X))* W & B Pubs.

Keyama, Hiroshi Hata. Adventures of My Dentist & Tooth Fairy Activity & Coloring Book. Keyama, Hiroshi Hata, tr. Hood, Karen Jean Matsko. Whispering Pine Press International, Inc. Staff, ed. 2010. (ENG.). 160p. (J). pap. 9.95 *(978-1-930948-76-1(X))* Whispering Pine Pr. International, Inc.

Keyes, Tina Misrasi. The Little Black Hen. Hege, Lynnita. 2013. 208p. (J). *(978-0-7399-2465-5(6))* Rod & Staff Pubs., Inc.

Keylock, Andy. Color Me: Trucks. Southon, Josephine. 2020. (ENG.). 96p. (J). (gr. 1-3). pap. 12.95 ***(978-1-4549-4130-9(8))*** Sterling Publishing Co., Inc.

Keylock, Andy & Veres, Laszlo. Football Spy: Band 13/Topaz (Collins Big Cat) Waddell, Martin. 2007. (Collins Big Cat Ser.). (ENG.). 40p. (J). (gr. 2-3). pap. 10.99 *(978-0-00-723086-0(9))* HarperCollins Pubs. Ltd. GBR. Dist: Independent Pubs. Group.

Keylon, Joe. The Drummer Who Lost His Beat. Bloom, Stephanie. 2005. 40p. (J). lib. bdg. 16.95 *(978-1-931969-47-5(7))* Bloom & Grow Bks.

Keynan, Yoni. The Quiet Things: An Original Screenplay. Shull, Daphna. 2018. (ENG.). 212p. (J). pap. 11.99 *(978-1-9860-0855-6(X))* CreateSpace Independent Publishing Platform.

Keys, Heather. Happy the Lion. Ahrenholz, Karin. 2019. (ENG.). 26p. (J). pap. 16.95 *(978-1-9822-2586-5(6)*, Balboa Pr.) Author Solutions, Inc.

Keys, Larry. Cat & Mouse in a Haunted House. Stilton, Geronimo. 2004. (Geronimo Stilton Ser.: 3). 128p. (J). (gr. 2-5). pap. 7.99 *(978-0-439-55965-2(0)*, Scholastic Paperbacks) Scholastic, Inc.

—The Curse of the Cheese Pyramid. Stilton, Geronimo. 2004. (Geronimo Stilton Ser.: 2). 128p. (J). (gr. 2-5). pap. 7.99 *(978-0-439-55964-5(2))* Scholastic, Inc.

Keys, Larry, et al. Field Trip to Niagara Falls. Stilton, Geronimo. 2005. (Geronimo Stilton Ser.: No. 24). 121p. (J). lib. bdg. 18.46 *(978-1-4242-0293-5(0))* Fitzgerald Bks.

Keys, Larry. I'm Too Fond of My Fur! Stilton, Geronimo. 2004. (Geronimo Stilton Ser.: 4). 128p. (J). (gr. 2-5). pap. 7.99 *(978-0-439-55966-9(9)*, Scholastic Paperbacks) Scholastic, Inc.

—Red Pizzas for a Blue Count. Stilton, Geronimo. 2004. (Geronimo Stilton Ser.: 7). 128p. (J). (gr. 2-5). pap. 7.99 *(978-0-439-55969-0(3))* Scholastic, Inc.

Keys, Larry, et al. Valentine's Day Disaster. Stilton, Geronimo. 2006. (Geronimo Stilton Ser.: No. 23). 122p. (J). lib. bdg. 18.46 *(978-1-4242-0292-8(2))* Fitzgerald Bks.

Keys, Larry, jt. illus. see Wolf, Matt.

Khalafova, Aytan. Casa Estrella: Aparece una Casa Misteriosa en la Comunidad Que Necesita Ayuda. Ochinero, John. 2019. (SPA.). 30p. (J). pap. 9.95 ***(978-1-6716-6886-7(3))*** Independently Published.

—Star House: A Mysterious House Shows up in a Community Seeking Assistance. Ochinero, John. 2019. (ENG.). 30p. (J). pap. 9.95 ***(978-1-7134-4627-9(8))*** Independently Published.

Khalinsky, Nathaniel. 3... 2... 1... Done! Gijsbers, Melissa. 2016. (ENG.). (J). pap. *(978-0-9946205-1-4(9))* Lilly Pilly Publishing.

Khan, Aadil. The Parables of Jesus. Sharpe Hamilton, Angela. 2018. (ENG.). 42p. (J). pap. 24.99 *(978-1-5456-4925-1(1))* Salem Author Services.

—The Taj Mahal: An Incredible Love Story. Hoskin, Rik. 2019. (Campfire Graphic Novels Ser.). (ENG.). 118p. (YA). (gr. 7). pap. 12.99 *(978-93-81182-59-8(0)*, Campfire) Steerforth Pr.

Khan, Afzal. What Is a Bully Lacking? Allen, Delores A. 2019. (ENG.). 30p. (J). pap. 16.99 ***(978-1-7283-3358-8(X))*** AuthorHouse.

Khan, Aziz. Dictionary of horses & ponies - internet Linked. Reid, Struan. rev. ed. 2004. 128p. (J). pap. 14.95 *(978-0-7945-0843-2(X)*, Usborne) EDC Publishing.

Khan, Nadir. Taye Tari's Animal Alphabet. Jones, Lance. 2018. (ENG.). 40p. (J). *(978-1-9993164-0-2(1))* Jones, Lance G Publishing Hse.

Khan, Ruqayyah. Jibreel's Heel & the Monk of Bostra: Two Great Stories in One Book. Ahmed, Raziah. 2020. (Noble Gifted Prophet Ser.: Vol. 4). (ENG.). 38p. (J). pap. 10.50 ***(978-1-6997-2030-1(4))*** Independently Published.

Khan, Ruqayyah & Ahmed, Raziah. Jibreel & the Pen & the Tablet: Two Great Stories in One Book! Ahmed, Raziah. 2019. (Noble, Gifted Prophet Book Ser.: Vol. 3). (ENG.). 30p. (J). pap. 9.50 *(978-1-7930-3388-8(9))* Independently Published.

Khan, Saffa. Like the Moon Loves the Sky: (Mommy Book for Kids, Islamic Children's Book, Read-Aloud Picture Book) Khan, Hena. 2020. (ENG.). 36p. (J). (gr. -1-k). 17.99 *(978-1-4521-8019-9(9))* Chronicle Bks. LLC.

Khan, Sophie. Can I Tell You about Stammering? A Guide for Friends, Family & Professionals. Cottrell, Sue. 2013. (Can I Tell You About... ? Ser.). (ENG.). 48p. (C). pap. 13.95 *(978-1-84905-415-7(0)*, 694233) Kingsley, Jessica Pubs. GBR. Dist: Hachette UK Distribution.

—Can I Tell You about Stuttering? A Guide for Friends, Family, & Professionals. Cottrell, Sue. 2013. (Can I Tell You About... ? Ser.). (ENG.). 48p. (C). pap. 13.95 *(978-1-84905-435-5(5)*, 694276) Kingsley, Jessica Pubs. GBR. Dist: Hachette UK Distribution.

Khatri, Mudassir. The Misadventures of Buck the Puppy Duck: The Case of the Missing Pooch, 6 vols., Vol. 1. Cowan, C. C. 2018. (ENG.). 40p. (J). pap. 12.00 *(978-0-9677385-0-5(4))* CCP Publishing & Entertainment.

Khatun, Jen. The Lion & the Mouse. Hoena, Blake. 2018. (Classic Fables in Rhythm & Rhyme Ser.). (ENG.). 24p. (C). (gr. k-2). 33.99 *(978-1-68410-308-9(8)*, 140699) Cantata Learning.

Khavnekar, Sagar. Burrito Has a Butterbody Dyslexic Edition: Dyslexic Font. Kothari, Anushi. 2020. (ENG.). 30p. (J). (gr. k-6). 19.99 ***(978-1-64372-544-4(0))***; pap. 15.99 ***(978-1-64372-545-1(9))*** MacLaren-Cochrane Publishing, Inc.

Khaya, Nkomo. Sunset Hike. Dineo, Dowd. 2019. (ENG.). 24p. (J). (gr. k-3). 21.00 *(978-0-368-42494-6(4))* dineo dowd.

Khe, Maria. The Adventures of Jimmy the Giraffe, Sydney the Shark & Gia the Grizzly Bear. Arikat, Amin. 2020. (ENG.). 64p. (J). ***(978-1-5255-6108-5(1))***; pap. ***(978-1-5255-6109-2(X))*** FriesenPress.

Kheiriyeh, Rashin. The Book Tree. Czajak, Paul. 2018. (ENG.). 32p. (J). (gr. -1-4). 17.99 *(978-1-78285-405-0(3))* Barefoot Bks., Inc.

—Ramadan. Eliot, Hannah. 2018. (Celebrate the World Ser.). (ENG.). 24p. (J). (gr. -1 — 1). bds. 8.99 *(978-1-5344-0635-3(2)*, Little Simon) Little Simon.

—Story Boat. Maclear, Kyo. 2020. (ENG.). 40p. (J). (gr. -1-2). 17.99 *(978-0-7352-6359-8(0)*, Tundra Bks.) Tundra Bks. CAN. Dist: Penguin Random Hse. LLC.

—There Was an Old Lady Who Swallowed a Fly. 2014. 32p. (J). 17.95 *(978-0-7358-4183-3(7))* North-South Bks., Inc.

—Tortoise & Hare. Kim, YeShil. 2014. (MySELF Bookshelf Ser.). (ENG.). 32p. (J). (gr. k-2). pap. 11.94 *(978-1-60357-700-7(9))*; lib. bdg. 25.27 *(978-1-59953-665-1(X))* Norwood Hse. Pr.

Kheiriyeh, Rashin. Saffron Ice Cream. Kheiriyeh, Rashin. 2018. (ENG.). 40p. (J). (gr. -1-3). 17.99 *(978-1-338-15052-0(9)*, Levine, Arthur A. Bks.) Scholastic, Inc.

Khmelovska, Natalie, jt. illus. see Bybyk, Steven.

Khory, Emil. Gemini Cricket: John Glenn - First Person to Orbit the Earth. Crotts, Barbara. 2011. 56p. pap. 10.03 *(978-1-4269-6213-4(4))* Trafford Publishing.

Khushi, Suzanne. One More Hug: Wish upon a Star for Sweet Dreams in This Cozy, Cuddly Story. Randall, Ronne. 2017. (ENG.). 26p. (J). 7.99 *(978-1-78670-346-0(7))* Igloo Bks. GBR. Dist: Simon & Schuster, Inc.

Kiaulevicius, Rolandas. Zoolidays. Glassman, Bruce. 2006. 32p. (J). (gr. -1-3). 15.95 *(978-1-60108-011-0(5))* Red Cygnet Pr.

Kibuishi, Kazu. Firelight. 2016. 197p. (J). *(978-1-4806-9909-0(8))* Baker & Taylor, CATS.

Kibuishi, Kazu. Amulet. Kibuishi, Kazu. (Amulet Ser.). (J). (gr. 3-7). 2018. 224p. 103.92 *(978-1-338-32818-9(2)*, Graphix); Bks. 1-7, Set. 2016. 90.93 *(978-1-338-04564-2(4))* Scholastic, Inc.

—Copper. Kibuishi, Kazu. 2010. (ENG.). 96p. (J). (gr. 3-7). pap. 12.99 *(978-0-545-09893-9(9)*, Graphix) Scholastic, Inc.

—Daisy Kutter: The Last Train. Kibuishi, Kazu. 2005. 192p. (YA). per. 10.95 *(978-0-9754193-2-8(3))* Viper Comics.

—Escape from Lucien. Kibuishi, Kazu. 2014. (Amulet Ser.: 6). 208p. (J). (gr. 3-7). pap. 12.99 *(978-0-545-43315-0(0)*, Graphix) Scholastic, Inc.

—Firelight. Kibuishi, Kazu. 2016. (Amulet Ser.: 7). (J). (gr. 3-7). (ENG.). 208p. 24.99 *(978-0-545-83966-2(1))*; 224p. pap. 12.99 *(978-0-545-43316-7(9))* Scholastic, Inc. (Graphix).

—The Last Council. Kibuishi, Kazu. 2011. (Amulet Ser.: 4). 224p. (J). (gr. 3-7). pap. 12.99 *(978-0-545-20887-1(4)*, Graphix) Scholastic, Inc.

—Prince of the Elves. Kibuishi, Kazu. 2012. (Amulet Ser.: 5). 208p. (J). (gr. 3-7). pap. 12.99 *(978-0-545-20889-5(0)*, Graphix) Scholastic, Inc.

—The Stonekeeper. Kibuishi, Kazu. 2008. (Amulet Ser.: 1). 192p. (J). (gr. 3-7). pap. 12.99 *(978-0-439-84681-3(1)*, Graphix) Scholastic, Inc.

—The Stonekeeper's Curse. Kibuishi, Kazu. 2009. (Amulet Ser.: 2). 224p. (J). (gr. 3-7). pap. 12.99 *(978-0-439-84683-7(8)*, Graphix) Scholastic, Inc.

Kichka, Michel. My Sister Is Sleeping. Busheri, Devora. 2020. (ENG.). 24p. (J). (gr. -1-2). 17.99 *(978-1-5415-4244-0(4)*, Kar-Ben Publishing) Lerner Publishing Group.

Kickingbird, Samantha. How the Blue-Tongued Skink Got His Blue Tongue. Langer Thompson, Mary. 2016. (ENG.). (J). pap. 12.99 *(978-0-9978612-0-4(7))* Mindstir Media.

—Learning ABCs with Jesus: A Teaching & Learning Tool. Amerson, Gladys. 2016. (ENG.). (J). pap. 9.99 *(978-0-9979788-6-5(4))* Mindstir Media.

—Sir Princess Petra: The Pen Pieyu Adventures. Robinson, Diane Mae. 2017. (Pen Pieyu Adventures Ser.: Vol. 2). (ENG.). 110p. (J). (gr. 1-5). *(978-1-988714-08-0(7))* Robinson, Diane Mae.

—Sir Princess Petra's Talent: The Pen Pieyu Adventures. Robinson, Diane Mae. 2017. (Pen Pieyu Adventures Ser.: Vol. 2). (ENG.). 106p. (J). (gr. 1-5). *(978-1-988714-00-4(1))* Robinson, Diane Mae.

Kickingbird, Samantha & Stier, Justin. Bello the Cello. Mathew, Dennis. 2019. (ENG.). 36p. (J). (gr. k-4). pap. 12.00 *(978-1-64516-670-2(8))*; 22.95 *(978-1-64440-055-5(3))* Primedia eLaunch LLC.

Kidby, Paul. Hatched. Coville, Bruce. 2017. (Enchanted Files Ser.: 2). (ENG.). 288p. (J). (gr. 3-7). pap. 7.99 *(978-0-385-39258-7(3)*, Yearling) Random Hse. Children's Bks.

—Trolled. Coville, Bruce. 2017. (Enchanted Files Ser.: 3). (ENG.). 288p. (J). (gr. 3-7). 16.99 *(978-0-385-39259-4(1)*, Random Hse. Bks. for Young Readers) Random Hse. Children's Bks.

Kidd, Diane. Pluto's Secret: An Icy World's Tale of Discovery. Weitekamp, Margaret & DeVorkin, David. 2015. (ENG.). 40p. (J). (gr. k-4). pap. 9.95 *(978-1-4197-1526-6(7)*, Abrams Bks. for Young Readers) Abrams, Inc.

—Pluto's Secret: an Icy World's Tale of Discovery: An Icy World's Tale of Discovery. Weitekamp, Margaret. 2013. (ENG.). 40p. (J). (gr. k-4). 16.95 *(978-1-4197-0423-9(0)*, Abrams Bks. for Young Readers) Abrams, Inc.

Kidd, Tom. Stonefather. Card, Orson Scott. 2008. 112p. 35.00 *(978-1-59606-194-1(4))* Subterranean Pr.

Kidney, Kevin. Taboo Table: Tiki Cuisine from Polynesian Restaurants of Yore. Berry, Jeff. 2005. (ENG.). 96p. (YA). spiral bd. 10.95 *(978-0-943151-99-1(6)*, bc12a7cf-f7fc-4377-9eee-2edc7f38699f) Slave Labor Bks.

Kido, Yukiko. In a Scary Old House. Ziefert, Harriet. 2006. (I'm Going to Read! Level 1 Ser.). (ENG.). 32p. (J). (gr. k-1). 16.19 *(978-1-4027-3406-9(9)*, 1261644) Sterling Publishing Co., Inc.

—Lower-Case Letters. Ziefert, Harriet. 2007. (I'm Going to Read® Ser.). 64p. (J). (gr. -1-1). pap. 5.95 *(978-1-4027-5055-7(2))* Sterling Publishing Co., Inc.

—Rhyming Words. Ziefert, Harriet. 2007. (I'm Going to Read® Ser.). 64p. (J). (gr. -1-1). pap. 5.95 *(978-1-4027-5059-5(5))* Sterling Publishing Co., Inc.

—Upper-Case Letters. Ziefert, Harriet. 2007. (I'm Going to Read® Ser.). 64p. (J). (gr. -1-1). pap. 5.95 *(978-1-4027-5054-0(4))* Sterling Publishing Co., Inc.

Kiedrowski, Steve. Guess Who Saves the Rain Forest? Hoch, Jeff. Hoch, Jeff, ed. Date not set. 39p. (J). (gr. k-5). pap. 7.00 *(978-0-9650629-3-0(7))* Coulee Region Pubns., Inc.

Kiefer, Karen. Kamehameha: The Warrior King of Hawai'i. Morrison, Susan Keyes. 2003. (ENG.). 104p. pap. 15.00 *(978-0-8248-2700-7(7)*, 3465) Univ. of Hawaii Pr.

Kiefer, Katja. Wir Gehen in Die Bibliothek - A Visit to the Library: Deutsch-Englische Ausgabe. Mörchen, Roland. 2010. (ENG.). 40p. (J). (gr. 3-7). 19.99 *(978-3-487-08843-3(6))* Olms, Georg Verlag AG DEU. Dist: Independent Pubs. Group.

Kiejna, Magdalenea. Christmas Lost & Found. Martini, T. J. 2017. (J). per. 15.99 *(978-0-9705018-7-5(0))* Wings, Inc.

Kiel, Casey K. Andrew Goes to the Chiropractor. Carlson, Geri L. 2007. (J). 21.99 *(978-1-59879-432-8(9))*; per. 15.99 *(978-1-59879-467-0(1))* Lifevest Publishing, Inc. (Lifevest).

Kiel, Casey Kizer. Maggie Seeks the Kingdom of God. Moore, Angela Hays. 2007. 32p. (J). 19.99 *(978-1-59879-323-9(3))* Lifevest Publishing, Inc.

Kieley, Rob. The Amazing Machine. Eggleton, Jill. (Sails Literacy Ser.). 24p. (gr. 3-18). 27.00 *(978-0-7578-6979-2(3))*;Pack. 57.00 *(978-0-7578-6995-2(5))* Rigby Education.

—The Amazing Machine: 6 Small Books. Eggleton, Jill. (Sails Literacy Ser.). 24p. (gr. 3-18). 25.00 *(978-0-7578-6987-7(4))* Rigby Education.

Kiely, Orla. Numbers. Kiely, Orla. 2012. (ENG.). 20p. (J). (gr. -1 — 1). bds. 12.99 *(978-0-8050-9492-3(X)*, 900080253, Holt, Henry & Co. Bks. For Young Readers) Holt, Henry & Co.

Kiely, Rob. Dinosaurs. Hinkler Books Staff. rev. ed. 2006. (ENG.). 6p. (J). (gr. 2-5). 9.95 *(978-1-74157-725-9(X))* Hinkler Bks. Pty. Ltd. AUS. Dist: Penton Overseas, Inc.

Kienzle, Bekah. Ricky, Buddy & Marshall: Pranks, Mischief & Adventure. Anderson, Marshall. 2019. (ENG.). 244p. (J). pap. 12.99 *(978-0-578-43586-2(1))* Anderson, Marshall.

Kiernan, Kenny. Fire in the Forest! Brooke, Samantha. 2012. 31p. (J). *(978-1-4242-5340-1(3))* Scholastic, Inc.

—Firefighter Rescue. King, Trey. 2015. (LEGO City Ser.). 32p. (J). (gr. -1-3). pap. 3.99 *(978-0-545-82555-9(5))* Scholastic, Inc.

—Kevin, the Money Master: How a Little Boy Learned to Master Money & How You Can Too! Wagner, Jessica. 2018. (Family Who Reads Together Stays Together Ser.: Vol. 1). (ENG.). 32p. (J). (gr. k-5). 18.99 *(978-1-947884-00-7(X))* Don't Stop Publishing.

—The Lego Movie. Salane, Jeffrey. 2013. (LEGO: the LEGO Movie Ser.). (ENG.). 64p. (J). (gr. 2-5). pap. 5.99 *(978-0-545-62462-6(2))* Scholastic, Inc.

—Look Out Below! Steele, Michael Anthony & Scholastic Editors. ed. 2012. (LEGO City Scholastic Readers Level 1 Ser.). lib. bdg. 13.55 *(978-0-606-26236-1(9))* Turtleback.

—Save the Day! King, Trey. 2013. (LEGO DC Super Heroes Ser.). (ENG.). 32p. (J). (gr. -1-3). pap. 3.99 *(978-0-545-48028-4(0))* Scholastic, Inc.

—Save the Day! 2013. (J). *(978-1-4844-0146-0(8))* Scholastic, Inc.

Kiernicki, Cindy. Lights & Music Bedtime Songs: Lights & Music Board Book. Wing, Scarlett. Cottage Door Press, ed. 2018. (ENG.). 12p. (J). (gr. -1-k). bds. 16.99 *(978-1-68052-346-1(5)*, 1003180) Cottage Door Pr.

Kiesler, Kate. Crab Moon. Horowitz, Ruth. 2004. (ENG.). 32p. (J). (gr. -1-3). pap. 7.99 *(978-0-7636-2313-5(X))* Candlewick Pr.

—The Great Frog Race: And Other Poems. George, Kristine O'Connell. 2005. (ENG.). 48p. (J). (gr. -1-3). reprint ed. 6.99 *(978-0-618-60478-4(2)*, 100436) Houghton Mifflin Harcourt Publishing Co.

—Hello, Harvest Moon. Fletcher, Ralph J. & Fletcher, Ralph. 2003. (ENG.). 32p. (J). (gr. -1-3). 17.99 *(978-0-618-16451-6(0)*, 111136) Houghton Mifflin Harcourt Publishing Co.

—Hello, Harvest Moon. Fletcher, Ralph. 2017. (ENG.). 32p. (J). (gr. -1-3). pap. 7.99 *(978-1-328-74049-6(8)*, 1677015, HMH Books For Young Readers) Houghton Mifflin Harcourt Publishing Co.

—Old Elm Speaks. George, Kristine O'Connell. 2007. (ENG.). 48p. (J). (gr. -1-3). 7.99 *(978-0-618-75242-3(0)*, 100524) Houghton Mifflin Harcourt Publishing Co.

Kightley, Rosalinda. Big Hug for Little Cub. Grover, Lorie Ann. 2014. 8p. (J). (— 1). bds. 7.99 *(978-0-545-53091-0(1)*, Cartwheel Bks.) Scholastic, Inc.

—I'm a Big Brother. Cole, Joanna. 2010. (ENG.). 32p. (J). (gr. -1-3). 7.99 *(978-0-06-190065-5(6)*, HarperFestival) HarperCollins Pubs.

—I'm a Big Sister. Cole, Joanna. 2010. (ENG.). 32p. (J). (gr. -1-3). 7.99 *(978-0-06-190062-4(1)*, HarperFestival) HarperCollins Pubs.

—Soy un Hermano Mayor: I'm a Big Brother (Spanish Edition), 1 vol. Cole, Joanna. 2010. (SPA.). 32p. (J). (gr. -1-k). 6.99 *(978-0-06-190066-2(4))* HarperCollins Pubs.

—Soy una Hermana Mayor: I'm a Big Sister (Spanish Edition), 1 vol. Cole, Joanna. 2010.Tr. of I am a Big Sister. (SPA.). 32p. (J). (gr. -1-k). 6.99 *(978-0-06-190063-1(X))* HarperCollins Pubs.

—Sparkly Christmas Angel. Watt, Fiona. 2007. (Luxury Touchy-Feely Board Bks). 10p. (J). (gr. -1-k). bds. 15.99 *(978-0-7945-1477-8(4)*, Usborne) EDC Publishing.

Kightly, Rosalinda. The Right Shoes for Me! Wang, Margaret. 2006. (ENG.). 12p. (J). (gr. -1-k). bds. 9.95 *(978-1-58117-494-6(2)*, Intervisual/Piggy Toes) Bendon, Inc.

Kiko. Who Lives Where? A Slide-And-Learn Book. Babin, Stephanie. 2019. (Slide-And-Learn Ser.: 2). (ENG.). 14p. (J). (gr. -1-k). bds. 12.99 *(978-2-408-00796-6(8))* Éditions Tourbillon FRA. Dist: Hachette Bk. Group.

Kilby, Don. Twilight Fairies, 1 vol. Hundal, Nancy. 2006. (ENG.). 32p. (J). (gr. k-3). per. 4.95 *(978-1-55041-961-0(7)*, 332ccce4-8c81-43cf-b802-2e266c530cbe) Fitzhenry & Whiteside, Ltd. CAN. Dist: Firefly Bks., Ltd.

Kilby, Don. On the Road. Kilby, Don. 2006. (Wheels at Work Ser.). 24p. (J). (gr. -1-2). 5.95 *(978-1-55337-986-7(1))* Kids Can Pr., Ltd. CAN. Dist: Hachette Bk. Group.

Kilby, Jak. Hindu Mandir. A&C Black Staff & Ganeri, Anita. 2004. 32p. pap. *(978-0-7136-5495-0(3)*, A&C Black) Bloomsbury Publishing Plc.

K

Killaire, B. M. The Adventures of Betty & Bo-Bob: A Tale of One & a Half Frogs. Killaire, B. M. Kwik, Penny Shannon, ed. 2012. 32p. pap. 24.95 *(978-1-4626-6621-8(3))* America Star Bks.

Kille, Steve. Boris the Dog. Soling, Cevin. 2015. (ENG.). 44p. 14.95 *(978-0-9767771-6-8(9))* Spectacle Films, Inc.

Killen, Nicola. Bobo & Co. Numbers. Killen, Nicola. ed. 2018. 10p. (J). bds. 9.99 *(978-1-4088-8002-9(4),* 9781408880029, Bloomsbury Children's Bks.) Bloomsbury Publishing USA.

Killen, Nicola. The Little Kitten. Killen, Nicola. 2020. (My Little Animal Friend Ser.). (ENG.). 32p. (J). (gr. -1-3). 16.99 ***(978-1-5344-6696-8(7),*** Simon & Schuster/Paula Wiseman Bks.) Simon & Schuster/Paula Wiseman Bks.

Killen, Nicola. The Little Rabbit. Killen, Nicola. 2019. (My Little Animal Friend Ser.). (ENG.). 32p. (J). (gr. -1-3). 15.99 *(978-1-5344-3828-6(9),* Simon & Schuster/Paula Wiseman Bks.) Simon & Schuster/Paula Wiseman Bks.

—The Little Reindeer. Killen, Nicola. 2017. (My Little Animal Friend Ser.). (ENG.). 32p. (J). (gr. -1-3). 17.99 *(978-1-4814-8686-6(1),* Simon & Schuster/Paula Wiseman Bks.) Simon & Schuster/Paula Wiseman Bks.

Killgore, Kodi. Feathers & Cheese. Tucker, G. Weldon. 2018. (ENG.). 54p. (J). pap. 14.99 *(978-1-7262-9941-1(4))* CreateSpace Independent Publishing Platform.

Killian, Sue. Once upon a Peanut: A true Story... Whelahan, Marlene. 2009. 24p. pap. 12.99 *(978-1-4389-5925-2(7))* AuthorHouse.

Killora, Ariana. Smarty Marty Steps up Her Game. Gutierrez, Amy. 2017. (ENG.). 132p. (J). (gr. 2-5). 13.95 *(978-1-944903-08-4(9),* Cameron Kids) Cameron + Co.

Killoran, Ariana. The One & Only Me: A Book about Genes. Inc., 23andMe. 2016. (ENG.). 32p. (J). (gr. -1-3). 15.95 *(978-0-9891537-1-3(1))* 23andMe.

—You Share Genes with Me. Inc., 23andMe. 2016. (ENG.). 18p. (J). (gr. -1-k). bds. 9.99 *(978-0-9891537-0-6(3))* 23andMe.

Killpack, David C. North American Box Turtles: Natural History & Captive Maintenance. Franklin, Carl J. 2003. (YA). 24.99 *(978-0-9741381-0-7(X))* Illumination Studios.

Kim. Colors All Around. 2008. (SPA & ENG.). 28p. (J). pap. 8.95 *(978-1-60448-009-2(2))* Lectura Bks.

Kim, Alex & Stone, Bryan. Explore the Wild West! With 25 Great Projects. Yasuda, Anita. 2012. (Explore Your World Ser.). 96p. (J). (gr. k-4). pap. 12.95 *(978-1-936749-71-3(8),* ae5c3af6-2f88-4db2-a595-817d1cc21fc6) Nomad Pr.

Kim, Anna. Danbi Leads the School Parade. Kim, Anna. 2020. 40p. (J). (gr. -1-2). 17.99 ***(978-0-451-47889-4(4),*** Viking Books for Young Readers) Penguin Young Readers Group.

Kim, Aram. Cat on the Bus. Kim, Aram. 2016. (ENG.). 32p. (J). (gr. -1-k). 16.95 *(978-0-8234-3647-7(0))* Holiday Hse., Inc.

Kim, Bo-young. The Shark That Taught Me English/El Tiburon Que Me Enseno Ingles. Markel, Michelle. 2008. (SPA & ENG.). 28p. (J). pap. 8.95 *(978-1-60448-003-0(3))* Lectura Bks.

—The Shark That Taught Me English/El Tiburon Que Me Enseno Ingles. Markel, Michelle. Guerrero, Ernesto, tr. 2008. (ENG & SPA.). 28p. (J). (gr. 1-2). 15.95 *(978-1-60448-002-3(5))* Lectura Bks.

Kim, Boo Young, et al. Stone Age Santa. O'Donnell, Kevin & Gon, Zang Sung. 2007. (ENG.). 128p. (J). (gr. 4-7). 11.95 *(978-1-58818-153-4(7))* Hill Street Pr., LLC.

Kim, Boyoun. My First Book of Patterns. George, Bobby, Jr. et al. 2017. (ENG.). 66p. (gr. -1 — 1). bds. 16.95 *(978-0-7148-7249-0(0))* Phaidon Pr., Inc.

Kim, Cecil & Kim, Joo-Kyung. A Happy Hat. 2014. 32p. (J). pap. *(978-1-4338-1337-5(8),* Magination Pr.) American Psychological Assn.

Kim, Derek Kirk. The Eternal Smile. Yang, Gene Luen. 2009. (ENG.). 176p. (YA). (gr. 9-12). pap. 18.99 *(978-1-59643-156-0(3),* 9781596431560, First Second Bks.) Roaring Brook Pr.

Kim, Derek Kirk. Vanishing Point. Kim, Derek Kirk. 2012. (Tune Ser.: 1). (ENG.). 160p. pap. 17.99 *(978-1-59643-516-2(X),* 900058926, First Second Bks.) Roaring Brook Pr.

Kim, Dong Soo. Twinkle, Twinkle! Lee, Mi-Ae. Cowley, Joy, ed. 2015. (Science Storybooks Ser.). (ENG.). 32p. (J). (gr. k-4). 10.00 *(978-1-925233-62-9(6),* Big and SMALL) ChoiceMaker Pty. Ltd., The AUS. Dist: Lerner Publishing Group.

Kim, Dong-soo. Twinkle Twinkle: Insect Life Cycle. Lee, Mi-Ae. Cowley, Joy, ed. 2015. (Science Storybooks Ser.). (ENG.). 32p. (gr. k-3). 7.99 *(978-1-925246-76-6(0));* 26.65 *(978-1-925246-24-7(8));* 26.65 *(978-1-925246-50-6(7))* ChoiceMaker Pty. Ltd., The AUS. (Big and SMALL). Dist: Lerner Publishing Group.

Kim, Eric. The Great Fishing Derby (Inuktitut/English) Ittimangnaq, Alex. ed. 2020. (ENG.). 40p. (J). pap. 10.95 ***(978-0-2287-0491-1(X))*** Inhabit Education CAN. Dist: Consortium Bk. Sales & Distribution.

Kim, Eric. Mamaqtuq! Cans, Jerry. ed. (ENG.). 36p. (J). 2019. 16.95 *(978-1-77227-230-7(2));* 2017. (gr. -1-1). bds. 16.95 *(978-1-77227-144-7(6))* Inhabit Media Inc. CAN. Dist: Consortium Bk. Sales & Distribution.

Kim, Eun Hee. Construyamos una Pir�mide: Las M�quinas Simples. Lee, Hee-Ju. 2018. (Click Click: Ciencia B�sica / Basic Science Ser.). (SPA.). 40p. (J). (gr. 2). pap. 17.99 ***(978-1-64101-213-3(7))*** Santillana USA Publishing Co., Inc.

Kim, Glenn. When the Sky Fell. Lynch, Mike & Barr, Brandon. 2009. (Sky Chronicles: 1). (ENG.). 368p. (YA). 18.95 *(978-0-9787782-3-1(5))* Silver Leaf Bks., LLC.

Kim, Hye-Won. Why Is It Rusty? Oxidation. Muhn, Joo-Yeong. 2017. (Science Storybooks Ser.). (ENG.). 32p. (J). (gr. k-4). lib. bdg. 27.99 *(978-1-925235-41-8(6),* Big and SMALL) ChoiceMaker Pty. Ltd., The AUS. Dist: Lerner Publishing Group.

Kim, Hyeon-ju. So Thirsty: A Water Story. Yun, Ji-yeon. 2020. (Green Earth Tales Ser.). (ENG.). 32p. (J). (gr. k-4). pap. 8.99 ***(978-1-925235-58-6(0));*** lib. bdg. 27.99 ***(978-1-925235-62-3(9))*** ChoiceMaker Pty. Ltd., The AUS. (Big and SMALL). Dist: Lerner Publishing Group.

Kim, IhHyeon. Ida's Present. Lee, HaeDa. 2014. (MySELF Bookshelf Ser.). (ENG.). 32p. (J). (gr. k-2). pap. 11.94 *(978-1-60357-694-9(0));* lib. bdg. 25.27 *(978-1-59953-659-0(5))* Norwood Hse. Pr.

Kim, Intae, photos by. Wind Drawing. 2003. 126p. pap. 50.00 *(978-0-9741052-0-8(1))* I-Mar.

Kim, Isabel Joy. Tangled in Beauty: Contemplative Nature Poems. Kim, Isabel Joy. Prasad, Siona. 2013. 74p. pap. 7.99 *(978-0-9912472-0-2(5))* Philokalos Pr.

Kim, Jaime. And Then Comes Summer. Brenner, Tom. 2017. (And Then Comes Ser.). 32p. (J). (gr. -1-3). 16.99 *(978-0-7636-6071-0(X))* Candlewick Pr.

—Around the Table That Grandad Built. Heuiser Hill, Melanie. 2019. (ENG.). 32p. (J). (gr. -1-2). 16.99 *(978-0-7636-9784-6(2))* Candlewick Pr.

—¿de dónde Eres? Where Are You from? (Spanish Edition) Méndez, Yamile Saied. 2019. (SPA.). 40p. (J). (gr. -1-3). 17.99 *(978-0-06-291525-2(8),* HarperCollins Español) HarperCollins Christian Publishing.

—Entonces Llega el Verano. Brenner, Tom. 2020. 32p. (J). (gr. -1-3). 6.99 *(978-1-5362-1169-6(9))* Candlewick Pr.

—I Am a Bird. Walrath, Dana. 2018. (ENG.). 40p. (J). (gr. -1-3). 17.99 *(978-1-4814-8002-4(2))* Simon & Schuster Children's Publishing.

—If You Were the Moon. Salas, Laura Purdie. 2017. (ENG.). 32p. (J). (gr. k-2). 19.99 *(978-1-4677-8009-4(X),* 9781467780094); E-Book 30.65 *(978-1-5124-2838-4(8))* Lerner Publishing Group. (Millbrook Pr.).

—Isle of You. LaRochelle, David. 2018. 32p. (J). (gr. -1-2). 16.99 *(978-0-7636-9116-5(X))* Candlewick Pr.

— La La La: A Story of Hope. Dicamillo, Kate. 2017. (ENG.). 72p. (J). (gr. -1-3). 17.99 *(978-0-7636-5833-5(2))* Candlewick Pr.

—Take Heart, My Child: A Mother's Dream. Earhardt, Ainsley. 2018. (ENG.). 34p. (J). (gr. -1-k). bds. 7.99 *(978-1-5344-2631-3(0),* Little Simon) Little Simon.

—Take Heart, My Child: A Mother's Dream. Earhardt, Ainsley. 2016. (ENG.). 32p. (J). (gr. -1-3). 18.99 *(978-1-4814-6622-6(4),* Aladdin) Simon & Schuster Children's Publishing.

—Welcome to Your World. Prasadam-Halls, Smriti. 2020. (ENG.). 32p. (J). (-k). 16.99 *(978-1-5362-0622-7(9))* Candlewick Pr.

—Where Are You From? Méndez, Yamile Saied. 2019. (ENG.). 40p. (J). (gr. -1-3). 17.99 *(978-0-06-283993-0(4))* HarperCollins Pubs.

Kim, Jay Jiyeon. Meet Arzeen, Citizen of the World. Shariati, Karen Allison. 2006. 45p. (J). *(978-0-9770475-0-5(4))* Arzana, Inc.

Kim, Jean. Wide-Awake Bear. Miller, Pat Zietlow. 2018. (ENG.). 40p. (J). (gr. -1-3). 17.99 *(978-0-06-235603-1(8))* HarperCollins Pubs.

Kim, Jeehyun. Worth the Wait. Cook, William. 2007. 32p. (J). per. 15.00 *(978-0-9791387-0-6(1));* per. 15.00 *(978-0-9791387-1-3(X))* Yadda Yadda Pr.

Kim, Ji-Ah. Las Se�ales Del Cuerpo: Salud y Enfermedad. Hong, Yun Jeong. 2018. (Click Click: Ciencia B�sica / Basic Science Ser.). (SPA.). 32p. (J). pap. 17.99 ***(978-1-64101-215-7(3))*** Santillana USA Publishing Co., Inc.

Kim, Ji-Hyuk. Animal Adventures. Peterson, Melissa & Wilder, Laura Ingalls. 2017. 102p. (J). *(978-1-5182-4227-4(8))* Harper & Row Ltd.

—Christmas Stories: Adpated from the Little House Books by Laura Ingalls Wilder. Henson, Heather & Wilder, Laura Ingalls. 2017. 103p. (J). *(978-1-5379-9556-4(1))* HarperCollins Pubs.

—Christmas Stories: Reillustrated Edition. Wilder, Laura Ingalls. 2017. (Little House Chapter Book Ser.: 5). (ENG.). 112p. (J). (gr. 1-5). pap. 4.99 *(978-0-06-237714-2(0))* HarperCollins Pubs.

—The Forget-Me-Not Summer. Howland, Leila. (Silver Sisters Ser.: 1). (ENG.). (J). (gr. 3-7). 2016. 368p. pap. 7.99 *(978-0-06-231870-1(5));* 2015. 352p. 16.99 *(978-0-06-231869-5(1))* HarperCollins Pubs.

—Laura & Nellie: Reillustrated Edition. Wilder, Laura Ingalls. 2017. (Little House Chapter Book Ser.: 4). (ENG.). 112p. (J). (gr. 1-5). pap. 4.99 *(978-0-06-237713-5(2))* HarperCollins Pubs.

—Pioneer Sisters: Reillustrated Edition. Wilder, Laura Ingalls. 2017. (Little House Chapter Book Ser.: 2). (ENG.). 112p. (J). (gr. 1-5). pap. 4.99 *(978-0-06-237710-4(8),* HarperCollins) HarperCollins Pubs. Ltd. GBR. Dist: HarperCollins Pubs.

—School Days: Reillustrated Edition. Wilder, Laura Ingalls. 2017. (Little House Chapter Book Ser.: 6). (ENG.). 112p. (J). (gr. 1-5). pap. 4.99 *(978-0-06-237711-1(6))* HarperCollins Pubs.

—Through Your Eyes: My Child's Gift to Me. Earhardt, Ainsley. 2017. (ENG.). 32p. (J). (gr. -1-3). 18.99 *(978-1-5344-0959-0(9),* Aladdin) Simon & Schuster Children's Publishing.

Kim, Ji-yeon. All Kinds of Nests. Choi, Eun-gyu. Cowley, Joy, ed. 2015. (Science Storybooks Ser.). (ENG.). 32p. (J). (gr. k-4). 10.00 *(978-1-925233-60-5(X),* Big and SMALL) ChoiceMaker Pty. Ltd., The AUS. Dist: Lerner Publishing Group.

—All Kinds of Nests: Birds. Choi, Eun-gyu. Cowley, Joy, ed. 2015. (Science Storybooks Ser.). (ENG.). 32p. (gr. k-3). 26.65 *(978-1-925246-22-3(1));* 7.99 *(978-1-925246-74-2(4));* 26.65 *(978-1-925246-48-3(5))* ChoiceMaker Pty. Ltd., The AUS. (Big and SMALL). Dist: Lerner Publishing Group.

Kim, Ji-yeong. Energy Makes Changes: Energy Transformation. Chocolate Tree, Chocolate. 2020. (Science Storybooks Ser.). (ENG.). 32p. (J). (gr. k-4). lib. bdg. 27.99 *(978-1-925235-55-5(6),* Big and SMALL) ChoiceMaker Pty. Ltd., The AUS. Dist: Lerner Publishing Group.

—Energy Makes Changes: Energy Transformation. Chocolate Tree. 2020. (Science Storybooks Ser.). (ENG.). 32p. (J). (gr. k-4). pap. 8.99 *(978-1-925235-51-7(3),* Big and SMALL) ChoiceMaker Pty. Ltd., The AUS. Dist: Lerner Publishing Group.

Kim, Jin-Woo. The Little Match Girl. Olmstead, Kathleen & Andersen, Hans. 2014. (J). *(978-1-4027-8348-7(5))* Sterling Publishing Co., Inc.

Kim, John Taesoo. Nova the Star Eater. Leslie, Lindsay. 2019. (ENG.). 32p. (J). 17.99 *(978-1-62414-693-0(7),* 900197961) Page Street Publishing Co.

Kim, Joo-Kyung, jt. illus. see Kim, Cecil.

Kim, Joung Un. Hen Hears Gossip. Mcdonald, Megan. 2008. 32p. (J). (gr. -1-k). lib. bdg. 17.89 *(978-0-06-113877-5(0),* Greenwillow Bks.) HarperCollins Pubs.

—Hen Hears Gossip. McDonald, Megan. 2008. (ENG.). 32p. (J). (gr. -1-k). 17.99 *(978-0-06-113876-8(2),* Greenwillow Bks.) HarperCollins Pubs.

—Neighbors: The Yard Critters Book 1. Held, George. 2011. (ENG.). 32p. 20.00 *(978-0-916754-25-9(1))* Filsinger & Co., Ltd.

—Neighbors: The Yard Critters Too. Held, George. 2013. (ENG.). 32p. 20.00 *(978-0-916754-26-6(X))* Filsinger & Co., Ltd.

—Sid's Surprise. Carter, Candace. 2005. (Green Light Readers Level 1 Ser.). (ENG.). 32p. (J). (gr. -1-3). pap. 4.99 *(978-0-15-205182-2(1),* 1195629) Houghton Mifflin Harcourt Publishing Co.

—Sid's Surprise. Carter, Candace. 2005. (Green Light Readers Level 1 Ser.). (gr. -1-3). 13.95 *(978-0-7569-5242-6(5))* Perfection Learning Corp.

—Why the Frog Has Big Eyes. Franco, Betsy & Franco-Feeney, Betsy. 2003. (Green Light Readers Level 2 Ser.). (ENG.). 24p. (J). (gr. -1-3). pap. 4.99 *(978-0-15-204834-1(0),* 1194598) Houghton Mifflin Harcourt Publishing Co.

Kim, Julie. Sweety, Vol. 3. Kim, Ju-Ri. 2008. (Sweety Ser.: Vol. 3). 196p. (YA). pap. 9.95 *(978-1-59697-233-9(5))* Infinity Studios LLC.

—Sweety, Vol. 4. Park, Je-Sung. 2007. (Sweety Ser.: Vol. 4). 200p. (YA). per. 9.95 *(978-1-59697-234-6(3))* Infinity Studios LLC.

—Sweety, Vol. 5. Park, Se-Jung. 2007. (Sweety Ser.: Vol. 5). 200p. (YA). per. 9.95 *(978-1-59697-235-3(1))* Infinity Studios LLC.

—Sweety. Park, Je-Sung. 2007. (Sweety Ser.: Vol. 7). 200p. (YA). Vol. 6. per. 9.95 *(978-1-59697-236-0(X));* Vol. 7. per. 9.95 *(978-1-59697-237-7(8))* Infinity Studios LLC.

Kim, Julie J. Mi Lugar Preferido: My Special Space. Meachen Rau, Dana. 2005. (Rookie Reader Español Ser.). 32p. (gr. k-2). 19.50 *(978-0-516-25250-6(X),* Children's Pr.) Scholastic Library Publishing.

—My Special Space. Meachen Rau, Dana. 2003. (Rookie Readers Ser.). 32p. (J). 19.50 *(978-0-516-22881-5(1),* Children's Pr.) Scholastic Library Publishing.

—Mysterious Spinners. Pfeffer, Wendy. 2005. 48p. (J). *(978-1-59336-315-4(X));* pap. *(978-1-59336-316-1(8))* Mondo Publishing.

Kim, Julie J. Rhymitis. Kim, Julie J., tr. Bramwell, Wendie & Normand, Bridgid. 2003. 32p. (J). pap. *(978-0-9741388-8-6(6))* Committee for Children.

Kim, Kang Won. INVU, 4 vols., Vol. 4. Kim, Kang Won. 2003. 192p. (YA). 9.99 *(978-1-59182-175-5(4))* TOKYOPOP, Inc.

Kim, Ki-Hwan. Dreams of Flight: Aircraft. Phil, Eun. 2020. (Science Storybooks Ser.). (ENG.). 32p. (J). (gr. k-4). pap. 8.99 *(978-1-925235-50-0(5));* lib. bdg. 27.99 *(978-1-925235-54-8(8))* ChoiceMaker Pty. Ltd., The AUS. (Big and SMALL). Dist: Lerner Publishing Group.

Kim, KyeMahn. Brown Bear's Dream. Kim, YunYeong. rev. ed. 2014. (MySELF Bookshelf Ser.). (ENG.). 32p. (J). (gr. k-2). pap. 11.94 *(978-1-60357-655-0(X));* lib. bdg. 25.27 *(978-1-59953-646-0(3))* Norwood Hse. Pr.

Kim, Lindsey. A Tiny Bud. Kim, Aerim. 2008. 80p. (J). 29.95 *(978-0-9789624-0-1(0))* Blue Lotus Wave.

Kim, Sarah. Little Belly Monster Makes a Pizza. John, Margaret. 2011. 36p. pap. *(978-0-9869424-0-2(5))* Belly Productions, Inc.

—Little Belly Monster Makes French Toast. John, Margaret. 2012. 40p. pap. *(978-0-9869424-2-6(1))* Belly Productions, Inc.

Kim, Sejung. I Love You More. Wing, Scarlett. Cottage Door Press, ed. 2020. (Love You Always Ser.). (ENG.). 18p. (J). (gr. -1-2). bds. 9.99 *(978-1-68052-818-3(1),* 1005310) Cottage Door Pr.

—Listen & Find - Animals. Auzou Publishing Staff. 2019. 16p. (J). bds. 11.95 *(978-2-7338-6741-9(5))* Auzou, Philippe Editions FRA. Dist: Consortium Bk. Sales & Distribution.

Kim, Seo. A Map into the World. Yang, Kao Kalia. 2019. (ENG.). 32p. (J). (gr. k-3). lib. bdg. 17.99 *(978-1-5415-3836-8(6),* Carolrhoda Bks.) Lerner Publishing Group.

Kim, So-yeong. Sleeping Beauty. Perrault, Charles. Cowley, Joy, ed. 2015. (World Classics Ser.). (ENG.). 32p. (gr. k-4). 26.65 *(978-1-925246-18-6(3));* 7.99 *(978-1-925246-70-4(1));* 26.65 *(978-1-925246-44-5(2))* ChoiceMaker Pty. Ltd., The AUS. (Big and SMALL). Dist: Lerner Publishing Group.

Kim, SookKyeong. Kanga & Anger. Kim, HoJeong. rev. ed. 2014. (MySELF Bookshelf Ser.). (ENG.). 32p. (J). (gr. k-2). pap. 11.94 *(978-1-60357-652-9(5));* lib. bdg. 25.27 *(978-1-59953-643-9(9))* Norwood Hse. Pr.

Kim, Soon-Ho. The Great Powers of Nature: Natural Disasters. Hong, Yun-Hui. 2017. (Science Storybooks Ser.). (ENG.). 32p. (J). (gr. k-4). lib. bdg. 27.99 *(978-1-925235-40-1(8),* Big and SMALL) ChoiceMaker Pty. Ltd., The AUS. Dist: Lerner Publishing Group.

Kim, Soyeon. Is This Panama? A Migration Story. Thornhill, Jan. 2013. (ENG.). 40p. (J). (gr. 3-3). 16.95 *(978-1-926973-88-3(7),* Owlkids) Owlkids Bks. Inc. CAN. Dist: Publishers Group West (PGW).

—A Last Goodbye. Kelsey, Elin. 2020. (ENG.). 32p. (J). (gr. 2-5). 18.95 *(978-1-77147-364-4(9))* Owlkids Bks. Inc. CAN. Dist: Publishers Group West (PGW).

—Sukaq & the Raven, 1 vol. Goose, Roy & McCluskey, Kerry. 2017. (ENG.). 36p. (J). (gr. k-2). 16.95 *(978-1-77227-139-3(X))* Inhabit Media Inc. CAN. Dist: Consortium Bk. Sales & Distribution.

—Wild Ideas: Let Nature Inspire Your Thinking. Kelsey, Elin. 2015. (ENG.). 32p. (J). (gr. k-5). 18.95 *(978-1-77147-062-9(3))* Owlkids Bks. Inc. CAN. Dist: Publishers Group West (PGW).

—You Are Never Alone. Kelsey, Elin. 2019. (ENG.). 32p. (J). 18.95 *(978-1-77147-315-6(0))* Owlkids Bks. Inc. CAN. Dist: Publishers Group West (PGW).

—You Are Stardust. Kelsey, Elin. 2012. (ENG.). 32p. (J). (gr. 1-4). 18.95 *(978-1-926973-35-7(6))* Owlkids Bks. Inc. CAN. Dist: Publishers Group West (PGW).

Kim, Sung-Min. The Toad Bridegroom & Other Fantastic Tales Retold. Seo & So, Chong-O. 2008. 125p. (J). *(978-0-9768086-7-1(6))* Rienner, Lynne Pubs.

Kim, Violet. Earth Day, Birthday!, 0 vols. Wright, Maureen. 2012. (ENG.). 32p. (J). (gr. k-3). 17.99 *(978-0-7614-6109-8(4),* 9780761461098, Two Lions) Amazon Publishing.

—If You're Going to a March. Freeman, Martha. 2018. (ENG.). 32p. (J). (gr. k). 16.95 *(978-1-4549-2993-2(6))* Sterling Publishing Co., Inc.

—The Little Gray Bunny. McGrath, Barbara Barbieri. 2013. (Holiday Books: Easter Ser.). 32p. (J). (gr. -1-1). 22.44 *(978-1-58089-394-7(5));* pap. 7.95 *(978-1-58089-395-4(3))* Charlesbridge Publishing, Inc.

Kim, Yeon Joo. Putting Faces to Names: The Art of Raphael. Yu, Myeong-Hwa. 2017. (Stories of Art Ser.). (ENG.). 36p. (J). (gr. 3-5). lib. bdg. 10.00 *(978-1-925235-25-8(4),* Big and SMALL) ChoiceMaker Pty. Ltd., The AUS. Dist: Lerner Publishing Group.

Kim, Yeong-Soon. This Hole, That Hole: Different Holes Found in Nature. Jang, Seon-Hye. 2017. (Science Storybooks Ser.). (ENG.). 32p. (J). (gr. k-4). lib. bdg. 27.99 *(978-1-925235-14-2(9),* Big and SMALL) ChoiceMaker Pty. Ltd., The AUS. Dist: Lerner Publishing Group.

Kim, Yon-Kyong. Mr. Moon & Miss Sun/the Herdsman & the Weaver. 2008. (Korean Folk Tales for Children Ser.: Vol. 2). (ENG.). 44p. (J). (gr. 2-5). lib. bdg. 14.50 *(978-0-930878-72-6(8))* Hollym International Corp.

—The Ogres' Magic Clubs - the Tiger & the Dried Persimmons. 2008. (Korean Folk Tales for Children Ser.: Vol. 5). (ENG.). 44p. (J). (gr. 2-5). lib. bdg. 14.50 *(978-0-930878-88-7(4))* Hollym International Corp.

—The Woodcutter & the Heavenly Maiden & the Fire Dogs. 2008. (Korean Folk Tales for Children Ser.: 1). (ENG.). 44p. (J). (gr. k-5). lib. bdg. 18.50 *(978-0-930878-71-9(X))* Hollym International Corp.

Kim, Yon-Kyong & Kang, Mi-Sun. The Son of the Cinnamon Tree/the Donkey's Egg. 2006. (Korean Folk Tales for Children Ser.: Vol. 10). (ENG.). 44p. (J). (gr. 2-5). lib. bdg. 14.50 *(978-0-930878-93-1(0))* Hollym International Corp.

Kim, Yon-Kyong, jt. illus. see Kang, Mi-Sun.

Kim, Yon-Kyong, jt. illus. see Pak, Mi-Son.

Kim, Yoon-Kyung. iD_eNTITY, Vol. 1. 2005. 200p. pap. 9.99 *(978-1-59532-345-3(7))* TOKYOPOP, Inc.

—Id_Entity, Vol. 2. rev. ed. 2005. 192p. pap. 9.99 *(978-1-59532-346-0(5))* TOKYOPOP, Inc.

—iD_eNTITY, Vol. 3. Son, Hee-Joon. 3rd rev. ed. 2005. 192p. pap. 9.99 *(978-1-59532-347-7(3))* TOKYOPOP, Inc.

Kim, Youn-Kyung. iD_eNTITY, 13 vols. Son, Hee-Joon. (Id_entity Ser.: Vol. 5). 192p. 5th rev. ed. 2006. per. 9.99 *(978-1-59532-349-1(X));* Vol. 4. 4th rev. ed. 2005. pap. 9.99 *(978-1-59532-348-4(1))* TOKYOPOP, Inc.

Kim, Youngsun. The Truth about Princesses, 1 vol. Allen, Nancy Kelly. 2010. (Fairy-Tale Superstars Ser.). (ENG.). 32p. (J). (gr. 1-3). lib. bdg. 27.99 *(978-1-4048-5747-6(8),* Picture Window Bks.) Capstone.

Kimbar, Murray. Josepha, 1 vol. McGugan, Jim. 2012. (ENG.). 32p. (J). (gr. 2-5). pap. 9.95 *(978-0-88995-461-8(5),* c5e26b5c-1347-4418-b0c5-73d51c42058f) Trifolium Bks., Inc. CAN. Dist: Firefly Bks., Ltd.

Kimbell, Emily & Kallis, Samantha. Warning! Journey to Forever #5. Oliver, Lin. 2019. (Fantastic Frame Ser.: 5). (ENG.). 128p. (J). (gr. 2-4). 7.99 *(978-1-5247-8699-1(3),* Penguin Workshop) Penguin Young Readers Group.

Kimber, Murray. Ancient Voices. Hovey, Kate. 2007. (ENG.). 40p. (J). (gr. 3-7). 11.99 *(978-1-4169-6818-4(0),* Simon & Schuster/Paula Wiseman Bks.) Simon & Schuster/Paula Wiseman Bks.

Kimberly, Nancy Wolfe. Hey. So, I'm a Baby. Borders, Mia. 2018. (ENG.). 28p. (J). pap. 19.95 *(978-1-5439-1989-9(8))* BookBaby.

Kimmel, Eric A. Wonders & Miracles: A Passover Companion. Kimmel, Eric A. 2004. (Wonders & Miracles Ser.). (ENG.). 144p. (J). 21.99 *(978-0-439-07175-8(5))* Scholastic, Inc.

Kimmel, Jimmy. The Serious Goose. Kimmel, Jimmy. 2019. (ENG.). 40p. (J). (gr. -1-2). 18.99 *(978-0-525-70775-2(1),* Random Hse. Bks. for Young Readers) Random Hse. Children's Bks.

Kimpimaki, Essi. Scientist Academy. Martin, Steve. 2018. (ENG.). 64p. (J). pap. 12.99 *(978-1-61067-668-7(8))* Kane Miller.

Kimura, Ken, jt. illus. see Murakami, Yasanuri.

Kinard, Brandi. I Just Want to Be Liked. Kay, Regina. 2013. (J). 19.95 *(978-1-56411-592-8(5),* CB Publishing & Design) UBUS Communications Systems.

Kinarney, Tom. Little Book of Saints. Wallace, Susan Helen. 2010. 24p. (J). (gr. 1-3). Vol. 5. 4.95 *(978-0-8198-4530-6(2));* Vol. 6. 4.95 *(978-0-8198-4531-3(0))* Pauline Bks. & Media.

—Little Book of Saints: Volume 4, 4. Wallace, Susan Helen. 2009. (J). 4.95 *(978-0-8198-4527-6(2))* Pauline Bks. & Media.

Kinarney, Tom, jt. illus. see Mattozzi, Patricia R.

Kincaid, Angela. Mythical Creatures: Sticker Book. Reed, Natasha. 2005. (Stickertastic Ser.). 24p. (J). (gr. -1-7). pap. *(978-1-84510-119-0(7))* Top That! Publishing PLC.

Kincaid, Olivia. Doy Gracias: (I Say Thanks) O'Neill, Juliana. 2018. (Xist Kids Spanish Bks.). (SPA.). 28p. (J). (gr. k-3). pap. 9.99 *(978-1-5324-0735-2(1))* Xist Publishing.

—I Say Thanks. O'Neill, Juliana. 2018. (Reading Stars Ser.). (ENG.). 28p. (J). (gr. k-3). pap. 9.99 *(978-1-5324-0922-6(2))* Xist Publishing.

—I Say Thanks / Doy Gracias. O'Neill, Juliana. 2018. (Xist Kids Bilingual Spanish English Ser.). (ENG & SPA.). 28p. (J). (gr. k-3). pap. 9.99 *(978-1-5324-0659-1(2))* Xist Publishing.

Kincannon, Karla M. Creativity & Divine Surprise: Finding the Place of Your Resurrection. Kincannon, Karla M. 2005. (ENG.). 221p. per. *(978-0-8358-9812-6(1),* 9780835898126) Upper Room Bks.

Kincheloe, Jayme & Kincheloe, Starlena. The Distracted Dino: Perfect for Young Children. Kincheloe, Jayme. 2018. (ENG.). 26p. (J). pap. 9.99 *(978-1-7178-2612-1(1))* Independently Published.

Kincheloe, Starlena, jt. illus. see Kincheloe, Jayme.

Kindersley, Anabel, jt. photos by see Kindersley, Barnabas.

Kindersley, Barnabas & Kindersley, Anabel, photos by. Celebraciones. 2005.Tr. of Celebrations. (SPA., (J). (gr. 1-4). 18.95 *(978-0-9628720-5-1(9))* Iaconi, Mariuccia Bk. Imports.

Kindert, Jennifer. Mommy's Bed. Scholastic, Inc. Staff & Black, Sonia. 2004. (Just for You Ser.). (ENG.). 32p. (gr. k-3). pap. 3.99 *(978-0-439-56857-9(9))* Scholastic, Inc.

Kindert, Jennifer C. Three Years & Eight Months. Smith, Icy. 2013. (J). *(978-0-9856237-8-4(0))* East West Discovery Pr.

Kindt, Kathleen G. J Is for Jupiter: A-Z of People, Places & Things in Jupiter, Florida. Brasch, Pamela. 2011. 52p. (J). pap. 19.95 *(978-0-9846071-7-4(X))* Middle River Pr.

Kindt, Matt. Be Confident in Who You Are, Vol. 1. Fox, Annie. 2008. (Middle School Confidential Ser.: Bk. 1). (ENG.). 96p. (YA). (gr. 6-18). pap. 9.99 *(978-1-57542-302-9(2),* 1285958) Free Spirit Publishing, Inc.

Kindt, Rita. Aunt Tami's Strawberry Farm. Ward, Terri & Ward, Tom. 2010. 38p. pap. 14.50 *(978-1-60693-935-2(1),* Eloquent Bks.) Strategic Book Publishing & Rights Agency (SBPRA).

King, Alice. Home Is Where the Heart Is: A Tale of Family Love. Alderson, Lisa. 2016. (ENG.). 26p. (J). bds. 8.95 *(978-1-78670-153-4(7))* Igloo Bks. GBR. Dist: Simon & Schuster, Inc.

King, Andy. Matter. Walker, Sally M. 2005. (Early Bird Energy Ser.). 48p. (J). (gr. 3-7). lib. bdg. 25.26 *(978-0-8225-5131-7(4),* Lerner Pubns.) Lerner Publishing Group.

King, Andy. Play-by-Play Field Events. King, Andy, photos by. Nitz, Kristin Wolden. 2004. (Play-by-Play Ser.). 80p. (J). (gr. 4-8). lib. bdg. 23.93 *(978-0-8225-3933-9(0))* Lerner Publishing Group.

—Play-by-Play Figure Skating. King, Andy, photos by. Freese, Joan. 2004. (Play-by-Play Ser.). 80p. (J). (gr. 4-8). lib. bdg. 23.93 *(978-0-8225-3934-6(9))* Lerner Publishing Group.

King, Andy, photos by. El Calor. Walker, Sally M. Translations.com Staff, tr. from ENG. 2007. (Libros de Energía para madrugadores (Early Bird Energy) Ser.). (SPA., 48p. (gr. 2-5). lib. bdg. 26.60 *(978-0-8225-7718-8(6))* Lerner Publishing Group.

—La Electricidad. Walker, Sally M. 2007. (Libros de Energía para madrugadores (Early Bird Energy) Ser.). (SPA., 48p. (J). (gr. 4-7). lib. bdg. 26.60 *(978-0-8225-7717-1(8),* Ediciones Lerner) Lerner Publishing Group.

—Electricity. Walker, Sally M. 2005. (Early Bird Energy Ser.). (ENG., 48p. (gr. 2-5). lib. bdg. 26.60 *(978-0-8225-2919-4(X),* Lerner Pubns.) Lerner Publishing Group.

—Gymnastics. Bragg, Linda Wallenberg. 2005. (Play-by-Play Ser.). 80p. (gr. 4-8). pap., lib. bdg. 23.93 *(978-0-8225-9877-0(9))* Lerner Publishing Group.

—Heat. Walker, Sally M. 2005. (Early Bird Energy Ser.). (ENG., 48p. (gr. 2-5). lib. bdg. 26.60 *(978-0-8225-2459-5(7),* Lerner Pubns.) Lerner Publishing Group.

—Hockey. Foley, Mike. 2005. (Play-by-Play Ser.). 80p. (J). (gr. 4-8). pap. 7.95 *(978-0-8225-9878-7(7))* Lerner Publishing Group.

—Light. Walker, Sally M. 2005. (Early Bird Energy Ser.). (ENG., 48p. (gr. 2-5). lib. bdg. 26.60 *(978-0-8225-2925-5(4),* Lerner Pubns.) Lerner Publishing Group.

—La Luz. Walker, Sally M. Translations.com Staff, tr. from ENG. 2007. (Libros de Energía para madrugadores (Early Bird Energy) Ser.). (SPA., 48p. (gr. 2-5). lib. bdg. 26.60 *(978-0-8225-7719-5(4))* Lerner Publishing Group.

—Magnetism. Walker, Sally M. 2005. (Early Bird Energy Ser.). (ENG., 48p. (gr. 2-5). lib. bdg. 26.60 *(978-0-8225-2932-3(7),* Lerner Pubns.) Lerner Publishing Group.

—El Magnetismo. Walker, Sally M. Translations.com Staff, tr. from ENG. 2007. (Libros de Energía para madrugadores (Early Bird Energy) Ser.). (SPA., 48p. (gr. 2-5). lib. bdg. 26.60 *(978-0-8225-7720-1(8))* Lerner Publishing Group.

—La Materia. Walker, Sally M. Translations.com Staff, tr. from ENG. 2007. (Libros de Energía para madrugadores (Early Bird Energy) Ser.). (SPA., 48p. (gr. 2-5). lib. bdg. 26.60 *(978-0-8225-7721-8(6))* Lerner Publishing Group.

—Palancas. Walker, Sally M. & Feldmann, Roseann. 2009. (Libros de Fisica para Madrugadores Ser.). (SPA., 47p. (J). (gr. 3-7). pap. 11.95 *(978-0-8225-2973-6(4))* Lerner Publishing Group.

—Planos Inclinados. Walker, Sally M. & Feldmann, Roseann. 2009. (Libros de Fisica para Madrugadores Ser.). (SPA., 47p. (J). (gr. 3-7). pap. 11.95 *(978-0-8225-2971-2(8))* Lerner Publishing Group.

—Play-by-Play Volleyball. Jensen, Julie. 2005. (Play-by-Play Ser.). 80p. (gr. 4-8). pap., lib. bdg. 23.93 *(978-0-8225-9882-4(5))* Lerner Publishing Group.

—Poleas. Walker, Sally M. & Feldmann, Roseann. 2005. (Libros de Física para Madrugadores (Early Bird Physics) Ser.). (SPA & ENG., 48p. (gr. 3-6). lib. bdg. 26.60 *(978-0-8225-2980-4(7),* Ediciones Lerner) Lerner Publishing Group.

—Softball. Nitz, Kristin Wolden. 2005. (Play-by-Play Ser.). 80p. (gr. 4-8). pap., lib. bdg. 23.93 *(978-0-8225-9875-6(2))* Lerner Publishing Group.

—El Sonido. Walker, Sally M. Translations.com Staff, tr. from ENG. 2007. (Libros de Energía para madrugadores (Early Bird Energy) Ser.). (SPA., 48p. (gr. 2-5). lib. bdg. 26.60 *(978-0-8225-7722-5(4))* Lerner Publishing Group.

—Sound. Walker, Sally M. 2005. (Early Bird Energy Ser.). 48p. (J). (gr. 3-7). lib. bdg. 25.26 *(978-0-8225-2634-6(4),* Lerner Pubns.) Lerner Publishing Group.

—Tornillos. Walker, Sally M. & Feldmann, Roseann. 2009. (Libros de Fisica para Madrugadores Ser.). (SPA., 47p. (J). (gr. 3-7). pap. 11.95 *(978-0-8225-2979-8(3))* Lerner Publishing Group.

—Trabajo. Walker, Sally M. & Feldmann, Roseann. 2005. (Libros de Física para Madrugadores (Early Bird Physics) Ser.). (SPA., 48p. (J). (gr. 3-6). lib. bdg. 26.65 *(978-0-8225-2984-2(X),* Ediciones Lerner) Lerner Publishing Group.

King, Bill. Mac King's Campfire Magic: 50 Amazing, Easy-To-Learn Tricks & Mind-Blowing Stunts Using Cards, String, Pencils, & Other Stuff from Your Knapsack. King, Mac. 2010. (ENG.). 176p. (J). (gr. -1-17). pap. 13.99 *(978-1-57912-829-6(7),* 81829, Black Dog & Leventhal Pubs. Inc.) Hachette Bks.

King, Brad. Brad King's Animal Coloring Book: Flamingos. King, Brad. 2019. (Brad King's Animal Coloring Book: Flamingos Ser.: Vol. 5). (ENG.). 30p. (J). pap. 9.95 ***(978-1-6880-0180-0(8))*** Independently Published.

King, Brad. Brad King's Animal Coloring Book: Lions. King, Brad. 2019. (Brad King's Animal Coloring Book: Lions Ser.: Vol. 4). (ENG.). 30p. (J). pap. 9.95 *(978-1-0799-5038-0(9))* Independently Published.

King, Cara. The Battle: Starting School Can Be Scary Sometimes! Kwok, Ashling. 2020. (ENG.). 32p. (J). (gr. -1-3). 18.99 ***(978-1-925820-40-9(8),*** 335054, EK Bks.) Exisle Publishing Pty Ltd. AUS. Dist: Hachette Bk. Group.

King, Cara. The Box Cars. Vescio, Robert. 2019. (ENG.). 32p. (J). (gr. -1-2). 17.99 *(978-1-925335-83-5(6),* 321973, EK Bks.) Exisle Publishing Pty Ltd. AUS. Dist: Hachette UK Distribution.

—Scaredy Book. Sillett, Devon. 2018. (ENG.). 32p. (J). (gr. -1-3). 17.99 *(978-1-925335-68-2(2),* EK Bks.) Exisle Publishing Pty Ltd. AUS. Dist: Hachette Bk. Group.

King-Chai, Sharon. Animalphabet. Donaldson, Julia. 2018. (ENG.). 52p. (J). (-k). 20.99 *(978-0-525-55415-8(7),* Dial Bks) Penguin Young Readers Group.

King, Cheryl. Alexee's Animals from A-Z, 1 vol. Eagan, Mary. 2010. 30p. 24.95 *(978-1-4489-3967-1(4))* PublishAmerica, Inc.

King, Chris. Aliens & UFOs. Hile, Lori. 2013. (Solving Mysteries with Science Ser.). (ENG.). 48p. (J). (gr. 3-6). pap. 9.95 *(978-1-4109-5504-3(4),* Raintree) Capstone.

—Backcourt Battle: An Up2U Character Education Adventure. Wallace, Rich. 2017. (Up2U Adventures Set 3 Ser.). (ENG.). 80p. (J). (gr. 2-5). lib. bdg. 29.93 *(978-1-5321-3028-1(7),* 25504, Calico Chapter Bks.) ABDO Publishing Co.

—Bigfoot & the Yeti, 1 vol. Colson, Mary. 2013. (Solving Mysteries with Science Ser.). (ENG.). 48p. (J). (gr. 3-6). pap. 9.95 *(978-1-4109-5505-0(2),* Raintree) Capstone.

—Ghosts & Haunted Houses, 1 vol. Bingham, Jane. 2013. (Solving Mysteries with Science Ser.). (ENG.). 48p. (J). (gr. 3-6). pap. 9.95 *(978-1-4109-5506-7(0),* Raintree) Capstone.

—Vampires & Werewolves, 1 vol. Bingham, Jane. 2013. (Solving Mysteries with Science Ser.). (ENG.). 48p. (J). (gr. 3-6). pap. 9.95 *(978-1-4109-5507-4(9),* Raintree) Capstone.

King, Chris, jt. illus. see Deverell, Richard.

King, Colin. Amazing Dragons: Fiendish Tales of Dastardly Deeds. Baxter, Nicola. 2012. 80p. (J). (gr. k-4). pap. 9.99 *(978-1-84322-836-3(X))* Anness Publishing GBR. Dist: National Bk. Network.

—Castles: Information for Young Readers - Level 1. Turnbull, Stephanie. 2007. (Usborne Beginners Ser.). 32p. (J). 4.99 *(978-0-7945-1335-1(2),* Usborne) EDC Publishing.

—Egyptians. Turnbull, Stephanie. 2007. (Usborne Beginners Ser.). 32p. (J). 4.99 *(978-0-7945-1344-3(1),* Usborne) EDC Publishing.

—Egyptians Kid Kit. Turnbull, Stephanie. 2005. 32p. (J). 9.99 *(978-1-58086-844-0(4),* Usborne) EDC Publishing.

—Elizabeth I Internet Referenced. Turnbull, Stephanie. 2004. 32p. (J). (gr. 1-18). pap. 4.95 *(978-0-7945-0808-1(1),* Usborne) EDC Publishing.

—Jigsaw Atlas of North America. 2006. (Usborne Jigsaw Bks.). 14p. (J). (gr. k-3). bds. 14.99 *(978-0-7945-1242-2(9),* Usborne) EDC Publishing.

—The Perils of Pirates & Other Dastardly Deeds: A Compendium of Swashbuckling Pirate Adventure Stories. Baxter, Nicola. 2012. 80p. (J). (gr. k-4). pap. 9.99 *(978-1-84322-802-8(5))* Anness Publishing GBR. Dist: National Bk. Network.

—See Inside Ships. Mason, Conrad. ed. 2011. (See Inside Board Books Ser.). 16p. (J). ring bd. 12.99 *(978-0-7945-3005-1(2),* Usborne) EDC Publishing.

—See Inside Your Body. Daynes, Katie. 2006. 15p. (J). (gr. -1-3). bds. 12.99 *(978-0-7945-1233-0(X),* Usborne) EDC Publishing.

—Ships. Bingham, Jane. 2004. (Young Reading Ser.). 64p. (J). (gr. 2-18). pap. 5.95 *(978-0-7945-0730-5(1),* Usborne) EDC Publishing.

—Ships. Bone, Emily. 2009. (Beginner's Science Ser.). 32p. (J). 4.99 *(978-0-7945-2507-1(5),* Usborne) EDC Publishing.

—The Story of Ships. Bingham, Jane. 2004. (Young Reading Ser.: Vol. 2). 62p. (J). (gr. 2-18). lib. bdg. 13.95 *(978-1-58086-700-9(6),* Usborne) EDC Publishing.

—The Story of Trains. Bingham, Jane. 2004. 64p. (J). (gr. 2-18). (Young Reading Series Two Ser.). pap. 5.95 *(978-0-7945-0737-4(9));* (Young Reading Ser.: Vol. 2). lib. bdg. 13.95 *(978-1-58086-702-3(2))* EDC Publishing. (Usborne).

—The Usborne Book of KnowHow. Amery, Heather et al. 2008. (Usborne Book Of... Ser.). 127p. (J). (gr. 4-7). 19.99 *(978-0-7945-2040-3(5),* Usborne) EDC Publishing.

King, Colin. Planes. King, Colin. Patchett, F. 2004. (Beginners Ser.). (ENG.). 32p. (J). (gr. 1-18). pap. 4.95 *(978-0-7945-0319-2(5),* Usborne) EDC Publishing.

King, Dave, photos by. Counting Book. Whittington, Melanie & Holtz, Lara Tankel, eds. 2003. 32p. (J). *(978-0-681-62667-6(4))* Dorling Kindersley.

King, Dave, jt. photos by see Burton, Jane.

King, Des'za'rae. My Favorite Shirt. Ijames, Ciara. 2019. (Brenda Kingsford Collection). (ENG.). 26p. (J). (gr. k-3). pap. 6.99 ***(978-0-578-51677-6(2))*** CI Publishing Group.

King, Elexis. Mrs. Betsy Fieldmouse Borrows an Egg. Bockman, Barbara. l.t. ed. 2016. (ENG.). (J). (gr. k-2). 19.95 *(978-1-61633-796-4(6));* pap. 10.95 *(978-1-61633-784-1(2))* Guardian Angel Publishing, Inc.

King, Elizabeth, photos by. Quinceanera: Celebrating Fifteen. King, Elizabeth. 2006. 40p. (YA). (gr. 8-11). reprint ed. 17.00 *(978-1-4223-5728-6(7))* DIANE Publishing Co.

King, Ingrid Fiksdahl. What Can I Be? Rand, Ann. 2016. (ENG.). 32p. (J). (gr. -1-1). 17.95 *(978-1-61689-472-6(5))* Princeton Architectural Pr.

King, Irene. Scary Mary. Dale, Elizabeth. 2019. (ENG.). 28p. (J). *(978-0-6483317-3-5(3))* Serenity Press.

King, Janet. Bluey, the Little Drip. King, Philip. 2011. 40p. pap. 14.95 *(978-1-60976-661-0(X),* Eloquent Bks.) Strategic Book Publishing & Rights Agency (SBPRA).

—I Love Outside. Gelsthorpe, Amy. 2018. (ENG.). 30p. (J). (gr. k-6). 17.99 *(978-1-365-86131-4(7));* pap. 13.99 *(978-1-365-86134-5(1))* Lulu Pr., Inc.

—I Love Outside Dyslexic Font. Gelsthorpe, Amy. 2018. (ENG.). 30p. (J). (gr. k-6). 21.99 *(978-1-365-86132-1(5));* pap. 15.99 *(978-1-365-86135-2(X))* Lulu Pr., Inc.

—Star Fishing. Gelsthorpe, Amy. 2017. (ENG.). (J). (gr. k-6). 17.99 *(978-1-365-86161-1(9));* pap. 13.99 *(978-1-365-86163-5(5))* Lulu Pr., Inc.

King, Janet. Star Fishing. Gelsthorpe, Amy. ed. 2017. (ENG.). 34p. (J). (gr. k-6). 17.99 ***(978-1-64372-026-5(0));*** pap. 13.99 ***(978-1-64372-263-4(8))*** MacLaren-Cochrane Publishing, Inc. (Huskies Pub).

—Star Fishing Dyslexic Edition: Dyslexic Font. Gelsthorpe, Amy. ed. 2017. (ENG.). 34p. (J). (gr. k-6). 19.99 ***(978-1-64372-264-1(6));*** pap. 15.99 ***(978-1-64372-265-8(4))*** MacLaren-Cochrane Publishing, Inc.

King, Janet. Star Fishing Dyslexic Font. Gelsthorpe, Amy. 2017. (ENG.). (J). (gr. k-6). 21.99 *(978-1-365-86162-8(7));* pap. 15.99 *(978-1-365-86164-2(3))* Lulu Pr., Inc.

King, Jerry. God Made the Skunk: And Other Animal Poems. Lewis, J. Patrick. 2005. 60p. (J). 14.95 *(978-0-9722820-1-7(7))* Doggerel Daze.

King, Jessie Marion. A House of Pomegranates. Wilde, Oscar. 2011. (Calla Editions Ser.). (ENG.). 208p. (J). (gr. 5). 35.00 *(978-1-60660-021-4(4))* Dover Pubns., Inc.

King, Jonathan. The Inkberg Enigma. King, Jonathan. 2020. (ENG.). 128p. (J). (gr. 2-5). pap. 14.99 ***(978-1-77657-266-3(1))*** Gecko Pr. NZL. Dist: Lerner Publishing Group.

King, Joseph. Granny & the Tractor. Menges, Thais D. 2012. 36p. pap. 10.95 *(978-1-60920-047-3(0))* Ajoyin Publishing, Inc.

King, Judy. When Summer Comes Again. King, Judy. 2013. 160p. (J). pap. *(978-1-884377-20-4(3))* Green Pastures Pr.

King, Philippa. Tibbs the Meditation Cat: Mindfulness for Kids. Collard, Patrizia. 2016. (ENG.). (J). pap. *(978-0-9553629-7-2(0))* North. Star Pr., Ltd.

King, Robin. The First Book of Electricity. Epstein, Sam & Epstein, Beryl. 2019. (ENG.). 74p. (J). (gr. 4-6). pap. 12.95 ***(978-0-578-58239-9(2))*** Living Library Pr.

King, Shannon. Daisy the Dachshund Gets Adopted. King, Shannon. 2018. (Daisy the Dachshund Ser.: Vol. 1). (ENG.). 28p. (J). (gr. k-4). pap. 12.99 *(978-0-692-04361-5(6))* Daisy Mae Bks.

—Daisy the Dachshund's Tail of Recovery. King, Shannon. 2019. (Daisy the Dachshund Children's Ser.: Vol. 2). (ENG.). 28p. (J). (gr. 1-6). pap. 12.99 *(978-0-578-46281-3(8))* Daisy Mae Bks.

King, Stephen Michael. All the Colours of Paradise. Millard, Glenda. 2020. (Kingdom of Silk Ser.: 04). 128p. 4.99 *(978-0-7333-2583-0(1))* ABC Bks. AUS. Dist: HarperCollins Pubs.

—Fizz & the Dog Academy Rescue. Gibbes, Lesley. 2017. (ENG.). 80p. (J). pap. 4.99 *(978-1-61067-613-7(0))* Kane Miller.

—Fizz & the Dog Academy Rescue. Gibbes, Lesley. 2017. 67p. (J). *(978-1-61067-640-3(8))* Kane Miller.

—Fizz & the Handbag Dognapper. Gibbes, Lesley. 2017. 67p. (J). *(978-1-61067-642-7(4))* Kane Miller.

—Fizz & the Handbag Dognapper. Gibbes, Lesley. 2017. (ENG.). 80p. (J). pap. 4.99 *(978-1-61067-615-1(7))* Kane Miller.

—Fizz & the Police Dog Tryouts. Gibbes, Lesley. 2017. (ENG.). 80p. (J). pap. 4.99 *(978-1-61067-612-0(2))* Kane Miller.

—Fizz & the Police Dog Tryouts. Gibbes, Lesley. 2017. 65p. (J). *(978-1-61067-639-7(4))* Kane Miller.

—Fizz & the Show Dog Jewel Thief. Gibbes, Lesley. 2017. 67p. (J). *(978-1-61067-641-0(6))* Kane Miller.

—Fizz & the Show Dog Jewel Thief. Gibbes, Lesley. 2017. (ENG.). 80p. (J). pap. 4.99 *(978-1-61067-614-4(9))* Kane Miller.

—Layla, Queen of Hearts. Millard, Glenda. 2019. (Kingdom of Silk Ser.: 02). 112p. (Orig.). mass mkt. 4.99 *(978-0-7333-1842-9(8))* ABC Bks. AUS. Dist: HarperCollins Pubs.

—Pea Pod Lullaby. Millard, Glenda. 2018. (ENG.). 40p. (J). (gr. -1-2). 16.99 *(978-1-5362-0197-0(9))* Candlewick Pr.

—Perry Angel's Suitcase. Millard, Glenda. 2020. (Kingdom of Silk Ser.: 03). 128p. pap. 4.99 *(978-0-7333-2255-6(7))* ABC Bks. AUS. Dist: HarperCollins Pubs.

—Piglet & Papa. Wild, Margaret. 2018. (ENG.). 32p. (J). (gr. -1-3). pap. 4.99 *(978-1-4197-2940-9(3),* Abrams Bks. for Young Readers) Abrams, Inc.

—Prudence Wants a Pet. Daly, Cathleen. 2011. (ENG.). 32p. (J). (gr. -1-2). 17.99 *(978-1-59643-468-4(6),* 900055550) Roaring Brook Pr.

—The Return of Gibblewort the Goblin, 3 bks. in 1. Kelleher, Victor. 2007. (Gibblewort the Goblin Ser.). 224p. (J). (gr. 2-4). pap. 14.99 *(978-1-74166-185-9(4))* Random Hse. Australia AUS. Dist: Independent Pubs. Group.

King, Stephen Michael. Mutt Dog! King, Stephen Michael. 2005. 32p. (J). *(978-1-86504-636-5(1));* pap. *(978-1-86504-637-2(X))* Scholastic, Inc. (Scholastic Pr.).

—You: A Story of Love & Friendship. King, Stephen Michael. 2011. (ENG.). 32p. (J). 14.99 *(978-0-06-206014-3(7),* Greenwillow Bks.) HarperCollins Pubs.

King, Steve. Molly's Sweet Shop. Canning, Laura A. 2012. 48p. pap. *(978-1-78148-772-3(3))* Grosvenor Hse. Publishing Ltd.

King, Sue. Tractors. Watt, Fiona. 2009. (Luxury Touchy-Feely Board Bks). 10p. (J). bds. 15.99 *(978-0-7945-2432-6(X),* Usborne) EDC Publishing.

King, Sue, jt. illus. see Cooper, Jenny.

King, Tara Calahan. Pastel para Enemigos. Munson, Derek. 2004.Tr. of Enemy Pie. (SPA.). 40p. (J). (gr. k-2). pap. 9.99 *(978-84-261-3378-6(9))* Juventud, Editorial ESP. Dist: Lectorum Pubns., Inc.

King, Travis. Old MacDonald's Farm. Ikids Staff. 2010. (ENG.). 20p. (J). (gr. -1-k). 14.99 *(978-1-60169-024-1(X))* Innovative Kids.

—10 Little Monkeys. Ikids Staff. 2009. (ENG.). 20p. (J). (gr. -1-k). 14.99 *(978-1-58476-938-5(6))* Innovative Kids.

King, W. B. Tom Cardiff's Circus. Garis, Howard Roger. 2005. reprint ed. pap. 28.95 *(978-1-4179-3393-8(3))* Kessinger Publishing, LLC.

Kingsley, Linda Kurtz. Bringing up Sophie. Kingsley, Linda Kurtz. 2010. 32p. (J). lib. bdg. 15.95 *(978-0-944727-25-6(5),* Turtle Bks.) Jason & Nordic Pubs.

—Signs of Jays. Kingsley, Linda Kurtz. 2008. 32p. (J). (ENG.). lib. bdg. 15.95 *(978-0-944727-23-2(9));* pap. 9.95 *(978-0-944727-22-5(0))* Jason & Nordic Pubs. (Turtle Bks.).

Kini, Kanyika. The Rumor. Ravishankar, Anushka. 2012. (ENG.). 32p. (J). (gr. -1-1). 17.95 *(978-1-77049-280-6(1),* Tundra Bks.) Tundra Bks. CAN. Dist: Penguin Random Hse. LLC.

Kinkade, Thomas. Away in a Manger. Public Domain, Public. 2009. (ENG.). 32p. (J). (gr. -1-3). pap. 7.99 *(978-0-06-078734-9(1))* HarperCollins Pubs.

—Away in a Manger. 2005. 32p. (J). lib. bdg. 17.89 *(978-0-06-078733-2(3))* HarperCollins Pubs.

—Away in a Manger. 2005. 32p. (J). 16.99 *(978-0-06-078730-1(9))* Zonderkidz.

Kinnaird, Ross. Doctor Grundy's Undies. McMillan, Dawn. 2019. (ENG.). 32p. (gr. 1-5). pap. 8.99 *(978-0-486-83248-7(1),* 832481) Dover Pubns., Inc.

—It's a Feudal, Feudal World: A Different Medieval History. Shapiro, Simon. 2nd ed. 2013. (ENG.). 48p. (J). (gr. 4-8). pap. 14.95 *(978-1-55451-552-3(1),* 9781554515523) Annick Pr., Ltd. CAN. Dist: Publishers Group West (PGW).

—Seagull Sid: And the Naughty Things His Seagulls Did! McMillan, Dawn. 2019. (ENG.). 32p. (gr. 1-5). pap. 8.99 *(978-0-486-83247-0(3),* 832473) Dover Pubns., Inc.

Kinnaird, Ross. 50 Body Questions: A Book That Spills Its Guts. Kyi, Tanya Lloyd. 2014. (50 Questions Ser.). (ENG.). 108p. (gr. 4-7). 36.19 ***(978-1-4844-2126-0(4));*** (J). 22.95 *(978-1-55451-613-1(7),* 9781554516131); 2nd ed. (J). pap. 14.95 *(978-1-55451-612-4(9),* 9781554516124) Annick Pr., Ltd. CAN. Dist: Children's Plus, Inc., Publishers Group West (PGW).

Kinnaird, Ross. 50 Burning Questions: A Sizzling History of Fire. Kyi, Tanya Lloyd. 2010. (50 Questions Ser.). (ENG.). 104p. (J). (gr. 3-18). pap. 12.95 *(978-1-55451-220-1(4),* 9781554512201) Annick Pr., Ltd. CAN. Dist: Publishers Group West (PGW).

—50 Climate Questions: A Blizzard of Blistering Facts. Christie, Peter. 2012. (50 Questions Ser.). (ENG.). 120p. (J). (gr. 3-8). 22.95 *(978-1-55451-375-8(8),* 9781554513758); pap. 14.95 *(978-1-55451-374-1(X),* 9781554513741) Annick Pr., Ltd. CAN. Dist: Publishers Group West (PGW).

—50 Poisonous Questions: A Book with Bite. Kyi, Tanya Lloyd. 2011. (50 Questions Ser.). (ENG.). 112p. (J). (gr. 4-7). 31.19 *(978-1-55451-281-2(6),* 9781554512812); 2nd ed. (gr. 3-18). pap. 12.95 *(978-1-55451-280-5(8),* 9781554512805) Annick Pr., Ltd. CAN. Dist: Children's Plus, Inc., Publishers Group West (PGW).

—50 Underwear Questions: A Bare-All History. Kyi, Tanya Lloyd. 2011. (50 Questions Ser.). (ENG.). 120p. (J). (gr. 3-18). pap. 12.95 *(978-1-55451-352-9(9),* 9781554513529) Annick Pr., Ltd. CAN. Dist: Publishers Group West (PGW).

Kinnear, Nicola. A Little Bit Brave. Kinnear, Nicola. 2020. (ENG.). 32p. (J). (gr. -1-2). 17.99 *(978-1-338-56327-6(0),* Orchard Bks.) Scholastic, Inc.

Kinneman, D. Michael. The Adventures of Jilly & Brad: Noises in the Attic. Hees, Miriam. 2003. 128p. (J). pap. 5.95 *(978-0-9718348-4-2(9))* Blooming Tree Pr.

Kinney, Davina. Lonnie the Loon Finds His Home. Renner, Barbara. 2020. (ENG.). 32p. (J). (gr. k-3). pap. 11.95 ***(978-0-9990586-6-4(5))*** Renner Writes.

—Lonnie the Loon Flies South for the Winter. Renner, Barbara. 2016. (ENG.). 22p. (J). (gr. k-3). pap. 11.95 ***(978-0-9990586-5-7(7))*** Renner Writes.

Kinney, Davina "Viv". Annie Aardvark, Mathematician. Olsen, Suzie. 2017. (ENG.). (J). pap. 9.99 *(978-0-9984337-0-7(5))* STEAM Publishing, LLC.

Kinney, Jo Hannah. When George Stopped Talking. Enos, Barbara. 2011. 20p. pap. 24.95 *(978-1-4626-4254-0(3))* America Star Bks.

Kinra, Richa. The Alley that Wanted to be a Street: Kirkland Morris. Morris, Kirkland. 2012. (ENG.). 27p. (J). pap. 11.95 *(978-1-4327-7844-6(7))* Outskirts Pr., Inc.

—Annabelle's Secret. Barth, Amy. 2009. (J). pap. 12.95 *(978-1-932690-95-8(6))* Loving Healing Pr., Inc.

K

—Annabelle's Secret: A Story about Sexual Abuse. Barth, Amy. 2011. 24p. (gr. 3-7). 28.95 *(978-1-61599-099-3(2))* Loving Healing Pr., Inc.

—Cinderella's Magical Wheelchair: An Empowering Fairy Tale. Kats, Jewel. 2012. (J). 24p. 29.95 *(978-1-61599-113-6(1))*; 20p. pap. 16.95 *(978-1-61599-112-9(3))* Loving Healing Pr., Inc.

—The Flip Flop Family. Vance, Colleen. 2013. (ENG.). (J). (gr. -1-3). 14.95 *(978-1-62086-275-9(1))* Mascot Bks., Inc.

Kinra, Richa. I See Me. Medrano, Rafael. 2020. (ENG.). 26p. (J). pap. 9.95 ***(978-1-7979-2762-6(0))*** Independently Published.

Kinra, Richa. Jiali's Traveling Heart. MacLean, Betty. 2013. 34p. (J). 17.95 *(978-1-60131-157-3(5)*, Castlebridge Bks.) Big Tent Bks.

—The Princess & the Ruby: An Autism Fairy Tale. Kats, Jewel. 2013. 42p. 26.95 *(978-1-61599-193-8(X))*; (J). (gr. 3-7). pap. 16.95 *(978-1-61599-175-4(1))* Loving Healing Pr., Inc.

—The Princess Panda Tea Party: A Cerebral Palsy Fairy Tale. 2014. 45p. (J). pap. 14.95 *(978-1-61599-219-5(7))* Loving Healing Pr., Inc.

—The Soap Bubble Frog. Lawson, Brandi. 2012. 32p. pap. 14.50 *(978-1-61897-784-7(9)*, Strategic Bk. Publishing) Strategic Book Publishing & Rights Agency (SBPRA).

—Will Was All Boy: A Story about Sexual Abuse. Barth, Amy. 2009. (J). pap. *(978-1-61599-000-9(3))* Loving Healing Pr., Inc.

Kinsella, Pat. Book 1: Crisis. Wolff, Tracy. 2016. (Mars Bound Ser.). (ENG.). 48p. (J). (gr. 3-7). lib. bdg. 29.93 *(978-1-62402-197-8(2)*, 24573, Spellbound) Magic Wagon.

—Book 2: Sabotage. Wolff, Tracy. 2016. (Mars Bound Ser.). (ENG.). 48p. (J). (gr. 3-7). lib. bdg. 29.93 *(978-1-62402-198-5(0)*, 24575, Spellbound) Magic Wagon.

—Book 3: Restoration. Wolff, Tracy. 2016. (Mars Bound Ser.). (ENG.). 48p. (J). (gr. 3-7). lib. bdg. 29.93 *(978-1-62402-199-2(9)*, 24577, Spellbound) Magic Wagon.

—Book 4: Arrival. Wolff, Tracy. 2016. (Mars Bound Ser.). (ENG.). 48p. (J). (gr. 3-7). lib. bdg. 29.93 *(978-1-62402-200-5(6)*, 24579, Spellbound) Magic Wagon.

—Houdini: The Life of the Great Escape Artist, 1 vol. Biskup, Agnieszka. 2011. (American Graphic Ser.). (ENG.). 32p. (gr. 3-9). (J). pap. 8.10 *(978-1-4296-6268-0(9))*; pap. 47.70 *(978-1-4296-6435-6(5)*, Capstone Pr.) Capstone.

—Jay-Z: Hip-Hop Icon, 1 vol. Gunderson, Jessica. 2012. (American Graphic Ser.). (ENG.). 32p. (gr. 3-9). (J). pap. 8.10 *(978-1-4296-7993-0(X))*; pap. 47.70 *(978-1-4296-8475-0(5))*; (J). lib. bdg. 31.32 *(978-1-4296-6017-4(1))* Capstone. (Capstone Pr.).

—Mars Bound (Set), 4 vols. Wolff, Tracy. 2016. (Mars Bound Ser.). 48p. (J). (gr. 3-7). lib. bdg. 114.00 *(978-1-62402-196-1(4)*, 24571, Spellbound) Magic Wagon.

—Soldier Dogs #1: Air Raid Search & Rescue. Sutter, Marcus. 2018. (Soldier Dogs Ser.: 1). (ENG.). 224p. (J). (gr. 3-7). 12.99 *(978-0-06-286866-4(7))*; pap. 7.99 *(978-0-06-284403-3(2))* HarperCollins Pubs. (HarperFestival).

—True Stories of the Revolutionary War. Raum, Elizabeth. 2012. (Stories of War Ser.). (ENG.). 32p. (gr. 3-4). pap. 47.70 *(978-1-4296-9343-1(6))*; (J). 31.32 *(978-1-4296-8674-7(X))*; (J). pap. 8.10 *(978-1-4296-9342-4(8))* Capstone. (Capstone Pr.).

—True Stories of World War II. Collins, Terry. 2012. (Stories of War Ser.). (ENG.). 32p. (gr. 3-4). pap. 47.70 *(978-1-4296-9347-9(9))*; (J). pap. 8.10 *(978-1-4296-9346-2(0))*; (J). lib. bdg. 31.32 *(978-1-4296-8623-5(5))* Capstone. (Capstone Pr.).

Kinsella, Pat, et al. True War Stories: Personal Accounts of History's Greatest Conflicts. Raum, Elizabeth et al. 2017. (J). *(978-1-4914-1965-6(2))* Capstone.

Kinsella, Pat & Byers, Michael. American Graphic. Gunderson, Jessica & Collins, Terry. 2012. (American Graphic Ser.). (ENG.). 32p. (gr. 3-4). pap. 477.00 *(978-1-4296-8478-1(X))*; (J). lib. bdg., lib. bdg., lib. bdg. 250.56 *(978-1-4296-8179-7(9))* Capstone. (Capstone Pr.).

Kinsley, Sean. Pick Me, Pick Me. Horton, Elizabeth. ed. 2008. (ENG.). 32p. (J). 14.95 *(978-0-9797460-0-0(0))* Lerue Pr., LLC.

Kinstle Nocera, Suzanne. A Day with Little Duke. Rode, Maureen. 2012. (J). *(978-0-9786675-1-1(4))* Gerardian Inkspot & Paint Society.

Kinzel, Sven. Der Muttwupp. Kinzel, Sven. Renner, Oliver. 2019. (GER.). 34p. (J). (gr. k-4). 14.99 *(978-1-63233-178-6(0))* Elfrig Publishing.

Kipin, Sara. Between the Water & the Woods. Snaith, Simone. 2019. 320p. (YA). (gr. 7). 18.99 *(978-0-8234-4020-7(6))* Holiday Hse., Inc.

—The Language of Thorns: Midnight Tales & Dangerous Magic. Bardugo, Leigh. 2017. (ENG.). 288p. (YA). 18.99 *(978-1-250-12252-0(X)*, 900173718) Imprint IND. Dist: Macmillan.

Kipling, J. Lockwood. Tales of the Punjab - Illustrated by John Lockwood Kipling. Steel, Flora Annie. 2020. (ENG.). 414p. (J). pap. ***(978-1-5287-1461-7(X))*** Read Bks.

Kipling, John Lockwood. The Jungle Book. Kipling, Rudyard. ed. 2015. (First Avenue Classics (tm) Ser.). (ENG.). 198p. (J). (gr. 3-8). E-Book 19.99 *(978-1-4677-5836-9(1)*, First Avenue Editions) Lerner Publishing Group.

—The Jungle Book - with Illustrations by John Lockwood Kipling & Others. Kipling, Rudyard. 2016. (ENG.). (J). (gr. 4-6). *(978-1-4733-3517-2(5))* Read Bks.

Kipling, Rudyard. Just So Stories. Kipling, Rudyard. 2017. (Alma Junior Classics Ser.). 224p. (J). pap. 9.99 *(978-1-84749-637-9(7)*, 351537) Alma Classics GBR. Dist: Bloomsbury Publishing Plc.

—Just So Stories: Children's Book. Kipling, Rudyard. 2018. (ENG.). 84p. (J). pap. 7.65 *(978-1-7310-4710-6(X))* Independently Published.

—Just So Stories - for Little Children - Written & Illustrated by Rudyard Kipling. Kipling, Rudyard. 2016. (ENG.). (J). *(978-1-4733-3518-9(3))* Read Bks.

Kiplinger Pandy, Lori. Another Way of Life. Collins, Arda. l.t. ed. 2005. 30p. (J). (gr. -1-3). per. 9.99 *(978-1-59879-023-8(4))* Lifevest Publishing, Inc.

—Besos y Abrazos Al Aire. Sample, Jewel. Tenorio-Gavin, Lucero, tr. l.t. ed. 2006. (SPA.). 30p. (J). 23.95 *(978-1-59879-291-1(1))* Lifevest Publishing, Inc.

—Flying Hugs & Kisses. l.t. ed. 2006. 32p. (J). 15.95 *(978-1-59879-119-8(2))* Lifevest Publishing, Inc.

—Flying Hugs & Kisses Activity Book. Sample, Jewel. 2007. 68p. (J). (gr. -1-3). per. 13.99 *(978-1-59879-377-2(2))* Lifevest Publishing, Inc.

—Goose Dreams. McWilliams Pittard, Irene. 2005. (J). 10.00 *(978-1-59971-142-3(7))* Aardvark Global Publishing.

Kirby, Jack. The a-Z of Marvel Monsters. 2017. (ENG.). 128p. (J). (gr. -1-17). 24.99 *(978-1-302-90863-8(4))* Marvel Worldwide, Inc.

Kirby, Jack, et al. Adventures into Fear Omnibus. 2020. (ENG.). 816p. (J). (gr. 4-17). 150.00 ***(978-1-302-92512-3(1))*** Marvel Worldwide, Inc.

—Amazing Fantasy Omnibus. 2020. (ENG.). 448p. (J). (gr. -1-17). 75.00 ***(978-1-302-92270-2(X))*** Marvel Worldwide, Inc.

Kirby, Jack, et al. Avengers vs. Fantastic Four. 2019. (ENG.). 384p. (YA). (gr. 4-17). pap. 34.99 *(978-1-302-92072-2(3))* Marvel Worldwide, Inc.

Kirby, Jack. Balder the Brave, Bk. 2. Lee, Stan. 2013. (Thor: Tales of Asgard Ser.). (ENG.). 24p. (J). (gr. 4-8). lib. bdg. 27.07 *(978-1-61479-169-0(4)*, 14760, Marvel Age) Spotlight.

—Boyhood of Thor! Lee, Stan. 2013. (Thor: Tales of Asgard Ser.). (ENG.). 24p. (J). (gr. 4-8). lib. bdg. 27.07 *(978-1-61479-170-6(8)*, 14761, Marvel Age) Spotlight.

Kirby, Jack, et al. Captain America: Evolutions of a Living Legend. 2019. (ENG.). 248p. (YA). (gr. -1-17). pap. 29.99 *(978-1-302-91848-4(6))* Marvel Worldwide, Inc.

Kirby, Jack. Challenge!, Bk. 3. Lee, Stan. 2013. (Thor: Tales of Asgard Ser.). (ENG.). 24p. (J). (gr. 4-8). lib. bdg. 27.07 *(978-1-61479-171-3(6)*, 14762, Marvel Age) Spotlight.

Kirby, Jack, et al. Fantastic Four Epic Collection: the Name Is Doom. 2020. 504p. (J). (gr. -1-17). pap. 39.99 ***(978-1-302-92203-0(3))*** Marvel Worldwide, Inc.

Kirby, Jack, et al. Inhumans: Beware the Inhumans. 2018. (ENG.). 352p. (J). (gr. -1-17). pap. 34.99 *(978-1-302-91081-5(7))* Marvel Worldwide, Inc.

Kirby, Jack. Kirby Is... Fantastic! King-Sized Hardcover. 2019. (ENG.). 400p. (YA). (gr. -1-17). 100.00 *(978-1-302-91773-9(0))* Marvel Worldwide, Inc.

Kirby, Jack, et al. M. O. D. O. K.: Head Trips. 2019. (ENG.). 456p. (gr. 10-17). pap. 39.99 *(978-1-302-92074-6(X))* Marvel Worldwide, Inc.

Kirby, Jack, et al. Marvel Comics: the World Outside Your Window. 2020. (ENG.). 320p. (YA). (gr. 8-17). pap. 34.99 ***(978-1-302-92353-2(6))*** Marvel Worldwide, Inc.

Kirby, Jack, et al. Marvel Masterworks: the Fantastic Four Vol. 21. 2019. (Marvel Masterworks: the Fantastic Four Ser.: 21). (ENG.). 352p. (YA). (gr. 4-17). 75.00 *(978-1-302-91819-4(2))* Marvel Worldwide, Inc.

Kirby, Jack, et al. Marvel-Verse: Captain America. 2020. 112p. (J). (gr. 5-9). pap. 9.99 ***(978-1-302-92513-0(X))*** Marvel Worldwide, Inc.

Kirby, Jack. Monsters Vol. 2: the Marvel Monsterbus by Stan Lee, Larry Lieber & Jack Kirby. 2017. 872p. (J). (gr. -1-17). 100.00 *(978-1-302-90862-1(6))* Marvel Worldwide, Inc.

—Quest for the Mystic Mountain! Lee, Stan. 2013. (Thor: Tales of Asgard Ser.). (ENG.). 24p. (J). (gr. 4-8). lib. bdg. 27.07 *(978-1-61479-172-0(4)*, 14763, Marvel Age) Spotlight.

Kirby, Jack. Steranko Is... Revolutionary! King-Size. 2020. (ENG.). 336p. (J). (gr. 4-17). 125.00 ***(978-1-302-92289-4(0))*** Marvel Worldwide, Inc.

Kirby, Jack. Thor: Tales of Asgard, 6 vols. Lee, Stan. 2013. (Thor: Tales of Asgard Ser.: 6). (ENG.). 24p. (J). (gr. 4-8). lib. bdg. 162.42 *(978-1-61479-168-3(6)*, 14759, Marvel Age) Spotlight.

Kirby, Jack, et al. Thor of the Realms. 2019. (ENG.). 272p. (YA). (gr. 8-17). pap. 29.99 *(978-1-302-91838-5(9))* Marvel Worldwide, Inc.

Kirby, Jack. Timely's Greatest: the Golden Age Simon & Kirby Omnibus. 2019. (ENG.). 840p. (YA). (gr. 4-17). 150.00 *(978-1-302-91934-4(2))* Marvel Worldwide, Inc.

—To the Death!, Bk. 6. Lee, Stan. 2013. (Thor: Tales of Asgard Ser.). (ENG.). 24p. (J). (gr. 4-8). lib. bdg. 27.07 *(978-1-61479-173-7(2)*, 14764, Marvel Age) Spotlight.

—When Speaks the Dragon! Lee, Stan. 2013. (Thor: Tales of Asgard Ser.). (ENG.). 24p. (J). (gr. 4-8). lib. bdg. 27.07 *(978-1-61479-174-4(0)*, 14765, Marvel Age) Spotlight.

Kirby, Jack. Marvel Visionaries: Jack Kirby. Kirby, Jack, text. 2019. (ENG.). 352p. (YA). (gr. 4-17). pap. 34.99 *(978-1-302-91969-6(5))* Marvel Worldwide, Inc.

Kirby, Jack & Buscema, John. Fantastic Four: Behold... Galactus! 2018. (ENG.). 312p. (J). (gr. 4-17). 50.00 *(978-1-302-91329-8(8))* Marvel Worldwide, Inc.

—Fantastic Four: Behold... Galactus! 2019. (ENG.). 312p. (YA). (gr. -1-17). pap. 24.99 *(978-1-302-91793-7(5))* Marvel Worldwide, Inc.

—Fantastic Four: Behold... Galactus! Marvel Select Edition. 2019. (ENG.). 232p. (YA). (gr. 4-17). 24.99 *(978-1-302-91887-3(7))* Marvel Worldwide, Inc.

Kirby, Jack & Wilson, Ron. Fantastic Four by John Byrne Omnibus Vol. 1. 2018. (ENG.). 1096p. (J). (gr. 4-17). 125.00 *(978-1-302-91328-1(X))* Marvel Worldwide, Inc.

Kirby, Jim. The Birth of Nanabosho, 1 vol. McLellan, Joseph. 2016. (ENG.). 32p. (J). pap. 10.95 *(978-0-921827-00-9(8)*, b884f8fe-3175-4bf4-96c3-5bb1a711f7a4) Pemmican Pubns., Inc. CAN. Dist: Firefly Bks., Ltd.

—Kawlija's Blueberry Promise, 1 vol. Guiboche, Audrey. 2015. (ENG.). 32p. (J). (gr. 1-2). mass mkt. 11.00 *(978-1-894717-55-7(4)*, ca8bac81-10d9-4a05-8feb-87e5400cb5dc) Pemmican Pubns., Inc. CAN. Dist: Firefly Bks., Ltd.

Kirchhoff, Art. The Adventures of Martin Luther. Bergt, Carolyn. 16p. (gr. -1-k). 20.00 *(978-0-570-00643-5(0)*, 22-2808) Concordia Publishing Hse.

—Behold the Lamb: An Introduction to the Signs & Symbols of the Church. Nielsen, Pamela & Luhmann, Edward Q. 2010. 48p. (J). 9.99 *(978-0-7586-1550-3(7))* Concordia Publishing Hse.

Kirchhoff, Arthur. Worshiping with Angels & Archangels: An Introduction to the Divine Service. Kinnaman, Scott A. 2005. 48p. 7.99 *(978-0-7586-1206-9(0))* Concordia Publishing Hse.

Kirchmeier, Jenn-Ann. The Tails of Brinkley the Berner: The Beginning. 2008. 32p. (J). 16.95 *(978-0-9793288-0-0(2))* Brinkley Bks., Inc.

Kirchner, Ben. The Constitution Decoded: A Guide to the Document That Shapes Our Nation. Kennedy, Katie. 2020. (ENG.). 208p. (J). (gr. 2-8). pap. 16.95 ***(978-1-5235-1044-3(7)**, 101044)* Workman Publishing Co., Inc.

Kirchoff, Arthur. The Adventures of Billie & Annie — Baby Bison. Meyer, Kay L. l.t. ed. 2004. 32p. (J). 6.00 *(978-0-9744536-0-6(9)*, 9780974453606) Meyer, Tjaden.

Kirichenko, Vladimir. El Sr Waldorf Viaja Al Salvaje Estado de Alaska. Terry, Barbara. 2020. (SPA.). 36p. (J). pap. 12.95 ***(978-1-64764-903-6(X))*** Waldorf Publishing.

Kirk, Andrea Cope. Beating the Bully. McLelland, Michael J. 2007. 16p. (J). 15.99 *(978-1-59955-006-0(7))* Cedar Fort, Inc./CFI Distribution.

Kirk, Daniel. Block City. Stevenson, Robert Louis. 2005. (ENG.). 32p. (J). (gr. -1-3). 19.99 *(978-0-689-86964-8(9)*, Simon & Schuster Bks. For Young Readers) Simon & Schuster Bks. For Young Readers.

—Dinosaur, Dinosaur. Lewis, Kevin. 2006. (J). *(978-0-439-78228-9(7)*, Orchard Bks.) Scholastic, Inc.

—Hello, Hello! Schlein, Miriam. 2011. (ENG.). 32p. (J). (gr. -1-1). pap. 16.99 *(978-1-4424-5229-9(3)*, Simon & Schuster Bks. For Young Readers) Simon & Schuster Bks. For Young Readers.

—Let's Go ABC! Things That Go, from a to Z. Greene, Rhonda Gowler. 2018. 40p. (J). 17.99 *(978-0-8027-3509-6(6)*, 900119732, Bloomsbury Children's Bks.) Bloomsbury Publishing USA.

—My Truck Is Stuck! Lewis, Kevin. 2006. (ENG.). 30p. (J). (gr. -1-k). bds. 7.99 *(978-0-7868-3739-7(X))* Hyperion Pr.

—Push! Dig! Scoop! A Construction Counting Rhyme. Greene, Rhonda Gowler. (J). 2017. 26p. bds. 7.99 *(978-1-68119-085-3(0)*, 900158430); 2016. 32p. 16.99 *(978-0-8027-3506-5(1)*, 900119729) Bloomsbury Publishing USA. (Bloomsbury USA Childrens).

—'Twas the Night Before Christmas. Moore, Clement. 2015. (ENG.). 32p. (J). (gr. -1-3). 16.95 *(978-1-4197-1233-3(0)*, Abrams Bks. for Young Readers) Abrams, Inc.

Kirk, Daniel. Honk Honk! Beep Beep! Kirk, Daniel. 2014. (ENG.). 32p. (J). (gr. -1-k). bds. 6.99 *(978-1-4231-8041-8(0))* Hyperion Bks. for Children.

Kirk, David. Oh So Brave Dragon: A Picture Book. Kirk, David. 2014. (ENG.). 40p. (J). (gr. -1-1). 17.99 *(978-1-250-01689-8(4)*, 900087097) Feiwel & Friends.

Kirk, Heather. My First Picture Numbers. 2012. (ENG.). 24p. (J). 9.95 *(978-1-84135-795-9(2))* Award Pubns. Ltd. GBR. Dist: Parkwest Pubns., Inc.

—Tiberius & the Chocolate Cake. Harvey, Keith. 2010. (Tiberius Tales Ser.). 24p. (J). (gr. -1-2). pap. 8.15 *(978-1-60754-836-2(4))*; lib. bdg. 25.60 *(978-1-60754-832-4(1))* Windmill Bks.

—Tiberius & the Friendly Dragon. Harvey, Keith. 2010. (Tiberius Tales Ser.). 24p. (J). (gr. -1-2). pap. 8.15 *(978-1-60754-834-8(8))*; lib. bdg. 25.60 *(978-1-60754-830-0(5))* Windmill Bks.

Kirk, Jacqueline. The Ant in the Cellar. Rosenblatt, Danielle. 2008. (J). per. 16.95 *(978-0-9801555-5-6(X))* Argus Enterprises International, Inc.

—The Ant in the Cellar. Rosenblatt, Danielle. 2008. 127p. per. 19.95 *(978-0-9788985-3-3(2))* W & B Pubs.

Kirk, Janice. The Christmas Redwood. Kirk, Janice. 2007. 56p. per. 18.95 *(978-0-60290-147-6(3))* Nassau-Street.com.

Kirk, Leonard, et al. Agents of Atlas: the Complete Collection Vol. 1. 2018. (ENG.). 488p. (YA). (gr. 8-17). pap. 39.99 *(978-1-302-91129-4(5))* Marvel Worldwide, Inc.

Kirk, Leonard. Attack of 50 Foot Girl! Parker, Jeff. 2014. (Avengers Ser.). (ENG.). 24p. (J). (gr. 2-6). lib. bdg. 27.07 *(978-1-61479-293-2(3)*, 38, Marvel Age) Spotlight.

—The Avenging Seven. Parker, Jeff. 2014. (Avengers Ser.). (ENG.). 24p. (J). (gr. 2-6). lib. bdg. 27.07 *(978-1-61479-294-9(1)*, 39, Marvel Age) Spotlight.

Kirk, Leonard, et al. Gambit: King of Thieves - the Complete Collection. 2019. 376p. (YA). (gr. -1-17). pap. 34.99 *(978-1-302-91778-4(1))* Marvel Worldwide, Inc.

Kirk, Leonard. Solo: a Star Wars Story Adaptation. 2019. (ENG.). 192p. (YA). (gr. -1-17). pap. 19.99 *(978-1-302-91572-8(X))* Marvel Worldwide, Inc.

—Squadron Supreme Vol. 3: Finding Namor. 2017. (ENG.). 136p. (YA). (gr. 8-17). pap. 17.99 *(978-1-302-90285-8(7))* Marvel Worldwide, Inc.

Kirk, Leonard, et al. Star Wars: Age of Resistance. 2020. (ENG.). 232p. (J). (gr. 4-17). 34.99 ***(978-1-302-91711-1(0))*** Marvel Worldwide, Inc.

Kirk, Leonard. Star Wars: Age of Resistance - Villains. 2019. 128p. (YA). (gr. 4-17). pap. 17.99 *(978-1-302-91730-2(7))* Marvel Worldwide, Inc.

—Star Wars: Han Solo - Imperial Cadet. 2019. (ENG.). 160p. (YA). pap. 17.99 *(978-1-302-91500-1(2))* Marvel Worldwide, Inc.

Kirk, Leonard, jt. illus. see Camuncoli, Giuseppe.

Kirk, Leonard, jt. illus. see Sprouse, Chris.

Kirk, Maria L. Heidi. Spyri, Johanna. ed. 2015. (First Avenue Classics (tm) Ser.). (ENG.). 192p. (YA). (gr. 3-8). E-Book 19.99 *(978-1-4677-5846-8(9)*, First Avenue Editions) Lerner Publishing Group.

Kirk, Maria L. Vinzi (Illustrated Edition) Spyri, Johanna. Stork, Elisabeth P., tr. 2019. (ENG.). 132p. (J). pap. ***(978-1-4068-9813-2(9))*** Echo Library.

Kirk, Maria L. & Hughes, Arthur. The Princess & Curdie. MacDonald, George. ed. 2011. 260p. pap. 10.95 *(978-1-59915-251-6(7))* Yesterday's Classics.

—The Princess & the Goblin. MacDonald, George. 2011. 260p. pap. 10.95 *(978-1-59915-250-9(9))* Yesterday's Classics.

Kirk, Phoebe. Carlos the Chameleon: A Story to Help Empower Children to Be Themselves. Reeves, Alice. 2018. (Truth & Tails Children's Bks.). (ENG.). 48p. (J). 15.95 *(978-1-78592-453-8(2)*, 696747) Kingsley, Jessica Pubs. GBR. Dist: Hachette UK Distribution.

—Molly the Mole: A Story to Help Children Build Self-Esteem. Reeves, Alice. 2018. (Truth & Tails Children's Bks.). (ENG.). 40p. (J). 15.95 *(978-1-78592-452-1(4)*, 696749) Kingsley, Jessica Pubs. GBR. Dist: Hachette UK Distribution.

—Vincent the Vixen: A Story to Help Children Learn about Gender Identity. Reeves, Alice. 2018. (Truth & Tails Children's Bks.). (ENG.). 48p. (J). 15.95 *(978-1-78592-450-7(8)*, 696746) Kingsley, Jessica Pubs. GBR. Dist: Hachette UK Distribution.

Kirk, Tim. Muggles & Magic: An Unofficial Guide to J. K. Rowling & the Harry Potter Phenomenon. Beahm, George. 2005. (J). lib. bdg. 19.95 *(978-1-57174-480-7(0))* Hampton Roads Publishing Co., Inc.

—Muggles & Magic: J.K. Rowling & the Harry Potter Phenomenon. Beahm, George. 2004. 416p. pap. 16.95 *(978-1-57174-412-8(6))* Hampton Roads Publishing Co., Inc.

—Passport to Narnia: A Newcomer's Guide. Beahm, George. 2005. (ENG.). 200p. (YA). (gr. 8-12). per. 12.95 *(978-1-57174-465-4(7))* Hampton Roads Publishing Co., Inc.

—Passport to Narnia: The Unofficial Guide. Beahm, George. 2005. (J). lib. bdg. 15.95 *(978-1-57174-481-4(9))* Hampton Roads Publishing Co., Inc.

—Twinkle: The Only Firefly Who Couldn't Light Up. Black, Cassandra. 3rd ed. 2012. (ENG.). 111p. (J). (gr. 4-7). pap. 12.99 *(978-0-9742739-3-8(7))* Lavender Bks.

Kirkbride, E. R. Azalea's Silver Web (Illustrated Edition) Peattie, Elia W. 2017. (ENG.). (J). pap. *(978-1-4068-8626-9(2))* Echo Library.

Kirkbride, Tom. The Gamacode: The Freeing of the Human Race! Kirkbride, Tom. 2019. (ENG.). 96p. (YA). (gr. 7-15). pap. 7.95 *(978-1-0956-9460-2(X))* Independently Published.

Kirkby, Joanne & Cooper, Sharon. Mosaic Picture Sticker Book. 2015. (Mosaic Sticker Bks.). (ENG.). 24+12p. (J). (gr. k-5). pap. 10.99 *(978-0-7945-3015-0(X)*, Usborne) EDC Publishing.

Kirkham, Jennifer. Missing in the Mountains: A Wren & Frog Adventure. Allison, Grant. Downs, Kate, ed. 2018. (Adventures of Wren & Frog Ser.: Vol. 1). (ENG.). 72p. (J). pap. 14.99 *(978-1-948657-05-1(8))* Summer Storm Publishing, LLC.

—Missing in the Mountains - Black & White Edition: A Wren & Frog Adventure. Allison, Grant. Downs, Kate, ed. 2018. (Wren & Frog Adventures Ser.: Vol. 1). (ENG.). 72p. (J). pap. 9.99 *(978-1-948657-06-8(6))* Summer Storm Publishing, LLC.

—Sailing into the Storm: A Wren & Frog Adventure: Book 0. Allison, Grant. Downs, Kate, ed. 2018. (Adventures of Wren & Frog Ser.). (ENG.). 30p. (J). pap. 9.99 *(978-1-948657-09-9(0))* Summer Storm Publishing, LLC.

Kirkland, Katherine. My Grandma & Me: Rhyming Devotions for You & Your Grandchild. Bowman, Crystal. 2012. (ENG.). 68p. (J). 14.99 *(978-1-4143-7170-2(5)*, 4606160, Tyndale Kids) Tyndale Hse. Pubs.

Kirkova, Milena. Lights Out, Night's Out. Boniface, William. 2011. (ENG.). 24p. (J). pap. 6.99 *(978-1-4494-0236-5(4))* Andrews McMeel Publishing.

—Where Does Love Come From? Accord Publishing Staff. 2011. (ENG.). 18p. (J). 9.99 *(978-1-4494-0839-8(7))* Andrews McMeel Publishing.

—Where Does Love Come From? Accord Publishing Staff. 2012. (ENG.). 18p. (J). bds. 5.99 *(978-1-4494-2884-6(3))* Andrews McMeel Publishing.

Kirkpatrick, Ian. If You Wave Your Wand: Stories for the Wildest Hearts. Decker, Stephanie a. 2018. (ENG.). 40p. (J). *(978-1-5255-3266-5(9))*; pap. *(978-1-5255-3267-2(7))* FriesenPress.

Kirkpatrick, Karen. The Boy Who Captured the Sun. Rodenbur, Susan. 2007. 32p. per. 12.95 *(978-1-59858-515-5(0))* Dog Ear Publishing, LLC.

Kirkpatrick, Katrina. Night Work. Gifune, Greg F. 2003. (ENG.). 278p. pap. 14.99 *(978-1-58124-094-8(5))* Fiction Works, The.

Kirkwood, Catherine. Looking for Tula. Kirkwood, Catherine. l.t. ed. 2013. (ENG.). 40p. (J). 19.95 *(978-1-929115-23-5(7))* Azro Pr., Inc.

Kirmse, Marguerite. Alfred Ollivant's Bob, Son of Battle: The Last Gray Dog of Kenmuir. Davis, Lydia & Ollivant, Alfred. 2014. 320p. (J). (gr. 3-7). 17.95 *(978-1-59017-729-7(0)*, NYR Children's Collection) New York Review of Bks., Inc., The.

—Lassie Come-Home. Knight, Eric. rev. ed. 2003. (ENG.). 256p. (J). (gr. 3-7). 26.99 *(978-0-8050-7206-8(3)*, 900018916, Holt, Henry & Co. Bks. For Young Readers) Holt, Henry & Co.

—Lassie Come-Home. Knight, Eric. 2007. (ENG.). 256p. (J). (gr. 3-7). per. 7.99 *(978-0-312-37131-9(4)*, 900044659) Square Fish.

Kirsch, Vincent X. Gingerbread for Liberty! How a German Baker Helped Win the American Revolution. Rockliff, Mara. 2015. (ENG.). 32p. (J). (gr. 1-4). 17.99 *(978-0-544-13001-2(4)*, 1543476, HMH Books For Young Readers) Houghton Mifflin Harcourt Publishing Co.

—The Hole Story of the Doughnut. Miller, Pat. 2016. (ENG.). 40p. (J). (gr. 1-4). 17.99 *(978-0-544-31961-5(3)*, 1582246, HMH Books For Young Readers) Houghton Mifflin Harcourt Publishing Co.

—Noah Webster & His Words. Ferris, Jeri Chase. (ENG.). 32p. (J). (gr. 1-4). 2015. 6.99 *(978-0-544-58242-2(X)*, 1613671, HMH Books For Young Readers); 2012. 16.99 *(978-0-547-39055-0(6)*, 1426556) Houghton Mifflin Harcourt Publishing Co.

Kirschner, Rafael & Glass House Graphics, Glass House. Down the Brain Drain. Hopper, Ada. 2020. (DATA Set Ser.: 8). (ENG.). 128p. (J). (gr. k-4). 17.99 ***(978-1-5344-1130-2(5))***; pap. 5.99 ***(978-1-5344-1129-6(1))*** Little Simon. (Little Simon).

Kirsten, Sevig. Kindness to Share from a to Z. Snow, Todd & Snow, Peggy. 2008. (ENG.). 32p. (J). pap. 10.99 *(978-1-934277-16-4(9))* Mam Green Publishing, Inc.

Kirton, Pamela T. Dino the Dog & His Day in the Country. Garr, Hillary. Date not set. 15.95 *(978-0-9637143-3-6(3))* Amicus Pr.

Kirwan, Wednesday. Eggs Are Everywhere: (Baby's First Easter Board Book, Easter Egg Hunt Book, Lift the Flap Book for Easter Basket) Chronicle Books. 2020. (ENG.). 10p. (J). (gr. -1 — 1). bds. 10.99 *(978-1-4521-7457-0(1))* Chronicle Bks. LLC.

—Henry's Bright Idea. Bradshaw, Lauren. 2016. (ENG.). 32p. (J). (gr. -1-1). 17.95 *(978-1-937359-94-2(8)*, Cameron Kids) Cameron + Co.

—A Little Bunny: Animal Shaped Board Book. Wren, Rosalee. Cottage Door Press, ed. 2018. (ENG.). 10p. (J). (gr. -1-k). bds. 4.99 *(978-1-68052-384-3(8)*, 1003491) Cottage Door Pr.

—Magnolia's Magnificent Map. Bradshaw, Lauren. 2018. (ENG.). 32p. (J). (gr. -1-3). 16.95 *(978-1-944903-12-1(7)*, Cameron Kids) Cameron + Co.

—The Night Dad Went to Jail: What to Expect When Someone You Love Goes to Jail, 1 vol. Higgins, Melissa. 2011. (Life's Challenges Ser.). (ENG.). 24p. (J). (gr. 2-3). lib. bdg. 26.65 *(978-1-4048-6679-9(5)*, Picture Window Bks.) Capstone.

—Night Dad Went to Jail: What to Expect When Someone You Love Goes to Jail. Higgins, Melissa. 2013. (Life's Challenges Ser.). (ENG.). 24p. (J). (gr. 2-3). 8.99 *(978-1-4795-2142-5(6)*, Picture Window Bks.) Capstone.

—Owl Love You. Heroux, Matthew. 2018. (ENG.). 32p. (J). (gr. -1-3). 16.95 *(978-1-944903-35-0(6)*, Cameron Kids) Cameron + Co.

—Santa Claus Is Green! How to Have an Eco-Friendly Christmas. Inches, Alison. 2009. (Little Green Book Ser.). (ENG.). 24p. (J). (gr. k-2). 18.69 *(978-1-4169-7223-5(4)*, Little Simon) Little Simon.

—Yeti, Turn Out the Light! Long, Greg & Edmundson, Chris. 2013. (ENG.). 36p. (J). (gr. -1-k). 12.99 *(978-1-4521-1158-2(8))* Chronicle Bks. LLC.

Kirwan, Wednesday. Baby Loves to Boogie! Kirwan, Wednesday. 2014. (ENG.). 30p. (J). (gr. -1 — 1). bds. 5.99 *(978-1-4814-0383-2(4)*, Little Simon) Little Simon.

—Baby Loves to Party! Kirwan, Wednesday. 2015. (ENG.). 30p. (J). (gr. -1 — 1). bds. 5.99 *(978-1-4814-2994-8(9)*, Little Simon) Little Simon.

—Baby Loves to Party! Rock! & Boogie! Baby Loves to Party!; Baby Loves to Rock!; Baby Loves to Boogie! Kirwan, Wednesday. ed. 2018. (ENG.). 88p. (J). (gr. -1 — 1). bds. 17.99 *(978-1-5344-3675-6(8)*, Little Simon) Little Simon.

—Baby Loves to Rock! Kirwan, Wednesday. 2013. (ENG.). 28p. (J). (gr. -1 — 1). bds. 5.99 *(978-1-4424-5989-2(1)*, Little Simon) Little Simon.

Kis, Gabor Norbert. The Great Orange. Vajda, Joseph. 2017. (ENG.). (gr. 1-4). *(978-1-78222-499-0(8))* Paragon Publishing, Rothersthorpe.

Kishimoto, Masashi. Naruto: Chapter Book, Vol. 1. Kishimoto, Masashi. 2008. (Naruto Ser.: 1). (ENG.). 80p. (J). (gr. 1-5). pap. 4.99 *(978-1-4215-2056-8(7))* Viz Media.

—Naruto: Chapter Book, Vol. 10. Kishimoto, Masashi. 2009. (ENG.). 80p. (J). pap. 4.99 *(978-1-4215-2320-0(5))* Viz Media.

—Naruto: Chapter Book, Vol. 11. Kishimoto, Masashi. 2010. (ENG.). 80p. (J). pap. 4.99 *(978-1-4215-3041-3(4))* Viz Media.

—Naruto: Chapter Book, Vol. 12. Kishimoto, Masashi. 2010. 80p. (J). pap. 4.99 *(978-1-4215-3042-0(2))* Viz Media.

—Naruto: Chapter Book, Vol. 13. Kishimoto, Masashi. 2010. (ENG.). 80p. (J). pap. 4.99 *(978-1-4215-3043-7(0))* Viz Media.

—Naruto: Chapter Book, Vol. 14. Kishimoto, Masashi. 2010. (ENG.). 80p. (J). pap. 4.99 *(978-1-4215-3044-4(9))* Viz Media.

—Naruto: Chapter Book, Vol. 15. Kishimoto, Masashi. 2010. 80p. (J). (gr. 1-4). pap. 4.99 *(978-1-4215-3045-1(7))* Viz Media.

—Naruto: Chapter Book, Vol. 16, 16. Kishimoto, Masashi. 2010. (Naruto Chapter Bks.). (ENG.). 80p. (J). (gr. 2-4). 17.44 *(978-1-4215-3046-8(5))* Viz Media.

—Naruto: Chapter Book, Vol. 2. Kishimoto, Masashi. 2008. (Naruto Ser.: 2). (ENG.). 80p. (J). (gr. 1-5). pap. 4.99 *(978-1-4215-2213-5(6))* Viz Media.

—Naruto: Chapter Book, Vol. 3. Kishimoto, Masashi. 2008. (Naruto Ser.: 3). (ENG.). 80p. (J). (gr. 1-5). pap. 4.99 *(978-1-4215-2214-2(4))* Viz Media.

—Naruto: Chapter Book, Vol. 4. Kishimoto, Masashi. 2008. (Naruto Ser.: 4). (ENG.). 80p. (J). (gr. 1-5). pap. 4.99 *(978-1-4215-2314-9(0))* Viz Media.

—Naruto: Chapter Book, Vol. 5. Kishimoto, Masashi. 2009. (ENG.). 80p. (J). (gr. 1). pap. 4.99 *(978-1-4215-2315-6(9))* Viz Media.

—Naruto: Chapter Book, Vol. 6. Kishimoto, Masashi. 2009. (ENG.). 80p. (J). pap. 4.99 *(978-1-4215-2316-3(7))* Viz Media.

—Naruto: Chapter Book, Vol. 7. Kishimoto, Masashi. 2009. (ENG.). 80p. (J). pap. 4.99 *(978-1-4215-2317-0(5))* Viz Media.

—Naruto: Chapter Book, Vol. 8. Kishimoto, Masashi. 2009. (Naruto Ser.: 8). (ENG.). 80p. (J). pap. 4.99 *(978-1-4215-2318-7(3))* Viz Media.

Kishimoto, Yuko. God Will Take Care of You. 2007. (ENG.). 16p. (J). pap. *(978-1-932381-18-4(X)*, 6160) Bible Visuals International, Inc.

Kishiro, Yukito. Battle Angel Alita, Vol. 1. Kishiro, Yukito. 2nd ed. 2003. (Battle Angel Alita Ser.: Vol. 1). (ENG.). 224p. (Orig.). pap. 9.95 *(978-1-56931-945-1(6))* Viz Media.

—Battle Angel Alita Last Order. Kishiro, Yukito. 2009. (ENG.). 216p. pap. 9.99 *(978-1-4215-2918-9(1))* Viz Media.

—Battle Angel Alita Last Order Vol. 4: Angel of Protest. Kishiro, Yukito. 2004. (Battle Angel Alita Last Order Ser.: Vol. 4). (ENG.). 200p. (YA). pap. 9.95 *(978-1-59116-281-0(5))* Viz Media.

—Battle Angel Alita, Vol. 3. Kishiro, Yukito. 2nd ed. 2004. (ENG.). 208p. pap. 9.95 *(978-1-59116-274-2(2))* Viz Media.

—Battle Angel Alita, Vol. 4. Kishiro, Yukito. 2nd ed. 2004. (ENG.). 216p. pap. 9.95 *(978-1-59116-275-9(0))* Viz Media.

—Fallen Angel, Vol. 8. Kishiro, Yukito. 2nd ed. 2005. (Battle Angel Alita Ser.). (ENG.). 232p. pap. 9.95 *(978-1-59116-279-7(3))* Viz Media.

Kiss, Andrew. Cool Woods: A Trip Around the World's Boreal Forest. Drake, Jane & Love, Ann. 2003. 80p. (J). (gr. 4-7). 19.95 *(978-0-88776-608-4(0)*, Tundra Bks.) Tundra Bks. CAN. Dist: Penguin Random Hse. LLC.

—A Mountain Alphabet. Ruurs, Margriet. 2009. (ABC Our Country Ser.). 32p. (J). (gr. 1-4). pap. 7.95 *(978-0-88776-940-5(3)*, Tundra Bks.) Tundra Bks. CAN. Dist: Penguin Random Hse. LLC.

—When We Go Camping. Ruurs, Margriet. 2004. (ENG.). 32p. (J). (gr. 1-4). pap. 8.95 *(978-0-88776-685-5(4)*, Tundra Bks.) Tundra Bks. CAN. Dist: Penguin Random Hse. LLC.

—Wild Babies. Ruurs, Margriet. 2003. 32p. (J). (gr. -1-3). 14.95 *(978-0-88776-627-5(7)*, Tundra Bks.) Tundra Bks. CAN. Dist: Penguin Random Hse. LLC.

Kiss, Gergely. Animals in the Outhouse. Frohlich, Anja. 2012. (ENG.). 28p. (J). (gr. k-3). 16.95 *(978-1-61608-659-6(9)*, 608659, Sky Pony Pr.) Skyhorse Publishing Co., Inc.

Kissenger, Beth. Mattie: At the Fair. Redditt, Delbert. 2019. (ENG.). 36p. (J). pap. 5.99 ***(978-1-7917-0420-9(4))*** Independently Published.

Kissi, Marta. The Adventures of Alfie Onion. French, Vivian. 2018. (ENG.). 192p. (J). pap. 5.99 *(978-1-61067-732-5(3))* Kane Miller.

Kissi, Marta. The Birthday Castle: Fort Builders Inc. 1. Romito, Dee. 2020. (Quix Ser.). (ENG.). 96p. (J). (gr. k-3). 17.99 ***(978-1-5344-5239-8(7))***; pap. 5.99 ***(978-1-5344-5238-1(9))*** Simon & Schuster Children's Publishing. (Aladdin).

Kissi, Marta. The Cherry Pie Princess. French, Vivian. 2018. (ENG.). 176p. (J). pap. 5.99 *(978-1-61067-733-2(1))* Kane Miller.

—Fairy Mom & Me. Kinsella, Sophie. (Fairy Mom & Me Ser.: 1). (ENG.). 160p. (J). (gr. 2-5). 2019. pap. 5.99 *(978-1-5247-6993-2(2)*, Yearling); 2018. 14.99 *(978-1-5247-6989-5(4)*, Delacorte Bks. for Young Readers) Random Hse. Children's Bks.

—Fairy Mom & Me #1. Kinsella, Sophie. 2018. (Fairy Mom & Me Ser.: 1). (ENG.). 160p. (J). (gr. 2-5). lib. bdg. 17.99 *(978-1-5247-7065-5(5)*, Delacorte Bks. for Young Readers) Random Hse. Children's Bks.

—Fairy Mom & Me #2: Fairy in Waiting. Kinsella, Sophie. 2020. (Fairy Mom & Me Ser.: 2). (ENG.). 160p. (J). (gr. 2-5). 5.99 *(978-1-5247-6994-9(0)*, Yearling) Random Hse. Children's Bks.

Kissi, Marta. Fairy Mom & Me #3: Fairy Unicorn Wishes. Kinsella, Sophie. 2020. (Fairy Mom & Me Ser.: 3). (ENG.). 176p. (J). (gr. 2-5). 5.99 ***(978-0-593-12051-4(5)***, Yearling); 14.99 *(978-0-593-12049-1(3)*, Delacorte Bks. for Young Readers) Random Hse. Children's Bks.

—Fairy Mom & Me #4: Fairy Mermaid Magic. Kinsella, Sophie. 2020. (Fairy Mom & Me Ser.: 4). (ENG.). 160p. (J). (gr. 2-5). 14.99 ***(978-0-593-12052-1(3)***, Delacorte Bks. for Young Readers) Random Hse. Children's Bks.

Kissi, Marta. Gabby Garcia's Ultimate Playbook. Palmer, Iva-Marie. 2017. (Gabby Garcia's Ultimate Playbook Ser.: 1). (ENG.). 304p. (J). (gr. 3-7). 12.99 *(978-0-06-239180-3(1)*, Tegen, Katherine Bks) HarperCollins Pubs.

—Gabby Garcia's Ultimate Playbook #2: MVP Summer. Palmer, Iva-Marie. 2018. (Gabby Garcia's Ultimate Playbook Ser.: 2). (ENG.). 304p. (J). (gr. 3-7). 12.99 *(978-0-06-239183-4(6)*, Tegen, Katherine Bks) HarperCollins Pubs.

—Gabby Garcia's Ultimate Playbook #3: Sidelined. Palmer, Iva-Marie. 2019. (Gabby Garcia's Ultimate Playbook Ser.: 3). (ENG.). 288p. (J). (gr. 3-7). 12.99 *(978-0-06-239186-5(0)*, Tegen, Katherine Bks) HarperCollins Pubs.

—Go Mo Go: Dinosaur Dash! Book 2, Bk. 2. Farah, Mo & Gray, Kes. 2018. (Go Mo Go Ser.). (ENG.). 96p. (J). (gr. k-2). pap. 9.99 *(978-1-4449-3401-4(5))* Hachette Children's Group GBR. Dist: Hachette Bk. Group.

—Go Mo Go: Monster Mountain Chase! Book 1. Farah, Mo & Gray, Kes. 2018. (Go Mo Go Ser.). 96p. (J). (gr. k-2). pap. 9.99 *(978-1-4449-3405-2(8))* Hachette Children's Group GBR. Dist: Hachette Bk. Group.

—Go Mo Go: Seaside Sprint! Book 3, Bk. 3. Farah, Mo & Gray, Kes. 2018. (Go Mo Go Ser.). 96p. (J). (gr. k-2). pap. 9.99 *(978-1-4449-3403-8(1))* Hachette Children's Group GBR. Dist: Hachette Bk. Group.

Kissi, Marta. Happy Tails Lodge: Fort Builders Inc. 2. Romito, Dee. 2020. (Quix Ser.). (ENG.). 96p. (J). (gr. k-3). 17.99 ***(978-1-5344-5242-8(7))***; pap. 5.99 ***(978-1-5344-5241-1(9))*** Simon & Schuster Children's Publishing. (Aladdin).

Kissi, Marta. Pennybaker School Is Headed for Disaster. Brown, Jennifer. 2017. 304p. (J). 16.99 *(978-1-68119-174-4(1)*, 900161366, Bloomsbury USA Childrens) Bloomsbury Publishing USA.

—Pennybaker School Is Revolting. Brown, Jennifer. 2018. (ENG.). 288p. (J). 16.99 *(978-1-68119-176-8(8)*, 900161358, Bloomsbury Children's Bks.) Bloomsbury Publishing USA.

—The Pennypackers Go on Vacation. Doan, Lisa. 2019. (ENG.). 272p. (J). 16.99 *(978-1-250-15411-8(1)*, 900184349) Roaring Brook Pr.

—Raise Your Hand. Tapper, Alice Paul. 2019. 32p. (J). (gr. -1-3). 17.99 *(978-1-5247-9120-9(2)*, Penguin Workshop) Penguin Young Readers Group.

—Trevor Lee & the Big Uh Oh! Blevins, Wiley. 2019. (ENG.). 160p. (J). (gr. 2-4). 14.99 *(978-1-947159-06-8(2)*, One Elm Books) Red Chair Pr.

—Trouble at Table 5 #1: the Candy Caper. Watson, Tom. 2020. (HarperChapters Ser.). (ENG.). 96p. (J). (gr. 1-5). 15.99 *(978-0-06-295341-4(9))*; pap. 5.99 *(978-0-06-295340-7(0))* HarperCollins Pubs. Ltd. GBR. (HarperCollins). Dist: HarperCollins Pubs.

—Trouble at Table 5 #2: Busted by Breakfast. Watson, Tom. 2020. (HarperChapters Ser.). (ENG.). 96p. (J). (gr. 1-5). 15.99 *(978-0-06-295344-5(3))*; pap. 5.99 *(978-0-06-295343-8(5))* HarperCollins Pubs. Ltd. GBR. (HarperCollins). Dist: HarperCollins Pubs.

Kissi, Marta. Trouble at Table 5 #3: the Firefly Fix. Watson, Tom. 2020. (HarperChapters Ser.). 96p. (J). (gr. 1-5). 15.99 ***(978-0-06-295347-6(8)***, HarperCollins) HarperCollins Pubs. Ltd. GBR. Dist: HarperCollins Pubs.

Kissi, Marta & Egmont, Hardie Grant. Project Best Friend. Perry, Chrissie. 2017. (Penelope Perfect Ser.: 1). (ENG.). 144p. (J). (gr. 2-5). 16.99 *(978-1-4814-6602-8(X)*, Simon & Schuster/Paula Wiseman Bks.) Simon & Schuster/Paula Wiseman Bks.

Kiste, Tori Lynn. Billy's Wish. Barnett, Wm. 2008. 28p. pap. 24.95 *(978-1-60563-330-5(5))* America Star Bks.

Kistler, Jeanni. A to Zebra. Holm, Deb. 2019. (ENG.). 32p. (J). pap. 16.99 *(978-1-5462-4091-4(8))* AuthorHouse.

Kiszla, B. Matthew, jt. illus. see Kiszla, Paula Ingram.

Kiszla, Paula Ingram & Kiszla, B. Matthew. When Eva Hollers. Pound, Brinkley Burks. 2019. (ENG.). 34p. (J). 23.95 ***(978-1-4808-8077-1(9))***; pap. 16.95 ***(978-1-4808-8076-4(0))*** Archway Publishing.

Kitamura, Satoshi. Beware of the Crocodile. Jenkins, Martin. 2019. (ENG.). 32p. (J). (gr. k-3). 16.99 *(978-0-7636-7538-7(5))* Candlewick Pr.

—The History of Money: From Bartering to Banking. Jenkins, Martin. 2014. (ENG.). 64p. (J). (gr. 4-7). 16.99 *(978-0-7636-6763-4(3))* Candlewick Pr.

—In the Attic. Oram, Hiawyn. 2012. 32p. (J). (gr. -1-k). pap. 13.99 *(978-1-84939-298-3(6))* Andersen Pr. GBR. Dist: Independent Pubs. Group.

—Once upon an Ordinary School Day. McNaughton, Colin. 2005. 32p. (J). (-k). pap. 14.99 *(978-1-84270-469-1(9))* Andersen Pr. GBR. Dist: Independent Pubs. Group.

—The Story of a Snail Who Discovered the Importance of Being Slow. Sepúlveda, Luis. Caistor, Nick, tr. 2017. (ENG.). 128p. (J). pap. 10.99 *(978-1-84688-413-9(6)*, 900184074) Alma Bks. GBR. Dist: Macmillan.

—The Yes. Bee, Sarah. 2015. (ENG.). 32p. (J). 16.00 *(978-0-8028-5449-0(4)*, Eerdmans Bks For Young Readers) Eerdmans, William B. Publishing Co.

Kitamura, Satoshi. Colours: Band 04/Blue (Collins Big Cat) Kitamura, Satoshi. 2007. (Collins Big Cat Ser.). (ENG.). 16p. (J). (gr. -1-1). pap. 7.99 *(978-0-00-718663-1(0))* HarperCollins Pubs. Ltd. GBR. Dist: Independent Pubs. Group.

—Cuando los Borregos No Pueden Dormir. Kitamura, Satoshi. 2nd ed. 2003. (Picture Books Collection). (SPA.). 26p. (J). (gr. k-3). pap. 12.95 *(978-84-372-2182-3(X))* Santillana USA Publishing Co., Inc.

—Me & My Cat? Kitamura, Satoshi. 2009. 32p. (J). (gr. k-k). pap. 12.95 *(978-1-84270-775-3(2))* Andersen Pr. GBR. Dist: Independent Pubs. Group.

—Millie's Marvellous Hat. Kitamura, Satoshi. 2009. (ENG.). 32p. (J). (gr. -1-3). 16.95 *(978-0-7613-5153-5(1)*, 9780761351535) Lerner Publishing Group.

—Por el Hilo se Saca el Ovillo. Kitamura, Satoshi. 2003. (Picture Books Collection). (SPA.). 32p. (J). (gr. k-3). 14.95 *(978-84-372-2357-5(1))* Altea, Ediciones, S.A. - Grupo Santillana ESP. Dist: Santillana USA Publishing Co., Inc.

—Pot-San's Tabletop Tales. Kitamura, Satoshi. 2013. (ENG.). 32p. (J). (gr. -1-k). 22.99 *(978-1-84939-378-2(8))* Andersen Pr. GBR. Dist: Independent Pubs. Group.

Kitchel, JoAnn E. Bach's Goldberg Variations. Celenza, Anna Harwell. 2016. (Once upon a Masterpiece Ser.: 3). 32p. (J). (gr. 1-4). lib. bdg. 16.95 *(978-1-58089-529-3(8))* Charlesbridge Publishing, Inc.

—Barabbas Goes Free. Rottmann, Erik. 2003. (Arch Bks.). (ENG.). 16p. (J). 1.99 *(978-0-570-07582-0(3))* Concordia Publishing Hse.

—Beethoven's Heroic Symphony. Celenza, Anna Harwell. 2016. (Once upon a Masterpiece Ser.: 4). 32p. (J). (gr. 1-4). lib. bdg. 16.95 *(978-1-58089-530-9(1))* Charlesbridge Publishing, Inc.

—The Farewell Symphony. Celenza, Anna Harwell. 2016. (Once upon a Masterpiece Ser.: 1). 32p. (J). (gr. 1-4). lib. bdg. 16.95 *(978-1-58089-527-9(1))* Charlesbridge Publishing, Inc.

—Pictures at an Exhibition. Celenza, Anna Harwell. 2016. (Once upon a Masterpiece Ser.: 2). 32p. (J). (gr. 1-4). lib. bdg. 16.95 *(978-1-58089-528-6(X))* Charlesbridge Publishing, Inc.

Kitchen, Bert. Predator & Prey: a Conversation in Verse. Buhrman-Deever, Susannah. 2019. 32p. (J). (gr. 1-4). 18.99 *(978-0-7636-9533-0(5))* Candlewick Pr.

Kitchen, Kenady a. The Beautiful, Brown, & Bionic Ballerina: LIFE Adventures of Madison the Bionic Ballerina. Zulueta, Chasney N. & Cothern, Madison Z. 2019. (Real Adventures of Madison the Bionic Ballerina Ser.: Vol. 2). (ENG.). 26p. (J). pap. 20.00 ***(978-1-0869-7196-5(5))*** Independently Published.

Kitchin, Megan. Funky Chicken a Bushy Tale of Crocs & Chooks: A Bushy Tale of Crocs & Chooks. 2014. (ENG.). 38p. (J). (gr. k-3). *(978-0-9874507-8-4(6))* Funkybooks.

—Funky Chicken Mission Incrocible. Collin, Chris. 2018. (ENG.). 34p. (J). pap. *(978-0-9942846-6-2(7))* Funkybooks.

Kitora, Tetsuo. La Rama. Paz Lozano, Octavio. 2005.Tr. of Branch. (SPA.). (J). (gr. k-2). pap. 10.95 *(978-968-494-046-8(7))* Centro de Informacion y Desarrollo de la Comunicacion y la Literatura MEX. Dist: Iaconi, Mariuccia Bk. Imports.

Kitsco, Victoria a. Dreamer. Lin, Patricia a. 2019. (ENG.). 44p. (J). pap. 13.00 *(978-1-7223-7476-1(4))* CreateSpace Independent Publishing Platform.

Kitson, Barry. Doctor Strange by Mark Waid Vol. 3: Herald. 2019. (ENG.). 136p. (YA). (gr. 8-17). pap. 17.99 *(978-1-302-91457-8(X))* Marvel Worldwide, Inc.

Kitson, Barry, et al. Spider-Man: New Ways to Live. 2019. (ENG.). 480p. (YA). (gr. 8-17). pap. 39.99 *(978-1-302-91562-9(2))* Marvel Worldwide, Inc.

Kitson, Rhys. Baby Bush Animals. Hart, Anna. 2020. (ENG.). 10p. (J). bds. ***(978-1-5037-5603-8(3)***, 12cdd91e-ca5d-491f-80cf-29be05bea327, p i kids) Phoenix International Publications, Inc.

Kittell DiOrio, Kathy. No More Garbage. Gilkey, Gail. Gilkey, Gail, ed. 2003. 32p. (J). (gr. k-2). lib. bdg. 14.95 *(978-0-9662983-4-5(9))* Windy Hill Pr.

Kitzing, Constanze V. Can't Catch Me! Kitzing, Constanze V. 2019. (ENG.). 32p. (J). (gr. -1 — 1). pap. *(978-1-78285-403-6(7))* Barefoot Bks., Ltd.

—Chilly Penguin. Kitzing, Constanze V. 2018. (ENG.). 24p. (J). (gr. -1). bds. 7.99 *(978-1-78285-406-7(1))* Barefoot Bks., Inc.

—I'm the Best! Kitzing, Constanze V. 2019. (ENG.). 32p. (J). (gr. -1 — 1). pap. *(978-1-78285-404-3(5))* Barefoot Bks., Ltd.

Kitzling, Constanze von. Are You Sleeping? Kitzling, Constanze von. 2019. (ENG.). 32p. (J). (gr. -1 — 1). pap. *(978-1-78285-402-9(9))* Barefoot Bks., Ltd.

Kitzmüller, Christian, jt. illus. see Bonadonna, Davide.

Kiuchi, Tatsuro. The Lotus Seed. Garland, Sherry. 2014. 32p. pap. 7.00 *(978-1-61003-219-3(5))* Center for the Collaborative Classroom.

Kiwak, Barbara. Bold Composer: A Story about Ludwig Van Beethoven. Josephson, Judith P. 2007. (Creative Minds Biographies Ser.). (ENG.). 64p. (gr. 4-8). lib. bdg. 22.60 *(978-0-8225-5987-0(0))* Lerner Publishing Group.

—Jazz Age Poet: A Story about Langston Hughes. Jones, Veda Boyd. 2005. (Creative Minds Biographies Ser.). (ENG.). 64p. (gr. 4-8). lib. bdg. 22.60 *(978-1-57505-757-6(3)*, Carolrhoda Bks.) Lerner Publishing Group.

—My Name Is Bilal. Mobin-Uddin, Asma. 2005. (ENG.). 32p. (J). (gr. 1-k). 17.99 *(978-1-59078-175-3(9))* Boyds Mills Pr.

—Saint Andre Bessette: Miracles in Montreal. Jablonski, Patricia Edward. 2010. (J). (gr. 4-7). pap. 7.95 *(978-0-8198-7140-4(0))* Pauline Bks. & Media.

—Saint Frances Xavier Cabrini: Cecchina's Dream. Dority, Victoria & Andes, Mary Lou. 2005. (Encounter the Saints Ser.: No. 20). 109p. (J). (gr. 3-7). per. 7.95 *(978-0-8198-7092-6(7))* Pauline Bks. & Media.

—Saint Katharine Drexel: The Total Gift. Wallace, Susan Helen. 2003. (Encounter the Saints Ser.: Vol. 15). 144p. (J). pap. 5.95 *(978-0-8198-7068-1(4)*, 332-365) Pauline Bks. & Media.

—Saint Teresa of Avila: Joyful in the Lord. Wallace, Susan Helen. 2008. (Encounter the Saints Ser.: No. 24). 106p. (J). (gr. 4-7). pap. 7.95 *(978-0-8198-7116-9(8))* Pauline Bks. & Media.

Kiwak, Barbara. Blessed Teresa of Calcutta: Missionary of Charity. Kiwak, Barbara, tr. Glavich, Mary Kathleen. 2003. (Encounter the Saints Ser.: Vol. 17). 136p. (J). pap. 7.95 *(978-0-8198-1160-8(2)*, 332-024) Pauline Bks. & Media.

Kizer, Fran. Playing: A Kid's Curriculum. Stone, Sandra J. 2nd ed. 2005. 234p. (Orig.). per. 18.95 *(978-1-59647-003-3(8))* Good Year Bks.

Kizlauskas, Diana. Jorge from Argentina: The Story of Pope Francis for Children. Monge, Marlyn & Wolfe, Jaymie Stuart. 2013. 64p. (J). pap. 8.95 *(978-0-8198-4006-6(8))* Pauline Bks. & Media.

KJA Artists Staff. Creepy-Crawlies: a 3D Pocket Guide. Candlewick Press Staff. 2013. (Panorama Pops Ser.). (ENG.). 30p. (J). (gr. -1-2). 8.99 *(978-0-7636-6662-0(9))* Candlewick Pr.

—Dinosaurs: a 3D Pocket Guide. Candlewick Press Staff. 2013. (Panorama Pops Ser.). (ENG.). 30p. (J). (gr. -1-2). 8.99 *(978-0-7636-6235-6(6))* Candlewick Pr.

—Mapping Earth from Space, 1 vol. Graf, Mike & Snedden, Robert. 2010. (Science Missions Ser.). (ENG.). 56p. (J). (gr. 6-10). 35.32 *(978-1-4109-3826-8(3)*, Raintree) Capstone.

Kjaergaard, Peter. Isabel & the Dragon Queen. Hillyard, Kenneth. 2018. (ENG.). 314p. (J). pap. *(978-1-84897-964-2(9))* Olympia Publishers.

Kjartansson, Stefan. Sometimes I Work in Atlanta: What I Do When I'm Not with You. 2004. 16p. (J). 10.95 *(978-0-9760259-0-0(6)*, SIWI-ATL-01) Relevant Ventures, LLC.

Kk, Raghava. The Sorcerer of Mandala. Kalyanaraman, D. 2016. (ENG.). (YA). (gr. 8-12). pap. 13.99 *(978-0-9890615-3-7(1))* Yali Publishing LLC.

Klaassen, Sandra. The Cat Who Decided: The Almost True Story of an Edinburgh Cat, 48 vols. Forrester, Margaret. 2007. (Young Kelpies Ser.). (ENG.). 112p. (J). per. *(978-0-86315-612-0(6))* Floris Bks.

Klanot, Makenna Karen. The Blue Penguin. Pirnot, Karen Hutchins. 2008. 44p. pap. 14.95 *(978-1-934246-79-5(4))* Peppertree Pr., The.

Klanot, Sameon Clay. The Colors of Myself. Pirnot, Dr Karen Hutchins & Pirnot, Karen Hutchins. 2010. 20p. pap. 12.95 *(978-1-936051-96-0(6))* Peppertree Pr., The.

Klanot, Taryn Lane. A Colorful Day. Pirnot, Karen Hutchins. 2008. 28p. pap. 12.95 *(978-0-9814894-9-0(4))* Peppertree Pr., The.

Klarczyk, Ophelie. Les Chroniques des Sang-M&#65533;l&#65533;s: 1. l'&#65533;veil Des &#65533;toiles. Lebourg, Joffrey. 2019. (Chroniques des Sang-M&#65533;l&#65533;s Ser.: Vol. 1). (FRE.). 230p. (J). pap. ***(978-2-9568623-3-8(2))*** Bekalle-Akwe (Henri Junior).

Klassen, Jon. Cats' Night Out. Stutson, Caroline. 2010. (ENG.). 32p. (J). (gr. -1-3). 18.99 *(978-1-4169-4005-0(7)*, Simon & Schuster/Paula Wiseman Bks.) Simon & Schuster/Paula Wiseman Bks.

—Circle. Barnett, Mac. 2019. (ENG.). 48p. (J). (gr. k-4). 15.99 *(978-0-7636-9608-5(0))* Candlewick Pr.

—The Dark. Snicket, Lemony. 2013. (ENG.). 40p. (J). (gr. -1-3). 18.99 *(978-0-316-18748-0(8))* Little, Brown Bks. for Young Readers.

—Extra Yarn. Barnett, Mac. 2012. (ENG.). 40p. (J). (gr. -1-3). 17.99 *(978-0-06-195338-5(5))* HarperCollins Pubs.

—The Hidden Gallery. Wood, Maryrose. (Incorrigible Children of Ashton Place Ser.: Bk. 2). (J). (gr. 3-7). 2011. 16.89

K

(978-0-06-179114-7(8)); Bk. 2. 2012. 336p. pap. 6.99 *(978-0-06-179113-0(X))* HarperCollins Pubs.

—House Held up by Trees. Kooser, Ted. 2012. (ENG.). 32p. (J). (gr. -1-3). 16.99 *(978-0-7636-5107-7(9))* Candlewick Pr.

—The Incorrigible Children of Ashton Place: Book I: The Mysterious Howling. Wood, Maryrose. (Incorrigible Children of Ashton Place Ser.: 1). (ENG.). (J). (gr. 3-7). 2015. 288p. pap. 7.99 *(978-0-06-236693-1(9))*; Bk. I. 2010. 272p. 16.99 *(978-0-06-179105-5(9))* HarperCollins Pubs. (Balzer & Bray).

—The Incorrigible Children of Ashton Place: Book II: The Hidden Gallery. Wood, Maryrose. (Incorrigible Children of Ashton Place Ser.: 2). (ENG.). (J). (gr. 3-7). 2015. 336p. pap. 6.99 *(978-0-06-236694-8(7))*; 2011. 320p. 16.99 *(978-0-06-179112-3(1)*, Balzer & Bray) HarperCollins Pubs.

—The Incorrigible Children of Ashton Place: Book III: The Unseen Guest. Wood, Maryrose. 2015. (Incorrigible Children of Ashton Place Ser.: 3). (ENG.). 352p. (J). (gr. 3-7). pap. 6.99 *(978-0-06-236695-5(5)*, Balzer & Bray) HarperCollins Pubs.

Klassen, Jon. Monster Tails: A Green-Eyed Boy Named Harvey. Scott, Kenlynn Dorothy. 2020. (Monster Tails Ser.: Vol. 1). (ENG.). 26p. (J). pap. 10.00 ***(978-1-6629-0049-5(X))*** Gatekeeper Pr.

Klassen, Jon. The Mysterious Howling. Wood, Maryrose. 2011. (Incorrigible Children of Ashton Place Ser.: Bk. 1). 288p. (J). (gr. 3-7). pap. 6.99 *(978-0-06-179110-9(5))* HarperCollins Pubs.

—The Nest. Oppel, Kenneth. (ENG.). (J). (gr. 5). 2016. 272p. pap. 8.99 *(978-1-4814-3233-7(8))*; 2015. 256p. 16.99 *(978-1-4814-3232-0(X))* Simon & Schuster Bks. For Young Readers. (Simon & Schuster Bks. For Young Readers).

—Pax. Pennypacker, Sara. 2016. (ENG.). (J). (gr. 3-3). 16.99 *(978-0-06-245703-5(9))* Blackstone Audio, Inc.

—Pax. Pennypacker, Sara. (ENG.). (J). (gr. 3-7). 2019. 304p. pap. 8.99 *(978-0-06-237702-9(7))*; 2016. 288p. 16.99 *(978-0-06-237701-2(9))* HarperCollins Pubs. (Balzer & Bray).

—Sam & Dave Dig a Hole. Barnett, Mac. 2014. 40p. (J). (gr. -1-3). 17.99 *(978-0-7636-6229-5(1))* Candlewick Pr.

—Square. Barnett, Mac. 2018. 48p. (J). (gr. k-4). 15.99 *(978-0-7636-9607-8(2))* Candlewick Pr.

—Triangle. Barnett, Mac. 2017. (ENG.). 48p. (J). (gr. k-4). 15.99 *(978-0-7636-9603-0(X))* Candlewick Pr.

—The Wolf, the Duck, & the Mouse. Barnett, Mac. 2017. (ENG.). 40p. (J). (gr. -1-3). 17.99 *(978-0-7636-7754-1(X))* Candlewick Pr.

Klassen, Jon. I Want My Hat Back. Klassen, Jon. (J). 2019. (ENG.). 32p. (-k). bds. 8.99 *(978-1-5362-0757-6(8))*; 2011. 40p. (gr. -1-3). 17.99 *(978-0-7636-5598-3(8))* Candlewick Pr.

—Jon Klassen's Hat Box. Klassen, Jon. 2019. (J). (gr. -1-3). 49.99 *(978-0-7636-6697-2(1))* Candlewick Pr.

—The Nest. Klassen, Jon. Oppel, Kenneth. ed. 2016. (ENG.). 272p. (J). (gr. 5). 18.40 *(978-0-606-39233-4(5))* Turtleback.

—This Is Not My Hat. Klassen, Jon. 2012. 40p. (J). (gr. -1-3). 17.99 *(978-0-7636-5599-0(6))* Candlewick Pr.

—We Found a Hat. Klassen, Jon. 2016. (ENG.). 56p. (J). (gr. -1-3). 17.99 *(978-0-7636-5600-3(3))* Candlewick Pr.

Klassen, Karen. You Are One. O'Leary, Sara. 2016. (You Are Ser.: 1). (ENG.). 24p. (J). (— 1). 14.95 *(978-1-77147-072-8(0)*, Owlkids) Owlkids Bks. Inc. CAN. Dist: Publishers Group West (PGW).

Klaus, Machelle. Winston Wonders about Capacity: A mathematical Story. Jones, Dee. 2010. 36p. pap. 14.95 *(978-1-60844-181-5(4))* Dog Ear Publishing, LLC.

Klauss, Anja. The Little Hippo: A Children's Book Inspired by Egyptian Art. Elschner, Géraldine. 2014. (Children's Books Inspired by Famous Artworks Ser.). (ENG.). 32p. (J). (gr. -1-3). 14.95 *(978-3-7913-7167-2(3))* Prestel Verlag GmbH & Co KG. DEU. Dist: Penguin Random Hse. LLC.

Klco, Gene, photos by. Loon Chick's First Flight. Klco, Gene. 2015. (ENG., 36p. (J). (gr. 1-2). pap. 17.95 *(978-1-933272-51-1(1))* Thunder Bay Pr.

Kleback, Amanda & Kleback, Brian. Hoo Hoo's Song. Kleback, Amanda. 2009. 24p. pap. 12.00 *(978-1-4389-1322-3(2))* AuthorHouse.

Kleback, Brian, jt. illus. see Kleback, Amanda.

Kleid, Neil. Xander Nash, Vol. 3. Talen, Hunter. 2010. (Xander Nash Ser.). (ENG.). 96p. (J). pap. 6.99 *(978-0-9828077-6-7(7))* Creation By Design.

Kleiman, Zalman. 5 Novelettes by Marcus Lehman Slipcased: Adopted Princess, Bustenai, Out of the Depths, Rabenu Gershom & Unpaid Ransom. Lehman, Marcus. Mindel, Nissan, tr. from GER. 2012. (ENG.). (YA). 64.95 *(978-0-8266-0033-2(6))* Kehot Pubn. Society.

Klein, Ellen Marie. I Have a Chuck. Johnson, Dawn M. 2013. 28p. pap. 24.95 *(978-1-62709-628-7(0))* America Star Bks.

Klein, Isabel. Bella Bella Brush. Tobias, Tamara. 2018. (ENG.). 34p. (J). (gr. k-2). *(978-0-692-13947-9(8))*; pap. *(978-0-692-13047-6(0))* Bella Bks.

Klein, Jean-Louis & Hubert, Marie-Luce. Face-to-Face with the Cat. Frattini, Stephane. 2004. (Face to Face Ser.). 28p. (J). 9.95 *(978-1-57091-454-6(0))* Charlesbridge Publishing, Inc.

Klein, Jean-Louis, jt. photos by see Hubert, Marie-Luce.

Klein, Laurie. The Buttermilk Biscuit Boy, 1 vol. Nelson, Amanda. 2014. (ENG.). 32p. (J). (gr. k-3). 16.99 *(978-1-4556-1970-2(1)*, Pelican Publishing) Arcadia Publishing.

Klein, Laurie Allen. Conoce Los Planetas, 1 vol. McGranaghan, John. 2011. (SPA.). 32p. (J). (gr. k-5). pap. 11.95 *(978-1-62855-411-3(8))* Arbordale Publishing.

—¡Ellos Ya Saben! Instintos de Los Animales, 1 vol. Yardi, Robin. 2015. (SPA & ENG.). 32p. (J). (gr. k-3). pap. 11.95 *(978-1-62855-644-5(7))* Arbordale Publishing.

—Fur & Feathers, 1 vol. Halfmann, Janet. 2010. (ENG.). 32p. (J). (gr. -1-4). 16.95 *(978-1-60718-075-3(8))*; pap. 8.95 *(978-1-60718-086-9(3))* Arbordale Publishing.

—The Ghost of Donley Farm, 1 vol. Johnson, Jaime Gardner. 2015. (ENG.). 32p. (J). (gr. k-3). 17.95 *(978-1-62855-451-9(7))*; pap. 9.95 *(978-1-62855-459-5(2))* Arbordale Publishing.

—If a Dolphin Were a Fish, 1 vol. Wlodarski, Loran. 2006. (ENG.). 32p. (J). (gr. -1-2). 15.95 *(978-0-9768823-2-9(9))* Arbordale Publishing.

—Little Skink's Tail, 1 vol. Halfmann, Janet. 2007. (ENG.). 32p. (J). (gr. -1-3). 15.95 *(978-0-9768823-8-1(8))* Arbordale Publishing.

—Meet the Planets, 1 vol. McGranaghan, John. 2011. (ENG.). 32p. (J). (gr. k-5). 16.95 *(978-1-60718-123-1(1))*; pap. 9.95 *(978-1-60718-869-8(4))* Arbordale Publishing.

—El Pronóstico Del Sistema Solar, 1 vol. Whitt, Kelly Kizer. 2012. (SPA & ENG.). 32p. (J). (gr. -1-4). 17.95 *(978-1-60718-676-6(0))*; pap. 9.95 *(978-1-62855-425-0(8))* Arbordale Publishing.

—Salvando Las Flores de Camelia, 1 vol. Sommer, Cindy. 2016. (SPA.). 32p. (J). (gr. k-3). pap. 11.95 *(978-1-62855-872-2(5))* Arbordale Publishing.

—Saving Kate's Flowers, 1 vol. Sommer, Cindy. 2016. (ENG & SPA.). 32p. (J). (gr. k-3). 17.95 *(978-1-62855-870-8(9))* Arbordale Publishing.

—Solar System Forecast, 1 vol. Whitt, Kelly Kizer. 2012. 32p. (J). (gr. -1-4). (ENG & SPA.). 17.95 *(978-1-60718-523-9(7))*; (SPA & ENG.). pap. 9.95 *(978-1-60718-532-1(6))* Arbordale Publishing.

—They Just Know: Animal Instincts, 1 vol. Yardi, Robin. 2015. (ENG.). 32p. (J). (gr. k-3). 17.95 *(978-1-62855-634-6(X))* Arbordale Publishing.

—Where Should Turtle Be?, 1 vol. Ring, Susan. 2009. (ENG.). 32p. (J). (gr. -1-3). 16.95 *(978-1-934359-89-1(0))* Arbordale Publishing.

Klein, Laurie Allen. La Larga y Corta Historia de Colo y Ruff. Klein, Laurie Allen. Lang, Diane. 2019. (SPA.). (J). *(978-1-60718-749-3(3))* Arbordale Publishing.

Klein, Nancy, jt. illus. see Guida, Liisa Chauncy.

Klein, Nancy, jt. illus. see Guida, Liisa.

Klein, Sierra. 'Twas an Evening in Bethlehem. Schmidt, Jenelle Leanne. 2019. (ENG.). 24p. (J). (gr. -1-3). 22.99 ***(978-0-9884512-1-6(2))*** Stormcave.

Klein Stahl, Miriam. Rad American Women A-Z: Rebels, Trailblazers, & Visionaries Who Shaped Our History ... & Our Future! Schatz, Kate. 2015. (City Lights/Sister Spit Ser.). (ENG.). 64p. (J). (gr. 2-11). 14.95 *(978-0-87286-683-6(1))* City Lights Bks.

Klein, Trish. Our Wintry Day Walk. Bouknight, Deena. 2007. (ENG.). 50p. pap. 12.00 *(978-1-55369-706-0(5))* Trafford Publishing.

Kleiner, Jr Norman. Tilly Comes Home. Sobon, Laurie. 2016. (ENG.). (J). 24.95 *(978-1-4575-5112-3(8))*; pap. 14.95 *(978-1-4575-5047-8(4))* Dog Ear Publishing, LLC.

Klemek, Ryan. Bedtime Stories. Gavin, Fred. Date not set. 64p. (J). (gr. k-3). pap. *(978-0-935668-00-1(4))* Gavin, Fred Enterprises.

Klenczar, Pamla Ladon. I'm Not Broken! Salatino, Jill R. 2019. (ENG.). 38p. (J). pap. 9.99 ***(978-1-6875-5051-4(4))*** Independently Published.

Klepacka, Aleksandra. The Alien Club. Sidoruk, Trel W. Sidoruk, Lauren, ed. 2016. (ENG.). (YA). (gr. 9-12). pap. 19.99 *(978-0-9971513-9-8(0))* Mo Peanuts Publishing.

Kleven, Dean. Little Einsteins. 2007. (Look & Find Ser.). (J). (gr. -1-3). 7.98 *(978-1-4127-7424-6(1))* Publications International, Ltd.

—My 1St Libraries Baby Enstein. Publications International Ltd. Staff & p i kids. 2014. (ENG.). 120p. (J). bds. 6.10 net. *(978-1-4508-1572-7(3)*, 17942164-061b-44d0-8042-8d9b4f113248) Phoenix International Publications, Inc.

Kleven, Elisa. Angels Watching over Me. Durango, Julia. 2007. (ENG.). 32p. (J). (gr. -1-3). 18.99 *(978-0-689-86252-6(0)*, Simon & Schuster Bks. For Young Readers) Simon & Schuster Bks. For Young Readers.

—One Little Chicken. Weber, Elka. 2011. 32p. (J). (gr. -1-2). 16.99 *(978-1-58246-374-2(3)*, Tricycle Pr.) Random Hse. Children's Bks.

Kleven, Elisa. The Puddle Pail. Kleven, Elisa. 2007. 32p. (J). (gr. -1-2). pap. 6.99 *(978-1-58246-206-6(2)*, Tricycle Pr.) Random Hse. Children's Bks.

—Welcome Home, Mouse. Kleven, Elisa. 2010. 32p. (J). (gr. -1-2). 15.99 *(978-1-58246-277-6(1)*, Tricycle Pr.) Random Hse. Children's Bks.

Klever, Elsa. Taxi Ride with Victor. Trofa, Sara. 2019. (ENG.). 40p. (J). (gr. -1-3). 14.95 *(978-3-7913-7406-2(0))* Prestel Verlag GmbH & Co KG. DEU. Dist: Penguin Random Hse. LLC.

Klick, Gloria. The Adventure of Mookin Munchkin. Wood, Barbie. 2013. 32p. pap. 24.95 *(978-1-63004-041-3(X))* America Star Bks.

Kligge, Elizabeth. Tae Kwon Do Classic Forms: 21 Hyung — Novice White Belt Through Advanced Black Belt. Hillson, Ted. 2003. 232p. (YA). spiral bd. 22.50 *(978-0-9729293-0-1(4))* Double Dagger Pr.

Klimko, Andrew. Bungalow 29. Ross, Jay. 2015. 92p. pap. 5.99 *(978-0-9771994-0-2(1))* Visor Bks.

Klimowski, Andrzej. Catlantis. Starobinets, Anna. Bugaeva, Jane, tr. from RUS. 2016. (ENG.). 136p. (J). (gr. 3-7). 16.95 *(978-1-68137-000-2(X)*, NYR Children's Collection) New York Review of Bks., Inc., The.

Kline, Michael. Double Trouble #2, 2. Press, J. 2013. (Doodles of Sam Dibble Ser.: 2). (ENG.). 128p. (J). (gr. 1-3). 17.44 *(978-0-448-46108-3(0))* Penguin Young Readers Group.

—Kids Write: Fantasy & Sci Fi, Mystery, Autobiography, Adventure & More! Olien, Rebecca. 2005. (Kids Can Ser.). (ENG.). 128p. (YA). (gr. 7-14). 14.95 *(978-0-8249-6775-8(5)*, Ideal Pubns.) Worthy Publishing.

—Peanut-Free Tea for Three. Mehra, Heather & McManama, Kerry. 2009. (J). *(978-0-9822150-1-2(0))* Parent Perks, Inc.

Kline, Michael. The Kids' Book of Weather Forecasting. Kline, Michael. Friestad, Kathleen M. et al. 2008. 160p. (J). 16.99 *(978-0-8249-6822-9(0)*, Ideal Pubns.) Worthy Publishing.

Kline, Michael P. In the Days of Dinosaurs: A Rhyming Romp Through Dino History. Temperley, Howard. 2004. (J). pap. 9.95 *(978-1-885593-81-8(3)*, Ideal Pubns.) Worthy Publishing.

—In The Days of the Dinosaurs. Temperley, Howard. 2008. (ENG.). 64p. (J). pap. 9.95 *(978-0-8249-6759-8(3)*, Ideal Pubns.) Worthy Publishing.

—The Kids' Multicultural Cookbook: Food & Fun Around the World. Cook, Deanna F. 2008. (ENG.). 160p. (J). (gr. k). 16.99 *(978-0-8249-6817-5(4)*, Ideal Pubns.) Worthy Publishing.

—Wordplay Cafe. 2006. (ENG.). 128p. (J). 14.95 *(978-0-8249-6773-4(9)*, Ideal Pubns.) Worthy Publishing.

Klineman, Harvey. Four in One: Four Favorites. Ganz, Yaffa. 2008. 24.99 *(978-1-59826-183-7(5))* Feldheim Pubs.

—Raise a Rabbit, Grow a Goose. Ganz, Yaffa. 2008. 30p. 14.99 *(978-1-59826-235-3(1))* Feldheim Pubs.

—Thirty-One Cakes: A Hashvas Aveida Adventure. Hodes, Loren. Rosenfeld, Devorah Leah, ed. 2003. (J). 10.95 *(978-1-929628-13-1(7))* Hachai Publishing.

Kling, Leslie. The Reindeer That Couldn't Fly. Chandler, Bill & Chandler, Marie. 2009. 48p. pap. 19.99 *(978-1-933817-40-8(2))* Profits Publishing.

Klingbeil, Kendall. GUARDIAN of DREAMS (1st Edition), Torrel, Wendy. l.t. ed. 2004. 32p. (J). 14.95 *(978-0-9746890-0-5(9))*; pap. 10.95 *(978-0-9746890-1-2(7))* White Tulip Publishing.

Klinting, Lars. Beaver the Tailor: A How-to Picture Book. Klinting, Lars. 2004. Orig. Title: Castor Syr.. 32p. (J). (gr. k-3). reprint ed. 17.00 *(978-0-7567-7213-0(3))* DIANE Publishing Co.

Kliros, Thea. Dracula. Stoker, Bram. abr. ed. 2011. (Dover Children's Thrift Classics Ser.). (ENG.). 96p. (J). (gr. 3-8). reprint ed. pap. 4.00 *(978-0-486-29567-1(2))* Dover Pubns., Inc.

—Favorite Uncle Wiggily Animal Bedtime Stories. Garis, Howard Roger. unabr. ed. 2011. (Dover Children's Thrift Classics Ser.). (ENG.). 64p. (J). (gr. 3-8). pap. 4.00 *(978-0-486-40101-0(4)*, 401014) Dover Pubns., Inc.

—Heidi: Adapted for Young Readers. Spyri, Johanna & Blaisdell, Robert. ed. 2011. (Dover Children's Thrift Classics Ser.). (ENG.). 80p. (J). (gr. 3-8). pap. 3.00 *(978-0-486-40166-9(9))* Dover Pubns., Inc.

—Kidnapped: Adapted for Young Readers. Stevenson, Robert Louis. abr. ed. 2011. (Dover Children's Thrift Classics Ser.). (ENG.). 96p. (J). (gr. 3-8). reprint ed. pap. 4.00 *(978-0-486-29354-7(8)*, 293548) Dover Pubns., Inc.

—The Little Mermaid & Other Fairy Tales. Andersen, Hans. 2011. (Dover Children's Thrift Classics Ser.). (ENG.). 96p. (J). (gr. 3-8). reprint ed. pap. 3.50 *(978-0-486-27816-2(6))* Dover Pubns., Inc.

—A Little Princess. Burnett, Frances Hodgson. abr. ed. 2012. (Dover Children's Thrift Classics Ser.). (ENG.). 96p. (J). (gr. 3-8). pap. 3.00 *(978-0-486-29171-0(5))* Dover Pubns., Inc.

—A Little Princess Coloring Book. Burnett, Frances Hodgson. abr. ed. 2013. (Dover Coloring Bks.). (ENG.). 48p. (J). (gr. 1-5). pap. 4.99 *(978-0-486-40561-2(3))* Dover Pubns., Inc.

—The Nutcracker. Hoffmann, E. T. A. 2003. 22p. (J). (gr. -1-1). 5.99 *(978-0-06-052745-7(5)*, HarperFestival) HarperCollins Pubs.

—The Prince & the Pauper. Twain, Mark et al. abr. ed. 2011. (Dover Children's Thrift Classics Ser.). (ENG.). 112p. (J). (gr. 3-8). reprint ed. pap. 4.00 *(978-0-486-29383-7(1))* Dover Pubns., Inc.

—The Secret Garden Coloring Book. Burnett, Frances Hodgson. 2014. (ENG.). 48p. (J). (gr. 4-7). pap. 4.99 *(978-0-486-27680-9(5))* Dover Pubns., Inc.

—Three Billy Goats Gruff. Public Domain, Public. 2003. (Once upon a Time Ser.). (ENG.). 20p. (J). (gr. -1-3). bds. 6.99 *(978-0-06-008237-6(2)*, HarperFestival) HarperCollins Pubs.

—Three Little Pigs. Public Domain, Public. 2003. (Once upon a Time Ser.). (ENG.). 20p. (J). (gr. -1-1). bds. 6.99 *(978-0-06-008236-9(4)*, HarperFestival) HarperCollins Pubs.

—Uncle Wiggily Bedtime Stories: In Easy-to-Read Type. Garis, Howard Roger. unabr. ed. 2011. (Dover Children's Thrift Classics Ser.). (ENG.). 80p. (J). (gr. 3-8). pap. 3.00 *(978-0-486-29372-1(6))* Dover Pubns., Inc.

—The Velveteen Rabbit Board Book. Williams, Margery. 2004. (ENG.). 22p. (J). (gr. -1-1). bds. 6.99 *(978-0-06-052746-4(3)*, HarperFestival) HarperCollins Pubs.

—The Velveteen Rabbit Coloring Book. Williams, Margery. 2013. (ENG.). 48p. (J). (gr. 2-5). pap. 4.99 *(978-0-486-25924-6(2))* Dover Pubns., Inc.

—The Wind in the Willows. Grahame, Kenneth. abr. ed. 2011. (Dover Children's Thrift Classics Ser.). (ENG.). 96p. (J). (gr. 3-8). pap. 4.00 *(978-0-486-28600-6(2)*, 286002) Dover Pubns., Inc.

Klise, Kate & Klise, M. Sarah. Regarding the Bathrooms: A Privy to the Past. Klise, Kate. 2008. (Regarding The ... Ser.: Bk. 4). 160p. (J). (gr. 3-7). pap. 6.99 *(978-0-15-206261-3(0)*, 1198771); (gr. 4-6). 21.19 *(978-0-15-205164-8(3))* Houghton Mifflin Harcourt Publishing Co.

—Regarding the Sink: Where, Oh Where, Did Waters Go? Klise, Kate. 2006. (Regarding the Fountain Ser.: Bk. 2). 127p. (J). (gr. 2-4). pap. 21.19 *(978-0-15-205019-1(1))* Harcourt Children's Bks.

Klise, M. Sarah. The Circus Goes to Sea. Klise, Kate. (Three-Ring Rascals Ser.: Book 3). (ENG.). (J). 2014. 160p. 15.95 *(978-1-61620-365-8(X)*, 73365); Volume 3. 2015. 144p. (gr. 2-5). pap. 6.95 *(978-1-61620-481-5(8)*, 73481) Algonquin Bks. of Chapel Hill.

—Dying to Meet You. Klise, Kate. 2010. (43 Old Cemetery Road Ser.: Bk. 1). (ENG.). 160p. (J). (gr. 3-7). pap. 6.99 *(978-0-547-39848-8(4)*, 1427649) Houghton Mifflin Harcourt Publishing Co.

—The Greatest Star on Earth. Klise, Kate. 2014. (Three-Ring Rascals Ser.: 2). (ENG.). 144p. (J). (gr. 2-5). 15.95 *(978-1-61620-245-3(9)*, 73245) Algonquin Bks. of Chapel Hill.

—Greetings from the Graveyard. Klise, Kate. (43 Old Cemetery Road Ser.). (ENG.). 160p. (J). (gr. 3-7). 2015. pap. 7.99 *(978-0-544-54010-1(7)*, 1608837); 2014. 16.99 *(978-0-544-10567-6(2)*, 1540173) Houghton Mifflin Harcourt Publishing Co. (HMH Books For Young Readers).

—Hollywood, Dead Ahead. Klise, Kate. (43 Old Cemetery Road Ser.: 5). (ENG.). 144p. (J). (gr. 3-7). 2014. pap. 7.99 *(978-0-544-33661-2(5)*, 1584183, HMH Books For Young Readers); 2013. 15.99 *(978-0-547-85283-6(5)*, 1501412) Houghton Mifflin Harcourt Publishing Co.

—Little Rabbit & the Meanest Mother on Earth. Klise, Kate. 2015. (ENG.). 32p. (J). (gr. -1-3). 6.99 *(978-0-544-45611-2(4)*, 1599396, HMH Books For Young Readers) Houghton Mifflin Harcourt Publishing Co.

—The Loch Ness Punster. Klise, Kate. 2016. (43 Old Cemetery Road Ser.: 7). (ENG.). 144p. (J). (gr. 3-7). pap. 6.99 *(978-0-544-81085-3(6)*, 1641667, HMH Books For Young Readers) Houghton Mifflin Harcourt Publishing Co.

—Over My Dead Body. Klise, Kate. 2011. (43 Old Cemetery Road Ser.: Bk. 2). (ENG.). 128p. (J). (gr. 3-7). pap. 6.99 *(978-0-547-57713-5(3)*, 1458461) Houghton Mifflin Harcourt Publishing Co.

—The Phantom of the Post Office. Klise, Kate. 2013. (43 Old Cemetery Road Ser.: 4). (ENG.). 160p. (J). (gr. 3-7). pap. 6.99 *(978-0-544-02281-2(5)*, 1528502) Houghton Mifflin Harcourt Publishing Co.

—Pop Goes the Circus! Klise, Kate. 2015. (Three-Ring Rascals Ser.: 4). (ENG.). 144p. (J). (gr. 2-5). pap. 5.95 *(978-1-61620-547-8(4)*, 73547); 15.95 *(978-1-61620-464-8(8)*, 73464) Algonquin Bks. of Chapel Hill.

—Regarding the Bees: A Lesson, in Letters, on Honey, Dating, & Other Sticky Subjects. Klise, Kate & Klise, Kate. 2009. (Regarding The ... Ser.: Bk. 5). (ENG.). 144p. (J). (gr. 3-7). pap. 6.99 *(978-0-15-206668-0(3)*, 1099002) Houghton Mifflin Harcourt Publishing Co.

—Secrets of the Circus. Klise, Kate. 2016. (Three-Ring Rascals Ser.: 5). (ENG.). 128p. (J). (gr. 2-5). pap. 5.95 *(978-1-61620-640-6(3)*, 73640); 15.95 *(978-1-61620-566-9(0)*, 73566) Algonquin Bks. of Chapel Hill.

—Stand Straight, Ella Kate: The True Story of a Real Giant. Klise, Kate. 2010. 32p. (J). (gr. 1-3). 17.99 *(978-0-8037-3404-3(2)*, Dial Bks) Penguin Young Readers Group.

—Till Death Do Us Bark. Klise, Kate. 2012. (43 Old Cemetery Road Ser.: 3). (ENG.). 144p. (J). (gr. 3-7). pap. 7.99 *(978-0-547-85081-8(6)*, 1501065) Houghton Mifflin Harcourt Publishing Co.

—Why Do You Cry? Not a Sob Story. Klise, Kate. rev. ed. 2006. (ENG.). 32p. (J). (gr. -1-2). 18.99 *(978-0-8050-7319-5(1)*, 9780805073195, Holt, Henry & Co. Bks. For Young Readers) Holt, Henry & Co.

Klise, M. Sarah, jt. illus. see Klise, Kate.

Klocek, Noah. Great Big Things. Hoefler, Kate. 2017. (ENG.). 40p. (J). (gr. -1-3). 17.99 *(978-0-544-77477-3(9)*, 1637144, HMH Books For Young Readers) Houghton Mifflin Harcourt Publishing Co.

Klocek, Noah. Dreamland. Klocek, Noah. 2018. (ENG.). 40p. (J). (gr. -1-2). 16.99 *(978-0-7636-9426-5(6))* Candlewick Pr.

Kloepper, Madeline. The Keeper of Wild Words: (Nature for Kids, Exploring Nature with Children) Smith, Brooke. 2020. (ENG.). 62p. (J). (gr. k-3). 18.99 *(978-1-4521-7073-2(8))* Chronicle Bks. LLC.

—Rooster Summer, 1 vol. Heidbreder, Robert. 2018. (ENG.). 64p. (J). (gr. 2-5). 16.95 *(978-1-55498-931-7(0))* Groundwood Bks. CAN. Dist: Publishers Group West (PGW).

Kloepper, Madeline, jt. illus. see Young, Cybèle.

Klofkorn, Lisa. Convection: A Current Event. Hoyt, Richard, photos by. Gould, Alan. rev. ed. 2005. (Great Explorations in Math & Science Ser.). 60p. (J). reprint ed. pap. 10.50 *(978-1-931542-05-0(8)*, GEMS) Univ. of California, Berkeley, Lawrence Hall of Science.

—Crime Lab Chemistry: Solving Mysteries with Chromatography. Beals, Kevin, photos by. Barber, Jacqueline et al. 2004. (Great Explorations in Math & Science Ser.). 104p. (J). pap. 10.50 *(978-0-924886-90-4(0)*, GEMS) Univ. of California, Berkeley, Lawrence Hall of Science.

—Early Adventures in Algebra: Featuring Zero the Hero. Krauss, Dan, photos by. Kopp, Jaine. 2004. (GEMS Guides Ser.). 132p. (J). pap. 16.00 *(978-0-924886-77-5(3)*, GEMS) Univ. of California, Berkeley, Lawrence Hall of Science.

—Moons of Jupiter. Hoyt, Richard & Bergman Publishing Co. Staff, photos by. Sutter, Debra et al. 2003. (Great Explorations in Math & Science Ser.). 116p. (J). pap., tchr. ed. 16.00 *(978-0-924886-87-4(0)*, GEMS) Univ. of California, Berkeley, Lawrence Hall of Science.

Klofkorn, Lisa, jt. illus. see Bevilacqua, Carol.

Klofkorn, Lisa, jt. illus. see Erickson, John.

Kloran, Mike. Zombies Love Brains. Drysdale, Colin M. 2016. (ENG.). 26p. (J). (gr. k-3). pap. *(978-1-909832-18-3(9))* Pictish Beast Pubns.

Klosowski, Carla. André the Five-Star Cat. Hammond, Alma. 2017. (Travel With Me Ser.). (ENG.). 48p. (J). pap. 14.95 *(978-0-9985362-3-1(7))* Sweetbeet Bks.

Klossner, John & Ricceri, David. Judaism's Great Debates. Schwartz, Barry L. & Levine, Mark H. 2012. 72p. (J). pap. *(978-0-87441-852-1(6))* Behrman Hse., Inc.

Klot, Masha. Lazlo Learns Recorder. Weber, Vicky. 2020. (ENG.). 32p. (J). (gr. 2-5). 18.99 ***(978-1-7342129-0-7(X))***; pap. 12.99 ***(978-1-7342129-1-4(8))*** Trunk Up Bks.

Klotz, Bryan. Lucy's Hero: Remembering Paul Wellstone. Shragg, Karen I. 2010. (ENG.). 32p. (J). (gr. 2-3). 18.95 *(978-0-9801045-7-8(2))*; pap. 12.95 *(978-0-9801045-8-5(0))* Raven Productions, Inc.

Klug, Dave. Space Station Science, Vol. Dyson, Marianne J. 2nd ed. 2004. 128p. (J). pap. 11.95 *(978-0-89317-059-2(3)*, WW-0593, Windward Publishing) Finney Co., Inc.

The check digit for ISBN-10 appears in parentheses after the full ISBN-13

Klug, David. Brainiac's Go Green! Activity Book. Conlon, Mara. 2008. (Activity Book Ser.). 127p. (J). (gr. k-5). 12.99 *(978-1-59359-806-8(8))* Peter Pauper Pr. Inc.
—Mega Magna Forms Safari Adventure. Bryan, Sarah Jane & Beilenson, Suzanne. 2008. (Activity Book Ser.). 48p. (J). (gr. -1-3). spiral bd. 19.95 *(978-1-59359-809-9(2))* Peter Pauper Pr. Inc.
Klug, Eric. The Monster in My Closet. Klug, Eric. 2007. 32p. (J). (gr. -1-3). 15.95 *(978-1-60108-007-3(7))* Red Cygnet Pr.
Klug, Frances Marie. Stories from Heaven, Vol. 33. Klug, Frances Marie, photos by. l.t. ed. 2004. (gr. 7-18). pap. 15.95 *(978-1-892957-33-7(7))* City of God, St. Joseph's Hill of Hope.
Klug, Leigh A. & Bryant, Carol W. Hamilton Troll Meets Chatterton Squirrel. Shields, Kathleen J. 2017. (Hamilton Troll Adventures Ser.: Vol. 4). (ENG.). 42p. (J). pap. 9.95 ***(978-1-941345-37-5(9))*** Erin Go Bragh Publishing.
Klug, Leigh A. & Bryant, Carol W. Hamilton Troll Meets Chatterton Squirrel. Shields, Kathleen J. 4th ed. 2013. 42p. 14.00 *(978-0-9882745-3-2(1))* Erin Go Bragh Publishing.
Klug, Leigh A. & Bryant, Carol W. Hamilton Troll Meets Dinosaurs. Shields, Kathleen J. 2017. (Hamilton Troll Adventures Ser.: Vol. 6). (ENG.). 36p. (J). pap. 9.95 ***(978-1-941345-39-9(5))*** Erin Go Bragh Publishing.
Klug, Leigh A. & Bryant, Carol W. Hamilton Troll Meets Dinosaurs. Shields, Kathleen J. 6th ed. 2013. 36p. 14.00 *(978-0-9882745-5-6(8))* Erin Go Bragh Publishing.
Klug, Leigh A. & Bryant, Carol W. Hamilton Troll Meets Elwood Woodpecker. Shields, Kathleen J. 2017. (Hamilton Troll Adventures Ser.: Vol. 5). (ENG.). 38p. (J). pap. 9.95 ***(978-1-941345-38-2(7))*** Erin Go Bragh Publishing.
Klug, Leigh A. & Bryant, Carol W. Hamilton Troll Meets Elwood Woodpecker. Shields, Kathleen J. 5th ed. 2013. 36p. 14.00 *(978-0-9882745-4-9(X))* Erin Go Bragh Publishing.
Klug, Leigh A. & Bryant, Carol W. Hamilton Troll Meets Pink Light Sprite. Shields, Kathleen J. 2017. (Hamilton Troll Adventures Ser.: Vol. 1).Tr. of Hamilton Troll Meets Pink Light Sprite. (ENG.). 46p. (J). pap. 12.95 ***(978-1-941345-34-4(4))*** Erin Go Bragh Publishing.
—Hamilton Troll Meets Skeeter Skunk. Shields, Kathleen J. 2017. (Hamilton Troll Adventures Ser.: Vol. 2).Tr. of Hamilton Troll Meets Skeeter Skunk. (ENG.). 54p. (J). pap. 12.95 ***(978-1-941345-35-1(2))*** Erin Go Bragh Publishing.
—Hamilton Troll Meets Whitaker Owl. Shields, Kathleen J. 2017. (Hamilton Troll Adventures Ser.: Vol. 7). (ENG.). 40p. (J). pap. 9.95 ***(978-1-941345-40-5(9))*** Erin Go Bragh Publishing.
Klug, Leigh A., jt. illus. see Bryant, Carol W.
Klund, Barbara. Tattoo You! Color & Make Your Own Temporary Tattoo Designs. Glossop, Jennifer. 2004. 30p. (J). (gr. k-4). reprint ed. pap. 8.00 *(978-0-7567-8260-3(0))* DIANE Publishing Co.
Klusza, Maureen. Handy Stories to Read & Sign. Napoli, Donna Jo & DeLuca, Doreen. 2009. (ENG.). 56p. (gr. k-3). pap. 19.95 *(978-1-56368-407-4(1))* Gallaudet Univ. Pr.
Knapp, Cheryl. Walking with God: The Young Person's Prayer Diary. Drake, Michelle. 2005. (ENG.). 224p. per. 12.99 *(978-0-927545-79-2(9))* YWAM Publishing.
Knapp, Tracy Adams. A Silent Night: A Child's Nativity Story. Havlicek, Cherisse M. 2018. (ENG.). 28p. (J). pap. 10.00 *(978-1-7326799-4-8(0))* Market Place Publishing.
Knarr, Jordan. The Code. Bradley, Steve. 2019. (Adventures of Chase & Bolts Ser.: Vol. 1). (ENG.). 32p. (J). (gr. k-3). pap. *(978-1-4866-1800-2(6))* Word Alive Pr.
Knaupp, Andrew & Koford, Adam. Heavenly Fathers Plan of Salvation Coloring Book. Rich, J. Milton. 2003. 108p. (J). per. 7.95 *(978-0-9726670-2-9(4))* Rich Publishing.
Kneebone, Simon. Pirate Pip's Party. Cronin, David. 2015. (ENG.). (J). (gr. k-4). pap. *(978-0-9944450-0-1(8))* BillingBear Bks.
Kneen, Maggie. The Christmas Hat. Wood, A. J. 2004. (ENG.). 24p. (J). *(978-1-55168-267-9(2))* Fenn, H. B. & Co., Ltd.
—Cockcrow to Starlight: A Day Full of Poetry. Godden, Rumer. 2003. (ENG.). 144p. (J). pap. 13.99 *(978-0-330-34302-2(5),* Pan) Pan Macmillan GBR. Dist: Trafalgar Square Publishing.
—The Owl Keeper. Brodien-Jones, Christine. 2011. (ENG.). 320p. (J). (gr. 3-7). 8.99 *(978-0-385-73815-6(3),* Yearling) Random Hse. Children's Bks.
—Some Pig! A Charlotte's Web Picture Book. 2006. (Charlotte's Web Ser.). 32p. (J). (gr. k-2). 17.89 *(978-0-06-078162-0(9))* HarperCollins Pubs.
—Summer at Forsaken Lake. Beil, Michael D. 2013. (ENG.). 336p. (J). (gr. 5). pap. 8.99 *(978-0-375-86496-4(2),* Yearling) Random Hse. Children's Bks.
—Thimbleberry Stories. Rylant, Cynthia. 2006. (ENG.). 64p. (J). (gr. -1-3). reprint ed. pap. 8.99 *(978-0-15-205645-2(9),* 1196974) Houghton Mifflin Harcourt Publishing Co.
—Wilbur's Adventure: A Charlotte's Web Picture Book. White, E. B. 2008. (Charlotte's Web Ser.). 32p. (J). (gr. k-2). lib. bdg. 17.89 *(978-0-06-078165-1(3))* HarperCollins Pubs.
Kneen, Maggie. Christmas in the Mouse House. Kneen, Maggie. Wood, Amanda. 2011. (ENG.). 16p. (J). (gr. -1-2). 14.99 *(978-0-7636-5287-6(3),* Templar) Candlewick Pr.
—The Christmas Surprise. Kneen, Maggie. 2006. 18p. (J). (gr. k-4). reprint ed. 16.00 *(978-0-7567-9837-6(X))* DIANE Publishing Co.
Kneupper, Setch. All in a Night's Work, 1 vol. Specter, Baron. 2012. (Graveyard Diaries). (ENG.). 128p. (J). (gr. 2-5). 29.93 *(978-1-61641-903-5(2),* 9184, Calico Chapter Bks.) ABDO Publishing Co.
—Approaching the Undead, 1 vol. Spector, Baron. 2012. (Graveyard Diaries). (ENG.). 128p. (J). (gr. 2-5). lib. bdg. 29.93 *(978-1-61641-899-1(0),* 9176, Calico Chapter Bks.) ABDO Publishing Co.
—How Not to Be Killed by a Zombie, 1 vol. Specter, Baron. 2012. (Graveyard Diaries). (ENG.). 128p. (J). (gr. 2-5). 29.93 *(978-1-61641-900-4(8),* 9178, Calico Chapter Bks.) ABDO Publishing Co.
—To Werewolf or Not to Werewolf, 1 vol. Specter, Baron. 2012. (Graveyard Diaries). (ENG.). 128p. (J). (gr. 2-5). 29.93 *(978-1-61641-901-1(6),* 9180, Calico Chapter Bks.) ABDO Publishing Co.
—Tracking Your Nightmare, 1 vol. Spector, Baron. 2012. (Graveyard Diaries). (ENG.). 128p. (J). (gr. 2-5). lib. bdg. 29.93 *(978-1-61641-898-4(2),* 9174, Calico Chapter Bks.) ABDO Publishing Co.
—Vampires Are Not Your Friends, 1 vol. Specter, Baron. 2012. (Graveyard Diaries). (ENG.). 128p. (J). (gr. 2-5). 29.93 *(978-1-61641-902-8(4),* 9182, Calico Chapter Bks.) ABDO Publishing Co.
Knife. Deep-Sea Dash. Packer. 2016. 93p. (J). *(978-1-61067-478-2(2))* Kane Miller.
—Rain Forest Rumble. Packer. 2016. 94p. (J). *(978-1-61067-479-9(0))* Kane Miller.
—Space Mash. Packer. 2016. 93p. (J). *(978-1-61067-477-5(4))* Kane Miller.
Knife & Packer. Desert Dustup: Wheelnuts! Knife & Packer. 2016. 96p. (J). pap. 6.99 *(978-1-61067-395-2(6))* Kane Miller.
—Spash Mash. Knife & Packer. 2016. 93p. (J). pap. 6.99 *(978-1-61067-397-6(2))* Kane Miller.
—Spooky Smackdown: Wheelnuts! Knife & Packer. 2016. 96p. (J). pap. 6.99 *(978-1-61067-396-9(4))* Kane Miller.
Knight, C. R. The World of the Great Forest: How Animals, Birds, Reptiles & Insects Talk, Think, Work & Live. Du Chaillu, Paul. 2004. reprint ed. pap. 31.95 *(978-1-4179-0914-8(5))* Kessinger Publishing, LLC.
Knight, Christopher G., photos by. Interrupted Journey: Saving Endangered Sea Turtles. Lasky, Kathryn. 2006. 48p. (J). (gr. 1-4). 7.99 *(978-0-7636-2883-3(2))* Candlewick Pr.
Knight, David. There's a Ginormous Albatross on My Roof. Knight, Brighde. 2017. (ENG.). (J). pap. *(978-0-9956006-7-6(8))* Blossom Spring Publishing.
Knight, Eve Lloyd. Rainbow Revolutions: Power, Pride, & Protest in the Fight for Queer Rights. Lawson, Jamie. 2020. (ENG.). 96p. (J). 19.95 ***(978-1-62371-952-4(6),*** Crocodile Bks.) Interlink Publishing Group, Inc.
Knight, Georgia. The Little House Mouse. Knight, Georgia. 2011. (ENG.). 42p. (J). pap. 6.99 *(978-0-9832355-1-4(1))* Grandfeather Pr.
Knight, Hilary. Eloise & Friends. Thompson, Kay. 2015. (Eloise Ser.). (ENG.). 26p. (J). (gr. -1-2). bds. 7.99 *(978-1-4814-5158-1(8),* Little Simon) Little Simon.
—Eloise at the Plaza. Thompson, Kay. 2015. (Eloise Ser.). (ENG.). 26p. (J). (gr. -1-2). bds. 8.99 *(978-1-4814-5159-8(6),* Little Simon) Little Simon.
—Kay Thompson's Eloise: The Absolutely Essential 50th Anniversary Edition: A Book for Precocious Grown-Ups. Thompson, Kay & Brenner, Marie. 2007. 84p. (J). reprint ed. 20.00 *(978-1-4223-6789-6(4))* DIANE Publishing Co.
—Nina in That Makes Me Mad!, 1 vol. Kroll, Steve. 2013. (Toon Bks.). (ENG.). 36p. (J). (gr. 1-2). lib. bdg. 29.93 *(978-1-61479-153-9(8),* 14845) Spotlight.
—Nina in That Makes Me Mad! TOON Level 2. Kroll, Steven. 2018. 36p. (J). (gr. -1-3). pap. 6.99 *(978-1-943145-32-4(6))* TOON Books / RAW Junior, LLC.
—On the Go with Eloise! Eloise Throws a Party!; Eloise Skates!; Eloise Visits the Zoo; Eloise & the Dinosaurs; Eloise's Pirate Adventure; Eloise at the Ball Game. Thompson, Kay. ed. 2019. (Eloise Ser.). (ENG.). 192p. (J). (gr. -1-1). pap. 17.99 *(978-1-5344-5054-7(8),* Simon Spotlight) Simon Spotlight.
Knight, Hilary. A Firefly in a Fir Tree: A Carol for Mice. Knight, Hilary. 2004. 32p. (J). (gr. -1-3). lib. bdg. 15.89 *(978-0-06-000992-2(6),* Tegen, Katherine Bks) HarperCollins Pubs.
Knight, Keith. Jake the Fake Goes for Laughs. Robinson, Craig & Mansbach, Adam. (Jake the Fake Ser.: 2). (J). (gr. 3-7). 2020. (ENG.). 192p. pap. 6.99 *(978-0-553-52358-4(9),* Yearling); 2019. 176p. 16.99 *(978-0-553-52355-3(4),* Crown Books For Young Readers); 2019. (ENG.). 176p. lib. bdg. 19.99 *(978-0-553-52356-0(2),* Crown Books For Young Readers) Random Hse. Children's Bks.
Knight, Keith. Jake the Fake Keeps His Cool. Robinson, Craig & Mansbach, Adam. 2020. (Jake the Fake Ser.: 3). (ENG.). 160p. (J). (gr. 3-7). 16.99 ***(978-0-553-52359-1(7),*** Crown Books For Young Readers) Random Hse. Children's Bks.
Knight, Keith. Jake the Fake Keeps It Real. Robinson, Craig & Mansbach, Adam. (Jake the Fake Ser.: 1). (J). (gr. 3-7). 2018. 160p. 6.99 *(978-0-553-52354-6(6),* Yearling); 2017. 144p. 13.99 *(978-0-553-52351-5(1),* Crown Books For Young Readers) Random Hse. Children's Bks.
Knight, Michael T. Because Daddy's Coming Home Today. Chatlos, Timothy J. 2012. 24p. (J). pap. 12.99 *(978-1-59755-300-1(X),* Advantage Childrens) Advantage Bks.
Knight, Paula. Alphabet. Law, Felicia. 2015. (Patchwork Ser.). (ENG.). 24p. (J). (gr. k-3). pap. 11.94 *(978-1-60357-805-9(6));* lib. bdg. 22.60 *(978-1-59953-715-3(X))* Norwood Hse. Pr.
—Busy Bee. Brown, J. A. 2003. (Funny Faces Ser.). 10p. (J). bds. 3.95 *(978-1-58925-715-3(4))* Tiger Tales.
—Colors. Law, Felicia. 2015. (Patchwork Ser.). (ENG.). 24p. (J). (gr. k-3). pap. 11.94 *(978-1-60357-799-1(8));* lib. bdg. 22.60 *(978-1-59953-709-2(5))* Norwood Hse. Pr.
—Family. Law, Felicia. 2015. (Patchwork Ser.). (ENG.). 24p. (J). (gr. k-3). pap. 11.94 *(978-1-60357-801-1(3));* lib. bdg. 22.60 *(978-1-59953-711-5(7))* Norwood Hse. Pr.
—Feelings. Law, Felicia. 2015. (Patchwork Ser.). (ENG.). 24p. (J). (gr. k-3). pap. 11.94 *(978-1-60357-802-8(1));* lib. bdg. 22.60 *(978-1-59953-712-2(5))* Norwood Hse. Pr.
—Lion's Mane. Brown, J. A. 2003. (Funny Faces Ser.). 10p. (J). 3.95 *(978-1-58925-718-4(9))* Tiger Tales.
—Numbers. Law, Felicia. 2015. (Patchwork Ser.). (ENG.). 24p. (J). (gr. k-3). pap. 11.94 *(978-1-60357-800-4(5));* lib. bdg. 22.60 *(978-1-59953-710-8(9))* Norwood Hse. Pr.
—Scaredy Duck. Brown, J. A. 2004. (Funny Faces Ser.). 10p. (J). 3.95 *(978-1-58925-716-0(2))* Tiger Tales.
—Shapes. Law, Felicia. 2015. (Patchwork Ser.). (ENG.). 24p. (J). (gr. k-3). pap. 11.94 *(978-1-60357-804-2(8));* lib. bdg. 22.60 *(978-1-59953-714-6(1))* Norwood Hse. Pr.
—Size. Law, Felicia. 2015. (Patchwork Ser.). (ENG.). 24p. (J). (gr. k-3). pap. 11.94 *(978-1-60357-803-5(X));* lib. bdg. 22.60 *(978-1-59953-713-9(3))* Norwood Hse. Pr.
Knight, Rhonda. Frankly, Frankie. Jones, Amber. 2019. (Helpville Learner Ser.: Vol. 1). (ENG.). 42p. (J). pap. 12.99 *(978-0-9980263-1-2(X))* Lady Knight Enterprises Publishing.
—Lumps of Koal. Knight, Alicia. 2019. (Helpville Learner Series 1 Ser.: Vol. 6). (ENG.). 46p. (J). pap. 12.99 *(978-0-9980263-6-7(0))* Lady Knight Enterprises Publishing.
—Somebody Save Scotty. Williams, Mignon. 2019. (Helpville Learner Series 1 Ser.: Vol. 2). (ENG.). 44p. (J). pap. 12.99 *(978-0-9980263-2-9(8))* Lady Knight Enterprises Publishing.
—There's No Place Like Home. Jones, Amber. 2019. (Helpville Learner Series 1 Ser.: Vol. 3). (ENG.). 46p. (J). pap. 12.99 *(978-0-9980263-3-6(6))* Lady Knight Enterprises Publishing.
Knight, Rhonda. James Stop Lion! Knight, Rhonda. Knight, Kayla. 2019. (Helpville Learner Series 1 Ser.: Vol. 5). (ENG.). 46p. (J). pap. 12.99 *(978-0-9980263-5-0(2))* Lady Knight Enterprises Publishing.
—Stronger Than You Think. Knight, Rhonda. 2019. (Helpville Learner Series 1 Ser.: Vol. 7). (ENG.). 48p. (J). pap. 12.99 *(978-0-9980263-7-4(9))* Lady Knight Enterprises Publishing.
Knight, Taryn. Embassy of the Dead. Mabbitt, Will. 2020. (Embassy of the Dead Ser.). (ENG.). 272p. (J). (gr. 3-7). 16.99 ***(978-1-5362-1047-7(1))*** Candlewick Pr.
Knight, Teresa Jane. Nina's Song - a Story by Lori: How a Little White Critter Changed the World. Fitzgerald, Lori. Birthistle, Anne, ed. 2019. (ENG.). 24p. (J). pap. 12.00 *(978-1-7219-4282-4(3))* CreateSpace Independent Publishing Platform.
Knight, Tom. The Big Bed. Laditan, Bunmi. 2018. (ENG.). 32p. (J). 17.99 *(978-0-374-30123-1(9),* 900138493, Farrar, Straus & Giroux (BYR)) Farrar, Straus & Giroux.
—Bone Soup: A Spooky, Tasty Tale. Capucilli, Alyssa Satin. 2018. (ENG.). 32p. (J). (gr. -1-3). 17.99 *(978-1-4814-8608-8(X),* Simon & Schuster/Paula Wiseman Bks.) Simon & Schuster/Paula Wiseman Bks.
Knight, Tom. Ferdinand Magellan (the First Names Series) Gourlay, Candy. 2020. (ENG.). 160p. (J). (gr. 3-7). 9.99 ***(978-1-4197-4678-9(2),*** 1279501, Abrams Bks. for Young Readers) Abrams, Inc.
Knight, Tom. Feúcho y Pablo. Quintero, Isabel. 2017. (Feucho y Pablo Ser.: 1). (SPA.). 112p. (J). (gr. 2-5). pap. 6.99 *(978-1-338-18787-8(2),* Scholastic en Espanol) Scholastic, Inc.
—Giddy-Up Buckaroos! Trent, Shanda. 2016. (ENG.). 32p. (J). (gr. -1-2). 16.99 *(978-1-68010-008-2(4))* Tiger Tales.
—Pirates in Pajamas. Crowe, Caroline. (ENG.). (J). (gr. -1-k). 2017. 28p. bds. 7.99 *(978-1-68010-516-2(7));* 2015. 32p. 16.99 *(978-1-58925-190-8(3))* Tiger Tales.
—Ugly Cat & Pablo. Quintero, Isabel. 2017. (J). (ENG.). 112p. (gr. 2-5). pap. 6.99 *(978-0-545-94091-7(5),* Scholastic Pr.); 88p. *(978-1-338-05396-8(5))* Scholastic, Inc.
—Ugly Cat & Pablo & the Missing Brother. Quintero, Isabel. 2018. (ENG.). 144p. (J). (gr. 2-5). pap. 6.99 *(978-0-545-94095-5(8),* Scholastic Paperbacks); lib. bdg. 14.99 *(978-0-545-94096-2(6),* Scholastic Pr.) Scholastic, Inc.
Knight, Tom, jt. illus. see Bitskoff, Aleksei.
Knight, Vanessa. Ben & His Friends. Longos, John J. 2004. (ENG.). 28p. pap. 15.50 *(978-1-4120-4349-6(2))* Trafford Publishing.
—Billy Bad Boy. Jones, Doughnie. 2004. (ENG.). 24p. pap. 8.49 *(978-1-4120-4282-6(8))* Trafford Publishing.
—Christmas Tails. Miller, Jennifer. 2009. 56p. pap. 17.26 *(978-1-4251-8987-7(3))* Trafford Publishing.
—Roger's Lion. De Charleroy, Charles, Jr. 2005. 20p. (J). (gr. -1-3). pap. 12.50 *(978-1-4120-7206-9(9))* Trafford Publishing.
—Tell Me, Tell Me, What You See. Howard, Jim & Welsh-Howard, Paula. 2009. 24p. (J). pap. *(978-1-926585-65-9(8),* CCB Publishing) CCB Publishing.
Knisley, Lucy. Love, Penelope. Rocklin, Joanne. 2018. (ENG.). 240p. (J). (gr. 3-7). 16.99 *(978-1-4197-2861-7(X),* Amulet Bks.) Abrams, Inc.
—Margaret & the Moon: How Margaret Hamilton Saved the First Lunar Landing. Robbins, Dean. 2017. 40p. (J). (gr. -1-3). 17.99 *(978-0-399-55185-7(9),* Knopf Bks. for Young Readers) Random Hse. Children's Bks.
Knold, Nijlon. The Adventures of Chickolet Pigolet: The Bribe of Frankenbeans. Branning, Debe. 2008. 48p. pap. 7.95 *(978-1-935137-40-5(9))* Guardian Angel Publishing, Inc.
Knopp-Kilpert, Inga. Moti the Mitzvah Mouse. Newman, Vivian Bonnie. 2017. (ENG.). 24p. (J). (gr. -1-k). 17.99 *(978-1-5124-2647-2(4),* 9781512426472); Vol. pap. 7.99 *(978-1-5124-2649-6(0),* 9781512426496) Lerner Publishing Group. (Kar-Ben Publishing).
Knorr, Laura. A Isn't for Fox: An Isn't Alphabet. Ulmer, Wendy. rev. ed. 2007. (ENG.). 32p. (J). (gr. 1-4). 16.95 *(978-1-58536-319-3(7),* 202123) Sleeping Bear Pr.
—K Is for Keystone: A Pennsylvania Alphabet. Kane, Kristen. 2003. (Discover America State by State Ser.). (ENG.). 40p. (J). 17.95 *(978-1-58536-104-5(6))* Sleeping Bear Pr.
—The Legend of Papa Noel: A Cajun Christmas Story. Dunham, Terri Hoover. 2006. (Myths, Legends, Fairy & Folktales Ser.). (ENG.). 32p. (J). (gr. 2-5). 17.95 *(978-1-58536-256-1(5),* 202072) Sleeping Bear Pr.
—Little Georgia. Crane, Carol. 2013. (Little State Ser.). (ENG.). 20p. (J). (gr. -1-k). 9.95 *(978-1-58536-203-5(4),* 202355) Sleeping Bear Pr.
—Little Louisiana. Prieto, Anita C. 2011. (My Little State Ser.). (ENG.). 20p. 9.95 *(978-1-58536-184-7(4))* Sleeping Bear Pr.
—P Is for Pelican: A Louisiana Alphabet. Prieto, Anita C. 2004. (Discover America State by State Ser.). (ENG.). 40p. (J). 17.95 *(978-1-58536-137-3(2))* Sleeping Bear Pr.
—Zero, Zilch, Nada: Counting to None. Ulmer, Wendy K. 2010. (ENG.). 32p. (J). (gr. -1-3). 16.95 *(978-1-58536-461-9(4))* Sleeping Bear Pr.
Knorr, Peter. The Storyteller of Damacus. Schami, Rafik. 2018. (ENG.). 48p. (J). 18.95 *(978-1-62371-971-5(2),* Crocodile Bks.) Interlink Publishing Group, Inc.
Knott, Simon. Newton's Wildlife Adventures: The Old Mill Pond. Correll, Stephanie. 2013. 24p. pap. *(978-1-910053-64-5(3))* Legend Pr.
Knott, Stephen. The Kitten Tales of Pumpkin & Parsnip 'Fairy Fields. Allman-Varty, Faye. 2008. 20p. pap. *(978-1-905553-28-0(5))* BookPublishingWorld.
Knotz, Sarah. Goodnight Miami. Baloyra, Patricia. 2012. (ENG.). 28p. (J). (gr. -1-3). 17.95 *(978-1-4507-9592-0(7))* Ampersand, Inc.
Knowles, Kent. Lucius & the Storm. Knowles, Kent. 2007. 32p. (J). (gr. -1-3). 15.95 *(978-1-60108-005-9(0))* Red Cygnet Pr.
Knowlton, Charlotte & Coates, Kathy. Cowgirl Alphabet, 1 vol. Knowlton, Laurie Lazzaro. 2011. (ABC Ser.). (ENG.). 32p. (J). (gr. k-3). 16.99 *(978-1-58980-669-6(7),* Pelican Publishing) Arcadia Publishing.
Knowlton, Dwight. The Little Red Racing Car: A Father/Son/Car Story. Knowlton, Dwight. 2013. (ENG.). (J). 21.99 *(978-0-9892949-0-4(0))* Carpe Viam Productions, LLC.
Knox, Anna Mae. Frank the Colorful Frog. Hutton, Gaila. 2011. 28p. pap. 24.95 *(978-1-4560-5607-0(7))* America Star Bks.
Knox, E. C. Don't Call Me Honey! Call Me Cherry Pie. Knox, E. C. 2011. 38p. pap. 14.50 *(978-1-60976-192-9(8),* Eloquent Bks.) Strategic Book Publishing & Rights Agency (SBPRA).
Knox, Susi Grell. Free As a Butterfly. Boone, Sheila. 2003. 32p. (J). (gr. -1-3). pap. 7.95 *(978-1-891577-80-2(8))* Image Pr., Inc.
Knudson, Dana. Archibald My Pet Pig. Griner, Jack. 2011. pap. 8.95 *(978-0-9836081-1-0(3))* Canoed Sun Publishing, LLC.
Knudtsen, Ken. Crowpsey / Rufus & Cleveland. Ferrara, Brian. 2005. (YA). per. 6.95 *(978-0-9753683-1-2(1))* Terminal Pr., LLC.
Knutson, Barbara. Cinco de Mayo. Lowery, Linda. 2005. (On My Own Holidays Ser.). 48p. (J). (gr. k-3). per. 6.95 *(978-1-57505-764-4(6));* (gr. 2-4). 25.26 *(978-1-57505-654-8(2))* Lerner Publishing Group.
—El Cinco de Mayo. Lowery, Linda. 2005. (Yo Solo - Festividades (on My Own - Holidays) Ser.). (SPA.). 48p. (J). (gr. 2-4). per. 6.95 *(978-0-8225-3119-7(4));* (gr. 3-7). lib. bdg. 25.26 *(978-0-8225-3118-0(6))* Lerner Publishing Group.
—The Color of Me. McDunn, Linda L. 2004. (ENG.). 32p. 16.95 *(978-0-8146-2952-9(0))* Liturgical Pr.
—Day of the Dead. Lowery, Linda. 2003. (On My Own Holidays Ser.). (ENG.). 48p. (gr. 2-4). (J). pap. 7.99 *(978-1-57505-581-7(3),* First Avenue Editions); lib. bdg. 25.26 *(978-0-87614-914-0(X))* Lerner Publishing Group.
—El Dia de los Muertos. Lowery, Linda. 2005. (Yo Solo Festividades Ser.).Tr. of Day of the Dead. (SPA.). 48p. (J). (gr. 2-4). per. 5.95 *(978-0-8225-3123-4(2))* Lerner Publishing Group.
—El Dia de los Muertos. Lowery, Linda. Translations.com Staff, tr. 2005. (Yo Solo - Festividades (on My Own - Holidays) Ser.).Tr. of Day of the Dead. (SPA & ENG.). 48p. (gr. 2-4). lib. bdg. 25.26 *(978-0-8225-3122-7(4))* Lerner Publishing Group.
Knutson, Barbara. Hanna's Cold Winter. Marx, Trish. 2020. (ENG.). 32p. (J). (gr. -1-3). pap. 11.95 ***(978-1-948959-13-1(5))*** Purple Hse. Pr.
Knutson, Barbara. Love & Roast Chicken: A Trickster Tale from the Andes Mountains. Knutson, Barbara. 2004. (ENG.). 40p. (J). (gr. k-3). 17.99 *(978-1-57505-657-9(7),* Carolrhoda Bks.) Lerner Publishing Group.
—Sungura & Leopard: A Swahili Trickster Tale. Knutson, Barbara. 2007. 26p. (J). (gr. -1-3). per. 6.95 *(978-0-8225-6801-8(2),* First Avenue Editions) Lerner Publishing Group.
Knuvers, Onno. At the Comma Store. Fuerst, Jeffrey B. 2013. (Reader's Theater Word Plays Ser.). (J). (gr. 1-2). *(978-1-4509-8921-3(7))* Benchmark Education Co.
Ko, Chin. Alexander Hamilton: a Plan for America. Albee, Sarah. 2018. (I Can Read Level 2 Ser.). (ENG.). 32p. (J). (gr. -1-3). 16.99 *(978-0-06-243291-9(5));* pap. 4.99 *(978-0-06-243290-2(7))* HarperCollins Pubs.
—George Washington: The First President. Albee, Sarah. 2017. 32p. (J). *(978-1-5182-5283-9(4))* HarperCollins Pubs.
—George Washington: the First President. Albee, Sarah. 2017. (I Can Read Level 2 Ser.). (ENG.). 32p. (J). (gr. -1-3). 16.99 *(978-0-06-243267-4(2))* HarperCollins Pubs.
—George Washington: the First President. Albee, Sarah. 2017. (I Can Read Level 2 Ser.). (ENG.). 32p. (J). (gr. -1-3). pap. 4.99 *(978-0-06-243266-7(4),* HarperCollins) HarperCollins Pubs. Ltd. GBR. Dist: HarperCollins Pubs.
—John F. Kennedy the Brave. Keenan, Sheila. 2017. 25p. (J). *(978-1-5182-4585-5(4))* Harper & Row Ltd.
—John F. Kennedy the Brave. Keenan, Sheila. 2017. (I Can Read Level 2 Ser.). (ENG.). 32p. (J). (gr. -1-3). pap. 4.99 *(978-0-06-243258-2(3))* HarperCollins Pubs.
—Long, Tall Lincoln. Dussling, Jennifer. 2017. (I Can Read Level 2 Ser.). (ENG.). 32p. (J). (gr. -1-3). pap. 4.99 *(978-0-06-243255-1(9))* HarperCollins Pubs.
—Martin Luther King Jr.: a Peaceful Leader. Albee, Sarah. 2018. (I Can Read Level 2 Ser.). (ENG.). 32p. (J). (gr. -1-3). 16.99 *(978-0-06-243276-6(1));* pap. 4.99 *(978-0-06-243275-9(3))* HarperCollins Pubs.
Ko, Hyung-Ju. Banned Book Club. Estrada, Ryan & Sook, Kim Hyun. 2020. 192p. (YA). pap. 15.00 *(978-1-945820-42-7(X))* Iron Circus Comics.
Kobak, Carrie. Tyrone: A Turtle Tale. Foley, Sue. 2010. (ENG.). 32p. (J). (gr. -1-5). 14.95 *(978-1-885003-88-1(9))* Reed, Robert D. Pubs.

K

Kobasic, Kevin. Blaze Loves to Race! (Blaze & the Monster Machines) Tillworth, Mary. 2016. (Step into Reading Ser.). (ENG.). 24p. (J). (gr. -1-1). pap. 4.99 (978-0-399-55888-7(8), Random Hse. Bks. for Young Readers) Random Hse. Children's Bks.

—Blaze's Biggest Race! (Blaze & the Monster Machines) Mangual, Cynthia Ines. 2017. (Step into Reading Ser.). (ENG.). 24p. (J). (gr. -1-1). pap. 4.99 (978-1-5247-1696-7(0)); lib. bdg. 12.99 (978-1-5247-1697-4(9)) Random Hse. Children's Bks. (Random Hse. Bks. for Young Readers).

—Bubble Trouble! (Blaze & the Monster Machines) Tillworth, Mary. 2016. (Step into Reading Ser.). (ENG.). 24p. (J). (gr. -1-1). 4.99 (978-1-101-93680-1(0), Random Hse. Bks. for Young Readers) Random Hse. Children's Bks.

—Nickelodeon Blaze & the Monster Machines: Wild Ride. 2018. (ENG.). 10p. (J). (gr. -1-k). bds. 9.99 (978-0-7944-4122-7(X), Reader's Digest Children's Bks.) Studio Fun International.

—Ready to Race! (Blaze & the Monster Machines) Random House. 2015. (Step into Reading Ser.). (ENG.). 24p. (J). (gr. -1-1). 4.99 (978-0-553-52460-4(7), Random Hse. Bks. for Young Readers) Random Hse. Children's Bks.

Kobayashi, Gavin. Whose Slippers Are Those? Kahalewai, Marilyn. 2005. 24p. (J). (gr. -1-3). 10.95 (978-1-57306-238-1(3)) Bess Pr., Inc.

Kobayashi, Yukiko. Where Has the Moon Gone? Arai, Hiroyuki. 2018. (ENG.). 24p. (J). (gr. -1-1). lib. bdg. 16.99 (978-1-57565-970-1(0), StarBerry) Astra Publishing Hse.

Kober, K. F. Paladin Audrey & the Dagger of Truth. Kober, A. E. & Kober, B. D. 2020. (Battle of Heartwood Ser.: Vol. 2). (ENG.). 116p. (J). pap. 7.99 (978-1-6606-3275-6(7)) Independently Published.

Kober, Shahar. Chicken in Charge. Lehrhaupt, Adam. 2019. (I Can Read Level 1 Ser.). (ENG.). 32p. (J). (gr. -1-3). 16.99 (978-0-06-236425-8(1)); pap. 4.99 (978-0-06-236424-1(3)) HarperCollins Pubs.

—Chicken in Mittens. Lehrhaupt, Adam. 2017. (I Can Read Level 1 Ser.). (ENG.). 32p. (J). (gr. -1-3). 16.99 (978-0-06-236415-9(4)); pap. 4.99 (978-0-06-236414-2(6)) HarperCollins Pubs.

—Chicken in School. Lehrhaupt, Adam. 2017. (ENG.). 40p. (J). (gr. -1-3). 17.99 (978-0-06-236413-5(8)) HarperCollins Pubs.

—Chicken in Space. Lehrhaupt, Adam. 2016. (ENG.). 40p. (J). (gr. -1-3). 17.99 (978-0-06-236412-8(X)) HarperCollins Pubs.

—Chicken on a Broom. Lehrhaupt, Adam. 2019. (I Can Read Level 1 Ser.). (ENG.). 32p. (J). (gr. -1-3). 16.99 (978-0-06-236422-7(7)); pap. 4.99 (978-0-06-236421-0(9)) HarperCollins Pubs.

—Chicken on Vacation. Lehrhaupt, Adam. 2018. (I Can Read Level 1 Ser.). (ENG.). 32p. (J). (gr. -1-3). 16.99 (978-0-06-236419-7(7)); pap. 4.99 (978-0-06-236418-0(9)) HarperCollins Pubs.

—The Cricket & the Ant: A Shabbat Story. Ben-Gur, Naomi. 2016. (ENG.). 32p. (J). (gr. -1-3). lib. bdg. 17.99 (978-1-4677-8935-6(6), 9781467789356, Kar-Ben Publishing) Lerner Publishing Group.

—Dreidel, Dreidel, Dreidel. 2014. (ENG.). 12p. (J). (gr. -1 — 1). bds. 4.99 (978-0-545-53364-5(3), Cartwheel Bks.) Scholastic, Inc.

—Engineer Ari & the Hanukkah Mishap, Vol. Cohen, Deborah Bodin. 2011. (ENG.). 32p. (J). (gr. k-3). pap. 7.95 (978-0-7613-5146-7(9), 9780761351467, Kar-Ben Publishing) Lerner Publishing Group.

—Engineer Ari & the Passover Rush. Cohen, Deborah Bodin. 2015. (ENG.). 32p. (J). (gr. k-3). lib. bdg. 17.95 (978-1-4677-3470-7(5)); E-Book 27.99 (978-1-4677-6201-4(6)) Lerner Publishing Group. (Kar-Ben Publishing).

—Engineer Ari & the Rosh Hashanah Ride, Vol. Cohen, Deborah Bodin. 2008. (ENG.). 32p. (J). (gr. k-3). pap. 7.95 (978-0-8225-8650-0(9), Kar-Ben Publishing) Lerner Publishing Group.

—Engineer Ari & the Sukkah Express. Cohen, Deborah Bodin. 2010. (Sukkot & Simchat Torah Ser.). (ENG.). 32p. (J). (gr. k-3). lib. bdg. 17.95 (978-0-7613-5126-9(4), Kar-Ben Publishing) Lerner Publishing Group.

—Giraffe's Long Good-Night: A Lift-The-Flap Book, 1 vol. 2020. (ENG.). 10p. (J). bds. 9.99 (978-1-4002-1753-3(9)) Nelson, Thomas Inc.

Kober, Shahar. How to... Brush Your Teeth. Lake Press. Cottage Door Press, ed. 2020. (How To... Ser.). (ENG.). 10p. (J). (gr. -1-2). bds. 9.99 (978-1-68052-926-5(9), 1005680) Cottage Door Pr.

Kober, Shahar. How to... Tell Time: Lake Press Activity Book. Lake Press. Cottage Door Press, ed. 2018. (Children's Interactive Daily Task Instructional Board Bks.). (ENG.). 10p. (J). (gr. -1-2). bds. 9.99 (978-1-68052-319-5(8), 1002950) Cottage Door Pr.

—How to... Tie Your Shoes: Lake Press Activity Book. Cottage Door Press & Lake Press. 2018. (ENG.). 10p. (J). (gr. -1-2). bds. 9.99 (978-1-68052-318-8(X), 1002940) Cottage Door Pr.

Kober, Shahar. The Ninth Night of Hanukkah. Perl, Erica S. 2020. (ENG.). 40p. (J). (gr. -1). 16.95 (978-1-4549-4088-3(3)) Sterling Publishing Co., Inc.

Kober, Shahar. The Passover Mouse. Nelkin Wieder, Joy. 2020. (ENG.). 32p. (J). (gr. -1-2). 20.99 (978-1-9848-9552-3(4), Doubleday Bks. for Young Readers) Random Hse. Children's Bks.

—Snakes & Ladders. Morpurgo, Michael. 2013. (Red Bananas Ser.). (ENG.). 48p. (J). (gr. -1-2). 17.44 (978-1-4052-6081-7(5)) Egmont Bks., Ltd. GBR. Dist: Children's Plus, Inc.

—The Ugly Dumpling. Campisi, Stephanie. 2016. (ENG.). 32p. (J). (-3). 15.95 (978-1-938063-67-1(8), Mighty Media Kids) Mighty Media Pr.

Koblish, Scott. Kiber the Cruel. Van Lente, Fred. 2010. (Iron Man Ser.: No. 3). (ENG.). 24p. (J). (gr. 2-6). lib. bdg. 27.07 (978-1-59961-772-5(2), 10036, Marvel Age) Spotlight.

—Northern Lights. Van Lente, Fred. 2010. (Iron Man Ser.: No. 3). (ENG.). 24p. (J). (gr. 2-6). lib. bdg. 27.07 (978-1-59961-773-2(0), 10037, Marvel Age) Spotlight.

—Rock Gods. David, Peter. 2013. (Wolverine: First Class Ser.). (ENG.). 24p. (J). (gr. 2-6). lib. bdg. 27.07 (978-1-61479-180-5(5), 15328, Marvel Age) Spotlight.

—Substitute. Van Lente, Fred. 2013. (Wolverine: First Class Ser.). (ENG.). 24p. (J). (gr. 2-6). lib. bdg. 27.07 (978-1-61479-181-2(3), 15329, Marvel Age) Spotlight.

Koch, Carla. Karol from Poland: The Life of Pope John Paul II for Children. Wilson, M. Leonora. rev. ed. 2006. 38p. (J). pap. 7.95 (978-0-8198-4209-1(5)) Pauline Bks. & Media.

Koch, Falynn. Science Comics: Bats: Learning to Fly. Koch, Falynn. 2017. (Science Comics Ser.). (ENG.). 128p. (J). pap. 12.99 (978-1-62672-408-2(3), 900156276, First Second Bks.) Roaring Brook Pr.

—Science Comics: Plagues: The Microscopic Battlefield. Koch, Falynn. 2017. (Science Comics Ser.). (ENG.). 128p. (J). pap. 12.99 (978-1-62672-752-6(X), 900172681, First Second Bks.) Roaring Brook Pr.

Koch Johnson, Amy. Reliff the Baker Elf: A Story of Friendship & Following Your Dreams. Kwedder, Rick. 2019. (ENG.). 36p. (J). pap. 9.99 (978-1-6974-5304-1(X)) Independently Published.

Koch, Miriam. Digby Differs. Koch, Miriam. Garlid, Ann, tr. from GER. 2013. 40p. 17.99 (978-1-4413-1306-5(0)) Peter Pauper Pr. Inc.

Koch, Nobu & Rizal, Clarissa. Mary's Wild Winter Feast. Lindoff, Hannah. 2014. (ENG.). 40p. pap. 14.95 (978-1-60223-232-7(6)) Univ. of Alaska Pr.

Koch, Pam. What Does My Mom Do? Ott, Lisa. 2019. (ENG.). 26p. (J). 19.99 (978-1-4575-6563-2(3)) Dog Ear Publishing, LLC.

Kochalka, James. The Glorkian Warrior Delivers a Pizza. Kochalka, James. 2014. (Glorkian Warrior Ser.: 1). (ENG.). 112p. (J). (gr. k-4). pap. 13.99 (978-1-59643-917-7(3), 900121318, First Second Bks.) Roaring Brook Pr.

Koci, Rudin. Glenn Gould: Sketches of Solitude. Kaufmann, Anne. 2013. (978-0-9868657-9-4(6)) Brownridge Publishing.

Kocsmiersky, Jenn. My Name Is Helen Keller. Uhlberg, Myron. 2020. 32p. (J). (gr. -1-3). 16.99 (978-0-8075-5322-0(0), 0807553220) Whitman, Albert & Co.

—Nina Soni, Former Best Friend. Sheth, Kashmira. (Nina Soni Ser.). (ENG.). (J). (gr. 2-5). 2020. 148p. pap. 7.99 (978-1-68263-205-5(9)); 2019. 152p. 15.95 (978-1-68263-057-0(9)) Peachtree Publishing Co. Inc.

Kocsmiersky, Jenn. Nina Soni, Sister Fixer. Sheth, Kashmira. 2020. (Nina Soni Ser.: 2). (ENG.). 128p. (J). (gr. 2-5). 15.99 (978-1-68263-054-9(4)) Peachtree Publishing Co. Inc.

Koda, Eric. Extraordinary X-Men Vol. 4: IvX. 2017. (ENG.). 112p. (YA). (gr. 8-17). pap. 16.99 (978-0-7851-9937-3(3)) Marvel Worldwide, Inc.

Kodaira, Machiyo. Hachiko Waits: Based on a True Story. Newman, Lesléa & Newman, Lesléa. 2008. (ENG.). 96p. (J). (gr. 3-5). pap. 7.99 (978-0-312-55806-2(6), 900057661) Square Fish.

Kodera, Craig. A Dream of Pilots, 1 vol. Handleman, Philip. 2009. (ENG.). 128p. (J). (gr. 3-7). 14.95 (978-1-58980-570-5(4), Pelican Publishing) Arcadia Publishing.

Kodman, Stansilawa. Grow: A Novel in Verse, 1 vol. Havill, Juanita. (ENG.). 160p. (J). (gr. 3-7). 2011. pap. 7.95 (978-1-56145-575-1(X)); 2008. 14.95 (978-1-56145-441-9(9)) Peachtree Publishing Co. Inc.

Koebel, Jessica, jt. illus. see McDermott, Lisa.

Koefler, Leatha. Churchmouse Tales: Puppet Book, 10 vols. Toler, Violet M. rev. ed. 2004. Orig. Title: Charlie Church Mouse. (J). (gr. -1-6). pap. 10.95 (978-0-9749749-0-3(0)) Wayside Pubns.

—Churchmouse Tales: Puppet Plays, 10 vols., Vol. 2. Toler, Violet M. 2nd rev. ed. 2004. Orig. Title: "Puppet Plays, Adventures of Charlie & His Friends". (J). (gr. -1-6). pap. 10.95 (978-0-9749749-1-0(9)) Wayside Pubns.

Koehler, Ed. Bible Puzzlers. Molski, Carol. 2007. (CPH Teaching Resource Ser.). (ENG.). 63p. (J). (gr. 4-7). per. 10.99 (978-0-7586-1332-5(6)) Concordia Publishing Hse.

—Bible Word Suduko. Molski, Carol. 2007. (CPH Teaching Resource Ser.). (ENG.). 64p. pap. 10.99 (978-0-7586-1344-8(X)) Concordia Publishing Hse.

—The Fiery Furnace. Busch, Melinda Kay. 2004. (Arch Bks.). 16p. (J). (gr. k-4). 1.99 (978-0-7586-0479-8(3)) Concordia Publishing Hse.

—Manualidades Faciles con Vasos de Papel. Stohs, Anita Reight. Beckmann, Ewaldo, tr. 2008. 64p. (J). pap. 9.99 (978-0-7586-1586-2(8)) Concordia Publishing Hse.

—Mary Magdalene's Easter Story. Hartman, Sara. 2005. (ENG.). 16p. (J). 1.99 (978-0-7586-0722-5(9)) Concordia Publishing Hse.

—The Mystery of the Moving Hand. Burgdorf, Larry. 2014. (Arch Bks.). (ENG.). 16p. (J). pap. 2.49 (978-0-7586-4603-3(8)) Concordia Publishing Hse.

—Praise God with Paper Cups: 45 Easy Bible Crafts; Grades 1-5. Stohs, Anita Reith. 2005. (CPH Teaching Resource Ser.). 64p. pap. 10.99 (978-0-7586-0842-0(X)) Concordia Publishing Hse.

Koehler, Ed, jt. illus. see Marxhausen, Benjamin.

Koehler, Ed, jt. illus. see Marxhausen, Ben.

Koehler, Fred. Flashlight Night. Esenwine, Matt Forrest. 2017. (ENG.). 32p. (J). (gr. -1-3). 16.95 (978-1-62979-493-8(7)) Boyds Mills Pr.

—One Day, the End: Short, Very Short, Shorter-Than-Ever Stories. Dotlich, Rebecca Kai. 2015. (ENG.). 32p. (J). (gr. -1-3). 17.99 (978-1-62091-451-9(4), 1396728) Boyds Mills Pr.

—Puppy, Puppy, Puppy. Sternberg, Julie. 2017. (ENG.). 32p. (J). (-k). 16.95 (978-1-62979-466-2(X)) Boyds Mills Pr.

—This Book Is Not about Dragons. Thomas, Shelley Moore. 2016. (ENG.). 32p. (J). (gr. -1-2). 16.95 (978-1-62979-168-5(7)) Boyds Mills Pr.

—What If ... ? Then We ... Short, Very Short, Shorter-Than-Ever Possibilities. Dotlich, Rebecca Kai. 2019. (ENG.). 32p. (J). (gr. k-4). 17.95 (978-1-62979-909-4(2)) Boyds Mills Pr.

Koehler, Mary. The Children are Happy Story CD with Animals from the Southwest. 2003. (J). cd-rom 5.00 (978-0-9744005-1-8(3)) In the Desert.

Koeller, Carol. Ah-Choo. Taylor-Butler, Christine. 2005. (My First Reader Ser.). (ENG.). 32p. (J). (gr. k-1). 18.50 (978-0-516-25175-2(9), Children's Pr.) Scholastic Library Publishing.

—Camino al Primer Grado. Cleveland, Alexandra et al. Franco, Sharon, tr. from ENG. 2004. (SPA.). 128p. (Orig.). (J). pap. 14.95 (978-0-943452-35-7(X)) Building Blocks, LLC.

—Easel Art. Wilmes, Liz & Wilmes, Dick. 2004. 128p. (J). pap. 12.95 (978-0-943452-25-8(2)) Building Blocks, LLC.

—Nick Is Sick. Riggs, Sandy. 2006. (Barron's Reader's Clubhouse Level 1 Ser.). (ENG.). 24p. (J). (gr. k-3). 16.19 (978-0-7641-3284-1(9), B.E.S. Publishing) Peterson's.

—Why I Thank You, God. Adams, Michelle Medlock. 2006. 20p. (J). (gr. -1). bds. 5.49 (978-0-7586-0911-3(6)) Concordia Publishing Hse.

Koeller, Carol. All about Adoption: How Families Are Made & How Kids Feel about It. Koeller, Carol, tr. Nemiroff, Marc A. & Annunziata, Jane. 2003. 48p. (J). (gr. k-3). 14.95 (978-1-59147-058-8(7)); pap. 9.95 (978-1-59147-059-5(5)) American Psychological Assn. (Magination Pr.).

Koelsch, Michael. Listos para Leer. Wells, Rosemary & Rosemary, Wells. Fernandez, Leire Amigo, tr. 2004. (SPA.). 32p. (J). (gr. k-1). 14.99 (978-84-241-8712-5(1)) Everest Editora ESP. Dist: Lectorum Pubns., Inc.

—El Mundo Que Nos Rodea. Wells, Rosemary & Rosemary, Wells. Fernandez, Leire Amigo, tr. 2004. (SPA.). 32p. (J). (gr. -1-1). 14.99 (978-84-241-8711-8(3)) Everest Editora ESP. Dist: Lectorum Pubns., Inc.

—Rock On. Christopher, Matt. 5th ed. 2004. (ENG.). 64p. (J). (gr. 1-4). pap. 8.99 (978-0-316-76265-6(2)) Little, Brown Bks. for Young Readers.

—Rock On, 5. Christopher, Matt. 2004. (Extreme Team Ser.: Vol. 5). (ENG.). 54p. (J). (gr. 3-6). 17.44 (978-0-316-76264-9(4)) Little Brown & Co.

—Wild Ride: Wild Ride. Christopher, Matt. 7th ed. 2005. (ENG.). 64p. (J). (gr. 1-4). pap. 8.99 (978-0-316-76263-2(6)) Little, Brown Bks. for Young Readers.

Koenig, Florence. Anna & Johanna. Elschner, Géraldine. 2018. (Children's Books Inspired by Famous Artworks Ser.). (ENG.). 32p. (J). (gr. -1-3). 14.95 (978-3-7913-7345-4(5)) Prestel Verlag GmbH & Co KG. DEU. Dist: Penguin Random Hse. LLC.

Koenig, James. The Little Indian Runner. Woommavovah, Mark E. L. 2019. (ENG.). 34p. (J). pap. 10.99 (978-1-0707-9218-7(7)) Independently Published.

Koenig, James. The Little Indian Runner. Woommavovah, Mark E. L. 2019. (ENG.). 34p. (J). (gr. k-2). 17.99 (978-0-578-51961-6(5)) Woommavovah, Mark.

—Seymour Monster Mcbean. Roosa, M. B. 2019. (ENG.). 38p. (J). (gr. k-2). 17.99 (978-0-578-60157-1(5)) Freelance Fridge, LLC.

—Seymour Monster Mcbean. Roosa, M. B. 2019. (ENG.). 38p. (J). pap. 10.99 (978-1-7026-5145-5(2)) Independently Published.

Koenig, James. What Would You Do at the Zoo? Roosa, M. B. 2018. (ENG.). 30p. (J). (gr. k-3). 17.99 (978-0-578-42245-9(X)) Freelance Fridge, LLC.

Koening, James. Halyn-Simone Engineer Kidd: Beach Klub House. Lewis, Idelle. 2016. (ENG.). (J). (gr. 1-6). 20.95 (978-1-4958-1135-7(2)) Infinity Publishing.

Koensgen, Joseph. The Beaver & the Muskrat. Smith, B. 2017. (ENG.). (J). pap. (978-1-4602-9924-1(8)) FriesenPress.

Koff, Deborah. Marissa the Tooth Fairy. Andersdatter, Karla Margaret. 2nd ed. 2005. (J). (978-0-9717611-2-4(4)) Depot Bks.

Koffsky, Ann. The Sun's Special Blessing: Happens Only Once in 28 Years - French Flap. Wasserman, Sand. 2009. 36p. 12.95 (978-1-934440-76-6(0), Pitspopany Pr.) Simcha Media Group.

—The Sun's Special Blessing: Happens Only Once in 28 Years - HC. Wasserman, Sand. 2009. 36p. 17.95 (978-1-934440-92-6(2), Pitspopany Pr.) Simcha Media Group.

Koffsky, Ann. Shabbat Shalom, Hey! Koffsky, Ann. 2015. (ENG.). 24p. (J). (gr. -1-k). lib. bdg. 9.99 (978-1-4677-4917-6(6), 9781467749176); E-Book 23.99 (978-1-4677-6208-3(3)) Lerner Publishing Group. (Kar-Ben Publishing).

Koffsky, Ann D. Creation Colors. 2019. (J). (978-1-68115-545-6(1), Apples & Honey Pr.) Behrman Hse., Inc.

—Kayla & Kugel. 2015. (J). (978-0-87441-898-9(4)); Vol. (ENG.). pap. (978-1-68115-502-9(8)) Behrman Hse., Inc.

—Kayla & Kugel's Almost-Perfect Passover, Vol. 2016. (ENG.). (J). pap. (978-1-68115-508-1(7)) Behrman Hse., Inc.

—My Cousin Tamar Lives in Israel. Abraham, Michelle Shapiro. 2006. 14p. (J). (gr. -1). pap. 6.95 (978-0-8074-0989-3(8)) URJ Pr.

—Teacher's Guide for to Learn Is to Do: A Tikkun Olam Roadmap. Halper, Sharon D. 2003. 46p. (gr. 4-6). pap., tchr. ed., tchr.'s training gde. ed. 12.00 (978-0-8074-0730-1(5), 208051) URJ Pr.

—To Learn Is to Do: A Tikkun Olam Road Map. Halper, Sharon. 2004. vi, 56p. (gr. 4-6). pap. 11.95 (978-0-8074-0729-5(1), 123935) URJ Pr.

Koford, Adam. The Book of Mormon on Trial Activity Learning Book. Koford, Adam, compiled by. 2003. 123p. (J). per. 14.95 (978-0-9726670-3-6(2)) Rich Publishing.

Koford, Adam, jt. illus. see Knaupp, Andrew.

Kofsky, Ann. Reaching Godward: Voices from Jewish Spiritual Guidance. Ochs, Carol. 2004. 250p. pap. 14.95 (978-0-8074-0866-7(2), 142612) URJ Pr.

Kofsky, Kristen. Coral Reefs A to Z Coloring Book. Pierce, Terry. 2003. 32p. 4.95 (978-1-57306-122-3(0)) Bess Pr., Inc.

—Father Damien. Williams, Laura E. 2009. (ENG.). 60p. (J). (gr. 4). pap. (978-1-59700-757-3(9)) Island Heritage Publishing.

—Surfing A to Z Coloring Book. Pierce, Terry. 2004. 24p. pap. 4.95 (978-1-57306-178-0(6)) Bess Pr., Inc.

Koge-Donbo. Pita-Ten Official Fan Book. Koge-Donbo. (Pita-Ten Ser.). 176p. Vol. 1. 2005. pap. 9.99 (978-1-59816-106-9(7)); Vol. 2. 2nd rev. ed. 2006. per. 9.99 (978-1-59816-107-6(5)) TOKYOPOP, Inc.

Kogo, Yoshi. Big Al & Shrimpy. Clements, Andrew. 2005. (ENG.). 40p. (J). (gr. -1-3). reprint ed. 7.99 (978-1-4169-0366-6(6), Atheneum Bks. for Young Readers) Simon & Schuster Children's Publishing.

Kohara, Kazuno. Ghosts in the House! Kohara, Kazuno. 2010. (ENG.). 32p. (J). (gr. -1-1). pap. 8.99 (978-0-312-60886-6(1), 900065181) Square Fish.

—Here Comes Jack Frost. Kohara, Kazuno. 2011. (ENG.). 32p. (J). (gr. -1-1). pap. 7.99 (978-0-312-60446-2(7), 900076478) Square Fish.

—The Midnight Library. Kohara, Kazuno. 2014. (ENG.). 32p. (J). (gr. -1-1). 16.99 (978-1-59643-985-6(8), 900128314) Roaring Brook Pr.

Kohen, Avigayil. Der Feyerdiger Shabes: An Emese Ertseylung. Peer, H. 2018. (YID.). 86p. (J). (978-1-68091-256-2(9)) Kinder Shpiel USA, Inc.

Kohler, Michelle. Santa Horse. Tapler, Judy. 2008. 36p. pap. 16.99 (978-1-4389-2290-4(6)) AuthorHouse.

Kohler, Ursula. The Dolls Nose. Haxhia, Miranda. 2007. 32p. (J). (POL & ENG.). pap. 16.95 (978-1-60195-097-0(7)); (ARA & ENG.). pap. 16.95 (978-1-60195-087-1(X)) International Step by Step Assn.

Kohn, Arnie. Dinosaurs. Spizzirri, Linda, ed. 32p. (J). (gr. 1-8). pap. 4.98 incl. audio (978-0-86545-019-6(6)) Spizzirri Pr., Inc.

—Prehistoric Sea Life. Spizzirri, Linda, ed. 32p. (J). (gr. 1-8). pap. 4.98 incl. audio (978-0-86545-020-2(X)) Spizzirri Pr., Inc.

Kohner, Elaine. Guided Meditations for Youth on Sacramental Life. Arsenault, Jane & Cedor, Jean. Stamschror, Robert P., ed. unabr. ed. 2003. (Quiet Place Apart Ser.). 40p. (YA). (gr. 9-12). pap. 9.95 incl. audio (978-0-88489-308-0(1)) Saint Mary's Press of Minnesota.

Kohrer, Ursula. The Doll's Nose. Haxhia, Miranda. 2014. (ARA.). (J). (978-0-9856237-4-6(8)) East West Discovery Pr.

Kohse, Lee. But Not Gino. Lyon, Shari. 2016. (ENG.). (J). 19.95 (978-1-943198-00-9(4)) Southwestern Publishing Hse., Inc.

Koji, Jeanette. A Really, Really, Scary Monster Story! Blume, Rebecca. l.t. ed. 2006. 32p. (J). 24.95 (978-0-9785427-0-2(3)) Liberty Artists Management.

Koji, Makoto. Lottie Perkins: Ballerina (Lottie Perkins, #2) Nannestad, Katrina. 2019. (Lottie Perkins Ser.: 02). 64p. 4.99 (978-0-7333-3910-3(7)) ABC Bks. AUS. Dist: HarperCollins Pubs.

—Lottie Perkins: Fashion Designer (Lottie Perkins, #4) Nannestad, Katrina. 2020. (Lottie Perkins Ser.: 04). 64p. 4.99 (978-0-7333-3912-7(3)) ABC Bks. AUS. Dist: HarperCollins Pubs.

—Lottie Perkins: Movie Star (Lottie Perkins, #1) Nannestad, Katrina. 2019. (Lottie Perkins Ser.: 01). 64p. 4.99 (978-0-7333-3909-7(3)) ABC Bks. AUS. Dist: HarperCollins Pubs.

—Lottie Perkins: Pop Singer (Lottie Perkins, #3) Nannestad, Katrina. 2020. (Lottie Perkins Ser.: 03). 64p. 4.99 (978-0-7333-3911-0(5)) ABC Bks. AUS. Dist: HarperCollins Pubs.

Koko, Danny. Junior Rabbit Travels to Pennsylvania. White, Jenny. 2018. (ENG.). 26p. (J). pap. 16.99 (978-1-5462-3996-3(0)) AuthorHouse.

Kolanovic, Dubravka. Baby Bear & the Big, Wide World. Patterson, Ellie. 2013. (J). (978-1-4351-4929-8(7)) Barnes & Noble, Inc.

—The Christmas Story for Little Angels. Dodd, Sarah J. & Stone, Julia. ed. 2015. (Little Angels Ser.). (ENG.). 32p. (J). (gr. -1-k). 7.99 (978-0-7459-7610-5(7)) Lion Hudson PLC GBR. Dist: Independent Pubs. Group.

—Count My Blessing 1 to 10. Cabral, Jeane. 2007. (Magnetic Counting Book Ser.). 10p. (978-1-84666-360-4(1), Tide Mill Pr.) Top That! Publishing PLC.

—Historias de la Biblia / My Bible Story Book. Piper, Sophie. 2018. (SPA.). 64p. (J). (gr. 2). 7.95 (978-1-945540-49-3(4)) Penguin Random House Grupo Editorial ESP. Dist: Penguin Random Hse. LLC.

—I Love You All Ways. Richmond, Marianne. 2019. 26p. (J). (-2). bds. 8.99 (978-1-4926-7515-0(6), Sourcebooks Jabberwocky) Sourcebooks, Inc.

—The Little Angels Christmas Story. Stone, Julia. 2016. (ENG.). 24p. (J). (gr. -1). 9.99 (978-1-61261-852-4(9)) Paraclete Pr., Inc.

—Little Bear's Special Friend. Freedman, Claire. 2007. (J). (978-0-545-06757-7(X)) Scholastic, Inc.

—The Little Raindrop. Gray, Joanna. 2014. (J). (978-1-4351-5254-0(9)) Barnes & Noble, Inc.

—The Little Raindrop. Gray, Joanna. 2014. (ENG.). 32p. (J). (gr. -1-k). 16.95 (978-1-62873-821-6(9), Sky Pony Pr.) Skyhorse Publishing Co., Inc.

—The Littlest Star. Littledale, Richard. ed. 2016. (ENG.). 32p. (J). pap. 8.99 (978-0-7459-7695-2(6)) Lion Hudson PLC GBR. Dist: Independent Pubs. Group.

—My Baptism Book. Piper, Sophie. 2007. (ENG.). 64p. (J). (gr. -1-1). 14.99 (978-1-55725-535-8(0), 5358) Paraclete Pr., Inc.

—My Bible Story Book. Piper, Sophie. ed. 2016. (ENG.). 64p. (J). (gr. -1-k). 9.99 (978-0-7459-6595-6(4)) Lion Hudson PLC GBR. Dist: Independent Pubs. Group.

—Nursery Rhyme Treasury. Davidson, Susanna. 2006. 96p. (J). 19.99 (978-0-7945-1281-1(X), Usborne) EDC Publishing.

—Recipe for How Much I Love You. Kartes, Danielle. 2020. (Baby Chef Ser.). 24p. (J). bds. 9.99 (978-1-7282-1414-6(9)) Sourcebooks, Inc.

Kolanovic, Dubravka. A Recipe for How Much I Miss You. Kartes, Danielle. 2020. (Baby Chef Ser.). (ENG.). 24p. (J). bds. 9.99 (978-1-7282-2113-7(7)) Sourcebooks, Inc.

Kolanovic, Dubravka. Safely Through the Night. Pasquali, Elena. 2008. (ENG.). 32p. (J). (gr. k-k). 16.95 *(978-0-7459-6048-7(0))* Lion Hudson PLC GBR. Dist: Independent Pubs. Group.
—Shine Moon Shine. Conway, David. 2008. 32p. (J). (gr. -1-2). 15.95 *(978-1-58925-073-4(7))* Tiger Tales.
—Under the Sleepy Moon. Parks, Luna. 2019. (ENG.). 16p. (J). (gr. 2-k). bds. 9.99 *(978-1-68010-588-9(4))* Tiger Tales.
—Wake up, Sleepy Head! Early Morning Poems. Ross, Mandy. 2004. (Poems for the Young Ser.). 32p. (J). (gr. 2-3). pap. *(978-1-904550-33-4(9))* Child's Play International Ltd.
—Welcome, Baby: Hello, Bunny. import ed. 2019. (Welcome, Baby Ser.). (ENG.). 14p. (J). (— 1). bds. 7.99 *(978-0-593-12361-4(1)*, Doubleday Bks. for Young Readers) Random Hse. Children's Bks.
—Welcome, Baby: Love You, Baby. import ed. 2019. (Welcome, Baby Ser.). (ENG.). 12p. (J). (— 1). bds. 9.99 *(978-0-593-12359-1(X)*, Doubleday Bks. for Young Readers) Random Hse. Children's Bks.
Kolanovic, Dubravka. Honey Hill Spinners: Dance Show. Kolanovic, Dubravka. 2009. (Honey Hill Ser.). (ENG.). 12p. (J). (gr. -1-k). bds. 7.99 *(978-0-230-71301-7(7))* Pan Macmillan GBR. Dist: Independent Pubs. Group.
—Honey Hill: Wipe-Clean Counting. Kolanovic, Dubravka. 2009. (Honey Hill Ser.). (ENG.). 12p. (J). (gr. -1-k). bds. 9.99 *(978-0-230-70914-0(1))* Pan Macmillan GBR. Dist: Independent Pubs. Group.
—Kindness Is Magic. Kolanovic, Dubravka. 2018. (Story Corner Ser.). (ENG.). 24p. (J). (gr. -1-k). lib. bdg. 19.99 *(978-1-68297-318-9(2))* QEB Publishing Inc.
—There's No Place Like Home. Kolanovic, Dubravka. 2017. (Story Corner Ser.). (ENG.). 24p. (J). (gr. -1-k). lib. bdg. 19.99 *(978-1-68297-184-0(8))* QEB Publishing Inc.
Kolanovic, Dubravka & Poole, Helen. Night-Night Boston. Sully, Katherine. 2016. (Night-Night Ser.). (ENG.). 20p. (J). (-1). bds. 9.99 *(978-1-4926-3937-4(0)*, 9781492639374, Sourcebooks Jabberwocky) Sourcebooks, Inc.
—Night-Night California. Sully, Katherine. 2016. (Night-Night Ser.). (ENG.). 20p. (J). (-1). bds. 9.99 *(978-1-4926-3939-8(7)*, 9781492639398, Sourcebooks Jabberwocky) Sourcebooks, Inc.
—Night-Night Chicago. Sully, Katherine. 2016. (Night-Night Ser.). (ENG.). 20p. (J). (-1). bds. 9.99 *(978-1-4926-3935-0(4)*, 9781492639350, Sourcebooks Jabberwocky) Sourcebooks, Inc.
—Night-Night Colorado. Sully, Katherine. 2016. (Night-Night Ser.). (ENG.). 20p. (J). (-1). bds. 9.99 *(978-1-4926-3938-1(9)*, 9781492639381, Sourcebooks Jabberwocky) Sourcebooks, Inc.
—Night-Night Florida. Sully, Katherine. 2016. (Night-Night Ser.). (ENG.). 20p. (J). (-1). bds. 9.99 *(978-1-4926-4218-3(5)*, 9781492642183, Sourcebooks Jabberwocky) Sourcebooks, Inc.
—Night-Night Georgia. Sully, Katherine. 2016. (ENG.). 20p. (J). (-1). bds. 9.99 *(978-1-4926-4216-9(9)*, 9781492642169, Sourcebooks Jabberwocky) Sourcebooks, Inc.
—Night-Night Kansas. Sully, Katherine. 2016. (ENG.). 20p. (J). (-1). bds. 9.99 *(978-1-4926-3941-1(9)*, 9781492639411, Sourcebooks Jabberwocky) Sourcebooks, Inc.
—Night-Night Michigan. Sully, Katherine. 2016. (Night-Night Ser.). (ENG.). 20p. (J). (-1). bds. 9.99 *(978-1-4926-3934-3(6)*, 9781492639343, Sourcebooks Jabberwocky) Sourcebooks, Inc.
—Night-Night Minnesota. Sully, Katherine. 2016. (Night-Night Ser.). (ENG.). 20p. (J). (-1). bds. 9.99 *(978-1-4926-3940-4(0)*, 9781492639404, Sourcebooks Jabberwocky) Sourcebooks, Inc.
—Night-Night New Jersey. Sully, Katherine. 2016. (Night-Night Ser.). (ENG.). 20p. (J). (-1). bds. 9.99 *(978-1-4926-3933-6(8)*, 9781492639336, Sourcebooks Jabberwocky) Sourcebooks, Inc.
—Night-Night New York City. Sully, Katherine. 2016. (Night-Night Ser.). (ENG.). 20p. (J). (-1). bds. 9.99 *(978-1-4926-3932-9(X)*, 9781492639329, Sourcebooks Jabberwocky) Sourcebooks, Inc.
—Night-Night Ohio. Sully, Katherine. 2016. (Night-Night Ser.). (ENG.). 20p. (J). (-1). bds. 9.99 *(978-1-4926-4220-6(7)*, 9781492642206, Sourcebooks Jabberwocky) Sourcebooks, Inc.
—Night-Night Pennsylvania. Sully, Katherine. 2016. (Night-Night Ser.). (ENG.). 20p. (J). (-1). bds. 9.99 *(978-1-4926-4219-0(3)*, 9781492642190, Sourcebooks Jabberwocky) Sourcebooks, Inc.
—Night-Night Texas. Sully, Katherine. 2016. (Night-Night Ser.). (ENG.). 20p. (J). (-1). bds. 9.99 *(978-1-4926-3936-7(2)*, 9781492639367, Sourcebooks Jabberwocky) Sourcebooks, Inc.
—Night-Night Wisconsin. Sully, Katherine. 2016. (Night-Night Ser.). (ENG.). 20p. (J). (-1). bds. 9.99 *(978-1-4926-4217-6(7)*, 9781492642176, Sourcebooks Jabberwocky) Sourcebooks, Inc.
Kolar, Bob. Alpha Oops! The Day Z Went First. Kontis, Alethea. ed. 2012. lib. bdg. 17.20 *(978-0-606-26928-5(2))* Turtleback.
—AlphaOops! H Is for Halloween. Kontis, Alethea. 2010. 40p. (J). (gr. -1-3). 15.99 *(978-0-7636-3966-2(4))* Candlewick Pr.
—AlphaOops! The Day Z Went First. Kontis, Alethea. 2012. 48p. (J). (gr. -1-3). pap. 6.99 *(978-0-7636-6084-0(1))* Candlewick Pr.
—The Boy & the Book. Slater, David Michael. 2015. 32p. (J). (-k). lib. bdg. 16.95 *(978-1-58089-562-0(X))* Charlesbridge Publishing, Inc.
—A Cat & a Dog. Masurel, Claire. 2003. (Cheshire Studio Book Ser.). 32p. (J). (gr. -1). 8.95 *(978-0-7358-1780-7(4))* North-South Bks., Inc.
—A Cat & a Dog / un Gato y un Perro. Masurel, Claire. 2018. (ENG.). 32p. (J). (gr. -1-2). pap. 8.95 *(978-0-7358-4354-7(6))* North-South Bks., Inc.
—Frank & Bean. Michalak, Jamie. 2019. (ENG.). 48p. (J). (gr. k-3). 15.99 *(978-0-7636-9559-0(9))* Candlewick Pr.
—Give Me Back My Bones! Norman, Kim. 2019. (ENG.). 40p. (J). (gr. -1-3). 16.99 *(978-0-7636-8841-7(X))* Candlewick Pr.
—Here We Go Digging for Dinosaur Bones. Lendroth, Susan. 2020. 32p. (J). (gr. -1-3). lib. bdg. 16.99 *(978-1-62354-104-0(2))* Charlesbridge Publishing, Inc.
—The Little Dump Truck. Cuyler, Margery. 2014. (Little Vehicles Ser.: 1). (ENG.). 24p. (J). (gr. -1-1). bds. 7.99 *(978-0-8050-9990-4(5)*, 900129326, Holt, Henry & Co. Bks. For Young Readers) Holt, Henry & Co.
—The Little Fire Truck. Cuyler, Margery. 2017. (Little Vehicles Ser.: 3). (ENG.). 32p. (J). 14.99 *(978-1-62779-805-1(6)*, 900160047, Holt, Henry & Co. Bks. For Young Readers) Holt, Henry & Co.
—The Little Ice Cream Truck. Cuyler, Margery. 2018. (Little Vehicles Ser.: 4). (ENG.). 32p. (J). 14.99 *(978-1-62779-806-8(4)*, 900160050, Holt, Henry & Co. Bks. For Young Readers) Holt, Henry & Co.
—The Little School Bus. Cuyler, Margery. (Little Vehicles Ser.: 2). (ENG.). (J). 2018. 24p. bds. 7.99 *(978-1-250-19645-3(0)*, 900194112); 2014. 32p. (gr. -1-1). 12.99 *(978-0-8050-9435-0(0)*, 9780805094350) Holt, Henry & Co. (Holt, Henry & Co. Bks. For Young Readers).
—Nothing Like a Puffin. Soltis, Sue. 2011. (ENG.). 40p. (J). (gr. -1-1). 16.99 *(978-0-7636-3617-3(7))* Candlewick Pr.
—Slickety Quick: Poems about Sharks. Brown, Skila. 2016. 32p. (J). (gr. 1-4). 16.99 *(978-0-7636-6543-2(6))* Candlewick Pr.
—Trucker & Train. Stark, Hannah. 2019. (ENG.). 40p. (J). (gr. -1-3). 17.99 *(978-0-544-80181-3(4)*, 1640534, Clarion Bks.) Houghton Mifflin Harcourt Trade & Reference Pubs.
—101 Dinosaurs: And Other Prehistoric Reptiles. Prince, April Jones. 2018. (ENG.). 14p. (J). (— 1). 8.99 *(978-1-338-19319-0(8))* Scholastic, Inc.
Kolar, Bob. Big Kicks. Kolar, Bob. 2008. (ENG.). 40p. (J). (gr. -1-1). 16.99 *(978-0-7636-3390-5(9))* Candlewick Pr.
Kolb, Andrew. All Aboard! Let's Ride a Train. Mara, Nichole. 2017. (ENG.). 10p. (J). (gr. -1 — 1). bds. 9.95 *(978-1-4197-2567-8(X)*, Abrams Appleseed) Abrams, Inc.
—All Aboard! the Airport Train. Mara, Nichole. 2019. (ENG.). 10p. (J). (gr. -1 — 1). bds. 9.99 *(978-1-4197-3678-0(7)*, Abrams Appleseed) Abrams, Inc.
—All Aboard! the Christmas Train. Mara, Nichole. 2018. (ENG.). 10p. (J). (gr. -1 — 1). bds. 9.99 *(978-1-4197-3295-9(1)*, Abrams Appleseed) Abrams, Inc.
—Spider-Man: Far from Home: Spider-Man Swings Through Europe! Glass, Calliope. 2019. (ENG.). 32p. (J). (gr. -1-k). 12.99 *(978-1-368-05028-9(X)*, Marvel Pr.) Disney Publishing Worldwide.
Kolding, Richard Max. Waking Up. Seese, Ellen. 2004. (ENG.). 24p. (gr. k-2). pap. 8.95 *(978-1-57874-041-3(X)*, Kaeden Bks.) Kaeden Corp.
—What Is Faith? Mueller, Virginia. 2013. (Happy Day Ser.). (ENG.). 16p. (J). pap. 2.49 *(978-1-4143-9293-6(1)*, 4608283) Tyndale Hse. Pubs.
Kolenko, Anja. Bonnie the Lucky Collie. Alhadeff, Vicky. 2018. (ENG.). 28p. (J). (gr. 3-4). pap. *(978-1-9164114-0-1(1))* City Collie Pr.
—Kitten Rescue Tales. Napper, Katherine & Alhadeff, Vicky. 2017. (ENG.). (J). (gr. k-6). pap. *(978-1-9998608-0-6(2))* Generation 2050.
—Los Cuentos Del Rescate Del Gatito. Alhadeff, Vicky & Napper, Katherine. 2017. (SPA.). (J). (gr. 1-6). pap. *(978-1-9998608-2-0(9))* Generation 2050.
—Making Rainbows. Gothard, Nicola. 2016. (ENG.). (J). (gr. 1-6). pap. *(978-0-9934631-8-1(5))* Generation 2050.
—Nimai & Syama a Black & White Tale. Alhadeff, Vicky. 2019. (ENG.). 22p. (J). pap. *(978-1-9164114-2-5(8))* City Collie Pr.
Kolesar, Slavka. The Promise Basket, 1 vol. Richardson, Bill. 2019. (ENG.). 32p. (J). (gr. k-3). 17.95 *(978-1-77306-089-7(9))* Groundwood Bks. CAN. Dist: Publishers Group West (PGW).
Kolesova, Juliana. The Brave Princess & Me, 1 vol. Kacer, Kathy. 2019. (ENG.). 32p. (J). (gr. 1-3). 18.95 *(978-1-77260-102-2(0))* Second Story Pr. CAN. Dist: Orca Bk. Pubs. USA.
Kolins, Scott, jt. illus. see Di Vito, Andrea.
Kolitsky, Joy. Escapade Johnson & Mayhem at Mount Moosilauke. Sullivan, Michael. 2007. (Escapade Johnson Ser.). (ENG.). 96p. (J). (gr. 2-4). per. 3.95 *(978-1-929945-70-2(1))* Big Guy Bks., Inc.
—Escapade Johnson & the Witches of Belknap County. Sullivan, Michael. 2008. (Escapade Johnson Ser.). (ENG.). 99p. (J). (gr. 2-4). pap. 3.95 *(978-1-929945-90-0(6))* Big Guy Bks., Inc.
Kollman, Carrie. Grand Entry. Compton, Dawn. 2004. 64p. pap. 12.95 *(978-1-932196-45-0(5))* WordWright.biz, Inc.
Kolnik, Paul, photos by. Dancing to America. Morris, Ann. 2004. 40p. (YA). (gr. 7-10). 16.00 *(978-0-7567-7577-3(9))* DIANE Publishing Co.
Kolpak, Nadiia. Tekatu Learns Obedience. Ross, Michelle. 2017. (ENG.). (J). (gr. k-5). pap. 12.95 *(978-1-946683-05-2(1))*; 17.99 *(978-1-946683-04-5(3))* Rapier Publishing Co., LLC.
Koltun, Amy. Meet Julius Carmichael: First Day Blues. Carroll, Jonathan. 2003. 96p. (J). (gr. 3-6). pap. 6.95 *(978-0-9724935-0-5(6))* Striking Presence Pubns.
Kolvanovic, Dubravka. Jingle Bells: A Collection of Songs & Carols. Tiger Tales Staff, ed. 2014. (ENG.). 22p. (J). (gr. -1-k). bds. 8.99 *(978-1-58925-568-5(2))* Tiger Tales.
—This Little Light of Mine. Tiger Tales. 2014. (ENG.). 22p. (J). (gr. -1-k). bds. 8.99 *(978-1-58925-569-2(0))* Tiger Tales.
Komai, Asuka. October Moon. 2009. (J). *(978-1-60108-017-2(4))* Red Cygnet Pr.
Komarck, Michael. Baby's Fraction Lunch. Hunt, Darleen L. 2003. (Sherman's Math Corner Ser.). (J). (gr. -1-3). *(978-1-929591-07-7(1))* Reading Rock, Inc.
—Bob's Busy Year: Months of the Year. Hunt, Darleen L. 2003. (Sherman's Math Corner Ser.). (J). (gr. -1-3). *(978-1-929591-03-9(9))* Reading Rock, Inc.
—Dad's Pancakes: Number Reduction. Hunt, Darleen L. 2003. (Sherman's Math Corner Ser.). (J). (gr. -1-3). *(978-1-929591-04-6(7))* Reading Rock, Inc.
—Dog & Cat Compare: Comparing Amounts. Hunt, Darleen L. 2003. (Sherman's Math Corner Ser.). (J). (gr. -1-3). *(978-1-929591-09-1(8))* Reading Rock, Inc.
—Dog's Dollars: Patterns. Hunt, Darleen L. 2003. (Sherman's Math Corner Ser.). (J). (gr. -1-3). *(978-1-929591-08-4(X))* Reading Rock, Inc.
—Ellen Elizabeth's Peanut Butter Jar: Counting. Hunt, Darleen L. 2003. (Sherman's Math Corner Ser.). (J). (gr. -1-3). *(978-1-929591-11-4(X))* Reading Rock, Inc.
—Harvey T. Crow Puts It All Together: Addition. Hunt, Darleen L. 2003. (Sherman's Math Corner Ser.). (J). (gr. -1-3). *(978-1-929591-02-2(0))* Reading Rock, Inc.
—Lyle & Mildred Are a Pair: Counting by 2's. Hunt, Darleen L. 2003. (Sherman's Math Corner Ser.). (J). (gr. -1-3). *(978-1-929591-00-8(4))* Reading Rock, Inc.
—Mr. Reed's Class Estimates: Estimating. Hunt, Darleen L. 2003. (Sherman's Math Corner Ser.). (J). (gr. -1-3). *(978-1-929591-06-0(3))* Reading Rock, Inc.
—Samanta Uses Patterns: Patterns. Hunt, Darleen L. 2003. (Sherman's Math Corner Ser.). (J). (gr. -1-3). *(978-1-929591-10-7(1))* Reading Rock, Inc.
—Samantha Visits Grandpa Geo: Shapes. Hunt, Darleen L. 2003. (Sherman's Math Corner Ser.). (J). (gr. -1-3). *(978-1-929591-01-5(2))* Reading Rock, Inc.
—Spider Inventories: Count & Record. Hunt, Darleen L. 2003. (Sherman's Math Corner Ser.). (J). (gr. -1-3). *(978-1-929591-05-3(5))* Reading Rock, Inc.
Komarudin. The Golden Feather: A Jataka Tale: A Story & Coloring Book. 2012. (CHI & ENG.). 30p. (J). *(978-1-60103-008-5(8))* Buddhist Text Translation Society.
Komedina, Tanya. Medieval Castle Sticker Book. Channing, Margot. ed. 2018. (Scribblers Fun Activity Ser.). 32p. (J). (gr. k-2). pap. 5.95 *(978-1-912537-17-4(6)*, Scribblers) Book Hse. GBR. Dist: Sterling Publishing Co., Inc.
Konak, Ipek. At the Hospital: Shine-A-light. Brown, Carron. 2018. (ENG.). 36p. (J). 12.99 *(978-1-61067-664-9(5))* Kane Miller.
Konatich, James. Twelve Treasures of the East: Legends & Folk Tales from Asia. Dutta-Yean, Tutu & Maire, Lucy Bedoya. Dutta-Yean, Tutu, ed. ed. 2005. (J). per. *(978-0-9768436-0-3(9)*, 20) Maire, Lucy Bedoya.
Kondeatis, Christos. Scenes from the Life of Jesus Christ: A Three-Dimensional Bible Storybook. Kondeatis, Christos. 2006. 10p. (J). (gr. k-4). reprint ed. 20.00 *(978-0-7567-9826-0(4))* DIANE Publishing Co.
Konecny, John. The Book Monster. Waisanen, Emily. 2012. 24p. pap. 8.99 *(978-1-937165-25-3(6))* Orange Hat Publishing.
—Dogs Don't Have Pockets. Raffaelli, Sean & Dreske, Erin. 2013. 24p. pap. 9.99 *(978-1-937165-55-0(8))* Orange Hat Publishing.
—Miller: The Mostly Misunderstood Mischief-Maker Who Went Missing. Thieme-Baeseman, Rebecca. 2012. 24p. pap. 9.99 *(978-1-937165-32-1(9))* Orange Hat Publishing.
—What If the Rain Were Bugs? Dewane, Patrick Ryan. 2013. 24p. 14.99 *(978-1-937165-39-0(6))* Orange Hat Publishing.
—Work Your Body Grow Your Brain. Boodey, Erin. 2012. 26p. 13.99 *(978-1-937165-23-9(X))* Orange Hat Publishing.
Konecny, John & Martin, Alliyah. STEM Adventures of Aleks & Lexi: Dylan the Butterfly. Martin Jung, Karen. 2016. (ENG.). (J). (gr. 2-6). pap. 12.95 *(978-1-943331-32-1(4))* Orange Hat Publishing.
Konewki, Ada. Danger Dad. Carter, Laura. 2019. (ENG.). 36p. (J). pap. *(978-0-9955109-2-0(X))* Wobbly Pr.
Kong, Benjamin. Hobo & the Frisbee. England, Daniel. England, Linh, ed. 2016. (ENG.). (J). pap. *(978-1-4602-8840-5(8))* FriesenPress.
Kong, Emilie. Halloween Is Here, Corduroy! Freeman, Don. 2007. (Corduroy Ser.). 16p. (J). (gr. -1-k). pap. 5.99 *(978-0-448-44563-2(8)*, Grosset & Dunlap) Penguin Young Readers Group.
Konicek-Moran, Kathleen. The Beaks of Birds. Konicek-Moran, Richard. 2019. (ENG.). 36p. (J). pap. 12.95 *(978-1-68140-352-6(8))* National Science Teachers Assn.
—From Flower to Fruit. Konicek-Moran, Richard. 2017. (ENG.). 30p. (J). (gr. k-2). pap. 11.95 *(978-1-941316-34-4(4))* National Science Teachers Assn.
Konietzko, Bryan & Gurihiru. Avatar: the Last Airbender - the Rift Part 2, Pt. 2. Yang, Gene Luen & DiMartino, Michael Dante. 2014. (Avatar: the Last Airbender Ser.). (ENG.). 80p. pap. 10.99 *(978-1-61655-296-1(4)*, Dark Horse Books) Dark Horse Comics.
Konigsburg, E. L. About the B'nai Bagels. Konigsburg, E. L. 2008. (ENG.). 208p. (J). (gr. 3-7). pap. 8.99 *(978-1-4169-5798-0(7)*, Atheneum Bks. for Young Readers) Simon & Schuster Children's Publishing.
—From the Mixed-Up Files of Mrs. Basil E. Frankweiler: Special Edition. Konigsburg, E. L. 2019. (ENG.). 176p. (J). (gr. 3-7). pap. 9.99 *(978-1-5344-3645-9(6)*, Atheneum Bks. for Young Readers) Simon & Schuster Children's Publishing.
—(george) Konigsburg, E. L. 2007. (ENG.). 192p. (J). (gr. 3-7). pap. 7.99 *(978-1-4169-4957-2(7)*, Atheneum Bks. for Young Readers) Simon & Schuster Children's Publishing.
Koniver, Laura. From the Ground Up. Koniver, Laura. 2012. 44p. (J). pap. 16.99 *(978-1-937848-03-3(5))* Do Life Right, Inc.
Könnecke, Ole. Anton Can Do Magic. Könnecke, Ole. Chidgey, Catherine. 2011. (Gecko Press Titles Ser.). (ENG.). 32p. 17.95 *(978-1-877467-37-0(5))* Gecko Pr. NZL. Dist: Lerner Publishing Group.
—The Big Book of Words & Pictures. Könnecke, Ole. 2012. (Gecko Press Titles Ser.). 22p. (J). (gr. -1-k). bds. 14.95 *(978-1-877579-05-9(X))* Gecko Pr. NZL. Dist: Lerner Publishing Group.
—The Big Book of Words & Pictures. Könnecke, Ole. 2017. (ENG.). 20p. (J). (gr. -1-k). bds. 14.99 *(978-1-77657-135-2(5))* Gecko Pr. NZL. Dist: Lerner Publishing Group.
—Sports Are Fantastic Fun! Könnecke, Ole. 2018. (ENG.). 56p. (J). (gr. -1-k). 19.99 *(978-1-77657-201-4(7))* Gecko Pr. NZL. Dist: Lerner Publishing Group.
Könnecke, Ole & Könnecke, Ole. The Big Book of Animals of the World. Könnecke, Ole & Könnecke, Ole. 2015. (ENG.). 20p. (J). (gr. -1-k). bds. 14.99 *(978-1-77657-012-6(X))* Gecko Pr. NZL. Dist: Lerner Publishing Group.
Könnecke, Ole, jt. illus. see Könnecke, Ole.
Kono, Erin Eitter. A Bit Is a Bite. Brimner, Larry Dane. 2007. (Rookie Reader Skill Set Ser.). (ENG.). 32p. (J). (gr. -1-3). pap. 4.95 *(978-0-531-17780-8(7)*, Children's Pr.) Scholastic Library Publishing.
—The Twelve Days of Christmas in Wisconsin. (Twelve Days of Christmas in America Ser.). (J). 2017. 22p. (-k). bds. 7.95 *(978-1-4549-2286-5(9))*; 2007. 40p. (gr. -1-3). 12.95 *(978-1-4027-3815-9(3))* Sterling Publishing Co., Inc.
Kono, Yara. El Camino. Satz, Mario. 2020. (SPA.). 40p. (J). (gr. 2-4). pap. 17.95 *(978-84-17440-26-8(7))* Akiara Bks. ESP. Dist: Independent Pubs. Group.
—Three Balls of Wool. Cristina, Henriqueta. Miller-Lachmann, Lyn, tr. 2017. 32p. (J). (gr. -1-4). 16.95 *(978-1-59270-220-6(1))* Enchanted Lion Bks., LLC.
Konola, Hanna. Art Masterclass with Claude Monet. Cotton, Katie. 2019. (Art Masterclass Ser.). (ENG.). 32p. (J). (gr. k-2). pap. 14.99 ***(978-1-78603-797-8(1)***, Wide Eyed Editions) Quarto Publishing Group UK GBR. Dist: Hachette Bk. Group.
Konopasek, Emily. 1, 2, 3 with Nephi & Me! Doxey, Heidi. 2015. 9.99 *(978-1-4621-1636-2(1)*, Horizon Pubs.) Cedar Fort, Inc./CFI Distribution.
Konopka, Jan. Alex & the Archangel. Williams, Rachel. 2005. (ENG.). 56p. pap. *(978-1-84401-614-3(5))* Athena Pr.
Konrad, Checinski. La Scarpetta Segreta Di Cenerentola / Cinderella's Secret Slipper: Bilingual Italian-English Edition. Alinka, Rutkowska. 2015. (ITA.). 38p. (J). 23.95 *(978-0-9831547-8-5(3))* Leaders Pr.
Konstantinov, Vitali. Loyola Kids Book of Heroes: Stories of Catholic Heroes & Saints Throughout History. Welborn, Amy. 2003. (ENG.). 208p. (J). (gr. 3-7). 17.95 *(978-0-8294-1584-1(X))* Loyola Pr.
Konye, Paul. Rosie & the Audition. Rushby, Pamela. 2009. 24p. pap. 10.67 *(978-1-4190-5524-9(0))* Rigby Education.
—Rosie Goes Home. Rushby, Pamela. 2009. (Rigby PM Stars Bridge Bks.). (ENG.). 24p. (gr. 2-3). pap. 8.25 *(978-1-4190-5529-4(1))* Rigby Education.
—Zap! Fab Things to Draw. Ashforth, Kate. 2014. (ENG.). (J). (gr. 4-7). pap. *(978-1-74363-385-4(8))* Hinkler Bks. Pty, Ltd.
Koo, Rob. Great Buddhist Stories. 2011. 32p. (J). pap. *(978-1-935523-22-2(8))* World Tribune Pr.
—More Great Buddhist Stories. 2012. (J). pap. *(978-1-935523-48-2(1))* World Tribune Pr.
Kooistra, Alex. Yoga Games for Children: Fun & Fitness with Postures, Movements & Breath. Bersma, Danielle & Visscher, Marjoke. 2003. (SmartFun Activity Bks.). (ENG.). 160p. (J). pap. 17.99 *(978-0-89793-389-6(3)*, Hunter Hse.) Turner Publishing Co.
Kook, Seol-Hui. Where Are You From? Oviparous/Viviparous Animals. Kim, In-Sook. 2017. (Science Storybooks Ser.). (ENG.). 32p. (J). (gr. k-4). lib. bdg. 27.99 *(978-1-925235-15-9(7)*, Big and SMALL) ChoiceMaker Pty. Ltd., The AUS. Dist: Lerner Publishing Group.
Koon, Cheng Puay. I Saved Two Tigers with a Really Magical Idea. Humphreys, Neil. 2018. (ENG.). 32p. pap. 9.90 *(978-981-4771-75-7(9))* Marshall Cavendish International (Asia) Private Ltd. SGP. Dist: National Bk. Network.
—Telling the Otters to Leave Home Was a Really Big Mistake. Humphreys, Neil. 2019. (ENG.). 32p. (J). (gr. -1-3). pap. 9.99 *(978-981-4828-76-5(9))* Marshall Cavendish International (Asia) Private Ltd. SGP. Dist: National Bk. Network.
Koon-chiu, Lo. Favorite Children's Stories from China & Tibet: (Chinese & Tibetan Fairy Tales) Hume, Lotta Carswell. 2018. 112p. (J). (gr. k-8). 9.99 *(978-0-8048-5018-6(6))* Tuttle Publishing.
Koontz, Piper & Koontz, Sharon. The Camp Creature. Buffington, Dianne. 2018. (ENG.). 32p. (J). pap. 16.95 *(978-1-9736-1784-6(6)*, WestBow Pr.) Author Solutions, Inc.
Koontz, Robin. Cinderella Zelda. Koontz, Robin. ed. 2011. (Little Birdie Readers Ser.). (ENG.). 24p. (gr. 2-3). pap. 8.95 *(978-1-61236-027-0(0)*, 9781612360270) Rourke Educational Media.
—Paul Bunyan. Koontz, Robin. 2012. (Little Birdie Bks.). (ENG.). 24p. (gr. 2-3). pap. 8.95 *(978-1-61810-326-0(1)*, 9781618103260) Rourke Educational Media.
—The Three Billy Goats & Gruff. Koontz, Robin. ed. 2011. (Little Birdie Readers Ser.). (ENG.). 24p. (gr. 2-3). pap. 8.95 *(978-1-61236-030-0(0)*, 9781612360300) Rourke Educational Media.
Koontz, Robin Michal. It Takes Three. Hayward, Linda. 2003. (Silly Millies Ser.: 3). 32p. (J). (gr. 1-3). pap. 5.95 *(978-0-7613-1798-2(8))*; lib. bdg. 17.90 *(978-0-7613-2902-2(1)*, Millbrook Pr.) Lerner Publishing Group.
—Whales: Read Well Level K Unit 18 Storybook. Dunn, Richard & Sprick, Jessica. 2003. (Read Well Level K Ser.). 20p. (J). *(978-1-57035-689-6(0)*, 55589) Cambium Education, Inc.
Koontz, Robin Michal. The King's New Clothes. Koontz, Robin Michal. ed. 2011. (Little Birdie Readers Ser.). (ENG.). 24p. (gr. 2-3). pap. 8.95 *(978-1-61236-028-7(9)*, 9781612360287) Rourke Educational Media.
—Lizzie Little, the Sky Is Falling! Koontz, Robin Michal. ed. 2011. (Little Birdie Readers Ser.). (ENG.). 24p. (gr. 2-3). pap. 8.95 *(978-1-61236-029-4(7)*, 9781612360294) Rourke Educational Media.
—Robin Hood. Koontz, Robin Michal. 2012. (Little Birdie Bks.). (ENG.). 24p. (gr. 2-3). pap. 8.95 *(978-1-61810-325-3(3)*, 9781618103253) Rourke Educational Media.
Koontz, Sharon, jt. illus. see Koontz, Piper.
Koopman, Caia. Umijoo: The Wondrous Tale of a Curious Girl & Her Journey under the Sea. Trenor, Casson. 2019. (ENG.). 66p. (J). (gr. 1-3). 24.95 *(978-1-7328605-0-6(5))* Shark & Siren Pr.

K

Koopmans, Loek. The Magical Wishing Fish: The Classic Grimm's Tale of the Fisherman & His Wife, 30 vols. Grimm, Jacob and Wilhelm. 2018. Orig. Title: Het Wensvisje. (ENG.). 24p. (J). 16.95 *(978-1-78250-524-2(5))* Floris Bks. GBR. Dist: Consortium Bk. Sales & Distribution.

Koopmans, Loek. Stella & the Berry Thief, 1 vol. Koopmans, Loek, tr. Mason, Jane B. 2004. (ENG.). 32p. (J). 16.95 *(978-0-7614-5123-5(4))* Marshall Cavendish Corp.

Koorang, Mundara. Little Platypus & the Fire Spirit. Koorang, Mundara. 2nd ed. 2011. (ENG.). 32p. (J). (gr. -1-k). pap. 17.95 *(978-0-85575-701-4(9))* Aboriginal Studies Pr. AUS. Dist: Independent Pubs. Group.

Kopald, Sue-Anne. Hey, Look at Me! Baby Days. Thomasson, Merry F. (Hey, Look at Me! Ser.). (J). *(978-1-882607-06-8(6))* Merrybooks & More.

Kopelke, Lisa. Super Oscar. De La Hoya, Oscar. Montejo, Andrea, tr. 2012. (SPA & ENG.). 32p. (J). (gr. -1-3). 7.99 *(978-1-4169-0612-4(6),* Simon & Schuster Bks. For Young Readers) Simon & Schuster Bks. For Young Readers.

Kopelke, Lisa. The Younger Brother's Survival Guide. Kopelke, Lisa. 2006. (ENG.). 32p. (J). (gr. -1-3). 17.99 *(978-0-689-86249-6(0),* Simon & Schuster Bks. For Young Readers) Simon & Schuster Bks. For Young Readers.

Kopervas, Gary & Hanes, Don. AbuLLard's ABC's of Branding: 26 Concepts That Capture the Essence of Good Brand Management. Wilcox, Jean K. & Cameron, E. Jane. unabr. ed. 2003. 64p. 19.95 *(978-0-9745612-0-2(7),* CPN-BMS-001) CattLeLogos Brand Management Systems.

Kopler, Joe. Lennie's Pennies. Garrett, Kelsey. 2012. (ENG.). 64p. pap. 19.95 *(978-1-4327-9606-8(2))* Outskirts Pr., Inc.

Kopp, Jenny. Cocoa's New Family: An Adoption Story. Reinhart, Tracie & Delcoglin, Gwendolyn. 2019. (ENG.). 48p. (J). pap. 13.99 *(978-1-0911-7447-4(4))* Independently Published.

Koppel, Shana. Dr. Mom's Super Duper Cookbook of Science You Can Eat: Molecular Gastronomy for Kids. Mom. 2019. (ENG.). 32p. (J). (gr. 1-6). pap. *(978-965-7043-00-4(X))* StellarNova.

—La Pequeña Nave Espacial. Mom. 2019. (SPA.). 26p. (J). (gr. k-6). pap. *(978-965-7043-02-8(6))* StellarNova.

—Stellarnova & the Jet Car. Mom. 2017. (ENG.). 132p. (J). (gr. 3-5). pap. *(978-965-92628-0-9(9))* StellarNova.

—StellarNova & the Mag Lev. Mom. 2018. (ENG.). 116p. (J). (gr. 3-5). pap. *(978-965-92628-4-7(1))* StellarNova.

Kopper, Lisa. Stories from the Ballet. Kopper, Lisa, tr. Greaves, Margaret. 2003. (ENG.). 72p. (J). pap. *(978-0-7112-2162-8(6))* ReiseArt Buchhandlung GmbH.

Kor, Paul. The Hawk & the Dove. Kor, Paul. 2019. (ENG.). 32p. (J). (gr. -1-3). 16.99 *(978-1-5253-0125-4(X))* Kids Can Pr., Ltd. CAN. Dist: Hachette Bk. Group.

Koraljka. The Puppy Who Wouldn't Share. Horan-Gross, Pia. 2018. (ENG.). 28p. (J). pap. *(978-0-6480135-4-9(5))* Thorpe-Bowker.

Korchemkina, Tatyana. My First Words: 15 CLEVER Mini-Books Box Set. Clever Publishing. 2019. (Clever Mini Board Bks.). (ENG.). 90p. (J). (gr. -1 — 1). bds. 24.99 *(978-1-948418-50-8(9))* Clever Media Group.

Korda, Lerryn. Into the Wild. Korda, Lerryn. 2010. (Playtime with Little Nye Ser.). (ENG.). 26p. (J). (gr. -1 — 1). 8.99 *(978-0-7636-4812-1(4))* Candlewick Pr.

—It's Vacation Time. Korda, Lerryn. 2010. (Playtime with Little Nye Ser.). (ENG.). 26p. (J). (— 1). 8.99 *(978-0-7636-4813-8(2))* Candlewick Pr.

—Millions of Snow. Korda, Lerryn. 2010. (Playtime with Little Nye Ser.). (ENG.). 32p. (J). (— 1). 8.99 *(978-0-7636-4651-6(2))* Candlewick Pr.

—So Cozy. Korda, Lerryn. 2015. (ENG.). 32p. (J). (— 1). 15.99 *(978-0-7636-7373-4(0))* Candlewick Pr.

Kordey, Igor. Soldier X. Macan, Darko. 2003. 144p. (YA). pap. 12.99 *(978-0-7851-1013-2(5))* Marvel Worldwide, Inc.

Kordich, Melinda. Bella-Blue Butterfly's Purple Surprise. Baumann, Jessica. 2013. 30p. pap. 9.99 *(978-1-937165-38-3(8))* Orange Hat Publishing.

Koren, Edward. Oops! Katz, Alan. 2008. (ENG.). 176p. (J). (gr. 2-5). 19.99 *(978-1-4169-0204-1(X),* McElderry, Margaret K. Bks.) McElderry, Margaret K. Bks.

—Poems I Wrote When No One Was Looking. Katz, Alan. 2011. (ENG.). 160p. (J). (gr. 2-5). 17.99 *(978-1-4169-3518-6(5),* McElderry, Margaret K. Bks.) McElderry, Margaret K. Bks.

Koren, Edward. Very Hairy Harry. Koren, Edward. 2003. *(978-0-06-057744-5(4));* (J). *(978-0-06-056868-9(2))* HarperCollins Pubs.

Koretz, Maria. Bozo Goes to Paris. Koretz, Maria. 2019. (Bozo Travels the World Ser.). (ENG.). 44p. (J). 19.99 ***(978-1-64713-187-6(1))*** Primedia eLaunch LLC.

Koretz, Maria M. Bozo Goes to Madagascar. Koretz, Maria M. 2020. (ENG.). 42p. (J). 19.99 ***(978-1-64945-748-6(0))*** Primedia eLaunch LLC.

—Bozo Goes to New Zealand. Koretz, Maria M. 2020. (Bozo Travels the World Ser.: Vol. 2). (ENG.). 42p. (J). 19.95 ***(978-1-64826-280-7(5))*** Primedia eLaunch LLC.

Korey, Woods. The Adventures of Mr. Bramble Bones: A Christmas to Remember. Bowden, M. Deborah. 2019. (Adventures of Mr. Bramble Bones Ser.: Vol. 5). (ENG.). 52p. (J). 21.99 ***(978-1-951263-07-2(3))*** Pen It! Pubns., LLC.

—Octavia & the Bug Problem. Maynard, Jeri Fay. 2020. (ENG.). 70p. (J). 25.99 ***(978-1-952011-71-9(X))*** Pen It! Pubns., LLC.

Korkin, Vladimir. Kniga Dlia Detskogo Sada. 2016. (RUS.). 128p. (J). *(978-5-353-06746-7(0))* RosmYn-Press, Izdatel'stvo.

Korkos, Alain. Be Your Own Rock & Mineral Expert. Pinet, Michele. Greenbaum, Fay, tr. from FRE. 2003. 40p. (J). (gr. 5-7). 14.95 *(978-0-8069-9580-9(7))* Sterling Publishing Co., Inc.

Korman, Justine. The Poky Little Puppy's First Christmas. Korman, Justine. 2014. 26p. (J). (-k). bds. 7.99 *(978-0-385-38473-5(4),* Golden Bks.) Random Hse. Children's Bks.

Kornacki, Christine. Marie-Grace & the Orphans, 3. Buckey, Sarah. 2011. (American Girl Mysteries Ser.). (ENG.). 104p. (J). (gr. 2-4). pap. 21.19 *(978-1-59369-654-2(X))* American Girl Publishing, Inc.

—The Sparkle Box. Hardie, Jill. 2018. 32p. (gr. -1-2). pap. 9.99 *(978-0-8249-5693-6(1))* Worthy Publishing.

Kornilov, Onga. The Adventures of Pretzel Bo. Phinizy. 2019. (ENG.). 70p. (J). pap. 22.99 *(978-1-7327547-2-0(1))* Pureheart UnLtd. media.

Kornmaneeroj, T., et al. The Lost Jewels of Nabooti. Montgomery, R. A. 2006. (Choose Your Own Adventure Ser.: No. 4). (ENG.). 144p. (J). (gr. 4-8). per. 6.99 *(978-1-933390-04-8(2),* CHCL04) Chooseco LLC.

Korobkina, Katya. Green Smoothie Magic. Boutenko, Victoria. 2013. 56p. (J). (gr. -1-3). 12.95 *(978-1-58394-601-5(2))* North Atlantic Bks.

Korolev, Nick. Sandy the Seagull, the Surfers & the Kites. Scott, Gini Graham. 2018. (Sandy the Seagull Ser.: 1). (ENG.). 44p. (J). (gr. k-3). pap. 14.95 *(978-1-943789-89-4(4))* Taylor and Seale Publishing.

Korrow, Chris. The Organic Bug Book, 1 vol. Korrow, Chris. 2013. (ENG.). 44p. (J). pap. 11.95 *(978-1-58420-145-8(2),* Lindisfarne Bks.) SteinerBooks, Inc.

Korthues, Barbara. Loopy. Jesset, Aurore. 2008. (ENG.). 32p. (J). (gr. -1-3). 16.95 *(978-0-7358-2175-0(5))* North-South Bks., Inc.

Korthues, Barbara, jt. illus. see Jesset, Aurore.

Kosaka, Fumi. Be Mine, Be Mine, Sweet Valentine. Weeks, Sarah. 2005. (ENG.). 20p. (J). (gr. -1-k). 9.99 *(978-0-694-01514-6(8),* HarperFestival) HarperCollins Pubs.

—If You'll Be My Valentine. Rylant, Cynthia. 2005. (ENG.). 32p. (J). (gr. -1-3). pap. 7.99 *(978-0-06-009271-9(8))* HarperCollins Pubs.

—Ordinary Mary's Extraordinary Deed, 1 vol. Pearson, Emily. 2017. 32p. (J). 7.99 *(978-1-4236-4887-1(0))* Gibbs Smith, Publisher.

—Ordinary Mary's Positively Extraordinary Day, 1 vol. Pearson, Emily. 2019. (ENG.). 32p. (J). (gr. 2-6). 16.99 *(978-1-4236-5181-9(2));* 8.99 *(978-1-4236-5345-5(9))* Gibbs Smith, Publisher.

Koschak, Brian. The Clone Wars: Destiny of Heroes. Gilroy, Henry. 2011. (Star Wars: Clone Wars Ser.: No. 2). (ENG.). 24p. (J). (gr. 6-12). 27.07 *(978-1-59961-843-2(5),* 13803, Graphic Novels) Spotlight.

—Hero of the Confederacy, Vol. 1. Gilroy, Henry. 2011. (Star Wars: Clone Wars Ser.: No. 2). (ENG.). 24p. (J). (gr. 6-12). 27.07 *(978-1-59961-841-8(9),* 13801, Graphic Novels) Spotlight.

—Hero of the Confederacy: A Hero Rises. Gilroy, Henry. 2011. (Star Wars: Clone Wars Ser.: No. 2). (ENG.). 24p. (J). (gr. 6-12). 27.07 *(978-1-59961-842-5(7),* 13802, Graphic Novels) Spotlight.

Kosec, Polona & Calderón, Marcela. The Mountain Jews & the Mirror, Vol. Feuerman, Ruchama King. 2015. (ENG.). 32p. (J). (gr. k-4). 7.99 *(978-1-4677-3896-5(4),* 9781467738965, Kar-Ben Publishing) Lerner Publishing Group.

Koshiba, Tetsuya. Remote, 3 vols., Vol. 1. Amagi, Seimaru. 2004. 192p. pap. 14.99 *(978-1-59182-740-5(X),* Tokyopop Adult) TOKYOPOP, Inc.

—Remote. rev. ed. 2005. Vol. 5. 216p. pap. 14.99 *(978-1-59532-032-2(6));* Vol. 6. 192p. pap. 14.99 *(978-1-59532-033-9(4))* TOKYOPOP, Inc. (Tokyopop Adult).

—Remote, Vol. 7. Amagi, Seimaru. 7th rev. ed. 2005. (Remote Ser.). 190p. (YA). per. 14.99 *(978-1-59532-810-6(6),* Tokyopop Adult) TOKYOPOP, Inc.

Kosinski, Colleen Rowan. Lilla's Sunflowers. 2016. 32p. (J). (gr. -1-k). 16.99 *(978-1-5107-0464-0(7),* Sky Pony Pr.) Skyhorse Publishing Co., Inc.

Kosir, Ana. The Pirate Kitty. Glover, Darryl. Austin, Britta, ed. 2008. 24p. (J). 16.95 *(978-0-9821387-0-0(9))* MagicStar Inc.

Kosits, Andrew. Tea Party at Chestertown. Maxson, H. A. & Young, Claudia H. 2003. (Magical History Tours Ser.). 55p. (J). per. 8.95 *(978-0-9741713-0-2(1))* Bay Oak Pubs., Ltd.

Kostecke, Nancy, jt. illus. see Fenton, Mary Frances.

Kostecki-Shaw, Jenny Sue. Luna & Me: The True Story of a Girl Who Lived in a Tree to Save a Forest. Kostecki-Shaw, Jenny Sue. 2015. (ENG.). 40p. (J). (gr. k-4). 18.99 *(978-0-8050-9976-8(X),* 900128928, Holt, Henry & Co. Bks. For Young Readers) Holt, Henry & Co.

—Papa Brings Me the World. Kostecki-Shaw, Jenny Sue. 2020. (ENG.). 40p. (J). 18.99 *(978-1-250-15925-0(3),* 900185620, Holt, Henry & Co. Bks. For Young Readers) Holt, Henry & Co.

—Same, Same but Different. Kostecki-Shaw, Jenny Sue. 2011. (ENG.). 40p. (J). (gr. -1-2). 18.99 *(978-0-8050-8946-2(2),* 900055610, Holt, Henry & Co. Bks. For Young Readers) Holt, Henry & Co.

Kostelyk, Jason. Bubba: A True Story about an Amazing Alligator. Nesci, Andrea Lynn & Nesci, Jim. l.t. ed. 2003. 24p. (J). pap. 12.50 *(978-0-9713197-6-9(6))* ECO Herpetological Pub. & Dist.

Kostenko, Max. Endling #2: the First. Applegate, Katherine. (Endling Ser.: 2). (ENG.). (J). (gr. 3-7). 2020. 416p. pap. 7.99 *(978-0-06-233557-9(X));* 2019. 400p. 17.99 *(978-0-06-233556-2(1))* HarperCollins Pubs. Ltd. GBR. (HarperCollins). Dist: HarperCollins Pubs.

Koster, Sonja. Perky Emigrates: The Adventures of Perky the Tortoise. Simmonds, Janet. 2018. (ENG.). 52p. (J). (gr. k-3). pap. *(978-0-9959554-0-0(9))* Simmonds, Janet.

Kostic, Dimitri. Fight for Rights. Winter, Barbara. 2007. 48p. (J). lib. bdg. 23.08 *(978-1-4242-1636-9(2))* Fitzgerald Bks.

Kostov, Pavel. Fascinating Facts for the Whole Family: Trivia about Human Body & Cute Animals (Cats, Dogs, Pandas, Horses & Pigs) Kostov, Nayden. Tabet, Jonathon, ed. 2017. (ENG.). 134p. (J). pap. *(978-99959-980-5-9(X))* Kostov, Nayden.

Koszowski, Allen, jt. illus. see Clark, Alan M.

Kosztelnik, Caroline. Rat-Catcher. Collins, Amanda. Hoekema, Sharai, ed. 2018. (Blade of the Capulets Ser.: Vol. 1). (ENG.). 242p. (J). pap. *(978-94-92375-17-9(6))* Fanflicks.

Kote, Geneviève. Cheers for Gymnastics. Meister, Cari. 2020. (Kids' Sports Stories Ser.). (ENG.). 32p. (J). (gr. k-2). pap. 5.95 *(978-1-5158-5877-5(4),* 142133); lib. bdg. 21.32 *(978-1-5158-4804-2(3),* 141419) Capstone. (Picture Window Bks.).

Kote, Genevieve. Friends, Fugues, & Fortune Cookies. Schusterman, Michelle. 2014. (I Heart Band Ser.: 2). 208p. (J). (gr. 3-7). 6.99 *(978-0-448-45684-3(2),* Grosset & Dunlap) Penguin Young Readers Group.

Kote, Geneviève. Soccer Dreams. Pryor, Shawn. 2020. (Kids' Sports Stories Ser.). (ENG.). 32p. (J). (gr. k-2). pap. 5.95 *(978-1-5158-5879-9(0),* 142135); lib. bdg. 21.32 *(978-1-5158-4808-0(6),* 141421) Capstone. (Picture Window Bks.).

Kote, Geneviève, jt. illus. see Erb, Amanda.

Koth, Brett. Best of Looney Tunes, Vol. 1. Kim, Chuck & Alvarez, Richard. 2016. (ENG.). 144p. (J). (gr. 4-7). pap. 12.99 *(978-1-4012-6359-1(3))* DC Comics.

Koth, Mona. Animals. Koth, Mona. Scott, Vicki. Cottage Door Press, ed. 2019. (Panda Panda Board Bks.). (ENG.). 24p. (J). (gr. -1-k). bds. 7.99 *(978-1-68052-770-4(3),* 1004800) Cottage Door Pr.

—Faces. Koth, Mona. Scott, Vicki. Cottage Door Press, ed. 2019. (Panda Panda Board Bks.). (ENG.). 24p. (J). (gr. -1-k). bds. 7.99 *(978-1-68052-771-1(1),* 1004810) Cottage Door Pr.

—Feelings. Koth, Mona. Scott, Vicki. Cottage Door Press, ed. 2019. (Panda Panda Board Bks.). (ENG.). 24p. (J). (gr. -1-k). bds. 7.99 *(978-1-68052-772-8(X),* 1004820) Cottage Door Pr.

—Love. Koth, Mona. Scott, Vicki. Cottage Door Press, ed. 2019. (Panda Panda Board Bks.). (ENG.). 24p. (J). (gr. -1-k). bds. 7.99 *(978-1-68052-769-8(X),* 1004790) Cottage Door Pr.

Kotick, Jennifer. Just for One Day. Hunter, B. J. Cottage, James P., ed. 2018. (ENG.). 34p. (J). pap. 12.99 *(978-1-7313-5344-3(8))* Independently Published.

Kotler, Arkady & Kotler, Elina. Seder in Herlin: And Other Stories. Kranzler, Gershon. 2003. 108p. (gr. 5-9). reprint ed. 13.95 *(978-0-8266-0343-2(2))* Merkos L'Inyonei Chinuch.

Kotler, Elina, jt. illus. see Kotler, Arkady.

Kotoyoshi, Yumisuke. Saber Marionette J, 3 vols., Vol. 2. Akahori, Satoru. 2nd rev. ed. 2003. 192p. 9.99 *(978-1-59182-387-2(0))* TOKYOPOP, Inc.

—Saber Marionette J, 3 vols., Vol. 3. Akahori, Satoru. Fukami, Yuko, tr. from JPN. rev. ed. 2003. 192p. 9.99 *(978-1-59182-388-9(9))* TOKYOPOP, Inc.

—Saber Marionette J, 5 vols. Akahori, Satoru. 2004. Vol. 4. 4th rev. ed. 168p. 9.99 *(978-1-59182-539-5(3));* Vol. 5. rev. ed. 208p. 9.99 *(978-1-59182-540-1(7))* TOKYOPOP, Inc.

Kotrous, Chad. Jayhawk Adventures, a Day at the Zoo. Goode, Teresa. 2006. 29p. (J). (gr. 1-3). pap. 5.95 *(978-0-9646898-5-5(5))* Leathers Publishing.

—Jayhawk Adventures, Jed's Birthday Surprise. Goode, Teresa. 2006. 27p. (J). (gr. 1-3). pap. 5.95 *(978-0-9646898-6-2(3))* Leathers Publishing.

—Wildcat Adventures: A Vacation in the Big Apple. Goode, Teresa. 2006. 31p. (J). pap. 5.95 *(978-1-890622-13-8(3))* Leathers Publishing.

Kouga, Yun. Earthian. Kouga, Yun. 2005. (Earthian Ser.). 408p. (YA). per. 14.99 *(978-1-59816-006-2(0),* TOKYOPOP Manga) TOKYOPOP, Inc.

—Loveless, 5 vols. Kouga, Yun. 2006. (Loveless (Tokyopop) Ser.: Vol. 1). 200p. pap. 9.99 *(978-1-59816-221-9(7))* TOKYOPOP, Inc.

Koultourides, Ariana. Bed Tales (Big Kid Books) Waisberg, Brigitte. 2018. (Big Kid Bks.: 3). (ENG.). 20p. (J). (gr. -1). bds. 7.99 *(978-1-55451-991-0(8))* Annick Pr., Ltd. CAN. Dist: Publishers Group West (PGW).

—Shirt Tales (Big Kid Books) Waisberg, Brigitte. 2018. (Big Kid Bks.: 2). (ENG.). 20p. (J). (gr. -1). bds. 7.99 *(978-1-55451-989-7(6))* Annick Pr., Ltd. CAN. Dist: Publishers Group West (PGW).

—Toilet Tales (Big Kid Books) Waisberg, Brigitte & von Königslöw, Andrea Wayne. 2018. (Big Kid Bks.: 1). (ENG.). 20p. (J). (gr. -1). bds. 7.99 *(978-1-55451-987-3(X))* Annick Pr., Ltd. CAN. Dist: Publishers Group West (PGW).

Koutsis, Nikos. Stretch Armstrong & the Flex Fighters. Wyatt, Chris & Burke, Kevin. 2018. (Stretch Armstrong Ser.). 80p. (J). (gr. 5-9). pap. 9.99 *(978-1-68405-250-9(5))* Idea & Design Works, LLC.

Kovaks, Tibor. Dahlia & the Angel. Blom, Tracy. 2018. (ENG.). 24p. (J). 16.00 *(978-0-9906871-2-2(0))* Blom Pubns.

Kovalcik, Terry. Cats! Cats! Cats!, 2. Evans, Mary. l.t. ed. 2005. (Sadlier Phonics Reading Program). 8p. (gr. -1-1). 23.00 net. *(978-0-8215-7348-8(9))* Sadlier, William H. Inc.

Kovalski, Maryann. Omar on Board, 1 vol. Kovalski, Maryann. 2005. (ENG.). 1p. (J). (gr. k-2). 9.95 *(978-1-55041-918-4(8),* 7d9c1192-3556-42ca-98d3-6d2aa997bf2f) Trifolium Bks., Inc. CAN. Dist: Firefly Bks., Ltd.

Kovar, Ben. Dark Tower Rising, 1 vol. Dahl, Michael. 2012. (Troll Hunters Ser.). (ENG.). 112p. (J). (gr. 5-9). lib. bdg. 25.32 *(978-1-4342-3308-0(1),* Stone Arch Bks.) Capstone.

—Fallen Star, 1 vol. Dahl, Michael. 2012. (Troll Hunters Ser.). (ENG.). 112p. (J). (gr. 5-9). lib. bdg. 25.32 *(978-1-4342-3310-3(3),* Stone Arch Bks.) Capstone.

—The Lava Crown, 1 vol. Dahl, Michael. 2012. (Troll Hunters Ser.). (ENG.). 112p. (J). (gr. 5-9). lib. bdg. 25.32 *(978-1-4342-3309-7(X),* Stone Arch Bks.) Capstone.

—Skyfall, 1 vol. Dahl, Michael. 2012. (Troll Hunters Ser.). (ENG.). 112p. (J). (gr. 5-9). lib. bdg. 25.32 *(978-1-4342-3307-3(3),* Stone Arch Bks.) Capstone.

—Troll Hunters, 1 vol. Dahl, Michael. 2012. (Troll Hunters Ser.). (ENG.). 320p. (J). (gr. 4-6). 12.95 *(978-1-4342-4590-8(X),* Stone Arch Bks.) Capstone.

Kove, Torill. John Jensen Feels Different. Hovland, Henrik & Bartlett, Don. 2011. (ENG.). 40p. (J). 16.00 *(978-0-8028-5399-8(4),* Eerdmans Bks For Young Readers) Eerdmans, William B. Publishing Co.

—Threads. 2018. (ENG.). 32p. (J). (gr. 2-6). 19.95 *(978-0-2281-0081-2(X),* 86c0cd34-0293-4512-8c77-e09165c64133) Firefly Bks., Ltd.

Kovinka, Maryna. James & the Sandals of Peace. Joseph, Terrica. 2018. (ENG.). 36p. (J). (gr. k-4). pap. 9.99 *(978-1-970016-35-2(3))* Fruit Springs, LLC.

—James & the Shield of Faith. Joseph, Terrica. 2018. (ENG.). 34p. (J). (gr. 1-4). 14.99 *(978-1-970016-36-9(1))* Fruit Springs, LLC.

—James & the Sword of the Spirit. Joseph, Terrica. 2018. (Armor of God Ser.: Vol. 2). (ENG.). 34p. (J). (gr. 2-3). 15.99 *(978-1-970016-38-3(8))* Fruit Springs, LLC.

—Joel: The Amazing Fisher of Men. Harrison, Gloria M. 2018. (ENG.). 36p. (J). pap. 9.99 *(978-1-949185-01-0(X))* Harrison, Gloria M.

Kowalchuk, Scott. Down Set Fight. Sims, Chris & Bowers, Chad. 2014. (ENG.). 144p. pap. 19.99 *(978-1-62010-116-2(5),* 9781620101162, Lion Forge) Oni Pr., Inc.

Kowalczyk, Abigail. Funny Boy: The Lost Keys. Ivankovich, Viktor. 2019. (Funny Boy Ser.: Vol. 1). (ENG.). 48p. (J). pap. 11.99 ***(978-1-6774-5979-7(4))*** Independently Published.

Kowitt, Holly. The Loser List. 2011. 213p. (J). pap. *(978-0-545-32900-2(0),* Scholastic Pr.) Scholastic, Inc.

—Revenge of the Loser. 2012. 233p. (J). *(978-0-545-42611-4(1),* Scholastic Pr.) Scholastic, Inc.

Kowitt, Holly. This Dance Is Doomed. Kowitt, Holly. 2020. (ENG.). 224p. (J). 16.99 *(978-1-250-09135-2(7),* 900159371) Feiwel & Friends.

Koyose, Junji. Who Made This Cake? Nakagawa, Chihiro. 2008. (ENG.). 32p. (J). (gr. k-2). 17.95 *(978-1-59078-595-9(9))* Boyds Mills Pr.

Koz, Paula. In the Company of Owls. Huggins, Peter. 2008. (ENG.). 96p. (J). 15.95 *(978-1-58838-036-4(X),* NewSouth Bks.) NewSouth, Inc.

—Shlemiel Crooks. Olswanger, Anna. 2009. (ENG.). 36p. (J). pap. 11.95 *(978-1-58838-236-8(2),* NewSouth Bks.) NewSouth, Inc.

Koz, Paula Goodman. Shlemiel Crooks. Olswanger, Anna. 2005. 36p. (J). (gr. 2-4). 15.95 *(978-1-58838-165-1(X))* NewSouth, Inc.

Kozak, Maria. Darling Daughter: What Will You Be? Marrero-Martinez, Gloria. 2006. (ENG.). 44p. per. 26.90 *(978-1-4259-4235-9(0))* AuthorHouse.

Koziara, Colleen. Thirteen Silver Moons. Koziara, Colleen. 2004. (J). per. *(978-0-9763205-0-0(9))* Mystical Willow Productions.

Kozjan, Drazen. Julia Gillian - And the Art of Knowing. Mcghee, Alison. 2009. (Julia Gillian Ser.). (ENG.). 304p. (J). (gr. 3-7). 6.99 *(978-0-545-03349-7(7),* Scholastic Paperbacks) Scholastic, Inc.

—Oh, How Sylvester Can Pester! And Other Poems More or Less about Manners. Kinerk, Robert. 2011. (ENG.). 32p. (J). (gr. -1-3). 16.99 *(978-1-4169-3362-5(X),* Simon & Schuster/Paula Wiseman Bks.) Simon & Schuster/Paula Wiseman Bks.

—Revolutionary Friends: General George Washington & the Marquis de Lafayette. Castrovilla, Selene. 2013. (ENG.). 40p. (J). (gr. 3-7). 16.99 *(978-1-59078-880-6(X),* Calkins Creek) Boyds Mills Pr.

Kozlowski, Tomasz. The Beast in My Belly. Kasdepke, Grzegorz. 2015. (ENG.). 48p. (J). (gr. k-4). 16.95 *(978-1-59270-160-5(4))* Enchanted Lion Bks., LLC.

Kraegel, Kenneth. Green Pants. Kraegel, Kenneth. 40p. (J). (gr. -1-2). 2020. 7.99 *(978-1-5362-0288-5(6));* 2017. 15.99 *(978-0-7636-8840-0(1))* Candlewick Pr.

—King Arthur's Very Great Grandson. Kraegel, Kenneth. 2012. 40p. (J). (gr. k-3). 16.99 *(978-0-7636-5311-8(X))* Candlewick Pr.

—The Song of Delphine. Kraegel, Kenneth. 2015. 40p. (J). (gr. k-3). 15.99 *(978-0-7636-7001-6(4))* Candlewick Pr.

Kraegel, Kenneth. This Is a Book of Shapes. Kraegel, Kenneth. 2020. (ENG.). 30p. (J). (-k). bds. 8.99 ***(978-1-5362-0701-9(2))*** Candlewick Pr.

Kraegel, Kenneth. Wild Honey from the Moon. Kraegel, Kenneth. 2019. (ENG.). 64p. (J). (gr. -1-3). 17.99 *(978-0-7636-8169-2(5))* Candlewick Pr.

Kraft, Erik P. Lenny & Mel. Kraft, Erik P. 2012. (Ready-For-Chapters Ser.). (ENG.). 64p. (J). (gr. 2-5). pap. 6.99 *(978-0-689-85891-8(4),* Aladdin) Simon & Schuster Children's Publishing.

—Lenny & Mel after-School Confidential. Kraft, Erik P. 2012. (Lenny & Mel Ser.). (ENG.). 64p. (J). (gr. 2-5). pap. 6.99 *(978-1-4424-6314-1(7),* Simon & Schuster/Paula Wiseman Bks.) Simon & Schuster/Paula Wiseman Bks.

—Lenny & Mel's Summer Vacation. Kraft, Erik P. 2012. (Ready-For-Chapters Ser.). (ENG.). 64p. (J). (gr. 2-5). pap. 6.99 *(978-0-689-86874-0(X),* Simon & Schuster/Paula Wiseman Bks.) Simon & Schuster/Paula Wiseman Bks.

Kraft, Jason. Cosmic Blackout! O'Ryan, Ray. 2017. (Galaxy Zack Ser.: 16). (ENG.). 128p. (J). (gr. k-4). 16.99 *(978-1-4814-9990-3(4));* pap. 5.99 *(978-1-4814-9989-7(0))* Little Simon. (Little Simon).

—A Haunted Halloween. O'Ryan, Ray. 2015. (Galaxy Zack Ser.: 11). (ENG.). 128p. (J). (gr. k-4). 17.99 *(978-1-4814-3491-1(8),* Little Simon) Little Simon.

—Operation Twin Trouble. O'Ryan, Ray. 2015. (Galaxy Zack Ser.: 12). (ENG.). 128p. (J). (gr. k-4). pap. 5.99 *(978-1-4814-4399-9(2),* Little Simon) Little Simon.

—Ready, Set, Blast Off! O'Ryan, Ray. 2017. (Galaxy Zack Ser.: 15). (ENG.). 128p. (J). (gr. k-4). pap. 5.99 *(978-1-4814-8595-1(4),* Little Simon) Little Simon.

—Return to Earth! O'Ryan, Ray. 2015. (Galaxy Zack Ser.: 10). (ENG.). 128p. (J). (gr. k-4). pap. 5.99 *(978-1-4814-2181-2(6),* Little Simon) Little Simon.

—Science Fair Disaster! O'Ryan, Ray. 2016. (Galaxy Zack Ser.: 13). (ENG.). 128p. (J). (gr. k-4). pap. 5.99 *(978-1-4814-5876-4(0),* Little Simon) Little Simon.

—Snow Place Like Home. O'Ryan, Ray. 2018. (Galaxy Zack Ser.: 17). (ENG.). 128p. (J). (gr. k-4). 16.99 *(978-1-5344-2906-2(9))*; pap. 5.99 *(978-1-5344-2905-5(0))* Little Simon. (Little Simon).

—Space Camp. O'Ryan, Ray. 2016. (Galaxy Zack Ser.: 14). (ENG.). 128p. (J). (gr. k-4). pap. 5.99 *(978-1-4814-6300-3(4),* Little Simon) Little Simon.

—Winter Colorland. Shaw, Natalie. 2017. (Crayola Ser.). (ENG.). 18p. (J). (gr. -1 — 1). bds. 8.99 *(978-1-5344-0213-3(6),* Simon Spotlight) Simon Spotlight.

Kraft, Jason, jt. illus. see Leyssenne, Mathieu.

Kraft, Joe. Gracie Blue Knows a Secret, 1 vol. Kraft, Andrea. 2009. 23p. pap. 19.95 *(978-1-61582-554-7(1))* PublishAmerica, Inc.

Kraft, Lauri. The Peaceful Lion. Brundige, Britt & Durant, Sybrina, eds. 2019. (ENG.). 30p. (J). pap. 12.99 ***(978-1-6794-7652-5(1))*** Independently Published.

Kraft, Lauri. The Peaceful Lion. Johnson, Sandi. Johnson, Britt, ed. l.t. ed. 2014. (ENG.). 28p. (J). (gr. k-5). pap. 12.99 *(978-1-929063-95-6(4),* 325) Moons & Stars Publishing For Children.

Krajenbrink Hulin, Yvonne. Gretchen & the Gremlins. Holst, Jerome Alphonse. 2012. 48p. pap. 15.95 *(978-0-9794133-5-3(4))* TV Acres Bks.

Krajewski, Nicole. Dig for Your Diamond: A Mandate to Excavate Your Own Piece of Heaven. Mosey, Caroline. 2020. (ENG.). 40p. (J). (gr. 2-4). 16.99 ***(978-1-64237-899-3(2))*** Gatekeeper Pr.

Krakow, Eric. Have You Heard? A Child's Introduction to the Ten Commandments, 1 vol. Glickman, Jeff. 2017. (ENG.). 32p. (J). (gr. -1-3). 14.99 *(978-0-7643-5395-6(0),* 7767) Schiffer Publishing, Ltd.

Kralapp, Karl. ABC Eat Local Wisconsin. Johnson, Rebekah. 2020. (ENG.). 32p. (J). 17.99 ***(978-1-64538-151-8(X))*** Orange Hat Publishing.

Kralapp, Karl E. Fish Food. Kralapp, Karl E. 28p. 2018. (ENG.). (J). 14.99 *(978-1-948365-37-6(5))*; 2013. pap. 9.99 *(978-1-937165-62-8(0))* Orange Hat Publishing.

Krall, Dan. Naughty Mabel. Lane, Nathan & Elliott, Devlin. 2015. (Naughty Mabel Ser.). (ENG.). 48p. (J). (gr. -1-3). 18.99 *(978-1-4814-3022-7(X),* Simon & Schuster Bks. For Young Readers) Simon & Schuster Bks. For Young Readers.

—Naughty Mabel Sees It All. Lane, Nathan & Elliott, Devlin. 2016. (Naughty Mabel Ser.). (ENG.). 48p. (J). (gr. -1-3). 17.99 *(978-1-4814-3024-1(6),* Simon & Schuster Bks. For Young Readers) Simon & Schuster Bks. For Young Readers.

—Oh, Nuts! Sauer, Tammi. 2012. (ENG.). 32p. (J). 17.89 *(978-1-59990-467-2(5),* 900065706); (gr. -1-6). 16.99 *(978-1-59990-466-5(7),* 900065648) Bloomsbury Publishing USA. (Bloomsbury USA Childrens).

—Skeleton Cat. Crow, Kristyn. 2012. (ENG.). 32p. (J). (gr. -1-1). pap. 6.99 *(978-0-545-15385-0(9),* Scholastic Pr.) Scholastic, Inc.

Krall, Dan. The Great Lollipop Caper. Krall, Dan. 2013. (ENG.). 48p. (J). (gr. -1-3). 16.99 *(978-1-4424-4460-7(6),* Simon & Schuster Bks. For Young Readers) Simon & Schuster Bks. For Young Readers.

—Sick Simon. Krall, Dan. (ENG.). 48p. (J). (gr. -1-3). 2020. 7.99 ***(978-1-5344-8342-2(X))***; 2015. 18.99 *(978-1-4424-9097-0(7))* Simon & Schuster Bks. For Young Readers. (Simon & Schuster Bks. For Young Readers).

Kralovansky, Susan. The Book That Jake Borrowed, 1 vol. Kralovansky, Susan. 2018. (ENG.). 32p. (J). (gr. k-3). 16.99 *(978-1-4556-2325-9(3),* Pelican Publishing) Arcadia Publishing.

—Twelve Cowboys Ropin', 1 vol. Kralovansky, Susan. 2015. (ENG.). 32p. (J). (gr. k-3). 16.99 *(978-1-4556-2081-4(5),* Pelican Publishing) Arcadia Publishing.

Kramer, Berri, photos by. Mbali: A story from South Africa. Kramer, Berri, text. 2nd ed. 2006. (J). per. *(978-0-9706901-1-1(8))* Rotaplast Pr.

Kramer, Brandie. Footlights & Fairy Dust: Matt & Maria Go to the Theatre. Tirabassi, Maren C. 2007. (ENG.). 48p. (J). (gr. 2-7). pap. 14.95 *(978-1-933002-26-2(3))* PublishingWorks.

Kramer, Connie, photos by. Cupcakes! A Sweet Treat with More Than 200 Stickers. Cooke, Brandy. 2011. (ENG.). 18p. (J). (gr. -1-k). bds. 6.99 *(978-1-4424-2825-6(2),* Little Simon) Little Simon.

Kramer, David. Monkey of the Month, 1 vol. Kramer, Adam. 2012. (ENG.). 40p. (J). (gr. -1-3). 16.99 *(978-0-7643-4156-4(1),* 9780764341564) Schiffer Publishing, Ltd.

Kramer, Ellen. It's Your Funeral. Riesbeck, Emily. 2020. 200p. (YA). pap. 15.00 *(978-1-945820-52-6(7))* Iron Circus Comics.

Kramer, Jaap. The Mystery of the Abandoned Mill. Prins, Piet. 2006. 127p. (J). pap. *(978-1-894666-48-0(8))* Inheritance Pubns.

—One Day at a Time, Margreet. Vogelaar, Alie. VanBrugge, Jeanne, tr. from DUT. 2004. Orig. Title: Elke Dag Genoeg, Margreet. 124p. *(978-0-9670728-6-9(7))* Early Foundations Pubs.

—The Sailing Sleuths. Prins, Piet. 2006. 137p. (J). pap. *(978-1-894666-46-6(1))* Inheritance Pubns.

—The Search for Sheltie. Prins, Piet. 2006. 137p. (J). pap. *(978-1-894666-43-5(7))* Inheritance Pubns.

—The Treasure of Rodensteyn Castle. Prins, Piet. 2006. 132p. (J). pap. *(978-1-894666-47-3(X))* Inheritance Pubns.

Kramer, Pat, photos by. Totem Poles for Kids: A Kids Own SuperGuide. Kramer, Pat. 48p. (J). pap. *(978-1-55153-626-2(9))* Altitude Publishing Canada Ltd.

Kramer, Sarah F. The Genereux Gateaux: The Generous Cakes. Kramer, Sarah F. Hall, Jill, ed. 2018. (ENG.). 34p. (J). (gr. k-6). 19.99 *(978-0-9991-99173-2(5))* Kramer, Sarah.

Kramin, Valerie. Into the Forest & down the Tower. Bugg, Ann T. 2012. 136p. pap. *(978-1-927044-24-7(3))* Writers AMuse Me.

Krampien, Celia. A Book of Bridges - Here to There & Me to You. Keely, Cheryl. 2017. (ENG.). 32p. (J). (gr. k-3). 16.99 *(978-1-58536-996-6(9),* 204231) Sleeping Bear Pr.

—My Family Four Floors Up. Stutson, Caroline. 2018. (ENG.). 32p. (J). (gr. -1-2). 16.99 *(978-1-58536-991-1(8),* 204406) Sleeping Bear Pr.

—Wings of Olympus: the Colt of the Clouds. George, Kallie. 2020. (Wings of Olympus Ser.: 2). (ENG.). 256p. (J). (gr. 3-7). 16.99 *(978-0-06-274154-7(3),* HarperCollins) HarperCollins Pubs. Ltd. GBR. Dist: HarperCollins Pubs.

Krasnoff, Lauren. When Ellie Sang a G. Birk, Jessica. 2019. (ENG.). 30p. (J). (gr. k-2). pap. ***(978-1-912384-09-9(4))*** Peculiarity Pr.

Krassa, Victoria. Grandma, How Do You Say I Love You? Unobagha, Uzo. 2007. 28p. (J). 16.95 *(978-0-9773180-0-1(1))* Adonoke Inc.

Krasulja, Zorica. Kelly's Cabin, 1 vol. Smith, Linda. 2006. (Orca Echoes Ser.). (ENG.). 64p. (J). (gr. 1-3). per. 6.95 *(978-1-55143-408-7(3))* Orca Bk. Pubs. USA.

Krati, Christina. El Plato Magico de Juanito. Lester, Donna Daun. Krowne, Lilian, tr. 2016. (SPA.). (J). pap. 14.99 *(978-0-9898633-9-1(5))* Nutrition Network Pubs., Inc.

Kratter, Paul. A Tiger Tale. Nagda, Ann Whitehead. (Soundprints' Amazing Animal Adventures! Ser.). (ENG.). 36p. (J). 2005. (gr. -1-2). 2.95 *(978-1-59249-044-8(1),* S7151); 2005. (gr. -1-2). 15.95 *(978-1-59249-042-4(5),* B7101); 2005. (gr. -1-2). pap. 6.95 *(978-1-59249-043-1(3),* S7101); 2005. (gr. -1-2). 19.95 *(978-1-59249-388-3(2),* BC7101); 2005. (gr. 2-2). 8.95 *(978-1-59249-389-0(0),* SC7101); 2003. (gr. -1-3). 9.95 *(978-1-59249-057-8(3),* PS7151) Soundprints.

—World above the Clouds: A Story of a Himalayan Ecosystem. Nagda, Ann Whitehead. 2005. (Wild Habitats Ser.: Vol. 18). (ENG.). 36p. (J). (gr. 1-4). 19.95 *(978-1-56899-880-0(5),* BC7017); 15.95 *(978-1-56899-878-7(3),* B7017); pap. 6.95 *(978-1-56899-879-4(1),* S7017) Soundprints.

Kratter, Paul. The Living Rain Forest: An Animal Alphabet. Kratter, Paul. rev. ed. 2010. 32p. (J). (gr. 1-4). pap. 7.95 *(978-1-58089-393-0(7))* Charlesbridge Publishing, Inc.

Kraulis, Julie. Whimsy's Heavy Things. Kraulis, Julie. 2013. (ENG.). 32p. (J). (gr. -1-1). 17.99 *(978-1-77049-403-9(0),* Tundra Bks.) Tundra Bks. CAN. Dist: Penguin Random Hse. LLC.

Krause, J. R. Dragon Night. Krause, J. R. 2019. (ENG.). 32p. (J). (gr. -1-2). 16.99 *(978-0-525-51424-4(4),* G.P. Putnam's Sons Books for Young Readers) Penguin Young Readers Group.

Krause, Ute. Oscar & the Very Hungry Dragon. Krause, Ute. 2015. (ENG.). 32p. (J). 8.95 *(978-0-7358-4230-4(2))* North-South Bks., Inc.

Krauss, Trisha. France. Candlewick Press Staff. 2015. (Panorama Pops Ser.). (ENG.). 30p. (J). (gr. k-4). 8.99 *(978-0-7636-7836-4(8))* Candlewick Pr.

—Maude: The Not-So-Noticeable Shrimpton. Child, Lauren. 2013. (ENG.). 32p. (J). (gr. k-3). 16.99 *(978-0-7636-6515-9(0))* Candlewick Pr.

—Rio de Janeiro: a 3D Keepsake Cityscape. Candlewick Press Staff. 2014. (Panorama Pops Ser.). (ENG.). 30p. (J). (gr. k-4). 8.99 *(978-0-7636-7029-0(4))* Candlewick Pr.

Kravanek, J. Elise. Holly the Christmas Collie. Draper, Melissa J. 2004. 63p. (J). *(978-0-9741081-3-1(8))* Acres Publishing.

Kravets, Ivan. The Legend of Blackbeard: Band 15/Emerald (Collins Big Cat) Bloor, Thomas. 2016. (Collins Big Cat Ser.). (ENG.). 48p. (J). pap. 9.95 *(978-0-00-814725-9(6))* HarperCollins Pubs. Ltd. GBR. Dist: Independent Pubs. Group.

Kravits, Ivan. The Shepherd's Story. Dunne, Jimmy. 2020. (ENG.). 32p. (J). (gr. k-5). 19.95 ***(978-0-8294-4890-0(X))*** Loyola Pr.

Krawczyk, Isabella. The Great (Grate) Book of Homophones. Mancuso, Kathleen. 2019. (ENG.). 34p. (J). pap. 12.95 ***(978-1-6970-9869-3(X))*** Independently Published.

Krawczyk, Sabine. Insects. Krawczyk, Sabine. Sautai, Raoul. 2012. (My First Discoveries Ser.). (ENG.). 36p. (J). (gr. -1-k). spiral bd. 13.99 *(978-1-85103-411-6(0))* Moonlight Publishing, Ltd. GBR. Dist: Independent Pubs. Group.

—Plantas. Krawczyk, Sabine. Delafosse, Claude. Barroso, Paz, tr. (Coleccion Mundo Maravilloso).Tr. of Plants. (SPA.). (J). (gr. 3-5). *(978-84-348-4501-5(6))* SM Ediciones.

Kray, Robert C. Bugs & Bugsicles: Insects in the Winter. Hansen, Amy S. 2010. (ENG.). 32p. (J). (gr. 2-k). pap. 11.95 *(978-1-59078-763-2(3))*; 17.95 *(978-1-59078-269-9(0))* Boyds Mills Pr.

Kraynak, George. Akio & the Moon Goddess. Falk, Elsa. 2011. 158p. 41.95 *(978-1-258-06311-5(5))* Literary Licensing, LLC.

Krebs, Patricia. On Your Mark, Get Set, Go! 2009. 32p. (J). 16.95 *(978-0-9796380-1-5(1))* Three Wishes Publishing Co.

—Zee: Adventure One: Borrowing China. Gilbert, Marcie. l.t. ed. 2006. 48p. (J). per. 16.99 *(978-0-9771566-0-3(5))* Librujas.

Krecskay, Stephen. Miss Tilly's Party. Thompson, Yvonne. 2004. (J). per. *(978-0-9749561-0-7(4))* My Sunshine Bks.

Kredel, Fritz. Slovenly Peter. Twain, Mark, tr. 2013. (Calla Editions Ser.). (ENG.). 48p. (gr. 5). 20.00 *(978-1-60660-048-1(6))* Dover Pubns., Inc.

—The Story of Beethoven. Kaufmann, Helen L. Meadowcroft, Enid Lamonte, ed. 2011. 192p. 42.95 *(978-1-258-10000-1(2))* Literary Licensing, LLC.

Kredensor, Diane. Buck's Tooth. Kredensor, Diane. 2015. (Pix Ser.). (ENG.). 64p. (J). (gr. 1-4). 12.99 *(978-1-4814-2382-3(7),* Aladdin) Simon & Schuster Children's Publishing.

—Superbuns! Kindness Is Her Superpower. Kredensor, Diane. 2019. (ENG.). 40p. (J). (gr. -1-3). 17.99 *(978-1-4814-9068-9(0),* Aladdin) Simon & Schuster Children's Publishing.

Krehbiel, Angie. Sierra, the Black Lab Who Loved to Eat: (a True Story) Unruh, Cindy. 2012. 32p. pap. 24.95 *(978-1-4626-5537-3(8))* America Star Bks.

Kreinberg, Sylvia. Volcano Bubbles, 1 vol. Giulieri, Anne. 2012. (Engage Literacy Blue Ser.). (ENG.). 32p. (gr. k-2). pap. 5.99 *(978-1-4296-8978-6(1),* Capstone Pr.) Capstone.

Kreinberg, Sylvia, photos by. The Castle, 1 vol. Giulieri, Anne. 2012. (Engage Literacy Magenta Ser.). (ENG., 32p. (gr. k-2). pap. 5.99 *(978-1-4296-8872-7(6),* Capstone Pr.) Capstone.

—Chocolate Banana Pops, 1 vol. Giulieri, Anne. 2012. (Engage Literacy Yellow Ser.). (ENG., 32p. (gr. k-2). pap. 5.99 *(978-1-4296-8836-9(X),* Capstone Pr.) Capstone.

—Here Is a Robot, 1 vol. Giulieri, Anne. 2012. (Engage Literacy Magenta Ser.). (ENG., 32p. (gr. k-2). pap. 5.99 *(978-1-4296-8848-2(3),* Capstone Pr.) Capstone.

—In My Car, 1 vol. Dale, Jay. 2012. (Engage Literacy Magenta Ser.). (ENG., 32p. (gr. k-2). pap. 5.99 *(978-1-4296-8850-5(5),* Capstone Pr.) Capstone.

—Look at the Picture, 1 vol. Giulieri, Anne. 2012. (Engage Literacy Magenta Ser.). (ENG., 32p. (gr. k-2). pap. 5.99 *(978-1-4296-8858-1(0),* Capstone Pr.) Capstone.

—Make a Monkey, 1 vol. Dale, Jay. 2012. (Engage Literacy Red Ser.). (ENG., 32p. (gr. k-2). pap. 5.99 *(978-1-4296-8946-5(3),* Capstone Pr.) Capstone.

—Make Two Crocodiles, 1 vol. Giulieri, Anne. 2012. (Engage Literacy Blue Ser.). (ENG., 32p. (gr. k-2). pap. 5.99 *(978-1-4296-8986-1(2),* Capstone Pr.) Capstone.

—My Birthday, 1 vol. Giulieri, Anne. 2012. (Engage Literacy Magenta Ser.). (ENG., 32p. (gr. k-2). pap. 5.99 *(978-1-4296-8868-0(8),* Capstone Pr.) Capstone.

—My Toy Box, 1 vol. Dale, Jay. 2012. (Engage Literacy Magenta Ser.). (ENG., 32p. (gr. k-2). pap. 5.99 *(978-1-4296-8860-4(2),* Capstone Pr.) Capstone.

Kreiswirth, Kinny & Lucas, Bonnie Gordon. All about Set. Groner, Judyth & Wikler, Madeline. (J). (gr. k-5). 26.78 *(978-1-58013-221-3(9),* Kar-Ben Publishing) Lerner Publishing Group.

Krejca, Gary. Generous Me. Pearson, Mary E. 2011. (Rookie Ready to Learn — All about Me! Ser.). 40p. (J). (gr. -1-k). lib. bdg. 25.00 *(978-0-531-26427-0(0))*; (ENG.). pap. 5.95 *(978-0-531-26652-6(4))* Scholastic Library Publishing. (Children's Pr.).

—Two Nice Mice. Gillis, Jennifer Blizin. 2006. (Barron's Reader's Clubhouse Level 2 Ser.). (ENG.). 24p. (J). (gr. k-3). 16.19 *(978-0-7641-3295-7(4),* B.E.S. Publishing) Peterson's.

Krejcova, Zdenka. Adventures of Saint Paul. Selucky, Oldrich. Trouvé, Marianne Lorraine, tr. from CZE. 2008. Orig. Title: Pavel, dobrudruh Viry. 96p. (J). (gr. 1-3). pap. *(978-0-8198-0786-1(9))* Pauline Bks. & Media.

Krekk, Gabriel. Walk Ride Rodeo: A Story about Amberley Snyder. Snyder, Amberley Lana. (ENG.). 34p. (J). (gr. k-6). 2018. 24.99 *(978-0-692-99640-9(0))*; 2017. pap. 17.99 *(978-0-692-99918-9(3))* Snyder Enterprises LLC.

Kreloff, Elliot. Big Box of Shapes. Blevins, Wiley. 2018. (Basic Concepts Ser.). (ENG.). 24p. (J). (gr. -1-1). pap. 6.99 *(978-1-63440-417-4(3),* Rocking Chair Kids) Red Chair Pr.

—Colors All Around. Blevins, Wiley. 2018. (Basic Concepts Ser.). (ENG.). 24p. (J). (gr. -1-1). pap. 6.99 *(978-1-63440-415-0(7),* Rocking Chair Kids) Red Chair Pr.

—Count on It. Blevins, Wiley. 2018. (Basic Concepts Ser.). (ENG.). 24p. (J). (gr. -1-1). pap. 6.99 *(978-1-63440-416-7(5),* Rocking Chair Kids) Red Chair Pr.

—Counting Duckies. 2010. 16p. (J). bds. *(978-1-60906-007-7(5))* Begin Smart LLC.

—Duck, Duck, Goose. Blevins, Wiley. 2018. (Basic Concepts Ser.). (ENG.). 24p. (J). (gr. -1-1). pap. 6.99 *(978-1-63440-419-8(X),* Rocking Chair Kids) Red Chair Pr.

—Matching Puzzle Cards - Numbers. 2012. (ENG.). 36p. (J). (gr. k-12). 9.99 *(978-1-60905-221-8(8))* Blue Apple Bks.

—My Little Baby. 2010. 12p. (J). bds. *(978-1-60906-008-4(3))* Begin Smart LLC.

—The Not-So-Right Day. Blevins, Wiley. 2018. (Basic Concepts Ser.). (ENG.). 24p. (J). (gr. -1-1). pap. 6.99 *(978-1-63440-418-1(1),* Rocking Chair Kids) Red Chair Pr.

—Splish-Splash, into the Bath! Danis, Naomi. 2007. 16p. (J). *(978-1-59354-609-0(2))* Handprint Bks.

—Where's Your Nose. 2010. 24p. (J). bds. *(978-1-60906-004-6(0))* Begin Smart LLC.

Kreloff, Elliot. Please Don't Make Me Fly! A Growing-Up Story of Self-Confidence. Kreloff, Elliot. 2017. (Growing Up Ser.). (ENG.). 32p. (J). (gr. -1-1). lib. bdg. 19.99 *(978-1-63440-179-1(4))*; E-Book 30.65 *(978-1-63440-183-8(2))* Red Chair Pr. (Rocking Chair Kids).

—Worth the Wait: A Growing-Up Story of Self-Esteem. Kreloff, Elliot. 2017. (Growing Up Ser.). (ENG.). 32p. (J). (gr. -1-1). lib. bdg. 19.99 *(978-1-63440-180-7(8))*; E-Book 30.65 *(978-1-63440-184-5(0))* Red Chair Pr. (Rocking Chair Kids).

Kreloff, Elliott. Big Box of Shapes. Blevins, Wiley. 2016. (Basic Concepts Ser.). (ENG.). 24p. (J). (gr. -1-1). lib. bdg. 14.99 *(978-1-63440-082-4(8),* Rocking Chair Kids) Red Chair Pr.

—Colors All Around. Blevins, Wiley. 2016. (Basic Concepts Ser.). (ENG.). 24p. (J). (gr. -1-1). lib. bdg. 14.99 *(978-1-63440-080-0(1),* Rocking Chair Kids) Red Chair Pr.

—Duck, Duck, Goose. Blevins, Wiley. 2016. (Basic Concepts Ser.). (ENG.). 24p. (J). (gr. -1-1). lib. bdg. 14.99 *(978-1-63440-084-8(4),* Rocking Chair Kids) Red Chair Pr.

—The Not-So-Right Day. Blevins, Wiley. 2016. (Basic Concepts Ser.). (ENG.). 24p. (J). (gr. -1-1). lib. bdg. 14.99 *(978-1-63440-083-1(6),* Rocking Chair Kids) Red Chair Pr.

Krementz, Jill, photos by. A Very Young Rider. Krementz, Jill. ed. 2006. 124p. (gr. 4-7). 24.95 *(978-0-9755516-2-2(0))* DreamHse. Publishing Inc.

Kremer, Warren & Robbins, Trina. Star Comics: Planet Terry - the Complete Collection. 2019. (ENG.). 424p. (J). (gr. -1-17). pap. 39.99 *(978-1-302-91864-4(8))* Marvel Worldwide, Inc.

Kremer, Warren & Romita, John. Star Comics: Top Dog - the Complete Collection. 2020. (ENG.). 336p. (J). (gr. -1-17). pap. 39.99 ***(978-1-302-92508-6(3))*** Marvel Worldwide, Inc.

Kremsner, Cynthia. My Puppy Gave to Me, 1 vol. Dannenbring, Cheryl. 2014. (Twelve Days of Christmas Ser.). (ENG.). 32p. (J). (gr. k-3). 16.99 *(978-1-4556-1943-6(4),* Pelican Publishing) Arcadia Publishing.

—Swashbarklers of the Sea, 1 vol. 2019. (ENG.). 32p. (J). (gr. -1-3). 16.99 *(978-1-4556-2414-0(4),* Pelican Publishing) Arcadia Publishing.

Kress, Camille. The High Holy Days. Kress, Camille. 2004. bds. 6.25 *(978-0-8074-0776-9(3),* 241856) URJ Pr.

—Purim! Kress, Camille. 2004. 10p. (gr. -1-k). bds. 5.95 *(978-0-8074-0654-0(6),* 102555) URJ Pr.

—A Tree Trunk Seder. Kress, Camille. 2004. (Camille Kress Library: Vol. 4). 7p. (gr. -1-k). bds. 6.25 *(978-0-8074-0735-6(6),* 101252) URJ Pr.

Kress, Sandra, photos by. Ollie & Moon in Paris. Kredensor, Diane. 2017. (Pictureback(R) Ser.). 32p. (J). (gr. -1-2). pap. 5.99 *(978-1-5247-1575-5(1),* Random Hse. Bks. for Young Readers) Random Hse. Children's Bks.

Krevi, Drew. I've Got This! White, Jeff. 2017. (Best of Buddies Ser.). (ENG.). 32p. (J). 12.99 *(978-1-4707-4855-5(X))* Group Publishing, Inc.

Kriebel, Jacqueline. You Are Brave. Chapeau, Chelsey. 2017. 26p. pap. 11.99 *(978-1-943871-42-1(6))* Painted Gate Publishing.

Krieger, Hannah. All My Friends Are Ghosts. Vidaurri, S. M. 2020. (ENG.). 160p. (J). pap. 14.99 *(978-1-68415-498-2(7))* Boom! Studios.

Krieger, Samantha. What Does It Mean to Be a Rainbow in Someone Else's Cloud? Rice, Nikki. 2019. (ENG.). 32p. (J). pap. 9.99 *(978-1-0976-0842-3(5))* Independently Published.

Kriembonga, Arief. Harriet's Monster Diary: Awfully Anxious (but I Squish It, Big Time) Melmed, Raun & Abramson, S. E. 2019. (Monster Diaries: 3). (ENG.). 116p. (J). pap. 12.99 *(978-1-64170-127-3(7),* 550127) Familius LLC.

Krilanovich, Nadia. Chicken, Chicken, Duck! Krilanovich, Nadia. (J). (gr. -1-2). 2016. 26p. bds. 7.99 *(978-0-553-53806-9(3))*; 2011. (ENG.). 32p. 14.99 *(978-1-58246-385-8(9))* Random Hse. Children's Bks. (Tricycle Pr.).

Krinsky, Rivka Siegel. The Greatest Ten. Surlin, Janice. 2016. (ENG.). 26p. (J). pap. 11.95 *(978-0-9981700-0-8(3))* Hummingbird Jewel Pr.

Kris. Jazz It Up. Sloan, Milo. 2017. (ENG.). 20p. (J). (gr. -1-k). bds. 8.99 *(978-1-4998-0478-2(4))* Little Bee Books Inc.

Krisanova, Darina. Making Princess Dresses. Fox, Julie G. Bulbeck, Leonora, ed. 2019. (ENG.). 30p. (J). pap. 9.99 *(978-1-7953-3948-3(9))* Independently Published.

Krishevski, E. Dan un Gad in Milhomeh Afn Oytser. Rozen, R. 2017. (YID.). 55p. (J). *(978-1-68091-159-6(7))* Kinder Shpiel USA, Inc.

—In Trit Fun Di Farkhapte Kinder. Rozen, R. 2018. (YID.). 58p. (J). *(978-1-68091-243-2(7))* Kinder Shpiel USA, Inc.

Krishnaswamy, Uma. Mangoes, Mischief, & Tales of Friendship: Stories from India. Soundar, Chitra. 2018. 192p. (J). (gr. 1-4). 16.99 *(978-1-5362-0067-6(0))* Candlewick Pr.

—Out of the Way! Out of the Way!, 1 vol. Krishnaswami, Uma. 2012. (ENG.). 28p. (J). (gr. -1-2). 17.95 *(978-1-55498-130-4(1))* Groundwood Bks. CAN. Dist: Publishers Group West (PGW).

Kristen, Mantooth. Danny Goes to the Doctor. Kristen, Mantooth. 2007. 24p. (J). 10.00 *(978-0-9800580-0-0(7))* Ballyhoo Printing.

Kristiansen, Teddy. M Is for Magic. Gaiman, Neil. 2007. 272p. (J). (gr. 5-9). 16.99 *(978-0-06-118642-4(2))* HarperCollins Pubs.

—M Is for Magic. Gaiman, Neil. 2008. (ENG.). 272p. (J). (gr. 5-9). pap. 7.99 *(978-0-06-118647-9(3),* HarperCollins) HarperCollins Pubs. Ltd. GBR. Dist: HarperCollins Pubs.

Kristie Kryssing. Bath Time Bears Have So Much Fun. Jennie Lyon Wood. 2009. 24p. pap. 12.99 *(978-1-4389-4420-3(9))* AuthorHouse.

Kristof Pincheira, Kyra. Where's Leon? Storybook & Reader's Guide CD-ROM, 1. Cassell, Jody. l.t. ed. 2006. 48p. (J). lib. bdg. 17.95 *(978-1-59494-013-2(4))* CPCC Pr.

Krit, Joey. Hooty & the Magic Power. Kamon. 2011. 36p. pap. 14.39 *(978-1-4634-1042-1(5))* AuthorHouse.

—Playtoon & the Antpod. Kamon. 2012. 28p. pap. 24.95 *(978-1-4626-7346-9(5))* PublishAmerica, Inc.

Krittendon, Kim & Johnson, Jim. Legend of the Blue Unicorn: Land of OSM. Johnson, Sandi et al. Johnson, Britt, ed. 2014. (Little Choo-Choo Bks.). (ENG.). 40p. (J). (gr. -1-6). 14.99 *(978-1-929063-09-3(1),* 109) Moons & Stars Publishing For Children.

Krizmanic, Tatjana. Ilian. Fordham, Walter. 2012. 42p. pap. *(978-0-9813889-5-3(7))* Publish Yourself.

—Stories to Nourish the Hearts of Our Children. Simms, Laura. 2013. 100p. pap. 19.99 *(978-0-9911692-1-4(2))* Simms, Laura Storyteller.

Krock, Libby Carruth. The Legend of OinkADoodleMoo. St. Jean, Alan. St. Jean, Alan, ed. 2013. 32p. 19.95 *(978-0-9777272-9-2(7))* Oren Village, LLC.

Kroeger, Vanesa. Dios Me Escucha: Oraciones en Rima para Ninos. Fernandez, Cecilia Fau. 2007. (SPA.). 48p. (J). lib. bdg. 8.99 *(978-0-7586-1248-9(6))* Concordia Publishing Hse.

Krogmann, Uta. The Junior Witch's Handbook: A Kid's Guide to White Magic, Spells, & Rituals. Van De Car, Nikki. 2020. 120p. (J). (gr. 3-7). 13.99 ***(978-0-7624-6930-7(7),*** Running Pr. Kids) Running Pr.

Krol, Malgosia. Quest-Terrestrials: Vol. 1. Krol, Malgosia. 2018. (ENG.). 40p. (J). pap. *(978-1-5255-2191-1(8))* FriesenPress.

Kroll, Felipe. End of Days: Doomsday Myths Around the World. Hoena, Blake. 2017. (Universal Myths Ser.). (ENG.). 48p. (J). (gr. 3-9). lib. bdg. 31.32 *(978-1-5157-6626-1(8),* 135197, Capstone Pr.) Capstone.

K

Krome, Mike. Christmas/Easter Flip-Over Book. Kovacs, Victoria. 2015. (Little Bible Heroes(tm) Ser.). (ENG.). 32p. (J). (gr. k-2). pap. 3.99 *(978-1-4336-8711-2(9),* 005742008, B&H Kids) B&H Publishing Group.

—Creation/Noah Flip-Over Book. Kovacs, Victoria. 2015. (Little Bible Heroes(tm) Ser.). (ENG.). 32p. (J). (gr. k-2). pap. 3.99 *(978-1-4336-8712-9(7),* 005742009, B&H Kids) B&H Publishing Group.

—David/Esther Flip-Over Book. Kovacs, Victoria. 2015. (Little Bible Heroes(tm) Ser.). (ENG.). 32p. (J). (gr. k-2). pap. 3.99 *(978-1-4336-8713-6(5),* 005742010, B&H Kids) B&H Publishing Group.

—Joseph/the Good Samaritan Flip-Over Book. Kovacs, Victoria. 2015. (Little Bible Heroes(tm) Ser.). (ENG.). 32p. (J). (gr. k-2). pap. 3.99 *(978-1-4336-8715-0(1),* 005742014, B&H Kids) B&H Publishing Group.

—Samuel/the Little Maid Flip-Over Book. Kovacs, Victoria. 2015. (Little Bible Heroes(tm) Ser.). (ENG.). 32p. (J). (gr. k-2). pap. 3.99 *(978-1-4336-8718-1(6),* 005742020, B&H Kids) B&H Publishing Group.

Krome, Mike & Ryley, David. Jesus' Miracles/Martha Flip-Over Book. Kovacs, Victoria. 2015. (Little Bible Heroes(tm) Ser.). (ENG.). 32p. (J). (gr. k-2). pap. 3.99 *(978-1-4336-8714-3(3),* 005742013, B&H Kids) B&H Publishing Group.

—Little Bible Heroes Storybook (padded) Kovacs, Victoria. 2016. (Little Bible Heroes(tm) Ser.). (ENG.). 264p. (J). 14.99 *(978-1-4336-9230-7(9),* 006109627, B&H Kids) B&H Publishing Group.

—Miriam/Daniel Flip-Over Book. Kovacs, Victoria. 2015. (Little Bible Heroes(tm) Ser.). (ENG.). 32p. (J). (gr. k-2). pap. 3.99 *(978-1-4336-8717-4(8),* 005742017, B&H Kids) B&H Publishing Group.

Krömer, Christiane. Anh's Anger. Silver, Gail. 2009. 40p. (J). (gr. -1-3). 16.95 *(978-1-888375-94-7(9),* Plum Blossom Bks.) Parallax Pr.

Kromer, Christiane. Anh's Anger. Silver, Gail. 2011. (J). *(978-1-935209-65-2(5),* Plum Blossom Bks.) Parallax Pr.

—Flower Girl Butterflies. Howard, Elizabeth Fitzgerald. 2004. 32p. (J). 16.89 *(978-0-688-17810-9(3))* HarperCollins Pubs.

Krömer, Christiane. King for a Day, 1 vol. Khan, Rukhsana. (ENG.). 32p. (J). 2019. (gr. 1-5). pap. 10.95 *(978-1-64379-056-5(0),* 88e3ab57-c591-490b-82b7-723b34a52180); 2014. 17.95 *(978-1-60060-659-5(8))* Lee & Low Bks., Inc.

Kromer, Christiane. Steps & Stones: An Anh's Anger Story. Silver, Gail. 2011. 40p. (J). (gr. -1-3). 16.95 *(978-1-935209-87-4(6),* Plum Blossom Bks.) Parallax Pr.

Krommes, Beth. The Barefoot Book of Earth Poems. Nicholls, Judith. 2016. (ENG.). 40p. (J). (gr. 1-5). pap. 9.99 *(978-1-78285-278-0(6))* Barefoot Bks., Inc.

—Before Morning. Sidman, Joyce. 2016. (ENG.). 48p. (J). (gr. -1-3). 17.99 *(978-0-547-97917-5(7),* 1523509, HMH Books For Young Readers) Houghton Mifflin Harcourt Publishing Co.

—Blue on Blue. White, Dianne. 2014. (ENG.). 48p. (J). (gr. k-3). 18.99 *(978-1-4424-1267-5(4),* Beach Lane Bks.) Beach Lane Bks.

—Butterfly Eyes & Other Secrets of the Meadow. Sidman, Joyce. 2006. (ENG.). 48p. (J). (gr. 3-7). 17.99 *(978-0-618-56313-5(X),* 595784) Houghton Mifflin Harcourt Publishing Co.

—The House in the Night. Swanson, Susan Marie. (ENG.). (J). 2011. 36p. (gr. k — 1). bds. 7.99 *(978-0-547-57769-2(9),* 1458661); 2008. 40p. (gr. -1-3). 17.99 *(978-0-618-86244-3(7),* 513213) Houghton Mifflin Harcourt Publishing Co.

—The Lamp, the Ice, & the Boat Called Fish: Based on a True Story. Martin, Jacqueline Briggs. 2005. (ENG.). 48p. (J). (gr. -1-3). 7.99 *(978-0-618-54895-8(5),* 410272) Houghton Mifflin Harcourt Publishing Co.

—The Sun in Me: Poems about the Planet. Nicholls, Judith. 2008. 40p. (J). (gr. -1). pap. 12.99 *(978-1-84686-161-1(6))* Barefoot Bks., Inc.

—The Sun in Me: Poems about the Planet. Nicholls, Judith, ed. 2003. 40p. (J). pap. 16.99 *(978-1-84148-058-9(4))* Barefoot Bks., Inc.

—Swirl by Swirl: Spirals in Nature. Sidman, Joyce. 2011. (ENG.). 40p. (J). (gr. -1-3). 17.99 *(978-0-547-31583-6(X),* 1415339) Houghton Mifflin Harcourt Publishing Co.

—Swirl by Swirl (board Book) Spirals in Nature. Sidman, Joyce. 2018. (ENG.). 30p. (J). (— 1). bds. 7.99 *(978-1-328-48543-4(9),* 1715778, HMH Books For Young Readers) Houghton Mifflin Harcourt Publishing Co.

Krone, Mike. Let's Be Friends. Sperry, Amanda. 2004. (Elements of Reading: Phonics Ser.). 8p. pap. 40.00 *(978-0-7398-9008-0(5))* Houghton Mifflin Harcourt Supplemental Pubs.

Kroneberger, Abigail Grace. The Sensory Room Kids Get in Sync. Kroneberger, Abigail Grace. 2008. 24p. per. 12.95 *(978-1-934246-98-6(0))* Peppertree Pr., The.

Kronheimer, Ann. The Golden Goose. King-Smith, Dick. 2006. (ENG.). 128p. (J). (gr. 3-7). 5.99 *(978-0-440-42030-9(X),* Yearling) Random Hse. Children's Bks.

—Johnny Clem's Civil War Story. Marsico, Katie. 2018. (Narrative Nonfiction: Kids in War Ser.). (ENG.). 32p. (J). (gr. 2-4). 27.99 *(978-1-5124-5678-3(0),* Lerner Pubns.) Lerner Publishing Group.

—Momcilo Gavric's World War I Story. Acton, Vanessa. 2018. (Narrative Nonfiction: Kids in War Ser.). (ENG.). 32p. (J). (gr. 2-4). 27.99 *(978-1-5124-5679-0(9),* Lerner Pubns.); pap. 9.99 *(978-1-5415-1193-4(X))* Lerner Publishing Group.

—Pretty Princesses: Beautiful Princesses to Color! 2014. (ENG.). 96p. (J). (gr. -1-2). 7.99 *(978-1-4424-8385-9(7),* Little Simon) Little Simon.

—Pride & Prejudice. Austen, Jane. 2013. (Jane Austen Ser.). (ENG.). 64p. pap. 6.95 *(978-1-906230-06-7(4))* Real Reads Ltd. GBR. Dist: Casemate Pubs. & Bk. Distributors, LLC.

—Sense & Sensibility. Austen, Jane. 2013. (Jane Austen Ser.). (ENG.). 64p. pap. 6.95 *(978-1-906230-11-1(0))* Real Reads Ltd. GBR. Dist: Casemate Pubs. & Bk. Distributors, LLC.

—Twilight Magic. Chapman, Linda. 2008. 149p. (J). pap. *(978-0-545-03160-8(5))* Scholastic, Inc.

Kronheimer, Ann. The Fairy Colouring Book. Kronheimer, Ann. 2014. (ENG.). 64p. (J). (gr. 1). pap. 8.99 *(978-1-78055-343-6(9))* O'Mara, Michael Bks., Ltd. GBR. Dist: Independent Pubs. Group.

—The Jungle Book Colouring Book. Kronheimer, Ann. 2018. (ENG.). 32p. (J). (gr. 1-4). pap. 7.99 *(978-1-78055-395-5(1))* O'Mara, Michael Bks., Ltd. GBR. Dist: Independent Pubs. Group.

Kroninger, Stephen. Psssst! It's Me ... the Bogeyman. Park, Barbara. 2018. (ENG.). 40p. (J). (gr. -1-4). 13.99 *(978-1-5344-4121-7(2),* Aladdin) Simon & Schuster Children's Publishing.

Kronreif, Kate. It's a Pumpkin! McClure, Wendy. 2020. (ENG.). 32p. (J). (gr. -1-3). 16.99 ***(978-0-8075-1216-6(8),*** 0807512168) Whitman, Albert & Co.

Krosoczka, Jarrett J. Chew, Chew, Gulp! Thompson, Lauren. 2011. (ENG.). 32p. (J). (gr. -1-k). 14.99 *(978-1-4169-9744-3(X),* McElderry, Margaret K. Bks.) McElderry, Margaret K. Bks.

—Chicken Talk. MacLachlan, Patricia. 2019. (ENG.). 32p. (J). (gr. -1-3). 17.99 *(978-0-06-239864-2(4),* Tegen, Katherine Bks) HarperCollins Pubs.

—The Force Oversleeps. 2017. 172p. (J). *(978-1-338-20871-9(3))* Scholastic, Inc.

—Hop, Hop, Jump! Thompson, Lauren. 2012. (ENG.). 32p. (J). (gr. -1-3). 16.99 *(978-1-4169-9745-0(8),* McElderry, Margaret K. Bks.) McElderry, Margaret K. Bks.

—Must. Push. Buttons! Good, Jason. 2015. (ENG.). 32p. (J). (gr. -1-1). 16.99 *(978-1-61963-095-6(8),* 900120245, Bloomsbury USA Childrens) Bloomsbury Publishing USA.

—Totally Tardy Marty. Perl, Erica S. 2015. (ENG.). 36p. (J). (gr. -1-3). 16.95 *(978-1-4197-1661-4(1),* Abrams Bks. for Young Readers) Abrams, Inc.

Krosoczka, Jarrett J. At Last, Jedi (Star Wars: Jedi Academy #9) Krosoczka, Jarrett J. Ignatow, Amy. 2020. (Star Wars: Jedi Academy Ser.: 9). (ENG.). 176p. (J). (gr. 3-7). 12.99 *(978-1-338-59751-6(5))* Scholastic, Inc.

—Baghead. Krosoczka, Jarrett J. 2004. (ENG.). 40p. (J). (gr. -1-2). reprint ed. pap. 7.99 *(978-0-553-11172-9(8),* Dragonfly Bks.) Random Hse. Children's Bks.

—Platypus Police Squad: Last Panda Standing. Krosoczka, Jarrett J. 2015. (Platypus Police Squad Ser.: 3). (ENG.). 256p. (J). (gr. 3-7). 12.99 *(978-0-06-207168-2(8),* Waldon Pond Pr.) HarperCollins Pubs.

—Platypus Police Squad: Never Say Narwhal. Krosoczka, Jarrett J. 2016. (Platypus Police Squad Ser.: 4). (ENG.). 256p. (J). (gr. 3-7). 12.99 *(978-0-06-207170-5(X),* Waldon Pond Pr.) HarperCollins Pubs.

—Platypus Police Squad: the Frog Who Croaked. Krosoczka, Jarrett J. 2013. (Platypus Police Squad Ser.: 1). (ENG.). 240p. (J). (gr. 3-7). 12.99 *(978-0-06-207164-4(5),* Waldon Pond Pr.) HarperCollins Pubs.

—Platypus Police Squad: the Ostrich Conspiracy. Krosoczka, Jarrett J. 2014. (Platypus Police Squad Ser.: 2). (ENG.). 240p. (J). (gr. 3-7). 13.99 *(978-0-06-207166-8(1),* Waldon Pond Pr.) HarperCollins Pubs.

—Revenge of the Sis. Krosoczka, Jarrett J. Ignatow, Amy. 2019. (Star Wars: Jedi Academy Ser.: 7). (ENG.). 176p. (J). (gr. 3-7). 12.99 *(978-1-338-29538-2(1))* Scholastic, Inc.

Kroug, Simon. Anytime Yoga: Fun & Easy Exercises for Concentration & Calm. Dez�, Ulrika. 2019. (ENG.). 64p. (J). (gr. -1-2). 16.95 *(978-1-61180-439-3(6),* Bala Kids) Shambhala Pubns., Inc.

Krovatin, Dan. A Matter of Conscience: The Trial of Anne Hutchinson. Nichols, Joan K. 2009. (Steck-Vaughn Stories of America Ser.). (ENG.). 112p. (gr. 3-8). pap. 14.20 *(978-0-8114-8073-4(9))* Houghton Mifflin Harcourt Publishing Co.

Krudop, Walter Lyon. At Ellis Island: A History in Many Voices. Peacock, Louise. 2007. (ENG.). 48p. (J). (gr. 2-5). 19.99 *(978-0-689-83026-6(2),* Atheneum Bks. for Young Readers) Simon & Schuster Children's Publishing.

—Black Whiteness: Admiral Byrd Alone in the Antarctic. Burleigh, Robert. 2011. (ENG.). 40p. (J). (gr. 2-5). pap. 19.99 *(978-1-4424-5334-0(6),* Atheneum Bks. for Young Readers) Simon & Schuster Children's Publishing.

—Crossing the Delaware: A History in Many Voices. Peacock, Louise. 2007. (ENG.). 48p. (J). (gr. 3-7). 12.99 *(978-1-4169-5890-1(8),* Simon & Schuster/Paula Wiseman Bks.) Simon & Schuster/Paula Wiseman Bks.

Krueger, Diane & Westenbroek, Ken. Blessly's Carrotnog Christmas Book & Coloring Book. Krueger, Diane. 2004. 14.99 *(978-0-9763695-1-6(6))* Hope Harvest Publishing.

Krueger, Peter. We Gather at This Table. Ostenso Moore, Anna V. 2020. (ENG.). 48p. (J). ***(978-1-64065-252-1(3),*** 815a8478-a047-4b4a-8ea3-db12a7a8eef1) Church Publishing, Inc.

Krug, Ken. No, Silly! Krug, Ken. 2015. (ENG.). 40p. (J). (gr. -1-3). 17.99 *(978-1-4814-0066-4(5),* Beach Lane Bks.) Beach Lane Bks.

Krüger, Simone. After the Rain. Koehn, Rebecca. 2020. (ENG.). 32p. (J). (gr. k-3). 17.99 *(978-1-5064-5451-1(8),* Beaming Books) Augsburg Fortress, Pubs.

Kruger, Simone. Memorial Day. Berne, Emma Carlson. 2018. (Holidays in Rhythm & Rhyme Ser.). (ENG.). 24p. (gr. k-2). lib. bdg. 33.99 *(978-1-68410-389-8(4),* 140366) Cantata Learning.

Kruger, Sydni. Nutcracker & Mouse-King. Hoffmann, E. T. A. Templeton, Alexander S., tr. 2017. (ENG.). (J). (gr. 3-7). pap. 7.99 *(978-0-9982464-1-3(7))* Alexander Stoll Templeton.

Kruk, Aurora. If a Monkey... Langford, Norman Robert. 2019. (ENG.). 28p. (J). pap. 9.99 *(978-1-7931-0151-8(5))* Independently Published.

Krum, Ronda. Jesus Lives! the Easter Story. Derico, Laura Ring. 2015. (Faith That Sticks Bks.). (ENG.). 26p. (J). pap. 3.99 *(978-1-4964-0310-0(X),* 4611985) Tyndale Hse. Pubs.

—Jesus Lives! the Easter Story. Derico, Laura Ring. 2014. (Happy Day Ser.). (ENG.). 16p. (J). pap. 2.49 *(978-1-4143-9415-2(2),* 4608405) Tyndale Hse. Pubs.

Krupa, Anna. What Am I Feeling? Defining Emotions. Flanagan, Katie. 2017. (ENG.). 44p. (J). pap. *(978-1-78623-991-4(4))* Grosvenor Hse. Publishing Ltd.

—What Am I Feeling? Feelings Journal. Flanagan, Katie. 2017. (ENG.). 76p. (J). pap. *(978-1-78623-992-1(2))* Grosvenor Hse. Publishing Ltd.

Krupa, Anna. What Else Am I Feeling? Defining More Emotions. Flanagan, Katie. 2020. (ENG.). 46p. (J). pap. ***(978-1-78623-695-1(8))*** Grosvenor Hse. Publishing Ltd.

Krupinski, Loretta. Como Crece una Semilla: How a Seed Grows (Spanish Edition), 1 vol. Jordan, Helene J. 2006. (Let's-Read-And-Find-Out Science 1 Ser.).Tr. of How a Seed Grows. (SPA.). 32p. (J). (gr. -1-3). pap. 6.99 *(978-0-06-088716-2(8),* HarperCollins Español) HarperCollins Christian Publishing.

—How a Seed Grows. Jordan, Helene J. 2015. (Let's-Read-And-Find-Out Science 1 Ser.). (ENG.). 32p. (J). (gr. -1-3). pap. 6.99 *(978-0-06-238188-0(1))* HarperCollins Pubs.

—Why Do Leaves Change Color? Maestro, Betsy. 2015. (Let's-Read-And-Find-Out Science 2 Ser.). (ENG.). 32p. (J). (gr. -1-3). pap. 6.99 *(978-0-06-238201-6(2))* HarperCollins Pubs.

Krupnek, Joann J. Sandbox Sandshoes. Eddy, Catherine J. 2009. 38p. pap. 10.95 *(978-0-9818488-5-3(0))* Ajoyin Publishing, Inc.

Krupp, Marian N. No-No & the Secret Touch: The Gentle Story of a Little Seal Who Learns to Stay Safe, Say "No" & Tell! Patterson, Sherri et al. unabr. ed. 70p. (J). (gr. 1-6). pap. 14.95 incl. audio *(978-0-9632276-2-1(9))* National Self-Esteem Resources & Development Ctr.

Krupp, Susan. Merlin's Kin. Everett, Jack & Coles, David. 2017. (ENG.). (J). pap. 13.95 *(978-1-946469-33-5(5))* Portals Publishing.

Kruse, Jason T. Arctic Attack. Greenberger, Robert & Loughridge, Lee. 2013. (Batman Ser.). (ENG.). 56p. (J). (gr. 3-6). pap. 4.95 *(978-1-4342-1728-8(0),* Stone Arch Bks.) Capstone.

Krüse, Tarsila. My Little Album of Dublin: An English & Irish Word Book. Saumande, Juliette. 2019. (ENG.). 32p. 20.00 *(978-1-84717-998-2(3))* O'Brien Pr., Ltd., The IRL. Dist: Casemate Pubs. & Bk. Distributors, LLC.

Krush, Beth. Senior Year. Emery, Anne. 2006. (YA). per. 11.95 *(978-1-59511-005-3(4))* Image Cascade Publishing.

Krush, Beth & Krush, Joe. The Borrowers. Norton, Mary. 2003. (Borrowers Ser.: 1). (ENG.). 192p. (J). (gr. 3-7). pap. 7.99 *(978-0-15-204737-5(9),* 1194281) Houghton Mifflin Harcourt Publishing Co.

—The Borrowers. Norton, Mary. l.t. ed. 2005. 215p. (J). (gr. 3). per. 10.95 *(978-0-7862-7954-8(0))* Thorndike Pr.

—The Borrowers. Norton, Mary. ed. 2003. (Odyssey Classic Ser.). 180p. (gr. 4-7). 17.20 *(978-0-613-63581-3(7))* Turtleback.

—The Borrowers Afield. Norton, Mary. 50th anniv. ed. 2003. (Borrowers Ser.: 2). (ENG.). 224p. (J). (gr. 3-7). pap. 7.99 *(978-0-15-204732-0(8),* 1194268) Houghton Mifflin Harcourt Publishing Co.

—The Borrowers Afloat. Norton, Mary. 2003. (Borrowers Ser.: 3). (ENG.). 192p. (J). (gr. 3-7). pap. 7.99 *(978-0-15-204733-7(6),* 1194271) Houghton Mifflin Harcourt Publishing Co.

—The Borrowers Aloft: Plus the Short Tale Poor Stainless. Norton, Mary. 50th anniv. ed. 2003. (Borrowers Ser.: 4). (ENG.). 224p. (J). (gr. 3-7). pap. 7.99 *(978-0-15-204734-4(4),* 1194274) Houghton Mifflin Harcourt Publishing Co.

Krush, Beth & Krush, Joe. Countdown at 37 Pinecrest Drive. Fleming, Susan. 2013. (37 Pinecrest Drive Ser.: Vol. 2). (ENG.). 134p. (J). pap. 10.00 ***(978-1-4848-5803-5(4))*** CreateSpace Independent Publishing Platform.

Krush, Beth & Krush, Joe. Gone-Away Lake. Enright, Elizabeth. 2006. 256p. (J). (gr. 4-8). reprint ed. pap. 6.00 *(978-1-4223-5436-0(9))* DIANE Publishing Co.

Krush, Beth & Krush, Joe. The Pig at 37 Pinecrest Drive. Fleming, Susan. 2013. (37 Pinecrest Drive Ser.: Vol. 1). (ENG.). 132p. (J). pap. 10.00 ***(978-1-4848-5801-1(8))*** CreateSpace Independent Publishing Platform.

Krush, Beth, jt. illus. see Krush, Joe.

Krush, Joe, et al. The Borrowers Avenged. Norton, Mary. 50th anniv. ed. 2003. (Borrowers Ser.: 5). (ENG.). 304p. (J). (gr. 3-7). pap. 7.99 *(978-0-15-204731-3(X),* 1194264) Houghton Mifflin Harcourt Publishing Co.

Krush, Joe & Krush, Beth. The Complete Adventures of the Borrowers. Norton, Mary. 2011. (ENG.). 1152p. (J). (gr. 3-7). 34.99 *(978-0-15-204915-7(0),* 1194842) Houghton Mifflin Harcourt Publishing Co.

—Miracles on Maple Hill. Sorensen, Virginia. 2003. (ENG.). 256p. (J). (gr. 3-7). pap. 7.99 *(978-0-15-204718-4(2),* 1194220) Houghton Mifflin Harcourt Publishing Co.

Krush, Joe, jt. illus. see Krush, Beth.

Krushak-Green, Laura. The Snow Baby. Hillert, Margaret. 21st ed. 2016. (BeginningtoRead Ser.). (ENG.). 32p. (J). (gr. -1-2). pap. 11.94 *(978-1-60357-945-2(1));* (gr. 1-2). 22.60 *(978-1-59953-804-4(0))* Norwood Hse. Pr.

Krutop, Lee. Ocean Creatures. 2008. (Jigsaw Bks.). 12p. (J). (gr. -1-3). bds. *(978-1-86503-923-7(3))* Five Mile Australia.

Krygsman, Joan. Rosa Rose. Priest, Robert. 2013. (ENG.). 56p. pap. 10.00 *(978-1-894987-73-8(X))* Wolsak & Wynn Pubs., Ltd. CAN. Dist: Independent Pubs. Group.

Krykorka, Vladyana. Baseball Bats for Christmas. Kusugak, Michael Arvaarluk. 2017. (ENG.). 24p. (J). (gr. 1-3). 9.95 *(978-1-55451-928-6(4))* Annick Pr., Ltd. CAN. Dist: Publishers Group West (PGW).

—Carl the Christmas Carp, 1 vol. Krykorka, Ian. 2016. (ENG.). 32p. (J). (gr. -1-k). 15.95 *(978-1-4598-1377-9(4))* Orca Bk. Pubs. USA.

—The Littlest Sled Dog, 1 vol. Kusugak, Michael. 2010. (ENG.). 32p. (J). (gr. -1-k). pap. 10.95 *(978-1-55469-174-6(5))* Orca Bk. Pubs. USA.

—Orphans in the Sky, 1 vol. Bushey, Jeanne. 2004. (ENG.). 32p. (J). (gr. k-1). 9.95 *(978-0-88995-291-1(4),* 71b62896-4f24-4e28-8513-28a5a303d3ce) Red Deer Pr. CAN. Dist: Firefly Bks., Ltd.

—A Promise Is a Promise. Munsch, Robert & Kusugak, Michael Arvaarluk. 2019. (Classic Munsch Ser.). (ENG.). 32p. (J). (gr. k-2). 6.95 *(978-1-77321-293-7(1))* Annick Pr., Ltd. CAN. Dist: Publishers Group West (PGW).

—A Promise Is a Promise. Kusugak, Michael Arvaarluk & Munsch, Robert. 2019. (Classic Munsch Ser.). (ENG.). 32p. (J). (gr. k-2). 19.95 *(978-1-77321-294-4(X))* Annick Pr., Ltd. CAN. Dist: Publishers Group West (PGW).

Krykorka, Vladyana & Ohi, Ruth. Next Stop!, 1 vol. Page, P. K. & Ellis, Sarah. 2005. (ENG.). 32p. (J). (gr. 1-2). pap. 6.95 *(978-1-55041-809-5(2),* 58baa977-9941-4c27-95a0-d4ce7540d026) éditeur, Annika Parance CAN. Dist: Firefly Bks., Ltd.

Krykorka, Vladyana L. A Grain of Sand, 1 vol. Page, P. K. 2003. (ENG.). 28p. (J). (gr. 1-4). 9.95 *(978-1-55041-801-9(7),* e06c5bcb-d171-4954-88d7-0ef5350041f6) Trifolium Bks., Inc. CAN. Dist: Firefly Bks., Ltd.

Krynauw, Theo. Go for Lift Off! How to Train Like an Astronaut. Williams, Dave & Cunti, Loredana. 2017. (Dr. Dave — Astronaut Ser.). (ENG.). 52p. (gr. 1-6). pap. 12.95 *(978-1-55451-914-9(4))* Annick Pr., Ltd. CAN. Dist: Publishers Group West (PGW).

Krysinski, Grzegorz, jt. illus. see Parisi, Andrea.

Krystoforski, Andrej. Alexander Graham Bell. MacLeod, Elizabeth. 2007. 32p. (J). (gr. 1-3). 14.95 *(978-1-55453-001-4(6))* Kids Can Pr., Ltd. CAN. Dist: Hachette Bk. Group.

—The Boy Who Loved Bananas. Elliott, George. 2005. 32p. (J). (gr. -1-2). 15.95 *(978-1-55337-744-3(3))* Kids Can Pr., Ltd. CAN. Dist: Hachette Bk. Group.

—From Then to Now: A Short History of the World. Moore, Christopher. 2011. 192p. (J). (gr. 5-18). 25.95 *(978-0-88776-540-7(8),* Tundra Bks.) Tundra Bks. CAN. Dist: Penguin Random Hse. LLC.

—Helen Keller. MacLeod, Elizabeth. 2007. (Kids Can Read Ser.). 32p. (J). (gr. 1-3). (ENG.). 3.95 *(978-1-55453-000-7(8));* 14.95 *(978-1-55337-999-7(3))* Kids Can Pr., Ltd. CAN. Dist: Hachette Bk. Group.

—In the Land of the Jaguar: South America & Its People. Gorrell, Gena K. 2007. 160p. (J). (gr. 4-7). 22.95 *(978-0-88776-756-2(7),* Tundra Bks.) Tundra Bks. CAN. Dist: Penguin Random Hse. LLC.

—Mystery of the Lake. Thomas, Cameron. 2004. (Jungle of Utt Ser.). 40p. (J). 16.95 *(978-0-921800-02-6(9))* MGT Developments, Ltd. CAN. Dist: Independent Pubs. Group.

—Shipwrecked on the Island of Skree. Thomas, Cameron. 2004. (Jungle of Utt Ser.). 48p. (J). 16.95 *(978-0-921800-01-9(0))* MGT Developments, Ltd. CAN. Dist: Independent Pubs. Group.

—Thomas Edison. MacLeod, Elizabeth. 2008. 32p. (J). (gr. 1-3). 14.95 *(978-1-55453-057-1(1));* (ENG.). pap. 11.99 *(978-1-55453-058-8(X))* Kids Can Pr., Ltd. CAN. Dist: Hachette Bk. Group.

—The Utt Jungle Airline: The Jungle of Utt. Thomas, Cameron. 2004. (Jungle of Utt Ser.). 48p. (J). 16.95 *(978-0-921800-03-3(7))* MGT Developments, Ltd. CAN. Dist: Independent Pubs. Group.

—The Wright Brothers. MacLeod, Elizabeth. 2008. (Kids Can Read Ser.). 32p. (J). (gr. 1-3). 14.95 *(978-1-55453-053-3(9));* (ENG.). pap. 3.95 *(978-1-55453-054-0(7))* Kids Can Pr., Ltd. CAN. Dist: Hachette Bk. Group.

Ku, Min Sung. Batman Origami: Amazing Folding Projects for the Dark Knight. Montroll, John. 2015. (DC Origami Ser.). (ENG.). 48p. (J). (gr. 3-7). lib. bdg. 28.65 *(978-1-4914-1786-7(2),* Stone Arch Bks.) Capstone.

—DC Origami. Montroll, John. 2015. (DC Origami Ser.). (ENG.). 48p. (gr. 4-5). 111.96 *(978-1-4914-1790-4(0),* Stone Arch Bks.) Capstone.

—Justice League Origami: Amazing Folding Projects for the JLA. Montroll, John. 2015. (DC Origami Ser.). (ENG.). 48p. (J). (gr. 3-7). lib. bdg. 28.65 *(978-1-4914-1789-8(7),* Stone Arch Bks.) Capstone.

—The Kid Who Saved Superman, 1 vol. Kupperberg, Paul & Loughridge, Lee. 2013. (Superman Ser.). (ENG.). 56p. (J). (gr. 3-6). pap. 4.95 *(978-1-4342-1937-4(2),* Stone Arch Bks.) Capstone.

—The Kid Who Saved Superman, 1 vol. Kupperberg, Paul. 2009. (Superman Ser.). (ENG.). 56p. (J). (gr. 3-6). lib. bdg. 26.65 *(978-1-4342-1936-7(4),* Stone Arch Bks.) Capstone.

—Superman Origami: Amazing Folding Projects for the Man of Steel. Montroll, John. 2015. (DC Origami Ser.). (ENG.). 48p. (J). (gr. 3-7). lib. bdg. 28.65 *(978-1-4914-1787-4(0),* Stone Arch Bks.) Capstone.

—Wonder Woman Origami: Amazing Folding Projects for the Warrior Princess. Montroll, John. 2015. (DC Origami Ser.). (ENG.). 48p. (J). (gr. 3-7). lib. bdg. 28.65 *(978-1-4914-1788-1(9),* Stone Arch Bks.) Capstone.

Kuang, Jiale, jt. illus. see Vallejo, Monserratt.

Kubasta, Vojtech. Once upon a Time: Folk & Fairy Tales of the World. Green, Roger Lancelyn, ed. 2011. 140p. 40.95 *(978-1-258-03324-8(0))* Literary Licensing, LLC.

Kubaszewska, Anna. Can You Stop the Rain? Novick, Rona Milch. 2020. (J). *(978-1-68115-555-5(9),* Apples & Honey Pr.) Behrman Hse., Inc.

—Counting Sheep. Fischer, Maggie. 2019. (ENG.). 10p. (J). (— 1). bds. 8.99 *(978-1-68412-840-2(4),* Silver Dolphin Bks.) Printers Row Publishing Group.

Kubert, Adam, et al. Avengers by Jonathan Hickman: the Complete Collection Vol. 1. 2020. (ENG.). 336p. (YA). (gr. 8-17). pap. 34.99 ***(978-1-302-92509-3(1))*** Marvel Worldwide, Inc.

Kubert, Adam, et al. Monsters Unleashed. 2018. (ENG.). 168p. (YA). (gr. 8-17). pap. 24.99 *(978-1-302-90485-2(X))* Marvel Worldwide, Inc.

—Monsters Unleashed: Monster-Size. 2017. (ENG.). 168p. (YA). (gr. 8-17). 50.00 *(978-1-302-90726-6(3))* Marvel Worldwide, Inc.

Kubert, Adam. Peter Parker: the Spectacular Spider-Man Vol. 1: Into the Twilight. 2017. 144p. (J). (gr. 4-17). pap. 17.99 *(978-1-302-90756-3(5))* Marvel Worldwide, Inc.

Kubert, Adam, et al. Ultimate X-Men, 2 vols., Vol. 2. Millar, Mark & Austen, Chuck. 2003. (Ultimate X-Men Ser.). 336p. (YA). 29.99 *(978-0-7851-1130-6(1))* Marvel Worldwide, Inc.

Kubert, Adam. Ultimate X-Men - Volume 3: World Tour. 2006. (ENG.). 192p. (J). (gr. -1-17). pap. 17.99 *(978-0-7851-0961-7(7))* Marvel Worldwide, Inc.

—Ultimate X-Men - Volume 4: Hellfire & Brimstone, 4 vols. 2006. (ENG.). 144p. (J). (gr. -1-17). pap. 12.99 *(978-0-7851-1089-7(5))* Marvel Worldwide, Inc.

Kubert, Adam & Kubert, Andy. Ultimate X-Men - Volume 1: The Tomorrow People, Vol. 1. 2006. (ENG.). 160p. (J). (gr. 4-17). pap. 14.99 *(978-0-7851-0788-0(6))* Marvel Worldwide, Inc.

Kubert, Adam, jt. illus. see Yu, Leinil Francis.

Kubert, Andy, et al. X-Men: Shattershot. 2019. 616p. (YA). (gr. 4-17). 75.00 *(978-1-302-92068-5(5))* Marvel Worldwide, Inc.

Kubert, Andy, jt. illus. see Kubert, Adam.

Kubert, Andy, jt. illus. see Quesada, Joe.

Kubert, Joe, et al. Conan Chronicles Epic Collection: the Battle of Shamla Pass. 2020. (ENG.). 472p. (gr. 12-17). pap. 44.99 *(978-1-302-92191-0(6))* Marvel Worldwide, Inc.

Kubic, Ginger. Just in Time. Butler, Dori Hillestad. Trissler, Rebecca Johns, ed. (Adventures of Storydog Ser.). (J). pap. *(978-0-9722690-2-5(9)*, 1002) Storydog, Inc.

—Subway Crush. Bonk, John J. Trissler, Rebecca Johns, ed. (Adventures of Storydog Ser.). 75p. (J). pap. *(978-0-9722690-1-8(0)*, 1001) Storydog, Inc.

Kubica, Donna. Tales. Moritz, Cassandra R. 2020. (Fractured World Ser.: Vol. 2). (ENG.). 56p. (J). pap. 7.00 ***(978-1-6573-2009-3(X))*** Independently Published.

Kubick, Dana. I Love You, Grandpa. French, Vivian. 2006. (ENG.). 32p. (J). (gr. -1-2). 5.99 *(978-0-7636-2748-5(8))* Candlewick Pr.

Kubina, Monica, jt. illus. see Widermann, Eva.

Kubinyi, Laszlo. The Diary of Elizabeth Bacon Custer: On the Plains with General Custer. Custer, Elizabeth Bacon. Plain, Nancy, ed. 2005. (In My Own Words Ser.). 64p. (gr. 6-6). lib. bdg. 32.36 *(978-0-7614-1647-0(1))* Cavendish Square Publishing LLC.

—Dig It! Riggs, Kate. 2013. (ENG.). 14p. (J). (gr. -1-k). bds. 7.99 *(978-1-56846-237-0(9)*, Creative Editions) Creative Co., The.

—Goldilocks, 1 vol. Roberts, Tom. 2005. (Rabbit Ears-A Classic Tale Ser.). (ENG.). 28p. (J). (gr. 2-6). 28.50 *(978-1-59197-748-3(7)*, 12950, Picture Bk.) Spotlight.

—Red Riding Hood, 1 vol. Roberts, Tom. 2005. (Rabbit Ears-A Classic Tale Ser.). (ENG.). 28p. (J). (gr. 2-6). 28.50 *(978-1-59197-752-0(5)*, 12954, Picture Bk.) Spotlight.

—The Revolutionary War. Beller, Susan Provost. 2003. (American Voices From Ser.). 160p. (gr. 6-6). 38.07 *(978-0-7614-1202-1(6))* Cavendish Square Publishing LLC.

—Skywriting: Poems to Fly. Lewis, J. Patrick. 2010. (ENG.). 32p. (J). (gr. 4-7). 17.95 *(978-1-56846-203-5(4)*, Creative Editions) Creative Co., The.

Kubinyi, Laszlo & Green, Julia. Survivors: the Gathering Darkness #1: a Pack Divided. Hunter, Erin. 2015. (Survivors: the Gathering Darkness Ser.: 1). (ENG.). 304p. (J). (gr. 3-7). 16.99 *(978-0-06-234333-8(5))* HarperCollins Pubs.

—Survivors: the Gathering Darkness #2: Dead of Night. Hunter, Erin. 2016. (Survivors: the Gathering Darkness Ser.: 2). (ENG.). 304p. (J). (gr. 3-7). 16.99 *(978-0-06-234337-6(8))* HarperCollins Pubs.

—Survivors: the Gathering Darkness #3: into the Shadows. Hunter, Erin. 2017. (Survivors: the Gathering Darkness Ser.: 3). (ENG.). 320p. (J). (gr. 3-7). 16.99 *(978-0-06-234341-3(6))* HarperCollins Pubs.

—Survivors: the Gathering Darkness #3: into the Shadows. Hunter, Erin. 2017. (Survivors: the Gathering Darkness Ser.: 3). (ENG.). 336p. (J). (gr. 3-7). pap. 7.99 *(978-0-06-234343-7(2)*, HarperCollins) HarperCollins Pubs. Ltd. GBR. Dist: HarperCollins Pubs.

—Survivors: the Gathering Darkness #4: Red Moon Rising. Hunter, Erin. (Survivors: the Gathering Darkness Ser.: 4). (ENG.). (J). (gr. 3-7). 2018. 320p. pap. 7.99 *(978-0-06-234347-5(5))*; 2017. 304p. 16.99 *(978-0-06-234345-1(9))*; 2017. 304p. lib. bdg. 17.89 *(978-0-06-234346-8(7))* HarperCollins Pubs.

—Survivors: the Gathering Darkness #5: the Exile's Journey. Hunter, Erin. (Survivors: the Gathering Darkness Ser.: 5). (ENG.). 320p. (J). (gr. 3-7). 2019. pap. 7.99 *(978-0-06-234351-2(3))*; 2018. 16.99 *(978-0-06-234349-9(1))*; 2018. lib. bdg. 17.89 *(978-0-06-234350-5(5))* HarperCollins Pubs.

Kubinyi, Laszlo, jt. illus. see Green, Julia.

Kubler, Annie. Baa, Baa, Black Sheep! American Sign Language. 2005. (Sign & Singalong Ser.). (ENG.). 12p. (J). (gr. k-1). bds. *(978-1-904550-41-9(X))* Child's Play International Ltd.

—Dress Up! 2012. (Mix & Match Babies Ser.). (ENG.). 12p. (J). bds. *(978-1-84643-485-3(8))* Child's Play International Ltd.

—Head, Shoulders, Knees & Toes... /Cabeza, Hombros, Piernas, Pies... 2009. (Baby Board Bks.). (ENG & SPA.). 12p. (J). bds. *(978-1-84643-311-5(8))* Child's Play International Ltd.

—Humpty Dumpty. 2010. (Baby Board Bks.). 12p. (J). bds. *(978-1-84643-339-9(8))* Child's Play International Ltd.

—If You're Happy & You Know It... /Si Te Sientes Bien Contento... 2009. (Baby Board Bks.). (ENG & SPA.). 12p. (J). bds. *(978-1-84643-310-8(X))* Child's Play International Ltd.

—I'm a Little Teapot. 2007. (Baby Board Bks.). 12p. (J). (gr. k-1). bds. *(978-1-84643-122-7(0))* Child's Play International Ltd.

—Itsy, Bitsy Spider: American Sign Language. 2005. (Sign & Singalong Ser.). (ENG.). 12p. (J). (gr. k-k). bds. *(978-1-904550-43-3(6))* Child's Play International Ltd.

—Las Ruedas Del Autobús Giran y Giran. (Classic Books with Holes 8x8 with CD Ser.). (SPA.). 16p. (J). 2019. *(978-1-78628-399-3(9))*; 2018. *(978-1-78628-166-1(X))*; 2018. pap. *(978-1-84643-965-0(5))*; 2018. bds. *(978-1-84643-968-1(X))* Child's Play International Ltd.

—The Mixed up Caterpillar. 2006. (Finger Puppet Bks.). (ENG.). 24p. (J). (gr. 1-1). *(978-1-84643-026-8(7))* Child's Play International Ltd.

—My First Signs: American Sign Language. 2005. (Baby Signing Ser.). (ENG.). 12p. (J). (gr. k-1). bds. *(978-1-904550-39-6(8))* Child's Play International Ltd.

—Pussy Cat, Pussy Cat. 2010. (Baby Board Bks.). 12p. (J). bds. *(978-1-84643-340-5(1))* Child's Play International Ltd.

—Ride On! 2012. (Mix & Match Babies Ser.). (ENG.). 12p. (J). bds. *(978-1-84643-483-9(1))* Child's Play International Ltd.

—Ring Around a Rosie. 2003. (Baby Board Bks.). (ENG.). 12p. (J). bds. *(978-0-85953-578-6(9))* Child's Play International Ltd.

—Round & Round the Garden. 2019. (Baby Board Bks.). 12p. (J). bds. *(978-1-78628-197-5(X))* Child's Play International Ltd.

—Row, Row, Row Your Boat. 2003. (Baby Board Bks.). 12p. (J). bds. *(978-0-85953-658-5(0))* Child's Play International Ltd.

—Sleeping Bunnies. 2019. (Baby Board Bks.). 12p. (J). bds. *(978-1-78628-198-2(8))* Child's Play International Ltd.

—Teddy Bear, Teddy Bear: American Sign Language. 2005. (Sign & Singalong Ser.). (ENG.). 12p. (J). (gr. k-1). bds. *(978-1-904550-40-2(1))* Child's Play International Ltd.

—Ten Little Fingers/Tengo Diez Deditos. 2009. (Baby Board Bks.). (ENG & SPA.). 12p. (J). bds. *(978-1-84643-312-2(6))* Child's Play International Ltd.

—This Little Piggy / Este Cochinito. 2009. (Baby Board Bks.). (ENG & SPA.). 12p. (J). bds. *(978-1-84643-313-9(4))* Child's Play International Ltd.

—Twinkle, Twinkle, Little Star. 2003. (Classic Books with Holes 8x8 Ser.). (ENG.). 16p. (J). (gr. -1-3). pap. *(978-0-85953-133-7(3))* Child's Play International Ltd.

—Twinkle, Twinkle, Little Star: American Sign Language. 2005. (Sign & Singalong Ser.). (ENG.). 12p. (J). (gr. k-k). bds. *(978-1-904550-42-6(8))* Child's Play International Ltd.

—What Can I Feel? 2011. (Small Senses Ser.). 12p. (J). spiral bd. *(978-1-84643-374-0(6))* Child's Play International Ltd.

—What Can I Hear? 2011. (Small Senses Ser.). 12p. (J). spiral bd. *(978-1-84643-377-1(0))* Child's Play International Ltd.

—What Can I See? 2011. (Small Senses Ser.). 12p. (J). spiral bd. *(978-1-84643-378-8(9))* Child's Play International Ltd.

—What Can I Smell? 2011. (Small Senses Ser.). 12p. (J). spiral bd. *(978-1-84643-376-4(2))* Child's Play International Ltd.

—What Can I Taste? 2011. (Small Senses Ser.). 12p. (J). spiral bd. *(978-1-84643-375-7(4))* Child's Play International Ltd.

—What Do I Feel? / ¿Qué Siento? Mlawer, Teresa, tr. ed. 2015. (Small Senses Bilingual Ser.: 5). (ENG & SPA.). 12p. (J). bds. *(978-1-84643-721-2(0))* Child's Play International Ltd.

—What Do I Hear? / ¿Qué Oigo? Mlawer, Teresa, tr. ed. 2015. (Small Senses Bilingual Ser.: 5). (ENG & SPA.). 12p. (J). bds. *(978-1-84643-724-3(5))* Child's Play International Ltd.

—What Do I See? / ¿Qué Veo? Mlawer, Teresa, tr. ed. 2015. (Small Senses Bilingual Ser.: 5). (ENG & SPA.). 12p. (J). bds. *(978-1-84643-725-0(3))* Child's Play International Ltd.

—What Do I Smell? / ¿Qué Huelo? Mlawer, Teresa, tr. ed. 2015. (Small Senses Bilingual Ser.: 5). (ENG & SPA.). 12p. (J). bds. *(978-1-84643-723-6(7))* Child's Play International Ltd.

—What Do I Taste? / ¿Qué Saboreo? Mlawer, Teresa, tr. ed. 2015. (Small Senses Bilingual Ser.: 5). (ENG & SPA.). 12p. (J). bds. *(978-1-84643-722-9(9))* Child's Play International Ltd.

—What's the Time, Mr Wolf? 2003. (Finger Puppet Bks.). 24p. (J). (gr. 1-1). *(978-0-85953-944-9(X))* Child's Play International Ltd.

—The Wheels on the Bus. 2019. (Baby Board Bks.). 12p. (J). bds. *(978-1-78628-196-8(1))* Child's Play International Ltd.

—The Wheels on the Bus Go Round & Round. (Classic Books with Holes 8x8 with CD Ser.). (ENG.). 16p. (J). 2007. (gr. -1-1). *(978-1-904550-66-2(5))*; 2003. *(978-0-85953-136-8(8))* Child's Play International Ltd.

—Work Out! 2012. (Mix & Match Babies Ser.). (ENG.). 12p. (J). bds. *(978-1-84643-484-6(X))* Child's Play International Ltd.

—Zoom, Zoom, Zoom! 2019. (Baby Board Bks.). 12p. (J). bds. *(978-1-78628-199-9(6))* Child's Play International Ltd.

Kubler, Annie. Wheels on the Bus, 15 vols. Kubler, Annie. 2005. 14p. (J). (ARA, ENG & MUL.). bds. *(978-1-84444-970-5(X))*; (BEN, ENG & MUL.). bds. *(978-1-84444-971-2(8))*; (CHI, ENG & MUL.). bds. *(978-1-84444-972-9(6))*; (CHI, ENG & MUL.). bds. *(978-1-84444-973-6(4))*; (ENG, FRE & MUL.). bds. *(978-1-84444-974-3(2))*; (ENG, HIN, MUL & GUJ.). bds. *(978-1-84444-975-0(0))*; (ENG, SOM & MUL.). bds. *(978-1-84444-978-1(5))*; (ENG, TUR & MUL.). bds. *(978-1-84444-980-4(7))*; (URD, ENG & MUL.). bds. *(978-1-84444-981-1(5))* Mantra Lingua.

—The Wheels on the Bus, 15 vols. Kubler, Annie. 14p. (J). 2005. (ENG, PER & MUL.). bds. *(978-1-84444-532-5(1))*; 2005. (SWA, ENG & MUL.). bds. *(978-1-84444-533-2(X))*; 2004. (ENG, TGL & MUL.). bds. *(978-1-84444-534-9(8))* Mantra Lingua.

Kubler, Annie & Dellow, Sarah. Hey Diddle Diddle. (Baby Board Bks.). 12p. (J). 2020. (ENG.). bds. ***(978-1-78628-408-2(1))***; 2007. (gr. 1-1). spiral bd. *(978-1-84643-121-0(2))* Child's Play International Ltd.

—Pat a Cake. 2020. (Baby Board Bks.). (ENG.). 12p. (J). bds. ***(978-1-78628-407-5(3))*** Child's Play International Ltd.

—Ten Little Fingers. 2020. (Baby Board Bks.). (ENG.). 12p. (J). bds. ***(978-1-78628-406-8(5))*** Child's Play International Ltd.

—This Little Piggy. 2020. (Baby Board Bks.). (ENG.). 12p. (J). bds. ***(978-1-78628-405-1(7))*** Child's Play International Ltd.

Kucharik, Elena. Bed Time Blessings. Mackall, Dandi Daley. 2012. (Little Blessings Ser.). (ENG.). 32p. (J). pap. 3.99 *(978-1-4143-7528-1(X)*, 4606518) Tyndale Hse. Pubs.

—Bedtime Stories & Prayers. Mackall, Dandi Daley & Bostrom, Kathleen Long. 2013. (Little Blessings Ser.). (ENG.). 128p. (J). 14.99 *(978-1-4143-8111-4(5)*, 4607101) Tyndale Hse. Pubs.

—Easter Stories & Prayers. Bostrom, Kathleen Long. 2015. (Little Blessings Ser.). (ENG.). 144p. (J). 7.99 *(978-1-4964-0280-6(4)*, 4611955) Tyndale Hse. Pubs.

—Is God Always with Me? Bowman, Crystal. 2006. (Little Blessings Ser.). (ENG.). 64p. (J). 9.99 *(978-1-4143-0287-4(8)*, 6002878) Tyndale Hse. Pubs.

—The One Year Devotions for Preschoolers. Bowman, Crystal. 2004. (Little Blessings Ser.). (ENG.). 384p. (J). 14.99 *(978-0-8423-8940-2(7)*, 6089407, Tyndale Kids) Tyndale Hse. Pubs.

—The One Year Devotions for Preschoolers 2. Barnhill, Carla. 2010. (Little Blessings Ser.). (ENG.). 384p. (J). 14.99 *(978-1-4143-3445-5(1)*, 4602435, Tyndale Kids) Tyndale Hse. Pubs.

—Questions from Little Hearts. Bostrom, Kathleen Long. 2009. (Little Blessings Ser.). (ENG.). 288p. (J). (gr. -1-k). 14.99 *(978-1-4143-2998-7(9)*, 4601988) Tyndale Hse. Pubs.

Kuder, Aaron. Fantastic Four by Dan Slott Vol. 2: Mr. & Mrs. Grimm, Vol. 2. 2019. (ENG.). 160p. (YA). pap. 15.99 *(978-1-302-91350-2(6))* Marvel Worldwide, Inc.

—Ghost Rider Vol. 1: King of Hell. 2020. (ENG.). 120p. (YA). (gr. 8-17). pap. 15.99 *(978-1-302-92005-0(7))* Marvel Worldwide, Inc.

Kuder, Aaron, et al. Guardians of the Galaxy by Gerry Duggan Omnibus. 2018. (Guardians of the Galaxy by Gerry Duggan Omnibus Ser.: 1). (ENG.). 408p. (YA). (gr. 8-17). 75.00 *(978-1-302-91315-1(8))* Marvel Worldwide, Inc.

Kudranski, Szymon. Fallen Angels Vol. 1. 2020. (ENG.). 176p. (YA). (gr. 8-17). pap. 17.99 *(978-1-302-91990-0(3))* Marvel Worldwide, Inc.

—The Punisher Vol. 2: War in Bagalia, Vol. 2. 2019. (ENG.). 112p. pap. 17.99 *(978-1-302-91348-9(4))* Marvel Worldwide, Inc.

Kudranski, Szymon, et al. Spider-Man: Miles Morales Omnibus. 2020. (ENG.). 856p. (YA). (gr. 4-17). 100.00 *(978-1-302-92288-7(2))* Marvel Worldwide, Inc.

Kuefler, Joseph. Caveboy Crush. Ferry, Beth. 2019. (ENG.). 48p. (J). (gr. -1-3). 17.99 *(978-1-4197-3656-8(6)*, 1242301) Abrams, Inc.

—Evangeline of the Bayou. Eldredge, Jan. 2018. (ENG.). 320p. (J). (gr. 3-7). 16.99 *(978-0-06-268034-1(X)*, Balzer & Bray) HarperCollins Pubs.

—The Night Is for Darkness. Stutzman, Jonathan. 2020. (ENG.). 40p. (J). (gr. -1-3). 17.99 *(978-0-06-291253-4(4)*, Balzer & Bray) HarperCollins Pubs.

Kuefler, Joseph. Beyond the Pond. Kuefler, Joseph. 2015. (ENG.). 40p. (J). (gr. -1-3). 17.99 *(978-0-06-236427-2(8))* HarperCollins Pubs.

—The Digger & the Flower. Kuefler, Joseph. 2018. (ENG.). 48p. (J). (gr. -1-3). 17.99 *(978-0-06-242433-4(5)*, Balzer & Bray) HarperCollins Pubs.

—Rulers of the Playground. Kuefler, Joseph. 2017. (ENG.). 48p. (J). (gr. -1-3). 17.99 *(978-0-06-242432-7(7))* HarperCollins Pubs.

Kueker, Donald. The Easter Story According to Matthew. 2007. 32p. (J). per. 7.49 *(978-0-7586-1008-9(4))* Concordia Publishing Hse.

Kuemer, Karl J., jt. illus. see Wyeth, Andrew N.

Kuether, James. Allosaurus. Sabelko, Rebecca. 2020. (World of Dinosaurs Ser.). (ENG.). 24p. (J). (gr. 3-7). pap. 7.99 ***(978-1-68103-835-3(8))***; lib. bdg. 25.95 ***(978-1-64487-290-1(0))*** Bellwether Media.

—Apatosaurus. Sabelko, Rebecca. 2020. (World of Dinosaurs Ser.). (ENG.). 24p. (J). (gr. 3-7). pap. 7.99 ***(978-1-68103-836-0(6))***; lib. bdg. 25.95 ***(978-1-64487-291-8(9))*** Bellwether Media.

—Argentinosaurus. Sabelko, Rebecca. 2021. (World of Dinosaurs Ser.). (ENG.). 24p. (J). (gr. 3-7). lib. bdg. 25.95 ***(978-1-64487-468-4(7))*** Bellwether Media.

—Iguanodon. Sabelko, Rebecca. 2021. (World of Dinosaurs Ser.). (ENG.). 24p. (J). (gr. 3-7). lib. bdg. 25.95 ***(978-1-64487-469-1(5))*** Bellwether Media.

—Oviraptor. Sabelko, Rebecca. 2020. (World of Dinosaurs Ser.). (ENG.). 24p. (J). (gr. 3-7). pap. 7.99 ***(978-1-68103-837-7(4))***; lib. bdg. 25.95 ***(978-1-64487-292-5(7))*** Bellwether Media.

—Parasaurolophus. Sabelko, Rebecca. 2020. (World of Dinosaurs Ser.). (ENG.). 24p. (J). (gr. 3-7). pap. 7.99 ***(978-1-68103-838-4(2))***; lib. bdg. 25.95 ***(978-1-64487-293-2(5))*** Bellwether Media.

—Spinosaurus. Sabelko, Rebecca. 2021. (World of Dinosaurs Ser.). (ENG.). 24p. (J). (gr. 3-7). lib. bdg. 25.95 ***(978-1-64487-470-7(9))*** Bellwether Media.

—Utahraptor. Sabelko, Rebecca. 2021. (World of Dinosaurs Ser.). (ENG.). 24p. (J). (gr. 3-7). lib. bdg. 25.95 ***(978-1-64487-471-4(7))*** Bellwether Media.

Kuga, Cain. Cowboy Bebop, 2 vols. Yadate, Hajime. 2003. pap. 44.99 *(978-1-59182-590-6(3))* TOKYOPOP, Inc.

Kuga, Cain. Cowboy Bebop: Shooting Star, 2 vols., Vol. 2. Kuga, Cain. Nakamura, Yuki, tr. from JPN. rev. ed. 2003. 192p. (gr. 8-18). pap. 9.99 *(978-1-59182-298-1(X))* TOKYOPOP, Inc.

—Cowboy Bebop Shooting Star, 2, 1. Kuga, Cain. 2003. 192p. (gr. 8-18). pap. 9.99 *(978-1-59182-297-4(1))* TOKYOPOP, Inc.

Kügler, Carson, jt. illus. see Kügler, Tina.

Kugler, Tina. No More Beige Food. Shirtliffe, Leanne. 2016. 32p. (J). (gr. -1-k). 16.99 *(978-1-63450-180-4(2)*, Sky Pony Pr.) Skyhorse Publishing Co., Inc.

Kügler, Tina. Who Ate My Book? Kügler, Tina. 2020. (Penguin Young Readers, Level 2 Ser.). (ENG.). 32p. (J). (gr. 1-2). 15.99 *(978-0-593-09469-3(7))*; pap. 4.99 *(978-0-593-09470-9(0))* Penguin Young Readers Group. (Penguin Young Readers).

Kügler, Tina & Kügler, Carson. In Mary's Garden. Kügler, Tina & Kügler, Carson. 2015. (ENG.). 32p. (J). (gr. 1-4). 17.99 *(978-0-544-27220-0(X)*, 1569327, HMH Books For Young Readers) Houghton Mifflin Harcourt Publishing Co.

—Snail & Worm: Meet My Friend. 2016. (Snail & Worm Ser.). (ENG.). 32p. (J). (gr. 1-4). 16.99 *(978-0-544-49412-1(1)*, 1604088, HMH Books For Young Readers) Houghton Mifflin Harcourt Publishing Co.

Kügler, Tina & Kügler, Tina. The Change Your Name Store. Shirtliffe, Leanne. 2014. (ENG.). 32p. (J). (gr. -1-k). 16.95 *(978-1-62873-608-3(9)*, Sky Pony Pr.) Skyhorse Publishing Co., Inc.

Kügler, Tina, jt. illus. see Kügler, Tina.

Kuhl, Anke. Tell Me: What Children Really Want to Know about Bodies, Sex, & Emotions. von der Gathen, Katharina. 2020. (ENG.). 208p. (J). (gr. 3-8). 17.99 *(978-1-77657-232-8(7))* Gecko Pr. NZL. Dist: Lerner Publishing Group.

Kuhlmann, Torben. Flight for Freedom: The Wetzel Family's Daring Escape from East Germany (Berlin Wall History for Kids Book; Nonfiction Picture Books) Fulton, Kristen. 2020. (ENG.). 56p. (J). (gr. k-3). 17.99 *(978-1-4521-4960-8(7))* Chronicle Bks. LLC.

Kuhlmann, Torben. Armstrong: The Adventurous Journey of a Mouse to the Moon. Kuhlmann, Torben. 2016. (Mouse Adventures Ser.). (ENG.). 128p. (J). (gr. 2-6). 19.95 *(978-0-7358-4262-5(0))* North-South Bks., Inc.

Kuhn, Andy. Hercules. Denton, Shannon Eric. 2008. (Short Tales Greek Myths Ser.). (ENG.). 32p. (J). (gr. 3-6). 27.07 *(978-1-60270-135-9(0)*, 13435, Short Tales) Magic Wagon.

—Michelangelo. Lynch, Brian. 2015. (Teenage Mutant Ninja Turtles Ser.). (ENG.). 24p. (J). (gr. 3-7). 27.07 *(978-1-61479-340-3(9)*, 17340, Graphic Novels) Spotlight.

—Robinson Crusoe: I Go to Sea. Dafoe, Daniel. 2008. (Short Tales Classics Ser.). (ENG.). 32p. (J). (gr. 2-6). 27.07 *(978-1-60270-121-2(0)*, 13393, Short Tales) Magic Wagon.

—Teenage Mutant Ninja Turtles Volume 4: Sins of the Fathers, Vol. 4. Waltz, Tom & Eastman, Kevin. 2013. (Teenage Mutant Ninja Turtles Ser.: 4). (ENG.). 104p. pap. 17.99 *(978-1-61377-568-4(7)*, 9781613775684) Idea & Design Works, LLC.

Kuhn, Bob. Big Red (75th Anniversary Edition) Kjelgaard, Jim. 2020. (ENG.). 272p. (J). (gr. 5). 17.99 *(978-0-8234-4265-2(9))* Holiday Hse., Inc.

Kuhn, Douglas W. Little Chick: Learns to Trust in the Lord, 1 vol. Kuhn, Tom B. 2009. 23p. pap. 24.95 *(978-1-60836-929-4(3))* America Star Bks.

Kuhn, Douglas Wolcik. Uncle Kyle's Magic Kite. Kuhn, Douglas Wolcik. 2012. 28p. pap. 24.95 *(978-1-4626-9699-4(6))* America Star Bks.

Kuhn, Dwight. Bugs. Kuhn, Dwight, photos by. Pascoe, Elaine. 2003. 48p. (J). 23.70 *(978-1-56711-458-4(X)*, Blackbirch Pr., Inc.) Cengage Gale.

Kuhn, Dwight, photos by. Animal Noses. Schwartz, David M. (Plants & Animals Ser.). 16p. (J). (gr. 1-3). pap. 2.99 *(978-1-57471-321-3(3)*, 3030) Creative Teaching Pr., Inc.

—Bean. Schwartz, David M. (Life Cycles Ser.). 16p. (J). (gr. 1-3). pap. 2.99 *(978-1-57471-580-4(1)*, 3060) Creative Teaching Pr., Inc.

—Fighting Fish. Schwartz, David M. (Life Cycles Ser.). 16p. (J). (gr. 1-3). pap. 2.99 *(978-1-57471-560-6(7)*, 3070) Creative Teaching Pr., Inc.

—Green Snake. Schwartz, David M. (Life Cycles Ser.). 16p. (J). (gr. 1-3). pap. 2.99 *(978-1-57471-557-6(7)*, 3067) Creative Teaching Pr., Inc.

—Look Once Look Again Collection Box Set. Schwartz, David M. 2005. (Look Once, Look Again! Ser.). (J). pap. 549.00 incl. audio compact disk *(978-1-59198-170-1(0)*, CTP 3269) Creative Teaching Pr., Inc.

—What in the Wild? Mysteries of Nature Concealed... And Revealed. Schy, Yael & Schwartz, David. 2010. 44p. (J). (gr. 1-4). 16.99 *(978-1-58246-310-0(7)*, Tricycle Pr.) Random Hse. Children's Bks.

—Where in the Wild? Camouflaged Creatures Concealed... & Revealed. Schwartz, David M. & Schy, Yael. 2011. 44p. (J). (gr. -1-2). pap. 8.99 *(978-1-58246-399-5(9)*, Tricycle Pr.) Random Hse. Children's Bks.

Kuhn, Jesse. Andy Acid, 26 vols. Cook, Sherry & Johnson, Terri. I.t. ed. 2006. (Quirkles — Exploring Phonics through Science Ser.: 1). 32p. (J). 7.99 *(978-1-933815-00-8(0)*, Quirkles, The) Creative 3, LLC.

—Botanist Bert, 26 vols. Cook, Sherry & Johnson, Terri. I.t. ed. 2006. (Quirkles — Exploring Phonics through Science Ser.: 2). 32p. (J). 7.99 *(978-1-933815-01-5(9)*, Quirkles, The) Creative 3, LLC.

—Colorful Caroline, 26 vols. Cook, Sherry & Johnson, Terri. I.t. ed. 2006. (Quirkles — Exploring Phonics through Science Ser.: 3). 32p. (J). 7.99 *(978-1-933815-02-2(7)*, Quirkles, The) Creative 3, LLC.

—Density Dan, 26 vols. Cook, Sherry & Johnson, Terri. I.t. ed. 2006. (Quirkles — Exploring Phonics through Science Ser.: 4). 32p. (J). 7.99 *(978-1-933815-03-9(5)*, Quirkles, The) Creative 3, LLC.

—Ellie Electricity, 26 vols. Cook, Sherry & Johnson, Terri. I.t. ed. 2006. (Quirkles — Exploring Phonics through Science Ser.: 5). 32p. (J). 7.99 *(978-1-933815-04-6(3)*, Quirkles, The) Creative 3, LLC.

—Friction Fred, 26 vols. Cook, Sherry & Johnson, Terri. I.t. ed. 2006. (Quirkles — Exploring Phonics through Science Ser.: 6). 32p. (J). 7.99 *(978-1-933815-05-3(1)*, Quirkles, The) Creative 3, LLC.

—Gilbert Gas, 26 vols. Cook, Sherry & Johnson, Terri. I.t. ed. 2006. (Quirkles — Exploring Phonics through Science Ser.: 7). 32p. (J). 7.99 *(978-1-933815-06-0(X)*, Quirkles, The) Creative 3, LLC.

—Hallie Heat, 26 vols. Cook, Sherry & Johnson, Terri. I.t. ed. 2006. (Quirkles — Exploring Phonics through Science

K

Ser.: 8). 32p. (J). 7.99 *(978-1-933815-07-7(8),* Quirkles, The) Creative 3, LLC.

—Inquisitive Inman, 26 vols. Cook, Sherry & Johnson, Terri. l.t. ed. 2006. (Quirkles — Exploring Phonics through Science Ser.: 9). 32p. (J). 7.99 *(978-1-933815-08-4(6),* Quirkles, The) Creative 3, LLC.

—Jazzy Jet, 26 vols. Cook, Sherry & Johnson, Terri. l.t. ed. 2006. (Quirkles — Exploring Phonics through Science Ser.: 10). 32p. (J). 7.99 *(978-1-933815-09-1(4),* Quirkles, The) Creative 3, LLC.

—Kitchen Chemistry Kai, 26 vols. Cook, Sherry & Johnson, Terri. l.t. ed. 2006. (Quirkles — Exploring Phonics through Science Ser.: 11). 32p. (J). 7.99 *(978-1-933815-10-7(8),* Quirkles, The) Creative 3, LLC.

—Mary Motion, 26 vols. Cook, Sherry & Johnson, Terri. l.t. ed. 2006. (Quirkles — Exploring Phonics through Science Ser.: 13). 32p. (J). 7.99 *(978-1-933815-12-1(4),* Quirkles, The) Creative 3, LLC.

—Nosey Nina, 26 vols. Cook, Sherry & Johnson, Terri. l.t. ed. 2006. (Quirkles — Exploring Phonics through Science Ser.: 14). 32p. (J). 7.99 *(978-1-933815-13-8(2),* Quirkles, The) Creative 3, LLC.

—Ollie Oxygen, 26 vols. Cook, Sherry & Johnson, Terri. l.t. ed. 2006. (Quirkles — Exploring Phonics through Science Ser.: 15). 32p. (J). 7.99 *(978-1-933815-14-5(0),* Quirkles, The) Creative 3, LLC.

—Pressure Pete, 26 vols. Cook, Sherry & Johnson, Terri. l.t. ed. 2006. (Quirkles — Exploring Phonics through Science Ser.: 16). 32p. (J). 7.99 *(978-1-933815-15-2(9),* Quirkles, The) Creative 3, LLC.

—Quincy Quake, 26. Cook, Sherry & Johnson, Terri. l.t. ed. 2006. (Quirkles — Exploring Phonics through Science Ser.: 17). 32p. (J). 7.99 *(978-1-933815-16-9(7),* Quirkles, The) Creative 3, LLC.

—Ronnie Rock, 26. Cook, Sherry & Johnson, Terri. l.t. ed. 2006. (Quirkles — Exploring Phonics through Science Ser.: 18). 32p. (J). 7.99 *(978-1-933815-17-6(5),* Quirkles, The) Creative 3, LLC.

—Susie Sound, 26. Cook, Sherry & Johnson, Terri. l.t. ed. 2006. 32p. (J). 7.99 *(978-1-933815-18-3(3),* Quirkles, The) Creative 3, LLC.

—Timothy Tornado, 26. Cook, Sherry & Johnson, Terri. l.t. ed. 2006. (Quirkles — Exploring Phonics through Science Ser.: 20). 32p. 7.99 *(978-1-933815-19-0(1),* Quirkles, The) Creative 3, LLC.

—Underwater Utley, 26. Cook, Sherry & Johnson, Martin. l.t. ed. 2006. (Quirkles — Exploring Phonics through Science Ser.: 21). 32p. (J). 7.99 *(978-1-933815-20-6(5),* Quirkles, The) Creative 3, LLC.

—Vinnie Volcano, 26. Cook, Sherry & Johnson, Terri. l.t. ed. 2006. (Quirkles — Exploring Phonics through Science Ser.: 22). 32p. (J). 7.99 *(978-1-933815-21-3(3),* Quirkles, The) Creative 3, LLC.

—Watery William, 26. Cook, Sherry & Johnson, Terri. l.t. ed. 2006. (Quirkles — Exploring Phonics through Science Ser.: 23). 32p. (J). 7.99 *(978-1-933815-22-0(1),* Quirkles, The) Creative 3, LLC.

—X. E. Ecology, 26. Cook, Sherry & Johnson, Terri. l.t. ed. 2006. (Quirkles — Exploring Phonics through Science Ser.: 24). 32p. (J). 7.99 *(978-1-933815-23-7(X),* Quirkles, The) Creative 3, LLC.

—Zany Science Zeke, 26. Cook, Sherry & Johnson, Terri. l.t. ed. 2006. (Quirkles — Exploring Phonics through Science Ser.: 26). 32p. (J). 7.99 *(978-1-933815-25-1(6),* Quirkles, The) Creative 3, LLC.

Kuhn, Rosemary. The Children Keep Their Promises. Kuhn, Rosemary. l.t. ed. 2016. (ENG.). (J). (gr. k-3). pap. 10.95 *(978-1-61633-787-2(7))* Guardian Angel Publishing, Inc.

—Christmas Comes to Koyuk. Kuhn, Rosemary. l.t. ed. 2017. (ENG.). (J). (gr. k-3). pap. 9.95 *(978-1-61633-884-8(9))* Guardian Angel Publishing, Inc.

—Joshua Meets the Good Shepherd. Kuhn, Rosemary. l.t. ed. 2018. (ENG.). 24p. (J). (gr. k-4). pap. 10.95 *(978-1-61633-958-6(6))* Guardian Angel Publishing, Inc.

Kuhwald, Caitlin. V Is for Voting. Farrell, Kate. 2020. (ENG.). 40p. (J). 18.99 *(978-1-250-23125-3(6),* 900209665, Holt, Henry & Co. Bks. For Young Readers) Holt, Henry & Co.

—Who Did It First? 50 Scientists, Artists, & Mathematicians Who Revolutionized the World. Leung, Julie. Hart, Alex, ed. 2019. (Who Did It First? Ser.: 1). (ENG.). 128p. (J). 18.99 *(978-1-250-21171-2(9),* 900203644, Holt, Henry & Co. Bks. For Young Readers) Holt, Henry & Co.

Kuijl, Eefje. Benji & the 24 Pound Banana Squash. Fox, Alan C. 2017. (Benji Ser.). (ENG.). 32p. (J). (gr. -1 — 1). 17.95 *(978-1-60537-344-7(3))* Clavis Publishing.

—Benji & the Giant Kite. Fox, Alan C. 2018. (Benji Ser.). (ENG.). 32p. (J). 17.95 *(978-1-60537-403-1(2))* Clavis Publishing.

Kuijle, Eefje. We Go Together. Drydahl, Link. 2019. (ENG.). 28p. (J). bds. 8.99 ***(978-1-926444-56-7(6))*** Rainstorm Pr.

Kujiradov, Misaho. Lumination, 3 vols., Vol. 2. Kujiradov, Misaho. Love, Courtney & Milky, D. J. Fujikawa, Kimiko & Johnson, Yuki N., trs. 2017. (ENG.). 192p. (YA). pap. 9.99 *(978-1-59182-670-5(5),* f80ebfc9-f52b-4931-909f-d475e5c22133) TOKYOPOP, Inc.

Kukahiko, Puni. Kou Lima. Honda, Liana. 2010. 22p. 8.00 *(978-0-87336-236-8(5))* Kamehameha Publishing.

—Kou Wawae. Honda, Liana. 2010. 22p. 8.00 *(978-0-87336-237-5(3))* Kamehameha Publishing.

Kukhareva, Nataly. What Is Worth Fighting for in These Woods: Fantasy & Adventure Book for Kids of All Ages, Bedtime Story Book for Preschool Children, Story about Friendship & Saving the Environment. Cooper, Amby. 2019. (Vol Ser.: Vol. 3). (ENG.). 46p. (J). pap. 9.99 *(978-1-0780-6751-5(1))* Independently Published.

—What We Almost Lost in These Woods: Bedtime Story for Little Girls & Boys, Storybook with Moral Lesson, Story about Animals in the Forest. Cooper, Amby. 2019. (Vol Ser.: Vol. 2). (ENG.). 44p. (J). pap. 9.99 *(978-1-0706-0362-9(7))* Independently Published.

Kukhtina, Margarita. Holiday Celebration Sticker Book: 1000 Clever Stickers. Clever Publishing. 2019. (Clever Stickers Ser.). (ENG.). 96p. (J). (gr. -1-17). pap. 9.99 *(978-1-949998-06-1(1))* Clever Media Group.

—The Holiday Season: 989 Things to Find. Clever Publishing. 2018. (Look & Find Ser.). (ENG.). 24p. (J). (gr. -1-1). 9.99 *(978-1-948418-31-7(2))* Clever Media Group.

—Holiday Season Sticker Book: 1000 Clever Stickers. Clever Publishing. 2018. (Clever Stickers Ser.). (ENG.). 96p. (J). (gr. -1-1). pap. 9.99 *(978-1-948418-01-0(0))* Clever Media Group.

—Our Animal Friends. Clever Publishing. 2018. (Look & Find Ser.). (ENG.). 24p. (J). (gr. -1-1). 9.99 *(978-1-948418-32-4(0))* Clever Media Group.

Kuklin, Susan. In Search of Safety: Voices of Refugees. Kuklin, Susan. 2020. 256p. (YA). (gr. 9). 24.99 *(978-0-7636-7960-6(7))* Candlewick Pr.

—We Are Here to Stay: Voices of Undocumented Young Adults. Kuklin, Susan. 2019. 192p. (YA). (gr. 9). 19.99 *(978-0-7636-7884-5(8))* Candlewick Pr.

Kuklin, Susan, photos by. Beyond Magenta: Transgender Teens Speak Out. Kuklin, Susan. 2015. 192p. (YA). (gr. 9). pap. 12.99 *(978-0-7636-7368-0(4))* Candlewick Pr.

Kukreja, Julie. Jesus, I Believe. Harrah, Judith. 2012. 34p. (J). pap. 10.99 *(978-1-937331-10-8(5))* ShadeTree Publishing, LLC.

Kulak, Jeff. Learn to Speak Fashion: A Guide to Creating, Showcasing, & Promoting Your Style. DeCarufel, Laura. 2012. (Learn to Speak Ser.). (ENG.). 96p. (J). (gr. 4-8). pap. 14.95 *(978-1-926973-42-5(9),* Owlkids) Owlkids Bks. Inc. CAN. Dist: Publishers Group West (PGW).

—Learn to Speak Film: A Guide to Creating, Promoting, & Screening Your Movies. Glassbourg, Michael. 2013. (Learn to Speak Ser.). (ENG.). 96p. (J). (gr. 4-8). pap. 14.95 *(978-1-926973-85-2(2),* Owlkids) Owlkids Bks. Inc. CAN. Dist: Publishers Group West (PGW).

—Learn to Speak Music: A Guide to Creating, Performing, & Promoting Your Songs. Crossingham, John. 2009. (Learn to Speak Ser.). (ENG.). 96p. (J). (gr. 4-7). pap. 22.95 *(978-1-897349-65-6(3),* Owlkids) Owlkids Bks. Inc. CAN. Dist: Publishers Group West (PGW).

—Starting from Scratch: What You Should Know about Food & Cooking, 0 vols. Elton, Sarah. 2014. (ENG.). 96p. (J). (gr. 4-6). 18.95 *(978-1-926973-96-8(8),* Owlkids) Owlkids Bks. Inc. CAN. Dist: Publishers Group West (PGW).

Kulihin, Vic. Super Hockey Infographics. Savage, Jeff. 2015. (Super Sports Infographics Ser.). (ENG.). 32p. (J). (gr. 3-5). pap. 8.99 *(978-1-4677-7577-9(0))* Lerner Publishing Group.

—US Culture Through Infographics. Higgins, Nadia. 2014. (Super Social Studies Infographics Ser.). (ENG.). 32p. (J). (gr. 3-5). pap. 8.99 *(978-1-4677-4565-9(0))* Lerner Publishing Group.

Kulihin, Vic, jt. illus. see Thompson, Bryon.

Kulikov, Boris. Albert Einstein. Krull, Kathleen. 2015. (Giants of Science Ser.). (ENG.). 144p. (J). (gr. 3-7). 7.99 *(978-0-14-751464-6(9),* Puffin Books) Penguin Young Readers Group.

—Barnum's Bones: How Barnum Brown Discovered the Most Famous Dinosaur in the World, 1 vol. Fern, Tracey E. 2012. (ENG.). 40p. (J). (gr. k-4). 18.99 *(978-0-374-30516-1(1),* 900065867, Farrar, Straus & Giroux (BYR)) Farrar, Straus & Giroux.

—Benjamin Franklin. Krull, Kathleen. 2014. (Giants of Science Ser.). 128p. (J). (gr. 3-7). pap. 7.99 *(978-0-14-751178-2(X),* Puffin Books) Penguin Young Readers Group.

—The Boy Who Cried Wolf. Hennessy, B. G. 2006. (ENG.). 40p. (J). (gr. -1-3). 18.99 *(978-0-689-87433-8(2),* Simon & Schuster Bks. For Young Readers) Simon & Schuster Bks. For Young Readers.

—The Boy Who Cried Wolf. Hennessy, B. G. 2011. (J). (gr. -1-2). 29.95 *(978-0-545-09452-8(6))* Weston Woods Studios, Inc.

—The Carnival of the Animals. Lithgow, John. 2004. (ENG.). 40p. (J). (gr. -1-3). 19.99 *(978-0-689-86721-7(2),* Simon & Schuster Bks. For Young Readers) Simon & Schuster Bks. For Young Readers.

—Carnival of the Animals. Lithgow, John. 2007. (ENG.). 40p. (J). (gr. -1-3). 8.99 *(978-0-689-87343-0(3),* Simon & Schuster Bks. For Young Readers) Simon & Schuster Bks. For Young Readers.

—The Castle on Hester Street. Heller, Linda. 25th ed. 2007. (ENG.). 40p. (J). (gr. -1-3). 18.99 *(978-0-689-87434-5(0),* Simon & Schuster Bks. For Young Readers) Simon & Schuster Bks. For Young Readers.

—Charles Darwin. Krull, Kathleen. 2015. (Giants of Science Ser.). 144p. (J). (gr. 3-7). 7.99 *(978-0-14-751463-9(0),* Puffin Books) Penguin Young Readers Group.

—Come Home, Angus. Downes, Patrick. 2016. (ENG.). 32p. (J). (gr. -1-k). 17.99 *(978-0-545-59768-5(4))* Scholastic, Inc.

—Fartiste. Krull, Kathleen & Brewer, Paul. 2008. (ENG.). 40p. (J). (gr. -1-3). 19.99 *(978-1-4169-2828-7(6),* Simon & Schuster Bks. For Young Readers) Simon & Schuster Bks. For Young Readers.

—How to Find an Elephant. Banks, Kate. 2017. (ENG.). 32p. (J). 16.99 *(978-0-374-33508-3(7),* 900147769, Farrar, Straus & Giroux (BYR)) Farrar, Straus & Giroux.

—Howard & the Mummy: Howard Carter & the Search for King Tut's Tomb. Fern, Tracey. 2018. (ENG.). 40p. (J). 17.99 *(978-0-374-30305-1(3),* 900153481, Farrar, Straus & Giroux (BYR)) Farrar, Straus & Giroux.

—I'm Brave! I'm Strong! I'm Five! Best, Cari. 2019. 32p. (J). (-k). 18.99 *(978-0-8234-4362-8(0),* Margaret Ferguson Books) Holiday Hse., Inc.

—Isaac Newton. Krull, Kathleen. 2008. (Giants of Science Ser.). 128p. (J). (gr. 3-7). 7.99 *(978-0-14-240820-9(4),* Puffin Books) Penguin Young Readers Group.

—Leonardo Da Vinci. Krull, Kathleen. 2005. (Giants of Science Ser.). (ENG.). 124p. (J). (gr. 5-9). 18.69 *(978-0-670-05920-1(X),* Viking) Penguin Publishing Group.

—Leonardo Da Vinci. Krull, Kathleen. 2008. (Giants of Science Ser.). 128p. (J). (gr. 3-7). 7.99 *(978-0-14-240821-6(2),* Puffin Books) Penguin Young Readers Group.

—Marie Curie. Krull, Kathleen. 2007. (Giants of Science Ser.). (ENG.). 142p. (J). (gr. 5-8). 18.69 *(978-0-670-05894-5(7))* Penguin Young Readers Group.

—Max's Math. Banks, Kate. 2015. (Max's Words Ser.: 4). (ENG.). 40p. (J). (gr. -1-3). 17.99 *(978-0-374-34875-5(8),* 900120932, Farrar, Straus & Giroux (BYR)) Farrar, Straus & Giroux.

—Max's Words. Banks, Kate. 2006. (Max's Words Ser.: 1). (ENG.). 32p. (J). (gr. -1-3). 18.99 *(978-0-374-39949-8(2),* 900028396, Farrar, Straus & Giroux (BYR)) Farrar, Straus & Giroux.

—Papa's Mechanical Fish. Fleming, Candace. 2013. (ENG.). 40p. (J). (gr. k-3). 18.99 *(978-0-374-39908-5(5),* 900050960, Farrar, Straus & Giroux (BYR)) Farrar, Straus & Giroux.

—Sandy's Circus: A Story about Alexander Calder. Stone, Tanya Lee. 2008. (ENG.). 40p. (J). (gr. 1-3). 17.99 *(978-0-670-06268-3(5),* Viking Books for Young Readers) Penguin Young Readers Group.

—Six Dots: a Story of Young Louis Braille. Bryant, Jen. 2016. 40p. (J). (gr. -1-3). 17.99 *(978-0-449-81337-9(1),* Knopf Bks. for Young Readers) Random Hse. Children's Bks.

Kulikov, Boris. Stay Curious! A Brief History of Stephen Hawking. Brewer, Paul & Krull, Kathleen. 2020. (ENG.). 40p. (J). (gr. -1-3). 17.99 ***(978-0-399-55028-7(3))***; lib. bdg. 20.99 ***(978-0-399-55029-4(1))*** Random Hse. Children's Bks. (Crown Books For Young Readers).

Kulikov, Boris. W Is for Webster: Noah Webster & His American Dictionary. Fern, Tracey. 2015. (ENG.). 40p. (J). 17.99 *(978-0-374-38240-7(9),* 9780374382407, Farrar, Straus & Giroux (BYR)) Farrar, Straus & Giroux.

Kulikovsky-Romanoff, Grand Duchess Olga Alexandrovna. The Adventures of Three White Bears. 2011. 26p. (J). pap. *(978-0-9716365-2-1(4),* St. Nicholas Pr.) CrossBearers Publishing.

Kulka, Joe. Gingerbread Man Superhero!, 1 vol. Enderle, Dotti. 2009. (ENG.). 32p. (J). (gr. k-3). 16.99 *(978-1-58980-521-7(6),* Pelican Publishing) Arcadia Publishing.

—Granny Gert & the Bunion Brothers, 1 vol. Enderle, Dotti. 2006. (ENG.). 32p. (J). (gr. k-3). 16.99 *(978-1-58980-373-2(6),* Pelican Publishing) Arcadia Publishing.

—Monkey Math. Brimner, Larry Dane. 2007. (Rookie Reader Skill Set Ser.). (ENG.). 32p. (J). (gr. k-2). pap. 4.95 *(978-0-531-13850-2(X))* Scholastic Library Publishing.

—The Spitting Twins. Jones, Andrea. 2004. 32p. (J). *(978-1-58394-095-2(2),* Frog Ltd.) North Atlantic Bks.

—We Both Read-Just Five More Minutes! Brown, Marcy & Haley, Dennis. 2008. (We Both Read Ser.). 44p. (J). (gr. -1-3). 7.99 *(978-1-60115-013-4(X))*; pap. 4.99 *(978-1-60115-014-1(8))* Treasure Bay, Inc.

—We Read Phonics-Talent Night. Orshoski, Paul. 2011. (We Read Phonics Ser.). 32p. (J). (gr. 1-3). 9.95 *(978-1-60115-339-5(2))*; pap. 4.99 *(978-1-60115-340-1(6))* Treasure Bay, Inc.

Kulka, Joe. The Christmas Coal Man. Kulka, Joe. 2015. (ENG.). 32p. (J). (gr. k-3). lib. bdg. 17.99 *(978-1-4677-1607-9(3),* 9781467716079); E-Book 27.99 *(978-1-4677-8808-3(2))* Lerner Publishing Group. (Carolrhoda Bks.).

—Undercover Ostrich. Kulka, Joe. 2019. (ENG.). 32p. (J). (gr. -1-3). 17.99 *(978-1-5124-9787-8(8),* Carolrhoda Bks.) Lerner Publishing Group.

—Vacation's Over! Return of the Dinosaurs. Kulka, Joe. 2010. (Carolrhoda Picture Bks.). (ENG.). 32p. (J). (gr. k-3). lib. bdg. 17.95 *(978-0-7613-5212-9(0))* Lerner Publishing Group.

—Wolf's Coming! Kulka, Joe. 2007. (ENG.). 32p. (J). (gr. -1-3). lib. bdg. 17.99 *(978-1-57505-930-3(4),* Carolrhoda Bks.) Lerner Publishing Group.

Kulp, Joy. Come Travel with Me: Chicago. Fisher, Michele. 2018. (ENG.). 64p. (J). (gr. -1-12). pap. 6.95 *(978-0-9986531-7-4(9))* Momosa Publishing LLC.

Kumakura, Yuichi. Jing Twilight Tales: King of Bandits, 6 vols. Kirsch, Alexis, tr. from JPN. rev. ed. 2005. 196p. pap. 14.99 *(978-1-59182-471-8(0),* Tokyopop Kids) TOKYOPOP, Inc.

Kumakura, Yuichi. Jing Vol. 6: King of Bandits, 7 vols. Kumakura, Yuichi. rev. ed. 2004. Vol. 4. 216p. pap. 14.99 *(978-1-59182-179-3(7))*; Vol. 5. 192p. pap. 14.99 *(978-1-59182-466-4(4))* TOKYOPOP, Inc. (Tokyopop Kids).

—Jing: Kind of Bandits Twilight Tales, 6 vols., Vol. 4. Kumakura, Yuichi. rev. ed. 2005. (Jing: King of Bandits-Twilight Tales Ser.). 192p. pap. 14.99 *(978-1-59532-417-7(8),* Tokyopop Kids) TOKYOPOP, Inc.

—Jing, King of Bandits, 7 vols., Vol. 3. Kumakura, Yuichi. 3rd rev. ed. 2003. 216p. pap. 14.99 *(978-1-59182-178-6(9),* Tokyopop Kids) TOKYOPOP, Inc.

—Jing, King of Bandits: Twilight Tales, 6 vols. Kumakura, Yuichi. 6th rev. ed. 2005. (Jing: King of Bandits-Twilight Tales Ser.). 171p. pap. 14.99 *(978-1-59532-419-1(4),* Tokyopop Kids) TOKYOPOP, Inc.

Kuman, Ivana. The Elephant in the Sukkah. Mandell, Sherri. 2019. (ENG.). 32p. (J). (gr. -1-2). 17.99 *(978-1-5415-2212-1(5),* 9781541522121); pap. 7.99 *(978-1-5415-2213-8(3),* 9781541522138) Lerner Publishing Group. (Kar-Ben Publishing).

—A Hoopoe Says Oop! Animals of Israel, Vol. Kiffel-Alcheh, Jamie. 2019. (ENG.). 12p. (J). (gr. -1 — 1). bds. 5.99 *(978-1-5415-0049-5(0),* Kar-Ben Publishing) Lerner Publishing Group.

Kumar, Aambadi. Brianna & the Water Tower. M, J. "E", ed. 2019. (Brianna's Dreams Ser.: Vol. 2). (ENG.). 38p. (J). pap. 15.95 ***(978-1-947656-96-3(1))*** Butterfly Typeface, The.

Kumar, Ambadi. All Dressed Up. Hardrick, Joseline Jean. 2020. (ENG.). 40p. (J). pap. 9.99 ***(978-1-6755-9750-7(2))*** Independently Published.

Kumar, Ambadi. Learning English with Tasha & Benji: Volume Two. Samantha, Weiland. 2017. (Learning English with Tasha & Benji Ser.: Vol. 2). (ENG.). (J). (gr. k-3). pap. 19.99 *(978-1-63535-228-3(2))* Samantha's Stories Inc.

—Learning with Tasha & Benji: This Is Tasha & This Is Benji. Weiland, Samantha. 2017. (Beginning Ser.: Vol. 1). (ENG.). (J). (gr. k-3). pap. 15.99 *(978-1-63535-906-0(6))* Future Bookworms LLC.

Kumar, Ambadi. Tou Abiye. Hardrick, Joseline Jean. 2020. (FRE.). 40p. (J). pap. 12.99 ***(978-1-6539-3570-3(7))*** Independently Published.

Kumar, Arun. Eeey Beey the Easter Bunny Story Book. Shaw, Jean. 2017. (ENG.). 30p. (J). pap. *(978-0-9557736-8-6(7))* Simply Me LLC.

Kumar, Arun. Surviving Middle School. Philendra, Vivek. 2019. (Surviving Middle School Ser.: Vol. 1). (ENG.). 80p. (J). pap. 5.38 ***(978-1-7032-8206-1(X))*** Independently Published.

Kumar, Naresh. The Dusk Society. Jones, Mark. 2011. (Campfire Graphic Novels Ser.). (ENG.). 88p. (YA). (gr. 3-7). pap. 11.99 *(978-93-80028-63-7(6),* Campfire) Steerforth Pr.

—Hamlet. Shakespeare, William. 2019. (Campfire Graphic Novels Ser.). (ENG.). 90p. (YA). (gr. 7). pap. 12.99 *(978-93-81182-51-2(5),* Campfire) Steerforth Pr.

—The Industrial Revolution. Helfand, Lewis. 2017. (Campfire Graphic Novels Ser.). (ENG.). 92p. (YA). (gr. 7). pap. 14.99 *(978-93-81182-28-4(0),* Campfire) Steerforth Pr.

—Kidnapped. Stevenson, Robert Louis. 2011. (Campfire Graphic Novels Ser.). (ENG.). 72p. (YA). (gr. 3-7). pap. 9.99 *(978-93-80028-52-1(0),* Campfire) Steerforth Pr.

—They Changed the World: Bell, Edison & Tesla. Helfand, Lewis. 2014. (Campfire Graphic Novels Ser.). (ENG.). 102p. (YA). (gr. 8-12). pap. 12.99 *(978-93-80741-87-1(1),* Campfire) Steerforth Pr.

—They Changed the World: Copernicus-Bruno-Galileo: A Graphic Biography. Hoskin, Rik. 2020. (Campfire Graphic Novels Ser.). (ENG.). 88p. (YA). (gr. 7). pap. 12.99 *(978-93-81182-96-3(5),* Campfire) Steerforth Pr.

Kumar, Surendhra. My Yummy Corn: The Story of a Little Mouse Who Did Not Listen to His Father. Padayatchi, Surendhra Kumar. 2018. (ENG.). 34p. (J). pap. 13.00 *(978-1-7268-9603-0(X))* Independently Published.

Kumar, Vinay. Wash & Dry. Holland, Trish. 2010. 24p. (J). *(978-1-60617-119-6(4))* Teaching Strategies, LLC.

Kumar, Vinod. The Hound of the Baskervilles. Doyle, A. Conan. 2011. (Campfire Graphic Novels Ser.). (ENG.). 72p. (YA). (gr. 5-12). pap. 9.99 *(978-93-80028-44-6(X),* Campfire) Steerforth Pr.

—A Journey to the Center of the Earth. Verne, Jules. 2011. (Campfire Graphic Novels Ser.). (ENG.). 72p. (YA). (gr. 5-12). pap. 9.99 *(978-93-80028-40-8(7),* Campfire) Steerforth Pr.

Kumata, Michelle Reiko. Flowers from Mariko. Noguchi, Rick & Jenks, Deneen. 2013. (ENG.). 32p. (J). (gr. 1-18). 16.95 *(978-1-58430-032-8(9))* Lee & Low Bks., Inc.

—Flowers from Mariko, 1 vol. Noguchi, Rick & Jenks, Deneen. 2016. (ENG.). 32p. (J). pap. 9.95 *(978-1-62014-315-5(1))* Lee & Low Bks., Inc.

Kumblekar, Nithin Rao. Chalk It Up: Imagine That! Spinner, Cala. 2017. (Crayola Ser.). (ENG.). 32p. (J). (gr. -1-k). 9.99 *(978-1-5344-0451-9(1),* Simon Spotlight) Simon Spotlight.

Kumer, Mark. The Book That I Love to Read. Fitzpatrick, Joe. 2012. 32p. (J). *(978-1-77093-145-9(7))* Flowerpot Children's Pr. Inc.

Kummer, Mark. The ABC's of Health. Alderman, Peter. 2017. (ENG.). 32p. (J). (gr. k-3). *(978-1-4867-1279-3(7))* Flowerpot Children's Pr. Inc.

—Guess How Much I Love Hockey. Caminelli, Harry. 2017. (Guess How Much I Love Ser.). (ENG.). 32p. (J). (gr. 1-3). 9.99 *(978-1-4867-1301-1(7),* 85b943e6-d3b2-42fa-ab16-a6709ae8d8a7) Flowerpot Pr.

—Guess How Much I Love Indiana. Paiva, Johannah Gilman. 2018. (Guess How Much I Love Ser.). (ENG.). 32p. (J). (gr. 1-3). 9.99 *(978-1-4867-1428-5(5),* 86738cda-24cd-4e09-9908-3780451e3db9) Flowerpot Pr.

—Guess How Much I Love Texas. Paiva, Johannah Gilman. 2017. (Guess How Much I Love Ser.). (ENG.). 32p. (J). (gr. 1-3). 9.99 *(978-1-4867-1280-9(0),* 92c5b757-f5ff-4afe-b393-a6cf683dd58c) Flowerpot Pr.

—I Am So Awesome: Read with Me. Fitzpatrick, Joe. 2014. (ENG.). 32p. (J). (gr. k-4). 7.99 *(978-1-4867-0005-9(5))* Flowerpot Children's Pr. Inc. CAN. Dist: Cardinal Pubs. Group.

—If You're Happy & You Know It. Everett, Melissa. 2017. (ENG.). 20p. (J). (gr. -1-2). bds. *(978-1-4867-1246-5(0))* Flowerpot Children's Pr. Inc.

—The Owl & the Kitty Cat. Everett, Melissa. 2013. (ENG.). 20p. (J). (gr. -1-3). 8.99 *(978-1-77093-535-8(5))* Flowerpot Children's Pr. Inc. CAN. Dist: Cardinal Pubs. Group.

—The Owl & the Kitty Cat. Everett, Melissa. 2017. (Re-Versed Rhymes Ser.). (ENG.). 24p. (J). (gr. -1-3). 6.99 *(978-1-4867-1260-1(6),* 8ea1f522-803e-4513-b454-c961f681e358) Flowerpot Pr.

—Pat-A-Cake. Everett, Melissa. 2013. (ENG.). 20p. (J). (gr. -1-1). 8.99 *(978-1-77093-521-1(5))* Flowerpot Children's Pr. Inc. CAN. Dist: Cardinal Pubs. Group.

—There Was a Crooked Man. Everett, Melissa. 2017. (ENG.). 24p. (J). (gr. -1-3). *(978-1-4867-1264-9(9))* Flowerpot Children's Pr. Inc.

Kun Rong, Yap, jt. illus. see Rong, Yap Kun.

Kunardi, Marco. Rick & Bobo: Two Brothers. One a Genius. One Not, 4 vols. Ventrillo, James & Ventrillo, Nick. 2009. 332p. (YA). pap. 13.95 *(978-0-615-28865-9(0))* Vanir Bks.

Kunce, Craig. Hope's Melody. Kunce, Jeanna. 2016. (ENG.). (J). (gr. k-3). pap. 14.00 *(978-1-944734-08-4(2))* Windhill Bks. LLC.

Kunce, Craig. Ellie Anders: The Impossible School Project. Kunce, Craig. 2017. (Ellie Anders Ser.: Vol. 1). (ENG.). (J). (gr. 1-5). pap. 14.00 *(978-1-944734-10-7(4))* Windhill Bks. LLC.

—Very, Very, Afraid! Kunce, Craig. 2016. (ENG.). (J). (gr. k-3). pap. 14.00 *(978-1-944734-02-2(3))* Windhill Bks. LLC.

Kunda, Shmuel. Boruch Learns His Brochos. Kunda, Shmuel. 2005. 40p. (J). 17.95 *(978-1-932443-41-7(X))* Judaica Pr., Inc., The.

Kundalic, Damir. Ferdinand Fox & the Hedgehog: A Rhyming Picture Book Story for Children Ages 3-6. Inglis, Karen. l.t. ed. 2018. (Ferdinand Fox Adventures Ser.). (ENG.). 30p. (J). (gr. k-1). pap. *(978-0-9954543-1-6(0))* Well Said Pr.

—Ferdinand Fox's Big Sleep Colouring Book. Inglis, Karen. 2013. 32p. pap. *(978-0-9569323-4-1(7))* Well Said Pr.

Kundiger, Marion S. Izzie of Fergus Falls: A Minnesota Childhood in The 1880s. Kundiger, Marion S. 2008. (ENG.). 56p. (J). 29.95 *(978-0-9659712-8-7(7))* Ravenstone Pr.

Kundu, Kunal. Collins Big Cat Phonics for Letters & Sounds - Living Fossils: Band 07/Turquoise, Bd. 7. Morgan, Sally. 2018. (Collins Big Cat Phonics Ser.). (ENG.). 24p. (J). (gr. 1-2). pap. 6.99 *(978-0-00-825180-2(0))* HarperCollins Pubs. Ltd. GBR. Dist: Independent Pubs. Group.

—A Jar of Sound: Bhil Art. Raghbeer, Anjali. 2012. (Art Tales from India Ser.). (ENG.). 24p. (J). 14.95 *(978-81-8328-188-1(5))* Wisdom Tree IND. Dist: SCB Distributors.

Kung, Chorkung. 12 Little Elves Visit Colorado. Madson, Trish. 2018. (12 Little Elves Ser.: 5). (ENG.). 32p. (J). (gr. 3-5). 16.99 *(978-1-64170-041-2(6)*, 550041) Familius LLC.

—12 Little Elves Visit Montana. Madson, Trish. 2018. (12 Little Elves Ser.: 6). (ENG.). 32p. (J). (gr. 3-5). 16.99 *(978-1-64170-042-9(4)*, 550042) Familius LLC.

Kunhardt, Dorothy. Junket Is Nice. Kunhardt, Dorothy. 2013. 72p. (J). (gr. -1-2). 16.95 *(978-1-59017-628-3(6)*, NYR Children's Collection) New York Review of Bks., Inc., The.

—Now Open the Box. Kunhardt, Dorothy. 2013. 60p. (J). (gr. -1-2). 16.95 *(978-1-59017-708-2(8)*, NYR Children's Collection) New York Review of Bks., Inc., The.

Kunkel, Dennis. Mosquito Bite. Siy, Alexandra. 32p. (J). (gr. 2-5). 2006. pap. 7.95 *(978-1-57091-592-5(X))*; 2005. 16.95 *(978-1-57091-591-8(1))* Charlesbridge Publishing, Inc.

Kunkel, Dennis, photos by. Hidden Worlds: Looking Through a Scientist's Microscope. Kramer, Stephen. 2003. (Scientists in the Field Ser.). (ENG., 64p. (J). (gr. 5-7). pap. 9.99 *(978-0-618-35405-4(0)*, 489120) Houghton Mifflin Harcourt Publishing Co.

—Hidden Worlds: Looking Through a Scientist's Microscope. Kramer, Stephen. 2005. 57p. (gr. 4-7). 20.00 *(978-0-7569-5188-7(7))* Perfection Learning Corp.

—Up Close with Bugs. Siy, Alexandra. 2018. 40p. (J). (gr. 2-5). pap. 8.99 *(978-0-8234-4036-8(2))* Holiday Hse., Inc.

—Up Close with Spiders. Siy, Alexandra. 2018. 48p. (J). (gr. 2-5). pap. 8.99 *(978-0-8234-4044-3(3))* Holiday Hse., Inc.

Kunkel, Dennis, jt. photos by see Siy, Alexandra.

Kunkel, Mike. Billy Batson & the Magic. Kunkel, Mike. 2015. (Billy Batson & the Magic of Shazam! Ser.). (ENG.). 32p. (J). (gr. 3-6). lib. bdg., lib. bdg., lib. bdg. 135.60 *(978-1-4965-0290-2(6)*, Stone Arch Bks.) Capstone.

—Brother vs. Brother!, 1 vol. Kunkel, Mike. 2014. (Billy Batson & the Magic of Shazam! Ser.). (ENG.). 32p. (J). (gr. 3-6). 22.60 *(978-1-4342-9228-5(2)*, Stone Arch Bks.) Capstone.

—Herobear & the Kid Vol. 1 the Inheritance. Kunkel, Mike. 2014. (Herobear & the Kid Ser.: 1). (ENG.). 128p. (J). (gr. 3). pap. 19.99 *(978-1-60886-366-2(2))* Boom! Studios.

—Magic Words!, 1 vol. Kunkel, Mike. 2014. (Billy Batson & the Magic of Shazam! Ser.). (ENG.). 32p. (J). (gr. 3-6). 22.60 *(978-1-4342-9209-4(6)*, Stone Arch Bks.) Capstone.

—The World's Mightiest Mortal!, 1 vol. Kunkel, Mike. 2014. (Billy Batson & the Magic of Shazam! Ser.). (ENG.). 32p. (J). (gr. 3-6). 22.60 *(978-1-4342-9226-1(6)*, Stone Arch Bks.) Capstone.

Kunnas, Mauri. Goodnight, Mr. Clutterbuck. Kunnas, Mauri. Timbers, Jill, tr. 2017. (ENG.). 12p. (J). (gr. -1-3). 18.00 *(978-0-914671-76-3(6)*, Elsewhere Editions) Steerforth Pr.

Künstler, Mort. The Revolutionary War: 1775-1783. Axelrod, Alan. 2016. (ENG.). 48p. (J). (gr. 2-7). 13.95 *(978-0-7892-1253-5(6)*, 791253, Abbeville Kids) Abbeville Pr., Inc.

—The Wild West: 1804-1890. 2016. (ENG.). 48p. (J). (gr. 2-6). 13.95 *(978-0-7892-1260-3(9)*, 791260, Abbeville Kids) Abbeville Pr., Inc.

—World War II: 1939-1945. 2016. (ENG.). 48p. (J). (gr. 2). 13.95 *(978-0-7892-1261-0(7)*, 791261, Abbeville Kids) Abbeville Pr., Inc.

Kunz, Rollin. The Adventure of Paperman - Heroes' Journey (Volume 3) Larner, Eric. 2018. (ENG.). 330p. (J). pap. 17.99 *(978-1-883651-91-6(3))* Winters Publishing.

Kuo, Cassey. Anna, Banana, & the Magic Show Mix-Up. Rissi, Anica Mrose. 2019. (Anna, Banana Ser.: 8). (ENG.). 160p. (J). (gr. 1-5). 16.99 *(978-1-5344-1722-9(2))*; pap. 5.99 *(978-1-5344-1721-2(4))* Simon & Schuster Bks. For Young Readers. (Simon & Schuster Bks. For Young Readers).

—Anna, Banana, & the Sleepover Secret. Rissi, Anica Mrose. 2018. (Anna, Banana Ser.: 7). (ENG.). 128p. (J). (gr. 1-5). 16.99 *(978-1-5344-1719-9(2))*; pap. 5.99 *(978-1-5344-1718-2(4))* Simon & Schuster Bks. For Young Readers. (Simon & Schuster Bks. For Young Readers).

Kuo, Ching-Pang. Bomji & Spotty's Frightening Adventure: A Story about How to Recover from a Scary Experience. Westcott, Anne & Hu, C. C. Alicia. 2017. (Hidden Strengths Therapeutic Children's Bks.). (ENG.). 40p. (C). pap. 15.95 *(978-1-78592-770-6(1)*, 696596) Kingsley, Jessica Pubs. GBR. Dist: Hachette UK Distribution.

—How Little Coyote Found His Secret Strength: A Story about How to Get Through Hard Times. Westcott, Anne & Hu, C. C. Alicia. 2017. (Hidden Strengths Therapeutic Children's Bks.). (ENG.). 32p. (C). pap. 15.95 *(978-1-78592-771-3(X)*, 696597) Kingsley, Jessica Pubs. GBR. Dist: Hachette UK Distribution.

—How Sprinkle the Pig Escaped the River of Tears: A Story about Finding Comfort after a Loss. Westcott, Anne & Hu, C. C. Alicia. 2017. (Hidden Strengths Therapeutic Children's Bks.). (ENG.). 40p. (C). pap. 15.95 *(978-1-78592-769-0(8)*, 696564) Kingsley, Jessica Pubs. GBR. Dist: Hachette UK Distribution.

Kuo, Julia. Daisy & Josephine. Gilbert, Melissa. 2014. (ENG.). 32p. (J). (gr. -1-3). 17.99 *(978-1-4424-4578-9(5)*, Simon & Schuster/Paula Wiseman Bks.) Simon & Schuster/Paula Wiseman Bks.

—Go, Little Green Truck! Schotter, Roni. 2016. (ENG.). 32p. (J). 16.99 *(978-0-374-30070-8(4)*, 900133842, Farrar, Straus & Giroux (BYR)) Farrar, Straus & Giroux.

—Heroism Begins with Her: Inspiring Stories of Bold, Brave, & Gutsy Women in the U. S. Military. Conkling, Winifred. 2019. (ENG.). 240p. (J). (gr. 3-7). 18.99 *(978-0-06-284741-6(4))* HarperCollins Pubs.

—A Place to Belong. Kadohata, Cynthia. (ENG.). (J). (gr. 5-9). 2020. 432p. pap. 8.99 *(978-1-4814-4665-5(7)*, Atheneum Bks. for Young Readers); 2019. 416p. 17.99 *(978-1-4814-4664-8(9)*, Atheneum/Caitlyn Dlouhy Books); 2019. 416p. E-Book *(978-1-4814-4666-2(5)*, Atheneum/Caitlyn Dlouhy Books) Simon & Schuster Children's Publishing.

—The Thing about Luck. Kadohata, Cynthia. (ENG.). (J). (gr. 5-9). 2014. 304p. pap. 8.99 *(978-1-4424-7465-9(3)*, Atheneum Bks. for Young Readers); 2013. 288p. 16.99 *(978-1-4169-1882-0(5))* Simon & Schuster Children's Publishing.

Kuo, Julia. Everyone Eats. Kuo, Julia. 2012. (ENG.). 22p. (J). (gr. -1). 9.95 *(978-1-897476-74-1(4))* Simply Read Bks. CAN. Dist: Ingram Publisher Services.

Kuo, Linda. A Visit to the Vet, Level 2. Andrus, Aubre. 2017. (Scholastic Reader, Level 2 Ser.). (ENG.). 32p. (J). (gr. 1-3). pap. 3.99 *(978-1-338-08761-1(4))* Scholastic, Inc.

Kuon, Vuthy. The Adventures of Roopster Roux: That's Not Punny, 1 vol. Lavette, Lavaille. Nguyen, Duke, ed. 2007. (Roopster Roux Ser.: Vol. 5). (ENG.). 32p. (J). (gr. 3-7). 16.95 *(978-1-58980-483-8(X)*, Pelican Publishing) Arcadia Publishing.

—Adventures of Roopster Roux: You're So Victor Vain, 1 vol. Lavette, Lavaille. 2007. (Roopster Roux Ser.). (ENG.). 32p. (J). (gr. 3-7). 16.95 *(978-1-58980-484-5(8)*, Pelican Publishing) Arcadia Publishing.

—The Rolling Stone: And Other Read Aloud Stories. Kimmel, Eric A. & Kang, Setha. 2004. 36p. (J). (gr. k-6). 15.95 *(978-0-9651661-2-6(0))* Providence Publishing.

Kuon, Vuthy & Nguyen, Duke. Herbert Hilligan & His Magical Adventure. Epner, Paul. 2003. 32p. (J). 15.95 *(978-0-9743335-0-2(6))* Imaginative Publishing, Ltd.

—Herbert Hilligan & His Magical Lunchbox. Epner, Paul. rev. ed. (Herbert Hilligan Ser.). 15.95 *(978-1-57168-549-0(9))* Eakin Pr.

—Herbert Hilligan's Lone Star Adventure. Epner, Paul. 2003. 32p. (J). 15.95 *(978-0-9743335-3-3(0))* Imaginative Publishing, Ltd.

—Herbert Hilligan's Prehistoric Adventure. Epner, Paul. 2003. 32p. (J). 15.95 *(978-0-9743335-1-9(4))* Imaginative Publishing, Ltd.

—Herbert Hilligan's Tropical Adventure. Epner, Paul. 2003. 32p. (J). 15.95 *(978-0-9743335-2-6(2))* Imaginative Publishing, Ltd.

Kupesic, Rajka. The Nutcracker. Kain, Karen. 2005. 32p. (J). (gr. k-12). 18.95 *(978-0-88776-696-1(X)*, Tundra Bks.) Tundra Bks. CAN. Dist: Penguin Random Hse. LLC.

Kupesic, Rajka. The White Ballets. Kupesic, Rajka, retold by. 2011. (ENG.). 42p. (J). (gr. -1-2). 19.95 *(978-0-88776-923-8(3)*, Tundra Bks.) Tundra Bks. CAN. Dist: Penguin Random Hse. LLC.

Kupferschmidt, Denise. The Twice & Always Princess. Coyne, Luann Tennant. 2020. (ENG.). 112p. (J). pap. 6.95 ***(978-1-5373-0569-1(7))*** CreateSpace Independent Publishing Platform.

Kupperberg, Alan & Vosburg, Mike. Marvel Masterworks: the Savage She-Hulk Vol. 2. 2019. (ENG.). 304p. (YA). 75.00 *(978-1-302-91718-0(8))* Marvel Worldwide, Inc.

Kupperman, Michael, jt. illus. see Helquist, Brett.

Kuprin, Igor. Felix's New Skirt. Brichzin, Kerstin. 2018. (ENG.). 40p. (J). (gr. k-2). 17.99 *(978-988-8341-58-0(8)*, Minedition) Neugebauer, Michael (Publishing) Limited HKG. Dist: Penguin Random Hse. LLC.

Kurelek, William. They Sought a New World: The Story of European Immigration to North America. Kurelek, William. Engelhart, Margaret S. 2005. 48p. (J). (gr. 4-8). reprint ed. 20.00 *(978-0-7567-8682-3(7))* DIANE Publishing Co.

Kuricheva, Natasha. The Nutcracker. Regan, Patrick. 2016. (ENG.). 26p. (J). bds. 9.99 *(978-1-4494-5586-6(7))* Andrews McMeel Publishing.

Kurihashi, Shinsuke. Record of the Last Hero, Vol. 3. Kurihashi, Shinsuke. Asamiya, Kia. 2007. (Junk Ser.). (ENG.). 200p. (YA). pap. 9.95 *(978-1-59796-109-7(4))* DrMaster Pubns. Inc.

Kurilla, RenÃe. Cosmo to the Rescue (My Pet Slime Book 2) Scheinmel, Courtney. 2020. (My Pet Slime Ser.). (ENG.). 160p. (J). 12.99 *(978-1-5248-5573-4(1))* Andrews McMeel Publishing.

—My Pet Slime (My Pet Slime Book 1) Scheinmel, Courtney. (My Pet Slime Ser.: 1). (ENG.). 160p. (J). 2020. pap. 6.99 *(978-1-5248-5520-8(0))*; 2019. 12.99 *(978-1-5248-5545-1(6))* Andrews McMeel Publishing.

Kurilla, Renée. Ada Lace Adventures Collection: Ada Lace, on the Case; Ada Lace Sees Red; Ada Lace, Take Me to Your Leader; Ada Lace & the Impossible Mission. Calandrelli, Emily. ed. 2018. (Ada Lace Adventure Ser.). (ENG.). 480p. (J). (gr. 1-5). pap. 27.99 *(978-1-5344-3004-4(0)*, Simon & Schuster Bks. For Young Readers) Simon & Schuster Bks. For Young Readers.

—Ada Lace & the Impossible Mission. Calandrelli, Emily. 2018. (Ada Lace Adventure Ser.: 4). (ENG.). 112p. (J). (gr. 1-5). pap. 6.99 *(978-1-5344-1684-0(6)*, Simon & Schuster Bks. For Young Readers) Simon & Schuster Bks. For Young Readers.

—Ada Lace & the Suspicious Artist. Calandrelli, Emily. 2019. (Ada Lace Adventure Ser.: 5). (ENG.). 112p. (J). (gr. 1-5). pap. 6.99 *(978-1-5344-1687-1(0)*, Simon & Schuster Bks. For Young Readers) Simon & Schuster Bks. For Young Readers.

—Ada Lace, on the Case. Calandrelli, Emily. 2017. (Ada Lace Adventure Ser.: 1). (ENG.). 128p. (J). (gr. 1-5). pap. 6.99 *(978-1-4814-8598-2(9)*, Simon & Schuster Bks. For Young Readers) Simon & Schuster Bks. For Young Readers.

—Ada Lace Sees Red. Calandrelli, Emily. 2017. (Ada Lace Adventure Ser.: 2). (ENG.). 144p. (J). (gr. 1-5). 17.99 *(978-1-4814-8602-6(0))*; pap. 6.99 *(978-1-4814-8601-9(2))* Simon & Schuster Bks. For Young Readers. (Simon & Schuster Bks. For Young Readers).

—Ada Lace, Take Me to Your Leader. Calandrelli, Emily. 2018. (Ada Lace Adventure Ser.: 3). (ENG.). 96p. (J). (gr. 1-5). 17.99 *(978-1-4814-8605-7(5))*; pap. 6.99 *(978-1-4814-8604-0(7))* Simon & Schuster Bks. For Young Readers. (Simon & Schuster Bks. For Young Readers).

—Berkley, the Terrible Sleeper. Sharmat, Mitchell. 2015. (Ready-To-Reads Ser.). (ENG.). 32p. (J). (gr. k-2). pap. 3.99 *(978-1-4814-3832-2(8)*, Simon Spotlight) Simon Spotlight.

Kurilla, Renée. Cosmo to the Rescue (My Pet Slime Book 2) Sheinmel, Courtney. 2020. (My Pet Slime Ser.: 2). (ENG.). 160p. (J). pap. 6.99 ***(978-1-5248-6294-7(0))*** Andrews McMeel Publishing.

Kurilla, Renee. Daisy's Decorating Dilemma. Dougherty, Brandi. 2018. (Wild Fairies Ser.: 1). 96p. (J). (gr. 1-4). 10.99 *(978-1-63565-132-4(8)*, 9781635651324, Rodale Kids) Random Hse. Children's Bks.

—I'm All Wrapped Up! Meet a Mummy. Knudsen, Shannon. 2014. (Monster Buddies Ser.). (ENG.). 24p. (J). (gr. k-2). lib. bdg. 23.99 *(978-0-7613-9188-3(6)*, 9780761391883, Millbrook Pr.) Lerner Publishing Group.

—Keep Calm! My Stress-Busting Tips. Bellisario, Gina. 2014. (Cloverleaf Books (tm) — My Healthy Habits Ser.). (ENG.). 24p. (J). (gr. k-2). lib. bdg. 25.32 *(978-1-4677-1354-2(6)*, 9781467713542, Millbrook Pr.) Lerner Publishing Group.

—Lily's Water Woes. Dougherty, Brandi. 2018. (Wild Fairies Ser.: 2). 96p. (J). (gr. 1-4). 10.99 *(978-1-63565-135-5(2)*, 9781635651355, Rodale Kids) Random Hse. Children's Bks.

—A Party for Clouds: Thunderstorms. Jensen, Belinda. 2016. (Bel the Weather Girl Ser.). (ENG.). 24p. (J). (gr. -1-3). 25.32 *(978-1-4677-7959-3(8)*, 9781467779593, Millbrook Pr.) Lerner Publishing Group.

Kurilla, Renée. The Pickwicks' Picnic: A Counting Adventure. Brendler, Carol. 2017. (ENG.). 40p. (J). (gr. -1-3). 16.99 *(978-0-544-83958-8(7)*, 1646081, Clarion Bks.) Houghton Mifflin Harcourt Trade & Reference Pubs.

—Poppy's Harvest Hullabaloo. Dougherty, Brandi. 2019. (J). *(978-1-63565-139-3(5))* Random Hse., Inc.

Kurilla, Renee. Raindrops on a Roller Coaster: Hail. Jensen, Belinda. 2016. (Bel the Weather Girl Ser.). (ENG.). 24p. (J). (gr. -1-3). 25.32 *(978-1-4677-7958-6(X)*, 9781467779586, Millbrook Pr.) Lerner Publishing Group.

—Right This Very Minute: A Table to Farm Book about Food & Farming. Detlefsen, Lisl H. 2019. (ENG.). 32p. (J). (gr. k-2). 17.99 *(978-1-948898-00-3(4))* Feeding Minds Pr.

—The Sky Stirs up Trouble: Tornadoes. Jensen, Belinda. 2016. (Bel the Weather Girl Ser.). (ENG.). 24p. (J). (gr. -1-3). 25.32 *(978-1-4677-7960-9(1)*, 9781467779609, Millbrook Pr.) Lerner Publishing Group.

—A Snowstorm Shows Off: Blizzards. Jensen, Belinda. 2016. (Bel the Weather Girl Ser.). (ENG.). 24p. (J). (gr. -1-3). 25.32 *(978-1-4677-7961-6(X)*, 9781467779616, Millbrook Pr.) Lerner Publishing Group.

—Spinning Wind & Water: Hurricanes. Jensen, Belinda. 2016. (Bel the Weather Girl Ser.). (ENG.). 24p. (J). (gr. -1-3). 25.32 *(978-1-4677-7962-3(8)*, 9781467779623, Millbrook Pr.) Lerner Publishing Group.

—Weather Clues in the Sky: Clouds. Jensen, Belinda. 2016. (Bel the Weather Girl Ser.). (ENG.). 24p. (J). (gr. -1-3). 25.32 *(978-1-4677-7963-0(6)*, 9781467779630, Millbrook Pr.) Lerner Publishing Group.

Kurisu, Jane. Funtime Riddles. Helmer, Marilyn. 2004. 31p. (J). lib. bdg. 15.38 *(978-1-4242-1184-5(0))* Fitzgerald Bks.

—Junk Drawer Jewelry. Warwick, Ellen & Di Salle, Rachel. 2006. (Kids Can Do It Ser.). 40p. (J). (gr. 3-7). 6.95 *(978-1-55337-966-9(7))* Kids Can Pr., Ltd. CAN. Dist: Hachette Bk. Group.

—My Pet Puppy. Baillie, Marilyn. 2005. (ENG.). 32p. (J). (gr. k-3). 6.95 *(978-1-55337-651-4(X))* Kids Can Pr., Ltd. CAN. Dist: Hachette Bk. Group.

Kurisu, Jane. The Jumbo Book of Drama. Kurisu, Jane, tr. Dunleavy, Deborah. 2004. (Jumbo Bks.). (ENG.). 208p. (J). (gr. 4-6). 14.95 *(978-1-55337-008-6(2))* Kids Can Pr., Ltd. CAN. Dist: Hachette Bk. Group.

Kuriyan, Priya. Dead As a Dodo. Coelho, Venita. 2015. 226p. (J). *(978-93-5009-844-8(X))* Hachette India.

—Princess Easy Pleasy. Sharma, Natasha. 2016. (ENG.). 40p. (J). 15.95 *(978-81-8190-385-3(4))* Karadi Tales Co. Pvt. Ltd. IND. Dist: Consortium Bk. Sales & Distribution.

Kurkela, Cassidy S. Lilies on the Moon. Kurkela, Robert W. 2005. 32p. (J). 16.95 *(978-0-9760220-0-8(1))* Kidzpoetz Publishing.

Kurkiala, Mira. Μαμά, τογνωρίζεις; Boutte, Sarah. 2019. (GRE.). 44p. (J). pap. 14.99 *(978-0-578-52568-6(2))* Boutte, Sarah.

Kurkoski, Bettina. The Rise of Scourge. Jolley, Dan & Hunter, Erin. ed. 2008. (Warriors Manga Ser.: 4). 82p. (J). (gr. 3-7). lib. bdg. 17.20 *(978-1-4178-3120-3(0))* Turtleback.

Kurkoski, Bettina M. Seekers: Kallik's Adventure. Hunter, Erin. 2011. (Seekers Manga Ser.). (ENG.). 112p. (J). (gr. 3-7). pap. 7.99 *(978-0-06-172383-4(5))* HarperCollins Pubs.

—Seekers: Toklo's Story. Hunter, Erin. 2010. (Seekers Manga Ser.). (ENG.). 112p. (J). (gr. 3-7). pap. 7.99 *(978-0-06-172380-3(0)*, HarperCollins) HarperCollins Pubs. Ltd. GBR. Dist: HarperCollins Pubs.

—Warriors: the Rise of Scourge. Hunter, Erin. 2008. (Warriors Graphic Novel Ser.: No. 3). (ENG.). 112p. (J). (gr. 3-7). pap. 7.99 *(978-0-06-147867-3(9)*, HarperCollins) HarperCollins Pubs. Ltd. GBR. Dist: HarperCollins Pubs.

Kurlansky, Mark. The Girl Who Swam to Euskadi: Euskadiraino Igerian Joan Zen Neska. Kurlansky, Mark. 2005. (ENG & BAQ.). 32p. (J). (gr. -1-3). 18.95 *(978-1-877802-54-6(9))* Ctr. for Basque Studies.

Kurosaki, Yoshisuke. Japanese Children's Favorite Stories. Sakade, Florence. anniv. ed. 2014. 112p. (J). (gr. 3-8). 17.95 *(978-4-8053-1260-5(2))* Tuttle Publishing.

—Little One-Inch & Other Japanese Children's Favorite Stories. Sakade, Florence. rev. ed. 2018. 48p. (J). (gr. -1-3). 9.99 *(978-0-8048-5059-9(3))* Tuttle Publishing.

Kurosaki, Yoshisuke. Peach Boy: And Other Japanese Children's Favorite Stories. Kurosaki, Yoshisuke. Sakade, Florence. 2008. 48p. (J). (gr. k-3). 12.95 *(978-4-8053-0996-4(2))* Tuttle Publishing.

Kurshid, Nida, jt. illus. see Godfrey, Neshelle.

Kurt D Williams and Jeff Baker. The Little Lost Allygator. Knapp, Rene & Berger, Marjorie B. 2012. 44p. pap. 24.95 *(978-1-4626-8155-6(7))* America Star Bks.

Kurth, Steve. Demeter & Persephone: Spring Held Hostage [a Greek Myth]. Fontes, Justine & Fontes, Ron. 2008. (Graphic Myths & Legends Ser.). (ENG.). 48p. (J). (gr. 4-8). per. 9.99 *(978-0-8225-6570-3(6)*, Graphic Universe™) Lerner Publishing Group.

—Hercules. Storrie, Paul D. 2007. (Graphic Myths & Legends Ser.). 48p. (J). 26.60 *(978-0-8225-3084-8(8))* Lerner Publishing Group.

—Hercules: The Twelve Labors [a Greek Myth]. Storrie, Paul D. (Graphic Myths & Legends Ser.). (ENG.). 48p. (gr. 4-8). 2015. 21.32 *(978-1-4677-5981-6(3)*, Lerner Digital); 2007. (J). per. 9.99 *(978-0-8225-6485-0(8)*, 9780822564850, Graphic Universe™) Lerner Publishing Group.

Kurth, Steve & Schulz, Barbara. Hercules: Los Doce Trabajos: un Mito Griego. Storrie, Paul D. 2007. (Mitos y leyendas en viñetas (Graphic Myths & Legends) Ser.). (SPA.). 48p. (J). (gr. 4-7). per. 8.95 *(978-0-8225-7967-0(7)*, Ediciones Lerner) Lerner Publishing Group.

Kurth, Steve, jt. illus. see Schulz, Barbara.

Kurth, Steven, et al. Avengers: the Initiative - the Complete Collection Vol. 2. 2017. (ENG.). 456p. (YA). (gr. 8-17). pap. 34.99 *(978-1-302-90687-0(9))* Marvel Worldwide, Inc.

Kurtz, Jane. Big, Bigger, Biggest: In English & Afaan Oromo. Goering, Noh & Ready Set Go Books. 2019. (ENG.). 32p. (J). pap. 9.99 ***(978-1-6974-8771-8(8))*** Independently Published.

—Too Brave: An Ethiopian Parable in Amharic & English. Goering, Noh. 2020. (ENG.). 32p. (J). pap. 9.99 ***(978-1-6596-2941-5(1))*** Independently Published.

—Too Brave: In English & Afaan Oromo. Goering, Noh & Ready Set Go Books. 2020. (ENG.). 32p. (J). pap. 9.99 ***(978-1-6542-8346-9(0))*** Independently Published.

Kurtz, John. Disney Princess: Look & Find. 2004. (Disney Princess Ser.). 24p. (J). 7.98 *(978-0-7853-7918-8(5)*, 7179200) Phoenix International Publications, Inc.

—The Little Engine: The Original Tale From 1920. Miller, Olive Beaupre. 2020. (Children's Classic Collections). 32p. (gr. -1-3). 12.99 *(978-1-63158-400-8(6)*, Racehorse Publishing) Skyhorse Publishing Co., Inc.

—Olivia Paper Dolls. Dreamworks Animation Publishing, LLC. 2015. (Dover Paper Dolls Ser.). (ENG.). 24p. (J). (gr. 2-5). 9.99 *(978-0-486-80278-7(7))* Dover Pubns., Inc.

—Olivia Sticker Paper Doll. Dreamworks Animation Publishing, LLC. 2015. (Dover Little Activity Books Stickers Ser.). (ENG.). 4p. (J). (gr. 2-5). 1.99 *(978-0-486-80277-0(9))* Dover Pubns., Inc.

—Olivia Stickers. Dreamworks Animation Publishing, LLC. 2015. (Dover Little Activity Books Stickers Ser.). (ENG.). 4p. (J). (gr. k-3). 1.99 *(978-0-486-80276-3(0))* Dover Pubns., Inc.

—Olivia's Big Day Coloring Book. Dreamworks Animation Publishing, LLC. 2015. (Dover Paper Dolls Ser.). (ENG.). 64p. (J). (gr. 2-5). pap. 6.99 *(978-0-486-80279-4(5))* Dover Pubns., Inc.

—Romy's Moon: A Romy the Cow Story. Kurtz, Sandrina. 2016. (ENG.). (J). 18.99 *(978-0-9982674-0-1(6))* Kurtz Art Studio Inc.

—Romy's Moon Coloring Book: A Romy the Cow Coloring Book. Kurtz, Sandrina. 2016. (ENG.). (J). pap. 5.99 *(978-0-9982674-6-3(5))* Kurtz Art Studio Inc.

—Vicki Cobb's Why Do I Dry Off? STEM Kids Discover the Science of Evaporation. Cobb, Vicki. 2020. (STEM Play Ser.). 40p. (J). (gr. 1-6). pap. 12.99 *(978-1-63158-347-6(6)*, Racehorse Publishing) Skyhorse Publishing Co., Inc.

—What Belongs? Shively, Julie. 2004. (Baby Looney Toons Ser.). (ENG.). 16p. (J). 6.95 *(978-0-8249-6561-7(2)*, Ideal Pubns.) Worthy Publishing.

—Winnie the Pooh's Many Adventures, Set. Marshall, Hallie. 2003. 176p. (J). 15.99 *(978-0-7868-3440-2(4))* Disney Pr.

Kurtz, John. You Can Be Brave: See How Magnolia Overcame Her Fear. Kurtz, Sandrina. 2020. 32p. (J). (gr. -1-1). 12.99 ***(978-1-5107-5498-0(9)**, Sky Pony Pr.)* Skyhorse Publishing Co., Inc.

—You Can Be Healthy: See How Violet Eats Well & Stays Active with Exercise. Kurtz, Sandrina. 2020. 32p. (J). (gr. -1-1). 12.99 ***(978-1-5107-5500-0(4)**, Sky Pony Pr.)* Skyhorse Publishing Co., Inc.

Kurtz, John. JATS Fairytale Classics - Goldilocks & the Three Bears. Kurtz, John. 2004. 24p. (J). lib. bdg. 8.00 *(978-1-4242-0635-3(9))* Fitzgerald Bks.

—JATS Fairytale Classics - Jack & the Beanstalk. Kurtz, John. 2004. 24p. (J). lib. bdg. 8.00 *(978-1-4242-0636-0(7))* Fitzgerald Bks.

Kurtz Kingsley, Linda. Blue Skies for Lupe. Kurtz Kingsley, Linda. 2015. (ENG.). 32p. (J). pap. *(978-1-60613-271-5(7))* Woodbine Hse.

Kurtz, Rory. Passage to Fortune: Searching for Saguenay. Gunderson, Jessica. 2016. (Discovering the New World Ser.). (ENG.). 96p. (J). (gr. 3-5). lib. bdg. 26.65 *(978-1-4965-3481-1(6)*, Stone Arch Bks.) Capstone.

—Passage to Fortune: Searching for Saguenay. Gunderson, Jessica. 2016. (Discovering the New World Ser.). (ENG.). 96p. (J). (gr. 3-5). pap. 7.95 *(978-1-4965-3482-8(4)*, Stone Arch Bks.) Capstone.

K

Kurtz Williams, David. The Very Best Story Ever Told: The Gospel with American Sign Language, Vol. Currie, Robin. 2018. (ENG.). 32p. (J). 16.99 *(978-1-5064-3811-5(3),* Beaming Books) Augsburg Fortress, Pubs.

Kurtzweil, Lee. My Private Parts Belong to Me! Feder, Yael. Setbon, Jessica, tr. 2019. (ENG.). 26p. (J). pap. ***(978-965-19-1071-5(2))*** Schocken Publishing Hse. Ltd.

Kurumada, Masami. Knights of the Zodiac, Vol. 5. Kurumada, Masami. 2004. (ENG.). 200p. pap. 7.95 *(978-1-59116-470-8(2))* Viz Media.

Kurup, Prakash. A-B-C in Action. Mehta, Poonam V. 2012. 36p. pap. 22.12 *(978-1-4669-2687-5(2))* Trafford Publishing.

Kuryla, Mary, jt. illus. see Yelchin, Eugene.

Kurzyca, Krystyna Emilia. Adventures with Bingo Borden. Anderson, Al. Agora Publications Staff, tr. 2010. 77p. (J). pap. 9.50 *(978-1-887250-46-7(8))* Agora Pubns., Inc.

—The Wise Enchanter: A Journey through the Alphabet, 1 vol. Davidow, Shelley. 2005. (ENG.). 159p. (J). (gr. 3-7). per. 17.95 *(978-0-88010-562-0(3))* SteinerBooks, Inc.

Kus, Lori. Deseamos Pescar. Owens, Lisa, ed. Vasquez, Christina Gales, tr. 2019. (SPA.). 26p. (J). pap. 10.95 *(978-1-0811-1764-1(8))* Independently Published.

—Nous Souhaitons Pêcher. Owens, Lisa, ed. Chilton, Sabine, tr. 2019. (FRE.). 26p. (J). pap. 13.99 *(978-1-0811-6851-3(X))* Independently Published.

Kus, Lori Ebaugh. We Wish to Fish. Gales, Wayne. Owens, Lisa, ed. 2019. (ENG.). 26p. (J). pap. 10.99 *(978-1-0736-5710-0(8))* Independently Published.

Kusaka, Akira. A Bowl Full of Peace: A True Story. Stelson, Caren. 2020. (ENG.). 40p. (J). (gr. 1-5). 17.99 *(978-1-5415-2148-3(X),* Carolrhoda Bks.) Lerner Publishing Group.

Kusaka, Hidenori. Pokémon Adventures, Vol. 8. Kusaka, Hidenori. 2010. 200p. (J). pap. 9.99 *(978-1-4215-3061-1(9))* Viz Media.

Kusaka, Michiru. Crazy Cat Goes to the Fais Do Do. RoAne, Janice. 2016. (ENG.). (J). (gr. 4-6). 19.99 *(978-0-9969750-5-6(5))* Roane Ink LLC.

Kusama, Yayoi & Weinstein, Ellen. Yayoi Kusama: From Here to Infinity! Suzuki, Sarah. 2017. (ENG.). 40p. (J). (gr. 8-17). 19.95 *(978-1-63345-039-4(2))* Museum of Modern Art.

Kushii, Tetsuo. Dinosaurs. Turnbull, Stephanie. 2006. (Usborne Beginners Ser.). 32p. (J). (gr. 2). lib. bdg. 12.99 *(978-1-58086-929-4(7),* Usborne) EDC Publishing.

Kushii, Tetsuo, et al. Spiders. Gilpin, Rebecca. 2006. (Beginners Nature: Level 1 Ser.). 32p. (J). (gr. k-2). 4.99 *(978-0-7945-1398-6(0),* Usborne) EDC Publishing.

Kushii, Tetsuo. Under the Sea. Patchett, Fiona. 2006. (Usborne Beginners Ser.). 32p. (J). (gr. 1). lib. bdg. 12.99 *(978-1-58086-931-7(9),* Usborne) EDC Publishing.

—Usborne Dinosaur Stencil Book. Pearcey, Alice. 2006. 14p. (J). (gr. -1-3). bds. 12.99 *(978-0-7945-1138-8(4),* Usborne) EDC Publishing.

Kushii, Tetsuo & Larkum, Adam. Bears. Helbrough, Emma. 2006. (Beginners Nature: Level 1 Ser.). 32p. (J). (gr. k-2). 4.99 *(978-0-7945-1393-1(X));* (gr. 1). lib. bdg. 12.99 *(978-1-58086-941-6(6))* EDC Publishing. (Usborne).

Kushii, Tetsuo & Wray, Zoe. Eggs & Chicks. Patchett, Fiona. 2007. (Usborne Beginners Ser.). 32p. (J). (gr. -1). 4.99 *(978-0-7945-1342-9(5),* Usborne) EDC Publishing.

—Under the Sea. Patchett, Fiona. 2006. (Beginners Nature: Level 1 Ser.). 32p. (J). (gr. k-2). 4.99 *(978-0-7945-1336-8(0),* Usborne) EDC Publishing.

Kushii, Tetsuo & Wright, David. Spiders. Gilpin, Rebecca. 2006. (Usborne Beginners Ser.). 32p. (J). (gr. 1). lib. bdg. 12.99 *(978-1-58086-946-1(7),* Usborne) EDC Publishing.

Kushii, Tetsuo, jt. illus. see Wray, Zoe.

Kushnareva, Julia. The Story of Rainbow Bear. Perri, Jessica. 2017. (ENG.). (J). 15.50 *(978-0-692-91830-2(2),* Wild Meadow) Perri, Jessica.

Kushner, Sarah. What You Have Now What Your Mommy Had Then. Shoemaker, Craig. 2004. 32p. 15.95 *(978-0-9713454-2-3(2))* Bennett/Novak & Co., Inc.

Kushnir, Hilli. Camp with Me ABC's: Lift-A-Tab Board Book. Downy, Rufus. Cottage Door Press, ed. 2018. (ENG.). 8p. (J). (gr. -1-k). bds. 8.99 *(978-1-68052-324-9(4),* 1003000) Cottage Door Pr.

—Five Funny Bunnies (board Book) Houghton Mifflin Harcourt, Houghton Mifflin & Gryta, Thomas. 2019. (ENG.). 12p. (J). (— 1). bds. 6.99 *(978-1-328-96603-2(8),* 1707383, HMH Books For Young Readers) Houghton Mifflin Harcourt Publishing Co.

—Five Silly Ghosts (board Book) Houghton Mifflin Company Editors & Gryta, Thomas. 2018. (ENG.). 12p. (J). (— 1). bds. 6.99 *(978-1-328-86659-2(9),* 1696027, HMH Books For Young Readers) Houghton Mifflin Harcourt Publishing Co.

—Now You Are Two: Little Bird Greetings. Birdsong, Minnie. 2019. (ENG.). 8p. (J). (gr. -1-k). bds. 6.99 *(978-1-68052-382-9(1),* 1003470) Cottage Door Pr.

Kushnir, Hilli. The Other Colors. Winget, Rosie. Cottage Door Press, ed. 2020. (Large Children's Interactive Lift-A-Flap Board Book Ser.). (ENG.). 10p. (J). (gr. -1-1). bds. 12.99 ***(978-1-68052-942-5(0),*** 1005850) Cottage Door Pr.

Kushnir, Hilli. Pat-A-Cake: Puppies. 2018. (Pat-A-Cake Ser.). (ENG.). 14p. (J). (— 1). bds. 7.99 *(978-1-68412-306-3(2),* Silver Dolphin Bks.) Printers Row Publishing Group.

—This Makes Me Angry: Dealing with Feelings Series. Carbone, Courtney. 2018. (Rodale Kids Curious Readers/Level 2 Ser.: 3). 32p. (J). (gr. -1-1). pap. 4.99 *(978-1-63565-071-6(2),* 9781635650716, Rodale Kids) Random Hse. Children's Bks.

—This Makes Me Happy: Dealing with Feelings Series. Carbone, Courtney. 2018. (Rodale Kids Curious Readers/Level 2 Ser.: 1). 32p. (J). (gr. -1-1). pap. 4.99 *(978-1-63565-038-9(0),* 9781635650389, Rodale Kids) Random Hse. Children's Bks.

—This Makes Me Jealous. Carbone, Courtney. 2019. (Rodale Kids Curious Readers/Level 2 Ser.: 6). 32p. (J). (gr. -1-1). pap. 4.99 *(978-1-63565-077-8(1),* 9781635650778, Rodale Kids) Random Hse. Children's Bks.

—This Makes Me Sad. Carbone, Courtney. 2018. (Dealing with Feelings Ser.). (ENG.). 32p. (J). (gr. 1-3). 17.44 *(978-1-5364-3729-4(8))* Rodale Pr., Inc.

—This Makes Me Sad: Dealing with Feelings Series. Carbone, Courtney. 2018. (Rodale Kids Curious Readers/Level 2 Ser.: 2). 32p. (J). (gr. -1-1). pap. 4.99 *(978-1-63565-040-2(2),* 9781635650402, Rodale Kids) Random Hse. Children's Bks.

—This Makes Me Silly: Dealing with Feelings Series. Carbone, Courtney. 2018. (Rodale Kids Curious Readers/Level 2 Ser.: 4). 32p. (J). (gr. -1-1). pap. 4.99 *(978-1-63565-074-7(7),* 9781635650747, Rodale Kids) Random Hse. Children's Bks.

Kusinitz, Nat. Sometimes the Spoon Runs Away with Another Spoon Coloring Book. Bunnell, Jacinta. 2010. (Reach & Teach Ser.). (ENG.). 32p. pap. 10.00 *(978-1-60486-329-1(3))* PM Pr.

Kuskin, Karla. Harrison Loved His Umbrella. Levine, Rhoda. 2016. 64p. (J). (-k). 14.95 *(978-1-59017-991-8(9),* NYR Children's Collection) New York Review of Bks., Inc., The.

—Traces. Fox, Paula. 2011. (ENG.). 32p. (gr. 2-4). 26.19 *(978-1-932425-43-7(8))* Boyds Mills Pr.

Kusunoki, Kei. Sengoku Nights, Vol. 1. Ohashi, Kaoru. 2006. 208p. pap. 9.99 *(978-1-59532-945-5(5))* TOKYOPOP, Inc.

Kutschbach, Doris. Claude Monet. Aston, Paul, tr. 2006. (Coloring Bks.). (ENG.). 32p. (J). (gr. 1-4). 8.95 *(978-3-7913-3713-5(0))* Prestel Verlag GmbH & Co KG. DEU. Dist: Penguin Random Hse. LLC.

—Coloring Book: Wassily Kandinsky. Aston, Paul, tr. 2006. (Coloring Bks.). (ENG.). 32p. (J). (gr. 1-4). 8.95 *(978-3-7913-3712-8(2))* Prestel Verlag GmbH & Co KG. DEU. Dist: Penguin Random Hse. LLC.

Kutsuwada, Chie. Hagakure: The Code of the Samurai, 1 vol. Tsunetomo, Yamamoto & Wilson, William Scott. 2011. (ENG.). 144p. pap. 14.95 *(978-4-7700-3120-4(3))* Kodansha International JPN. Dist: Penguin Random Hse. LLC.

Kuumba, Mshindo. A Day at the Four Seasons: "Finding the Ingredients" Pitt, Roosevelt, Jr. 2005. (Food Adventures with Charles the Chef Ser.). (J). per. 12.95 *(978-0-9760745-0-2(8))* AMARA Entertainment.

Kuumba, Mshindo & Bey, Elihu "Adofo". Chris Obiyah's Rites of Passage: The Kandake's Amulet. Peaks, Taifa, ed. 2018. (Chris Obiyah's Rites of Passage Ser.: Vol. 1). (ENG.). 148p. (J). pap. 12.99 *(978-1-7262-4416-9(4))* CreateSpace Independent Publishing Platform.

Kuusisto, Toni, et al. My Little Pony: Friendship Is Magic Volume 16. Anderson, Ted & Whitley, Jeremy. 2019. (My Little Pony Ser.: 16). 120p. (J). (gr. 4-7). pap. 17.99 *(978-1-68405-428-2(1))* Idea & Design Works, LLC.

—My Little Pony: Friendship Is Magic Volume 18. Maggs, Sam & Zahler, Thom. 2020. (My Little Pony Ser.: 18). 120p. (J). (gr. 4-7). pap. 17.99 *(978-1-68405-615-6(2))* Idea & Design Works, LLC.

Kuvarzina, Anya. Make a Face. Alegria, Ricardo. 2017. (ENG.). 32p. (J). (-k). pap. 15.99 *(978-1-57687-850-7(3),* powerHouse Bks.) powerHse. Bks.

Kuzma, Jakub. Alena & the Favorite Thing. Anderson, Eric B. 2008. 36p. (J). (ENG.). 18.95 *(978-0-9798659-2-3(1));* pap. 13.95 *(978-0-9798659-3-0(X))* Edgecliff Pr. LLC.

Kuznet?s?ova, E. Tetradki Pod Dozhdem. Goll?a?vkin, V. V. 2017. (RUS.). 125p. (J). *(978-5-353-07704-6(0))* RosmYn-Press, Izdatel'stvo.

Kvasnosky, Laura McGee. The Big Picture. Kvasnosky, Laura McGee. 2010. (Zelda & Ivy Ser.). 48p. (J). (gr. k-4). 14.99 *(978-0-7636-4180-1(4))* Candlewick Pr.

—Keeping Secrets. Kvasnosky, Laura McGee. 2009. (Zelda & Ivy Ser.). 48p. (J). (gr. k-4). 15.99 *(978-0-7636-4179-5(0))* Candlewick Pr.

—Really Truly Bingo. Kvasnosky, Laura McGee. 2008. (ENG.). 32p. (J). (gr. k-k). 15.99 *(978-0-7636-3210-6(4))* Candlewick Pr.

—The Runaways. Kvasnosky, Laura McGee. 2006. (Zelda & Ivy Ser.). (ENG.). 48p. (J). (gr. k-4). 14.99 *(978-0-7636-2689-1(9))* Candlewick Pr.

—Zelda & Ivy - Keeping Secrets. Kvasnosky, Laura McGee. 2013. (Candlewick Sparks Ser.). (ENG.). 48p. (J). (gr. k-4). pap. 4.99 *(978-0-7636-6636-1(X))* Candlewick Pr.

—Zelda & Ivy & the Boy Next Door. Kvasnosky, Laura McGee. 2014. (Candlewick Sparks Ser.). 40p. (J). (gr. k-4). pap. 4.99 *(978-0-7636-7182-2(7))* Candlewick Pr.

—Zelda & Ivy One Christmas. Kvasnosky, Laura McGee. 2013. (Candlewick Sparks Ser.). 40p. (J). (gr. k-4). pap. 3.99 *(978-0-7636-6865-5(6))* Candlewick Pr.

—Zelda & Ivy: the Big Picture: Candlewick Sparks. Kvasnosky, Laura McGee. 2013. (Candlewick Sparks Ser.). (ENG.). 48p. (J). (gr. k-4). pap. 4.99 *(978-0-7636-6637-8(8))* Candlewick Pr.

—Zelda & Ivy: the Runaways: Candlewick Sparks. Kvasnosky, Laura McGee. 2013. (Candlewick Sparks Ser.). (ENG.). 48p. (J). (gr. k-4). pap. 4.99 *(978-0-7636-6635-4(1))* Candlewick Pr.

Kvasnosky, Laura McGee & McGee, Kate Harvey. Little Wolf's First Howling. Kvasnosky, Laura McGee. 2017. (ENG.). 32p. (J). (gr. -1-2). 16.99 *(978-0-7636-8971-1(8))* Candlewick Pr.

Kveta. Smoke: A Wolf's Story, 1 vol. Kveta, tr. Banner, Melanie Jane. 2003. (ENG.). 160p. (J). (gr. 4-7). pap. 9.95 *(978-1-55041-322-9(8),* c44ddae4-6a13-4952-9625-2719a5453c0d) Fitzhenry & Whiteside, Ltd. CAN. Dist: Firefly Bks., Ltd.

Kvirikashvili, Lika. Dreaming Athens. Fox, Julie G. 2019. (ENG.). 38p. (J). pap. 9.99 *(978-1-7962-1652-3(6))* Independently Published.

—Goodbye, Emma. Fox, Julie G. Nel, René, ed. 2019. (ENG.). 30p. (J). pap. 9.99 *(978-1-0906-6887-5(2))* Independently Published.

—The Rugby Museum - Colour Me: The Webb Ellis Rugby Football Museum Colouring Book. Jackson, Paul & Fuxman, Julie G. 2019. (ENG.). 26p. (J). pap. 6.99 *(978-1-7980-0201-8(9))* Independently Published.

—Tommy the Learned Cat Learns to Be a Chef. Fox, Julie G. 2019. (ENG.). 36p. (J). pap. 9.99 *(978-1-7977-7681-1(9))* Independently Published.

Kvirikashvili, Lika, jt. illus. see Bera, Aparna.

Kwag, Jin-yeong. Typhoon Holidays: Taiwan. Hsu, Yi Ling. 2015. (Global Kids Storybooks Ser.). (ENG.). 32p. (J). (gr. 1-4). pap. 8.99 *(978-1-925233-43-8(X),* Big and SMALL) ChoiceMaker Pty. Ltd., The AUS. Dist: Lerner Publishing Group.

—Typhoon Holidays: Taiwan. Hsu, Yi Ling. Cowley, Joy, ed. 2015. (Global Kids Storybooks Ser.). (ENG.). 32p. (gr. 1-4). 26.65 *(978-1-925246-04-9(3));* 26.65 *(978-1-925246-30-8(2));* 7.99 *(978-1-925246-56-8(6))* ChoiceMaker Pty. Ltd., The AUS. (Big and SMALL). Dist: Lerner Publishing Group.

Kwakkenbos, Frans. Unlocking the Secret of Otherland: A Story & Activity Book for Children Living Abroad. Janssen-Mathes, Mieke M. E. 2007. 96p. pap. *(978-90-6832-587-4(6))* Royal Tropical Institute Pr. (KIT (Koninklijk Instituut voor de Tropen).

Kwas, Susan Estelle. Wild Birds. Ryder, Joanne. 2003. 40p. (J). (gr. -1-2). 16.99 *(978-0-06-027738-3(6))* HarperCollins Pubs.

Kwasny, Karl. Everything You Need to Know about NIGHTMARES! & How to Defeat Them: The Nightmares! Handbook. Segel, Jason & Miller, Kirsten. 2017. (Nightmares! Ser.). (ENG.). 240p. (J). (gr. 3-7). 16.99 *(978-0-385-74431-7(5));* lib. bdg. 19.99 *(978-0-375-99160-8(3))* Random Hse. Children's Bks. (Delacorte Bks. for Young Readers).

—Nightmares! Segel, Jason & Miller, Kirsten. (J). (gr. 3-7). 2015. (Nightmares! Ser.: 1). (ENG.). 400p. 7.99 *(978-0-385-74426-3(9),* Yearling); 2014. 368p. 16.99 *(978-0-385-74425-6(0),* Delacorte Bks. for Young Readers) Random Hse. Children's Bks.

—Nightmares! the Lost Lullaby. Segel, Jason & Miller, Kirsten. (Nightmares! Ser.: 3). (ENG.). (J). (gr. 3-7). 2017. 352p. pap. 7.99 *(978-0-385-74430-0(7),* Yearling); 2016. 336p. lib. bdg. 19.99 *(978-0-375-99159-2(X),* Delacorte Bks. for Young Readers) Random Hse. Children's Bks.

—The Sleepwalker Tonic. Segel, Jason & Miller, Kirsten. 2015. (Nightmares! Ser.: 2). (ENG.). 368p. (J). (gr. 3-7). 16.99 *(978-0-385-74427-0(7));* lib. bdg. 19.99 *(978-0-375-99158-5(1))* Random Hse. Children's Bks. (Delacorte Bks. for Young Readers).

—The Sleepwalker Tonic. Segel, Jason & Miller, Kirsten. ed. 2016. (Nightmares! Ser.: 2). (ENG.). 384p. (J). (gr. 3-7). 18.40 *(978-0-606-39350-8(1))* Turtleback.

—The Year of Shadows. Legrand, Claire. 2013. (ENG.). 416p. (J). (gr. 3-7). 16.99 *(978-1-4424-4294-8(8),* Simon & Schuster Bks. For Young Readers) Simon & Schuster Bks. For Young Readers.

Kwaymullina, Ambelin. Bush Bash. Morgan, Sally. 2019. (ENG.). 24p. (J). (— 1). pap. 11.99 *(978-1-921894-14-5(8))* Little Hare Bks. AUS. Dist: Independent Pubs. Group.

—Joey Counts to Ten. Morgan, Sally. 2018. (ENG.). 24p. (J). (gr. -1-k). pap. 12.99 *(978-1-76050-294-2(4))* Little Hare Bks. AUS. Dist: Independent Pubs. Group.

Kwee, Natalie. If You Love Books, You Could Be... Dennis, Elizabeth. 2020. (If You Love Ser.). (ENG.). 32p. (J). (gr. k-2). 17.99 ***(978-1-5344-7102-3(2));*** pap. 4.99 ***(978-1-5344-7101-6(4))*** Simon Spotlight. (Simon Spotlight).

Kwee, Natalie. If You Love Cooking, You Could Be... Dennis, Elizabeth. 2019. (If You Love Ser.). (ENG.). 32p. (J). (gr. k-2). 17.99 *(978-1-5344-5454-5(3));* pap. 4.99 *(978-1-5344-5455-2(1))* Simon Spotlight. (Simon Spotlight).

—If You Love Dolphins, You Could Be... Nakamura, May. 2019. (If You Love Ser.). (ENG.). 32p. (J). (gr. k-2). 17.99 *(978-1-5344-4469-0(6));* pap. 4.99 *(978-1-5344-4468-3(8))* Simon Spotlight. (Simon Spotlight).

—If You Love Fashion, You Could Be... Ready-To-Read Level 2. Nakamura, May. 2019. (If You Love Ser.). (ENG.). 32p. (J). (gr. k-2). 17.99 *(978-1-5344-4877-3(2));* pap. 4.99 *(978-1-5344-4876-6(4))* Simon Spotlight. (Simon Spotlight).

Kwee, Natalie. If You Love Robots, You Could Be... Nakamura, May. 2020. (If You Love Ser.). (ENG.). 32p. (J). (gr. k-2). 17.99 ***(978-1-5344-6523-7(5));*** pap. 4.99 ***(978-1-5344-6522-0(7))*** Simon Spotlight. (Simon Spotlight).

Kwee, Natalie. If You Love Video Games, You Could Be... Feldman, Thea. 2019. (If You Love Ser.). (ENG.). 32p. (J). (gr. k-2). 17.99 *(978-1-5344-4399-0(1));* pap. 4.99 *(978-1-5344-4398-3(3))* Simon Spotlight. (Simon Spotlight).

Kwiat, Ernie. Abby Caddaby up & Down. 2013. (J). *(978-0-7636-6741-2(2))* Candlewick Pr.

—Love: From Sesame Street. Sesame Workshop Staff. 2018. (Sesame Street Scribbles Ser.: 0). (ENG.). 32p. (J). (-3). 12.99 *(978-1-4926-7749-9(3),* Sourcebooks Jabberwocky) Sourcebooks, Inc.

—Sesame Street: Boo! Guess Who, Elmo! 2015. (Guess Who! Book Ser.). (ENG.). 10p. (J). (gr. -1-k). bds. 10.99 *(978-0-7944-3475-5(4))* Reader's Digest Assn., Inc., The.

Kwon, Elisa & rem. Vampire Kisses: Blood Relatives, Volume III, Vol. 3. Schreiber, Ellen. 2009. (Vampire Kisses: Blood Relatives Ser.: Vol. 3). (ENG.). 192p. (YA). (gr. 8-18). pap. 9.99 *(978-0-06-134083-3(9),* Tegen, Katherine Bks) HarperCollins Pubs.

Kwon, Min. Snow Biz, Vol. 5. 2006. (Serenity Ser.: Vol. 5). 96p. (YA). (gr. 7-12). per. 7.97 *(978-1-59310-874-8(5),* Barbour Bks.) Barbour Publishing, Inc.

Kwon, Sa-Woo. El niño de la Pegatina Amarilla. Sunmi, Hwang. 2016. (SPA.). 104p. (J). (gr. 2-4). pap. 9.95 *(978-607-8469-23-9(1))* Nostra Ediciones MEX. Dist: Independent Pubs. Group.

Kwon, Yeong-mook. Ah I'm Full. Jo, Eun-sook. Cowley, Joy, ed. 2015. (Science Storybooks Ser.). (ENG.). 32p. (J). (gr. k-4). 10.00 *(978-1-925233-59-9(6),* Big and SMALL) ChoiceMaker Pty. Ltd., The AUS. Dist: Lerner Publishing Group.

—Ah I'm Full: Food Chain. Jo, Eun-sook. Cowley, Joy, ed. 2015. (Science Storybooks Ser.). (ENG.). 32p. (gr. k-3). 26.65 *(978-1-925246-21-6(3));* 7.99 *(978-1-925246-73-5(6));* 26.65 *(978-1-925246-47-6(7))* ChoiceMaker Pty. Ltd., The AUS. (Big and SMALL). Dist: Lerner Publishing Group.

Kwong, Alvina. The Giraffe That Ate the Moon: Babl Children's Books in Chinese & English. Rangel, Aralie. 2018. (ENG.). 28p. (J). (gr. k-1). 14.99 *(978-1-68304-280-8(8))* Babl Books, Incorporated.

Kwong, Alvina. Happy Trails with Abby & Taz. Brown, Christina. 2019. (ENG.). 26p. (J). (gr. -1-3). pap. 9.99 ***(978-1-61254-387-1(1))*** Brown Books Publishing Group.

—Maddy Lou & Mack at the State Fair of Texas. Granzow, Krystal. 2019. (ENG.). 26p. (J). (gr. -1-3). pap. 10.99 ***(978-1-61254-398-7(7))*** Brown Books Publishing Group.

Kwong, Alvina. My Imagination. Estes-Hill, Katrina. 2007. 32p. (J). (gr. -1-2). 15.95 *(978-0-9745715-6-0(3))* KRBY Creations, LLC.

—Sand Mouse's Soup: A Story about Sharing Every Day of the Week in Hawaii. BeachHouse Publishing. 2016. (ENG.). 18p. (J). (gr. -1-1). bds. 7.95 *(978-1-933067-73-5(X))* Beachhouse Publishing, LLC.

Kyak, Martha. Nattiq & the Land of Statues, 1 vol. Landry, Barbara. 2020. (ENG.). 24p. (J). (gr. k-2). 18.95 *(978-1-55498-891-4(8))* Groundwood Bks. CAN. Dist: Publishers Group West (PGW).

Kyger, Michelle. Wild Styles: Cats of the Mill Mountain Zoo. Bradford, M. H. 2019. (ENG.). 32p. (J). pap. 9.99 ***(978-1-7257-1805-0(7))*** CreateSpace Independent Publishing Platform.

Kyle, Fleming. Hockey Wars 2: The New Girl. Lawrence, Sam & Jackson, Ben. 2019. (Hockey Wars Ser.: Vol. 2). (ENG.). 172p. (J). (gr. 3-7). 21.99 *(978-1-988656-28-1(1))* Indie Publishing Group.

Kyle, Margaret. After the Beginning. Pogue, Carolyn & Price, Ian. 2006. (ENG.). 32p. 18.95 *(978-1-896836-83-6(6),* Copperhouse) Wood Lake Publishing, Inc. CAN. Dist: Westminster John Knox Pr.

—The Bible in the Hunger Games: A "Bibleizing" Study Guide. Chapman, Patricia. 2012. (ENG.). 52p. (J). (gr. 17-17). pap. 9.95 *(978-1-77064-565-3(9))* Wood Lake Publishing, Inc. CAN. Dist: Westminster John Knox Pr.

—52 More Crafts: For the Church Year. Payne-Krzyzanowski, Anna et al. 2008. (ENG.). 64p. pap. 16.95 *(978-1-55145-570-9(6))* Wood Lake Publishing, Inc. CAN. Dist: Westminster John Knox Pr.

Kylee Matson. Meet Repeat Pete: A Pirate with Repetitive Behaviour. Matson, Kylee. Margaret Whiskin, ed. 2019. (ENG.). 48p. (J). (gr. 3-5). pap. ***(978-0-646-99845-9(5))*** Amazing Smart Kids.

Kyong-Nan, Nani. Korean Children's Day. Suyenaga, Ruth et al. 2005. (Multicultural Celebrations Ser.). 32p. (J). 4.95 *(978-1-59373-011-6(X))* Bunker Hill Publishing, Inc.

—Korean Children's Day. Suyenaga, Ruth. 2004. 23p. (J). (gr. 4-8). reprint ed. pap. 15.00 *(978-0-7567-7068-6(8))* DIANE Publishing Co.

Kyoung-Sim, Jeong. Korean Children's Favorite Stories: Fables, Myths & Fairy Tales. So-Un, Kim. 2020. 64p. (J). (gr. k-5). 14.99 *(978-0-8048-5020-9(8))* Tuttle Publishing.

—Three Korean Fairy Tales: Beloved Stories & Legends Retold for Children. So-Un, Kim. 2019. 96p. (J). (gr. 1-7). 15.99 *(978-0-8048-5227-2(8))* Tuttle Publishing.

—The Tigers of the Kumgang Mountains: A Korean Folktale. So-Un, Kim. 2005. (ENG.). 1p. (J). (gr. 4-11). 16.95 *(978-0-8048-3653-1(1))* Tuttle Publishing.

Kyoung-Sim, Jeong. Korean Children's Favorite Stories. Kyoung-Sim, Jeong. So-Un, Kim. 2004. 96p. (J). (gr. k-8). 18.95 *(978-0-8048-3591-6(8))* Tuttle Publishing.

Kyung-ah, Choi. Snow Drop. Kyung-ah, Choi, creator. 2005. Vol. 8. rev. ed. 208p. pap. 9.99 *(978-1-59532-044-5(X));* Vol. 9. 9th rev. ed. 192p. pap. 9.99 *(978-1-59532-045-2(8))* TOKYOPOP, Inc.

Kyung, Hyewon. Bigger Than You. Kyung, Hyewon. 2018. (ENG.). 32p. (J). (gr. -1-3). 17.99 *(978-0-06-268312-0(8),* Greenwillow Bks.) HarperCollins Pubs.

—Save Your Friends! Kyung, Hyewon. 2019. (ENG.). 32p. (J). (gr. -1-3). 16.99 *(978-0-06-268315-1(2),* Greenwillow Bks.) HarperCollins Pubs.

L

L a S, Alex. Magnificent Sir Johnny & Biggest Diamond. L a S, Alex. 2019. (1 Ser.: Vol. 4). (ENG.). 32p. (J). pap. 11.90 *(978-1-0965-9710-0(1))* Independently Published.

—Magnificent Sir Johnny & Tom the Reasonable. L a S, Alex. 2018. (1 Ser.: Vol. 3). (ENG.). 58p. (J). pap. 14.90 *(978-1-7309-3875-7(2))* Independently Published.

L a Severin. When It Snows. J M Severin. 2020. (ENG.). 26p. (J). pap. 11.99 ***(978-1-6593-0459-6(8))*** Independently Published.

L, Frankye. Bernie's' Christmas Conundrum. McDougal, Sandra. 2018. (ENG.). 24p. (J). (gr. k-1). pap. *(978-1-9996577-7-2(2))* Little Goblins' Bks.

L, Joe. Times Three. May, Maggie. 2011. 36p. pap. 24.95 *(978-1-4626-2504-8(5))* America Star Bks.

La Baleine, Lili. In Every House on Every Street. Hitchman, Jess. 2019. (ENG.). 32p. (J). (gr. -1-2). 17.99 *(978-1-68010-172-0(2))* Tiger Tales.

La Beree, Brian. Herbert the Tadpole in the Big Change. Bodrogi, Michael. 2003. 48p. (J). (gr. -1-4). 15.95 *(978-1-878398-61-1(X),* Blue Note Bks.) Blue Note Pubns.

—Herbert the Tadpole in the Big Change: Color-Me Version. 2007. 48p. (J). 6.95 *(978-0-9800736-0-7(X))* Sophrose Entertainment Inc.

La Fave, Kim. Ben & the Scaredy-Dog. Ellis, Sarah. 2018. (ENG.). 32p. (J). (gr. -1-1). 17.95 *(978-1-77278-044-4(8))* Pajama Pr. CAN. Dist: Ingram Publisher Services.

—Ben Says Goodbye. Ellis, Sarah. 2016. (ENG.). 32p. (J). (gr. -1-1). 16.95 *(978-1-927485-79-8(7))* Pajama Pr. CAN. Dist: Ingram Publisher Services.

—Fishing with Gubby. Kent, Gary. unabr. ed. 2010. (ENG.). 48p. (J). 19.95 *(978-1-55017-497-7(5))* Harbour Publishing Co., Ltd. CAN. Dist: Publishers Group West (PGW).

La Forest, Courtney. The Magic Eraser #1. Starmer, Aaron. 2020. (Locker 37 Ser.: 1). (ENG.). 224p. (J). (gr. 3-7). 16.99 ***(978-0-593-09428-0(X))***; pap. 8.99 ***(978-0-593-22285-0(7))*** Penguin Young Readers Group. (Penguin Workshop).

—The Rewindable Clock #2. Starmer, Aaron. 2020. (Locker 37 Ser.: 2). (ENG.). 224p. (J). (gr. 3-7). 16.99 ***(978-0-593-09430-3(1))***; pap. 8.99 ***(978-0-593-22286-7(5))*** Penguin Young Readers Group. (Penguin Workshop).

La Grange, Myrtle. Bogwaddle Pond. Jordan, Annie Laurie. 2004. 25p. pap. 24.95 *(978-1-4137-2013-6(7))* PublishAmerica, Inc.

La Porte, Laurena. Big Plans: How Not to Hatch an Egg - in English & Amharic. La Porte, Theresa & Ready Set Go Books. 2019. (ENG.). 36p. (J). pap. 11.99 ***(978-1-7059-7742-2(1))*** Independently Published.

—Big Plans: How Not to Hatch an Egg in English & Tigrinya. La Porte, Theresa & Ready Set Go Books. 2020. (ENG.). 36p. (J). pap. 11.99 ***(978-1-6542-0128-9(6))*** Independently Published.

Laaker, Terry. Charlie & the Rodent Queen. Goody, C. A. l.t. ed. 2003. (Charlie's Great Adventures: No. 3). 88p. per. 5.95 *(978-0-9702546-2-7(8),* 623-876-1518) GoodyGoody Bks.

—Charlie the Spy: Charlie's Great Adventure #6. 2008. 104p. (J). pap. 5.95 *(978-0-9702546-7-2(9))* GoodyGoody Bks.

—The Quest for the Golden Taco: Pepe's Great Adventure #1. Goody, C. A. 2017. (ENG.). (J). pap. 5.95 *(978-0-9995920-0-7(9))* GoodyGoody Bks.

LaBaff, Stephanie. Genetics & Evolution Science Fair Projects, Revised & Expanded Using the Scientific Method. Gardner, Robert. 2010. (Biology Science Projects Using the Scientific Method Ser.). 160p. (gr. 5-6). 36.94 *(978-0-7660-3422-8(4))* Enslow Publishing, LLC.

—Science Fair Projects about the Properties of Matter, Revised & Expanded Using the Scientific Method. Gardner, Robert. 2010. (Physics Science Projects Using the Scientific Method Ser.). 160p. (gr. 5-6). 36.94 *(978-0-7660-3417-4(8))* Enslow Publishing, LLC.

LaBaff, Stephanie & LaBaff, Tom. Earth Science Fair Projects, Revised & Expanded Using the Scientific Method. Calhoun, Yael. 2010. (Earth Science Projects Using the Scientific Method Ser.). 160p. (gr. 5-6). 36.94 *(978-0-7660-3425-9(9))* Enslow Publishing, LLC.

—Electricity & Magnetism Science Fair Projects, Revised & Expanded Using the Scientific Method. Gardner, Robert. 2010. (Physics Science Projects Using the Scientific Method Ser.). 160p. (gr. 5-6). 36.94 *(978-0-7660-3418-1(6))* Enslow Publishing, LLC.

—Planet Earth Science Fair Projects, Revised & Expanded Using the Scientific Method. Gardner, Robert. 2010. (Earth Science Projects Using the Scientific Method Ser.). 160p. (gr. 5-6). 36.94 *(978-0-7660-3423-5(2))* Enslow Publishing, LLC.

LaBaff, Stephanie, jt. illus. see LaBaff, Tom.

LaBaff, Tom. Awesome Animal Science Projects. Benbow, Ann & Mably, Colin. 2009. (Real Life Science Experiments Ser.). 48p. (gr. 3-3). lib. bdg. 26.27 *(978-0-7660-3148-7(9))* Enslow Publishing, LLC.

—Draw Aliens & Space Objects in 4 Easy Steps: Then Write a Story. LaBaff, Stephanie. 2012. (Drawing in 4 Easy Steps Ser.). 48p. (gr. 3-3). lib. bdg. 26.27 *(978-0-7660-3841-7(6))* Enslow Publishing, LLC.

—Draw Aliens & Space Objects in 4 Easy Steps: Then Write a Story. Labaff, Stephanie. 2012. (Drawing in 4 Easy Steps Ser.). 48p. (gr. 3-3). pap. 10.53 *(978-1-4644-0014-8(8),* Enslow Elementary) Enslow Publishing, LLC.

—Draw Animals in 4 Easy Steps: Then Write a Story. LaBaff, Stephanie. 2012. (Drawing in 4 Easy Steps Ser.). 48p. (gr. 3-3). 26.27 *(978-0-7660-3840-0(8))* Enslow Publishing, LLC.

—Draw Animals in 4 Easy Steps: Then Write a Story. Labaff, Stephanie. 2012. (Drawing in 4 Easy Steps Ser.). 48p. (gr. 3-3). pap. 10.53 *(978-1-4644-0013-1(X),* Enslow Elementary) Enslow Publishing, LLC.

—Draw Cartoon People in 4 Easy Steps: Then Write a Story. Labaff, Stephanie. 2012. (Drawing in 4 Easy Steps Ser.). 48p. (gr. 3-3). pap. 10.53 *(978-1-4644-0016-2(4),* Enslow Elementary) Enslow Publishing, LLC.

—Draw Pirates in 4 Easy Steps: Then Write a Story. LaBaff, Stephanie. 2012. (Drawing in 4 Easy Steps Ser.). 48p. (gr. 3-3). 26.27 *(978-0-7660-3839-4(4))*; pap. 10.53 *(978-1-4644-0012-4(1),* Enslow Elementary) Enslow Publishing, LLC.

—Draw Princesses in 4 Easy Steps: Then Write a Story. LaBaff, Stephanie. 2012. (Drawing in 4 Easy Steps Ser.). 48p. (gr. 3-3). 26.27 *(978-0-7660-3838-7(6))* Enslow Publishing, LLC.

—Draw Princesses in 4 Easy Steps: Then Write a Story. Labaff, Stephanie. 2012. (Drawing in 4 Easy Steps Ser.). 48p. (gr. 3-3). pap. 10.53 *(978-1-4644-0011-7(3),* Enslow Elementary) Enslow Publishing, LLC.

—Draw Superheroes in 4 Easy Steps: Then Write a Story. LaBaff, Stephanie. 2012. (Drawing in 4 Easy Steps Ser.). 48p. (gr. 3-3). 26.27 *(978-0-7660-3842-4(4))*; pap. 10.53 *(978-1-4644-0015-5(6),* Enslow Elementary) Enslow Publishing, LLC.

—Energizing Science Projects with Electricity & Magnetism. Gardner, Robert. 2006. (Fantastic Physical Science Experiments Ser.). 48p. (gr. 3-3). lib. bdg. 26.27 *(978-0-7660-2584-4(5),* Enslow Elementary) Enslow Publishing, LLC.

—Jazzy Science Projects with Sound & Music. Gardner, Robert. 2006. (Fantastic Physical Science Experiments Ser.). 48p. (gr. 3-3). lib. bdg. 26.27 *(978-0-7660-2588-2(8),* Enslow Elementary) Enslow Publishing, LLC.

—Master the Scientific Method with Fun Life Science Projects. Benbow, Ann & Mably, Colin. 2010. (Real Life Science Experiments Ser.). 48p. (gr. 3-3). lib. bdg. 26.27 *(978-0-7660-3151-7(9))* Enslow Publishing, LLC.

—Nature's Secret Habitats Science Projects. Benbow, Ann & Mably, Colin. 2010. (Real Life Science Experiments Ser.). 48p. (gr. 3-3). lib. bdg. 26.27 *(978-0-7660-3150-0(0))* Enslow Publishing, LLC.

—Never Eat Soggy Waffles: Fun Mnemonic Memory Tricks. Murphy, Patricia J. 2009. (Prime (Elementary) Ser.). 48p. (gr. 3-3). lib. bdg. 26.27 *(978-0-7660-2710-7(4))* Enslow Publishing, LLC.

—Ready for Addition. Wingard-Nelson, Rebecca. 2014. (Ready for Math Ser.). 48p. (gr. 3-3). pap. 10.53 *(978-1-4644-0433-7(X),* Enslow Elementary) Enslow Publishing, LLC.

—Ready for Division. Wingard-Nelson, Rebecca. 2014. (Ready for Math Ser.). 48p. (gr. 3-3). lib. bdg. 26.27 *(978-0-7660-4249-0(9),* Enslow Elementary) Enslow Publishing, LLC.

—Ready for Fractions & Decimals. Wingard-Nelson, Rebecca. 2014. (Ready for Math Ser.). 48p. (gr. 3-3). 26.27 *(978-0-7660-4247-6(2))*; pap. 10.53 *(978-1-4644-0437-5(2),* Enslow Elementary) Enslow Publishing, LLC.

—Ready for Multiplication. Wingard-Nelson, Rebecca. 2014. (Ready for Math Ser.). 48p. (gr. 3-3). 26.27 *(978-0-7660-4248-3(0))*; pap. 10.53 *(978-1-4644-0439-9(9),* Enslow Elementary) Enslow Publishing, LLC.

—Ready for Subtraction. Wingard-Nelson, Rebecca. 2014. (Ready for Math Ser.). 48p. (gr. 3-3). lib. bdg. 26.27 *(978-0-7660-4246-9(4),* Enslow Elementary) Enslow Publishing, LLC.

—Ready for Word Problems & Problem Solving. Wingard-Nelson, Rebecca. 2014. (Ready for Math Ser.). 48p. (gr. 3-3). 26.27 *(978-0-7660-4250-6(2))*; pap. 10.53 *(978-1-4644-0443-6(7),* Enslow Elementary) Enslow Publishing, LLC.

—Sensational Human Body Science Projects. Benbow, Ann & Mably, Colin. 2010. (Real Life Science Experiments Ser.). 48p. (gr. 3-3). lib. bdg. 26.27 *(978-0-7660-3149-4(7))* Enslow Publishing, LLC.

—Weather Science Fair Projects, Revised & Expanded Using the Scientific Method. Gardner, Robert. 2010. (Earth Science Projects Using the Scientific Method Ser.). 160p. (gr. 5-6). 36.94 *(978-0-7660-3424-2(0))* Enslow Publishing, LLC.

LaBaff, Tom & LaBaff, Stephanie. Chemistry Science Fair Projects Using Inorganic Stuff. Gardner, Robert. rev. exp. ed. 2010. (Chemistry Science Projects Using the Scientific Method Ser.). 160p. (gr. 5-6). 36.94 *(978-0-7660-3413-6(5))* Enslow Publishing, LLC.

—Environmental Science Fair Projects, Revised & Expanded Using the Scientific Method. Rybolt, Thomas R. & Mebane, Robert C. 2010. (Earth Science Projects Using the Scientific Method Ser.). 160p. (gr. 5-6). 36.94 *(978-0-7660-3426-6(7))* Enslow Publishing, LLC.

—Organic Chemistry Science Fair Projects, Revised & Expanded Using the Scientific Method. Gardner, Robert & Conklin, Barbara Gardner. 2010. (Chemistry Science Projects Using the Scientific Method Ser.). 160p. (gr. 5-6). 36.94 *(978-0-7660-3414-3(3))* Enslow Publishing, LLC.

—Plastics & Polymers Science Fair Projects. Goodstein, Madeline P. rev. exp. ed. 2010. (Chemistry Science Projects Using the Scientific Method Ser.). 160p. (gr. 5-6). 36.94 *(978-0-7660-3412-9(7))* Enslow Publishing, LLC.

—Water Science Fair Projects, Revised & Expanded Using the Scientific Method. Goodstein, Madeline P. 2010. (Chemistry Science Projects Using the Scientific Method Ser.). 160p. (gr. 5-6). 36.94 *(978-0-7660-3411-2(9))* Enslow Publishing, LLC.

Labaff, Tom & LaBaff, Tom. Lively Plant Science Projects. Benbow, Ann & Mably, Colin. 2009. (Real Life Science Experiments Ser.). 48p. (gr. 3-3). lib. bdg. 26.27 *(978-0-7660-3146-3(2))* Enslow Publishing, LLC.

LaBaff, Tom, jt. illus. see LaBaff, Stephanie.

LaBaff, Tom, jt. illus. see LaBaff, Tom.

Labarre, Natalie. Incredible Jobs You've (Probably) Never Heard Of. Labarre, Natalie. 2020. (ENG.). 48p. (J). (gr. 5). 19.99 *(978-1-5362-1219-8(9),* Nosy Crow) Candlewick Pr.

Labat, Yancey. Date with Disaster! Fontana, Shea. 2020. (DC Super Hero Girls Ser.). (ENG.). 128p. (J). (gr. 2-6). lib. bdg. 31.99 ***(978-1-5158-7437-9(0),*** 202142, Stone Arch Bks.) Capstone.

Labat, Yancey. Date with Disaster! Fontana, Shea. 2018. (ENG.). 128p. (J). (gr. 3-7). pap. 9.99 *(978-1-4012-7878-6(7),* DC Zoom) DC Comics.

Labat, Yancey. DC Super Hero Girls: Midterms. Wolfram, Amy. 2020. 144p. (J). (gr. 3-7). pap. 9.99 ***(978-1-4012-9852-4(4))*** DC Comics.

—DC Super Hero Girls: Weird Science. Deibert, Amanda. 2020. 168p. (J). (gr. 3-7). pap. 9.99 ***(978-1-4012-9846-3(X))*** DC Comics.

—Finals Crisis. Fontana, Shea. 2020. (DC Super Hero Girls Ser.). (ENG.). 128p. (J). (gr. 2-6). lib. bdg. 31.99 ***(978-1-5158-7432-4(X),*** 202136, Stone Arch Bks.) Capstone.

—Hits & Myths. Fontana, Shea. 2020. (DC Super Hero Girls Ser.). (ENG.). 128p. (J). (gr. 2-6). lib. bdg. 31.99 ***(978-1-5158-7433-1(8),*** 202137, Stone Arch Bks.) Capstone.

Labat, Yancey. How Many Jelly Beans? A Giant Book of Giant Numbers! Menotti, Andrea. 2012. (ENG.). 28p. (J). (gr. -1-1). 18.99 *(978-1-4521-0206-1(6))* Chronicle Bks. LLC.

Labat, Yancey. Summer Olympus. Fontana, Shea. 2020. (DC Super Hero Girls Ser.). (ENG.). 128p. (J). (gr. 2-6). lib. bdg. 31.99 ***(978-1-5158-7434-8(6),*** 202138, Stone Arch Bks.) Capstone.

Labat, Yancey. The Worst-Case Scenario: Mars (an Ultimate Adventure Novel) Borgenicht, David & Khan, Hena. 2011. (Worst Case Scenario Ser.: WORS). (ENG.). 208p. (J). (gr. 4-7). 12.99 *(978-0-8118-7124-2(X))* Chronicle Bks. LLC.

Labat, Yancey, jt. illus. see Garbowska, Agnes.

Labat, Yancey C. Fun Foods for Holidays! 2007. 56p. (J). *(978-0-439-83229-8(2))* Scholastic, Inc.

—It's Party Time! 2006. 56p. (J). *(978-0-439-83227-4(6))* Scholastic, Inc.

—Let's Have a Cookout! 2007. 56p. (J). *(978-0-439-83228-1(4))* Scholastic, Inc.

—Make, Draw, & Design Your Own Book. Gaylord, Susan Kapuscinski & Jabbour, Joyce. 2006. 48p. (J). *(978-0-439-81339-6(5))* Scholastic, Inc.

—Pizza-Zazz & Lotsa Pasta. 2006. 56p. (J). *(978-0-439-83187-1(3))* Scholastic, Inc.

—Rise & Shine! It's Breakfast Time! 2006. 56p. (J). *(978-0-439-83223-6(3))* Scholastic, Inc.

—S'mores, Shakes & Chocolate Cakes: Chocolate, Chocolate All Day Long. 2006. 56p. (J). *(978-0-439-83226-7(8))* Scholastic, Inc.

—The Space Explorer's Guide to the Universe. Doyle, Bill. 2003. (Space University Ser.). 48p. (J). *(978-0-439-55739-9(9))* Scholastic, Inc.

Labbé, Jesse. Glubbery Gray, the Knight-Eating Beast, 1 vol. Kander, Beth & Kenyon, Bret. 2010. (ENG.). 40p. (J). (gr. k-3). 17.99 *(978-1-58980-867-6(3),* Pelican Publishing) Arcadia Publishing.

Labeda, Patricia R. Miko & the Mystery Friend. Labeda, Patricia R. 2007. 73p. (J). (gr. 4-7). per. 10.99 *(978-1-59879-415-1(9),* Lifevest) Lifevest Publishing, Inc.

Laberis, S. El Cumpleanos. Koons, Linda. 2016. (Early Rising Readers Ser.). (SPA.). 16p. (J). (gr. 1-1). 6.67 *(978-1-4788-3749-7(7))* Newmark Learning LLC.

—Yo Estoy Feliz. Lindeen, Mary. 2016. (Early Rising Readers Ser.). (SPA.). 16p. (J). (gr. 1-1). 6.67 *(978-1-4788-3762-6(4))* Newmark Learning LLC.

Laberis, Steph. Can I Join Your Club? Kelly, John. 2017. (ENG.). 32p. (J). ***(978-1-84869-435-4(0))*** Kane Miller.

—Grump in the Night (Grumpy Cat) Sisler, Celeste. 2020. (Pictureback(R) Ser.). 24p. (J). (gr. -1-2). 5.99 ***(978-1-9848-5137-6(3),*** Random Hse. Bks. for Young Readers) Random Hse. Children's Bks.

Laberis, Steph. A Is for Awful: a Grumpy Cat ABC Book (Grumpy Cat) Webster, Christy. 2017. (Little Golden Book Ser.). 24p. (J). (gr. -1-1). 4.99 *(978-0-399-55783-5(0),* Golden Bks.) Random Hse. Children's Bks.

—The Little Grumpy Cat That Wouldn't (Grumpy Cat) Golden Books. 2016. (Little Golden Book Ser.). 24p. (J). (gr. -1-1). 4.99 *(978-0-399-55354-7(1),* Golden Bks.) Random Hse. Children's Bks.

—Love & Grumpiness (Grumpy Cat) Berrios, Frank. 2019. (Pictureback(R) Ser.). 24p. (J). (gr. -1-2). 6.99 *(978-0-593-11912-9(6),* Random Hse. Bks. for Young Readers) Random Hse. Children's Bks.

—My Little Golden Book about Dinosaurs. Shealy, Dennis R. 2017. (Little Golden Book Ser.). 24p. (J). (-k). 4.99 *(978-0-385-37861-1(0),* Golden Bks.) Random Hse. Children's Bks.

—My Little Golden Book about Sharks. Bader, Bonnie. 2016. (Little Golden Book Ser.). (ENG.). 24p. (J). (-k). 4.99 *(978-1-101-93092-2(6),* Golden Bks.) Random Hse. Children's Bks.

—Yawn! a Grumpy Cat Bedtime Story (Grumpy Cat) Foxe, Steve. 2018. (Little Golden Book Ser.). 24p. (J). (-k). 4.99 *(978-1-5247-2055-1(0),* Golden Bks.) Random Hse. Children's Bks.

Laberis, Stephanie. After Dark: Poems about Nocturnal Animals. Harrison, David L. 2020. 32p. (J). (gr. k-4). 17.99 *(978-1-62979-717-5(0),* Wordsong) Boyds Mills Pr.

—Animal Inn 3-Books-In-1! A Furry Fiasco; Treasure Hunt; the Bow-Wow Bus. Jacobs, Paul DuBois & Swender, Jennifer. 2017. (Animal Inn Ser.). (ENG.). 304p. (J). (gr. 2-5). pap. 8.99 *(978-1-5344-0964-4(5),* Aladdin) Simon & Schuster Children's Publishing.

—Animal Inn Fur-Tastic Collection Books 1-4: A Furry Fiasco; Treasure Hunt; the Bow-Wow Bus; Bright Lights, Big Kitty! Jacobs, Paul DuBois & Swender, Jennifer. ed. 2017. (Animal Inn Ser.). (ENG.). 448p. (J). (gr. 2-5). pap. 23.99 *(978-1-4814-9690-2(5),* Aladdin) Simon & Schuster Children's Publishing.

—The Bow-Wow Bus. Swender, Jennifer & Jacobs, Paul DuBois. 2017. (Animal Inn Ser.: 3). (ENG.). 112p. (J). (gr. 2-5). pap. 5.99 *(978-1-4814-6229-7(6),* Simon & Schuster/Paula Wiseman Bks.) Simon & Schuster/Paula Wiseman Bks.

—Bright Lights, Big Kitty! Jacobs, Paul DuBois & Swender, Jennifer. 2017. (Animal Inn Ser.: 4). (ENG.). 112p. (J). (gr. 2-5). pap. 5.99 *(978-1-4814-6232-7(6),* Aladdin) Simon & Schuster Children's Publishing.

Laberis, Stephanie. Frockodile. Willis, Jeanne. 2019. 32p. (J). (ENG.). (gr. -1-k). 16.99 ***(978-1-4449-0823-7(5),*** Hodder Children's Books); pap. 9.99 *(978-1-4449-0824-4(3))* Hachette Children's Group GBR. Dist: Hachette Bk. Group.

Laberis, Stephanie. Fur, Feather, Fin — All of Us Are Kin. Lang, Diane. 2018. (ENG.). 48p. (J). (gr. -1-3). 18.99 *(978-1-4814-4709-6(2),* Beach Lane Bks.) Beach Lane Bks.

—A Furry Fiasco. Swender, Jennifer & Jacobs, Paul DuBois. 2016. (Animal Inn Ser.: 1). (ENG.). 112p. (J). (gr. 2-5). pap. 5.99 *(978-1-4814-6223-5(7),* Aladdin) Simon & Schuster Children's Publishing.

—How Could a Bear Sleep Here? Gonzalez, Julie. 2018. 32p. (J). (gr. -1-3). 17.99 *(978-0-8234-3679-8(9))* Holiday Hse., Inc.

—Just So Willow. Shacter, Sara. 2019. 32p. (J). (gr. -1-1). 16.95 *(978-1-4549-2741-9(0))* Sterling Publishing Co., Inc.

—Like a Lizard. Sayre, April Pulley. 2019. 32p. (J). (gr. -1-3). 17.95 *(978-1-62979-211-8(X))* Boyds Mills Pr.

Laberis, Stephanie. Peppermint Post. Hale, Bruce. 2020. 32p. (J). (gr. -1-3). 17.99 ***(978-0-06-284717-1(1),*** HarperCollins) HarperCollins Pubs. Ltd. GBR. Dist: HarperCollins Pubs.

—Pipsqueaks, Slowpokes, & Stinkers: Celebrating Animal Underdogs. Stewart, Melissa. (ENG.). 32p. (J). 2020. (gr. -1-3). 8.99 ***(978-1-68263-202-4(4))***; 2018. (gr. k-3). 16.95 *(978-1-56145-936-0(4))* Peachtree Publishing Co. Inc.

Laberis, Stephanie. Pretty Kitty. Beaumont, Karen. 2018. (ENG.). 32p. (J). 17.99 *(978-0-8050-9232-5(3),* 900066528, Holt, Henry & Co. Bks. For Young Readers) Holt, Henry & Co.

—Prudence the Part-Time Cow. Shaffer, Jody Jensen. 2017. (ENG.). 32p. (J). 16.99 *(978-1-62779-615-6(0),* 900156975, Holt, Henry & Co. Bks. For Young Readers) Holt, Henry & Co.

Laberis, Stephanie. The Sea Knows. McGinty, Alice B. & Havis, Alan B. 2020. (ENG.). 48p. (J). (gr. -1-3). 17.99 ***(978-1-5344-3822-4(X),*** Simon & Schuster/Paula Wiseman Bks.) Simon & Schuster/Paula Wiseman Bks.

Laberis, Stephanie. Treasure Hunt. Swender, Jennifer & Jacobs, Paul DuBois. 2016. (Animal Inn Ser.: 2). (ENG.). 112p. (J). (gr. 2-5). pap. 5.99 *(978-1-4814-6226-6(1),* Aladdin) Simon & Schuster Children's Publishing.

—Treasure Hunt. Swender, Jennifer & Jacobs, Paul DuBois. 2016. (Animal Inn Ser.: 2). (ENG.). 112p. (J). (gr. 2-5). 16.99 *(978-1-4814-6227-3(X),* Simon & Schuster/Paula Wiseman Bks.) Simon & Schuster/Paula Wiseman Bks.

—Unhappy Birthday, Grumpy Cat! (Grumpy Cat) Berrios, Frank. 2019. (Step into Reading Ser.). 32p. (J). (gr. -1-1). 4.99 *(978-1-9848-5030-0(X),* Random Hse. Bks. for Young Readers) Random Hse. Children's Bks.

—When Numbers Met Letters. Barr, Lois. 2020. 40p. (J). (gr. -1-2). 18.99 *(978-0-8234-4052-8(4))* Holiday Hse., Inc.

—Whooooo Done It? Jacobs, Paul DuBois & Swender, Jennifer. 2018. (Animal Inn Ser.: 5). (ENG.). 96p. (J). (gr. 2-5). 17.99 *(978-1-4814-9963-7(7))*; pap. 5.99 *(978-1-4814-9962-0(9))* Simon & Schuster Children's Publishing. (Aladdin).

Labourot, Thomas. Elenora Mandragora: Daughter of Merlin. Gauthier, Severine. 2017. (Eleanor Mandragore Ser.). 64p. (J). (gr. 4-7). 14.99 *(978-1-68405-008-6(1))* Idea & Design Works, LLC.

Labrecque, Candida & Labrecque, Candida. A Riverside Walk with Grandma. Labrecque, Candida. l.t. ed. 2006. 23p. (J). per. 11.95 *(978-1-59879-137-2(0))* Lifevest Publishing, Inc.

Labrecque, Candida, jt. illus. see Labrecque, Candida.

Labrosse, Darcia. If You Could Wear My Sneakers, 1 vol. Fitch, Sheree. 20th ed. 2017. (ENG.). 36p. (J). (gr. 1-3). 22.95 *(978-1-77108-469-7(3),* fd7ef13e-100f-4f51-a811-85f5f8ad7e03) Nimbus Publishing, Ltd. CAN. Dist: Baker & Taylor Publisher Services (BTPS).

Lacámara, Laura. Alicia's Fruity Drinks / Las Aguas Frescas de Alicia. Ruiz-Flores, Lupe. Baeza Ventura, Gabriela, tr. from ENG. 2012. (SPA & ENG.). (J). 17.95 *(978-1-55885-705-6(2),* Piñata Books) Arte Publico Pr.

—Mamá the Alien: Mamá la Extraterrestre, 1 vol. Laínez, René Colato. 2016. (ENG & SPA.). 32p. (J). (gr. 1-4). 18.95 *(978-0-89239-298-8(3),* 83eca5c4-d439-4329-a3e1-dcfd94994e8f) Lee & Low Bks., Inc.

—The Runaway Piggy/El Cochinito Fugitivo. Luna, James & Villarroel, Carolina. 2010. (SPA.). 32p. (J). (gr. -1-3). 16.95 *(978-1-55885-586-1(6),* Piñata Books) Arte Publico Pr.

Lacamara, Laura. Dalia's Wondrous Hair / el Maravilloso Cabello de Dalia. Lacamara, Laura. Baeza Ventura, Gabriela, tr. from SPA. 2014. (ENG & SPA.). (J). 17.95 *(978-1-55885-789-6(3),* Piñata Books) Arte Publico Pr.

Lacapa, Michael. The Good Rainbow Road. Ortiz, Simon J. 2nd ed. 2010. (ENG.). 80p. pap. 10.95 *(978-0-8165-2935-3(3))* University of Arizona Pr.

Lacapria, Sr Ellen. Christmas, the Mystery & the Wonder. Russell, Michael E. 2016. (ENG.). (J). (gr. k-6). pap. 19.99 *(978-0-692-75285-2(4))* Thomas More Publishing.

Lacava, Domenico. Il Mistero Della Casa Abbandonata. Bordi, Giuseppe. 2019. (Raganelle Ser.: Vol. 1). (ITA.). 118p. (J). pap. 10.57 ***(978-1-7127-8246-0(0))*** Independently Published.

Lacera, Megan. ¡Los Zombis No Comen Verduras!, 1 vol. Lacera, Jorge. 2019. (SPA.). 40p. (J). (gr. 4-3). 19.95 *(978-1-62014-851-8(X),* 47c9b521-2e5b-4d78-990f-eada10dbcc15, Children's Book Press) Lee & Low Bks., Inc.

—Zombies Don't Eat Veggies!, 1 vol. Lacera, Jorge. 2019. (ENG.). 40p. (J). (gr. -1-3). 19.95 *(978-1-62014-794-8(7),* 8306284d-73b9-4af2-8de3-52b674ef9d71, Children's Book Press) Lee & Low Bks., Inc.

Lacey, Mike. Abraham Lincoln: The Life of America's Sixteenth President. Jeffery, Gary & Petty, Kate. 2005. (Graphic Biographies Ser.). (ENG.). 48p. (gr. 5-8). pap. 14.05 *(978-1-4042-5164-9(2))* Rosen Publishing Group, Inc., The.

—The Bermuda Triangle: Strange Happenings at Sea. West, David. 2006. (Graphic Mysteries Ser.). (ENG.). 48p. (gr. 5-8). pap. 14.05 *(978-1-4042-0806-3(2))*; (YA). lib. bdg. 35.45 *(978-1-4042-0795-0(3))* Rosen Publishing Group, Inc., The.

—Hurricanes. Jeffrey, Gary. 2007. (Graphic Natural Disasters Ser.). (ENG.). 48p. (J). (gr. 5-9). lib. bdg. 35.45 *(978-1-4042-1991-5(9))* Rosen Publishing Group, Inc., The.

—Incredible Space Missions. Jeffrey, Gary. 2008. (Graphic Discoveries Ser.). (ENG.). 48p. (J). (gr. 5-9). lib. bdg. 35.45 *(978-1-4042-1090-5(3))* Rosen Publishing Group, Inc., The.

—Incredible Space Missions: By Gary Jeffrey: Illustrated by Mike Lacey. Jeffrey, Gary. 2008. (Graphic Nonfiction Ser.). (ENG.). 48p. (gr. 3-8). pap. 14.05 *(978-1-4042-9595-7(X))* Rosen Publishing Group, Inc., The.

—The Three Musketeers, 1 vol. Dumas, Alexandre. 2010. (Calico Illustrated Classics Ser.). (ENG.). 112p. (J). (gr. 2-5). 29.93 *(978-1-60270-751-1(0),* 4003, Calico Chapter Bks.) ABDO Publishing Co.

—Who Was Beatrix Potter? Fabiny, Sarah. 2015. 105p. (J). *(978-1-4806-8934-3(3),* Grosset & Dunlap) Penguin Publishing Group.

—Who Was Beatrix Potter? Fabiny, Sarah & Who HQ. 2015. (Who Was? Ser.). 112p. (J). (gr. 3-7). 5.99 *(978-0-448-48305-4(X),* Penguin Workshop) Penguin Young Readers Group.

L

—Who Was Susan B. Anthony? Belviso, Meg et al. 2014. (Who Was? Ser.). (ENG.). 112p. (J). (gr. 3-7). 5.99 *(978-0-448-47963-7(X)*, Penguin Workshop) Penguin Young Readers Group.

Lacey, Rochae J. Fur Friends Forever. Humphrey Balentine, Latezeon. 2020. (ENG.). 28p. (J). pap. 15.99 ***(978-1-970133-71-4(6))***; 26.99 ***(978-1-970133-83-7(X))*** EduMatch.

Lachuk, Dani. Saint Thomas More: Courage, Conscience, & the King. Wallace, Susan Helen & Jablonski, Patricia E. 2014. (ENG.). 144p. (J). pap. 8.95 *(978-0-8198-9021-4(9))* Pauline Bks. & Media.

Lackritz, Arielle Hana. The Choice of a Lifetime. Lackritz, Arielle Hana. 2019. (ENG.). 60p. (J). pap. 9.00 ***(978-0-578-58440-9(9))*** Horn, Jonathan.

Lacombe, Benjamin. Curiosity House: the Shrunken Head. Oliver, Lauren & Chester, H. C. (Curiosity House Ser.: 1). (ENG.). (J). (gr. 3-7). 2016. 384p. pap. 6.99 *(978-0-06-227082-5(6))*; 2015. 368p. 16.99 *(978-0-06-227081-8(8))* HarperCollins Pubs.

—Lin Yi's Lantern: A Moon Festival Tale. Williams, Brenda. 2009. (ENG.). 32p. (J). (gr. -1-5). 16.99 *(978-1-84686-147-5(0))* Barefoot Bks., Inc.

Lacombe, Benjamin. Lin Yi's Lantern. Lacombe, Benjamin. Williams, Brenda. 2012. 32p. (J). (gr. k-3). pap. 8.99 *(978-1-84686-793-4(2))* Barefoot Bks., Inc.

Lacombe, Michel, et al. Star Wars Legends Epic Collection: the Rebellion Vol. 4. 2020. (ENG.). 496p. (J). (gr. 4-17). pap. 44.99 ***(978-1-302-92505-5(9))*** Marvel Worldwide, Inc.

Lacome, Julie. Walking Through the Jungle Big Book. Lacome, Julie. 2004. (ENG.). 32p. (J). (gr. k-k). pap. 24.99 *(978-0-7636-2471-2(3))* Candlewick Pr.

Lacome, Susie. My First 200 Words: Learning Is Fun with Teddy the Bear! Baxter, Nicola. 2016. 24p. (J). (gr. -1-12). pap. 7.99 *(978-1-86147-759-0(7)*, Armadillo) Anness Publishing GBR. Dist: National Bk. Network.

—My First 200 Words in French: Learning Is Fun with Teddy the Bear! Dopffer, Guillaume & Nicola, Baxter. 2016. 24p. (J). (gr. -1-12). pap. 7.99 *(978-1-86147-760-6(0)*, Armadillo) Anness Publishing GBR. Dist: National Bk. Network.

—My First Words: At Home. Baxter, Nicola. 2016. 24p. (J). (gr. -1-12). pap. 7.99 *(978-1-86147-769-9(4)*, Armadillo) Anness Publishing GBR. Dist: National Bk. Network.

—My First Words: Nature. Baxter, Nicola. 2016. 24p. (J). (gr. -1-12). pap. 7.99 *(978-1-86147-770-5(8)*, Armadillo) Anness Publishing GBR. Dist: National Bk. Network.

—Out & About: Name 200 Things in the World Around You! Baxter, Nicola. 2016. 24p. (J). (gr. -1-12). pap. 7.99 *(978-1-86147-777-4(5)*, Armadillo) Anness Publishing GBR. Dist: National Bk. Network.

—Teddy Bear's Fun to Learn First 1000 Words. Baxter, Nicola. 2013. 96p. (J). (gr. -1-k). 12.99 *(978-1-84322-955-1(2))* Anness Publishing GBR. Dist: National Bk. Network.

—1000 First Words in French. Dopffer, Guillaume. 2013. 96p. (J). (gr. k-4). 12.99 *(978-1-84322-957-5(9))* Anness Publishing GBR. Dist: National Bk. Network.

—1000 First Words in German. Kenkmann, Andrea. 2013. (ENG.). 96p. (J). (gr. k-4). 12.99 *(978-1-84322-958-2(7))* Anness Publishing GBR. Dist: National Bk. Network.

—1000 First Words in Spanish. Budds, Sam. 2013. 96p. (J). (gr. k-4). 12.99 *(978-1-84322-959-9(5))* Anness Publishing GBR. Dist: National Bk. Network.

LaCoste, Gary. I Can Do Anything! White, Jeff. 2017. (Best of Buddies Ser.). (ENG.). 32p. (J). 12.99 *(978-1-4707-4851-7(7))* Group Publishing, Inc.

—Poems from under My Bed: LOL Halloween Rhymes. Katz, Alan. 2013. 47p. (J). pap. *(978-0-545-48295-0(X))* Scholastic, Inc.

—TJ Zaps a Nightmare: Stopping Blackmail Bullying #5, 1 vol. Mullarkey, Lisa. 2012. (TJ Trapper, Bully Zapper Ser.). (ENG.). 80p. (J). (gr. 2-5). lib. bdg. 29.93 *(978-1-61641-909-7(1)*, 14796, Calico Chapter Bks.) ABDO Publishing Co.

—TJ Zaps the Freeze Out: Stopping the Silent Treatment #3, 1 vol. Mullarkey, Lisa. 2012. (TJ Trapper, Bully Zapper Ser.). (ENG.). 80p. (J). (gr. 2-5). lib. bdg. 29.93 *(978-1-61641-907-3(5)*, 14792, Calico Chapter Bks.) ABDO Publishing Co.

—TJ Zaps the New Kid: Stopping a Social Bully #1, 1 vol. Mullarkey, Lisa. 2012. (TJ Trapper, Bully Zapper Ser.). (ENG.). 80p. (J). (gr. 2-5). lib. bdg. 29.93 *(978-1-61641-905-9(9)*, 14788, Calico Chapter Bks.) ABDO Publishing Co.

—TJ Zaps the One-Upper: Stopping One-Upping & Cell Phone Bullying #2, 1 vol. Mullarkey, Lisa. 2012. (TJ Trapper, Bully Zapper Ser.). (ENG.). 80p. (J). (gr. 2-5). lib. bdg. 29.93 *(978-1-61641-906-6(7)*, 14790, Calico Chapter Bks.) ABDO Publishing Co.

—TJ Zaps the Rumor Mill: Stopping Gossip #4, 1 vol. Mullarkey, Lisa. 2012. (TJ Trapper, Bully Zapper Ser.). (ENG.). 80p. (J). (gr. 2-5). lib. bdg. 29.93 *(978-1-61641-908-0(3)*, 14794, Calico Chapter Bks.) ABDO Publishing Co.

—TJ Zaps the Smackdown: Stopping a Physical Bully #6, 1 vol. Mullarkey, Lisa. 2012. (TJ Trapper, Bully Zapper Ser.). (ENG.). 80p. (J). (gr. 2-5). lib. bdg. 29.93 *(978-1-61641-910-3(5)*, 14798, Calico Chapter Bks.) ABDO Publishing Co.

Lacy, Leticia. Lucky: The Adventures of an Unlucky Leprechaun. Coughlin, Bart. 2019. (ENG.). 32p. (J). (gr. -1-2). 9.99 *(978-1-9848-3056-2(2)*, Random Hse. Bks. for Young Readers) Random Hse. Children's Bks.

Ladan, Haila. Bazi Ba Angusht Ha. Rahmandust, Mustafá. 2017. (PER.). (J). *(978-600-01-0559-4(2))* Kanun-e Parvaresh Fekr-ye Kudakan Va Nujavanan.

Ladatko, Ekaterina. I Dig Bathtime. Jorden, Brooke. 2018. (ENG.). 16p. (J). (gr. -1-2). bds. 8.99 *(978-1-64170-030-6(0)*, 550030) Familius LLC.

Ladd, Dave & Anderson, Stephanie. Animals Are Delicious. Hutt, Sarah. 2016. (ENG.). 48p. (J). (gr. -1 — 1). 17.95 *(978-0-7148-7144-8(3))* Phaidon Pr., Inc.

Ladd, David & Anderson, Stephanie. Animals Are Delicious. Hutt, Sarah. 2016. (ENG.). 48p. 17.95 *(978-0-7148-7123-3(0))* Phaidon Pr., Inc.

Ladd, London. Frederick's Journey: the Life of Frederick Douglass. Rappaport, Doreen. 2015. (Big Words Book Ser.: 8). (ENG.). 48p. (J). (gr. 1-3). 17.99 *(978-1-4231-1438-3(8))* Disney Pr.

Ladd, London. Frederick's Journey: the Life of Frederick Douglass. Rappaport, Doreen. 2018. (Big Words Book Ser.: 8). 48p. (J). (gr. -1-3). 8.99 ***(978-1-4847-4959-3(6))*** Little, Brown Bks. for Young Readers.

Ladd, London. Lend a Hand: Poems About Giving. Frank, John. 2014. (ENG.). 32p. (J). 17.95 *(978-1-60060-970-1(8))* Lee & Low Bks., Inc.

—March On! The Day My Brother Martin Changed the World. Farris, Christine King. 2011. (J). (gr. 2-7). 29.95 *(978-0-545-10689-4(3))* Weston Woods Studios, Inc.

—Midnight Teacher: Lilly Ann Granderson & Her Secret School, 1 vol. Halfmann, Janet. 2018. (ENG.). 40p. (J). (gr. 2-7). 19.95 *(978-1-62014-163-2(9)*, b995d129-540b-4294-8d87-9a90814ba79a) Lee & Low Bks., Inc.

—Under the Freedom Tree. VanHecke, Susan. 2019. 32p. (J). (gr. 1-4). pap. 7.99 *(978-1-58089-551-4(4))* Charlesbridge Publishing, Inc.

—Under the Freedom Tree. van Hecke, Susan. 2014. 32p. (J). (gr. 1-4). lib. bdg. 16.95 *(978-1-58089-550-7(6))* Charlesbridge Publishing, Inc.

Ladecka, Anna. Mommy & Daddy Love You. Kim, Cecil. 2014. (MySELF Bookshelf Ser.). (ENG.). 32p. (J). (gr. k-2). pap. 11.94 *(978-1-60357-691-8(6))*; lib. bdg. 25.27 *(978-1-59953-656-9(0))* Norwood Hse. Pr.

Laden, Nina. An Ant's Day Off. Becker, Bonny. 2017. (ENG.). 32p. (J). (gr. -1-3). 13.99 *(978-1-5344-0949-1(1)*, Simon & Schuster Bks. For Young Readers) Simon & Schuster Bks. For Young Readers.

LaDuca, Michael. The Don't-Give-Up Kid: And Learning Disabilities. Gehret, Jeanne. 4th ed. 2009. (Coping Ser.). (ENG.). 32p. (J). (gr. 1-3). 17.95 *(978-0-9821982-0-9(5))* Verbal Images Pr.

—Eagle Eyes: A Child's Guide to Paying Attention. Gehret, Jeanne. 4th ed. 2009. (Coping Ser.). (ENG.). 32p. (J). (gr. 1-3). 17.95 *(978-0-9821982-1-6(3))* Verbal Images Pr.

—Princess Cupcake Jones Saddles Up! Fields, Ylleya. 2018. (Princess Cupcake Jones Ser.). (ENG.). 32p. (J). (gr. k-2). 16.95 *(978-0-9909986-6-2(5))* Belle Publishing.

Ladwig, Tim. The Beatitudes: From Slavery to Civil Rights. Weatherford, Carole Boston. 2009. (ENG.). 36p. (J). (gr. 3-7). 17.00 *(978-0-8028-5352-3(8)*, Eerdmans Bks For Young Readers) Eerdmans, William B. Publishing Co.

—Especially Heroes. Kroll, Virginia L. 2004. 32p. (J). 16.00 *(978-0-8028-5221-2(1))* Eerdmans, William B. Publishing Co.

—Good King Wenceslas. Neale, John M. 2005. (ENG.). 32p. (J). (gr. k-17). 17.00 *(978-0-8028-5209-0(2)*, Eerdmans Bks For Young Readers) Eerdmans, William B. Publishing Co.

—The Lord's Prayer. 2004. 32p. pap. 8.50 *(978-0-8028-5238-0(6))*; (J). (gr. -1-3). 17.00 *(978-0-8028-5180-2(0))* Eerdmans, William B. Publishing Co.

—Probity Jones & the Fear Not Angel. Wangerin, Walter, Jr. 2005. 32p. (J). (gr. 1-4). 16.95 *(978-1-55725-457-3(5))* Paraclete Pr., Inc.

—Tonight You Are My Baby Board Book: Mary's Christmas Gift. Norris, Jeannine Q. 2010. (HarperBlessings Ser.). (ENG.). 30p. (J). (gr. -1-k). bds. 7.99 *(978-0-06-147999-1(3)*, HarperFestival) HarperCollins Pubs.

—What Does the Sky Say? Carlstrom, Nancy White. 2004. 32p. (J). (gr. -1-3). 17.00 *(978-0-8028-5208-3(4))* Eerdmans, William B. Publishing Co.

—When Daddy Prays. Grimes, Nikki. 2004. 32p. (J). (ENG.). pap. 8.00 *(978-0-8028-5266-3(1))*; 16.00 *(978-0-8028-5152-9(5))* Eerdmans, William B. Publishing Co.

Lady Josephine. Madeline & Friends: Fruits & Veggies vs Candy. Hassan, Masood. 2010. *(978-0-9812600-6-8(3))* Sapphira Pubns.

Ladybird Books Staff. Peppa Pig & the Lost Christmas List. Candlewick Press Staff. 2012. (Peppa Pig Ser.). (ENG.). 32p. (J). (gr. k-k). 12.99 *(978-0-7636-6276-9(3)*, Candlewick Entertainment) Candlewick Pr.

Ladybird Books Staff, jt. illus. see Candlewick Press Staff.

Laëtitia, Aynié. Amy's Diary #1: Space Alien... Almost? Grisseaux, Veronique & Desjardins, India. 2019. (Amy's Diary Ser.: 1). (ENG.). 96p. (J). 14.99 *(978-1-5458-0215-1(7)*, 900198753) Papercutz.

—Amy's Diary #2: The World's Upside Down. Grisseaux, Veronique & Desjardins, India. 2019. (Amy's Diary Ser.: 2). (ENG.). 96p. (YA). 14.99 *(978-1-62991-857-0(1)*, 900185412); pap. 9.99 *(978-1-62991-856-3(3)*, 900185413) Papercutz.

—Space Alien... Almost? Grisseaux, Veronique & Desjardins, India. 2019. (Amy's Diary Ser.: 1). (ENG.). 96p. (J). pap. 9.99 *(978-1-5458-0214-4(9)*, 900198772) Papercutz.

Lafan, Algie. The Infinite Odyssey. Dingler, Jay. 2004. 540p. (YA). pap. 25.00 *(978-0-9754539-0-2(4))* Gray Jay Bks.

Lafarge, Kelly. An Ugly Black Bird, 1 vol. Lawson, Barbara. 2009. 35p. pap. 24.95 *(978-1-61546-656-6(8))* America Star Bks.

Lafave, Kim. Amos's Sweater, 1 vol. Lunn, Janet. 2nd ed. 2007. (ENG.). 32p. (J). (gr. -1-k). pap. 7.95 *(978-0-88899-845-3(7))* Groundwood Bks. CAN. Dist: Publishers Group West (PGW).

LaFave, Kim. Angels Inc., 1 vol. McBay, Bruce. 2008. (ENG.). 71p. (J). (gr. 1-3). pap. 7.95 *(978-1-896580-30-2(0))* Tradewind Bks. CAN. Dist: Orca Bk. Pubs. USA.

—At the Circus. McFarlane, Sheryl. 2006. (What's That Sound? Ser.). (ENG.). 20p. (J). (gr. -1-k). bds. 6.95 *(978-1-55041-959-7(5)*, 3e1c945a-a212-45c0-850d-56aa1da1c70f) Trifolium Bks., Inc. CAN. Dist: Firefly Bks., Ltd.

—Ben over Night, 1 vol. Ellis, Sarah. 2005. (ENG.). 32p. (J). (gr. -1-1). 10.95 *(978-1-55041-807-1(6)*, 0e84cead-52c1-40e8-bd0e-975d5935d88e) Fitzhenry & Whiteside, Ltd. CAN. Dist: Firefly Bks., Ltd.

—Big Ben. Ellis, Sarah. ed. 2004. (J). (gr. -1-1). spiral bd. *(978-0-616-11108-6(8))*; spiral bd. *(978-0-616-11109-3(6))* Canadian National Institute for the Blind/Institut National Canadien pour les Aveugles.

—A Bumblebee Sweater, 1 vol. Waterton, Betty. 2007. (ENG.). 32p. (J). (gr. -1-1). 18.95 *(978-1-55455-028-9(9)*, b4c51848-09d0-4118-be11-659baf34b523) Fitzhenry & Whiteside, Ltd. CAN. Dist: Firefly Bks., Ltd.

—Fire Fighters. Bourgeois, Paulette. 2005. 32p. (J). lib. bdg. 15.38 *(978-1-4242-1189-0(1))* Fitzgerald Bks.

—Garbage Collectors. Bourgeois, Paulette. 2004. 32p. (J). lib. bdg. 15.38 *(978-1-4242-1190-6(5))* Fitzgerald Bks.

—Garbage Collectors. Bourgeois, Paulette. 2003. (Kids Can Read Level 3 Ser.). (ENG.). 32p. (J). (gr. k-3). 16.19 *(978-1-55337-573-9(4))* Kids Can Pr., Ltd. CAN. Dist: Children's Plus, Inc.

Lafave, Kim. Grandpa's Girls, 1 vol. Campbell, Nicola. 2011. (SAL.). 32p. (J). (gr. -1-2). 18.95 *(978-1-55498-084-0(4))* Groundwood Bks. CAN. Dist: Publishers Group West (PGW).

LaFave, Kim. Un Perro Muy Diferente. Harris, Dorothy Joan. Rioja, Alberto Jimenez, tr. from ENG. 2006. (SPA.). 28p. (J). (gr. 5-6). pap. 7.99 *(978-1-933032-04-7(9))* Lectorum Pubns., Inc.

—Police Officers. Bourgeois, Paulette. 2004. (Kids Can Read Level 3 Ser.). (ENG.). 32p. (J). (gr. k-3). 16.19 *(978-1-55337-742-9(7))* Kids Can Pr., Ltd. CAN. Dist: Children's Plus, Inc.

—Police Workers. Bourgeois, Paulette. 2004. 32p. (J). lib. bdg. 15.38 *(978-1-4242-1191-3(3))* Fitzgerald Bks.

—Postal Workers. Bourgeois, Paulette. 2005. 32p. (J). lib. bdg. 15.38 *(978-1-4242-1192-0(1))* Fitzgerald Bks.

—Postal Workers. Bourgeois, Paulette. 2005. (Kids Can Read Ser.). (ENG.). 32p. (J). (gr. 1-3). 3.95 *(978-1-55337-747-4(8))* Kids Can Pr., Ltd. CAN. Dist: Hachette Bk. Group.

—Shi-Shi-Etko, 1 vol. Campbell, Nicola. 2005. (ENG.). 32p. (J). (gr. -1-2). 18.95 *(978-0-88899-659-6(4))* Groundwood Bks. CAN. Dist: Publishers Group West (PGW).

Lafave, Kim. Shin-Chi's Canoe. Campbell, Nicola I. 2008. (ENG.). 40p. (J). (gr. -1-2). 18.95 *(978-0-88899-857-6(0))* Groundwood Bks. CAN. Dist: Publishers Group West (PGW).

LaFave, Kim. We'll All Go Exploring, 1 vol. Thompson, Richard & Spicer, Maggee. 2003. (ENG.). 32p. (J). (gr. -1-k). 5.95 *(978-1-55041-732-6(0)*, 93b8a88e-b5d4-4d33-be08-4b23a8ae3422) Fitzhenry & Whiteside, Ltd. CAN. Dist: Firefly Bks., Ltd.

LaFerriere, Suzanne. Gracey's Desire. Castle, Jan And Kare. 2008. 28p. pap. 17.99 *(978-1-4389-2433-5(X))* AuthorHouse.

LaFever, Greg. The Legend of Ohio. Mackall, Dandi Daley. 2005. (Legend Ser.). (ENG.). 40p. (J). (gr. k-5). 17.95 *(978-1-58536-244-8(1))* Sleeping Bear Pr.

Laff, Becky. Joseph the Dreamer. Laff, Becky. 2016. (ENG.). 48p. (J). (gr. k-4). 17.99 *(978-1-4677-7845-9(1)*, 9781467778459, Kar-Ben Publishing) Lerner Publishing Group.

LaFleur, David. Stop That Bull, Theseus! McMullan, Kate. 2003. (Myth-o-Mania Ser.: Bk. 5). (ENG.). 160p. (J). (gr. 3-7). 9.99 *(978-0-7868-0861-8(6))* Hyperion Bks. for Children.

Lafond, Pascale. The Story of Christmas. Flowerpot Press, ed. 2019. (ENG.). 16p. (J). (gr. k-2). bds. 5.99 *(978-1-4867-1821-4(3)*, 85bbdd07-afc2-472c-ba7e-cbac870bd34d) Flowerpot Pr.

Lafontaine, Thierry. The Genius Factor - How to Capture an Invisible Cat. Tobin, Paul. 2016. (ENG.). 272p. (J). 16.99 *(978-1-61963-840-2(1)*, 900150260, Bloomsbury USA Childrens) Bloomsbury Publishing USA.

—The Genius Factor: How to Capture an Invisible Cat. Tobin, Paul. 2017. (ENG.). 288p. (J). pap. 7.99 *(978-1-68119-278-9(0)*, 900165496, Bloomsbury USA Childrens) Bloomsbury Publishing USA.

—How to Outsmart a Billion Robot Bees. Tobin, Paul. 2018. (ENG.). 336p. (J). pap. 8.99 *(978-1-68119-604-6(2)*, 9781681196046, Bloomsbury USA Childrens) Bloomsbury Publishing USA.

Lafontaine, Thierry & Abey, Katie. How to Outsmart a Billion Robot Bees. Tobin, Paul. 2017. (ENG.). 320p. (J). 16.99 *(978-1-61963-897-6(5)*, 900151196, Bloomsbury USA Childrens) Bloomsbury Publishing USA.

Lafrance, Daniel. War Brothers: The Graphic Novel. McKay, Sharon E. 2013. (ENG.). 176p. (YA). (gr. 9-12). 2nd ed. 27.95 *(978-1-55451-489-2(4)*, 9781554514892); 3rd ed. pap. 18.95 *(978-1-55451-488-5(6)*, 9781554514885) Annick Pr., Ltd. CAN. Dist: Publishers Group West (PGW).

Lafrance, David. L' Oiseau Tatoué. Chiasson, Herménéglide. 2004. (Poetry Ser.). (FRE.). 36p. (J). (gr. 7). pap. *(978-2-89021-675-4(6))* Diffusion du livre Mirabel (DLM).

LaFrance, Debbie. Elf Dog. Redmond, Pamela Woods. 2005. 44p. (J). 15.95 *(978-0-9760767-0-4(5))* Redmond, Pamela.

Lafrance, Marie. Bunny the Brave War Horse: Based on a True Story. MacLeod, Elizabeth. 2014. (ENG.). 32p. (J). (gr. 1-3). 16.95 *(978-1-77138-024-9(1))* Kids Can Pr., Ltd. CAN. Dist: Hachette Bk. Group.

—The Firehouse Light. Nolan, Janet. 2010. (ENG.). 32p. (J). (gr. k-3). 15.99 *(978-1-58246-298-1(4)*, Tricycle Pr.) Random Hse. Children's Bks.

—The First Gift. Gadot, A. S. 2006. (ENG.). 24p. (J). (gr. -1-3). lib. bdg. 15.95 *(978-1-58013-146-9(8)*, Kar-Ben Publishing) Lerner Publishing Group.

—The First Gift, Vol. 2006. (ENG.). 24p. (J). (gr. 2). per. 6.95 *(978-1-58013-149-0(2)*, Kar-Ben Publishing) Lerner Publishing Group.

—Oscar Lives Next Door: A Story Inspired by Oscar Peterson's Childhood. Farmer, Bonnie. 2015. (ENG.). 32p. (J). (gr. k-4). 16.95 *(978-1-77147-104-6(2)*, Owlkids) Owlkids Bks. Inc. CAN. Dist: Publishers Group West (PGW).

—The Stranger's Farewell: English-Dari Edition. Bazger Salam, Palwasha. 2017. (Hoopoe Teaching-Stories Ser.). (ENG.). (J). (gr. 1-6). pap. 9.99 *(978-1-946270-20-7(2)*, Hoopoe Bks.) I S H K.

—The Stranger's Farewell: English-Pashto Edition. Salam, Palwasha Bazger. 2017. (Hoopoe Teaching-Stories Ser.). (ENG.). (J). (gr. 2-6). pap. 9.99 *(978-1-944493-65-3(4)*, Hoopoe Bks.) I S H K.

—Tam Ti Delam: Initiation du Jeune Public Au Patrimoine de la Chanson Québécoise. Leclerc, Félix & Vigneault, Gilles. 2019. (ENG.). 44p. (J). (gr. k-2). 16.95 *(978-2-924774-27-4(6))* La Montagne Secrete CAN. Dist: Independent Pubs. Group.

—The True Tale of a Giantess: The Story of Anna Swan. Renaud, Anne. 2018. (ENG.). 32p. (J). (gr. -1-3). 17.99 *(978-1-77138-376-9(3))* Kids Can Pr., Ltd. CAN. Dist: Hachette Bk. Group.

—The Tweedles Go Electric, 1 vol. Kulling, Monica. 2014. (ENG.). 32p. (J). (gr. -1-2). 16.95 *(978-1-55498-167-0(0))* Groundwood Bks. CAN. Dist: Publishers Group West (PGW).

—The Tweedles Go Online, 1 vol. Kulling, Monica. 2015. (ENG.). 32p. (J). (gr. -1-2). 16.95 *(978-1-55498-353-7(3))* Groundwood Bks. CAN. Dist: Publishers Group West (PGW).

Lagan, Jamie Hatley. The Christmas Eve Mouse: Who Lived in the Little Red House. Horvath, Evelyn R. 2019. (ENG.). 76p. (J). pap. 15.99 ***(978-1-6997-3303-5(1))*** Independently Published.

Lagares, Luciano. But It's True. Gemmen, Heather. 2004. (Tough Stuff for Kids Ser.). 36p. (J). (gr. 4-7). pap., pap. 5.99 *(978-0-7814-4033-2(5)*, 0781440335) Cook, David C.

Lagarrigue, Carolina, jt. illus. see Di Prospero, Francisco.

Lagarrigue, Jerome. Freedom on the Menu: The Greensboro Sit-Ins. Weatherford, Carole Boston. 2004. (ENG.). 32p. (J). (gr. 1-3). 21.19 *(978-0-8037-2860-8(3))* Penguin Young Readers Group.

—Freedom on the Menu: The Greensboro Sit-Ins. Weatherford, Carole Boston. 2007. (gr. 4-7). 16.00 *(978-0-7569-8160-0(3))* Perfection Learning Corp.

—Freedom Summer. Wiles, Deborah. 2005. (ENG.). 32p. (J). (gr. -1-3). reprint ed. 7.99 *(978-0-689-87829-9(X)*, Aladdin) Simon & Schuster Children's Publishing.

—Freedom Summer: Celebrating the 50th Anniversary of the Freedom Summer. Wiles, Deborah. 50th anniv. ed. 2014. (ENG.). 32p. (J). (gr. -1-3). 17.99 *(978-1-4814-2298-7(7)*, Atheneum Bks. for Young Readers) Simon & Schuster Children's Publishing.

—My Man Blue. Grimes, Nikki. 2015. 32p. pap. 7.00 *(978-1-61003-533-0(X))* Center for the Collaborative Classroom.

—Poetry for Young People: Maya Angelou. Wilson, Edwin Graves, ed. 2013. (Poetry for Young People Ser.). (ENG.). 48p. (J). (gr. 3). 16.95 *(978-1-4549-0329-1(5))* Sterling Publishing Co., Inc.

Lagarrigue, Jerome Lagarrigue. Freedom on the Menu: The Greensboro Sit-Ins. Weatherford, Carole Boston. 2007. (ENG.). 32p. (J). (gr. -1-3). pap. 6.99 *(978-0-14-240894-0(8)*, Puffin Books) Penguin Young Readers Group.

Lago, Alexis. Mi Isla y Yo: La Naturaleza de Cuba. Silva Lee, Alfonso. Hayskar, Bonnie J., ed. 2010. (SPA.). 32p. (J). pap. 9.95 *(978-1-929165-22-3(6))* PANGAEA.

—Mi Isla y Yo: La Naturaleza de Puerto Rico. Silva Lee, Alfonso. Hayskar, Bonnie J., ed. 2007. (SPA.). 32p. (J). pap. 8.95 *(978-1-929165-19-3(6))* PANGAEA.

—Mi Isla y Yo: La Naturaleza de Republica Dominicana. Silva Lee, Alfonso. Hayskar, Bonnie, ed. 2010. (SPA.). 32p. (J). pap. 9.95 *(978-1-929165-25-4(0))* PANGAEA.

—Mi isla y yo/My Island & I: La naturaleza de Puerto Rico/The Nature of Puerto Rico. Silva Lee, Alfonso. Hayskar, Bonnie J., ed. 2003. (SPA & ENG.). 32p. (J). pap. 9.95 *(978-1-929165-12-4(9))* PANGAEA.

—Mon Ile et Moi: La Nature d'Haiti: Lanati an Ayti: Peym Avem. Silva Lee, Alfonso. Hayskar, Bonnie, ed. Hilaire, Jean Vilmond, tr. 2010. (FRE & CRP.). 32p. (J). pap. 9.95 *(978-1-929165-28-5(5))* PANGAEA.

—My Island & I: The Nature of the Caribbean. Silva Lee, Alfonso. Hayskar, Bonnie J., ed. 2010. 32p. (J). pap. 9.95 *(978-1-929165-14-8(5))* PANGAEA.

Lago, Angela. El Cuento del Joven Marinero. Dinesen, Isak. 2008. (Coleccion Clasicos Ser.).Tr. of Skibsdrengens Fortlling. (SPA.). 26p. (J). (gr. 4-7). 12.99 *(978-968-16-8075-6(8))* Fondo de Cultura Economica USA.

LaGrange, Tiffany. The Adventure of a Lifetime! Medley, Shari. 2009. 24p. pap. 10.95 *(978-1-936051-20-5(6))* Peppertree Pr., The.

—Animals & Stuff. Shaber, Mark. 2008. 32p. pap. 12.95 *(978-1-934246-10-8(7))* Peppertree Pr., The.

—Bunko's Journey. Bender, Randy L. 2008. 44p. pap. 13.95 *(978-0-9818683-2-5(0))* Peppertree Pr., The.

—Camp Charlie, the Adventures of Grandma Lipstick. Snyder, Karen. 2013. 20p. pap. 12.95 *(978-1-61493-218-5(2))* Peppertree Pr., The.

—Just Molly & Me & Nikki Make Three. Tarsy, Jean. 2008. 36p. pap. 12.95 *(978-0-9820479-6-5(7))* Peppertree Pr., The.

—Making Beautiful Music. Stilwell, Norma Mintum. 2011. 28p. pap. 14.95 *(978-1-936343-92-8(4))* Peppertree Pr., The.

—Mona Lisa's Makeover. Snyder, Karen. 2010. 24p. pap. 12.95 *(978-1-936343-15-7(0))* Peppertree Pr., The.

—Mrs Owl's Nest of Rhymes. Howell, Julie Ann. 2008. 24p. pap. 12.95 *(978-0-9818683-8-7(X))* Peppertree Pr., The.

—My Abc Blue Book. Lagrange, Tiffany. 2008. 32p. pap. 12.95 *(978-1-934246-38-2(7))* Peppertree Pr., The.

—My Abc Pink Book. Lagrange, Tiffany. 2008. 32p. pap. 12.95 *(978-0-9814894-3-8(5))* Peppertree Pr., The.

—Numbers All in a Row. Reeves, Pamela. 2008. 24p. pap. 12.95 *(978-0-9820479-5-8(9))* Peppertree Pr., The.

—The Pepper Tree, How the Seeds Were Planted! Howell, Julie. 2007. 28p. per. 12.95 *(978-1-934246-51-1(4))* Peppertree Pr., The.

—The Pepper Tree, How the Seeds Were Planted! Howell, Julie Ann. 2008. 28p. pap. 12.95 *(978-0-9820479-0-3(8))* Peppertree Pr., The.

—The Pepper Tree, How the Seeds Were Planted. Howell, Julie Ann. 2012. 28p. 24.95 *(978-1-61493-059-4(7))* Peppertree Pr., The.

—Safari Smooches. Snyder, Karen. 2011. 24p. pap. 12.95 *(978-1-936343-95-9(9))* Peppertree Pr., The.

—Talking to the Moon. Bootsma, Verner. 2007. 32p. per. 12.95 *(978-1-934246-70-2(0))* Peppertree Pr., The.

—United We Stand, a Story about Two Bullies. Reeves, Pamela. 2009. 24p. pap. 12.95 *(978-1-936051-36-6(2))* Peppertree Pr., The.

—Weather or Not? Falcon, David. 2009. 28p. pap. 12.95 *(978-1-936051-24-3(9))* Peppertree Pr., The.

Laguna, Fabio. Everything That Glitters Is Guy! Random House. 2017. (Pictureback(R) Ser.). (ENG.). 16p. (J). (gr. -1-2). pap. 5.99 *(978-1-5247-1732-2(0)*, Random Hse. Bks. for Young Readers) Random Hse. Children's Bks.

—Pet Problem! (DreamWorks Trolls) Lewman, David. 2017. (Pictureback(R) Ser.). (ENG.). 16p. (J). (gr. -1-2). pap. 4.99 *(978-1-5247-6640-5(2)*, Random Hse. Bks. for Young Readers) Random Hse. Children's Bks.

—Scooby-Doo in over the Boardwalk, 1 vol. Kupperberg, Paul. 2013. (Scooby-Doo Graphic Novels Ser.). (ENG.). 24p. (J). (gr. 2-6). lib. bdg. 27.07 *(978-1-61479-052-5(3)*, 585, Graphic Novels) Spotlight.

—Scooby-Doo in Read All about It!, 1 vol. Kupperberg, Paul. 2013. (Scooby-Doo Graphic Novels Ser.). (ENG.). 24p. (J). (gr. 2-6). lib. bdg. 27.07 *(978-1-61479-053-2(1)*, 586, Graphic Novels) Spotlight.

—Scooby-Doo in Yankee Doodle Danger, 1 vol. Rozum, John. 2013. (Scooby-Doo Graphic Novels Ser.). (ENG.). 24p. (J). (gr. 2-6). lib. bdg. 27.07 *(978-1-61479-054-9(X)*, 587, Graphic Novels) Spotlight.

Laguna, Fabio, et al. Shazam!: Becoming Shazam. West, Alexandra. 2019. (I Can Read Level 3 Ser.). (ENG.). 32p. (J). (gr. -1-3). pap. 4.99 *(978-0-06-289086-3(7))* HarperCollins Pubs.

Laguna, Fabio. The Sound of Spring. Lewman, David. 2018. (Step into Reading: Step 2 Ser.). (ENG.). 24p. (J). (gr. -1-1). 17.44 *(978-1-5364-3064-6(1))* Random Hse. Bks. for Young Readers.

—Trolls Holiday Big Golden Book (DreamWorks Trolls) Lewman, David. 2017. (Big Golden Book Ser.). 32p. (J). (gr. -1-2). 10.99 *(978-1-5247-7212-3(7)*, Golden Bks.) Random Hse. Children's Bks.

—Trolls. la Fiesta de Arcoíris / Rainbow Party (DreamWorks) Penguin Random House Grupo Editorial. 2016. (SPA.). 128p. (J). (gr. -1-k). pap. 9.95 *(978-607-31-4960-0(3)*, Altea) Penguin Random House Grupo Editorial ESP. Dist: Penguin Random Hse. LLC.

—Trolls. Ramón Sale de Su Cueva / Out of Branch's Bunker (DreamWorks) Grupo Editorial, Penguin Random House. 2016. (SPA.). 28p. (J). (gr. -1-k). pap. 6.95 *(978-607-31-4957-0(3)*, Altea) Penguin Random House Grupo Editorial ESP. Dist: Penguin Random Hse. LLC.

Laguna, Fabio & Andreu, Meritxell. Belle Is My Babysitter (Disney Princess) Saxon, Victoria & Posner-Sanchez, Andrea. 2016. (Little Golden Book Ser.). (ENG.). 24p. (J). (-k). 4.99 *(978-0-7364-3502-4(6)*, Golden/Disney) Random Hse. Children's Bks.

Laguna, Fabio & Batson, Alan. Color Day Party! Random House. 2019. (Step into Reading Ser.). (ENG.). 48p. (J). (gr. -1-2). 12.99 *(978-0-525-64762-1(7))*; pap. 5.99 *(978-0-525-64761-4(9))* Random Hse. Children's Bks. (Random Hse. Bks. for Young Readers).

—The Sound of Spring (DreamWorks Trolls) Lewman, David. 2018. (Step into Reading Ser.). (ENG.). 24p. (J). (gr. -1-1). pap. 4.99 *(978-1-5247-6920-8(7)*, Random Hse. Bks. for Young Readers) Random Hse. Children's Bks.

Laguna, Fabio & Cagol, Andrea. Frosty the Snowman Big Golden Book (Frosty the Snowman) Capozzi, Suzy. 2014. (Big Golden Book Ser.). (ENG.). 48p. (J). (gr. -1-2). 9.99 *(978-0-385-38877-1(2)*, Golden Bks.) Random Hse. Children's Bks.

Laguna, Fabio & Colletti, Marco. A Royal Spring (Disney Princess) Depken, Kristen L. 2016. (Step into Reading Ser.). (ENG.). 24p. (J). (gr. -1-1). 4.99 *(978-0-7364-3452-2(6)*, RH/Disney) Random Hse. Children's Bks.

Laguna, Fabio & Gallego, James. Fang-Tastic! (Disney Junior: Henry Hugglemonster) Posner-Sanchez, Andrea. 2015. (Little Golden Book Ser.). (ENG.). 24p. (J). (-k). 4.99 *(978-0-7364-3348-8(1)*, Golden/Disney) Random Hse. Children's Bks.

—The Hugglefish (Disney Junior: Henry Hugglemonster) Posner-Sanchez, Andrea. 2015. (Little Golden Book Ser.). (ENG.). 24p. (J). (-k). 4.99 *(978-0-7364-3360-0(0)*, Golden/Disney) Random Hse. Children's Bks.

Laguna, Fabio & Matta, Gabriella. Drop the Beat! Lewman, David. 2017. 24p. (J). *(978-1-5379-5751-7(1))* Random Hse., Inc.

—Frosty's Favorite Things! (Frosty the Snowman) Man-Kong, Mary. 2017. (ENG.). 16p. (J). (-k). bds. 7.99 *(978-1-5247-1962-3(5)*, Random Hse. Bks. for Young Readers) Random Hse. Children's Bks.

Laguna, Fabio, jt. illus. see Batson, Alan.

Laguna, Fabio, jt. illus. see Dalton, Alex.

Laguna, Fabio, jt. illus. see Golden Books Staff.

Laguna, Fabio, jt. illus. see Random House.

Laguna, Fabio, jt. illus. see RH Disney Staff.

Lahdensuo, Debbie. I Wish I Was... Teys, Jo-Anne. 2005. 36p. (J). pap. *(978-0-9757001-1-2(1))* Love Song Publishing.

Lai, Hsin-Shih. The Bremen Town Musicians, 1 vol. GRIMM. Bell, Anthea, ed. Bell, Anthea, tr. 2007. (ENG.). 32p. (J). (gr. -1-3). 17.95 *(978-0-88010-583-5(6)*, Bell Pond Bks.) SteinerBooks, Inc.

—Thumbelina, 1 vol. Andersen, Hans. 2008.Tr. of Tommelise. (ENG.). 56p. (J). 19.95 *(978-0-88010-592-7(5)*, Bell Pond Bks.) SteinerBooks, Inc.

Lai, Remy. Fly on the Wall. Lai, Remy. 2020. (ENG.). 336p. (J). 16.99 *(978-1-250-31411-6(9)*, 900199489, Holt, Henry & Co. Bks. For Young Readers) Holt, Henry & Co.

—Pie in the Sky. Lai, Remy. 2019. (ENG.). 384p. (J). 21.99 *(978-1-250-31409-3(7)*, 900199487); pap. 12.99 *(978-1-250-31410-9(0)*, 900199488) Holt, Henry & Co. (Holt, Henry & Co. Bks. For Young Readers).

Lai, Trevor. Tomo Takes Flight. Lai, Trevor. 2017. (Tomo's Adventure Ser.). (ENG.). 40p. (J). 17.99 *(978-1-250-08546-7(2)*, 900157206) Imprint IND. Dist: Macmillan.

Laidley, Victoria, jt. illus. see Antonello, Marisa.

Lailah, Daniel, photos by. Kids Cooking Made Easy. Schapira, Leah & Dwek, Victoria. 2013. (ENG., 144p. (J). pap. 15.99 *(978-1-4226-1435-8(2))* Mesorah Pubns., Ltd.

Laínez, René Colato & Graullera Ramírez, Fabiola. René Has Two Last Names/René Tiene Dos Apellidos. Laínez, René Colato. 2009. (SPA & ENG.). 32p. (J). (gr. -1-3). 16.95 *(978-1-55885-530-4(0))* Arte Publico Pr.

Laing, Sarah. The Curioseum: Collected Stories of the Odd & Marvellous. Jansen, Adrienne, ed. 2014. (ENG.). 160p. (J). (gr. 4-7). pap. 24.99 *(978-1-877385-92-6(1))* Te Papa Pr. NZL. Dist: Independent Pubs. Group.

Laird, Alastair. Inviting Harmony: A Story of Belonging in Australia. Lee, Cary. 2017. (ENG.). (J). (gr. k-2). *(978-0-6480084-0-8(1))* Creatively Sunny Moon.

Laiso, Emilio. Marvel's Spider-Man: Velocity. 2020. (ENG.). 112p. (YA). (gr. 4-17). pap. 15.99 *(978-1-302-91922-1(9))* Marvel Worldwide, Inc.

Laiso, Emilio, et al. Rogue One: Volume 1. Houser, Jody. 2018. (Star Wars: Rogue One Ser.). (ENG.). 32p. (J). (gr. 6-12). lib. bdg. 27.07 *(978-1-5321-4168-3(8)*, 28584, Graphic Novels) Spotlight.

Laiso, Emilio. Star Wars: Doctor Aphra Vol. 5: Worst among Equals. 2019. 144p. (YA). pap. 24.99 *(978-1-302-91487-5(1))* Marvel Worldwide, Inc.

—Star Wars: Rogue One Adaptation. 2017. (ENG.). 144p. (J). (gr. 4-17). pap. 19.99 *(978-0-7851-9457-6(6))* Marvel Worldwide, Inc.

Laiso, Emilio & Rosenberg, Rachelle. Rogue One: Volume 2. Houser, Jody. 2018. (Star Wars: Rogue One Ser.). (ENG.). 24p. (J). (gr. 6-12). lib. bdg. 27.07 *(978-1-5321-4169-0(6)*, 28585, Graphic Novels) Spotlight.

—Rogue One: Volume 6. Houser, Jody. 2018. (Star Wars: Rogue One Ser.). (ENG.). 24p. (J). (gr. 6-12). lib. bdg. 27.07 *(978-1-5321-4173-7(4)*, 28589, Graphic Novels) Spotlight.

—Rogue One: Volume 4. Houser, Jody. 2018. (Star Wars: Rogue One Ser.). (ENG.). 24p. (J). (gr. 6-12). lib. bdg. 27.07 *(978-1-5321-4171-3(8)*, 28587, Graphic Novels) Spotlight.

—Rogue One: Volume 5. Houser, Jody. 2018. (Star Wars: Rogue One Ser.). (ENG.). 24p. (J). (gr. 6-12). lib. bdg. 27.07 *(978-1-5321-4172-0(6)*, 28588, Graphic Novels) Spotlight.

Laitinen, Anna. Breathe & Be: A Book of Mindfulness Poems. Coombs, Kate. 2017. (ENG.). 32p. (J). 17.95 *(978-1-62203-937-1(8)*, 900220831) Sounds True, Inc.

Laiug, Naucie, jt. illus. see Walker, John.

Lajeunesse, Nicolas. Silent Words. Fournier, Chantal. deluxe ed. 2013. (ENG.). 52p. 26.95 *(978-1-62253-096-0(9))*; pap. 10.95 *(978-1-62253-098-4(5))* Evolved Publishing.

Lake, Carron M. Ian & Igor: Inquisitive Island Iguanas. Myers, Chloricia Lake. 2019. (ENG.). 40p. (J). *(978-1-5255-3413-3(0))*; pap. *(978-1-5255-3414-0(9))* FriesenPress.

Lake, Joyce. Tammy the Sea Turtle. Lake, Joyce. 2nd ed. 2018. (ENG.). 43p. (J). 14.99 *(978-0-9986381-8-8(8)*, Happy Dolphin Pr.) Glass Onion Publishing.

Lake, Oliver. Beauty & the Beast: Les Petits Fairytales. Belle, Trixie & Caruso-Scott, Melissa. 2013. (Petits Fairytales Ser.). (ENG.). 26p. (J). (gr. -1 — 1). bds. 7.99 *(978-0-8050-9788-7(0)*, 9780805097887, Holt, Henry & Co. Bks. For Young Readers) Holt, Henry & Co.

—Cinderella: Les Petits Fairytales. Caruso-Scott, Melissa & Belle, Trixie. 2012. (Petits Fairytales Ser.). (ENG.). 26p. (J). (gr. -1 — 1). bds. 7.99 *(978-0-8050-9624-8(8)*, 900086241, Holt, Henry & Co. Bks. For Young Readers) Holt, Henry & Co.

—The Little Mermaid: Les Petits Fairytales. Belle, Trixie & Caruso-Scott, Melissa. 2013. (Petits Fairytales Ser.). (ENG.). 26p. (J). (gr. -1 — 1). bds. 7.99 *(978-0-8050-9789-4(9)*, 9780805097894, Holt, Henry & Co. Bks. For Young Readers) Holt, Henry & Co.

—Rapunzel. Belle, Trixie & Caruso-Scott, Melissa. 2013. (Petits Fairytales Ser.). (ENG.). 26p. (J). (gr. -1 — 1). bds. 7.99 *(978-0-8050-9790-0(2)*, 900119520, Holt, Henry & Co. Bks. For Young Readers) Holt, Henry & Co.

—Sleeping Beauty: Les Petits Fairytales. Belle, Trixie & Caruso-Scott, Melissa. 2013. (Petits Fairytales Ser.). (ENG.). 26p. (J). (gr. -1 — 1). bds. 7.99 *(978-0-8050-9791-7(0)*, 900119521, Holt, Henry & Co. Bks. For Young Readers) Holt, Henry & Co.

—Snow White: Les Petits Fairytales. Mack, Tracy et al. 2012. (Petits Fairytales Ser.). (ENG.). 26p. (J). (gr. -1 — 1). bds. 7.99 *(978-0-8050-9623-1(X)*, 900086239, Holt, Henry & Co. Bks. For Young Readers) Holt, Henry & Co.

Lakes, Lofton & Metu. The Dream Team. 2007. 48p. (YA). pap. *(978-0-9799320-0-7(9))* Pinkney, Gail.

Lalalimola. Can You Tickle a Tiger's Tummy? Nicholson, Sue. 2017. (Little Know-It-All Ser.). (ENG.). 48p. (J). (gr. -1-2). 12.95 *(978-1-68297-200-7(3))* QEB Publishing Inc.

—Can You Touch a Rainbow? Nicholson, Sue. 2017. (Little Know-It-All Ser.). (ENG.). 48p. (J). (gr. -1-2). 12.95 *(978-1-68297-201-4(1))* QEB Publishing Inc.

—If Everything Were Blue. Eliot, Hannah. 2015. (ENG.). 16p. (J). (gr. -1-k). bds. 8.99 *(978-1-4814-3539-0(6)*, Little Simon) Little Simon.

—If Everything Were Pink. Eliot, Hannah. 2015. (ENG.). 16p. (J). (gr. -1-k). bds. 8.99 *(978-1-4814-3538-3(8)*, Little Simon) Little Simon.

Lalara, Alfred. When We Go Walkabout. Lalara, Rhoda. 2017. (ENG.). 32p. (J). (gr. -1-1). pap. 13.99 *(978-1-76063-127-7(2))* Allen & Unwin AUS. Dist: Independent Pubs. Group.

Laliberete, Louise-Andree. Dimples Delight. Wishinsky, Frieda. 2005. (SPA.). 61p. (J). lib. bdg. 20.00 *(978-1-4242-1252-1(9))* Fitzgerald Bks.

Laliberté, Louise-Andrée. A Bee in Your Ear, 1 vol. Wishinsky, Frieda. 2004. (Orca Echoes Ser.). (ENG.). 64p. (J). (gr. 1-3). pap. 6.95 *(978-1-55143-324-0(9))* Orca Bk. Pubs. USA.

Laliberte, Louise-Andree. A Bee in Your Ear. Wishinsky, Frieda. 2004. 64p. (J). lib. bdg. 20.00 *(978-1-4242-1255-2(3))* Fitzgerald Bks.

Laliberté, Louise-Andrée. Dimples Delight, 1 vol. Wishinsky, Frieda. 2005. (Orca Echoes Ser.). (ENG.). 64p. (J). (gr. 1-3). per. 6.95 *(978-1-55143-362-2(1))* Orca Bk. Pubs. USA.

—A Frog in My Throat, 1 vol. Wishinsky, Frieda. 2008. (Orca Echoes Ser.). (ENG.). 64p. (J). (gr. 1-3). pap. 6.95 *(978-1-55143-632-6(9))* Orca Bk. Pubs. USA.

—A Noodle up Your Nose, 1 vol. Wishinsky, Frieda. 2004. (Orca Echoes Ser.). (ENG.). 64p. (J). (gr. 1-3). pap. 6.95 *(978-1-55143-294-6(3))* Orca Bk. Pubs. USA.

Laliberte, Mario. Match, Sort & Play. 2007. (Hands-on Bks.). 48p. (J). (gr. -1-k). spiral bd. *(978-2-7641-1936-5(4))* Tormont Pubns.

Lalich, Nadine. Finding Happiness: A Magical Tale about the Power of Positive Thinking. Lalich, Nadine. 2017. (ENG.). 68p. (gr. -1-4). reprint ed. per. 14.95 *(978-0-9711776-0-4(0))* Nadine Lalich.

Lalla, Christine, photos by. This Is My Digger. Oxlade, Chris. 2008. (Mega Machine Drivers Ser.). 30p. (J). (gr. k). lib. bdg. 28.50 *(978-1-59771-104-3(7))* Sea-To-Sea Pubns.

—This Is My Tractor. Oxlade, Chris. 2008. (Mega Machine Drivers Ser.). 30p. (J). (gr. k). lib. bdg. 28.50 *(978-1-59771-106-7(3))* Sea-To-Sea Pubns.

Lally, Cory. The Adventures of Pea-Shooter: Into the Forbidden Forest. Serino, Robert. 2012. 32p. pap. 24.95 *(978-1-4626-8019-1(4))* America Star Bks.

LaLonde, Deanna L. The Golden Metis. Ell, Flynn J. 2015. (ENG.). 32p. (J). (gr. 9). pap. 11.95 *(978-1-894717-20-5(1)*, 3e1a6a3f-8327-4358-944a-383c60f62901) Pemmican Pubns., Inc. CAN. Dist: Firefly Bks., Ltd.

Lalonde, Johnathan. Hide Tommy Turkey. Lalonde, Carolyn. 2005. 20p. (J). 9.60 *(978-1-4120-4893-4(1))* Trafford Publishing.

Lalonde, Nicolle. Our Big Little Place. Conan, James A. 2019. 36p. (J). (gr. k-2). 18.95 *(978-1-77321-317-0(2))* Annick Pr., Ltd. CAN. Dist: Publishers Group West (PGW).

Lam, Amy. Big Bear & Little Bear: Buttons. Cowley, Joy. 2013. (ENG.). 8p. pap. *(978-1-927186-33-6(1)*, Joy Cowley Club) Flying Start Bks.

—Big Bear & Little Bear: Cold Feet. Cowley, Joy. 2013. (ENG.). 8p. pap. *(978-1-927186-27-5(7)*, Joy Cowley Club) Flying Start Bks.

—Big Bear & Little Bear: Cookies. Cowley, Joy. 2013. (ENG.). 8p. pap. *(978-1-927186-29-9(3)*, Joy Cowley Club) Flying Start Bks.

—Big Bear & Little Bear: Egg. Cowley, Joy. 2013. (ENG.). 8p. pap. *(978-1-927186-32-9(3)*, Joy Cowley Club) Flying Start Bks.

—Big Bear & Little Bear: Ice Cream. Cowley, Joy. 2013. (ENG.). 8p. pap. *(978-1-927186-21-3(8)*, Joy Cowley Club) Flying Start Bks.

—Big Bear & Little Bear: Jackets. Cowley, Joy. 2013. (ENG.). 8p. pap. *(978-1-927186-26-8(9)*, Joy Cowley Club) Flying Start Bks.

—Big Bear & Little Bear: Lemonade. Cowley, Joy. 2013. (ENG.). 8p. pap. *(978-1-927186-28-2(5)*, Joy Cowley Club) Flying Start Bks.

—Big Bear & Little Bear: Lollipop. Cowley, Joy. 2013. (ENG.). 8p. pap. *(978-1-927186-30-5(7)*, Joy Cowley Club) Flying Start Bks.

—Big Bear & Little Bear: Puddle. Cowley, Joy. 2013. (ENG.). 8p. pap. *(978-1-927186-34-3(X)*, Joy Cowley Club) Flying Start Bks.

—Big Bear & Little Bear: Race. Cowley, Joy. 2013. (ENG.). 8p. pap. *(978-1-927186-22-0(6)*, Joy Cowley Club) Flying Start Bks.

—Big Bear & Little Bear: Singing. Cowley, Joy. 2013. (ENG.). 8p. pap. *(978-1-927186-25-1(0)*, Joy Cowley Club) Flying Start Bks.

—Big Bear & Little Bear: Story. Cowley, Joy. 2013. (ENG.). 8p. pap. *(978-1-927186-23-7(4)*, Joy Cowley Club) Flying Start Bks.

—Big Bear & Little Bear: Wind. Cowley, Joy. 2013. (ENG.). 8p. pap. *(978-1-927186-20-6(X)*, Joy Cowley Club) Flying Start Bks.

Lam, Gracia. Awake Beautiful Child. Rosenthal, Amy Krouse. 2015. 32p. (J). (gr. -1-k). 17.95 *(978-1-938073-92-2(4)*, 2cb9fc8c-749d-49b4-9d1f-c002be0fe1ff) McSweeney's Publishing.

Lam, Jon & Libranda, Kevin. Future Fight Firsts. 2020. (ENG.). 112p. (YA). (gr. 8-17). pap. 15.99 *(978-1-302-92300-6(5))* Marvel Worldwide, Inc.

Lam, Maple. Frenemies in the Family: Famous Brothers & Sisters Who Butted Heads & Had Each Other's Backs. Krull, Kathleen. 2018. 240p. (J). (gr. 3-7). 17.99 *(978-0-399-55124-6(7))*; (ENG.). lib. bdg. 20.99 *(978-0-399-55125-3(5))* Random Hse. Children's Bks. (Crown Books For Young Readers).

Lam, Maple. Shake My Sillies Out. Raffi. 2020. (Raffi Songs to Read Ser.). 32p. (J). (— 1). bds. 7.99 ***(978-0-593-12223-5(2)***, Knopf Bks. for Young Readers) Random Hse. Children's Bks.

Lam, Maple. Two Girls Want a Puppy. Cordell, Ryan & Cordell, Evie. 2015. (ENG.). 32p. (J). (gr. -1-3). 17.99 *(978-0-06-229261-2(7))* HarperCollins Pubs.

—What Can You Do with a Toolbox? Colaneri, John & Carrino, Anthony. 2018. (ENG.). 32p. (J). (gr. -1-3). 17.99 *(978-1-5344-0296-6(9)*, Simon & Schuster/Paula Wiseman Bks.) Simon & Schuster/Paula Wiseman Bks.

Lam, Maple. My Little Sister & Me. Lam, Maple. 2016. (ENG.). 40p. (J). (gr. -1-3). 17.99 *(978-0-06-239697-6(8))* HarperCollins Pubs.

Lam, Michelle. How to Train Your Dragon the Hidden World the Movie Storybook. ed. 2019. (How to Train Your Dragon: Hidden World Ser.). (ENG.). 32p. (J). (gr. -1-3). 7.99 *(978-1-5344-3813-2(0)*, Simon Spotlight) Simon Spotlight.

Lamar, Andrew. I Saw a Starburst to Flames. Lamar, J. R. 2019. (ENG.). 138p. (J). (gr. k-6). 24.99 *(978-1-7336364-0-7(4))*; pap. 16.99 *(978-1-7336364-1-4(2))* Jollyrhymes.

Lamar, J. R. I Found Some Ancient Hieroglyphs: Jolly Rhymes from Around the World. Lamar, J. R. 2019. (ENG.). 60p. (J). (gr. 2-6). 19.99 ***(978-1-7336364-3-8(9))***; pap. 11.99 ***(978-1-7336364-5-2(5))*** Jollyrhymes.

LaMarca, Luke. The Curious Demise of a Contrary Cat. Berry, Lynne. 2006. (ENG.). 40p. (J). (gr. -1-3). 17.99 *(978-1-4169-0211-9(2)*, Simon & Schuster Bks. For Young Readers) Simon & Schuster Bks. For Young Readers.

—The Day Ray Got Away. Johnson, Angela. 2010. (ENG.). 40p. (J). (gr. k-3). 16.99 *(978-0-689-87375-1(1)*, Simon & Schuster Bks. For Young Readers) Simon & Schuster Bks. For Young Readers.

—Stick Tac Toe: Forever Foes! 2018. (ENG.). 60p. (J). (gr. -1-17). 7.99 *(978-1-4521-6402-1(9))* Chronicle Bks. LLC.

LaMarche, Jim. Albert. Napoli, Donna Jo. 2005. (ENG.). 32p. (J). (gr. -1-3). reprint ed. pap. 7.99 *(978-0-15-205249-2(6)*, 1195814) Houghton Mifflin Harcourt Publishing Co.

—The Carpenter's Gift: A Christmas Tale about the Rockefeller Center Tree. Rubel, David. 2011. (ENG.). 48p. (J). (gr. k-4). 17.99 *(978-0-375-86922-8(0)*, Random Hse. Bks. for Young Readers) Random Hse. Children's Bks.

—Ivy Takes Care. Wells, Rosemary. 208p. (J). (gr. 3-7). 2015. pap. 6.99 *(978-0-7636-7660-5(8))*; 2013. 15.99 *(978-0-7636-5352-1(7))* Candlewick Pr.

—The King of Bees, 1 vol. Laminack, Lester L. 2018. (ENG.). 32p. (J). (gr. -1-3). 17.95 *(978-1-56145-953-7(4))* Peachtree Publishing Co. Inc.

—The Little Fir Tree. Brown, Margaret Wise. 32p. (J). (gr. -1-1). 2005. lib. bdg. 16.89 *(978-0-06-028190-8(1))*; 2005. (ENG.). 15.99 *(978-0-06-028189-2(8))*; Vol. 2009. (ENG.). pap. 7.99 *(978-0-06-443529-1(6))* HarperCollins Pubs.

—Puma Dreams. Johnston, Tony. 2019. (ENG.). 48p. (J). (gr. -1-3). 17.99 *(978-1-5344-2979-6(4)*, Simon & Schuster Bks. For Young Readers) Simon & Schuster Bks. For Young Readers.

—The Rainbabies. Melmed, Laura Krauss. 2004. (ENG.). 32p. (J). (gr. -1-3). pap. 7.99 *(978-0-688-15113-3(2))* HarperCollins Pubs.

—A Story for Bear. Haseley, Dennis. 2018. (ENG.). 32p. (J). (gr. -1-3). pap. 7.99 *(978-1-328-74048-9(X)*, 1677013, HMH Books For Young Readers) Houghton Mifflin Harcourt Publishing Co.

—Winter Is Coming. Johnston, Tony. 2014. (ENG.). 40p. (J). (gr. -1-3). 18.99 *(978-1-4424-7251-8(0)*, Simon & Schuster Bks. For Young Readers) Simon & Schuster Bks. For Young Readers.

LaMarche, Jim. Pond. LaMarche, Jim. 2016. (ENG.). 40p. (J). (gr. -1-3). 18.99 *(978-1-4814-4735-5(1)*, Simon & Schuster/Paula Wiseman Bks.) Simon & Schuster/Paula Wiseman Bks.

Lamb, Braden, et al. Adventure Time Vol. 17. Hastings, Christopher et al. 2019. (Adventure Time Ser.). (ENG.). 112p. (J). (gr. 4-7). pap. 14.99 *(978-1-68415-331-2(X))* Boom! Studios.

Lamb, Braden & Paroline, Shelli. Making Scents. Yorinks, Arthur. 2017. (ENG.). 112p. (J). 15.99 *(978-1-59643-452-3(X)*, 9781596434523, First Second Bks.) Roaring Brook Pr.

—One Day a Dot: The Story of You, the Universe, & Everything. Lendler, Ian. 2018. (ENG.). 40p. (J). 17.99 *(978-1-62672-244-6(7)*, 900146577, First Second Bks.) Roaring Brook Pr.

Lamb, Braden, jt. illus. see Paroline, Shelli.

Lamb, Janie. Around Our Feeder with George the Groundhog & Friends. Renshaw, Douglas. 2008. 48p. pap. 24.95 *(978-1-60610-657-0(0))* America Star Bks.

Lamb, Karen. Jolly Music Player: Beginners: (Physical CD) Rowsell, Cyrilla & Vinden, David. 2018. (ENG.). (J). cd-rom 43.95 *(978-1-84414-491-4(7)*, Jolly Music) Jolly Learning, Ltd. GBR. Dist: American International Distribution Corp.

—Jolly Music Player: Level 1: (Physical CD) Rowsell, Cyrilla & Vinden, David. 2018. (ENG.). (J). cd-rom 43.95 *(978-1-84414-492-1(5)*, Jolly Music) Jolly Learning, Ltd. GBR. Dist: American International Distribution Corp.

—Jolly Music Player: Level 2. Rowsell, Cyrilla & Vinden, David. 2018. (ENG.). (J). cd-rom 43.95 *(978-1-84414-493-8(3)*, Jolly Music) Jolly Learning, Ltd. GBR. Dist: American International Distribution Corp.

—Jolly Music Player: Level 3. Rowsell, Cyrilla & Vinden, David. 2018. (ENG.). (J). cd-rom 43.95 *(978-1-84414-494-5(1)*, Jolly Music) Jolly Learning, Ltd. GBR. Dist: American International Distribution Corp.

—The Music Handbook - Level 4. Rowsell, Cyrilla & Vinden, David. 2019. (ENG.). (J). spiral bd. 59.95 *(978-1-84414-573-7(5)*, Jolly Music) Jolly Learning, Ltd. GBR. Dist: American International Distribution Corp.

—The Music Handbook, Level 2: Teaching Music Skills to Children Through Singing. Rowsell, Cyrilla & Vinden, David. 2012. (ENG.). 212p. (J). spiral bd. 59.95 incl. audio compact disk *(978-1-84414-265-1(5)*, Jolly Learning) Jolly Learning, Ltd. GBR. Dist: American International Distribution Corp.

Lamb, Michael. Ace Canary & Dud Clutch. Lamb, Phillip C. 2011. 40p. pap. 24.95 *(978-1-4626-0401-2(3))* America Star Bks.

Lamb, Rosy. Paul Meets Bernadette. Lamb, Rosy. 2013. 40p. (J). (gr. -1-3). 14.00 *(978-0-7636-6130-4(9))* Candlewick Pr.

Lamb, Sandra. Je Suis Ballerine! Coulman, Valerie. Duchesne, Christiane, tr. from ENG. (FRE.). 32p. (J). pap. 6.95 *(978-2-922435-05-4(9))* Editions Homard CAN. Dist: Univ. of Toronto Pr.

Lamb, Stacey. ABC. 2009. (Sticker Bks). 24p. (J). pap. 6.99 *(978-0-7945-2362-6(5)*, Usborne) EDC Publishing.

—Dinosaurs. Taplin, Sam. ed. 2011. (First Sticker Books Ser.). 16p. (J). pap. 6.99 *(978-0-7945-2994-9(1)*, Usborne) EDC Publishing.

—My ABC Bible, 1 vol. Bowman, Crystal. 2012. (ENG.). 56p. (J). 5.99 *(978-0-310-73037-8(6))* Zonderkidz.

—My ABC Prayers, 1 vol. Bowman, Crystal. 2012. (ENG.). 56p. (J). 5.99 *(978-0-310-73039-2(2))* Zonderkidz.

Lamb, Stacey, et al. My First Christmas Activity Book. 2013. (ENG.). 50p. (J). pap. 11.99 *(978-0-7945-3182-9(2)*, Usborne) EDC Publishing.

Lamb, Stacey. Wipe Clean 123 Book. ed. 2011. (Wipe-Clean Bks). 20p. (J). pap. 7.99 *(978-0-7945-3075-4(3)*, Usborne) EDC Publishing.

—Wipe Clean Alphabet Book. ed. 2011. (Wipe-Clean Bks). 20p. (J). pap. 7.99 *(978-0-7945-3099-0(0)*, Usborne) EDC Publishing.

—Wipe-Clean Doodles. ed. 2013. (Wipe-Clean Bks). 20p. (J). pap. 7.99 *(978-0-7945-3312-0(4)*, Usborne) EDC Publishing.

—Wipe-Clean Dot-To-Dot. ed. 2013. (Wipe-Clean Bks). 20p. (J). pap. 7.99 *(978-0-7945-3278-9(0)*, Usborne) EDC Publishing.

—Wipe Clean First Letters. ed. 2011. (Wipe-Clean Bks). 20p. (J). pap. 7.99 *(978-0-7945-3100-3(8)*, Usborne) EDC Publishing.

—Wipe-Clean Mazes. ed. 2012. (Wipe-Clean Bks). 20p. (J). pap. 7.99 *(978-0-7945-3257-4(8)*, Usborne) EDC Publishing.

—Wipe Clean Ready for Writing. ed. 2011. (Wipe-Clean Bks). 20p. (J). pap. 7.99 *(978-0-7945-3076-1(1)*, Usborne) EDC Publishing.

—123 Sticker Book. 2009. (Sticker Bks). 24p. (J). pap. 6.99 *(978-0-7945-2361-9(7)*, Usborne) EDC Publishing.

Lamb, Stacey. Shapes Sticker Book. Lamb, Stacey. 2009. (Sticker Bks). 16p. (J). pap. 6.99 *(978-0-7945-2501-9(6)*, Usborne) EDC Publishing.

Lamb, Stacy. First Puzzles. 2014. (Usborne Wipe-Clean Ser.). (ENG.). 22p. (J). pap. 7.99 *(978-0-7945-2524-8(5)*, Usborne) EDC Publishing.

Lamb, Susan Condie. Miss Dorothy & Her Bookmobile. Houston, Gloria. 2011. (ENG.). 32p. (J). (gr. 1-4). 16.99 *(978-0-06-029155-6(9))* HarperCollins Pubs.

—Prairie Primer: A to Z. Stutson, Caroline. 2006. 29p. (J). (gr. -1-2). reprint ed. 16.00 *(978-1-4223-5585-5(3))* DIANE Publishing Co.

Lamb, T. S. Asim the Awesome Possum: Asim Gets His Awesome. Oddo, Jennifer M. 2012. 36p. 16.95 *(978-0-9855906-2-8(9))* Pie Plate Publishing Co.

Lambdin, Victor R. Viking Tales (Yesterday's Classics) Hall, Jennie. 2005. 168p. (J). per. 8.95 *(978-1-59915-004-8(2))* Yesterday's Classics.

Lambe, Steve. Follow the Ninja! (Teenage Mutant Ninja Turtles) Golden Books. 2015. (Little Golden Book Ser.). (ENG.). 24p. (J). (-k). 4.99 *(978-0-553-51204-5(8)*, Golden Bks.) Random Hse. Children's Bks.

—Frog Fight! (Teenage Mutant Ninja Turtles) Golden Books. 2016. (Little Golden Book Ser.). (ENG.). 24p. (J). (-k). 4.99 *(978-0-553-53907-3(8)*, Golden Bks.) Random Hse. Children's Bks.

—How to Merit in Monsters: Strange Scout Tales #1. Cody, Matthew. 2018. (Strange Scout Tales Ser.: 1). 128p. (J). (gr. 2-5). 12.99 *(978-1-63565-059-4(3)*, 9781635650594, Rodale Kids) Random Hse. Children's Bks.

—The Loch Ness Lock-In: Strange Scout Tales #2. Cody, Matthew. 2018. (Strange Scout Tales Ser.: 2). 128p. (J). (gr. 2-5). 12.99 *(978-1-63565-060-0(7)*, 9781635650600, Rodale Kids) Random Hse. Children's Bks.

—Scaredy Monster (Scaredy Monster Book 1) Hashimoto, Meika. 2020. (Scaredy Monster Ser.). (ENG.). 104p. (J). 12.99 *(978-1-5248-5522-2(7))* Andrews McMeel Publishing.

Lambe, Steve, jt. illus. see Childrens Books Staff.

Lambe, Steve, jt. illus. see Golden Books Staff.

Lambelet, Anne. Greystone Secrets #1: the Strangers. Haddix, Margaret Peterson. (Greystone Secrets Ser.: 1). (ENG.). (J). (gr. 3-7). 2020. 432p. pap. 8.99 *(978-0-06-283838-4(5))*; 2019. 416p. 17.99 *(978-0-06-283837-7(7))*; 2019. 432p. E-Book *(978-0-06-283839-1(3))* HarperCollins Pubs. (Tegen, Katherine Bks).

Lambert, Celeste. 8 Boys & 8 Beasts, 1 vol. Lambert, George J. 2010. 24p. 24.95 *(978-1-4489-5901-3(2))* PublishAmerica, Inc.

Lambert, Jonathan. Charlie Chimp's Christmas: A Pop-up Extravaganza of Festive Friends. Faulkner, Keith. 2006. 12p. (J). (gr. -1-3). reprint ed. 10.00 *(978-1-4223-5446-9(6))* DIANE Publishing Co.

—To Grandpa, with Love. 2018. (Special Delivery Bks.). (ENG.). 8p. (J). (— 1). bds. 6.49 *(978-1-68412-271-4(6)*, Silver Dolphin Bks.) Printers Row Publishing Group.

Lambert, Jonny. Good Trick Walking Stick. Bestor, Sheri M. 2016. (ENG.). 32p. (J). (gr. 1-3). 16.99 *(978-1-58536-943-0(8)*, 204033) Sleeping Bear Pr.

—I Love You More & More. Benson, Nicky. 2016. (ENG.). 24p. (J). (gr. -1-k). bds. 9.99 *(978-1-58925-227-1(6))* Tiger Tales.

—Soar High, Dragonfly. Bestor, Sheri M. 2019. (ENG.). 32p. (J). (gr. k-3). 16.99 *(978-1-58536-410-7(X)*, 204659) Sleeping Bear Pr.

—Soar High Dragonfly. Bestor, Sheri M. 2019. (ENG.). 32p. (J). (gr. k-3). 8.99 *(978-1-5341-1056-4(9)*, 204764) Sleeping Bear Pr.

Lambert, Jonny. The Great AAA-OOO! Lambert, Jonny. 2016. (ENG.). 32p. (J). (gr. -1-2). 16.99 *(978-1-68010-032-7(7))* Tiger Tales.

—Jonny Lambert's Animal 123. Lambert, Jonny. 2018. (Jonny Lambert Illustrated Ser.). (ENG.). 24p. (J). (— 1). bds. 12.99 *(978-1-4654-7845-0(0)*, DK Children) Dorling Kindersley Publishing, Inc.

—Jonny Lambert's Animal ABC. Lambert, Jonny. 2018. (Jonny Lambert Illustrated Ser.). (ENG.). 24p. (J). (— 1). bds. 12.99 *(978-1-4654-7571-8(0)*, DK Children) Dorling Kindersley Publishing, Inc.

—Let's All Creep Through Crocodile Creek. Lambert, Jonny. 2019. (ENG.). 32p. (J). (gr. -1-2). 17.99 *(978-1-68010-152-2(8))* Tiger Tales.

—Look Out! It's a Dragon! Lambert, Jonny. 2018. (ENG.). 32p. (J). (gr. -1-2). 16.99 *(978-1-68010-081-5(5))* Tiger Tales.

—The Only Lonely Panda. Lambert, Jonny. 2017. (ENG.). 32p. (J). (gr. -1-2). 16.99 *(978-1-68010-065-5(3))* Tiger Tales.

—Special You. Lambert, Jonny. 2016. (ENG.). 24p. (J). (gr. -1-k). bds. 9.99 *(978-1-58925-238-7(1))* Tiger Tales.

—Tiger Tiger. Lambert, Jonny. 2017. (ENG.). 32p. (J). (gr. -1-2). 16.99 *(978-1-68010-044-0(0))* Tiger Tales.

Lambert, Joseph. Annie Sullivan & the Trials of Helen Keller. Lambert, Joseph. 2018. (Center for Cartoon Studies Presents Ser.). 96p. (J). (gr. 5-9). 17.99 *(978-1-368-02230-9(8))* Hyperion Bks. for Children.

Lambert, Sally Anne. Gator Gumbo: A Spicy-Hot Tale. Fleming, Candace. 2004. (ENG.). 32p. (J). (gr. -1-3). 18.99 *(978-0-374-38050-2(3)*, 9780374380502, Farrar, Straus & Giroux (BYR)) Farrar, Straus & Giroux.

—The Story of the Easter Bunny. Tegen, Katherine. (ENG.). 40p. (J). (gr. -1-3). 2007. pap. 7.99 *(978-0-06-058781-9(4))*; 2005. 12.99 *(978-0-06-050711-4(X))* HarperCollins Pubs.

—The Story of the Easter Bunny Board Book. Tegen, Katherine. 2017. (ENG.). 32p. (J). (gr. -1-3). bds. 7.99 *(978-0-06-238155-2(5)*, HarperFestival) HarperCollins Pubs.

—The Story of the Leprechaun. Tegen, Katherine Brown. 2011. (J). lib. bdg. 14.89 *(978-0-06-143085-5(4))* HarperCollins Pubs.

—The Story of the Leprechaun. Tegen, Katherine. 2011. (ENG.). 40p. (J). (gr. -1-3). 12.99 *(978-0-06-143086-2(2))* HarperCollins Pubs.

—The Yippy, Yappy Yorkie in the Green Doggy Sweater. Macomber, Debbie & Carney, Mary Lou. 2011. (ENG.). 32p. (J). (gr. -1-2). 17.99 *(978-0-06-165096-3(X))* HarperCollins Pubs.

Lambert, Stephen. Little Book of Horses & Ponies. Khan, Sarah. 2010. (Miniature Editions Ser.). 64p. (YA). (gr. 3-18). 6.99 *(978-0-7945-2791-4(4)*, Usborne) EDC Publishing.

—El Reloj de Mi Abuela. MacCaughrean, Geraldine et al. 2003. (SPA.). 32p. (J). (gr. k-2). 14.99 *(978-84-241-8643-2(5))* Everest Editora ESP. Dist: Lectorum Pubns., Inc.

—El Viaje en Tren. Crebbin, June. Rubio, Esther, tr. 2004. (SPA.). (J). 7.95 *(978-1-930332-76-8(9))* Lectorum Pubns., Inc.

Lambert, Tredel. Jack Fly. Lambert, Tredel. Lambert, Jessica. 2018. (Hip-Hop Heroz Ser.: Vol. 1). (ENG.). 48p. (J). (gr. k-5). pap. *(978-0-9808886-0-7(3))* Platinum Rouge.

Lambert, Tredel. No Chainz Hip-Hop Heroz: Kids Learn about Money & Wealth Development Skills. Lambert, Tredel. Lambert, Jessica. 2020. (Hip Hop Heroz Ser.: Vol. 2). (ENG.). 56p. (J). pap. ***(978-0-9808886-3-8(8))*** Platinum Rouge.

Lambiase, Lauren. Glove of Their Own. Conkling, Keri. 2008. 32p. 15.95 *(978-0-9760469-5-0(4))* Franklin Mason Pr.

—A Glove of Their Own. Moldovan, Deborah et al. 2015. (ENG.). 32p. pap. 9.95 *(978-1-63047-415-7(0))* Morgan James Publishing.

Lambil, Willy. Bluecoats - Greenhorn, Vol. 4. Cauvin, Raoul. 4th ed. 2011. (Bluecoats Ser.: 4). (ENG.). 48p. (gr. 3-17). pap. 11.95 *(978-1-84918-066-5(0))* CineBook GBR. Dist: National Bk. Network.

—The Bluecoats Vol. 12: the David. Cauvin, Raoul. 2019. (Bluecoats Ser.: 12). (ENG.). 48p. pap. 11.95 *(978-1-84918-430-4(5))* CineBook GBR. Dist: National Bk. Network.

—The Blues in the Mud. Cauvin, Raoul. 2014. (Bluecoats Ser.: 7). (ENG.). 48p. pap. 11.95 *(978-1-84918-183-9(7))* CineBook GBR. Dist: National Bk. Network.

—Bronco Benny. Cauvin, Raoul. 2013. (Bluecoats Ser.: 6). (ENG.). 48p. pap. 11.95 *(978-1-84918-146-4(2))* CineBook GBR. Dist: National Bk. Network.

—The Navy Blues. Cauvin, Raoul. 2009. (Bluecoats Ser.: 2). (ENG.). 46p. (J). (gr. 4-7). pap. 11.95 *(978-1-905460-82-3(1))* CineBook GBR. Dist: National Bk. Network.

—Robertsonville Prison, Volume 1. Cauvin, Raoul. 2009. (Bluecoats Ser.: 1). (ENG.). 46p. (J). (gr. -1-17). pap. 11.95 *(978-1-905460-71-7(6))* CineBook GBR. Dist: National Bk. Network.

—Rumberley. Cauvin, Raoul. 2012. (Bluecoats Ser.: 5). (ENG.). 48p. (J). (gr. 3-8). pap. 11.95 *(978-1-84918-108-2(X))* CineBook GBR. Dist: National Bk. Network.

Lambo, Don. Magic Fingers. Mulcahy, Lucille. 2012. 124p. 40.95 *(978-1-258-23435-5(1))*; pap. 25.95 *(978-1-258-24669-3(4))* Literary Licensing, LLC.

Lambson, Elizabeth. Just Like You. Gill, Janie S. Date not set. 5.95 *(978-0-89868-430-8(7))*; pap. 3.95 *(978-0-89868-429-2(3))* ARO Publishing Co.

—Socks. Spaht-Gill, Janie. (J). 5.95 *(978-0-89868-301-1(7))* ARO Publishing Co.

Lamere, Jill. Upside Down. Lamere, Jill. 2005. (J). bds. 12.95 *(978-0-9772320-0-0(X))* Minikin Pr.

Laming, Marc, et al. Star Wars: Age of Rebellion. 2020. (ENG.). 224p. (YA). (gr. 4-17). 34.99 *(978-1-302-91707-4(2))* Marvel Worldwide, Inc.

Laming, Marc. Star Wars: Target Vader. 2020. 136p. (YA). (gr. 4-17). pap. 17.99 *(978-1-302-91858-3(3))* Marvel Worldwide, Inc.

Laming, Marc & Martin, Frank. The Force Awakens: Volume 3. Wendig, Chuck. 2017. (Star Wars: the Force Awakens Ser.). (ENG.). 24p. (J). (gr. 6-12). lib. bdg. 27.07 *(978-1-5321-4024-2(X)*, 25456, Graphic Novels) Spotlight.

Laming, Marc, jt. illus. see Walker, Kev.

Lammie, Leslie. Pajama Pirates. Kramer, Andrew. 2010. (ENG.). 40p. (J). (gr. k-3). 16.99 *(978-0-06-125194-8(1))* HarperCollins Pubs.

Lammle, Leslie. Once upon a Saturday. Lammle, Leslie. 2009. 32p. (J). (gr. k-2). lib. bdg. 18.89 *(978-0-06-125191-7(7))*; (ENG.). 17.99 *(978-0-06-125190-0(9))* HarperCollins Pubs.

—Princess Wannabe. Lammle, Leslie. 2014. (ENG.). 40p. (J). (gr. -1-3). 17.99 *(978-0-06-125197-9(6))* HarperCollins Pubs.

Lamont, Priscilla. Animal Rescue Team: Gator on the Loose! Stauffacher, Sue. 2011. (Animal Rescue Team Ser.: 1). 160p. (J). (gr. 3-7). 6.99 *(978-0-375-85131-5(3)*, Yearling) Random Hse. Children's Bks.

—Animal Rescue Team: Hide & Seek. Stauffacher, Sue. 2011. (Animal Rescue Team Ser.: 3). 160p. (J). (gr. 3-7). 5.99 *(978-0-375-85133-9(X)*, Yearling) Random Hse. Children's Bks.

—Animal Rescue Team: Show Time. Stauffacher, Sue. 2011. (Animal Rescue Team Ser.: 4). 160p. (J). (gr. 3-7). 5.99 *(978-0-375-85134-6(8)*, Yearling) Random Hse. Children's Bks.

—Fairy Tales: A Beautiful Collection of Favorite Fairy Tales. Parragon Books & Cottage Door Press, eds. 2018. (Hardcover Storybook Treasury Ser.). (ENG.). 192p. (J). (gr. -1-3). 12.99 *(978-1-68052-463-5(1)*, 2000620, Parragon Books) Cottage Door Pr.

—Gator on the Loose!, 1. Stauffacher, Sue. 2011. (Animal Rescue Team Ser.). (ENG.). 160p. (J). (gr. 2-5). lib. bdg. 18.69 *(978-0-375-95847-2(9)*, Knopf Bks. for Young Readers) Random Hse. Children's Bks.

—Goose & Duck. George, Jean Craighead. 2008. (I Can Read Level 2 Ser.). (ENG.). 48p. (J). (gr. k-3). 16.99 *(978-0-06-117076-8(3))* HarperCollins Pubs.

—Hide & Seek, 3. Stauffacher, Sue. 2012. (Animal Rescue Team Ser.). (ENG.). 160p. (J). (gr. 2-5). lib. bdg. 18.69 *(978-0-375-95849-6(5)*, Knopf Bks. for Young Readers) Random Hse. Children's Bks.

—The Lion Nursery Bible. Pasquali, Elena. ed. (ENG.). 192p. (J). (gr. -1-k). 2015. 14.99 *(978-0-7459-7601-3(8))*; 2014. 14.99 *(978-0-7459-6399-0(4))* Lion Hudson PLC GBR. Dist: Independent Pubs. Group.

—Lulu & the Cat in the Bag. McKay, Hilary. (Lulu Ser.: 3). (ENG.). 112p. (J). (gr. 1-5). 2014. pap. 5.99 *(978-0-8075-4805-9(7)*, 807548057); 2013. 13.99 *(978-0-8075-4804-2(9)*, 807548049) Whitman, Albert & Co.

—Lulu & the Dog from the Sea. McKay, Hilary. (Lulu Ser.: Book 2). (ENG.). 112p. (J). (gr. 1-5). 2014. pap. 5.99 *(978-0-8075-4821-9(9)*, 807548219); 2013. 13.99 *(978-0-8075-4820-2(0)*, 807548200) Whitman, Albert & Co.

—Lulu & the Duck in the Park. McKay, Hilary. (Lulu Ser.: Book 1). (ENG.). (J). (gr. 1-5). 2012. 104p. 13.99 *(978-0-8075-4808-0(1)*, 807548081); Bk. 1. 2014. 112p. 5.99 *(978-0-8075-4809-7(X)*, 080754809X) Whitman, Albert & Co.

—Lulu & the Hedgehog in the Rain. McKay, Hilary. 2014. (Lulu Ser.: 5). (ENG.). 128p. (J). (gr. 1-5). 13.99 *(978-0-8075-4812-7(X)*, 080754812X) Whitman, Albert & Co.

—Lulu & the Rabbit Next Door. McKay, Hilary. 2014. (Lulu Ser.: Book 4). (ENG.). 112p. (J). (gr. 1-5). 13.99 *(978-0-8075-4816-5(2)*, 807548162) Whitman, Albert & Co.

Lamont, Priscilla. Max & Mo's Science Fair Surprise. Lakin, Patricia. 2020. (Max & Mo Ser.). (ENG.). 32p. (J). (gr. -1-1). 17.99 ***(978-1-5344-6322-6(4))***; pap. 4.99 ***(978-1-5344-6323-3(2))*** Simon Spotlight. (Simon Spotlight).

Lamont, Priscilla. Mother Goose Treasury: A Beautiful Collection of Favorite Nursery Rhymes. Parragon Books & Cottage Door Press, eds. 2018. (Hardcover Storybook Treasury Ser.). (ENG.). 192p. (J). (gr. -1-2). 12.99 *(978-1-68052-461-1(5)*, 2000600, Parragon Books) Cottage Door Pr.

—Secrets of the Garden: Food Chains & the Food Web in Our Background. Zoehfeld, Kathleen Weidner. 2014. 40p. (J). (gr. k-3). 7.99 *(978-0-385-75364-7(0)*, Dragonfly Bks.) Random Hse. Children's Bks.

—Special Delivery! Stauffacher, Sue. 2010. (Animal Rescue Team Ser.: 2). 176p. (J). (gr. 3-7). 12.99 *(978-0-375-85848-2(2)*, Knopf Bks. for Young Readers) Random Hse. Children's Bks.

—Special Delivery! Animal Rescue Team. Stauffacher, Sue. 2011. (Animal Rescue Team Ser.: 2). 176p. (J). (gr. 3-7). 6.99 *(978-0-375-85132-2(1)*, Yearling) Random Hse. Children's Bks.

—Tom & Sofia Start School. Barkow, Henriette. 2004. (J). (BEN, ENG & MAL.). *(978-1-84444-573-8(9))*; (MAL & ENG.). 32p. pap. *(978-1-84444-587-5(9))*; (SPA & ENG.). 32p. pap. *(978-1-84444-586-8(0))*; (SOM & ENG.). 32p. pap. *(978-1-84444-585-1(2))*; (ENG & VIE.). 32p. pap. *(978-1-84444-584-4(4))*; (URD & ENG.). 32p. pap. *(978-1-84444-583-7(6))*; (ENG & TUR.). 32p. pap. *(978-1-84444-582-0(8))*; (TAM & ENG.). 32p. pap. *(978-1-84444-581-3(X))*; (ENG & TGL.). 32p. pap. *(978-1-84444-580-6(1))*; (ENG & RUS.). 32p. pap. *(978-1-84444-579-0(8))*; (ENG & POR.). 32p. pap. *(978-1-84444-577-6(1))*; (ENG & POL.). 32p. pap. *(978-1-84444-576-9(3))*; (ENG & PAN.). 32p. pap. *(978-1-84444-575-2(5))*; (ENG & KUR.). 32p. pap. *(978-1-84444-574-5(7))*; (ENG & JPN.). 32p. pap. *(978-1-84444-572-1(0))*; (ENG & ITA.). 32p. pap. *(978-1-84444-571-4(2))*; (ENG & HIN.). 32p. pap. *(978-1-84444-570-7(4))*; (ENG & GUJ.). 32p. pap. *(978-1-84444-569-1(0))*; (ENG & GRE.). 32p. pap. *(978-1-84444-568-4(2))*; (ENG & GER.). 32p. pap. *(978-1-84444-567-7(4))*; (FRE & ENG.). 32p. pap. *(978-1-84444-566-0(6))*; (ENG & PER.). 32p. pap. *(978-1-84444-565-3(8))*; (ENG & CHI.). 32p. pap. *(978-1-84444-564-6(X))*; (CHI & ENG.). 32p. pap. *(978-1-84444-563-9(1))*; (ENG & BEN.). 32p. pap. *(978-1-84444-562-2(3))*; (ENG & ARA.). 32p. pap. *(978-1-84444-561-5(5))*; (ENG & ALB.). 32p. pap. *(978-1-84444-560-8(7))* Mantra Lingua.

Lamontagne, Jayce. Chinook & Winter, 1 vol. Hunter, Rhonda. 2017. (ENG.). 40p. (J). (gr. 2-4). pap. 10.95 *(978-1-926506-01-2(4)*, 33c8a013-2ae3-492b-874e-3f5d42bd7279) Pemmican Pubns., Inc. CAN. Dist: Firefly Bks., Ltd.

Lamoreaux, M. A. The Princess & the Pea: The Graphic Novel, 1 vol. Andersen, Hans. 2009. (Graphic Spin Ser.). (ENG.). 40p. (J). (gr. 3-6). pap. 5.95 *(978-1-4342-1743-1(4)*, Stone Arch Bks.) Capstone.

Lamoreaux, M. A. & Lamoreaux, Michelle. The Legend of Johnny Appleseed. Stone Arch Books Staff. 2010. (Graphic Spin Ser.). (ENG.). 40p. (J). (gr. 3-6). pap. 5.95 *(978-1-4342-2266-4(7)*, Stone Arch Bks.) Capstone.

—The Princess & the Pea: The Graphic Novel, 1 vol. Andersen, Hans. 2009. (Graphic Spin Ser.). (ENG.). 40p. (J). (gr. 3-6). lib. bdg. 25.32 *(978-1-4342-1594-9(6)*, Stone Arch Bks.) Capstone.

Lamoreaux, Michelle. Are You Fur Real?, Bk. 4. Taddonio, Lea. 2018. (Camp Nowhere Ser.). (ENG.). 48p. (J). (gr. 3-7). lib. bdg. 29.93 *(978-1-5321-3261-2(1)*, 28477, Spellbound) Magic Wagon.

—Beauty & the Basement, 1 vol. Snowe, Olivia. 2014. (Twicetold Tales Ser.). (ENG.). 128p. (J). (gr. 3-6). 8.95 *(978-1-4342-9830-0(2)*, Stone Arch Bks.) Capstone.

—Book 1: Hair Today, Gone Tomorrow. Taddonio, Lea. 2018. (Camp Nowhere Ser.). (ENG.). 48p. (J). (gr. 3-7). lib. bdg. 29.93 *(978-1-5321-3258-2(1)*, 28471, Spellbound) Magic Wagon.

—Book 2: off on the Wrong Foot. Taddonio, Lea. 2018. (Camp Nowhere Ser.). (ENG.). 48p. (J). (gr. 3-7). lib. bdg. 29.93 *(978-1-5321-3259-9(X)*, 28473, Spellbound) Magic Wagon.

—Book 3: I'm Squatching You. Taddonio, Lea. 2018. (Camp Nowhere Ser.). (ENG.). 48p. (J). (gr. 3-7). lib. bdg. 29.93 *(978-1-5321-3260-5(3)*, 28475, Spellbound) Magic Wagon.

—Camp Nowhere (Set), 4 vols. Taddonio, Lea. 2018. (Camp Nowhere Ser.). 48p. (J). (gr. 3-7). lib. bdg. 114.00 *(978-1-5321-3257-5(3)*, 28469, Spellbound) Magic Wagon.

—Cassie & the Woolf, 1 vol. Snowe, Olivia. 2013. (Twicetold Tales Ser.). (ENG.). 128p. (J). (gr. 3-6). lib. bdg. 25.32 *(978-1-4342-3786-6(9)*, Stone Arch Bks.) Capstone.

—Dandelion & the Witch, 1 vol. Snowe, Olivia. 2014. (Twicetold Tales Ser.). (ENG.). 128p. (J). (gr. 3-6). 25.32 *(978-1-4342-9147-9(2)*, Stone Arch Bks.) Capstone.

—The Girl & the Seven Thieves, 1 vol. Snowe, Olivia. (Twicetold Tales Ser.). (ENG.). 128p. (J). (gr. 3-6). 2014. pap. 5.95 *(978-1-4342-9555-2(9))*; 2013. 8.95 *(978-1-4342-6280-6(4))*; 2013. lib. bdg. 25.32 *(978-1-4342-6018-5(6))* Capstone. (Stone Arch Bks.).

—The Glass Voice, 1 vol. Snowe, Olivia. 2014. (Twicetold Tales Ser.). (ENG.). 128p. (J). (gr. 3-6). 25.32 *(978-1-4342-9148-6(0)*, Stone Arch Bks.) Capstone.

—Hansen & Gracie, 1 vol. Snowe, Olivia. 2014. (Twicetold Tales Ser.). (ENG.). 128p. (J). (gr. 3-6). pap. 5.95 *(978-1-4342-9150-9(2)*, Stone Arch Bks.) Capstone.

—A Home in the Sky, 1 vol. Snowe, Olivia. (Twicetold Tales Ser.). (ENG.). 128p. (J). (gr. 3-6). 2014. pap. 5.95 *(978-1-4342-9554-5(0))*; 2013. 8.95 *(978-1-4342-6279-0(0))*; 2013. lib. bdg. 25.32 *(978-1-4342-5041-4(5))* Capstone. (Stone Arch Bks.).

—The Legend of Johnny Appleseed. Capstone Press Staff. 2010. (Graphic Spin Ser.). (ENG.). 40p. (J). (gr. 3-6). lib. bdg. 25.32 *(978-1-4342-1895-7(3)*, Stone Arch Bks.) Capstone.

—Made You Look: How Advertising Works & Why You Should Know. Graydon, Shari. 2nd rev. ed. 2013. (ENG.). 160p. (J). (gr. 6-12). 26.95 *(978-1-55451-561-5(0)*, 9781554515615); pap. 16.95 *(978-1-55451-560-8(2)*, 9781554515608) Annick Pr., Ltd. CAN. Dist: Publishers Group West (PGW).

—The Sealed-Up House, 1 vol. Snowe, Olivia. (Twicetold Tales Ser.). (ENG.). 128p. (J). (gr. 3-6). 2014. pap. 5.95 *(978-1-4342-9556-9(7))*; 2013. 8.95 *(978-1-4342-6281-3(2))*; 2013. lib. bdg. 25.32 *(978-1-4342-6019-2(4))* Capstone. (Stone Arch Bks.).

Lamoreaux, Michelle, jt. illus. see Lamoreaux, M. A.

L'amour, Sandrine. Mi Primera Biblia para Memorizar, 1 vol. Vium-Olesen, Jacob. 2019. (SPA.). 48p. (J). bds. 12.99 *(978-1-4041-1012-0(7))* Grupo Nelson.

Lamoureux, Hampton & Faul, Tara. Fire & Chaos: Book 3 of the Traveler's League. Soares, Sue, ed. 2019. (Traveler's League Ser.: Vol. 3). (ENG.). 198p. (J). pap. 9.99 *(978-1-7321815-6-4(X))* Goss, Nicholas.

Lampe, Kate. But What If There's No Chimney? Thompson, Emily Weisner & Hussey, Mandy. 2016. (ENG.). 24p. (J). (gr. 17). 12.00 *(978-0-253-02392-6(0)*, 978-0-253-02392-6) Indiana Univ. Pr.

Lamug, Ken. Ghastly Ghosts. Bateman, Teresa. 2019. (ENG.). 32p. (J). (gr. -1-3). 16.99 *(978-0-8075-2864-8(1)*, 807528641) Whitman, Albert & Co.

Lanan, Jessica. Finding Narnia: The Story of C. S. Lewis & His Brother Warnie. McAlister, Caroline. 2019. (ENG.). 48p. (J). 19.99 *(978-1-62672-658-1(2)*, 900165434) Roaring Brook Pr.

—Good Fortune in a Wrapping Cloth. Schoettler, Joan. 2011. (ENG.). (J). 17.95 *(978-1-885008-40-4(6)*, Shen's Bks.) Lee & Low Bks., Inc.

—Just Right: Searching for the Goldilocks Planet. Manley, Curtis. 2019. (ENG.). 48p. (J). 18.99 *(978-1-250-15533-7(9)*, 900184622) Roaring Brook Pr.

LANAN, Jessica. A Kid of Their Own. Lambert, Megan Dowd. 2020. 32p. (J). (gr. -1-3). lib. bdg. 16.99 *(978-1-58089-879-9(3))* Charlesbridge Publishing, Inc.

Lanan, Jessica. Out of School & into Nature: The Story of Anna Comstock. Slade, Suzanne. 2017. (ENG.). 32p. (J). (gr. 1-4). 16.99 *(978-1-58536-986-7(1)*, 204225) Sleeping Bear Pr.

—The Story I'll Tell, 1 vol. Ling, Nancy Tupper. 2015. (ENG.). 32p. (J). (gr. 3-3). 17.95 *(978-1-62014-160-1(4))* Lee & Low Bks., Inc.

Lanan, Jessica. The Fisherman & the Whale. Lanan, Jessica. 2019. (ENG.). 48p. (J). (gr. -1-3). 17.99 *(978-1-5344-1574-4(2),* Simon & Schuster Bks. For Young Readers) Simon & Schuster Bks. For Young Readers.

Lanas, Mattias. ResQ & the Baby Orangutan. Pell, Eva. 2019. (ResQ: Saving One Animal at a Time Ser.). (ENG.). 160p. (J). (gr. 3-6). pap. 13.95 *(978-1-943431-48-9(5))* Tumblehome Learning.

Lancaster, Derek. Cock-a-Doodle-Doo, I Love You. Wixom, Jason Kay & Wixom, Tedi Tuttle. 2nd ed. 2003. (Ralph Rooster Ser.: Vol. 1). 16p. (J). (gr. -1-2). 6.95 *(978-1-885227-05-8(1))* TNT Bks.

Lancett, James. Drawing Lab: Superheroes. 2018. (ENG.). 128p. (J). pap. 12.99 *(978-1-78888-159-3(1),* 0de8b883-5a8d-4dd7-8715-87721416c6f0) Arcturus Publishing GBR. Dist: Baker & Taylor Publisher Services (BTPS).

Land Eagle. The Storyteller. Packard, Mary. 2009. 196p. (J). *(978-1-4351-1557-6(0))* Metro Bks.

Land, Greg. Hulk: Return to Planet Hulk. 2018. (Totally Awesome Hulk (2016) Ser.: 5). (ENG.). 136p. (J). (gr. 4-17). pap. 15.99 *(978-1-302-90996-3(7))* Marvel Worldwide, Inc.

Land, Greg, et al. Sojourn, Vol. 4. Marz, Ron. 2003. (Sojourn Ser.: Vol. 4). 160p. (YA). pap. 15.95 *(978-1-931484-91-6(0))* CrossGeneration Comics, Inc.

—Sojourn: The Sorcerer's Tale, Vol. 5. Edginton, Ian. 2004. (Sojourn Ser.). 160p. (YA). pap. 15.95 *(978-1-59314-038-0(X))* CrossGeneration Comics, Inc.

Land, Greg. Symbiote Spider-Man. 2019. (ENG.). 144p. (YA). (gr. 4-17). pap. 15.99 *(978-1-302-91904-7(0))* Marvel Worldwide, Inc.

Land, Greg. Symbiote Spider-Man: Alien Reality. 2020. (ENG.). 120p. (J). (gr. 4-17). pap. 15.99 ***(978-1-302-92145-3(2))*** Marvel Worldwide, Inc.

Land, Greg, et al. Uncanny X-Men by Kieron Gillen: the Complete Collection Vol. 2. 2020. (ENG.). 496p. (YA). (gr. 8-17). pap. 39.99 *(978-1-302-92277-1(7))* Marvel Worldwide, Inc.

—The Warrior's Tale, Vol. 3. Marz, Ron. (Sojourn Traveler Ser.: Vol. 3). 160p. (YA). 2004. pap. 9.95 *(978-1-59314-043-4(6));* 2003. (gr. 7-18). pap. 15.95 *(978-1-931484-65-7(1))* CrossGeneration Comics, Inc.

Land, Greg. Weapons of Mutant Destruction. 2017. (ENG.). 144p. (YA). (gr. 8-17). pap. 17.99 *(978-1-302-91085-3(X))* Marvel Worldwide, Inc.

Land, Greg & Jay, Leisten. From the Ashes. Marz, Ron. 2003. (Sojourn Traveler Ser.: Vol. 1). 192p. (YA). (gr. 7-18). pap. 9.95 *(978-1-59314-013-7(4))* CrossGeneration Comics, Inc.

Land, Greg, jt. illus. see Asrar, Mahmud.

Land, Matthew. The Dragon Stoorworm, 37 vols. Breslin, Theresa. 2014. (Traditional Scottish Tales Ser.). (ENG.). 24p. (J). pap. 11.95 *(978-1-78250-117-6(7),* Kelpies) Floris Bks. GBR. Dist: Consortium Bk. Sales & Distribution.

—The 12 Days O Yule, 76 vols. Rennie, Susan. 2015. (Traditional Scottish Tales Ser.). (ENG.). 32p. (J). 11.95 *(978-1-78250-208-1(4),* Kelpies) Floris Bks. GBR. Dist: Consortium Bk. Sales & Distribution.

Landa, Dan. Max & the Meanies. Landa, Liz. 2019. (ENG.). 36p. (J). (gr. 4-6). pap. 15.00 ***(978-1-60571-472-1(0),*** Shires Press) Northshire Pr.

Landau, Donna. Round & Round the Garden, Finger Games in English & Spanish. MansBach, Sara. Arroyave, Heidy, tr. 2007. 42p. spiral bd. *(978-0-9785477-2-1(1))* BladeRunner Publishing.

Landau, Elaine. Tyrannosaurus Rex. Landau, Elaine. rev. ed. 2007. (True Bks.). (ENG.). 48p. (J). (gr. 3-5). pap. 6.95 *(978-0-531-15472-4(6),* Children's Pr.) Scholastic Library Publishing.

—Velociraptor. Landau, Elaine. rev. ed. 2007. (True Bks.). (ENG.). 48p. (J). (gr. 3-5). pap. 6.95 *(978-0-531-15473-1(4),* Children's Pr.) Scholastic Library Publishing.

—Your Pet Cat. Landau, Elaine. rev. ed. 2007. (True Bks.). (ENG.). 48p. (J). (gr. 3-5). pap. 6.95 *(978-0-531-15464-9(5),* Children's Pr.) Scholastic Library Publishing.

Landau, Helena Von & Meister, Charles. Our Little Frankish Cousin of Long Ago. Stein, Evaleen. 2007. 92p. per. 8.95 *(978-1-59915-244-8(4))* Yesterday's Classics.

Landau, Natasha. Misha Loves to Sing. 2004. (J). *(978-0-615-12595-4(6))* Tikva Corp.

Landazábal, Andrés F. The Fabulous World That God Made, Vol. Ellis, Joyce K. 2019. (ENG.). 32p. (J). (gr. k-3). 17.99 *(978-1-5064-4857-2(7),* Beaming Books) Augsburg Fortress, Pubs.

Landels, Angela. The First Dog to Be Somebody's Best Friend: A Likely Story in Two Bits & a Decide. Stacey, Tom. 2007. (ENG.). 46p. 15.95 *(978-1-905299-34-8(6),* Stacey International) Stacey Publishing GBR. Dist: Casemate Pubs. & Bk. Distributors, LLC.

Landers, Ace & White, Dave. Drag Race! 2009. (Scholastic Reader Ser.). 32p. (J). *(978-0-545-11039-6(4))* Scholastic, Inc.

Landers, Jeri. The Journey of Bushky Bushybottom. Landers, Jeri. 2008. 40p. (J). 21.00 *(978-0-9765303-1-2(7))* Ocher Moon Pr.

Landes, William-Alan, photos by. Assignments in Musical Theatre: Acting & Directing. Landes, William-Alan, ed. Wheeler, Jacque & Laughlin, Haller. unabr. ed. 2003. (Musical Theatre Ser.). 192p. (Orig.). (YA). (gr. 8-12). pap. 28.00 *(978-0-88734-676-7(6))* Players Pr., Inc.

Landgraf, Ken, et al. Marvel Masterworks: Thor Vol. 19. 2020. (ENG.). 288p. (YA). (gr. 4-17). 75.00 *(978-1-302-92234-4(3))* Marvel Worldwide, Inc.

Landgraf, Kenneth. Robinson Crusoe: With a Discussion of Resourcefulness. Dafoe, Daniel. 2003. (Values in Action Illustrated Classics Ser.). 190p. (J). *(978-1-59203-035-4(1))* Learning Challenge, Inc.

Landinez, Jairo Linares. El Globito Azul. Arrieta, Luisa Noguera. 2003. (Coleccion OA Infantil Ser.). (SPA.). 69p. (J). (gr. -1-7). pap. *(978-958-30-0878-8(8))* Panamericana Editorial.

—Un Pescado en la Olla! Silva, Luna. 2003. (Primer Acto: Teatro Infantil y Juvenil Ser.). (SPA.). 54p. (J). (gr. -1-7). pap. *(978-958-30-0996-9(2))* Panamericana Editorial.

Landini, Stefano. The Punisher: War Machine Vol. 2. 2018. (Punisher: War Machine (2017) Ser.: 2). (ENG.). 136p. (gr. 10-17). pap. 15.99 *(978-1-302-91073-0(6))* Marvel Worldwide, Inc.

Landmann, Bimba. Clare & Francis. Visconti, Guido. 2004. 40p. 20.00 *(978-0-8028-5269-4(6))* Eerdmans, William B. Publishing Co.

—The Genius of Leonardo. (J). 12.99 *(978-1-84148-482-2(2))* Barefoot Bks., Inc.

—Genius of Leonardo. Visconti, Guido. 2016. (ENG.). 40p. (J). (gr. 1-5). pap. 10.99 *(978-1-78285-277-3(8))* Barefoot Bks., Inc.

—Grandfather Whisker's Table. Jo, Eun-jeong. 2017. (J). 10.00 *(978-0-8028-5474-2(5),* Eerdmans Bks For Young Readers) Eerdmans, William B. Publishing Co.

—In Search of the Little Prince: The Story of Antoine de Saint-Exupéry. 2014. (ENG.). 34p. (J). 17.00 *(978-0-8028-5435-3(4),* Eerdmans Bks For Young Readers) Eerdmans, William B. Publishing Co.

Landmann, Bimba. I Am Marc Chagall. Landmann, Bimba. 2006. (Eerdmans Books for Young Readers). 34p. (J). (gr. 2). 18.00 *(978-0-8028-5305-9(6),* Eerdmans Bks For Young Readers) Eerdmans, William B. Publishing Co.

Landolt, Gredna. Carolina's Gift: A Story of Peru. Diaz, Katacha. (ENG.). 32p. (J). (gr. k-3). 2005. 8.95 *(978-1-56899-699-8(3),* SC8005); 2003. 15.95 *(978-1-56899-695-0(0),* B8005) Soundprints.

Landreau, Sarah. When Father Sun Moved to the Sky. Orsinger-Olson, Ann Kathryn. 2017. (ENG.). (J). 15.99 *(978-0-9994330-2-7(4))* Lemonade Bks.

Landry, Brittani. Help, I'm Being Bullied! Johnson, Stephanie S. 2018. (Adventures of Jeremy Jackson, Wisdom Seeker Ser.: Vol. 1). (ENG.). 32p. (J). (gr. k-6). pap. 11.99 *(978-1-940461-77-9(4))* Bayou Publishing.

Landry, Douglas. Maggie Mae Moose. Maxfield, Deanna. 2011. 28p. (J). pap. 8.95 *(978-0-9743407-0-8(7))* ASMedia Publishing.

Landry, Leo. Emily's Magic Words: Please, Thank You, & More. Post, Peggy & Senning, Cindy P. 2007. (ENG.). 32p. (J). (gr. -1-1). 15.99 *(978-0-06-111680-3(7),* Collins) HarperCollins Pubs.

—Let's Sign, Baby! A Fun & Easy Way to Talk with Baby. Ault, Kelly. abr. ed. 2010. (ENG.). 40p. (J). (gr. k — 1). bds. 9.99 *(978-0-547-31596-6(1),* 1415353) Houghton Mifflin Harcourt Publishing Co.

Landry, Leo. Grin & Bear It. Landry, Leo. 48p. (J). (gr. k-3). 2014. pap. 5.95 *(978-1-57091-746-2(9));* 2011. 12.95 *(978-1-57091-745-5(0))* Charlesbridge Publishing, Inc.

—Home Run, Touchdown, Basket, Goal! Sports Poems for Little Athletes. Landry, Leo. 2019. (ENG.). 32p. (J). 17.99 *(978-1-62779-349-0(6),* 900147060, Holt, Henry & Co. Bks. For Young Readers) Holt, Henry & Co.

Landry, Noemie Gionet. AbbeyLoo & Gus the Talking Toad. Cortez, Tammy. 2015. (ENG.). 32p. (J). pap. 9.95 *(978-1-943274-38-3(X),* 9781943274383) Waldorf Publishing.

Landry, Noémie Gionet. Making It Happen. Arrow, Emily. 2019. (My Feelings, My Choices Ser.). (ENG.). 24p. (J). (gr. -1-2). pap. 7.95 *(978-1-68410-432-1(7),* 141227) Cantata Learning.

Lands, Meghan. Move It, Miss Macintosh! Janousky, Peggy Robbins. 2016. (ENG.). 32p. (J). (gr. -1-2). 9.95 *(978-1-55451-862-3(8))* Annick Pr., Ltd. CAN. Dist: Publishers Group West (PGW).

—Wannabe Farms. McCann, Brian. 2020. (ENG.). 168p. (J). (gr. 3-7). 18.99 *(978-1-5247-9300-5(0),* Penguin Workshop) Penguin Young Readers Group.

Landsberg, Bryan. Rosie the Riveter: A Cultural Icon. Shoup, Kate. 2018. (American Legends & Folktales Ser.). 32p. (gr. 3-3). lib. bdg. 28.50 *(978-1-5026-3693-5(X))* Cavendish Square Publishing LLC.

Landseer, Sir Edwin. Landseer's Dogs & Their Stories (Illustrated Edition) Tytler, Sarah. 2016. (ENG.). (J). pap. *(978-1-4068-8144-8(9))* Echo Library.

Landstrom, Olaf. Benito y el Chupon. Lindgren, Barbro. rev. ed. 2006. (Castillo de la Lectura Preschool Ser.). (ENG.). 40p. (J). (gr. -1-k). pap. 6.95 *(978-970-20-0847-7(6))* Castillo, Ediciones, S. A. de C. V. MEX. Dist: Macmillan.

Landstrom, Olof. Benny's Had Enough! Lindgren, Barbro. Dyssegaard, Elisabeth Kallick, tr. from SWE. 2005. 28p. (J). (gr. -1-1). reprint ed. 6.95 *(978-91-29-66338-9(5))* R & S Bks. SWE. Dist: Macmillan.

—Boris's Glasses. Cohen, Peter. Sandin, Joan, tr. from SWE. 2003. 28p. (J). (gr. k-3). 15.00 *(978-91-29-65942-9(6))* R & S Bks. SWE. Dist: Macmillan.

—Four Hens & a Rooster. Landstrom, Lena. Sandin, Joan, tr. from SWE. 2005. 28p. (J). (gr. -1-3). 16.00 *(978-91-29-66336-5(9))* R & S Bks. SWE. Dist: Macmillan.

—Oink, Oink Benny. Lindgren, Barbro & Lindgren, B. L. Dyssegaard, Elisabeth Kallick, tr. from SWE. 2008. 28p. (J). (gr. -1-1). 16.00 *(978-91-29-66855-1(7))* R & S Bks. SWE. Dist: Macmillan.

—Wallace's Lists. Bottner, Barbara & Kruglik, Gerald. 2004. (ENG.). 40p. (J). (gr. -1-2). 16.99 *(978-0-06-000224-4(7),* Tegen, Katherine Bks) HarperCollins Pubs.

—Wallace's Lists. Bottner, Barbara & Kruglik, Gerald. 2011. (J). (gr. 1-3). 29.95 *(978-0-545-04275-8(5))* Weston Woods Studios, Inc.

Landy, Ariel. The Spacesuit: How a Seamstress Helped Put Man on the Moon. Donald, Alison. 2019. (ENG.). 36p. (J). (gr. -1-3). 17.99 *(978-1-84886-415-3(9))* Maverick Arts Publishing GBR. Dist: Lerner Publishing Group.

—This Is the Church. Cunningham, Sarah Raymond. 2020. (ENG.). 32p. (J). (gr. -1-3). 17.99 *(978-1-5064-4532-8(2),* Beaming Books) Augsburg Fortress, Pubs.

Lane, Adam J. B. Odd Gods. Slavin, David & Weitzman, Daniel. 2019. (Odd Gods Ser.: 1). (ENG.). 224p. (J). (gr. 3-7). 13.99 *(978-0-06-283953-4(5),* HarperCollins) HarperCollins Pubs. Ltd. GBR. Dist: HarperCollins Pubs.

—Odd Gods: the Oddyssey. Slavin, David. 2020. (Odd Gods Ser.: 2). (ENG.). 224p. (J). (gr. 3-7). 13.99 *(978-0-06-283955-8(1),* HarperCollins) HarperCollins Pubs. Ltd. GBR. Dist: HarperCollins Pubs.

Lane, Cannon. A Tale of Tails: A Grand Animal Anthology. Seidel, Charleen. 2020. (ENG.). 24p. (J). pap. 12.99 ***(978-1-947773-72-1(0),*** Yawn Publishing LLC) Yawn's Bks. & More, Inc.

Lane, Charly. All about Me. Make Believe Ideas Ltd. 2019. (ENG.). 48p. (J). (gr. -1-7). spiral bd. *(978-1-78947-076-5(5))* Make Believe Ideas.

—I Love You, Little One. Make Believe Ideas Ltd. 2019. (ENG.). 26p. (J). bds. *(978-1-78947-176-2(1))* Make Believe Ideas.

—Mini Board Book Stack: Spring. Make Believe Ideas Ltd. 2019. (Seasonal Stack Ser.). (ENG.). 36p. (J). bds. *(978-1-78843-533-8(8))* Make Believe Ideas.

—My Year in Kindergarten. Make Believe Ideas Ltd. 2019. (ENG.). 48p. (J). spiral bd. *(978-1-78947-075-8(7))* Make Believe Ideas.

Lane, Charly. Super Cute. Make Believe Ideas Ltd. 2020. (ENG.). 86p. (J). (gr. -1-7). ***(978-1-78947-394-0(2))*** Make Believe Ideas.

Lane, Cody R. Frantic the Frog. Johnson, Cindy B. 2004. 27p. pap. 24.95 *(978-1-4137-2954-2(1))* America Star Bks.

Lane, Dakota. Gothic Lolita: A Mystical Thriller. Lane, Dakota. 2008. (ENG.). 208p. (YA). (gr. 7-18). 17.99 *(978-1-4169-1396-2(3),* Atheneum Bks. for Young Readers) Simon & Schuster Children's Publishing.

Lane, Janelda. The Boy Who Dreamed Big. Carter, Alton. 2018. (ENG.). 32p. (J). (gr. k-6). pap. 14.99 *(978-1-7321189-6-6(5))* Monocle Pr.

—The Boy Who Went to the Library. Carter, Alton. 2018. (ENG.). 32p. (J). pap. 14.99 *(978-1-7321189-7-3(3))* Monocle Pr.

Lane, Kim. The Complete Book of the Microscope. Rogers, Kirsteen. Dowswell, Paul, ed. rev. ed. 2005. (Complete Bks.). 96p. (J). pap. 14.99 *(978-0-7945-1558-4(4),* Usborne) EDC Publishing.

—Pasta & Pizza: For Beginners. Allman, Howard, photos by. Watt, Fiona. rev. ed. 2004. (Cooking School Ser.). 48p. (J). (gr. 5). lib. bdg. 15.95 *(978-1-58086-567-8(4))* EDC Publishing.

—What Shall I Grow? Allman, Howard, photos by. Gibson, Ray. Watt, Fiona, ed. 2006. (What Shall I Do Today? Ser.). 32p. (J). (gr. 2). lib. bdg. 15.95 *(978-1-58086-548-7(8))* EDC Publishing.

Lane, Lily. Sunny Day Point N Match: Hardcover Board Book. Winget, Rosie. 2015. (Look Look Baby Ser.). (ENG.). 14p. (J). (gr. -1-k). bds. 8.99 *(978-1-68052-012-5(1),* 1000130) Cottage Door Pr.

Lane, Nancy. Call the Horse Lucky. Havill, Juanita. 2010. (ENG.). 24p. (J). (gr. k-3). 16.95 *(978-0-940719-10-1(X))* Gryphon Pr., The.

—Cookie's Fortune. Graham-Barber, Lynda. 2017. (ENG.). 24p. (J). (gr. -1-2). 17.95 *(978-0-940719-39-2(8))* Gryphon Pr., The.

—Finding Chance. Benson, Linda. 2006. 112p. (J). *(978-1-59336-696-4(5))* Mondo Publishing.

—KokoCat, Inside & Out. Graham-Barber, Lynda. 2012. (ENG.). 24p. (J). (gr. k). 16.95 *(978-0-940719-12-5(6))* Gryphon Pr., The.

Lane, Queen. It's Christmas Time (Babytown Storybook) Lane, Queen, creator. 2005. (BABYTOWN Ser.: Bk. 4). 36p. (J). spiral bd. 15.00 *(978-0-9772738-1-2(4))* Quebla.

Lane, Queen & Boykin, Brian. No No Baby (Babytown Storybook) 2005. (BABYTOWN Ser.: Bk. 1). 30p. (J). spiral bd. 15.00 *(978-0-9772738-0-5(6))* Quebla.

Lane, Ranae. Follow God. Comley, Kathryn. 2004. (J). bds. 9.99 *(978-1-4183-0009-8(8))* Christ Inspired, Inc.

—Know & Remember all These Things. Comley, Kathryn. 2004. (J). bds. *(978-1-4183-0011-1(X))* Christ Inspired, Inc.

—That's How I Found God. Comley, Kathryn. 2004. (J). bds. 9.99 *(978-1-4183-0014-2(4))* Christ Inspired, Inc.

Lang, Allison. Ashie: Lost in the Hurricane. Cohen, Pamela June. 2008. 40p. pap. 24.95 *(978-1-60474-961-8(X))* America Star Bks.

Láng, Anna. Good Morning Yoga: Relaxing Poses for Children. Pajalunga, Lorena Valentina. 2018. (ENG.). 40p. (J). (gr. -1). 14.95 *(978-88-544-1295-8(3))* White Star ITA. Dist: Sterling Publishing Co., Inc.

Láng, Anna. The Great Book of Dinosaurs. Magrin, Federica. 2020. (Great Book Of... Ser.: 1). (ENG.). 64p. (J). (gr. 2). 19.95 ***(978-1-4549-4111-8(1))*** Sterling Publishing Co., Inc.

—The Great Book of Dragons. Magrin, Federica. 2020. (Great Book Of... Ser.: 2). (ENG.). 64p. (J). (gr. 2). 19.95 ***(978-1-4549-4112-5(X))*** Sterling Publishing Co., Inc.

—The Great Book of Fantastic Creatures. D'Anna, Giuseppe. 2020. (Great Book Of... Ser.: 3). (ENG.). 64p. (J). (gr. 2). 19.95 ***(978-1-4549-4113-2(8))*** Sterling Publishing Co., Inc.

—The Great Book of Monsters of the Deep. D'Anna, Giuseppe. 2020. (Great Book Of... Ser.: 4). (ENG.). 64p. (J). (gr. 2). 19.95 ***(978-1-4549-4114-9(6))*** Sterling Publishing Co., Inc.

Láng, Anna. My Favorite Prayers. 2020. (ENG.). 40p. (J). (gr. 1). 14.95 *(978-88-544-1669-7(X))* White Star ITA. Dist: Sterling Publishing Co., Inc.

Lang, Annie. Guess What I Heard Today. Lang, Annie. 2019. (ENG.). 40p. (J). pap. 9.50 *(978-1-0994-5808-8(0))* Independently Published.

Lang, Carole. The Adventures of Willy & Billy Bk. 1: The Lake Lure Chronicles - Book 1. Klett, David. l.t. ed. 2006. 32p. (J). lib. bdg. 17.95 *(978-0-9779325-0-4(8))* Five Oaks Pr.

Lang, Cecily. Una Cesta de Cumpleanos para Tia Abuela. Mora, Pat. (SPA.). (J). (gr. k-2). pap. 3.16 net. *(978-0-395-78817-2(X),* HMS088) Houghton Mifflin Harcourt Publishing Co.

Lang, Gary. The Glass Heart. Killion, Kathleen. 2005. 19.95 *(978-0-9723067-2-0(2))* Imagine That Enterprises.

Lang, Glenna. My Shadow. Stevenson, Robert Louis. 2019. (ENG.). 32p. (gr. 1-18). 17.95 *(978-0-87923-788-2(0))* Godine, David R. Pub.

Lang, Glenna. Looking Out for Sarah. Lang, Glenna. 2003. 32p. (J). (gr. -1-3). pap. 7.95 *(978-1-57091-607-6(1))* Charlesbridge Publishing, Inc.

Lang, Mark. Capturing Joy: The Story of Maud Lewis. Bogart, Jo Ellen. 2011. 32p. (J). (gr. 3-7). pap. 8.95 *(978-1-77049-262-2(3),* Tundra Bks.) Tundra Bks. CAN. Dist: Penguin Random Hse. LLC.

—Tales of Court & Castle. Bodger, Joan. 2003. (ENG.). 96p. (J). (gr. 3-7). pap. 9.95 *(978-0-88776-614-5(5),* Tundra Bks.) Tundra Bks. CAN. Dist: Penguin Random Hse. LLC.

Lang, Max. Grumpy Monkey. Lang, Suzanne. (Grumpy Monkey Ser.). (ENG.). 32p. (J). 2019. (— 1). bds. 8.99 *(978-0-593-12399-7(9));* 2018. (gr. -1-2). 17.99 *(978-0-553-53786-4(5));* 2018. (gr. -1-2). 20.99 *(978-0-553-53787-1(3))* Random Hse. Children's Bks. (Random Hse. Bks. for Young Readers).

—Grumpy Monkey Party Time! Lang, Suzanne. 2019. (Grumpy Monkey Ser.). (ENG.). 44p. (J). (gr. -1-2). 17.99 *(978-0-593-11862-7(6));* lib. bdg. 20.00 *(978-0-593-11863-4(4))* Random Hse. Children's Bks. (Random Hse. Bks. for Young Readers).

—Hooray for Kids! Lang, Suzanne. 2016. 40p. (J). (gr. -1-2). 17.99 *(978-0-553-53783-3(0),* Random Hse. Bks. for Young Readers) Random Hse. Children's Bks.

Langan, Bob. Destiny, Valor & a Lizard Named Louie. Ambrosio, Michael. 2004. 128p. pap. 5.95 *(978-0-9716085-3-5(9))* LionX Publishing.

Langcaon, Jeff. My Grandpa's Battleship Missouri Tour. 2007. (J). 14.95 *(978-1-56647-831-1(6))* Mutual Publishing LLC.

Langdo, Bryan. Cat & Dog. Minarik, Else Holmelund. 2005. (My First I Can Read Ser.). (ENG.). 32p. (J). (gr. -1 — 1). 16.99 *(978-0-06-074247-8(X))* HarperCollins Pubs.

—Do You Sing Twinkle? A Story about Remarriage & New Family. Levins, Sandra. 2009. 32p. (J). (gr. -1-3). 14.95 *(978-1-4338-0539-4(1));* pap. 9.95 *(978-1-4338-0551-6(0))* American Psychological Assn. (Magination Pr.).

—The Gift: The Life & Times of Birdie Mae Hayes #1. Agee, Jeri Anne. 2018. (Life & Times of Birdie Mae Hayes Ser.: 1). (ENG.). 112p. (J). (gr. 2-5). 13.99 *(978-1-5107-2453-2(2),* Sky Pony Pr.) Skyhorse Publishing Co., Inc.

—The Gift: The Life & Times of Birdie Mae Hayes #1. Agee, Jeri Anne. 2018. (Life & Times of Birdie Mae Hayes Ser.: 1). (ENG.). 112p. (J). (gr. 2-5). pap. 4.99 *(978-1-5107-2454-9(0),* Sky Pony Pr.) Skyhorse Publishing Co., Inc.

—Henry the Cat: The Life & Times of Birdie Mae Hayes #2. Agee, Jeri Anne. 2018. (Life & Times of Birdie Mae Hayes Ser.: 2). (ENG.). 104p. (J). (gr. 2-5). pap. 4.99 *(978-1-5107-2456-3(7),* Sky Pony Pr.) Skyhorse Publishing Co., Inc.

—Henry the Cat: The Life & Times of Birdie Mae Hayes #2. Agee, Jeri Anne. 2018. (Life & Times of Birdie Mae Hayes Ser.: 2). (ENG.). 104p. (J). (gr. 2-5). 13.99 *(978-1-5107-2455-6(9),* Sky Pony Pr.) Skyhorse Publishing Co., Inc.

—Hero Dad, 0 vols. Hardin, Melinda. 2010. (ENG.). 24p. (J). (gr. -1-3). 12.99 *(978-0-7614-5713-8(5),* 9780761457138, Two Lions) Amazon Publishing.

—Hero Mom, 0 vols. Hardin, Melinda. 2013. 24p. (ENG.). (J). (gr. -1-3). 12.99 *(978-1-4778-1645-5(3),* 9781477816455, Two Lions); pap. 12.99 *(978-1-4778-6645-0(0))* Amazon Publishing.

—King Calm: Mindful Gorilla in the City. Miles, Brenda & Sweet, Susan D. 2016. 32p. (J). *(978-1-4338-2272-8(5),* Magination Pr.) American Psychological Assn.

Langdo, Bryan. Latkes for Santa Claus. Emaus, Janie. 2020. 40p. (J). (gr. -1-1). 16.99 ***(978-1-5107-5988-6(3),*** Sky Pony Pr.) Skyhorse Publishing Co., Inc.

Langdo, Bryan. The Leaf That Wouldn't Leave. Trinco, Trish. 2008. (ENG.). 32p. (J). 16.95 *(978-0-931674-90-7(5),* Waldman House Pr.) TRISTAN Publishing, Inc.

—The Miracle of Easter. Malone, Jean M. 2010. (Penguin Young Readers, Level 3 Ser.). (ENG.). 48p. (J). (gr. 1-3). 4.99 *(978-0-448-45265-4(0),* Penguin Young Readers) Penguin Young Readers Group.

—Mr. Tanner. Chapin, Harry. 2017. (ENG.). 40p. (J). (gr. k-2). 17.99 *(978-0-9913866-8-0(X))* Ripple Grove Pr.

—Mummy Math: An Adventure in Geometry. Neuschwander, Cindy. 2009. (Matt & Bibi Math Adventures Ser.). (ENG.). 32p. (J). (gr. 2-5). pap. 8.99 *(978-0-312-56117-8(2),* 900058847) Square Fish.

—No Room at the Inn: The Nativity Story. Malone, Jean M. 2009. (All Aboard Reading: Station Stop 2 Ser.). 48p. (J). (gr. 1-3). 16.19 *(978-0-448-45217-3(0))* Penguin Young Readers Group.

—Pastry School in Paris: An Adventure in Capacity. Neuschwander, Cindy. 2009. (Matt & Bibi Math Adventures Ser.). (ENG.). 32p. (J). (gr. 2-6). 18.99 *(978-0-8050-8314-9(6),* 900044295, Holt, Henry & Co. Bks. For Young Readers) Holt, Henry & Co.

—Salad Pie. BooydeGraaff, Wendy. 2016. (ENG.). 44p. (J). (gr. k-7). 17.99 *(978-0-9913866-4-2(7))* Ripple Grove Pr.

—Sometimes I'm Scared. Annunziata, Jane & Nemiroff, Marc. 2009. 32p. pap. 9.95 *(978-1-4338-0550-9(2));* (J). (gr. -1-3). 14.95 *(978-1-4338-0449-6(2))* American Psychological Assn. (Magination Pr.).

—There's a Cat in Our Class! A Tale about Getting Along. Ransom, Jeanie Franz. 2016. 32p. (J). *(978-1-4338-2262-9(8),* Magination Pr.) American Psychological Assn.

—Was It the Chocolate Pudding? A Story for Little Kids about Divorce. Levins, Sandra. 2005. 40p. (J). 14.95 *(978-1-59147-308-4(X));* (gr. -1-3). per. 9.95 *(978-1-59147-309-1(8))* American Psychological Assn. (Magination Pr.).

Langdo, Bryan. Tornado Slim & the Magic Cowboy Hat. Langdo, Bryan. 2019. (ENG.). 32p. (J). (gr. k-4). pap. 9.99 *(978-1-5420-1543-1(X),* 9781542015431, Two Lions) Amazon Publishing.

Langdo, Bryan, jt. illus. see Hirschmann, Kris.

Lange, Astrid. Alte Meister Neu Entdecken: Eine Spurensuche in der Gemaldegalerie Alte Meister und der Skulpturensammlung Bis 1800. Blei-Hoch, Claudia. 2020. (GER.). 64p. (J). 15.95 ***(978-3-95498-523-4(3))*** Sandstein Kommunikation GmbH DEU. Dist: ISD.

L

Lange, Francois. The Itty-Bitty Icky Committee/Heroes of the Heart. Lindsay, Debbie. 2013. (ENG.). 80p. pap. 27.97 (978-1-4525-7329-8(8), Balboa Pr.) Author Solutions, Inc.

Langelier-Lebeda, Suzanne. Green Golly & Her Golden Flute. Torgan, Keith & Siesel, Barbara. 2013. 58p. pap. 19.99 (978-1-936172-61-0(5)) Elfrig Publishing.

Langfield, Kym. Solo Dan. Raffa-Mulligan, Teena. 2020. (ENG.). 32p. (J). (gr. k-3). **(978-0-6486998-8-0(9))**; pap. **(978-0-6486998-9-7(7))** Daisy Lane Publishing.

Langford, Alton. Seagull by the Shore: The Story of a Herring Gull. Birch, Vanessa Giancamilli. (Smithsonian Oceanic Collection Ser.). (ENG.). (J). (gr. -1-3). 2011. 31p. pap. 4.95 (978-1-60727-540-4(6)); 2010. 32p. 16.95 (978-1-60727-089-8(7)); 2010. 32p. pap. 6.95 (978-1-60727-090-4(0)) Soundprints.

Langille, Elaine. Down in the Tropics. Hann, Harry Henry & Johnson, Nancy. 2013. 48p. pap. 14.99 (978-0-9891323-0-5(7)) Goin' Native, Inc.

Langley, Bats. Alice's Adventures In #Wonderland. Carroll, Lewis. Farthing, Penny, ed. 2018. (ENG.). 152p. (J). (gr. 5-9). 18.95 (978-1-949116-10-6(7)) Woodhall Pr.

—Groggle's Monster Valentine. Murray, Diana. 2017. (ENG.). 32p. (J). (gr. -1-k). 9.99 (978-1-5107-0508-1(2), Sky Pony Pr.) Skyhorse Publishing Co., Inc.

Langley, Bill & Dias, Ron. 101 Dalmatians (Disney 101 Dalmatians) Korman, Justine. 2007. (Little Golden Book Ser.). (ENG.). 24p. (J). (gr. -1-2). 4.99 (978-0-7364-2420-2(2), Golden/Disney) Random Hse. Children's Bks.

Langley, Bill, jt. illus. see Wakeman, Bill.

Langley, Gene. The Return of the Alaskan: Mailboat in the Outpost. Herron, Edward A. 2011. 190p. 42.95 (978-1-258-09093-7(7)) Literary Licensing, LLC.

Langley, Jonathan. Farmyard Read & Play Set, 3 vols. Rosen, Michael. 2008. (ENG.). 96p. (J). (gr. -1-k). bds. 19.95 (978-0-00-725969-4(7)) HarperCollins Pubs. Ltd. GBR. Dist: Independent Pubs. Group.

—Ronquidos! Rosen, Michael.Tr. of Snore!. (SPA.). (J). (gr. 1-3). (978-958-04-4646-0(6)) Norma S.A.

Langlois, Florence. The Extraordinary Gift. Langlois, Florence. Goodman, John, tr. from FRE. 2005. 48p. (J). (gr. -1-2). reprint ed. 15.00 (978-0-7567-8942-8(7)) DIANE Publishing Co.

Langlois, Suzane. Smarty pants. Sydor, Colleen. 2nd rev. ed. 2003. 32p. (J). (gr. 1-5). (978-1-894222-62-4(8)) Lobster Pr.

Langridge, Roger. Criminy. Langridge, Roger. Ferrier, Ryan. 2018. (ENG.). 96p. (J). (gr. 5-9). pap. 12.99 (978-1-5067-0744-0(0)) Dark Horse Comics.

—Meet the Muppets. Langridge, Roger. 2009. (Muppet Show Ser.). (ENG.). 112p. (J). 24.99 (978-1-60886-527-7(4)) Boom! Studios.

—The Muppet Show Comic Book: The Treasure of Peg-Leg Wilson. Langridge, Roger. 2010. (Muppet Show Ser.). (ENG.). 112p. (J). 24.99 (978-1-60886-530-7(4)); (gr. 4-7). pap. 9.99 (978-1-60886-504-8(5)) Boom! Studios.

—The Muppet Show Comic Book: Muppet Mash. Langridge, Roger. 2011. (Muppet Show Ser.). 128p. pap. 9.99 (978-1-60886-611-3(4)) Boom! Studios.

—On the Road. Langridge, Roger. 2011. (Kaboom! Graphic Novels Ser.). (ENG.). 112p. (J). (gr. 4-7). 26.19 (978-1-60886-516-1(9)) Boom! Studios.

—Snarked Vol. 2: Ships & Sealing Wax. Langridge, Roger. 2012. (Snarked Ser.). (ENG.). 112p. (J). (gr. 4). pap. 14.99 (978-1-60886-276-4(3)) Boom! Studios.

Langridge, Roger & Mebberson, Amy. Family Reunion. Langridge, Roger. 2010. (Muppet Show Ser.). (ENG.). 112p. (J). pap. 9.99 (978-1-60886-587-1(8)) Boom! Studios.

Langrish, Bob. My Little Book of Horses & Ponies. Swinney, Nicola Jane. 2016. 64p. (J). (978-1-4351-6349-2(4)) Barnes & Noble, Inc.

Langrish, Bob, et al, photos by. Dream Horses. 2004. (ENG., 64p. (J). (gr. 2-8). pap. 10.95 (978-1-58017-574-6(0), 67574) Storey Publishing, LLC.

Langrish, Bob, photos by. Dreaming of Horses. Swinney, Nicola. 2019. (ENG., 96p. (J). (gr. 3-5). pap. 12.95 (978-0-2281-0209-0(X), ba64ac2c-f5ce-4e04-9a22-6fef0f024239) Firefly Bks., Ltd.

—The Foaling Primer: A Step-By-Step Guide to Raising a Healthy Foal. McFarland, Cynthia. 2005. (ENG., 160p. pap. 19.95 (978-1-58017-608-8(9), 67608) Storey Publishing, LLC.

Langston, Joanne M. Winnie & Tate. Crinklaw, Nancy L. 2017. (ENG.). (J). pap. 15.95 (978-1-882190-58-4(0)) Polar Bear & Co.

Langston, Laura. Jim Henson's Labyrinth: a Discovery Adventure. 2019. (ENG.). 24p. (J). 14.99 (978-1-68415-238-4(0), Archaia Entertainment) Boom! Studios.

Langtiw, Ron. Kirin Rise the Cast of Shadows. Cruz, Ed. 2017. (ENG.). (J). pap. 16.99 (978-1-946003-00-3(X)) Kirin Rise Studios, LLC.

Langton, Bruce. Count on Us: A Tennessee Number Book. Shoulders, Michael. 2003. (Count Your Way Across the U. S. A. Ser.). (ENG.). 40p. (J). 16.95 (978-1-58536-131-1(3)) Sleeping Bear Pr.

—Discover Ohio, 2 bks. Schonberg, Marcia. 2003. (ENG.). 40p. (J). 27.95 (978-1-58536-225-7(5)) Sleeping Bear Pr.

—Discover Tennessee: Count on Us; V is for Volunteer, 2 bks. Shoulders, Michael. 2003. (ENG.). 40p. (J). 27.95 (978-1-58536-228-8(X)) Sleeping Bear Pr.

—Full Count: A Baseball Number Book. Herzog, Brad. 2009. (ENG.). 40p. (J). (gr. k-6). 17.95 (978-1-58536-429-9(0)) Sleeping Bear Pr.

—Hands as Warm as Toast. Himle, Lisa. 2006. 32p. (J). (gr. -1-3). 17.95 (978-1-58726-298-2(3), Mitten Pr.) Ann Arbor Editions LLC.

—P Is for Putt: A Golf Alphabet. Herzog, Brad. (Alphabet-Sports Ser.). (ENG.). 40p. 2009. (gr. k-6). pap. 7.95 (978-1-58536-476-3(2)); 2005. (J). (gr. -1-5). 16.95 (978-1-58536-252-3(2)) Sleeping Bear Pr.

—P Is for Putt: A Golf Alphabet. Herzog, Brad. 2015. (Av2 Fiction Readalong 2016 Ser.). (ENG.). (J). (gr. 1-4). lib. bdg. 34.28 (978-1-4896-3759-8(1), AV2 by Weigl) Weigl Pubs., Inc.

—Win One for the Gipper: America's Football Hero. Wargin, Kathy-jo. 2004. (ENG.). 40p. (J). (gr. k-6). 16.95 (978-1-58536-221-9(2)) Sleeping Bear Pr.

Langton, Bruce. H Is for Hawkeye: An Iowa Alphabet. Langton, Bruce, tr. Pierce, Patricia A. 2003. (Discover America State by State Ser.). (ENG.). 40p. (J). 17.95 (978-1-58536-114-4(3)) Sleeping Bear Pr.

Langton, Bruce, jt. illus. see Larson, Katherine.

Langton, Roger. The Bible in Pictures for Toddlers. Lindvall, Ella K. adapted ed. 2003. (ENG.). 144p. (J). 9.99 (978-0-8024-3058-8(9)) Moody Pubs.

—Classic Folk Tales: 80 Traditional Stories from Around the World. Baxter, Nicola. 2013. (ENG.). 96p. (J). (gr. 7-12). pap. 9.99 (978-1-84322-855-4(6)) Anness Publishing GBR. Dist: National Bk. Network.

Langton, Roger. Children's Stories from the Bible: A Collection of over 20 Tales from the Old & New Testament, Retold for Younger Readers. Langton, Roger. Baxter, Nicola. 2013. 80p. (J). (gr. 5-12). pap. 9.99 (978-1-84322-982-7(X), Armadillo) Anness Publishing GBR. Dist: National Bk. Network.

Langton, Roger W. A Little Life of Jesus - To Read & Treasure. Rock, Lois. 2nd ed. 2015. (ENG.). 352p. (J). (gr. -1-k). pap. 8.99 (978-0-7459-6567-3(9)) Lion Hudson PLC GBR. Dist: Independent Pubs. Group.

Lanino, Deborah. Maria's Comet. Hopkinson, Deborah. 2003. (ENG.). 32p. (J). (gr. -1-3). 8.99 (978-0-689-85678-5(4), Simon & Schuster/Paula Wiseman Bks.) Simon & Schuster/Paula Wiseman Bks.

Lankester Brisley, Joyce. Adventures of the Little Wooden Horse. Moray Williams, Ursula. 2020. (ENG.). 272p. (J). (gr. 2). 9.99 **(978-1-5290-4241-2(0)**, Macmillan Children's Bks.) Pan Macmillan GBR. Dist: Independent Pubs. Group.

Lanning, Andrea J. The Imposturous Egg. Lanning, Andrea J. Corcacas, Maria, photos by. 2012. 32p. (978-0-9571677-0-4(9)); pap. (978-0-9571677-4-2(1)) Ginnal Creatives Ltd.

Lanos, Henri & Shepperson, Claude Allin. When the Sleeper Wakes (Illustrated)/ the First Men in the Moon (Illustrated). / the Sea Lady: A Tissue of Moonshine (Illustrated) / the Food of the Gods & How It Came to Earth. Barry, ed. 2019. (H. G. Wells: Notable Works: Vol. 2). (ENG.). 706p. (J). pap. 39.95 **(978-1-6984-9037-3(2))** Independently Published.

Lanot, Harvey. The 50 States, by a Seven-Year-Old. Ramtri, Rocco. 2019. (ENG.). 44p. (J). pap. (978-1-78830-168-8(4)) Olympia Publishers.

Lanoue, Michelle. The Dinosaur & Ladybug in Heels Christmas Nativity Story. Lanoue, Michelle. 2018. (ENG.). 32p. (J). (gr. k-4). 17.99 (978-0-692-11265-6(0)) Lanoue, Michelle.

Lanoue, Michelle. The Dinosaur & Ladybug in Heels Christmas Nativity Story. Lanoue, Michelle. ed. 2019. (ENG.). 26p. (J). (gr. k-6). pap. 13.99 **(978-1-64372-305-1(7)**, Huskies Pub) MacLaren-Cochrane Publishing, Inc.

Lanoue, Michelle. The Dinosaur & Ladybug in Heels Farm Adventure. Lanoue, Michelle. 2014. (ENG.). 32p. (J). (gr. k-4). 17.99 (978-0-692-10170-4(5)) Lanoue, Michelle.

Lanoue, Michelle. The Dinosaur & Ladybug in Heels Farm Adventure. Lanoue, Michelle. ed. 2020. (ENG.). 30p. (J). (gr. k-6). 17.99 **(978-1-64372-048-7(1))**; pap. 13.99 **(978-1-64372-310-5(3))** MacLaren-Cochrane Publishing, Inc. (Huskies Pub).

Lanphear, Dave, jt. illus. see Cariello, Sergio.

Lanquetin, Anne-Sophie. Not All Princesses Dress in Pink. Yolen, Jane & Stemple, Heidi E. Y. 2010. (ENG.). 32p. (J). (gr. -1-3). 17.99 (978-1-4169-8018-6(0), Simon & Schuster Bks. For Young Readers) Simon & Schuster Bks. For Young Readers.

Lanza, Barbara. Time to Fly: A Fairy Lane Book. Lanza, Barbara. 2005. (ENG.). 32p. (J). (gr. 4-7). 19.95 (978-0-9724853-7-1(6)) Keene Publishing.

Lanza, Marco, photos by. The Kids' Cookbook: Recipes from Around the World. Gioffre, Rosalba et al. Wilson, Alison & Farrell, Helen, eds. 2008. (ENG., 120p. (J). (gr. 2-18). 19.95 (978-88-88166-96-4(3)) McRae Bks. Srl ITA. Dist: Independent Pubs. Group.

Lanzon, Paul. Curse of the Mudchalk Devil. Lanzon, Phil. 2019. (ENG.). 300p. (YA). (gr. 7-12). pap. 16.99 (978-1-910903-19-3(1)) AudioGO.

Lanzrein, Helen. All Things Bright & Beautiful: A Collection of Prayer & Verse. 2007. (Padded Board Bks.). 24p. (J). (gr. -1). bds. 7.95 (978-1-58925-799-3(5)) Tiger Tales.

Lao, Ione. Minhoca Pa�ca: Na Dan�a das Profiss�es. Lao, Ione. 2018. (POR.). 36p. (J). pap. 10.00 **(978-1-9829-2707-3(0))** Independently Published.

Lapadula, Thomas. Thomas & the Dinosaur (Thomas & Friends) Golden Books. 2015. (Little Golden Book Ser.). (ENG.). 24p. (J). (-k). 4.99 (978-0-553-49681-9(6), Golden Bks.) Random Hse. Children's Bks.

—Thomas at the Animal Park (Thomas & Friends) Random House. 2014. (ENG.). 10p. (J). (— 1). 10.99 (978-0-385-38469-8(6), Random Hse. Bks. for Young Readers) Random Hse. Children's Bks.

LaPadula, Tom. Clifford for President. McVeigh, Mark et al. 2004. (Clifford's Big Red Reader Ser.). (ENG.). 32p. (J). (gr. -1-3). pap. 3.99 (978-0-439-69391-2(8)) Scholastic, Inc.

—How to Draw Military Machines: Step-By-step Instructions for 18 High-powered Vehicles. 2018. (Learn to Draw Ser.). (ENG.). 32p. (J). (gr. 1-3). pap. 5.99 (978-1-63322-754-5(5), Walter Foster Jr) Quarto Publishing Group USA.

LaPadula, Tom, et al. Learn to Draw Cars, Planes & Moving Machines: Step-By-Step Instructions for More Than 25 High-Powered Vehicles. Walter Foster Jr. Creative Team. 2015. (Learn to Draw: Expanded Edition Ser.). (ENG.). 64p. (J). (gr. 3-5). 33.32 (978-1-939581-69-3(9), Walter Foster Jr) Quarto Publishing Group USA.

LaPadula, Tom. Learn to Draw Tanks, Aircraft & Armored Vehicles: Learn to Draw 23 Favorite Subjects, Step by Easy Step, Shape by Simple Shape! 2013. 40p. (J). (978-1-936309-83-2(1)) Quarto Publishing Group USA.

—Thanks a Lot, Robo-Turkey! Banks, Steven. ed. 2005. (Adventures of Jimmy Neutron Ser.: 10). 24p. (J). lib. bdg. 15.00 (978-1-59054-787-8(X)) Fitzgerald Bks.

Lapegüe, Matias. Calamity Jane: Frontierswoman. Klepeis, Alicia Z. 2016. (American Legends & Folktales Ser.). 32p. (gr. 3-3). pap. 10.58 (978-1-5026-2200-6(9)); lib. bdg. 28.50 (978-1-5026-2202-0(5)) Cavendish Square Publishing LLC.

—Davy Crockett. Coddington, Andrew. 2016. (American Legends & Folktales Ser.). 32p. (gr. 3-3). 28.50 (978-1-5026-2193-1(2)) Cavendish Square Publishing LLC.

—Jesse James. Cunningham, Meghan Engsberg. 2016. (American Legends & Folktales Ser.). 32p. (gr. 3-3). 28.50 (978-1-5026-2197-9(5)) Cavendish Square Publishing LLC.

Laperla, Artur. The Epic Origin of Super Potato. Laperla, Artur. 2018. (Super Potato Ser.). 56p. (J). (gr. 2-5). 27.99 (978-1-5124-4021-8(3), Graphic Universe™) Lerner Publishing Group.

Laperla, Artur. Super Potato & the Castle of Robots: Book 5. Laperla, Artur. 2020. (Super Potato Ser.). 64p. (J). (gr. 2-5). (ENG.). pap. 8.99 **(978-1-7284-1293-1(5))**; lib. bdg. 27.99 **(978-1-5124-4025-6(6))** Lerner Publishing Group. (Graphic Universe™).

Laperla, Artur. Super Potato & the Mutant Animal Mayhem. Laperla, Artur. MacTyre, Norwyn. 2020. (Super Potato Ser.). 56p. (J). (gr. 2-5). 27.99 (978-1-5124-4024-9(8), Graphic Universe™) Lerner Publishing Group.

—Super Potato & the Mutant Animal Mayhem: Book 4. Laperla, Artur. 2020. (Super Potato Ser.). (ENG.). 56p. (J). (gr. 2-5). pap. 8.99 (978-1-5415-8701-4(4), Graphic Universe™) Lerner Publishing Group.

—Super Potato's Galactic Breakout. Laperla, Artur. 2019. (Super Potato Ser.). (ENG.). 56p. (J). (gr. 2-5). 27.99 (978-1-5124-4022-5(1), Graphic Universe™) Lerner Publishing Group.

—Super Potato's Mega Time-Travel Adventure. Laperla, Artur. 2019. (Super Potato Ser.). 56p. (J). (gr. 2-5). 27.99 (978-1-5124-4023-2(X), 9781512440232, Graphic Universe™) Lerner Publishing Group.

—Super Potato's Mega Time-Travel Adventure: Book 3. Laperla, Artur. 2019. (Super Potato Ser.). (ENG.). 56p. (J). (gr. 2-5). pap. 8.99 (978-1-5415-7287-4(4), 9781541572874, Graphic Universe™) Lerner Publishing Group.

LaPierre, Karina. Nugrl90, 0 vols. Dellasega, Cheryl. 2007. (Bloggrls Ser.: 1). (ENG.). 192p. (YA). (gr. 7-11). pap. 9.99 (978-0-7614-5396-3(2), 9780761453963, Skyscape) Amazon Publishing.

LaPierre, Richard. The Thinking Toolbox: Thirty-Five Lessons That Will Build Your Reasoning Skills. Bluedorn, Nathaniel & Bluedorn, Hans. 2005. 234p. per. 25.00 (978-0-9745315-1-9(0), 4000) Christian Logic.

Lapointe, Claude. Un Ordenador Nada Ordinario. Lapointe, Claude, tr. Kahn, Michéele. Trapero, Florentino, tr. 2003. (SPA.). 124p. (J). (gr. 3-5). pap. 10.95 (978-84-204-4767-4(6)) Santillana USA Publishing Co., Inc.

Lapovich, Melanie, jt. illus. see Kennedy, Nick.

Lapuss, Stephane. Minions - Evil Panic, Vol. 2. Collin, Renaud. 2016. (Minions Ser.: 2). (ENG.). 48p. (J). (gr. 3-7). 14.99 (978-1-78276-556-1(5)) Titan Bks. Ltd. GBR. Dist: Penguin Random Hse. LLC.

Lara, David. La Gran Rata de Sumatra. Fleischman, Sid. rev. ed. 2006. (Castillo de la Lectura Roja Ser.). 152p. (YA). (gr. 7). pap. 8.95 (978-970-20-0855-2(7)) Castillo, Ediciones, S. A. de C. V. MEX. Dist: Macmillan.

Lara, Pablo. El Instinto de la Luz. Londo. 2018. (SPA.). 126p. (J). pap. 6.99 (978-1-7238-2477-7(1)) Independently Published.

—El Retorno de la Luz. Londo. 2018. (SPA.). 124p. (J). pap. 6.99 (978-1-7915-6174-1(8)) Independently Published.

—El Tiempo Muerto. Londo. 2018. (SPA.). 122p. (J). pap. 6.99 (978-1-7915-0853-1(7)) Independently Published.

Larade, April. Pilot, Swaydy & Friends. May, Maggie. 2011. 30p. pap. 24.95 (978-1-4560-8499-8(2)) America Star Bks.

Laraque, Keira. Silly Celly: A Story in Rhyme. Batista, N. Lenaure. 2017. (Silly Celly Ser.: Vol. 1). (ENG.). (J). (gr. k-3). 18.95 (978-0-692-81697-4(6)) Billionaire Butterfly, LLC.

Larder, Dawn M. An Introduction to Women's Collegiate Bowling. Trapp, Heather & Davis, Wayne L. 2020. (Bowling Ser.: Vol. 1). (ENG.). 116p. (YA). 27.99 **(978-1-940803-39-5(X))**; pap. 18.99 **(978-1-940803-40-1(3))** LoGiudice Publishing.

Lardot, Christopher. Clothes & Fashion Sticker Book IR. Brocklehurst, Ruth. ed. 2013. (Clothes & Fashion Sticker Book Ser.). 31p. (J). pap. 9.99 (978-0-7945-3235-2(7), Usborne) EDC Publishing.

Lardy, Philippe. A Wreath for Emmett Till. Nelson, Marilyn. 2009. (ENG.). 48p. (YA). (gr. 7). pap. 8.99 (978-0-547-07636-2(3), 1042024) Houghton Mifflin Harcourt Publishing Co.

LaReau, Jenna. Rocko & Spanky Call It Quits. LaReau, Kara. 2008. (Rocko & Spanky Ser.). 40p. (J). 16.00 (978-0-15-216611-3(4)) Harcourt Children's Bks.

—Top Secret: A Handbook of Codes, Ciphers & Secret Writing. Janeczko, Paul B., ed. 2006. (ENG.). 144p. (J). (gr. 4-7). per. 9.99 (978-0-7636-2972-4(3)) Candlewick Pr.

Largie, A. D. Hip Hop History for Kids: Rap for Kids. Largie, A. D. 2019. (Hip Hop Kids Book Ser.: Vol. 1). (ENG.). 30p. (J). pap. 12.95 **(978-1-7126-5118-6(8))** Independently Published.

LaRiccia, Mike. Harvey's Woods: the Royal Adventures. Dauer, Marty. 2007. 52p. per. 16.95 (978-1-4241-7924-4(6)) America Star Bks.

Larimore, J. C. Real Food for Littles. Miller, Risse. 2017. (ENG.). 30p. (J). pap. 13.95 (978-1-4808-5643-1(6)) Archway Publishing.

Larin, Max. Hippo Can't Wait: (childrens Books about Patience) Gordon, Michael. 2018. (ENG.). 30p. (J). pap. 12.99 (978-1-7267-3448-6(X)) Independently Published.

Larina, Lida. Charlie Meets Santa. Purchase, Elizabeth. 2015. (ENG.). (J). pap. (978-0-9949564-1-5(X)) Elizabeth Purchase.

Larina, Lidiya. I Know Nature: Lift-The-flap Book. Clever Publishing. 2018. (Clever Questions Ser.). (ENG.). 16p. (J). (gr. -1-1). bds. 9.99 (978-1-948418-35-5(5)) Clever Media Group.

Larina, Tatjana. A Frog Is in My Shoe. Moore, Rose. Moore, Rose, ed. 2019. (ENG.). 38p. pap. 16.95 (978-0-9965097-8-7(X)) BookBaby.

Larivière Chaput, Elaine. What Would You Do?, 1 vol. 2015. (ENG.). 32p. (J). mass mkt. 10.95 (978-1-894717-48-9(1), 762f51f1-b606-4fc3-85f8-92cd1f765729) Pemmican Pubns., Inc. CAN. Dist: Firefly Bks., Ltd.

Lark, Casi, photos by. Busy Horsies. Schindel, John. 2007. (Busy Book Ser.). 20p. (J). (gr. k — 1). bds. 7.99 (978-1-58246-223-3(2), Tricycle Pr.) Random Hse. Children's Bks.

Lark, Michael, et al. Daredevil by Ed Brubaker & Michael Lark Omnibus Vol. 2. 2017. (ENG.). 472p. (YA). (gr. 8-17). 75.00 (978-1-302-90859-1(6)) Marvel Worldwide, Inc.

—Secret Avengers by Ed Brubaker: the Complete Collection. 2018. (ENG.). 304p. (YA). (gr. 8-17). pap. 34.99 (978-1-302-91219-2(4)) Marvel Worldwide, Inc.

Larkin, Catherine. Harry Scores A Hat Trick, Pawns, Pucks, & Scoliosis: The Sequel to Stand Tall, Harry. Mahony, Mary. Pasternack, Susan, ed. 2003. 130p. (YA). (gr. 5-8). per. 14.95 (978-0-9658879-3-9(6)) Redding Pr.

Larkin, Eric. Farmer Will Allen & the Growing Table. Martin, Jacqueline Briggs. 2013. (Food Heroes Ser.). (ENG.). 32p. (J). (gr. k). 17.95 (978-0-9836615-3-5(7)) READERS to EATERS.

Larkin, Eric-Shabazz. A Moose Boosh: A Few Choice Words about Food. 2014. (ENG.). 96p. (J). (gr. 4-7). 18.95 (978-0-9836615-5-9(3)) READERS to EATERS.

Larkin, Paige A. Pearlie. Stroud-Peace, Glenda. 2009. 48p. pap. 16.95 (978-1-60844-033-7(8)) Dog Ear Publishing, LLC.

Larkin, Tara. I Will Own a Castle. Brown, Stacy. 2018. (ENG.). 40p. (J). pap. (978-1-5255-1498-2(9)) FriesenPress.

Larkins, Christina. Beauty & the Beast: A Favorite Story in Rhythm & Rhyme. Peale, Jonathan. 2020. (Fairy Tale Tunes Ser.). (ENG.). 20p. (J). (gr. -1-3). bds. 7.99 (978-1-5158-6095-2(7), 142375) Cantata Learning.

Larkins, Mona. Dear Grandchild, When You Come for a Visit. Robinson, Linda M. 2005. 37p. (J). (gr. -1-4). 15.99 (978-0-9740841-4-5(X)) K&B Products.

—Mother Duck Knows the Way. Thomas, Kate. 2005. 32p. (J). 8.95 (978-1-58374-122-1(4)) Chicago Spectrum Pr.

Larkins, Mona & Anderson, Jan. Bullies Beware! Day-Bivins, Pat. 2006. (ENG.). 32p. (J). (gr. -1). 16.95 (978-0-9742806-5-3(8)) Heart to Heart Publishing, Inc.

Larkum, A. Cars. Daynes, Katie. 2005. 64p. (J). (gr. 2-18). pap. 5.95 (978-0-7945-0999-6(1), Usborne) EDC Publishing.

Larkum, Adam. The American Revolution. Ohlin, Nancy. 2016. (Blast Back! Ser.). (ENG.). 112p. (J). (gr. 2-5). pap. 5.99 (978-1-4998-0122-4(X)) Little Bee Books Inc.

—Ancient Egypt. Ohlin, Nancy. 2016. (Blast Back! Ser.). (ENG.). 112p. (J). (gr. 2-5). pap. 5.99 (978-1-4998-0116-3(5)) Little Bee Books Inc.

—Ancient Greece. Ohlin, Nancy. 2016. (Blast Back! Ser.). (ENG.). 112p. (J). (gr. 2-5). pap. 5.99 (978-1-4998-0118-7(1)) Little Bee Books Inc.

—Chocolate. Daynes, Katie. 2004. 48p. (J). (gr. 2-18). pap. 5.95 (978-0-7945-0759-6(X), Usborne) EDC Publishing.

—The Civil War. Ohlin, Nancy. 2016. (Blast Back! Ser.). (ENG.). 112p. (J). (gr. 2-5). pap. 5.99 (978-1-4998-0120-0(3)) Little Bee Books Inc.

—The Story of Toilets, Telephones & Other Useful Inventions. Daynes, Katie. 2005. (Usborne Young Reading: Series One Ser.). 48p. (J). (gr. 2). lib. bdg. 13.95 (978-1-58086-983-6(1), Usborne) EDC Publishing.

—The Titanic. Ohlin, Nancy. 2016. (Blast Back! Ser.). (ENG.). 112p. (J). (gr. 2-5). pap. 5.99 (978-1-4998-0273-3(0)) Little Bee Books Inc.

—Vikings. Turnbull, Stephanie. 2006. (Beginners Social Studies: Level 2 Ser.). 32p. (J). (gr. 1-3). 4.99 (978-0-7945-1254-5(2), Usborne) EDC Publishing.

—Vikings. Ohlin, Nancy. 2017. (Blast Back! Ser.). (ENG.). 112p. (J). (gr. 2-5). 16.99 (978-1-4998-0386-0(9)) Little Bee Books Inc.

—What's Happening to Me? Firth, Alex. Meredith, Susan, ed. 2007. 48p. (J). (gr. 4-7). pap. 6.99 (978-0-7945-1514-0(2), Usborne) EDC Publishing.

—Why Shouldn't I Eat Junk Food? Knighton, Kate. 2008. (Usborne Ser.). 48p. (J). (gr. 4-7). pap. 6.99 (978-0-7945-1953-7(9), Usborne) EDC Publishing.

—World History Sticker Atlas. Dalby, Elizabeth. 2006. (Sticker Atlases Ser.). 24p. (J). (gr. 1-4). pap. 8.99 (978-0-7945-1244-6(5), Usborne) EDC Publishing.

Larkum, Adam, jt. illus. see Donaera, Patrizia.

Larkum, Adam, jt. illus. see Kushii, Tetsuo.

Larkum, Adam, jt. illus. see Sage, Molly.

Larned, Phillip. The Magic Muffin, 1 vol. Larned, S. 2010. 22p. pap. 24.95 (978-1-4489-8138-0(7)) PublishAmerica, Inc.

Laroche, Bridget. Thunder & the Pirates. Valeska, Jon & Fripp, Jean. Fripp, Jean, ed. 2004. 32p. (J). (gr. k-4). 5.99 (978-0-9701008-9-4(2)) Bicast, Inc.

Laroche, Giles. Now You See Them, Now You Don't: Creatures That Know How to Hide. Harrison, David L. 2016. 32p. (J). (gr. k-4). lib. bdg. 17.95 (978-1-58089-610-8(3)) Charlesbridge Publishing, Inc.

—A Place to Start a Family: Poems about Creatures That Build. Harrison, David. 2018. 32p. (J). (gr. k-4). 17.99 (978-1-58089-748-8(7)) Charlesbridge Publishing, Inc.

—A Place to Start a Family: Poems about Creatures That Build. Harrison, David L. 2019. 32p. (J). (gr. k-4). pap. 9.99 (978-1-62354-162-0(X)) Charlesbridge Publishing, Inc.

—¿Qué Hacen las Ruedas Todo el Día? Prince, April Jones. 2013.Tr. of What Do Wheels Do All Day. (ENG.). 32p. (J). (— 1). bds. 5.99 (978-0-547-99625-7(X), 1525533) Houghton Mifflin Harcourt Publishing Co.

—What Do Wheels Do All Day? Prince, April Jones. 2006. (ENG.). 32p. (J). (gr. -1-3). 17.99 *(978-0-618-56307-4(5),* 593931) Houghton Mifflin Harcourt Publishing Co.

LaRoe, Misty Bailey. Oops Was Bullied? Hey, Why Did You Hurt Me That Way? King, Sharon. 2013. (ENG.). 32p. (J). pap. 16.95 *(978-1-4787-1364-7(X))* Outskirts Pr., Inc.

Laronde, Gary. Hector Saves the Moon. Bauld, Jane Scoggins. 2019. (ENG.). 46p. (J). pap. 13.95 *(978-1-7951-4890-0(X))* Independently Published.

—Hector Saves the Moon, Vol. 2. Bauld, Jane Scoggins. 2003. (Hector's Escapades Ser.). 34p. (J). (gr. -1-3). per. 7.95 *(978-1-57168-312-0(7))* Eakin Pr.

—Hector Visits His Country Cousin, Vol. 3. Bauld, Jane Scoggins. 2003. (Hector's Escapades Ser.). 25p. (gr. -1). per. 7.95 *(978-1-57168-676-3(2))* Eakin Pr.

Larosa, Lewis. Punisher Max - Volume 1: In the Beginning. 2006. (ENG.). 144p. (gr. 13-17). pap. 14.99 *(978-0-7851-1391-1(6))* Marvel Worldwide, Inc.

Larranaga, Ana. Little Turtles. Ikids Staff. 2008. (iBaby Float-Alongs Ser.). (ENG.). 6p. (J). (gr. -1). 12.99 *(978-1-58476-808-1(8))* Innovative Kids.

—Matching Puzzle Cards - Animals. 2012. (ENG.). 36p. (J). (gr. k-12). 9.99 *(978-1-60905-225-6(0))* Blue Apple Bks.

—Tiny Tugboats. Ikids Staff. 2008. (iBaby Float-Alongs Ser.). (ENG.). 6p. (J). (gr. -1). 12.99 *(978-1-58476-807-4(X))* Innovative Kids.

—Wiggle My Ears. Powell, Richard. 2004. (Wrigglers Ser.). 8p. (J). bds. 5.95 *(978-1-58925-692-7(1))* Tiger Tales.

—Zoo Faces. Schultz, Lucy & Shultz, Lucy. 2007. (ENG.). 12p. (J). (gr. -1 — 1). bds. 6.99 *(978-1-58476-556-1(9),* IKIDS) Innovative Kids.

Larranaga, Ana Martin. Baby Dolphins. Jugran, Jan. 2006. (ENG.). 6p. (J). (gr. -1 — 1). 14.99 *(978-1-58476-490-8(2),* IKIDS) Innovative Kids.

Larrañaga, Ana Martín. Colors - E-Z Page Turners. Page, Liza & Innovative Kids Staff. 2008. (ENG.). 12p. (J). (gr. -1 — 1). bds. 5.99 *(978-1-58476-655-1(7))* Innovative Kids.

Larrañaga, Ana Martín. Counting: E-Z Page Turners. Innovative Kids Staff. 2008. (ENG.). 12p. (J). (gr. -1 — 1). bds. 5.99 *(978-1-58476-657-5(3))* Innovative Kids.

Larranaga, Ana Martin. Farm Faces: A Book of Masks. Ikids Staff. 2006. (ENG.). 12p. (J). (gr. -1 — 1). bds. 6.99 *(978-1-58476-471-7(6),* IKIDS) Innovative Kids.

—Goodnight Faces: A Book of Masks. Jugran, Jan. 2007. (ENG.). 12p. (J). (gr. -1 — 1). bds. 6.99 *(978-1-58476-672-8(7),* IKIDS) Innovative Kids.

—Hugs. Jugran, Jan. 2007. (ENG.). 12p. (J). (gr. -1 — 1). 9.99 *(978-1-58476-620-9(4),* IKIDS) Innovative Kids.

Larrañaga, Ana Martín. I Love You All Day Long. 2012. (ENG.). 12p. (J). (gr. -1 — 1). 9.99 *(978-1-60169-269-6(2))* Innovative Kids.

Larranaga, Ana Martin. Ibaby - Goodnight, Baby: Tuck All the Babies into Their Beds. Ikids Staff. 2006. (ENG.). 12p. (J). (gr. -1 — 1). 9.99 *(978-1-58476-482-3(1),* IKIDS) Innovative Kids.

—Ibaby - Rub-a-Dub-Dub. Jugran, Jan. 2007. (ENG.). 6p. (J). (gr. -1 — 1). 14.99 *(978-1-58476-555-4(0),* IKIDS) Innovative Kids.

Larrañaga, Ana Martín. Mommies & Babies. Page, Liza & Innovative Kids Staff. 2008. (ENG.). 12p. (J). (gr. -1 — 1). bds. 5.99 *(978-1-58476-656-8(5))* Innovative Kids.

Larrañaga, Ana Martín. Opposites. Page, Liza & Innovative Kids Staff. 2008. (ENG.). 12p. (J). (gr. -1 — 1). bds. 5.99 *(978-1-58476-654-4(9))* Innovative Kids.

Larranaga, Ana Martin. Pig. Rivers-Moore, Debbie. 2012. (Come Out & Play! Bks.). (ENG.). 10p. (J). (gr. -1-k). bds. 2.99 *(978-0-7641-6519-1(4),* B.E.S. Publishing) Peterson's.

—Pony. Rivers-Moore, Debbie. 2012. (Come Out & Play! Bks.). (ENG.). 10p. (J). (gr. -1-k). bds. 2.99 *(978-0-7641-6520-7(8),* B.E.S. Publishing) Peterson's.

—Puppy. Rivers-Moore, Debbie. 2012. (Come Out & Play! Bks.). (ENG.). 10p. (J). (gr. -1-k). bds. 2.99 *(978-0-7641-6521-4(6),* B.E.S. Publishing) Peterson's.

—Shapes. Ikids Staff. 2009. (ENG.). 12p. (J). (gr. -1 — 1). bds. 5.99 *(978-1-58476-937-8(8))* Innovative Kids.

—Trucks. Ikids Staff. 2009. (ENG.). 12p. (J). (gr. -1 — 1). bds. 5.99 *(978-1-58476-936-1(X))* Innovative Kids.

Larrañaga, Ana Martín. Who Said Boo? A Lift-the-Flap Book. Root, Phyllis. 2005. (ENG.). 14p. (J). (gr. -1-k). bds. 5.99 *(978-0-689-85408-8(0),* Little Simon) Little Simon.

Larrañaga, Ana Martín & Larrañaga, Ana Martín. Airplane Flight! A Lift-The-Flap Adventure. Hill, Susanna Leonard. 2009. (ENG.). 12p. (J). (gr. -1-k). bds. 7.99 *(978-1-4169-7832-9(1),* Little Simon) Little Simon.

Larrañaga, Ana Martín, jt. illus. see Larrañaga, Ana Martín.

Larranaga, Ana Martin, jt. illus. see Parsons, Jackie.

Larraz, Pepe, et al. Avengers: No Surrender. 2018. (Avengers: No Surrender Ser.: 1). (ENG.). 400p. (YA). (gr. 8-17). pap. 34.99 *(978-1-302-91146-1(5))* Marvel Worldwide, Inc.

Larraz, Pepe. House of X/Powers of X. 2019. 304p. (YA). (gr. 8-17). 60.00 *(978-1-302-91570-4(3))* Marvel Worldwide, Inc.

—Uncanny Avengers: Unity Vol. 4: Red Skull. 2017. (ENG.). 136p. (J). (gr. 4-17). pap. 17.99 *(978-1-302-90644-3(5))* Marvel Worldwide, Inc.

Larraz, Pepe & Silva, R. B. House of X/Powers of X. 2020. (ENG.). 1p. (YA). (gr. 8-17). pap. 44.99 ***(978-1-302-91571-1(1))*** Marvel Worldwide, Inc.

Larrazz, Pepe & Ribic, Esad. Thor: Worthy Origins. 2017. (ENG.). 136p. (YA). (gr. 8-17). pap. 17.99 *(978-0-7851-8476-8(7))* Marvel Worldwide, Inc.

Larrison, Charity. Ziji: The Puppy Who Learned to Meditate. Rinpoché, Yongey Mingyur & Hayden, Torey. 2017. (ENG.). 56p. (J). 16.95 *(978-1-61429-471-9(2))* Wisdom Pubns.

Larroca, Salvador. Doctor Doom Vol. 1: Pottersville. 2020. 120p. (YA). (gr. 8-17). pap. 15.99 *(978-1-302-92089-0(8))* Marvel Worldwide, Inc.

—Namor: Sea & Sand. Jemas, Bill & Watson, Andi. 2004. (Marvel Heroes Ser.). 144p. (YA). pap. 12.99 *(978-0-7851-1241-9(3))* Marvel Worldwide, Inc.

—Star Wars Vol. 10: The Escape. 2019. 136p. (J). (gr. 4-17). pap. 17.99 *(978-1-302-91449-3(9))* Marvel Worldwide, Inc.

—Star Wars Vol. 5: Yoda's Secret War. 2017. 144p. (J). (gr. 4-17). pap. 17.99 *(978-1-302-90265-0(2))* Marvel Worldwide, Inc.

—Star Wars Vol. 6: Out among the Stars. 2017. (ENG.). 112p. (J). (gr. 4-17). pap. 19.99 *(978-1-302-90553-8(8))* Marvel Worldwide, Inc.

—Star Wars Vol. 7: The Ashes of Jedha. 2018. (ENG.). 136p. (J). (gr. 4-17). pap. 17.99 *(978-1-302-91052-5(3))* Marvel Worldwide, Inc.

—Star Wars Vol. 9: Hope Dies. 2018. (Star Wars (2015) Ser.: 9). (ENG.). 120p. (J). (gr. 4-17). pap. 19.99 *(978-1-302-91054-9(X))* Marvel Worldwide, Inc.

—Uncanny X-Men: Wolverine & Cyclops Vol. 1. 2019. (ENG.). 136p. (YA). pap. 19.99 *(978-1-302-91582-7(7))* Marvel Worldwide, Inc.

Larroca, Salvador & Delgado, Edgar. Shadows & Secrets: Volume 1. Gillen, Kieron. 2016. (Star Wars: Darth Vader Set 2 Ser.). (ENG.). 24p. (J). (gr. 6-12). lib. bdg. 27.07 *(978-1-61479-547-6(9),* 24381, Graphic Novels) Spotlight.

—Shadows & Secrets: Volume 2. Gillen, Kieron. 2016. (Star Wars: Darth Vader Set 2 Ser.). (ENG.). 24p. (J). (gr. 6-12). lib. bdg. 27.07 *(978-1-61479-548-3(7),* 24382, Graphic Novels) Spotlight.

—Shadows & Secrets: Volume 3. Gillen, Kieron. 2016. (Star Wars: Darth Vader Set 2 Ser.). (ENG.). 24p. (J). (gr. 6-12). lib. bdg. 27.07 *(978-1-61479-549-0(5),* 24383, Graphic Novels) Spotlight.

—Shadows & Secrets: Volume 4. Gillen, Kieron. 2016. (Star Wars: Darth Vader Set 2 Ser.). (ENG.). 24p. (J). (gr. 6-12). lib. bdg. 27.07 *(978-1-61479-550-6(9),* 24384, Graphic Novels) Spotlight.

—Shadows & Secrets: Volume 5. Gillen, Kieron. 2016. (Star Wars: Darth Vader Set 2 Ser.). (ENG.). 24p. (J). (gr. 6-12). lib. bdg. 27.07 *(978-1-61479-551-3(7),* 24385, Graphic Novels) Spotlight.

—Shadows & Secrets: Volume 6. Gillen, Kieron. 2016. (Star Wars: Darth Vader Set 2 Ser.). (ENG.). 24p. (J). (gr. 6-12). lib. bdg. 27.07 *(978-1-61479-552-0(5),* 24386, Graphic Novels) Spotlight.

—The Shu-Torun War: Volume 2. Gillen, Kieron. 2018. (Star Wars: Darth Vader Ser.). (ENG.). 24p. (J). (gr. 6-12). lib. bdg. 27.07 *(978-1-5321-4163-8(7),* 28579, Graphic Novels) Spotlight.

—The Shu-Torun War: Volume 3. Gillen, Kieron. 2018. (Star Wars: Darth Vader Ser.). (ENG.). 24p. (J). (gr. 6-12). lib. bdg. 27.07 *(978-1-5321-4164-5(5),* 28580, Graphic Novels) Spotlight.

—The Shu-Torun War: Volume 4. Gillen, Kieron. 2018. (Star Wars: Darth Vader Ser.). (ENG.). 24p. (J). (gr. 6-12). lib. bdg. 27.07 *(978-1-5321-4165-2(3),* 28581, Graphic Novels) Spotlight.

—The Shu-Torun War: Volume 5. Gillen, Kieron. 2018. (Star Wars: Darth Vader Ser.). (ENG.). 24p. (J). (gr. 6-12). lib. bdg. 27.07 *(978-1-5321-4166-9(1),* 28582, Graphic Novels) Spotlight.

—Star Wars: Darth Vader Set 2 (Set), 6 vols. Gillen, Kieron. 2016. (Star Wars: Darth Vader Set 2 Ser.). (ENG.). 24p. (J). (gr. 6-12). lib. bdg. 162.42 *(978-1-61479-546-9(0),* 24380, Graphic Novels) Spotlight.

—Vader. Gillen, Kieron. 2016. (Star Wars: Darth Vader Ser.). (ENG.). (J). (gr. 6-12). 24p. lib. bdg. 27.07 *(978-1-61479-521-6(5),* 21421); 24p. lib. bdg. 27.07 *(978-1-61479-523-0(1),* 21423); Vol. 1. 36p. lib. bdg. 27.07 *(978-1-61479-520-9(7),* 21420); Vol. 3. 24p. lib. bdg. 27.07 *(978-1-61479-522-3(3),* 21422); Vol. 5. 24p. lib. bdg. 27.07 *(978-1-61479-524-7(X),* 21424); Vol. 6. 24p. lib. bdg. 27.07 *(978-1-61479-525-4(8),* 21425) Spotlight. (Graphic Novels).

—Vader down: Volume 2. Gillen, Kieron. 2016. (Star Wars: Vader Down Ser.). (ENG.). 24p. (J). (gr. 6-12). lib. bdg. 27.07 *(978-1-61479-562-9(2),* 24396, Graphic Novels) Spotlight.

—Vader down: Volume 4. Gillen, Kieron. 2016. (Star Wars: Vader Down Ser.). (ENG.). 24p. (J). (gr. 6-12). lib. bdg. 27.07 *(978-1-61479-564-3(9),* 24398, Graphic Novels) Spotlight.

—Vader down: Volume 6. Gillen, Kieron. 2016. (Star Wars: Vader Down Ser.). (ENG.). 24p. (J). (gr. 6-12). lib. bdg. 27.07 *(978-1-61479-566-7(5),* 24400, Graphic Novels) Spotlight.

Larroca, Salvador & Immonen, Stuart. Rebel Jail: Volume 5. Aaron, Jason. 2017. (Star Wars: Rebel Jail Ser.). (ENG.). 24p. (J). (gr. 6-12). lib. bdg. 27.07 *(978-1-5321-4145-4(9),* 27018, Graphic Novels) Spotlight.

Larroca, Salvador & Scott, Greg. Fantastic Four: Heroes Return - the Complete Collection Vol. 2. 2020. (ENG.). 496p. (YA). (gr. 4-17). pap. 39.99 *(978-1-302-92340-2(4))* Marvel Worldwide, Inc.

Larroca, Salvador & Yardin, David. X-Men by Peter Milligan Vol. 1: Dangerous Liaisons. 2019. (ENG.). 320p. (YA). (gr. 8-17). pap. 34.99 *(978-1-302-91650-3(5))* Marvel Worldwide, Inc.

Larroca, Salvador, jt. illus. see Alburquerque, Alberto Jimenez.

Larsen, Alison. My Turtle. Larsen, Alison. 2006. 24p. (J). (gr. -1-3). per. 11.95 *(978-1-60002-095-7(X),* 3963) Mountain Valley Publishing, LLC.

—What Makes You Smile? Larsen, Alison. 2006. 23p. (J). (gr. -1-3). per. 13.95 *(978-1-60002-094-0(1))* Mountain Valley Publishing, LLC.

Larsen, Angela Sage. Petalwink Learns to Fly. Larsen, Angela Sage. 2010. 32p. (J). lib. bdg. 12.95 *(978-1-936086-20-7(4))* Rising Star Studios, LLC.

Larsen, Christine. By Night Vol. 1. Allison, John. 2019. (ENG.). 112p. (YA). pap. 14.99 *(978-1-68415-282-7(8))* Boom! Studios.

—By Night Vol. 2. Allison, John. 2019. (ENG.). 112p. (YA). pap. 14.99 *(978-1-68415-399-2(9))* Boom! Studios.

—By Night Vol. 3. Allison, John. 2020. (By Night Ser.: 3). (ENG.). 112p. (YA). pap. 14.99 *(978-1-68415-483-8(9))* Boom! Studios.

—The Five Stages of Andrew Brawley. Hutchinson, Shaun David. 2015. (ENG.). 304p. (YA). (gr. 7). 17.99 *(978-1-4814-0310-8(9),* Simon Pulse) Simon Pulse.

Larsen, Dan. Return to Winterville. Wood, Francis Eugene. Pickett, Elizabeth & Dean, Tina, eds. 2004. 96p. (YA). per. 14.95 net. *(978-0-9746372-1-1(1))* Tip-Of-The-Moon Publishing Co.

—The SnowPeople. Wood, Francis. 2003. 96p. (YA). per. 14.95 *(978-0-9746372-0-4(3))* Tip-Of-The-Moon Publishing Co.

Larsen, Eric, jt. illus. see Michael, Joan.

Larsen, Erik, et al. Amazing Spider-Man Epic Collection: Assassin Nation. 2019. (ENG.). 480p. (YA). (gr. -1-17). pap. 39.99 *(978-1-302-91811-8(7))* Marvel Worldwide, Inc.

Larsen, Kate. Love & Chicken Nuggets. Kelsey, Annie. 2017. (Pippa Morgan's Diary Ser.: 2). (ENG.). 176p. (J). (gr. 3-7). pap. 9.99 *(978-1-4926-4794-2(2),* Sourcebooks Jabberwocky) Sourcebooks, Inc.

Larsen, Ramonita. Yes, I Can Do It/Sí, lo Puedo Hacer. Larsen, Ramonita. l.t. ed. 2006. 18p. (J). per. 10.99 *(978-1-59879-292-8(X))* Lifevest Publishing, Inc.

Larson, Abigail. Monster Goose Nursery Rhymes, 1 vol. Herz, Henry et al. 2015. (Mother Goose Ser.). (ENG.). 32p. (J). (gr. k-3). 16.99 *(978-1-4556-2032-6(7),* Pelican Publishing) Arcadia Publishing.

—When You Give an Imp a Penny, 1 vol. Herz, Henry et al. 2016. (ENG.). 32p. (J). (gr. k-3). 16.99 *(978-1-4556-2144-6(7),* Pelican Publishing) Arcadia Publishing.

Larson, Amanda. The Adventures of Baylee Beagle: Coloring & Puzzle Book. 2005. (J). act. bk. ed. 5.00 *(978-0-9767096-3-3(5))* Maxim Pr.

—The Adventures of Baylee Beagle — Annabelle Beagle. Gildea, Kathy. 2005. 28p. (J). 7.95 *(978-0-9767096-1-9(9))* Maxim Pr.

—The Adventures of Baylee Beagle — Hurricane Hound. Gildea, Kathy. 2005. 28p. (J). 7.95 *(978-0-9767096-2-6(7))* Maxim Pr.

Larson, Caleb A. It's Your Ball after All. Larson, Melissa J. 2007. 20p. per. 24.95 *(978-1-4241-9046-1(0))* America Star Bks.

Larson, D. J. Pigsley Brew. Larson, D. J. 2003. 39p. (J). (gr. k-2). pap. 5.95 *(978-0-9728234-0-1(9))* Don't Look Publishing.

Larson, Elysia. I Am Not a Sloth. Hill, Janice. 2019. (ENG.). 26p. (J). pap. 9.13 ***(978-1-0756-4997-4(8))*** Independently Published.

Larson, Emory Leigh. Tommy Tractor & the Christmas Donkey. Ayers, Sanda. 2019. (Tommy Tractor Adventures Ser.: Vol. 5). (ENG.). 28p. (J). pap. 9.50 ***(978-1-6731-7057-3(9))*** Independently Published.

—Tommy Tractor Likes Colors. Ayers, Sanda. 2019. (Tommy Tractor Adventures Ser.: Vol. 4). (ENG.). 28p. (J). pap. 9.95 ***(978-1-0863-9431-3(3))*** Independently Published.

Larson, Hope. Intergalactic P. S. 3. L'Engle, Madeleine. 2018. (Wrinkle in Time Quintet Ser.). (ENG.). 112p. (J). 13.99 *(978-0-374-31072-1(6),* 900194248, Farrar, Straus & Giroux (BYR)) Farrar, Straus & Giroux.

—Intergalactic P. S. 3: A Wrinkle in Time Story. L'Engle, Madeleine. 2019. (Wrinkle in Time Quintet Ser.). (ENG.). 112p. (J). pap. 6.99 *(978-1-250-30849-8(6),* 900194249) Square Fish.

—A Wrinkle in Time. L'Engle, Madeleine. 2012. (ENG.). 392p. (J). (gr. 5-9). 24.99 *(978-0-374-38615-3(3),* 900068987, Farrar, Straus & Giroux (BYR)) Farrar, Straus & Giroux.

Larson, Hope. All Summer Long. Larson, Hope. 2018. (Eagle Rock Ser.: 1). (ENG.). 176p. (J). 21.99 *(978-0-374-30485-0(8),* 900160974); pap. 12.99 *(978-0-374-31071-4(8),* 900194119) Farrar, Straus & Giroux. (Farrar, Straus & Giroux (BYR)).

—All Together Now. Larson, Hope. 2020. (Eagle Rock Ser.: 2). (ENG.). 192p. (J). 21.99 *(978-0-374-31162-9(5),* 900195864); pap. 12.99 *(978-0-374-31365-4(2),* 900215357) Farrar, Straus & Giroux. (Farrar, Straus & Giroux (BYR)).

—Chiggers. Larson, Hope. 2008. (ENG.). 176p. (J). (gr. 5-9). pap. 12.99 *(978-1-4169-3587-2(8),* Simon & Schuster/Paula Wiseman Bks.) Simon & Schuster Children's Publishing.

—Mercury. Larson, Hope. 2010. (ENG.). 240p. (J). (gr. 7-18). pap. 16.99 *(978-1-4169-3588-9(6),* Atheneum Bks. for Young Readers) Simon & Schuster Children's Publishing.

Larson, J. E. Hades Speaks! A Guide to the Underworld by the Greek God of the Dead. Shecter, Vicky Alvear. 2014. (Secrets of the Ancient Gods Ser.). (ENG.). 128p. (J). (gr. 4-7). 16.95 *(978-1-62091-598-1(7))* Boyds Mills Pr.

—Thor Speaks! A Guide to the Realms by the Norse God of Thunder. Shecter, Vicky Alvear. 2015. (Secrets of the Ancient Gods Ser.). (ENG.). 128p. (J). (gr. 4-7). 16.95 *(978-1-62091-599-8(5))* Boyds Mills Pr.

Larson, Jennifer S., photos by. The Craft-a-Day Book: 30 Projects to Make with Recycled Materials. Cornell, Kari A. 2018. (ENG., 168p. (J). (gr. 6-12). 39.99 *(978-1-5124-1313-7(5),* Twenty-First Century Bks.) Lerner Publishing Group.

—Dig In! 12 Easy Gardening Projects Using Kitchen Scraps. Cornell, Kari A. 2018. (ENG., 64p. (J). (gr. 4-8). 31.99 *(978-1-5124-3065-3(X),* Millbrook Pr.) Lerner Publishing Group.

—The Nitty-Gritty Gardening Book: Fun Projects for All Seasons. Cornell, Kari A. 2015. (ENG., 48p. (J). (gr. 4-8). lib. bdg. 26.65 *(978-1-4677-2647-4(8),* Millbrook Pr.) Lerner Publishing Group.

Larson, Joan. Yetsa's Sweater, 1 vol. Olsen, Sylvia. 2013. (ENG.). 40p. (J). (gr. 1-3). 9.95 *(978-1-55039-202-9(6))* Sono Nis Pr. CAN. Dist: Orca Bk. Pubs. USA.

Larson, Katherine. Break-in at the Basilica: Adventures with Sister Philomena, Special Agent to the Pope. Ahern, Dianne. 2006. (J). *(978-0-9679437-8-7(7))* En Route Bks. & Media.

—Lost in Peter's Tomb: Adventures with Sister Philomena, Special Agent to the Pope. Ahern, Dianne. 2006. (J). pap. *(978-0-9679437-9-4(5))* En Route Bks. & Media.

—M Is for Melody: A Music Alphabet. Wargin, Kathy-jo. 2006. (Art & Culture Ser.). (ENG.). 40p. (J). (gr. 1-4). 16.95 *(978-1-58536-215-8(8),* 202129) Sleeping Bear Pr.

—M Is for Melody: A Music Alphabet. Wargin, Kathy-jo. rev. ed. 2006. (Art & Culture Ser.). (ENG.). 40p. (J). (gr. 1-4). pap. 9.99 *(978-1-58536-332-2(4),* 202295) Sleeping Bear Pr.

—Today I Made My First Reconciliation. Ahern, Dianne. 2004. 56p. 19.95 *(978-0-9679437-3-2(6))* En Route Bks. & Media.

Larson, Katherine & Langton, Bruce. A Is for Arches: A Utah Alphabet. Hall, Rebecca. 2003. (Discover America State by State Ser.). (ENG.). 40p. (J). (gr. 1-3). 17.95 *(978-1-58536-096-3(1),* 201976) Sleeping Bear Pr.

Larson, Lisa K. Claudius Saves the Pumpkin Patch. Kirby, Ruth M. 2008. 20p. pap. 24.95 *(978-1-60703-827-6(7))* America Star Bks.

Larson, Maria Burgaleta. The ABC's of Fruits & Vegetables & Beyond: Delicious Alphabet Poems Plus Food, Facts & Fun for Everyone. Charney, Steve & Goldbeck, David. 2007. 112p. (J). (gr. -1-4). per. 16.95 *(978-1-886101-07-4(8))* Ceres Pr.

Larson, Melissa. Iver & Ellsworth. Robinson, Casey W. 2018. (ENG.). 40p. (J). (gr. k-2). 17.99 *(978-0-9990249-1-1(4))* Ripple Grove Pr.

Larson, Sannel. Mr. Beaver Plans a Party: Illustrated Children's Book. Zutautas, Susan. 2016. (ENG.). (J). pap. *(978-0-9939172-1-9(6))* Zutautas, Susan.

Larsson, Therese, jt. illus. see Blaise, Aaron.

Larter, John & Bianco, Mike. Penguin Brothers, Vol. 1. Blaylock, Josh. 2005. 144p. (YA). pap. 10.95 *(978-1-932796-20-9(7))* Devil's Due Publishing, Inc.

LaRue, Athena Mariah. Danny the Fisherman, 1 vol. Stanley, Dan. 2010. 46p. 24.95 *(978-1-4512-9695-2(9))* PublishAmerica, Inc.

Lascelles, Desireah, jt. illus. see Rempel, Billi-Jo.

Lasher, Mary Ann, jt. illus. see Baum, Ann.

Lashley, Ken, et al. X-Men Gold Vol. 1: Back to the Basics, Vol. 1. 2017. (ENG.). 144p. (YA). (gr. 8-17). pap. 15.99 *(978-1-302-90730-3(1))* Marvel Worldwide, Inc.

Laskey, Shannon. Go for It! Start Smart, Have Fun, & Stay Inspired in Any Activity. Anton, Carrie, ed. 2008. (American Girl Library). (ENG.). 64p. (YA). (gr. 3-18). pap. 9.95 *(978-1-59369-423-4(7))* American Girl Publishing, Inc.

—3-D Studio. Falligant, Erin, ed. 2008. 48p. (J). 17.95 *(978-1-59369-414-2(8))* American Girl Publishing, Inc.

Lasky, David. El Deafo. Bell, Cece. 2014. (ENG.). (J). (gr. 3-7). lib. bdg. 22.05 *(978-1-62765-651-1(0))* Perfection Learning Corp.

Lasley, Tony. April's Journal: A Journal for Children. Reinoso, Marta. 13.95 incl. audio *(978-0-9676203-0-5(9))* Reinoso, Marta.

Lassal. 108 Word Search Puzzles with the American Sign Language Alphabet, Volume 05: ASL Fingerspelling Word Search Games. Lassal, . 2017. (ASL Word Search Ser.: Vol. 5). (ENG.). 126p. (J). (gr. 3-5). pap. *(978-3-86469-022-8(6))* LegendaryMedia.

Lassal. 108 Word Search Puzzles with the American Sign Language Alphabet, Volume 04 (Bundle Volumes 01+02+03) ASL Fingerspelling Word Search Games. Lassal. 2017. (ASL Word Search Ser.: Vol. 4). (ENG.). (J). (gr. 3-5). pap. *(978-3-86469-020-4(X))* LegendaryMedia.

Lassen, Caitlin Bryce. Ziggy: The Pig Who Loved Sushi. Mountain-Pazell, Rebecca. 2019. (ENG.). 45p. (J). pap. 12.95 *(978-1-9772-0849-1(5))* Outskirts Pr., Inc.

Lassen, Christian R. Ocean Friends. Book Company Staff. 2003. (Puzzles Ser.). (J). bds. 14.95 *(978-1-74047-381-1(7))* Book Co. Publishing Pty, Ltd., The AUS. Dist: Penton Overseas, Inc.

—Treasures of the Sea: Birthday & Address Book. Book Company Staff. 2003. (Stationery Ser.). (J). 14.95 *(978-1-86309-793-2(7))* Book Co. Publishing Pty, Ltd., The AUS. Dist: Penton Overseas, Inc.

Lassen, Christian Riese. Moon Dance. 2005. 16p. (J). (gr. -1-3). bds. 8.95 *(978-1-74047-591-4(7),* Penton Kids) Penton Overseas, Inc.

Lasson, Matt. Santa Heads South: Casey's Christmas Surprise. Jordan, L. W. 2008. 40p. per. 24.95 *(978-1-60441-374-8(3))* America Star Bks.

Last, Ian & Smith, Diana. How to Draw. 2005. (Art Tricks Ser.). 48p. (J). (gr. 4-7). *(978-1-84510-676-8(8))* Top That! Publishing PLC.

Laster, Brenda. The Valley of the Christmas Trees: A Legend. Rucker, David. 2007. 41p. (J). (gr. -1-3). 14.95 *(978-1-931643-94-8(6))* Seven Locks Pr.

Lat. Kampung Boy. Lat. rev. ed. 2006. Orig. Title: The Kampung Boy. (ENG.). 144p. (J). (gr. 7-8). pap. 19.99 *(978-1-59643-121-8(0),* 900031942, First Second Bks.) Roaring Brook Pr.

L'Atelier Cartographik. Hello World: A Celebration of Languages & Curiosities. Litton, Jonathan. 2016. (ENG.). 16p. (J). (gr. 2-6). 19.99 *(978-1-944530-00-6(2),* 360 Degrees) Tiger Tales.

Latham, Karen & Latham, Rebecca. V Is for Viking: A Minnesota Alphabet. Wargin, Kathy-jo. 2003. (Discover America State by State Ser.). (ENG.). 40p. (J). 17.95 *(978-1-58536-125-0(9))* Sleeping Bear Pr.

Latham, Rebecca, jt. illus. see Latham, Karen.

Latham, Sarah. The Day an Angel Ran into My Room. Valenzuela, Anabelle. 2012. 56p. 30.50 *(978-1-61897-794-6(6),* Strategic Bk. Publishing) Strategic Book Publishing & Rights Agency (SBPRA).

Lathrop, Dorothy P. A Little Boy Lost (Illustrated Edition) Hudson, W. H. 2019. (ENG.). 104p. (J). pap. ***(978-1-4068-9835-4(X))*** Echo Library.

Lathrop, Dorothy P. The Three Mulla-Mulgars (the Three Royal Monkeys) de la Mare, Walter. 2013. (ENG.). 288p. (J). (gr. 3-6). pap. 12.95 *(978-0-486-49380-0(6))* Dover Pubns., Inc.

Latimer, Alex. Just So Stories. Kipling, Rudyard. 2008. (Puffin Classics Ser.). (ENG.). (J). (gr. 5). lib. bdg. 15.60 *(978-1-61383-686-6(4))* Perfection Learning Corp.

Latimer, Alex. Am I Yours?, 1 vol. Latimer, Alex. (ENG.). 32p. (J). (gr. -1-3). 2020. pap. 7.99 *(978-1-68263-172-0(9));* 2018. 16.95 *(978-1-68263-044-0(7))* Peachtree Publishing Co. Inc.

L

—The Boy Who Cried Ninja, 1 vol. Latimer, Alex. 2011. (ENG.). 32p. (J). (gr. -1-3). 15.95 (978-1-56145-579-9(2)) Peachtree Publishing Co. Inc.
—The Boy Who Cried Ninja. Latimer, Alex. 2014. (ENG.). (J). (gr. k-3). lib. bdg. 18.55 (978-1-62765-364-0(3)) Perfection Learning Corp.
—Lion vs. Rabbit, 1 vol. Latimer, Alex. (ENG.). 32p. (J). (gr. -1-3). 2017. pap. 7.95 (978-1-56145-898-1(8)); 2013. 15.95 (978-1-56145-709-0(4)) Peachtree Publishing Co. Inc.
—Lula & the Sea Monster, 1 vol. Latimer, Alex. 2019. (ENG.). 32p. (J). (gr. -1-3). 16.95 (978-1-68263-122-5(2)) Peachtree Publishing Co. Inc.
—Never Follow a Dinosaur, 1 vol. Latimer, Alex. 2016. (ENG.). 32p. (J). (gr. -1-3). 16.95 (978-1-56145-704-5(3)) Peachtree Publishing Co. Inc.
—Penguin's Hidden Talent, 1 vol. Latimer, Alex. 2012. (ENG.). 32p. (J). 15.95 (978-1-56145-629-1(2)) Peachtree Publishing Co. Inc.
—Pig & Small, 1 vol. Latimer, Alex. (ENG.). 32p. (J). (gr. -1-3). 2018. pap. 7.95 (978-1-68263-036-5(6)); 2014. 15.95 (978-1-56145-797-7(3)) Peachtree Publishing Co. Inc.
—Stay! A Top Dog Story, 1 vol. Latimer, Alex. 2015. (ENG.). 32p. (J). (gr. -1-3). 16.95 (978-1-56145-884-4(8)) Peachtree Publishing Co. Inc.
Latimer, Miriam. Build-a-Story Cards. Barefoot Books & Barefoot Books Staff. 2018. (ENG.). 36p. (J). (gr. -1-4). ring bd. 12.99 (978-1-78285-383-1(9)) Barefoot Bks., Inc.
—Choose to Recycle. Bewley, Elizabeth. 2009. 10p. 7.95 (978-1-58117-904-0(9), Intervisual/Piggy Toes) Bendon, Inc.
—Dayenu! A Favorite Passover Song. Traditional Staff. 2012. (ENG.). 12p. (J). (gr. -1-k). bds. 7.99 (978-0-545-31236-3(1), Cartwheel Bks.) Scholastic, Inc.
—El Desayuno Del Principe. Oppenheim, Joanne F. & Barefoot Books. 2014. 32p. (J). (gr. -1-2). pap. 7.99 (978-1-78285-076-2(7)) Barefoot Bks., Inc.
—Dr. Potts, My Pets Have Spots! Hull, Rod. 2017. 32p. (J). (gr. -1-2). 16.99 (978-1-78285-319-0(7)); (ENG.). pap. 8.99 (978-1-78285-324-4(3)) Barefoot Bks., Inc.
—The Gingerbread Man. Tiger Tales. 2016. (My First Fairy Tales Ser.). (ENG.). 32p. (J). (gr. -1-2). pap. 7.99 (978-1-58925-477-0(5)) Tiger Tales.
—El Hermanito de Ruby. White, Kathryn. 2013. 32p. (J). pap. 8.99 (978-1-78285-026-7(0)) Barefoot Bks., Inc.
—The Prince's Bedtime. Oppenheim, Joanne F. 32p. (J). (gr. -1-3). 2007. pap. 7.99 (978-1-84686-106-2(3)); 2006. (ENG.). 16.99 (978-1-84148-597-3(7)) Barefoot Bks., Inc.
—The Prince's Bedtime. Oppenheim, Joanne. 2019. (ENG.). 32p. (J). (gr. -1-2). pap. (978-1-78285-419-7(3)) Barefoot Bks., Ltd.
—The Prince's Breakfast. Oppenheim, Joanne F. & Barefoot Books Staff. 2014. 32p. (J). (gr. -1-2). 16.99 (978-1-78285-074-8(0)); 9.99 (978-1-78285-075-5(9)) Barefoot Bks., Inc.
—The Prince's Breakfast. Oppenheim, Joanne. 2019. (ENG.). 32p. (J). (gr. -1-2). pap. (978-1-78285-417-3(7)) Barefoot Bks., Ltd.
—El Principe No Duerme. Oppenheim, Joanne F. & Barefoot Books Staff. 2014. 32p. (J). (gr. -1-1). pap. 7.99 (978-1-78285-077-9(5)) Barefoot Bks., Inc.
—Ruby's Baby Brother. White, Kathryn. 2013. 32p. (J). 16.99 (978-1-84686-864-1(5)); (gr. -1-2). pap. 8.99 (978-1-84686-950-1(1)) Barefoot Bks., Inc.
—Ruby's School Walk. White, Kathryn. 2010. 32p. (J). (gr. -1-2). 16.99 (978-1-84686-275-5(2)) Barefoot Bks., Inc.
—Ruby's School Walk. White, Kathryn. 2012. 29p. (J). (gr. -1-1). pap. 22.44 (978-1-84686-786-6(X)) Barefoot Bks., Ltd. GBR. Dist: Children's Plus, Inc.
—Ruby's Sleepover. White, Kathryn. 32p. (J). 2013. (gr. -1-2). pap. 8.99 (978-1-84686-758-3(4)); 2012. (ENG.). 16.99 (978-1-84686-593-0(X)) Barefoot Bks., Inc.
—Shopping with Dad. Harvey, Matt. 2008. 32p. (J). (gr. -1-3). 16.99 (978-1-84686-172-7(1)) Barefoot Bks., Inc.
—The Sunflower Sword. Sperring, Mark. 2011. (Andersen Press Picture Bks). (ENG.). 32p. (J). (gr. -1-3). 16.95 (978-0-7613-7486-2(8)) Lerner Publishing Group.
Latimer, Miriam. Shopping with Dad. Latimer, Miriam. Harvey, Matt. 2010. 32p. (J). (gr. -1-2). pap. 7.99 (978-1-84686-449-0(6)) Barefoot Bks., Inc.
—Shrinking Sam. Latimer, Miriam. 2007. 32p. (J). (gr. -1-3). 16.99 (978-1-84686-038-6(5)) Barefoot Bks., Inc.
Latimer, Muriam. The Prince's Bedtime. Latimer, Muriam. Oppenheim, Joanne F. 2007. 32p. (J). (gr. -1-2). 9.99 (978-1-84686-096-6(2)) Barefoot Bks., Inc.
Latimer, Patrick. Wild Violet! Latimer, Alex. 2018. 32p. (J). (gr. -1-k). pap. 9.99 (978-1-84365-382-0(6), Pavilion) Pavilion Bks. GBR. Dist: Independent Pubs. Group.
—Woolf. Latimer, Alex. 2018. 32p. (J). (gr. k-2). pap. 9.99 (978-1-84365-340-0(0), Pavilion Children's Books) Pavilion Bks. GBR. Dist: Penguin Random Hse. LLC.
Latimor, Miriam. Emily's Tiger. Latimor, Miriam. 2011. 32p. (J). (gr. -1-2). pap. 7.99 (978-1-84686-594-7(8)) Barefoot Bks., Inc.
Latino, Kyle. Savage Beard of She Dwarf. Latino, Kyle. 2020. (Savage Beard of She Dwarf Ser.). (ENG.). 144p. (YA). pap. 19.99 (978-1-62010-738-6(4), Lion Forge) Oni Pr., Inc.
Latorre, Adolfo. Cornbread Runs for Class President, Taylor, Vincent. Griffin, Kasana & Griggs, Charles, eds. 2004. (Cornbread Ser.: 1). 96p. (J). per. 4.99 (978-0-9704512-4-8(5)) TriEclipse, Inc.
Lätti, Leo. Cristoforo Colombo e la Pasta Al Pomodoro - Christopher Columbus & the Pasta with Tomato Sauce: A Bilingual Picture Book (Italian-English Text) Bach, Nancy. 2013. 30p. pap. (978-1-938712-06-7(4)) Roxby Media Ltd.
—Galileo Galilei e la Torre Di Pisa - Galileo Galilei & the Pisa Tower: A Bilingual Picture Book about the Italian Astronomer (Italian-English Text) Bach, Nancy. 2013. 26p. pap. (978-1-938712-07-4(2)) Roxby Media Ltd.
—Giuseppe Verdi, Compositore d'Opera Italiano - Giuseppe Verdi, Italian Opera Composer: A Bilingual Picture Book (Italian-English Text) Bach, Nancy. 2013. 28p. pap. (978-1-938712-12-8(9)) Roxby Media Ltd.
—Maria Montessori & Her Quiet Revolution: A Picture Book about Maria Montessori & Her School Method. Bach, Nancy. 2013. 24p. pap. (978-1-938712-10-4(2)) Roxby Media Ltd.
—Ottavia e I Gatti Di Roma - Octavia & the Cats of Rome: A Bilingual Picture Book in Italian & English. Cerulli, Claudia. 2013. 40p. pap. (978-1-938712-11-1(0)) Roxby Media Ltd.
Lattie, Tim. Battle Extravagonzo #1. Tobin, Paul. 2019. (Plants vs. Zombies Ser.). (ENG.). 28p. (J). (gr. 3-7). lib. bdg. 27.07 (978-1-5321-4380-9(X), 32883, Graphic Novels) Spotlight.
—Battle Extravagonzo #2. Tobin, Paul. 2019. (Plants vs. Zombies Ser.). (ENG.). 28p. (J). (gr. 3-7). lib. bdg. 27.07 (978-1-5321-4381-6(8), 32884, Graphic Novels) Spotlight.
—Battle Extravagonzo #3. Tobin, Paul. 2019. (Plants vs. Zombies Ser.). (ENG.). 28p. (J). (gr. 3-7). lib. bdg. 27.07 (978-1-5321-4382-3(6), 32885, Graphic Novels) Spotlight.
—Plants vs. Zombies: Garden Warfare Volume 2. Tobin, Paul. 2018. (ENG.). 88p. (J). (gr. 3-7). 10.99 (978-1-5067-0548-4(0), Dark Horse Books) Dark Horse Comics.
Lattie, Tim, jt. illus. see Rainwater, Matt J.
Lattimore, Eleanor Frances. Little Pear. Lattimore, Eleanor Frances. 2006. (ENG.). 128p. (J). (gr. 1-4). pap. 7.99 (978-0-15-205502-8(9), 1196550) Houghton Mifflin Harcourt Publishing Co.
—Little Pear & His Friends. Lattimore, Eleanor Frances. 2006. (ENG.). 144p. (J). (gr. 1-4). pap. 10.95 (978-0-15-205490-8(1), 1196517) Houghton Mifflin Harcourt Publishing Co.
Latts, Sarah. L' il Red in the Great White North. Richard, Zachary. 2017. (ENG.). (J). (gr. -1-3). pap. 14.95 (978-1-946160-13-3(X)) Univ. of Louisiana at Lafayette Pr.
Latushkin, Valentin. The Picture Book Dictionary: The Essential Source for Bilingual Families, English-Spanish Edition. Laud, Valerie. l.t. ed. 2005. (ENG & SPA.). 96p. (J). (978-0-9747387-0-3(0)) EKADOO Publishing Group.
Latyk, Oliver. The Little Boy Star: An Allegory of the Holocaust. Hausfater, Rachel et al. 2nd ed. 2017. (ENG.). 32p. (J). (gr. k-3). pap. 19.95 (978-1-59687-542-5(9), ipicturebooks) ibooks, Inc.
Latyk, Olivier. Cars. Krasinski, Géraldine. 2019. (AllAbout Ser.). (ENG.). 22p. (J). (gr. -1-k). 14.99 (978-2-408-00790-4(9)) Editions Tourbillon FRA. Dist: Hachette Bk. Group.
—Follow the Red Balloon. 2015. (J). (978-1-4351-5986-0(1)) Barnes & Noble, Inc.
—Jeannette Claus Saves Christmas. Rees, Douglas. 2010. (ENG.). 40p. (J). (gr. k-3). 16.99 (978-1-4169-2686-3(0), McElderry, Margaret K. Bks.) McElderry, Margaret K. Bks.
—Letters I Know. Prasadam-Halls, Smriti. 2019. (Start Little, Learn Big Wipe-Clean Writing Practice Board Book Ser.). (ENG.). 14p. (J). (gr. -1-1). bds. 8.99 (978-1-68052-589-2(1), 2002310, Parragon Books) Cottage Door Pr.
—Lift-The-Flap Colors. Prasadam-Halls, Smriti. 2019. (Start Little, Learn Big Children's Interactive Lift-A-Flap Board Book Ser.). (ENG.). 12p. (J). (gr. -1-k). bds. 8.99 (978-1-68052-593-9(X), 2002350, Parragon Books) Cottage Door Pr.
—The Little Boy Star: An Allegory of the Holocaust. Hausfater, Rachel. Zimmerman, Joelle, tr. from FRE. 2006. (ENG.). 32p. (J). (gr. 4-7). 16.95 (978-1-59687-172-4(5)) iBks., Inc.
—El Nino Estrella. Hausfater-Douieb, Rachel. 2005. (SPA.). 32p. (J). 20.99 (978-84-263-5007-7(0)) Vives, Luis Editorial (Edelvives) ESP. Dist: Lectorum Pubns., Inc.
—Numbers I Know. Prasadam-Halls, Smriti. 2019. (Start Little, Learn Big Wipe-Clean Writing Practice Board Book Ser.). (ENG.). 14p. (J). (gr. -1-k). bds. 8.99 (978-1-68052-590-8(5), 2002320, Parragon Books) Cottage Door Pr.
Lau, Benny. Socks Heaven. 2003. (ENG.). 32p. (J). (-k). 15.50 (978-962-86816-5-5(6)) Zephyr Pr.
Lau, Kevin. Sunn. Roman, Steven A. Preiss, Byron, ed. 2003. 192p. pap. 9.95 (978-0-7434-7504-4(6)) ibooks, Inc.
Lau, Lisa. Luna the Cat & the Halloween Pumpkin. Hutton, Samantha V. 2019. (ENG.). 46p. (J). pap. 10.50 (978-1-7918-7612-8(9)) Independently Published.
Lau, Sarah. When I Grow Up. Letic, Anica. 2018. (ENG.). 24p. (J). (978-1-5255-1840-9(2)); pap. (978-1-5255-1841-6(0)) FriesenPress.
Laub, Frima & Uhlig, Elizabeth. Between the Shadows. Laub, Frima. 2009. 81p. (J). pap. 12.95 (978-0-9815345-2-7(X)) Marble Hse. Editions.
Laubscher, André, jt. illus. see Lomofsky, Lynne.
Laud, Julia. My First Book of Indonesian Words: An ABC Rhyming Book of Indonesian Language & Culture. Hibbs, Linda. 32p. (J). (gr. -1-3). 2020. 10.99 (978-0-8048-5311-8(8)); 2016. (ENG.). 12.95 (978-0-8048-4557-1(3)) Tuttle Publishing.
Laudec. Cedric Vol. 4: Hot & Cold. Cauvin, Raoul. 2013. (Cedric Ser.: 4). (ENG.). 48p. pap. 11.95 (978-1-84918-158-7(6)) CineBook GBR. Dist: National Bk. Network.
—What Got into Him?, Vol. Cauvin, Raoul. 2011. (Cedric Ser.: 3). (ENG.). 48p. (gr. 3-17). pap. 11.95 (978-1-84918-081-8(4)) CineBook GBR. Dist: National Bk. Network.
Laudec, Calvinaoul. Cedric 1 - High-Risk Class. Cauvin, Raoul. 2008. (Cedric Ser.: 1). (ENG.). 48p. pap. 11.95 (978-1-905460-68-7(6)) CineBook GBR. Dist: National Bk. Network.
Laudiero, Spencer. Eleanor Wyatt, Princess & Pirate. MacFarlane, Rachael. 2018. (Eleanor Wyatt & Harrison Dwight Ser.). (ENG.). 32p. (J). 17.99 (978-1-250-13857-6(4), 900179124) Imprint IND. Dist: Macmillan.
—Harrison Dwight, Ballerina & Knight. MacFarlane, Rachael. 2019. (Eleanor Wyatt & Harrison Dwight Ser.). (ENG.). 40p. (J). 17.99 (978-1-250-13858-3(2), 900179125) Imprint IND. Dist: Macmillan.
Lauffray, Mathieu. The Emerald Maze, Vol. 3. Dorison, Xavier. 2012. (Long John Silver Ser.: 3). (ENG.). 56p. pap. 13.95 (978-1-84918-105-1(5)) CineBook GBR. Dist: National Bk. Network.
—Lady Vivian Hastings. Dorison, Xavier. Saincantin, Jerome, tr. 2011. (Long John Silver Ser.: 1). (ENG.). 56p. pap. 13.95 (978-1-84918-062-7(8)) CineBook GBR. Dist: National Bk. Network.
—Long John Silver Vol. 4: Guiana-Capac. Dorison, Xavier. 2014. (Long John Silver Ser.: 4). (ENG.). 64p. pap. 15.95 (978-1-84918-175-4(6)) CineBook GBR. Dist: National Bk. Network.
—Neptune Vol. 2: Long John Silver. Dorison, Xavier. 2011. (Long John Silver Ser.: 2). (ENG.). 56p. pap. 13.95 (978-1-84918-072-6(5)) CineBook GBR. Dist: National Bk. Network.
Laufman, Derek. Buggin' Out! Cadenhead, MacKenzie & Ryan, Sean. 2019. (Marvel Super Hero Adventures Ser.). (ENG.). 80p. (J). (gr. 1-5). lib. bdg. 27.07 (978-1-5321-4312-0(5), 31842, Chapter Bks.) Spotlight.
—Deck the Malls! Cadenhead, MacKenzie & Ryan, Sean. 2019. (Marvel Super Hero Adventures Ser.). (ENG.). 80p. (J). (gr. 1-5). lib. bdg. 27.07 (978-1-5321-4313-7(3), 31843, Chapter Bks.) Spotlight.
—Marvel Super Hero Adventures Buggin' Out! An Early Chapter Book. Cadenhead, MacKenzie. 2018. (Super Hero Adventures Chapter Bks.: 3). (ENG.). 80p. (J). (gr. 1-3). pap. 4.99 (978-1-368-00857-0(7), Marvel Pr.) Disney Publishing Worldwide.
—Marvel Super Hero Adventures Mighty Marvels! An Early Chapter Book. Cadenhead, MacKenzie & Ryan, Sean. 2019. (Super Hero Adventures Chapter Bks.: 4). (ENG.). 80p. (J). (gr. 1-3). pap. 4.99 (978-1-368-00858-7(5), Marvel Pr.) Disney Publishing Worldwide.
—Marvel Super Hero Adventures (Set), 4 vols. Cadenhead, MacKenzie & Ryan, Sean. 2019. (Marvel Super Hero Adventures Ser.). (ENG.). 80p. (J). (gr. 1-5). lib. bdg. 108.28 (978-1-5321-4311-3(7), 31841, Chapter Bks.) Spotlight.
—Marvel's Super Hero Adventures Spider-Man: a Tangled Web. Roth, Megan. 2018. (Magnetic Hardcover Ser.). (ENG.). 10p. (J). (gr. -1-k). 12.99 (978-0-7944-4010-7(X), Reader's Digest Children's Bks.) Studio Fun International.
—Mighty Marvels! Cadenhead, MacKenzie & Ryan, Sean. 2019. (Marvel Super Hero Adventures Ser.). (ENG.). 80p. (J). (gr. 1-5). lib. bdg. 27.07 (978-1-5321-4314-4(1), 31844, Chapter Bks.) Spotlight.
Laufman, Derek & Brizuela, Dario. Marvel Super Hero Adventures: These Are the Avengers. West, Alexandra. 2019. (World of Reading Level 1 Ser.). (ENG.). 32p. (J). (gr. -1-3). lib. bdg. 27.07 (978-1-5321-4402-8(4), 33807) Spotlight.
Laufman, Derek & Marvel Press Artist. World of Reading Super Hero Adventures: Meet Ant-Man & the Wasp (Level 1) West, Alexandra C. 2018. (World of Reading Ser.). (ENG.). 32p. (J). (gr. -1-k). pap. 4.99 (978-1-368-02354-2(1), Marvel Pr.) Disney Publishing Worldwide.
Laufman, Derek, jt. illus. see Marvel Press Artist.
Laughbaum, Steve & Crutchfield, Jim. Tennessee Trailblazers. Sparkman, Winette. 56p. (J). pap., wbk. ed., act. bk. ed. 6.95 (978-0-9634824-1-9(6)) March Media, Inc.
Laughead, Mike. The Big Catch: A Robot & Rico Story, 1 vol. Suen, Anastasia. 2009. (Robot & Rico Ser.). (ENG.). 32p. (J). (gr. 1-2). pap. 6.25 (978-1-4342-1751-6(5), Stone Arch Bks.) Capstone.
—The Comet of Doom, 1 vol. Perritano, John. 2014. (Kid Squad Saves the World Ser.). (ENG.). 112p. (J). (gr. 3-6). 29.93 (978-1-62402-038-4(0), 1473, Calico Chapter Bks.) ABDO Publishing Co.
—Dino Hunt: A Robot & Rico Story. Suen, Anastasia. 2010. (Robot & Rico Ser.). (ENG.). 32p. (J). (gr. 1-2). pap. 6.25 (978-1-4342-2300-5(0), Stone Arch Bks.) Capstone.
—A Dress for Me!, 0 vols. Fliess, Sue. 2012. (ENG.). 24p. (J). (gr. k-3). 12.99 (978-0-7614-6148-7(5), 9780761461487, Two Lions) Amazon Publishing.
—The Egyptian Prophecy. Perritano, John. 2014. (Kid Squad Saves the World Ser.). (ENG.). 112p. (J). (gr. 2-5). 29.93 (978-1-62402-039-1(9), 1475, Calico Chapter Bks.) ABDO Publishing Co.
—Find the Farter. Sourcebooks & Hart, Phyllis F. 2019. 40p. (J). 14.99 (978-1-4926-8567-8(4)) Sourcebooks, Inc.
—La Gran Pesca. Suen, Anastasia & Heck, Claudia M. 2012. (Robot y Rico/Robot & Rico Ser.).Tr. of Big Catch. (ENG.). 32p. (J). (gr. 1-2). pap. 5.05 (978-1-4342-3920-4(9)); lib. bdg. 22.65 (978-1-4342-3781-1(8)) Capstone. (Stone Arch Bks.).
—La Noche de Terror. Suen, Anastasia. Heck, Claudia M., tr. 2012. (Robot y Rico/Robot & Rico Ser.).Tr. of Scary Night. (ENG.). 32p. (J). (gr. 1-2). pap. 5.05 (978-1-4342-3918-1(7)); lib. bdg. 22.65 (978-1-4342-3779-8(6)) Capstone. (Stone Arch Bks.).
—The Pirate Map: A Robot & Rico Story. Suen, Anastasia. 2010. (Robot & Rico Ser.). (ENG.). 32p. (J). (gr. 1-2). pap. 6.25 (978-1-4342-2301-2(9), Stone Arch Bks.) Capstone.
—Un Premio Adentro. Suen, Anastasia. Heck, Claudia M., tr. 2012. (Robot y Rico/Robot & Rico Ser.).Tr. of Prize Inside. (ENG.). 32p. (J). (gr. 1-2). pap. 5.05 (978-1-4342-3919-8(5)); lib. bdg. 22.65 (978-1-4342-3780-4(X)) Capstone. (Stone Arch Bks.).
—A Prize Inside: A Robot & Rico Story, 1 vol. Suen, Anastasia. 2009. (Robot & Rico Ser.). (ENG.). 32p. (J). (gr. 1-2). 22.65 (978-1-4342-1627-4(6)); pap. 6.25 (978-1-4342-1749-3(3)) Capstone. (Stone Arch Bks.).
—The Scary Night: A Robot & Rico Story, 1 vol. Suen, Anastasia. 2009. (Robot & Rico Ser.). (ENG.). 32p. (J). (gr. 1-2). 22.65 (978-1-4342-1628-1(4)); pap. 6.25 (978-1-4342-1752-3(3)) Capstone. (Stone Arch Bks.).
—Shoes for Me! Fliess, Sue. 2018. (ENG.). 26p. (J). (gr. -1-1). pap. 9.99 (978-1-4778-1069-9(2), 9781477810699, Two Lions) Amazon Publishing.
—Skate Trick: A Robot & Rico Story, 1 vol. Suen, Anastasia. 2009. (Robot & Rico Ser.). (ENG.). 32p. (J). (gr. 1-2). pap. 6.25 (978-1-4342-1750-9(7), Stone Arch Bks.) Capstone.
—The Snickerblooms & the Age Bug, 1 vol. Perritano, John. 2014. (Kid Squad Saves the World Ser.). (ENG.). 112p. (J). (gr. 2-5). 29.93 (978-1-62402-041-4(0), 1479, Calico Chapter Bks.) ABDO Publishing Co.
—Snow Games: A Robot & Rico Story. Suen, Anastasia. 2010. (Robot & Rico Ser.). (ENG.). 32p. (J). (gr. 1-2). pap. 6.25 (978-1-4342-2302-9(7)); lib. bdg. 22.65 (978-1-4342-1869-8(4)) Capstone. (Stone Arch Bks.).
—Test Drive: A Robot & Rico Story. Suen, Anastasia. 2010. (Robot & Rico Ser.). (ENG.). 32p. (J). (gr. 1-2). pap. 6.25 (978-1-4342-2303-6(5), Stone Arch Bks.) Capstone.
—Trucos en la Patineta. Suen, Anastasia. Heck, Claudia M., tr. 2012. (Robot y Rico/Robot & Rico Ser.).Tr. of Skate Trick. 32p. (J). (gr. 1-2). (ENG.). 24p. (J). pap. 5.05 (978-1-4342-3917-4(9)); (MUL, SPA & ENG.). lib. bdg. 21.32 (978-1-4342-3778-1(8)) Capstone. (Stone Arch Bks.).
—What If You Need to Call 911?, 1 vol. Guard, Anara. 2011. (Danger Zone Ser.). (ENG.). 24p. (J). (gr. k-2). lib. bdg. 26.65 (978-1-4048-6682-9(5), Picture Window Bks.) Capstone.
Laugherty, Jeanne M. The Circumstantial Wallowing of Allister the Alligator. Pelkey II, James R. 2018. (ENG.). 28p. (J). pap. 10.00 (978-0-9981870-0-6(3)) Dreighton Pubns.
Launay, Melissa. My Mama Earth. Katz, Susan B. 2012. (ENG.). 24p. (J). 16.99 (978-1-84686-418-6(6)) Barefoot Bks., Inc.
Laune, Paul. A Figure in Hiding, No. 16. Dixon, Franklin W. 2005. (Hardy Boys Ser.). (ENG.). 228p. (J). (gr. 3-9). 17.95 (978-1-55709-274-8(5)) Applewood Bks.
—The Lone Ranger Traps the Smugglers. Striker, Fran. 2011. 224p. 44.95 (978-1-258-09845-2(8)) Literary Licensing, LLC.
—Wilbur & Orville Wright: Boys with Wings. Stevenson, Augusta. 2011. 192p. (gr. 2-5). 42.95 (978-1-258-07857-7(0)) Literary Licensing, LLC.
—William Henry Harrison, Young Tippecanoe: Childhood of Famous Americans Series. Peckham, Howard Henry. 2011. 190p. 42.95 (978-1-258-07766-2(3)) Literary Licensing, LLC.
—A Yankee Flier in the Far East. Avery, Al. 2011. 224p. 44.95 (978-1-258-06349-8(2)) Literary Licensing, LLC.
Laura, Ana. La Princesa Que Se Cansó. Laura, Ana. 2019. (SPA.). 30p. (J). pap. 10.00 (978-1-0955-3226-3(X)) Independently Published.
Laura, Bachynski. The Diaries of Polly Aster. Tannas, Kathy. 2018. (ENG.). 252p. (J). pap. (978-1-77354-079-5(3)) PageMaster Publication Services, Inc.
Laura Lee, Cundiff. The Last Little Polar Bear: A Global Change Adventure Story. Foresman, Timothy. 2007. 60p. (J). per. 19.95 (978-0-9776906-2-6(8)) Blueline Publishing.
Laurel, Hylton. The Cowboy Frog. Laurel, Hylton. 2003. 24p. (J). (gr. k-5). pap. 5.95 (978-1-875641-85-7(8)) Magabala Bks. AUS. Dist: Independent Pubs. Group.
Laurel, Jaime. My First Book of Tagalog Words: An ABC Rhyming Book of Filipino Language & Culture. Romulo, Liana. 2018. 32p. (J). (gr. -1-3). 10.99 (978-0-8048-5014-8(3)) Tuttle Publishing.
Laurence, Laurence, jt. illus. see Pirie, Lauren.
Laurent, Fabien. Art Through the Ages. Furon, Frédéric & Virgona, Mady. 2018. (J). (978-1-4413-2799-4(1)) Peter Pauper Pr. Inc.
Laurente, Lourdes. The Faraway Kingdom of Oop Loop la Pink. Bradley, Adrian. 2013. 36p. pap. 10.95 (978-0-9910180-0-0(1)) Someday Ranch.
Laures, Blayne. Daisy & the Shepherd. McPherson, Betsy. 2019. (ENG.). 44p. (J). (gr. k-6). 26.95 (978-1-61493-644-2(7)) Peppertree Pr., The.
Lauresa, Tomlinson. Elaytay's Adventures in Space & Time - (pt3) Which Time May Be. Lauresa, Tomlinson. 2019. (ENG.). (YA). (gr. 7-12). 246p. 18.99 (978-1-950421-23-7(6)); 236p. pap. 11.99 (978-1-950421-10-7(4)) Young of Heart Publishing.
Laurice, Skye. Hunter's Super Night. Ellen, Laurel. 2019. (ENG.). 48p. (J). pap. (978-1-5255-5001-0(2)) FriesenPress.
Lauricella, Domenic. Ecological Footprints. Jakab, Cheryl. 2011. (Environment in Focus Ser.). 32p. (gr. 4-4). 29.50 (978-1-60870-088-2(7)) Cavendish Square Publishing LLC.
—Food Supplies. Jakab, Cheryl. 2011. (Environment in Focus Ser.). 32p. (gr. 4-4). 29.50 (978-1-60870-090-5(9)) Cavendish Square Publishing LLC.
—Natural Wonders. Jakab, Cheryl. 2011. (Environment in Focus Ser.). 32p. (gr. 4-4). 29.50 (978-1-60870-092-9(5)) Cavendish Square Publishing LLC.
—Pollution. Jakab, Cheryl. 2011. (Environment in Focus Ser.). 32p. (gr. 4-4). 29.50 (978-1-60870-089-9(5)) Cavendish Square Publishing LLC.
Laurie, Caple. Fiddleheads to Fir Trees: Leaves in All Seasons, 1 vol. Linden, Joanne. 2013. (ENG.). 32p. (J). 12.00 (978-0-87842-606-5(X)) Mountain Pr. Publishing Co., Inc.
Laurie, Cook. Amelia Asks Why. 2007. (J). 3.99 (978-0-9726075-4-4(4)) EPI Bks.
Laurie, Jane. Twisted Fairy Tales. McHugh, Maura. 2013. (ENG.). 144p. (J). (gr. 6-11). 19.99 (978-0-7641-6588-7(7), B.E.S. Publishing) Peterson's.
Laurie, Linda. A Most Amazing Zoo. Flynn, Linda. 2020. (ENG.). 44p. (J). (gr. k-1). pap. (978-1-910542-48-4(2)) Chapeltown.
Laurie, Marshall. The Flood of Kindness: Inspired by Hurricane Katrina. Webster, DeAnte. 2017. (ENG.). 34p. (J). (gr. 2-5). 16.95 (978-0-692-94964-1(X)) Blessed Bk. Publishing.
Lauritano, Michael. Magic Mail: (Birthday Gift, Holiday Gift, Magic-Themed Interactive Gift, Kid's Magic Kit, Children's Magic Book) Jay, Joshua. 2020. (ENG.). 30p. (J). (gr. 3-7). 19.99 (978-1-4521-5916-4(5)) Chronicle Bks. LLC.
—Snowmobile: Bombardier's Dream Machine. Older, Jules. 2012. 64p. (J). (gr. 3-6). 21.19 (978-1-58089-334-3(1)); pap. 6.95 (978-1-58089-335-0(X)) Charlesbridge Publishing, Inc.

Lauritano, Michael & Love, Mike. Mayflower: The Ship That Started a Nation. Siegel, Rebecca. 2020. (ENG.). 64p. (J). (gr. 2-6). 19.95 *(978-0-7112-4825-0(7)*, 330713, Words & Pictures) Quarto Publishing Group UK GBR. Dist: Hachette UK Distribution.
Lauso, Judith. Maz, You're Up! Mazeroski, Kelly. 2010. 24p. (J). pap. 12.95 *(978-0-936340-18-0(5))* Historical Society of Western Pennsylvania.
Laustroer, Jonas. The Elephant's Child. Kipling, Rudyard. 2018. (ENG.). 64p. (J). (gr. k-2). 19.99 *(978-988-8341-67-2(7)*, Minedition) Neugebauer, Michael (Publishing) Limited HKG. Dist: Penguin Random Hse. LLC.
Lauter, Richard. Little Women. (Young Collector's Illustrated Classics Ser.). 192p. (J). 9.95 *(978-1-56156-371-5(4))* Kidsbooks, LLC.
—Little Women: With a Discussion of Family. Alcott, Louisa May. 2003. (Values in Action Illustrated Classics Ser.). 191p. (J). *(978-1-59203-032-3(7))* Learning Challenge, Inc.
—The Secret Garden: With a Discussion of Compassion. Burnett, Frances Hodgson. 2003. (Values in Action Illustrated Classics Ser.). 191p. (J). *(978-1-59203-037-8(8))* Learning Challenge, Inc.
Lauter, Richard. The Adventures of Huckleberry Finn: With a Discussion of Friendship. Lauter, Richard, tr. Twain, Mark. 2003. (Values in Action Illustrated Classics Ser.). (J). *(978-1-59203-042-2(4))* Learning Challenge, Inc.
Lauve, Celia & Shepherd, Rosalie M. Clarence Thomas: Fighter with Words, 1 vol. Collins, David R. 2003. (ENG.). 32p. (J). (gr. 1-3). 16.99 *(978-1-56554-862-6(0)*, Pelican Publishing) Arcadia Publishing.
Laval, Thierry. Look & Find at Home. Laval, Thierry. 2017. (Mini Look & Find Ser.). (ENG.). 14p. (J). (gr. -1-k). 9.95 *(978-0-531-23082-4(1)*, Children's Pr.) Scholastic Library Publishing.
—Look & Find at School. Laval, Thierry. 2017. (Mini Look & Find Ser.). (ENG.). 14p. (J). (gr. -1-k). 9.95 *(978-0-531-23081-7(3)*, Children's Pr.) Scholastic Library Publishing.
—Look & Find on the Farm. Laval, Thierry. 2017. (Mini Look & Find Ser.). (ENG.). 14p. (J). (gr. -1-k). 9.95 *(978-0-531-23080-0(5)*, Children's Pr.) Scholastic Library Publishing.
—Look & Find on Vacation. Laval, Thierry. 2017. (Mini Look & Find Ser.). (ENG.). 14p. (J). (gr. -1-k). 9.95 *(978-0-531-23083-1(X)*, Children's Pr.) Scholastic Library Publishing.
Lavallee, Barbara. All You Need for a Snowman. Schertle, Alice. 2007. (ENG.). 32p. (J). (gr. -1-3). pap. 7.99 *(978-0-15-206115-9(0)*, 1198369) Houghton Mifflin Harcourt Publishing Co.
—All You Need for a Snowman (board Book) Schertle, Alice. 2019. (ENG.). 28p. (J). (— 1). bds. 8.99 *(978-0-358-08701-4(5)*, 1746696, HMH Books For Young Readers) Houghton Mifflin Harcourt Publishing Co.
—Groucho's Eyebrows: An Alaskan Cat Tale. Brown, Tricia. 2012. (ENG.). 32p. (J). (gr. -1-1). pap. 11.99 *(978-0-88240-892-7(5)*, Alaska Northwest Bks.) West Margin Pr.
—Papa, Do You Love Me? Joosse, Barbara M. 2005. (Mama Ser.: MAMA). (ENG.). 36p. (J). (gr. -1-7). 15.99 *(978-0-8118-4265-5(7))* Chronicle Bks. LLC.
—The Sourdough Man: An Alaska Folktale. Stihler, Chérie B. 2010. (Paws IV Ser.). 32p. (J). (gr. -1-2). pap. 10.99 *(978-1-57061-594-8(2)*, Little Bigfoot) Sasquatch Bks.
Lavandeira, Sandra. Celebra el Dia de San Patricio con Samantha y Lola. Ada, Alma Flor & Campoy, F. Isabel. 2006. (Cuentos para Celebrar / Stories to Celebrate Ser.). (SPA.). 30p. (J). pap. 11.95 *(978-1-63113-883-6(9))* Santillana USA Publishing Co., Inc.
—Celebra el Dia De3 San Patricio con Samantha y Lola. Flor Ada, Alma. 2006. (Cuentos para Celebrar / Stories to Celebrate Ser.). (SPA.). 30p. (J). (gr. k-6). per. 11.95 *(978-1-59820-117-8(4)*, Alfaguara) Santillana USA Publishing Co., Inc.
—Cuentopos de Gulubu. Walsh, Maria Elena. 2003. (SPA.). 120p. (J). (gr. 3-5). 14.95 *(978-950-511-630-0(6))* Alfaguara S.A. de Ediciones ARG. Dist: Santillana USA Publishing Co., Inc.
—Dailan Kifki. Walsh, Maria Elena. 2003. (SPA.). 248p. (YA). (gr. 5-8). 18.95 *(978-950-511-629-4(2))* Alfaguara S.A. de Ediciones ARG. Dist: Santillana USA Publishing Co., Inc.
Lavandeira, Sandra. Good Citizenship. Lucas, Kathryn. 2008. (Fácil de Leer / Easy to Read Ser.). (ENG.). 16p. (J). pap. 5.99 ***(978-1-59820-558-9(7)***, Santillana Texto) Santillana USA Publishing Co., Inc.
—I Don't Need an Umbrella! White, Amy. 2008. (Fácil de Leer / Easy to Read Ser.). (ENG.). 16p. (J). pap. 5.99 ***(978-1-59820-571-8(4)***, Santillana Texto) Santillana USA Publishing Co., Inc.
Lavandeira, Sandra. No Necesito Paraguas. White, Amy. Kratky, Lada J., tr. 2009. (Colección Fácil de Leer Ser.). (SPA.). 16p. (gr. k-2). pap. 5.99 *(978-1-60396-419-7(3))* Ediciones Alfaguara ESP. Dist: Santillana USA Publishing Co., Inc.
Lavar, Vanda. Tucker's Tale. Walsh, Christopher. 2009. 28p. pap. 11.95 *(978-1-935137-21-4(2))* Guardian Angel Publishing, Inc.
Lavarello, Jose Maria. Aquello Que Tanto Queria Susana. Ramon, Elisa. 2004.Tr. of What Susana Loved Dearly. (SPA.). (J). pap. 7.99 *(978-84-236-6702-4(2))* Edebé ESP. Dist: Lectorum Pubns., Inc.
—Cuentame un Cuento, No. 2. (SPA.). 366p. (J). (gr. k-3). *(978-84-480-1124-6(4)*, TM2346) Timun Mas, Editorial S.A. ESP. Dist: Lectorum Pubns., Inc.
—Que Llueva, Que Llueva. Zubizarreta, Paxti. 2nd ed. (SPA.). 31p. (J). pap. 7.99 *(978-84-236-3678-5(X))* Edebé ESP. Dist: Lectorum Pubns., Inc.
Lavater, Warja. Tell. 2019. (ENG.). 22p. (J). (gr. -1-2). 20.00 *(978-3-314-10492-3(8))* North-South Bks., Inc.
Lavender, Todd. Creak in the Night - Mystery of the Crypts. Freeman, J. Miller. 2012. 74p. pap. 9.99 *(978-0-9850410-1-4(3))* Akmaeon Publishing, LLC.
Lavender, Todd. Farmer Fred & His Hen So Red. Lavender, Todd. 2012. 48p. pap. 9.99 *(978-0-9850410-0-7(5))* Akmaeon Publishing, LLC.
Laver, Sarah, 8th. Where's Jesus. Jeffs, Stephanie. 2004. 32p. 13.95 *(978-0-8294-1728-9(1))* Loyola Pr.
Laverdet, Marcel. Les Vikings Heros des Mers. Laverdet, Marcel. Ragache, Gilles. 2010. (Mythes et Legendes Ser.: Vol. 2920932). (FRE.). 96p. (J). pap. *(978-2-01-292093-4(4))* Hachette Jeunesse.
Lavers, Ralph. Redskin Morning & Other Stories. Grant, Joan Marshall. 2010. (J). pap. *(978-1-59731-555-5(9))* Perennis, Sophia.
—Scarlet Fish & Other Stories. Grant, Joan Marshall. 2010. (J). pap. *(978-1-59731-554-8(0))* Perennis, Sophia.
Lavina, Zulema Scotto & Hamilton, Piky. Disney the Little Mermaid. Castellucci, Cecil. 2020. (ENG.). 72p. (J). (gr. 3-7). pap. 12.99 *(978-1-5067-1572-8(9)*, Dark Horse Books) Dark Horse Comics.
LaViolette, Renee, jt. illus. see Keimig, Candice.
Laviosa, Mattia Francesco. All Bottled up! (Shimmer & Shine) Tillworth, Mary. 2017. (Pictureback(R) Ser.). (ENG.). 16p. (J). (gr. -1-2). pap. 5.99 *(978-1-5247-1718-6(5)*, Random Hse. Bks. for Young Readers) Random Hse. Children's Bks.
—Santa's Christmas Genies (Shimmer & Shine) James, Hollis. 2016. (Big Golden Book Ser.). (ENG.). 32p. (J). (gr. -1-2). 9.99 *(978-0-399-55121-5(2)*, Golden Bks.) Random Hse. Children's Bks.
Lavis, Steve. All Aboard to Work - Choo-Choo! Roth, Carol. 2013. (AV2 Fiction Readalong Ser.). (ENG.). (J). (gr. -1-3). 34.28 *(978-1-62127-866-5(2)*, AV2 by Weigl) Weigl Pubs., Inc.
—You're Too Small! Roddie, Shen. 2004. 32p. (J). 6.95 *(978-1-58925-385-8(X))*; tchr. ed. 15.95 *(978-1-58925-038-3(9))* Tiger Tales.
Lavoie, Lewis. Amazing Dinosaurs Designed by God. Butt, Kyle. 2009. (A. P. Reader Ser.). (ENG.). 32p. (J). (gr. 4-7). pap. 4.99 *(978-1-60063-015-6(4))* Apologetics Pr., Inc.
Lavoradori, Alberto. Duck Avenger New Adventures, Book 1. Sisti, Alessandro et al. 2017. (Duck Avenger Ser.: 1). 200p. pap. 24.99 *(978-1-63140-864-9(X))* Idea & Design Works, LLC.
Lavreys, Debbie. The Little Hamster, 114 vols. Van Der Linden, Elly. 2007. (ENG.). 12p. (gr. -1-k). *(978-0-86315-605-2(3))* Floris Bks.
—The Prickly Hedgehog, 114 vols. Van Der Linden, Elly. 2007. (ENG.). 12p. (J). (gr. -1-k). *(978-0-86315-603-8(7))* Floris Bks.
—The Woolly Sheep, 114 vols. Van Der Linden, Elly. 2007. (ENG.). 12p. (gr. -1-k). *(978-0-86315-604-5(5))* Floris Bks.
Lavrova, Daria. The Mealtime Monster. Williams, Jessica. 2018. (ENG.). 32p. (J). (gr. k-2). *(978-1-7753456-4-0(5))*; pap. *(978-1-7753456-0-2(2))* All Write Here Publishing.
Law, Felicia, et al. Castaway Code: Sequencing in Action. Law, Felicia & Way, Steve. 2010. (Mandrill Mountain Math Mysteries Ser.). 32p. (J). (gr. 2-6). 25.60 *(978-1-60754-817-1(8))*; pap. 10.55 *(978-1-60754-822-5(4))* Windmill Bks.
Law, Stephanie Pui-Mun. The Hotel under the Sand. Baker, Kage. 2009. (ENG.). 179p. (J). (gr. 2-7). pap. 8.00 *(978-1-892391-89-6(9)*, c1c9c70c-9bed-423d-86dc-37c75f7551f4) Tachyon Pubns.
Laween. The Little Pine Cone. Schenck, Ella Syfers. 2018. (ENG.). 42p. (J). (gr. k-3). 19.99 *(978-0-9996633-0-1(5))* Blynbeek Publishing.
Lawn, John. Abraham Lincoln: Road to the White House. Brandt, Keith & Macken, JoAnn Early. 2007. 53p. (J). *(978-0-439-88005-3(X))* Scholastic, Inc.
—Daniel Boone: Frontier Explorer. Brandt, Keith & Macken, JoAnn Early. 2008. 55p. (J). pap. *(978-0-439-02020-6(4))* Scholastic, Inc.
Lawrason, June. The Birthday Girl. Little, Jean. 2004. 64p. (J). lib. bdg. 20.00 *(978-1-4242-1256-9(1))* Fitzgerald Bks.
Lawrence, C. H. Aladdin or, the Wonderful Lamp. 2012. (Shape Bks.). (ENG.). 16p. pap. 9.95 *(978-1-59583-454-6(0)*, 9781595834546, Green Tiger Pr.) Laughing Elephant.
Lawrence, C. H., jt. illus. see Adams, Frank.
Lawrence, David. The Egyptians. Platt, Richard. 2011. (How They Made Things Work! Ser.). 32p. (J). (gr. 2-5). lib. bdg. 28.50 *(978-1-59771-287-3(6))* Sea-To-Sea Pubns.
—The Greeks. Platt, Richard. 2011. (How They Made Things Work! Ser.). 32p. (J). (gr. 2-5). lib. bdg. 28.50 *(978-1-59771-288-0(4))* Sea-To-Sea Pubns.
—In the Renaissance. Platt, Richard. 2011. (How They Made Things Work! Ser.). 32p. (YA). (gr. 2-5). lib. bdg. 28.50 *(978-1-59771-289-7(2))* Sea-To-Sea Pubns.
Lawrence, George. The Voyage of the Beetle: A Journey Around the World with Charles Darwin & the Search for the Solution to the Mystery of Mysteries, as Narrated by Rosie, an Articulate Beetle. Weaver, Anne H. 2007. (ENG.). 80p. (J). (gr. 5-8). 19.95 *(978-0-8263-4304-8(X))* Univ. of New Mexico Pr.
Lawrence, George. The Voyage of the Beetle: A Journey Around the World with Charles Darwin & the Search for the Solution to the Mystery of Mysteries, As Narrated by Rosie, an Articulate Beetle. Lawrence, George, tr. Weaver, Anne H. 2004. (Roman Mysteries Ser.). 80p. (J). (gr. 5-8). lib. bdg. 26.90 *(978-0-7613-2923-7(4)*, Millbrook Pr.) Lerner Publishing Group.
Lawrence, Jack. Dragons - Riders of Berk, Vol. 2. Furman, Simon & Nazif, Iwan. 2016. (Dragons: Riders of Berk Ser.: 2). 112p. (J). (gr. 3-7). pap. 12.99 *(978-1-78585-176-6(4))* Titan Bks. Ltd. GBR. Dist: Penguin Random Hse. LLC.
—The Ice Castle, Vol. 3. Titan Comics, Titan. 2015. (Riders of Berk Ser.). (ENG.). 64p. (J). (gr. 3-7). pap. 6.99 *(978-1-78276-078-8(4))* Titan Bks. Ltd. GBR. Dist: Penguin Random Hse. LLC.
Lawrence, Jack, et al. Party with Fiesta! Marz, Ron & Rodriguez, David A. 2017. (Skylanders: SuperChargers Ser.). (ENG.). 24p. (J). (gr. 1-5). lib. bdg. 27.07 *(978-1-5321-4038-9(X)*, 25443, Graphic Novels) Spotlight.
—Skylanders: Spyro & Friends: Biting Back. Marz, Ron & Rodriguez, David A. 2018. (Skylanders Ser.). 80p. (J). (gr. 4-7). 12.99 *(978-1-68405-128-1(2))* Idea & Design Works, LLC.
Lawrence, Jack, jt. illus. see Nazif, Iwan.
Lawrence, Jack, jt. illus. see Yardley, Tracy.
Lawrence, John. Fish. Taylor-Butler, Christine. 2013. (True Book: Animal Kingdom Ser.). (ENG.). 48p. (J). (gr. 3-5). 31.00 *(978-0-531-21752-8(3)*, Children's Pr.) Scholastic Library Publishing.
—His Dark Materials: Lyra's Oxford. Pullman, Philip. (His Dark Materials Ser.). (ENG.). (J). (gr. 5). 2017. 80p. 7.99 *(978-0-399-55545-9(5)*, Yearling); 2003. 64p. 12.99 *(978-0-375-82819-5(2)*, Knopf Bks. for Young Readers) Random Hse. Children's Bks.
—His Dark Materials: Once upon a Time in the North. Pullman, Philip. 2017. (His Dark Materials Ser.). (ENG.). 144p. (J). (gr. 5). 7.99 *(978-0-399-55544-2(7)*, Yearling) Random Hse. Children's Bks.
—Lyra's Oxford. Pullman, Philip. 2006. (His Dark Materials Ser.). 49p. (YA). reprint ed. 11.00 *(978-1-4223-5410-0(5))* DIANE Publishing Co.
—Sea Horse: Read & Wonder: the Shyest Fish in the Sea. Butterworth, Chris. 2009. (Read & Wonder Ser.). (ENG.). 32p. (J). (gr. -1-3). pap. 7.99 *(978-0-7636-4140-5(5))* Candlewick Pr.
—Sea Horse: The Shyest Fish in the Sea. Butterworth, Christine. (Read, Listen, & Wonder Ser.). (ENG.). 32p. (J). 2010. (gr. -1-3). pap. 9.99 *(978-0-7636-4868-8(X))*; 2006. (gr. k-2). 22.44 *(978-0-7636-2989-2(8))* Candlewick Pr.
—Treasure Island. Stevenson, Robert Louis. 2009. (ENG.). 272p. (J). (gr. 4-7). 24.99 *(978-0-7636-4445-1(5))* Candlewick Pr.
Lawrence, John. This Little Chick. Lawrence, John. 2013. (ENG.). 32p. (J). (gr. -1-1). 17.44 *(978-0-7636-6350-6(6))* Candlewick Pr.
Lawrence, Kim. I Love You to the Moon & Back. Precious Moments & Hill, Susanna Leonard. 2019. 40p. (J). (-3). 9.99 *(978-1-4926-7932-5(1)*, Sourcebooks Jabberwocky) Sourcebooks, Inc.
Lawrence, Margaret & Thorgeirsson, Sigmundur. When Pumpkins Fly. Lawrence, Margaret. 2020. (ENG.). 32p. (J). 16.95 *(978-1-77227-249-3(3))* Inhabit Media Inc. CAN. Dist: Consortium Bk. Sales & Distribution.
Lawrence, Mike. The Incredible Adventures of Cinnamon Girl. Keil, Melissa. (ENG.). 352p. (YA). (gr. 7-12). 2018. pap. 9.95 *(978-1-68263-041-9(2))*; 2016. 17.95 *(978-1-56145-905-6(4))* Peachtree Publishing Co. Inc.
—Muddy Max: The Mystery of Marsh Creek. Rusch, Elizabeth. 2014. (ENG.). 224p. (J). pap. 9.99 *(978-1-4494-3561-5(0))* Andrews McMeel Publishing.
Lawrence, Muriel. Miguel & the Pirates: A Tale of Mission Santa Cruz. Roberts, Helen M. 2011. 28p. 35.95 *(978-1-258-02882-4(4))* Literary Licensing, LLC.
Lawrence, Sarah. Astronaut in Training. Kingfisher Editors. 2018. (ENG.). 48p. (J). pap. 8.99 *(978-0-7534-7442-6(5)*, 900192222, Kingfisher) Roaring Brook Pr.
—Coder in Training. Ard, Cath. 2020. (ENG.). 48p. (J). pap. 8.99 *(978-0-7534-7524-9(3)*, 900207588, Kingfisher) Roaring Brook Pr.
—Doctor in Training. Ard, Cath. 2019. (ENG.). 48p. (J). pap. 8.99 *(978-0-7534-7470-9(0)*, 900196714, Kingfisher) Roaring Brook Pr.
—Engineer in Training. Ard, Cath. 2019. (ENG.). 48p. (J). pap. 8.99 *(978-0-7534-7469-3(7)*, 900196713, Kingfisher) Roaring Brook Pr.
—Firefighter in Training. Ard, Cath. 2019. (ENG.). 48p. (J). pap. 8.99 *(978-0-7534-7497-6(2)*, 900198771, Kingfisher) Roaring Brook Pr.
—Una Pijamada Difícil (a Tricky Sleepover) Greve, Meg. 2017. (Beginning Chapter Bks.: Vol. 9781683422). (SPA.). 48p. (gr. k-3). pap. 8.95 *(978-1-68342-249-5(X)*, 9781683422495) Rourke Educational Media.
—Scientist in Training. Kingfisher Editors. 2018. (ENG.). 48p. (J). pap. 8.99 *(978-0-7534-7443-3(3)*, 900192223, Kingfisher) Roaring Brook Pr.
—Sports Star in Training. Ard, Cath. 2020. (ENG.). 48p. (J). pap. 8.99 *(978-0-7534-7523-2(5)*, 900207584, Kingfisher) Roaring Brook Pr.
Lawrence, Tate, jt. illus. see Carlos, Uribe.
Lawrey, Derek. Oscar & Willie: Silly Oscar's Days of the Week. Hetherington, Lisa. 2012. (ENG.). 26p. (J). pap. 9.99 *(978-0-9839963-0-9(X))* Hetherington Hall.
Lawrie, Chris, jt. illus. see Lawrie, Robin.
Lawrie, Robin. Cuda of the Celts. Ashe, Susan. 2005. (Yellow Go Bananas Ser.). (ENG.). 48p. (J). (gr. 3-4). lib. bdg. *(978-0-7787-2720-0(3))* Crabtree Publishing Co.
—The Dancing Flame. Overell, J. J. 2003. (Overell Bks.). (ENG.). 128p. (C). per. 13.00 *(978-0-7188-3036-6(9))* Lutterworth Pr., The GBR. Dist: ISD.
—Great Irish Legends for Children, 1 vol. Carroll, Yvonne. 2005. (ENG.). 64p. (J). (gr. k-3). 18.99 *(978-1-58980-345-9(0)*, Pelican Publishing) Arcadia Publishing.
—Great Irish Legends for Children. Carroll, Yvonne. 2005. (ENG.). 64p. (J). pap. 20.95 incl. audio compact disk *(978-0-7171-3872-2(0))* M.H. Gill & Co. U. C. IRL. Dist: Dufour Editions, Inc.
—Nid Fy Mai I. Huws, Emily. 2005. (WEL.). 64p. pap. *(978-1-84512-025-2(6))* Cymdeithas Lyfrau Ceredigion.
—Palaces, Peasants & Plagues - England in the 14th Century: Band 18/Pearl (Collins Big Cat) Platt, Richard. 2014. (Collins Big Cat Ser.). (ENG.). 80p. (J). (gr. 5). pap. 11.95 *(978-0-00-753016-8(1))* HarperCollins Pubs. Ltd. GBR. Dist: Independent Pubs. Group.
Lawrie, Robin & Lawrie, Chris. Chain Reaction. 32p. pap. *(978-0-237-52110-3(5))* Evans Brothers, Ltd.
—Fear 3.1. 32p. (J). pap. *(978-0-237-52107-3(5))* Evans Brothers, Ltd.
—Muddy Mayhem. 32p. (J). pap. *(978-0-237-52105-9(9))* Evans Brothers, Ltd.
—Winged Avenger. 32p. pap. *(978-0-237-52106-6(7))* Evans Brothers, Ltd.
Laws, Jerl L. The Princess Escape. Tyler-Laws, Sadiya. 2017. (ENG.). (J). (gr. 2-4). 18.99 *(978-0-9992446-1-6(2))* Tyler Laws Pr.
Lawson, Denise A. Black Bear Goes to Washington. Lawson, Denise A. 2018. (Black Bear Ser.: Vol. 1). (ENG.). 30p. (J). (gr. k-3). 18.99 *(978-1-7322303-1-6(5))* Brown & Lowe Bks.
—Meet Monique. Lawson, Denise A. 2019. (ENG.). 24p. (J). (gr. k-3). 15.99 *(978-1-7322303-0-9(7))* Brown & Lowe Bks.
Lawson, Devin. Digibots Classroom Adventures. Holmes, Kimberly. 2004. (J). *(978-0-9755725-0-4(4)*, 1238415) Digibots Corp.
Lawson, Glory. Forest Communities: Living in Harmony with Fire. Whizpops, The. 2017. (J). 14.00 *(978-0-87842-674-4(4))* Mountain Pr. Publishing Co., Inc.
Lawson, Greg, photos by. Natural States. ltd. ed. 2005. 208p. (ENG., 135.00 *(978-0-9762197-6-7(X))*; 135.00 *(978-0-9762197-7-4(8))* Oakana Hse.
Lawson, Heather. The Enchanted Garden. Magnan, Karen. 2019. (ENG.). 82p. (J). pap. 6.00 *(978-1-0781-2537-6(6))* Independently Published.
Lawson, J. Chip the Buffalo: Based on a True Story. Beerntsen, Tammy, photos by. Lawson, Cheri. 2006. 32p. (J). lib. bdg. 14.95 *(978-1-930580-61-9(4)*, Luminary Media Group) Pine Orchard, Inc.
Lawson, Jeremy, jt. illus. see Brizuela, Dario.
Lawson, Keri, photos by. Randy Grows a Garden for Julia. Taylor, "Grandma" Mary. 2005. (J). 12.50 *(978-1-58597-321-7(1))* Leathers Publishing.
Lawson, Michael. Larry's Colouring Book. 2017. (Larry the London Bus & Friends Ser.: Vol. 10). (ENG.). (J). pap. *(978-0-9933455-8-6(1))* Larry the London Bus and Friends Ltd.
Lawson, Nan. The Confidence Code for Girls: Taking Risks, Messing up, & Becoming Your Amazingly Imperfect, Totally Powerful Self. Kay, Katty et al. 2018. (ENG.). 320p. (J). (gr. 3-7). 14.99 *(978-0-06-279698-1(4))* HarperCollins Pubs.
Lawson, Peter. Fishing Boat. Goldsack, Gaby. 2009. (Turn the Wheel Ser.). (ENG.). 10p. (J). (gr. -1-k). bds. 5.95 *(978-0-7892-1025-8(8)*, Abbeville Kids) Abbeville Pr., Inc.
—My Pumpkin. Noonan, Julia. 2005. (My First Reader Ser.). (ENG.). 32p. (J). (gr. k-1). lib. bdg. 18.50 *(978-0-516-24876-9(6)*, Children's Pr.) Scholastic Library Publishing.
—Pull the Lever: Who's at Nursery? Baxter, Nicola. 2014. (ENG.). 8p. (J). (gr. -1-1). bds. 6.99 *(978-1-86147-393-6(1)*, Armadillo) Anness Publishing GBR. Dist: National Bk. Network.
—Who's on the Farm? Wolfe, Jane & Baxter, Nicola. 2013. (ENG.). 8p. bds. 6.99 *(978-1-84322-652-9(9)*, Armadillo) Anness Publishing GBR. Dist: National Bk. Network.
Lawson, Rob. Duke Finds a Home. 2006. (Duke's Tails Ser.). 32p. (J). *(978-0-9779308-0-7(7))* Bush Brothers & Co.
Lawson, Robert. Adam of the Road (Puffin Modern Classics) Gray, Elizabeth Janet. 2006. (Puffin Modern Classics Ser.). (ENG.). 320p. (J). (gr. 3-7). 7.99 *(978-0-14-240659-5(7)*, Puffin Books) Penguin Young Readers Group.
—Ferdinand Book & Toy Set. Leaf, Munro. 2017. (ENG.). 32p. (J). (-k). 18.99 *(978-0-425-29180-1(4)*, Viking Books for Young Readers) Penguin Young Readers Group.
—Just for Fun: A Collection of Stories & Verses. 2013. (Dover Children's Classics Ser.). (ENG.). 64p. (gr. 2-5). pap. 6.99 *(978-0-486-49720-4(8))* Dover Pubns., Inc.
—The Little Woman Wanted Noise. Teal, Val. 2013. (ENG.). 48p. (J). (gr. -1-2). 14.95 *(978-1-59017-711-2(8)*, NYR Children's Collection) New York Review of Bks., Inc., The.
Lawson, Robert. Mr. Popper's Penguins. Atwater, Richard & Atwater, Florence. 2020. 158p. pap. 18.95 ***(978-4-87187-096-2(0))*** Ishi Pr. International.
Lawson, Robert. The Story of Ferdinand. Leaf, Munro. (ENG.). (J). 2018. 34p. (-k). bds. 13.99 *(978-1-9848-3559-8(9)*, Viking Books for Young Readers); 2017. 34p. (-k). bds. 8.99 *(978-0-425-29111-5(1)*, Viking Books for Young Readers); 2011. 32p. (gr. -1-k). pap. 4.99 *(978-0-448-45694-2(X)*, Grosset & Dunlap) Penguin Young Readers Group.
—Wee Gillis. Leaf, Munro. ed. 2006. (ENG.). 80p. (J). (gr. -1-2). 16.95 *(978-1-59017-206-3(X)*, NYR Children's Collection) New York Review of Bks., Inc., The.
Lawson, Robert. Rabbit Hill (Puffin Modern Classics) Lawson, Robert. 2007. (Puffin Modern Classics Ser.). (ENG.). 128p. (J). (gr. 3-7). 6.99 *(978-0-14-240796-7(8)*, Puffin Books) Penguin Young Readers Group.
Lawson, Robert & Spatrisano, Kimberly. Road Wrangler: Cowboys on Wheels. Novara, Joe. 2007. 112p. (J). pap. 8.95 *(978-1-58980-507-1(0)*, Pelican Publishing) Arcadia Publishing.
—Wa-Tonka! Camp Cowboys, 1 vol. Novara, Joe. 2006. (ENG.). 120p. (J). (gr. 3-6). per. 8.95 *(978-1-58980-354-1(X)*, Pelican Publishing) Arcadia Publishing.
Lawton, Abigail. Molly Meets Meow-Meow: A Book about Finding Friends. E.B.N.S. 2019. (ENG.). 34p. (J). pap. 20.99 *(978-1-7283-2023-6(2))* AuthorHouse.
Lawton, Catherine. Something Is Coming to Our World: How a Backyard Bird Sees Christmas. Lawton, Catherine. 2018. (ENG.). 34p. (J). pap. 10.99 *(978-1-945099-11-3(9))* CLADACH Publishing.
Lawton, Val. Emily's Magical Journey with Toothena the Tooth Fairy. Clark, CoraMarie. 2007. (ENG.). 32p. (J). *(978-0-9783779-0-8(7))* Strategix Ltd.
Lay, Helen. Wakey-Wakey, Blue Moon! Lay, Brandy. 2019. (ENG.). 26p. (J). pap. 9.99 ***(978-1-6938-6387-5(1))*** Independently Published.
Layne, Aliza. Beetle & the Hollowbones. Layne, Aliza. 2020. (ENG.). 256p. (J). (gr. 3-7). 21.99 ***(978-1-5344-4153-8(0))***; pap. 12.99 ***(978-1-5344-4154-5(9))*** Simon & Schuster Children's Publishing. (Atheneum Bks. for Young Readers).
Layne, Deborah, jt. illus. see Ettlinger, Doris.
Layton, Bob, jt. illus. see Zeck, Mike.
Layton, Neal. Danny Mcgee Drinks the Sea. Stanton, Andy. 2017. (ENG.). 32p. (J). (gr. -1-3). 17.99 *(978-1-5247-1736-0(3))*; lib. bdg. 20.99 *(978-1-5247-1737-7(1))* Random Hse. Children's Bks. (Schwartz & Wade Bks.).

L

—Deadly! The Truth about the Most Dangerous Creatures on Earth. Davies, Nicola. (Animal Science Ser.). (ENG.). 64p. (J). (gr. 3-7). 2015. pap. 7.99 *(978-0-7636-7971-2(2))*; 2013. 14.99 *(978-0-7636-6231-8(3))* Candlewick Pr.

—Don't Make Me Laugh, Liam. Oldfield, Jenny. (ENG.). 128p. (J). pap. 8.95 *(978-0-340-85107-4(4))* Macmillan Pubs., Ltd. GBR. Dist: Trafalgar Square Publishing.

—Drop Dead, Danielle. Oldfield, Jenny. (ENG.). 112p. mass mkt. *(978-0-340-85106-7(6)*, Coronet) Hodder & Stoughton.

—Extreme Animals: The Toughest Creatures on Earth. Davies, Nicola. 2006. (Nicola Davies' Animal Science Ser.). (ENG.). 64p. (J). (gr. 3-5). 22.44 *(978-0-7636-3067-6(5))* Candlewick Pr.

—Extreme Animals: The Toughest Creatures on Earth. Davies, Nicola. 2009. (Animal Science Ser.). (ENG.). 64p. (J). (gr. 3-7). pap. 7.99 *(978-0-7636-4127-6(8))* Candlewick Pr.

—Get Lost, Lola. Oldfield, Jenny. (ENG.). 112p. mass mkt. 7.99 *(978-0-340-85104-3(X)*, Coronet) Hodder & Stoughton GBR. Dist: Trafalgar Square Publishing.

—Jennifer Jones Won't Leave Me Alone. Wishinsky, Frieda. 2005. (Carolrhoda Picture Bks.). 32p. (J). (gr. -1-3). per. 6.95 *(978-1-57505-921-1(5))*; (gr. k-2). 15.95 *(978-0-87614-921-8(2))* Lerner Publishing Group.

—Just the Right Size: Why Big Animals Are Big & Little Animals Are Little. Davies, Nicola. 2011. (Animal Science Ser.). (ENG.). 64p. (J). (gr. 3-7). pap. 7.99 *(978-0-7636-5300-2(4))* Candlewick Pr.

—Look! I Wrote a Book! (and You Can Too!) Lloyd-Jones, Sally. 2019. 40p. (J). (gr. -1-3). 17.99 *(978-0-399-55818-4(7))*; (ENG.). lib. bdg. 20.99 *(978-0-399-55819-1(5))* Random Hse. Children's Bks. (Schwartz & Wade Bks.).

—Nothing Scares Us. Wishinsky, Frieda. (Carolrhoda Picture Books Ser.). 32p. (J). 2004. (gr. 1-4). pap. 6.25 *(978-1-57505-669-2(0))*; 2003. (gr. -1-3). 15.95 *(978-1-57505-490-2(6)*, Carolrhoda Bks.) Lerner Publishing Group.

—Poop: A Natural History of the Unmentionable. Davies, Nicola. 2011. (Animal Science Ser.). (ENG.). 64p. (J). (gr. 3-7). pap. 7.99 *(978-0-7636-4128-3(6))* Candlewick Pr.

—That Rabbit Belongs to Emily Brown. Cowell, Cressida. 2007. (ENG.). 40p. (gr. -1-3). 16.99 *(978-1-4231-0645-6(8))* Hyperion Pr.

—Uncle Gobb & the Dread Shed. Rosen, Michael. 2015. 208p. (J). (gr. 2-4). 17.99 *(978-1-4088-5130-2(X)*, 900146180, Bloomsbury Children's Bks.) Bloomsbury Publishing USA.

—What's Eating You? Parasites — the Inside Story. Davies, Nicola. 2009. (Animal Science Ser.). (ENG.). 64p. (J). (gr. 3-7). pap. 7.99 *(978-0-7636-4521-2(4))* Candlewick Pr.

—Wicked Poems. McGough, Roger. ed. 2004. 208p. (gr. 2-4). pap. 15.00 *(978-0-7475-6195-8(8))* Bloomsbury Publishing Plc GBR. Dist: Independent Pubs. Group.

—Zartog's Remote. Brennan, Herbie. 2003. (Middle Grade Fiction Ser.). 96p. (J). (gr. 3-6). 14.95 *(978-1-57505-507-7(4)*, Carolrhoda Bks.) Lerner Publishing Group.

Layton, Neal. Friends for a Day. Layton, Neal. 2018. 32p. (J). (gr. -1-k). pap. 9.99 *(978-1-4449-2825-9(2))* Hachette Children's Group GBR. Dist: Hachette Bk. Group.

—Hot Hot Hot. Layton, Neal. 2004. (ENG.). 32p. (J). (gr. -1-3). 15.99 *(978-0-7636-2148-3(X))* Candlewick Pr.

—The Mammoth Academy. Layton, Neal. 2010. (ENG.). 176p. (J). (gr. 4-6). 21.19 *(978-0-312-60882-8(9))* Square Fish.

—The Tree. Layton, Neal. 2017. (ENG.). 40p. (J). (-k). 17.99 *(978-0-7636-8952-0(1))* Candlewick Pr.

Lazar, Ligia. Coloring Book Happy Vegetables. Tudosa-Fundureanu, Lucia. Chabvepi-Tudosa, Patricia, tr. 2012. 50p. pap. 11.95 *(978-1-936629-17-6(8))* Reflection Publishing.

Lazar, Ralph. Rory Branagan: Detective #1. Clover, Andrew. 2020. (Rory Branagan: Detective Ser.: 1). (ENG.). 352p. (J). (gr. 2-7). pap. 9.99 *(978-1-5247-9364-7(7)*, Penguin Workshop) Penguin Young Readers Group.

Lazar, Ralph. Rory Branagan: Detective: the Dog Squad #2. Clover, Andrew. 2020. (Rory Branagan: Detective Ser.: 2). (ENG.). 368p. (J). (gr. 2). pap. 9.99 ***(978-1-5247-9366-1(3)***, Penguin Workshop) Penguin Young Readers Group.

Lazewnik, Sara. Guess-the-Ending Mitzvah Book. Finkelstein, Ruth. 2004. 26p. (J). (gr. k-3). 9.95 *(978-0-9628157-4-4(8))* Finkelstein, Ruth.

Lazo, Hayley. Alcatraz vs. the Evil Librarians. Sanderson, Brandon. 2016. (Alcatraz Versus the Evil Librarians Ser.: 1). (ENG.). 320p. (J). 17.99 *(978-0-7653-7894-1(9)*, 900141060, Starscape) Doherty, Tom Assocs., LLC.

Lazuli, Lilly. The Dessert Diaries, 4 vols. Dower, Laura. 2016. (Dessert Diaries). (ENG.). 160p. (J). (gr. 4-8). lib. bdg., lib. bdg., lib. bdg. 106.60 *(978-1-4965-3140-7(X)*, Stone Arch Bks.) Capstone.

—For Emme, Baked with Love. Dower, Laura. 2016. (Dessert Diaries). (ENG.). 160p. (J). (gr. 4-8). pap. 5.95 *(978-1-4965-4142-0(1))*; lib. bdg. 26.65 *(978-1-4965-3122-3(1))* Capstone. (Stone Arch Bks.).

—Gabi & the Great Big Bakeover. Dower, Laura. (ENG.). 160p. (J). 2017. pap. *(978-1-4747-2213-1(X))*; 2016. (gr. 4-8). lib. bdg. 26.65 *(978-1-4965-3119-3(1))* Capstone. (Stone Arch Bks.).

—Kiki Takes the Cake. Dower, Laura. 2016. (Dessert Diaries). (ENG.). 160p. (J). (gr. 4-8). lib. bdg. 26.65 *(978-1-4965-3120-9(5)*, Stone Arch Bks.) Capstone.

—Maggie's Magic Chocolate Moon. Dower, Laura. 2016. (Dessert Diaries). (ENG.). 160p. (J). (gr. 4-8). pap. 5.95 *(978-1-4965-4141-3(3))*; lib. bdg. 26.65 *(978-1-4965-3121-6(3))* Capstone. (Stone Arch Bks.).

Lazzati, Laura, jt. illus. see Aón, Carlos.

Lazzell, R. H. Camping Catastrophe! Mccormick, Scott. 2016. (Mr. Pants Ser.: 4). 128p. (J). (gr. k-3). 14.99 *(978-0-525-42812-1(7)*, Dial Bks) Penguin Young Readers Group.

—It's Go Time! McCormick, Scott. 2014. (Mr. Pants Ser.: 1). (ENG.). 128p. (J). (gr. 1-3). 14.99 *(978-0-8037-4007-5(7)*, Dial Bks) Penguin Young Readers Group.

—Mr. Pants: It's Go Time! Mccormick, Scott. 2015. (Mr. Pants Ser.: 1). (ENG.). 128p. (J). (gr. 1-3). pap. 7.99 *(978-0-14-751710-4(9)*, Puffin Books) Penguin Young Readers Group.

—Mr. Pants: Trick or Feet! Mccormick, Scott. 2015. (Mr. Pants Ser.: 3). (ENG.). 128p. (J). (gr. k-3). 14.99 *(978-0-525-42811-4(9)*, Dial Bks) Penguin Young Readers Group.

—Slacks, Camera, Action! McCormick, Scott. 2015. (Mr. Pants Ser.: 2). 128p. (J). (gr. k-3). 14.99 *(978-0-8037-4009-9(3)*, Dial Bks) Penguin Young Readers Group.

Lê, Christine & Lê, Michel. The Hawai'i Snowman. 2008. (J). 14.95 *(978-1-56647-879-3(0))* Mutual Publishing LLC.

Le Coultre, Marcel, jt. illus. see Broders, Roger.

Le Duo, Le. People of Peace: 40 Inspiring Icons. Mirza, Sandrine. 2018. (40 Inspiring Icons Ser.). (ENG.). 88p. (J). (gr. 2-5). 14.99 ***(978-1-78603-144-0(2)***, Wide Eyed Editions) Quarto Publishing Group UK GBR. Dist: Hachette Bk. Group.

Le Fevebvre, Severine. Tom Sawyer, No. 4. Twain, Mark. 2011. (ENG.). 144p. (J). (gr. 3-9). 17.95 *(978-1-59707-152-9(8)*, 9781597071529) Papercutz.

Le Feyer, Diane. Be a Star! Alexander, Heather. 2015. (Amazing Stardust Friends Ser.: 2). (ENG.). 96p. (J). (gr. 1-3). pap. 4.99 *(978-0-545-75754-6(1))* Scholastic, Inc.

—Brendan & the Blarney Stone. Walsh, Stephen & O'Donovan, Marita. 2017. (Tales from Leprechaun Land Ser.). (ENG.). 32p. (J). pap. 14.00 *(978-1-84717-723-0(9))* O'Brien Pr., Ltd., The IRL. Dist: Casemate Pubs. & Bk. Distributors, LLC.

—God's Words to Dream On: Bedtime Bible Stories & Prayers, 1 vol. Stortz, Diane. 2019. (ENG.). 224p. (J). 16.99 *(978-1-4002-0935-4(8))* Nelson, Thomas Inc.

—I Am: The Names of God for Little Ones, 1 vol. Stortz, Diane. 2018. 24p. (J). bds. 9.99 *(978-1-4003-1079-1(2))* Nelson, Thomas Inc.

—My Little Bible, 1 vol. Thomas Nelson, Thomas. 2016. (ENG.). 96p. (J). 6.99 *(978-0-7180-4018-5(X))* Nelson, Thomas Inc.

—My Little Bible & Prayers, 1 vol. Thomas Nelson Publishing Staff. 2019. (ENG.). 192p. (J). 10.99 *(978-1-4002-1120-3(4))* Nelson, Thomas Inc.

—My Little Prayers, 1 vol. Thomas Nelson, Thomas. 2016. (ENG.). 96p. (J). 6.99 *(978-0-7180-4019-2(8))* Nelson, Thomas Inc.

—Poacher Panic, 1 vol. Burchett, Jan & Vogler, Sara. 2012. (Wild Rescue Ser.). (ENG.). 152p. (J). (gr. 3-6). lib. bdg. 25.32 *(978-1-4342-3286-1(7)*, Stone Arch Bks.) Capstone.

—Polar Meltdown, 1 vol. Burchett, Jan & Vogler, Sara. 2012. (Wild Rescue Ser.). (ENG.). 152p. (J). (gr. 3-6). 9.95 *(978-1-4342-4594-6(2)*, Stone Arch Bks.) Capstone.

—Rainforest Rescue, 1 vol. Burchett, Jan & Vogler, Sara. 2012. (Wild Rescue Ser.). (ENG.). 152p. (J). (gr. 3-6). lib. bdg. 25.32 *(978-1-4342-3768-2(0)*, Stone Arch Bks.) Capstone.

—Safari Survival, 1 vol. Burchett, Jan & Vogler, Sara. 2013. (Wild Rescue Ser.). (ENG.). 152p. (J). (gr. 3-6). 9.95 *(978-1-4342-4890-9(9)*, Stone Arch Bks.) Capstone.

—Step into the Spotlight! Alexander, Heather. 2015. (Amazing Stardust Friends Ser.: 1). (ENG.). 96p. (J). (gr. 1-3). pap. 4.99 *(978-0-545-75752-2(5))* Scholastic, Inc.

—Vinnie Goes to Vegas. Walsh, Stephen & O'Donovan, Marita. 2017. (Tales from Leprechaun Land Ser.). (ENG.). 32p. (J). pap. 14.00 *(978-1-84717-724-7(7))* O'Brien Pr., Ltd., The IRL. Dist: Casemate Pubs. & Bk. Distributors, LLC.

Le Feyer, Diane & Kennedy, Sam. Ocean S. O. S. Burchett, Jan & Vogler, Sara. 2012. (Wild Rescue Ser.). (ENG.). 152p. (J). (gr. 3-6). lib. bdg. 25.32 *(978-1-4342-3771-2(0)*, Stone Arch Bks.) Capstone.

Le Goff, Hervé. L' Ours Qui Voulait Son Doudou. Beigel, Christine. 2011. (Petites Histoires du Soir Ser.: Vol. 3934726). (FRE.). (J). pap. *(978-2-01-393472-5(6))* Gautier-Languereau.

Le Grand, Claire. Paolo from Rome. Husar, Stephane. 2014. (AV2 Fiction Readalong Ser.: Vol. 134). (ENG.). 32p. (J). (gr. -1-3). lib. bdg. 34.28 *(978-1-4896-2274-7(8)*, AV2 by Weigl) Weigl Pubs., Inc.

Le, Guo. The Dragon's Tears. 2004. (ENG & POR.). 24p. (J). pap. *(978-1-85269-693-1(1))*; pap. *(978-1-85269-700-6(8))* Mantra Lingua.

—The Dragon's Tears. Gregory, Manju. 2004. (ENG & ARA.). 24p. (J). pap. *(978-1-85269-686-3(9))*; pap. *(978-1-85269-687-0(7))*; pap. *(978-1-85269-688-7(5))*; pap. *(978-1-85269-691-7(5))*; pap. *(978-1-85269-692-4(3))*; pap. *(978-1-85269-694-8(X))*; pap. *(978-1-85269-695-5(8))*; pap. *(978-1-85269-696-2(6))*; pap. *(978-1-85269-697-9(4))*; pap. *(978-1-85269-698-6(2))*; pap. *(978-1-85269-699-3(0))*; pap. *(978-1-85269-787-7(3))*; pap. *(978-1-85269-805-8(5))*; pap. *(978-1-85269-810-2(1))* Mantra Lingua.

—Dragon's Tears. Gregory, Manju. 2004. (ENG & CHI.). 24p. (J). pap. *(978-1-84444-477-9(5))* Mantra Lingua.

—The Dragon's Tears: Les Larmes du Dragon. Gregory, Manju. 2004. (ENG & FRE.). 24p. (J). pap. *(978-1-85269-689-4(3))* Mantra Lingua.

—The Dragon's Tears: Lotet e Kucedres. Gregory, Manju. 2004. (ENG & ALB.). 24p. (J). pap. *(978-1-85269-685-6(0))* Mantra Lingua.

Le Huche, Magali. City Kitty Cat. Webb, Steve. 2015. (ENG.). 32p. (J). (gr. -1-3). 17.99 *(978-1-4814-4331-9(3)*, Simon & Schuster Bks. For Young Readers) Simon & Schuster Bks. For Young Readers.

—Happy Zappa Cat. Webb, Steve. 2014. (ENG.). 32p. 15.99 *(978-0-85707-620-5(5)*, Simon & Schuster Children's) Simon & Schuster, Ltd. GBR. Dist: Simon & Schuster, Inc.

—Poppy & the Brass Band: With 16 Musical Instrument Sounds! 2017. (ENG.). 24p. (J). (gr. -1-1). 15.95 *(978-1-63322-402-5(3)*, Walter Foster Jr) Quarto Publishing Group USA.

—Poppy & the Orchestra: With 16 Musical Instrument Sounds! 2017. (ENG.). 24p. (J). (gr. -1-1). 15.95 *(978-1-63322-401-8(5)*, Walter Foster Jr) Quarto Publishing Group USA.

—This Is a Good Story. Lehrhaupt, Adam. 2017. (ENG.). 40p. (J). (gr. k-3). 17.99 *(978-1-4814-2935-1(3)*, Simon & Schuster/Paula Wiseman Bks.) Simon & Schuster/Paula Wiseman Bks.

Le Huche, Magali. Poppy & Mozart: With 16 Musical Sounds! Le Huche, Magali. 2018. (ENG.). 24p. (J). (gr. -1-1). 15.95 *(978-1-63322-600-5(X)*, Walter Foster Jr) Quarto Publishing Group USA.

—Poppy & Vivaldi: With 16 Musical Sounds! Le Huche, Magali. 2018. (ENG.). 24p. (J). (gr. -1-1). 15.95 *(978-1-63322-599-2(2)*, Walter Foster Jr) Quarto Publishing Group USA.

le Joly Sénoville, Tinou. My First Communion. Thoms, Susan Collins. 2017. 44p. (J). (gr. k). 12.95 *(978-1-4549-1453-2(X))* Sterling Publishing Co., Inc.

Le, Khoa. The Fish Who Found the Sea. Watts, Alan. 2020. (ENG.). 32p. (J). 17.99 *(978-1-68364-289-3(9)*, 900220032) Sounds True, Inc.

—Flash & Gleam: Light in Our World. Fliess, Sue. 2020. (ENG.). 32p. (J). (gr. k-2). lib. bdg. 19.99 *(978-1-5415-5770-3(0)*, Millbrook Pr.) Lerner Publishing Group.

—Miriam at the River. Yolen, Jane. 2020. (ENG.). 32p. (J). (gr. k-3). 17.99 *(978-1-5415-4400-0(5)*, Kar-Ben Publishing) Lerner Publishing Group.

Le, Leonard Rolland. Second world war - internet Linked. Dowswell, Paul. 2005. 128p. (J). 19.99 *(978-0-7945-1044-2(2)*, Usborne) EDC Publishing.

Le, Loanne. The Fake Doughnut. Chedekel, Evelyn. 2013. 24p. 16.95 *(978-0-9888974-0-3(7))* BugaBk. llc.

Le Mair, Henriette Willebeek. A Gallery of Children. Milne, A. A. 2006. 79p. (J). (gr. k-4). reprint ed. 20.00 *(978-1-4223-5106-2(8))* DIANE Publishing Co.

Lê, Michel, jt. illus. see Lê, Christine.

Le Ray, Marina. Hey, Diddle, Diddle, 1 vol. Reasoner, Charles. 2014. (Charles Reasoner Nursery Rhymes Ser.). (ENG.). 10p. (J). (gr. -1 — 1). bds. 4.99 *(978-1-4795-3807-2(8)*, Picture Window Bks.) Capstone.

—Hickory, Dickory, Dock. Reasoner, Charles. 2014. (Charles Reasoner Nursery Rhymes Ser.). (ENG.). 10p. (J). (gr. -1 — 1). bds. 4.99 *(978-1-4795-3805-8(1)*, Picture Window Bks.) Capstone.

—Hide-And-Ghost Seek... Matthews, Rupert. 2013. (J). *(978-1-4351-4895-6(9))* Barnes & Noble, Inc.

—Itsy Bitsy Spider, 1 vol. Reasoner, Charles. 2013. (Charles Reasoner Nursery Rhymes Ser.). (ENG.). 10p. (J). (gr. -1 — 1). bds. 4.99 *(978-1-4795-1691-9(0)*, Picture Window Bks.) Capstone.

—Jack & Jill, 1 vol. Reasoner, Charles. 2014. (Charles Reasoner Nursery Rhymes Ser.). (ENG.). 10p. (J). (gr. -1 — 1). bds. 4.99 *(978-1-4795-3806-5(X)*, Picture Window Bks.) Capstone.

—Little Bo Peep, 1 vol. Reasoner, Charles. 2014. (Charles Reasoner Nursery Rhymes Ser.). (ENG.). 10p. (J). (gr. -1 — 1). bds. 4.99 *(978-1-4795-3804-1(3)*, Picture Window Bks.) Capstone.

—Row, Row, Row Your Boat; and, Ride, Ride, Ride Your Bike. 2013. (ENG.). 24p. (J). *(978-0-7787-1149-0(8))* Crabtree Publishing Co.

—Twinkle, Twinkle, Little Star, 1 vol. Reasoner, Charles. 2013. (Charles Reasoner Nursery Rhymes Ser.). (ENG.). 10p. (J). (gr. -1 — 1). bds. 4.99 *(978-1-4795-1693-3(7)*, Picture Window Bks.) Capstone.

Le Rolland, Leonard. The Complete Book of Chess. Dalby, Elizabeth. 2006. (Chess Guides). 96p. (J). (gr. 5). lib. bdg., act. bk. ed. 25.95 *(978-1-58086-517-3(8))* EDC Publishing.

—Martin Luther King Jr. Jones, Rob Lloyd. 2006. (Usborne Famous Lives Gift Bks.). 64p. (J). (gr. 2-5). 8.99 *(978-0-7945-1260-6(7)*, Usborne) EDC Publishing.

—Seas & Oceans Sticker Atlas. Clarke, Phillip. 2006. 24p. (J). pap. 8.95 *(978-0-7945-1218-7(6)*, Usborne) EDC Publishing.

—The Usborne Book of Really Awful Jokes: About School & Other Stuff. Howell, Laura, ed. 2005. (Usborne Ser.). 288p. (J). (gr. -1-7). per. 10.95 *(978-0-7945-0578-3(3)*, Usborne) EDC Publishing.

—The Usborne Book of Silly Jokes. Howell, Laura, ed. 2003. (Jokes Ser.). 96p. (J). (gr. 4-7). pap. 6.95 *(978-0-7945-0395-6(0)*, Usborne) EDC Publishing.

Le-Tan, Pierre. Puss in Boots, 1 vol. Metaxas, Eric. 2007. (Rabbit Ears-A Classic Tale Ser.). (ENG.). 36p. (J). (gr. 2-6). 28.50 *(978-1-59961-311-6(5)*, 12964, Picture Bk.) Spotlight.

—What the Dormouse Said: Lessons for Grown-Ups from Children's Books. Gash, Amy. 2004. (ENG.). 160p. (J). pap. 9.95 *(978-1-56512-451-6(0)*, 72451) Algonquin Bks. of Chapel Hill.

Le Tandé, Prisca. Here Comes Santacorn. McLean, Danielle. import ed. 2020. (Llamacorn & Friends Ser.). (ENG.). 18p. (J). (— 1). bds. 9.99 ***(978-0-593-30633-8(3)***, Random Hse. Bks. for Young Readers) Random Hse. Children's Bks.

Le Tandé, Prisca. I Believe in Bunnycorns. McLean, Danielle. import ed. 2020. (Llamacorn & Friends Ser.). (ENG.). 18p. (J). (— 1). bds. 9.99 *(978-0-593-12643-1(2)*, Random Hse. Bks. for Young Readers) Random Hse. Children's Bks.

—I Love My Llamacorn. McLean, Danielle. 2019. (Llamacorn & Friends Ser.). (ENG.). 18p. (J). (— 1). bds. 9.99 *(978-0-593-12206-8(2)*, Random Hse. Bks. for Young Readers) Random Hse. Children's Bks.

Le Tandé, Prisca. My Magical Mermicorn. McLean, Danielle. import ed. 2020. (Llamacorn & Friends Ser.). (ENG.). 18p. (J). (— 1). bds. 9.99 ***(978-0-593-17835-5(1)***, Random Hse. Bks. for Young Readers) Random Hse. Children's Bks.

Le Tandé, Prisca. 45 Games... Going Away. Auzou Publishing Staff, ed. 2018. 52p. (J). 6.99 *(978-2-7338-5624-6(3))* Auzou, Philippe Editions FRA. Dist: Consortium Bk. Sales & Distribution.

Le Tord, Bijou. A Bird or Two: A Story about Henri Matisse. Le Tord, Bijou. 2004. 32p. (gr. 2-7). 18.00 *(978-0-8028-5184-0(3))* Eerdmans, William B. Publishing Co.

—A Mountain Is to Climb. Le Tord, Bijou. Date not set. 40p. (J). 5.99 *(978-0-06-443591-8(1))* HarperCollins Pubs.

Lea, Corinne. Goobadabers. Powell, Gregg E. 2011. 24p. pap. 24.95 *(978-1-4626-0734-1(9))* America Star Bks.

Lea, Henry, jt. illus. see Lea, Jenny.

Lea, Jenny & Lea, Henry. Malela: A Childhood Long Ago. 2014. 42p. (J). *(978-1-4931-4231-6(3))* Xlibris Corp.

Leach, Elizabeth. The Mystery of the Haunted House. Night, Willow. 2020. (Sycamore Street Mysteries Ser.: Vol. 1). (ENG.). 110p. (J). pap. 5.99 ***(978-1-393-56670-0(7))*** Draft2Digital.

Leach, Garry & Firmansyah, Miralti. Imperfect: A Story of Body Image. Awada, Dounya. 2019. (Zuiker Teen Topics Ser.). (ENG.). 96p. (YA). (gr. 6). 12.99 *(978-1-947378-07-0(4))* Zuiker Pr.

Leach, Wendy. Someday We Will: A Book for Grandparents & Grandchildren. Webb, Pam. 2020. (ENG.). 32p. (J). (gr. -1-3). 17.99 *(978-1-5064-5400-9(3)*, Beaming Books) Augsburg Fortress, Pubs.

Leadlove, Ben. Louie the Loon & the Moon. Lowe, Tom. 2011. 28p. pap. 11.00 *(978-1-61170-030-5(2))* Robertson Publishing.

Leaf, Jess. The Great Big Surprise. Leaf, Eva. 2018. (ENG.). 40p. (J). (gr. -1). pap. 13.99 *(978-1-910786-81-9(0)*, c6d90c1e-f546-44ee-9178-68837d0561ed, Sarah Grace Publishing) Malcolm Down Publishing Ltd. GBR. Dist: Baker & Taylor Publisher Services (BTPS).

Leake, Kate. Smelly Feet Sandwich: And Other Silly Poems. Zobel-Nolan, Allia. 2008. 22p. (J). (gr. -1-2). 7.95 *(978-1-58925-836-5(3))* Tiger Tales.

Lear, Edward, jt. illus. see Gorey, Edward.

Learner, Vickie. Harriet Higby. Howard-Hess, Susan. 2006. (ENG.). 20p. (gr. k-2). pap. 8.95 *(978-1-57874-093-2(2)*, Kaeden Bks.) Kaeden Corp.

Leary, Catherine. Are We There Yet? Williams, Rozanne Lanczak. 2005. (Science Mini Units Ser.). 8p. (J). pap. 2.49 *(978-1-59198-151-0(4)*, 4251) Creative Teaching Pr., Inc.

—Cat Can't Write: A Cat & Dog Story. Williams, Rozanne Lanczak. (Learn to Write Ser.). 16p. (J). 2007. (gr. -1-3). pap. 8.99 *(978-1-59198-344-6(4))*; 2006. (gr. k-2). pap. 3.49 *(978-1-59198-293-7(6)*, 6187) Creative Teaching Pr., Inc.

—Cat's Fairy Tale: A Cat & Dog Story. Williams, Rozanne Lanczak. 2006. (Learn to Write Ser.). 16p. (J). (gr. k-2). pap. 3.49 *(978-1-59198-294-4(4)*, 6191) Creative Teaching Pr., Inc.

—Cat's Fairy Tale: A Cat & Dog Story. Williams, Rozanne Lanczak. Maio, Barbara, ed. 2006. (J). per. 8.99 *(978-1-59198-348-4(7))* Creative Teaching Pr., Inc.

—Granny's Coming 'Round the Mountain' Scelsa, Greg. Faulkner, Stacey, ed. 2006. (J). pap. 2.99 *(978-1-59198-350-7(9))* Creative Teaching Pr., Inc.

Leary, Catherine, jt. illus. see Christensen, David.

Leascenco, Ecaterina. Does the Cat Have Your Tongue? Karner, Mimi Anne. 2020. (ENG.). 32p. (J). pap. 9.99 ***(978-1-6874-0853-2(X))*** Independently Published.

Lease, Janice m. Rudy the Roadrunner. Lease, Janice M. 2009. 48p. pap. 19.95 *(978-0-9800762-3-3(4))* Cinnamon Ridge Publishing.

Leasman, Nancy Packard. A Kitty Named Indra/Una Gata Llamada Indra. Tanner, Dawn Leasman. l.t. ed. 2003. (SPA & ENG.). 36p. (J). per. 6.95 *(978-0-9741725-0-7(2))* Leatherwood Publishing.

Leatham, Marc Vincent. The Story of the Five Squirrels. Leatham, Marc Vincent. 2007. (J). (gr. -1-3). per. 15.99 *(978-1-59879-275-1(X))* Lifevest Publishing, Inc.

Leathers, Philippa. The Black Rabbit. Leathers, Philippa. (ENG.). 40p. (J). (gr. -1-2). 2016. 7.99 *(978-0-7636-8879-0(7))*; 2013. 14.00 *(978-0-7636-5714-7(X))* Candlewick Pr.

—How to Catch a Mouse. Leathers, Philippa. 2015. (ENG.). 40p. (J). (gr. -1-2). 15.99 *(978-0-7636-6912-6(1))* Candlewick Pr.

—The Tiptoeing Tiger. Leathers, Philippa. 2018. (ENG.). 32p. (J). (gr. -1-2). 15.99 *(978-0-7636-8843-1(6))* Candlewick Pr.

Lebarre, Erika. Jesus Visits Mary & Martha - Arch Books. 2017. (ENG.). (J). pap. 2.99 *(978-0-7586-5738-1(2))* Concordia Publishing Hse.

Lebedev, Aleksandr. Bible Stories. 2006. (Play & Learn Puzzle Bks.). 12p. (J). 12.95 *(978-0-88271-385-4(X))* Regina Pr., Malhame & Co.

—Life of Jesus Puzzle Book. Brierley, Jane. 2006. (Play & Learn Puzzle Bks.). (J). 12.95 *(978-0-88271-854-5(1))* Regina Pr., Malhame & Co.

LeBlanc, Andre. La Biblia Ilustrada. Hoth, Iva. 2012.Tr. of Picture Bible. (SPA.). 800p. (J). 19.99 *(978-1-4143-6307-3(9)*, 4605297) Tyndale Hse. Pubs.

LeBlanc, Giselle, jt. illus. see Collier, Kevin Scott.

LeBlanc, Marc. The Angel Who Didn't Fit In. Rogers-Busboom, Kimberly. 2010. 32p. (J). lib. bdg. 16.99 *(978-0-9823145-3-1(1))* Dirks Publishing, LLC.

LeBlanc, Nancy. Finn Finds Fun! Gardner, Graham. 2015. 32p. (J). (gr. -1-2). 17.95 *(978-1-939930-41-5(3)*, Belle Isle Bks.) Brandylane Pubs., Inc.

—The Santa Beacon. Gardner, Graham. 2012. 40p. (J). 19.95 *(978-0-9859358-0-1(4)*, Belle Isle Bks.) Brandylane Pubs., Inc.

Leblond, Valériane. Little Honey Bee, Vol. Lewis, Caryl. 2019. (ENG.). 32p. (J). 10.00 *(978-1-78461-561-1(7))* Y Lolfa GBR. Dist: Casemate Pubs. & Bk. Distributors, LLC.

LeBreton, Zachary. Rhyming with the Little Ones, 1 vol. LeBreton, Heather. 2009. 31p. pap. 24.95 *(978-1-60749-114-9(1))* America Star Bks.

Lebrun, Maxime. My First Wild Activity Book. Ross, Isabel Otter-Barry. 2018. (ENG.). 32p. (J). (gr. k-k). pap. 12.99 *(978-1-62686-957-8(X)*, Silver Dolphin Bks.) Printers Row Publishing Group.

—Slide-A-Story: Who's in the Barn? Roth, Megan. 2018. (ENG.). 12p. (J). (— 1). bds. 8.99 *(978-1-68412-232-5(5)*, Silver Dolphin Bks.) Printers Row Publishing Group.

—This Is NOT a Dragon Party. Flaherty, Mike. 2019. 32p. (J). (gr. -1). 16.95 *(978-1-4549-2233-9(8))* Sterling Publishing Co., Inc.

Lebrun, Maxime, jt. illus. see Heinsz, Joshua.

Lechler, Louan. When the Bear Came Back: The Whole Story. Wooten, Terry. 2006. (J). per. 9.49 *(978-1-893972-27-8(5))* Wordsmith Pr.

Lechner, John. Sticky Burr: Adventures in Burrwood Forest. Lechner, John. 2008. 56p. (J). (gr. 1-4). pap. 7.99 *(978-0-7636-3567-1(7))* Candlewick Pr.

Lechon, Daniel. The Desert Is My Mother/el Desierto Es Mi Madre. Mora, Pat. 97th ed. 2008. (SPA & ENG.). 32p. (J). (gr. -1-2). pap. 7.95 *(978-1-55885-158-0(5)*, Piñata Books) Arte Publico Pr.

—The Desert is My Mother/El Desierto Es Mi Madre: CD & Book Set. Mora, Pat. 2008. 32p. (J). pap. 18.95 *(978-0-9815686-2-1(9))* Lorito Bks., Inc.

Lechón, Daniel. Kikiriki / Quiquiriquí. De Anda, Diane. Hernández, Karina, tr. from ENG. 2004. (ENG & SPA.). 32p. 16.95 *(978-1-55885-382-9(0)*, Piñata Books) Arte Publico Pr.

Lechon, Daniel. My Tata's Guitar / la guitarra de mi Tata. Brammer, Ethriam Cash. (ENG & SPA.). 32p. (J). 16.95 *(978-1-55885-369-0(3)*, Piñata Books) Arte Publico Pr.

Lechowick, Silvija. Tale of Little Zero & Bully 9. Lechowick, Silvija. 2018. (Scientific Fairytales for Children Ser.: 1). (ENG.). 28p. (J). (gr. k-7). 22.97 *(978-0-9989929-0-7(9))* BookBaby.

Lecia, Balian, jt. illus. see Lorna, Balian.

Lecuona, Vania. El Monstruo Del Cajon. Cerdeira, Pamela. 2019. (SPA.). 76p. (J). (gr. -1-3). 12.95 *(978-607-748-144-7(0)*, Uranito) Ediciones Urano de México MEX. Dist: Spanish Pubs., LLC.

—Simon y el Sauce Lloron. Coronado, Ingrid. 2019. (SPA.). 80p. (J). (gr. -1-3). 12.95 *(978-607-748-142-3(4)*, Uranito) Ediciones Urano de México MEX. Dist: Spanish Pubs., LLC.

Ledbetter, John'el. The Tickle Man. Curry, Cicero. 2013. 44p. 24.95 *(978-1-63004-279-0(X))*; pap. 24.95 *(978-1-63000-015-8(9))* America Star Bks.

Ledbetter, Maggui. The Blanket of Miracles. Bulla, Lynda. 2016. (ENG.). (J). 24.00 *(978-1-61009-254-8(6))*; pap. 16.00 *(978-1-61009-218-0(X))* Oak Tree Publishing.

Lederhos, Anne. Kitten up a Tree. Abel, Melanie. 2008. 24p. (J). pap. 15.95 *(978-0-9791606-4-6(2))* E & E Publishing.

Lederman, Marsha. Virginia: An Alphabetical Journey Through History. Shepard, Betty Bruce. 2007. 32p. (J). (gr. -1-3). 17.95 *(978-1-893622-14-2(2)*, VSP Bks.) Vacation Spot Publishing.

Ledesma, Sophie. Monsters: A Magic Lens Hunt for Creatures of Myth, Legend, Fairy Tale, & Fiction. Potard, Céline. 2019. (ENG.). 32p. (J). (gr. 1-5). 21.99 *(978-1-9999680-6-9(9))* What on Earth Bks GBR. Dist: Ingram Publisher Services.

Ledesma, Sophie. Stomp, Stomp! Otter, Isabel. 2020. (ENG.). 12p. (J). (-k). bds. 8.99 ***(978-1-68010-644-2(9))*** Tiger Tales.

Ledger, Bill. En el Dentista. Lindeen, Mary. 2016. (Early Rising Readers Ser.). (SPA.). (J). (gr. -1). 6.67 *(978-1-4788-3683-4(0))* Newmark Learning LLC.

—I See the Dentist. Lindeen, Mary. 2015. (Early Rising Readers Ser.). (J). (gr. -1-k). 5.83 *(978-1-4788-1584-6(1))* Newmark Learning LLC.

—Mrs. MacDonald's Garden: Set Of 6. Fuerst, Jeffrey B. 2014. (Shared Reading Foundations Ser.). (J). (gr. 1). 36.00 net. *(978-1-4900-0054-1(2))* Benchmark Education Co.

—Mrs. MacDonald's Garden Book Set. Fuerst, Jeffrey B. 2014. (Shared Reading Foundations Ser.). (J). (gr. 1). 72.00 net. *(978-1-4900-0024-4(0))* Benchmark Education Co.

—Pies for Simple Simon. Fuerst, Jeffrey B. 2009. (Reader's Theater Nursery Rhymes & Songs Set B Ser.). 48p. (J). pap. *(978-1-60859-165-7(4))* Benchmark Education Co.

—Red Roses, Blue Violets, And... ? Grudzina, Rebecca. 2009. (Reader's Theater Nursery Rhymes & Songs Set B Ser.). 48p. (J). pap. *(978-1-60859-167-1(0))* Benchmark Education Co.

—Simple Simon. Fuerst, Jeffrey B. 2010. (Rising Readers Ser.). (J). 3.49 *(978-1-60719-706-5(5))* Newmark Learning LLC.

—Technology Breakdown. Parkes, Brenda & Fuerst, Jeffrey B. 2015. (Shared Reading Contemporary Tales Ser.). (J). (gr. k-1). *(978-1-4900-2118-8(3))* Benchmark Education Co.

—Technology Breakdown: Big Book Edition. Parkes, Brenda & Fuerst, Jeffrey B. 2015. (Shared Reading Contemporary Tales Ser.). (J). (gr. k-1). *(978-1-4900-2113-3(2))* Benchmark Education Co.

—This Little Piggy. Harris, Brooke. 2010. (Rising Readers Ser.). (J). 3.49 *(978-1-60719-696-9(4))* Newmark Learning LLC.

—What Is Papa Cooking? Set Of 6. Parkes, Brenda. 2014. (Shared Reading Foundations Ser.). (J). (gr. 1). 36.00 net. *(978-1-4900-0042-8(9))* Benchmark Education Co.

—What Is Papa Cooking? Book Set. Parkes, Brenda. 2014. (Shared Reading Foundations Ser.). (J). (gr. 1). 72.00 net. *(978-1-4900-0012-1(7))* Benchmark Education Co.

—What Is That Sound? Set Of 6. Fuerst, Jeffrey B. 2014. (Shared Reading Foundations Ser.). (J). (gr. 1). 36.00 net. *(978-1-4900-0041-1(0))* Benchmark Education Co.

—What Is That Sound? Book Set. Fuerst, Jeffrey B. 2014. (Shared Reading Foundations Ser.). (J). (gr. 1). 72.00 net. *(978-1-4900-0011-4(9))* Benchmark Education Co.

Ledger, Craig. Tripawd Toffee: Adventures of a 3 - Legged Cat. Song, Miss Anna R. 2018. (ENG.). 30p. (J). pap. *(978-1-9999463-1-9(6))* Anna R Song.

Ledger, Faye. Buggy Buggy. Hall, Shirley. 2010. 20p. 12.00 *(978-1-4520-6787-2(2))* AuthorHouse.

Ledoyen, Sam. Colin Kaepernick. Hoena, B. A. 2020. (Athletes Who Made a Difference Ser.). (ENG.). 32p. (J). (gr. 3-6). 27.99 ***(978-1-5415-7817-3(1)***, Graphic Universe™) Lerner Publishing Group.

LeDoyen, Sam. Colin Kaepernick: Athletes Who Made a Difference. Hoena, Blake. 2020. (Athletes Who Made a Difference Ser.). (ENG.). 32p. (J). (gr. 3-6). pap. 8.99 ***(978-1-7284-0293-2(X)***, Graphic Universe™) Lerner Publishing Group.

Ledoyen, Sam. Serena Williams. Hoena, B. A. 2020. (Athletes Who Made a Difference Ser.). 32p. (J). (gr. 3-6). 27.99 ***(978-1-5415-7818-0(X)***, Graphic Universe™) Lerner Publishing Group.

LeDoyen, Sam. Serena Williams: Athletes Who Made a Difference. Hoena, Blake. 2020. (Athletes Who Made a Difference Ser.). (ENG.). 32p. (J). (gr. 3-6). pap. 8.99 ***(978-1-7284-0296-3(4)***, Graphic Universe™) Lerner Publishing Group.

Ledoyen, Sam, jt. illus. see Wolski, Igor.

Ledwidge, Natacha. Emily Windsnap & the Castle in the Mist. Kessler, Liz. 2012. (Emily Windsnap Ser.: 3). (ENG.). 208p. (J). (gr. 3-7). pap. 6.99 *(978-0-7636-6017-8(5))* Candlewick Pr.

Ledwidge, Natacha & Gibb, Sarah. Emily Windsnap & the Castle in the Mist. Kessler, Liz. 2007. (Emily Windsnap Ser.: 3). (ENG.). 208p. (J). (gr. 3-7). 15.99 *(978-0-7636-3330-1(5))* Candlewick Pr.

Ledwidge, Natacha, jt. illus. see Gibb, Sarah.

Ledwon, Peter, jt. illus. see Mets, Marilyn.

Ledyard, Addie. The New-Year's Bargain (Illustrated Edition) Coolidge, Susan. 2019. (ENG.). 104p. (J). pap. *(978-1-4068-9090-7(1))* Echo Library.

—What Katy Did. Coolidge, Susan. 2013. 132p. pap. *(978-1-909735-03-3(5))* Aziloth Bks.

—What Katy Did. Coolidge, Susan. 284p. 2010. 35.16 *(978-1-163-85079-4(9))*; 2010. pap. 23.16 *(978-1-163-77965-1(2))*; 2007. 43.95 *(978-0-548-53870-8(0))*; 2007. per. 28.95 *(978-0-548-48700-6(6))* Kessinger Publishing, LLC.

Lee, Hye Ran . El jardín secreto. Burnett, Frances Hodgson. 2014. (SPA.). 360p. (J). pap. 16.99 *(978-607-01-1877-7(4))* Santillana Ediciones Generales, S.A. de C.V. MEX. Dist: Santillana USA Publishing Co., Inc.

Lee, Alan. Black Ships Before Troy. Sutcliff, Rosemary. 2017. (ENG.). 128p. (J). (gr. 2-5). 19.99 *(978-1-84780-995-7(2)*, Frances Lincoln Children's Bks.) Quarto Publishing Group UK GBR. Dist: Hachette Bk. Group.

Lee, Albert, photos by. Changing from Boys to Men: The Importance of Mentoring African American Boys. Ferguson, Eric T. 2016. (ENG., (J). (gr. k-6). pap. 12.99 *(978-0-692-72880-2(5))* Kingdom Builders Pubn.

Lee, Alexander T. The Achiever's Alphabet. Bolden, Christian J. 2017. (ENG.). 64p. (J). pap. 13.99 *(978-0-692-96171-1(2))* Bolden, Christian.

Lee, Anais. A Hat for Melinda: Fighting Leukemia Together. Tucker, Seletha Marie Head. 2013. *(978-1-62086-164-6(X))* Mascot Bks., Inc.

—The Toy-Gobbling Monster. V, Vasanthi. 2013. (ENG.). (J). 14.95 *(978-1-62086-330-5(8))* Mascot Bks., Inc.

Lee Ann, Mbil Art. Justice for a Texas Marshall: Marshall Morris Is at It Again! Ira, First Editing & DeLuca, Robert John. 2018. (ENG.). 168p. (J). pap. 8.99 *(978-1-7320596-0-3(8))* DeLuca, Robert John.

Lee, Annette S. The Forever Sky. Peacock, Thomas. 2019. (ENG.). 32p. (J). 16.95 *(978-1-68134-098-2(4))* Minnesota Historical Society Pr.

Lee, April. Don't Let the Beasties Escape This Book! Berry, Julie. 2019. (ENG.). 40p. (J). (gr. k-2). 17.99 *(978-1-947440-04-3(7)*, J. Paul Getty Museum) Getty Pubns.

Lee, Bill. Ko'eku Tohi Lau Fika. Thompson, Richard & Thompson, Ofa. l.t. ed. 2003. (TON.). 24p. (J). (gr. -1-18). 5.00 *(978-0-9678979-1-2(2))* Friendly Isles Pr.

Lee, Brian. A Castle. 2005. (What's Inside? Ser.). (J). *(978-0-7607-6568-5(5))* backpackbook.

—A Construction Site. 2005. (What's Inside Ser.). (J). *(978-0-7607-6570-8(7))* backpackbook.

—Let's Explore a Castle. Harris, Nicholas. 2010. 36p. (J). (gr. k-3). 13.99 *(978-0-8437-1395-4(X))* Hammond World Atlas Corp.

—Let's Explore a Pirate Ship. Harris, Nicholas. 2010. 36p. (J). 13.99 *(978-0-8437-1378-7(X))* Hammond World Atlas Corp.

—A Pirate Ship. 2005. (What's Inside? Ser.). *(978-0-7607-6809-9(9))* backpackbook.

—The World of Dinosaurs. 2005. (J). *(978-0-7607-6569-2(3))* backpackbook.

Lee, Brittney. Frozen Anna Loves Elsa. Rubiano, Brittany. 2015. (ENG.). 14p. (J). (gr. -1-k). bds. 9.99 *(978-1-4847-2470-5(4))* Disney Pr.

—Loser/Queen. Anderson, Jodi Lynn. 2010. (ENG.). 272p. (YA). (gr. 7-18). pap. 9.99 *(978-1-4169-9646-0(X)*, Simon & Schuster Bks. For Young Readers) Simon & Schuster Bks. For Young Readers.

—Mary Blair's Unique Flair: The Girl Who Became One of the Disney Legends. Novesky, Amy. 2019. (ENG.). 40p. (J). (gr. 1-3). 17.99 *(978-1-4847-5720-8(3))* Disney Pr.

Lee, Calee M. St. Patrick's Journey. Lee, Calee M. 2019. (Peg Saints Ser.). (ENG.). 32p. (J). (gr. -1-5). pap. 9.99 *(978-1-5324-0756-7(4))* Xist Publishing.

Lee, Calee M. & Lee, Jacob G. Saint Patrick's Journey. Lee, Calee M. 2019. (Peg Saints Ser.). (ENG.). 32p. (J). (gr. -1-5). 9.99 *(978-1-5324-1129-8(4))* Xist Publishing.

Lee, Catherine. Saving Jackson's Tooth. Shnall, Jeff. Lemonier, Edee, ed. 2019. (ENG.). 42p. (J). (gr. k-4). ***(978-1-9991101-6-0(0))***; pap. ***(978-1-9991101-0-9(2))*** Beech Avenue Publishing.

Lee, Cedar. A Search for the Northern Lights. Rusch, Elizabeth & Rusch, Izzi. 2020. 40p. (J). (gr. 2-5). 17.99 *(978-1-5132-6290-1(4)*, West Margin Pr.) West Margin Pr.

Lee, Chi-ching. Romance of the Three Kingdoms Manga: The Oath in the Peach Orchard, 23 vols., Vol. 1. Ahlstrom, Peter, ed. Kirsch, Alexis, tr. from CHI. 2003. (YA). pap. 9.95 *(978-1-932592-00-9(8)*, ROM1101) Romancing Cathay.

Lee, Chin. The Pawed Piper. Robinson, Michelle. 2019. (ENG.). 32p. (J). (-k). 16.99 *(978-1-5362-0165-9(0))* Candlewick Pr.

Lee, Christopher. In a Spooky Haunted House: A Pop-Up Adventure. Stern, Joel. 2020. (ENG.). 14p. (J). (gr. -1-k). bds. 12.99 ***(978-1-5344-6036-2(5)***, Little Simon) Little Simon.

Lee, Christopher. Sunny's Tow Truck Saves the Day! Pace, Anne Marie. 2019. (ENG.). 24p. (J). (gr. -1-1). 14.99 *(978-1-4197-3191-4(2))* Abrams, Inc.

Lee, Dara Lashia. Astrid & Apollo. Bidania, V. T. 2020. (Astrid & Apollo Ser.). (ENG.). (J). (gr. k-2). 93.28 ***(978-1-5158-6126-3(0)***, 177562); pap., pap., pap. 27.80 ***(978-1-5158-6135-5(X)***, 177563) Capstone. (Picture Window Bks.).

—Astrid & Apollo & the Fishing Flop. Bidania, V. T. 2020. (Astrid & Apollo Ser.). (ENG.). 64p. (J). (gr. k-2). pap. 6.95 ***(978-1-5158-6127-0(9)***, 193756); lib. bdg. 23.32 ***(978-1-5158-6123-2(6)***, 142399) Capstone. (Picture Window Bks.).

—Astrid & Apollo & the Happy New Year. Bidania, V. T. 2020. (Astrid & Apollo Ser.). (ENG.). 64p. (J). (gr. k-2). pap. 6.95 ***(978-1-5158-6129-4(5)***, 193758); lib. bdg. 23.32 ***(978-1-5158-6125-6(2)***, 142401) Capstone. (Picture Window Bks.).

—Astrid & Apollo & the Soccer Celebration. Bidania, V. T. 2020. (Astrid & Apollo Ser.). (ENG.). 64p. (J). (gr. k-2). pap. 6.95 ***(978-1-5158-6133-1(3)***, 193762); lib. bdg. 23.32 ***(978-1-5158-6124-9(4)***, 142400) Capstone. (Picture Window Bks.).

—Astrid & Apollo & the Starry Campout. Bidania, V. T. 2020. (Astrid & Apollo Ser.). (ENG.). 64p. (J). (gr. k-2). pap. 6.95 ***(978-1-5158-6131-7(7)***, 193760); lib. bdg. 23.32 ***(978-1-5158-6122-5(8)***, 142398) Capstone. (Picture Window Bks.).

Lee, Deborah. The Invisible Boy. Hollingsworth, Alyssa. 2020. (ENG.). 320p. (J). 16.99 *(978-1-250-15572-6(X)*, 900184754) Roaring Brook Pr.

Lee, Dom. Baseball Saved Us, 1 vol. Mochizuki, Ken. 97th ed. 2018. (ENG.). 30p. (J). (gr. k-3). pap. 10.95 *(978-1-880000-19-9(9)*, 4610bf3e-a077-439d-a4d2-9bdd62df73da) Lee & Low Bks., Inc.

—Baseball Saved Us. Mochizuki, Ken. (Picture Book Readalong Ser.). pap. 39.95 incl. audio compact disk *(978-1-59112-917-2(6))*; 2004. (J). (gr. -1-2). 25.95 incl. audio *(978-1-59112-456-6(5))* Live Oak Media.

—Be Water, My Friend: The Early Years of Bruce Lee, 1 vol. Mochizuki, Ken. 2006. (ENG.). 32p. (J). (gr. 1-6). pap. 10.95 *(978-1-62014-164-9(7)*, b82caee0-28b3-4626-b19c-0c1f057ba38f) Lee & Low Bks., Inc.

—El Beisbol Nos Salvo, 1 vol. Mochizuki, Ken. González, Tomás, tr. 2018. (Reissue Ser.). (SPA.). 32p. (J). (gr. k-3). pap. 10.95 *(978-1-880000-22-9(9)*, bfdd393c-1533-46c3-9943-4e8844bf2144) Lee & Low Bks., Inc.

—Sixteen Years in Sixteen Seconds: The Sammy Lee Story, 1 vol. Yoo, Paula. 2010. (ENG.). 32p. (J). (gr. 3-6). 24.94 *(978-1-58430-247-6(X))* Lee & Low Bks., Inc.

—The Story of Olympic Diver Sammy Lee, 1 vol. Yoo, Paula. 2020. (Story Of Ser.). (ENG.). 80p. (J). (gr. 3-7). pap. 9.95 *(978-1-64379-014-5(5)*, 3fb3a7e9-9ffc-4ea1-ac29-6f281312042f) Lee & Low Bks., Inc.

Lee, Ella Dolbear. The Wonderful Story of Jesus. 2004. reprint ed. pap. 20.95 *(978-1-4179-3177-4(9))* Kessinger Publishing, LLC.

Lee, Fran. My Vacation Album: Includes: Reusable Camera, Film, Batteries & Glue Stick. Elton, Candice & Elton, Richard. 2003. (ENG.). 28p. (J). spiral bd. 19.95 *(978-1-58685-280-1(9))* Gibbs Smith, Publisher.

—Riding on a Range: Western Activities for Kids. Drinkard, Lawson. ed. 2003. (ENG.). 64p. (YA). pap. 9.99 *(978-1-58685-036-4(9))* Gibbs Smith, Publisher.

Lee, Fran. Backyard Birding for Kids, 1 vol. Lee, Fran. 2005. (ENG.). 64p. (J). pap. 9.99 *(978-1-58685-411-9(9))* Gibbs Smith, Publisher.

Lee, Frances Cook. Sliding in the Snow: Winter Activities for Kids, 1 vol. Dymock, Melissa. 2015. (ENG.). 64p. (J). pap. 9.99 *(978-1-4236-3893-3(X))* Gibbs Smith, Publisher.

Lee, Frank. Steve Longenecker's Wilderness Emergency Medical Aid Book for Kids & Their Adults. Longnecker, Steve. 2005. 176p. (YA). (gr. 5-18). pap. 16.95 *(978-1-889596-18-1(3))* Milestone Pr., Inc.

Lee, George Douglas. Oppy Stops the Hopping Popper. Lee, George Douglas. Lee, Brenda Donaloio, ed. 2012. 30p. pap. 10.95 *(978-0-9848486-1-4(4))* Electric Theatre Radio Hour.

—Twyla the Truffle Pig. Lee, George Douglas. Lee, Brenda Donaloio, ed. 2012. 34p. pap. 10.95 *(978-0-9848486-0-7(6))* Electric Theatre Radio Hour.

—The Wolf Who Cried Boy. Lee, George Douglas. Lee, Brenda Donaloio, ed. 2012. 46p. pap. 15.95 *(978-0-9848486-2-1(2))* Electric Theatre Radio Hour.

Lee, George T. Petie the Parrot's Amazing Adventures: P. D. Q., 1 vol. Hannaford, Linda S. 2010. 16p. pap. 24.95 *(978-1-61582-767-1(6))* PublishAmerica, Inc.

Lee, Grace. Disney Junior Fancy Nancy: My Fanciest Things, Bk. 1. Tucker, Krista. 2018. (Disney Junior Fancy Nancy Ser.). (ENG.). 40p. (J). (gr. -1-3). 15.99 *(978-0-06-274855-3(6))* HarperCollins Pubs.

—Elena of Avalor Elena & the Secret of Avalor. Gerber, Craig. 2016. (ENG.). 48p. (J). (gr. 1-3). 15.99 *(978-1-4847-1554-3(3))* Disney Pr.

Lee, Grace. Frozen 2: Forest of Shadows. Benko, Kamilla. 2019. (ENG.). 416p. (J). (gr. 3-7). 14.99 ***(978-1-368-04363-2(1))*** Disney Pr.

Lee, Grace. The Magic Is in You. Hosten, Colin & Vitale, Brooke. 2018. (ENG.). 40p. (J). (gr. 1-3). 16.99 *(978-1-368-02461-7(0))* Disney Pr.

Lee, Grace & Cagol, Andrea. Frozen (Disney Frozen) Saxon, Victoria. 2015. (Little Golden Book Ser.). (ENG.). 24p. (J). (-k). 4.99 *(978-0-7364-3471-3(2)*, Golden/Disney) Random Hse. Children's Bks.

Lee, Grace & Disney Storybook Artists. Sofia the First Little Golden Book Favorites (Disney Junior: Sofia the First) Posner-Sanchez, Andrea. 2015. (ENG.). 80p. (J). (-k). 7.99 *(978-0-7364-3406-5(2)*, Golden/Disney) Random Hse. Children's Bks.

Lee, Grace & Disney Storybook Artists Staff. Sofia's Royal World (Disney Junior: Sofia the First) Posner-Sanchez, Andrea. 2014. (Big Golden Book Ser.). (ENG.). 64p. (J). (gr. -1-2). 9.99 *(978-0-7364-3262-7(0)*, Golden/Disney) Random Hse. Children's Bks.

Lee, Gyeong-Gook. Contacto: la Electricidad / Contact: Electricity. Kim, Mi-Gyeong. 2018. (Click Click: Ciencia Básica / Basic Science Ser.). (SPA.). 32p. (J). (gr. 3-7). pap. 16.99 *(978-1-947783-63-8(7)*, Altea) Penguin Random House Grupo Editorial ESP. Dist: Penguin Random Hse. LLC.

Lee, Han & Wu, Stacie. My New School: Blonde Boy. Anderson, Pamela. 2004. (J). 12.95 *(978-1-932555-05-9(6))* Watch Me Grow Kids.

—My New School: Blonde Girl. Anderson, Pamela. 2004. (J). 12.95 *(978-1-932555-04-2(8))* Watch Me Grow Kids.

—My New School: Brunette Boy. Anderson, Pamela. 2004. (J). 12.95 *(978-1-932555-07-3(2))* Watch Me Grow Kids.

—My New School: Brunette Girl. Anderson, Pamela. 2004. (J). 12.95 *(978-1-932555-06-6(4))* Watch Me Grow Kids.

Lee, Hanlim & WU, Stacie. My New School: Afro Boy. Anderson, Pamela Dell. 2003. 24p. (J). 12.95 *(978-1-932555-01-1(3))* Watch Me Grow Kids.

—My New School: Afro Girl. Anderson, Pamela Dell. 2003. 24p. (J). 12.95 *(978-1-932555-00-4(5))* Watch Me Grow Kids.

—My New School: Asian/Latin Boy. Anderson, Pamela Dell. 2003. 24p. (J). 12.95 *(978-1-932555-03-5(X))* Watch Me Grow Kids.

—My New School: Latin/Asian Girl. Anderson, Pamela Dell. 2003. 24p. (J). 12.95 *(978-1-932555-02-8(1))* Watch Me Grow Kids.

Lee, Harper. Turkey's Eggcellent Easter. Silvano, Wendi. 2019. (Turkey Trouble Ser.: 4). (ENG.). 40p. (J). (gr. -1-2). 9.99 *(978-1-5420-4037-2(X)*, 9781542040372, Two Lions) Amazon Publishing.

Lee, Harper. The Emperor's Cool Clothes. Lee, Harper. 2018. (ENG.). 32p. (J). (gr. -1-2). pap. 9.99 *(978-1-5420-4259-8(3)*, 9781542042598, Two Lions) Amazon Publishing.

Lee, Harper, jt. illus. see Harper, Lee.

Lee, Haylen. Planet of Success: An Inspirational Book about Attitude Adn Character. Woods, Shirley. 2006. 41p. (J). per. 9.95 *(978-1-60002-183-1(2)*, 4207) Mountain Valley Publishing, LLC.

Lee, Ho Baek. Bee-Bim Bop! Park, Linda Sue. (ENG.). 32p. (J). (gr. -1-3). 2008. pap. 7.99 *(978-0-547-07671-3(1)*, 1042030); 2005. 17.99 *(978-0-618-26511-4(2)*, 111270) Houghton Mifflin Harcourt Publishing Co.

Lee, Huy Voun. Fire Drill. Jacobs, Paul DuBois & Swender, Jennifer. 2010. (ENG.). 32p. (J). (gr. -1-2). 17.99 *(978-0-8050-8953-0(5)*, 900055716, Holt, Henry & Co. Bks. For Young Readers) Holt, Henry & Co.

Lee, Hye-Seong. The Call of Samuel: From 1 Samuel 3:1-10. 2003. 29p. (J). 13.50 *(978-0-9659164-9-3(9))* Fountain Publishing.

Lee, Hyeon-joo. There It Is! Observation - Objects. Kim, Soo-hyeon. Cowley, Joy, ed. 2015. (Step up - Creative Thinking Ser.). (ENG.). 32p. (J). (gr. -1-2). 26.65 *(978-1-925246-09-4(4))*; 26.65 *(978-1-925246-35-3(3))*; 7.99 *(978-1-925246-61-2(2))* ChoiceMaker Pty. Ltd., The AUS. (Big and SMALL). Dist: Lerner Publishing Group.

Lee, Hyeon-Ju. The Happiest Tree: a Story of Growing Up. Lee, Hyeon-Ju. 2019. (ENG.). 40p. (J). 18.99 *(978-1-250-14567-3(8)*, 900181073) Feiwel & Friends.

Lee, Hyeong-Jin. Animal Talk: Animal Communication. Jang, Seon-Hye. 2017. (Science Storybooks Ser.). (ENG.). 32p. (J). (gr. k-4). lib. bdg. 27.99 *(978-1-925235-13-5(0)*, Big and SMALL) ChoiceMaker Pty. Ltd., The AUS. Dist: Lerner Publishing Group.

Lee, Hyeongjin. Shooting Stars Soccer Team. Kim, YoeongAh. rev. ed. 2014. (MySELF Bookshelf Ser.). (ENG.). 32p. (J). (gr. k-2). pap. 11.94 *(978-1-60357-657-4(6))* Norwood Hse. Pr.

—The Shooting Stars Soccer Team. Kim, YoeongAh. rev. ed. 2014. (MySELF Bookshelf Ser.). (ENG.). 32p. (J). (gr. k-2). lib. bdg. 25.27 *(978-1-59953-648-4(X))* Norwood Hse. Pr.

Lee, Imani K. The Origin of the Forever Four! F4 Clever! Clever! Lee, Glenn E. 2005. (YA). per. 19.99 *(978-0-9768429-4-1(7))* Genius In A Bottle Technology Corp.

Lee, Imani K. & Lee, Shaka S. Clever! Clever! & the Book of Forever. 2005. 17p. (YA). per. 9.99 *(978-0-9768429-2-7(0))* Genius In A Bottle Technology Corp.

Lee, Ioe. Power Reading: Comic Book/Treasure Island. Cole, Bob. 2005. 70p. (J). (gr. 4-6). vinyl bd. *(978-1-883186-78-4(1)*, PPCLC3) National Reading Styles Institute, Inc.

Lee, Jack. Three Dogs & a Horse Named Blue. Lee, Patty. 2009. 80p. pap. 10.49 *(978-1-4389-9685-1(3))* AuthorHouse.

—Wild Animals: What is That I Ask? Lee, Patty. 2013. 30p. pap. 14.00 *(978-1-4349-3518-2(3)*, RoseDog Bks.) Dorrance Publishing Co., Inc.

Lee, Jacob G., jt. illus. see Lee, Calee M.

Lee, Jacqui. I Am Josephine (and I Am a Living Thing) Thornhill, Jan. 2019. (ENG.). 32p. (J). (gr. k-2). pap. 9.95 *(978-1-77147-353-8(3))* Owlkids Bks. Inc. CAN. Dist: Publishers Group West (PGW).

—Murilla Gorilla & the Hammock Problem. Lloyd, Jennifer. 2014. (Murilla Gorilla Ser.: 3). (ENG.). 42p. (J). (gr. -1-3). 9.95 *(978-1-927018-47-7(1))* Simply Read Bks. CAN. Dist: Ingram Publisher Services.

—Murilla Gorilla & the Lost Parasol. Lloyd, Jennifer. 2013. (Murilla Gorilla Ser.: 2). (ENG.). 42p. (J). (gr. -1-3). 9.95 *(978-1-927018-23-1(4))* Simply Read Bks. CAN. Dist: Ingram Publisher Services.

—Murilla Gorilla, Jungle Detective. Lloyd, Jennifer. 2013. (Murilla Gorilla Ser.: 1). (ENG.). 42p. (J). (gr. -1-3). 9.95

L

(978-1-927018-15-6(3)) Simply Read Bks. CAN. Dist: Ingram Publisher Services.

—Taffy Time. Lloyd, Jennifer. 2015. (ENG.). 40p. (J). (gr. -1-3). 16.95 *(978-1-927018-62-0(5))* Simply Read Bks. CAN. Dist: Ingram Publisher Services.

Lee, Jade Winston. I Can, Too! Alderson, Niki. 2019. (ENG.). 30p. (J). pap. 9.49 *(978-1-9796-6485-1(4))* CreateSpace Independent Publishing Platform.

Lee, Janet K. Sea Sirens. Chu, Amy. 2019. (Trot & Cap'n Bill Adventure Ser.: 1). 144p. (J). (gr. 3-7). 20.99 *(978-0-451-48016-3(3))*; pap. 12.99 *(978-0-451-48017-0(1))* Penguin Young Readers Group. (Viking Books for Young Readers).

—Sky Island. Chu, Amy. 2020. (Trot & Cap'n Bill Adventure Ser.: 2). 160p. (J). (gr. 3-7). 20.99 *(978-0-451-48023-1(6))*; pap. 12.99 *(978-0-451-48024-8(4))* Penguin Young Readers Group. (Viking Books for Young Readers).

Lee, Jared. The Amusement Park from the Black Lagoon. Thaler, Mike. 2016. (Black Lagoon Adventures Set 4 Ser.). (ENG.). 64p. (J). (gr. 2-6). lib. bdg. 27.07 *(978-1-61479-600-8(9))*, 24333, Chapter Bks.) Spotlight.

—April Fools' Day from the Black Lagoon. Thaler, Mike. 2008. (J). *(978-0-545-01767-1(X))* Scholastic, Inc.

—April Fools' Day from the Black Lagoon, 1 vol. Thaler, Mike. 2012. (Black Lagoon Adventures Ser.: No. 2). (ENG.). 64p. (J). (gr. 2-6). 27.07 *(978-1-59961-959-0(8))*, 3603, Chapter Bks.) Spotlight.

—The Art Teacher from the Black Lagoon, 1 vol. Thaler, Mike. 2012. (Black Lagoon Ser.: No. 2). (ENG.). 32p. (J). (gr. k-4). lib. bdg. 27.07 *(978-1-59961-952-1(0))*, 3627, Picture Bk.) Spotlight.

—The Author Visit from the Black Lagoon, 1 vol. Thaler, Mike. 2012. (Black Lagoon Adventures Ser.: No. 2). (ENG.). 64p. (J). (gr. 2-6). 27.07 *(978-1-59961-960-6(1))*, 3604, Chapter Bks.) Spotlight.

—Back-to-School Fright from the Black Lagoon. Thaler, Mike. 2012. (Black Lagoon Adventures Ser.: No. 2). (ENG.). 64p. (J). (gr. 2-6). 27.07 *(978-1-59961-961-3(X))*, 3605, Chapter Bks.) Spotlight.

—Believe It! Bible Basics That Won't Break Your Brain. James, Steven. 2006. 76p. (YA). pap. 11.99 *(978-0-7847-1393-8(6))*, 42171) Standard Publishing.

—The Big Foot in the End Zone. Doyle, Bill. 2012. (Scream Team Ser.). (ENG.). 96p. (J). (gr. 2-5). pap. 4.99 *(978-0-545-47977-6(0))*, Scholastic Paperbacks) Scholastic, Inc.

—The Big Game from the Black Lagoon. Thaler, Mike. 2016. (Black Lagoon Adventures Set 4 Ser.). (ENG.). 64p. (J). (gr. 2-6). lib. bdg. 27.07 *(978-1-61479-601-5(7))*, 24334, Chapter Bks.) Spotlight.

—Black Lagoon Adventures Set 4 (Set), 10 vols. Thaler, Mike. 2016. (Black Lagoon Adventures Set 4 Ser.). (ENG.). 64p. (J). (gr. 2-6). lib. bdg. 270.70 *(978-1-61479-599-5(1))*, 24332, Chapter Bks.) Spotlight.

—Black Lagoon Adventures Set 5 (Set), 5 vols. Thaler, Mike. 2019. (Black Lagoon Adventures Ser.). (ENG.). 64p. (J). (gr. 2-6). lib. bdg. 135.35 *(978-1-5321-4416-5(4))*, 33821, Chapter Bks.) Spotlight.

—The Book Fair from the Black Lagoon. Thaler, Mike. 2006. pap. *(978-0-439-88348-1(2))* Scholastic, Inc.

—The Bully from the Black Lagoon. Thaler, Mike. 2008. (From the Black Lagoon Ser.). (gr. -1-3). 14.00 *(978-0-7569-8834-0(9))* Perfection Learning Corp.

—The Bully from the Black Lagoon. Thaler, Mike. (J). 2008. (ENG.). 32p. (gr. -1-3). pap. 3.99 *(978-0-545-06521-4(6))*, Cartwheel Bks.); 2004. *(978-0-439-68072-1(7))* Scholastic, Inc.

—The Bully from the Black Lagoon, 1 vol. Thaler, Mike. 2012. (Black Lagoon Ser.: No. 2). (ENG.). 32p. (J). (gr. k-4). lib. bdg. 27.07 *(978-1-59961-953-8(9))*, 3628, Picture Bk.) Spotlight.

—The Cafeteria Lady from the Black Lagoon, 1 vol. Thaler, Mike. 2012. (Black Lagoon Ser.: No. 2). (ENG.). 32p. (J). (gr. k-4). lib. bdg. 27.07 *(978-1-59961-954-5(7))*, 3629, Picture Bk.) Spotlight.

—The Christmas Party from the Black Lagoon. Thaler, Mike. 2006. 64p. (J). pap. *(978-0-439-87160-0(3))* Scholastic, Inc.

—Church Harvest Mess-Tivall, 1 vol. Thaler, Mike. 2010. (Tales from the Back Pew Ser.). (ENG.). 32p. (J). (gr. k-2). 3.99 *(978-0-310-71595-5(4))* Zonderkidz.

—Church Summer Cramp, 1 vol. Thaler, Mike. 2009. (Tales from the Back Pew Ser.). (ENG.). 32p. (J). (gr. 1-4). pap. 3.99 *(978-0-310-71592-4(X))* Zonderkidz.

—The Class Election from the Black Lagoon. Thaler, Mike. 2004. (Black Lagoon Adventures Ser.: 3). (ENG.). 64p. (J). (gr. 2-5). 4.99 *(978-0-439-55716-0(X))*, Scholastic Paperbacks) Scholastic, Inc.

—The Class Election from the Black Lagoon. Thaler, Mike. 2011. (Black Lagoon Adventures Ser.: No. 1). (ENG.). 64p. (J). (gr. 2-6). 27.07 *(978-1-59961-810-4(9))*, 3596, Chapter Bks.) Spotlight.

—The Class from the Black Lagoon. Thaler, Mike. 2009. (ENG.). 32p. (J). (gr. -1-3). pap. 3.99 *(978-0-545-08544-1(6))*, Cartwheel Bks.) Scholastic, Inc.

—The Class Picture Day from the Black Lagoon. Thaler, Mike. 2016. (Black Lagoon Adventures Set 4 Ser.). (ENG.). 64p. (J). (gr. 2-6). lib. bdg. 27.07 *(978-1-61479-602-2(5))*, 24335, Chapter Bks.) Spotlight.

—The Class Trip from the Black Lagoon. Thaler, Mike. 2004. (Black Lagoon Adventures Ser.: 1). (ENG.). 64p. (J). (gr. 2-5). pap. 3.99 *(978-0-439-42927-6(7))*, Scholastic Paperbacks) Scholastic, Inc.

—The Class Trip from the Black Lagoon. Thaler, Mike. 2011. (Black Lagoon Adventures Ser.: No. 1). (ENG.). 64p. (J). (gr. 2-6). 27.07 *(978-1-59961-811-1(7))*, 3597, Chapter Bks.) Spotlight.

—The Computer Teacher from the Black Lagoon. Thaler, Mike. 2007. (J). *(978-0-439-87133-4(6))* Scholastic, Inc.

—The Computer Teacher from the Black Lagoon, 1 vol. Thaler, Mike. 2012. (Black Lagoon Ser.: No. 2). (ENG.). 32p. (J). (gr. k-4). lib. bdg. 27.07 *(978-1-59961-955-2(5))*, 3630, Picture Bk.) Spotlight.

—The Custodian from the Black Lagoon. Thaler, Mike. 2014. (Black Lagoon Ser.). (ENG.). 32p. (J). (gr. -1-4). lib. bdg. 27.07 *(978-1-61479-196-6(1))*, 3636, Picture Bk.) Spotlight.

—El Dia Que Jordan Se Enfermo: Jordan's Silly Sick Day. Fontes, Justine. 2005. (Rookie Reader Español Ser.). 32p. (gr. k-2). 19.50 *(978-0-516-24445-7(0))*, Children's Pr.) Scholastic Library Publishing.

—Earth Day from the Black Lagoon. Thaler, Mike. 2016. (Black Lagoon Adventures Set 4 Ser.). (ENG.). 64p. (J). (gr. 2-6). lib. bdg. 27.07 *(978-1-61479-603-9(3))*, 24336, Chapter Bks.) Spotlight.

—The Field Day from the Black Lagoon. Thaler, Mike. 2008. (From the Black Lagoon Ser.). 64p. (gr. 2-5). 14.00 *(978-0-7569-8801-2(2))* Perfection Learning Corp.

—The Field Day from the Black Lagoon. Thaler, Mike. 2008. (Black Lagoon Adventures Ser.: 6). (ENG.). 64p. (J). (gr. 2-5). pap. 4.99 *(978-0-439-68076-9(X))* Scholastic, Inc.

—The Field Day from the Black Lagoon. Thaler, Mike. 2011. (Black Lagoon Adventures Ser.: No. 1). (ENG.). 64p. (J). (gr. 2-6). 27.07 *(978-1-59961-812-8(5))*, 3598, Chapter Bks.) Spotlight.

—Friday the 13th from the Black Lagoon. Thaler, Mike. 2016. (Black Lagoon Adventures Set 4 Ser.). (ENG.). 64p. (J). (gr. 2-6). lib. bdg. 27.07 *(978-1-61479-604-6(1))*, 24337, Chapter Bks.) Spotlight.

—Groundhog Day from the Black Lagoon. Thaler, Mike. 2015. 64p. (J). *(978-0-545-78520-4(0))* Scholastic, Inc.

—Groundhog Day from the Black Lagoon. Thaler, Mike. 2016. (Black Lagoon Adventures Set 4 Ser.). (ENG.). 64p. (J). (gr. 2-6). lib. bdg. 27.07 *(978-1-61479-605-3(X))*, 24338, Chapter Bks.) Spotlight.

—The Gym Teacher from the Black Lagoon, 1 vol. Thaler, Mike. 2011. (Black Lagoon Ser.: No. 1). (ENG.). 32p. (J). (gr. k-4). lib. bdg. 27.07 *(978-1-59961-794-7(3))*, 3620, Picture Bk.) Spotlight.

—The Gym Teacher from the Black Lagoon. Thaler, Mike. (J). (gr. -1-3). 2009. pap. 18.95 incl. audio compact disk *(978-0-545-19706-9(6))*; 2008. (ENG.). 32p. pap. 3.99 *(978-0-545-06931-1(9))* Weston Woods Studios, Inc.

—Hubie Cool: Super Spy. Thaler, Mike. 2019. (Black Lagoon Adventures Ser.). (ENG.). 64p. (J). (gr. 2-6). lib. bdg. 27.07 *(978-1-5321-4417-2(2))*, 33822, Chapter Bks.) Spotlight.

—Hubie Cool: Superhero. Thaler, Mike. 2019. (Black Lagoon Adventures Ser.). (ENG.). 64p. (J). (gr. 2-6). lib. bdg. 27.07 *(978-1-5321-4418-9(0))*, 33823, Chapter Bks.) Spotlight.

—Hubie Cool: Vampire Hunter. Thaler, Mike. 2019. (Black Lagoon Adventures Ser.). (ENG.). 64p. (J). (gr. 2-6). lib. bdg. 27.07 *(978-1-5321-4419-6(9))*, 33824, Chapter Bks.) Spotlight.

—In the Big Inning Bible Riddles from the Back Pew. Thaler, Mike. 2010. (Tales from the Back Pew Ser.). (ENG.). 32p. (J). (gr. k-2). 17.44 *(978-0-310-71597-9(0))* Zonderkidz.

—Jordan's Silly Sick Day. Fontes, Justine. 2008. (Rookie Readers: Level C (Pb) Ser.). (ENG.). (J). (gr. 1-2). lib. bdg. 15.55 *(978-0-7569-5392-8(8))* Perfection Learning Corp.

—The Librarian from the Black Lagoon. Thaler, Mike. unabr. ed. 2007. (J). (gr. k-2). pap. 14.95 incl. audio *(978-0-439-02773-1(X))* Scholastic, Inc.

—The Librarian from the Black Lagoon, 1 vol. Thaler, Mike. 2011. (Black Lagoon Ser.: No. 1). (ENG.). 32p. (J). (gr. k-4). lib. bdg. 27.07 *(978-1-59961-795-4(1))*, 3621, Picture Bk.) Spotlight.

—The Little League Team from the Black Lagoon. Thaler, Mike. 2009. (Black Lagoon Chapter Bks.: 10). (ENG.). 64p. (J). (gr. 2-5). 4.99 *(978-0-439-87162-4(X))*, Scholastic Paperbacks) Scholastic, Inc.

—The Little League Team from the Black Lagoon. Thaler, Mike. 2011. (Black Lagoon Adventures Ser.: No. 1). (ENG.). 64p. (J). (gr. 2-6). 27.07 *(978-1-59961-813-5(3))*, 3599, Chapter Bks.) Spotlight.

—The Music Teacher from the Black Lagoon, 1 vol. Thaler, Mike. 2011. (Black Lagoon Ser.: No. 1). (ENG.). 32p. (J). (gr. k-4). lib. bdg. 27.07 *(978-1-59961-796-1(X))*, 3622, Picture Bk.) Spotlight.

—The New Kid from the Black Lagoon, 1 vol. Thaler, Mike. 2012. (Black Lagoon Ser.: No. 2). (ENG.). 32p. (J). (gr. k-4). lib. bdg. 27.07 *(978-1-59961-956-9(3))*, 3631, Picture Bk.) Spotlight.

—The New Puppy from the Black Lagoon. Thaler, Mike. 2019. (Black Lagoon Adventures Ser.). (ENG.). 64p. (J). (gr. 2-6). lib. bdg. 27.07 *(978-1-5321-4420-2(2))*, 33825, Chapter Bks.) Spotlight.

—New Year's Eve Sleepover from the Black Lagoon, 1 vol. Thaler, Mike. 2014. (Black Lagoon Adventures Ser.). (ENG.). 64p. (J). (gr. 2-6). lib. bdg. 27.07 *(978-1-61479-204-8(6))*, 3613, Chapter Bks.) Spotlight.

—The Planet Without Pronouns. Martin, Justin McCory. 2004. (Grammar Tales Ser.). (ENG.). 16p. (J). (gr. 3-7). pap. 3.25 *(978-0-439-45820-7(X))* Scholastic, Inc.

—The Pool Party from the Black Lagoon. Thaler, Mike. 2019. (Black Lagoon Adventures Ser.). (ENG.). 64p. (J). (gr. 2-6). lib. bdg. 27.07 *(978-1-5321-4421-9(0))*, 33826, Chapter Bks.) Spotlight.

—The Principal from the Black Lagoon. Thaler, Mike. 2009. (From the Black Lagoon Ser.). 14.00 *(978-1-60686-507-1(2))* Perfection Learning Corp.

—The Principal from the Black Lagoon. Thaler, Mike. 2008. (Black Lagoon Adventures Ser.). (ENG.). 32p. (J). (gr. -1-3). pap. 3.99 *(978-0-545-06932-8(7))*, Cartwheel Bks.) Scholastic, Inc.

—The Principal from the Black Lagoon, 1 vol. Thaler, Mike. 2011. (Black Lagoon Ser.: No. 1). (ENG.). 32p. (J). (gr. k-4). lib. bdg. 27.07 *(978-1-59961-797-8(8))*, 3623, Picture Bk.) Spotlight.

—The Reading Challenge from the Black Lagoon. Thaler, Mike. 2016. (Black Lagoon Adventures Set 4 Ser.). (ENG.). 64p. (J). (gr. 2-6). lib. bdg. 27.07 *(978-1-61479-606-0(8))*, 24339, Chapter Bks.) Spotlight.

—The School Bus Driver from the Black Lagoon. Thaler, Mike. 2012. (Black Lagoon Ser.: No. 2). (ENG.). 32p. (J). (gr. k-4). lib. bdg. 27.07 *(978-1-59961-957-6(1))*, 3632, Picture Bk.) Spotlight.

—The School Carnival from the Black Lagoon. Thaler, Mike. 2005. 64p. (J). pap. *(978-0-439-80075-4(7))* Scholastic, Inc.

—The School Carnival from the Black Lagoon, 1 vol. Thaler, Mike. 2012. (Black Lagoon Adventures Ser.: No. 2). (ENG.). 64p. (J). (gr. 2-6). 27.07 *(978-1-59961-962-0(8))*, 3606, Chapter Bks.) Spotlight.

—The School Nurse from the Black Lagoon, 1 vol. Thaler, Mike. 2011. (Black Lagoon Ser.: No. 1). (ENG.). 32p. (J). (gr. k-4). lib. bdg. 27.07 *(978-1-59961-798-5(6))*, 3624, Picture Bk.) Spotlight.

—The School Nurse from the Black Lagoon. Thaler, Mike. 2009. (Black Lagoon (8x8) - Reissues Ser.). (ENG.). (J). (gr. -1-3). lib. bdg. 14.60 *(978-1-61383-261-5(3))* Perfection Learning Corp.

—School Play from the Black Lagoon, 1 vol. Thaler, Mike. 2014. (Black Lagoon Adventures Ser.). (ENG.). 64p. (J). (gr. 2-6). lib. bdg. 27.07 *(978-1-61479-205-5(4))*, 3614, Chapter Bks.) Spotlight.

—School Riddles from the Black Lagoon. Thaler, Mike. 2007. (J). pap. *(978-0-545-01758-9(0))* Scholastic, Inc.

—The School Secretary from the Black Lagoon. Thaler, Mike. 2006. (J). *(978-0-439-80077-8(3))* Scholastic, Inc.

—The Science Fair from the Black Lagoon. Thaler, Mike. 2005. (Black Lagoon Adventures Ser.: 4). (ENG.). 64p. (J). (gr. 2-5). pap. 3.99 *(978-0-439-55717-7(8))*, Scholastic Paperbacks) Scholastic, Inc.

—The Science Fair from the Black Lagoon. Thaler, Mike. 2011. (Black Lagoon Adventures Ser.: No. 1). (ENG.). 64p. (J). (gr. 2-6). 27.07 *(978-1-59961-814-2(1))*, 3600, Chapter Bks.) Spotlight.

—The Secret Santa from the Black Lagoon. Thaler, Mike. 2016. (Black Lagoon Adventures Set 4 Ser.). (ENG.). 64p. (J). (gr. 2-6). lib. bdg. 27.07 *(978-1-61479-607-7(6))*, 24340, Chapter Bks.) Spotlight.

—The Snow Day from the Black Lagoon. Thaler, Mike. 2008. 63p. (J). pap. *(978-0-545-01766-4(1))* Scholastic, Inc.

—The Spring Dance from the Black Lagoon. Thaler, Mike. 2009. 62p. (J). *(978-0-545-07223-6(9))* Scholastic, Inc.

—The Spring Dance from the Black Lagoon, 1 vol. Thaler, Mike. 2012. (Black Lagoon Adventures Ser.: No. 2). (ENG.). 64p. (J). (gr. 2-6). 27.07 *(978-1-59961-963-7(6))*, 3607, Chapter Bks.) Spotlight.

—St. Patrick's Day from the Black Lagoon. Thaler, Mike. 2011. 61p. (J). *(978-0-545-27328-2(5))* Scholastic, Inc.

—The Substitute Teacher from the Black Lagoon. Thaler, Mike. 2014. (Black Lagoon Ser.). (ENG.). 32p. (J). (gr. -1-4). 27.07 *(978-1-61479-199-7(6))*, 3639, Picture Bk.) Spotlight.

—The Summer Camp from the Black Lagoon. Thaler, Mike. 2016. (Black Lagoon Adventures Set 4 Ser.). (ENG.). 64p. (J). (gr. 2-6). lib. bdg. 27.07 *(978-1-61479-608-4(4))*, 24341, Chapter Bks.) Spotlight.

—The Summer Vacation from the Black Lagoon, 1 vol. Thaler, Mike. 2012. (Black Lagoon Adventures Ser.: No. 2). (ENG.). 64p. (J). (gr. 2-6). 27.07 *(978-1-59961-964-4(4))*, 3608, Chapter Bks.) Spotlight.

—The Talent Show from the Black Lagoon. Thaler, Mike. 2004. (Black Lagoon Adventures Ser.: 2). (ENG.). 64p. (J). (gr. 2-5). 4.99 *(978-0-439-43894-0(2))*, Scholastic Paperbacks) Scholastic, Inc.

—The Talent Show from the Black Lagoon. Thaler, Mike. 2011. (Black Lagoon Adventures Ser.: No. 1). (ENG.). 64p. (J). (gr. 2-6). 27.07 *(978-1-59961-815-9(X))*, 3601, Chapter Bks.) Spotlight.

—The Teacher from the Black Lagoon. Thaler, Mike. 2008. (From the Black Lagoon Ser.). (gr. -1-3). 14.00 *(978-0-7569-8779-4(2))* Perfection Learning Corp.

—The Teacher from the Black Lagoon. Thaler, Mike. 2008. (Black Lagoon Adventures Ser.). (ENG.). 32p. (J). (gr. -1-3). pap. 3.99 *(978-0-545-06522-1(4))*, Cartwheel Bks.) Scholastic, Inc.

—The Teacher from the Black Lagoon, 1 vol. Thaler, Mike. 2011. (Black Lagoon Ser.: No. 1). (ENG.). 32p. (J). (gr. k-4). lib. bdg. 27.07 *(978-1-59961-799-2(4))*, 3625, Picture Bk.) Spotlight.

—The Teacher from the Black Lagoon. Thaler, Mike. 2004. (J). (gr. k-3). 18.95 *(978-1-55592-495-9(6))* Weston Woods Studios, Inc.

—The Thanksgiving Day from the Black Lagoon. Thaler, Mike. 2009. 64p. (J). *(978-0-545-16812-0(0))* Scholastic, Inc.

—There Was a Cold Lady Who Swallowed Some Snow! Colandro, Lucille. (There Was an Old Lad Ser.). (J). 2003. (ENG.). 32p. (gr. -1-3). pap. 6.99 *(978-0-439-56703-9(3))*; 2003. 32p. (gr. k-3). pap. 5.95 *(978-0-439-47109-1(5))*, Cartwheel Bks.); 2006. (ENG.). (gr. -1-3). audio compact disk 9.99 *(978-0-439-89556-9(1))* Scholastic, Inc.

—There Was an Old Lady Who Swallowed a Bat! Colandro, Lucille. 2005. (There Was an Old Lad Ser.). (ENG.). 32p. (J). (gr. -1-3). pap. 6.99 *(978-0-439-73766-1(4))*, Cartwheel Bks.) Scholastic, Inc.

—There Was an Old Lady Who Swallowed a Bell! Colandro, Lucille. 2008. (There Was an Old Lad Ser.). (ENG.). 32p. (J). (gr. -1-3). pap. 6.99 *(978-0-545-04361-8(1))*, Cartwheel Bks.) Scholastic, Inc.

—There Was an Old Lady Who Swallowed a Chick! Colandro, Lucille. (There Was an Old Lad Ser.). (ENG.). (J). (gr. -1-k). 2011. audio compact disk 10.99 *(978-0-545-27367-1(6))*; 2010. 32p. pap. 6.99 *(978-0-545-16181-7(9))*, Cartwheel Bks.) Scholastic, Inc.

—There Was an Old Lady Who Swallowed a Chick! Colandro, Lucille. ed. 2010. (There Was an Old Lady... Ser.). lib. bdg. 17.20 *(978-0-606-06821-5(X))* Turtleback.

—There Was an Old Lady Who Swallowed a Clover. Colandro, Lucille. 2012. (ENG.). 32p. (J). (gr. -1-k). pap. 6.99 *(978-0-545-35222-2(3))*, Cartwheel Bks.) Scholastic, Inc.

—There Was an Old Lady Who Swallowed a Fly! Colandro, Lucille. 2014. (There Was an Old Lad Ser.). (ENG.). 32p. (J). (gr. -1-1). 6.99 *(978-0-545-68292-3(4))*, Cartwheel Bks.) Scholastic, Inc.

—There Was an Old Lady Who Swallowed a Rose! Colandro, Lucille. 2012. (There Was an Old Lad Ser.). (ENG.). 32p. (J). (gr. -1-k). pap. 6.99 *(978-0-545-35223-9(1))* Scholastic, Inc.

—There Was an Old Lady Who Swallowed a Rose! Colandro, Lucille. ed. 2012. (There Was an Old Lady... Ser.). lib. bdg. 17.20 *(978-0-606-26734-2(4))* Turtleback.

—There Was an Old Lady Who Swallowed a Shell! Colandro, Lucille. (There Was an Old Lad Ser.). (J). 2008. (ENG.). 32p. (gr. -1-3). pap. 6.99 *(978-0-439-87380-2(0))*, Cartwheel Bks.); 2006. *(978-0-439-81536-9(3))* Scholastic, Inc.

—There Was an Old Lady Who Swallowed Some Books! Colandro, Lucille. 2012. (ENG.). 32p. (J). (gr. -1-k). 6.99 *(978-0-545-40287-3(5))*, Cartwheel Bks.) Scholastic, Inc.

—There Was an Old Lady Who Swallowed Some Books! Colandro, Lucille. ed. 2012. (There Was an Old Lady... Ser.). lib. bdg. 17.20 *(978-0-606-26208-8(3))* Turtleback.

—There Was an Old Lady Who Swallowed Some Leaves! Colandro, Lucille. 2010. (There Was an Old Lad Ser.). (ENG.). 32p. (J). (gr. -1-k). pap. 6.99 *(978-0-545-24198-4(7))*, Cartwheel Bks.) Scholastic, Inc.

—There Was an Old Pirate Who Swallowed a Map! Colandro, Lucille. 2018. (There Was an Old Lad Ser.). (ENG.). 64p. (J). (gr. -1-3). 8.99 *(978-1-338-12994-6(5))*, Cartwheel Bks.) Scholastic, Inc.

—Trick or Treat from the Black Lagoon. Thaler, Mike. 2016. (Black Lagoon Adventures Set 4 Ser.). (ENG.). 64p. (J). (gr. 2-6). lib. bdg. 27.07 *(978-1-61479-609-1(2))*, 24342, Chapter Bks.) Spotlight.

—Vacation Bible Snooze, 1 vol. Thaler, Mike. 2010. (Tales from the Back Pew Ser.). (ENG.). 32p. (J). (gr. k-2). 3.99 *(978-0-310-71596-2(2))* Zonderkidz.

—Valentine's Day from the Black Lagoon, 1 vol. Thaler, Mike. 2014. (Black Lagoon Adventures Ser.). (ENG.). 64p. (J). (gr. 2-6). lib. bdg. 27.07 *(978-1-61479-209-3(7))*, 3618, Chapter Bks.) Spotlight.

—The Vice Principal from the Black Lagoon. Thaler, Mike. 2007. (J). pap. *(978-0-439-87132-7(8))* Scholastic, Inc.

—You're Different & That's Super. Kressley, Carson. 2005. (ENG.). 64p. (J). (gr. -1-3). 14.99 *(978-1-4169-0070-2(5))*, Simon & Schuster Bks. For Young Readers) Simon & Schuster Bks. For Young Readers.

—The Zombie at the Finish Line, 4. Doyle, Bill. 2013. (Scream Team Ser.). (ENG.). 96p. (J). (gr. 2-4). 17.44 *(978-0-545-47978-3(9))* Scholastic, Inc.

—The 100th Day of School from the Black Lagoon. Thaler, Mike. 2012. 64p. (J). pap. *(978-0-545-37325-8(5))* Scholastic, Inc.

Lee, Jared. Jordan's Silly Sick Day. Lee, Jared, tr. Fontes, Justine. 2004. (Rookie Readers Ser.). 31p. (J). 19.50 *(978-0-516-25897-3(4))*, Children's Pr.) Scholastic Library Publishing.

Lee, Jared, jt. illus. see Gordon, Mike.

Lee, Jared D. The Amusement Park from the Black Lagoon. Thaler, Mike. 2014. 64p. (J). *(978-0-545-61641-6(7))* Scholastic, Inc.

—The Author Visit from the Black Lagoon. Thaler, Mike. 2010. 61p. (J). *(978-0-545-27327-5(7))* Scholastic, Inc.

—The Big Game from the Black Lagoon. Thaler, Mike. 2013. 63p. (J). pap. *(978-0-545-61639-3(5))* Scholastic, Inc.

—The Class Picture Day from the Black Lagoon. Thaler, Mike. 2012. 64p. (J). pap. *(978-0-545-47666-9(6))* Scholastic, Inc.

—The Dentist from the Black Lagoon. Thaler, Mike. 2014. (Black Lagoon Ser.). (ENG.). 32p. (J). (gr. -1-4). 27.07 *(978-1-61479-197-3(X))*, 3637, Picture Bk.) Spotlight.

—Earth Day from the Black Lagoon. Thaler, Mike. 2013. 64p. (J). *(978-0-545-47669-0(0))* Scholastic, Inc.

—Friday the 13th from the Black Lagoon. Thaler, Mike. 2017. 64p. (J). *(978-0-545-61638-6(7))* Scholastic, Inc.

—Hubie Cool: Super Spy. Thaler, Mike. 2016. 64p. (J). *(978-0-545-85076-6(2))* Scholastic, Inc.

—Hubie Cool: Vampire Hunter. Thaler, Mike. 2015. 64p. (J). pap. *(978-0-545-85075-9(4))* Scholastic, Inc.

—Meatloaf Monster from the School Cafeteria. Thaler, Mike. 2012. (J). pap. *(978-0-545-48570-8(3))* Scholastic, Inc.

—The New Puppy from the Black Lagoon. Thaler, Mike. 2017. 64p. (J). *(978-1-338-24461-8(2))* Scholastic, Inc.

—The Pool Party from the Black Lagoon. Thaler, Mike. 2016. 64p. (J). pap. *(978-0-545-85073-5(8))* Scholastic, Inc.

—The Reading Challenge from the Black Lagoon. Thaler, Mike. 2015. 64p. (J). pap. *(978-0-545-78521-1(9))* Scholastic, Inc.

—The Secret Santa from the Black Lagoon. Thaler, Mike. 2014. 64p. (J). *(978-0-545-78519-8(7))* Scholastic, Inc.

—The Summer Vacation from the Black Lagoon. Thaler, Mike. 2010. 62p. (J). *(978-0-545-07224-3(7))* Scholastic, Inc.

—There Was a Cold Lady Who Swallowed Some Snow! Colandro, Lucille. 2017. (There Was an Old Lady [Colandro] Ser.). (ENG.). 32p. (J). (— 1). bds. 6.99 *(978-1-338-15187-9(8))*, Cartwheel Bks.) Scholastic, Inc.

—There Was an Old Lady Who Swallowed a Bat! Colandro, Lucille. (There Was an Old Lad Ser.). (ENG.). (J). (gr. -1 — 1). 2017. 32p. bds. 6.99 *(978-1-338-13580-0(5))*, Cartwheel Bks.); 2009. audio compact disk 10.99 *(978-0-545-16353-8(6))* Scholastic, Inc.

—There Was an Old Lady Who Swallowed a Bell! Colandro, Lucille. (There Was an Old Lad Ser.). (ENG.). (J). 2016. 32p. bds. 6.99 *(978-0-545-94615-5(8))*, Cartwheel Bks.); 2008. (gr. -1-3). audio compact disk 9.99 *(978-0-545-09238-8(8))* Scholastic, Inc.

—There Was an Old Lady Who Swallowed a Birthday Cake! Colandro, Lucille. 2019. (There Was an Old Lad Ser.). (ENG.). 32p. (J). (gr. -1 — 1). bds. 6.99 *(978-1-338-25374-0(3))*, Cartwheel Bks.) Scholastic, Inc.

—There Was an Old Lady Who Swallowed a Chick!: a Board Book. Colandro, Lucille. 2017. (There Was an Old Lad Ser.). (ENG.). 32p. (J). (— 1). bds. 6.99 *(978-1-338-21038-5(6))* Scholastic, Inc.

—There Was an Old Lady Who Swallowed a Frog! Colandro, Lucille. (J). 2015. *(978-0-545-83213-7(6))*; 2014. (ENG.). 32p. pap. 6.99 *(978-0-545-69138-3(9))*, Cartwheel Bks.) Scholastic, Inc.

—There Was an Old Lady Who Swallowed a Turkey! Colandro, Lucille. 2016. (There Was an Old Lad Ser.). (ENG.). 32p. (J). (gr. -1-1). 6.99 *(978-0-545-93190-8(8))*, Cartwheel Bks.) Scholastic, Inc.

—There Was an Old Lady Who Swallowed Some Books! Colandro, Lucille. 2012. (J). *(978-0-545-48186-1(4))* Scholastic, Inc.
—There Was an Old Mermaid Who Swallowed a Shark! Colandro, Lucille. 2018. (There Was an Old Lad Ser.). (ENG.). 64p. (J). (gr. -1-3). 8.99 *(978-1-338-12993-9(7)*, Cartwheel Bks.) Scholastic, Inc.
—This Is the House That Monsters Built. Metzger, Steve. 2016. 32p. (J). (gr. -1-k). pap. 9.99 *(978-0-545-61112-1(1))* Scholastic, Inc.
—Trick or Treat from the Black Lagoon. Thaler, Mike. 2015. 64p. (J). *(978-0-545-85072-8(X))* Scholastic, Inc.
Lee, Jason. The Black History Colouring Book. Albert-Steven, Marcus. 2018. (ENG.). 26p. (J). pap. *(978-1-912551-40-8(3))* Conscious Dreams Publishing.
—Dolly May & the Magical Enchanted Garden. Coleman Nelson, Carrol. 2019. (ENG.). 48p. (J). (gr. 3). pap. *(978-1-912551-60-6(8))* Conscious Dreams Publishing.
—Mum, I Want to Pee! Milling, Sharon. 2018. (ENG.). 22p. (J). pap. *(978-1-912551-14-9(4))* Conscious Dreams Publishing.
—Renae's Magical Wellington Boots. Jones, Adenike. 2018. (ENG.). 70p. (J). pap. *(978-1-912551-19-4(5))* Conscious Dreams Publishing.
Lee, Jeannie, jt. illus. see Whitten, Samantha.
Lee, Jen. The Adventures of Molly Mermaid: (English & Spanish Combo) Sanford, Jason Robert. 2019. (Molly Mermaid Ser.: Vol. 1). (ENG.). 26p. (J). pap. 9.99 ***(978-1-6958-7451-0(X))*** Independently Published.
Lee, Jenn Manley & Chow, Candice. #7 the Book Bandit: A Mystery with Geometry. Thielbar, Melinda. 2011. (Manga Math Mysteries Set II Ser.). pap. 39.62 *(978-0-7613-8364-2(6)*, Graphic Universe™) Lerner Publishing Group.
Lee, Jennifer A. & Chow, Candice. The Book Bandit No. 7: A Mystery with Geometry. Thielbar, Melinda. 2011. (Manga Math Mysteries Ser.: 7). (ENG.). 48p. (J). (gr. 3-5). pap. 6.95 *(978-0-7613-8136-5(8)*, 9780761381365, Graphic Universe™) Lerner Publishing Group.
Lee, Jessica, jt. illus. see A Lee, Michael.
Lee, Jim, et al. X-Men Epic Collection: Dissolution & Rebirth. 2019. 488p. (YA). (gr. 4-17). pap. 39.99 *(978-1-302-91847-7(8))* Marvel Worldwide, Inc.
Lee, Jo-Shin. Still a Family. Sturgis, Brenda Reeves. 2017. (ENG.). 32p. (J). (gr. -1-3). 16.99 *(978-0-8075-7707-3(3)*, 807577073) Whitman, Albert & Co.
Lee, Jody A. The Monster's Legacy. Norton, Andre. 2017. (ENG.). 160p. (YA). (gr. 7). pap. 13.99 *(978-1-5344-1247-7(6)*, Atheneum Bks. for Young Readers) Simon & Schuster Children's Publishing.
Lee, Joe. The Day My Peanut Butter Lost Its Stick. Tait, Elena. 2008. 24p. pap. 12.99 *(978-1-4389-1936-2(0))* AuthorHouse.
—I'm with Poppy!! Markette, Paul Scott. 2010. 24p. pap. 12.99 *(978-1-4520-6276-1(5))* AuthorHouse.
—Megan's Monster. Harris, M. S. Ed Rebecca a. & Harris, M. S. Ed. 2009. 28p. pap. 15.00 *(978-1-4490-2822-0(5))* AuthorHouse.
—Power Reading: Classics/Treasure Island. Cole, Bob. 2004. 94p. (J). (gr. 5-6). vinyl bd. 39.95 *(978-1-883186-59-3(5)*, PPCL3) National Reading Styles Institute, Inc.
—Putting on the Brakes: Understanding & Taking Control of Your ADD or ADHD. Quinn, Patricia O. & Stern, Judith M. 2nd ed. 2008. 80p. (J). (gr. 3-7). pap. 12.95 *(978-1-4338-0387-1(9))*; 16.95 *(978-1-4338-0386-4(0))* American Psychological Assn. (Magination Pr.).
—Putting on the Brakes Activity Book for Kids with ADD or ADHD. Quinn, Patricia O. & Stern, Judith M. 2nd ed. 2009. 96p. (J). (gr. 3-8). pap. 14.95 *(978-1-4338-0441-0(7)*, Magination Pr.) American Psychological Assn.
Lee, Joo-Yun. See, Hear, & Feel! Sensory Organs. Jeong, Min-Ji. 2017. (Science Storybooks Ser.). (ENG.). 32p. (J). (gr. k-4). lib. bdg. 27.99 *(978-1-925235-37-1(8)*, Big and SMALL) ChoiceMaker Pty. Ltd., The AUS. Dist: Lerner Publishing Group.
Lee, Jubal. The Totally Ninja Raccoon Joke Book. Coolidge, Kevin. 2018. (ENG.). 66p. (J). (gr. k-4). pap. 5.99 *(978-1-64467-429-1(7))* From My Shelf Bks. & Gifts.
—The Totally Ninja Raccoons & the Catmas Caper. Coolidge, Kevin. 2016. (Totally Ninja Raccoons Ser.: Vol. 5). (ENG.). (J). (gr. 2-4). pap. 6.99 *(978-0-692-80112-3(X))* From My Shelf Bks. & Gifts.
—The Totally Ninja Raccoons Meet the Little Green Men. Coolidge, Kevin. 2017. (Totally Ninja Raccoons Ser.: Vol. 7). (ENG.). (J). (gr. 2-5). pap. 6.99 *(978-1-64136-434-8(3))* From My Shelf Bks. & Gifts.
Lee, Jumin. Mermaids. Heinrichs, Cynthia. 2011. (ENG.). 32p. (J). (gr. -1-3). 16.95 *(978-1-897476-37-6(X))* Simply Read Bks. CAN. Dist: Ingram Publisher Services.
Lee, Jung Hwa. Adrenalin, 4 vols. Lee, Jung Hwa. (Adrenalin Ser.: Vol. 2). 192p. (YA). Vol. 2. 2006. per. 9.95 *(978-1-59697-001-4(4))*; Vol. 3. 2007. per. 9.95 *(978-1-59697-002-1(2))*; Vol. 4. 2007. per. 9.99 *(978-1-59697-003-8(0))* Infinity Studios LLC.
Lee, Kang-Woo. Rebirth, 11 vols., Vol. 5. Lee, Kang-Woo. 5th rev. ed. 2003. 184p. pap. 9.99 *(978-1-59182-220-2(3))* TOKYOPOP, Inc.
—Rebirth, Vol. 14. Lee, Kang-Woo. Woo & Yi, Kang-u. rev. ed. 2005. 192p. pap. 9.99 *(978-1-59532-029-2(6))* TOKYOPOP, Inc.
—Rebirth, Vol. 15. Lee, Kang-Woo. 15th rev. ed. 2005. (Rebirth Ser.). 200p. per. 9.99 *(978-1-59532-030-8(X))* TOKYOPOP, Inc.
Lee, Karen. Un día Non, 1 vol. Fisher, Doris & Sneed, Dani. 2006. (SPA.). 32p. (J). (gr. -1-3). 17.95 *(978-1-60718-694-6(2))* Arbordale Publishing.
—Mi día Par, 1 vol. Fisher, Doris & Sneed, Dani. 2007. (SPA.). 32p. (J). (gr. -1-3). 17.95 *(978-1-60718-692-2(6))* Arbordale Publishing.
—My Even Day, 1 vol. Fisher, Doris & Sneed, Dani. 2007. (ENG.). 32p. (J). (gr. -1-3). pap. 8.95 *(978-1-934359-22-8(X)*, 9781934359228); Vol. 2. 15.95 *(978-0-9777423-3-2(4))* Arbordale Publishing.
—My Half Day, 1 vol. Sneed, Dani & Fisher, Doris. 2008. (Basic Math Numbers Ser.). (ENG.). 32p. (J). (gr. -1-3). 16.95 *(978-1-934359-14-3(9))*; pap. 8.95 *(978-1-934359-29-7(7))* Arbordale Publishing.
—One Odd Day, 1 vol. Fisher, Doris & Sneed, Dani. 2006. (Basic Math Numbers Ser.). (ENG.). 32p. (J). (gr. -1-3). 15.95 *(978-0-9768823-3-6(7))*; Vol. 1. pap. 8.95 *(978-1-934359-33-4(5))* Arbordale Publishing.
—Seth & Savannah Build a Speech. Ingalls, Ann. 2012. (Writing Builders Ser.). 32p. (J). (gr. 2-4). pap. 11.94 *(978-1-60357-391-7(7))*; lib. bdg. 25.27 *(978-1-59953-511-1(4))* Norwood Hse. Pr.
Lee, Karen. ABC Safari, 1 vol. Lee, Karen. 2007. (ENG.). 32p. (J). (gr. -1-3). 15.95 *(978-0-9777423-0-1(X))*; pap. 8.95 *(978-0-9777423-6-3(9))* Arbordale Publishing.
—Aventura Safari (ABC Safari in Portuguese) Lee, Karen. Sacciotto, Adriana & Wiedemann, Tatiana, trs. 2019. (POR.). 32p. (J). (gr. -1-1). pap. 11.95 *(978-1-64351-397-3(4))* Arbordale Publishing.
—Mushy Mashed Bananas. Lee, Karen. 2012. 24p. pap. *(978-1-4602-0136-7(1))* FriesenPress.
Lee, Kary. Dizzy. Nyikos, Stacy. l.t. ed. 2006. 32p. (J). (gr. -1-3). 15.95 *(978-0-9764199-2-1(0)*, 888-867-1927) Stonehorse Publishing, LLC.
Lee, Kathy. Look Up! Young, Sandy de. 2017. (ENG.). (J). pap. 9.25 *(978-1-948227-00-1(2))* Colorfield Creative, LLC.
—The New Adventures of A. R. Achnid (Revised Edition) Smith, Sandi. 2017. (ENG.). (J). 19.99 *(978-0-9983183-7-0(X))* Mindstir Media.
Lee, Katie. Monarch Butterfly of Aster Way. Ring, Elizabeth. (ENG.). 32p. (J). (gr. -1-2). 2005. pap. 7.65 *(978-1-931465-40-3(1)*, S5017); Incl. toy. 2003. 9.95 *(978-1-56899-573-1(3)*, PB5067) Soundprints.
—Orca Song. Armour, Michael C. (ENG.). 32p. (J). (gr. -1-2). pap. 6.95 *(978-1-59249-479-8(X)*, S4004) Soundprints.
—Sea Turtle Journey: The Story of a Loggerhead Turtle. Jay, Lorraine A. 2011. (Smithsonian Oceanic Collection Ser.). (ENG.). 32p. (J). (gr. -1-3). 19.95 *(978-1-60727-660-9(7))* Soundprints.
Lee, Kim. The Magic in Believing: The Tooth Fairies. Webb, Carla. (Magic in Believing Ser.). 36p. (J). (gr. k-5). *(978-0-9705726-0-8(3))* Ageless Treasures.
Lee, Kong. Hiss! Pop! Boom! Celebrating Chinese New Year. Morrissey, Tricia. 2006. (ENG.). 32p. (J). (gr. -1-3). 12.95 *(978-0-9715940-7-4(4))* ThingsAsian Pr.
Lee, Leslie W., jt. illus. see Lee, Melicent Humason.
Lee, Linda. Pat, the Cat. Strong, Frances Dinkins. 2003. 24p. (J). pap. *(978-0-9720267-1-0(1))* Learning Abilities Bks.
Lee, Marc. Back Burn. Bowen, Carl. 2016. (Firestormers Ser.). (ENG.). 112p. (J). (gr. 4-8). lib. bdg. 26.65 *(978-1-4965-3305-0(4)*, Stone Arch Bks.) Capstone.
—Bone Yard. Bowen, Carl. 2016. (Firestormers Ser.). (ENG.). 112p. (J). (gr. 4-8). lib. bdg. 26.65 *(978-1-4965-3306-7(2)*, Stone Arch Bks.) Capstone.
—Fire Front. Bowen, Carl. 2016. (Firestormers Ser.). (ENG.). 112p. (J). (gr. 4-8). lib. bdg. 26.65 *(978-1-4965-3308-1(9)*, Stone Arch Bks.) Capstone.
—Firestormers, 4 vols. Bowen, Carl. 2016. (Firestormers Ser.). (ENG.). 112p. (J). (gr. 4-8). lib. bdg., lib. bdg., lib. bdg. 106.60 *(978-1-4965-3321-0(6)*, Stone Arch Bks.) Capstone.
—Firestormers: Elite Firefighting Crew. Bowen, Carl. 2016. (ENG.). 224p. (J). (gr. 4-8). pap. 8.95 *(978-1-62370-756-9(0)*, Capstone Young Readers) Capstone.
—Hot Spot. Bowen, Carl. 2016. (Firestormers Ser.). (ENG.). 112p. (J). (gr. 4-8). lib. bdg. 26.65 *(978-1-4965-3307-4(0)*, Stone Arch Bks.) Capstone.
Lee, Maxine. Hard Hat Cat! Kiffel-Alcheh, Jamie. 2020. (ENG.). 24p. (J). (gr. -1-2). 17.99 *(978-1-5415-4635-6(0)*, Kar-Ben Publishing) Lerner Publishing Group.
—Hippo's Hiccups. 2016. (Pardon Me! Ser.: 4). 14p. (J). spiral bd. *(978-1-84643-751-9(2))* Child's Play International Ltd.
—A Hot Day. Hawes, Alison. 2016. (Cambridge Reading Adventures Ser.). (ENG.). 16p. pap. 7.37 *(978-1-316-60069-6(6))* Cambridge Univ. Pr.
—Today I'm a Construction Worker. Polansky, Marisa. 2018. (Today I'm A... Ser.). (ENG.). 14p. (J). bds. 8.99 *(978-0-374-30441-6(6)*, 900159319, Farrar, Straus & Giroux (BYR)) Farrar, Straus & Giroux.
—Today I'm a Dancer. Polansky, Marisa. 2018. (Today I'm A... Ser.). (ENG.). 14p. (J). bds. 8.99 *(978-0-374-30440-9(8)*, 9780374304409, Farrar, Straus & Giroux (BYR)) Farrar, Straus & Giroux.
—Today I'm a Racecar Driver. Polansky, Marisa. 2018. (Today I'm A... Ser.). (ENG.). 14p. (J). bds. 8.99 *(978-0-374-30439-3(4)*, 9780374304393, Farrar, Straus & Giroux (BYR)) Farrar, Straus & Giroux.
—Today I'm a Veterinarian. Polansky, Marisa. 2018. (Today I'm A... Ser.). (ENG.). 14p. (J). bds. 8.99 *(978-0-374-30442-3(4)*, 9780374304423, Farrar, Straus & Giroux (BYR)) Farrar, Straus & Giroux.
—Zebra's Sneeze. 2016. (Pardon Me! Ser.: 4). 14p. (J). spiral bd. *(978-1-84643-753-3(9))* Child's Play International Ltd.
Lee, Maxine. Pi-Rat! Lee, Maxine. 2013. (ENG.). 32p. (J). (gr. -1-2). 14.99 *(978-1-58925-143-4(1))* Tiger Tales.
Lee, Meikele. If I Were Deployed. Burch, Nicole. 2019. (ENG.). 28p. (J). pap. 9.99 ***(978-1-7007-9200-6(8))*** Independently Published.
Lee, Melicent Humason & Lee, Leslie W. Indians of the Oaks. 2nd ed. 2007. xiv, 244p. (J). pap. *(978-0-937808-50-4(4))* San Diego Museum of Man.
Lee, Myung Jin. Ragnarok, 10 vols., Vol. 9. Lee, Myung Jin. rev. ed. 2004. 192p. pap. 9.99 *(978-1-59182-208-0(4))* TOKYOPOP, Inc.
Lee, Myung Jin. Lights Out, Vol. 2. Lee, Myung Jin, creator. 2nd rev. ed. 2006. 192p. pap. 14.99 *(978-1-59532-361-3(9)*, Tokyopop Adult) TOKYOPOP, Inc.
Lee, Na Hyeon. Traveler of the Moon, 3 vols. Lee, Na Hyeon. (Traveler of the Moon Ser.: Vol. 2). 176p. Vol. 2. 2005. pap. 9.95 *(978-1-59697-062-5(6))*; Vol. 3. 2007. pap. 9.95 *(978-1-59697-063-2(4))* Infinity Studios LLC.
Lee, Nikita. Bessie Bump Gets a New Family. Meredith, Amberley. 2010. 26p. pap. 13.95 *(978-1-60911-901-0(0)*, Eloquent Bks.) Strategic Book Publishing & Rights Agency (SBPRA).
Lee, Oh. Where the Winds Meet: Mongolia. Joo, Mi-hwa. 2015. (Global Kids Storybooks Ser.). (ENG.). 32p. (J). (gr. 1-4). pap. 8.99 *(978-1-925233-49-0(9)*, Big and SMALL) ChoiceMaker Pty. Ltd., The AUS. Dist: Lerner Publishing Group.
Lee, Paige. The School Mice & the New Baby: Book 7 for Both Boys & Girls Ages 6-11 Grades: 1-5. Higham, Nancy. Cavanagh, Larry, ed. 2018. (School Mice (TM) Series Book Ser.: Vol. 7). (ENG.). 64p. (J). (gr. 1-5). pap. 12.99 *(978-1-55323-894-2(X)*, ExamWise) Total Recall Learning, Inc.
Lee, Pat, jt. illus. see Wrightson, Bernie.
Lee, Paul. Hank Aaron: Brave in Every Way. Golenbock, Peter. 2005. (ENG.). 32p. (J). (gr. -1-3). reprint ed. pap. 7.99 *(978-0-15-205250-8(X)*, 1195816) Houghton Mifflin Harcourt Publishing Co.
—Lego Minifigures. Petranek, Michael. 2018. (Lego Ser.). (ENG.). 12p. (J). (gr. -1-3). bds. 12.99 *(978-1-338-24964-4(9))* Scholastic, Inc.
—A Voice of Her Own: The Story of Phillis Wheatley, Slave Poet. Lasky, Kathryn. 2012. (Candlewick Biographies Ser.). (ENG.). 48p. (J). (gr. 3-7). 14.99 *(978-0-7636-6427-5(8))*; pap. 4.99 *(978-0-7636-6091-8(4))* Candlewick Pr.
Lee, Paul, jt. illus. see Arlon, Penelope.
Lee, Roslyn. Pick-a-WooWoo- Grandma's Great Advice: The Art of Listening, 16 vols., Vol. 4. Harper, Julie Ann. 2009. 32p. pap. *(978-0-9803669-3-8(3))* Pick-a-Woo Woo Pubs.
Lee, Ru. Witch Class, Vol. 3. Lee, Ru. 2006. (Witch Class Ser.: Vol. 3). 192p. (YA). per. 9.95 *(978-1-59697-083-0(9))* Infinity Studios LLC.
Lee, Sarah Ann. The Buggy That Boogied Away. Lee, Betsy B. 2006. 24p. (J). pap. 6.95 *(978-0-9720267-7-2(0))* Learning Abilities Bks.
Lee, Shaka S., jt. illus. see Lee, Imani K.
Lee, So-Young. Arcana. Lee, So-Young. 3rd rev. ed. 2005. (Arcana (Tokyopop) Ser.: Vol. 3). 192p. pap. 9.99 *(978-1-59532-483-2(6))* TOKYOPOP, Inc.
Lee, So-Young. Arcana, Vol. 1. Lee, So-Young, creator. 2005. 208p. pap. 9.99 *(978-1-59532-481-8(X))* TOKYOPOP, Inc.
Lee, Songhee. The Biggest Burp: A Dining Primer. Coscia, Alexandra. 2019. (ENG.). 28p. (J). 20.00 *(978-1-7335291-0-5(1))* Coscia, Alexandra.
Lee, Soo. Enter the Dumpling, Vol. 1. Goh, Colin & Woo, Yen Yen. 2013. (ENG.). 144p. (J). pap. 12.99 *(978-0-9881899-0-4(9)*, 6c4a244a-3a8f-4e58-a54f-f5a3830824c4) Yumcha Studios LLC.
Lee, Stacie. Four Frogs in a Glass Pond: With a Special Section on How to Win a Frog Jumping Contest! Blodgett, Laura. 2018. (ENG.). 42p. (J). pap. 10.99 *(978-1-7315-4314-1(X))* Independently Published.
Lee, SunNeko. Los Miserables. Silvermoon, Crystal & Hugo, Víctor. 2016. (Clasicos Manga Ser.). (SPA.). 338p. (YA). (gr. 7). pap. 19.99 ***(978-84-679-2208-0(7))*** Norma Editorial, S.A. ESP. Dist: Independent Pubs. Group.
—Zita, la Viajera Espacial. Hatke, Ben & Hugo, Victor. 2018. (Zita Ser.). (SPA.). 192p. (J). (gr. 4-7). 17.99 ***(978-84-679-3201-0(5))*** Norma Editorial, S.A. ESP. Dist: Independent Pubs. Group.
Lee, Susan. How the Winter Frog Came to Was: Or, How to Get a Nice Surprise on Thanksgiving! Hurley, Wes. 2007. 36p. per. 24.95 *(978-1-4241-8395-1(2))* America Star Bks.
Lee, Suzy. Ask Me. Waber, Bernard. 2015. (ENG.). 40p. (J). (gr. -1-3). 16.99 *(978-0-547-73394-4(1)*, 1484489, HMH Books For Young Readers) Houghton Mifflin Harcourt Publishing Co.
—Open This Little Book. Klausmeier, Jesse. 2013. (ENG.). 40p. (J). (gr. -1-3). 16.99 *(978-0-8118-6783-2(8))* Chronicle Bks. LLC.
—This Beautiful Day. Jackson, Richard. 2017. (ENG.). 40p. (J). (gr. -1-3). 15.99 *(978-1-4814-4139-1(6)*, Atheneum/Caitlyn Dlouhy Books) Simon & Schuster Children's Publishing.
Lee, Suzy. Lines. Lee, Suzy. 2017. (ENG.). 40p. (J). (gr. -1-k). 17.99 *(978-1-4521-5665-1(4))* Chronicle Bks. LLC.
Lee, Tae E. A Medieval Tale. Pulido, Brian. 2003. (Lady Death Ser.: Vol. 1). 160p. (YA). (gr. 7-18). pap. 9.95 *(978-1-931484-72-5(4))* CrossGeneration Comics, Inc.
Lee, Tania. Topsy Turvy History of New Orleans & Ten Tiny Turtles: 300 Years & Slowly Counting... Lee, Tania. Rathlé, Simone. 2018. (ENG.). 35p. (J). 16.95 *(978-0-692-98877-0(7))* simoneink, llc.
Lee, Travaglini. The Amazing Adventures of Zion the Lion: Book 1: How Zion Almost Lost His Tail. Emmanuel, Sophie. 2018. (ENG.). 26p. (J). pap. *(978-0-9919270-0-5(1))* Emmanuel, Sophia.
Lee, Tricia Ting. The Adventures of Henry Hamper & the Flying Fish. Libby, Lori Ann. 2010. 34p. pap. 13.95 *(978-1-60911-493-0(0)*, Eloquent Bks.) Strategic Book Publishing & Rights Agency (SBPRA).
Lee, Uk-Bae. When Spring Comes to the DMZ. Lee, Uk-Bae. 2019. 40p. (J). (gr. -1-3). 17.95 *(978-0-87486-972-9(2))* Plough Publishing Hse.
Lee, Virginia. Persephone. Clayton, Sally Pomme. 2009. (ENG.). 28p. (J). (gr. 2-5). 18.00 *(978-0-8028-5349-3(8)*, Eerdmans Bks For Young Readers) Eerdmans, William B. Publishing Co.
Lee, Wei-Chun. Little Lotus & the Loving-Kindness Cup. Tidwell, Susan. 2012. 77p. (J). 6.95 *(978-1-932293-72-2(8))* Buddha's Light Publications USA Corp.
Lee, Wendy W. The Apple Tree's Discovery, Vol. Schram, Peninnah & Davis, Rachayl Eckstein. 2012. (ENG.). 24p. (J). (gr. -1-2). pap. 7.95 *(978-0-7613-5132-0(9)*, 9780761351320); lib. bdg. 16.95 *(978-0-7613-5130-6(2))* Lerner Publishing Group. (Kar-Ben Publishing).
Lee, Williams. The Adventures of Old Henry: Nobody Cares. Brouillette, Peter. 2004. (J). per. 19.99 *(978-0-9760419-3-1(6))* ThatsMyLife Co.
Lee, Xiongpao. The African Interior Mission. Allen, C. William. 2006. 232p. (J). pap. 20.00 *(978-0-9653308-5-5(0))* Africana Homestead Legacy Pubs., Inc.
Lee, Y. J. The Little Moon Princess. Lee, Y. J. 2010. (ENG.). 32p. (J). (gr. -1-3). 16.99 *(978-0-06-154736-2(0))* HarperCollins Pubs.
Lee, Yeong-Rim. El Viaje Del Polen: la Reproducci�n de Las Plantas. Kim, Mi-Gyeong. 2018. (Click Click: Ciencia B�sica / Basic Science Ser.). (SPA.). 32p. (J). pap. 17.99 ***(978-1-64101-214-0(5))*** Santillana USA Publishing Co., Inc.
Lee, Yuan. The Parthenon: The Height of Greek Civilization. Mann, Elizabeth. 2006. (Wonders of the World Book Ser.). (ENG.). 48p. (J). (gr. 4-8). 22.95 *(978-1-931414-15-9(7)*, 64d92e5c-b1bb-462a-9837-369748e1fc29) Mikaya Pr.
Leeann, Chris. Adventures with Annie. Merideth, Misty Marksberry & Keen, Tammi Croteau. 2018. (Adventures of Super Liam Ser.: Vol. 2). (ENG.). 40p. (J). pap. 14.95 *(978-1-9856-5065-7(7))* CreateSpace Independent Publishing Platform.
—Adventures with Annie Coloring Book. Merideth, Misty Marksberry & Keen, Tammi Croteau. 2018. (Adventures of Super Liam Ser.: Vol. 2). (ENG.). 26p. (J). pap. 6.95 *(978-1-9856-5113-5(0))* CreateSpace Independent Publishing Platform.
Leech, Jacob. It's Me, Penny! The Hot Air Balloon Adventure. Guerrero, Rhonda. 2011. 28p. pap. 24.95 *(978-1-4489-7070-4(9))* America Star Bks.
Leech, John. Annotated Christmas Carol: A Christmas Carol in Prose. Dickens, Charles. annot. ed. 2004. (Annotated Bks.: 0). (ENG.). 288p. 29.95 *(978-0-393-05158-2(7)*, 5158) Norton, W. W. & Co., Inc.
Leech, John. A Christmas Carol: A Facsimile of the Original 1843 Edition in Full Color. Dickens, Charles. 2016. (ENG.). 186p. (J). (gr. 1-6). 19.95 ***(978-1-64594-038-8(1))*** Athanatos Publishing Group.
Leech, John. A Christmas Carol: Compact Pocket Edition of 1843 Original. Dickens, Charles. 2018. (ENG.). 74p. (J). pap. 4.50 *(978-1-947844-82-7(2))* Athanatos Publishing Group.
—A Christmas Carol: With Original Illustrations. Dickens, Charles. 2016. (ENG.). (J). (gr. 1-4). pap. 9.00 *(978-1-936830-89-3(2))* Athanatos Publishing Group.
—A Christmas Carol: With Original Illustrations in Full Color. Dickens, Charles. 2016. (ENG.). (J). (gr. 1-4). 17.00 *(978-1-936830-88-6(4))* Athanatos Publishing Group.
Leech, John & Rackham, Arthur. A Christmas Carol (Large Print Edition) Complete & Unabridged 1843 Edition (Illustrated) Mnemosyne Books, ed. l.t. ed. 2019. (Mnemosyne Classics Ser.: Vol. 2). (ENG.). 158p. (J). pap. 7.99 ***(978-1-7094-1920-1(2))*** Independently Published.
Leeds, Marjorie M. The Adventures of Giggles & Owen: Adventure Three - Unlimited Pawsibilities. Terrill Holdman, Shirley. 2013. 50p. pap. 17.95 *(978-1-4575-2175-1(X))* Dog Ear Publishing, LLC.
Leedy, Loreen. There's a Frog in My Throat! 440 Animal Sayings a Little Bird Told Me. Street, Pat. 2004. (ENG.). 48p. (J). (gr. 1-4). reprint ed. pap. 8.99 *(978-0-8234-1819-0(7))* Holiday Hse., Inc.
Leedy, Loreen. Mapping Penny's World. Leedy, Loreen. rev. ed. 2003. (Penny Ser.). (ENG.). 32p. (J). (gr. k-3). pap. 8.99 *(978-0-8050-7262-4(4)*, 900018972) Square Fish.
—Seeing Symmetry. Leedy, Loreen. 2012. (ENG.). 32p. (J). (gr. 1-4). 17.95 *(978-0-8234-2360-6(3))* Holiday Hse., Inc.
—Shocking Truth about Energy. Leedy, Loreen. 2011. (ENG.). 32p. (J). (gr. k-3). pap. 7.95 *(978-0-8234-2388-0(3))* Holiday Hse., Inc.
Leeflang-Oudenarden, C. Tina's Island Home. Van Walsum-Quispel, J. M. 36p. (J). (gr. k-5). 12.95 *(978-0-87592-053-5(5))* Scroll Pr., Inc.
Leek, Kenny. How to Be a Human Bean. Markels, Bobby. Date not set. 24p. (J). (gr. 3-18). reprint ed. pap. 4.50 *(978-1-880991-01-5(2))* Stone Publishing Co.
Leeks, David. Big Book of Science. Cullen, Dave. 2004. 48p. (J). 7.99 *(978-1-85854-532-5(3))* Brimax Books Ltd. GBR. Dist: Byeway Bks.
—Big Book of Transport. Richard, John. 2004. 48p. (J). 7.99 *(978-1-85854-550-9(1))* Brimax Books Ltd. GBR. Dist: Byeway Bks.
—My First Atlas. Cullen, Dave & Williams, Simon. 2004. 48p. (J). 5.99 *(978-1-85854-709-1(1))* Brimax Books Ltd. GBR. Dist: Byeway Bks.
—My First Atlas. Cullen, Dave. 2004. 48p. (J). 7.99 *(978-1-85854-425-0(4))* Brimax Books Ltd. GBR. Dist: Byeway Bks.
Leeper, Chris & Leeper, Chris. Jeshi the Gorilla. Grey, Chelsea Gillian. (Internet Interactive Ser.). (ENG.). 36p. (J). (gr. -1-2). 8.95 *(978-1-59249-417-0(X)*, SD6504) Soundprints.
Leeper, Chris, jt. illus. see Leeper, Chris.
Leeper, Christopher. Ema the Rhinoceros. Shriver, Chelsea & Grey, Chelsea Gillian. 2005. (African Wildlife Foundation Kids Ser.). (ENG.). 36p. (J). (gr. -1-2). 9.95 *(978-1-59249-180-3(4)*, PS6550) Soundprints.
—Norman the Lion. Galvin, Laura Gates. (African Wildlife Foundation Ser.). (ENG.). 36p. (J). (gr. -1-2). 2005. 2.95 *(978-1-59249-191-9(X)*, S6553); 2004. 8.95 *(978-1-59249-208-4(8)*, SD6503); 2004. 9.95 *(978-1-59249-192-6(8)*, PS6553) Soundprints.
—River Otter at Autumn Lane. Galvin, Laura Gates. 2005. (Smithsonian's Backyard Ser.). (ENG.). 32p. (J). (gr. -1-2). 19.95 *(978-1-931465-63-2(0)*, BC5023); 15.95 *(978-1-931465-61-8(4)*, B5023) Soundprints.
—River Otter at Autumn Lane. Galvin, Laura. 2003. (ENG.). 32p. (J). (gr. -1-3). 9.95 *(978-1-931465-66-3(5)*, PB5073) Soundprints.
Leeper, Christopher J., et al. Alphabet of African Animals. Galvin, Laura Gates. 2011. (Alphabet Bks.). (ENG.). 40p. (J). (gr. -1-3). 17.95 *(978-1-60727-574-9(0))* Soundprints.
Leeper, Christopher J. Jeshi the Gorilla. Grey, Chelsea Gillian. 2005. (Meet Africa's Animals Ser.). (ENG.). 32p. (J). (gr. -1-2). 2.95 *(978-1-59249-418-7(8)*, S6554) Soundprints.

L

—River Otter at Autumn Lane. Galvin, Laura Gates. 2011. (Smithsonian's Backyard Ser.). (ENG.). 32p. (J). (gr. -1-3). 8.95 (978-1-60727-642-5(9)); 19.95 (978-1-60727-641-8(0)) Soundprints.

Leeper, Christopher J. Ema the Rhinoceros. Leeper, Christopher J., tr. Shriver, Chelsea & Grey, Chelsea Gillian. 2005. (African Wildlife Foundation Ser.). (ENG.). 36p. (J). (gr. -1-2). 14.95 (978-1-59249-177-3(4), H6500); pap. 6.95 (978-1-59249-178-0(2), S6500) Soundprints.

—Norman the Lion. Leeper, Christopher J., tr. Galvin, Laura Gates. 2005. (African Wildlife Foundation Ser.). (ENG.). 36p. (J). (gr. -1-2). 14.95 (978-1-59249-189-6(8), H6503); pap. 6.95 (978-1-59249-190-2(1), S6503) Soundprints.

Leer, Korrie. The Big Sibling Getaway. Leer, Korrie. 2020. 32p. (J). (gr. -1-3). 16.99 **(978-0-8075-2831-0(5),** 0807528315) Whitman, Albert & Co.

Leer, Rebecca. A Spoon for Every Bite. Hayes, Joe. 2005. (SPA.). 32p. (J). (gr. 1-4). reprint ed. pap. 8.95 (978-0-938317-93-7(8)) Cinco Puntos Pr.

Lees, Harry H. John Wanamaker: Boy Merchant. Burt, Olive Woolley. 2011. 192p. 42.95 (978-1-258-08290-1(X)) Literary Licensing, LLC.

Lees, Jeanette. Australian Animal Walkabout. Weaver, Karen. 2017. (ENG.). (J). (978-0-6480432-2-5(3)) Serenity Press.

—Bumble Bee Rock Around the Clock. Weaver, Karen. 2018. (ENG.). (J). (978-0-6481906-6-0(8)) Serenity Press.

Leeson, Pat and Tom, photos by. It's Nice to Be a Mountain Lion. Woodward, Molly. 2018. (ENG.). 20p. (J). bds. 8.99 (978-1-59714-429-2(0)) Heyday.

Leeson, Tom and Pat, et al, photos by. Cascade Babies. 2013. 26p. (J). 8.95 (978-1-56037-330-8(X)) Farcountry Pr.

Leeson, Tom and Pat, photos by. It's Nice to Be an Otter. Woodward, Molly. 2016. (ENG.). 20p. (J). bds. 8.99 (978-1-59714-335-6(9)) Heyday.

Lefebure, Ingrid. Ella & the Worry Doll. Canale, Allison. 2013. (ENG.). (J). (gr. -1-3). 14.95 (978-1-62086-332-9(4)) Mascot Bks., Inc.

Lefebvre, Bénédicte. Catholic Saints for Children. du Bouëtiez, Anne-Sophie. 2015. (ENG.). 96p. (J). (gr. -1-6). pap. 16.99 (978-1-62164-041-7(8)) Ignatius Pr.

Lefebvre, Patrick, photos by. Cool in School Communication Game: Gb362. Eisenberg, Rebecca & Kjesbo, Rynette. 2011. (J). 64.95 net. (978-1-58650-994-1(2)) Super Duper Pubns.

Leff, Tova. Azoi Vi Ess Past Fahr a Princessen (Fit for a Princess) Rotman, Risa. Flohr, Perel, tr. 2012.Tr. of Fit for a Princess. 32p. (J). 10.95 (978-1-929628-66-7(8)) Hachai Publishing.

—Big Small or Just One Wall: A Book about Shuls. Fajnland, Leibel. Rosenfeld, D. L., ed. 2011. 36p. (J). 12.95 (978-1-929628-59-9(5)) Hachai Publishing.

—On This Night: The Steps of the Seder in Rhyme. Steiner, Nancy. 2013. 32p. (J). 10.95 (978-1-929628-51-3(X)) Hachai Publishing.

—Ten Tzedakah Pennies. Klein-Higger, Joni. 2005. 30p. (J). 10.95 (978-1-929628-19-3(6)) Hachai Publishing.

—What Did Pinny Do? An Upsherin Story. Sitner, Nechama. 2013. 36p. (J). 12.95 (978-1-929628-72-8(2)) Hachai Publishing.

Leffler, Dub. Once There Was a Boy. Leffler, Dub. 2016. 40p. (J). (gr. -1-k). 18.99 (978-1-921248-37-5(8)) Magabala Bks. AUS. Dist: Independent Pubs. Group.

Leffler, Silke. Emma in Buttonland. Rylance, Ulrike. Morby, Connie Stradling, tr. 2013. 120p. (J). (gr. 1-5). 12.95 (978-1-62087-992-4(1), 620992, Sky Pony Pr.) Skyhorse Publishing Co., Inc.

—I Have a Little Problem, Said the Bear. Janisch, Heinz. 2012. (ENG.). 32p. (J). (gr. -1-3). pap. 8.95 (978-0-7358-4094-2(6)) North-South Bks., Inc.

—Peter Pan. Barrie, J. M. 2016. (ENG.). 176p. 25.00 (978-0-7358-4259-5(0)) North-South Bks., Inc.

Legasey Pappas, Monique. The St. Patrick's Day Festival: Creative Pet Show. Legasey, Sharon Ross. 2019. (ENG.). 46p. (J). 29.99 **(978-1-7283-3984-9(7));** pap. 16.99 **(978-1-7283-3982-5(0))** AuthorHouse.

Legdani, Sanaa. Little Detectives: the Magic Kingdom of Unicorns: A Look-And-Find Book. 2020. (Little Detectives Ser.). 14p. (J). (gr. -1-1). bds. 9.99 (978-2-89802-157-2(1), CrackBoom! Bks.) Chouette Publishing CAN. Dist: Publishers Group West (PGW).

—Southern California Monsters: A Search & Find Book. 2018. (ENG.). 22p. (J). (gr. -1). bds. 9.99 (978-2-924734-08-7(8)) City Monsters Bks. CAN. Dist: Publishers Group West (PGW).

Legdani, Sanaa, jt. illus. see Baretti, Sonia.

Legdani, Sanaa, jt. illus. see Brignaud, Pierre.

Legdani, Sanaa, jt. illus. see Gardie, Amandine.

Legdani, Sanaa, jt. illus. see Kary.

Legdani, Sanaa, jt. illus. see Nelvana Ltd.

Legdani, Sanaa, jt. illus. see Paradis.

Legdani, Sanaa, jt. illus. see ROI Visual Staff.

Legdani, Sanaa, jt. illus. see Sechao, Annie.

Legendre, Philippe. Animals Around the World. Osle, Janessa & Walter Foster Jr. Creative Team. 2015. (I Can Draw Ser.). (ENG.). 48p. (J). (gr. -1-3). 30.65 (978-1-939581-56-3(7), Walter Foster Jr) Quarto Publishing Group USA.

—Planes, Trains & Moving Machines. Osle, Janessa & Walter Foster Jr. Creative Team. 2015. (I Can Draw Ser.). (ENG.). 48p. (J). (gr. -1-3). 30.65 (978-1-939581-58-7(3), Walter Foster Jr) Quarto Publishing Group USA.

—Sea Creatures & Other Favorite Animals: Learn to Draw Land & Sea Animals Step by Step! Osle, Janessa & Walter Foster Jr. Creative Team. 2015. (I Can Draw Ser.). (ENG.). 48p. (J). (gr. -1-3). 30.65 (978-1-939581-57-0(5), Walter Foster Jr) Quarto Publishing Group USA.

Léger, Michael. Emily Carr's Attic, 1 vol. Léger, Diane Carmel. 2008. (ENG.). 32p. (J). (gr. -1-k). pap. 13.95 (978-1-55143-958-7(1)) Orca Bk. Pubs. USA.

Leger, Michel. La Butte À Pétard. Leger, Diane Carmel. 2004. (FRE.). 122p. (J). pap. (978-2-89682-064-1(7)) Bouton d'or Acadie.

Legg, Barbara. Born under a Star, 1 vol. Buchholz, Erwin. 2009. 44p. pap. 24.95 (978-1-61546-130-1(2)) America Star Bks.

Legge, David. Kisses for Daddy. Watts, Frances. 2008. (ENG.). 24p. (J). bds. (978-1-921272-56-1(2)) Little Hare Bks. AUS. Dist: HarperCollins Pubs. Australia.

—Kisses for Daddy. Watts, Frances. 2010. (ENG.). 26p. (J). (gr. -1-k). bds. 7.99 (978-1-4169-8721-5(5), Little Simon) Little Simon.

—Kisses for Daddy Gift Pack: Book & Soft Toy. Watts, Frances. 2007. 22p. (978-1-921049-48-4(0)) Little Hare Bks. AUS. Dist: HarperCollins Pubs. Australia.

Leggitt, Marjorie. Arches & Canyonlands National Parks - In the Land of Standing Rocks. Graf, Mike. 2012. (Adventures with the Parkers Ser.: 10). (ENG.). 112p. pap. 12.95 (978-0-7627-7962-8(4), Falcon Guides) Globe Pequot Pr., The.

—Do Seals Ever ... ?, Vol. Hodgkins, Fran. 2017. (ENG.). 32p. (J). (gr. -1-3). 16.95 (978-1-60893-467-6(5)) Down East Bks.

—Glacier National Park: Going to the Sun. Graf, Mike. 2012. (Adventures with the Parkers Ser.: 7). (ENG.). 96p. pap. 12.95 (978-0-7627-7964-2(0), Falcon Guides) Globe Pequot Pr., The.

—Grand Canyon National Park: Tail of the Scorpion. Graf, Mike. 2012. (Adventures with the Parkers Ser.: 2). (ENG.). 96p. pap. 14.95 (978-0-7627-7965-9(9), Falcon Guides) Globe Pequot Pr., The.

—Great Smokies National Park: Ridge Runner Rescue. Graf, Mike. 2012. (Adventures with the Parkers Ser.: 6). (ENG.). 96p. pap. 12.95 (978-0-7627-7966-6(7), Falcon Guides) Globe Pequot Pr., The.

—Kupe & the Corals. Padilla-Gamino, Jacqueline L. 2014. (Long Term Ecological Research Ser.). (ENG.). 32p. (J). (gr. 3-7). 15.95 (978-1-58979-753-6(1)) Taylor Trade Publishing.

—Seeking the Wolf Tree, Vol. Cleavitt, Natalie. 2015. (Long Term Ecological Research Ser.). (ENG.). 32p. (J). (gr. 3-7). 15.95 (978-1-63076-145-5(1)) Taylor Trade Publishing.

—Yellowstone National Park: Eye of the Grizzly. Graf, Mike. 2012. (Adventures with the Parkers Ser.: 4). (ENG.). 96p. pap. 12.95 (978-0-7627-7972-7(1), Falcon Guides) Globe Pequot Pr., The.

—Yosemite National Park: Harrowing Ascent of Half Dome. Graf, Mike. 2012. (Adventures with the Parkers Ser.: 3). (ENG.). 96p. pap. 12.95 (978-0-7627-7973-4(X), Falcon Guides) Globe Pequot Pr., The.

Leghima, Marie. Un Tazon de Tristeza para Leiza. Kochka. 2020. (SPA.). 32p. (J). (gr. -1-2). 12.95 **(978-84-9145-331-4(8),** Picarona Editorial) Ediciones Obelisco ESP. Dist: Spanish Pubs., LLC.

Legnazzi, Claudia. Habia una Vez una Nube. Montes, Graciela. 2006. 23p. (J). (gr. -1-3). 8.95 (978-1-59820-214-4(6), Alfaguara) Santillana USA Publishing Co., Inc.

Legramandi, Francesco. Bizarro Day! (DC Super Friends) Wrecks, Billy. 2013. (Step into Reading Ser.). (ENG.). 32p. (J). (gr. k-3). pap. 4.99 (978-0-307-98119-6(3), Random Hse. Bks. for Young Readers) Random Hse. Children's Bks.

Legramandi, Francesco. A Day at the Cafe: a Scratch-And-Sniff Book (Butterbean's Cafe) Depken, Kristen L. 2020. (ENG.). 24p. (J). (gr. -1-2). 9.99 **(978-0-593-12189-4(9),** Random Hse. Bks. for Young Readers) Random Hse. Children's Bks.

Legramandi, Francesco. Dumbo Deluxe Step into Reading (Disney Dumbo) Webster, Christy. 2019. (Step into Reading Ser.). (ENG.). 24p. (J). (gr. k-2). 5.99 (978-0-7364-3951-0(X)); 12.99 (978-0-7364-8268-4(7)) Random Hse. Children's Bks. (RH/Disney).

—A Fairy-Tale Fall. Jordan, Apple. 2010. (Step into Reading Ser.). (ENG.). 32p. (J). (gr. k-3). pap. 4.99 (978-0-7364-2674-9(4), RH/Disney) Random Hse. Children's Bks.

—Harley Quinn's Brain-Squeezers! (DC Super Hero Girls) Lee, C. 2017. (ENG.). 64p. (J). (gr. 2-4). 5.99 (978-1-5247-6395-4(0), Random Hse. Bks. for Young Readers) Random Hse. Children's Bks.

Legramandi, Francesco, et al. Marvel Spider-Man: I'm Ready to Read. PI Kids. 2020. (Play-A-Sound Ser.). (ENG.). 24p. (J). **(978-1-5037-5502-4(9),** 4b84e56b-cf55-4a77-aa78-970d08aedb45, p i kids) Phoenix International Publications, Inc.

Legramandi, Francesco. Princess Hearts (Disney Princess) Weinberg, Jennifer Liberts. 2012. (Step into Reading Ser.). (ENG.). 32p. (J). (gr. -1-1). pap. 4.99 (978-0-7364-3013-5(X), RH/Disney) Random Hse. Children's Bks.

Legramandi, Francesco. Switched up! (DC Super Hero Girls) Sharpe, Tess & Matta, Gabriella. 2020. (ENG.). 144p. (J). (gr. 1-4). 6.99 **(978-1-9848-9506-6(0));** 12.99 **(978-1-9848-9507-3(9))** Random Hse. Children's Bks. (Random Hse. Bks. for Young Readers).

Legramandi, Francesco & Matta, Gabriella. Baboons! (Disney Junior: the Lion Guard) Jordan, Apple. 2017. (Little Golden Book Ser.). (ENG.). 24p. (J). (-k). 4.99 (978-0-7364-3563-5(8), Golden/Disney) Random Hse. Children's Bks.

—The Bean Team (Butterbean's Cafe) Huntley, Tex. 2019. (Step into Reading Ser.). (ENG.). 24p. (J). (gr. -1-1). 12.99 (978-1-9848-9446-5(3)); pap. 5.99 (978-1-9848-9445-8(5)) Random Hse. Children's Bks. (Random Hse. Bks. for Young Readers).

—Christmas Friends Forever! (Sunny Day) Random House. 2019. (ENG.). 22p. (J). (gr. -1-2). bds. 6.99 (978-1-9848-9444-1(7), Random Hse. Bks. for Young Readers) Random Hse. Children's Bks.

—Easter 1, 2, 3! (Butterbean's Cafe) Random House. 2020. (ENG.). 22p. (J). (— 1). bds. 6.99 (978-0-593-12397-3(2), Random Hse. Bks. for Young Readers) Random Hse. Children's Bks.

—Eye in the Sky (Disney Junior: the Lion Guard) Jordan, Apple. 2016. (Little Golden Book Ser.). (ENG.). 24p. (J). (-k). 4.99 (978-0-7364-3500-0(X), Golden/Disney) Random Hse. Children's Bks.

—Good Night, Princess! (Disney Princess) Posner-Sanchez, Andrea. 2012. (Pictureback(R) Ser.). (ENG.). 16p. (J). (gr. -1-2). pap. 4.99 (978-0-7364-2851-4(8), RH/Disney) Random Hse. Children's Bks.

—I Love My Dad (Disney Princess) Liberts, Jennifer. 2017. (Step into Reading Ser.). (ENG.). 24p. (J). (gr. -1-1). pap. 4.99 (978-0-7364-3755-4(X)); lib. bdg. 12.99 (978-0-7364-9022-1(1)) Random Hse. Children's Bks. (RH/Disney).

—Pretty As a Pumpkin! (Sunny Day) Random House. 2019. (ENG.). 22p. (J). (— 1). bds. 6.99 (978-1-9848-4879-6(8), Random Hse. Bks. for Young Readers) Random Hse. Children's Bks.

—Princesses & Puppies (Disney Princess) Liberts, Jennifer. 2016. (Step into Reading Ser.). (ENG.). 24p. (J). (gr. -1-1). pap. 4.99 (978-0-7364-3660-1(X), RH/Disney) Random Hse. Children's Bks.

—Teacup: Belle's Star Pup (Disney Princess: Palace Pets) Random House Disney Staff & Redbank, Tennant. 2015. (Stepping Stone Book(TM) Ser.). (ENG.). 64p. (J). (gr. 1-4). 5.99 (978-0-7364-3345-7(7), RH/Disney) Random Hse. Children's Bks.

—Three Royal Birthdays! (Disney Princess) Posner-Sanchez, Andrea. 2015. (Pictureback(R) Ser.). (ENG.). 24p. (J). (gr. -1-2). 5.99 (978-0-7364-3403-4(8), RH/Disney) Random Hse. Children's Bks.

—Too Many Termites (Disney Junior: the Lion Guard) Katschke, Judy. 2017. (Little Golden Book Ser.). (ENG.). 24p. (J). (-k). 4.99 (978-0-7364-3689-2(8), Golden/Disney) Random Hse. Children's Bks.

Legramandi, Francesco & Scolari, Silvano. Night of the Vulture! (Marvel: Spider-Man) Berrios, Frank. 2017. (Little Golden Book Ser.). (ENG.). 24p. (J). (-k). 4.99 (978-1-5247-1728-5(2), Golden Bks.) Random Hse. Children's Bks.

Legramandi, Francesco, jt. illus. see Cagol, Andrea.

Legramandi, Francesco, jt. illus. see Matta, Gabriella.

Lehman, A. C. Girl Scouts in Arizona & New Mexico. Roy, Lillian Elizabeth. 2011. 250p. 46.95 (978-1-258-05940-8(1)) Literary Licensing, LLC.

Lehman, Barbara. The Plan. Paul, Alison. 2015. (ENG.). 32p. (J). (gr. -1-3). 17.99 (978-0-544-28333-6(3), 1571292, HMH Books For Young Readers) Houghton Mifflin Harcourt Publishing Co.

Lehman, Barbara. The Red Book. Lehman, Barbara. 2004. (ENG.). 32p. (J). (gr. -1-3). 16.99 (978-0-618-42858-8(5), 510240, HMH Books For Young Readers) Houghton Mifflin Harcourt Publishing Co.

Lehman, Charles. First Pitch. Sabino, David. 2018. (Game Day Ser.). (ENG.). 40p. (J). (gr. k-2). 17.99 (978-1-5344-3242-0(6)); pap. 4.99 (978-1-5344-3241-3(8)) Simon Spotlight. (Simon Spotlight).

—Jump Shot. Sabino, David. 2018. (Game Day Ser.). (ENG.). 40p. (J). (gr. k-2). 17.99 (978-1-5344-3245-1(0)); pap. 4.99 (978-1-5344-3244-4(2)) Simon Spotlight. (Simon Spotlight).

—Tessie Tames Her Tongue: A Book about Learning When to Talk & When to Listen. Martin, Melissa. 2017. (ENG.). 36p. (J). (gr. k-4). 14.99 (978-1-63198-133-3(1)) Free Spirit Publishing, Inc.

Lehman, Denise. Before I Knew You. Lee, Shelley R. Lee, Shelley R., ed. 2006. (J). lib. bdg. 20.00 (978-0-9786757-0-7(3)) Lee, Shelley.

Lehmkuhl, Pat. Miranda & Starlight: (the Starlight Books, 1) Revised Edition, 6 vols. Hill, Janet Muirhead. 2nd rev. ed. 2003. (Starlight Bks.: 1). 168p. (J). (gr. 3-7). per. 9.00 (978-0-9714161-4-7(1)) Raven Publishing Inc. of Montana.

—Starlight, Star Bright: (the Starlight Books, 3), 6 vols. 2003. (Starlight Bks.: Bk. 3). 192p. (J). (gr. 3-7). per. 12.00 (978-0-9714161-2-3(5)) Raven Publishing Inc. of Montana.

Lehner-Rhoades, Shirley. Can I Have Some Cake Too? Nazareth, Melanie. 2013. 32p. (J). pap. 14.95 (978-1-935914-28-0(6)) River Sanctuary Publishing.

Lehner, Zach. Out of the Woods, Bk. 2. Smith, Greg & Tanner, Michael. 2018. (Junior Braves of the Apocalypse Ser.: 2). (ENG.). 192p. 19.99 (978-1-62010-519-1(5)); pap. 14.99 (978-1-62010-527-6(6)) Oni Pr., Inc. (Lion Forge).

Lehrer, Damon. Rocket Boy. 2016. (ENG.). 32p. (J). 17.95 (978-1-56792-587-6(1)) Godine, David R. Pub.

Lehto, Christine. I'm Only a Little Bunny. Jenks, Patricia. 2013. 34p. 15.99 (978-1-937165-48-2(5)) Orange Hat Publishing.

Leibold, Lauren. Parts of the (Church) Body. Strater, Amanda. 2018. (ENG.). 30p. (J). pap. 13.95 (978-1-9736-3756-1(1), WestBow Pr.) Author Solutions, Inc.

Leick, Bonnie. Alien Invaders. Cooper, Lynne. 2010. (ENG.). 32p. (J). (gr. 4-7). 16.95 (978-1-934960-83-7(7), Raven Tree Pr.,Csi) Continental Sales, Inc.

—Baby Bear Eats the Night, 0 vols. Pearson, Anthony. 2012. (ENG.). 32p. (J). (gr. k-3). 16.99 (978-0-7614-6103-6(5), 9780761461036, Two Lions) Amazon Publishing.

—Beautiful Moon. Jeffers, Dawn. 2010. (ENG.). 32p. (J). (gr. -1-3). pap. 7.95 (978-1-934960-06-6(3), Raven Tree Pr.,Csi) Continental Sales, Inc.

—Goodnight, Little Monster, 0 vols. Ketteman, Helen. 2010. (Little Monster Ser.: 1). (ENG.). 32p. (J). (gr. -1-k). 16.99 (978-0-7614-5683-4(X), 9780761456834, Two Lions) Amazon Publishing.

—Impetuous R. , Secret Agent. Conly, Jane Leslie. 2008. (ENG.). 240p. (gr. 3-7). 16.99 (978-1-4231-0418-6(8)) Hyperion Pr.

—It's Halloween, Little Monster. Ketteman, Helen. 2020. (Little Monster Ser.: 3). (ENG.). 32p. (J). (gr. -1-2). 17.99 (978-1-5420-9208-1(6), 9781542092081, Two Lions) Amazon Publishing.

—Where the Mild Things Are: A Very Meek Parody. Send-up, Maurice. 2009. (ENG.). 40p. (J). (gr. -1-3). 16.99 (978-1-4169-9551-7(X), Simon & Schuster Bks. For Young Readers) Simon & Schuster Bks. For Young Readers.

—47 Strings: Tessa's Special Code. Carey, Becky. Stidwell O'Boyle, Carrie, ed. 2012. (ENG.). 36p. 16.95 (978-0-9849245-6-1(6)) Little Creek Press.

Leidemer, Adam. The Puppy Who Wasn't. Ritner, Amelia. 2012. 24p. 24.95 (978-1-4626-6221-0(8)) America Star Bks.

Leigh, Jenna. Emma & Starfire: A Story of the Star Horses. Marie, Lauren. 2019. (ENG.). 32p. (J). (gr. 1-3). pap. 13.95 (978-1-945805-84-4(6)); 25.95 (978-1-949290-23-3(9)) Bedazzled Ink Publishing Co.

Leigh, Rob, jt. illus. see Research & Education Association Editors.

Leigh, Tom. Angus & Sadie. Voigt, Cynthia. (ENG.). 208p. (J). (gr. 3-7). 2008. pap. 6.99 (978-0-06-074584-4(3)); 2005. 16.99 (978-0-06-074582-0(7)) HarperCollins Pubs.

—The Count's Hanukkah Countdown, Vol. Balsley, Tilda & Fischer, Ellen. 2012. (ENG.). 24p. (J). (gr. -1-1). 7.99 (978-0-7613-7557-9(0), 9780761375579, Kar-Ben Publishing) Lerner Publishing Group.

—Elmo Says... (Sesame Street) Albee, Sarah. 2009. (Big Bird's Favorites Board Bks.). (ENG.). 24p. (J). (gr. k — 1). bds. 4.99 (978-0-375-84540-6(2), Random Hse. Bks. for Young Readers) Random Hse. Children's Bks.

—Grover & Big Bird's Passover Celebration. Balsley, Tilda & Fischer, Ellen. 2013. (ENG.). 24p. (J). (gr. -1-1). lib. bdg. 16.99 (978-0-7613-8491-5(X), 9780761384915); Vol. 7.99 (978-0-7613-8492-2(8), 9780761384922) Lerner Publishing Group. (Kar-Ben Publishing).

—Grover Goes to Israel, Vol. Sussman, Joni Kibort. 2019. (ENG.). 12p. (J). (gr. -1 — 1). bds. 5.99 (978-1-5415-2920-5(0), Kar-Ben Publishing) Lerner Publishing Group.

—Grover's Hanukkah Party. Sussman, Joni Kibort. 2019. (ENG.). 12p. (J). (gr. -1 — 1). bds. 5.99 (978-1-5415-2923-6(5), Kar-Ben Publishing) Lerner Publishing Group.

—Hello, Cat, Hello, Dog. Albee, Sarah. 2006. (Step-By-Step Readers Ser.). (J). pap. (978-1-59939-054-3(X), Reader's Digest Young Families, Inc.) Studio Fun International.

—I'm Sorry, Grover: A Rosh Hashanah Tale. Balsley, Tilda & Fischer, Ellen. 2013. (ENG.). 24p. (J). (gr. -1-k). lib. bdg. 16.95 (978-0-7613-7560-9(0), 9780761375609); Vol. 6.95 (978-0-7613-7561-6(9), 9780761375616) Lerner Publishing Group. (Kar-Ben Publishing).

—It's a Mitzvah, Grover! Balsley, Tilda & Fischer, Ellen. 2013. (ENG.). 24p. (J). (gr. -1-1). lib. bdg. 16.95 (978-0-7613-7562-3(7)); Vol. 6.95 (978-0-7613-7563-0(5), 9780761375630) Lerner Publishing Group. (Kar-Ben Publishing).

—Off to the Moon! Marbury, Stephanie. 2006. 20p. (J). (978-1-59939-100-7(7), Reader's Digest Young Families, Inc.) Studio Fun International.

—Pinocchio: A Tale of Honesty. 2006. (J). 6.99 (978-1-59939-005-5(1)) Cornerstone Pr.

—A Seder for Grover, Vol. Sussman, Joni Kibort. 2019. (ENG.). 12p. (J). (gr. -1 — 1). bds. 5.99 (978-1-5415-2921-2(9), Kar-Ben Publishing) Lerner Publishing Group.

—Shalom Everybodeee! Grover's Adventures in Israel. Balsley, Tilda & Fischer, Ellen. 2016. (ENG.). 24p. (J). (gr. -1-2). 16.99 (978-0-7613-7558-6(9), 9780761375586, Kar-Ben Publishing) Lerner Publishing Group.

—Shanah Tovah, Grover! Sussman, Joni Kibort. 2019. (ENG.). 12p. (J). (gr. -1 — 1). bds. 6.99 (978-1-5415-2922-9(7), 9781541529229, Kar-Ben Publishing) Lerner Publishing Group.

Leigh, Tom, jt. illus. see Swanson, Maggie.

Leighton, Robert. Bugged: How Insects Changed History. Albee, Sarah. 2014. (ENG.). 176p. (J). (gr. 3-6). pap. 17.99 (978-0-8027-3422-8(7), 900095581, Bloomsbury USA Childrens) Bloomsbury Publishing USA.

—Poop Happened! A History of the World from the Bottom Up. Albee, Sarah. 2010. (ENG.). 176p. (YA). (gr. 5-9). pap. 18.99 (978-0-8027-2077-1(3), 9780802720771, Bloomsbury USA Childrens) Bloomsbury Publishing USA.

—What's Going on down There? A Boy's Guide to Growing Up. Gravelle, Karen. 2017. 160p. (J). pap. 13.99 (978-1-68119-361-8(2), 900171548, Bloomsbury USA Childrens) Bloomsbury Publishing USA.

Leijs, Tommie. Playtime Adventures. Vinsh, Aara J. 2011. 48p. pap. 24.95 (978-1-4560-9982-4(5)) America Star Bks.

Leijten, Aileen. Bella & Bean. Dotlich, Rebecca Kai. 2009. (ENG.). 40p. (J). (gr. -1-3). 19.99 (978-0-689-85616-7(4), Atheneum Bks. for Young Readers) Simon & Schuster Children's Publishing.

—City Hall: The Heart of Los Angeles. Bloom, Susan & Bertram, Debbie. 2015. (ENG.). 100p. (J). 9.95 (978-1-931290-24-1(5)) Tallfellow Pr.

—Leaping Lily: A Ballet Story. Marsoli, Lisa Ann. 2005. (J). bds. 14.99 (978-0-9767325-3-2(X)) Toy Quest.

Leiper, Kate. An Illustrated Treasury of Scottish Castle Legends, 10 vols. Breslin, Theresa. 2019. (ENG.). 176p. (J). 24.95 (978-1-78250-595-2(4)) Floris Bks. GBR. Dist: Consortium Bk. Sales & Distribution.

—An Illustrated Treasury of Scottish Folk & Fairy Tales, 10 vols. Breslin, Theresa. 2012. (ENG.). 160p. (J). 24.95 (978-0-86315-907-7(9)) Floris Bks. GBR. Dist: Consortium Bk. Sales & Distribution.

—An Illustrated Treasury of Scottish Mythical Creatures, 5 vols. Breslin, Theresa. 2015. (ENG.). 192p. (J). 24.95 (978-1-78250-195-4(9)) Floris Bks. GBR. Dist: Consortium Bk. Sales & Distribution.

—A Wee Bird Was Watching. Polwart, Karine. 2018. (ENG.). 32p. pap. 10.95 (978-1-78027-532-1(3), BC Bks.) Birlinn, Ltd. GBR. Dist: Casemate Pubs. & Bk. Distributors, LLC.

Leipsic, Regina. Zane & the Armadillo. Knesek, Marian. 2012. 26p. 24.95 (978-1-4626-6685-0(X)) America Star Bks.

Leist, Christina. Nutz!, 1 vol. Schwartz, Virginia Frances. 2012. (ENG.). 152p. (J). (gr. 4-7). pap. 12.95 (978-1-896580-87-6(4)) Tradewind Bks. CAN. Dist: Orca Bk. Pubs. USA.

—On My Bike, 1 vol. Winters, Kari-Lynn. 2017. (On My ... Ser.). (ENG.). 24p. (J). (gr. -1-k). bds. 12.95

(978-1-926890-13-5(2)) Tradewind Bks. CAN. Dist: Orca Bk. Pubs. USA.

—On My Skis, 1 vol. Winters, Kari-Lynn. 2017. (On My ... Ser.). (ENG.). 24p. (J). (gr. -1-k). bds. 12.95 *(978-1-926890-03-6(5))* Tradewind Bks. CAN. Dist: Orca Bk. Pubs. USA.

—On My Swim, 1 vol. Winters, Kari-Lynn. 2018. (ENG.). 24p. (J). (gr. -1-k). 12.95 *(978-1-926890-16-6(7))* Tradewind Bks. CAN. Dist: Orca Bk. Pubs. USA.

—On My Walk, 1 vol. Winters, Kari-Lynn. 2010. (ENG.). 32p. (J). (gr. -1-k). 16.95 *(978-1-896580-61-6(0))* Tradewind Bks. CAN. Dist: Orca Bk. Pubs. USA.

Leist, Kara Suzanne. The Littlest Star. Kieffer, Elise Lael. 2005. (J). 14.99 *(978-1-59971-086-0(2))* Aardvark Global Publishing.

Leja, Nela. Sam the Black Cat. Leja, Nela. Leja, Mary. 2019. (ENG.). 42p. (J). pap. *(978-1-989388-00-6(0))* TaleFeather Publishing.

Leland, Toni M. Christa Joins a Horse Club: Second in Christa Duncan Series. Leland, Toni M. 2004. Orig. Title: Christa Joins 4-H. (J). pap. 6.95 *(978-1-887932-49-3(6),* SmallHorse Pr.) Equine Graphics Publishing Group.

Leliwa, Anna. Une Surprise Pour Dolly: Dolly's Winter Surprise. Thorpe, Rochelle O'Neal. Brovender, Jacqueline Grenez, tr. 2017. (FRE.). (J). pap. 11.95 *(978-1-935706-48-9(9))* Wiggles Pr.

Leloup, Geneviève. Too Princessy! Reidy, Jean. 2013. (Too! Bks.). (ENG.). 26p. (J). (gr. -1 — 1). bds. 7.99 *(978-1-59990-955-4(3),* 9781599909554, Bloomsbury USA Childrens) Bloomsbury Publishing USA.

Lemaire, Bonnie. Epic Life. Daugherty, Jon. 2020. (ENG.). 46p. (J). ***(978-0-2288-3237-9(3))***; pap. ***(978-1-7771823-0-4(1))*** Tellwell Talent.

Lemaire, Bonnie. Lilly Loves Beards. Gardner, Carol Thompson. 2019. (ENG.). 36p. (J). *(978-0-2288-1133-6(3))*; pap. *(978-0-2288-1132-9(5))* Tellwell Talent.

Lemaire, Bonnie. The Mindfulness Room. Lynch, Amanda Loraine. Davis, Candice L., ed. 2019. (ENG.). 48p. (J). pap. 19.95 ***(978-0-578-53381-0(2))*** Rethinking Resiliency, LLC.

Lemaire, Bonnie. When Jungle Jim Comes to Visit Fred the Snake. Cotton, Peter B. 2013. 48p. 24.95 *(978-0-9883370-4-6(5))* Fig & The Vine, LLC, The.

Lemaire, Bonnie. The 5-Minute Mindfulness Journal for Kids. Lynch, Amanda Loraine. Davis, Candice, ed. 2020. (ENG.). 100p. (J). pap. 15.83 ***(978-1-7345026-3-3(0))*** Rethinking Resiliency, LLC.

Lemaitre, Pascal. Always. McGhee, Alison. 2009. (ENG.). 40p. (J). (gr. -1-3). 15.99 *(978-1-4169-7481-9(4),* Simon & Schuster/Paula Wiseman Bks.) Simon & Schuster/Paula Wiseman Bks.

Lemaitre, Pascal. Artist Ted. Beaty, Andrea. 2012. (ENG.). 32p. (J). (gr. -1-3). 19.99 *(978-1-4169-5374-6(4),* McElderry, Margaret K. Bks.) McElderry, Margaret K. Bks.

—Bulldog's Big Day. McMullan, Kate. 2011. (J). *(978-0-545-17156-4(3),* Orchard Bks.) Scholastic, Inc.

—Come with Me. McGhee, Holly M. 2017. 40p. (J). (gr. k-3). 17.99 *(978-1-5247-3905-8(7),* G.P. Putnam's Sons Books for Young Readers) Penguin Young Readers Group.

Lemaitre, Pascal. Do Not Ever Be a Babysitter! Muntean, Michaela. 2020. (ENG.). 40p. (J). (gr. -1-3). 17.99 *(978-1-338-28390-7(1),* Scholastic Pr.) Scholastic, Inc.

—Do Not Open This Book. Muntean, Michaela. 2006. (ENG.). 40p. (J). (gr. -1-3). 17.99 *(978-0-439-69839-9(1),* Scholastic Pr.) Scholastic, Inc.

Lemaitre, Pascal. Doctor Ted. Beaty, Andrea. 2008. (ENG.). 32p. (J). (gr. -1-3). 17.99 *(978-1-4169-2820-1(0),* McElderry, Margaret K. Bks.) McElderry, Margaret K. Bks.

—Firefighter Ted. Beaty, Andrea. 2009. (ENG.). 32p. (J). (gr. -1-3). 18.99 *(978-1-4169-2821-8(9),* McElderry, Margaret K. Bks.) McElderry, Margaret K. Bks.

Lemaitre, Pascal. Hush, Baby Ghostling. Beaty, Andrea. 2009. (ENG.). 32p. (J). (gr. -1-3). 14.99 *(978-1-4169-2545-3(7),* McElderry, Margaret K. Bks.) McElderry, Margaret K. Bks.

—The Lion or the Mouse? Morrison, Toni & Morrison, Slade. 2014. (Who's Got Game? Ser.: 2). (ENG.). 36p. pap. 16.99 *(978-1-4767-9268-2(2),* Scribner) Scribner.

—Listen. McGhee, Holly M. 2019. (ENG.). 32p. (J). 17.99 *(978-1-250-31812-1(2),* 900200072) Roaring Brook Pr.

Lemaitre, Pascal. Me! Me! Mine! Katz, Alan. 2011. (ENG.). 16p. (J). (gr. -1-1). bds. 7.99 *(978-1-4169-8993-6(5),* Little Simon) Little Simon.

—A Pet Named Sneaker. Heilbroner, Joan. 2013. (Beginner Books(R) Ser.). 48p. (J). (gr. k-3). 8.99 *(978-0-307-97580-5(0),* Random Hse. Bks. for Young Readers) Random Hse. Children's Bks.

—Squirrels on Skis. Ray, J. Hamilton. 2013. (Beginner Books(R) Ser.). 64p. (J). (gr. k-3). 9.99 *(978-0-449-81081-1(X),* Random Hse. Bks. for Young Readers) Random Hse. Children's Bks.

—Supercat-Prepack 8. McMullan, Kate. (ENG.). 1p. (J). bds. 55.60 *(978-0-7611-2802-1(6),* 22802) Workman Publishing Co., Inc.

—Supercat to the Rescue. McMullan, Kate. (ENG.). 1p. (J). bds. 55.60 *(978-0-7611-3234-9(1),* 23234) Workman Publishing Co., Inc.

Lemaitre, Pascal. You Are the Pea, & I Am the Carrot. Elkins, J. 2013. (ENG.). 32p. (J). (gr. -1-2). 16.95 *(978-1-4197-0850-3(3),* Abrams Bks. for Young Readers) Abrams, Inc.

Lemanski, Mike. Design Line: Planes, Trains, & Automobiles. Oxlade, Chris. 2014. (ENG.). 16p. (J). (gr. k-12). 17.99 *(978-0-7636-7121-1(5),* Big Picture Press) Candlewick Pr.

Lemaster, Michael. Corn for Tomorrow: A Story from Glengary. Lemaster, Kevin. 2009. 28p. pap. 13.99 *(978-1-4343-8548-2(5))* AuthorHouse.

LeMay, Meagan. Emma's First Agate, 1 vol. Magnuson, James. 2014. (ENG.). 32p. (J). (gr. 1-2). pap. 7.95 *(978-1-59193-443-1(5),* Adventure Pubns.) AdventureKEEN.

Lemay, Violet. Babies Around the World. Puck. 2017. (ENG.). 20p. (J). (gr. -1 — 1). bds. 7.95 *(978-1-938093-87-6(9),* 809387, Duo Pr. Llc (US)) Duo Pr. LLC.

—Bookstore Babies. Puck. 2019. (ENG.). 22p. (J). bds. 7.95 *(978-1-947458-50-5(7),* 805850, Duo Pr. Llc (US)) Duo Pr. LLC.

—Doodle Texas. Pohlen, Jerome. 2013. (ENG.). 120p. (J). (gr. k-5). pap. 12.95 *(978-1-938093-05-0(4),* 809305) Duo Pr. LLC.

—How a City Works. Ward, D. J. 2018. (Let's-Read-And-Find-Out Science 2 Ser.). (ENG.). 40p. (J). (gr. -1-3). 17.99 *(978-0-06-247031-7(0))*; pap. 6.99 *(978-0-06-247030-0(2))* HarperCollins Pubs.

—Lindsay's Joyride. Hurford, Molly. 2019. (Shred Girls Ser.: 1). 256p. (J). (gr. 3-7). 13.99 *(978-1-63565-277-2(4),* Rodale Kids) Random Hse. Children's Bks.

—New York Baby: A Local Baby Book. Puck. 2012. (Local Baby Bks.). (ENG.). 22p. (J). (gr. k — 1). bds. 8.95 *(978-0-9838121-4-2(4),* 801214) Duo Pr. LLC.

—The Obamas: a Lift-The-Flap Book. 2019. (ENG.). 22p. (J). (gr. -1-k). bds. 9.95 *(978-1-947458-82-6(5),* 805882, Duo Pr. Llc (US)) Duo Pr. LLC.

—San Francisco Baby: A Local Baby Book. Shea, Tess & Pohlen, Jerome. 2013. (Local Baby Bks.). (ENG.). 22p. (— 1). bds. 8.95 *(978-1-938093-16-6(X),* 809316) Duo Pr. LLC.

—Shred Girls: Lindsay's Joyride. Hurford, Molly. 2019. (Shred Girls Ser.: 1). (ENG.). 256p. (J). (gr. 3-7). lib. bdg. 16.99 *(978-1-9848-9425-0(0),* Rodale Kids) Random Hse. Children's Bks.

—Writers & Their Pets: True Stories of Famous Authors & Their Animal Friends. Krull, Kathleen. 2019. (ENG.). 192p. (J). (gr. 2-5). 14.95 *(978-1-947458-52-9(3),* 805852, Duo Pr. Llc (US)) Duo Pr. LLC.

LeMay, Violet. Yes I Can! A Girl & Her Wheelchair. Barrett, Kendra J. et al. 2018. (J). *(978-1-4338-2869-0(3),* Magination Pr.) American Psychological Assn.

Lemay, Violet. 100 Pablo Picassos. 2015. (ENG.). 32p. (J). (gr. k-5). 14.99 *(978-1-938093-32-6(1),* 809332) Duo Pr. LLC.

Lember, Barbara Hirsch, photos by. If You Find a Rock. Christian, Peggy. 2008. (ENG., 32p. (J). (gr. -1-3). pap. 7.99 *(978-0-15-206354-2(4),* 1199032) Houghton Mifflin Harcourt Publishing Co.

Lemke, Horst. Around the World in Eighty Dishes. Van der Linde, Polly & Van der Linde, Tasha. 88p. (J). (gr. k-7). 12.95 *(978-0-87592-007-8(1))* Scroll Pr., Inc.

—Places & Faces. 32p. (J). (gr. -1). 14.95 *(978-0-87592-041-2(1))* Scroll Pr., Inc.

—Ride with Me Through ABC. Bond, Susan. 32p. (J). (gr. -1). 14.95 *(978-0-87592-043-6(8))* Scroll Pr., Inc.

Lemniscates, Carme. Grandma's Gardens. Clinton, Hillary & Clinton, Chelsea. 2020. 40p. (J). (gr. -1-3). 18.99 *(978-0-593-11535-0(X),* Philomel Bks.) Penguin Young Readers Group.

—I Am a Warrior Goddess. Adams, Jennifer. 2018. (I Am a Warrior Goddess Ser.: 1). (ENG.). 32p. (J). 17.95 *(978-1-68364-005-9(5),* 900220842) Sounds True, Inc.

—Los Jardines de la Abuela. Clinton, Hillary & Clinton, Chelsea. 2020. (SPA.). 40p. (J). (gr. -1-3). 18.99 *(978-0-593-11538-1(4),* Philomel Bks.) Penguin Young Readers Group.

Lemniscates, Carme. Birds. Lemniscates, Carme. 2019. (ENG.). 40p. (J). (-k). 14.99 *(978-1-5362-0178-9(2))* Candlewick Pr.

—Seeds. Lemniscates, Carme. 2020. 40p. (J). (-k). 14.99 *(978-1-5362-0844-3(2))* Candlewick Pr.

—Trees. Lemniscates, Carme. 2017. (ENG.). 40p. (J). (-k). 14.99 *(978-0-7636-9001-4(5))* Candlewick Pr.

Lemoine, Georges. Lullaby. Le Clézio, J. M. G. 2007. (FRE.). 72p. (J). (gr. 5-10). pap. *(978-2-07-061258-1(9))* Gallimard, Editions.

Lemon, Darnell C. My Friend Pup-Pup: Mi Amigo Pup-Pup. Anderson, Cynthia Y. 2019. (ENG.). 34p. (J). (gr. k-5). 16.99 ***(978-1-7327901-1-7(6))*** Wolfy International Corp.

Lemon, Nancy. How to Make a Mountain. Huntington, Amy. 2020. (J). *(978-1-4521-7588-1(8))* Chronicle Bks. LLC.

—What John Marco Saw. Barrows, Annie. 2019. (ENG.). 44p. (J). (gr. -1-k). 17.99 *(978-1-4521-6336-9(7))* Chronicle Bks. LLC.

Lemon, Nancy. Emma & Muse. Lemon, Nancy. 2018. (ENG.). 32p. (J). (gr. -1-k). 16.99 *(978-0-8075-1994-3(4),* 807519944) Whitman, Albert & Co.

Lemon Ribbon Studio. Hello from Around the World Locked Diary. Mudpuppy. 2018. (ENG.). 192p. (J). (gr. -1-7). 10.99 *(978-0-7353-5643-6(2))* Mudpuppy Pr.

Lemus, Kristina. Catch me if you Can. Mau, Connie. l.t. ed. 2006. 28p. (J). 14.95 *(978-0-9778843-0-8(9))* Mau, C. Publishing Co.

Lenart, Claudia. Hansel & Gretel: A Fairy Tale with a Down Syndrome Twist. Kats, Jewel. 2014. 37p. (J). *(978-1-61599-251-5(0))* Loving Healing Pr., Inc.

—Prince Preemie: A Tale of a Tiny Puppy Who Arrives Early. Kats, Jewel. 2016. 28p. (J). pap. *(978-1-61599-306-2(1))* Loving Healing Pr., Inc.

—Seasons of Joy: Every Day Is for Outdoor Play. 2017. 27p. (J). pap. *(978-1-61599-317-8(7))* Loving Healing Pr., Inc.

Lendler, Ian. The Stratford Zoo Midnight Revue Presents Romeo & Juliet. Lendler, Ian. 2015. (Stratford Zoo Ser.). (ENG.). 96p. (J). (gr. 2-5). pap. 13.99 *(978-1-59643-916-0(5),* 9781596439160, First Second Bks.) Roaring Brook Pr.

Lendway, Andy. From A to Zamboni, the Alphabet Hockey Style! Flyers Edition. Grocki, Jennifer. 2007. 32p. (J). 16.95 *(978-0-9793833-0-4(7))* Team Kidz, Inc.

Lenehan, Mary & Weber, Rich. Flight: First Vehicles. Mott, Professor. 8p. (J). (gr. -1-3). 14.99 *(978-1-890647-36-0(5))* TOMY International, Inc.

Leng, Qin. Away, 1 vol. Sher, Emil. 2017. (ENG.). 32p. (J). (gr. -1-2). 18.95 *(978-1-55498-483-1(1))* Groundwood Bks. CAN. Dist: Publishers Group West (PGW).

—The Best Thing about Kindergarten. Lloyd, Jennifer. 2013. 36p. (J). (gr. -1-1). 16.95 *(978-1-897476-82-6(5))* Simply Read Bks. CAN. Dist: Ingram Publisher Services.

—The Better Tree Fort, 1 vol. Kerrin, Jessica Scott. 2018. (ENG.). 32p. (J). (gr. -1-2). 17.95 *(978-1-55498-863-1(2))* Groundwood Bks. CAN. Dist: Publishers Group West (PGW).

—The Better Tree Fort. Kerrin, Jessica Scott. 2018. (ENG.). 32p. E-Book *(978-1-55498-864-8(0))* Groundwood Bks.

—Dear Baobab, 1 vol. Foggo, Cheryl. 2011. (ENG.). 24p. (J). (gr. 1-3). 15.95 *(978-1-897187-91-3(2))* Second Story Pr. CAN. Dist: Orca Bk. Pubs. USA.

—A Family Is a Family Is a Family, 1 vol. O'Leary, Sara. 2016. (ENG.). 32p. (J). (gr. -1-2). 17.95 *(978-1-55498-794-8(6))* Groundwood Bks. CAN. Dist: Publishers Group West (PGW).

—Fifteen Dollars & Thirty-Five Cents: A Story about Choices, 1 vol. Cole, Kathryn. 2015. (I'm a Great Little Kid Ser.). (ENG.). 24p. (J). (gr. 1-3). 15.95 *(978-1-927583-82-1(9))* Second Story Pr. CAN. Dist: Orca Bk. Pubs. USA.

—A Flock of Shoes. Tsiang, Sarah. 3rd ed. 2010. (ENG.). 32p. (J). (gr. -1-k). pap. 8.95 *(978-1-55451-248-5(4),* 9781554512485) Annick Pr., Ltd. CAN. Dist: Publishers Group West (PGW).

—God's Little Lambs, My First Bible, 1 vol. Stiegemeyer, Julie. 2018. (ENG.). 32p. (J). bds. 9.99 *(978-0-310-76159-4(X))* Zonderkidz.

—Going Places. Potter, Ellen. 2017. 108p. (J). *(978-1-101-93961-1(3))* Knopf, Alfred A. Inc.

—Good Night, Good Night. Lee, Dennis. 2018. (ENG.). 26p. (J). (gr. -1-k). bds. 10.50 *(978-1-4434-1165-3(5))* HarperCollins Pubs.

—Hana Hashimoto, Sixth Violin. Uegaki, Chieri. 2014. (ENG.). 30p. (J). (gr. -1-3). 16.99 *(978-1-894786-33-1(5))* Kids Can Pr., Ltd. CAN. Dist: Hachette Bk. Group.

—Happy Birthday, Alice Babette, 1 vol. Kulling, Monica. 2016. (ENG.). 32p. (J). (gr. -1-3). 16.95 *(978-1-55498-820-4(9))* Groundwood Bks. CAN. Dist: Publishers Group West (PGW).

—Harry & Walter. Stinson, Kathy. 2018. (ENG.). 32p. (J). (gr. k-2). pap. 9.95 *(978-1-55451-801-2(6))* Annick Pr., Ltd. CAN. Dist: Publishers Group West (PGW).

—A History of Just about Everything: 180 Events, People & Inventions That Changed the World. MacLeod, Elizabeth & Wishinsky, Frieda. 2013. (ENG.). 124p. (J). (gr. 3-7). 21.95 *(978-1-55453-775-4(4))* Kids Can Pr., Ltd. CAN. Dist: Hachette Bk. Group.

—An Inuit Puppy Story, 1 vol. Uluadluak, Donald. 2012. (Kamik Ser.: 1). (ENG.). 32p. (J). (gr. 1-3). 10.95 *(978-1-927095-11-9(5))* Inhabit Media Inc. CAN. Dist: Consortium Bk. Sales & Distribution.

—Kamik Joins the Pack, 1 vol. Baker, Darryl. 2016. (Kamik Ser.: 3). (ENG.). 32p. (J). (gr. k-2). pap. 10.95 *(978-1-77227-125-6(X))* Inhabit Media Inc. CAN. Dist: Consortium Bk. Sales & Distribution.

—Kamik's First Sled, 1 vol. Sulurayok, Matilda. 2015. (Kamik Ser.: 2). (ENG.). 32p. (J). (gr. k-2). 10.95 *(978-1-77227-020-4(2))* Inhabit Media Inc. CAN. Dist: Consortium Bk. Sales & Distribution.

—Me on the Map. Sweeney, Joan. 2018. 32p. (J). (gr. -1-2). 12.99 *(978-1-5247-7200-0(3),* Knopf Bks. for Young Readers); pap. 7.99 *(978-1-5247-7201-7(1),* Dragonfly Bks.) Random Hse. Children's Bks.

—Nala's Magical Mitsiaq: A Story of Inuit Adoption, 1 vol. Noah, Jennifer. 2013. (ENG.). 32p. (J). (gr. 1-3). 10.95 *(978-1-927095-26-3(3))* Inhabit Media Inc. CAN. Dist: Consortium Bk. Sales & Distribution.

—Never Give Up: A Story about Self-Esteem, 1 vol. Cole, Kathryn. 2015. (I'm a Great Little Kid Ser.). (ENG.). 24p. (J). (gr. 1-3). 15.95 *(978-1-927583-60-9(8))* Second Story Pr. CAN. Dist: Orca Bk. Pubs. USA.

—Norman, Speak!, 1 vol. Adderson, Caroline. 2014. (ENG.). 32p. (J). (gr. -1-2). 17.95 *(978-1-55498-322-3(3))* Groundwood Bks. CAN. Dist: Publishers Group West (PGW).

—Not Just Another Princess Story. 2015. (ENG.). 62p. (J). 16.95 *(978-1-927018-57-6(9))* Simply Read Bks. CAN. Dist: Ingram Publisher Services.

—Ordinary, Extraordinary Jane Austen: The Story of Six Novels, Three Notebooks, a Writing Box, & One Clever Girl. Hopkinson, Deborah. 2018. (ENG.). 40p. (J). (gr. -1-3). 17.99 *(978-0-06-237330-4(7),* Balzer & Bray) HarperCollins Pubs.

—Piper Green & the Fairy Tree. Potter, Ellen. 2015. (Piper Green & the Fairy Tree Ser.: 1). (ENG.). 112p. (J). (gr. 2-4). pap. 5.99 *(978-0-553-49926-1(2),* Yearling) Random Hse. Children's Bks.

—Piper Green & the Fairy Tree: Going Places. Potter, Ellen. 2017. (Piper Green & the Fairy Tree Ser.). (ENG.). (J). (gr. 2-4). 20.95 *(978-1-4301-2680-5(9))* Live Oak Media.

—Piper Green & the Fairy Tree: Going Places (1 CD Set) Potter, Ellen. 2017. (Piper Green & the Fairy Tree Ser.). (ENG.). (J). 15.95 *(978-1-4301-2679-9(5))* Live Oak Media.

—Piper Green & the Fairy Tree: Pie Girl. Potter, Ellen. 2017. (Piper Green & the Fairy Tree Ser.: 5). 144p. (J). (gr. 2-4). pap. 5.99 *(978-1-101-93968-0(0),* Yearling) Random Hse. Children's Bks.

—Piper Green & the Fairy Tree: Pie Girl (1 CD Set) Potter, Ellen. 2017. (Piper Green & the Fairy Tree Ser.). (ENG.). (J). (gr. 2-4). 15.95 *(978-1-4301-2792-5(9))* Live Oak Media.

—Piper Green & the Fairy Tree: Pie Girl (1 Paperback/1 CD Set) Potter, Ellen. 2018. (Piper Green & the Fairy Tree Ser.). (ENG.). (J). (gr. 2-4). 20.95 *(978-1-4301-2793-2(7))* Live Oak Media.

—Piper Green & the Fairy Tree: Going Places. Potter, Ellen. 2017. (Piper Green & the Fairy Tree Ser.: 4). (ENG.). 128p. (J). (gr. 2-4). lib. bdg. 17.99 *(978-1-101-93962-8(1),* Knopf Bks. for Young Readers) Random Hse. Children's Bks.

—Piper Green & the Fairy Tree: Pie Girl. Potter, Ellen. 2017. (Piper Green & the Fairy Tree Ser.: 5). (ENG.). 144p. (J). (gr. 2-4). lib. bdg. 17.99 *(978-1-101-93966-6(4),* Yearling) Random Hse. Children's Bks.

—Piper Green & the Fairy Tree: the Sea Pony. Potter, Ellen. 2016. (Piper Green & the Fairy Tree Ser.: 3). (ENG.). 128p. (J). (gr. 2-4). 14.99 *(978-0-553-49931-5(9),* Knopf Bks. for Young Readers) Random Hse. Children's Bks.

—Piper Green And The Fairy Tree Too Much Good Luck. Potter, Ellen. 2015. (Piper Green & the Fairy Tree Ser.: 2). 128p. (J). (gr. 2-4). 14.99 *(978-0-553-49927-8(0),* Knopf Bks. for Young Readers) Random Hse. Children's Bks.

—Ready, Set ... Baby! Rusch, Elizabeth. 2017. (ENG.). 32p. (J). (gr. -1-3). 17.99 *(978-0-544-47272-3(1),* 1601681, HMH Books For Young Readers) Houghton Mifflin Harcourt Publishing Co.

—Reptile Flu: A Story about Communication, 1 vol. Cole, Kathryn. 2015. (I'm a Great Little Kid Ser.). (ENG.). 24p. (J). (gr. 1-3). 15.95 *(978-1-927583-61-6(6))* Second Story Pr. CAN. Dist: Orca Bk. Pubs. USA.

—Sign up Here: A Story about Friendship, 1 vol. Cole, Kathryn. 2016. (I'm a Great Little Kid Ser.). (ENG.). 24p. (J). (gr. 1-3). 15.95 *(978-1-927583-90-6(X))* Second Story Pr. CAN. Dist: Orca Bk. Pubs. USA.

—A Tattle-Tell Tale: A Story about Getting Help, 1 vol. Cole, Kathryn. 2016. (I'm a Great Little Kid Ser.). (ENG.). 24p. (J). (gr. 1-3). 15.95 *(978-1-927583-92-0(6))* Second Story Pr. CAN. Dist: Orca Bk. Pubs. USA.

—That Uh-Oh Feeling: A Story about Touch, 1 vol. Cole, Kathryn. 2016. (I'm a Great Little Kid Ser.). (ENG.). 24p. (J). (gr. 1-3). 15.95 *(978-1-927583-91-3(8))* Second Story Pr. CAN. Dist: Orca Bk. Pubs. USA.

—A Walk on the Shoreline. Hainnu, Rebecca. 2020. 40p. (J). 10.95 *(978-1-77227-269-7(8))* Inhabit Media Inc. CAN. Dist: Consortium Bk. Sales & Distribution.

—A Walk on the Tundra, 1 vol. Hainnu, Rebecca & Ziegler, Anna. 2018. (ENG.). 40p. (J). (gr. 3-5). 10.95 *(978-1-77227-185-0(3))* Inhabit Media Inc. CAN. Dist: Consortium Bk. Sales & Distribution.

Leng, Qin. I Am Small. Leng, Qin. 2018. (ENG.). 40p. (J). (gr. -1-2). 16.99 *(978-1-5253-0115-5(2))* Kids Can Pr., Ltd. CAN. Dist: Hachette Bk. Group.

Lenman, Jamie. Daring, Deadly, Brilliant, Brave: History's Toughest People. Turner, Tracey. 2012. 110p. (J). *(978-1-4351-4760-7(X))* Barnes & Noble, Inc.

—Hard As Nails in Ancient Egypt. Turner, Tracey. 2015. (Hard As Nails in History Ser.). (ENG.). 64p. (J). (gr. 4-5). *(978-0-7787-1511-5(6))* Crabtree Publishing Co.

—Hard As Nails in Ancient Greece. Turner, Tracey. 2015. (Hard As Nails in History Ser.). (ENG.). 64p. (J). (gr. 4-5). *(978-0-7787-1512-2(4))* Crabtree Publishing Co.

—Hard As Nails in Ancient Rome. Turner, Tracey. 2015. (Hard As Nails in History Ser.). (ENG.). 64p. (J). (gr. 4-5). *(978-0-7787-1513-9(2))* Crabtree Publishing Co.

—Hard as Nails Warriors. Turner, Tracey. 2015. (Hard As Nails in History Ser.). (ENG.). 64p. (J). (gr. 4-5). pap. *(978-0-7787-1517-7(5))* Crabtree Publishing Co.

Lennhoff, Andrew. I Love You Every Minute. Stone, Amy Wingrove. 2006. pap. 18.00 *(978-0-8059-9119-2(0),* RoseDog Bks.) Dorrance Publishing Co., Inc.

Lenoir, Jane. Alaska: Be Brave, 4 vols. Sargent, Daina. l.t. ed. 2004. (Double Trouble Ser.: 4). 48p. (J). pap. 10.95 *(978-1-59381-121-1(7))*; lib. bdg. 23.60 *(978-1-59381-120-4(9))* Ozark Publishing.

—Arkansas: Dream Big. Sargent, Daina. l.t. ed. 2004. (Double Trouble Ser.). 48p. (J). pap. 10.95 *(978-1-59381-123-5(3))*; lib. bdg. *(978-1-59381-122-8(5))* Ozark Publishing.

—Baldy Eagle: Honor. Sargent, Dave. 2003. (Feather Tales Ser.: 1). 42p. (J). pap. 6.95 *(978-1-56763-720-5(5))* Ozark Publishing.

—Bashful: (Dusty Dun) Be Brave. Sargent, Dave & Sargent, Pat. 2003. (Saddle up Ser.: Vol. 1). 42p. (J). pap. 10.95 *(978-1-56763-684-0(5))*; lib. bdg. 23.60 *(978-1-56763-683-3(7))* Ozark Publishing.

—Berry Picking Time Vol. 3: (Apache) Be Brave, 20 vols. Sargent, Dave et al. l.t. ed. 2003. (Story Keeper Ser.: 3). 42p. (J). Vol. 3. lib. bdg. 23.60 *(978-1-56763-907-0(0),* 1228136); vol. 3. pap. 6.95 *(978-1-56763-908-7(9),* 1228136) Ozark Publishing.

—The Black Panther, 6 vols., Vol. 2. Sargent, Pat. 2003. (Barney the Bear Killer Ser.: Vol. 2). 137p. (J). pap. 10.95 *(978-1-56763-966-7(6))*; lib. bdg. 26.25 *(978-1-56763-965-0(8))* Ozark Publishing.

—Blackie Crow: Tell the Truth, 20 vols. Sargent, Dave. 2003. (Feather Tales Ser.: No. 2). 42p. (J). Vol. 2. lib. bdg. 20.95 *(978-1-56763-721-2(3))*; vol. 2. pap. 6.95 *(978-1-56763-722-9(1))* Ozark Publishing.

—Bo: (Linebacked Orange Dun) Be Happy, 30 vols., Vol. 4. Sargent, Dave & Sargent, Pat. 2003. (Saddle up Ser.: Vol. 4). 42p. (J). lib. bdg. 23.60 *(978-1-56763-685-7(3))*; mass mkt. 10.95 *(978-1-56763-686-4(1))* Ozark Publishing.

—Bob White: Use Good Judgement, 20 vols., Vol. 3. Sargent, David M. 2003. (Feather Tales Ser.: No. 3). 42p. (J). lib. bdg. 20.95 *(978-1-56763-723-6(X))* Ozark Publishing.

—Bob White: Use Good Judgement, 20 vols., Vol. 3. Sargent, Dave & Sargent, David M. 2003. (Feather Tales Ser.: No. 3). 42p. (J). pap. 10.95 *(978-1-56763-724-3(8))* Ozark Publishing.

—The Bobcat, 6 vols., Vol. 5. Sargent, Pat. 2003. (Barney the Bear Killer Ser.: Vol. 5). 136p. (J). pap. 10.95 *(978-1-56763-972-8(0))*; lib. bdg. 26.25 *(978-1-56763-971-1(2))* Ozark Publishing.

—Bogart Blue Jay: Be Thoughtful, 19, vol. 4. Sargent, Dave. 2003. (Feather Tales Ser.: 4). 42p. (J). pap. *(978-1-56763-726-7(4))* Ozark Publishing.

—Bogart Blue Jay: Be Thoughtful, 20 vols., Vol. 4. Sargent, Dave & Sargent, David M. 2nd ed. 2003. (Feather Tales Ser.: 3). 42p. (J). lib. bdg. 20.95 *(978-1-56763-725-0(6))* Ozark Publishing.

—Brandy: (Blue Roan) Beauty Is Inside, 30 vols., Vol. 5. Sargent, Dave & Sargent, Pat. 2003. (Saddle up Ser.: Vol. 5). 42p. (J). lib. bdg. 23.60 *(978-1-56763-799-1(X))*; mass mkt. 10.95 *(978-1-56763-800-4(7))* Ozark Publishing.

—The Bundle Keeper: (Pawnee) Be Responsible, 20 vols., Vol. 18. Sargent, Dave et al. l.t. ed. 2004. (Story Keeper Ser.: 18). 48p. (J). pap. 10.95 *(978-1-56763-938-4(0))* Ozark Publishing.

—Buttons: (Muddy Dun) Have Courage, Vol. 9. Sargent, Dave & Sargent, Pat. 2003. (Saddle up Ser.: Vol. 9). 42p. (J). pap. 10.95 *(978-1-56763-688-8(8))*; lib. bdg. 23.60 *(978-1-56763-687-1(X))* Ozark Publishing.

—Buzz Buzzard: Obey the Rules, 19 vols., Vol. 5. Sargent, Dave & Sargent, David M. 2003. (Feather Tales Ser.: 5).

L

42p. (J). pap. 10.95 *(978-1-56763-728-1(0))*; 2nd ed. lib. bdg. 20.95 *(978-1-56763-727-4(2))* Ozark Publishing.

—The Cheetah, 6 vols., Vol. 6. Sargent, Pat L. l.t. ed. 2004. (Barney the Bear Killer Ser.: No. 6). 146p. (YA). pap. 10.95 *(978-1-56763-974-2(7))* Ozark Publishing.

—Chick: (Chocolate Chestnut) Be Loyal, 30 vols., Vol. 16. Sargent, Dave & Sargent, Pat. 2003. (Saddle up Ser.: Vol. 16). 42p. (J). pap. 10.95 *(978-1-56763-678-9(0))*; lib. bdg. 23.60 *(978-1-56763-677-2(2))* Ozark Publishing.

—The Chuck Wagon: Don't Be Stubborn, 10 vols., Vol. 7. Sargent, Dave & Sargent, Pat. 2005. (Colorado Cowboys Ser.: 10). 32p. (J). pap. 10.95 *(978-1-59381-099-3(7))*; lib. bdg. 23.60 *(978-1-59381-098-6(9))* Ozark Publishing.

—Cindy Sparrow: Respect the Property of Others, 19 vols., Vol. 6. Sargent, Dave & Sargent, David M. 2003. (Feather Tales Ser.: 6). 42p. (J). pap. 10.95 *(978-1-56763-730-4(2))*; 2nd ed. lib. bdg. 20.95 *(978-1-56763-729-8(9))* Ozark Publishing.

—The Colorado Blizzard: Be Determined, 10 vols., Vol. 8. Sargent, Dave & Sargent, Pat. (Colorado Cowboys Ser.: 10). 32p. (J). 2005. pap. 10.95 *(978-1-59381-027-6(X))*; 2004. (gr. 3-8). lib. bdg. 23.60 *(978-1-59381-026-9(1))* Ozark Publishing.

—Colors & the Number 1, 11 vols. Sargent, Daina. (Learn to Read Ser.: 11). 24p. (J). 2005. pap. 10.95 *(978-1-59381-031-3(8))*; 2004. lib. bdg. 20.95 *(978-1-59381-030-6(X))* Ozark Publishing.

—Colors & the Number 10, 11 vols. Sargent, Daina. 2004. (Learn to Read Ser.: 11). 24p. (J). pap. 10.95 *(978-1-59381-049-8(0))*; per. 9.95 *(978-1-59381-527-1(1))*; lib. bdg. 20.95 *(978-1-59381-048-1(2))* Ozark Publishing.

—Colors & the Number 10/Los Colores y el Número 10, 11 vols. Sargent, Daina. 2005. (Learn to Read Ser.: 11). (ENG & SPA.). 24p. (J). pap. 10.95 *(978-1-59381-147-1(0))*; lib. bdg. 20.95 *(978-1-59381-146-4(2))* Ozark Publishing.

—Colors & the Number 1/Los Colores y el Número 1, 11 vols. Sargent, Daina. 2004. (Learn to Read Ser.: 11). (SPA & ENG.). 24p. (J). pap. 10.95 *(978-1-59381-129-7(2))* Ozark Publishing.

—Colors & the Number 2, 11 vols. Sargent, Daina. 2004. (Learn to Read Ser.: 11). 24p. (J). pap. 10.95 *(978-1-59381-033-7(4))*; per. 10.95 *(978-1-59381-529-5(8))*; lib. bdg. 20.95 *(978-1-59381-032-0(6))* Ozark Publishing.

—Colors & the Number 2/Los Colores y el Número 2, 11 vols. Sargent, Daina. 2004. (Learn to Read Ser.: 11).Tr. of Los colores y el Número 2. (SPA & ENG.). 24p. (J). pap. 10.95 *(978-1-59381-131-0(4))*; lib. bdg. 20.95 *(978-1-59381-130-3(6))* Ozark Publishing.

—Colors & the Number 3, 11 vols. Sargent, Daina. 2004. (Learn to Read Ser.: 11). 24p. (J). pap. 10.95 *(978-1-59381-035-1(0))*; pap. 10.95 *(978-1-59381-530-1(1))* Ozark Publishing.

—Colors & the Number 3/Los Colores y el Número 3, 11 vols. Sargent, Daina. 2004. (Learn to Read Ser.: 11).Tr. of Los colores y el el Número 3. (SPA & ENG.). 24p. (J). pap. 10.95 *(978-1-59381-133-4(0))*; lib. bdg. 20.95 *(978-1-59381-132-7(2))* Ozark Publishing.

—Colors & the Number 4, 11 vols. Sargent, Daina. (Learn to Read Ser.). 24p. (J). 2005. pap. 10.95 *(978-1-59381-037-5(7))*; 2004. per. 10.95 *(978-1-59381-531-8(X))* Ozark Publishing.

—Colors & the Number 4/Los colores y el Número 4, 11 vols. Sargent, Daina. 2004. (Learn to Read Ser.: 11).Tr. of Los colores y el Número 4. (SPA & ENG.). 24p. (J). pap. 10.95 *(978-1-59381-135-8(7))*; lib. bdg. 20.95 *(978-1-59381-134-1(9))* Ozark Publishing.

—Colors & the Number 5, 11 vols. Sargent, Daina. 2004. (Learn to Read Ser.: 11). 24p. (J). pap. 10.95 *(978-1-59381-039-9(3))*; per. 10.95 *(978-1-59381-532-5(8))* Ozark Publishing.

—Colors & the Number 5/Los colores y el Número 5, 11 vols. Sargent, Daina. 2004. (Learn to Read Ser.: 11).Tr. of Los colores y el Número 5. (SPA & ENG.). 24p. (J). pap. 10.95 *(978-1-59381-137-2(3))*; lib. bdg. 20.95 *(978-1-59381-136-5(5))* Ozark Publishing.

—Colors & the Number 6, 11 vols. Sargent, Daina. 2004. (Learn to Read Ser.: 11). 24p. (J). pap. 10.95 *(978-1-59381-041-2(5))*; per. 10.95 *(978-1-59381-533-2(6))*; lib. bdg. 20.95 *(978-1-59381-040-5(7))* Ozark Publishing.

—Colors & the Number 6/Los Colores y el Número 6, 11 vols. Sargent, Daina. 2005. (Learn to Read Ser.: 11). (ENG & SPA.). 24p. (J). pap. 10.95 *(978-1-59381-139-6(X))* Ozark Publishing.

—Colors & the Number 7, 11 vols. Sargent, Daina. 2004. (Learn to Read Ser.: 11). 24p. (J). pap. 10.95 *(978-1-59381-043-6(1))*; per. 10.95 *(978-1-59381-534-9(4))*; lib. bdg. 20.95 *(978-1-59381-042-9(3))* Ozark Publishing.

—Colors & the Number 7/Los Colores y el Número 7, 11 vols. Sargent, Daina. 2004. (Learn to Read Ser.: 11).Tr. of Los colores y el Número 7. (SPA & ENG.). 24p. (J). pap. 10.95 *(978-1-59381-141-9(1))*; lib. bdg. 20.95 *(978-1-59381-140-2(3))* Ozark Publishing.

—Colors & the Number 8, 11 vols. Sargent, Daina. 2004. (Learn to Read Ser.: 11). 24p. (J). pap. 10.95 *(978-1-59381-045-0(8))*; lib. bdg. 20.95 *(978-1-59381-044-3(X))* Ozark Publishing.

—Colors & the Number 8/Los Colores y el Número 8, 11 vols. Sargent, Daina. 2004. (Learn to Read Ser.: 11).Tr. of Los colores y el Número 8. (SPA & ENG.). 24p. (J). pap. 10.95 *(978-1-59381-143-3(8))*; lib. bdg. 20.95 *(978-1-59381-142-6(X))* Ozark Publishing.

—Colors & the Number 9, 11 vols. Sargent, Daina. 2004. (Learn to Read Ser.: 11). 24p. (J). pap. 10.95 *(978-1-59381-047-4(4))*; lib. bdg. 20.95 *(978-1-59381-046-7(6))* Ozark Publishing.

—Colors & the Number 9/Los Colores y el Número 9, 11 vols. Sargent, Daina. 2004. (Learn to Read Ser.: 11).Tr. of Los colores y el Número 9. (SPA & ENG.). 24p. (J). pap. 10.95 *(978-1-59381-145-7(4))*; lib. bdg. 20.95 *(978-1-59381-144-0(6))* Ozark Publishing.

—Counting Coup Vol. 4: (Cheyenee) Be Proud, 20 vols. Sargent, Dave et al. l.t. ed. 2003. (Story Keeper Ser.). 42p. (J). lib. bdg. 23.60 *(978-1-56763-909-4(7))* Ozark Publishing.

—Cricket: (Seal Brown) Do Your Best, 30. Sargent, Dave & Sargent, Pat. 2003. (Saddle up Ser.: Vol. 20). 42p. (J). 20. lib. bdg. 22.60 *(978-1-56763-649-9(7))*; Vol. 20. pap. 10.95 *(978-1-56763-650-5(0))* Ozark Publishing.

—Dinky Duck: Be Prompt, 19 vols., Vol. 7. Sargent, Dave & Sargent, David M., Jr. 2003. (Feather Tales Ser.: 7). 42p. (J). pap. 10.95 *(978-1-56763-732-8(9))*; 2nd ed. lib. bdg. 20.95 *(978-1-56763-731-1(0))* Ozark Publishing.

—The Drought: Have Faith, 10 vols., Vol. 9. Sargent, Dave & Sargent, Pat. 2005. (Colorado Cowboys Ser.: 10). 32p. (J). pap. 10.95 *(978-1-59381-103-7(9))*; lib. bdg. 23.60 *(978-1-59381-102-0(0))* Ozark Publishing.

—Duke: (Dappled Palomino) Good Behavior, 30 vols., Vol. 23. Sargent, Dave & Sargent, Pat. 2003. (Saddle up Ser.: Vol. 23). 42p. (J). pap. 10.95 *(978-1-56763-682-6(9))*; lib. bdg. 23.60 *(978-1-56763-681-9(0))* Ozark Publishing.

—Dusty: (Grey Sabino) Be Helpful, 30 vols., Vol. 24. Sargent, Dave & Sargent, Pat. 2003. (Saddle up Ser.: Vol. 24). 42p. (J). pap. 10.95 *(978-1-56763-808-0(2))*; lib. bdg. 23.60 *(978-1-56763-807-3(4))* Ozark Publishing.

—Fields of Golden Corn Vol. 6: (Navajo) Be Energetic, 20 vols. Sargent, Dave et al. l.t. ed. 2003. (Story Keeper Ser.: 6). 42p. (J). pap. 10.95 *(978-1-56763-914-8(3))*; lib. bdg. 23.60 *(978-1-56763-913-1(5))* Ozark Publishing.

—Fierce Warriors Vol. 7: (Comanche) Learn Skills, 20 vols. Sargent, Dave et al. l.t. ed. 2004. (Story Keeper Ser.: 7). 48p. (J). pap. 10.95 *(978-1-56763-916-2(X))* Ozark Publishing.

—The Fire: A Second Chance, 10 vols., Vol. 10. Sargent, Dave & Sargent, Pat. 2005. (Colorado Cowboys Ser.: 10). 32p. (J). pap. 10.95 *(978-1-59381-105-1(5))* Ozark Publishing.

—Freckles: (Flea-bitten Grey) Be Proud of Old Glory, 30 vols., Vol. 26. Sargent, Dave & Sargent, Pat. 2003. (Saddle up Ser.: Vol. 26). 42p. (J). pap. 10.95 *(978-1-56763-810-3(4))*; lib. bdg. 23.60 *(978-1-56763-809-7(0))* Ozark Publishing.

—Ginger: (Lilac Roan) Be Likeable, 30 vols., Vol. 27. Sargent, Dave & Sargent, Pat. 2003. (Saddle up Ser.: Vol. 27). 42p. (J). pap. 10.95 *(978-1-56763-812-7(0))*; lib. bdg. 23.60 *(978-1-56763-811-0(2))* Ozark Publishing.

—Glenda Goose: Sharing, 19 vols., Vol. 8. Sargent, Dave & Sargent, David M., Jr. 2003. (Feather Tales Ser.: 8). 42p. (J). pap. 10.95 *(978-1-56763-734-2(5))*; 2nd ed. lib. bdg. 20.95 *(978-1-56763-733-5(7))* Ozark Publishing.

—Goober: (Silver Dapple) Appreciate Others, 30 vols., Vol. 29. Sargent, Dave & Sargent, Pat. 2003. (Saddle up Ser.: Vol. 29). 42p. (J). lib. bdg. 23.60 *(978-1-56763-689-5(6))* Ozark Publishing.

—Goober: (Silver Dapple) Appreciate Others, 30 vols., Vol. 29. Sargent, Dave & Sargent, Pat. 2004. (Saddle up Ser.: Vol. 29). 42p. (J). pap. 10.95 *(978-1-56763-690-1(X))* Ozark Publishing.

—Grady: (Dappled Grey) Proud to Be an American, 30 vols., Vol. 30. Sargent, Dave & Sargent, Pat. 2003. (Saddle up Ser.: Vol. 30). 42p. (J). lib. bdg. 23.60 *(978-1-56763-813-4(9))* Ozark Publishing.

—Grady: Proud to Be an American, 30 vols. Sargent, Dave & Sargent, Pat. 2003. (Saddle up Ser.: Vol. 30). 42p. (J). pap. 10.95 *(978-1-56763-814-1(7))* Ozark Publishing.

—The Grizzly, 6 vols., Vol. 1. Sargent, Pat L. 2004. (Barney the Bear Killer Ser.: No. 1). 129p. (YA). pap. 10.95 *(978-1-56763-964-3(X))* Ozark Publishing.

—Gus: (Slate Grullo) Be Thankful, 30 vols., Vol. 32. Sargent, Dave & Sargent, Pat. 2003. (Saddle up Ser.: Vol. 32). 42p. (J). lib. bdg. 23.60 *(978-1-56763-693-2(4))*; pap. 10.95 *(978-1-56763-694-9(2))* Ozark Publishing.

—A Hole in the Sun: (Choctaw) Be Independent, 20, Vol. 1. Sargent, Dave et al. l.t. ed. 2003. (Story Keeper Ser.: 1). 42p. (J). pap. 6.95 *(978-1-56763-904-9(6))*; lib. bdg. 23.60 *(978-1-56763-903-2(8))* Ozark Publishing.

—Hondo: (Silver Dun) Look for Good in Others, 30 vols., Vol. 34. Sargent, Dave & Sargent, Pat. 2003. (Saddle up Ser.: Vol. 34). 42p. (J). pap. 10.95 *(978-1-56763-802-8(3))*; lib. bdg. 23.60 *(978-1-56763-801-1(5))* Ozark Publishing.

—Hoot: (Grullo) Be Creative, 30. Sargent, Dave & Sargent, Pat. 2003. (Saddle up Ser.: Vol. 35). 42p. (J). 35. pap. 6.95 *(978-1-56763-696-3(9))*; Vol. 35. lib. bdg. 23.60 *(978-1-56763-695-6(0))* Ozark Publishing.

—Hoot Owl: Mind Your Mamma, 19 vols., Vol. 9. Sargent, Dave & Sargent, David, Jr. 2003. (Feather Tales Ser.: 9). 42p. (J). pap. 10.95 *(978-1-56763-736-6(1))* Ozark Publishing.

—Hoot Owl: Mind Your Mamma, 20 vols., Vol. 9. Sargent, Dave & Sargent, David M., Jr. 2nd ed. 2003. (Feather Tales Ser.: 9). 42p. (J). lib. bdg. *(978-1-56763-735-9(3))* Ozark Publishing.

—Hummer Hummingbird: Being Small Is Okay, 19. Sargent, Dave & Sargent, David, Jr. 2003. (Feather Tales Ser.: 10). (J). 10. 42p. pap. 6.95 *(978-1-56763-738-0(8))*; Vol. 10. 2nd ed. 24p. lib. bdg. 20.95 *(978-1-56763-737-3(X))* Ozark Publishing.

—Introduction to Colors & Niumbers, 11 vols. Sargent, Daina. 2005. (Learn to Read Ser.: 11). 24p. (J). pap. 10.95 *(978-1-59381-051-1(2))* Ozark Publishing.

—Introduction to Colors & Numbers, 11 vols. Sargent, Daina. (Learn to Read Ser.: 11). 24p. (J). 2005. per. 10.95 *(978-1-59381-528-8(X))*; 2004. lib. bdg. 20.95 *(978-1-59381-050-4(4))* Ozark Publishing.

—Introduction to Colors & Numbers (BL) Introduccion a los colores y a los Numeros, 11 vols. Sargent, Daina. 2004. (Learn to Read Ser.: 11). (SPA & ENG.). 24p. (J). lib. bdg. 20.95 *(978-1-59381-148-8(9))* Ozark Publishing.

—Introduction to Colors & Numbers/Introduccion a los Colores Numeros, 11 vols. Sargent, Daina. l.t. ed. 2005. (Learn to Read Ser.: 11). (SPA & ENG.). 24p. (J). pap. 10.95 *(978-1-59381-149-5(7))* Ozark Publishing.

—The Jaguar, 8 vols. Sargent, Pat L. 2007. (Barney the Bear Killer Ser.: 8). 164p. (YA). lib. bdg. 26.25 *(978-1-59381-424-3(0))* Ozark Publishing.

—Kansas: Conquer Fear. Sargent, Daina. l.t. ed. 2004. (Double Trouble Ser.). 48p. (J). pap. 10.95 *(978-1-59381-125-9(X))*; lib. bdg. 23.60 *(978-1-59381-124-2(1))* Ozark Publishing.

—Keeping Ghosts Away Vol. 8: (Creek) Be Respectful, 20 vols. Sargent, Dave et al. l.t. ed. 2003. (Story Keeper Ser.: Vol. 8). 42p. (J). pap. 10.95 *(978-1-56763-918-6(6)*, 1228135) Ozark Publishing.

—Kitty Hawk: Stealing, 20. Sargent, Dave & Sargent, David, Jr. 2003. (Feather Tales Ser.: 11). 42p. (J). 11. pap. 6.95 *(978-1-56763-740-3(X))*; Vol. 11. 2nd ed. lib. bdg. 20.95 *(978-1-56763-739-7(6))* Ozark Publishing.

—Knocking the Rice Vol. 9: (Chippewa) Be Powerful, 20 vols. Sargent, Dave et al. l.t. ed. 2003. (Story Keeper Ser.: 9). 42p. (J). pap. 10.95 *(978-1-56763-920-9(8))*; lib. bdg. 23.60 *(978-1-56763-919-3(4))* Ozark Publishing.

—Ladder at the Door Vol. 10: (Hopi) Be Curious, 20 vols. Sargent, Dave et al. l.t. ed. 2004. (Story Keeper Ser.: 10). 48p. (J). pap. 10.95 *(978-1-56763-922-3(4))*; lib. bdg. 23.60 *(978-1-56763-921-6(6))* Ozark Publishing.

—Land of the Sun Vol. 11: (Ute) Respect Elders, 20 vols., Vol. 11. Sargent, Dave et al. l.t. ed. 2004. (Story Keeper Ser.: 11). 48p. (J). lib. bdg. 23.60 *(978-1-56763-923-0(2))*; pap. 10.95 *(978-1-56763-924-7(0))* Ozark Publishing.

—Lily: (Lilac Dun) A Second Chance, 30 vols., Vol. 38. Sargent, Dave & Sargent, Pat. 2003. (Saddle up Ser.: Vol. 38). 42p. (J). pap. 10.95 *(978-1-56763-698-7(5))*; lib. bdg. 23.60 *(978-1-56763-697-0(7))* Ozark Publishing.

—Little One Vol. 12: (Cherokee) Be Inventive, 20 vols. Sargent, Dave et al. l.t. ed. 2003. (Story Keeper Ser.: Vol. 12). 42p. (J). pap. 10.95 *(978-1-56763-926-1(7))*; Vol. 12. lib. bdg. 23.60 *(978-1-56763-925-4(9))* Ozark Publishing.

—Mack: (Medicine Hat Paint) Be a Leader, 30 vols., Vol. 39. Sargent, Dave & Sargent, Pat. 2003. (Saddle up Ser.: Vol. 39). 42p. (J). pap. 10.95 *(978-1-56763-700-7(0))* Ozark Publishing.

—Missouri: Teamwork. Sargent, Daina. l.t. ed. 2004. (Double Trouble Ser.). 48p. (J). pap. 10.95 *(978-1-59381-127-3(6))*; lib. bdg. 23.60 *(978-1-59381-126-6(8))* Ozark Publishing.

—Nick: (Linebacked Claybank Dun) Crime Does Not Pay, 30 vols., Vol. 42. Sargent, Dave & Sargent, Pat. 2003. (Saddle up Ser.: Vol. 42). 42p. (J). pap. 10.95 *(978-1-56763-702-1(7))*; lib. bdg. 23.60 *(978-1-56763-701-4(9))* Ozark Publishing.

—Nubbin: (Linebacked Apricot Dun) Freedom, 30 vols., Vol. 43. Sargent, Dave & Sargent, Pat. 2003. (Saddle up Ser.: Vol. 43). 42p. (J). pap. 10.95 *(978-1-56763-704-5(3))*; lib. bdg. 23.60 *(978-1-56763-703-8(5))* Ozark Publishing.

—On the Banks of the Wallowa River: (Nez Perce) Use Your Talent, 20 vols., Vol. 13. Sargent, Dave et al. l.t. ed. 2004. (Story Keeper Ser.: 13). 48p. (J). pap. 10.95 *(978-1-56763-928-5(3))*; lib. bdg. 23.60 *(978-1-56763-927-8(5))* Ozark Publishing.

—Once upon a Totem Pole Vol. 14: (Haida) Be Creative, 20 vols. Sargent, Dave et al. l.t. ed. 2003. (Story Keeper Ser.: 14). 42p. (J). pap. 10.95 *(978-1-56763-930-8(5))*; Vol. 14. lib. bdg. 23.60 *(978-1-56763-929-2(1))* Ozark Publishing.

—Pammie Pigeon: Keep Your Cool, 19 vols., Vol. 12. Sargent, Dave & Sargent, David M., Jr. 2003. (Feather Tales Ser.: 12). 42p. (J). pap. 10.95 *(978-1-56763-742-7(6))*; 2nd ed. lib. bdg. 20.95 *(978-1-56763-741-0(8))* Ozark Publishing.

—Penny Penguin: Be Kind to Others, 20 vols., Vol. 13. Sargent, Dave & Sargent, David M., Jr. 2nd ed. 2003. (Feather Tales Ser.: 13). 42p. (J). lib. bdg. 20.95 *(978-1-56763-743-4(4))* Ozark Publishing.

—Pete: (Pink-skinned Palomino) Be a Hero, 30 vols., Vol. 46. Sargent, Dave & Sargent, Pat. 2003. (Saddle up Ser.: Vol. 46). 42p. (J). lib. bdg. 23.60 *(978-1-56763-707-6(8))* Ozark Publishing.

—Pete: Pink-skinned Palomino) Be a Hero, 30 vols., Vol. 46. Sargent, Dave & Sargent, Pat. 2003. (Saddle up Ser.: Vol. 46). 42p. (J). pap. 10.95 *(978-1-56763-708-3(6))* Ozark Publishing.

—Petie Pelican: Be Proud of Yourself, 19 vols., Vol. 14. Sargent, Dave & Sargent, David M., Jr. 2003. (Feather Tales Ser.: 14). 42p. (J). pap. 10.95 *(978-1-56763-746-5(9))* Ozark Publishing.

—Petie Pelican: Be Proud of Yourself, 20 vols., Vol. 14. Sargent, Dave & Sargent, David, Jr. 2nd ed. 2003. (Feather Tales Ser.: 14). 42p. (J). lib. bdg. 20.95 *(978-1-56763-745-8(0))* Ozark Publishing.

—Pinkie Flamingo: Leaving Home, 19 vols., Vol. 15. Sargent, Dave & Sargent, David, Jr. 2003. (Feather Tales Ser.: 15). 42p. (J). pap. 10.95 *(978-1-56763-748-9(5))*; 2nd ed. lib. bdg. 20.95 *(978-1-56763-747-2(7))* Ozark Publishing.

—Ranger: (Olive Grullo) Be Honest, 30 vols., Vol. 48. Sargent, Dave & Sargent, Pat. 2003. (Saddle up Ser.: Vol. 48). 42p. (J). pap. 10.95 *(978-1-56763-710-6(8))*; lib. bdg. 23.60 *(978-1-56763-709-0(4))* Ozark Publishing.

—Rascal: (Red Dun) Responsible Leadership, 30 vols., Vol. 49. Sargent, Dave & Sargent, Pat. 2003. (Saddle up Ser.: Vol. 49). 42p. (J). pap. 10.95 *(978-1-56763-712-0(4))* Ozark Publishing.

—Rays of the Sun Vol. 15: (shoshone) Learn Lessons, 20 vols. Sargent, Dave et al. l.t. ed. 2004. (Story Keeper Ser.: 15). 48p. (J). pap. 10.95 *(978-1-56763-932-2(1))* Ozark Publishing.

—Rays of the Sun Vol. 15: (Shoshone) Learn Lessons, 20 vols. Sargent, Dave et al. l.t. ed. 2004. (Story Keeper Ser.: 15). 48p. (J). lib. bdg. 23.60 *(978-1-56763-931-5(3))* Ozark Publishing.

—Rocky: (Blue-eyed Palomino) Be Free, 30 vols., Vol. 51. Sargent, Dave & Sargent, Pat. 2003. (Saddle up Ser.: Vol. 51). 42p. (J). lib. bdg. 23.60 *(978-1-56763-713-7(2))* Ozark Publishing.

—Rusty: (Red Roan) Be Strong & Brave, 30 vols., Vol. 52. Sargent, Dave & Sargent, Pat. 2003. (Saddle up Ser.: Vol. 52). 42p. (J). pap. 10.95 *(978-1-56763-804-2(X))*; lib. bdg. 23.60 *(978-1-56763-803-5(1))* Ozark Publishing.

—Sandy Sea Gull: Making Friends, 20 vols., Vol. 16. Sargent, Dave & Sargent, David, Jr. 2nd ed. 2003. (Feather Tales Ser.: 16). 42p. (J). lib. bdg. 20.95 *(978-1-56763-749-6(3))* Ozark Publishing.

—Sonny: (Linebacked Yellow Dun) Have Orderly Manners, 30 vols., Vol. 54. Sargent, Dave & Sargent, Pat. 2003. (Saddle up Ser.: Vol. 54). 42p. (J). lib. bdg. 23.60 *(978-1-56763-715-1(9))* Ozark Publishing.

—Sonny: (Linebacked Yllow Dun) Have Orderly Manners, 30 vols., Vol. 54. Sargent, Dave & Sargent, Pat. 2003. (Saddle up Ser.: Vol. 54). 42p. (J). pap. 10.95 *(978-1-56763-716-8(7))* Ozark Publishing.

—Speedy Roadrunner: Helping Others, 19 vols., Vol. 17. Sargent, Dave & Sargent, David M., Jr. 2003. (Feather Tales Ser.: 17). 42p. (J). pap. 10.95 *(978-1-56763-752-6(3))*; 2nd ed. lib. bdg. 20.95 *(978-1-56763-751-9(5))* Ozark Publishing.

—Storky Stork: Be Trustworthy, 19 vols., Vol. 18. Sargent, Dave. 2003. (Feather Tales Ser.: 18). 42p. (J). pap. 10.95 *(978-1-56763-754-0(X))* Ozark Publishing.

—Storky Stork: Be Trustworthy, 20 vols., Vol. 18. Sargent, Dave & Sargent, David, Jr. 2nd ed. 2003. (Feather Tales Ser.: 18). 42p. (J). lib. bdg. 20.95 *(978-1-56763-753-3(1))* Ozark Publishing.

—A Strand of Wampum Vol. 2: Be Honest, 20 vols. Sargent, Dave et al. l.t. ed. 2003. (Story Keeper Ser.: 2). 42p. (J). lib. bdg. 23.60 *(978-1-56763-905-6(4))* Ozark Publishing.

—Summer Milky Way: (Blackfeet) Be Compassionate, 20 vols., Vol. 16. Sargent, Dave et al. l.t. ed. 2004. (Story Keeper Ser.). 48p. (J). lib. bdg. 23.60 *(978-1-56763-933-9(X))*; pap. 10.95 *(978-1-56763-934-6(8))* Ozark Publishing.

—Sweetpea: (Purple Corn Welsh) Be Happy, 30 vols., Vol. 58. Sargent, Dave & Sargent, Pat. 2003. (Saddle up Ser.: Vol. 58). 42p. (J). pap. 10.95 *(978-1-56763-816-5(3))*; lib. bdg. 23.60 *(978-1-56763-815-8(5))* Ozark Publishing.

—Tattoos of Honor Vol. 17: (Osage) Be Gentle & Giving, 20 vols. Sargent, Dave et al. l.t. ed. 2004. (Story Keeper Ser.: Vol. 17). 42p. (J). pap. 10.95 *(978-1-56763-936-0(4))*; lib. bdg. 23.60 *(978-1-56763-935-3(6))* Ozark Publishing.

—The Timber Wolf, 6 vols., Vol. 3. Sargent, Pat. 2003. (Barney the Bear Killer Ser.: Vol. 3). 123p. (J). pap. 10.95 *(978-1-56763-968-1(2))*; lib. bdg. 26.25 *(978-1-56763-967-4(4))* Ozark Publishing.

—Tin Wren: Be Nice, 19 vols., Vol. 19. Sargent, Dave & Sargent, David, Jr. 2003. (Feather Tales Ser.: No. 19). 42p. (J). pap. 10.95 *(978-1-56763-756-4(6))*; 2nd ed. lib. bdg. 20.95 *(978-1-56763-755-7(8))* Ozark Publishing.

—Tom Turkey: Don't Bully, 19. Sargent, Dave & Sargent, David, Jr. 2003. (Feather Tales Ser.: 20). 42p. (J). 20. pap. 6.95 *(978-1-56763-758-8(2))*; Vol. 20. 2nd ed. lib. bdg. 20.95 *(978-1-56763-757-1(4))* Ozark Publishing.

—Topper: Son of Barney, 8. Sargent, Pat L. 2007. (Barney the Bear Killer Ser.: 7). 147p. (YA). lib. bdg. 25.25 *(978-1-56763-425-9(7))* Ozark Publishing.

—Tornado & Sweep, Bk. II. Sargent, Dave. Bowen, Debbie, ed. Zapata, Miguel, tr. from ENG. (SPA.). (Orig.). (J). (gr. k-6). pap. 6.95 *(978-1-56763-123-4(1))*; pap. 6.95 *(978-1-56763-126-5(6))* Ozark Publishing.

—Truth, Power & Freedom Vol. 19: (Sioux) Show Respect, 20 vols., Vol. 19. Sargent, Dave et al. l.t. ed. 2004. (Story Keeper Ser.: 19). 42p. (J). pap. 10.95 *(978-1-56763-940-7(2))* Ozark Publishing.

—Valley Oak Acorns: (Maidu) Be Helpful, 20 vols., Vol. 20. Sargent, Dave & Sargent, Pat. l.t. ed. 2005. (Story Keeper Ser.: 20). 42p. (J). (gr. -1 — 1). lib. bdg. 23.60 *(978-1-56763-941-4(0))* Ozark Publishing.

—Valley Oaks Acorns Vol. 20: (Maidu) Be Helpful, 20 vols. Sargent, Dave et al. l.t. ed. 2004. (Story Keeper Ser.: 20). 48p. (J). pap. 10.95 *(978-1-56763-942-1(9))* Ozark Publishing.

—Whiskers: (Roan) Pride & Peace, 30 vols., Vol. 59. Sargent, Dave & Sargent, Pat. 2003. (Saddle up Ser.: Vol. 59). 42p. (J). pap. 10.95 *(978-1-56763-806-6(9))* Ozark Publishing.

—Zeb: (Zebra Dun) Be Prepared, 30 vols., Vol. 60. Sargent, Dave & Sargent, Pat. 2003. (Saddle up Ser.: Vol. 60). 42p. (J). pap. 10.95 *(978-1-56763-718-2(3))*; lib. bdg. 23.60 *(978-1-56763-717-5(5))* Ozark Publishing.

Lenoir, Maarten. Frog Moves Out of the Rain Forest. Potts, Nikki. 2020. (Habitat Hunter Ser.). (ENG.). 32p. (J). (gr. -1-2). pap. 8.95 *(978-1-9771-2021-2(0)*, 142311); lib. bdg. 29.32 *(978-1-9771-1423-5(7)*, 141551) Capstone. (Picture Window Bks.).

—Goat Moves Out of the Barnyard. Potts, Nikki. 2020. (Habitat Hunter Ser.). (ENG.). 32p. (J). (gr. -1-2). pap. 8.95 *(978-1-9771-2019-9(9)*, 142309); lib. bdg. 29.32 *(978-1-9771-1421-1(0)*, 141549) Capstone. (Picture Window Bks.).

—Habitat Hunter. Potts, Nikki. 2020. (Habitat Hunter Ser.). (ENG.). (J). (gr. -1-2). 175.92 *(978-1-9771-1431-0(8)*, 29796); pap., pap., pap. 53.70 *(978-1-9771-2078-6(4)*, 30101) Capstone. (Picture Window Bks.).

—Meerkat Moves Out of the Desert. Potts, Nikki. 2020. (Habitat Hunter Ser.). (ENG.). 32p. (J). (gr. -1-2). pap. 8.95 *(978-1-9771-2017-5(2)*, 142307); lib. bdg. 29.32 *(978-1-9771-1419-8(9)*, 141548) Capstone. (Picture Window Bks.).

—Owl Moves Out of the Forest. Potts, Nikki. 2020. (Habitat Hunter Ser.). (ENG.). 32p. (J). (gr. -1-2). pap. 8.95 *(978-1-9771-2022-9(9)*, 142312); lib. bdg. 29.32 *(978-1-9771-1424-2(5)*, 141552) Capstone. (Picture Window Bks.).

—Penguin Moves Out of the Antarctic. Potts, Nikki. 2020. (Habitat Hunter Ser.). (ENG.). 32p. (J). (gr. -1-2). pap. 8.95 *(978-1-9771-2020-5(2)*, 142310); lib. bdg. 29.32 *(978-1-9771-1422-8(9)*, 141550) Capstone. (Picture Window Bks.).

—Shark Moves Out of the Ocean. Potts, Nikki. 2020. (Habitat Hunter Ser.). (ENG.). 32p. (J). (gr. -1-2). pap. 8.95 *(978-1-9771-2018-2(0)*, 142308); lib. bdg. 29.32 *(978-1-9771-1420-4(2)*, 141547) Capstone. (Picture Window Bks.).

—Taking a Spin. Arrow, Emily. 2019. (My Feelings, My Choices Ser.). (ENG.). 24p. (J). (gr. -1-2). 33.99 *(978-1-68410-406-2(8)*, 141216) Cantata Learning.

Lenoir, Sue. The Bundle Keeper: (Pawnee) Be Responsible, 20 vols., Vol. 18. Sargent, Dave et al. 2004. (Story Keeper Ser.: No. 18). 42p. (J). lib. bdg. 23.60 *(978-1-56763-937-7(2))* Ozark Publishing.
—A Strand of Wampum Vol. 2: Be Honest, 20 vols. Sargent, Dave et al. l.t. ed. 2003. (Story Keeper Ser.: 2). 42p. (J). pap. 10.95 *(978-1-56763-906-3(2))* Ozark Publishing.
Lenox, August. Roy Rogers' Bullet & Trigger: Wild Horse Roundup. Beecher, Elizabeth. 2011. 28p. pap. 35.95 *(978-1-258-03850-2(1))* Literary Licensing, LLC.
Lensch, Chris. Comportamiento y Modales en la Cafetería. Tourville, Amanda Doering. 2011. (¡Así Debemos Ser!: Buenos Modales, Buen Comportamiento/Way to Be!: Manners Ser.).Tr. of Manners in the Lunchroom. (ENG.). 24p. (J). (gr. -1-2). lib. bdg. 27.32 *(978-1-4048-6695-9(7),* Picture Window Bks.) Capstone.
—Coral Reef: Hide & Seek. 2005. (ENG.). 10p. (J). bds. 7.95 *(978-1-58117-362-8(8),* Intervisual/Piggy Toes) Bendon, Inc.
—Manners at a Friend's House, 1 vol. Tourville, Amanda Doering. 2009. (Way to Be!: Manners Ser.). (ENG.). 24p. (J). (gr. -1-2). pap. 7.95 *(978-1-4048-5306-5(5));* lib. bdg. 27.32 *(978-1-4048-5305-8(7))* Capstone. (Picture Window Bks.).
—Manners at School, 1 vol. Finn, Carrie. (Way to Be!: Manners Ser.). 2010. (ENG.). 32p. 8.99 *(978-1-4048-6511-2(X));* 2009. 24p. (gr. -1-2). pap. 0.63 *(978-1-4048-5991-3(8));* 2009. 24p. (gr. -1-2). pap. 2.76 *(978-1-4048-6050-6(9))* Capstone. (Picture Window Bks.).
—Manners at School [Scholastic]. Finn, Carrie. 2010. (Way to Be!: Manners Ser.). 24p. pap. 0.55 *(978-1-4048-6584-6(5),* Picture Window Bks.) Capstone.
—Manners at the Table. Finn, Carrie. (Way to Be!: Manners Ser.). 24p. (gr. -1-2). 2009. pap. 0.63 *(978-1-4048-5992-0(6));* 2007. (ENG.). (J). per. 7.95 *(978-1-4048-3553-5(9))* Capstone. (Picture Window Bks.).
—Manners in Public. Finn, Carrie. (Way to Be!: Manners Ser.). 24p. (gr. -1-2). 2009. pap. 0.63 *(978-1-4048-5993-7(4));* 2007. (ENG.). (J). per. 7.95 *(978-1-4048-3555-9(5))* Capstone. (Picture Window Bks.).
—Manners in the Library. Finn, Carrie. (Way to Be!: Manners Ser.). 24p. (gr. -1-2). 2009. pap. 0.63 *(978-1-4048-5994-4(2));* 2007. (ENG.). (J). lib. bdg. 27.32 *(978-1-4048-3152-0(5),* 1265722); 2007. (ENG.). (J). per. 7.95 *(978-1-4048-3557-3(1),* 1265722) Capstone. (Picture Window Bks.).
—Manners in the Lunchroom. Doering Tourville, Amanda. 2009. (Way to Be!: Manners Ser.). 24p. (gr. -1-2). pap. 2.76 *(978-1-4048-6051-3(7));* (ENG.). (J). 27.32 *(978-1-4048-5308-9(1))* Capstone. (Picture Window Bks.).
—Manners on the Playground. Finn, Carrie. (Way to Be!: Manners Ser.). 24p. (gr. -1-2). 2009. pap. 0.63 *(978-1-4048-5995-1(0));* 2009. pap. 2.76 *(978-1-4048-6053-7(3));* 2007. (ENG.). (J). per. 7.95 *(978-1-4048-3559-7(8))* Capstone. (Picture Window Bks.).
—Manners on the School Bus, 1 vol. Doering Tourville, Amanda. 2009. (Way to Be!: Manners Ser.). 24p. (gr. -1-2). (ENG.). (J). pap. 7.95 *(978-1-4048-5312-6(X));* pap. 2.76 *(978-1-4048-6052-0(5))* Capstone. (Picture Window Bks.).
—Manners on the Telephone. Finn, Carrie. (Way to Be!: Manners Ser.). 24p. (gr. -1-2). 2009. pap. 0.63 *(978-1-4048-5996-8(9));* 2007. (ENG.). (J). per. 7.95 *(978-1-4048-3561-0(X))* Capstone. (Picture Window Bks.).
—Manners with a Library Book, 1 vol. Tourville, Amanda Doering. 2009. (Way to Be!: Manners Ser.). (ENG.). 24p. (J). (gr. -1-2). lib. bdg. 27.32 *(978-1-4048-5314-0(6),* Picture Window Bks.) Capstone.
—Manners with a Library Book, 1 vol. Doering Tourville, Amanda. 2009. (Way to Be!: Manners Ser.). (ENG.). 24p. (J). (gr. -1-2). pap. 7.95 *(978-1-4048-5315-7(4),* Picture Window Bks.) Capstone.
—Who's Hiding Inside? Dinosaurs. Perez, Jessica. 2005. (Who's Hiding Inside Ser.). 12p. (J). bds. 7.95 *(978-1-58117-246-1(X),* Intervisual/Piggy Toes) Bendon, Inc.
Lenski, Lois. Betsy-Tacy. Lovelace, Maud Hart. 60th anniv. ed. 2007. (Betsy-Tacy Ser.: 1). (ENG.). 144p. (J). (gr. 2-5). pap. 6.99 *(978-0-06-440096-1(4),* HarperCollins) HarperCollins Pubs. Ltd. GBR. Dist: HarperCollins Pubs.
—A Letter to Popsey. La Rue, Mabel Guinnip. 2011. 28p. pap. 35.95 *(978-1-258-06342-9(5))* Literary Licensing, LLC.
Lenski, Lois. Cowboy Small. Lenski, Lois. 2006. (Lois Lenski Bks.). 32p. (J). (gr. -1-2). bds. 6.99 *(978-0-375-83570-4(9),* Random Hse. Bks. for Young Readers) Random Hse. Children's Bks.
—The Little Airplane. Lenski, Lois. 2003. 56p. (J). (gr. -1-k). reprint ed. 11.95 *(978-0-375-81079-4(X),* Random Hse. Bks. for Young Readers) Random Hse. Children's Bks.
—Policeman Small. Lenski, Lois. 2006. (Lois Lenski Bks.). 32p. (J). (— 1). bds. 6.99 *(978-0-375-83569-8(5),* Random Hse. Bks. for Young Readers) Random Hse. Children's Bks.
—Strawberry Girl 60th Anniversary Edition. Lenski, Lois. 60th anniv. ed. 2005. (ENG.). 208p. (J). (gr. 5-18). pap. 7.99 *(978-0-06-440585-0(0),* HarperCollins) HarperCollins Pubs. Ltd. GBR. Dist: HarperCollins Pubs.
Lent, Blair. Tikki Tikki Tembo. Mosel, Arlene. 2008. (gr. k-2). 16.95 *(978-0-7569-8457-1(2))* Perfection Learning Corp.
—Tikki Tikki Tembo. Mosel, Arlene. 2007. (ENG.). 48p. (J). (gr. -1-3). 8.99 *(978-0-312-36748-0(1),* 900042353) Square Fish.
—Tikki Tikki Tembo Book & CD Storytime Set. Mosel, Arlene. unabr. ed. 2012. (Macmillan Young Listeners Story Time Sets Ser.). (ENG.). (J). 12.99 *(978-1-4272-3211-3(3),* 900121709) Macmillan Audio.
Lenton, Steve. Fairytale Frankie & the Mermaid Escapade. Gormley, Greg. 2018. (Fairytale Frankie Ser.). (ENG.). 32p. (J). (gr. -1-k). pap. 9.99 ***(978-1-4083-3388-4(0),*** Orchard Bks.) Hachette Children's Group GBR. Dist: Hachette Bk. Group.
Lenton, Steven. Dilly the Donkey. Woollard, Elli. 2019. (ENG.). 32p. (J). (gr. -1-k). pap. 12.99 ***(978-1-5098-0792-5(6),*** Macmillan Children's Bks.) Pan Macmillan GBR. Dist: Independent Pubs. Group.
Lenton, Steven. Dinosaurs Don't Draw. Woollard, Elli. ed. 2018. (ENG.). 32p. (J). (gr. -1-k). 19.99 *(978-1-4472-5482-9(1),* Macmillan Children's Bks.) Pan Macmillan GBR. Dist: Independent Pubs. Group.
—Fairy Tale Frankie & the Tricky Witch. Gormley, Greg. 2016. (ENG.). 32p. (J). (gr. -1-1). 17.99 *(978-1-4814-6625-7(9),* Aladdin) Simon & Schuster Children's Publishing.
—The Great Gran Plan. Woollard, Elli. 2019. (ENG.). 32p. (J). 17.99 *(978-1-250-18603-4(X),* 900191471, Holt, Henry & Co. Bks. For Young Readers) Holt, Henry & Co.
—The Hundred & One Dalmatians. Smith, Dodie & Bently, Peter. 2019. (ENG.). 32p. (J). (gr. -1-3). 16.99 *(978-1-4197-3632-2(9),* Abrams Bks. for Young Readers) Abrams, Inc.
—Shifty Mcgifty & Slippery Sam. Corderoy, Tracey. 2013. (ENG.). 32p. (J). (gr. -1-3). 14.99 *(978-0-7636-6838-9(9),* Nosy Crow) Candlewick Pr.
—Teddy Bear, Teddy Bear: And Other Favorite Nursery Rhymes. Tiger Tales. 2013. (ENG.). 22p. (J). (gr. -1-k). bds. 8.95 *(978-1-58925-601-9(8))* Tiger Tales.
Lentz, Bob. Basic Training: A Few Good Manners. Lemke, Donald. 2019. (Basic Training Ser.). (ENG.). 30p. (J). (gr. -1 — 1). bds. 7.99 *(978-1-68446-065-6(4),* 140523, Capstone Editions) Capstone.
—Basic Training: Call of Doodie. Lemke, Donald. 2018. (Basic Training Ser.). (ENG.). 30p. (J). (gr. -1 — 1). bds. 7.99 *(978-1-68446-008-3(5),* 138937, Picture Window Bks.) Capstone.
—Book-O-Beards. Lemke, Donald. 2015. (Wearable Bks.). (ENG.). 12p. (J). (gr. -1-1). bds. 7.99 *(978-1-62370-183-3(X),* Capstone Young Readers) Capstone.
—Book-O-Hats. Lemke, Donald. 2015. (Wearable Bks.). (ENG.). 12p. (J). (gr. -1-1). bds. 7.99 *(978-1-62370-184-0(8),* Capstone Young Readers) Capstone.
—Book-O-Masks. Lemke, Donald. 2015. (Wearable Bks.). (ENG.). 12p. (J). (gr. -1-1). bds. 7.99 *(978-1-62370-185-7(6),* Capstone Young Readers) Capstone.
—Book-O-Teeth. Lemke, Donald B. 2015. (Wearable Bks.). (ENG.). 12p. (J). (gr. -1-1). bds. 7.99 *(978-1-62370-186-4(4),* Capstone Young Readers) Capstone.
—Fish & Fowl: Easy & Awesome Sandwiches for Kids. Deering, Alison. 2017. (Between the Bread Ser.). (ENG.). 48p. (J). (gr. 4-8). lib. bdg. 31.99 *(978-1-5157-3920-3(1),* 133828, Capstone Pr.) Capstone.
—Jackie Robinson: Gran Pionero del Béisbol. Glaser, Jason. 2006. (Biografías Gráficas Ser.). (SPA.). 32p. (J). (gr. 3-9). 31.32 *(978-0-7368-6602-6(7))* Capstone.
—More Meat Please! Delicious Sandwiches for Meat-Eating Kids. Deering, Alison. 2017. (Between the Bread Ser.). (ENG.). 48p. (J). (gr. 4-8). lib. bdg. 31.99 *(978-1-5157-3921-0(X),* 133829, Capstone Pr.) Capstone.
—Sandwiches! More Than You've Ever Wanted to Know about Making & Eating America's Favorite Food. Deering, Alison. ed. 2017. (ENG.). 144p. (J). (gr. 4-8). pap. 15.95 *(978-1-62370-816-0(8),* 133830, Capstone Young Readers) Capstone.
Lenz, Deborah. Sarah's Wings. Helmer, Marilyn. 2017. (ENG.). (J). pap. 9.13 *(978-0-9988339-4-1(0))* Dancing With Bear Publishing.
Lenz, Mary. Remember the Love. Jue, Thea. 2013. 36p. pap. 13.95 *(978-0-9827753-3-2(4))* Interdimensional Pr.
LEO, Inc Staff. Aldebaran Vol. 1, 3 vols., Vol. 1. LEO, Inc Staff. Leo. 2008. (Aldebaran Ser.: 1). (ENG.). 104p. pap. 19.95 *(978-1-905460-57-1(0))* CineBook GBR. Dist: National Bk. Network.
Leon, Andreu. Sian & the Winterwife: A Fairy Tale. Weston, Avalon. Booth, Kevin, ed. 2016. (ENG.). (J). (gr. 3-6). pap. *(978-0-9932298-4-8(0))* Poble Sec Bks.
Leon, Gabriela. El Juego de Pelota Mixteca. Del Angel, Varinia. rev. ed. 2006. (Otra Escalera Ser.). (SPA & ENG.). 24p. (J). (gr. 2-4). pap. 9.95 *(978-968-5920-66-7(4))* Castillo, Ediciones, S. A. de C. V. MEX. Dist: Macmillan.
Leon, John Paul, jt. illus. see Jeanty, Georges.
Leon, Karen. As the Crow Flies. Higgins, Kitty. ed. 2004. (Reader's Theater Ser.). (J). pap. *(978-1-4108-2304-5(0),* A23040) Benchmark Education Co.
—Battle for the Ballot. Howard, Annabelle. ed. 2004. (Reader's Theater Ser.). (J). pap. *(978-1-4108-2305-2(9),* A23059) Benchmark Education Co.
—The Big Cheese. Howard, Annabelle. ed. 2004. (Reader's Theater Ser.). (J). pap. *(978-1-4108-2294-9(X),* A2294X) Benchmark Education Co.
—The Corps of Discovery. Flounders, Anne. ed. 2004. (Reader's Theater Ser.). (J). pap. *(978-1-4108-2310-6(5),* A23105) Benchmark Education Co.
—The Fifth Grade Votes. Kramer, Alan & Kramer, Candice. ed. 2004. (Reader's Theater Ser.). (J). pap. *(978-1-4108-2307-6(5),* A23075) Benchmark Education Co.
—Jackie Robinson: Breaking Baseball's Barriers. Kramer, Alan. ed. 2004. (Reader's Theater Ser.). (J). pap. *(978-1-4108-2301-4(6),* A23016) Benchmark Education Co.
—Lost City of the Inca. Meissner, David. ed. 2004. (Reader's Theater Ser.). (J). pap. *(978-1-4108-2308-3(3),* A23083) Benchmark Education Co.
—Our New Home. Wall, Suzy. ed. 2004. (Reader's Theater Ser.). (J). pap. *(978-1-4108-2299-4(0),* A22990) Benchmark Education Co.
—Why Coyote Stopped Imitating His Friends. Kramer, Candice. ed. 2004. (Reader's Theater Ser.). (J). pap. *(978-1-4108-2302-1(4),* A23024) Benchmark Education Co.
Leon, Loni & Huston, Kyle. Can you Imagine..., 1. Leon, Loni. 2006. 49p. (J). 21.95 *(978-0-9728556-0-0(2))* Sullivan, Kelley Enterprises.
Leon, Nico. Agents of Atlas: Pandemonium. 2020. 120p. (YA). (gr. 8-17). pap. 15.99 *(978-1-302-92011-1(1))* Marvel Worldwide, Inc.
—Ms. Marvel Vol. 10: Time & Again, Vol. 10. 2019. (Ms. Marvel (2014) Ser.: 10). 144p. (YA). (gr. 8-17). pap. 19.99 *(978-1-302-91269-7(0))* Marvel Worldwide, Inc.
—Ms. Marvel Vol. 5. 2019. 272p. (YA). (gr. 8-17). 34.99 *(978-1-302-91735-7(8))* Marvel Worldwide, Inc.
—She-Hulk Vol. 1: Deconstructed. 2017. (ENG.). 136p. (YA). (gr. 8-17). pap. 17.99 *(978-1-302-90567-5(8))* Marvel Worldwide, Inc.
Leon, Nico & Sorrentino, Andrea. War of the Realms: Spider-Man/Daredevil. 2019. (ENG.). 128p. (YA). (gr. 4-17). pap. 15.99 *(978-1-302-91928-3(8))* Marvel Worldwide, Inc.
Leonard, Andre. Dinosaur Hunters in the Forest. Mason, Paul. 2018. (Dinosaurs Rule Ser.). (ENG.). 32p. (J). (gr. 3-6). lib. bdg. 27.99 *(978-1-5415-0104-1(7),* Hungry Tomato ®) Lerner Publishing Group.
—Dinosaur Predators on the Plain. Mason, Paul. 2018. (Dinosaurs Rule Ser.). (ENG.). 32p. (J). (gr. 3-6). lib. bdg. 27.99 *(978-1-5415-0101-0(2),* Hungry Tomato ®) Lerner Publishing Group.
—Dinosaur Slayers by the Shore. Mason, Paul. 2018. (Dinosaurs Rule Ser.). (ENG.). 32p. (J). (gr. 3-6). lib. bdg. 27.99 *(978-1-5415-0103-4(9),* Hungry Tomato ®) Lerner Publishing Group.
—Dinosaur Stalkers in the Swamp. Mason, Paul. 2018. (Dinosaurs Rule Ser.). (ENG.). 32p. (J). (gr. 3-6). lib. bdg. 27.99 *(978-1-5415-0102-7(0),* Hungry Tomato ®) Lerner Publishing Group.
Leonard, Barbara. All New Crafts for Halloween. Ross, Kathy. 2003. (All New Holiday Crafts for Kids Ser.). 48p. lib. bdg. 23.90 *(978-0-7613-2554-3(9),* Millbrook Pr.) Lerner Publishing Group.
Leonard, Barbara & Holm, Sharon. All New Crafts for Halloween. Ross, Kathy. 2003. (All New Holiday Crafts for Kids Ser.). (ENG.). 48p. (gr. k-3). pap. 7.95 *(978-0-7613-1577-3(2),* Millbrook Pr.) Lerner Publishing Group.
Leonard, Barry. Alphabet Connections: English-Spanish: 26 Picture Cards. Leonard, Barry, ed. 2004. 26p. (J). (gr. k-4). reprint ed. 15.00 *(978-0-7567-7825-5(5))* DIANE Publishing Co.
Leonard, David. The Extreme Team: Skateboard Moves. Christopher, Matt. 2018. (Matt Christopher Sports Readers Ser.). (ENG.). 32p. (J). (gr. 1-4). lib. bdg. 27.07 *(978-1-5321-4257-4(9),* 31057) Spotlight.
—Good Night Aerospace Museum. Gamble, Adam & Jasper, Mark. 2018. (Good Night Our World Ser.). 20p. (J). (— 1). bds. 9.95 *(978-1-60219-679-7(6))* Good Night Bks.
—Good Night Moose. Gamble, Adam & Jasper, Mark. 2020. (Good Night Our World Ser.). (ENG.). 20p. (J). (— 1). bds. 9.95 *(978-1-60219-782-4(2))* Good Night Bks.
—Good Night Nashville. Gamble, Adam & Jasper, Mark. 2018. (Good Night Our World Ser.). 20p. (J). (— 1). bds. 9.95 *(978-1-60219-773-2(3))* Good Night Bks.
—If You Were a Kid Discovering Dinosaurs. Gregory, Josh. 2017. (If You Were a Kid Ser.). (ENG.). 32p. (J). (gr. 2-4). pap. 7.95 *(978-0-531-23948-3(9));* lib. bdg. 26.00 *(978-0-531-23747-2(8))* Scholastic Library Publishing. (Children's Pr.).
Leonard, David. Inky the Octopus: Based on a Real-Life Aquatic Escape! Guendelsberger, Erin. 2020. 32p. (J). (-6). 8.99 ***(978-1-7282-2301-8(6))*** Sourcebooks, Inc.
Leonard, David. Inky the Octopus: Bound for Glory. Guendelsberger, Erin. 2018. 32p. (J). (-6). 17.99 *(978-1-4926-5414-8(0),* Sourcebooks Jabberwocky) Sourcebooks, Inc.
—Murphy's Ticket: The Goofy Start & Glorious End of the Chicago Cubs Billy Goat Curse. Herzog, Brad. 2017. (ENG.). 32p. (J). (gr. 1-4). 16.99 *(978-1-58536-387-2(1),* 204331) Sleeping Bear Pr.
Leonard, Erskine. Prison to Palace. Pozdol, MaryBeth. 2004. 189p. (J). ring bd. 29.95 *(978-1-889723-43-3(6))* Family Harvest Church.
Leonard, Herb, jt. illus. see Leonhard, Herb.
Leonard, Kaycee. Chee Choo's Adventures, 1 vol. Bassler, Joni. 2007. (ENG.). 33p. 24.95 *(978-1-4241-8773-7(7))* America Star Bks.
Leonard, Michael. Bluegrass Breeze. Rhema, Dan. 2004. (J). per. 19.95 *(978-0-9729835-1-8(1))* Mesquite Tress Pr., LLC.
—One Tiny Twig, 1. Rhema, Dan. 2003. 32p. (J). per. 19.95 *(978-0-9729835-0-1(3))* Mesquite Tress Pr., LLC.
Leonard, Richard & Alcala, Alfredo. I Am Not Afraid! Level 2. Mann, Kenny. 2020. (ENG.). 34p. (J). pap. 9.95 ***(978-1-899694-76-1(5))*** ibooks, Inc.
Leonard, Terry. Let's Get Going! The Step-by-Step Guide to Successful Outings with Children, 1 vol. Weisner, Candace. 2003. (ENG.). 184p. (J). (gr. 1-5). pap. 9.95 *(978-0-88995-193-8(4),* c9820627-15f2-4157-bbd3-0bbff9163105) Red Deer Pr. CAN. Dist: Firefly Bks., Ltd.
Leonard, Tom. Crab. Pallotta, Jerry. 2019. 32p. (J). (gr. -1-2). lib. bdg. 17.99 *(978-1-57091-144-6(4))* Charlesbridge Publishing, Inc.
Leonard, Tom, et al. Extraordinary Migrations. Cooper, Sharon Katz. 2015. (Extraordinary Migrations Ser.). (ENG.). 24p. (J). (gr. k-3). lib. bdg., lib. bdg., lib. bdg. 109.28 *(978-1-4795-6247-3(5),* Picture Window Bks.) Capstone.
Leonard, Tom. Here Is Antarctica. Dunphy, Madeleine. 2008. (Web of Life Ser.). (ENG.). 32p. (J). (gr. -1-3). 16.95 *(978-0-9777539-4-9(8))* Web of Life Children's Bks.
—Here Is the African Savanna. Dunphy, Madeleine. 2006. (Web of Life Ser.). (ENG.). 32p. (J). (gr. -1-3). 16.95 *(978-0-9773795-3-8(1));* pap. 9.95 *(978-0-9773795-2-1(3))* Web of Life Children's Bks.
—Here Is the Coral Reef. Dunphy, Madeleine. 2006. (Web of Life Ser.). (ENG.). 32p. (J). (gr. -1-3). 16.95 *(978-0-9773795-5-2(8));* pap. 9.95 *(978-0-9773795-4-5(X))* Web of Life Children's Bks.
—Honeybees. Neye, Emily. 2016. (Step into Reading Ser.). (ENG.). 32p. (J). (gr. -1-1). pap. 3.99 *(978-0-307-26217-2(0),* Random Hse. Bks. for Young Readers) Random Hse. Children's Bks.
—One Small Place by the Sea. Brenner, Barbara. 2004. (One Small Place Ser.). (ENG.). 32p. (J). (gr. k-3). 16.99 *(978-0-688-17182-7(6))* HarperCollins Pubs.
—One Small Place in a Tree. Brenner, Barbara. 2004. (ENG.). 32p. (J). (gr. k-3). 17.99 *(978-0-688-17180-3(X))* HarperCollins Pubs.
—The Sea Mammal Alphabet Book. Pallotta, Jerry. 2019. 32p. (J). (gr. -1-2). lib. bdg. 17.99 *(978-1-57091-146-0(0))* Charlesbridge Publishing, Inc.
—The Sea Mammal Alphabet Book. Boss, Karen & Pallotta, Jerry. 2019. 32p. (J). (gr. -1-2). pap. 7.99 *(978-1-57091-149-1(5))* Charlesbridge Publishing, Inc.
—When Penguins Cross the Ice: The Emperor Penguin Migration. Cooper, Sharon Katz. 2015. (Extraordinary Migrations Ser.). (ENG.). 24p. (J). (gr. k-3). pap. 8.95 *(978-1-4795-6102-5(9),* Picture Window Bks.) Capstone.
—When Penguins Cross the Ice: The Emperor Penguin Migration. Cooper, Sharon Katz. 2015. (Extraordinary Migrations Ser.). (ENG.). 24p. (J). (gr. k-3). lib. bdg. 27.32 *(978-1-4795-6078-3(2),* Picture Window Bks.) Capstone.
—When Whales Cross the Sea: The Gray Whale Migration. Cooper, Sharon Katz. 2015. (Extraordinary Migrations Ser.). (ENG.). 24p. (J). (gr. k-3). lib. bdg. 27.32 *(978-1-4795-6079-0(0),* Picture Window Bks.) Capstone.
—Whiskers. Daly-Weir, Catherine. 2015. (Step into Reading Ser.). (ENG.). 32p. (J). (gr. -1-1). pap. 3.99 *(978-0-307-26214-1(6),* Random Hse. Bks. for Young Readers) Random Hse. Children's Bks.
—Who Will Plant a Tree? Pallotta, Jerry. 2010. (ENG.). 32p. (J). (gr. -1-2). 15.95 *(978-1-58536-502-9(5))* Sleeping Bear Pr.
Leonardi, Rick. Darth Vader & the Lost Command. Blackman, Haden. 2012. (Star Wars: Darth Vader & the Lost Command Ser.). (ENG.). 24p. (J). (gr. 6-12). 27.07 *(978-1-59961-980-4(6),* 13805, Graphic Novels) Spotlight.
Leonardi, Rick, et al. Darth Vader & the Lost Command. Blackman, Haden. 2012. (Star Wars: Darth Vader & the Lost Command Ser.). (ENG.). 24p. (J). (gr. 6-12). 27.07 *(978-1-59961-983-5(0),* 13808, Graphic Novels) Spotlight.
Leonardi, Rick. Darth Vader & the Lost Command, Vol. 2. Blackman, Haden. 2012. (Star Wars: Darth Vader & the Lost Command Ser.). (ENG.). 24p. (J). (gr. 6-12). 27.07 *(978-1-59961-981-1(4),* 13806, Graphic Novels) Spotlight.
Leonardi, Rick, et al. Darth Vader & the Lost Command, Vol. 3. Blackman, Haden. 2012. (Star Wars: Darth Vader & the Lost Command Ser.). (ENG.). 24p. (J). (gr. 6-12). 27.07 *(978-1-59961-982-8(2),* 13807, Graphic Novels) Spotlight.
Leonardi, Rick. Lost Command. Blackman, Haden. 2012. (Star Wars: Darth Vader & the Lost Command Ser.). (ENG.). 24p. (J). (gr. 6-12). 27.07 *(978-1-59961-984-2(9),* 13809, Graphic Novels) Spotlight.
Leonardi, Rick, et al. X-Men Milestones: X-Tinction Agenda. 2019. (ENG.). 328p. (YA). (gr. 4-17). pap. 34.99 *(978-1-302-91968-9(7))* Marvel Worldwide, Inc.
Leonardo, Todd. Nobody Knew What to Do: A Story about Bullying. McCain, Becky Ray. 2017. (ENG.). 24p. (J). (gr. -1-3). pap. 7.99 *(978-0-8075-5713-6(7),* 807557137) Whitman, Albert & Co.
Leone, Fabio & Lopez, Michelle. Bob, Tab, & I - Go up, up, up - Rob, Ron, & I: StartUp Unit 5 Lap Book. Soto, Luisa et al. 2015. (Start up Core Phonics Ser.). (J). (gr. k). *(978-1-4900-2594-0(4))* Benchmark Education Co.
Leone, Jason. the Enchantress of Caratunk. Manna, Elizabeth, photos by. 2003. 30p. (J). (gr. 1-5). pap. 9.95 *(978-0-9729807-0-8(9))* Murray, David M.
Leone, Sergio. Peggy Finds the Theater. Hughes, Virginia. 2011. 186p. 42.95 *(978-1-258-10513-6(6))* Literary Licensing, LLC.
Leone, Tony, et al. Unbored: The Essential Field Guide to Serious Fun. Larsen, Elizabeth Foy & Glenn, Joshua. 2012. 352p. 29.00 *(978-1-60819-641-8(0),* 900076932) Bloomsbury Publishing USA.
—UNBORED Adventure: 70 Seriously Fun Activities for Kids & Their Families. Glenn, Joshua & Larsen, Elizabeth Foy. 2015. 176p. pap. 16.00 *(978-1-63286-096-5(1),* 900146828) Bloomsbury Publishing USA.
—UNBORED Games: Serious Fun for Everyone. Glenn, Joshua & Larsen, Elizabeth Foy. 2014. 176p. pap. 16.00 *(978-1-62040-706-6(X),* 900136507) Bloomsbury Publishing USA.
Leonello, Tanya. Pterodactyl Show & Tell. Krasnesky, Thad. 2018. (ENG.). 32p. (J). (gr. k-2). 17.95 *(978-1-936261-34-5(0))* Flashlight Pr.
—Walter & the Wallet. Bloom, Billy. 2017. (ENG.). (J). (gr. k-5). pap. 9.99 *(978-1-63233-115-1(2))* Elfrig Publishing.
Leong, Sloane. Epic Athletes: Serena Williams. Wetzel, Dan. 2019. (Epic Athletes Ser.: 3). (ENG.). 176p. (J). 16.99 *(978-1-250-29578-1(5),* 900195301, Holt, Henry & Co. Bks. For Young Readers) Holt, Henry & Co.
—Epic Athletes: Serena Williams. Wetzel, Dan. 2020. (Epic Athletes Ser.: 3). (ENG.). 192p. (J). pap. 7.99 *(978-1-250-25072-8(2),* 900198023) Square Fish.
Leong, Sonia. Manga Shakespeare: Romeo & Juliet. Shakespeare, William. 2007. (ENG.). 208p. (J). (gr. 2-8). pap. 14.99 *(978-0-8109-9325-9(2),* Abrams Bks. for Young Readers) Abrams, Inc.
Leonhard, Herb. Billy's Mountain. Richardson, Steve. 2007. 52p. 14.95 *(978-0-9786422-0-4(1))* Impossible Dreams Publishing Co.
—The Cajun Fisherman & His Wife, 1 vol. Morgan, Connie. 2018. (ENG.). 32p. (gr. k-3). 16.99 *(978-1-4556-2366-2(0),* Pelican Publishing) Arcadia Publishing.
—The Faerie Garden Coloring Book. 2004. 24p. (J). 3.50 *(978-0-9763555-0-2(7))* Prancing Pony, The.
—Hercules on the Bayou, 1 vol. Collins Morgan, Connie. 2016. (ENG.). 32p. (J). (gr. k-3). 16.99

L

(978-1-4556-2185-9(4), Pelican Publishing) Arcadia Publishing.

—The Hiding Game, 1 vol. Strauss, Gwen. 2017. (ENG.). 40p. (J). (gr. 2-5). 17.99 *(978-1-4556-2265-8(6)*, Pelican Publishing) Arcadia Publishing.

—I Know a Librarian Who Chewed on a Word, 1 vol. Knowlton, Laurie. 2012. (ENG.). 32p. (J). (gr. k-3). 16.99 *(978-1-58980-892-8(4)*, Pelican Publishing) Arcadia Publishing.

—Kendall & Kyleah. Hill, Janet Muirhead. 2012. (J). pap. 13.00 *(978-1-937849-05-4(8))* Raven Publishing Inc. of Montana.

—Kendall's Storm. Hill, Janet Muirhead. 2011. (J). pap. 12.00 *(978-0-9820893-0-9(9))* Raven Publishing Inc. of Montana.

—Kyleah's Tree. Hill, Janet Muirhead. 2011. (J). pap. 12.00 *(978-0-9827377-9-8(3))* Raven Publishing Inc. of Montana.

—Matthew's Box. Reish, Kathleen. 2005. 48p. (J). 21.95 *(978-0-9762664-0-2(7)*, 3000) KBR Mutt's Pubns.

—The Quest Begins: Magic Bag Trilogy Book One. Watts, James. 2011. 410p. (YA). 24.95 *(978-1-936824-04-5(3))* Etcetera Pr. LLC.

—The Runaway Beignet, 1 vol. Morgan, Connie & Morgan, Connie Collins. 2014. (ENG.). 32p. (J). (gr. k-3). 16.99 *(978-1-4556-1912-2(4)*, Pelican Publishing) Arcadia Publishing.

—A Southern Child's Garden of Verses, 1 vol. Davis, David. 2010. (ENG.). 40p. (J). (gr. k-k). 17.99 *(978-1-58980-764-8(2)*, Pelican Publishing) Arcadia Publishing.

—Southern Mother Goose, 1 vol. Davis, David. 2013. (ENG.). 40p. (J). (gr. k-4). 17.99 *(978-1-4556-1760-9(1)*, Pelican Publishing) Arcadia Publishing.

—St. Patrick & the Three Brave Mice, 1 vol. Stengel, Joyce A. 2009. (ENG.). 32p. (J). (gr. k-3). 16.99 *(978-1-58980-663-4(8)*, Pelican Publishing) Arcadia Publishing.

—Way Out West on My Little Pony, 1 vol. Peck, Jan. 2010. (ENG.). 32p. (J). (gr. k-3). 16.99 *(978-1-58980-697-9(2)*, Pelican Publishing) Arcadia Publishing.

Leonhard, Herb. Sir Norman & the Dreaming Dragon. Leonhard, Herb. 2008. (ENG.). 32p. (J). 17.95 *(978-0-9763555-1-9(5))* Prancing Pony, The.

Leonhard, Herb & Leonard, Herb. Leonardo's Monster, 1 vol. Sutcliffe, Jane. 2010. (ENG.). 32p. (J). (gr. k-3). 16.99 *(978-1-58980-838-6(X)*, Pelican Publishing) Arcadia Publishing.

Leonhard, Herb, jt. illus. see Champagne, Tony.

Leoni, Nancy. Toby Goes to Camp, 1 vol. Leoni, Nancy. 2009. 21p. pap. 24.95 *(978-1-61546-417-3(4))* America Star Bks.

Leonidou, Niki. Fall. Corriols, Carmen. 2015. (Early Rising Readers Ser.). (J). (gr. -1-k). 5.83 *(978-1-4788-2155-7(8))* Newmark Learning LLC.

—Guess Who Lives on My Street: Set Of 6. Parkes, Brenda. 2014. (Shared Reading Foundations Ser.). (J). (gr. 1). 36.00 net. *(978-1-4900-0032-9(1))* Benchmark Education Co.

—Guess Who Lives on My Street Book Set. Parkes, Brenda. 2014. (Shared Reading Foundations Ser.). (J). (gr. 1). 72.00 net. *(978-1-4900-0002-2(X))* Benchmark Education Co.

—Kids Have Fun - Yes, Cubs! - Val Is a Vet: StartUp Unit 8 Lap Book. Johnson, Tiffany et al. 2015. (Start up Core Phonics Ser.). (J). (gr. k). *(978-1-4900-2597-1(9))* Benchmark Education Co.

—Los Abrigos. Lindeen, Mary. 2016. (Early Rising Readers Ser.). (SPA.). (J). (gr. -1). 6.67 *(978-1-4788-3650-6(4))* Newmark Learning LLC.

—El Otono. Corriols, Carmen. 2016. (Early Rising Readers Ser.). (SPA.). 16p. (J). (gr. 1-1). 6.67 *(978-1-4788-4185-2(0))* Newmark Learning LLC.

—El Picnic. Koons, Linda. 2016. (Early Rising Readers Ser.). (SPA.). (J). (gr. -1). 6.67 *(978-1-4788-3649-0(0))* Newmark Learning LLC.

—La Princesa y el Guisante. Strom, Laura Layton. 2016. (Jump into Genre Ser.). (SPA.). (J). (gr. 2). 5.25 *(978-1-4788-3614-8(8))* Newmark Learning LLC.

—Rapunzel. Strom, Laura Layton. 2016. (Jump into Genre Ser.). (SPA.). (J). (gr. 2). 5.25 *(978-1-4788-3615-5(6))* Newmark Learning LLC.

—Rikki-Tikki-Tavi - 6 Pack: Set of 6 with Common Core Teacher Materials. 2015. (Classic Tales Ser.). (J). (gr. k-1). 39.00 *(978-1-5125-8363-2(4))* Benchmark Education Co.

—Rumpelstiltskin - 6 Pack: Set of 6 with Common Core Teacher Materials. 2015. (Classic Tales Ser.). (J). (gr. k-1). 39.00 *(978-1-5125-8364-9(2))* Benchmark Education Co.

—What Can We Share? Set Of 6. Parkes, Brenda. 2014. (Shared Reading Foundations Ser.). (J). (gr. 1). 36.00 net. *(978-1-4900-0028-2(3))* Benchmark Education Co.

—What Can We Share? Book Set. Parkes, Brenda. 2014. (Shared Reading Foundations Ser.). (J). (gr. 1). 72.00 net. *(978-1-4509-9998-4(0))* Benchmark Education Co.

Leonidou, Niki, jt. illus. see Czernichowska, Joanna.

Leonov, Anatoliy. Colors for Panda Bear Bo: Learning Colors for Kids. Khomenok, Alya. Khomenok, Olga, tr. 2019. (ENG.). 32p. (J). pap. 9.99 ***(978-1-0891-3043-7(0))*** Independently Published.

—Colors for Panda Bear Bo for Preschoolers. Khomenok, Alya. Khomenok, Olga, tr. 2019. (ENG.). 34p. (J). pap. 9.99 ***(978-1-6895-3573-1(3))*** Independently Published.

Leonova, Valeria. Better Day Coming: A Dream, a Journey, a New Beginning. Armen, Rose Maiolo. 2018. (ENG.). 48p. (J). (gr. 1-6). 19.95 *(978-0-692-06994-3(1))* Armen, Rose Maiolo.

—Brave Kayla: A Story about Being Brave at the Doctor. Spray, Michelle. 2018. (ENG.). 26p. (J). pap. 9.95 *(978-1-7270-9388-9(7))* CreateSpace Independent Publishing Platform.

—Breakfast Surprise. Aisha, Tempestt. 2018. (Maddy Ser.: Vol. 1). (ENG.). 32p. (J). (gr. k-3). 22.00 *(978-0-692-14985-0(6))* Williams, Tempestt.

—I Have Scoliosis Too: A Story of Friendship & Hope Throughout Scoliosis. Spray, Michelle. Munn, Monica, ed. 2019. (ENG.). 34p. (J). pap. 9.95 *(978-1-0744-8996-0(9))* Independently Published.

—Just Like Mommy. Aisha, Tempestt. 2017. (Maddy Ser.: Vol. 1). (ENG.). 34p. (J). (gr. k-2). 20.00 *(978-0-692-12044-6(0))* Williams, Tempestt.

Leonova, Valeria. Waiting for the Mailman: An Alzheimer's Story. Spray, Michelle. Munn, Monica, ed. 2020. (ENG.). 30p. (J). pap. 9.95 ***(978-1-6607-7963-5(4))*** Independently Published.

Lepere, Leslie W. The Longest, Darkest Night!, Second Edition. Lewis, Peter B. 2nd ed. 2020. (ENG.). 56p. (J). (gr. k-4). pap. 12.95 ***(978-0-9980365-6-4(0))*** Audisee Sound & Music.

Leplar, Anna. All the Gold in the World. Leeson, Robert. 2004. 96p. bds. 8.95 *(978-0-7136-4059-5(6)*, A&C Black) Bloomsbury Publishing Plc GBR. Dist: Consortium Bk. Sales & Distribution.

—The Wind in the Willows. Grahame, Kenneth. 256p. (J). *(978-1-4054-3774-5(X))* Parragon, Inc.

LePlatt, Betsy. Mosquito, 1 vol. Kroll, Virginia. 2011. (ENG.). 32p. (J). (gr. k-3). 16.99 *(978-1-58980-883-6(5)*, Pelican Publishing) Arcadia Publishing.

L'Eplattenier, Michelle. It's Okay to Talk to God. Neuls, Lillian. 2008. 12p. pap. 24.95 *(978-1-60703-855-9(2))* America Star Bks.

Lepley, Kathy. Frozen in Motion: Alaska's Glaciers. Hocker, Katherine M. Brubaker, Jill, ed. 2006. 54p. (J). spiral bd. 8.95 *(978-0-930931-76-6(9))* Alaska Geographic Assn.

Lepp, Kevin. Ben Franklin's Big Shock. Jango-Cohen, Judith. 2006. (On My Own Science Ser.). 48p. (J). (gr. k-3). per. 5.95 *(978-0-8225-6450-8(5)*, First Avenue Editions); lib. bdg. 25.26 *(978-1-57505-873-3(1)*, Millbrook Pr.) Lerner Publishing Group.

—Salvar a la Campana de la Libertad. Figley, Marty Rhodes. 2005. (Yo Solo - Historia (On My Own - History) Ser.). (SPA.). 48p. (J). (gr. 3-7). lib. bdg. 25.26 *(978-0-8225-3094-7(5)*, Ediciones Lerner); (gr. 2-5). per. 6.95 *(978-0-8225-3095-4(3))* Lerner Publishing Group.

—Saving the Liberty Bell. Figley, Marty Rhodes. 2004. (On My Own History Ser.). (ENG.). 48p. (J). (gr. 2-4). pap. 7.99 *(978-1-57505-696-8(8)*, First Avenue Editions) Lerner Publishing Group.

Lepp, Royden. Barnabas Goes Swimming, 1 vol. Lepp, Royden. 2008. (I Can Read! / Barnabas Ser.). (ENG.). 32p. (J). (gr. -1-1). pap. 4.99 *(978-0-310-71584-9(9))* Zonderkidz.

—Barnabas Helps a Friend, 1 vol. Lepp, Royden. 2008. (I Can Read! / Barnabas Ser.). (ENG.). 32p. (J). (gr. -1-1). pap. 4.99 *(978-0-310-71585-6(7))* Zonderkidz.

—God Loves You Barnabas, 1 vol. Lepp, Royden. 2008. (I Can Read! / Barnabas Ser.). (ENG.). 32p. (J). (gr. -1-1). pap. 4.99 *(978-0-310-71587-0(3))* Zonderkidz.

—Happy Birthday Barnabas, 1 vol. Lepp, Royden. 2008. (I Can Read! / Barnabas Ser.). (ENG.). 32p. (J). (gr. -1-1). pap. 4.99 *(978-0-310-71586-3(5))* Zonderkidz.

—Secrets of the Cell, Vol. 2. Lepp, Royden. 2017. (Rust Ser.: 2). (ENG.). 144p. (J). (gr. 8-12). pap. 14.99 *(978-1-60886-895-7(8)*, Archaia Entertainment) Boom! Studios.

—Visitor In the Field, Vol. 1. Lepp, Royden. 2016. (Rust Ser.: 1). (ENG.). 176p. (J). (gr. 8-12). pap. 14.99 *(978-1-60886-894-0(X)*, Archaia Entertainment) Boom! Studios.

Lepretre, Jean-Marc. Monster Machines! on the Farm. Vandewièle, Agnès. 2013. (ENG.). 18p. (J). (gr. -1-1). bds. 12.99 *(978-1-4022-9247-7(3)*, Sourcebooks Jabberwocky) Sourcebooks, Inc.

Lerangis, Peter. The Colossus Rises, No. 1. Lerangis, Peter. 2012. (Seven Wonders Ser.). 112p. (J). (gr. 3-7). 2.99 *(978-0-06-223889-4(2))* HarperCollins Pubs.

Leray, Marjolaine. Little Red Hood. Leray, Marjolaine. Ardizzone, Sarah. Ardizzone, Sarah, tr. 2013. 40p. (J). (gr. -1). 12.99 *(978-1-907912-00-9(2))* Phoenix Yard Bks. GBR. Dist: Independent Pubs. Group.

Lerch, Steffie. The Surprise Doll. Gipson, Morrell. 2005. 46p. (J). (gr. -1-2). reprint ed. 15.00 *(978-1-930900-18-9(X))* Purple Hse. Pr.

Lerot-Calvo, Florence. I'm Learning Japanese! A Language Adventure for Young People. Galan, Christian. 2010. 128p. (gr. 3-8). 19.95 *(978-4-8053-1074-8(X))* Tuttle Publishing.

Leroy, Benjamin. A Big Help. Fehr, Daniel. 2018. (ENG.). 36p. (J). 15.95 *(978-84-17123-21-5(0))* NubeOcho Ediciones ESP. Dist: Consortium Bk. Sales & Distribution.

—Una Gran Ayuda. Fehr, Daniel. 2018. (SPA.). 36p. (J). 15.95 *(978-84-17123-20-8(2))* NubeOcho Ediciones ESP. Dist: Consortium Bk. Sales & Distribution.

Lervold, Erik. The Dung Beetle Bandits, 1 vol. Reynolds, Aaron. 2007. (Graphic Sparks Ser.). (ENG.). 40p. (J). (gr. 2-5). lib. bdg. 23.99 *(978-1-59889-317-5(3)*, Stone Arch Bks.) Capstone.

—The Dung Beetle Bandits: Tiger Moth. Reynolds, Aaron. 2007. (Graphic Sparks Ser.). (ENG.). 40p. (J). (gr. 2-5). pap. 5.95 *(978-1-59889-412-7(9)*, Stone Arch Bks.) Capstone.

—The Fortune Cookies of Weevil: Tiger Moth. Reynolds, Aaron. 2007. (Graphic Sparks Ser.). (ENG.). 40p. (J). (gr. 2-5). pap. 5.95 *(978-1-59889-413-4(7)*, Stone Arch Bks.) Capstone.

—Insect Ninja: Tiger Moth. Reynolds, Aaron. 2006. (Graphic Sparks Ser.). (ENG.). 40p. (J). (gr. 2-5). per. 5.95 *(978-1-59889-228-4(2)*, Stone Arch Bks.) Capstone.

—Kung Pow Chicken: Tiger Moth. Reynolds, Aaron. 2008. (Graphic Sparks Ser.). (ENG.). 40p. (J). (gr. 2-5). pap. 5.95 *(978-1-4342-0505-6(3)*, Stone Arch Bks.) Capstone.

—The Pest Show on Earth: Tiger Moth, 1 vol. Reynolds, Aaron. 2008. (Graphic Sparks Ser.). (ENG.). 40p. (J). (gr. 2-5). per. 5.95 *(978-1-4342-0504-9(5)*, Stone Arch Bks.) Capstone.

—Tiger Moth: Adventures of an Insect Ninja, 1 vol. Reynolds, Aaron. 2011. (Tiger Moth Ser.). (ENG.). 128p. (J). (gr. 2-5). pap. 7.95 *(978-1-4342-3032-4(5)*, Stone Arch Bks.) Capstone.

—Tiger Moth & the Dragon Kite Contest, 1 vol. Reynolds, Aaron. 2006. (Tiger Moth Ser.). (ENG.). 40p. (J). (gr. 2-5). lib. bdg. 23.99 *(978-1-59889-056-3(5))*; per. 5.95 *(978-1-59889-229-1(0))* Capstone. (Stone Arch Bks.).

Lesage, Maria. Broken Crayons, 1 vol. Dingwell, Patsy. 2020. (ENG.). 32p. (J). pap. 14.95 ***(978-1-77366-063-9(2)***, 6ddb0013-8d78-448b-b5ca-8cbb468ad050) Acorn Pr., The CAN. Dist: Baker & Taylor Publisher Services (BTPS).

Leschnikoff, Nancy. My First Christmas Stories & Poems. Berry-Byrd, Holly. Cottage Door Press, ed. ed. 2020. (Children's First Padded Board Illustrated Treasury Ser.). (ENG.). 26p. (J). (gr. -1 — 1). 9.99 ***(978-1-68052-989-0(7)***, 1006160) Cottage Door Pr.

Leschnikoff, Nancy. What's Happening to Me? (Girls Edition) Meredith, Susan. 2006. 48p. (J). pap. 6.99 *(978-0-7945-1267-5(4)*, Usborne) EDC Publishing.

Lesko, Marco, et al. Harley at Bat! (DC Super Heroes: Batman) Kaplan, Arie. 2020. (Step into Reading Ser.). (ENG.). 32p. (J). (gr. -1-1). pap. 5.99 ***(978-0-593-12802-2(8))***; lib. bdg. 14.99 ***(978-0-593-12803-9(6))*** Random Hse. Children's Bks. (Random Hse. Bks. for Young Readers).

Lesley, Georgia. The Train. Callaghan, Jodie. 2020. (ENG.). 32p. (J). (gr. 1-3). 17.95 ***(978-1-77260-129-9(2))*** Second Story Pr. CAN. Dist: Orca Bk. Pubs. USA.

Leslie, Melissa. Joey Discovers Astronomy. Ferraro, Lynn. 2005. (ENG.). 23p. per. 12.99 *(978-1-4134-9624-6(5))* Xlibris Corp.

—Joey's Day of Discovery. Ferraro, Lynn. 2005. (ENG.). 21p. per. 12.99 *(978-1-4134-9622-2(9))* Xlibris Corp.

Lesnick, Tina. Dragonfly Flight. Nettrour, Nelani. l.t. ed. 2003. 62p. (J). pap. 11.94 *(978-1-932657-02-9(9))* Third Millennium Pubns.

Lesnie, Phil. Once a Shepherd. Millard, Glenda. 2014. 32p. (J). (gr. -1-3). 16.99 *(978-0-7636-7458-8(3))* Candlewick Pr.

Lesniewski, Matthew. Les Stroud's: Survivorman: the Horn of Providence. 2017. (ENG.). (J). (gr. 1-6). pap. 19.99 *(978-1-948216-66-1(3))* TidalWave.

Less, Sally. Isaac the Frog. Irvin, Christine. 2004. 14p. (J). 7.95 *(978-0-9706654-9-2(0))* Sprite Pr.

Lessac, Frané. Capital! Washington D. C. from a to Z. Melmed, Laura Krauss. 2006. (ENG.). 48p. (J). (gr. 1-6). 7.99 *(978-0-06-113614-6(X)*, Collins) HarperCollins Pubs.

—Clouds. Rockwell, Anne. 2008. (Let's-Read-And-Find-Out Science 1 Ser.). (ENG.). 40p. (J). (gr. -1-3). pap. 5.99 *(978-0-06-445220-5(4))* HarperCollins Pubs.

—The Day of the Elephant. Wilson, Barbara K. 32p. 2007. pap. *(978-0-207-20059-5(9))*; 2005. *(978-0-207-20055-7(6))* HarperCollins Pubs. Australia.

—The Donkey of Gallipoli: A True Story of Courage in World War I. Greenwood, Mark. 2008. (ENG.). 32p. (J). (gr. 1-4). 17.99 *(978-0-7636-3913-6(3))* Candlewick Pr.

—The Greatest Liar on Earth. Greenwood, Mark. 2012. (ENG.). 32p. (J). (gr. 2-5). 16.99 *(978-0-7636-6155-7(4))* Candlewick Pr.

—New York, New York! The Big Apple from a to Z. Melmed, Laura Krauss. (ENG.). 48p. (J). (gr. 1-6). 2008. pap. 7.99 *(978-0-06-054877-3(0)*, Collins); 2005. 16.99 *(978-0-06-054874-2(6))* HarperCollins Pubs.

—Pattan's Pumpkin: A Traditional Flood Story from Southern India. Chitra Soundar. 2017. (J). *(978-3-692-74397-4(1))* Candlewick Pr.

—We Are Grateful: Otsaliheliga. Sorell, Traci. 2018. (ENG.). 32p. (J). (gr. -1-2). 17.99 *(978-1-58089-772-3(X))* Charlesbridge Publishing, Inc.

—The Wonderful Towers of Watts. Zelver, Patricia. 2005. (ENG.). 32p. (J). (gr. k-k). pap. 10.99 *(978-1-59078-255-2(0))* Boyds Mills Pr.

Lessac, Frané. A Is for Australian Animals. Lessac, Frané. 2018. (ENG.). 48p. (J). (gr. 2-4). 16.99 *(978-0-7636-9484-5(3))* Candlewick Pr.

—Island Counting 1 2 3. Lessac, Frané. 2007. 24p. (J). (— 1). bds. 8.99 *(978-0-7636-3518-3(9))* Candlewick Pr.

Lessac, Frané & Lessac, Frané. The Fire Children: A West African Folk Tale. 2015. (ENG.). 32p. (J). (gr. -1-2). pap. 9.99 *(978-1-84780-652-9(X)*, Frances Lincoln Children's Bks.) Quarto Publishing Group UK GBR. Dist: Hachette Bk. Group.

—Midnight: A True Story of Loyalty in World War I. Greenwood, Mark. 2015. (ENG.). 32p. (J). (gr. k-4). 16.99 *(978-0-7636-7466-3(4))* Candlewick Pr.

—Under the Southern Cross. Lessac, Frané & Lessac, Frané. 2019. (ENG.). 32p. (J). (gr. k-3). 16.99 *(978-1-5362-0226-7(6))* Candlewick Pr.

Lessac, Frané, jt. illus. see Lessac, Frané.

Lester, Alison. Magic Beach. Lester, Alison. 2006. (ENG.). 32p. (J). (gr. -1-k). pap. 11.99 *(978-1-74114-488-8(4))* Allen & Unwin AUS. Dist: Independent Pubs. Group.

—Noni the Pony. Lester, Alison. 2012. (Noni the Pony Ser.). (ENG.). 32p. (J). (gr. -1-k). 15.99 *(978-1-4424-5959-5(X)*, Beach Lane Bks.) Beach Lane Bks.

—Noni the Pony. Lester, Alison. 2019. (Noni the Pony Ser.). (ENG.). 28p. (J). (gr. -1-k). bds. 7.99 *(978-1-5344-5355-5(5)*, Little Simon) Little Simon.

—Noni the Pony Goes to the Beach. Lester, Alison. 2015. (Noni the Pony Ser.). (ENG.). 32p. (J). (gr. -1-3). 17.99 *(978-1-4814-4625-9(8)*, Beach Lane Bks.) Beach Lane Bks.

—Noni the Pony Rescues a Joey. Lester, Alison. 2019. (Noni the Pony Ser.). (ENG.). 32p. (J). (-3). 17.99 *(978-1-5344-4370-9(3)*, Beach Lane Bks.) Beach Lane Bks.

Lester, Helen & Munsinger, Lynn. Boris & the Worrisome Wakies. Lester, Helen & Munsinger, Lynn. 2017. (ENG.). 32p. (J). (gr. -1-3). 16.99 *(978-0-544-64094-8(2)*, 1620832, HMH Books For Young Readers) Houghton Mifflin Harcourt Publishing Co.

Lester, Mike. The Butt Book. Bennett, Artie. 2010. (ENG.). 32p. (J). (gr. k-2). 17.99 *(978-1-59990-311-8(3)*, 900054082, Bloomsbury USA Childrens) Bloomsbury Publishing USA.

—Funny Bugs. Rothman, Cynthia Anne. l.t. ed. 2005. (Little Books & Big Bks.: Vol. 4). 8p. (gr. k-2). 23.00 net. *(978-0-8215-7513-0(9))* Sadlier, William H. Inc.

—Las Sombras. Calvert, Deanna. 2005. (Rookie Reader Español Ser.). (SPA.). 23p. (J). (gr. k-2). per. 4.95 *(978-0-516-24697-0(6)*, Children's Pr.) Scholastic Library Publishing.

—The Really Rotten Princess. Snodgrass, Lady Cecily. 2012. (Ready-To-Read Level 2 Ser.). (ENG.). 32p. (J). (gr. k-2). 16.19 *(978-1-4424-3326-7(4)*, Simon Spotlight) Simon & Schuster Children's Publishing.

—The Really Rotten Princess. Snodgrass, Lady Cecily. 2012. (Really Rotten Princess Ser.). (ENG.). 32p. (J). (gr. k-2). pap. 3.99 *(978-1-4424-3325-0(6)*, Simon Spotlight) Simon Spotlight.

Lester, Mike. The Really Rotten Princess & the Awful, Icky Election. Snodgrass, Lady Cecily. 2020. (Really Rotten Princess Ser.). (ENG.). 32p. (J). (gr. k-2). 17.99 ***(978-1-5344-7929-6(5))***; pap. 4.99 ***(978-1-5344-7928-9(7))*** Simon Spotlight. (Simon Spotlight).

Lester, Mike. The Really Rotten Princess & the Cupcake Catastrophe. Snodgrass, Lady Cecily. 2013. (Really Rotten Princess Ser.). (ENG.). 32p. (J). (gr. k-2). 17.99 *(978-1-4424-8974-5(X))*; pap. 3.99 *(978-1-4424-8973-8(1))* Simon Spotlight. (Simon Spotlight).

—Shadows. Calvert, Deanna. 2004. (Rookie Readers Ser.). 23p. (J). 12.60 *(978-0-7569-4333-2(7))* Perfection Learning Corp.

—Las Sombras: Shadows. Calvert, Deanna. 2005. (Rookie Reader Español Ser.). (SPA.). 24p. (gr. k-2). 19.50 *(978-0-516-24448-8(5)*, Children's Pr.) Scholastic Library Publishing.

—When Charlie McButton Lost Power. Collins, Suzanne. 2009. 32p. 16.00 *(978-1-60686-529-3(3))* Perfection Learning Corp.

—When Charlie Mcbutton Lost Power. Collins, Suzanne. 2007. 32p. (J). (gr. -1-3). pap. 7.99 *(978-0-14-240857-5(3)*, Puffin Books) Penguin Young Readers Group.

Lester, Roseanna. Sheldon Zab the Crab. Kucej, Kristine. 2009. 24p. pap. 11.49 *(978-1-4389-6204-7(5))* AuthorHouse.

—The Story of Rocco on Satterwhite Ridge: Spring Surprises. Thomas, Amy T. 2009. 16p. pap. 8.49 *(978-1-4389-3142-5(5))* AuthorHouse.

Leszek, Cedryll. Harold the Owl Who Couldn't Sleep. Leadbetter, Lesley. 2012. 30p. (J). pap. *(978-1-921869-89-1(5)*, Digital Publishing Centre) Interactive Pubns. Pty, Ltd.

Leth, Kate, jt. illus. see Farina, Katy.

Lethcoe, Jason. Gus Beezer with Spider-Man. Simone, Gail. 2006. (Marvelous Adventures of Gus Beezer Ser.). (ENG.). 24p. (J). (gr. 2-6). lib. bdg. 27.07 *(978-1-59961-047-4(7)*, 11342, Marvel Age) Spotlight.

—Gus Beezer with Spider-Man: Along Came a Spidey! Simone, Gail. 2006. (Marvelous Adventures of Gus Beezer Ser.). (ENG.). 24p. (J). (gr. 2-6). lib. bdg. 27.07 *(978-1-59961-048-1(5)*, 11343, Marvel Age) Spotlight.

—Gus Beezer with the X-Men: X Marks the Mutant. Simone, Gail. 2006. (Marvelous Adventures of Gus Beezer Ser.). (ENG.). 24p. (J). (gr. 2-6). lib. bdg. 27.07 *(978-1-59961-050-4(7)*, 11345, Marvel Age) Spotlight.

—You Wish. 2007. 215p. (J). *(978-1-4287-1806-7(0)*, Grosset & Dunlap) Penguin Publishing Group.

Lethcoe, Jason. Amazing Adventures from Zoom's Academy. Lethcoe, Jason. 2005. (ENG.). 160p. (J). (gr. 4-7). pap. 12.95 *(978-0-345-48355-3(3)*, Ballantine Bks.) Random House Publishing Group.

Lethcoe, Jason J. Gus Beezer with the Hulk. Simone, Gail. 2006. (Marvelous Adventures of Gus Beezer Ser.). (ENG.). 24p. (J). (gr. 2-6). lib. bdg. 27.07 *(978-1-59961-049-8(3)*, 11344, Marvel Age) Spotlight.

Letheby, Lavinia. Baby Jake's Birthday: Learn 9 Ways to Spell the Long a Sound. Sandelin, Karen. 2018. (ENG.). 38p. (J). pap. *(978-0-6483102-4-2(8))* Clever Speller Pty, Limited.

—Stuck in the Mud: Learn 6 Ways to Spell the Short U Sound. Sandelin, Karen L. 2019. (ENG.). 40p. (J). pap. *(978-0-6483102-0-4(5))* Clever Speller Pty, Limited.

Letherland, Lucy. Atlas of Adventures: A Collection of Natural Wonders, Exciting Experiences & Fun Festivities from the Four Corners of the Globe. Williams, Rachel. 2015. (Atlas Of Ser.). (ENG.). 96p. (J). (gr. 2-5). 35.00 *(978-1-84780-695-6(3)*, Wide Eyed Editions) Quarto Publishing Group UK GBR. Dist: Hachette Bk. Group.

—Atlas of Animal Adventures: A Collection of Nature's Most Unmissable Events, Epic Migrations & Extraordinary Behaviours. Williams, Rachel & Hawkins, Emily. 2016. (Atlas Of Ser.). (ENG.). 96p. (J). (gr. 1-4). 35.00 *(978-1-84780-841-7(7)*, Wide Eyed Editions) Quarto Publishing Group UK GBR. Dist: Hachette Bk. Group.

—Atlas of Dinosaur Adventures: Step into a Prehistoric World. Hawkins, Emily. 2017. (Atlas Of Ser.). (ENG.). 96p. (J). (gr. 1-4). 35.00 *(978-1-78603-035-1(7)*, Wide Eyed Editions) Quarto Publishing Group UK GBR. Dist: Hachette Bk. Group.

—Atlas of Miniature Adventures: A Pocket-Sized Collection of Small-scale Wonders. Hawkins, Emily. 2017. (Atlas Of Ser.). (ENG.). 64p. (J). (gr. 1-4). 9.99 *(978-1-84780-910-0(3)*, Wide Eyed Editions) Quarto Publishing Group UK GBR. Dist: Hachette Bk. Group.

—Atlas of Miniature Adventures: A Pocket-Sized Collection of Small-scale Wonders - Because Bigger Isn't Always Better. Hawkins, Emily. 2016. (Atlas Of Ser.). (ENG.). 64p. (J). 9.99 *(978-1-84780-909-4(X)*, Wide Eyed Editions) Quarto Publishing Group UK GBR. Dist: Littlehampton Bk Services, Ltd.

Letherland, Lucy. Atlas of Record-Breaking Adventures: A Collection of the BIGGEST, FASTEST, LONGEST, TOUGHEST, TALLEST & MOST DEADLY Things from Around the World. Hawkins, Emily. 2020. (Atlas Of Ser.). (ENG.). 96p. (J). (gr. 1-7). 35.00 ***(978-0-7112-5565-4(2)***, Wide Eyed Editions) Quarto Publishing Group UK GBR. Dist: Hachette Bk. Group.

LeTourneau, Anthony & Carlson, Josh. A Child's ABCs of Praise. Wiens, Patti. Spieler, Leah, ed. 2004. 60p. (J). pap. 14.99 *(978-0-9761408-0-1(2))* Creative Marketing Concepts, Inc.

LeTourneau, Anthony Alex. The Good Fun! Book: 12 Months of Parties That Celebrate Service. Duncan, Karen & Issa, Kate Hannigan. 2010. 64p. (J). (gr. 2-6). 15.95 *(978-0-9792918-5-2(2))* Blue Marlin Pubns.

—Hanni & Beth: Safe & Sound. 2007. (J). (gr. k-3). 17.95 *(978-0-9792918-0-7(1))* Blue Marlin Pubns.

—In the Shadow of the Mammoth. Clark, Patricia Nikolina. (J). 2005. 14.99 *(978-0-9674602-8-4(X))*; 2003. 190p. pap. 6.99 *(978-0-9674602-4-6(7))* Blue Marlin Pubns.

—Johnny Joins the Army. Beyers, Andrea. 2008. (Flower Kingdom Ser.: Vol. 2). 40p. (J). 16.95 *(978-0-9800754-1-0(6))* RockTuff.

LeTourneau, Anthony Alex, jt. illus. see Bone, Thomas H.

Letourneau, Marie. Is a Worry Worrying You? Wolff, Ferida & Savitz, Harriet May. 2005. (ENG.). 32p. (J). (gr. -1-3). per. 7.99 *(978-1-933718-05-7(6))*; (gr. k-5). 15.95 *(978-0-9749303-2-9(6))* Tanglewood Pr.

LeTourneau, Marie. The Tiptoe Guide to Tracking Fairies. Paquette, Ammi-Joan. 2010. (ENG.). 32p. (J). (gr. -1-3). pap. 8.95 *(978-1-933718-50-7(1))* Tanglewood Pr.

—The Tiptoe Guide to Tracking Mermaids. Paquette, Ammi-Joan. 2012. (ENG.). 32p. (J). (gr. k-5). 16.95 *(978-1-933718-59-0(5))* Tanglewood Pr.

Letria, André. A Donkey Reads, 1 vol. 2011. (ENG.). 32p. (J). (gr. k-3). 16.95 *(978-1-59572-255-3(6))*; pap. 6.95 *(978-1-59572-256-0(4))* Star Bright Bks., Inc.

—If I Were a Book. Letria, José Jorge. 2014. (ENG.). 64p. 12.95 *(978-1-4521-2144-4(3))* Chronicle Bks. LLC.

—Ocean: A Visual Miscellany. Henriques, Ricardo. 2018. (ENG.). 48p. (J). (gr. 3-7). 18.99 *(978-1-4521-5526-5(7))* Chronicle Bks. LLC.

Let's Draw Studio Staff. Four's a Crowd. Chanda, J-P. ed. 2005. (Teenage Mutant Ninja Turtles Ser.: No. 7). 24p. lib. bdg. 15.00 *(978-1-59054-832-5(9))* Fitzgerald Bks.

Letts, Nancy. I Know Him. Smeltzer, Matthew. 2018. (ENG.). 18p. (J). (gr. k-6). pap. 10.00 *(978-1-61286-336-8(1))* Avid Readers Publishing Group.

Leturgie, Morris. Kid Lucky. Leturgie, Jean. 2018. (Lucky Luke Ser.: 69). (ENG.). 48p. pap. 11.95 *(978-1-84918-406-9(2))* CineBook GBR. Dist: National Bk. Network.

Letzig, Michael. Trick-Or-Treat Countdown. Hubbard, Patricia. 2018. 24p. (J). (— 1). bds. 7.99 *(978-0-8234-4033-7(8))* Holiday Hse., Inc.

Leue, Mary. The Hermit's Handbook. Leue, Mary, photos by. Barry, Jack. Leue, Mary, ed. 2004. (Philaterra Ser.). 208p. pap. 12.95 *(978-1-878115-14-0(6))* Down-To-Earth-Bks.

Leung, Andrew. The Royal Waker-Upper. Masters, Elaine. 2003. (ENG.). 39p. (J). *(978-0-89610-992-6(5))* Island Heritage Publishing.

Leung, Hilary. The Pirate Girl's Treasure: An Origami Adventure. Leung, Peyton. 2012. (ENG.). 32p. (J). (gr. -1-3). 16.95 *(978-1-55453-660-3(X))* Kids Can Pr., Ltd. CAN. Dist: Hachette Bk. Group.

Leung, Hilary. Two Tough Trucks. Leung, Hilary. Schwartz, Corey Rosen & Gomez, Rebecca J. 2019. (ENG.). 40p. (J). (gr. -1-k). 17.99 *(978-1-338-23654-5(7),* Orchard Bks.) Scholastic, Inc.

Leung, Raymond. African Animal Tracks: A Folding Pocket Guide to the Tracks & Signs of Familiar Species, Vol. Kavanagh, James & Waterford Press Staff. 2016. (Wildlife & Nature Identification Ser.). (ENG.). 12p. 7.95 *(978-1-58355-037-3(2))* Waterford Pr., Inc.

—African Birds: A Folding Pocket Guide to Familiar Species, Vol. Kavanagh, James & Waterford Press Staff. 2016. (Wildlife & Nature Identification Ser.). (ENG.). 12p. 7.95 *(978-1-58355-033-5(X))* Waterford Pr., Inc.

—African Wildlife: A Folding Pocket Guide to Familiar Species, Vol. Kavanagh, James & Press, Waterford. 2018. (Wildlife & Nature Identification Ser.). (ENG.). 12p. 7.95 *(978-1-58355-032-8(1))* Waterford Pr., Inc.

—African Wildlife Nature Activity Book, Vol. Kavanagh, James & Waterford Press Staff. 2nd rev. ed. 2011. (Wildlife & Nature Identification Ser.). (ENG.). 32p. (J). (gr. -1-12). pap. 6.95 *(978-1-58355-574-3(9))* Waterford Pr., Inc.

—Arctic Wildlife Nature Activity Book, Vol. Kavanagh, James & Waterford Press Staff. 2nd ed. 2011. (Wildlife & Nature Identification Ser.). (ENG.). 32p. (J). (gr. -1-12). pap. 6.95 *(978-1-58355-575-0(7))* Waterford Pr., Inc.

—Australia Birds: A Folding Pocket Guide to Familiar Species, Vol. Kavanagh, James & Waterford Press Staff. 2016. (Wildlife & Nature Identification Ser.). (ENG.). 12p. 7.95 *(978-1-58355-036-6(4))* Waterford Pr., Inc.

—Birds Nature Activity Book. Kavanagh, James. 2nd ed. 2011. (Nature Activity Book Ser.). 32p. (J). (gr. 4-7). 6.95 *(978-1-58355-577-4(3))* Western National Parks Assn.

—California Trees & Wildflowers: A Folding Pocket Guide to Familiar Plants, Vol. Kavanagh, James & Waterford Press Staff. 2017. (Wildlife & Nature Identification Ser.). (ENG.). 12p. 7.95 *(978-1-58355-071-7(2))* Waterford Pr., Inc.

—Colorado Birds: A Folding Pocket Guide to Familiar Species, Vol. Kavanagh, James & Waterford Press Staff. rev. ed. 2017. (Wildlife & Nature Identification Ser.). (ENG.). 12p. (gr. 8). 7.95 *(978-1-58355-068-7(2))* Waterford Pr., Inc.

—Ducks Nature Activity Book. Kavanagh, James & Waterford Press Staff. 2nd ed. 2011. (Nature Activity Book Ser.). (ENG.). 32p. (J). (gr. -1-12). pap. 6.95 *(978-1-58355-579-8(X))* Waterford Pr., Inc.

—Freshwater Fishing: A Waterproof Folding Guide to What a Novice Needs to Know, Vol. Kavanagh, James & Waterford Press Staff. 2016. (Outdoor Skills & Preparedness Ser.). (ENG.). 2p. 7.95 *(978-1-58355-535-4(8))* Waterford Pr., Inc.

—Grasslands Wildlife: A Folding Pocket Guide to Familiar Species Found in Prairie Grasslands, Vol. Kavanagh, James & Waterford Press Staff. 2010. (Wildlife & Nature Identification Ser.). (ENG.). 2p. 7.95 *(978-1-58355-510-1(2))* Waterford Pr., Inc.

—Great Lakes Wildlife Nature Activity Book. Kavanagh, James & Waterford Press Staff. 2nd ed. 2011. (Nature Activity Book Ser.). (ENG.). 32p. (J). (gr. -1-8). pap. 6.95 *(978-1-58355-580-4(3))* Waterford Pr., Inc.

—Hawaii Trees & Wildflowers: A Folding Pocket Guide to Familiar Species, Vol. Kavanagh, James & Waterford Press Staff. 2017. (Wildlife & Nature Identification Ser.). (ENG.). 12p. 7.95 *(978-1-58355-509-5(9))* Waterford Pr., Inc.

—Kansas Birds: A Folding Pocket Guide to Familiar Species, Vol. Kavanagh, James & Waterford Press Staff. 2016. (Wildlife & Nature Identification Ser.). (ENG.). 12p. 7.95 *(978-1-58355-047-2(X))* Waterford Pr., Inc.

—Michigan Birds: A Folding Pocket Guide to Familiar Species, Vol. Kavanagh, James & Waterford Press Staff. rev. ed. 2017. (Wildlife & Nature Identification Ser.). (ENG.). 12p. 7.95 *(978-1-58355-070-0(4))* Waterford Pr., Inc.

—My First Arctic Nature, Vol. Kavanagh, James & Waterford Press Staff. 2011. (Nature Activity Book Ser.). (ENG.). 32p. (J). (gr. -1-8). pap., act. bk. ed. 6.95 *(978-1-58355-586-6(2))* Waterford Pr., Inc.

—My First Deserts Nature, Vol. Kavanagh, James & Waterford Press Staff. 2011. (Nature Activity Book Ser.). (ENG.). 32p. (J). (gr. -1-8). pap., act. bk. ed. 6.95 *(978-1-58355-587-3(0))* Waterford Pr., Inc.

—My First Grasslands Nature, Vol. Kavanagh, James & Waterford Press Staff. 2011. (Nature Activity Book Ser.). (ENG.). 32p. (J). (gr. -1-6). pap., act. bk. ed. 6.95 *(978-1-58355-589-7(7))* Waterford Pr., Inc.

—My First Seashores, Vol. Kavanagh, James & Waterford Press Staff. 2013. (Nature Activity Book Ser.). (ENG.). 32p. (J). (gr. -1-12). pap., act. bk. ed. 6.95 *(978-1-58355-590-3(0))* Waterford Pr., Inc.

—My First Wetlands Nature. Kavanagh, James. 2011. (Nature Activity Book Ser.). 32p. (J). (gr. 2-4). act. bk. ed. 6.95 *(978-1-58355-591-0(9))* Western National Parks Assn.

—New York City Birds: A Folding Pocket Guide to Familiar Species in the Metropolitan Area, Vol. Kavanagh, James & Waterford Press Staff. 2017. (Wildlife & Nature Identification Ser.). (ENG.). 2p. 7.95 *(978-1-58355-012-0(7))* Waterford Pr., Inc.

—Oklahoma Birds: A Folding Pocket Guide to Familiar Species, Vol. Kavanagh, James & Waterford Press Staff. 2017. (Wildlife & Nature Identification Ser.). (ENG.). 12p. (gr. 9). 7.95 *(978-1-58355-008-3(9))* Waterford Pr., Inc.

—Pennsylvania Birds: A Folding Pocket Guide to Familiar Species, Vol. Kavanagh, James & Waterford Press Staff. 2017. (Wildlife & Nature Identification Ser.). (ENG.). 12p. (gr. 9). 7.95 *(978-1-58355-009-0(7))* Waterford Pr., Inc.

—Pond Life, Vol. Kavanagh, James & Waterford Press Staff. 2nd rev. ed. 2016. (Nature Activity Book Ser.). (ENG.). 32p. (J). (gr. -1-8). 6.95 *(978-1-58355-582-8(X))* Waterford Pr., Inc.

—Seashore Wildlife. Kavanagh, James & Waterford Press Staff. 2nd ed. 2013. (Nature Activity Book Ser.). (ENG.). 32p. (J). (gr. -1-8). pap., act. bk. ed. 6.95 *(978-1-58355-584-2(6))* Waterford Pr., Inc.

Leupin, Herbert. Tales from the Brothers Grimm. Grimm. 2015. 160p. (J). (gr. -1-3). 29.95 *(978-0-7358-4228-1(0))* North-South Bks., Inc.

Leutwiler, Anita. Excuse Me, Is This India? Ravishankar, Anushka. 2003. 24p. (J). 14.95 *(978-81-86211-56-4(X))* Tara Publishing IND. Dist: Consortium Bk. Sales & Distribution.

Level, Brian, jt. illus. see Sandoval, Gerardo.

Levens, Megan. Mysticons Volume 1. Leth, Kate. 2018. (ENG.). 80p. (J). (gr. 3-7). pap. 10.99 *(978-1-5067-0647-4(9))* Dark Horse Comics.

—Mysticons Volume 2. Leth, Kate. 2019. (ENG.). 80p. (J). (gr. 3-7). pap. 10.99 *(978-1-5067-0876-8(5))* Dark Horse Comics.

Leveque, Lyne. Count Your Way Through Kenya. Haskins, James & Benson, Kathleen. 2006. (Count Your Way Ser.). 24p. (J). (gr. -1-3). lib. bdg. 19.93 *(978-1-57505-884-9(7),* Millbrook Pr.) Lerner Publishing Group.

LeVert, Mireille. Down at the Sea Hotel: A Greg Brown Song. Brown, Greg. 2007. (ENG.). 36p. (J). (gr. -1-2). 16.95 *(978-2-923163-34-5(6))* La Montagne Secrete CAN. Dist: Independent Pubs. Group.

Levert, Mireille. Tina & the Penguin. Dyer, Heather. 2004. 32p. (J). (gr. k-3). pap. 5.95 *(978-1-55337-767-2(2))* Kids Can Pr., Ltd. CAN. Dist: Hachette Bk. Group.

Levesque, Haude. Bird Brains: The Wild & Wacky World of Birds. Hyman, Jeremy. 2017. (ENG.). 80p. (J). (gr. 3-7). 14.95 *(978-1-63322-153-6(9),* Moondance) Quarto Publishing Group USA.

—If You Were Raised by a Dinosaur. Brooklyn, Isabella. 2013. 80p. (J). (gr. 2-5). pap. 9.95 *(978-1-62354-015-9(1))* Charlesbridge Publishing, Inc.

LeVesque, Sherry, jt. photos by see Cavanaugh, Wendy.

Levey, Emma. Hattie Peck. 2016. (ENG.). 32p. (J). (gr. -1-k). 16.99 *(978-1-63450-170-5(5),* Sky Pony Pr.) Skyhorse Publishing Co., Inc.

—Mine, Mine, Mine Said the Porcupine. English, Alex. 2019. (Early Bird Readers — Blue (Early Bird Stories (tm)) Ser.). (ENG.). 32p. (J). (gr. -1-2). 27.99 *(978-1-5415-4173-3(1),* Lerner Pubns.) Lerner Publishing Group.

—See You Later, Alligator. Hopgood, Sally. 2016. (ENG.). 32p. (J). (gr. -1-k). 16.99 *(978-1-5107-0484-8(1),* Sky Pony Pr.) Skyhorse Publishing Co., Inc.

—Where Is the Bear? De la Bédoyère, Camilla. Kelly, Richard, ed. 2017. (ENG.). 24p. (J). pap. 9.95 *(978-1-78209-984-0(0))* Miles Kelly Publishing, Ltd. GBR. Dist: Parkwest Pubns., Inc.

—Yuck! Said the Yak. English, Alex. 2019. (Early Bird Readers — Green (Early Bird Stories (tm)) Ser.). (ENG.). 32p. (J). (gr. k-3). 27.99 *(978-1-5415-4202-0(9),* 9781541542020); pap. 7.99 *(978-1-5415-7410-6(9),* 9781541574106) Lerner Publishing Group. (Lerner Pubns.).

Levin, Jack E. Our Police. Levin, Jack E. 2018. (ENG.). 40p. (J). (gr. -1-3). 18.99 *(978-1-5344-2950-5(6),* Aladdin) Simon & Schuster Children's Publishing.

—Proverbs for Young People. Levin, Jack E. 2015. (ENG.). 72p. (J). (gr. -1-3). 18.99 *(978-1-4814-5945-7(7),* Aladdin) Simon & Schuster Children's Publishing.

Levin, Jack E. & Levin, Norma R. My Dog Spot. Levin, Jack E. & Levin, Norma R. 2016. (ENG.). 40p. (J). (gr. -1-3). 17.99 *(978-1-4814-6907-4(X),* Aladdin) Simon & Schuster Children's Publishing.

Levin, Lon. Monster Boy & the Classroom Pet, 1 vol. Emerson, Carl. 2008. (Monster Boy Ser.). (ENG.). 32p. (J). (gr. k-4). 28.50 *(978-1-60270-234-9(9),* 11516, Looking Glass Library) Magic Wagon.

—Monster Boy & the Halloween Parade, 1 vol. Emerson, Carl. 2010. (Monster Boy Ser.). (ENG.). 32p. (J). (gr. k-4). 28.50 *(978-1-60270-777-1(4),* 11530, Looking Glass Library) Magic Wagon.

—Monster Boy & the Scary Scouts, 1 vol. Emerson, Carl. 2010. (Monster Boy Ser.). (ENG.). 32p. (J). (gr. k-4). 28.50 *(978-1-60270-778-8(2),* 11532, Looking Glass Library) Magic Wagon.

—Monster Boy at the Library, 1 vol. Emerson, Carl. 2008. (Monster Boy Ser.). (ENG.). 32p. (J). (gr. k-4). 28.50 *(978-1-60270-235-6(7),* 11518, Looking Glass Library) Magic Wagon.

—Monster Boy's Art Project, 1 vol. Emerson, Carl. 2010. (Monster Boy Ser.). (ENG.). 32p. (J). (gr. k-4). 28.50 *(978-1-60270-780-1(4),* 11536, Looking Glass Library) Magic Wagon.

—Monster Boy's Field Trip, 1 vol. Emerson, Carl. 2008. (Monster Boy Ser.). (ENG.). 32p. (J). (gr. k-4). 28.50 *(978-1-60270-236-3(5),* 11520, Looking Glass Library) Magic Wagon.

—Monster Boy's First Day of School, 1 vol. Emerson, Carl. 2008. (Monster Boy Ser.). (ENG.). 32p. (J). (gr. k-4). 28.50 *(978-1-60270-237-0(3),* 11522, Looking Glass Library) Magic Wagon.

—Monster Boy's Gym Class, 1 vol. Emerson, Carl. 2010. (Monster Boy Ser.). (ENG.). 32p. (J). (gr. k-4). 28.50 *(978-1-60270-781-8(2),* 11538, Looking Glass Library) Magic Wagon.

—Monster Boy's School Lunch, 1 vol. Emerson, Carl. 2008. (Monster Boy Ser.). (ENG.). 32p. (J). (gr. k-4). 28.50 *(978-1-60270-238-7(1),* 11524, Looking Glass Library) Magic Wagon.

—Monster Boy's Soccer Game, 1 vol. Emerson, Carl. 2008. (Monster Boy Ser.). (ENG.). 32p. (J). (gr. k-4). 28.50 *(978-1-60270-239-4(X),* 11526, Looking Glass Library) Magic Wagon.

—Monster Boy's Valentine, 1 vol. Emerson, Carl. 2010. (Monster Boy Ser.). (ENG.). 32p. (J). (gr. k-4). 28.50 *(978-1-60270-782-5(0),* 11540, Looking Glass Library) Magic Wagon.

Levin, Lorena. Simba's Adventures. Sonis, Gaby. 2016. (ENG.). 44p. (J). pap. 9.99 *(978-0-692-99275-3(8),* ML Networks) Sonis, Gabriela.

Levin, Norma R., jt. illus. see Levin, Jack E.

Levin, Tom. The Magical Fruit. Levin, Tom. 2019. (ENG.). 34p. (J). pap. 9.99 *(978-1-7930-0078-1(6))* Independently Published.

Levina, Margarita. Polly Profiterole's Little Town: Good Enough to Eat. Gordon, Maggie May. 2020. (ENG.). 36p. (J). (gr. -1-k). pap. 11.99 ***(978-1-912678-18-1(7))*** Little Steps Bks AUS. Dist: Independent Pubs. Group.

Levine, Jennifer. When Kayla Was Kyle. Fabrikant, Amy. 2013. 32p. pap. 8.95 *(978-1-61286-154-8(7))* Avid Readers Publishing Group.

Levine, Lenora D. Special Words: A Story about Multicultural Families & Their Pets. Gomes, Linda Nunes. 2007. (YA). per. 12.99 *(978-1-934400-02-9(5))* Rock Village Publishing.

Levins, Tim. Amazo & the Planetary Reboot. Snider, Brandon T. 2017. (Justice League Ser.). (ENG.). 88p. (J). (gr. 2-6). lib. bdg. 26.65 *(978-1-4965-5156-6(7),* 136169, Stone Arch Bks.) Capstone.

—Batman Undercover. Weissburg, Paul. 2013. (Dark Knight Ser.). (ENG.). 88p. (J). (gr. 3-7). pap. 5.95 *(978-1-4342-4213-6(7),* Stone Arch Bks.) Capstone.

—Batman vs. Catwoman, 1 vol. Bright, J. E. 2013. (DC Super Heroes Ser.). (ENG.). 56p. (J). (gr. 3-6). lib. bdg. 26.65 *(978-1-4342-6013-0(5),* Stone Arch Bks.) Capstone.

—Bizarro & the Doppelgängers of Doom. Snider, Brandon T. 2018. (Justice League Ser.). (ENG.). 88p. (J). (gr. 2-6). lib. bdg. 26.65 *(978-1-4965-5982-1(7),* 137332, Stone Arch Bks.) Capstone.

—Black Adam & the Eternity War. Fridolfs, Derek. 2018. (Justice League Ser.). (ENG.). 88p. (J). (gr. 2-6). lib. bdg. 26.65 *(978-1-4965-5981-4(9),* 137330, Stone Arch Bks.) Capstone.

—Cyborg Superman. Bright, J. E. 2013. (Man of Steel Ser.). (ENG.). 88p. (J). (gr. 3-7). pap. 5.95 *(978-1-4342-4219-8(6),* Stone Arch Bks.) Capstone.

—Darkseid & the Fires of Apokolips. Fridolfs, Derek. 2017. (Justice League Ser.). (ENG.). 88p. (J). (gr. 2-6). lib. bdg. 26.65 *(978-1-4965-5157-3(5),* 136170, Stone Arch Bks.) Capstone.

—Day of the Bizarros! Bird, Benjamin & Siegel, Jerry. 2015. (Amazing Adventures of Superman! Ser.). (ENG.). 32p. (J). (gr. k-2). pap. 3.95 *(978-1-4795-6522-1(9),* Stone Arch Bks.) Capstone.

—Gorilla Grodd & the Primate Protocol. Snider, Brandon T. 2018. (Justice League Ser.). (ENG.). 88p. (J). (gr. 2-6). lib. bdg. 26.65 *(978-1-4965-5979-1(7),* 137328, Stone Arch Bks.) Capstone.

—How to Draw the Joker, Lex Luthor, & Other DC Super-Villains. Sautter, Aaron. 2015. (Drawing DC Super Heroes Ser.). (ENG.). 32p. (J). (gr. 3-9). lib. bdg. 28.65 *(978-1-4914-2155-0(X),* Stone Arch Bks.) Capstone.

—How to Draw Wonder Woman, Green Lantern, & Other DC Super Heroes. Sautter, Aaron. 2015. (Drawing DC Super Heroes Ser.). (ENG.). 32p. (J). (gr. 3-9). lib. bdg. 28.65 *(978-1-4914-2154-3(1),* Stone Arch Bks.) Capstone.

—Injustice Gang & the Deadly Nightshade. Fridolfs, Derek. 2017. (Justice League Ser.). (ENG.). 88p. (J). (gr. 2-6). lib. bdg. 26.65 *(978-1-4965-5158-0(3),* 136171, Stone Arch Bks.) Capstone.

—The Joker & Harley Quinn's Justice League Jailhouse. Simonson, Louise. 2018. (Justice League Ser.). (ENG.). 88p. (J). (gr. 2-6). lib. bdg. 26.65 *(978-1-4965-5980-7(0),* 137329, Stone Arch Bks.) Capstone.

—Justice League. Snider, Brandon T. et al. 2017. (Justice League Ser.). (ENG.). 88p. (J). (gr. 2-6). 103.96 *(978-1-4965-5181-8(8),* 27022, Stone Arch Bks.) Capstone.

—Justice League. Fridolfs, Derek. 2017. (Justice League Ser.). (ENG.). 88p. (J). (gr. 2-6). pap., pap., pap. 23.80 *(978-1-4965-5644-8(5),* 27376, Stone Arch Bks.) Capstone.

—Magic Monsters! Bird, Benjamin. 2015. (Amazing Adventures of Superman! Ser.). (ENG.). 32p. (J). (gr. k-2). pap. 3.95 *(978-1-4795-6525-2(3),* Stone Arch Bks.) Capstone.

—Mxy's Magical Mayhem. Korte, Steve. 2013. (Man of Steel Ser.). (ENG.). 88p. (J). (gr. 3-7). pap. 5.95 *(978-1-4342-4826-8(7),* Stone Arch Bks.) Capstone.

—Poison Ivy's Rainforest Revenge. Stephens, Sarah Hines. 2017. (Batman & Robin Adventures Ser.). (ENG.). 88p. (J). (gr. 2-6). lib. bdg. 26.65 *(978-1-4965-5352-2(7),* 136292, Stone Arch Bks.) Capstone.

—The Riddler's Battleship Blitz. Bright, J. E. 2017. (Batman & Robin Adventures Ser.). (ENG.). 88p. (J). (gr. 2-6). lib. bdg. 26.65 *(978-1-4965-5348-5(9),* 136290, Stone Arch Bks.) Capstone.

—Supergirl's Pet Problem! Bird, Benjamin. 2015. (Amazing Adventures of Superman! Ser.). (ENG.). 32p. (J). (gr. k-2). pap. 3.95 *(978-1-4795-6523-8(7),* Stone Arch Bks.) Capstone.

Levins, Tim & DC Comics Staff. Batman Undercover. Weissburg, Paul. 2013. (Dark Knight Ser.). (ENG.). 88p. (J). (gr. 3-7). 26.65 *(978-1-4342-4094-1(0),* Stone Arch Bks.) Capstone.

Levins, Tim & Lokus, Rex. Starro & the Cybersporе. Snider, Brandon T. 2017. (Justice League Ser.). (ENG.). 88p. (J). (gr. 2-6). lib. bdg. 26.65 *(978-1-4965-5160-3(5),* 136173, Stone Arch Bks.) Capstone.

Levins, Tim & Vecchio, Luciano. A Buried Starship. Dahl, Michael. 2017. (Superman Tales of the Fortress of Solitude Ser.). (ENG.). 40p. (J). (gr. 4-8). lib. bdg. 24.65 *(978-1-4965-4395-0(5),* Stone Arch Bks.) Capstone.

—The Last City of Krypton. Dahl, Michael. 2017. (Superman Tales of the Fortress of Solitude Ser.). (ENG.). 40p. (J). (gr. 4-8). lib. bdg. 24.65 *(978-1-4965-4394-3(7),* Stone Arch Bks.) Capstone.

—Rays of Doom. Dahl, Michael. 2017. (Superman Tales of the Fortress of Solitude Ser.). (ENG.). 40p. (J). (gr. 4-8). lib. bdg. 24.65 *(978-1-4965-4396-7(3),* Stone Arch Bks.) Capstone.

—The Robot That Barked. Dahl, Michael. 2017. (Superman Tales of the Fortress of Solitude Ser.). (ENG.). 40p. (J). (gr. 4-8). lib. bdg. 24.65 *(978-1-4965-4397-4(1),* Stone Arch Bks.) Capstone.

Levins, Tim, jt. illus. see Cavallaro, Mike.

Levins, Tim, jt. illus. see Doescher, Erik.

Levitas, Alex. Pick-A-Woowoo: Have You Ever Wondered about Angels? Alexandria, Chris. 2013. 34p. *(978-1-921883-50-7(2))* Pick-a-Woo Woo Pubs.

—Pick-A-Woowoo - Have You Ever Wondered about Angels? Alexandria, Chris. 2013. 34p. pap. *(978-1-921883-36-1(7))* Pick-a-Woo Woo Pubs.

Levitas, Alexander. Faiga Finds the Way. Brandeis, Batsheva. 2005. (Fun to Read Book Ser.). 120p. (J). pap. 9.95 *(978-1-929628-28-5(5))* Hachai Publishing.

—The Place That I Love. Cohen, R. G. 2006. 30p. (J). 10.95 *(978-1-929628-29-2(3))* Hachai Publishing.

—¡Tú También Puedes! La Vida de Barack Obama. Benatar, Raquel. 2009.Tr. of Yes, you can too! the Life of Barack Obama. (SPA & ENG.). 40p. (J). (gr. 4-9). 16.95 *(978-1-56492-365-3(7))* Laredo Publishing Co., Inc.

Levithan, David & Farmer, Jonathan, photos by. Every You, Every Me. Levithan, David. 2012. 256p. (YA). (gr. 7). pap. 9.99 *(978-0-375-85451-4(7),* Ember) Random Hse. Children's Bks.

LeVitt, Mike. Ghsots of Whitner. LeVitt, J. A. 2004. 84p. (J). per. 10.95 *(978-1-932196-47-4(1))* WordWright.biz, Inc.

Levy, David B. My Visit with Periwinkle. Inches, Alison. 2003. (Blue's Clues Ser.). (ENG.). 24p. (J). pap. 3.99 *(978-0-689-85230-5(4),* Simon Spotlight/Nickelodeon) Simon Spotlight/Nickelodeon.

Levy-Holm, Lori Ann. Look at Me, Look at Me- Can You Guess My Specialty? Christie, Barbara. 2015. 28p. (J). *(978-0-18-219883-2(9))* Figueroa Pr.

Levy, Jane. The 50 State Fossils: A Guidebook for Aspiring Paleontologists, 1 vol. Wang, Yinan. 2018. (ENG.). 72p. (gr. 3-6). 18.99 *(978-0-7643-5557-8(0),* 9830) Schiffer Publishing, Ltd.

Levy, Pamela R. Hector Afloat. Shreeve, Elizabeth. 2004. 71p. (J). lib. bdg. 15.00 *(978-1-4242-0902-6(1))* Fitzgerald Bks.

—Hector Afloat. Shreeve, Elizabeth. 2004. (Ready-For-Chapters Ser.: 3). (ENG.). 64p. (J). (gr. 1-4). pap. 6.99 *(978-0-689-86416-2(7),* Simon & Schuster/Paula Wiseman Bks.) Simon & Schuster/Paula Wiseman Bks.

—Hector Finds a Fortune. Shreeve, Elizabeth. 2004. 68p. (J). lib. bdg. 15.00 *(978-1-4242-0903-3(X))* Fitzgerald Bks.

—Hector Finds a Fortune. Shreeve, Elizabeth. 2004. (Adventures of Hector Fuller Ser.). 68p. (J). (gr. 1-4). 11.65 *(978-0-7569-5527-4(0))* Perfection Learning Corp.

—Hector Springs Loose. Shreeve, Elizabeth. 2004. (Adventures of Hector Fuller Ser.). 67p. (J). (gr. 1-4). 11.65 *(978-0-7569-5528-1(9))* Perfection Learning Corp.

—Hector Springs Loose. Shreeve, Elizabeth. 2004. (Ready-For-Chapters Ser.). (ENG.). 80p. (J). (gr. 1-4). pap. 3.99 *(978-0-689-86414-8(0),* Simon & Schuster/Paula Wiseman Bks.) Simon & Schuster/Paula Wiseman Bks.

—Here Comes Peter Cottontail! Nelson, Steve & Rollins, Jack. 2007. (ENG.). 26p. (J). bds. 12.99 *(978-0-8249-6701-7(1),* Ideal Pubns.) Worthy Publishing.

—Here Comes Peter Cottontail, Set. Nelson, Steve & Rollins, Jack. 2007. (ENG.). 26p. 16.99 *(978-0-8249-6689-8(9),* Ideal Pubns.) Worthy Publishing.

—The Story of Chanukah. Silberg, Francis Barry. 2017. (ENG.). 24p. (J). (gr. -1-k). bds. 7.99 *(978-0-8249-1665-7(4))* Worthy Publishing.

L

—Walking Home Alone. Baker, Ginger. 2003. (Books for Young Learners). (ENG.). 16p. (J). 5.75 net. *(978-1-57274-604-6(1)*, 2534, Bks. for Young Learners) Owen, Richard C. Pubs., Inc.

Levy, Ruth. Animals. Morris, Ting & Morris, Neil. 2006. (Sticky Fingers Ser.). 32p. (J). lib. bdg. 28.50 *(978-1-59771-025-1(3))* Sea-To-Sea Pubns.

Levy, Ruth & Cowne, Joanne. Dinosaurs. Morris, Ting & Morris, Neil. 2006. (Sticky Fingers Ser.). 32p. (J). lib. bdg. 28.50 *(978-1-59771-029-9(6))* Sea-To-Sea Pubns.

Levy, Shaun & Jamieson, Eden. The Fortieth Horse. Fiddick, Calay. 2006. 32p. (J). *(978-1-55306-876-1(9)*, Epic Pr.) Essence Publishing.

Lew-McCabe, Minette. Make Your Own Hawaii Landmarks. 2007. *(978-1-59700-381-0(6))* Island Heritage Publishing.

Lew, Steph. Best Sisters! (Nella the Princess Knight) Glass, George. 2019. (Pictureback(R) Ser.). (ENG.). 24p. (J). (-k). pap. 5.99 *(978-0-525-64725-6(2)*, Random Hse. Bks. for Young Readers) Random Hse. Children's Bks.

Lew, Steph. Can't Catch Santa! Cunningham, Emily. 2020. (ENG.). 20p. (J). bds. ***(978-1-5037-5466-9(9)***, a0a550e3-5032-4be0-be89-65cc7c7f13c7, p i kids) Phoenix International Publications, Inc.

Lew, Steph. The Great Egg Race! (Nella the Princess Knight) Carbone, Courtney. 2018. (Pictureback(R) Ser.). (ENG.). 16p. (J). (gr. -1-2). pap. 5.99 *(978-1-5247-6885-0(5)*, Random Hse. Bks. for Young Readers) Random Hse. Children's Bks.

—I Am a Panda. Garnett, Jaye. Cottage Door Press, ed. 2020. (Finger Puppet Board Book Smithsonian Kids Ser.). (ENG.). 12p. (J). (gr. -1-k). bds. 6.99 *(978-1-68052-813-8(0)*, 1005260) Cottage Door Pr.

—I Am a Tiger. Garnett, Jaye. Cottage Door Press, ed. 2020. (Finger Puppet Board Book Smithsonian Kids Ser.). (ENG.). 12p. (J). (gr. -1 — 1). bds. 6.99 *(978-1-68052-812-1(2)*, 1005250) Cottage Door Pr.

—Nickelodeon Nella the Princess Knight: Looking for a Friend: Sliding Tab. 2018. (Sliding Tab Ser.). (ENG.). 12p. (J). (gr. -1-k). bds. 10.99 *(978-0-7944-4175-3(0)*, Reader's Digest Children's Bks.) Studio Fun International.

—Sparkle Fest Showdown! (Nella the Princess Knight) Matheis, Mickie. 2017. (Pictureback(R) Ser.). (ENG.). 24p. (J). (gr. -1-2). pap. 5.99 *(978-1-5247-1723-0(1)*, Random Hse. Bks. for Young Readers) Random Hse. Children's Bks.

—Trink at the Rink! (Nella the Princess Knight) Matheis, Mickie. 2019. (Pictureback(R) Ser.). (ENG.). 24p. (J). (gr. -1-2). 5.99 *(978-1-9848-4897-0(6)*, Random Hse. Bks. for Young Readers) Random Hse. Children's Bks.

Lew, Stephen, jt. illus. see Random House.

Lew-Vriethoff, Joanne. Another Day As Emily. Spinelli, Eileen. 2015. 240p. (J). (gr. 3-7). 7.99 *(978-0-449-80989-1(7)*, Yearling) Random Hse. Children's Bks.

—Bear on the Loose! Lysiak, Hilde & Lysiak, Matthew. 2017. (Hilde Cracks the Case Ser.: 2). (ENG.). 96p. (J). (gr. 1-3). pap. 4.99 *(978-1-338-14158-0(9))*; lib. bdg. 15.99 *(978-1-338-14159-7(7))* Scholastic, Inc.

—Beautiful. McAnulty, Stacy. 2016. 32p. (J). (gr. -1-1). 16.95 *(978-0-7624-5781-6(3)*, Running Pr. Kids) Running Pr.

Lew-Vriethoff, Joanne. Bonitas. Mcanulty, Stacy. 2018. (SPA.). 32p. (J). (gr. -1-k). 17.50 ***(978-84-679-2886-0(7))*** Norma Editorial, S.A. ESP. Dist: Independent Pubs. Group.

Lew-Vriethoff, Joanne. Brave. McAnulty, Stacy. 2017. 32p. (J). (gr. -1-3). 16.99 *(978-0-7624-5782-3(1)*, Running Pr. Kids) Running Pr.

—The Dancing Pancake. Spinelli, Eileen. 2011. 256p. (J). (gr. 3-7). 7.99 *(978-0-375-85348-7(0)*, Yearling) Random Hse. Children's Bks.

—A Day with Parkinson's. Hultquist, A. 2016. (ENG.). 32p. (J). (gr. -1-3). 16.99 *(978-0-8075-5581-1(9)*, 807555819) Whitman, Albert & Co.

—Do You Know Dewey? Exploring the Dewey Decimal System. Cleary, Brian P. 2012. (ENG.). 32p. (J). (gr. 2-5). lib. bdg. 22.65 *(978-0-7613-6676-8(8)*, Millbrook Pr.) Lerner Publishing Group.

—Fire! Fire! Lysiak, Hilde & Lysiak, Matthew. 2017. (Hilde Cracks the Case Ser.: 3). (ENG.). 96p. (J). (gr. 1-3). pap. 4.99 *(978-1-338-14161-0(9))*; lib. bdg. 24.99 *(978-1-338-14162-7(7))* Scholastic, Inc.

—Hero Dog! Lysiak, Hilde & Lysiak, Matthew. 2017. (Hilde Cracks the Case Ser.: 1). (ENG.). 112p. (J). (gr. 1-3). pap. 4.99 *(978-1-338-14155-9(4))* Scholastic, Inc.

—I Am Famous. Cattie, Becky & Luebbe, Tara. 2018. (ENG.). 32p. (J). (gr. -1-k). 16.99 *(978-0-8075-3440-3(4)*, 807534404) Whitman, Albert & Co.

—I See You. Genhart, Michael. 2017. 40p. (J). 15.95 *(978-1-4338-2758-7(1)*, Magination Pr.) American Psychological Assn.

—I Used to Be Famous. Luebbe, Tara & Cattie, Becky. 2019. (ENG.). 32p. (J). (gr. -1-3). 16.99 *(978-0-8075-3443-4(9)*, 807534439) Whitman, Albert & Co.

—I'm Big! Schafer, Milton. 2006. (J). *(978-1-4156-8150-3(3)*, Dial) Penguin Publishing Group.

—The Invisible Leash: A Story Celebrating Love after the Loss of a Pet. Karst, Patrice. 2019. (Invisible String Ser.). 32p. (J). (gr. -1-3). 17.99 *(978-0-316-52485-8(9))* Little Brown & Co.

—The Invisible String. Karst, Patrice. 2018. 40p. (J). (gr. -1-3). 8.99 *(978-0-316-48623-1(X))* Little, Brown Bks. for Young Readers.

—The Invisible String Workbook: Creative Activities to Comfort, Calm, & Connect. Karst, Patrice & Wyss, Dana. 2019. (Invisible String Ser.). 112p. (J). (gr. -1-17). pap. 12.99 *(978-0-316-52491-9(3))* Little, Brown Bks. for Young Readers.

—The Invisible Web: A Story Celebrating Love & Universal Connection. Karst, Patrice. 2020. (Invisible String Ser.). 32p. (J). (gr. -1-3). 17.99 *(978-0-316-52496-4(4))* Little Brown & Co.

—Joey Daring, Caring, & Curious. Craver, Marcella Marino. 2014. 32p. (J). *(978-1-4338-1652-9(0))*; pap. *(978-1-4338-1653-6(9))* American Psychological Assn. (Magination Pr.).

—Love. McAnulty, Stacy. 2018. (ENG.). 32p. (J). (gr. -1-3). 17.99 *(978-0-7624-6212-4(4)*, Running Pr. Kids) Running Pr.

—The Magician's Hat. Mitchell, Malcolm. 2018. (ENG.). 32p. (J). (gr. -1-3). 17.99 *(978-1-338-11454-6(9))* Scholastic, Inc.

—The Punctuation Station. Cleary, Brian P. (ENG.). 32p. (J). (gr. k-3). 2018. pap. 8.99 *(978-1-5415-1492-8(0)*, Millbrook Pr.); 2010. lib. bdg. 16.95 *(978-0-8225-7852-9(2)*, 1306583) Lerner Publishing Group.

—Summerhouse Time. Spinelli, Eileen. 2009. (ENG.). 224p. (J). (gr. 3-7). 6.99 *(978-0-440-42224-2(8)*, Yearling) Random Hse. Children's Bks.

—Thief Strikes! Lysiak, Hilde & Lysiak, Matthew. 2019. (Hilde Cracks the Case Ser.: 6). (ENG.). 96p. (J). (gr. 1-3). pap. 4.99 *(978-1-338-28391-4(X))*; lib. bdg. 24.99 *(978-1-338-28392-1(8))* Scholastic, Inc.

Lew-Vriethoff, Joanne. Too Sticky! Sensory Issues with Autism. Malia, Jen. 2020. (ENG.). 32p. (J). (gr. -1-3). 16.99 ***(978-0-8075-8026-4(0)***, 807580260) Whitman, Albert & Co.

Lew-Vriethoff, Joanne. Tornado Hits! Lysiak, Hilde & Lysiak, Matthew. 2018. (Hilde Cracks the Case Ser.: 5). (ENG.). 96p. (J). (gr. 1-3). pap. 4.99 *(978-1-338-26677-1(2))*; lib. bdg. 15.99 *(978-1-338-26678-8(0))* Scholastic, Inc.

—UFO Spotted! Lysiak, Hilde & Lysiak, Matthew. 2018. (Hilde Cracks the Case Ser.: 4). (ENG.). 96p. (J). (gr. 1-3). pap. 4.99 *(978-1-338-14164-1(3))*; lib. bdg. 15.99 *(978-1-338-14165-8(1))* Scholastic, Inc.

—Who Will I Be? Huntsman, Abby. 2018. (ENG.). 32p. (J). (gr. -1-3). 18.99 *(978-0-06-284004-2(5))* HarperCollins Pubs.

Lewellen, Emily. Piano & Laylee & the Cyberbully. Curatola Knowles, Carmela N. 2011. (J). pap. *(978-1-56484-279-4(7))* International Society for Technology in Education.

—Piano & Laylee Go Online. Curatola Knowles, Carmela N. 2011. (J). pap. *(978-1-56484-277-0(0))* International Society for Technology in Education.

—Piano & Laylee Learn about Acceptable Use Policies. Curatola Knowles, Carmela N. 2011. (J). 40p. *(978-1-56484-296-1(7))*; 34p. pap. *(978-1-56484-281-7(9))* International Society for Technology in Education.

Lewin, Betsy. A Barnyard Collection: Click, Clack, Moo & More. Cronin, Doreen. 2010. (Click Clack Book Ser.). (ENG.). 128p. (J). (gr. -1-3). 19.99 *(978-1-4424-1263-7(1)*, Atheneum Bks. for Young Readers) Simon & Schuster Children's Publishing.

—A Busy Day at the Farm. Cronin, Doreen. 2009. (Click Clack Book Ser.). (ENG.). 16p. (J). (gr. -1-k). pap. 6.99 *(978-1-4169-5518-4(6)*, Little Simon) Little Simon.

—Clic, Clac, Plif, Plaf: Una Aventura de Contar. Cronin, Doreen. 2006. (J). (gr. -1-k). per. 6.99 *(978-1-933032-03-0(0))* Lectorum Pubns., Inc.

—Clic, Clac, Plif, Plaf: Una Aventura de Contar. Cronin, Doreen. Rioja, Alberto Jimenez, tr. from ENG. 2006. (J). (gr. 5-6). 12.99 *(978-1-933032-11-5(1))* Lectorum Pubns., Inc.

—Click, Clack, 123. Cronin, Doreen. 2010. (Click Clack Book Ser.). (ENG.). 24p. (J). (gr. -1 — 1). bds. 8.99 *(978-1-4169-9125-0(5)*, Little Simon) Little Simon.

—Click, Clack, ABC. Cronin, Doreen. 2010. (Click Clack Book Ser.). (ENG.). 24p. (J). (gr. -1 — 1). bds. 7.99 *(978-1-4169-9124-3(7)*, Little Simon) Little Simon.

—Click, Clack, Boo! A Tricky Treat. Cronin, Doreen. 2019. (Click Clack Book Ser.). (ENG.). 40p. (J). (gr. -1). bds. 7.99 *(978-1-5344-5012-7(2)*, Little Simon) Little Simon.

—Click, Clack, Boo! A Tricky Treat. Cronin, Doreen. 2013. 40p. (J). (gr. -1-2). 17.99 *(978-1-4424-6553-4(0))* Simon & Schuster Children's Publishing.

—Click, Clack, Boo! Lap Edition. Cronin, Doreen. 2020. (Click Clack Book Ser.). (ENG.). 40p. (J). (gr. -1). bds. 12.99 *(978-1-5344-5013-4(0)*, Little Simon) Little Simon.

—Click, Clack, Boo!/Ready-To-Read: A Tricky Treat. Cronin, Doreen. 2018. (Click Clack Book Ser.). (ENG.). 40p. (J). (gr. k-2). 17.99 *(978-1-5344-1380-1(4))*; pap. 4.99 *(978-1-5344-1379-5(0))* Simon Spotlight. (Simon Spotlight).

—Click, Clack, Go! Click, Clack, Moo; Giggle, Giggle, Quack; Dooby Dooby Moo; Click, Clack, Boo!; Click, Clack, Peep!; Click, Clack, Surprise! Cronin, Doreen. ed. 2019. (Click Clack Book Ser.). (ENG.). 224p. (J). (gr. k-2). pap. 17.99 *(978-1-5344-5091-2(2)*, Simon Spotlight) Simon Spotlight.

—Click, Clack, Ho! Ho! Ho! Cronin, Doreen. 2015. (Click Clack Book Ser.). (ENG.). 40p. (J). (gr. -1-2). 17.99 *(978-1-4424-9673-6(8))* Simon & Schuster Children's Publishing.

Lewin, Betsy. Click, Clack, Ho! Ho! Ho! Cronin, Doreen. 2020. (Doreen Cronin: Click, Clack & More Ser.). (ENG.). 40p. (J). (gr. -1-3). 27.07 ***(978-1-5321-4464-6(4)***, 35154, Picture Bk.) Spotlight.

Lewin, Betsy. Click, Clack, Holiday Pack: Click, Clack, Moo I Love You!; Click, Clack, Peep!; Click, Clack, Boo!; Click, Clack, Ho, Ho, Ho! Cronin, Doreen. ed. 2018. (Click Clack Book Ser.). (ENG.). 160p. (J). (gr. -1-3). 71.99 *(978-1-5344-3980-1(3)*, Atheneum Bks. for Young Readers) Simon & Schuster Children's Publishing.

—Click, Clack, Moo. Cronin, Doreen. ed. 2018. 30p. (J). (gr. 1-4). 13.89 *(978-1-64310-126-2(9))* Penworthy Co., LLC, The.

—Click, Clack, Moo: A Book & Play Set, Set. Cronin, Doreen. 2009. (Click Clack Book Ser.). (ENG.). 16p. (J). (gr. -1-k). bds. 14.99 *(978-1-4169-5516-0(X)*, Little Simon) Little Simon.

—Click, Clack, Moo: Cows That Type. Cronin, Doreen & Simon and Schuster/LeapFrog Staff. 2008. (J). 13.99 *(978-1-59319-936-4(8))* LeapFrog Enterprises, Inc.

—Click, Clack, Moo: Cows That Type. Cronin, Doreen. (Click Clack Book Ser.). (ENG.). (J). (gr. -1-3). 2011. 32p. pap. 9.99 *(978-1-4424-3370-0(1))*; 2010. 34p. bds. 7.99 *(978-1-4424-0889-0(8))* Little Simon. (Little Simon).

—Click, Clack, Moo: Cows That Type. Cronin, Doreen. 2016. (J). *(978-0-605-96664-2(8)*, Simon Spotlight) Simon Spotlight.

Lewin, Betsy. Click, Clack, Moo 20th Anniversary Edition: Cows That Type. Cronin, Doreen. ed. 2020. (Click Clack Book Ser.). (ENG.). 32p. (J). (gr. -1-3). 17.99 ***(978-1-5344-6302-8(X)***, Atheneum/Caitlyn Dlouhy Books) Simon & Schuster Children's Publishing.

Lewin, Betsy. Click, Clack, Moo I Love You! Cronin, Doreen. 2017. (Click Clack Book Ser.). (ENG.). 40p. (J). (gr. -1-3). 17.99 *(978-1-4814-4496-5(4)*, Atheneum/Caitlyn Dlouhy Books) Simon & Schuster Children's Publishing.

Lewin, Betsy. Click, Clack, Moo I Love You! Cronin, Doreen. 2020. (Doreen Cronin: Click, Clack & More Ser.). (ENG.). 36p. (J). (gr. -1-3). 27.07 ***(978-1-5321-4465-3(2)***, 35155, Picture Bk.) Spotlight.

Lewin, Betsy. Click, Clack, Moo/Ready-To-Read: Cows That Type. Cronin, Doreen. 2016. (Click Clack Book Ser.). (ENG.). 32p. (J). (gr. k-2). pap. 4.99 *(978-1-4814-6540-3(6)*, Simon Spotlight) Simon Spotlight.

—Click, Clack, Peep! Cronin, Doreen. 2015. (Click Clack Book Ser.). (ENG.). 40p. (J). (gr. -1-3). 17.99 *(978-1-4814-2411-0(4))* Simon & Schuster Children's Publishing.

Lewin, Betsy. Click, Clack, Peep! Cronin, Doreen. 2020. (Doreen Cronin: Click, Clack & More Ser.). (ENG.). 40p. (J). (gr. -1-3). 27.07 ***(978-1-5321-4466-0(0)***, 35156, Picture Bk.) Spotlight.

Lewin, Betsy. Click, Clack, Peep!/Ready-To-Read. Cronin, Doreen. 2019. (Click Clack Book Ser.). (ENG.). 40p. (J). (gr. k-2). 17.99 *(978-1-5344-1386-3(3))*; pap. 4.99 *(978-1-5344-1385-6(5))* Simon Spotlight. (Simon Spotlight).

—Click, Clack, Quack to School! Cronin, Doreen. 2018. (Click Clack Book Ser.). (ENG.). 40p. (J). (gr. -1-3). 17.99 *(978-1-5344-1449-5(5)*, Atheneum/Caitlyn Dlouhy Books) Simon & Schuster Children's Publishing.

Lewin, Betsy. Click, Clack, Quack to School! Cronin, Doreen. 2020. (Doreen Cronin: Click, Clack & More Ser.). (ENG.). 40p. (J). (gr. -1-3). 27.07 ***(978-1-5321-4467-7(9)***, 35157, Picture Bk.) Spotlight.

Lewin, Betsy. Click, Clack, Quackity-Quack: A Typing Adventure. Cronin, Doreen. 2008. (Click Clack Book Ser.). (ENG.). 14p. (J). (gr. -1-k). 14.99 *(978-1-4169-5517-7(8)*, Little Simon) Little Simon.

—Click, Clack, Quackity-Quack: An Alphabetical Adventure. Cronin, Doreen. 2006. (Doreen Cronin: Click-Clack & More Ser.). (ENG.). (J). (gr. k-3). lib. bdg. 27.07 *(978-1-59961-089-4(2)*, 5417, Picture Bk.) Spotlight.

—Click, Clack! Ready-To-Read Value Pack: Click, Clack, Moo; Giggle, Giggle, Quack; Dooby Dooby Moo; Click, Clack, Boo!; Click, Clack, Peep!; Click, Clack, Surprise! Cronin, Doreen. 2019. (Click Clack Book Ser.). (ENG.). 224p. (J). (gr. k-2). pap. 17.96 *(978-1-5344-5768-3(2)*, Simon Spotlight) Simon Spotlight.

—Click, Clack, Splish, Splash: A Counting Adventure, 1 vol. Cronin, Doreen. 2006. (Doreen Cronin: Click-Clack & More Ser.). (ENG.). 24p. (J). (gr. k-3). lib. bdg. 27.07 *(978-1-59961-090-0(6)*, 5418, Picture Bk.) Spotlight.

—Click, Clack, Surprise! Cronin, Doreen. 2016. (Click Clack Book Ser.). (ENG.). 40p. (J). (gr. -1-3). 17.99 *(978-1-4814-7031-5(0)*, Atheneum/Caitlyn Dlouhy Books) Simon & Schuster Children's Publishing.

Lewin, Betsy. Click, Clack, Surprise! Cronin, Doreen. 2020. (Doreen Cronin: Click, Clack & More Ser.). (ENG.). 40p. (J). (gr. -1-3). 27.07 ***(978-1-5321-4468-4(7)***, 35158, Picture Bk.) Spotlight.

Lewin, Betsy. Click, Clack, Surprise!/Ready-To-Read. Cronin, Doreen. 2019. (Click Clack Book Ser.). (ENG.). 40p. (J). (gr. k-2). 17.99 *(978-1-5344-1383-2(9))*; pap. 4.99 *(978-1-5344-1382-5(0))* Simon Spotlight. (Simon Spotlight).

—Cowgirl Kate & Cocoa. Silverman, Erica. 2006. (Cowgirl Kate & Cocoa Ser.). (ENG.). 44p. (J). (gr. 1-4). pap. 5.95 *(978-0-15-205660-5(2)*, 1197019) Houghton Mifflin Harcourt Publishing Co.

—Cowgirl Kate & Cocoa. Silverman, Erica. 2007. (Cowgirl Kate & Cocoa Ser.). (gr. 1-4). 15.95 *(978-0-7569-8043-6(7))* Perfection Learning Corp.

—Cowgirl Kate & Cocoa: Horse in the House. Silverman, Erica. 2010. (Cowgirl Kate & Cocoa Ser.). (ENG.). 44p. (J). (gr. 1-4). pap. 5.99 *(978-0-547-31672-7(0)*, 1415362) Houghton Mifflin Harcourt Publishing Co.

—Cowgirl Kate & Cocoa: Partners. Silverman, Erica. 2007. (Cowgirl Kate & Cocoa Ser.). (ENG.). 44p. (J). (gr. 1-4). pap. 5.95 *(978-0-15-206010-7(3)*, 1198050) Houghton Mifflin Harcourt Publishing Co.

—Cowgirl Kate & Cocoa: Rain or Shine. Silverman, Erica. 2009. (Cowgirl Kate & Cocoa Ser.). (ENG.). 44p. (J). (gr. 1-4). pap. 5.99 *(978-0-15-206602-4(0)*, 1099022) Houghton Mifflin Harcourt Publishing Co.

—Cowgirl Kate & Cocoa: Spring Babies. Silverman, Erica. 2011. (Cowgirl Kate & Cocoa Ser.: 6). (ENG.). 40p. (J). (gr. 1-4). pap. 5.99 *(978-0-547-56685-6(9)*, 1455223) Houghton Mifflin Harcourt Publishing Co.

—Dooby Dooby Moo. Cronin, Doreen. 2010. (Click Clack Book Ser.). (ENG.). 40p. (J). (gr. -1-k). bds. 7.99 *(978-1-4424-0890-6(1)*, Little Simon) Little Simon.

—Dooby Dooby Moo. Cronin, Doreen. 2006. (Click Clack Book Ser.). (ENG.). 40p. (J). (gr. -1-3). 18.99 *(978-0-689-84507-9(3)*, Atheneum Bks. for Young Readers) Simon & Schuster Children's Publishing.

—Dooby Dooby Moo, 1 vol. Cronin, Doreen. 2006. (Doreen Cronin: Click-Clack & More Ser.). (ENG.). 40p. (J). (gr. k-3). lib. bdg. 27.07 *(978-1-59961-423-6(5)*, 5423, Picture Bk.) Spotlight.

—Dooby Dooby Moo. Cronin, Doreen. 2011. (J). (gr. -1-3). 29.95 *(978-0-545-04281-9(X))* Weston Woods Studios, Inc.

—Dooby Dooby Moo/Ready-To-Read. Cronin, Doreen. 2017. (Click Clack Book Ser.). (ENG.). 40p. (J). (gr. k-2). 16.99 *(978-1-5344-0177-8(6))*; pap. 4.99 *(978-1-5344-0176-1(8))* Simon Spotlight. (Simon Spotlight).

Lewin, Betsy. Doreen Cronin: Click, Clack & More Set 2 (Set), 6 vols. Cronin, Doreen. 2020. (Doreen Cronin: Click, Clack & More Ser.). (ENG.). 36p. (J). (gr. -1-3). 162.42 ***(978-1-5321-4463-9(6))***, 35153, Picture Bk.) Spotlight.

Lewin, Betsy. Duck for President. Cronin, Doreen. 2004. (Click Clack Book Ser.). (ENG.). 32p. (J). (gr. -1-3). 17.99 *(978-0-689-86377-6(2)*, Atheneum Bks. for Young Readers) Simon & Schuster Children's Publishing.

—Duck for President. Cronin, Doreen. 2006. (Doreen Cronin: Click-Clack & More Ser.). (ENG.). 32p. (J). (gr. k-3). lib. bdg. 27.07 *(978-1-59961-091-7(4)*, 5419, Picture Bk.) Spotlight.

Lewin, Betsy. Duck Stays in the Truck. Cronin, Doreen. 2020. (Click Clack Book Ser.). (ENG.). 32p. (J). (gr. k-2). 17.99 ***(978-1-5344-5415-6(2))***; pap. 4.99 ***(978-1-5344-5414-9(4))*** Simon Spotlight. (Simon Spotlight).

Lewin, Betsy. Farmer Brown's Barnyard: A Bestselling Board Book Gift Set, Set. Cronin, Doreen. gif. ed. 2008. (Click Clack Book Ser.). (ENG.). 106p. (J). (gr. -1-k). 18.99 *(978-1-4169-5521-4(6)*, Little Simon) Little Simon.

—Favorite Stories from Cowgirl Kate & Cocoa: Partners. Silverman, Erica. ed. 2013. (Cowgirl Kate & Cocoa — Green Light Readers Ser.). (ENG.). 22p. (J). (gr. -1-3). lib. bdg. 13.55 *(978-0-606-33983-4(3))* Turtleback.

—Favorite Stories from Cowgirl Kate & Cocoa: Rain or Shine. Silverman, Erica. 2013. (Green Light Readers Level 2 Ser.). (ENG.). 24p. (J). (gr. 1-4). pap. 4.99 *(978-0-544-10502-7(8)*, 1540804) Houghton Mifflin Harcourt Publishing Co.

—Favorite Stories from Cowgirl Kate & Cocoa: Horse in the House (reader) Silverman, Erica. 2018. (Green Light Readers Level 2 Ser.). (ENG.). 32p. (J). (gr. -1-3). 12.99 *(978-1-328-90089-0(4)*, 1700130); pap. 3.99 *(978-1-328-89580-6(7)*, 1699663) Houghton Mifflin Harcourt Publishing Co. (HMH Books For Young Readers).

—Fraidy Cats. Krensky, Stephen. 2015. (Scholastic Reader, Level 2 Ser.). (ENG.). 32p. (J). (gr. -1-3). pap. 3.99 *(978-0-545-79966-9(X)*, Cartwheel Bks.) Scholastic, Inc.

—Giggle, Giggle, Quack. Cronin, Doreen. 2011. (Click Clack Book Ser.). (ENG.). 34p. (J). (gr. -1-k). bds. 7.99 *(978-1-4424-0891-3(X)*, Little Simon) Little Simon.

—Giggle, Giggle, Quack. Cronin, Doreen. ed. 2018. 30p. (J). (gr. 1-4). 13.89 *(978-1-64310-125-5(0))* Penworthy Co., LLC, The.

—Giggle, Giggle, Quack. Cronin, Doreen. 2006. (Doreen Cronin: Click-Clack & More Ser.). (ENG.). 32p. (J). (gr. k-3). lib. bdg. 27.07 *(978-1-59961-092-4(2)*, 5420, Picture Bk.) Spotlight.

—Jaja Jiji, Cuac. Cronin, Doreen. Jimenez, Alberto, tr. from ENG. 2003.Tr. of Giggle, Giggle, Quack. (SPA.). (J). 15.00 *(978-1-930332-46-1(7))* Lectorum Pubns., Inc.

—Mousequerade Ball: A Counting Tale. Mortensen, Lori. 2016. 32p. (J). 16.99 *(978-1-61963-422-0(8)*, 900135731, Bloomsbury USA Childrens) Bloomsbury Publishing USA.

—Partners. Silverman, Erica. 2007. (Cowgirl Kate & Cocoa Ser.). pap. 7.93 *(978-1-4189-5237-2(0))* Houghton Mifflin Harcourt Trade & Reference Pubs.

—Partners. Silverman, Erica. 2007. (Cowgirl Kate & Cocoa Ser.). (gr. 1-4). 15.95 *(978-0-7569-8042-9(9))* Perfection Learning Corp.

—Pato para Presidente. Cronin, Doreen. 2008.Tr. of Duck for President. (SPA.). (J). (gr. k-2). pap. 7.99 *(978-1-930332-74-4(2)*, LC32509) Lectorum Pubns., Inc.

Lewin, Betsy. Pool Party! Cronin, Doreen. 2020. (Click Clack Book Ser.). (ENG.). 32p. (J). (gr. k-2). 17.99 ***(978-1-5344-5418-7(7))***; pap. 4.99 ***(978-1-5344-5417-0(9))*** Simon Spotlight. (Simon Spotlight).

Lewin, Betsy. Pum, Cuac, Muu: Una Loca Aventura. Cronin, Doreen & Jiménez Rioja, Alberto. 2008. (SPA.). (J). pap. 8.99 *(978-1-933032-54-2(5))*; 36p. 16.99 *(978-1-933032-53-5(7))* Lectorum Pubns., Inc.

—The Red-Hot Rattoons. Winthrop, Elizabeth. 2006. (ENG.). 224p. (J). (gr. 3-6). pap. 17.99 *(978-0-8050-7986-9(6)*, 9780805079869, Holt, Henry & Co. Bks. For Young Readers) Holt, Henry & Co.

—School Days. Silverman, Erica. 2008. (Cowgirl Kate & Cocoa Ser.). (ENG.). 48p. (J). (gr. 1-4). pap. 5.95 *(978-0-15-206130-2(4)*, 1198404) Houghton Mifflin Harcourt Publishing Co.

—So, What's It Like to Be a Cat? Kuskin, Karla. (ENG.). (J). (gr. -1-3). 2008. 40p. 8.99 *(978-0-689-85930-4(9))*; 2005. 32p. 19.99 *(978-0-689-84733-2(5))* Simon & Schuster Children's Publishing. (Atheneum Bks. for Young Readers).

—So, What's It Like to Be a Cat? Kuskin, Karla. 2008. (ENG.). (J). (gr. -1-3). lib. bdg. 18.60 *(978-1-61383-753-5(4))* Perfection Learning Corp.

Lewin, Betsy. Thump, Quack, Moo. Cronin, Doreen. 2020. (Doreen Cronin: Click, Clack & More Ser.). (ENG.). 36p. (J). (gr. -1-3). 27.07 ***(978-1-5321-4469-1(5)***, 35159, Picture Bk.) Spotlight.

Lewin, Betsy. Thump, Quack, Moo: A Whacky Adventure. Cronin, Doreen. 2008. (Click Clack Book Ser.). (ENG.). 42p. (J). (gr. -1-2). 17.99 *(978-1-4169-1630-7(X)*, Atheneum Bks. for Young Readers) Simon & Schuster Children's Publishing.

—Two Eggs, Please. Weeks, Sarah. 2007. (ENG.). 32p. (J). (gr. -1-1). reprint ed. 7.99 *(978-1-4169-2714-3(X)*, Atheneum Bks. for Young Readers) Simon & Schuster Children's Publishing.

Lewin, Betsy. Good Night, Knight. Lewin, Betsy. 2015. (I Like to Read Ser.). (ENG.). 24p. (J). (gr. -1-3). 14.95 *(978-0-8234-3206-6(8))*; 6.99 *(978-0-8234-3315-5(3))* Holiday Hse., Inc.

—Where Is Tippy Toes? Lewin, Betsy. 2010. (ENG.). 32p. (J). (gr. -1-2). 16.99 *(978-1-4169-3808-8(7)*, Atheneum Bks. for Young Readers) Simon & Schuster Children's Publishing.

Lewin, Betsy & Lewin, Ted. Gorilla Walk Gorilla Walk, 1 vol. 2014. (Adventures Around the World Ser.). (ENG.). 48p. (J). pap. 11.95 *(978-1-62014-182-3(5))* Lee & Low Bks., Inc.

—Top to Bottom down under Top to Bottom down Under, 1 vol. 2014. (Adventures Around the World Ser.). (ENG.). 48p. (J). pap. 11.95 *(978-1-62014-184-7(1))* Lee & Low Bks., Inc.

Lewin, Betsy, jt. illus. see Lewin, Ted.

Lewin, Betsy, jt. illus. see Menchin, Scott.

Lewin, Ted. Island of the Blue Dolphins. O'Dell, Scott. gif. ed. 2010. (ENG.). 192p. (J). (gr. 3-7). 22.00 *(978-0-547-42483-5(3),* 1431561) Houghton Mifflin Harcourt Publishing Co.

—One Green Apple. Bunting, Eve. 2006. (ENG.). 32p. (J). (gr. -1-3). 17.99 *(978-0-618-43477-0(1),* 100359) Houghton Mifflin Harcourt Publishing Co.

—Pennies in a Jar, 1 vol. Chaconas, Dori. 2007. (ENG.). 36p. (J). (gr. 1-5). 16.95 *(978-1-56145-422-8(2))* Peachtree Publishing Co. Inc.

—Peppe the Lamplighter. Bartone, Elisa. 2015. 32p. pap. 7.00 *(978-1-61003-612-2(3))* Center for the Collaborative Classroom.

Lewin, Ted. Lost City: The Discovery of Machu Picchu. Lewin, Ted. 2012. (ENG.). 48p. (J). (gr. 2-5). pap. 8.99 *(978-0-14-242580-0(X),* Puffin Books) Penguin Young Readers Group.

—What Am I? Where Am I? Lewin, Ted. 2014. (I Like to Read Ser.). (ENG.). 24p. (J). (gr. -1-3). 7.99 *(978-0-8234-3180-9(0))* Holiday Hse., Inc.

Lewin, Ted & Lewin, Betsy. Balarama: A Royal Elephant. Lewin, Ted & Lewin, Betsy. 2009. (Adventures Around the World Ser.). (ENG.). 56p. (J). (gr. 1-6). 19.95 *(978-1-60060-265-8(7))* Lee & Low Bks., Inc.

Lewin, Ted, jt. illus. see Lewin, Betsy.

Lewis, Anthony. Amber Brown Horses Around. Danziger, Paula et al. 2015. (Amber Brown Ser.: 12). (ENG.). 224p. (J). (gr. 2-5). 6.99 *(978-0-14-751552-0(1),* Puffin Books) Penguin Young Readers Group.

—Amber Brown Is on the Move. Danziger, Paula et al. 2014. (Amber Brown Ser.: 11). (ENG.). 192p. (J). (gr. 2-5). pap. 6.99 *(978-0-14-751223-9(9),* Puffin Books) Penguin Young Readers Group.

—Ant Attack! Ants. James, Anne. 2006. (Science Solves It! ® Ser.). (ENG.). 32p. (J). (gr. k-2). pap. 5.95 *(978-1-57565-117-0(3))* Astra Publishing Hse.

—!Ataque de las Hormigas! James, Anne. Ramirez, Alma B., tr. from ENG. 2008. (Science Solves It! en Espanol Ser.). (SPA.). 32p. (J). (gr. -1-3). pap. 5.95 *(978-1-57565-278-8(1))* Astra Publishing Hse.

—¿Baño o Cama? Nilsen, Anna. Morell, Ivonne Bonsfill, tr. 2010. (SPA.). 12p. (J). 12.95 *(978-84-92691-23-4(9))* Roca Editorial ESP. Dist: Spanish Pubs., LLC.

—Carrots or Peas? Nilsen, Anna. 2008. (Pick & Choose Ser.). 12p. (J). (gr. -1). spiral bd. *(978-1-84643-242-2(1))* Child's Play International Ltd.

—The Color-Day Coach: Baking. 2018. (Makers Make It Work Ser.). (ENG.). 32p. (J). (gr. k-3). 25.32 *(978-1-63592-013-0(2))* Astra Publishing Hse.

—The Color-Day Coach: Baking. Herman, Gail. 2018. (Makers Make It Work Ser.). (ENG.). 32p. (J). (gr. k-3). pap. 5.99 *(978-1-57565-993-0(X))* Astra Publishing Hse.

—Emergency, Call 911. Slater, Teddy. 2010. 16p. (J). *(978-0-545-24601-9(6))* Scholastic, Inc.

—Fire Prevention. Slater, Teddy. 2010. 16p. (J). *(978-0-545-24603-3(2))* Scholastic, Inc.

—First Dinosaur Picture Atlas. Burnie, David. 2020. (Kingfisher First Reference Ser.). (ENG.). 48p. (J). 16.99 *(978-0-7534-7536-2(7),* 900211376, Kingfisher) Roaring Brook Pr.

—First Picture Atlas. Chancellor, Deborah. 2020. (ENG.). 48p. (J). 16.99 *(978-0-7534-7632-1(0),* 900226423, Kingfisher) Roaring Brook Pr.

—Five Little Ducks: American Sign Language. 2013. (Hands-On Songs Ser.). (ENG.). 12p. (J). (gr. -1). bds. *(978-1-84643-630-7(3))* Child's Play International Ltd.

—Frank & Beans, 1 vol. Wargin, Kathy-jo. 2010. (I Can Read! / Frank & Beans Ser.). (ENG.). 32p. (J). pap. 4.99 *(978-0-310-71847-5(3))* Zondervan.

—Frank & Beans & the Scary Campout, 1 vol. Wargin, Kathy-jo. 2010. (I Can Read! / Frank & Beans Ser.). (ENG.). 32p. (J). pap. 4.99 *(978-0-310-71850-5(3))* Zondervan.

—Getting Ready: American Sign Language. ed. 2006. (Sign About Ser.). (ENG.). 12p. (J). (gr. -1). bds. *(978-1-84643-029-9(1))* Child's Play International Ltd.

—Going Out: American Sign Language. ed. 2006. (Sign About Ser.). (ENG.). 12p. (J). (gr. -1). bds. *(978-1-84643-032-9(1))* Child's Play International Ltd.

Lewis, Anthony. Hands-On Songs Board Book Set Of 5. 2020. (Social & Emotional Learning Sets Ser.). (ENG.). 60p. (J). bds., bds., bds. ***(978-1-78628-533-1(9))*** Child's Play International Ltd.

Lewis, Anthony. Human Body Lift-The-Flap. Brooks, Susie. 2014. (Lift-The-Flap Tab Bks.). (ENG.). 16p. (J). (gr. k-1). bds. 9.99 *(978-0-7534-7060-2(8),* 900118664, Kingfisher) Roaring Brook Pr.

—Humpty Dumpty: American Sign Language. 2013. (Hands-On Songs Ser.). (ENG.). 12p. (J). bds. *(978-1-84643-627-7(3))* Child's Play International Ltd.

—Jack & Jill: American Sign Language. 2013. (Hands-On Songs Ser.). (ENG.). 12p. (J). (gr. -1). bds. *(978-1-84643-629-1(X))* Child's Play International Ltd.

—The Lion Book of Prayers to Read & Know, 1 vol. Piper, Sophie. 2010. (ENG.). 96p. (J). 12.99 *(978-0-8254-7898-7(7),* Lion Children's) Lion Hudson PLC GBR. Dist: Kregel Pubns.

—The Lion Read & Know Bible. Piper, Sophie. ed. 2016. (ENG.). 384p. (J). (gr. -1-k). pap. 9.99 *(978-0-7459-7659-4(X));* (gr. k-2). 14.99 *(978-0-7459-7639-6(5))* Lion Hudson PLC GBR. Dist: Independent Pubs. Group.

—Little Ocean Explorers. 2007. (Little Explorers Ser.). 14p. (J). (gr. 1-1). spiral bd. *(978-1-84643-039-8(9))* Child's Play International Ltd.

—Look Inside Bible Times. Rock, Lois. ed. 2016. (ENG.). 8p. (J). (gr. k-2). 16.99 *(978-0-7459-7614-3(X))* Lion Hudson PLC GBR. Dist: Independent Pubs. Group.

—Meal Time: American Sign Language. 2006. (Sign About Ser.). (ENG.). 12p. (J). (gr. -1). bds. *(978-1-84643-030-5(5))* Child's Play International Ltd.

—The Mess. Jensen, Patricia. (My First Reader Ser.). (ENG.). 32p. (J). (gr. k-1). 2004. pap. 3.95 *(978-0-516-24634-5(8));* 2003. 18.50 *(978-0-516-22932-4(X))* Scholastic Library Publishing. (Children's Pr.).

—My First Biography: Benjamin Franklin. Bauer, Marion Dane. 2011. (My First Biography Ser.). (ENG.). 32p. (J). (gr. -1-3). 16.19 *(978-0-545-23256-2(2))* Scholastic, Inc.

—Old Macdonald: American Sign Language. 2013. (Hands-On Songs Ser.). (ENG.). 12p. (J). (gr. -1). bds. *(978-1-84643-628-4(1))* Child's Play International Ltd.

—¿Osito o Tren? Nilsen, Anna. Morell, Ivonne Bonsfill, tr. 2010. (SPA.). 12p. (J). 12.95 *(978-84-92691-25-8(5))* Roca Editorial ESP. Dist: Spanish Pubs., LLC.

—Play Time: American Sign Language. 2006. (Sign About Ser.). (ENG.). 12p. (J). (gr. -1). bds. *(978-1-84643-031-2(3))* Child's Play International Ltd.

—Rescued by a Dog Called Flow. Goodhart, Pippa. 2006. 121p. (J). (gr. 4-7). pap. 6.95 *(978-1-903015-47-6(2))* Barn Owl Bks, London GBR. Dist: Independent Pubs. Group.

—Stranger Danger. Slater, Teddy. 2010. 16p. (J). *(978-0-545-24605-7(9))* Scholastic, Inc.

—Take a Pause, Paul: A Book about Commas. Powell, Marie. 2015. (Punctuation Station Ser.). (ENG.). 16p. (J). (gr. k-2). 17.95 *(978-1-60753-731-1(1))* Amicus Publishing.

—The Tallest Bridge in the World: A Story about Social Anxiety Disorder. Burns, Ellen Flanagan. 2017. 64p. (J). *(978-1-4338-2760-0(3),* Magination Pr.) American Psychological Assn.

—¿Viento o Lluvia? Nilsen, Anna. Morell, Ivonne Bonsfill, tr. 2010. (SPA.). 12p. (J). 12.95 *(978-84-92691-29-6(8))* Roca Editorial ESP. Dist: Spanish Pubs., LLC.

—We Love You Baby. Davidson, Alice Joyce. 2004. (J). 9.99 *(978-1-890647-09-4(8))* TOMY International, Inc.

—What Is That? A Book about Question Marks. Powell, Marie. 2015. (Punctuation Station Ser.). (ENG.). 16p. (J). (gr. k-2). 17.95 *(978-1-60753-732-8(X))* Amicus Publishing.

—The Wheels on the Bus: American Sign Language. 2013. (Hands-On Songs Ser.). (ENG.). 12p. (J). bds. *(978-1-84643-626-0(5))* Child's Play International Ltd.

—¿Zanahorias o Guisantes? Nilsen, Anna. Morell, Ivonne Bonsfill, tr. 2010. (SPA.). 12p. (J). 12.95 *(978-84-92691-27-2(1))* Roca Editorial ESP. Dist: Spanish Pubs., LLC.

Lewis, Anthony, jt. illus. see Dehennin, Stephanie.

Lewis, Anthony, jt. illus. see Farías, Carolina.

Lewis, Aura. Steve Jobs. Sanchez Vegara, Maria Isabel. ed. 2020. (Little People, BIG DREAMS Ser.: 47). (ENG.). 32p. (J). (gr. -1-2). 15.99 ***(978-0-7112-4577-8(0),*** Frances Lincoln Children's Bks.) Quarto Publishing Group UK GBR. Dist: Hachette Bk. Group.

Lewis, Aura. We the People: The United States Constitution Explored & Explained. Lewis, Aura. Sargent, Evan. 2020. (ENG.). 128p. (J). (gr. 5-9). 24.99 ***(978-0-7112-5404-6(4),*** 335935, Wide Eyed Editions) Quarto Publishing Group UK GBR. Dist: Hachette UK Distribution.

Lewis, Brandi. Jesse Sphynxman. Lewis, Brandi. 2018. (Jesse Sphynxman Ser.: Vol. 2). (ENG.). 38p. (J). pap. 12.99 *(978-1-7308-6891-7(6))* Independently Published.

—Jesse Sphynxman Is Breaking Bald. Lewis, Brandi. 2018. (Jesse Sphynxman Is Breaking Bald Ser.: Vol. 1). (ENG.). 32p. (J). pap. 12.99 *(978-1-7294-3248-8(4))* Independently Published.

—Life of a Crunchy Kid: Dairy. Lewis, Brandi. 2018. (Life of a Crunchy Kid Ser.: Vol. 2). (ENG.). 32p. (J). pap. 12.99 *(978-1-7292-7259-6(2))* Independently Published.

Lewis, Brandi D. Life of a Crunchy Kid: Flu Season. Lewis, Brandi D. 2018. (Life of a Crunchy Kid Ser.: Vol. 1). (ENG.). 26p. (J). pap. 12.99 *(978-1-7267-8286-9(7))* Independently Published.

Lewis, Buddy. Bash & the Chocolate Milk Cows. Cole, Burton W. 2015. (ENG.). 224p. (J). (gr. 3-7). pap. 8.99 *(978-1-4336-8530-9(2),* 005699442, B&H Kids) B&H Publishing Group.

Lewis, Corey. Peng! Action Sports Adventures. Lewis, Corey. 2020. (Peng! Ser.). (ENG.). 136p. (J). pap. 14.99 ***(978-1-62010-757-7(0),*** Lion Forge) Oni Pr., Inc.

Lewis, Cynthia. Perk up Your Ears: Discover Your Sense of Hearing. Cobb, Vicki. 2003. (Five Senses Ser.). (ENG.). 32p. (gr. 3-5). pap. 7.95 *(978-0-7613-1981-8(6),* Millbrook Pr.) Lerner Publishing Group.

Lewis, Drew. The Adventures of Big Sil Philadelphia, Pa: Children's Book / Picture Book. Thomas, Nick, photos by. Bennett, A. J. 2016. (Adventures of Big Sil Ser.: Vol. 3). (ENG.). (J). pap. 7.99 *(978-0-9967352-4-7(0))* Big Sil LLC.

—The Adventures of Big Sil Philadelphia, Pa: Children's Book Picture Book. Thomas, Nick, photos by. Bennett, A. J. 2016. (Adventures of Big Sil Ser.: Vol. 3). (ENG.). (J). 19.99 *(978-0-9967352-5-4(9))* Big Sil LLC.

Lewis, E. B. Across the Alley. Michelson, Richard. 2006. (ENG.). 32p. (J). (gr. -1-3). 18.99 *(978-0-399-23970-0(7),* G.P. Putnam's Sons Books for Young Readers) Penguin Young Readers Group.

—The Bat Boy & His Violin. Curtis, Gavin. 2015. 32p. pap. 8.00 *(978-1-61003-618-4(2))* Center for the Collaborative Classroom.

—Bippity Bop Barbershop. Tarpley, Natasha Anastasia. 2009. (ENG.). 32p. (gr. -1-3). pap. 8.99 *(978-0-316-03382-4(0))* Little, Brown Bks. for Young Readers.

—Circle Unbroken. Raven, Margot Theis. 2007. (ENG.). 48p. (J). (gr. -1-3). per. 9.99 *(978-0-312-37603-1(0),* 900048323) Square Fish.

Lewis, E. B. Coming on Home Soon. Woodson, Jacqueline. 2009. (JPN.). 31p. (J). (gr. k-3). ***(978-4-89572-699-3(1))*** Mitsumura Kyouiku Tosho Co., Ltd.

Lewis, E. B. Coming on Home Soon. Woodson, Jacqueline. 2004. (ENG.). 32p. (J). (gr. k-3). 17.99 *(978-0-399-23748-5(8),* G.P. Putnam's Sons Books for Young Readers) Penguin Young Readers Group.

—D Is for Drinking Gourd: An African American Alphabet. Sanders, Nancy I. 2007. (ENG.). 40p. (J). (gr. k-6). 17.95 *(978-1-58536-293-6(X))* Sleeping Bear Pr.

—Danitra Brown, Class Clown. Grimes, Nikki. 2005. 32p. (J). lib. bdg. 17.89 *(978-0-688-17291-6(1));* (ENG.). (gr. 3). 16.99 *(978-0-688-17290-9(3),* Amistad) HarperCollins Pubs.

Lewis, E. B. Dark Was the Night: Blind Willie Johnson's Journey to the Stars. Golio, Gary. 2020. 32p. (J). (gr. k-3). 17.99 ***(978-1-5247-3888-4(3),*** Nancy Paulsen Books) Penguin Young Readers Group.

Lewis, E. B. Each Kindness. Woodson, Jacqueline. 2012. (ENG.). 32p. (J). (gr. k-3). 17.99 *(978-0-399-24652-4(5),* Nancy Paulsen Books) Penguin Young Readers Group.

—The First Step: How One Girl Put Segregation on Trial. Goodman, Susan E. 2016. 40p. (J). 17.99 *(978-0-8027-3739-7(0),* 900135323); (ENG.). (gr. 1-3). E-Book 12.59 *(978-0-8027-3741-0(2))* Bloomsbury Publishing USA. (Bloomsbury USA Childrens).

—Homegrown House. Wong, Janet S. 2009. (ENG.). 40p. (J). (gr. -1-3). 19.99 *(978-0-689-84718-9(1),* McElderry, Margaret K. Bks.) McElderry, Margaret K. Bks.

—I Love My Hair! Tarpley, Natasha Anastasia. 2014. 32p. pap. 7.00 *(978-1-61003-348-0(5))* Center for the Collaborative Classroom.

—I Love My Hair! Tarpley, Natasha Anastasia. 2003. (ENG.). 22p. (J). (gr. -1 — 1). bds. 7.99 *(978-0-316-52558-9(8))* Little, Brown Bks. for Young Readers.

—Joe-Joe's First Flight. Tarpley, Natasha Anastasia. 2003. (ENG.). 40p. (J). (gr. k-2). lib. bdg. 21.19 *(978-0-375-91053-1(0))* Random House Publishing Group.

—Keeping the Night Watch. Smith, Hope Anita. 2014. (ENG.). (J). (gr. 5-8). lib. bdg. 20.60 *(978-1-62765-440-1(2))* Perfection Learning Corp.

—Keeping the Night Watch. Smith, Hope Anita. 2014. (ENG.). 80p. (J). (gr. 5-8). pap. 10.99 *(978-0-312-65936-3(9),* 900070521) Square Fish.

—The Legend of the Cape May Diamond. Noble, Trinka Hakes. rev. ed. 2007. (Legend (Sleeping Bear) Ser.). (ENG.). 40p. (J). (gr. 3-7). 17.95 *(978-1-58536-279-0(4))* Sleeping Bear Pr.

—Lizzie Demands a Seat! Elizabeth Jennings Fights for Streetcar Rights. Anderson, Beth. 2020. (ENG.). 32p. (J). (gr. 2-5). 17.99 *(978-1-62979-939-1(4),* Calkins Creek) Boyds Mills Pr.

—My Best Friend. Rodman, Mary Ann. 2007. (ENG.). 32p. (J). (gr. -1-3). pap. 7.99 *(978-0-14-240806-3(9),* Puffin Books) Penguin Young Readers Group.

—My Best Friend. Rodman, Mary Ann. 2007. (gr. -1-3). 16.00 *(978-0-7569-8151-8(4))* Perfection Learning Corp.

—My Rows & Piles of Coins. Mollel, Tololwa M. 2019. (ENG.). 32p. (J). (gr. -1-3). pap. 8.99 *(978-0-358-12447-4(6),* 1753728, HMH Books For Young Readers) Houghton Mifflin Harcourt Publishing Co.

—Night Boat to Freedom. Raven, Margot Theis. 2008. (ENG.). 40p. (J). (gr. 1-4). pap. 10.99 *(978-0-312-55018-9(9),* 900055951) Square Fish.

—Preaching to the Chickens: The Story of Young John Lewis. Asim, Jabari. 2016. (ENG.). 32p. (J). (gr. k-3). 17.99 *(978-0-399-16856-7(7),* Nancy Paulsen Books) Penguin Young Readers Group.

—The Secret World of Walter Anderson. Bass, Hester. 2014. (Candlewick Biographies Ser.). (ENG.). 48p. (J). (gr. 3-7). 14.99 *(978-0-7636-7116-7(9))* Candlewick Pr.

—The Secret World of Walter Anderson. Bass, Hester & Anderson, Walter Inglis. 2009. 48p. (J). (gr. 1-4). 17.99 *(978-0-7636-3583-1(9))* Candlewick Pr.

—The Secret World of Walter Anderson. Bass, Hester. 2014. (Candlewick Biographies Ser.). (ENG.). (J). (gr. 3-7). lib. bdg. 15.60 *(978-1-62765-775-4(4))* Perfection Learning Corp.

—Seeds of Freedom: The Peaceful Integration of Huntsville, Alabama. Bass, Hester. 32p. (J). (gr. k-3). 2018. 7.99 *(978-0-7636-9516-3(5));* 2015. 16.99 *(978-0-7636-6919-5(9))* Candlewick Pr.

—This Little Light of Mine. Public Domain, Public. 2005. (ENG.). 32p. (J). (gr. -1-3). 19.99 *(978-0-689-83179-9(X),* Simon & Schuster Bks. For Young Readers) Simon & Schuster Bks. For Young Readers.

—Under the Baobab Tree, 1 vol. Stiegemeyer, Julie. 2012. (ENG.). 32p. (J). 16.99 *(978-0-310-72561-9(5))* Zonderkidz.

—Virgie Goes to School with Us Boys. Howard, Elizabeth Fitzgerald. 2005. (gr. k-3). 18.00 *(978-0-7569-5088-0(0))* Perfection Learning Corp.

—Virgie Goes to School with Us Boys. Howard, Elizabeth Fitzgerald. 2005. (ENG.). 32p. (J). (gr. k-3). reprint ed. 7.99 *(978-0-689-87793-3(5),* Aladdin) Simon & Schuster Children's Publishing.

Lewis, Gina J. Wings. Jarrell, Reggie. 2019. (ENG.). 44p. (J). pap. 9.95 ***(978-1-7133-0015-1(X))*** Independently Published.

Lewis, H. B. Mi Pinguino Oliver. Kimmel, Elizabeth Cody. 2004.Tr. of My Penguin Osbert. (SPA.). (J). 15.99 *(978-84-88342-68-3(3))* S.A. Kokinos ESP. Dist: Lectorum Pubns., Inc.

—My Penguin Osbert. Kimmel, Elizabeth Cody. 2004. (ENG.). 40p. (J). (gr. -1-3). 16.99 *(978-0-7636-1699-1(0))* Candlewick Pr.

—My Penguin Osbert. Kimmel, Elizabeth Cody. 2005. 40p. pap. *(978-1-84428-565-5(0))* Walker Bks., Ltd.

—My Penguin Osbert in Love. Kimmel, Elizabeth Cody. 2010. (ENG.). 48p. (J). (gr. -1-3). 7.99 *(978-0-7636-5001-8(3))* Candlewick Pr.

—My Penguin Osbert in Love, Set. Kimmel, Elizabeth Cody & Buck, Lewis. 2008. (ENG.). 48p. (J). (gr. -1-3). 16.99 *(978-0-7636-3032-4(2))* Candlewick Pr.

Lewis, Jackie. Play Ball. Weir, Christina & DeFilippis, Nunzio. 2012. (ENG.). 144p. 14.99 *(978-1-934964-79-8(4),* 9781934964798, Lion Forge) Oni Pr., Inc.

Lewis, Jan. ABC: Turn the Wheels; Find the Words. 2016. 10p. bds. 14.99 *(978-1-86147-712-5(0),* Armadillo) Anness Publishing GBR. Dist: National Bk. Network.

—Animals. 2017. 14p. (J). (gr. -1-12). 11.99 *(978-1-86147-727-9(9),* Armadillo) Anness Publishing GBR. Dist: National Bk. Network.

—Animals: Turn the Wheels Find the Pictures. 2016. 10p. bds. 14.99 *(978-1-86147-713-2(9),* Armadillo) Anness Publishing GBR. Dist: National Bk. Network.

—Ask Me about Animals: Lift the Flaps & Find the Answers! 2016. 14p. (J). (gr. -1-12). 10.99 *(978-1-86147-774-3(0),* Armadillo) Anness Publishing GBR. Dist: National Bk. Network.

—Ask Me about Colours: Lift the Flaps & Find the Answers! 2016. 14p. (J). (gr. -1-12). 10.99 *(978-1-86147-775-0(9),* Armadillo) Anness Publishing GBR. Dist: National Bk. Network.

—At School. 2017. 14p. (J). (gr. -1-12). 11.99 *(978-1-86147-726-2(0),* Armadillo) Anness Publishing GBR. Dist: National Bk. Network.

—Baby's Bible Stories: The Birth of Jesus. Armadillo Publishing Staff. 2015. (ENG.). 24p. (J). (gr. -1 — 1). bds. 6.99 *(978-1-86147-484-1(9),* Armadillo) Anness Publishing GBR. Dist: National Bk. Network.

—The Elves & the Shoemaker. Read, Lorna & Ladybird Books Staff. 2015. (First Favourite Tales Ser.). (ENG.). 32p. (J). (-k). 9.99 *(978-1-4093-0628-3(3))* Penguin Bks., Ltd. GBR. Dist: Independent Pubs. Group.

—The Emperor's New Clothes. 2015. 24p. (J). (gr. -1-2). bds. 6.99 *(978-1-86147-413-1(X),* Armadillo) Anness Publishing GBR. Dist: National Bk. Network.

—Fairy Palace: You Are Invited to a Party in the Fairy Palace! 2015. 10p. (J). (gr. k-3). bds. 7.99 *(978-1-86147-315-8(X),* Armadillo) Anness Publishing GBR. Dist: National Bk. Network.

—First Fairy Tales: Cinderella. 2013. (ENG.). 24p. (J). (gr. -1-k). bds. 6.99 *(978-1-86147-334-9(6),* Armadillo) Anness Publishing GBR. Dist: National Bk. Network.

—First Fairy Tales: Sleeping Beauty. 2013. (ENG.). 24p. (J). (gr. -1-k). bds. 6.99 *(978-1-86147-338-7(9),* Armadillo) Anness Publishing GBR. Dist: National Bk. Network.

—First Fairy Tales: The Ugly Duckling. 2013. (ENG.). 24p. (J). (gr. -1-k). bds. 6.99 *(978-1-86147-333-2(8),* Armadillo) Anness Publishing GBR. Dist: National Bk. Network.

—First Fairy Tales: Three Little Pigs. 2013. (ENG.). 24p. (J). (gr. -1-k). bds. 6.99 *(978-1-86147-331-8(1),* Armadillo) Anness Publishing GBR. Dist: National Bk. Network.

—First Prayers for Little Ones: Prayers for Every Day, Special Occasions & the Family. 2016. 48p. (J). (gr. -1-12). 9.99 *(978-1-86147-716-3(3),* Armadillo) Anness Publishing GBR. Dist: National Bk. Network.

—How to Be a Pirate in 7 Days or Less. Rees, Lesley. 2006. (How to be A Ser.). 32p. (J). (gr. k-3). 12.95 *(978-0-7534-6041-2(6),* Kingfisher) Roaring Brook Pr.

—I Want to Know about the Bible, 1 vol. Goodings, Christina. (ENG.). 48p. (J). 2010. 14.99 *(978-0-8254-7896-3(0),* Lion Children's); 2012. pap. 8.99 *(978-0-7459-6217-7(3))* Lion Hudson PLC GBR. Dist: Kregel Pubns., Independent Pubs. Group.

—Lift-The-Flap Word House: 200 Things to Find, See & Say. 2016. (ENG.). 10p. (J). (gr. -1-12). bds. 7.99 *(978-1-86147-778-1(3),* Armadillo) Anness Publishing GBR. Dist: National Bk. Network.

—Look & Learn with Little Dino: Action Words. 2014. (ENG.). 24p. (J). (gr. k-2). bds. 6.99 *(978-1-86147-382-0(6),* Armadillo) Anness Publishing GBR. Dist: National Bk. Network.

—Look & Learn with Little Dino: Busy Day. 2014. (ENG.). 24p. (J). (gr. k-2). bds. 6.99 *(978-1-86147-379-0(6),* Armadillo) Anness Publishing GBR. Dist: National Bk. Network.

—Look & Learn with Little Dino: Count 123. 2014. (ENG.). 24p. (J). (gr. -1-1). bds. 6.99 *(978-1-86147-381-3(8),* Armadillo) Anness Publishing GBR. Dist: National Bk. Network.

—Love from Santa, 6 vols. ed. 2013. (ENG.). 60p. (J). (gr. -1-2). bds. 7.99 *(978-1-86147-313-4(3),* Armadillo) Anness Publishing GBR. Dist: National Bk. Network.

—Magical Fairy Tales: Aladdin & the Lamp; the Ugly Duckling; the Emperor's New Clothes; Puss in Boots. 2016. 48p. bds. 9.99 *(978-1-86147-700-2(7),* Armadillo) Anness Publishing GBR. Dist: National Bk. Network.

—Mother Goose Action Rhymes: Old MacDonald Had a Farm; One, Two, Buckle My Shoe; Round & Round the Garden; This Little Pig. 2004. 90p. (J). vinyl bd. *(978-1-902272-32-0(3))* Tucker Slingsby, Ltd.

—Mother Goose Rhymes: One, Two, Buckle My Shoe. 2015. 24p. bds. 6.99 *(978-1-86147-637-1(X),* Armadillo) Anness Publishing GBR. Dist: National Bk. Network.

—My Big Book of Fairy Tales in Rhyme! Tucker Slingsby Ltd., Staff. 2004. 224p. (J). *(978-1-902272-31-3(5))* Tucker Slingsby, Ltd.

—My Busy Day. 2017. 14p. (J). (gr. -1-12). pap. 11.99 *(978-1-86147-723-1(6))* Anness Publishing, Inc.

—My Favourite Nursery Rhyme Collection, Set. 2017. (ENG.). 1p. bds. 14.99 *(978-1-86147-740-8(6),* Armadillo) Anness Publishing GBR. Dist: National Bk. Network.

—My First 123. 2014. (ENG.). 24p. (J). (gr. -1-k). bds. 6.99 *(978-1-86147-371-4(0),* Armadillo) Anness Publishing GBR. Dist: National Bk. Network.

—My First 123: Learn to Count from 1 To 100! 2015. 48p. pap. 9.99 *(978-1-86147-425-4(3),* Armadillo) Anness Publishing GBR. Dist: National Bk. Network.

—My First ABC. 2014. (ENG.). 24p. (J). (gr. -1-k). bds. 6.99 *(978-1-86147-372-1(9),* Armadillo) Anness Publishing GBR. Dist: National Bk. Network.

—My First ABC: Learn the Alphabet with 300 Words & Pictures. 2016. 48p. (J). (gr. -1-12). pap. 9.99 *(978-1-86147-728-6(7),* Armadillo) Anness Publishing GBR. Dist: National Bk. Network.

—My First Animals. 2014. (ENG.). 24p. (J). (gr. -1-k). bds. 6.99 *(978-1-86147-373-8(7),* Armadillo) Anness Publishing GBR. Dist: National Bk. Network.

—My First Animals: Over 200 Animals to Name & Learn About. Armadillo, Jeffrey. 2015. 48p. bds. 9.99 *(978-1-86147-652-4(3),* Armadillo) Anness Publishing GBR. Dist: National Bk. Network.

—My First Bible Stories: Adam & Eve, Noah's Ark, Moses, Joseph, David & Goliath, Jesus. 2016. 48p. (J). (gr.

L

-1-12). bds. 9.99 *(978-1-86147-737-8(6)*, Armadillo) Anness Publishing GBR. Dist: National Bk. Network.

—My First Colours. 2014. (ENG.). 24p. (J). (gr. -1-k). bds. 6.99 *(978-1-86147-374-5(5)*, Armadillo) Anness Publishing GBR. Dist: National Bk. Network.

—My First Learning Library: 3 Great Books: First Abc First 123 First Words, 3 vols. 2014. (ENG.). 72p. (J). (gr. -1-1). bds., bds., bds. 9.99 *(978-1-86147-387-5(7)*, Armadillo) Anness Publishing GBR. Dist: National Bk. Network.

—My First Words: Over 300 Everyday Words & Pictures. 2015. 48p. bds. 9.99 *(978-1-86147-627-2(2)*, Armadillo) Anness Publishing GBR. Dist: National Bk. Network.

—Old MacDonald Had a Farm. 2015. 24p. bds. 6.99 *(978-1-86147-468-1(7)*, Armadillo) Anness Publishing GBR. Dist: National Bk. Network.

—On the Farm: A Friendly Story with Flaps to Lift. 2016. (ENG.). 10p. (J). (gr. -1-12). bds. 7.99 *(978-1-86147-779-8(1)*, Armadillo) Anness Publishing GBR. Dist: National Bk. Network.

—On the Farm: Pull the Tab to Make the Words Appear! 2017. 14p. (J). (gr. -1-12). 11.99 *(978-1-86147-722-4(8))* Anness Publishing, Inc.

—Performance. 2012. (First Time Ser.). 24p. (J). *(978-1-84643-487-7(4))* Child's Play International Ltd.

—The Pied Piper of Hamelin. 2006. (First Fairy Tales Ser.). 30p. (J). (gr. -1-3). lib. bdg. 28.50 *(978-1-59771-072-5(5))* Sea-To-Sea Pubns.

—Pirate Ship: Lift the Flaps to Follow the Clues & Discover the Fabulous Treasure. 2016. (ENG.). 10p. (J). (gr. -1-12). bds. 7.99 *(978-1-86147-767-5(8)*, Armadillo) Anness Publishing GBR. Dist: National Bk. Network.

—Playtime Rhymes: My Mother Goose Collection. 2018. 24p. (J). (gr. -1-12). bds. 6.99 *(978-1-86147-694-4(9)*, Armadillo) Anness Publishing GBR. Dist: National Bk. Network.

—The Princess & the Pea. 2015. 24p. bds. 6.99 *(978-1-86147-467-4(9)*, Armadillo) Anness Publishing GBR. Dist: National Bk. Network.

—Round & Round the Garden. 2015. 24p. bds. 6.99 *(978-1-86147-636-4(1)*, Armadillo) Anness Publishing GBR. Dist: National Bk. Network.

—Santa's Christmas Box of Books: A Festive Box of Fun Picture Books. 2017. (ENG.). 1p. bds. 14.99 *(978-1-86147-738-5(4)*, Armadillo) Anness Publishing GBR. Dist: National Bk. Network.

—Santa's Workshop: The Inside Story! 2015. 10p. (J). (gr. k-4). bds. 7.99 *(978-1-86147-314-1(1)*, Armadillo) Anness Publishing GBR. Dist: National Bk. Network.

—School. 2012. (First Time Ser.). (ENG.). 24p. (J). *(978-1-84643-491-4(2))* Child's Play International Ltd.

—Small Bad Wolf. Taylor, Sean. 2004. (I Am Reading Ser.). 45p. (J). (gr. -1-3). 11.60 *(978-0-7569-5400-0(2))* Perfection Learning Corp.

—This Little Pig. Armadillo Publishing Staff. 2015. (ENG.). 24p. bds. 6.99 *(978-1-86147-486-5(5)*, Armadillo) Anness Publishing GBR. Dist: National Bk. Network.

—Toby's Trousers. Cassidy, Anne. 2005. (Reading Corner Ser.). 24p. (J). (gr. k-3). lib. bdg. 22.80 *(978-1-59771-009-1(1))* Sea-To-Sea Pubns.

—Words: Turn the Wheels, Find the Pictures. 2015. 10p. bds. 14.99 *(978-1-86147-660-9(4)*, Armadillo) Anness Publishing GBR. Dist: National Bk. Network.

—123: Turn the Wheels - Learn to Count! 2015. 10p. (J). (gr. -1-12). bds. 14.99 *(978-1-86147-661-6(2)*, Armadillo) Anness Publishing GBR. Dist: National Bk. Network.

Lewis, Jan. Look & Learn with Little Dino: Colour Fun. Lewis, Jan. 2014. (ENG.). 24p. (J). (gr. -1-2). bds. 6.99 *(978-1-86147-380-6(X)*, Armadillo) Anness Publishing GBR. Dist: National Bk. Network.

—Princess Fairy Tales: Cinderella, the Princess & the Pea, Sleeping Beauty, the Little Mermaid. Lewis, Jan. 2015. 48p. bds. 9.99 *(978-1-86147-423-0(7)*, Armadillo) Anness Publishing GBR. Dist: National Bk. Network.

Lewis, Jasmine. Donut & Her Daddy. Cook, Iyeesha. 2018. (ENG.). 36p. (J). pap. 13.99 *(978-1-7320698-0-0(8))* I C Legacy LLC.

Lewis, Jenn. Valentine the Porcupine Dances Funny. Brown, Derrick. 2011. (ENG.). 44p. 20.00 *(978-1-935904-18-2(3)*, Write Fuzzy) Write Bloody Publishing.

Lewis, Jesse. The Stone Heart. Foster, D. S. 2012. (J). pap. 12.99 *(978-1-937331-14-6(8))* ShadeTree Publishing, LLC.

Lewis, Josh. A Day at the Dinosaur Museum. Adams, Tom. 2017. (ENG.). 14p. (J). (gr. 2-4). 18.99 *(978-0-7636-9687-0(0)*, Templar) Candlewick Pr.

—The Giving Farmer. Pizzo, Erika. 2018. (ENG.). 24p. (J). (gr. -1-2). 10.99 *(978-0-8307-7606-1(0)*, 145330) Cook, David C.

—The Saving Farmer. Pizzo, Erika. 2018. (ENG.). 24p. (J). (gr. -1-2). 10.99 *(978-0-8307-7641-2(9)*, 146442) Cook, David C.

Lewis Jr, Daryl M. The 3Ds' Christmas. 2007. 30p. (J). 9.99 *(978-0-9776987-2-1(6))* Blackberry Pubns.

Lewis, K. E. Arturo & the Bienvenido Feast, 1 vol. Broyles, Anne. Cortes, Maru, tr. 2017. (ENG & SPA.). 32p. (J). (gr. -1-3). 16.99 *(978-1-4556-2283-2(4)*, Pelican Publishing) Arcadia Publishing.

—Arturo & the Navidad Birds, 1 vol. Broyles, Anne. 2013. (ENG & SPA.). 32p. (J). (gr. k-3). 16.99 *(978-1-4556-1801-9(2)*, Pelican Publishing) Arcadia Publishing.

—City Fun. Hillert, Margaret. 2016. (BeginningtoRead Ser.). (ENG.). 32p. (J). (gr. -1-2). pap. 11.94 *(978-1-60357-975-9(3))*; 21st ed. (gr. k-2). 22.60 *(978-1-59953-813-6(X))* Norwood Hse. Pr.

—Will It Blow? Become a Volcano Detective at Mount St. Helens. Rusch, Elizabeth. 2017. 48p. (J). (gr. 1-4). pap. 14.99 *(978-1-63217-110-8(4)*, Little Bigfoot) Sasquatch Bks.

Lewis, Karen. Grandmother Fish: A Child's First Book of Evolution. Tweet, Jonathan. 2016. (ENG.). 40p. (J). 17.99 *(978-1-250-11323-8(7)*, 900170789) Feiwel & Friends.

Lewis, Kellie. Please Pass the Manners! Mealtime Tips for Everyone. Schaefer, Lola. 2009. (ENG.). 12p. (J). (gr. -1-1). 7.99 *(978-1-4169-4826-1(0)*, Little Simon) Little Simon.

Lewis, Kim. I'll Always Be Your Friend. McBratney, Sam. 2004. (ENG.). 32p. (J). (gr. -1-3). pap. 6.99 *(978-0-06-055548-1(3)*, Harper Trophy) HarperCollins Pubs.

Lewis, Kim. Seymour & Henry. Lewis, Kim. 2009. (ENG.). 32p. (J). (gr. k-k). 15.99 *(978-0-7636-4243-3(6))* Candlewick Pr.

Lewis, Kim & Graef, Renee. Kirsten's Short Story Collection. Shaw, Janet. 2006. (American Girls Collection). 213p. (J). (gr. 3-8). 12.95 *(978-1-59369-323-7(0))* American Girl Publishing, Inc.

Lewis, Liza. Silly Sounds: Ready, Set... Go! 2020. (Silly Sounds Ser.). (ENG.). 12p. (J). (gr. -1-k). bds. 14.99 *(978-1-68412-704-7(1)*, Silver Dolphin Bks.) Printers Row Publishing Group.

Lewis-MacDougall, Patricia Ann, jt. illus. see Fiegenschuh, Emily.

Lewis, Marcia. Comfy, Cozy: A Bedtime Story. Lenihan, Kelly. 2018. (ENG.). 50p. (J). 20.00 *(978-0-9979578-1-5(6))* Artisan Bookworks.

Lewis, Maud. Christmas with the Rural Mail, 1 vol. 2017. (ENG.). 32p. (J). (gr. -1-k). pap. 12.95 *(978-1-55109-530-1(0)*, 3b92ffe7-b0e9-4f57-953c-36ca982ff525) Nimbus Publishing, Ltd. CAN. Dist: Baker & Taylor Publisher Services (BTPS).

—Maud Lewis 1,2,3, 1 vol. LaRamee-Jones, Shanda & McDougall, Carol. 2017. (ENG.). 20p. (J). (gr. -1 — 1). bds. 12.95 *(978-1-77108-521-2(5)*, aa7e2577-a4c7-447c-bfd0-98824caada61) Nimbus Publishing, Ltd. CAN. Dist: Baker & Taylor Publisher Services (BTPS).

Lewis, Naomi C. The New Neighbors. Ellis, Julie. 2009. (Rigby PM Stars Bridge Bks.). (ENG.). 16p. (gr. 2-3). pap. 8.70 *(978-1-4190-5507-2(0))* Rigby Education.

Lewis, Paul Owen. Storm Boy, 1 vol. Lewis, Paul Owen. 2008. (ENG.). 32p. (J). (gr. -1-3). pap. 8.95 *(978-1-55285-268-2(7))* Whitecap Bks., Ltd. CAN. Dist: Graphic Arts Ctr. Publishing Co.

Lewis, R. J. The Ballerina with Webbed Feet/la Bailarina Palmipeda. Van Scoyoc, Pam. Teichman, Diane E., tr. from ENG. l.t. ed. 2004. (ENG & SPA.). 40p. (J). (gr. k-2). lib. bdg. 16.98 *(978-0-9663629-2-3(6))* By Grace Enterprises.

—I Could Catch a Whale/ Yo Podría Pescar una Ballena. Van Scoyoc, Pam. Santillan-Cruz, Sylvia R., tr. l.t. ed. 2005. (ENG & SPA.). 32p. (J). (gr. k-2). lib. bdg. 16.98 *(978-0-9663629-5-4(0))* By Grace Enterprises.

Lewis, Rebecca. Tilli's Tale. Williams, Barbara A. 2004. 48p. (J). per. *(978-1-932077-52-0(9))* Athena Pr.

Lewis, Robin Baird. Bunny Angel. Gallagher, Jennifer. 2020. (ENG.). 40p. (J). ***(978-1-5255-6673-8(3))***; pap. ***(978-1-5255-6674-5(1))*** FriesenPress.

Lewis, Robin Baird. Parfois Grand, Parfois Petit. Stinson, Kathy. Homel, David, tr. from ENG. 2006. (FRE.). 23p. (J). (gr. -1-2). reprint ed. pap. 5.00 *(978-1-4223-5663-0(9))* DIANE Publishing Co.

—Red Is Best. Stinson, Kathy. (ENG.). (J). (gr. -1 — 1). 6th ed. 2011. 26p. bds. 7.99 *(978-1-55451-364-2(2)*, 9781554513642); 7th ed. 2006. 32p. 19.95 *(978-1-55451-052-8(X)*, 9781554510528); 9th anniv. ed. 2006. 32p. pap. 6.95 *(978-1-55451-051-1(1)*, 9781554510511) Annick Pr., Ltd. CAN. Dist: Publishers Group West (PGW).

Lewis, Rosario Aguilera. Nicio y el Incendio Cedar. Aguilera, Gina. Aguilera, Francisco Enrique, tr. 2010. (SPA.). 42p. (J). pap. 13.00 *(978-0-9842392-1-4(9))* Jennie's Music Room Bks.

Lewis, Stephen. Monster Eyeballs. Wilson, Jacqueline. 2nd ed. 2016. (Reading Ladder Ser.). (ENG.). 48p. (J). (gr. k-2). pap. 7.99 *(978-1-4052-8199-7(5))* Egmont Bks., Ltd. GBR. Dist: Independent Pubs. Group.

—Nine Bright Pennies. Slater, Teddy & Scholastic, Inc. Staff. 2005. (ENG.). 16p. (J). (gr. -1-1). pap. 2.99 *(978-0-439-69020-1(X))* Scholastic, Inc.

—Seven Magic Hats. Charlesworth, Liza. 2005. (ENG.). 16p. (J). (gr. -1-1). pap. 2.99 *(978-0-439-69018-8(8))* Scholastic, Inc.

—Snow Friends. Jones, Milo. 2010. 16p. (J). pap. *(978-0-545-24823-5(X))* Scholastic, Inc.

Lewis, Steve. Magic on the Map #3: Texas Treasure, 3. Sheinmel, Courtney & Turetsky, Bianca. 2020. (Magic on the Map Ser.: 3). 128p. (J). (gr. 2-5). 5.99 *(978-1-9848-9569-1(9)*, Random Hse. Bks. for Young Readers) Random Hse. Children's Bks.

Lewis, Stevie. A Cast Is the Perfect Accessory: (and Other Lessons I've Learned) Gutknecht, Allison. 2014. (ENG.). 160p. (J). (gr. 2-5). 16.99 *(978-1-4424-8396-5(2))*; pap. 5.99 *(978-1-4424-8395-8(4))* Simon & Schuster Children's Publishing. (Aladdin).

—Don't Wear Polka-Dot Underwear with White Pants: (and Other Lessons I've Learned) Gutknecht, Allison. 2013. (ENG.). 160p. (J). (gr. 2-5). pap. 6.99 *(978-1-4424-8392-7(X)*, Aladdin) Simon & Schuster Children's Publishing.

—Don't Wear Polka-Dot Underwear with White Pants: (and Other Lessons I've Learned) Gutknecht, Allison. 2013. (ENG.). 160p. (J). (gr. 2-5). 15.99 *(978-1-4424-8393-4(8)*, Simon & Schuster/Paula Wiseman Bks.) Simon & Schuster/Paula Wiseman Bks.

—Finding Serendipity. Banks, Angelica. 2015. (Tuesday Mcgillycuddy Adventures Ser.). (ENG.). 288p. (J). (gr. 3-7). 16.99 *(978-1-62779-154-0(X)*, 900138447, Holt, Henry & Co. Bks. For Young Readers) Holt, Henry & Co.

—Finding Serendipity. Banks, Angelica. 2016. (Tuesday Mcgillycuddy Adventures Ser.). (ENG.). 304p. (J). pap. 8.99 *(978-1-250-07337-2(5)*, 900150766) Square Fish.

—Lost in the Library: A Story of Patience & Fortitude. Funk, Josh. 2018. (New York Public Library Book Ser.). (ENG.). 40p. (J). 17.99 *(978-1-250-15501-6(0)*, 900184517, Holt, Henry & Co. Bks. For Young Readers) Holt, Henry & Co.

—Magic on the Map #1: Let's Mooove! Sheinmel, Courtney & Turetsky, Bianca. 2019. (Magic on the Map Ser.: 1). 128p. (J). (gr. 2-5). 5.99 *(978-1-63565-166-9(2)*, Random Hse. Bks. for Young Readers) Random Hse. Children's Bks.

Lewis, Stevie. Magic on the Map #4: Escape from Camp California. Sheinmel, Courtney & Turetsky, Bianca. 2020. (Magic on the Map Ser.: 4). 128p. (J). (gr. 2-5). pap. 5.99 ***(978-1-9848-9572-1(9))***; (ENG.). lib. bdg. 12.99 ***(978-1-9848-9573-8(7))*** Random Hse. Children's Bks. (Random Hse. Bks. for Young Readers).

Lewis, Stevie. Moon! Earth's Best Friend. McAnulty, Stacy. 2019. (Our Universe Ser.: 3). (ENG.). 40p. (J). 18.99 *(978-1-250-19934-8(4)*, 900194811, Holt, Henry & Co. Bks. For Young Readers) Holt, Henry & Co.

—Never Wear Red Lipstick on Picture Day: (and Other Lessons I've Learned) Gutknecht, Allison. 2014. (ENG.). 176p. (J). (gr. 2-5). 16.99 *(978-1-4814-2959-7(0))*; pap. 6.99 *(978-1-4814-2958-0(2))* Simon & Schuster Children's Publishing. (Aladdin).

—Pizza Is the Best Breakfast: (and Other Lessons I've Learned) Gutknecht, Allison. 2015. (ENG.). 176p. (J). (gr. 2-5). pap. 6.99 *(978-1-4814-2961-0(2)*, Aladdin) Simon & Schuster Children's Publishing.

—Prince & Knight. Haack, Daniel. (ENG.). (J). (gr. -1-1). 2020. 26p. bds. 8.99 *(978-1-4998-1095-0(4))*; 2018. 40p. 17.99 *(978-1-4998-0552-9(7))* Little Bee Books Inc.

—The Show Must Go On. Sheinmel, Courtney & Turetsky, Bianca. 2019. (Magic on the Map Ser.: 2). 128p. (J). (gr. 2-5). 5.99 *(978-1-63565-169-0(7)*, Random Hse. Bks. for Young Readers) Random Hse. Children's Bks.

—A Smart Girl's Guide, Travel: Everything You Need to Know about Adventuring near & Far. Andrus, Aubre. 2019. (ENG.). 96p. (J). pap. *(978-1-68337-123-6(2))* American Girl Publishing, Inc.

—Sun! One in a Billion. McAnulty, Stacy. 2018. (Our Universe Ser.: 2). (ENG.). 40p. (J). 17.99 *(978-1-250-19932-4(8)*, 900194804, Holt, Henry & Co. Bks. For Young Readers) Holt, Henry & Co.

Lewis, Stevie. Baby Shark! Lewis, Stevie. 2020. (ENG.). 24p. (J). bds. 8.99 *(978-1-250-26318-6(2)*, 900221681, Holt, Henry & Co. Bks. For Young Readers) Holt, Henry & Co.

Lewis, T. Tillena Lou's Day in the Sun. Tharp, Barbara et al. Denk, James, ed. 2nd ed. 2013. (My World & Me Ser.). (ENG.). 32p. (J). (gr. k-2). pap. *(978-1-888997-44-6(3)*, BioEd) Baylor College of Medicine.

Lewis, Wayne. Ted & the Combine Harvester. Lougher, Jenny. 2007. 23p. pap. *(978-1-905553-27-3(7))* BookPublishingWorld.

Lewitt and Him Staff & Anon. Locomotive. Tuwim, Julian & Anon. 2017. (ENG.). 47p. (J). (gr. -1-5). 16.95 *(978-0-500-65097-4(7)*, 565097) Thames & Hudson.

Ley, Mary. Tri-Son: The Little Triathlete. Ley, Mary. 2003. per. *(978-0-9707547-1-4(X))* Woodburn Graphics, Inc.

Leybler, Nehameh. Hershi Lernt Zikh Farmestn MIT Gefiln. Gold, R. & Marmorshteyn, M. H. 2018. (YID.). (J). *(978-1-68091-229-6(1))* Kinder Shpiel USA, Inc.

Leyhane, Vici & Baggott, Stella. Sticker Dolly Dressing Dolls. Watt, Fiona. 2006. (Usborne Activities Ser.). 23p. (J). pap. 8.99 *(978-0-7945-1389-4(1)*, Usborne) EDC Publishing.

—Sticker Dolly Dressing Princesses. Watt, Fiona. 2007. (Sticker Dolly Dressing Ser.). 32p. (J). pap. 8.99 *(978-0-7945-1390-0(5)*, Usborne) EDC Publishing.

Leyhane, Vici, jt. illus. see Baggott, Stella.

Leyland, Scott. Molly & Corry: Satellite Sleuths. Hart, Chris. 2018. (Molly & Corry Ser.: Vol. 2). (ENG.). 222p. (J). pap. *(978-1-9998113-0-3(5))* Nitere Publishing.

—Molly & Corry Boot Up! The Friendship Paradox. Hart, Chris A. 2017. (Molly & Corry Ser.: Vol. 1). (ENG.). 216p. (J). pap. *(978-0-9956568-1-9(9))* Nitere Publishing.

Leyris, Ad�le. Blink! Boyle, Doe. 2020. (Imagine This! Ser.). 32p. (J). (gr. -1-3). 17.99 ***(978-0-8075-0667-7(2)***, 0807506672) Whitman, Albert & Co.

Leyssenne, Mathieu & Kraft, Jason. The Ultimate Pirate Handbook. Hamilton, Libby. 2015. (ENG.). 20p. (J). (gr. k-3). 19.99 *(978-0-7636-7963-7(1)*, Templar) Candlewick Pr.

Leyva, Barbara. Henry & the Magic Window. Leyva, Barbara. l.t. ed. 2003. 50p. (J). 3.50 *(978-0-9729056-0-2(X)*, 0, Balticbard Publishing) Leyva, Barbara.

Leyva, Juan Camilo. Nettey Loves Shoeboxes. Delisle, Annette Gonzalez. 2011. 28p. pap. 9.99 *(978-1-61170-015-2(9))* Robertson Publishing.

Lhamo, Choki & Loday, Gyelsey, photos by. Bhutan: An Odyssey in Shangri-la with Choki & Gyelsey. Hawley, Michael. 2nd ed. 2003. 216p. lib. bdg. 10000.00 *(978-0-9742469-0-1(5)*, Big Bks. for Little People) Friendly Planet.

L'Hirondelle, Cheryl. Nieve. Griggs, Terry. 2010. (ENG.). 264p. (J). (gr. 4-10). pap. 14.95 *(978-1-897231-87-6(3))* Biblioasis CAN. Dist: Consortium Bk. Sales & Distribution.

Lhomme, Sandrine. The Earth Has Caught Cold. Galliez, Roxane Marie. 2009. 24p. (J). (gr. -1-3). 9.99 *(978-0-8416-7140-9(0))* Hammond World Atlas Corp.

—Farewell Sadness. Galliez, Roxane Marie. 2010. 24p. (J). 9.99 *(978-0-8416-7139-3(7))* Hammond World Atlas Corp.

Lhomme, Sandrine. Sammy the Snail's Amazing Day, 1 vol. Lhomme, Sandrine. Piu, Amandine. 2012. (My Baby Stories Ser.). (ENG.). 24p. (J). (gr. -1). bds. 9.95 *(978-2-7338-1981-4(X))* Auzou, Philippe Editions FRA. Dist: Consortium Bk. Sales & Distribution.

L'Hommedieu, Arthur John. Children of the Sun. L'Hommedieu, Arthur John. 24p. (J). (gr. k-11). spiral bd. 10.99 *(978-0-85953-939-5(3))* Child's Play International Ltd. GBR. Dist: Child's Play-International.

Li, Amy. Monster Counting. Tyler, Madeline. 2020. (Monster Math Ser.). (ENG.). 24p. (J). (gr. -1-2). pap. 7.99 *(978-1-5415-8920-9(3))*; lib. bdg. 26.65 *(978-1-5415-7927-9(5))* Lerner Publishing Group. (Lerner Pubns.).

—Monster Measuring. Tyler, Madeline. 2020. (Monster Math Ser.). (ENG.). 24p. (J). (gr. -1-2). pap. 7.99 *(978-1-5415-8923-0(8))*; lib. bdg. 26.65 *(978-1-5415-7928-6(3))* Lerner Publishing Group. (Lerner Pubns.).

—Monster Patterns. Tyler, Madeline. 2020. (Monster Math Ser.). (ENG.). 24p. (J). (gr. -1-2). pap. 7.99 *(978-1-5415-8921-6(1))*; lib. bdg. 26.65 *(978-1-5415-7929-3(1))* Lerner Publishing Group. (Lerner Pubns.).

—Monster Shapes. Tyler, Madeline. 2020. (Monster Math Ser.). (ENG.). 24p. (J). (gr. -1-2). pap. 7.99 *(978-1-5415-8922-3(X))*; lib. bdg. 26.65 *(978-1-5415-7930-9(5))* Lerner Publishing Group. (Lerner Pubns.).

Li-Chee-Ming, Linda. Tiny World: Felting! Li-Chee-Ming, Linda. Odd Dot. 2019. (Tiny World Ser.: 3). (ENG.). 32p. (J). pap. 14.99 *(978-1-250-20385-4(6)*, 900200608, Odd Dot) St. Martin's Pr.

Li, Cornelia. My Family, Your Family! Cole, Kathryn. 2020. (ENG.). 16p. (J). (gr. -1 — 1). bds. 10.95 ***(978-1-77260-133-6(0))*** Second Story Pr. CAN. Dist: Orca Bk. Pubs. USA.

—Nature's Light Spectacular: 12 Stunning Scenes of Earth's Greatest Shows. Flint, Katy. 2020. (Glow in the Dark Ser.). (ENG.). 24p. (J). (gr. -1-3). ***(978-0-7112-5197-7(5)***, Wide Eyed Editions) Quarto Publishing Group UK.

Li, Cornelia. The Trouble with Time Travel. Martin, Stephen W. 2019. (ENG.). 24p. (J). (gr. k-5). 16.95 *(978-1-77147-332-3(0))* Owlkids Bks. Inc. CAN. Dist: Publishers Group West (PGW).

Li, Deborah. Tricia & the Blue Cap. l.t. ed. 2003. 28p. (J). 7.95 net. *(978-0-9706654-5-4(8))* Sprite Pr.

Li, Ellen. A Girl Like Tilly. Bates, Helen. 2016. (ENG.). 72p. (C). 15.95 *(978-1-78592-163-6(0)*, 694041) Kingsley, Jessica Pubs. GBR. Dist: Hachette UK Distribution.

Li, Hui. Astronauts: With Stem Projects for Kids. Klepeis, Alicia. 2019. (Gutsy Girls Ser.). 112p. (J). (gr. 3-5). (ENG.). 19.95 *(978-1-61930-778-0(2)*, 2f00c9f9-d6ca-4635-900e-a941ee73a2e0); pap. 14.95 *(978-1-61930-781-0(2)*, c558ede6-f2cb-49a6-ac43-36a437b9ec9a) Nomad Pr.

—Energy. Diehn, Andi. 2018. (Picture Book Science Ser.). (ENG.). 32p. (J). (gr. k-3). 19.95 *(978-1-61930-639-4(5)*, eca583dd-2c0c-4769-990c-c8572d14a646) Nomad Pr.

—Engineers: With Stem Projects for Kids. Taylor, Diane. 2019. (Gutsy Girls Ser.). 112p. (J). (gr. 3-5). (ENG.). 19.95 *(978-1-61930-782-7(0)*, 07903f7b-9ef8-4d94-a2a6-2669860ab4c6); pap. 14.95 *(978-1-61930-785-8(5)*, 3ff272d6-65c0-409e-b4a9-93159b61b228) Nomad Pr.

—Forces. Diehn, Andi. 2018. (Picture Book Science Ser.). (ENG.). 32p. (J). (gr. k-3). 19.95 *(978-1-61930-636-3(0)*, 2b02db9d-1805-4bed-afbb-2c5ed98b6ef5) Nomad Pr.

—Matter. Diehn, Andi. 2018. (Picture Book Science Ser.). (ENG.). 32p. (J). (gr. k-3). 19.95 *(978-1-61930-642-4(5)*, 60fb786f-dc09-481a-9a75-329cff5308fb) Nomad Pr.

—Paleontologists: With Stem Projects for Kids. Gibson, Karen Bush. 2019. (Gutsy Girls Ser.). 112p. (J). (gr. 3-5). 19.95 *(978-1-61930-790-2(1)*, eb31c6c6-0d76-4b50-b22e-c19cd4bba0c8); pap. 14.95 *(978-1-61930-793-3(6)*, ed1886f2-df16-439a-a393-1c5d8373805c) Nomad Pr.

—Programmers: With Stem Projects for Kids. Gibson, Karen Bush. 2019. (Gutsy Girls Ser.). 112p. (J). (gr. 3-5). (ENG.). 19.95 *(978-1-61930-786-5(3)*, 57135b37-1124-4d93-adc5-f35db481a178); pap. 14.95 *(978-1-61930-789-6(8)*, be68c475-2d17-4ce3-b968-6cd0c833e947) Nomad Pr.

—Running Across America: A True Story of Dreams, Determination, & Heading for Home. McGillivray, Dave & Feehrer, Nancy. 2019. (ENG.). 32p. (J). 16.95 *(978-1-61930-875-6(4)*, 48d31823-aa82-4fb9-a8dc-65c1ef23e6e5) Nomad Pr.

—Waves. Diehn, Andi. 2018. (Picture Book Science Ser.). (ENG.). 32p. (J). (gr. k-3). 19.95 *(978-1-61930-633-2(6)*, 28eb7c98-95c2-4a3e-981b-5e7d40ef0ede) Nomad Pr.

Li, Maggie. What Do Scientists Do All Day? Wilsher, Jane. 2020. (ENG.). 64p. (J). (gr. -1-2). ***(978-0-7112-4978-3(4)***, Wide Eyed Editions) Quarto Publishing Group UK.

Li, Sophie. Mulan's Lunar New Year. Yim, Natasha. 2018. (ENG.). 48p. (J). (gr. 1-3). 17.99 *(978-1-368-02326-9(6))* Disney Pr.

Li, Wai-Yant, jt. illus. see Ching, Kai Yun.

Li, Xiaojun. Selvakumar Knew Better. Kroll, Virginia. 2009. (Selvakumar Knew Better Ser.). 32p. (J). (gr. -1-3). pap. 8.95 *(978-1-885008-36-7(8)*, Shen's Bks.) Lee & Low Bks., Inc.

Li, Yishan. Will Supervillains Be on the Final? Liberty Vocational. Novik, Naomi. 2011. 192p. (YA). pap. 10.99 *(978-0-345-51656-5(7)*, Del Rey) Random House Publishing Group.

Lia, Simone. The Secret Time Machine & the Gherkin Switcheroo. Lia, Simone. 2020. (ENG.). 192p. (J). (gr. 2-4). 14.99 ***(978-1-5362-0740-8(3))*** Candlewick Pr.

Lia, Simone. They Didn't Teach THIS in Worm School! Lia, Simone. 2018. (ENG.). 192p. (J). (gr. 2-4). 14.99 *(978-0-7636-9536-1(X))* Candlewick Pr.

Liam Michel Liam. Notebook Journal: Paper Notebook, Diary, Journal, Planner or Sketchbook - Size 6 X 9 - 120 Pages - Office Equipment - Great Gift ... Liam Michel Liam. 2019. (ENG.). 122p. (J). pap. 6.00 ***(978-1-6731-0437-0(1))***; pap. 6.00 ***(978-1-6731-0697-8(8))***; pap. 6.00 ***(978-1-6731-1407-2(5))***; pap. 6.00 ***(978-1-6731-1492-8(X))***; pap. 6.00 ***(978-1-6731-1497-3(0))***; pap. 6.00 ***(978-1-6731-1647-2(7))***; pap. 6.00 ***(978-1-6731-1687-8(6))*** Independently Published.

—Notebook Journal: Wood Design Paper Notebook, Diary, Journal, Planner or Sketchbook - Size 6 X 9 - 120 Pages - Office Equipment - Great Gift ... Liam Michel Liam. 2019. (ENG.). 122p. (J). pap. 6.00 ***(978-1-6730-9869-3(X))*** Independently Published.

—Notebook Journal: Wood Moustaches Paper Notebook, Diary, Journal, Planner or Sketchbook - Size 6 X 9 - 120 Pages - Office Equipment - Great Gift ... Liam Michel Liam. 2019. (ENG.). 122p. (J). pap. 6.00 ***(978-1-6731-0229-1(8))*** Independently Published.

Liance, Bruno. Nina: Jazz Legend & Civil-Rights Activist Nina Simone. Bri�re-Haquet, Alice. 2017. (ENG.). 40p. (J). (gr. -1-3). lib. bdg. 16.99 *(978-1-58089-827-0(0))* Charlesbridge Publishing, Inc.

Liang, Mindy. Donde Esta Mi Casa? Carmi, Tali. 2017. (Historias Hora de Dormir para Los Ninos Ser.: Vol. 3). (SPA.). (J). (gr. k-3). *(978-965-7724-23-1(6))* Valcal Software Ltd.

—God's Fruit in Me. Rozier, Vince. 2018. (ENG.). 28p. (J). pap. 9.25 *(978-0-9913224-6-6(0))* Step One Publishing.

—Terry el Trepador Encuentra Nuevos Amigos. Carmi, Tali. 2017. (Historias Hora de Dormir para Los Ninos Ser.: Vol. 1). (SPA.). (J). (gr. k-3). *(978-965-7724-21-7(X))* Valcal Software Ltd.

—Terry el Trepador y el Huevo Perdido. Carmi, Tali. 2017. (SPA.). (J). (gr. k-3). *(978-965-7724-22-4(8))* Valcal Software Ltd.

—Terry Treetop & the Christmas Star. Carmi, Tali. Rider, Taira, tr. 2017. (ENG.). 42p. (J). (gr. k-3). *(978-965-7724-27-9(9))* Valcal Software Ltd.

—Terry Treetop & the Lost Egg. Carmi, Tali. 2017. (Terry Treetop Ser.: Vol. 2). (ENG.). (J). (gr. k-3). *(978-965-92331-5-1(9))* Valcal Software Ltd.

Liang, Xiao Long. Battle of Red Cliffs. Dong Chen, Wei. 2013. (Three Kingdoms Ser.: 11). (ENG.). 176p. (gr. 5-12). pap. 9.99 *(978-89-98341-24-4(7))* JR Comics KOR. Dist: Lerner Publishing Group.

—Blood & Renewal. Chen, Wei Dong. 2015. (Outlaws of the Marsh Ser.). (ENG.). 176p. (YA). (gr. 6-12). pap. 9.99 *(978-89-98341-90-9(5))* Lerner Publishing Group.

—Heroes & Chaos, Vol. 1. Chen, Wei Dong. 2013. (Three Kingdoms Ser.: 1). (ENG.). 176p. (gr. 5-12). pap. 9.99 *(978-89-94208-89-3(5))* JR Comics KOR. Dist: Lerner Publishing Group.

—Rage & Rebellion, Vol. 11. Chen, Wei Dong. 2015. (Outlaws of the Marsh Ser.). (ENG.). 176p. (YA). (gr. 6-12). pap. 9.99 *(978-89-98341-95-4(6))* Lerner Publishing Group.

—The Timely Rain. Chen, Wei Dong. 2015. (Outlaws of the Marsh Ser.). (ENG.). 176p. (YA). (gr. 6-12). pap. 9.99 *(978-89-98341-91-6(3))* Lerner Publishing Group.

—Wagers & Vows. Dong Chen, Wei. 2013. (Three Kingdoms Ser.: 12). (ENG.). 176p. (gr. 5-12). pap. 9.99 *(978-89-98341-25-1(5))* JR Comics KOR. Dist: Lerner Publishing Group.

Liang, Xiao Long. The Brotherhood Restored, Vol. 7. Liang, Xiao Long. Chen, Wei Dong. 2013. (Three Kingdoms Ser.: 7). (ENG.). 176p. (gr. 5-12). pap. 9.99 *(978-89-94208-67-1(4))* JR Comics KOR. Dist: Lerner Publishing Group.

—Three Kingdoms, Vol. 9. Liang, Xiao Long. Chen, Wei Dong. 2013. (Three Kingdoms Ser.: 9). (ENG.). 176p. (gr. 5-12). pap. 9.99 *(978-89-98341-22-0(0))* JR Comics KOR. Dist: Lerner Publishing Group.

Liang, Zhu Chen. A New Year's Reunion: A Chinese Story. Yu, Li Qiong. 2011. (ENG.). 40p. (J). (gr. -1-2). 15.99 *(978-0-7636-5881-6(2))* Candlewick Pr.

Liao, Jimmy. Filbert, the Good Little Fiend. Oram, Hiawyn. 2013. (ENG.). 32p. (J). (gr. -1-2). 15.99 *(978-0-7636-5870-0(7))* Candlewick Pr.

—The World Champion of Staying Awake. Taylor, Sean. 2011. (ENG.). 32p. (J). (gr. -1-2). 15.99 *(978-0-7636-4957-9(0))* Candlewick Pr.

Liao, Yivian. Activity Story Book: Sunshine & Her Big Blarney Smile. Hale, Linda. 2013. 26p. pap. *(978-1-927915-03-5(1))* Chase Enterprises.

—Sunshine & Her Big Blarney Smile. Hale, Linda. 2013. 26p. pap. *(978-1-927915-02-8(3))* Chase Enterprises.

Liautaud, Judy. Lulu Turns on the Night Light. Liautaud, Judy. 2013. 24p. pap. 12.95 *(978-1-883841-19-5(4))* City Creek Pr., Inc.

Libenson, Terri. Adventures in Middle School 2-Book Box Set: Invisible Emmie & Positively Izzy. Libenson, Terri. 2018. (Emmie & Friends Ser.). (ENG.). 416p. (J). (gr. 3-7). pap. 25.98 *(978-0-06-289749-7(7),* Balzer & Bray) HarperCollins Pubs.

—Becoming Brianna. Libenson, Terri. 2020. (Emmie & Friends Ser.). (ENG.). 320p. (J). (gr. 3-7). 22.99 *(978-0-06-289454-0(4));* pap. 12.99 *(978-0-06-289453-3(6))* HarperCollins Pubs. (Balzer & Bray).

—Invisible Emmie. Libenson, Terri. 2017. (Emmie & Friends Ser.). (ENG.). 192p. (J). (gr. 3-7). 22.99 *(978-0-06-248494-9(X),* Balzer & Bray) HarperCollins Pubs.

—Just Jaime. Libenson, Terri. 2019. (Emmie & Friends Ser.). (ENG.). 256p. (J). (gr. 3-7). 22.99 *(978-0-06-285107-9(1),* Balzer & Bray) HarperCollins Pubs.

—Positively Izzy. Libenson, Terri. 2018. (Emmie & Friends Ser.). (ENG.). 224p. (J). (gr. 3-7). 22.99 *(978-0-06-248497-0(4),* Balzer & Bray) HarperCollins Pubs.

Libenson, Terri. You-Niquely You: an Emmie & Friends Interactive Journal. Libenson, Terri. 2020. (Emmie & Friends Ser.). (ENG.). 144p. (J). (gr. 3-7). pap. 12.99 ***(978-0-06-299838-5(2),*** Balzer & Bray) HarperCollins Pubs.

Liberatore, Laura. El Oso Meloso y Su Pandilla. Cisneros, Diego A. 2018. (SPA.). 26p. (J). 22.95 *(978-1-4808-5750-6(5));* pap. 16.95 *(978-1-4808-5751-3(3))* Archway Publishing.

—The Sweet Mellow Bear & His Gang. Cisneros, Diego A. Cisneros, Luis G., tr. 2018. (ENG.). 26p. (J). 22.95 *(978-1-4808-5514-4(6));* pap. 16.95 *(978-1-4808-5512-0(X))* Archway Publishing.

Libertelli, Clarissa. My Life with Scoliosis. Guerrero, Elsie. 2019. (ENG.). 30p. (J). (gr. k-6). 19.99 ***(978-1-7327573-5-6(6))*** Elsie Publishing Co.

Librach, Wendi. Abagail's Adventure. LaVigne, Carin. House, Racquel, ed. 2019. (ENG.). 46p. (J). pap. 10.99 ***(978-1-0729-1976-6(1))*** Independently Published.

Libranda, Kevin. Royals Vol. 2: Judgment Day. 2018. (ENG.). 112p. (YA). (gr. 8-17). pap. 19.99 *(978-1-302-90695-5(X))* Marvel Worldwide, Inc.

Libranda, Kevin, jt. illus. see Izaakse, Sean.

Libranda, Kevin, jt. illus. see Lam, Jon.

Licht, Jake. Super Caydan to the Rescue! Licht, Traci. 2019. (Boy Who Wanted to Save the World Ser.: Vol. 2). (ENG.). 28p. (J). pap. 12.95 ***(978-1-0795-4645-3(6))*** Independently Published.

Lichtenheld, Tom. A Bailar y Contar en la Fiesta. Litwin, Eric. 2017. (José el Chévere Ser.: 2). (SPA.). 40p. (J). (gr. -1-k). 17.99 *(978-1-338-18786-1(4),* Scholastic en Espanol) Scholastic, Inc.

—Buenas Noches, Construccion. Buenas Noches, Diversion. Rinker, Sherri Duskey. Lázaro, Georgina & Mlawer, Teresa, trs. 2019. (SPA.). 32p. (J). (gr. -1 — 1). 16.99 *(978-1-4521-7037-4(1))* Chronicle Bks. LLC.

—Camp Buccaneer. Smallcomb, Pam. ed. 2005. 58p. (J). lib. bdg. 15.00 *(978-1-59054-897-4(3))* Fitzgerald Bks.

—Dance Party Countdown. Litwin, Eric. 2017. (Groovy Joe Ser.: 2). (ENG.). 40p. (J). (gr. -1-k). 17.99 *(978-0-545-88379-5(2),* Orchard Bks.) Scholastic, Inc.

—Duck! Rabbit! Rosenthal, Amy Krouse. (J). 2014. (ENG.). 40p. (gr. -1-k). bds. 7.99 *(978-1-4521-3733-9(1));* 2009. 16.99 *(978-0-8118-6332-0(9))* Chronicle Bks. LLC.

—Exclamation Mark. Rosenthal, Amy Krouse. 2013. (ENG.). 56p. (J). (gr. -1-3). 17.99 *(978-0-545-43679-3(6),* Scholastic Pr.) Scholastic, Inc.

—Friendshape. Rosenthal, Amy Krouse. 2015. 40p. (J). (gr. -1-k). 16.99 *(978-0-545-43682-3(6),* Scholastic Pr.) Scholastic, Inc.

—Goodnight, Goodnight, Construction Site. Rinker, Sherri Duskey. (ENG.). (J). 2017. 30p. bds. 7.99 *(978-1-4521-1173-5(1));* 2016. 16p. (gr. -1-7). 12.99 *(978-1-4521-5463-3(5));* 2015. 66p. (gr. -1 — 1). 15.99 *(978-1-4521-4698-0(5))* Chronicle Bks. LLC.

—Goodnight, Goodnight, Construction Site: Glow in the Dark Edition. Rinker, Sherri Duskey. 2016. (ENG.). 32p. (J). (gr. -1 — 1). 18.99 *(978-1-4521-5215-8(2))* Chronicle Bks. LLC.

—Goodnight, Goodnight Construction Site (Hardcover Books for Toddlers, Preschool Books for Kids) Rinker, Sherri Duskey. 2011. (ENG.). 32p. (J). (gr. -1-1). 16.99 *(978-0-8118-7782-4(5))* Chronicle Bks. LLC.

—Goodnight Goodnight Construction Site Sound Book: (Construction Books for Kids, Books with Sound for Toddlers, Children's Truck Books, Read Aloud Books) Rinker, Sherri Duskey. 2014. (ENG.). 12p. (J). (gr. -1 — 1). 12.99 *(978-1-4521-2824-5(3))* Chronicle Bks. LLC.

—I Wish You More (Encouragement Gifts for Kids, Uplifting Books for Graduation) Rosenthal, Amy Krouse. 2015. (ENG.). 40p. (J). (gr. k-3). 14.99 *(978-1-4521-2699-9(2))* Chronicle Bks. LLC.

—Ice Cream & Dinosaurs. Litwin, Eric. 2016. (Groovy Joe Ser.: 1). (ENG.). 40p. (J). (gr. -1-k). 17.99 *(978-0-545-88378-8(4),* Orchard Bks.) Scholastic, Inc.

—If You're Groovy & You Know It, Hug a Friend! Litwin, Eric. 2018. (Groovy Joe Ser.: 3). (ENG.). 32p. (J). (gr. -1-k). 9.99 *(978-0-545-88380-1(6),* Orchard Bks.) Scholastic, Inc.

—It's Not Fair! Rosenthal, Amy Krouse. 2008. (ENG.). 40p. (J). (gr. -1-3). 16.99 *(978-0-06-115257-3(9))* HarperCollins Pubs.

—Let's Go! Rinker, Sherri Duskey. 2017. (ENG.). 10p. (J). (gr. -1 — 1). bds. 8.99 *(978-1-4521-6476-2(2))* Chronicle Bks. LLC.

—Mighty, Mighty Construction Site. Rinker, Sherri Duskey. 2017. (ENG.). 40p. (J). 16.99 *(978-1-4521-5216-5(0))* Chronicle Bks. LLC.

—Mighty, Mighty Construction Site Sound Book. Rinker, Sherri Duskey. 2019. (ENG.). 12p. (J). (gr. -1 — 1). bds. 12.99 *(978-1-4521-6507-3(6))* Chronicle Bks. LLC.

Lichtenheld, Tom. Moo Moo, I Love You. Rosenthal, Amy Krouse. 2020. (ENG.). 48p. (J). (gr. -1-3). 17.99 ***(978-1-4197-4706-9(1),*** 1701601, Abrams Bks. for Young Readers) Abrams, Inc.

Lichtenheld, Tom. The OK Book. Rosenthal, Amy Krouse. 2007. (ENG.). 40p. (J). (gr. -1-2). 12.99 *(978-0-06-115255-9(2))* HarperCollins Pubs.

—One Big Pair of Underwear. Gehl, Laura. 2018. (Classic Board Bks.). (ENG.). 36p. (J). (gr. -1-k). bds. 7.99 *(978-1-5344-2036-6(3),* Little Simon) Little Simon.

—Palo y Piedra/Stick & Stone Bilingual Board Book. Ferry, Beth. 2019. (Stick & Stone Ser.). (ENG.). 38p. (J). (— 1). bds. 5.99 *(978-0-358-08698-7(1),* 1746636, HMH Books For Young Readers) Houghton Mifflin Harcourt Publishing Co.

—Shark vs. Train. Barton, Chris. (J). (gr. -1 — 1). 2015. 20p. bds. 6.99 *(978-0-316-37814-7(3));* 2010. 48p. 18.99 *(978-0-316-00762-7(5))* Little, Brown Bks. for Young Readers.

—Sing. Raposo, Joe. 2013. (ENG.). 40p. (J). (gr. -1-3). 16.99 *(978-0-8050-9071-0(1),* 900061330, Holt, Henry & Co. Bks. For Young Readers) Holt, Henry & Co.

—Steam Train, Dream Train. Rinker, Sherri Duskey. 2018. (ENG.). 32p. (J). (gr. -1 — 1). bds. 7.99 *(978-1-4521-5217-2(9))* Chronicle Bks. LLC.

—Steam Train, Dream Train Colors. Rinker, Sherri Duskey. 2016. (ENG.). 20p. (J). (gr. -1 — 1). bds. 7.99 *(978-1-4521-4915-8(1))* Chronicle Bks. LLC.

—Steam Train, Dream Train Counting. Rinker, Sherri Duskey. 2016. (ENG.). 20p. (J). (gr. -1 — 1). bds. 7.99 *(978-1-4521-4914-1(3))* Chronicle Bks. LLC.

—Steam Train, Dream Train Sound Book. Rinker, Sherri Duskey. 2015. (ENG.). 12p. (J). (gr. -1-k). 12.99 *(978-1-4521-2825-2(1))* Chronicle Bks. LLC.

—Stick & Stone. Ferry, Beth. (Stick & Stone Ser.). (ENG.). (J). 2017. 38p. (— 1). bds. 7.99 *(978-1-328-71432-9(2),* 1673785); 2015. 48p. (gr. -1-3). 17.99 *(978-0-544-03256-9(X),* 1530246) Houghton Mifflin Harcourt Publishing Co. (HMH Books For Young Readers).

—Ten Rules of the Birthday Wish. Ferry, Beth. 2019. (ENG.). 48p. (J). (gr. -1-3). 17.99 *(978-1-5247-4154-9(X),* G.P. Putnam's Sons Books for Young Readers) Penguin Young Readers Group.

—Yes Day! Rosenthal, Amy Krouse. 2009. (ENG.). 40p. (J). (gr. -1-3). 14.99 *(978-0-06-115259-7(5))* HarperCollins Pubs.

—Zero the Hero. Holub, Joan. 2012. (ENG.). 40p. (J). (gr. 1-5). 18.99 *(978-0-8050-9384-1(2),* 900074413, Holt, Henry & Co. Bks. For Young Readers) Holt, Henry & Co.

Lichtenheld, Tom. Cloudette. Lichtenheld, Tom. 2011. (ENG.). 40p. (J). (gr. -1-2). 18.99 *(978-0-8050-8776-5(1),* 900050160, Holt, Henry & Co. Bks. For Young Readers) Holt, Henry & Co.

—Everything I Know about Cars. Lichtenheld, Tom. 2005. (ENG.). 40p. (J). (gr. -1-3). 19.99 *(978-0-689-84382-2(8),* Simon & Schuster Bks. For Young Readers) Simon & Schuster Bks. For Young Readers.

—Everything I Know about Pirates. Lichtenheld, Tom. 2003. (ENG.). 40p. (J). (gr. -1-3). pap. 7.99 *(978-0-689-86009-6(9),* Simon & Schuster Bks. For Young Readers) Simon & Schuster Bks. For Young Readers.

Lichtenheld, Tom, jt. illus. see Rosenthal, Amy Krouse.

Lichtschein, Udi. The Little Innovator: A Moral for the Young Innovator, the Future Inventor & Entrepreneur. Manor, Eliezer. 2019. (ENG.). 42p. (J). (gr. k-6). 25.95 *(978-1-948858-75-5(4))* Strategic Book Publishing & Rights Agency (SBPRA).

Lickens, Alice. My Great Outdoors Book: The Kids' Guide to Being Outside. Jeffery, Josie. 2018. (ENG.). 80p. (J). (gr. 2-5). pap. 9.99 *(978-1-78240-605-1(0),* Ivy Kids) Ivy Group, The GBR. Dist: Hachette Bk. Group.

Lida, Toshitsugu. Wolf's Rain, Vol. 1. Bones & Nobumoto, Keiko. 2004. (ENG.). 184p. pap. 9.99 *(978-1-59116-591-0(1))* Viz Media.

—Wolf's Rain, Vol. 2. Bones. 2005. (ENG.). 184p. pap. 9.99 *(978-1-59116-718-1(3))* Viz Media.

Lidard, Kelly & Seeley, Douglas A. Chincoteague Daisy Chain. Seeley, Bonnie L. 2003. 32p. (J). bds. 12.95 *(978-0-9728380-0-9(7))* Seelcraft Publishing.

Lidberg, Micah. Rise & Fall. 2012. (Leporello Ser.). 20p. (gr. k). pap. 16.00 *(978-1-907704-30-7(2))* Nobrow Ltd. GBR. Dist: Penguin Random Hse. LLC.

Liddell, Daniel & Basta, Mary. California Native American Tribes: Mohave Tribe, 28 booklets. Boule, Mary Null. (California Native American Tribes). 52p. (J). (gr. 3-6). pap. 7.95 *(978-1-877599-73-6(5))* Merryant Pubs.

—Native Americans of North America, Set, 11. 2003. (Native Americans of North America). 48p. (J). (gr. 3-6). pap. 6.45 *(978-1-877599-61-3(1))* Merryant Pubs.

—Navajo People: SW Region, Set. Boule, Mary Null. (Native Americans of North America Ser.). 50-60p. (J). (gr. 3-6). pap. 7.95 *(978-1-877599-59-0(X))* Merryant Pubs.

Liddelow, Angelique. The Doodle Bug Story. Ford, J. Nell. 2010. (ENG.). 32p. (YA). 24.99 ***(978-1-4535-4893-6(9))*** Xlibris Corp.

Liddiard, Merrilee. Leif & the Fall. Grant, Allison Sweet & Grant, Adam. 2020. (ENG.). 32p. (J). (gr. k-3). 17.99 ***(978-1-9848-1549-1(0),*** Dial Bks) Penguin Young Readers Group.

Liddiard, Merrilee. Out of Place. Blecher, Jennifer. 2019. (ENG.). 304p. (J). (gr. 3-7). 16.99 *(978-0-06-274859-1(9),* Greenwillow Bks.) HarperCollins Pubs.

—A Scarf for Keiko. Malaspina, Ann. 2019. (ENG.). 32p. (J). (gr. k-4). 17.99 *(978-1-5415-2164-3(1),* Kar-Ben Publishing) Lerner Publishing Group.

—When Charley Met Emma, Vol. Webb, Amy. 2019. (ENG.). 32p. (J). (gr. -1-k). 16.99 *(978-1-5064-4872-5(0),* Beaming Books) Augsburg Fortress, Pubs.

Liddiment, Carol. How Many Donkeys? An Arabic Counting Tale. MacDonald, Margaret Read & Taibah, Nadia Jameel. 2012. (J). 34.28 *(978-1-61913-148-4(X))* Weigl Pubs., Inc.

—How Many Donkeys? An Arabic Counting Tale. MacDonald, Margaret Read & Taibah, Nadia Jameel. 2012. (Alphabet Bks.). (ENG.). 32p. (J). (gr. -1-1). 21.19 *(978-0-8075-3424-3(2))* Whitman, Albert & Co.

—The Wooden Sword. Stampler, Ann Redisch. 2013. (AV2 Fiction Readalong Ser.: Vol. 100). (ENG.). (J). (gr. k-3). 34.28 *(978-1-62127-900-6(6),* AV2 by Weigl) Weigl Pubs., Inc.

—The Wooden Sword: A Jewish Folktale from Afghanistan. 2012. (ENG.). 32p. (J). (gr. k-3). 16.99 *(978-0-8075-9201-4(3),* 807592013) Whitman, Albert & Co.

Lidston, Colin. A Book of Values & Character Ideals for Home & School. Byrnes, John Carroll. 2016. (ENG.). (J). (gr. 1-6). pap. 6.99 *(978-1-62720-085-1(1))* Apprentice Hse.

Lie, Vivian. Pink Feathers,Murky Pools & a Witch: A Lellaland Adventure. Masters, H. 2003. 52p. pap. *(978-1-84401-098-1(8))* Athena Pr.

Lieb, Claudia. The Incredible yet True Adventures of Alexander Von Humboldt: The Greatest Inventor-Naturalist-Scientist-Explorer Who Ever Lived. Mehnert, Volker. 2019. 112p. 17.95 *(978-1-61519-631-9(5),* 779631) Experiment LLC, The.

Liebeck, Lisa. Count with Balloons. Rembisz, Linda. 2009. 28p. pap. 12.49 *(978-1-4490-1989-1(7))* AuthorHouse.

Lieber, Larry, jt. illus. see Romita, John.

Lieberherr, Ruth. The Knotties, 1 vol. Mellon, Nancy. 2012. (ENG.). 32p. (J). pap. 11.95 *(978-1-62148-003-7(8))* SteinerBooks, Inc.

—Winter, Awake!, 1 vol. Kroll, Linda. rev. ed. 2003. (ENG.). 32p. (J). pap. 11.95 *(978-0-88010-528-6(3))* SteinerBooks, Inc.

Lieberherr, Ruth. The Boy Without a Name. Lieberherr, Ruth. 2018. (ENG.). 38p. (J). (gr. k-6). 24.95 *(978-1-7328877-3-2(X))* Lieberherr, Ruth.

—Der Bub Ohne Namen. Lieberherr, Ruth. 2018. (GER.). 38p. (J). (gr. 1-6). 24.95 *(978-1-7328877-1-8(3));* 24.95 *(978-1-7328877-2-5(1))* Lieberherr, Ruth.

—The Caterpillar & the Butterfly. Lieberherr, Ruth. 2nd ed. 2019. (ENG.). 30p. (J). (gr. k-6). 24.95 *(978-1-7328877-5-6(6));* pap. 15.95 *(978-1-7328877-4-9(8))* Lieberherr, Ruth.

—Die Raupe und der Schmetterling. Lieberherr, Ruth. 2nd ed. 2019. (GER.). 30p. (J). (gr. k-6). pap. 15.95 *(978-1-7328877-6-3(4));* 24.95 ***(978-1-7328877-7-0(2))*** Lieberherr, Ruth.

Lieberman, Roy. Relay. Lieberman, Roy. 2019. (ENG.). 36p. (J). (gr. k-3). 14.99 *(978-1-7338376-0-6(4));* pap. 9.99 *(978-1-7338376-1-3(2))* Coolidge Corner Pr.

Liebert, Marjorie. The Kid from the Other Side. Liebert, Burt. l.t. ed. 2003. 192p. (YA). (gr. 5-7). pap. 7.95 *(978-0-9727499-0-9(X))* Creative Works.

Liebl, Noah. Try a Papaya. Phipps, Lisa. 2019. (ENG.). 44p. (J). pap. 10.99 ***(978-1-6900-3499-5(8))*** Independently Published.

Liebman, Kate. The Fallen Star. Hecht, Tracey. 2018. (Nocturnals Ser.: 3). (ENG.). 208p. (J). (gr. 3-7). pap. 8.99 *(978-1-944020-07-1(1),* Fabled Films Pr. LLC) Fabled Films LLC.

—The Hidden Kingdom. Hecht, Tracey. (Nocturnals Ser.: 4). (ENG.). 208p. (J). (gr. 3-7). 2019. pap. 8.99 *(978-1-944020-13-2(6));* 2018. 15.99 *(978-1-944020-11-8(X))* Fabled Films LLC. (Fabled Films Pr. LLC).

—The Mysterious Abductions. Hecht, Tracey. 2016. (Nocturnals Ser.: 1). (ENG.). 232p. (J). (gr. 3-7). 15.99 *(978-1-944020-00-2(4),* Fabled Films Pr. LLC) Fabled Films LLC.

—The Ominous Eye. Hecht, Tracey. 2016. (Nocturnals Ser.: 2). (ENG.). 208p. (J). (gr. 3-7). 15.99 *(978-1-944020-03-3(9),* Fabled Films Pr. LLC) Fabled Films LLC.

Liebman, Simean. The Pigeon with the Sticky Stuck Neck. Arthur, Anne. 2004. (J). per. 7.99 *(978-0-9753320-0-9(7))* Riverbank Publishing.

Lieder, Rick. Among a Thousand Fireflies. Frost, Helen. 2016. 32p. (J). (gr. -1-2). 15.99 *(978-0-7636-7642-1(X))* Candlewick Pr.

—Among a Thousand Fireflies. Frost, Helen. 2019. 32p. (J). (gr. -1-2). 6.99 *(978-1-5362-0562-6(1))* Candlewick Pr.

—Hello, I'm Here! Frost, Helen. 2019. 32p. (J). (-k). 16.99 *(978-0-7636-9858-4(X))* Candlewick Pr.

—Step Gently Out. Frost, Helen. 2018. 32p. (J). (-k). 6.99 *(978-0-7636-9517-0(3))* Candlewick Pr.

—Sweep up the Sun. Frost, Helen. 2015. 32p. (J). (-k). 15.99 *(978-0-7636-6904-1(0))* Candlewick Pr.

—Sweep up the Sun. Frost, Helen. 2018. 32p. (J). (-k). 6.99 *(978-0-7636-9673-3(0))* Candlewick Pr.

—Wake Up! Frost, Helen. 2017. 32p. (J). (gr. -1-2). 15.99 *(978-0-7636-8149-4(0))* Candlewick Pr.

Lieder, Rick, photos by. Step Gently Out. Frost, Helen. 2012. 32p. (J). (gr. k-k). 15.99 *(978-0-7636-5601-0(1))* Candlewick Pr.

Liedtke, Gabriele. Scott the Shot: Helping Children Understand the Main Reason for Receiving Shots. Raber, James Briggs. Duman, Crystal, ed. 2019. (ENG.). 32p. (J). (gr. k-3). pap. 9.99 ***(978-0-578-45861-8(6))*** James Briggs Raber.

Liefeld, Rob. X-Force: Big Guns. Nicieza, Fabián. 2004. (X-Force Ser.). 136p. pap. 15.99 *(978-0-7851-1483-3(1))* Marvel Worldwide, Inc.

Lieffering, Jan. Frank & Fiona Build a Fictional Story. Lynette, Rachel. 2014. (Writing Builders Ser.). (ENG.). 32p. (J). (gr. 2-4). pap. 11.94 *(978-1-60357-561-4(8));* lib. bdg. 25.27 *(978-1-59953-587-6(4))* Norwood Hse. Pr.

Liegey, Daniel. I Was Born to Be a Brother. Michels-Gualtieri, Zaydek G. 2005. (ENG.). 32p. (J). (gr. -1-3). 9.95 incl. lp *(978-1-930775-10-7(5))* Platypus Media, L.L.C.

Liem, Fanny. The Message in the Mirror. Denise, Katrina. 2017. (ENG.). (J). (gr. 2-5). 16.95 *(978-0-692-84082-5(6))* Katrina Denise.

Lierz, Heidi. Stop Those Germs. Heigert, Joyce. 2020. (ENG.). 18p. (J). pap. 12.95 ***(978-1-64531-969-6(5))*** Newman Springs Publishing, Inc.

Lies, Brian. Deep in the Swamp. Bateman, Donna M. 2007. 32p. (J). (gr. -1-3). 16.95 *(978-1-57091-596-3(2));* pap. 7.95 *(978-1-57091-597-0(0))* Charlesbridge Publishing, Inc.

—Finklehopper Frog. Livingston, Irene. 2008. 32p. (J). (gr. -1-2). pap. 7.95 *(978-1-58246-234-9(8),* Tricycle Pr.) Random Hse. Children's Bks.

—Lucky Duck. Weiss, Ellen. 2004. (Ready-to-Read Ser.). 31p. (J). (gr. -1-1). 11.65 *(978-0-7569-5618-9(8))* Perfection Learning Corp.

—Malcolm at Midnight. Beck, W. H. 2015. (ENG.). 272p. (J). (gr. 3-7). pap. 7.99 *(978-0-544-33666-7(6),* 1584188, HMH Books For Young Readers) Houghton Mifflin Harcourt Publishing Co.

—Malcolm under the Stars. Beck, W. H. 2016. (ENG.). 272p. (J). (gr. 3-7). pap. 7.99 *(978-0-544-81312-0(X),* 1641907, HMH Books For Young Readers) Houghton Mifflin Harcourt Publishing Co.

—More. Springman, I. C. (ENG.). 40p. (J). (gr. -1-3). 2019. pap. 7.99 *(978-0-358-11790-2(9),* 1750732, HMH Books For Young Readers); 2012. 17.99 *(978-0-547-61083-2(1),* 1464468) Houghton Mifflin Harcourt Publishing Co.

—Popcorn! Landau, Elaine. 2003. 32p. (J). (gr. 1-4). pap. 7.95 *(978-1-57091-443-0(5))* Charlesbridge Publishing, Inc.

Lies, Brian. Bats at the Library. Lies, Brian. 2008. (Bat Book Ser.). (ENG.). 32p. (J). (gr. -1-3). 18.99 *(978-0-618-99923-1(X),* 1027891) Houghton Mifflin Harcourt Publishing Co.

—Bats in the Band. Lies, Brian. 2014. (Bat Book Ser.). (ENG.). 32p. (J). (gr. -1-3). 17.99 *(978-0-544-10569-0(9),* 1540826, HMH Books For Young Readers) Houghton Mifflin Harcourt Publishing Co.

—The Rough Patch. Lies, Brian. 2018. (ENG.). 40p. (J). (gr. -1-3). 17.99 *(978-0-06-267127-1(8),* Greenwillow Bks.) HarperCollins Pubs.

Lies, Gregory. My Two Great Great Aunts. Eck, Brenda. 2017. (ENG.). (J). (gr. k-2). 20.00 *(978-1-939054-67-8(2))* Rowe Publishing.

Liese, Charles. Me & Caleb Again. Meyer, Franklyn E. 2006. (J). kivar 16.95 *(978-0-9789388-1-9(X))* Hester Publishing.

Liessner, Richard. The Foot Prince. Liessner, Richard. 2006. 24p. (J). 9.95 *(978-0-9766129-5-7(X))* Raindrop Bks.

Liest, Christina. The Graveyard Hounds, 1 vol. Hughes, Vi. 2009. (ENG.). 167p. (J). (gr. 4-7). pap. 12.95 *(978-1-896580-49-4(1))* Tradewind Bks. CAN. Dist: Orca Bk. Pubs. USA.

Lietha, Dan, et al. Dinosaur Pak & Stak. 2007. (J). 10.99 *(978-0-89051-486-3(0),* Master Books) New Leaf Publishing Group.

L

Liew, David. The Never-Ending Game. Dirani, Mo & Goh, Hwee. 2019. (Plano Adventures Ser.). (ENG.). 60p. pap. 8.99 *(978-981-4828-96-3(3))* Marshall Cavendish International (Asia) Private Ltd. SGP. Dist: National Bk. Network.

—The Ray Keepers: The Plano Adventures. Dirani, Mo & Goh, Hwee. 2019. (Plano Adventures Ser.). (ENG.). 60p. (J). (gr. k-4). pap. 8.99 *(978-981-4828-69-7(6))* Marshall Cavendish International (Asia) Private Ltd. SGP. Dist: National Bk. Network.

—Trouble in Murktown. Dirani, Mo & Goh, Hwee. 2019. (Plano Adventures Ser.). (ENG.). 52p. (J). (gr. k-4). pap. 8.99 *(978-981-4828-48-2(3))* Marshall Cavendish International (Asia) Private Ltd. SGP. Dist: National Bk. Network.

Liew, Sonny, et al. Fairy Tales I Just Made Up: Snarky Bedtime Stories for Weirdo Children. Friesen, Ray. 2015. (ENG.). 80p. (J). (gr. 3-7). 18.95 *(978-0-9802314-4-1(2))* Don't Eat Any Bugs Prodns.

Liew, Sonny. The Shadow Hero. Yang, Gene Luen. 2014. (ENG.). 176p. (YA). (gr. 7-12). pap. 18.99 *(978-1-59643-697-8(2)*, 900073186, First Second Bks.) Roaring Brook Pr.

—The Shadow Hero. Yang, Gene Luen. ed. 2014. (YA). lib. bdg. 30.60 *(978-0-606-35521-6(9))* Turtleback.

Life, Kay. My Red Balloon. Bunting, Eve. 2005. (ENG.). 32p. (J). (gr. k-2). 15.95 *(978-1-59078-263-7(1))* Boyds Mills Pr.

Ligasan, Darryl. Allie's Basketball Dream, 1 vol. Barber, Barbara E. 2013. (ENG.). 32p. (J). (gr. 1-4). pap. 10.95 *(978-1-880000-72-4(5)*, 5afbec81-97a1-4090-b753-a171ed4e8b62) Lee & Low Bks., Inc.

Ligertwood, Scott. What a Beautiful Name. Ligertwood, Scott. Ligertwood, Brooke et al. 2020. (ENG.). 40p. (J). (gr. -1-2). 17.99 ***(978-0-593-19270-2(2)**, WaterBrook Pr.)* Crown Publishing Group, The.

Light, Carol. Oops, a Curious Horse Big Book. Gansle, Sherry. 2003. 56p. (J). *(978-0-9745803-6-4(8))* Little Big Tomes.

—Oops, a Curious Horse Little Book. Gansle, Sherry. 2003. 52p. (J). *(978-0-9745803-7-1(6))* Little Big Tomes.

—Oops, a Curious Horse Story Book Reader. Gansle, Sherry. 2003. 58p. (J). *(978-0-9745803-5-7(X))* Little Big Tomes.

—Oops, a Curious Horse Story Telling Board. 2003. (J). *(978-0-9745803-4-0(1))* Little Big Tomes.

Light, Carol. Chickensing Big Book. Light, Carol. 2003. (J). *(978-0-9745803-2-6(5))* Little Big Tomes.

—Chickensing Little Book. Light, Carol. 2003. 108p. (J). *(978-0-9745803-3-3(3))* Little Big Tomes.

—Chickensing Story Book Reader. Light, Carol. 2003. 60p. (J). *(978-0-9745803-1-9(7))* Little Big Tomes.

Light, Karen. The Amazing World of Aviation. Camacho-Ruiz, Jacqueline. 2019. (ENG.). 42p. (J). pap. 9.97 *(978-1-7324916-7-0(4)*, Fig Factor Media LLC) JJR Marketing Consultants LLC.

—Big Karma & Little Kosmo Help Each Other. Ross, Karyn. 2019. (ENG.). 26p. (J). pap. 12.99 *(978-1-0979-5948-8(1))* Independently Published.

Light, Karen. Gros Karma et Petit Kosmo S'entraident. Ross, Karyn. Czerwice, Jarek, tr. 2019. (FRE.). 26p. (J). pap. 12.99 ***(978-1-6917-1745-3(2))*** Independently Published.

—Grote Karme en Kleine Kosmo Helpen Elkaar. Witter, Isabel & Witter-Vliege, Sylvia, trs. 2019. (DUT.). 26p. (J). pap. 12.99 ***(978-1-6939-1051-7(9))*** Independently Published.

—Store Karma Og Lille Kosmo Hjaelper Hinanden. Ross, Karyn. Jamvig, Tine, tr. 2019. (DAN.). 26p. (J). pap. 12.99 ***(978-1-6940-6283-3(X))*** Independently Published.

Light, Kelly. Elvis & the Underdogs. Lee, Jenny. 2013. (Elvis & the Underdogs Ser.: 1). (ENG.). 304p. (J). (gr. 3-7). 16.99 *(978-0-06-223554-1(0))* HarperCollins Pubs.

—Elvis & the Underdogs: Secrets, Secret Service, & Room Service. Lee, Jenny. (Elvis & the Underdogs Ser.: 2). (ENG.). 352p. (J). (gr. 3-7). 2015. pap. 6.99 *(978-0-06-223557-2(5))*; 2014. 16.99 *(978-0-06-223556-5(7))* HarperCollins Pubs.

—The Quirks & the Quirkalicious Birthday. Soderberg, Erin. 2015. (Quirks Ser.). (ENG.). 208p. (J). (gr. 3-6). 13.99 *(978-1-61963-370-4(1)*, 9781619633704, Bloomsbury USA Childrens) Bloomsbury Publishing USA.

—We Read Phonics-Who Took the Cookbook? Orshoski, Paul. 2012. 32p. (J). 9.95 *(978-1-60115-347-0(3))*; pap. 4.99 *(978-1-60115-348-7(1))* Treasure Bay, Inc.

Light, Kelly. Louise & Andie: The Art of Friendship. Light, Kelly. 2016. (ENG.). 40p. (J). (gr. -1-3). 17.99 *(978-0-06-234440-3(4))* HarperCollins Pubs.

—Louise & the Class Pet. Light, Kelly. 2018. (I Can Read Level 1 Ser.). (ENG.). 32p. (J). (gr. -1-3). 16.99 *(978-0-06-236369-5(7))*; pap. 4.99 *(978-0-06-236368-8(9))* HarperCollins Pubs. (Balzer & Bray).

—Louise Loves Art. Light, Kelly. 2014. (ENG.). 40p. (J). (gr. -1-3). 17.99 *(978-0-06-224817-6(0)*, Balzer & Bray) HarperCollins Pubs.

—Louise Loves Bake Sales. Light, Kelly. 2018. (I Can Read Level 1 Ser.). (ENG.). 32p. (J). (gr. -1-3). 16.99 *(978-0-06-236366-4(2))*; pap. 4.99 *(978-0-06-236365-7(4))* HarperCollins Pubs. (Balzer & Bray).

Light, Steve. Have You Seen My Monster? Light, Steven. 2015. (ENG.). 48p. (J). (-k). 16.99 *(978-0-7636-7513-4(X))* Candlewick Pr.

Light, Steve. Black Bird Yellow Sun. Light, Steve. 2018. 16p. (J). (— 1). bds. 7.99 *(978-0-7636-9067-0(8))* Candlewick Pr.

—Builders & Breakers. Light, Steve. 2018. 40p. (J). (gr. -1-2). 16.99 *(978-0-7636-9872-0(5))* Candlewick Pr.

—Have You Seen My Dragon? Light, Steve. 2014. (ENG.). 48p. (J). (-k). 16.99 *(978-0-7636-6648-4(3))* Candlewick Pr.

—Have You Seen My Lunch Box? Light, Steve. 2017. (ENG.). 18p. (J). (-k). bds. 6.99 *(978-0-7636-9068-7(6))* Candlewick Pr.

—I Am Happy: A Touch-and-Feel Book of Feelings. Light, Steve. 2005. 10p. (J). (gr. k-4). reprint ed. 13.00 *(978-0-7567-9630-3(X))* DIANE Publishing Co.

—Lucky Lazlo. Light, Steve. 2016. (ENG.). 32p. (J). (gr. -1-2). 16.99 *(978-0-7636-8825-7(8))* Candlewick Pr.

—Mama Tiger Tiger Cub. Light, Steve. 2019. 16p. (J). (— 1). bds. 7.99 *(978-1-5362-0677-7(6))* Candlewick Pr.

—Swap! Light, Steve. 2016. (ENG.). 40p. (J). (gr. -1-2). 16.99 *(978-0-7636-7990-3(9))* Candlewick Pr.

—Up Cat down Cat. Light, Steve. 2020. (ENG.). 16p. (J). (— 1). bds. 7.99 *(978-1-5362-1031-6(5))* Candlewick Pr.

—Zephyr Takes Flight. Light, Steve. 2012. (ENG.). 40p. (J). (gr. -1-3). 16.99 *(978-0-7636-5695-9(X))* Candlewick Pr.

Lightburn, Ron. How Smudge Came, 1 vol. Gregory, Nan. 2003. (ENG.). 32p. (J). pap. 6.95 *(978-0-88995-161-7(6)*, e2874e57-e203-4cd1-a3b5-9783e6e3cf1f) Red Deer Pr. CAN. Dist: Firefly Bks., Ltd.

—Juba This, Juba That. Becker, Helaine. 2011. (ENG.). 24p. (J). (gr. k-k). 17.95 *(978-0-88776-975-7(6)*, Tundra Bks.) Tundra Bks. CAN. Dist: Penguin Random Hse. LLC.

—Pumpkin People, 1 vol. Lightburn, Sandra. ed. 2008. (ENG.). 32p. (J). (gr. -1-k). 17.95 *(978-1-55109-681-0(1)*, 1b78c7f4-cdcc-4745-8c6e-2a1d4e526912) Nimbus Publishing, Ltd. CAN. Dist: Baker & Taylor Publisher Services (BTPS).

—Roll On: Rick Hansen Wheels Around the World, 1 vol. Manson, Ainslie. 2013. (ENG.). 40p. (J). (gr. k-5). pap. 10.95 *(978-1-77100-268-4(9))* Greystone Books Ltd. CAN. Dist: Publishers Group West (PGW).

Lightfield Studios, jt. illus. see AlohaHawaii.

Lightfoot, Martha. The Great Big Busy Wheels Activity Book: Includes 4 Adventure Stories. Bently, Peter et al. 2019. (ENG.). 192p. (J). (gr. k-2). pap. 12.99 ***(978-1-78603-407-6(7))*** QEB Publishing Inc.

Lightfoot, Martha. The Lion's Share. 2009. (Finger Puppet Bks.). 24p. (J). (gr. -1-1). *(978-1-84643-248-4(0))* Child's Play International Ltd.

Lightfoot, Tammy. Happy Being Gluten Free: Marley the Celiac Seal. Lightfoot Svendsen, Tiana. 2019. (ENG.). 30p. (J). pap. 9.95 ***(978-1-0962-9831-1(7))*** Independently Published.

Lightheart, Judith. Not Funny, Said the Bunny. Lightheart, Judith. 2018. (ENG.). (J). (gr. k-2). 36p. 18.99 *(978-0-9995526-2-9(7))*; 38p. pap. 8.99 *(978-0-9995526-1-2(9))* Park Ave Pr.

Ligi, Raffaella. The Lion Picture Bible, 1 vol. Dodd, Sarah J. ed. 2015. (ENG.). 384p. (J). (gr. k-2). 13.99 *(978-0-7459-6303-7(X))* Lion Hudson PLC GBR. Dist: Independent Pubs. Group.

—Lion Picture Bible. Dodd, Sarah J. gif. ed. 2016. (ENG.). 384p. (J). (gr. k-2). 19.99 *(978-0-7459-7627-3(1))* Lion Hudson PLC GBR. Dist: Independent Pubs. Group.

—See Inside Fairyland. Davidson, Susanna. 2007. (See Inside Board Bks). 14p. (J). (gr. -1-k). bds. 12.99 *(978-0-7945-1570-6(3)*, Usborne) EDC Publishing.

Lignell, Brent. Listen to the Raindrops: Featuring the Storm Song. Lignell, Kirk. 2007. 32p. (J). (gr. -1-3). 17.95 *(978-1-932399-15-8(1))* Huron River Pr.

Liguori, Kathy. The Ducks of Congress Park. Losey, Tori. 2004. 36p. (J). *(978-0-925168-97-9(1))* North Country Bks., Inc.

Likhon, Mahmudul Hasan. Spiggle Spider's Scary Adventure. Brunner, Leanna. 2017. (Spiggle Ser.: Vol. 1). (ENG.). (J). 14.99 *(978-1-64204-867-4(4))*; pap. 8.99 *(978-1-64204-865-0(8))* Primedia eLaunch LLC.

Lilaz, The. Wolfie's All Hallows' Eve. Mechenes, Jessica & Mechenes, Matthew. 2019. (Eeeeww!! Eerie Tales Ser.: Vol. 2). (ENG.). 26p. (J). pap. 9.98 ***(978-1-6996-8205-0(4))*** Independently Published.

Liles-Amponsah, Alyssa. The Beauty of My Skin. Cline Walton, Cecily. 2019. (ENG.). 30p. (J). pap. 9.99 *(978-1-7324712-6-9(6))* 13th & Joan.

Liles, Dot. Austin & Charlie Adventures Across America. Parker, Linda & Langdon, Katie. 2018. (ENG.). 38p. (J). (gr. k-6). pap. 14.50 *(978-1-946539-16-8(3))* Strategic Book Publishing & Rights Agency (SBPRA).

Lilje, Karen. The Little Red Hen. Orford, Margie. 2011. (Best Loved Tales for Africa Ser.). 32p. (J). (gr. k-2). pap. 10.95 *(978-1-77009-821-3(6))* Jacana Media ZAF. Dist: Independent Pubs. Group.

Lill, Debra. Music & Drum: Voices of War & Peace, Hope & Dreams. Robb, Laura. 2005. 32p. (J). reprint ed. 17.00 *(978-0-7567-9580-1(X))* DIANE Publishing Co.

Lillie, Briena. The Adventures of Goldie & Oscar: Goldie Finds a Home. Lillie, Briena, ed. Stay, Norma. 2019. (Adventures of Goldie & Oscar Ser.: Vol. 1). (ENG.). 44p. (J). pap. 12.99 *(978-1-0946-8853-4(3))* Independently Published.

Lillington, Joe. Ancient Warriors. Volant, Iris. 2018. (ENG.). 64p. (J). (gr. 2). 19.95 *(978-1-911171-93-5(3))* Flying Eye Bks. GBR. Dist: Penguin Random Hse. LLC.

—Ride on, Will Cody! A Legend of the Pony Express. Rose, Caroline Starr. 2017. (ENG.). 32p. (J). (gr. k-2). 16.99 *(978-0-8075-7068-5(0)*, 807570680) Whitman, Albert & Co.

Lilly, Kenneth. The Animal Atlas: A Pictorial Guide to the World's Wildlife. DK. 2020. (ENG.). 64p. (J). (gr. 4-7). 20.00 *(978-1-4654-9097-1(3)*, DK Children) Dorling Kindersley Publishing, Inc.

—Atlas Visual de los Animales. Taylor, Barbara. 2nd ed. (Colección Atlas Visual). (SPA.). 64p. (YA). (gr. 5-8). *(978-84-216-1815-8(6)*, BU4894) Bruño, Editorial ESP. Dist: Lectorum Pubns., Inc.

Lilly, Matthew. Charged Up: The Story of Electricity. Bailey, Jacqui. 2004. (Science Works). (ENG.). 32p. (J). (gr. 3-6). per. 7.95 *(978-1-4048-1129-4(X)*, Picture Window Bks.) Capstone.

—Cracking Up: A Story about Erosion. Bailey, Jacqui. 2006. (Science Works). (ENG.). 32p. (J). (gr. 3-6). per. 7.95 *(978-1-4048-1996-2(7)*, Picture Window Bks.) Capstone.

—A Drop in the Ocean: The Story of Water. Bailey, Jacqui. 2004. (Science Works). (ENG.). 32p. (J). (gr. 3-6). per. 7.95 *(978-1-4048-1127-0(3)*, Picture Window Bks.) Capstone.

—Sun up, Sun Down: The Story of Day & Night, 1 vol. Bailey, Jacqui. 2004. (Science Works). (ENG.). 32p. (J). (gr. 3-6). per. 7.95 *(978-1-4048-1128-7(1)*, Picture Window Bks.) Capstone.

Lillywhite, Karlee. Little Bear & the Mirror. Du Toit, Lydia Du. 2019. (ENG.). 24p. (J). (gr. k-5). pap. ***(978-0-9922236-9-4(5))*** Mirror Word Publishing.

Lilova, Maya. Cheese & Cucumbers & Lollipops. Boisselle, Laila. 2018. (ENG.). 42p. (J). (gr. 3-6). pap. *(978-9948-24-380-9(3))* Boisselle, Laila Ingram Spark.

—Cheese & Cucumbers & Lollipops. Boisselle, Laila. 2018. (ENG.). 42p. (J). (gr. 3-6). *(978-0-9779716-9-5(4))* Boisselle, Laila Ingram Spark.

Lim, Gang Hyuk. War of the Realms: New Agents of Atlas. 2019. (ENG.). 112p. (YA). (gr. 8-17). pap. 15.99 *(978-1-302-91877-4(X))* Marvel Worldwide, Inc.

Lim, Hwei. Jon's Tricky Journey: A Story for Inuit Children with Cancer & Their Families, 1 vol. McCarthy, Patricia. ed. 2017. (ENG.). 70p. (J). (gr. -1-k). pap. 19.95 *(978-1-77227-145-4(4))* Inhabit Media Inc. CAN. Dist: Consortium Bk. Sales & Distribution.

—Narwhal, 1 vol. Awa, Solomon. 2016. (Animals Illustrated Ser.). (ENG.). 24p. (J). (gr. -1-k). 12.95 *(978-1-77227-080-8(6))* Inhabit Media Inc. CAN. Dist: Consortium Bk. Sales & Distribution.

Lim, Hwei. On the Side of the Angels (English) Amaujaq Kusugak, Jose. 2020. (Qinuisaarniq Ser.). (ENG.). 56p. (J). pap. 10.95 ***(978-1-77450-203-7(8))*** Inhabit Education CAN. Dist: Consortium Bk. Sales & Distribution.

Lim, Hwei. Our First Caribou Hunt, 1 vol. Noah, Jennifer & Giroux, Chris. 2015. (ENG.). 32p. (J). (gr. k-2). 10.95 *(978-1-77227-022-8(9))* Inhabit Media Inc. CAN. Dist: Consortium Bk. Sales & Distribution.

Lim, Kara. Demon Diary. Lee, Jee-Hyung. rev. ed. 192p. Vol. 2. 2003. (gr. 8-18). pap. 9.99 *(978-1-59182-155-7(X))*; Vol. 4. 2003. pap. 9.99 *(978-1-59182-157-1(6))*; Vol. 5. 2004. pap. 9.99 *(978-1-59182-430-5(3))*; Vol. 6. 2004. pap. 9.99 *(978-1-59182-431-2(1))* TOKYOPOP, Inc.

—Demon Diary, 7 vols., Vol. 7. Jee-Hyung, Lee. rev. ed. 2004. 192p. pap. 9.99 *(978-1-59182-432-9(X))* TOKYOPOP, Inc.

Lim, Koi. The Judging Frog! Mawo, Nathalie. 2019. (ENG.). 40p. (J). pap. 9.99 ***(978-1-7191-7832-7(1))*** CreateSpace Independent Publishing Platform.

Lim, Ron, et al. Captain America: the Winter Soldier: Falcon Takes Flight. Davis, Adam et al. 2017. (World of Reading Level 2 Ser.). (ENG.). 32p. (J). (gr. k-3). lib. bdg. 27.07 *(978-1-5321-4061-7(4)*, 25432) Spotlight.

Lim, Ron. Infinity War. 2006. (ENG.). 400p. (J). (gr. 4-17). 29.99 *(978-0-7851-2105-3(6))* Marvel Worldwide, Inc.

Lim, Ron, et al. Infinity War Omnibus. 2019. (ENG.). 1352p. (J). (gr. 4-17). 125.00 *(978-1-302-91596-4(7))* Marvel Worldwide, Inc.

Lim, Ron, et al. Silver Surfer Epic Collection: Resurrection. 2020. (ENG.). 456p. (J). (gr. 4-17). pap. 44.99 ***(978-1-302-92507-9(5))*** Marvel Worldwide, Inc.

Lim, Ron, et al. Silver Surfer Epic Collection: Thanos Quest. 2018. (ENG.). 480p. (J). (gr. 4-17). pap. 39.99 *(978-1-302-91186-7(4))* Marvel Worldwide, Inc.

—World of Reading Level 1 Set 2 (Set), 8 vols. 2015. (World of Reading Level 1 Ser.). (ENG.). 32p. (J). (gr. -1-3). lib. bdg. 216.56 *(978-1-61479-357-1(3)*, 18192) Spotlight.

Lim, Ron & Millet, Jason. Reloaded Vol. I: In the Name of Patriotism. Rieber, John Ney. 2005. 144p. pap. 12.95 *(978-1-932796-23-0(1))* Devil's Due Publishing, Inc.

Lim, Ron & Pinto, Marcelo. Guardians of the Galaxy: the Story of the Guardians. Palacios, Tomas. 2017. (World of Reading Level 2 Ser.). (ENG.). 32p. (J). (gr. k-3). lib. bdg. 27.07 *(978-1-5321-4063-1(0)*, 25434) Spotlight.

—Guardians of the Galaxy: These Are the Guardians, 1 vol. Wong, Clarissa. 2015. (World of Reading Level 1 Ser.). (ENG.). 32p. (J). (gr. -1-3). 27.07 *(978-1-61479-360-1(3)*, 18195) Spotlight.

Lim, Ron & Rosenberg, Rachelle. Ant-Man: This Is Ant-Man. Wyatt, Chris. 2017. (World of Reading Level 1 Ser.). (ENG.). 32p. (J). (gr. -1-3). lib. bdg. 27.07 *(978-1-5321-4048-8(7)*, 25419) Spotlight.

—Falcon: Fear of Flying. Lambert, Nancy. 2017. (World of Reading Level 2 Ser.). (ENG.). 32p. (J). (gr. k-3). lib. bdg. 27.07 *(978-1-5321-4062-4(2)*, 25433) Spotlight.

Lim, Ron, jt. illus. see Bagley, Mark.

Lim, Ron, jt. illus. see Perez, George.

Lim, Ronald, et al. Escape from Black Panther. 2016. 32p. (J). *(978-1-4844-8092-2(9))* Little Brown & Co.

—Hulk to the Rescue. Davis, Adam. 2015. (Passport to Reading: Level 2 Ser.). (ENG.). 32p. (J). (gr. k-2). 16.19 *(978-1-4844-5268-4(2))* Little Brown & Co.

—Marvel Guardians of the Galaxy. 2017. 32p. (J). *(978-1-5182-4191-8(3))* Little Brown & Co.

—Meet the Team! 2017. 32p. (J). *(978-1-5182-4190-1(5))* Little Brown & Co.

—The Path to Enlightenment. 2016. (Marvel Characters Ser.). (ENG.). 24p. (J). (gr. k-2). 17.44 *(978-1-4844-9685-5(X))* Little, Brown Bks. for Young Readers.

—The Return of Rocket & Groot. 2017. (J). *(978-1-5379-5840-8(2))* Little Brown & Co.

Lim, Ronald. Thor vs. Hulk. 2017. 31p. (J). *(978-1-5364-2522-2(2))* Little Brown & Co.

Lim, Ronald & Rosenberg, Rachelle. This Is Ant-Man. 2015. 31p. (J). *(978-1-4844-5652-1(1))* Disney Pr.

Lim, Ronald & Troy, Andy. Knowhere to Run: Starring Star-Lord. Wyatt, Chris. 2015. (Marvel Heroes Chapter Bks.). (ENG.). 128p. (J). (gr. 1-3). 18.69 *(978-1-4844-4394-1(2))* Disney Pr.

Lim, Tze-Chiang. Barnabas the Magical Cat. Panagiotidis, Maria. 2018. (ENG.). 26p. (J). pap. 9.50 *(978-1-9850-3259-0(7))* CreateSpace Independent Publishing Platform.

Lima Araujo, Andre. Spidey #7: Weekdays. Thompson, Robbie. 2017. (Spidey Ser.). (ENG.). 24p. (J). (gr. 2-8). lib. bdg. 27.07 *(978-1-5321-4155-3(6)*, 27028, Marvel Age) Spotlight.

Lima, Dijjo & Furuzono, Carlos. Go Slow. Manning, Matthew K. 2016. (EOD Soldiers Ser.). (ENG.). 40p. (J). (gr. 4-8). lib. bdg. 26.65 *(978-1-4965-3109-4(4)*, Stone Arch Bks.) Capstone.

—Two Sides. Manning, Matthew K. 2016. (EOD Soldiers Ser.). (ENG.). 40p. (J). (gr. 4-8). lib. bdg. 26.65 *(978-1-4965-3107-0(8)*, Stone Arch Bks.) Capstone.

Lima, Dijjo, jt. illus. see Lima, Rico.

Lima, Graca. A Heart Alone in the Land of Darkness. Rozen, Beti. 2nd ed. 2004. Orig. Title: A Heart Alone in theLand of Darkness. 48p. 15.95 *(978-0-9642333-2-4(0))* Sem Fronteiras Pr., Ltd.

—Stolen Spirit. Rozen, Beti. 2nd ed. 2004. 32p. (gr. 3-7). pap. *(978-0-9642333-1-7(2))* Sem Fronteiras Pr., Ltd.

Lima, Rico, et al. The List. Manning, Matthew K. 2016. (EOD Soldiers Ser.). (ENG.). 40p. (J). (gr. 4-8). lib. bdg. 26.65 *(978-1-4965-3110-0(8)*, Stone Arch Bks.) Capstone.

Lima, Rico & Bello, Thiago Dal. The Mist. Manning, Matthew K. 2016. (EOD Soldiers Ser.). (ENG.). 40p. (J). (gr. 4-8). lib. bdg. 26.65 *(978-1-4965-3108-7(6)*, Stone Arch Bks.) Capstone.

Lima, Rico & Lima, Dijjo. EOD Soldiers, 4 vols. Manning, Matthew K. 2016. (EOD Soldiers Ser.). (ENG.). 40p. (J). (gr. 4-8). lib. bdg., lib. bdg., lib. bdg. 106.60 *(978-1-4965-3415-6(8)*, Stone Arch Bks.) Capstone.

Lima, Sidney. Flights. McGregor, Don. 4th rev. ed. 2006. (Zorro Ser.). (ENG.). 96p. (J). pap. 7.95 *(978-1-59707-026-3(2))* Papercutz.

Lima, Sidney, jt. illus. see Henrique, Paulo.

Limanowka, Jacek. Around the World with the Travelling Angels. Harris, Helen. 2019. (ENG.). 48p. (J). pap. ***(978-1-922355-52-2(6))*** Tablo Publishing.

Limmer, Hannes. Lo Que los Ninos Quieren Saber. Leipe, Ulla. (SPA.). 180p. (YA). 11.95 *(978-84-241-5501-8(7)*, EV867) Everest Editora ESP. Dist: Continental Bk. Co., Inc.

Lin, Albert & Smith, Crystal. Questions for Kids: A Book to Discover a Child's Imagination & Knowledge. Smith, Michael. 2003. 208p. (J). (gr. k-4). pap. 9.95 *(978-0-9669437-1-9(6))* East West Discovery Pr.

Lin, Albert, jt. illus. see Smith, Crystal.

Lin, Arthur & Veno, Joe. Good Night Children's Museum. Gamble, Adam & Jasper, Mark. 2018. (Good Night Our World Ser.). 20p. (J). (— 1). bds. 9.95 *(978-1-60219-578-3(1))* Good Night Bks.

Lin, Bofeng. Me & My Hair. Givens, Tiffeny S. 2019. (ENG.). 26p. (J). pap. 9.50 *(978-1-7202-6908-3(4))* Independently Published.

Lin, Grace. The Jade Necklace. Yee, Paul. 2006. 29p. (J). (gr. 4-8). reprint ed. 16.00 *(978-1-4223-5135-2(1))* DIANE Publishing Co.

—One Year in Beijing. Wang, Xiaohong. 2006. 32p. (J). (gr. -1-3). 16.95 *(978-0-9747302-5-7(4))* Chinasprout, Inc.

—Red Is a Dragon. Thong, Roseanne Greenfield. 2014. 40p. pap. 7.00 *(978-1-61003-333-6(7))* Center for the Collaborative Classroom.

—Red Is a Dragon: A Book of Colors. Thong, Roseanne. 2008. (ENG.). 40p. (J). (gr. -1-17). pap. 7.99 *(978-0-8118-6481-7(2))* Chronicle Bks. LLC.

—Round Is a Mooncake: A Book of Shapes. Thong, Roseanne. 2014. (ENG.). 40p. (J). (gr. -1-k). 7.99 *(978-1-4521-3644-8(0))* Chronicle Bks. LLC.

—The Seven Chinese Sisters. Tucker, Kathy. 2003. (ENG.). 32p. (J). (gr. -1-3). per. 6.99 *(978-0-8075-7310-5(8)*, 807573108) Whitman, Albert & Co.

—When You Grow up to Vote: How Our Government Works for You. Roosevelt, Eleanor & Markel, Michelle. 2018. (ENG.). 96p. (J). 19.99 *(978-1-62672-879-0(8)*, 900176491) Roaring Brook Pr.

Lin, Grace. Dim Sum for Everyone! Lin, Grace. (J). (gr. -1-2). 2014. 24p. bds. 6.99 *(978-0-385-75488-0(4)*, Knopf Bks. for Young Readers); 2003. 32p. 7.99 *(978-0-440-41770-5(8)*, Dragonfly Bks.) Random Hse. Children's Bks.

—Fortune Cookie Fortunes. Lin, Grace. 2006. (ENG.). 32p. (J). (gr. -1-2). 7.99 *(978-0-440-42192-4(6)*, Dragonfly Bks.) Random Hse. Children's Bks.

—Mulan: Before the Sword. Lin, Grace. 2020. (ENG.). 384p. (J). (gr. 3-7). 16.99 *(978-1-368-02033-6(X))* Disney Pr.

—Our Seasons. Lin, Grace. McKneally, Ranida T. 2007. 32p. (J). (gr. k-3). pap. 7.95 *(978-1-57091-361-7(7))* Charlesbridge Publishing, Inc.

Lin, Melanie, jt. illus. see Amber, Holly.

Lin, Yali. The Fishy Fountain No. 6: A Mystery with Multiplication & Division. Thielbar, Melinda. 2011. (Manga Math Mysteries Ser.: 6). (ENG.). 48p. (J). (gr. 3-5). pap. 6.95 *(978-0-7613-8135-8(X)*, 9780761381358, Graphic Universe™) Lerner Publishing Group.

—#6 the Fishy Fountain: A Mystery with Multiplication & Division. Thielbar, Melinda. 2011. (Manga Math Mysteries Set II Ser.). pap. 39.62 *(978-0-7613-8363-5(8)*, Graphic Universe™) Lerner Publishing Group.

Lin, Zhang. The Dragon with the One-Coin Hoard. Gorbski, Jeff. 2020. (ENG.). 48p. (J). pap. ***(978-1-78830-424-5(1))*** Olympia Publishers.

Linares, Jairo. Cuentos de Fantasmas. Panamericana Staff, ed. 2003. (Coleccion el Pozo y el Pendulo Ser.). (SPA.). 138p. (YA). (gr. 4-7). pap. *(978-958-30-1066-8(9))* Panamericana Editorial.

—Pinocho. 2004. (Literatura Juvenil (Panamericana Editorial) Ser.).Tr. of Pinocchio. (SPA.). 283p. (J). (gr. 4-7). pap. *(978-958-30-0803-0(6)*, PV30464) Centro de Informacion y Desarrollo de la Comunicacion y la Literatura MEX. Dist: Lectorum Pubns., Inc.

Linci, Yume. Le Char Saboté: Les Aventures de Mei et Noé. Lise, Isa. 2019. (Aventures de Mei et Noé Ser.: Vol. 8). (FRE.). 178p. (J). pap. 35.00 *(978-1-7953-1415-2(X))* Independently Published.

Linci, Yume. Les Oiseaux Disparus - Renaissance: Les Aventures de Mei et No� Lise, Isa. 2019. (Aventures de Mei et No� Ser.: Vol. 14). (FRE.). 280p. (J). pap. 51.25 ***(978-1-6949-4331-6(3))*** Independently Published.

Linci, Yume. Safari Au Kenya: Les Aventures de Mei et Noé. Lise, Isa. 2019. (Aventures de Mei et Noé Ser.: Vol. 9). (FRE.). 182p. (J). pap. 35.00 *(978-1-0909-3595-3(1))* Independently Published.

Lincoln, Hazel. Little Snow Bear, 30 vols. Lincoln, Hazel. 2004. (ENG.). 32p. (J). 17.95 *(978-0-86315-454-6(9))* Floris Bks. GBR. Dist: SteinerBooks, Inc.

Lincoln, Kelly. Charlie the Catfish: The Adventures of Coal & Andy. Dean, Mark M. 2017. (ENG.). 40p. (J). (gr. 2-6). 16.99 *(978-0-692-96396-8(0))* Monday Creek Publishing.

Lind, Jenny. Navajo Coyote Tales, 1 vol. 2007. (ENG.). 50p. (J). (gr. 2-2). reprint ed. pap. 9.99 *(978-0-941270-52-6(1))* Gibbs Smith, Publisher.

Lind, Kathleen & Simonis, Cheryl. Best Friends. Lind, Kathleen. 2005. (J). 4.95 *(978-1-58597-305-7(X))* Leathers Publishing.

Linda, Graves & Graves, Linda. Sister Bear: A Norse Tale, 0 vols. Yolen, Jane. 2011. (ENG.). 32p. (J). (gr. k-3). 17.99 *(978-0-7614-5958-3(8)*, 9780761459583, Two Lions) Amazon Publishing.

Lindahl, Larry, photos by. The Insider's Guide to Sedona. Andres, Dennis Michael. 2003. 222p. per. 16.95 *(978-0-9721202-1-0(1)*, 825-694) Meta Adventures Publishing & DIA Publishing.

Lindauer, Alexa. ResQ Takes on the Takhi. Pell, Eva J. 2020. (ResQ: Saving One Animal at a Time Ser.). 190p. (J). (gr. 4-8). pap. 13.95 *(978-1-943431-56-4(6))* Tumblehome Learning.

Lindblad, Stefan. Strange Creatures. Orme, David. 2010. (Fact to Fiction Grafx Ser.). 36p. pap. 7.45 *(978-0-7891-7994-4(6))* Perfection Learning Corp.

Linde, Hermann. The Green Snake & the Beautiful Lily, 1 vol. Goethes Fairy Tale Staff. Allen, Joan deRis, ed. Heuscher, Julius E., tr. 2006. (ENG.). 53p. (J). (gr. 3-7). 25.00 *(978-0-88010-570-5(4))* SteinerBooks, Inc.

Lindeberg, Kevin. The Art of Boiling Water. Grundy, Bruce. 2020. (ENG.). 46p. (J). ***(978-1-5289-8867-4(1))***; pap. ***(978-1-5289-8866-7(3))*** Austin Macauley Pubs. Ltd.

Linden, Martijn van der. The Prince Child. Rinck, Maranke. 2004. (ENG & GER.). 32p. (J). (gr. -1-3). 16.95 *(978-1-932425-15-4(2))* Lemniscaat USA.

Linden, Theresa. Breastplate of Righteousness. Linden, Theresa. 2020. (Armor of God Ser.: Vol. 2). (ENG.). 122p. (J). pap. 8.00 ***(978-1-7349929-0-8(5))*** Silver Fire Publishing.

Lindenbaum, Pija. Mirabelle. Lindgren, Astrid. Dyssegaard, Elisabeth Kallick, tr. from SWE. 2003. 32p. (J). 15.00 *(978-91-29-65821-7(7))* R & S Bks. SWE. Dist: Macmillan.

Linderholm, Grace. Langston's Moon. Edwards, Dorothy. 2018. (Nana Ser.: Vol. 1). (ENG.). 36p. (J). (gr. k-1). pap. 9.99 *(978-0-9987995-0-6(5))* Bell & Murry.

Lindgren, Eric. Who Am I ? Colby, Tami Lynn. 2019. (ENG.). 26p. (J). pap. 12.99 ***(978-1-0871-7553-9(4))*** Independently Published.

Lindman. Flicka, Ricka, Dicka & the Little Dog. Lindman. 2013. (Flicka, Ricka, Dicka Ser.). (ENG.). 32p. (J). (gr. k-3). 9.99 *(978-0-8075-2509-8(X)*, 080752509X) Whitman, Albert & Co.

—Flicka, Ricka, Dicka & the Strawberries. Lindman. 2013. (Flicka, Ricka, Dicka Ser.). (ENG.). 32p. (J). (gr. -1-3). 9.99 *(978-0-8075-2512-8(X)*, 080752512X) Whitman, Albert & Co.

—Flicka, Ricka, Dicka & the Three Kittens. Lindman. 2013. (Flicka, Ricka, Dicka Ser.). (ENG.). 32p. (J). (gr. -1-3). 9.99 *(978-0-8075-2515-9(4)*, 807525154) Whitman, Albert & Co.

—Flicka, Ricka, Dicka Bake a Cake. Lindman. 2013. (Flicka, Ricka, Dicka Ser.). (ENG.). 32p. (J). (gr. -1-3). 9.99 *(978-0-8075-2506-7(5)*, 807525065) Whitman, Albert & Co.

Lindman, Amy Sorvaag. Vegetable Soup - The Fruit Bowl. Jones, Susan Smith & Warren, Dianne. rev. ed. 2006. 64p. (J). (gr. -1-3). per. 14.95 *(978-0-9652736-0-2(1))* Oasis Pubns.

Lindman, Maj. Flicka, Ricka, Dicka & the New Dotted Dresses. Lindman, Maj. 2012. (Flicka, Ricka, Dicka Ser.). (ENG.). 32p. (J). (gr. k-3). 9.99 *(978-0-8075-2484-8(0)*, 807524840) Whitman, Albert & Co.

—Flicka, Ricka, Dicka & Their New Skates. Lindman, Maj. 2011. (Flicka, Ricka, Dicka Ser.). (ENG.). 32p. (J). (gr. -1-3). 9.99 *(978-0-8075-2491-6(3)*, 807524913) Whitman, Albert & Co.

—Flicka, Ricka, Dicka Go to Market. Lindman, Maj. 2012. (ENG.). 32p. (J). (gr. -1-3). 9.99 *(978-0-8075-2478-7(6)*, 807524786) Whitman, Albert & Co.

Lindmark, Margaret. Braids - Trencitas. Contreras, Kathleen. 2009. (ENG & SPA.). 32p. (J). (gr. -1-3). 14.99 *(978-1-933032-27-6(8))* Lectorum Pubns., Inc.

—Fatima. Lipp, Frederick. 2006. 32p. (J). pap. *(978-1-59336-302-4(8))* Mondo Publishing.

—Mark Twain. Lázaro León, Georgina. 2019. (SPA.). 32p. (J). (gr. 4-6). 14.99 *(978-1-63245-762-2(8))* Lectorum Pubns., Inc.

Lindmark, Margaret. Sweet Memories/Dulces Recuerdos. Lindmark, Margaret. Contreras, Kathleen. 2014. (SPA & ENG.). 32p. (J). (gr. 2-4). pap. 14.99 *(978-1-933032-91-7(X))* Lectorum Pubns., Inc.

Lindner, Ellen. Little Rock Nine. Poe, Marshall. 2008. (Turning Points Ser.). (ENG.). 128p. (J). (gr. 3-7). pap. 7.99 *(978-1-4169-5066-0(4)*, Simon & Schuster/Paula Wiseman Bks.) Simon & Schuster/Paula Wiseman Bks.

Lindro. To Live a Truer Life: A Story of the Hopedale Community. Hughes, Lynn Gordon. 2003. 32p. (J). 10.00 *(978-0-9725017-2-9(X))* Blackstone Editions.

Lindsay, Anne, photos by. Before It Wriggles Away. Wong, Janet S. 2006. (Meet the Author Ser.). (ENG., 32p. (J). 14.95 *(978-1-57274-861-3(3)*, 735, Meet the Author) Owen, Richard C. Pubs., Inc.

Lindsay, Ashling. The Night Box. Greig, Louise. 2018. (ENG.). 32p. (J). (gr. -1-3). 17.99 *(978-1-328-85093-5(5)*, 1693450, Clarion Bks.) Houghton Mifflin Harcourt Trade & Reference Pubs.

Lindsay, Ashling & Montano, Irene. River Stories. Knapman, Timothy. 2020. (ENG.). 32p. (J). 19.99 ***(978-1-4052-9254-2(7))*** Egmont Bks., Ltd. GBR. Dist: HarperCollins Pubs.

Lindsay, Jahnoy. She-Hulk Vol. 3: Jen Walters Must Die. 2018. (ENG.). 112p. (YA). (gr. 8-17). pap. 15.99 *(978-1-302-90569-9(4))* Marvel Worldwide, Inc.

Lindsay, Marion. Bella Donna: Too Many Spells. Symes, Ruth. 2016. (ENG.). 192p. (J). (gr. 1-5). pap. 7.99 *(978-1-63450-155-2(1)*, Sky Pony Pr.) Skyhorse Publishing Co., Inc.

—The Case of the Feathered Mask. Webb, Holly. 2016. (Mysteries of Maisie Hitchins Ser.: 4). (ENG.). 176p. (J). (gr. 3-7). 15.99 *(978-0-544-61993-7(5)*, 1619222, HMH Books For Young Readers) Houghton Mifflin Harcourt Publishing Co.

—The Case of the Feathered Mask: The Mysteries of Maisie Hitchins, Book 4. Webb, Holly. 2017. (Mysteries of Maisie Hitchins Ser.: 4). (ENG.). 176p. (J). (gr. 3-7). pap. 5.99 *(978-0-544-94884-6(X)*, 1660308, HMH Books For Young Readers) Houghton Mifflin Harcourt Publishing Co.

—The Case of the Phantom Cat. Webb, Holly. (Mysteries of Maisie Hitchins Ser.: 3). (ENG.). 176p. (J). (gr. 3-7). 2016. pap. 5.99 *(978-0-544-81084-6(8)*, 1641531); 2015. 15.99 *(978-0-544-58243-9(8)*, 1613672) Houghton Mifflin Harcourt Publishing Co. (HMH Books For Young Readers).

—The Case of the Secret Tunnel. Webb, Holly. 2016. (Mysteries of Maisie Hitchins Ser.: 5). (ENG.). 176p. (J). (gr. 3-7). 15.99 *(978-0-544-81554-4(8)*, 1642499, HMH Books For Young Readers) Houghton Mifflin Harcourt Publishing Co.

—The Case of the Vanishing Emerald. Webb, Holly. 2016. (Mysteries of Maisie Hitchins Ser.: 2). (ENG.). 176p. (J). (gr. 3-7). pap. 6.99 *(978-0-544-66851-5(0)*, 1625474, HMH Books For Young Readers) Houghton Mifflin Harcourt Publishing Co.

—Ready, Steady, Ghost! Baguley, Elizabeth. 2014. (ENG.). 32p. (J). (gr. -1-k). 16.99 *(978-1-4231-8039-5(9))* Hyperion Bks. for Children.

—Unicorns & Germs. Citro, Asia. 2018. (Zoey & Sassafras Ser.: 6). 96p. (J). (gr. 1-5). pap. 5.99 *(978-1-943147-47-2(7)*, e495f648-9a38-4303-85db-0c5f3d636da2) Innovation Pr., The.

Lindsay, Marion. The Case of the Stolen Sixpence. Lindsay, Marion. Webb, Holly. ed. 2015. (Mysteries of Maisie Hitchins Ser.: 1). (ENG.). 176p. (J). (gr. 3-7). pap. 6.99 *(978-0-544-58234-7(9)*, 1613663, HMH Books For Young Readers) Houghton Mifflin Harcourt Publishing Co.

Lindsay, Norman. The Magic Pudding. Lindsay, Norman. 2016. (ENG.). 184p. (J). (gr. 4-7). pap. 9.99 *(978-1-59017-994-9(3)*, NYRB Kids) New York Review of Bks., Inc., The.

Lindsay, Pattie. Seasons in Our Garden. Robinson, Julie. 2017. 28p. (J). spiral bd. *(978-0-692-71414-0(6))* Robinson, Julia.

Lindsay, Sierra. Spindly the Spider. Lindsay, Sierra. 2012. 20p. pap. 10.99 *(978-0-9836641-9-2(6))* Kids At Heart Publishing, LLC.

Lindsey, Jessica. Eager Beavers. Burt, Vicky. 2012. 28p. pap. 13.99 *(978-1-937129-39-2(X))* Faithful Life Pubs.

—Hot Dog or Egg Sandwich? Burt, Vickie. 2013. 28p. pap. 13.99 *(978-1-937129-87-3(X))* Faithful Life Pubs.

—The Supper Surprise. Burt, Vickie. l.t. ed. 2016. (Granny B Ser.: Vol. 4). (ENG.). (J). (gr. k-6). pap. 13.99 *(978-1-63073-154-0(4))* Faithful Life Pubs.

Lindsey, Michael. The Catarbie Conspiracy: A Conspiracy... A Stuggle... An Adventure! deSouza, Sabrina. 2nd ed. 2008. (Houkura Ser.: 1). (ENG.). 400p. pap. 4.99 *(978-0-9805090-0-7(9)*, 9780980509007) Houkura AUS. Dist: Baker & Taylor Publisher Services (BTPS).

Lindsey, Robin, photos by. Leopard & Silkie: One Boy's Quest to Save the Seal Pups. Peterson, Brenda. 2012. (My Readers Ser.). (ENG., 32p. (J). (gr. -1-3). 17.99 *(978-0-8050-9167-0(X)*, 900064714, Holt, Henry & Co. Bks. For Young Readers) Holt, Henry & Co.

—Seal Pup Rescue. Peterson, Brenda. 2013. (My Readers Ser.). (ENG., 32p. (J). (gr. k-2). pap. 4.99 *(978-1-250-02776-4(4)*, 900104565) Square Fish.

Lindsley, Jennifer. The Fifolet, 1 vol. Downing, Johnette. 2015. (Cajun Tall Tales Ser.). (ENG.). 32p. (J). (gr. k-3). 16.99 *(978-1-4556-2036-4(X)*, Pelican Publishing) Arcadia Publishing.

—Mumbo Jumbo, Stay Out of the Gumbo, 1 vol. Downing, Johnette. 2017. (ENG.). 32p. (J). (gr. -1-3). 16.99 *(978-1-4556-2300-6(8)*, Pelican Publishing) Arcadia Publishing.

—Rolling down the Avenue, 1 vol. Brian, Marion Rea. 2016. (ENG.). 32p. (J). pap. 9.95 *(978-1-4556-2179-8(X)*, Pelican Publishing) Arcadia Publishing.

Lindstrom, Alice. Fox & Bird. Wyatt, Edwina. 2019. (ENG.). 32p. (J). (gr. -1-k). 18.99 ***(978-1-76050-146-4(8))*** Little Hare Bks. AUS. Dist: Independent Pubs. Group.

—A Stage Full of Shakespeare Stories. McAllister, Angela. 2018. (ENG.). 128p. (J). (gr. 2-4). 22.99 ***(978-1-78603-115-0(9)***, Frances Lincoln Children's Bks.) Quarto Publishing Group UK GBR. Dist: Hachette Bk. Group.

Lindstrom, Brita, jt. illus. see Peterson, Sara.

Lindström, Emma. Robin & the White Rabbit. Lindström, Emma. Brunnström, Åse. 2017. (ENG.). 48p. (C). 16.95 *(978-1-78592-290-9(4)*, 696515) Kingsley, Jessica Pubs. GBR. Dist: Hachette UK Distribution.

Lindstrom, Eva. Bertil & the Bathroom Elephants. Lindahl, Inger. Dyssegaard, Elisabeth Kallick, tr. 2003. 28p. (J). 15.00 *(978-91-29-65944-3(2))* R & S Bks. SWE. Dist: Macmillan.

Lindstrom, Eva. Everyone Walks Away. Lindstrom, Eva. 2019. (ENG.). 32p. (J). (gr. k-2). 17.99 *(978-1-77657-186-4(X))* Gecko Pr. NZL. Dist: Lerner Publishing Group.

—My Dog Mouse. Lindstrom, Eva. 2017. (ENG.). 32p. (J). (gr. -1-1). 16.99 *(978-1-77657-148-2(7))* Gecko Pr. NZL. Dist: Lerner Publishing Group.

Lindwall, Erika. The Moose & the Goose. Lindwall, Erika. 2013. 32p. pap. 11.95 *(978-1-940728-01-8(0)*, Simple Faith Bks.) Sunrise Mountain Bks.

Line Art Staff. Tennessee Jeopardy! Answers & Questions about Our State! Marsh, Carole. 2004. 32p. (J). (gr. 3-8). pap. 7.95 *(978-0-7933-9812-6(6))* Gallopade International.

Line, Scribble. Santa's Kitchen. Stanford, Lance. 2019. (ENG.). 40p. (J). pap. 12.99 ***(978-1-7040-4796-6(X))*** Independently Published.

Lineberger, Joy. Mr. Nubbins Goes to School. Spencer, Jill C. 2018. (ENG.). 26p. (J). (gr. k-3). pap. 14.99 *(978-1-946171-28-3(X))* Kids At Heart Publishing, LLC.

Lineberger, Judy. Ick the Stick: Yes, I Can Read! Nature Series, Book 1. D'Agata, Tabatha Jean. 2006. (Yes, I Can Read! Ser.: 1). 24p. (J). pap. 6.95 *(978-1-934138-01-4(0))* Bouncing Ball Bks., Inc.

—Storm Tunes: Yes, I Can Read! Nature Series, Book 2. D'Agata, Tabatha Jean. 2006. (Yes, I Can Read! Ser.: Bk. 2). 30p. (J). pap. 6.95 *(978-1-934138-02-1(9))* Bouncing Ball Bks., Inc.

Linen, Mark. Half a Rabbit. Washington, Janice Hutto. 2016. (ENG.). (J). 20.00 *(978-0-692-70761-6(1))* Kingdom Builders Pubn.

Linenthal, Peter. Look at Baby's House. 2008. 18p. (J). (gr. k — 1). bds. 7.99 *(978-0-525-42061-3(4)*, Dutton Books for Young Readers) Penguin Young Readers Group.

Linenthal, Peter. That's Our Custodian! Linenthal, Peter, photos by. Morris, Ann. 2003. (That's Our School Ser.). (ENG.). 32p. (gr. k-3). lib. bdg. 22.60 *(978-0-7613-2401-0(1)*, Millbrook Pr.) Lerner Publishing Group.

—That's Our Gym Teacher! Linenthal, Peter, photos by. Morris, Ann. 2003. (That's Our School Ser.). (ENG.). 32p. (gr. k-3). lib. bdg. 22.60 *(978-0-7613-2403-4(8)*, Millbrook Pr.) Lerner Publishing Group.

—That's Our Librarian! Linenthal, Peter, photos by. Morris, Ann. 2003. (That's Our School Ser.). (ENG.). 32p. (gr. k-3). lib. bdg. 22.60 *(978-0-7613-2400-3(3)*, Millbrook Pr.) Lerner Publishing Group.

—That's Our Nurse! Linenthal, Peter, photos by. Morris, Ann. 2003. (That's Our School Ser.). (ENG.). 32p. (gr. k-3). lib. bdg. 22.60 *(978-0-7613-2402-7(X)*, Millbrook Pr.) Lerner Publishing Group.

Linenthal, Peter, photos by. Grandma Esther Remembers. Morris, Ann. 32p. (J). (gr. 3-6). 16.95 *(978-1-58013-225-1(1)*, Kar-Ben Publishing) Lerner Publishing Group.

—Grandma Hekmat Remembers: An Arab-American Family Story. Morris, Ann. 2003. (What Was It Like, Grandma? Ser.). (ENG., 32p. (gr. 2-5). lib. bdg. 22.60 *(978-0-7613-2864-3(5)*, Millbrook Pr.) Lerner Publishing Group.

—Grandma Hekmat Remembers: An Egyptian - American Family Story. Morris, Ann. 2003. 32p. (J). (gr. 5-18). pap. 7.95 *(978-0-7613-1944-3(1)*, Millbrook Pr.) Lerner Publishing Group.

Linero, Sol. I Spy the 50 States. Rosart, Sharyn. 2018. (ENG.). 102p. (J). (gr. -1-k). bds. 16.99 *(978-1-84780-991-9(X)*, Wide Eyed Editions) Quarto Publishing Group UK GBR. Dist: Hachette Bk. Group.

—50 Cities of the U. S. A. Explore America's Cities with 50 Fact-Filled Maps. Balkan, Gabrielle. 2017. (50 States Ser.). (ENG.). 112p. (J). (gr. 2-5). 30.00 *(978-1-84780-870-7(0)*, 1094089, Wide Eyed Editions) Quarto Publishing Group UK GBR. Dist: Hachette UK Distribution.

—The 50 States: Explore the U. S. A. with 50 Fact-Filled Maps! Balkan, Gabrielle. 2015. (50 States Ser.). (ENG.). 112p. (J). (gr. 2-5). 30.00 *(978-1-84780-711-3(9)*, 315236, Wide Eyed Editions) Quarto Publishing Group UK GBR. Dist: Hachette Bk. Group.

—The 50 States: Activity Book: Maps of the 50 States of the USA. Balkan, Gabrielle. 2016. (50 States Ser.). (ENG.). 32p. (J). (gr. 3-6). pap., act. bk. ed. 10.99 *(978-1-84780-862-2(X)*, Wide Eyed Editions) Quarto Publishing Group UK GBR. Dist: Hachette Bk. Group.

—The 50 States: Activity Book - Custom: Maps of the 50 States of the USA. Balkan, Gabrielle. 2016. (ENG.). (J). (gr. 3-6). pap. 9.99 *(978-1-84780-997-1(9)*, Wide Eyed Editions) Quarto Publishing Group UK GBR. Dist: Hachette Bk. Group.

—The 50 States: Fun Facts: Celebrate the People, Places & Food of the U. S. a! Balkan, Gabrielle. 2016. (50 States Ser.). (ENG.). 12p. (J). (gr. 3-6). 19.99 *(978-1-84780-869-1(7)*, Wide Eyed Editions) Quarto Publishing Group UK GBR. Dist: Hachette Bk. Group.

Ling Kang, Yong. Making a Whole Person (English) Traditional Inuit Education. Ittusardjuat, Monica. 2020. (Qinuisaarniq Ser.). (ENG.). 26p. (J). 18.95 ***(978-1-77450-205-1(4))*** Inhabit Education CAN. Dist: Consortium Bk. Sales & Distribution.

Lingas, Leo. Escape from East Berlin. Downey, Glen. 2007. 48p. (J). lib. bdg. 23.08 *(978-1-4242-1635-2(4))* Fitzgerald Bks.

Lingenfelter, Jim. Fall Is Fun, 1 vol. Meister, Cari. 2010. (First Graphics: Seasons Ser.). (ENG.). 24p. (gr. 1-3). (J). pap. 6.29 *(978-1-4296-5623-8(9))*; pap. 35.70 *(978-1-4296-5692-4(1))*; (J). lib. bdg. 24.65 *(978-1-4296-4731-1(0))* Capstone.

—Spring Is Special, 1 vol. Meister, Cari. 2010. (First Graphics: Seasons Ser.). (ENG.). 24p. (gr. 1-3). (J). pap. 6.29 *(978-1-4296-5621-4(2))*; pap. 35.70 *(978-1-4296-5693-1(X))*; (J). lib. bdg. 24.65 *(978-1-4296-4729-8(9))* Capstone.

—Summer Is Super. Meister, Cari. 2010. (First Graphics: Seasons Ser.). (ENG.). 24p. (gr. 1-2). pap. 35.70 *(978-1-4296-5694-8(8))*; (J). lib. bdg. 24.65 *(978-1-4296-4730-4(2))* Capstone.

—Winter Is Wonderful. Meister, Cari. 2010. (First Graphics: Seasons Ser.). (ENG.). 24p. (gr. 1-2). pap. 35.70 *(978-1-4296-5695-5(6))*; (J). lib. bdg. 24.65 *(978-1-4296-4732-8(9))* Capstone.

Linhares, Arthur. The Misadventures of Sprinkles the Cupcake Fairy. Dunn, Staci L. 2019. (1 Ser.: Vol. 1). (ENG.). 26p. (J). pap. 12.99 *(978-1-0936-6109-5(7))* Independently Published.

Liniers. Written & Drawn by Henrietta. 2015. (ENG.). 64p. (J). (gr. k). 12.95 *(978-1-935179-90-0(X))* TOON Books / RAW Junior, LLC.

Linke, Donald Q., Jr. IJustWantTo SLEEP for KIDS. Benett, Janet M. Kater, Mary, ed. 2005. (J). 56.97 net. *(978-0-9744357-0-1(8))* IJustWantToSleep, Inc.

Linley, Adam. Awesome Experiments with Living Things. Canavan, Thomas. 2017. (Mind-Blowing Science Experiments Ser.). 32p. (gr. 4-5). pap. 63.00 *(978-1-5382-0728-4(1))* Stevens, Gareth Publishing LLLP.

—Cool Experiments with Heat & Cold. Canavan, Thomas. 2017. (Mind-Blowing Science Experiments Ser.). 32p. (gr. 4-5). pap. 63.00 *(978-1-5382-0729-1(X))* Stevens, Gareth Publishing LLLP.

—Fantastic Experiments with Forces. Canavan, Thomas. 2017. (Mind-Blowing Science Experiments Ser.). 32p. (gr. 4-5). pap. 63.00 *(978-1-5382-0731-4(1))* Stevens, Gareth Publishing LLLP.

—Magnificent Experiments with Materials. Canavan, Thomas. 2017. (Mind-Blowing Science Experiments Ser.). 32p. (gr. 4-5). pap. 63.00 *(978-1-5382-0732-1(X))* Stevens, Gareth Publishing LLLP.

—Super Experiments with Light & Sound. Canavan, Thomas. 2017. (Mind-Blowing Science Experiments Ser.). 32p. (gr. 4-5). pap. 63.00 *(978-1-5382-0733-8(8))* Stevens, Gareth Publishing LLLP.

Linn, Laurent. Draw the Line. Linn, Laurent. 2016. (ENG.). 528p. (YA). (gr. 7). 17.99 *(978-1-4814-5280-9(0)*, McElderry, Margaret K. Bks.) McElderry, Margaret K. Bks.

Linn, Laurent, jt. illus. see Nelson, Mary Beth.

Linn, Matthew. We All Matter. Tawandra, Angel & McGowan, Jacqueline. 2017. (ENG.). (J). 19.95 *(978-1-4787-8318-3(4))*; pap. 12.95 *(978-1-4787-8317-6(6))* Outskirts Pr., Inc.

Linnea Teljas-Puranen. Fall Asleep with Me: A Children's Book about Falling Asleep with Someone Else Than Mom. Ida Theren. Giovanna Olmos, tr. 2016. (ENG.). (J). pap. *(978-91-982176-8-1(2))* Nära förlag.

Linnet, Paul. Snowball. Hendra, Sue. 2019. (ENG.). 24p. (J). (-k). bds. 8.99 *(978-0-593-09593-5(6)*, Grosset & Dunlap) Penguin Young Readers Group.

Linnet, Paul, jt. illus. see Hendra, Sue.

Linsdell, Jo. Jasmine at Work. Rochelle, Maria. 2013. 34p. pap. 9.99 *(978-0-9913342-1-6(3))* Draper Publishing.

—Jasmine at Work (Coloring Book) Rochelle, Maria. 2014. (ENG.). 34p. (J). pap. 7.39 *(978-0-9913342-2-3(1))* Draper Publishing.

—Jasmine's Got Talent! Rochelle, Maria. 2015. (ENG.). 34p. (J). pap. 10.00 *(978-0-9913342-6-1(4))* Draper Publishing.

Linsley, Paul. The Conifer Court Competition. Linsley, Sonja Paschal. 2006. 26p. (J). 18.95 *(978-0-9766062-1-5(6)*, HGP 2005-2) Higher Ground Pr.

—Know Your Shapes! (Teenage Mutant Ninja Turtles: Half-Shell Heroes) Smith, Geof. 2016. (ENG.). 24p. (J). (gr. -1-k). bds. 4.99 *(978-1-101-93497-5(2)*, Random Hse. Bks. for Young Readers) Random Hse. Children's Bks.

Linsley, Paul Adam. May I Have the First Dance? Linsley, Sonja Paschal. 2005. 24p. (J). 19.95 net. *(978-0-9766062-0-8(8))* Higher Ground Pr.

Linstead, Kathy. Garden of Friends: The Beginning. Stonesmith, Christina. 2020. (ENG.). 34p. (J). pap. 13.99 ***(978-1-7960-0960-6(1))*** Xlibris Corp.

Lintern, Tom. The Tooth Fairy Meets el Ratón Pérez. Laínez, René Colato. 2010. 32p. (J). (gr. -1-2). 16.99 *(978-1-58246-296-7(8)*, Tricycle Pr.) Random Hse. Children's Bks.

Linton, J. D., jt. illus. see Barnard, Frederick.

Linton, Jonathan. The Dance. Evans, Richard Paul. 2014. (ENG.). 32p. (J). (gr. -1). 16.99 *(978-1-4814-3112-5(9)*, Simon & Schuster/Paula Wiseman Bks.) Simon & Schuster/Paula Wiseman Bks.

—The Spyglass: A Book about Faith. Evans, Richard Paul. 2014. (ENG.). 32p. (J). (gr. -1-3). 16.99 *(978-1-4814-3109-5(9)*, Simon & Schuster/Paula Wiseman Bks.) Simon & Schuster/Paula Wiseman Bks.

—The Tower: A Story of Humility. Evans, Richard Paul. 2014. (ENG.). 32p. (J). (gr. -1-3). 16.99 *(978-1-4814-3111-8(0)*, Simon & Schuster/Paula Wiseman Bks.) Simon & Schuster/Paula Wiseman Bks.

Linton, Vera. Skoob. Howell, Kathy. 2004. (J). per. 6.95 *(978-1-59571-026-0(4))* Word Association Pubs.

Linville, S. Olga. Olga's Cats: An ABC Book. Anjou, Colette. 2005. 28p. (J). (gr. -1-3). per. 15.95 *(978-0-9748933-5-8(8))* E & E Publishing.

Lio, Pela. Expanding Dog: A Betsy the Dog Book. Darminio, Debbie O'Neil. 2019. (Betsy the Dog Ser.: Vol. 1). (ENG.). 30p. (J). (gr. k-3). 16.99 *(978-1-7338162-1-2(6))* Climb Your Moutain Publishing.

Lionni, Leo. A Color of His Own. Lionni, Leo. 2006. 40p. (J). (gr. -1-k). reprint ed. 12.95 *(978-0-375-83697-8(7)*, Knopf Bks. for Young Readers) Random Hse. Children's Bks.

—Frederick. Lionni, Leo. Mlawer, Teresa, tr. 2005. (SPA.). 32p. (gr. 1-2). pap. 9.99 *(978-1-930332-81-2(5))* Lectorum Pubns., Inc.

—Geraldine, the Music Mouse. Lionni, Leo. 2016. 32p. (J). (gr. -1-2). 17.99 *(978-0-394-84238-7(3))*; (ENG.). 20.99 *(978-0-394-94238-4(8))* Random Hse. Children's Bks. (Knopf Bks. for Young Readers).

—Inch by Inch. Lionni, Leo. unabr. ed. 2006. (J). (gr. -1-1). 18.95 *(978-0-439-90585-5(0)*, WPCD699) Weston Woods Studios, Inc.

—Pezzettino. Lionni, Leo. 2006. 40p. (J). (gr. -1-3). lib. bdg. 17.99 *(978-0-394-93156-2(4)*, Pantheon) Knopf Doubleday Publishing Group.

—Su Propio Color (a Color of His Own, Spanish-English Bilingual Edition) Lionni, Leo. 2016. (ENG.). 30p. (J). (gr. -1-k). bds. 7.99 *(978-0-553-53873-1(X)*, Knopf Bks. for Young Readers) Random Hse. Children's Bks.

—Tillie & the Wall. Lionni, Leo. 2014. (ENG.). 32p. (J). (gr. -1-2). 17.99 *(978-0-394-82155-9(6)*, Knopf Bks. for Young Readers) Random Hse. Children's Bks.

Lionni, Leo & Gerardi, Jan. A Little Book about Colors (Leo Lionni's Friends) Lionni, Leo. 2019. (Leo Lionni's Friends Ser.). 28p. (J). (— 1). bds. 8.99 *(978-0-525-58229-8(0)*, Random Hse. Bks. for Young Readers) Random Hse. Children's Bks.

Lionni, Leo & Hamilton, Julie. A Little Book about ABCs (Leo Lionni's Friends) Lionni, Leo. 2019. (Leo Lionni's Friends Ser.). 28p. (J). (— 1). bds. 8.99 *(978-0-525-58228-1(2)*, Random Hse. Bks. for Young Readers) Random Hse. Children's Bks.

—A Little Book about Spring (Leo Lionni's Friends) Lionni, Leo. 2019. (Leo Lionni's Friends Ser.). 28p. (J). (— 1). bds. 8.99 *(978-0-525-58227-4(4)*, Random Hse. Bks. for Young Readers) Random Hse. Children's Bks.

L

Lipchenko, Oleg. Alice's Adventures in Wonderland. Carroll, Lewis. 2009. 104p. (J). (gr. 5-12). 22.95 *(978-0-88776-932-0(2),* Tundra Bks.) Tundra Bks. CAN. Dist: Penguin Random Hse. LLC.

—The Hunting of the Snark: An Agony in Eight Fits. Carroll, Lewis. 2012. (ENG.). 48p. (J). (gr. 5-12). 17.95 *(978-1-77049-407-7(3),* Tundra Bks.) Tundra Bks. CAN. Dist: Penguin Random Hse. LLC.

Lipe, Barbara. Once upon A Monday. Roberts, Mary. 2004. 48p. (J). per. 19.95 *(978-0-9744412-0-7(1))* DinRo.

Lipking, Ron. The Secret of the Silver Key. Perry, Phyllis J. 2003. (Fribble Mouse Library Mystery Ser.). 90p. (J). pap. 16.95 *(978-1-932146-03-5(2))* Highsmith Inc.

—The Secrets of the Rock. Perry, Phyllis J. 2004. (Fribble Mouse Library Mystery Ser.). 96p. (J). 16.95 *(978-1-932146-22-6(9),* 1237661) Highsmith Inc.

Lipniewska, Dominika. 100 Christmas Coloring Book. 2017. (ENG.). 18p. (J). (gr. -1-17). pap. 12.95 *(978-1-84976-511-4(1))* Tate Publishing, Ltd. GBR. Dist: Hachette Bk. Group.

Lipow, Dan, photos by. I Love Our Earth. Martin, Bill, Jr. et al. 2009. 32p. (J). (gr. -1-2). pap. 7.95 *(978-1-58089-107-3(1))* Charlesbridge Publishing, Inc.

—I Love Our Earth / Amo Nuestra Tierra. Martin, Bill, Jr. & Sampson, Michael. ed. 2013. (Charlesbridge Bilingual Bks.). 32p. (J). (gr. -1-2). pap. 7.95 *(978-1-58089-557-6(3))* Charlesbridge Publishing, Inc.

Lipp, Tony. Rhyming Ricky Rutherford. Reid, Robin L. 2012. 24p. pap. 24.95 *(978-1-4626-8896-8(9))* America Star Bks.

Lippincott, Gary A. Hiding Glory. Chester, Laura. 2007. (ENG.). 160p. (J). (gr. 3-7). 18.95 *(978-1-59543-616-0(2))* Willow Creek Pr., Inc.

—Jennifer Murdley's Toad. Coville, Bruce. 2007. (Magic Shop Book Ser.: 3). (ENG.). 176p. (J). (gr. 5-7). pap. 7.99 *(978-0-15-206246-0(7),* 1198731) Houghton Mifflin Harcourt Publishing Co.

—Jeremy Thatcher, Dragon Hatcher: A Magic Shop Book. Coville, Bruce. 20th ed. 2007. (Magic Shop Book Ser.: 2). (ENG.). 176p. (J). (gr. 5-7). pap. 7.99 *(978-0-15-206252-1(1),* 1198750) Houghton Mifflin Harcourt Publishing Co.

—Marvel the Marvelous. Chester, Laura. 2008. (ENG.). 176p. (J). 18.95 *(978-1-59543-841-6(6))* Willow Creek Pr., Inc.

—The Skull of Truth: A Magic Shop Book. Coville, Bruce. 2007. (Magic Shop Book Ser.: 4). (ENG.). 208p. (J). (gr. 5-7). pap. 7.99 *(978-0-15-206084-8(7),* 1198275) Houghton Mifflin Harcourt Publishing Co.

Lips, Callie. Lupe Says. Jones, T. L. 2016. (ENG.). (J). 17.99 *(978-0-9907449-4-8(9))* Cedar Loft Publishing.

Lipscomb, Phillip and Zachary. Adventures of the Cabin Kids: 88 Mountain View Cir. (New Edition) Lipscomb, Zachary. 2019. (ENG.). 24p. (J). pap. 8.99 *(978-1-64550-287-6(2))* Matchstick Literary.

Lipscombe, Nick, jt. illus. see Biggin, Gary.

Lirius, Adelina. The Secret Garden. Brill, Calista & Burnett, Frances Hodgson. 2020. (ENG.). 40p. (J). (gr. -1-3). 17.99 *(978-0-06-293754-4(5),* HarperCollins) HarperCollins Pubs. Ltd. GBR. Dist: HarperCollins Pubs.

Lis, Jan. Tyrone the Terrible: The Chameleon Who Decided He Was an Alligator. Lis, Jan. 2020. (ENG.). 54p. (J). (gr. 1-5). pap. 9.99 ***(978-1-951970-15-4(2))*** Elk Lake Publishing, Inc.

Lisa Byers. Singled Out in Center Field: Diamonds Are A Girl's Best Friend - Book One. Robyn Washburn. 2009. 80p. pap. 12.00 *(978-1-4389-6245-0(2))* AuthorHouse.

Lisansky, Sue. Cinderella. 2011. (First Fairy Tales Ser.). (ENG.). 20p. (J). (gr. -1-3). pap. 4.99 *(978-1-934004-19-7(7))* Byeway Bks.

Liselle, Naomi. When I Go to Sleep. Liselle, Naomi. 2019. (ENG.). 36p. (J). pap. 10.00 *(978-1-7324805-8-2(3))* Horn, Jonathan.

Lisette, Soleil. Cool Kids Cook: Fresh & Fit, 1 vol. de Las Casas, Dianne & Eliana, Kid. 2014. (Cool Kids Cook Ser.). (ENG.). 64p. (J). (gr. 3-7). 14.95 *(978-1-4556-1892-7(6),* Pelican Publishing) Arcadia Publishing.

Lishchenko, Lenny. Families, 1 vol. McCluskey, Kerry & Mike, Jesse Unaapik. 2017. (ENG.). 28p. (J). (gr. k-2). pap. 10.95 *(978-1-77227-161-4(6))* Inhabit Media Inc. CAN. Dist: Consortium Bk. Sales & Distribution.

—In My Anaana's Amautik. Sammurtok, Nadia. 2020. (ENG.). 24p. (J). 16.95 *(978-1-77227-252-9(3))* Inhabit Media Inc. CAN. Dist: Consortium Bk. Sales & Distribution.

Lishchenko, Lenny. Nuliajuk, 1 vol. Rasmussen, Knud. 2017. (Nunavummi Ser.). (ENG.). 28p. (gr. 3-3). 7.95 ***(978-1-77266-578-9(9))*** Inhabit Education CAN. Dist: Consortium Bk. Sales & Distribution.

Lishchenko, Lenny. The Origin of Day & Night, 1 vol. Rumbolt, Paula Ikuutaq. 2018. (ENG.). 32p. (J). (gr. k-2). 16.95 *(978-1-77227-180-5(2))* Inhabit Media Inc. CAN. Dist: Consortium Bk. Sales & Distribution.

Lishchenko, Lenny. A Summer Day in the Community (Inuktitut/English) Kelly, Masiana. ed. 2020. (ENG.). 40p. (J). pap. 10.95 ***(978-0-2287-0493-5(6))*** Inhabit Education CAN. Dist: Consortium Bk. Sales & Distribution.

Lishinski, Jamie. Let Your Light Shine. Lishinski, Ann King. Morello, Charles, ed. 2003. (J). pap. 9.95 *(978-0-9709575-0-4(5))* Singing River Pubns.

Lisi, Margaret. Count on the Farm. Lisi, Branden. 2006. (J). lib. bdg. 15.95 *(978-0-9771472-0-5(7))* Count On Learning.

Liska, Eliska. Jayde the Jaybird. Buble, Brandee. 2015. (One of a Kind Ser.: 2). (ENG.). 32p. (J). 15.95 ***(978-1-927018-69-9(2))*** Simply Read Bks. CAN. Dist: Ingram Publisher Services.

Liska, Eliska. My Granny Loves Hockey. Weber, Lori. 2014. 32p. (J). (gr. -1-3). 16.95 *(978-1-927018-43-9(9))* Simply Read Bks. CAN. Dist: Ingram Publisher Services.

—O'Shae the Octopus. Buble, Brandee. 2014. 32p. (J). (gr. -1-3). 15.95 *(978-1-927018-56-9(0))* Simply Read Bks. CAN. Dist: Ingram Publisher Services.

Lisowski, Gabriel. Hardlucky: The Story of a Boy Who Learns How to Think Before He Acts. Chaikin, Miriam. 2012. 40p. (J). (gr. -1-3). 16.95 *(978-1-61608-963-4(6),* 608963, Sky Pony Pr.) Skyhorse Publishing Co., Inc.

Liss, Ira & Sorensen, Peter. Planetary Intelligence: 101 Easy Steps to Energy, Well-Being, & Natural Light. Hein, Simeon. 2006. 152p. per. 9.95 *(978-0-9715863-5-2(7),* 303 440-7393) Mount Baldy Pr., Inc.

Lissiat, Amy. The Short & Incredibly Happy Life of Riley. Thompson, Colin. 2006. 32p. (J). *(978-0-7344-0806-8(4),* Lothian Children's Bks.) Hachette Australia.

Listokin, David & Connally, Perry L., Sr. Puffy the Watermelon. Switzer, Vern. 2004. 24p. (J). 15.95 *(978-0-9753542-0-9(5))* Rural Farm Productions.

Liston, Chloe. Tinsel & Heart: Story by Michael Henry Jones. Ellis, James. 2015. (ENG.). (J). pap. 10.95 *(978-1-68181-275-5(4))* Strategic Book Publishing & Rights Agency (SBPRA).

Litchfield, David. Earth! My First 4. 54 Billion Years. McAnulty, Stacy. 2017. (Our Universe Ser.: 1). (ENG.). 40p. (J). 17.99 *(978-1-250-10808-1(X),* 900165029, Holt, Henry & Co. Bks. For Young Readers) Holt, Henry & Co.

—Hats off to Mr. Pockles! Lloyd-Jones, Sally. 2019. (ENG.). 40p. (J). (gr. -1-3). 17.99 *(978-0-399-55815-3(2),* Schwartz & Wade Bks.) Random Hse. Children's Bks.

—Miss Muffet, or What Came After. Singer, Marilyn. 2016. (ENG.). 40p. (J). (gr. 1-4). 16.99 *(978-0-547-90566-2(1),* 1511586) Houghton Mifflin Harcourt Publishing Co.

—Ocean! Waves for All. McAnulty, Stacy. 2020. (Our Universe Ser.: 4). (ENG.). 40p. (J). 18.99 *(978-1-250-10809-8(8),* 900165032, Holt, Henry & Co. Bks. For Young Readers) Holt, Henry & Co.

—Remarkables. Mantchev, Lisa. 2019. (ENG.). 40p. (J). (gr. -1-3). 17.99 *(978-1-4814-9717-6(0),* Simon & Schuster/Paula Wiseman Bks.) Simon & Schuster/Paula Wiseman Bks.

—War Is Over. Almond, David. 2020. (ENG.). 128p. (J). (gr. 4-7). 16.99 *(978-1-5362-0986-0(4))* Candlewick Pr.

—When Paul Met Artie: The Story of Simon & Garfunkel. Neri, G. 2018. 48p. (J). (gr. 4-7). 17.99 *(978-0-7636-8174-6(1))* Candlewick Pr.

Litchfield, Jo. Baby Brother Look & Say. 2008. (Look & Say Board Bks). 12p. (J). bds. 7.99 *(978-0-7945-2101-1(0),* Usborne) EDC Publishing.

—Baby Sister Look & Say. 2008. (Look & Say Board Bks). 12p. (J). bds. 7.99 *(978-0-7945-2102-8(9),* Usborne) EDC Publishing.

—Backyard. Durber, Matt. 2007. (Look & Say Board Bks). 10p. (J). (gr. -1-k). bds. 7.99 *(978-0-7945-1692-5(0),* Usborne) EDC Publishing.

—Box of Trucks. 2004. (Boxed Jigsaws Ser.). 10p. (J). 11.99 *(978-0-7945-0916-3(9),* Usborne) EDC Publishing.

—Daisy Doctor. Brooks, Felicity. 2005. 24p. (J). pap. 6.95 *(978-0-7945-0724-4(7),* Usborne) EDC Publishing.

—Daisy the Doctor. Brooks, Felicity. 2008. (Jobs People Do Ser.). 23p. (J). (gr. 4-7). pap. 6.99 *(978-0-7945-2214-8(9),* Usborne) EDC Publishing.

—Dinosaurios. Brooks, Felicity. 2004. (Titles in Spanish Ser.). (SPA.). 10p. (J). 4.95 *(978-0-7460-6111-4(0),* Usborne) EDC Publishing.

—Everyday Words in Spanish. Brooks, Felicity. rev. ed. 2004. (Everyday Words Ser.). 48p. (J). pap. 9.95 *(978-0-7945-0881-4(2),* Usborne) EDC Publishing.

—Farms lift & Look. Brooks, Felicity. 2005. 12p. (J). 9.95 *(978-0-7945-0932-3(0),* Usborne) EDC Publishing.

—First Book of Christmas Carols. 2004. (First Book of Christmas Carols Ser.). 24p. (J). 9.95 *(978-0-7945-0596-7(1),* Usborne) EDC Publishing.

—First Picture 123. 2005. (First Picture Board Books Ser.). 16p. (J). 11.95 *(978-0-7945-0939-2(8),* Usborne) EDC Publishing.

—First Picture Abc. 2005. (First Picture Board Books Ser.). 16p. (J). 11.95 *(978-0-7945-0907-1(X),* Usborne) EDC Publishing.

—First Picture Nursery Rhymes. 2005. (Usborne First Book Ser.). 16p. (J). (gr. -1-k). per. 11.99 *(978-0-7945-1014-5(0),* Usborne) EDC Publishing.

—First Picture Spanish. Brooks, Felicity & MacKinnon, Mairi. 2006. (First Picture Flap Bks.). 18p. (J). (gr. 1-4). bds. 14.99 *(978-0-7945-1384-9(0),* Usborne) EDC Publishing.

—First Shapes. MMStudios, photos by. Brooks, Felicity. 2007. (Usborne Look & Say Ser.). 12p. (J). (gr. -1-k). bds. 14.99 *(978-0-7945-1450-1(2),* Usborne) EDC Publishing.

—Frank the Farmer. Brooks, Felicity. (Jobs People Do Ser.). 23p. (J). 2005. (gr. -1-7). pap. 6.95 *(978-0-7945-0723-7(9));* 2007. (gr. 4-7). pap. 6.99 *(978-0-7945-1621-5(1))* EDC Publishing. (Usborne).

—Fred the Firefighter. Brooks, Felicity. (Jobs People Do Ser.). (J). 2004. (ENG.). 24p. pap. 6.95 *(978-0-7945-0725-1(5));* 2006. 23p. (gr. -1). pap. 6.99 *(978-0-7945-1496-9(0))* EDC Publishing. (Usborne).

—La Granja Minilibros Usborne. Brooks, Felicity. 2005. (SPA.). 10p. (J). 4.95 *(978-0-7460-6110-7(2),* Usborne) EDC Publishing.

—Jobs People Do. Brooks, Felicity. 2008. (Jobs People Do Ser.). 143p. (J). (gr. -1-3). 22.99 *(978-0-7945-1998-8(9),* Usborne) EDC Publishing.

—The Runaway Orange. Brooks, Felicity, ed. 2004. (Easy Reading Ser.). (ENG.). 1p. (J). (gr. -1-3). pap. 5.95 *(978-0-7460-3029-5(0))* EDC Publishing.

—School Look & Say. Brooks, Felicity. 2005. 10p. (J). 7.95 *(978-0-7945-1015-2(9),* Usborne) EDC Publishing.

—Tessa the Teacher. Brooks, Felicity. 2006. 24p. (J). per. 6.99 *(978-0-7945-0937-8(1),* Usborne) EDC Publishing.

—Trains lift & Look. Brooks, Felicity. 2005. 12p. (J). 9.99 *(978-0-7945-0935-4(5),* Usborne) EDC Publishing.

—The Usborne Very First Dictionary. Young, Caroline & Brooks, Felicity. 2005. 64p. (J). (gr. -1-3). 11.95 *(978-0-7945-1002-2(7),* Usborne) EDC Publishing.

—Very First Words in Spanish. 2009. (Very First Words in Spanish Ser.). (SPA & ENG.). 18p. (J). (gr. -1). bds. 7.99 *(978-0-7945-2446-3(X),* Usborne) EDC Publishing.

—Vicky the Vet. Brooks, Felicity. 2004. (Jobs People Do Ser.). 24p. (J). pap. 6.95 *(978-0-7945-0726-8(3));* (gr. -1). lib. bdg. 14.95 *(978-1-58086-699-6(9))* EDC Publishing. (Usborne).

—Vicky the Vet Kid Kit. Brooks, Felicity. 2007. (Kid Kits Ser.). 23p. (J). pap. 15.99 *(978-1-60130-008-9(5),* Usborne) EDC Publishing.

Litchfield, Jo. Christmas. Litchfield, Jo. 2005. (Usborne Look & Say Ser.). 10p. (J). (gr. -1-k). bds. 9.95 *(978-0-7945-1173-9(2),* Usborne) EDC Publishing.

—First Words Look & Say. Litchfield, Jo. 2005. 18p. (J). 14.99 *(978-0-7945-1024-4(8),* Usborne) EDC Publishing.

Litchfield, Jo & Allen, Francesca. First Picture Fairytales. MMStudios, photos by. 2007. (First Picture Board Bks.). 16p. (J). (gr. -1-k). bds. 11.99 *(978-0-7945-1460-0(X),* Usborne) EDC Publishing.

—First Picture Nursery Rhymes With. 2006. 18p. (J). bds. 18.99 *(978-0-7945-1489-1(8),* Usborne) EDC Publishing.

—Home. Litchfield, Jo. 2006. (Usborne Look & Say Ser.). 12p. (J). (gr. -1-k). bds. 7.99 *(978-0-7945-1425-9(1),* Usborne) EDC Publishing.

—Jobs. Litchfield, Jo. 2006. (Usborne Look & Say Ser.). 10p. (J). (gr. -1-k). bds. 7.99 *(978-0-7945-1353-5(0),* Usborne) EDC Publishing.

Litchfield, Jo & Jones, Stephanie. First 1,2,3. Allman, Howard, photos by. 2006. (Usborne Look & Say Ser.). 20p. (J). (gr. -1-k). bds. 14.95 *(978-0-7945-1219-4(4),* Usborne) EDC Publishing.

Litten, Kristyna. Angel's Great Escape: A Christmas Story. Rowson, Kirstie. 2016. (ENG.). 36p. (J). pap. *(978-0-9928408-1-5(3))* And So We Begin Ltd.

—Bike on, Bear! Liu, Cynthea. 2015. (ENG.). 32p. (J). (gr. -1-2). 17.99 *(978-1-4814-0506-5(3),* Aladdin) Simon & Schuster Children's Publishing.

—Gracie Laroo, 4 vols. Qualey, Marsha. 2017. (Gracie Laroo Ser.). (ENG.). 40p. (J). (gr. k-2). 82.60 *(978-1-5158-1455-9(6),* 26747, Picture Window Bks.) Capstone.

—Gracie Laroo at Pig Jubilee. Qualey, Marsha. 2017. (Gracie Laroo Ser.). (ENG.). 40p. (J). (gr. k-2). lib. bdg. 21.32 *(978-1-5158-1442-9(4),* 135712, Picture Window Bks.) Capstone.

—Gracie Laroo Goes to School. Qualey, Marsha. 2017. (Gracie Laroo Ser.). (ENG.). 40p. (J). (gr. k-2). lib. bdg. 21.32 *(978-1-5158-1440-5(8),* 135710, Picture Window Bks.) Capstone.

—Gracie Laroo on the Big Screen. Qualey, Marsha. 2017. (Gracie Laroo Ser.). (ENG.). 40p. (J). (gr. k-2). lib. bdg. 21.32 *(978-1-5158-1441-2(6),* 135711, Picture Window Bks.) Capstone.

—Gracie Laroo Sets Sail. Qualey, Marsha. 2017. (Gracie Laroo Ser.). (ENG.). 40p. (J). (gr. k-2). lib. bdg. 21.32 *(978-1-5158-1439-9(4),* 135709, Picture Window Bks.) Capstone.

—I'll Love You till the Cows Come Home. Cristaldi, Kathryn. 2018. (ENG.). 32p. (J). (gr. -1-3). 17.99 *(978-0-06-257420-6(5))* HarperCollins Pubs.

Litten, Kristyna. The Mouse's Apples. Stickley, Frances. 2020. (ENG.). 32p. (J). (gr. -1-3). 17.99 ***(978-1-7284-1580-2(2))*** Lerner Publishing Group.

Litten, Kristyna. Pins & Needles. Krensky, Stephen. 2014. (Penguin Core Concepts Ser.). 32p. (J). (gr. -1-k). 3.99 *(978-0-448-46209-7(5),* Grosset & Dunlap) Penguin Young Readers Group.

—This Day in June. Pitman, Gayle E. 2013. 32p. (J). *(978-1-4338-1658-1(X));* pap. *(978-1-4338-1659-8(8))* American Psychological Assn. (Magination Pr.).

Litten, Kristyna. Blue & Bertie. Litten, Kristyna. 2016. (ENG.). 32p. (J). (gr. -1-3). 17.99 *(978-1-4814-6154-2(0),* Simon & Schuster Bks. For Young Readers) Simon & Schuster Bks. For Young Readers.

—Hong Kong & Macau: a 3D Keepsake Cityscape. Litten, Kristyna. 2013. (Panorama Pops Ser.). (ENG.). 30p. (J). (gr. k-4). 8.99 *(978-0-7636-6416-9(2))* Candlewick Pr.

—Rome: a 3D Keepsake Cityscape. Litten, Kristyna. 2013. (Panorama Pops Ser.). (ENG.). 15p. (J). (gr. k-12). 8.99 *(978-0-7636-6415-2(4))* Candlewick Pr.

Litteral, Christopher. Sammy the Sea Turtle, 1 vol. Kruse, Robyn A. 2010. 18p. 24.95 *(978-1-4489-4020-2(6))* PublishAmerica, Inc.

Little Airplane Productions. Go, Wonder Pets! Selig, Josh. 2008. (Wonder Pets! Ser.). (ENG.). 26p. (J). bds. 5.99 *(978-1-4169-4723-3(X),* Simon Spotlight/Nickelodeon) Simon Spotlight/Nickelodeon.

Little Airplane Productions & Fogarty, Alexandria. Baby Beaver Rescue. 2009. (Wonder Pets! Ser.). (ENG.). 24p. (J). (gr. -1-2). pap. 3.99 *(978-1-4169-8499-3(2),* Simon Spotlight/Nickelodeon) Simon Spotlight/Nickelodeon.

Little Airplane Productions & Scanlon, Michael. Off to School! 2009. (Wonder Pets! Ser.). (ENG.). 24p. (J). (gr. -1-1). 16.19 *(978-1-4169-7197-9(1))* Simon & Schuster, Inc.

Little Airplane Productions Staff. How We Met! Scanlon, Michael. 2010. (Wonder Pets! Ser.). (ENG.). 24p. (J). pap. 3.99 *(978-1-4424-0654-4(2),* Simon Spotlight/Nickelodeon) Simon Spotlight/Nickelodeon.

Little, Elaine, photos by. My Family. Kinkade, Sheila. 2006. (Global Fund for Children Bks.). 32p. (J). (gr. -1-3). 7.95 *(978-1-57091-691-5(8));* 16.95 *(978-1-57091-662-5(4))* Charlesbridge Publishing, Inc.

Little, Gary. My Story as Told by Sacagawea. Lohof, Arle & Jensen, Joyce. 2006. 32p. (J). (gr. 1-2). 3.95 *(978-0-9711667-3-8(0))* Outlook Publishing, Inc.

Little, James. H Is for Howdy: And Other Lone Star Letters. Bright Sky Press, Bright Sky et al. 2016. (ENG.). 24p. (J). 15.95 *(978-1-942945-34-5(5),* fd45f5f1-be54-4927-a95e-10d265d8269b) Night Heron Media.

—H Is for Howdy: the Coloring Book: And Other Lone Star Letters. Freeburn, Eva & Gow, Lawson. 2016. (ENG.). 24p. (J). pap. 9.95 *(978-1-942945-45-1(0),* b34825af-00ae-48c2-ae41-b268ee985ee8) Night Heron Media.

—How to Make a Monster's Birthday Cake: A Second Serving of Poppin' Poetry. Arnold, Daniela. 2018. (J). *(978-1-942945-64-2(7))* Night Heron Media.

—Smitty Tackles Bullying. Smith, Wade. 2017. (ENG.). 24p. (J). 19.95 *(978-1-942945-49-9(3),* 5dba8b3a-fdea-424e-a9fb-76798021751b) Night Heron Media.

Little, Jeanette. In Disguise! Undercover with Real Women Spies. Hunter, Ryan Ann. 2013. (ENG.). 176p. (J). (gr. 3-7). pap. 9.99 *(978-1-58270-382-4(5))* Aladdin/Beyond Words.

Little, Kelli Ann. Rockabet: Classic Edition. Polark, Kelly. 2013. 32p. pap. 10.49 *(978-0-9888462-0-3(9))* Big Smile Pr., LLC.

Little, Marc. Yes &... I Am a Princess! Little, Julie. 2017. (Yes & Ser.: Vol. 1). (ENG.). (J). pap. 7.99 *(978-1-4951-8552-6(4))* Independent Pub.

Littlechild, George. What's the Most Beautiful Thing You Know about Horses? Van Camp, Richard. 2013. (ENG.). 32p. (J). pap. 11.95 *(978-0-89239-185-1(5))* Lee & Low Bks., Inc.

Littlechild, George. This Land Is My Land, 1 vol. Littlechild, George. 2014. (ENG.). 32p. (J). pap. 11.95 *(978-0-89239-184-4(7),* Children's Book Press) Lee & Low Bks., Inc.

Littlejohn, Anna. Divided Loyalties. Upham, Linda. 2007. 188p. per. *(978-0-7552-0302-4(X))* Authors OnLine, Ltd.

Littlejohn, Brad. A Is for All Aboard!, 1 vol. Kluth, Paula & Kluth, Victoria. 2009. (ENG.). 32p. (J). 16.95 *(978-1-59857-071-7(4))* Brookes Publishing.

LittlePinkPebble. Queen Amina of Zari: Queens of Africa Book 1. Judybee. 2011. 28p. pap. *(978-1-908218-43-8(6))* MX Publishing, Ltd.

—Queen Esther: Queens of Africa Book 4. Judybee. 2011. 28p. pap. *(978-1-908218-52-0(5))* MX Publishing, Ltd.

—Queen Idi: Queens of Africa Book 5. Judybee. 2011. 24p. pap. *(978-1-908218-55-1(X))* MX Publishing, Ltd.

—Queen Maked: Queens of Africa Book 2. Judybee. 2011. 28p. pap. *(978-1-908218-46-9(0))* MX Publishing, Ltd.

—Queen Moremi: Queens of Africa Book 3. Judybee. 2011. 28p. pap. *(978-1-908218-49-0(5))* MX Publishing, Ltd.

—The Zoo Crew Play Ball. Judybee. 2011. 40p. pap. *(978-1-78092-000-9(8))* MX Publishing, Ltd.

Littler, Jamie. Disaster Diaries: Brainwashed! McGeddon, R. 2016. 187p. (J). pap. *(978-1-250-09093-5(8))* ETT Imprint.

Littler, Jamie, jt. illus. see McGeddon, R.

Littler, Phil. The Three Frilly Goats Fluff. Guillain, Adam & Guillain, Charlotte. 2015. (Tadpoles: Fairytale Twists Ser.). (ENG.). 32p. (J). (gr. 1-2). *(978-0-7787-1935-9(9))* Crabtree Publishing Co.

Littlewood, Karin. Chanda & the Mirror of Moonlight. Bateson-Hill, Margaret. 2003. (Folk Tales Ser.). 32p. (J). (gr. 3-4). *(978-1-84089-217-8(X))* Zero to Ten, Ltd.

—Los Colores de Casa. Hoffman, Mary. 2003. (SPA.). 28p. (J). (gr. k-2). 20.99 *(978-84-8452-223-2(7),* MON32674) Fundacion Intermon ESP. Dist: Lectorum Pubns., Inc.

—The Day the Rains Fell. Faundez, Anne. 2010. (ENG.). 32p. (J). (gr. k-2). pap. 15.99 *(978-1-84853-015-7(3),* Tamarind) Transworld Publishers Ltd. GBR. Dist: Independent Pubs. Group.

—Home Now. Beake, Lesley. 2007. 32p. (J). (ENG.). (gr. -1-3). pap. 6.95 *(978-1-58089-163-9(2));* (gr. k-3). 16.95 *(978-1-58089-162-2(4))* Charlesbridge Publishing, Inc.

—Lucy & the Big Bad Wolf. Jungman, Ann. 2005. 120p. (J). (gr. -1-6). pap. 4.95 *(978-1-903015-39-1(1))* Barn Owl Bks, London GBR. Dist: Independent Pubs. Group.

—Tara's Tree House. Dunmore, Helen. 2005. (Yellow Go Bananas Ser.). (ENG.). 48p. (J). (gr. 3-4). *(978-0-7787-2743-9(2));* lib. bdg. *(978-0-7787-2721-7(1))* Crabtree Publishing Co.

Littlewood, Karin. Immi's Gift, 1 vol. Littlewood, Karin. 2010. (ENG.). 32p. (J). (gr. -1-3). 15.95 *(978-1-56145-545-4(8))* Peachtree Publishing Co. Inc.

Littlewort, Lizza. The Magic Fish. Orford, Margie. 2012. (Best Loved Tales for Africa Ser.). 32p. (J). (gr. k-2). pap. 9.95 *(978-1-77009-822-0(4))* Jacana Media ZAF. Dist: Independent Pubs. Group.

Litwin, Mike. ABC - I - I Like: StartUp Unit 1 Lap Book. Wilkens, Karen & Johnson, Tiffany. 2015. (Start up Core Phonics Ser.). (J). (gr. k). *(978-1-4900-2590-2(1))* Benchmark Education Co.

—Girl in Charge. Fosberry, Jennifer. 2016. 32p. (J). (-4). 16.99 *(978-1-4926-4173-5(1),* 9781492641735, Sourcebooks Jabberwocky) Sourcebooks, Inc.

—Isabella: Girl on the Go. Fosberry, Jennifer. 2012. (ENG.). 32p. (J). (gr. k-3). 16.99 *(978-1-4022-6648-5(0),* Sourcebooks Jabberwocky) Sourcebooks, Inc.

—Isabella: Star of the Story. Fosberry, Jennifer. 2013. 32p. (J). (-3). 16.99 *(978-1-4022-7936-2(1),* 9781402279362, Sourcebooks Jabberwocky) Sourcebooks, Inc.

Litwin, Mike. Isabella: Girl in Charge. Fosberry, Jennifer. 2020. 32p. (J). (-4). 8.99 ***(978-1-7282-2146-5(3),*** Sourcebooks Jabberwocky) Sourcebooks, Inc.

—Isabella: Star of the Story. Fosberry, Jennifer. 2020. 32p. (J). (-3). 8.99 ***(978-1-7282-2303-2(2),*** Sourcebooks Jabberwocky) Sourcebooks, Inc.

Litwin, Mike. My Name Is Not Alexander. Fosberry, Jennifer. 2011. (ENG.). 32p. (J). (gr. k-3). 16.99 *(978-1-4022-5433-8(4),* Sourcebooks Jabberwocky) Sourcebooks, Inc.

—My Name Is Not Isabella. Fosberry, Jennifer. 2008. 32p. (J). (gr. -1-3). lib. bdg. 19.99 *(978-0-9802000-7-2(5))* Monkey Barrel Pr.

Litwin, Mike. My Name Is Not Isabella. Fosberry, Jennifer. 32p. (J). (-3). 2020. 8.99 ***(978-1-7282-2302-5(4));*** 2010. (ENG.). 16.99 *(978-1-4022-4395-0(2))* Sourcebooks, Inc. (Sourcebooks Jabberwocky).

Litwin, Mike. Nosotras Podemos Jugar. Craddock, Petra. 2016. (Early Rising Readers Ser.). (SPA.). 16p. (J). (gr. 1-1). 6.67 *(978-1-4788-3766-4(7))* Newmark Learning LLC.

Litz, Marnie Saebz. Saint Brendan & the Voyage Before Columbus. McGrew, Michael. 2005. 32p. 9.95 *(978-0-8091-6705-0(0),* 6705-0) Paulist Pr.

Litzinger, Rosanne. Chicken Soup by Heart. Hershenhorn, Esther. 2010. (ENG.). 40p. (J). (gr. -1-3). 16.99 *(978-1-4424-2197-4(5),* Simon & Schuster Bks. For Young Readers) Simon & Schuster Bks. For Young Readers.

—The Frog Princess: A Tlingit Legend from Alaska. Kimmel, Eric A. 2005. (ENG.). 32p. (J). (gr. -1-3). 16.95 *(978-0-8234-1618-9(6))* Holiday Hse., Inc.

—The Matzo Ball Boy, Vol. Shulman, Lisa. 2007. 32p. (J). (gr. -1-2). pap. 6.99 *(978-0-14-240769-1(0)*, Puffin Books) Penguin Young Readers Group.

—Snail's Good Night. Paul, Ann Whitford. 2008. (Holiday House Readers: Level 1 Ser.). (ENG.). 32p. (J). (gr. -1-3). 14.95 *(978-0-8234-1912-8(6))* Holiday Hse., Inc.

Liu, Carloe. Always with You, 1 vol. Walters, Eric. 2019. (ENG.). 32p. (J). 24.95 *(978-1-77108-738-4(2)*, 443cc515-bce8-4ff6-beba-3f7c8e46f608) Nimbus Publishing, Ltd. CAN. Dist: Baker & Taylor Publisher Services (BTPS).

Liu, Chun & Melaranci, Elisabetta. Belle: The Charming Gift. O'Ryan, Ellie. 2017. (Disney Princess Ser.). (ENG.). 96p. (J). (gr. 2-6). lib. bdg. 27.07 *(978-1-5321-4120-1(3)*, 26993, Chapter Bks.) Spotlight.

Liu, Davy. The Giant Leaf: Take a Giant Leaf of Faith. Liu, Davy. 2009. (CHI.). (J). 1995.00 *(978-0-9825050-0-7(0))* Kendu Films.

Liu, Jia. Arithmechicks Add Up: A Math Story. Stephens, Ann Marie. 2019. 32p. (J). (gr. -1-3). 17.99 *(978-1-62979-807-3(X))* Boyds Mills Pr.

—Bedtime for Beasties. Staub, Leslie. 2019. 32p. (J). (gr. -1-3). 17.95 *(978-1-59078-930-8(X))* Boyds Mills Pr.

—Bugs in Danger: Our Vanishing Bees, Butterflies, & Beetles. Kurlansky, Mark. 2019. 176p. (J). 19.99 *(978-1-5476-0085-4(3)*, 900198112, Bloomsbury Children's Bks.) Bloomsbury Publishing USA.

—Earth's Record Breakers. Higgins, Nadia. 2018. (What Shapes Our Earth? Ser.). (ENG.). 24p. (gr. 1-3). 33.99 *(978-1-68410-314-0(2)*, 140696); lib. bdg. 33.99 incl. audio compact disk *(978-1-68410-135-1(2)*, 31858) Cantata Learning.

—The Story of Earth. Higgins, Nadia. 2018. (What Shapes Our Earth? Ser.). (ENG.). 24p. (gr. 1-3). lib. bdg. 33.99 incl. audio compact disk *(978-1-68410-129-0(8)*, 31857) Cantata Learning.

—Tectonic Plates Are on the Move. Higgins, Nadia. 2018. (What Shapes Our Earth? Ser.). (ENG.). 24p. (C). (gr. 1-3). lib. bdg. 33.99 incl. audio compact disk *(978-1-68410-144-3(1)*, 31859) Cantata Learning.

—Terrific Tongues! Gianferrari, Maria. 2018. 32p. (J). (gr. -1-3). 17.99 *(978-1-62091-784-8(X))* Boyds Mills Pr.

Liu, Jia. What Shapes Our Earth? Higgins, Nadia. 2018. (What Shapes Our Earth? Ser.). (ENG.). (J). 135.96 ***(978-1-5158-4624-6(5)***, 29693) Cantata Learning.

Liu, Jia. Wind & Water Shape the Land. Higgins, Nadia. 2018. (What Shapes Our Earth? Ser.). (ENG.). 24p. (C). (gr. 1-3). lib. bdg. 33.99 incl. audio compact disk *(978-1-68410-121-4(2)*, 31856) Cantata Learning.

Liu, Kimi. Mira. Trujillo, Rafael E. 2009. (SPA.). 10p. (J). 5.99 *(978-0-9765007-3-5(6))* Big-head fish.

—Mira: La Granja. Trujillo, Rafael E. 2009. (SPA.). 10p. (J). 5.99 *(978-0-9765007-4-2(4))* Big-head fish.

—La ultima ola de Marianela. Trujillo, Rafael E. 2009. (SPA.). 16p. (J). 17.00 *(978-0-9765007-6-6(0))* Big-head fish.

Liu, Siyu. A Thousand Peaks: Poems from China. Liu, Siyu, tr. Protopopescu, Orel O. 2003. (CHI & ENG.). 52p. (gr. 7-18). 19.95 *(978-1-881896-24-1(2)*, THPE) Pacific View Pr.

Liu, Xun. As If... As If... Qin, Wenjun. 2018. 36p. (J). (gr. 2-3). 16.95 *(978-1-76036-061-0(9)*, 9363efa8-1b9a-456e-bf92-588701dbaa53) Starfish Bay Publishing Pty Ltd. AUS. Dist: Baker & Taylor Publisher Services (BTPS).

Liu, Zhen. Good Night Portland Maine. Gamble, Adam & Jasper, Mark. 2020. (Good Night Our World Ser.). (ENG.). 20p. (J). (— 1). bds. 9.95 *(978-1-60219-880-7(2))* Good Night Bks.

LiveLearn, Robert. Hamster on the Run. Richter, Debra A. 2011. 24p. pap. 24.95 *(978-1-4626-3897-0(X))* America Star Bks.

—Hamster on the Run, Let's Play in the Snow. Richter, Debra A. 2012. 28p. pap. 24.95 *(978-1-4626-5064-4(3))* America Star Bks.

Liversidge, Cassie. Ice Cream! Grow Your Own Ingredients. 2015. (ENG.). 40p. (J). (gr. -1-3). 12.99 *(978-1-63220-405-9(3)*, Sky Pony Pr.) Skyhorse Publishing Co., Inc.

Lividini, Dante. Dawn of Time: Creation Myths Around the World. Yomtov, Nel. 2017. (Universal Myths Ser.). (ENG.). 48p. (J). (gr. 3-9). lib. bdg. 31.32 *(978-1-5157-6629-2(2)*, 135200, Capstone Pr.) Capstone.

Livingston, Francis. Davy Crockett: Young Pioneer. Santrey, Laurence & Macken, JoAnn Early. 2008. 55p. (J). pap. *(978-0-439-02048-0(4))* Scholastic, Inc.

—Paul Revere, Son of Liberty. Brandt, Keith & Macken, JoAnn Early. 2007. 50p. (J). *(978-0-439-02017-6(4))* Scholastic, Inc.

Livingston, Jessica. My First Trip to the Bank. Kawa, Katie. 2012. (My First Adventures Ser.). (ENG.). 24p. (J). (gr. k-2). pap. 8.15 *(978-1-4339-6238-7(1))*; lib. bdg. 23.60 *(978-1-4339-6236-3(5))* Stevens, Gareth Publishing LLLP.

—My First Trip to the Bank: Mi Primera Visita Al Banco. Kawa, Katie. 2012. (My First Adventures / Mis primeras aventuras Ser.). (ENG & SPA.). 24p. (J). (gr. k-2). lib. bdg. 23.60 *(978-1-4339-6625-5(5))* Stevens, Gareth Publishing LLLP.

—My First Trip to the Dentist. Kawa, Katie. 2012. (My First Adventures Ser.). (ENG.). 24p. (J). (gr. k-2). pap. 8.15 *(978-1-4339-6243-1(8))*; lib. bdg. 23.60 *(978-1-4339-6241-7(1))* Stevens, Gareth Publishing LLLP.

—My First Trip to the Dentist: Mi Primera Visita Al Dentista. Kawa, Katie. 2012. (My First Adventures / Mis primeras aventuras Ser.). (ENG & SPA.). 24p. (J). (gr. k-2). lib. bdg. 23.60 *(978-1-4339-6627-9(1))* Stevens, Gareth Publishing LLLP.

—My First Trip to the Doctor. Kawa, Katie. 2012. (My First Adventures Ser.). (ENG.). 24p. (J). (gr. k-2). pap. 8.15 *(978-1-4339-6247-9(0))*; lib. bdg. 23.60 *(978-1-4339-6245-5(4))* Stevens, Gareth Publishing LLLP.

—My First Trip to the Library. Kawa, Katie. 2012. (My First Adventures Ser.). (ENG.). 24p. (J). (gr. k-2). pap. 8.15 *(978-1-4339-6251-6(9))*; lib. bdg. 23.60 *(978-1-4339-6249-3(7))* Stevens, Gareth Publishing LLLP.

—My First Trip to the Library: Mi Primera Visita a la Biblioteca. Kawa, Katie. 2012. (My First Adventures / Mis primeras aventuras Ser.). (ENG & SPA.). 24p. (J). (gr. k-2). lib. bdg. 23.60 *(978-1-4339-6631-6(X))* Stevens, Gareth Publishing LLLP.

—My First Trip to the Post Office. Kawa, Katie. 2012. (My First Adventures Ser.). (ENG.). 24p. (J). (gr. k-2). 23.60 *(978-1-4339-6253-0(5))*; pap. 8.15 *(978-1-4339-6255-4(1))* Stevens, Gareth Publishing LLLP.

—My First Trip to the Post Office: Mi Primera Visita Al Correo. Kawa, Katie. 2012. (My First Adventures / Mis primeras aventuras Ser.). (ENG & SPA.). 24p. (J). (gr. k-2). lib. bdg. 23.60 *(978-1-4339-6633-0(6))* Stevens, Gareth Publishing LLLP.

—My First Trip to the Zoo. Kawa, Katie. 2012. (My First Adventures Ser.). (ENG.). 24p. (J). (gr. k-2). pap. 8.15 *(978-1-4339-6259-2(4))*; lib. bdg. 23.60 *(978-1-4339-6257-8(8))* Stevens, Gareth Publishing LLLP.

Livingston, Mary A. Percy Learns to Fly. Schetter, Patricia. 2013. (ENG.). (J). (gr. k-6). pap. 11.99 *(978-0-9844660-2-3(9))* ABTA Pubns. & Products.

Livingston, Mary A. No Place for Ugly Birds. Livingston, Mary A. 2013. (ENG.). 32p. (J). 19.99 *(978-0-9847756-7-5(6))*; pap. 11.99 *(978-0-9847756-8-2(4))* Red Tail Publishing.

Livingston, Tim. Buddy & the Magic Chicken Tree, 2 bks. Livingston, Mary A. & Shufelberger, Amanda. 2014th ed. 2014. (ENG.). 34p. (J). 19.99 *(978-0-9635757-3-9(2))* Red Tail Publishing.

—Buddy, the Wayward Wolverine. Livingston, Mary A. & Shufelberger, Amanda. 2013. (ENG.). 32p. (J). 19.99 *(978-0-9847756-5-1(X))* Red Tail Publishing.

—Buddy, the Wayward Wolverine. Shufelberger, Amanda & Livingston, Mary A. 2013. (ENG.). 32p. (J). pap. 11.99 *(978-0-9847756-6-8(8))* Red Tail Publishing.

Livingston, Timothy J. FireStorm in the Forest: When a Forest Burns. Livingston, Timothy J. Livingston, Mary A. 2006. 32p. (J). 19.99 *(978-0-9635757-1-5(6))* Red Tail Publishing.

Liwska, Renata. The Christmas Quiet Book. Underwood, Deborah. (ENG.). 32p. (J). (gr. -1-3). 2017. pap. 7.99 *(978-1-328-74056-4(0)*, 1677029, HMH Books For Young Readers); 2012. 12.99 *(978-0-547-55863-9(5)*, 1453618) Houghton Mifflin Harcourt Publishing Co.

—Crafty Llama. Kerr, Mike. 2018. 32p. (J). 16.99 *(978-1-68119-121-8(0)*, 900159672, Bloomsbury Children's Bks.) Bloomsbury Publishing USA.

—The Loud Book! Underwood, Deborah. (ENG.). 32p. (J). (gr. -1-3). 2018. pap. 7.99 *(978-1-328-86929-6(6)*, 1696691, HMH Books For Young Readers); 2011. 12.99 *(978-0-547-39008-6(4)*, 1426459) Houghton Mifflin Harcourt Publishing Co.

—The Loud Book! Padded Board Book. Underwood, Deborah. 2015. (ENG.). 32p. (J). (— 1). bds. 8.99 *(978-0-544-43064-8(6)*, 1595739, HMH Books For Young Readers) Houghton Mifflin Harcourt Publishing Co.

—Once upon a Memory. Laden, Nina. 2013. 40p. (J). (gr. -1-3). 17.99 *(978-0-316-20816-1(7))* Little, Brown Bks. for Young Readers.

—Places to Be. Barnett, Mac. 2017. (ENG.). 32p. (J). (gr. -1-3). 17.99 *(978-0-06-228621-5(8))* HarperCollins Pubs.

—A Puppy Is for Loving, 1 vol. Labatt, Mary. 2007. (Orca Echoes Ser.). (ENG.). 64p. (J). (gr. 1-3). per. 6.95 *(978-1-55143-477-3(6))* Orca Bk. Pubs. USA.

—The Quiet Book. Underwood, Deborah. (ENG.). 32p. (J). 2016. (gr. -1-3). pap. 6.99 *(978-0-544-80904-8(1)*, 1641353, HMH Books For Young Readers); 2013. (— 1). bds. 8.99 *(978-0-544-05667-1(1)*, 1533572); 2010. (gr. -1-3). 12.95 *(978-0-547-21567-9(3)*, 1060743) Houghton Mifflin Harcourt Publishing Co.

—The Quiet Book. Underwood, Deborah. ed. 2016. (ENG.). 32p. (J). (gr. -1-3). lib. bdg. 17.96 net. *(978-1-64310-087-6(4))* Penworthy Co., LLC, The.

—Waiting for Snow. Arnold, Marsha Diane. 2016. (ENG.). 32p. (J). (gr. -1-3). 14.99 *(978-0-544-41687-1(2)*, 1594762, HMH Books For Young Readers) Houghton Mifflin Harcourt Publishing Co.

Liwska, Renata. Red Wagon. Liwska, Renata. 2013. 32p. (J). (gr. -1 — 1). bds. 7.99 *(978-0-399-16239-8(9)*, Philomel Bks.) Penguin Young Readers Group.

Liz, Laura. Camo Cocinar Princesas. Martinez Castillo, Ana. 2018. (SPA.). 56p. (J). 16.95 *(978-84-946926-3-5(1))* NubeOcho Ediciones ESP. Dist: Consortium Bk. Sales & Distribution.

—How to Cook a Princess. Martinez Castillo, Ana. 2018. (ENG.). 56p. (J). 16.95 *(978-84-946926-4-2(X))* NubeOcho Ediciones ESP. Dist: Consortium Bk. Sales & Distribution.

Liz, Pichon. Three Horrid Little Pigs. Liz, Pichon. 2010. (ENG.). 32p. (J). pap. 7.95 *(978-1-58925-423-7(6))* Tiger Tales.

Liz Warren. Kimmy Finds Her Key. Harris-Wyrick, Wayne. 2013. 28p. pap. 11.99 *(978-0-9852661-8-9(X))* 4RV Pub.

Lizana, Lorenzo. The Adventures of Thumbs up Johnnie Banker Bill's Guide to Common Cents: Banker Bill's Guide to Common Cents. Bain, Michelle. 2007. (J). 14.95 *(978-0-9761421-9-5(8))* Pixie Stuff LLC.

—The Adventures of Thumbs up Johnnie Jimmy Jam Germ & the Happy Handshake: Jimmy Jam Germ & the Happy Handshake Version 2. Bain, Michelle. 2007. (J). 14.95 *(978-0-9761421-7-1(1))* Pixie Stuff LLC.

—The Adventures of Thumbs up Johnnie Johnnie Finds A Buddy: Johnnie Finds A Buddy Color Version 2. Bain, Michelle. 2007. (J). 14.95 *(978-0-9761421-6-4(3))* Pixie Stuff LLC.

—The Adventures of Thumbs up Johnnie Johnnie's Missing Boot! Johnnie's Missing Boot! Bain, Michelle. 2007. (J). 14.95 *(978-0-9761421-8-8(X))* Pixie Stuff LLC.

—The Adventures of Thumbs up Johnnie Rules of Thumb for Going Green: Rules of Thumb for Going Green. Bain, Michelle. 2008. 18p. (J). pap. 5.95 *(978-0-9795832-4-7(1))* Pixie Stuff LLC.

—The Adventures of Thumbs up Johnnie Thumbs up to Red, White & Blue! Thumbs up to Red, White & Blue! Bain, Michelle. 2007. 48p. (J). 14.95 *(978-0-9795832-2-3(5))* Pixie Stuff LLC.

—The Adventures of Thumbs up Johnnie Zipp, Little Digit & the Happy Signs: Zipp, Little Digit & the Happy Signs. Bain, Michelle. 2007. (J). 14.95 *(978-0-9795832-0-9(9))* Pixie Stuff LLC.

—Las aventuras de Juanito el Pulgarcito Juanito encuentra un Compañerito: Juanito encuentra un Compañerito. Bain, Michelle. 2006.Tr. of Johnnie Finds a Buddy. (SPA.). (J). 16.95 *(978-0-9761421-4-0(7))* Pixie Stuff LLC.

—Las aventuras de Juanito el Pulgarcito Liborio el Microbio y el apretón de Manos: Liborio el Microbio y el apretón de Manos. Bain, Michelle. 2007.Tr. of Jimmy Jam Germ & the Happy Handshake!. (SPA.). (J). pap. 16.95 *(978-0-9795832-1-6(7))* Pixie Stuff LLC.

—Las aventuras de Juanito el Pulgarcito Zipp, Pequeño Dígito, las señales y las Señas: Zipp, Pequeño Dígito, las señales y las Señas. Bain, Michelle. 2007.Tr. of Zipp, Digit & the Happy Signs!. (SPA.). 28p. (J). *(978-0-9795832-3-0(3))* Pixie Stuff LLC.

Lizano, Marc. Hidden: a Child's Story of the Holocaust. Dauvillier, Loïc. 2014. (ENG.). 80p. (J). (gr. 1-5). 17.99 *(978-1-59643-873-6(8)*, 900111569, First Second Bks.) Roaring Brook Pr.

Ljungberg, Jon. The Bully: A Discussion & Activity Story. Toews, Rita. 2011. 40p. (J). pap. 11.95 *(978-1-59850-102-5(X))* Youthlight, Inc.

—The Bully: A Discussion & Activity Story. Toews, Rita Y. l.t. ed. 2004. (ENG.). 40p. (J). *(978-0-9736224-0-9(7))* Birds Hill Publishing.

Ljungkvist, Laura. Yoo-Hoo, Ladybug! Fox, Mem. 2013. (ENG.). 32p. (J). (gr. -1-3). 17.99 *(978-1-4424-3400-4(7))* Simon & Schuster Children's Publishing.

Llamas, Kristin. Sedrick the Snake. Jostand, Jeffrey Jay. 2008. 32p. pap. 24.95 *(978-1-4241-9944-0(1))* America Star Bks.

Llamzon, Francis. The Adventures of Junior & Rubble: The Oil Monster- Part 2: the Oil Monster- Part 2. Robinson, Ramon. 2019. (Adventures of Junior & Rubble Ser.: Vol. 2). (ENG.). 30p. (J). pap. 9.99 *(978-1-0979-8487-9(7))* Independently Published.

Llanera, Russell. Sharing Is Caring (Tetun Edition) - Ajuda Malu No Hanoin Malu. Knox, Cynthia. 2020. (TET.). 20p. (J). pap. ***(978-1-922331-50-2(3))*** Library For All Limited.

Llapashtica, Mentor. Dorothy & the Glasses. Brezinova, Ivona. 2007. 32p. (J). (ARA & ENG.). pap. 12.95 *(978-1-60195-088-8(8))*; (POL & ENG.). pap. 12.95 *(978-1-60195-099-4(3))* International Step by Step Assn.

Llewellyn-Pollack, Jennifer. The Presents' Presents! De Grosbois, Teresa. 2018. (ENG.). 24p. (J). pap. *(978-1-926643-16-8(X))* Small Shifts Bks. & Media, Inc.

—The Presents' Presents. De Grosbois, Teresa. 2019. (Small Shift Ser.). (ENG.). 24p. (J). *(978-1-926643-15-1(1))* Small Shifts Bks. & Media, Inc.

Llewhellin, Gareth. Always There Bear. Granger, Trudi. (ENG.). (J). (-k). 2015. 32p. 16.99 *(978-1-63220-434-9(7))*; 2018. 24p. bds. 8.99 *(978-1-5107-3561-3(5))* Skyhorse Publishing Co., Inc. (Sky Pony Pr.).

—Dive into the Sea! 2016. (ENG.). 12p. (J). (gr. -1-k). bds. 7.99 *(978-1-4998-0297-9(8))* Little Bee Books Inc.

—A Surprise for Bunny. Little Bee Books. 2018. (ENG.). 12p. (J). (gr. -1-k). bds. 8.99 *(978-1-4998-0669-4(8))* Little Bee Books Inc.

—Sweet Dreams, Kitty. Little Bee Books. 2018. (ENG.). 12p. (J). (gr. -1-k). bds. 8.99 *(978-1-4998-0689-2(2))* Little Bee Books Inc.

—100 Things to Make Baby Smile. Little, Sally. 2020. (ENG.). 20p. (J). (— 1). bds. 6.99 *(978-1-68412-961-4(3)*, Silver Dolphin Bks.) Printers Row Publishing Group.

Llewhellin, Gareth, jt. illus. see Barnes, Kim.

Lloyd-Diviny, Karen. Zoo Album. Morecroft/Mackay et al. 2004. (ENG.). 48p. (J). (gr. 3). 17.95 *(978-1-59270-032-5(2))* Enchanted Lion Bks., LLC.

Lloyd, James. 77 Things You Absolutely Have to Do Before You Finish College. Bondy, Halley. 2014. (ENG.). 192p. (gr. 9-17). pap. 14.99 *(978-1-936976-00-3(5)*, Zest Bks.) Lerner Publishing Group.

Lloyd, Megan. Betsy Ross. White, Becky. 2019. (I Like to Read Ser.). 32p. (J). (gr. -1-3). pap. 7.99 *(978-0-8234-4523-3(2))* Holiday Hse., Inc.

—A Big Boy Now. Spinelli, Eileen. 2012. (ENG.). 32p. (J). (gr. -1-3). 16.99 *(978-0-06-008673-2(4))* HarperCollins Pubs.

—Earthquakes. Branley, Franklyn M. 2015. (Let's-Read-And-Find-Out Science 2 Ser.). (ENG.). 40p. (J). (gr. -1-3). pap. 6.99 *(978-0-06-238202-3(0))* HarperCollins Pubs.

—Earthquakes. Branley, Franklyn M. rev. ed. 2005. (Let's-Read-and-Find-Out Science Ser.). 40p. (J). (gr. k-4). (ENG.). 15.99 *(978-0-06-028008-6(5))*; lib. bdg. 16.89 *(978-0-06-028009-3(3))* HarperCollins Pubs.

—The Little Old Lady Who Was Not Afraid of Anything. Williams, Linda. 2019. (ENG.). 32p. (J). (gr. -1-3). 17.99 *(978-0-690-04584-0(0))*; pap. 7.99 *(978-0-06-443183-5(5))*; lib. bdg. 18.89 *(978-0-690-04586-4(7))* HarperCollins Pubs. Ltd. GBR. (HarperCollins). Dist: HarperCollins Pubs.

—The Mixed-up Rooster. Edwards, Pamela Duncan. 2006. 32p. (J). (gr. -1-1). 15.99 *(978-0-06-028999-7(6)*, Tegen, Katherine Bks) HarperCollins Pubs.

—Thanksgiving at the Tappletons' Spinelli, Eileen. 2005. (gr. -1-3). 17.00 *(978-0-7569-5762-9(1))* Perfection Learning Corp.

—This Is the Feast. Shore, Diane Z. (ENG.). 32p. (J). (gr. -1-3). 2011. pap. 7.99 *(978-0-06-443850-6(3))*; 2008. 16.99 *(978-0-06-623794-7(7))* HarperCollins Pubs.

—Volcanoes. Branley, Franklyn M. 2008. (Let's-Read-And-Find-Out Science 2 Ser.). (ENG.). 40p. (J). (gr. k-4). pap. 5.99 *(978-0-06-445189-5(5))* HarperCollins Pubs.

Lloyd, Sam. Dino-Baby. Sperring, Mark. 2013. (ENG.). 32p. (J). (gr. -1-1). 14.99 *(978-1-61963-151-9(2)*, 900123359); lib. bdg. 15.89 *(978-1-61963-152-6(0)*, 9781619631526) Bloomsbury Publishing USA. (Bloomsbury USA Childrens).

—Dino-Daddy. Sperring, Mark. 2015. (ENG.). 32p. (J). (gr. -1-1). 18.99 *(978-1-4088-4969-9(0)*, 900152991, Bloomsbury Children's Bks.) Bloomsbury Publishing USA.

Lloyd, Sam. Inspector Croc Investigates. 2014. (J). ***(978-1-4351-5627-2(7))*** Barnes & Noble, Inc.

Lloyd, Sam. Yikes, Ticklysaurus! Butchart, Pamela. 2015. 32p. (J). (gr. -1-1). 18.99 *(978-1-4088-3969-0(5)*, 900153460, Bloomsbury Children's Bks.) Bloomsbury Publishing USA.

Lloyd, Sam. Mr. Pusskins: A Love Story. Lloyd, Sam. 2006. (ENG.). 32p. (J). (gr. -1-3). 19.99 *(978-1-4169-2517-0(1)*, Atheneum Bks. for Young Readers) Simon & Schuster Children's Publishing.

Lloyd, Sam, jt. illus. see Lloyd, Sam R.

Lloyd, Sam R. & Lloyd, Sam. Mr. Pusskins & Little Whiskers: Another Love Story. Lloyd, Sam R. & Lloyd, Sam. 2008. (ENG.). 32p. (J). (gr. -1-3). 19.99 *(978-1-4169-5796-6(0)*, Atheneum Bks. for Young Readers) Simon & Schuster Children's Publishing.

Lloyd-Thompson, Megan. The Weaver's Surprise, Vol. Knisely, Tom. 2019. (ENG.). 32p. (J). (gr. -1-3). 16.95 *(978-0-8117-3821-7(3))* Stackpole Bks.

Lo Cascio, Maria Cristina. Jesus Speaks to Me on My First Holy Communion. Burrin, Angela M. 2009. 39p. (J). (gr. 1-5). 12.95 *(978-1-59325-149-9(1))* Word Among Us Pr.

—Stories of Fairytale Castles. Lester, Anna. 2007. (Young Reading Series 1 Gift Bks). 48p. (J). (gr. 4-7). 8.99 *(978-0-7945-1679-6(3)*, Usborne) EDC Publishing.

Lo, Joanne. Herstory: A Hong Kong Mother. Tso, Anna. 2019. (Hong Kong Reader Ser.: Vol. 5). (ENG.). 22p. (J). 19.95 *(978-1-948210-05-8(3))* Alpha Academic Pr.

—Taming Babel. Tso, Anna. 2018. (Hong Kong Children's Book Ser.: Vol. 4). (ENG.). 20p. (J). (gr. 3-6). 19.95 *(978-1-948210-04-1(5))* Alpha Academic Pr.

—Unforgettable Neighbours. Tso, Anna. 2018. (Hong Kong Reader Ser.: Vol. 3). (ENG.). 20p. (J). (gr. 3-6). 19.95 *(978-1-948210-03-4(7))* Alpha Academic Pr.

Lo, Junsunn. La Maison Au Lait. Dumeix, Sandra. 2019. (FRE.). 118p. (J). pap. 21.00 *(978-1-0979-1705-1(3))* Independently Published.

Lo Raso, Carlo. Front-Page News. 2010. (Ready-To-Read Level 1 Ser.). (ENG.). 24p. (J). (gr. -1-1). 16.19 *(978-1-4169-8569-3(7))* Simon & Schuster, Inc.

Lo Raso, Carlo, et al. My Little Pony Phonics Fun/[stories by Joanne Mattern]; [phonics Scope & Sequence by Cathy Toohey; Pictures by Carlo Lo Rosa ... [et Al.], 12 vols. Mattern, Joanne & Toohey, Cathy. 2008. (J). *(978-0-06-123171-1(1))*; *(978-0-06-123173-5(8))*; *(978-0-06-123174-2(6))*; *(978-0-06-123175-9(4))*; *(978-0-06-123176-6(2))*; *(978-0-06-123178-0(9))*; *(978-0-06-123179-7(7))*; *(978-0-06-123180-3(0))*; *(978-0-06-123181-0(9))*; *(978-0-06-123182-7(7))*; *(978-0-06-123183-4(5))*; *(978-0-06-123184-1(3))* HarperCollins Pubs. (Harper Trophy).

Lo Raso, Carlo. Watch Me Draw the Backyardigans' Incredible Adventures. 2012. (J). *(978-1-936309-42-9(4))* Quarto Publishing Group USA.

Lo, Rich. Father's Chinese Opera. Lo, Rich. 2014. 40p. (J). (gr. -1-k). 16.95 *(978-1-62873-610-6(0)*, Sky Pony Pr.) Skyhorse Publishing Co., Inc.

Lo, Talthau, photos by. The Disobedient Ducklings. Lo, Yer Jenny. 2008. 44p. pap. 24.95 *(978-1-60441-576-6(2))* America Star Bks.

Lobato, Arcadio. Volando por las Palabras. 2004.Tr. of Flying through Words. (SPA.). 48p. (J). 10.50 *(978-84-263-5018-3(6))* Vives, Luis Editorial (Edelvives) ESP. Dist: Lectorum Pubns., Inc.

Lobbecke, Eric. The Koala Bounces Back. Thomson, Jimmy. 2012. (ENG.). 32p. (J). (gr. k-2). 16.99 *(978-1-74275-007-1(9))* Random Hse. Australia AUS. Dist: Independent Pubs. Group.

Lobel, Adrianne, jt. illus. see Lobel, Arnold.

Lobel, Anita. All the World's a Stage. Davidson, Rebecca Piatt. 2003. 32p. (J). 16.89 *(978-0-06-029627-8(5))* HarperCollins Pubs.

Lobel, Anita. The Night Before Christmas. Moore, Clement C. 2020. (ENG.). 32p. (J). (gr. -1-3). 17.99 ***(978-1-5344-6967-9(2)***, Simon & Schuster/Paula Wiseman Bks.) Simon & Schuster/Paula Wiseman Bks.

—On Market Street. Lobel, Arnold. 2020. (ENG.). 40p. (J). (gr. -1-3). 17.99 ***(978-1-5344-6815-3(3)***, Simon & Schuster/Paula Wiseman Bks.) Simon & Schuster/Paula Wiseman Bks.

Lobel, Anita. On Market Street 25th Anniversary Edition. Lobel, Arnold. 25th anniv. ed. 2006. (ENG.). 40p. (J). (gr. -1-3). pap. 7.99 *(978-0-688-08745-6(0)*, Greenwillow Bks.) HarperCollins Pubs.

—So Happy! Henkes, Kevin. 2005. (ENG.). 32p. (J). (gr. -1-3). 16.99 *(978-0-06-056483-4(0)*, Greenwillow Bks.) HarperCollins Pubs.

Lobel, Anita. Animal Antics: A to Z. Lobel, Anita. 2005. 32p. (J). lib. bdg. 16.89 *(978-0-06-051815-8(4))* HarperCollins Pubs.

—Hello, Day! Lobel, Anita. 2008. (ENG.). 40p. (J). (gr. -1 — 1). 16.99 *(978-0-06-078765-3(1)*, Greenwillow Bks.) HarperCollins Pubs.

Lobel, Arnold. I'll Fix Anthony. Viorst, Judith. 2020. (ENG.). 32p. (J). (gr. -1-3). 17.99 *(978-1-5344-0481-6(3)*, Atheneum Bks. for Young Readers) Simon & Schuster Children's Publishing.

—Miss Suzy. Young, Miriam. (J). 40th anniv. ed. 2004. 44p. 18.95 *(978-1-930900-28-8(7))*; 50th ed. 2014. (ENG.). 40p. (gr. -1-3). 18.95 *(978-1-930900-75-2(9))* Purple Hse. Pr.

Lobel, Arnold. Days with Frog & Toad. Lobel, Arnold. 2004. (I Can Read Level 2 Ser.). (ENG.). 64p. (J). (gr. -1-3). pap. 4.99 *(978-0-06-444058-5(3))*; 25th ed. 16.99 *(978-0-06-023963-3(8))* HarperCollins Pubs. Ltd. GBR. (HarperCollins). Dist: HarperCollins Pubs.

—Frog & Toad: a Complete Reading Collection: Frog & Toad Are Friends, Frog & Toad Together, Days with Frog & Toad, Frog & Toad All Year. Lobel, Arnold. 2020. (I Can Read Level 2 Ser.). (ENG.). 256p. (J). (gr. -1-3). pap. 19.99 *(978-0-06-298342-8(3)*, HarperCollins) HarperCollins Pubs. Ltd. GBR. Dist: HarperCollins Pubs.

—Frog & Toad: a Little Book of Big Thoughts. Lobel, Arnold. 2020. (ENG.). 48p. (J). (gr. -1-3). 12.99 *(978-0-06-298341-1(5)*, HarperCollins) HarperCollins Pubs. Ltd. GBR. Dist: HarperCollins Pubs.

—Frog & Toad Are Friends. Lobel, Arnold. 2003. (I Can Read Level 2 Ser.). (ENG.). 64p. (J). (gr. -1-3). pap. 4.99 *(978-0-06-444020-2(6)*, HarperCollins) HarperCollins Pubs.

—Frog & Toad Are Friends. Lobel, Arnold. 2017. (I Can Read Level 2 Ser.). (ENG.). 72p. (J). (gr. -1-3). 9.99 *(978-0-06-257273-8(3)*, HarperCollins) HarperCollins Pubs. Ltd. GBR. Dist: HarperCollins Pubs.

—The Frog & Toad Collection Box Set: Includes 3 Favorite Frog & Toad Stories!, Set. Lobel, Arnold. 2004. (I Can Read Level 2 Ser.). (ENG.). 192p. (J). (gr. k-3). pap. 14.99 *(978-0-06-058086-5(0)*, HarperCollins) HarperCollins Pubs. Ltd. GBR. Dist: HarperCollins Pubs.

—Frog & Toad Storybook Favorites: Includes 4 Stories Plus Stickers! Lobel, Arnold. 2019. (I Can Read Level 2 Ser.). (ENG.). 256p. (J). (gr. -1-3). 13.99 *(978-0-06-288312-4(7)*, HarperCollins) HarperCollins Pubs. Ltd. GBR. Dist: HarperCollins Pubs.

—Prince Bertram the Bad. Lobel, Arnold. 2019. (ENG.). 32p. (J). 18.99 *(978-1-250-14366-2(7)*, 900180540, Holt, Henry & Co. Bks. For Young Readers) Holt, Henry & Co.

—Sapo y Sepo, Inseparables. Lobel, Arnold. 2003.Tr. of Frog & Toad Together. (SPA.). 68p. (J). (gr. -1-3). 12.95 *(978-84-204-3047-8(1))* Ediciones Alfaguara ESP. Dist: Lectorum Pubns., Inc., Santillana USA Publishing Co., Inc.

—Sapo y Sepo Son Amigos. Lobel, Arnold. 2003.Tr. of Frog & Toad Are Friends. (SPA.). 66p. (J). (gr. k-3). pap. 12.95 *(978-968-19-0714-3(0))* Aguilar, Altea, Taurus, Alfaguara, S.A. de C.V MEX. Dist: Santillana USA Publishing Co., Inc.

Lobel, Arnold & Lobel, Adrianne. The Frogs & Toads All Sang. Lobel, Arnold & Lobel, Adrianne. 2009. (ENG.). 32p. (J). (gr. -1-2). 16.99 *(978-0-06-180022-1(8)*, HarperCollins) HarperCollins Pubs. Ltd. GBR. Dist: HarperCollins Pubs.

Lobo, Erik. The Monster Lie. Hanson, Lynne. 2016. (ENG.). (J). pap. 14.99 *(978-0-692-69750-4(0))* Creekside Publishing.

Lobo, Mari. The Amazing Life of Azaleah Lane. Smith, Nikki Shannon. 2020. (Azaleah Lane Ser.). (ENG.). (J). (gr. k-2). 29.90 ***(978-1-5158-4472-3(2)***, 29332); 112p. 14.95 *(978-1-5158-4464-8(1)*, 140571) Capstone. (Picture Window Bks.).

—Judge Juliette. Gehl, Laura. 2020. (ENG.). 32p. (J). (gr. -1-2). 16.95 ***(978-1-4549-3432-5(8))*** Sterling Publishing Co., Inc.

Lobo, Mari. Noses. Garnett, Jaye. Cottage Door Press, ed. 2019. (Peek-A-Flap Ser.). (ENG.). 12p. (J). (gr. -1-1). bds. 8.99 *(978-1-68052-701-8(0)*, 1004340) Cottage Door Pr.

Lobo, Mari, et al. Ohio Books for Kids Gift Set. James, Eric et al. 2020. (ENG.). (J). 29.99 ***(978-1-7282-4188-3(X))*** Sourcebooks, Inc.

Lobo, Mari. Trompas. Garnett, Jaye. Cottage Door Press, ed. 2020. (Peek-A-Flap Children's Interactive Lift-a-Flap Board Bks.). (ENG.). 12p. (J). (gr. -1-1). bds. 8.99 ***(978-1-64638-078-7(9)***, 1004340-SLA) Cottage Door Pr.

Loboguerrero Donald, Laura. Searching for Aliens. Donald Liebisch, Diana Jean. Donald Liebisch, Diana Jean, tr. 2019. (Searching for Aliens Ser.: Vol. 1). (ENG.). 56p. (J). pap. 12.90 *(978-1-0807-7929-1(9))* Independently Published.

Locatelli, Ellen. Filastrocche Italiane- Italian Nursery Rhymes. 2013. 54p. *(978-1-938712-08-1(0))* Roxby Media Ltd.

Locke, Barbara K. Oliver's Ghost: A Spooky Tale from Nantucket. Bouton, Warren Hussey. 2003. (J). per. 5.95 *(978-0-9700555-3-8(6))* Hither Creek Pr.

Locke, Barbara Kauffmann. The Captain's Return: A Spooky Tale from Nantucket. Bouton, Warren Hussey. 2004. (J). per. 5.95 *(978-0-9700555-4-5(4))* Hither Creek Pr.

Locke, Gary. Bird, Bird, Bird! A Chirping Chant. Sayre, April Pulley. 2007. (American City Ser.). (ENG.). 32p. (J). (gr. k-3). 16.95 *(978-1-55971-978-0(8))* Cooper Square Publishing Llc.

—Raymie, Dickie, & the Bean: Why I Love & Hate My Brothers. Romano, Ray. 2007. 30p. (J). 18.00 *(978-1-4223-6806-0(8))* DIANE Publishing Co.

Locke, Margo. Lillie's Smile. Doolittle, Sara. 2011. 32p. (J). pap. 18.99 *(978-0-9827611-6-8(3)*, Catch the Spirit of Appalachia) Ammons Communications, Ltd.

Locke, Terry. Spencer Hurley & the Aliens: Book One: the Abduction, Vol. 1. Locke, Terry. Hucks, Robin, ed. 2008. (Spencer Hurley & the Aliens Ser.: 1). 256p. (J). per. 8.99 *(978-0-9786940-1-2(5))* Dream Workshop Publishing Co., LLC, The.

Locker, Thomas. Rembrandt & Titus: Artist & Son. Comora, Madeleine. 2005. (ENG.). 32p. (J). (gr. 3-5). 17.95 *(978-1-55591-490-5(X))* Fulcrum Publishing.

Locker, Thomas. Hudson: The Story of a River. Locker, Thomas. Baron, Robert C. 2004. (ENG.). 32p. (J). (gr. 3). 17.95 *(978-1-55591-512-4(4))* Fulcrum Publishing.

Lockhart, David. Hercules & Other Tales from Greek Myths. Coolidge, Olivia E. 2011. 120p. 39.95 *(978-1-258-02308-9(3))* Literary Licensing, LLC.

Lockhart, Louise. The Dictionary of Difficult Words: With More Than 400 Perplexing Words to Test Your Wits! Solomon, Jane. ed. 2019. (ENG.). 112p. (J). (gr. 2-17). ***(978-1-78603-811-1(0))*** Frances Lincoln Childrens Bks.

Lockhart, Lynne N. The Secret of Heron Creek, 1 vol. Meacham, Margaret. 2009. (ENG.). 136p. (Orig.). (J). (gr. 2-18). pap. 7.95 *(978-0-87033-414-6(X)*, 9780870334146, Cornell Maritime Pr./Tidewater Pubs.) Schiffer Publishing, Ltd.

Lockhart, Lynne N. Rambling Raft, 1 vol. Lockhart, Lynne N. Lockhart, Barbara M. 2009. (ENG.). 30p. (J). (gr. -1-3). 7.95 *(978-0-87033-392-7(5)*, 3706, Cornell Maritime Pr./Tidewater Pubs.) Schiffer Publishing, Ltd.

Lockhart-Smith, Cara. Let's Explore Berwick-Upon-Tweed, 84 vols. Lockhart-Smith, Cara. English, Anne Bruce. 2003. (Let's Explore Ser.). (ENG.). 180p. pap. 9.95 *(978-1-84282-029-2(X)*, b79329bf-4c82-4255-b732-007f5a3d7516) Luath Pr. Ltd. GBR. Dist: Independent Pubs. Group.

Lockman, Vic. Catechism for Young Children Coloring Book. Lockman, Vic. 2003. 24p. (J). (gr. -1-3). *(978-0-936175-41-6(9))* Lockman, Vic.

Lockspeiser, Nancy Flanders. Flexible You: 21 Stretches a Day for a 9-Lives Body: a Cat's Quick Guide to Stretching & Self-Massage. Lockspeiser, Nancy Flanders. 2004. 48p. spiral bd. 14.94 *(978-0-9752922-0-4(X))* Catamount Publishing LLC.

Lockwood, C. C., photos by. Tales of Mike the Tiger: Facts & Fun for Everyone. Baker, David G. & Stewart, Margaret Taylor. 2006. (ENG., 144p. (gr. 4-7). 19.95 *(978-0-8071-3118-3(0)*, 1181) Louisiana State Univ. Pr.

Locsinto, Lucas. The Adventures of Seek & Save Volume 3: The Village. Swanepoel, Sharon. 2011. (J). *(978-0-9772647-6-6(9))* God's Glory Media.

Loday, Gyelsey, jt. photos by see Lhamo, Choki.

Lodge, Ali. The Leopard & the Sky God. 2007. (Usborne First Reading: Level 3 Ser.). 48p. (J). (gr. -1-3). 8.99 *(978-0-7945-1838-7(9)*, Usborne) EDC Publishing.

—Moonlight Animals. Golding, Elizabeth. 2011. (ENG.). 12p. (J). (gr. -1-3). 12.95 *(978-0-7624-4316-1(2)*, Running Pr. Kids) Running Pr.

—Moonlight Ocean. Golding, Elizabeth. 2012. (ENG.). 12p. (J). (gr. -1-3). 12.95 *(978-0-7624-4486-1(X)*, Running Pr. Kids) Running Pr.

—My First Farmyard Tales: Eight Exciting Picture Stories for Little Ones. Baxter, Nicola. 2013. (ENG.). 16p. (J). (gr. -1-2). bds. 13.99 *(978-1-84322-990-2(0)*, Armadillo) Anness Publishing GBR. Dist: National Bk. Network.

—Noah's Ark: Baby's First Pop-up! Lodge, Yvette. gif. ed. 2006. 8p. (J). 19.95 *(978-1-57791-217-0(9))* Brighter Minds Children's Publishing.

Lodge, Alison. My First Book about the Prophet Muhammad: Teachings for Toddlers & Young Children. Khan, Sara. 2020. (ENG.). 26p. (J). (gr. -1-k). bds. 9.95 *(978-0-86037-702-3(4))* Islamic Foundation, Ltd. GBR. Dist: Consortium Bk. Sales & Distribution.

—My First Book about the Qur'an. Khan, Sara. 2017. (ENG.). 26p. (J). (gr. -1-k). bds. 9.95 *(978-0-86037-618-7(4))* Kube Publishing Ltd. GBR. Dist: Consortium Bk. Sales & Distribution.

Lodge, Alison. Clever Chameleon. Lodge, Alison. Lodge, Ali. 2005. 24p. (J). 15.99 *(978-1-84148-347-4(8))* Barefoot Bks., Inc.

Lodge, Bernard. Songs for Survival: Songs & Chants from Tribal Peoples Around the World. Siegen-Smith, Nikki, ed. 2005. 80p. (J). (gr. k-4). reprint ed. 19.00 *(978-0-7567-9404-0(8))* DIANE Publishing Co.

Lodge, Jo. Baby's First Playbook: Farm. 2016. (ENG.). 10p. (J). (— 1). bds. 16.99 *(978-1-5098-0808-3(6))* Pan Macmillan GBR. Dist: Independent Pubs. Group.

—Giraffe, Giraffe What Will You Wear Today? 2020. (Wiggle & Giggle Ser.: 6). (ENG.). 10p. (J). (gr. -1-k). bds. 10.99 *(978-1-5098-7522-1(0)*, Campbell Bks.) Pan Macmillan GBR. Dist: Independent Pubs. Group.

Lodge, Jo. Roar! Roar! I'm a Dinosaur! Lodge, Jo. 2019. (ENG.). 10p. (J). (gr. -1 — 1). 8.99 *(978-1-338-54781-8(X)*, Cartwheel Bks.) Scholastic, Inc.

—1, 2, 3, ¡Ya! Lodge, Jo. 2009. (SPA.). 12p. (J). bds. *(978-84-263-7278-9(3))* Vives, Luis Editorial (Edelvives).

Lodge, Katherine. Peach Tree Street, Vol. 2. Miranda, Anne. l.t. ed. 2005. (Little Books & Big Bks.: Vol. 10). 8p. (gr. k-2). 23.00 net. *(978-0-8215-7519-2(8))* Sadlier, William H. Inc.

Lodge, Nettie. Kindy Kitchen. Rosman, Jessica. 2016. 128p. pap. 19.99 *(978-0-7333-3438-2(5))* ABC Bks. AUS. Dist: HarperCollins Pubs.

Lodwick, Sarah. A Christmas Eve Victory. Spangenberg, Greg. l.t. ed. 2006. 32p. (J). 16.99 *(978-1-59879-140-2(0))* Lifevest Publishing, Inc.

—Churchy & the Light on Christmas Eve. Spangenberg, Greg. l.t. ed. 2006. 40p. (J). (gr. -1-7). 14.99 *(978-1-59879-017-7(X))* Lifevest Publishing, Inc.

Loebel, Bonnie. Duckling's First Adventure. Perry, Shelly. 2006. (ENG.). 56p. (J). per. 9.95 *(978-0-9787740-3-5(5))* Peppertree Pr., The.

Loebel-Fried, Caren. Naupaka: By Nona Beamer: Illustrations by Caren Loebel-Fried: Hawaiian Translation by Kaliko Beamer-Trapp: Music by Keola Beamer. Beamer, Winona Desha et al. 2008. (J). 14.95 *(978-1-58178-089-5(3))* Bishop Museum Pr.

Loebel-Fried, Caren. A Perfect Day for an Albatross, 1 vol. Loebel-Fried, Caren, creator. 2017. (ENG.). 40p. (J). (gr. -1-3). 15.95 *(978-1-943645-27-5(2)*, 8c1c5155-05dc-4004-9d41-27178a0e7649) WunderMill, Inc.

Loebel-Fried, Caren Keala. Pua Polu: The Pretty Blue Hawaiian Flower. Beamer, Winona Desha & Beamer-Trapp, Kaliko. 2005. (HAW & ENG.). 36p. (J). audio compact disk 14.95 *(978-1-58178-041-3(9))* Bishop Museum Pr.

Loeffelholz, Sarah. Can You Just Imagine. 2007. 40p. (J). 14.95 *(978-0-9786850-1-0(6))* Overdue Bks.

—My Favorite Food. Robey, Stephanie. 2006. (J). 14.95 *(978-0-9786850-0-3(8))* Overdue Bks.

Loeffler, Trade. Zig & Wikki in Something Ate My Homework. Spiegelman, Nadja. (Zig & Wikki Ser.). (ENG.). 40p. (J). (gr. -1-3). 2013. pap. 6.99 *(978-1-935179-38-2(1))*; 2010. 12.95 *(978-1-935179-02-3(0))* TOON Books / RAW Junior, LLC.

—Zig & Wikki in the Cow. Spiegelman, Nadja. 2012. (Zig & Wikki Ser.). (ENG.). 40p. (J). (gr. -1-3). 12.95 *(978-1-935179-15-3(2))* TOON Books / RAW Junior, LLC.

—Zig & Wikki in the Cow: TOON Level 3. Spiegelman, Nadja. 2018. (Zig & Wikki Ser.). (ENG.). 40p. (J). (gr. -1-3). pap. 6.99 *(978-1-943145-25-6(3))* TOON Books / RAW Junior, LLC.

Loehle, Richard. Michael's Racing Machine. Lowery, Lawrence F. 2014. (I Wonder Why Ser.). (ENG.). 36p. (J). (gr. k-3). pap. 11.95 *(978-1-941316-05-4(0))* National Science Teachers Assn.

Loehr, Jenny. Eek! I Hear a Squeak & the Scurrying of Little Feet. Carlson, Lavelle. 2006. (ENG.). 28p. (J). (gr. -1-3). 19.95 incl. audio compact disk *(978-0-9725803-8-0(7))* Children's Publishing.

—I Can Do That. Lederer, Susan. 2008. 28p. (J). per. 19.95 *(978-0-9789347-0-5(9))* Children's Publishing.

—I Can Say That. Lederer, Suzy. l.t. ed. 2006. 32p. (J). (gr. -1-3). 19.95 incl. audio compact disk *(978-0-9725803-7-3(9))* Children's Publishing.

Loehr, Patrick. Mucumber McGee & the Half-Eaten Hot Dog. Loehr, Patrick. 2007. 32p. (J). (gr. -1-3). lib. bdg. 16.89 *(978-0-06-082328-3(3)*, Tegen, Katherine Bks) HarperCollins Pubs.

Loescher, Claire. Kameko & the Monkey-King. Addey, Melissa. 2018. (ENG.). 48p. (J). (gr. k-1). *(978-1-910940-65-5(8))* Letterpress Publishing.

—Kameko & the Monkey-King. Addey, Melissa. 2018. (ENG.). 48p. (J). pap. *(978-1-910940-66-2(6))* Letterpress Publishing.

Loewer, Jean. The Moonflower, 1 vol. Loewer, Peter. rev. ed. 2019. (ENG.). 32p. (J). (gr. 1-5). pap. 7.95 *(978-1-68263-101-0(X))* Peachtree Publishing Co. Inc.

LoFaro, Jerry. El Tesoro de Los Cuentos de Hadas. Publications International Ltd. Staff, ed. 2004. (SPA & ESP.). 384p. (J). 15.98 *(978-1-4127-0165-5(1)*, 3995001) Phoenix International Publications, Inc.

LoFaro, Jerry, et al. Treasury of Fairy Tales. Goldenburg, Dorothea & Killian, Bette. 2004. 320p. (J). 15.98 *(978-0-7853-7771-9(9)*, 3049205) Phoenix International Publications, Inc.

Löfdahl, Maja. Ming & Her Poppy. Sullivan, Deirdre. 2017. (ENG.). 32p. (J). (gr. -1-1). 16.99 *(978-1-5107-2943-8(7)*, Sky Pony Pr.) Skyhorse Publishing Co., Inc.

—Ming Goes to School. Sullivan, Deirdre. 2016. (ENG.). 32p. (J). (gr. -1-k). 16.99 *(978-1-5107-0050-5(1)*, Sky Pony Pr.) Skyhorse Publishing Co., Inc.

Loflin, Van Zandt Roberta. Red Beans & Rice. Weiland, Jeanette. 2020. (ENG.). 32p. (J). (gr. -1-5). 19.95 ***(978-1-7336341-4-4(2))*** Schadt, Susan Pr., LLC.

Lofting, Hugh. Doctor Dolittle the Complete Collection: Doctor Dolittle the Complete Collection, Vol. 1; Doctor Dolittle the Complete Collection, Vol. 2; Doctor Dolittle the Complete Collection, Vol. 3; Doctor Dolittle the Complete Collection, Vol. 4. Lofting, Hugh. ed. 2019. (Doctor Dolittle the Complete Collection). (ENG.). 3264p. (J). (gr. 3-7). pap. 59.99 *(978-1-5344-5034-9(3)*, Aladdin) Simon & Schuster Children's Publishing.

—Doctor Dolittle the Complete Collection, Vol. 1: The Voyages of Doctor Dolittle; the Story of Doctor Dolittle; Doctor Dolittle's Post Office. Lofting, Hugh. 2019. (Doctor Dolittle the Complete Collection: 1). (ENG.). 720p. (J). (gr. 3-7). pap. 14.99 *(978-1-5344-4890-2(X)*, Aladdin) Simon & Schuster Children's Publishing.

—Doctor Dolittle the Complete Collection, Vol. 1: The Voyages of Doctor Dolittle; the Story of Doctor Dolittle; Doctor Dolittle's Post Office. Lofting, Hugh. 2019. (Doctor Dolittle the Complete Collection: 1). (ENG.). 720p. (J). (gr. 3-7). 24.99 *(978-1-5344-4891-9(8)*, Aladdin) Simon & Schuster Children's Publishing.

—Doctor Dolittle the Complete Collection, Vol. 2: Doctor Dolittle's Circus; Doctor Dolittle's Caravan; Doctor Dolittle & the Green Canary. Lofting, Hugh. 2019. (Doctor Dolittle the Complete Collection: 2). (ENG.). 880p. (J). (gr. 3-7). 24.99 *(978-1-5344-4894-0(2))*; pap. 14.99 *(978-1-5344-4893-3(4))* Simon & Schuster Children's Publishing. (Aladdin).

—Doctor Dolittle the Complete Collection, Vol. 3: Doctor Dolittle's Zoo; Doctor Dolittle's Puddleby Adventures; Doctor Dolittle's Garden. Lofting, Hugh. 2019. (Doctor Dolittle the Complete Collection: 3). (ENG.). 784p. (J). (gr. 3-7). 24.99 *(978-1-5344-4897-1(7))*; pap. 14.99 *(978-1-5344-4896-4(9))* Simon & Schuster Children's Publishing. (Aladdin).

—Doctor Dolittle the Complete Collection, Vol. 4: Doctor Dolittle in the Moon; Doctor Dolittle's Return; Doctor Dolittle & the Secret Lake; Gub-Gub's Book. Lofting, Hugh. 2019. (Doctor Dolittle the Complete Collection: 4). (ENG.). 880p. (J). (gr. 3-7). 24.99 *(978-1-5344-4900-8(0)*, Aladdin) Simon & Schuster Children's Publishing.

—Doctor Dolittle the Complete Collection, Vol. 4: Doctor Dolittle in the Moon; Doctor Dolittle's Return; Doctor Dolittle & the Secret Lake; Gub-Gub's Book. Lofting, Hugh. 2019. (Doctor Dolittle the Complete Collection: 4). (ENG.). 880p. (J). (gr. 3-7). pap. 14.99 *(978-1-5344-4899-5(3)*, Aladdin) Simon & Schuster Children's Publishing.

—Doctor Dolittle the Complete Collection Volumes 1-4: Doctor Dolittle the Complete Collection, Volume 1; Docotor Dolittle the Complete Collection, Volume 2; Doctor Dolittle the Complete Collection, Volume 3; Doctor Dolittle the Complete Collection, Volume 4. Lofting, Hugh. ed. 2019. (Doctor Dolittle the Complete Collection). (ENG.). 3264p. (J). (gr. 3-7). 99.99 *(978-1-5344-5035-6(1)*, Aladdin) Simon & Schuster Children's Publishing.

Lofting, Hugh. The Story of Doctor Dolittle (Illustrated) Book 1 of the Doctor Dolittle Series. Lofting, Hugh. Mnemosyne Books, ed. 2020. (Doctor Dolittle Ser.: Vol. 1). (ENG.). 124p. (J). pap. 5.99 ***(978-1-6593-2091-6(7))*** Independently Published.

Lofting, Hugh. The Story of Doctor Dolittle, Original Version. Lofting, Hugh. 2010. (ENG.). 204p. (J). pap. 25.95 *(978-4-87187-305-5(6))* Ishi Pr. International.

Loftis, Cory, jt. illus. see RH Disney Staff.

Logan, C. P. Goodnight Greensboro. Hall, Dana a. 2018. (ENG.). 38p. (J). (gr. k-2). 21.95 *(978-0-578-40551-3(2))* Hall, Dana.

Logan, Desiree. Princesses Do Not Wear Tattoos. Parker, Lisa L. Gray. 2011. 48p. pap. 24.95 *(978-1-4560-3281-4(X))* America Star Bks.

Logan, Laura. HeartShaper Bible Storybook: Bible Stories to Fill Young Hearts with God's Word. DeVries, Catherine & Etue, Kate. 2018. (HeartSmart Ser.). (ENG.). 224p. (J). (gr. -1-k). 16.99 *(978-0-7814-1273-5(0)*, 134428) Cook, David C.

—I Can Play It Safe. Feigh, Alison. 2008. (ENG.). 32p. (J). (gr. -1-3). 14.99 *(978-1-57542-285-5(9))* Free Spirit Publishing, Inc.

—Nonna Tell Me a Story: Lidia's Christmas Kitchen. Bastianich, Lidia. 2010. 56p. (J). (gr. -1-3). 15.95 *(978-0-7624-3692-7(1)*, Running Pr. Kids) Running Pr.

—Ten Easter Eggs. Bodach, Vijaya. 2015. (ENG.). 22p. (J). (gr. -1-k). 8.99 *(978-0-545-74730-1(9)*, Cartwheel Bks.) Scholastic, Inc.

—That's My Mommy! Hodgman, Ann. 2013. (ENG.). 22p. bds. *(978-1-58925-645-3(X))* Tiger Tales.

—You Poked My Heart! Cooke, Brandy. 2016. (ENG.). 16p. (J). (gr. -1-1). bds. 5.99 *(978-1-4998-0310-5(9))* Little Bee Books Inc.

Logan, Laura. Little Butterfly. Logan, Laura. 2016. (ENG.). 32p. (J). (gr. -1-3). 14.99 *(978-0-06-228126-5(7))* HarperCollins Pubs.

Logan, Stephanie, jt. illus. see Noah, Ian.

Logsdon, Catherine. Home in the Big Backyard. Thompson, Karla Harney. 2016. (ENG.). (J). 20.99 *(978-1-4984-9386-4(6))*; pap. 9.99 *(978-1-4984-9385-7(8))* Salem Author Services.

Loh, Martin. Malaysian Children's Favourite Stories. Lyons, Kay. 2014. (ENG.). 64p. (J). (gr. 2-6). pap. 12.95 *(978-0-8048-4401-7(1))* Tuttle Publishing.

Löhlein, Henning. Fish Food. Mansfield, Any. 2015. (ENG.). 14p. (J). (gr. -1-k). 9.99 *(978-1-4998-0044-9(4))* Little Bee Books Inc.

Lohmann, Renate. The Bitty Twins on the Go. Hirsch, Jennifer. 2006. (J). *(978-1-59369-188-2(2))* American Girl Publishing, Inc.

—The Lucky Boots. 2006. (Famous Fables Ser.). (J). 6.99 *(978-1-59939-027-7(2))* Cornerstone Pr.

—The Queen & the Mouse: A Story about Friendship. Lang, Andrew. 2006. (J). *(978-1-59939-081-9(7)*, Reader's Digest Young Families, Inc.) Studio Fun International.

—The Wild Swans: A Tale of Persistence. Andersen, Hans. 2006. (J). *(978-1-59939-093-2(0)*, Reader's Digest Young Families, Inc.) Studio Fun International.

Lohmann, Stephanie. Keeper at the Inn. McCurdy, Steve. 2007. 36p. 17.95 *(978-0-9761179-2-6(4))* StoryMaster Pr.

Lohr, Tyrel, jt. illus. see Watson, Travis.

Lohse, Otha Zackariah Edward. The Assassination of Abraham Lincoln, 1 vol. Olson, Kay Melchisedech & Melchisedech Olson, Kay. 2005. (Graphic History Ser.). (ENG.). 32p. (J). (gr. 3-9). 31.32 *(978-0-7368-3831-3(7)*, Capstone Pr.) Capstone.

—The Assassination of Abraham Lincoln, 1 vol. Olson, Kay Melchisedech. 2005. (Graphic History Ser.). (ENG.). 32p. (J). (gr. 3-9). per. 8.10 *(978-0-7368-5241-8(7)*, Capstone Pr.) Capstone.

Lohse, Otha Zackariah Edward & Schulz, Barbara. The Curse of King Tut's Tomb, 1 vol. Burgan, Michael & Hoena, Blake A. 2005. (Graphic History Ser.). (ENG.). 32p. (J). (gr. 3-9). 31.32 *(978-0-7368-3833-7(3)*, Capstone Pr.) Capstone.

Lohstoeter, Lori. Beatrice's Goat. McBrier, Page. 2004. (ENG.). 40p. (J). (gr. -1-3). reprint ed. 8.99 *(978-0-689-86990-7(8)*, Aladdin) Simon & Schuster Children's Publishing.

—Cesar Chavez: A Hero for Everyone. Soto, Gary. 2003. (Milestone Ser.). (ENG.). 80p. (J). (gr. 2-5). pap. 6.99 *(978-0-689-85922-9(8)*, Simon & Schuster/Paula Wiseman Bks.) Simon & Schuster/Paula Wiseman Bks.

—How the Leopard Got His Spots, 1 vol. Kipling, Rudyard. 2005. (Rabbit Ears-A Classic Tale Ser.). (ENG.). 36p. (J). (gr. 2-6). 28.50 *(978-1-59679-344-6(9)*, 12945, Picture Bk.) Spotlight.

Loiacono, Melanie. The Rabbit Ears Diaries. Loiacono, Mikayla. l.t. ed. 2016. (ENG.). (J). pap. 10.95 *(978-1-61633-824-4(5))* Guardian Angel Publishing, Inc.

Lois, Collins. Crumbdog. Lois, Collins. 2019. (ENG.). 46p. (J). pap. *(978-1-912576-05-0(8))* Boughton, George Publishing.

Lois, Lowry. The Willoughbys. Lois, Lowry. 2008. (Willoughbys Ser.). (ENG.). 176p. (J). (gr. 1-4). 17.99 *(978-0-618-97974-5(3)*, 1025183, HMH Books For Young Readers) Houghton Mifflin Harcourt Publishing Co.

Loiselet, Camille. Bedtime. 2018. (My First Interactive Board Book Ser.). (ENG.). 10p. (J). bds. 9.99 *(978-2-7338-5914-8(5))* Auzou, Philippe Editions FRA. Dist: Consortium Bk. Sales & Distribution.

Loizedda, Danilo, et al. Operation: Secret Recipe. Stilton, Geronimo & Heim, Julia. 2017. 107p. (J). *(978-1-5379-1881-5(8))* Scholastic, Inc.

Loki & Splink. The Little Flower Bulb: Helping Children Bereaved by Suicide. Gormally, Eleanor. 2011. (ENG.). 32p. (J). (gr. -1-3). pap. 21.95 *(978-1-84730-260-1(2))* Veritas Pubns. IRL. Dist: Casemate Pubs. & Bk. Distributors, LLC.

Lokus, Rex & Sánchez, Alvaro Iglesias. Milton Hershey's Sweet Idea: A Chocolate Kingdom. Cooper, Sharon Katz. 2015. (Story Behind the Name Ser.). (ENG.). 32p. (J). (gr. 2-4). lib. bdg. 29.32 *(978-1-4795-7137-6(7)*, Picture Window Bks.) Capstone.

Lokus, Rex, jt. illus. see Levins, Tim.

Lokus, Rex, jt. illus. see Smith, Tod.

Lola & Ivanke. Trucks. Krensky, Stephen. 2009. (Ready-To-Reads Ser.). (ENG.). 32p. (J). (gr. -1-1). pap. 4.99 *(978-1-4169-0236-2(8)*, Simon Spotlight) Simon Spotlight.

Lollar, Cathy. I Can Do It! Quantrell, Angie. 2003. 9.99 *(978-1-56309-626-6(9))* Woman's Missionary Union.

Lolli, Matteo. Marauders by Gerry Duggan Vol. 1. 2020. 176p. (YA). (gr. 8-17). pap. 17.99 *(978-1-302-91994-8(6))* Marvel Worldwide, Inc.

Lolos, Vasilis & Atiyeh, Michael. Akaneiro. Aclin, Justin. Marshall, Dave, ed. 2013. (ENG.). 72p. 14.99 *(978-1-61655-194-0(1))* Dark Horse Comics.

Loman, Sam. Magical Unicorn Christmas Activity Book. 2019. (Dover Children's Activity Bks.). (ENG.). 96p. (J). (gr. 1-4). pap. 9.99 *(978-0-486-83226-5(0)*, 832260) Dover Pubns., Inc.

—Magical Unicorn Spot the Differences. 2019. (ENG.). 96p. (J). (gr. -1-3). pap. 9.99 *(978-0-486-83229-6(5)*, 832295) Dover Pubns., Inc.

—Make a Mobile: Magical Unicorns. Stones, Annabel & Savery, Annabel. 2019. (ENG.). 8p. (J). bds. 9.99 *(978-1-78950-034-9(6)*, d52da961-9ba7-4bad-82a1-c7d5ffee885b) Arcturus Publishing GBR. Dist: Baker & Taylor Publisher Services (BTPS).

—Super-Cute Baby Animals Activity Book. Regan, Lisa. 2020. (Super-Cute Activity Bks.: 2). (ENG.). 96p. (J). pap. 9.99 *(978-1-83857-606-6(1)*, 5156c52e-0762-4c8c-a2ab-32b00333fcd4) Arcturus Publishing GBR. Dist: Baker & Taylor Publisher Services (BTPS).

—Super-Cute Kittens & Puppies Activity Book. Regan, Lisa. 2020. (Super-Cute Activity Bks.: 3). (ENG.). 96p. (J). pap. 9.99 *(978-1-83857-607-3(X)*, f75cc832-e689-416a-a5ee-6878f0b562f9) Arcturus Publishing GBR. Dist: Baker & Taylor Publisher Services (BTPS).

Loman, Sam. The Amazing Angels Activity Book. Loman, Sam. 2019. (ENG.). 96p. (J). pap. 9.99 *(978-1-78950-667-9(0)*, 2d42dc81-94a7-460a-8d43-87adc1c1e066) Arcturus Publishing GBR. Dist: Baker & Taylor Publisher Services (BTPS).

—The Horses & Ponies Activity Book. Loman, Sam. 2019. (ENG.). 96p. (J). pap. 9.99 *(978-1-78950-021-9(4)*, 016416c8-8b03-4d97-854d-edc8a57cd08b) Arcturus Publishing GBR. Dist: Baker & Taylor Publisher Services (BTPS).

—The Magical Fairies Activity Book. Loman, Sam. 2019. (ENG.). 96p. (J). pap. 9.99 *(978-1-78950-524-5(0)*, 292a3bc9-be99-47e0-a163-b3f9951a6e0c) Arcturus Publishing GBR. Dist: Baker & Taylor Publisher Services (BTPS).

—The Magical Unicorn Activity Book. Loman, Sam. 2019. (ENG.). 176p. (J). pap. 16.99 *(978-1-78950-829-1(0)*, 8ebdf3f7-d733-48d9-b46b-f0de90788ca3) Arcturus Publishing GBR. Dist: Baker & Taylor Publisher Services (BTPS).

—The Magical Unicorn Puzzle & Activity Book. Loman, Sam. 2019. (ENG.). 96p. (J). pap. 9.99 *(978-1-78950-466-8(X)*, 496e4e74-1700-441f-b41a-a1399caa33e1) Arcturus Publishing GBR. Dist: Baker & Taylor Publisher Services (BTPS).

Lomax, Don. Gulf War Journal: Book Two - Ground War. Lomax, Don. 2017. (ENG.). (YA). pap. 16.99 *(978-1-63529-988-5(8))* Caliber Comics.

Lombardi, Kristine A. The Belonging Tree. Cocca-Leffler, Maryann. 2020. (ENG.). 40p. (J). 18.99 *(978-1-250-30513-8(6)*, 900197497, Holt, Henry & Co. Bks. For Young Readers) Holt, Henry & Co.

Lombardi, Kristine A. Mr. Biddles. Lombardi, Kristine A. 2017. (ENG.). 40p. (J). (gr. -1-3). 17.99 *(978-0-06-244114-0(0))* HarperCollins Pubs.

Lombardi, Steven. Try. Lato, Greg. Cannella, Nicole, ed. 2017. (ENG.). (J). (gr. k-4). 16.95 *(978-0-692-91633-9(4))* Lato, Greg.

Lombardo, Constance. Everybody Says Meow. Lombardo, Constance. 2019. (ENG.). 32p. (J). (gr. -1-3). 17.99 *(978-0-06-268988-7(6))* HarperCollins Pubs.

—Mr. Puffball: Escape from Castaway Island. Lombardo, Constance. 2018. (Mr. Puffball Ser.: 3). (ENG.). 240p. (J). (gr. 3-7). 12.99 *(978-0-06-232071-1(8))* HarperCollins Pubs.

—Mr. Puffball: Stunt Cat Across America. Lombardo, Constance. 2016. (Mr. Puffball Ser.: 2). (ENG.). 240p. (J). (gr. 3-7). 12.99 *(978-0-06-232068-1(8)*, Tegen, Katherine Bks) HarperCollins Pubs.

—Mr. Puffball: Stunt Cat to the Stars. Lombardo, Constance. 2015. (Mr. Puffball Ser.: 1). (ENG.). 240p. (J). (gr. 3-7). 12.99 *(978-0-06-232065-0(3))* HarperCollins Pubs.

Lombardo, Giulia. Challenging Picture Puzzles: Over 75 Timed Puzzles to Test Your Skills. 2017. (Challenging... Bks.). (ENG.). 96p. (J). (gr. 3-7). pap. 7.99 *(978-1-4380-0979-7(8)*, B.E.S. Publishing) Peterson's.

—Challenging Spot the Difference: Over 60 Timed Puzzles to Test Your Skills. 2017. (Challenging... Bks.). (ENG.). 96p. (J). (gr. 3-7). pap. 7.99 *(978-1-4380-0980-3(1)*, B.E.S. Publishing) Peterson's.

—City Atlas. Magrin, Federica. 2019. (ENG.). 96p. (J). (gr. 3). 16.95 *(978-88-544-1463-1(8))* White Star ITA. Dist: Sterling Publishing Co., Inc.

Lombardo, Giulia. Tobia e la Grande Catastrofe Delle Patate. Wonders, Junia. 2019. (ITA.). 38p. (J). (gr. k-3). ***(978-3-907130-11-7(1))*** Yves, Gmür Verlag, Gmür.

Lombardo, Giulia. Travel the Animal World: An Atlas of Amazing Creatures. 2019. (ENG.). 96p. (J). (gr. 3). 16.95 *(978-88-544-1526-3(X))* White Star ITA. Dist: Sterling Publishing Co., Inc.

—Zachary & the Great Potato Catastrophe. Wonders, Junia. 2018. (ENG.). (J). (gr. k-3). 36p. *(978-3-907130-01-8(4))*; 38p. pap. ***(978-3-907130-00-1(6))*** Yves, Gmür Verlag, Gmür.

Lombardo, Giulia & Parchow, Marc. Amazing Puzzles: 155+ Timed Puzzles to Test Your Skill. Golding, Elizabeth. 2018. (Challenging... Bks.). (ENG.). 196p. (J). (gr. 3-7). pap. 12.99 *(978-1-4380-1206-3(3)*, B.E.S. Publishing) Peterson's.

—Incredible Puzzles: 145+ Timed Puzzles to Test Your Skill. Golding, Elizabeth. 2018. (Challenging... Bks.). (ENG.). 196p. (J). (gr. 3-7). pap. 12.99 *(978-1-4380-1207-0(1)*, B.E.S. Publishing) Peterson's.

Lombardo, Irina. Let There Be Llamas! Kroll, Virginia. 2006. 31p. (J). pap. 11.95 *(978-0-8198-4519-1(1))* Pauline Bks. & Media.

Lombardo, Irina, jt. illus. see Curreli, Augusta.

Lombardo, Serena. May Saves the Day. Gehl, Laura. 2020. (ENG.). 32p. (J). (gr. -1-2). 17.99 ***(978-1-68446-102-8(2)***, 141336, Capstone Editions) Capstone.

Lombardo, Serena, jt. illus. see Brooks, Patrick.

Lomenech Gill, Olivia. Where My Wellies Take Me. Morpurgo, Michael & Morpurgo, Clare. 2013. (ENG.). 110p. (J). (gr. 1-4). 29.99 *(978-0-7636-6629-3(7)*, Templar) Candlewick Pr.

Lomofsky, Lynne & Laubscher, André. Taking the Cows Home. Schermbrucker, Reviva. 2011. (ENG.). 24p. (J). (gr. k-2). pap. 6.95 *(978-1-77009-862-6(3))* Jacana Media ZAF. Dist: Independent Pubs. Group.

Lomp, Stephan. Catch Me If You Can. Jin, Cindy. 2017. (ENG.). 16p. (J). (gr. -1 — 1). bds. 6.99 *(978-1-4814-9218-8(7)*, Little Simon) Little Simon.

—A Crash of Rhinos: And Other Wild Animal Groups. Danylyshyn, Greg. 2016. (ENG.). 40p. (J). (gr. -1-3). 17.99 *(978-1-4814-3150-7(1)*, Little Simon) Little Simon.

—Follow That Car. Feather, Lucy. 2020. (ENG.). 32p. (J). (gr. -1-3). 12.99 *(978-0-358-21220-1(0)*, 1765190, HMH Books For Young Readers) Houghton Mifflin Harcourt Publishing Co.

—Indestructibles: Baby Animals. 2017. (Indestructibles Ser.). (ENG.). 12p. (J). pap. 5.95 *(978-0-7611-9308-1(1)*, 19308) Workman Publishing Co., Inc.

—Indestructibles: Baby, Let's Eat! 2018. (Indestructibles Ser.). (ENG.). 12p. (J). pap. 5.95 *(978-1-5235-0207-3(X)*, 100207) Workman Publishing Co., Inc.

—Indestructibles: Home Sweet Home. 2018. (Indestructibles Ser.). (ENG.). 12p. (J). pap. 5.95 *(978-1-5235-0208-0(8)*, 100208) Workman Publishing Co., Inc.

—Indestructibles: Love You, Baby. 2017. (Indestructibles Ser.). (ENG.). 12p. (J). pap. 5.95 *(978-1-5235-0122-9(7)*, 100122) Workman Publishing Co., Inc.

—Indestructibles: Te Amo, Bebé / Love You, Baby. 2020. (Indestructibles Ser.). (SPA.). 12p. (J). (— 1). pap. 5.95 *(978-1-5235-0988-1(0)*, 100988) Workman Publishing Co., Inc.

—Indestructibles: Things That Go! Chew Proof · Rip Proof · Nontoxic · 100% Washable (Book for Babies, Newborn Books, Vehicle Books, Safe to Chew) Pixton, Amy. 2017. (Indestructibles Ser.). (ENG.). 12p. (J). pap. 5.95 *(978-0-7611-9362-3(6)*, 19362) Workman Publishing Co., Inc.

—Indestructibles: Welcome, Baby. 2017. (Indestructibles Ser.). (ENG.). 12p. (J). pap. 5.95 *(978-1-5235-0123-6(5)*, 100123) Workman Publishing Co., Inc.

Lonaytis, Olga. Grandpa Mouse & Little Mouse: A Tale about Respect for Elders. Grimm, Jacob & Grimm, Wilhelm K. 2006. (J). *(978-1-59939-088-8(4)*, Reader's Digest Young Families, Inc.) Studio Fun International.

London, Claire. Peek-A-Boo! I Love You! Skwish, Emily & P. I. Kids Staff. 2017. (Baby's First Look & Find Ser.). (ENG.). 10p. (J). *(978-1-5037-2734-2(3)*, e8e6dd8d-d204-40c6-aff3-f004c659afed, p i kids) Phoenix International Publications, Inc.

London Ladd, London. Lend a Hand: Poems about Giving, 1 vol. Frank, John. 2019. (ENG.). 32p. (J). (gr. 1-5). pap. 10.95 *(978-1-62014-829-7(3)*, ceaabfcd-9f60-4b4d-bd13-1340b393443c) Lee & Low Bks., Inc.

London, Sean. Bella Bella. London, Jonathan. 2016. (Aaron's Wilderness Ser.: 2). (ENG.). 180p. (gr. 3-5). (J). pap. 12.99 *(978-0-88240-923-8(9))*; (YA). 23.99 *(978-1-943328-33-8(1))* West Margin Pr. (West Winds Pr.).

—Desolation Canyon. London, Jonathan. 2015. (Aaron's Wilderness Ser.: 1). (ENG.). 168p. (gr. 3-5). (YA). 23.99 *(978-1-941821-60-2(X))*; (J). pap. 12.99 *(978-1-941821-29-9(4))* West Margin Pr. (West Winds Pr.).

—Grizzly Peak. London, Jonathan. 2017. (Aaron's Wilderness Ser.). (ENG.). 174p. (YA). 24.99 *(978-1-943328-85-7(4))*; (gr. 3-7). pap. 12.99 *(978-1-943328-77-2(3))* West Margin Pr. (West Winds Pr.).

—Pup the Sea Otter. London, Jonathan. 2019. (ENG.). 32p. (J). (gr. k-3). 11.99 *(978-1-5132-6284-0(X)*, West Margin Pr.) West Margin Pr.

Lonechild, Michael. Hidden Buffalo, 1 vol. Wiebe, Rudy. 2006. (ENG.). 32p. (J). (gr. 2-4). pap. 9.95 *(978-0-88995-334-5(1)*, 6d9682cb-b7e1-479e-aac3-a77e292ef652) Trifolium Bks., Inc. CAN. Dist: Firefly Bks., Ltd.

Lonergan Iorio, John. Another Tree in the Yard. Sera, Lucia. 2004. 32p. (J). per. 16.95 *(978-1-932653-36-6(8))* Vocalis, Ltd.

Lonergan, Kirrili. Dandelions. McKelvey, Katrina. 2015. (ENG.). 32p. (J). (gr. -1-4). 17.99 *(978-1-921966-82-8(3))* Exisle Publishing Pty Ltd. AUS. Dist: Hachette Bk. Group.

—Grey-Glasses-itis: Life's Brighter When You're Not Wearing Grey Glasses! Jenkins, Lynn. 2019. (Lessons of a LAC Ser.). (ENG.). 32p. (J). (gr. -1-3). 17.99 *(978-1-925335-95-8(X)*, 331987, EK Bks.) Exisle Publishing Pty Ltd. AUS. Dist: Hachette Bk. Group.

—Lessons of a LAC: It Can Be Hard to Stop Worrying When You're a Little Anxious Creature! Jenkins, Lynn. 2nd ed. 2018. (Lessons of a LAC Ser.). (ENG.). 32p. (J). (gr. -1-3). pap. 17.99 *(978-1-925335-82-8(8)*, EK Bks.) Exisle Publishing Pty Ltd. AUS. Dist: Hachette Bk. Group.

—Ollie's Treasure: Happiness Is Easy to Find If You Just Know Where to Look! Jenkins, Lynn. 2nd ed. 2019. (ENG.). 32p. (J). (gr. -1-3). pap. 14.99 *(978-1-925820-26-3(2)*, EK Bks.) Exisle Publishing Pty Ltd. AUS. Dist: Hachette Bk. Group.

—Perfect Petunias: The 'perfect' Book for Little Perfectionists Everywhere! Jenkins, Lynn. 2018. (Lessons of a LAC Ser.). (ENG.). 32p. (J). (gr. -1-3). 17.99 *(978-1-925335-58-3(5)*, 321613, EK Bks.) Exisle Publishing Pty Ltd. AUS. Dist: Hachette Bk. Group.

Lonergan, Kirrili. Tree: A Gentle Story of Love & Loss. Jenkins, Lynn. 2020. (Lessons of a LAC Ser.). (ENG.). 32p. (J). (gr. -1-2). 18.99 ***(978-1-925820-12-6(2)***, 336585, EK Bks.) Exisle Publishing Pty Ltd. AUS. Dist: Hachette UK Distribution.

Lonergan, Kirrili. Up to Something. McKelvey, Katrina. 2019. (ENG.). 32p. (J). (gr. -1-3). 17.99 *(978-1-925335-70-5(4)*, 321548, EK Bks.) Exisle Publishing Pty Ltd. AUS. Dist: Hachette Bk. Group.

Long, Carlos. Why Am I at the Red Table? Kamins, Julie Firstenberg. 2008. 32p. (J). 13.95 *(978-0-9771566-9-6(9))* Librujas.

Long, Chad Michael. The Lycan Journal. Long, Chad Michael, . 2nd ed. 2007. 141p. (YA). per. 12.95 *(978-0-615-18961-1(X))* Long Stories LLC.

Long, Corey. Use Your Imagination. Robinson, Vickie J. 2008. 24p. pap. 24.95 *(978-1-60703-825-2(0))* America Star Bks.

Long, Daniel. Heartbeat. Boyle, Doe. 2020. (Imagine This! Ser.). 32p. (J). (gr. -1-3). 17.99 ***(978-0-8075-3190-7(1)***, 0807531901) Whitman, Albert & Co.

Long, Dave. The Marvelous Fountain: And other stories my grandma told Me. Filipi, Carmen. 2007.Tr. of Fuente Maravillosa y otros cuentos que me conto mi Abuela. (ENG & SPA.). 55p. (J). per. 14.95 *(978-0-9797814-0-7(X))* Hispanic Institute of Social Issues.

Long, DeWayne Lee. The Little Crooked Christmas Tree. Parker, Robert H. 2012. 32p. (J). pap. 15.00 *(978-0-9837382-9-9(7)*, Catch the Spirit of Appalachia) Ammons Communications, Ltd.

Long, Ethan. Bulldozer's Shapes: Goodnight, Goodnight, Construction Site. Rinker, Sherri Duskey & Lichtenheld, Tom. 2019. (ENG.). 20p. (J). (gr. -1 — 1). bds. 6.99 *(978-1-4521-5321-6(3))* Chronicle Bks. LLC.

—Bunny Race! Maccarone, Grace. 2009. (J). *(978-0-545-11290-1(7))* Scholastic, Inc.

—Cement Mixer's ABC: Goodnight, Goodnight, Construction Site (Alphabet Book for Kids, Board Books for Toddlers, Preschool Concept Book) Rinker, Sherri Duskey. 2018. (ENG.). 20p. (J). (gr. -1 — 1). bds. 6.99 *(978-1-4521-5318-6(3))* Chronicle Bks. LLC.

—Count on Culebra. Paul, Ann Whitford. 2010. (ENG.). 40p. (J). (gr. -1-k). pap. 6.95 *(978-0-8234-2310-1(7))* Holiday Hse., Inc.

—Crash! Bang! Boo! McGee, Joe. 2019. (Junior Monster Scouts Ser.: 2). (ENG.). 112p. (J). (gr. 2-5). 16.99 *(978-1-5344-3680-0(4))*; pap. 5.99 *(978-1-5344-3679-4(0))* Simon & Schuster Children's Publishing. (Aladdin).

—Drooling & Dangerous. Amato, Mary. (Riot Brothers Ser.: 2). (ENG.). (J). (gr. 1-4). 2020. 160p. pap. 7.99 *(978-0-8234-4527-1(5))*; 2017. 192p. 12.95 *(978-0-8234-3866-2(X))* Holiday Hse., Inc.

—Dump Truck's Colors: Goodnight, Goodnight, Construction Site. Rinker, Sherri Duskey & Lichtenheld, Tom. 2018. (ENG.). 20p. (J). (gr. -1 — 1). bds. 6.99 *(978-1-4521-5320-9(5))* Chronicle Bks. LLC.

—Excavator's 123: Goodnight, Goodnight, Construction Site (Counting Books for Kids, Learning to Count Books, Goodnight Book) Rinker, Sherri Duskey. 2019. (ENG.). 20p. (J). (gr. -1 — 1). bds. 6.99 *(978-1-4521-5316-2(7))* Chronicle Bks. LLC.

—Fiesta Fiasco. Paul, Ann Whitford. 2012. pap. 18.95 *(978-1-4301-1099-6(6))* Live Oak Media.

—Greedy Apostrophe: A Cautionary Tale. Carr, Jan. 2009. (ENG.). 32p. (J). (gr. 1-3). pap. 7.99 *(978-0-8234-2205-0(4))* Holiday Hse., Inc.

—In, over & on the Farm. 2015. (J). Non-ISBN Publisher.

—It's Raining Bats & Frogs! McGee, Joe. 2020. (Junior Monster Scouts Ser.: 3). (ENG.). 112p. (J). (gr. 2-5). 16.99 *(978-1-5344-3683-1(9))*; pap. 5.99 *(978-1-5344-3682-4(0))* Simon & Schuster Children's Publishing. (Aladdin).

—The Luckiest St. Patrick's Day Ever! Slater, Teddy. (J). 2008. (ENG.). 32p. (gr. -1-3). pap. 5.99 *(978-0-545-03943-7(6)*, Cartwheel Bks.); 2007. *(978-0-439-86648-4(0))* Scholastic, Inc.

—Manana, Iguana. Paul, Ann Whitford. 2005. (ENG.). 32p. (J). (gr. -1-3). 7.99 *(978-0-8234-1980-7(0))* Holiday Hse., Inc.

—The Monster Squad. McGee, Joe. 2019. (Junior Monster Scouts Ser.: 1). (ENG.). 112p. (J). (gr. 2-5). 16.99 *(978-1-5344-3677-0(4))*; pap. 5.99 *(978-1-5344-3676-3(6))* Simon & Schuster Children's Publishing. (Aladdin).

—Nuttiest Knock-Knocks Ever. Rissinger, Matt & Yates, Philip. 2008. (Jokes & Riddles Ser.). (ENG.). 96p. (J). (gr. k-3). 17.44 *(978-1-4027-4256-9(8))* Sterling Publishing Co., Inc.

—Our Teacher Is a Vampire & Other (Not) True Stories. Amato, Mary. (ENG.). 256p. (J). (gr. 3-7). 2017. pap. 6.99 *(978-0-8234-3769-6(8))*; 2016. 16.95 *(978-0-8234-3553-1(9))* Holiday Hse., Inc.

—Snarf Attack, Underfoodle, & the Secret of Life: The Riot Brothers Tell All. Amato, Mary. (Riot Brothers Ser.: 1). (ENG.). 160p. (J). (gr. 1-4). 2020. pap. 7.99 *(978-0-8234-4526-4(7))*; 2017. 12.95 *(978-0-8234-3865-5(1))* Holiday Hse., Inc.

—Stick Dog Wants a Hot Dog. Watson, Tom. 2013. 200p. (J). *(978-0-06-229593-4(4))* Harper & Row Ltd.

—Stinky & Successful. Amato, Mary. 2020. (Riot Brothers Ser.: 3). 160p. (J). (gr. 1-4). pap. 7.99 *(978-0-8234-4528-8(3))* Holiday Hse., Inc.

—Super Schnoz & the Gates of Smell. Urey, Gary. (Super Schnoz Ser.: 1). (ENG.). 160p. (J). (gr. 3-7). 2015. pap. 6.99 *(978-0-8075-7560-4(7)*, 807575607); 2013. 14.99 *(978-0-8075-7555-0(0)*, 807575550) Whitman, Albert & Co.

—Take the Mummy & Run. Amato, Mary. 2020. (Riot Brothers Ser.: 4). 240p. (J). (gr. 1-4). pap. 7.99 *(978-0-8234-4529-5(1))* Holiday Hse., Inc.

—The Tighty Whitey Spider: And More Wacky Animal Poems I Totally Made Up. Nesbitt, Kenn. 2010. (ENG.). 128p. (J). (gr. 1-6). 11.99 *(978-1-4022-3833-8(9)*, Sourcebooks Jabberwocky) Sourcebooks, Inc.

—The Ultimate Top Secret Guide to Taking over the World. Nesbitt, Kenn. 2011. (ENG.). 208p. (J). (gr. 4-8). pap. 10.99 *(978-1-4022-3834-5(7)*, Sourcebooks Jabberwocky) Sourcebooks, Inc.

—The Zombie Nite Cafe. Kutner, Merrily. 2007. (ENG.). 32p. (J). (gr. -1-3). 16.95 *(978-0-8234-1963-0(0))* Holiday Hse., Inc.

Long, Ethan. Big Cat. Long, Ethan. 2016. (I Like to Read Ser.). (ENG.). 24p. (J). (gr. -1-3). 7.99 *(978-0-8234-3539-5(3))*; 14.95 *(978-0-8234-3538-8(5))* Holiday Hse., Inc.

—Clara & Clem Take a Ride. Long, Ethan. 2012. (Penguin Young Readers, Level 1 Ser.). 32p. (J). (gr. k-1). mass mkt. 4.99 *(978-0-448-46264-6(8)*, Penguin Young Readers) Penguin Young Readers Group.

—Clara & Clem under the Sea. Long, Ethan. 2014. (Penguin Young Readers, Level 1 Ser.). 32p. (J). (gr. k-1). pap. 4.99 *(978-0-448-47812-8(9)*, Penguin Young Readers) Penguin Young Readers Group.

—The Croaky Pokey! Long, Ethan. 2011. (ENG.). 32p. (J). (gr. -1-k). 14.95 *(978-0-8234-2291-3(7))* Holiday Hse., Inc.

—Hello, World! Happy County Book 1. Long, Ethan. 2020. (Happy County Ser.: 1). (ENG.). 48p. (J). 18.99 *(978-1-250-19175-5(0)*, 900192824, Holt, Henry & Co. Bks. For Young Readers) Holt, Henry & Co.

—Max & Milo Go to Sleep! Long, Ethan. Long, Heather. 2013. (ENG.). 32p. (J). (gr. -1-3). 14.99 *(978-1-4424-5143-8(2)*, Aladdin) Simon & Schuster Children's Publishing.

—Max & Milo the Mixed-Up Message. Long, Ethan. Long, Heather. 2013. (ENG.). 32p. (J). (gr. -1-3). 14.99 *(978-1-4424-5140-7(8)*, Simon & Schuster/Paula Wiseman Bks.) Simon & Schuster/Paula Wiseman Bks.

—Sun & Moon Together: Happy County Book 2. Long, Ethan. 2020. (Happy County Ser.: 2). (ENG.). 48p. (J). 18.99 *(978-1-250-19174-8(2)*, 900192823, Holt, Henry & Co. Bks. For Young Readers) Holt, Henry & Co.

—Up, Tall & High. Long, Ethan. 2012. (ENG.). 44p. (J). (gr. -1-2). 17.99 *(978-0-399-25611-0(3)*, G.P. Putnam's Sons Books for Young Readers) Penguin Young Readers Group.

Long, Ethan & Frawley, Keith. Super Schnoz Boxed Set #1-3. Urey, Gary. 2017. (Super Schnoz Ser.). (ENG.). 480p. (J). (gr. 3-7). 19.99 *(978-0-8075-9989-1(1)*, 807599891) Whitman, Albert & Co.

Long, Ethan, jt. illus. see Watson, Tom.

Long, Jennifer. Cricket's Capers. Cobb, Laney. 2014. (Cricket & Izzy Ser.: Vol. 1). (ENG.). 34p. (J). (gr. -1-3). pap. 10.99 *(978-0-692-17740-2(X))* Cobbs Creations.

Long, John. Gogo Fish! The Story of the Western Australian State Fossil Emblem. Long, John. Ruse, Jill. 2004. 40p. (J). pap. *(978-1-920843-08-3(6))* Art Gallery of Western Australia, The.

Long, John & Ruse, Jill. Gogo Fish! The Story of the Western Australian State Fossil Emblem. Long, John. 2004. 40p. (J). *(978-1-920843-10-6(8))* Art Gallery of Western Australia, The.

Long, Laurel. The Legend of Holly Claus. Ryan, Brittney. 2004. (Julie Andrews Collection). 544p. (J). (gr. 4-18). 16.99 *(978-0-06-058511-2(0))*; lib. bdg. 17.89 *(978-0-06-058514-3(5))* HarperCollins Pubs. (Julie Andrews Collection).

Long, Laurel. The Twelve Days of Christmas. Long, Laurel. 2014. (ENG.). 32p. (J). (gr. -1-2). pap. 8.99 *(978-0-14-751286-4(7)*, Puffin Books) Penguin Young Readers Group.

Long Liang, Xiao. Etched in Blood. Chen, Wei Dong. 2013. (Three Kingdoms Ser.: 5). 176p. (YA). (gr. 5-12). lib. bdg. 29.27 *(978-89-94208-98-5(4))* Lerner Publishing Group.

—The Family Plot. Chen, Wei Dong. 2013. (Three Kingdoms Ser.: 2). 176p. (YA). (gr. 5-12). lib. bdg. 29.27 *(978-89-94208-92-3(5))* Lerner Publishing Group.

—The Fortunate Sons. Dong Chen, Wei. 2013. (Three Kingdoms Ser.: 8). (ENG.). 176p. (gr. 5-12). pap. 9.99 *(978-89-98341-21-3(2))* JR Comics KOR. Dist: Lerner Publishing Group.

—Heroes & Chaos. Chen, Wei Dong. 2013. (Three Kingdoms Ser.: 1). 176p. (YA). (gr. 5-12). lib. bdg. 29.27 *(978-89-94208-90-9(9))* Lerner Publishing Group.

—Revenge & Betrayal. Chen, Wei Dong. 2013. (Three Kingdoms Ser.: 4). 176p. (YA). (gr. 5-12). lib. bdg. 29.27 *(978-89-94208-96-1(8))* Lerner Publishing Group.

—To Pledge Allegiance. Chen, Wei Dong. 2013. (Three Kingdoms Ser.: 3). 176p. (YA). (gr. 5-12). lib. bdg. 29.27 *(978-89-94208-94-7(1))* Lerner Publishing Group.

—War of Words. Dong Chen, Wei. 2013. (Three Kingdoms Ser.: 10). (ENG.). 176p. (gr. 5-12). pap. 9.99 *(978-89-98341-23-7(9))* JR Comics KOR. Dist: Lerner Publishing Group.

Long, Loren. Amor. de la Peña, Matt. 2018. 40p. (J). (gr. -1-3). 17.99 *(978-0-525-51880-8(0)*, G.P. Putnam's Sons Books for Young Readers) Penguin Young Readers Group.

—The Day the Animals Came: A Story of Saint Francis Day. Weller, Frances Ward. 2006. 35p. (J). (gr. k-4). reprint ed. 17.00 *(978-1-4223-5396-7(6))* DIANE Publishing Co.

—Good Day, Good Night. Brown, Margaret Wise. 2017. (ENG.). 40p. (J). (gr. -1-3). 18.99 *(978-0-06-238310-5(8))* HarperCollins Pubs.

—Good Day, Good Night Board Book. Brown, Margaret Wise. 2019. (ENG.). 34p. (J). (gr. -1 — 1). bds. 8.99 *(978-0-06-238312-9(4)*, HarperFestival) HarperCollins Pubs.

—I Dream of Trains. Johnson, Angela. 2003. (ENG.). 32p. (J). (gr. k-2). 19.99 *(978-0-689-82609-2(5)*, Simon & Schuster Bks. For Young Readers) Simon & Schuster Bks. For Young Readers.

—If I Was the Sunshine. Fogliano, Julie. 2019. (ENG.). 48p. (J). (gr. -1-3). 17.99 *(978-1-4814-7243-2(7)*, Atheneum Bks. for Young Readers) Simon & Schuster Children's Publishing.

Long, Loren, et al. Kat's Maps. Scieszka, Jon. 2011. (Jon Scieszka's Trucktown Ser.). (ENG.). 24p. (J). (gr. -1-1). 15.99 *(978-1-4169-4159-0(2)*, Simon Spotlight) Simon Spotlight.

Long, Loren. The Little Engine That Could. Piper, Watty & Penguin / LeapFrog. 2008. (J). 13.99 *(978-1-59319-938-8(4))* LeapFrog Enterprises, Inc.

—The Little Engine That Could: Loren Long Edition. Piper, Watty. 2005. (Little Engine That Could Ser.). 48p. (J). (gr.

L

-1-2). 17.99 *(978-0-399-24467-4(0)*, Philomel Bks.) Penguin Young Readers Group.

—Love. de la Peña, Matt. 2018. 40p. (J). (gr. -1-3). 17.99 *(978-1-5247-4091-7(8)*, G.P. Putnam's Sons Books for Young Readers) Penguin Young Readers Group.

Long, Loren. The Night Before Christmas. Moore, Clement C. 2020. (ENG.). 40p. (J). (gr. -1-3). 18.99 ***(978-0-06-286946-3(9)***, HarperCollins) HarperCollins Pubs. Ltd. GBR. Dist: HarperCollins Pubs.

Long, Loren. Nightsong. Berk, Ari. 2012. (ENG.). 48p. (J). (gr. -1-3). 17.99 *(978-1-4169-7886-2(0)*, Simon & Schuster Bks. For Young Readers) Simon & Schuster Bks. For Young Readers.

—Of Thee I Sing: A Letter to My Daughters. Obama, Barack. 2010. (ENG.). 40p. (J). (gr. k-12). 17.99 *(978-0-375-83527-8(X)*, Knopf Bks. for Young Readers) Random Hse. Children's Bks.

—Toy Boat. de Sève, Randall & de Sève, Randall. 2014. 30p. (J). (gr. -1 — 1). bds. 7.99 *(978-0-399-16797-3(8)*, Philomel Bks.) Penguin Young Readers Group.

—The Toy Boat. de Sève, Randall & de Sève, Randall. 2007. 40p. (J). (gr. -1-2). 17.99 *(978-0-399-24374-5(7)*, Philomel Bks.) Penguin Young Readers Group.

—Wind Flyers. Johnson, Angela. 2007. (ENG.). 32p. (J). (gr. k-4). 17.99 *(978-0-689-84879-7(X)*, Simon & Schuster Bks. For Young Readers) Simon & Schuster Bks. For Young Readers.

Long, Loren. Blastin' the Blues. Long, Loren. Bildner, Phil. (Sluggers Ser.: 5). (ENG.). 448p. (J). (gr. 3-7). 2011. pap. 8.99 *(978-1-4169-1891-2(4))*; 2010. 15.99 *(978-1-4169-1867-7(1))* Simon & Schuster Bks. For Young Readers. (Simon & Schuster Bks. For Young Readers).

—Game 3. Long, Loren. Bildner, Phil. 2008. (ENG.). 208p. (J). (gr. 2-5). 10.99 *(978-1-4169-1865-3(5)*, Simon & Schuster Bks. For Young Readers) Simon & Schuster Bks. For Young Readers.

—Great Balls of Fire. Long, Loren. Bildner, Phil. 2009. (Sluggers Ser.: 3). (ENG.). 224p. (J). (gr. 3-7). pap. 7.99 *(978-1-4169-1889-9(2)*, Simon & Schuster Bks. For Young Readers) Simon & Schuster Bks. For Young Readers.

—Home of the Brave. Long, Loren. Bildner, Phil. (Sluggers Ser.: 6). (ENG.). 336p. (J). (gr. 3-7). 2011. pap. 9.99 *(978-1-4169-1892-9(2))*; 2010. 15.99 *(978-1-4169-1868-4(X))* Simon & Schuster Bks. For Young Readers. (Simon & Schuster Bks. For Young Readers).

—Horsin' Around. Long, Loren. Bildner, Phil. 2009. (Sluggers Ser.: 2). (ENG.). 224p. (J). (gr. 3-7). pap. 8.99 *(978-1-4169-1888-2(4)*, Simon & Schuster Bks. For Young Readers) Simon & Schuster Bks. For Young Readers.

—Little Tree. Long, Loren. 2015. 40p. (J). (gr. k-3). 17.99 *(978-0-399-16397-5(2)*, Philomel Bks.) Penguin Young Readers Group.

—Magic in the Outfield. Long, Loren. Bildner, Phil. 2009. (Sluggers Ser.: 1). (ENG.). 160p. (J). (gr. 3-7). pap. 9.99 *(978-1-4169-1884-4(1)*, Simon & Schuster Bks. For Young Readers) Simon & Schuster Bks. For Young Readers.

—Mi Barco/Toy Boat. Long, Loren. de Sève, Randall & -Long, Sève. 2008. (SPA.). 40p. (gr. k-1). 21.99 *(978-84-261-3657-2(5))* Juventud, Editorial ESP. Dist: Lectorum Pubns., Inc.

—Otis. Long, Loren. (Otis Ser.). (J). (gr. -1 — 1). 2011. 34p. bds. 8.99 *(978-0-399-25600-4(8))*; 2009. 40p. 17.99 *(978-0-399-25248-8(7))* Penguin Young Readers Group. (Philomel Bks.).

—Otis & the Kittens. Long, Loren. 2016. (Otis Ser.). 40p. (J). (gr. -1-3). 17.99 *(978-0-399-16398-2(0)*, Philomel Bks.) Penguin Young Readers Group.

—Otis & the Puppy. Long, Loren. 2013. (Otis Ser.: 3). 40p. (J). (gr. -1-2). 17.99 *(978-0-399-25469-7(2)*, Philomel Bks.) Penguin Young Readers Group.

—Otis & the Puppy: Board Book. Long, Loren. 2014. (Otis Ser.: 3). 36p. (J). (gr. -1-k). bds. 8.99 *(978-0-399-17196-3(7)*, Philomel Bks.) Penguin Young Readers Group.

—Otis & the Scarecrow. Long, Loren. 2014. (Otis Ser.). 40p. (J). (gr. k-3). 17.99 *(978-0-399-16396-8(4)*, Philomel Bks.) Penguin Publishing Group.

—Otis & the Tornado. Long, Loren. 2011. (Otis Ser.: 2). 40p. (J). (gr. -1-2). 18.99 *(978-0-399-25477-2(3)*, Philomel Bks.) Penguin Young Readers Group.

—An Otis Christmas. Long, Loren. 2013. (Otis Ser.: Bk. 4). 40p. (J). (gr. -1-2). 17.99 *(978-0-399-16395-1(6)*, Philomel Bks.) Penguin Publishing Group.

—An Otis Christmas. Long, Loren. 2016. (Otis Ser.). 38p. (J). (gr. -1-2). bds. 8.99 *(978-0-399-54811-6(4)*, Philomel Bks.) Penguin Young Readers Group.

—Otis Gives Thanks. Long, Loren. 2017. (Otis Ser.). (ENG.). 30p. (J). (— 1). bds. 8.99 *(978-1-5247-4115-0(9)*, Philomel Bks.) Penguin Young Readers Group.

—Otis (Spanish Edition) Long, Loren. 2013. (Otis Ser.). (SPA.). 40p. (J). (gr. -1-k). 7.99 *(978-0-14-751124-9(0)*, Puffin Books) Penguin Young Readers Group.

—Otis's Busy Day. Long, Loren. 2014. (Otis Ser.). (ENG.). 32p. (J). (gr. k-1). pap. 4.99 *(978-0-448-48130-2(8)*, Penguin Young Readers) Penguin Young Readers Group.

—There's a Hole in the Log on the Bottom of the Lake. Long, Loren. 2018. (ENG.). 40p. (J). (gr. -1-3). 17.99 *(978-0-399-16399-9(9)*, Philomel Bks.) Penguin Young Readers Group.

—Water, Water Everywhere. Long, Loren. Bildner, Phil. (Sluggers Ser.: 4). (ENG.). (J). (gr. 3-7). 2010. 288p. pap. 9.99 *(978-1-4169-1890-5(6))*; 2009. 272p. 14.99 *(978-1-4169-1866-0(3))* Simon & Schuster Bks. For Young Readers. (Simon & Schuster Bks. For Young Readers).

—What Does Otis See? Long, Loren. 2015. (Otis Ser.). 32p. (J). (gr. k-1). 4.99 *(978-0-448-48758-8(6)*, Penguin Young Readers) Penguin Young Readers Group.

—When I Heard the Learn'd Astronomer. Long, Loren. Whitman, Walt. 2004. (ENG.). 32p. (J). (gr. k-4). 18.99 *(978-0-689-86397-4(7)*, Simon & Schuster Bks. For Young Readers) Simon & Schuster Bks. For Young Readers.

Long, Loren, jt. illus. see Hurd, Clement.

Long, Marian. Windsor Heights Book 1. Long, Lisa. Beery, Lindsay, ed. 2017. (Windsor Heights Ser.: 1). (ENG.). 208p. (gr. 3-12). pap. 14.99 *(978-0-9753566-0-9(7))* Windsor Heights Bks.

—Windsor Heights Book 2: To the Country. Long, Lisa. Beery, Lindsay, ed. 2017. (Windsor Heights Ser.: 2). (ENG.). 205p. (gr. 3-12). pap. 14.99 *(978-0-9753566-1-6(5))* Windsor Heights Bks.

—Windsor Heights Book 3: Moon & Midnight. Long, Lisa. Beery, Lindsay, ed. 2017. (Windsor Heights Ser.: 3). (ENG.). 220p. (gr. 3-12). pap. 14.99 *(978-0-9753566-2-3(3))* Windsor Heights Bks.

—Windsor Heights Book 4: The Auction. Long, Lisa. Beery, Lindsay, ed. 2017. (Windsor Heights Ser.: 4). (ENG.). 226p. (gr. 3-12). pap. 14.99 *(978-0-9753566-3-0(1))* Windsor Heights Bks.

—Windsor Heights Book 5: The Great Gift. Long, Lisa. Beery, Lindsay, ed. 2017. (Windsor Heights Ser.: 5). (ENG.). 209p. (gr. 3-12). pap. 14.99 *(978-0-9753566-4-7(X))* Windsor Heights Bks.

—Windsor Heights Book 6: Sugar & Cheyenne. Long, Lisa. Beery, Lindsay, ed. 2017. (Windsor Heights Ser.: 6). (ENG.). 210p. (gr. 3-12). pap. 14.99 *(978-0-9753566-6-1(6))* Windsor Heights Bks.

—Windsor Heights Book 7: Dazzle. Long, Lisa. Beery, Lindsay, ed. 2017. (Windsor Heights Ser.: 7). (ENG.). 193p. (gr. 3-12). pap. 14.99 *(978-0-9753566-7-8(4))* Windsor Heights Bks.

—Windsor Heights Book 8: The Black Gelding, bk. 8. Long, Lisa. Beery, Lindsay, ed. 2017. (Windsor Heights Ser.: 8). (ENG.). 225p. (gr. 3-12). pap. 14.99 *(978-0-9753566-8-5(2))* Windsor Heights Bks.

Long, Marian. Windsor Heights Coloring Book Vol 1: Volume I. Long, Marian. 2017. (Windsor Heights Ser.: 1). (ENG.). 84p. (gr. 3-12). pap., act. bk. ed. 14.99 *(978-0-9753566-5-4(8))* Windsor Heights Bks.

—Windsor Heights Coloring Book Vol 2: Volume II, vol. 2. Long, Marian. 2017. (Windsor Heights Ser.: 2). (ENG.). 84p. (gr. 3-12). pap., act. bk. ed. 14.99 *(978-0-9753566-9-2(0))* Windsor Heights Bks.

Long, Martha. A Keepsake Book of Love & Marriage: An enchanting way to say, I love You. Ramirez, Jeannette. 2007. 172p. (YA). 12.95 *(978-0-9794946-0-4(5))* Losantiville Pr., Inc.

Long, Matty. Super Happy Magic Forest. Long, Matty. 2016. (ENG.). 32p. (J). (gr. -1-3). 17.99 *(978-0-545-86059-8(8)*, Scholastic Pr.) Scholastic, Inc.

—Super Slug of Doom: A Super Happy Magic Forest Story. Long, Matty. 2017. (ENG.). 32p. (J). (gr. -1-3). 17.99 *(978-1-338-05435-4(X)*, Scholastic Pr.) Scholastic, Inc.

Long, May, jt. illus. see Chu, Kate.

Long, Olivia. Billy Bumble Is Missing! Long, Olivia. Date not set. (Kaleidoscope Ser.). 32p. (J). (gr. -1-4). *(978-1-880042-02-1(9))* Shelf-Life Bks.

—The Boy & the Dog. Long, Olivia. Date not set. (Pets & Their People Ser.). 32p. (J). (gr. k-5). *(978-1-880042-07-6(X))* Shelf-Life Bks.

—The Dandelion Queen. Long, Olivia. Date not set. (Our Precious Planet Ser.). 32p. (J). (gr. -1-4). 9.95 *(978-1-880042-08-3(8)*, SL12461) Shelf-Life Bks.

—Diary of a Dog. Long, Olivia. Date not set. (Pets & Their People Ser.). 32p. (J). (gr. -1-4). 9.95 *(978-1-880042-06-9(1)*, SL12456) Shelf-Life Bks.

—The Elephant Who Forgot. Long, Olivia. Date not set. (Kaleidoscope Ser.). 32p. (J). (gr. -1-4). *(978-1-880042-05-2(3))* Shelf-Life Bks.

—A Horse of a Different Color. Long, Olivia. Date not set. (Kaleidoscope Ser.). 32p. (J). (gr. -1-4). 9.95 *(978-1-880042-01-4(0)*, SL12451) Shelf-Life Bks.

—Hortense, the Happy Hippo. Long, Olivia. Date not set. (Kaleidoscope Ser.). 32p. (J). (gr. -1-4). *(978-1-880042-03-8(7))* Shelf-Life Bks.

—The Impossible Peacock. Long, Olivia. Date not set. (Kaleidoscope Ser.). 32p. (J). (gr. -1-4). *(978-1-880042-04-5(5))* Shelf-Life Bks.

—There's a Dinosaur in My Bathtub! Long, Olivia. Date not set. (World of Dinosaurs Ser.). 32p. (J). (gr. -1-4). *(978-1-880042-11-3(8))* Shelf-Life Bks.

—Thunderbirds & Thunderbeings. Long, Olivia. Date not set. (Our Precious Planet Ser.). 32p. (J). (gr. -1-4). *(978-1-880042-10-6(X))* Shelf-Life Bks.

—Too Many Kittens. Long, Olivia. Date not set. (Pets & Their People Ser.). 32p. (J). (gr. -1-4). *(978-1-880042-09-0(6))* Shelf-Life Bks.

—Why Don't Cats Lay Eggs? Long, Olivia. Date not set. (Our Precious Planet Ser.). 32p. (J). (gr. -1-4). *(978-1-880042-12-0(6))* Shelf-Life Bks.

Long, Paulette Rich. Is There a Monster in My Closet? Paiva, Johannah Gilman. 2014. (ENG.). 32p. (J). (gr. -1-3). 7.99 *(978-1-4867-0002-8(0))* Flowerpot Children's Pr. Inc. CAN. Dist: Cardinal Pubs. Group.

—The Mouse & the Star. Condenzio, Mary. 2008. 13p. pap. 24.95 *(978-1-60441-449-3(9))* America Star Bks.

Long, Sylvia. Any Bear Can Wear Glasses: The Spectacled Bear & other Curious Creatures. Long, Matthew & Long, Thomas. 2005. 24p. (J). (gr. k-4). reprint ed. 17.00 *(978-0-7567-9763-8(2))* DIANE Publishing Co.

—Because You Are My Baby. Ward, Jennifer. 2007. (ENG.). 32p. (J). (gr. -1-1). 15.95 *(978-0-87358-911-6(4))* Cooper Square Publishing Llc.

—A Beetle Is Shy. Aston, Dianna Hutts. 2016. (ENG.). 40p. (J). (gr. k-3). 16.99 *(978-1-4521-2712-5(3))* Chronicle Bks. LLC.

—A Butterfly Is Patient. Aston, Dianna Hutts. 2015. (ENG.). 40p. (J). (gr. k-3). pap. 7.99 *(978-1-4521-4124-4(X))* Chronicle Bks. LLC.

—A Butterfly Is Patient. Hutts Aston, Dianna. 2011. (ENG.). 40p. (J). (gr. k-5). 16.99 *(978-0-8118-6479-4(0))* Chronicle Bks. LLC.

—An Egg Is Quiet. Aston, Dianna Hutts. 2006. (J). 16.95 *(978-0-8118-5554-9(6))* Chronicle Bks. LLC.

—An Egg Is Quiet: (Nature Books for Kids, Children's Books Ages 3-5, Award Winning Children's Books) Hutts Aston, Dianna. 2006. (ENG.). 36p. (J). (gr. -1-7). 16.99 *(978-0-8118-4428-4(5))* Chronicle Bks. LLC.

—A Nest Is Noisy. Aston, Dianna Hutts. 2015. (ENG.). 40p. (J). (gr. k-3). 16.99 *(978-1-4521-2713-2(1))* Chronicle Bks. LLC.

—A Nest Is Noisy. Aston, Dianna Hutts. 2017. (ENG.). 40p. (J). pap. 7.99 *(978-1-4521-6135-8(6))* Chronicle Bks. LLC.

—A Rock Is Lively. Aston, Dianna Hutts. (ENG.). 40p. (J). (gr. k-3). 2015. pap. 7.99 *(978-1-4521-4555-6(5))*; 2012. 16.99 *(978-1-4521-0645-8(2))* Chronicle Bks. LLC.

—A Seed Is Sleepy. Hutts Aston, Dianna. 2007. (ENG.). 40p. (J). (gr. k-5). 16.99 *(978-0-8118-5520-4(1))* Chronicle Bks. LLC.

—Sylvia Long's Big Book for Small Children. 2018. (ENG.). 112p. (J). (gr. -1 — 1). 22.99 *(978-0-8118-3441-4(7))* Chronicle Bks. LLC.

—Sylvia Long's Thumbelina. 2010. (ENG.). 58p. (J). (gr. k-5). 17.99 *(978-0-8118-5522-8(8))* Chronicle Bks. LLC.

Long, Sylvia. Twinkle, Twinkle, Little Star: (Twinkle Star Books for Baby, Board Books with Light Stars, Good Night Books) Long, Sylvia. 2006. (ENG.). 26p. (J). (gr. -1-7). bds. 6.99 *(978-0-8118-5230-2(X))* Chronicle Bks. LLC.

Long, Taillefer. Bryce Bumps His Head: A Sierra the Search Dog Novel. Calkins, Robert. 2016. (Sierra the Search Dog Ser.). (ENG.). (J). (gr. 2-6). pap. 10.95 *(978-0-9971911-1-0(2))* Callout Pr.

—Howard B. Wigglebottom on Yes or No: A Fable about Trust. Binkow, Howard & Ana, Reverend. 2013. (Howard B. Wigglebottom Ser.). (ENG.). 32p. (J). (gr. -1-3). 15.00 *(978-0-9826165-8-1(9)*, We Do Listen) We Do Listen Foundation.

Longabough, Kristen. The Bat Who Wore Glasses. Goss, Michael Anthony. 2005. (J). pap. *(978-1-933156-13-2(9))*; per. 16.99 *(978-1-933156-06-4(6))* GSVQ Publishing. (VisionQuest Kids).

Longfellow, Jay. Children's Limericks from a to Z. Longfellow, Chris. 2017. (ENG.). (J). pap. 11.95 *(978-1-4787-8467-8(9))* Outskirts Pr., Inc.

Longfoot, Stephanie. All Things Bright & Beautiful. Taylor, Caroline. 2004. (My First Prayers Ser.). 10p. (J). bds. 3.99 *(978-1-85854-238-6(3))* Brimax Books Ltd. GBR. Dist: Byeway Bks.

—All Things Wise & Wonderful. Taylor, Caroline. 2004. (My First Prayers Ser.). 10p. (J). bds. 3.99 *(978-1-85854-239-3(1))* Brimax Books Ltd. GBR. Dist: Byeway Bks.

—Lord God Made Us All. Taylor, Caroline. 2004. (My First Prayers Ser.). 10p. (J). bds. 3.99 *(978-1-85854-243-0(X))* Brimax Books Ltd. GBR. Dist: Byeway Bks.

Longhi, Katya. La Abejita Amarilla. Swift, Ginger. Cottage Door Press, ed. 2020. (Chunky Lift-A-Flap Board Book Ser.). (SPA.). 12p. (J). (gr. -1 — 1). bds. 7.99 ***(978-1-64638-057-2(6)***, 1000660-SLA) Cottage Door Pr.

Longhi, Katya. Autumn in the Forest. Finch, Rusty. Cottage Door Press, ed. 2019. (Lift-A-Flap Surprise Pop-up Board Bks.). (ENG.). 10p. (J). (gr. -1-1). bds. 9.99 *(978-1-68052-489-5(5)*, 1003640) Cottage Door Pr.

—Big Red & the Terrible Tomato Hornworm: Bloomers Island. Carbone, Courtney & Wylie, Cynthia. 2018. (Bloomers Island Ser.: 3). 32p. (J). (gr. -1-3). pap. 4.99 *(978-1-63565-110-2(7)*, 9781635651102, Rodale Kids) Random Hse. Children's Bks.

—Bless This Child: Keepsake Greeting Card Board Book. Birdsong, Minnie. Cottage Door Press, ed. ed. 2017. (Little Bird Greetings Keepsake Book Ser.). (ENG.). 8p. (J). (gr. -1-2). bds. 6.99 *(978-1-68052-204-4(3)*, 1000591) Cottage Door Pr.

—Counting Change. Heos, Bridget. 2015. (Math World Ser.). 24p. (J). lib. bdg. 27.10 *(978-1-60753-462-4(2))* Amicus Publishing.

—Do You Really Want a Bird? Heos, Bridget & Powell, Marie. 2013. (Do You Really Want a Pet? Ser.). (ENG.). 24p. (gr. 1-4). 27.10 *(978-1-60753-205-7(0))* Amicus Publishing.

—Do You Really Want a Cat? Heos, Bridget. 2013. (Do You Really Want a Pet? Ser.). (ENG.). 24p. (gr. 1-4). 27.10 *(978-1-60753-203-3(4))* Amicus Publishing.

—Do You Really Want a Dog? Heos, Bridget. 2013. (Do You Really Want a Pet? Ser.). (ENG.). 24p. (gr. 1-4). 27.10 *(978-1-60753-204-0(2))* Amicus Publishing.

—Do You Really Want a Guinea Pig? Heos, Bridget. 2015. (Do You Really Want a Pet? Ser.). (ENG.). 24p. (J). (gr. 1-3). 19.95 *(978-1-60753-749-6(4))* Amicus Publishing.

—Do You Really Want a Hamster? Heos, Bridget. 2013. (Do You Really Want a Pet? Ser.). (ENG.). 24p. (gr. 1-4). 27.10 *(978-1-60753-206-4(9))* Amicus Publishing.

—Do You Really Want a Horse? Heos, Bridget. 2013. (Do You Really Want a Pet? Ser.). (ENG.). 24p. (gr. 1-4). 27.10 *(978-1-60753-207-1(7))* Amicus Publishing.

—Do You Really Want a Lizard? Heos, Bridget. 2015. (Do You Really Want a Pet? Ser.). (ENG.). 24p. (J). (gr. 1-3). 19.95 *(978-1-60753-750-2(8))* Amicus Publishing.

—Do You Really Want a Rabbit? Heos, Bridget. 2013. (Do You Really Want a Pet? Ser.). (ENG.). 24p. (gr. 1-4). 27.10 *(978-1-60753-208-8(5))* Amicus Publishing.

—Do You Really Want a Snake? Heos, Bridget. 2015. (Do You Really Want a Pet? Ser.). (ENG.). 24p. (J). (gr. 1-3). 19.95 *(978-1-60753-751-9(6))* Amicus Publishing.

—Do You Really Want a Turtle? Heos, Bridget. 2015. (Do You Really Want a Pet? Ser.). (ENG.). 24p. (J). (gr. 1-3). 19.95 *(978-1-60753-752-6(4))* Amicus Publishing.

—Elephant. Perkins, Wendy. 2015. (J). pap. *(978-1-68152-074-2(5))* Amicus Publishing.

—Good Night, Good Morning. Fischer, Maggie. 2019. (ENG.). 16p. (J). (— 1). bds. 8.99 *(978-1-68412-519-7(7)*, Silver Dolphin Bks.) Printers Row Publishing Group.

—Great Garden Party. Wylie, Cynthia & Carbone, Courtney. 2018. (Bloomers Island Ser.). 32p. (J). (gr. -1-3). 17.99 *(978-1-63565-069-3(0)*, 9781635650693, Rodale Kids) Random Hse. Children's Bks.

—Jesus Calling: the Story of Christmas (board Book), 1 vol. Young, Sarah. 2018. (Jesus Calling® Ser.). 0000024p. (J). bds. 12.99 *(978-1-4002-1030-5(5))* Nelson, Thomas Inc.

—Jesus Calling: the Story of Christmas (picture Book), 1 vol. Young, Sarah. 2018. (Jesus Calling® Ser.). (ENG.). 32p. (J). 17.99 *(978-1-4002-1029-9(1))* Nelson, Thomas Inc.

—Jesus Calling: the Story of Easter (board Book), 1 vol. Young, Sarah. 2020. (Jesus Calling® Ser.). 24p. (J). bds. 12.99 *(978-1-4002-1034-3(8))* Nelson, Thomas Inc.

—Jesus Calling: the Story of Easter (picture Book), 1 vol. Young, Sarah. 2020. (Jesus Calling® Ser.). (ENG.). 32p. (J). 17.99 *(978-1-4002-1032-9(1))* Nelson, Thomas Inc.

—Little Bible Playbook: the Story of Easter. 2020. (Little Bible Playbook Ser.). (ENG.). 10p. (J). (gr. -1-k). bds. 7.99 *(978-0-7944-4491-4(1)*, Studio Fun International) Printers Row Publishing Group.

—Little Blessings for Little Children: Padded Board Book. Bunting, Rose. 2017. (Love You Always Ser.). (ENG.). 18p. (J). (gr. -1-1). bds. 9.99 *(978-1-68052-186-3(1)*, 1001840) Cottage Door Pr.

—Little Yellow Bee: Chunky Lift a Flap Board Book. Swift, Ginger. Cottage Door Press, ed. 2016. (Chunky Lift-A-Flap Board Book Ser.). (ENG.). 12p. (J). (gr. -1-k). bds. 7.99 *(978-1-68052-083-5(0)*, 1000660) Cottage Door Pr.

—Making Graphs. Heos, Bridget. 2015. (Math World Ser.). 24p. (J). lib. bdg. 27.10 *(978-1-60753-463-1(0))* Amicus Publishing.

—Manners at a Friend's House. Heos, Bridget. 2015. (Monstrous Manners Ser.). (ENG.). 24p. (J). (gr. 1-3). 19.95 *(978-1-60753-743-4(5))* Amicus Publishing.

—Manners at a Restaurant. Heos, Bridget. 2015. (Monstrous Manners Ser.). (ENG.). 24p. (J). (gr. 1-3). 19.95 *(978-1-60753-744-1(3))* Amicus Publishing.

—Manners at School. Heos, Bridget. 2015. (Monstrous Manners Ser.). (ENG.). 24p. (J). (gr. 1-3). 19.95 *(978-1-60753-745-8(1))* Amicus Publishing.

—Manners at the Store. Heos, Bridget. 2015. (Monstrous Manners Ser.). (ENG.). 24p. (J). (gr. 1-3). 19.95 *(978-1-60753-746-5(X))* Amicus Publishing.

—Manners on Vacation. Heos, Bridget. 2015. (Monstrous Manners Ser.). (ENG.). 24p. (J). (gr. 1-3). 19.95 *(978-1-60753-747-2(8))* Amicus Publishing.

—Manners with Technology. Heos, Bridget. 2015. (Monstrous Manners Ser.). (ENG.). 24p. (J). (gr. 1-3). 19.95 *(978-1-60753-748-9(6))* Amicus Publishing.

—Measure It. Heos, Bridget. 2015. (Math World Ser.). 24p. (J). lib. bdg. 27.10 *(978-1-60753-464-8(9))* Amicus Publishing.

—Pete Moss & the Super Strong Spinach. Wylie, Cynthia & Carbone, Courtney. 2018. (Bloomers Island Ser.: 1). 32p. (J). (gr. -1-3). pap. 4.99 *(978-1-63565-052-5(6)*, 9781635650525, Rodale Kids) Random Hse. Children's Bks.

—Rosey Posey & the Perfectly Pink Radish. Wylie, Cynthia & Carbone, Courtney. 2018. (Bloomers Island Ser.: 2). 32p. (J). (gr. -1-3). pap. 4.99 *(978-1-63565-054-9(2)*, 9781635650549, Rodale Kids) Random Hse. Children's Bks.

—Spring in the Forest. Wing, Scarlett & Finch, Rusty. 2019. (Lift-A-Flap Surprise Pop-up Board Bks.). (ENG.). 10p. (J). (gr. -1-1). bds. 9.99 *(978-1-68052-482-6(8)*, 1003620) Cottage Door Pr.

—Summer in the Forest. Finch, Rusty. Cottage Door Press, ed. 2019. (Lift-A-Flap Surprise Pop-up Board Bks.). (ENG.). 10p. (J). (gr. -1-1). bds. 9.99 *(978-1-68052-483-3(6)*, 1003630) Cottage Door Pr.

—Telling Time. Heos, Bridget. 2015. (Math World Ser.). 24p. (J). lib. bdg. 27.10 *(978-1-60753-461-7(4))* Amicus Publishing.

—Violet & the Eggplant Painting Problem. Carbone, Courtney & Wylie, Cynthia. 2018. (Bloomers Island Ser.: 4). 32p. (J). (gr. -1-3). pap. 4.99 *(978-1-63565-112-6(3)*, 9781635651126, Rodale Kids) Random Hse. Children's Bks.

—Winter in the Forest. Finch, Rusty. Cottage Door Press, ed. 2019. (Lift-A-Flap Surprise Pop-up Board Bks.). (ENG.). 10p. (J). (gr. -1-1). bds. 9.99 *(978-1-68052-490-1(9)*, 1003650) Cottage Door Pr.

Longhi, Katya, jt. illus. see Demidova, Olga.

Longman, Mary. The Little Duck Sikihpsis. Cuthand, Beth. Cuthand, Stan, tr. ed. 2013. (ENG.). 34p. 18.00 *(978-1-894778-10-7(3))* Theytus Bks., Ltd. CAN. Dist: Univ. of Toronto Pr.

—Sikihpsis. Cuthand, Beth. Cuthand, Stan, tr. ed. 2007. (Little Duck Ser.). (ENG.). 28p. 17.00 *(978-1-894778-44-2(8))* Theytus Bks., Ltd. CAN. Dist: Univ. of Toronto Pr.

Longman, Stanley. Corah's Magical Excursions in the Night. Longman, Stanley. 2018. (ENG.). 120p. (YA). pap. 20.00 *(978-0-9981627-8-2(7))* Bilbo Bks.

Longmore, Nickolai. The Little Princess. Snider, Lori L. 2005. 32p. (J). 3.99 *(978-0-9771700-0-5(4))* Mystic Arts, LLC.

—Nighttime Adventures Counting Sheep. Rock, Michelle L. 2006. 32p. (J). 3.99 net. *(978-0-9771700-1-2(2))* Mystic Arts, LLC.

Longo, Jason. Mommy Did You Know... An Adoption Story. Giroir, Constance H. 2005. 22p. per. 17.32 *(978-1-59926-397-7(1))* Xlibris Corp.

—Otto's Colorful Campus Tour - Syracuse University A-Z. 2004. (J). 9.99 *(978-1-933069-04-3(X))* Odd Duck Ink, Inc.

Longo, Tiziana. Estamos Juntos. Lindeen, Mary. 2016. (Early Rising Readers Ser.). (SPA.). 16p. (J). (gr. 1-1). 6.67 *(978-1-4788-3737-4(3))* Newmark Learning LLC.

—Go! Go! Go! McGillian, Jamie. 2015. (Early Rising Readers Ser.). (J). (gr. -1-k). 5.83 *(978-1-4788-1599-0(X))* Newmark Learning LLC.

—¡Vamos! ¡Vamos! ¡Vamos! McGillian, Jamie. 2016. (Early Rising Readers Ser.). (SPA.). (J). (gr. -1). 6.67 *(978-1-4788-3657-5(1))* Newmark Learning LLC.

—We Can Be. Lindeen, Mary. 2015. (Early Rising Readers Ser.). (J). (gr. -1-k). 5.83 *(978-1-4788-1694-2(5))* Newmark Learning LLC.

—The Wind in the Willows. Grahame, Kenneth. 2018. (ENG.). 256p. (J). 19.99 *(978-1-78888-386-3(1),* 08275abc-56b6-4a67-9d48-45d8c4042f22) Arcturus Publishing GBR. Dist: Baker & Taylor Publisher Services (BTPS).

Longoria, Rheanna R. I'm Sorry Story. McAllister, Melody. 2020. (ENG.). 48p. (J). 26.99 ***(978-1-970133-62-2(7))***; pap. 17.99 ***(978-1-970133-49-3(X))*** EduMatch.

Longson, Philip. The Tale of Tam Linn, 37 vols. Don, Lari. 2014. (Traditional Scottish Tales Ser.). (ENG.). 32p. (J). pap. 11.95 *(978-1-78250-134-3(7),* Kelpies) Floris Bks. GBR. Dist: Consortium Bk. Sales & Distribution.

Longua, Katie. Debian Perl: Digital Detective Book One. Hilario, Melanie & Davis, Lauren. 2019. (ENG.). 208p. (J). pap. 12.99 *(978-1-5493-0332-6(5),* d24fd2dc-512e-4419-8b7b-f1a391782acd, Lion Forge) Oni Pr., Inc.

Lonsdale, Mary. First Words Sticker Book. 2003. 12p. (J). bds. *(978-1-85854-658-2(3))* Autumn Publishing, Ltd.

—My Big Book of Numbers. Lebron, Karen. 2004. 48p. (J). 5.99 *(978-1-85854-317-8(7))* Brimax Books Ltd. GBR. Dist: Byeway Bks.

—My Prayers for Everyday. 2004. 10p. (J). bds. 7.99 *(978-1-85854-438-0(6))* Brimax Books Ltd. GBR. Dist: Byeway Bks.

—Whatever the Weather: When the Snow Comes. 2004. (Whatever the Weather Ser.). 10p. (J). bds. 4.99 *(978-1-85854-103-7(4))* Brimax Books Ltd. GBR. Dist: Byeway Bks.

—Whatever the Weather: When the Sun Shines. 2004. (Whatever the Weather Ser.). 10p. (J). bds. 4.99 *(978-1-85854-105-1(0))* Brimax Books Ltd. GBR. Dist: Byeway Bks.

—Whatever the Weather: When the Wind Blows. 2004. (Whatever the Weather Ser.). 10p. (J). bds. 4.99 *(978-1-85854-102-0(6))* Brimax Books Ltd. GBR. Dist: Byeway Bks.

Loomis, Jennifer A., photos by. Wildlife in the Rocky Mountains. Loomis, Jennifer A. unabr. ed. 2005. 100p. (J). 24.95 *(978-0-88045-159-8(9))* Stemmer Hse. Pubs.

Looney, Bill. Dinosaurs for Kids. Ham, Ken. 2009. (ENG.). 64p. (YA). 14.99 *(978-0-89051-555-6(7),* Master Books) New Leaf Publishing Group.

—Dragons: Legends & Lore of Dinosaurs. Hodge, Bodie & Welch, Laura, eds. 2009. 24p. (J). 18.99 *(978-0-89051-558-7(1),* Master Books) New Leaf Publishing Group.

—The Flood of Noah: Legends & Lore of Survival. 2014. 24p. (J). 18.99 *(978-0-89051-801-4(7),* Master Books) New Leaf Publishing Group.

—God Is Really, Really Real: 30 Easily Taught Bible Doctrines. Davenport, Jeff. 2015. (ENG.). 96p. (J). 15.99 *(978-0-89221-738-0(3))* New Leaf Publishing Group.

—Inside Noah's Ark 4 Kids. Dudley, Becki. 2017. (ENG.). 12p. (J). bds. 12.99 *(978-1-68344-072-7(2),* Master Books) New Leaf Publishing Group.

—Noah, Didn't It Rain. Golden, William Lee. 2008. 29p. (J). (gr. -1-3). 13.99 incl. audio compact disk *(978-0-89221-683-3(2))* New Leaf Publishing Group.

—Not Too Small at All: A Mouse Tale. Townsend, Stephanie Z. 2008. (ENG.). 30p. (J). (gr. -1). 13.99 *(978-0-89051-524-2(7),* Master Books) New Leaf Publishing Group.

—The Vince Vance Rock & Roll Reader: Bedtime Stories, Poems, Songs, Jokes, Pictures & Other Real Cool Stuff for Kids of All Ages. Rice, Bob, photos by. Vance, Vince. Pennington, Carole, ed. 2003. 182p. (J). (gr. 3-8). per. *(978-0-9652918-0-4(4))* Fullerton Bks., Inc.

—What Ever Happened to the Wooly Mammoth: Life at the End of the Great Ice Age. Oard, Beverly & Oard, Michael. 2007. 72p. (J). 15.99 *(978-0-89051-508-2(5),* Master Books) New Leaf Publishing Group.

Loper, Carol J. The Miracle of Life. Loper, Ami M. 2007. (J). *(978-0-9678798-1-9(7))* Biblical Standards Pubns.

Lopes, Tom. In a Word: 750 Words & Their Fascinating Stories & Origins. Baker, Rosalie. 2003. (ENG.). 250p. (J). 17.95 *(978-0-8126-2710-7(5))* Cricket Bks.

López, Àlex. Basketball Break. Joven, C. C. 2017. (Sports Illustrated Kids Starting Line Readers Ser.). (ENG.). 32p. (J). (gr. -1-1). lib. bdg. 22.65 *(978-1-4965-4253-3(3),* Stone Arch Bks.) Capstone.

—The Boy Who Cried Vampire: A Graphic Novel. Harper, Benjamin. 2017. (Far Out Fables Ser.). (ENG.). 40p. (J). (gr. 3-6). pap. 4.95 *(978-1-4965-5425-3(6),* 136358); lib. bdg. 25.32 *(978-1-4965-5421-5(3),* 136354) Capstone. (Stone Arch Bks.).

—Do Robots Get Space Sick? Baker, Theo. 2017. (Galaxy Games Ser.). (ENG.). 48p. (gr. 3-5). 25.64 *(978-1-68342-338-6(0),* 9781683423386) Rourke Educational Media.

Lopez, Alex. The Emperor's New Clothes: An Interactive Fairy Tale Adventure. Braun, Eric Mark. 2020. (You Choose: Fractured Fairy Tales Ser.). (ENG.). 112p. (J). (gr. 3-7). pap. 6.95 *(978-1-4966-5811-1(6),* 142243); lib. bdg. 32.65 *(978-1-5435-9011-1(X),* 141367) Capstone.

López, Àlex. Gas Giant Jump. Baker, Theo. 2017. (Galaxy Games Ser.). (ENG.). 48p. (gr. 3-5). 25.64 *(978-1-68342-336-2(4),* 9781683423362); pap. 8.95 *(978-1-68342-432-1(8),* 9781683424321) Rourke Educational Media.

Lopez, Alex. The Ghost Emperor's New Clothes: A Graphic Novel. Harper, Benjamin. 2020. (Far Out Fairy Tales Ser.). (ENG.). 40p. (J). (gr. 3-6). pap. 5.95 ***(978-1-4965-9908-7(X),*** 201319); lib. bdg. 25.32 ***(978-1-4965-9686-4(2),*** 199254) Capstone. (Stone Arch Bks.).

López, Àlex. Goldilocks & the Three Bears: An Interactive Fairy Tale Adventure. Braun, Eric. 2015. (You Choose: Fractured Fairy Tales Ser.). (ENG.). 112p. (J). (gr. 3-7). lib. bdg. 32.65 *(978-1-4914-5855-6(0),* Capstone Pr.) Capstone.

Lopez, Alex. Hansel & Gretel. Gunderson, Jessica. 2020. (Fairy Tales Ser.). (ENG.). 32p. (J). (gr. k-2). pap. 6.95 ***(978-1-5158-7273-3(4),*** 201233); lib. bdg. 21.32 ***(978-1-5158-7120-0(7),*** 199342) Capstone. (Picture Window Bks.).

Lopez, Alex. John Henry, Steel-Drivin' Elf: A Graphic Novel. Harper, Benjamin. 2019. (Far Out Folktales Ser.). (ENG.). 40p. (J). (gr. 3-6). lib. bdg. 25.32 *(978-1-4965-7844-0(9),* 139310, Stone Arch Bks.) Capstone.

López, Àlex. Moon of Deception. Baker, Theo. 2017. (Galaxy Games Ser.). (ENG.). 48p. (gr. 3-5). pap. 8.95 *(978-1-68342-433-8(6),* 9781683424338) Rourke Educational Media.

Lopez, Alex. The Princess & the Pea: An Interactive Fairy Tale Adventure. Hoena, Blake. 2020. (You Choose: Fractured Fairy Tales Ser.). (ENG.). 112p. (J). (gr. 3-7). pap. 6.95 *(978-1-4966-5814-2(0),* 142246); lib. bdg. 32.65 *(978-1-5435-9014-2(4),* 141371) Capstone.

—Robin Hood, Time Traveler: A Graphic Novel. Harper, Benjamin. 2020. (Far Out Classic Stories Ser.). (ENG.). 40p. (J). (gr. 3-6). pap. 5.95 *(978-1-4965-9194-4(1),* 142207); lib. bdg. 25.32 *(978-1-4965-8688-9(3),* 141431) Capstone. (Stone Arch Bks.).

López, Àlex. Sleeping Beauty, Magic Master: A Graphic Novel. Peters, Stephanie True. 2016. (Far Out Fairy Tales Ser.). (ENG.). 40p. (J). (gr. 3-6). lib. bdg. 25.32 *(978-1-4965-3784-3(X),* Stone Arch Bks.) Capstone.

—Soccer Score. Joven, C. C. 2017. (Sports Illustrated Kids Starting Line Readers Ser.). (ENG.). 32p. (J). (gr. -1-1). pap. 3.95 *(978-1-4965-4258-8(4));* lib. bdg. 22.65 *(978-1-4965-4251-9(7))* Capstone. (Stone Arch Bks.).

—Space Face Off. Baker, Theo. 2017. (Galaxy Games Ser.). (ENG.). 48p. (gr. 3-5). 25.64 *(978-1-68342-335-5(6),* 9781683423355); pap. 8.95 *(978-1-68342-431-4(X),* 9781683424314) Rourke Educational Media.

Lopez, Alex. Thumbelina, Wrestling Champ: A Graphic Novel. Rayo, Alberto. 2019. (Far Out Fairy Tales Ser.). (ENG.). 40p. (J). (gr. 3-6). pap. 5.95 *(978-1-4965-8445-8(7),* 140970); lib. bdg. 25.32 *(978-1-4965-8396-3(5),* 140687) Capstone. (Stone Arch Bks.).

López, Alex, jt. illus. see Jennings, C. S.

Lopez, Anuki. Rapunzel. Fandel, Jennifer Lee. 2020. (Fairy Tales Ser.). (ENG.). 32p. (J). (gr. k-2). pap. 6.95 ***(978-1-5158-7274-0(2),*** 201235); lib. bdg. 21.32 ***(978-1-5158-7118-7(5),*** 199339) Capstone. (Picture Window Bks.).

Lopez, Ayesha. Cinderella: An Interactive Fairy Tale Adventure. Braun, Eric & Gunderson, Jessica. 2015. (You Choose: Fractured Fairy Tales Ser.). (ENG.). 112p. (J). (gr. 3-7). lib. bdg. 32.65 *(978-1-4914-5854-9(2),* Capstone Pr.) Capstone.

—Mira Como Voy! Schmauss, Judy Kentor. 2016. (Early Rising Readers Ser.). (SPA.). 16p. (J). (gr. 1-1). 6.67 *(978-1-4788-3718-3(7))* Newmark Learning LLC.

—MIS Esquis. Schmauss, Judy Kentor. 2016. (Early Rising Readers Ser.). (SPA.). 16p. (J). (gr. 1-1). 6.67 *(978-1-4788-3725-1(X))* Newmark Learning LLC.

—My Skis. Schmauss, Judy Kentor. 2015. (Early Rising Readers Ser.). (J). (gr. -1-k). 5.83 *(978-1-4788-1696-6(1))* Newmark Learning LLC.

—The Sun Is up. Pink a Band. Llewellyn, Claire. 2016. (Cambridge Reading Adventures Ser.). (ENG.). 16p. pap. 7.37 *(978-1-107-54987-6(6))* Cambridge Univ. Pr.

—Watch Me Go. Schmauss, Judy Kentor. 2015. (Early Rising Readers Ser.). (J). (gr. -1-k). 5.83 *(978-1-4788-2159-5(0))* Newmark Learning LLC.

—The Wooden Bowl. 2016. (Spring Forward Ser.). (J). (gr. 1). *(978-1-4900-9377-2(X))* Benchmark Education Co.

Lopez, Baldo Lazaro. Love Is the Most Important Thing in the Universe. Phillip, Christopher. 2019. (ENG.). 48p. (J). (gr. k-6). pap. 13.50 *(978-1-946539-83-0(X))* Strategic Book Publishing & Rights Agency (SBPRA).

Lopez, Carlos. Amber's Sick Day. Woodard, Sarah. 2019. (ENG.). 58p. (J). pap. 12.50 ***(978-1-6887-3651-1(4))*** Independently Published.

—Carlos Makes a Discovery. Woodard, Sarah. 2019. (ENG.). 64p. (J). pap. 14.50 ***(978-1-7072-4133-0(3))*** Independently Published.

Lopez, Carlos. Gabby's Special Day. Woodard, Sarah. 2019. (ENG.). 44p. (J). pap. 10.50 *(978-1-0752-6873-1(7))* Independently Published.

Lopez, Carlos. Joey's Big Decision. Woodard, Sarah. 2019. (ENG.). 56p. (J). pap. 12.00 ***(978-1-6972-7844-6(2))*** Independently Published.

—Leila's Goal. Woodard, Sarah. 2019. (ENG.). 50p. (J). pap. 11.50 ***(978-1-6770-8065-6(5))*** Independently Published.

Lopez, Carlos. The Sad Dragon. Woodard, Sarah. 2019. (ENG.). 42p. (J). pap. 10.50 *(978-1-0814-5536-1(5))* Independently Published.

Lopez, Claudia Navarro. La Nina Que Tenia el Mar Adentro. Chavez, Ricardo & Aguileta, Gabriela. rev. ed. 2005. (Castillo de la Lectura Verde Ser.). (SPA & ENG.). 136p. (J). (gr. -1-7). pap. 7.95 *(978-970-20-0176-8(5))* Castillo, Ediciones, S. A. de C. V. MEX. Dist: Macmillan.

Lopez, Daniela J. & Whyte, Christen A. Afros, Braids, & Curls: A Coloring Book for Curly Girls. Lopez, Daniela J. 2019. (ENG.). 56p. (J). (gr. k-6). pap. 10.00 ***(978-0-578-59508-5(7))*** Lopez, Daniela J.

Lopez, David. Mr. & Mrs. X Vol. 2: Gambit & Rogue Forever. 2019. (ENG.). 136p. (YA). (gr. 8-17). pap. 17.99 *(978-1-302-91352-6(2))* Marvel Worldwide, Inc.

—A New World/Un Nuevo Mundo: Spanish/English Edition. Barron's Educational Series & Rabley, Stephen. 2010. (Let's Read! Spanish-English Ser.). (ENG.). 32p. (J). (gr. k-3). 17.44 *(978-0-7641-4471-4(5),* B.E.S. Publishing) Peterson's.

López del Hierro, Fernando. Depeche Mode: The Unauthorized Biography. Romero, Soledad. 2020. (Band Bios Ser.). 40p. (J). (-3). 14.99 *(978-1-7282-1094-0(1))* Sourcebooks, Inc.

Lopez, Frank, et al. Doctor Strange, Sorcerer Supreme Omnibus Vol. 2. 2018. (ENG.). 1056p. (YA). (gr. 8-17). 125.00 *(978-1-302-91178-2(3))* Marvel Worldwide, Inc.

Lopez, Julian, jt. illus. see Molina, Jorge.

Lopez, Kenneth. Paloma's Secret. Hood, Mia & Fabrikant, Amy. 2019. (ENG.). 40p. (J). pap. 10.99 *(978-1-7218-1997-3(5))* CreateSpace Independent Publishing Platform.

—Paloma's Secret. Hood, Mia & Fabrikant, Amy. 2019. (ENG.). 40p. (J). pap. 10.99 *(978-1-7337582-0-8(8))* Pebbles Pr.

Lopez, Kenneth. El Secreto de Paloma. Hood, Mia & Fabrikant, Amy. 2019. (SPA.). 40p. (J). pap. 10.99 ***(978-1-7337582-1-5(6))*** Pebbles Pr.

Lopez, Laia. Ula y Hop Hacen un Amigo / Ula & Hop Make a Friend. Lilliput, Eric. 2019. (Ula y Hop Ser.). (SPA.). 128p. (J). (gr. 1-4). pap. 13.95 *(978-607-31-7935-5(9),* Alfaguara) Penguin Random House Grupo Editorial ESP. Dist: Penguin Random Hse. LLC.

López, Laia. Ula y Hop Resuelven un Misterio / Ula & Hop Solve a Mystery. Lilliput, Eric. 2020. (Ula y Hop Ser.). (SPA.). 128p. (J). (gr. 1-4). pap. 13.95 ***(978-607-31-8888-3(9),*** Alfaguara) Penguin Random House Grupo Editorial ESP. Dist: Penguin Random Hse. LLC.

Lopez, Laia. Ula y Hop Van a la Escuela / Ula & Hop Go to School. Lilliput, Eric. 2020. (Ula y Hop Ser.). (SPA.). 128p. (J). (gr. 1-4). pap. 13.95 *(978-607-31-8375-8(5),* Alfaguara) Penguin Random House Grupo Editorial ESP. Dist: Penguin Random Hse. LLC.

Lopez, Loretta. I Remember Abuelito: A Day of the Dead Story. Levy, Janice & Arisa, Miguel. 2012.Tr. of Yo Recuerdo a Abuelito - Un Cuento del Dia de los Muertos. (SPA & ENG.). (J). *(978-1-61913-114-9(5))* Weigl Pubs., Inc.

—I Remember Abuelito: A Day of the Dead Story. Levy, Janice. Arisa, Miguel, tr. 2007.Tr. of Yo Recuerdo a Abuelito - Un Cuento del Dia de los Muertos. (ENG & SPA.). 32p. (J). (gr. -1-3). 6.99 *(978-0-8075-3517-2(6),* 807535176) Whitman, Albert & Co.

—Say Hola to Spanish. Elya, Susan Middleton. 2013. (Say Hola to Spanish Ser.). (ENG, MUL & SPA.). (J). (gr. k-3). lib. bdg. 21.05 *(978-1-68065-229-1(X))* Perfection Learning Corp.

—Say Hola to Spanish at the Circus. Elya, Susan Middleton. 2013. (ENG.). 32p. (J). (gr. -1-5). pap. 8.95 *(978-1-58430-042-7(6))* Lee & Low Bks., Inc.

—Say Hola to Spanish, Otra Vez (Again!) Elya, Susan Middleton. 2013. (SPA & ENG.). 32p. (J). (gr. -1-5). pap. 10.95 *(978-1-880000-64-9(4));* pap. 9.95 *(978-1-880000-83-0(0))* Lee & Low Bks., Inc.

Lopez, Luis. Two Kittens Come Home. Demaio, Carlo a. 2018. (Two Kittens Book Ser.: Vol. 1). (ENG.). 32p. (J). pap. 10.99 *(978-1-7322583-7-2(6))* DeMaio, Carlo A.

Lopez, Luz-Maria. How the Gods Created the Finger People, 1 vol. Moore, Elizabeth & Couvillon, Alice. 2011. (SPA.). 32p. (J). (gr. k-3). 18.99 *(978-1-58980-889-8(4),* Pelican Publishing) Arcadia Publishing.

Lopez, Lyle. Timmy & the Baseball Birthday Party. Dzidrums, Christine. 2012. 50p. pap. 6.99 *(978-0-9835393-8-4(3))* Creative Media Publishing.

Lopez, Lyle & Dzidrums, Joseph. Fair Youth: Emylee of Forest Springs. Dzidrums, Christine. 2012. (ENG.). 120p. (YA). pap. 9.99 *(978-1-938438-05-9(1))* Creative Media Publishing.

—Timmy Adopts a Girl Dog. Dzidrums, Christine. 2012. (ENG.). 48p. (J). pap. 6.99 *(978-1-938438-03-5(5))* Creative Media Publishing.

Lopez, Maria Joao. Mary & the Little Shepherds of Fatima. Monge, Marilyn. 2017. (ENG.). 34p. (J). 14.95 *(978-0-8198-4959-5(6))* Pauline Bks. & Media.

Lopez, Merce. Poetry for Kids: William Shakespeare. Shakespeare, William & Tassi, Marguerite. Tassi, Marguerite, ed. 2018. (Poetry for Kids Ser.). (ENG.). 48p. (J). (gr. 3-7). 14.95 *(978-1-63322-504-6(6),* 302412, Moondance) Quarto Publishing Group USA.

Lopez, Michael, et al. Bloodstone & the Legion of Monsters. 2017. (ENG.). 312p. (YA). (gr. 8-17). pap. 34.99 *(978-1-302-90802-7(2))* Marvel Worldwide, Inc.

Lopez, Michelle. El Columpio Sube y Baja. Craddock, Petra. 2016. (Early Rising Readers Ser.). (SPA.). 16p. (J). (gr. 1-1). 6.67 *(978-1-4788-4219-4(9))* Newmark Learning LLC.

Lopez, Michelle, jt. illus. see Leone, Fabio.

López, Nivio. Companero de Suenos. López, Nivio, tr. Almena, Fernando & Artigot, Manuel. 6th ed. (SPA.). 217p. (J). (gr. 4-6). pap. *(978-84-216-1567-6(X),* BU5118) Bruño, Editorial ESP. Dist: Lectorum Pubns., Inc.

López, Oscar J. Sing along with Abuelita Rosa: Hispanic Lullabies = Canciones de Cuna. 2006. (ENG & SPA.). 13p. (J). *(978-0-9788379-0-7(8))* Baby Abuelita Productions, Inc.

López, Pablo Ortega. Isabela Captura un Congo. López, Pablo Ortega, ed. Rowan, Karen. Seely, Contee, ed. 2011. 76p. (YA). pap. 5.95 *(978-0-9824687-1-5(7))* Fluency Fast Language Classes, Inc.

Lopez, Patricia. A Dog Named Pom Pom & Friends. Lopez, Patricia. l.t. ed. 2011. (ENG.). 34p. pap. 15.99 *(978-1-4610-4886-2(9))* CreateSpace Independent Publishing Platform.

Lopez, Paul. The Adventures of Melon & Turnip. Howell, Trisha Adelena. 2004. 32p. 15.95 *(978-1-931210-04-1(7))* Howell Canyon Pr.

—In the Jungle. Robinson, Fay. 2004. (Treasure Tree Ser.). 32p. (J). *(978-0-7166-1604-7(1))* World Bk., Inc.

—Into the Rain Forest. Robinson, Fay. 2012. 32p. (J). pap. *(978-0-7166-1652-8(1))* World Bk., Inc.

Lopez, Paul & Hong, Denise. Why I Love My Mom: The Ultimate Gift of the Heart. Hong, Denise & Hong, Andrew. 2004. 32p. (J). lib. bdg. 17.95 *(978-0-9746503-4-0(X))* Platinum Bks.

Lopez, Rafael. Book Fiesta! Celebrate Children's Day/Book Day; Celebremos el Dia de Los Ninos/el Dia de Los Libros (Bilingual Spanish-English) Mora, Pat. 2009. (ENG.). 40p. (J). (gr. -1-3). 17.99 *(978-0-06-128877-7(2),* HarperCollins Español) HarperCollins Christian Publishing.

—Book Fiesta! Celebrate Children's Day/Book Day; Celebremos el Dia de Los Ninos/el Dia de Los Libros (Bilingual Spanish-English) Mora, Pat. 2016. (ENG.). 40p. (J). (gr. -1-3). pap. 7.99 *(978-0-06-128878-4(0))* HarperCollins Pubs.

López, Rafael. Bravo! (Bilingual Board Book - Spanish Edition) Poems about Amazing Hispanics / Poemas Sobre Hispanos Extraordinarios. Engle, Margarita. 2020. (ENG.). 28p. (J). bds. 8.99 *(978-1-250-23081-2(0),* 900209517, Holt, Henry & Co. Bks. For Young Readers) Holt, Henry & Co.

—The Cazuela That the Farm Maiden Stirred. Vamos, Samantha R. 2011. 32p. (J). (gr. k-3). 17.95 *(978-1-58089-242-1(6))* Charlesbridge Publishing, Inc.

—Drum Dream Girl: How One Girl's Courage Changed Music. Engle, Margarita. 2015. (ENG.). 48p. (J). (gr. -1-3). 17.99 *(978-0-544-10229-3(0),* 1540161, HMH Books For Young Readers) Houghton Mifflin Harcourt Publishing Co.

—Maybe Something Beautiful: How Art Transformed a Neighborhood. Campoy, F. Isabel & Howell, Theresa. 2016. (ENG.). 40p. (J). (gr. -1-3). 17.99 *(978-0-544-35769-3(8),* 1587128, HMH Books For Young Readers) Houghton Mifflin Harcourt Publishing Co.

—My Name Is Celia: The Life of Celia Cruz. Brown, Monica. 2004.Tr. of Me Llamo Celia - La Vida de Celia Cruz. (ENG, MUL & SPA.). 32p. (J). (gr. k-3). 15.95 *(978-0-87358-872-0(X))* Cooper Square Publishing Llc.

—My Name is Celia (Me Llamo Celia) The Life of Celia Cruz (La Vida de Celia Cruz) Brown, Monica. 2015. (ENG, MUL & SPA.). 32p. (J). (gr. k-3). pap. 7.95 *(978-1-58979-998-1(4))* Jaffe Book Solutions.

—Quizás Algo Hermoso (Maybe Something Beautiful Spanish Edition) Cómo el Arte Transformó un Barrio. Campoy, F. Isabel & Howell, Theresa. 2018. (SPA.). 40p. (J). (gr. -1-3). 17.99 *(978-1-328-90406-5(7),* 1700744, HMH Books For Young Readers) Houghton Mifflin Harcourt Publishing Co.

Lopez, Rafael. Tito Puente, Mambo King/Tito Puente, Rey Del Mambo: Bilingual Spanish-English Children's Book. Brown, Monica. 2013. (ENG.). 32p. (J). (gr. -1-3). 17.99 *(978-0-06-122783-7(8),* HarperCollins Español) HarperCollins Christian Publishing.

López, Rafael. We've Got the Whole World in Our Hands / Tenemos el Mundo Entero en Las Manos. 2018. (ENG & SPA.). 40p. (J). (gr. -1-k). 17.99 *(978-1-338-29950-2(6),* Scholastic en Espanol) Scholastic, Inc.

—Yum! Mmmm! Que Rico! America's Sproutings, 1 vol. Mora, Pat. 2007. 32p. (J). (gr. -1-3). lib. bdg. 16.95 *(978-1-58430-271-1(2))* Lee & Low Bks., Inc.

—Yum! ¡Mmmm! ¡Qué Rico! Americas' Sproutings, 1 vol. Mora, Pat. 2016. (ENG.). 32p. (J). (gr. k-6). pap. 10.95 *(978-1-60060-892-6(2),* 9745600f-b0ee-42d1-b0ed-27d19f0b41fc) Lee & Low Bks., Inc.

—Yum! ¡MmMm! ¡Qué Rico! Brotes de las Américas. Mora, Pat. 2009.Tr. of Yum! ¡MmMm! ¡Qué rico! America's Sproutings. (SPA.). 32p. (J). 17.95 *(978-1-60060-430-0(7))* Lee & Low Bks., Inc.

López, Rafael. We've Got the Whole World in Our Hands. López, Rafael, adapted by. 2018. 40p. (J). (gr. -1-k). 17.99 *(978-1-338-17736-7(2),* Scholastic Pr.) Scholastic, Inc.

López, Rafael & Flor Ada, Alma. Yum! Mmmm! Qué Rico! Brotes de las Américas, 1 vol. Mora, Pat et al. 2007.Tr. of Yum! ¡MmMm! ¡Qué rico! America's Sproutings. (SPA.). 32p. (J). (gr. k-6). pap. 10.95 *(978-1-60060-268-9(1),* 78416424-b9a1-4307-8978-bc3da9f9d1ad) Lee & Low Bks., Inc.

López, Rafael & López, Rafael. The Cazuela That the Farm Maiden Stirred. Vamos, Samantha R. 2013. (ENG.). 32p. (J). (gr. k-3). pap. 8.95 *(978-1-58089-243-8(4))* Charlesbridge Publishing, Inc.

—Dancing Hands: How Teresa Carreño Played the Piano for President Lincoln. Engle, Margarita. 2019. (ENG.). 40p. (J). (gr. -1-3). 17.99 *(978-1-4814-8740-5(X))* Simon & Schuster Children's Publishing.

—The Day You Begin. Woodson, Jacqueline. 2018. (ENG.). 32p. (J). (gr. k-3). 18.99 *(978-0-399-24653-1(3),* Nancy Paulsen Books) Penguin Young Readers Group.

—El día en Que Descubres Quién Eres. Woodson, Jacqueline. 2018. (SPA.). 32p. (J). (gr. k-3). 18.99 *(978-1-9848-1207-0(6),* Nancy Paulsen Books) Penguin Young Readers Group.

—Just Ask! Be Different, Be Brave, Be You. Sotomayor, Sonia. 2019. (ENG.). 32p. (J). (gr. -1-3). 17.99 *(978-0-525-51412-1(0),* Philomel Bks.) Penguin Young Readers Group.

—Nuestra California. Ryan, Pam Muñoz. 2008.Tr. of Our California. 48p. (J). (gr. 1-4). 17.95 *(978-1-58089-226-1(4))* Charlesbridge Publishing, Inc.

—Our California. Ryan, Pam Muñoz. 2008. 48p. (J). (gr. 1-4). 18.95 *(978-1-58089-116-5(0));* per. 9.95 *(978-1-58089-117-2(9))* Charlesbridge Publishing, Inc.

—¡Solo Pregunta! Sé Diferente, Sé Valiente, Sé Tú. Sotomayor, Sonia. 2019. (SPA.). 32p. (J). (gr. -1-3). 17.99 *(978-0-525-51550-0(X),* Philomel Bks.) Penguin Young Readers Group.

López, Rafael, jt. illus. see López, Rafael.

López, Rafael, jt. illus. see Mora, Pat.

López, Real Anna. Luca's Bridge/el Puente de Luca. Llanos, Mariana. ed. 2019. (ENG.). 40p. (J). 16.95 *(978-0-9987999-5-7(5))* Penny Candy Bks., LLC.

Lopez, Ricard, jt. illus. see Ricardicus.

Lopez Rubio, Ayesha. All Kinds of Bodies. Heneghan, Judith. 2020. (J). ***(978-0-7787-6801-2(5))*** Crabtree Publishing Co.

—All Kinds of Families. Ganeri, Anita. 2020. 32p. (J). ***(978-0-7787-6802-9(3))*** Crabtree Publishing Co.

—All Kinds of Feelings. Heneghan, Judith. 2020. 32p. (J). ***(978-0-7787-6803-6(1))*** Crabtree Publishing Co.

Lopez, Seija. Toot & Poot - Adventures of Amazing Fart Friends: The Unifart Forest. Butvidas, Bryan. 2019. (ENG.). 34p. (J). pap. 9.50 ***(978-1-7915-4605-2(6))*** Independently Published.

Lopez, Shana. Shakespeare's a Midsummer Night's Dream for Kids: 3 Short Melodramatic Plays for 3 Group Sizes. Kelso, Brendan. 2008. (ENG.). 54p. pap. 9.99 *(978-1-4196-8552-1(X))* CreateSpace Independent Publishing Platform.

L

—Shakespeare's Julius Caesar for Kids: 3 Short Melodramatic Plays for 3 Group Sizes. Kelso, Brendan P. Sidaris-Green, Hannah, ed. 2009. (Playing with Plays Ser.). (ENG.). 44p. pap. 9.99 *(978-1-4392-1355-1(0))* CreateSpace Independent Publishing Platform.

Lopez, Willie. Jack Crow Said Hello, 1 vol. Simmons, Lynn Sheffield. 2003. (ENG.). 128p. (J). (gr. 3-7). 10.95 *(978-1-58980-218-6(7),* Pelican Publishing) Arcadia Publishing.

Lopez, Xan. Barro de Medellin/ Mud of Medellin. Gómez Cerda, Alfredo. 2010. (SPA.). 146p. (YA). (gr. 5-8). *(978-84-263-6849-2(2))* Vives, Luis Editorial (Edelvives).

Lopiz, Violeta, jt. illus. see Vidali, Valerio.

Lopresti, Aaron, et al. Mystic: The Mathemagician, Vol. 6. Bedard, Tony. 2004. (Mystic Ser.). 160p. (YA). pap. 15.95 *(978-1-59314-039-7(8))* CrossGeneration Comics, Inc.

Lopresti, Sarah H., jt. illus. see Lucas, Stacey L.

Lopshire, Robert & Cummings, Art. The Big Aqua Book of Beginner Books. Lopshire, Robert et al. 2017. (Beginner Books(R) Ser.). (ENG.). 256p. (J). (gr. -1-2). 16.99 *(978-1-5247-6442-5(6),* Random Hse. Bks. for Young Readers) Random Hse. Children's Bks.

Lora, Miren Asiain. Hello, Earth! Poems to Our Planet. Sidman, Joyce. 2020. (ENG.). 68p. (J). ***(978-0-8028-5528-2(8),*** Eerdmans Bks For Young Readers) Eerdmans, William B. Publishing Co.

Lora, Miren Asiain. The Mermaid Atlas: Merfolk of the World. Claybourne, Anna. 2020. (ENG.). 48p. (J). (gr. 2-6). 19.99 *(978-1-78627-585-1(6),* King, Laurence Publishing) Orion Publishing Group, Ltd. GBR. Dist: Hachette Bk. Group.

Loram, James. Let's Rock 'n' Roll: Sound Book Wood Button Module. Crowe, Carmen. 2016. (Early Bird Sound Bks.). (ENG.). 10p. (J). (gr. -1-k). bds. 12.99 *(978-1-68052-133-7(0),* 1001500) Cottage Door Pr.

—A Monster Alphabet: The ABCs of Screams! Olson, Gillia M. 2016. (Alphabet Connection Ser.). (ENG.). 32p. (J). (gr. -1-2). lib. bdg. 27.99 *(978-1-4795-6887-1(2),* Picture Window Bks.) Capstone.

Loram, James & Jevons, Chris. Alphabet Connection. Jaycox, Jaclyn et al. 2016. (Alphabet Connection Ser.). (ENG.). 32p. (J). (gr. -1-2). lib. bdg., lib. bdg., lib. bdg. 109.28 *(978-1-4795-8005-7(8),* Picture Window Bks.) Capstone.

—Alphabet Connection: The ABCs of Prehistoric Beasts! Hasselius, Michelle M. et al. 2016. (Alphabet Connection Ser.). (ENG.). 32p. (J). (gr. -1-2). pap., pap., pap. 31.80 *(978-1-5158-0403-1(8),* Picture Window Bks.) Capstone.

LoRaso, Carlo. My Little Pony: A Very Minty Christmas. Lange, Nikki Bataille. gif. ed. 2005. 22p. (J). (gr. -1-1). bds. 13.99 *(978-1-57791-191-3(1))* Brighter Minds Children's Publishing.

Lorbiecki, Marybeth & Heinzen, Kory S. Escaping Titanic: A Young Girl's True Story of Survival, 1 vol. Lorbiecki, Marybeth. 2012. (Na Ser.). (ENG.). 32p. (J). (gr. k-5). pap. 8.95 *(978-1-4048-7235-6(3),* Picture Window Bks.) Capstone.

Lord, Jeremy. Meet Weary Dunlop. Saxby, Claire. 2015. (Meet... Ser.). 32p. (J). (gr. -1-k). 21.99 *(978-0-85798-536-1(1))* Random Hse. Australia AUS. Dist: Independent Pubs. Group.

—Meet... Weary Dunlop. Saxby, Claire. 2016. 36p. (J). (gr. k-2). 15.99 *(978-0-85798-587-3(6))* Random Hse. Australia AUS. Dist: Independent Pubs. Group.

Lord, John Vernon. The Giant Jam Sandwich. Lord, John Vernon. Burroway, Janet. 2009. (ENG.). 28p. (J). (gr. -1-3). bds. 7.99 *(978-0-547-15077-2(6),* 1051726) Houghton Mifflin Harcourt Publishing Co.

Lord, Leonie. Ding Dong! Gorilla!, 1 vol. Robinson, Michelle. 2013. (ENG.). 32p. (J). (gr. -1-3). 15.95 *(978-1-56145-730-4(2))* Peachtree Publishing Co. Inc.

—The Super Swooper Dinosaur. Waddell, Martin. 2013. (J). *(978-1-4351-5000-3(7))* Barnes & Noble, Inc.

Lordon, Claire. Fall in the Country. Tarsky, Sue. 2019. (Taking a Walk Ser.). (ENG.). 32p. (J). (gr. -1-3). 16.99 *(978-0-8075-7729-5(4),* 807577294) Whitman, Albert & Co.

—Spring in the Woods. Tarsky, Sue. 2019. (Taking a Walk Ser.). (ENG.). 32p. (J). (gr. -1-3). 16.99 *(978-0-8075-7730-1(8),* 807577308) Whitman, Albert & Co.

—Summer at the Seashore. Tarsky, Sue. 2019. (Taking a Walk Ser.). (ENG.). 32p. (J). (gr. -1-3). 16.99 *(978-0-8075-7731-8(6),* 807577316) Whitman, Albert & Co.

—Winter in the City. Tarsky, Sue. 2019. (Taking a Walk Ser.). (ENG.). 32p. (J). (gr. -1-3). 16.99 *(978-0-8075-7728-8(6),* 807577286) Whitman, Albert & Co.

Lore, Erin. Timmy the Dragon. l.t. ed. 2007. 32p. (J). 8.95 *(978-0-9741562-7-9(2))* Yarrow Pr.

Loredo, Armando. Little Worm: A Story about Worry. Pierce, Laura Ann Elpers. 2019. (ENG.). 26p. (J). (gr. -1-2). pap. 9.99 ***(978-1-61254-397-0(9))*** Brown Books Publishing Group.

Loren, John. Frankenstein Doesn't Wear Earmuffs! Loren, John. 2020. (ENG.). 40p. (J). (gr. -1-3). 17.99 ***(978-0-06-294114-5(3),*** HarperCollins) HarperCollins Pubs. Ltd. GBR. Dist: HarperCollins Pubs.

Lorena Maldonado, Gina. Happy Little Elephant: Sound Book Wood Module with Handle. Rose, Robin. Cottage Door Press, ed. 2017. (Early Bird Sound Bks.). (ENG.). 10p. (J). (gr. -1-k). bds. 9.99 *(978-1-68052-160-3(8),* 1001580) Cottage Door Pr.

Lorentowicz, Irena. Cavalry Hero: Casimir Pulaski. Adams, Dorothy. 2018. 195p. (J). (gr. 8-18). pap. 14.95 *(978-1-932350-74-6(8))* Bethlehem Bks.

Lorenz, Albert. A Three-Minute Speech: Lincoln's Remarks at Gettysburg. Armstrong, Jennifer. 2003. (Milestone Ser.). (ENG.). 96p. (J). pap. 4.99 *(978-0-689-85622-8(9),* Simon & Schuster/Paula Wiseman Bks.) Simon & Schuster/Paula Wiseman Bks.

—The True Story Behind Lincoln's Gettysburg Address. Armstrong, Jennifer. 2013. (ENG.). 96p. (J). (gr. 2-5). 15.99 *(978-1-4424-9388-9(7));* pap. 5.99 *(978-1-4424-9387-2(9))* Simon & Schuster/Paula Wiseman Bks. (Simon & Schuster/Paula Wiseman Bks.).

Lorenz, Jinye, Sr. Grandfather, the Tiger & Ryong. Lorenz, Jinye, Sr. Lorenz, Virginia O., Sr., ed. ltd. ed. 2005. 65p. (J). spiral bd. 14.95 *(978-1-888350-10-4(5))* Lighted Lamp Pr.

Lorenzet, Eleonora. Claire's Cursed Camping Trip. Brandes, Wendy L. 2016. (Summer Camp Ser.). (ENG.). 96p. (J). (gr. 4-6). lib. bdg. 24.65 *(978-1-4965-2600-7(7),* Stone Arch Bks.) Capstone.

—Emily's Pranking Problem. Brandes, Wendy L. 2016. (Summer Camp Ser.). (ENG.). 96p. (J). (gr. 4-6). lib. bdg. 24.65 *(978-1-4965-2599-4(X),* Stone Arch Bks.) Capstone.

—MJ's Camp Crisis. Brandes, Wendy L. 2016. (Summer Camp Ser.). (ENG.). 96p. (J). (gr. 4-6). lib. bdg. 24.65 *(978-1-4965-2598-7(1),* Stone Arch Bks.) Capstone.

—Nina's Not Boy Crazy! (She Just Likes Boys) Brandes, Wendy L. 2016. (Summer Camp Ser.). (ENG.). 96p. (J). (gr. 4-6). lib. bdg. 24.65 *(978-1-4965-2601-4(5),* Stone Arch Bks.) Capstone.

—Summer Camp, 4 vols. Brandes, Wendy L. 2016. (Summer Camp Ser.). (ENG.). 96p. (J). (gr. 4-6). lib. bdg., lib. bdg., lib. bdg. 98.60 *(978-1-4965-2749-3(6),* Stone Arch Bks.) Capstone.

Lorenzetti, Doreen. Bridgetender's Boy. Barth, Linda J. 2004. *(978-0-930973-35-3(6));* pap. *(978-0-930973-34-6(8))* Delaware &Lehigh National Heritage Corridor, Inc. (Canal History & Technology Pr.).

—Cathy Williams, Buffalo Soldier, 1 vol. Solomon, Sharon. 2010. (ENG.). 32p. (J). (gr. k-3). 16.99 *(978-1-58980-801-0(0),* Pelican Publishing) Arcadia Publishing.

Lorenzetti, Marco. The Story of the Betrothed. Eco, Umberto. 2017. (Save the Story Ser.: 10). (ENG.). 104p. (J). (gr. 3-7). 19.95 *(978-1-78269-022-1(0),* Pushkin Children's Bks.) Steerforth Pr.

Lorenzo, David Rodriguez. Moldilocks & the Three Scares. Marie, Lynne. 2019. 40p. (J). (gr. -1-3). 16.95 *(978-1-4549-3061-7(6))* Sterling Publishing Co., Inc.

Lorenzo, Gloria. Mountain Miracle: A Navtivity Story. Correa, Alvaro. 2008. 94p. (J). (gr. -1). pap. 14.95 *(978-1-933271-23-1(X))* Circle Pr.

Lorenzo, Veronica Di & Bertelè, Luca. Moana. Ferrari, Alessandro. 2020. (Disney Princesses Ser.). (ENG.). 52p. (J). (gr. 2-6). lib. bdg. 28.50 ***(978-1-5321-4563-6(2),*** 35210, Graphic Novels) Spotlight.

Loring-Fisher, Jo. Maisie's Scrapbook. Narh, Samuel. 2019. 32p. (J). (gr. -1-2). 17.99 *(978-1-911373-57-5(9))* Lantana Publishing GBR. Dist: Lerner Publishing Group.

Lorna, Balian & Lecia, Balian. The Aminal, 1 vol. Lorna, Balian. 2012. (ENG.). 48p. (J). pap. 7.95 *(978-1-59572-363-5(3))* Star Bright Bks., Inc.

Lorne, Patrick, photos by. Face-to-Face with the Ladybug: Little Garden Monster. Tracqui, Valérie. 2004. (Face-to-Face Ser.). 28p. (J). (gr. -1-2). 9.95 *(978-1-57091-453-9(2))* Charlesbridge Publishing, Inc.

Lornie, June. Alice's Adventures in Wonderland. Carroll, Lewis. 2013. 104p. pap. *(978-1-78201-037-1(8))* Evertype.

Losa, Ann. What Do You Say? Gillis, Jennifer Blizin. 2006. (Reader's Clubhouse Level 2 Reader Ser.). (ENG.). 24p. (J). (gr. k-1). pap. 3.99 *(978-0-7641-3298-8(9),* B.E.S. Publishing) Peterson's.

Losantos, Cristina. Beauty & the Beast: La Bella y la Bestia. 2007. (Bilingual Fairy Tales Ser.: BILI). (ENG.). 32p. (J). (gr. -1-3). pap. 6.95 *(978-0-8118-5970-7(3))* Chronicle Bks. LLC.

—Beauty & the Beast (La Bella y la Bestia) 2013. (Bilingual Fairy Tales Ser.). (SPA & ENG.). 32p. (J). (gr. 1-4). lib. bdg. 28.50 *(978-1-60753-355-9(3))* Amicus Publishing.

—El the Pied Piper / Flautista de Hamelin: A Bilingual Book. 2008. (Bilingual Fairy Tales Ser.: BILI).Tr. of Flautista de Hamelin. (ENG.). 32p. (J). (gr. -1-3). 14.95 *(978-0-8118-6028-4(0))* Chronicle Bks. LLC.

Loschiavo, Richard William. Life's Lessons for Children: (and for Teachers & Parents, Too!) Loschiavo, Janice. 2016. (ENG.). (J). (gr. 3-6). pap. 16.95 *(978-1-938812-82-8(4))* Full Court Pr.

Loseby, Eleanor. Craig. Meador, K. 2018. (A-Z Book for Boys Ser.: Vol. 3). (ENG.). 32p. (J). pap. 14.99 *(978-1-7262-6400-6(9))* CreateSpace Independent Publishing Platform.

Losh, Eric. Insectaside. Reffett, Frances. l.t. ed. 2006. 28p. (J). 8.00 net. *(978-0-9785886-0-1(6))* Chicory Pr.

Lossing, Abbey. 50 Trailblazers of the 50 States: Celebrate the Lives of Inspiring People Who Paved the Way from Every State in America! Megdal, Howard. 2019. (50 States Ser.). (ENG.). 112p. (J). (gr. 7-11). 24.99 *(978-1-78603-967-5(2),* 308401, Wide Eyed Editions) Quarto Publishing Group UK GBR. Dist: Hachette UK Distribution.

Lostimolo, Stephanie. BeBa & the Curious Creature Catchers. Griffin, Lydia. l.t. ed. 2006. 32p. (J). 16.95 *(978-0-9770516-0-1(9))* Laffin Minor Pr.

Lostrom, Sam. The Blue Hare. Webster, Hugh. 2019. (ENG.). 166p. (J). pap. *(978-1-9993714-0-1(2))* Natural Storytelling.

Loter, Inc. The Big Ballet Show (Dora the Explorer) Golden Books. 2012. (Little Golden Book Ser.). 24p. (J). (gr. k-k). 4.99 *(978-0-307-93094-1(7),* Golden Bks.) Random Hse. Children's Bks.

—Clubhouse Christmas. Amerikaner, Susan & Disney Book Group. 2008. (ENG.). 12p. (J). (gr. -1-k). bds. 6.99 *(978-1-4231-1253-2(9))* Disney Pr.

—Disney Junior Mickey & Minnie. Broderick, Kathy et al. 2019. (ENG.). 160p. (J). pap., pap. *(978-1-5037-4407-3(8),* af327b04-a29a-4b48-8595-652ad5147e10, p i kids) Phoenix International Publications, Inc.

Loter Inc. Disney Mickey & Friends: Scaredy-Mouse. Acampora, Courtney. 2018. (ENG.). 8p. (J). (gr. -1-k). bds. 9.99 *(978-0-7944-4162-3(9),* Reader's Digest Children's Bks.) Studio Fun International.

Loter, Inc. Disney Mickey Mouse Clubhouse: Guess Who, Mickey! Mitter, Matt. 2nd ed. 2017. (Guess Who Ser.). (ENG.). 10p. (J). (gr. -1-k). bds. 10.99 *(978-0-7944-4091-6(6),* Reader's Digest Children's Bks.) Studio Fun International.

—Disney Mickey Road Trip. Froeb, Lori C. 2020. (Lift-The-Flap Ser.). (ENG.). 12p. (J). (gr. -1-k). bds. 9.99 *(978-0-7944-4505-8(5),* Studio Fun International) Printers Row Publishing Group.

Loter Inc. Disney Minnie's Easter Adventure. Fischer, Maggie. 2019. (ENG.). 12p. (J). (gr. -1-k). bds. 9.99 *(978-0-7944-4235-4(8),* Studio Fun International) Printers Row Publishing Group.

Loter, Inc. Mickey Mouse Clubhouse: Minnie-Rella. Marsoli, Lisa Ann & Mendoza, Ashley. 2018. (World of Reading Level 1 Ser.). (ENG.). 32p. (J). (gr. -1-3). lib. bdg. 27.07 *(978-1-5321-4191-1(2),* 28533) Spotlight.

—Mickey Mouse Clubhouse: Minnie's Summer Vacation. Scollon, Bill & Ring, Susan. 2018. (World of Reading Level Pre-1 Ser.). (ENG.). 32p. (J). (gr. -1-2). lib. bdg. 27.07 *(978-1-5321-4182-9(3),* 28528) Spotlight.

—Mickey Mouse Roadster Racers: Mickey's Perfecto Day! Stoner, Sherri & Mendoza, Ashley. 2019. (World of Reading Level 1 Ser.). (ENG.). 32p. (J). (gr. -1-3). lib. bdg. 27.07 *(978-1-5321-4403-5(2),* 33808) Spotlight.

—Minnie: a Walk in the Park. Gold, Gina & Heftler, Jennifer. 2018. (World of Reading Level Pre-1 Ser.). (ENG.). 32p. (J). (gr. -1-2). lib. bdg. 27.07 *(978-1-5321-4183-6(1),* 31062) Spotlight.

Loter, Inc. & Disney Storybook Art Team. Disney Mickey Mouse Clubhouse: Songs to Go. pi kids. 2014. (Play-A-Song Ser.). (ENG.). 14p. (J). bds., bds. *(978-1-4127-8848-9(X),* c5c24b7a-522b-4d11-97a0-db7037ad57d3, p i kids) Phoenix International Publications, Inc.

Loter, Inc. & McGee, Warner. Disney Junior Mickey: I'm Ready to Read: Mickey. Keast, Jennifer H. 2019. (Play-A-Sound Ser.). (ENG.). 24p. (J). *(978-1-5037-4697-8(6),* 7049acc4-9681-4d0e-8273-36f7035afa8d, p i kids) Phoenix International Publications, Inc.

Loter Inc. Staff. Minnie: Case of the Missing Sparkle-Izer. Scollon, Bill. 2014. (World of Reading Level Pre-1 Ser.). (ENG.). 32p. (J). (gr. -1-2). lib. bdg. 27.07 *(978-1-61479-248-2(8),* 1762) Spotlight.

Loter, John. Disney Mickey's Christmas Carol. 2018. (ENG.). 12p. (J). (gr. -1-k). 9.99 *(978-0-7944-4179-1(3),* Studio Fun International) Printers Row Publishing Group.

—Finding Dory: Including Dory, Nemo, Marlin, & All Your Favorite Characters! Disney Enterprises Inc., Staff. 2017. (Learn to Draw Favorite Characters: Expanded Edition Ser.). (ENG.). 64p. (J). (gr. 3-5). 33.32 *(978-1-942875-18-5(5),* Walter Foster Jr) Quarto Publishing Group USA.

Loter, John, jt. illus. see Horne, Philip.

Lott, Sheena. Island Santa, 1 vol. McFarlane, Sheryl. 2012. (ENG.). 32p. (J). (gr. k). 19.95 *(978-0-9880536-0-1(8))* Queen Alexandra Foundation for Children CAN. Dist: Orca Bk. Pubs. USA.

—Kah-Lan the Adventurous Sea Otter, 1 vol. Autio, Karen. 2016. (ENG.). 64p. (J). (gr. 1-3). 9.95 *(978-1-55039-244-9(1))* Sono Nis Pr. CAN. Dist: Orca Bk. Pubs. USA.

—A Morning to Polish & Keep, 1 vol. Lawson, Julie. 2nd ed. 2015. (ENG.). 32p. (J). (gr. 1-3). pap. 8.95 *(978-0-88995-521-9(2),* 580f087f-2a71-467e-8f32-6d33e1210523) Red Deer Pr. CAN. Dist: Firefly Bks., Ltd.

Lott, Sheena. Neekah's Knitting Needles. Olsen, Sylvia. 2020. (ENG.). 40p. (J). (gr. 1-3). 21.95 ***(978-1-55039-255-5(7))*** Sono Nis Pr. CAN. Dist: Orca Bk. Pubs. USA.

Lott, Sheena. Salmon Forest. Ellis, Sarah & Suzuki, David. 2006. (ENG.). 32p. (J). (gr. k-3). pap. 9.95 *(978-1-55365-163-5(4))* Greystone Books Ltd. CAN. Dist: Publishers Group West (PGW).

Lotter, Megan. The Chalk Giraffe. Paxton, Kirsty. 2020. (ENG.). 32p. (J). (gr. -1-1). 17.95 *(978-1-68446-096-0(4),* 141333, Capstone Editions) Capstone.

Lotti, Alice. When an Elephant Falls in Love. Cali, Davide. 2016. (ENG.). 32p. (J). (gr. k-3). 14.99 *(978-1-4521-4727-7(2))* Chronicle Bks. LLC.

Lou, Cindy. The King of Ing Wants to Sing. Lou, Cindy, text. 2008. (J). 12.00 *(978-1-935332-00-8(7))* Kite Tales Publishing.

Lou Who, Carrie. Today Is My Birthday & I Have Nothing to Wear! Klitzner, Irene & Adams, Peggy. 2011. 48p. 18.95 *(978-0-9846496-0-0(3),* 6489124b-2620-4158-8a22-983304de3041) Attitude Pie Publishing.

Loubet, Denis. Through the Moongate. the Story of Richard Garriott, Origin Systems Inc. & Ultima: Part 1 - from Akalabeth to Ultima VI. Przygienda, Andreas & McGeachie, Ellouise, trs. 2020. (Video Games Ser.: Vol. 1). (ENG.). 224p. (J). pap. 16.99 ***(978-1-0710-0685-6(1))*** Independently Published.

Louchard, Anne. This Way, That Way. Louchard, Anne. 2017. (ENG.). 18p. (J). (gr. -1-k). bds. 9.99 *(978-988-8341-41-2(3),* Minedition) Neugebauer, Michael (Publishing) Limited HKG. Dist: Penguin Random Hse. LLC.

Loucks-Christenson, Lisa, photos by. 2005, Year One Dancer & Daedee: The Eagle Nest Coffee Bar & Cafe. Loucks-Christenson, Lisa. 2020. 1. 65.00 *(978-0-9771365-0-6(7),* Waiting Room to Heaven) Bk. Entree(TM).

Loufane. When Pigs Fly! Boonen, Stefan. 2004. 32p. (J). 6.95 *(978-1-58925-384-1(1))* Tiger Tales.

Lougheed, Robert. Mustang: Wild Spirit of the West. Henry, Marguerite. 2016. (ENG.). 240p. (J). (gr. 3-7). 19.99 *(978-1-4814-5222-9(3),* Simon & Schuster/Paula Wiseman Bks.) Simon & Schuster/Paula Wiseman Bks.

—San Domingo. Henry, Marguerite. 2016. (ENG.). 288p. (J). (gr. 3-7). 19.99 *(978-1-4814-6211-2(3),* Aladdin) Simon & Schuster Children's Publishing.

Loughran, P. J. Turning 15 on the Road to Freedom: My Story of the 1965 Selma Voting Rights March. 2015. (ENG.). 128p. (YA). (gr. 7). 19.99 *(978-0-8037-4123-2(5),* Dial Bks) Penguin Young Readers Group.

Loughrey, Anita, et al. International Primary Science Student's Book 4. Morrison, Karen et al. Pilling, Anne & Robinson, Pete, eds. 2015. (Collins International Primary Science Ser.). (ENG.). 96p. (gr. 3). pap., stu. ed. 12.95 *(978-0-00-758620-2(5))* HarperCollins Pubs. Ltd. GBR. Dist: Independent Pubs. Group.

—International Primary Science Student's Book 6. Morrison, Karen et al. Pilling, Anne & Robinson, Pete, eds. ed. 2015. (Collins International Primary Science Ser.). (ENG.). 96p. (J). (gr. 5). pap. 12.95 *(978-0-00-758627-1(2))* HarperCollins Pubs. Ltd. GBR. Dist: Independent Pubs. Group.

Loughridge, Stuart. Grandfather's Story Cloth. Gerdner, Linda & Langford, Sarah. 2008. (Grandfather's Story Cloth Ser.). 32p. (J). (gr. 2-4). 16.95 *(978-1-885008-34-3(1),* Shen's Bks.) Lee & Low Bks., Inc.

Louhi, Kristiina. Tundra Mouse Mountain. Jalonen, Riitta. Ledgard, J. M., tr. from FIN. 2006. (Picture books from around the World Seri Ser.). (ENG.). 56p. (J). (gr. k-2). 20.95 *(978-1-905341-05-4(9))* WingedChariot Pr. GBR. Dist: Independent Pubs. Group.

Louie, Ron. Animals Sing Aloha. Arita, Vera. 2009. (ENG.). 20p. (J). (gr. -1-1). bds. 7.95 *(978-1-933067-29-2(2))* Beachhouse Publishing, LLC.

Louie, Wes. Track Star! Montgomery, R. A. 2009. (Choose Your Own Adventure Ser.: No. 31). (ENG.). 144p. (J). (gr. 4-8). pap. 6.99 *(978-1-933390-31-4(X))* Chooseco LLC.

—U. N. Adventure: Mission to Molowa. Montgomery, Ramsey. 2009. (ENG.). 144p. (J). (gr. 4-8). pap. 6.99 *(978-1-933390-32-1(8))* Chooseco LLC.

—Zombie Penpal. McMurtry, Ken. 2010. (ENG.). 144p. (J). (gr. 4-8). pap. 7.99 *(978-1-933390-34-5(4))* Chooseco LLC.

Louie, Wes & Cannella, Marco. Island of Time. Montgomery, R. A. 2009. (ENG.). 144p. (J). (gr. 4-8). pap. 6.99 *(978-1-933390-28-4(X))* Chooseco LLC.

Louis, Catherine. Liu & the Bird: A Journey in Chinese Calligraphy. Kazeroid, Sibylle, tr. 2006. 40p. (J). (gr. -1-3). 16.95 *(978-0-7358-2050-0(3))* North-South Bks., Inc.

—What the Rat Told Me. Sellier, Marie. 2014. 32p. (J). (gr. k-3). 7.95 *(978-0-7358-4158-1(6))* North-South Bks., Inc.

Louis, Catherine & Fei, Wang. Legend of the Chinese Dragon. Sellier, Marie. Kazeroid, Sibylle, tr. 2008. 40p. (J). (gr. -1-3). 15.95 *(978-0-7358-2152-1(6))* North-South Bks., Inc.

Louis, Rhead. Treasure Island & Kidnapped (Unabridged & Fully Illustrated) Stevenson, Robert Louis. 2020. (ENG.). 418p. (J). ***(978-1-78943-101-8(8));*** pap. ***(978-1-78943-100-1(X))*** Benediction Classics.

—Treasure Island (Unabridged & Fully Illustrated) Stevenson, Robert Louis. 2020. (ENG.). 198p. (J). pap. ***(978-1-78943-102-5(6))*** Benediction Classics.

—Treasure Island (Unabridged & Fully Illustrated) Stevenson, Robert Louis. 2020. (ENG.). 200p. (J). ***(978-1-78943-103-2(4))*** Benediction Classics.

Louise, Cristina & McIlroy, Michelle. Where Is Paco Now? Louise, Cristina & McIlroy, Michelle. 2012. (SPA & ENG.). (J). *(978-1-934370-26-1(6),* Campanita Bks.) Editorial Campana.

Louise, Finnoula. Cookies Cookies: A Year of Holiday Treats. Louise, Finnoula. 2011. 20p. (J). bds. 11.95 *(978-0-9827951-1-8(4))* Woodglen Publishing LLC.

Louise, Karen. The Deep. Winton, Tim. 32p. (YA). pap. 13.95 *(978-1-86368-210-7(4))* Fremantle Pr. AUS. Dist: Independent Pubs. Group.

Louissaint, Louis. Makso. Heurtelou, Maude. (CRP.). 24p. (J). (gr. k-2). pap. 8.50 *(978-1-58432-005-0(2))* Educa Vision Inc.

loundraw. I Want to Eat Your Pancreas (Light Novel) Sumino, Yoru. 2018. (ENG.). 260p. (YA). pap. 14.99 *(978-1-64275-033-1(6),* 900199469) Seven Seas Entertainment, LLC.

Lounsbury, Jennica. Ella's Umbrella. Shannon Strand, Courtney. 2020. (ENG.). 32p. (J). (gr. k-2). 18.99 ***(978-1-7342789-0-3(0))*** Kicky Cane Pr.

Louren�o, Estrela. Sasha & Puck & the Brew for Brainwash. Nayeri, Daniel. 2020. (Elixir Fixers Ser.). (ENG.). 128p. (J). (gr. 1-5). pap. 5.99 ***(978-0-8075-7257-3(8),*** 0807572578) Whitman, Albert & Co.

Lourenco, Estrela. Sasha & Puck & the Brew for Brainwash. Nayeri, Daniel. 2020. (Elixir Fixers Ser.). (ENG.). 128p. (J). (gr. 1-5). 14.99 ***(978-0-8075-7246-7(2),*** 807572462) Whitman, Albert & Co.

Lourenço, Estrela. Sasha & Puck & the Cure for Courage. Nayeri, Daniel. 2019. (Elixir Fixers Ser.: 3). (ENG.). 128p. (J). (gr. 1-5). 14.99 *(978-0-8075-7245-0(4),* 807572454) Whitman, Albert & Co.

Lourenco, Estrela. Sasha & Puck & the Cure for Courage. Nayeri, Daniel. 2020. (Elixir Fixers Ser.). (ENG.). 128p. (J). (gr. 1-5). pap. 5.99 ***(978-0-8075-7255-9(1),*** 807572551) Whitman, Albert & Co.

Lourido, Alfonso. Sending a Pig to Grammy. Moore, Rose et al. Moore, Rose, ed. 2019. (ENG.). 40p. pap. 16.95 *(978-0-9965097-1-8(2))* BookBaby.

Lovas, Pamela. Science Fair Crisis. Fridolfs, Derek. 2019. (DC Comics: Secret Hero Society Ser.: 4). (ENG.). 176p. (J). (gr. 3-7). 12.99 *(978-1-338-27328-1(0))* Scholastic, Inc.

Lovass-Nagy, Nicole. I Wish I Had a Tail. Lepage, Michaele L. 2008. 20p. pap. 12.49 *(978-1-4343-4721-3(4))* AuthorHouse.

Love, Dakota & Love, Rose. I Love Our Little Garden. Love, Rose. 2019. (ENG.). 30p. (J). pap. 11.99 ***(978-1-6797-2551-7(3))*** Independently Published.

Love, Ethan C. Max & Me. Love, Ethan C. 2018. (ENG.). 28p. (J). (gr. 3-5). pap. *(978-0-6480675-7-3(2))* Nenge Books.

Love, Jeffrey Alan. Norse Myths: Tales of Odin, Thor & Loki. Crossley-Holland, Kevin. 2017. (ENG.). 240p. (J). (gr. 5). 27.99 *(978-0-7636-9500-2(9))* Candlewick Pr.

Love, Jeremy, et al. Frontline Vol. 4: Oneshots. McKeever, Sean et al. 2004. 160p. (YA). pap. 15.95 *(978-1-932796-16-2(9))* Devil's Due Publishing, Inc.

Love, Jessica. Juli�n Is a Mermaid. Love, Jessica. 2018. (ENG.). 40p. (J). (gr. -1-3). 16.99 *(978-0-7636-9045-8(7))* Candlewick Pr.

Love, Judy. The Baby Shower. Bunting, Eve. 2007. 28p. (J). (gr. -1-2). 15.95 *(978-1-58089-139-4(X))* Charlesbridge Publishing, Inc.

—The Big Test. Danneberg, Julie. 2011. (Julie Danneberg Ser.). 32p. (J). (gr. k-2). 22.44 *(978-1-58089-360-2(0))* Charlesbridge Publishing, Inc.

Love, Judy. Big Test Jitters. Danneberg, Julie. 2020. (Jitters Ser.: 6). 32p. (J). (gr. 1-4). pap. 7.99 ***(978-1-58089-073-1(3))*** Charlesbridge Publishing, Inc.

Love, Judy. Can I Bring My Pterodactyl to School, Ms. Johnson? Grambling, Lois G. 2006. (Prehistoric Pets Ser.: 1). 32p. (J). (gr. k-3). 7.95 *(978-1-58089-141-7(1))* Charlesbridge Publishing, Inc.

—Can I Bring Saber to New York, Ms. Mayor? Grambling, Lois G. 2014. (Prehistoric Pets Ser.: 3). 32p. (J). (gr. k-3). 17.95 *(978-1-58089-570-5(0))* Charlesbridge Publishing, Inc.

—Can I Bring Woolly to the Library, Ms. Reeder? Grambling, Lois G. 2012. 32p. (J). 16.95 *(978-1-60734-074-4(7))*; (Prehistoric Pets Ser.: 2). pap. 7.95 *(978-1-58089-282-7(5))*; (Prehistoric Pets Ser.: 2). lib. bdg. 16.95 *(978-1-58089-281-0(7))* Charlesbridge Publishing, Inc.

—Field-Trip Fiasco. Danneberg, Julie. 2015. (Jitters Ser.: 5). 32p. (J). (gr. k-3). 16.95 *(978-1-58089-671-9(5))* Charlesbridge Publishing, Inc.

—First Year Letters. Danneberg, Julie. 2014. 32p. pap. 7.00 *(978-1-61003-320-6(5))* Center for the Collaborative Classroom.

—First Year Letters. Danneberg, Julie. 2003. (Mrs. Hartwell's Classroom Adventures Ser.: 3). 32p. (J). (gr. 1-4). 16.95 *(978-1-58089-084-7(9))*; pap. 7.95 *(978-1-58089-085-4(7))* Charlesbridge Publishing, Inc.

—Jake's 100th Day of School, 1 vol. Laminack, Lester L. (ENG.). 32p. (J). (gr. k-3). 2008. pap. 8.95 *(978-1-56145-463-1(X))*; 2006. 16.95 *(978-1-56145-355-9(2))* Peachtree Publishing Co. Inc.

—Last Day Blues. Danneberg, Julie. 2006. (Jitters Ser.: 2). (ENG.). 32p. (J). (gr. k-3). 7.99 *(978-1-58089-104-2(7))* Charlesbridge Publishing, Inc.

Love, Judy, et al. Poetry Speaks to Children. Paschen, Elise. Collins, Billy et al, eds. 2005. (Poetry Speaks Experience Ser.: 0). (ENG.). 112p. (gr. k-3). 19.95 *(978-1-4022-0329-9(2)*, Sourcebooks MediaFusion) Sourcebooks, Inc.

Love, Judy. Que Nervios! el Primer Dia de Escuela. Danneberg, Julie. 2006. (Jitters Ser.). 32p. (J). (gr. k-3). pap. 7.99 *(978-1-58089-126-4(8))* Charlesbridge Publishing, Inc.

Love, Judy, jt. illus. see Cartwright, Shannon.

Love, Mike. Build Your Own Dinosaur Museum, 1 vol. Jacoby, Jenny & Lonely Planet Kids. 2018. (Build Your Own Ser.). (ENG.). 24p. (J). (gr. 1-3). 18.99 *(978-1-78868-128-5(2))* Lonely Planet Global Ltd. IRL. Dist: Hachette Bk. Group.

Love, Mike, et al. Let's Explore... City, 1 vol. Webb, Christina et al. 2017. (Let's Explore Ser.). (ENG.). 48p. (J). (gr. 1-3). pap. 9.99 *(978-1-78657-230-1(3)*, 5380) Lonely Planet Global Ltd. IRL. Dist: Hachette Bk. Group.

—Let's Explore... Desert, 1 vol. Webb, Christina et al. 2017. (Let's Explore Ser.). (ENG.). 48p. (J). (gr. 1-3). pap. 9.99 *(978-1-78657-314-8(8)*, 5400) Lonely Planet Global Ltd. IRL. Dist: Hachette Bk. Group.

Love, Mike. Sherlock Holmes. Doyle, Arthur Conan. 2014. 46p. (J). *(978-1-4351-5822-1(9))* Barnes & Noble, Inc.

Love, Mike, jt. illus. see Farkus, Ruldolf.

Love, Mike, jt. illus. see Lauritano, Michael.

Love, Rose, jt. illus. see Love, Dakota.

Love, Willie a. The Pawsome Christmas Surprise. Pugh-Love, Val. 2015. (ENG.). (J). (gr. k-6). pap. 15.99 *(978-0-692-68624-9(X))* Pugh, Val.

Loveheart, Lucy & Clibbon, Lucy. The Fairyspotters Guide. Meg, Magic. 2007. (ENG.). 24p. (J). (gr. 2-4). *(978-1-84089-297-0(8))* Zero to Ten, Ltd.

Lovell, Edith. Sheep of Many Colors: Coloring Book. Guzman, Maria Del C. 2013. 26p. pap. 5.99 *(978-0-9855639-4-3(X))* Guzman, Maria del C.

Lovell, Katie. Build a Picture Cars Sticker Book. Brooks, Felicity. 2013. (Build a Picture Sticker Bks.). (ENG.). (J). (gr. -1-3). 6.99 *(978-0-7945-3376-2(0)*, Usborne) EDC Publishing.

—Build a Picture Tractors Sticker Book. Brooks, Felicity. ed. 2013. (Build a Picture Sticker Bks). 24p. (J). pap. 6.99 *(978-0-7945-3319-9(1)*, Usborne) EDC Publishing.

—Christmas Stencil Cards. 2007. (Christmas Stencil Cards Ser.). 16p. (J). 9.99 *(978-0-7945-1896-7(6)*, Usborne) EDC Publishing.

—Dinosaur Fun. Watt, Fiona. 2009. (Preschool Activities Ser.). 24p. (J). (gr. -1). spiral bd. 12.99 *(978-0-7945-2133-2(9)*, Usborne) EDC Publishing.

Lovell, Katie, jt. illus. see Harrison, Erica.

Lovelock, Brian. Construction. Sutton, Sally. (J). 2015. (ENG.). 32p. (-k). bds. 7.99 *(978-0-7636-7975-0(5))*; 2014. 34p. (gr. -1-2). 16.99 *(978-0-7636-7325-3(0))* Candlewick Pr.

—Construction Board Book Boxed Set. Sutton, Sally. 2016. (ENG.). (J). (-k). bds. 19.99 *(978-0-7636-9260-5(3))* Candlewick Pr.

—Construir una Carretera (Roadwork) Sutton, Sally. 2013. (SPA.). 28p. (J). (-k). bds. 7.99 *(978-0-7636-6494-7(4))* Candlewick Pr.

—Construyendo. Sutton, Sally. 2015. (SPA.). 32p. (J). (gr. -1-2). bds. 6.99 *(978-0-7636-7976-7(3))* Candlewick Pr.

—Demolicion. Sutton, Sally. 2014. (SPA.). 22p. (J). (-k). bds. 6.99 *(978-0-7636-7031-3(6))* Candlewick Pr.

—Demolition. Sutton, Sally. (ENG.). (J). 2014. 22p. (-k). bds. 7.99 *(978-0-7636-6493-0(6))*; 2012. 32p. (gr. -1-2). 16.99 *(978-0-7636-5830-4(8))* Candlewick Pr.

—Did My Mother Do That? Holt, Sharon. 2010. (ENG.). 32p. (J). (gr. -1-2). 15.99 *(978-0-7636-4685-1(7))* Candlewick Pr.

—Dig, Dump, Roll. Sutton, Sally. (ENG.). (J). 2019. 28p. (-k). bds. 7.99 *(978-1-5362-0902-0(3))*; 2018. 32p. (gr. -1-2). 16.99 *(978-1-5362-0391-2(2))* Candlewick Pr.

—Flight of the Honey Bee. Huber, Raymond. (Read & Wonder Ser.). (ENG.). 32p. (J). (gr. -1-2). 2015. 7.99 *(978-0-7636-7648-3(9))*; 2013. 16.99 *(978-0-7636-6760-3(9))* Candlewick Pr.

—Flight of the Honey Bee. Huber, Raymond. 2015. (Read & Wonder Ser.). (ENG.). (J). (gr. -1-2). lib. bdg. 17.60 *(978-1-62765-713-6(4))* Perfection Learning Corp.

—Gecko. Huber, Raymond. 2019. (ENG.). 32p. (J). (gr. k-4). 16.99 *(978-0-7636-9885-0(7))* Candlewick Pr.

—Roadwork. Sutton, Sally. (ENG.). (J). 2017. 32p. 7.99 *(978-0-7636-9870-6(9))*; 2011. 28p. bds. 7.99 *(978-0-7636-4653-0(9))* Candlewick Pr.

—Wheels. Sutton, Sally. 2020. (ENG.). 32p. (J). (-k). 16.99 *(978-1-5362-1108-5(7))* Candlewick Pr.

Loveridge, Matt. The Art Show Attacks! Chabert, Jack. 2018. (Eerie Elementary Ser.: 9). (ENG.). 96p. (J). (gr. 1-3). lib. bdg. 15.99 *(978-1-338-18198-2(X))* Scholastic, Inc.

—The Art Show Attacks! A Branches Book. Chabert, Jack. 2018. (Eerie Elementary Ser.: 9). (ENG.). 96p. (J). (gr. 1-3). pap. 4.99 *(978-1-338-18197-5(1))* Scholastic, Inc.

—Can You Find? An ABC Book. McKay, Sindy. 2016. (We Both Read Ser.). (ENG.). 44p. (J). (gr. k-3). 17.44 *(978-1-4844-8052-6(X))* Treasure Bay, Inc.

—Can You Find?/Puedes Hallario? Spanish/English Bilingual (We Both Read - Level Pk-K) An ABC Book. McKay, Sindy. 2016. (We Both Read - Level Pk -K Ser.). (ENG & SPA.). (J). pap. 4.99 *(978-1-60115-072-1(5))* Treasure Bay, Inc.

—Classes Are Canceled! Chabert, Jack. 2017. (Eerie Elementary Ser.: 7). (ENG.). 96p. (J). (gr. 1-3). 24.99 *(978-1-338-18183-8(1))*; pap. 4.99 *(978-1-338-18180-7(7))* Scholastic, Inc.

—Dinosaur Disaster. Lubar, David. 2013. (Looniverse Ser.: 3). (ENG.). 96p. (J). (gr. 1-3). 15.99 *(978-0-545-49605-6(5))* Scholastic, Inc.

—The End of Orson Eerie? Chabert, Jack. 2019. (Eerie Elementary Ser.: 10). (ENG.). 96p. (J). (gr. 1-3). pap. 4.99 *(978-1-338-31856-2(X))* Scholastic, Inc.

—The Hall Monitors Are Fired! Chabert, Jack. 2018. (Eerie Elementary Ser.: 8). (ENG.). 96p. (J). (gr. 1-3). pap. 4.99 *(978-1-338-18188-3(2))*; lib. bdg. 24.99 *(978-1-338-18191-3(2))* Scholastic, Inc.

—Meltdown Madness. Lubar, David. 2013. (Looniverse Ser.: 2). (ENG.). 96p. (J). (gr. 1-3). pap. 4.99 *(978-0-545-49604-9(7))* Scholastic, Inc.

Loveridge, Matt, et al. Pucks, Clubs, & Baseball Gloves: Reading & Writing Sports Poems, 1 vol. Ipcizade, Catherine et al. 2014. (Poet in You Ser.). (ENG.). 32p. (J). (gr. 2-4). pap. 9.95 *(978-1-4795-2947-6(8))*; lib. bdg. 27.99 *(978-1-4795-2196-8(5))* Capstone. (Picture Window Bks.).

Loveridge, Matt. Stranger Things. Lubar, David. 2013. (Looniverse Ser.: 1). (ENG.). 96p. (J). (gr. 1-3). pap. 4.99 *(978-0-545-49602-5(0))* Scholastic, Inc.

—This Old Band. Wissinger, Tamera Will. 2014. (ENG.). 32p. (J). (gr. -1-k). 16.95 *(978-1-62873-595-6(3)*, Sky Pony Pr.) Skyhorse Publishing Co., Inc.

Lovero, Ernesto. Aftermath of World War II: Bridges Edition. Sherman, Patrice. 2015. (Prime Plus Ser.). (YA). (gr. 6-8). pap. *(978-1-4900-1954-3(5))* Benchmark Education Co.

—Aftermath of World War II: Bridges Edition Set of 6 with Common Core Indicators. Sherman, Patrice. 2015. (Prime Plus Ser.). (YA). (gr. 6-8). 69.00 net. *(978-1-4900-2050-1(0))* Benchmark Education Co.

—Causes of World War II: Bridges Edition. Burgan, Michael. 2015. (Prime Plus Ser.). (YA). (gr. 6-8). pap. *(978-1-4900-1952-9(9))* Benchmark Education Co.

—Causes of World War II: Bridges Edition Set of 6 with Common Core Indicators. Burgan, Michael. 2015. (Prime Plus Ser.). (YA). (gr. 6-8). 69.00 net. *(978-1-4900-2048-8(9))* Benchmark Education Co.

Lovero, Ernesto, jt. illus. see Nowakoski, Marcin.

Lovesin, Polona. I Love You Because ... Joyce, Melanie. 2016. (ENG.). 24p. (J). (gr. -1-1). 16.99 *(978-1-4998-0212-2(9))* Little Bee Books Inc.

Lovett, Louise Sheppa. A Happy Day. Lovett, Louise Sheppa, . 2008. 32p. (J). 18.50 *(978-0-9793419-0-8(6))* Tish & Co. LLC.

Lovett, Nate. All Fired up! (Paw Patrol) Golden Books Staff. 2016. (ENG.). 64p. (J). (gr. -1-2). pap. 4.99 *(978-1-101-93167-7(1)*, Golden Bks.) Random Hse. Children's Bks.

—All Paws on Deck! (Paw Patrol) Golden Books. 2014. (ENG.). 128p. (J). (gr. -1-2). pap. 7.99 *(978-0-385-38446-9(7)*, Golden Bks.) Random Hse. Children's Bks.

—Daring Dino Rescue! (Rusty Rivets) Behling, Steve. 2017. (Big Golden Book Ser.). (ENG.). 48p. (J). (gr. -1-2). 9.99 *(978-1-5247-1678-3(2)*, Golden Bks.) Random Hse. Children's Bks.

—Fix It up! (Rusty Rivets) Golden Books. 2017. (Deluxe Paint Box Book Ser.). (ENG.). 128p. (J). (gr. -1-2). pap. 7.99 *(978-1-5247-1674-5(X)*, Golden Bks.) Random Hse. Children's Bks.

Lovett, Nate. Let's Visit the Doctor (PAW Patrol) Random House. 2020. (Pictureback(R) Ser.). (ENG.). 24p. (J). (gr. -1-2). 5.99 ***(978-0-593-17271-1(X)***, Random Hse. Bks. for Young Readers) Random Hse. Children's Bks.

Lovett, Nate. Mission Paw. Sullivan, Steve & Guerdat, Andy. 2017. 24p. (J). *(978-1-5182-4195-6(6))* Random Hse., Inc.

—Mission PAW (PAW Patrol) Random House. 2017. (Step into Reading Ser.). (ENG.). 24p. (J). (gr. -1-1). pap. 4.99 *(978-1-5247-6413-5(2)*, Random Hse. Bks. for Young Readers) Random Hse. Children's Bks.

—Nickelodeon PAW Patrol: Pups Save Adventure Bay! 2019. (ENG.). 10p. (J). (gr. -1-k). bds. 9.99 *(978-0-7944-4236-1(6)*, Studio Fun International) Printers Row Publishing Group.

—Night of the Ghost Pirate (Paw Patrol) Golden Books. 2015. (ENG.). 64p. (J). (gr. -1-2). pap. 4.99 *(978-0-553-52390-4(2)*, Golden Bks.) Random Hse. Children's Bks.

—Potty Patrol (PAW Patrol) Random House. 2020. (ENG.). 22p. (J). (— 1). bds. 9.99 *(978-0-593-12258-7(5)*, Random Hse. Bks. for Young Readers) Random Hse. Children's Bks.

—Puppy Dance Party! (PAW Patrol) James, Hollis. 2019. (Pictureback(R) Ser.). (ENG.). 24p. (J). (gr. -1-2). 5.99 *(978-1-9848-4935-9(2)*, Random Hse. Bks. for Young Readers) Random Hse. Children's Bks.

—Sea Patrol to the Rescue! (PAW Patrol) Random House. 2018. (Pictureback(R) Ser.). (ENG.). 24p. (J). (gr. -1-2). pap. 5.99 *(978-1-5247-6875-1(8)*, Random Hse. Bks. for Young Readers) Random Hse. Children's Bks.

Lovett, Nate, jt. illus. see Golden Books Staff.

Lovett, Nate, jt. illus. see Golden Books.

Lovett, Nathaniel, jt. illus. see Golden Books Staff.

Lovett, Tracy M. Buck's Rodeo. Lovett, Tracy M. 2012. 470p. pap. 16.50 *(978-0-9819736-6-1(3))* Inclement Pr.

Lovice, Ommi. Truth Series: Christmas Tree, Not for Me!; Ho, Ho, Ho, Santa Must Go!; the Truth about Christmas. Thompson, T. F. 2018. (Truth Ser.: Vol. 1). (ENG.). 36p. (J). (gr. k-6). 18.00 *(978-0-692-16998-8(9))* Milner, Ommi.

Løvlie, Jenny. The Girls. Ace, Lauren. 2019. (ENG.). 32p. (J). (gr. -1-2). 17.99 *(978-1-9848-9651-3(2)*, Rodale Kids) Random Hse. Children's Bks.

—In My Heart. Porter, Mackenzie. 2020. (ENG.). 26p. (J). (gr. -1). bds. 7.99 *(978-1-5344-5433-0(0)*, Little Simon) Little Simon.

Lovlie, Jenny. Kitty & the Moonlight Rescue. Harrison, Paula. 2019. (Kitty Ser.: 1). (ENG.). 128p. (J). (gr. 1-5). 15.99 *(978-0-06-293472-7(4))*; pap. 5.99 *(978-0-06-293471-0(6))* HarperCollins Pubs. (Greenwillow Bks.).

—Kitty & the Sky Garden Adventure. Harrison, Paula. 2020. (Kitty Ser.: 3). (ENG.). 128p. (J). (gr. 1-5). 15.99 *(978-0-06-293549-6(6))*; pap. 5.99 *(978-0-06-293548-9(8))* HarperCollins Pubs. (Greenwillow Bks.).

—Kitty & the Tiger Treasure. Harrison, Paula. 2019. (Kitty Ser.: 2). (ENG.). 128p. (J). (gr. 1-5). 15.99 *(978-0-06-293476-5(7))*; pap. 5.99 *(978-0-06-293474-1(0))* HarperCollins Pubs. (Greenwillow Bks.).

Lovlie, Jenny. Kitty & the Treetop Chase. Harrison, Paula. 2020. (Kitty Ser.: 4). (ENG.). 128p. (J). (gr. 1-5). 15.99 ***(978-0-06-293577-9(1))***; pap. 5.99 ***(978-0-06-293576-2(3))*** HarperCollins Pubs. (Greenwillow Bks.).

—The Mouse Before Christmas. Turner, Tracey. 2020. (ENG.). 40p. (J). ***(978-1-5037-5495-9(2)***, bc86b9b5-1cd9-4163-9fae-bb3afc7b7daf, Sunbird Books) Phoenix International Publications, Inc.

Lovsin, Polona. Daddies Are Awesome. Costain, Meredith. (ENG.). (J). 2017. 28p. bds. 7.99 *(978-1-250-10720-6(2)*, 900164822); 2016. 32p. 17.99 *(978-1-62779-452-7(2)*, 900151265) Holt, Henry & Co. (Holt, Henry & Co. Bks. For Young Readers).

—I Love You, Daddy: Full of Love & Hugs! Joyce, Melanie. 2016. (ENG.). 26p. (J). bds. 7.99 *(978-1-78440-562-5(0))* Igloo Bks. GBR. Dist: Simon & Schuster, Inc.

—I Love You, Mommy: Full of Love & Hugs! Joyce, Melanie. 2014. (ENG.). 26p. (J). bds. 7.99 *(978-1-78440-561-8(2))* Igloo Bks. GBR. Dist: Simon & Schuster, Inc.

—Little One, God Loves You, 1 vol. Hilliker, Amy Warren. 2016. (ENG.). 14p. (J). bds. 6.99 *(978-0-310-75307-0(4))* Zonderkidz.

—Little One, God Loves You Gift Set, 1 vol. Hilliker, Amy Warren. 2020. 14p. (J). 19.99 *(978-0-310-76858-6(6))* Zonderkidz.

—Little One, God Made You Special, 1 vol. Hilliker, Amy Warren. 2016. (ENG.). 14p. (J). bds. 8.99 *(978-0-310-75300-1(7))* Zonderkidz.

—The Littlest Bunny. Shields, Gillian. 2015. 32p. (J). *(978-1-4351-5967-9(5))* Barnes & Noble, Inc.

—Mi Abuela. Kraljic, Helena. 2018. (SPA.). 32p. (J). 18.95 *(978-84-9145-132-7(3)*, Picarona Editorial) Ediciones Obelisco ESP. Dist: Spanish Pubs., LLC.

—Mi Abuelo. Kraljic, Helena. 2018. (SPA.). 32p. (J). 18.95 *(978-84-9145-131-0(5)*, Picarona Editorial) Ediciones Obelisco ESP. Dist: Spanish Pubs., LLC.

—Mommies Are Amazing. Costain, Meredith. 2018. (ENG.). 28p. (J). bds. 7.99 *(978-1-250-10721-3(0)*, 900164823, Holt, Henry & Co. Bks. For Young Readers) Holt, Henry & Co.

Low, Alan M. Black Tortoise & the Dynasty Dragon. Wacker, Eileen. 2012. (Fujimini Adventure Ser.: Vol. 5). (ENG.). 40p. (J). (gr. -1-3). 10.99 *(978-1-4675-1741-6(0))* Oncekids.

Low, Dane. Alex & the Immortals. Dunn, Tracy. Garnsworthy, Marlo, ed. 2019. (Immortal Realms Ser.: Vol. 1). (ENG.). 216p. (J). pap. 9.99 ***(978-1-6786-2897-0(2))*** Independently Published.

Low, J. H. The Hyena & the Monster. Low, J. H. 2016. (ENG.). 32p. 10.00 *(978-981-4721-69-1(7))* Marshall Cavendish International (Asia) Private Ltd. SGP. Dist: National Bk. Network.

—The Lazy Hyena. Low, J. H. 2016. (ENG.). 32p. 10.00 *(978-981-4721-70-7(0))* Marshall Cavendish International (Asia) Private Ltd. SGP. Dist: National Bk. Network.

—Lost in the Gardens. Low, J. H. 2015. (ENG.). 48p. 10.00 *(978-981-4677-10-3(8))* Marshall Cavendish International (Asia) Private Ltd. SGP. Dist: National Bk. Network.

—There Is Nothing Buried Here. Low, J. H. 2016. (ENG.). 32p. 10.00 *(978-981-4721-67-7(0))* Marshall Cavendish International (Asia) Private Ltd. SGP. Dist: National Bk. Network.

—A Thief in the Night. Low, J. H. 2016. (ENG.). 32p. 10.00 *(978-981-4721-68-4(9))* Marshall Cavendish International (Asia) Private Ltd. SGP. Dist: National Bk. Network.

—The Visitor from Far Far Away. Low, J. H. 2016. (ENG.). 32p. 10.00 *(978-981-4721-71-4(9))* Marshall Cavendish International (Asia) Private Ltd. SGP. Dist: National Bk. Network.

Low, Stephen. A Dog & His Bone. Brock, Mister. 2018. (ENG.). 42p. (J). pap. 13.99 *(978-1-948026-18-5(X))* Write Integrity Pr.

Low, William. Me & Momma & Big John. Rockliff, Mara. 2012. 32p. (J). (gr. -1-2). 16.99 *(978-0-7636-4359-1(9))* Candlewick Pr.

—The Sinking of the Vasa: A Shipwreck of Titanic Proportions. Freedman, Russell. 2018. (ENG.). 44p. (J). 18.99 *(978-1-62779-866-2(8)*, 900161274, Holt, Henry & Co. Bks. For Young Readers) Holt, Henry & Co.

—Young Fu of the Upper Yangtze. Lewis, Elizabeth Foreman. 2008. (ENG.). 320p. (YA). (gr. 5-9). pap. 8.99 *(978-0-312-38007-6(0)*, 900050531) Square Fish.

Low, William. Henry & the Kite Dragon. Low, William, tr. Hall, Bruce Edward & Hall, Bruce. 2004. 40p. (J). (gr. 1-4). 17.99 *(978-0-399-23727-0(5)*, Philomel Bks.) Penguin Young Readers Group.

Low, William & Cobalt Illustrations Studio Staff. Daytime Nighttime. Low, William & Cobalt Illustrations Studio Staff. 2015. (ENG.). 28p. (J). (gr. -1-3). bds. 7.99 *(978-1-62779-172-4(8)*, 900139185, Holt, Henry & Co. Bks. For Young Readers) Holt, Henry & Co.

—Feathered Dinosaurs. Guiberson, Brenda Z. 2016. (ENG.). 40p. (J). 17.99 *(978-0-8050-9828-0(3)*, 9780805098280, Holt, Henry & Co. Bks. For Young Readers) Holt, Henry & Co.

—The Last Days of Jesus: His Life & Times. O'Reilly, Bill. 2014. (ENG.). 320p. (J). (gr. 5-12). 19.99 *(978-0-8050-9877-8(1)*, 9780805098778, Holt, Henry & Co. Bks. For Young Readers) Holt, Henry & Co.

—Old Penn Station. Low, William & Cobalt Illustrations Studio Staff. 2007. (ENG.). 40p. (J). (gr. k-4). 19.99 *(978-0-8050-7925-8(4)*, 900031604, Holt, Henry & Co. Bks. For Young Readers) Holt, Henry & Co.

—Los Últimos Días de Jesús. O'Reilly, Bill. Uxó, Carlos, tr. 2015.Tr. of Last Days of Jesus. (SPA.). 320p. (J). (gr. 5). 25.99 *(978-1-62779-278-3(3)*, 9781627792783, Holt, Henry & Co. Bks. For Young Readers) Holt, Henry & Co.

Lowe, David. Alphabet of Sports. Schwaeber, Barbie Heit. (Alphabet Bks.). (ENG.). 40p. 2011. (J). (gr. -1-3). 9.95 *(978-1-60727-446-9(9))*; 2009. 9.95 *(978-1-59249-994-6(5))*; 2008. (J). (gr. k-2). 15.95 *(978-1-59249-769-0(1))* Soundprints.

Lowe, Frank Allen. The King's Silverware. Riddle, Sharon Kay & Sanders, Nancy/Ida. 2007. 32p. (J). pap. 15.00 *(978-0-9761583-5-6(3))* Olive Leaf Pubns.

Lowe, Greg, photos by. Cook It in a Cup! Quick Meals & Treats Kids Can Cook in Silicone Cups. Myall, Julia. 2008. (ENG., 64p. (J). (gr. 1-9). 18.99 *(978-0-8118-5956-1(8))* Chronicle Bks. LLC.

Lowe, Hayley. A Time to Wean. Susan, Marlene. 2018. (ENG.). 28p. (J). pap. 11.99 *(978-0-692-08080-1(5))* Corolishine Bks.

Lowe, Isabel. The Truth at Last about the Little Red Hen. Price, Hugh. 2003. 16p. (J). pap. *(978-1-877228-19-3(2))* Steele Roberts Aotearoa Ltd.

Lowe, Jason, photos by. Fun Food. Rosenbaum, Stephanie. Williams, Chuck, ed. 2006. (ENG., 128p. 19.95 *(978-0-7432-7856-0(9)*, Free Pr.) Free Pr.

Lowe, Sylbil & Russ, Sylvia. I'm Just Like You: The Story of Women Girl. Worrell, Princess. 2018. (I'm Just Like You Ser.: Vol. 1). (ENG.). 30p. (J). pap. 15.00 ***(978-1-7270-6314-1(7))*** CreateSpace Independent Publishing Platform.

Lowe, Tony. Troggle the Troll. Falk, Nicholas. 2013. 48p. (J). (-k). pap. 11.99 *(978-1-74275-601-1(8))* Random Hse. Australia AUS. Dist: Independent Pubs. Group.

Lowe, Wes. Augustine of Hippo. Carr, Simonetta. 2009. (ENG.). 62p. (J). 18.00 *(978-1-60178-073-7(7))* Reformation Heritage Bks.

—Sarky Puddleboat. Branson, Eve. 2011. 44p. (J). 14.99 *(978-1-4520-9754-1(2)*, 1d1b72af-0c10-4df7-ba8f-0db2b62e1ebb) AuthorHouse.

Lowe, Wesley. Ajàyí Gb' Ìtum' Ìlù. ¿Ládò¿Ù, F¿Lák¿'. 2013. 34p. *(978-0-9866435-1-4(3))* Adubi Publishing.

—Ajayi lo Si Ile-Eko. Oladosu, Folake. 2018. (Ajayi Ser.: Vol. 2). (YOR.). 34p. (J). (gr. k-4). *(978-0-9866435-3-8(X))*; pap. *(978-0-9866435-2-1(1))* Adubi Publishing.

Lowe, Wesley. Ajayi lo Si Oko Isu. Oladosu, Folake. 2020. (Ajayi Ser.: Vol. 3). (YOR.). 34p. (J). (gr. k-4). ***(978-0-9866435-5-2(6))***; pap. ***(978-0-9866435-4-5(8))*** Adubi Publishing.

Lowe, Wesley. Alexander Trout's Amazing Adventure. Richardson, Steve. 2008. 75p. 16.95 *(978-0-9786422-2-8(8))* Impossible Dreams Publishing Co.

—Apollo 13: How Three Brave Astronauts Survived a Space Disaster. Zoehfeld, Kathleen Weidner. 2015. (Totally True Adventures Ser.). 112p. (J). (gr. 2-5). pap. 5.99 *(978-0-385-39125-2(0)*, Random Hse. Bks. for Young Readers) Random Hse. Children's Bks.

—Growing Trees. Stamper, Judith Bauer. 2010. (J). *(978-1-60617-127-1(5))* Teaching Strategies, LLC.

—The Race Around the World (Totally True Adventures) How Nellie Bly Chased an Impossible Dream... Castaldo, Nancy. 2015. (Totally True Adventures Ser.). (ENG.). 112p. (J). (gr. 2-5). 4.99 *(978-0-553-52278-5(7)*, Random Hse. Bks. for Young Readers) Random Hse. Children's Bks.

—The $25,000 Flight: How Lindbergh Set a Daring Record... Houran, Lori Haskins. 2014. (Totally True Adventures Ser.). 112p. (J). (gr. 2-5). 4.99 *(978-0-385-38284-7(7)*, Random Hse. Bks. for Young Readers) Random Hse. Children's Bks.

Lowell, Shelley. This Is the Land of Two Suns: Paintings & Poetry. Lowell, Shelley. 2000th ltd. ed. 2005. 32p. per. 20.00 *(978-0-9765344-0-2(1))* Lowell, Shelley.

Lowen, Lauren. Adjectives Say Incredible! Dahl, Michael. 2019. (Word Adventures: Parts of Speech Ser.). (ENG.). 32p. (J). (gr. k-3). pap. 7.95 *(978-1-5158-4060-2(3)*, 140054); lib. bdg. 27.99 *(978-1-5158-3871-5(4)*, 139590) Capstone. (Picture Window Bks.).

—Interjections Say Yay! Dahl, Michael. 2019. (Word Adventures: Parts of Speech Ser.). (ENG.). 32p. (J). (gr. k-3). pap. 7.95 *(978-1-5158-4108-1(1)*, 140146); lib. bdg. 27.99 *(978-1-5158-4100-5(6)*, 140140) Capstone. (Picture Window Bks.).

—Nouns Say What's That? Dahl, Michael. 2019. (Word Adventures: Parts of Speech Ser.). (ENG.). 32p. (J). (gr. k-3). pap. 7.95 *(978-1-5158-4058-9(1)*, 140052); lib. bdg.

27.99 (978-1-5158-3869-2(2), 139588) Capstone. (Picture Window Bks.).

—Pronouns Say You & Me! Dahl, Michael. 2019. (Word Adventures: Parts of Speech Ser.). (ENG.). 32p. (J). (gr. k-3). pap. 7.95 (978-1-5158-4105-0(7), 140143); lib. bdg. 27.99 (978-1-5158-4097-8(2), 140135) Capstone. (Picture Window Bks.).

Lowen, Lauren, jt. illus. see Chiodi, Maira Kistemann.

Lowenstein, Anna. Don't Call Me Cookie. Pasiadis, Vanessa. 2010. 178p. pap. 21.00 (978-1-60911-470-1(1), Strategic Bk. Publishing) Strategic Book Publishing & Rights Agency (SBPRA).

Lowenstein, Sallie. Sir Kyle & Lady Madeline. Lowenstein, Sallie, . 2007. 32p. (J). 18.95 (978-0-9658486-6-4(3)) Lion Stone Bks.

Lowenstein, Sallie. Waiting for Eugene. Lowenstein, Sallie. 2005. 208p. (J). 19.00 (978-0-9658486-5-7(5)) Lion Stone Bks.

Lowery, Mike. Ancient Egypt. Jennings, Ken. 2015. (Ken Jennings' Junior Genius Guides). (ENG.). 160p. (J). (gr. 3-5). 19.99 (978-1-4814-2953-5(1), Little Simon) Little Simon.

—Bubble in the Bathtub. Nesbø, Jo. Chace, Tara, tr. from NOR. 2011. (Doctor Proctor's Fart Powder Ser.). (ENG.). 432p. (J). (gr. 3-7). 17.99 (978-1-4169-7974-6(3), Aladdin) Simon & Schuster Children's Publishing.

—Bubble in the Bathtub. Nesbo, Jo. Chace, Tara F., tr. 2011. (Doctor Proctor's Fart Powder Ser.). (ENG.). 448p. (J). (gr. 3-7). pap. 7.99 (978-1-4169-7975-3(1), Aladdin) Simon & Schuster Children's Publishing.

—Chef Gino's Taste Test Challenge: 90 Winning Recipes That Any Kid Can Cook. Campagna, Gino. 2017. 192p. (J). (gr. 3-7). 18.99 (978-1-62336-886-9(3), 9781623368869, Rodale Kids) Random Hse. Children's Bks.

—Clever Hans: The True Story of the Counting, Adding, & Time-Telling Horse. Kokias, Kerri. 2020. 32p. (J). (gr. -1-3). 17.99 (978-0-525-51498-5(8), G.P. Putnam's Sons Books for Young Readers) Penguin Young Readers Group.

—The Day Dad Joined My Soccer Team. Fergus, Maureen. 2018. (ENG.). 32p. (J). (gr. -1-2). 16.99 (978-1-77138-654-8(1)) Kids Can Pr., Ltd. CAN. Dist: Hachette Bk. Group.

—Dinosaurs. Jennings, Ken. 2016. (Ken Jennings' Junior Genius Guides). (ENG.). 160p. (J). (gr. 3-5). pap. 7.99 (978-1-4814-2955-9(8), Little Simon) Little Simon.

—Doctor Proctor's Fart Powder. Nesbo, Jo. Chace, Tara F., tr. 2010. (Doctor Proctor's Fart Powder Ser.). (ENG.). 288p. (J). (gr. 3-7). pap. 7.99 (978-1-4169-7973-9(5), Aladdin) Simon & Schuster Children's Publishing.

—Doctor Proctor's Fart Powder, 1. Nesbø, Jo. Chace, Tara, tr. 2010. (Doctor Proctor's Fart Powder Ser.). (ENG.). 160p. (J). (gr. 4-6). 18.69 (978-1-4169-7972-2(7), Aladdin) Simon & Schuster Children's Publishing.

—Doctor Proctor's Fart Powder Collection: Doctor Proctor's Fart Powder; Bubble in the Bathtub; Who Cut the Cheese?; the Magical Fruit; Silent (but Deadly) Night. Nesbø, Jo. ed. 2018. (Doctor Proctor's Fart Powder Ser.). (ENG.). 1888p. (J). (gr. 3-7). pap. 40.99 (978-1-5344-1872-1(5), Aladdin) Simon & Schuster Children's Publishing.

—The Gingerbread Man & the Leprechaun Loose at School. Murray, Laura. 2018. (ENG.). 32p. (J). (-k). 17.99 (978-1-101-99694-2(3), G.P. Putnam's Sons Books for Young Readers) Penguin Young Readers Group.

—The Gingerbread Man Loose at Christmas. Murray, Laura & McPike, Elizabeth. 2015. 32p. (J). (gr. k-k). bds. 17.99 (978-0-399-16866-6(4), G.P. Putnam's Sons Books for Young Readers) Penguin Young Readers Group.

—The Gingerbread Man Loose in the School. Murray, Laura. 2011. 32p. (J). (gr. k-3). 16.99 (978-0-399-25052-1(2), G.P. Putnam's Sons Books for Young Readers) Penguin Young Readers Group.

—The Gingerbread Man Loose on the Fire Truck. Murray, Laura. 2013. 32p. (J). (gr. k-3). 17.99 (978-0-399-25779-7(9), G.P. Putnam's Sons Books for Young Readers) Penguin Young Readers Group.

—Greek Mythology. Jennings, Ken. 2014. (Ken Jennings' Junior Genius Guides). (ENG.). 160p. (J). (gr. 3-5). 12.99 (978-1-4814-2615-2(X)); 18.99 (978-1-4424-9849-5(8)); pap. 7.99 (978-1-4424-7330-0(4)) Little Simon. (Little Simon).

—How to Be a T. Rex. North, Ryan. 2018. (ENG.). 32p. (J). (gr. -1-3). 17.99 (978-0-399-18624-0(7), Dial Bks) Penguin Young Readers Group.

—How to Talk to Your Computer. Simon, Seymour. 2019. (Let's-Read-And-Find-Out Science 2 Ser.). (ENG.). 40p. (J). (gr. -1-3). 17.99 (978-0-06-249087-2(7)); pap. 7.99 (978-0-06-249086-5(9)) HarperCollins Pubs.

—The Human Body. Jennings, Ken. 2015. (Ken Jennings' Junior Genius Guides). (ENG.). 160p. (J). (gr. 3-5). pap. 9.99 (978-1-4814-0173-9(4), Little Simon) Little Simon.

—The Impossible Crime. Barnett, Mac. 2018. (Mac B. , Kid Spy Ser.: 2). (ENG.). 160p. (J). (gr. 2-5). 12.99 (978-1-338-14368-3(9), Orchard Bks.) Scholastic, Inc.

—Knot Cannot. Stone, Tiffany. 2020. 32p. (J). (gr. -1-3). 17.99 (978-0-7352-3080-4(3), Dial Bks) Penguin Young Readers Group.

—Mac Cracks the Code (Mac B. , Kid Spy #4) Barnett, Mac. 2019. (Mac B. , Kid Spy Ser.: 4). (ENG.). 176p. (J). (gr. 2-5). 12.99 (978-1-338-59423-2(0), Orchard Bks.) Scholastic, Inc.

—Mac Undercover. Barnett, Mac. 2018. (Mac B. , Kid Spy Ser.: 1). (ENG.). 160p. (J). (gr. 2-5). 12.99 (978-1-338-14359-1(X), Orchard Bks.) Scholastic, Inc.

—The Magical Fruit. Nesbø, Jo. Chace, Tara F., tr. from NOR. 2013. (Doctor Proctor's Fart Powder Ser.). (ENG.). 320p. (J). (gr. 3-7). 17.99 (978-1-4424-9342-1(9), Aladdin) Simon & Schuster Children's Publishing.

—Maps & Geography. Jennings, Ken. 2014. (Ken Jennings' Junior Genius Guides). (ENG.). 160p. (J). (gr. 3-5). pap. 7.99 (978-1-4424-7328-7(2), Little Simon) Little Simon.

—My Cat Book: A Keepsake Journal for My Pet. Running Press. 2018. 80p. (J). (gr. 2-17). pap. 12.99 (978-0-7624-9163-6(9), Running Pr. Kids) Running Pr.

—My Dog Book: A Keepsake Journal for My Pet. Running Press. 2018. 80p. (J). (gr. 2-17). pap. 12.99 (978-0-7624-9164-3(7), Running Pr. Kids) Running Pr.

—Random Body Parts: Gross Anatomy Riddles in Verse. Bulion, Leslie. (ENG.). 48p. (J). (gr. 3-6). 2019. pap. 7.95 (978-1-68263-103-4(6)); 2015. 14.95 (978-1-56145-737-3(X)) Peachtree Publishing Co. Inc.

—Silent (but Deadly) Night. Nesbø, Jo. 2017. (Doctor Proctor's Fart Powder Ser.). (ENG.). 368p. (J). (gr. 3-7). 17.99 (978-1-5344-0999-6(8), Aladdin) Simon & Schuster Children's Publishing.

—Silent (but Deadly) Night. Nesbo, Jo. 2018. (Doctor Proctor's Fart Powder Ser.). (ENG.). 368p. (J). (gr. 3-7). pap. 8.99 (978-1-5344-1000-8(7), Simon & Schuster/Paula Wiseman Bks.) Simon & Schuster/Paula Wiseman Bks.

—Simple Machines. Ward, D. J. 2015. (Let's-Read-And-Find-Out Science 2 Ser.). (ENG.). 40p. (J). (gr. -1-3). pap. 6.99 (978-0-06-232147-3(1)) HarperCollins Pubs.

—A Squiggly Story. Larsen, Andrew. 2016. (ENG.). 32p. (J). (gr. -1-2). 16.99 (978-1-77138-016-4(0)) Kids Can Pr., Ltd. CAN. Dist: Hachette Bk. Group.

—U. S. Presidents. Jennings, Ken. 2014. (Ken Jennings' Junior Genius Guides). (ENG.). 160p. (J). (gr. 3-5). pap. 7.99 (978-1-4424-7332-4(0), Little Simon) Little Simon.

—Unscripted by Lainey McBride. Howie, Betsy. 2012. 183p. (J). (978-0-545-39705-6(7)) Scholastic, Inc.

—The Way Downtown: Adventures in Public Transit. Gertsberg, Inna. 2017. (ENG.). 44p. (J). (gr. -1-3). 17.99 (978-1-77138-552-7(9)) Kids Can Pr., Ltd. CAN. Dist: Hachette Bk. Group.

—What Can a Crane Pick Up? Kai Dotlich, Rebecca. 2014. 28p. (J). (-k). bds. 6.99 (978-0-385-75383-8(7), Knopf Bks. for Young Readers) Random Hse. Children's Bks.

—Who Cut the Cheese? Nesbø, Jo. Chace, Tara, tr. from NOR. 2012. (Doctor Proctor's Fart Powder Ser.). (ENG.). 464p. (J). (gr. 3-7). 17.99 (978-1-4424-3307-6(8), Aladdin) Simon & Schuster Children's Publishing.

—Who Cut the Cheese? Nesbo, Jo. Chace, Tara F., tr. 2012. (Doctor Proctor's Fart Powder Ser.). (ENG.). 464p. (J). (gr. 3-7). pap. 8.99 (978-1-4424-3308-3(6), Aladdin) Simon & Schuster Children's Publishing.

Lowes, Tom. Casey's Four Holiday Celebrations. I.t. ed. 2003. 38p. (J). 16.95 (978-0-9722099-9-1(9), C4HC) Caseys World Bks.

—Casey's Unexpected Friend. Stormer, Kate. I.t. ed. 2003. 38p. (J). 16.95 (978-0-9722099-7-7(2), CUF) Caseys World Bks.

—The Rescue of Little Red. Stormer, Kate. 2005. 91p. (J). (gr. 3-5). per. 5.99 (978-0-9765872-0-0(3)) Caseys World Bks.

—A Stranger in Casey's World. Stormer, Kate. I.t. ed. 2004. 32p. (J). 16.95 (978-0-9647663-1-0(0)) Caseys World Bks.

—Teddy's TV Troubles. Cantor, Joanne. 2004. 36p. (J). mass mkt. 16.95 (978-0-9647663-7-2(X)) HenschelHAUS Publishing, Inc.

Lowrie, Derrick. Caught Red-Handed - Me Pescaron con Las Manos en la Maza. Smith, Vickie A. 2018. (MUL.). 68p. (J). pap. 16.95 (978-1-64140-977-3(0)) Christian Faith Publishing.

Lowry, Judith. Home to Medicine Mountain. Santiago, Chiori. 2013. (ENG.). 32p. (J). (gr. 1-18). pap. 12.95 (978-0-89239-176-9(6)) Lee & Low Bks., Inc.

Loxton, Daniel. Evolution: How We & All Living Things Came to Be. Loxton, Daniel. 2010. (ENG.). 56p. (J). (gr. 3-8). 18.95 (978-1-55453-430-2(5)) Kids Can Pr., Ltd. CAN. Dist: Hachette Bk. Group.

Loxton, Daniel & Smith, Jim W. W. Ankylosaur Attack. Loxton, Daniel. 2011. (Tales of Prehistoric Life Ser.). (ENG.). 32p. (J). (gr. -1-2). 16.95 (978-1-55453-631-3(6)) Kids Can Pr., Ltd. CAN. Dist: Hachette Bk. Group.

—Plesiosaur Peril, 0 vols. Loxton, Daniel. 2014. (Tales of Prehistoric Life Ser.). (ENG.). 32p. (J). (gr. -1-2). 16.95 (978-1-55453-633-7(2)) Kids Can Pr., Ltd. CAN. Dist: Hachette Bk. Group.

—Pterosaur Trouble. Loxton, Daniel. 2013. (Tales of Prehistoric Life Ser.). (ENG.). 32p. (J). (gr. -1-2). 16.95 (978-1-55453-632-0(4)) Kids Can Pr., Ltd. CAN. Dist: Hachette Bk. Group.

Loy, Jessica. Weird & Wild Animal Facts. Loy, Jessica. 2015. (ENG.). 40p. (J). (gr. -1-3). 17.99 (978-0-8050-7945-6(9), 900031889, Holt, Henry & Co. Bks. For Young Readers) Holt, Henry & Co.

Loy, Nikki. David & Goliath. Page, Nick & Page, Claire. 2006. (Read with Me (Make Believe Ideas) Ser.). 31p. (J). (gr. k-2). (978-1-84610-173-1(5)) Make Believe Ideas.

—The Good Samaritan. Page, Nick & Page, Claire. 2006. (Read with Me (Make Believe Ideas) Ser.). 31p. (J). (gr. k-2). (978-1-84610-174-8(3)) Make Believe Ideas.

—Read with Me Jonah the Moaner: Sticker Activity Book. Page, Nick & Page, Claire. 2006. (Read with Me (Make Believe Ideas) Ser.). 12p. (J). (gr. k-2). pap. (978-1-84610-183-0(2)) Make Believe Ideas.

Loyal Kids, Loyal. How to Be a Virus Warrior. The Parent-Child Dino Research Team, The Parent-Child. 2020. (ENG.). 32p. (J). (gr. -1-1). pap. 7.99 **(978-1-913639-25-9(8))** Little Steps Bks AUS. Dist: Lerner Publishing Group.

Loyd, Mark. Big Ben: A Little Known Story. Loyd, Mark. ed. 2005. (J). (978-0-9773317-1-0(7)) Too Fun Publishing.

Loza, Nicolle N. Babies Have All the Fun. Lis, Jen E. 2018. (ENG.). 38p. (J). pap. 11.99 (978-1-7325487-0-1(6)) Scholarly Hour.

Lozano, Alexis. Thump Thump. Montoya, Amanda. 2019. (ENG.). 30p. (J). pap. 14.99 (978-0-578-45106-0(9)) Montoya, Amanda.

Lozano, Andres. Animal Championships, 1 vol. Lonely Planet Kids & Baker, Kate. 2020. (ENG.). 16p. (J). (gr. 1-3). 18.99 (978-1-78868-929-8(1), Lonely Planet Kids) Lonely Planet Global Ltd. IRL. Dist: Hachette Bk. Group.

Lozano, Andrés. Cities in Layers. Steele, Philip. 2020. (ENG.). 64p. (J). (gr. 3-7). 22.00 (978-1-5362-0310-3(6), Big Picture Press) Candlewick Pr.

Lozano, Andres. Curiositree: Human World: A Visual History of Humankind. Wood, A. J. & Jolley, Mike. 2018. (Curiositree Ser.). (ENG.). 112p. (J). (gr. 4-6). 27.99 **(978-1-84780-992-6(8)**, Wide Eyed Editions) Quarto Publishing Group UK GBR. Dist: Hachette Bk. Group.

Lozano, Andres. Life on Earth: Dinosaurs: With 100 Questions & 70 Lift-Flaps! Alexander, Heather. 2017. (Life on Earth Ser.). (ENG.). 16p. (J). (gr. -1-1). bds. 14.99 (978-1-84780-904-9(9), Wide Eyed Editions) Quarto Publishing Group UK GBR. Dist: Hachette Bk. Group.

Lozano, Andrés. Peeking under the City. Porter, Esther. 2016. (What's Beneath Ser.). (ENG.). 32p. (J). (gr. -1-3). lib. bdg. 27.99 (978-1-4795-8665-3(X), Picture Window Bks.) Capstone.

Lozano, Andres & Lozano, Andrés. Peeking under the Hood. Porter, Esther. 2016. (What's Beneath Ser.). (ENG.). 32p. (J). (gr. -1-3). lib. bdg. 27.99 (978-1-4795-8667-7(6), Picture Window Bks.) Capstone.

Lozano, Andrés, jt. illus. see Lozano, Andres.

Lozano, Luciano. Boys Dance! (American Ballet Theatre) Allman, John Robert. 2020. (American Ballet Theatre Ser.). (ENG.). 40p. (J). (gr. -1-2). 17.99 **(978-0-593-18114-0(X))**; lib. bdg. 20.99 **(978-0-593-18115-7(8))** Random Hse. Children's Bks. (Doubleday Bks. for Young Readers).

Lozano, Luciano. I (Don't) Like Snakes. Davies, Nicola. (Read & Wonder Ser.). (ENG.). 32p. (J). (gr. k-4). 2018. 7.99 (978-1-5362-0323-3(8)); 2015. 15.99 (978-0-7636-7831-9(7)) Candlewick Pr.

—Mayhem at the Museum: A Book in Pictures. 2020. 40p. (J). (gr. -1-2). 17.99 (978-0-593-09354-2(2), Penguin Workshop) Penguin Young Readers Group.

—Miles of Smiles. Orloff, Karen Kaufman. 2016. 32p. (J). (gr. -1-1). 14.95 (978-1-4549-1699-4(0)) Sterling Publishing Co., Inc.

—Mister H. Nesquens, Daniel & Schimel, Lawrence. 2015. (ENG.). 61p. (J). 14.00 (978-0-8028-5440-7(0), Eerdmans Bks For Young Readers) Eerdmans, William B. Publishing Co.

—Operation Alphabet. MacCuish, Al. 2011. (Ministry of Letters Ser.: 0). (ENG.). 64p. (J). (gr. -1-k). 19.95 (978-0-500-51584-6(0), 551584) Thames & Hudson.

—The Sun Shines Everywhere. Hoberman, Mary Ann. 2019. 32p. (J). (gr. -1-3). 17.99 (978-0-316-52384-4(4)) Little, Brown Bks. for Young Readers.

—When Neil Armstrong Built a Wind Tunnel. Weakland, Mark. 2017. (Leaders Doing Headstands Ser.). (ENG.). 32p. (J). (gr. 1-4). lib. bdg. 28.65 (978-1-5158-1575-4(7), 136245, Picture Window Bks.) Capstone.

Lozano, Omar. Be a Star, Wonder Woman! Dahl, Michael. (DC Super Heroes Ser.). (ENG.). (J). (gr. -1-2). 2018. 30p. bds. 7.99 (978-1-68436-222-6(9), 138938); 2017. 32p. lib. bdg. 22.65 (978-1-5158-1402-3(5), 135195); 2017. 32p. 15.95 (978-1-62370-875-7(3), 135196) Capstone. (Stone Arch Bks.).

—The Computer Meltdown. Sonneborn, Scott. 2015. (North Police Ser.). (ENG.). 32p. (J). (gr. k-2). lib. bdg. 21.32 (978-1-4795-6485-9(0), Picture Window Bks.) Capstone.

—The Crystal Quest. Sutton, Laurie S. 2019. (You Choose Stories: Wonder Woman Ser.). (ENG.). 112p. (J). (gr. 2-6). pap. 6.95 (978-1-4965-8441-0(4), 140966); lib. bdg. 32.65 (978-1-4965-8351-2(5), 140645) Capstone. (Stone Arch Bks.).

—Double Trouble. Snider, Brandon T. 2020. (Amazing Adventures of Batman! Ser.). (ENG.). 32p. (J). (gr. k-2). pap. 5.95 (978-1-5158-5882-9(0), 142138); lib. bdg. 25.32 (978-1-5158-4823-3(X), 141605) Capstone. (Picture Window Bks.).

—Family Is a Superpower. Dahl, Michael. 2019. (DC Super Heroes Ser.). (ENG.). 32p. (J). (gr. -1-2). lib. bdg. 16.95 (978-1-68446-035-9(2), 139805, Capstone Editions) Capstone.

Lozano, Omar. Far Out Fairy Tales. Powell, Martin & Rayo, Alberto. (Far Out Fairy Tales Ser.). (ENG.). (J). (gr. 3-6). 2020. pap., pap., pap. 95.20 **(978-1-4965-9925-4(X)**, 201359); 2020. 405.12 **(978-1-4965-9766-3(4)**, 199570); 2019. 303.84 (978-1-4965-8397-0(3), 29357) Capstone. (Stone Arch Bks.).

Lozano, Omar. Good Morning, Superman! Dahl, Michael. 2017. (DC Super Heroes Ser.). (ENG.). 32p. (J). (gr. -1-2). lib. bdg. 22.65 (978-1-5158-0970-8(6), Stone Arch Bks.) Capstone.

—The Heart of Hades. Sutton, Laurie S. 2019. (You Choose Stories: Wonder Woman Ser.). (ENG.). 112p. (J). (gr. 2-6). pap. 6.95 (978-1-4965-8438-0(4), 140963); lib. bdg. 32.65 (978-1-4965-8348-2(5), 140642) Capstone. (Stone Arch Bks.).

—Jak & the Magic Nano-Beans: a Graphic Novel. Bowen, Carl. 2016. (Far Out Fairy Tales Ser.). (ENG.). 40p. (J). (gr. 3-6). lib. bdg. 25.32 (978-1-4965-2510-9(8), Stone Arch Bks.) Capstone.

—Jet-Powered Justice. Dahl, Michael. 2018. (Wonder Woman Tales of Paradise Island Ser.). (ENG.). 40p. (J). (gr. 4-8). lib. bdg. 24.65 (978-1-5158-3023-8(3), 138653, Stone Arch Bks.) Capstone.

—The Legendary Lasso. Dahl, Michael. 2018. (Wonder Woman Tales of Paradise Island Ser.). (ENG.). 40p. (J). (gr. 4-8). lib. bdg. 24.65 (978-1-5158-3020-7(9), 138650, Stone Arch Bks.) Capstone.

Lozano, Omar. The Little Werewolf: A Graphic Novel. Peters, Stephanie. 2020. (Far Out Fairy Tales Ser.). (ENG.). 40p. (J). (gr. 3-6). pap. 5.95 **(978-1-4965-9906-3(3)**, 201317); lib. bdg. 25.32 **(978-1-4965-9684-0(6)**, 199251) Capstone. (Stone Arch Bks.).

Lozano, Omar. Meet the South Police. Sonneborn, Scott. 2015. (North Police Ser.). (ENG.). 32p. (J). (gr. k-2). lib. bdg. 21.32 (978-1-4795-6486-6(9), Picture Window Bks.) Capstone.

—Movie Magic Madness. Steele, Michael Anthony. 2019. (You Choose Stories: Wonder Woman Ser.). (ENG.). 112p. (J). (gr. 2-6). pap. 6.95 (978-1-4965-8440-3(6), 140965); lib. bdg. 32.65 (978-1-4965-8350-5(7), 140644) Capstone. (Stone Arch Bks.).

—The Mystery of Santa's Sleigh. Sonneborn, Scott. (ENG.). 32p. (J). 2016. pap. (978-1-4747-0031-3(4)); 2015. lib. bdg. 21.32 (978-1-4795-6484-2(2)) Capstone. (Picture Window Bks.).

—Myth Monster Mayhem. Korte, Steve. 2019. (You Choose Stories: Wonder Woman Ser.). (ENG.). 112p. (J). (gr. 2-6). pap. 6.95 (978-1-4965-8439-7(2), 140964); lib. bdg. 32.65 (978-1-4965-8349-9(3), 140643) Capstone. (Stone Arch Bks.).

—Ninja-Rella: A Graphic Novel. Comeau, Joey. 2015. (Far Out Fairy Tales Ser.). (ENG.). 40p. (J). (gr. 3-6). lib. bdg. 25.32 (978-1-4342-9647-4(4), Stone Arch Bks.) Capstone.

Lozano, Omar. Ninja cienta: Una Novela Gráfica. Comeau, Joey. 2020. (Cuentos de Hadas Futuristas Ser.).Tr. of Ninja-Rella: a Graphic Novel. (SPA.). 40p. (J). (gr. 3-6). pap. 5.95 **(978-1-4965-9958-2(6)**, 201604); lib. bdg. 25.32 **(978-1-4965-9812-7(1)**, 200700) Capstone. (Stone Arch Bks.).

Lozano, Omar. The North Police. Sonneborn, Scott. 2015. (North Police Ser.). (ENG.). 32p. (J). (gr. k-2). lib. bdg., lib. bdg., lib. bdg. 85.28 (978-1-4795-7929-7(7), Picture Window Bks.) Capstone.

—Rapunzel vs. Frankenstein: A Graphic Novel. Powell, Martin. 2019. (Far Out Fairy Tales Ser.). (ENG.). 40p. (J). (gr. 3-6). pap. 5.95 (978-1-4965-8444-1(9), 140969); lib. bdg. 25.32 (978-1-4965-8395-6(7), 140686) Capstone. (Stone Arch Bks.).

—The Reindeer Games. Sonneborn, Scott. (ENG.). 32p. (J). 2016. pap. (978-1-4747-0034-4(9)); 2015. lib. bdg. 21.32 (978-1-4795-6487-3(7)) Capstone. (Picture Window Bks.).

—The Silver Spurs of Oz: A Graphic Novel. Schultz, Erica. 2020. (Far Out Classic Stories Ser.). (ENG.). 40p. (J). (gr. 3-6). pap. 5.95 (978-1-4965-9195-1(X), 142208); lib. bdg. 25.32 (978-1-4965-8690-2(5), 141432) Capstone. (Stone Arch Bks.).

—Sweet Dreams, Supergirl. Dahl, Michael. 2018. (DC Super Heroes Ser.). (ENG.). 32p. (J). (gr. -1-2). lib. bdg. 21.99 (978-1-5158-2439-8(X), 137531, Stone Arch Bks.) Capstone.

—Sweet Dreams, Supergirl. Dahl, Michael. 2019. (DC Super Heroes Ser.). (ENG.). 30p. (J). (gr. -1-2). bds. 7.99 (978-1-68436-232-5(6), 139250, Capstone Young Readers) Capstone.

—The Tiara & the Titan. Dahl, Michael. 2018. (Wonder Woman Tales of Paradise Island Ser.). (ENG.). 40p. (J). (gr. 4-8). lib. bdg. 24.65 (978-1-5158-3021-4(7), 138651, Stone Arch Bks.) Capstone.

—The Unbreakable Bracelets. Dahl, Michael. 2018. (Wonder Woman Tales of Paradise Island Ser.). (ENG.). 40p. (J). (gr. 4-8). lib. bdg. 24.65 (978-1-5158-3022-1(5), 138652, Stone Arch Bks.) Capstone.

—Wonder Woman Tales of Paradise Island. Dahl, Michael. 2018. (Wonder Woman Tales of Paradise Island Ser.). (ENG.). 40p. (J). (gr. 4-8). 95.96 (978-1-5158-3024-5(1), 28531, Stone Arch Bks.) Capstone.

—You Choose Stories: Wonder Woman. Korte, Steve et al. 2019. (You Choose Stories: Wonder Woman Ser.). (ENG.). (J). (gr. 2-6). 130.60 (978-1-4965-8352-9(3), 29347); pap., pap., pap. 27.80 (978-1-4965-8522-6(4), 29688) Capstone. (Stone Arch Bks.).

Lozano, Omar & Brizuela, Dario. Bane Drain. Snider, Brandon T. 2020. (Amazing Adventures of Batman! Ser.). (ENG.). 32p. (J). (gr. k-2). pap. 5.95 (978-1-5158-5884-3(7), 142140); lib. bdg. 25.32 (978-1-5158-4825-7(6), 141607) Capstone. (Picture Window Bks.).

Lozano, Omar, jt. illus. see Brizuela, Dario.

Lozano, Omar, jt. illus. see Frampton, Otis.

Ltd, Duck Egg Blue. World's Coolest Jobs: Discover 40 Awesome Careers!, 1 vol. Lonely Planet Kids & Brett, Anna. 2020. (ENG.). 96p. (J). (gr. 1-3). pap. 9.99 (978-1-78868-925-0(9), Lonely Planet Kids) Lonely Planet Global Ltd. IRL. Dist: Hachette Bk. Group.

Ltd, Dynamo. Amelia's Maze Adventure, 1 vol. Morgan, Sally et al. 2017. (ENG.). 96p. (J). (gr. 1-3). pap. 9.99 (978-1-78657-436-7(5), 5374) Lonely Planet Global Ltd. IRL. Dist: Hachette Bk. Group.

—Marco's Maze Mission, 1 vol. Morgan, Sally et al. 2017. (ENG.). 96p. (J). (gr. 1-3). pap. 9.99 (978-1-78657-687-3(2), 5510) Lonely Planet Global Ltd. IRL. Dist: Hachette Bk. Group.

Lu, Bao. 100 First Words. Redwing, Jack. Cottage Door Press, ed. 2020. (John Deere 100 Firsts Children's Interactive Board Book Ser.). (ENG.). 22p. (J). (gr. -1-k). bds. 9.99 **(978-1-68052-937-1(4)**, 1005800) Cottage Door Pr.

Lu, Marisa. Nadia Hears the Shahadah. Baten, Kim. 2018. (ENG.). 30p. (J). (gr. -1-2). 14.95 (978-1-59784-934-0(0), Tughra Bks.) Blue Dome, Inc.

Lu, Nick. Bumper-To-Bumper Cars & Trucks Flash Cards. 2017. (ENG.). 20p. (J). 14.99 (978-1-4521-5503-6(8)) Chronicle Bks. LLC.

—Bumper-To-Bumper Stroller Cars. 2017. (ENG.). 10p. (J). 9.99 (978-1-4521-5504-3(6)) Chronicle Bks. LLC.

Lu, Oamul. Snowy Farm. Shaw, Calvin. 2019. (ENG.). 32p. (J). (gr. -1-3). 17.99 (978-1-5344-1047-3(3), Simon & Schuster/Paula Wiseman Bks.) Simon & Schuster/Paula Wiseman Bks.

Lu, Wei. Mixter Twizzle's Breakfast. Macaulay, Regan W. H. 2018. (ENG.). 44p. (J). (gr. k-3). pap. (978-1-987976-49-6(5)) Mirror World Publishing.

Lubach, Peter. What Is the Moon Made Of? And Other Questions Kids Have about Space, 1 vol. Bowman, Donna H. (Kids' Questions Ser.). (ENG.). 24p. (J). (gr. k-2). 2011. pap. 7.49 (978-1-4048-6726-0(0)); 2009. lib. bdg. 27.32 (978-1-4048-5529-8(7)) Capstone. (Picture Window Bks.).

Lubach, Vanessa. Dr Jekyll & Mr Hyde. Stevenson, Robert Louis. 2014. (Classics of Science Fiction Ser.). (ENG.). 64p. pap. 6.95 (978-1-906230-15-9(3)) Real Reads Ltd. GBR. Dist: Casemate Pubs. & Bk. Distributors, LLC.

—Jane Eyre. 2009. (Real Reads Ser.). 64p. (J). (gr. 4-8). 32.25 (978-1-60754-667-2(1)) Windmill Bks.

—Wuthering Heights. Brontë, Emily. 2009. (Real Reads Ser.). 64p. (J). (gr. 4-8). 32.25 (978-1-60754-670-2(1)) Windmill Bks.

Lubera, Logan. The Impending Storm: The Imperium Saga: Fall of the Imperium Trilogy, 3 vols., Vol. 1. Bowyer, Clifford B. 2003. (Imperium Saga: 1). (ENG.). 463p. (YA). 27.95 *(978-0-9744354-4-2(9)*, BK0001) Silver Leaf Bks., LLC.

Luberoff, William. My First Prayer Book. Cavanaugh, Karen. 2007. (Catholic Classics Ser.). 32p. (J). 3.95 *(978-0-88271-216-1(0))* Regina Pr., Malhame & Co.

—My Mass Book. Cavanagh, Karen & Hoagland, Victor, eds. 2008. (ENG.). 32p. (gr. -1-3). pap. 2.95 *(978-0-88271-542-1(9)*, RG10356) Regina Pr., Malhame & Co.

—The Rosary. Hoagland, Victor & Cavanagh, Karen, eds. 2003. (ENG.). 32p. (gr. -1-3). pap. 2.95 *(978-0-88271-456-1(2)*, RG10350) Regina Pr., Malhame & Co.

Lubitsky, Maribeth Jenkins. Go-bez Nibe: Very Clever Firefly, 1 vol. Angelo, Tony. 2010. 48p. 24.95 *(978-1-4489-5184-0(4))* PublishAmerica, Inc.

Luca, Bogdan. They Shoot! They Score! Life's Lessons on Ice. Macdonald, Kelly. 2005. 32p. 9.99 *(978-0-9736893-0-3(7))* MacDonald, Kelly CAN. Dist: Hushion Hse. Publishing, Ltd.

Lucas, Bonnie Gordon, jt. illus. see Kreiswirth, Kinny.

Lucas, David. Christmas at the Toy Museum. Lucas, David. 2012. (ENG.). 32p. (J). (gr. -1-2). 15.99 *(978-0-7636-5868-7(5))* Candlewick Pr.

—I Was Made for You. Lucas, David. 2018. (ENG.). 32p. (J). (gr. -1-3). 17.99 *(978-1-5415-3559-6(6))* Lerner Publishing Group.

—The Lying Carpet. Lucas, David. 2013. (ENG.). 80p. (J). (gr. 4-7). pap. 10.99 *(978-1-84939-017-0(7))* Andersen Pr. GBR. Dist: Independent Pubs. Group.

—Peanut. Lucas, David. 2008. (ENG.). 32p. (J). (gr. k-k). 15.99 *(978-0-7636-3925-9(7))* Candlewick Pr.

Lucas, Diane. Adopting Jake. Black, Angie. 2010. 32p. pap. 12.95 *(978-1-935268-47-5(3))* Halo Publishing International.

—Boog the Bug, 1 vol. Genaille, Cynthia & Wheeler, Jordan. 2015. (ENG.). 32p. (J). (gr. -1-k). mass mkt. 10.95 *(978-1-894717-46-5(5)*, 6e78ea3c-8d38-4f29-9c90-ecef7a35c2d1) Pemmican Pubns., Inc. CAN. Dist: Firefly Bks., Ltd.

—Chickadee Trust, 1 vol. St. Cyr, Angel. 2015. (ENG.). 32p. (J). (gr. 2-4). mass mkt. 10.95 *(978-1-894717-67-0(8)*, 3db21e67-57b6-4a13-a447-642c869fdd1e) Pemmican Pubns., Inc. CAN. Dist: Firefly Bks., Ltd.

—He Wore a Purple Robe. Sena, Barbara T. 2016. (Faith Heroes Ser.: Vol. 2). (ENG.). (J). (gr. 3-6). 24.99 *(978-0-692-78537-9(X))* BTSena Pubns.

—Is Today the Day? Sheehan, Linda Clarke. 2006. (ENG.). 34p. pap. 14.95 *(978-1-4120-5259-7(9))* Trafford Publishing.

—It's Time for Holi! Roy Shah, Amita. 2011. 24p. pap. 13.95 *(978-1-60844-943-9(2))* Dog Ear Publishing, LLC.

—Ka-Boom. Rininger, Alyce. 2012. 46p. pap. 13.95 *(978-1-61244-069-9(X))* Halo Publishing International.

—Keep Out!, 1 vol. Boudreau, Hélène. ed. 2010. (ENG.). 80p. (J). (gr. 1-3). pap. 8.95 *(978-1-55109-753-4(2))* Nimbus Publishing, Ltd. CAN. Dist: Orca Bk. Pubs. USA.

—Milton the Square Shell Turtle. Tatro, MaryAnn. 2013. 24p. pap. 11.95 *(978-1-61244-106-1(8))* Halo Publishing International.

—The Seed Sower, Walter's Special Garden. Anderson, Debra. 2012. 24p. pap. 11.95 *(978-1-61244-097-2(5))* Halo Publishing International.

—Stella Saves the Game. E.A. Budd. 2012. 24p. pap. 12.95 *(978-1-61244-059-0(2))* Halo Publishing International.

Lucas, Gareth. Fun on the Farm. Tiger Tales. 2020. (ENG.). 12p. (J). (-k). bds. 9.99 *(978-1-68010-602-2(3))* Tiger Tales.

—The Happy Snappy Crab. Tiger Tales. 2019. (ENG.). 12p. (J). (gr. 2-k). bds. 9.99 *(978-1-68010-584-1(1))* Tiger Tales.

—Roar! Roar! Dinosaur. 2020. (Squishy Sounds Ser.). (ENG.). 10p. (J). (gr. -1-k). 14.99 *(978-1-68412-709-2(2)*, Silver Dolphin Bks.) Printers Row Publishing Group.

—The Very Noisy Farm. 2020. (Squishy Sounds Ser.). (ENG.). 10p. (J). (gr. -1-k). bds. 14.99 *(978-1-68412-710-8(6)*, Silver Dolphin Bks.) Printers Row Publishing Group.

—Woof! Says Dog. Elliot, Rachel. 2019. (ENG.). 10p. (J). (— 1). bds. 14.99 *(978-1-68412-708-5(4)*, Silver Dolphin Bks.) Printers Row Publishing Group.

Lucas, Karen. Amazing Attitudes. Fonseca, Carol M. & Nolley, Sheree. 2016. (ENG.). (J). pap. 8.95 *(978-1-4575-4768-3(6))* Dog Ear Publishing, LLC.

—Amazing Attitudes. Fonseca, Carol & Nolley, Sheree. 2016. (ENG.). (J). 18.95 *(978-1-4575-4997-7(2))* Dog Ear Publishing, LLC.

Lucas, Margeaux. Abby's Asthma & the Big Race. Golding, Theresa. 2013. (AV2 Fiction Readalong Ser.). (ENG.). (J). (gr. k-3). 34.28 *(978-1-62127-863-4(8)*, AV2 by Weigl) Weigl Pubs., Inc.

—The Aliens Have Landed at Our School. Nesbitt, Kenn. 2006. (Giggle Poetry Ser.). (ENG.). 96p. (J). (gr. 1-7). per. 9.99 *(978-0-689-04864-7(5)*, Running Pr.) Running Pr.

—Alpha Betti. Morton, Carlene. 2007. (ENG.). (J). (gr. -1-3). 17.95 *(978-1-932146-69-1(5)*, Upstart Bks.) Highsmith Inc.

—Cuando Sea Grande. Kittinger, Jo S. 2005. (Rookie Reader Español Ser.). (SPA.). 23p. (J). (gr. k-2). per. 4.95 *(978-0-516-24692-5(5)*, Children's Pr.) Scholastic Library Publishing.

—Cuando sea Grande: When I Grow Up. Kittinger, Jo S. 2005. (Rookie Reader Español Ser.). 24p. (gr. k-2). 19.50 *(978-0-516-24443-3(4)*, Children's Pr.) Scholastic Library Publishing.

—Dancing Dinos at the Beach. Lucas, Sally. 2010. (Step into Reading Ser.). 32p. (J). (gr. -1-1). pap. 4.99 *(978-0-375-85640-2(4)*, Random Hse. Bks. for Young Readers) Random Hse. Children's Bks.

—Great Green Gator Graduation. Dadey, Debbie. 2006. (Swamp Monster in Third Grade Ser.). 58p. (J). pap. *(978-0-439-79401-5(3))* Scholastic, Inc.

—Max & His Map. Harkrader, Lisa. 2016. (Spring Forward Ser.). (J). (gr. 1). *(978-1-4900-9371-0(0))* Benchmark Education Co.

—My Best Friend Is Moving. Parker, David. 2007. (J). *(978-0-545-00389-6(X))* Scholastic, Inc.

—The Nose Knows: Sense of Smell. Weiss, Ellen. 2006. (Science Solves It! ® Ser.). (ENG.). 32p. (J). (gr. k-2). pap. 5.95 *(978-1-57565-120-0(3))* Astra Publishing Hse.

—Our Class Works Together. Parker, David. 2007. (J). *(978-0-545-00384-1(9))* Scholastic, Inc.

—P Is for Passover, Vol. Stone, Tanya Lee. 2003. (ENG.). 32p. (J). (gr. -1-k). mass mkt. 5.99 *(978-0-8431-0238-3(1)*, Price Stern Sloan) Penguin Young Readers Group.

—Rachel's Roses. Wolff, Ferida. 2019. (ENG.). 112p. (J). (gr. 2-5). 15.99 *(978-0-8234-4365-9(5))* Holiday Hse., Inc.

—Regina Jonas: The Girl Who Persisted. Sasso, Sandy Eisenberg. 2018. (J). *(978-1-68115-540-1(0)*, Apples & Honey Pr.) Behrman Hse., Inc.

—Room 9 Writes a Report. Williams, Rozanne Lanczak. 2006. (Learn to Write Ser.). 16p. (J). (gr. k-2). pap. 3.49 *(978-1-59198-297-5(9)*, 6193) Creative Teaching Pr., Inc.

—Room 9 Writes a Report. Williams, Rozanne Lanczak. Maio, Barbara, ed. 2006. (J). per. 8.99 *(978-1-59198-357-6(6))* Creative Teaching Pr., Inc.

—Sharing My Room. Parker, David. 2007. (J). *(978-0-545-00386-5(5))* Scholastic, Inc.

—Signing at School: Sign Language for Kids, 1 vol. Clay, Kathryn & Vonne, Mira. 2013. (Time to Sign Ser.). (ENG.). 32p. (J). (gr. -1-2). 27.99 *(978-1-62065-052-3(5))* Capstone.

—We Can All Play. Parker, David. 2007. (J). *(978-0-545-00390-2(3))* Scholastic, Inc.

Lucas, Nya a. Only a Boy Named David. Scott, Shannon. 2019. (ENG.). 120p. (J). (gr. 1-6). pap. 14.95 *(978-1-4796-1115-7(8))* TEACH Services, Inc.

Lucas, Simon. Felix the Fox & His Awesome Odd Socks. Dodd, Katie. 2020. (ENG.). 32p. (J). (gr. k-1). pap. ***(978-1-9997429-9-7(0))*** Beercott Bks.

Lucas, Stacey L., et al. Sara Safety, School Safety Pamphlet. LaBerge, Margaret M. 2004. (J). pap. *(978-0-9755561-0-8(X))* Reading Resc.

Lucas, Stacey L. & Lopresti, Sarah H. Sara Safety, Personal Safety: Kid's Activity Book. LaBerge, Margaret M. 2004. 21p. (J). pap. *(978-0-9755561-2-2(6))* Reading Resc.

Lucas, Trevor. You Are Loved. Gholson, Tijuana a. Brown, Alesha R., ed. 2019. (ENG.). 18p. (J). pap. 9.99 *(978-1-970097-01-6(9))* MAX Publishing, LLC.

Lucco, Kristine. Let's Visit Easter Island! Adventures of Bella & Harry. Manzione, Lisa. 2019. (Adventures of Bella & Harry Ser.: 23). (ENG.). 48p. (J). (gr. k-5). 16.95 *(978-1-937616-83-0(5))* Bella & Harry, LLC.

—Let's Visit Jerusalem! Adventures of Bella & Harry. Manzione, Lisa. ed. 2013. (Adventures of Bella & Harry Ser.: 10). (ENG.). 48p. (J). (gr. k-5). 16.95 *(978-1-937616-00-7(2))* Bella & Harry, LLC.

—Let's Visit London! Adventures of Bella & Harry. Manzione, Lisa. ed. 2011. (Adventures of Bella & Harry Ser.: 3). (ENG.). 48p. (J). (gr. k-5). 16.95 *(978-1-937616-03-8(7))* Bella & Harry, LLC.

—Let's Visit Machu Picchu! Adventures of Bella & Harry. Manzione, Lisa. 2018. (Adventures of Bella & Harry Ser.: 21). (ENG.). 48p. (J). (gr. k-5). 16.95 *(978-1-937616-81-6(9))* Bella & Harry, LLC.

—Let's Visit Paris! Adventures of Bella & Harry. Manzione, Lisa. ed. 2011. (Adventures of Bella & Harry Ser.: 1). (ENG.). 48p. (J). (gr. k-5). 16.95 *(978-1-937616-01-4(0))* Bella & Harry, LLC.

—Let's Visit Prague! Adventures of Bella & Harry. Manzione, Lisa. 2018. (Adventures of Bella & Harry Ser.: 22). (ENG.). 48p. (J). (gr. k-5). 16.95 *(978-1-937616-82-3(7))* Bella & Harry, LLC.

—Let's Visit Saint Petersburg! Adventures of Bella & Harry. Manzione, Lisa. ed. 2014. (Adventures of Bella & Harry Ser.: 13). (ENG.). 48p. (J). (gr. k-5). 16.95 *(978-1-937616-53-3(3))* Bella & Harry, LLC.

Lucero, Arlette. Chili Today, Hot Tamale & Other Tummy Tales. Fajardo, Renee & Ruby, Carl. Fajardo, Renee et al, eds. 2004. 110p. (YA). (gr. 4-8). pap. 14.00 *(978-0-9724472-2-5(9))* Just Enjoyable Memorable Story Bks.

—Ole Posole & Other Tummy Tales. Fajardo, Renee & Ruby, Carl. Fajardo, Renee & Winograd, Ed, eds. 2005. 110p. (YA). (gr. 4-8). pap. 14.00 *(978-0-9724472-3-2(7))* Just Enjoyable Memorable Story Bks.

Lucero, Jessica. Skulls. Marquitz, Tim. Milner, Isaac, ed. 2011. pap. 13.25 *(978-1-61572-354-6(4))* Damnation Bks.

Luchsinger, Linda. Waddling to the Pond. Poet, Jonny. 2011. 40p. pap. 24.95 *(978-1-4560-4033-8(2))* America Star Bks.

Luciana, Rebeca. Kiwi. Isern, Susanna. 2019. (ENG.). 32p. (J). (gr. -1-k). 16.95 *(978-84-16566-93-8(3))* Ediciones La Fragatina ESP. Dist: Independent Pubs. Group.

Luciani, Rebeca. Jatakas: Seis Cuentos Budistas. Millà, Marta. 2018. (Pequeño Fragmenta Ser.). (SPA.). 40p. (J). (gr. 2-4). pap. 17.95 *(978-84-15518-66-2(8))* Fragmenta Editorial ESP. Dist: Independent Pubs. Group.

—Mira's Curly Hair. Al Serkal, Maryam. 2019. (ENG.). 32p. (J). (gr. -1-2). 17.99 *(978-1-911373-61-2(7))* Lantana Publishing GBR. Dist: Lerner Publishing Group.

Luciano, Fleitas. Fae Hunter. Wilson, Sarah K. L. 2019. (Tangled Fae Ser.: Vol. 1). (ENG.). 222p. (YA). ***(978-1-9992872-1-4(5))*** Wilson, Sarah K. L.

Lucini, Carmen. Tungaira: Miss Primeras Poesias. Plaza, José María & María, Plaza José. (SPA.). 96p. (J). 8.99 *(978-84-392-8115-3(3)*, EV4870) Gaviota Ediciones ESP. Dist: Lectorum Pubns., Inc.

Lucini, Chata. El Palacio de los Tres Ojos. Gisbert, Joan Manuel. 2006. (SPA.). 127p. (J). (gr. 4-7). pap. 10.99 *(978-84-263-4614-8(6))* Vives, Luis Editorial (Edelvives) ESP. Dist: Lectorum Pubns., Inc.

Lucke, Deb. The Pilgrims' First Thanksgiving, 1 vol. Gunderson, Jessica. (Thanksgiving Ser.). (ENG.). 24p. (J). (gr. k-3). 2011. pap. 8.95 *(978-1-4048-6720-8(1))*; 2010. lib. bdg. 27.99 *(978-1-4048-6285-2(4))* Capstone. (Picture Window Bks.).

Lucke, Deb. The Book of Time Outs: A Mostly True History of the World's Biggest Troublemakers. Lucke, Deb. 2008. (ENG.). 32p. (J). (gr. 1-4). 15.99 *(978-1-4169-2829-4(4)*, Simon & Schuster Bks. For Young Readers) Simon & Schuster Bks. For Young Readers.

Luckemeyer, Norma. Johnny Coalboy. Witschen, Kay. 2003. (J). per. 5.95 *(978-0-9741352-0-5(8))* Dwitt Publishing.

Lucken, Gary. Create with Code: Build Your Own Website. Hatter, Clyde et al. 2017. 93p. (J). *(978-1-338-14634-9(3))* Scholastic, Inc.

Lucky, Liza. Las Primeras 100 Palabras - Libro de Imágenes. Lucky, Liza. 2018. (SPA.). 30p. (J). pap. 9.99 *(978-1-7200-7264-5(7))* Independently Published.

LuckySports. Adventures in SportsLand - the Golf Bully (with accompanying CD) The Golf Bully. LuckySports, . 2008. 32p. (J). pap. 19.95 *(978-0-935938-29-6(X))* Stogo, Malcolm Assocs.

Lucot, Erica. I Sette Pesci: The Seven Fishes. Pursh, Eric. 2005. (J). per. *(978-0-9727319-3-5(8)*, Blacktypewriter Pr.) Pittsburgh Literary Arts Network LLC.

Ludlam, Jamie. And Jake Makes Three. Whitaker, Sue. 2013. 108p. pap. *(978-1-907978-16-6(X))* ETA Publishing Hse.

—And Jake Makes Three & the Secret of Badlands. Whitaker, Sue. 2013. 92p. pap. *(978-1-907978-26-5(7))* ETA Publishing Hse.

—And Jake Makes Three in the Snow. Whitaker, Sue. 2013. 104p. pap. *(978-1-907978-21-0(6))* ETA Publishing Hse.

—And Jake Makes Three in the Vampires Den. Whitaker, Sue. Thomas-Brown, Cauline, ed. 2013. 86p. pap. *(978-1-907978-31-9(3))* ETA Publishing Hse.

Ludlow, Hal. A Sweet Girl Graduate (Illustrated Edition) Meade, L. T. 2019. (ENG.). 180p. (J). pap. ***(978-1-4068-9840-8(6))*** Echo Library.

Ludlow, Patricia. Creation Myths: How the World Began, in 15 Origin Legends. 2020. 80p. (J). (gr. -1-12). 15.00 *(978-1-86147-866-5(6)*, Armadillo) Anness Publishing GBR. Dist: National Bk. Network.

Ludlow, Patricia D. Casting the Gods Adrift: A Tale of Ancient Egypt. McCaughrean, Geraldine. 2003. (ENG.). 112p. (J). (gr. 4-7). 15.95 *(978-0-8126-2684-1(2))* Cricket Bks.

Ludovise, Jamie. Parker Buck Saves Up. Balch, Rj. 2019. (Money Hero Ser.: Vol. 1). (ENG.). 30p. (J). pap. 9.99 ***(978-1-0870-5328-8(5))*** Independently Published.

Ludvigsen, Henning. Project U. L. F. Clark, Stuart. 2007. (Project U.L.F. Ser.: 1). (ENG.). 418p. (YA). 27.95 *(978-0-9787782-0-0(0)*, BK0021) Silver Leaf Bks., LLC.

Ludwig, Emilie. I Hear Music Everywhere. Jackson, Betty Whitaker. 2019. (ENG.). 36p. (J). pap. 10.00 ***(978-1-7080-7976-5(9))*** Independently Published.

Ludy, Mark. When I Was a Boy... I Dreamed. Matott, Justin. 2004. (ENG.). 32p. (J). (gr. -1-4). *(978-0-9664276-2-2(9))* Green Pastures Publishing, Inc.

—When I Was a Girl ... I Dreamed. Matott, J. P. & Baker, Margaret. 2005. (ENG.). 32p. (J). (gr. -1-4). *(978-0-9664276-3-9(7))* Green Pastures Publishing, Inc.

Ludy, Mark. Jujo: The Youngest Tribesman. Ludy, Mark. 2007. (ENG.). 32p. (J). (gr. k-2). 16.95 *(978-0-9664276-5-3(3))* Scribble & Sons.

Lue Sue, Majella. Penina Levine Is a Hard-boiled Egg. O'Connell, Rebecca. 2009. (ENG.). 192p. (J). (gr. 3-7). pap. 18.99 *(978-0-312-55026-4(X)*, 9780312550264) Square Fish.

Luebs, Robin. Who Said Coo? Ruddell, Deborah. 2010. (ENG.). 40p. (J). (gr. -1-2). 17.99 *(978-1-4169-8510-5(7)*, Beach Lane Bks.) Beach Lane Bks.

Luebs, Robin. Please Pick Me up, Mama! Luebs, Robin. 2009. (ENG.). 40p. (J). (gr. -1-k). 15.99 *(978-1-4169-7977-7(8)*, Beach Lane Bks.) Beach Lane Bks.

Lueck, Sabrina. Carl Prescott & the Sleeping One. Brinkley, Adele, ed. 2019. (ENG.). 248p. (J). pap. 11.99 *(978-1-7909-9233-1(8))* Independently Published.

Luecke, Amber Leigh. Daffy Dreams of a Family. Chambers, Tamara & Edmonds, H. Lionel. 2018. (Sequel to Daffy's Beautiful Day Ser.). (ENG.). 34p. (J). pap. 13.00 *(978-0-692-11886-3(1))* Chambers, Ta'mara.

—Seed's Journey Home: Book 2: Orange Gate. Tipene, Tania. 2018. (ENG.). 48p. (J). pap. 14.99 *(978-0-9998845-1-5(4))* Nurture Wellness now.

Luedecke, Bev. Birthday Beastie: All about Counting. Hall, Kirsten. 2003. (Beastieville Ser.). 32p. (J). 19.50 *(978-0-516-22891-4(9)*, Children's Pr.) Scholastic Library Publishing.

—Buried Treasure: All about Using a Map. Hall, Kirsten. 2003. (Beastieville Ser.). 32p. (J). 19.50 *(978-0-516-22894-5(3)*, Children's Pr.) Scholastic Library Publishing.

—Double Trouble: All about Colors. Hall, Kirsten. 2003. (Beastieville Ser.). 32p. (J). (gr. -1-1). 19.50 *(978-0-516-22892-1(7)*, Children's Pr.) Scholastic Library Publishing.

—First Day of School: All about Shapes & Sizes. Hall, Kirsten. 2004. (Beastieville Ser.). (ENG.). 32p. (J). (gr. k-1). pap. 3.95 *(978-0-516-24654-3(2)*, Children's Pr.) Scholastic Library Publishing.

—Good Times: All about the Seasons. Hall, Kirsten. 2004. (Beastieville Ser.). (J). 19.50 *(978-0-516-23648-3(2)*, Children's Pr.) Scholastic Library Publishing.

—Help! All about Telling Time. Hall, Kirsten. (Beastieville Ser.). 32p. (J). (gr. k-1). 2004. (ENG.). pap. 3.95 *(978-0-516-24655-0(0))*; 2003. 19.50 *(978-0-516-22890-7(0))* Scholastic Library Publishing. (Children's Pr.).

—Hide-And-Seek: All about Location. Hall, Kirsten. 2004. (Beastieville Ser.). (J). 19.50 *(978-0-516-23649-0(0)*, Children's Pr.) Scholastic Library Publishing.

—Hide-and-Seek: All about Location. Hall, Kirsten. 2005. (Beastieville Ser.). (ENG.). 32p. (J). (gr. k-1). pap. 3.95 *(978-0-516-25519-4(3)*, Children's Pr.) Scholastic Library Publishing.

—Let's Trade: All about Trading. Hall, Kirsten. (Beastieville Ser.). (J). (gr. k-1). 2005. (ENG.). 32p. pap. 3.95 *(978-0-516-25520-0(7))*; 2004. 19.50 *(978-0-516-22999-7(0))* Scholastic Library Publishing. (Children's Pr.).

—Little Lies: All about Math. Hall, Kirsten. (Beastieville Ser.). 32p. (J). (gr. k-1). 2004. (ENG.). pap. 3.95 *(978-0-516-24656-7(9))*; 2003. 19.50 *(978-0-516-22896-9(X))* Scholastic Library Publishing. (Children's Pr.).

—A Perfect Day: All about the Five Senses. Hall, Kirsten. (Beastieville Ser.). (J). (gr. k-1). 2005. (ENG.). 32p. pap. 3.95 *(978-0-516-25521-7(5))*; 2004. 19.50 *(978-0-516-24437-2(X))* Scholastic Library Publishing. (Children's Pr.).

—Slider's Pet: All about Nature. Hall, Kirsten. 2004. (Beastieville Ser.). (J). 19.50 *(978-0-516-22898-3(6)*, Children's Pr.) Scholastic Library Publishing.

—Tug-of-War: All about Balance. Hall, Kirsten. 2004. (Beastieville Ser.). 31p. (J). 19.50 *(978-0-516-22899-0(4)*, Children's Pr.) Scholastic Library Publishing.

—Vote for Me: All about Civics. Hall, Kirsten. 2003. (Beastieville Ser.). 32p. (J). 19.50 *(978-0-516-22897-6(8)*, Children's Pr.) Scholastic Library Publishing.

—What a Mess! All about Numbers. Hall, Kirsten. 2004. (Beastieville Ser.). (J). 19.50 *(978-0-516-23670-4(9)*, Children's Pr.) Scholastic Library Publishing.

Lueder, Duff. Does Money Grow on Trees? Farming Is Fun. Sheffer, Jane. 2017. (ENG.). (J). pap. 12.99 *(978-0-9973189-3-7(7))* Growing Senses Pubns.

—Pollinating Your Toolbox. Sheffer, Jane. 2018. (ENG.). 44p. (J). pap. 13.95 *(978-0-9973189-7-5(X))* Growing Senses Pubns.

Lueer, Carmen A. A Bunny Tail. Nees, Diane L. 2012. 44p. pap. 24.95 *(978-1-4626-9191-3(9))* America Star Bks.

Lueth, Nathan. The Empty Room. Mikkelsen, Jon. 2008. (We Are Heroes Ser.). (ENG.). 40p. (J). (gr. 5-9). lib. bdg. 23.99 *(978-1-4342-0791-3(9)*, Stone Arch Bks.) Capstone.

—Kids Against Hunger. Mikkelsen, Jon. 2008. (We Are Heroes Ser.). (ENG.). 40p. (J). (gr. 5-9). lib. bdg. 23.99 *(978-1-4342-0790-6(0)*, Stone Arch Bks.) Capstone.

—Race for Home. Mikkelsen, Jon. 2008. (We Are Heroes Ser.). (ENG.). 40p. (J). (gr. 5-9). lib. bdg. 23.99 *(978-1-4342-0786-9(2)*, Stone Arch Bks.) Capstone.

—Skateboard Buddy. Mikkelsen, Jon. 2008. (We Are Heroes Ser.). (ENG.). 40p. (J). (gr. 5-9). lib. bdg. 23.99 *(978-1-4342-0788-3(9)*, Stone Arch Bks.) Capstone.

—Storm Shelter. Mikkelsen, Jon. 2008. (We Are Heroes Ser.). (ENG.). 40p. (J). (gr. 5-9). lib. bdg. 23.99 *(978-1-4342-0787-6(0)*, Stone Arch Bks.) Capstone.

Luevano, Raul. Harriet the Ferret, 1 vol. Gifford, Dorinda. 2009. 20p. pap. 24.95 *(978-1-59129-405-4(3))* America Star Bks.

Lufkin, Raymond. We Were There with the California Forty-Niners. Holt, Stephen & Lewis, Oscar. 2011. 186p. 42.95 *(978-1-258-05988-0(6))* Literary Licensing, LLC.

Lugo, Patrick. Little Monk & the Mantis: A Bug, a Boy, & the Birth of a Kung Fu Legend. Fusco, John. 32p. (J). (gr. -1-3). 2016. 8.95 *(978-0-8048-4650-9(2))*; 2012. (ENG.). 16.95 *(978-0-8048-4221-1(3))* Tuttle Publishing.

Lugo, Udayana. Goodnight Basketball. Dahl, Michael. 2020. (Sports Illustrated Kids Bedtime Bks.). (ENG.). 32p. (J). (gr. -1-2). 17.99 ***(978-1-68446-200-1(2)***, 200231, Capstone Editions) Capstone.

—The Great & the Terrible: The World's Most Glorious & Notorious Rulers & How They Got Their Names. O'Sullivan, Joanne. 2020. (ENG.). 176p. (J). (gr. 3-7). 17.99 ***(978-0-7624-9661-7(4)***, Running Pr. Kids) Running Pr.

Luhrs, Henry. Dale Evans & Danger in Crooked Canyon. Hale, Helen. 2011. 280p. 47.95 *(978-1-258-02056-9(4))* Literary Licensing, LLC.

Luigart-Stayner, Becky, photos by. Southern Cakes: Sweet & Irresistible Recipes for Everyday Celebrations. McDermott, Nancie. 2007. (ENG., 168p. (gr. 8-17). pap. 19.95 *(978-0-8118-5370-5(5))* Chronicle Bks. LLC.

Luisa, Gioffre-Suzuki. Worst Case of Paskett-Itis. Asselin, Kristine Carlson. 2013. 24p. pap. 12.99 *(978-0-9889617-0-8(9))* 4RV Pub.

Luiz, Fernando. Babies Love the Little Things. 2009. (ENG.). 10p. (J). (gr. -1). 7.95 *(978-1-58117-846-3(8)*, Intervisual/Piggy Toes) Bendon, Inc.

—Color Train, Color Train! Kelly, Martin. 2009. 20p. bds. 12.99 *(978-0-8249-1437-0(6)*, Ideal Pubns.) Worthy Publishing.

—How to Be a Princess: A Girly Girl Book. 2009. 12p. (J). bds. 6.95 *(978-1-58117-850-0(6)*, Intervisual/Piggy Toes) Bendon, Inc.

Luizada, A. Legends of Queen Esther. Simhoni, S. Lask, I. M., tr. 2011. 62p. 36.95 *(978-1-258-09389-1(8))* Literary Licensing, LLC.

Lujan, Rodrigo. ¡Es la Hora de los Esqueletos! / It's Skeleton Time! 2017. (ENG & SPA.). 32p. (J). (gr. -1-3). pap. 5.99 *(978-1-338-18785-4(6)*, Scholastic en Espanol) Scholastic, Inc.

Lujan, Tonita. Little Boy with Three Names: Stories of Taos Pueblo. Clark, Ann Nolan. 2005. 75p. (J). (gr. 2-6). reprint ed. pap. 15.00 *(978-0-7567-9717-1(9))* DIANE Publishing Co.

Lukas, Mary. Five Blessings. Drogo, Susette. 2008. 24p. (J). pap. 15.00 *(978-0-9800611-8-5(0))* Orr Bks.

Lukashevsky, Ashley. Antiracist Baby Board Book. Kendi, Ibram X. 2020. (ENG.). 24p. (J). (— 1). bds. 8.99 *(978-0-593-11041-6(2)*, Kokila) Penguin Young Readers Group.

Lukashevsky, Ashley. Antiracist Baby Picture Book. Kendi, Ibram X. 2020. (ENG.). 32p. (J). (— 1). 8.99 ***(978-0-593-11050-8(1)***, Kokila) Penguin Young Readers Group.

Lukashevsky, Ashley. Beyond the Gender Binary. Vaid-Menon, Alok. 2020. (Pocket Change Collective Ser.). (ENG.). 64p. (YA). (gr. 7). pap. 8.99 *(978-0-593-09465-5(4)*, Penguin Workshop) Penguin Young Readers Group.

—Imaginary Borders. Martinez, Xiuhtezcatl. 2020. (Pocket Change Collective Ser.). (ENG.). 64p. (YA). (gr. 7). pap. 8.99 *(978-0-593-09413-6(1)*, Penguin Workshop) Penguin Young Readers Group.

—The New Queer Conscience. Eli, Adam. 2020. (Pocket Change Collective Ser.). (ENG.). 64p. (YA). (gr. 7). pap.

L

8.99 *(978-0-593-09368-9(2)*, Penguin Workshop) Penguin Young Readers Group.

—This Is What I Know about Art. Drew, Kimberly. 2020. (Pocket Change Collective Ser.). (ENG.). 64p. (YA). (gr. 7). pap. 8.99 *(978-0-593-09518-8(9)*, Penguin Workshop) Penguin Young Readers Group.

Lukatz, Casey. Coconut's Guide to Life: Life Lessons from a Girl's Best Friend. Chobanian, Elizabeth & American Girl Publishing Staff, eds. 2003. (Coconut Ser.). (ENG.). 32p. (J). 5.95 *(978-1-58485-771-6(4))* American Girl Publishing, Inc.

—Coconut's Guide to Life: Life Lessons from a Girl's Best Friend. Chobanian, Elizabeth, ed. 2003. (Coconut Ser.). 32p. (J). 21.95 *(978-1-58485-772-3(2))* American Girl Publishing, Inc.

—Top-Secret Code Book: Tricky, Fun Codes for You & Your Friends. Maring, Therese, ed. 2005. (American Girl Today Ser.). (ENG.). 32p. (J). (gr. 4-7). per. 5.95 *(978-1-59369-018-2(5)*, American Girl) American Girl Publishing, Inc.

Lukehart, Teriann. Katie the Camel's Christmas Surprise. Ault, Paula. 2017. (ENG.). (J). pap. 12.95 *(978-1-64079-500-6(6))* Christian Faith Publishing.

lukel, Onur. No Veggies for Me. Pierro, Rita. 2011. 32p. pap. 24.95 *(978-1-4626-4554-1(2))* America Star Bks.

Lukens, Lizzie Joy. Where's Mommy's Mommy? Lukens, Lizzie. 2017. (ENG.). 36p. (J). (gr. k-6). pap. 8.99 *(978-0-692-97943-3(3))* Lizzie Joy Lukens.

Lukesh, Ronald E. My Favorite Dog & Cat Story: My Favorite Dog Story/My Favorite Cat Story. Lukesh, Jean A. 2013. 38p. (J). pap. 14.95 *(978-0-9888021-0-0(4))* Field Mouse Productions.

Lukowiak, Michael. Yuri Whiskerin's True Tale of the Invasion of the Shrews. Whiskerin, Yuri. 2016. (ENG.). (J). 19.95 *(978-0-9839877-6-5(9))* Terabyte Pr. LLC.

Lum, Bernice. The Attractive Truth about Magnetism. Swanson, Jennifer. 2012. (LOL Physical Science Ser.). (ENG.). 32p. (gr. 3-4). pap. 47.70 *(978-1-4296-9297-7(9))*; (J). pap. 8.10 *(978-1-4296-9296-0(0))* Capstone. (Capstone Pr.).

—Fully Woolly. Warwick, Ellen. 2007. (Planet Girl Ser.). 80p. (J). (gr. 5-9). 12.95 *(978-1-55337-798-6(2))* Kids Can Pr., Ltd. CAN. Dist: Hachette Bk. Group.

—The Gripping Truth about Forces & Motion. Biskup, Agnieszka. 2012. (LOL Physical Science Ser.). (ENG.). 32p. (gr. 3-4). pap. 47.70 *(978-1-4296-9299-1(5))*; (J). pap. 8.10 *(978-1-4296-9298-4(7))*; (J). lib. bdg. 27.99 *(978-1-4296-8601-3(4))* Capstone. (Capstone Pr.).

—Injeanuity. Warwick, Ellen. 2006. (Planet Girl Ser.). 80p. (J). (gr. 7-12). 12.95 *(978-1-55337-681-1(1))* Kids Can Pr., Ltd. CAN. Dist: Hachette Bk. Group.

—LOL Physical Science. Swanson, Jennifer et al. 2012. (LOL Physical Science Ser.). (ENG.). 32p. (gr. 3-4). pap. 190.80 *(978-1-4296-9305-9(3))*; (J). pap., pap., pap. 31.80 *(978-1-4296-9304-2(5))* Capstone. (Capstone Pr.).

—Mighty Maddie. Murphy, Stuart J. 2004. (MathStart Ser.). 40p. (J). 15.99 *(978-0-06-053159-1(2))*; (ENG.). (gr. -1-3). pap. 6.99 *(978-0-06-053161-4(4))* HarperCollins Pubs.

—The Shocking Truth about Electricity, 1 vol. Swanson, Jennifer Ann. 2012. (LOL Physical Science Ser.). (ENG.). 32p. (J). (gr. 3-6). pap. 8.10 *(978-1-4296-9300-4(2)*, Capstone Pr.) Capstone.

—The Shocking Truth about Electricity. Swanson, Jennifer. 2012. (LOL Physical Science Ser.). (ENG.). 32p. (gr. 3-4). pap. 47.70 *(978-1-4296-9301-1(0)*, Capstone Pr.) Capstone.

—The Solid Truth about Matter, 1 vol. Weakland, Mark Andrew. 2012. (LOL Physical Science Ser.). (ENG.). 32p. (J). (gr. 3-6). pap. 8.10 *(978-1-4296-9302-8(9)*, Capstone Pr.) Capstone.

—The Solid Truth about Matter. Weakland, Mark. 2012. (LOL Physical Science Ser.). (ENG.). 32p. (gr. 3-4). pap. 47.70 *(978-1-4296-9303-5(7)*, Capstone Pr.) Capstone.

—Stuff to Hold Your Stuff. Warwick, Ellen. 2006. (Planet Girl Ser.). 80p. (J). (gr. 5-9). 12.95 *(978-1-55337-745-0(1))* Kids Can Pr., Ltd. CAN. Dist: Hachette Bk. Group.

—3 Little Firefighters. Murphy, Stuart J. 2003. (MathStart 1 Ser.). (ENG.). 40p. (J). (gr. -1-3). pap. 5.99 *(978-0-06-000120-9(8))* HarperCollins Pubs.

Lum, Bernice. Stuff for Your Space. Lum, Bernice, tr. Warwick, Ellen. 2004. (Kids Can Do It Ser.). 40p. (J). (gr. 3-7). 6.95 *(978-1-55337-399-5(5))* Kids Can Pr., Ltd. CAN. Dist: Hachette Bk. Group.

Lum, J. Checkers & Dot at the Beach. Torres, J. 2013. (Checkers & Dot Ser.). (ENG.). 16p. (J). (— 1). bds. 7.95 *(978-1-77049-444-2(8)*, Tundra Bks.) Tundra Bks. CAN. Dist: Penguin Random Hse. LLC.

—Checkers & Dot at the Zoo. Torres, J. 2012. (Checkers & Dot Ser.). 16p. (J). (gr. k — 1). bds. 7.95 *(978-1-77049-442-8(1)*, Tundra Bks.) Tundra Bks. CAN. Dist: Penguin Random Hse. LLC.

—Checkers & Dot on the Farm. Torres, J. 2013. (Checkers & Dot Ser.). (ENG.). 16p. (J). (— 1). bds. 7.95 *(978-1-77049-443-5(X)*, Tundra Bks.) Tundra Bks. CAN. Dist: Penguin Random Hse. LLC.

Lumb, Steve. Dance to the Beat: Band 03/Yellow (Collins Big Cat) Afzal, Uz. 2005. (Collins Big Cat Ser.). (ENG.). 16p. (J). (gr. k-1). pap. 7.99 *(978-0-00-718576-4(6))* HarperCollins Pubs. Ltd. GBR. Dist: Independent Pubs. Group.

—My Party: Band 00/Lilac (Collins Big Cat) Kelly, Maoliosa. 2005. (Collins Big Cat Ser.). (ENG.). 16p. (J). (gr. -1-k). pap. 7.99 *(978-0-00-718533-7(2))* HarperCollins Pubs. Ltd. GBR. Dist: Independent Pubs. Group.

Lumbers, Fiona. The Hairdo That Got Away. Coelho, Joseph. 2019. (ENG.). 32p. (J). (gr. -1-3). 17.99 *(978-1-5415-7841-8(4))* Lerner Publishing Group.

—I Like Bees, I Don't Like Honey! Bishop, Sam. 2018. (ENG.). 32p. (J). pap. 8.95 *(978-0-571-33419-3(9)*, Faber & Faber Children's Bks.) Faber & Faber, Inc.

—Luna Loves Library Day. Coelho, Joseph. 2018. (ENG.). 32p. (J). 12.99 *(978-1-61067-675-5(0))* Kane Miller.

Lumbers, Fiona. Clem & Crab. Lumbers, Fiona. 2020. (ENG.). 32p. (J). (gr. -1-3). 17.99 *(978-1-5415-9619-1(6))* Lerner Publishing Group.

Lumer, Marc. Babel. Burston, Chaim & Naiditch, Dov. 2016. (J). *(978-1-68115-514-2(1))* Behrman Hse., Inc.

—Can You Hear a Coo, Coo?, Vol. Kiffel-Alcheh, Jamie. 2018. (ENG.). 12p. (J). (gr. -1 — 1). bds. 5.99 *(978-1-5124-4443-8(X)*, Kar-Ben Publishing) Lerner Publishing Group.

—Hashem Is Truly Everywhere. Altein, Chani. Rosenfeld, D. L. & Leverton, Yossi, eds. 2011. 28p. (J). 12.95 *(978-1-929628-57-5(9))* Hachai Publishing.

—The Search for the Stones. Blitz, Shmuel & Zakon, Miriam Stark. 2009. 96p. (J). *(978-1-4226-0934-7(0)*, Shaar Pr.) Mesorah Pubns., Ltd.

—The Torah Book of Opposites. Segal, Nechamy. 2012. 12p. (J). pap. 7.95 *(978-1-929628-67-4(6))* Hachai Publishing.

—When Miracles Happened- Wondrous Stories of Tzaddikim. 2009. 22p. (J). *(978-1-56871-484-4(X))* Targum Pr., Inc.

Lumley, Stef, photos by. London Sticker Book. Dickins, Rosie. Clarke, Phillip, ed. 2006. (Usborne Sticker Bks.). 15p. (J). (gr. 2-5). pap. 8.99 *(978-0-7945-1284-2(4)*, Usborne) EDC Publishing.

Lumsden, Colin. Apostles. 2003. (Bible Colour & Learn Ser.). 32p. pap. 2.50 *(978-1-903087-51-0(1))* DayOne Pubns. GBR. Dist: Send The Light Distribution LLC.

—Hebrews Men of Faith. 2003. (Bible Colour & Learn Ser.). 32p. pap. 2.50 *(978-1-903087-52-7(X))* DayOne Pubns. GBR. Dist: Send The Light Distribution LLC.

—John the Baptist. 2003. (Bible Colour & Learn Ser.). 32p. pap. 2.50 *(978-1-903087-44-2(9))* DayOne Pubns. GBR. Dist: Send The Light Distribution LLC.

—Miracles of Jesus. 2003. (Bible Colour & Learn Ser.). 32p. pap. 2.50 *(978-1-903087-48-0(1))* DayOne Pubns. GBR. Dist: Send The Light Distribution LLC.

—Parables of Jesus. 2003. (Bible Colour & Learn Ser.). 32p. pap. 2.50 *(978-1-903087-47-3(3))* DayOne Pubns. GBR. Dist: Send The Light Distribution LLC.

—People in the Life of Jesus. 2003. (Bible Colour & Learn Ser.). 32p. pap. 2.50 *(978-1-903087-49-7(X))* DayOne Pubns. GBR. Dist: Send The Light Distribution LLC.

—People in the Life of Paul. 2003. (Bible Colour & Learn Ser.). 32p. pap. 2.50 *(978-1-903087-50-3(3))* DayOne Pubns. GBR. Dist: Send The Light Distribution LLC.

—Story of Mary. 2003. (Bible Colour & Learn Ser.). 32p. pap. 2.50 *(978-1-903087-43-5(0))* DayOne Pubns. GBR. Dist: Send The Light Distribution LLC.

—Story of Paul. 2003. (Bible Colour & Learn Ser.). 32p. pap. 2.50 *(978-1-903087-46-6(5))* DayOne Pubns. GBR. Dist: Send The Light Distribution LLC.

—Story of Peter. 2003. (Bible Colour & Learn Ser.). 32p. pap. 2.50 *(978-1-903087-45-9(7))* DayOne Pubns. GBR. Dist: Send The Light Distribution LLC.

Lumsden, Matt. Crow No More. Burggraaf, Deborah. 2011. 28p. (J). pap. 10.95 *(978-0-9845161-8-6(2))* Protective Hands Communications.

Luna, Jose. El Queso y la Rata: With English Subtitles. Luna, Jose. 2006. (J). per. *(978-1-934379-00-4(X))* Printmedia Bks.

Luna, Lauren. The Stories True of Gabby Cockatoo. Houston, Alecia. 2010. 24p. pap. 11.25 *(978-1-60911-446-6(9)*, Strategic Bk. Publishing) Strategic Book Publishing & Rights Agency (SBPRA).

Luna, Margarita. Angela en el Cielo de Saturno. Baranda, Maria. rev. ed. 2006. (Castillo de la Lectura Naranja Ser.). (SPA & ENG.). 131p. (J). (gr. 4-7). pap. 7.95 *(978-968-5920-86-5(9))* Castillo, Ediciones, S. A. de C. V. MEX. Dist: Macmillan.

—La Isla de los Pollos. Estrada, Jorge Antonio. rev. ed. 2006. (Castillo de la Lectura Blanca Ser.). (SPA & ENG.). 48p. (J). (gr. k-2). pap. 6.95 *(978-968-5920-38-4(9))* Castillo, Ediciones, S. A. de C. V. MEX. Dist: Macmillan.

Luna, Tom & Alvarez, Laura. The Spots on the Jaguar: A Counting Book. Luna, Tom. 2005. (SPA & ENG.). 20p. (J). *(978-0-9716580-4-2(8))* Lectura Bks.

Lunch Lab, LLC., Llc. Fizzy's Lunch Lab: Escape from Greasy World. Michalak, Jamie. 2015. (Fizzy's Lunch Lab Ser.). (ENG.). 48p. (J). (gr. 1-4). pap. 5.99 *(978-0-7636-7546-2(6)*, Candlewick Entertainment) Candlewick Pr.

Lunch Lab LLC, Lunch Lab. Nelly Nitpick, Kid Food Critic. Candlewick Press Staff. 2015. (Fizzy's Lunch Lab Ser.). (ENG.). 48p. (J). (gr. 1-4). pap. 5.99 *(978-0-7636-6885-3(0)*, Candlewick Entertainment) Candlewick Pr.

Lunch Lab Staff. Fizzy's Lunch Lab: Super Supper Throwdown. Candlewick Press Staff. 2014. (Fizzy's Lunch Lab Ser.). (ENG.). 64p. (J). (gr. 1-4). pap. 5.99 *(978-0-7636-6883-9(4)*, Candlewick Entertainment) Candlewick Pr.

Lund, Brian. G Is for Golden Boy: A Manitoba Alphabet. Verstraete, Larry. 2009. (Discover Canada Province by Province Ser.). (ENG.). 40p. (J). (gr. k-8). 17.95 *(978-1-58536-364-3(2))* Sleeping Bear Pr.

Lund, Nancy M. Chippy: The sea lion that lost its Way. Haller, Christine A. 2006. 20p. (J). 11.95 *(978-0-9771129-0-6(X))* Oxbow Bks.

Lundgren, Shai & Wharton, Sigrid. Saying Goodbye: A Story about Learning to Let Go. Cooper, Lisa. 2019. (ENG.). 40p. 24.58 *(978-1-5434-0932-1(6))*; pap. 18.26 *(978-1-5434-0931-4(8))* Xlibris Corp.

Lundie, Isobel. Ada Lovelace. Pierce, Nick. 2019. (Women in Science Ser.). (ENG.). 32p. (J). (gr. 2-3). pap. 9.95 *(978-0-531-23951-3(9))*; lib. bdg. 29.00 *(978-0-531-23534-8(3))* Scholastic Library Publishing. (Watts, Franklin).

—Ghost Stories. Townsend, John. ed. 2018. (Shivers Ser.). (ENG.). 128p. (J). (gr. 2). pap. 7.95 *(978-1-912233-52-6(5)*, Scribo) Book Hse. GBR. Dist: Sterling Publishing Co., Inc.

—Hip! Hip! Hooray! Santa! ed. 2019. (Booktacular Ser.). 30p. (J). (— 1). 9.95 *(978-1-912904-47-1(0)*, Scribblers) Book Hse. GBR. Dist: Sterling Publishing Co., Inc.

—The Long-Lost Secret Diary of the World's Worst Hollywood Director. Collins, Tim. 2020. (Long-Lost Secret Diary Ser.). (ENG.). 216p. (J). pap. 9.99 *(978-1-63163-380-5(5)*, 1631633805); lib. bdg. 28.50 *(978-1-63163-379-9(1)*, 1631633791) North Star Editions. (Jolly Fish Pr.).

Lundie, Isobel. The Long-Lost Secret Diary of the World's Worst Olympic Athlete. Collins, Tim. 2020. (Long-Lost Secret Diary Ser.). (ENG.). 200p. (J). pap. 9.99 ***(978-1-63163-446-8(1)***, 1631634461); lib. bdg. 28.50 ***(978-1-63163-445-1(3)***, 1631634453) North Star Editions. (Jolly Fish Pr.).

—The Long-Lost Secret Diary of the World's Worst Samurai. Collins, Tim. 2020. (Long-Lost Secret Diary Ser.). (ENG.). 200p. (J). pap. 9.99 ***(978-1-63163-450-5(X)***, 163163450X); lib. bdg. 28.50 ***(978-1-63163-449-9(6)***, 1631634496) North Star Editions. (Jolly Fish Pr.).

Lundie, Isobel. The Long-Lost Secret Diary of the World's Worst Tomb Hunter. Collins, Tim. 2020. (Long-Lost Secret Diary Ser.). (ENG.). (J). 216p. pap. 7.95 *(978-1-63163-384-3(8)*, 1631633848); lib. bdg. 28.50 *(978-1-63163-383-6(X)*, 163163383X) North Star Editions. (Jolly Fish Pr.).

—Pirate Stories. Townsend, John. ed. 2018. (Shivers Ser.). (ENG.). 128p. (J). (gr. 2). pap. 7.95 *(978-1-912233-51-9(7)*, Scribo) Book Hse. GBR. Dist: Sterling Publishing Co., Inc.

—Rachel Carson. Rooney, Anne. 2019. (Women in Science Ser.). (ENG.). 32p. (J). (gr. 2-3). lib. bdg. 29.00 *(978-0-531-23537-9(8)*, Watts, Franklin) Scholastic Library Publishing.

—Scarlet Hood. Evans, Mark. ed. 2018. 64p. (J). (gr. 2). pap. 8.95 *(978-1-912233-34-2(7))* Book Hse. GBR. Dist: Sterling Publishing Co., Inc.

Lundie, Isobel. Wherever You Go, I Want You to Know. Kruger, Melissa B. 2020. (ENG.). 24p. (J). ***(978-1-78498-535-6(X))*** Good Bk. Co., The.

Lundie, Isobel. Women in Science - Jane Goodall. Woolf, Alex. 2019. (Women in Science Ser.). (ENG.). 32p. (J). (gr. 2-3). pap. 9.95 *(978-0-531-23952-0(7))*; lib. bdg. 29.00 *(978-0-531-23535-5(1))* Scholastic Library Publishing. (Watts, Franklin).

—Women in Science - Rachel Carson. Rooney, Anne. 2019. (Women in Science Ser.). (ENG.). 32p. (J). (gr. 2-3). pap. 9.95 *(978-0-531-23954-4(3)*, Watts, Franklin) Scholastic Library Publishing.

—Women in Science - Temple Grandin. Cardona, Ruby. 2019. (Women in Science Ser.). (ENG.). 32p. (J). (gr. 2-3). lib. bdg. 29.00 *(978-0-531-23536-2(X)*, Watts, Franklin) Scholastic Library Publishing.

Lundie, Isobel & Beach, Bryan. The Science of Buildings: The Sky-Scraping Story of Structures. Woolf, Alex. 2019. (Science of Engineering Ser.). (ENG.). 32p. (J). (gr. 3-3). lib. bdg. 29.00 *(978-0-531-13194-7(7)*, Watts, Franklin) Scholastic Library Publishing.

Lundie, Isobel & Scrace, Carolyn. Draw, Paint, & Stick. 2020. (ENG.). 160p. (J). (gr. k). 12.95 *(978-1-912904-85-3(3)*, Scribblers) Book Hse. GBR. Dist: Sterling Publishing Co., Inc.

—Who's That Hiding in the Barn? Pierce, Nick. ed. 2019. (ENG.). 14p. (J). (gr. -1). bds. 6.95 *(978-1-912904-45-7(4)*, Scribblers) Book Hse. GBR. Dist: Sterling Publishing Co., Inc.

—Who's That Present For? Pierce, Nick. ed. 2019. 14p. (J). (gr. -1). bds. 6.95 *(978-1-912904-46-4(2)*, Scribblers) Book Hse. GBR. Dist: Sterling Publishing Co., Inc.

Lundie, Isobel, jt. illus. see Beach, Bryan.

Lundquist, David R., photos by. Clarabelle: Making Milk & So Much More. Peterson, Cris. 2013. (ENG., 32p. (J). (gr. 4-7). pap. 8.99 *(978-1-62091-590-5(1))* Boyds Mills Pr.

—Popcorn Country: The Story of America's Favorite Snack. Peterson, Cris. 2019. 32p. (J). (gr. -1-3). 17.95 *(978-1-62979-892-9(4))* Boyds Mills Pr.

—Seed, Soil, Sun: Earth's Recipe for Food. Peterson, Cris. (ENG., 32p. (J). (gr. k-3). 2012. pap. 8.95 *(978-1-59078-947-6(4))*; 2010. 17.95 *(978-1-59078-713-7(7))* Boyds Mills Pr.

Lundquist, Mary. The Amazing Idea of You. Wild, Charlotte Sullivan. 2019. (ENG.). 40p. (J). 17.99 *(978-1-68119-183-6(0)*, 900162074, Bloomsbury Children's Bks.) Bloomsbury Publishing USA.

—Animal Babies Like to Play. Adams, Jennifer. 2019. (ENG.). 32p. (J). (gr. -1-3). 17.99 *(978-0-06-239447-7(9)*, Balzer & Bray) HarperCollins Pubs.

—Bloom: An Ode to Spring. Diesen, Deborah. 2017. (ENG.). 32p. (J). 16.99 *(978-0-374-30250-4(2)*, 900147219, Farrar, Straus & Giroux (BYR)) Farrar, Straus & Giroux.

—One Little Two Little Three Little Children. DiPucchio, Kelly. 2016. (ENG.). 32p. (J). (gr. -1-3). 17.99 *(978-0-06-234866-1(3))* HarperCollins Pubs.

Lundquist, Mary. Cat & Bunny. Lundquist, Mary. 2015. (ENG.). 32p. (J). (gr. -1-3). 17.99 *(978-0-06-228780-9(X))* HarperCollins Pubs.

Lundquist, Robert. Heather's Amazing Discovery: A True Story of Paleontology. Griffiths, Deborah. 2013. pap. *(978-0-9696612-0-7(7))* Courtenay & District Museum.

Lundy, Christy. Earthrise: Apollo 8 & the Photo That Changed the World. Gladstone, James. 2018. (ENG.). 32p. (J). (gr. 2-5). 16.95 *(978-1-77147-316-3(9))* Owlkids Bks. Inc. CAN. Dist: Publishers Group West (PGW).

Lunelli, Giuliano. Puss in Boots. Perrault, Charles. Bell, Anthea, tr. 2003. 24p. (J). (gr. 3-5). reprint ed. 18.00 *(978-0-7567-6600-9(1))* DIANE Publishing Co.

Lunik, Alejandra. What Can You Do? White, Amy. 2008. (Fácil de Leer / Easy to Read Ser.). (ENG.). 16p. (J). pap. 5.99 ***(978-1-59820-559-6(5)***, Santillana Texto) Santillana USA Publishing Co., Inc.

Lunn, Corey. Peekaboo Presents. Night & Day Studios. 2015. (Peekaboo Ser.). (ENG.). 20p. (J). (— 1). bds. 7.99 *(978-0-7636-7567-7(9)*, Candlewick Entertainment) Candlewick Pr.

—Peekaboo Wild. Night & Day Studios. 2016. (Peekaboo Ser.). (ENG.). 20p. (J). (— 1). bds. 7.99 *(978-0-7636-7568-4(7)*, Candlewick Entertainment) Candlewick Pr.

Lunn, Naomi. The Fight Before Christmas. McCormack, Chris. 2013. 44p. (J). pap. *(978-0-9572875-4-9(2))* Batmack Ltd.

Lunsford, Robert. George Washington & the Magic Hat: George Washington & the Magic Hat, 1 vol. Kalb, Deborah. 2016. (President & Me Ser.: 1). (ENG.). 144p. (gr. 3-6). pap. 12.99 *(978-0-7643-5110-5(9)*, 7365) Schiffer Publishing, Ltd.

—John Adams & the Magic Bobblehead: John Adams & the Magic Bobblehead, 1 vol. Kalb, Deborah. 2018. (President & Me Ser.: 2). (ENG.). 144p. (gr. 3-6). pap. 12.99 *(978-0-7643-5556-1(2)*, 9948) Schiffer Publishing, Ltd.

Lunzer, Lee. Betty Grable Paper Dolls. Lunzer, Lee. 2007. (ENG.). 16p. pap. 12.00 *(978-0-9790668-7-0(5))* Paper Studio Pr.

Lunzer, Lee, jt. illus. see Valliant, Regina.

Luo, Keyi. Colorful Childhood. 2004. (CHI.). (J). pap. 27.50 *(978-1-932002-47-8(2)*, Cozy Publishing Hse.) Cozy Graphics Corp.

Luo, Shiyin Sean. By the Light of the Moon. Goss, Leon. 2005. (J). pap. *(978-1-933156-12-5(0))*; per. 16.99 *(978-1-933156-05-7(8))* GSVQ Publishing. (VisionQuest Kids).

Lupton, David. Goodbye Brecken. 2012. 32p. (J). pap. *(978-1-4338-1290-3(8)*, Magination Pr.) American Psychological Assn.

—Prokofiev's Peter & the Wolf. Hahm, Ji-seul. 2016. (Music Storybooks Ser.). (ENG.). 44p. (J). (gr. 3-5). 29.32 *(978-1-925247-39-8(2)*, Big and SMALL) ChoiceMaker Pty. Ltd., The AUS. Dist: Lerner Publishing Group.

Luraschi, Anna. Christmas Poems. Taplin, Sam. 2006. (Christmas Poems Ser.). 95p. (J). 12.99 *(978-0-7945-1471-6(5)*, Usborne) EDC Publishing.

—Illustrated Stories for Christmas. Chandler, Samuel. Spatz, Caroline, ed. 2010. (Illustrated Stories Ser.). 351p. (YA). (gr. 3-18). 14.99 *(978-0-7945-2687-0(X)*, Usborne) EDC Publishing.

—The Nutcracker. 2007. 24p. (J). 9.99 *(978-0-7945-1515-7(0)*, Usborne) EDC Publishing.

—The Usborne Book of Bedtime Rhymes. Taplin, Sam. 2008. (Usborne Book Of... Ser.). 12p. (J). (gr. -1-3). bds. 12.99 *(978-0-7945-1898-1(2)*, Usborne) EDC Publishing.

Lush, Debbie. Hot Like Fire. Bloom, Valerie. 2009. (J). (gr. 4-7). pap. 11.95 *(978-0-7475-9973-9(4))* Bloomsbury Publishing Plc GBR. Dist: Independent Pubs. Group.

Lusky, Gretel. Primer. Krajewski, Thomas & Muro, Jennifer. 2020. (ENG.). 160p. (J). (gr. 7). pap. 9.99 ***(978-1-4012-9657-5(2))*** DC Comics.

Lustig, Loretta. The Little Red Hen: A Tale about Cooperation. 2006. (J). 6.99 *(978-1-59939-018-5(3))* Cornerstone Pr.

Luterio, Edward. Let's Color Some Sharks! Luterio, Edward. 2020. (ENG.). 26p. (J). pap. 5.95 ***(978-1-6562-9599-6(7))*** Independently Published.

Luthardt, Kevin. Zoom!, 1 vol. Adams, Diane. (ENG.). 32p. (J). 2013. (gr. -1-1). pap. 7.95 *(978-1-56145-683-3(7))*; 2005. (gr. k-1). 15.95 *(978-1-56145-332-0(3))* Peachtree Publishing Co. Inc.

Luthardt, Kevin. Flying!, 1 vol. Luthardt, Kevin. (ENG.). 32p. (J). (gr. -1-1). 2013. 7.95 *(978-1-56145-724-3(8))*; 2009. 15.95 *(978-1-56145-430-3(3))* Peachtree Publishing Co. Inc.

—Larabee, 1 vol. Luthardt, Kevin. (ENG.). 32p. (J). 2009. (gr. -1-1). pap. 7.95 *(978-1-56145-482-2(6))*; 2004. (gr. k-1). 15.95 *(978-1-56145-300-9(5))* Peachtree Publishing Co. Inc.

—Peep!, 1 vol. Luthardt, Kevin. (ENG.). 36p. (J). (gr. -1-1). 2012. pap. 7.95 *(978-1-56145-682-6(9))*; 2003. 15.95 *(978-1-56145-046-6(4))* Peachtree Publishing Co. Inc.

—When Edgar Met Cecil, 1 vol. Luthardt, Kevin. 2013. (ENG.). 32p. (J). (gr. -1-3). 15.95 *(978-1-56145-706-9(X))* Peachtree Publishing Co. Inc.

Luther, Rowan. Little Puddle Cat. LaBadie, Sally J. 2019. (ENG.). 24p. (J). ***(978-1-5255-6454-3(4))***; pap. ***(978-1-5255-6455-0(2))*** FriesenPress.

Luthi, Morgan. Wall- E: Out There. Carlson, Bryce. 2010. (ENG.). 112p. (J). (gr. 3-6). pap. 9.99 *(978-1-60886-568-0(1))* Boom! Studios.

—Wall E Vol. 1: Recharge. Wheeler, Shannon & Torres, J. 2010. (ENG.). 112p. (J). 24.99 *(978-1-60886-554-3(1))* Boom! Studios.

Luthi, Morgan & Barks, Carl. Wall-E Vol. 1: Recharge. Wheeler, Shannon & Barks, Carl. Torres, J. 2010. (ENG.). 112p. (J). pap. 9.99 *(978-1-60886-512-3(6))* Boom! Studios.

Lütje, Susanne. Best Grandma in the World! Zabini, Eleni & Livanios, Eleni. 2015. 16p. (J). bds. 7.95 *(978-0-7358-4225-0(6))* North-South Bks., Inc.

—Best Grandpa in the World! Zabini, Eleni & Livanios, Eleni. 2015. 16p. (J). bds. 7.95 *(978-0-7358-4237-3(X))* North-South Bks., Inc.

Lutz, Nancie Anne. Patsy & Freckles Make Christmas Cookies. Lutz, Nancie Anne. 2005. 25p. (J). *(978-0-9760064-1-1(3))* Dollworks.

—Patsy Ann Back Again. Lutz, Nancie Anne. 2005. 25p. (J). pap. 14.50 *(978-0-9760064-0-4(5))* Dollworks.

—Patsy Ann Paperdoll: Including Photographs of Patsy's Original Clothes. Lutz, Nancie Anne. 2005. 10p. (J). 14.50 *(978-0-9760064-2-8(1))* Dollworks.

Lutz, Patrick & Neal, Lindsay. Jules, the Lightning Bug. Singh, Amulya. 2019. (ENG.). 18p. (J). (gr. k-4). pap. 7.00 ***(978-0-578-53459-6(2))*** Singh, Amulya.

Lutz, Will. The Mega Monster Guidebook: A Guide for Learning the Monsters of the World. Lutz, Will. 2019. (Volume 1 Ser.: Vol. 1). (ENG.). 40p. (J). (gr. k-5). 22.00 ***(978-0-578-56281-0(2))*** Lutz, William.

Luu, Bao. Earth Hour: A Lights-Out Event for Our Planet. Heffernan, Nanette. 2020. 32p. (J). (gr. -1-2). lib. bdg. 16.99 *(978-1-58089-942-0(0))* Charlesbridge Publishing, Inc.

—Hoot! Meow! Roar! Let's Listen to Animals Around the World! Cottage Door Press & Parragon Books, eds. 2019. (ENG.). 10p. (J). (gr. -1-2). bds. 12.99 *(978-1-68052-682-0(0)*, 2002840, Parragon Books) Cottage Door Pr.

—The Seed of Compassion: Lessons from the Life & Teachings of His Holiness the Dalai Lama. His Holiness The Dalai Lama, His Holiness. 2020. (ENG.). 40p. (J). (gr.

-1-3). 18.99 *(978-0-525-55514-8(5)*, Kokila) Penguin Young Readers Group.

Luu, Cindy. The Knot Guide for the Mother of the Bride. Roney, Carley. 2005. (ENG.). 108p. (gr. 8-17). 16.95 *(978-0-8118-4636-3(9))* Chronicle Bks. LLC.

Lux, Eldon. Iris Wall, Cracker Cowgirl, 1 vol. Rey, Carol. 2012. (ENG.). 32p. (J). (gr. k-3). 16.99 *(978-1-4556-1525-4(0)*, Pelican Publishing) Arcadia Publishing.

Luxbacher, Irene. Aunt Pearl, 1 vol. Kulling, Monica. 2019. (ENG.). 32p. (J). (gr. k-2). 18.95 *(978-1-77306-153-5(4))* Groundwood Bks. CAN. Dist: Publishers Group West (PGW).

Luxbacher, Irene. The Imaginary Garden. Larsen, Andrew. (ENG.). 32p. (J). (gr. -1-2). 2020. pap. 10.99 ***(978-1-5253-0539-9(5))***; 2009. 16.95 *(978-1-55453-279-7(5))* Kids Can Pr., Ltd. CAN. Dist: Hachette Bk. Group.

Luxbacher, Irene. Treasure, 1 vol. Messier, Mireille. 2019. (ENG.). 32p. (J). (gr. -1-k). 19.95 *(978-1-4598-1734-0(6))* Orca Bk. Pubs. USA.

—Trésor, 1 vol. Messier, Mireille. 2019. (FRE.). 32p. (J). (gr. -1-k). 19.95 *(978-1-4598-2327-3(3))* Orca Bk. Pubs. USA.

Luxbacher, Irene. Mattoo, Let's Play! Luxbacher, Irene. 2010. 32p. (J). (gr. -1-2). 16.95 *(978-1-55453-424-1(0))* Kids Can Pr., Ltd. CAN. Dist: Hachette Bk. Group.

—123 I Can Build! Luxbacher, Irene. 2009. (Starting Art Ser.). 24p. (J). (gr. -1-2). 14.95 *(978-1-55453-315-2(5))*; (gr. k-3). pap. 21.19 *(978-1-55453-316-9(3))* Kids Can Pr., Ltd. CAN. Dist: Hachette Bk. Group, Children's Plus, Inc.

—123 I Can Draw! Luxbacher, Irene. 2008. (Starting Art Ser.). 24p. (J). (gr. -1-2). 14.95 *(978-1-55453-039-7(3))* Kids Can Pr., Ltd. CAN. Dist: Hachette Bk. Group.

—123 I Can Make Prints! Luxbacher, Irene. 2008. (Starting Art Ser.). 24p. (J). (gr. -1-2). 14.95 *(978-1-55453-040-3(7))* Kids Can Pr., Ltd. CAN. Dist: Hachette Bk. Group.

Luxich, Matt. Invasion of the Gym Class Zombies. Nickel, Scott. 2008. (Graphic Sparks Ser.). (ENG.). 40p. (J). (gr. 2-5). pap. 5.95 *(978-1-4342-0503-2(7)*, Stone Arch Bks.) Capstone.

—Secret of the Summer School Zombies, 1 vol. Nickel, Scott. 2008. (Graphic Sparks Ser.). (ENG.). 40p. (J). (gr. 2-5). 23.99 *(978-1-4342-0760-9(9))*; pap. 5.95 *(978-1-4342-0856-9(7))* Capstone. (Stone Arch Bks.).

Luyken, Corinna. Adrian Simcox Does NOT Have a Horse. Campbell, Marcy. 2018. 40p. (J). (-k). 17.99 *(978-0-7352-3037-8(4)*, Dial Bks) Penguin Young Readers Group.

—Weird Little Robots. Crimi, Carolyn. 2019. (ENG.). 240p. (J). (gr. 3-7). 16.99 *(978-0-7636-9493-7(2))* Candlewick Pr.

Luyken, Corinna. The Book of Mistakes. Luyken, Corinna. 2017. 56p. (J). (gr. -1-3). 18.99 *(978-0-7352-2792-7(6)*, Dial Bks) Penguin Young Readers Group.

Luykx, Th. D. Oil Comes to Us. Wyler, Rose & McSpadden, Warren W. 2011. 32p. pap. 35.95 *(978-1-258-10512-9(8))* Literary Licensing, LLC.

Luzano, Tony. I Just Want to Be Super. Katz, Andrew. 2020. 32p. (J). (gr. -1). 15.95 *(978-2-89802-193-0(8)*, CrackBoom! Bks.) Chouette Publishing CAN. Dist: Publishers Group West (PGW).

Luzgin, Helen. Whisper the Baby Butterfly. Hines, Connie. 2018. (ENG.). 26p. (J). pap. 13.95 *(978-1-4808-6836-6(1))* Archway Publishing.

Luzniak, Greg, et al. Venom: Carnage Unleashed. 2017. (ENG.). 440p. (J). (gr. 4-17). pap. 34.99 *(978-1-302-90796-9(4))* Marvel Worldwide, Inc.

LV Studio. Pat the Zoo (Pat the Bunny) Golden Books. 2012. (Touch-And-Feel Ser.). 16p. (J). (gr. k — 1). 14.99 *(978-0-307-97797-7(8)*, Golden Bks.) Random Hse. Children's Bks.

Ly, Erik. Bullied. Langteau, Scott. 2018. (ENG.). 56p. (J). 17.95 *(978-0-692-14333-9(5)*, 9780692143339) Shake the Moon Bks.

Lý, Thu Hà. Indebted As Lord Chom/No Nhu Chua Chom: The Legend of the Forbidden Street. Song Hà. Smith, William, tr. from VIE. 2006. (ENG & VIE.). 32p. (J). (gr. 1-4). 16.95 *(978-0-9701654-6-6(3))* East West Discovery Pr.

Ly, Youme Nguyen. Peace, Bugs, & Understanding: An Adventure in Sibling Harmony. Silver, Gail. 2014. 48p. (J). (gr. -1-3). 16.95 *(978-1-937006-63-1(8)*, Plum Blossom Bks.) Parallax Pr.

Lyall, Dennis. The American Revolution. Rife, Douglas M. & Capaldi, Gina. 2009. (ENG.). 44p. (J). (gr. 3-17). 19.99 *(978-1-58476-612-4(3))* Innovative Kids.

—Letters for Freedom: the Civil War. Rife, Douglas M. & Capaldi, Gina. 2011. (ENG.). 44p. (J). (gr. 3-17). 19.99 *(978-1-60169-018-0(5))* Innovative Kids.

—Marshall: A Nantucket Sea Rescue. Stewart, Whitney. 2008. (ENG.). 32p. (J). (gr. -1-2). 2.95 *(978-1-59249-856-7(6))*; 6.95 *(978-1-59249-855-0(8))*; 10.95 *(978-1-59249-857-4(4))* Soundprints.

—The Upside-Down Voyage. Wulffson, Don L. 2005. (J). *(978-1-59336-334-5(6))*; pap. *(978-1-59336-335-2(4))* Mondo Publishing.

Lybeck, Bertil. The Wonderful Adventure of Nils Holgersson. Lagerlöf, Selma. Norlen, Paul, tr. 2018. (ENG.). 224p. pap. 14.00 *(978-0-241-20609-6(X)*, Penguin Classics) Penguin Publishing Group.

Lydenberg, Annica. The Other Side of Lost. Kirby, Jessi. 2018. (ENG.). 320p. (J). (gr. 9). 17.99 *(978-0-06-242424-2(6)*, HarperTeen) HarperCollins Pubs.

Lydes, Mariette. The Cloak of Dreams: Chinese Fairy Tales. Balázs, Béla & Balázs, Béla. 2010. (Oddly Modern Fairy Tales Ser.: 3). (ENG.). 208p. 24.95 *(978-0-691-14711-6(6)*, 32167) Princeton Univ. Pr.

Lye, Michael. Choices: Stories for Assembly & P. S. H. E. Aspland, G. 2013. (ENG.). 64p. pap. 15.95 *(978-1-85741-077-8(7))* Southgate Pubs. GBR. Dist: Parkwest Pubns., Inc.

—Geography in the School Grounds. Hare, Ralph. 2013. (ENG.). 72p. pap. 15.95 *(978-1-85741-023-5(8))* Southgate Pubs. GBR. Dist: Parkwest Pubns., Inc.

—Home Stories: Talking about Personal, Social & Health Issues at Home. Aspland, Gordon. 2013. (ENG.). 30p. pap. 11.95 *(978-1-85741-130-0(7))* Southgate Pubs. GBR. Dist: Parkwest Pubns., Inc.

Lyford, Cabot. Arthur the Moose. Lyford, Cabot. l.t. ed. 2004. 32p. (J). lib. bdg. *(978-0-9748145-0-6(4))* Castlebay, Inc.

Lyle, Avis. The Bumpy Pumpkin. Inman, George, Jr. et al. 2004. (ENG.). 18p. (J). 12.95 *(978-0-9754696-0-6(6))* Bumpy Pumpkin.

Lyle, Kevin, jt. illus. see Chaisty, Chris.

Lyle, Tom, et al. Mutant X: the Complete Collection Vol. 2. 2019. 472p. (YA). (gr. 4-17). pap. 39.99 *(978-1-302-92062-3(6))* Marvel Worldwide, Inc.

Lyles, Christopher. Good-Bye, Jeepers: What to Expect When Your Pet Dies, 1 vol. Loewen, Nancy. 2011. (Life's Challenges Ser.). (ENG.). 24p. (J). (gr. 2-3). lib. bdg. 26.65 *(978-1-4048-6680-5(9)*, Picture Window Bks.) Capstone.

—Grow Grateful. Foster-Lasser, Sage & Lasser, Jon. 2018. 32p. (J). *(978-1-4338-2903-1(7)*, Magination Pr.) American Psychological Assn.

—Grow Happy. Lasser, Jon & Foster-Lasser, Sage. 2017. 32p. (J). 15.95 *(978-1-4338-2331-2(4)*, Magination Pr.) American Psychological Assn.

—Grow Kind. Lasser, Jon & Foster-Lasser, Sage. 2020. (J). *(978-1-4338-3050-1(7)*, Magination Pr.) American Psychological Assn.

—Lucy & Lila. Fletcher, Alison. 2016. (ENG.). 32p. (J). (gr. -1-3). 16.99 *(978-1-4998-0156-9(4))* Little Bee Books Inc.

—Once upon a Time: Writing Your Own Fairy Tale, 1 vol. Loewen, Nancy. 2009. (Writer's Toolbox Ser.). (ENG.). 32p. (J). (gr. 2-4). pap. 8.95 *(978-1-4048-5336-2(7)*, Picture Window Bks.) Capstone.

—Saying Good-Bye to Uncle Joe: What to Expect When Someone You Love Dies, 1 vol. Loewen, Nancy. 2011. (Life's Challenges Ser.). (ENG.). 24p. (J). (gr. 2-3). lib. bdg. 26.65 *(978-1-4048-6677-5(9)*, Picture Window Bks.) Capstone.

—Share a Scare: Writing Your Own Scary Story, 1 vol. Loewen, Nancy. 2009. (Writer's Toolbox Ser.). (ENG.). 32p. (J). (gr. 2-4). pap. 8.95 *(978-1-4048-5700-1(1)*, Picture Window Bks.) Capstone.

—Show Me a Story: Writing Your Own Picture Book, 1 vol. Loewen, Nancy. 2009. (Writer's Toolbox Ser.). (ENG.). 32p. (J). (gr. 2-4). pap. 8.95 *(978-1-4048-5342-3(1))*; lib. bdg. 27.99 *(978-1-4048-5341-6(3))* Capstone. (Picture Window Bks.).

—Sincerely Yours: Writing Your Own Letter, 1 vol. Loewen, Nancy. 2009. (Writer's Toolbox Ser.). (ENG.). 32p. (J). (gr. 2-4). pap. 8.95 *(978-1-4048-5339-3(1)*, Picture Window Bks.) Capstone.

—When You Look Out the Window: How Phyllis Lyon & Del Martin Built a Community. Pitman, Gayle E. 2017. 40p. (J). *(978-1-4338-2736-5(0)*, Magination Pr.) American Psychological Assn.

—Words, Wit, & Wonder: Writing Your Own Poem, 1 vol. Loewen, Nancy. 2010. (Writer's Toolbox Ser.). (ENG.). 32p. (J). (gr. 2-4). pap. 8.95 *(978-1-4048-5345-4(6)*, Picture Window Bks.) Capstone.

Lyles, Christopher, et al. Writer's Toolbox: Learn How to Write Letters, Fairy Tales, Scary Stories, Journals, Poems, & Reports, 1 vol. Loewen, Nancy. 2009. (Writer's Toolbox Ser.). (ENG.). 192p. (J). (gr. 2-4). pap. 14.95 *(978-1-4048-5905-0(5)*, Picture Window Bks.) Capstone.

Lyles, Christopher & Ouren, Todd. It's All about You: Writing Your Own Journal, 1 vol. Loewen, Nancy. 2009. (Writer's Toolbox Ser.). (ENG.). 32p. (J). (gr. 2-4). pap. 8.95 *(978-1-4048-5698-1(6))*; lib. bdg. 27.99 *(978-1-4048-5520-5(3))* Capstone. (Picture Window Bks.).

Lyles, Christopher, jt. illus. see Beacon, Dawn.

Lyles, Christopher, jt. illus. see Doerrfeld, Cori.

Lyman, Bradford Trent. Choices. Withers, Vanessa Lyman. 2019. (ENG.). 34p. (J). pap. 21.99 ***(978-1-7960-6199-4(9))*** Xlibris Corp.

Lyman, Mitzi. The Reading Rabbit. Yager, Jan. 32p. (J). 2014. (ENG.). 25.95 *(978-1-938998-00-3(6))*; 2013. pap. 17.95 *(978-1-938998-01-0(4))* Hannacroix Creek Bks., Inc.

Lyn, Jami. Cabo & Coral Go Surfing! Wahn, Udo. 2007. 48p. (J). pap. 17.95 *(978-0-615-17598-0(8))* Caboandcoral.com.

Lynch, Dan. Kid Scripts: Just What the Doctor Ordered. Kachmann, Rudy. 2005. (ENG.). 48p. (J). spiral bd. 12.95 *(978-1-893270-38-1(6))* Evangel Author Services.

Lynch, Emily S. Talking Is Hard for Me! Encouraging Communication in Children with Speech-Language Difficulties. Reinert, Linda M. 2013. (ENG.). 54p. pap. 18.95 *(978-1-60613-192-3(3))* Woodbine Hse.

Lynch, Jason. Worthwhile. Kirkpatrick, Taylor. 2003. 32p. (J). 15.95 *(978-0-9725420-0-5(0))* Chapman Pr., LLC.

Lynch, Jay. Mo & Jo: Fighting Together Forever, 1 vol. Lynch, Jay. Haspiel, Dean. 2013. (Toon Bks.). (ENG.). 40p. (J). (gr. 2-3). lib. bdg. 29.93 *(978-1-61479-152-2(X)*, 14844) Spotlight.

Lynch, Jay, jt. illus. see Cammuso, Frank.

Lynch, Josh. White House Winners: What You Don't Know about the Presidents. Scholastic & Tracosas, L. J. 2017. (ENG.). 64p. (J). (gr. 1-3). 10.99 *(978-1-338-12997-7(X))* Scholastic, Inc.

—White House Winners: What You Don't Know about the Presidents. Tracosas, L. J. 2017. 64p. (J). *(978-1-338-15978-3(X))* Scholastic, Inc.

Lynch, Kelly. Mighty Mike Repairs a Playground, 1 vol. Lynch, Casey. 2011. (Mighty Mike Ser.). (ENG.). 32p. (J). (gr. k-4). 28.50 *(978-1-61641-132-9(5)*, 11450, Looking Glass Library) Magic Wagon.

Lynch, P. J. The Bee-Man of Orn. Stockton, Frank Richard. 2006. 44p. (J). (gr. k-4). reprint ed. 18.00 *(978-1-4223-5505-3(5))* DIANE Publishing Co.

—A Christmas Carol. Dickens, Charles. 2006. (ENG.). 160p. (Orig.). (J). (gr. 5-6). 19.99 *(978-0-7636-3120-8(5))* Candlewick Pr.

—The Christmas Miracle of Jonathan Toomey. Wojciechowski, Susan. 2015. (ENG.). 40p. (J). (gr. 1-4). 17.99 *(978-0-7636-7822-7(8))* Candlewick Pr.

—The Dog Who Lost His Bark. Colfer, Eoin. 2019. (ENG.). 144p. (J). (gr. 2-5). 16.99 *(978-1-5362-0442-1(0))* Candlewick Pr.

—Fairy Tales of Ireland. Yeats, W. B. 2019. (ENG.). 160p. (J). 6.99 *(978-0-00-825304-2(8)*, HarperCollins Children's Bks.) HarperCollins Pubs. Ltd. GBR. Dist: HarperCollins Pubs.

—The Gift of the Magi. Henry, O. 2008. (ENG.). 40p. (J). (gr. 5-9). 17.99 *(978-0-7636-3530-5(8))* Candlewick Pr.

—Grandad's Prayers of the Earth. Wood, Douglas. 2009. 32p. pap. 6.99 *(978-0-7636-1865-0(9))*; (ENG.). (J). (gr. 1-4). pap. 8.99 *(978-0-7636-4675-2(X))* Candlewick Pr.

—Grandad's Prayers of the Earth. Wood, Douglas. 2004. 28p. (J). (gr. k-4). reprint ed. 17.00 *(978-0-7567-7101-0(3))* DIANE Publishing Co.

—Lincoln & His Boys. Wells, Rosemary. 96p. (J). (gr. 3-7). 2015. pap. 8.99 *(978-0-7636-8069-5(9))*; 2008. (ENG.). 16.99 *(978-0-7636-3723-1(8))* Candlewick Pr.

—No One but You. Wood, Douglas. 2011. 32p. (J). (gr. 1-4). 17.99 *(978-0-7636-3848-1(X))* Candlewick Pr.

—Patrick & the President. Tubridy, Ryan. 2017. (ENG.). 40p. (J). (gr. 1-4). 16.99 *(978-0-7636-8949-0(1))* Candlewick Pr.

—The Snow Queen. Andersen, Hans. 2014. Orig. Title: Snedronningen. 48p. (J). (gr. k-2). pap. 10.99 *(978-1-84270-901-6(1))* Andersen Pr. GBR. Dist: Independent Pubs. Group.

—The Steadfast Tin Soldier. Andersen, Hans & Lewis, Naomi. 2005.Tr. of Standhaftige Tinsoldat. 32p. (J). (gr. -1-4). pap. 11.99 *(978-1-84270-443-1(5))* Andersen Pr. GBR. Dist: Independent Pubs. Group.

—The Story of Britain from the Norman Conquest to the European Union. Dillon, Patrick. 2011. (ENG.). 352p. (J). (gr. 5-18). 21.99 *(978-0-7636-5122-0(2))* Candlewick Pr.

—When Jessie Came Across the Sea. Hest, Amy. 2003. (ENG.). 40p. (J). (gr. 1-4). pap. 7.99 *(978-0-7636-1274-0(X))* Candlewick Pr.

Lynch, P. J. The Boy Who Fell off the Mayflower, or John Howland's Good Fortune. Lynch, P. J. 64p. (J). (gr. 2-5). 2018. 9.99 *(978-1-5362-0296-0(7))*; 2015. (ENG.). 18.99 *(978-0-7636-6584-5(3))* Candlewick Pr.

Lynch, P. J. The Haunted Lake. Lynch, P. J. 2020. (ENG.). 48p. (J). (gr. 2-5). 17.99 ***(978-1-5362-0013-3(1))*** Candlewick Pr.

Lynch, Stephanie. The Tale of Squabbit. Young, Rachel & Young, Jackie. 2011. 42p. pap. 15.00 *(978-1-60911-360-5(8)*, Eloquent Bks.) Strategic Book Publishing & Rights Agency (SBPRA).

Lynch, Stuart. Always Hug a Unicorn. Make Believe Ideas Ltd. 2019. (Read & Play Ser.). (ENG.). 12p. (J). (gr. -1-7). *(978-1-78843-659-5(8))* Make Believe Ideas.

—Be Clever Little Fox. Make Believe Ideas Ltd. 2019. (ENG.). 12p. (J). bds. *(978-1-78947-006-2(4))* Make Believe Ideas.

—Be Fabulous Like a Flamingo. Make Believe Ideas Ltd. 2019. (ENG.). 12p. (J). (gr. -1-7). bds. *(978-1-78947-174-8(5))* Make Believe Ideas.

Lynch, Stuart. La Bella y la Bestia. un Cuento Sobre la Empat�a / Beauty & the Beast. a Story about Empathy. Anderton, Helen. 2020. (Cuentos con Valores Ser.: 1). (SPA.). 20p. (J). (-k). bds. 10.95 ***(978-1-64473-174-1(6)***, Beascoa) Penguin Random House Grupo Editorial ESP. Dist: Penguin Random Hse. LLC.

Lynch, Stuart. Butt Out! Make Believe Ideas Ltd. 2019. (ENG.). 14p. (J). (gr. -1-7). bds. *(978-1-78843-987-9(2))* Make Believe Ideas.

Lynch, Stuart. Caperucita Roja. un Cuento Sobre la Autoestima / Little Red Riding Hood. a Story about Self-Esteem. Anderton, Helen. 2020. (Cuentos con Valores Ser.: 3). (SPA.). 20p. (J). (-k). bds. 10.95 ***(978-1-64473-172-7(X)***, Beascoa) Penguin Random House Grupo Editorial ESP. Dist: Penguin Random Hse. LLC.

—Christmas Activity Book. Make Believe Ideas Ltd. 2019. (ENG.). 32p. (J). (gr. -1-7). pap. ***(978-1-78843-933-6(3))*** Make Believe Ideas.

—Clump the Lump of Coal. Make Believe Ideas Ltd & Best, Elanor. 2020. (ENG.). 26p. (J). bds. ***(978-1-78947-720-7(4))*** Make Believe Ideas.

Lynch, Stuart. Dinosaur Island Activity Book. Make Believe Ideas Ltd. 2019. (Balloon Stickers Ser.). (ENG.). 66p. (J). (gr. -1-7). pap. *(978-1-78843-669-4(5))* Make Believe Ideas.

Lynch, Stuart. Dinosaur Math Missions. Make Believe Ideas Ltd. 2020. (ENG.). 66p. (J). pap. ***(978-1-78947-785-6(9))*** Make Believe Ideas.

Lynch, Stuart. Dinosaur Stencil Art. Make Believe Ideas Ltd. 2019. (ENG.). 50p. (J). spiral bd. *(978-1-78947-036-9(6))* Make Believe Ideas.

—Dinosaurs Activity Book. Make Believe Ideas Ltd. 2019. (Scratch & Sparkle Ser.). (ENG.). 36p. (J). pap. *(978-1-78843-675-5(X))* Make Believe Ideas.

Lynch, Stuart. Don't Look Inside. Make Believe Ideas Ltd & Greening, Rosie. 2020. (ENG.). 12p. (J). bds. ***(978-1-78947-369-8(1))*** Make Believe Ideas.

—Farmyard Activity Book. Make Believe Ideas Ltd. 2020. (Balloon Stickers Ser.). (ENG.). 66p. (J). (gr. -1-7). pap. ***(978-1-78947-352-0(7))*** Make Believe Ideas.

Lynch, Stuart. Goodnight Little Groovicorns. Make Believe Ideas Ltd. 2019. (ENG.). 14p. (J). bds. *(978-1-78843-991-6(0))* Make Believe Ideas.

—If You Want to Be a Groovicorn. Make Believe Ideas Ltd. 2019. (ENG.). 12p. (J). bds. *(978-1-78843-993-0(7))* Make Believe Ideas.

—It's Nice to Be a Narwhal. Make Believe Ideas Ltd. 2019. (ENG.). 12p. (J). (gr. -1-7). bds. *(978-1-78843-998-5(8))* Make Believe Ideas.

Lynch, Stuart. Little Dino's Noisy Day. Make Believe Ideas Ltd. 2020. (ENG.). 16p. (J). pap. ***(978-1-78947-850-1(2))*** Make Believe Ideas.

—The Magic of Christmas. Make Believe Ideas Ltd & Greening, Rosie. 2020. (ENG.). 12p. (J). bds. ***(978-1-78947-719-1(0))*** Make Believe Ideas.

Lynch, Stuart. Meet the Groovicorns. Make Believe Ideas Ltd. 2019. (Playhouse Boxset Ser.). (ENG.). 10p. (J). (gr. -1-7). *(978-1-78843-618-2(0))* Make Believe Ideas.

—Mrs Bee's ABC. Make Believe Ideas Ltd. 2019. (Trace & Flap Ser.). (ENG.). 14p. (J). (gr. -1-1). bds. *(978-1-78843-625-0(3))* Make Believe Ideas.

Lynch, Stuart. Never Feed a Grumpy Elf. Make Believe Ideas Ltd & Greening, Rosie. 2020. (Felt Teeth Ser.). (ENG.). 12p. (J). bds. ***(978-1-78947-717-7(4))*** Make Believe Ideas.

Lynch, Stuart. Never Touch a Dinosaur. Make Believe Ideas Ltd. 2019. (Read & Play Ser.). (ENG.). 12p. (J). (gr. -1-7). *(978-1-78843-660-1(1))* Make Believe Ideas.

Lynch, Stuart. Never Touch a Dinosaur! Make Believe Ideas Ltd & Greening, Rosie. 2020. (Never Touch A Ser.). (ENG.). 12p. (J). bds. ***(978-1-78947-883-9(9))*** Make Believe Ideas.

Lynch, Stuart. Never Touch a Dinosaur! Make Believe Ideas Ltd. 2019. (ENG.). 72p. (J). (gr. -1-7). pap. *(978-1-78947-026-0(9))* Make Believe Ideas.

Lynch, Stuart. Never Touch a Grumpy Elf! Make Believe Ideas Ltd & Greening, Rosie. 2020. (Never Touch A Ser.). (ENG.). 12p. (J). (gr. -1-7). bds. ***(978-1-78843-925-1(2))*** Make Believe Ideas.

—Never Touch a Grumpy Elf! Make Believe Ideas Ltd. 2020. (ENG.). 40p. (J). (gr. -1-7). pap. ***(978-1-78947-716-0(6))*** Make Believe Ideas.

—Never Touch a Monster! Make Believe Ideas Ltd & Greening, Rosie. 2020. (Never Touch A Ser.). (ENG.). 12p. (J). bds. ***(978-1-78947-882-2(0))*** Make Believe Ideas.

—Never Touch a Panda! Make Believe Ideas Ltd & Greening, Rosie. 2020. (Never Touch A Ser.). (ENG.). 12p. (J). bds. ***(978-1-78947-745-0(X))*** Make Believe Ideas.

—Never Touch a Polar Bear! Make Believe Ideas Ltd & Greening, Rosie. 2020. (Never Touch A Ser.). (ENG.). 12p. (J). bds. ***(978-1-78947-888-4(X))*** Make Believe Ideas.

—Never Touch a Porcupine! Make Believe Ideas Ltd & Greening, Rosie. 2020. (ENG.). 12p. (J). bds. ***(978-1-78947-887-7(1))*** Make Believe Ideas.

—Never Touch a Porcupine! Make Believe Ideas Ltd. 2020. (ENG.). 32p. (J). (gr. -1-7). pap. ***(978-1-78947-791-7(3))*** Make Believe Ideas.

—Never Touch a Shark! Make Believe Ideas Ltd & Greening, Rosie. 2020. (Never Touch A Ser.). (ENG.). 12p. (J). bds. ***(978-1-78947-886-0(3))*** Make Believe Ideas.

—Never Touch a Shark! Make Believe Ideas Ltd. 2020. (Never Touch A Ser.). (ENG.). 72p. (J). (gr. -1-7). ***(978-1-78947-390-2(X))*** Make Believe Ideas.

—Never Touch a T. Rex. Make Believe Ideas Ltd & Greening, Rosie. 2020. (Never Touch A Ser.). (ENG.). 32p. (J). (gr. -1-1). pap. ***(978-1-78947-380-3(2))***; ***(978-1-78947-381-0(0))*** Make Believe Ideas.

—Never Touch a T. Rex. Greening, Rosie. 2020. (Never Touch A Ser.). (ENG.). 32p. (J). (gr. -1-7). ***(978-1-78947-502-9(3))***; pap. ***(978-1-78947-501-2(5))*** Make Believe Ideas.

—Never Touch a Tiger! Make Believe Ideas Ltd & Greening, Rosie. 2020. (Never Touch A Ser.). (ENG.). 12p. (J). bds. ***(978-1-78947-889-1(8))*** Make Believe Ideas.

Lynch, Stuart. Never Touch the Dinosaurs. Make Believe Ideas Ltd. 2019. (ENG.). 14p. (J). (gr. -1-7). bds. *(978-1-78843-983-1(X))* Make Believe Ideas.

Lynch, Stuart. Never Touch the Monsters. Make Believe Ideas Ltd & Greening, Rosie. 2020. (Never Touch A Ser.). (ENG.). 14p. (J). bds. ***(978-1-78947-706-1(9))*** Make Believe Ideas.

—Rapunzel. un Cuento Sobre el Perdón / Rapunzel. a Story about Forgiveness. Anderton, Helen. 2020. (Cuentos con Valores Ser.: 4). (SPA.). 20p. (J). (-k). bds. 10.95 ***(978-1-64473-173-4(8)***, Beascoa) Penguin Random House Grupo Editorial ESP. Dist: Penguin Random Hse. LLC.

—Shark Reef Activity Book. Make Believe Ideas Ltd. 2020. (ENG.). 66p. (J). (gr. -1-7). pap. ***(978-1-78947-795-5(6))*** Make Believe Ideas.

—Sharks Activity Book. Make Believe Ideas Ltd. 2020. (Scratch & Sparkle Ser.). (ENG.). 36p. (J). pap. ***(978-1-78947-391-9(8))*** Make Believe Ideas.

—Space Activity Book. Make Believe Ideas Ltd. 2020. (ENG.). 36p. (J). pap. ***(978-1-78947-797-9(2))*** Make Believe Ideas.

—Unicorn Math Missions. Make Believe Ideas Ltd. 2020. (ENG.). 66p. (J). pap. ***(978-1-78947-787-0(5))*** Make Believe Ideas.

—Unicorn Mysteries. Make Believe Ideas Ltd & Best, Elanor. 2020. (ENG.). 48p. (J). pap. ***(978-1-78947-395-7(0))*** Make Believe Ideas.

Lynch, Stuart. Unicorns Activity Book. Make Believe Ideas Ltd. 2019. (Balloon Stickers Ser.). (ENG.). 66p. (J). (gr. -1-7). pap. *(978-1-78843-668-7(7))* Make Believe Ideas.

Lynch, Tara. Mister Cool. Jones, Birdy. 2015. (ENG.). 34p. (J). (gr. 1-4). 16.95 *(978-1-57687-719-7(1)*, powerHouse Bks.) powerHse. Bks.

Lynch, Tim. Christmas on the Broken Road Farm. Lynch, Lauren Boehm. 2019. (ENG.). 26p. (J). pap. 10.00 ***(978-1-0817-3345-2(4))*** Independently Published.

—Coloring on the Broken Road Farm. Lynch, Lauren Boehm. 2019. (ENG.). 66p. (J). pap. 8.00 ***(978-1-0817-4134-1(1))*** Independently Published.

—Snutter Butter Kittens. Lynch, Lauren Boehm. 2019. (ENG.). 26p. (J). pap. 10.50 ***(978-1-7986-6437-7(2))*** Independently Published.

Lynch, Tim & Boehm Sr, William Michel. Night Critters. Lynch, Lauren Boehm. 2019. (ENG.). 26p. (J). pap. 9.50 ***(978-1-0822-0510-1(9))*** Independently Published.

Lynch, Timothy & Boatright, Emily Belle. Coloring on the Broken Road Farm. Lynch, Lauren Boehm. 2016. (ENG.). (J). pap. 9.99 *(978-1-62868-194-9(2))* Fountain Blue Publishing.

Lynch, Todd, jt. illus. see Breckenridge, Trula.

Lynch, Tom. Around the World. Coy, John & Reonegro, Antonio. 2005. (ENG.). 32p. (J). (gr. 1-7). 17.95 *(978-1-58430-244-5(5))* Lee & Low Bks., Inc.

Lynch, Wayne. Baby Sea Turtle, 1 vol. Lang, Aubrey. 2007. (Nature Babies Ser.). (ENG.). 32p. (J). (gr. k-3). 16.95 *(978-1-55041-728-9(2)*, bd5d0bd2-27ea-490d-8048-71af4afe56c3) Fitzhenry & Whiteside, Ltd. CAN. Dist: Firefly Bks., Ltd.

L

—Baby Sea Turtle, 1 vol. Lang, Aubrey. 2007. (Nature Babies Ser.). (ENG.). 36p. (J). (gr. k-3). pap. 7.95 *(978-1-55041-746-3(0),* 62f1a238-ef42-4d93-9d7a-9de52dd283a7) Trifolium Bks., Inc. CAN. Dist: Firefly Bks., Ltd.

Lynch, Wayne, photos by. Baby Black Bear, 1 vol. Lang, Aubrey. 2008. (Nature Babies Ser.). (ENG., 36p. (J). (gr. k-3). pap. 7.95 *(978-1-55455-097-5(1),* 9c7320e4-99d2-418c-8e38-29c947c171b2) Fitzhenry & Whiteside, Ltd. CAN. Dist: Firefly Bks., Ltd.

—Baby Elephant, 1 vol. Lang, Aubrey. 2004. (Nature Babies Ser.). (ENG., 36p. (J). (gr. k-3). pap. 7.95 *(978-1-55041-717-3(7),* b46c4953-3d0d-4e96-b8ab-1727afcf48c2) Trifolium Bks., Inc. CAN. Dist: Firefly Bks., Ltd.

—Baby Elephant, 1 vol. Lang, Aubrey. 2003. (Nature Babies Ser.). (ENG., 36p. (J). (gr. k-3). 16.95 *(978-1-55041-715-9(0),* 3546fde1-ccac-4366-839a-29eff8c07749) éditeur, Annika Parance CAN. Dist: Firefly Bks., Ltd.

—Baby Fox, 1 vol. Lang, Aubrey. 2003. (Nature Babies Ser.). (ENG., 36p. (J). (gr. k-3). pap. 7.95 *(978-1-55041-724-1(X),* 474fe554-dcfa-4b56-a18d-3dd3bae99f43) Trifolium Bks., Inc. CAN. Dist: Firefly Bks., Ltd.

—Baby Grizzly, 1 vol. Lang, Aubrey. 2006. (Nature Babies Ser.). (ENG., (J). (gr. k-3). 32p. pap. 7.95 *(978-1-55041-579-7(4),* 0765b8f0-b40e-4692-a7e3-1e86720660da); 36p. 21.19 *(978-1-55041-577-3(8),* f6a3a84e-5320-47b2-9a55-a0b489d85486) Fitzhenry & Whiteside, Ltd. CAN. Dist: Firefly Bks., Ltd., Children's Plus, Inc.

—Baby Ground Squirrel, 1 vol. Lang, Aubrey. 2004. (Nature Babies Ser.). (ENG., 36p. (J). (gr. k-3). pap. 7.95 *(978-1-55041-799-9(1),* b81c53f6-709c-4cc2-8df4-a85c940cd612) Trifolium Bks., Inc. CAN. Dist: Firefly Bks., Ltd.

—Baby Ground Squirrel, 1 vol. Lang, Aubrey. 2004. (Nature Babies Ser.). (ENG., 36p. (J). (gr. k-3). 16.95 *(978-1-55041-797-5(5),* 88a6fe54-8f9f-40c9-bc95-52939cb5c80e) éditeur, Annika Parance CAN. Dist: Firefly Bks., Ltd.

—Baby Koala, 1 vol. Lang, Aubrey. 2004. (Nature Babies Ser.). (ENG., 36p. (J). (gr. k-3). pap. 7.95 *(978-1-55041-876-7(9),* 3e37bc07-9542-45f5-8080-97b857e8fd1b) Clockwise Pr. CAN. Dist: Firefly Bks., Ltd.

—Baby Koala, 1 vol. Lang, Aubrey. 2004. (Nature Babies Ser.). (ENG., 36p. (J). (gr. k-3). 16.95 *(978-1-55041-874-3(2),* 8febdb11-aaad-49d9-8d76-6aceb0daed95) Trifolium Bks., Inc. CAN. Dist: Firefly Bks., Ltd.

—Baby Lion, 1 vol. Lang, Aubrey. 2003. (Nature Babies Ser.). (ENG., 36p. (J). (gr. k-3). 16.95 *(978-1-55041-711-1(8),* eefef011-c8f6-4d7e-a688-a848207c2ece) Clockwise Pr. CAN. Dist: Firefly Bks., Ltd.

—Baby Lion, 1 vol. Lang, Aubrey. 2004. (Nature Babies Ser.). (ENG., 36p. (J). (gr. k-3). pap. 7.95 *(978-1-55041-713-5(4),* 03fd9412-88ff-4daa-a980-0bcfbbec8132) Fitzhenry & Whiteside, Ltd. CAN. Dist: Firefly Bks., Ltd.

—Baby Mountain Sheep, 1 vol. Lang, Aubrey. 2007. (Nature Babies Ser.). (ENG., 36p. (J). (gr. k-3). 7.95 *(978-1-55455-043-2(2),* 6deec32a-d37c-4852-9d9c-0a9a1e1c3d92); 16.95 *(978-1-55455-042-5(4),* 3eea2ae0-93cd-4674-a882-46ef99c02b84) Trifolium Bks., Inc. CAN. Dist: Firefly Bks., Ltd.

—Baby Owl, 1 vol. Lang, Aubrey. 2004. (Nature Babies Ser.). (ENG., 36p. (J). (gr. k-3). 16.95 *(978-1-55041-796-8(7),* 51cd5abe-0798-434c-97e9-1a8525e97416); pap. 7.95 *(978-1-55041-798-2(3),* 4c6efa6f-0bcb-43c0-8ce9-c767c3653b27) Trifolium Bks., Inc. CAN. Dist: Firefly Bks., Ltd.

—Baby Polar Bear, 1 vol. Lang, Aubrey. 2008. (Nature Babies Ser.: 15). (ENG., 36p. (J). (gr. k-3). pap. 7.95 *(978-1-55455-102-6(1),* 954af2a7-6b31-401c-81ba-04aec91a31cc) Trifolium Bks., Inc. CAN. Dist: Firefly Bks., Ltd.

—Baby Porcupine, 1 vol. Lang, Aubrey. 2005. (Nature Babies Ser.). (ENG., 36p. (J). (gr. k-3). 16.95 *(978-1-55041-560-5(3),* e5636941-e868-4a1e-a772-6344ae381a07); pap. 7.95 *(978-1-55041-562-9(X),* 75589ef0-15ed-42d5-95e4-b0f98b0fa0ba) Trifolium Bks., Inc. CAN. Dist: Firefly Bks., Ltd.

—Baby Seal, 1 vol. Lang, Aubrey. 2004. (Nature Babies Ser.). (ENG., 36p. (J). (gr. k-3). pap. 7.95 *(978-1-55041-726-5(6),* a224862a-f658-4ffc-b144-b77d1286af7a) Trifolium Bks., Inc. CAN. Dist: Firefly Bks., Ltd.

—Baby Sloth, 1 vol. Lang, Aubrey. 2004. (Nature Babies Ser.). (ENG., 36p. (J). (gr. k-3). pap. 7.95 *(978-1-55041-827-9(0),* a9a62cab-c605-4971-a51a-a7b258b18c5d) Trifolium Bks., Inc. CAN. Dist: Firefly Bks., Ltd.

—Sonoran Desert. 2008. (J). *(978-1-55971-984-1(2));* pap. *(978-1-55971-985-8(0))* T&N Children's Publishing. (NorthWord Bks. for Young Readers).

Lynch, Wayne, photos by. The Arctic. Lynch, Wayne. 2007. (Our Wild World Ser.). (ENG., 64p. (J). (gr. 3-7). pap. 8.95 *(978-1-55971-961-2(3))* Cooper Square Publishing Llc.

—Arctic Alphabet: Exploring the North from A to Z. Lynch, Wayne. 2006. 32p. (J). (gr. k-4). reprint ed. 20.00 *(978-1-4223-5190-1(4))* DIANE Publishing Co.

—The Everglades. Lynch, Wayne. 2007. (Our Wild World Ser.). (ENG., 64p. (J). (gr. 3-7). 16.95 *(978-1-55971-970-4(2));* pap. 9.95 *(978-1-55971-971-1(0))* Cooper Square Publishing Llc.

—Scoop on Poop!, 1 vol. Lynch, Wayne. 2019. (ENG., 32p. (J). (gr. 4-7). 14.95 *(978-1-927083-53-6(2),* d6c7b241-3a73-46e4-a21e-abe203d03bf7) Fifth Hse. Pubs. CAN. Dist: Firefly Bks., Ltd.

Lyndon, Janice. The Mark of the Wagari. Little, Lorna. 2004. 28p. (J). *(978-1-875641-97-0(1))* Magabala Bks.

Lyndon, Tracy S. The Secret of Wattensaw Bayou. Hubbs, M. E. 2013. 170p. pap. 12.95 *(978-1-934610-76-3(3))* Bluewater Pubns.

Lyne, Alison. Bo & the Christmas Bandit, 1 vol. Simmons, Lynn. 2009. (Bo Ser.). (ENG.). 128p. (J). (gr. 3-6). pap. 8.95 *(978-1-58980-723-5(5),* Pelican Publishing) Arcadia Publishing.

—Petite Rouge: A Cajun Twist to an Old Tale, 1 vol. Hébert-Collins, Sheila. 2015. (ENG.). 32p. (J). (gr. k-3). 16.99 *(978-1-58980-602-3(6),* Pelican Publishing) Arcadia Publishing.

Lyne, Alison D. Thanksgiving Day Alphabet, 1 vol. Vidrine, Beverly Barras. 2006. (ABC Ser.). (ENG.). 32p. (J). (gr. k-3). 8.95 *(978-1-58980-338-1(8),* Pelican Publishing) Arcadia Publishing.

Lyne, Alison Davis. Bo & the Roaring Pines, 1 vol. Simmons, Lynn Sheffield. 2008. (Bo Ser.). (ENG.). 120p. (J). (gr. 3-6). pap. 8.95 *(978-1-58980-522-4(4),* Pelican Publishing) Arcadia Publishing.

—Easter Day Alphabet, 1 vol. Vidrine, Beverly Barras. 2003. (ABC Ser.). (ENG.). 32p. (J). (gr. k-k). pap. 8.95 *(978-1-58980-076-2(1),* Pelican Publishing) Arcadia Publishing.

—G Is for Grits: A Southern Alphabet, 1 vol. Bethea, Nikole Brooks. 2012. (ABC Ser.). (ENG.). 32p. (J). (gr. k-3). 16.99 *(978-1-4556-1698-5(2),* Pelican Publishing) Arcadia Publishing.

—Halloween Alphabet, 1 vol. Vidrine, Beverly Barras. 2004. (ABC Ser.). (ENG.). 32p. (J). (gr. k-1). pap. 8.95 *(978-1-58980-242-1(X),* Pelican Publishing) Arcadia Publishing.

—Jacques et la Canne à Sucre: A Cajun Jack & the Beanstalk, 1 vol. Hébert-Collins, Sheila. 2004. (Cajun Tall Tales Ser.). (ENG.). 32p. (J). (gr. k-3). pap. 16.99 *(978-1-58980-191-2(1),* Pelican Publishing) Arcadia Publishing.

—Kudzu Chaos, 1 vol. Lambe, Jennifer Holloway & National Geographic Learning Staff. 2003. (ENG.). 32p. (J). (gr. k-3). 16.99 *(978-1-58980-157-8(1),* Pelican Publishing) Arcadia Publishing.

Lyne, Alison Davis. Little Things Aren't Little ... When You're Little, 1 vol. Lyne, Alison Davis. Burrows, Mark. 2013. (ENG.). 32p. (J). (gr. -1-k). 16.99 *(978-1-4556-1791-3(1),* Pelican Publishing) Arcadia Publishing.

Lyne, William Rayford. Galisteo: Thothmes III's Colony in America, C. 1626 B. C.: the Tanoan-Egyptian Djed Festival Stone. Lyne, William Rayford, photos by. 2011. (ENG.). 250p. pap. 25.00 *(978-0-9637467-3-3(1))* Creatopia Productions - Lamy, New Mexico.

Lynn, Andrea. Kayla the Vegan. Mitchell, Stewart. 2019. (ENG.). 66p. (J). pap. 5.99 *(978-1-0735-4529-2(6))* Independently Published.

Lynn, Bei. Gus, the Dinosaur Bus. Liu, Julia. 2013. (ENG.). 32p. (J). (gr. -1-3). 16.99 *(978-0-547-90573-0(4))* Houghton Mifflin Harcourt Publishing Co.

Lynn, Bei. Bibbit Jumps. Lynn, Bei. 2020. (ENG.). 78p. (J). (gr. k-3). 18.99 ***(978-1-77657-277-9(7))*** Gecko Pr. NZL. Dist: Lerner Publishing Group.

Lynn, Galsterer. The Adventures Begin. Haller, Reese. 2005. (Fred the Mouse Ser.). 108p. (J). (gr. -1-3). per. 4.97 *(978-0-9616046-8-4(9))* Personal Power Pr.

Lynn, Rick. Lewis & Clark's Journey of Discovery: A Guide for Young Explorers. Conant, Susan Sens. 2004. 48p. (J). pap. *(978-0-9725584-1-9(1))* Little Blue Pr.

Lynn, Ronny. My Filipino Word Book: English - Tagalog - Ilokano. Fancy, Robin Lyn & Welch, Vala Jeanne. Gasmen, Imelda Fines, ed. 2007. 28p. (J). (gr. -1-3). 10.95 *(978-1-57306-276-3(6))* Bess Pr., Inc.

Lynn, Sweat. Wake up, Baby! Oppenheim, Joanne. 2015. (ENG.). 34p. (J). pap. 11.95 *(978-1-899694-56-3(0),* ipicturebooks) ibooks, Inc.

Lynn, Tammy. Happy Birthday Puppy: An I See Puppy Book. Lynn, Tammy. Stewart, Elaine, ed. 2006. 12p. (J). bds. 6.99 *(978-0-9774277-0-3(6),* 0-9774277-0-6) I See Puppy, LLP.

Lynn, Valerie. Be Everything You Can Be: Book 2. Seader, Karen. 2018. (In Your Heart Lives a Rainbow Ser.: Vol. 2). (ENG.). 38p. (J). (gr. k-2). 18.95 *(978-0-9857824-4-3(7))* In Your Heart Lives a Rainbow.

—In Your Heart Lives a Rainbow: Book 1. Seader, Karen. 2018. (In Your Heart Lives a Rainbow Ser.: Vol. 1). (ENG.). 38p. (J). (gr. k-2). 18.95 *(978-0-9857824-3-6(9))* In Your Heart Lives a Rainbow.

—Ride the Rainbow: Book 3. Seader, Karen. 2018. (In Your Heart Lives a Rainbow Ser.: Vol. 3). (ENG.). 38p. (J). (gr. k-2). 18.95 *(978-0-9857824-5-0(5))* In Your Heart Lives a Rainbow.

Lynne, Kimberlee. The Frog & the Mouse. 2011. (First Steps in Music Ser.). 32p. (J). (gr. k-2). 17.95 *(978-1-57999-802-8(X))* G I A Pubns., Inc.

Lyon, Aj. Ladybugs Like Popcorn & Other Short Stories for Kids. Lyon, Carley. 2019. (ENG.). 40p. (J). pap. 5.50 *(978-1-5086-0638-3(2))* CreateSpace Independent Publishing Platform.

Lyon, Belinda. My Book of Princess Stories. Baxter, Nicola. 2012. 80p. (J). (gr. k-4). pap. 9.99 *(978-1-84322-801-1(7))* Anness Publishing GBR. Dist: National Bk. Network.

Lyon, Carol. How & Why Stories: World Tales Kids Can Read & Tell. Hamilton, Martha & Weiss, Mitch. 2005. (World Storytelling from August House Ser.). (ENG.). 96p. (J). (gr. 1-7). pap. 15.95 *(978-0-87483-561-8(5))* August Hse. Pubs., Inc.

—Through the Grapevine: World Tales Kids Can Read & Tell. Hamilton, Martha & Weiss, Mitch. (ENG.). 128p. (J). (gr. 1-6). 2006. pap. 15.95 *(978-0-87483-624-0(7));* 2005. 24.95 *(978-0-87483-625-7(5))* August Hse. Pubs., Inc.

Lyon, Chris. Calligraphy: From Beginner to Expert. Young, Caroline. 2006. (Usborne Guide Ser.). 48p. (J). (gr. 6). lib. bdg. 16.99 *(978-1-58086-934-8(3),* Usborne) EDC Publishing.

Lyon, Chris, et al. Diggers & Cranes. Young, Caroline. rev. ed. 2006. (Usborne Big Machines Ser.). 32p. (J). (gr. k-3). per. 6.95 *(978-0-7945-0840-1(5),* Usborne) EDC Publishing.

Lyon, Chris. Trucks. Castor, Harriet. 2006. (Big MacHines Ser.). 32p. (J). (gr. k). lib. bdg. 14.95 *(978-1-58086-847-1(9))* EDC Publishing.

Lyon, Chris, et al. Trucks. Castor, Harriet. rev. ed. 2004. (Usborne Big Machines Ser.). 31p. (J). (gr. -1). per. 6.95 *(978-0-7945-0839-5(1),* Usborne) EDC Publishing.

Lyon, Chris. The Usborne Book of Machines That Work. Young, Caroline & Castor, Harriet. 2004. (Young MacHines Ser.). 95p. (J). (gr. k). lib. bdg. 22.95 *(978-1-58086-031-4(1),* Usborne) EDC Publishing.

Lyon, Chris & Biggin, Gary. Bulldozers & Other Construction Machines. Butterfield, Moira. 32p. (J). mass mkt. 8.99 *(978-0-590-24556-2(2))* Scholastic, Inc.

Lyon, Chris & Gower, Teri. Tractors. Young, Caroline. 2004. (Young MacHines Ser.). 32p. (J). (gr. k). lib. bdg. 14.95 *(978-1-58086-616-3(6),* Usborne) EDC Publishing.

Lyon, David. Flight of the Buzby Bee. Lyon, David. 2005. 32p. (J). 16.95 *(978-0-9741328-0-8(2))* Lyon, Ernest Media Productions.

Lyon, Gabriela. Small History of a Disagreement. Fuentes, Claudio. Amado, Elisa, tr. 2020. (ENG.). 56p. (J). (gr. 2-7). 18.95 ***(978-1-77164-707-6(8),*** Greystone Bks.) Greystone Books Ltd. CAN. Dist: Publishers Group West (PGW).

Lyon, Lea. It Rained Warm Bread: Moishe Moskowitz's Story of Hope. Moskowitz-Sweet, Gloria & Smith, Hope Anita. 2019. (ENG.). 160p. (J). 16.99 *(978-1-250-16572-5(5),* 900187113, Holt, Henry & Co. Bks. For Young Readers) Holt, Henry & Co.

—The Miracle Jar: A Hanukkah Story. Penn, Audrey. 2009. (ENG.). 32p. (J). (gr. -1-3). pap. 8.95 *(978-1-933718-26-2(9))* Tanglewood Pr.

Lyon, Lea. Keep Your Ear on the Ball, 1 vol. Lyon, Lea. Petrillo, Genevieve. 2007. (ENG.). 32p. (J). (gr. -1-3). 16.95 *(978-0-88448-296-3(0))* Tilbury Hse. Pubs.

Lyon, Lea07/. Keep Your Ear on the Ball, 1 vol. Petrillo, Genevieve & Lyon, Lea. 2009. (ENG.). 32p. (J). (gr. 2-6). pap. 8.95 *(978-0-88448-324-3(X),* 884324) Tilbury Hse. Pubs.

Lyon, Tammie. Best Club. Manushkin, Fran. 2016. (Katie Woo Ser.). (ENG.). 32p. (J). (gr. k-2). lib. bdg. 21.32 *(978-1-4795-9639-3(6),* Picture Window Bks.) Capstone.

Lyon, Tammie. The Best Pet? Manushkin, Fran. 2020. (Pedro Ser.). (ENG.). 32p. (J). (gr. k-2). pap. 5.95 ***(978-1-5158-7316-7(1),*** 201599); lib. bdg. 21.32 ***(978-1-5158-7082-1(0),*** 199057) Capstone. (Picture Window Bks.).

Lyon, Tammie. Best Season Ever, 1 vol. Manushkin, Fran. 2010. (Katie Woo Ser.). (ENG.). 32p. (J). (gr. k-2). lib. bdg. 21.32 *(978-1-4048-5730-8(3),* Picture Window Bks.) Capstone.

—The Big Lie, 1 vol. Manushkin, Fran. 2009. (Katie Woo Ser.). (ENG.). 32p. (J). (gr. k-2). 21.32 *(978-1-4048-5497-0(5),* Picture Window Bks.) Capstone.

—The Big Stink. Manushkin, Fran. 2018. (Pedro Ser.). (ENG.). 32p. (J). (gr. k-2). lib. bdg. 21.32 *(978-1-5158-2820-4(4),* 137985, Picture Window Bks.) Capstone.

—Boo, Katie Woo!, 1 vol. Manushkin, Fran. 2010. (Katie Woo Ser.). (ENG.). 32p. (J). (gr. k-2). lib. bdg. 21.32 *(978-1-4048-5987-6(X));* pap. 5.95 *(978-1-4048-6366-8(4))* Capstone. (Picture Window Bks.).

—Boss of the World, 1 vol. Manushkin, Fran. 2009. (Katie Woo Ser.). (ENG.). 32p. (J). (gr. k-2). 21.32 *(978-1-4048-5493-2(2),* Picture Window Bks.) Capstone.

—Bugs in My Hair?! Stier, Catherine. 2012. (J). 34.28 *(978-1-61913-111-8(0))* Weigl Pubs., Inc.

—Bugs in My Hair?!, 1 vol. Stier, Catherine. 2010. (ENG.). 32p. (J). (gr. -1-3). pap. 6.99 *(978-0-8075-0909-8(4),* 807509094) Whitman, Albert & Co.

—Cartwheel Katie. Manushkin, Fran. 2015. (Katie Woo Ser.). (ENG.). 32p. (J). (gr. k-2). 21.32 *(978-1-4795-5894-0(X),* Picture Window Bks.) Capstone.

—El Club de Los Misterios de Pedro. Manushkin, Fran. 2018. (Pedro en Español Ser.). (SPA.). 32p. (J). (gr. k-2). lib. bdg. 21.32 *(978-1-5158-2512-8(4),* 137571, Picture Window Bks.) Capstone.

—Cowgirl Katie, 1 vol. Manushkin, Fran. 2014. (Katie Woo Ser.). (ENG.). 32p. (J). (gr. k-2). lib. bdg. 21.32 *(978-1-4795-2174-6(4),* Picture Window Bks.) Capstone.

—Daddy Can't Dance. Manushkin, Fran. 2018. (Katie Woo Ser.). (ENG.). 32p. (J). (gr. k-2). lib. bdg. 21.32 *(978-1-5158-2266-0(4),* 136885, Picture Window Bks.) Capstone.

—Double or Nothing: 3-D Printing. 2018. (Makers Make It Work Ser.). (ENG.). 32p. (J). (gr. k-3). 25.32 *(978-1-63592-014-7(0))* Astra Publishing Hse.

—Double or Nothing: 3D Printing. Daly, Catherine. 2018. (Makers Make It Work Ser.). (ENG.). 32p. (J). (gr. k-3). pap. 5.99 *(978-1-57565-989-3(1))* Astra Publishing Hse.

—Eloise & the Big Parade. McClatchy, Lisa. 2007. (Eloise Ser.). (ENG.). 32p. (J). (gr. -1-1). pap. 4.99 *(978-1-4169-3523-0(1),* Simon Spotlight) Simon Spotlight.

—Eloise & the Dinosaurs. McClatchy, Lisa. 2017. (Eloise Ser.). (ENG.). 32p. (J). (gr. -1-1). 16.99 *(978-1-4814-9980-4(7),* Simon Spotlight) Simon Spotlight.

—Eloise & the Dinosaurs. McClatchy, Lisa. 2007. (Eloise Ser.). (ENG.). 32p. (J). (gr. -1-1). pap. 3.99 *(978-0-689-87453-6(7),* Simon Spotlight) Simon Spotlight.

—Eloise & the Snowman. McClatchy, Lisa. 2006. (Eloise Ser.). (ENG.). 32p. (J). (gr. -1-1). pap. 4.99 *(978-0-689-87451-2(0),* Simon Spotlight) Simon Spotlight.

—Eloise & the Snowman, 1 vol. McClatchy, Lisa. 2015. (Kay Thompson's Eloise Ser.). (ENG.). 32p. (J). (gr. -1-2). 27.07 *(978-1-61479-402-8(2),* 18187) Spotlight.

—Eloise & the Very Secret Room, 1 vol. Weiss, Ellen. 2015. (Kay Thompson's Eloise Ser.). (ENG.). 32p. (J). (gr. -1-2). 27.07 *(978-1-61479-403-5(0),* 18188) Spotlight.

—Eloise at the Wedding. 2006. (Eloise Ser.). (ENG.). 32p. (J). (gr. -1-1). pap. 4.99 *(978-0-689-87449-9(9),* Simon Spotlight) Simon Spotlight.

—Eloise Breaks Some Eggs. 2018. (Eloise Ser.). (ENG.). 32p. (J). (gr. -1-1). 16.99 *(978-1-4814-7680-5(7),* Simon Spotlight) Simon Spotlight.

—Eloise Breaks Some Eggs. 2005. (Eloise Ser.). (ENG.). 32p. (J). (gr. -1-1). pap. 3.99 *(978-0-689-87368-3(9),* Simon Spotlight) Simon Spotlight.

—Eloise Decorates for Christmas. McClatchy, Lisa. 2007. (Eloise Ser.). (ENG.). 32p. (J). (gr. -1-1). pap. 4.99 *(978-1-4169-4978-7(X),* Simon Spotlight) Simon Spotlight.

—Eloise Skates! McClatchy, Lisa. 2008. (Eloise Ser.). (ENG.). 32p. (J). (gr. -1-1). pap. 3.99 *(978-1-4169-6406-3(1))* Simon & Schuster, Inc.

—Eloise Throws a Party! 2018. (Eloise Ser.). (ENG.). 32p. (J). (gr. -1-1). 17.99 *(978-1-5344-2038-0(X),* Simon Spotlight) Simon Spotlight.

—Eloise Throws a Party! 2008. (Eloise Ser.). (ENG.). 32p. (J). (gr. -1-1). pap. 4.99 *(978-1-4169-6172-7(0),* Simon Spotlight) Simon Spotlight.

—Eloise Visits the Zoo. McClatchy, Lisa. 2018. (Eloise Ser.). (ENG.). 32p. (J). (gr. -1-1). 17.99 *(978-1-5344-2039-7(8),* Simon Spotlight) Simon Spotlight.

—Eloise Visits the Zoo. McClatchy, Lisa. 2009. (Eloise Ser.). (ENG.). 32p. (J). (gr. -1-1). pap. 4.99 *(978-1-4169-8642-3(1),* Simon Spotlight) Simon Spotlight.

—Eloise's Pirate Adventure. McClatchy, Lisa. 2017. (Eloise Ser.). (ENG.). 32p. (J). (gr. -1-1). 16.99 *(978-1-4814-9979-8(3),* Simon Spotlight) Simon Spotlight.

—Eloise's Mother's Day Surprise. McClatchy, Lisa. (Eloise Ser.). (ENG.). 32p. (J). (gr. -1-1). 2018. 17.99 *(978-1-4814-7678-2(5));* 2009. pap. 4.99 *(978-1-4169-7889-3(5))* Simon Spotlight. (Simon Spotlight).

—Eloise's New Bonnet. McClatchy, Lisa. 2007. (Eloise Ser.). (ENG.). 32p. (J). (gr. -1-1). pap. 3.99 *(978-0-689-87452-9(9),* Simon Spotlight) Simon Spotlight.

—Eloise's Pirate Adventure. McClatchy, Lisa. 2007. (Eloise Ser.). (ENG.). 32p. (J). (gr. -1-1). pap. 4.99 *(978-1-4169-4979-4(8),* Simon Spotlight) Simon Spotlight.

—Eloise's Summer Vacation. McClatchy, Lisa. 2007. (Eloise Ser.). (ENG.). 32p. (J). (gr. -1-1). pap. 4.99 *(978-0-689-87454-3(5),* Simon Spotlight) Simon Spotlight.

—¡en la Cima Del Mundo! Manushkin, Fran. 2019. (Pedro en Español Ser.). (SPA.). 32p. (J). (gr. k-2). pap. 4.95 *(978-1-5158-4694-9(6),* 141321); lib. bdg. 21.32 *(978-1-5158-4660-4(1),* 141259) Capstone. (Picture Window Bks.).

—Fly High, Katie, 1 vol. Manushkin, Fran. 2014. (Katie Woo Ser.). (ENG.). 32p. (J). (gr. k-2). lib. bdg. 21.32 *(978-1-4795-2175-3(2),* Picture Window Bks.) Capstone.

—The Gingerbread Bear. Dennis, Robert. 2012. (J). *(978-0-545-46767-4(5),* Cartwheel Bks.) Scholastic, Inc.

—El Golazo de Pedro. Manushkin, Fran. 2018. (Pedro en Español Ser.). (SPA.). 32p. (J). (gr. k-2). lib. bdg. 21.32 *(978-1-5158-2511-1(6),* 137570, Picture Window Bks.) Capstone.

—Goodbye to Goldie, 1 vol. Manushkin, Fran. 2009. (Katie Woo Ser.). (ENG.). 32p. (J). (gr. k-2). 21.32 *(978-1-4048-5495-6(9),* Picture Window Bks.) Capstone.

—La Gran Peste. Manushkin, Fran. 2019. (Pedro en Español Ser.). (SPA.). 32p. (J). (gr. k-2). pap. 4.95 *(978-1-5158-4693-2(8),* 141320); lib. bdg. 21.32 *(978-1-5158-4657-4(1),* 141256) Capstone. (Picture Window Bks.).

—A Happy Day, 1 vol. Manushkin, Fran. 2009. (Katie Woo Ser.). (ENG.). 32p. (J). (gr. k-2). 21.32 *(978-1-4048-5496-3(7),* Picture Window Bks.) Capstone.

—Harriet Tubman. Bauer, Marion Dane. 2010. (My First Biography Ser.). (ENG.). 32p. (J). (gr. -1-3). 16.19 *(978-0-545-23257-9(0))* Scholastic, Inc.

—¡Pedro Se Vuelve Salvaje! Manushkin, Fran. 2020. (Pedro en Español Ser.).Tr. of Pedro Goes Wild!. (SPA.). 32p. (J). (gr. k-2). pap. 5.95 *(978-1-5158-5724-2(7),* 142091); lib. bdg. 21.32 *(978-1-5158-5722-8(0),* 142089) Capstone. (Picture Window Bks.).

—It Doesn't Need to Rhyme, Katie: Writing a Poem with Katie Woo, 1 vol. Manushkin, Fran. 2013. (Katie Woo: Star Writer Ser.). (ENG.). 32p. (J). (gr. k-2). pap. 6.95 *(978-1-4795-1923-1(5));* lib. bdg. 21.32 *(978-1-4048-8128-0(X))* Capstone. (Picture Window Bks.).

—Just Like Always. Perry, Anne M. (Rookie Ready to Learn Ser.). (J). 2011. 40p. pap. 5.95 *(978-0-531-26675-5(3));* 2011. 40p. (gr. -1-k). lib. bdg. 23.00 *(978-0-531-26370-9(3));* 2005. (ENG.). 32p. (gr. 1-2). 19.50 *(978-0-516-25154-7(6))* Scholastic Library Publishing. (Children's Pr.).

—Katie & the Class Pet, 1 vol. Manushkin, Fran. 2011. (Katie Woo Ser.). (ENG.). 32p. (J). (gr. k-2). pap. 5.95 *(978-1-4048-6856-4(9));* lib. bdg. 21.32 *(978-1-4048-6520-4(9))* Capstone. (Picture Window Bks.).

—Katie Blows Her Top. Manushkin, Fran. 2018. (Katie Woo Ser.). (ENG.). 32p. (J). (gr. k-2). lib. bdg. 21.32 *(978-1-5158-2265-3(6),* 136884, Picture Window Bks.) Capstone.

—Katie Finds a Job, 1 vol. Manushkin, Fran. 2011. (Katie Woo Ser.). (ENG.). 32p. (J). (gr. k-2). pap. 5.95 *(978-1-4048-6614-0(0));* lib. bdg. 21.32 *(978-1-4048-6513-6(6))* Capstone. (Picture Window Bks.).

—Katie Goes Camping, 1 vol. Manushkin, Fran. 2010. (Katie Woo Ser.). (ENG.). 32p. (J). (gr. k-2). lib. bdg. 21.32 *(978-1-4048-5731-5(1),* Picture Window Bks.) Capstone.

—Katie in the Kitchen, 1 vol. Manushkin, Fran. 2010. (Katie Woo Ser.). (ENG.). 32p. (J). (gr. k-2). lib. bdg. 21.32 *(978-1-4048-5724-7(9),* Picture Window Bks.) Capstone.

—Katie Saves Thanksgiving, 1 vol. Manushkin, Fran. 2010. (Katie Woo Ser.). (ENG.). 32p. (J). (gr. k-2). lib. bdg. 21.32 *(978-1-4048-5988-3(8));* pap. 5.95 *(978-1-4048-6367-5(2))* Capstone. (Picture Window Bks.).

—Katie Saves the Earth, 1 vol. Manushkin, Fran. 2013. (Katie Woo Ser.). (ENG.). 32p. (J). (gr. k-2). pap. 5.95 *(978-1-4048-8046-7(1));* lib. bdg. 21.32 *(978-1-4048-7652-1(9))* Capstone. (Picture Window Bks.).

—Katie Woo & Friends, 1 vol. Manushkin, Fran. 2012. (Katie Woo Ser.). (ENG.). 96p. (J). (gr. k-2). pap. 4.95 *(978-1-4048-7909-6(9)*, Picture Window Bks.) Capstone.
—Katie Woo & Her Big Ideas, 1 vol. Manushkin, Fran. 2013. (Katie Woo Ser.). (ENG.). 96p. (J). (gr. k-2). pap. 4.95 *(978-1-4795-2026-8(8)*, Picture Window Bks.) Capstone.
—Katie Woo Book Club Kit. Manushkin, Fran. 2013. (Katie Woo Ser.). (ENG.). 576p. (J). (gr. k-2). pap., pap., pap. 29.70 *(978-1-4795-5120-0(1)*, Picture Window Bks.) Capstone.
—Katie Woo Celebrates, 1 vol. Manushkin, Fran. 2013. (Katie Woo Ser.). (ENG.). 96p. (J). (gr. k-2). pap. 4.95 *(978-1-4048-8100-6(X)*, Picture Window Bks.) Capstone.
—Katie Woo Collection. Manushkin, Fran. 2016. (Katie Woo Ser.). (ENG.). 288p. (J). (gr. k-2). 9.99 *(978-1-4795-9318-7(4)*, Picture Window Bks.) Capstone.
—Katie Woo, Don't Be Blue, 1 vol. Manushkin, Fran. 2013. (Katie Woo Ser.). (ENG.). 96p. (J). (gr. k-2). pap. 4.95 *(978-1-4048-8101-3(8)*, Picture Window Bks.) Capstone.
—Katie Woo, Every Day's an Adventure, 1 vol. Manushkin, Fran. 2014. (Katie Woo Ser.). (ENG.). 96p. (J). (gr. k-2). pap. 4.95 *(978-1-4795-5211-5(9)*, Picture Window Bks.) Capstone.
—Katie Woo Has the Flu, 1 vol. Manushkin, Fran. 2011. (Katie Woo Ser.). (ENG.). 32p. (J). (gr. k-2). pap. 5.95 *(978-1-4048-6854-0(2))*; lib. bdg. 21.32 *(978-1-4048-6518-1(7))* Capstone. (Picture Window Bks.).
—Katie Woo Loves School, 1 vol. Manushkin, Fran. 2013. (Katie Woo Ser.). (ENG.). 96p. (J). (gr. k-2). pap. 4.95 *(978-1-4795-2027-5(6)*, Picture Window Bks.) Capstone.
—Katie Woo Rules the School, 1 vol. Manushkin, Fran. 2011. (Katie Woo Ser.). (ENG.). 96p. (J). (gr. k-2). pap. 4.95 *(978-1-4048-7908-9(0)*, Picture Window Bks.) Capstone.
—Katie Woo: Star Writer. Manushkin, Fran. 2013. (Katie Woo: Star Writer Ser.). (ENG.). 32p. (J). (gr. k-2). pap., pap., pap. 35.70 *(978-1-4795-1991-0(X))*; lib. bdg., lib. bdg., lib. bdg. 106.60 *(978-1-4048-8082-5(8))* Capstone. (Picture Window Bks.).
—Katie Woo, Super Scout. Manushkin, Fran. 2015. (Katie Woo Ser.). (ENG.). 32p. (J). (gr. k-2). 21.32 *(978-1-4795-6178-0(9)*, Picture Window Bks.) Capstone.
—Katie Woo Tries Something New. Manushkin, Fran. 2015. (Katie Woo Ser.). (ENG.). 96p. (J). (gr. k-2). pap. 4.95 *(978-1-4795-6182-7(7)*, Picture Window Bks.) Capstone.
—Katie Woo, We Love You! Manushkin, Fran. ed. 2018. (Katie Woo Ser.). (ENG.). 96p. (J). (gr. k-2). pap. 4.95 *(978-1-5158-2277-6(X)*, 136893, Picture Window Bks.) Capstone.
—Katie Woo, Where Are You?, 1 vol. Manushkin, Fran. 2011. (Katie Woo Ser.). (ENG.). 32p. (J). (gr. k-2). pap. 5.95 *(978-1-4048-6853-3(4))*; lib. bdg. 21.32 *(978-1-4048-6517-4(9))* Capstone. (Picture Window Bks.).
—Katie Woo's Big Idea Journal: A Place for Your Best Stories, Drawings, Doodles, & Plans, 1 vol. Manushkin, Fran. 2014. (Katie Woo Ser.). (ENG.). 144p. (J). (gr. k-2). 9.95 *(978-1-62370-166-6(X)*, Capstone Young Readers) Capstone.
—Katie's Happy Mother's Day. Manushkin, Fran. 2015. (Katie Woo Ser.). (ENG.). 32p. (J). (gr. k-2). 21.32 *(978-1-4795-6179-7(7)*, Picture Window Bks.) Capstone.
—Katie's Lucky Birthday, 1 vol. Manushkin, Fran. 2011. (Katie Woo Ser.). (ENG.). 32p. (J). (gr. k-2). pap. 5.95 *(978-1-4048-6612-6(4))*; lib. bdg. 21.32 *(978-1-4048-6514-3(4))* Capstone. (Picture Window Bks.).
—Katie's New Shoes, 1 vol. Manushkin, Fran. 2011. (Katie Woo Ser.). (ENG.). 32p. (J). (gr. k-2). pap. 5.95 *(978-1-4048-6855-7(0))*; lib. bdg. 21.32 *(978-1-4048-6519-8(5))* Capstone. (Picture Window Bks.).
—Katie's Noisy Music. Manushkin, Fran. 2015. (Katie Woo Ser.). (ENG.). 32p. (J). (gr. k-2). 21.32 *(978-1-4795-5893-3(1)*, Picture Window Bks.) Capstone.
—Katie's Spooky Sleepover. Manushkin, Fran. 2016. (Katie Woo Ser.). (ENG.). 32p. (J). (gr. k-2). lib. bdg. 21.32 *(978-1-4795-9640-9(X)*, Picture Window Bks.) Capstone.
—Keep Dancing, Katie, 1 vol. Manushkin, Fran. 2014. (Katie Woo Ser.). (ENG.). 32p. (J). (gr. k-2). 21.32 *(978-1-4795-5187-3(2)*, Picture Window Bks.) Capstone.
—Let's Hear It for Almigal. Kupfer, Wendy. 2012. (ENG.). 32p. (J). (gr. k-2). 16.99 *(978-0-9838294-0-9(3))* Handfinger Pr.
—Letters to God, 1 vol. Doughtie, Patrick & Doughtie, Heather. 2016. (Letters to God Ser.). (ENG.). 32p. (J). 16.99 *(978-0-310-75395-7(3))* Zonderkidz.
—Look at You, Katie Woo!, 1 vol. Manushkin, Fran. 2011. (Katie Woo Ser.). (ENG.). 112p. (J). (gr. k-2). pap. 7.95 *(978-1-4048-6596-9(9)*, Picture Window Bks.) Capstone.
—Make-Believe Class, 1 vol. Manushkin, Fran. 2010. (Katie Woo Ser.). (ENG.). 32p. (J). (gr. k-2). lib. bdg. 21.32 *(978-1-4048-5732-2(X)*, Picture Window Bks.) Capstone.
—Moo, Katie Woo! Manushkin, Fran. 2013. (J). pap. 35.70 *(978-1-4048-8093-1(3))*; (ENG.). 32p. pap. 5.95 *(978-1-4048-8047-4(X))*; (ENG.). 32p. lib. bdg. 21.32 *(978-1-4048-7653-8(7))* Capstone. (Picture Window Bks.).
—Moving Day, 1 vol. Manushkin, Fran. 2010. (Katie Woo Ser.). (ENG.). 32p. (J). (gr. k-2). pap. 5.95 *(978-1-4048-6059-9(2))*; lib. bdg. 21.32 *(978-1-4048-5733-9(8))* Capstone. (Picture Window Bks.).
—My Pup, 0 vols. O'Hair, Margaret. 2010. (ENG.). 24p. (J). (gr. -1-2). bds. 7.99 *(978-0-7614-5644-5(9)*, 9780761456445, Two Lions) Amazon Publishing.
—My Whirling, Twirling Motor. Saunders, Merriam. 2019. (J). *(978-1-4338-2936-9(3)*, Magination Pr.) American Psychological Assn.
—A Nervous Night, 1 vol. Manushkin, Fran. 2010. (Katie Woo Ser.). (ENG.). 32p. (J). (gr. k-2). pap. 5.95 *(978-1-4048-6060-5(6))*; lib. bdg. 21.32 *(978-1-4048-5725-4(7))* Capstone. (Picture Window Bks.).
—No More Teasing, 1 vol. Manushkin, Fran. 2009. (Katie Woo Ser.). (ENG.). 32p. (J). (gr. k-2). 21.32 *(978-1-4048-5492-5(4)*, Picture Window Bks.) Capstone.
—No Valentines for Katie, 1 vol. Manushkin, Fran. 2010. (Katie Woo Ser.). (ENG.). 32p. (J). (gr. k-2). lib. bdg. 21.32 *(978-1-4048-5986-9(1))*; pap. 5.95 *(978-1-4048-6365-1(6))* Capstone. (Picture Window Bks.).
—On Top of the World. Manushkin, Fran. 2018. (Pedro Ser.). (ENG.). 32p. (J). (gr. k-2). lib. bdg. 21.32 *(978-1-5158-2823-5(9)*, 137988, Picture Window Bks.) Capstone.
Lyon, Tammie. Pedro. Manushkin, Fran. (Pedro Ser.). (ENG.). (J). (gr. k-2). 2020. 341.12 ***(978-1-5158-7085-2(5)***, 199070); 2020. pap., pap., pap. 95.20 ***(978-1-5158-7343-3(9)***, 201800); 2019. 298.48 *(978-1-5158-4454-9(4)*, 29330); 2019. pap., pap., pap. 83.30 *(978-1-5158-4610-9(5)*, 29671) Capstone. (Picture Window Bks.).
Lyon, Tammie. Pedro & the Shark. Manushkin, Fran. 2017. (Pedro Ser.). (ENG.). 32p. (J). (gr. k-2). lib. bdg. 21.32 *(978-1-5158-0873-2(4)*, Picture Window Bks.) Capstone.
—Pedro, Candidato a Presidente. Manushkin, Fran. 2018. (Pedro en Español Ser.). (SPA.). 32p. (J). (gr. k-2). lib. bdg. 21.32 *(978-1-5158-2508-1(6)*, 137567, Picture Window Bks.) Capstone.
—Pedro el Ninja. Manushkin, Fran. 2018. (Pedro en Español Ser.). (SPA.). 32p. (J). (gr. k-2). lib. bdg. 21.32 *(978-1-5158-2510-4(8)*, 137568, Picture Window Bks.) Capstone.
—Pedro el Pirata. Manushkin, Fran. 2018. (Pedro en Español Ser.). (SPA.). 32p. (J). (gr. k-2). lib. bdg. 21.32 *(978-1-5158-2514-2(0)*, 137573, Picture Window Bks.) Capstone.
—Pedro en Español. Manushkin, Fran. (Pedro en Español Ser.).Tr. of Pedro. (SPA.). (J). (gr. k-2). 2020. 298.48 *(978-1-5158-5749-5(2)*, 29925); 2020. pap., pap., pap. 83.30 *(978-1-5158-5750-1(6)*, 29926); 2019. 255.84 *(978-1-5158-4689-5(X)*, 29725); 2019. pap., pap., pap. 59.40 *(978-1-5158-4705-2(5)*, 29747) Capstone. (Picture Window Bks.).
—Pedro, First-Grade Hero. Manushkin, Fran. 2016. (Pedro Ser.). (ENG.). 96p. (J). (gr. k-2). pap. 4.95 *(978-1-5158-0112-2(8)*, Picture Window Bks.) Capstone.
—Pedro for President. Manushkin, Fran. 2016. (Pedro Ser.). (ENG.). 32p. (J). (gr. k-2). lib. bdg. 21.32 *(978-1-5158-0087-3(3)*, Picture Window Bks.) Capstone.
—Pedro Goes Buggy. Manushkin, Fran. 2016. (Pedro Ser.). (ENG.). 32p. (J). (gr. k-2). lib. bdg. 21.32 *(978-1-5158-0085-9(7)*, Picture Window Bks.) Capstone.
Lyon, Tammie. Pedro Goes to Mars. Manushkin, Fran. 2020. (Pedro Ser.). (ENG.). 32p. (J). (gr. k-2). pap. 5.95 ***(978-1-5158-7315-0(3)***, 201598); lib. bdg. 21.32 ***(978-1-5158-7081-4(2)***, 199038) Capstone. (Picture Window Bks.).
Lyon, Tammie. Pedro Goes Wild! Manushkin, Fran. 2019. (Pedro Ser.). (ENG.). 32p. (J). (gr. k-2). 21.32 *(978-1-5158-4450-1(1)*, 140565, Picture Window Bks.) Capstone.
—Pedro Keeps His Cool. Manushkin, Fran. 2019. (Pedro Ser.). (ENG.). 32p. (J). (gr. k-2). pap. 5.95 *(978-1-5158-4564-5(8)*, 141152); lib. bdg. 21.32 *(978-1-5158-4451-8(X)*, 140566) Capstone. (Picture Window Bks.).
—Pedro No Pierde la Calma. Manushkin, Fran. 2020. (Pedro en Español Ser.).Tr. of Pedro Keeps His Cool. (SPA.). 32p. (J). (gr. k-2). pap. 5.95 *(978-1-5158-5725-9(5)*, 142093); lib. bdg. 21.32 *(978-1-5158-5723-5(9)*, 142090) Capstone. (Picture Window Bks.).
Lyon, Tammie. Pedro on the Go. Manushkin, Fran. ed. 2020. (Pedro Ser.). (ENG.). 96p. (J). (gr. k-2). pap. 4.95 ***(978-1-5158-7268-9(8)***, 201186, Picture Window Bks.) Capstone.
Lyon, Tammie. Pedro the Ninja. Manushkin, Fran. 2017. (Pedro Ser.). (ENG.). 32p. (J). (gr. k-2). lib. bdg. 21.32 *(978-1-5158-1904-2(3)*, 136538, Picture Window Bks.) Capstone.
—Pedro y el Monstruo. Manushkin, Fran. 2019. (Pedro en Español Ser.). (SPA.). 32p. (J). (gr. k-2). pap. 4.95 *(978-1-5158-4696-3(2)*, 141323); lib. bdg. 21.32 *(978-1-5158-4658-1(X)*, 141257) Capstone. (Picture Window Bks.).
—Pedro y el Tiburón. Manushkin, Fran. 2018. (Pedro en Español Ser.). (SPA.). 32p. (J). (gr. k-2). lib. bdg. 21.32 *(978-1-5158-2507-4(8)*, 137566, Picture Window Bks.) Capstone.
—Pedro y Su Suerte. Manushkin, Fran. 2019. (Pedro en Español Ser.). (SPA.). 32p. (J). (gr. k-2). pap. 4.95 *(978-1-5158-4695-6(4)*, 141322); lib. bdg. 21.32 *(978-1-5158-4659-8(8)*, 141258) Capstone. (Picture Window Bks.).
—Pedro y Sus Bichos. Manushkin, Fran. 2018. (Pedro en Español Ser.). (SPA.). 32p. (J). (gr. k-2). lib. bdg. 21.32 *(978-1-5158-2509-8(4)*, 137569, Picture Window Bks.) Capstone.
—Pedro's Big Break. Manushkin, Fran. 2018. (Pedro Ser.). (ENG.). 32p. (J). (gr. k-2). lib. bdg. 21.32 *(978-1-5158-2822-8(0)*, 137987, Picture Window Bks.) Capstone.
—Pedro's Big Goal. Manushkin, Fran. 2016. (Pedro Ser.). (ENG.). 32p. (J). (gr. k-2). lib. bdg. 21.32 *(978-1-5158-0086-6(5)*, Picture Window Bks.) Capstone.
—Pedro's Monster. Manushkin, Fran. 2018. (Pedro Ser.). (ENG.). 32p. (J). (gr. k-2). lib. bdg. 21.32 *(978-1-5158-2821-1(2)*, 137986, Picture Window Bks.) Capstone.
—Pedro's Mystery Club. Manushkin, Fran. 2016. (Pedro Ser.). (ENG.). 32p. (J). (gr. k-2). lib. bdg. 21.32 *(978-1-5158-0084-2(9)*, Picture Window Bks.) Capstone.
—Pedro's Tricky Tower. Manushkin, Fran. 2017. (Pedro Ser.). (ENG.). 32p. (J). (gr. k-2). lib. bdg. 21.32 *(978-1-5158-1903-5(5)*, 136537, Picture Window Bks.) Capstone.
—Piggy Bank Problems, 1 vol. Manushkin, Fran. 2013. (Katie Woo Ser.). (ENG.). 32p. (J). (gr. k-2). pap. 5.95 *(978-1-4048-8048-1(8))*; lib. bdg. 21.32 *(978-1-4048-7654-5(5))* Capstone. (Picture Window Bks.).
—Pirate Pedro. Manushkin, Fran. 2017. (Pedro Ser.). (ENG.). 32p. (J). (gr. k-2). lib. bdg. 21.32 *(978-1-5158-0872-5(6)*, Picture Window Bks.) Capstone.
—The Princess & the Peanut Allergy. McClure, Wendy. 2012. (J). *(978-1-61913-127-9(7))* Weigl Pubs., Inc.
—The Princess & the Peanut Allergy. McClure, Wendy. 2019. 32p. (J). (gr. -1-3). pap. 7.99 *(978-0-8075-6619-0(5)*, 807566195) Whitman, Albert & Co.
—Princess with a Purpose. Chapman, Kelly. ldr.'s ed. 2009. pap. 12.99 *(978-0-7369-2743-7(3))* Harvest Hse. Pubs.
—Red, White, & Blue & Katie Woo!, 1 vol. Manushkin, Fran. 2010. (Katie Woo Ser.). (ENG.). 32p. (J). (gr. k-2). lib. bdg. 21.32 *(978-1-4048-5985-2(3))*; pap. 5.95 *(978-1-4048-6364-4(8))* Capstone. (Picture Window Bks.).
—Rocket Rivals. Harkrader, Lisa. 2019. (Makers Make It Work Ser.). (ENG.). 32p. (J). (gr. k-3). 25.32 *(978-1-63592-118-2(X))* Astra Publishing Hse.
—Rosie Saves the World. Herman, Debbie. 2017. (ENG.). 32p. (J). (gr. -1-2). 17.99 *(978-1-5124-2085-2(9)*, 9781512420852, Kar-Ben Publishing) Lerner Publishing Group.
—Sincerely, Katie: Writing a Letter with Katie Woo, 1 vol. Manushkin, Fran. 2013. (Katie Woo: Star Writer Ser.). (ENG.). 32p. (J). (gr. k-2). pap. 6.95 *(978-1-4795-1921-7(9))*; lib. bdg. 21.32 *(978-1-4048-8126-6(3))* Capstone. (Picture Window Bks.).
—Star of the Show, 1 vol. Manushkin, Fran. 2011. (Katie Woo Ser.). (ENG.). 32p. (J). (gr. k-2). pap. 5.95 *(978-1-4048-6613-3(2))*; lib. bdg. 21.32 *(978-1-4048-6515-0(2))* Capstone. (Picture Window Bks.).
—Stick to the Facts, Katie: Writing a Research Paper with Katie Woo, 1 vol. Manushkin, Fran. 2013. (Katie Woo: Star Writer Ser.). (ENG.). 32p. (J). (gr. k-2). pap. 6.95 *(978-1-4795-1925-5(1))*; lib. bdg. 21.32 *(978-1-4048-8130-3(1))* Capstone. (Picture Window Bks.).
—Too Much Rain, 1 vol. Manushkin, Fran. 2009. (Katie Woo Ser.). (ENG.). 32p. (J). (gr. k-2). 21.32 *(978-1-4048-5494-9(0)*, Picture Window Bks.) Capstone.
—La Torre Embromada de Pedro. Manushkin, Fran. 2018. (Pedro en Español Ser.). (SPA.). 32p. (J). (gr. k-2). lib. bdg. 21.32 *(978-1-5158-2513-5(2)*, 137572, Picture Window Bks.) Capstone.
—The Tricky Tooth, 1 vol. Manushkin, Fran. 2011. (Katie Woo Ser.). (ENG.). 32p. (J). (gr. k-2). pap. 5.95 *(978-1-4048-6611-9(6))*; lib. bdg. 21.32 *(978-1-4048-6516-7(0))* Capstone. (Picture Window Bks.).
—What Do You Think, Katie? Writing an Opinion Piece with Katie Woo, 1 vol. Manushkin, Fran. 2013. (Katie Woo: Star Writer Ser.). (ENG.). 32p. (J). (gr. k-2). pap. 6.95 *(978-1-4795-1926-2(X))*; lib. bdg. 21.32 *(978-1-4048-8131-0(X))* Capstone. (Picture Window Bks.).
—What Happens Next, Katie? Writing a Narrative with Katie Woo, 1 vol. Manushkin, Fran. 2013. (Katie Woo: Star Writer Ser.). (ENG.). 32p. (J). (gr. k-2). pap. 6.95 *(978-1-4795-1924-8(3)*, Picture Window Bks.) Capstone.
—What's in Your Heart, Katie? Writing in a Journal with Katie Woo, 1 vol. Manushkin, Fran. 2013. (Katie Woo: Star Writer Ser.). (ENG.). 32p. (J). (gr. k-2). pap. 6.95 *(978-1-4795-1922-4(7))*; lib. bdg. 21.32 *(978-1-4048-8127-3(1))* Capstone. (Picture Window Bks.).
—Who Needs Glasses?, 1 vol. Manushkin, Fran. 2013. (Katie Woo Ser.). (ENG.). 32p. (J). (gr. k-2). pap. 5.95 *(978-1-4048-8049-8(6))*; lib. bdg. 21.32 *(978-1-4048-7655-2(3))* Capstone. (Picture Window Bks.).
Lyon, Tammie. Adiós a Goldie. Lyon, Tammie. Manushkin, Fran. 2012. (Katie Woo en Español Ser.). (SPA.). 32p. (J). (gr. k-2). pap. 6.95 *(978-1-4048-7676-7(6))*; lib. bdg. 21.32 *(978-1-4048-7524-1(7))* Capstone. (Picture Window Bks.).
—Basta de Burlas, 1 vol. Lyon, Tammie. Manushkin, Fran. 2012. (Katie Woo en Español Ser.). (SPA.). 32p. (J). (gr. k-2). pap. 6.95 *(978-1-4048-7677-4(4))*; lib. bdg. 21.32 *(978-1-4048-7525-8(5))* Capstone. (Picture Window Bks.).
—La Gran Mentira, 1 vol. Lyon, Tammie. Manushkin, Fran. 2012. (Katie Woo en Español Ser.). (SPA.). 32p. (J). (gr. k-2). pap. 6.95 *(978-1-4048-7678-1(2))*; lib. bdg. 21.32 *(978-1-4048-7522-7(0))* Capstone. (Picture Window Bks.).
—La Jefa Del Mundo, 1 vol. Lyon, Tammie. Manushkin, Fran. 2012. (Katie Woo en Español Ser.). (SPA.). 32p. (J). (gr. k-2). pap. 6.95 *(978-1-4048-7679-8(0))*; lib. bdg. 21.32 *(978-1-4048-7523-4(9))* Capstone. (Picture Window Bks.).
—¡Soy Optimista! Lyon, Tammie. Parker, David. 2011. (SPA.). (J). *(978-0-545-27356-5(0))* Scholastic, Inc.
Lyon, Tammie, jt. illus. see Lyon, Tammie Speer.
Lyon, Tammie Speer. Grumbly Bunnies. Welch, Willy. 2004. 32p. (J). 15.95 *(978-1-58089-086-1(5))* Charlesbridge Publishing, Inc.
—Hickory Dickory Dock! gif. ed. 2006. 10p. (J). (gr. -1-k). bds. 10.95 *(978-1-57791-213-2(6))* Brighter Minds Children's Publishing.
—Mary Had a Little Lamb. 2006. 8p. (J). bds. 10.95 *(978-1-57791-210-1(1))* Brighter Minds Children's Publishing.
—Now I Lay Me down to Sleep. 2006. 8p. (J). bds. 10.95 *(978-1-57791-211-8(X))* Brighter Minds Children's Publishing.
—This Little Piggy. gif. ed. 2006. 10p. (J). bds. 10.95 *(978-1-57791-212-5(8))* Brighter Minds Children's Publishing.
Lyon, Tammie Speer & Lyon, Tammie. Eloise & the Very Secret Room. Weiss, Ellen. 2006. (Eloise Ser.). (ENG.). 32p. (J). (gr. -1-1). pap. 4.99 *(978-0-689-87450-5(2)*, Simon Spotlight) Simon Spotlight.
—Eloise Goes to the Beach. Fry, Sonali & Knight, Hilary. 2007. (Eloise Ser.). (ENG.). 12p. (J). (gr. -1-2). 9.99 *(978-1-4169-3344-1(1)*, Little Simon) Little Simon.
Lyona. I Will Fight Monsters for You. Balmes, Santi. 2015. (ENG.). 32p. (J). (gr. -1-3). 16.99 *(978-0-8075-9056-0(8)*, 807590568) Whitman, Albert & Co.
Lyons, Chris, jt. illus. see Benoit, Renné.
Lyons, Sarah Rose. Community Heroes: A Guide to Being Brave in the Face of Coronavirus. Lyons, Ren�e. 2020. (ENG.). 24p. (J). (gr. k-5). pap. 9.99 ***(978-1-949979-99-2(7))*** Clemson Univ. Pr.
—H�roes de la Comunidad: Una Gu�a para Enfrentar con Seguridad Al Coronavirus. Lyons, Ren�e. 2020. (SPA.). 24p. (J). (gr. k-5). pap. 9.99 ***(978-1-949979-98-5(9))*** Clemson Univ. Pr.
L¿pez, Anuki. Katt vs. Dogg. Patterson, James & Grabenstein, Chris. 2019. (ENG.). 320p. (J). (gr. 3-7). 13.99 *(978-0-316-41156-1(6)*, Jimmy Patterson) Little Brown & Co.

M

M

M, Baby, jt. illus. see D, Baby.
M, Deanna. BJ's Big Dream. Leverette, Sonia Cunningham. (ENG.). (J). (gr. k-3). 2017. 20.00 *(978-0-692-98525-0(5))*; 2016. pap. 10.00 *(978-0-9981230-0-4(5))* Hadassah's Crown Publishing, LLC.
M., Dhanya. The Story of Esther. Paiva, Johannah Gilman. 2017. (5 Minute Bible Stories Ser.). (ENG.). 20p. (J). (gr. 1-3). bds. 8.99 *(978-1-4867-1316-5(5)*, 466ce790-4342-46eb-9d2a-b96303b4a05c) Flowerpot Pr.
—The Story of Ruth. Paiva, Johannah Gilman. 2017. (5 Minute Bible Stories Ser.). (ENG.). 20p. (J). (gr. 1-3). bds. 8.99 *(978-1-4867-1315-8(7)*, 3543f8b0-7d50-4cb3-bd4c-ed319d07b222) Flowerpot Pr.
M, Elle. She's Just Like Me: Celebrating Diversity. Robertson, Tammy. 2017. (J). 19.99 *(978-1-945384-19-6(0))* Hawaii Way Publishing.
M, Found. Tails of the Caygeon Cats. Coulter, Lynn. 2018. (ENG.). 56p. (J). (gr. k-4). pap. 12.95 *(978-0-9996048-3-0(X))* CreateSpace Independent Publishing Platform.
M, J. "E". Moon Ridge Valley. M, J. "E", ed. Williams, Iris M. 2018. (Moon Ridge Valley Ser.: Vol. 1). (ENG.). 148p. (J). pap. 10.95 *(978-1-947656-77-2(5))* Butterfly Typeface, The.
M J, Goulart. Genevieve: Fashion Princess. M J, Goulart. 2016. (ENG.). (J). (gr. k-4). 13.95 *(978-0-9980932-2-2(X))* Goulart-Johnston, Michelle.
M. J. Studios Staff. The Incredible Dionsaur. Nichols, V. 128p. (J). (gr. k-6). pap., act. bk. ed. 2.95 *(978-1-879424-64-7(9))* Nickel Pr.
M M, Shanith. The Jet of Justice. Lake, Angie. ed. 2020. (Danny Dingle's Fantastic Finds Ser.: 3). (ENG.). 256p. (J). (gr. 3-7). 7.99 *(978-1-78226-572-6(4)*, f2c9ccf6-4fca-4682-a3b5-83bf1e48fd2e) Sweet Cherry Publishing GBR. Dist: Baker & Taylor Publisher Services (BTPS).
—The Mighty Iron Foot. Lake, Angie. ed. 2020. (Danny Dingle's Fantastic Finds Ser.: 4). (ENG.). 248p. (J). (gr. 3-7). 7.99 *(978-1-78226-573-3(2)*, c3dfede5-21f0-4ee2-b4a0-8ab6d2a57564) Sweet Cherry Publishing GBR. Dist: Baker & Taylor Publisher Services (BTPS).
—Super-Sonic Submarine. Lake, Angie. ed. 2019. (Danny Dingle's Fantastic Finds Ser.: 2). (ENG.). 296p. (J). (gr. 3-7). 7.99 *(978-1-78226-571-9(6)*, 2ba45f80-6cd6-425b-bff6-3f9a17865207) Sweet Cherry Publishing GBR. Dist: Baker & Taylor Publisher Services (BTPS).
M M, Shanith & Sati, Suruchi. The Metal-Mobile. Lake, Angie. ed. 2019. (Danny Dingle's Fantastic Finds Ser.: 1). (ENG.). 240p. (J). (gr. 3-7). 7.99 *(978-1-78226-570-2(8)*, bc6d58a6-d7b4-46a9-a111-2c3b613dc796) Sweet Cherry Publishing GBR. Dist: Baker & Taylor Publisher Services (BTPS).
Ma, C. J. Animal Rescuers. Ma, C. J. 2016. (ENG.). (J). pap. 11.99 *(978-1-61170-242-2(9))* Robertson Publishing.
Ma Van As, Yaoyao. Kudo Kids: the Mystery of the Masked Medalist. Shibutani, Alex et al. 2020. (Kudo Kids Ser.: 1). (ENG.). 272p. (J). (gr. 3-7). 16.99 ***(978-0-593-11373-8(X)***, Razorbill) Penguin Young Readers Group.
Ma, Wenhai. Tang Monk Disciples Monkey King. 2005. (Adventures of Monkey King Ser.: No. 3). 32p. (J). 16.95 *(978-1-57227-084-8(5))* Pan Asia Pubns. (USA), Inc.
—Tang Monk Disciples Monkey King: English/Chinese. 2005. (Adventures of Monkey King Ser.: No. 3). (ENG & CHI.). 32p. (J). 16.95 *(978-1-57227-086-2(1))* Pan Asia Pubns. (USA), Inc.
—Tang Monk Disciples Monkey King: English/Vietnamese. Do, Kim-Thu, tr. from ENG. 2005. (Adventures of Monkey King Ser.: No. 3). (ENG & VIE.). 32p. (J). 16.95 *(978-1-57227-087-9(X))* Pan Asia Pubns. (USA), Inc.
Ma, Winnie. Circles of Round. Sturup, Signe. 2013. 40p. (J). (gr. k-3). 16.95 *(978-1-927018-18-7(8))* Simply Read Bks. CAN. Dist: Ingram Publisher Services.
Maa'Dhoor, Lilian. Palabrerías: Retahílas, trabalenguas, Colmos y otros juegos de palabras. Hernandez, Eufemia. 2015. 48p. (J). (gr. k-3). pap. 10.99 *(978-970-58-0212-6(2))* Consejo Estatal Electoral MEX. Dist: Santillana USA Publishing Co., Inc.
Maas, Dorothy. Mr Dawson Had an Elephant. Work, Rhoda O. 2011. 128p. 40.95 *(978-1-258-07973-4(9))* Literary Licensing, LLC.

Maas, Jason A. Cows Can't Jump. Reisman, Dave. 2008. (ENG.). 44p. (J). 11.99 *(978-0-9801433-1-7(4))*; pap. 7.99 *(978-0-9801433-0-0(6))* Jumping Cow Pr.

Mabbitt, Will. I Can Only Draw Worms. Mabbitt, Will. 2019. (ENG.). 32p. (J). (-k). 14.99 *(978-1-5247-8822-3(8)*, Penguin Workshop) Penguin Young Readers Group.

Mabe, Ryan. Little Spooky Troop & the Buried Treasure. St John, Stewart. 2018. (ENG.). 34p. (J). (gr. k-3). 19.99 *(978-0-9830463-9-4(5))* Wonkybot Publishing.

Mabee, Andrea, photos by. Dory Glory: Building A Boat from Stem to Stern. Mabee, Andrea. 2005. 67p. (YA). per. 15.95 *(978-0-9630074-1-4(6))* Bass Cove Bks.

Maberry, Maranda. Do Not Open This Math Book: Addition + Subtraction. McKellar, Danica. 2018. 160p. (J). (gr. 1-4). pap. 18.99 *(978-1-101-93398-5(4)*, Crown Books For Young Readers) Random Hse. Children's Bks.

Maberry, Maranda, jt. illus. see Peterson, Stacy.

Mabey, Coline. A Christmas Kindness. Gevry, C. C. 2012. 24p. pap. 11.99 *(978-0-9852661-4-1(7))* 4RV Pub.

Mabire, Grégoire. The Street Cat Gang. Metzmeyer, Catherine. ed. 2018. 32p. (J). (gr. -1). 16.95 *(978-1-912233-76-2(2)*, Scribblers) Book Hse. GBR. Dist: Sterling Publishing Co., Inc.

—Tooth Monsters. Martinello, Jessica. ed. 2019. 32p. (J). (gr. -1-1). 16.95 *(978-1-912537-75-4(3)*, Scribblers) Book Hse. GBR. Dist: Sterling Publishing Co., Inc.

Mabrey, Charles. What Are Dreams? Williams, Sandra T. 2018. (ENG.). 30p. (J). pap. 11.99 *(978-1-947773-11-0(9))* Yawn's Bks. & More, Inc.

Mac. The Hawww Monster: A Book about Bad Breath. Mac. 2018. (ENG.). 26p. (J). pap. 9.13 *(978-1-7172-3626-5(X))* CreateSpace Independent Publishing Platform.

Mac, David. Kawaii Seashell Composition Notebook. David, Designs by. 2019. (Kawaii Seashell Composition Notebook Ser.: Vol. 1). (ENG.). 122p. (J). pap. 7.99 *(978-1-0988-5218-4(4))* Independently Published.

MacAdam, Dean. Here We Come, Construction Fun!, 1 vol. Greene, Rhonda Gowler. 2018. (ENG.). 24p. (J). bds. 9.99 *(978-0-310-76389-5(4))* Zonderkidz.

MacAdam, Ian Paul. Donkey Oatie's Fashion Statement. Rath, Tom H. 2012. 32p. pap. *(978-0-9866065-7-1(X))* Wood Islands Prints.

MacAdam, Reegory. Donkey Oatie's Impossible Dream. Rath, Tom H. 2012. 24p. pap. *(978-0-9866065-5-7(3))* Wood Islands Prints.

Macale, Leitaya. You're a Star: A 'by Children, for Children' Book. Macale, Leitaya. 2019. (You're Special Inspirational Bks.: Vol. 3). (ENG.). 20p. (J). (gr. k-2). pap. ***(978-0-473-47947-3(8))*** Sunsmile Bks.

—You're Wonderful: A 'by Children, for Children' Book. Macale, Leitaya. 2019. (You're Special Inspirational Bks.: Vol. 2). (ENG.). 20p. (J). (gr. k-2). pap. ***(978-0-9951238-1-6(0))*** Sunsmile Bks.

Macaluso, James. The Man with the Twisted Lip - Lego - the Adventures of Sherlock Holmes. Doyle, A. Conan. 2014. (ENG.). pap. *(978-1-78092-698-8(7))* MX Publishing, Ltd.

Macari, Mario Duilio. Funny Riddles for Kids: Squeaky Clean Easy Kid Riddles Drawn As Funny Kid's Cartoons in A Cool Comicbook Style. Macari, Mario Duilio, ed. 2007. 104p. (J). per. 10.00 *(978-0-9766755-0-1(1))* Cartoonmario.com.

Macaulay, David. Mammoth Science: The Big Ideas That Explain Our World. DK. 2020. (ENG.). 160p. (J). (gr. 3-7). 19.99 ***(978-1-4654-9146-6(5)***, DK Children) Dorling Kindersley Publishing, Inc.

Macaulay, David. Building Big. Macaulay, David. 2006. 192p. reprint ed. 30.00 *(978-1-4223-5328-8(1))* DIANE Publishing Co.

Macbeth, Seth. Kooper's Tale. Koffman, Donna Carol & Segel, Lawrence. 2016. (ENG.). (J). (gr. 4-5). pap. *(978-1-55483-998-8(X))* Insomniac Pr.

MacCarthy, Patricia. Forget-me-not Fairies Story Collection. Musgrove, Marianne. 2013. (ENG.). 192p. (J). (gr. -1-3). *(978-1-74308-536-3(2))* Hinkler Bks. Pty. Ltd.

MacCarthy, Patricia. Ocean Parade: A Counting Book. MacCarthy, Patricia. 2005. 24p. (J). (gr. -1-3). reprint ed. 12.00 *(978-0-7567-8983-1(4))* DIANE Publishing Co.

MacCormick Secure Center, Residents. Another Sad Inning: Incarcerated Youth Reveal Their Trials, Tribulations & Loves. MacCormick SEcure Center, Residents. 2003. 90p. (YA). per. 17.00 *(978-0-9740184-1-6(4)*, MAC-2) Durland Alternatives Library.

MacDonald, Bruce. Two Fables of Aesop. Hamilton, Martha & Weiss, Mitch. 2005. (ENG.). 16p. (J). 5.75 *(978-1-57274-718-0(8)*, 2788, Bks. for Young Learners) Owen, Richard C. Pubs., Inc.

—Why Animals Never Got Fire: A Story of the Couer d'Alene Indians. Hamilton, Martha & Weiss, Mitch. 2005. (ENG.). 12p. (J). 5.75 *(978-1-57274-715-9(3)*, 2793, Bks. for Young Learners) Owen, Richard C. Pubs., Inc.

MacDonald, Clarke. Captain Lilly & the New Girl, 1 vol. Bellingham, Brenda. 2016. (Formac First Novels Ser.). (ENG.). 64p. (J). (gr. 1-5). 5.95 *(978-0-88780-855-5(7)*, 63115bd8-fe0d-4da3-a70c-a3a84a4d5b97) Formac Publishing Co., Ltd. CAN. Dist: Lerner Publishing Group.

—Lilly & the Hullabaloo, 1 vol. Bellingham, Brenda. 2008. (Formac First Novels Ser.). (ENG.). 64p. (gr. 2-5). (J). 5.95 *(978-0-88780-752-7(6)*, 752); (YA). 14.95 *(978-0-88780-754-1(2)*, 754) Formac Publishing Co., Ltd. CAN. Dist: Formac Lorimer Bks. Ltd.

—Lilly & the Snakes. Bellingham, Brenda. 2007. (Formac First Novels Ser.: 37). (GER.). 64p. (J). (gr. 2-5). 14.95 *(978-0-88780-727-5(5)*, 727); 4.95 *(978-0-88780-723-7(2)*, 723) Formac Publishing Co., Ltd. CAN. Dist: Formac Lorimer Bks. Ltd.

—Lilly Babysits Her Brother, 1 vol. Bellingham, Brenda. 2013. (Formac First Novels Ser.). (ENG.). 60p. (J). (gr. 2-3). 14.95 *(978-1-4595-0286-4(8)*, 0286); pap. 5.95 *(978-1-4595-0287-1(6)*, 0287) Formac Publishing Co., Ltd. CAN. Dist: Formac Lorimer Bks. Ltd.

—Lilly Makes a Friend. Bellingham, Brenda. 2004. 62p. (J). lib. bdg. 12.00 *(978-1-4242-1221-7(9))* Fitzgerald Bks.

—Lilly Makes a Friend, 1 vol. Bellingham, Brenda. 2004. (Formac First Novels Ser.: 29). (ENG.). 64p. (J). (gr. 1-5). 4.95 *(978-0-88780-624-7(4)*, 624); 14.95 *(978-0-88780-625-4(2)*, 625) Formac Publishing Co., Ltd. CAN. Dist: Formac Lorimer Bks. Ltd.

—Lilly Takes the Lead. Bellingham, Brenda. 2006. (Formac First Novels Ser.: 34). (ENG.). 64p. (gr. 2-5). 14.95 *(978-0-88780-703-9(8)*, 703); (J). 4.95 *(978-0-88780-701-5(1)*, 701) Formac Publishing Co., Ltd. CAN. Dist: Formac Lorimer Bks. Ltd.

—Lilly Traps the Bullies, 1 vol. Bellingham, Brenda. (Formac First Novels Ser.). (ENG.). 64p. (J). 2016. (gr. 1-5). pap. 5.95 *(978-0-88780-959-0(6)*, f9f29cff-e652-45db-a245-cf4dff61ddb6); 2011. (gr. 2-3). 14.95 *(978-0-88780-961-3(8)*, 961) Formac Publishing Co., Ltd. CAN. Dist: Lerner Publishing Group, Formac Lorimer Bks. Ltd.

—Lilly's Special Gift. Bellingham, Brenda. 2005. (Formac First Novels Ser.: 32). (ENG.). 64p. (gr. 2-5). 14.95 *(978-0-88780-665-0(1)*, 665) Formac Publishing Co., Ltd. CAN. Dist: Formac Lorimer Bks. Ltd.

MacDonald, Clarke & Kaulbach, Kathy. Lilly's Special Gift, 1 vol. Bellingham, Brenda. 2005. (Formac First Novels Ser.: 32). (ENG.). 64p. (gr. 2-5). 4.95 *(978-0-88780-664-3(3)*, 664) Formac Publishing Co., Ltd. CAN. Dist: Formac Lorimer Bks. Ltd.

MacDonald Denton, Kady. Elephant Child. Ellis, Mary. 2010. (ENG.). 128p. (J). (gr. 2-4). pap. 7.99 *(978-0-00-712820-4(7)*, HarperCollins Children's Bks.) HarperCollins Pubs. Ltd. GBR. Dist: HarperCollins Pubs.

MacDonald, John. Miracle: The True Story of the Wreck of the Sea Venture. Karwoski, Gail Langer. 2004. (Junior Library Guild Selection Ser.). 64p. (J). (gr. 4-18). 17.95 *(978-1-58196-015-0(8)*, Darby Creek) Lerner Publishing Group.

—Tsunami: The True Story of an April Fools' Day Disaster. Karwoski, Gail Langer. 2006. (ENG.). 64p. (J). (gr. 5-12). lib. bdg. 17.95 *(978-1-58196-044-0(1)*, Darby Creek) Lerner Publishing Group.

MacDonald, Judy. Human Body A to Z. Galvin, Laura Gates. 2012. (ENG.). 40p. 9.95 *(978-1-60727-296-0(2))* Soundprints.

MacDonald, Norma. The Great Lizard Trek. Bradshaw, Felicity. 2018. 32p. (J). (gr. 1-6). 19.95 *(978-1-4863-0882-8(1))* CSIRO Publishing AUS. Dist: Stylus Publishing, LLC.

MacDonald, Ross. American Gothic: The Life of Grant Wood. Wood, Susan. 2017. (ENG.). 40p. (J). (gr. k-2). 18.95 *(978-1-4197-2533-3(5)*, Abrams Bks. for Young Readers) Abrams, Inc.

—Boys of Steel: The Creators of Superman. Nobleman, Marc Tyler. 2013. 40p. (J). (gr. 5-6). 7.99 *(978-0-449-81063-7(1)*, Dragonfly Bks.) Random Hse. Children's Bks.

—Grumpy Grandpa. Henson, Heather. 2009. (ENG.). 40p. (J). (gr. -1-3). 16.99 *(978-1-4169-0811-1(0)*, Atheneum Bks. for Young Readers) Simon & Schuster Children's Publishing.

—Hey Batta Batta Swing! The Wild Old Days of Baseball. Cook, Sally & Charlton, James. 2007. (ENG.). 56p. (J). (gr. 1-5). 19.99 *(978-1-4169-1207-1(X)*, McElderry, Margaret K. Bks.) McElderry, Margaret K. Bks.

—Hit the Road, Jack. Burleigh, Robert. 2012. (ENG.). 48p. (J). (gr. -1-3). 17.95 *(978-1-4197-0399-7(4)*, Abrams Bks. for Young Readers) Abrams, Inc.

MacDonald, Ross. The Upper Case: Trouble in Capital City. Lazar, Tara. 2019. (Private I Ser.). (ENG.). 32p. (J). (gr. -1-3). 17.99 ***(978-1-368-02765-6(2))*** Little, Brown Bks. for Young Readers.

MacDonald, Shona Shirley. The Moon Spun Round: W. B. Yeats for Children. Yeats, W. B. Doody, Noreen, ed. 2016. (ENG.). 64p. 30.00 *(978-1-84717-738-4(7))* O'Brien Pr., Ltd., The IRL. Dist: Casemate Pubs. & Bk. Distributors, LLC.

MacDonald, Stacy. Hope. Guins, Brenda. 2018. (ENG.). 20p. (J). 21.95 *(978-1-64191-999-9(X))*; pap. 11.95 *(978-1-64114-670-8(2))* Christian Faith Publishing.

MacDonald, Stella. Dead Hairy. Thomas, Debbie. unabr. ed. 2011. (ENG.). 256p. (J). pap. 14.95 *(978-1-85635-678-7(7))* Mercier Pr., Ltd., The IRL. Dist: Dufour Editions, Inc.

—G. F. Woz Ere. Fitzmaurice, Gabriel. 2009. (ENG.). 96p. (J). pap. 12.95 *(978-1-85635-622-0(1))* Mercier Pr., Ltd., The IRL. Dist: Dufour Editions, Inc.

—Jungle Tangle. Thomas, Debbie. 2013. (ENG.). 320p. (J). pap. 14.95 *(978-1-78117-116-5(5))* Mercier Pr., Ltd., The IRL. Dist: Dufour Editions, Inc.

—Monkie Business. Thomas, Debbie. 2014. (ENG.). 320p. (J). pap. 9.99 *(978-1-78117-170-7(X))* Mercier Pr., Ltd., The IRL. Dist: Casemate Pubs. & Bk. Distributors, LLC.

MacDonald, Suse. Alphabet Animals: A Slide-And-Peek Adventure. MacDonald, Suse. 2008. (ENG.). 28p. (J). (gr. -1-k). 14.99 *(978-1-4169-5045-5(1)*, Little Simon) Little Simon.

—Circus Opposites: An Interactive Extravaganza! MacDonald, Suse. 2010. (ENG.). 20p. (J). (gr. -1-2). 12.99 *(978-1-4169-7154-2(8)*, Little Simon) Little Simon.

—Dino Shapes. MacDonald, Suse. 2014. (ENG.). 20p. (J). (gr. -1-2). bds. 8.99 *(978-1-4814-0093-0(2)*, Little Simon) Little Simon.

—Fish, Swish! Splash, Dash! Counting Round & Round. MacDonald, Suse. 2007. (ENG.). 30p. (J). (gr. -1-k). 12.99 *(978-1-4169-3605-3(X)*, Little Simon) Little Simon.

—Shape by Shape. MacDonald, Suse. 2009. (ENG.). 24p. (J). (gr. -1-3). 17.99 *(978-1-4169-7147-4(5)*, Little Simon) Little Simon.

MacDonall, Angus. Classic Myths. Judd, Mary Catherine. 2007. 172p. per. *(978-1-4065-4675-0(5))* Dodo Pr.

MacDougall, Larry. Hare & the Big Green Lawn. Robey, Katharine Crawford. 2006. (ENG.). 32p. (J). (gr. -1-3). 15.95 *(978-0-87358-889-8(4))* Cooper Square Publishing Llc.

MacDougall, Larry, jt. illus. see Fiegenschuh, Emily.

Mace, Joyce. Ella the Elephant. Mace, Isabelle. 2018. (ENG.). 28p. (J). pap. 10.00 *(978-1-7329995-0-3(3))* OutFlow Publishing.

MacEachern, Stephen. Earth-Friendly Buildings Bridges & More: The Eco-Journal of Corry Lapont. Kaner, Etta. 2012. (ENG.). 64p. (J). (gr. 3-7). 18.95 *(978-1-55453-570-5(0))* Kids Can Pr., Ltd. CAN. Dist: Hachette Bk. Group.

—Gotcha! 18 Amazing Ways to Freak Out Your Friends. Acer, David. 2008. (ENG.). 48p. (J). (gr. 3-7). 16.95 *(978-1-55453-194-3(2))* Kids Can Pr., Ltd. CAN. Dist: Hachette Bk. Group.

MacEachern, Stephen. The Kids Guide to Money Cent$ MacEachern, Stephen, tr. Thomas, Keltie. 2004. (ENG.). 56p. (J). 8.95 *(978-1-55337-391-9(X))*; (gr. 4-6). 8.95 *(978-1-55337-390-2(1))* Kids Can Pr., Ltd. CAN. Dist: Hachette Bk. Group.

Macedo, David. Chug & Thug: The Alug Bugs. Seede, Gemal. 2015. (ENG.). 36p. (J). (gr. k-3). *(978-1-7752871-2-4(2))* Mumin Media Inc.

—Chug & Thug: The Alug Bugs; Mid-East Edition. Seede, Gemal. 2015. (ENG.). 36p. (J). (gr. k-3). *(978-1-7752871-4-8(9))* Mumin Media Inc.

—Chug & Thug Ride Trike. Seede, Gemal K. 2018. (Chug & Thug Ser.: Vol. 2). (ENG.). 36p. (J). (gr. k-3). *(978-1-7752871-0-0(6))* Mumin Media Inc.

Macejko, Jeanne Ann. A Jillion Giraffes. Macejko, Jeanne Ann. 2018. (ENG.). 26p. (J). pap. 10.95 *(978-1-7290-7246-2(1))* Independently Published.

—A Million Chameleons: Color Your Own. Macejko, Jeanne Ann. 2019. (ENG.). 30p. (J). pap. 6.95 *(978-1-0962-1184-6(X))* Independently Published.

Macejko, Jeanne Anne. A Million Chameleons. 2004. (J). pap. 10.95 *(978-1-888836-13-4(X))* Shenango River Bks.

MacFarlane, Heather. Tom's MRI Space Adventure. Kumer, Ed D. Leslie. 2018. (ENG.). 28p. (J). pap. 16.95 *(978-1-4808-6169-5(3))* Archway Publishing.

MacFarlane, John. Horace the Great Harmonica King. Mayerhofer, Felix. 2006. 31p. (J). (gr. -1-7). per. 16.95 *(978-1-60002-255-5(3)*, 4313) Mountain Valley Publishing, LLC.

MacGregor, Doug. The Incredible Tongue Twister That Swallowed My Sister: Another Santa Story by Doug MacGregor. MacGregor, Doug. ltd. ed. 2006. 40p. (J). per. *(978-0-9654843-5-0(1))* MacGregor, Doug.

Mach, Delphine & Aki. The Weather Girls. Mach, Delphine & Aki. 2018. (ENG.). 32p. (J). 16.99 *(978-1-62779-620-0(7)*, 900156981, Holt, Henry & Co. Bks. For Young Readers) Holt, Henry & Co.

Machas, Dimi. Tsaani: The Grizzly Bear Story. 2nd ed. 2005. 28p. (YA). 10.00 *(978-0-9767217-0-3(8))* Chickaloon Village Publishing.

Machell, Dawn. An All-American ABC. Make Believe Ideas Ltd. 2019. (All American ABC Ser.). (ENG.). 26p. (J). (gr. -1-7). bds. *(978-1-78843-627-4(X))* Make Believe Ideas.

—Animal Friends. Ford, Emily et al. 2018. (ENG.). 12p. (J). (gr. -1 — 1). bds. 7.99 *(978-1-68412-185-4(X)*, Silver Dolphin Bks.) Printers Row Publishing Group.

Machell, Dawn. Bible Stories. Make Believe Ideas Ltd. 2020. (ENG.). 12p. (J). bds. ***(978-1-78947-877-8(4))*** Make Believe Ideas.

—Christmas. Make Believe Ideas Ltd. 2020. (ENG.). 42p. (J). (gr. -1-7). pap. ***(978-1-78947-715-3(8))*** Make Believe Ideas.

—Christmas Activity Book. Make Believe Ideas Ltd. 2019. (ENG.). 36p. (J). (gr. -1-7). pap. ***(978-1-78843-934-3(1))*** Make Believe Ideas.

Machell, Dawn. The Christmas Star. Make Believe Ideas Ltd. 2019. (ENG.). 12p. (J). bds. *(978-1-78843-926-8(0))* Make Believe Ideas.

Machell, Dawn. Cuddlycorn! Make Believe Ideas Ltd. 2020. (ENG.). 12p. (J). (gr. -1-7). bds. ***(978-1-78947-852-5(9))*** Make Believe Ideas.

Machell, Dawn. Dino Fun. Make Believe Ideas Ltd. 2019. (ENG.). 8p. (J). *(978-1-78947-078-9(1))* Make Believe Ideas.

—Easter Egg Hunt. Make Believe Ideas Ltd. 2019. (Seasonal Tabbed Ser.). (ENG.). 14p. (J). bds. *(978-1-78843-538-3(9))* Make Believe Ideas.

—Easter Parade Peekaboo! Make Believe Ideas Ltd. 2019. (Seasonal Peekaboo Ser.). (ENG.). 12p. (J). bds. *(978-1-78843-537-6(0))* Make Believe Ideas.

Machell, Dawn. Farm Fun. Make Believe Ideas Ltd. 2020. (ENG.). 8p. (J). (gr. -1-6). ***(978-1-78947-752-8(2))*** Make Believe Ideas.

—Five Sparkly Mermaids. Make Believe Ideas Ltd & Hainsby, Christie. 2020. (ENG.). 14p. (J). bds. ***(978-1-78947-367-4(5))*** Make Believe Ideas.

—Halloween. Make Believe Ideas Ltd. 2020. (ENG.). 42p. (J). (gr. -1-7). pap. ***(978-1-78947-707-8(7))*** Make Believe Ideas.

Machell, Dawn. Halloween Activity Book. Make Believe Ideas Ltd. 2019. (ENG.). (J). 36p. pap. *(978-1-78843-897-1(3))*; 32p. (gr. -1-7). pap. *(978-1-78843-898-8(1))* Make Believe Ideas.

Machell, Dawn. Halloween Party. Make Believe Ideas Ltd. 2020. (ENG.). 12p. (J). bds. ***(978-1-78947-689-7(5))*** Make Believe Ideas.

Machell, Dawn. Halloween Peek-A-Boo. Make Believe Ideas Ltd. 2019. (ENG.). 12p. (J). bds. *(978-1-78843-918-3(X))* Make Believe Ideas.

Machell, Dawn. Hide & Seek ABC. Make Believe Ideas Ltd. 2020. (Hide & Seek Ser.). (ENG.). 44p. (J). bds. ***(978-1-78947-589-0(9))*** Make Believe Ideas.

Machell, Dawn. I Love You, Ted. Make Believe Ideas Ltd. 2019. (ENG.). 14p. (J). bds. *(978-1-78947-004-8(8))* Make Believe Ideas.

Machell, Dawn. I-Spy-A-Saurus. Make Believe Ideas Ltd & Hainsby, Christie. 2020. (ENG.). 12p. (J). bds. ***(978-1-78947-374-2(8))*** Make Believe Ideas.

—Mermaids. Make Believe Ideas Ltd. 2020. (ENG.). 86p. (J). (gr. -1-7). pap. ***(978-1-78947-789-4(1))*** Make Believe Ideas.

Machell, Dawn. Mermaids & Narwhals. Make Believe Ideas Ltd. 2019. (ENG.). 86p. (J). (gr. -1-7). pap. *(978-1-78947-032-1(3))* Make Believe Ideas.

—My Awesome Dinosaur Book. Make Believe Ideas Ltd. 2019. (ENG.). 30p. (J). bds. *(978-1-78947-073-4(0))* Make Believe Ideas.

Machell, Dawn. My Awesome Magical Creatures Book. Make Believe Ideas Ltd. 2020. (ENG.). 28p. (J). bds. ***(978-1-78947-368-1(3))*** Make Believe Ideas.

Machell, Dawn. My Easter Activity Book. Make Believe Ideas Ltd. 2019. (Seasonal Activity Book Ser.). (ENG.). 42p. (J). (gr. -1-7). pap. *(978-1-78843-536-9(2))* Make Believe Ideas.

—My First Bible Stories. Make Believe Ideas Ltd. 2019. (My First Bible Stories Ser.). (ENG.). 40p. (J). bds. *(978-1-78843-535-2(4))* Make Believe Ideas.

Machell, Dawn. My Mermaid Purse. Make Believe Ideas Ltd. 2020. (ENG.). 72p. (J). (gr. -1-1). pap. ***(978-1-78947-393-3(4))*** Make Believe Ideas.

Machell, Dawn. My Rainbow Purse. Make Believe Ideas Ltd. 2019. (ENG.). 72p. (J). (gr. -1-7). pap. *(978-1-78947-030-7(7))* Make Believe Ideas.

Machell, Dawn. My Snowflake Purse. Make Believe Ideas Ltd. 2019. (ENG.). 48p. (J). (gr. -1-7). pap. ***(978-1-78843-935-0(X))*** Make Believe Ideas.

—My Unicorn Puppet Theater. Make Believe Ideas Ltd. 2020. (ENG.). 8p. (J). (gr. -1-7). bds. ***(978-1-78947-731-3(X))*** Make Believe Ideas.

—The Nativity. Make Believe Ideas Ltd. 2020. (ENG.). 12p. (J). bds. ***(978-1-78947-878-5(2))*** Make Believe Ideas.

Machell, Dawn. Noah's Ark & Other Bible Stories: 100 Puffy Stickers, 1 vol. Make Believe Ideas, Ltd., Ltd. 2019. (ENG.). 54p. (J). pap. 9.99 *(978-1-4002-1590-4(0))* Nelson, Thomas Inc.

—Nosy Bear. Make Believe Ideas Ltd. 2019. (Nosy Bear Ser.). (ENG.). 12p. (J). bds. *(978-1-78843-658-8(X))* Make Believe Ideas.

—Ocean Fun. Make Believe Ideas Ltd. 2019. (ENG.). 8p. (J). *(978-1-78947-079-6(X))* Make Believe Ideas.

—Old MacDonald Had a Farm. Make Believe Ideas Ltd. 2019. (Read & Play Ser.). (ENG.). 12p. (J). (gr. -1-7). *(978-1-78843-661-8(X))* Make Believe Ideas.

Machell, Dawn. Old MacDonald Had a Farm. Make Believe Ideas Ltd. 2020. (Playhouse Boxset Ser.). (ENG.). 10p. (J). (gr. -1-7). ***(978-1-78947-379-7(9))*** Make Believe Ideas.

Machell, Dawn. Peekaboo, I Love You. Make Believe Ideas Ltd. 2019. (Seasonal Peekaboo Ser.). (ENG.). 12p. (J). bds. *(978-1-78947-177-9(X))* Make Believe Ideas.

Machell, Dawn. Squidge-O-Saurus! Make Believe Ideas Ltd. 2020. (ENG.). 12p. (J). (gr. -1-7). bds. ***(978-1-78947-854-9(5))*** Make Believe Ideas.

—Squishy Stickers Unicorn World. Make Believe Ideas Ltd. 2020. (ENG.). 66p. (J). (gr. -1-7). pap. ***(978-1-78947-793-1(X))*** Make Believe Ideas.

Machell, Dawn. Super Sticker Activity: Baby Animals. 2016. (Super Sticker Activity Ser.). (ENG.). 32p. (J). (gr. -1 — 1). 5.99 *(978-1-62686-648-5(1)*, Silver Dolphin Bks.) Printers Row Publishing Group.

—Super Sticker Activity: Christmas. 2016. (Super Sticker Activity Ser.). (ENG.). 32p. (J). (gr. -1 — 1). pap. 5.99 *(978-1-62686-665-2(1)*, Silver Dolphin Bks.) Printers Row Publishing Group.

—Super Sticker Activity: Dinos. 2016. (Super Sticker Activity Ser.). (ENG.). 32p. (J). (gr. -1). 5.99 *(978-1-62686-649-2(X)*, Silver Dolphin Bks.) Printers Row Publishing Group.

—Super Sticker Activity: Farm. 2016. (Super Sticker Activity Ser.). (ENG.). 32p. (J). (gr. -1). 5.99 *(978-1-62686-647-8(3)*, Silver Dolphin Bks.) Printers Row Publishing Group.

—Super Sticker Activity: Things That Go. 2016. (Super Sticker Activity Ser.). (ENG.). 32p. (J). (gr. -1). 5.99 *(978-1-62686-650-8(3)*, Silver Dolphin Bks.) Printers Row Publishing Group.

—Super Sticker Activity: Tricks & Treats. 2016. (Super Sticker Activity Ser.). (ENG.). 32p. (J). (gr. -1 — 1). 5.99 *(978-1-62686-705-5(4)*, Silver Dolphin Bks.) Printers Row Publishing Group.

—Trace & Lift 123. Make Believe Ideas Ltd. 2019. (Trace & Lift Ser.). (ENG.). 16p. (J). bds. *(978-1-78843-613-7(X))* Make Believe Ideas.

—Trace & Lift ABC. Make Believe Ideas Ltd. 2019. (Trace & Lift Ser.). (ENG.). 16p. (J). bds. *(978-1-78843-612-0(1))* Make Believe Ideas.

—Trick or Treat. Make Believe Ideas Ltd. 2019. (ENG.). 14p. (J). bds. *(978-1-78843-919-0(8))* Make Believe Ideas.

Machell, Dawn. Unicorn Fun. Make Believe Ideas Ltd. 2020. (ENG.). 8p. (J). ***(978-1-78947-750-4(6))*** Make Believe Ideas.

—Unicorn's Magical Wishes. Make Believe Ideas Ltd. 2020. (ENG.). 16p. (J). (gr. -1-1). pap. ***(978-1-78947-844-0(8))*** Make Believe Ideas.

Machell, Dawn. 100 Animal Words. 2018. (ENG.). 24p. (J). (— 1). bds. 6.99 *(978-1-68412-023-9(3)*, Silver Dolphin Bks.) Printers Row Publishing Group.

Machell, Dawn & Illustrator, West Yorkshire. 100 Farm Words. 2017. (ENG.). 24p. (J). (gr. -1 — 1). bds. 6.99 *(978-1-68412-040-6(3)*, Silver Dolphin Bks.) Printers Row Publishing Group.

—100 First Words. 2017. (ENG.). 24p. (J). (gr. -1 — 1). bds. 6.99 *(978-1-68412-022-2(5)*, Silver Dolphin Bks.) Printers Row Publishing Group.

Machen Pritchard, M. Ann. Phil the Pill & Friends: Making Positive Choices. Machen Pritchard, M. Ann. 2005. 75p. (J). per. 11.99 *(978-0-9772210-0-4(8)*, Phil the Pill & Friends) MAMP Creations.

Maciá, Raquel Garcia. Jumping Jenny. Bari, Ellen. 2011. (Kar-Ben Favorites Ser.). (ENG.). 32p. (J). (gr. k-3). lib. bdg. 17.95 *(978-0-7613-5141-2(8)*, Kar-Ben Publishing) Lerner Publishing Group.

Maciborski, Charmaine. Baby, Please Go to Sleep. Prendergast, R. L. 2013. 16p. (J). pap. *(978-0-9784548-4-5(7))* Dekko Publishing.

MacInnes, Cat. Netball Gems: Hooked on Netball. Gibbs, L. & Hellard, B. 2016. (Netball Gems Ser.: 1). 144p. (J). (gr. 4-7). 8.99 *(978-0-85798-763-1(1))* Random Hse. Australia AUS. Dist: Independent Pubs. Group.

MacInnes, Kayla. Woo Hoo. McWood, Allison. 2019. (ENG.). 32p. (J). pap. ***(978-1-9992475-1-5(5))*** Annelid Pr.

Macintosh, Tessa, photos by. Caribou Feed My Soul, 1 vol. Willett, Mindy & Enzoe, Peter. 2010. (Land Is Our Storybook Ser.). (ENG., 32p. (J). (gr. 5-8). 16.95 *(978-1-897252-67-3(6)*, 1f611a9a-304f-42ad-b6b0-edbad7c89ecc) Fifth Hse. Pubs. CAN. Dist: Firefly Bks., Ltd.

—Le Caribou Nourrit Notre Âme, 1 vol. Enzoe, Peter & Willett, Mindy. 2012. (Land Is Our Storybook Ser.: 6). (FRE., 32p. (J). 19.95 *(978-1-927083-05-5(2)*, 62902e87-d9e4-4583-9e45-afaf59572978) Fifth Hse. Pubs. CAN. Dist: Firefly Bks., Ltd.

—Come & Learn with Me, 1 vol. Jumbo, Sheyenne & Willett, Mindy. 2009. (Land Is Our Storybook Ser.). (ENG., 32p. (J). (gr. 5-8). 16.95 *(978-1-897252-57-4(9)*, 2a17106c-b31c-43db-a5fb-6413f420a63f) Fifth Hse. Pubs. CAN. Dist: Firefly Bks., Ltd.

Macintosh, Tessa, photos by. Comme on Se Sent Bien Ici! Zhik Gwaa'an, Nakhwatthaiitat Gwiinzii, 1 vol. André, Julie-Ann & Willett, Mindy. 2011. (Land Is Our Storybook Ser.). (FRE., 32p. (J). 19.95 *(978-1-897252-85-7(4)*, 45294afe-267a-4bea-8947-cb950d60b279) Fifth Hse. Pubs. CAN. Dist: Firefly Bks., Ltd.

Macintosh, Tessa, photos by. Le Delta, C'est Mon Chez Moi: Ehdiitat Shanankat T'agoonch'uu - Uvanga Nunatarmuitmi Aimayuaqtunga, 1 vol. McLeod, Tom & Willett, Mindy. 2011. (Land Is Our Storybook Ser.). (FRE., 32p. (J). 19.95 *(978-1-897252-84-0(6)*, fea16f1a-3b20-42fe-a314-24d9bb8d542c) Fifth Hse. Pubs. CAN. Dist: Firefly Bks., Ltd.

—The Delta Is My Home, 1 vol. McLeod, Tom & Willett, Mindy. 2008. (Land Is Our Storybook Ser.). (ENG., 32p. (J). (gr. 5-8). 16.95 *(978-1-897252-32-1(3)*, 16be51b4-8247-4cd7-aaad-b92486f0ed59) Fifth Hse. Pubs. CAN. Dist: Firefly Bks., Ltd.

—Living Stories: Godi Weghàà Ets' Eèda, 1 vol. Highway, Tomson et al. ed. 2009. (Land Is Our Storybook Ser.). (ENG., 32p. (J). (gr. 5-8). 16.95 *(978-1-897252-47-5(1)*, a10bfaf7-8d66-4efe-a5c4-ccba079a985e) Trifolium Bks., Inc. CAN. Dist: Firefly Bks., Ltd.

—No Borders, 1 vol. Willett, Mindy & Enyagotailak, Darla. 2013. (Land Is Our Storybook Ser.: 8). (ENG., 40p. (J). (gr. 5-8). 19.95 *(978-1-927083-07-9(9)*, 775dcdc2-f27a-4a02-852a-ba2e6937af3d) Fifth Hse. Pubs. CAN. Dist: Firefly Bks., Ltd.

Macintosh, Tessa, photos by. Nos Histoires Sont Vivantes: God Weghàà Ets' Eèda, 1 vol. Zoe, Therese et al. 2011. (Land Is Our Storybook Ser.). (FRE., 32p. (J). 19.95 *(978-1-897252-99-4(4)*, 213c2bb6-7f63-4b04-b329-8141260d2770) Fifth Hse. Pubs. CAN. Dist: Firefly Bks., Ltd.

Macintosh, Tessa, photos by. Proud to Be Inuvialuit: Quviahuktunga Inuvialuugama, 1 vol. Willett, Mindy & Pokiak, James. 2010. (Land Is Our Storybook Ser.: 5). (ENG., 32p. (J). (gr. 4-6). 16.95 *(978-1-897252-59-8(5)*, b72f5ecb-b765-4f65-904a-fc59b290e151) Fifth Hse. Pubs. CAN. Dist: Firefly Bks., Ltd.

Macintosh, Tessa & Macintosh, Tessa, photos by. Viens Avec Moi, Nous Apprendrons Ensemble! Éwo, Séh Keddh, 1 vol. Willett, Mindy. 2011. (Land Is Our Storybook Ser.). (FRE., 26p. (J). (gr. 1-2). 19.95 *(978-1-897252-98-7(6)*, 968f188a-c95b-4311-9346-95e22c36e451) Fifth Hse. Pubs. CAN. Dist: Firefly Bks., Ltd.

Macintosh, Tessa, jt. photos by see Macintosh, Tessa.

Macintosh, Tessa, jt. photos by see Mactinosh, Tessa.

Mack, David, et al. Daredevil by Brian Michael Bendis Omnibus Vol. 1. 2020. 848p. (YA). (gr. 8-17). 100.00 *(978-1-302-92166-8(5))* Marvel Worldwide, Inc.

—411. Gandhi, Arun et al. 2004. (Marvel Heroes Ser.). 96p. (YA). pap. 11.99 *(978-0-7851-1255-6(3))* Marvel Worldwide, Inc.

Mack, Jeff. Boo, Bunny! Board Book. Galbraith, Kathryn O. 2012. (ENG.). 32p. (J). (gr. -1 — 1). bds. 5.99 *(978-0-547-81850-4(5)*, 1496581) Houghton Mifflin Harcourt Publishing Co.

—Cindy Moo. Mortensen, Lori. 2012. (ENG.). 32p. (J). (gr. -1-2). 16.99 *(978-0-06-204393-1(5))* HarperCollins Pubs.

—Creepy-Crawly Birthday. Howe, James. (Bunnicula & Friends Ser.: 6). (ENG.). 48p. (J). (gr. 1-3). 2008. pap. 4.99 *(978-0-689-85753-9(5))*; 2007. 16.99 *(978-0-689-85728-7(4))* Simon Spotlight. (Simon Spotlight).

—The Fright Before Christmas, 5. Howe, James. 2006. (Ready-To-Read Level 2 Ser.: 5). (ENG.). 42p. (J). (gr. 1-3). 16.99 *(978-0-689-86939-6(8)*, Simon Spotlight) Simon & Schuster Children's Publishing.

—The Fright Before Christmas. Howe, James. 2007. (Bunnicula & Friends Ser.: 5). (ENG.). 48p. (J). (gr. 1-3). pap. 4.99 *(978-0-689-86941-9(X)*, Simon Spotlight) Simon Spotlight.

—Good News, Bad News. 2012. (ENG.). 40p. (J). (gr. -1-1). 16.99 *(978-1-4521-0110-1(8))* Chronicle Bks. LLC.

—Hot Fudge. Howe, James. 2006. (Bunnicula & Friends Ser.). 42p. (gr. k-4). 14.00 *(978-0-7569-7224-0(8))* Perfection Learning Corp.

—Hot Fudge. Howe, James. 2006. (Bunnicula & Friends Ser.: 2). (ENG.). 48p. (J). (gr. 1-3). pap. 4.99 *(978-0-689-85750-8(0)*, Simon Spotlight) Simon Spotlight.

—How Do You Say I Love You, Dewey Dew? Staub, Leslie. 2017. (ENG.). 32p. (J). (gr. -1-3). 17.95 *(978-1-62979-497-6(X))* Boyds Mills Pr.

—Hurry! Hurry! Bunting, Eve. (ENG.). (J). 2014. 40p. (gr. -1 — 1). pap. 6.99 *(978-0-544-22733-0(6)*, 1563549, HMH Books For Young Readers); 2009. 32p. (gr. k — 1). bds. 6.99 *(978-0-15-206686-4(1)*, 1098963) Houghton Mifflin Harcourt Publishing Co.

—Icky Sticky Chameleon. Bentley, Dawn. 2005. 18p. (J). 9.95 *(978-1-58117-086-3(6)*, Intervisual/Piggy Toes) Bendon, Inc.

—If My Love Were a Fire Truck. Reynolds, Luke. 2017. 32p. (J). (gr. -1-2). 16.99 *(978-1-101-93740-2(8)*, Doubleday Bks. for Young Readers) Random Hse. Children's Bks.

—If My Love Were a Fire Truck: A Daddy's Love Song. Reynolds, Luke. 2018. 26p. (J). (— 1). bds. 7.99 *(978-0-525-58066-9(2)*, Doubleday Bks. for Young Readers) Random Hse. Children's Bks.

—Mr. Duck Means Business. Sauer, Tammi. 2011. (ENG.). 32p. (J). (gr. -1-3). 19.99 *(978-1-4169-8522-8(0)*, Simon & Schuster/Paula Wiseman Bks.) Simon & Schuster/Paula Wiseman Bks.

—Rabbit-Cadabra! Howe, James. (Bunnicula & Friends Ser.: 4). (ENG.). 48p. (J). (gr. 1-3). 2007. pap. 4.99 *(978-0-689-85752-2(7))*; 2006. 16.99 *(978-0-689-85727-0(6))* Simon Spotlight. (Simon Spotlight).

—Scared Silly. Howe, James. 2006. (Bunnicula & Friends Ser.). 42p. (gr. 1-3). 14.00 *(978-0-7569-7225-7(6))* Perfection Learning Corp.

—Scared Silly, 3. Howe, James. 2005. (Ready-To-Read Level 3 Ser.: 3). (ENG.). 36p. (J). (gr. 1-3). 16.19 *(978-0-689-85726-3(8)*, Simon Spotlight) Simon & Schuster Children's Publishing.

—Scared Silly. Howe, James. 2006. (Bunnicula & Friends Ser.: 3). (ENG.). 48p. (J). (gr. 1-3). pap. 4.99 *(978-0-689-85751-5(9)*, Simon Spotlight) Simon Spotlight.

—Time for (Earth) School, Dewey Dew. Staub, Leslie. 2016. (ENG.). 32p. (J). (gr. -1-3). 16.95 *(978-1-59078-958-2(X))* Boyds Mills Pr.

—The Vampire Bunny. Howe, James. 2005. (Bunnicula & Friends Ser.). 41p. (J). (gr. 1-3). 11.65 *(978-0-7569-6832-8(1))* Perfection Learning Corp.

—The Vampire Bunny. Howe, James. 2005. (Bunnicula & Friends Ser.: 1). (ENG.). 48p. (J). (gr. 1-3). pap. 4.99 *(978-0-689-85749-2(7)*, Simon Spotlight) Simon Spotlight.

Mack, Jeff. Clueless Mcgee. Mack, Jeff. 2012. (Clueless Mcgee Ser.: 1). 240p. (J). (gr. 3-7). 13.99 *(978-0-399-25749-0(7)*, Philomel Bks.) Penguin Young Readers Group.

—Clueless McGee & the Inflatable Pants, Bk. 2. Mack, Jeff. 2013. (Clueless Mcgee Ser.: 2). 256p. (J). (gr. 3-7). 13.99 *(978-0-399-25750-6(0)*, Philomel Bks.) Penguin Young Readers Group.

—Hippo & Rabbit. Mack, Jeff. 2011. (Scholastic Reader Level 1 Ser.). (ENG.). 32p. (J). (gr. -1-2). pap. 3.99 *(978-0-545-27445-6(1)*, Cartwheel Bks.) Scholastic, Inc.

—Hippo & Rabbit in Brave Like Me. Mack, Jeff. 2011. (Scholastic Reader Level 1 Ser.). (ENG.). 32p. (J). (gr. -1-2). pap. 3.99 *(978-0-545-28360-1(4)*, Cartwheel Bks.) Scholastic, Inc.

—Hush Little Polar Bear. Mack, Jeff. (ENG.). (J). (gr. -1-1). 2013. 36p. bds. 7.99 *(978-1-59643-945-0(9)*, 900123718); 2008. 40p. 17.99 *(978-1-59643-368-7(X)*, 9781596433687) Roaring Brook Pr.

—Look! Mack, Jeff. 2015. (ENG.). 32p. (J). (gr. -1-k). 16.99 *(978-0-399-16205-3(4)*, Philomel Bks.) Penguin Young Readers Group.

—Mr. Monkey Bakes a Cake. Mack, Jeff. (Mr. Monkey Ser.: 1). (ENG.). 64p. (J). (gr. -1-3). 2019. 7.99 *(978-1-5344-6670-8(3))*; 2018. 8.99 *(978-1-5344-0431-1(7))* Simon & Schuster Bks. For Young Readers. (Simon & Schuster Bks. For Young Readers).

—Mr. Monkey Takes a Hike. Mack, Jeff. 2019. (Mr. Monkey Ser.: 3). (ENG.). 64p. (J). (gr. -1-3). 8.99 *(978-1-5344-0433-5(3)*, Simon & Schuster Bks. For Young Readers) Simon & Schuster Bks. For Young Readers.

—Mr. Monkey Visits a School. Mack, Jeff. 2018. (Mr. Monkey Ser.: 2). (ENG.). 64p. (J). (gr. -1-3). 8.99 *(978-1-5344-0429-8(5)*, Simon & Schuster Bks. For Young Readers) Simon & Schuster Bks. For Young Readers.

—Playtime? Mack, Jeff. 2016. (ENG.). 32p. (J). (-k). 16.99 *(978-0-399-17598-5(9)*, Philomel Bks.) Penguin Young Readers Group.

—The Things I Can Do. Mack, Jeff. 2013. (ENG.). 32p. (J). (gr. -1-1). 16.99 *(978-1-59643-675-6(1)*, 900071111) Roaring Brook Pr.

—Who Needs a Bath? Mack, Jeff. 2015. (ENG.). 40p. (J). (gr. -1-3). 17.99 *(978-0-06-222028-8(4))* HarperCollins Pubs.

—Who Wants a Hug? Mack, Jeff. 2015. (ENG.). 40p. (J). (gr. -1-3). 17.99 *(978-0-06-222026-4(8))* HarperCollins Pubs.

Mack, Jeff. The Vampire Bunny. Mack, Jeff, tr. Henson, Heather et al. 2004. (Bunnicula & Friends Ser.: 1). (ENG.). 48p. (J). (gr. 1-3). 17.99 *(978-0-689-85724-9(1)*, Simon Spotlight) Simon Spotlight.

Mack, Kathryn. Super Cyclist. Carl, Dave. 2010. (ENG.). (J). pap. 12.00 *(978-0-9785160-8-6(7))* Etcetera Pr. LLC.

Mack, Steve. Cake & I Scream! ... Being Bossy Isn't Sweet. Genhart, Michael. 2017. 32p. (J). *(978-1-4338-2759-4(X)*, Magination Pr.) American Psychological Assn.

—The Grouchies. Wagenbach, Debbie. 2009. 32p. (J). (gr. -1-3). 14.95 *(978-1-4338-0543-1(X))*; pap. 9.95 *(978-1-4338-0553-0(7))* American Psychological Assn. (Magination Pr.).

—I Love Engineering: Explore with Sliders, Lift-The-flaps, a Wheel, & More! Wortche, Allison. 2020. (ENG.). 14p. (J). (— 1). bds. 8.99 *(978-0-358-17004-4(4)*, 1758713, HMH Books For Young Readers) Houghton Mifflin Harcourt Publishing Co.

—I Love Genetics: Explore with Sliders, Lift-The-flaps, a Wheel, & More! Wortche, Allison. 2020. (ENG.). 14p. (J). (— 1). bds. 8.99 *(978-0-358-16901-7(1)*, 1758439, HMH Books For Young Readers) Houghton Mifflin Harcourt Publishing Co.

—I Love Science. Wortche, Allison. 2019. (ENG.). 14p. (J). (— 1). bds. 8.99 *(978-1-328-52937-4(1)*, 1722032, HMH Books For Young Readers) Houghton Mifflin Harcourt Publishing Co.

—I Love Space. Wortche, Allison. 2019. (ENG.). 14p. (J). (— 1). bds. 8.99 *(978-1-328-52936-7(3)*, 1722031, HMH Books For Young Readers) Houghton Mifflin Harcourt Publishing Co.

—Jurassic Poop: What Dinosaurs (and Others) Left Behind. Berkowitz, Jacob. 2006. 40p. (J). (gr. 3-7). (ENG.). 6.95 *(978-1-55337-867-9(9))*; 14.95 *(978-1-55337-860-0(1))* Kids Can Pr., Ltd. CAN. Dist: Hachette Bk. Group.

—Listen! Israel's All Around, Vol. Kiffel-Alcheh, Jamie. 2019. (ENG.). 12p. (J). (gr. -1 — 1). bds. 5.99 *(978-1-5415-0969-6(2)*, Kar-Ben Publishing) Lerner Publishing Group.

—Mac & Geeeez! ...being Real Is What It's All About. Genhart, Michael. 2017. 32p. (J). *(978-1-4338-2723-5(9)*, Magination Pr.) American Psychological Assn.

—Peanut Butter & Jellyous: ...sometimes Friendships Get Sticky. Genhart, Michael. 2017. 32p. (J). *(978-1-4338-2337-4(3)*, Magination Pr.) American Psychological Assn.

—Stickley Makes a Mistake! A Frog's Guide to Trying Again. Miles, Brenda. 2016. 32p. (J). *(978-1-4338-2264-3(4)*, Magination Pr.) American Psychological Assn.

—Stickley Sticks to It! A Frog's Guide to Getting Things Done. Miles, Brenda. 2014. 32p. (J). *(978-1-4338-1910-0(4)*, Magination Pr.) American Psychological Assn.

—Tikkun Olam Ted, Vol. Newman, Vivian Bonnie. 2013. (ENG.). 12p. (J). (gr. -1 — 1). bds. 5.95 *(978-0-7613-9040-4(5)*, 9780761390404, Kar-Ben Publishing) Lerner Publishing Group.

—Whiskers & Tails: Animal Flip a Flap Board Book. Partridge, Rose. Cottage Door Press, ed. 2017. (Flip a Flap Ser.). (ENG.). 10p. (J). (gr. -1-k). bds. 8.99 *(978-1-68052-161-0(6)*, 1001590) Cottage Door Pr.

—3 Falafels in My Pita: A Counting Book of Israel, Vol. Friedman, Maya. 2015. (ENG.). 12p. (J). (gr. -1 — 1). bds. 5.95 *(978-1-4677-3472-1(1)*, 9781467734721, Kar-Ben Publishing) Lerner Publishing Group.

Mack, Tim. It's Time for Bed, 1 vol. Mearns, Ceoporah & Debicki, Jeremy. 2019. 36p. (J). 16.95 *(978-1-77227-227-7(2))* Inhabit Media Inc. CAN. Dist: Consortium Bk. Sales & Distribution.

—What's My Superpower?, 1 vol. Johnston, Aviaq. 2017. (ENG.). 36p. (J). (gr. -1-k). 16.95 *(978-1-77227-140-9(3))* Inhabit Media Inc. CAN. Dist: Consortium Bk. Sales & Distribution.

Mack, Travis. I'm Living My Dream: An inspirational Rhyme for all Ages in English & Spanish. Spencer, Mignon. 2008.Tr. of Hago mi sueno Realidad. (ENG & SPA.). 32p. (J). 12.99 *(978-0-9763871-2-1(3))* Solomon's Bks.

Mackall, Debbie. What Happens When I'm Asleep? Mackall, Deborah. 2008. (ENG.). 32p. (J). (gr. -1-k). 15.95 *(978-0-9762273-1-1(2))* Dimensions in Media, Inc.

Mackall, Deborah. Be Still! The Story of a Little Bird & How He Found His Purpose. Mackall, Deborah. 2nd ed. 2008. (ENG.). 32p. (J). (gr. -1-k). 15.95 *(978-0-9762273-3-5(9))* Dimensions in Media, Inc.

Mackay, Dustin. Superfail. Brunner, Max. 2017. 208p. (J). (gr. 3-7). 13.99 *(978-0-7624-6229-2(9)*, Running Pr. Kids) Running Pr.

MacKay, Elly. Beach Baby, 1 vol. Elmquist, Laurie. 2016. (ENG.). 24p. (J). (gr. -1 — 1). bds. 10.95 *(978-1-4598-0954-3(8))* Orca Bk. Pubs. USA.

—Best Gifts, 1 vol. Skrypuch, Marsha Forchuk. 2nd rev. ed. 2013. (ENG.). 32p. (J). (gr. 1-4). 18.95 *(978-1-55455-283-2(4)*, 44346ed9-e389-44cd-ad47-8cb536f1d88d) éditeur, Annika Parance CAN. Dist: Firefly Bks., Ltd.

—Fall Leaves. Holland, Loretta. 2014. (ENG.). 32p. (J). (gr. -1-3). 16.99 *(978-0-544-10664-2(4)*, 1540825, HMH Books For Young Readers) Houghton Mifflin Harcourt Publishing Co.

—If You Hold a Seed. 2013. 32p. (J). (gr. -1-1). 16.99 *(978-0-7624-4721-3(4)*, Running Pr. Kids) Running Pr.

Mackay, Hugh. Brown Bear, 1 vol. Perry, Laurie. 2010. 22p. pap. 24.95 *(978-1-4489-5702-6(8))* PublishAmerica, Inc.

Mackay, John. Classic Children's Games from Scotland. Ross, Kendric. 128p. pap. 10.95 *(978-1-899827-12-1(9))* Scottish Children's Pr. GBR. Dist: Gatewood Pr.

Mackay, Louis. What Makes a Tornado Twist? And Other Questions about Weather. Carson, Mary Kay. 2014. (Good Question! Ser.). (ENG.). 32p. (J). (gr. 1). pap. 6.95 *(978-1-4549-0683-4(9))* Sterling Publishing Co., Inc.

Mackay, Stephanie. San Francisco Monsters. 2017. (ENG.). 22p. (J). (gr. -1). bds. 9.99 *(978-2-924734-03-2(7))* City Monsters Bks. CAN. Dist: Publishers Group West (PGW).

—Thank You a Latte! Teacher Appreciation Gift Cards to Customize, Tear Out, & Give. 2020. (Books for Teachers Ser.). (ENG.). 20p. (J). 7.95 *(978-1-64604-027-8(9))* Ulysses Pr.

Mackay, Stephanie & Drouot, Lucile Danis. Chicago Monsters. Laforest, Carine. 2017. (ENG.). 22p. (J). (gr. -1). bds. 9.99 *(978-2-924734-01-8(0))* City Monsters Bks. CAN. Dist: Publishers Group West (PGW).

MacKenzie, Emily. Stanley the Amazing Knitting Cat. MacKenzie, Emily. 2016. 32p. (J). *(978-1-4088-6047-2(3)*, 253325, Bloomsbury Children's Bks.) Bloomsbury Publishing Plc.

Mackenzie, Robert. Jack & the Beanstalk. Cech, John. 2015. (Classic Fairy Tale Collection). (ENG.). 32p. (J). (gr. -1-2). pap. 6.95 *(978-1-4549-1677-2(X))* Sterling Publishing Co., Inc.

MacKenzie, Sibyl. St. Francis & the Animals: A Mother Bird's Story. Gallery, Phil. 2018. (ENG.). 32p. (J). (gr. -1). 17.99 *(978-1-61261-973-6(8))* Paraclete Pr., Inc.

Mackey, Cindy. Blu. Mackey, Cindy. 2018. (ENG.). 54p. (J). (gr. k-4). pap. 11.99 *(978-1-7322739-0-0(1))* Cyrano Bks.

Mackey, Kaitlin L. Little Bear & Honey Bee. MacKey, Esther L. 2012. 28p. 14.95 *(978-1-937260-10-1(0))* Sleepytown Pr.

Mackie, Clare. Crazy Creature Capers. Reidy, Hannah. 2003. (Crazy Creatures Ser.). 26p. (J). pap. *(978-1-84089-222-2(6))* Zero to Ten, Ltd.

—Crazy Creature Colors. Reidy, Hannah. 2003. (Crazy Creatures Ser.). 26p. (J). pap. *(978-1-84089-221-5(8))* Zero to Ten, Ltd.

—Crazy Creature Contrasts. Reidy, Hannah. 2003. (Crazy Creatures Ser.). 26p. (J). pap. *(978-1-84089-223-9(4))* Zero to Ten, Ltd.

—Crazy Creatures Counting. Reidy, Hannah. 2003. (Crazy Creatures Ser.). 26p. (J). pap. *(978-1-84089-220-8(X))* Zero to Ten, Ltd.

—Nonsense. Rosen, Michael. 2003. (ENG.). 48p. pap. *(978-0-7500-2671-0(5)*, Wayland) Hachette Children's Group.

Mackie, Marie-Anne. The Adventures of Hamish the Sea Eagle. MacKie, Ian. 2013. 24p. *(978-1-78148-614-6(X))* Grosvenor Hse. Publishing Ltd.

Mackie, Melissa. Finn & Puss. Vescio, Robert. 2017. (ENG.). 32p. (J). (gr. -1-2). 17.99 *(978-1-925335-50-7(X)*, EK Bks.) Exisle Publishing Pty Ltd. AUS. Dist: Hachette Bk. Group.

MacKinnon, Catherine-Anne. Babies Baby Flashcards. 2007. (Baby Flashcards Ser.). 16p. (J). (gr. -1-k). 9.99 *(978-0-7945-1571-3(1)*, Usborne) EDC Publishing.

—Cuddly Baby: Snuggletime. Watt, Fiona. 2006. 10p. (J). (gr. -1-k). bds. 8.99 *(978-0-7945-1070-1(1)*, Usborne) EDC Publishing.

—I Love You, Baby. Watt, Fiona. 2008. (Snuggletime Touchy-Feely Ser.). 10p. (J). (gr. -1-k). bds. 8.99 *(978-0-7945-2071-7(5)*, Usborne) EDC Publishing.

—Sleepy Baby. Watt, Fiona. 2006. (Snuggletime Board Bks.). 10p. (J). (gr. -1). bds., bds. 8.99 *(978-0-7945-1071-8(X)*, Usborne) EDC Publishing.

—Snuggletime Busy Baby. Watt, Fiona. 2005. 10p. (J). (gr. -1-k). per., bds. 8.99 *(978-0-7945-1054-1(X)*, Usborne) EDC Publishing.

MacKinnon, Catherine-Anne. Animals Baby Flashcards. MacKinnon, Catherine-Anne. 2007. (Baby Flashcards Ser.). 16p. (J). (gr. -1-k). 9.99 *(978-0-7945-1498-3(7)*, Usborne) EDC Publishing.

MacKinnon, Patsy. King of Keji, 1 vol. Coates, Jan. 2015. (ENG.). 32p. (J). (gr. 1-3). pap. 12.95 *(978-1-77108-281-5(X)*, 45f03fb9-05c9-4c90-9f1b-84f8ef433257) Nimbus Publishing, Ltd. CAN. Dist: Baker & Taylor Publisher Services (BTPS).

MacKinstry, Elizabeth. The Fairy Ring. Wiggin, Kate Douglas & Smith, Nora Archibald. 2008. 680p. pap. 20.95 *(978-1-59915-298-1(3))* Yesterday's Classics.

Mackintosh, David. Archie & the Bear. Louise, Zanni. 2018. (ENG.). 32p. (J). (gr. -1-3). 17.99 *(978-1-328-97341-2(7)*, 1708137, Clarion Bks.) Houghton Mifflin Harcourt Trade & Reference Pubs.

MacKintosh, David. Poor Fish! Godwin, Jane. 2019. (Puffin Nibbles Ser.). 80p. (J). (gr. k-3). pap. 9.99 ***(978-0-14-130665-0(3)**, Puffin)* Penguin Random Hse. AUS. Dist: Independent Pubs. Group.

Mackintosh, David. There's a Bug on My Arm That Won't Let Go. Mackintosh, David. 2020. (ENG.). 32p. (J). pap. 6.99 *(978-0-00-835797-9(8)*, HarperCollins Children's Bks.) HarperCollins Pubs. Ltd. GBR. Dist: HarperCollins Pubs.

—Waiting for Chicken Smith. Mackintosh, David. 2019. (ENG.). 32p. (J). (gr. -1-2). 16.99 *(978-1-5362-0771-2(3))* Candlewick Pr.

—What's up Mumu? Mackintosh, David. 2015. (ENG.). 32p. (J). 17.99 *(978-0-00-812469-4(8)*, HarperCollins Children's Bks.) HarperCollins Pubs. Ltd. GBR. Dist: HarperCollins Pubs.

Mackintosh, Michelle. Undercover. Badger, Meredith. 2007. (Fairy School Drop-Out Ser.). 144p. (J). *(978-1-921098-71-0(6))* Hardie Grant Egmont Pty, Ltd.

MacLean, Amber. China's Daughters. Williams, Suzanne. 2011. (J). *(978-1-881896-34-0(X))* Pacific View Pr.

Maclean, Andrew. Siff a Saff: A Straeon Eraill. Davies, Helen Emanuel. 2005. (WEL.). 64p. pap. *(978-0-86381-364-1(X))* Gwasg Carreg Gwalch.

MacLean, Colin and Moira. Baby's First Bible. ed. 2016. (ENG.). 20p. (J). (gr. -1 — 1). bds. 9.99 *(978-0-7944-3849-4(0))* Studio Fun International.

—Baby's First Bible CarryAlong: A CarryAlong Treasury. ed. 2016. (Carry along Treasury Ser.: 1). (ENG.). 20p. (J). (gr. -1 — 1). bds. 14.99 *(978-0-7944-3835-7(0)*, Reader's Digest Children's Bks.) Studio Fun International.

MacLean, Kerry Lee. Mindful Monkey, Happy Panda. Alderfer, Lauren. 2011. (ENG.). 32p. (J). (gr. -1-3). 16.95 *(978-0-86171-683-8(3))* Wisdom Pubns.

MacLean, Kerry Lee. Peaceful Piggy Bedtime. Maclaren, Sophie. 2020. (ENG.). 32p. (J). 17.95 ***(978-1-61429-674-4(X))*** Wisdom Pubns.

MacLean, Kerry Lee. Peaceful Piggy Meditation. MacLean, Kerry Lee. 2016. (ENG.). 32p. (J). (gr. -1-3). 12.99 *(978-0-8075-6389-2(7)*, 807563897) Whitman, Albert & Co.

—Peaceful Piggy Yoga. MacLean, Kerry Lee. (ENG.). 32p. (J). (gr. -1-3). 2016. 12.99 *(978-0-8075-6388-5(9)*, 807563889); 2014. 6.99 *(978-0-8075-6383-0(8)*, 807563838) Whitman, Albert & Co.

—Peacefully Piggy Meditation. MacLean, Kerry Lee. 2004. (ENG.). 32p. (J). (gr. -1-3). 6.99 *(978-0-8075-6381-6(1)*, 807563811) Whitman, Albert & Co.

MacLean, Moira. Baby's First Easter. Froeb, Lori C. 2019. (First Bible Collection). (ENG.). 10p. (J). (gr. -1 — 1). 9.99 *(978-0-7944-4118-0(1)*, Studio Fun International) Printers Row Publishing Group.

Maclean, Moira. Bible Adventures & Activities. Wright, Sally Ann. 2012. 144p. (J). pap. 11.95 *(978-0-8198-1199-8(8))* Pauline Bks. & Media.

MacLean, Moira. First COLL of Bible Stories & Stickers: Daniel, Jonah, Jesus & Other Stories. Reynolds, Annette. 2004. 16p. pap. 8.95 *(978-1-59325-045-4(2))* Word Among Us Pr.

—First COLL of Bible Stories & Stickers: Noahn, Samson, Jesus & Other Stories. Reynolds, Annette. 2004. 16p. pap. 8.95 *(978-1-59325-044-7(4))* Word Among Us Pr.

—Knock, Knock! Who's There at Christmas? Howie, Vickie. 2004. 20p. (J). bds. 9.49 *(978-0-7586-0649-5(4))* Concordia Publishing Hse.

—The Look & See Bible. Wright, Sally Ann. 2006. (Children's Bibles & Bible Story Collections). 94p. (J). (gr. -1-3). 12.95 *(978-0-8091-6735-7(2)*, 6735-2) Paulist Pr.

—My First Christmas Sticker Book. Wright, Sally Ann. 2007. (J). (gr. -1-3). 6.95 *(978-0-8198-4852-9(2))* Pauline Bks. & Media.

MacLean, Roz. This Is a Job for Mommy! An a-Z Adventure. Tracy, Keegan Connor. 2019. (ENG.). 32p. (J). (-4). 9.95 *(978-1-77374-016-4(4))* Promontory Pr. CAN. Dist: Independent Pubs. Group.

MacLeod, Alastair. The Boy Who Picked Dandelions. MacLeod, Helen Louise. 2019. (ENG.). 48p. (J). pap. 10.35 ***(978-1-6964-7415-3(9))*** Independently Published.

M

MacLeod, C. Anne. Mr. Grumbles: Bedtime Stories for the Young. Pryse-Phillips, William. 2020. (ENG.). 56p. (J). ***(978-1-5255-6259-4(2))***; pap. ***(978-1-5255-6260-0(6))*** FriesenPress.

MacLeod, Gavin. Action Robots: A Pop-up Book Showing How They Work. Reeve, Tim. 2004. 14p. (YA). (gr. 4-10). reprint ed. 17.00 *(978-0-7567-7284-0(2))* DIANE Publishing Co.

MacLure, Ashley. Beyond the Science Lab. Lindsey, Jason. 2012. 82p. pap. 16.95 *(978-0-9854248-4-8(2))* Pinwheel Bks.

MacMenamin, John. Islands. Raine, Bonnie. 2003. 48p. (J). per. *(978-1-931456-74-6(7))* Athena Pr.

—Two of Our Friends Are Doves. Coon, Thomas & Coon, Helene. 2003. 64p. (J). per. *(978-1-932077-17-9(0))* Athena Pr.

Macmillan Children's Books, Editors of. The Nutcracker - A Coloring Book. 2018. (Classic Coloring Book Ser.). (ENG.). 96p. (J). (gr. 1-3). pap. 12.99 *(978-1-68412-381-0(X)*, Silver Dolphin Bks.) Printers Row Publishing Group.

MacMillan, Eric G. Khala Maninge - the Little Elephant That Cried a Lot: An African Fable. MacMillan, Ian C. 2nd ed. 2003. lib. bdg. 5.00 *(978-0-9729698-0-2(2))* Maninge Mali.

Macnaughton, Tina. Are You Sad, Little Bear? A Book about Learning to Say Goodbye. Rivett, Rachel. ed. (ENG.). 32p. (J). 2020. (gr. -1-k). 10.99 ***(978-0-7459-7893-2(2)***, Lion Children's); 2013. (-k). 8.99 *(978-0-7459-6430-0(3))* Lion Hudson PLC GBR. Dist: Independent Pubs. Group.

Macnaughton, Tina. An Arkful of Animal Prayers, 1 vol. Piper, Sophie. 2009. 64p. (J). 9.95 *(978-0-8254-7840-6(5)*, Lion Children's) Lion Hudson PLC GBR. Dist: Kregel Pubns.

—An Arkful of Animal Stories. Goodwin, John. 2008. 32p. (J). (gr. k-3). 13.95 *(978-0-8198-0782-3(6))* Pauline Bks. & Media.

—Bedtime Blessing. Davies, Becky. 2016. (ENG.). 24p. (J). (gr. -1-k). bds. 8.99 *(978-1-58925-205-9(5))* Tiger Tales.

—Cuddles for Mommy. Brown, Ruby. 2016. (ENG.). 32p. (J). (gr. -1-3). 16.99 *(978-1-4998-0203-0(X))* Little Bee Books Inc.

—Good Night, I Love You. McLean, Danielle. 2018. (ENG.). 16p. (J). (gr. -1-k). bds. 9.99 *(978-1-68010-540-7(X))* Tiger Tales.

—One Christmas Adventure. Butler, M. Christina. 2019. (ENG.). 32p. (J). (gr. -1-2). 17.99 *(978-1-68010-155-3(2))* Tiger Tales.

Macnaughton, Tina. One Christmas Wish. Butler, M. Christina. 2020. (ENG.). 32p. (J). (gr. -1-2). 17.99 ***(978-1-68010-212-3(5))*** Tiger Tales.

Macnaughton, Tina. One Cozy Christmas. Butler, M. Christina. 2017. (ENG.). 32p. (J). (gr. -1-2). 16.99 *(978-1-68010-068-6(8))* Tiger Tales.

—One Noisy Night. Butler, M. Christina. 2016. (ENG.). 32p. (J). (gr. -1-2). 16.99 *(978-1-68010-034-1(3))* Tiger Tales.

—One Snowy Rescue. Butler, M. Christina. 2015. (ENG.). 32p. (J). (gr. -1-2). 16.99 *(978-1-58925-196-0(2))* Tiger Tales.

—One Special Christmas. Butler, M. Christina. 2013. (ENG.). 32p. (J). (gr. -1-2). 14.99 *(978-1-58925-145-8(8))* Tiger Tales.

—Snow Friends. Butler, M. Christina. 2016. (ENG.). 16p. (J). (— 1). bds. 9.99 *(978-1-5107-1116-7(3)*, Sky Pony Pr.) Skyhorse Publishing Co., Inc.

—Snuggles with Daddy. Brown, Ruby. 2017. (ENG.). 24p. (J). (gr. -1-k). bds. 13.99 *(978-1-76012-762-6(0))* Hardie Grant Egmont Pty, Ltd. AUS. Dist: Independent Pubs. Group.

—Where Snowflakes Fall. Freedman, Claire. 2012. 24p. (J). *(978-1-4351-4321-0(3))* Barnes & Noble, Inc.

MacNaughton, Wendy. The Gutsy Girl: Escapades for Your Life of Epic Adventure. Paul, Caroline. 2016. 160p. (gr. 5-8). 18.00 *(978-1-63286-123-8(2)*, 900148432) Bloomsbury Publishing USA.

MacNeil, Chris. The Chipster's Sister. Wollman, Jessica. 2005. (Penelope Fritter: Super-Sitter Ser.: 1). (ENG.). 128p. (J). (gr. 3-7). pap. 7.99 *(978-1-4169-0089-4(6)*, Simon & Schuster/Paula Wiseman Bks.) Simon & Schuster/Paula Wiseman Bks.

MacNeil, Colin, jt. illus. see Estes, John.

MacNeill, Aimee. My Friends. Parmar, Nicole. McCormack, Olivia, ed. 2019. (ENG.). 32p. (J). pap. 9.13 ***(978-1-6923-3391-1(7))*** Independently Published.

—Swimming. Parmar, Nicole. McCormack, Olivia, ed. 2019. (ENG.). 34p. (J). pap. 9.13 ***(978-1-6880-4531-6(7))*** Independently Published.

—Welcome to the World. Parmar, Nicole. McCormack, Olivia, ed. 2019. (ENG.). 36p. (J). pap. 9.13 ***(978-1-6938-7234-1(X))*** Independently Published.

Macomber, C. R. The Snuggly House. Warner, Gaylee. 2015. (ENG.). 32p. (J). 25.95 *(978-1-4808-5235-8(X))* Archway Publishing.

Macon, Summer. ABCs of Kindness. Hegarty, Patricia. import ed. 2019. (ENG.). 22p. (J). (— 1). bds. 8.99 *(978-0-593-12307-2(7)*, Rodale Kids) Random Hse. Children's Bks.

Maçon, Summer. Up & down Mom. Child's Play. 2020. (Child's Play Library). (ENG.). 36p. (J). *(978-1-78628-340-5(9))* Child's Play International Ltd.

Macon, Summer. 123s of Thankfulness. Hegarty, Patricia. import ed. 2020. (ENG.). 22p. (J). (— 1). bds. 8.99 ***(978-0-593-17450-0(X)***, Rodale Kids) Random Hse. Children's Bks.

Maconachie, Roy, photos by. Cape Town. Bowden, Rob. 2006. (Global Cities Ser.). 61p. (gr. 5-8). 30.00 *(978-0-7910-8856-2(1)*, Chelsea Hse.) Facts On File, Inc.

Macor, Jim. Frazier Fir, A Christmas Fable. Macor, Jim. 2007. 32p. (J). 17.95 *(978-0-9785551-3-9(9))* Zuber Publishing.

MacPherson, Bruce. Josefina Javelina: A Hairy Tale. Lowell, Susan. 2005. (ENG.). 32p. (J). (gr. -1-3). 15.95 *(978-0-87358-790-7(1))* Cooper Square Publishing Llc.

—Thank You, Aunt Tallulah! Coyle, Carmela Lavigna. 2006. (ENG.). 32p. (J). (gr. -1-3). 15.95 *(978-0-87358-891-1(6))* Cooper Square Publishing Llc.

Macpherson, Carol. Littlestar, 1 vol. Grandmother Littlewolf. 2010. (ENG.). 19p. pap. 24.95 *(978-1-4489-8619-4(2))* America Star Bks.

MacPherson, Dougal. Introducing Teddy: A Gentle Story about Gender & Friendship. Walton, Jessica. 2016. (ENG.). 32p. (J). 17.99 *(978-1-68119-210-9(1)*, 900164037); E-Book 12.59 *(978-1-68119-211-6(X))* Bloomsbury Publishing USA. (Bloomsbury USA Childrens).

MacPherson, Lauren. Anxious Aidan Is Agitated. Gough, Patricia. 2019. (Anxious Aidan Ser.: Vol. 1). (ENG.). 36p. (J). pap. 15.00 ***(978-1-0891-9840-6(X))*** Independently Published.

Macquignon, Stephen. Ferdinand Frog's Flight. Mayer, Marvin. 2011. 32p. pap. 15.55 *(978-0-9832740-0-1(2))* 4RV Pub.

—Why Am I Me? Harris-Wyrick, Wayne. 2011. 32p. pap. 17.99 *(978-0-9828346-2-6(4))* 4RV Pub.

MacRae, Jock. Hook, Line & Sinker: Everything Kids Want to Know about Fishing! Labignan, Italo. rev. ed. 2007. (ENG.). 48p. (J). (gr. 2-7). pap. 14.95 *(978-1-55263-549-0(X))* Leaf Storm Pr.

—The Kids Book of Canada. Greenwood, Barbara. 2007. (Kids Book Of Ser.). (ENG.). 60p. (J). (gr. 3-7). 14.99 *(978-1-55453-226-1(4))* Kids Can Pr., Ltd. CAN. Dist: Hachette Bk. Group.

Mactavious, Dwayne. Arona's First Garden. George, Keiyia & Fahie, Elena, eds. 2019. (ENG.). 32p. (J). pap. 14.99 ***(978-1-7067-0023-4(7))*** Independently Published.

Mactinosh, Tessa & Macintosh, Tessa, photos by. Sharing Our Truths/Tapwe, 1 vol. Beaver, Henry & Willett, Mindy. 2019. (This Land Is Our Storybook Ser.). (ENG., 40p. (J). (gr. 3-7). lib. bdg. 19.95 *(978-1-927083-52-9(4)*, 95108597-5758-4b92-9ae7-93c4a3f234f7) Fifth Hse. Pubs. CAN. Dist: Firefly Bks., Ltd.

Macvean, Alexandra H. Meagan's Wish. Rains, Charlotte J. 2019. (ENG.). 28p. (J). pap. 10.99 *(978-1-9792-0817-8(4))* CreateSpace Independent Publishing Platform.

—Meagan's Wish. Rains, Charlotte J. 2019. (ENG.). 32p. (J). pap. 10.98 *(978-1-7932-5313-2(7))* Independently Published.

—Meagan's Wish. Rains, Charlotte J. 2019. (ENG.). 32p. (J). 15.98 *(978-0-578-48057-2(3))* Rains, Charlotte.

Macy, Carolyn. Hawaiian Night Before Christmas, 1 vol. Macy, Carolyn. 2008. (Night Before Christmas Ser.). (ENG.). 32p. (J). (gr. 1-3). 16.99 *(978-1-58980-598-9(4)*, Pelican Publishing) Arcadia Publishing.

Mada Design Inc. Kung Fu Panda. Chihak, Sheena & Loki. 2008. (I Can Find It Ser.). 22p. (J). 7.99 *(978-0-696-23484-2(X))* Meredith Bks.

Mada Design, Inc Staff. Superman Versus Bizarro. Stratheam, Chris. 2010. (I Can Read Level 2 Ser.). (ENG.). 32p. (J). (gr. -1-3). pap. 3.99 *(978-0-06-188516-7(9))* HarperCollins Pubs.

Mada Design Staff. Batman Classic: Gotham's Villains Unleashed! Sazaklis, John. 2009. (ENG.). 24p. (J). (gr. -1-3). pap. 3.99 *(978-0-06-187856-5(1)*, HarperFestival) HarperCollins Pubs.

—Heads or Tails. Sudduth, Brent & Meredith Books Staff. 2008. 20p. (J). pap. 3.99 *(978-0-696-23959-5(0))* Meredith Bks.

—Superman Classic: Superman & the Mayhem of Metallo. Stephens, Sarah Hines. 2010. (Superman Classics). (ENG.). 24p. (J). (gr. -1-3). pap. 3.99 *(978-0-06-188529-7(0)*, HarperFestival) HarperCollins Pubs.

—Superman Versus Mongul. Teitelbaum, Michael. 2011. (I Can Read Level 2 Ser.). (ENG.). 32p. (J). (gr. -1-3). pap. 3.99 *(978-0-06-188518-1(5))* HarperCollins Pubs.

Madan, Fredric C. & Ernst, Clara. Greer Garson Paper Dolls. Madan, Fredric C. 2007. (ENG.). 16p. pap. 12.00 *(978-0-9790668-6-3(7))* Paper Studio Pr.

Madaras, Diana & Nielsen, Ric. Kitty Humbug's Christmas Tail. Madaras, Diana. 2009. 24p. 17.99 *(978-1-892344-56-4(4))* Palomino Publishing.

Madden, Chris. Mountains: Explore Earth's Majestic Mountain Habitats. Guillain, Charlotte. 2020. (World of Wonder Ser.). (ENG.). 64p. (J). (gr. 3-6). 18.95 ***(978-0-7112-4354-5(9)***, Words & Pictures) Quarto Publishing Group UK GBR. Dist: Hachette Bk. Group.

Madden, Chris. We Travel So Far... Knowles, Laura. 2018. (ENG.). 64p. (J). (gr. 2-5). 19.95 *(978-1-77085-985-2(3)*, 97c110c3-21f2-4fb0-b9a7-d791636263e9) Firefly Bks., Ltd.

Madden, Colleen. All I Want for Christmas Is You. Carey, Mariah. 2015. 32p. (J). (gr. -1-2). 17.99 *(978-0-399-55139-0(5)*, Doubleday Bks. for Young Readers) Random Hse. Children's Bks.

Madden, Colleen, et al. Beauty & the Beast Stories Around the World: 3 Beloved Tales. Meister, Cari. 2016. (Multicultural Fairy Tales Ser.). (ENG.). 32p. (J). (gr. k-2). pap. 6.95 *(978-1-5158-0414-7(3)*, Picture Window Bks.) Capstone.

—La Bella y la Bestia: 3 Cuentros Predilectos de Alrededor Del Mundo. Meister, Cari. 2020. (Cuentos Multiculturales Ser.).Tr. of Beauty & the Beast Stories Around the World. (SPA.). 32p. (J). (gr. k-2). pap. 6.95 *(978-1-5158-6072-3(8)*, 142292); lib. bdg. 27.99 *(978-1-5158-5714-3(X)*, 142075) Capstone. (Picture Window Bks.).

—Cuentos Multiculturales. Meister, Cari. 2020. (Cuentos Multiculturales Ser.).Tr. of Multicultural Fairy Tales. (SPA.). (J). (gr. k-2). pap., pap., pap. 41.70 *(978-1-5158-6082-2(5)*, 30090, Picture Window Bks.) Capstone.

Madden, Colleen. The Great Hunger. Krichilsky, Lauren. 2017. (Text Connections Guided Close Reading Ser.). (J). (gr. 2). *(978-1-4900-1862-1(X))* Benchmark Education Co.

—Green Fever. Brunstetter, Wanda E. 2013. (Double Trouble Ser.: 4). (ENG.). 160p. (J). (gr. 3-5). pap. 5.99 *(978-1-62416-286-2(X)*, Barbour Bks.) Barbour Publishing, Inc.

—Happy Sparkling Halloween. Spurr, Elizabeth. 2010. (Sparkling Stories Ser.). (ENG.). 14p. (J). (gr. k-k). bds. 5.95 *(978-1-4027-7138-5(X))* Sterling Publishing Co., Inc.

—Happy Sparkling Hanukkah. Spurr, Elizabeth. 2011. (J). *(978-1-4027-9660-9(9))* Sterling Publishing Co., Inc.

Madden, Colleen, et al. Little Red Riding Hood Stories Around the World: 3 Beloved Tales, 1 vol. Gunderson, Jessica. 2014. (Multicultural Fairy Tales Ser.). (ENG.). 32p. (J). (gr. k-2). lib. bdg. 27.99 *(978-1-4795-5435-5(9)*, Picture Window Bks.) Capstone.

Madden, Colleen. Making New Friends. Blumenstock, Jacqueline & Pool, David. 2nd ed. 2005. 32p. (J). lib. bdg. 14.95 *(978-0-9764647-1-6(3))* Big Brown Box, Inc., The.

—The Mysterious Talent Show Mystery, 4. Abbott, Tony. 2013. (Goofballs Ser.: No. 4). (ENG.). 112p. (J). (gr. 2-4). 17.44 *(978-1-60684-167-9(X))* Egmont Bks., Ltd. GBR. Dist: Children's Plus, Inc.

—One Wordy Bird. Royce, Brenda Scott. 2019. (PAW Pals Ser.). (ENG.). 128p. (J). (gr. 1-3). pap. 5.99 *(978-0-7944-4109-8(2)*, Studio Fun International) Printers Row Publishing Group.

—What If Everybody Thought That? Javernick, Ellen. 2019. (What If Everybody? Ser.: 3). 32p. (J). (gr. -1-3). 14.99 *(978-1-5420-9137-4(3)*, 9781542091374, Two Lions) Amazon Publishing.

—Yeabsolutely. George, Shannan. 2016. (ENG.). (J). pap. 11.99 *(978-0-9855074-0-4(3))* Parker Girl Publishing.

—Your Life As a Private on the Lewis & Clark Expedition, 1 vol. Gunderson, Jessica Sarah. 2012. (Way It Was Ser.). (ENG.). 32p. (J). (gr. 2-5). pap. 8.95 *(978-1-4048-7746-7(0)*, Picture Window Bks.) Capstone.

—Your Life As a Private on the Lewis & Clark Expedition, 1 vol. Gunderson, Jessica. 2012. (Way It Was Ser.). (ENG.). 32p. (J). (gr. 2-5). lib. bdg. 27.32 *(978-1-4048-7370-4(8)*, Picture Window Bks.) Capstone.

Madden, Colleen. The 12 Days of First Grade. Lettice, Jenna. 2020. (12 Days Of Ser.). (ENG.). 24p. (J). (gr. -1-2). pap. 4.99 ***(978-1-9848-9674-2(1)***, Random Hse. Bks. for Young Readers) Random Hse. Children's Bks.

Madden, Colleen. The 12 Days of Kindergarten. Lettice, Jenna. 2017. (12 Days Of Ser.). (ENG.). 24p. (J). (gr. -1-2). pap. 4.99 *(978-0-399-55733-0(4)*, Random Hse. Bks. for Young Readers) Random Hse. Children's Bks.

—The 12 Days of Preschool. Lettice, Jenna. 2018. (12 Days Of Ser.). (ENG.). 24p. (J). (gr. -1-2). pap. 4.99 *(978-1-5247-6660-3(7)*, Random Hse. Bks. for Young Readers) Random Hse. Children's Bks.

—The 12 Days of Thanksgiving. Lettice, Jenna. 2018. (12 Days Of Ser.). 24p. (J). (gr. -1-2). pap. 4.99 *(978-1-5247-6658-0(5)*, Random Hse. Bks. for Young Readers) Random Hse. Children's Bks.

—The 12 Days of Valentine's. Lettice, Jenna. 2017. (12 Days Of Ser.). 24p. (J). (gr. -1-2). pap. 4.99 *(978-0-399-55735-4(0)*, Random Hse. Bks. for Young Readers) Random Hse. Children's Bks.

Madden, Colleen, jt. illus. see Chano, Teresa Ramos.

Madden, Colleen M. Diva Duck Dreams, 1 vol. Levy, Janice. 2012. (Diva Duck Ser.). (ENG.). 32p. (J). (gr. -1-4). 28.50 *(978-1-61641-886-1(9)*, 5191, Looking Glass Library) Magic Wagon.

—Diva Duck Goes to Hollywood, 1 vol. Levy, Janice. 2012. (Diva Duck Ser.). (ENG.). 32p. (J). (gr. -1-4). 28.50 *(978-1-61641-887-8(7)*, 5193, Looking Glass Library) Magic Wagon.

—Diva Duck Travels the World, 1 vol. Levy, Janice. 2012. (Diva Duck Ser.). (ENG.). 32p. (J). (gr. -1-4). 28.50 *(978-1-61641-888-5(5)*, 5195, Looking Glass Library) Magic Wagon.

—Flip-Flop & the Absolutely Awful New Baby, 1 vol. Levy, Janice. 2011. (Flip-Flop Adventure Ser.). (ENG.). 32p. (J). (gr. -1-4). 28.50 *(978-1-61641-651-5(3)*, 7768, Looking Glass Library) Magic Wagon.

—Flip-Flop & the BFFs, 1 vol. Levy, Janice. 2011. (Flip-Flop Adventure Ser.). (ENG.). 32p. (J). (gr. -1-4). 28.50 *(978-1-61641-652-2(1)*, 7770, Looking Glass Library) Magic Wagon.

—Flip-Flop & the Bully Frogs Gruff, 1 vol. Levy, Janice. 2011. (Flip-Flop Adventure Ser.). (ENG.). 32p. (J). (gr. -1-4). 28.50 *(978-1-61641-653-9(X)*, 7772, Looking Glass Library) Magic Wagon.

—Humble Pie. Brunstetter, Wanda E. 2014. 158p. (J). *(978-1-63058-967-7(5))* Barbour Publishing, Inc.

—The Library Gingerbread Man. Enderle, Dotti. 2010. 32p. (J). (gr. -1). 17.95 *(978-1-60213-048-7(5)*, Upstart Bks.) Highsmith Inc.

—School Rules for Diva Duck, 1 vol. Levy, Janice. 2012. (Diva Duck Ser.). (ENG.). 32p. (J). (gr. -1-4). 28.50 *(978-1-61641-889-2(3)*, 5197, Looking Glass Library) Magic Wagon.

—Showtime for Flip-Flop, 1 vol. Levy, Janice. 2011. (Flip-Flop Adventure Ser.). (ENG.). 32p. (J). (gr. -1-4). 28.50 *(978-1-61641-654-6(8)*, 7774, Looking Glass Library) Magic Wagon.

—What If a Stranger Approaches You?, 1 vol. Guard, Anara. 2011. (Danger Zone Ser.). (ENG.). 24p. (J). (gr. k-2). pap. 7.49 *(978-1-4048-7031-4(8))*; lib. bdg. 26.65 *(978-1-4048-6683-6(3))* Capstone. (Picture Window Bks.).

—What If Everybody Did That?, 0 vols. Javernick, Ellen. 2010. 32p. (J). (gr. -1-2). 12.99 *(978-0-7614-5686-5(4)*, 9780761456865, Two Lions) Amazon Publishing.

—The 12 Days of Halloween. Lettice, Jenna. 2017. (12 Days Of Ser.). 24p. (J). (gr. -1-2). pap. 4.99 *(978-0-399-55731-6(8)*, Random Hse. Bks. for Young Readers) Random Hse. Children's Bks.

Madden-Lunsford, Lucy. Nothing Fancy about Kathryn & Charlie. Madden-Lunsford, Kerry. 2013. (ENG.). 36p. (J). pap. 14.95 *(978-0-9828528-0-4(0))* Mockingbird Publishing.

Madden, Myles. Grandma Got Stuck in the Bathtub. Horton, Alice F. 2018. (Oh Grandma!! Ser.: Vol. 1). (ENG.). 36p. (J). pap. 15.00 *(978-1-5482-6040-8(1))* CreateSpace Independent Publishing Platform.

Maddison, Kevin. Book of Roman Pop-Up Board Games. Fields, Sadie & Tango Books Staff. 2004. (Pop-Up Board Games Ser.). (ENG.). 10p. (J). (gr. -1-2). 24.99 *(978-1-85707-597-7(8))* Tango Bks. GBR. Dist: Independent Pubs. Group.

Maddison, Kevin & Stephen, Lib. Snakes; the Tree That Blinked; the Tree Billy Goats Gruff, 18 Bks., Pack. Wernham, Sara. 2004. (ENG.). (J). pap. 42.00 *(978-1-84414-090-9(3)*, Jolly Learning) Jolly Learning, Ltd. GBR. Dist: American International Distribution Corp.

Maddison, Kevin, jt. illus. see Stephen, Lib.

Maddison, Lucy. I'm Telling on You! Poems about Brothers & Sisters. Moses, Brian. 2003. (ENG.). 60p. (J). pap. *(978-0-330-36867-4(2)*, Pan) Pan Macmillan.

—The Practical Joker's Handbook 2. Dinneen, John. (ENG.). 80p. (J). pap. 4.95 *(978-0-330-35524-7(4)*, Pan) Pan Macmillan GBR. Dist: Trafalgar Square Publishing.

Maddock, Monika. Horsing Around. Arena, Jacqueline. 2005. (Girlz Rock! Ser.). (J). pap. *(978-1-59336-703-9(1))* Mondo Publishing.

—Pool Pals. Smith Dinbergs, Holly. 2005. (Girlz Rock! Ser.). (J). pap. *(978-1-59336-705-3(8))* Mondo Publishing.

—School Play Stars. Mullins, Julie. 2005. (Girlz Rock! Ser.). (J). pap. *(978-1-59336-706-0(6))* Mondo Publishing.

Maddocks, Maria. Animal Parade. Zobel-Nolan, Allia. 2008. 10p. (J). (gr. -1). 12.95 *(978-1-932915-63-1(X))* Sandvik Innovations, LLC.

—Baby's First Bible, 1 vol. Piper, Sophie. ed. 2014. (ENG.). 40p. (J). (— 1). bds. 9.99 *(978-0-7459-6411-9(7))* Lion Hudson PLC GBR. Dist: Kregel Pubns.

—Diggers & Dumpers. Wilding, Valerie. 2006. (Green Bananas Ser.). (ENG.). 48p. (J). (gr. -1-k). lib. bdg. *(978-0-7787-1030-1(0))* Crabtree Publishing Co.

—Our Ballet Recital. Piggy Toes Press. 2005. (ENG.). 12p. (J). (gr. -1-3). 12.95 *(978-1-58117-425-0(X)*, Intervisual/Piggy Toes) Bendon, Inc.

—Two Little Ballerinas: A Girly Girl Book. 2009. (ENG.). 10p. (J). 9.95 *(978-1-58117-871-5(9)*, Intervisual/Piggy Toes) Bendon, Inc.

Maddox, Anna. Happiness: A Lesson with Lulu. Jones, Robert. 2018. (Lessons with Lulu Ser.: Vol. 1). (ENG.). 34p. (J). (gr. 1-6). pap. 12.99 *(978-1-939267-74-0(9))* Healthy Life Pr., LLC.

Mader, C. Roger. Stowaway in a Sleigh. 2016. (ENG.). 32p. (J). (gr. -1-3). 17.99 *(978-0-544-48174-9(7)*, 1602693, HMH Books For Young Readers) Houghton Mifflin Harcourt Publishing Co.

Mader, C. Roger. Lost Cat. Mader, C. Roger. 2013. (ENG.). 32p. (J). (gr. -1-3). 17.99 *(978-0-547-97458-3(2)*, 1522533) Houghton Mifflin Harcourt Publishing Co.

—Tiptop Cat. Mader, C. Roger. 2014. (ENG.). 40p. (J). (gr. -1-3). 17.99 *(978-0-544-14799-7(5)*, 1547591, HMH Books For Young Readers) Houghton Mifflin Harcourt Publishing Co.

Maderna, Victoria. Ronan the Librarian. Luebbe, Tara & Cattie, Becky. 2020. (ENG.). 32p. (J). 17.99 *(978-1-250-18921-9(7)*, 900192191) Roaring Brook Pr.

Madhav, Vishnu. Agra. Lake, Ken & Lake, Angie. 2016. (Diaries of Robin's Travels Ser.). (ENG.). 96p. (J). (gr. 1-5). 5.99 *(978-1-78226-053-0(6)*, f0382746-373a-4494-bc7e-7ac5b4bf9d4a) Sweet Cherry Publishing GBR. Dist: Baker & Taylor Publisher Services (BTPS).

—Istanbul. Lake, Ken & Lake, Angie. 2016. (Diaries of Robin's Travels Ser.). (ENG.). 96p. (J). (gr. 1-5). 5.99 *(978-1-78226-250-3(4)*, 834a201e-91e8-4833-9232-e1b54928cbb8) Sweet Cherry Publishing GBR. Dist: Baker & Taylor Publisher Services (BTPS).

—Las Vegas. Lake, Ken & Lake, Angie. 2016. (Diaries of Robin's Travels Ser.). (ENG.). 96p. (J). (gr. 1-5). 5.99 *(978-1-78226-251-0(2)*, e6d181e7-f69e-4de2-b8e2-02ae61e19fab) Sweet Cherry Publishing GBR. Dist: Baker & Taylor Publisher Services (BTPS).

—Rio de Janeiro. Lake, Ken & Lake, Angie. 2016. (Diaries of Robin's Travels Ser.). (ENG.). 96p. (J). (gr. 1-5). 5.99 *(978-1-78226-252-7(0)*, a07c757c-71a0-4eff-b91d-fd633fcfbd1a) Sweet Cherry Publishing GBR. Dist: Baker & Taylor Publisher Services (BTPS).

—St. Petersburg. Lake, Ken & Lake, Angie. 2016. (Diaries of Robin's Travels Ser.). (ENG.). 96p. (J). (gr. 1-5). 5.99 *(978-1-78226-052-3(8)*, e6a6f84f-cc65-42ad-8e39-aab02b92a3f2) Sweet Cherry Publishing GBR. Dist: Baker & Taylor Publisher Services (BTPS).

—Venice. Lake, Ken & Lake, Angie. 2016. (Diaries of Robin's Travels Ser.). (ENG.). 96p. (J). (gr. 1-5). 5.99 *(978-1-78226-051-6(X)*, 20197875-8fce-40aa-bd52-fb30c93115fd) Sweet Cherry Publishing GBR. Dist: Baker & Taylor Publisher Services (BTPS).

Madill, Douglas. Why Me, Lord? For victims of sexual & physical Abuse, 1 vol. Bissell, Sybil A. 2nd l.t. ed. 2004. Orig. Title: Why Me, Lord? for Victims of Sexual & Physical Abuse. (ENG.). 36p. pap. 7.95 *(978-0-9747516-0-3(X)*, 1001) Heart Communications.

Madle, Shaun. The Adventures of Eric the Spider. Madle, Elaine. 2018. (ENG.). 40p. (J). pap. *(978-1-912562-29-9(4))* Clink Street Publishing.

Madley, Vanita. Welcome Home, Baby Buddy. Bradley, Dianne. 2019. (My Story Keepsake Ser.: Vol. 1). (ENG.). 48p. (J). pap. 14.99 ***(978-1-0998-9067-3(5))*** Independently Published.

Madley, Vanita. Ashley Loves Blue. Madley, Vanita. Bradley, Dianne, ed. 2019. (My Story Keepsake (Debut) Ser.: Vol. 1). (ENG.). 38p. (J). pap. 9.99 *(978-1-0968-7585-7(3))* Independently Published.

—The Big Catch. Madley, Vanita. Bradley, Dianne, ed. 2019. (My Story Keepsake (Adventure Collection) Ser.: Vol. 2). (ENG.). 38p. (J). pap. 11.99 *(978-1-0968-0453-6(0))* Independently Published.

—For the Love of Vanilla: (an Adventure in Recipes Tale) Madley, Vanita. Bradley, Dianne, ed. 2019. (My Story Keepsake (Adventure Collection) Ser.: Vol. 2). (ENG.). 38p. (J). pap. 11.99 *(978-1-0968-5049-6(4))* Independently Published.

—Jenny's Super, Spectacular Sleepover. Madley, Vanita. Bradley, Dianne, ed. 2019. (My Story Keepsake

(Adventure Collection) Ser.: Vol. 2). (ENG.). 38p. (J). pap. 11.99 *(978-1-0968-7337-2(0))* Independently Published.
—The Legend of Mathis & His Super Shoes. Madley, Vanita. Bradley, Dianne, ed. (My Story Keepsake (Debut) Ser.: Vol. 2). (ENG.). 38p. (J). 2019. pap. 9.99 *(978-1-0968-9179-6(4))*; 2018. pap. 11.99 *(978-1-9769-2120-9(1))* Independently Published.
—Sophina's Rainbow Cupcakes. Madley, Vanita. Bradley, Dianne, ed. 2019. (My Story Keepsake (Debut Ser.: Vol. 1). (ENG.). 38p. (J). pap. 9.99 *(978-1-0968-7867-4(4))* Independently Published.
—Teeny, Tiny Baby Fits Rattle Jenny's Baby Wits. Madley, Vanita. Bradley, Dianne, ed. 2019. (My Story Keepsake (Debut) Ser.: Vol. 1). (ENG.). 38p. (J). pap. 9.99 *(978-1-0968-8274-9(4))* Independently Published.
—Xander Can't Compute: (a Camping Crisis Story) Madley, Vanita. Bradley, Dianne, ed. 2019. (My Story Keepsake (Adventure Collection) Ser.: Vol. 2). (ENG.). 38p. (J). pap. 11.99 *(978-1-0968-1050-6(6))* Independently Published.
Madonna, Marissa. There's a Hole in the Bucket! 2013. (First Steps in Music Ser.). 32p. (J). (gr. k-2). 16.95 *(978-1-57999-970-4(0))* G I A Pubns., Inc.
Madrid, Erwin. Amy Namey in Ace Reporter. Mcdonald, Megan. 2014. (Judy Moody & Friends Ser.: 3). 64p. (J). (gr. -1-1). 12.99 *(978-0-7636-5715-4(8))* Candlewick Pr.
—April Fools', Mr. Todd! Mcdonald, Megan. 2017. (Judy Moody & Friends Ser.: 8). 64p. (J). (gr. -1-1). 12.99 *(978-0-7636-8200-2(4))* Candlewick Pr.
—April Fools', Mr. Todd! Mcdonald, Megan. ed. 2017. (Judy Moody & Friends Ser.: 8). (ENG.). (J). (gr. -1-1). lib. bdg. 14.75 *(978-0-606-39835-0(X))* Turtleback.
—The Best Bat. Howard, Ryan & Howard, Krystle. 2015. (Little Rhino Ser.: 2). (ENG.). 112p. (J). (gr. 2-5). pap. 4.99 *(978-0-545-67493-5(X)*, Scholastic Paperbacks) Scholastic, Inc.
—Disaster Strikes #1: Earthquake Shock. Kennedy, Marlane. 2014. (Disaster Strikes Ser.: 1). (ENG.). 128p. (J). (gr. 2-5). pap. 4.99 *(978-0-545-53044-6(X)*, Scholastic Paperbacks) Scholastic, Inc.
—Disney Parks Presents: Jungle Cruise: Purchase Includes a CD with Narration! Walt Disney Imagineering & Jungle Cruise Skippers. 2018. (ENG.). 32p. (J). (gr. -1-k). 18.99 *(978-1-4847-0985-6(3))* Disney Pr.
—A Dolphin Named Star. Berne, Emma Carlson. 2019. (Seaside Sanctuary Ser.). (ENG.). 112p. (J). (gr. 3-7). lib. bdg. 25.99 *(978-1-4965-7859-4(7)*, 139398, Stone Arch Bks.) Capstone.
—Dugout Hero. Howard, Ryan & Howard, Krystle. 2015. (Little Rhino Ser.: 3). (ENG.). 112p. (J). (gr. 2-5). pap. 4.99 *(978-0-545-67496-6(4)*, Scholastic Paperbacks) Scholastic, Inc.
—Frank Pearl in the Awful Waffle Kerfuffle. Mcdonald, Megan. 2014. (Judy Moody & Friends Ser.: 4). 64p. (J). (gr. -1-1). 12.99 *(978-0-7636-5717-8(4))* Candlewick Pr.
—Judy Moody & Friends: Countdown to Trouble. Mcdonald, Megan. 2019. (Judy Moody & Friends Ser.). 200p. (J). (gr. -1-1). pap. 8.99 *(978-1-5362-0553-4(2))* Candlewick Pr.
—Judy Moody & Friends: Jessica Finch in Pig Trouble. McDonald, Megan. 2014. (Judy Moody & Friends Ser.: 1). (ENG.). 64p. (J). (gr. -1-1). pap. 4.99 *(978-0-7636-7027-6(8))* Candlewick Pr.
—Judy Moody & Friends: Judy Moody, Tooth Fairy. Mcdonald, Megan. 2017. (Judy Moody & Friends Ser.: 9). 64p. (J). (gr. -1-1). 12.99 *(978-0-7636-9167-7(4))*; pap. 4.99 *(978-0-7636-9168-4(2))* Candlewick Pr.
—Judy Moody & Friends: Mrs. Moody in the Birthday Jinx. Mcdonald, Megan. 2016. (Judy Moody & Friends Ser.: 7). 64p. (J). (gr. -1-1). 12.99 *(978-0-7636-8198-2(9))* Candlewick Pr.
—Judy Moody & Friends: Not-So-Lucky Lefty. Mcdonald, Megan. 2018. (Judy Moody & Friends Ser.: 10). 64p. (J). (gr. -1-1). 12.99 *(978-0-7636-9605-4(6))* Candlewick Pr.
—Judy Moody & Friends: Not-So-Lucky Lefty. McDonald, Megan. 2018. (Judy Moody & Friends Ser.: 10). 64p. (J). (gr. -1-1). pap. 4.99 *(978-0-7636-9847-8(4))* Candlewick Pr.
—Judy Moody & Friends: One, Two, Three, ROAR! Books 1-3. Mcdonald, Megan. 2017. (Judy Moody & Friends Ser.). 200p. (J). (gr. -1-1). pap. 8.99 *(978-0-7636-9576-7(9))* Candlewick Pr.
—Judy Moody & Friends: Prank You Very Much. Mcdonald, Megan. 2020. (Judy Moody & Friends Ser.: 12). 64p. (J). (gr. -1-1). 12.99 *(978-1-5362-0007-2(7))*; pap. 4.99 *(978-1-5362-0008-9(5))* Candlewick Pr.
—Judy Moody & Friends: Rocky Zang in the Amazing Mr. Magic. Mcdonald, Megan. 2014. (Judy Moody & Friends Ser.). (ENG.). 64p. (J). (gr. -1-1). lib. bdg. 15.80 *(978-1-62765-371-8(6))* Perfection Learning Corp.
—Judy Moody & Friends: Searching for Stinkodon. Mcdonald, Megan. 2019. (Judy Moody & Friends Ser.: 11). 64p. (J). (gr. -1-1). 12.99 *(978-0-7636-9997-0(7))*; pap. 4.99 *(978-0-7636-9998-7(5))* Candlewick Pr.
—Juniper Berry. Kozlowsky, M. P. 2012. (ENG.). 240p. (J). (gr. 3-7). pap. 7.99 *(978-0-06-199870-6(2))* HarperCollins Pubs.
—Mrs. Moody in the Birthday Jinx. Mcdonald, Megan. ed. 2016. (Judy Moody & Friends Ser.: 7). (ENG.). 64p. (J). (gr. -1-1). 14.75 *(978-0-606-39092-7(8))* Turtleback.
—My New Team. Howard, Ryan & Howard, Krystle. 2015. (Little Rhino Ser.: 1). (ENG.). 112p. (J). (gr. 2-5). pap. 4.99 *(978-0-545-67490-4(5)*, Scholastic Paperbacks) Scholastic, Inc.
—Oil-Soaked Wings. Berne, Emma Carlson. 2019. (Seaside Sanctuary Ser.). (ENG.). 112p. (J). (gr. 3-7). lib. bdg. 25.99 *(978-1-4965-7861-7(9)*, 139400, Stone Arch Bks.) Capstone.
—Orca in Open Water. Berne, Emma Carlson. 2019. (Seaside Sanctuary Ser.). (ENG.). 112p. (J). (gr. 3-7). lib. bdg. 25.99 *(978-1-4965-7862-4(7)*, 139401, Stone Arch Bks.) Capstone.
—Outback All-Stars. Earhart, Kristin. 2016. 130p. (J). *(978-1-5182-2515-4(2))* Scholastic, Inc.
—The Prairie Thief. Wiley, Melissa. (ENG.). 224p. (J). (gr. 3-7). 2013. pap. 7.99 *(978-1-4424-4057-9(0))*; 2012. 15.99 *(978-1-4424-4056-2(2))* McElderry, Margaret K. Bks. (McElderry, Margaret K. Bks.).
—Rudolph the Red-Nosed Reindeer. Feldman, Thea. 2016. (ENG.). 22p. (J). bds. 10.99 *(978-1-250-12323-7(2)*, 900174036, Holt, Henry & Co. Bks. For Young Readers) Holt, Henry & Co.
—Rudolph the Red-Nosed Reindeer: the Classic Story: Deluxe 50th-Anniversary Edition. Feldman, Thea. 50th ed. 2014. (Rudolph the Red-Nosed Reindeer Ser.). (ENG.). 40p. (J). (gr. -1-3). 12.99 *(978-1-250-04760-1(9)*, 900132420) Square Fish.
—The Scary Places Map Book: Seven Terrifying Tours. Hennessy, B. G. 2012. 32p. (J). (gr. k-4). 15.99 *(978-0-7636-4541-0(9))* Candlewick Pr.
—Stink Moody in Master of Disaster. Mcdonald, Megan. 2015. (Judy Moody & Friends Ser.: 5). 64p. (J). (gr. -1-1). 12.99 *(978-0-7636-7218-8(1))* Candlewick Pr.
—Triple Pet Trouble. Mcdonald, Megan. 2015. (Judy Moody & Friends Ser.: 6). 64p. (J). (gr. -1-1). 12.99 *(978-0-7636-7443-4(5))* Candlewick Pr.
Madrigal, Julia, jt. illus. see Sarin, Max.
Madsen, James. The Endangereds. Cousteau, Philippe & Aslan, Austin. 2020. (ENG.). 352p. (J). (gr. 3-7). 16.99 ***(978-0-06-289416-8(1)***, HarperCollins) HarperCollins Pubs. Ltd. GBR. Dist: HarperCollins Pubs.
Madsen, James. Surviving Bear Island. Greci, Paul. 2017. (ENG.). 192p. (J). (gr. 4-7). pap. 6.95 *(978-0-692-97736-1(8))* Move Bks., LLC.
Madsen, Jim. Adventure Bible Storybook, 1 vol. DeVries, Catherine. 2009. (Adventure Bible Ser.). (ENG.). 288p. (J). 16.99 *(978-0-310-71637-2(3))* Zonderkidz.
—Aventuras en 5 Minutos de la Biblia Aventura, 1 vol. Zondervan. 2019. (Adventure Bible Ser.). (SPA.). 182p. (J). 12.99 *(978-0-8297-6973-9(0))* Vida Pubs.
—The Crossing. Napoli, Donna Jo. 2011. (ENG.). 40p. (J). (gr. -1-3). 19.99 *(978-1-4169-9474-9(2)*, Atheneum Bks. for Young Readers) Simon & Schuster Children's Publishing.
—Family Huddle. Manning, Peyton et al. 2009. (J). *(978-0-545-21351-6(7)*, Scholastic Pr.) Scholastic, Inc.
—The Jungle Book: Rikki-Tikki-Tavi Moves In. Kipling, Rudyard. 2007. (Easy Reader Classics Ser.). (ENG.). 32p. (J). (gr. k-3). lib. bdg. 27.07 *(978-1-59961-336-9(0)*, 6213) Spotlight.
—The Little Shepherd Girl: A Christmas Story. Henry, Juliann. 2007. 32p. (J). (gr. -1-3). 14.99 *(978-0-7814-4513-9(2))* Cook, David C.
—Tuki & Moka: A Tale of Two Tamarins. Young, Judy. 2013. (ENG.). 32p. 16.99 *(978-1-58536-795-5(8))* Sleeping Bear Pr.
—What Was Your Dream, Dr. King? And Other Questions About... Martin Luther King, Jr. Carson, Mary Kay. 2013. (Good Question! Ser.). (ENG.). 32p. (J). (gr. 2). pap. 6.95 *(978-1-4027-9045-4(7))* Sterling Publishing Co., Inc.
—Wing & Claw #1: Forest of Wonders. Park, Linda Sue. (Wing & Claw Ser.: 1). (ENG.). 352p. (J). (gr. 3-7). 2017. pap. 6.99 *(978-0-06-232739-0(9))*; 2016. 16.99 *(978-0-06-232738-3(0))* HarperCollins Pubs.
—Wing & Claw #2: Cavern of Secrets. Park, Linda Sue. (Wing & Claw Ser.: 2). (J). (gr. 3-7). 2018. 336p. pap. 6.99 *(978-0-06-232742-0(9))*; 2017. 320p. 16.99 *(978-0-06-232741-3(0))* HarperCollins Pubs.
—Wing & Claw #3: Beast of Stone. Park, Linda Sue. (Wing & Claw Ser.: 3). (ENG.). 368p. (J). (gr. 3-7). 2019. pap. 6.99 *(978-0-06-232745-1(3))*; 2018. 16.99 *(978-0-06-232744-4(5))* HarperCollins Pubs.
—5-Minute Adventure Bible Stories, 1 vol. DeVries, Catherine. 2017. (Adventure Bible Ser.). (ENG.). 192p. (J). 12.99 *(978-0-310-75970-6(6))* Zonderkidz.
—5-Minute Adventure Bible Stories, Polar Exploration Edition, 1 vol. Zondervan Staff. 2019. (Adventure Bible Ser.). (ENG.). 192p. (J). 12.99 *(978-0-310-76536-3(6))* Zonderkidz.
Madsen, Laura. Brisk's New Home. Madsen, Manda and Laura. 2019. (ENG.). 38p. (J). pap. 9.99 *(978-1-7978-9293-1(2))* Independently Published.
Madsen, Michelle. Buffy the Vampire Slayer, 4 vols., Vol. 4. Whedon, Joss et al. Allie, Scott & Hahn, Sierra, eds. 2013. (ENG.). 320p. 29.99 *(978-1-61655-127-8(5))* Dark Horse Comics.
—Predators & Prey, 8 vols., Vol. 5. Espenson, Jane et al. 2009. (ENG.). 144p. pap. 15.99 *(978-1-59582-342-7(5))* Dark Horse Comics.
Madueira, Joe, et al. Avenging Spider-Man: the Complete Collection. 2019. (ENG.). 504p. (YA). (gr. 8-17). pap. 39.99 *(978-1-302-91618-3(1))* Marvel Worldwide, Inc.
—X-Men: Onslaught Aftermath. 2019. (ENG.). 488p. (J). (gr. 4-17). pap. 39.99 *(978-1-302-91651-0(3))* Marvel Worldwide, Inc.
Madzel, D. E., jt. illus. see Robinson-Chavez, Kathryn A.
Mae, Louisa. Chester Chipmunk Will Not Sleep. George, Kathleen. 2020. (ENG.). 32p. (J). (gr. -1-3). 21.95 ***(978-1-947860-77-3(1)***, Belle Isle Bks.) Brandylane Pubs., Inc.
Maeda, Matsuo. The Turtle & the Warrior. Arai, Shizuko. 2014. (J). 8.95 *(978-1-935523-69-7(4))* World Tribune Pr.
Maeda, Toshio. Adventure Kid - the Original Manga 1 Vol. 1: User Friendly. Maeda, Toshio. 2003. 208p. pap. 16.95 *(978-1-58664-878-7(0)*, CMX 63501G, Manga 18) Central Park Media Corp.
Maeno, Itoko. Gift of Flowers. Paine, Penelope C. 2006. 24p. per. 5.95 *(978-0-9707944-5-1(2))* Paper Posie.
—Gift of Love. Paine, Penelope C. 2006. 24p. per. 5.95 *(978-0-7909-7443-9(6))* Paper Posie.
—Gift of Taste. Paine, Penelope C. 2006. 24p. per. 5.95 *(978-0-9707944-6-8(0))* Paper Posie.
Maertens, Iris. Nikki et la Révolution des Serviettes. Revah, Irma. 2019. (Aventures de Nikki Ser.: Vol. 1). (FRE.). 38p. (J). pap. 9.50 *(978-1-7938-4881-9(5))* Independently Published.
Maes, Ame. Tomorrow I Am a Big Sister, but Today I Am Me. Munoz, Ruby. 2008. 24p. pap. 24.95 *(978-1-60672-862-8(8))* America Star Bks.
Maese, Fares. Soccer Longshot, 1 vol. Renner, C. J. et al. 2011. (Sports Illustrated Kids Graphic Novels Ser.). (ENG.). 56p. (J). (gr. 3-8). lib. bdg. 26.65 *(978-1-4342-2241-1(1)*, Stone Arch Bks.) Capstone.
Maese, Fares & Aburto, Jesus. Soccer Longshot, 1 vol. Renner, C. J. et al. 2011. (Sports Illustrated Kids Graphic Novels Ser.). (ENG.). 56p. (J). (gr. 3-8). pap. 7.19 *(978-1-4342-3402-5(9)*, Stone Arch Bks.) Capstone.
Maestro, Giulio. Eight Ate: A Feast of Homonym Riddles. Terban, Marvin. 2007. (ENG.). 64p. (J). (gr. -1-3). pap. 7.99 *(978-0-618-76676-5(6)*, 100537) Houghton Mifflin Harcourt Publishing Co.
—Guppies in Tuxedos: Funny Eponyms. Terban, Marvin. 2008. (ENG.). 64p. (J). (gr. 5-7). pap. 7.95 *(978-0-547-03188-0(2)*, 1033417) Houghton Mifflin Harcourt Publishing Co.
—In a Pickle: And Other Funny Idioms. Terban, Marvin. 2007. (ENG.). 64p. (J). (gr. -1-3). pap. 8.99 *(978-0-618-83001-5(4)*, 100561) Houghton Mifflin Harcourt Publishing Co.
—Liberty or Death: The American Revolution: 1763-1783. Maestro, Betsy. 2005. 64p. (J). lib. bdg. 17.89 *(978-0-688-08803-3(1))*; (ENG.). (gr. 2-7). 18.99 *(978-0-688-08802-6(3))* HarperCollins Pubs.
—Mad As a Wet Hen! And Other Funny Idioms. Terban, Marvin. 2007. (ENG.). 64p. (J). (gr. -1-3). pap. 8.99 *(978-0-618-83003-9(0)*, 100562) Houghton Mifflin Harcourt Publishing Co.
—A More Perfect Union: The Story of Our Constitution. Maestro, Betsy. 2008. (American Story Ser.). (ENG.). 48p. (J). (gr. 2-7). pap. 8.99 *(978-0-688-10192-3(5)*, HarperCollins) HarperCollins Pubs. Ltd. GBR. Dist: HarperCollins Pubs.
—The New Americans: Colonial Times: 1620-1689. Maestro, Betsy. 2004. (American Story Ser.). (ENG.). 48p. (J). (gr. 2-7). pap. 7.99 *(978-0-06-057572-4(7))* HarperCollins Pubs.
—The Story of Clocks & Calendars. Maestro, Betsy. 2004. (ENG.). 48p. (J). (gr. 2-7). pap. 9.99 *(978-0-06-058945-5(0))* HarperCollins Pubs.
—Too Hot to Hoot: Funny Palindrome Riddles. Terban, Marvin. 2008. (ENG.). 64p. (J). (gr. 3-7). pap. 8.95 *(978-0-618-19165-9(8)*, 1013224) Houghton Mifflin Harcourt Publishing Co.
—Your Foot's on My Feet! And Other Tricky Nouns. Terban, Marvin. 2008. (ENG.). 64p. (J). (gr. 3-7). pap. 8.99 *(978-0-618-19166-6(6)*, 1013225) Houghton Mifflin Harcourt Publishing Co.
Mafaridik, Nasaya. Planet Omar: Accidental Trouble Magnet. Mian, Zanib. 2020. (Planet Omar Ser.: 1). (ENG.). 224p. (J). (gr. 3-7). 13.99 *(978-0-593-10921-2(X)*, G.P. Putnam's Sons Books for Young Readers) Penguin Young Readers Group.
Mafigiri, Christian. Bernie & the Lonely Rhino. Karimi, Faith. 2018. (ENG.). 32p. (J). 14.95 *(978-0-578-40480-6(X))* Bernie's Bks.
—Bernie & the Lonely Rhino. Karimi, Faith. 2018. (ENG.). 32p. (J). pap. 11.95 *(978-0-692-19120-0(8))* Bernie's Bks.
Magagna, Anna Marie. My Book about God's World. Mays, Blanche, ed. 2011. 28p. pap. 35.95 *(978-1-258-10454-2(7))* Literary Licensing, LLC.
Magaldi, Anita. Los Duendes de Las Horas. Londono, Margarita. 2019. (Torre Roja Ser.). (SPA.). 55p. (J). pap. ***(978-958-8774-15-2(2))*** Norma Ediciones, S.A.
Magalinska, Ingrid. Charlie's Perfect Day. Likins, Kim. I.t. ed. 2003. 32p. (J). bds. *(978-0-9729987-0-3(5))* Island Friends LLC.
Magallanes, Alejandro. Con Cuatro Alcanza. Hernandez, Claudia et al. rev. ed. 2006. (Otra Escalera Ser.). (ENG.). 36p. (J). pap. 8.95 *(978-970-20-0811-8(5))* Castillo, Ediciones, S. A. de C. V. MEX. Dist: Macmillan.
—Quien Es Criminal? un Recorrido Por el Delito, la Ley, la Justicia y el Castigo en Mexico: Desde el Virreinato Hasta el Siglo XX. Guerra, Elisa Speckman. rev. ed. 2006. (Castillo de la Lectura Roja Ser.). 84p. (YA). (gr. 8-10). pap. 14.95 *(978-970-20-0829-3(8))* Castillo, Ediciones, S. A. de C. V. MEX. Dist: Macmillan.
—Ruge! Baranda, Maria. 2009. (SPA.). (J). (gr. -1-k). bds. *(978-968-5389-65-5(9))* El Naranjo, Ediciones.
Magallanes, Marco & Finnegan, Marco. Lizard in a Zoot Suit. Finnegan, Marco. 2020. 144p. (YA). (gr. 7-12). 31.99 *(978-1-5415-2365-4(2)*, Graphic Universe™) Lerner Publishing Group.
Magaril, Mikhail. The Feather Merchants, & Other Tales of the Fools of Chelm. Sanfield, Steve. 2005. 102p. (J). (gr. 3-6). reprint ed. 16.00 *(978-0-7567-8554-3(5))* DIANE Publishing Co.
Magdalena-Brown, Maria. My Little Book of Burrowing Owls, Vol. Irvin-Marston, Hope. 2nd ed. 2004. (ENG.). 32p. (J). pap. 7.95 *(978-0-89317-054-7(2)*, WW-0542, Windward Publishing) Finney Co., Inc.
Magdalena Brown, Maria. My Little Book of Burrowing Owls (My Little Book Of...) Marston, Hope Irvin. 2020. (My Little Books Of Ser.). (ENG.). 32p. (J). (gr. -1-12). pap. 7.95 *(978-1-63076-374-9(8))* Muddy Boots Pr.
Magdalena-Brown, Maria. My Little Book of Painted Turtles, Vol. Irvin-Marston, Hope. 2nd ed. 2004. (ENG.). 32p. (J). pap. 7.95 *(978-0-89317-055-4(0)*, WW-0550, Windward Publishing) Finney Co., Inc.
Magdalena Brown, Maria. My Little Book of Painted Turtles (My Little Book Of...) Marston, Hope Irvin. 2020. (My Little Books Of Ser.). (ENG.). 32p. (J). (gr. -1-12). pap. 7.95 *(978-1-63076-372-5(1))* Muddy Boots Pr.
Magdalena-Brown, Maria. My Little Book of River Otters, Vol. Irvin-Marston, Hope. 2nd ed. 2004. (ENG.). 32p. (J). pap. 7.95 *(978-0-89317-051-6(8)*, WW-0518, Windward Publishing) Finney Co., Inc.
Magdalena Brown, Maria. My Little Book of River Otters (My Little Book Of...) Marston, Hope Irvin. 2020. (My Little Books Of Ser.). (ENG.). 32p. (J). (gr. -1-12). pap. 7.95 *(978-1-63076-364-0(0))* Muddy Boots Pr.
Magdalena-Brown, Maria. My Little Book of Timber Wolves. Irvin-Marston, Hope. 2nd ed. 2004. 32p. (J). pap. 7.95 *(978-0-89317-052-3(6)*, WW-0526, Windward Publishing) Finney Co., Inc.
Magdalena Brown, Maria. My Little Book of Whitetails. Marston, Hope Irvin. 2020. (My Little Book Ser.). (ENG.). 32p. (J). (gr. -1-12). pap. 7.95 *(978-1-63076-366-4(7))* Muddy Boots Pr.
Magdalena-Brown, Maria. My Little Book of Whitetails, Vol. Irvin-Marston, Hope. 2004. (ENG.). 32p. (J). pap. 7.95 *(978-0-89317-050-9(X)*, WW-050X, Windward Publishing) Finney Co., Inc.
—My Little Book of Wood Ducks, Vol. Irvin-Marston, Hope. 2nd ed. 2004. 32p. (J). pap. 7.95 *(978-0-89317-053-0(4)*, WW-0534, Windward Publishing) Finney Co., Inc.
Magdy, Esraa. Vivi's Quest: Nana Camp. Weissman, Seth Michael. 2019. (Vivi's Quest Ser.: Vol. 2). (ENG.). 38p. (J). pap. 11.99 ***(978-1-7109-6059-4(0))*** Independently Published.
Magee, Christopher. A Writer's Guide to Powerful Paragraphs. Pellegrino, Victor C. 2003. 187p. (YA). (gr. 7-18). pap. 18.95 *(978-0-945045-05-2(0))* Maui Arthoughts Co.
Magee, Melanie. Mud Puddle Hunting Day. Grant, Callie. 2013. (ENG.). 20p. (J). bds. 8.99 *(978-0-9854090-0-5(2))* Blanchard, Graham.
Magellan, Mauro. Anole Invasion. Magellan, Marta. 2018. (ENG.). 34p. (J). (gr. k-5). pap. 9.99 *(978-1-63233-186-1(1))* Eifrig Publishing.
Magellan, Mauro. Dragonflies: Water Angels & Brilliant Bioindicators. Magellan, Marta. 2020. (ENG.). 34p. (J). (gr. k-5). pap. 9.99 ***(978-1-63233-258-5(2))*** Eifrig Publishing.
Magellan, Mauro. Python Catchers: Saving the Everglades, Vol. Magellan, Marta. 2020. (ENG.). 32p. (J). (gr. k-4). 16.95 *(978-1-68334-049-2(3))* Pineapple Pr., Inc.
Magellan, Mauro. Max the Apartment Cat. Magellan, Mauro. 2013. 36p. pap. 12.95 *(978-0-89334-887-8(2))* Green Dragon Bks.
Magenta, Emma. Orlando on a Thursday. Magenta, Emma. 2010. (ENG.). 32p. (J). (gr. -1-2). 15.99 *(978-0-7636-4560-1(5))* Candlewick Pr.
Magerl, Caroline. Do-Wrong Ron. Herrick, Steven. 2005. (ENG.). 132p. (J). (gr. 1-5). pap. 11.99 *(978-1-86508-661-3(4))* Allen & Unwin AUS. Dist: Independent Pubs. Group.
—The Naming of Tishkin Silk. Millard, Glenda. 2019. (Kingdom of Silk Ser.: 01). 96p. mass mkt. 4.99 *(978-0-7333-1314-1(0))* ABC Bks. AUS. Dist: HarperCollins Pubs.
—Rose & the Wish Thing. Random House Disney Staff. 2016. (ENG.). 40p. (J). (gr. -1-2). 16.99 *(978-0-553-53617-1(6)*, Doubleday Bks. for Young Readers) Random Hse. Children's Bks.
Magerl, Caroline. Maya & the Lost Cat. Magerl, Caroline. 2019. (ENG.). 40p. (J). (gr. -1-2). 16.99 *(978-1-5362-0423-0(4))* Candlewick Pr.
Maggiorini, Mauricio. Green Was My Forest. Iturralde, Edna. Powell, Jessica Emst, tr. 2018. (Young Eco Fiction Ser.: 2).Tr. of Verde Fue Mi Selva. (ENG.). 136p. (YA). pap. 14.99 *(978-1-942134-60-2(6))* Mandel Vilar Pr.
Magic Eye Studios. Rally Race. Porter, Alan J. 2011. (Kaboom! Graphic Novels Ser.). (ENG.). 112p. (J). (gr. 4-7). 26.19 *(978-1-60886-517-8(7))* Boom! Studios.
Magic Eye Studios, jt. illus. see Pastrovicchio, Lorenzo.
Magic Eye Studios Staff, et al. Prilla's Talent, No. 1. Petrucha, Stefan. 2010. (Disney Fairies Ser.: 1). (ENG.). 80p. (J). (gr. 1-6). 12.99 *(978-1-59707-187-1(0))* Papercutz.
Magic Mike. The Very Unluckily Lucky Quaroo. Magic Mike. 2017. (ENG.). (J). (gr. 4-6). *(978-0-9950687-8-0(X))* MagicWayMedia Inc.
Maginn, Traci. Gilbert! Front & Center! McCord, Marianne. 2003. 24p. (J). per. 5.95 *(978-0-9743352-0-9(7))* Jades Publishing.
Maglio-Macullar, Andrea. The Cat That Purred. Plantedosi, John J. 2014. (ENG.). (J). pap. 11.95 *(978-1-56548-540-2(8))* New City Press of the Focolare.
—El Rosario para Ni?os. 2007. (ENG & SPA.). (J). (gr. k-5). pap. 14.95 *(978-1-59276-395-5(2))* Our Sunday Visitor, Publishing Div.
Magnaye, Blok. Who Do You Think You Are? 20 Psychology Tests to Explore Your Growing Mind. Harman, Alice. 2020. (ENG.). 96p. (J). (gr. 4-7). 22.99 ***(978-1-78603-648-3(7)***, 308165, Wide Eyed Editions) Quarto Publishing Group UK GBR. Dist: Hachette UK Distribution.
Magniat, Jeffrey. Allosaurus. Mattern, Joanne. 2009. (Let's Read about Dinosaurs Ser.). 24p. (gr. -1-3). pap. 8.15 *(978-0-8368-9418-9(9)*, Weekly Reader Leveled Readers) Stevens, Gareth Publishing LLLP.
—Ankylosaurus. Mattern, Joanne. 2009. (Let's Read about Dinosaurs Ser.). 24p. (gr. -1-3). pap. 8.15 *(978-0-8368-9419-6(7)*, Weekly Reader Leveled Readers) Stevens, Gareth Publishing LLLP.
—Apatosaurus. Mattern, Joanne. 2007. (Let's Read about Dinosaurs Ser.). 24p. (gr. k-3). pap. 8.15 *(978-0-8368-7702-1(0))*; lib. bdg. 22.00 *(978-0-8368-7695-6(4))* Stevens, Gareth Publishing LLLP. (Weekly Reader Leveled Readers).
—Apatosaurus/Apatosaurio. Mattern, Joanne. 2007. (Let's Read about Dinosaurs/ Conozcamos a los dinosaurios Ser.). (ENG & SPA.). 24p. (gr. k-3). lib. bdg. 23.00 *(978-0-8368-8018-2(8)*, Weekly Reader Leveled Readers) Stevens, Gareth Publishing LLLP.
—Diplodocus. Mattern, Joanne. 2009. (Let's Read about Dinosaurs Ser.). 24p. (gr. -1-3). (J). lib. bdg. 23.00 *(978-0-8368-9416-5(2))*; pap. 8.15 *(978-0-8368-9420-2(0))* Stevens, Gareth Publishing LLLP. (Weekly Reader Leveled Readers).
—Giganotosaurus. Mattern, Joanne. 2007. (Let's Read about Dinosaurs Ser.). 24p. (gr. k-3). pap. 8.15 *(978-0-8368-7703-8(9)*, Weekly Reader Leveled Readers) Stevens, Gareth Publishing LLLP.
—Giganotosaurus/Gigantosaurio. Mattern, Joanne. 2007. (Let's Read about Dinosaurs/ Conozcamos a los dinosaurios Ser.). (ENG & SPA.). 24p. (J). (gr. k-3). lib. bdg. 23.00 *(978-0-8368-8019-9(6)*, Weekly Reader Leveled Readers) Stevens, Gareth Publishing LLLP.

M

—Oviraptor. Mattern, Joanne. 2009. (Let's Read about Dinosaurs Ser.). 24p. (gr. -1-3). (J). lib. bdg. 23.00 *(978-0-8368-9417-2(0))*; pap. 8.15 *(978-0-8368-9421-9(9))* Stevens, Gareth Publishing LLLP. (Weekly Reader Leveled Readers).

—Stegosaurus. Mattern, Joanne. 2007. (Let's Read about Dinosaurs Ser.). 24p. (gr. k-3). lib. bdg. 22.00 *(978-0-8368-7697-0(0)*, Weekly Reader Leveled Readers) Stevens, Gareth Publishing LLLP.

—Stegosaurus/Estegosaurio. Mattern, Joanne. 2007. (Let's Read about Dinosaurs/ Conozcamos a los dinosaurios Ser.). (ENG & SPA.). 24p. (gr. k-3). lib. bdg. 23.00 *(978-0-8368-8020-5(X)*, Weekly Reader Leveled Readers) Stevens, Gareth Publishing LLLP.

—Triceratops. Mattern, Joanne. 2007. (Let's Read about Dinosaurs Ser.). 24p. (gr. k-3). pap. 8.15 *(978-0-8368-7705-2(5))*; lib. bdg. 23.00 *(978-0-8368-7698-7(9))* Stevens, Gareth Publishing LLLP. (Weekly Reader Leveled Readers).

—Triceratops/Triceratops. Mattern, Joanne. 2007. (Let's Read about Dinosaurs/ Conozcamos a los dinosaurios Ser.). (ENG & SPA.). 24p. (gr. k-3). lib. bdg. 23.00 *(978-0-8368-8021-2(8)*, Weekly Reader Leveled Readers) Stevens, Gareth Publishing LLLP.

—Tyrannosaurus Rex. Mattern, Joanne. 2007. (Let's Read about Dinosaurs Ser.). 24p. (gr. k-3). pap. 8.15 *(978-0-8368-7706-9(3)*, Weekly Reader Leveled Readers) Stevens, Gareth Publishing LLLP.

—Tyrannosaurus Rex/Tiranosaurio Rex. Mattern, Joanne. 2007. (Let's Read about Dinosaurs/ Conozcamos a los dinosaurios Ser.). (ENG & SPA.). 24p. (J). (gr. k-3). lib. bdg. 23.00 *(978-0-8368-8022-9(6)*, Weekly Reader Leveled Readers) Stevens, Gareth Publishing LLLP.

—Velociraptor. Mattern, Joanne. 2007. (Let's Read about Dinosaurs Ser.). 24p. (gr. k-3). pap. 8.15 *(978-0-8368-7707-6(1)*, Weekly Reader Leveled Readers) Stevens, Gareth Publishing LLLP.

—Velociraptor/Velociraptor. Mattern, Joanne. 2007. (Let's Read about Dinosaurs/ Conozcamos a los dinosaurios Ser.). (ENG & SPA.). 24p. (gr. k-3). lib. bdg. 23.00 *(978-0-8368-8023-6(4)*, Weekly Reader Leveled Readers) Stevens, Gareth Publishing LLLP.

Magnisi, Angelica, jt. illus. see Magnisi, Sabrina.

Magnisi, Sabrina & Magnisi, Angelica. Miss Sabrina's Learn the Hail Mary As You Color the Rosary: A Guide for Children 6 - 9 & Up! Magnisi, Sabrina. 2005. 104p. (J). per. *(978-1-933593-30-2(X))* Puarose Publishing.

Magno, Carlos. Movie Prequel: Rising Storm. Barber, John. 2012. (Transformers: Dark of the Moon Movie Prequel Ser.). (ENG.). 24p. (J). (gr. 2-6). 27.07 *(978-1-59961-977-4(6)*, 14857, Graphic Novels) Spotlight.

—Movie Prequel - Rising Storm. Barber, John. 2012. (Transformers: Dark of the Moon Movie Prequel Ser.). (ENG.). 24p. (J). (gr. 2-6). 27.07 *(978-1-59961-975-0(X)*, 14855); 27.07 *(978-1-59961-976-7(8)*, 14856) Spotlight. (Graphic Novels).

—Rising Storm, Vol. 4. Barber, John. 2012. (Transformers: Dark of the Moon Movie Prequel Ser.). (ENG.). 24p. (J). (gr. 2-6). 27.07 *(978-1-59961-978-1(4)*, 14858, Graphic Novels) Spotlight.

Magno, Carlos & Guice, Butch. Invaders Vol. 1: War Ghost, Vol. 1. 2019. (ENG.). 112p. (YA). (gr. 8-17). pap. 17.99 *(978-1-302-91749-4(8))* Marvel Worldwide, Inc.

—Invaders Vol. 2: Dead in the Water. 2020. (Invaders - 2018 Ser.: 2). 112p. (YA). (gr. 8-17). pap. 17.99 *(978-1-302-91750-0(1))* Marvel Worldwide, Inc.

Magno, Ryan. Sasquatch for Dinner. Robledo, Ronald J. Robledo, Victoria, ed. 2013. 32p. 18.99 *(978-0-578-12711-8(3))* One Little Spark.

Magnuson, Diana. Home on the Range. Smithsonian Institution Staff. Schwaeber, Barbie H., ed. 2007. (ENG.). 32p. (J). (gr. -1-3). 9.85 *(978-1-59249-686-0(5))* Soundprints.

—Hope Weavers. Ehrmantraut, Brenda. 2009. (J). *(978-0-9729833-8-9(4))* Bubble Gum Pr.

—Jack & the Beanstalk: Classic Tales Edition. Adams, Alison. 2011. (Classic Tales Ser.). (J). *(978-1-936258-68-0(4))* Benchmark Education Co.

—Sacagawea. Krensky, Stephen. ed. 2005. 32p. (J). lib. bdg. 15.00 *(978-1-59054-954-4(6))* Fitzgerald Bks.

—There's a Bear in My Chair. Magoun, James. 2004. (ENG.). 20p. (gr. k-2). pap. 8.95 *(978-1-57874-080-2(0)*, Kaeden Bks.) Kaeden Corp.

Magnuson, Natalie. La Gallinita Roja, 1 vol. Jones, Christianne C. Abello, Patricia, tr. 2006. (Read-It! Readers en Español: Cuentos Folclóricos Ser.).Tr. of Little Red Hen. (SPA.). 32p. (J). (gr. k-3). 21.32 *(978-1-4048-1650-3(X)*, Picture Window Bks.) Capstone.

—The Little Red Hen, 1 vol. Jones, Christianne C. 2011. (My First Classic Story Ser.). (ENG.). 32p. (J). (gr. k-3). pap. 7.10 *(978-1-4048-7356-8(2)*, Picture Window Bks.) Capstone.

Magoon, Scott. Big Mean Mike. Knudsen, Michelle. (ENG.). 40p. (J). (gr. -1-3). 2020. 7.99 *(978-0-7636-6813-6(3))*; 2012. 15.99 *(978-0-7636-4990-6(2))* Candlewick Pr.

—Chopsticks. Rosenthal, Amy Krouse. 2012. (Spoon Ser.: 2). 40p. (J). (gr. -1-3). 16.99 *(978-1-4231-0796-5(9))* Hyperion Pr.

—I Have a Balloon. Bernstein, Ariel. 2017. (ENG.). 40p. (J). (gr. -1-3). 17.99 *(978-1-4814-7250-0(X)*, Simon & Schuster/Paula Wiseman Bks.) Simon & Schuster/Paula Wiseman Bks.

—I Will Not Eat You. Lehrhaupt, Adam. 2016. (ENG.). 40p. (J). (gr. -1-3). 17.99 *(978-1-4814-2933-7(7)*, Simon & Schuster Bks. For Young Readers) Simon & Schuster Bks. For Young Readers.

—The Knights Before Christmas. Holub, Joan. 2015. (ENG.). 32p. (J). (gr. k-3). 16.99 *(978-0-8050-9932-4(8)*, 900126311, Holt, Henry & Co. Bks. For Young Readers) Holt, Henry & Co.

—Misunderstood Shark. Dyckman, Ame. 2018. (ENG.). 48p. (J). (gr. -1-k). 17.99 *(978-1-338-11247-4(3)*, Orchard Bks.) Scholastic, Inc.

—Misunderstood Shark: Friends Don't Eat Friends. Dyckman, Ame. 2019. (ENG.). 48p. (J). (gr. -1-k). 17.99 *(978-1-338-11388-4(7)*, Orchard Bks.) Scholastic, Inc.

—Mostly Monsterly. Sauer, Tammi. 2010. (ENG.). 40p. (J). (gr. -1-3). 18.99 *(978-1-4169-6110-9(0)*, Simon & Schuster/Paula Wiseman Bks.) Simon & Schuster/Paula Wiseman Bks.

—The Nuts: Bedtime at the Nut House. Litwin, Eric. 2014. (ENG.). 32p. (J). (gr. -1-3). 18.99 *(978-0-316-32244-7(X))* Little, Brown Bks. for Young Readers.

—The Nuts: Keep Rolling! Litwin, Eric. 2017. 32p. (J). (gr. -1-3). 18.99 *(978-0-316-32251-5(2))* Little, Brown Bks. for Young Readers.

—The Nuts: Sing & Dance in Your Polka-Dot Pants. Litwin, Eric. 2015. 48p. (J). (gr. -1-3). 18.99 *(978-0-316-32250-8(4))* Little Brown & Co.

—Rescue & Jessica: A Life-Changing Friendship. Kensky, Jessica & Downes, Patrick. 2018. 32p. (J). (gr. k-4). 16.99 *(978-0-7636-9604-7(8))* Candlewick Pr.

—Rover Throws a Party: Inspired by NASA's Curiosity on Mars. Gray, Kristin L. 2020. 40p. (J). (gr. -1-2). 17.99 *(978-0-525-64648-8(5))*; (ENG.). lib. bdg. 20.99 *(978-0-525-64649-5(3))* Random Hse. Children's Bks. (Knopf Bks. for Young Readers).

—Spoon. Rosenthal, Amy Krouse. 2009. (Spoon Ser.: 1). (ENG.). 40p. (J). (gr. -1-k). 16.99 *(978-1-4231-0685-2(7))* Hyperion Pr.

—Ugly Fish. LaReau, Kara. 2006. (ENG.). 40p. (J). (gr. -1-3). 17.99 *(978-0-15-205082-5(5)*, 1195349) Houghton Mifflin Harcourt Publishing Co.

—Where Is My Balloon? Bernstein, Ariel. 2019. (ENG.). 40p. (J). (gr. -1-3). 17.99 *(978-1-5344-1451-8(7)*, Simon & Schuster Bks. For Young Readers) Simon & Schuster Bks. For Young Readers.

Magoon, Scott. The Boy Who Cried Bigfoot! Magoon, Scott. 2013. (ENG.). 48p. (J). (gr. -1-3). 18.99 *(978-1-4424-1257-6(7)*, Simon & Schuster Bks. For Young Readers) Simon & Schuster/Paula Wiseman Bks.

—Breathe. Magoon, Scott. 2014. (ENG.). 40p. (J). (gr. -1-3). 18.99 *(978-1-4424-1258-3(5)*, Simon & Schuster/Paula Wiseman Bks.) Simon & Schuster/Paula Wiseman Bks.

Magoon, Scott. Linus the Little Yellow Pencil. Magoon, Scott. 2019. 32p. (J). (gr. -1-k). 16.99 ***(978-1-368-00627-9(2))*** Little, Brown Bks. for Young Readers.

Magsamen, Sandra. Beecause I Love You. Magsamen, Sandra. 2017. (Made with Love Ser.). 14p. (J). (— 1). 7.99 *(978-1-338-11090-6(X)*, Cartwheel Bks.) Scholastic, Inc.

—Bible Stories for Little Hearts. Magsamen, Sandra. 2019. (ENG.). 10p. (J). (gr. -1 — 1). bds. 6.99 *(978-1-338-58942-9(3)*, Cartwheel Bks.) Scholastic, Inc.

—Good Night, My Love. Magsamen, Sandra. 2018. (ENG.). 10p. (J). (gr. -1 — 1). bds. 7.99 *(978-1-338-11093-7(4)*, Cartwheel Bks.) Scholastic, Inc.

—I Love Old MacDonald's Farm. Magsamen, Sandra. 2018. (ENG.). 12p. (J). (gr. -1 — 1). 6.99 *(978-1-338-32398-6(9)*, Cartwheel Bks.) Scholastic, Inc.

—I Love to Gobble You Up! Magsamen, Sandra. 2018. (Made with Love Ser.). (ENG.). 10p. (J). (gr. -1 — 1). 7.99 *(978-1-338-11092-0(6)*, Cartwheel Bks.) Scholastic, Inc.

—I Love You, Honey Bunny. Magsamen, Sandra. 2016. (Made with Love Ser.). 12p. (J). (— 1). bds. 7.99 *(978-1-338-11084-5(5)*, Cartwheel Bks.) Scholastic, Inc.

—I Love You Snow Much. Magsamen, Sandra. 2015. (ENG.). 10p. (J). (gr. -1 — 1). bds. 7.99 *(978-0-316-37876-5(3))* Little, Brown Bks. for Young Readers.

—I Love You Snow Much. Magsamen, Sandra. 2017. (Made with Love Ser.). (ENG.). 10p. (J). (— 1). 7.99 *(978-1-338-11086-9(1)*, Cartwheel Bks.) Scholastic, Inc.

—I Ruff You (Made with Love) Magsamen, Sandra. 2016. (ENG.). 12p. (J). (gr. -1-k). bds. 7.99 *(978-1-338-11082-1(9)*, Cartwheel Bks.) Scholastic, Inc.

—I'M Wild about You! Magsamen, Sandra. 2016. (Heart-Felt Bks.). 10p. (J). (— 1). 7.99 *(978-0-545-46839-8(6)*, Cartwheel Bks.) Scholastic, Inc.

—Itsy-Bitsy I Love You! Magsamen, Sandra. 2016. (Heart-Felt Bks.). 10p. (J). (— 1). 7.99 *(978-0-545-46841-1(8)*, Cartwheel Bks.) Scholastic, Inc.

—Mama Loves Her Little Goose! Magsamen, Sandra. 2018. (ENG.). 10p. (J). (gr. -1 — 1). 6.99 *(978-1-338-30577-7(8)*, Cartwheel Bks.) Scholastic, Inc.

—Mama Loves Her Little Llama. Magsamen, Sandra. 2020. (ENG.). (J). (gr. -1 — 1). 7.99 *(978-1-338-62917-0(4)*, Cartwheel Bks.) Scholastic, Inc.

—Merry Christmas, Little One! Magsamen, Sandra. 2018. (ENG.). 10p. (J). (gr. -1 — 1). 8.99 *(978-1-338-24309-3(8)*, Cartwheel Bks.) Scholastic, Inc.

—Our Little Deer (Made with Love) Magsamen, Sandra. 2016. (ENG.). 12p. (J). 7.99 *(978-1-338-11081-4(0)*, Cartwheel Bks.) Scholastic, Inc.

—Our Little Love Bug! Magsamen, Sandra. 2018. 12p. (J). (gr. -1 — 1). bds. 8.99 *(978-1-338-24318-5(7)*, Cartwheel Bks.) Scholastic, Inc.

—Peek-A-Boo, I Love You! Magsamen, Sandra. 2017. 12p. (J). (gr. -1 — 1). bds. 7.99 *(978-1-338-11088-3(8)*, Cartwheel Bks.) Scholastic, Inc.

—Peek-a-Boooo! Magsamen, Sandra. 2018. (Heart-Felt Bks.). 12p. (J). (gr. -1 — 1). bds. 7.99 *(978-0-545-92798-7(6)*, Cartwheel Bks.) Scholastic, Inc.

—Peep, Peep, I Love You! Magsamen, Sandra. 2018. (ENG.). 10p. (J). (gr. -1 — 1). 7.99 *(978-1-338-24314-7(4)*, Cartwheel Bks.) Scholastic, Inc.

—Twinkle, Twinkle, You're My Star. Magsamen, Sandra. 2018. (ENG.). (J). (gr. -1 — 1). bds. 7.99 *(978-1-338-24312-3(8)*, Cartwheel Bks.) Scholastic, Inc.

—Whooo Loves You? Magsamen, Sandra. 2017. (Made with Love Ser.). (ENG.). 10p. (J). (gr. -1 — 1). 7.99 *(978-1-338-11087-6(X)*, Cartwheel Bks.) Scholastic, Inc.

—You Are a Gift to Me! Magsamen, Sandra. 2020. (ENG.). 22p. (J). (gr. -1 — 1). bds. 7.99 *(978-1-338-58943-6(1)*, Cartwheel Bks.) Scholastic, Inc.

—You Are My Sunshine. Magsamen, Sandra. 2018. (ENG.). 6p. (J). (gr. -1 — 1). 7.99 *(978-1-338-30576-0(X)*, Cartwheel Bks.) Scholastic, Inc.

Maguire, Gail. Elvin the Elf. Hardy Kushner, Synthia. 2018. (ENG.). 26p. (J). 18.99 *(978-1-7329442-0-6(2))* Hardy Ink LLC.

Maguire, Jake. The Turnarounders & the Arbuckle Rescue. Heneghan, Lou. 2013. 496p. pap. *(978-0-9573523-1-5(X))* Natus Publishing.

Maguire, Kerry. Oh, the Places He Went: A Story about Dr. Seuss. Weidt, Maryann N. 2007. (Creative Minds Biographies Ser.). (ENG.). 64p. (gr. 4-8). 9.99 *(978-0-87614-627-9(2))* Lerner Publishing Group.

—Saber-Toothed Cats. Goodman, Susan E. (On My Own Science Ser.). 48p. (J). 2006. (ENG.). (gr. 2-4). per. 7.99 *(978-1-57505-851-1(0)*, First Avenue Editions); 2005. (gr. 3-7). lib. bdg. 25.26 *(978-1-57505-759-0(X))* Lerner Publishing Group.

Maguire, Kevin, et al. Captain America: the Adventures of Captain America. 2018. (ENG.). 304p. (YA). (gr. 8-17). pap. 34.99 *(978-1-302-91036-5(1))* Marvel Worldwide, Inc.

Maguire, Rachel & Kelley, Nichole. Galactic Hot Dogs 1: Cosmoe's Wiener Getaway. Brallier, Max. (Galactic Hot Dogs Ser.: 1). (ENG.). 304p. (J). (gr. 3-7). 2020. 19.99 ***(978-1-5344-7797-1(7))***; 2020. pap. 9.99 ***(978-1-5344-7796-4(9))***; 2016. 14.99 *(978-1-4814-8098-7(7))* Simon & Schuster Children's Publishing. (Aladdin).

—Galactic Hot Dogs 2: The Wiener Strikes Back. Brallier, Max. (Galactic Hot Dogs Ser.: 2). (ENG.). 288p. (J). (gr. 3-7). 2020. 19.99 ***(978-1-5344-7800-8(0))***; 2020. pap. 9.99 ***(978-1-5344-7799-5(3))***; 2016. 13.99 *(978-1-4814-2496-7(3))* Simon & Schuster Children's Publishing. (Aladdin).

—Galactic Hot Dogs 3: Revenge of the Space Pirates. Brallier, Max. (Galactic Hot Dogs Ser.: 3). (ENG.). 320p. (J). (gr. 3-7). 2020. 19.99 ***(978-1-5344-7803-9(5))***; 2020. pap. 9.99 ***(978-1-5344-7802-2(7))***; 2017. 13.99 *(978-1-4814-2498-1(X))* Simon & Schuster Children's Publishing. (Aladdin).

—Galactic Hot Dogs Collection: Cosmoe's Wiener Getaway; the Wiener Strikes Back; Revenge of the Space Pirates. Brallier, Max. ed. 2020. (Galactic Hot Dogs Ser.). (ENG.). 912p. (J). (gr. 3-7). pap. 29.99 ***(978-1-5344-7812-1(4)***, Aladdin) Simon & Schuster Children's Publishing.

Maguire, Rachel & Kelley, Nichole. Galactic Hot Dogs Collection: Galactic Hot Dogs 1; Galactic Hot Dogs 2; Galactic Hot Dogs 3. Brallier, Max. ed. 2017. (Galactic Hot Dogs Ser.). (ENG.). 912p. (J). (gr. 3-7). 41.99 *(978-1-4814-9802-9(9)*, Aladdin) Simon & Schuster Children's Publishing.

Maguire, Thomas Aquinas. The Wild Swans. Andersen, Hans Christian. 2012. (ENG.). 104p. (J). (gr. k). 24.95 *(978-1-897476-36-9(1))* Simply Read Bks. CAN. Dist: Ingram Publisher Services.

Mah, Anna. It's Cool to Be Clever: The story of Edson C. Hendricks, the genius who invented the design for the Internet. Jones, Leanne. 2011. 40p. *(978-1-897435-63-2(0))* Agio Publishing Hse.

Mah, Derek. Monsterology: Fabulous Lives of the Creepy, the Revolting, & the Undead. Slade, Arthur. 2005. 96p. (J). (gr. 4-7). pap. 8.95 *(978-0-88776-714-2(1)*, Tundra Bks.) Tundra Bks. CAN. Dist: Penguin Random Hse. LLC.

—Villainology: Fabulous Lives of the Big, the Bad, & the Wicked. Slade, Arthur. 2007. 96p. (J). (gr. 4-7). per. 9.95 *(978-0-88776-809-5(1)*, Tundra Bks.) Tundra Bks. CAN. Dist: Penguin Random Hse. LLC.

Mahajan, Subrata. Apley Towers. King, Myra. 2016. (Apley Towers Ser.). (ENG.). (J). Bks. 1-3. *(978-1-78226-300-5(4))*; Bks. 4-6. *(978-1-78226-301-2(2))* Sweet Cherry Publishing.

—Bringing Out the Best, 1 vol. King, Myra. 2016. (Apley Towers Ser.: 5). (ENG.). 204p. (J). 7.99 *(978-1-78226-281-7(4)*, 63109856-68f6-4400-89c1-2d9c23e381da) Sweet Cherry Publishing GBR. Dist: Baker & Taylor Publisher Services (BTPS).

—Good Enough, 1 vol. King, Myra. 2016. (Apley Towers Ser.: 6). (ENG.). 191p. (J). 7.99 *(978-1-78226-282-4(2)*, 405cab1c-3f9f-4bf8-80aa-3bf54f804f5c) Sweet Cherry Publishing GBR. Dist: Baker & Taylor Publisher Services (BTPS).

—Made Powerful, 1 vol. King, Myra. 2016. (Apley Towers Ser.: 2). (ENG.). 202p. (J). 7.99 *(978-1-78226-278-7(4)*, 822c7922-1c5c-4b3e-a6ec-1b65de9935eb) Sweet Cherry Publishing GBR. Dist: Baker & Taylor Publisher Services (BTPS).

—Restless Warrior, 1 vol. King, Myra. 2016. (Apley Towers Ser.: 4). (ENG.). 187p. (J). 7.99 *(978-1-78226-280-0(6)*, eee6d53e-6bae-4d92-be59-0ff8437c7aac) Sweet Cherry Publishing GBR. Dist: Baker & Taylor Publisher Services (BTPS).

—Siren's Song, 1 vol. King, Myra. 2016. (Apley Towers Ser.: 3). (ENG.). 215p. (J). 7.99 *(978-1-78226-279-4(2)*, 178f841d-3cc0-4ff8-b2fb-9351ac945b0b) Sweet Cherry Publishing GBR. Dist: Baker & Taylor Publisher Services (BTPS).

Mahal, Susan. Felicity's Cooking Studio. Athan, Polly et al. 2007. (American Girl Ser.). 55p. (J). (gr. 3-7). 15.95 *(978-1-59369-266-7(8))* American Girl Publishing, Inc.

Mahan, Ben. All about Holidays. Kain, Kathleen. 2004. (Treasure Tree Ser.). 32p. (J). *(978-0-7166-1644-3(0))* World Bk., Inc.

—All about Holidays: With Inspector McQ. Kain, Kathleen. 2004. (Early Literacy Library). 32p. (J). (gr. 2-5). 219.00 *(978-0-7166-1647-4(5))* World Bk., Inc.

—Hi, I'm Blackbeary: The Fruit of the Spirit Is Peace. Carlson, Melody. 2004. (Beary Patch Bears Ser.). 96p. bds. 6.99 *(978-1-58134-182-9(2))* Crossway.

—Molly the Great Misses the Bus: A Book about Being on Time. Marshall, Shelley. 2010. (Character Education with Super Ben & Molly the Great Ser.). 24p. (J). (gr. k-2). 23.60 *(978-0-7660-3518-8(2))*; pap. 9.35 *(978-0-7660-3743-4(6))* Enslow Publishing, LLC. (Enslow Elementary).

—Molly the Great Respects the Flag: A Book about Being a Good Citizen. Marshall, Shelley. 2010. (Character Education with Super Ben & Molly the Great Ser.). 24p. (J). (gr. k-2). 23.60 *(978-0-7660-3519-5(0))*; pap. 9.35 *(978-0-7660-3744-1(4))* Enslow Publishing, LLC. (Enslow Elementary).

—Molly the Great Tells the Truth: A Book about Honesty. Marshall, Shelley. 2010. (Character Education with Super Ben & Molly the Great Ser.). 24p. (J). (gr. k-2). 23.60 *(978-0-7660-3520-1(4))*; pap. 9.35 *(978-0-7660-3745-8(2)*, Enslow Elementary) Enslow Publishing, LLC.

—Molly the Great's Messy Bed: A Book about Responsibility. Marshall, Shelley. 2010. (Character Education with Super Ben & Molly the Great Ser.). 24p. (J). (gr. k-2). 23.60 *(978-0-7660-3517-1(4))*; pap. 9.35 *(978-0-7660-3742-7(8)*, Enslow Elementary) Enslow Publishing, LLC.

—The Story of Ronald Reagan. Pingry, Patricia A. 2006. (ENG.). 26p. (J). (gr. -1-k). bds. 7.69 *(978-0-8249-6621-8(X)*, Ideal Pubns.) Worthy Publishing.

—Super Ben's Brave Bike Ride: A Book about Courage. Marshall, Shelley. 2010. (Character Education with Super Ben & Molly the Great Ser.). 24p. (J). (gr. k-2). 23.60 *(978-0-7660-3515-7(8))*; pap. 9.35 *(978-0-7660-3740-3(1)*, Enslow Elementary) Enslow Publishing, LLC.

—Super Ben's Broken Cookie: A Book about Sharing. Marshall, Shelley. 2010. (Character Education with Super Ben & Molly the Great Ser.). 24p. (J). (gr. k-2). pap. 9.35 *(978-0-7660-3739-7(8)*, Enslow Elementary) Enslow Publishing, LLC.

—Super Ben's Dirty Hands: A Book about Healthy Habits. Marshall, Shelley. 2010. (Character Education with Super Ben & Molly the Great Ser.). 24p. (J). (gr. k-2). 23.60 *(978-0-7660-3513-3(1))*; pap. 9.35 *(978-0-7660-3738-0(X)*, Enslow Elementary) Enslow Publishing, LLC.

Mahan, Benton. Friends Forever. Scelsa, Greg & Debney, John. Faulkner, Stacey, ed. 2006. (J). pap. 2.99 *(978-1-59198-322-4(3))* Creative Teaching Pr., Inc.

—The Mouse Who Cried Cat, Vol. 4263. Williams, Rozanne Lanczak. 2005. (Reading for Fluency Ser.). 16p. (J). pap. 3.49 *(978-1-59198-163-3(8)*, 4263) Creative Teaching Pr., Inc.

—My Picture Story. Williams, Rozanne Lanczak. 2006. (Learn to Write Ser.). 8p. (J). (gr. k-2). pap. 3.49 *(978-1-59198-281-4(2)*, 6175) Creative Teaching Pr., Inc.

—My Picture Story. Williams, Rozanne Lanczak. Maio, Barbara & Faulkner, Stacey, eds. 2006. (J). per. 6.99 *(978-1-59198-332-3(0))* Creative Teaching Pr., Inc.

—Patty Cat: Short Vowel A. deRubertis, Barbara. 2006. (Let's Read Together ® Ser.). (ENG.). 32p. (J). (gr. -1-2). pap. 5.95 *(978-1-57565-000-5(2))* Astra Publishing Hse.

—Today Is Somebody's Birthday. Williams, Rozanne Lanczak. 2005. (Reading for Fluency Ser.). 8p. (J). pap. 2.49 *(978-1-59198-140-4(9)*, 4240) Creative Teaching Pr., Inc.

—Tuckerbean on the Moon, 1 vol. Kalz, Jill. 2009. (Read-It! Readers: Adventures of Tuckerbean Ser.). (ENG.). 24p. (J). (gr. -1-3). 21.32 *(978-1-4048-5234-1(4)*, Picture Window Bks.) Capstone.

Mahan, Cornell. Kellie's K-9 Kollection: Angel's Christmas Story. Harris, Kellie. 2018. (ENG.). 32p. (J). pap. 12.00 *(978-1-944583-26-2(2))* Laurel Rose Publishing.

Maharaj, Amar, jt. illus. see Maharaj, Christina.

Maharaj, Christina & Maharaj, Amar. The Tarot Cards: Wand of Creation: Book 3. Maharaj, Christina. 2019. (Tarot Cards Ser.: Vol. 3). (ENG.). 282p. (J). pap. 10.99 *(978-1-0908-8592-0(X))* Independently Published.

Mahardhika, Irfan. Ghost Wars: Rise of the Nanimals. Levin, Benjamin. 2018. (ENG.). 114p. (J). pap. 9.99 *(978-0-9997310-4-8(1))* Shrimlife Pr.

Mahardhika, Stevie. Ty the Turtle in the Land of the Can'ts. Rutledge, Susan. 2nd ed. 2019. (ENG.). 70p. (J). 21.99 *(978-1-950019-06-9(3))*; pap. 14.99 ***(978-1-950019-09-0(8))*** Willow Bend Pr.

Mahbab, Mustashrik. Manga Shakespeare: Julius Caesar. Shakespeare, William. 2008. (ENG.). 208p. (YA). (gr. 7-11). pap. 14.99 *(978-0-8109-7072-4(4)*, Amulet Bks.) Abrams, Inc.

Maher, Adele & Cline, Mike. Franky Fox's Fun with English Readers Level A1. Maher, Adele. 2007. 228p. (J). 26.99 *(978-0-9777419-5-3(8))* Lingo Pr. LLC.

Maher, Alex. Diego in the Dark: Being Brave at Night. Stierle, Cynthia. 2008. (Go, Diego, Go! Ser.). (ENG.). 16p. (J). (gr. -1-2). pap. 6.99 *(978-1-4169-5935-9(1)*, Simon Spotlight/Nickelodeon) Simon Spotlight/Nickelodeon.

—Diego's Sea Turtle Adventure. Ricci, Christine. 2006. 26p. (J). *(978-0-7172-9870-9(1))* Scholastic, Inc.

—El Safari de Diego. 2007. (Go, Diego, Go! Ser.).Tr. of Diego's Safari Rescue. (SPA.). 24p. (J). (gr. -1-2). pap. 3.99 *(978-1-4169-5998-4(X)*, Libros Para Ninos) Libros Para Ninos.

Maher, Bob. Emma & Topsy's Story: The Art of Loving & Letting Go. Edwards, Linda M. 2010. 20p. pap. 10.95 *(978-1-60911-808-2(1)*, Eloquent Bks.) Strategic Book Publishing & Rights Agency (SBPRA).

Maher, Terre. A Maze Me: Poems for Girls. Nye, Naomi Shihab. (ENG.). 128p. (YA). (gr. 8). 2014. pap. 10.99 *(978-0-06-058191-6(3))*; 2005. 17.99 *(978-0-06-058189-3(1))* HarperCollins Pubs. (Greenwillow Bks.).

Mahfoud, Michael. Hamster World Attacks. Atallah, John. Wade, Samar, ed. 2018. (ENG.). 88p. (J). pap. 7.95 ***(978-1-7278-8666-5(6))*** CreateSpace Independent Publishing Platform.

—Hamster World Attacks: The Cryptic Fire Stone. Atallah, John. Wade, Samar, ed. 2018. (Hamster World Ser.: Vol. 1). (ENG.). 84p. (J). pap. 16.95 ***(978-1-6967-8012-4(8))*** Independently Published.

Mahjouri. The Science of Sleep. Mahjouri. 2014. (ENG.). pap. 9.99 *(978-1-941006-04-7(3))* SoGo Creation.

Mahomet, John. Escape from Kingsland: Colored, 3rd Edition. Mistry, Kamlesh. 2019. (ENG.). 146p. (J). pap. 30.00 *(978-1-0968-7067-8(3))* Independently Published.

—The Humorous Hunt: Colored, 3rd Edition. Mistry, Kamlesh. 2019. (Kingsland Ser.: Vol. 1). (ENG.). 56p. (J). pap. 15.00 *(978-1-0971-1863-2(0))* Independently Published.
—King Dudley & the Golden Mystery: Colored, 3rd Edition. Mistry, Kamlesh. 2019. (Kingsland Ser.: Vol. 2). (ENG.). 86p. (J). pap. 20.00 *(978-1-0973-6877-8(7))* Independently Published.
Mahoney, Catherine. If Only I Could Bark. Weingarth, Debra. 2014. (J). *(978-0-9904469-0-3(5))* City Girl Gone Country.
Mahoney, Daniel & Wood, Hannah. Ocean Wonders. Ranson, Erin. Top That! Staff, ed. 2007. (Sparkling Slide Nature Bks.). (ENG.). 12p. (J). (gr. -1). 9.99 *(978-1-84666-167-9(6))* Top That! Publishing PLC GBR. Dist: Independent Pubs. Group.
Mahoney, Daniel, jt. illus. see Mahoney, Daniel J.
Mahoney, Daniel J. The Happy Hippos. Charlesworth, Liza & Scholastic, Inc. Staff. 2005. (ENG.). 16p. (J). (gr. -1-1). pap. 2.99 *(978-0-439-69023-2(4))* Scholastic, Inc.
—I See a Monster! Young, Laurie. 2007. (Touch & Feel Ser.). 12p. (gr. -1-k). 15.95 *(978-1-58117-574-5(4),* Intervisual/Piggy Toes) Bendon, Inc.
—I See a Monster. 2008. (ENG.). 12p. (J). bds. 5.95 *(978-1-58117-729-9(1),* Intervisual/Piggy Toes) Bendon, Inc.
Mahoney, Daniel J. & Mahoney, Daniel. I See a Monster! Young, Laurie. 2006. (ENG.). 12p. (J). (gr. -1-k). bds. 10.95 *(978-1-58117-483-0(7),* Intervisual/Piggy Toes) Bendon, Inc.
Mahoney, Daniel J., jt. illus. see Wood, Hannah.
Mahoney, Trish. God Made Me & You: Celebrating God's Design for Ethnic Diversity. Linne, Shai. 2018. (ENG.). (J). 15.99 *(978-1-948130-13-4(0))* New Growth Pr.
Mahurin, Matt. Grumbles from the Forest: Fairy-Tale Voices with a Twist. Yolen, Jane & Dotlich, Rebecca Kai. 2013. (ENG.). 40p. (J). (gr. 2-5). 16.95 *(978-1-59078-867-7(2),* Wordsong) Boyds Mills Pr.
Mai Long. Tam & Cam/Tam Cam: The Ancient Vietnamese Cinderella Story. Minh Quoc. Smith, William, tr. from VIE. 2006. (ENG & VIE.). 32p. (J). (gr. 1-4). 16.95 *(978-0-9701654-4-2(7))* East West Discovery Pr.
Mai-Wyss, Tatjana. Audrey (Cow) Bar-el, Dan. 2014.Tr. of Cow. (ENG.). 234p. (J). (gr. 2-5). 17.99 *(978-1-77049-602-6(5),* Tundra Bks.) Tundra Bks. CAN. Dist: Penguin Random Hse. LLC.
—Audrey (Cow) Bar-El, Dan. 2016. (ENG.). 240p. (J). (gr. 2-4). pap. 9.99 *(978-1-77049-603-3(3),* Tundra Bks.) Tundra Bks. CAN. Dist: Penguin Random Hse. LLC.
—Bunny's Book Club. Silvestro, Annie. 2017. 40p. (J). (gr. -1-2). 17.99 *(978-0-553-53758-1(X),* Doubleday Bks. for Young Readers) Random Hse. Children's Bks.
—Bunny's Book Club Goes to School. Silvestro, Annie. 2019. (ENG.). 40p. (J). (gr. -1-2). 17.99 *(978-0-525-64464-4(4),* Doubleday Bks. for Young Readers) Random Hse. Children's Bks.
—My Teacher Dances on the Desk. Gagliano, Eugene. 2009. (ENG.). 48p. (J). (gr. k-6). pap. 6.95 *(978-1-58536-446-6(0))* Sleeping Bear Pr.
—One Fine Shabbat. Barash, Chris. ed. 2016. (ENG.). 12p. (J). (gr. -1 — 1). E-Book 23.99 *(978-1-4677-9614-9(X));* Vol. bds. 5.99 *(978-1-4677-5871-0(X),* 9781467758710) Lerner Publishing Group. (Kar-Ben Publishing).
—That's Not How You Play Soccer, Daddy!, 1 vol. Shahan, Sherry. 2007. (ENG.). 32p. (J). (gr. -1-3). 15.95 *(978-1-56145-416-7(8),* Peachtree Junior) Peachtree Publishing Co. Inc.
—A Tree for Emmy. Rodman, Mary Ann. (ENG.). 32p. (J). (gr. -1-3). 2018. pap. 7.95 *(978-1-68263-037-2(4));* 2009. 15.95 *(978-1-56145-475-4(3))* Peachtree Publishing Co. Inc.
—The Twelve Days of Christmas in South Carolina. Long, Melinda. (Twelve Days of Christmas in America Ser.). (J). (-k). 2016. 22p. bds. 7.95 *(978-1-4549-2058-8(0));* 2010. 40p. 12.95 *(978-1-4027-6672-5(6))* Sterling Publishing Co., Inc.
—Whole-Y Cow! Fractions Are Fun. Souders, Taryn. 2010. (ENG.). 40p. (J). (gr. 1-4). 15.95 *(978-1-58536-460-2(6),* 202182) Sleeping Bear Pr.
Maia, Chavez Larkin. My Mom's Not Cool. Rubi, Nicholas. 2008. 24p. (J). per. 12.95 *(978-0-9776906-4-0(4))* Blueline Publishing.
Maiborada, Tanya. The Hunting of the Great Bear: A Native American Folktale. Malaspina, Ann. 2013. (Folktales from Around the World Ser.). (ENG.). 24p. (J). (gr. k-3). 28.50 *(978-1-62323-616-8(9),* 206383) Child's World, Inc., The.
Maichin, Christine. Little Big Sister on the Move. McCoy, Amy B. 2019. (Little Big Sister Ser.: Vol. 2). (ENG.). 248p. (J). pap. 9.99 ***(978-1-7330362-0-7(2))*** McCoy, Amy.
Maiden, D. W. & Govoni, Dennis, photos by. Insects & Spiders. Walls, Suzanne L. 2012. 64p. (J). pap. 14.95 *(978-0-9841960-9-8(9))* Chantilly Books.
Maidment, Mikaila. Otter Lee Brave, 1 vol. Brown, Rena Cherry. 2012. (ENG.). 48p. (J). (gr. -1-3). 16.99 *(978-0-7643-4155-7(3),* 4632) Schiffer Publishing, Ltd.
Maidment, Stella. The Star Child. Whelan, Olwyn. 2004. 40p. (J). 14.95 *(978-1-84458-039-2(3))* Avalon Publishing.
Maier, Albert. Brave Jack: Book 4: Stroon with Cool Raccoon Brown. Fez. 2007. (ENG.). 50p. pap. 26.50 *(978-1-4120-3962-8(2))* Trafford Publishing.
Maier, Christof. Vier Fäuste, Bohnen und Patronen. Marscalli, Maria. 2019. (GER.). 68p. (J). pap. 5.49 *(978-1-7967-4787-4(4))* Independently Published.
—Vier Fäuste Haben Niemals Angst. Schmidt, Hedda. 2019. (GER.). 68p. (J). pap. 5.99 *(978-1-7962-9762-1(3))* Independently Published.
Maier, Ximena. La Casa de los Miedos. Alcantara, Ricardo. 2009. (SPA.). 141p. (J). (gr. 3-5). pap. *(978-84-263-7269-7(4))* Vives, Luis Editorial (Edelvives).
Maier, Ximena. Cuento para Susana. Maier, Ximena, tr. Aldecoa, Josefina. 2003. (AlfaGuay Ser.). (SPA.). 80p. *(978-84-204-6611-8(5))* Ediciones Alfaguara.
Maihack, Mike. Geeks, Girls, & Secret Identities. Jung, Mike. 2012. (J). (ENG.). 320p. (gr. 3-7). 17.99 *(978-0-545-33548-5(5));* pap. *(978-0-545-33549-2(3))* Scholastic, Inc. (Levine, Arthur A. Bks.).
Maihack, Mike. Fallen Empires. Maihack, Mike. 2019. (Cleopatra in Space Ser.: 5). (ENG.). 208p. (J). (gr. 3-7). 24.99 *(978-1-338-20413-1(0));* pap. 14.99 *(978-1-338-20412-4(2))* Scholastic, Inc. (Graphix).
—The Golden Lion, Bk. 4. Maihack, Mike. 2017. (Cleopatra in Space Ser.: 4). (ENG.). 208p. (J). (gr. 3-7). 22.99 *(978-0-545-83871-9(1));* pap. 14.99 *(978-0-545-83872-6(X))* Scholastic, Inc. (Graphix).
—The Thief & the Sword. Maihack, Mike. 2015. (Cleopatra in Space Ser.: 2). (ENG.). 192p. (J). (gr. 3-7). 22.99 *(978-0-545-52844-3(5),* Graphix) Scholastic, Inc.
Maijala, Marika. The Piano, 1 vol. Virta, Juha. 2018. 32p. (J). (gr. -1-4). 16.99 *(978-1-4236-4926-7(5))* Gibbs Smith, Publisher.
—Where's Your Creativity? Rosen, Aaron & Watts, Riley. 2018. (ENG.). 32p. (J). (gr. -1-k). 16.95 *(978-1-84976-509-1(X))* Tate Publishing, Ltd. GBR. Dist: Hachette Bk. Group.
Mailer, Maggie. Lara's First Christmas, 1 vol. Howell, Alice O. 2004. (ENG.). 96p. (J). pap. 9.95 *(978-0-88010-553-8(4),* Bell Pond Bks.) SteinerBooks, Inc.
Mailey, Maria C. & Neuburger, Jenny. I'm Good, I'm Beautiful, I'm Smart. Goss, Leon. 2005. (J). per. *(978-1-933156-02-6(3),* VisionQuest Kids) GSVQ Publishing.
Mailhot, Eileen. Oh Mylanta! They Said, There's No Santa! Gaudreau, Ryan D. 2018. (ENG.). 28p. (J). pap. 13.99 *(978-1-7329482-9-7(1))* Mindstir Media.
Main, Valerie. The Kirby Boys' Adventure. Beaudin, Karen. 2016. (ENG.). (J). 41.99 *(978-1-4984-9408-3(0));* pap. 31.99 *(978-1-4984-9407-6(2))* Salem Author Services.
Maincent, Karine. How to Survive on a Desert Island: Operation Robinson!, 1 vol. Tribaudeau, Denis. 2019. (ENG.). 64p. (J). (gr. 3-6). pap. 14.99 *(978-0-7643-5706-0(9),* 16272) Schiffer Publishing, Ltd.
Maines, Sherry a. A Day in the Life of Me! Maines, Sherry a. 2019. (ENG.). 50p. (J). (gr. 1-3). pap. 11.99 ***(978-0-578-53654-5(4))*** Sherry A. Maines.
Maione, Heather. The Cats in the Doll Shop. McDonough, Yona Zeldis. 2012. (ENG.). 128p. (J). (gr. 2-4). 18.69 *(978-0-670-01279-4(3))* Penguin Young Readers Group.
—The Doll Shop Downstairs. McDonough, Yona Zeldis. 2011. (ENG.). 144p. (J). (gr. 2-5). 5.99 *(978-0-14-241691-4(6),* Puffin Books) Penguin Young Readers Group.
—How Oliver Olson Changed the World. Mills, Claudia. 2011. (ENG.). 128p. (J). (gr. 2-5). pap. 6.99 *(978-0-312-67282-9(9),* 900072371) Square Fish.
—Remembering Mrs. Rossi. Hest, Amy. 2007. (Annie & Leo Ser.). (ENG.). 192p. (J). (gr. 4-6). 21.19 *(978-0-7636-2163-6(3))* Candlewick Pr.
—Remembering Mrs. Rossi. Hest, Amy. 2010. 192p. (J). (gr. 3-7). 6.99 *(978-0-7636-4089-7(1))* Candlewick Pr.
Maione, Heather, jt. illus. see Maione, Heather Harms.
Maione, Heather Harms. Annie Glover Is Not a Tree Lover. Maione, Heather Harms. Beard, Darleen Bailey. 2009. (ENG.). 128p. (J). (gr. 2-5). 18.99 *(978-0-374-30351-8(7),* 9780374303518, Farrar, Straus & Giroux (BYR)) Farrar, Straus & Giroux.
Maione, Heather Harms & Maione, Heather. Princess Bess Gets Dressed. Cuyler, Margery. 2009. (ENG.). 32p. (J). (gr. -1-3). 18.99 *(978-1-4169-3833-0(8),* Simon & Schuster Bks. For Young Readers) Simon & Schuster Bks. For Young Readers.
Mair, Jacqueline. Folktales of America: Stockings of Buttermilk: Traditional Stories from the United States of America. Philip, Neil. 2018. (ENG.). 128p. (J). (gr. 3-7). 13.99 *(978-1-86147-859-7(3),* Armadillo) Anness Publishing GBR. Dist: National Bk. Network.
—Folktales of Mexico: Horse Hooves & Chicken Feet: Traditional Mexican Stories. Philip, Neil. 2018. 96p. (J). (gr. 3-7). 13.99 *(978-1-86147-857-3(7),* Armadillo) Anness Publishing GBR. Dist: National Bk. Network.
—Indian Folk Tales: Eighteen Stories of Magic, Fate, Bravery & Wonder. Ness, Caroline & Philip, Neil. 2019. 128p. (J). (gr. -1-12). 15.00 *(978-1-86147-858-0(5),* Armadillo) Anness Publishing GBR. Dist: National Bk. Network.
Maisch, Klara. The Stubborn Gal: The True Story of an Undefeated Sled Dog Racer. O'Neill, Dan. 2015. (ENG.). 32p. 15.95 *(978-1-60223-272-3(5))* Univ. of Alaska Pr.
Maisey-Shinnick, Toni. My Mum's a Princess. Eckersley, Carol. 2019. (ENG.). 28p. (J). pap. 10.00 ***(978-1-7328957-3-7(2))*** Sentimental Bloke Holdings International.
Maiste, Piia. Anna's Teeth. Petrone, Epp. 2013. 94p. pap. *(978-9949-511-27-3(5))* Petrone Print.
Maizel, Karen. Big Brother Now: A Story about Me & Our New Baby. Sheldon, Annette. 2008. 32p. (J). (gr. -1-1). 14.95 *(978-1-4338-0381-9(X));* pap. 9.95 *(978-1-4338-0382-6(8))* American Psychological Assn. (Magination Pr.).
—Big Sister Now: A Story about Me & Our New Baby. Sheldon, Annette. 2005. 32p. (J). (gr. -1-1). per. 9.95 *(978-1-59147-244-5(X));* 14.95 *(978-1-59147-243-8(1))* American Psychological Assn. (Magination Pr.).
—Jake Goes Fishing, 1 vol. Bowman, Crystal. 2007. (I Can Read! / the Jake Ser.). (ENG.). 32p. (J). (gr. -1-3). pap. 4.99 *(978-0-310-71454-5(0))* Zonderkidz.
—Jake Helps Out, 1 vol., Level 2. Bowman, Crystal. 2007. (Jake Ser.). (ENG.). 32p. (J). (gr. -1-3). pap. 4.99 *(978-0-310-71457-6(5))* Zonderkidz.
—Jake Plays Ball, 1 vol. Bowman, Crystal. 2007. (I Can Read! / the Jake Ser.). (ENG.). 32p. (J). (gr. -1-3). pap. 4.99 *(978-0-310-71455-2(9))* Zonderkidz.
—Jake's Brave Night, 1 vol. Bowman, Crystal. 2007. (I Can Read! / the Jake Ser.). (ENG.). 32p. (J). (gr. -1-3). pap. 4.99 *(978-0-310-71456-9(7))* Zonderkidz.
—Package. Bauer, Roger. l.t. ed. 2005. (ENG.). 8p. (gr. k-2). pap. 7.95 *(978-1-879835-84-9(3),* Kaeden Bks.) Kaeden Corp.
—Time for a Bath! World of Discovery II. Mader, Jan. l.t. ed. 2005. (ENG.). 8p. (gr. k-1). pap. 7.95 *(978-1-879835-46-7(0),* Kaeden Bks.) Kaeden Corp.
Maizels, Jennie. The Great Grammar Book. Petty, Kate. 2018. (ENG.). 14p. (J). (gr. 2-5). 24.99 *(978-0-7636-9575-0(0))* Candlewick Pr.
—Pop-Up Shakespeare. The Reduced Shakespeare Co., The Reduced. 2017. (ENG.). 10p. (J). (gr. 2-5). 19.99 *(978-0-7636-9874-4(1))* Candlewick Pr.
Maizels, Jennie. Pop-Up New York. Maizels, Jennie. 2014. (ENG.). 12p. (J). (gr. k-4). 19.99 *(978-0-7636-7162-4(2))* Candlewick Pr.
Majan, Daniel. Bobby & Mandee's Monster Tips for a Happy Halloween. Kahn, Robert. 2020. (ENG.). 50p. (J). pap. 18.99 ***(978-1-7960-8668-3(1))*** Xlibris Corp.
—A Penny's Worth. Burke, Nicole. 2019. (ENG.). 24p. (J). pap. 15.99 ***(978-1-5245-7583-0(6))*** Xlibris Corp.
Majewski, Dawn. Borya & the Burps: An Eastern European Adoption Story. McNamara, Joan. 2005. 30p. (J). (gr. -1 — 1). 18.00 *(978-0-944934-31-9(5))* Perspectives Pr., Inc.
—Sam's Sister. Bond, Juliet C. 2004. (J). 18.00 *(978-0-944934-30-2(7))* Perspectives Pr., Inc.
Majewski, Julie. Color with Max! Activity & Coloring Book. Majewski, Anthony M. T. & Maximus. 2010. 16p. (J). pap., act. bk. ed. 4.99 *(978-0-615-38985-1(6))* Emarketing Of Michigan, LLC.
Major, Rebekah. What Do You See in Me I am Who I am. Major, Gail Baccelli. 2013. (ENG.). 32p. (J). pap. 9.95 *(978-1-939289-22-3(X),* Little Creek Bks.) Jan-Carol Publishing, INC.
Major, Rebekah. Mama Wrex. Major, Rebekah. 2014. (ENG.). (J). pap. 10.95 *(978-1-939289-46-9(7),* Little Creek Bks.) Jan-Carol Publishing, INC.
Major, Sarah. Alphabet Tales. Major, Sarah. 2010. 139p. (J). pap. 19.95 *(978-0-9829873-3-9(1))* Child1st Pubns., LLC.
—Easy-For-Me Children's Readers Set C. Major, Sarah. 2012. pap. 52.95 *(978-1-936981-49-6(1))* Child1st Pubns., LLC.
—Right-Brained Addition & Subtraction: A Forget Memorization Book. Major, Sarah. 2013. (ENG.). 182p. (J). pap. 28.95 *(978-1-936981-54-0(8))* Child1st Pubns., LLC.
—Right-Brained Place Value: A Forget Memorization Book. Major, Sarah. 2013. 224p. (J). pap. 29.95 *(978-1-936981-55-7(6))* Child1st Pubns., LLC.
—SnapWords® Mini-Lessons: How to Teach Each SnapWord Integrating Spelling, Writing, & Phonics Concepts. Major, Sarah. 2013. (ENG.). (J). pap. 14.95 *(978-1-936981-56-4(4))* Child1st Pubns., LLC.
—Writing the Visual, Kinesthetic, & Auditory Alphabet. Major, Sarah. 2007. 30p. (J). pap. 9.99 *(978-0-9829873-2-2(3))* Child1st Pubns., LLC.
Majors, Sarah. Easy-For-Me Reading Teaching Manual: A Snap for the Teacher... a Cinch for the Child. Majors, Sarah. 2nd ed. 2013. (ENG.). 92p. (J). pap. 19.95 *(978-1-936981-57-1(2))* Child1st Pubns., LLC.
Majumder, Ankur & Soni, M. S. Ruhi. Polar Bear Pete's Perfect Performance. Peterson, M. S. Natasha Celeste. 2017. (ENG.). 28p. (J). pap. *(978-0-9952330-3-4(9))* Peterson, Natasha.
Majumder, Ankur, jt. illus. see Patachitra, Studio.
Mak, Anneliese. Sasha & Puck & the Cordial Cordial. Nayeri, Daniel. 2019. (Elixir Fixers Ser.: 2). (ENG.). 128p. (J). (gr. 1-5). pap. 5.99 *(978-0-8075-7250-4(0),* 807572500); 14.99 *(978-0-8075-7243-6(8),* 807572438) Whitman, Albert & Co.
—Sasha & Puck & the Potion of Luck. Nayeri, Daniel. 2019. (Elixir Fixers Ser.: 1). (ENG.). 128p. (J). (gr. 1-5). pap. 5.99 *(978-0-8075-7249-8(7),* 807572497); 14.99 *(978-0-8075-7242-9(X),* 080757242X) Whitman, Albert & Co.
Mak, Ding Sang. Everyday Life: Through Chinese Peasant Art. Morrissey, Tricia. 2009. (ENG.). 36p. (J). (gr. -1-5). pap. 9.95 *(978-1-934159-18-7(2))* ThingsAsian Pr.
Mak, Kam. My Chinatown: One Year in Poems. Mak, Kam. 2016. (ENG.). 32p. (J). (gr. -1-3). pap. 7.99 *(978-0-06-443732-5(9))* HarperCollins Pubs.
Maka, Stephen, photos by. Life in a Wetland. Stewart, Melissa. 2003. (Ecosystems in Action Ser.). (ENG., 72p. (gr. 5-9). lib. bdg. 26.60 *(978-0-8225-4687-0(6))* Lerner Publishing Group.
Makansi, Elena. The Secret of the Santa Box. Fenoglio, Christopher. (ENG.). 32p. (J). (gr. 2). 2018. pap. 9.95 *(978-1-7321391-4-5(8));* 2017. 16.95 *(978-0-9963901-6-3(2))* TreeHse. Publishing Group.
Makartichan, Karine. Three Pampered Pugs: The Patriotic Pet Contest. Kitabjian, Sandra. 2019. (ENG.). 30p. (J). (gr. k-2). 18.99 ***(978-0-578-60451-0(5));*** pap. 10.99 ***(978-0-578-59816-1(7))*** Sandra Kitabjian.
Make Believe Ideas Ltd. Christmas Fun. Make Believe Ideas Ltd. 2020. (Sticker Book Ser.). (ENG.). 48p. (J). (gr. -1-7). pap. ***(978-1-78947-703-0(4))*** Make Believe Ideas.
—Clay Modeling. Make Believe Ideas Ltd. 2020. (ENG.). 12p. (J). (gr. 2-5). pap. ***(978-1-78947-399-5(3))*** Make Believe Ideas.
—Halloween Treats. Make Believe Ideas Ltd. 2020. (Sticker Book Ser.). (ENG.). 48p. (J). (gr. -1-7). pap. ***(978-1-78947-702-3(6))*** Make Believe Ideas.
—I Love Hearts. Make Believe Ideas Ltd. 2020. (ENG.). 48p. (J). pap. ***(978-1-78947-419-0(1))*** Make Believe Ideas.
—I Love Unicorns Coloring. Make Believe Ideas Ltd. 2020. (ENG.). 64p. (J). (gr. -1-7). ***(978-1-78947-447-3(7))*** Make Believe Ideas.
—Mega Dino File. Make Believe Ideas Ltd. 2017. (ENG.). 36p. (J). ***(978-1-78692-770-5(5))*** Make Believe Ideas.
Make Believe Ideas Ltd. My Super Sparkly Sticker Purse. Make Believe Ideas Ltd. 2020. (ENG.). 48p. (J). (gr. -1-7). pap. *(978-1-78947-323-0(3))* Make Believe Ideas.
Make Believe Ideas Ltd. Puffy Stickers Designer Diva. Make Believe Ideas Ltd. 2020. (Puffy Stickers Ser.). (ENG.). 54p. (J). (gr. -1-7). pap. ***(978-1-78947-658-3(5))*** Make Believe Ideas.
—Puffy Stickers I Love Unicorns. Make Believe Ideas Ltd. 2020. (ENG.). 54p. (J). (gr. -1-7). pap. ***(978-1-78947-657-6(7))*** Make Believe Ideas.
—Shake Touch Play. Make Believe Ideas Ltd. 2020. (ENG.). 12p. (J). bds. ***(978-1-78947-365-0(9))*** Make Believe Ideas.
Make Believe Ideas Ltd. Space. Make Believe Ideas Ltd. 2019. (ENG.). 40p. (J). *(978-1-78947-173-1(7))* Make Believe Ideas.
—Sparkling Unicorns. Make Believe Ideas Ltd. 2019. (ENG.). 40p. (J). *(978-1-78692-852-8(3))* Make Believe Ideas.
Make Believe Ideas Ltd. Sticker Activity Book My Rainbow Purse. Make Believe Ideas Ltd. 2020. (ENG.). 48p. (J). (gr. -1-7). pap. ***(978-1-78947-656-9(9))*** Make Believe Ideas.
—Sticker Activity Book My Unicorn Purse. Make Believe Ideas Ltd. 2020. (ENG.). 48p. (J). (gr. -1-7). pap. ***(978-1-78947-655-2(0))*** Make Believe Ideas.
—Super-Cute Coloring. Make Believe Ideas Ltd. 2020. (ENG.). 64p. (J). (gr. -1-7). ***(978-1-78947-446-6(9))*** Make Believe Ideas.
Make Believe Ideas Ltd. 5 Minute Enchanting Tales. Make Believe Ideas Ltd. 2019. (ENG.). 192p. (J). (gr. -1-7). *(978-1-78947-290-5(3))* Make Believe Ideas.
—1000 Easter Stickers. Make Believe Ideas Ltd. 2020. (ENG.). 48p. (J). (gr. -1-7). pap. *(978-1-78947-288-2(1))* Make Believe Ideas.
Maker, Mark. Daddy Drew Me Upside Down. Maker, Mark. 2018. (ENG.). 42p. (J). (gr. k-6). pap. 11.59 *(978-1-988159-23-2(7))* Guardian Publishing.
Maki, Tab. Timmy the Tiny Troubled Turtle, 1 vol. Syrstad, Suzi. 2009. 13p. pap. 24.95 *(978-1-61546-455-5(7))* PublishAmerica, Inc.
Maki, Yoko. Aishiteruze Baby, Vol. 3. Maki, Yoko. 2006. (Aishiteruze Baby Ser.). (ENG.). 208p. pap. 8.99 *(978-1-4215-0570-1(3))* Viz Media.
Makis, Sidney. Icy the Iceberg. Friend, Larry. 2008. 28p. pap. 13.95 *(978-1-4327-3777-1(5))* Outskirts Pr., Inc.
Makonin, Anna. Fishing with Dad: The Little Dinosaur with Big Ideas. Makonin, Anna. 2018. (ENG.). 36p. (J). *(978-0-9938188-2-0(X))* Nutnay Pr.
—Puddles or Lunch? The Little Dinosaur Who Stomps in Puddles. Makonin, Anna. 2014. (ENG.). 40p. (J). *(978-0-9938188-1-3(1))* Nutnay Pr.
Makowski, Robin Lee. Dogs. 2004. (J). *(978-1-59203-088-0(2))* Learning Challenge, Inc.
—Sea Creatures. 2004. (J). *(978-1-59203-090-3(4))* Learning Challenge, Inc.
Makuc, Lucy. Christmas Drawing Wonderland! Besel, Jennifer M. 2013. (My First Sketchpads Ser.). (ENG.). (J). (gr. 1-3). 40p. pap. 4.95 *(978-1-4765-3447-3(0));* 24p. 25.99 *(978-1-4765-3092-5(0))* Capstone. (Capstone Pr.).
—Drawing a Christmas Wonderland: A Step-by-Step Sketchpad. Besel, Jennifer M. 2014. (My First Sketchpads Ser.). (ENG.). 48p. (J). (gr. 1-3). pap. 5.95 *(978-1-4914-1748-5(X),* 127182, Capstone Pr.) Capstone.
—Halloween Drawing Spooktacular! Besel, Jennifer M. 2013. (My First Sketchpads Ser.). (ENG.). (J). (gr. 1-3). 40p. pap. 4.95 *(978-1-4765-3446-6(2));* 24p. 25.99 *(978-1-4765-3091-8(2))* Capstone. (Capstone Pr.).
—Holiday Sketchbook. Besel, Jennifer M. 2013. (Holiday Sketchbook Ser.). (ENG.). (J). (gr. 1-3). 40p. pap., pap., pap. 19.80 *(978-1-4765-3653-8(8));* 24p. lib. bdg., lib. bdg., lib. bdg. 103.96 *(978-1-4765-3652-1(X))* Capstone. (Capstone Pr.).
Makuc, Lucy. ¿Qué Soy? Hillert, Margaret. 2020. (Beginning-To-Read: Spanish Easy Stories Ser.). (SPA.). 32p. (J). (-2). 22.60 ***(978-1-68450-868-6(1));*** pap. 11.94 ***(978-1-68404-546-4(0))*** Norwood Hse. Pr.
Makuc, Lucy. Thanksgiving Drawing Feast! Besel, Jennifer M. 2013. (Holiday Sketchbook Ser.). (ENG.). (J). (gr. 1-3). 40p. pap. 4.95 *(978-1-4765-3448-0(9));* 24p. 25.99 *(978-1-4765-3093-2(9))* Capstone. (Capstone Pr.).
—Valentine's Day Drawing Treat! Besel, Jennifer M. 2013. (Holiday Sketchbook Ser.). (ENG.). (J). (gr. 1-3). 40p. pap. 4.95 *(978-1-4765-3449-7(7));* 24p. 25.99 *(978-1-4765-3094-9(7))* Capstone. (Capstone Pr.).
Makuc, Lucy & Dynamo Limited Staff. Drawing Faces: A Step-By-Step Sketchbook, 1 vol. Bolte, Mari. 2014. (My First Sketchbook Ser.). (ENG.). 24p. (J). (gr. 1-3). lib. bdg. 25.99 *(978-1-4914-0284-9(9),* Capstone Pr.) Capstone.
—Drawing Monsters: A Step-By-Step Sketchbook, 1 vol. Bolte, Mari. 2014. (My First Sketchbook Ser.). (ENG.). 24p. (J). (gr. 1-3). lib. bdg. 25.99 *(978-1-4914-0282-5(2),* Capstone Pr.) Capstone.
—Drawing Pets: A Step-By-Step Sketchbook, 1 vol. Bolte, Mari. 2014. (My First Sketchpads Ser.). (ENG.). 24p. (J). (gr. 1-3). lib. bdg. 25.99 *(978-1-4914-0281-8(4),* Capstone Pr.) Capstone.
—Drawing Vehicles: A Step-By-Step Sketchbook, 1 vol. Bolte, Mari. 2014. (My First Sketchpads Ser.). (ENG.). 24p. (J). (gr. 1-3). lib. bdg. 25.99 *(978-1-4914-0283-2(0),* Capstone Pr.) Capstone.
—My First Sketchbook, 1 vol. Bolte, Mari. 2014. (My First Sketchbook Ser.). (ENG.). 24p. (J). (gr. 1-3). lib. bdg., lib. bdg., lib. bdg. 103.96 *(978-1-4914-0285-6(7),* Capstone Pr.) Capstone.
Malak, Annabel. Cinderella. (Classic Stories Ser.). 48p. (J). (gr. -1-2). incl. audio *(978-2-921997-75-1(4))* Coffragants.
—Goldilocks & the Three Bears. (Classic Stories Ser.). 48p. (J). audio, audio compact disk *(978-2-921997-84-3(3))* Coffragants.
—Little Red Riding Hood. Sorgini, Linda. 2011. (ENG.). 16p. cd-rom 12.95 *(978-2-89558-408-7(7),* 9782895584087) Editions Alexandre Stanke CAN. Dist: Baker & Taylor Publisher Services (BTPS).
—The Three Little Pigs. Biddle, Charles, Jr. 2011. (ENG.). 16p. pap. 12.95 *(978-2-89558-409-4(5),* 9782895584094) Editions Alexandre Stanke CAN. Dist: Baker & Taylor Publisher Services (BTPS).
Malakar, Nilanjan. Flux: Celestial Genesis. White, W. L., III. 2020. (Flux Ser.: 1). (ENG.). 146p. (YA). pap. 24.99 ***(978-1-0983-1477-4(8))*** BookBaby.
—Flux: Sequence of Astrometry. White, W. L., III. 2020. (Flux Ser.: 2). (ENG.). 170p. (YA). pap. 24.99 ***(978-1-0983-1479-8(4))*** BookBaby.
Malam, John. Ancient Egypt. Malam, John. 2004. (Picturing the Past Ser.). 32p. (J). 15.95 *(978-1-59270-021-9(7))* Enchanted Lion Bks., LLC.
—Library: From Ancient Scrolls to the Worldwide Web: A Building Works Book. Malam, John. 2006. 32p. (J). (gr. 4-18). reprint ed. 17.00 *(978-1-4223-5173-4(4))* DIANE Publishing Co.

M

—Theater: From First Rehearsal to Opening Night! a Building Works Book. Malam, John. 2006. 32p. (J). (gr. k-4). 17.00 *(978-1-4223-5179-6(3))* DIANE Publishing Co.

Malan, David. What Is the Story of Dracula? Burgan, Michael & Who HQ. 2020. (What Is the Story Of? Ser.). (ENG.). 112p. (J). (gr. 3-7). 6.99 ***(978-1-5247-8845-2(7))***; 15.99 ***(978-1-5247-8846-9(5))*** Penguin Young Readers Group. (Penguin Workshop).

Malan, David. What Is the Story of Frankenstein? Keenan, Sheila & Who HQ. 2019. (What Is the Story Of? Ser.). 112p. (J). (gr. 3-7). 6.99 *(978-1-5247-8842-1(2))*; 15.99 *(978-1-5247-8843-8(0))* Penguin Young Readers Group. (Penguin Workshop).

—Where Is the Tower of London? Pascal, Janet B. & Who HQ. 2018. (Where Is? Ser.). 112p. (J). (gr. 3-7). 5.99 *(978-1-5247-8606-9(3))*; lib. bdg. 15.99 *(978-1-5247-8608-3(X))* Penguin Young Readers Group. (Penguin Workshop).

Maland, Nick. Big Blue Whale. Davies, Nicola. 2008. (Read, Listen, & Wonder Ser.). (ENG.). 32p. (J). (gr. -1-3). pap. 8.99 *(978-0-7636-3822-1(6))* Candlewick Pr.

—Big Blue Whale. Davies, Nicola. 2015. 32p. pap. 7.00 *(978-1-61003-542-2(9))* Center for the Collaborative Classroom.

—Colour in the Queen: Celebrate the Queen's Life with 15 Frameable Prints. 2016. (ENG.). 32p. (J). (gr. -1-2). pap. 9.99 *(978-1-84780-884-4(0))*, Frances Lincoln Children's Bks.) Quarto Publishing Group UK GBR. Dist: Hachette Bk. Group.

—Mr. Tiger, Betsy, & the Blue Moon. Gardner, Sally. 2020. (ENG.). 192p. (J). (gr. 3-7). 16.99 *(978-0-593-09516-4(2))*, Penguin Workshop) Penguin Young Readers Group.

—Oliver Who Would Not Sleep! Bergman, Mara. 2007. (J). *(978-0-439-92827-4(3))*, Levine, Arthur A. Bks.) Scholastic, Inc.

—Snip Snap! What's That? Bergman, Mara. 2005. (ENG.). 32p. (J). (gr. -1-3). 17.99 *(978-0-06-077754-8(0))*, Greenwillow Bks.) HarperCollins Pubs.

—Wishing for Tomorrow: The Sequel to a Little Princess. McKay, Hilary. (ENG.). 288p. (J). (gr. 3-7). 2011. pap. 6.99 *(978-1-4424-0170-9(2))*; 2010. 16.99 *(978-1-4424-0169-3(9))* McElderry, Margaret K. Bks. (McElderry, Margaret K. Bks.).

—You've Got Dragons, 1 vol. Cave, Kathryn. 2020. (ENG.). 32p. (J). (gr. 1-5). pap. 8.99 *(978-1-68263-171-3(0))* Peachtree Publishing Co. Inc.

Malara, Nicholas. Sasha & the Dragon. Wolfe, Laura E. I.t. ed. 2017. (ENG.). 32p. (J). 19.95 *(978-1-944967-27-7(3))* Ancient Faith Publishing.

Malasomma, Roberta. The Big Buna Bash. Arnold, Sara C. 2020. (ENG.). 36p. (J). (gr. k-4). 22.95 ***(978-1-951565-01-5(0))***; pap. 13.95 ***(978-1-951565-02-2(9))*** Brandylane Pubs., Inc.

Malatesta. The Juggler of Our Lady. France, Anatole & Ziolkowski, Jan M. 2018. (Juggling the Middle Ages Ser.). (ENG.). 78p. (J). 19.95 *(978-0-88402-434-7(2))*, 30447) Dumbarton Oaks.

Malbon, Mandy. A Puppy Named Cowboy. Gagnier, Susan Arce. 2018. (I Read, You Read Ser.: Vol. 1). (ENG.). 48p. (J). pap. 14.95 *(978-0-9993302-3-4(3))* Gagnier Enterprises.

Malbrough, Michael & Fisher, G. W. Fire Proves Iron: Grounded Stars. Malbrough, Page. 2004. 80p. (YA). per. 9.95 *(978-0-9758883-0-8(7))* Malbrough, Michael.

Malbrough, Mike. Warren & Dragon 100 Friends. Bernstein, Ariel. 2018. (Warren & Dragon Ser.: 1). 96p. (J). (gr. k-3). 14.99 *(978-0-425-28844-3(7))*, Viking Books for Young Readers) Penguin Young Readers Group.

—Warren & Dragon 100 Friends. Bernstein, Ariel. 2018. (Warren & Dragon Ser.: 1). 96p. (J). (gr. k-3). 5.99 *(978-0-425-28846-7(3))*, Puffin Books) Penguin Young Readers Group.

—Warren & Dragon Scary Sleepover. Bernstein, Ariel. 2019. 96p. (J). (gr. k-3). 5.99 *(978-0-451-48107-8(0))*, Puffin Books); 14.99 *(978-0-451-48105-4(4))*, Viking Books for Young Readers) Penguin Young Readers Group.

—Warren & Dragon Volcano Deluxe. Bernstein, Ariel. 2019. 96p. (J). (gr. k-3). 5.99 *(978-0-451-48104-7(6))*, Puffin Books); 14.99 *(978-0-451-48102-3(X))*, Viking Books for Young Readers) Penguin Young Readers Group.

—Weekend with Chewy. Bernstein, Ariel. 2018. (Warren & Dragon Ser.: 2). 96p. (J). (gr. k-3). 5.99 *(978-0-425-28849-8(8))*, Puffin Books); 14.99 *(978-0-425-28845-0(5))*, Viking Books for Young Readers) Penguin Young Readers Group.

—You Made Me a Dad. Sala, Laurenne. 2019. (ENG.). 32p. (J). (gr. -1-3). 15.99 *(978-0-06-239694-5(3))* HarperCollins Pubs.

Malbrough, Mike. Marigold Bakes a Cake. Malbrough, Mike. 2017. (ENG.). 40p. (J). (gr. -1-2). 17.99 *(978-1-5247-3738-2(0))*, Philomel Bks.) Penguin Young Readers Group.

—Marigold Finds the Magic Words. Malbrough, Mike. 2019. (ENG.). 40p. (J). (gr. -1-2). 17.99 *(978-1-5247-3743-6(7))*, Philomel Bks.) Penguin Young Readers Group.

Maldonado, Gina Lorena. Follow the Dots: 123. 2018. (Follow the Dots Ser.). (ENG.). 10p. (J). (— 1). bds. 8.99 *(978-1-68412-178-6(7))*, Silver Dolphin Bks.) Printers Row Publishing Group.

—Follow the Dots: ABC. 2018. (Follow the Dots Ser.). (ENG.). 10p. (J). (— 1). bds. 8.99 *(978-1-68412-177-9(9))*, Silver Dolphin Bks.) Printers Row Publishing Group.

—Go Away! & Let's Make a Rocket. Dale, Elizabeth. 2020. (Early Bird Readers — Red (Early Bird Stories (tm)) Ser.). (ENG.). 32p. (J). (gr. -1-2). pap. 7.99 *(978-1-5415-8730-4(8))*, Lerner Pubns.) Lerner Publishing Group.

—Trick or Treat on Animal Street. Fischer, Maggie. 2018. (ENG.). 14p. (J). (gr. -1-k). bds. 8.99 *(978-1-68412-433-6(6))*, Silver Dolphin Bks.) Printers Row Publishing Group.

Maldonado, Luis. Friends Having Fun. Maldonado, Luis, . 2007. 48p. (J). 3.95 *(978-0-9790699-1-8(2))* Empty Harbor Productions, LLC.

Male, Alan. Crocodile Crossing. Bull, Schuyler. 2005. (Amazing Animal Adventures Ser.). (ENG.). 36p. (J). (gr. -1-2). 15.95 *(978-1-59249-051-6(4))*, B7104); (gr. -1-2). pap. 6.95 *(978-1-59249-052-3(2))*, S7104); (gr. -1-2). 19.95 *(978-1-59249-390-6(4))*, BC7104); (gr. 2-2). 8.95 *(978-1-59249-391-3(2))*, SC7104) Soundprints.

—Crocodile Crossing. Bull, Schuyler M. 2003. (Soundprints' Amazing Animal Adventures! Ser.). (ENG.). 36p. (J). (gr. -1-3). 9.95 *(978-1-59249-060-8(3))*, PS7154); 2.95 *(978-1-59249-053-0(0))*, S7154) Soundprints.

Malecky, Aiden. Clarence Christopher Purdy. Doane, Bonnie. 2020. (ENG.). 42p. (J). 24.95 ***(978-1-0980-2837-4(6))***; pap. 14.95 ***(978-1-0980-2835-0(X))*** Christian Faith Publishing.

Maleev, Alex, et al. Civil War: The Road to Civil War. 2007. (ENG.). 160p. (YA). (gr. 8-17). 14.99 *(978-0-7851-1974-6(4))* Marvel Worldwide, Inc.

Maleev, Alex. Daredevil: Out, 5. Bendis, Brian Michael. 2003. 208p. (YA). pap. 19.99 *(978-0-7851-1074-3(7))* Marvel Worldwide, Inc.

—Daredevil by Brian Michael Bendis & Alex Maleev Omnibus Vol. 2. 2020. 656p. (YA). (gr. 8-17). 100.00 *(978-1-302-92167-5(3))* Marvel Worldwide, Inc.

—International Iron Man. 2017. (ENG.). 160p. (YA). (gr. 8-17). pap. 24.99 *(978-0-7851-9979-3(9))* Marvel Worldwide, Inc.

—Marvel Knights Daredevil by Bendis & Maleev: Underboss. 2018. (Marvel Knights Ser.: 1). (ENG.). 152p. (YA). (gr. 8-17). pap. 17.99 *(978-1-302-91403-5(0))* Marvel Worldwide, Inc.

Maleev, Alexander, et al. Batman Vol. 1: No Man's Land. Gale, Bob & Grayson, Devin K. rev. ed. 2006. (Batman Ser.: Vol. 1). (ENG.). 200p. (YA). 17.99 *(978-1-56389-564-7(1))* DC Comics.

Malekoff, Stephanie & Warner, Chalene. The Jumping Fish. Wrzosek, Jennifer. 2020. (ENG.). 36p. (J). pap. ***(978-1-5255-7126-8(5))***; ***(978-1-5255-7125-1(7))*** FriesenPress.

Malenfant, Isabelle. Morris Micklewhite & the Tangerine Dress, 1 vol. Baldacchino, Christine. 2014. (ENG.). 32p. (J). (gr. -1-2). 16.95 *(978-1-55498-347-6(9))* Groundwood Bks. CAN. Dist: Publishers Group West (PGW).

—Once upon a Balloon, 1 vol. Galbraith, Bree. 2013. (ENG.). 32p. (J). (gr. -1-k). 19.95 *(978-1-4598-0324-4(8))* Orca Bk. Pubs. USA.

—Pinny in Fall, 1 vol. Schwartz, Joanne. 2018. (ENG.). 32p. (J). (gr. k-2). 16.95 *(978-1-77306-106-1(2))* Groundwood Bks. CAN. Dist: Publishers Group West (PGW).

—Pinny in Summer, 1 vol. Schwartz, Joanne. 2016. (ENG.). 32p. (J). (gr. -1-2). 16.95 *(978-1-55498-782-5(2))* Groundwood Bks. CAN. Dist: Publishers Group West (PGW).

Malépart, Céline. Les Bisous. Stanké, Claudie. 2004. (Picture Bks.). (FRE.). 32p. (J). (gr. -1). *(978-2-89021-694-5(2))*; pap. *(978-2-89021-693-8(4))* Diffusion du livre Mirabel (DLM).

—Earth-Friendly Crafts: Clever Ways to Reuse Everyday Items. Ross, Kathy. 2011. (ENG.). 48p. (gr. 2-5). pap. 7.95 *(978-0-7613-7409-1(4))*, Millbrook Pr.) Lerner Publishing Group.

—L' Héritage de Julien. Tremblay, Alain Ulysse. 2004. (Roman Jeunesse Ser.). (FRE.). 96p. (J). (gr. 4-7). pap. *(978-2-89021-682-2(9))* Diffusion du livre Mirabel (DLM).

Malepart, Celine. When Pigs Fly: A Piggy Pop-up Book! 2008. (ENG.). 12p. 16.95 *(978-1-58117-671-1(6))*, Intervisual/Piggy Toes) Bendon, Inc.

Malet, Oriol, jt. illus. see Bonilla, Rocío.

Malik, Shehzil. A Girl Called Genghis Khan: The Story of Maria Toorpakai Wazir. Lord, Michelle. 2019. (People Who Shaped Our World Ser.: 5). 48p. (J). (gr. k). 16.95 *(978-1-4549-3136-2(1))* Sterling Publishing Co., Inc.

Malin, Jon & Izaakse, Sean. Thunderbolts Vol. 2: No Going Back. 2017. (ENG.). 144p. (YA). (gr. 8-17). pap. 17.99 *(978-0-7851-9669-3(2))* Marvel Worldwide, Inc.

Malkowski, Melissa. Larry the Turtle When Everyone Helps, Everyone Wins! Kleemann, Linda. 2005. (J). pap. 7.95 *(978-0-9776487-0-2(2))* Fencepost Communications Inc.

Mallam, Sally. L' Homme et le Renard: French-Arabic Edition. Shah, Idries. 2018. (Hoopoe Teaching-Stories Ser.). (FRE.). 40p. (J). (gr. k-2). pap. 9.99 ***(978-1-949358-47-6(X))***, Hoopoe Bks.) I S H K.

Mallam, Sally. The Man & the Fox. Shah, Idries. 2006. 32p. (J). (gr. -1). 18.00 *(978-1-883536-43-5(X))*; pap. 7.99 *(978-1-883536-60-2(X))* I S H K. (Hoopoe Bks.).

—The Man & the Fox: English-Dari Edition. Shah, Idries. 2017. (Hoopoe Teaching-Stories Ser.). (ENG.). (J). (gr. k-6). pap. 9.99 *(978-1-946270-13-9(X))*, Hoopoe Bks.) I S H K.

—The Man & the Fox: English-Pashto Edition. Shah, Idries. 2017. (Hoopoe Teaching-Stories Ser.). (ENG & PUS.). (J). (gr. k-6). pap. 9.99 *(978-1-944493-58-5(1))*, Hoopoe Bks.) I S H K.

—The Man & the Fox: English-Urdu Bilingual Edition. Shah, Idries. 2016. (URD & ENG.). (J). (gr. k-6). pap. 9.99 *(978-1-942698-82-1(8))*, Hoopoe Bks.) I S H K.

Mallam, Sally. Dende Maro: The Golden Prince. Mallam, Sally. 2009. 40p. (J). (gr. k-18). 17.99 *(978-1-933779-48-5(9))*, Hoopoe Bks.) I S H K.

Mallari, K. S. Happy to Be Me: Positive Affirmations for Little Girls. Mazor, Sarah. 2019. (Bedtime with a Smile Picture Bks.: Vol. 1). (ENG.). 40p. (J). pap. 12.98 *(978-1-7962-0336-3(X))* Independently Published.

Mallari, Kathleen Sue. Cassandra & the Strange Tale of the Blue-Footed Boobies. Lester, Michael H. 2019. (ENG.). 46p. (J). pap. 12.95 *(978-1-7310-2077-2(5))* Independently Published.

Mallari, Raymon. Lucky to Have a Friend Like You: A Lesson to Learn. Dillingham, Marquita Corine. 2018. (Death Ser.: Vol. 1). (ENG.). 94p. (J). pap. 10.00 *(978-1-9856-7972-6(8))* CreateSpace Independent Publishing Platform.

Mallea, Cristian. Bigfoot & Adaptation, 1 vol. Collins, Terry. 2011. (Monster Science Ser.). (ENG.). 32p. (J). (gr. 3-9). lib. bdg. 31.32 *(978-1-4296-6579-7(3))*, Capstone Pr.) Capstone.

—Encountering Aliens: Eyewitness Accounts, 1 vol. Kincade, Chris. 2014. (Eyewitness to the Unexplained Ser.). (ENG.). 32p. (J). (gr. 3-9). 31.32 *(978-1-4914-0244-3(X))*, Capstone Pr.) Capstone.

—George Washington: The Rise of America's First President. Biskup, Agnieszka. 2012. (American Graphic Ser.). (ENG.). 32p. (gr. 3-4). pap. 47.70 *(978-1-4296-9335-6(5))*, Capstone Pr.); (J). lib. bdg. 31.32 *(978-1-4296-8621-1(9))* Capstone.

—George Washington: The Rise of America's First President, 1 vol. Biskup, Agnieszka Józefina. 2012. (American Graphic Ser.). (ENG.). 32p. (J). (gr. 3-9). pap. 8.10 *(978-1-4296-9334-9(7))* Capstone.

—Mummies & Sound, 1 vol. Wacholtz, Anthony. 2013. (Monster Science Ser.). (ENG.). 32p. (gr. 3-9). (J). pap. 8.10 *(978-1-62065-818-5(6))*; 47.70 *(978-1-62065-819-2(4))*; (J). 31.32 *(978-1-4296-9930-3(2))* Capstone. (Capstone Pr.).

—Robert E. Lee: The Story of the Great Confederate General. Collins, Terry. (American Graphic Ser.). (ENG.). 32p. (gr. 3-4). 2011. pap. 47.70 *(978-1-4296-6436-3(3))*; 2010. (J). lib. bdg. 31.32 *(978-1-4296-5475-3(9))* Capstone. (Capstone Pr.).

Mallea, Cristian & Gervasio. Monster Science. Collins, Terry et al. 2013. (Monster Science Ser.). (ENG.). 32p. (J). (gr. 3-9). lib. bdg., lib. bdg., lib. bdg. 281.88 *(978-1-4765-0427-8(X))*, Capstone Pr.) Capstone.

Mallea, Cristian Javier. Bigfoot y Adaptación. Collins, Terry Lee. 2019. (Ciencias Monstruosas Ser.). (SPA.). 32p. (J). (gr. 3-9). lib. bdg. 31.32 *(978-1-5435-8264-2(8))*, 141274) Capstone.

Mallet, Lisa & Parchow, Marc. Challenging Mazes: 80 Timed Mazes to Test Your Skill! 2016. (Challenging... Bks.). (ENG.). 96p. (J). (gr. 3-7). pap. 7.99 *(978-1-4380-0788-5(4))*, B.E.S. Publishing) Peterson's.

Mallett, Keith. How Jelly Roll Morton Invented Jazz. Winter, Jonah. 2015. (ENG.). 32p. (J). (gr. k-3). 17.99 *(978-1-59643-963-4(7))*, 900126199) Roaring Brook Pr.

—Sing a Song: How Lift Every Voice & Sing Inspired Generations. Lyons, Kelly Starling. 2019. 32p. (J). (gr. k-3). 17.99 *(978-0-525-51609-5(3))*, Nancy Paulsen Books) Penguin Young Readers Group.

Mallett, Lisa. Forty-Eight Funny Faces: Use the Cling-On Stickers to Make Funny Faces! Golding, Elizabeth. 2015. (ENG.). 56p. (J). (gr. -1-2). pap. 8.99 *(978-1-4380-0599-7(7))*, B.E.S. Publishing) Peterson's.

—God Loves Me, My First Bible, 1 vol. Beck, Susan Elizabeth. 2017. (ENG.). 34p. (J). bds. 9.99 *(978-0-310-75931-7(5))* Zonderkidz.

Mallette, Dania. God Says I've Changed Your Dna: Walk As Children of the Light. _Meli, Ayani & D., Jessie. 2013. 24p. pap. 12.00 *(978-0-9846315-7-5(7))* JWD Publishing.

—The Three Keys. Dimarco, Tony. 2010. 146p. pap. 9.95 *(978-0-9818391-2-7(6))* Panoply Pubns.

Mallol, Judit. Blaire. Castle, Jennifer. 2018. (American Girl: Girl of the Year 2019 Ser.: 1). (ENG.). 192p. (J). (gr. 3-7). pap. 7.99 *(978-1-338-26711-2(6))* Scholastic, Inc.

Mallory, Edgar. Hand Me down House. Norfleet, Mary Crockett. 2011. 98p. 38.95 *(978-1-258-07946-8(1))* Literary Licensing, LLC.

Malloy, Brigid. Bear Goes to the Donut Shop. Malloy, Brigid. 2018. (ENG.). 40p. (J). (gr. k-3). 18.99 *(978-1-948365-69-7(3))* Orange Hat Publishing.

Malloy, Kalle. Jingle Bats. Jennings, Sharon. 72p. pap. *(978-1-897039-22-9(0))* High Interest Publishing (HIP).

Malone, Kyle. Miles Grand Adventures: The Denver Broncos Mascot's A-to-Z Journey Around Colorado. Merliatt, James & Frainier, Tamara. 2004. 32p. (J). 19.95 *(978-0-9759579-2-9(9))* Denver Broncos.

Malone, Nola Langner. Earrings! Viorst, Judith. 2010. (ENG.). 32p. (J). (gr. 1-5). 18.99 *(978-1-4424-1281-1(X))*, Atheneum Bks. for Young Readers) Simon & Schuster Children's Publishing.

Malone, Peter. Agrippina: "Atrocious & Ferocious" Bridges, Shirin Yim. 2011. (Thinking Girl's Treasury of Dastardly Dames Ser.). (ENG.). 32p. (J). (gr. 3-8). 18.95 *(978-0-9834256-1-8(2))* Goosebottom Bks. LLC.

—The Boston Tea Party. Freedman, Russell. (ENG.). 40p. (J). (gr. 2-5). 2012. 17.95 *(978-0-8234-2266-1(6))*; 2013. pap. 7.99 *(978-0-8234-2915-8(6))* Holiday Hse., Inc.

—Catherine de' Medici: "The Black Queen" Havemeyer, Janie. 2011. (Thinking Girl's Treasury of Dastardly Dames Ser.). (ENG.). 32p. (J). (gr. 3-8). 18.95 *(978-0-9834256-3-2(9))* Goosebottom Bks. LLC.

—Cixi: "The Dragon Empress" Yim, Natasha. 2011. (Thinking Girl's Treasury of Dastardly Dames Ser.). 32p. (J). (gr. 3-8). 18.95 *(978-0-9834256-5-6(5))* Goosebottom Bks. LLC.

—Cleopatra: "Serpent of the Nile" Pack, Mary Fisk. 2011. (Thinking Girl's Treasury of Dastardly Dames Ser.). (ENG.). 32p. (J). (gr. 3-8). 18.95 *(978-0-9834256-0-1(4))* Goosebottom Bks. LLC.

—The Forest Child. Edwards, Richard. 2004. 28p. (J). reprint ed. *(978-0-7567-7850-7(6))* DIANE Publishing Co.

—Marie Antoinette "Madame Deficit" Hockinson, Liz. 2011. (Thinking Girl's Treasury of Dastardly Dames Ser.). (ENG.). 32p. (J). (gr. 3-8). 18.95 *(978-0-9834256-4-9(7))* Goosebottom Bks. LLC.

—Mary Tudor: "Bloody Mary" Maurer, Gretchen. 2011. (Thinking Girl's Treasury of Dastardly Dames Ser.). (ENG.). 32p. (J). (gr. 3-8). 18.95 *(978-0-9834256-2-5(0))* Goosebottom Bks. LLC.

—Njinga the Warrior Queen. Havemeyer, Janie. 2011. (Thinking Girl's Treasury of Dastardly Dames Ser.). 32p. (J). (gr. 3-8). 18.95 *(978-0-9834256-6-3(3))* Goosebottom Bks. LLC.

—The Nutcracker. Spinner, Stephanie. (ENG.). 40p. (J). (gr. -1-2). 2015. lib. bdg. 20.99 *(978-0-553-52465-9(8))*; 2008. 17.99 *(978-0-375-84464-5(3))* Random Hse. Children's Bks. (Knopf Bks. for Young Readers).

Malone, Peter. Sergei Prokofiev's Peter & the Wolf: With a Fully-Orchestrated & Narrated CD. Malone, Peter. Prokofiev, Sergei. 2004. (ENG.). 40p. (J). (gr. -1-2). 19.99 *(978-0-375-82430-2(8))*, Knopf Bks. for Young Readers) Random Hse. Children's Bks.

Malone, Rebecca. Buenas Noches, Perrito Bueno/Goodnight, Good Dog - Bilingual Board Book. Ray, Mary Lyn. 2020. (ENG.). 30p. (J). (— 1). bds. 5.99 *(978-0-358-21224-9(3))*, 1765191, HMH Books For Young Readers) Houghton Mifflin Harcourt Publishing Co.

—Goodnight, Good Dog. Ray, Mary Lyn. 2015. (ENG.). 32p. (J). (gr. -1-3). 16.99 *(978-0-544-28612-2(X))*, 1571592, HMH Books For Young Readers) Houghton Mifflin Harcourt Publishing Co.

—Goodnight, Good Dog (padded Board Book) Ray, Mary Lyn. 2018. (ENG.). 30p. (J). (— 1). bds. 8.99 *(978-1-328-85242-7(3))*, 1694366, HMH Books For Young Readers) Houghton Mifflin Harcourt Publishing Co.

Malone, Shearry. Absolutely Alfie & the First Week Friends. Warner, Sally. 2017. (Absolutely Alfie Ser.: 2). (ENG.). 144p. (J). (gr. 1-3). 5.99 *(978-1-101-99991-2(8))*, Puffin Books); 14.99 *(978-1-101-99989-9(6))*, Viking Books for Young Readers) Penguin Young Readers Group.

—Absolutely Alfie & the Furry, Purry Secret. Warner, Sally. 2017. (Absolutely Alfie Ser.: 1). (ENG.). 144p. (J). (gr. 1-3). 5.99 *(978-1-101-99988-2(8))*, Puffin Books) Penguin Young Readers Group.

—Absolutely Alfie & the Princess Wars, 4. Warner, Sally. 2018. (Absolutely Alfie Ser.). (ENG.). 142p. (J). (gr. 1-3). 18.69 *(978-1-5364-4646-3(7))*, Puffin) Penguin Publishing Group.

—Absolutely Alfie & the Princess Wars. Warner, Sally. 2018. (Absolutely Alfie Ser.: 4). (ENG.). 144p. (J). (gr. 1-3). 5.99 *(978-1-101-99997-4(7))*, Puffin Books) Penguin Young Readers Group.

—Absolutely Alfie & the Worst Best Sleepover. Warner, Sally. 2018. (Absolutely Alfie Ser.: 3). (ENG.). 144p. (J). (gr. 1-3). 5.99 *(978-1-101-99994-3(2))*, Puffin Books); 14.99 *(978-1-101-99992-9(6))*, Viking Books for Young Readers) Penguin Young Readers Group.

—Henry Is Kind: A Story of Mindfulness, 1 vol. Ryden, Linda. 2018. (ENG.). 32p. (J). (gr. k-5). 16.95 *(978-0-88448-661-9(3))*, 884661) Tilbury Hse. Pubs.

Maloney, Cynthia, photos by. How Does God Listen? Lindahl, Kay. 2005. (ENG., 32p. (J). pap. 8.99 *(978-1-59473-084-9(9))*, e076fb37-2c1b-4b6b-a357-57f161ddad03, Skylight Paths Publishing) LongHill Partners, Inc.

Malsawmthar, Nancy. This Is Us. Dusolle, Karla. 2020. (ENG.). 34p. (J). pap. ***(978-1-922374-88-2(1))*** Library For All Limited.

Malteste. Carnet Blanc Absinthe Parisienne. 2016. (Bnf Affiches Ser.). (FRE.). (J). pap. *(978-2-01-116958-7(5))* Hachette Groupe Livre.

—Carnet Ligne Absinthe Parisienne. 2016. (Bnf Affiches Ser.). (FRE.). (J). pap. *(978-2-01-116935-8(6))* Hachette Groupe Livre.

Maltman Dinwoodie, Heather. The Splendiddly Fazztabulous Grandmas. Sellen, Sandi. 2013. 32p. pap. *(978-1-77069-893-2(0))* Word Alive Pr.

Malungila, Jason. La Qu�te du Grand-Changeur: R�cit de l'homme Qui Voulait Cr�e un Monde des Reves. Malungila, Yves. 2019. (FRE.). 278p. (J). pap. 15.00 ***(978-1-0889-8733-9(8))*** Independently Published.

Malvern, Corinne. The Night Before Christmas. Moore, Clement C. (J). 2014. 26p. (-k). bds. 7.99 *(978-0-385-38474-2(2))*; 2011. 24p. (gr. -1-k). 4.99 *(978-0-375-86359-2(1))* Random Hse. Children's Bks. (Golden Bks.).

—Nurse Nancy. Jackson, Kathryn. 2005. (Little Golden Book Ser.). (ENG.). 24p. (J). (gr. -1-2). 4.99 *(978-0-375-83262-8(9))*, Golden Bks.) Random Hse. Children's Bks.

Malvezi, Irene. Draw Water & Other Things. Nissen Samuels, Linda. 2010. 48p. (J). pap. 15.98 *(978-1-905941-15-5(3))* Sigel Pr.

Malyon, Serena. Mouse Guard Alphabet Book. Petersen, David. 2017. (Mouse Guard Ser.: 1). (ENG.). 64p. (J). (gr. -1). 16.99 *(978-1-68415-010-6(8))*, Archaia Entertainment) Boom! Studios.

Mamada, Mineko. Which Is Round? Which Is Bigger? Mamada, Mineko. 2013. (ENG.). 24p. (J). (gr. -1-1). 16.95 *(978-1-55453-973-4(0))* Kids Can Pr., Ltd. CAN. Dist: Hachette Bk. Group.

Mamata, Sue. Black, White & Beautiful. Harris, Amber. 2007. 25p. pap. 24.95 *(978-1-4241-8932-8(2))* PublishAmerica, Inc.

Mammano, Julie. Rhinos Who Play Baseball. Mammano, Julie. 2006. 24p. (J). (gr. k-4). reprint ed. 14.00 *(978-0-7567-9995-3(3))* DIANE Publishing Co.

Man, Alex. Christmas Greeting Cards Coloring Book: This Unique 'christmas Greeting Card Coloring Book' Includes 30 Handmade Greeting Cards to Cut-Out & Color. & an Accompanying Set of 30 Envelopes to Cut-Out, Color, & Glue. Man, Alex. 2018. (ENG.). 126p. (J). pap. 8.56 *(978-1-7907-5637-7(5))* Independently Published.

Man, Alex. Halloween Dark Spooky Activity Book: Spooktacular Activity Book Contains More Than 55 Great Activities. Black & White Edition. Suitable for Ages 4-11. Man, Alex. 2019. (Halloween Ser.: Vol. 3). (ENG.). 118p. (J). pap. 8.93 ***(978-1-7007-3183-8(1))*** Independently Published.

Man, Alex. Happy Easter Activity Book: Activity Book for Kids, Fun Puzzles, Coloring Pages, Mazes & More. Suitable for Ages 4 - 10. Black & White Version. Man, Alex. 2019. (Easter Activity Book Ser.: Vol. 1). (ENG.). 84p. (J). pap. 7.95 *(978-1-0916-0981-5(0))* Independently Published.

—Ho Ho Ho Merry Christmas Coloring Book: More Than 70 Coloring Pages for the Whole Family. Man, Alex. 2018. (ENG.). 154p. (J). pap. 9.03 *(978-1-7913-7659-8(2))* Independently Published.

—Horses Coloring Book: The Ultimate Coloring Book for Horse Lovers. Man, Alex. 2019. (ENG.). 64p. (J). pap. 6.92 *(978-1-0776-8191-0(7))* Independently Published.

—How to Draw Sea Animals & More. Black & White Version: (volume 8) Man, Alex. 2018. (How to Draw Ser.: Vol. 8). (ENG.). 60p. (J). pap. 6.98 *(978-1-7919-6172-5(X))* Independently Published.

Man, Alex. Jewish High Holidays Activity Book: Including Rosh Hashanah, Yom Kippur, Sukkot, Shemini Atzeret/Simchat Torah (Black & White Version) Man, Alex. 2019. (ENG.). 144p. (J). pap. 8.72 ***(978-1-6898-5683-6(1))*** Independently Published.

—Jewish High Holidays Coloring Book: Including Rosh Hashanah, Yom Kippur, Sukkot, Shemini Atzeret/Simchat Torah (Jewish Holidays for Children) Man, Alex. 2019. (ENG.). 102p. (J). pap. 8.59 ***(978-1-6891-4758-3(X))*** Independently Published.

Man, Alex. The Mystery Egg: A Magical Story about a Girl, an Unusual Friendship & an Egg. Man, Alex. 2019. (ENG.). 40p. (J). pap. 9.83 *(978-1-0923-7852-9(9))* Independently Published.

—The Mystery Egg - Coloring Book: A Prehistoric Magical Story & Coloring Book. Man, Alex. 2019. (Mystery Egg Ser.: Vol. 2). (ENG.). 76p. (J). pap. 6.97 *(978-1-0936-7434-7(2))* Independently Published.

—Oliver the Cute Octopus - First Day of School: Enhance Your Child Confidence to Interact with Other Kids (Children's Moral Bedtime Story) Man, Alex. 2019. (Oliver the Cute Octopus Ser.: Vol. 1). (ENG.). 28p. (J). pap. 9.76 *(978-1-0924-2374-8(5))* Independently Published.

Man, Alex. The Purr-Fect Cat Activity Book: A Fun Activity Book for Cats & Kitten Lovers with Puzzles, Coloring Pages, How to Draw, Mazes & Much More! Suitable for Ages 4 - 8. (Black & White Version). (Cat) Man, Alex. 2020. (ENG.). 82p. (J). pap. 7.21 ***(978-1-6573-9285-4(6))*** Independently Published.

—The Purr-Fect Guide to Drawing Cats in an Easy & Simple Way: (a Step- by- Step Guide to Draw) Book 9 (How to Draw. a Step by Step Guide.) Man, Alex. 2020. (ENG.). 66p. (J). pap. 6.91 ***(978-1-6581-3222-0(X))*** Independently Published.

Man, Alex. Spring Coloring Book: Great Coloring Book for Hours of Relaxation, Mindful Calm, & Fun. Man, Alex. 2019. (ENG.). 72p. (J). pap. 6.67 *(978-1-0932-4833-3(5))* Independently Published.

—Unicorn Activity Book: A Fun Activity Book for Kids & Unicorn Lovers W/ Puzzles, Coloring Pages, Word Search, Mazes & Much More! Suitable for Ages 4 - 8. (Black & White Version) Man, Alex. 2019. (Unicorns Ser.: Vol. 2). (ENG.). 80p. (J). pap. 6.79 *(978-1-0814-2967-6(4))* Independently Published.

—Unicorn Activity Book: A Fun Activity Book for Kids & Unicorn Lovers W/ Puzzles, Coloring Pages, Word Search, Mazes & Much More! Suitable for Ages 4 - 8. (Color Version) Man, Alex. 2019. (Unicorns Ser.: Vol. 3). (ENG.). 78p. (J). pap. 15.65 *(978-1-0819-0481-4(X))* Independently Published.

Manak, Dave. Sabrina Animated. Gallagher, Mike. 2011. (Archie & Friends All-Stars Ser.: 13). (ENG.). 128p. (J). (gr. 4-7). pap. 9.95 *(978-1-879794-80-1(2))* Archie Comic Pubns., Inc.

Manapov, Masha. Ariba. Manapov, Masha. 2019. 40p. (J). 17.95 *(978-1-59270-300-5(3))* Enchanted Lion Bks., LLC.

Manarino, Mark. Sourpuss Sue. McKenna, Jacqueline & Manarino-Leggett, Priscilla. 2011. 24p. pap. 24.95 *(978-1-4560-8939-9(0))* America Star Bks.

Manasau, Amos. The Curse of the Laulau Tree. Mesibere, Ellen. 2012. 34p. pap. *(978-9980-945-67-9(2))* Univ. of Papua New Guinea Pr.

—Wagabuibui, the Four Eyed Eagle. Charles, Novalyn. 2012. 38p. pap. *(978-9980-945-66-2(4))* Univ. of Papua New Guinea Pr.

Manasco, Katharine. An Exceptional Children's Guide to Touch: Teaching Social & Physical Boundaries to Kids. Manasco, Mckinley Hunter. 2012. (ENG.). 72p. 17.95 *(978-1-84905-871-1(7)*, 694463) Kingsley, Jessica Pubs. GBR. Dist: Hachette UK Distribution.

—The Way to A: Empowering Children with Autism Spectrum & Other Neurological Disorders to Monitor & Replace Aggression & Tantrum Behavior. Manasco, Hunter. 2006. 19p. spiral bd., wbk. ed. 18.95 *(978-1-931282-87-1(0))* Autism Asperger Publishing Co.

Manav, Begum. I Like Me & I Love Me: A Self-Love & Like Book of Affirmations for Children. Zaitley, Abby. 2019. (ENG.). 34p. (J). pap. ***(978-1-9992673-0-8(3))*** One Door Pr.

Mancek, Marjan. Let's Go to Work. Brunel, Aude. 2007. 32p. (J). (POL & ENG.). pap. 16.95 *(978-1-60195-101-4(9))*; (ARA & ENG.). pap. 16.95 *(978-1-60195-089-5(6))* International Step by Step Assn.

Manchess, Gregory. Giving Thanks. London, Jonathan. 2011. 32p. (J). (gr. -1-2). pap. 6.99 *(978-0-7636-5594-5(5))* Candlewick Pr.

—The Last River: John Wesley Powell & the Colorado River Exploring Expedition. Waldman, Stuart. 2015. (ENG.). 48p. (J). (gr. 4-8). pap. 12.95 *(978-1-931414-58-6(0)*, e999c5e6-d64b-4269-92cc-9b0cbe2f0365) Mikaya Pr.

—Magellan's World. Waldman, Stuart. 2007. (Great Explorers Ser.). (ENG.). 48p. (J). (gr. 4-8). 22.95 *(978-1-931414-19-7(X)*, d791e557-6143-40be-b887-e8739022f002) Mikaya Pr.

—Nanuk, Lord of the Ice. Heinz, Brian J. 2005. (J). *(978-0-936335-13-1(0))*; pap. *(978-0-936335-14-8(9))* Ballyhoo BookWorks, Inc.

Manchester, Peter. Fishes in the Sea, 1 vol. Downey, Shirley. 2008. (ENG.). 24p. (J). pap. 12.95 *(978-0-9686586-3-5(6)*, 756f5dbd-3953-4e7e-9396-95924c4de7c0) Muddle Puddle Bks. CAN. Dist: Baker & Taylor Publisher Services (BTPS).

Mancine, Amie. Brown Bunny's Bird & Flower Book. Mancine, Barbara. 2018. (ENG.). 24p. (J). 22.95 *(978-1-4808-5877-0(3))*; pap. 12.45 *(978-1-4808-5878-7(1))* Archway Publishing.

Mandarino, Gene. Losing Papou: One Child's Journey Towards Understanding & Accepting Death. Garrick, Lainie. l.t. ed. 2003. 32p. (J). *(978-0-9765725-0-3(8))* printONDEMANDpublisher.com.

Mandell, Rebecca. The Cloud Catcher. Mandell, Frederick. 2018. (ENG.). 28p. (J). 19.99 *(978-1-7323398-8-0(0))* Mindstir Media.

Mander, Sanna. Design Line: History of Women's Fashion. Slee, Natasha. 2015. (ENG.). 16p. (J). (gr. 5). 17.99 *(978-0-7636-7962-0(3)*, Big Picture Press) Candlewick Pr.

Manders, John. Case of the Psychic Hamster. McMahon, P. J. 2005. 153p. (J). lib. bdg. 15.38 *(978-1-4242-0404-5(6))* Fitzgerald Bks.

—The Case of the Psychic Hamster: Secret File #4. McMahon, P. J. 4th ed. 2005. (Freaky Joe Club Ser.: 4). (ENG.). 160p. (J). (gr. 2-5). pap. 8.99 *(978-0-689-86263-2(6)*, Simon & Schuster/Paula Wiseman Bks.) Simon & Schuster/Paula Wiseman Bks.

—Case of the Singing Sea Dragons. McMahon, P. J. 2005. 153p. (J). lib. bdg. 15.38 *(978-1-4242-0406-9(2))* Fitzgerald Bks.

—Case of the Smiling Shark. McMahon, P. J. 2004. 116p. (J). lib. bdg. 15.38 *(978-1-4242-0402-1(X))* Fitzgerald Bks.

—The Case of the Smiling Shark: Secret File #2. McMahon, P. J. 2004. (Freaky Joe Club Ser.: 2). (ENG.). 128p. (J). (gr. 2-5). pap. 7.99 *(978-0-689-86261-8(X)*, Aladdin) Simon & Schuster Children's Publishing.

—Finnegan & Fox: The Ten-Foot Cop. Wilbur, Helen L. 2013. (ENG.). 32p. (J). (gr. 1-4). 19.99 *(978-1-58536-784-9(2)*, 202354) Sleeping Bear Pr.

—First-Base Hero: A Lift-the-Flap Pop-up Book. Hernandez, Keith. 2005. 12p. (J). (gr. k-4). reprint ed. 13.00 *(978-0-7567-8543-7(X))* DIANE Publishing Co.

—Goldie Socks & the Three Libearians. Hopkins, Jackie Mims. 2007. (J). *(978-1-932146-68-4(7))*; (gr. -1-3). 17.95 *(978-1-932146-98-1(9))* Highsmith Inc. (Upstart Bks.).

—Henry & the Buccaneer Bunnies. Crimi, Carolyn. 2009. 40p. (J). (gr. -1-3). pap. 7.99 *(978-0-7636-4540-3(0))* Candlewick Pr.

—Jack & the Giant Barbecue, 0 vols. Kimmel, Eric A. 2012. (ENG.). 32p. (J). (gr. 1-3). 17.99 *(978-0-7614-6128-9(0)*, 9780761461289, Two Lions) Amazon Publishing.

—Joe Bright & the Seven Genre Dudes. Hopkins, Jackie Mims. 2010. (J). 36p. (gr. 1-5). 17.95 *(978-1-60213-051-7(5))*; *(978-1-60213-049-4(3))* Highsmith Inc. (Upstart Bks.).

—Lewis & Clark: A Prairie Dog for the President. Redmond, Shirley Raye. 2003. (Step into Reading Ser.). 48p. 14.00 *(978-0-7569-1697-8(6))* Perfection Learning Corp.

—Lewis & Clark: A Prairie Dog for the President. Redmond, Shirley Raye. 2003. (Step into Reading Ser.: No. 3). 48p. (J). (gr. k-3). pap. 4.99 *(978-0-375-81120-3(6)*, Random Hse. Bks. for Young Readers) Random Hse. Children's Bks.

—Minnie's Diner: A Multiplying Menu. Dodds, Dayle Ann. 2007. 40p. (J). (gr. k-3). pap. 7.99 *(978-0-7636-3313-4(5))* Candlewick Pr.

—The Mystery of the Morphing Hockey Stick. McMahon, Patricia. 2004. 138p. (J). lib. bdg. 15.38 *(978-1-4242-0403-8(8))* Fitzgerald Bks.

—The Mystery of the Morphing Hockey Stick. McMahon, P. J. 3rd ed. 2004. (Freaky Joe Club Ser.: 3). (ENG.). 144p. (J). (gr. 2-5). pap. 8.99 *(978-0-689-86262-5(8)*, Aladdin) Simon & Schuster Children's Publishing.

—Mystery of the Swimming Gorilla. McMahon, P. J. 2004. 106p. (J). lib. bdg. 15.38 *(978-1-4242-0401-4(1))* Fitzgerald Bks.

—The Mystery of the Swimming Gorilla, 1. McMahon, P. J. 2004. (Freaky Joe Club Ser.: 1). (ENG.). 105p. (J). (gr. 3-6). 16.19 *(978-0-689-86260-1(1))* Simon & Schuster, Inc.

—P Is for Pirate: A Pirate Alphabet. Bunting, Eve. 2014. (ENG.). 40p. (J). (gr. 2-5). 16.95 *(978-1-58536-815-0(6)*, 203668) Sleeping Bear Pr.

—The Perfect Nest. Friend, Catherine. 2018. 40p. (J). (gr. -1-2). 7.99 *(978-0-7636-9975-8(6))* Candlewick Pr.

—Pete & Fremont. Tripp, Jenny. 2008. (ENG.). 192p. (J). (gr. 3-7). pap. 12.95 *(978-0-15-206238-5(6))* Houghton Mifflin Harcourt Publishing Co.

—Santa's Reindeer Games. Berger, Samantha. 2011. (J). *(978-0-545-36866-7(9))* Scholastic, Inc.

—Stinker & the Onion Princess. Griffin, Kitty & Combs, Kathy. 2005. (J). *(978-0-8037-2976-6(6)*, Dial) Penguin Publishing Group.

—What You Never Knew about Beds, Bedrooms, & Pajamas. Lauber, Patricia. 2008. (ENG.). 40p. (J). (gr. 1-4). 6.99 *(978-1-4169-6738-5(9)*, Simon & Schuster Bks. For Young Readers) Simon & Schuster Bks. For Young Readers.

—What You Never Knew about Fingers, Forks, & Chopsticks. Lauber, Patricia. 2009. (ENG.). 36p. (J). (gr. 1-5). pap. 12.99 *(978-1-4424-0937-8(1)*, Simon & Schuster Bks. For Young Readers) Simon & Schuster Bks. For Young Readers.

—Where's My Mummy? Crimi, Carolyn. 32p. (J). (gr. -1-3). 2009. 7.99 *(978-0-7636-4337-9(8))*; 2008. 15.99 *(978-0-7636-3196-3(5))* Candlewick Pr.

—2030: A Day in the Life of Tomorrow's Kids. Daly, James & Zuckerman, Amy. 2009. (ENG.). 32p. (J). (gr. 1-3). 17.99 *(978-0-525-47860-7(4)*, Dutton Books for Young Readers) Penguin Young Readers Group.

Mandracchia, Charles, 8th. Showtoonz, Mandracchia, Charles, 8th, creator. 2nd l.t. ed. 2005. 38p. (J). per. 995.00 net. *(978-0-9721957-2-0(6)*, Mandracchia Bks.) Mandracchia, Charles.

Mandrake, Tom. Alice's Adventures in Wonderland: Down the Rabbit-Hole. Carroll, Lewis. 2008. (Short Tales Classics Ser.). (ENG.). 32p. (J). (gr. 2-6). 27.07 *(978-1-60270-119-9(9)*, 13389, Short Tales) Magic Wagon.

Mandrake, Tom, et al. Marvel Knights Punisher by Garth Ennis: the Complete Collection Vol. 3. 2019. (ENG.). 400p. (gr. 10-17). pap. 39.99 *(978-1-302-91865-1(6))* Marvel Worldwide, Inc.

Mandrake, Tom & Zezelj, Danijel. The Call of Duty Vol. 2: The Precinct, 2 vols. Jones, Bruce & Austen, Chuck. 2003. (Call Ser.). 128p. (YA). pap. 9.99 *(978-0-7851-0974-7(9))* Marvel Worldwide, Inc.

Mandy, Stanley. Bella: The Birthday Party. Mandy, Stanley. 2010. (ENG.). 32p. (J). (gr. -1-k). 9.95 *(978-1-58925-850-1(9))* Tiger Tales.

—Bella: The Fairy Ball. Mandy, Stanley. 2010. (ENG.). 32p. (J). (gr. -1-k). 9.95 *(978-1-58925-851-8(7))* Tiger Tales.

Maneki, Tanya. The Clumsy Groundhog. Blum, Ingo. 2019. (Riverboat Series Chapter Book Ser.: Vol. 2). (ENG.). 98p. (J). (gr. 1-3). pap. *(978-3-947410-73-6(5))* Blum, Ingo Planet-Oh Concepts.

—The River Raft. Blum, Ingo. 2019. (Riverboat Series Chapter Book Ser.: Vol. 1). (ENG.). 66p. (J). (gr. 1-3). pap. *(978-3-947410-71-2(9))* Blum, Ingo Planet-Oh Concepts.

—Riverboat: The River Raft. Blum, Ingo. 2018. (Riverboat Ser.: Vol. 1). (ENG.). 50p. (J). (gr. k-3). *(978-3-947410-60-6(3))* Blum, Ingo Planet-Oh Concepts.

—Riverboat - a Very Special Ant. Blum, Ingo. 2018. (Riverboat Ser.: Vol. 3). (ENG.). 50p. (J). (gr. k-3). *(978-3-947410-64-4(6))* Blum, Ingo Planet-Oh Concepts.

—A Very Special Ant. Blum, Ingo. 2019. (Riverboat Series Chapter Book Ser.: Vol. 3). (ENG.). 100p. (J). (gr. 1-3). pap. *(978-3-947410-75-0(1))* Blum, Ingo Planet-Oh Concepts.

Maneki, Tanya. With Love. Brewer Gant, Kirsten. 2020. (ENG.). 32p. (J). pap. 11.99 ***(978-1-6590-9392-6(9))*** Independently Published.

Manet & Dor. Le Corbeau / the Raven - Edition Bilingue Illustree: Fran. Barry, ed. 2018. (FRE.). 60p. (J). pap. 14.99 *(978-1-7292-6236-8(8))* Independently Published.

Manetti, Francesco. What Could It Be? Nayar, Nandini. 2013. (ENG.). 28p. (J). (gr. -1). 11.95 *(978-81-8190-285-6(8))* Karadi Tales Co. Pvt, Ltd. IND. Dist: Consortium Bk. Sales & Distribution.

Maney, Melissa. Roxie y Los Ciervos. Smith, Ivy. 2011. (SPA.). 32p. (J). 19.99 *(978-0-9847756-3-7(3))*; pap. 11.99 *(978-0-9847756-4-4(1))* Red Tail Publishing.

—Stickers VIP. Smith, Ivy. 2011. (ENG.). 30p. (J). pap. 11.99 *(978-0-9847756-0-6(9))* Red Tail Publishing.

Manfre, Joey. Patch Land Adventures Book 2 Camping at Mimi's Ranch. Swick, Carmen D. Lambert, Page, ed. 2012. 40p. pap. 12.99 *(978-0-9831380-1-3(X))* Presbeau Publishing, Inc.

Manfre, Joey. Patch Land Adventures Coloring Book & Activity Sheets. Swick, Carmen. 2020. (ENG.). 34p. (J). (gr. k-3). pap. 5.00 ***(978-0-9831380-5-1(2))*** Presbeau Publishing, Inc.

Manfredi, Alessandra. The Great Book of Emotions. 2020. (ENG.). 48p. (J). (gr. 3). 14.95 ***(978-88-544-1670-3(3))*** White Star ITA. Dist: Sterling Publishing Co., Inc.

Manfredi, Federica. Kat & Mouse Vol. 1: Teacher Torture, 1 vol. De Campi, Alex. 2008. (Tokyopop Ser.). (ENG.). 96p. (J). (gr. 2-6). 28.50 *(978-1-59961-564-6(9)*, 14807, Graphic Novels) Spotlight.

—Kat & Mouse Vol. 2: Tripped, 1 vol. De Campi, Alex. 2008. (Tokyopop Ser.). (ENG.). 96p. (J). (gr. 2-6). 28.50 *(978-1-59961-565-3(7)*, 14808, Graphic Novels) Spotlight.

—Kat & Mouse Vol. 3: The Ice Storm, 1 vol. De Campi, Alex. 2008. (Tokyopop Ser.). (ENG.). 96p. (J). (gr. 2-6). 28.50 *(978-1-59961-566-0(5)*, 14809, Graphic Novels) Spotlight.

Manfredi, Frederica. Kat & Mouse, Vol. 4. De Campi, Alex. 2017. (ENG.). 192p. (YA). pap. 5.99 *(978-1-4278-1175-2(X)*, 48bbcd82-ae96-43fc-8267-32d4aef78904) TOKYOPOP, Inc.

Mangal, Sakshi. Fernando & the Thames Barge. Samuels, Jo. 2018. (ENG.). 32p. (J). pap. *(978-1-5255-3111-8(5))* FriesenPress.

—Hail to the Snail. Bruneau, Sandra. 2018. (ENG.). 28p. (J). *(978-1-77370-665-8(9))*; pap. *(978-1-77370-666-5(7))* Tellwell Talent.

—Hide-And-Seek: A First Book of Position Words. Ornot, R. D. 2019. (ENG.). 3p. (J). (gr. -1-2). 16.99 *(978-1-77138-794-1(7))* Kids Can Pr., Ltd. CAN. Dist: Hachette Bk. Group.

—How to Get along with Snakes. Naus, Matt. 2018. (ENG.). 28p. (J). *(978-0-2288-0015-6(3))*; pap. *(978-0-2288-0014-9(5))* Tellwell Talent.

Mangal, Sakshi. The Incredible Adventures of Zazou Lerou: The Trouble with Bubbles. Hyland, Alexandra. 2020. (ENG.). 28p. (J). ***(978-0-2288-1991-2(1))***; pap. ***(978-0-2288-1990-5(3))*** Tellwell Talent.

Mangal, Sakshi. Little Milly & the Great Lakes: Bess & the Boil. McInenly, Kelly. 2019. (Little Milly & the Great Lakes Ser.: Vol. 3). (ENG.). 26p. (J). pap. *(978-0-2288-0876-3(6))* Tellwell Talent.

—Little Milly & the Great Lakes: Marj & the Medal. McInenly, Kelly. 2019. (Little Milly & the Great Lakes Ser.: Vol. 1). (ENG.). 26p. (J). pap. *(978-0-2288-0896-1(0))* Tellwell Talent.

—Little Milly & the Great Lakes: Peg & the Party Line. McInenly, Kelly. 2019. (Little Milly & the Great Lakes Ser.: Vol. 2). (ENG.). 26p. (J). pap. *(978-0-2288-0895-4(2))* Tellwell Talent.

Mangal, Sakshi. Little Tree's Big Dream: A Christmas Story. Albert, M. J. 2019. (ENG.). 28p. (J). ***(978-1-5255-6153-5(7))***; pap. ***(978-1-5255-6154-2(5))*** FriesenPress.

—The Monkey Who Ate Meatballs. Casstevens, Allyson L. 2019. (ENG.). 24p. (J). ***(978-1-5255-4009-7(2))***; pap. ***(978-1-5255-4010-3(6))*** FriesenPress.

Mangal, Sakshi. Pitter-Patter Raindrops. Jesani, Zoiya. 2019. (ENG.). 30p. (J). *(978-1-77370-653-5(5))*; pap. *(978-1-77370-652-8(7))* Tellwell Talent.

—Seed School: Growing up Amazing. Holub, Joan. 2018. (ENG.). 32p. (J). (gr. -1-2). 16.95 *(978-1-63322-374-5(4)*, 225463, Seagrass) Quarto Publishing Group USA.

—Stories & Poems from a Grandmother's Heart. Mirza, Kishwar. 2019. (ENG.). 48p. (J). *(978-1-5255-3101-9(8))*; pap. *(978-1-5255-3102-6(6))* FriesenPress.

Mangal, Sakshi. The Strength Match: Who's the Real King of the Jungle? Lynn, Jamie. 2020. (Jamie Bo Bamie Ser.). (ENG.). 28p. (J). ***(978-1-5255-4510-8(8))***; pap. ***(978-1-5255-4511-5(6))*** FriesenPress.

—The Struggle for Fenland: Quietly We Fall. Byron, M. 2019. (Struggle for Fenland Ser.). (ENG.). 136p. (J). ***(978-1-5255-4573-3(6))***; pap. ***(978-1-5255-4574-0(4))*** FriesenPress.

Mangal, Sakshi. The Tale of the Little Green Tomato. Pelletier, Christina. 2019. (ENG.). 24p. (J). *(978-0-2288-0665-3(8))*; pap. *(978-0-2288-0664-6(X))* Tellwell Talent.

Mangal, Sakshi. Two Sisters Too Many. Pritchard-Vignjevic, Ashley Katherine. 2019. (ENG.). 22p. (J). pap. ***(978-0-2288-1323-1(9))*** Tellwell Talent.

Mangal, Sakshi. Winston Wiggles. Cline, Megan. 2019. (ENG.). 28p. (J). *(978-1-5255-4144-5(7))*; pap. *(978-1-5255-4145-2(5))* FriesenPress.

—Winston Winks. Cline, Megan. 2018. (ENG.). 28p. (J). *(978-1-5255-3482-9(3))*; pap. *(978-1-5255-3483-6(1))* FriesenPress.

Mangal, Sakshi. Winston's Wet. Cline, Megan. 2019. (ENG.). 28p. (J). ***(978-1-5255-5066-9(7))***; pap. ***(978-1-5255-5067-6(5))*** FriesenPress.

Mangano, Lorrie. Daddy & Me. McCarthy, Michele. 2019. (ENG.). 28p. (J). pap. 13.99 *(978-1-68314-757-2(X))* Redemption Pr.

Mangano, Tom. Dora. Beinstein, Phoebe. 2003. (Dora the Explorer Ser.). (ENG & SPA.). 12p. (J). bds. 7.99 *(978-0-689-85484-2(6)*, Simon Spotlight/Nickelodeon) Simon Spotlight/Nickelodeon.

Mangano, Tom, et al. Dora's Rainbow Picnic. Ricci, Christine. 2007. (J). pap. *(978-1-4127-8927-1(3))* Publications International, Ltd.

Mangano, Tom. Dora's World Adventure! 2006. (Dora the Explorer Ser.). (ENG.). 24p. (J). (gr. -1-2). pap. 3.99 *(978-1-4169-2447-0(7)*, Simon Spotlight/Nickelodeon) Simon Spotlight/Nickelodeon.

—Puppy Takes a Bath. Ricci, Christine. 2006. (Dora the Explorer Ser.: 10). (ENG.). 24p. (J). (gr. 3-7). pap. 3.99 *(978-1-4169-1483-9(8)*, Simon Spotlight/Nickelodeon) Simon Spotlight/Nickelodeon.

Mangano, Tom & Miller, Victoria. Where Is Baby Jaguar? Driscoll, Laura. 2011. (Dora & Diego Ser.). (ENG.). 24p. (J). pap. 3.99 *(978-1-4424-1398-6(0)*, Simon Spotlight/Nickelodeon) Simon Spotlight/Nickelodeon.

Mangelsen, Thomas D. & Cooper, Deborah. Searching for Grizzlies. Mangelsen, Thomas D., photos by. Hirschi, Ron. 2005. (J). *(978-1-4156-2797-6(5))* Boyds Mills Pr.

Mangiarotti, Adriana, jt. illus. see Ora, Vania.

Mangiat, Jeff. Snakes. Scott, L. K. 2008. (ENG.). 24p. (J). (gr. 3-18). 19.95 *(978-1-58117-799-2(2)*, Intervisual/Piggy Toes) Bendon, Inc.

Mangiat, Jeffrey. Allosaurus. Mattern, Joanne. 2009. (Let's Read about Dinosaurs Ser.). 24p. (J). (gr. -1-3). lib. bdg. 23.00 *(978-0-8368-9414-1(6)*, Weekly Reader Leveled Readers) Stevens, Gareth Publishing LLLP.

—Ankylosaurus. Mattern, Joanne. 2009. (Let's Read about Dinosaurs Ser.). 24p. (J). (gr. -1-3). lib. bdg. 23.00 *(978-0-8368-9415-8(4)*, Weekly Reader Leveled Readers) Stevens, Gareth Publishing LLLP.

Mangiatordi, Vitale. The Unbeatable Squirrel Girl: Squirrel Meets World. Hale, Shannon & Hale, Dean. 2017. (Squirrel Girl Novel Ser.: 1). (ENG.). 336p. (J). (gr. 3-7). 13.99 *(978-1-4847-8154-8(6)*, Marvel Pr.) Disney Publishing Worldwide.

Mangione, Olivia. The Creep. Balcom, Annette. 2018. (ENG.). 22p. (J). pap. 12.95 *(978-1-7325075-1-7(1))* McMillan, Carol.

Mangis Sink, Theresa. Big Heart: A Story of a Girl & Her Horse. Slaughter, Michael R. 2019. (ENG.). 164p. (YA). (gr. 7-9). pap. 13.99 ***(978-1-951263-93-5(6))*** Pen It! Pubns., LLC.

Mangoro, Lynda Louise. Martina Mctripaw & the Goldmeister General. Levy, Rachel Julia. 2018. (ENG.). 24p. (J). pap. 5.95 *(978-0-9743626-9-4(7))* Hope Through Healing Pubns.

Mangrum, Kaylea J. How to Draw Step-By-Step Using the Alphabet. Mangrum, Kaylea J. 2013. 38p. pap. 12.49 *(978-0-9883009-4-1(X))* Mangrum, Kaylea J.

—How to Draw Step-By-Step with Special Kids. Mangrum, Kaylea J. 2013. 38p. pap. 12.49 *(978-0-9883009-3-4(1))* Mangrum, Kaylea J.

—Tucker Goes to Kindergarten. Mangrum, Kaylea J. Bartch, Lea. 2013. 54p. pap. 14.99 *(978-0-9883009-5-8(8))* Mangrum, Kaylea J.

Mangum, James A. The Fairy the Chupacabra & Those Marfa Lights: A West Texas Fable. Mangum, James A. Spires, Sidney. 2008. 32p. (J). 17.95 *(978-0-9798391-5-3(7))* Texas Bk. Pubs. Assn.

Mangum, Nicole. Aunt Mittie: Goes to Church. Moore-Johnson, Melinda Marie. 2019. (Aunt Mittie Ser.). (ENG.). 26p. (J). (gr. 1-3). pap. 9.99 *(978-1-7336754-9-9(3))* Liberation's Publishing.

—Summer Vacation. Moore-Johnson, Melinda M. 2018. (Aunt Mittie's Ser.: Vol. 1). (ENG.). 24p. (J). pap. 12.99 *(978-1-7320846-4-3(5))* Liberation's Publishing.

Manier, Grant. Grant the Jigsaw Giraffe: Different Is More. Coy Manier, Julie. 2017. (J). 16.95 *(978-1-941515-83-9(5))* LongTale Publishing, LLC.

Manikandan, jt. illus. see Jones, K. L.

Manion, Moira. The Vineyard Book. Johnston, Jack. 2005. 48p. (J). 25.00 *(978-0-9629880-0-4(6))* ACME Pr.

Manjula Padmanabhan. Unprincess! 2005. 98p. (J). *(978-0-14-333495-8(6)*, Puffin) Penguin Publishing Group.

Mankamyer, Laura. The Adventures of the Stonycreek Gang. Mankamyer, Laura. l.t. ed. 2003. 84p. (J). 12.99 *(978-0-9728431-4-0(0))* Mankamyer, Laura.

Manley, Andy. Gracie the Gopher & the Christmas Bunny. England, Michael. 2019. (ENG.). 38p. (J). pap. 10.99 *(978-1-7335503-0-7(5))* Endurance Pr.

—Gracie the Gopher & the Silly Man. England, Michael. 2018. (Gracie the Gopher Ser.: Vol. 1). (ENG.). 42p. (J). pap. 10.99 *(978-0-9988756-3-7(5))* Endurance Pr.

Manley, Mike, et al. Acts of Vengeance: Avengers. 2020. (ENG.). 504p. (YA). (gr. 8-17). pap. 39.99 *(978-1-302-92273-3(4))* Marvel Worldwide, Inc.

Mann, Bethany. Show Off: How to Do Absolutely Everything. One Step at a Time. Stephens, Sarah Hines. 2009. (ENG.). 224p. (J). (gr. 5-9). pap. 18.99 *(978-0-7636-4599-1(0))* Candlewick Pr.

Mann, Brooke Malia. Miracles of Jesus. 2019. (J). 16.99 *(978-1-62972-522-2(6))* Deseret Bk. Co.

M

Mann, Jennifer K. Percy, Dog of Destiny. McGhee, Alison. 2017. (ENG.). 32p. (J). (gr. -1-3). 16.95 *(978-1-59078-984-1(9))* Boyds Mills Pr.
—Turkey Tot. Shannon, George. (ENG.). 32p. (J). (gr. -1-k). 2014. 6.99 *(978-0-8234-3175-5(4))*; 2013. 16.95 *(978-0-8234-2379-8(4))* Holiday Hse., Inc.
Mann, Jennifer K. The Camping Trip. Mann, Jennifer K. 2020. (ENG.). 56p. (J). (gr. -1-2). 17.99 *(978-1-5362-0736-1(5))* Candlewick Pr.
—I Will Never Get a Star on Mrs. Benson's Blackboard. Mann, Jennifer K. 40p. (J). (gr. k-3). 2017. 6.99 *(978-0-7636-9299-5(9))*; 2015. 16.99 *(978-0-7636-6514-2(2))* Candlewick Pr.
—Josie's Lost Tooth. Mann, Jennifer K. 2018. 40p. (J). (gr. k-3). 16.99 *(978-0-7636-9694-8(3))* Candlewick Pr.
—Sam & Jump. Mann, Jennifer K. 2016. (ENG.). 32p. (J). (gr. -1-2). 15.99 *(978-0-7636-7947-7(X))* Candlewick Pr.
—Two Speckled Eggs. Mann, Jennifer K. 2014. (ENG.). 32p. (J). (gr. k-3). 14.99 *(978-0-7636-6168-7(6))* Candlewick Pr.
Mann, Lawrence. Stellarcadia. Grasso, Julie Anne. 2014. (Cardamom Ser.: Bk. 3). 128p. (J). pap. *(978-0-9873725-6-7(4))* Grasso, Julie Anne AUS. Dist: INT Bks.
Mann, William A. The Anhinga Tree. Maddock-Cowart, Donna. 2012. 74p. pap. 9.95 *(978-0-9836484-3-7(3))* Miglior Pr.
Manna, Francesco. Fantastic Four: Prodigal Sun. 2019. 112p. (YA). (gr. 8-17). pap. 15.99 *(978-1-302-91980-1(6))* Marvel Worldwide, Inc.
Manna, Francesco & Brown, Garry. Marvel Comics: Timeless Tales. 2019. (ENG.). 136p. (YA). (gr. -1-17). pap. 19.99 *(978-1-302-91755-5(2))* Marvel Worldwide, Inc.
Manna, Giovanni. The Barefoot Book of Giants, Ghosts, & Goblins. Matthews, John. 2008. 80p. (J). 21.99 *(978-1-84686-235-9(3))* Barefoot Bks., Inc.
—The Barefoot Book of Knights. Matthews, John. 80p. (J). 2009. (ENG.). 19.99 *(978-1-84686-307-3(4))*; 2005. (gr. 4-7). 15.99 *(978-1-84148-205-7(6))* Barefoot Bks., Inc.
—Knights. Matthews, John. 2014. (Barefoot Bks.). 79p. (J). (gr. 3-6). 15.99 *(978-1-78285-165-3(8))* Barefoot Bks., Inc.
—Swing High, Swing Low. Coward, Fiona. 2005. (ENG.). 32p. (J). 16.99 *(978-1-84148-170-8(X))* Barefoot Bks., Inc.
—A Year in the Woods. Thoreau, Henry David. 2017. (ENG.). 32p. (J). (gr. 4-7). 18.99 *(978-1-56846-305-6(7))*, Creative Editions) Creative Co., The.
—You & Me. Blackstone, Stella. 2009. (ENG.). 32p. (J). 14.99 *(978-1-84686-336-3(8))* Barefoot Bks., Inc.
Mannaa, Ruaida. Farah Rocks. Darraj, Susan Muaddi. 2020. (Farah Rocks Ser.). (ENG.). (J). (gr. 3-6). 31.90 ***(978-1-4965-8343-7(4)***, 29324, Stone Arch Bks.) Capstone.
Mannaa, Ruaida. Farah Rocks Fifth Grade. Darraj, Susan Muaddi. 2020. (Farah Rocks Ser.). (ENG.). 144p. (J). (gr. 3-6). 15.95 *(978-1-4965-8339-0(6)*, 140529, Stone Arch Bks.) Capstone.
Mannaa, Ruaida. Farah Rocks Summer Break. Darraj, Susan Muaddi. 2020. (Farah Rocks Ser.). (ENG.). 144p. (J). (gr. 3-6). 15.95 ***(978-1-4965-8340-6(X)***, 140530, Stone Arch Bks.) Capstone.
Mannello, Emanuela. Star Signs for Little Astrologers. Rossa, Paloma. Cottage Door Press, ed. 2020. (ENG.). 26p. (J). (gr. -1-2). 14.99 *(978-1-68052-707-0(X)*, 1004400) Cottage Door Pr.
Manni, Mia (Maio). Flora & the Silver Coins. Deluca, Laura. 2011. 40p. pap. 24.95 *(978-1-4560-7752-5(X))* America Star Bks.
Manning, Eddie. Family Favourites. McKay-Lawton, Toni. 2007. (Just in Rhyme Ser.). (ENG.). 12p. (J). (gr. -1-3). pap. *(978-1-84167-028-7(6))* Ransom Publishing Ltd.
—In Bloom. McKay-Lawton, Toni. 2007. (Just in Rhyme Ser.). (ENG.). 12p. (J). (gr. -1-3). pap. *(978-1-84167-030-0(8))* Ransom Publishing Ltd.
—In the Garden. McKay-Lawton, Toni. 2007. (Just in Rhyme Ser.). (ENG.). 12p. (J). (gr. -1-3). pap. *(978-1-84167-029-4(4))* Ransom Publishing Ltd.
—Under the Sea. McKay-Lawton, Toni. 2007. (Just in Rhyme Ser.). (ENG.). 12p. (J). (gr. -1-3). pap. *(978-1-84167-027-0(8))* Ransom Publishing Ltd.
Manning, Jane. Baa-Choo! Weeks, Sarah. 2006. (I Can Read Level 1 Ser.). (ENG.). 32p. (J). (gr. k-3). pap. 4.99 *(978-0-06-443740-0(X))* HarperCollins Pubs.
—Beetle Mcgrady Eats Bugs! McDonald, Megan. 2005. (ENG.). 32p. (J). (gr. k-5). 17.99 *(978-0-06-001354-7(0)*, Greenwillow Bks.) HarperCollins Pubs.
—The Green Dog: Green Algae. Luke, Melinda. 2006. (Science Solves It! ® Ser.). (ENG.). 32p. (J). (gr. 1-3). pap. 5.95 *(978-1-57565-115-6(7))* Astra Publishing Hse.
—Jumping off Library Shelves. Hopkins, Lee Bennett. 2015. (ENG.). 32p. (J). (gr. k-4). 17.95 *(978-1-59078-924-7(5)*, 1396014, Wordsong) Boyds Mills Pr.
—Little Elfie One. Jane, Pamela. 2015. (ENG.). 32p. (J). (gr. -1-3). 17.99 *(978-0-06-220673-2(7)*, Balzer & Bray) HarperCollins Pubs.
Manning, Jane. Little Goblins Ten. Jane, Pamela. 2020. 32p. (J). (gr. -1-3). pap. 4.99 ***(978-0-06-176801-9(4)***, HarperCollins) HarperCollins Pubs. Ltd. GBR. Dist: HarperCollins Pubs.
Manning, Jane. Little Goblins Ten. Jane, Pamela. 2011. (ENG.). 32p. (J). (gr. -1-3). 16.99 *(978-0-06-176798-2(0))* HarperCollins Pubs.
—Mac & Cheese. Weeks, Sarah. 2010. (I Can Read Level 1 Ser.). (ENG.). 32p. (J). (gr. -1-3). pap. 4.99 *(978-0-06-117081-2(X))* HarperCollins Pubs.
—Mac & Cheese. Weeks, Sarah. 2010. (I Can Read Level 1 Ser.). (ENG.). 32p. (J). (gr. -1-3). 16.99 *(978-0-06-117079-9(8)*, HarperCollins) HarperCollins Pubs. Ltd. GBR. Dist: HarperCollins Pubs.
—Mac & Cheese & the Perfect Plan. Weeks, Sarah. 2012. 32p. (J). lib. bdg. 17.89 *(978-0-06-117083-6(6))*; (ENG.). 16.99 *(978-0-06-117082-9(8))*; (ENG.). pap. 4.99 *(978-0-06-117084-3(4))* HarperCollins Pubs.
—A Pet for Me: Poems. Hopkins, Lee Bennett. 2003. (I Can Read Bks.). (ENG.). 48p. (J). (gr. k-3). 15.99 *(978-0-06-029111-2(7))* HarperCollins Pubs.
—Pip Squeak. Weeks, Sarah. 2008. (I Can Read Level 1 Ser.). (ENG.). 32p. (J). (gr. k-3). pap. 4.99 *(978-0-06-075638-3(1))* HarperCollins Pubs.
—Snoring Beauty. Bardhan-Quallen, Sudipta. 2014. (J). *(978-0-06-087405-6(8))* Harper & Row Ltd.
—Snoring Beauty. Bardhan-Quallen, Sudipta. 2014. (ENG.). 32p. (J). (gr. -1-3). 17.99 *(978-0-06-087403-2(1))* HarperCollins Pubs.
—There's No Place Like School: Classroom Poems. Prelutsky, Jack. 2010. (ENG.). 32p. (J). (gr. k-5). 16.99 *(978-0-06-082338-2(0)*, Greenwillow Bks.) HarperCollins Pubs.
Manning, Jane. Cat Nights. Manning, Jane. 2008. 32p. (J). lib. bdg. 17.89 *(978-0-06-113889-8(4)*, Greenwillow Bks.) HarperCollins Pubs.
—Millie Fierce. Manning, Jane. 2012. (Millie Fierce Ser.). 32p. (J). (gr. -1-2). 17.99 *(978-0-399-25642-4(3)*, Philomel Bks.) Penguin Young Readers Group.
Manning, Jane K. The Green Dog. Luke, Melinda. 2006. (Science Solves It Ser.). 32p. (J). pap. 7.99 *(978-0-15-356581-6(0))* Houghton Mifflin Harcourt School Pubs.
—The Just-So Woman. Blackwood, Gary L. 2006. (I Can Read Bks.). 48p. (J). (gr. -1-3). lib. bdg. 16.89 *(978-0-06-057728-5(2))* HarperCollins Pubs.
—Look Behind! Tales of Animal Ends. Schaefer, Lola M. & Miller, Heather Lynn. 2008. 32p. (J). (gr. -1-3). lib. bdg. 17.89 *(978-0-06-088394-2(4)*, Greenwillow Bks.) HarperCollins Pubs.
—Pip Squeak. Weeks, Sarah. 2007. (I Can Read Bks.). 32p. (J). (gr. -1-3). lib. bdg. 16.89 *(978-0-06-075637-6(3)*, Geringer, Laura Book) HarperCollins Pubs.
Manning, Jane K. Fast 'n Snappy. Manning, Jane K., tr. Schnetzler, Pattie L. 2004. (Carolrhoda Picture Books Ser.). 32p. (J). (gr. k-3). 16.95 *(978-1-57505-539-8(2))* Lerner Publishing Group.
Manning, Kris. Upside down Pig. Gray, Bev. 2019. (ENG.). 38p. (J). pap. 12.99 *(978-1-5332-4123-8(6))* CreateSpace Independent Publishing Platform.
Manning, Lisa C. Falcons in the City. Manning, Lisa C. 2013. (ENG.). 40p. (J). pap. 14.95 *(978-1-59299-886-9(0))* Inkwater Pr.
Manning, Mary. The Bear & the Fern. Miletsky, Jay. 2018. (ENG.). 28p. (J). 17.95 ***(978-0-692-15613-1(5))*** New Paige Pr., LLC.
Manning, Mary. Carolyn Quimby. Copp, Raymond. 2013. 110p. pap. 30.95 *(978-1-4575-2364-9(7))* Dog Ear Publishing, LLC.
—Hey Diddle Diddle. Everett, Melissa. 2017. (ENG.). 24p. (J). (gr. -1-3). *(978-1-4867-1258-8(4))* Flowerpot Children's Pr. Inc.
—Hey Diddle Diddle. Everett, Melissa. 2013. (ENG.). 20p. (J). (gr. -1-3). 8.99 *(978-1-77093-536-5(3))* Flowerpot Children's Pr. Inc. CAN. Dist: Cardinal Pubs. Group.
—I Wish I Was a Little. Everett, Melissa. Paiva, Johannah Gilman, ed. 2014. (ENG.). 20p. (J). 8.99 *(978-1-77093-844-1(3))* Flowerpot Children's Pr. Inc. CAN. Dist: Cardinal Pubs. Group.
—I Wish I Was a Little. Everett, Melissa. Paiva, Johannah Gilman, ed. 2017. (ENG.). 24p. (J). (gr. k-3). *(978-1-4867-1257-1(6))* Flowerpot Children's Pr. Inc.
—Jack & the Beanstalk: An English Folktale. Malaspina, Ann. 2013. (Folktales from Around the World Ser.). (ENG.). 24p. (J). (gr. k-3). 28.50 *(978-1-62323-615-1(0)*, 206382) Child's World, Inc., The.
—Us. Boylan, Frank. 2018. (ENG.). 20p. (J). (gr. -1-2). bds. 7.99 *(978-1-4867-1545-9(1)*, a4951003-26d4-46e9-a1fb-22080109acda) Flowerpot Pr.
Manning, Maurie. The Hot Shots. Aboff, Marcie. 2003. (ENG.). 56p. (J). (gr. 6-8). pap. 7.97 net. *(978-0-7652-3275-5(8)*, Celebration Pr.) Savvas Learning Co.
—Water Everywhere! Taylor-Butler, Christine. 2011. (Rookie Ready to Learn - First Science Ser.). 40p. (J). (gr. -1-k). lib. bdg. 23.00 *(978-0-531-26504-8(8)*, Children's Pr.) Scholastic Library Publishing.
Manning, Maurie J. Dear Child. Farrell, John. 2008. (ENG.). 32p. (J). (gr. -1 — 1). 16.95 *(978-1-59078-495-2(2))* Boyds Mills Pr.
—Getting to Know Ruben Plotnick. Rosenbluth, Roz. 2005. (ENG.). 32p. (J). (gr. k-2). 15.95 *(978-0-9729225-5-5(5))* Flashlight Pr.
—Looking for Home. Berry, Eileen M. 2006. 75p. (J). (gr. -1-3). per. *(978-1-59166-493-2(4))* BJU Pr.
—Sorry! Ludwig, Trudy. 2006. 32p. (J). (gr. 1-4). 17.99 *(978-1-58246-173-1(2)*, Tricycle Pr.) Random Hse. Children's Bks.
—Tommy's Race. Hambrick, Sharon. 2004. (Fig Street Kids Ser.). 95p. (J). (gr. 1-2). 7.49 *(978-1-59166-286-0(9))* BJU Pr.
—Tommy's Rocket. Hambrick, Sharon. 2003. (Fig Street Kids Ser.). 83p. (J). (gr. 1-2). 7.49 *(978-1-59166-186-3(2))* BJU Pr.
—Water Everywhere! Taylor-Butler, Christine. 2005. (Rookie Reader Skill Set Ser.). (ENG.). 24p. (J). (gr. 1-2). per. 4.95 *(978-0-516-25285-8(2)*, Children's Pr.) Scholastic Library Publishing.
Manning, Maurie J. Kitchen Dance. Manning, Maurie J. 2008. (ENG.). 32p. (J). (gr. -1-3). 17.99 *(978-0-618-99110-5(7)*, 1027359) Houghton Mifflin Harcourt Publishing Co.
Manning, Maurie J. The Giant King. Manning, Maurie J., tr. Pelley, Kathleen. 2003. (New Child & Family Press Titles Ser.). 32p. (gr. -1-4). 14.95 *(978-0-87868-880-7(3)*, 8803, Child & Family Pr.) Child Welfare League of America, Inc.
—Tommy's Clubhouse. Manning, Maurie J., tr. Hambrick, Sharon. 2003. (Fig Street Kids Ser.). 78p. (J). (gr. 1-2). pap. 7.49 *(978-1-57924-993-9(0))* BJU Pr.
Manning, Mick & Granstrom, Brita. What Mr Darwin Saw. 2014. (ENG.). 48p. (J). (gr. 1-4). pap. 9.95 *(978-1-84780-107-4(2)*, Frances Lincoln Children's Bks.) Quarto Publishing Group UK GBR. Dist: Hachette Bk. Group.
Mannings, Garrett. Kara's Prayer. Andem, Shakara. Martin, Perry, ed. 2019. (ENG.). 34p. (J). pap. 9.99 ***(978-1-6866-6521-9(0))*** Independently Published.
Manny. Willow, Too Soon, Too Late. storiesbypj.com. 2010. (ENG.). 26p. pap. 10.92 *(978-0-9841194-3-1(4))* Cowan, Pricilla J.
Manoj, Bhargav. Las Aventuras de Carolina: Y el Dragón Esmeralda. Oberst, Eric Russell. 2019. (Las Aventuras de Carolina Ser.: Vol. 2). (SPA.). 190p. (J). (gr. 4-6). 24.99 *(978-0-578-52703-1(0))* Painted Leaf Publishing.
Manolessou, Katherina. T. Veg: The Story of a Carrot-Crunching Dinosaur. Prasadam-Halls, Smriti. 2017. (ENG.). 30p. (J). (gr. -1-3). 16.95 *(978-1-4197-2494-7(0)*, Abrams Bks. for Young Readers) Abrams, Inc.
Manolis, Tim. Dragonflies of North America: A Color & learn Book for All Ages, with Activities. Biggs, Kathy. l.t. ed. 2007. (ENG.). 48p. (J). *(978-0-9677934-4-3(0))* Azalea Creek Publishing.
—Dragonflies of North America: A Color & Learn Book for All Ages, with Activities. Biggs, Kathy. l.t. ed. 2007. 48p. (J). cd-rom *(978-0-9677934-5-0(9))* Azalea Creek Publishing.
Manousos, Dave. Life Is Good & Other Reasons for Rhyme. Manousos, Dave. 2008. 36p. pap. 16.95 *(978-1-59858-590-2(8))* Dog Ear Publishing, LLC.
Mansell, Dom. Dress Code: Doodlebug & Dandelion. Dell, Pamela. 2020. (ENG.). 24p. (J). pap. ***(978-1-922331-18-2(X))*** Library For All Limited.
Mansfield, Andy. Backyard Explorer, 1 vol. Baxter, Nicola & Lonely Planet Kids. 2017. (ENG.). 72p. (J). (gr. 1-3). 12.99 *(978-1-78657-319-3(9)*, 5405) Lonely Planet Global Ltd. IRL. Dist: Hachette Bk. Group.
—Boredom Buster, 1 vol. Baxter, Nicola & Lonely Planet Kids. 2016. (ENG.). 128p. (J). (gr. 1-3). pap. 11.99 *(978-1-76034-106-0(1)*, 5190) Lonely Planet Global Ltd. IRL. Dist: Hachette Bk. Group.
—First Phrases - French, 1 vol. Lonely Planet Kids. 2020. (First Words Ser.). (ENG.). 168p. (J). (gr. 1-3). pap. 14.99 *(978-1-83869-093-9(X)*, Lonely Planet Kids) Lonely Planet Global Ltd. IRL. Dist: Hachette Bk. Group.
Mansfield, Andy. First Phrases - Italian. Lonely Planet Kids. 2020. (First Words Ser.). (ENG.). 168p. (J). (gr. 1-3). pap. 14.99 ***(978-1-83869-419-7(6))*** Lonely Planet Global Ltd. IRL. Dist: Hachette Bk. Group.
Mansfield, Andy. First Phrases - Spanish, 1 vol. Lonely Planet Kids. 2020. (First Words Ser.). (ENG.). 168p. (J). (gr. 1-3). pap. 14.99 *(978-1-83869-089-2(1)*, Lonely Planet Kids) Lonely Planet Global Ltd. IRL. Dist: Hachette Bk. Group.
—The Incredible Cabinet of Wonders, 1 vol. Lonely Planet Kids & Fullman, Joe. 2017. (ENG.). 28p. (J). (gr. 4-7). 21.99 *(978-1-78701-104-5(6)*, 5676) Lonely Planet Global Ltd. IRL. Dist: Hachette Bk. Group.
—My Family Height Chart, 1 vol. Lonely Planet Kids. 2017. (ENG.). 18p. (J). (gr. 1-3). 14.99 *(978-1-78657-689-7(9)*, 5512) Lonely Planet Global Ltd. IRL. Dist: Hachette Bk. Group.
—My Family Travel Map, 1 vol. Baxter, Nicola & Lonely Planet Kids. 2016. (My Family Travel Map Ser.). (ENG.). 16p. (J). (gr. 1-3). 14.99 *(978-1-76034-101-5(0)*, 5185) Lonely Planet Global Ltd. IRL. Dist: Hachette Bk. Group.
—My Travel Journal, 1 vol. Baxter, Nicola & Lonely Planet Kids. 2016. (ENG.). 72p. (J). (gr. 1-3). 12.99 *(978-1-76034-100-8(2)*, 5184) Lonely Planet Global Ltd. IRL. Dist: Hachette Bk. Group.
—What's That in the Water? A Pop-Up Mystery. Norris, Eryl. 2015. (ENG.). 18p. (J). (gr. -1-1). 9.99 *(978-1-4998-0139-2(4))* Little Bee Books Inc.
—Who's Who in the Woods? Norris, Eryl. 2015. (ENG.). 18p. (J). (gr. -1-1). 9.99 *(978-1-4998-0140-8(8))* Little Bee Books Inc.
Mansfield, Andy. Find the Dots. Mansfield, Andy. 2017. (ENG.). 14p. (J). (gr. -1-2). 15.00 *(978-0-7636-9558-3(0))* Candlewick Pr.
—Pop-Up London, 1 vol. Mansfield, Andy. Lonely Planet Kids. 2016. (Pop-Up Cities Ser.). (ENG.). 8p. (J). (gr. -1-k). 9.99 *(978-1-76034-339-2(0)*, 5339) Lonely Planet Global Ltd. IRL. Dist: Hachette Bk. Group.
—Pop-Up New York, 1 vol. Mansfield, Andy. Lonely Planet Kids. 2016. (Pop-Up Cities Ser.). (ENG.). 8p. (J). (gr. -1-k). 9.99 *(978-1-76034-337-8(4)*, 5337) Lonely Planet Global Ltd. IRL. Dist: Hachette Bk. Group.
—Pop-Up Paris, 1 vol. Mansfield, Andy. Lonely Planet Kids. 2016. (Pop-Up Cities Ser.). (ENG.). 8p. (J). (gr. -1-k). 9.99 *(978-1-76034-335-4(8)*, 5335) Lonely Planet Global Ltd. IRL. Dist: Hachette Bk. Group.
—See the Stripes. Mansfield, Andy. 2018. (ENG.). 14p. (J). (gr. -1-2). 15.00 *(978-0-7636-9895-9(4))* Candlewick Pr.
Mansfield, Andy, jt. illus. see Flintham, Thomas.
Mansfield, Andy, jt. illus. see Iwohn, Sebastien.
Mansilla, Magalí. STEAM Stories: the Backyard Build (Engineering) Litton, Jonathan. 2018. (STEAM Stories Ser.). (ENG.). 24p. (J). (gr. -1-1). 12.95 ***(978-1-78603-281-2(3))*** QEB Publishing Inc.
—STEAM Stories: the Picnic Problem (Math) Litton, Jonathan. 2018. (STEAM Stories Ser.). (ENG.). 24p. (J). (gr. -1-1). 12.95 ***(978-0-7112-3986-9(X))*** QEB Publishing Inc.
Mansmann, Leslie. When I'm with You. Elder, Elizabeth. ed. 2003. (ENG.). 32p. (J). 15.95 *(978-0-9671662-8-5(4))* Islandport Pr., Inc.
Manson, Beverlie. Dreamland Fairies: Magical Bedtime Stories from Fairyland. Baxter, Nicola. 2012. 80p. (J). (gr. k-4). pap. 9.99 *(978-1-84322-806-6(8))* Anness Publishing GBR. Dist: National Bk. Network.
—The Little Mermaid. 2017. 24p. (J). (gr. -1-12). pap. 7.99 *(978-1-86147-828-3(3)*, Armadillo) Anness Publishing GBR. Dist: National Bk. Network.
—My Treasury of Fairies & Elves: A Collection of 20 Magical Stories. Baxter, Nicola. 2012. 240p. (J). (gr. k-4). 18.99 *(978-1-84322-835-6(1))* Anness Publishing GBR. Dist: National Bk. Network.
—My Treasury of Traditional Princess Fairytales. Anness, P. L. 2015. 160p. 16.99 *(978-1-86147-370-7(2)*, Armadillo) Anness Publishing GBR. Dist: National Bk. Network.
—Rapunzel. 2017. 24p. (J). (gr. -1-12). pap. 7.99 *(978-1-86147-827-6(5)*, Armadillo) Anness Publishing GBR. Dist: National Bk. Network.
—Stories to Share: The Twelve Dancing Princesses. 2017. 24p. (J). (gr. -1-12). pap. 7.99 *(978-1-86147-829-0(1)*, Armadillo) Anness Publishing GBR. Dist: National Bk. Network.
—A Visit from the Tooth Fairy: Magical Stories & a Special Message from the Little Friend Who Collects Your Baby Teeth. Baxter, Nicola. 2013. (ENG.). 40p. (J). (gr. k-4). 14.99 *(978-1-84322-987-2(0)*, Armadillo) Anness Publishing GBR. Dist: National Bk. Network.
Manson, Christopher. Black Swan/White Crow. Lewis, J. Patrick. 2007. (ENG.). 32p. (J). (gr. 2-5). 9.99 *(978-1-4169-6158-1(5)*, Simon & Schuster/Paula Wiseman Bks.) Simon & Schuster/Paula Wiseman Bks.
—Good King Wenceslas. 2004. 25p. (J). (gr. k-4). reprint ed. 15.00 *(978-0-7567-8226-9(0))* DIANE Publishing Co.
—Over the River & Through the Wood. Child, Lydia Maria. 2014. 32p. (J). 14.95 *(978-0-7358-4191-8(8))* North-South Bks., Inc.
—Till Year's Good End. Nikola-lisa, W. 2009. (ENG.). 36p. (J). (gr. 1-4). 12.99 *(978-1-4424-0225-6(3)*, Atheneum Bks. for Young Readers) Simon & Schuster Children's Publishing.
Manson, Davien. Who, Me? Smith, Scott. 2nd ed. 2017. (ENG.). 28p. (gr. -1-1). 12.99 *(978-0-9986381-4-0(5)*, Happy Dolphin Pr.) Glass Onion Publishing.
Mansur, Elisabeth Fahmi. Shuba & the Cyclone. Chandpai - Dhamrai Bangladeshi Students Staff. Kelly, Victoria, ed. 2011. (ENG.). 36p. (J). 17.95 *(978-0-9842146-6-2(6))* Concinnity Initiatives.
Mantell, Ahuva & Sperling, S. David. The Gift of Wisdom: The Books of Prophets & Writings. Steinbock, Steven E. 2004. (J). (gr. 4-6). pap. 13.95 *(978-0-8074-0752-3(6)*, 123944) URJ Pr.
Mantha, John. Harry Houdini. MacLeod, Elizabeth. 2009. (Kids Can Read Ser.). 32p. (J). (gr. 1-3). 14.95 *(978-1-55453-298-8(1))* Kids Can Pr., Ltd. CAN. Dist: Hachette Bk. Group.
—The Kids Book of Aboriginal Peoples in Canada. Silvey, Diane. 2012. (Kids Book Of Ser.). (ENG.). 64p. (J). (gr. 3-7). 14.95 *(978-1-55453-930-7(7))* Kids Can Pr., Ltd. CAN. Dist: Hachette Bk. Group.
—The Kids Book of Canada's Railway: And How the CPR Was Built. Hodge, Deborah. 2008. (Kids Book Of Ser.). (ENG.). 48p. (J). (gr. 3-7). pap. 15.99 *(978-1-55453-256-8(6))* Kids Can Pr., Ltd. CAN. Dist: Hachette Bk. Group.
—The Kids Book of Canadian Exploration. Owens, Ann-Maureen & Yealland, Jane. 2008. (Kids Book Of Ser.). (ENG.). 56p. (J). (gr. 3-7). pap. 14.95 *(978-1-55453-257-5(4))* Kids Can Pr., Ltd. CAN. Dist: Hachette Bk. Group.
—The Kids Book of Canadian History. Hacker, Carlotta. 2009. (Kids Book Of Ser.). (ENG.). 72p. (J). (gr. 3-7). 14.99 *(978-1-55453-328-2(7))* Kids Can Pr., Ltd. CAN. Dist: Hachette Bk. Group.
—The Kids Book of Canadian Prime Ministers. Hancock, Pat. 2005. (Kids Book Of Ser.). 56p. (J). (gr. 3-7). 19.95 *(978-1-55337-740-5(0))* Kids Can Pr., Ltd. CAN. Dist: Hachette Bk. Group.
—The Kids Book of World Religions. Glossop, Jennifer. 2013. (Kids Book Of Ser.). (ENG.). 64p. (J). (gr. 3-7). pap. 14.95 *(978-1-55453-981-9(1))* Kids Can Pr., Ltd. CAN. Dist: Hachette Bk. Group.
—Lucy Maud Montgomery. MacLeod, Elizabeth. 2008. 32p. (J). (gr. 1-3). 14.95 *(978-1-55453-055-7(5))* Kids Can Pr., Ltd. CAN. Dist: Hachette Bk. Group.
—Marie Curie. MacLeod, Elizabeth. 2009. (Kids Can Read Ser.). (ENG.). 32p. (J). (gr. 1-3). 11.99 *(978-1-55453-297-1(3))* Kids Can Pr., Ltd. CAN. Dist: Hachette Bk. Group.
—The Old Ways, 1 vol. Chapman, Susan. 2014. (ENG.). 32p. (J). (gr. k-3). 17.95 *(978-1-927083-16-1(8)*, 27d66706-4444-4b63-987d-010d24f17d03) Fifth Hse. Pubs. CAN. Dist: Firefly Bks., Ltd.
—Samuel de Champlain. MacLeod, Elizabeth. 2008. (Kids Can Read Level 3 Ser.). 32p. (J). (gr. k-3). 16.19 *(978-1-55453-049-6(0))* Kids Can Pr., Ltd. CAN. Dist: Children's Plus, Inc.
—Time of the Thunderbird. Silvey, Diane. 2008. (ENG.). 88p. (J). (gr. 6-5). pap. 11.99 *(978-1-55002-792-1(1)*, Sandcastle Bks.) Dundurn CAN. Dist: Ingram Publisher Services.
—What Was Pearl Harbor? Demuth, Patricia Brennan & Who HQ. 2013. (What Was? Ser.). (ENG.). 112p. (J). (gr. 3-7). pap. 5.99 *(978-0-448-46462-6(4)*, Penguin Workshop) Penguin Young Readers Group.
—What Was the Battle of Gettysburg? O'Connor, Jim & Who Hq. 2013. (What Was... Ser.). (ENG.). 106p. (J). (gr. 3-7). 16.80 *(978-1-5311-8708-8(0))* Perfection Learning Corp.
—What Was the Battle of Gettysburg? Who HQ & O'Connor, Jim. 2013. (What Was? Ser.). (ENG.). 112p. (J). (gr. 3-7). pap. 5.99 *(978-0-448-46286-8(9)*, Penguin Workshop) Penguin Young Readers Group.
Mantilla, Maria Fernanda. Amores Eternos. Arciniega, Triunfo. 2003. (Primer Acto: Teatro Infantil y Juvenil Ser.). (SPA.). 55p. (J). (gr. -1-7). pap. *(978-958-30-0998-3(9))* Panamericana Editorial.
Mantle, Ben. Bunnies on the Bus. Ardagh, Philip. 2020. (ENG.). 32p. (J). (gr. -1-2). 16.99 *(978-1-5362-1116-0(8))* Candlewick Pr.
—Busy Bug Book. Watt, Fiona. ed. 2011. (Pull-Back Books Ser.). 10p. (J). ring bd. 24.99 *(978-0-7945-2941-3(0)*, Usborne) EDC Publishing.
—A Cooked-Up Fairy Tale. Klostermann, Penny Parker. 2017. (ENG.). 40p. (J). (gr. -1-2). 17.99 *(978-1-101-93232-2(5))*; lib. bdg. 20.99 *(978-1-101-93233-9(3))* Random Hse. Children's Bks. (Random Hse. Bks. for Young Readers).
—Five Little Pumpkins. Tiger Tales. 2010. (ENG.). 24p. (J). (gr. -1-k). bds. 8.95 *(978-1-58925-856-3(8))* Tiger Tales.
—Follow the Track All the Way Back. Knapman, Timothy. 2017. (ENG.). 32p. (J). (-k). 16.99 *(978-0-7636-9573-6(4))* Candlewick Pr.
—Hug! Tiger Tales. 2013. (ENG.). 16p. (J). (-k). bds. 8.95 *(978-1-58925-637-8(9))* Tiger Tales.

—The Land of Roar. McLachlan, Jenny. 2020. (Land of Roar Ser.: 1). (ENG.). 304p. (J). (gr. 3-7). 16.99 *(978-0-06-298271-1(0)*, HarperCollins) HarperCollins Pubs. Ltd. GBR. Dist: HarperCollins Pubs.

—Little Red Reading Hood. Rowland, Lucy. 2018. (ENG.). 32p. (J). (gr. -1-k). pap. 12.99 *(978-1-5098-2522-6(3))* Pan Macmillan GBR. Dist: Independent Pubs. Group.

—Peek-A-Boo! Tiger Tales Staff. 2013. (ENG.). 16p. (J). bds. *(978-1-58925-636-1(0))* Tiger Tales.

—Rudy's Windy Christmas. Baugh, Helen. 2015. (ENG.). 32p. (J). (gr. -1-3). 16.99 *(978-0-8075-7173-6(3)*, 807571733) Whitman, Albert & Co.

—There Was an Old Dragon Who Swallowed a Knight. Klostermann, Penny Parker. 2020. (ENG.). 32p. (J). (— 1). bds. 8.99 *(978-1-9848-9242-3(8)*, Random Hse. Bks. for Young Readers) Random Hse. Children's Bks.

—Trick or Treat: 12 Board Books, 12 vols. 2011. (J). *(978-1-4508-1914-5(1))* Phoenix International Publications, Inc.

—Trick or Treat: 12 Board Books, 12 vols. 2011. (J). *(978-1-4508-2461-3(7)); (978-1-4508-2465-1(X)); (978-1-4508-2458-3(7)); (978-1-4508-2459-0(5)); (978-1-4508-2460-6(9)); (978-1-4508-2457-6(9)); (978-1-4508-2462-0(5)); (978-1-4508-2468-2(4)); (978-1-4508-2464-4(1)); (978-1-4508-2463-7(3)); (978-1-4508-2467-5(6)); (978-1-4508-2466-8(8))* Publications International, Ltd.

Mantle, Ben. The Spooky Wheels on the Bus. Mantle, Ben. Mills, J. Elizabeth. 2010. (ENG.). 24p. (J). (gr. -1-k). pap. 3.99 *(978-0-545-17480-0(5))* Scholastic, Inc.

Mantle, Benjamin. This Is Not That Kind of Book. Healy, Christopher. 2019. (ENG.). 40p. (J). (gr. -1-2). lib. bdg. 20.99 *(978-0-525-58030-0(1)*, Random Hse. Bks. for Young Readers) Random Hse. Children's Bks.

Manton, Jimmy. Goddesses & Sirens. Demarco, Stacey. 2013. (ENG.). 176p. (YA). (gr. 7). 19.99 *(978-1-58270-381-7(7)*, Beyond Words) Simon & Schuster.

—Gods & Titans. Demarco, Stacey. 2013. (ENG.). 160p. (YA). (gr. 7). 19.99 *(978-1-58270-380-0(9)*, Beyond Words) Simon & Schuster.

Mantzke, Jurgen. The Adventures of the Rocky Mountain Tea Twerps. Hartman, Moreta. 2003. 56p. 18.95 *(978-0-9743937-0-4(3))* Hallelujah Acres Publishing.

Manu, jt. illus. see Chandu.

Manuzak, Lisa. Gobi: a Little Dog with a Big Heart, 1 vol. Leonard, Dion. 2017. (ENG.). 32p. (J). 16.99 *(978-0-7180-7529-3(3))* Nelson, Thomas Inc.

—Gobi for Little Ones: The Race for Home, 1 vol. Leonard, Dion. 2018. (ENG.). 24p. (J). bds. 9.99 *(978-0-7180-7530-9(7))* Nelson, Thomas Inc.

—The Lost Lamb & the Good Shepherd. Mackall, Dandi Daley. 2016. (Flipside Stories Ser.). (ENG.). 48p. (J). 14.99 *(978-1-4964-1121-1(8)*, 4612796) Tyndale Hse. Pubs.

—Magic Animal Rescue 1: Maggie & the Flying Horse. Baker, E. D. 2017. 128p. (J). 16.99 *(978-1-68119-312-0(4)*, 900165678); (ENG.). pap. 5.99 *(978-1-68119-141-6(5)*, 900159887) Bloomsbury Publishing USA. (Bloomsbury USA Childrens).

—Magic Animal Rescue Bind-Up Books 1-3 Bks. 1-3: Maggie & the Flying Horse, Maggie & the Wish Fish, & Maggie & the Unicorn. Baker, E. D. 2017. (ENG.). 368p. (J). 10.99 *(978-1-68119-934-4(3)*, 900193211, Bloomsbury USA Childrens) Bloomsbury Publishing USA.

—PrayerWorks: Prayer Strategy & Training for Kids. Kendrick, Stephen et al. 2015. (ENG.). 128p. (J). (gr. 3-6). 12.99 *(978-1-4336-8869-0(7)*, 005765908, B&H Kids) B&H Publishing Group.

—Tooth Bandits. Hay, Sam. 2016. (Stella & the Night Sprites Ser.: 2). (ENG.). 96p. (J). (gr. 1-3). 15.99 *(978-0-545-82001-1(4))* Scholastic, Inc.

—A Walk in the Forest: Wheels of Wonder Book. Garnett, Jaye. Cottage Door Press, ed. 2017. (Smithsonian Kids Ser.). (ENG.). 10p. (J). (gr. -1-2). bds. 9.99 *(978-1-68052-236-5(1)*, 1002220) Cottage Door Pr.

—Zacchaeus & Jesus. Mackall, Dandi Daley. 2016. (Flipside Stories Ser.). (ENG.). 48p. (J). 14.99 *(978-1-4964-1119-8(6)*, 4612794) Tyndale Hse. Pubs.

Manwill, Melissa. A Girl Named Misty: The True Story of Misty Copeland. Lyons, Kelly Starling. 2018. (American Girl: a Girl Named Ser.). (ENG.). 48p. (J). (gr. 2-5). pap. 4.99 *(978-1-338-19305-3(8))* Scholastic, Inc.

—A Little Fawn. Wren, Rosalee. Cottage Door Press, ed. 2019. (ENG.). 10p. (J). (gr. -1-k). bds. 4.99 *(978-1-68052-629-5(4)*, 1004220) Cottage Door Pr.

Manwill, Melissa A. When Penny Met POTUS. Ruiz, Rachel. 2016. (Fiction Picture Bks.). (ENG.). 32p. (J). (gr. -1-3). lib. bdg. 27.99 *(978-1-5158-0218-1(3)*, Picture Window Bks.) Capstone.

Manwiller, S. A. The Adventures of Jack & Max: What Jack & Max Love. Manwiller, S. A. 2013. (ENG.). 30p. 19.99 *(978-0-9838427-4-3(4))* Sevenhorns Publishing.

Manwiller, S. A. & Overley, Kristen V. The Adventures of Jack & Max: The Truliest Meaning of Christmas. Manwiller, S. A. 2013. (ACH & ENG.). 38p. 24.99 *(978-0-9838427-7-4(9))* Sevenhorns Publishing.

Manz, Ronnette Benoit. Oakley the Lonely Oak Tree. Maurer, M. S. Valerie. 2018. (ENG.). 38p. (J). pap. *(978-1-7752825-0-1(3))* Maurer, Valerie.

Manzano, Summer. The Hopping Frog & the Flipping Waterlily. Sevaru, Molly. 2018. (ENG.). 18p. (J). pap. *(978-9980-89-988-0(3))* Library For All Limited.

Manzel, Michael. Moby's Tale. 2004. 248p. (YA). pap. 19.95 *(978-0-9746345-0-0(6))* River of Life Publishing.

Manzo, Jr Franklin. Andy's Surprise! What a Moose, Ayuh! Caverly, Tim. 2019. (Allagash Tails Collection: Vol. 8). (ENG.). 28p. (J). pap. 10.99 ***(978-1-7322456-6-2(5))*** Leicester Bay Bks.

Mape, Michael. The Flying Fox & the Cockatoo. Baia, Edward. 2013. 22p. pap. *(978-9980-86-507-6(5))* Univ. of Papua New Guinea Pr.

Mape, Michael & Ella, Peter Leo. Isokau Akuaku: A Traditional Story from Central Province. Baia, Edward. 2013. 30p. pap. *(978-9980-86-494-9(X))* Univ. of Papua New Guinea Pr.

Mar, Sandra. Why Dragons Cannot Go Shopping. Rioux, Jacqueline. 2018. (ENG.). 34p. (J). *(978-1-78324-083-8(0))* Wordzworth Publishing.

Mara, Leilani. The Little Blue Dragon with Three Heads. Blackburn, Diane. 2020. (Little Blue Dragon Ser.: Vol. 1). (ENG.). 24p. (J). ***(978-0-2288-2840-2(6))***; pap. ***(978-0-2288-2839-6(2))*** Tellwell Talent.

Mara, S. M. Steven Universe Vol. 8: To Be Happy. Robbin, Taylor. 2020. (Steven Universe Ser.). (ENG.). 112p. (J). pap. 14.99 ***(978-1-68415-626-9(2))*** Boom! Studios.

Maraja. Alice in Wonderland Picture Book. 2013. (Shape Bks.). (ENG.). 16p. (J). pap. 9.95 *(978-1-59583-701-1(9))* Laughing Elephant.

Marantz, Larissa. Clyde Goes to School. Marantz, Keith. 2020. (Clyde the Hippo Ser.). 32p. (J). (-k). 8.99 *(978-0-593-09446-4(8))*; pap. 4.99 *(978-0-593-09445-7(X))* Penguin Young Readers Group. (Penguin Workshop).

—Clyde Lied. Marantz, Keith. 2020. (Clyde the Hippo Ser.). 32p. (J). (-k). 8.99 *(978-0-593-09452-5(2))*; pap. 4.99 *(978-0-593-09451-8(4))* Penguin Young Readers Group. (Penguin Workshop).

—Clyde Likes to Slide. Marantz, Keith. 2020. (Clyde the Hippo Ser.). 32p. (J). (-k). 8.99 *(978-0-593-09449-5(2))*; pap. 4.99 *(978-0-593-09448-8(4))* Penguin Young Readers Group. (Penguin Workshop).

Marantz, Larissa & DiPaolo, Katharine. What's with Dad? Willson, Sarah. 2006. (Ready-To-Read Level 3 Ser.). (ENG.). 32p. (J). (gr. 1-3). 16.19 *(978-1-4169-0669-8(X))* Simon & Schuster, Inc.

Marble, Abigail. My Secret Bully. Ludwig, Trudy. 32p. (J). (gr. 1-4). 2015. 7.99 *(978-0-553-50940-3(3)*, Dragonfly Bks.); 2005. 16.99 *(978-1-58246-159-5(7)*, Tricycle Pr.) Random Hse. Children's Bks.

—Two for Joy. Amateau, Gigi. 2015. 96p. (J). (gr. 2-5). 14.99 *(978-0-7636-3010-2(1))* Candlewick Pr.

Marbury, Ja'Nitta. All Mixed Up. Marbury, Ja'Nitta. 2003. 22p. (J). pap. 22.50 *(978-0-9718307-3-8(8))* Shades of Me Publishing.

Marc, Sylvain. The Case of the Fatal Phantom, 3 vols. Kennedy, Emma. 2012. (Wilma Tenderfoot Ser.: 3). (ENG.). 351p. (J). (gr. 3-6). 17.95 *(978-0-8037-3542-2(1))* Penguin Young Readers Group.

Marcellin, Jean. Boats Through the Ages. Crabbé, Raoul & Barwell, Eve. 6th ed. 2013. (ENG & FRE.). 25p. *(978-0-245-50382-5(X))* Harrap, Larousse Pubs.

Marcellino, Ann. Black Widow (Marvel) Webster, Christy. 2020. (Little Golden Book Ser.). (ENG.). 24p. (J). (-k). 4.99 *(978-0-593-12215-0(1)*, Golden Bks.) Random Hse. Children's Bks.

Marcellino, Fred. Ouch! Babbitt, Natalie. pap. 18.95 incl. audio compact disk *(978-1-59112-350-7(X))*; pap. incl. audio compact disk *(978-1-59112-558-7(8))* Live Oak Media.

—The Pelican Chorus: And Other Nonsense. Lear, Edward. 2017. (ENG.). 40p. (J). (gr. -1-3). 17.99 *(978-1-4814-7049-0(3)*, Atheneum/Caitlyn Dlouhy Books) Simon & Schuster Children's Publishing.

—Puss in Boots. Perrault, Charles. Arthur, Malcolm, tr. from ENG. 2011. (ENG.). 32p. (J). (gr. -1-3). pap. 8.99 *(978-0-312-65945-5(8)*, 900070543) Square Fish.

—A Rat's Tale. Seidler, Tor. 2008. (ENG.). 192p. (J). (gr. 3-7). pap. 11.99 *(978-0-374-40031-6(8)*, 9780374400316, Farrar, Straus & Giroux (BYR)) Farrar, Straus & Giroux.

—The Steadfast Tin Soldier. 2017.Tr. of Standhaftige Tinsoldat. (ENG.). 32p. (J). (gr. -1-3). 17.99 *(978-1-4814-7662-1(9)*, Atheneum/Caitlyn Dlouhy Books) Simon & Schuster Children's Publishing.

—The Trumpet of the Swan. White, E. B. 2020. (ENG.). 272p. (J). (gr. 3-7). pap. 7.99 *(978-0-06-440867-7(1)*, HarperCollins) HarperCollins Pubs. Ltd. GBR. Dist: HarperCollins Pubs.

—The Wainscott Weasel. 2014. (ENG.). 208p. (J). (gr. 2-7). 16.99 *(978-1-4814-1010-6(5)*, Atheneum Bks. for Young Readers) Simon & Schuster Children's Publishing.

Marcellino, Fred & Puybaret, Eric. Arrivederci, Crocodile. Marcellino, Fred. 2019. (ENG.). 40p. (J). (gr. -1-3). 17.99 *(978-1-5344-0401-4(5)*, Atheneum Bks. for Young Readers) Simon & Schuster Children's Publishing.

Marcero, Deborah. Jess's Story. Heppermann, Christine & Koertge, Ron. 2016. (Backyard Witch Ser.: 2). (ENG.). 192p. (J). (gr. 3-7). 16.99 *(978-0-06-233841-9(2)*, Greenwillow Bks.) HarperCollins Pubs.

—Maya's Story. Heppermann, Christine & Koertge, Ron. (Backyard Witch Ser.: 3). (ENG.). 192p. (J). (gr. 3-7). 2018. pap. 5.99 *(978-0-06-233845-7(5))*; 2017. 16.99 *(978-0-06-233844-0(7))* HarperCollins Pubs. (Greenwillow Bks.).

—Sadie's Story. Heppermann, Christine & Koertge, Ron. (Backyard Witch Ser.: 1). (ENG.). 176p. (J). (gr. 3-7). 2016. pap. 5.99 *(978-0-06-233839-6(0))*; 2015. 16.99 *(978-0-06-233838-9(2))* HarperCollins Pubs. (Greenwillow Bks.).

—Twinderella, a Fractioned Fairy Tale. Schwartz, Corey Rosen. 2017. 32p. (J). (gr. -1-3). 17.99 *(978-0-399-17633-3(0)*, G.P. Putnam's Sons Books for Young Readers) Penguin Young Readers Group.

—Ursa's Light. 2016. (J). *(978-1-4413-1881-7(X))* Peter Pauper Pr. Inc.

Marcero, Deborah. In a Jar. Marcero, Deborah. 2020. (ENG.). 40p. (J). (gr. -1-2). 17.99 *(978-0-525-51459-6(7)*, G.P. Putnam's Sons Books for Young Readers) Penguin Young Readers Group.

March, Chloe. My First 100 Words Book: A Lift-the-Flap, Pull-Tab Learning Book. Haney Perez, Jessica. 2005. (Learn to Read Ser.). 10p. (J). 10.95 *(978-1-58117-210-2(9)*, Intervisual/Piggy Toes) Bendon, Inc.

March, Guillermo, et al. Japones en Vinetas: Curso Basico de Japones a Traves del Manga. Bernabe, Marc. 5th ed. 2004. (SPA.). 293p. (YA). (gr. 8). per. 34.95 *(978-1-59497-074-0(2))* Public Square Bks.

March, Marc. How the Earth Became Round. March, Mason. 2019. (ENG.). 46p. (J). (gr. k-4). 17.99 ***(978-0-578-52163-3(6))*** AHRWEILER, ERIC.

March, Molly. The Silver Lining. Spottiswoode, Amanda. 2016. (ENG.). 224p. (J). (gr. 4-7). pap. 12.95 ***(978-1-77203-132-4(1)***, Wandering Fox) Heritage Hse. CAN. Dist: Orca Bk. Pubs. USA.

—Up in Arms, 1 vol. Spottiswoode, Amanda. 2017. (ENG.). 224p. (J). (gr. 4-7). pap. 12.95 ***(978-1-77203-202-4(6)***, Wandering Fox) Heritage Hse. CAN. Dist: Orca Bk. Pubs. USA.

Marchand, Barbara. Neekna & Chemai, 1 vol. Armstrong, Jeannette. 3rd ed. 2019. (Schchechmala Children's Ser.). (ENG.). 52p. (YA). (gr. 4-7). pap. 14.95 ***(978-1-926886-43-5(7))*** Theytus Bks., Ltd. CAN. Dist: Orca Bk. Pubs. USA.

Marchand, V. Smoker. A River Lost. Bragg, Lynn E. 2009. (Act Ser.). (ENG.). 32p. (Orig.). (gr. 2-8). pap. 11.95 *(978-0-88839-383-8(0))* Hancock Hse. Pubs.

Marchese, Stephen. The Flights of Marceau: Week Two. 2007. (ENG.). 60p. (J). 16.95 *(978-0-9797495-1-3(4))* Majestic Eagle Publishing.

Marchesi, Stephen. Box Turtle at Silver Pond Lane. Korman, Susan. 2005. (Smithsonian's Backyard Ser.). (ENG.). 32p. (J). (gr. -1-2). 15.95 *(978-1-56899-860-2(0)*, B5020) Soundprints.

—Box Turtle at Silver Pond Lane: Smithsonians Backyard. Korman, Susan. 2005. (Smithsonian's Backyard Ser.). (ENG.). 32p. (J). (gr. -1-2). pap. 6.95 *(978-1-56899-935-7(6)*, S5020) Soundprints.

—Deborah Saves the Day. Rottmann, Erik. 2008. (Arch Bks.). 16p. (J). (gr. k-4). pap. 1.99 *(978-0-7586-1457-5(8))* Concordia Publishing Hse.

—Dorothy Day: A Catholic Life of Action. Shaw, Maura D. 2004. (Spiritual Biographies for Young Readers Ser.). (ENG.). 32p. (J). 12.99 *(978-1-59473-011-5(3)*, 9135644c-888c-415d-a4b2-abbdcd24b83e, Skylight Paths Publishing) LongHill Partners, Inc.

—The Flights of Marceau: Week One. 2007. (ENG.). 56p. (J). 16.95 *(978-0-9797495-0-6(6))* Majestic Eagle Publishing.

—Gandhi: India's Great Soul. Shaw, Maura D. 2003. (ENG.). 32p. (J). (gr. 1-3). 12.95 *(978-1-893361-91-1(8)*, cae3cea7-a255-4b12-be7a-5ba52b13badc, Skylight Paths Publishing) LongHill Partners, Inc.

—Glow-In-The-Dark Constellations. 2006. (J). *(978-1-59412-171-5(0))* Mud Puddle, Inc.

—Hurricanes: Weathering the Storm. Hojem, Benjamin. 2010. (All Aboard Science Reader Station Stop 3 Ser.). (ENG.). 48p. (J). (gr. 2-4). 16.19 *(978-0-448-45466-5(1))* Penguin Young Readers Group.

—Let's Read About — Pocahontas. Weinberger, Kimberly. 2003. (Scholastic First Biographies Ser.). (J). pap. *(978-0-439-56148-8(5))* Scholastic, Inc.

Marchesi, Stephen. ¿Por Qué Tenemos el día de Acción de Gracias. Hillert, Margaret. 2020. (Beginning-To-Read: Spanish Easy Stories Ser.). (SPA.). 32p. (J). (-2). 22.60 ***(978-1-68450-879-2(7))***; pap. 11.94 ***(978-1-68404-535-8(5))*** Norwood Hse. Pr.

Marchesi, Stephen. Race to the Rescue. Brown, Joe. 2009. (J). *(978-0-545-13473-6(0))* Scholastic, Inc.

—Thich Nhat Hanh: Buddhism in Action. Shaw, Maura D. 2003. (Spiritual Biographies for Young Readers Ser.). (ENG.). 32p. (J). (gr. 1-3). 12.95 *(978-1-893361-87-4(X)*, 129628dd-3095-464c-9e68-a7a267cccba7, Skylight Paths Publishing) LongHill Partners, Inc.

—What Are the Summer Olympics? Herman, Gail & Who HQ. 2016. (What Was? Ser.). 112p. (J). (gr. 3-7). 5.99 *(978-0-448-48834-9(5)*, Penguin Workshop) Penguin Young Readers Group.

—What Is the World Cup? Bader, Bonnie & Who HQ. 2018. (What Was? Ser.). 112p. (J). (gr. 3-7). 5.99 *(978-0-515-15821-2(6)*, Penguin Workshop) Penguin Young Readers Group.

—What Was the Berlin Wall? Medina, Nico & Who HQ. 2019. (What Was? Ser.). 112p. (J). (gr. 3-7). 5.99 *(978-1-5247-8967-1(4))*; 15.99 *(978-1-5247-8968-8(2))* Penguin Young Readers Group. (Penguin Workshop).

—What Was the Wild West? Pascal, Janet B. & Who HQ. 2017. (What Was? Ser.). (ENG.). 112p. (J). (gr. 3-7). 5.99 *(978-0-399-54424-8(0)*, Penguin Workshop) Penguin Young Readers Group.

—What Were the Negro Leagues? Johnson, Varian & Who HQ. 2019. (What Was? Ser.). 112p. (J). (gr. 3-7). 5.99 *(978-1-5247-8998-5(4))*; 15.99 *(978-1-5247-8999-2(2))* Penguin Young Readers Group. (Penguin Workshop).

—Who Is Dolly Parton? Kelley, True & Who HQ. 2014. (Who Was? Ser.). 112p. (J). (gr. 3-7). 5.99 *(978-0-448-47892-0(7)*, Penguin Workshop) Penguin Young Readers Group.

—Who Is J. K. Rowling? Pollack, Pam et al. 2012. (Who Was? Ser.). 112p. (J). (gr. 3-7). pap. 5.99 *(978-0-448-45872-4(1)*, Penguin Workshop) Penguin Young Readers Group.

—Who Is Ralph Lauren? Who HQ & O'Connor, Jane. 2017. (Who Was? Ser.). 112p. (J). (gr. 3-7). 5.99 *(978-1-5247-8402-7(8))*; lib. bdg. 15.99 *(978-1-5247-8403-4(6))* Penguin Young Readers Group. (Penguin Workshop).

—Who Was Claude Monet? Waldron, Ann & Who HQ. 2009. (Who Was? Ser.). (ENG.). 112p. (J). (gr. 3-7). pap. 5.99 *(978-0-448-44985-2(4)*, Penguin Workshop) Penguin Young Readers Group.

—Who Was H. J. Heinz? Burgan, Michael & Who HQ. 2019. (Who Was? Ser.). 112p. (J). (gr. 3-7). 5.99 *(978-0-448-48865-3(5))*; lib. bdg. 15.99 *(978-1-5247-9095-0(8))* Penguin Young Readers Group. (Penguin Workshop).

—Who Was Jesus? Morgan, Ellen & Who HQ. 2015. (Who Was? Ser.). (ENG.). 112p. (J). (gr. 3-7). 5.99 *(978-0-448-48320-7(3)*, Penguin Workshop) Penguin Young Readers Group.

—Who Was Maurice Sendak? Pascal, Janet B. & Who HQ. 2013. (Who Was? Ser.). 112p. (J). (gr. 3-7). pap. 5.99 *(978-0-448-46500-5(0)*, Penguin Workshop) Penguin Young Readers Group.

—Who Was Muhammad Ali? Buckley, James, Jr. et al. 2014. (Who Was? Ser.). 112p. (J). (gr. 3-7). 5.99 *(978-0-448-47955-2(9)*, Penguin Workshop) Penguin Young Readers Group.

—Who Was Neil Armstrong? Edwards, Roberta & Who HQ. (Who Was? Ser.). (ENG.). 112p. (J). (gr. 3-7). 2018. 9.99 *(978-1-5247-9207-7(1))*; 2008. pap. 5.99 *(978-0-448-44907-4(2))* Penguin Young Readers Group. (Penguin Workshop).

—Who Was Nelson Mandela? Pollack, Pam & Belviso, Meg. 2014. (Who Was... ? Ser.). (ENG.). (J). (gr. 3-7). lib. bdg. 15.60 *(978-1-62765-404-3(6))* Perfection Learning Corp.

—Who Was Nelson Mandela? Pollack, Pam & Who HQ. 2014. (Who Was? Ser.). (ENG.). 112p. (J). (gr. 3-7). 5.99 *(978-0-448-47933-0(8)*, Penguin Workshop) Penguin Young Readers Group.

—Who Was P. T. Barnum? Anderson, Kirsten & Who HQ. 2019. (Who Was? Ser.). 112p. (J). (gr. 3-7). 5.99 *(978-0-448-48848-6(5))*; 15.99 *(978-1-5247-9222-0(5))* Penguin Young Readers Group. (Penguin Workshop).

—Who Was Pete Seeger? MacCarry, Noel & Who HQ. 2017. (Who Was? Ser.). 112p. (J). (gr. 3-7). 5.99 *(978-0-448-48475-4(7)*, Penguin Workshop) Penguin Young Readers Group.

—Who Was Roald Dahl? Kelley, True & Who HQ. 2012. (Who Was? Ser.). 112p. (J). (gr. 3-7). pap. 5.99 *(978-0-448-46146-5(3)*, Penguin Workshop) Penguin Young Readers Group.

—Who Was Rosa Parks? McDonough, Yona Zeldis & Who HQ. 2010. (Who Was? Ser.). (ENG.). 112p. (J). (gr. 3-7). pap. 5.99 *(978-0-448-45442-9(4)*, Penguin Workshop) Penguin Young Readers Group.

—Why We Have Thanksgiving. Hillert, Margaret. 2016. (BeginningtoRead Ser.). (ENG.). 32p. (J). (gr. 1-2). 22.60 *(978-1-59953-809-9(1))* Norwood Hse. Pr.

Marchetti, Angela. A Donkey's Tale. Gorla, Stefano. 2013. 64p. (J). pap. 9.95 *(978-0-8198-1901-7(8))* Pauline Bks. & Media.

Marchus, Linda. The Gorilla Who Wanted to Dance. Marchus, Linda. 2003. 32p. (J). lib. bdg. 15.95 *(978-0-9723122-1-9(8))* Wee Read Publishing.

Marcin, Piwowarski, jt. illus. see Piwowarski, Marcin.

Marco, Harvey, jt. illus. see Niednagel, David.

Marcolla, Bernardo. Me & You & the Universe. Marcolla, Bernardo. 2020. (ENG.). 36p. (J). (gr. k-3). 16.99 ***(978-1-63198-522-5(1)***, 85225) Free Spirit Publishing, Inc.

Marconi, Gloria. Bela & the Gold Medallion. Preston, James, photos by. Smith, Loretta. 2012. 32p. pap. 13.00 *(978-1-930357-27-3(3))* Do The Write Thing Foundation of DC.

Marcos, Pablo. Clara Barton & the American Red Cross. Marko, Eve. 2005. (Heroes of America Ser.). 237p. (gr. 3-8). 27.07 *(978-1-59679-255-5(8)*, Abdo & Daughters) ABDO Publishing Co.

—Daniel Boone. Nemerson, Roy. 2005. (Heroes of America Ser.). 239p. (gr. 3-8). lib. bdg. 27.07 *(978-1-59679-256-2(6)*, Abdo & Daughters) ABDO Publishing Co.

—Jackie Robinson. Hanft, Joshua E. 2005. (Heroes of America Ser.). 238p. (gr. 3-8). lib. bdg. 27.07 *(978-1-59679-259-3(0)*, Abdo & Daughters) ABDO Publishing Co.

—King Solomon's Mines. Haggard, H. Rider. 2005. (Great Illustrated Classics Ser.). 239p. (J). (gr. 3-8). 21.35 *(978-1-59679-244-9(2)*, Abdo & Daughters) ABDO Publishing Co.

—A Little Princess: The Story of Sara Crewe. Burnett, Frances Hodgson. Warren, Eliza, ed. 2006. 239p. (YA). reprint ed. 10.00 *(978-0-7567-9835-2(3))* DIANE Publishing Co.

—Martin Luther King, Jr. Boyd, Herb. 2005. (Heroes of America Ser.). 239p. (gr. 3-8). 27.07 *(978-1-59679-258-6(2)*, Abdo & Daughters) ABDO Publishing Co.

—Sherlock Holmes & the Case of the Hound of the Baskervilles. Doyle, A. Conan. Vogel, Malvina G., ed. 2006. 237p. (YA). (gr. 4-8). 10.00 *(978-0-7567-9834-5(5))* DIANE Publishing Co.

Marden, Priscilla. Oliver, a Story about Adoption - Updated. Wickstrom, Lois. 2020. (ENG.). 24p. (J). pap. 9.99 ***(978-1-6586-4235-4(X))*** Independently Published.

Marderosian, Mark. Christmas Wishes. Herman, Gail. 2004. (J). *(978-0-439-66763-0(1))* Scholastic, Inc.

Mardinly, Berdan. Fresh Tarhana Soup - English. Mardinly, Berdan. 2008. (ENG.). 16p. (J). pap. 5.50 *(978-1-935125-05-1(2))* Robertson Publishing.

Mardon, John. Bats in the Garbage, 1 vol. Jennings, Sharon. 2003. (First Flight Level 4 Ser.). (ENG.). 64p. (J). (gr. 2-3). pap. 4.95 *(978-1-55041-723-4(1)*, 25c4d0ad-71ba-44d7-8360-265fade47744) éditeur, Annika Parance CAN. Dist: Firefly Bks., Ltd.

Marecic, Ivan. A Mousekeeper Christmas: Early Reader. Copeland, Jenny. 2018. (Mousekeeper Christmas Ser.: Vol. 2). (ENG.). 78p. (J). (gr. k-3). 21.99 *(978-0-9992968-3-7(3))* Crazy Red Head Publishing.

Marek, Jane. The Professor's Telescope. Moreau, Chris. 2006. (YA). 10.95 *(978-0-9785399-0-0(7))*; cd-rom 7.95 *(978-0-9785399-2-4(3))* Windows of Discovery.

Maren, Julie. Celia Cruz, Queen of Salsa. Chambers, Veronica. 2008. (J). (gr. -1-3). 28.95 incl. audio compact disk *(978-1-4301-0284-7(5))*; 25.95 incl. audio *(978-1-4301-0281-6(0))*; pap. 16.95 incl. audio *(978-1-4301-0280-9(2))* Live Oak Media.

—Celia Cruz, Queen of Salsa. Chambers, Veronica. 2007. (ENG.). 40p. (J). (gr. k-3). pap. 7.99 *(978-0-14-240779-0(8)*, Puffin Books) Penguin Young Readers Group.

—Celia Cruz, Queen of Salsa. Chambers, Veronica. 2007. (gr. 2-5). 17.00 *(978-0-7569-8153-2(0))* Perfection Learning Corp.

—An Orange in January. Aston, Dianna Hutts. 2007. 32p. (J). (gr. -1-3). 17.99 (978-0-8037-3146-2(9), Dial Bks) Penguin Young Readers Group.

Marent, Thomas, photos by. All in a Rainforest Day. Senisi, Ellen B. (J). 2016. (gr. -1-3). 45.99 (978-0-9912337-2-4(7)); 2016. (ENG., (gr. -1-3). pap. 7.95 (978-0-9912337-1-7(9)); 2014. (ENG., 32p. 17.95 (978-0-9912337-0-0(0)) EdTechLens.

—Weird Butterflies & Moths. Orenstein, Ronald. 2016. (ENG., 64p. (J). (gr. 5-8). pap. 9.95 (978-1-77085-814-5(8), e98fc3f8-b0d0-4c68-90b0-ab2f408b8b27) Firefly Bks., Ltd.

Maresca, Beth Anne. Megan Owlet. 2015. 32p. (J). (gr. -1-k). 16.99 (978-1-63220-404-2(5), Sky Pony Pr.) Skyhorse Publishing Co., Inc.

Maresky, David & Denomm�-Warren, Madison & Brooke. Awesome Inside + Out. Denomm�, Margot L. 2019. (ENG.). (J). (gr. k-6). 26p. (978-0-9920340-2-3(7)); 28p. pap. (978-0-9920340-3-0(5)) Denomme, Margot Lynn.

Marfil, Darwin. Scarlett. Beckett, Risa. 2018. (ENG.). 32p. (J). 16.99 (978-1-64293-002-3(4)) Post Hill Pr.

Margeson, John. Balls! Rosen, Michael J. 2006. 72p. (J). (gr. 4-8). 18.95 (978-1-58196-030-3(1), Darby Creek) Lerner Publishing Group.

—Balls! Round 2. Rosen, Michael J. 2008. (Darby Creek Exceptional Titles Ser.). (ENG.). 80p. (J). (gr. 4-8). 18.95 (978-1-58196-066-2(2), Darby Creek) Lerner Publishing Group.

—Rufus the Scrub Does Not Wear a Tutu. McEwan, Jamie. 2006. 64p. (J). (gr. 2-3). 14.95 (978-1-58196-060-0(3), Darby Creek) Lerner Publishing Group.

—Scrubs Forever! McEwan, Jamie. 2008. (Darby Creek Exceptional Titles Ser.). (ENG.). 64p. (J). (gr. 2-5). lib. bdg. 14.95 (978-1-58196-069-3(7), Darby Creek) Lerner Publishing Group.

—Whitewater Scrubs. McEwan, Jamie. 2005. (ENG.). 80p. (J). (gr. 2-4). 14.99 (978-1-58196-038-9(7), Darby Creek) Lerner Publishing Group.

Margie & Jimbo. My Fridge: My First Book of Food. duopress labs. 2017. (ENG.). 20p. (J). (gr. -1-k). bds. 7.95 (978-1-946064-00-4(9), 806400) Duo Pr. LLC.

Margie & Jimbo, Margie &. My Fridge: My First Book of Food. duopress labs, duopress. 2017. (ENG.). 20p. (J). (gr. -1-k). E-Book (978-1-946064-81-3(5), 806400E) Duo Pr. LLC.

Margiotta, Kristen. Gustav Gloom & the Nightmare Vault #2. Castro, Adam-Troy. 2014. (Gustav Gloom Ser.: 2). 248p. (J). (gr. 3-7). 7.99 (978-0-448-48329-0(7), Grosset & Dunlap) Penguin Young Readers Group.

Margo, Marie. 45 Games... While You Wait! Auzou Publishing Staff, ed. 2018. 52p. (J). 6.99 (978-2-7338-5622-2(7)) Auzou, Philippe Editions FRA. Dist: Consortium Bk. Sales & Distribution.

Margolis, Al. Boy in the Hoodie. Fontaine, Renee. 2012. 34p. (J). 19.95 (978-1-61863-105-3(5)) Bookstand Publishing.

—Fucious: The True Story of the Ugly Duckling. Mastrud, Karen. 2012. 32p. (J). 24.95 (978-1-61863-414-6(3)) Bookstand Publishing.

—Gabe's Nantucket Adventure: Daffodils, Dogs, & Cars. Thorpe, Rochelle O'Neal. Nakell, Eugenie, ed. l.t. ed. 2010. 28p. (YA). pap. 7.95 (978-1-935706-02-1(0)) Wiggles Pr.

—Grandpa Wins the Big Game. Sylte, Darren. 2019. (ENG.). 38p. (J). (gr. k-6). pap. 17.95 (978-1-63498-814-8(0)) Bookstand Publishing.

—The Playground Bully Blues. Ladin, Marc J. 2010. 26p. pap. 14.95 (978-1-60844-377-2(9)) Dog Ear Publishing, LLC.

—Presents for Phoebe: Growing Independent. Rhode, Paul. 2011. 24p. (YA). pap. 9.95 (978-1-935706-05-2(5)) Wiggles Pr.

—Seana's New Accessory. Faircloth, M. L. 2012. 26p. 19.95 (978-1-61863-407-8(0)) Bookstand Publishing.

—Stories for Dreamers. Dultz, Dorothy. 2013. 68p. (J). pap. 9.95 (978-1-61863-425-2(9)) Bookstand Publishing.

—Timothy Toot... Finds A Hat. Tait, Barbara. 2011. 32p. (J). 24.95 (978-1-58909-917-3(6)) Bookstand Publishing.

—Timothy Toot... Goes Fishing. Tait, Barbara. 2011. 28p. (J). 24.95 (978-1-58909-879-4(X)) Bookstand Publishing.

—Virgil: The Bully from Cyberspace. Sanchez, Lorrie Christel & Blank, Carol. 2013. 54p. (J). 20.99 (978-0-9891338-0-7(X)) Utterly Global.

—Virgil: The Bully from Cyberspace Teacher Edition. Sanchez, Lorrie Christel & Blank, Carol. 2013. 88p. 99.00 (978-0-9891338-1-4(8)) Utterly Global.

Margolis, Al & Young, Bill. The Little Plum Tree. Rodhe, Paul & Wallas Reidy, Sarah. 2010. 24p. (J). pap. 9.95 (978-1-935706-06-9(3)) Wiggles Pr.

Margolis, Alan. Sophia & the Missing Socks. Davis, Anthony Quinn. 2019. (ENG.). 26p. (J). (gr. k-3). 19.50 (978-0-578-59378-4(5)) Anthony Quinn Davis.

Margolis, Lois. David's Tractor. Spinelli, Jami. l.t. ed. 2006. (J). 32p. 20.99 (978-1-59879-242-3(3)); 27p. (gr. -1-3). per. 11.99 (978-1-59879-241-6(5)) Lifevest Publishing, Inc.

Marhaj, Lina. La Talab Ma Al-Dik! Abd-Allah, Hassan. 2018. (ARA.). 24p. (J). (978-614-03-2026-0(7)) Dar al saqi.

Mari, Ian Robert, photos by. We Catch Them Falling. Ratto, Linda Lee. 2004. 225p. (YA). per. (978-1-932496-08-6(4)) Penman Publishing, Inc.

Maria, Dalbaeva. The Tale of Wilhanna: A Horse's Magical Birthday. Halverson, Kristen. 2018. (ENG.). 34p. (J). (gr. 1-5). 21.99 (978-0-692-10176-6(4)) The Tale of Noel: The Holiday Horse Angel, The.

Maria, Lisa. Meet Zammy's New Friends: The Adventures of Zammy the Giant Sheepadoodle. Pitner, Todd. 2020. (ENG.). 28p. (J). (978-952-7065-58-7(5)); pap. (978-952-7065-60-0(7)) Castalia Hse.

Maria, Vrednicu. Ștefănel Șmecherel învață Să Mănânce Sănătos. Iren, Alexoi. 2019. (RUM.). 30p. (J). pap. (978-606-9036-24-2(7)) Berg.

MARIADIAMANTES. Amelia Earhart. Sanchez Vegara, Maria Isabel. 2016. (Little People, BIG DREAMS Ser.: 3). (ENG.). 32p. (J). (gr. -1-2). 15.99 (978-1-84780-888-2(3), Frances Lincoln Children's Bks.) Quarto Publishing Group UK GBR. Dist: Hachette Bk. Group.

Mariana, Hnatenko. Owly & Magellanic Penguin Go to the Moon. Anderson, Mariya & Anderson, Oliver. 2020. (ENG.). 50p. (J). 24.99 (978-0-578-66904-5(8)) Anderson, Mariya.

Marichal, Carlos. El Mu�eco Del Tintero. Marichal Lugo, Poli & Marichal Lugo, Tere, eds. 2020. (SPA.). 50p. (J). pap. 12.00 (978-1-6533-0947-4(4)) Independently Published.

Marichal, Poli. Julia: Cuando Los Grandes Eran Pequenos. Lazaro, Georgina. 2006. (SPA.). 30p. (YA). (gr. 8-10). 14.99 (978-1-930332-58-4(0)) Lectorum Pubns., Inc.

Marie, Berri. My Name Was Fear. Shadrick, Crystal Star. Stone, Karen, ed. 2013. 60p. pap. 12.95 (978-1-935186-41-0(8)) Waldenhouse Pubs., Inc.

Marie, Denise. Paxton Passes Out. Marie, Denise. 2018. (ENG.). 36p. (J). (gr. 3-6). pap. 12.95 (978-1-7329164-0-1(3)) Donkey Penguin.

Marie, Paula Braxton. The Light in the Dark, 1. Keyes, Eric, 3rd et al. l.t. ed. 2004. (ENG.). 40p. (J). pap. 14.99 (978-0-9722795-5-0(5), Highest Good Pubns.) GEM Bk. Club.

Marie, Shiela a. The Challah That Took over the House. Berg, Melissa. 2019. (ENG.). 64p. (J). (gr. k-4). (978-1-9995167-5-8(3)) Heartlab Pr.

Marier, Chuck. Old MacDonald's Farm: Read Well Level K Unit 7 Storybook. Gunn, Barbara. 2004. (Read Well Level K Ser.). 20p. (J). (978-1-57035-679-7(3)) Cambium Education, Inc.

Marin, Danny. You Wouldn't Like Me Without My Coffee. Millsaps, Grace & Murphy, Ryan. 2014. (ENG.). 40p. (J). (gr. k-2). 17.95 (978-0-9904093-0-4(9)) Millfree Mursaps Media.

Marin, Jorge. Fairy Tale Pets. Corderoy, Tracey. 2017. (ENG.). 32p. (J). pap. (978-1-84869-442-2(3)) Tiger Tales.

Marin, Liz. Rachel Beth & the Day the Towers Came Down, 1 vol. Marin, Dale Diane. 2009. 27p. pap. 24.95 (978-1-60813-328-4(1)) America Star Bks.

Marin, Mary Rodriguez. Tulia y la Tecla Magica. Baranda, Maria. rev. ed. 2006. (Castillo de la Lectura, Serie Naranja). (SPA & ENG.). 160p. (J). (gr. 4-7). pap. 7.95 (978-970-20-0177-5(3)) Castillo, Ediciones, S. A. de C. V. MEX. Dist: Macmillan.

Marina, Saumell. Henry's Discovery. Schmidt, Kimberly K. 2018. (ENG.). 50p. (J). (gr. k-1). 21.95 (978-0-9864009-2-6(0)) Schmidt, Kimberly K.

MariNaomi. Distant Stars. MariNaomi. 2020. (Life on Earth Ser.). 272p. (YA). (gr. 9-12). 29.32 (978-1-5124-4912-9(1), Graphic Universe™) Lerner Publishing Group.

—Gravity's Pull. MariNaomi. 2019. (Life on Earth Ser.). 224p. (YA). (gr. 9-12). 29.32 (978-1-5124-4911-2(3), Graphic Universe™) Lerner Publishing Group.

—Losing the Girl. MariNaomi. 2018. (Life on Earth Ser.). 280p. (YA). (gr. 9-12). 29.32 (978-1-5124-4910-5(5), Graphic Universe™) Lerner Publishing Group.

—Losing the Girl: Book 1, Bk. 1. MariNaomi. 2018. (Life on Earth Ser.). (ENG.). 280p. (YA). (gr. 9-12). pap. 11.99 (978-1-5415-1044-9(5), Graphic Universe™) Lerner Publishing Group.

Marini, Enrico. Rapaces. Dufaux, Jean. 2004. (SPA.). Vol. 1. 56p. pap. 17.95 (978-1-59497-003-0(3)); Vol. 2. 56p. pap. 17.95 (978-1-59497-004-7(1)); Vol. 3. 64p. pap. 17.95 (978-1-59497-005-4(X)) Public Square Bks.

Mariniello, Cecco. Air Show. Suen, Anastasia. 2006. 30p. (J). (gr. k-4). reprint ed. 16.00 (978-1-4223-5669-2(8)) DIANE Publishing Co.

Marino, Carla. You Are Special Too: A Book for Brothers & Sisters of Children Diagnosed with Asperger Syndrome. Santomauro, Josie. 2009. (ENG.). 32p. (C). pap. 9.95 (978-1-84310-656-2(6), 695505) Kingsley, Jessica Pubs. GBR. Dist: Hachette UK Distribution.

—Your Special Friend: A Book for Peers of Children Diagnosed with Asperger Syndrome. Santomauro, Josie. 2009. (ENG.). 32p. (C). pap. 12.95 (978-1-84310-661-6(2), 695508) Kingsley, Jessica Pubs. GBR. Dist: Hachette UK Distribution.

Marino, Danielle. Limitless: Unearth Your Superhero Self. Klepetar, Ian. 2018. (ENG.). 40p. (J). 15.95 (978-0-9998865-2-6(5)) Limitless Bks.

Marino, Gianna. Don't Let Them Disappear. Clinton, Chelsea. 2019. 40p. (J). (gr. -1-3). 17.99 (978-0-525-51432-9(5), Philomel Bks.) Penguin Young Readers Group.

—How Do You Do? Theule, Larissa. 2019. 40p. (J). 17.99 (978-1-61963-807-5(X), 900149147, Bloomsbury Children's Bks.) Bloomsbury Publishing USA.

—No Dejes Que Desaparezcan. Clinton, Chelsea. 2019. (SPA.). 40p. (J). (gr. -1-3). 17.99 (978-0-593-11329-5(2), Philomel Bks.) Penguin Young Readers Group.

Marino, Gianna. If I Had a Horse. Marino, Gianna. 2018. (ENG.). 40p. (J). 18.99 (978-1-62672-908-7(5), 900177399) Roaring Brook Pr.

—Night Animals. Marino, Gianna. 2015. (ENG.). 40p. (J). (gr. -1-k). 16.99 (978-0-451-46954-0(2), Viking Books for Young Readers) Penguin Young Readers Group.

Marino, Illustrator, Natalie, Natalie, jt. illus. see Marino, Natalie.

Marino, Michael F. Thanksgiving at Grandma's. Olson, Nancy. 2009. 24p. pap. 10.95 (978-1-4251-8909-9(1)) Trafford Publishing.

Marino, Natalie. Andre's Great Day. Triche, Trina. 2017. (ENG.). (YA). 21.99 (978-1-5456-1380-1(X)); pap. 11.49 (978-1-5456-1379-5(6)) Salem Author Services.

—Guess What Happened to Me, Auntie Kate! Arden, Lynne. 2008. 52p. pap. 18.95 (978-1-59858-733-3(1)) Dog Ear Publishing, LLC.

—The Misadventures of Tood & Taboon. Wood, Natasha Tabon and Angela. 2016. (ENG.). (J). pap. 12.99 (978-1-4984-9048-1(4)) Salem Author Services.

—Sam Learns about Forgiveness. Davis, Jean. 2019. (ENG.). 28p. (J). 29.99 (978-1-5456-5719-5(X)); pap. 19.99 (978-1-5456-5718-8(1)) Salem Author Services.

—Tinabright. Hutchinson, Sharon G. 2016. (ENG.). (J). pap. 9.99 (978-1-4984-9221-8(5)) Salem Author Services.

—Zinyama Village Road. Karim, Janet Z. 2016. (ENG.). (J). pap. 11.99 (978-1-4984-9343-7(2)) Salem Author Services.

Marino, Natalie & Marino, Illustrator, Natalie, Natalie. A Place in the Sky. Singer, Maurene et al. 2005. 52p. (J). 16.00 (978-0-9759382-0-1(7)) Carousel Pubns., Inc.

Marinoni, Antonio. My Mastodon. Lowell, Barbara. 2020. (ENG.). 32p. (J). (gr. 1-3). 19.99 (978-1-56846-327-8(8), Creative Editions) Creative Co., The.

Marinsky, Jane. The Goat-Faced Girl: A Classic Italian Folktale. Sharpe, Leah Marinsky. 2009. (ENG.). 32p. (J). (gr. 1-4). 16.95 (978-1-56792-393-3(3)) Godine, David R. Pub.

marion, designs & proctor, brian. Ellen G Goes Fishing. Crews, G. 2007. 28p. pap. 4.99 (978-0-9795236-0-1(5)) Crews Pubns., LLC.

Marion, V. Kenneth, jt. illus. see Roberts, Jeremy.

Mariscal, Javier. Senor Mundo & Me: A Happy Birthday Story. Summers, Kim. 2004. 31p. (J). (gr. k-4). 20.00 (978-0-7567-7759-3(3)) DIANE Publishing Co.

Marjoribanks, Karen & Edwards, William M. Chloe's New Baby Brother. Thiel, Annie. 2006. (Playdate Kids Ser.). 32p. (J). (gr. -1-3). 14.95 (978-1-933721-01-9(4)) Playdate Kids Publishing.

Marjoribanks, Karen, jt. illus. see Edwards, William M.

Marjorie, Leggitt. Olympic National Park: Touch of the Tide Pool, Crack of the Glacier. Graf, Mike. 2012. (Adventures with the Parkers Ser.: 5). (ENG.). 96p. pap. 12.95 (978-0-7627-7969-7(1), Falcon Guides) Globe Pequot Pr., The.

—Rocky Mountain National Park: Peril on Long's Peak. Graf, Mike. 2012. (Adventures with the Parkers Ser.: 8). (ENG.). 96p. pap. 12.95 (978-0-7627-7970-3(5), Falcon Guides) Globe Pequot Pr., The.

Mark, Alicia. The Dancing Flamingos of Lake Chimichanga: Silly Birds. Beckstrand, Karl. l.t. ed. 2019. (ENG.). 26p. (J). 26.55 (978-1-951599-03-4(9)) Premio Publishing & Gozo Bks., LLC.

Mark, Alycia. Ma MacDonald Flees the Farm: It's Not a Pretty Picture ... Book. Beckstrand, Karl. l.t. ed. 2019. (Careers for Kids Ser.: Vol. 2). (ENG.). 34p. (J). 26.55 (978-1-951599-02-7(0)) Premio Publishing & Gozo Bks., LLC.

Mark Bergin. Draw Cats & Kittens. Bergin, Mark. 2017. (Step-By-Step Ser.). 32p. (gr. 3-8). 31.35 (978-1-911242-21-5(0)) Book Hse. GBR. Dist: Black Rabbit Bks.

—Draw Horses. Bergin, Mark. 2017. (Step-By-Step Ser.). 32p. (gr. 3-8). 31.35 (978-1-911242-23-9(7)) Book Hse. GBR. Dist: Black Rabbit Bks.

—Draw Tanks & Other Military Vehicles. Bergin, Mark. 2017. (Step-By-Step Ser.). 32p. (gr. 3-8). 31.35 (978-1-911242-24-6(5)) Book Hse. GBR. Dist: Black Rabbit Bks.

Mark, Bergin. Inca Town. Macdonald, Fiona. 2017. (Time Traveler's Guide Ser.). 48p. (gr. 3-7). 37.10 (978-1-911242-01-7(6)) Book Hse. GBR. Dist: Black Rabbit Bks.

—Roman Town. Martell, Hazel Mary. 2017. (Time Traveler's Guide Ser.). 48p. (gr. 3-7). 37.10 (978-1-911242-02-4(4)) Book Hse. GBR. Dist: Black Rabbit Bks.

Mark Bergin. The Story of Magellan. Macdonald, Fiona. 2017. (Explorers Ser.). 32p. (gr. 3-6). 31.35 (978-1-910706-90-9(6)) Book Hse. GBR. Dist: Black Rabbit Bks.

—The Story of Marco Polo. Macdonald, Fiona. 2017. (Explorers Ser.). 32p. (gr. 3-6). 31.35 (978-1-910706-91-6(4)) Book Hse. GBR. Dist: Black Rabbit Bks.

—The Story of the Race to the Moon. Green, Jen. 2017. (Explorers Ser.). 32p. (gr. 3-6). 31.35 (978-1-910706-92-3(2)) Book Hse. GBR. Dist: Black Rabbit Bks.

Mark, Steve. Cliques, Phonies & Other Baloney. Romain, Trevor & Verdick, Elizabeth. rev. ed. 2018. (Laugh & Learn® Ser.). (ENG.). 128p. (J). (gr. 3-8). pap. 9.99 (978-1-63198-242-2(7)) Free Spirit Publishing, Inc.

—Get Organized Without Losing It. Fox, Janet S. 2017. (Laugh & Learn® Ser.). (ENG.). 112p. (J). (gr. 3-7). pap. 9.99 (978-1-63198-173-9(0)) Free Spirit Publishing, Inc.

—How to Do Homework Without Throwing Up. Romain, Trevor. 2017. (Laugh & Learn® Ser.). (ENG.). 80p. (J). (gr. 3-8). pap. 9.99 (978-1-63198-066-4(1)) Free Spirit Publishing, Inc.

—How to Take the Ache Out of Mistakes. Braun, Eric & Feltes Taylor, Kimberly. 2019. (Laugh & Learn® Ser.). (ENG.). 128p. (J). (gr. 2-6). pap. 9.99 (978-1-63198-308-5(3), 83085) Free Spirit Publishing, Inc.

—Rosie the Response Boat. Benson, Kristy et al. 2016. (ENG.). 20p. (J). (gr. -1-k). bds. 8.95 (978-0-9892846-7-7(0)) Ensign Benson Bks., LLC.

—Stress Can Really Get on Your Nerves. Romain, Trevor & Verdick, Elizabeth. rev. ed. 2018. (Laugh & Learn® Ser.). (ENG.). 104p. (J). (gr. 3-8). pap. 9.99 (978-1-63198-245-3(1)) Free Spirit Publishing, Inc.

Mark, Steve, jt. illus. see Romain, Trevor.

Markel, Marilyn, jt. illus. see Alarid, Carilyn.

Markham, Patricia. All Day All Night: Read & Color Series. Markham, Patricia. 2018. (Read & Color Ser.: Vol. 1). (ENG.). 28p. (J). pap. 9.99 (978-1-9853-7483-6(8)) CreateSpace Independent Publishing Platform.

Marklew, Gilly. Great Irish Heroes. Waters, Fiona. 2007. (ENG.). 66p. (J). 23.95 (978-0-7171-3793-0(7)) M.H. Gill & Co. U. C. IRL. Dist: Dufour Editions, Inc.

Marklew, Gilly. History Quick Reads, No. 5. Oakden, David. 2018. (History Quick Reads Ser.). (ENG.). 58p. (J). pap. 9.99 (978-1-871173-41-3(8)) BookLife Publishing Ltd. GBR. Dist: Independent Pubs. Group.

—History Quick Reads, No. 8. Childs, Alan. 2018. (History Quick Reads Ser.). (ENG.). 60p. (J). pap. 9.99 (978-1-871173-44-4(2)) BookLife Publishing Ltd. GBR. Dist: Independent Pubs. Group.

Marko, Cyndi. The Birdy Snatchers. Marko, Cyndi. 2014. (Kung Pow Chicken Ser.: 3). (ENG.). 80p. (J). (gr. k-2). pap. 4.99 (978-0-545-61068-1(0)) Scholastic, Inc.

—Bok! Bok! Boom! Marko, Cyndi. 2014. (Kung Pow Chicken Ser.: 2). (ENG.). 80p. (J). (gr. k-2). 15.99 (978-0-545-61064-3(8)); pap. 4.99 (978-0-545-61063-6(X)) Scholastic, Inc.

—Heroes on the Side. Marko, Cyndi. 2014. (Kung Pow Chicken Ser.: 4). (ENG.). 80p. (J). (gr. k-2). pap. 4.99 (978-0-545-61074-2(5)) Scholastic, Inc.

—Let's Get Cracking! Marko, Cyndi. 2014. (Kung Pow Chicken Ser.: 1). (ENG.). 80p. (J). (gr. k-2). pap. 4.99 (978-0-545-61061-2(3)) Scholastic, Inc.

—This Little Piggy: An Owner's Manual. Marko, Cyndi. 2017. (Pix Ser.). (ENG.). 64p. (J). (gr. 1-4). 14.99 (978-1-4814-6826-8(X), Aladdin) Simon & Schuster Children's Publishing.

Markovitch, Evegeny, jt. illus. see Pollack, Gadi.

Markowitz, Dan, jt. illus. see Dress, Robert.

Marks, Alan. Black Beauty. Sewell, Anna. 2006. (Usborne Young Reading Ser.). 64p. (J). (gr. 2-5). 8.99 (978-0-7945-1193-7(7), Usborne) EDC Publishing.

—Black Beauty (Picture Book) Sebag-Montefiore, Mary. 2008. (Picture Book Classics Ser.). 24p. (J). 9.99 (978-0-7945-2250-6(5), Usborne) EDC Publishing.

—The Canterville Ghost. Wilde, Oscar. 2005. (Young Reading Ser.: Vol. 2). 64p. (J). (gr. 2-18). lib. bdg. 13.95 (978-1-58086-781-8(2), Usborne) EDC Publishing.

—A Christmas Carol. 2013. (ENG.). 24p. (J). 18.99 (978-0-7945-2910-9(0), Usborne) EDC Publishing.

—The Enchanted Castle. Sims, Lesley. 2007. (Young Reading Series 2 Gift Bks). 62p. (J). (gr. 4-7). 8.99 (978-0-7945-1347-4(6), Usborne) EDC Publishing.

—Family Pack. Markle, Sandra. 32p. (J). (gr. -1-3). 2019. pap. 7.99 (978-1-58089-218-6(3)); 2011. 15.95 (978-1-58089-217-9(5)) Charlesbridge Publishing, Inc.

—Finding Home. Markle, Sandra. 2010. 32p. (J). (gr. -1-3). pap. 7.95 (978-1-58089-123-3(3)) Charlesbridge Publishing, Inc.

—Heidi. Spyri, Johanna. 2006. 63p. (J). (gr. 2). 8.99 (978-0-7945-1237-8(2), Usborne) EDC Publishing.

—Hip-Pocket Papa. Markle, Sandra. 32p. (J). (gr. -1-3). 2019. pap. 7.99 (978-1-57091-709-7(4)); 2010. 15.95 (978-1-57091-708-0(6)) Charlesbridge Publishing, Inc.

—The Little Mermaid. 2005. 48p. (J). (gr. 4-7). 8.95 (978-0-7945-1122-7(8), Usborne) EDC Publishing.

—Moonfleet: A Classic Tale of Smuggling. Falkner, John Meade. 2007. (Young Reading Series 3 Gift Bks). 63p. (J). (gr. 4-7). 8.99 (978-0-7945-1906-3(7), Usborne) EDC Publishing.

—A Mother's Journey. Markle, Sandra. 32p. (J). (gr. -1-3). 2006. pap. 7.95 (978-1-57091-622-9(5)); 2005. 16.95 (978-1-57091-621-2(7)) Charlesbridge Publishing, Inc.

—A Mother's Journey. Markle, Sandra. 2006. (gr. 4-7). 16.95 (978-0-7569-6967-7(0)) Perfection Learning Corp.

—Pilot Mom. Duble, Kathleen Benner. 2004. 32p. (J). (gr. k-3). 15.95 (978-1-57091-555-0(5)) Charlesbridge Publishing, Inc.

—The Princess Who Hid in a Tree: An Anglo-Saxon Story. Holderness, Jackie. 2019. (ENG.). 40p. 20.00 (978-1-85124-518-5(9)) Bodleian Library GBR. Dist: Chicago Distribution Ctr.

—The Railway Children. Sebag-Montefiore, Mary. 2007. (Young Reading Series 2 Gift Bks). 60p. (J). (gr. 4-7). 8.99 (978-0-7945-1615-4(7), Usborne) EDC Publishing.

—Rare & Blue: Finding Nature's Treasures. Van Hoven, Constance. 2020. (ENG.). 48p. (J). (gr. k-4). lib. bdg. 18.99 (978-1-62354-097-5(6)) Charlesbridge Publishing, Inc.

—Rickie & Henri: A True Story. Goodall, Jane. 2017. (Minedition Classic Ser.). (ENG.). 64p. (J). (gr. k-2). 12.00 (978-988-8341-35-1(9), Minedition) Neugebauer, Michael (Publishing) Limited HKG. Dist: Penguin Random Hse. LLC.

—Snow School. Markle, Sandra. 2013. 32p. (J). (gr. -1-3). lib. bdg. 16.95 (978-1-58089-410-4(0)) Charlesbridge Publishing, Inc.

—Spirit of the Forest: Tree Tales from Around the World. East, Helen & Maddern, Eric. 2003. (ENG.). 48p. (J). pap. (978-0-7112-1879-6(X)) ReiseArt Buchhandlung GmbH.

—Spooks' Surprise. Dolby, Karen. 2003. (Young Puzzle Adventures Ser.). 32p. (J). (gr. 1-18). lib. bdg. 12.95 (978-1-58086-492-3(9)) EDC Publishing.

—The Stories of Knights. 2004. (Young Reading Series One Ser.). 48p. (J). (gr. 2-18). pap. 5.95 (978-0-7945-0755-8(7), Usborne) EDC Publishing.

—Stories of Knights & Castles. Milbourne, Anna. Doherty, Gillian, ed. 2007. (Stories for Young Children Ser.). 96p. (J). 16.99 (978-0-7945-1466-2(9), Usborne) EDC Publishing.

—Storm. Crossley-Holland, Kevin. 2nd ed. 2016. (Reading Ladder Ser.). (ENG.). 48p. (J). (gr. k-2). 7.99 (978-1-4052-8236-9(3)) Egmont Bks., Ltd. GBR. Dist: Independent Pubs. Group.

—The Story of Heidi. 2007. (Picture Book Classics Ser.). 24p. (J). (gr. -1-3). 9.99 (978-0-7945-1716-8(1), Usborne) EDC Publishing.

—The Story of Robin Hood. Jones, Rob Lloyd. 2010. (Picture Book Classics Ser.). 24p. (J). 9.99 (978-0-7945-2859-1(7), Usborne) EDC Publishing.

—Waiting for Ice. Markle, Sandra. 2012. 32p. (J). (gr. -1-3). 15.95 (978-1-58089-255-1(8)) Charlesbridge Publishing, Inc.

Marks, Carolyn. I Can't Sit Still. Carlstrom, Kimberly. 2018. (ENG.). 32p. (J). pap. 10.95 (978-1-948282-35-2(6)) Yorkshire Publishing Group.

Marks, Elizabeth. Growing Together Across the Autism Spectrum: A Kid's Guide to Living with, Learning from, & Loving a Parent with Autism Spectrum Disorder. Marks, Elizabeth. 2015. (ENG.). 47p. (J). pap. 19.95 (978-1-942197-08-9(X)) Autism Asperger Publishing Co.

Marks, Hannah. Hamster Sitter Wanted. Gunaratnam, Tracy. 2019. (ENG.). 32p. (J). (gr. -1-3). 17.99 (978-1-84886-359-0(4)) Maverick Arts Publishing GBR. Dist: Lerner Publishing Group.

—Let's Dance. Bowie, David. 2020. 32p. (J). (gr. -1-3). 17.99 *(978-0-7624-6808-9(4),* Running Pr. Kids) Running Pr.
—The Panda Problem. Underwood, Deborah. 2019. (ENG.). 48p. (J). (gr. -1-2). 17.99 *(978-0-7352-2850-4(7),* Dial Bks) Penguin Young Readers Group.
—Stop-and-Go Devotional: 52 Devotions for Busy Families, 1 vol. Stortz, Diane. 2019. 224p. (J). 17.99 *(978-1-4003-1758-5(4))* Nelson, Thomas Inc.
Markus, James, photos by. The Last Bedtime Story: That We Read Each Night. Gray, Carol. 2013. (ENG.). 32p. (J). pap. 9.95 *(978-1-935567-43-1(8),* 9781935567431) Sensory Resources.
Marlette, Andy. Gator Alphabet ABC. Bianchi, Mike & Novak, Marisol. 2004. 32p. (J). (gr. -1-k). 6.95 *(978-1-58261-403-8(2))* Sports Publishing, LLC.
—Harry Loves Greens. Baldwin, Laura. 2012. 30p. (J). pap. 10.00 *(978-1-61153-013-1(X))* Light Messages Publishing.
—Harry Loves Turnips (Not!) Baldwin, Laura. 2012. 30p. (J). pap. 10.00 *(978-1-61153-023-0(7))* Light Messages Publishing.
—Swampmeet: A Gator Counting Book. Bianchi, Mike & Novak, Marisol. 2004. 32p. (J). (gr. -1-k). 6.95 *(978-1-58261-780-0(5))* Sports Publishing, LLC.
Marley, Alea. A Day So Gray. Lamba, Marie. 2019. (ENG.). 32p. (J). (gr. -1-3). 17.99 *(978-1-328-69599-4(9),* 1671314, Clarion Bks.) Houghton Mifflin Harcourt Trade & Reference Pubs.
—Goodnight, Little Dancer. Adams, Jennifer. 2020. (ENG.). 32p. (J). 14.99 *(978-1-250-31004-0(0),* 900198612) Roaring Brook Pr.
—Goodnight, Little Superhero. Adams, Jennifer. 2020. (ENG.). 32p. (J). 14.99 *(978-1-250-31005-7(9),* 900198613) Roaring Brook Pr.
—Loretta's Gift. Miller, Pat Zietlow. 2018. (ENG.). 40p. (J). (gr. -1-3). 17.99 *(978-1-4998-0681-6(7))* Little Bee Books Inc.
—The Many Colors of Harpreet Singh. Kelkar, Supriya. 2019. 32p. (J). (gr. -1-2). 16.95 *(978-1-4549-3184-3(1))* Sterling Publishing Co., Inc.
Marlin, Kathryn. God Made Kittens. Bennett, Marian. 2014. (Happy Day Ser.). (ENG.). 16p. (J). pap. 2.49 *(978-1-4143-9479-4(9),* 4608469) Tyndale Hse. Pubs.
—God Made Seasons. Shearer, Amelia. 2014. (Happy Day Ser.). (ENG.). 16p. (J). pap. 2.49 *(978-1-4143-9481-7(0),* 4608471) Tyndale Hse. Pubs.
—God's Baby Animals. Redford, Margorie & Rice, Courtney. 2014. (Happy Day Ser.). (ENG.). 16p. (J). pap. 2.49 *(978-1-4143-9418-3(7),* 4608408) Tyndale Hse. Pubs.
—My Bible Says. Redford, Marjorie. 2013. (Happy Day Ser.). (ENG.). 16p. (J). pap. 2.49 *(978-1-4143-9301-8(6),* 4608291) Tyndale Hse. Pubs.
Marlin, Kathryn & Julien, Terry. God Always Cares. Beveridge, Amy. 2014. (Happy Day Ser.). (ENG.). 16p. (J). pap. 2.49 *(978-1-4143-9417-6(9),* 4608407) Tyndale Hse. Pubs.
Marlin, Lissy. The Addams Family: a Frightful Welcome. West, Alexandra. 2019. (I Can Read Level 3 Ser.). (ENG.). 32p. (J). (gr. -1-3). pap. 4.99 *(978-0-06-294677-5(3))* HarperCollins Pubs.
—The Addams Family: an Original Picture Book: Includes Lyrics to the Iconic Song! Mizzy, Vic. 2019. (Addams Family Ser.). (ENG.). 32p. (J). (gr. -1-3). 17.99 *(978-0-06-294679-9(X))* HarperCollins Pubs.
—The Addams Family: Meet the Family. West, Alexandra. 2019. (I Can Read Level 2 Ser.). (ENG.). 32p. (J). (gr. -1-3). pap. 4.99 *(978-0-06-294675-1(7))* HarperCollins Pubs.
—Bring Back the Bees. Smith, Emma Bland. 2018. (Maddy Mcguire, CEO Ser.). (ENG.). 112p. (J). (gr. 2-5). lib. bdg. 29.93 *(978-1-5321-3183-7(6),* 28461, Calico Chapter Bks.) ABDO Publishing Co.
—Crafting for a Cause. Smith, Emma Bland. 2018. (Maddy Mcguire, CEO Ser.). (ENG.). 112p. (J). (gr. 2-5). lib. bdg. 29.93 *(978-1-5321-3184-4(4),* 28463, Calico Chapter Bks.) ABDO Publishing Co.
—Ghost of a Chance. Schmid, Susan Maupin. 2017. (100 Dresses Ser.: 2). 320p. (J). (gr. 3-7). 16.99 *(978-0-553-53373-6(8),* Random Hse. Bks. for Young Readers) Random Hse. Children's Bks.
—Jonah & the Fish. Mackall, Dandi Daley. 2016. (Flipside Stories Ser.). (ENG.). 48p. (J). 14.99 *(978-1-4964-1120-4(X),* 4612795) Tyndale Hse. Pubs.
—Maddy Mcguire, CEO (Set), 4 vols. Smith, Emma Bland. 2018. (Maddy Mcguire, CEO Ser.). 112p. (J). (gr. 2-5). lib. bdg. 114.00 *(978-1-5321-3182-0(8),* 28459, Calico Chapter Bks.) ABDO Publishing Co.
Marlin, Lissy. The Magic Misfits: The Second Story. Harris, Neil Patrick & Azam, Alec. 2018. xii, 312p. (J). ***(978-0-316-52639-5(8)); (978-0-316-48724-5(4))*** Little Brown & Co.
Marlin, Lissy. Mira Forecasts the Future. Andrews, Kell. 2016. 40p. (J). (gr. k-3). 14.95 *(978-1-4549-1698-7(2))* Sterling Publishing Co., Inc.
—Nikki Tesla & the Ferret-Proof Death Ray (Elements of Genius #1) Keating, Jess. 2020. (Elements of Genius Ser.: 1). (ENG.). 288p. (J). (gr. 3-7). pap. 7.99 *(978-1-338-29520-7(9),* Scholastic Pr.) Scholastic, Inc.
—Pet Camp. Smith, Emma Bland. 2018. (Maddy Mcguire, CEO Ser.). (ENG.). 112p. (J). (gr. 2-5). lib. bdg. 29.93 *(978-1-5321-3185-1(2),* 28465, Calico Chapter Bks.) ABDO Publishing Co.
—Pop-Up Movie Theater. Smith, Emma Bland. 2018. (Maddy Mcguire, CEO Ser.). (ENG.). 112p. (J). (gr. 2-5). lib. bdg. 29.93 *(978-1-5321-3186-8(0),* 28467, Calico Chapter Bks.) ABDO Publishing Co.
—The Starlight Slippers. Schmid, Susan Maupin. 2018. (100 Dresses Ser.: 3). 336p. (J). (gr. 3-7). 16.99 *(978-0-553-53377-4(0),* Random Hse. Bks. for Young Readers) Random Hse. Children's Bks.
Marlin, Lissy & Hilton, Kyle. The Magic Misfits. Harris, Neil Patrick. (Magic Misfits Ser.: 1). (ENG.). (J). (gr. 3-7). 2018. 288p. pap. 7.99 *(978-0-316-35557-5(7));* 2017. 272p. 16.99 *(978-0-316-39182-5(4));* 2017. 336p. 29.00 *(978-0-316-43984-8(3))* Little, Brown Bks. for Young Readers.
—The Magic Misfits: the Second Story. Harris, Neil Patrick. 2019. (Magic Misfits Ser.: 2). (ENG.). 352p. (J). (gr. 3-7). pap. 7.99 *(978-0-316-39184-9(0))* Little, Brown Bks. for Young Readers.
Marlin, Lissy, jt. illus. see Hilton, Kyle.
Marlow, Layn. I'll Catch You If You Fall. Sperring, Mark. (ENG.). 32p. (J). (gr. -1-3). 2019. 7.99 *(978-1-5344-5209-1(5));* 2016. 18.99 *(978-1-4814-5206-9(1))* Simon & Schuster Bks. For Young Readers. (Simon & Schuster Bks. For Young Readers).
—A T-Wit for a T-Woo. Farley, Charlie. 2019. 32p. (J). (gr. -1-k). 14.99 *(978-1-4083-4649-5(4));* pap. 9.99 *(978-1-4083-4650-1(8))* Hachette Children's Group GBR. (Orchard Bks.). Dist: Hachette Bk. Group.
Marlow, Wayne. La Charla:: Entendiendo la Pubertad, la Pornografía, el Sexo y el Matrimonio. Chelliah, Joel. 2019. (SPA.). 34p. (J). (gr. 2-5). 20.00 *(978-1-945454-13-4(X))* Holloway, Greg.
Marlowe, Susan B. Goodnight, Boone. Greene, Melanie W. et al. 2012. (J). *(978-1-933251-80-6(8))* Parkway Pubs., Inc.
Marly. Nina, Leo et Jean de la Fontaine: Nina et Leo À la Rencontre des Auteurs. Marine, Laura. 2018. (Nina et léo À la Rencontre des Auteurs Ser.: Vol. 1). (FRE.). 60p. (J). pap. *(978-2-9602250-0-6(7))* Laure éditions.
Marman, Richard. Mcalister's Spark. Marman, Richard. 2013. 364p. pap. *(978-1-909302-21-1(X))* Abela Publishing.
Maroh, Julie. You Brought Me the Ocean. Sanchez, Alex. 2020. 208p. (YA). (gr. 9). pap. 16.99 ***(978-1-4012-9081-8(7))*** DC Comics.
Marohn, James. Juaquinito: A Manatee Hero. Handelsman, Valerie. 2009. (ENG.). 32p. (J). (gr. k-5). pap. 7.95 *(978-0-9748884-3-9(5))* Little Thoughts For Little Ones Publishing, Inc.
Maroney, Biddy, jt. illus. see Day, Sonny.
Maronie, Cortez P. The Day My Sister Gave Me the Hiccups. Blassingame, Stephanie T. 2019. (ENG.). 32p. (J). 20.00 ***(978-1-0878-4858-7(X))*** Indy Pub.
Marques, Gabriel T. A Real Life Huper Sero: Oops, I Mean Super Hero! Huu, Andre L. 2018. (ENG.). 34p. (J). (gr. k-2). 17.95 *(978-0-578-40283-3(1))* Huu, Andre.
Marques, Sidnei. Gary the Go-Cart: Carbon Comes Out of the Closet. Denson, B. B. 2017. (Gary the Go-Cart Ser.: Vol. 2). (ENG.). (J). (gr. k-3). 18.77 *(978-0-9975883-3-0(0))* Desideramus Publishing.
Marquez, David, et al. Invincible Iron Man by Brian Michael Bendis. 2018. (ENG.). 328p. (YA). (gr. 8-17). 39.99 *(978-1-302-90448-7(5))* Marvel Worldwide, Inc.
—Miles Morales: with Great Power. 2019. 280p. (J). (gr. 4-7). pap. 12.99 *(978-1-302-91977-1(6))* Marvel Worldwide, Inc.
Marquez, David & Bagley, Mark. Miles Morales: Great Responsibility. 2020. 256p. (J). (gr. 4-7). pap. 12.99 *(978-1-302-92114-9(2))* Marvel Worldwide, Inc.
Marquez, David & Pichelli, Sara. Fantastic Four: Fantastic Origins. 2019. (ENG.). 136p. (YA). (gr. 8-17). pap. 15.99 *(978-0-7851-5642-0(9))* Marvel Worldwide, Inc.
Marquez, David & Sorrentino, Andrea. Avengers by Jason Aaron Vol. 3: War of the Vampires. 2019. (ENG.). 136p. (YA). pap. 17.99 *(978-1-302-91461-5(8))* Marvel Worldwide, Inc.
Marquez, David, jt. illus. see Pichelli, Sara.
Marquez, Erick. The Binky Fairy. Shaw-Lott, Karen. 2009. 12p. pap. 11.00 *(978-1-60844-271-3(3))* Dog Ear Publishing, LLC.
Marquez, Francisca. Dig Those Dinosaurs. Houran, Lori Haskins. 2013. (ENG.). 24p. (J). (gr. -1-2). 15.99 *(978-0-8075-1579-2(5))* Whitman, Albert & Co.
—Dig Those Dinosaurs. Houran, Lori Haskins. 2013. (AV2 Fiction Readalong Ser.: Vol. 55). (ENG.). (J). (gr. -1-2). 32.71 *(978-1-62127-875-7(1),* AV2 by Weigl) Weigl Pubs., Inc.
—How to Spy on a Shark. Houran, Lori Haskins. 2019. (ENG.). 24p. (J). (-3). pap. 7.99 *(978-0-8075-3406-9(4),* 807534064) Whitman, Albert & Co.
—A Trip into Space: An Adventure to the International Space Station. Houran, Lori Haskins. 2019. 24p. (J). (gr. -1-3). pap. 7.99 *(978-0-8075-8093-6(7),* 807580937) Whitman, Albert & Co.
Marquez, Sofia. Pepe Perez Mexican Mouse: Pepe Perez Comes to the United States: Book 1, 1 vol. Marquez, Sofia. 2009. 20p. pap. 24.95 *(978-1-61546-496-8(4))* America Star Bks.
Marquis, KariAnn. Seven Friends, 1 vol. Greeley, David. 2010. 38p. 24.95 *(978-1-4489-4101-8(6))* PublishAmerica, Inc.
Marrinan, Chris. Spartans. McLeese, Don. ed. 2009. (Warriors Graphic Illustrated Ser.). (ENG.). 32p. (J). (gr. 4-8). pap. 9.95 *(978-1-60694-545-2(9),* 9781606945452) Rourke Educational Media.
Marriot, Pat. El Dedo Magico. Dahl, Roald.Tr. of Magic Finger. (SPA.). 74p. (J). (gr. 3-5). 9.95 *(978-968-19-0621-4(7))* Aguilar Editorial MEX. Dist: Santillana USA Publishing Co., Inc.
Marriott, Brian. Granny Butterfly's Birthday. French, Jean. 2017. (Granny Butterfly Ser.: Vol. 2). (ENG.). (J). pap. *(978-1-78623-258-8(8))* Grosvenor Hse. Publishing Ltd.
Marriott, Lauren. Doodle Cat Is Bored. Patrick, Kat. 2017. (Doodle Cat Ser.). (ENG.). 32p. (J). ***(978-1-925321-88-3(6))*** Scribe Pubns. AUS. Dist: Consortium Bk. Sales & Distribution.
Marriott, Pat. El Dedo Magico. Dahl, Roald. 2003.Tr. of Magic Finger. (SPA.). 74p. (gr. 3-5). pap. 11.95 *(978-958-24-0178-8(8))* Santillana COL. Dist: Santillana USA Publishing Co., Inc.
Marroquin-Burr, Kristina. Learn to Draw Angry Birds Space. 2014. 64p. (J). (gr. 3-5). 33.27 *(978-1-939581-33-4(8))* Quarto Publishing Group USA.
Marroquin, Melissa. Who Sees Your Scrunchy Face? Conlin, Christine. 2016. (ENG.). (J). 18.95 *(978-1-59298-658-3(7))* Beaver's Pond Pr., Inc.
Marrucchi, Elisa. Beautiful Brides. Lagonegro, Melissa. 2011. (Step into Reading Ser.). (ENG.). 32p. (J). (gr. k-3). pap. 4.99 *(978-0-7364-2685-5(X),* RH/Disney) Random Hse. Children's Bks.
—Happy Birthday, Princess! (Disney Princess) Liberts, Jennifer. 2016. (Step into Reading Ser.). (ENG.). 24p. (J). (gr. -1-1). pap. 4.99 *(978-0-7364-3664-9(2),* RH/Disney) Random Hse. Children's Bks.
—Sealed with a Kiss. Lagonegro, Melissa. 2005. (Step into Reading Ser.). (ENG.). 32p. (J). (gr. k-3). per. 4.99 *(978-0-7364-2363-2(X),* RH/Disney) Random Hse. Children's Bks.
—Sweet & Spooky Halloween (Disney Princess) RH Disney. 2007. (Pictureback(R) Ser.). (ENG.). 24p. (J). (gr. -1-2). pap. 3.99 *(978-0-7364-2453-0(9),* RH/Disney) Random Hse. Children's Bks.
—Teachers' Pets (Disney Princess) Man-Kong, Mary. 2011. (Step into Reading Ser.). (ENG.). 32p. (J). (gr. k-3). pap. 3.99 *(978-0-7364-2778-4(3),* RH/Disney) Random Hse. Children's Bks.
—Winter Wishes. Jordan, Apple J. 2006. (Step into Reading Ser.). (ENG.). 32p. (J). (gr. k-3). per. 4.99 *(978-0-7364-2409-7(1),* RH/Disney) Random Hse. Children's Bks.
Mars, E., jt. illus. see Squire, M H.
Mars, W. T. The Friendly Frontier: The Story of the Canadian-American Border. Meyer, Edith Patterson. 2011. 304p. 48.95 *(978-1-258-09384-6(7))* Literary Licensing, LLC.
Marschall, Felicia. The Night the Chimneys Fell. Figley, Marty Rhodes. 2011. (On My Own History Ser.). 48p. (J). pap. 39.62 *(978-0-7613-7622-4(4),* First Avenue Editions) Lerner Publishing Group.
—The Night the Chimneys Fell. Figley, Marthy Rhodes & Figley, Marty Rhodes. 2011. 48p. (J). pap. 6.95 *(978-0-7613-3939-7(6),* First Avenue Editions) Lerner Publishing Group.
Marschell, Hannah. My Beautiful Bow: An Adoption Story. Goldman Marshall, Lauren. 2010. 36p. pap. 14.95 *(978-1-60844-395-6(7))* Dog Ear Publishing, LLC.
Marsden, Ken. Lucy's Grade School Adventure. Hansen, Jennifer. 2006. (J). *(978-0-9774822-7-6(8))* Crosam Pr.
Marsden, Suzanne. Eraser Cookies. Schnurr, Rosina G. 2020. (ENG.). 130p. (J). pap. ***(978-0-2288-1175-6(9))*** Tellwell Talent.
Marsee, Kimberly. Daughter of the King: Daughter of the King: Book with Audio CD. Tucker, Terra. ed. 2007. 48p. (J). 19.95 *(978-0-9794578-0-7(7))* Tucker, Terra.
Marsh, Amanda. Sunny & Tug Go to the Beach: The Adventures of Sunny & Tug. Doyle, Krista. 2019. (Adventures of Sunny & Tug Ser.: Vol. 2). (ENG.). 28p. (J). pap. 14.95 ***(978-1-7187-3466-1(2))*** CreateSpace Independent Publishing Platform.
Marsh, Ariel. The Last Tree. Churchill, Michelle. 2019. (Impardia Ser.: Vol. 1). (ENG.). 304p. (J). pap. ***(978-1-989473-24-5(5))*** Engen Bks.
Marsh, Bobbi. Gaylord Goose. Christensen, Bob. 2011. 28p. pap. 12.95 *(978-1-61493-014-3(7))* Peppertree Pr., The.
Marsh, Bobbie. The Princess Mermaid & the Missing Sea Shells. Dipinto, Michael J. 2013. 36p. pap. 15.95 *(978-1-61493-151-5(8))* Peppertree Pr., The.
Marsh, Carole, photos by. The Mystery of Blackbeard the Pirate. Marsh, Carole. 2009. (Real Kids, Real Places Ser.). 150p. (J). 18.99 *(978-0-635-06992-4(X),* Marsh, Carole Mysteries) Gallopade International.
Marsh, Dilleen. What Happens When People Die? Marsh, Dilleen, tr. 2003. (J). 12.95 *(978-1-57008-954-1(X))* Deseret Bk. Co.
Marsh, Jakob. EZ Times Table: An easy visual way to learn multiplication & division by playing with patterns & making friends with Numbers. Biesanz, Thomas. 2nd rev. ed. 2008. (ENG.). 80p. (J). per. 12.95 *(978-0-9799636-1-2(3))* Growth-Ink.
Marsh, Julia. The Osprey Nest. Spidell, Mary. 2019. (Sidewalk Chalk Artists Ser.: Vol. 3). (ENG.). 74p. (J). pap. 10.00 *(978-1-0750-7006-8(6))* Independently Published.
Marsh, Nancy. Path Winds Home. DeVos, Janie. l.t. ed. 2005. 32p. 16.95 *(978-0-9743758-0-9(2))* Red Engine Pr.
Marsh, Rob. Gold in the Hills: Stories of Riches in Oklahoma's Mountains. Watson, Andy. 2019. (ENG.). 36p. (J). pap. 12.99 *(978-1-7967-6873-2(1))* Independently Published.
Marsh, Sarah. The Adventures of Kingston: The Pitbull Who Found His Strength in God. Lee, Blake. 2017. (ENG.). (J). pap. 12.95 *(978-1-64114-792-7(X))* Christian Faith Publishing.
Marshal, Natalie. In the Wild. 2018. (Touch & Feel Surprises Ser.). (ENG.). 10p. (J). (— 1). bds. 8.99 *(978-1-68412-168-7(X),* Silver Dolphin Bks.) Printers Row Publishing Group.
Marshall, Allana C. I Wandered Lonely As a Cloud: Daffodills. Wordsworth, William & Schlieve, Ngj. 2017. (It's a Classic, Baby Ser.). (ENG.). 28p. (J). 16.95 *(978-1-947032-50-7(X))* Pemberley Publishing.
Marshall, Carol, jt. illus. see Walt Disney Studio.
Marshall, Dan. Lydia Darragh: Quaker Patriot. Rand, Carol. (J). 15.95 *(978-0-945912-33-0(1))* Pippin Pr.
Marshall, Denise. Snow White & Rose Red: A Grimms' Fairy Tale, 1 vol. Brothers Grimm. 2008. (ENG.). 28p. (J). 17.95 *(978-0-88010-591-0(7),* Bell Pond Bks.) SteinerBooks, Inc.
Marshall, Felicia. Beautiful Shades of Brown: The Art of Laura Wheeler Waring. Churnin, Nancy. 2020. (ENG.). 32p. (J). (gr. 1-4). 18.99 *(978-1-939547-65-1(2))* Creston Bks.
—Harriet Tubman & the Freedom Train. Gayle, Sharon. ed. 2005. (Ready-to-Read Ser.). 32p. (J). lib. bdg. 15.00 *(978-1-59054-960-5(0))* Fitzgerald Bks.
—Harriet Tubman & the Freedom Train. Gayle, Sharon. 2003. (Ready-To-read SOFA Ser.). (ENG.). 32p. (J). (gr. 1-3). pap. 4.99 *(978-0-689-85480-4(3),* Simon Spotlight) Simon Spotlight.
—Keepers. Watts, Jeri Hanel. 2013. (ENG.). 32p. (J). (gr. -1-5). pap. 10.95 *(978-1-58430-013-7(2))* Lee & Low Bks., Inc.
—Loved Best. McKissack, Patricia C. 2005. (ENG.). 64p. (J). (gr. 2-5). pap. 5.99 *(978-0-689-86151-2(6),* Simon & Schuster/Paula Wiseman Bks.) Simon & Schuster/Paula Wiseman Bks.
—The Night the Chimneys Fell. Figley, Marty Rhodes. 2009. (On My Own History Ser.). (ENG.). 48p. (gr. 2-4). 25.26 *(978-0-8225-7894-9(8))* Lerner Publishing Group.
—Robert Smalls Sails to Freedom. Brown, Susan Taylor. 2006. (On My Own History Ser.). 48p. (J). (gr. 3-7). pap. 6.95 *(978-0-8225-6051-7(8),* First Avenue Editions); (ENG.). (gr. 2-4). lib. bdg. 25.26 *(978-1-57505-872-6(3))* Lerner Publishing Group.
—Secret Holes. Flood, Pansie Hart. 2004. 128p. (J). (gr. 3-6). 15.95 *(978-0-87614-923-2(9),* Carolrhoda Bks.) Lerner Publishing Group.
—Sometimey Friend. Flood, Pansie Hart. 2005. 124p. (J). (gr. 3-7). 15.95 *(978-1-57505-866-5(9))* Lerner Publishing Group.
—Sylvia & Miz Lula Maye. Flood, Pansie Hart. 2003. (Middle Grade Fiction Ser.). 120p. (J). (gr. 3-6). 15.95 *(978-0-87614-204-2(8),* Carolrhoda Bks.) Lerner Publishing Group.
Marshall, H. Keene, jt. illus. see Miller, Bryan.
Marshall, Heidi Amenda. Petra's Adventure in Nievenheim. Marshall, Heidi Amenda. l.t. ed. 2003. 57p. (J). per. 7.99 *(978-0-9747445-0-6(6))* Landfall Co., The.
Marshall, Ian. Not Again, Frannie! A Frannie Flotnick Adventure. Turkovitz, Karen. Ryan, Linda et al, eds. unabr. ed. 2003. (YA). pap. 12.95 *(978-0-9679115-6-4(7))* Five Degrees of Frannie.
Marshall, James. Cinderella. Karlin, Barbara. unabr. ed. 2006. (J). (gr. -1-4). 29.95 *(978-0-439-84888-6(1),* WHCD671); 18.95 *(978-0-439-84890-9(3),* WPCD671) Weston Woods Studios, Inc.
—Miss Nelson Has a Field Day, 1 vol. Allard, Harry G., Jr. 2012. (ENG.). 32p. (J). (gr. -1-3). 10.99 *(978-0-547-75376-8(4),* 1487728) Houghton Mifflin Harcourt Publishing Co.
—Miss Nelson Is Back, 1 vol. Allard, Harry G., Jr. 2011. (ENG.). 32p. (J). (gr. -1-3). 10.99 *(978-0-547-57718-0(4),* 1458493) Houghton Mifflin Harcourt Publishing Co.
—Miss Nelson Is Missing!, 1 vol. Allard, Harry. 2007. (ENG.). 32p. (J). (gr. -1-3). 10.99 *(978-0-618-85281-9(6),* 416986) Houghton Mifflin Harcourt Publishing Co.
—The Piggy in the Puddle. Pomerantz, Charlotte. 2018. (Classic Board Bks.). (ENG.). 32p. (J). (gr. -1-k). bds. 7.99 *(978-1-5344-0660-5(3),* Little Simon) Little Simon.
Marshall, Jamie. The Poopy Pekinese. Howell, Trisha Adelena. 2005. 32p. (J). 15.95 *(978-1-931210-09-6(8))* Howell Canyon Pr.
—The Stinky Shepherd. Howell, Trisha Adelena. 2005. 32p. (J). 15.95 *(978-1-931210-25-6(X))* Howell Canyon Pr.
Marshall, Janet. A Nantucket Nanny. Manley, Molly. 2005. (Little Limericks Ser.). (ENG.). 24p. (J). (gr. k-3). 12.95 *(978-1-889833-96-5(7),* Commonwealth Editions) Applewood Bks.
—On a Vineyard Veranda. Manley, Molly. 2007. (Little Limericks Ser.). (ENG.). 24p. (J). (gr. k-3). 12.95 *(978-1-933212-46-3(2),* Commonwealth Editions) Applewood Bks.
Marshall, Julia. The Daring Coast Guard Rescue of the Pendleton Crew. Barbo, Theresa Mitchell & Webster, W. Russell. 2013. Orig. Title: The Daring Coast Guard Rescue of the Pendleton Crew. (ENG.). 128p. (J). (gr. 4-7). 14.99 *(978-1-62619-095-5(X),* History Pr., The) Arcadia Publishing.
—Louisiana, the Jewel of the Deep South, 1 vol. Downing, Johnette. 2015. (ENG.). 32p. (J). (gr. k-3). 16.99 *(978-1-4556-2096-8(3),* Pelican Publishing) Arcadia Publishing.
—When Hurricane Katrina Hit Home. Karwoski, Gail Langer. 2013. Orig. Title: When Hurricane Katrina Hit Home. (ENG.). 192p. (gr. 4-7). 15.99 *(978-1-62619-083-2(6),* History Pr., The) Arcadia Publishing.
Marshall, Laurie. Take Me with You When You Go. Venable, Alan. 2008. 112p. (J). 12.95 *(978-0-9777082-7-7(6))* One Monkey Bks.
Marshall, Natalie. Babies Love Easter: Chunky Lift a Flap Board Book. Redd, R. I. Cottage Door Press, ed. 2017. (Chunky Lift a Flap Board Book Ser.). (ENG.). 12p. (J). (gr. -1-k). bds. 7.99 *(978-1-68052-286-0(8),* 1002710) Cottage Door Pr.
—Colors in the Ocean. 2017. (Touch & Learn Bks.). (ENG.). 12p. (J). (gr. -1 — 1). bds. 5.99 *(978-1-4380-5001-0(1),* B.E.S. Publishing) Peterson's.
—Farm Friends. 2017. (Touch & Learn Bks.). (ENG.). 12p. (J). (gr. -1 — 1). bds. 5.99 *(978-1-4380-5002-7(X),* B.E.S. Publishing) Peterson's.
—In the Forest. 2018. (Touch & Feel Surprises Ser.). (ENG.). 10p. (J). (— 1). bds. 8.99 *(978-1-68412-169-4(8),* Silver Dolphin Bks.) Printers Row Publishing Group.
—Millie-Mae: In Autumn. 2014. (J). *(978-1-4351-5612-8(9))* Barnes & Noble, Inc.
—My Peekaboo Animals. Edwards, Nicola. 2020. (ENG.). 12p. (J). (-k). bds. 10.99 *(978-1-68010-604-6(X))* Tiger Tales.
—Seaside Sandcastle! 2014. (J). *(978-1-4351-5505-3(X))* Barnes & Noble, Inc.
—Small Smaller Smallest. Fletcher, Corina. 2015. (ENG.). 12p. (J). (— 1). bds. 8.95 *(978-1-4549-1559-1(5))* Sterling Publishing Co., Inc.
—Tiny Creatures: Touch & Feel Book. 2015. (J). *(978-1-4351-5935-8(7))* Barnes & Noble, Inc.
—You're My Little Christmas Wish. Edwards, Nicola. 2019. (You're My Little Ser.). (ENG.). 18p. (J). (— 1). bds. 8.99 *(978-1-68412-675-0(4),* Silver Dolphin Bks.) Printers Row Publishing Group.
—You're My Little Cuddle Bug. Edwards, Nicola. 2018. (You're My Little Ser.). (ENG.). 18p. (J). (gr. -1 — 1). bds. 8.99 *(978-1-68412-258-5(9),* Silver Dolphin Bks.) Printers Row Publishing Group.
—You're My Little Honey Bunny. 2019. (You're My Little Ser.). (ENG.). 18p. (J). (— 1). bds. 8.99 *(978-1-68412-618-7(5),* Silver Dolphin Bks.) Printers Row Publishing Group.
—You're My Little Pumpkin Pie. 2018. (You're My Little Ser.). (ENG.). 18p. (J). (— 1). bds. 8.99 *(978-1-68412-434-3(4),* Silver Dolphin Bks.) Printers Row Publishing Group.
—Zoo Fun: A Lift the Flap Guessing Book. 2013. (J). *(978-1-4351-4930-4(0))* Barnes & Noble, Inc.

M

Marshall, Natalie. Five Little Pumpkins. Marshall, Natalie. 2017. (Fingers & Toes Nursery Rhymes Ser.). (ENG.). 12p. (J). (gr. -1 — 1). bds. 6.99 *(978-1-338-09117-5(4),* Cartwheel Bks.) Scholastic, Inc.

—Slide & Surprise in the Ocean. Marshall, Natalie. 2020. (ENG.). 12p. (J). (gr. -1-k). bds. 7.99 *(978-1-338-36004-2(3),* Cartwheel Bks.) Scholastic, Inc.

—This Little Piggy: A Fingers & Toes Nursery Rhyme Book. Marshall, Natalie. 2015. (ENG.). 12p. (J). (— 1). bds. 6.99 *(978-0-545-76761-3(X),* Cartwheel Bks.) Scholastic, Inc.

Marshall, Setsu. The Adventures of Tommy Toad. Rundstrom, Teressa. 2004. 40p. (J). per. *(978-1-932062-41-0(6))* Hability Solution Services, Inc.

Marshall, Todd, et al. Stegosaurus up Close: Plated Dinosaur. Dodson, Peter & Library Association Staff. 2011. (Zoom in on Dinosaurs! Ser.). 24p. (gr. k-2). 23.95 *(978-0-7660-3334-4(1))* Enslow Publishing, LLC.

—Tyrannosaurus Rex up Close: Meat-Eating Dinosaur. Dodson, Peter & Library Association Staff. 2011. (Zoom in on Dinosaurs! Ser.). 24p. (gr. k-2). 23.95 *(978-0-7660-3336-8(8))* Enslow Publishing, LLC.

Marshall, Todd & Bindon, John. Diplodocus up Close: Long-Necked Dinosaur. Dodson, Peter & Library Association Staff. 2011. (Zoom in on Dinosaurs! Ser.). 24p. (gr. k-2). 23.95 *(978-0-7660-3333-7(3))* Enslow Publishing, LLC.

Marshall, Todd & Fields, Laura. Triceratops up Close: Horned Dinosaur. Dodson, Peter & Library Association Staff. 2011. (Zoom in on Dinosaurs! Ser.). 24p. (gr. k-2). 23.95 *(978-0-7660-3335-1(X))* Enslow Publishing, LLC.

Marshmallow Creative. I Love Engines! (Thomas & Friends) Random House. 2019. (ENG.). 22p. (J). (— 1). bds. 6.99 *(978-0-593-12090-3(6),* Random Hse. Bks. for Young Readers) Random Hse. Children's Bks.

—My First Thomas & Friends. Golden Books. 2019. (ENG.). 22p. (J). (— 1). bds. 6.99 *(978-1-9848-4838-3(0),* Random Hse. Bks. for Young Readers) Random Hse. Children's Bks.

Marsico, Katie. A Baby Lobster Grows Up. Marsico, Katie. 2007. (Scholastic News Nonfiction Readers Ser.). (ENG.). 24p. (J). (gr. 1-2). 22.00 *(978-0-531-17475-3(1))* Scholastic Library Publishing.

—A Ladybug Larva Grows Up. Marsico, Katie. 2007. (Scholastic News Nonfiction Readers Ser.). (ENG.). 24p. (J). (gr. 1-2). 22.00 *(978-0-531-17478-4(6))* Scholastic Library Publishing.

—A Peachick Grows Up. Marsico, Katie. 2007. (Scholastic News Nonfiction Readers Ser.). (ENG.). 24p. (J). (gr. 1-2). 22.00 *(978-0-531-17480-7(8))* Scholastic Library Publishing.

Marsollier, Cam. Sticky Brains. Libin, Nicole. 2020. (ENG.). 40p. (J). ***(978-1-5255-5685-2(1))***; pap. ***(978-1-5255-5686-9(X))*** FriesenPress.

Marstall, Bob. Butternut Hollow Pond. Heinz, Brian. 2006. (ENG.). 32p. (J). (gr. 2-6). pap. 7.99 *(978-0-8225-5993-1(5),* First Avenue Editions) Lerner Publishing Group.

—Crows! Strange & Wonderful. Pringle, Laurence. 2010. (Strange & Wonderful Ser.). (ENG.). 32p. (J). (gr. 2-4). pap. 9.99 *(978-1-59078-724-3(2))* Boyds Mills Pr.

—On Bird Hill, 1 vol. Yolen, Jane. 2017. (On Bird Hill & Beyond Ser.: 1). (ENG.). 32p. (J). (gr. -1-2). 8.95 *(978-1-943645-30-5(2),* aa55fc37-f980-4745-8834-da1bdfa64785) WunderMill, Inc.

—On Duck Pond. Yolen, Jane. 2019. (On Bird Hill & Beyond Ser.: 2). (ENG.). 32p. (J). 8.95 *(978-1-943645-36-7(1),* 38b9b133-d35f-47ac-99d5-5f231af4fae7, Cornell Lab Publishing Group, The) WunderMill, Inc.

—On Gull Beach. Yolen, Jane. (On Bird Hill & Beyond Ser.: 3). (ENG.). 36p. (J). 2019. 8.95 *(978-1-943645-35-0(3),* f250f7a4-642f-4ab5-8591-2869dfbad189); 2018. (gr. -1-2). 16.95 *(978-1-943645-18-3(3),* 6db3d5fc-48cc-41e2-b07c-5850f2c6b126) WunderMill, Inc. (Cornell Lab Publishing Group, The).

Marstall, Robert. B Is for Blue Planet: An Earth Science Alphabet. Strother, Ruth. 2011. (Sleeping Bear Alphabets Ser.). (ENG.). 40p. (J). (gr. k-6). lib. bdg. 16.95 *(978-1-58536-454-1(1))* Sleeping Bear Pr.

Marston, Elaine. Maybell & Water Rat. Mallard, Pauline. 2018. (ENG.). 22p. (J). (gr. k-2). pap. *(978-1-78963-019-0(3),* Choir Pr., The) Action Publishing Technology Ltd.

Marston, J. D., photos by. The Poems for Pequenines (Poemas Para Pequenines) 2004. (Baby Einstein Ser.). (SPA., 12p. (J). bds. *(978-970-718-159-5(1),* Silver Dolphin en Español) Advanced Marketing, S. de R. L. de C. V.

Marston, Mick. A Beginner's Projects in Coding. Scott, Marc. 2020. (ENG.). 64p. (J). 14.99 *(978-1-5476-0276-6(7),* 900209457, Bloomsbury Children's Bks.) Bloomsbury Publishing USA.

Marta, Diana M. Firebug & the Mind Spark. Kisinger, E. Jean. 2012. 42p. pap. 12.50 *(978-0-615-58954-1(5))* Firebug Fairy Tales.

Martchenko, Michael. Andrew's Loose Tooth. Munsch, Robert. 2019. (ENG.). 32p. (J). pap. 7.99 *(978-0-590-12435-5(8))* Scholastic Canada, Ltd. CAN. Dist: Publishers Group West (PGW).

—Angela's Airplane. Munsch, Robert. 2018. (Classic Munsch Ser.). 28p. (J). (gr. k-2). 6.95 *(978-1-77321-076-6(9))* Annick Pr., Ltd. CAN. Dist: Publishers Group West (PGW).

—L' Anniversaire. Munsch, Robert. 2003. (Droles D'Histories Ser.).Tr. of Moira's Birthday. (FRE.). 24p. (J). (gr. k-18). pap. *(978-2-89021-114-8(2))* Diffusion du livre Mirabel (DLM).

—Boo! Munsch, Robert. 2019. (ENG.). 32p. (J). pap. 7.99 *(978-0-439-96126-4(2))* Scholastic Canada, Ltd. CAN. Dist: Publishers Group West (PGW).

—The Boy in the Drawer. Munsch, Robert. 2019. (Classic Munsch Ser.). 28p. (J). (gr. k-2). pap. 6.95 *(978-1-77321-102-2(1))* Annick Pr., Ltd. CAN. Dist: Publishers Group West (PGW).

—The Boy in the Drawer. Munsch, Robert. ed. 2019. (Classic Munsch Ser.). (ENG.). 28p. (J). (gr. k-2). 19.95 *(978-1-77321-103-9(X))* Annick Pr., Ltd. CAN. Dist: Publishers Group West (PGW).

—Boy Soup. Lesynski, Loris. 2nd ed. 2008. (ENG.). 32p. (J). (gr. -1-2). 18.95 *(978-1-55451-143-3(7),* 9781554511433) Annick Pr., Ltd. CAN. Dist: Publishers Group West (PGW).

—Class Clown. Munsch, Robert. 2019. (ENG.). 32p. (J). pap. 7.99 *(978-0-439-93594-4(6))* Scholastic Canada, Ltd. CAN. Dist: Publishers Group West (PGW).

—A Classic Munsch - ABC. Munsch, Robert. 2018. (Classic Munsch Concepts Ser.). (ENG.). 32p. (J). (gr. -1). bds. 12.99 *(978-1-77321-092-6(0))* Annick Pr., Ltd. CAN. Dist: Publishers Group West (PGW).

—Classic Munsch 123. Munsch, Robert. 2019. (Classic Munsch Concepts Ser.). (ENG.). 32p. (J). (gr. -1-k). bds. 12.99 *(978-1-77321-246-3(X))* Annick Pr., Ltd. CAN. Dist: Publishers Group West (PGW).

—Classic Munsch Moods. Munsch, Robert. 2019. (Classic Munsch Concepts Ser.). (ENG.). 34p. (J). (gr. -1-k). bds. 12.99 *(978-1-77321-300-2(8))* Annick Pr., Ltd. CAN. Dist: Publishers Group West (PGW).

—The Dark. Munsch, Robert. 2019. (Classic Munsch Ser.). (ENG.). 32p. (J). pap. 6.95 *(978-1-77321-104-6(8))* Annick Pr., Ltd. CAN. Dist: Publishers Group West (PGW).

—The Dark. Munsch, Robert. 2019. (Classic Munsch Ser.). (ENG.). 32p. (J). 19.95 *(978-1-77321-105-3(6))* Annick Pr., Ltd. CAN. Dist: Publishers Group West (PGW).

—David's Father. Munsch, Robert. 2018. (Classic Munsch Ser.). (ENG.). 32p. (J). (gr. k-2). 6.95 *(978-1-77321-078-0(5))* Annick Pr., Ltd. CAN. Dist: Publishers Group West (PGW).

—Le Dodo. Munsch, Robert. 2003. (Droles D'Histories Ser.).Tr. of Mortimer. (FRE.). 24p. (J). (gr. k-18). pap. *(978-2-89021-055-4(3))* Diffusion du livre Mirabel (DLM).

—Down the Drain! Munsch, Robert. 2020. (ENG.). 32p. (J). pap. 7.99 *(978-0-545-98600-7(1))* Scholastic Canada, Ltd. CAN. Dist: Publishers Group West (PGW).

—The Enormous Suitcase. Munsch, Robert. 2019. (ENG.). 32p. (J). pap. 7.99 *(978-1-4431-6318-7(X))* Scholastic Canada, Ltd. CAN. Dist: Publishers Group West (PGW).

—Enough, 1 vol. Forchuk Skrypuch, Marsha. 2003. (ENG.). 32p. (J). (gr. 2-4). pap. 9.95 *(978-1-55041-884-2(X),* 1fcfbf3a-f1b0-418a-aaa8-7c1cd6ec6770) Clockwise Pr. CAN. Dist: Firefly Bks., Ltd.

—Espera y Verás. Munsch, Robert. 2004. (SPA.). 24p. (J). (gr. -1-2). pap. 7.95 *(978-1-55037-872-6(4),* 9781550378726) Annick Pr., Ltd. CAN. Dist: Publishers Group West (PGW).

—The Fire Station. Munsch, Robert. (Classic Munsch Ser.). (ENG.). (J). 2018. 28p. (gr. k-2). 19.95 *(978-1-77321-081-0(5))*; 5th ed. 2012. 24p. (gr. -1-k). bds. 7.99 *(978-1-55451-423-6(1),* 9781554514236) Annick Pr., Ltd. CAN. Dist: Publishers Group West (PGW).

—Give Me Back My Dad! Munsch, Robert. 2020. (ENG.). 32p. (J). pap. 7.99 *(978-1-4431-0764-8(6))*; 19.99 ***(978-1-4431-0763-1(8),*** North Winds Pr) Scholastic Canada, Ltd. CAN. Dist: Publishers Group West (PGW).

—I Did It Because... How a Poem Happens. Lesynski, Loris. 3rd ed. 2006. (ENG.). 64p. (J). (gr. 2-5). pap. 9.95 *(978-1-55451-017-7(1),* 9781554510177) Annick Pr., Ltd. CAN. Dist: Publishers Group West (PGW).

—I Have to Go! Munsch, Robert. 2019. (Classic Munsch Ser.). 24p. (J). pap. 6.95 *(978-1-77321-106-0(4))* Annick Pr., Ltd. CAN. Dist: Publishers Group West (PGW).

—I Have to Go! Munsch, Robert. 2019. (Classic Munsch Ser.). (ENG.). 24p. (J). 19.95 *(978-1-77321-107-7(2))* Annick Pr., Ltd. CAN. Dist: Publishers Group West (PGW).

—I'm So Embarassed! Munsch, Robert. 2019. (ENG.). 32p. (J). pap. 7.99 *(978-0-439-95239-2(5))* Scholastic Canada, Ltd. CAN. Dist: Publishers Group West (PGW).

—Kiss Me, I'm Perfect! Munsch, Robert. 2008. (J). (gr. -1-3). 11.65 *(978-0-7569-9007-7(6))* Perfection Learning Corp.

—Makeup Mess. Munsch, Robert. ed. 2004. (J). (gr. k-3). spiral bd. *(978-0-616-11124-6(X))* Canadian National Institute for the Blind/Institut National Canadien pour les Aveugles.

—Makeup Mess. Munsch, Robert. 2019. (ENG.). 32p. (J). pap. 7.99 *(978-0-439-98896-4(9))* Scholastic Canada, Ltd. CAN. Dist: Publishers Group West (PGW).

—Marvellous Munsch! Munsch, Robert. 2019. (ENG.). 184p. (J). 24.99 *(978-1-4431-4863-4(6))* Scholastic Canada, Ltd. CAN. Dist: Publishers Group West (PGW).

—Matthew & the Midnight Pirates, 1 vol. Morgan, Allen. 2005. (First Flight Level 3 Ser.). (ENG.). 40p. (J). (gr. k-3). lib. bdg. 11.95 *(978-1-55041-902-3(1),* 4757829b-f633-44da-b324-3ada7670aaef) Fitzhenry & Whiteside, Ltd. CAN. Dist: Firefly Bks., Ltd.

—Matthew & the Midnight Wrestlers, 1 vol. Morgan, Allen. 2005. (First Flight Level 3 Ser.). (ENG.). 40p. (J). (gr. k-3). lib. bdg. 11.95 *(978-1-55041-915-3(3),* 354c9091-1e9a-482b-86c0-bbd1228f8727); per. 4.95 *(978-1-55041-916-0(1),* 14aa35f0-a4a1-41d9-a1e3-785f758dfead) Trifolium Bks., Inc. CAN. Dist: Firefly Bks., Ltd.

—Mmm, Cookies! Munsch, Robert. 2019. (ENG.). 32p. (J). pap. 7.99 *(978-0-590-51694-5(9))* Scholastic Canada, Ltd. CAN. Dist: Publishers Group West (PGW).

—Moira's Birthday. Munsch, Robert. 2019. (Classic Munsch Ser.). (ENG.). 32p. (J). pap. 6.95 *(978-1-77321-108-4(0))* Annick Pr., Ltd. CAN. Dist: Publishers Group West (PGW).

—Moose! Munsch, Robert. 2019. (ENG.). 30p. (J). bds. 9.99 *(978-1-4431-4292-2(1))* Scholastic Canada, Ltd. CAN. Dist: Publishers Group West (PGW).

—Moose! Munsch, Robert. 2015. 28p. (J). pap. *(978-0-545-82631-0(4))* Scholastic, Inc.

—More Pies! Munsch, Robert. 2020. (ENG.). 32p. (J). pap. 7.99 *(978-0-7791-1363-7(2))* Scholastic Canada, Ltd. CAN. Dist: Publishers Group West (PGW).

—More Pies. Munsch, Robert. ed. 2004. (J). (gr. k-3). spiral bd. *(978-0-616-14590-6(X))* Canadian National Institute for the Blind/Institut National Canadien pour les Aveugles.

—Mortimer. Munsch, Robert. (Classic Munsch Ser.). (J). 2018. 28p. (gr. k-2). 6.95 *(978-1-77321-082-7(3))*; 2007. (SPA.). 24p. (gr. -1-2). pap. 7.95 *(978-1-55451-109-9(7),* 9781554511099) Annick Pr., Ltd. CAN. Dist: Publishers Group West (PGW).

Martchenko, Michael. Moving Day! Munsch, Robert. 2020. (ENG.). 32p. (J). 19.99 ***(978-1-4431-6398-9(8),*** North Winds Pr); pap. 7.99 ***(978-1-4431-6399-6(6))*** Scholastic Canada, Ltd. CAN. Dist: Publishers Group West (PGW).

Martchenko, Michael. Munsch Mini-Treasury One. Munsch, Robert. 5th ed. 2010. (Munsch for Kids Ser.). (ENG.). 144p. (J). (gr. -1-2). 18.95 *(978-1-55451-273-7(5),* 9781554512737) Annick Pr., Ltd. CAN. Dist: Publishers Group West (PGW).

—Munsch Mini-Treasury Two. Munsch, Robert. 4th ed. 2010. (Munsch for Kids Ser.). (ENG.). 136p. (J). (gr. -1-2). 18.95 *(978-1-55451-274-4(3),* 9781554512744) Annick Pr., Ltd. CAN. Dist: Publishers Group West (PGW).

Martchenko, Michael, et al. Munsch More! A Robert Munsch Collection. Munsch, Robert. 2004. (ENG.). 184p. (J). 24.99 *(978-0-439-96135-6(1),* North Winds Pr) Scholastic Canada, Ltd. CAN. Dist: Publishers Group West (PGW).

Martchenko, Michael. Murmel, Murmel, Murmel. Munsch, Robert. 2018. (Classic Munsch Ser.). (ENG.). 28p. (J). (gr. k-2). 6.95 *(978-1-77321-084-1(X))* Annick Pr., Ltd. CAN. Dist: Publishers Group West (PGW).

—The Paper Bag Princess. Munsch, Robert. (Classic Munsch Ser.). (ENG.). (J). (gr. -1-2). 2018. 32p. 19.95 *(978-1-77321-030-8(0))*; 2018. 32p. pap. 6.95 *(978-1-77321-029-2(7))*; 10th ed. 2009. 28p. bds. 7.99 *(978-1-55451-211-9(5),* 9781554512119) Annick Pr., Ltd. CAN. Dist: Publishers Group West (PGW).

—The Paper Bag Princess 40th Anniversary Edition. Munsch, Robert. ed. 2020. (ENG.). 36p. (J). (gr. k-2). 19.95 *(978-1-77321-343-9(1))* Annick Pr., Ltd. CAN. Dist: Publishers Group West (PGW).

—Pigs. Munsch, Robert. 2018. (Classic Munsch Ser.). 32p. (J). (gr. -1-2). (ENG.). 19.95 *(978-1-77321-032-2(7))*; pap. 6.95 *(978-1-77321-031-5(9))* Annick Pr., Ltd. CAN. Dist: Publishers Group West (PGW).

—Pyjama Day! Munsch, Robert. 2019. (ENG.). 32p. (J). pap. 7.99 *(978-1-4431-3917-5(3))* Scholastic Canada, Ltd. CAN. Dist: Publishers Group West (PGW).

—Roar! Munsch, Robert. 2019. (ENG.). 32p. (J). pap. 7.99 *(978-0-545-98020-3(8))* Scholastic Canada, Ltd. CAN. Dist: Publishers Group West (PGW).

—Shoe Shakes. Lesynski, Loris. 2007. (ENG.). 32p. (J). (gr. -1-k). pap. 9.95 *(978-1-55451-105-1(4),* 9781554511051) Annick Pr., Ltd. CAN. Dist: Publishers Group West (PGW).

—Show & Tell. Munsch, Robert. 2019. (Classic Munsch Ser.). (ENG.). 32p. (J). 19.95 *(978-1-77321-113-8(7))* Annick Pr., Ltd. CAN. Dist: Publishers Group West (PGW).

—Silver Threads, 1 vol. Skrypuch, Marsha Forchuk. 2004. (ENG.). 32p. (J). (gr. 4-6). pap. 8.95 *(978-1-55041-903-0(X),* 263764ab-d98e-4f6e-8437-6e5fc0656f8e) Fitzhenry & Whiteside, Ltd. CAN. Dist: Firefly Bks., Ltd.

—Smelly Socks. Munsch, Robert. 2019. (ENG.). 32p. (J). pap. 7.99 *(978-0-439-96707-5(4))* Scholastic Canada, Ltd. CAN. Dist: Publishers Group West (PGW).

—Smelly Socks. Munsch, Robert. 2005. (ENG.). 32p. (J). (gr. -1-3). pap. 4.99 *(978-0-439-64948-3(X),* Cartwheel Bks.) Scholastic, Inc.

—Something Good. Munsch, Robert. 2018. (Classic Munsch Ser.). (ENG.). 32p. (J). (gr. k-2). 6.95 *(978-1-77321-086-5(6))* Annick Pr., Ltd. CAN. Dist: Publishers Group West (PGW).

—Stephanie's Ponytail. Munsch, Robert. (Classic Munsch Ser.). (ENG.). (J). (gr. -1-2). 2018. 32p. 19.95 *(978-1-77321-036-0(X))*; 2018. 24p. pap. 6.95 *(978-1-77321-035-3(1))*; 17th ed. 2007. 24p. 2.49 *(978-1-55451-114-3(3),* 9781554511143) Annick Pr., Ltd. CAN. Dist: Publishers Group West (PGW).

—Thomas' Snowsuit. Munsch, Robert. (Classic Munsch Ser.). (J). (gr. -1-2). 2018. (ENG.). 24p. 19.95 *(978-1-77321-038-4(6))*; 2018. 24p. pap. 6.95 *(978-1-77321-037-7(8))*; 6th ed. 2011. 22p. bds. 7.99 *(978-1-55451-363-5(4),* 9781554513635) Annick Pr., Ltd. CAN. Dist: Publishers Group West (PGW).

—Too Much Stuff! Munsch, Robert. 2020. (ENG.). 32p. (J). pap. 7.99 *(978-1-4431-0245-2(8))* Scholastic Canada, Ltd. CAN. Dist: Publishers Group West (PGW).

—Uncle Farley's False Teeth, 1 vol. Walsh, Alice. 2019. (ENG.). 32p. (J). pap. 10.95 *(978-1-77108-719-3(6),* ccf74940-c59a-45c5-bb01-70309a1ab77b) Nimbus Publishing, Ltd. CAN. Dist: Baker & Taylor Publisher Services (BTPS).

—Wait & See. Munsch, Robert. 2019. (Classic Munsch Ser.). (ENG.). 28p. (J). 19.95 *(978-1-77321-115-2(3))* Annick Pr., Ltd. CAN. Dist: Publishers Group West (PGW).

—We Share Everything! Munsch, Robert. 2019. (ENG.). 32p. (J). 7.99 *(978-0-590-51450-7(4))* Scholastic Canada, Ltd. CAN. Dist: Publishers Group West (PGW).

—Zoom! Munsch, Robert. 2019. (ENG.). 32p. (J). pap. 7.99 *(978-0-7791-1432-0(9))* Scholastic Canada, Ltd. CAN. Dist: Publishers Group West (PGW).

—50 below Zero. Munsch, Robert. 2019. (Classic Munsch Ser.). (ENG.). 24p. (J). pap. 6.95 *(978-1-77321-100-8(5))* Annick Pr., Ltd. CAN. Dist: Publishers Group West (PGW).

—50 below Zero. Munsch, Robert. 2019. (Classic Munsch Ser.). (ENG.). 24p. (J). 19.95 *(978-1-77321-101-5(3))* Annick Pr., Ltd. CAN. Dist: Publishers Group West (PGW).

Martchenko, Michael. Matthew & the Midnight Firefighter, 1 vol. Martchenko, Michael, tr. Morgan, Allen. 2004. (First Flight Level 3 Ser.). (ENG.). 40p. (J). (gr. k-3). lib. bdg. 5.95 *(978-1-55041-875-0(0),* e3fe4f01-f9af-4129-9c51-fd2c00c200b8) Fitzhenry & Whiteside, Ltd. CAN. Dist: Firefly Bks., Ltd.

Martel, June Atsuko. Brandy's New Home. Martel, June Atsuko. 2019. (ENG.). 38p. (J). pap. 12.95 ***(978-1-6906-6336-2(7))*** Independently Published.

Martello, Annapaola & Carnero, Carmen. Captain Marvel Vol. 2: Falling Star. 2020. 136p. (YA). (gr. 8-17). pap. 17.99 *(978-1-302-91688-6(2))* Marvel Worldwide, Inc.

Marten, Luanne. Measuring Length. Vogel, Julia. 2012. (Simple Measurement Ser.). (ENG.). 24p. (J). (gr. -1-2). 27.07 *(978-1-61473-279-2(5),* 204984) Child's World, Inc., The.

—Measuring Temperature. Vogel, Julia. 2012. (Simple Measurement Ser.). (ENG.). 24p. (J). (gr. -1-2). 27.07 *(978-1-61473-280-8(9),* 204985) Child's World, Inc., The.

—Measuring Time: The Calendar. Vogel, Julia. 2012. (Simple Measurement Ser.). (ENG.). 24p. (J). (gr. -1-2). 27.07 *(978-1-61473-281-5(7),* 204986) Child's World, Inc., The.

—Measuring Time: The Clock. Vogel, Julia. 2012. (Simple Measurement Ser.). (ENG.). 24p. (J). (gr. -1-2). 27.07 *(978-1-61473-282-2(5),* 204987) Child's World, Inc., The.

—Measuring Volume. Vogel, Julia. 2012. (Simple Measurement Ser.). (ENG.). 24p. (J). (gr. -1-2). 27.07 *(978-1-61473-283-9(3),* 204988) Child's World, Inc., The.

—Measuring Weight. Vogel, Julia. 2012. (Simple Measurement Ser.). (ENG.). 24p. (J). (gr. -1-2). 27.07 *(978-1-61473-284-6(1),* 204989) Child's World, Inc., The.

—Sophie & Sadie Build a Sonnet. StJohn, Amanda. 2011. (Poetry Builders Ser.). 32p. (J). (gr. 2-4). lib. bdg. 25.27 *(978-1-59953-440-4(1))* Norwood Hse. Pr.

Martha, Day Zschock. Forest Friends Scratch & Sketch (Trace Along) 2019. (ENG.). (J). 14.99 *(978-1-4413-3080-2(1))* Peter Pauper Pr. Inc.

—Llamas & Friends Scratch & Sketch (Trace Along) 2019. (ENG.). (J). 14.99 *(978-1-4413-3079-6(8))* Peter Pauper Pr. Inc.

—New York City Scratch & Sketch (Trace Along) 2019. (ENG.). (J). 14.99 *(978-1-4413-3081-9(X))* Peter Pauper Pr. Inc.

—Scratch & Sketch Puppies (Trace Along) 2018. (ENG.). (J). 14.99 *(978-1-4413-2923-3(4))* Peter Pauper Pr. Inc.

—Scratch & Sketch Sloths & Friends (Trace Along) 2018. (ENG.). (J). 14.99 *(978-1-4413-2924-0(2))* Peter Pauper Pr. Inc.

Marti, Romina. Bears Make Dens. Raum, Elizabeth. 2018. (Animal Builders Ser.). (ENG.). 24p. (J). (gr. k-3). pap. 8.99 *(978-1-68152-152-7(0))* Amicus.

—Beavers Build Lodges. Raum, Elizabeth. 2018. (Animal Builders Ser.). (ENG.). 24p. (J). (gr. k-3). pap. 8.99 *(978-1-68152-149-7(0))* Amicus.

—Bees Build Beehives. Raum, Elizabeth. 2018. (Animal Builders Ser.). (ENG.). 24p. (J). (gr. k-3). pap. 8.99 *(978-1-68152-150-3(4))* Amicus.

—Birds Build Nests. Raum, Elizabeth. 2018. (Animal Builders Ser.). (ENG.). 24p. (J). (gr. k-3). pap. 8.99 *(978-1-68152-151-0(2))* Amicus.

Martí, Romina. How Deep in the Ocean? Ocean Animal Habitats. Davies, Monika. 2019. (J). lib. bdg. *(978-1-68151-384-3(6),* Amicus Illustrated) Amicus Publishing.

—How Far Home? Animal Migrations. Davies, Monika. 2019. (J). lib. bdg. *(978-1-68151-385-0(4),* Amicus Illustrated) Amicus Publishing.

—How Far Underground? Burrowing Animals. Davies, Monika. 2019. (J). lib. bdg. *(978-1-68151-386-7(2),* Amicus Illustrated) Amicus Publishing.

—How High in the Rainforest? Rainforest Animal Habitats. Davies, Monika. 2019. (J). lib. bdg. *(978-1-68151-387-4(0),* Amicus Illustrated) Amicus Publishing.

—How High in the Sky? Flying Animals. Davies, Monika. 2019. (J). lib. bdg. *(978-1-68151-388-1(9),* Amicus Illustrated) Amicus Publishing.

—How High up the Mountain? Mountain Animal Habitats. Davies, Monika. 2019. (J). lib. bdg. *(978-1-68151-389-8(7),* Amicus Illustrated) Amicus Publishing.

—Los Castores y Sus Madrigueras. Raum, Elizabeth. 2018. (SPA.). 24p. (J). lib. bdg. *(978-1-68151-278-5(5))* Amicus Publishing.

Marti, Romina. Orangutans Build Tree Nests. Raum, Elizabeth. 2018. (Animal Builders Ser.). 24p. (J). (gr. k-3). pap. 9.99 *(978-1-68152-153-4(9))* Amicus.

Martin, Alice, et al. When Two Saints Meet. Hunger, Bill. Ripley, Jill, ed. 100p. (Orig.). (YA). (gr. 6-12). pap. 9.95 *(978-0-9625782-0-5(7))* Two Saints Publishing.

Martin, Alison J. Charlie, the Brave Monkey. Martin, Alison J. 2013. 24p. pap. 13.97 *(978-1-62516-155-0(7),* Strategic Bk. Publishing) Strategic Book Publishing & Rights Agency (SBPRA).

Martin, Alliyah, jt. illus. see Konecny, John.

Martin, Amy. The Frizz. Fogwell, Jasmine. 2018. (ENG.). 34p. (J). *(978-0-9952650-0-4(3))*; pap. *(978-0-9952650-1-1(1))* Fogwell, Jasmine.

—Music Is ... Stosuy, Brandon. 2016. (ENG.). 32p. (J). (gr. -1 — 1). bds. 8.99 *(978-1-4814-7702-4(1),* Little Simon) Little Simon.

Martin, Amy. The Quest for the Golden Bracelet. Fogwell, Jasmine. 2019. (ENG.). 290p. (J). (gr. 4-6). pap. ***(978-0-9952650-4-2(6))*** Fogwell, Jasmine.

Martin, Anne E. A Tail & Two Kitties. Martin, Anne E. 2007. 40p. (J). (gr. -1-3). per. 13.99 *(978-1-59879-340-6(3))* Lifevest Publishing, Inc.

—There's A Ladybug in My House. Martin, Anne E. l.t. ed. 2006. 45p. (J). per. 12.99 *(978-1-59879-165-5(6))* Lifevest Publishing, Inc.

Martin, Anrilize. The Adventures of Homer the Roamer. Mach, Tom. 2017. (ENG.). (J). pap. 10.95 *(978-0-692-82104-6(X))* Hill Song Pr.

Martin, Ashley P. Big Star. Martin, Ethan. 2017. (ENG.). (J). (gr. 1-5). pap. *(978-1-910615-51-5(X))* Pure Indigo Ltd.

Martin, Brian. If Winning Isn't Everything, Why Do I Hate to Lose? Smith, Bryan. 2015. (ENG.). 32p. (J). pap. 10.95 *(978-1-934490-85-3(7))* Boys Town Pr.

—The Misadventures of Michael Mcmichaels: The Angry Alligator, Vol. 1. Penn, Tony. 2016. (ENG.). 96p. (J). pap. 7.95 *(978-1-934490-94-5(6))* Boys Town Pr.

—The Misadventures of Michael Mcmichaels Vol 2: The Borrowed Bracelet, Vol. 2. Penn, Tony. 2016. (ENG.).

88p. (J). (gr. 3-6). pap. 7.95 *(978-1-944882-03-7(0))* Boys Town Pr.

Martin, Brian. Pause Power: Learning to Stay Calm When Your Buttons Get Pushed. Law, Jennifer. 2020. (ENG.). 32p. (J). (gr. -1-2). pap. 10.95 ***(978-1-944882-49-5(9))*** Boys Town Pr.

Martin, Caroline & Davies, Nic. Girl 2 Girl: The Swap Book You Share with Your Friends. Reader, Jenny. 2003. 96p. (J). pap. *(978-0-439-56743-5(2))* Scholastic, Inc.

Martin, Cecile L. K. The Shark's Tooth. Rash, Ron. 2015. (Young Palmetto Bks.). (ENG.). 40p. (J). pap. 12.99 *(978-1-61117-527-1(5))* Univ. of South Carolina Pr.

Martin, Chris. Can I Tell You About ADHD? A Guide for Friends, Family & Professionals. Yarney, Susan. 2013. (Can I Tell You About...? Ser.). (ENG.). 64p. (J). pap. 13.95 *(978-1-84905-359-4(6)*, 694728) Kingsley, Jessica Pubs. GBR. Dist: Hachette UK Distribution.

Martin, Christine. Bluetooth & the World Wide Web. Hardcastle, E. Rachael. 2019. (Bluetooth & Friends Ser.: Vol. 1). (ENG.). 154p. (J). (gr. 4-6). pap. 10.49 *(978-1-9999688-3-0(2)*, Curious Cat Bks.) Legacy Bound.

Martin, Courtney. Ballots for Belva: The True Story of a Woman's Race for the Presidency. Bardhan-Quallen, Sudipta. 2015. (ENG.). 32p. (J). (gr. k-5). pap. 10.99 *(978-1-4197-1627-0(1)*, Abrams Bks. for Young Readers) Abrams, Inc.

—Follow the Drinking Gourd: Come along the Underground Railroad. Coleman, Wim & Perrin, Pat. 2014. (Setting the Stage for Fluency Ser.). (ENG.). 40p. (J). (gr. 3-5). pap. 8.99 *(978-1-939656-10-0(9))* Red Chair Pr.

Martin, Courtney Autumn, et al. Life in Color: A Coloring Book of Teenage Confusion, Creativity, & Discovery. 2016. (ENG.). 96p. (YA). (gr. 9-11). pap. 12.95 *(978-1-63079-059-2(1)*, Switch Pr.) Capstone.

Martin, Cynthia. Adventures in Sound with Max Axiom, Super Scientist. Sohn, Emily. 2007. (Graphic Science Ser.). (ENG.). 32p. (J). (gr. 3-9). 31.32 *(978-0-7368-6836-5(4))*; per. 8.10 *(978-0-7368-7889-0(0))* Capstone.

—Adventures in Sound with Max Axiom Super Scientist: 4D an Augmented Reading Science Experience. Sohn, Emily. 2018. (Graphic Science 4D Ser.). (ENG.). 32p. (J). (gr. 3-9). lib. bdg. 34.65 *(978-1-5435-2944-9(5)*, 138533, Capstone Pr.) Capstone.

—Adventures in Sound with Max Axiom Super Scientist: An Augmented Reading Science Experience. Sohn, Emily. 2018. (Graphic Science 4D Ser.). (ENG.). 32p. (J). (gr. 3-9). pap. 7.95 *(978-1-5435-2955-5(0)*, 138555, Capstone Pr.) Capstone.

—Alley of Shadows, 1 vol. Brezenoff, Steve. 2008. (Vortex Bks.). (ENG.). 112p. (J). (gr. 5-9). pap. 7.19 *(978-1-59889-922-1(8)*, Stone Arch Bks.) Capstone.

Martin, Cynthia, et al. Amazing Spider-Man Epic Collection: Venom. 2018. (Amazing Spider-Man Epic Collection: 18). (ENG.). 504p. (J). (gr. 4-17). pap. 39.99 *(978-1-302-91142-3(2))* Marvel Worldwide, Inc.

Martin, Cynthia. Arachne. 2008. (Short Tales Greek Myths Ser.). (ENG.). 32p. (J). (gr. 3-6). 27.07 *(978-1-60270-134-2(2)*, 13433, Short Tales) Magic Wagon.

—The Attractive Story of Magnetism with Max Axiom, Super Scientist. Gianopoulos, Andrea. 2008. (Graphic Science Ser.). (ENG.). 32p. (J). (gr. 3-9). pap. 8.10 *(978-1-4296-1769-7(1))* Capstone.

—The Attractive Story of Magnetism with Max Axiom Super Scientist: 4D an Augmented Reading Science Experience. Gianopoulos, Andrea. 2018. (Graphic Science 4D Ser.). (ENG.). 32p. (J). (gr. 3-9). lib. bdg. 34.65 *(978-1-5435-2950-0(X)*, 138539, Capstone Pr.) Capstone.

—The Attractive Story of Magnetism with Max Axiom Super Scientist: An Augmented Reading Science Experience. Gianopoulos, Andrea. 2018. (Graphic Science 4D Ser.). (ENG.). 32p. (J). (gr. 3-9). pap. 7.95 *(978-1-5435-2961-6(5)*, 138561, Capstone Pr.) Capstone.

—Booker T. Washington: Great American Educator, 1 vol. Braun, Eric. 2006. (Graphic Biographies Ser.). (ENG.). 32p. (J). (gr. 3-9). per. 8.10 *(978-0-7368-6190-8(4)*, Capstone Pr.) Capstone.

—George Washington: Leading a New Nation. Doeden, Matt. 2005. (Graphic Biographies Ser.). (ENG.). 32p. (J). (gr. 3-9). 31.32 *(978-0-7368-4963-0(7))* Capstone.

—Hedy Lamarr & a Secret Communication System, 1 vol. Robbins, Trina. 2006. (Inventions & Discovery Ser.). (ENG.). 32p. (J). (gr. 3-9). 8.10 *(978-0-7368-9641-2(4)*, Capstone Pr.) Capstone.

—How to Draw Comic Heroes, 1 vol. Sautter, Aaron. 2007. (Drawing Cool Stuff Ser.). (ENG.). 32p. (J). (gr. 3-9). 28.65 *(978-1-4296-0074-3(8)*, Capstone Pr.) Capstone.

—A Journey into Adaptation with Max Axiom, Super Scientist: 4D an Augmented Reading Science Experience. Biskup, Agnieszka Józefina. 2019. (Graphic Science 4D Ser.). (ENG.). 32p. (J). (gr. 3-9). pap. 7.95 *(978-1-5435-6002-2(4)*, 140063); lib. bdg. 34.65 *(978-1-5435-5869-2(0)*, 139792) Capstone.

—Knights, 1 vol. Lee, Adrienne. 2013. (Legendary Warriors Ser.). (ENG.). 32p. (J). (gr. 3-9). 27.32 *(978-1-4765-3115-1(3)*, Capstone Pr.) Capstone.

—Legendary Warriors. Lee, Adrienne. 2013. (Legendary Warriors Ser.). (ENG.). 32p. (J). (gr. 3-9). lib. bdg., lib. bdg., lib. bdg. 136.60 *(978-1-4765-3628-6(7)*, Capstone Pr.) Capstone.

—The Pony Express, 1 vol. Dunn, Joeming W. 2008. (Graphic History Ser.). (ENG.). 32p. (J). (gr. 3-8). 29.93 *(978-1-60270-184-7(9)*, 9060, Graphic Planet - Fiction) Magic Wagon.

—The Salem Witch Trials, 1 vol. Dunn, Joeming W. 2008. (Graphic History Ser.). (ENG.). 32p. (J). (gr. 3-8). 29.93 *(978-1-60270-186-1(5)*, 9064, Graphic Planet - Fiction) Magic Wagon.

—Samurai, 1 vol. Lee, Adrienne. 2013. (Legendary Warriors Ser.). (ENG.). 32p. (J). (gr. 3-9). 27.32 *(978-1-4765-3113-7(7)*, Capstone Pr.) Capstone.

—Shellshocked. Hammer, Cully et al. Hilty, Joan, ed. rev. ed. 2006. (ENG.). 144p. (YA). pap. 12.99 *(978-1-4012-0965-0(3))* DC Comics.

—The Tempest, 1 vol. Conner, Daniel. 2008. (Graphic Shakespeare Ser.). (ENG.). 48p. (J). (gr. 5-10). 31.35 *(978-1-60270-194-6(6)*, 9150, Graphic Planet - Fiction) Magic Wagon.

Martin, Cynthia, et al. Theodore Roosevelt: Bear of a President, 1 vol. Olson, Nathan. 2007. (Graphic Biographies Ser.). (ENG.). 32p. (J). (gr. 3-9). per. 8.10 *(978-0-7368-7901-9(3)*, 1264944, Capstone Pr.) Capstone.

Martin, Cynthia. Twelfth Night, 1 vol. Goodwin, Vincent & Shakespeare, William. 2008. (Graphic Shakespeare Ser.). (ENG.). 48p. (J). (gr. 5-10). 31.35 *(978-1-60270-195-3(4)*, 9152, Graphic Planet - Fiction) Magic Wagon.

—Understanding Global Warming with Max Axiom, Super Scientist, 1 vol. Biskup, Agnieszka. 2008. (Graphic Science Ser.). (ENG.). 32p. (J). (gr. 3-9). per. 8.10 *(978-1-4296-1767-3(5)*, Capstone Pr.) Capstone.

—Understanding Global Warming with Max Axiom Super Scientist: 4D an Augmented Reading Science Experience. Biskup, Agnieszka. 2018. (Graphic Science 4D Ser.). (ENG.). 32p. (J). (gr. 3-9). lib. bdg. 34.65 *(978-1-5435-2953-1(4)*, 138542, Capstone Pr.) Capstone.

—Understanding Global Warming with Max Axiom Super Scientist: An Augmented Reading Science Experience. Biskup, Agnieszka. 2018. (Graphic Science 4D Ser.). (ENG.). 32p. (J). (gr. 3-9). pap. 7.95 *(978-1-5435-2964-7(X)*, 138564, Capstone Pr.) Capstone.

—Vikings, 1 vol. Lee, Adrienne. 2013. (Legendary Warriors Ser.). (ENG.). 32p. (J). (gr. 3-9). 27.32 *(978-1-4765-3116-8(1)*, Capstone Pr.) Capstone.

—White Fang, 1 vol. London, Jack. 2007. (Graphic Classics Ser.). (ENG.). 32p. (J). (gr. 3-8). 29.93 *(978-1-60270-055-0(9)*, 9028, Graphic Planet - Fiction) Magic Wagon.

—The World of Food Chains with Max Axiom, Super Scientist. O'Donnell, Liam. 2016. (Graphic Science Ser.). (ENG.). 32p. (J). (gr. 3-9). pap. 8.10 *(978-1-5157-4642-3(9))*; lib. bdg. 31.32 *(978-1-5157-4648-5(8))* Capstone.

—The World of Food Chains with Max Axiom Super Scientist: 4D an Augmented Reading Science Experience. O'Donnell, Liam. 2018. (Graphic Science 4D Ser.). (ENG.). 32p. (J). (gr. 3-9). lib. bdg. 34.65 *(978-1-5435-2951-7(8)*, 138540, Capstone Pr.) Capstone.

—The World of Food Chains with Max Axiom Super Scientist: An Augmented Reading Science Experience. O'Donnell, Liam. 2018. (Graphic Science 4D Ser.). (ENG.). 32p. (J). (gr. 3-9). pap. 7.95 *(978-1-5435-2962-3(3)*, 138562, Capstone Pr.) Capstone.

Martin, Cynthia. Comprender el Calentamiento Global con Max Axiom, Supercientífico. Martin, Cynthia. Biskup, Agnieszka. Strictly Spanish Translation Services Staff, tr. from ENG. 2012. (Ciencia Gráfica Ser.). (SPA.). 32p. (J). (gr. 3-9). lib. bdg. 31.32 *(978-1-4296-9235-9(9))* Capstone.

Martin, Cynthia & Beatty, Terry. The Story of the Star-Spangled Banner, 1 vol. Jacobson, Ryan. 2006. (Graphic History Ser.). (ENG.). 32p. (J). (gr. 3-9). 31.32 *(978-0-7368-5493-1(2))* Capstone.

Martin, Cynthia & Dominguez, Richard. Graphic Science 4D: 4D an Augmented Reading Science Experience. O'Donnell, Liam et al. 2018. (Graphic Science 4D Ser.). (ENG.). 32p. (J). (gr. 3-9). 346.50 *(978-1-5435-2954-8(2)*, 28452, Capstone Pr.) Capstone.

Martin, Cynthia & Milgrom, Al. The Whirlwind World of Hurricanes with Max Axiom, Super Scientist: 4D an Augmented Reading Science Experience. Krohn, Katherine. 2019. (Graphic Science 4D Ser.). (ENG.). 32p. (J). (gr. 3-9). pap. 7.95 *(978-1-5435-7547-7(1)*, 141079); lib. bdg. 34.65 *(978-1-5435-7250-6(2)*, 140591) Capstone.

Martin, Cynthia & Schoonover, Brent. Nathan Hale: Revolutionary Spy, 1 vol. Olson, Nathan & Glaser, Jason. 2006. (Graphic Biographies Ser.). (ENG.). 32p. (J). (gr. 3-9). per. 8.10 *(978-0-7368-6199-1(8)*, Capstone Pr.) Capstone.

Martin, Cynthia & Schultz, Barbara. Sacagawea: Journey into the West, 1 vol. Gunderson, Jessica Sarah. 2006. (Graphic Biographies Ser.). (ENG.). 32p. (J). (gr. 3-9). 31.32 *(978-0-7368-6499-2(7))* Capstone.

Martin, Cynthia & Schulz, Barbara. A Journey Through the Digestive System with Max Axiom, Super Scientist, 1 vol. Sohn, Emily. 2009. (Graphic Science Ser.). (ENG.). 32p. (J). (gr. 3-9). pap. 8.10 *(978-1-4296-3452-6(9)*, Capstone Pr.) Capstone.

—A Journey Through the Digestive System with Max Axiom, Super Scientist: 4D an Augmented Reading Science Experience. Sohn, Emily Beth. 2019. (Graphic Science 4D Ser.). (ENG.). 32p. (J). (gr. 3-9). pap. 7.95 *(978-1-5435-6031-2(8)*, 140078); lib. bdg. 34.65 *(978-1-5435-5876-0(3)*, 139801) Capstone.

—A Refreshing Look at Renewable Energy with Max Axiom, Super Scientist: 4D an Augmented Reading Science Experience. Krohn, Katherine. 2019. (Graphic Science 4D Ser.). (ENG.). 32p. (J). (gr. 3-9). pap. 7.95 *(978-1-5435-7544-6(7)*, 141076); lib. bdg. 34.65 *(978-1-5435-7248-3(0)*, 140589) Capstone.

—Sacagawea: Journey into the West, 1 vol. Gunderson, Jessica Sarah. 2006. (Graphic Biographies Ser.). (ENG.). 32p. (J). (gr. 3-9). per. 8.10 *(978-0-7368-9663-4(5))* Capstone.

—The Solid Truth about States of Matter with Max Axiom, Super Scientist, 1 vol. Biskup, Agnieszka. 2009. (Graphic Science Ser.). (ENG.). 32p. (J). (gr. 3-9). pap. 8.10 *(978-1-4296-3451-9(0))* Capstone.

—The Solid Truth about States of Matter with Max Axiom, Super Scientist. Biskup, Agnieszka. 2008. (Life Cycles Ser.). 24p. 289.10 *(978-1-4296-2451-0(5))* Capstone.

—The Solid Truth about States of Matter with Max Axiom, Super Scientist: 4D an Augmented Reading Science Experience. Biskup, Agnieszka Józefina. 2019. (Graphic Science 4D Ser.). (ENG.). 32p. (J). (gr. 3-9). pap. 7.95 *(978-1-5435-6007-7(5)*, 140068); lib. bdg. 34.65 *(978-1-5435-5874-6(7)*, 139799) Capstone.

Martin, Cynthia & Timmons, Anne. Elizabeth Blackwell: America's First Woman Doctor, 1 vol. Robbins, Trina. 2006. (Graphic Biographies Ser.). (ENG.). 32p. (J). (gr. 3-9). per. 8.10 *(978-0-7368-9660-3(0)*, Capstone Pr.) Capstone.

—Hedy Lamarr & a Secret Communication System, 1 vol. Robbins, Trina. 2006. (Inventions & Discovery Ser.). (ENG.). 32p. (J). (gr. 3-9). 31.32 *(978-0-7368-6479-4(2)*, Capstone Pr.) Capstone.

—Jane Goodall: Animal Scientist, 1 vol. Krohn, Katherine. 2006. (Graphic Biographies Ser.). (ENG.). 32p. (J). (gr. 3-9). 31.32 *(978-0-7368-5485-6(1)*, Capstone Pr.) Capstone.

—The Powerful World of Energy with Max Axiom, Super Scientist, 1 vol. Biskup, Agnieszka. 2009. (Graphic Science Ser.). (ENG.). 32p. (J). (gr. 3-9). pap. 8.10 *(978-1-4296-3450-2(2))* Capstone.

—The Powerful World of Energy with Max Axiom, Super Scientist: 4D an Augmented Reading Science Experience. Biskup, Agnieszka Józefina. 2019. (Graphic Science 4D Ser.). (ENG.). 32p. (J). (gr. 3-9). pap. 7.95 *(978-1-5435-6006-0(7)*, 140066); lib. bdg. 34.65 *(978-1-5435-5873-9(9)*, 139798) Capstone.

Martin, Dana. Johnstown Flood: An Up2U Historical Fiction Adventure, 1 vol. Mullarkey, John & Mullarkey, Lisa. 2013. (Up2U Adventures Ser.). (ENG.). 80p. (J). (gr. 2-5). lib. bdg. 29.93 *(978-1-61641-967-7(9)*, 15217, Calico Chapter Bks.) ABDO Publishing Co.

Martin, David Lozell. King Bartholomew & the Jesters Riddle. Mastromonaco, Pina. 2005. 32p. (J). (gr. -1-7). 15.95 *(978-0-9744307-1-3(4))* Merry Lane Pr.

Martin, David Lozell. Lucy & Bob: Brand New Readers. Martin, David Lozell. 2006. (Brand New Readers Ser.). (ENG.). 48p. (J). (gr. -1-3). pap. 5.99 *(978-0-7636-2722-5(4))* Candlewick Pr.

Martin, Don. My Day at the Zoo. Mademann Vaughan, Kathryn. 2004. (J). per. 19.95 *(978-0-9747447-1-1(9))* Chaser Media LLC.

Martin, Elizabeth B. I'm Not a Silly Goose. Martin, Elizabeth B., . ed. 2014. (ENG.). (J). 9.99 *(978-0-9910543-1-2(8))* Martin, Elizabeth B.

Martin, Frank, jt. illus. see Laming, Marc.

Martin, Frank, jt. illus. see Ross, Luke.

Martin, Fred. Condor Caper. Heimbuch, Carol Jo. 2008. 128p. pap. 11.50 *(978-1-59330-560-4(5))* Aventine Pr.

Martin, Gillian. Dragon River. Saunders, Rob. 2020. (ENG.). 114p. (J). pap. ***(978-1-78132-927-6(3))*** SilverWood Bks.

Martin, Iain C. Complete Theory Fun Factory. 2004. (ENG.). 96p. pap. 27.99 *(978-0-85162-181-4(3)*, 0851621813) Boosey & Hawkes, Inc.

—Fun Factory Violin Book. 2004. (ENG.). 32p. pap. 15.99 *(978-0-85162-183-8(X)*, 085162183X) Leonard, Hal Corp.

Martin Isidro, Oscar. La Llegada Del Hombre Lobo. Prieto Hernandez, Alvaro. 2015. (Terror�fico Mundo de Bobby Ser.: Vol. 1). (SPA.). 146p. (J). pap. *(978-84-923998-7-1(2))* Martín, Óscar Studio, S.L.

Martin, James R. Old King Stinky Toes. Graham, Baxter. 2005. 32p. (J). 15.95 *(978-0-9764791-0-9(9))* Drumstick Media.

Martin, Jan. Spies. Orme, David. 2010. (Fact to Fiction Grafx Ser.). 36p. pap. 7.45 *(978-0-7891-7998-2(9))* Perfection Learning Corp.

Martin, Jean-Francois. The Memory of an Elephant: An Unforgettable Journey. Strady, Sophie. 2014. (ENG.). 38p. (J). (gr. k-3). 18.99 *(978-1-4521-2903-7(7))* Chronicle Bks. LLC.

Martin, John. Dorothea Creamer. Stiegemeyer, Julie. 2012. (Hero of Faith Ser.). (ENG.). 47p. (J). pap. 7.99 *(978-0-7586-3077-3(8))* Concordia Publishing Hse.

—Double Trouble. Incomprehensible, Vordak T. & Seegert, Scott. 2012. (Vordak the Incomprehensible Ser.: No. 3). (ENG.). 192p. (J). (gr. 5). 13.99 *(978-1-60684-372-7(9)*, Darby Creek) Lerner Publishing Group.

Martin, John F. In the Hands of the Enemy. Sheely, Robert. Kilcoyne, Hope L., ed. 2003. (Adventures in America Ser.: Vol. 8). 75p. (gr. 4). 14.95 *(978-1-893110-31-1(1))* Silver Moon Pr.

—Seeking Safety. Weber, Judith Eichler. 2006. (Adventures in America Ser.). (J). *(978-1-893110-46-5(X))* Silver Moon Pr.

Martin, Jorge. Boing! A Very Noisy ABC. McCanna, Tim. 2018. (ENG.). 32p. (J). (gr. -1-3). 17.99 *(978-1-4814-8755-9(8)*, Simon & Schuster/Paula Wiseman Bks.) Simon & Schuster/Paula Wiseman Bks.

—A Cat Is Better. Singleton, Linda Joy. 2017. (ENG.). 32p. (J). (gr. -1-3). 16.99 *(978-1-4998-0278-8(1))* Little Bee Books Inc.

—Fairy Tale Pets. Corderoy, Tracey. 2017. (ENG.). 32p. (J). (gr. -1-2). 16.99 *(978-1-68010-064-8(5))* Tiger Tales.

—Little Taco Truck. Valentine, Tanya. 2019. 40p. (J). (gr. -1-2). 17.99 *(978-1-5247-6585-9(6))*; (ENG.). 20.99 *(978-1-5247-6586-6(4))* Random Hse. Children's Bks. (Schwartz & Wade Bks.).

Martin, Jorge. Fingerprint Fun. Martin, Jorge. 2016. (ENG.). 32p. (J). (gr. -1-1). pap. 7.99 *(978-1-78055-304-7(8))* O'Mara, Michael Bks., Ltd. GBR. Dist: Independent Pubs. Group.

Martin-Jourdenais, Norma Jean. 12 Easy Knitting Projects. Blanchette, Peg & Thibault, Terri. 2008. (ENG.). 64p. (J). (gr. 3-7). 12.95 *(978-0-8249-6784-0(4)*, Ideal Pubns.) Worthy Publishing.

Martin, Joyce. The Amazing Animal ABC Book. Mock, Jean. 2005. (J). *(978-0-9767210-1-7(5))* JM2 Publishing Co.

—The Amazing Animal ABC Book the Study Guide. Mock, Jean. 2005. *(978-0-9767210-2-4(3))* JM2 Publishing Co.

Martin, Julie. Great Lakes Rhythm & Rhyme. Rodgers, Denise. 2004. 58p. (J). per. 14.95 incl. audio compact disk *(978-0-938682-81-3(4))* River Road Pubns., Inc.

—A Little Bit of Nonsense. Rodgers, Denise. (J). (gr. k-7). 16.95 *(978-0-9708382-0-9(4))* Creative Writing Pr., Inc.

Martin-Laranaga, Ana. Flap My Wings. Powell, Richard. 2003. 10p. (J). 5.95 *(978-1-58925-690-3(5))* Tiger Tales.

Martín-Larrañaga, Ana. Butterfly at Home. 2007. (Butterfly Bks.). bds. 5.95 *(978-1-58925-804-4(5))* Tiger Tales.

—Butterfly in the Garden. 2007. (Butterfly Bks.). (J). bds. 5.95 *(978-1-58925-803-7(7))* Tiger Tales.

—Butterfly in the Town. 2007. (Butterfly Bks.). (J). bds. 5.95 *(978-1-58925-805-1(3))* Tiger Tales.

—Butterfly on the Farm. 2007. (Butterfly Bks.). (J). bds. 5.95 *(978-1-58925-802-0(9))* Tiger Tales.

Martin Larranaga, Ana. If You See a Cow. Powell, Richard & Powell, Richard. 2015. (ENG.). 12p. (J). (gr. -1 — 1). 4.99 *(978-1-4998-0112-5(2))* Little Bee Books Inc.

—If You See a Tiger. Powell, Richard & Powell, Richard. 2015. (ENG.). 12p. (J). (gr. -1 — 1). 4.99 *(978-1-4998-0113-2(0))* Little Bee Books Inc.

Martín-Larrañaga, Ana. Wag My Tail. Powell, Richard. 2003. 10p. (J). 5.95 *(978-1-58925-691-0(3))* Tiger Tales.

Martín Larrañaga, Ana. What's in the Box? Powell, Richard. 2004. (Ana's Mini Movers Ser.). 12p. (J). 5.95 *(978-1-58925-742-9(1))* Tiger Tales.

—What's in the Egg? Powell, Richard. 2004. (Ana's Mini Movers Ser.). 14p. (J). 5.95 *(978-1-58925-739-9(1))* Tiger Tales.

—Who Lives Here? Powell, Richard. 2004. (Ana's Mini Movers Ser.). 14p. (J). 5.95 *(978-1-58925-741-2(3))* Tiger Tales.

—Whose Hat Is That? Powell, Richard. 2004. (Ana's Mini Movers Ser.). 12p. (J). 5.95 *(978-1-58925-740-5(5))* Tiger Tales.

Martin, Laura & Kennedy, Seamus. The Hippity Dippity Witch. O' Byrne, Lorraine. 2012. 138p. pap. *(978-1-78176-391-9(7))* FeedARead.com.

Martin, Laura, jt. illus. see Cassaday, John.

Martin, Laura, jt. illus. see Deodato, Mike.

Martin, Laura, jt. illus. see Stelfreeze, Brian.

Martin, Leire. Ava in Code Land. Hitchman, Jess & Cullen, Gavin. 2020. (ENG.). 96p. (J). 18.99 *(978-1-250-31661-5(8)*, 900199822) Feiwel & Friends.

—An Egg-Cellent Costume Party! (My Little Pony) Ventura, Bonnie. 2018. (Little Golden Book Ser.). (ENG.). 24p. (J). (gr. -1-1). 4.99 *(978-0-525-57858-1(7)*, Golden Bks.) Random Hse. Children's Bks.

—Penny & Clover, Follow That Ball! Perl, Erica S. 2020. (Lucky Dogs Ser.). (ENG.). 32p. (J). (gr. k-1). 15.99 *(978-1-5247-9345-6(0))*; pap. 4.99 *(978-1-5247-9344-9(2))* Penguin Young Readers Group. (Penguin Young Readers).

—Penny & Clover, up & Over! Perl, Erica S. 2020. (Lucky Dogs Ser.). (ENG.). 32p. (J). (gr. k-1). 15.99 *(978-1-5247-9342-5(6)*, Penguin Young Readers) Penguin Young Readers Group.

—Penny & Clover, up & Over. Perl, Erica S. 2020. (Lucky Dogs Ser.). (ENG.). 32p. (J). (gr. k-1). pap. 4.99 *(978-1-5247-9341-8(8)*, Penguin Young Readers) Penguin Young Readers Group.

—Unicorn Club. Senior, Suzy. (ENG.). 32p. (J). (gr. -1-2). 2020. pap. 4.99 ***(978-1-68010-479-0(9))***; 2019. 17.99 *(978-1-68010-176-8(5))* Tiger Tales.

Martin, Lyn. Busy Bees on Broadway. DeLand, M. Maitland. 2011. 32p. 15.95 *(978-1-60832-063-9(4))* Greenleaf Book Group.

Martin, M. J. Jazzmin's Jamboree. Danby, Aaron. 2005. 40p. 13.95 *(978-0-9730583-3-8(1))* Lion & Mouse Tales, Inc. CAN. Dist: Hushion Hse. Publishing, Ltd.

Martin, M. J. & Danby, Aaron. The Elusive Mr. Zee. 2004. 32p. 11.95 *(978-0-9730583-2-1(3))* Lion & Mouse Tales, Inc. CAN. Dist: Hushion Hse. Publishing, Ltd.

Martin, Marc. Every Child a Song: A Celebration of Children's Rights. Davies, Nicola. 2020. (ENG.). 32p. (J). 17.95 ***(978-1-62371-872-5(4)***, Crocodile Bks.) Interlink Publishing Group, Inc.

Martin, Marilyn. The Merriest, the Bleariest Bears: A Story Book & an Activity Book. Atkinson, Doreen M. 2019. (ENG.). 54p. (J). pap. *(978-1-7752962-1-8(0))* Tellwell Talent.

Martin, Marilyn & Bates, Jean. Grandmas Precious Memories. Yusuf, Katharine. 2018. (ENG.). 34p. (J). (gr. k-3). 16.95 *(978-0-9994765-0-5(5))* Prairie Moon Pubs.

—Grandma's Precious Memories. Yusuf, Katharine. 2018. (ENG.). 34p. (J). (gr. k-3). pap. 12.95 *(978-0-9994765-1-2(3))* Prairie Moon Pubs.

Martin, Mark. Underwhere. Eastman, Kevin & Jenkins, Paul. 2018. 144p. (J). (gr. 4-7). pap. 14.99 *(978-1-68405-204-2(1))* Idea & Design Works, LLC.

Martin, Matthew. The Christmas Peg. Williams, Cameron. 2018. 32p. (J). (gr. -1-k). 14.99 *(978-0-14-378576-7(1))* Random Hse. Australia AUS. Dist: Independent Pubs. Group.

—The Marvellous Funambulist of Middle Harbour & Other Sydney Firsts. Bell, Hilary. 2016. 48p. (J). 24.99 *(978-1-74223-440-3(2)*, UNSW Press) NewSouth Publishing AUS. Dist: Independent Pubs. Group.

Martin, Matthew. The New Kid: Very Popular Me. O'Loghlin, James. 2019. (ENG.). 224p. (J). (gr. 3-5). 11.99 ***(978-1-76055-483-5(9)***, Pan) Pan Macmillan Australia Pty, Ltd. AUS. Dist: Independent Pubs. Group.

Martin, McDonald. The Perfect Pet: Finding a pet that is dear to your Heart. Cantor, Don & Cantor, Michael. 2010. 30p. (J). pap. 9.95 *(978-0-9823906-6-5(1))* Wiggles Pr.

Martin, M.E. Herobrine Episode 19: Minecraft Zombie Horde. Martin, M.E. 2018. (Herobrine Comic Book Ser.: Vol. 19). (ENG.). 48p. (J). pap. 14.99 *(978-1-7918-4397-7(2))* Independently Published.

—Herobrine Episode 20: Minecraft Wolf. Martin, M.E. 2018. (Herobrine Comic Book Ser.: Vol. 20). (ENG.). 50p. (J). pap. 14.99 *(978-1-7929-5315-6(1))* Independently Published.

Martin, Miles J. Around the Clock: A Story about Telling Time. Jackson, Lora Z. 2011. 58p. 36.95 *(978-1-258-06483-9(9))* Literary Licensing, LLC.

Martin, Molly. Smokey & Bobtail: A Tale of Two Kitties. Brown, Brina. Brown, M., ed. 2018. (ENG.). 40p. (J). pap. 10.00 *(978-1-7275-1416-2(5))* CreateSpace Independent Publishing Platform.

Martin, Oshane. Bubblegum Boy. Sims, Renita. 2019. (ENG.). 34p. (J). pap. 14.95 ***(978-1-64214-612-7(9))*** Page Publishing Inc.

Martin, Pauline. The Bureau of Misplaced Dads. Veillé, Eric. 2015. (ENG.). 34p. (J). (gr. -1-2). 16.95 *(978-1-77138-238-0(4))* Kids Can Pr., Ltd. CAN. Dist: Hachette Bk. Group.

Martin, Pedro. Don't Know Much about Dinosaurs. Davis, Kenneth C. 2004. (Picture Bks.: No. 7). 48p. (J). 15.99 *(978-0-06-028619-4(9))* HarperCollins Pubs.

—Don't Know Much about the Presidents. Davis, Kenneth C. rev. ed. 2009. (Don't Know Much About Ser.). (ENG.). 64p. (J). (gr. k-4). pap. 6.99 *(978-0-06-171823-6(8))* HarperCollins Pubs.

—Don't Know Much about the Solar System. Davis, Kenneth C. 2004. (Don't Know Much About Ser.). (ENG.). 48p. (J). (gr. 1-4). pap. 7.99 *(978-0-06-446230-3(7))* HarperCollins Pubs.

—Hamster Champs. Murphy, Stuart J. 2005. (MathStart 3 Ser.). (ENG.). 40p. (J). (gr. 2). pap. 5.99 *(978-0-06-055773-7(7))* HarperCollins Pubs.

—The Presidents. Davis, Kenneth C. 2003. (Don't Know Much About Ser.). (ENG.). 64p. (J). (gr. 1-4). reprint ed. pap. 6.99 *(978-0-06-446231-0(5))* HarperCollins Pubs.

Martin, Pedro, jt. illus. see Murphy, Stuart J.

Martin, Peter. The Short March to Wisdom. Yung Dong, Venerable & Jacobs, Marjorie. 2015. 64p. (J). pap. 0.00 *(978-1-943211-00-5(0))* Fo Guang Shan International Translation Ctr.

Martin, Philippe, photos by. Creatures Close Up. Watts, Gillian. 2016. (ENG., 64p. (J). (gr. 3-7). pap. 9.95 *(978-1-77085-782-7(6),* 94a941be-e462-4cee-aa0a-3c1b6aeccc8d) Firefly Bks., Ltd.

Martin, Richard. Black Beauty: And a Discussion of Kindness. Sewell, Anna. 2003. (Values in Action Illustrated Classics Ser.). 191p. (J). *(978-1-59203-028-6(9))* Learning Challenge, Inc.

Martin, Shawn. Peter's Christmas Eve Adventure, 1 vol. Organ, Betty. 2010. (ENG.). 32p. (J). (gr. k-3). *(978-1-897174-68-5(3))* Breakwater Bks., Ltd.

Martin, Sherry. Welcome Home, Indigeaux: A Louisiana Adventure. Woods, Wendy. 2013. (ENG.). (J). (gr. -1-3). 14.95 *(978-1-62086-246-9(8))* Mascot Bks., Inc.

Martin, Stephanie. The Red Caterpillar on College Street. Cooper, Afua. Date not set. 400p. (J). (gr. -1-3). pap. *(978-0-920813-87-4(9))* Sister Vision Pr.

Martin, Stuart. Fly Away Home. Edgecombe, Jane. 2003. (J). 15.95 *(978-1-74047-152-7(0))* Book Co. Publishing Pty, Ltd., The AUS. Dist: Penton Overseas, Inc.

—Puddle Pen Bible Stories, 1 vol. David, Juliet. 2010. (Candle Puddle Pen Ser.). 10p. (J). (gr. -1). bds. 12.99 *(978-0-8254-7394-4(2),* Candle Bks.) Lion Hudson PLC GBR. Dist: Kregel Pubns.

Martin, Susan. Doug E Do. Tuey. 2006. 76p. pap. 16.95 *(978-1-4241-0295-2(2))* PublishAmerica, Inc.

Martin, Tom. Abraham Lincoln: Defender of the Union! Shulman, Mark. 2019. (Show Me History! Ser.). (ENG.). 96p. (J). (gr. 3-7). 12.99 *(978-1-68412-544-9(8),* Portable Pr.) Printers Row Publishing Group.

Martin Vidal, Beatriz. Bird. 2015. 32p. (J). 16.95 *(978-1-927018-64-4(1))* Simply Read Bks. CAN. Dist: Ingram Publisher Services.

Martin, W. Lyon. Rabbit's Song. Tucker, S. J. & Herring, Trudy. 2009. (ENG.). 32p. (J). lib. bdg. 16.95 *(978-0-9796834-7-3(5),* Magical Child Bks.) Shades of White.

Martin, W. Lyon. Aidan's First Full Moon Circle: A Magical Child Story. Martin, W. Lyon. 2008. 32p. (J). (gr. -1-1). lib. bdg. 16.95 *(978-0-9796834-4-2(0))* Shades of White.

—An Ordinary Girl, A Magical Child. Martin, W. Lyon. 2008. (ENG.). 48p. (J). lib. bdg. 16.95 *(978-0-9796834-3-5(2),* Magical Child Bks.) Shades of White.

Martin, Wendy. The Story Circle / el Circulo de Cuentos. Gonzales Betrand, Diane. 2016. (ENG, MUL & SPA.). 32p. (J). (gr. k-3). 17.95 *(978-1-55885-826-8(1),* Piñata Books) Arte Publico Pr.

Martin, Whitney. Cory's Stories: A Kid's Book about Living with ADHD. Kraus, Jeanne. 2004. 32p. (J). 14.95 *(978-1-59147-148-6(6));* pap. 9.95 *(978-1-59147-154-7(0))* American Psychological Assn. (Magination Pr.).

—Finding the Right Spot: When Kids Can't Live with Their Parents. Levy, Janice. 2004. 48p. (J). 14.95 *(978-1-59147-073-1(0));* pap. 9.95 *(978-1-59147-074-8(9))* American Psychological Assn. (Magination Pr.).

—Ginny Morris & Dads New Girlfriend. Gallagher, Mary Collins. 2006. (Ginny Morris Ser.). 64p. (J). (gr. 3-7). 14.95 *(978-1-59147-386-2(1));* per. 9.95 *(978-1-59147-387-9(X))* American Psychological Assn. (Magination Pr.).

—Let George Do It! Foreman, George & Manushkin, Fran. 2017. (ENG.). 32p. (J). (gr. -1-3). 13.99 *(978-1-5344-0946-0(7),* Simon & Schuster Bks. For Young Readers) Simon & Schuster Bks. For Young Readers.

—Nine Is Not an Even Number. Gallagher, Mary Collins. 2005. 48p. (J). 14.95 *(978-1-59147-157-8(5));* pap. 9.95 *(978-1-59147-158-5(3))* American Psychological Assn. (Magination Pr.).

—An Undone Fairy Tale. Lendler, Ian. 2005. (ENG.). 32p. (J). (gr. 1-5). 19.99 *(978-0-689-86677-7(1),* Simon & Schuster Bks. For Young Readers) Simon & Schuster Bks. For Young Readers.

Martin, Zac a. A Small Dogs Tale. Harley, M. F. 2019. (ENG.). 44p. (J). pap. 9.48 *(978-1-0714-2331-8(2))* Independently Published.

Martina, Luca. La Lama Delle Lacrime - 2 Sogni Oscuri. Martina, Luca. 2018. (Saga Della Lama Delle Lacrime Ser.: Vol. 2). (ITA.). 296p. (J). pap. 10.99 *(978-1-7315-7017-8(1))* Independently Published.

Martincic, Miriam. The Wreck of the Good Ship Lollipop: A Rhyming Picture Book for Good Children & Bad Parents. Gillespie, William Kemp. 2018. (Flap Books: Kid's Lit with Four Lines a Page Ser.: Vol. 1). (ENG.). 62p. (J). (gr. k-6). pap. 24.00 ***(978-0-9801392-5-9(2))*** Spineless Bks.

Martineau, Luke. Every Boy's Alphabet. Bingham, Kate. Holland, Kate, ed. 2019. (ENG.). 56p. (J). (gr. k-2). 21.99 *(978-1-912654-54-3(7))* Graffeg Limited GBR. Dist: Independent Pubs. Group.

—Every Girl's Alphabet. Bingham, Kate. Holland, Kate, ed. 2019. (ENG.). 56p. (J). (gr. k-2). 21.99 *(978-1-912654-53-6(9))* Graffeg Limited GBR. Dist: Independent Pubs. Group.

Martineau, Philip James. The Big Race Old. Sheppard, Kristen. 2018. (ENG.). 30p. (J). (gr. k-6). pap. 13.99 *(978-1-365-86193-2(7))* Lulu Pr., Inc.

Martines, Donna. My ABCs: An ABC Book for Any Age. Spray, Michelle. Pasternack, Susan, ed. I.t. ed. 2006. 64p. (J). per. 8.95 *(978-0-9714160-4-8(4))* Bk. Shelf.

Martinez, Alitha, et al. Iron Man: the Mask in the Iron Man Omnibus. 2019. (ENG.). 688p. (YA). (gr. 8-17). 75.00 *(978-1-302-92065-4(0))* Marvel Worldwide, Inc.

—Miles Morales Vol. 2: Bring on the Bad Guys. 2020. 112p. (YA). (gr. 4-17). pap. 15.99 *(978-1-302-91479-0(0))* Marvel Worldwide, Inc.

Martinez, Alitha. The Quest for Dragon Mountain. Mayhall, Robin. 16th rev. ed. 2010. (Twisted Journeys ® Ser.: 16). (ENG.). (J). (gr. 4-7). pap. 45.32 *(978-0-7613-6999-8(6))* Lerner Publishing Group.

—Superb Vol. 3: The Youth Are Getting Restless. Walker, David F. 2019. (ENG.). 144p. (YA). pap. 14.99 *(978-1-941302-86-6(6),* e130ca16-9918-4128-841a-cdfd409e19f6, Lion Forge) Oni Pr., Inc.

Martínez, Andrés Vera. Little White Duck: A Childhood in China. Martínez, Andrés Vera. 2012. (ENG.). 108p. (J). (gr. 4-7). pap. 9.99 *(978-0-7613-8115-0(5),* 9780761381150, Graphic Universe™) Lerner Publishing Group.

Martínez, Andrés Vera & Martínez, Andrés Vera. Babe Ruth. Delsante, Vito. 2009. (Before They Were Famous Ser.). (ENG.). 128p. (J). (gr. 3-7). pap. 10.99 *(978-1-4169-5071-4(0),* Simon & Schuster/Paula Wiseman Bks.) Simon & Schuster/Paula Wiseman Bks.

Martínez, Andrés Vera, jt. illus. see Martínez, Andrés Vera.

Martinez, Andrew, photos by. Don't Mess with Me: The Weird Lives of Venomous Sea Creatures, 1 vol. Erickson, Paul. 2018. (How Nature Works: 0). (ENG., 48p. (J). (gr. 3-7). 17.95 *(978-0-88448-551-3(X),* 884551) Tilbury Hse. Pubs.

Martinez, April. Toto's Tale. Hays, K. D. & Weidman, Meg. 2010. 248p. (J). pap. 14.99 *(978-1-936144-61-7(1),* Zumaya Thresholds) Zumaya Pubns. LLC.

Martinez, Aydee Lopez. Countdown to the Last Tortilla. Reyes, Maria de la Luz. 2019. (ENG.). 40p. (J). (gr. 3-6). 17.99 ***(978-0-9972790-2-3(8))*** REYES, MARIA DE LA LUZ.

Martinez, David J. The Mansion on Champagnolle. Nahte, Ethan. 2019. (Weird Tales Investigators Ser.: Vol. 1). (ENG.). 52p. (J). pap. 5.50 *(978-1-7982-2919-4(6))* Independently Published.

Martinez, David R. Hurry-Up Harry. Ernst, Robert A. 2018. (Dr. Bob's Tales Ser.: Vol. 1). (ENG.). 128p. (J). 17.95 *(978-0-9998318-1-6(X))* Discoveries Publishing llc.

—Miss Little Bea Sharp. Rosen, M. S. Jessica. 2017. (ENG.). 34p. (J). pap. 15.00 *(978-0-9996760-0-4(8))* Free Spirit Artworks, LLC.

Martinez, Eduardo. H Is for Harvey. Beasley, Julie. 2018. (ENG.). 40p. 16.95 *(978-0-87565-705-9(2))* Texas Christian Univ. Pr.

Martinez, Edward. Farmers Market. Parks, Carmen. ed. 2003. (Green Light Readers Level 2 Ser.). (ENG.). 24p. (J). (gr. -1-3). pap. 4.99 *(978-0-15-204841-9(3),* 1194619) Houghton Mifflin Harcourt Publishing Co.

—Farmers Market/Día de Mercado. Parks, Carmen. Flor Ada, Alma & Campoy, F. Isabel, trs. 2010. (Green Light Readers Level 2 Ser.). (ENG.). 28p. (J). (gr. -1-3). pap. 4.99 *(978-0-547-36900-6(X),* 1422975) Houghton Mifflin Harcourt Publishing Co.

—Tomás Rivera. Medina, Jane & National Geographic Learning Staff. 2004. (Green Light Readers Level 2 Ser.). (ENG.). 24p. (J). (gr. -1-3). pap. 4.99 *(978-0-15-205145-7(7),* 1195527, HMH Books For Young Readers) Houghton Mifflin Harcourt Publishing Co.

—Tomás Rivera. Medina, Jane. 2004. (Green Light Reader Level 2 Ser.). 24p. (J). (gr. k-2). 16.19 *(978-0-15-205146-4(5))* Houghton Mifflin Harcourt Publishing Co.

Martinez, Emily. Jenae. Kempf, Julia. 2019. (ENG.). 50p. (J). pap. 12.95 *(978-1-0949-1896-9(2))* Independently Published.

Martinez, Emma. 100 Words in the Wild: Tiered Shaped Board Book. Byrd, Redd. Cottage Door Press, ed. 2017. (Discover & Learn Ser.). (ENG.). 12p. (J). (gr. -1-1). bds. 12.99 *(978-1-68052-182-5(9),* 1001800) Cottage Door Pr.

Martinez, Enrique. Un Cambio de Piel. Remolina, Tere. (Barril Sin Fondo Ser.). (SPA.). (J). (gr. 3-5). pap. *(978-968-6465-20-4(0))* Casa de Estudios de Literatura y Talleres Artisticos Amaquemecan A.C. MEX. Dist: Lectorum Pubns., Inc.

—El Deseo de Aurelio. Martínez, Rafael. 2006. (la Orilla del Viento Ser.). (SPA.). 48p. (J). (gr. 8-10). pap. *(978-968-16-7988-0(1))* Fondo de Cultura Economica.

—Loteria de Adivinanzas. Angel Lome, Emilio. 2010. (Serie Morada Ser.). (SPA.). 46p. (J). pap. 6.95 *(978-1-64101-137-2(8))* Santillana USA Publishing Co., Inc.

—Loteria de Adivinanzas: Lottery of Riddles. Lome, Emilio Angel. 2013. (ENG & SPA.). (J). pap. 7.00 *(978-607-01-1720-6(4),* Alfaguara) Santillana USA Publishing Co., Inc.

—Lottery of Riddles. Lome, Emilio Angel. 2011. 46p. (gr. 2-5). pap. 6.95 *(978-968-19-0663-4(2))* Aguilar, Altea, Taurus, Alfaguara, S.A. de C.V MEX. Dist: Santillana USA Publishing Co., Inc.

—Los Pelusos, Cuentos Policiacos. Diaz, Enrique Perez. 2003. (SPA.). 95p. (J). (gr. 3-5). pap. 8.95 *(978-968-19-1018-1(4))* Santillana USA Publishing Co., Inc.

—Solo para Muchachos. Boullosa, Carmen. 2003. (SPA.). 60p. (J). (gr. 4-7). 11.95 *(978-968-19-0325-1(0))* Aguilar, Altea, Taurus, Alfaguara, S.A. de C.V MEX. Dist: Santillana USA Publishing Co., Inc.

Martinez, Enrique & Graullera, Fabiola. Del Otro Lado de los Suenos. Alberto, Eliseo. 2003. (SPA.). 32p. (J). (gr. k-3). 12.95 *(978-968-19-0473-9(7))* Aguilar, Altea, Taurus, Alfaguara, S.A. de C.V MEX. Dist: Santillana USA Publishing Co., Inc.

—Jose Marti: Cuatro cuentos Infantiles. Marti, Jose. (SPA.). 28p. (J). (gr. 3-5). 9.95 *(978-970-29-0522-6(2))* Santillana, Editorial, S.A. de C.V. MEX. Dist: Santillana USA Publishing Co., Inc.

—El Pais de las Sombras. Alvarez, Leticia Herrera. 2003. (SPA.). 48p. (J). (gr. 3-5). pap. 7.95 *(978-968-19-0535-4(0))* Santillana USA Publishing Co., Inc.

Martinez, Gabriel. Cenzontle/Mockingbird (YA Edition) Songs of Empowerment (Poetry * Drama) Garcia Ordaz, Daniel. 2018. (ENG.). 104p. (J). pap. 30.00 *(978-1-7328106-0-0(5))* El Zarape Pr.

Martinez, Gayle Denise. Lean on Me, Lee. Valdez, Joseph G. 2012. 24p. pap. *(978-1-77067-670-1(8))* FriesenPress.

Martinez, Gil. La Princesa de Largos Cabellos. Van Haeringen, Annemarie. De Sterck, Goedele, tr. 2007. (Los Especiales de A la Orilla del Viento Ser.). (SPA.). 27p. (J). *(978-968-16-8471-6(0))* Fondo de Cultura Economica.

Martinez, Heather. Albert: The Little Tree with Big Dreams. Golden Books et al. 2016. (Big Golden Book Ser.). (ENG.). 32p. (J). (gr. -1-2). 9.99 *(978-0-399-55120-8(4),* Golden Bks.) Random Hse. Children's Bks.

—The Big Halloween Scare. Banks, Steven. 2003. (SpongeBob SquarePants Ser.: Vol. 1). (ENG.). 32p. (J). (gr. k-2). pap. 3.99 *(978-0-689-84196-5(5),* Simon Spotlight/Nickelodeon) Simon Spotlight/Nickelodeon.

—Camp Spongebob. Reisner, Molly & Ostrow, Kim. 2005. (Spongebob Squarepants Ser.). 32p. (gr. k-2). 14.00 *(978-0-7569-5424-6(X))* Perfection Learning Corp.

—Christmas with Krabby Klaws. David, Erica. 2010. (SpongeBob SquarePants Ser.). (ENG.). 16p. (J). pap. 5.99 *(978-1-4424-0805-0(7),* Simon Spotlight/Nickelodeon) Simon Spotlight/Nickelodeon.

—Dino Parade! (Blaze & the Monster Machines) Tillworth, Mary. 2017. (Little Golden Book Ser.). (ENG.). 24p. (J). (-k). 4.99 *(978-0-399-55795-8(4),* Golden Bks.) Random Hse. Children's Bks.

—The Golden Gecko. Arps, Melissa & Lagonegro, Melissa. 2017. (Little Golden Book Ser.). (ENG.). 24p. (J). (-k). 4.99 *(978-0-7364-3721-9(5),* Golden/Disney) Random Hse. Children's Bks.

—Happy Birthday, SpongeBob! Chanda, J-P. 2005. (SpongeBob SquarePants Ser.). (ENG.). 24p. (J). pap. 3.99 *(978-0-689-87674-5(2),* Simon Spotlight/Nickelodeon) Simon Spotlight/Nickelodeon.

—I Am a Princess. Carbone, Courtney. 2016. (J). *(978-1-5182-1626-8(9),* Golden Bks.) Random Hse. Children's Bks.

—I Am a Princess (Star Wars) Carbone, Courtney. 2016. (Little Golden Book Ser.). (ENG.). 24p. (J). (-k). 4.99 *(978-0-7364-3605-2(7),* Golden Bks.) Random Hse. Children's Bks.

—Ice-Cream Dreams. Krulik, Nancy. 2004. 22p. (J). lib. bdg. 15.00 *(978-1-4242-0975-0(7))* Fitzgerald Bks.

—Ice-Cream Dreams. 2004. (SpongeBob SquarePants Ser.). (ENG.). 24p. (J). pap. 3.99 *(978-0-689-86861-0(8),* Simon Spotlight/Nickelodeon) Simon Spotlight/Nickelodeon.

—New Student Starfish. Miglis, Jenny. 2003. (SpongeBob SquarePants Ser.). (ENG.). 64p. (J). pap. 3.99 *(978-0-689-86164-2(8),* Simon Spotlight/Nickelodeon) Simon Spotlight/Nickelodeon.

—Plankton's Christmas Surprise! (SpongeBob SquarePants) Random House. 2013. (Pictureback(R) Ser.). (ENG.). 16p. (J). (gr. -1-2). 4.99 *(978-0-449-81851-0(9),* Random Hse. Bks. for Young Readers) Random Hse. Children's Bks.

—Ready, Set, Tow! 2018. (J). *(978-1-5444-0206-2(6),* Golden Bks.) Random Hse. Children's Bks.

—Sponge in Space! (SpongeBob SquarePants) Golden Books Staff. 2012. (Little Golden Book Ser.). (ENG.). 24p. (J). (gr. k-k). 4.99 *(978-0-307-92990-7(6),* Golden Bks.) Random Hse. Children's Bks.

—SpongeBob Airpants: The Lost Episode. Richards, Kitty. 2003. (SpongeBob SquarePants Ser.). (ENG.). 64p. (J). pap. 3.99 *(978-0-689-86163-5(X),* Simon Spotlight/Nickelodeon) Simon Spotlight/Nickelodeon.

—The SpongeBob Movie: Sponge on the Run: Welcome to Camp Coral! (SpongeBob SquarePants) Lewman, David. 2020. (Little Golden Book Ser.). (ENG.). 24p. (J). (gr. -1-2). 4.99 *(978-0-593-12752-0(8),* Golden Bks.) Random Hse. Children's Bks.

—SpongeBob Rocks! Chipponeri, Kelli. 2006. (SpongeBob SquarePants Ser.: 9). (ENG.). 32p. (J). (gr. -1-3). pap. 3.99 *(978-1-4169-1314-6(9),* Simon Spotlight/Nickelodeon) Simon Spotlight/Nickelodeon.

—Star Wars: the Phantom Menace (Star Wars) Carbone, Courtney. 2015. (Little Golden Book Ser.). (ENG.). 24p. (J). (-k). 4.99 *(978-0-7364-3542-0(5),* Golden Bks.) Random Hse. Children's Bks.

—Where the Pirates Arrgh! (SpongeBob SquarePants) Wygand, Melissa. 2013. (Little Golden Book Ser.). (ENG.). 24p. (J). (-k). 3.99 *(978-0-307-98174-5(6),* Golden Bks.) Random Hse. Children's Bks.

Martinez, Heather, jt. illus. see Random House Disney Staff.

Martinez, Ivanova. Celebrate Halloween & the Day of the Dead with Cristina & Her Blue Bunny. Flor Ada, Alma. 2006. (Cuentos para Celebrar / Stories to Celebrate Ser.). 30p. (gr. k-6). per. 11.95 *(978-1-59820-132-1(8))* Santillana USA Publishing Co., Inc.

Martinez, J-P Loppo. Dody the Dog Has a Rainbow. Derrick, Patricia. 2007. 32p. 18.95 incl. audio compact disk *(978-1-933818-10-8(7))* Animalations.

—Farley the Ferret of Farkleberry Farm. Derrick, Patricia. 2007. 32p. (J). (gr. -1-3). 18.95 incl. audio compact disk *(978-1-933818-12-2(3))* Animalations.

—Montgomery the Moose Can Shake His Caboose. Derrick, Patricia & Sibbett, Joyce. 2007. 32p. (J). (gr. -1). 18.95 incl. audio compact disk *(978-1-933818-18-4(2))* Animalations.

—Mr. Walrus & the Old School Bus. Derrick, Patricia. 2007. 32p. 18.95 incl. audio compact disk *(978-1-933818-13-9(1))* Animalations.

—Rathbone the Rat. Derrick, Patricia & O'Neil, Shirley. 2007. 32p. (J). (gr. -1-3). 18.95 incl. audio compact disk *(978-1-933818-17-7(4))* Animalations.

—Rickity & Snickity at the Balloon Fiesta. Derrick, Patricia. 2007. 32p. (J). (gr. -1-3). 18.95 incl. audio compact disk *(978-1-933818-11-5(5))* Animalations.

—Riley the Rhinoceros. Derrick, Patricia. 2007. 32p. (J). 18.95 incl. audio compact disk *(978-1-933818-15-3(8))* Animalations.

—Sly the Dragonfly. Derrick, Patricia. 2007. 32p. (J). (gr. -1-3). 18.95 incl. audio compact disk *(978-1-933818-16-0(6))* Animalations.

Martinez, Jorge. Androcles & the Lion. Sommer, Carl. 2014. (Sommer-Time Story Classics Ser.). (ENG.). 32p. (J). (gr. k-4). 16.95 *(978-1-57537-075-0(1))* Advance Publishing, Inc.

Martínez, Jorge, et al. Dare to Dream! Sommer, Carl. 2007. (Another Sommer-Time Story Ser.). (ENG.). 48p. (J). 23.95 incl. audio compact disk *(978-1-57537-723-0(3));* (gr. -1-3). 9.95 *(978-1-57537-024-8(7));* (gr. -1-3). 16.95 incl. audio compact disk *(978-1-57537-523-6(0));* (gr. k-4). lib. bdg. 16.95 *(978-1-57537-073-6(5))* Advance Publishing, Inc.

Martinez, Jorge, et al. Dare to Dream! Sommer, Carl. 2014. (J). pap. *(978-1-57537-951-7(1))* Advance Publishing, Inc.

Martínez, Jorge, et al. Dare to Dream! ¡Atrévete a Soñar! Sommer, Carl. ed. 2009. 48p. (J). 26.95 incl. audio compact disk *(978-1-57537-176-4(6))* Advance Publishing, Inc.

—Dream. Sommer, Carl. 2009. (Quest for Success Ser.). (ENG.). 56p. (YA). pap. 4.95 *(978-1-57537-276-1(2));* lib. bdg. 12.95 *(978-1-57537-251-8(7))* Advance Publishing, Inc.

—Dream (Sueña) Sommer, Carl. ed. 2009. (Quest for Success Bilingual Ser.). (SPA & ENG.). 104p. (YA). (gr. 6-18). lib. bdg. 14.95 *(978-1-57537-226-6(6))* Advance Publishing, Inc.

Martinez, Jorge. The Emperor & the Seed. Sommer, Carl. 2016. (J). *(978-1-57537-946-3(5))* Advance Publishing, Inc.

Martínez, Jorge. The Richest Poor Kid. Sommer, Carl. 2007. (Another Sommer-Time Story Ser.). (ENG.). 48p. (J). 23.95 incl. audio compact disk *(978-1-57537-724-7(1));* (gr. -1-3). 9.95 *(978-1-57537-025-5(5));* (gr. -1-3). 16.95 incl. audio compact disk *(978-1-57537-524-3(9));* (gr. k-4). 16.95 *(978-1-57537-074-3(3))* Advance Publishing, Inc.

Martinez, Jorge. The Richest Poor Kid. Sommer, Carl. 2014. (J). pap. *(978-1-57537-965-4(1))* Advance Publishing, Inc.

—The Ugly Princess. Sommer, Carl. 2016. 32p. (J). *(978-1-57537-948-7(1))* Advance Publishing, Inc.

Martinez, Laura. Optimizing an Octopus: An Engineering Everything Adventure. Hunt, Emily & Pantoya, Michelle. 2018. (Engineering Everything Ser.). (ENG.). 96p. (J). 14.95 *(978-1-68283-033-8(0))* Texas Tech Univ. Pr.

Martinez, Leovigildo. The Twenty-Five Mixtec Cats. Gollub, Matthew. 2004. (J). *(978-1-889910-30-7(9))* Tortuga Pr.

—The Twenty-Five Mixtec Cats. Gollub, Matthew W. 2nd rev. ed. 2004. (ENG.). 32p. (J). (gr. 2-4). 15.95 *(978-1-889910-28-4(7))* Tortuga Pr.

—Uncle Snake. Gollub, Matthew. 2004. (ENG.). 32p. (J). (gr. 2-4). pap. 6.95 *(978-1-889910-32-1(5));* 2nd ed. 15.95 *(978-1-889910-31-4(7))* Tortuga Pr.

Martinez, Logan. Kitties Don't Eat Quesadillas: An a-To-Z Picture Book for Picky Eaters. Adams Martinez, Patty. 2019. (ENG.). 36p. (J). (gr. k-2). pap. 6.99 ***(978-1-7332949-1-1(0));*** (Kitties Don't Eat Quesadillas Ser.: Vol. 1). 19.99 ***(978-1-7332949-0-4(2))*** Martinez, Patty & Logan.

Martinez, Michael. Nobody Likes Me: What Am I Doing Wrong? Williams, Justine. 2013. 20p. pap. 10.95 *(978-1-62212-778-8(1),* Strategic Bk. Publishing) Strategic Book Publishing & Rights Agency (SBPRA).

Martinez, Natali. Nerdel's ABC Book. Kesselman, Robin & Kesselman, Marc. 2009. 38p. (J). 16.99 *(978-0-9823357-2-7(5))* Nerdel Co., The.

Martinez-Neal, Juana. Babymoon. Barrett, Hayley. 2019. (ENG.). 32p. (J). (-k). 16.99 *(978-0-7636-8852-3(5))* Candlewick Pr.

—Fry Bread: A Native American Family Story. Noble Maillard, Kevin. 2019. (ENG.). 48p. (J). 18.99 *(978-1-62672-746-5(5),* 900172345) Roaring Brook Pr.

—Leillie the Different Elephant. Garza, Lois Ann. 2011. 36p. pap. 11.95 *(978-1-60047-592-4(2))* Wasteland Pr.

—La Madre Goose: Nursery Rhymes for Los Niños. Elya, Susan Middleton. 2016. 32p. (J). (gr. k-3). 16.99 *(978-0-399-25157-3(X),* G.P. Putnam's Sons Books for Young Readers) Penguin Young Readers Group.

—The Messy One, 1 vol. Jones, Christianne C. (Little Boost Ser.). (ENG.). 32p. (J). (gr. -1-1). 2012. 7.95 *(978-1-4048-7417-6(8));* 2011. lib. bdg. 23.99 *(978-1-4048-6651-5(5))* Capstone. (Picture Window Bks.).

—La Princesa & the Pea. Elya, Susan Middleton. 2017. 32p. (J). (gr. -1-3). 17.99 *(978-0-399-25156-6(1),* G.P. Putnam's Sons Books for Young Readers) Penguin Young Readers Group.

—Swashby & the Sea. Ferry, Beth. 2020. (ENG.). 32p. (J). (gr. -1-3). 17.99 *(978-0-544-70737-5(0),* 1628687, HMH Books For Young Readers) Houghton Mifflin Harcourt Publishing Co.

Martinez-Neal, Juana. Alma & How She Got Her Name. Martinez-Neal, Juana. 2018. 32p. (J). (gr. -1-3). 15.99 *(978-0-7636-9355-8(3))* Candlewick Pr.

—Alma y Cómo Obtuvo Su Nombre. Martinez-Neal, Juana. 2018. 32p. (J). (gr. -1-3). 15.99 *(978-0-7636-9358-9(8))* Candlewick Pr.

Martinez Ricci, Andres. Electricity Is Everywhere Site CD+Book. Higgins, Nadia. 2010. (Science Rocks! Set 2 Site CD+Book Ser.). 32p. lib. bdg. 84.14 incl. cd-rom *(978-1-61641-008-7(6))* ABDO Publishing Co.

—Excited about Energy Site CD+Book. Higgins, Nadia. 2010. (Science Rocks! Set 2 Site CD+Book Ser.). 32p. lib. bdg. 84.14 incl. cd-rom *(978-1-61641-009-4(4))* ABDO Publishing Co.
—Marvelous Motion Site CD+Book. Higgins, Nadia. 2010. (Science Rocks! Set 2 Site CD+Book Ser.). 32p. lib. bdg. 84.14 incl. cd-rom *(978-1-61641-010-0(8))* ABDO Publishing Co.
—Mighty Magnet Site CD+Book. Higgins, Nadia. 2010. (Science Rocks! Set 2 Site CD+Book Ser.). 32p. lib. bdg. 84.14 incl. cd-rom *(978-1-61641-011-7(6))* ABDO Publishing Co.
—Stupendous Sound Site CD+Book. Higgins, Nadia. 2010. (Science Rocks! Set 2 Site CD+Book Ser.). 32p. lib. bdg. 84.14 incl. cd-rom *(978-1-61641-012-4(4))* ABDO Publishing Co.
—Super Shadows Site CD+Book. Higgins, Nadia. 2010. (Science Rocks! Set 2 Site CD+Book Ser.). 32p. lib. bdg. 84.14 incl. cd-rom *(978-1-61641-013-1(2))* ABDO Publishing Co.
Martinez, Rocio. The Fox & the Crow. 2007. (First Reading Level 1 Ser.). 32p. (J). (gr. -1-3). 8.99 *(978-0-7945-1813-4(3),* Usborne) EDC Publishing.
—Las Adventuras de Pepe. Ballesteros, Jose Manuel & Manuel, Ballesteros Pastor José. (SPA.). 156p. (J). *(978-84-392-8118-4(8))* Gaviota Ediciones ESP. Dist: Lectorum Pubns., Inc.
—Por Qué? Munrriz, Mercedes & Munárriz Guezala, Mercedes. 2003. (SPA.). 16p. (J). *(978-84-667-2627-6(6))* Grupo Anaya, S.A. ESP. Dist: Lectorum Pubns., Inc.
—La Princesa Que No Sabia Estornudar. Canas, José & José, Cañas Torregrosa. (Leer Es Vivir Serie Teatro).Tr. of Princess Who Couldn't Sneeze. (SPA.). 48p. (J). 5.56 *(978-84-241-7716-4(9))* Everest Editora ESP. Dist: Lectorum Pubns., Inc.
—Qué Es? Munrriz, Mercedes & Munárriz Guezala, Mercedes. 2003. (SPA.). 16p. (J). *(978-84-667-2626-9(8))* Grupo Anaya, S.A. ESP. Dist: Lectorum Pubns., Inc.
Martinez, Rosemary. The Twin Kangaroo Treasure Hunt, a Gay Parenting Story. Martinez Jover, Carmen. 2013. 32p. pap. *(978-607-00-6545-3(X))* Martínez Jover, María del Carmen Dorotea.
Martínez Ruppel, Fernando. La Iliada Contada para Niños. Rigiroli, Victoria. 2017. (SPA.). 64p. (J). (gr. 4-7). pap. 9.95 *(978-987-718-239-2(4))* Ediciones Lea S.A. ARG. Dist: Independent Pubs. Group.
Martinez, Sergio. Best of All. Lucado, Max. 2003. (Max Lucado's Wemmicks Ser.: 4). (ENG.). 32p. (J). 16.99 *(978-1-58134-501-8(1))* Crossway.
—From Colonies to Country with George Washington. Hedstrom-Page, Deborah. 2007. (My American Journey Ser.). 82p. (J). (gr. 3-9). 9.99 *(978-0-8054-3265-7(5))* B&H Publishing Group.
—From Log Cabin to White House with Abraham Lincoln. Hedstrom-Page, Deborah. 2007. (My American Journey Ser.). 82p. (J). (gr. 3-9). 9.99 *(978-0-8054-3269-5(8))* B&H Publishing Group.
—From Settlement to City with Benjamin Franklin. Hedstrom-Page, Deborah. 2007. (My American Journey Ser.). 84p. (J). (gr. 3-9). 9.99 *(978-0-8054-3267-1(1))* B&H Publishing Group.
—From Slavery to Freedom with Harriet Tubman. Hedstrom-Page, Deborah. 2007. (My American Journey Ser.). 84p. (J). (gr. 3-9). 9.99 *(978-0-8054-3268-8(X))* B&H Publishing Group.
Martinez, Sergio. Los Hijos Del Rey / the Children of King. Lucado, Max. 2020. (SPA.). 32p. (J). (gr. k-3). pap. 9.99 ***(978-1-64473-180-2(0))*** Penguin Random House Grupo Editorial ESP. Dist: Penguin Random Hse. LLC.
Martinez, Sergio. The Prayer of Jabez for Young Hearts. Wilkinson, Bruce & Suggs, Robb. 2004. 32p. (J). (gr. -1-3). 15.99 *(978-0-8499-7932-3(3))* Nelson, Thomas Inc.
—Punchinello & the Most Marvelous Gift. Lucado, Max. 2004. (Max Lucado's Wemmicks Ser.: 5). (ENG.). 32p. (J). 15.99 *(978-1-58134-546-9(1));* 2003. 28p. bds. 6.99 *(978-1-58134-562-9(3))* Crossway.
—Punchinello & the Most Marvelous Gift: And, Your Special Gift. Lucado, Max. 2007. (J). *(978-1-58134-877-4(0))* Crossway.
—You Are Mine. Lucado, Max. import ed. 2005. 28p. bds. *(978-1-85985-546-1(6),* Candle Bks.) Lion Hudson PLC.
Martinez, Sirac. Aaaachooo! Palmer Ph D, Cristina Casas. 2019. (ENG.). 34p. (J). pap. 11.99 ***(978-1-7112-4390-0(6))*** Independently Published.
Martinez, Sonia. Meet Mary MacKillop. Murphy, Sally. 2nd ed. 2014. (Meet... Ser.). (ENG.). 32p. (J). (gr. k). 13.99 *(978-1-74275-722-3(7))* Random Hse. Australia AUS. Dist: Independent Pubs. Group.
Martinez, Teresa. The Halloween Tree. Montanari, Susan. 2019. (ENG.). 32p. (J). (-3). 10.99 *(978-1-4926-7335-4(8),* Sourcebooks Jabberwocky) Sourcebooks, Inc.
—It's Not a Bed, It's a Time Machine. Rapkin, Mickey. 2019. (It's Not a Book Series, It's an Adventure Ser.). (ENG.). 32p. (J). 17.99 *(978-1-250-16762-0(0),* 900187570) Imprint IND. Dist: Macmillan.
—It's Not a School Bus, It's a Pirate Ship. Rapkin, Mickey. 2020. (It's Not a Book Series, It's an Adventure Ser.). (ENG.). 32p. (J). 18.99 *(978-1-250-22977-9(4),* 900209272) Imprint IND. Dist: Macmillan.
—Mario & the Hole in the Sky: How a Chemist Saved Our Planet. Rusch, Elizabeth. 2019. 40p. (J). (gr. 1-4). lib. bdg. 16.99 *(978-1-58089-581-1(6))* Charlesbridge Publishing, Inc.
—Mario y el Agujero en el Cielo: C�mo un Qu�mico Salv� Nuestro Planeta. Rusch, Elizabeth. Calvo, Carlos E., tr. 2019. (SPA.). 40p. (J). (gr. 1-4). lib. bdg. 16.99 *(978-1-58089-582-8(4))* Charlesbridge Publishing, Inc.
—Mary, Queen of Scots: Escape from the Castle, 34 vols. Breslin, Theresa. 2018. (Traditional Scottish Tales Ser.). (ENG.). 32p. (J). 11.95 *(978-1-78250-512-9(1),* Kelpies) Floris Bks. GBR. Dist: Consortium Bk. Sales & Distribution.
—Robert the Bruce: The King & the Spider, 25 vols. MacPherson, Molly. 2019. (Traditional Scottish Tales Ser.). (ENG.). 24p. (J). 11.95 *(978-1-78250-558-7(X),* Kelpies) Floris Bks. GBR. Dist: Consortium Bk. Sales & Distribution.
—William Wallace: The Battle to Free Scotland, 30 vols. MacPherson, Molly. 2020. (Traditional Scottish Tales Ser.). (ENG.). 32p. (J). pap. 11.95 *(978-1-78250-629-4(2),* Kelpies) Floris Bks. GBR. Dist: Consortium Bk. Sales & Distribution.
Martinez, Tito. Mariana y el Albiqueno. Lantigua, Yanette. 2015. 24p. (J). (gr. -1-2). pap. 12.95 *(978-9942-05-249-0(6),* Alfaguara Infantil) Santillana Ecuador ECU. Dist: Santillana USA Publishing Co., Inc.
—Mariana y el Albiqueno. Lantigua, Yanette. 2015. (Serie Verde / Album Ilustrado Ser.). (SPA.). 24p. (J). pap. 12.95 *(978-9942-19-333-9(2))* Santillana USA Publishing Co., Inc.
Martinez Vicente, Silvia. Todos Los Monstruos Que Encontré en Tu Jardín. Garvi, Elena. 2018. (SPA.). 304p. (J). pap. 11.42 *(978-1-7928-1953-7(6))* Independently Published.
Martinez y Luis San Vicente, Enrique. Cuentos de Todo y de Nada. Sastrias, Marta. 2003. (SPA.). 82p. (J). (gr. 3-5). *(978-968-19-0551-4(2))* Aguilar, Altea, Taurus, Alfaguara, S.A. de C.V.
Martini, Angela. Ballerina Weather Girl. Stout, Shawn K. 2013. (Not-So-Ordinary Girl Ser.: 1). (ENG.). 192p. (J). (gr. 1-5). pap. 6.99 *(978-1-4424-7401-7(7),* Aladdin) Simon & Schuster Children's Publishing.
—Ballerina Weather Girl. Stout, Shawn K. 2013. (Not-So-Ordinary Girl Ser.: 1). (ENG.). 192p. (J). (gr. 1-5). 15.99 *(978-1-4424-7402-4(5),* Simon & Schuster/Paula Wiseman Bks.) Simon & Schuster/Paula Wiseman Bks.
—Best Friends Forever! Golosi, Rosanne. 2005. 64p. (J). *(978-0-439-80072-3(2))* Scholastic, Inc.
—Fiona Finkelstein, Big-Time Ballerina!! Stout, Shawn K. 2010. (ENG.). 192p. (J). pap. 4.99 *(978-1-4169-7109-2(2),* Simon & Schuster/Paula Wiseman Bks.) Simon & Schuster/Paula Wiseman Bks.
—Fiona Finkelstein Meets Her Match!! Stout, Shawn K. 2010. (Fiona Finkelstein Ser.). (ENG.). 150p. (J). (gr. 1-5). 17.44 *(978-1-4169-7928-9(X))* Simon & Schuster, Inc.
—I Heard a Rumor. Krulik, Nancy. 2007. (How I Survived Middle School Ser.: No. 3). 105p. (J). *(978-0-439-90091-1(3))* Scholastic, Inc.
—Miss Matched. Stout, Shawn K. 2013. (Not-So-Ordinary Girl Ser.: 2). (ENG.). 176p. (J). (gr. 1-5). pap. 5.99 *(978-1-4424-7404-8(1),* Aladdin) Simon & Schuster Children's Publishing.
—Miss Matched. Stout, Shawn K. 2013. (Not-So-Ordinary Girl Ser.: 2). (ENG.). 160p. (J). (gr. 1-5). 15.99 *(978-1-4424-7405-5(X),* Simon & Schuster/Paula Wiseman Bks.) Simon & Schuster/Paula Wiseman Bks.
—Oops! I Did It (Again)! Wasserman, Robin. 2003. 96p. (J). *(978-0-439-55608-8(2))* Scholastic, Inc.
—Perfect World: I Was Soooo Embarrassed! Bligh, Deirdre. 2005. 62p. (J). *(978-0-439-80069-3(2))* Scholastic, Inc.
Martiniere, Stephan. Robonocchio. Lofficier, Randy & Lofficier, Jean-Marc. Pijuán Aragón, Miren, tr. 2004. (SPA.). 128p. (YA). per. 14.95 *(978-1-932983-25-8(2),* Black Coat Pr.) HollywoodComics.com, LLC.
—Robonocchio. Lofficier, Randy & Lofficier, Jean-Marc. 2004. (FRE.). 128p. (YA). per. 14.95 *(978-1-932983-04-3(X),* Black Coat Pr.) HollywoodComics.com, LLC.
Martino, Anita. Free to Be Gluten Free! Spergel, Heather. 2013. (ENG.). 48p. (J). 19.99 *(978-1-938501-18-0(7))* Turn the Page Publishing.
Martino, Stefano, et al. Other Side #1. Houser, Jody. 2019. (Stranger Things Ser.). (ENG.). 24p. (J). (gr. 6-12). lib. bdg. 27.07 *(978-1-5321-4387-8(7),* 32890, Graphic Novels) Spotlight.
—Other Side #2. Houser, Jody. 2019. (Stranger Things Ser.). (ENG.). 24p. (J). (gr. 6-12). lib. bdg. 27.07 *(978-1-5321-4388-5(5),* 32891, Graphic Novels) Spotlight.
—Other Side #3. Houser, Jody. 2019. (Stranger Things Ser.). (ENG.). 24p. (J). (gr. 6-12). lib. bdg. 27.07 *(978-1-5321-4389-2(3),* 32892, Graphic Novels) Spotlight.
—Other Side #4. Houser, Jody. 2019. (Stranger Things Ser.). (ENG.). 24p. (J). (gr. 6-12). lib. bdg. 27.07 *(978-1-5321-4390-8(7),* 32893, Graphic Novels) Spotlight.
—Stranger Things (Set), 4 vols. Houser, Jody. 2019. (Stranger Things Ser.). (ENG.). 24p. (J). (gr. 6-12). lib. bdg. 162.42 *(978-1-5321-4386-1(9),* 32889, Graphic Novels) Spotlight.
Martins, Ann-Kathrin & Fowler, Romana. I Don't Want to Be Grumpy Anymore! Fowler, Leona. 2011. 19p. (J). 12.95 *(978-1-58909-804-6(8))* Bookstand Publishing.
Martins, Elsa. Physics Animated! Jorden, Tyler. 2019. (ENG.). 14p. (J). bds. 14.99 *(978-1-64170-132-7(3),* 550132) Familius LLC.
Martins, Marlene. Dylan Dolphin Learns to Swim. Bullock, Laura. 2019. (ENG.). 34p. (J). pap. 9.99 ***(978-1-7956-0177-1(9))*** Independently Published.
Martinsen, Sarah. Charlie & the Blanket Toss. Brown, Tricia. 2015. (ENG.). 32p. (J). pap. 11.99 *(978-1-941821-66-4(9),* Alaska Northwest Bks.) West Margin Pr.
Marton, Eleonora. Sock Story. Smouha, C. K. 2019. (ENG.). 32p. (J). 14.95 *(978-1-908714-59-6(X))* Cicada Bks. GBR. Dist: Consortium Bk. Sales & Distribution.
Marton, Jirina. Arctic Adventures: Tales from the Lives of Inuit Artists, 1 vol. Rivera, Raquel. 2007. (ENG.). 48p. (J). (gr. 2-18). 18.95 *(978-0-88899-714-2(0))* Groundwood Bks. CAN. Dist: Publishers Group West (PGW).
—Fergie Tries to Fly. Cocks, Nancy. 2003. 16p. pap. *(978-2-89507-275-1(2))* Novalis Publishing.
—Where, Oh Where, Is Fergie? Cocks, Nancy. 2003. 16p. pap. *(978-2-89507-273-7(6))* Novalis Publishing.
—You Can Count on Fergie. Cocks, Nancy. 2003. 16p. pap. *(978-2-89507-272-0(8))* Novalis Publishing.
Martorell, Antonio & Rodriguez, Edel. Island Treasures: Growing up in Cuba. Ada, Alma Flor. 2015. (ENG.). 240p. (J). (gr. 3-7). pap. 8.99 *(978-1-4814-2900-9(0))* Simon & Schuster Children's Publishing.
Martowiredjo, Salim. Indonesian Children's Favorite Stories. Suyenaga, Joan. 2015. (ENG.). 64p. (J). (gr. k-8). pap. 11.95 *(978-0-8048-4511-3(5))* Tuttle Publishing.
—Indonesian Children's Favorite Stories: Fables, Myths & Fairy Tales. Suyenaga, Joan. 2020. 64p. (J). (gr. k-5). 14.99 *(978-0-8048-5150-3(6))* Tuttle Publishing.
Marts, Doreen. Look at Me! Look at Me! Williamson, Rose. 2014. (ENG.). 32p. (J). (gr. -1-k). 16.95 *(978-1-62914-617-1(X),* Sky Pony Pr.) Skyhorse Publishing Co., Inc.
Marts, Doreen & Mulryan, Doreen. This Is My Country. Bullard, Lisa. 2016. (Cloverleaf Books (tm) — Where I Live Ser.). (ENG.). 24p. (J). (gr. k-2). lib. bdg. 25.32 *(978-1-4677-9524-1(0),* 9781467795241, Millbrook Pr.) Lerner Publishing Group.
Marts, Doreen Mulryan. Check, Please!, 3 vols. Stern, A. J. 2010. (Frankly, Frannie Ser.: 3). 128p. (J). (gr. 1-3). pap. 5.99 *(978-0-448-45352-1(5),* Grosset & Dunlap) Penguin Young Readers Group.
—Doggy Day Care, 2 vols. Stern, A. J. 2010. (Frankly, Frannie Ser.: 2). 128p. (J). (gr. 1-3). pap. 4.99 *(978-0-448-45350-7(9),* Grosset & Dunlap) Penguin Young Readers Group.
—Fashion Frenzy. Stern, A. J. 2011. (Frankly, Frannie Ser.: 6). 128p. (J). (gr. 1-3). pap. 5.99 *(978-0-448-45544-0(7),* Grosset & Dunlap) Penguin Young Readers Group.
—Frankly, Frannie, 1 vol. Stern, A. J. 2010. (Frankly, Frannie Ser.: 1). 128p. (J). (gr. 1-3). pap. 5.99 *(978-0-448-45348-4(7),* Grosset & Dunlap);1. (ENG.). (gr. 2-5). 18.69 *(978-0-448-45349-1(5))* Penguin Young Readers Group.
—Funny Business, 4 vols. Stern, A. J. 2011. (Frankly, Frannie Ser.: 4). 128p. (J). (gr. 1-3). pap. 5.99 *(978-0-448-45540-2(4),* Grosset & Dunlap);4. (ENG.). (gr. 2-5). 18.69 *(978-0-448-45541-9(2))* Penguin Young Readers Group.
—Here Comes the... Trouble! Stern, A. J. 2012. (Frankly, Frannie Ser.: 9). 128p. (J). (gr. 1-3). pap. 5.99 *(978-0-448-45752-9(0),* Grosset & Dunlap);9. (ENG.). (gr. 2-5). 18.69 *(978-0-448-45753-6(9))* Penguin Young Readers Group.
—Miss Fortune, 7 vols. Stern, A. J. 2012. (Frankly, Frannie Ser.: 7). 128p. (J). (gr. 1-3). pap. 5.99 *(978-0-448-45748-2(2),* Grosset & Dunlap) Penguin Young Readers Group.
—My Pumpkin. Karr, Lily. 2014. (ENG.). 12p. (J). (gr. -1 — 1). bds. 4.99 *(978-0-545-49332-1(3),* Cartwheel Bks.) Scholastic, Inc.
—Principal for the Day. Stern, A. J. 2011. (Frankly, Frannie Ser.: 5). 128p. (J). (gr. 1-3). pap. 5.99 *(978-0-448-45542-6(0),* Grosset & Dunlap);5. (ENG.). (gr. 2-5). 18.69 *(978-0-448-45543-3(9))* Penguin Young Readers Group.
—Rocking Out! Stern, A. J. 2012. (Frankly, Frannie Ser.: 8). 128p. (J). (gr. 1-3). pap. 5.99 *(978-0-448-45750-5(4),* Grosset & Dunlap) Penguin Young Readers Group.
Marts, Doreen Mulryan. Even Monsters Say Good Night. Marts, Doreen Mulryan. 2015. (ENG.). 32p. (J). (gr. -1-2). 14.95 *(978-1-62370-256-4(9),* Capstone Young Readers) Capstone.
Marttila, Andrew, jt. photos by see Shaw, Hannah.
Martyr, Paula. New Tales from Alice's Wonderland: Dinah Plays Hide & Seek. Brown, Michele. 24p. (J). pap. 7.99 *(978-0-233-99535-9(8))* Andre Deutsch GBR. Dist: Trafalgar Square Publishing.
—New Tales from Alice's Wonderland: The Queen of Hearts & the Wibbly Wobbly Jelly. Brown, Michele. 24p. (J). pap. 7.95 *(978-0-233-99536-6(6))* Andre Deutsch GBR. Dist: Trans-Atlantic Pubns., Inc.
Martz, John. Black & Bittern Was Night. Heidbreder, Robert. 2013. (ENG.). 32p. (J). (gr. -1-3). 16.95 *(978-1-55453-302-2(3))* Kids Can Pr., Ltd. CAN. Dist: Hachette Bk. Group.
—Do Frogs Drink Hot Chocolate? How Animals Keep Warm. Kaner, Etta. 2018. (ENG.). 32p. (J). (gr. k-4). 17.95 *(978-1-77147-292-0(8))* Owlkids Bks. Inc. CAN. Dist: Publishers Group West (PGW).
—How to Give Your Cat a Bath: In Five Easy Steps. Winstanley, Nicola. 2019. (ENG.). 40p. (J). (gr. -1-2). 17.99 *(978-0-7352-6354-3(X),* Tundra Bks.) Tundra Bks. CAN. Dist: Penguin Random Hse. LLC.
Marucchi, Leigh Norridge. Hilmy the Hippo Learns Not to Lie. Norridge, Rae. 2007. (ENG.). 28p. 7.95 *(978-0-86037-344-5(4))* Kube Publishing Ltd. GBR. Dist: Consortium Bk. Sales & Distribution.
Maruda, Trotsky. Line & Circle. Maruda, Trotsky. 2004. 32p. (J). (ALB & ENG.). pap. *(978-1-84444-000-9(1));* (ARA & ENG.). pap. *(978-1-84444-002-3(8));* (BEN & ENG.). pap. *(978-1-84444-003-0(6));* (CZE & ENG.). pap. *(978-1-84444-005-4(2));* (ENG & PER.). pap. *(978-1-84444-006-1(0));* (PAN & ENG.). pap. *(978-1-84444-012-2(5));* (SER & ENG.). pap. *(978-1-84444-016-0(8));* (SOM & ENG.). pap. *(978-1-84444-017-7(6));* (ENG & TUR.). pap. *(978-1-84444-019-1(2));* (URD & ENG.). pap. *(978-1-84444-020-7(6));* (VIE & ENG.). pap. *(978-1-84444-021-4(4))* Mantra Lingua.
Marudu, Trotsky. Line & Circle. Menon, Radhika. 2004. (ENG & SPA.). 24p. (J). *(978-1-84444-018-4(4))* Mantra Lingua.
Maruyama, Ed, photos by. Games of Survival: Traditional Inuit Games for Elementary School Students, 1 vol. Issaluk, Johnny. 2013. (ENG., 62p. (J). (gr. 3-6). 12.95 *(978-1-927095-21-8(2))* Inhabit Media Inc. CAN. Dist: Consortium Bk. Sales & Distribution.
Maruyama, Jerrod. Box of Mixed Emotions. Candau, Brittany. 2015. (J). ***(978-1-4847-3220-5(0))*** Disney Publishing Worldwide.
—Disney: Alice Wants to Grow. PI Kids. 2020. (My First Stories Ser.). (ENG.). 32p. (J). ***(978-1-5037-5441-6(3),*** b4e18a8c-68a3-4a79-92fd-ce1fa9e0ba50, p i kids) Phoenix International Publications, Inc.
—Disney: Louie Likes Basketball: a Story about Sharing. PI Kids. 2020. (Growing up Stories Ser.). (ENG.). 34p. (J). ***(978-1-5037-5488-1(X),*** d2d8e648-c630-4e11-a244-1425327eb327, p i kids) Phoenix International Publications, Inc.
—Disney: Mowgli's First Dance. PI Kids. 2020. (My First Stories Ser.). (ENG.). 32p. (J). ***(978-1-5037-5442-3(1),*** 93bd6b0b-6250-4bd1-9067-6dd2fb34fb3f, p i kids) Phoenix International Publications, Inc.
—Disney: The Aristocats' Show. PI Kids. 2020. (My First Stories Ser.). (ENG.). 32p. (J). ***(978-1-5037-5444-7(8),*** e6a624fb-f104-4ed5-97c7-6ef1b93ac3f7, p i kids) Phoenix International Publications, Inc.
—Disney: Tinker Bell's Best Birthday Party. PI Kids. 2020. (My First Stories Ser.). (ENG.). 32p. (J). ***(978-1-5037-5443-0(X),*** d1b91056-4ad8-48a1-ba79-e38318371587, p i kids) Phoenix International Publications, Inc.
Maruyama, Jerrod. Toy Story 4 Toy Box: Words to Play By. Francis, Suzanne. 2019. (ENG.). 120p. (J). (gr. -1-k). 12.99 *(978-1-368-04584-1(7))* Disney Pr.
Maruyama, Yoko. The Forgotten Crayon. Maruyama, Yoko. 2020. (ENG.). 32p. (J). (gr. k-2). 17.99 ***(978-988-8341-98-6(7),*** Minedition) Neugebauer, Michael (Publishing) Limited HKG. Dist: Penguin Random Hse. LLC.
Maruyama, Yoko. Little Santa. Maruyama, Yoko. 2017. (ENG.). 40p. (J). (gr. -1-k). 17.99 *(978-988-8341-46-7(4),* Minedition) Neugebauer, Michael (Publishing) Limited HKG. Dist: Penguin Random Hse. LLC.
Marvel Artist Staff. Breakout!, 1 vol. Siglain, Michael. 2012. (Avengers: Earth's Mightiest Heroes! Ser.). (ENG.). 24p. (J). (gr. k-5). lib. bdg. 27.07 *(978-1-61479-001-3(9),* 2885, Marvel Age) Spotlight.
—Hulk Versus the World, 1 vol. Rudnick, Elizabeth. 2012. (Avengers: Earth's Mightiest Heroes! Ser.). (ENG.). 24p. (J). (gr. k-5). lib. bdg. 27.07 *(978-1-61479-002-0(7),* 2886, Marvel Age) Spotlight.
—Iron Man Is Born, 1 vol. Rudnick, Elizabeth. 2012. (Avengers: Earth's Mightiest Heroes! Ser.). (ENG.). 24p. (J). (gr. k-5). lib. bdg. 27.07 *(978-1-61479-003-7(5),* 2887, Marvel Age) Spotlight.
—The Man in the Ant Hill, 1 vol. Castro, Nachie. 2012. (Avengers: Earth's Mightiest Heroes! Ser.). (ENG.). 24p. (J). (gr. k-5). lib. bdg. 27.07 *(978-1-61479-004-4(3),* 2888, Marvel Age) Spotlight.
—Thor the Mighty, 1 vol. Rudnick, Elizabeth. 2012. (Avengers: Earth's Mightiest Heroes! Ser.). (ENG.). 24p. (J). (gr. k-5). lib. bdg. 27.07 *(978-1-61479-005-1(1),* 2889, Marvel Age) Spotlight.
Marvel Press Artist. Avengers Storybook Collection. Marvel Press Book Group. 2018. (Storybook Collection). (ENG.). 304p. (J). (gr. 1-3). 16.99 *(978-1-4847-2957-1(9),* Marvel Pr.) Disney Publishing Worldwide.
—Black Panther: the Battle for Wakanda. Snider, Brandon T. 2018. (Mighty Marvel Chapter Book Ser.). (ENG.). 128p. (J). (gr. 3-7). pap. 5.99 *(978-1-368-02014-5(3),* Marvel Pr.) Disney Publishing Worldwide.
—Guardians of the Galaxy: Gamora's Galactic Showdown. Snider, Brandon T. 2017. (Mighty Marvel Chapter Book Ser.). (ENG.). 128p. (J). (gr. 3-7). pap. 5.99 *(978-1-4847-3213-7(8),* Marvel Pr.) Disney Publishing Worldwide.
—Marvel's Spider-Man: the Ultimate Spider-Man. Marsham, Liz. 2017. (ENG.). 24p. (J). (gr. 1-3). pap. 4.99 *(978-1-368-00310-0(9),* Marvel Pr.) Disney Publishing Worldwide.
—Thor Double Feature Read-Along Storybook & CD. Marvel Press Book Group. 2017. (Read-Along Storybook & CD Ser.). (ENG.). 64p. (J). (gr. 1-3). pap. 8.99 *(978-1-368-00861-7(5),* Marvel Pr.) Disney Publishing Worldwide.
—World of Reading: Black Panther: This Is Black Panther (Level 1) Level 1. West, Alexandra C. 2018. (World of Reading Ser.). (ENG.). 32p. (J). (gr. -1-k). pap. 4.99 *(978-1-368-00853-2(4),* Marvel Pr.) Disney Publishing Worldwide.
—World of Reading Marvel Meet the Super Heroes! (Pre-Level 1 Boxed Set), Set. Marvel Press Book Group. 2017. (World of Reading Ser.). (ENG.). 144p. (J). (gr. -1-k). pap. 12.99 *(978-1-368-00852-5(6),* Marvel Pr.) Disney Publishing Worldwide.
—World of Reading This Is Captain Marvel (Level 1) Marvel Press Book Group. 2019. (World of Reading Ser.). (ENG.). 32p. (J). (gr. -1-k). pap. 4.99 *(978-1-368-02669-7(9),* Marvel Pr.) Disney Publishing Worldwide.
—World of Reading: This Is Miles Morales. Marvel Press Book Group. 2018. (World of Reading Ser.). (ENG.). 32p. (J). (gr. -1-k). pap. 4.99 *(978-1-368-02863-9(2),* Marvel Pr.) Disney Publishing Worldwide.
—5-Minute Marvel Stories. Marvel Press Book Group et al. 2019. (5-Minute Stories Ser.). (ENG.). 192p. (J). (gr. 1-3). 12.99 *(978-1-368-02667-3(2),* Marvel Pr.) Disney Publishing Worldwide.
Marvel Press Artist & di Salvo, Roberto. World of Reading This Is Thor (Level 1) Level 1. West, Alexandra C. 2017. (World of Reading Ser.). (ENG.). 32p. (J). (gr. -1-k). pap. 4.99 *(978-1-368-01128-0(4),* Marvel Pr.) Disney Publishing Worldwide.
Marvel Press Artist & Laufman, Derek. World of Reading Marvel Super Hero Adventures: These Are the Avengers (Level 1) West, Alexandra C. 2018. (World of Reading Ser.). (ENG.). 32p. (J). (gr. -1-k). pap. 4.99 *(978-1-368-02353-5(3),* Marvel Pr.) Disney Publishing Worldwide.
Marvel Press Artist, jt. illus. see Laufman, Derek.
Marvel Press Artist, jt. illus. see Richardson, Owen.
Marvel Press Book Group. Spider-Man: an Amazing Book & Magnetic Play Set: Book & Magnetic Play Set. Marvel Press Book Group. 2016. (Magnetic Dress-Up Book Ser.). (ENG.). 32p. (J). (gr. -1-k). 15.99 *(978-1-4847-6168-7(5),* Marvel Pr.) Disney Publishing Worldwide.
Marvel Staff. Drawmaster Marvel Avengers: Captain America Super Stencil Kit: 4 Easy Steps to Draw Your Heroes. 2019. (Drawmaster Ser.). (ENG.). 24p. (J). (gr. k). 11.99 *(978-2-89802-134-3(2),* CrackBoom! Bks.) Chouette Publishing CAN. Dist: Publishers Group West (PGW).
—Drawmaster Marvel Spider-Man: Super Stencil Kit: 4 Easy Steps to Draw Your Heroes. 2019. (Drawmaster Ser.). (ENG.). 24p. (J). (gr. k). 11.99 *(978-2-89802-086-5(9),*

M

CrackBoom! Bks.) Chouette Publishing CAN. Dist: Publishers Group West (PGW).

Marvel Strike Force Development Team. Marvel Strike Force: the Art of the Game. 2019. (ENG.). 240p. (YA). (gr. -1-17). 50.00 *(978-1-302-91906-1(7))* Marvel Worldwide, Inc.

Marvin, Fred. Seven Animals Wag Their Tales. Bogot, Howard I. et al. 2005. 48p. (J). (gr. -1-1). pap. 9.95 *(978-1-930143-01-2(X))*; (gr. k-3). 16.95 *(978-1-930143-00-5(1))* Simcha Media Group. (Devora Publishing).

Marxhausen, Ben & Koehler, Ed. Heaven is a Wonderful Place. Marxhausen, Joanne. 2nd ed. 2004. 48p. (J). (gr. -1-4). 9.49 *(978-0-7586-0681-5(8))* Concordia Publishing Hse.

Marxhausen, Benjamin & Koehler, Ed. El Cielo Es un Lugar Maravilloso. Marxhausen, Joanne. 2008. (SPA.). 48p. (J). (gr. -1). pap. 7.99 *(978-0-7586-1587-9(6))* Concordia Publishing Hse.

Mary Connors. Princess Bonnie & the Dragon. Claire Hamelin Bruyere. 2009. 16p. pap. 8.49 *(978-1-4389-8731-6(5))* AuthorHouse.

Mary Jean. Saint Hyacinth of Poland: The Story of the Apostle of the North. Windeatt, Mary F. 2009. (ENG.). 208p. (J). (gr. 1-8). reprint ed. pap. 13.95 *(978-0-89555-422-2(4))* TAN Bks.

Marzan, Jose, Jr. One Small Step, Vol. 3. Vaughan, Brian K. & Rambo, Pamela. MacDonald, Heidi, ed. rev. ed. 2004. 168p. pap. 14.99 *(978-1-4012-0201-9(2))*, Vertigo) DC Comics.

Marzano, Elisa. The Adventures of Petit Piton: Petit Piton, Beetle & the Ball of Poop. Tazzi, Fausto. 2018. (ENG.). 38p. (J). pap. 14.90 *(978-1-7902-8881-6(9))* Independently Published.

Marzel, Pepi. My First Yiddish Word Book. Sussman, Joni Kibort. 2009. (Israel Ser.). 32p. (J). (gr. -1-3). bds. 17.95 *(978-0-8225-8755-2(6)*, Kar-Ben Publishing) Lerner Publishing Group.

Marzel, Pépi. My First Yiddish Word Book, Vol. Sussman, Joni Kibort. 2014. (ENG.). 32p. (J). (gr. -1-2). pap. 12.95 *(978-1-4677-5175-9(8)*, Kar-Ben Publishing) Lerner Publishing Group.

Marzel, Pépi & Marzel, Pépi. My First Hebrew Word Book, Vol. Groner, Judyth. 2005. (ENG.). 32p. (J). (gr. -1-2). lib. bdg. 18.99 *(978-1-58013-126-1(3)*, Kar-Ben Publishing) Lerner Publishing Group.

Marzel, Pépi, jt. illus. see Marzel, Pépi.

Marzo, Bridget. Tiz & Ott's Big Draw. 2015. (ENG.). 32p. (J). (gr. -1-3). 15.95 *(978-1-84976-310-3(0))* Tate Publishing, Ltd. GBR. Dist: Hachette Bk. Group.

Más, Alicia. I Love Daddy Every Day. Otter, Isabel. import ed. 2020. (Every Day Together Book Ser.). (ENG.). 32p. (J). (gr. -1-2). 10.99 *(978-0-593-12305-8(0)*, Rodale Kids) Random Hse. Children's Bks.

Mas, Maribel. El Auto del Sr. Pulga. Barbot, Daniel. 2004. (SPA.). 28p. (J). pap. 6.99 *(978-980-257-260-1(8))* Ekare, Ediciones VEN. Dist: Lectorum Pubns., Inc.

Masciullo, Lucia. Daisy All Alone. Hamer, Michelle. 2015. 144p. (J). (gr. 3-7). 8.99 *(978-0-14-330764-8(9))* Penguin Random Hse. AUS. Dist: Independent Pubs. Group.

—Enough Apples. Kane, Kim. 2019. (ENG.). 32p. (J). (gr. -1-k). 18.99 *(978-1-76012-491-5(5))* Little Hare Bks. AUS. Dist: Independent Pubs. Group.

—The Letty Stories, 4 bks. in 1. Lloyd, Alison. ed. 2016. (Our Australian Girl Ser.). 480p. (J). (gr. 3-7). 23.99 *(978-0-670-07805-9(0))* Penguin Random Hse. AUS. Dist: Independent Pubs. Group.

—Marly & the Goat, Bk. 3. Pung, Alice. 3rd ed. 2016. (Our Australian Girl Ser.: 3). 144p. (J). (gr. 3-7). 8.99 *(978-0-14-330851-5(3))* Penguin Random Hse. AUS. Dist: Independent Pubs. Group.

—Marly's Business. Pung, Alice. 2016. (Our Australian Girl Ser.: 2). 144p. (J). (gr. 3-7). 7.99 *(978-0-14-330850-8(5))* Penguin Random Hse. AUS. Dist: Independent Pubs. Group.

—The Nellie Stories. Matthews, Penny. 2016. (Our Australian Girl Ser.). 480p. (J). (gr. 3-7). 24.99 *(978-0-670-07915-5(4))* Penguin Random Hse. AUS. Dist: Independent Pubs. Group.

—Our Australian Girl: The Ruby Stories. Matthews, Penny;Masciullo. 2019. (Our Australian Girl Ser.). 496p. (J). (gr. 3-7). 24.99 *(978-0-14-378868-3(X))* Random Hse. Australia AUS. Dist: Independent Pubs. Group.

Mase, Naokata. The Rainy Trip Surprise. Mase, Naokata. Perry, Mia Lynn, tr. 2006. 24p. (J). (gr. -1-1). 19.95 incl. audio compact disk *(978-1-74126-436-4(7))* R.I.C. Pubns. AUS. Dist: SCB Distributors.

Masefield, Judith. The Box of Delights. Masefield, John. 2007. (Kay Harker Ser.). (ENG.). 312p. (J). (gr. 4-7). 18.95 *(978-1-59017-251-3(5)*, NYR Children's Collection) New York Review of Bks., Inc., The.

Masel, Christy. Gorp's Dream: A Tale of Diversity, Tolerance, & Love in Pumpernickel Park. 2003. 36p. (J). 14.95 *(978-0-9724249-0-5(3))* Gorp Group Pr., The.

—Gorp's Dream: A Tale of Diversity, Tolerance, & Love in Pumpernickel Park. Chessen, Sherri. 2003. (ENG.). 36p. (J). pap. 7.95 *(978-0-9724249-1-2(1))* Gorp Group Pr., The.

Mash, Brittany. Konnichiwa & Hello: Celebrating Diversity. Robertson, Tammy. 2014. (J). 19.99 *(978-1-945384-07-3(7))* Hawaii Way Publishing.

Mashburn Bland, Lynn. A Toe That I Know. Mashburn, Leigh Ann. 2020. (ENG.). 26p. (J). pap. 11.00 ***(978-1-59755-566-1(5)***, Advantage BibleStudy) Advantage Bks.

Mashburn, Marcus M. Vision in the Storm. Cabose, Rachel Whitaker. 2018. 127p. (J). pap. *(978-0-8163-6421-3(4))* Pacific Pr. Publishing Assn.

Masheris, Bob. Circus Fun. Hillert, Margaret. 2016. (BeginningtoRead Ser.). (ENG.). 32p. (J). (gr. -1-2). pap. 11.94 *(978-1-60357-937-7(0))*; (gr. k-2). 22.60 *(978-1-59953-796-2(6))* Norwood Hse. Pr.

—Play It Smart: Playground Safety, 1 vol. Urban Donahue, Jill. 2008. (How to Be Safe! Ser.). (ENG.). 24p. (J). (gr. k-2). 27.32 *(978-1-4048-4823-8(1)*, Picture Window Bks.) Capstone.

Mashima, Hiro. Rave Master, Vol. 14. rev. ed. 2005. 200p. pap. 14.99 *(978-1-59532-019-3(9)*, Tokyopop Kids) TOKYOPOP, Inc.

Mashima, Hiro. Rave Master, 21 vols. Mashima, Hiro. 2003. Vol. 3. rev. ed. 192p. (gr. 8-18). pap. 14.99 *(978-1-59182-210-3(6))*; Vol. 5. 5th rev. ed. pap. 14.99 *(978-1-59182-212-7(2))*; Vol. 6. rev. ed. 192p. pap. 14.99 *(978-1-59182-213-4(0))* TOKYOPOP, Inc. (Tokyopop Kids).

—Rave Master, 18 vols., Vol. 7. Mashima, Hiro. Dunn, Brian, tr. from JPN. rev. ed. 2004. 200p. pap. 14.99 *(978-1-59182-517-3(2)*, Tokyopop Kids) TOKYOPOP, Inc.

—Rave Master, 21 vols., Vol. 11. Mashima, Hiro. Bourque, Jeremiah, tr. from JPN. rev. ed. 2004. 192p. (YA). pap. 14.99 *(978-1-59182-521-0(0)*, Tokyopop Kids) TOKYOPOP, Inc.

—Rave Master. Mashima, Hiro. Vol. 13. rev. ed. 2005. 192p. pap. 14.99 *(978-1-59532-018-6(0))*; Vol. 15. rev. ed. 2005. 192p. pap. 14.99 *(978-1-59532-020-9(2))*; Vol. 17. 17th rev. ed. 2005. 192p. pap. 14.99 *(978-1-59532-022-3(9))*; Vol. 18. 18th rev. ed. 2005. 200p. per. 14.99 *(978-1-59532-023-0(7))*; Vol. 19. 19th rev. ed. 2006. 174p. (YA). pap. 14.99 *(978-1-59532-024-7(5))*; Vol. 20. rev. ed. 2006. 191p. pap. 14.99 *(978-1-59532-025-4(3))*; Vol. 22. 22nd rev. ed. 2006. 180p. per. 9.99 *(978-1-59532-626-3(X))*; Vol. 24. 2007. 192p. pap. 9.99 *(978-1-59532-628-7(6))*; Vol. 25. 2007. 192p. pap. 9.99 *(978-1-59532-629-4(4))* TOKYOPOP, Inc. (Tokyopop Kids).

Mashima, Hiro. Rave Master, Vol. 16. Mashima, Hiro, creator. rev. ed. 2005. (Rave Master Ser.). 192p. pap. 14.99 *(978-1-59532-021-6(0)*, Tokyopop Kids) TOKYOPOP, Inc.

Masi, Jérôme. Music Legends: 40 Inspiring Icons. Guilleminot, Hervé. 2018. (40 Inspiring Icons Ser.). (ENG.). 88p. (J). (gr. 2-5). 14.99 ***(978-1-78603-145-7(0)***, Wide Eyed Editions) Quarto Publishing Group UK GBR. Dist: Hachette Bk. Group.

Masi, P. J. Alex Anklebone & Andy the Dog. Stevenson, Richard. 2005. (ENG.). 32p. (J). (gr. -1-17). *(978-1-896209-57-9(2))* Bayeux Arts, Inc.

Masiello, Ralph. Beasts. Brockway, Stephanie. 2011. 144p. (J). (gr. 4-7). 15.95 *(978-1-57091-718-9(3))* Charlesbridge Publishing, Inc.

—The Flag We Love. Ryan, Pam Muñoz. 10th anniv. ed. 2006. 32p. (J). (gr. k-3). 17.95 *(978-1-57091-707-3(8))* Charlesbridge Publishing, Inc.

—The Icky Bug Counting Book. Pallotta, Jerry. 2004. (Jerry Pallotta's Counting Bks.). 30p. (J). (-k). bds. 7.95 *(978-1-57091-624-3(1))* Charlesbridge Publishing, Inc.

Masiello, Ralph. Bug Drawing Book: Simple Steps Make Anyone an Artist. Masiello, Ralph. 2004. (Ralph Masiello's Drawing Bks.). (ENG.). 32p. (J). (gr. k-3). 16.95 *(978-1-57091-525-3(3))* Charlesbridge Publishing, Inc.

—Bug Drawing Book: Simple Steps to Make Anyone an Artist. Masiello, Ralph. 2004. (Ralph Masiello's Drawing Bks.). 32p. (J). (gr. k-3). pap. 7.95 *(978-1-57091-526-0(1))* Charlesbridge Publishing, Inc.

—Fantastic Fruits: A Grimal Grove Coloring Book. Masiello, Ralph. 2020. 32p. (J). (gr. k-4). pap. 6.99 *(978-1-62354-141-5(7))* Charlesbridge Publishing, Inc.

—Ralph Masiello's Alien Drawing Book. Masiello, Ralph. 2019. (Ralph Masiello's Drawing Bks.). (ENG.). 32p. (J). (gr. k-3). pap. 7.99 *(978-1-57091-770-7(1))* Charlesbridge Publishing, Inc.

—Ralph Masiello's Ancient Egypt Drawing Book. Masiello, Ralph. 2008. (Ralph Masiello's Drawing Bks.). (ENG.). 40p. (J). (gr. 3-7). pap. 7.95 *(978-1-57091-534-5(2))* Charlesbridge Publishing, Inc.

—Ralph Masiello's Christmas Drawing Book. Masiello, Ralph. 2013. (Ralph Masiello's Drawing Bks.). 32p. (J). (gr. k-3). 17.95 *(978-1-57091-543-7(1))*; pap. 7.95 *(978-1-57091-544-4(X))* Charlesbridge Publishing, Inc.

—Ralph Masiello's Dinosaur Drawing Book. Masiello, Ralph. 2005. (Ralph Masiello's Drawing Bks.). 48p. (J). (gr. k-3). per. 7.95 *(978-1-57091-528-4(8))* Charlesbridge Publishing, Inc.

—Ralph Masiello's Dragon Drawing Book. Masiello, Ralph. 2007. (Ralph Masiello's Drawing Bks.). (ENG.). 64p. (J). (gr. 3-7). pap. 9.95 *(978-1-57091-532-1(6))* Charlesbridge Publishing, Inc.

—Ralph Masiello's Fairy Drawing Book. Masiello, Ralph. 2013. (Ralph Masiello's Drawing Bks.). 32p. (J). (gr. -1-3). lib. bdg. 22.44 *(978-1-57091-539-0(3))*; (gr. k-3). pap. 7.95 *(978-1-57091-540-6(7))* Charlesbridge Publishing, Inc.

—Ralph Masiello's Farm Drawing Book. Masiello, Ralph. 2012. (Ralph Masiello's Drawing Bks.). (J). 32p. (gr. k-3). 16.95 *(978-1-57091-537-6(7))*; 32p. (gr. k-3). pap. 7.95 *(978-1-57091-538-3(5))*; (gr. 1-4). pap. 16.95 *(978-1-60734-082-9(8))* Charlesbridge Publishing, Inc.

—Ralph Masiello's Halloween Drawing Book. Masiello, Ralph. 2012. (Ralph Masiello's Drawing Bks.). 32p. (J). (gr. k-3). pap. 7.95 *(978-1-57091-542-0(3))* Charlesbridge Publishing, Inc.

—Ralph Masiello's Ocean Drawing Book. Masiello, Ralph. 2006. (Ralph Masiello's Drawing Bks.). 32p. (J). (gr. k-3). pap. 7.95 *(978-1-57091-530-7(X)*, 1258410) Charlesbridge Publishing, Inc.

—Ralph Masiello's Robot Drawing Book. Masiello, Ralph. 2011. (Ralph Masiello's Drawing Bks.). (ENG.). 32p. (J). (gr. 1-4). 7.95 *(978-1-57091-536-9(9))*; 16.95 *(978-1-57091-535-2(0))* Charlesbridge Publishing, Inc.

Masiello, Ralph, photos by. The Icky Bug Alphabet Book. Pallotta, Jerry. 32p. (J). (gr. -1-1). 10.95 *(978-0-933341-95-1(4))* Quinlan Pr.

Mask, Cynthia. Moon of the Wishing Night. Lamar, Gail Renfroe. 2004. 32p. (J). 17.95 *(978-1-57966-047-5(9)*, River City Kids) River City Publishing.

Maslen, John R. Long Vowels, Set. Maslen, Bobby Lynn. 2006. (Bob Bks.: No. 5). (ENG.). 16p. (J). (gr. -1-1). 16.99 *(978-0-439-86541-8(7)*, Scholastic Paperbacks) Scholastic, Inc.

Maslen, John R. Beginning Readers, Set. Maslen, John R. Maslen, Bobby Lynn. 2006. (Bob Bks.). (ENG.). 12p. (J). (gr. -1-1). 16.99 *(978-0-439-84500-7(9)*, Scholastic Paperbacks) Scholastic, Inc.

—Compound Words, Set. Maslen, John R. Maslen, Bobby Lynn. 2006. (Bob Bks.). (ENG.). 24p. (J). (gr. -1-1). 17.99 *(978-0-439-84506-9(8)*, Scholastic Paperbacks) Scholastic, Inc.

—Word Families, Set. Maslen, John R. Maslen, Bobby Lynn. 2006. (Bob Bks.). (ENG.). 16p. (J). (gr. -1-1). 16.99 *(978-0-439-84509-0(2)*, Scholastic Paperbacks) Scholastic, Inc.

Maslen, John R. & Hendra, Sue. Alphabet. Kertell, Lynn Maslen. 2008. (Bob Bks.). (ENG.). (J). (gr. -1-k). 16.99 *(978-0-545-01921-7(4)*, Cartwheel Bks.) Scholastic, Inc.

Maslen, John R., jt. illus. see Hendra, Sue.

Maslo, Lina. Free As a Bird: The Story of Malala. Maslo, Lina. 2018. (ENG.). 40p. (J). (gr. -1-3). 17.99 *(978-0-06-256077-3(8)*, Balzer & Bray) HarperCollins Pubs.

—Through the Wardrobe: How C. S. Lewis Created Narnia. Maslo, Lina. 2020. 48p. (J). (gr. -1-3). 17.99 *(978-0-06-279856-5(1)*, Balzer & Bray) HarperCollins Pubs.

Masnaghetti, Sandra. The Secret of Castle Rock. Stamer, Mary. 2018. (ENG.). 72p. (J). pap. 10.99 *(978-1-7913-9722-7(0))* Independently Published.

Mason, Abi. The Soggy Saga of Samuel Sprat. Winbolt-Lewis, Martin. 2013. 24p. pap. *(978-1-78222-152-4(2))* Paragon Publishing, Rothersthorpe.

Mason, Alfonso & Mason, Ruth. English - French Counting Book, 1 vol. Baker, Mary E. 2010. 28p. pap. 24.95 *(978-1-4489-4347-0(7))* PublishAmerica, Inc.

—English - Spanish Counting Book. Baker, Mary. 2008. 24p. pap. 24.95 *(978-1-60672-035-6(X))* America Star Bks.

Mason, Bergetta. Turtle Games. Mason, Craig. 2003. 32p. (J). 4.99 *(978-0-9729153-0-4(3))* 1 Sleeve Publishing.

Mason, Conrad. Illustrated Animal Stories. Sims, Lesley, ed. 2009. (Illustrated Stories Ser.). 352p. (YA). (gr. 3-18). 19.99 *(978-0-7945-2235-3(1)*, Usborne) EDC Publishing.

—Illustrated Classics for Girls. Sims, Lesley. 2009. (Illustrated Stories Ser.). 384p. (YA). (gr. 3-18). 19.99 *(978-0-7945-2419-7(2)*, Usborne) EDC Publishing.

Mason, Janeen. Color, Color, Where Are You, Color? Koski, Mary B. 2004. (ENG.). (J). 28p. bds. 7.95 *(978-1-930650-34-3(5))*; 32p. (gr. 1-3). 14.95 *(978-1-930650-35-0(3))* mTrellis Publishing, Inc.

—Fish Facts, 1 vol. Swinney, Geoff. 2011. (ENG.). 48p. (J). (gr. k-3). 17.99 *(978-1-58980-908-6(4)*, Pelican Publishing) Arcadia Publishing.

—For Baby (For Bobbie) Denver, John. 2009. (ENG.). 32p. (J). (gr. -1-6). 19.95 *(978-1-58469-120-4(4))*; pap. 8.95 *(978-1-58469-121-1(2))* Sourcebooks, Inc. (Dawn Pubns.).

—Going Around the Sun: Some Planetary Fun, 1 vol. Berkes, Marianne Collins. 2012. (ENG.). 32p. (J). (gr. -1-4). 16.95 *(978-1-58469-099-3(2))*; pap. 8.95 *(978-1-58469-100-6(X))* Sourcebooks, Inc. (Dawn Pubns.).

—Kissimmee Pete & the Hurricane, 1 vol. Day, Jan. 2008. (ENG.). 32p. (J). (gr. 1-3). 16.99 *(978-1-58980-544-6(5)*, Pelican Publishing) Arcadia Publishing.

—Kissimmee Pete, Cracker Cow Hunter, 1 vol. Day, Jan. 2005. (ENG.). 32p. (J). (gr. k-3). 16.99 *(978-1-58980-325-1(6)*, Pelican Publishing) Arcadia Publishing.

—Pirate Pink & Treasures of the Reef, 1 vol. Day, Jan. 2003. (Pirate Pink Ser.). (ENG.). 32p. (J). (gr. -1-3). 16.99 *(978-1-58980-086-1(9)*, Pelican Publishing) Arcadia Publishing.

—The World's Greatest Explorer, 1 vol. Day, Jan. 2009. (ENG.). 32p. (J). (gr. k-3). 16.99 *(978-1-58980-603-0(4)*, Pelican Publishing) Arcadia Publishing.

Mason, Janeen. Ocean Commotion: Caught in the Currents, 1 vol. Mason, Janeen, . 2019. (Ocean Commotion Ser.). (ENG.). 34p. (J). (gr. k-3). 9.95 *(978-1-4556-2490-4(X)*, Pelican Publishing) Arcadia Publishing.

Mason, Janeen. The Gift of the Magpie, 1 vol. Mason, Janeen. 2011. (ENG.). 32p. (J). (gr. k-3). 16.99 *(978-1-58980-861-4(4)*, Pelican Publishing) Arcadia Publishing.

—Ocean Commotion: Life on the Reef, 1 vol. Mason, Janeen. 2010. (ENG.). 32p. (J). (gr. k-3). 16.99 *(978-1-58980-783-9(9)*, Pelican Publishing) Arcadia Publishing.

—Ocean Commotion: Sea Turtles, 1 vol. Mason, Janeen. 2006. (ENG.). 32p. (J). (gr. k-3). 16.99 *(978-1-58980-434-0(1)*, Pelican Publishing) Arcadia Publishing.

Mason, Mark. Classroom Plays for Social Studies America in the 1800s, 4 vols. McCullough, L. E. 2003. 48p. (J). per. 7.99 *(978-1-56472-242-3(2))* Edupress, Inc.

—Classroom Plays for Social Studies American Biographies, 4. McCullough, L. E. 2003. 48p. (J). per. 7.99 *(978-1-56472-243-0(0))* Edupress, Inc.

—Classroom Plays for Social Studies Ancient Civilizations, 4 vols. McCullough, L. E. 2003. 48p. (J). per. 7.99 *(978-1-56472-240-9(6))* Edupress, Inc.

—Classroom Plays for Social Studies Early America, 4 vols. McCullough, L. E. 2003. 48p. (J). per. 7.99 *(978-1-56472-241-6(4))* Edupress, Inc.

—Following Directions 1-2. Schwartz, Linda. Scott, Kelly, ed. 2004. 64p. (J). pap. 10.99 *(978-1-59198-042-1(9)*, 3397) Creative Teaching Pr., Inc.

—Following Directions 3-4. Schwartz, Linda. Martin, Kelly, ed. 2004. 64p. (J). pap. 10.99 *(978-1-59198-043-8(7)*, 3398) Creative Teaching Pr., Inc.

—Primary Math Quiz Whiz, Vol. 428. Schwartz, Linda. VanBlaricum, Pam, ed. 2004. 128p. (J). (gr. 1-3). pap. 14.99 *(978-0-88160-371-2(6)*, LW-428) Creative Teaching Pr., Inc.

—Primary Science Quiz Whiz, Vol. 429. Schwartz, Linda. VanBlaricum, Pam, ed. 2004. 128p. (J). (gr. 1-3). pap. 14.99 *(978-0-88160-372-9(4)*, LW-429) Creative Teaching Pr., Inc.

Mason, Mark & Willardson, David. Leap into Literacy Fall. Geiser, Traci Ferguson & Boylan, Maureen McCourt. Cernek, Kim, ed. 2003. 160p. (J). (gr. k-2). pap. 17.99 *(978-1-57471-960-4(2)*, 3376) Creative Teaching Pr., Inc.

Mason Rast, Barbara J. A Frog Went A-Wandering. Mason Rast, Barbara J. 2017. (ENG.). (J). (gr. k-2). 18.99 *(978-0-692-96859-8(8))* Golden Door Pr.

Mason, Roberta Black. Tangle-Leina? I'll Tangle-Leina Them. Turner, Diane. 2008. 48p. pap. 24.95 *(978-1-60563-586-6(3))* America Star Bks.

Mason, Rose. Fitz Goes to the Pool. Wimperly, Tracey. 2019. (Fridays with Fitz Ser.). (ENG.). 44p. (J). ***(978-1-5255-4784-3(4))***; pap. ***(978-1-5255-4785-0(2))*** FriesenPress.

Mason, Ruth, jt. illus. see Mason, Alfonso.

Mason, Sue. Dick & His Cat. Adams, Katie. 2014. (Traditional Tales Ser.). (ENG.). 16p. (J). (gr. -1-k). pap. 6.95 *(978-1-62521-550-5(9)*, Capstone Classroom) Capstone.

—George & the Dragonfly. Blackford, Andy. 2011. (ENG.). 32p. (J). (gr. -1-k). pap. *(978-1-84089-624-4(8))* Zero to Ten, Ltd.

—The Perfect Prince. Harrison, Paul. 2009. (ENG.). 32p. (J). (gr. -1-k). pap. *(978-1-84089-534-6(9))* Zero to Ten, Ltd.

Mason, Susan. The Little Turkle. Van Dyken, Deborah. 2019. (ENG.). 32p. (J). 16.95 *(978-1-949467-04-8(X)*, Blair) Carolina Wren Pr.

Mason, Suzie. Cats / Gatos. Falligant, Erin. 2018. (Pets! / ILas Mascotas! Ser.). (MUL.). 24p. (J). (gr. -1-2). lib. bdg. 33.99 *(978-1-68410-248-8(0)*, 138446) Cantata Learning.

—Dogs / Perros. Williams, Gail. (Pets! / ILas Mascotas! Ser.). (MUL.). (J). (gr. -1-2). 2020. 20p. bds. 7.99 *(978-1-5158-6094-5(9)*, 142374); 2018. 24p. lib. bdg. 33.99 *(978-1-68410-249-5(9)*, 138447) Cantata Learning.

—Fish / Peces. Williams, Gail. 2018. (Pets! / ILas Mascotas! Ser.). (MUL.). 24p. (J). (gr. -1-2). lib. bdg. 33.99 *(978-1-68410-250-1(2)*, 138448) Cantata Learning.

—Frogs / Ranas. Anderson, J. L. 2018. (Pets! / ILas Mascotas! Ser.). (MUL.). 24p. (J). (gr. -1-2). lib. bdg. 33.99 *(978-1-68410-251-8(0)*, 138449) Cantata Learning.

—Guinea Pigs / Cobayos. Falligant, Erin. 2018. (Pets! / ILas Mascotas! Ser.). (MUL.). 24p. (J). (gr. -1-2). lib. bdg. 33.99 *(978-1-68410-252-5(9)*, 138450) Cantata Learning.

—I Love You All Year Through. Stansbie, Stephanie. 2019. (ENG.). 32p. (J). (-k). 17.99 *(978-1-9848-5149-9(7)*, Random Hse. Bks. for Young Readers) Random Hse. Children's Bks.

—I Love You, Little One. Tiger Tales. 2019. (ENG.). 12p. (J). (gr. 2-k). bds. 9.99 *(978-1-68010-585-8(X))* Tiger Tales.

—I've Loved You since Forever. Kotb, Hoda. 2018. (ENG.). 32p. (J). (gr. -1-3). 18.99 *(978-0-06-284174-2(2))* HarperCollins Pubs.

—I've Loved You since Forever Board Book. Kotb, Hoda. 2019. (ENG.). 32p. (J). (gr. -1-3). bds. 8.99 *(978-0-06-284175-9(0)*, HarperFestival) HarperCollins Pubs.

—Rabbits / Conejos. Anderson, J. L. 2018. (Pets! / ILas Mascotas! Ser.). (MUL.). 24p. (J). (gr. -1-2). lib. bdg. 33.99 *(978-1-68410-253-2(7)*, 138451) Cantata Learning.

—You Are My Happy. Kotb, Hoda. 2019. (ENG.). 32p. (J). (gr. -1-k). 18.99 *(978-0-06-288789-4(0))* HarperCollins Pubs.

Mason, Trisha. Be Brave, Be Brave, Be Brave: A True Story of Fatherhood & Native American Heritage. Falcon, F. Anthony. 2019. (ENG.). 32p. (J). (gr. -1-2). 17.99 *(978-1-57687-914-6(3)*, powerHouse Bks.) powerHse. Bks.

Mason, Turning Bear. The Cost of Eggs: Hill House Farm Series. Smith, Sandra S. 2012. 24p. 24.95 *(978-1-4626-4928-0(9))* America Star Bks.

Mason, Tyla. What Can I Do When I Grow Up: A Children's Career Guide. The School of Life, The School. 2020. 160p. (J). 19.99 *(978-1-912891-20-7(4))* First Church Iam, The Schl. of Life Ministry of Solehealism, The GBR. Dist: Consortium Bk. Sales & Distribution.

Massardier, Greg. Boo & Bear. Massardier, Greg, tr. Wyley, Enda. 2003. (Panda Cubs Ser.: 1). (ENG.). 48p. (J). pap. 9.95 *(978-0-86278-806-3(4))* O'Brien Pr., Ltd., The IRL. Dist: Casemate Pubs. & Bk. Distributors, LLC.

Massari, Alida. Angels in the Bible for Little Ones, 1 vol. Nolan, Allia Zobel. 2017. (ENG.). 32p. (J). bds. 9.99 *(978-0-310-75043-7(1))* Zonderkidz.

—Bible & Me. Rock, Lois. ed. 2016. (ENG.). 128p. (J). (gr. k-3). 14.99 *(978-0-7459-6495-9(8))* Lion Hudson PLC GBR. Dist: Independent Pubs. Group.

—La Biblia y Yo / the Bible & Me. Rock, Lois. 2018. (SPA.). 128p. (J). (gr. 2-4). 14.95 *(978-1-945540-54-7(0))* Penguin Random House Grupo Editorial ESP. Dist: Penguin Random Hse. LLC.

—Children of the Bible. McAllister, Margaret. ed. 2019. (ENG.). 48p. (J). (gr. 2-4). pap. 12.99 *(978-0-7459-7829-1(0))* Lion Hudson PLC GBR. Dist: Independent Pubs. Group.

—The Marvelous Mud House: A Story of Finding Fullness & Joy. Graney, April. 2017. (ENG.). 32p. (J). (gr. -1-3). 14.99 *(978-1-4627-4099-4(5)*, 005793053, B&H Kids) B&H Publishing Group.

—Mujeres de la Biblia (Women of the Bible) McAllister, Margaret. 2014. (ENG & SPA.). (J). 13.99 *(978-1-55883-172-8(X))* Libros Desafío.

Massari, Alida. Nicanor's Gate. Kimmel, Eric A. 2020. (ENG.). 24p. (J). (gr. -1-2). 17.99 ***(978-1-5415-7452-6(4)***, Kar-Ben Publishing) Lerner Publishing Group.

Massari, Alida. Stories of the Saints, 1 vol. McAllister, Margaret. ed. 2015. (ENG.). 48p. (J). (gr. 2-4). 12.99 *(978-0-7459-6445-4(1))* Lion Hudson PLC GBR. Dist: Independent Pubs. Group.

—The Story of Easter. Joslin, Mary. ed. 2015. (ENG.). 32p. (J). (gr. k-2). pap. 8.99 *(978-0-7459-6486-7(9))* Lion Hudson PLC GBR. Dist: Independent Pubs. Group.

—Under the Sabbath Lamp. Herman, Michael. 2017. (ENG.). 32p. (J). (gr. -1-2). 17.99 *(978-1-5124-0841-6(7)*, 9781512408416, Kar-Ben Publishing) Lerner Publishing Group.

—Women of the Bible. McAllister, Margaret. 2013. (ENG.). 48p. (J). 16.99 *(978-1-61261-372-7(1))* Paraclete Pr., Inc.

Masse, Alexandria. Everyone Can Learn Math. Aspinall, Alice. 2nd ed. 2019. (ENG.). 32p. (J). (gr. k-4). 26.99 ***(978-1-970133-43-1(0))***; pap. 17.99 ***(978-1-970133-41-7(4))*** EduMatch.

Masse, Alexandria. Everyone Can Learn Math. Aspinall, Alice. 2018. (ENG.). 28p. (J). *(978-1-5255-3374-7(6))*; pap. *(978-1-5255-3375-4(4))* FriesenPress.

Masse, Jos�e. Good Night, Oliver Wizard. Dotlich, Rebecca Kai. 2019. 32p. (J). (gr. -1-2). 17.99 *(978-1-62979-337-5(X))* Boyds Mills Pr.

—Thunder Underground. Yolen, Jane. 2017. (ENG.). 32p. (J). (gr. k-4). 17.99 *(978-1-59078-936-0(9)*, Wordsong) Boyds Mills Pr.

Masse, Josée. The Care & Keeping of You 2: The Body Book for Older Girls. Natterson, Cara. ed. 2013. lib. bdg. 24.50 *(978-0-606-31576-0(4))* Turtleback.

—Echo Echo: Reverso Poems about Greek Myths. Singer, Marilyn. 2016. (ENG.). 32p. (J). (gr. 1-4). 17.99 *(978-0-8037-3992-5(3)*, Dial Bks) Penguin Young Readers Group.

—Follow Follow: A Book of Reverso Poems. Singer, Marilyn. 2013. (ENG.). 32p. (J). (gr. 1-4). 16.99 *(978-0-8037-3769-3(6)*, Dial Bks) Penguin Young Readers Group.

—Frog & Friends. Bunting, Eve. 2011. (I Am a Reader: Frog & Friends Ser.). (ENG.). 40p. (J). (gr. -1-1). lib. bdg. 16.19 *(978-1-58536-548-7(3))*; (gr. k-3). pap. 3.99 *(978-1-58536-689-7(7))* Sleeping Bear Pr.

—Frog & Friends: Outdoor Surprises. Bunting, Eve. 2013. (I AM a READER!: Frog & Friends Ser.). (ENG.). 48p. (J). (gr. 1-2). 9.95 *(978-1-58536-807-5(5)*, 202361); pap. 3.99 *(978-1-58536-808-2(3)*, 202370) Sleeping Bear Pr.

—Frog & Friends Celebrate Thanksgiving, Christmas, & New Year's Eve. Bunting, Eve. 2015. (I AM a READER!: Frog & Friends Ser.). (ENG.). 40p. (J). (gr. 1-2). 9.99 *(978-1-58536-897-6(0)*, 203949) Sleeping Bear Pr.

—Frog Saves the Day. Bunting, Eve. 2013. (I AM a READER!: Frog & Friends Ser.). (ENG.). 40p. (J). (gr. 1-2). 9.99 *(978-1-58536-809-9(1)*, 202895); pap. 3.99 *(978-1-58536-810-5(5)*, 202896) Sleeping Bear Pr.

—Frog's Lucky Day. Bunting, Eve. 2014. (I Am a Reader!: Frog & Friends Ser.). (ENG.). 40p. (J). (gr. 1-2). 9.99 *(978-1-58536-892-1(X)*, 203014) Sleeping Bear Pr.

—The Magic Cake Shop. Hashimoto, Meika. 2012. (ENG.). 176p. (J). (gr. 4-6). lib. bdg. 21.19 *(978-0-375-96822-8(9))* Random House Publishing Group.

—Mirror Mirror: A Book of Reverso Poems. Singer, Marilyn. 2010. (ENG.). 32p. (J). (gr. 1-4). 17.99 *(978-0-525-47901-7(5)*, Dutton Books for Young Readers) Penguin Young Readers Group.

—Motherbridge of Love. Xinran, Xinran & Mother's Bridge of Love Staff. 2013. 32p. (J). (gr. k-3). pap. 7.99 *(978-1-78285-040-3(6))* Barefoot Bks., Inc.

—Motherbridge of Love. Xinran, Xinran et al. 2007. (ENG.). 32p. (J). (gr. -1-5). 16.99 *(978-1-84686-047-8(4))* Barefoot Bks., Inc.

—My Give Thanks Bible, 1 vol. Thomas Nelson, Thomas. 2015. (ENG.). 32p. (J). bds. 9.99 *(978-0-310-74942-4(5))* Zonderkidz.

—The Princess Who Had Almost Everything. Levert, Mireille. 2008. (ENG.). 32p. (J). (gr. -1-3). 19.95 *(978-0-88776-887-3(3)*, Tundra Bks.) Tundra Bks. CAN. Dist: Penguin Random Hse. LLC.

Masse, Josée & Archer, Micha. Lola's Fandango. Witte, Anna. 2011. 48p. (J). 16.99 *(978-1-84686-174-1(8))* Barefoot Bks., Inc.

Massegu, Marcel P. Navajo Code Talkers: Top Secret Messengers of World War II. Hoena, Blake. 2019. (Amazing World War II Stories Ser.). (ENG.). 32p. (J). (gr. 3-9). pap. 7.95 *(978-1-5435-7549-1(8)*, 141081); lib. bdg. 34.65 *(978-1-5435-7314-5(2)*, 140619) Capstone.

Masseva, Bistra. Dario & the Whale. Malone, Cheryl Lawton. 2016. (ENG.). 32p. (J). (gr. -1-3). 16.99 *(978-0-8075-1463-4(2)*, 807514632) Whitman, Albert & Co.

—Elephants Walk Together. Malone, Cheryl Lawton. 2017. (ENG.). 32p. (J). (gr. k-2). 16.99 *(978-0-8075-1960-8(X)*, 080751960X) Whitman, Albert & Co.

Massey, Cal. My Name Is Oney Judge. Turner, Diane D. 2010. (J). pap. *(978-0-88378-321-4(5))* Third World Press.

Massey, Ed, photos by. Casper, the Friendly Service Dog. Massey, Wayland. 2011. 28p. pap. 14.95 *(978-1-936343-73-7(8))* Peppertree Pr., The.

Massey Foister, Heather. Tiger & Lily Together. Hopper, Sarah. 2020. (ENG.). 36p. (J). pap. 15.95 ***(978-1-68433-557-2(4))*** Black Rose Writing.

Massey, Jane. Animales de la Granja. (Coloca y Siente). (SPA.). 10p. (J). (gr. k-2). bds. *(978-968-5308-67-0(5)*, Silver Dolphin en Español) Advanced Marketing, S. de R. L. de C. V.

—Animales de la Selva. (Coloca y Siente). (SPA.). 10p. (J). (gr. k-2). bds. *(978-968-5308-68-7(3)*, Silver Dolphin en Español) Advanced Marketing, S. de R. L. de C. V.

—Eat, Sleep, Poop. Penfold, Alexandra. 2016. (ENG.). 40p. (J). (-k). 16.99 *(978-0-385-75503-0(1)*, Knopf Bks. for Young Readers) Random Hse. Children's Bks.

—Florence Frizzball. Freedman, Claire. 2018. (ENG.). 32p. (J). 7.99 *(978-1-4711-4454-7(2)*, Simon & Schuster Children's) Simon & Schuster, Ltd. GBR. Dist: Simon & Schuster, Inc.

—I Love You, Blankie. Haft, Sheryl. 2015. (ENG.). 22p. (J). (gr. -1 — 1). bds. 8.99 *(978-0-316-28356-4(8))* Little, Brown Bks. for Young Readers.

—Mascotas. (Coloca y Siente). (SPA.). 10p. (J). (gr. k-2). bds. *(978-968-5308-66-3(7)*, Silver Dolphin en Español) Advanced Marketing, S. de R. L. de C. V.

—My Mommy Is Magic. Richards, Dawn. 2015. (ENG.). 32p. (J). (gr. -1-k). 8.99 *(978-0-7641-6757-7(X)*, B.E.S. Publishing) Peterson's.

—Night-Night, Emily! Freedman, Claire. 2005. 32p. (J). 6.95 *(978-1-58925-390-2(6))* Tiger Tales.

—Potty Hero. 2016. (J). *(978-0-545-92773-4(0))* Scholastic, Inc.

—Potty Star. 2015. (J). *(978-0-545-92772-7(2))* Scholastic, Inc.

—Ten Little Fingers, Two Small Hands. Dempsey, Kristy. (Mini Bee Board Bks.). (ENG.). (J). (gr. -1-k). 2018. 26p. bds. 7.99 *(978-1-4998-0671-7(X))*; 2016. 32p. 16.99 *(978-1-4998-0229-0(3))* Little Bee Books Inc.

—Ten Little Toes, Two Small Feet. Dempsey, Kristy. (Mini Bee Board Bks.). (ENG.). 32p. (J). (gr. -1-k). 2018. bds. 7.99 *(978-1-4998-0672-4(8))*; 2016. 16.99 *(978-1-4998-0236-8(6))* Little Bee Books Inc.

Massey, Jane. Night-Night, Emily! Massey, Jane, tr. Freedman, Claire. 2003. 32p. (J). (gr. -1-1). tchr. ed. 15.95 *(978-1-58925-032-1(X))* Tiger Tales.

Massey, Jane, jt. illus. see Pedler, Caroline.

Massey, Luke, photos by. Falcons in the City: The Story of a Peregrine Family. Earley, Chris. 2016. (ENG., 48p. (J). (gr. 4-8). pap. 9.95 *(978-1-77085-803-9(2)*, af6e8002-865c-43a0-a5f4-18625a6f7d29) Firefly Bks., Ltd.

Massey, Mitch & Kelleher, Michael. League of Super Groovy Crimefighters Trade Paperback. Campbell, Jan-Ives. 2003. (YA). per. 12.95 *(978-0-9744216-0-5(X))* Ancient Studios.

Massey, Ron, photos by. Fart Bubbles: A Book of Wacky Poems. Lashe, Tyla. 2017. (ENG., (J). pap. 10.00 *(978-0-9986624-3-5(7))* A Beautiful, Wonderful Me LLC.

Massini, Luca, jt. illus. see Calvetti, Leonello.

Massini, Sarah. Books Always Everywhere. Blatt, Jane. 2013. (J). *(978-0-385-37535-1(2))* Random Hse., Inc.

—The Girl & the Dinosaur. Hughes, Hollie. 2020. (ENG.). 32p. (J). 17.99 *(978-1-5476-0322-0(4)*, 900211339, Bloomsbury Children's Bks.) Bloomsbury Publishing USA.

—Kiss It Better. Prasadam-Halls, Smriti. 2017. 32p. (J). bds. 7.99 *(978-1-68119-164-5(4)*, 9781681191645, Bloomsbury USA Childrens) Bloomsbury Publishing USA.

—Love Always Everywhere. 2014. (ENG.). 32p. (J). (gr. -1-2). 16.99 *(978-0-385-37552-8(2)*, Random Hse. Bks. for Young Readers) Random Hse. Children's Bks.

—Oodles of Noodles. Hendry, Diana. 2008. (Tiger Tales Ser.). 32p. (J). (gr. -1-2). 15.95 *(978-1-58925-075-8(3))* Tiger Tales.

—A Recipe for Playtime. Bently, Peter. 2019. 32p. (J). (gr. -1-k). pap. 9.99 *(978-1-4449-2725-2(6))* Hachette Children's Group GBR. Dist: Hachette Bk. Group.

—The Star in the Jar. Hay, Sam. 2018. (ENG.). 32p. (J). (-3). 17.99 *(978-1-4926-6220-4(8)*, Sourcebooks Jabberwocky) Sourcebooks, Inc.

—Tulip & Rex Write a Story. Capucilli, Alyssa Satin. 2015. (ENG.). 32p. (J). (gr. -1-3). 17.99 *(978-0-06-209416-2(5)*, Tegen, Katherine Bks) HarperCollins Pubs.

Massini, Sarah. The Boy & the Bear. Massini, Sarah. 2019. (ENG.). 32p. (J). (-k). 16.99 *(978-1-5362-0814-6(0)*, Nosy Crow) Candlewick Pr.

Massironi, Daniela. Frankie the Frog. 2014. (J). *(978-1-4351-5573-2(4))* Barnes & Noble, Inc.

—Freddie the Fish. 2014. (J). *(978-1-4351-5574-9(2))* Barnes & Noble, Inc.

—Happy Peeps-Oween! Posner-Sanchez, Andrea. 2017. (Pictureback(R) Ser.). 16p. (J). (-k). pap. 4.99 *(978-1-5247-6507-1(4)*, Random Hse. Bks. for Young Readers) Random Hse. Children's Bks.

—Peeps at School. Posner-Sanchez, Andrea. 2018. 24p. (J). *(978-1-5490-4055-9(3))* Random Hse., Inc.

—The Sweetest Easter (Peeps) Posner-Sanchez, Andrea. 2017. (Pictureback(R) Ser.). (ENG.). 16p. (J). (-k). pap. 4.99 *(978-1-5247-1905-0(6)*, Random Hse. Bks. for Young Readers) Random Hse. Children's Bks.

Massironi, Daniela. Time for Christmas. Rainstorm Publishing, ed. 2018. (Holiday Lift-The-Flap Ser.). (ENG.). 12p. (J). bds. 7.99 ***(978-1-77402-145-3(5))*** Rainstorm Pr.

—Time for Easter. Rainstorm Publishing, ed. 2018. (Holiday Lift-The-Flap Ser.). (ENG.). 12p. (J). bds. 7.99 ***(978-1-926444-80-2(9))*** Rainstorm Pr.

—Time for Halloween. Rainstorm Publishing, ed. 2018. (Holiday Lift-The-Flap Ser.). (ENG.). 12p. (J). bds. 7.99 ***(978-1-77402-144-6(7))*** Rainstorm Pr.

Massivebrain.com. The Tree & the Light. Strange, J. R. 2013. 48p. pap. 11.99 *(978-0-9887214-0-1(6))* Firesidenook.

Masslich, Lisa LaGrow. Lost Lady: The Lady Elgin Tragedy. Hollander, M. Paul. 2018. (ENG.). 194p. (J). pap. 11.95 *(978-1-9835-6389-8(7))* CreateSpace Independent Publishing Platform.

Masso, Acacia. A Bird, a Girl, & a Rescue: Book Two of the Rwendigo Tales. Myhre, J. A. 2016. (ENG.). 144p. (J). pap. 15.99 *(978-1-942572-69-5(7))* New Growth Pr.

Masson, Annick. I Can't Do Anything! Robberecht, Thierry. 2013. 32p. (J). *(978-1-4338-1309-2(2))* American Psychological Assn.

—No, No, No! Callier, Marie-Isabelle. 2013. 32p. pap. 9.95 *(978-1-4338-1312-2(2))*; (J). *(978-1-4338-1311-5(4))* American Psychological Assn. (Magination Pr.).

Mastantuono, Corrado & Cavazzano, Giorgio. Angry Birds Comics: Flight School. Tobin, Paul & Korhonen, Kari. 2017. (Angry Birds Ser.). 80p. (J). (gr. 4-7). 12.99 *(978-1-68405-001-7(4))* Idea & Design Works, LLC.

Masters, Jason. Captain America by Ta-Nehisi Coates Vol. 3: The Legend of Steve. 2020. (Captain America by Ta-Nehisi Coates Ser.: 3). (ENG.). 136p. (YA). (gr. 8-17). pap. 19.99 *(978-1-302-91441-7(3))* Marvel Worldwide, Inc.

Masters, Lizzie. The Bedtime Book. Wright, Devin. 2nd ed. 2018. (ENG.). 26p. (J). *(978-0-6399841-2-4(6))*; pap. *(978-0-6399841-3-1(4))* Seraph Creative.

Masters, Lizzie. The Bedtime Journal. Wright, Devin. 2019. (ENG.). 48p. (J). pap. ***(978-0-620-83797-2(7))*** Seraph Creative.

Masters, Lizzie. Colouring Book - the Name of Yahweh, Angels & the Garden of My Heart. Masters, Lindi. 2018. (ENG.). 28p. (J). pap. *(978-0-6399841-6-2(9))* Seraph Creative.

—The Name of Yahweh, Angels & the Garden of My Heart. Masters, Lindi. 2nd ed. 2018. (ENG.). 26p. (J). *(978-0-9946974-6-2(5))*; pap. *(978-0-9946974-7-9(3))* Seraph Creative.

—The Other Christmas Story. Masters, Lindi. 2018. (ENG.). 52p. (J). pap. *(978-0-6399842-5-4(8))* Seraph Creative.

—Realms of the Kingdom, Mountains & the Throne of Grace. Masters, Lindi. 2nd ed. 2018. (ENG.). 32p. (J). *(978-0-9946974-9-3(X))*; pap. *(978-0-6399841-0-0(X))* Seraph Creative.

—The Remember Book. Wright, Devin. 2019. (ENG.). 28p. (J). pap. *(978-0-620-83577-0(X))* Seraph Creative.

—The Remember Journal. Wright, Devin. 2019. (ENG.). 48p. (J). pap. *(978-0-620-83798-9(5))* Seraph Creative.

—Scrolls, Courts & the Seven Spirits of God. Masters, Lindi. 2nd ed. 2018. (ENG.). 26p. (J). *(978-0-6399842-1-6(5))*; pap. *(978-0-6399842-2-3(3))* Seraph Creative.

Mastin, Ian. The Lamb: PowerPoint Booklet. Cross, John R. 2007. (J). spiral bd. *(978-1-890082-62-8(7))* GoodSeed International.

Mastrangelo, Judy. What Do Bunnies Do All Day? Mastrangelo, Judy. 32p. (J). pap. 4.95 *(978-0-8249-5370-6(3)*, Ideal Pubns.) Worthy Publishing.

Mastrangelo, Madison. In the Beginning: The Story of Creation. Elliot, Rachel. Parragon Books & Cottage Door Press, eds. 2019. (ENG.). 32p. (J). (gr. -1-3). 9.99 *(978-1-68052-552-6(2)*, 2001400, Parragon Books) Cottage Door Pr.

Mastroserio, Rocke. The Action Heroes Archives, Vol. 2. Kaler, David et al. rev. ed. 2007. (DC Archive Editions Ser.). (ENG.). 388p. (YA). 75.00 *(978-1-4012-1346-6(4))* DC Comics.

Masuda, Coco. Issun Boshi, or One-Inch Boy - 6 Pack: Set of 6 with Common Core Teacher Materials. 2015. (Classic Tales Ser.). (J). (gr. k-1). 39.00 *(978-1-5125-8347-2(2))* Benchmark Education Co.

Masukawa, Masako. The White Mouse: a Folk Tale from the Panchatantra: Band 13/Topaz (Collins Big Cat) Casey, Dawn. 2016. (Collins Big Cat Ser.). (ENG.). 32p. (J). pap. 9.99 *(978-0-00-814721-1(3))* HarperCollins Pubs. Ltd. GBR. Dist: Independent Pubs. Group.

Mata, Anthony. Akiti the Hunter (Softcover) The First African Action Hero. Bolaji, Ajayi. 2017. (African Action Heroes Ser.: Vol. 1). (ENG.). (J). (gr. k-3). pap. *(978-1-910882-58-0(5))* Abela Publishing.

Mata, Nina. Fettuccine & Four-Leaf Clovers: A Readers' Theater Script & Guide, 1 vol. Wallace, Nancy K. 2015. (Readers' Theater: How to Put on a Production Ser.). 32p. (J). (gr. 3-6). 28.50 *(978-1-62402-112-1(3)*, 18166, Looking Glass Library) Magic Wagon.

Mata, Nina. I Promise. James, Lebron. 2020. (ENG.). 40p. (J). (gr. -1-3). 19.99 ***(978-0-06-297106-7(9)***, HarperCollins) HarperCollins Pubs. Ltd. GBR. Dist: HarperCollins Pubs.

Mata, Nina. Medals & Memorials: A Readers' Theater Script & Guide, 1 vol. Wallace, Nancy K. 2015. (Readers' Theater: How to Put on a Production Ser.). 32p. (J). (gr. 3-6). 28.50 *(978-1-62402-115-2(8)*, 18172, Looking Glass Library) Magic Wagon.

—Princedom of Pea: A Readers' Theater Script & Guide. Wallace, Nancy K. 2013. (Readers' Theater: How to Put on a Production Ser.). (ENG.). 32p. (J). (gr. 2-6). lib. bdg. 28.50 *(978-1-61641-988-2(1)*, 549, Looking Glass Library) Magic Wagon.

—She's Got This. Hernandez, Laurie. 2018. (ENG.). 32p. (J). (gr. -1-3). 18.99 *(978-0-06-284058-5(4)*, HarperCollins) HarperCollins Pubs. Ltd. GBR. Dist: HarperCollins Pubs.

—Snow White & the Seven Dorks: A Readers' Theater Script & Guide. Wallace, Nancy K. 2013. (Readers' Theater: How to Put on a Production Ser.). (ENG.). 32p. (J). (gr. 2-6). lib. bdg. 28.50 *(978-1-61641-990-5(3)*, 553, Looking Glass Library) Magic Wagon.

Mata, Nina. Ty's Travels: All Aboard! Lyons, Kelly Starling. 2020. (My First I Can Read Ser.). (ENG.). 32p. (J). (gr. -1-3). 16.99 ***(978-0-06-295112-0(2))***; pap. 4.99 ***(978-0-06-295107-6(6))*** HarperCollins Pubs. Ltd. GBR. (HarperCollins). Dist: HarperCollins Pubs.

—Ty's Travels: Zip, Zoom! Lyons, Kelly Starling. 2020. (My First I Can Read Ser.). 32p. (J). (gr. -1-3). 16.99 ***(978-0-06-295110-6(6))***; pap. 4.99 ***(978-0-06-295109-0(2))*** HarperCollins Pubs. Ltd. GBR. (HarperCollins). Dist: HarperCollins Pubs.

Mata, Nina. Ways to Make Sunshine. Watson, Renée. 2020. (Ryan Hart Novel Ser.: 1). (ENG.). 192p. (J). 16.99 *(978-1-5476-0056-4(X)*, 900196518, Bloomsbury Children's Bks.) Bloomsbury Publishing USA.

—What Does It Mean to Be American? DiOrio, Rana & Yoran, Elad. 2019. (What Does It Mean to Be... ? Ser.: 0). (ENG.). 40p. (J). (-3). 17.99 *(978-1-4926-8380-3(9)*, Little Pickle Pr.) Sourcebooks, Inc.

Matchette, Karen. Scooby-Doo in Ready-to-Werewolf, 1 vol. Busch, Robbie. 2010. (Scooby-Doo Graphic Novels Ser.: No. 1). (ENG.). 24p. (J). (gr. 2-6). 27.07 *(978-1-59961-696-4(3)*, 564, Graphic Novels) Spotlight.

—Scooby-Doo in Screechy Keen, 1 vol. Griep, Terrence, Jr. 2010. (Scooby-Doo Graphic Novels Ser.: No. 1). (ENG.). 24p. (J). (gr. 2-6). 27.07 *(978-1-59961-697-1(1)*, 565, Graphic Novels) Spotlight.

Mate, Nikki. Airshow. Hewitt, Mark A. 2017. (ENG.). (J). (gr. -1-3). 15.95 *(978-1-61296-936-7(4))* Black Rose Writing.

Mate, Rae. Crocodiles Play! Heidbreder, Robert. 2009. (ENG.). 32p. (J). (gr. -1-3). 16.95 *(978-1-894965-86-6(8))* Simply Read Bks. CAN. Dist: Ingram Publisher Services.

—Crocodiles Say... Heidbreder, Robert. 2005. (ENG.). 32p. (J). (gr. -1-3). 16.95 *(978-1-894965-42-2(6))* Simply Read Bks. CAN. Dist: Ingram Publisher Services.

Maté, Rae. Crocs in a Box. Heidbreder, Robert. 2020. (ENG.). 96p. (J). (gr. k-1). 19.95 ***(978-1-926890-06-7(X))*** Tradewind Bks. CAN. Dist: Orca Bk. Pubs. USA.

Mate, Rae. Pussycat, Pussycat, Where Have You Been? Bar-el, Dan. 2011. (ENG.). 32p. (J). (gr. -1-3). 16.95 *(978-1-897476-46-8(9))* Simply Read Bks. CAN. Dist: Ingram Publisher Services.

Mateo, Rosario. Un Agente Oportuno: Cuando la Penicilina Entra en Accion. Mariscal, Libia Barajas. rev. ed. 2006. (Otra Escalera Ser.). (SPA & ENG.). 24p. (J). (gr. 2-4). pap. 9.95 *(978-968-5920-64-3(8))* Castillo, Ediciones, S. A. de C. V. MEX. Dist: Macmillan.

Mateo, Rosario & Sada, Margarita. Venir del Mar. Caban, Jose Alberto. rev. ed. 2006. (Otra Escalera Ser.). (SPA & ENG.). 24p. (J). (gr. 2-4). pap. 9.95 *(978-968-5920-74-2(5))* Castillo, Ediciones, S. A. de C. V. MEX. Dist: Macmillan.

Matera, Adele, jt. illus. see Florean, Arianna.

Maters, Ingrid. Samaya: The Deaf Baby Elephant. De Silva-Nijkamp, Tineke. 2005. 33p. (J). *(978-955-599-438-5(2))* Sarvodaya Bk. Publishing Services.

Matesic, Ella. Sharing Seeds of Kindness. Matesic, Kathy. 2018. (ENG.). 48p. (J). (gr. 2-3). pap. *(978-0-9959067-0-9(X))* Matesic, Kathy.

Mateu, Francesca. The Little Mermaid. RH Disney Staff & Calmenson, Stephanie. 2003. (Pictureback(R) Ser.). (ENG.). 24p. (J). (gr. -1-2). pap. 3.99 *(978-0-7364-2128-7(9)*, RH/Disney) Random Hse. Children's Bks.

Mateu, Xavier Vives. Aladdin. Weiss, Bobbi Jg. 2020. (Disney Classics Ser.). (ENG.). 48p. (J). (gr. 2-6). lib. bdg. 28.50 ***(978-1-5321-4533-9(0)***, 35179, Graphic Novels) Spotlight.

—The Little Mermaid. Anderson, Tom. 2020. (Disney Princesses Ser.). (ENG.). 48p. (J). (gr. 2-6). lib. bdg. 28.50 ***(978-1-5321-4562-9(4)***, 35209, Graphic Novels) Spotlight.

Matheny, Jean, jt. illus. see Sherlock, Jean.

Matheny, Jean Sherlock. I Want to Be a Christian: The Story of Blessed Kateri Tekakwitha. Paddock, Susan Star. Jaurequi, Leticia & Gomez, Elisa, trs. 2004. (J). *(978-0-9747571-8-6(7))* Catholic World Mission.

Matheny, Melody. Rock, Stream, Tree. Zito, Ann R. 2010. 52p. pap. 11.00 *(978-1-4520-7822-9(X))* AuthorHouse.

Mather, Daniel. Who Is Steven Spielberg? Spinner, Stephanie & Who HQ. 2013. (Who Was? Ser.). 112p. (J). (gr. 3-7). 5.99 *(978-0-448-47935-4(4)*, Penguin Workshop) Penguin Young Readers Group.

Mather-Smith, Charles. Inside Our Earth. Arnov Jr., Boris & Mindlin, Helen Mather-Smith. 2011. 160p. 41.95 *(978-1-258-07682-5(9))* Literary Licensing, LLC.

Matherne, Noelle E. Roxy the Therapy Dog Gets a Helper. Flint, Pam. 2019. (ENG.). 52p. (J). ***(978-1-5255-5691-3(6))***; pap. ***(978-1-5255-5692-0(4))*** FriesenPress.

Mathers, Petra. Button Up! Wrinkled Rhymes. Schertle, Alice. 2013. (ENG.). 40p. (J). (gr. -1-3). pap. 7.99 *(978-0-544-02269-0(6)*, 1528491) Houghton Mifflin Harcourt Publishing Co.

—The Frogs Wore Red Suspenders. Prelutsky, Jack. 2005. (ENG.). 64p. (J). (gr. k-5). reprint ed. pap. 7.99 *(978-0-06-073776-4(X)*, Greenwillow Bks.) HarperCollins Pubs.

—In Aunt Giraffe's Green Garden. Prelutsky, Jack. 2007. 64p. (J). (gr. -1-3). lib. bdg. 18.89 *(978-0-06-623869-2(2))* HarperCollins Pubs.

—Strange Mr. Satie: Composer of the Absurd. Anderson, M. T. 2016. 48p. (J). (gr. 2-5). 7.99 *(978-0-7636-8775-5(8))* Candlewick Pr.

Mathers, Petra. The McElderry Book of Mother Goose: Revered & Rare Rhymes. Mathers, Petra, compiled by. 2012. (ENG.). 96p. (J). (gr. k-5). 21.99 *(978-0-689-85605-1(9)*, McElderry, Margaret K. Bks.) McElderry, Margaret K. Bks.

Matheson, Christie. Bird Watch. Matheson, Christie. 2019. (ENG.). 48p. (J). (gr. -1-3). 17.99 *(978-0-06-239340-1(5)*, Greenwillow Bks.) HarperCollins Pubs.

—Plant the Tiny Seed. Matheson, Christie. 2017. (ENG.). 40p. (J). (gr. -1-3). 16.99 *(978-0-06-239339-5(1)*, Greenwillow Bks.) HarperCollins Pubs.

—Tap the Magic Tree. Matheson, Christie. 2013. (ENG.). 40p. (J). (gr. -1-3). 16.99 *(978-0-06-227445-8(7)*, Greenwillow Bks.) HarperCollins Pubs.

—Tap the Magic Tree Board Book. Matheson, Christie. 2016. (ENG.). 42p. (J). (gr. -1-3). bds. 7.99 *(978-0-06-227446-5(5)*, Greenwillow Bks.) HarperCollins Pubs.

—Touch the Brightest Star. Matheson, Christie. 2015. (ENG.). 40p. (J). (gr. -1-3). 15.99 *(978-0-06-227447-2(3)*, Greenwillow Bks.) HarperCollins Pubs.

—Touch the Brightest Star Board Book. Matheson, Christie. 2017. (ENG.). 42p. (J). (gr. -1-3). bds. 7.99 *(978-0-06-227448-9(1)*, Greenwillow Bks.) HarperCollins Pubs.

Mathew, Gillian. The Gift of Gold. Kowen, Dorothy. 2011. (ENG.). 24p. (J). 13.95 *(978-1-77009-796-4(1))* Jacana Media ZAF. Dist: Independent Pubs. Group.

Mathieu, Joe. Big Mike's Police Car. McGuire, Leslie. 2003. (Please Read to Me Ser.). (ENG.). 24p. (J). (gr. -1-3). 16.19 *(978-0-375-82334-3(4))* Random House Publishing Group.

—Dogs Don't Wear Sneakers. Numeroff, Laura Joffe. 2014. 40p. pap. 8.00 *(978-1-61003-344-2(2))* Center for the Collaborative Classroom.

—Don't Be Silly, Mrs. Millie!, 0 vols. Cox, Judy. 2010. (ENG.). 34p. (J). (gr. k-3). pap. 6.99 *(978-0-7614-5727-5(5)*, 9780761457275, Two Lions) Amazon Publishing.

—Elmo's Lucky Day (Sesame Street) Posner-Sanchez, Andrea. 2020. (ENG.). 22p. (J). (-k). bds. 6.99 *(978-0-593-12247-1(X)*, Random Hse. Bks. for Young Readers) Random Hse. Children's Bks.

—Elmo's Merry Christmas/Oscar's Grouchy Christmas (Sesame Street) Webster, Christy. 2016. (Pictureback(R) Ser.). (ENG.). 24p. (J). (-k). 4.99 *(978-1-101-93923-9(0)*, Random Hse. Bks. for Young Readers) Random Hse. Children's Bks.

—Elmo's Super-Duper Birthday (Sesame Street) Kleinberg, Naomi. 2016. (Pictureback(R) Ser.). (ENG.). 24p. (J). (gr. -1-2). pap. 5.99 *(978-0-399-55216-8(2)*, Random Hse. Bks. for Young Readers) Random Hse. Children's Bks.

—Grover's Eight Nights of Light (Sesame Street) Shepherd, Jodie. 2017. (Pictureback(R) Ser.). (ENG.). 24p. (J). (gr. -1-2). pap. 6.99 *(978-1-5247-2073-5(9)*, Random Hse. Bks. for Young Readers) Random Hse. Children's Bks.

—Happy Birthday, Mrs. Millie!, 0 vols. Cox, Judy. 2012. (ENG.). 32p. (J). (gr. k-3). 16.99 *(978-0-7614-6126-5(4)*, 9780761461265, Two Lions) Amazon Publishing.

—Have You Seen My Dinosaur? Surgal, Jon. 2010. (Beginner Books(R) Ser.). (ENG.). 48p. (J). (gr. -1-1). 9.99 *(978-0-375-85639-6(0)*, Random Hse. Bks. for Young Readers) Random Hse. Children's Bks.
—Hello, Dragons! Hola, Dragones! Rodecker, Ron. 2005. (ENG & SPA.). 10p. (J). (gr. -1-2). reprint ed. 10.00 *(978-0-7567-8937-4(0))* DIANE Publishing Co.
—It's Passover, Grover! (Sesame Street) Shepherd, Jodie. 2019. (Pictureback(R) Ser.). (ENG.). 24p. (J). (-k). pap. 6.99 *(978-0-525-64722-5(8)*, Random Hse. Bks. for Young Readers) Random Hse. Children's Bks.
—Knock, Knock! Who's There? (Sesame Street) A Lift-The-Flap Board Book. Ross, Anna. 2018. (ENG.). 22p. (J). (— 1). bds. 6.99 *(978-1-5247-7032-7(9)*, Random Hse. Bks. for Young Readers) Random Hse. Children's Bks.
—Let's Visit Sesame Street. November, Deborah et al. 2010. (ENG.). 24p. (J). bds. 14.99 *(978-0-7944-2101-4(6))* Reader's Digest Assn., Inc., The.
—Moose Crossing, 0 vols. Greene, Stephanie. 2010. (Moose & Hildy Ser.: 2). (ENG.). 64p. (J). (gr. 1-2). pap. 9.99 *(978-0-7614-5699-5(6)*, 9780761456995, Two Lions) Amazon Publishing.
—Moose's Big Idea, 0 vols. Greene, Stephanie. 2010. (Moose & Hildy Ser.: 1). (ENG.). 64p. (J). (gr. 1-4). pap. 6.99 *(978-0-7614-5698-8(8)*, 9780761456988, Two Lions) Amazon Publishing.
—Mrs. Millie Goes to Philly!, 0 vols. Cox, Judy. 2013. (ENG.). 32p. (J). (gr. -1-2). pap. 9.99 *(978-1-4778-1680-6(1)*, 9781477816806, Two Lions) Amazon Publishing.
—The Nose Book. Perkins, Al. 2017. (Big Bright & Early Board Book Ser.). 24p. (J). (— 1). bds. 6.99 *(978-0-553-53863-2(2)*, Random Hse. Bks. for Young Readers) Random Hse. Children's Bks.
—The Nose Book. Dr. Seuss Enterprises Staff & Perkins, Al. 2003. (Bright & Early Board Books(TM) Ser.). (ENG.). 24p. (J). (— 1). bds. 4.99 *(978-0-375-82493-7(6)*, Random Hse. Bks. for Young Readers) Random Hse. Children's Bks.
—Pick a Pumpkin, Mrs. Millie!, 0 vols. Cox, Judy. 2009. (ENG.). 32p. (J). (gr. -1-3). 15.99 *(978-0-7614-5573-8(6)*, 9780761455738, Two Lions) Amazon Publishing.
—Pig Pickin', 0 vols. Greene, Stephanie. 2013. (Moose & Hildy Ser.: 3). (ENG.). 68p. (J). (gr. -1-3). pap. 9.99 *(978-1-4778-1684-4(4)*, 9781477816844, Two Lions) Amazon Publishing.
—The Runaway Egg (Sesame Street) Kleinberg, Naomi. 2018. (Pictureback(R) Ser.). (ENG.). 24p. (J). (gr. -1-2). pap. 6.99 *(978-1-5247-6905-5(3)*, Random Hse. Bks. for Young Readers) Random Hse. Children's Bks.
—Sesame Street 5-Minute Stories (Sesame Street) 2017. (ENG.). 160p. (J). (gr. -1-2). 12.99 *(978-1-5247-1989-0(7)*, Random Hse. Bks. for Young Readers) Random Hse. Children's Bks.
—The Sesame Street Dictionary (Sesame Street) Over 1,300 Words & Their Meanings Inside! Hayward, Linda. 2004. (ENG.). 256p. (J). (gr. -1-2). 24.99 *(978-0-375-82810-2(9)*, Random Hse. Bks. for Young Readers) Random Hse. Children's Bks.
—Sesame Street: Guess Who, Easter Elmo! Mitter, Matt. 2nd ed. 2018. (Guess Who! Book Ser.). (ENG.). 10p. (J). (gr. -1-k). 10.99 *(978-0-7944-4197-5(1)*, Reader's Digest Children's Bks.) Studio Fun International.
—The Show-Off, 0 vols. Greene, Stephanie. 2013. (Moose & Hildy Ser.: 4). (ENG.). 64p. (J). (gr. 1-4). pap. 9.99 *(978-1-4778-1686-8(0)*, 9781477816868, Two Lions) Amazon Publishing.
—Too Many Cats. Houran, Lori Haskins. 2009. (Step into Reading: Step 1 Ser.). (ENG.). 32p. (J). (gr. -1-1). lib. bdg. 16.19 *(978-0-375-95197-8(0))* Random House Publishing Group.
—Too Many Cats. Houran, Lori Haskins. 2009. (Step into Reading Ser.). (ENG.). 32p. (J). (gr. -1-1). pap. 4.99 *(978-0-375-85197-1(6)*, Random Hse. Bks. for Young Readers) Random Hse. Children's Bks.
—The Tooth Book. Seuss, Dr. 2017. (Big Bright & Early Board Book Ser.). 24p. (J). (— 1). bds. 6.99 *(978-0-553-53864-9(0)*, Random Hse. Bks. for Young Readers) Random Hse. Children's Bks.
—The Tooth Book. Seuss. 2003. (Bright & Early Board Books(TM) Ser.). (ENG.). 24p. (J). (— 1). bds. 4.99 *(978-0-375-82492-0(8)*, Random Hse. Bks. for Young Readers) Random Hse. Children's Bks.
—We're Different, We're the Same (Sesame Street) Kates, Bobbi. 2017. (ENG.). 40p. (J). (gr. -1-2). 9.99 *(978-1-5247-7056-3(6)*, Random Hse. Bks. for Young Readers) Random Hse. Children's Bks.
—Who Are the People in Your Neighborhood? Kleinberg, Naomi. 2009. (ENG.). 14p. (J). (gr. k — 1). bds. 7.99 *(978-0-375-85138-4(0)*, Random Hse. Bks. for Young Readers) Random Hse. Children's Bks.
—Who's Afraid of Monsters? (Sesame Street) Tillworth, Mary. 2016. (Pictureback(R) Ser.). (ENG.). 24p. (J). (gr. -1-2). 5.99 *(978-1-101-93840-9(4)*, Random Hse. Bks. for Young Readers) Random Hse. Children's Bks.
Mathieu, Joe & Ruiz, Aristides. Tree's Company. Golden Books Staff. 2011. (ENG.). 12p. (J). (gr. -1-2). 6.99 *(978-0-375-86559-6(4)*, Golden Bks.) Random Hse. Children's Bks.
Mathieu, Joe, jt. illus. see Ruiz, Aristides.
Mathieu, Joe, jt. illus. see Urbanovic, Jackie.
Mathieu, Joseph, jt. illus. see Ruiz, Aristides.
Mathieu, Middy. I Love Ladybugs! Fisher, Meaghan. 2012. 16p. pap. 6.99 *(978-1-938768-00-2(0))* Gypsy Pubns.
—What Would You Do If You Were Left at the Zoo? Hand, Renne. 2012. 24p. pap. 8.99 *(978-1-938768-06-4(X))* Gypsy Pubns.
Mathieu, Sue. Sesame Street Elmo's Favorite Places. Monica, Carol. 2017. (Lift-The-Flap Ser.). (ENG.). 10p. (J). (gr. -1-k). 11.99 *(978-0-7944-4059-6(2))* Studio Fun International.
Mathis, Leslie. Be Satisfied with Who You Are. Fyne, Olga M. 2013. 24p. pap. 9.99 *(978-1-61286-142-5(3))* Avid Readers Publishing Group.
—The Bedtime of the Sky & Other Sleepy-Bye Stories. Wolfe, Carolyn. 2010. 32p. pap. 11.25 *(978-1-935105-57-2(4))* Avid Readers Publishing Group.
—Coyotebat. Hazelwood, K. D. 2010. 68p. pap. 14.99 *(978-1-935105-52-7(3))* Avid Readers Publishing Group.
—Dollygal, Peacock, & the Serpent. Darlene, Cannon. 2011. 108p. pap. 19.95 *(978-1-61286-001-5(X))* Avid Readers Publishing Group.
—Fluffy, a Puppy with a Purpose. Patterson, Eric. 2013. 146p. pap. 6.99 *(978-1-61286-150-0(4))* Avid Readers Publishing Group.
—The Unhappy Little Dragon: Lessons Begin. Wolfe, Carolyn. 2009. 38p. pap. 12.99 *(978-1-935105-42-8(6))* Avid Readers Publishing Group.
Mathis, Shawn. My First Ubie the Ubinator Coloring Book: Alphabet Wonders. Robert, Robert Lee. 2017. (Alphabet Wonders Ser.: Vol. 1). (ENG.). (J). pap. 9.99 *(978-0-9986232-1-4(0))* Rolest P. Inc.
—My First Ubie the Ubinator Coloring Book: Wonders of Numbers. Styles, Robert. 2017. (Wonders of Numbers Ser.: Vol. 1). (ENG.). (J). pap. 9.99 *(978-0-9986232-0-7(2))* Rolest P. Inc.
Mathis, Teresa, jt. illus. see Tom, Darcy.
Mathur, Vinita. Biscotti Moon. Gray Palmer, Victoria. 2019. (ENG.). 32p. (J). (gr. k-2). 19.50 ***(978-1-5439-3873-9(6))*** Surfside Six Publishing.
Mathy, Vincent. Boo! Scared You! Includes 10 Big & Scary Flaps. Babin, Stephanie. 2019. (Big Flaps Ser.: 2). (ENG.). 22p. (J). (gr. -1 — 1). 14.99 *(978-2-408-01281-6(3))* Éditions Tourbillon FRA. Dist: Hachette Bk. Group.
—Colors Matching Game Book: 4 Activities In 1! Babin, Stéphanie. 2020. (Matching Game Bks.: 3). (ENG.). 12p. (J). (gr. -1-k). bds. 16.99 *(978-2-408-01614-2(2))* Éditions Tourbillon FRA. Dist: Hachette Bk. Group.
—Ha-Ha! Made You Laugh! Includes 10 Big & Funny Flaps. Babin, Stephanie. 2019. (Big Flaps Ser.: 1). (ENG.). 22p. (J). (gr. -1-k). 14.99 *(978-2-408-00795-9(X))* Éditions Tourbillon FRA. Dist: Hachette Bk. Group.
—Who's Hiding with Penguin? 2016. (ENG.). 10p. (J). (gr. -1 — 1). bds. 8.99 *(978-1-4521-5661-3(1))* Chronicle Bks. LLC.
—Who's Hiding with Tiger? 2016. (ENG.). 10p. (J). (gr. -1 — 1). bds. 8.99 *(978-1-4521-5662-0(X))* Chronicle Bks. LLC.
Matic, Jaclyn. My New Friend, Squatchette: A True Story As Told to Robert E. Wood. Wood, Robert E. 2018. (ENG.). 36p. (J). *(978-1-5255-2215-4(9))*; pap. *(978-1-5255-2216-1(7))* FriesenPress.
Matijasevich, Astrid. Big Bill's Bed. Eggleton, Jill. 2003. (Rigby Sails Early Ser.). (ENG.). 16p. (gr. 1-2). pap. 6.95 *(978-0-7578-8731-4(7))* Houghton Mifflin Harcourt Publishing Co.
—Flea & Big Bill. Eggleton, Jill. 2003. (Rigby Sails Early Ser.). (ENG.). 16p. (gr. 1-2). pap. 6.95 *(978-0-7578-8722-2(8))* Houghton Mifflin Harcourt Publishing Co.
—Flea Goes Out! Eggleton, Jill. 2003. (Rigby Sails Early Ser.). (ENG.). 16p. (gr. 1-2). pap. 6.95 *(978-0-7578-8737-6(6))* Houghton Mifflin Harcourt Publishing Co.
Matine, Laura. The Upside-Down Fish. Louise, Kate. 2015. 32p. (J). (gr. -1-k). 16.95 *(978-1-62914-628-7(5)*, Sky Pony Pr.) Skyhorse Publishing Co., Inc.
Matiuzzo, Nick. Noise in the Night. Sullivan-Ringe, Laurie. 2008. 37p. pap. 24.95 *(978-1-60672-476-7(2))* America Star Bks.
Matje, Martin. Stuart Goes to School. Pennypacker, Sara. 2005. (ENG.). 64p. (J). (gr. -1-3). reprint ed. pap. 5.99 *(978-0-439-30183-1(1))* Scholastic, Inc.
Matkovich, Gregory. Red, 1 vol. Lloyd, Ashley. 2009. 19p. pap. 24.95 *(978-1-61546-913-0(3))* PublishAmerica, Inc.
Matlashevsky, Angela. God's Plan Under the Cherry Tree. Kloster, Bonnie Louise. l.t. ed. 2019. (ENG.). 16p. (J). (gr. k-3). pap. 9.95 ***(978-1-61633-987-6(X))*** Guardian Angel Publishing, Inc.
Matlashevsky, Angela. My Super Family: A Book for Blended Families. Orchard, Heather. 2018. (Healing Hearts Ser.: Vol. 1). (ENG.). 36p. (J). (gr. k-4). pap. 14.99 *(978-0-692-18461-5(9))* Healing Heart's Publishing Co.
Matlashevsky, Angela. What's My Angle? Kloster, Bonnie Louise. l.t. ed. 2019. (ENG.). 20p. (J). (gr. k-3). pap. 10.95 ***(978-1-61633-995-1(0))*** Guardian Angel Publishing, Inc.
—Yellowstone Yeti: Case of the Gushless Geyser. Vroom, Craig. 2019. (Lucky Penny Detective Adventures Ser.: Vol. 2). (ENG.). 46p. (J). pap. 14.95 ***(978-1-6778-2725-1(4))*** Independently Published.
Mato. Pokémon Adventures (Gold & Silver), Vol. 9. Kusaka, Hidenori. 2010. (Pokemon Ser.: 9). (ENG.). 224p. (J). pap. 9.99 *(978-1-4215-3062-8(7))* Viz Media.
—Pokémon Adventures (Red & Blue), Vol. 1. Kusaka, Hidenori. 2nd ed. 2009. (Pokemon Ser.: 1). (ENG.). 200p. (J). pap. 9.99 *(978-1-4215-3054-3(6))* Viz Media.
—Pokémon Adventures (Red & Blue), Vol. 2. Kusaka, Hidenori. 2nd ed. 2009. (Pokemon Ser.: 2). (ENG.). 200p. (J). pap. 9.99 *(978-1-4215-3055-0(4))* Viz Media.
—Pokémon Adventures (Red & Blue), Vol. 3. Kusaka, Hidenori. 2nd ed. 2009. (Pokemon Ser.: 3). (ENG.). 240p. (J). pap. 9.99 *(978-1-4215-3056-7(2))* Viz Media.
—Pokémon Adventures (Red & Blue), Vol. 4. Kusaka, Hidenori. 2nd ed. 2009. (Pokemon Ser.: 4). (ENG.). 216p. (J). pap. 9.99 *(978-1-4215-3057-4(0))* Viz Media.
—Pokémon Adventures (Red & Blue), Vol. 5. Kusaka, Hidenori. 2nd ed. 2010. (Pokemon Ser.: 5). (ENG.). 208p. (J). pap. 9.99 *(978-1-4215-3058-1(9))* Viz Media.
—Pokémon Adventures (Red & Blue), Vol. 6. Kusaka, Hidenori. 2nd ed. 2010. (Pokemon Ser.: 6). (ENG.). 208p. (J). pap. 9.99 *(978-1-4215-3059-8(7))* Viz Media.
—Pokémon Adventures (Red & Blue), Vol. 7. Kusaka, Hidenori. 2nd ed. 2010. (Pokemon Ser.: 7). (ENG.). 200p. (J). pap. 9.99 *(978-1-4215-3060-4(0))* Viz Media.
Matoh, Sanami. Fake, 7 vols. Matoh, Sanami. rev. ed. 2003. 192p. Vol. 3. pap. 9.99 *(978-1-59182-328-5(5))*; Vol. 4. pap. 9.99 *(978-1-59182-329-2(3))* TOKYOPOP, Inc.
—Fake, 7 vols., Vol. 5. Matoh, Sanami. Rymer, Nan, tr. from JPN. rev. ed. 2004. 192p. pap. 9.99 *(978-1-59182-330-8(7))* TOKYOPOP, Inc.
Matoso, Madalena. At Our House. Minhós Martins, Isabel & Minhós Martins, Isabel. 2013. (ENG.). 28p. 12.95 *(978-1-84976-049-2(7))* Tate Publishing, Ltd. GBR. Dist: Hachette Bk. Group.
—Lines, Squiggles, Letters, Words. Rocha, Ruth. 2016. 40p. (J). (gr. -1-k). 16.95 *(978-1-59270-208-4(2))* Enchanted Lion Bks., LLC.
—What's That Noise? Martins, Isabel Minhós & Martins, Isabel Minhós. 2016. (ENG.). 40p. (J). (gr. -1-2). 19.95 *(978-1-84976-429-2(8))* Tate Publishing, Ltd. GBR. Dist: Hachette Bk. Group.
—When I Was Born. Martins, Isabel Minhós & Martins, Isabel Minhós. 2011. (ENG.). 32p. (gr. -1-3). 12.95 *(978-1-85437-958-0(5))* Tate Publishing, Ltd. GBR. Dist: Hachette Bk. Group.
Matricardi, Luca. Frank the Skunk. Mounts, Samia. 2008. (ENG.). 150p. (J). (gr. 4-6). pap. 9.95 *(978-0-9798841-0-8(1))* 4N Publishing LLC.
Matsick, Anni. The Boy Who Opened Our Eyes. Sussman, Elaine. 2017. 38p. (J). *(978-1-68265-353-1(6))* Sussman Sales Co.
Matson, Kurt. Mother, I'm Bored! Hummel, Michelle. 2019. (ENG.). 26p. (J). pap. 9.99 *(978-1-0908-9399-4(X))* Independently Published.
Matson, Laurie. Jaz-O & 'G' in Key West. Matson, Laurie. l.t. ed. 2003. (J). 4.95 *(978-0-9673704-5-3(0))* Seastory Pr.
Matsoureff, Atanas. The Lost Island. Johnson, E. Pauline & Johnson-Tekahionwake, E. Pauline. 2004. (ENG.). 40p. (J). (gr. -1-3). 16.95 *(978-1-894965-07-1(8))* Simply Read Bks. CAN. Dist: Ingram Publisher Services.
Matsubuchi, Akemi, photos by. What Grows Here? Indoors: Favorite Houseplants for Every Situation, 1 vol. Hole, Jim. rev. ed. 2007. (What Grows Here? Ser.: 4). (ENG., 288p. per. 18.95 *(978-1-894728-06-5(8)*, e6b2957c-c11f-478b-aec3-2020aa1e62f1) Hole's Greenhouses & Gardens, Ltd. CAN. Dist: Lone Pine Publishing USA.
Matsuhashi, Toshimitsu, photos by. Life-Size Aquarium. Komiya, Teruyuki. 2010. (ENG., 48p. (gr. -1-2). 18.95 *(978-1-934734-59-9(4))* Seven Footer Pr.
Matsumoto, Nina. Sparks!, Bk. 1. Boothby, Ian. 2018. (ENG.). 192p. (J). (gr. 2-5). 24.99 *(978-1-338-02947-5(9))*; pap. 12.99 *(978-1-338-02946-8(0))* Scholastic, Inc. (Graphix).
Matsunaga, Judd. King's Kids Coloring Book. Fleming, Jesse, photos by. Date not set. (SPA.). 32p. (J). *(978-0-9703880-4-9(7))* King's Kids Trading Cards, Inc.
Matsunaga, Judd & Fleming, Jesse. King's Kids Coloring Book. Date not set. 32p. (J). *(978-0-9703880-3-2(9))* King's Kids Trading Cards, Inc.
Matsuoka, Mei. The Great Balloon Hullaballoo. Bently, Peter. 2014. (ENG.). 32p. (J). (gr. -1-3). 16.95 *(978-1-4677-3449-3(7)*, 9781467734493) Lerner Publishing Group.
—The Great Dog Bottom Swap. Bently, Peter. 2011. (ENG.). 32p. (J). (gr. -1-k). pap. 12.99 *(978-1-84270-988-7(7))* Andersen Pr. GBR. Dist: Independent Pubs. Group.
—The Great Sheep Shenanigans. Bently, Peter. 2012. (Andersen Press Picture Bks). (ENG.). 32p. (J). (gr. -1-3). 16.95 *(978-0-7613-8990-3(3))* Lerner Publishing Group.
Matsuoka, Tatsuhide. Jump! Matsuoka, Tatsuhide. 2019. (ENG.). 36p. (J). (gr. -1-1). bds. 12.99 *(978-1-77657-231-1(9))* Gecko Pr. NZL. Dist: Lerner Publishing Group.
Matsuoka, Yasushi. Papa Surfs: A Children's Book about What Surfing Teaches You. Popescu, George Alex. 2019. (ENG.). 32p. (J). pap. 9.99 *(978-1-7946-1246-4(7))* Independently Published.
Matsuoka, Yoko. If Chocolate Were Purple. Barton, Jen. gif. ed. 2013. (ENG.). 28p. (J). pap., instr.'s hndbk. ed. 10.89 *(978-0-615-78343-7(0)*, Flickerfawn) Barton Bks.
Matsuzawa, Yoji, photos by. Gensundai Suizokukan. Sakanakun. 2010. (JPN., 48p. (J). *(978-4-09-217253-1(2))* Shogakukan.
Matta, Gabriella & Legramandi, Francesco. I Am a Princess (Disney Princess) Posner-Sanchez, Andrea. 2012. (Little Golden Book Ser.). (ENG.). 24p. (J). (gr. k-k). 4.99 *(978-0-7364-2906-1(9)*, Golden/Disney) Random Hse. Children's Bks.
—The Imaginary Okapi (Disney Junior: the Lion Guard) Katschke, Judy. 2017. (Little Golden Book Ser.). (ENG.). 24p. (J). (-k). 4.99 *(978-0-7364-3719-6(3)*, Golden/Disney) Random Hse. Children's Bks.
—The Sweetest Spring. Jordan, Apple. 2008. (Step into Reading Ser.). (ENG.). 32p. (J). (gr. k-3). pap. 3.99 *(978-0-375-84810-0(X)*, RH/Disney) Random Hse. Children's Bks.
Matta, Gabriella, jt. illus. see Laguna, Fabio.
Matta, Gabriella, jt. illus. see Legramandi, Francesco.
Matta, Gabriella, jt. illus. see Random House Disney Staff.
Mattassi, Ezio. Pepito the Penguin, 1 vol. Mattassi, Ezio. 2009. 15p. pap. 24.95 *(978-1-61582-731-2(5))* PublishAmerica, Inc.
Matter, Philippe. Cherche et Trouve Mini-Loup. 2010. (Mini-Loup Ser.: Vol. 2258408). (FRE.). (J). *(978-2-01-225840-2(9))* Hachette Jeunesse.
Mattes-Ruggiero, Lynn. Where Did Grandma Go? Scanlon, Cara. 2008. (J). *(978-1-930596-85-6(5))* Amherst Pr.
—Where Did Grandpa Go? Scanlon, Cara. 2008. (J). *(978-1-930596-86-3(3))* Amherst Pr.
Matteson, Angela. Grumbles from the Town: Mother-Goose Voices with a Twist. Yolen, Jane & Dotlich, Rebecca Kai. 2016. (ENG.). 40p. (J). (gr. k-4). 17.95 *(978-1-59078-922-3(9)*, Wordsong) Boyds Mills Pr.
—In the Middle of the Night: Poems from a Wide-Awake House. Salas, Laura Purdie. 2019. (ENG.). 32p. (J). (gr. -1-3). 17.95 *(978-1-62091-630-8(4)*, Wordsong) Boyds Mills Pr.
Matthes, Justice. The Red Sock Christmas. Frazier, Kelly. 2008. 25p. pap. 24.95 *(978-1-60610-704-1(6))* America Star Bks.
Mattheson, Jenny. The Great Tulip Trade. Brust, Beth Wagner. 2005. (Step into Reading Ser.). 48p. (J). (gr. 1-3). 11.65 *(978-0-7569-5160-3(7))* Perfection Learning Corp.
—The Great Tulip Trade. Brust, Beth Wagner. 2005. (Step into Reading Ser.: Vol. 3). (ENG.). 48p. (J). (gr. k-3). pap. 4.99 *(978-0-375-82573-6(8)*, Random Hse. Bks. for Young Readers) Random Hse. Children's Bks.
—No Bows!, 1 vol. Duke, Shirley Smith. 2006. (ENG.). 32p. (J). (gr. k-1). 15.95 *(978-1-56145-356-6(0))* Peachtree Publishing Co. Inc.
Matthew, Hughes. Billy Beechum & the Hooticat's Secret. McNair, Mike. 2016. (Billy Beechum Trilogy Ser.: Vol. 1). (ENG.). (J). (gr. 3-5). pap. 14.99 *(978-1-940310-52-7(0))* 4RV Pub.
Matthews, Amanda L. Bailey Becomes a Therapy Dog. Rivera, Lorna A. 2019. (ENG.). 26p. (J). (gr. k-4). 19.99 ***(978-0-578-51929-6(1))*** Lorna A Rivera.
Matthews, Ashley. Maya Visits a Hospital: Love is the Best Medicine, 110 vols. Bucki, Jo Dee & O'Malley, John. Hicks, Mindy, ed. l.t. ed. 2007. 32p. (J). per. 4.95 *(978-0-9769069-0-2(2))* TAOH Inspired Education, LLC.
Matthews, Bonnie. Blue Cheese Breath & Stinky Feet: How to Deal with Bullies. DePino, Catherine S. 2004. 48p. (J). 14.95 *(978-1-59147-111-0(7))*; pap. 9.95 *(978-1-59147-112-7(5))* American Psychological Assn. (Magination Pr.).
—What to Do When Bad Habits Take Hold: A Kid's Guide to Overcoming Nail Biting & More. Huebner, Dawn. 2008. 72p. (J). (gr. 6-12). pap. 15.95 *(978-1-4338-0383-3(6)*, Magination Pr.) American Psychological Assn.
—What to Do When You Dread Your Bed: A Kid's Guide to Overcoming Problems with Sleep. Huebner, Dawn. 2008. (What to Do Guides for Kids Ser.). 96p. (J). (gr. 1-7). per. 15.95 *(978-1-4338-0318-5(6)*, Magination Pr.) American Psychological Assn.
—What to Do When You Grumble Too Much: A Kid's Guide to Overcoming Negativity. Huebner, Dawn. 2006. ("What to Do" Guides for Kids Ser.). 88p. (J). (gr. 4-7). per. 15.95 *(978-1-59147-450-0(7)*, Magination Pr.) American Psychological Assn.
—What to Do When Your Brain Gets Stuck: A Kid's Guide to Overcoming Ocd. Huebner, Dawn. 2007. 96p. (J). (gr. 3-7). per. 15.95 *(978-1-59147-805-8(7)*, Magination Pr.) American Psychological Assn.
—What to Do When Your Temper Flares: A Kid's Guide to Overcoming Problems with Anger. Huebner, Dawn. 2007. (What-to-Do Guides for Kids Ser.). 88p. (J). (gr. 3-7). per. 15.95 *(978-1-4338-0134-1(5)*, 4418005, Magination Pr.) American Psychological Assn.
Matthews, Derek. God Made Animals. Taylor, Jane & Macleod, Una. 2015. (Board Books God Made Ser.). (ENG.). 16p. (J). bds. 3.99 *(978-1-85792-290-5(5)*, 956bfda0-ce0e-4f33-bbf4-6a8a1be7b0a7) Christian Focus Pubns. GBR. Dist: Baker & Taylor Publisher Services (BTPS).
—God Made Me. Taylor, Jane & Macleod, Una. 2015. (Board Books God Made Ser.). (ENG.). 16p. (J). bds. 3.99 *(978-1-85792-289-9(1)*, aa8240de-b6fd-423b-9e26-ed9d90883b58) Christian Focus Pubns. GBR. Dist: Baker & Taylor Publisher Services (BTPS).
—Snappy Little Halloween. Steer, Dugald A. 2004. 20p. (J). (gr. k-4). reprint ed. 13.00 *(978-0-7567-7403-5(9))* DIANE Publishing Co.
Matthews, Elizabeth. Different Like Coco. Matthews, Elizabeth. 2007. 40p. (J). (gr. k-4). 16.99 *(978-0-7636-2548-1(5))* Candlewick Pr.
Matthews, Jenny, photos by. Living in Bangladesh. Thomson, Ruth. 2006. (Living In- Ser.). 32p. (J). (gr. 4-7). lib. bdg. 27.10 *(978-1-59771-045-9(8))* Sea-To-Sea Pubns.
Matthews, Jenny, photos by. Children Growing up with War. Matthews, Jenny. 2014. (ENG., 48p. (J). (gr. 5). 17.99 *(978-0-7636-6942-3(3))* Candlewick Pr.
Matthews, Joe. Stickmen's Guide to Engineering. Farndon, John. 2018. (Stickmen's Guides to STEM Ser.). (ENG.). 32p. (J). (gr. 3-6). lib. bdg. 27.99 *(978-1-5415-0061-7(X)*, Hungry Tomato ®) Lerner Publishing Group.
—Stickmen's Guide to Math. Farndon, John. 2018. (Stickmen's Guides to STEM Ser.). (ENG.). 32p. (J). (gr. 3-6). lib. bdg. 27.99 *(978-1-5415-0062-4(8)*, Hungry Tomato ®) Lerner Publishing Group.
—Stickmen's Guide to Science. Farndon, John. 2018. (Stickmen's Guides to STEM Ser.). (ENG.). 32p. (J). (gr. 3-6). lib. bdg. 27.99 *(978-1-5415-0059-4(8)*, Hungry Tomato ®) Lerner Publishing Group.
—Stickmen's Guide to Technology. Farndon, John. 2018. (Stickmen's Guides to STEM Ser.). (ENG.). 32p. (J). (gr. 3-6). lib. bdg. 27.99 *(978-1-5415-0060-0(1)*, Hungry Tomato ®) Lerner Publishing Group.
Matthews, John. The Everyday Easter Dress. Matthews, Elli. 2011. 24p. pap. 24.95 *(978-1-4560-9411-9(4))* America Star Bks.
Matthews, Kelly & Matthews, Nichole. Just Beyond: the Scare School. Stine, R. L. 2019. (Just Beyond Ser.). (ENG.). 144p. (J). pap. 9.99 *(978-1-68415-416-6(2))* Boom! Studios.
—Pandora's Legacy. Leopard, Bones. 2018. (ENG.). 112p. (J). pap. 9.99 *(978-1-68415-287-2(9))* Boom! Studios.
Matthews, Kelly & Matthews, Nichole. Volume 1: the Scare School. Stine, R.I. 2020. (Just Beyond Ser.). (ENG.). 28p. (J). (gr. 4-8). lib. bdg. 28.50 ***(978-1-5321-4489-9(X)***, 35218, Graphic Novels) Spotlight.
—Volume 2: a Strange Discovery. Stine, R.I. 2020. (Just Beyond Ser.). (ENG.). 28p. (J). (gr. 4-8). lib. bdg. 28.50 ***(978-1-5321-4490-5(3)***, 35219, Graphic Novels) Spotlight.
—Volume 3: a Monster's Lunch. Stine, R.I. 2020. (Just Beyond Ser.). (ENG.). 28p. (J). (gr. 4-8). lib. bdg. 28.50 ***(978-1-5321-4491-2(1)***, 35220, Graphic Novels) Spotlight.
—Volume 4: No Escape. Stine, R.I. 2020. (Just Beyond Ser.). (ENG.). 24p. (J). (gr. 4-8). lib. bdg. 28.50 ***(978-1-5321-4492-9(X)***, 35221, Graphic Novels) Spotlight.
Matthews, Melanie. Circus Train, 0 vols. Judd, Jennifer Cole. 2015. (ENG.). 24p. (J). (gr. -1-2). 14.99 *(978-1-4778-2634-8(3)*, 9781477826348, Two Lions) Amazon Publishing.
—Merry Christmas, Santa Claus! Coppage, J. L. 2018. 16p. (J). (-k). bds. 6.99 *(978-1-5247-8782-0(5)*, Grosset & Dunlap) Penguin Young Readers Group.

—Trick or Treat on My Street. Coppage, J. L. 2017. 16p. (J). (-k). bds. 6.99 *(978-0-515-15975-2(1),* Grosset & Dunlap) Penguin Young Readers Group.

Matthews, Nichole, jt. illus. see Matthews, Kelly.

Matthews, Rodney. Greek & Norse Legends. 2004. (Myths & Legends Ser.). 112p. (J). (gr. 6). lib. bdg. 20.95 *(978-1-58086-603-3(4))* EDC Publishing.

—Greek Myths & Legends. Evans, Cheryl & Millard, Anne. 2006. (Myths & Legends Ser.). 64p. (J). (gr. 6). lib. bdg. 18.95 *(978-1-58086-553-1(4))* EDC Publishing.

—Tales of King Arthur. rev. ed. 2007. (Usborne Classics Retold Ser.). 139p. (J). (gr. 4-7). per. 4.99 *(978-0-7945-1483-9(9),* Usborne) EDC Publishing.

Matthews, W. Fairy Tales from Spain: [illustrated Edition]. Escomez, J. Munoz. 2019. (ENG.). 152p. (J). (gr. k-4). pap. *(978-605-7876-37-9(7))* Uhrayoglu, Murat E Kitap Projesi.

Matthews, W. Fairy Tales from Spain: [illustrated Edition]. Escomez, J. Munoz. 2019. (ENG.). 152p. (J). (gr. k-4). ***(978-605-7748-58-4(1))*** Uhrayoglu, Murat E Kitap Projesi.

Matthews, Wendy Mary. The Feather. Matthews, Wendy Mary. 2019. (ENG.). 30p. (J). (gr. 2-4). *(978-0-473-45181-3(6))* Wendy Matthews Bks.

Mattotti, Lorenzo. Hansel & Gretel. Gaiman, Neil. 2014. (ENG.). (J). (gr. 2-7). 56p. 16.95 *(978-1-935179-62-7(4));* 60p. 29.95 *(978-1-935179-65-8(9))* TOON Books / RAW Junior, LLC.

Mattozzi, Patricia. Santa's Prayer. Andes, Mary Lou. 2007. (J). (gr. -1-k). bds. 11.95 incl. cd-rom *(978-0-8198-7100-8(1))* Pauline Bks. & Media.

—Stations of the Cross for Children. Will, Julianne M. 2005. 32p. (J). (gr. -1-3). pap. 3.95 *(978-1-59276-153-1(4))* Our Sunday Visitor, Publishing Div.

Mattozzi, Patricia R. The Jesus Garden: An Easter Legend. Bosco, Antoinette. 2004. 44p. (J). 14.95 *(978-0-8198-3979-4(5),* 332-155) Pauline Bks. & Media.

—Little Book of Saints, 2 bks. Muldoon, Kathleen M. 2005. 24p. (J). Vol. 2. pap. 3.95 *(978-0-8198-4511-5(6),* 332-187); Vol. I. pap. 3.95 *(978-0-8198-4510-8(8),* 332-186) Pauline Bks. & Media.

Mattozzi, Patricia R. & Kinarney, Tom. My First Book of Saints. Muldoon, Kathleen M. & Wallace, Susan Helen. 2012. 128p. (J). 12.95 *(978-0-8198-4917-5(0))* Pauline Bks. & Media.

Mattucci, Sandra. Levi the Lightning Bug's Amazing Discovery. Mattucci, Sandra. 2012. 36p. 19.99 *(978-1-936453-08-5(8))* Bezalel Bks.

Matulay, Laszlo. We Were There at the First Airplane Flight. Sutton, Felix. 2013. (ENG.). 192p. (J). (gr. 3-8). pap. 6.99 *(978-0-486-49258-2(3))* Dover Pubns., Inc.

—We Were There at the First Airplane Flight. Sutton, Felix & Loening, Grover. 2011. 194p. 42.95 *(978-1-258-09600-7(5))* Literary Licensing, LLC.

Matusic, Greg. The Elephant in the Room: A Lockdown Story. Stenard, Alicia Cyr. 2019. (ENG.). 32p. (J). (gr. k-2). 16.99 ***(978-1-7339929-6-1(0))*** St. Cyr Pr.

Matuszak, Dagmara. Julio César. Rebscher, Susanne. Schleper, Frank, tr. from GER. 2009. (SPA.). 32p. (YA). (gr. 5-18). *(978-84-263-7255-0(4))* Vives, Luis Editorial (Edelvives).

Matvienko, Valery. El Bañador de Colores de Jimena la Jirafita: Aprende Los Colores. Cuento para niños de 2 años. (Spanish Edition Large Print) Gutierrez, Pedro & Winn, Melissa. 2019. (SPA.). 38p. (J). pap. 9.99 *(978-1-0934-4595-4(5))* Independently Published.

—A Hug & a Kiss Is Every Baby's Bliss. un Beso y un Abrazo Es lo Que Necesita el Bebé: A Cute Bilingual Book for Toddlers English & Spanish Edition. Children's Book That Parents Love. Cuentos para Dormir. Cuento para niños de 2 años. Libro en Español. Gutierrez, Pedro. Yanez, Alfonso, ed. 2019. (ENG.). 42p. (J). pap. 9.99 *(978-1-0978-6170-5(8))* Independently Published.

Matyjaszek, Kasia. Black Beauty. Sewell, Anna & Ladybird Books Staff. 2015. (Ladybird Classics Ser.). 72p. (J). (gr. k-3). 10.99 *(978-1-4093-1124-9(4))* Penguin Bks., Ltd. GBR. Dist: Independent Pubs. Group.

—I Am Actually a Penguin. Taylor, Sean. 2018. (ENG.). 32p. (J). (-k). 16.99 *(978-1-5362-0278-6(9),* Templar) Candlewick Pr.

—This Bonny Baby: A Mirror Board Book, 96 vols. 2017. (ENG.). 12p. (J). 9.95 *(978-1-78250-465-8(6),* Kelpies) Floris Bks. GBR. Dist: Consortium Bk. Sales & Distribution.

Matyschenko, Tanya. Frogs by the Dozen. Bollen, Christine. l.t. ed. 2006. 24p. (J). per. 9.99 *(978-1-59879-115-0(X))* Lifevest Publishing, Inc.

Matyuschenko, Tanya. An Angel in My Garden, 1 vol. Bollen, Christina. 2009. 47p. pap. 24.95 *(978-1-60813-661-2(2))* America Star Bks.

—Flying with the Geese, 1 vol. Bollen, Christine. 2010. 34p. 24.95 *(978-1-4489-4401-9(5))* PublishAmerica, Inc.

Matzen, Deon C. Chipper, the Heroic Chipmunk. Martin, Martha M. 2004. 32p. (J). (gr. -1-3). 16.95 *(978-0-9758580-0-4(9))* M & B Publishing.

Mauchline, Sarah. Posie Pixie & the Copper Kettle. Hill, Sarah. O'Gorman, Sarah, ed. 2013. 52p. pap. *(978-1-909302-20-4(1))* Abela Publishing.

—Posie Pixie & the Lost Matchbox. Hill, Sarah. O'Gorman, Sarah, ed. 2013. 60p. pap. *(978-1-909302-31-0(7))* Abela Publishing.

Maunder, Brian. Polly's Little Kite. Maunder, Brian. 2014. (ENG.). 44p. (J). (gr. -1-3). pap. 11.95 *(978-1-56548-528-0(9))* New City Press of the Focolare.

Maununen, Irina. The Rabbit Who Wants to Fall Asleep: A New Way of Getting Children to Sleep. Ehrlin, Carl-Johan Forssén. 2015. (ENG.). 32p. (J). (gr. -1-2). 15.99 *(978-0-399-55413-1(0),* Crown Books For Young Readers) Random Hse. Children's Bks.

Maurel, Aude. Who Left the Light On? Marnier, Richard. Ramadan, Emma, tr. 2018. (ENG.). 30p. (J). (gr. -1-1). 21.99 *(978-1-63206-189-8(9))* Restless Bks.

Maurer, Ashley. Jennie Jenkins. 2015. (First Steps in Music Ser.). 32p. (J). (— 1). 17.95 *(978-1-62277-139-4(7))* G I A Pubns., Inc.

Maurey, Katty. David Jumps In. Woo, Alan. 2020. (ENG.). 32p. (J). (gr. -1-2). 17.99 *(978-1-77138-845-0(5))* Kids Can Pr., Ltd. CAN. Dist: Hachette Bk. Group.

—The Man Who Loved Libraries: The Story of Andrew Carnegie. Larsen, Andrew. 2017. (ENG.). 32p. (J). (gr. 1-5). 16.95 *(978-1-77147-267-8(7))* Owlkids Bks. Inc. CAN. Dist: Publishers Group West (PGW).

—The Specific Ocean. Maclear, Kyo. 2015. (ENG.). 32p. (J). (gr. -1-3). 17.95 *(978-1-894786-35-5(1))* Kids Can Pr., Ltd. CAN. Dist: Hachette Bk. Group.

Mauricet, et al. Crossovers. Rodi, Rob. 2003. (Crossovers Ser.: Vol. 1). 160p. (YA). pap. 15.95 *(978-1-931484-85-5(6))* CrossGeneration Comics, Inc.

Mauricet. The Vampire from the Marshes. Vanholme, Virginie. 2008. (Scared to Death Ser.: 1). (ENG.). 46p. pap. 11.95 *(978-1-905460-47-2(3))* CineBook GBR. Dist: National Bk. Network.

Mauricet, jt. illus. see Charm, Derek.

Mauro, Tony. Cold Case. Leonard, Julia Platt. 2011. (ENG.). 288p. (J). (gr. 3-7). 15.99 *(978-1-4424-2009-0(X),* Simon & Schuster/Paula Wiseman Bks.) Simon & Schuster/Paula Wiseman Bks.

Maurri, Marnie. Doodle Girl & the Monkey Mystery. Smith, Suzanne & Taylor, Lindsay. 2016. (ENG.). 32p. (J). pap. 9.99 *(978-1-4711-2318-4(9),* Simon & Schuster Children's) Simon & Schuster, Ltd. GBR. Dist: Simon & Schuster, Inc.

—Doodle Girl Summer Sticker Activity. Smith, Suzanne & Taylor, Lindsay. 2018. (ENG.). 24p. (J). 9.99 *(978-1-4711-2320-7(0),* Simon & Schuster Children's) Simon & Schuster, Ltd. GBR. Dist: Simon & Schuster, Inc.

—The Magical Ice Palace: A Doodle Girl Adventure. Smith, Suzanne & Taylor, Lindsay. 2018. (ENG.). 32p. (J). 9.99 *(978-1-4711-2319-1(7),* Simon & Schuster Children's) Simon & Schuster, Ltd. GBR. Dist: Simon & Schuster, Inc.

Maury, William. The Sisters Boxed Set: Vol. #1-3. Cazenove, Christophe. 2019. (Sisters Ser.). (ENG.). 288p. (J). pap. 29.99 *(978-1-5458-0132-1(0),* 900191731) Papercutz.

—Super Sisters. Cazenove, Christophe. 2020. (Sisters Ser.). (ENG.). 96p. (J). 14.99 *(978-1-62991-867-9(9),* 900185390); pap. 9.99 *(978-1-62991-866-2(0),* 900185391) Papercutz.

Maval Publishing Inc. Staff. Como el Viento Paso a Ser Tormenta. Hernandez, Mary L.Tr. of How the Tornado Got It's Wind. (SPA.). (J). (gr. -1-3). pap. 7.50 *(978-1-59134-015-7(2))* Maval Publishing, Inc.

Mavlian, Vatche. Spider-Man & Wolverine, 4 vols., Vol. 4. Matthews, Brett & Marvel Comics Staff. 2004. (Spider-Man Legends Ser.). 144p. (YA). pap. 13.99 *(978-0-7851-1297-6(9))* Marvel Worldwide, Inc.

Mavor, Salley. My Bed Rocks on the Water. Bond, Rebecca. 2020. (ENG.). 40p. (J). (gr. -1-3). 18.99 *(978-0-544-94906-5(4),* 1660320, HMH Books For Young Readers) Houghton Mifflin Harcourt Publishing Co.

Mavronis, Michelle. The Adventures of Rocky, Croaker & Spot. Gesser, Bernadette. 2008. 20p. pap. 24.95 *(978-1-60703-178-9(7))* America Star Bks.

Mawhinney, Art. Archie Babies. Kunkel, Mike. 2011. (Archie & Friends All-Stars Ser.: 11). (ENG.). 128p. (J). (gr. 2-5). pap. 9.95 *(978-1-879794-72-6(1))* Archie Comic Pubns., Inc.

—The Avengers. Harmening, Derek. 2018. (Look & Find Ser.). (ENG.). 24p. (J). *(978-1-5037-3405-0(6),* 4d723637-44b3-43b1-a2de-dbbb2191cb6c, p i kids) Phoenix International Publications, Inc.

—Diego Saves the Sloth! Romay, Alexis. 2007. (Go, Diego, Go! Ser.: 4). (ENG.). 24p. (J). (gr. -1-2). pap. 3.99 *(978-1-4169-3470-7(7),* Simon Spotlight/Nickelodeon) Simon Spotlight/Nickelodeon.

—Diego's Arctic Rescue. 2009. (Go, Diego, Go! Ser.). (ENG.). 24p. (J). (gr. -1-2). pap. 3.99 *(978-1-4169-8504-4(2),* Simon Spotlight/Nickelodeon) Simon Spotlight/Nickelodeon.

—Diego's Birthday Surprise. Bergen, Lara. 2008. (Go, Diego, Go! Ser.: 8). (ENG.). 24p. (J). (gr. -1-1). pap. 3.99 *(978-1-4169-5431-6(7),* Simon Spotlight/Nickelodeon) Simon Spotlight/Nickelodeon.

—Diego's Halloween Party. Lindner, Brooke. 2008. (Go, Diego, Go! Ser.). (ENG.). 16p. (J). (gr. -1-k). bds. 5.99 *(978-1-4169-5497-2(X),* Simon Spotlight/Nickelodeon) Simon Spotlight/Nickelodeon.

—Diego's Ocean Adventure: A Book of Facts about Ocean Animals. Sollinger, Emily. 2008. (Go, Diego, Go! Ser.). (ENG.). 16p. (J). (gr. -1-2). pap. 6.99 *(978-1-4169-4781-3(7),* Simon Spotlight/Nickelodeon) Simon Spotlight/Nickelodeon.

—Diego's Wolf Pup Rescue. 2006. (Go, Diego, Go! Ser.: 1). (ENG.). 24p. (J). (gr. -1-2). pap. 3.99 *(978-1-4169-1559-1(1),* Simon Spotlight/Nickelodeon) Simon Spotlight/Nickelodeon.

—Dinosaurs. 2011. 24p. (J). *(978-1-4508-3384-4(5))* Phoenix International Publications, Inc.

Mawhinney, Art, et al. Disney: Look & Find 4-Book Collection. 2019. (Look & Find Ser.). (ENG.). 96p. (J). *(978-1-5037-4204-8(0),* debb924e-3213-4407-b18e-9341aee70852, p i kids) Phoenix International Publications, Inc.

—Disney Frozen. 2020. (Look & Find Ser.). (ENG.). 96p. (J). *(978-1-5037-4822-4(7),* ca23b2a8-6fa8-4b0b-b44b-29baec8b6ce4, p i kids) Phoenix International Publications, Inc.

Mawhinney, Art. Disney Marvel Guardians of the Galaxy. 2018. (Look & Find Ser.). (ENG.). 24p. (J). *(978-1-5037-4505-6(8),* bdf17aa3-8535-404e-841c-c312cf6d7dde, p i kids) Phoenix International Publications, Inc.

—Disney Moana. 2016. (Look & Find Ser.). (ENG.). 24p. (J). *(978-1-5037-0790-0(3),* 4f4dad61-4ba2-4677-a5f8-7d9de086697c, p i kids) Phoenix International Publications, Inc.

—Disney Princess: Dream Big Princess. Wage, Erin Rose. 2018. (Look & Find Ser.). (ENG.). 24p. (J). *(978-1-5037-3570-5(2),* 67f97617-1466-47f4-b657-42bda77362b0, p i kids) Phoenix International Publications, Inc.

Mawhinney, Art, et al. Disney Princess: Enchanted Collection. Wage, Erin Rose & Wagner, Veronica, eds. 2019. (ENG.). 80p. (J). *(978-1-5037-5075-3(2),* 7611126d-cd3f-4482-bb72-4fe760e18dee, p i kids) Phoenix International Publications, Inc.

Mawhinney, Art. Disney Ralph Breaks the Internet. 2018. (Look & Find Ser.). (ENG.). 24p. (J). *(978-1-5037-3934-5(1),* f11552c0-5fc8-4c77-83cb-4d2946112344); *(978-1-5037-3651-1(2),* 41fb42ec-f302-46bb-8d88-e0f020e7e17a) Phoenix International Publications, Inc. (p i kids).

—Dora & Diego Help the Dinosaur. ed. 2011. (Dora & Diego Ser.). (ENG.). 24p. (J). pap. 3.99 *(978-1-4424-1400-6(6),* Simon Spotlight/Nickelodeon) Simon Spotlight/Nickelodeon.

—Dora & Diego to the Rescue! 2010. (Go, Diego, Go! Ser.). (ENG.). 48p. (J). pap. 5.99 *(978-1-4424-0660-5(7),* Simon Spotlight/Nickelodeon) Simon Spotlight/Nickelodeon.

Mawhinney, Art. DreamWorks Trolls. PI Kids. 2020. (Look & Find Ser.). (ENG.). 18p. (J). ***(978-1-5037-5468-3(5),*** e17391a9-d0d5-426b-bdcd-848d754b4404, p i kids) Phoenix International Publications, Inc.

—DreamWorks Trolls: Write-And-Erase Look & Find. PI Kids. 2020. (Look & Find Ser.). (ENG.). 20p. (J). ***(978-1-5037-5486-7(3),*** 025e5713-e112-41b5-981f-fbfa627300a8, p i kids) Phoenix International Publications, Inc.

—DreamWorks Trolls World Tour. 2020. (Look & Find Ser.). (ENG.). 24p. (J). ***(978-1-5037-5231-3(3),*** 73cd2bc2-cda3-4177-95e5-1a7c69338d8f, p i kids) Phoenix International Publications, Inc.

Mawhinney, Art. Frozen & Frozen 2. 2020. (Look & Find Ser.). (ENG.). 48p. (J). *(978-1-5037-4359-5(4),* 8f576cea-2b26-4939-93b4-6fb0e6bc675d, p i kids) Phoenix International Publications, Inc.

—Look & Find Disney Princess Worlds of Wonder. 2006. (Look & Find Books). (J). pap. 24.98 *(978-1-4127-6490-2(4))* Publications International, Ltd.

—Look & Find Open Season. 2007. 32p. (J). (gr. -1-3). lib. bdg. 7.98 *(978-1-4127-8889-2(7))* Publications International, Ltd.

—Marvel. 2016. (Look & Find Ser.). (ENG.). 24p. (J). *(978-1-5037-0696-5(6),* 04c7f56f-1f2e-4c21-8be5-c586c38c4b58, p i kids) Phoenix International Publications, Inc.

—Marvel: Best of Marvel. Harmening, Derek et al. 2019. (Look & Find Ser.). (ENG.). 48p. (J). *(978-1-5037-4789-0(1),* 5d44e654-918f-4ed1-abfc-38bc8e7f254b, p i kids) Phoenix International Publications, Inc.

—Marvel: Look & Find 4-Book Collection. Harmening, Derek & Beck, Riley. 2019. (Look & Find Ser.). (ENG.). 96p. (J). *(978-1-5037-4203-1(2),* 4de57b33-25a2-49ea-827e-e1c86e188896, p i kids) Phoenix International Publications, Inc.

—Marvel Spider-Man. Harmening, Derek. 2017. (Look & Find Ser.). (ENG.). 24p. (J). *(978-1-5037-1524-0(8),* 977c8916-5ca6-465d-ace6-367e24903fb5); *(978-1-5037-1523-3(X),* 0141f2c8-9804-4e21-be7d-0fe5ddf5aae7) Phoenix International Publications, Inc. (p i kids).

—Marvel Spider-Man: Web-Slinging Adventure. Harmening, Derek & Halpern, Rachel. 2019. (Look & Find Ser.). (ENG.). 16p. (J). bds. *(978-1-5037-4791-3(3),* ce34b134-4be9-4d63-832f-be5e5a0672fe, p i kids) Phoenix International Publications, Inc.

—Roadwork! Lagonegro, Melissa & Random House Disney Staff. 2008. (Step into Reading Ser.). (ENG.). 32p. (J). (gr. k-3). pap. 3.99 *(978-0-7364-2516-2(0),* RH/Disney) Random Hse. Children's Bks.

—Star Wars: the Force Awakens Search & Find. 2019. (Search & Find Ser.). (ENG.). 48p. (J). (gr. -1-k). 9.99 *(978-0-7944-4376-4(1),* Studio Fun International) Printers Row Publishing Group.

—Star Wars: the Last Jedi Search & Find. 2019. (Search & Find Ser.). (ENG.). 48p. (J). (gr. -1-k). 9.99 *(978-0-7944-4385-6(0),* Studio Fun International) Printers Row Publishing Group.

—Star Wars: the Last Jedi Search & Find Mass Market Edition. 2019. (Search & Find Ser.). (ENG.). 48p. (J). (gr. -1-k). 6.99 *(978-0-7944-4378-8(8),* Studio Fun International) Printers Row Publishing Group.

—Transformers. Burroughs, Caleb. 2007. (Look & Find (Publications International) Ser.). 16p. (J). (gr. -1-3). 7.98 *(978-1-4127-8673-7(8))* Publications International, Ltd.

—Trees for the Okapis: Little Green Nickelodeon. Aguirre, Jorge. 2010. (Go Diego Go! Ser.). (ENG.). 24p. (J). (gr. -1-1). 17.44 *(978-1-4169-9090-1(9))* Simon & Schuster, Inc.

Mawhinney, Art & Disney Storybook Art Team. Disney Frozen: Adventures on Ice. PI Kids. 2020. (ENG.). 80p. (J). ***(978-1-5037-5457-7(X),*** ef50d0c4-bdfe-41e3-a9df-1922e62d9051, p i kids) Phoenix International Publications, Inc.

Mawhinney, Art & Disney Storybook Artists Staff. Fairies. 2007. (Look & Find Ser.). 7.98 *(978-1-4127-7423-9(3))* Publications International, Ltd.

Mawhinney, Art & Roldan, Meg. Disney Incredibles 2. 2018. (Look & Find Ser.). (ENG.). 24p. (J). *(978-1-5037-3045-8(X),* 83720810-e30b-48b7-b9ad-b38cb37b5519, p i kids) Phoenix International Publications, Inc.

—The Incredibles 2. P. I. Kids Staff. 2018. (Look & Find Ser.). (ENG.). 24p. (J). *(978-1-5037-3044-1(1),* 529a997d-6410-407f-bee9-b25ebb1c8a64, p i kids) Phoenix International Publications, Inc.

Mawhinney, Art, jt. illus. see DiCicco, Sue.

Mawson. The Tales of Henry Tuffin - Henry's Sore Foot & a New Arrival. Adams, Keith. Hewitt, Geoff, ed. 2013. 20p. pap. *(978-1-78222-105-0(0))* Paragon Publishing, Rothersthorpe.

Mawson, Alan. The Tales of Henry Tuffin - Henry Goes to School. Adams, Keith. Hewitt, Geoff, ed. 2013. 20p. pap. *(978-1-78222-103-6(4))* Paragon Publishing, Rothersthorpe.

—The Tales of Henry Tuffin - Henry's Christmas. Adams, Keith. Geoff Hewitt, ed. 2013. 32p. pap. *(978-1-78222-172-2(7))* Paragon Publishing, Rothersthorpe.

—The Tales of Henry Tuffin - the Day the Light Went Out. Adams, Keith. Hewitt, Geoff, ed. 2013. 20p. pap. *(978-1-78222-104-3(2))* Paragon Publishing, Rothersthorpe.

Max. El Ruiseñor. Bailer, Darice et al. 2007. (SPA & ENG.). 28p. (J). *(978-0-545-03029-8(3))* Scholastic, Inc.

Max and Sid. Animal 123. 2015. (Tiny Touch Ser.). (ENG.). 12p. (J). (gr. -1 — 1). bds. 4.99 *(978-1-4998-0000-5(2))* Little Bee Books Inc.

—Animal Babies. Little Bee Books. 2015. (Tiny Touch Ser.). (ENG.). 12p. (J). (gr. -1 — 1). bds. 4.99 *(978-1-4998-0058-6(4))* Little Bee Books Inc.

—Animal Colors. Little Bee Books. 2015. (Tiny Touch Ser.). (ENG.). 12p. (J). (gr. -1 — 1). bds. 4.99 *(978-1-4998-0057-9(6))* Little Bee Books Inc.

—Animal Homes. 2015. (Tiny Touch Ser.). (ENG.). 12p. (J). (gr. -1 — 1). bds. 4.99 *(978-1-4998-0023-4(1))* Little Bee Books Inc.

—Counting. 2016. (What Can You Spot? Ser.). (ENG.). 18p. (J). (gr. -1 — 1). bds. 7.99 *(978-1-4998-0269-6(2))* Little Bee Books Inc.

—Learning. 2016. (What Can You Spot? Ser.). (ENG.). 18p. (J). (gr. -1 — 1). bds. 7.99 *(978-1-4998-0270-2(6))* Little Bee Books Inc.

—My First Animals. 2016. (My First Ser.). (ENG.). 12p. (J). (gr. -1 — 1). bds. 5.99 *(978-1-4998-0185-9(8))* Little Bee Books Inc.

—My First Sounds. 2016. (My First Ser.). (ENG.). 12p. (J). (gr. -1 — 1). bds. 5.99 *(978-1-4998-0187-3(4))* Little Bee Books Inc.

—My First Vehicles. 2016. (My First Ser.). (ENG.). 12p. (J). (gr. -1 — 1). bds. 5.99 *(978-1-4998-0188-0(2))* Little Bee Books Inc.

Max, Iman. Dangers of the Deep, Vol. 2. Titan Comics Staff & Furman, Simon. 2014. (Riders of Berk Ser.). (ENG.). 64p. (J). (gr. 3-7). pap. 6.99 *(978-1-78276-077-1(6))* Titan Bks. Ltd. GBR. Dist: Penguin Random Hse. LLC.

—Pluck & Perfection. Terrell, Brandon. 2016. (Time Machine Magazine Ser.). (ENG.). 128p. (J). (gr. 3-6). lib. bdg. 22.65 *(978-1-4965-2595-6(7),* Stone Arch Bks.) Capstone.

—Valor & Victory. Terrell, Brandon. 2016. (Time Machine Magazine Ser.). (ENG.). 128p. (J). (gr. 3-6). lib. bdg. 22.65 *(978-1-4965-2594-9(9),* Stone Arch Bks.) Capstone.

Max, Iman & Garcia, Eduardo. Grit & Gold. Terrell, Brandon. 2016. (Time Machine Magazine Ser.). (ENG.). 128p. (J). (gr. 3-6). lib. bdg. 22.65 *(978-1-4965-2597-0(3))* Capstone.

—Harmony & Hoops. Terrell, Brandon. 2016. (Time Machine Magazine Ser.). (ENG.). 128p. (J). (gr. 3-6). lib. bdg. 22.65 *(978-1-4965-2596-3(5))* Capstone.

Max, Iman, jt. illus. see St. Pierre, Joe.

Max, Larin. When I Am Angry: Kids Books about Anger, Ages 3 5, Children's Books. Michael, Gordon. 2019. (Self-Regulation Skills Ser.: Vol. 2). (ENG.). 30p. (J). (gr. k-1). 14.99 ***(978-1-7344674-0-6(1))*** Kids Bk. Pr.

Max, Max. Thumbelina/Pulgarcita. ed. 2004. (Bilingual Fairy Tales Ser.: BILI). (ENG.). 32p. (J). (gr. -1-7). 14.99 *(978-0-8118-3927-3(3))* Chronicle Bks. LLC.

Maxey, David. Cindy Big Hair: A Twisted (and Teased & Braided) Cinderella Story. Auerbach, Annie. 2005. 16p. (J). 12.95 *(978-1-58117-387-1(3),* Intervisual/Piggy Toes) Bendon, Inc.

Maxner, Pearl. The Hawaiian Bat: Ope'ape'a. Coste, Marion. 2005. (ENG.). 40p. (gr. 4-18). 14.99 *(978-0-8248-2797-7(X),* 2133) Univ. of Hawaii Pr.

Maxwell, Cassandre. Silent Night: A Christmas Story. McCullough, L. E. 2006. 24p. (J). 7.95 *(978-0-88271-009-9(5))* Regina Pr., Malhame & Co.

—We Three Kings: A Christmas Story. McCullough, L. E. 2006. 24p. (J). 7.95 *(978-0-88271-010-5(9))* Regina Pr., Malhame & Co.

Maxwell, Helena. Big Boys Cry. Moncrieff, Charlotte. 2019. (ENG.). 32p. (J). *(978-1-913136-11-6(6))* Clink Street Publishing.

Maxwell, Jeremy. Ferdie the Fay Meets Flutterey the Butterfly: A Forest Fable. Robinson, Zan D. (Ferdie the Fay Adventure Ser.: No. 1). 52p. (Orig.). (J). (gr. -1-4). *(978-0-9635587-4-9(9))* Connors, E. W. Publishing Co.

Maxwell, Robert W. The Weeb Book. Maxwell, Robert W. 2009. 60p. pap. 20.00 *(978-1-59925-140-0(X))* Solid Ground Christian Bks.

May, Ashley. Jumpy the Turtle. Jeffords, Stephanie & Branum, Anita. 2012. 92p. pap. 20.00 *(978-1-936750-80-1(5))* Yorkshire Publishing Group.

May, Dan. Passage to Monterey. May, Dan, tr. Romeyn, Debra. 2003. (Adventures of Juan & Mariano Ser.: No. 1). 39p. (J). pap. 9.95 *(978-0-9729016-0-4(4))* Gossamer Bks.

May, Edwina L. Finding Home: My Arf-O-Biography. Langson, Bridgett Bell. 2018. (ENG.). 118p. (J). pap. 7.99 *(978-0-9994376-0-5(7),* Tale Wag Pr.) Langson, Bridgett Bell.

May, Gillie. A contar con la sopa de Beto: Fiction-to-Fact Big Book. Schieber, Jennifer. enl. ed. 2004. (SPA.). (J). pap. 26.00 *(978-1-4108-2361-8(X),* 2361X) Benchmark Education Co.

May, Gin. The Plumber & the Wishing Well. Maher, Liam. 2012. 24p. (gr. k-3). 19.95 *(978-1-61633-269-3(7));* pap. 10.95 *(978-1-61633-268-6(9))* Guardian Angel Publishing, Inc.

May, Gretchen. Little I's Butterflies. Roberts, Laura. Cole, Cindy, ed. 2018. (Little I's Butterflies Ser.: Vol. 1). (ENG.). 48p. (J). 17.99 *(978-0-578-43509-1(8))* Roberts, Laura.

May, Kate. Wish Fish. Hay, Sam. 2011. (My Phonics Readers: Level 2 Ser.). 24p. (J). (gr. -1-1). 24.25 *(978-1-84898-508-7(8))* Sea-To-Sea Pubns.

May, Kyla. Cat Show Queen. Johnson, Rebecca. 2015. (Juliet, Nearly a Vet Ser.: 10). 96p. (J). (gr. 3-5). 9.99 *(978-0-14-330872-0(6))* Penguin Random Hse. AUS. Dist: Independent Pubs. Group.

M

—The Dog Rules. La Rue, Coco. 2011. (ENG.). 128p. (J). (gr. 2-5). pap. 4.99 *(978-0-545-28261-1(6)*, Scholastic Paperbacks) Scholastic, Inc.

—Juliet, Nearly a Vet: Collection One: 4 Books in One. Johnson, Rebecca. 2018. (Juliet, Nearly a Vet Ser.: 1). 384p. (J). (gr. 3-5). pap. 14.99 *(978-0-14-378691-7(1))* Random Hse. Australia AUS. Dist: Independent Pubs. Group.

—Juliet, Nearly a Vet, Collection Two, 4 Bks. Johnson, Rebecca. 2018. (Juliet, Nearly a Vet Ser.: 2). 368p. (J). (gr. 3-5). pap. 14.99 *(978-0-14-378692-4(X))* Random Hse. Australia AUS. Dist: Independent Pubs. Group.

—A New Pig in Town. La Rue, Coco. 2013. 127p. (J). pap. *(978-0-545-46607-3(5))* Scholastic, Inc.

—Outback Adventure. Johnson, Rebecca. 2015. (Juliet, Nearly a Vet Ser.: 9). 96p. (J). (gr. 3-5). 9.99 *(978-0-14-330871-3(8))* Penguin Random Hse. AUS. Dist: Independent Pubs. Group.

—Pug Blasts Off. 2019. 72p. (J). *(978-1-338-50034-9(1))* Scholastic, Inc.

May, Kyla. Paws for a Cause: a Branches Book (Diary of a Pug #3) May, Kyla. 2020. (Diary of a Pug Ser.: 3). (ENG.). 80p. (J). (gr. k-2). pap. 4.99 *(978-1-338-53009-4(7))* Scholastic, Inc.

—Pug Blasts Off. May, Kyla. Sander, Sonia. 2019. (Diary of a Pug Ser.: 1). (ENG.). 80p. (J). (gr. k-2). 24.99 *(978-1-338-53004-9(6))* Scholastic, Inc.

—Pug's Snow Day. May, Kyla. 2019. (Diary of a Pug Ser.: 2). (ENG.). 80p. (J). (gr. k-2). 24.99 *(978-1-338-53007-0(0))* Scholastic, Inc.

May, Lisa. Bubble Trouble: Using Mindfulness to Help Kids with Grief. Krantz, Heather. 2018. (ENG.). 40p. (J). (gr. k-4). 16.99 *(978-0-9987037-6-3(1)*, Herow Pr.) Krantz, Heather.

—Heart Bubbles: Exploring Compassion with Kids. Krantz, Heather. 2017. (ENG.). (J). (gr. k-4). 16.99 *(978-0-9987037-2-5(9)*, Herow Pr.) Krantz, Heather.

—Sleep Bubbles: Using Mindfulness to Help Kids Sleep. Krantz, Heather. 2018. (ENG.). 42p. (J). (gr. k-4). 16.99 *(978-0-9987037-4-9(5)*, Herow Pr.) Krantz, Heather.

May, Margaret Cavers. Christmas with Maddy. Cavers, Charlene M. 2018. (Maddy Chronicles Ser.). (ENG.). 24p. (J). *(978-1-5255-4243-5(5))*; pap. *(978-1-5255-4244-2(3))* FriesenPress.

—Maddy the Dragonslayer. Cavers, Charlene M. 2017. (ENG.). 24p. (J). *(978-1-5255-1924-6(7))*; pap. *(978-1-5255-1925-3(5))* FriesenPress.

—Maddy's First Winter. Cavers, Charlene M. 2018. (Maddy Chronicles Ser.). (ENG.). 32p. (J). *(978-1-5255-3227-6(8))*; pap. *(978-1-5255-3228-3(6))* FriesenPress.

May, Sandy. For the Love of Sapphire: The Promise. Mitchell, Gwendolyn. 2008. 27p. pap. 24.95 *(978-1-60813-029-0(0))* America Star Bks.

May, Steve. The Recess Bully. Ruiz, Rachel. 2017. (Superhero Harry Ser.). (ENG.). 48p. (J). (gr. k-2). pap. 8.95 *(978-1-4795-9860-1(7)*, 135317); lib. bdg. 23.32 *(978-1-4795-9856-4(9)*, 135309) Capstone. (Picture Window Bks.).

—The Runaway Robot. Ruiz, Rachel. 2017. (Superhero Harry Ser.). (ENG.). 48p. (J). (gr. k-2). pap. 8.95 *(978-1-4795-9859-5(3)*, 135316); lib. bdg. 23.32 *(978-1-4795-9855-7(0)*, 135308) Capstone. (Picture Window Bks.).

—The Superhero Project. Ruiz, Rachel. 2017. (Superhero Harry Ser.). (ENG.). 48p. (J). (gr. k-2). pap. 8.95 *(978-1-4795-9862-5(3)*, 135319); lib. bdg. 23.32 *(978-1-4795-9858-8(5)*, 135311) Capstone. (Picture Window Bks.).

—The Wild Field Trip. Ruiz, Rachel. 2017. (Superhero Harry Ser.). (ENG.). 48p. (J). (gr. k-2). pap. 8.95 *(978-1-4795-9861-8(5)*, 135318); lib. bdg. 23.32 *(978-1-4795-9857-1(7)*, 135310) Capstone. (Picture Window Bks.).

Maybank, Jem. The World Jesus Knew: A Curious Kid's Guide to Life in First-Century Palestine, Vol. Olson, Marc. 2017. (Curious Kids' Guides Ser.: 1). (ENG.). 64p. (J). (gr. 4-6). 19.99 *(978-1-5064-2500-9(3)*, Sparkhouse Family) Augsburg Fortress, Pubs.

—The World of the Old Testament: A Curious Kid's Guide to the Bible's Most Ancient Stories, Vol. Olson, Marc. 2019. (Curious Kids' Guides Ser.: 2). (ENG.). 64p. (J). (gr. 4-9). 19.99 *(978-1-5064-5059-9(8)*, Beaming Books) Augsburg Fortress, Pubs.

Maybank, Jemima. The World of the First Christians: A Curious Kid's Guide to the Early Church. Olson, Marc. 2020. (Curious Kids' Guides). (ENG.). 64p. (J). (gr. 3-7). 19.99 *(978-1-5064-6049-9(6)*, Beaming Books) Augsburg Fortress, Pubs.

Mayberry, Maranda. My Day of Ballet. Feldman, Thea. 2007. (Magnix Imagination Activity Bks.). 6p. (J). (gr. -1-3). bds. 5.99 *(978-1-932915-41-9(9))* Sandvik Innovations, LLC.

Maydak, Michael. There's a Babirusa in My Bathtub: Fact & Fancy about Curious Creatures. Schur, Maxine Rose. 2009. 32p. (J). (gr. 2-7). pap. 8.95 *(978-1-58469-118-1(2))* Dawn Pubns.

Maydak, Michael S. Discovering Sharks & Rays. Field, Nancy H. 2003. (Discovering Nature Library). 40p. (J). (gr. 2-6). pap. 7.95 *(978-0-941042-33-8(2))* Dog-Eared Pubns.

—Lifetimes. Rice, David L. 2015. 32p. pap. 9.00 *(978-1-61003-549-1(6))* Center for the Collaborative Classroom.

—Millions of Monarchs. Roop, Connie & Roop, Peter. 2003. 30p. (J). *(978-0-439-43965-7(5))* Scholastic, Inc.

—Salmon Stream. Reed-jones, Carol. 2004. (Sharing Nature with Children Book Ser.). 32p. (J). (gr. 4-7). 16.95 *(978-1-58469-014-6(3))* Dawn Pubns.

—There's a Babirusa in My Bathtub: Fact & Fancy about Curious Creatures, 1 vol. Schur, Maxine Rose. 2009. (ENG.). 32p. (J). (gr. 2-7). 16.99 *(978-1-58469-117-4(4)*, Dawn Pubns.) Sourcebooks, Inc.

—The Web at Dragonfly Pond. Ellis, Brian. 2006. (ENG.). 32p. (J). (gr. 1-7). 16.99 *(978-1-58469-078-8(X))*; pap. 8.99 *(978-1-58469-079-5(8))* Sourcebooks, Inc. (Dawn Pubns.).

—Wild Stickers - Sharks & Rays. 2003. 4p. (J). 2.50 *(978-0-941042-34-5(0))* Dog-Eared Pubns.

Maydak, Michael S. & Morrison, Cathy. Water Cycle Books for Kids: A Nature & Science Book Set for Kids. McKinney, Barbara Shaw et al. 2020. (ENG.). (J). (-6). pap. 26.89 ***(978-1-7282-4202-6(9)***, Dawn Pubns.) Sourcebooks, Inc.

Maydak, Mike. Gone Extinct! Parker, Katie. 2009. (ENG.). 24p. (J). (gr. k-17). 19.99 *(978-1-58476-941-5(6))* Innovative Kids.

Maydani, Shahrzad. Duérmete, Bebé (Hush a Bye, Baby) Capucilli, Alyssa Satin. Romay, Alexis, tr. 2020. (New Books for Newborns Ser.). (SPA.). 16p. (J). (gr. -1 — 1). bds. 7.99 ***(978-1-5344-6550-3(2)***, Libros Para Ninos) Libros Para Ninos.

Maydani, Shahrzad. Hush a Bye, Baby. Capucilli, Alyssa Satin. 2017. (New Books for Newborns Ser.). (ENG.). 16p. (J). (— 1). bds. 8.99 *(978-1-5344-0139-6(3)*, Little Simon) Little Simon.

—Poetree. Reynolds, Shauna LaVoy. 2019. 32p. (J). (gr. -1-3). 17.99 *(978-0-399-53912-1(3)*, Dial Bks) Penguin Young Readers Group.

Maye, Warren L. Mommy Says! Beek, Rosheena. 2nd ed. 2013. (ENG.). 24p. pap. *(978-1-927750-20-9(2))* Bermuda National Trust.

Mayer, Bill. All Aboard! All Aboard! 2008. (ENG.). 40p. (J). (gr. -1-2). 17.99 *(978-0-689-85249-7(5)*, McElderry, Margaret K. Bks.) McElderry, Margaret K. Bks.

—Brer Rabbit & Boss Lion. Kessler, Brad & Harris, Joel Chandler. 2004. (Rabbit Ears-A Classic Tale Ser.). (ENG.). 40p. (J). (gr. 2-6). 28.50 *(978-1-59197-760-5(6)*, 12921, Picture Bk.) Spotlight.

—Hide & Sheep. Beaty, Andrea. 2011. (ENG.). 32p. (J). (gr. -1-3). 15.99 *(978-1-4169-2544-6(9)*, McElderry, Margaret K. Bks.) McElderry, Margaret K. Bks.

—The Monster Who Did My Math, 1 vol. Schnitzlein, Danny. (ENG.). 32p. (J). 2012. pap. 7.95 *(978-1-56145-668-0(3))*; 2007. 16.95 *(978-1-56145-420-4(6))* Peachtree Publishing Co. Inc.

—On My Very First School Day I Met... Stiles, Norman. 2005. (ENG.). 32p. (J). (gr. -1-3). 9.95 *(978-1-59687-182-3(2))* IBks., Inc.

—On My Very First School Day I Met... Stiles, Norman. 2005. 32p. (J). (gr. -1). 9.95 *(978-0-689-03924-9(7)*, Milk & Cookies) ibooks, Inc.

—Super Bugs. Meadows, Michelle. 2016. 40p. (J). (gr. -1-k). 16.99 *(978-0-545-68756-0(X))* Scholastic, Inc.

—Teeny Weenies: Freestyle Frenzy: And Other Stories. Lubar, David. 2019. (Teeny Weenies Ser.: 2). (ENG.). 128p. (J). 12.99 *(978-1-250-17350-8(7)*, 900188883, Starscape) Doherty, Tom Assocs., LLC.

—Teeny Weenies: the Intergalactic Petting Zoo: And Other Stories. Lubar, David. 2019. (Teeny Weenies Ser.: 1). (ENG.). 128p. (J). 12.99 *(978-1-250-17342-3(6)*, 900188882, Starscape) Doherty, Tom Assocs., LLC.

—Warrior Queens: True Stories of Six Ancient Rebels Who Slayed History. Shecter, Vicky Alvear. 2019. 160p. (J). (gr. 4-7). 17.99 *(978-1-62979-679-6(4))* Boyds Mills Pr.

Mayer, Danuta. Tenzin's Deer. Soros, Barbara. (ENG.). 32p. (J). (gr. 2-4). 2007. pap. 7.99 *(978-1-84686-130-7(6))*; 2005. 16.99 *(978-1-905236-57-2(3))* Barefoot Bks., Inc.

—Tenzin's Deer: A Tibetan Tale. Soros, Barbara. 2003. 32p. (J). (gr. 2-5). 16.99 *(978-1-84148-811-0(9))* Barefoot Bks., Inc.

Mayer, Hy. Top o' the World (Illustrated) A Once upon a Time Tale. E Swan, Mark. 2019. (ENG.). 124p. (J). pap. 5.99 *(978-1-0924-3138-5(1))* Independently Published.

Mayer-Johnson. Full Schedule: A Picture Symbol Activity Book. McIlquham, Mary Caroline. 2005. 338p. spiral bd. 44.95 *(978-0-9768379-0-9(0))* Symtext Media.

Mayer, Jonathan. Anatomy of a Dragon. Doeden, Matt. 2013. (World of Dragons Ser.). (ENG.). 32p. (J). (gr. 3-9). lib. bdg. 27.32 *(978-1-62065-145-2(9)*, Capstone Pr.) Capstone.

—Dragon Behavior, 1 vol. Doeden, Matt. 2013. (World of Dragons Ser.). (ENG.). 32p. (J). (gr. 3-9). lib. bdg. 27.32 *(978-1-62065-144-5(0)*, Capstone Pr.) Capstone.

Mayer, Jonathan & Pellegrino, Rich. The World of Dragons. Doeden, Matt. 2013. (World of Dragons Ser.). (ENG.). 32p. (J). (gr. 3-9). lib. bdg., lib. bdg., lib. bdg. 109.28 *(978-1-62065-147-6(5)*, Capstone Pr.) Capstone.

Mayer, Marianna & Mayer, Mercer. One Frog Too Many. Mayer, Marianna & Mayer, Mercer. 2003. (Boy, a Dog, & a Frog Ser.). (ENG.). 32p. (J). (gr. -1-k). 7.99 *(978-0-8037-2885-1(9)*, Dial Bks) Penguin Young Readers Group.

Mayer, Marianna, jt. illus. see Mayer, Mercer.

Mayer, Melody & Olson, Ed. The Crucifixion Part 1 ... the Road to the Cross Pt. I, Vol. 11: New Testament Volume 11 Life of Christ Part 11. Greiner, Ruth B. 2011. 36p. (J). pap. *(978-1-932381-41-2(4)*, 1011) Bible Visuals International, Inc.

—The Crucifixion Part 2 Christ Sacrifice Our Salvation Pt. 2, Vol. 12: New Testament Volume 12 LIfe of Christ Part 12. Greiner, Ruth B. 2011. 36p. (J). pap. *(978-1-932381-42-9(2)*, 1012) Bible Visuals International, Inc.

—Judgment the Wrath of God Vol. 44: New Testament Volume 44 Revelation Part 3. Greiner, Ruth B. 2010. 36p. (J). pap. *(978-1-932381-30-6(9)*, 1044) Bible Visuals International, Inc.

Mayer, Mercer, et al. Altogether, One at a Time. Konigsburg, E. L. 3rd ed. 2008. (ENG.). 112p. (J). (gr. 3-7). pap. 6.99 *(978-1-4169-5501-6(1)*, Atheneum Bks. for Young Readers) Simon & Schuster Children's Publishing.

Mayer, Mercer. The Great Brain. Fitzgerald, John D. 2004. (Great Brain Ser.: 1). (ENG.). 208p. (J). (gr. 3-7). 7.99 *(978-0-14-240058-6(0)*, Puffin Books) Penguin Young Readers Group.

—Me & My Little Brain. Fitzgerald, John D. 2004. (Great Brain Ser.: 3). (ENG.). 160p. (J). (gr. 3-7). 7.99 *(978-0-14-240064-7(5)*, Puffin Books) Penguin Young Readers Group.

—Me & My Little Brain. Fitzgerald, John D. 2004. (Great Brain Ser.). 137p. (gr. 3-7). 16.00 *(978-0-7569-2541-3(X))* Perfection Learning Corp.

—More Adventures of the Great Brain. Fitzgerald, John D. 2004. (Great Brain Ser.: 2). (ENG.). 176p. (J). (gr. 3-7). pap. 7.99 *(978-0-14-240065-4(3)*, Puffin Books) Penguin Young Readers Group.

—Outside My Window. Skorpen, Liesel Moak. 2004. 32p. (J). (gr. -1-3). 16.89 *(978-0-06-050775-6(6))* HarperCollins Pubs.

Mayer, Mercer. Bedtime Stories - Little Critter. Mayer, Mercer. 2013. (Little Critter Ser.). (ENG.). 144p. (J). (gr. -1-3). pap. 11.99 *(978-0-06-223640-1(7)*, HarperFestival) HarperCollins Pubs.

—The Best Teacher Ever No. 6. Mayer, Mercer. 2008. (Little Critter Ser.). (ENG.). 24p. (J). (gr. -1-2). pap. 3.99 *(978-0-06-053960-3(7)*, HarperFestival) HarperCollins Pubs.

—The Best Yard Sale. Mayer, Mercer. 2010. (Little Critter Ser.). 24p. (J). (gr. -1-2). pap. 3.99 *(978-0-06-147799-7(0)*, HarperFestival) HarperCollins Pubs.

—A Boy, a Dog, & a Frog. Mayer, Mercer. 2003. (Boy, a Dog, & a Frog Ser.). (ENG.). 32p. (J). (gr. -1-k). 6.99 *(978-0-8037-2880-6(8)*, Dial Bks) Penguin Young Readers Group.

—The Bravest Knight. Mayer, Mercer. 2007. 32p. (J). (gr. -1-3). 17.99 *(978-0-8037-3206-3(6)*, Dial Bks) Penguin Young Readers Group.

—East of the Sun & West of the Moon. Mayer, Mercer. 2017. (ENG.). 32p. (J). (gr. k-3). 13.99 *(978-1-5344-1240-8(9)*, Aladdin) Simon & Schuster Children's Publishing.

—Frog Goes to Dinner. Mayer, Mercer. 2003. (Boy, a Dog, & a Frog Ser.). (ENG.). 32p. (J). (gr. -1-k). 6.99 *(978-0-8037-2884-4(0)*, Dial Bks) Penguin Young Readers Group.

—Frog on His Own. Mayer, Mercer. 2003. (Boy, a Dog, & a Frog Ser.). (ENG.). 32p. (J). (gr. -1-k). 7.99 *(978-0-8037-2883-7(2)*, Dial Bks) Penguin Young Readers Group.

—Frog, Where Are You? Mayer, Mercer. 2003. (Boy, a Dog, & a Frog Ser.). (ENG.). 32p. (J). (gr. -1-k). 7.99 *(978-0-8037-2881-3(6)*, Dial Bks) Penguin Young Readers Group.

—A Green, Green Garden. Mayer, Mercer. 2011. (My First I Can Read Ser.). (ENG.). 32p. (J). (gr. -1-3). 16.99 *(978-0-06-083562-0(1))* HarperCollins Pubs.

—Happy Mother's Day! Mayer, Mercer. 2009. (Little Critter Ser.). (ENG.). 20p. (J). (gr. -1-2). pap. 6.99 *(978-0-06-053970-2(4)*, HarperFestival) HarperCollins Pubs.

—It's Earth Day!, No. 5. Mayer, Mercer. 2008. (Little Critter Ser.: No. 5). (ENG.). 24p. (J). (gr. -1-2). pap. 3.99 *(978-0-06-053959-7(3)*, HarperFestival) HarperCollins Pubs.

—Just a Day at the Pond. Mayer, Mercer. 2008. (Little Critter Ser.). (ENG.). 24p. (J). (gr. -1-2). pap. 3.99 *(978-0-06-053961-0(5)*, HarperFestival) HarperCollins Pubs.

—Just a Little Critter Collection. Mayer, Mercer. 2005. 176p. (J). (gr. -1-2). 9.99 *(978-0-375-83255-0(6)*, Golden Bks.) Random Hse. Children's Bks.

—Just a Little Luck. Mayer, Mercer. 2011. (Little Critter Ser.). (ENG.). 24p. (J). (gr. -1-2). pap. 3.99 *(978-0-06-147800-0(8)*, HarperFestival) HarperCollins Pubs.

—Just Me & My Mom/Just Me & My Dad (Little Critter) Mayer, Mercer. 2014. (Pictureback(R) Ser.). 48p. (J). (gr. -1-2). 4.99 *(978-0-385-37175-9(6)*, Random Hse. Bks. for Young Readers) Random Hse. Children's Bks.

—Little Critter 12-Book Phonics Fun! Includes 12 Mini-Books Featuring Short & Long Vowel Sounds. Mayer, Mercer. 2012. (My First I Can Read Ser.). (ENG.). 144p. (J). (gr. -1-k). pap. 14.99 *(978-0-06-147825-3(3))* HarperCollins Pubs.

—Little Critter: 5-Minute Little Critter Stories: Includes 12 Classic Stories! Mayer, Mercer. 2017. (Little Critter Ser.). (ENG.). 192p. (J). (gr. -1-3). 12.99 *(978-0-06-265525-7(6)*, HarperFestival) HarperCollins Pubs.

—Little Critter: a Green, Green Garden. Mayer, Mercer. 2011. (My First I Can Read Ser.). (ENG.). 32p. (J). (gr. -1-3). pap. 4.99 *(978-0-06-083561-3(3)*, HarperCollins) HarperCollins Pubs. Ltd. GBR. Dist: HarperCollins Pubs.

—Little Critter: Bedtime Storybook Boxed Set: 5 Favorite Critter Tales! Mayer, Mercer. 2018. (Little Critter Ser.). (ENG.). 120p. (J). (gr. -1-3). pap. 11.99 *(978-0-06-265524-0(8)*, HarperFestival) HarperCollins Pubs.

—Little Critter: Bye-Bye, Mom & Dad. Mayer, Mercer. 2004. (Little Critter Ser.). (ENG.). 24p. (J). (gr. -1-2). pap. 3.99 *(978-0-06-053945-0(3)*, HarperFestival) HarperCollins Pubs.

—Little Critter Collector's Quintet: Critters Who Care, Going to the Firehouse, This Is My Town, Going to the Sea Park, to the Rescue. Mayer, Mercer. 2017. (My First I Can Read Ser.). (ENG.). 160p. (J). (gr. -1-3). pap. 19.99 *(978-0-06-265349-9(0)*, HarperCollins) HarperCollins Pubs. Ltd. GBR. Dist: HarperCollins Pubs.

—Little Critter: Exploring the Great Outdoors. Mayer, Mercer. 2019. (My First I Can Read Ser.). (ENG.). 32p. (J). (gr. -1-3). 16.99 *(978-0-06-243145-5(5))* HarperCollins Pubs.

—Little Critter: Exploring the Great Outdoors. Mayer, Mercer. 2019. (My First I Can Read Ser.). (ENG.). 32p. (J). (gr. -1-3). pap. 4.99 *(978-0-06-243144-8(7)*, HarperCollins) HarperCollins Pubs. Ltd. GBR. Dist: HarperCollins Pubs.

—Little Critter Fall Storybook Favorites: Includes 7 Stories Plus Stickers! Mayer, Mercer. 2019. (Little Critter Ser.). (ENG.). 192p. (J). (gr. -1-3). 13.99 *(978-0-06-289460-1(9))* HarperCollins Pubs.

—Little Critter: First Day of School No. 3. Mayer, Mercer. 2009. (Little Critter Ser.). (ENG.). 20p. (J). (gr. -1-2). pap. 6.99 *(978-0-06-053969-6(0)*, HarperFestival) HarperCollins Pubs.

—Little Critter: Going to the Firehouse. Mayer, Mercer. 2008. (My First I Can Read Ser.). (ENG.). 32p. (J). (gr. -1-3). 16.99 *(978-0-06-083546-0(X))* HarperCollins Pubs.

—Little Critter: Going to the Firehouse. Mayer, Mercer. 2008. (My First I Can Read Ser.). (ENG.). 32p. (J). (gr. -1-3). pap. 4.99 *(978-0-06-083545-3(1)*, HarperCollins) HarperCollins Pubs. Ltd. GBR. Dist: HarperCollins Pubs.

—Little Critter: Going to the Sea Park. Mayer, Mercer. 2017. (My First I Can Read Ser.). (ENG.). 40p. (J). (gr. -1-3). 9.99 *(978-0-06-257281-3(4))* HarperCollins Pubs.

—Little Critter: Going to the Sea Park. Mayer, Mercer. 2009. (My First I Can Read Ser.). (ENG.). 32p. (J). (gr. -1-3). pap. 4.99 *(978-0-06-083553-8(2))* HarperCollins Pubs.

—Little Critter: Good for Me & You. Mayer, Mercer. 2004. (Little Critter Ser.). (ENG.). 24p. (J). (gr. -1-2). pap. 3.99 *(978-0-06-053948-1(8)*, HarperFestival) HarperCollins Pubs.

—Little Critter: Grandma, Grandpa, & Me. Mayer, Mercer. 2007. (Little Critter Ser.). (ENG.). 24p. (J). (gr. -1-2). pap. 3.99 *(978-0-06-053951-1(8)*, HarperFestival) HarperCollins Pubs.

—Little Critter: Happy Halloween, Little Critter! Mayer, Mercer. 2004. (Little Critter Ser.). (ENG.). 16p. (J). (gr. -1-1). pap. 6.99 *(978-0-06-053971-9(2)*, HarperFestival) HarperCollins Pubs.

—Little Critter: Happy Valentine's Day, Little Critter! Mayer, Mercer. 2005. (Little Critter Ser.). (ENG.). 20p. (J). (gr. -1-3). pap. 6.99 *(978-0-06-053973-3(9)*, HarperFestival) HarperCollins Pubs.

—Little Critter: It's Easter, Little Critter! Mayer, Mercer. 2007. (Little Critter Ser.). (ENG.). 20p. (J). (gr. -1-1). pap. 6.99 *(978-0-06-053974-0(7)*, HarperFestival) HarperCollins Pubs.

—Little Critter: Just a Baby Bird. Mayer, Mercer. 2016. (My First I Can Read Ser.). (ENG.). 32p. (J). (gr. -1-3). pap. 4.99 *(978-0-06-147821-5(0))* HarperCollins Pubs.

—Little Critter: Just a Kite. Mayer, Mercer. 2014. (My First I Can Read Ser.). (ENG.). 32p. (J). (gr. -1-3). 16.99 *(978-0-06-207197-2(1))* HarperCollins Pubs.

—Little Critter: Just a Kite. Mayer, Mercer. 2014. (My First I Can Read Ser.). (ENG.). 32p. (J). (gr. -1-3). pap. 4.99 *(978-0-06-147814-7(8)*, HarperCollins) HarperCollins Pubs. Ltd. GBR. Dist: HarperCollins Pubs.

—Little Critter: Just a Little Love. Mayer, Mercer. 2013. (My First I Can Read Ser.). (ENG.). 32p. (J). (gr. -1-3). 16.99 *(978-0-06-207196-5(3))*; pap. 4.99 *(978-0-06-147815-4(6))* HarperCollins Pubs.

—Little Critter: Just a Little Music. Mayer, Mercer. 2009. (Little Critter Ser.). (ENG.). 24p. (J). (gr. -1-3). pap. 3.99 *(978-0-06-053962-7(3)*, HarperFestival) HarperCollins Pubs.

—Little Critter: Just a Little Sick. Mayer, Mercer. 2009. (My First I Can Read Ser.). (ENG.). 32p. (J). (gr. -1-3). 16.99 *(978-0-06-083556-9(7))*; pap. 4.99 *(978-0-06-083555-2(9))* HarperCollins Pubs.

—Little Critter: Just a School Project. Mayer, Mercer. 2004. (Little Critter Ser.). (ENG.). 24p. (J). (gr. -1-2). pap. 3.99 *(978-0-06-053946-7(1)*, HarperFestival) HarperCollins Pubs.

—Little Critter: Just a Snowman. Mayer, Mercer. 2004. (Little Critter Ser.). (ENG.). 24p. (J). (gr. -1-2). pap. 3.99 *(978-0-06-053947-4(X)*, HarperFestival) HarperCollins Pubs.

—Little Critter: Just a Special Day. Mayer, Mercer. 2014. (My First I Can Read Ser.). (ENG.). 32p. (J). (gr. -1-3). pap. 4.99 *(978-0-06-147817-8(2)*, HarperCollins) HarperCollins Pubs. Ltd. GBR. Dist: HarperCollins Pubs.

—Little Critter: Just a Special Thanksgiving. Mayer, Mercer. 2015. (Little Critter Ser.). (ENG.). 24p. (J). (gr. -1-3). pap. 4.99 *(978-0-06-147811-6(3)*, HarperFestival) HarperCollins Pubs.

—Little Critter: Just a Teacher's Pet. Mayer, Mercer. 2015. (My First I Can Read Ser.). (ENG.). 32p. (J). (gr. -1-3). pap. 4.99 *(978-0-06-147819-2(9)*, HarperCollins) HarperCollins Pubs. Ltd. GBR. Dist: HarperCollins Pubs.

—Little Critter: Just an Adventure at Sea. Mayer, Mercer. 2017. (My First I Can Read Ser.). (ENG.). 32p. (J). (gr. -1-3). pap. 4.99 *(978-0-06-243140-0(4))* HarperCollins Pubs.

—Little Critter: Just Big Enough. Mayer, Mercer. 2013. (Little Critter Ser.). (ENG.). 24p. (J). (gr. -1-2). pap. 3.99 *(978-0-06-147805-5(9)*, HarperFestival) HarperCollins Pubs.

—Little Critter: Just Critters Who Care. Mayer, Mercer. 2010. (My First I Can Read Ser.). (ENG.). 32p. (J). (gr. -1-3). 16.99 *(978-0-06-083560-6(5))* HarperCollins Pubs.

—Little Critter: Just Critters Who Care. Mayer, Mercer. 2010. (My First I Can Read Ser.). (ENG.). 32p. (J). (gr. -1-3). pap. 4.99 *(978-0-06-083559-0(1)*, HarperCollins) HarperCollins Pubs. Ltd. GBR. Dist: HarperCollins Pubs.

—Little Critter: Just Fishing with Grandma. Mayer, Mercer. Mayer, Gina. 2015. (Little Critter Ser.). (ENG.). 24p. (J). (gr. -1-3). pap. 3.99 *(978-0-06-147808-6(3)*, HarperFestival) HarperCollins Pubs.

—Little Critter: Just Helping My Dad. Mayer, Mercer. 2011. (My First I Can Read Ser.). (ENG.). 32p. (J). (gr. -1-3). pap. 4.99 *(978-0-06-083563-7(X))* HarperCollins Pubs.

—Little Critter: Just My Best Friend. Mayer, Mercer. 2019. (My First I Can Read Ser.). (ENG.). 32p. (J). (gr. -1-3). 16.99 *(978-0-06-243147-9(1))* HarperCollins Pubs.

—Little Critter: Just My Best Friend. Mayer, Mercer. 2019. (My First I Can Read Ser.). (ENG.). 32p. (J). (gr. -1-3). pap. 4.99 *(978-0-06-243146-2(3)*, HarperCollins) HarperCollins Pubs. Ltd. GBR. Dist: HarperCollins Pubs.

—Little Critter: Just My Lost Treasure. Mayer, Mercer. 2014. (Little Critter Ser.). (ENG.). 24p. (J). (gr. -1-3). pap. 3.99 *(978-0-06-147806-2(7)*, HarperFestival) HarperCollins Pubs.

—Little Critter: Just One More Pet. Mayer, Mercer. 2013. (Little Critter Ser.). (ENG.). 24p. (J). (gr. -1-2). pap. 3.99 *(978-0-06-147807-9(5)*, HarperFestival) HarperCollins Pubs.

—Little Critter: Just Pick Us, Please! Mayer, Mercer. 2017. (My First I Can Read Ser.). (ENG.). 32p. (J). (gr. -1-3). 16.99

(978-0-06-243143-1(9)); pap. 4.99 *(978-0-06-243142-4(0))* HarperCollins Pubs.

—Little Critter: Just Saving My Money. Mayer, Mercer. 2010. (My First I Can Read Ser.). (ENG.). 32p. (J). (gr. -1-3). pap. 4.99 *(978-0-06-083557-6(5))* HarperCollins Pubs.

—Little Critter: Just Storybook Favorites. Mayer, Mercer. 2020. (Little Critter Ser.). (ENG.). 176p. (J). (gr. -1-3). 13.99 *(978-0-06-293161-0(X)*, HarperFestival) HarperCollins Pubs.

—Little Critter: Merry Christmas, Little Critter! Mayer, Mercer. 2004. (Little Critter Ser.). (ENG.). 16p. (J). (gr. -1-1). pap. 6.99 *(978-0-06-053972-6(0)*, HarperFestival) HarperCollins Pubs.

—Little Critter: My Trip to the Hospital, No. 5. Mayer, Mercer. 2005. (Little Critter Ser.). (ENG.). 24p. (J). (gr. -1-2). pap. 3.99 *(978-0-06-053949-8(6)*, HarperFestival) HarperCollins Pubs.

—Little Critter: My Trip to the Science Museum. Mayer, Mercer. 2017. (Little Critter Ser.). (ENG.). 24p. (J). (gr. -1-3). pap. 3.99 *(978-0-06-147809-3(1)*, HarperFestival) HarperCollins Pubs.

—Little Critter: Snowball Soup. Mayer, Mercer. 2007. (My First I Can Read Ser.). (ENG.). 32p. (J). (gr. -1-3). pap. 4.99 *(978-0-06-083543-9(5))* HarperCollins Pubs.

—Little Critter Storybook Collection. Mayer, Mercer. 2005. (Little Critter Ser.). (ENG.). 176p. (J). (gr. -1-3). 11.99 *(978-0-06-082009-1(8)*, HarperFestival) HarperCollins Pubs.

—Little Critter: the Fall Festival. Mayer, Mercer. 2009. (My First I Can Read Ser.). (ENG.). 32p. (J). (gr. -1-3). pap. 4.99 *(978-0-06-083551-4(6))* HarperCollins Pubs.

—Little Critter: the Lost Dinosaur Bone. Mayer, Mercer. 2007. (Little Critter Ser.). (ENG.). 24p. (J). (gr. -1-3). pap. 3.99 *(978-0-06-053952-8(6)*, HarperFestival) HarperCollins Pubs.

—Little Critter: This Is My Town. Mayer, Mercer. 2008. (My First I Can Read Ser.). (ENG.). 32p. (J). (gr. -1-3). pap. 4.99 *(978-0-06-083549-1(4))* HarperCollins Pubs.

—Little Critter: to the Rescue! Mayer, Mercer. 2008. (My First I Can Read Ser.). (ENG.). 32p. (J). (gr. -1-3). pap. 4.99 *(978-0-06-083547-7(8)*, HarperCollins) HarperCollins Pubs. Ltd. GBR. Dist: HarperCollins Pubs.

—Little Critter: We Are Moving. Mayer, Mercer. 2012. (Little Critter Ser.). (ENG.). 24p. (J). (gr. -1-2). pap. 3.99 *(978-0-06-147803-1(2)*, HarperFestival) HarperCollins Pubs.

—Octopus Soup, 0 vols. Mayer, Mercer. 2011. (ENG.). 24p. (J). (gr. k-3). 16.99 *(978-0-7614-5812-8(3)*, 9780761458128, Two Lions) Amazon Publishing.

—Snowball Soup. Mayer, Mercer. 2007. (My First I Can Read Bks.). (ENG.). 32p. (J). (gr. -1-k). 16.99 *(978-0-06-083544-6(3))* HarperCollins Pubs.

—To the Rescue! Mayer, Mercer. 2008. (My First I Can Read Bks.). (ENG.). 32p. (J). (gr. -1-3). 16.99 *(978-0-06-083548-4(6))* HarperCollins Pubs.

—What Do You Do with a Kangaroo? Mayer, Mercer. 2008. (ENG.). (J). (gr. -1-3). audio compact disk 9.99 *(978-0-545-07457-5(6))* Scholastic, Inc.

Mayer, Mercer & Mayer, Marianna. A Boy, a Dog, a Frog, & a Friend. Mayer, Mercer & Mayer, Marianna. 2003. (Boy, a Dog, & a Frog Ser.). (ENG.). 32p. (J). (gr. -1-k). 6.99 *(978-0-8037-2882-0(4)*, Dial Bks) Penguin Young Readers Group.

Mayer, Mercer, jt. illus. see Mayer, Marianna.

Mayer, Sandra. Bye-Bye, Train. Chanko, Pamela. 2018. (Rookie Toddler Ser.). (ENG.). 12p. (J). (gr. -1 — 1). bds. 6.95 *(978-0-531-12701-8(X)*, Children's Pr.) Scholastic Library Publishing.

—I Love Dinosaurs. Miller, Amanda. 2018. (Rookie Toddler Ser.). (ENG.). 12p. (J). (gr. -1 — 1). bds. 6.95 *(978-0-531-22888-3(6)*, Children's Pr.) Scholastic Library Publishing.

—I Love Kittens. Falk, Laine. 2017. (Rookie Toddler Ser.). (ENG.). 12p. (J). (gr. -1 — 1). bds. 6.95 *(978-0-531-22687-2(5)*, Children's Pr.) Scholastic Library Publishing.

—I Love Puppies. Miller, Amanda. 2017. (Rookie Toddler Ser.). (ENG.). 12p. (J). (gr. -1 — 1). bds. 6.95 *(978-0-531-22686-5(7)*, Children's Pr.) Scholastic Library Publishing.

—Silly Monsters at Mealtime. Acer, Kerilyn. 2019. (Rookie Toddler Ser.). (ENG.). 12p. (J). (gr. -1 — 1). bds. 6.95 *(978-0-531-12928-9(4)*, Children's Pr.) Scholastic Library Publishing.

—Silly Monsters in the Bath. Chanko, Pamela. 2019. (Rookie Toddler Ser.). (ENG.). 12p. (J). (gr. -1 — 1). bds. 6.95 *(978-0-531-12927-2(6)*, Children's Pr.) Scholastic Library Publishing.

Mayer-Skumanz, Lene. One Cat's Special Christmas. Gantschev, Ivan. 2018. (Minedition Classic Ser.). (ENG.). 32p. (J). (gr. k-2). 12.00 *(978-988-8341-68-9(5)*, Minedition) Neugebauer, Michael (Publishing) Limited HKG. Dist: Penguin Random Hse. LLC.

Mayer, Uwe. The Stinking Story of Garbage. Daynes, Katie. (Usborne Young Reading: Series Two Ser.). (J). 2006. 64p. (gr. 4-7). per. 5.99 *(978-0-7945-1247-7(X))*; 2007. 62p. (gr. -1-3). 8.99 *(978-0-7945-1750-2(1))* EDC Publishing. (Usborne).

—Usborne the Children's Book of Art: Internet Linked. Dickins, Rosie. Armstrong, Carrie, ed. 2006. 64p. (J). (gr. 5-9). 14.99 *(978-0-7945-1223-1(2)*, Usborne) EDC Publishing.

Mayer, Uwe & McNee, Ian. The Story of Painting. Wheatley, Abigail. Riley, Janis, ed. 2007. (Story of Painting Ser.). 96p. (J). (gr. 4-7). pap. 10.99 *(978-0-7945-1678-9(5)*, Usborne) EDC Publishing.

Mayer, Uwe, jt. illus. see Chen, Kuo Kang.

Mayer, Uwe, jt. illus. see Donaera, Patrizia.

Mayer, Uwe, jt. illus. see Guille, Rosanne.

Mayer, Uwe, jt. illus. see Silver, Maggie.

Mayerik, Val, et al. Decades: Marvel in the 70s - Legion of Monsters. 2019. (ENG.). 248p. (YA). (gr. 8-17). pap. 24.99 *(978-1-302-91661-9(0))* Marvel Worldwide, Inc.

Mayes, Steven. Introducing... Max, 1 vol. Mayes, Rosey. 2010. 16p. 24.95 *(978-1-4489-3895-7(3))* PublishAmerica, Inc.

Mayfield, Helen. The Enchanted Deer. 77p. (Orig.). (J). (gr. 6-18). pap. 4.00 *(978-1-884993-03-9(6))* Koldarana Pubns.

—The Island of the Three Sapphires. Robbins, Neal. 98p. (J). (gr. 6-18). pap. 4.00 *(978-1-884993-04-6(4))* Koldarana Pubns.

Mayhew, James. Barefoot Books Stories from the Opera. Husain, Shahrukh & Barefoot Books. 2015. 96p. (J). (gr. 2-6). 16.99 *(978-1-78285-253-7(0))* Barefoot Bks., Inc.

—Classic Poems to Read Aloud. Berry, James. 2003. (Classic Collections). (ENG.). 256p. (J). (gr. 2-5). pap. 8.99 *(978-0-7534-5688-0(5)*, 9780753456880, Kingfisher) Roaring Brook Pr.

—Gaspard the Fox. Soanes, Zeb. 2018. (Gaspard the Fox Ser.). (ENG.). 36p. (J). (gr. -1-k). 19.99 *(978-1-912213-54-2(0))* Graffeg Limited GBR. Dist: Independent Pubs. Group.

—Gaspard the Fox Postcard Pack. Soanes, Zeb. 2018. (ENG.). 12p. (J). (gr. k-2). 18.95 *(978-1-912654-20-8(2))* Graffeg Limited GBR. Dist: Independent Pubs. Group.

—Shakespeare's Storybook: Folk Tales That Inspired the Bard. Ryan, Patrick. (ENG.). (J). 2009. 21.99 *(978-1-84686-271-7(X))*; 2006. 80p. (gr. 4-7). pap. 16.99 *(978-1-905236-86-2(7))* Barefoot Bks., Inc.

Mayhew, Mike. Rebel Jail: Volume 1. Aaron, Jason. 2017. (Star Wars: Rebel Jail Ser.). (ENG.). 24p. (J). (gr. 6-12). lib. bdg. 27.07 *(978-1-5321-4141-6(6)*, 27014, Graphic Novels) Spotlight.

Mayhew, Sara E. First Emperor. Low, Vicki. 2007. 48p. (J). lib. bdg. 23.08 *(978-1-4242-1626-0(5))* Fitzgerald Bks.

Maylin, Grace B., photos by. There Will Come Another: A Lesson from the Trees. Maylin, Grace B. 2007. per. *(978-0-9792384-0-6(4))* Maylin, Grace.

Maynard, Barbara, jt. illus. see Rousseff, Minnie.

Maynard, Marc. Weather. Litchfield, Jo. 2008. (Usborne Look & Say Ser.). 12p. (J). (gr. -1-3). bds. 7.99 *(978-0-7945-1989-6(X)*, Usborne) EDC Publishing.

Maynard, Tiya Caniel. I Threw Rocks As a Kid. Caniel, Jay. 2019. (ENG.). 40p. (J). pap. 9.99 ***(978-0-692-17816-4(3))*** Maynard, Vernal Hugo.

Mayne, Michael. A Wild Ride. Biggs, Pauline. 2004. 20p. (J). per. 12.95 *(978-0-9760129-0-0(1))* The Publishing Place LLC.

Mayo, Diana. The Children of Lir: A Celtic Legend. Casey, Dawn. 2004. 32p. (J). pap. *(978-1-85269-897-3(7))*; pap. *(978-1-85269-892-8(6))*; pap. *(978-1-85269-887-4(X))*; pap. *(978-1-85269-878-2(0))*; pap. *(978-1-85269-873-7(X))*; (ARA.). pap. *(978-1-85269-872-0(1))*; pap. *(978-1-85269-868-3(3))*; pap. *(978-1-85269-867-6(5))*; pap. *(978-1-85269-863-8(2))*; pap. *(978-1-85269-858-4(6))*; pap. *(978-1-85269-853-9(5))*; pap. *(978-1-85269-848-5(9))*; (PAN.). pap. *(978-1-85269-843-0(8))*; pap. *(978-1-85269-838-6(1))*; pap. *(978-1-85269-828-7(4))*; pap. *(978-1-85269-823-2(3))*; pap. *(978-1-85269-818-8(7))* Mantra Lingua.

—The Gingerbread Man. Lupton, Hugh. 2003. 24p. (J). (gr. k-3). 14.99 *(978-1-84148-056-5(8))* Barefoot Bks., Inc.

—Isis & Osiris. 2004. (J). (ALB & ENG.). *(978-1-84444-313-0(2))*; (ARA & ENG.). *(978-1-84444-314-7(0))*; (CHI & ENG.). *(978-1-84444-316-1(7))*; (PER & ENG.). *(978-1-84444-318-5(3))*; (GER.). 30p. *(978-1-84444-320-8(5))*; (GUJ & ENG.). *(978-1-84444-321-5(3))*; (ITA & ENG.). *(978-1-84444-322-2(1))*; (POR & ENG.). *(978-1-84444-324-6(8))*; (SER & ENG.). *(978-1-84444-325-3(6))*; (SOM & ENG.). *(978-1-84444-326-0(4))*; (SPA.). 30p. *(978-1-84444-327-7(2))*; (TAM & ENG.). *(978-1-84444-328-4(0))*; (TUR & ENG.). *(978-1-84444-329-1(9))*; (VIE & ENG.). *(978-1-84444-331-4(0))*; (ENG & FRE.). 32p. pap. *(978-1-84444-319-2(1))* Mantra Lingua.

—My Little Picture Bible. DK. 2008. (ENG.). 80p. (J). (gr. -1 — 1). 7.99 *(978-0-7566-3997-6(2)*, DK Children) Dorling Kindersley Publishing, Inc.

—My Very First Bible. Dorling Kindersley Publishing Staff. 2019. (ENG.). 80p. (J). (gr. 2-4). 14.99 *(978-1-4654-8133-7(8)*, DK Children) Dorling Kindersley Publishing, Inc.

—Pandora's Box. Barkow, Henriette. 2004. (ENG & ARA.). 32p. (J). pap. *(978-1-85269-898-0(5))*; pap. *(978-1-85269-894-2(2))*; pap. *(978-1-85269-893-5(4))*; pap. *(978-1-85269-889-8(6))*; pap. *(978-1-85269-884-3(5))*; pap. *(978-1-85269-879-9(9))*; pap. *(978-1-85269-874-4(8))*; pap. *(978-1-85269-869-0(1))*; pap. *(978-1-85269-864-5(0))*; pap. *(978-1-85269-859-1(4))*; pap. *(978-1-85269-854-6(3))*; pap. *(978-1-85269-849-2(7))*; pap. *(978-1-85269-844-7(6))*; pap. *(978-1-85269-839-3(X))*; pap. *(978-1-85269-834-8(9))*; pap. *(978-1-85269-829-4(2))*; pap. *(978-1-85269-824-9(1))*; pap. *(978-1-85269-819-5(5))* Mantra Lingua.

—Pandora's Box: English Only. Barkow, Henriette. 2004. (ENG.). 32p. (J). pap. *(978-1-84444-380-2(9))* Mantra Lingua.

—The Tiger & the Wise Man. Fusek Peters, Andrew. (Traditional Tales with a Twist Ser.). 32p. (J). 2010. (gr. -1-2). *(978-1-84643-346-7(0))*; 2004. (gr. 2-3). *(978-1-904550-07-5(X))* Child's Play International Ltd.

—Winter King, Summer Queen. Lister, Mary. 2007. 32p. (J). (gr. -1-3). pap. 9.99 *(978-1-84686-009-6(1))*; (ENG.). pap. 7.99 *(978-1-84686-080-5(6))* Barefoot Bks., Inc.

Mayo, Diana. Yawning Yoga. Jordan, Laurie. 2020. 32p. (J). (-3). 8.99 ***(978-1-7282-2307-0(5)***, Little Pickle Pr.) Sourcebooks, Inc.

Mayo, Diana & Mistry, Nilesh. Isis & Osiris. Casey, Dawn. 2004. (ENG & BEN.). 32p. (J). pap. *(978-1-84444-315-4(9))*; pap. *(978-1-84444-323-9(X))*; pap. *(978-1-84444-330-7(2))*; pap. *(978-1-84444-433-5(3))*; pap. *(978-1-84444-434-2(1))*; pap. *(978-1-84444-435-9(X))* Mantra Lingua.

Mayo, Frank. An Alligator Adventure in Florida. Wilsdon, Christina. 2006. 26p. (J). 7.99 *(978-1-59939-010-9(8))* Cornerstone Pr.

—King Midas & the Golden Touch: A Tale about Greed. 2006. (J). 6.99 *(978-1-59939-022-2(1))* Cornerstone Pr.

Mays, Victor. Patrick Henry: Firebrand of the Revolution. Campion, Nardi Reeder. 2011. 272p. 47.95 *(978-1-258-04065-9(4))* Literary Licensing, LLC.

Maytorena de Barron, Martha. My Best Friend Is a Giraffe. Pottinger, Heidi Lee. 2018. (My Best Friend Is... Ser.: Vol. 1). (ENG.). 26p. (J). pap. 19.99 *(978-1-5393-4956-3(X))* CreateSpace Independent Publishing Platform.

Mazali, Gustavo. Albert Einstein: a Curious Mind. Albee, Sarah. 2020. (I Can Read Level 2 Ser.). (ENG.). 32p. (J). (gr. -1-3). pap. 4.99 ***(978-0-06-243269-8(9)***, HarperCollins) HarperCollins Pubs. Ltd. GBR. Dist: HarperCollins Pubs.

Mazali, Gustavo. Ben Franklin Thinks Big. Keenan, Sheila. 2018. (I Can Read Level 2 Ser.). (ENG.). 32p. (J). (gr. -1-3). 16.99 *(978-0-06-243264-3(8))*; pap. 4.99 *(978-0-06-243263-6(X))* HarperCollins Pubs.

—Biblia de Historias Del Gran Plan de Dios: La Revelación Del Plan de Dios, 1 vol. Fodor, Cecile Olesen. 2019. (SPA.). 108p. (J). 16.99 *(978-1-4041-0987-2(0))* Grupo Nelson.

—Celebrate Fourth of July with Champ, the Scamp. Flor Ada, Alma. 2006. (Cuentos para Celebrar / Stories to Celebrate Ser.). 30p. (J). (gr. k-6). per. 11.95 *(978-1-59820-131-4(X))* Santillana USA Publishing Co., Inc.

—A Day with Daddy. Gikow, Louise. 2004. (My First Reader Ser.). (ENG.). 32p. (J). (gr. k-1). pap. 3.95 *(978-0-516-25501-9(0)*, Children's Pr.) Scholastic Library Publishing.

—Desastre en la Cocina. Muñoz, Isabel. 2012. (Eric & Julieta Ser.). (ENG & SPA.). 24p. (J). (gr. -1-3). pap. 3.99 *(978-0-545-35581-0(8)*, Scholastic en Espanol) Scholastic, Inc.

—En el Museo. Muñoz, Isabel. ed. 2011. (Eric & Julieta Ser.).Tr. of At the Museum. (ENG & SPA.). 24p. (J). (gr. -1-3). pap. 3.99 *(978-0-545-34512-5(X)*, Scholastic en Espanol) Scholastic, Inc.

—Harriet Tubman: Freedom Fighter. Hohn, Nadia L. 2018. (I Can Read Level 2 Ser.). (ENG.). 32p. (J). (gr. -1-3). 16.99 *(978-0-06-243285-8(0))* HarperCollins Pubs.

—Harriet Tubman: Freedom Fighter. Hohn, Nadia L. 2018. (I Can Read Level 2 Ser.). (ENG.). 32p. (J). (gr. -1-3). pap. 4.99 *(978-0-06-243284-1(2)*, HarperCollins) HarperCollins Pubs. Ltd. GBR. Dist: HarperCollins Pubs.

—Heaven Is a Wonderful Place. Burrin, Angela. 2019. (ENG.). 32p. (J). 14.95 *(978-1-59325-358-5(3))* Word Among Us Pr.

—Helen Keller: the World at Her Fingertips. Albee, Sarah. 2019. (I Can Read Level 2 Ser.). (ENG.). 32p. (J). (gr. -1-3). 16.99 *(978-0-06-243282-7(6))*; pap. 4.99 *(978-0-06-243281-0(8))* HarperCollins Pubs.

—It's Mine (Es Mío) Muñoz, Isabel. ed. 2006. (Eric & Julieta Ser.). (ENG & SPA.). 24p. (J). (gr. -1-3). pap. 3.99 *(978-0-439-78370-5(4))* Scholastic, Inc.

—Jane Goodall: a Champion of Chimpanzees. Albee, Sarah. 2020. (I Can Read Level 2 Ser.). (ENG.). 32p. (J). (gr. -1-3). 16.99 *(978-0-06-243279-7(6))* HarperCollins Pubs.

—Jane Goodall: a Champion of Chimpanzees. Albee, Sarah. 2020. (I Can Read Level 2 Ser.). (ENG.). 32p. (J). (gr. -1-3). pap. 4.99 *(978-0-06-243278-0(8)*, HarperCollins) HarperCollins Pubs. Ltd. GBR. Dist: HarperCollins Pubs.

—Just Like Mom. Muñoz, Isabel. 2005. 22p. (J). pap. *(978-0-439-78844-1(7))* Scholastic, Inc.

—Lee y Juega: Es Tiempo para Amar y Reír, 1 vol. Stancliff, David. 2019. (SPA.). 48p. (J). bds. 12.99 *(978-1-4041-1014-4(3))* Grupo Nelson.

—My First Handy Bible. Olesen, Cecilie. 2006. (ENG.). 64p. (gr. -1-k). bds. 12.99 *(978-1-59052-608-8(2)*, Multnomah Bks.) Crown Publishing Group, The.

—My Time with God. Fodor, Cecilie. 2018. (ENG.). (J). bds. 11.95 *(978-0-8091-6790-6(5))* Paulist Pr.

—Now What? Muñoz, Isabel. ed. 2006. (Eric & Julieta Ser.).Tr. of ¿Ahora Que?. (SPA & ENG.). 24p. (J). (gr. -1-3). pap. 3.99 *(978-0-439-78372-9(0))* Scholastic, Inc.

—Read & Play Baby Bible, 1 vol. 2016. (ENG.). 46p. (J). bds. 9.99 *(978-0-310-75780-1(0))* Zonderkidz.

—Thomas Edison: Lighting the Way. Houran, Lori Haskins. 2019. (I Can Read Level 2 Ser.). (ENG.). 32p. (J). (gr. -1-3). 16.99 *(978-0-06-243288-9(5))*; pap. 4.99 *(978-0-06-243287-2(7))* HarperCollins Pubs.

—Trucks & Diggers. Brooks, Felicity & Durber, Matt. 2008. (Magnet Bks.). 10p. (J). (gr. -1-3). bds. 19.99 *(978-0-7945-1907-0(5)*, Usborne) EDC Publishing.

—Where Is Eric? (¿Donde Está Eric?) Muñoz, Isabel. 2006. (Eric & Julieta Ser.). (ENG & SPA.). 24p. (J). (gr. -1-3). pap. 3.99 *(978-0-439-78371-2(2))* Scholastic, Inc.

—The White Elephant 4 Voyagers. McCaughrean, Geraldine. 2017. (Cambridge Reading Adventures Ser.). (ENG.). 40p. pap. 10.11 *(978-1-108-40588-1(6))* Cambridge Univ. Pr.

Maze, Deborah & Williams, Garth. The World of Little House. Collins, Carolyn Strom & Eriksson, Christina Wyss. 2015. (Little House Nonfiction Ser.). (ENG.). 160p. (J). (gr. 3). 29.99 *(978-0-06-243049-6(1))* HarperCollins Pubs.

Mazeika, Katie. Computer Decoder: Dorothy Vaughn, Computer Scientist. Diehn, Andi. 2019. (Picture Book Biography Ser.). 32p. (J). (gr. k-3). 16.95 *(978-1-61930-556-4(9)*, a9c7b5db-9f65-4c9f-bd43-2fdb4e84b143); pap. 9.95 *(978-1-61930-765-0(0)*, 31f0edb7-0fb1-4483-b3a0-8f77f87dd11b) Nomad Pr.

—Fossil Huntress: Mary Leakey, Paleontologist. Diehn, Andi. 2019. (Picture Book Biography Ser.). 32p. (J). (gr. k-3). 16.95 *(978-1-61930-770-4(7)*, 2f3d9fe9-c7d7-4113-a8e4-26db6d649589); pap. 9.95 *(978-1-61930-773-5(1)*, 6f3eb50e-2725-4cb2-b7bc-a835bca6493a) Nomad Pr.

—Human Computer: Mary Jackson, Engineer. Diehn, Andi. 2019. (Picture Book Biography Ser.). 32p. (J). (gr. k-3). 16.95 *(978-1-61930-774-2(X)*, b08f0d76-53aa-4608-819b-ed45d26ce264); pap. 9.95 *(978-1-61930-777-3(4)*, 460ddec6-2b24-4743-8d9c-2f20d96c7640) Nomad Pr.

—The Magic Trapdoor. Nelson, M. R. 2018. (Magic Trapdoor Ser.). (ENG.). 32p. (J). (gr. k-3). 5.99 *(978-1-5324-0935-6(4))*; pap. 5.99 *(978-1-5324-0822-9(6))* Xist Publishing.

—Space Adventurer: Bonnie Dunbar, Astronaut. Diehn, Andi. 2019. (Picture Book Biography Ser.). 32p. (J). (gr. k-3). 16.95 *(978-1-61930-766-7(9)*, ef167057-202a-468c-90a1-afdee0391983); pap. 9.95 *(978-1-61930-769-8(3)*, de43edcd-a3ab-4024-bff4-63bd8aeafbfa) Nomad Pr.

—Spit Nests, Puke Power, & Other Brilliant Bird Adaptations. Perdew, Laura. 2020. (Picture Book Science Ser.). 32p. (J). (gr. k-3). (ENG.). 19.95 *(978-1-61930-949-4(1)*, 2914ecdc-bc7e-4d05-b80a-06c7f354ab87); pap. 9.95 *(978-1-61930-952-4(1)*, 12c3d2ed-6e32-4eb2-86e6-9e6dff94cfd5) Nomad Pr.

—Stink Fights, Earwax, & Other Marvelous Mammal Adaptations. Perdew, Laura. 2020. (Picture Book Science Ser.). 32p. (J). (gr. k-3). (ENG.). 19.95 *(978-1-61930-957-9(2)*, 2de25913-24d6-4918-87dc-f0a5e5188202); pap. 9.95 *(978-1-61930-960-9(2)*, 127877c9-ed30-41be-ad13-82c4bcc8fbb4) Nomad Pr.

—Water-Walking, Sidewinding, & Other Remarkable Reptile Adaptations. Perdew, Laura. 2020. (Picture Book Science Ser.). 32p. (J). (gr. k-3). (ENG.). 19.95 *(978-1-61930-945-6(9)*, 7fc312d0-f1bc-4045-b01a-32198045291f); pap. 9.95 *(978-1-61930-948-7(3)*, 17feb765-67a2-426d-9e04-169568556e61) Nomad Pr.

Mazellan, Ron. A Is for Abraham: A Jewish Family Alphabet. Michelson, Richard. 2008. (ENG.). 40p. (J). (gr. 1-4). 17.95 *(978-1-58536-322-3(7)*, 202126) Sleeping Bear Pr.

—Finding Daddy: A Story of the Great Depression. Harper, Jo & Harper, Josephine. 2005. (ENG.). 48p. (J). (gr. k). 16.95 *(978-1-890515-31-7(0))* Turtle Bks.

—The Harmonica. Johnston, Tony. 2004. (ENG.). 32p. (J). (gr. 2-4). 22.44 *(978-1-57091-547-5(4))* Charlesbridge Publishing, Inc.

—Irena's Jars of Secrets, 1 vol. Vaughan, Marcia. 2011. (ENG.). 40p. (J). 18.95 *(978-1-60060-439-3(0))* Lee & Low Bks., Inc.

—Kids' Questions about Church & the Future. Fawcett, Cheryl & Newman, Robert C. 2003. 79p. pap. *(978-1-59402-084-1(1))* Regular Baptist Pr.

—Kids' Questions about God & Jesus. Fawcett, Cheryl & Newman, Robert C. 2003. 71p. pap. *(978-1-59402-081-0(7))* Regular Baptist Pr.

—We Will Walk. 2005. 16p. (J). pap. *(978-0-7367-2919-2(4))* Zaner-Bloser, Inc.

—You Can Be a Friend. Dungy, Tony & Dungy, Lauren. 2011. (ENG.). 32p. (J). (gr. -1-2). 17.99 *(978-1-4169-9771-9(7)*, Little Simon Inspirations) Little Simon Inspirations.

Mazellan, Ron. The Harmonica. Mazellan, Ron. Johnston, Tony. 2008. (ENG.). 32p. (J). (gr. 2-5). pap. 7.95 *(978-1-57091-489-8(3))* Charlesbridge Publishing, Inc.

Mazerac, Joseph. ANDY, Book 1: The Rise of David. Mazerac, Joseph. 2007. (ENG.). 96p. 9.99 *(978-0-9792770-0-9(0))* Old Time Stories.

Mazhar, Jay. Ants Don't Talk, Do They? Sharer, John. 2020. (ENG.). 76p. (J). pap. 10.95 ***(978-0-9961142-0-2(3))*** Wompetias Pr.

Mazhar, Jay. A Boy at Heart. Vento, Ray M. 2018. (Sam Caruso Stories Ser.: Vol. 3). (ENG.). 34p. (J). (gr. 3-5). 14.95 *(978-0-9856890-5-6(6))* Ray.

Mazibuko, Luthando. How Riley Rescued the Hufffy Woofer. Garrott, Dawn E. 2015. (How Riley Ser.). (ENG.). 67p. (J). (gr. 2-7). pap. 12.00 *(978-1-61851-092-1(4))* Baha'i Publishing.

—How Riley Tamed the Invisible Monster. Garrott, Dawn E. 2009. (How Riley Ser.). (ENG.). 65p. (J). (gr. 2-7). pap. 9.95 *(978-0-87743-709-3(2))* Baha'i Publishing.

Mazibuko, Luthando. John Birks Dizzy Gillespie: A Man, a Trumpet, & a Journey to Bebop. Engle, Susan. 2020. (Change Maker Ser.). (ENG.). 90p. (J). pap. 9.95 ***(978-1-61851-155-3(6))*** Baha'i Publishing.

Mazibuko, Luthando. Mema Says Good-Bye. Jaskwhich, Cynthia Sheperd. 2010. (J). *(978-0-87743-710-9(6))* Baha'i Publishing Trust, U.S.

Mazille, Capucine. My Take-Along Bible. Davidson, Alice Joyce. 2004. 20p. (J). bds. 11.99 *(978-0-89221-577-5(1))* New Leaf Publishing Group.

—Red Riding Hood's Math Adventure. Harcourt, Lalie & Wortzman, Rickie. 2006. 19p. (J). (gr. k-4). reprint ed. 15.00 *(978-0-7567-9957-1(0))* DIANE Publishing Co.

Mazon, Alyssa. Ducklings on the Run. Summerhill, Abby & Summerhill, Noni. 2019. (ENG.). 34p. (J). (gr. k-3). pap. 10.95 ***(978-1-7322135-7-9(7))*** Legacies & Memories.

—Patitos Al Escape. Summerhill, Abby & Summerhill, Noni (Gail). 2020. (SPA.). 34p. (J). (gr. k-3). pap. 10.95 ***(978-1-7347007-0-1(X))*** Legacies & Memories.

Mazumdar, Sintu. Ben Brown & the Return of the Nephilim. Thorp, Michael C. 2010. 172p. (YA). pap. *(978-0-473-15580-3(X))* Free House Publishing.

Mazzara, Aurelio, et al. Champions: déjà Vu All over Again & Again. Marz, Ron & Rodriguez, David A. 2018. (Skylanders Ser.). (ENG.). 24p. (J). (gr. 1-5). lib. bdg. 27.07 *(978-1-5321-4244-4(7)*, 28572, Graphic Novels) Spotlight.

—Marvel Spider-Man: 8-Book Library & Electronic Reader. 2019. (Me Reader Ser.). (ENG.). 192p. (J). *(978-1-5037-4792-0(1)*, eaab1a2f-edc6-4c47-93b6-809c4b13914d, p i kids) Phoenix International Publications, Inc.

Mazzara, Aurelio. Starcadia Quest: Heart of a Star. Roberts, James. 2020. 80p. (J). (gr. 4-7). pap. 9.99 *(978-1-68405-646-0(2))* Idea & Design Works, LLC.

Mazzarello, Marco. Disney Comics & Stories: Friends Forever. Stabile, Vito et al. 2019. (DISNEY COMICS & STORIES Ser.). (ENG.). 152p. (J). (gr. 4-7). pap. 14.99 *(978-1-68405-504-3(0))* Idea & Design Works, LLC.

M

Mazzei, Miriam. Does It Still Hurt. Pinto, Marie Parks. 2012. 30p. pap. 16.95 *(978-1-938812-02-6(6))* Full Court Pr.

—I Am Not Broken. Pinto, Marie Parks. 2012. (ENG.). 30p. pap. 16.95 *(978-1-938812-00-2(X))* Full Court Pr.

—Where Is Daddy? Pinto, Marie Parks. 2012. 30p. pap. 16.95 *(978-1-938812-06-4(9))* Full Court Pr.

Mazzola, Frank, Jr. The Ocean Alphabet Board Book. Pallotta, Jerry. 2003. 28p. (J). (-k). bds. 7.95 *(978-1-57091-524-6(5))* Charlesbridge Publishing, Inc.

Mazzon, Michelle, jt. illus. see Castellan, Andrea "Casty".

Mazzucchelli, David, jt. illus. see Hernandez, Gilbert.

Mazzucco, Jennifer. The Pig Who Went Home on Sunday: An Appalachian Folktale. Davis, Donald. (ENG.). 40p. (J). (gr. -1-3). 2007. 8.95 *(978-0-87483-851-0(7))*; 2005. 16.95 *(978-0-87483-571-7(2))* August Hse. Pubs., Inc.

Mbairamadji, Koffi. African Savannah Stories, Volume 1. Mbairamadji, Koffi. 2006. 40p. (J). per. 17.49 *(978-1-59879-277-5(6))* Lifevest Publishing, Inc.

Mbamalu, Stanley. Winter & Me! From the Crunchety-Crunch & Other Season Sounds Collection. Hayes, Gail. 2020. (ENG.). 34p. (J). pap. 12.95 ***(978-1-886853-28-7(2))*** Handle Your Business Girl Publishing.

Mbd, Dion. My Heart Song. Solana, Sister. 2018. (ENG.). 32p. (J). (gr. k-4). pap. 12.95 *(978-1-61493-629-9(3))* Peppertree Pr., The.

Mboya, Sharif. Heart Fealt Doses of Reality. Mboya, Sharif. 2004. 148p. (YA). per. 14.99 *(978-0-9754024-5-0(5))* Doses of Reality, Inc.

Mc Kelvey, Shawn. Timothy's Tic. Hurwitz, Kathleen A. 2008. 40p. (gr. -1 — 1). 16.99 *(978-1-4389-1924-9(7))* AuthorHouse.

McAdam, Matt. To the Spider in My House. Rubinstein, Samuel L. 2019. (ENG.). 26p. (J). pap. 15.00 ***(978-1-9876-5364-9(5))*** CreateSpace Independent Publishing Platform.

McAdams, Caleb. Shubert. McAdams, Susan. 2008. 16p. per. 24.95 *(978-1-4241-9756-9(2))* America Star Bks.

McAdoo, Grami & McAdoo, O'Pa. In the Wake of Suicide: A Child's Journey. Kaulen, Diane Bouman. 2008. (J). (gr. 3-5). 14.95 *(978-0-9764026-5-7(3))* Longhorn Creek Pr.

McAdoo, O'Pa, jt. illus. see McAdoo, Grami.

McAliley, Susan, et al. Kit's Cooking Studio. Hirsch, Jennifer & Jones, Michelle. Witkowski, Teri, ed. 2007. (American Girl Ser.). 55p. (J). (gr. 3-7). 15.95 *(978-1-59369-267-4(6))* American Girl Publishing, Inc.

—Meet Julie 1974, 1. Mcdonald, Megan. 2007. (American Girls Collection: Julie Stories Ser.). (ENG.). 104p. (J). (gr. 2-4). pap. 21.19 *(978-1-59369-257-5(9))* American Girl Publishing, Inc.

McAliley, Susan & Hunt, Robert. Happy New Year, Julie, Bk. 3. Mcdonald, Megan. 2007. (American Girl Ser.). (ENG.). 88p. (J). (gr. 3-7). 12.95 *(978-1-59369-292-6(7))* American Girl Publishing, Inc.

McAliley, Susan, jt. illus. see Rane, Walter.

McAlister, Rachel. Goodnight, Constellations. Running Press. 2019. 20p. (J). (gr. -1 — 1). bds. 9.99 *(978-0-7624-9460-6(3)*, Running Pr. Kids) Running Pr.

—Koala Is Not a Bear. Gray, Kristin L. 2019. 32p. (J). (gr. -1-2). 16.95 *(978-1-4549-2745-7(3))* Sterling Publishing Co., Inc.

—My First Horoscope. Running Press, Running. 2020. 26p. (J). (gr. -1 — 1). bds. 9.99 *(978-0-7624-9630-3(4)*, Running Pr. Kids) Running Pr.

McAlister, Sydney. Christmas in Lake Meadow. McAlister, Brandon. 2017. (ENG.). 36p. (J). pap. 9.99 *(978-1-7288-4897-6(0))* Independently Published.

McAllan, Marina. Hey Diddle Diddle: The Story. Egan, Cecilia. 2015. (The Nursery Rhyme Story Ser.: 1). (ENG.). (J). pap. *(978-1-925110-65-4(6)*, Leaves of Gold Pr.) Quillpen Pty. Ltd.

—Humpty Dumpty: The Story. Egan, Cecilia. 2015. (The Nursery Rhyme Story Ser.: 2). (ENG.). (J). pap. *(978-1-925110-66-1(4)*, Leaves of Gold Pr.) Quillpen Pty. Ltd.

—Little Miss Muffet: The Story. Egan, Cecilia. 2015. (The Nursery Rhyme Story Ser.: 3). (ENG.). (J). pap. *(978-1-925110-67-8(2)*, Leaves of Gold Pr.) Quillpen Pty. Ltd.

McAllister, Chris. Bullfrog Pops!, 1 vol. Walton, Rick. 2005. 32p. (J). (gr. 3-3). pap. 7.99 *(978-1-58685-840-7(8))* Gibbs Smith, Publisher.

—Bullfrog Pops! Adventures in Verbs & Objects, 1 vol. Walton, Rick. 2011. (ENG.). 36p. (J). (gr. 2-3). pap. 7.99 *(978-1-4236-2079-2(8))* Gibbs Smith, Publisher.

McAllister, Ian, photos by. A Bear's Life, 1 vol. Read, Nicholas. 2017. (My Great Bear Rainforest Ser.: 2). (ENG., 32p. (J). (gr. 1-3). 19.95 *(978-1-4598-1270-3(0))* Orca Bk. Pubs. USA.

—The Great Bear Sea: Exploring the Marine Life of a Pacific Paradise, 1 vol. Read, Nicholas. 2013. (ENG., 128p. (J). (gr. 4-7). pap. 19.95 *(978-1-4598-0019-9(2))* Orca Bk. Pubs. USA.

—My Great Bear Rainforest Bundle, 1 vol. Read, Nicholas. 2020. (My Great Bear Rainforest Ser.). (ENG., 128p. (J). (gr. 1-3). 69.95 *(978-1-4598-2278-8(1))* Orca Bk. Pubs. USA.

—The Salmon Bears: Giants of the Great Bear Rainforest, 1 vol. Read, Nicholas. 2010. (ENG., 96p. (J). (gr. 4-7). 18.95 *(978-1-55469-205-7(9))* Orca Bk. Pubs. USA.

—The Sea Wolves: Living Wild in the Great Bear Rainforest, 1 vol. Read, Nicholas. 2010. (ENG., 128p. (J). (gr. 4-7). pap. 19.95 *(978-1-55469-206-4(7))* Orca Bk. Pubs. USA.

—The Seal Garden, 1 vol. Read, Nicholas. 2018. (My Great Bear Rainforest Ser.: 3). (ENG., 32p. (J). (gr. 1-3). 19.95 *(978-1-4598-1267-3(0))* Orca Bk. Pubs. USA.

—A Whale's World, 1 vol. Read, Nicholas. 2018. (My Great Bear Rainforest Ser.: 4). (ENG., 32p. (J). (gr. 1-3). 19.95 *(978-1-4598-1273-4(5))* Orca Bk. Pubs. USA.

—Wolf Island, 1 vol. Read, Nicholas. 2017. (My Great Bear Rainforest Ser.: 1). (ENG., 32p. (J). (gr. 1-3). 19.95 *(978-1-4598-1264-2(6))* Orca Bk. Pubs. USA.

McAndrew, Phil. Caveboy Dave: More Scrawny Than Brawny. Reynolds, Aaron. 2016. (Caveboy Dave Ser.: 1). 256p. (J). (gr. 3-7). bds. 13.99 *(978-0-14-751658-9(7)*, Viking Books for Young Readers) Penguin Young Readers Group.

—Monster Science: Could Monsters Survive (and Thrive!) in the Real World? Becker, Helaine. 2016. (ENG.). 96p. (J). (gr. 3-7). 18.95 *(978-1-77138-054-6(3))* Kids Can Pr., Ltd. CAN. Dist: Hachette Bk. Group.

—Not So Faboo. Reynolds, Aaron. 2018. (Caveboy Dave Ser.: 2). 256p. (J). (gr. 3-7). 20.99 *(978-0-451-47548-0(8))*; pap. 12.99 *(978-0-14-751659-6(5))* Penguin Young Readers Group. (Viking Books for Young Readers).

McAskill, Diana. Boo & Oscar in the Terrible Trouble on the Tobique. Koenig, Wendy L. 2019. (Boo & Oscar Ser.: Vol. 2). (ENG.). 26p. (J). pap. 10.00 *(978-1-0959-0186-1(9))* Independently Published.

—Boo et Oscar Dans le Terrible de Trouble Sur la Tobique. Koenig, Wendy L. 2019. (Boo & Oscar Ser.: Vol. 2). (FRE.). 26p. (J). pap. 10.00 *(978-1-0708-1403-2(2))* Independently Published.

McAskin, Denice. Comprehension Crosswords Grade 4, 6 vols. Hemminger, Marcia. 2003. 32p. (J). 4.99 *(978-1-56472-188-4(4))* Edupress, Inc.

McAteer, Thomas. Basil's New Home: The Garden Rabbit Series - Part One. Vetter Squires, Diane. 2009. 28p. pap. 13.99 *(978-1-4490-0675-4(2))* AuthorHouse.

—Sandy's Vision. Bednar, Martin. 2014. (ENG.). (J). (gr. -1-3). 19.95 *(978-1-62086-861-4(X))* Mascot Bks., Inc.

McBee, Scott. At the Seashore. Koeppel, Ruth. 2009. (ENG.). 10p. (J). (gr. -1-1). 12.99 *(978-1-58476-817-3(7))* Innovative Kids.

—In the Wild. Koeppel, Ruth. 2009. (ENG.). 10p. (J). (gr. -1-1). 15.99 *(978-1-58476-816-6(9))* Innovative Kids.

McBeth, Glen. Create an Animation with Scratch. Wood, Kevin. 2018. (Project Code Ser.). (ENG.). 32p. (J). (gr. 4-7). pap. 9.99 *(978-1-5415-2513-9(2))*; lib. bdg. 29.32 *(978-1-5415-2436-1(5)*, Lerner Pubns.) Lerner Publishing Group.

—Create Computer Games with Scratch. Wood, Kevin. 2018. (Project Code Ser.). (ENG.). 32p. (J). (gr. 4-7). pap. 9.99 *(978-1-5415-2514-6(0))*; lib. bdg. 29.32 *(978-1-5415-2439-2(X)*, Lerner Pubns.) Lerner Publishing Group.

—Create Music with Scratch. Wood, Kevin. 2018. (Project Code Ser.). (ENG.). 32p. (J). (gr. 4-7). pap. 9.99 *(978-1-5415-2515-3(9))*; lib. bdg. 29.32 *(978-1-5415-2437-8(3)*, Lerner Pubns.) Lerner Publishing Group.

—Create Your Own Story with Scratch. Wood, Kevin. 2018. (Project Code Ser.). (ENG.). 32p. (J). (gr. 4-7). pap. 9.99 *(978-1-5415-2512-2(4))*; lib. bdg. 29.32 *(978-1-5415-2438-5(1)*, Lerner Pubns.) Lerner Publishing Group.

McBeth, T. L. Big Words Small Stories: the Missing Donut. Henderson, Judith. 2018. (ENG.). 56p. (J). (gr. k-3). 12.99 *(978-1-77138-788-0(2))* Kids Can Pr., Ltd. CAN. Dist: Hachette Bk. Group.

—Big Words Small Stories: the Traveling Dustball. Henderson, Judith. 2019. (ENG.). 56p. (J). (gr. k-3). 12.99 *(978-1-77138-789-7(0))* Kids Can Pr., Ltd. CAN. Dist: Hachette Bk. Group.

—Ducks! Underwood, Deborah. 2020. (ENG.). 40p. (J). 17.99 *(978-1-250-12709-9(2)*, 900175376, Holt, Henry & Co. Bks. For Young Readers) Holt, Henry & Co.

—Ogilvy. Underwood, Deborah. 2019. (ENG.). 40p. (J). 17.99 *(978-1-250-15176-6(7)*, 900183400, Holt, Henry & Co. Bks. For Young Readers) Holt, Henry & Co.

—Stegothesaurus. Heos, Bridget. 2018. (ENG.). 40p. (J). 17.99 *(978-1-250-13488-2(9)*, 900177994, Holt, Henry & Co. Bks. For Young Readers) Holt, Henry & Co.

McBeth, T. L. Randy, the Badly Drawn Horse. McBeth, T. L. 2020. (ENG.). 40p. (J). 18.99 *(978-1-250-18590-7(4)*, 900191444, Holt, Henry & Co. Bks. For Young Readers) Holt, Henry & Co.

—Robot in Love. McBeth, T. L. 2018. (ENG.). 40p. (J). 17.99 *(978-1-250-18593-8(9)*, 900191448, Holt, Henry & Co. Bks. For Young Readers) Holt, Henry & Co.

McBride, Angus. Egypt. Heinrichs, Ann. 2012. (Enchantment of the World Ser.). (ENG.). 144p. (J). (gr. 5-9). lib. bdg. 40.00 *(978-0-531-25309-0(0)*, Children's Pr.) Scholastic Library Publishing.

McBride, Angus. Puss in Boots. McBride, Angus, tr. 2004. (ENG.). 26p. (J). (gr. 1-3). pap. 6.47 net. *(978-0-7685-0327-2(2)*, Dominie Elementary) Savvas Learning Co.

McBride, Earvin, Jr. The Adventurous Cyborg. McBride, Earvin, Jr. 2nd unabr. ed. 2003. (Amazing Sci-Fi & Adventure Heroes Ser.). 43p. (YA). (gr. 7-12). 4.95 *(978-1-892511-06-5(1))* MacBride, E. J. Pubn., Inc.

—The Bowdery Rodeo Cowboys of Texas. McBride, Earvin, Jr. 2nd unabr. ed. 2003. (Earvin MacBride's Amazing Sci-Fi & Adventure Heroes Ser.). 329p. (J). (gr. 7-12). pap. 4.95 *(978-1-892511-07-2(X))* MacBride, E. J. Pubn., Inc.

—Earvin MacBride's Amazing Sci-Fi & Adventure Heroes, 7 vols. McBride, Earvin, Jr. 2nd unabr. ed. 2003. (J). (gr. 7-12). pap. 25.95 *(978-1-892511-05-8(3))* MacBride, E. J. Pubn., Inc.

—The Eerie Adventures of Detective Omar Mendez. McBride, Earvin, Jr. 2nd unabr. ed. 2003. (Earvin MacBride's Amazing Sci-Fi & Adventure Heroes Ser.). 329p. (J). (gr. 7-12). pap. 5.95 *(978-1-892511-08-9(8))* MacBride, E. J. Pubn., Inc.

—Space - M. D. 3001. McBride, Earvin, Jr. 2nd unabr. ed. 2003. (Earvin MacBride's Amazing Sci-Fi & Adventure Heroes Ser.). 329p. (J). (gr. 7-12). pap. 4.95 *(978-1-892511-09-6(6))* MacBride, E. J. Pubn., Inc.

McBride, Jureesa L. Little Shirley Barker Wants to Be a Teacher. McBride, Jureesa L. 2019. (ENG.). 40p. (J). pap. 10.00 *(978-1-0804-3469-5(0))* Independently Published.

McBride, Marc. Isle of the Dead, 3. Rodda, Emily. 2004. (Dragons of Deltora Ser.: 3). (ENG.). 195p. (J). (gr. 5-8). 17.44 *(978-0-439-63375-8(3))* Scholastic, Inc.

—The Sister of the South, 4. Rodda, Emily. 2005. (Dragons of Deltora Ser.: 4). (ENG.). 205p. (J). (gr. 5-8). 17.44 *(978-0-439-63376-5(1))* Scholastic, Inc.

McCabb, Jamie. Spike the Friendly Caterpillar. Martin, Anne E. l.t. ed. 2006. 53p. (J). per. 9.99 *(978-1-59879-127-3(3))* Lifevest Publishing, Inc.

McCabe, Dennis. Haunted Halloween: Color & Create with Spooky Stickers. 2004. 10p. (J). (gr. -1-18). bds. 4.99 *(978-1-57151-730-2(8))* Playhouse Publishing.

McCabe, Jane M. The Miracle of Sandy Duck: A True Story. Maxwell, Wayne F., Jr. 2003. 32p. (gr. k-4). lib. bdg. 15.00 *(978-0-9747023-0-8(7))* Pegasus Pubns.

McCabe, Steve. The Golden Key: Classic fairy Tales. MacDonald, George. 2008. 104p. (J). pap. *(978-0-88835-045-9(7))* Meany, P. D. Pubs.

McCafferty, Jan. Cake Test. Goodhart, Pippa. 2nd ed. 2016. (Reading Ladder Ser.). (ENG.). 48p. (J). (gr. k-2). pap. 7.99 *(978-1-4052-8223-9(1))* Egmont Bks., Ltd. GBR. Dist: Independent Pubs. Group.

—Chilling Out. Harper, Meg. 2005. (Saint Jenni Ser.). (ENG.). 96p. (J). (gr. 2-4). per. 9.99 *(978-0-7459-4896-6(0)*, Lion Books) Lion Hudson PLC GBR. Dist: Independent Pubs. Group.

—Don't Be Greedy, Graham. Cox, Phil Roxbee. Tyler, Jenny, ed. 2006. (Cautionary Tales Ser.). 24p. (J). (gr. -1). lib. bdg. 15.99 *(978-1-58086-972-0(6))*; pap. 7.99 *(978-0-7945-1361-0(1))* EDC Publishing. (Usborne).

—Drawing Cartoons: Internet-Linked. Milbourne, Anna. 2006. (Art School Ser.). 64p. (J). (gr. 5). lib. bdg. 16.95 *(978-1-58086-507-4(0))* EDC Publishing.

—Fairy Things to Make & Do Kid Kit. Gilpin, Rebecca. 2004. (Kid Kits Ser.). 32p. (J). 15.99 *(978-1-58086-727-6(8))*; 15.99 *(978-1-58086-731-3(6))* EDC Publishing. (Usborne).

—The Games Player of Zob: Band 15/Emerald (Collins Big Cat) Shipton, Paul. 2007. (Collins Big Cat Ser.). (ENG.). 48p. (J). (gr. 3-4). pap. 10.99 *(978-0-00-723094-5(X))* HarperCollins Pubs. Ltd. GBR. Dist: Independent Pubs. Group.

—Say Please, Louise! Roxbee Cox, Phil. Tyler, Jenny, ed. 2007. (Cautionary Tales Ser.). 23p. (J). (gr. -1-3). per. 7.99 *(978-0-7945-1726-7(9)*, Usborne) EDC Publishing.

—Super Hero. Harper, David R. & Harper, Meg. ed. 2004. (Saint Jenni Ser.). (ENG.). 96p. (J). (gr. 2-4). pap. 8.99 *(978-0-7459-4895-9(2)*, Lion Books) Lion Hudson PLC GBR. Dist: Independent Pubs. Group.

—Wanda's Washing Machine. McQuinn, Anna. 2005. 20p. (J). (gr. -1-2). 12.95 *(978-1-58925-768-9(5))* Tiger Tales.

McCaffery, William. The Flea Circus. 2013. (J). *(978-0-307-97997-1(0))*; lib. bdg. *(978-0-375-97132-7(7))* Random Hse. Children's Bks.

McCaffrey, Susie. Ancient world - internet Linked. Chandler, Fiona. rev. ed. 2004. 96p. (J). pap. 14.95 *(978-0-7945-0816-6(2)*, Usborne) EDC Publishing.

McCaig, Dave & Brosseau, Pat. The Other Side. Aaron, Jason. rev. ed. 2007. (ENG.). 144p. pap. 12.99 *(978-1-4012-1350-3(2)*, Vertigo) DC Comics.

McCain, Kevin. Daddy Promises. Arquette, Kerry. 2005. 32p. (J). pap. 7.49 *(978-0-7586-0905-2(1))* Concordia Publishing Hse.

McCall, Anthony. And They Fell Fast Asleep. Cox, Roy. 2012. 48p. pap. 15.95 *(978-1-61493-045-7(7))* Peppertree Pr., The.

McCall, William L. My Very Special Brother. Hill, Genita. 2007. 40p. per. 24.95 *(978-1-4241-8852-9(0))* America Star Bks.

McCalla, Darrell. From Lands of the Night, 1 vol. Mollel, Tololwa. 2020. (ENG.). 32p. (J). (gr. 1-4). pap. 12.95 ***(978-0-88995-581-3(6)***, 29c578ce-e327-4bcb-aad1-d53bd3084666) Red Deer Pr. CAN. Dist: Firefly Bks., Ltd.

McCalla, Darrell. From the Lands of the Night, 1 vol. Mollel, Tololwa. 2013. (ENG.). 32p. (J). (gr. 2-5). 18.95 *(978-0-88995-498-4(4)*, adc8b392-89e4-4246-8c49-8b5039f06865) Trifolium Bks., Inc. CAN. Dist: Firefly Bks., Ltd.

McCallum, Brenda. I Am Not a Princess!, 1 vol. Burt, Bethany. 2016. (ENG.). 40p. (J). 16.99 *(978-0-7643-5212-6(1)*, 7563) Schiffer Publishing, Ltd.

McCallum, Jodie. God's Christmas Gift. Navillus, Nell. 2006. (J). *(978-1-58173-595-6(2))* Sweetwater Pr.

—Happy Birthday, Jesus. Navillus, Nell. 2007. (J). *(978-1-60261-264-8(1))* Cliff Road Bks.

McCann, Brandi. Hey, Skedaddle! Musk, Angel. Wagner, Debra, ed. 2018. (ENG.). 46p. (J). pap. 9.99 *(978-1-7287-1108-9(8))* Independently Published.

McCann, Caroline. Heart Stockings. Hewlett, Stefanie & Foulk, Allison. 2015. (J). pap. 7.99 *(978-1-62972-159-0(X))* Deseret Bk. Co.

McCann, Emily. Animal Doodles. McCann, Emily. 2011. (Doodle On! Ser.). (ENG.). 160p. (J). (gr. k-4). 15.99 *(978-0-230-74485-1(0))* Pan Macmillan GBR. Dist: Independent Pubs. Group.

McCann, Emma. The Blizzard Challenge. Grylls, Bear. 2017. 117p. (J). pap. *(978-1-61067-763-9(3))* Kane Miller.

—The Desert Challenge. Grylls, Bear. 2017. 115p. (J). pap. *(978-1-61067-764-6(1))* Kane Miller.

—The Earthquake Challenge. Grylls, Bear. 2019. 117p. (J). pap. *(978-1-61067-930-5(X))* Kane Miller.

—The Jungle Challenge. Grylls, Bear. 2017. 117p. (J). *(978-1-61067-768-4(4))* Kane Miller.

—The River Challenge. Grylls, Bear. 2019. 117p. (J). pap. 4.99 *(978-1-61067-929-9(6))* Kane Miller.

—The Sea Challenge. Grylls, Bear. 2017. 118p. (J). pap. *(978-1-61067-769-1(2))* Kane Miller.

—The Volcano Challenge. Grylls, Bear. 2019. 131p. (J). pap. 4.99 *(978-1-61067-935-0(0))* Kane Miller.

McCann, Gerald. We Were There at the Opening of the Erie Canal. Meadowcroft, Enid Lamonte & Vigilante, Sylvester. 2011. 192p. 42.95 *(978-1-258-09742-4(7))* Literary Licensing, LLC.

McCann, Martin. Cooper's Pack — New York City: New York City, Vol. 1. Rudd, Brandon Kyle. 2007. 72p. (J). per. 14.95 *(978-0-9794882-0-7(6))* Cooper's Pack.

—Cooper's Pack Travel Guide to Alaska. Rudd, Brandon Kyle. 2011. (Cooper's Pack Ser.). (ENG.). 72p. (J). (gr. 1-6). pap. 12.95 *(978-0-9794882-3-8(0))* Cooper's Pack.

—Cooper's Pack Travel Guide to New York City. Rudd, Brandon Kyle. rev. ed. 2012. (ENG.). 72p. (J). (gr. 1-6). pap. 12.95 *(978-0-9794882-5-2(7))* Cooper's Pack.

McCann, Shawn. Catch the Wind. 2008. 38p. (J). pap. *(978-1-59298-244-8(1))* Beaver's Pond Pr., Inc.

—Why the Owl Has Big Ears. 2005. 32p. (J). (gr. -1-3). 8.75 *(978-0-9771466-0-4(X))* Goulasche Pr.

McCarter, Zack. Wellington's Windows. Randall, MarilynMae. 2003. 146p. (J). per. 15.00 *(978-0-9713589-6-6(6))* Ubaviel's Gifts.

McCarthy, Brianna. If Dominican Were a Color. Recio, Sili. 2020. (ENG.). 32p. (J). (gr. -1-3). 17.99 *(978-1-5344-6179-6(5)*, Simon & Schuster Bks. For Young Readers) Simon & Schuster Bks. For Young Readers.

McCarthy, Brianna. Si Quisqueya Fuera un Color (If Dominican Were a Color) Recio, Sili. 2020. (SPA.). 32p. (J). (gr. -1-3). 17.99 ***(978-1-5344-7709-4(8)***, Simon & Schuster Bks. For Young Readers) Simon & Schuster Bks. For Young Readers.

McCarthy, Courtney Watson. ABC Pop-Up. McCarthy, Courtney Watson. 2017. (ENG.). 32p. (J). (gr. k-4). 29.99 *(978-0-7636-9007-6(4))* Candlewick Pr.

McCarthy-Evans, Colleen. The Three Sunflowers Los Tres Girasoles. Lucy, Janet. Flores, Arturo, tr. 2017. (SPA.). (J). pap. 14.95 *(978-1-940654-93-5(9))* Seven Seas Pr.

McCarthy, Hailey. Leopold the Lion: Escapes from the Zoo. Tomlins, Ann Marie. 2017. (ENG.). (J). pap. *(978-1-987852-10-3(9))* Wood Islands Prints.

—Nature Girl. Macdonaly, Cyril y. 2018. (ENG.). 92p. (J). (gr. k-5). pap. *(978-1-987852-13-4(3))* Wood Islands Prints.

—Where Foxes Roam. Tomlins, Ann Marie. 2018. (ENG.). 38p. (J). (gr. 2-5). pap. *(978-1-987852-18-9(4))* Wood Islands Prints.

—Where Foxes Roam 2nd Ed: Prince Edward Island & Panmure Island. Tomlins, Ann Marie. 2nd ed. 2019. (ENG.). 38p. (J). (gr. k-6). pap. *(978-1-987852-19-6(2))* Wood Islands Prints.

McCarthy, Heather. My Laundry Basket Adventures. Yamaner, Jill. 2020. (ENG.). 18p. (J). 24.95 ***(978-0-578-22287-5(6))***; pap. 14.95 ***(978-0-578-22288-2(4))*** Happy Kamperz.

McCarthy, Kate. The Little Girl with a Loud Voice. McCarthy, Terry. 2013. 26p. pap. *(978-0-646-90439-9(6))* McCarthy, Kate.

McCarthy, Kevin. 20th Century Wars. Smith, Robert W. Hoffman, Nancy, ed. ed. 2006. (Spotlight on America Ser.). (ENG.). 96p. (gr. 5-9). pap. 13.99 *(978-1-4206-3219-4(1))* Teacher Created Resources, Inc.

McCarthy, Mary. A Closer Look. McCarthy, Mary. 2007. (ENG.). 40p. (J). (gr. -1-k). 17.99 *(978-0-06-124073-7(7)*, Greenwillow Bks.) HarperCollins Pubs.

McCarthy, Mary Toia. The Taming of the Halloween Monster: The Saga of the Gallant Platoon. Kaspee. 2003. 16p. 9.50 *(978-1-4120-0729-0(1))* Trafford Publishing.

McCarthy, Meghan. All That Trash: The Story of the 1987 Garbage Barge & Our Problem with Stuff. McCarthy, Meghan. 2018. (ENG.). 48p. (J). (gr. -1-3). 17.99 *(978-1-4814-7752-9(8)*, Simon & Schuster/Paula Wiseman Bks.) Simon & Schuster/Paula Wiseman Bks.

—City Hawk: The Story of Pale Male. McCarthy, Meghan. 2007. (ENG.). 40p. (J). (gr. -1-3). 18.99 *(978-1-4169-3359-5(X)*, Simon & Schuster/Paula Wiseman Bks.) Simon & Schuster/Paula Wiseman Bks.

—Daredevil: The Daring Life of Betty Skelton. McCarthy, Meghan. 2013. (ENG.). 48p. (J). (gr. -1-3). 17.99 *(978-1-4424-2262-9(9)*, Simon & Schuster/Paula Wiseman Bks.) Simon & Schuster/Paula Wiseman Bks.

—Earmuffs for Everyone! How Chester Greenwood Became Known As the Inventor of Earmuffs. McCarthy, Meghan. 2015. (ENG.). 48p. (J). (gr. -1-3). 17.99 *(978-1-4814-0637-6(X)*, Simon & Schuster/Paula Wiseman Bks.) Simon & Schuster/Paula Wiseman Bks.

—Firefighters' Handbook. McCarthy, Meghan. 2019. (ENG.). 48p. (J). (gr. -1-3). 17.99 *(978-1-5344-1733-5(8)*, Simon & Schuster Bks. For Young Readers) Simon & Schuster Bks. For Young Readers.

—Pop! The Invention of Bubble Gum. McCarthy, Meghan. 2010. (ENG.). 40p. (J). (gr. -1-3). 18.99 *(978-1-4169-7970-8(0)*, Simon & Schuster/Paula Wiseman Bks.) Simon & Schuster/Paula Wiseman Bks.

—Seabiscuit the Wonder Horse. McCarthy, Meghan. 2008. (ENG.). 40p. (J). (gr. -1-3). 19.99 *(978-1-4169-3360-1(3)*, Simon & Schuster/Paula Wiseman Bks.) Simon & Schuster/Paula Wiseman Bks.

—The Wildest Race Ever: The Story of the 1904 Olympic Marathon. McCarthy, Meghan. 2016. (ENG.). 48p. (J). (gr. -1-3). 18.99 *(978-1-4814-0639-0(6)*, Simon & Schuster/Paula Wiseman Bks.) Simon & Schuster/Paula Wiseman Bks.

McCarthy, Pat, jt. illus. see Brodie, Neale.

McCarthy, Steve. A Sailor Went to Sea, Sea, Sea: Favourite Rhymes from an Irish Childhood. Webb, Sarah. 2017. (ENG.). 64p. (J). 27.00 *(978-1-84717-794-0(8))* O'Brien Pr., Ltd., The IRL. Dist: Casemate Pubs. & Bk. Distributors, LLC.

—Sally Go Round the Stars: Favourite Rhymes from an Irish Childhood. Webb, Sarah & Ranson, Claire. 2014. (ENG.). 64p. (J). pap. 17.00 *(978-1-84717-675-2(5))* O'Brien Pr., Ltd., The IRL. Dist: Casemate Pubs. & Bk. Distributors, LLC.

McCarthy, Steven. Sally Go Round the Stars: Favourite Rhymes for an Irish Childhood. Webb, Sarah & Ranson, Claire. 2011. (ENG.). 64p. (J). 26.00 *(978-1-84717-211-2(3))* O'Brien Pr., Ltd., The IRL. Dist: Casemate Pubs. & Bk. Distributors, LLC.

McCartney, Jen. Luke & His Amazing Space Bed. Sheridan, Luke. 2010. (ENG.). 32p. (J). (gr. -1-3). 17.95 *(978-0-9814536-6-8(X)*, Cambridge House Pr.) Sterling & Ross Pubs.

MCCARTNEY, Margaret. This Is a Book to Read with a Worm. Wheeler-Toppen, Jodi. 2020. 32p. (J). (gr. k-3). lib. bdg. 16.99 *(978-1-58089-897-3(1))* Charlesbridge Publishing, Inc.

M

McCartney, Margaret. We're Not Gonna Take It: A Children's Picture Book. Snider, Dee. 2020. (LyricPop Ser.). 32p. (J). 16.95 *(978-1-61775-788-4(8))* Akashic Bks.
McCartney, Michael David. A Real Name for Puppy. Alderton, Sylvia. 2006. (J). *(978-1-930566-58-3(1),* WestWind Pr.) Scott, D.& F. Publishing, Inc.
McCarty, Peter. Frozen Girl: The Discovery of an Incan Mummy. Getz, David. 2018. (ENG.). 80p. (J). pap. 6.99 *(978-1-250-14363-1(2),* 9781250143631) Square Fish.
—Hermanos Bajo Cero. Seidler, Tor & Tor, Seidler. 2004. (Punto de Encuentro (Editorial Everest) Ser.).Tr. of Brothers Below Zero. (SPA.). 118p. (J). (gr. 5-12). pap., pap. 11.99 *(978-84-241-8076-8(3))* Everest Editora ESP. Dist: Lectorum Pubns., Inc.
—Purple Death: The Mysterious Spanish Flu Of 1918. Getz, David. 2017. (ENG.). 96p. (J). pap. 8.99 *(978-1-250-13909-2(0),* 900179222) Square Fish.
—The Tree in the Courtyard: Looking Through Anne Frank's Window. Gottesfeld, Jeff. 2016. 40p. (J). (gr. k-3). 17.99 *(978-0-385-75397-5(7));* (ENG.). lib. bdg. 20.99 *(978-0-385-75398-2(5))* Random Hse. Children's Bks. (Knopf Bks. for Young Readers).
McCarty, Peter. Bunny Dreams. McCarty, Peter. 2016. (ENG.). 40p. (J). 16.99 *(978-0-8050-9687-3(6),* 9780805096873, Holt, Henry & Co. Bks. For Young Readers) Holt, Henry & Co.
—Chloe. McCarty, Peter. 2012. (ENG.). 40p. (J). (gr. -1-1). 16.99 *(978-0-06-114291-8(3));* lib. bdg. 17.89 *(978-0-06-114292-5(1))* HarperCollins Pubs.
—Fabian Escapes. McCarty, Peter. rev. ed. 2007. (ENG.). 40p. (J). (gr. -1-1). 21.99 *(978-0-8050-7713-1(8),* 9780805077131, Holt, Henry & Co. Bks. For Young Readers) Holt, Henry & Co.
—Fall Ball. McCarty, Peter. 2013. (ENG.). 32p. (J). (gr. -1-3). 16.99 *(978-0-8050-9253-0(6),* 900068283, Holt, Henry & Co. Bks. For Young Readers) Holt, Henry & Co.
—First Snow. McCarty, Peter. 2015. (ENG.). 40p. (J). (gr. -1-3). 16.99 *(978-0-06-218996-7(4))* HarperCollins Pubs.
—Henry in Love. McCarty, Peter. 2009. (ENG.). 48p. (J). (gr. -1-1). 16.99 *(978-0-06-114288-8(3))* HarperCollins Pubs.
—Hondo & Fabian. McCarty, Peter. 2007. (ENG.). 40p. (J). (gr. -1-1). per. 8.99 *(978-0-312-36747-3(3),* 900042352) Square Fish.
—Jeremy Draws a Monster. McCarty, Peter. 2009. (Jeremy & the Monster Ser.). (ENG.). 40p. (J). (gr. -1-1). 18.99 *(978-0-8050-6934-1(8),* 9780805069341, Holt, Henry & Co. Bks. For Young Readers) Holt, Henry & Co.
—The Monster Returns. McCarty, Peter. 2012. (Jeremy & the Monster Ser.). (ENG.). 40p. (J). (gr. -1-1). 16.99 *(978-0-8050-9030-7(4),* 900059285, Holt, Henry & Co. Bks. For Young Readers) Holt, Henry & Co.
McCaslin, Anna. The Owl Who Thinks He Is an Eagle. Ferer, Whitney H. 2003. 20p. (J). 14.95 *(978-0-9729975-0-8(4),* OWL1) Graphically Speaking, Inc.
McCatherty, Jan. Posy & the Trouble with Draglings. Faraway, Lara. 2013. (Fairythorn Tales Ser.). (ENG.). 124p. (J). (gr. k-3). pap. 8.99 *(978-1-84877-970-9(4))* Bonnier Publishing GBR. Dist: Independent Pubs. Group.
McCaughey, Nadine. Freddie the Rock & Roll Cat. McWood, Allison. 2018. (ENG.). 34p. (J). pap. *(978-0-9782729-6-8(X))* Annelid Pr.
—Nog the Christmas Manatee. McWood, Allison. 2018. (ENG.). 28p. (J). pap. *(978-0-9782729-9-9(4))* Annelid Pr.
—The Polka-Dotted Snake. McWood, Allison. 2019. (ENG.). 28p. (J). pap. *(978-0-9782729-8-2(6))* Annelid Pr.
—Rosalie's Animal Zoo. McWood, Allison. 2017. (ENG.). 28p. (J). pap. *(978-0-9782729-4-4(3))* Annelid Pr.
—Snuggles the Misunderstood Shark. McWood, Allison. 2019. (ENG.). 32p. (J). pap. *(978-1-9994377-4-9(8))* Annelid Pr.
McCauley, Adam. Basketball Bats / Goof-Off Goalie. Hicks, Betty. 2009. (Gym Shorts Ser.). (ENG.). 128p. (J). (gr. 2-4). pap. 21.19 *(978-0-312-58247-0(1),* 900062060) Square Fish.
—Cheesie Mack Is Cool in a Duel. Cotler, Steve. (Cheesie Mack Ser.: 2). 240p. (J). (gr. 3-7). 2013. 7.99 *(978-0-375-86395-0(8),* Yearling); 2012. 15.99 *(978-0-375-86438-4(5),* Random Hse. Bks. for Young Readers) Random Hse. Children's Bks.
—Cheesie Mack Is Not a Genius or Anything. 1. Cotler, Steve. 2012. (Cheesie Mack Ser.). (ENG.). 240p. (J). (gr. 4-6). lib. bdg. 21.19 *(978-0-375-96437-4(1))* Random House Publishing Group.
—Cheesie Mack Is Not a Genius or Anything. Cotler, Steve. (Cheesie Mack Ser.: 1). 240p. (J). (gr. 3-7). 2012. 6.99 *(978-0-375-86394-3(X),* Yearling); 2011. 15.99 *(978-0-375-86437-7(7),* Random Hse. Bks. for Young Readers) Random Hse. Children's Bks.
—Da Wild, Da Crazy, Da Vinci. Scieszka, Jon. 2006. (Time Warp Trio Ser.: No. 14). 72p. (gr. 4-7). 15.00 *(978-0-7569-6677-5(9))* Perfection Learning Corp.
—Hey Kid, Want to Buy a Bridge? Scieszka, Jon. 2005. (Time Warp Trio Ser.: No. 11). 74p. (gr. 4-7). 15.00 *(978-0-7569-5988-3(8))* Perfection Learning Corp.
—Hey Kid, Want to Buy a Bridge? #11. Scieszka, Jon. 2004. (Time Warp Trio Ser.: 11). (ENG.). 80p. (J). (gr. 2-4). pap. 5.99 *(978-0-14-240089-0(0),* Puffin Books) Penguin Young Readers Group.
—Marco? Polo! 16. Scieszka, Jon. 2006. (Time Warp Trio Ser.: 16). (ENG.). 80p. (J). (gr. 2-4). 17.44 *(978-0-670-06104-4(2))* Penguin Young Readers Group.
—Marco? Polo! Scieszka, Jon. 2008. (Time Warp Trio Ser.: No. 16). 90p. (J). (gr. 4-6). 12.65 *(978-0-7569-8923-1(X))* Perfection Learning Corp.
—Marco? Polo! #16, No. 16. Scieszka, Jon. 2008. (Time Warp Trio Ser.: 16). 96p. (J). (gr. 2-4). 5.99 *(978-0-14-241177-3(9),* Puffin Books) Penguin Young Readers Group.
—Me Oh Maya. Scieszka, Jon. 2005. (Time Warp Trio Ser.: 13). 96p. (J). (gr. 2-4). 5.99 *(978-0-14-240300-6(8),* Puffin Books) Penguin Young Readers Group.
—Me Oh Maya. Scieszka, Jon. 2005. (Time Warp Trio Ser.: No. 13). 69p. (gr. 2-6). 15.00 *(978-0-7569-5060-6(0))* Perfection Learning Corp.
—Oh Say, I Can't See #15, No. 15. Scieszka, Jon. 2007. (Time Warp Trio Ser.: 15). 80p. (J). (gr. 2-4). 5.99 *(978-0-14-240808-7(5),* Puffin Books) Penguin Young Readers Group.
—Sam Samurai. Scieszka, Jon. 2004. (Time Warp Trio Ser.: 10). 96p. (J). (gr. 2-4). pap. 5.99 *(978-0-14-240088-3(2),* Puffin Books) Penguin Young Readers Group.
—Sam Samurai. Scieszka, Jon. 2006. (Time Warp Trio Ser.: No. 10). 85p. (gr. 4-7). 15.00 *(978-0-7569-6779-6(1))* Perfection Learning Corp.
—See You Later, Gladiator. Scieszka, Jon. 2004. (Time Warp Trio Ser.: 9). 96p. (J). (gr. 2-4). pap. 5.99 *(978-0-14-240117-0(X),* Puffin Books) Penguin Young Readers Group.
—See You Later, Gladiator. Scieszka, Jon. 2004. (Time Warp Trio Ser.: No. 9). 87p. (J). (gr. 4-7). 12.65 *(978-0-7569-5986-9(1))* Perfection Learning Corp.
—Sideways Stories from Wayside School. Sachar, Louis. 2019. (Wayside School Ser.). (ENG.). 176p. (J). (gr. 3-7). pap. 7.99 *(978-0-380-69871-4(4),* HarperCollins) HarperCollins Pubs. Ltd. GBR. Dist: HarperCollins Pubs.
—Smarty Marty's Got Game ¡en Español! Gutierrez, Amy. 2017. (ENG.). 40p. (J). (gr. -1-3). 17.95 *(978-1-944903-28-2(3),* Cameron Kids) Cameron + Co.
—Swimming with Sharks / Track Attack. Hicks, Betty. 2010. (Gym Shorts Ser.). (ENG.). 128p. (J). (gr. 2-4). pap. 21.19 *(978-0-312-60237-6(5),* 900064236) Square Fish.
—Viking It & Liking It. Scieszka, Jon. 2004. (Time Warp Trio Ser.: 12). 96p. (J). (gr. 2-4). pap. 5.99 *(978-0-14-240002-9(5),* Puffin Books) Penguin Young Readers Group.
—Viking It & Liking It. Scieszka, Jon. 2004. (Time Warp Trio Ser.: No. 12). 73p. (gr. 2-6). 15.00 *(978-0-7569-2589-5(4))* Perfection Learning Corp.
—The Wayside School 3-Book Box Set: Sideays Stories from Wayside School, Wayside School Is Falling down, Wayside School Gets a Little Stranger, 3 vols., Set. Sachar, Louis. 2019. (Wayside School Ser.). (ENG.). 608p. (J). (gr. 3-7). pap. 23.97 *(978-0-380-79171-2(4),* HarperCollins) HarperCollins Pubs. Ltd. GBR. Dist: HarperCollins Pubs.
—Wayside School Gets a Little Stranger. Sachar, Louis. rev. ed. 2004. (Wayside School Ser.). (ENG.). 160p. (J). (gr. 3-7). pap. 6.99 *(978-0-380-73149-7(5))* HarperCollins Pubs.
—Wayside School Gets a Little Stranger. Sachar, Louis. 2019. (Wayside School Ser.). (ENG.). 208p. (J). (gr. 3-7). pap. 7.99 *(978-0-380-72381-2(6),* HarperCollins) HarperCollins Pubs. Ltd. GBR. Dist: HarperCollins Pubs.
—Wayside School Is Falling Down. Sachar, Louis. rev. ed. 2004. (Wayside School Ser.). (ENG.). 160p. (J). (gr. 3-7). pap. 6.99 *(978-0-380-73150-3(9))* HarperCollins Pubs.
—Wayside School Is Falling Down. Sachar, Louis. 2019. (Wayside School Ser.). (ENG.). 224p. (J). (gr. 3-7). pap. 7.99 *(978-0-380-75484-7(3),* HarperCollins) HarperCollins Pubs. Ltd. GBR. Dist: HarperCollins Pubs.
McCauley, Adam & Adam, Mccauley. Da Wild, Da Crazy, Da Vinci, No. 14. Scieszka, Jon. 2006. (Time Warp Trio Ser.: 14). 96p. (J). (gr. 2-4). 5.99 *(978-0-14-240465-2(9),* Puffin Books) Penguin Young Readers Group.
McCauley, Marlene & Children's Art-Friends of Kateri. Song of Kateri: Princess of the Eucharist. McCauley, Marlene. McCauley, R. Allan, ed. unabr. ed. 2005. 300p. (YA). (gr. 4-7). per. 14.95 *(978-0-9633633-2-9(8))* Grace Hse. Publishing.
McCaw, Robert, photos by. Birds A to Z. McCaw, Robert. Earley, Chris G. 2009. 32p. (J). (gr. 1-5). 19.95 *(978-1-55407-554-6(8),* fb066d01-f6f6-4747-acb0-dfa192c94485); pap. 7.95 *(978-1-55407-500-3(9),* ef8f88c1-8124-4ad8-b741-d35bdad16b58) Firefly Bks., Ltd.
McClain, Tania. Big Jake Plants a Garden: Big Jake Adventures. McClain, Charles. Southern Lion Books, ed. 2013. 26p. (J). *(978-1-935272-21-2(7))* Southern Lion Bks.
McClaine, Les. The Middle Man: Volume 1. Grillo-Marxuach, Javier. 2006. 112p. per. 9.95 *(978-0-9754193-7-3(4))* Viper Comics.
—TinkerActive Workbooks: 2nd Grade Math. Sidat, Enil & Odd Dot. 2019. (TinkerActive Workbooks Ser.: 3). (ENG.). 128p. (J). pap. 12.99 *(978-1-250-30723-1(6),* 900197983, Odd Dot) St. Martin's Pr.
McClatchie, Matthew. BJ & the Green Monstah. Dirsa, Tom. 2016. (ENG.). (J). pap. *(978-1-927510-76-6(7))* Dream Write Publishing, Ltd.
McCleary, Twila. Meesha, Guardian of Grand Mountain: Book One of the Guardian Series. Juckes, Deborah Sioux. 2005. (Guardian Ser.: Bk. 1). (YA). pap. 12.95 *(978-0-9767748-0-8(1))* Red Earth Publishing.
—Meesha, Guardian of Grand Mountain: Book One of the Guardian Series. Juckes, Deborah Sioux. 2005. (YA). 18.95 *(978-0-9767748-1-5(X))* Red Earth Publishing.
McClellan, David. The Eighth Day. Salerni, Dianne K. (Eighth Day Ser.: 1). (ENG.). (J). (gr. 3-7). 2015. 336p. pap. 6.99 *(978-0-06-227216-4(0));* 2014. 320p. 16.99 *(978-0-06-227215-7(2))* HarperCollins Pubs.
—The Guardian Herd: Stormbound. Alvarez, Jennifer Lynn. (Guardian Herd Ser.: 2). (ENG.). (J). (gr. 3-7). 2016. 368p. pap. 6.99 *(978-0-06-228610-9(2));* 2015. 320p. 16.99 *(978-0-06-228609-3(9))* HarperCollins Pubs.
—The Guardian Herd: Windborn. Alvarez, Jennifer Lynn. (Guardian Herd Ser.: 4). (ENG.). (J). (gr. 3-7). 2017. 432p. pap. 7.99 *(978-0-06-228616-1(1));* 2016. 368p. 16.99 *(978-0-06-228615-4(3))* HarperCollins Pubs.
—Windborn. Alvarez, Jennifer Lynn. ed. 2017. (Guardian Herd Ser.: 4). (ENG.). (J). (gr. 3-7). lib. bdg. 17.20 *(978-0-606-40048-0(6))* Turtleback.
McClellan, Maddy. Friday the Scaredy Cat. McMahon, Kara. 2011. (Friday the Scaredy Cat Ser.). (ENG.). 24p. (J). (gr. -1-1). 15.99 *(978-1-4424-3612-1(3));* pap. 3.99 *(978-1-4424-2293-3(9))* Simon Spotlight. (Simon Spotlight).
—Pirate!: Band 15/Emerald (Collins Big Cat), Bd. 15. Gates, Susan. 2007. (Collins Big Cat Ser.). (ENG.). 48p. (J). (gr. 3-4). pap. 10.99 *(978-0-00-723095-2(8))* HarperCollins Pubs. Ltd. GBR. Dist: Independent Pubs. Group.
—Playdates Are Not Scary! McMahon, Kara. 2015. (Friday the Scaredy Cat Ser.). (ENG.). 24p. (J). (gr. -1-1). pap. 3.99 *(978-1-4814-3591-8(4),* Simon Spotlight) Simon Spotlight.
—The Scariest Day Ever ... So Far. McMahon, Kara. 2013. (Friday the Scaredy Cat Ser.). (ENG.). 24p. (J). (gr. -1-1). 16.99 *(978-1-4424-6694-4(4));* pap. 3.99 *(978-1-4424-6693-7(6))* Simon Spotlight. (Simon Spotlight).
McClelland, Maddy. Mop Top. Graves, Sue. 2008. (Tadpoles Ser.). (ENG.). 24p. (J). (gr. -1-3). pap. *(978-0-7787-3888-6(4));* lib. bdg. *(978-0-7787-3857-2(4))* Crabtree Publishing Co.
McClements, George. Dinosaur Woods: Can Seven Clever Critters Save Their Forest Home? McClements, George. 2009. (ENG.). 40p. (J). (gr. -1-2). 19.99 *(978-1-4169-8626-3(X),* Beach Lane Bks.) Beach Lane Bks.
—Night of the Veggie Monster. McClements, George. (ENG.). 32p. (J). (gr. -1-1). 2014. 7.99 *(978-1-61963-180-9(6),* 900125204); 2008. 17.99 *(978-1-59990-061-2(0),* 900044531) Bloomsbury Publishing USA. (Bloomsbury USA Childrens).
McClements, George & Kardos, Stéphane. Spider-Man: Far from Home: Peter & Ned's Ultimate Travel Journal. Chhibber, Preeti. 2019. (ENG.). 192p. (J). (gr. 3-7). 12.99 *(978-1-368-04698-5(3),* Marvel Pr.) Disney Publishing Worldwide.
McCliggott, Timothy M. A Report on Quibnoida. McCliggott, Timothy M. 2007. 52p. (YA). pap. 17.00 *(978-0-8059-7289-4(7))* Dorrance Publishing Co., Inc.
McClintic, Ben, jt. illus. see Woods, Christopher.
Mcclintock, Barbara. Animal Fables from Aesop. Aesop, Aesop. 2012. (ENG.). 48p. (J). 17.95 *(978-0-87923-913-8(1))* Godine, David R. Pub.
McClintock, Barbara. A Child's Garden of Verses. Stevenson, Robert Louis. 2011. (ENG.). 80p. (J). (gr. -1-3). 17.99 *(978-0-06-028228-8(2))* HarperCollins Pubs.
—The Gingerbread Man. Aylesworth, Jim. (StoryPlay Ser.). (ENG.). (J). 2017. 40p. (gr. -1-k). 5.99 *(978-1-338-18734-2(1));* 2010. 32p. (gr. k — 1). bds. 6.99 *(978-0-545-23514-3(6))* Scholastic, Inc. (Cartwheel Bks.).
Mcclintock, Barbara. Mary & the Mouse, the Mouse & Mary. Donofrio, Beverly. 2014. (Mary & the Mouse Ser.). 32p. (J). (gr. -1-2). 7.99 *(978-0-385-38872-6(1),* Dragonfly Bks.) Random Hse. Children's Bks.
McClintock, Barbara. My Grandfather's Coat. Aylesworth, Jim. 2014. (ENG.). 32p. (J). (gr. -1-3). 17.99 *(978-0-439-92545-7(2),* Scholastic Pr.) Scholastic, Inc.
—Nothing Stopped Sophie: The Story of Unshakable Mathematician Sophie Germain. Bardoe, Cheryl. 2018. 40p. (J). (gr. -1-3). 18.99 *(978-0-316-27820-1(3))* Little Brown & Co.
Mcclintock, Barbara. A Tale of Two Bad Mice, 1 vol. Potter, Beatrix. 2007. (Rabbit Ears-A Classic Tale Ser.). (ENG.). 40p. (J). (gr. 2-6). 28.50 *(978-1-59961-314-7(X),* 12967, Picture Bk.) Spotlight.
—The Twelve Dancing Princesses. Grimm, Jacob & Grimm, Wilhelm. 2017. (J). *(978-0-439-89402-9(6),* Scholastic Pr.) Scholastic, Inc.
—Twelve Kinds of Ice. Obed, Ellen Bryan. 2015. (ENG.). 64p. (J). (gr. 1-4). 6.99 *(978-0-544-55554-9(6),* 1610460, HMH Books For Young Readers) Houghton Mifflin Harcourt Publishing Co.
McClintock, Barbara. Where's Mommy? Donofrio, Beverly. 2014. (Mary & the Mouse Ser.). 32p. (J). (gr. -1-2). 17.99 *(978-0-375-84423-2(6),* Schwartz & Wade Bks.) Random Hse. Children's Bks.
Mcclintock, Barbara. Adèle & Simon. Mcclintock, Barbara. 2006. (Adele & Simon Ser.). (ENG.). 40p. (J). (gr. -1-3). 18.99 *(978-0-374-38044-1(9),* 900028406, Farrar, Straus & Giroux (BYR)) Farrar, Straus & Giroux.
McCloskey, Daniel. Charlie Sparrow & the Book of Flight. Anderson, D. F. 2018. (Tales of Tree City Ser.: Vol. 2). (ENG.). 170p. (J). (gr. 1-4). pap. *(978-0-9918003-7-7(0))* Underdog Bks.
—Charlie Sparrow & the Secret of Flight. Anderson, D. F. 2nd ed. 2018. (Tales of Tree City Ser.: Vol. 1). (ENG.). 86p. (J). (gr. 1-4). pap. *(978-0-9918003-5-3(4))* Underdog Bks.
McCloskey, Kevin. A Dog Named Pavlov: Un Perro Llamado Pavlov. Campbell, Howard. 2010. 44p. (J). pap. 12.95 *(978-0-9790350-4-3(X))* Stanley Publishing Co.
McCloskey, Robert. Henry Reed, Inc., Set. Robertson, Keith. abr. ed. (J). (gr. 4-7). 24.95 incl. audio *(978-0-670-36800-6(8))* Live Oak Media.
—The Man Who Lost His Head. Bishop, Claire Huchet. 2009. (ENG.). 64p. (J). (gr. -1-3). 17.95 *(978-1-59017-332-9(5),* NYR Children's Collection) New York Review of Bks., Inc., The.
McCloskey, Robert. Homer Price (Puffin Modern Classics) McCloskey, Robert. 2005. (Puffin Modern Classics Ser.). 160p. (J). (gr. 3-7). 7.99 *(978-0-14-240415-7(2),* Puffin Books) Penguin Young Readers Group.
McCloskey, Shanda. Fire Truck vs. Dragon. Barton, Chris. 2020. 40p. (J). (gr. -1-3). 17.99 *(978-0-316-52213-7(9))* Little, Brown Bks. for Young Readers.
McClure, Gillian. Dog on Wheels Goes Snowboarding. McClure, Gillian. 2020. 32p. (J). (gr. -1-k). pap. 10.99 *(978-1-909991-79-8(1))* Troika Bks. GBR. Dist: Independent Pubs. Group.
McClure, Jessica. Is Nothing Something? Kids' Questions & Zen Answers about Life, Death, Family, Friendship, & Everything in Between. Hanh, Thich Nhat. 2014. 40p. (J). (gr. -1-3). 16.95 *(978-1-937006-65-5(4),* Plum Blossom Bks.) Parallax Pr.
—Once upon a Tree. Kisiel, Soren & Jarock, Dawn. 2017. 40p. (J). (gr. -1-3). 16.95 *(978-1-941529-74-4(7),* Plum Blossom Bks.) Parallax Pr.
McClure, Nikki. All in a Day. Rylant, Cynthia. (ENG.). (J). (gr. -1 — 1). 2017. 30p. bds. 8.95 *(978-1-4197-2612-5(9),* Abrams Appleseed); 2009. 32p. 18.95 *(978-0-8109-8321-2(4),* Abrams Bks. for Young Readers) Abrams, Inc.
—The Golden Thread: A Song for Pete Seeger. Meloy, Colin. 2018. (ENG.). 48p. (J). (gr. -1-3). 18.99 *(978-0-06-236825-6(7),* Balzer & Bray) HarperCollins Pubs.
—May the Stars Drip Down. Chatelain, Jeremy. 2014. (ENG.). 40p. (J). (gr. -1-2). 17.95 *(978-1-4197-1024-7(9),* Abrams Bks. for Young Readers) Abrams, Inc.
McClure, Tom. Dirtiest Hair in the World. McAllen, Bob. 2008. (ENG.). 44p. (J). (gr. k-3). lib. bdg. 17.99 *(978-1-934277-24-9(X))* Mam Green Publishing, Inc.
McClurkan, Rob. Captain Bling's Christmas Plunder. Colby, Rebecca. 2017. (ENG.). 32p. (J). (gr. k-2). 16.99 *(978-0-8075-1063-6(7),* 807510637) Whitman, Albert & Co.
McClurkan, Rob. Captain Marvel: Beware the Flerken! Glass, Calliope. 2020. (ENG.). 32p. (J). (gr. -1-k). 12.99 ***(978-1-368-05497-3(8),*** Marvel Pr.) Disney Publishing Worldwide.
McClurkan, Rob. Christmas Cookies for Santa. Berry Byrd, Holly. Cottage Door Press, ed. 2019. (Touch & Feel Board Book Ser.). (ENG.). 10p. (J). (gr. -1-k). bds. 9.99 *(978-1-68052-708-7(8),* 1004410) Cottage Door Pr.
—The Colorful Story of Comics. Lakin, Patricia. 2016. (History of Fun Stuff Ser.). (ENG.). 48p. (J). (gr. 1-3). pap. 3.99 *(978-1-4814-7144-2(9),* Simon Spotlight) Simon Spotlight.
—Crayola! the Secrets of the Cool Colors & Hot Hues. Williams, Bonnie. 2018. (Science of Fun Stuff Ser.). (ENG.). 40p. (J). (gr. 1-3). 17.99 *(978-1-5344-1776-2(1));* pap. 4.99 *(978-1-5344-1775-5(3))* Simon Spotlight. (Simon Spotlight).
—Lucy Loves Goosey. Singleton, Linda Joy. 2017. (ENG.). 32p. (J). (gr. -1-3). 16.99 *(978-1-4998-0396-9(6))* Little Bee Books Inc.
—Pulling Back the Curtain on Magic! Higginson, Sheila Sweeny. 2015. (Science of Fun Stuff Ser.). (ENG.). 48p. (J). (gr. 1-3). 16.99 *(978-1-4814-3702-8(X),* Simon Spotlight) Simon Spotlight.
—Sloth to the Rescue. Shirtliffe, Leanne. 2019. 32p. (J). (gr. -1-3). 17.99 *(978-0-7624-9159-9(0),* Running Pr. Kids) Running Pr.
—The Sugary Secrets Behind Candy. O'Ryan, Ellie. 2015. (Science of Fun Stuff Ser.). (ENG.). 48p. (J). (gr. 1-3). pap. 3.99 *(978-1-4814-5626-5(1),* Simon Spotlight) Simon Spotlight.
McClurkan, Rob. Aw, Nuts! McClurkan, Rob. 2014. (ENG.). 32p. (J). (gr. -1-3). 17.99 *(978-0-06-231729-2(6))* HarperCollins Pubs.
—Playdates Rule! McClurkan, Rob. 2017. 32p. (J). 16.99 *(978-1-68119-369-4(8),* 900171776, Bloomsbury USA Childrens) Bloomsbury Publishing USA.
McClurkan, Rob, jt. illus. see Ho, Jannie.
McCluskey, Cindy. Chess for Children. Chandler, Murray & Milligan, Helen. 2004. (ENG.). 112p. (YA). (gr. k-7). 16.95 *(978-1-904600-06-0(9))* Gambit Pubns., Ltd. GBR. Dist: Two Rivers Distribution.
McCluskey, Gary. The Christmas Cats Care for the Bear. Wilson, Constance Corcoran. 2016. (Christmas Cats Ser.: Vol. 5). (ENG.). (J). (gr. k-4). 12.99 *(978-0-9863898-3-2(8))* Quad City Pr.
McCollam, Maggie. Victoria Hurts Whitney Baker's Feelings. 2019. (Victoria Ser.: Vol. 2). (ENG.). 24p. (J). pap. 11.99 *(978-1-7276-3290-3(7))* CreateSpace Independent Publishing Platform.
McConkey, Barbara. Tulowly the Possum. Trowbridge, Terri. I.t. ed. 2005. 24p. (J). 9.95 *(978-0-9766418-0-3(1))* Sidewalk Publishing.
McConnell, Clem. I Speak to Myself: Encouraging Words for Children. McConnell, Clem. 2007. 32p. (J). per. 5.00 *(978-0-9673490-0-8(1))* Positive Strokes.
McConnell, Garrett. Lying on the Bed with a Monkey on Her Head. Gainey, Tonda R. 2018. (ENG.). 22p. (J). 21.95 *(978-1-64003-854-7(X));* pap. 11.95 *(978-1-64003-853-0(1))* Covenant Bks.
McConnell, Greg. The Search for Shehakim: Mahana & Tarila. Brown, S. L. 2020. (ENG.). 78p. (J). pap. ***(978-1-5255-6175-7(8)); (978-1-5255-6174-0(X))*** FriesenPress.
McConnell, Jack. The Cooking of Mexico. Locricchio, Matthew. 2nd rev. ed. 2012. (Superchef Ser.). 96p. (gr. 6-6). 36.64 *(978-1-60870-555-9(2))* Cavendish Square Publishing LLC.
—The Cooking of Brazil. Locricchio, Matthew. 2006. (Superchef Ser.). 80p. (gr. 6-6). 35.21 *(978-0-7614-1732-3(X))* Cavendish Square Publishing LLC.
—The Cooking of Brazil. 2nd rev. ed. 2012. (Superchef Ser.). 96p. (gr. 6-6). 36.64 *(978-1-60870-549-8(8))* Cavendish Square Publishing LLC.
—The Cooking of China. Locricchio, Matthew. 2003. (Superchef Ser.). 80p. (gr. 6-6). 35.21 *(978-0-7614-1214-4(X))* Cavendish Square Publishing LLC.
—The Cooking of China. Locricchio, Matthew. 2nd rev. ed. 2012. (Superchef Ser.). 96p. (gr. 6-6). 36.64 *(978-1-60870-550-4(1))* Cavendish Square Publishing LLC.
—The Cooking of France. Locricchio, Matthew. 2003. (Superchef Ser.). 80p. (gr. 6-6). 35.21 *(978-0-7614-1216-8(6))* Cavendish Square Publishing LLC.
—The Cooking of Greece. 2nd rev. ed. 2012. (Superchef Ser.). 96p. (gr. 6-6). 36.64 *(978-1-60870-552-8(8))* Cavendish Square Publishing LLC.
—The Cooking of Italy. Locricchio, Matthew. (Superchef Ser.). (gr. 6-6). 2003. 80p. 35.21 *(978-0-7614-1215-1(8));* 2nd rev. ed. 2012. 96p. 36.64 *(978-1-60870-554-2(4))* Cavendish Square Publishing LLC.
—The Cooking of Mexico. Locricchio, Matthew. 2003. (Superchef Ser.). 80p. (gr. 6-6). 35.21 *(978-0-7614-1217-5(4))* Cavendish Square Publishing LLC.
McConnell, Jack B. The Cooking of India. Locricchio, Matthew. 2006. (Superchef Ser.). 80p. (gr. 6-6). 35.21 *(978-0-7614-1730-9(3))* Cavendish Square Publishing LLC.

McConnell, James. Edgar Allan Poe. Poe, Edgar Allen. 2004. (Great American Short Stories Ser.). 80p. (gr. 4-7). lib. bdg. 24.00 *(978-0-8368-4254-8(5)*, Gareth Stevens Learning Library) Stevens, Gareth Publishing LLLP.

—Edith Wharton. Wharton, Edith. 2004. (Great American Short Stories Ser.). 80p. (gr. 4-7). lib. bdg. 25.00 *(978-0-8368-4256-2(1)*, Gareth Stevens Learning Library) Stevens, Gareth Publishing LLLP.

—Nathaniel Hawthorne. Hawthorne, Nathaniel. 2004. (Great American Short Stories Ser.). 80p. (gr. 4-7). lib. bdg. 25.00 *(978-0-8368-4252-4(9)*, Gareth Stevens Learning Library) Stevens, Gareth Publishing LLLP.

McConnell, Nathan Alan. [growing up Aspie] the Boy Who Lost His Stims. McConnell, Nathan Alan. Bravo, Oscar, ed. 2018. (ENG.). 30p. (J). pap. 12.00 *(978-1-7202-6335-7(3))* Independently Published.

McConnell, Sarah. Chewy Hughie: Band 07/Turquoise (Collins Big Cat) Clarke, Jane. 2006. (Collins Big Cat Ser.). (ENG.). 136p. (J). (gr. 2-2). pap. 8.99 *(978-0-00-718692-1(4))* HarperCollins Pubs. Ltd. GBR. Dist: Independent Pubs. Group.

—Dixie. Gilman, Grace. 2011. (I Can Read Level 1 Ser.). (ENG.). 32p. (J). (gr. -1-3). 16.99 *(978-0-06-171914-1(5))*; pap. 4.99 *(978-0-06-171913-4(7))* HarperCollins Pubs.

—Dixie & the Big Bully. Gilman, Grace. 2013. (I Can Read Level 1 Ser.). (ENG.). 32p. (J). (gr. -1-3). 16.99 *(978-0-06-208637-2(5))* HarperCollins Pubs.

—Dixie & the Good Deeds. Gilman, Grace. 2013. (I Can Read Level 1 Ser.). (ENG.). 32p. (J). (gr. -1-3). 16.99 *(978-0-06-208657-0(X))*; pap. 4.99 *(978-0-06-208643-3(X))* HarperCollins Pubs.

—Dixie & the School Trip. Gilman, Grace. 2012. (I Can Read Level 1 Ser.). (ENG.). 32p. (J). (gr. -1-3). 16.99 *(978-0-06-208609-9(X))*; pap. 4.99 *(978-0-06-208608-2(1))* HarperCollins Pubs.

—Dixie Loves School Pet Day. Gilman, Grace. 2011. (I Can Read Level 1 Ser.). (ENG.). 32p. (J). (gr. -1-3). 16.99 *(978-0-06-171912-7(9))*; pap. 4.99 *(978-0-06-171911-0(0))* HarperCollins Pubs.

—I've Got Music! Molitoris, Cathy. 2006. (J). *(978-0-439-88620-8(1))* Scholastic, Inc.

McConville, Linda. A Most Slanticulis Christmas. Smedley, Beaufort. 2018. (ENG.). 104p. (J). pap. *(978-1-9993215-0-5(2))* Beaufort Smedley Bks.

McCook, Eileen. Great Adventure Kids Coloring Book: Bible Story Coloring Book. Cavins, Emily. 2008. (Great Adventures: Kids Ser.). 48p. pap. 7.95 *(978-1-934217-64-1(6))* Ascension Pr.

McCool, Arlene. The Proud Christmas Tree. Lawless, Mary Ann. 2006. (J). 12.95 *(978-0-9772795-0-0(2))* Tuesday's Child.

McCool, Lindsay Sarles & Aviles, Martha. Active Minds Inside My Body: Learn What Makes You Work! Burroughs, Caleb. 2021. (ENG.). 10p. (J). bds. ***(978-1-64269-251-8(4)***, a9c6398e-9f3b-402a-b053-271721a0cf1a, Sequoia Publishing & Media LLC) Phoenix International Publications, Inc.

McCorkindale, Bruce & Youtsey, Scott. Sikulu & Harambe by the Zambezi River: An African Vversion of the Good Samaritan Story. Oguneye, Kunle. 2008. 32p. (J). (gr. -1-5). 14.99 *(978-0-9777382-4-3(8))* Blue Brush Media.

McCorkle, Mark. Kim Possible Cine-Manga, 9 vols., Vol. 7. Schooley, Bob. 2004. 96p. pap. 14.99 *(978-1-59182-570-8(9)*, Tokyopop Kids) TOKYOPOP, Inc.

—Kim Possible Cine-Manga: Animal Attraction & All the News, 9 vols., Vol. 5. Schooley, Bob. 2004. 96p. pap. 14.99 *(978-1-59182-568-5(7)*, Tokyopop Kids) TOKYOPOP, Inc.

—Kim Possible Cine-Manga: Sink or Swim & Number One, 9 vols., Vol. 6. Schooley, Bob. 2004. 96p. pap. 14.99 *(978-1-59182-569-2(5)*, Tokyopop Kids) TOKYOPOP, Inc.

McCormick, Jeanne K. The Secret Hat. Losey, Peggy. 2019. (ENG.). 36p. (J). 19.99 ***(978-0-578-49629-0(1))*** Secret Hat, L.L.C., The.

McCormick, Joey. Adventure Time Vol. 16. Cannon, Kevin. 2019. (Adventure Time Ser.: 16). (ENG.). 112p. (J). (gr. 4-7). pap. 14.99 *(978-1-68415-272-8(0))* Boom! Studios.

McCoskey, Rachel. The Oregon Trail: Ollie's Great Adventure. Dundy, Melanie Richardson. 2018. (ENG.). 66p. (J). (gr. 4-6). 21.95 *(978-0-578-43146-8(7))*; pap. 12.95 *(978-0-578-42274-9(3))* M D C T Publishing.

McCould-Carr, Daniel. The Gum Chums in Decay in the Fruit Garden. Binns, Kesha Naomi. 2nd ed. 2019. (ENG.). 28p. (J). pap. *(978-1-78645-288-7(X))* Beaten Track Publishing.

McCoy, Derrick. Starchild's Adventures on Earth. McCoy, Angie. 2011. 24p. pap. 24.95 *(978-1-4560-5053-5(2))* America Star Bks.

McCoy, Glenn. The Legend of Spud Murphy. Colfer, Eoin. 2005. (Eoin Colfer's Legend Of... Ser.). 95p. (gr. 2-6). 16.00 *(978-0-7569-6514-3(4))* Perfection Learning Corp.

McCoy, Glenn. No Funciona la Tele! McCoy, Glenn. 2016. (Serie Amarilla Ser.). (SPA.). 40p. (J). pap. 10.99 *(978-607-01-3355-8(2))* Santillana USA Publishing Co., Inc.

McCoy, John. Families Are Forever. Shemin, Craig. 2006. 34p. (J). (gr. -1-2). 16.95 *(978-0-9728666-6-8(3))* As Simple As That Publishing.

—Families Are Forever. Shemin, Craig. l.t. ed. 2003. 34p. 9.95 *(978-0-9728666-0-6(4)*, 1) As Simple As That Publishing.

—Families Are Forever. Shemin, Craig. l.t. ed. 2004. 34p. 9.95 *(978-0-9728666-1-3(2)*, 1) As Simple As That Publishing.

McCoy, Travis. Origami Orchestra. Elliott, Ammie. 2019. (Dreamscape Ser.: Vol. 1). (ENG.). 40p. (J). 21.99 ***(978-1-64237-845-0(3))***; pap. 17.99 ***(978-1-64237-844-3(5))*** Gatekeeper Pr.

McCoy, Virginia. The Rabbits' Race, 1 vol. Delaronde, Deborah L. ed. 2016. (ENG.). 50p. (J). (gr. 4-7). 18.95 *(978-1-894778-76-3(6))* Theytus Bks., Ltd. CAN. Dist: Orca Bk. Pubs. USA.

McCracken, Jaime, photos by. A Show & Tell Lesson. Pugh, Tracey D. l.t. ed. 2006. 32p. (J). 12.95 *(978-1-59879-105-1(2))* Lifevest Publishing, Inc.

McCranie, Stephen. The Biggest, Bestest Time Ever! Mal & Chad Book 1. McCranie, Stephen. 2011. (Mal & Chad Ser.: 1). 224p. (J). (gr. 3-7). 10.99 *(978-0-399-25221-1(5)*, Philomel Bks.) Penguin Young Readers Group.

—Food Fight!, 2 vols. McCranie, Stephen. 2nd ed. 2012. (Mal & Chad Ser.: 2). 224p. (J). (gr. 3-7). 10.99 *(978-0-399-25657-8(1)*, Philomel Bks.) Penguin Young Readers Group.

—Mal & Chad: Belly Flop! McCranie, Stephen. 3rd ed. 2012. (Mal & Chad Ser.: 3). (ENG.). 224p. (J). (gr. 3-7). pap. 10.99 *(978-0-399-25658-5(X)*, Philomel Bks.) Penguin Young Readers Group.

—Space Boy, 5. McCranie, Stephen. 2019. (ENG.). 224p. (J). (gr. 7). 10.99 *(978-1-5067-1399-1(8))* Dark Horse Comics.

—Stephen Mccranie's Space Boy Volume 2. McCranie, Stephen. 2018. (ENG.). 240p. (J). (gr. 5-9). pap. 10.99 *(978-1-5067-0680-1(0))* Dark Horse Comics.

—Stephen Mccranie's Space Boy Volume 3. McCranie, Stephen. 2019. (ENG.). 240p. (J). (gr. 5-9). pap. 10.99 *(978-1-5067-0842-3(0))* Dark Horse Comics.

—Stephen Mccranie's Space Boy Volume 6. McCranie, Stephen. 2020. (ENG.). 1p. (J). (gr. 5). pap. 10.99 *(978-1-5067-1400-4(5)*, Dark Horse Books) Dark Horse Comics.

McCranie, Stephen. Stephen Mccranie's Space Boy Volume 7, Vol. 7. McCranie, Stephen. 2020. 232p. (J). (gr. 5). pap. 10.99 ***(978-1-5067-1401-1(3)***, Dark Horse Books) Dark Horse Comics.

McCray, Ed. Jill Chill & the Baron of Glacier Mountain: Wonder Tales from the Book of Ed. McCray, Ed. Brewer, Tammy & Harms, Cathy, eds. 2003. 150p. (J). mass mkt. 14.95 *(978-1-929515-26-4(X)*, Solovisions) Comic Library International.

McCrea, John, et al. Spider-Man's Tangled Web Omnibus. 2017. (ENG.). 560p. (YA). (gr. 8-17). 100.00 *(978-1-302-90682-5(8))* Marvel Worldwide, Inc.

McCrea, John. Theseus: Battling the Minotaur [a Greek Myth]. Limke, Jeff. 2008. (Graphic Myths & Legends Ser.). (ENG.). 48p. (J). (gr. 4-8). pap. 9.99 *(978-0-8225-8517-6(0)*, Graphic Universe™) Lerner Publishing Group.

McCrea, John. Yondu: My Two Yondus. 2020. 112p. (YA). (gr. 8-17). pap. 15.99 ***(978-1-302-92109-5(6))*** Marvel Worldwide, Inc.

McCreary, Jane. On the Trail of Bigfoot in Washington. Wilsdon, Christina. 2006. 26p. (J). 7.99 *(978-1-59939-012-3(4))* Cornerstone Pr.

McCreery, Crash. El Chupacabras. Rubin, Adam. 2018. (ENG & SPA.). 48p. (J). (gr. -1-3). 17.99 *(978-0-399-53929-9(8)*, Dial Bks) Penguin Young Readers Group.

McCroskey, Christine. Lying Awake. Furbush, Helen. l.t. ed. 2004. 32p. (J). (gr. 1-6). 15.95 *(978-0-9741787-0-7(5)*, 1239134) Harbor Island Bks.

McCubbin, David. Alien Invasion. Kettle, Phil. 2019. (Spike! Ser.). (ENG.). 44p. (J). (gr. k-8). pap. *(978-0-6485557-0-4(4)*, Brolly Bks.) Borghesi & Adam Pubs. Pty Ltd.

—The Snowboard Race. Kettle, Phil. 2019. (Spike! Ser.). (ENG.). 44p. (J). (gr. k-3). pap. *(978-0-6485557-1-1(2)*, Brolly Bks.) Borghesi & Adam Pubs. Pty Ltd.

—Tennis Champ. Kettle, Phil. 2019. (Spike! Ser.). (ENG.). 44p. (J). (gr. k-7). pap. *(978-0-6485557-2-8(0)*, Brolly Bks.) Borghesi & Adam Pubs. Pty Ltd.

McCue, Lisa. The Babysitters. Chaconas, Dori. 2014. (Cork & Fuzz Ser.: 6). 32p. (J). (gr. 1-3). pap. 4.99 *(978-0-448-48050-3(6)*, Penguin Young Readers) Penguin Young Readers Group.

—Best Friends No. 1. Chaconas, Dori. 2010. (Cork & Fuzz Ser.: 1). 32p. (J). (gr. 1-3). mass mkt. 4.99 *(978-0-14-241593-1(6)*, Penguin Young Readers) Penguin Young Readers Group.

—Busy Bunnies. 2nd ed. 2020. (ENG.). 14p. (J). (— 1). bds. 5.99 *(978-0-7944-4226-2(9)*, Studio Fun International) Printers Row Publishing Group.

—The Collectors, 4 vols. Chaconas, Dori. 2010. (Cork & Fuzz Ser.: 4). 32p. (J). (gr. 1-3). mass mkt. 4.99 *(978-0-14-241714-0(9)*, Penguin Young Readers) Penguin Young Readers Group.

—Corduroy Goes to the Beach. Hennessy, B. G. 2006. (Corduroy Ser.). (ENG.). 20p. (J). (gr. 1-k). 11.99 *(978-0-670-06052-8(6)*, Viking Books for Young Readers) Penguin Young Readers Group.

—Corduroy Goes to the Doctor (lg Format) Freeman, Don. 2005. (Corduroy Ser.). 14p. (J). (gr. -1 — 1). bds. 5.99 *(978-0-670-06031-3(3)*, Viking Books for Young Readers) Penguin Young Readers Group.

—Corduroy's Day. Freeman, Don. 2005. (Corduroy Ser.). (ENG.). 14p. (J). (gr. -1 — 1). bds. 6.99 *(978-0-670-06030-6(5)*, Viking Books for Young Readers) Penguin Young Readers Group.

—Corduroy's Fourth of July. 2007. (Corduroy Ser.). (ENG.). 16p. (J). (gr. -1 — 1). bds. 5.99 *(978-0-670-06159-4(X)*, Viking Books for Young Readers) Penguin Young Readers Group.

—Corduroy's Thanksgiving. 2006. (Corduroy Ser.). (ENG.). 16p. (J). (gr. -1 — 1). bds. 5.99 *(978-0-670-06108-2(5)*, Viking Books for Young Readers) Penguin Young Readers Group.

—Corduroy's Tiny Treasury, 5 bks., Set. Freeman, Don. 2010. (Corduroy Ser.). 30p. (J). (gr. -1 — 1). bds. 9.99 *(978-0-670-01230-5(0)*, Viking Books for Young Readers) Penguin Young Readers Group.

—Corduroy's Valentine's Day. 2004. (Corduroy Ser.). (ENG.). 16p. (J). (gr. -1 — 1). bds. 5.99 *(978-0-670-03640-0(4)*, Viking Books for Young Readers) Penguin Young Readers Group.

—Cork & Fuzz. Chaconas, Dori. 2005. (Cork & Fuzz Ser.: 1). 32p. (J). (gr. 1-3). 13.99 *(978-0-670-03602-8(1)*, Viking Books for Young Readers) Penguin Young Readers Group.

—Easter Parade. Berlin, Irving. 2003. 32p. (J). 16.89 *(978-0-06-029126-6(5))* HarperCollins Pubs.

—Easter Surprises. Schaefer, Lola. 2009. (ENG.). 18p. (J). (gr. -1-1). 7.99 *(978-1-4169-6476-6(2)*, Little Simon) Little Simon.

—Finders Keepers, 5 vols. Chaconas, Dori. 2011. (Cork & Fuzz Ser.: 5). 32p. (J). (gr. 1-3). mass mkt. 4.99 *(978-0-14-241869-7(2)*, Penguin Young Readers) Penguin Young Readers Group.

—Good Sports. Chaconas, Dori. 2010. (Cork & Fuzz Ser.: 3). 32p. (J). (gr. 1-3). mass mkt. 4.99 *(978-0-14-241713-3(0)*, Penguin Young Readers) Penguin Young Readers Group.

—Happy Hanukkah, Corduroy. Freeman, Don. 2009. (Corduroy Ser.). (ENG.). 16p. (J). (gr. -1 — 1). bds. 6.99 *(978-0-670-01127-8(4)*, Viking Books for Young Readers) Penguin Young Readers Group.

—How Do I Love You? Kimmelman, Leslie. 2005. 32p. (J). lib. bdg. 16.89 *(978-0-06-001201-4(3))* HarperCollins Pubs.

—Little Bear. Namm, Diane. (My First Reader Ser.). (ENG.). 32p. (J). (gr. k-1). 2004. pap. 3.95 *(978-0-516-24633-8(X))*; 2003. 18.50 *(978-0-516-22931-7(1))* Scholastic Library Publishing. (Children's Pr.).

—Mama Loves: Step Into Reading. Goode, Molly. 2015. (Step into Reading Ser.). 32p. (J). (gr. -1-1). 4.99 *(978-0-553-53896-0(9)*, Random Hse. Bks. for Young Readers) Random Hse. Children's Bks.

—My First Mother Goose Nursery Rhymes. Editors of Studio Fun International. 2018. (ENG.). 20p. (J). (gr. -1 — 1). bds. 8.99 *(978-0-7944-4163-0(7)*, Reader's Digest Children's Bks.) Studio Fun International.

—Polar Bear Babies. Ring, Susan. 2016. (Step into Reading Ser.). 32p. (J). (gr. -1-1). 4.99 *(978-0-399-54954-0(4)*, Random Hse. Bks. for Young Readers) Random Hse. Children's Bks.

—The Puppy Who Wanted a Boy. Thayer, Jane. 2005. (ENG.). 32p. (J). (gr. -1-3). pap. 7.99 *(978-0-06-052698-6(X))* HarperCollins Pubs.

—Short & Tall. Chaconas, Dori. 2006. (Penguin Young Readers: Level 3 Ser.: 2). (ENG.). 32p. (J). (gr. 1-3). 16.19 *(978-0-670-05985-0(4)*, Viking) Penguin Publishing Group.

—Short & Tall No. 2, 2 vols. Chaconas, Dori. 2010. (Cork & Fuzz Ser.: 2). 32p. (J). (gr. 1-3). mass mkt. 4.99 *(978-0-14-241594-8(4)*, Penguin Young Readers) Penguin Young Readers Group.

—Snot Stew. Wallace, Bill. 2nd ed. 2008. (ENG.). 96p. (J). (gr. 3-7). pap. 6.99 *(978-1-4169-5804-8(5)*, Aladdin) Simon & Schuster Children's Publishing.

—Snuggle Bunnies. Falken, L. C. 2018. (ENG.). 18p. (J). (gr. -1 — 1). bds. 6.99 *(978-0-7944-4069-5(X)*, Reader's Digest Children's Bks.) Studio Fun International.

—Spring Is Here, Corduroy! Freeman, Don. 2007. (Corduroy Ser.). (ENG.). 16p. (J). (gr. -1-k). 6.99 *(978-0-448-44461-1(5)*, Grosset & Dunlap) Penguin Young Readers Group.

—The Story of Peter Rabbit. Potter, Beatrix. 2nd ed. 2019. (ENG.). 20p. (J). (gr. -1-1). bds. 10.99 *(978-0-7944-4227-9(7)*, Studio Fun International) Printers Row Publishing Group.

—The Swimming Lesson. Chaconas, Dori. 2014. (Cork & Fuzz Ser.: 7). 32p. (J). (gr. 1-3). pap. 4.99 *(978-0-448-48051-0(4)*, Penguin Young Readers) Penguin Young Readers Group.

—Wait a Minute. Chaconas, Dori. 2015. (Cork & Fuzz Ser.: 9). (ENG.). 32p. (J). (gr. 1-3). pap. 4.99 *(978-0-14-750856-0(8)*, Penguin Young Readers) Penguin Young Readers Group.

McCue, Lisa, jt. illus. see Barasch, Lynne.

McCue, Lisa, jt. illus. see Freeman, Don.

McCue, Patrick. Some Things Are Made to Smoke. Knapp-Grosz, Tamara & Loyd, Elizabeth. 2004. 20p. (J). pap. *(978-1-893974-23-4(5)*, Design Pr. Bks.) Savannah College of Art & Design Exhibitions.

McCullen, Sam. Ella the Superstar: Band 05/Green (Collins Big Cat) Whybrow, Ian. 2007. (Collins Big Cat Ser.). (ENG.). 24p. (J). (gr. 1-2). pap. 8.99 *(978-0-00-718681-5(9))* HarperCollins Pubs. Ltd. GBR. Dist: Independent Pubs. Group.

McCulley Seibold, Sheri. The 12 Joys of Christmas. Seibold, Thomas K. 2016. (ENG.). (J). 20.00 *(978-0-9981591-0-2(7))* Sheri McCulley Studio.

McCulloch, Jessica Clark. The Tales of Polly & Lilly: Cupcake Baking Day. Flores, Julie Park. 2019. (Tales of Polly & Lilly Ser.: Vol. 2). (ENG.). 28p. (J). pap. 9.25 ***(978-1-7037-0117-3(8))*** Independently Published.

McCulloch, Ryan. Figley's Little White Lie: Mutasia. McCulloch, Ryan. Cotsakos, Suzanne. 2017. (Mutasia Ser.: 2). (ENG.). 48p. (J). (gr. k-2). 15.99 *(978-0-9856002-0-4(9))* Mutasian Entertainment, LLC.

McCullough, Anita. Rookie Ranger Meets the Big Five. Thompson, Ann, photos by. Joya Cultural, Enterprises & Enterprises, Joya Cultural. 2015. (Rookie Ranger Ser.: Vol. 1). (ENG.). 28p. (J). pap. 11.99 *(978-0-9904135-2-3(7))* Joya Cultural Enterprises Inc.

McCullough, Liam. How Alice's Bad Day Turned Good. McCullough, Annette. McIntyre, Kim, ed. 2018. (ENG.). 52p. (J). *(978-1-5255-3446-1(7))*; pap. *(978-1-5255-3447-8(5))* FriesenPress.

McCullough, Marilyn. Two by Two: Noah's Story in Rhyme. Kilpatrick, Leanne. 2013. 28p. pap. *(978-0-906672-67-9(8))* Oleander Pr., The.

McCullough, Sharon Pierce. Bunbun. (J). 12.99 *(978-1-84148-455-6(5))* Barefoot Bks., Inc.

McCully, Emily Arnold. Ballywhinney Girl. Bunting, Eve. 2012. (ENG.). 32p. (J). (gr. -1-3). 16.99 *(978-0-547-55843-1(0)*, 1453506) Houghton Mifflin Harcourt Publishing Co.

—Black Is Brown Is Tan. Adoff, Arnold. 2004. (ENG.). 40p. (J). (gr. -1-3). reprint ed. pap. 7.99 *(978-0-06-443644-1(6))* HarperCollins Pubs.

—Dare the Wind: The Record-Breaking Voyage of Eleanor Prentiss & the Flying Cloud. Fern, Tracey E. 2014. (ENG.). 540p. (J). (gr. k-3). 17.99 *(978-0-374-31699-0(6)*, 900051870, Farrar, Straus & Giroux (BYR)) Farrar, Straus & Giroux.

—In Like a Lion, Out Like a Lamb. Bauer, Marion Dane. 2011. (ENG.). 32p. (J). (gr. -1-3). 16.95 *(978-0-8234-2238-8(0))* Holiday Hse., Inc.

—In Like a Lion Out Like a Lamb. Bauer, Marion Dane. 2012. (ENG.). 32p. (J). (gr. -1-3). pap. 7.99 *(978-0-8234-2432-0(4))* Holiday Hse., Inc.

—That's What Leprechauns Do. Bunting, Eve. 2009. (ENG.). 32p. (J). (gr. -1-3). pap. 7.99 *(978-0-547-07673-7(8)*, 1042034) Houghton Mifflin Harcourt Publishing Co.

McCully, Emily Arnold. Clara: The (Mostly) True Story of the Rhinoceros Who Dazzled Kings, Inspired Artists, & Won the Hearts of Everyone... While She Ate Her Way up & down a Continent. McCully, Emily Arnold. 2016. (ENG.). 48p. (J). (gr. -1-3). 17.99 *(978-0-553-52246-4(9)*, Schwartz & Wade Bks.) Random Hse. Children's Bks.

—First Snow. McCully, Emily Arnold. 2003. (ENG.). 32p. (J). (gr. -1-3). 17.99 *(978-0-06-623852-4(8))* HarperCollins Pubs.

—Little Ducks Go. McCully, Emily Arnold. 2014. (I Like to Read Ser.). (ENG.). 24p. (J). (gr. -1-3). 14.95 *(978-0-8234-2941-7(5))* Holiday Hse., Inc.

—My Heart Glow: Alice Cogswell, Thomas Gallaudet, & the Birth of American Sign Language. McCully, Emily Arnold. 2008. (ENG.). 40p. (gr. 1-4). 15.99 *(978-1-4231-0028-7(X))* Hyperion Pr.

—Pete Likes Bunny. McCully, Emily Arnold. 2016. (I Like to Read Ser.). (ENG.). 24p. (J). (gr. -1-3). 6.99 *(978-0-8234-3687-3(X))* Holiday Hse., Inc.

—Picnic. McCully, Emily Arnold. 2003. 32p. (J). (gr. -1-k). 16.89 *(978-0-06-623855-5(2))*; (ENG.). 17.99 *(978-0-06-623854-8(4))* HarperCollins Pubs.

—Sam & the Big Kids. McCully, Emily Arnold. 2014. (I Like to Read Ser.). (ENG.). 24p. (J). (gr. -1-3). 7.99 *(978-0-8234-3060-4(X))* Holiday Hse., Inc.

—School. McCully, Emily Arnold. 2005. 32p. (J). lib. bdg. 16.89 *(978-0-06-623857-9(9))* HarperCollins Pubs.

—Wonder Horse: The True Story of the World's Smartest Horse. McCully, Emily Arnold. 2010. (ENG.). 32p. (J). (gr. -1-3). 17.99 *(978-0-8050-8793-2(1)*, 900050752, Holt, Henry & Co. Bks. For Young Readers) Holt, Henry & Co.

—3, 2, 1, Go! McCully, Emily Arnold. 2015. (I Like to Read Ser.). (ENG.). 24p. (J). (gr. -1-3). 14.95 *(978-0-8234-3288-2(2))* Holiday Hse., Inc.

McCune, Mark. Modern Fables. Gibbons, Ted & Wilcox, S. Michael. 2010. (J). 14.99 *(978-1-59955-307-8(4))* Cedar Fort, Inc./CFI Distribution.

McCurdy, Michael. Johnny Tremain. Forbes, Esther. l.t. ed. 2005. (ENG.). 440p. (YA). pap. 10.95 *(978-0-7862-7178-8(7))* Thorndike Pr.

—Lucy's Christmas. Hall, Donald. 2007. (ENG.). 40p. (J). (gr. 1). pap. 10.95 *(978-1-56792-342-1(9))* Godine, David R. Pub.

—Lucy's Summer. Hall, Donald. 2015. (ENG.). 40p. (J). (gr. 1-18). pap. 10.95 *(978-1-56792-348-3(8))* Godine, David R. Pub.

—Tarzan. San Souci, Robert D. & Burroughs, Edgar Rice. 2004. 31p. (J). (gr. k-4). reprint ed. 16.00 *(978-0-7567-7576-6(0))* DIANE Publishing Co.

—The Train They Call the City of New Orleans. Goodman, Steve. pap. 16.95 incl. audio *(978-1-59112-899-1(4))*; pap. incl. audio *(978-1-59112-901-1(X))*; pap. 18.95 incl. audio compact disk *(978-1-59112-903-5(6))*; pap. incl. audio compact disk *(978-1-59112-905-9(2))* Live Oak Media.

—The Train They Call the City of New Orleans. Goodman, Steve. 2003. 16.99 *(978-3-00-100280-8(8)*, Putnam Juvenile) Penguin Publishing Group.

McCurdy, Michael. Walden Then & Now: An Alphabetical Tour of Henry Thoreau's Pond. McCurdy, Michael. 2010. (ENG.). 32p. (J). (gr. k-12). 16.95 *(978-1-58089-253-7(1))* Charlesbridge Publishing, Inc.

McCurdy, Scott. Gusto Gambini the Great. Stewart, Bonnie. 2018. (ENG.). 36p. (J). pap. 11.98 *(978-1-5452-7397-5(9))* CreateSpace Independent Publishing Platform.

McCurоy, Michael. American Fairy Tales: From Rip Van Winkle to the Rootabaga Stories. Philip, Neil, ed. 2004. 160p. (J). (gr. k-4). reprint ed. pap. 13.00 *(978-0-7567-8068-5(3))* DIANE Publishing Co.

McDaniel, Carren. Three Lost Pups. McDaniel, Carren. 2019. (Benjamin to the Rescue Ser.: Vol. 4). (ENG.). 40p. (J). pap. 11.00 *(978-1-0902-1394-5(8))* Independently Published.

McDaniel, Rick. Tuttle Stories. Murcray, Rod. 2012. 40p. pap. 14.95 *(978-1-61897-654-3(0)*, Strategic Bk. Publishing) Strategic Book Publishing & Rights Agency (SBPRA).

McDaniel, Thomas. Does This Belong Here? A Twiggyleaf Adventure. Goodwin, Carol. l.t. ed. 2003. 32p. (J). 14.95 *(978-0-9741072-1-9(2))* CornerWind Media, L.L.C.

—The Great Acorn: A Twiggyleaf Adventure. Goodwin, Carol. l.t. ed. 2004. 32p. (J). 14.95 *(978-0-9741072-2-6(0))* CornerWind Media, L.L.C.

—Tippy Needs A Home: A Twiggyleaf Adventure. Goodwin, Carol. l.t. ed. 32p. (J). 2004. 14.95 *(978-0-9741072-3-3(9))*; 2003. per. 14.95 *(978-0-09-741072-2(1))* CornerWind Media, L.L.C.

—What's the Hurry, Furry? A Twiggyleaf Adventure. Goodwin, Carol. l.t. ed. 2003. 32p. (J). 14.95 *(978-0-9741072-0-2(4))* CornerWind Media, L.L.C.

McDaniel, Veronica P. Mrs. Popsicle's Popsicle Day. Levy, Barbara W. 2019. (ENG.). 32p. (J). pap. 9.99 *(978-1-0950-2291-7(1))* Independently Published.

McDaniels, Preston. The Bear. Rylant, Cynthia. (Lighthouse Family Ser.: 8). (ENG.). 48p. (J). (gr. 1-5). 2019. pap. 5.99 *(978-1-4814-6029-3(3))*; 2018. 15.99 *(978-1-4814-6028-6(5))* Beach Lane Bks. (Beach Lane Bks.).

—The Eagle. Rylant, Cynthia. 2004. (Lighthouse Family Ser.: 3). (ENG.). 64p. (J). (gr. 1-5). 15.99 *(978-0-689-86243-4(1)*, Simon & Schuster Bks. For Young Readers) Simon & Schuster Bks. For Young Readers.

—The Eagle. Rylant, Cynthia. 2005. (Lighthouse Family Ser.: 3). (ENG.). 64p. (J). (gr. 1-5). pap. 5.99 *(978-0-689-86311-0(X)*, Simon & Schuster Bks. For

Young Readers) Simon & Schuster Bks. For Young Readers.

—The Lighthouse Family Collection: The Storm; the Whale; the Eagle; the Turtle; the Octopus; the Otter; the Sea Lion; the Bear. Rylant, Cynthia. ed. 2018. (Lighthouse Family Ser.). (ENG.). 464p. (J). (gr. 1-5). 129.99 *(978-1-5344-3213-0(2)*, Beach Lane Bks.) Beach Lane Bks.

—The Lighthouse Family Paperback Collection: The Storm; the Whale; the Eagle; the Turtle; the Octopus; the Otter; the Sea Lion; the Bear. Rylant, Cynthia. ed. 2019. (Lighthouse Family Ser.). (ENG.). 464p. (J). (gr. 1-5). pap. 47.99 *(978-1-5344-4054-8(2)*, Beach Lane Bks.) Beach Lane Bks.

—The Octopus. Rylant, Cynthia. 2005. (Lighthouse Family Ser.: 5). (ENG.). 64p. (J). (gr. 1-5). 15.99 *(978-0-689-86246-5(6)*, Simon & Schuster Bks. For Young Readers) Simon & Schuster Bks. For Young Readers.

—The Otter. Rylant, Cynthia. 2016. (Lighthouse Family Ser.: 6). (ENG.). 48p. (J). (gr. 1-5). 15.99 *(978-1-4814-6045-3(5)*, Beach Lane Bks.) Beach Lane Bks.

—Phineas L. MacGuire ... Blasts Off! Dowell, Frances O'Roark. 2011. (From the Highly Scientific Notebooks of Phineas L. MacGuire Ser.). (ENG.). 224p. (J). (gr. 3-7). pap. 7.99 *(978-1-4424-2204-9(1)*, Atheneum Bks. for Young Readers) Simon & Schuster Children's Publishing.

—Phineas L. MacGuire ... Blasts Off! Dowell, Frances O'Roark. 2008. (From the Highly Scientific Notebooks of Phineas L. MacGuire Ser.). (ENG.). 208p. (J). (gr. 3-7). 16.99 *(978-1-4169-2689-4(5))* Simon & Schuster, Inc.

—Phineas L. MacGuire ... Erupts! The First Experiment. Dowell, Frances O'Roark. (From the Highly Scientific Notebooks of Phineas L. MacGuire Ser.). (ENG.). 176p. (J). (gr. 3-7). 2007. pap. 7.99 *(978-1-4169-4734-9(5))*; 2006. 18.99 *(978-1-4169-0195-2(7))* Simon & Schuster Children's Publishing. (Atheneum Bks. for Young Readers).

—Phineas L. MacGuire ... Gets Cooking! Dowell, Frances O'Roark. (From the Highly Scientific Notebooks of Phineas L. MacGuire Ser.). (ENG.). (J). (gr. 3-7). 2015. 224p. pap. 6.99 *(978-1-4814-0100-5(9))*; 2014. 208p. 16.99 *(978-1-4814-0099-2(1)*, Atheneum Bks. for Young Readers) Simon & Schuster Children's Publishing.

—Phineas L. MacGuire ... Gets Slimed! Dowell, Frances O'Roark. 2010. (From the Highly Scientific Notebooks of Phineas L. MacGuire Ser.). (ENG.). 224p. (J). (gr. 3-7). pap. 7.99 *(978-1-4169-9775-7(X)*, Atheneum Bks. for Young Readers) Simon & Schuster Children's Publishing.

—Phineas L. MacGuire ... Gets Slimed! Dowell, Frances O'Roark. 2007. (From the Highly Scientific Notebooks of Phineas L. MacGuire Ser.). (ENG.). 208p. (J). (gr. 3-7). 16.99 *(978-1-4169-0196-9(5))* Simon & Schuster, Inc.

—Phineas L. MacGuire... Gets Slimed! Dowell, Frances O'Roark. l.t. ed. 2008. (From the Highly Scientific Notebooks of Phineas L. MacGuire Ser.). 159p. (J). (gr. 3-7). 22.95 *(978-1-4104-0440-4(4))* Thorndike Pr.

—The Sea Lion. Rylant, Cynthia. (Lighthouse Family Ser.: 7). (ENG.). 48p. (J). (gr. 1-5). 2018. pap. 5.99 *(978-1-4814-6026-2(9))*; 2017. 15.99 *(978-1-4814-6025-5(0))* Beach Lane Bks. (Beach Lane Bks.).

—The Squire & the Scroll: A Tale of the Rewards of a Pure Heart. Bishop, Jennie. 2009. (ENG.). 32p. (J). 15.99 *(978-1-59317-382-1(2))* Warner Pr., Inc.

—The Squire & the Scroll: A Tale of the Rewards of a Pure Heart. 2004. (ENG.). 32p. (J). 12.99 *(978-1-59317-079-0(3))* Warner Pr., Inc.

—The Storm. Rylant, Cynthia. 2003. (Lighthouse Family Ser.: 1). (ENG.). 80p. (J). (gr. 1-5). pap. 5.99 *(978-0-689-84882-7(X)*, Simon & Schuster Bks. For Young Readers) Simon & Schuster Bks. For Young Readers.

—The Three Gifts of Christmas. Bishop, Jennie. 2009. 32p. (J). (gr. 3-18). 15.99 incl. audio compact disk *(978-1-59317-378-4(4))* Warner Pr., Inc.

—The Turtle. Rylant, Cynthia. 2006. (Lighthouse Family Ser.). 47p. (J). (gr. -1-3). 11.65 *(978-0-7569-6611-9(6))* Perfection Learning Corp.

—The Turtle. Rylant, Cynthia. (Lighthouse Family Ser.: 4). (ENG.). 48p. (J). (gr. 1-5). 2006. pap. 5.99 *(978-0-689-86312-7(8))*; 2005. 15.99 *(978-0-689-86244-1(X))* Simon & Schuster Bks. For Young Readers. (Simon & Schuster Bks. For Young Readers).

—The Whale. Rylant, Cynthia. (Lighthouse Family Ser.: 2). (ENG.). 64p. (J). (gr. 1-5). 2004. pap. 5.99 *(978-0-689-84883-4(8))*; 2003. 17.99 *(978-0-689-84881-0(1))* Simon & Schuster Bks. For Young Readers. (Simon & Schuster Bks. For Young Readers).

McDaniels, Preston. A Perfect Snowman. McDaniels, Preston. 2007. (ENG.). 40p. (J). (gr. -1-3). 18.99 *(978-1-4169-1026-8(3)*, Simon & Schuster Bks. For Young Readers) Simon & Schuster Bks. For Young Readers.

McDee, Katie. Bridget & Bo Build a Blog. St. John, Amanda. 2012. (Writing Builders Ser.). 32p. (J). (gr. 2-4). lib. bdg. 25.27 *(978-1-59953-507-4(6))* Norwood Hse. Pr.

—Bridget & Bo Build a Blog. StJohn, Amanda. 2012. (Writing Builders Ser.). 32p. (J). (gr. 2-4). pap. 11.94 *(978-1-60357-387-0(9))* Norwood Hse. Pr.

—How Do We Know about Dinosaurs? A Fossil Mystery, 1 vol. Olien, Rebecca. 2011. (First Graphics: Science Mysteries Ser.). (ENG.). 24p. (J). (gr. k-3). pap. 6.29 *(978-1-4296-7173-6(4)*, Capstone Pr.); (gr. 1-2). pap. 35.70 *(978-1-4296-7177-4(7))* Capstone.

—Where Do the Birds Go? A Migration Mystery, 1 vol. Olien, Rebecca. 2011. (First Graphics: Science Mysteries Ser.). (ENG.). 24p. (J). (gr. k-3). pap. 6.29 *(978-1-4296-7175-0(0))*; (gr. 1-2). pap. 35.70 *(978-1-4296-7179-8(3))* Capstone.

McDee, Katie, jt. illus. see Scott, Korey.

Mcdermot, Jessie. Clover. Coolidge, Susan. 2007. (ENG.). 168p. per. *(978-1-4065-1524-4(8))* Dodo Pr.

McDermott, Gerald. Gerald McDermott & You, 1 vol. Stott, Jon C. 2004. (Author & YOU Ser.). 128p. pap. 35.00 *(978-1-59158-175-8(3)*, LU1753, Libraries Unlimited) ABC-CLIO, LLC.

McDermott, Gerald. Arrow to the Sun: A Pueblo Indian Tale. McDermott, Gerald. 2004. 37p. (J). (gr. k-3). reprint ed. pap. 14.00 *(978-0-7567-7103-4(X))* DIANE Publishing Co.

—The Light of the World. McDermott, Gerald. 2006. 32p. (J). 16.99 *(978-0-525-47488-3(9)*, Dutton Juvenile) Penguin Publishing Group.

McDermott, Lisa & Koebel, Jessica. A Christmas Penguin's Wish. Hill, Lenny M. 2020. (ENG.). 32p. (J). ***(978-1-5255-6829-9(9))***; pap. ***(978-1-5255-6830-5(2))*** FriesenPress.

McDermott, Robert. The Christmas Letter. Wood, Christine, photos by. Wood, Francis Eusene. Wood, Christine & Marken, Jon, eds. 2007. pap. 9.95 *(978-0-9746372-6-6(2))* Tip-Of-The-Moon Publishing Co.

McDermott, Robert W. Autumn's Reunion: A Story of Thanksgiving. Wood, Francis Eugene. Dean, Tina & Marken, Jon, eds. 2006. 47p. pap. 8.00 *(978-0-9746372-2-8(X))* Tip-Of-The-Moon Publishing Co.

McDevitt, Mary Kate. What the World Needs Now Is Love. Bacharach, Burt & David, Hal. 2017. (ENG.). 32p. (J). (gr. k-4). 9.99 *(978-1-5247-8598-7(9)*, Penguin Workshop) Penguin Young Readers Group.

—Words That Built a Nation: Voices of Democracy That Have Shaped America's History. Miller, Marilyn et al. 2018. 208p. (J). (gr. 5). 18.99 *(978-1-63565-188-1(3)*, 9781635651881, Rodale Kids) Random Hse. Children's Bks.

McDivitt, Krista. And Away They Went: A Saskatchewan Adventure. McDivitt, Krista. Slobodian, Michael. 2019. (ENG.). 34p. (J). *(978-0-2288-1312-5(3))* Tellwell Talent.

McDonald, Amanda. Friday Night at the Zoo, 1 vol. McDonald, Regina. 2010. 16p. 24.95 *(978-1-4489-4090-5(7))* PublishAmerica, Inc.

McDonald, Candice Hartsough. Oliver at the Window. Shreeve, Elizabeth. 2009. (ENG.). 32p. (J). (gr. -1 — 1). 16.95 *(978-1-59078-548-5(7))* Boyds Mills Pr.

McDonald, Carissa. Elsie's Story: This Story Has No Hero. Murphy, Michael. 2018. (ENG.). 42p. (J). pap. 10.50 *(978-0-692-17801-0(5))* Murphy, Michael.

McDonald, Danielle. Ballet Backflip. Costain, Meredith. 2017. 144p. (J). pap. 5.99 *(978-1-61067-521-5(5))* Kane Miller.

—Double Dare You. Costain, Meredith. 2017. (Ella Diaries Ser.: 1). 144p. (J). pap. 5.99 *(978-1-61067-520-8(7))* Kane Miller.

—Dreams Come True. Costain, Meredith. 2017. (Ella Diaries Ser.: 4). 144p. (J). pap. 5.99 *(978-1-61067-523-9(1))* Kane Miller.

—Fun Bums. 2014. (ENG.). 14p. (J). (gr. -1-k). bds. 5.99 *(978-1-74297-594-8(1))* Hardie Grant Egmont Pty, Ltd. AUS. Dist: Independent Pubs. Group.

—I Heart Pets: The Ella Diaries. Costain, Meredith. 2017. 144p. (J). pap. 5.99 *(978-1-61067-522-2(3))* Kane Miller.

—Pony School Showdown. Costain, Meredith. 2016. 143p. (J). *(978-1-61067-568-0(1))* Kane Miller.

—Pony School Showdown: The Ella Diaries. Costain, Meredith. 2017. 144p. (J). pap. 5.99 *(978-1-61067-524-6(X))* Kane Miller.

McDonald, Jake. Color Me: Dinosaurs. Taylor, Emma. 2020. (ENG.). 96p. (J). (gr. 1-3). pap. 12.95 ***(978-1-4549-4129-3(4))*** Sterling Publishing Co., Inc.

McDonald, Jake. Doodle Magic: Animals. Griffiths, Margaret. 2016. (Doodle Magic Ser.). (ENG.). 64p. (J). (gr. k). spiral bd. 14.95 *(978-1-62686-480-1(2)*, Silver Dolphin Bks.) Readerlink Distribution Services, LLC.

—My First Alphabet Dot-To-Dot: Over 50 Fantastic Puzzles. Golding, Elizabeth. 2019. (My First Activity Bks.). (ENG.). 64p. (J). (gr. -1-2). pap. 6.99 *(978-1-4380-1270-4(5)*, B.E.S. Publishing) Peterson's.

McDonald, Jill. A Farmer's Life for Me. Law, Jessica. 2013. 24p. (J). pap. 6.99 *(978-1-78285-025-0(2))* Barefoot Bks., Inc.

—Ghoulish Gang. 2008. (ENG.). 12p. (J). 9.95 *(978-1-58117-782-4(8)*, Intervisual/Piggy Toes) Bendon, Inc.

—A Hole in the Bottom of the Sea. Law, Jessica. 2013. 24p. (J). (gr. -1-2). 9.99 *(978-1-84686-862-7(9))*; (gr. k-3). 16.99 *(978-1-84686-861-0(0))*; (ENG.). (gr. k-3). pap. 6.99 *(978-1-84686-948-8(X))* Barefoot Bks., Inc.

—Over in the Meadow. Books, Barefoot. 2012. 24p. (J). (gr. -1-2). 9.99 *(978-1-84686-747-7(9))* Barefoot Bks., Inc.

—Who's in the Farmyard? Gershator, Phyllis. 2012. 24p. (J). (gr. -1-k). bds. 14.99 *(978-1-84686-574-9(3))* Barefoot Bks., Inc.

—Who's in the Forest? Gershator, Phyllis. 2010. 24p. (J). (gr. -1-k). bds. 14.99 *(978-1-84686-476-6(3))* Barefoot Bks., Inc.

—Who's in the Garden? Gershator, Phillis. 2010. 24p. (J). (gr. -1-k). bds. 14.99 *(978-1-84686-403-2(8))* Barefoot Bks., Inc.

McDonald, Jill. Over in the Meadow Puzzle. Mcdonald, Jill. Fatus, Sophie. 2012. (J). (gr. -1-1). 14.99 *(978-1-84686-746-0(0))* Barefoot Bks., Inc.

McDonald, Jill. Shapes: A Play-with-Me BK. McDonald, Jill. 2007. (ENG.). 10p. bds. 6.95 *(978-1-58117-604-9(X)*, Intervisual/Piggy Toes) Bendon, Inc.

McDonald, Jill & Reed, Susan. Over in the Meadow. McDonald, Jill. 2011. (ENG.). 24p. (J). (gr. 1-4). 16.99 *(978-1-84686-543-5(3))* Barefoot Bks., Inc.

Mcdonald, Joe, photos by. Snakes: Biggest! Littlest! Markle, Sandra. 2011. (Biggest! Littlest! Ser.). (ENG., 32p. (J). (gr. k-2). pap. 10.95 *(978-1-59078-874-5(5))* Boyds Mills Pr.

McDonald, Kel. Misfits of Avalon Volume 3: the Future in the Wind. McDonald, Kel. 2017. (Misfits of Avalon Ser.: 3). (ENG.). 216p. (J). (gr. 2-5). pap. 14.99 *(978-1-61655-749-2(4))* Dark Horse Comics.

McDonald, Kim. The Gold of Angel Island. Martin, Brian. 2007. 46p. (J). *(978-0-9798059-0-5(2))* Lunchbox Stories Inc.

—The Lost Ring. Martin, Brian. 2007. 42p. (J). *(978-0-9798059-1-2(0))* Lunchbox Stories Inc.

McDonald, Marion & Brown, Marion. The Missing Mom. McDonald, Marion. 2012. 30p. pap. 9.00 *(978-1-4349-8628-3(4)*, RoseDog Bks.) Dorrance Publishing Co., Inc.

McDonald, Mercedes. For a Girl Becoming. Harjo, Joy. 2nd ed. 2009. (Sun Tracks Ser.: 66). (ENG.). 48p. (gr. -1). 17.95 *(978-0-8165-2797-7(0))* University of Arizona Pr.

—Hello Night/Hola Noche. Costales, Amy. 2007. (MUL.). 24p. (J). (gr. -1 — 1). 14.95 *(978-0-87358-927-7(0))* Cooper Square Publishing Llc.

McDonald, Patrick. Patrick & Hatrick, 1 vol. Borer, Christopher. 2010. 44p. pap. 24.95 *(978-1-4489-7978-3(1))* PublishAmerica, Inc.

McDonald, Steve. Fantastic Cities: A Coloring Book of Amazing Places Real & Imagined (Adult Coloring Books, City Coloring Books, Coloring Books for Adults) 2015. (ENG.). 60p. pap. 14.95 *(978-1-4521-4957-8(7))* Chronicle Bks. LLC.

McDonald, Suzi. Henry & the Oranges: Henry's Wild Adventures. Hart, Janice. 2010. 32p. pap. 13.00 *(978-1-60860-911-6(1)*, Eloquent Bks.) Strategic Book Publishing & Rights Agency (SBPRA).

McDonald, Trevy. The Speech Family. McDonald, Charles. 2007. (J). 15.00 *(978-0-9670712-3-7(2))* zReyomi Publishing.

McDonnell, Janet. Adopted & Loved Forever. Dellinger, Annetta. 2nd ed. 2009. 32p. (J). 12.99 *(978-0-7586-1591-6(4))* Concordia Publishing Hse.

—Blossom Plays Possum: (Because She's Shy) Jones, Birdy. 2017. 32p. (J). 15.95 *(978-1-4338-2735-8(2)*, Magination Pr.) American Psychological Assn.

—Bye Bye Pesky Fly. Mullady, Lysa. 2018. 32p. (J). *(978-1-4338-2855-3(3)*, Magination Pr.) American Psychological Assn.

—Gary Asks for Help. Chikowore, Nyasha. 2019. 32p. (J). *(978-1-4338-2946-8(0)*, Magination Pr.) American Psychological Assn.

—God Makes Me His Child in Baptism. Wittenback, Janet. rev. ed. 2007. 32p. (J). (gr. -1-k). pap. 6.49 *(978-0-7586-1305-9(9))* Concordia Publishing Hse.

—What to Do When Fear Interferes: A Kid's Guide to Overcoming Phobias. Freeland, Claire A.B. & Toner, Jacqueline B. 2019. (J). pap. *(978-1-4338-2974-1(6)*, Magination Pr.) American Psychological Assn.

—What to Do When Mistakes Make You Quake: A Kid's Guide to Accepting Imperfection. Freeland, Claire A.B. & Toner, Jacqueline B. 2015. 96p. (J). pap. *(978-1-4338-1930-8(9)*, Magination Pr.) American Psychological Assn.

—What to Do When You Don't Want to Be Apart: A Kid's Guide to Overcoming Separation Anxiety. Lavallee, Kristen & Schneider, Silvia. 2017. 88p. (J). pap. *(978-1-4338-2713-6(1)*, Magination Pr.) American Psychological Assn.

—What to Do When You Feel Too Shy: A Kid's Guide to Overcoming Social Anxiety. Freeland, Claire A.B. & Toner, Jacqueline B. 2016. 96p. (J). pap. *(978-1-4338-2276-6(8)*, Magination Pr.) American Psychological Assn.

McDonnell, Kevin. Turtle in the Tuba: Read Well Level K Unit 8 Storybook. Jones, Shelley V. & Sprick, Marilyn. 2004. (Read Well Level K Ser.). 20p. *(978-1-57035-672-8(6))* Cambium Education, Inc.

McDonnell, Patrick. Silly Wonderful You. Rinker, Sherri Duskey. 2016. (ENG.). 40p. (J). (gr. -1-3). 17.99 *(978-0-06-227105-1(9))* HarperCollins Pubs.

Mcdonnell, Patrick. The Skunk. Barnett, Mac. 2015. (ENG.). 40p. (J). (gr. -1-3). 17.99 *(978-1-59643-966-5(1)*, 900126271) Roaring Brook Pr.

McDonnell, Peter. Landing at Ellis Island. Karapetkova, Holly. ed. 2009. (Eye on History Graphic Illustrated Ser.). (ENG.). 32p. (gr. 4-8). pap. 9.95 *(978-1-60694-552-0(1)*, 9781606945520) Rourke Educational Media.

—The Pilgrims & the First Thanksgiving, 1 vol. Englar, Mary. 2006. (Graphic History Ser.). (ENG.). 32p. (J). (gr. 3-9). 8.10 *(978-0-7368-9656-6(2))*; 31.32 *(978-0-7368-5492-4(4))* Capstone. (Capstone Pr.).

—Riding with Paul Revere. Karapetkova, Holly. 2009. (Eye on History Graphic Illustrated Ser.). (ENG.). 32p. (gr. 4-8). pap. 9.95 *(978-1-60694-551-3(3)*, 9781606945513) Rourke Educational Media.

—El Viaje del Mayflower. Lassieur, Allison. 2006. (Historia Gráficas Ser.). (SPA.). 32p. (J). (gr. 3-9). 31.32 *(978-0-7368-6613-2(2))* Capstone.

McDonough, Amanda. Garden Friends: Fun for Little Fingers. 2018. (Pull-Ups Bks.). (ENG.). 8p. (J). (gr. -1 — 1). bds. 6.99 *(978-1-4380-5053-9(4)*, B.E.S. Publishing) Peterson's.

—Woodland Babies: Fun for Little Fingers. 2018. (Pull-Ups Ser.). (ENG.). 8p. (J). (gr. -1 — 1). bds. 6.99 *(978-1-4380-5054-6(2)*, B.E.S. Publishing) Peterson's.

McDonough, Mati. How Do I Love Thee? Browning, Elizabeth Barrett. 2016. (ENG.). 32p. (J). (gr. -1-3). 16.95 *(978-1-937359-83-6(2)*, Cameron Kids) Cameron + Co.

McDougald, Sheryl. Alison's Fishing Birds. Haig-Brown, Roderick. 2017. (ENG.). 48p. (J). 21.95 *(978-1-987915-19-8(4))* Caitlin Pr., Inc. CAN. Dist: Independent Pubs. Group.

McDuffie, Seth. Across Grandma's Garden. Angelucci, Karen & McDuffie, Lauren. 2012. (ENG.). 40p. (J). 15.95 ***(978-1-935001-93-5(0)***, Joey Bks.) Acclaim Pr., Inc.

McElfatrick, Claire. The Book of Brilliant Bugs. French, Jess. 2020. (ENG.). 80p. (J). (gr. 1-3). 16.99 *(978-1-4654-8982-1(7)*, DK Children) Dorling Kindersley Publishing, Inc.

—The Magic & Mystery of Trees. Green, Jen. 2019. (ENG.). 80p. (J). (gr. 2-4). 16.99 *(978-1-4654-7936-5(8)*, DK Children) Dorling Kindersley Publishing, Inc.

McElhinney, Glenn. Frankenkids, No. 5. Graves, Annie. 2015. (Nightmare Club Ser.: 5). (ENG.). 64p. (J). (gr. 2-5). lib. bdg. 25.32 *(978-1-4677-4352-5(6)*, 9781467743525, Darby Creek) Lerner Publishing Group.

—Guinea Pig Killer, No. 4. Graves, Annie. 2015. (Nightmare Club Ser.: 4). (ENG.). 64p. (J). (gr. 2-5). pap. 6.99 *(978-1-4677-6044-7(7)*, 9781467760447); lib. bdg. 25.32 *(978-1-4677-4351-8(8)*, 9781467743518) Lerner Publishing Group. (Darby Creek).

—The Hatching, No. 8. Graves, Annie. 2015. (Nightmare Club Ser.: 8). (ENG.). 64p. (J). (gr. 2-5). lib. bdg. 25.32 *(978-1-4677-4354-9(2)*, 9781467743549, Darby Creek) Lerner Publishing Group.

—Help! My Brother's a Zombie. Graves, Annie. ed. 2015. (Nightmare Club Ser.). (ENG.). 64p. (J). (gr. 2-5). E-Book 6.99 *(978-1-4677-7871-8(0)*, 9781467778718, Darby Creek) Lerner Publishing Group.

—Mirrored, No. 3. Graves, Annie. 2015. (Nightmare Club Ser.: 3). (ENG.). 64p. (J). (gr. 2-5). pap. 6.99 *(978-1-4677-6047-8(1)*, 9781467760478, Darby Creek) Lerner Publishing Group.

—The Wolfling's Bite, No. 6. Graves, Annie. 2015. (Nightmare Club Ser.: 6). (ENG.). 64p. (J). (gr. 2-5). lib. bdg. 25.32 *(978-1-4677-4353-2(4)*, 9781467743532, Darby Creek) Lerner Publishing Group.

McElligott, Matthew. Bean Thirteen. McElligott, Matthew. 2007. 32p. (J). (gr. k-3). 15.99 *(978-0-399-24535-0(9)*, G.P. Putnam's Sons Books for Young Readers) Penguin Young Readers Group.

—Benjamin Franklinstein Lives! McElligott, Matthew. Tuxbury, Larry David. 2011. (Benjamin Franklinstein Ser.: 1). (ENG.). (J). 144p. (gr. 3-7). 7.99 *(978-0-14-241935-9(4)*, Puffin Books);1. 128p. (gr. 4-6). 22.44 *(978-0-399-25229-7(0))* Penguin Young Readers Group.

—Benjamin Franklinstein Meets the Fright Brothers, 2. McElligott, Matthew. Tuxbury, Larry David. 2012. (Benjamin Franklinstein Ser.: 2). (ENG.). 160p. (J). (gr. 4-6). 22.44 *(978-0-399-25480-2(3))* Penguin Young Readers Group.

—Even Aliens Need Snacks. McElligott, Matthew. 2014. (ENG.). 40p. (J). (gr. k-3). pap. 8.99 *(978-0-8027-3652-9(1)*, 900128206, Bloomsbury USA Childrens) Bloomsbury Publishing USA.

—Even Monsters Need Haircuts. McElligott, Matthew. (J). 2015. 32p. (gr. -1-2). bds. 6.99 *(978-0-8027-3839-4(7)*, 9780802738394); 2012. (ENG.). 40p. (gr. k-8). pap. 8.99 *(978-0-8027-2801-2(4)*, 900081563) Bloomsbury Publishing USA. (Bloomsbury USA Childrens).

—The Lion's Share. McElligott, Matthew. (ENG.). (J). (gr. k-8). 2012. 40p. pap. 8.99 *(978-0-8027-2360-4(8)*, 900078463); 2009. 32p. 17.99 *(978-0-8027-9768-1(7)*, 900051430) Bloomsbury Publishing USA. (Bloomsbury USA Childrens).

—The Lion's Share. McElligott, Matthew. 2012. (ENG.). (J). (gr. k-8). lib. bdg. 19.60 *(978-1-68065-139-3(0))* Perfection Learning Corp.

McElmurry, Jill. El Camioncito Azul. Schertle, Alice. 2013. (Little Blue Truck Ser.).Tr. of Little Blue Truck. (SPA.). 30p. (J). (— 1). bds. 7.99 *(978-0-547-98397-4(2)*, 1524121, HMH Books For Young Readers) Houghton Mifflin Harcourt Publishing Co.

—Good Night, Little Blue Truck. Schertle, Alice. 2019. (Little Blue Truck Ser.). (ENG.). 32p. (J). (gr. -1-3). 17.99 *(978-1-328-85213-7(X)*, 1711385, HMH Books For Young Readers) Houghton Mifflin Harcourt Publishing Co.

—It's a Miracle! A Hanukkah Storybook, Vol. Spinner, Stephanie. 2007. (ENG.). 48p. (J). (gr. -1-3). 7.99 *(978-1-4169-5001-1(X)*, Aladdin) Simon & Schuster Children's Publishing.

—Little Blue Truck. Schertle, Alice. (Little Blue Truck Ser.). (ENG.). (J). 2015. 30p. (— 1). bds. 12.99 *(978-0-544-05685-5(X)*, 1533603, HMH Books For Young Readers); 2010. 32p. (gr. -1-3). 26.99 *(978-0-547-48248-4(5)*, 1439681); 2008. 32p. (gr. -1-3). 17.99 *(978-0-15-205661-2(0)*, 1197021) Houghton Mifflin Harcourt Publishing Co.

—Little Blue Truck Farm Sticker Fun! Schertle, Alice. 2013. (Little Blue Truck Ser.). (ENG.). 24p. (J). (gr. -1-3). 5.99 *(978-0-544-06687-8(1)*, 1535019) Houghton Mifflin Harcourt Publishing Co.

—Little Blue Truck Leads the Way. Schertle, Alice. (Little Blue Truck Ser.). (ENG.). (J). 2016. 38p. (— 1). bds. 12.99 *(978-0-544-70899-0(7)*, 1628910, HMH Books For Young Readers); 2012. 40p. (gr. -1-3). 26.99 *(978-0-547-85060-3(3)*, 1501044); 2009. 40p. (gr. -1-3). 17.99 *(978-0-15-206389-4(7)*, 1199129); 2015. 38p. (— 1). bds. 8.99 *(978-0-544-56805-1(2)*, 1611971, HMH Books For Young Readers) Houghton Mifflin Harcourt Publishing Co.

—Little Blue Truck (padded Board Book) Schertle, Alice. 2020. (Little Blue Truck Ser.). (ENG.). 30p. (J). (— 1). bds. 9.99 *(978-0-358-21178-5(6)*, 1764302, HMH Books For Young Readers) Houghton Mifflin Harcourt Publishing Co.

—Little Blue Truck's Christmas. Schertle, Alice. 2014. (Little Blue Truck Ser.). (ENG.). 24p. (J). (— 1). 15.99 *(978-0-544-32041-3(7)*, 1582526, HMH Books For Young Readers) Houghton Mifflin Harcourt Publishing Co.

—Little Blue Truck's Halloween. Schertle, Alice. 2016. (Little Blue Truck Ser.). (ENG.). 16p. (J). (— 1). bds. 12.99 *(978-0-544-77253-3(9)*, 1636990, HMH Books For Young Readers) Houghton Mifflin Harcourt Publishing Co.

—Little Blue Truck's Springtime. Schertle, Alice. 2018. (Little Blue Truck Ser.). (ENG.). 16p. (J). (gr. -1 — 1). bds. 13.99 *(978-0-544-93809-0(7)*, 1658575, HMH Books For Young Readers) Houghton Mifflin Harcourt Publishing Co.

—Pirate Princess. Bardhan-Quallen, Sudipta. 2012. (ENG.). 40p. (J). (gr. -1-3). 17.99 *(978-0-06-114242-0(5))* HarperCollins Pubs.

—Sharing the Bread: An Old-Fashioned Thanksgiving Story. Miller, Pat Zietlow. 2015. (ENG.). 32p. (J). (gr. -1-3). 17.99 *(978-0-307-98182-0(7)*, Schwartz & Wade Bks.) Random Hse. Children's Bks.

—The Tree Lady: The True Story of How One Tree-Loving Woman Changed a City Forever. Hopkins, H. Joseph. 2013. (ENG.). 32p. (J). (gr. k-5). 17.99 *(978-1-4424-1402-0(2)*, Beach Lane Bks.) Beach Lane Bks.

McElmurry, Jill. Little Blue Truck's Beep-Along Book. McElmurry, Jill. Schertle, Alice. 2015. (Little Blue Truck Ser.). (ENG.). 8p. (J). (— 1). bds. 12.99 *(978-0-544-56812-9/5)*, 1611972, HMH Books For Young Readers) Houghton Mifflin Harcourt Publishing Co.

McElmurry, Jill, jt. illus. see Szekeres, Cyndy.

McElrath-Eslick, Lori. Barefoot: Poems for Naked Feet. Weisburd, Stefi. 2008. (ENG.). 32p. (J). (gr. k-k). 16.99 *(978-1-59078-306-1/9)*, Wordsong) Boyds Mills Pr.

—Does God Know How to Tie Shoes? Carlstrom, Nancy White. 2009. (ENG.). 12p. (J). (gr. -1). bds. 8.00 *(978-0-8028-5366-0/8))* Eerdmans, William B. Publishing Co.

—The Good Fire Helmet. Hoppey, Tim. 2010. (ENG.). 32p. (J). (gr. 3). 16.95 *(978-1-934617-06-9/7)*, Alma Little) Elva Resa Publishing, LLC.

—If Jesus Came to My House. Thomas, Joan G. 2008. (HarperBlessings Ser.). (ENG.). 40p. (J). (gr. -1-3). 16.99 *(978-0-06-083942-0/2))* HarperCollins Pubs.

McElroy, Gerry. Nipper of Drayton Hall. Lewis, Amey. 2015. (Young Palmetto Bks.). (ENG.). 40p. (J). (gr. 5-5). 19.99 *(978-1-61117-625-4/5))* Univ. of South Carolina Pr.

McElroy, Kim. No More Night Mares: A Dream of Freedom. Van Zant, Dawn. 2005. (J). pap. 9.99 *(978-0-9761768-1-7/5))* Wild Heart Ranch, Inc.

McElvane, Catherine. Chipi Chipis, Small Shells of the Sea. Patterson, Irania. 2005.Tr. of Chipi Chipis, Caracolitos del Mar. (SPA.). 44p. (J). per. 12.99 *(978-1-59494-006-4/1))* CPCC Pr.

McEntee, Bill, jt. illus. see O'Kane, George.

McErlean, Michael. Patrick Mcstup's Mixed-Up Family Christmas Part 1. McErlean, Patrick. 2019. (ENG.). 200p. (YA). pap. 12.99 ***(978-1-64237-779-8/1))***; (Patrick Mcstup's Mixed-Up Family Ser.: Vol. 1). 19.99 ***(978-1-64237-778-1/3))*** Gatekeeper Pr.

McEvenue, Tim. Hats off to the President: A White House Mystery. Walsh, Brendan & Benchmark Education Co., LLC. 2014. (Text Connections Ser.). (J). (gr. 3). *(978-1-4509-9660-0/4))* Benchmark Education Co.

—Hats off to the President - a White House Mystery: Set Of 6. Walsh, Brendan. 2014. (Text Connections Ser.). (J). (gr. 3). 49.00 net. *(978-1-4900-0136-4/0))* Benchmark Education Co.

McEwan, Alison. Kentucky Magic! Connelly, Susan. 2019. (ENG.). 16p. (J). pap. *(978-1-78623-502-2/1))* Grosvenor Hse. Publishing Ltd.

McEwan, Joseph. Who's Home? Faulkner, Keith. 12p. (J). (gr. -1). pap. 4.99 *(978-1-881445-33-3/X))* Sandvik Publishing.

McEwan, Sandy. The Kilted Mice at Christmas. Aitchison, Mandy. 2017. (ENG.). (J). pap. *(978-1-78623-894-8/2))* Grosvenor Hse. Publishing Ltd.

McEwen, Katharine. Escape from Silver Street Farm. Davies, Nicola. 2013. (Silver Street Farm Ser.). (ENG.). 80p. (J). (gr. 2-5). 12.99 *(978-0-7636-6133-5/3))* Candlewick Pr.

—El Gato Que Desapareció Misteriosamente. Ahlberg, Allan. Abio, Carlos & Villegas, Mercedes, trs. 2009. (SPA.). 80p. (J). (gr. 2-4). pap. *(978-607-11-0111-2/5))* Aguilar, Altea, Taurus, Alfaguara, S.A. de C.V.

—I Love You, Little Monkey. Durant, Alan. 2007. (ENG.). 32p. (J). (gr. -1-1). 15.99 *(978-1-4169-2481-4/7)*, Simon & Schuster Bks. For Young Readers) Simon & Schuster Bks. For Young Readers.

—Send for a Superhero! Rosen, Michael. 2014. (ENG.). 40p. (J). (gr. -1-2). 16.99 *(978-0-7636-6438-1/3))* Candlewick Pr.

—That's Not Right! Durant, Alan. 2004. (Flying Foxes Ser.). 48p. (J). (gr. k-2). 13.10 *(978-0-7569-3057-8/X))* Perfection Learning Corp.

—That's Not Right. Durant, Alan. 2003. (Flying Foxes Ser.). (ENG.). 48p. (J). *(978-0-7787-1532-0/9))*; lib. bdg. *(978-0-7787-1486-6/1))* Crabtree Publishing Co.

—Welcome to Silver Street Farm. Davies, Nicola. 2012. (Silver Street Farm Ser.). (ENG.). 80p. (J). (gr. 2-5). 12.99 *(978-0-7636-5831-1/6))* Candlewick Pr.

—Welcome to Silver Street Farm. Davies, Nicola. 2013. (Silver Street Farm Ser.). (ENG.). 80p. (J). (gr. 2-5). pap. 5.99 *(978-0-7636-6443-5/X))* Candlewick Pr.

—Who's Hiding at the Beach? Nosy Crow. 2019. (Who's Hiding Ser.). (ENG.). 10p. (J). (-k). bds. 9.99 *(978-1-5362-0585-5/0)*, Nosy Crow) Candlewick Pr.

—Who's Hiding in the Rain Forest? Nosy Crow. 2020. (Who's Hiding Ser.). (ENG.). 10p. (J). (-k). bds. 9.99 *(978-1-5362-1010-1/2)*, Nosy Crow) Candlewick Pr.

—Who's Hiding in the Woods? Nosy Crow. 2019. (Who's Hiding Ser.). (ENG.). 10p. (J). (-k). bds. 9.99 *(978-1-5362-0820-7/5)*, Nosy Crow) Candlewick Pr.

—Who's Hiding on the Farm? Nosy Crow. 2019. (Who's Hiding Ser.). (ENG.). 10p. (J). (-k). bds. 9.99 *(978-1-5362-0586-2/9)*, Nosy Crow) Candlewick Pr.

—Who's Hiding on the River? Nosy Crow. 2019. (Who's Hiding Ser.). (ENG.). 10p. (J). (-k). bds. 9.99 *(978-1-5362-0821-4/3)*, Nosy Crow) Candlewick Pr.

—Who's Hiding on the Savanna? Nosy Crow. 2020. (Who's Hiding Ser.). (ENG.). 10p. (J). (-k). bds. 9.99 *(978-1-5362-1217-4/2)*, Nosy Crow) Candlewick Pr.

McEwen, Katharine. Bear Hug. McEwen, Katharine. 2014. (ENG.). 32p. (J). (gr. -1-2). 15.99 *(978-0-7636-6630-9/0)*, Templar) Candlewick Pr.

McFadden, Joline. When the Bees Fly Home. 1 vol. Cheng, Andrea. 2005. (ENG.). 32p. (J). (gr. 3-6). 16.95 *(978-0-88448-238-3/3))* Tilbury Hse. Pubs.

McFall, Christie. America Underground. McFall, Christie. 2004. 80p. (J). (gr. 4-8). reprint ed. 14.00 *(978-0-7567-7712-8/7))* DIANE Publishing Co.

McFarland, Clive. One Leaf, Two Leaves, Count with Me! Micklos, John, Jr. & Micklos, John. 2017. 32p. (J). (— 1). 16.99 *(978-0-399-54471-2/2)*, Nancy Paulsen Books) Penguin Young Readers Group.

McFarland, Clive. Caterpillar Dreams. McFarland, Clive. 2017. (ENG.). 32p. (J). (gr. -1-3). 17.99 *(978-0-06-238636-6/0))* HarperCollins Pubs.

—The Fox & the Wild. McFarland, Clive. 2017. (ENG.). 40p. (J). (gr. -1-2). 16.99 *(978-0-7636-9648-1/X)*, Templar) Candlewick Pr.

McFarland, Jim. Widget. McFarland, Lyn Rossiter. ed. 2004. (J). (gr. -1-k). spiral bd. *(978-0-616-11121-5/5))*; spiral bd. *(978-0-616-11122-2/3))* Canadian National Institute for the Blind/Institut National Canadien pour les Aveugles.

—Widget. McFarland, Lyn Rossiter. 2006. (ENG.). 32p. (J). (gr. -1-1). per. 8.99 *(978-0-374-48386-9/8)*, 900034724) Square Fish.

McFarland, Michael. Baylor's Song. Smither, Michael Wesley. 2020. (ENG.). 30p. (J). (gr. k-4). pap. 14.95 ***(978-1-68433-515-2/9))*** Black Rose Writing.

McFarland, Richard. Grandfather's Wrinkles. England, Kathryn. 2007. (ENG.). 32p. (J). (gr. k-3). 15.95 *(978-0-9729225-9-3/8))* Flashlight Pr.

McFarland, Shea. Ellie Finds a New Home. Carmichael, Heather. 2008. (ENG.). 36p. pap. 16.99 *(978-1-4389-2976-7/5))* AuthorHouse.

McFee, Ann Marie. Koli's Birthday Adventure: Koli the Great White Shark. Werner, Tamra. 2017. (ENG.). (J). (gr. k-4). 19.99 *(978-0-692-94041-9/3))*; pap. 12.99 *(978-0-692-94044-0/8))* Werner, Tamra.

McFeeley, Dan. Westward, Ha-Ha!, 1800-1850. Levy, Elizabeth & Havlan, J. R. 2003. 160p. (J). pap. *(978-0-590-12257-3/6))* Scholastic, Inc.

McFeeley, Daniel. Dr. Laura Schlessinger's Where's God? Schlessinger, Laura. 2003. 40p. (J). (gr. -1-2). lib. bdg. 16.89 *(978-0-06-051910-0/X))* HarperCollins Pubs.

McFerrin, Grady. Boats on the Bay. Harvey, Jeanne Walker. 2018. (ENG.). 40p. (J). (gr. -1-3). 17.95 *(978-1-944903-33-6/X)*, Cameron Kids) Cameron + Co.

McG, Shane. Tiger's Roar. Rance, Alex. 2019. (ENG.). 32p. (J). (gr. k-3). 16.99 *(978-1-76052-391-6/7))* Allen & Unwin AUS. Dist: Independent Pubs. Group.

—Zelda's Big Adventure. Alafaci, Marie. 2017. (ENG.). 32p. (J). (gr. -1-3). 16.99 *(978-1-328-66081-7/8)*, 1667182, Clarion Bks.) Houghton Mifflin Harcourt Trade & Reference Pubs.

—10 Little Hermit Crabs. Fox, Lee. 2012. (ENG.). 32p. (J). (-k). pap. 8.99 *(978-1-74237-952-4/4))* Allen & Unwin AUS. Dist: Independent Pubs. Group.

McGairy, James, jt. illus. see Aldous, Kate.

McGann, James. The Tailor & the Mouse. Feierabend, John M. 2012. (First Steps in Music Ser.). (ENG.). 32p. (J). (gr. -1-k). 16.95 *(978-1-57999-903-2/4))* G I A Pubns., Inc.

McGann, Oisín. Beyond the Cherry Tree. O'Brien, Joe. 2011. (ENG.). 224p. (J). pap. 12.95 *(978-1-84717-212-9/1))* O'Brien Pr., Ltd., The IRL. Dist: Casemate Pubs. & Bk. Distributors, LLC.

McGann, Oisín. Mad Grandad & the Kleptoes. McGann, Oisín. 2018. (Mad Grandad Ser.). (ENG.). 64p. 11.00 *(978-1-78849-046-7/0))* O'Brien Pr., Ltd., The IRL. Dist: Casemate Pubs. & Bk. Distributors, LLC.

—Mad Grandad's Flying Saucer. McGann, Oisín. 2003. (Flyers Ser.: 11). (ENG.). 64p. (J). pap. 9.95 *(978-0-86278-822-3/6))* O'Brien Pr., Ltd., The IRL. Dist: Dufour Editions, Inc.

McGannon, Cj. The Riding Lesson. Williamson, Susan. 2018. (ENG.). 40p. (J). pap. 12.99 *(978-1-945990-54-0/6))* High Tide Pubns.

McGary, Norman. The Adventures of Andy Ant: Lawn Mower on the Loose. O'Nan, Gerald D. 2014. (ENG.). 28p. (gr. -1-4). pap. 9.95 *(978-1-61448-673-2/5))* Morgan James Publishing.

—The Adventures of Andy Ant: The Swimming Hole Disaster. O'Nan, Lawrence W. & O'Nan, Gerald D. 2014. (ENG.). 34p. (gr. -1-4). pap. 9.95 *(978-1-61448-799-9/5))* Morgan James Publishing.

McGaw, Laurie. Avram's Gift. Blumberg, Margie. (ENG.). 48p. 2005. (YA). pap. 11.95 *(978-0-9624166-3-7/0))*; 2003. (J). (gr. 3-18). 15.95 *(978-0-9624166-2-0/2))* MB Publishing, LLC.

—A Little Something. Bosak, Susan V. 2008. 32p. (J). *(978-1-896232-06-5/X)*, TCP Pr.) Communication Project, The.

—Something to Remember Me By: A Story about Love & Legacies. Bosak, Susan V. 2003. 32p. pap. *(978-1-896232-02-7/7))*; (gr. 1-6). *(978-1-896232-01-0/9))* Communication Project, The. (TCP Pr.).

McGeddon, R. Zombies! 2016. (Disaster Diaries). 178p. (J). pap. *(978-1-250-09086-7/5))* ETT Imprint.

McGeddon, R. Brainwashed! McGeddon, R. 2016. (Disaster Diaries). (ENG.). 208p. (J). 9.99 *(978-1-250-09091-1/1)*, 9781250090911) Imprint IND. Dist: Macmillan.

McGeddon, R. & Littler, Jamie. Aliens! McGeddon, R. 2016. (Disaster Diaries: 2). (ENG.). 208p. (J). 9.99 *(978-1-250-09088-1/1)*, 900159291) Imprint IND. Dist: Macmillan.

—Zombies! McGeddon, R. 2016. (Disaster Diaries: 1). (ENG.). 192p. (J). 9.99 *(978-1-250-09084-3/9)*, 900159287) Imprint IND. Dist: Macmillan.

McGee, Bridgette. Some Sciencey Thing, Like Humidity & the Moon: Book of Explosions 8. Creative Youth Center, Grand Rapids. 2019. (ENG.). 168p. (J). pap. 12.00 *(978-1-7976-6958-8/3))* Independently Published.

McGee, Cara. Black Canary: Ignite. Cabot, Meg. 2019. (ENG.). 144p. (J). (gr. 3-7). pap. 9.99 *(978-1-4012-8620-0/8)*, DC Zoom) DC Comics.

—Over the Garden Wall Vol. 3, Vol. 3. Sjursen-Lien, Kiernan et al. 2018. (Over the Garden Wall Ser.: 3). (ENG.). 112p. (J). (gr. 4-7). pap. 14.99 *(978-1-68415-060-1/4))* Boom! Studios.

McGee, Cara, et al. Steven Universe: Welcome to Beach City. Sorese, Jeremy et al. 2019. (Steven Universe Ser.). (ENG.). 112p. (J). pap. 14.99 *(978-1-68415-466-1/9))* Boom! Studios.

McGee, Cara & Campbell, Jim. Over the Garden Wall Vol. 4. Sjursen-Lien, Kiernan et al. 2018. (Over the Garden Wall Ser.: 4). (ENG.). 112p. (J). (gr. 4-7). pap. 14.99 *(978-1-68415-185-1/6))* Boom! Studios.

McGee, E. Alan, jt. photos by see Dawson, Sandy.

McGee, John F. Gorillas. Dennard, Deborah. 2003. (Our Wild World Ser.). (ENG.). 48p. (J). (gr. 2-5). pap. 7.95 *(978-1-55971-843-1/9))* Cooper Square Publishing Llc.

McGee, Kate Harvey, jt. illus. see Kvasnosky, Laura McGee.

McGee, Rick. Eleven Chickens in a Boat: A Story of Faith, Fear, & Feathers! 2013. (J). *(978-1-56722-974-5/3))* Word Aflame Pr.

McGee, Thomas. Multables, Inc. Osborne, Amy, ed. 3p. (J). (gr. 2-5). 13.99 *(978-0-9645004-0-2/X))* Multables, Inc.

McGee, Warner. ABC Animals (Dora the Explorer) Golden Books. 2013. (Color Plus Card Stock Ser.). (ENG.). 48p. (J). (gr. -1-2). pap. 3.99 *(978-0-307-98218-6/1)*, Golden Bks.) Random Hse. Children's Bks.

—Ariel's Song. 2007. (Play a Tune Tale Ser.). 16p. (gr. -1-k). 12.98 *(978-1-4127-8829-8/3))* Publications International, Ltd.

—Christmas Is Coming! (Dora the Explorer) Golden Books Staff. 2011. (ENG.). 64p. (J). (gr. -1-2). pap. 4.99 *(978-0-375-87393-5/7)*, Golden Bks.) Random Hse. Children's Bks.

—Deep-Sea Countdown. Spelvin, Justin. 2006. (Backyardigans Ser.). (ENG.). 26p. (J). (gr. -1). bds. 5.99 *(978-1-4169-1484-6/6)*, Simon Spotlight/Nickelodeon) Simon Spotlight/Nickelodeon.

—Diego & the Baby Sea Turtles. Rao, Lisa. 2008. (Go, Diego, Go! Ser.: 8). (ENG.). 24p. (J). pap. 3.99 *(978-1-4169-5450-7/3)*, Simon Spotlight/Nickelodeon) Simon Spotlight/Nickelodeon.

—Diego rescata al bebé manatí (Diego's Manatee Rescue) Higginson, Sheila Sweeny. 2009. (Go, Diego, Go! Ser.). (SPA.). 24p. (J). pap. 3.99 *(978-1-4169-7983-8/2)*, Libros Para Ninos) Libros Para Ninos.

—Diego Saves a Butterfly. 2007. (Go, Diego, Go! Ser.: 3). (ENG.). 24p. (J). (gr. -1-1). pap. 3.99 *(978-1-4169-3364-9/6)*, Simon Spotlight/Nickelodeon) Simon Spotlight/Nickelodeon.

—Diego's Egyptian Expedition. 2009. (Go, Diego, Go! Ser.). (ENG.). 24p. (J). pap. 3.99 *(978-1-4169-6870-2/9)*, Simon Spotlight/Nickelodeon) Simon Spotlight/Nickelodeon.

—Diego's Family Christmas. Fernandez, Rafael. 2008. (Go, Diego, Go! Ser.). (ENG.). 16p. (J). (gr. -1-k). bds. 5.99 *(978-1-4169-5836-9/3)*, Simon Spotlight/Nickelodeon) Simon Spotlight/Nickelodeon.

—Extreme Rescue: Crocodile Mission. David, Erica. 2009. (Go, Diego, Go! Ser.). (ENG.). 24p. (J). pap. 3.99 *(978-1-4169-8515-0/8)*, Simon Spotlight/Nickelodeon) Simon Spotlight/Nickelodeon.

—Frosty the Snowman. Pil et al. 2011. (J). *(978-1-4508-2604-4/0))* Publications International, Ltd.

—Legend Hunters! Ricci, Christine. 2007. (Backyardigans Ser.: 9). (ENG.). 24p. (J). (gr. -1-1). 16.19 *(978-1-4169-4058-6/8))* Simon & Schuster, Inc.

—Mission to Mars. 2006. (Backyardigans Ser.: 4). (ENG.). 24p. (J). (gr. -1-2). pap. 3.99 *(978-1-4169-1486-0/2)*, Simon Spotlight/Nickelodeon) Simon Spotlight/Nickelodeon.

—Monster Halloween Party. 2007. (Backyardigans Ser.). (ENG.). 14p. (J). (gr. -1-k). bds. 6.99 *(978-1-4169-3435-6/9)*, Simon Spotlight/Nickelodeon) Simon Spotlight/Nickelodeon.

—Run, Run, Koala! 2010. (Go Diego Go! Ser.). (ENG.). 24p. (J). (gr. -1-1). 16.19 *(978-1-4169-9937-9/X))* Simon & Schuster, Inc.

Mcgee, Warner & MJ Illustrations Staff. Dora's Chilly Day (Dora the Explorer) Rosebrough, Ellen. 2013. (Pictureback(R) Ser.). (ENG.). 16p. (J). (gr. -1-2). 3.99 *(978-0-449-81950-0/7)*, Random Hse. Bks. for Young Readers) Random Hse. Children's Bks.

McGee, Warner, jt. illus. see Loter, Inc.

McGee, Warner, jt. illus. see Moore, Saxton.

McGeehan, Dan. Bicycles Before the Store. Lynette, Rachel. 2012. (Before the Store Ser.). (ENG.). 32p. (J). (gr. 2-5). lib. bdg. 29.93 *(978-1-60973-676-7/1)*, 201248) Child's World, Inc., The.

—The Bizarre Origins of Kangaroo Court & Other Idioms. Ringstad, Arnold. 2012. (Idioms Ser.). (ENG.). 32p. (J). (gr. 3-6). 14.21 *(978-1-61473-231-0/0)*, 204938) Child's World, Inc., The.

—Bread Before the Store. Shaffer, Jody Jensen. 2012. (Before the Store Ser.). (ENG.). 32p. (J). (gr. 2-5). lib. bdg. 29.93 *(978-1-60973-629-3/X)*, 201250) Child's World, Inc., The.

—The Compelling Histories of Long Arm of the Law & Other Idioms. Ringstad, Arnold. 2012. (Idioms Ser.). (ENG.). 32p. (J). (gr. 3-6). 14.21 *(978-1-61473-232-7/9)*, 204939) Child's World, Inc., The.

—Footballs Before the Store. Lynette, Rachel. 2012. (Before the Store Ser.). (ENG.). 32p. (J). (gr. 2-5). lib. bdg. 29.93 *(978-1-60973-675-0/3)*, 201251) Child's World, Inc., The.

—Ice Cream Before the Store. Bernard, Jan. 2012. (Before the Store Ser.). (ENG.). 32p. (J). (gr. 2-5). lib. bdg. 29.93 *(978-1-60973-677-4/X)*, 201252) Child's World, Inc., The.

—Opposites. Rosa-Mendoza, Gladys. Cifuentes, Carolina, ed. 2004. (English-Spanish Foundations Ser.: Vol. 5).Tr. of Opuestos. (ENG & SPA.). 20p. (J). (gr. -1-4). bds. 6.95 *(978-0-9679748-6-6/0))* Me+Mi Publishing.

—Opposites/Opuestos. Rosa-Mendoza, Gladys. Cifuentes, Carolina, ed. 2008. (English-Spanish Foundations Ser.). (gr. -1-k). bds. 6.95 *(978-1-931398-04-6/6))* Me+Mi Publishing.

—Orange Juice Before the Store. Jacobson, Ryan. 2012. (Before the Store Ser.). (ENG.). 32p. (J). (gr. 2-5). lib. bdg. 29.93 *(978-1-60973-678-1/8)*, 201253) Child's World, Inc., The.

—The Over-the-Top Histories of Chew the Scenery & Other Idioms. Ringstad, Arnold. 2012. (Idioms Ser.). (ENG.). 32p. (J). (gr. 3-6). 14.21 *(978-1-61473-234-1/5)*, 204941) Child's World, Inc., The.

—Peanut Butter Before the Store. Bernard, Jan. 2012. (Before the Store Ser.). (ENG.). 32p. (J). (gr. 2-5). lib. bdg. 29.93 *(978-1-60973-679-8/6)*, 201254) Child's World, Inc., The.

—Pencils Before the Store. Lynette, Rachel. 2012. (Before the Store Ser.). (ENG.). 32p. (J). (gr. 2-5). lib. bdg. 29.93 *(978-1-60973-680-4/X)*, 201255) Child's World, Inc., The.

—The Shocking Stories Behind Lightning in a Bottle & Other Idioms. Ringstad, Arnold. 2012. (Idioms Ser.). (ENG.). 32p. (J). (gr. 3-6). 14.21 *(978-1-61473-236-5/1)*, 204943) Child's World, Inc., The.

—Shoes Before the Store. Jacobson, Ryan. 2012. (Before the Store Ser.). (ENG.). 32p. (J). (gr. 2-5). lib. bdg. 29.93 *(978-1-60973-681-1/8)*, 201256) Child's World, Inc., The.

—Soda Pop Before the Store. Lynette, Rachel. 2012. (Before the Store Ser.). (ENG.). 32p. (J). (gr. 2-5). lib. bdg. 29.93 *(978-1-60973-682-8/6)*, 201257) Child's World, Inc., The.

—The Thrilling Sources of Push the Envelope & Other Idioms. Ringstad, Arnold. 2012. (Idioms Ser.). (ENG.). 32p. (J). (gr. 3-6). 14.21 *(978-1-61473-237-2/X)*, 204944) Child's World, Inc., The.

—Toilet Paper Before the Store. Lynette, Rachel. 2012. (Before the Store Ser.). (ENG.). 32p. (J). (gr. 2-5). lib. bdg. 29.93 *(978-1-60973-683-5/4)*, 201258) Child's World, Inc., The.

—Toothpaste Before the Store. Bernard, Jan. 2012. (Before the Store Ser.). (ENG.). 32p. (J). (gr. 2-5). lib. bdg. 29.93 *(978-1-60973-684-2/2)*, 201259) Child's World, Inc., The.

—The Unbelievable Origins of Snake Oil & Other Idioms. Ringstad, Arnold. 2012. (Idioms Ser.). (ENG.). 32p. (J). (gr. 3-6). 14.21 *(978-1-61473-238-9/8)*, 204945) Child's World, Inc., The.

McGeehan, Dan & Moore, David, Jr. Being Safe around Water. Lindeen, Mary & Kesselring, Susan. 2011. (Be Safe Ser.). (ENG.). 24p. (J). (gr. k-3). lib. bdg. 14.21 *(978-1-60954-298-6/3)*, 200078) Child's World, Inc., The.

—Being Safe at Home. Lindeen, Mary & Kesselring, Susan. 2011. (Be Safe Ser.). (ENG.). 24p. (J). (gr. k-3). lib. bdg. 14.21 *(978-1-60954-299-3/1)*, 200079) Child's World, Inc., The.

McGeehan, Dan & Moore, David. Being Safe in Your Neighborhood. Lindeen, Mary & Kesselring, Susan. 2011. (Be Safe Ser.). (ENG.). 24p. (J). (gr. k-3). lib. bdg. 14.21 *(978-1-60954-370-9/X)*, 200081) Child's World, Inc., The.

—Being Safe on Wheels. Lindeen, Mary & Kesselring, Susan. 2011. (Be Safe Ser.). (ENG.). 24p. (J). (gr. k-3). lib. bdg. 14.21 *(978-1-60954-371-6/8)*, 200082) Child's World, Inc., The.

—Being Safe with Fire. Lindeen, Mary & Kesselring, Susan. 2011. (Be Safe Ser.). (ENG.). 24p. (J). (gr. k-3). lib. bdg. 14.21 *(978-1-60954-372-3/6)*, 200083) Child's World, Inc., The.

—Being Safe with Weather. Lindeen, Mary & Kesselring, Susan. 2011. (Be Safe Ser.). (ENG.). 24p. (J). (gr. k-3). lib. bdg. 14.21 *(978-1-60954-374-7/2)*, 200085) Child's World, Inc., The.

McGehee, Claudia. Creekfinding: A True Story. Martin, Jacqueline Briggs. 2017. (ENG.). 36p. (J). 16.95 *(978-0-8166-9802-8/3))* Univ. of Minnesota Pr.

McGehee, Claudia. A Tallgrass Prairie Alphabet. McGehee, Claudia. 2004. (Bur Oak Book Ser.). (ENG.). 32p. (J). 17.95 *(978-0-87745-897-5/9))* Univ. of Iowa Pr.

McGhee, Chelsea. The Fox Behind the Chatterbox. Matalonis, Anne. 2008. 32p. pap. 17.95 *(978-1-59858-783-8/8))* Dog Ear Publishing, LLC.

McGhee, Katie Mariah & Herrera, Aaron Jeremiah. The Case of the Missing Chimpanzee from Classroom C2. McGhee, Katie Mariah. 2012. 28p. 24.95 *(978-1-4560-0039-4/X))* America Star Bks.

McGhee, Kerry. Princess Alice & the Dreadful Dragon. Bernhardt, William. 2007. 27p. (J). 19.99 *(978-1-930709-65-2/X))* HAWK Publishing Group.

McGhee, Stuart. The Magic Custard Factory. Perree, Leyland. 2016. (ENG.). 32p. (J). (gr. 1-3). pap. *(978-0-9932915-8-6/9))* GLUE Publishing.

McGill, Erin. I Do Not Like Al's Hat. McGill, Erin. 2017. (ENG.). 32p. (J). (gr. -1-3). 17.99 *(978-0-06-245576-5/1)*, Greenwillow Bks.) HarperCollins Pubs.

—I Do Not Like That Name. McGill, Erin. 2019. (ENG.). 32p. (J). (gr. -1-3). 17.99 *(978-0-06-245577-2/X)*, Greenwillow Bks.) HarperCollins Pubs.

McGill, Joshua. Proton Gator & Friends Coloring Book. Simone, Val Edward. 2011. 32p. (J). pap. 5.99 *(978-1-935296-27-0/2))* Morningside Publishing, LLC.

McGillivray, Alan, jt. illus. see Welch, Kathleen.

McGilp, Tina. Jack & Too Many Goats. Howell, B. M. 2019. (ENG.). 34p. (J). pap. *(978-1-989027-11-0/3))* Cavern of Dreams Publishing Hse.

—The Very Best Me. Oliver, - Linda. 2019. (ENG.). 32p. (J). pap. *(978-1-989027-10-3/5))* Cavern of Dreams Publishing Hse.

McGinley-Nally, Sharon. Pigs at Odds: Fun with Math & Games. Axelrod, Amy. 2003. (ENG.). 40p. (J). (gr. -1-4). 8.99 *(978-0-689-86144-4/3)*, Aladdin) Simon & Schuster Children's Publishing.

—Pigs in the Corner: Fun with Math & Dance. Axelrod, Amy. 2005. (ENG.). 40p. (J). (gr. -1-4). 8.99 *(978-1-4169-0335-2/6)*, Simon & Schuster/Paula Wiseman Bks.) Simon & Schuster/Paula Wiseman Bks.

McGinnis, Ben. Avoiding Injuries. Pinchbeck, Chris, photos by. Goodbody, Slim. 2007. (Slim Goodbody Good Health Guides). 32p. (J). (gr. 2-6). lib. bdg. 27.00 *(978-0-8368-7739-7/X)*, Gareth Stevens Learning Library) Stevens, Gareth Publishing LLLP.

—Cats. Goodbody, Slim & Burstein, John. 2008. (Slim Goodbody's Inside Guide to Pets Ser.). 32p. (gr. 2-6). lib. bdg. 27.00 *(978-0-8368-8954-3/1)*, Gareth Stevens Learning Library) Stevens, Gareth Publishing LLLP.

—Dogs. Goodbody, Slim & Burstein, John. 2008. (Slim Goodbody's Inside Guide to Pets Ser.). 32p. (gr. 2-6). lib. bdg. 27.00 *(978-0-8368-8955-0/X)*, Gareth Stevens Learning Library) Stevens, Gareth Publishing LLLP.

—Eating Right. Pinchbeck, Chris, photos by. Goodbody, Slim. 2007. (Slim Goodbody's Good Health Guides Ser.). 32p. (J). (gr. 2-6). lib. bdg. 27.00 *(978-0-8368-7740-3/3)*, Gareth Stevens Learning Library) Stevens, Gareth Publishing LLLP.

—Exercising. Pinchbeck, Chris, photos by. Goodbody, Slim. 2007. (Slim Goodbody Good Health Guides). 32p. (J). (gr. 2-6). lib. bdg. 27.00 *(978-0-8368-7741-0/1)*, Gareth Stevens Learning Library) Stevens, Gareth Publishing LLLP.

—Goldfish. Goodbody, Slim & Burstein, John. 2008. (Slim Goodbody's Inside Guide to Pets Ser.). 32p. (J). (gr. 2-6). lib. bdg. 27.00 *(978-0-8368-8956-7/8)*, Gareth Stevens Learning Library) Stevens, Gareth Publishing LLLP.

—Guinea Pigs. Goodbody, Slim & Burstein, John. 2008. (Slim Goodbody's Inside Guide to Pets Ser.). 32p. (J). (gr. 2-6). lib. bdg. 27.00 *(978-0-8368-8957-4(6)*, Gareth Stevens Learning Library) Stevens, Gareth Publishing LLLP.

—Keeping Clean. Pinchbeck, Chris, photos by. Goodbody, Slim. 2007. (Slim Goodbody Good Health Guides). 32p. (J). (gr. 2-6). lib. bdg. 27.00 *(978-0-8368-7742-7(X)*, Gareth Stevens Learning Library) Stevens, Gareth Publishing LLLP.

—Keeping Safe. Pinchbeck, Chris, photos by. Goodbody, Slim. 2007. (Slim Goodbody Good Health Guides). 32p. (gr. 2-6). lib. bdg. 27.00 *(978-0-8368-7743-4(8)*, Gareth Stevens Learning Library) Stevens, Gareth Publishing LLLP.

—Rabbits. Goodbody, Slim & Burstein, John. 2008. (Slim Goodbody's Inside Guide to Pets Ser.). 32p. (gr. 2-6). lib. bdg. 27.00 *(978-0-8368-8958-1(4)*, Gareth Stevens Learning Library) Stevens, Gareth Publishing LLLP.

—Staying Well. Pinchbeck, Chris, photos by. Goodbody, Slim. 2007. (Slim Goodbody's Good Health Guides Ser.). 32p. (J). (gr. 2-6). lib. bdg. 27.00 *(978-0-8368-7744-1(6)*, Gareth Stevens Learning Library) Stevens, Gareth Publishing LLLP.

McGinnis, Steve. Darling the Curly Tailed Reindoe Saves Christmas: The Continuing Adventures of Darling the Curly Tailed Reindoe. Campbell, Cheryl. 2010. (ENG.). 36p. (J). (gr. k-3). 18.95 *(978-0-9828689-2-8(8)*, BQB Publishing) Boutique of Quality Books Publishing Co., Inc.

—Grrranimals: Unforgettable Land & Water Creatures. Peabody, Phineas. 2018. (ENG.). 30p. (J). pap. 17.95 *(978-0-9963323-8-5(3))*; (Grranimals: I Love Animals Ser.: Vol. 1). 17.95 *(978-0-9963323-9-2(1))* Peabody Publishing Co.

McGinty, Ian. Adventure Time Vol. 13. Hastings, Christopher. 2017. (Adventure Time Ser.: 13). (ENG.). 112p. (J). (gr. 4-7). pap. 14.99 *(978-1-68415-051-9(5))* Boom! Studios.

—Adventure Time Vol. 14. Tamaki, Mariko. 2018. (Adventure Time Ser.: 14). (ENG.). 112p. (J). (gr. 4-7). pap. 14.99 *(978-1-68415-144-8(9))* Boom! Studios.

—Adventure Time Vol. 15. Dawson, Delilah S. 2018. (Adventure Time Ser.: 15). (ENG.). 112p. (J). (gr. 4-7). pap. 14.99 *(978-1-68415-203-2(8))* Boom! Studios.

—Glint Book One: The Cloud Raiders. Sattin, Samuel. 2019. (ENG.). 160p. (J). pap. 12.99 *(978-1-5493-0299-2(X)*, ffca3439-73a3-4310-9b34-186ca95db5c5, Lion Forge) Oni Pr., Inc.

—Gotta Warn the Unicorns! #7. Krulik, Nancy. 2019. (Princess Pulverizer Ser.: 7). 144p. (J). (gr. 1-3). 6.99 *(978-1-5247-9156-8(3))*; 15.99 *(978-1-5247-9157-5(1))* Penguin Young Readers Group. (Penguin Workshop).

McGinty, Ian, et al. Hello Kitty - It's about Time. Chabot, Jacob. 2015. 64p. (J). pap. 7.99 *(978-1-4215-7769-2(0))* Viz Media.

—Hello Kitty: Work of Art. Chabot, Jacob. 2014. 64p. (J). pap. 7.99 *(978-1-4215-7542-1(6))* Viz Media.

McGinty, Ian. Sonic & the Tales of Deception. Black, Jake. 2018. (Sonic the Hedgehog Ser.). (ENG.). 64p. (J). (gr. 2-5). 6.99 *(978-1-5247-8474-4(5)*, Penguin Young Readers Licenses) Penguin Young Readers Group.

—Yo-Ho, Yo ... NO! #8. Krulik, Nancy. 2020. (Princess Pulverizer Ser.: 8). 144p. (J). (gr. 1-3). 6.99 *(978-1-5247-9159-9(8))*; 15.99 *(978-1-5247-9160-5(1))* Penguin Young Readers Group. (Penguin Workshop).

McGinty, Ian, jt. illus. see Green, K. C.

McGinty, Lupi. Lil' Red Pepper. Wold, Bruce. 2018. (ENG.). 24p. (J). 15.95 *(978-1-59298-661-3(7))* Beaver's Pond Pr., Inc.

McGinty, Mick. Whales. Rosenthal, Sue. 2003. (Magic School Bus Fact Finder Ser.). (ENG.). 96p. (J). pap. 4.99 *(978-0-439-38174-1(6))* Scholastic, Inc.

McGivern, Kevin. Copa90 - Our World Cup: A Fans' Guide to 2018. Puffin Staff. 2018. 176p. (J). (gr. 4-11). 21.99 *(978-0-14-138772-7(6))* Penguin Bks., Ltd. GBR. Dist: Independent Pubs. Group.

McGoldrick, Bernita. Pretty Pretty Picky Penelope. McGoldrick, Bernita. 2010. 32p. pap. 12.95 *(978-1-935268-49-9(X))* Halo Publishing International.

McGowan, Dennis E. Sammy Makes New Friends. McGowan, Denise R. 2019. (ENG.). 34p. (J). pap. 9.99 *(978-1-7933-0388-2(6))* Independently Published.

McGowan, Linda. Unicorn & the Master's Glory. Linda McGowan, Linda. 2019. (ENG.). 36p. (J). (gr. k-5). 19.95 *(978-1-7336947-2-8(2))* McGowan, Linda G. LLC dba LM.

McGrath, Liz. The Ghouls Come Haunting One by One, 1 vol. McDermott, Tom. 2010. (ENG.). 32p. (J). (gr. k-k). 16.99 *(978-1-58980-786-0(3)*, Pelican Publishing) Arcadia Publishing.

McGrath, Michael, jt. illus. see Hyatt, Sean.

McGrath, Michael O'Neill. Patrons & Protectors: In Times of Need. 2003. (Patrons & Protectors Ser.: Vol. 3). 58p. (J). 18.95 *(978-1-56854-410-6(3))* Liturgy Training Pubns.

McGrath, Raymond. Dad & the Bike Race. Eggleton, Jill. 2003. (Rigby Sails Sailing Solo Ser.). (ENG.). 24p. (gr. 1-2). pap. 9.05 *(978-0-7578-3963-4(0))* Houghton Mifflin Harcourt Publishing Co.

—Fearless Phil: 3-in-1 Package. Eggleton, Jill. (Sails Literacy Ser.). 24p. (gr. 3-18). 57.00 *(978-0-7578-6996-9(3))* Rigby Education.

—Fearless Phil: 6 Small Books. Eggleton, Jill. (Sails Literacy Ser.). 24p. (gr. 3-18). 25.00 *(978-0-7578-6988-4(2))* Rigby Education.

—Fearless Phil: Big Book Only. Eggleton, Jill. (Sails Literacy Ser.). 24p. (gr. 3-18). 27.00 *(978-0-7578-6980-8(7))* Rigby Education.

McGrath, Raymond. The Little Ghost Who Lost Her Boo! Bickell, Elaine. 2020. (ENG.). 32p. (J). (gr. -1-3). 17.99 ***(978-0-593-20215-9(5)***, Philomel Bks.) Penguin Young Readers Group.

McGrath, Raymond. The Moon: Individual Title Six-Packs. (Sails Literacy Ser.). 16p. (gr. k-18). 27.00 *(978-0-7635-4426-3(4))* Rigby Education.

—My Alien: Individual Title Six-Packs. (Sails Literacy Ser.). 16p. (gr. k-18). 27.00 *(978-0-7635-4394-5(2))* Rigby Education.

—Where Are You, Mouse? Eggleton, Jill. 2003. (Rigby Sails Early Ser.). (ENG.). 16p. (gr. 1-2). pap. 6.95 *(978-0-7578-8741-3(4))* Houghton Mifflin Harcourt Publishing Co.

McGrath, Ryan. Swamp Band Lullaby. Joachimowski, Paula L. 2008. 32p. 17.99 *(978-1-59879-433-5(7))* Lifevest Publishing, Inc.

McGrath, Tom, et al. How to Draw Dragons, Trolls, & Other Dangerous Monsters. Sautter, A. J. 2016. (Drawing Fantasy Creatures Ser.). (ENG.). 32p. (J). (gr. 3-9). lib. bdg. 28.65 *(978-1-4914-8023-6(8)*, Capstone Pr.) Capstone.

McGrath, Tom & Juta, Jason. Fantasy Field Guides, 1 vol. Sautter, A. J. 2014. (Fantasy Field Guides). (ENG.). 32p. (J). (gr. 3-9). lib. bdg., lib. bdg., lib. bdg. 114.60 *(978-1-4914-0705-9(0)*, Capstone Pr.) Capstone.

McGraw, Jinay. Kindergarten Rich: Our Future Leaders. Perkins, Wendy. 2019. (ENG.). 64p. (J). pap. *(978-1-4602-2421-2(3))* FriesenPress.

McGraw, Sheila. I Promise I'll Find You. Ward, Heather P. 2005. 32p. (J). (gr. -1-2). pap. 6.95 *(978-1-55209-094-7(9)*, b2e9cb1c-7dfd-493e-91f4-412e01a76868) Firefly Bks., Ltd.

—Je T'aimerai Toujours. Munsch, Robert. 2019. (FRE.). 32p. (J). (gr. -1-1). bds. 9.95 *(978-0-2281-0185-7(9)*, 6ab89ad4-88f7-4e82-95fa-03dba2bfd807) Firefly Bks., Ltd.

—Love You Forever. Munsch, Robert. 2018. (ENG.). 32p. (J). (gr. -1-1). bds. 8.95 *(978-0-2281-0104-8(2)*, 694870f9-82d1-4291-a216-fc7f96a10cd2) Firefly Bks., Ltd.

—Love You Forever Pop-Up Edition. Munsch, Robert. 2017. (ENG.). 14p. (J). (gr. -1-1). 24.95 *(978-1-77085-965-4(9)*, 865aede3-8fe2-43eb-ba9e-f4c8a4c707b7) Firefly Bks., Ltd.

McGregor, Barbara. Mega Magna Forms Princess. Bryan, Sarah Jane & Bellenson, Suzanne. 2008. (Activity Book Ser.). 48p. (J). (gr. -1-3). spiral bd. 19.95 *(978-1-59359-808-2(4))* Peter Pauper Pr. Inc.

—The Wedding Planner's Daughter. Paratore, Coleen Murtagh. 2006. (Wedding Planner's Daughter Ser.). (ENG.). 208p. (J). (gr. 3-8). reprint ed. pap. 7.99 *(978-1-4169-1854-7(X)*, Simon & Schuster Bks. For Young Readers) Simon & Schuster Bks. For Young Readers.

McGregor, Jody. Brave Little Bear: Too Big Not to Share. Schembri, Xenia. 2018. (ENG.). 18p. (J). pap. ***(978-0-9946321-2-8(6))*** Reeve, Ocean Publishing.

McGregor, Malcolm. 100 Animals to Spot at the Zoo. Clarke, Phillip, ed. 2009. (Spotter's Cards Ser.). 52p. (J). 9.99 *(978-0-7945-2254-4(8)*, Usborne) EDC Publishing.

McGregor, Malcolm & Jackson, Ian. Animals Sticker Book. Clarke, Phillip & Khan, Sarah. Rogers, Kirsteen, ed. 2007. (Spotter's Guides Sticker Bks). 24p. (J). (gr. -1-3). pap. 8.99 *(978-0-7945-1744-1(7)*, Usborne) EDC Publishing.

McGregor, Tony L. The "I Love You" Story. Kelley, Walter P. 2004. (J). *(978-0-9729569-4-9(8))* BuTo, Ltd. Co.

McGrellis, Cynthia. The Longest Shortcut. Ayder, Earl. 2005. 40p. pap. 8.53 *(978-0-7578-9857-0(2))* Rigby Education.

McGrone, Indya. Zoey & Cloey & the Monster's Grub - Tub. McGrone, Indya. 2020. (ENG.). 32p. (J). (gr. k-2). 18.99 ***(978-0-578-65781-3(3))*** Children's Poetic Pr.

McGrory, Anik. Amazing Monty. Hurwitz, Johanna. 2013. (Monty Ser.: 3). 112p. (J). (gr. k-4). pap. 5.99 *(978-0-7636-6561-6(4))* Candlewick Pr.

—Magical Monty. Hurwitz, Johanna. 2013. (Monty Ser.: 4). 112p. (J). (gr. k-4). pap. 5.99 *(978-0-7636-6457-2(X))* Candlewick Pr.

—Magical Monty. Hurwitz, Johanna. 2013. (Monty Ser.). (ENG.). (J). (gr. k-4). lib. bdg. 16.60 *(978-1-62765-368-8(6))* Perfection Learning Corp.

—Mighty Monty: More First-Grade Adventures. Hurwitz, Johanna. 2010. (Monty Ser.: 2). 112p. (J). (gr. 1-4). pap. 5.99 *(978-0-7636-4786-5(1))* Candlewick Pr.

—Mostly Monty. Hurwitz, Johanna & McCrory, Anik. 2008. (Monty Ser.: 1). (ENG.). 96p. (J). (gr. 1-4). pap. 5.99 *(978-0-7636-4062-0(X))* Candlewick Pr.

—Mostly Monty, 1. Hurwitz, Johanna. 2008. (Monty Ser.: 1). (ENG.). 86p. (J). (gr. k-3). 18.69 *(978-0-7636-2831-4(X))* Candlewick Pr.

—Mountain of Blintzes, 0 vols. Goldin, Barbara Diamond. 2010. (ENG.). 32p. (J). (gr. -1-2). pap. 6.99 *(978-0-7614-5790-9(9)*, 9780761457909, Two Lions) Amazon Publishing.

—You See a Circus, I See... Downs, Mike. 2006. 32p. (J). (gr. -1-3). pap. 7.95 *(978-1-58089-155-4(1))* Charlesbridge Publishing, Inc.

McGrory, Paul. Threadneedle 01. Price, Robin. 2016. (ENG.). 32p. (J). pap. *(978-1-906132-86-6(0))* Mogzilla.

McGuckie, Cierra Jade. Mami, Que Es una Carcel? Stanglin, Jackie A. 2007. (J). (gr. -1-3). 40p. 13.99 *(978-1-59879-428-1(0))*; 36p. 19.99 *(978-1-59879-429-8(9))* Lifevest Publishing, Inc.

—What Is Jail, Mommy? Stanglin, Jackie A. l.t. ed. 2006. 40p. (J). 21.99 *(978-1-59879-252-2(0))*; (gr. -1-3). 13.99 *(978-1-59879-248-5(2))* Lifevest Publishing, Inc.

McGuiness, Dan. Hotdog! #1. Do, Anh. 2020. (ENG.). 128p. (J). (gr. 2-4). pap. 5.99 *(978-1-338-58720-3(X))* Scholastic, Inc.

—Party Time! Do, Anh. 2020. (ENG.). 128p. (J). (gr. 2-4). pap. 5.99 *(978-1-338-58721-0(8))* Scholastic, Inc.

McGuinness, Áine. Marco: Master of Disguise. Boland, Gerry. 2012. (Rather Remarkable Grizzly Bear Ser.: 2). (ENG.). 64p. (J). 12.95 *(978-1-84717-273-0(3))* O'Brien Pr., Ltd., The IRL. Dist: Casemate Pubs. & Bk. Distributors, LLC.

—Marco Moves In. Boland, Gerry. 2012. (Rather Remarkable Grizzly Be Ser.). (ENG.). 64p. (J). 12.95 *(978-1-84717-229-7(6))* O'Brien Pr., Ltd., The IRL. Dist: Dufour Editions, Inc.

McGuinness, Ed. Avengers by Jason Aaron Vol. 6: Starbrand Reborn. 2020. (ENG.). 136p. (YA). (gr. 8-17). pap. 15.99 ***(978-1-302-92094-4(4))*** Marvel Worldwide, Inc.

McGuinness, Ed, et al. Deadpool by Joe Kelly: the Complete Collection Vol. 1. 2019. (ENG.). 432p. (YA). (gr. 8-17). pap. 39.99 *(978-1-302-92061-6(8))* Marvel Worldwide, Inc.

—Hulk by Loeb & Mcguinness Omnibus. 2019. (ENG.). 912p. (YA). (gr. -1-17). 100.00 *(978-1-302-91805-7(2))* Marvel Worldwide, Inc.

McGuinness, Ed. Marvel Monograph: the Art of Ed Mcguinness ¿ Deadpool & His Amazing Friends. 2019. (Marvel Monograph Ser.). (ENG.). 112p. (YA). (gr. 8-17). pap. 19.99 *(978-1-302-91763-0(3))* Marvel Worldwide, Inc.

McGuinness, Jane. What's Next? Knapman, Timothy. 2019. (ENG.). 32p. (J). (-k). 16.99 *(978-1-5362-0989-1(9))* Candlewick Pr.

McGuinness, Jane. Prickly Hedgehogs! McGuinness, Jane. 2018. (ENG.). 32p. (J). (-k). 16.99 *(978-0-7636-9880-5(6))* Candlewick Pr.

McGuinness-Kelly, Tracy-Lee. Bad Cat. McGuinness-Kelly, Tracy-Lee. 2006. 29p. (J). (gr. k-4). reprint ed. 16.00 *(978-0-7567-9823-9(X))* DIANE Publishing Co.

McGuinness, Tracey, jt. illus. see McGuinness, Tracy.

McGuinness, Tracy. Brainiac's Bug Book: Creepy Crawly Activities. Tenah, Ann. 2005. (Activity Journals Ser.). 128p. 12.99 *(978-0-88088-362-7(6))* Peter Pauper Pr. Inc.

—Math Smarts: Tips, Tricks, & Secrets for Making Math More Fun! Long, Lynette. 2004. (AmericanGirl Library). (ENG.). 64p. (J). pap. 8.95 *(978-1-58485-875-1(3))* American Girl Publishing, Inc.

McGuinness, Tracy & McGuinness, Tracey. School Smarts Projects. Raymer, Dottie. 2007. (American Girl Library). (ENG.). 96p. (J). (gr. 3-7). pap. 8.95 *(978-1-59369-005-2(3)*, American Girl) American Girl Publishing, Inc.

McGuire, Bill. Buzz Beaker & the Cave Creatures. Meister, Cari. 2010. (Buzz Beaker Bks.). (ENG.). 32p. (J). (gr. 2-3). pap. 6.25 *(978-1-4342-2797-3(9))*; 22.65 *(978-1-4342-2060-8(5))* Capstone. (Stone Arch Bks.).

—Buzz Beaker & the Cool Caps, 1 vol. Meister, Cari. 2011. (Buzz Beaker Bks.). (ENG.). 32p. (J). (gr. 2-3). pap. 6.25 *(978-1-4342-3055-3(4)*, Stone Arch Bks.) Capstone.

—Buzz Beaker & the Growing Goo, 1 vol. Meister, Cari. 2011. (Buzz Beaker Bks.). (ENG.). 32p. (J). (gr. 2-3). pap. 6.25 *(978-1-4342-3056-0(2))*; lib. bdg. 22.65 *(978-1-4342-2527-6(5))* Capstone. (Stone Arch Bks.).

—Buzz Beaker & the Outer Space Trip. Meister, Cari. 2010. (Buzz Beaker Bks.). (ENG.). 32p. (J). (gr. 2-3). pap. 6.25 *(978-1-4342-2800-0(2)*, Stone Arch Bks.) Capstone.

—Buzz Beaker & the Putt-Putt Contest. Meister, Cari. 2010. (Buzz Beaker Bks.). (ENG.). 32p. (J). (gr. 2-3). pap. 6.25 *(978-1-4342-2799-7(5))*; 22.65 *(978-1-4342-2062-2(1))* Capstone. (Stone Arch Bks.).

—Buzz Beaker & the Race to School, 1 vol. Meister, Cari. 2011. (Buzz Beaker Bks.). (ENG.). 32p. (J). (gr. 2-3). pap. 6.25 *(978-1-4342-3057-7(0)*, Stone Arch Bks.) Capstone.

—Buzz Beaker & the Speed Secret. Meister, Cari. 2010. (Buzz Beaker Bks.). (ENG.). 32p. (J). (gr. 2-3). pap. 6.25 *(978-1-4342-2798-0(7))*; 22.65 *(978-1-4342-2061-5(3))* Capstone. (Stone Arch Bks.).

—Buzz Beaker & the Super Fast Car, 1 vol. Meister, Cari. 2011. (Buzz Beaker Bks.). (ENG.). 32p. (J). (gr. 2-3). pap. 6.25 *(978-1-4342-3058-4(9)*, Stone Arch Bks.) Capstone.

McGuire, Bryan, jt. illus. see Menix, Cinda.

McGuire, Erin. Alabama Spitfire: the Story of Harper Lee & to Kill a Mockingbird. Hegedus, Bethany. 2018. (ENG.). 40p. (J). (gr. -1-3). 17.99 *(978-0-06-245670-0(9))* HarperCollins Pubs.

—Bite-Sized Magic. Littlewood, Kathryn. (Bliss Bakery Trilogy Ser.: 3). (ENG.). 432p. (J). (gr. 3-7). 2015. pap. 7.99 *(978-0-06-208427-9(5))*; 2014. 16.99 *(978-0-06-208426-2(7))* HarperCollins Pubs. (Tegen, Katherine Bks).

—Breadcrumbs. Ursu, Anne. (ENG.). (J). (gr. 3-7). 2013. 336p. pap. 7.99 *(978-0-06-201506-8(0))*; 2011. 320p. 16.99 *(978-0-06-201505-1(2))* HarperCollins Pubs. (Waldon Pond Pr.).

—Breadcrumbs. Ursu, Anne. 2012. 320p. 55.00 *(978-0-449-01400-4(2))* Random Hse., Inc.

—French Ducks in Venice. Freymann-Weyr, Garret. 2011. (ENG.). 56p. (J). (gr. k-4). 16.99 *(978-0-7636-4173-3(1))* Candlewick Pr.

—Jelly Bean. Lord, Cynthia. 2014. (Shelter Pet Squad Ser.: 1). (ENG.). 128p. (J). (gr. 1-3). 16.99 *(978-0-545-63596-7(9))*; (gr. 2-5). pap. 5.99 *(978-0-545-63597-4(7))* Scholastic, Inc. (Scholastic Pr.).

—Lucky for Good. Patron, Susan. 2012. (ENG.). 224p. (J). (gr. 3-7). pap. 7.99 *(978-1-4169-9059-8(3)*, Atheneum Bks. for Young Readers) Simon & Schuster Children's Publishing.

—Merlin. Lord, Cynthia. 2015. (Shelter Pet Squad Ser.: 2). (ENG.). 128p. (J). (gr. 1-4). 16.99 *(978-0-545-63599-8(3))* Scholastic, Inc.

—The Real Boy. Ursu, Anne. 2015. (ENG.). 352p. (J). (gr. 3-7). pap. 6.99 *(978-0-06-201508-2(7)*, Waldon Pond Pr.) HarperCollins Pubs.

—Sleeping Beauty. Rylant, Cynthia. 2017. (ENG.). 40p. (J). (gr. -1-k). 16.99 *(978-1-4231-2108-4(2))* Disney Pr.

—A Whale in Paris. Presley, Daniel & Polders, Claire. (ENG.). 256p. (J). (gr. 5). 2019. pap. 7.99 *(978-1-5344-1916-2(0))*; 2018. 17.99 *(978-1-5344-1915-5(2))* Simon & Schuster Children's Publishing. (Atheneum Bks. for Young Readers).

McGuire, Erin K. Lucky for Good, 3. Patron, Susan. 2011. (Lucky Ser.). (ENG.). 224p. (J). (gr. 4-6). 21.19 *(978-1-4169-9058-1(5))* Simon & Schuster, Inc.

McGuire, Miranda. Dystopia 2153: Escape from the Rathouse. Liberman, W. L. 2018. (ENG.). 76p. (J). pap. *(978-1-987834-08-6(9))* TEACH Magazine.

McGuire, Robert. The Furry-Legged Teapot, 0 vols. Myers, Tim J. 2013. (ENG.). 32p. (J). (gr. k-3). pap. 9.99 *(978-1-4778-1026-2(9)*, 9781477810262, Two Lions) Amazon Publishing.

—The Last Black King of the Kentucky Derby: The Story of Jimmy Winkfield. Hubbard, Crystal. 2008. (ENG.). 40p. (J). (gr. 1-6). 17.95 *(978-1-58430-274-2(7))* Lee & Low Bks., Inc.

—The White Elephant. Fleischman, Sid. 2006. 112p. (J). (gr. 3-6). lib. bdg. 16.89 *(978-0-06-113137-0(7))*; 15.99 *(978-0-06-113136-3(9))* HarperCollins Pubs. (Greenwillow Bks.).

McGuirk, Leslie. Gobble, Gobble, Tucker! McGuirk, Leslie. 2014. 32p. (J). (-k). bds. 7.99 *(978-0-7636-6887-7(7))* Candlewick Pr.

—Ho, Ho, Ho, Tucker! McGuirk, Leslie. 2010. (Candlewick Storybook Animations Ser.). (ENG.). 32p. (J). (-k). 8.99 *(978-0-7636-5043-8(9))* Candlewick Pr.

—Lucky Tucker. McGuirk, Leslie. 2008. (ENG.). 24p. (J). (gr. -1-k). pap. 5.99 *(978-0-7636-3389-9(5))* Candlewick Pr.

—The Moogees Move House. McGuirk, Leslie. 2012. 32p. (J). (gr. -1-2). 14.99 *(978-0-7636-5558-7(9))* Candlewick Pr.

—Tucker Digs Easter! McGuirk, Leslie. 2017. 28p. (J). (-k). bds. 7.99 *(978-0-7636-8536-2(4))* Candlewick Pr.

—Tucker's Spooky Halloween. McGuirk, Leslie. (Candlewick Storybook Animations Ser.). (J). 2011. (ENG.). 32p. (gr. k-k). 8.99 *(978-0-7636-5113-8(3))*; 2009. (ENG.). 32p. (gr. k-k). 14.99 *(978-0-7636-4469-7(2))*; 2007. 28p. (gr. -1-k). bds. 7.99 *(978-0-7636-3181-9(7))* Candlewick Pr.

—Wiggens Learns His Manners at the Four Seasons Restaurant. McGuirk, Leslie. Von Bidder, Alex. 2009. 32p. (J). (gr. -1-2). 16.99 *(978-0-7636-4014-9(X))* Candlewick Pr.

McHaffie, Natalie. C-Growl: The Daring Little Airplane. McHaffie, Natalie. 2004. 32p. 14.95 *(978-1-55125-015-1(2))* Vanwell Publishing, Ltd. CAN. Dist: Casemate Pubs. & Bk. Distributors, LLC.

McHale, Conor. Ancient Ireland Colouring Book: From Newgrange to the Vikings. McHale, Conor. 2014. (ENG.). 32p. (J). pap. 12.00 *(978-1-84717-629-5(1))* O'Brien Pr., Ltd., The IRL. Dist: Casemate Pubs. & Bk. Distributors, LLC.

McHargue, D., et al. Ana Frank. Brown, Jonatha A. & Goff, Elizabeth Hudson. 2007. (Biografías Gráficas (Graphic Biographies) Ser.). (SPA.). 32p. (gr. 5-8). lib. bdg. 28.00 *(978-0-8368-7880-6(9))* Stevens, Gareth Publishing LLLP.

McHargue, D. The Battle of Gettysburg. Anderson, Dale & O'Hern, Kerri. 2006. (Graphic Histories Ser.). 32p. (gr. 5-8). lib. bdg. 28.00 *(978-0-8368-6204-1(X))* Stevens, Gareth Publishing LLLP.

—The Battle of the Alamo. Riehecky, Janet & O'Hern, Kerri. 2006. (Graphic Histories Ser.). 32p. (gr. 5-8). lib. bdg. 28.00 *(978-0-8368-6201-0(5))* Stevens, Gareth Publishing LLLP.

—Nelson Mandela. Holland, Gini & O'Hern, Kerri. 2006. (Graphic Biographies Ser.). 32p. (gr. 5-8). lib. bdg. 27.00 *(978-0-8368-6197-6(3))* Stevens, Gareth Publishing LLLP.

McHeffey, Adam. The Dyno-Mite Dog Show, 0 vols. Bonnett-Rampersaud, Louise. 2015. (Secret Knock Club Ser.: 1). (ENG.). 112p. (J). (gr. 1-4). pap. 9.99 *(978-0-7614-6325-2(9)*, 9780761463252, Two Lions) Amazon Publishing.

—The Great Sleep-Under, 0 vols. Bonnett-Rampersaud, Louise. 2016. (Secret Knock Club Ser.: 4). (ENG.). 96p. (J). (gr. 1-4). pap. 9.99 *(978-1-5039-5063-4(8)*, 9781503950634, Two Lions) Amazon Publishing.

McHeffey, Adam. Asiago, 0 vols. McHeffey, Adam. 2012. (ENG.). 32p. (J). (gr. -1-k). 16.99 *(978-0-7614-6138-8(8)*, 9780761461388, Two Lions) Amazon Publishing.

McHose, Jean. Tommy Wilson, Junior Veterinarian: The Case of the Wounded Jack Rabbit. Smith, Maggie Caldwell. 2005. 104p. (J). (gr. 3-6). pap. 7.95 *(978-1-889159-14-0(X))* Magpie Pr., Pine Mountain Club, CA.

McHugh, Kevin. Webster's Best Day Ever. McEvoy, Mack. 2019. (ENG.). 34p. (J). *(978-0-6484803-0-3(5))* Serenity Press.

—What on Earth Is under My Bed? Quinn, Laura. 2017. (ENG.). (J). pap. *(978-0-6481906-4-6(1))* Serenity Press.

McIlhany. A Toddler's Abc of Blessings. Prus, Jennifer. 2012. 20p. pap. 9.95 *(978-1-61633-256-3(5))* Guardian Angel Publishing, Inc.

McIlroy, Michelle, jt. illus. see Louise, Cristina.

McInerney, Kunyi June-Anne. Bush Games & Knucklebones. Kartinyeri, Doris. 2003. 32p. (J). pap. *(978-1-875641-81-9(5))* Magabala Bks.

McInerny, Judi. Gabrielle's Violin. Santiago, Ruth E. 2017. (ENG.). (J). pap. 11.99 *(978-1-4984-9268-3(1))* Salem Author Services.

McIntosh, Gabe. Parasaurolophus. Bailey, Gerry. 2011. (Smithsonian Prehistoric Zone Ser.). (ENG.). 32p. (J). (gr. k-3). *(978-0-7787-1799-7(2))*; pap. *(978-0-7787-1812-3(3))* Crabtree Publishing Co.

—Parasaurolophus Escapes. Bentley, Dawn. 2006. (Smithsonian's Prehistoric Pals Ser.). (ENG.). 36p. (J). 2.95 *(978-1-59249-645-7(8))*; (gr. -1-3). pap. 6.95 *(978-1-59249-643-3(1))* Soundprints.

McIntosh, Gabe, jt. illus. see Scalf, Christopher.

McIntosh, Gabe, jt. illus. see Scalf, Chris.

McIntosh, Iain. Mystery of Meerkat Hill. McCall Smith, Alexander. 2013. (Precious Ramotswe Mysteries for Young Readers Ser.: 2). (ENG.). 112p. (J). (gr. 2-5). pap. 7.99 *(978-0-345-80446-4(5)*, Anchor) Knopf Doubleday Publishing Group.

—The Mystery of Meerkat Hill: A Precious Ramotswe Mystery for Young Readers. McCall Smith, Alexander. 2013. (Precious Ramotswe Mysteries for Young Readers Ser.: 2). (ENG.). 112p. (J). (gr. 2-5). 12.99 *(978-0-345-80458-7(9))*; lib. bdg. 13.99 *(978-0-345-80616-1(6))* Knopf Doubleday Publishing Group. (Anchor).

McIntosh, Jason D. The Adventures of Largo & Shelby. Randall, Joanne M. 2018. (Adventures of Largo Ser.: Vol. 1). (ENG.). 28p. (J). (gr. k-5). pap. 12.95 *(978-0-692-08633-9(1))* Leap Year Marketing.

McInturff, Linda & Brownlie, Ian. One Day. Cunningham, Edie. 2004. 28p. (J). pap. *(978-1-932381-09-2(0)*, 6340) Bible Visuals International, Inc.

McInturff, Linda & Pope, Patricia. I Love to Tell the Story: A Visualized Gospel Song. 2010. 16p. (J). pap. *(978-1-932381-96-2(1)*, 6220) Bible Visuals International, Inc.

M

McInturff, Linda & Tweed, Sean. The Light of the World Is Jesus. 2004. 16p. (J). pap. *(978-1-932381-08-5(2))* Bible Visuals International, Inc.

McInturff, Sheri. Hip Hop Anonymous. Noble, Debbie. 2016. (ENG.). (J). pap. 11.99 *(978-1-945620-14-0(5))* Hear My Heart Publishing.

McIntyre, Coleen. Baking with Friends: Recipies, Tips & Fun Facts for Teaching Kids to Bake. Davis, Sharon & Patton, Charlene. Beatty, Nicholas, ed. 2010. 78p. (J). *(978-0-9712368-2-0(8))* Goops Unlimited.

McIntyre, Connie, jt. illus. see Gage, Amy Glaser.

McIntyre, Georgina. Sammy Goes Flying. Elliott, Odette. 2011. (ENG.). 32p. (J). (gr. -1-k). pap. 15.99 *(978-1-84853-050-8(1))* Transworld Publishers Ltd. GBR. Dist: Independent Pubs. Group.

McIntyre, Louise. Flowers for Grandpa Dan: A Gentle Story to Help Children Understand Alzheimer's Disease. McIntyre, Connie. 2004. 20p. (J). 12.95 *(978-0-9677685-5-7(1))*; lib. bdg. 17.95 *(978-0-9677685-6-4(X))* Grannie Annie Family Story Celebration, The.

McIntyre, Sarah. Adventures of Riley: Dolphins in Danger. Lumry, Amanda & Hurwitz, Laura. 2005. 36p. 15.95 *(978-0-9748411-1-3(0))* Eaglemont Pr.

—Adventures of Riley: Mission to Madagascar. Lumry, Amanda & Hurwitz, Laura. 2005. 36p. (gr. 2-3). 15.95 *(978-0-9748411-2-0(9))* Eaglemont Pr.

—Amazon River Rescue. Lumry, Amanda & Hurwitz, Laura. 2004. (Adventures of Riley Ser.). 36p. 15.95 *(978-0-9662257-9-2(1))* Eaglemont Pr.

—Cakes in Space. Reeve, Philip. 2015. (Not-So-Impossible Tale Ser.). (ENG.). 224p. (J). (gr. 2-5). 12.99 *(978-0-385-38792-7(X)*, Random Hse. Bks. for Young Readers) Random Hse. Children's Bks.

—Carnival in a Fix. Reeve, Philip. 2017. (Not-So-Impossible Tale Ser.). (ENG.). 224p. (J). (gr. 2-5). 12.99 *(978-0-385-38800-9(4)*, Random Hse. Bks. for Young Readers) Random Hse. Children's Bks.

—Morris the Mankiest Monster. Andreae, Giles. 2011. 32p. (J). (gr. -1-k). pap. 14.95 *(978-0-552-55935-5(0))* Transworld Publishers Ltd. GBR. Dist: Independent Pubs. Group.

—Oliver & the Sea Monkeys. Reeve, Philip. 2016. (Not-So-Impossible Tale Ser.). (ENG.). 224p. (J). (gr. 2-5). pap. 6.99 *(978-0-385-38789-7(X)*, Yearling) Random Hse. Children's Bks.

—Oliver & the Seawigs. Reeve, Philip. 2014. (Not-So-Impossible Tale Ser.). (ENG.). 208p. (J). (gr. 2-5). 12.99 *(978-0-385-38788-0(1)*, Random Hse. Bks. for Young Readers) Random Hse. Children's Bks.

—Pugs of the Frozen North. Reeve, Philip. 2016. (Not-So-Impossible Tale Ser.). (ENG.). 224p. (J). (gr. 2-5). 12.99 *(978-0-385-38796-5(2)*, Random Hse. Bks. for Young Readers) Random Hse. Children's Bks.

—Tigers in Terai. Lumry, Amanda & Hurwitz, Laura. 2nd rev. ed. 2007. (Adventures of Riley (Unnumbered) Ser.). 36p. (J). (gr. -1-3). 15.95 *(978-1-60040-003-2(5))* Centro Bks., LLC.

—Tigers in Terai. Lumry, Amanda & Hurwitz, Laura. (Adventures of Riley Ser.). 36p. 2003. 15.95 *(978-0-9662257-7-8(5))*; 2nd ed. 2007. *(978-0-9748411-6-8(1))* Eaglemont Pr.

McIntyre, Sarah. The New Neighbors. McIntyre, Sarah. 2019. (ENG.). 32p. (J). (gr. -1-2). 17.99 *(978-1-5247-8996-1(8)*, Penguin Workshop) Penguin Young Readers Group.

McIntyre, Sasha, et al. Franklin's Pond Phantom. Jennings, Sharon. 2005. 32p. (J). lib. bdg. 15.38 *(978-1-4242-1181-4(6))* Fitzgerald Bks.

McIsaac, James. Les Holocaustes: �galement Sous le Titre Perrine et Charlot �; Ville-Marie. Daveluy, Marie Claire. 2019. (FRE.). 140p. (J). pap. 10.99 ***(978-1-6959-3122-0(X))*** Independently Published.

—Michel et Josephte Dans la Tourmente. Daveluy, Marie Claire. 2019. (FRE.). 220p. (J). pap. 14.99 ***(978-1-6960-1755-8(6))*** Independently Published.

—Les Petits Patriotes du Richelieu. Daveluy, Marie Claire. 2019. (FRE.). 210p. (J). pap. 14.99 ***(978-1-6960-1516-5(2))*** Independently Published.

McKay, Ann Marie. Hungry Mr. Gator. McLaughlin, Julie. 2005. (J). 15.99 *(978-0-933101-24-1(4))* Legacy Pubns.

—Mr. Gator Hits the Beach. McLaughlin, Julie. 2009. 32p. (J). 16.99 *(978-0-933101-56-2(2))* Legacy Pubns.

—Mr. Gator's up the Creek. McLaughlin, Julie. 2005. (J). 16.99 *(978-0-933101-23-4(6))* Legacy Pubns.

McKay, Donald. The Story of Mark Twain. Howard, Joan. Meadowcroft, Enid Lamonte, ed. 2011. 186p. 42.95 *(978-1-258-05565-3(1))* Literary Licensing, LLC.

McKay-Fleming, Kimberly. Granny's Giant Bannock, 1 vol. Wastasecoot, Brenda Isabel. 2015. (ENG.). 40p. (J). (gr. 1-4). mass mkt. 10.95 *(978-1-894717-49-6(X)*, 5b91bb70-1377-468d-b71e-833f2ffd9715) Pemmican Pubns., Inc. CAN. Dist: Firefly Bks., Ltd.

—I Loved Her, 1 vol. Ansloos, Sheeza. 2015. (ENG.). 32p. (J). (gr. 2-3). mass mkt. 10.95 *(978-1-894717-59-5(7)*, 922612d4-7fa3-4260-ac6e-febf86c4e032) Pemmican Pubns., Inc. CAN. Dist: Firefly Bks., Ltd.

—A Journey Through the Circle of Life. Gillespie, Desiree. 2015. (ENG.). 32p. (J). (gr. 1-2). mass mkt. 10.95 *(978-1-894717-45-8(7)*, d445d0be-36ff-4ba3-88dc-653d221d65a6) Pemmican Pubns., Inc. CAN. Dist: Firefly Bks., Ltd.

McKay, Hannah. The Scrawny Christmas Tree. Mullaney, Joanne. 2017. (ENG.). 24p. (J). pap. 15.99 *(978-1-5434-6877-9(2))* Xlibris Corp.

McKay, Lisa. Kenney Kookaburra's Lost Laugh: A Story from Waratah Glen. Morell, Corina. 2016. (Waratah Glen Ser.: Vol. 2). (ENG.). 42p. (J). pap. ***(978-1-925529-47-0(9))*** MoshPit Publishing.

McKay, Sindy & Johnson, Meredith. Kecko the Gecko. 2018. (We Both Read Ser.). (ENG.). 40p. (J). (gr. k-3). 17.44 *(978-1-5364-3154-4(0))* Treasure Bay, Inc.

McKay, Siobhan. Sharing Me: Helping Young Children Deal with Divorce. Alsop, Bonnie. 2013. 24p. pap. 11.50 *(978-1-62212-232-5(1)*, Strategic Bk. Publishing) Strategic Book Publishing & Rights Agency (SBPRA).

McKay, Traci. My Happy Gift. Langdown, Leanne Shea. 2011. 26p. pap. 6.99 *(978-1-61667-300-0(1))* Raider Publishing International.

McKean, Dave. Coraline. Gaiman, Neil. movie tie-in ed. 2008. (ENG.). 176p. (J). (gr. 3). pap. 6.99 *(978-0-06-164969-1(4)*, HarperFestival) HarperCollins Pubs.

—Coraline. Gaiman, Neil. 2004. (ENG.). 224p. (J). (gr. 3-7). pap. 9.99 *(978-0-06-057591-5(3)*, HarperCollins) HarperCollins Pubs. Ltd. GBR. Dist: HarperCollins Pubs.

—Coraline. Gaiman, Neil. 2007. 151p. (J). (gr. 6-8). 60.00 *(978-1-59606-147-7(2))* Subterranean Pr.

—Coraline: Reading Group Guide. Gaiman, Neil. *(978-0-06-056878-8(X))* HarperCollins Pubs.

—Coraline 10th Anniversary Edition. Gaiman, Neil. 10th anniv. ed. 2012. (HarperClassics Ser.). (ENG.). 208p. (J). (gr. 3-7). pap. 7.99 *(978-0-380-80734-5(3)*, HarperCollins) HarperCollins Pubs. Ltd. GBR. Dist: HarperCollins Pubs.

—Crazy Hair. Gaiman, Neil. (ENG.). 40p. (J). (gr. -1-3). 2015. pap. 6.99 *(978-0-06-057910-4(2))*; 2009. 18.99 *(978-0-06-057908-1(0))* HarperCollins Pubs. Ltd. GBR. (HarperCollins). Dist: HarperCollins Pubs.

—The Day I Swapped My Dad for Two Goldfish. Gaiman, Neil. 2004. 64p. (J). lib. bdg. 17.89 *(978-0-06-058702-4(4))* HarperCollins Pubs.

—The Day I Swapped My Dad for Two Goldfish. Gaiman, Neil. (ENG.). 64p. (J). (gr. k-3). 2006. pap. 7.99 *(978-0-06-058703-1(2))*; 2004. 17.99 *(978-0-06-058701-7(6))* HarperCollins Pubs. Ltd. GBR. (HarperCollins). Dist: HarperCollins Pubs.

—Death: The Time of Your Life. Gaiman, Neil et al. Kahan, Bob, ed. rev. ed. 2006. (ENG.). 96p. (YA). pap. 12.99 *(978-1-56389-333-9(9))* DC Comics.

—The Graveyard Book. Gaiman, Neil. 2008. 552p. (J). pap. 17.99 *(978-0-06-170912-8(3))* HarperCollins Pubs.

—The Graveyard Book. Gaiman, Neil. (ENG.). 320p. (J). (gr. 5). 2018. pap. 8.99 *(978-0-06-053094-5(4))*; 2008. 17.99 *(978-0-06-053092-1(8))*; 2008. lib. bdg. 18.89 *(978-0-06-053093-8(6))* HarperCollins Pubs. Ltd. GBR. (HarperCollins). Dist: HarperCollins Pubs.

—The Graveyard Book: a Harper Classic. Gaiman, Neil. 2017. (Harper Classic Ser.). (ENG.). 368p. (J). (gr. 3-7). 16.99 *(978-0-06-266703-8(3)*, HarperCollins) HarperCollins Pubs. Ltd. GBR. Dist: HarperCollins Pubs.

—The Graveyard Book Commemorative Edition. Gaiman, Neil. 2014. (ENG.). 352p. (J). (gr. 5-7). pap. 9.99 *(978-0-06-234918-7(X)*, HarperCollins) HarperCollins Pubs. Ltd. GBR. Dist: HarperCollins Pubs.

—Joe Quinn's Poltergeist. Almond, David. 2019. (ENG.). 80p. (J). (gr. 7). 17.99 *(978-1-5362-0160-4(X))* Candlewick Pr.

—Los Lobos de la Pared. Gaiman, Neil. 2006.Tr. of Wolves in the Wall. (SPA.). 64p. 22.95 *(978-1-59497-222-5(2))* Public Square Bks.

—MirrorMask (children's Edition) Gaiman, Neil. ed. 2005. (ENG.). 80p. (J). (gr. 5). 16.99 *(978-0-06-082109-8(4)*, HarperCollins) HarperCollins Pubs. Ltd. GBR. Dist: HarperCollins Pubs.

Mckean, Dave. Mouse Bird Snake Wolf. Almond, David. 2013. (ENG.). 80p. (J). (gr. 2-5). 17.99 *(978-0-7636-5912-7(6))* Candlewick Pr.

McKean, Dave. Phoenix. Said, S. F. 2016. (ENG.). 496p. (J). (gr. 5). 19.99 *(978-0-7636-8850-9(9))* Candlewick Pr.

—The Savage. Almond, David. 2008. (ENG.). 80p. (J). (gr. 7). 17.99 *(978-0-7636-3932-7(X))* Candlewick Pr.

—Slog's Dad. Almond, David. 2011. (ENG.). 64p. (J). (gr. 5-18). 15.99 *(978-0-7636-4940-1(6))* Candlewick Pr.

—Varjak Paw. Said, S. F. 2005. (ENG.). 256p. (J). (gr. 3-7). reprint ed. pap. 7.99 *(978-0-440-42076-7(8)*, Yearling) Random Hse. Children's Bks.

—The Wolves in the Walls. Gaiman, Neil. (ENG.). 56p. (J). (gr. k). 2003. 17.99 *(978-0-380-97827-4(X))*; 2005. reprint ed. pap. 7.99 *(978-0-380-81095-6(6))* HarperCollins Pubs. Ltd. GBR. (HarperCollins). Dist: HarperCollins Pubs.

McKean, Dave. Mirrormask. McKean, Dave. ed. 2005. 80p. (J). lib. bdg. 17.89 *(978-0-06-082110-4(8))* HarperCollins Pubs.

McKean, Kaley. Howl Like a Wolf! Learn to Think, Move, & Act Like 15 Amazing Animals. Yale, Kathleen. 2018. (ENG.). 80p. (J). 18.95 *(978-1-61212-905-1(6)*, 622905) Storey Publishing, LLC.

McKee, Darren. Colors of Spring. Neusner, Dena Wallenstein. 2003. (Barney Ser.). (ENG.). 32p. (J). pap., act. bk. ed. 3.99 *(978-1-58668-305-4(5))* Scholastic, Inc.

—Musical Mystery Scooby Doo! Fertig, Michael P. 2007. (Scooby Doo Ser.). (J). (gr. -1-3). 12.98 *(978-1-4127-7429-1(2))* Publications International, Ltd.

—Zach Apologizes. Mulcahy, William. 2012. (Zach Rules Ser.). (ENG.). 32p. (J). (gr. -1-3). 12.99 *(978-1-57542-389-0(8))* Free Spirit Publishing, Inc.

—Zach Hangs in There. Mulcahy, William. 2017. (Zach Rules Ser.). (ENG.). 32p. (J). (gr. k-3). 12.99 *(978-1-63198-162-3(5))* Free Spirit Publishing, Inc.

—Zach Makes Mistakes. Mulcahy, William. 2016. (Zach Rules Ser.). (ENG.). 32p. (J). 12.99 *(978-1-63198-110-4(2))* Free Spirit Publishing, Inc.

—Zach Stands Up. Mulcahy, William. 2018. (Zach Rules Ser.). (ENG.). 36p. (J). (gr. k-3). 12.99 *(978-1-63198-293-4(1))* Free Spirit Publishing, Inc.

McKee, David. The King of Quizzical Island. Snell, Gordon. 2009. (ENG.). 40p. (J). (gr. -1-3). 16.99 *(978-0-7636-3857-3(9))* Candlewick Pr.

—Sir Ned & the Nasties. McKee, Brett. 2017. 32p. (J). (-k). 21.99 *(978-1-78344-534-9(3))* Andersen Pr. GBR. Dist: Independent Pubs. Group.

—Sir Ned & the Nasties. 2018. 32p. (J). (-k). pap. 9.99 *(978-1-78344-567-7(X))* Andersen Pr. GBR. Dist: Independent Pubs. Group.

McKee, David. Charlotte's Piggy Bank. McKee, David. 2004. 32p. (J). pap. 12.95 *(978-1-84270-331-1(5))* Andersen Pr. GBR. Dist: Independent Pubs. Group.

—Denver. McKee, David. 2012. 32p. (J). (gr. -1-k). pap. 10.99 *(978-1-84939-389-8(3))* Andersen Pr. GBR. Dist: Independent Pubs. Group.

—Elmer, Level 4.9. McKee, David. 3rd ed. 2003. (Picture Books Collection). (SPA.). 32p. (J). (gr. k-3). 12.95 *(978-84-372-2186-1(2))* Altea, Ediciones, S.A. - Grupo Santillana ESP. Dist: Santillana USA Publishing Co., Inc.

—Elmer. McKee, David. (Historias Para Dormir Ser.). (SPA.). 32p. (J). (gr. k-3). pap. 9.95 *(978-968-19-1029-7(X))* Santillana USA Publishing Co., Inc.

—Elmer & Aunt Zelda. McKee, David. 2017. (Elmer Ser.). (ENG.). 32p. (J). (gr. -1-3). 17.99 *(978-1-5124-3945-8(2))* Lerner Publishing Group.

—Elmer & Butterfly. McKee, David. 2015. (Elmer Ser.). (ENG.). 32p. (J). (gr. -1-3). 16.95 *(978-1-4677-6326-4(8)*, 9781467763264); E-Book 27.99 *(978-1-4677-6327-1(6))* Lerner Publishing Group.

—Elmer & Grandpa Eldo. McKee, David. 2016. (Elmer Ser.). (ENG.). 32p. (J). (gr. -1-3). 17.99 *(978-1-5124-0569-9(8)*, 9781512405699) Lerner Publishing Group.

—Elmer & Rose. McKee, David. 2010. (Elmer Ser.). (ENG.). 32p. (J). (gr. -1-3). 17.99 *(978-0-7613-5493-2(X)*, 9780761354932) Lerner Publishing Group.

—Elmer & Super El. McKee, David. 2012. (Elmer Ser.). (ENG.). 32p. (J). (gr. -1-3). 16.95 *(978-0-7613-8989-7(X)*, 9780761389897) Lerner Publishing Group.

—Elmer & the Birthday Quake. McKee, David. 2013. (Elmer Ser.). (ENG.). 32p. (J). (gr. -1-3). 16.95 *(978-1-4677-1117-3(9)*, 9781467711173) Lerner Publishing Group.

—Elmer & the Flood. McKee, David. 2015. (Elmer Ser.). (ENG.). 32p. (J). (gr. -1-3). 17.99 *(978-1-4677-9312-4(4)*, 9781467793124); E-Book 27.99 *(978-1-4677-9314-8(0))* Lerner Publishing Group.

—Elmer & the Hippos. McKee, David. 2010. (Elmer Ser.). (ENG.). 32p. (J). (gr. -1-3). 17.99 *(978-0-7613-6442-9(0)*, 9780761364429) Lerner Publishing Group.

—Elmer & the Lost Teddy. McKee, David. 2004. (Elmer Bks.). 32p. (J). 9.99 *(978-0-06-075243-9(2))* HarperCollins Pubs.

—Elmer & the Monster. McKee, David. 2014. (Elmer Ser.). (ENG.). 32p. (J). (gr. -1-3). 16.95 *(978-1-4677-4200-9(7)*, 9781467742009) Lerner Publishing Group.

—Elmer & the Race. McKee, David. 2016. (Elmer Ser.). (ENG.). 32p. (J). (gr. -1-3). 17.99 *(978-1-5124-1624-4(X)*, 9781512416244) Lerner Publishing Group.

—Elmer & the Rainbow. McKee, David. 2011. (Elmer Ser.). (ENG.). 32p. (J). (gr. -1-3). 17.99 *(978-0-7613-7410-7(8)*, 9780761374107) Lerner Publishing Group.

—Elmer & the Tune. McKee, David. 2017. (Elmer Ser.). (ENG.). 32p. (J). (gr. -1-3). 17.99 *(978-1-5124-8124-2(6)*, 9781512481242) Lerner Publishing Group.

—Elmer & the Whales. McKee, David. 2014. (Elmer Ser.). (ENG.). 32p. (J). (gr. -1-3). 16.95 *(978-1-4677-3453-0(5)*, 9781467734530) Lerner Publishing Group.

—Elmer & Wilbur. McKee, David. 2004. (Elmer Bks.). 32p. (J). 9.99 *(978-0-06-075239-2(4))* HarperCollins Pubs.

Mckee, David. Elmer Board Book. Mckee, David. 2014. (ENG.). 32p. (J). (gr. -1 — 1). bds. 7.99 *(978-0-06-232405-4(5)*, HarperFestival) HarperCollins Pubs.

McKee, David. Elmer in the Snow. McKee, David. 2004. (Elmer Bks.). 32p. (J). 9.99 *(978-0-06-075240-8(8))* HarperCollins Pubs.

Mckee, David. Elmer Padded Board Book. Mckee, David. 2018. (ENG.). 32p. (J). (gr. -1 — 1). bds. 9.99 *(978-0-06-274160-8(8)*, HarperFestival) HarperCollins Pubs.

McKee, David. Elmer's Birthday. McKee, David. 2019. (Elmer Ser.). (ENG.). 32p. (J). (gr. -1-3). 17.99 *(978-1-5415-7764-0(7))* Lerner Publishing Group.

—Elmer's Opposites. McKee, David. 2012. (ENG.). 10p. (J). (gr. -1-2). bds. 7.95 *(978-0-7613-8998-9(9)*, 9780761389989) Lerner Publishing Group.

—Elmer's Special Day. McKee, David. 2009. (Elmer Ser.). (ENG.). 32p. (J). (gr. -1-3). 17.99 *(978-0-7613-5154-2(X)*, 9780761351542) Lerner Publishing Group.

—Elmer's Walk. McKee, David. 2018. (Elmer Ser.). (ENG.). 32p. (J). (gr. -1-3). 17.99 *(978-1-5415-3554-1(5))* Lerner Publishing Group.

—George's Invisible Watch. McKee, David. McKee, Brett. 2013. 32p. (J). (gr. -1-k). pap. 8.99 *(978-1-84270-864-4(3))* Andersen Pr. GBR. Dist: Independent Pubs. Group.

—Isabel's Noisy Tummy. McKee, David. 2013. 32p. (J). (gr. -1-k). pap. 10.99 *(978-1-84939-689-9(2))* Andersen Pr. GBR. Dist: Independent Pubs. Group.

—Melric: The Magician Who Lost His Magic. McKee, David. 2013. (Melric Ser.). (ENG.). 32p. (J). (gr. -1-k). 16.99 *(978-1-84939-439-0(3))* Andersen Pr. GBR. Dist: Independent Pubs. Group.

—Melric & the Dragon. McKee, David. 2016. (Melric Ser.: 4). 32p. (J). (-k). pap. 13.99 *(978-1-78344-210-2(7))*; (ENG.). (gr. -1-k). 16.99 *(978-1-78344-162-4(3))* Andersen Pr. GBR. Dist: Independent Pubs. Group.

—Melric & the Petnapping. McKee, David. 2014. (Melric Ser.). (ENG.). 32p. (J). (gr. -1-k). 16.99 *(978-1-78344-008-5(2))* Andersen Pr. GBR. Dist: Independent Pubs. Group.

—Melric the Magician Who Lost His Magic. McKee, David. 2013. (Melric Ser.). 32p. (J). (gr. -1-k). pap. 12.99 *(978-1-84939-525-0(X))* Andersen Pr. GBR. Dist: Independent Pubs. Group.

—Zebra's Hiccups. McKee, David. 2009. (ENG.). 32p. (J). (gr. k-k). pap. 10.99 *(978-1-84270-923-8(2))* Andersen Pr. GBR. Dist: Independent Pubs. Group.

McKee, Karen & Griffin, Georgene. Hot Wings. 2004. (J). *(978-1-59203-091-0(2))* Learning Challenge, Inc.

McKeever, John. Once upon a Time in Norfolk. King, Isabelle. 2018. (ENG.). 192p. pap. 16.95 *(978-0-7509-8415-7(5))* History Pr. Ltd.,The GBR. Dist: Independent Pubs. Group.

McKelvie, Jamie. Young Avengers by Gillen & Mckelvie: the Complete Collection. Gillen, Kieron. 2020. 360p. (YA). (gr. 8-17). pap. 34.99 ***(978-1-302-92568-0(7))*** Marvel Worldwide, Inc.

McKenna, Brenton E. Ubby's Underdogs: The Legend of the Phoenix Dragon. McKenna, Brenton E. 2019. (Ubby's Underdogs Ser.: 1). 178p. (J). pap. 14.99 *(978-1-921248-31-3(9))* Magabala Bks. AUS. Dist: Independent Pubs. Group.

McKenna, Bridgett. Tumbleweed Christmas. McClure, Beverly Stowe. 2011. 24p. pap. 13.99 *(978-0-9832740-4-9(5))* 4RV Pub.

McKenna, Lou. Math's Mate Orange: Student Pad. Wright, Joe. Tutos, Joanna, ed. 2013. 72p. pap. *(978-1-921535-55-0(5))* Educational Advantage Pty, Ltd, The.

—Math's Mate Rose: Student Pad. Wright, Joseph B. Tutos, Joanna, ed. 2013. 72p. pap. *(978-1-921535-56-7(3))* Educational Advantage Pty, Ltd, The.

McKenna, Mark, et al. Banana Tail. 2003. 32p. (J). 12.95 *(978-0-9727681-3-9(0))* Active Media Publishing, LLC.

McKenna, Mark. Timebreakers. Bedard, Tony. 2005. (Exiles Ser.). 168p. (YA). pap. 17.99 *(978-0-7851-1730-8(X))* Marvel Worldwide, Inc.

McKenna, Nancy Durrell, photos by. Nuevo Libro del Embarazo y Nacimiento: Guia Practica y Completa para Todos los Futuros Padres. Stoppard, Miriam. (SPA., 255p. pap. 20.99 *(978-958-04-5849-4(9))* Norma S.A. COL. Dist: Distribuidora Norma, Inc.

McKenna, Sharon Michelle. Good Morning, Sunshine: A Grandpa Story. 2006. 32p. (J). (gr. -1-3). 15.95 *(978-1-60108-003-5(4))* Red Cygnet Pr.

McKenna, Terry. Armor. Clarke, Catriona. 2007. (Usborne Beginners Ser.). 32p. (J). (gr. -1-3). 4.99 *(978-0-7945-1578-2(9)*, Usborne) EDC Publishing.

—Celts: Information for Young Readers - Level 2. Pratt, Leonie. 2007. (Usborne Beginners Ser.). 32p. (J). 4.99 *(978-0-7945-1580-5(0)*, Usborne) EDC Publishing.

—Pirates. Clarke, Catriona. 2006. (Beginners Social Studies: Level 2 Ser.). 32p. (J). (gr. 1-3). 4.99 *(978-0-7945-1332-0(8)*, Usborne) EDC Publishing.

McKenney, J. David. Careful What You Wish For. Petroff, Shani. 2010. (Bedeviled Ser.: 3). 240p. (J). (gr. 3-7). pap. 6.99 *(978-0-448-45113-8(1)*, Grosset & Dunlap) Penguin Young Readers Group.

—Love Struck, 4. Petroff, Shani. 2011. (Bedeviled Ser.: 4). 240p. (J). (gr. 6-8). 18.69 *(978-0-448-45114-5(X)*, Grosset & Dunlap) Penguin Publishing Group.

McKenney, Linda. The Diamond Shop Heist: Tales from Sintar. McKenney, Sean. 2018. (Tales from Sintar Ser.: Vol. 1). (ENG.). 38p. (YA). (gr. 7-12). pap. 12.00 *(978-0-692-18742-5(1))* Celebration Media.

McKenney, Marlon. Alice in Wonderland Remixed. McKenney, Marlon. 2018. (ENG.). 52p. (J). (gr. k-4). 20.00 *(978-1-7322051-0-9(8))*; 2nd ed. pap. 9.99 *(978-1-7322051-2-3(4))* Conscious Culture Publishing.

McKenny, Stewart & Moy, Philip. Wanted - The Super Friends. Fisch, Sholly. 2012. (DC Super Friends Ser.). (ENG.). 32p. (J). (gr. 2-3). lib. bdg. 22.60 *(978-1-4342-4543-4(8)*, Stone Arch Bks.) Capstone.

McKenzie, Heath. Better Out Than In: Number Twos. Wallace, Adam. 2013. (Better Out Than In Ser.). 120p. (J). pap. 14.09 *(978-0-9874635-3-1(5))* JoJo Publishing AUS. Dist: Baker & Taylor Publisher Services (BTPS).

—The Droid of Doom. Metz, Melinda. 2016. (S. M. A. R. T. S. Ser.). (ENG.). 128p. (J). (gr. 3-6). pap. 9.95 *(978-1-4965-3017-2(9)*, Stone Arch Bks.) Capstone.

—Eu Amo Você, Livro. Hathorn, Libby. Dalla, Juliana, tr. from ENG. 2012.Tr. of I love Your Book. (POR.). 36p. pap. *(978-1-921869-82-2(8)*, IP Kidz) Interactive Pubns. Pty, Ltd.

—Good Night, Truck. Odgers, Sally. 2016. (ENG.). 32p. (J). 16.99 *(978-1-250-07019-7(8)*, 900148342) Feiwel & Friends.

—Mac O'Beasty, Bk. 2. Wallace, Adam. 2009. (ENG.). 40p. (J). pap. 15.97 *(978-0-9805564-5-2(7))* JoJo Publishing AUS. Dist: Baker & Taylor Publisher Services (BTPS).

—The Mars Mission Mayhem. Metz, Melinda. 2016. (S. M. A. R. T. S. Ser.). (ENG.). 128p. (J). (gr. 3-6). pap. 9.95 *(978-1-4965-3018-9(7)*, Stone Arch Bks.) Capstone.

—Nerdy Ninjas vs the Really Really Bad Guys. Whamhower, Shogun. 2012. 137p. (J). *(978-0-545-53736-0(3))* Scholastic, Inc.

—A New Friend for Marmalade. Reynolds, Alison. 2014. (ENG.). 40p. (J). (gr. -1-1). 15.99 *(978-1-4814-2046-4(1)*, Little Simon) Little Simon.

—S. M. A. R. T. S. & the 3-D Danger. Metz, Melinda. 2015. (S. M. A. R. T. S. Ser.). (ENG.). 128p. (J). (gr. 3-6). 22.65 *(978-1-4965-0465-4(8)*, Stone Arch Bks.) Capstone.

—S. M. A. R. T. S. & the Droid of Doom. Metz, Melinda. 2016. (S. M. A. R. T. S. Ser.). (ENG.). 128p. (J). (gr. 3-6). lib. bdg. 22.65 *(978-1-4965-3015-8(2)*, Stone Arch Bks.) Capstone.

—S. M. A. R. T. S. & the Invisible Robot. Metz, Melinda. 2015. (S. M. A. R. T. S. Ser.). (ENG.). 128p. (J). (gr. 3-6). 22.65 *(978-1-4965-0463-0(1)*, Stone Arch Bks.) Capstone.

—S. M. A. R. T. S. & the Mars Mission Mayhem. Metz, Melinda. 2016. (S. M. A. R. T. S. Ser.). (ENG.). 128p. (J). (gr. 3-6). lib. bdg. 22.65 *(978-1-4965-3016-5(0)*, Stone Arch Bks.) Capstone.

—S. M. A. R. T. S. & the Missing UFO. Metz, Melinda. 2015. (S. M. A. R. T. S. Ser.). (ENG.). 128p. (J). (gr. 3-6). lib. bdg. 22.65 *(978-1-4965-0466-1(6)*, Stone Arch Bks.) Capstone.

—S. M. A. R. T. S. & the Poison Plates. Metz, Melinda. 2015. (S. M. A. R. T. S. Ser.). (ENG.). 128p. (J). (gr. 3-6). 22.65 *(978-1-4965-0464-7(X)*, Stone Arch Bks.) Capstone.

—Sausage Curls. Cordina, Annette. 2012. (ENG.). 40p. (J). 23.49 *(978-0-9871448-8-1(X))* JoJo Publishing AUS. Dist: Baker & Taylor Publisher Services (BTPS).

—A Year with Marmalade. Reynolds, Alison. 2013. (ENG.). 40p. (J). (gr. -1-1). 15.99 *(978-1-4424-8105-3(6)*, Little Simon) Little Simon.

McKenzie, Josie. Mrs. Potter's Cat. Abbott, D. K. 2007. 28p. per. 24.95 *(978-1-4241-8345-6(6))* America Star Bks.

McKeown, Ashley. My Dog Is the Tooth Fairy. Viele, Steven. 2018. (ENG.). 26p. (J). (gr. k-4). 18.99 *(978-1-7323550-0-2(2))*; pap. 13.99 *(978-1-7323550-2-6(9))* Lollypop Bks.

McKeown, Christian. Nightmare in the Woods. Anglen, Becca. 2007. 36p. (J). pap. 9.00 *(978-0-8059-7655-7(8))* Dorrance Publishing Co., Inc.

McKeown, David. Scotty's Dream: Book & CD. Fant, Donna. Axford, Elizabeth C., ed. 2004. (ENG.). 16p. (J). audio compact disk 14.99 *(978-1-931844-17-8(8),* PP1034) Piano Pr.

McKeown, Mark. Llamas Stencil Art. Make Believe Ideas Ltd. 2019. (Scratch & Sparkle Ser.). (ENG.). 50p. (J). spiral bd. *(978-1-78843-676-2(8))* Make Believe Ideas.

McKerral, Lynn. Tess Baker: With the Right Ingredients Anything Is Possible. LeRoux, Kathy. 2020. (ENG.). 36p. (J). ***(978-0-2288-2752-8(3))***; pap. ***(978-0-2288-2751-1(5))*** Tellwell Talent.

McKie, Roy. ¡Diez Manzanas en la Cabeza! (Ten Apples up on Top! Spanish Edition) Seuss. 2019. (Beginner Books(R) Ser.). (SPA.). 72p. (J). (gr. -1-2). 9.99 *(978-1-9848-3114-9(3))*; lib. bdg. 12.99 *(978-1-9848-9497-7(8))* Random Hse. Children's Bks. (Random Hse. Bks. for Young Readers).

—The Many Mice of Mr. Brice. Seuss, Dr. 2015. (Big Bright & Early Board Book Ser.). 24p. (J). (— 1). bds. 6.99 *(978-0-553-49733-5(2),* Random Hse. Bks. for Young Readers) Random Hse. Children's Bks.

McKig, Susan. Let's Praise & Play: Children's Christian Mini-Piano Book. Advance Cal-Tech Inc. Staff. Kung, Edward, ed. 36p. (J). (gr. -1-6). *(978-0-943759-00-5(5))* Advance Cal Tech, Inc.

McKillip Thornburgh, Rebecca, jt. illus. see Molnar, Albert.

McKimmie, Chris. Maisie Moo & Invisible Lucy. McKimmie, Chris. 2008. (ENG.). 32p. (J). (gr. k-2). 19.99 *(978-1-74175-134-5(9))* Allen & Unwin AUS. Dist: Independent Pubs. Group.

—Scarlett & the Scratchy Moon. McKimmie, Chris. 2015. (ENG.). 32p. (J). (gr. -1-1). 19.99 *(978-1-74331-515-6(5))* Allen & Unwin AUS. Dist: Independent Pubs. Group.

—Two Peas in a Pod. McKimmie, Chris. 2010. (ENG.). 32p. (J). (gr. -1-k). 23.99 *(978-1-74237-304-1(6))* Allen & Unwin AUS. Dist: Independent Pubs. Group.

McKinley, John. Camping Catastrophe! Klein, Abby. 2008. (Ready, Freddy! Ser.: Bk. 14). 95p. (J). (gr. -1-3). 11.65 *(978-0-7569-8837-1(3))* Perfection Learning Corp.

—Camping Catastrophe! Klein, Abby. 2008. (Ready, Freddy! Ser.: 14). (ENG.). 96p. (J). (gr. -1-3). 5.99 *(978-0-439-89594-1(4),* Blue Sky Pr., The) Scholastic, Inc.

—Don't Sit on My Lunch! Klein, Abby. 2005. (Ready, Freddy! Ser.: 4). (ENG.). 96p. (J). (gr. -1-3). 5.99 *(978-0-439-55602-6(3),* Blue Sky Pr., The) Scholastic, Inc.

—Gingerbread Jitters. Klein, Abby. 2016. 85p. (J). pap. *(978-0-545-93174-8(6))* Scholastic, Inc.

—Halloween Parade. Klein, Abby. 2009. (Ready, Freddy! Reader List: No. 3). 32p. (J). *(978-0-545-14174-1(5))* Scholastic, Inc.

—The Haunted Hayride. Klein, Abby. 2016. 90p. (J). *(978-0-545-93172-4(X))* Scholastic, Inc.

—Homework Hassles. Klein, Abby. 2004. (Ready, Freddy! Ser.: 3). (ENG.). 96p. (J). (gr. -1-3). 5.99 *(978-0-439-55600-2(7),* Blue Sky Pr., The) Scholastic, Inc.

—The King of Show-and-Tell. Klein, Abby. 2004. (Ready, Freddy! Ser.: 2). (ENG.). 96p. (J). (gr. -1-3). 5.99 *(978-0-439-55598-2(1),* Blue Sky Pr., The) Scholastic, Inc.

—Looking for Leprechauns. Klein, Abby. 2009. (Ready, Freddy! Reader List: No. 2). (J). pap. *(978-0-545-09933-2(1),* Scholastic) Scholastic, Inc.

—Monster Academy. Yolen, Jane & Stemple, Heidi E. Y. 2018. (ENG.). 32p. (J). (gr. -1-3). 17.99 *(978-1-338-09881-5(0),* Blue Sky Pr., The) Scholastic, Inc.

—The One Hundredth Day of School! Klein, Abby. 2008. (Ready, Freddy! Ser.: Bk. 13). 94p. (J). (gr. -1-3). 11.65 *(978-0-7569-8836-4(5))* Perfection Learning Corp.

—The Pumpkin Elf Mystery. Klein, Abby. 2007. (Ready, Freddy! Ser.: Bk. 11). 95p. (J). (gr. -1-3). 11.65 *(978-0-7569-8301-7(0))* Perfection Learning Corp.

—The Reading Race. Klein, Abby. 2013. (Ready, Freddy! Ser.: 27). (ENG.). 96p. (J). (gr. 2-5). pap. 5.99 *(978-0-545-55044-4(0))* Scholastic, Inc.

—Second Grade Rules! Klein, Abby. 2014. 85p. (J). pap. *(978-0-545-69031-7(5))* Scholastic, Inc.

—Secret Santa Surprise! Klein, Abby. 2015. 86p. (J). *(978-0-545-86357-5(0))* Scholastic, Inc.

—Stop That Hamster! Klein, Abby. 2008. (Ready, Freddy! Ser.: Bk. 12). 95p. (gr. -1-3). 16.00 *(978-0-7569-8300-0(2))* Perfection Learning Corp.

—Thanks for Giving. Klein, Abby. 2009. (Ready, Freddy! Reader List: No. 4). 32p. (J). pap. *(978-0-545-14176-5(1))* Scholastic, Inc.

—Thanksgiving Turkey Trouble. Klein, Abby. 2008. (Ready, Freddy! Ser.: Bk. 15). 95p. (gr. -1-3). 16.00 *(978-0-7569-8838-8(1))* Perfection Learning Corp.

—Tooth Trouble. Klein, Abby. 2004. (Ready, Freddy! Ser.: 1). (ENG.). 96p. (J). (gr. -1-3). 5.99 *(978-0-439-55596-8(5),* Blue Sky Pr., The) Scholastic, Inc.

McKinley, Kay, photos by. Un Desfile de Patrones. Freese, Joan. 2007. (Matemáticas en Nuestro Mundo (Math in Our World) Ser.). (SPA., 24p. (gr. 1-2). lib. bdg. 23.00 *(978-0-8368-8491-3(4),* Weekly Reader Leveled Readers) Stevens, Gareth Publishing LLLP.

—Midiendo para una Búsqueda del Tesoro. Marrewa, Jennifer. 2008. (Matemáticas en Nuestro Mundo - Nivel 2 (Math in Our World - Level 2) Ser.). (SPA., 24p. (gr. 1-4). lib. bdg. 23.00 *(978-0-8368-9025-9(6),* Weekly Reader Leveled Readers) Stevens, Gareth Publishing LLLP.

—Patterns on Parade. Freese, Joan. 2007. (Math in Our World Ser.). 24p. (gr. 1-2). lib. bdg. 23.00 *(978-0-8368-8473-9(6),* Weekly Reader Leveled Readers) Stevens, Gareth Publishing LLLP.

—Usamos Matemáticas en la Fiesta del Salon. Rauen, Amy & Ayers, Amy. 2007. (Matemáticas en Nuestro Mundo (Math in Our World) Ser.). (SPA., 24p. (gr. 1-2). lib. bdg. 23.00 *(978-0-8368-8493-7(0),* Weekly Reader Leveled Readers) Stevens, Gareth Publishing LLLP.

—Using Math at the Class Party. Rauen, Amy. 2007. (Math in Our World Ser.). 24p. (gr. 1-2). lib. bdg. 23.00 *(978-0-8368-8475-3(2),* Weekly Reader Leveled Readers) Stevens, Gareth Publishing LLLP.

—Using Money on a Shopping Trip. Marrewa, Jennifer. 2008. (Math in Our World: Level 2 Ser.). 24p. (gr. 1-4). lib. bdg. 23.00 *(978-0-8368-9004-4(3),* Weekly Reader Leveled Readers) Stevens, Gareth Publishing LLLP.

—Vamos a Usar Dinero en un Viaje de Compras. Marrewa, Jennifer. 2008. (Matemáticas en Nuestro Mundo - Nivel 2 (Math in Our World - Level 2) Ser.). (SPA., 24p. (gr. 1-4). lib. bdg. 23.00 *(978-0-8368-9022-8(1),* Weekly Reader Leveled Readers) Stevens, Gareth Publishing LLLP.

McKinney, Brandon. Loki. Worley, Rob M. 2010. (Short Tales Norse Myths Ser.). (ENG.). 32p. (J). (gr. 1-4). 27.07 *(978-1-60270-567-8(4),* 13463, Short Tales) Magic Wagon.

McKinney, Malachy. Pep, Polish & Paint. Harper, Helena. 2011. (ENG.). 40p. (J). pap. 8.86 *(978-0-9570530-0-7(2))* Harper Bks. GBR. Dist: Gardners Bks. Ltd.

McKinnon, Darrell A. Naynuk the Special Gecko. McKinnon, Darrell A. Thomas, Joan, ed. 2017. (Naynuk the Special Gecko Ser.: Vol. 1). (ENG.). 46p. (YA). (gr. 7-12). pap. 8.99 *(978-0-9989938-0-5(8))* Ravishing Gecko Publishing.

McKinnon, Gay. The Smallest Carbon Footprint in the Land & Other Eco-Tales. Morgan, Anne. 2012. 82p. pap. *(978-1-922120-23-6(5),* IP Kidz) Interactive Pubns. Pty, Ltd.

McKinnon, Heidi. Baz & Benz. McKinnon, Heidi. 2020. (ENG.). 40p. (J). (gr. -1-3). 17.99 ***(978-1-5344-6802-3(1),*** Simon & Schuster Bks. For Young Readers) Simon & Schuster Bks. For Young Readers.

McKinnon, Heidi. I Just Ate My Friend. McKinnon, Heidi. (ENG.). 40p. (J). (gr. -1-3). 2019. 7.99 *(978-1-5344-6668-5(1))*; 2018. 17.99 *(978-1-5344-1032-9(5))* Simon & Schuster Bks. For Young Readers. (Simon & Schuster Bks. For Young Readers).

McKinnon, James. Koala Country: A Story of an Australian Eucalyptus Forest. Dennard, Deborah. 2005. (Wild Habitats Ser.: Vol. 17). (ENG.). 36p. (J). (gr. 1-4). 15.95 *(978-1-56899-887-9(2),* B7018) Soundprints.

McKinnon, Joy. The Angel Explains Christmas Blessings. Mancil, Arlene. 2008. 16p. pap. 24.95 *(978-1-60813-297-3(8))* America Star Bks.

McKinnon, Margie & McKinnon, Tom W. Repair for Kids: A Children's Program for Recovery from Incest & Childhood Sexual Abuse. McKinnon, Margie & McKinnon, Tom W. 2008. 92p. (J). pap. 34.95 *(978-1-932690-57-6(3))* Loving Healing Pr., Inc.

McKinnon, Tom W., jt. illus. see McKinnon, Margie.

McKinsey, McKinsey. Zeeko, Coloring - Story Book. Brady, Nita. 2020. (ENG.). 28p. (J). pap. 6.95 ***(978-1-950768-10-3(4))*** ProsePress.

McKinsey, Ruth. The Little House Who Didn't Lose Hope Second Edition. Brady, Nita. 2020. (ENG.). 32p. (J). (gr. k-6). 14.95 ***(978-1-950768-20-2(1))***; pap. 8.95 ***(978-1-950768-19-6(8))*** ProsePress.

—The Little House Who Didn't Lose Hope Second Edition Coloring - Story Book. Brady, Nita. 2020. (ENG.). 26p. (J). (gr. k-6). pap. 6.95 ***(978-1-950768-21-9(X))*** ProsePress.

—Zeeko: The Bunny Who Lost His Way. Brady, Nita. 2019. (ENG.). 34p. (J). (gr. k-6). pap. 12.95 ***(978-1-950768-05-9(8))*** ProsePress.

McKinsey, Ruth. What's Going on at Noah's Farm? McKinsey, Ruth. 2020. (ENG.). 82p. (J). (gr. k-6). pap. 14.95 ***(978-1-950768-11-0(2))*** ProsePress.

McKissock, Charmaine, jt. illus. see Peecock, Simon.

McKone, Mike, et al. Avengers Academy: the Complete Collection Vol. 1. 2018. (ENG.). 400p. (YA). (gr. 8-17). pap. 34.99 *(978-1-302-90946-8(0))* Marvel Worldwide, Inc.

—Spider-Man: Brand New Day - the Complete Collection Vol. 4. 2018. 504p. (YA). (gr. 8-17). pap. 39.99 *(978-1-302-90799-0(9))* Marvel Worldwide, Inc.

McKone, Mike, jt. illus. see Calafiore, Jim.

McKowen, Scott. The Adventures & the Memoirs of Sherlock Holmes. Doyle, A. Conan. 2004. (Sterling Unabridged Classics Ser.). 576p. (J). (gr. 5). 14.95 *(978-1-4027-1453-5(X))* Sterling Publishing Co., Inc.

—The Adventures of Huckleberry Finn. Twain, Mark. 2006. (Sterling Unabridged Classics Ser.). 320p. (J). (gr. 5-7). 14.95 *(978-1-4027-2600-2(7))* Sterling Publishing Co., Inc.

—The Adventures of Tom Sawyer. Twain, Mark. 2004. (Sterling Unabridged Classics Ser.). 224p. (J). (gr. 5). 9.95 *(978-1-4027-1460-3(2))* Sterling Publishing Co., Inc.

—Alice's Adventures in Wonderland. Carroll, Lewis. 2005. (Sterling Unabridged Classics Ser.). 136p. (J). (gr. 5-9). 9.95 *(978-1-4027-2502-9(7))* Sterling Publishing Co., Inc.

—Anne of Avonlea. Montgomery, L. M. 2008. (Sterling Unabridged Classics Ser.). 256p. (J). 9.95 *(978-1-4027-5428-9(0))* Sterling Publishing Co., Inc.

—Anne of Green Gables. Montgomery, L. M. 2004. (Sterling Unabridged Classics Ser.). 312p. (J). (gr. 5). 9.95 *(978-1-4027-1451-1(3))* Sterling Publishing Co., Inc.

—Around the World in 80 Days. Verne, Jules. 2008. (Sterling Unabridged Classics Ser.). 224p. (J). 9.95 *(978-1-4027-5427-2(2))* Sterling Publishing Co., Inc.

—Black Beauty. Sewell, Anna. 2004. (Sterling Unabridged Classics Ser.). 208p. (J). (gr. 5). 9.95 *(978-1-4027-1452-8(1))* Sterling Publishing Co., Inc.

—The Call of the Wild & White Fang. London, Jack. 2004. (Sterling Unabridged Classics Ser.). 312p. (J). (gr. 5). 9.95 *(978-1-4027-1455-9(6))* Sterling Publishing Co., Inc.

—A Christmas Carol. Dickens, Charles. 2009. (Sterling Unabridged Classics Ser.). 96p. (Orig.). (J). (gr. 5). 9.95 *(978-1-4027-6690-9(4))* Sterling Publishing Co., Inc.

—Dracula. Stoker, Bram. 2010. (Sterling Unabridged Classics Ser.). 416p. (J). (gr. 5-18). 14.95 *(978-1-4027-7324-2(2))* Sterling Publishing Co., Inc.

—Grimm's Fairy Tales. Grimm, Jacob & Grimm, Wilhelm. 2009. (Sterling Unabridged Classics Ser.). 288p. (J). (gr. 5). 9.95 *(978-1-4027-6702-9(1))* Sterling Publishing Co., Inc.

—Journey to the Center of the Earth. Verne, Jules. 2007. (Sterling Unabridged Classics Ser.). 256p. (J). 9.95 *(978-1-4027-4337-5(8),* 1272698) Sterling Publishing Co., Inc.

—The Jungle Book. Kipling, Rudyard. Rowe, John, ed. 2007. (Sterling Unabridged Classics Ser.). 352p. (J). 14.95 *(978-1-4027-4340-5(8))* Sterling Publishing Co., Inc.

—The Legend of Sleepy Hollow & Other Stories. Irving, Washington. 2013. (Sterling Unabridged Classics Ser.). 96p. (J). (gr. 5). 9.95 *(978-1-4549-0871-5(8))* Sterling Publishing Co., Inc.

—A Little Princess. Burnett, Frances Hodgson. 2004. (Sterling Unabridged Classics Ser.). 208p. (J). (gr. 5). 9.95 *(978-1-4027-1454-2(8))* Sterling Publishing Co., Inc.

—Little Women. Alcott, Louisa May. 2004. (Sterling Unabridged Classics Ser.). 536p. (J). (gr. 5). 14.95 *(978-1-4027-1458-0(0))* Sterling Publishing Co., Inc.

—The Merry Adventures of Robin Hood. Pyle, Howard. 2004. (Sterling Unabridged Classics Ser.). 344p. (J). (gr. 5). 14.95 *(978-1-4027-1456-6(4))* Sterling Publishing Co., Inc.

—Oliver Twist. Dickens, Charles. 2008. (Sterling Unabridged Classics Ser.). 464p. (J). 14.95 *(978-1-4027-5425-8(6))* Sterling Publishing Co., Inc.

—Peter Pan. Barrie, J. M. 2008. (Sterling Unabridged Classics Ser.). 160p. (J). 9.95 *(978-1-4027-5426-5(4))* Sterling Publishing Co., Inc.

—Pinocchio. Collodi, Carlo. 2014. (Sterling Unabridged Classics Ser.). 184p. (J). (gr. 5). 9.95 *(978-1-4549-1220-0(0))* Sterling Publishing Co., Inc.

—Pollyanna. Porter, Eleanor H. 2013. (Sterling Unabridged Classics Ser.). 208p. (J). (gr. 5). 9.95 *(978-1-4027-9718-7(4))* Sterling Publishing Co., Inc.

—Robinson Crusoe. Dafoe, Daniel. 2011. (Sterling Unabridged Classics Ser.). 288p. (J). 9.95 *(978-1-4027-8406-4(6))* Sterling Publishing Co., Inc.

—The Secret Garden. Burnett, Frances Hodgson. 2004. (Sterling Unabridged Classics Ser.). 248p. (J). (gr. 5). 9.95 *(978-1-4027-1459-7(9))* Sterling Publishing Co., Inc.

—The Stories of Edgar Allan Poe. Poe, Edgar Allen. 2010. (Sterling Unabridged Classics Ser.). 344p. (J). (gr. 5-18). 14.95 *(978-1-4027-7325-9(0))* Sterling Publishing Co., Inc.

—The Story of King Arthur & His Knights. Pyle, Howard. 2005. (Sterling Unabridged Classics Ser.). (ENG.). 320p. (J). (gr. 5-9). 14.95 *(978-1-4027-2503-6(5),* 1252056) Sterling Publishing Co., Inc.

—The Strange Case of Dr. Jekyll & Mr. Hyde. Stevenson, Robert Louis. 2011. (Sterling Unabridged Classics Ser.). 96p. (J). 9.95 *(978-1-4027-8402-6(3))* Sterling Publishing Co., Inc.

—The Swiss Family Robinson. Wyss, Johann David. 2006. (Sterling Unabridged Classics Ser.). 352p. (J). (gr. 5-7). 14.95 *(978-1-4027-2602-6(3))* Sterling Publishing Co., Inc.

—Treasure Island. Stevenson, Robert Louis. 2004. (Sterling Unabridged Classics Ser.). 232p. (J). (gr. 5). 9.95 *(978-1-4027-1457-3(2))* Sterling Publishing Co., Inc.

—The Voyages of Doctor Dolittle. Lofting, Hugh. 2012. (Sterling Unabridged Classics Ser.). 256p. (J). (gr. 5). 9.95 *(978-1-4027-9721-7(4))* Sterling Publishing Co., Inc.

McKowen, Scott, jt. illus. see Baum, L. Frank.

McKowen, Scott, jt. illus. see Grahame, Kenneth.

McLachlan, J. P. Twilla & the Fuzzy Finger. McLachlan, Joni. 2012. 20p. pap. *(978-0-9878035-2-8(2))* Insomniac Pr.

McLachlan, Josephine. Maddy Wylde. McLachlan, Josephine. 2018. (ENG.). 158p. (J). pap. 7.99 *(978-1-7267-0113-6(1))* Independently Published.

McLachlin, Michelle. F@#k It I'm Writing: A Companion Journal for the Mad Writer in White Floral. McLachlin, Michelle. 2020. (F@#k It I'm Writing Ser.: Vol. 4). (ENG.). 102p. (J). pap. 6.50 ***(978-1-6544-9603-6(0))*** Independently Published.

Mclanson, Matt. Dark Ryder. Brown, Liz. 2004. (New Series Canada). 91p. (J). pap. *(978-1-897039-02-1(6))* High Interest Publishing (HIP).

McLaren, Chesley. Pippa by Design: A Story of Ballet & Costumes. Logan, Claudia. 2019. (ENG.). 192p. (J). 16.99 *(978-0-374-35956-0(3),* 900078776, Farrar, Straus & Giroux (BYR)) Farrar, Straus & Giroux.

—Princess Lessons. Cabot, Meg. 2003. (Princess Diaries Guidebook Ser.). (ENG.). 144p. (YA). (gr. 8-18). 15.99 *(978-0-06-052677-1(7),* HarperTeen) HarperCollins Pubs.

McLaren, Duncan. Esther: The Brave Queen. Mackenzie, Carine. 2008. (Bible Time Ser.). (ENG.). 32p. (J). (gr. -1-2). pap. 4.50 *(978-1-84550-195-2(0),* 3a633117-1151-4322-8aac-7d0065bd7217) Christian Focus Pubns. GBR. Dist: Baker & Taylor Publisher Services (BTPS).

—Gideon: Soldier of God. MacKenzie, Carine. 2014. (Bible Time Ser.). (ENG.). 32p. (J). (gr. -1-2). pap. 4.50 *(978-1-84550-196-9(9),* 12f9178d-14f2-48f9-9d17-6fdd7df2c34a) Christian Focus Pubns. GBR. Dist: Baker & Taylor Publisher Services (BTPS).

—Hannah: The Mother Who Prayer. MacKenzie, Carine. 2013. (Bible Time Ser.). (ENG.). 32p. (J). (gr. -1-2). pap. 4.50 *(978-1-84550-163-1(2),* 5372f378-0fbe-4d23-bc12-c966a17e3cd3) Christian Focus Pubns. GBR. Dist: Baker & Taylor Publisher Services (BTPS).

—John: The Baptist. MacKenzie, Carine. 2013. (Bible Time Ser.). (ENG.). 32p. (J). (gr. -1-2). pap. 4.50 *(978-1-84550-164-8(0),* 9bf1065e-4c32-44ca-9d6b-c073888b18ed) Christian Focus Pubns. GBR. Dist: Baker & Taylor Publisher Services (BTPS).

—Jonah: The Runaway Preacher. Mackenzie, Carine. 2013. (Bible Time Ser.). (ENG.). 32p. (J). (gr. -1-2). pap. 4.50 *(978-1-84550-165-5(9),* 4e6a8d6b-d494-4d78-954c-788b58ced69e) Christian Focus Pubns. GBR. Dist: Baker & Taylor Publisher Services (BTPS).

—Joshua: The Brave Leader. Mackenzie, Carine. 2012. (Bible Time Ser.). (ENG.). 32p. (J). (gr. -1-2). pap. 4.50 *(978-1-84550-166-2(7),* a60c8948-a8eb-44f0-8548-36f6638ae27b) Christian Focus Pubns. GBR. Dist: Baker & Taylor Publisher Services (BTPS).

—Martha & Mary: Friends of Jesus. Mackenzie, Carine. 2014. (Bible Time Ser.). (ENG.). 32p. (J). (gr. -1-2). pap. 4.50 *(978-1-84550-167-9(5),* ffc96adc-c3a4-4d8b-b6a8-e59ecc5c5948) Christian Focus Pubns. GBR. Dist: Baker & Taylor Publisher Services (BTPS).

—Mary: Mother of Jesus. MacKenzie, Carine. 2012. (Bible Time Ser.). (ENG.). 32p. (J). (gr. -1-2). pap. 4.50 *(978-1-84550-168-6(3),* e0d9ae2d-fd36-46c1-8389-34ab09c21754) Christian Focus Pubns. GBR. Dist: Baker & Taylor Publisher Services (BTPS).

—Nehemiah: Builder for God. MacKenzie, Carine & Ross, Neil M. 2014. (Bible Time Ser.). (ENG.). 32p. (J). (gr. -1-2). pap. 4.50 *(978-1-84550-169-3(1),* c185c074-c081-4ab6-8e93-e5a38b42fedb) Christian Focus Pubns. GBR. Dist: Baker & Taylor Publisher Services (BTPS).

—Peter: The Apostle. MacKenzie, Carine. 2014. (Bible Time Ser.). (ENG.). 32p. (J). (gr. -1-2). pap. 4.50 *(978-1-84550-170-9(5),* 16798b96-df80-416b-87e8-9538ff5ba81d) Christian Focus Pubns. GBR. Dist: Baker & Taylor Publisher Services (BTPS).

—Peter: The Fisherman. MacKenzie, Carine. 2014. (Bible Time Ser.). (ENG.). 32p. (J). (gr. -1-2). pap. 4.50 *(978-1-84550-171-6(3),* 3328658f-1630-4857-94a0-e3278d56e7c2) Christian Focus Pubns. GBR. Dist: Baker & Taylor Publisher Services (BTPS).

—Rebekah: The Mother of Twins. Mackenzie, Carine. 2012. (Bible Time Ser.). (ENG.). 32p. (J). (gr. -1-2). pap. 4.50 *(978-1-84550-172-3(1),* c123322f-a013-4fcb-ba6a-c6345b65beee) Christian Focus Pubns. GBR. Dist: Baker & Taylor Publisher Services (BTPS).

—Ruth: The Harvest Girl. MacKenzie, Carine. 2012. (Bible Time Ser.). (ENG.). 32p. (J). (gr. -1-2). pap. 4.50 *(978-1-84550-173-0(X),* c16d3e16-00b4-417b-bfec-b9e86731d0de) Christian Focus Pubns. GBR. Dist: Baker & Taylor Publisher Services (BTPS).

—Simon Peter: The Disciple. MacKenzie, Carine. 2014. (Bible Time Ser.). (ENG.). 32p. (J). (gr. -1-2). pap. 4.50 *(978-1-84550-174-7(8),* 82b5abe8-64fa-4a40-b8ce-6da3758f81d5) Christian Focus Pubns. GBR. Dist: Baker & Taylor Publisher Services (BTPS).

McLaughlin, David & Rocheleau, Paul, photos by. The Unfolding History of the Berkshires. McLaughlin, David. 2007. 92p. (J). pap. 18.95 *(978-0-9763500-5-7(X))* Pentacle Pr.

McLaughlin, Jessica. Bella's Big Wish. Davis, Ronda. 2019. (Adventures of Bella Noelle Ser.: Vol. 1). (ENG.). 46p. (J). pap. 14.95 ***(978-1-7021-1162-1(8))*** Independently Published.

—Bella's Big Wish Coloring Book. Davis, Ronda. 2019. (Adventures of Bella Noelle Ser.: Vol. 1). (ENG.). 46p. (J). pap. 12.95 ***(978-1-6712-3132-0(5))*** Independently Published.

McLaughlin, Julie. The Art of the Possible: An Everyday Guide to Politics. Keenan, Edward. 2020. (ENG.). 64p. (J). (gr. 5-8). pap. 10.95 *(978-1-77147-413-9(0))* Owlkids Bks. Inc. CAN. Dist: Publishers Group West (PGW).

McLaughlin, Julie. For Which We Stand: How Our Government Works & Why It Matters. Foster, Jeff. 2020. (ENG.). 176p. (J). (gr. 3-7). pap. 12.99 ***(978-1-338-64308-4(8))*** Scholastic, Inc.

McLaughlin, Julie. Little Cloud: The Science of a Hurricane. Wagstaffe, Johanna. 2020. (ENG.). 32p. (J). (gr. 1-3). 19.95 *(978-1-4598-2184-2(X))* Orca Bk. Pubs. USA.

—Meatless? A Fresh Look at What You Eat. Elton, Sarah. 2017. (ENG.). 48p. (J). (gr. 4-8). 16.95 *(978-1-926818-43-6(1))* Owlkids Bks. Inc. CAN. Dist: Publishers Group West (PGW).

—The Someday Birds. Pla, Sally J. (ENG.). (J). (gr. 3-7). 2018. 352p. pap. 6.99 *(978-0-06-244577-3(4))*; 2017. 336p. 16.99 *(978-0-06-244576-6(6))* HarperCollins Pubs.

—Wishing Day. Myracle, Lauren. 2016. (Wishing Day Ser.: 1). (ENG.). 336p. (J). (gr. 3-7). 16.99 *(978-0-06-234206-5(1),* Tegen, Katherine Bks) HarperCollins Pubs.

McLaughlin, Kimber. Sandra's Bee Restaurant. McLaughlin, Leona. 2019. (ENG.). 26p. (J). pap. 9.25 ***(978-1-0870-7267-8(0))*** Independently Published.

McLaughlin, Linda. What Would a Dinosaur Eat for Lunch? Gomlick, Judy. 2016. (ENG.). (J). pap. 15.95 *(978-1-4787-0864-3(6))* Outskirts Pr., Inc.

McLaughlin, Nadine. Sebastian's Roo. Kochakji, Erin. 2016. (ENG.). (J). pap. 12.99 *(978-0-692-79724-2(6))* Graphics North.

McLaughlin, Tom. Captain Buckleboots on the Naughty Step. Sperring, Mark. 2011. (ENG.). 32p. (J). (gr. -1-1). 22.44 *(978-0-7641-4678-7(5),* B.E.S. Publishing) Peterson's.

—Catch That Rat. Hart, Caryl. 2013. (ENG.). 32p. (J). pap. 8.99 *(978-1-84738-931-2(7),* Simon & Schuster Children's) Simon & Schuster, Ltd. GBR. Dist: Simon & Schuster, Inc.

—The Sheep Won't Sleep! Joblins, Curtis. 2016. (ENG.). 32p. (J). (— 1). pap. 9.99 *(978-1-4052-6711-3(9))* Egmont Bks., Ltd. GBR. Dist: Independent Pubs. Group.

McLaughlin, Tom. Up, up & Away. McLaughlin, Tom. 2016. 32p. (J). *(978-1-4088-7015-0(0),* 292009, Bloomsbury Children's Bks.) Bloomsbury Publishing Plc.

McLaughlin, Zack. What Eats What in a Forest Food Chain, 1 vol. Amstutz, Lisa J. 2012. (Food Chains Ser.). (ENG.). 24p. (J). (gr. 2-4). 26.65 *(978-1-4048-7388-9(0))*; pap. 8.95 *(978-1-4048-7692-7(8))* Capstone. (Picture Window Bks.).

—What Eats What in an Ocean Food Chain, 1 vol. Slade, Suzanne. 2012. (Food Chains Ser.). (ENG.). 24p. (J). (gr. 2-4). pap. 8.95 *(978-1-4048-7696-5(0),* Picture Window Bks.) Capstone.

M

McLean, Andrew. Bob the Railway Dog: The True Story of an Adventurous Dog. Fenton, Corinne. 2016. (ENG.). 32p. (J). (gr. k-3). 16.99 *(978-0-7636-8097-8(4))* Candlewick Pr.

McLean, Rachael. Bedtime. Kim, W. Harry & Clever Publishing. 2019. (Animal Families Ser.). (ENG.). 20p. (J). (gr. -1 — 1). bds. 8.99 *(978-1-948418-69-0(X)*, 331764) Clever Media Group.

—Being a Team Player Online. Lovett, Amber. 2020. (Create & Share: Thinking Digitally Ser.). (ENG.). 24p. (J). (gr. 1-4). pap. 12.79 *(978-1-5341-6144-3(9)*, 214576); lib. bdg. 28.50 *(978-1-5341-5914-3(2)*, 214575) Cherry Lake Publishing.

—Building a Digital Footprint. Matteson, Adrienne. 2020. (Create & Share: Thinking Digitally Ser.). (ENG.). 24p. (J). (gr. 1-4). pap. 12.79 *(978-1-5341-6139-9(2)*, 214556); lib. bdg. 28.50 *(978-1-5341-5909-9(6)*, 214555) Cherry Lake Publishing.

—Busy Baby Animals: Spin the Wheel to Learn about Baby Animals! Clever Publishing. 2020. (Clever Wheels Ser.). (ENG.). 8p. (J). (gr. -1 — 1). bds. 8.99 *(978-1-949998-36-8(3))* Clever Media Group.

—Busy Christmas. Clever Publishing. 2019. (Clever Wheels Ser.). (ENG.). 8p. (J). (gr. -1 — 1). bds. 8.99 *(978-1-949998-35-1(5))* Clever Media Group.

—Clean-Up Time. Kim, W. Harry & Clever Publishing. 2019. (Animal Families Ser.). (ENG.). 20p. (J). (gr. -1 — 1). bds. 8.99 *(978-1-948418-70-6(3)*, 331765) Clever Media Group.

—Creating Digital Videos. Lovett, Amber. 2020. (Create & Share: Thinking Digitally Ser.). (ENG.). 24p. (J). (gr. 1-4). pap. 12.79 *(978-1-5341-6142-9(2)*, 214568); lib. bdg. 28.50 *(978-1-5341-5912-9(6)*, 214567) Cherry Lake Publishing.

—Manes & Tails - Horses & Unicorns. Copper, Jenny. 2019. (Paint with Water Ser.). (ENG.). 32p. (J). (gr. -1-2). 12.99 *(978-1-78700-959-2(9))* Top That! Publishing PLC GBR. Dist: Independent Pubs. Group.

—Recording Podcasts. Fontichiaro, Kristin. 2020. (Create & Share: Thinking Digitally Ser.). (ENG.). 24p. (J). (gr. 1-4). pap. 12.79 *(978-1-5341-6143-6(0)*, 214572); lib. bdg. 28.50 *(978-1-5341-5913-6(4)*, 214571) Cherry Lake Publishing.

—Respecting Others Online. Truesdell, Ann. 2020. (Create & Share: Thinking Digitally Ser.). (ENG.). 24p. (J). (gr. 1-4). pap. 12.79 *(978-1-5341-6137-5(6)*, 214548); lib. bdg. 28.50 *(978-1-5341-5907-5(X)*, 214547) Cherry Lake Publishing.

—Roars & Claws - Animals. Copper, Jenny. 2019. (Paint with Water Ser.). (ENG.). 32p. (J). (gr. -1-2). 12.99 *(978-1-78958-145-4(1))* Top That! Publishing PLC GBR. Dist: Independent Pubs. Group.

—Scales & Tails - Dinosaurs. Copper, Jenny. 2019. (Paint with Water Ser.). (ENG.). 32p. (J). (gr. -1-2). 12.99 *(978-1-78700-961-5(0))* Top That! Publishing PLC GBR. Dist: Independent Pubs. Group.

—Searching Online. Fontichiaro, Kristin. 2020. (Create & Share: Thinking Digitally Ser.). (ENG.). 24p. (J). (gr. 1-4). pap. 12.79 *(978-1-5341-6138-2(4)*, 214552); lib. bdg. 28.50 *(978-1-5341-5908-2(8)*, 214551) Cherry Lake Publishing.

—Sharing Photos Online. Lovett, Amber. 2020. (Create & Share: Thinking Digitally Ser.). (ENG.). 24p. (J). (gr. 1-4). pap. 12.79 *(978-1-5341-6141-2(4)*, 214564); lib. bdg. 28.50 *(978-1-5341-5911-2(8)*, 214563) Cherry Lake Publishing.

—Staying Safe Online. Matteson, Adrienne. 2020. (Create & Share: Thinking Digitally Ser.). (ENG.). 24p. (J). (gr. 1-4). pap. 12.79 *(978-1-5341-6140-5(6)*, 214560); lib. bdg. 28.50 *(978-1-5341-5910-5(X)*, 214559) Cherry Lake Publishing.

—Time to Learn. Kim, W. Harry & Clever Publishing. 2019. (Animal Families Ser.). (ENG.). 20p. (J). (gr. -1 — 1). bds. 8.99 *(978-1-948418-71-3(1))* Clever Media Group.

—Wheels & Steel - Machines. Copper, Jenny. 2019. (Paint with Water Ser.). (ENG.). 32p. (J). (gr. -1-2). 12.99 *(978-1-78958-144-7(3))* Top That! Publishing PLC GBR. Dist: Independent Pubs. Group.

McLean, Rachael. My Best Friend Is a Dragon: A Lift-The-Flap Book. McLean, Rachael. 2020. 14p. (J). (-k). bds. 7.99 *(978-0-593-09399-3(2)*, Penguin Workshop) Penguin Young Readers Group.

McLeer, Michael. Hip-Hop Alphabet. Abrams, Howie. 2019. (ENG.). 32p. (J). 14.99 *(978-1-68261-866-0(8))* Permuted Press.

McLeer, Michael Kaves. Hip-Hop Alphabet 2. Abrams, Howie. 2019. (ENG.). 32p. (J). 14.99 *(978-1-68261-845-5(5))* Permuted Press.

McLellan, Stu. The House of the Nine Doors: Band 12/Copper (Collins Big Cat) Don, Lari. 2015. (Collins Big Cat Ser.). (ENG.). 32p. (J). (gr. 3-3). pap. 9.99 *(978-0-00-812772-5(7))* HarperCollins Pubs. Ltd. GBR. Dist: Independent Pubs. Group.

McLellan, Stu. Jolly Phonic Little Word Books: In Print Letters (AE) Wernham, Sara. 2020. (ENG.). (J). pap. 28.00 ***(978-1-84414-714-4(2)***, Jolly Phonics) Jolly Learning, Ltd. GBR. Dist: American International Distribution Corp.

McLellan, Stu. Play Card Games in French. Bougard, Marie-Thérèse. 2018. (Play Card Games Ser.). (ENG.). 48p. (J). (gr. 1-4). pap. 15.99 *(978-1-909767-90-4(5))* B Small Publishing GBR. Dist: Independent Pubs. Group.

—Play Card Games in Spanish. Bougard, Marie-Thérèse. 2018. (Play Card Games Ser.). (ENG.). 48p. (J). (gr. 1-4). pap. 15.99 *(978-1-909767-91-1(3))* B Small Publishing GBR. Dist: Independent Pubs. Group.

McLelland, Kate. Press Out & Color: Christmas Ornaments. Nosy Crow. 2017. (ENG.). 20p. (J). (gr. 2-5). 15.99 *(978-0-7636-9618-4(8)*, Nosy Crow) Candlewick Pr.

—Press Out & Color: Easter Eggs. Nosy Crow. 2018. (ENG.). 20p. (J). (gr. 2-5). 15.99 *(978-0-7636-9692-4(7)*, Nosy Crow) Candlewick Pr.

—Press Out & Color: Unicorns. Nosy Crow. 2019. (ENG.). 24p. (J). (gr. 2-5). 12.99 *(978-1-5362-0708-8(X)*, Nosy Crow) Candlewick Pr.

—There Was a Wee Lassie Who Swallowed a Midgie, 50 vols. Colby, Rebecca. 2014. (ENG.). 24p. (J). 11.95 *(978-1-78250-048-3(0)*, Kelpies) Floris Bks. GBR. Dist: Consortium Bk. Sales & Distribution.

—What's Inside? Smith, Miranda. 2019. (ENG.). 12p. (J). (gr. -1-k). 21.99 *(978-1-4052-8863-7(9))* Egmont Bks., Ltd. GBR. Dist: Independent Pubs. Group.

—Where's My Llama? Davies, Becky. 2020. (ENG.). 10p. (J). (— 1). bds. 8.99 *(978-1-68412-978-2(8)*, Silver Dolphin Bks.) Printers Row Publishing Group.

McLennan, Connie. Domítila: A Cinderella Tale from the Mexican Tradition, 1 vol. 2014. (Cinderella Ser.). (ENG.). 32p. (J). (gr. 2-5). pap. 10.95 *(978-1-885008-43-5(0)*, d2baee7f-f2ee-4c16-92de-0ebf1d12d259, Shen's Bks.) Lee & Low Bks., Inc.

McLennan, Connie. Domítila: Cuento de la Cenicienta Basado en la Tradición Mexicana, 1 vol. 2020. (Cinderella Ser.). (SPA.). 32p. (J). (gr. 2-5). pap. 10.95 ***(978-1-64379-453-2(1)***, 0d374a2a-cff6-422b-a8ee-8c7bb6182525, Shen's Bks.) Lee & Low Bks., Inc.

McLennan, Connie. A Floresta Tropical Se Espalhou Por Toda Parte (the Rainforest Grew All Around in Portuguese) Mitchell, Susan K. Sacciotto, Adriana & Wiedemann, Tatiana, trs. 2019. (POR.). 32p. (J). (gr. k-3). pap. 11.95 *(978-1-64351-327-0(3))* Arbordale Publishing.

—Octavia & Her Purple Ink Cloud, 1 vol. Rathmell, Donna & Rathmell, Doreen. 2006. (ENG.). 32p. (J). (gr. -1-2). 15.95 *(978-0-9764943-5-5(3))*; pap. 9.95 *(978-1-60718-586-4(5))* Arbordale Publishing.

—The Rainforest Grew All Around, 1 vol. Mitchell, Susan K. 2007. (ENG.). 32p. (J). (gr. -1-2). 16.95 *(978-0-9768823-6-7(1))*; pap. 8.95 *(978-0-9777423-8-7(5)*, 9780977742387) Arbordale Publishing.

—Ready, Set ... Wait! What Animals Do Before a Hurricane, 1 vol. Zelch, Patti R. 2010. (ENG.). 32p. (J). (gr. -1-4). 16.95 *(978-1-60718-072-2(3))*; pap. 8.95 *(978-1-60718-083-8(9))* Arbordale Publishing.

—River Beds: Sleeping in the World's Rivers, 1 vol. Karwoski, Gail Langer. 2008. (ENG.). 32p. (J). (gr. -1-3). 16.95 *(978-0-9777423-4-9(2))*; pap. 8.95 *(978-1-934359-31-0(9))* Arbordale Publishing.

—Scottish Alphabet, 1 vol. Pittman, Rickey. 2008. (ABC Ser.). (ENG.). 32p. (J). (gr. 1-3). 16.99 *(978-1-58980-596-5(8)*, Pelican Publishing) Arcadia Publishing.

—Water Beds: Sleeping in the Ocean, 1 vol. Karwoski, Gail Langer. 2005. (ENG.). 32p. (J). (gr. -1-3). 15.95 *(978-0-9764943-1-7(0))*; pap. 9.95 *(978-1-934359-01-3(7)*, 9781934359013) Arbordale Publishing.

—The Wishing Tree. Thong, Roseanne Greenfield. 2004. (Wishing Tree Ser.). 32p. (J). (gr. -1-3). 16.95 *(978-1-885008-26-8(0)*, Shen's Bks.) Lee & Low Bks., Inc.

McLeod, Bob. SuperHero ABC. McLeod, Bob. (ENG.). 40p. (J). (gr. -1-3). 2008. pap. 7.99 *(978-0-06-074516-5(9))*; 2006. 17.99 *(978-0-06-074514-1(2))*; 2006. lib. bdg. 18.89 *(978-0-06-074515-8(0))* HarperCollins Pubs.

McLeod, Chum. An Alien in My House, 1 vol. Nanji, Shenaaz. 2003. (ENG.). 24p. (J). (gr. 1-3). 15.95 *(978-1-896764-77-1(0))* Second Story Pr. CAN. Dist: Orca Bk. Pubs. USA.

—TLC Grow with Me! Rovetch, L. Bob. 2005. (J). *(978-1-58987-114-4(6))* Kindermusik International.

McLeod, Cinders. Earn It! McLeod, Cinders. 2017. 32p. (J). (-k). 16.99 *(978-0-399-54444-6(5)*, Nancy Paulsen Books) Penguin Young Readers Group.

—Save It! McLeod, Cinders. 2019. (ENG.). 32p. (J). (-k). 16.99 *(978-1-9848-1240-7(8)*, Nancy Paulsen Books) Penguin Young Readers Group.

—Spend It! McLeod, Cinders. 2019. 32p. (J). (-k). 16.99 *(978-0-399-54446-0(1)*, Nancy Paulsen Books) Penguin Young Readers Group.

McLeod, David. Trixie - the Christmas Cow. Hastings, Leon. 2012. 18p. pap. *(978-1-84903-192-9(4))* Schiel & Denver Publishing Ltd.

McLeod, Herbert. Big Daddy Chinaberry: Love Given - Love Returned. McLeod, Rona. 2012. 24p. pap. 24.95 *(978-1-4626-7700-9(2))* America Star Bks.

McLeod, Kagan, jt. illus. see Zhao, Amei.

McLeod, Kris Aro. Catch a Kiss. Diesen, Deborah. 2016. (ENG.). 32p. (J). (gr. k-2). 15.99 *(978-1-58536-961-4(6)*, 204037) Sleeping Bear Pr.

—Lizzie & the Last Day of School. Noble, Trinka Hakes. 2015. (ENG.). 32p. (J). (gr. k-2). 15.99 *(978-1-58536-895-2(4)*, 203811) Sleeping Bear Pr.

McLeod, Madalyn. Étoile. Aab, Richard. 2018. (ENG.). 38p. (J). 16.99 *(978-0-9998571-3-7(4))*; pap. 9.99 *(978-0-9998571-4-4(2))* Ascend Pr.

McLimans, David. Gone Wild. McLimans, David. 2016. (ENG.). 32p. (J). bds. 7.99 *(978-1-61963-954-6(8)*, 900152939, Bloomsbury USA Childrens) Bloomsbury Publishing USA.

McLoughlin, Wayne. Here Is the Wetland. Dunphy, Madeleine. 2007. (Web of Life Ser.). (ENG.). 32p. (J). (gr. -1-3). 16.95 *(978-0-9773795-9-0(0))*; pap. 9.95 *(978-0-9773795-8-3(2))* Web of Life Children's Bks.

—Warriors: Cats of the Clans. Hunter, Erin. 2008. (Warriors Field Guide Ser.: No. 2). (ENG.). 112p. (J). (gr. 3-7). 16.99 *(978-0-06-145856-9(2)*, HarperCollins) HarperCollins Pubs. Ltd. GBR. Dist: HarperCollins Pubs.

—Warriors: Code of the Clans. Hunter, Erin. 2009. (Warriors Field Guide Ser.: No. 3). (ENG.). 176p. (J). (gr. 3-7). 16.99 *(978-0-06-166009-2(4))*; lib. bdg. 17.89 *(978-0-06-166010-8(8))* HarperCollins Pubs.

—Warriors: Dawn of the Clans Box Set: Volumes 1 To 3. Hunter, Erin. 2016. (Warriors: Dawn of the Clans Ser.). (ENG.). 1088p. (J). (gr. 3-7). pap. 20.97 *(978-0-06-234325-3(4))* HarperCollins Pubs.

—Warriors Super Edition: Bluestar's Prophecy. Hunter, Erin. 2009. (Warriors Super Edition Ser.: 2). (ENG.). 544p. (J). (gr. 3-7). 17.99 *(978-0-06-158247-9(6))* HarperCollins Pubs.

—Warriors Super Edition: Bluestar's Prophecy. Hunter, Erin. 2019. (Warriors Super Edition Ser.: 2). (ENG.). 576p. (J). (gr. 3-7). pap. 7.99 *(978-0-06-158250-9(6)*, HarperCollins) HarperCollins Pubs. Ltd. GBR. Dist: HarperCollins Pubs.

—Warriors Super Edition: SkyClan's Destiny. Hunter, Erin. (Warriors Super Edition Ser.: 3). (ENG.). 528p. (J). (gr. 3-7). 2011. pap. 7.99 *(978-0-06-169996-2(9))*; 2010. 17.99 *(978-0-06-169994-8(2))* HarperCollins Pubs.

—Warriors: Tales from the Clans. 2014. (Warriors Novella Ser.). (ENG.). 320p. (J). (gr. 3-7). pap. 7.99 *(978-0-06-229085-4(1))* HarperCollins Pubs.

—Warriors: the Ultimate Guide. Hunter, Erin. 2013. (Warriors Field Guide Ser.). (ENG.). 256p. (J). (gr. 3-7). 19.99 *(978-0-06-224533-5(3))* HarperCollins Pubs.

—Warriors: the Untold Stories. Hunter, Erin. 2013. (Warriors Novella Ser.). (ENG.). 320p. (J). (gr. 3-7). pap. 7.99 *(978-0-06-223292-2(4))* HarperCollins Pubs.

McLoughlin, Wayne & Douglas, Allen. Thunder Rising. Hunter, Erin. 2014. (Warriors: Dawn of the Clans Ser.: 2). 368p. (J). (gr. 3-7). pap. 7.99 *(978-0-06-206352-6(9))* HarperCollins Pubs.

—Warriors: Dawn of the Clans #1: the Sun Trail. Hunter, Erin. (Warriors: Dawn of the Clans Ser.: 1). (ENG.). (J). (gr. 3-7). 2014. 368p. pap. 7.99 *(978-0-06-206348-9(0))*; 2013. 352p. 16.99 *(978-0-06-206346-5(4))* HarperCollins Pubs.

—Warriors: Dawn of the Clans #1: the Sun Trail. Hunter, Erin. 2016. (Warriors: Dawn of the Clans Ser.: 1). (ENG.). 368p. (J). (gr. 3-7). pap. 7.99 *(978-0-06-241000-9(8)*, HarperCollins) HarperCollins Pubs. Ltd. GBR. Dist: HarperCollins Pubs.

—Warriors: Dawn of the Clans #2: Thunder Rising. Hunter, Erin. 2013. (Warriors: Dawn of the Clans Ser.: 2). (ENG.). 352p. (J). (gr. 3-7). 16.99 *(978-0-06-206350-2(2))* HarperCollins Pubs.

—Warriors: Dawn of the Clans #2: Thunder Rising. Hunter, Erin. 2016. (Warriors: Dawn of the Clans Ser.: 2). (ENG.). 368p. (J). (gr. 3-7). pap. 7.99 *(978-0-06-241001-6(6)*, HarperCollins) HarperCollins Pubs. Ltd. GBR. Dist: HarperCollins Pubs.

—Warriors: Dawn of the Clans #2: Thunder Rising. Hunter, Erin. 2013. (Warriors: Dawn of the Clans Ser.: 2). (ENG.). 352p. (J). (gr. 3-7). lib. bdg. 17.89 *(978-0-06-206351-9(0))* HarperCollins Pubs.

—Warriors: Dawn of the Clans #3: the First Battle. Hunter, Erin. (Warriors: Dawn of the Clans Ser.: 3). (ENG.). 352p. (J). (gr. 3-7). 2016. pap. 7.99 *(978-0-06-241002-3(4))*; 2014. 16.99 *(978-0-06-206353-3(7))* HarperCollins Pubs.

—Warriors: Dawn of the Clans #4: the Blazing Star. Hunter, Erin. 2016. (Warriors: Dawn of the Clans Ser.: 4). (ENG.). 336p. (J). (gr. 3-7). pap. 7.99 *(978-0-06-241003-0(2))* HarperCollins Pubs.

—Warriors: Dawn of the Clans #5: a Forest Divided. Hunter, Erin. 2015. (Warriors: Dawn of the Clans Ser.: 5). (ENG.). 384p. (J). (gr. 3-7). 16.99 *(978-0-06-206362-5(6))* HarperCollins Pubs.

—Warriors: Dawn of the Clans #6: Path of Stars. Hunter, Erin. 2015. (Warriors: Dawn of the Clans Ser.: 6). (ENG.). 352p. (J). (gr. 3-7). 16.99 *(978-0-06-206366-3(9))* HarperCollins Pubs.

McMahon, Bob. Apple Days: A Rosh Hashanah Story, Vol. Soffer, Allison Sarnoff. 2014. (ENG.). 32p. (J). (gr. -1-2). 7.95 *(978-1-4677-1204-0(3)*, 9781467712040, Kar-Ben Publishing) Lerner Publishing Group.

—La Doctora. Schmauss, Judy Kentor. 2016. (Early Rising Readers Ser.). (SPA.). 16p. (J). (gr. 1-1). 6.67 *(978-1-4788-3750-3(0))* Newmark Learning LLC.

—Hannah's Hanukkah Hiccups. Silva, Shanna. 2018. (J). *(978-1-68115-537-1(0)*, Apples & Honey Pr.) Behrman Hse., Inc.

—Mira Al Raton. Koons, Linda. 2016. (Early Rising Readers Ser.). (SPA.). 16p. (J). (gr. 1-1). 6.67 *(978-1-4788-3757-2(8))* Newmark Learning LLC.

—Soccer Time! Pierce, Terry. 2019. (Step into Reading Ser.). (ENG.). 32p. (J). (gr. -1-1). pap. 4.99 *(978-0-525-58203-8(7)*, Random Hse. Bks. for Young Readers) Random Hse. Children's Bks.

McMahon, Bob. Cookie & Broccoli: Ready for School! McMahon, Bob. 2020. 80p. (J). (gr. k-3). 12.99 ***(978-0-593-10907-6(4)***, Dial Bks) Penguin Young Readers Group.

McMahon, Bob. Something Rotten at Village Market. McMahon, Bob, tr. Fertig, Dennis. 2003. 60p. 11.60 net. *(978-0-7398-5170-8(5))* Steck-Vaughn.

McMahon, Brad. Sinbad: Legend of the Seven Seas Pop-up. Auerbach, Annie. 2003. (Media Favorites!! Ser.). 10p. (J). 9.95 *(978-1-58117-171-6(4)*, Intervisual/Piggy Toes) Bendon, Inc.

McMahon, James P. Mister Pudge. McMahon, Kathleen A. 2009. 20p. pap. 8.50 *(978-1-4251-8704-0(8))* Trafford Publishing.

McMahon, Kelly. Comprehension Crosswords Grade 1, 6 vols. Shiotsu, Vicky. 2003. 32p. (J). 4.99 *(978-1-56472-185-3(X))* Edupress, Inc.

—Comprehension Crosswords Grade 2, 6 vols. Shiotsu, Vicky. 2003. 32p. (J). 4.99 *(978-1-56472-186-0(8))* Edupress, Inc.

—Phonics - The Gerbil Plays Guitar on the Girafee, Bk. 3. Crane, Kathy Dickerson. Klistoff, Lorin & Coan, Sharon, eds. ed. 2004. (Phonics (Teacher Created Resources) Ser.). (ENG.). 176p. pap. 17.99 *(978-0-7439-3017-8(7))* Teacher Created Resources, Inc.

McMahon, Michael. Two Rainbows. Masson, Sophie. 2018. (ENG.). 48p. (J). (gr. -1-k). 17.99 *(978-1-76012-779-4(5))* Little Hare Bks. AUS. Dist: Independent Pubs. Group.

McMahon, Scoot. Wrapped up Vol. 1. Scheidt, Dave. 2018. (ENG.). 160p. (J). pap. 12.99 *(978-1-941302-47-7(5)*, cbe38b61-c12c-4bb0-9441-309ae342a384, Lion Forge) Oni Pr., Inc.

—Wrapped up Vol. 2. Scheidt, Dave. 2018. (ENG.). 144p. (J). pap. 12.99 *(978-1-941302-70-5(X)*, 41dfa637-7f8b-4c36-9590-b8766c99c3ec, Lion Forge) Oni Pr., Inc.

McMahon, Wm. Franklin, photos by. We Came from Vietnam. Stanek, Muriel. 2004. 46p. (J). (gr. k-4). reprint ed. *(978-0-7567-7795-1(X))* DIANE Publishing Co.

McMann, Zoe. Katie Cow. McMann, Kat. 2019. (ENG.). 26p. (J). pap. 21.99 ***(978-1-7960-5669-3(3))*** Xlibris Corp.

—Rosie Horse. McMann, Kat. 2019. (ENG.). 26p. (J). pap. 21.99 ***(978-1-7960-5705-8(3))*** Xlibris Corp.

—Tate Cat. McMann, Kat. 2019. (ENG.). 26p. (J). pap. 21.99 ***(978-1-7960-5479-8(8))*** Xlibris Corp.

McManus, Blanche. Alice's Adventures in Wonderland & Through the Looking-Glass - with Sixteen Full-Page Illustrations by Blanche Mcmanus. Carroll, Lewis. 2016. (ENG.). (J). *(978-1-4733-3502-8(7))* Read Bks.

McManus, Shawn. Captain Cold & the Blizzard Battle, 1 vol. Sonneborn, Scott & Loughridge, Lee. 2012. (DC Super-Villains Ser.). (ENG.). 56p. (J). (gr. 3-6). pap. 5.95 *(978-1-4342-3897-9(0))*; lib. bdg. 26.65 *(978-1-4342-3796-5(6))* Capstone. (Stone Arch Bks.).

—Joker on the High Seas, 1 vol. Bright, J. E. & Loughridge, Lee. 2012. (DC Super-Villains Ser.). (ENG.). 56p. (J). (gr. 3-6). pap. 5.95 *(978-1-4342-3895-5(4))*; lib. bdg. 26.65 *(978-1-4342-3794-1(X))* Capstone. (Stone Arch Bks.).

—Meteor of Doom, 1 vol. Kupperberg, Paul. 2009. (Superman Ser.). (ENG.). 56p. (J). lib. bdg. 26.65 *(978-1-4342-1568-0(7)*, Stone Arch Bks.) Capstone.

—Parasite's Power Drain, 1 vol. Fein, Eric. (Superman Ser.). (ENG.). 56p. (J). (gr. 3-6). 2013. pap. 4.95 *(978-1-4342-2261-9(6))*; 2010. lib. bdg. 26.65 *(978-1-4342-1882-7(1))* Capstone. (Stone Arch Bks.).

—Sinestro & the Ring of Fear, 1 vol. Sutton, Laurie S. & Loughridge, Lee. 2012. (DC Super-Villains Ser.). (ENG.). 56p. (J). (gr. 3-6). pap. 5.95 *(978-1-4342-3899-3(7)*, Stone Arch Bks.) Capstone.

—Two-Face's Double Take, 1 vol. Manning, Matthew K. 2010. (Batman Ser.). (ENG.). 56p. (J). (gr. 3-6). lib. bdg. 26.65 *(978-1-4342-1878-0(3)*, Stone Arch Bks.) Capstone.

McManus, Shawn. Two-Face's Double Take. McManus, Shawn. Manning, Matthew K. & Loughridge, Lee. 2013. (Batman Ser.). (ENG.). 56p. (J). (gr. 3-6). pap. 4.95 *(978-1-4342-2264-0(0)*, Stone Arch Bks.) Capstone.

McMaster, Anne & Tiwi College Students. Barramundi Fishing Story, Arlaminga: Reading Tracks. James, Margaret. 2018. (Reading Tracks Ser.: Vol. 16). (ENG.). 36p. (YA). (gr. 7-12). *(978-1-925855-32-6(5)*, Reading Tracks) Honey Ant Readers.

McMaster, Madeleine. Indestructible. McMaster, C. 2019. (ENG.). 30p. (J). 19.90 *(978-0-9891166-4-0(6))* Pilgrim Voyage Pr.

McMaugh, Kimberly. Southpaw. Baird, Noah. 2013. 40p. pap. 13.95 *(978-1-938101-35-9(9))* Indigo Sea Pr., LLC.

McMenemy, Sarah. Bees in the City, 1 vol. Cheng, Andrea. 2017. (ENG.). 36p. (J). (gr. 2-6). 17.95 *(978-0-88448-520-9(X)*, 884520) Tilbury Hse. Pubs.

—Berlin: a 3D Keepsake Cityscape. Candlewick Press Staff. 2014. (Panorama Pops Ser.). (ENG.). 30p. (J). (gr. k-4). 8.99 *(978-0-7636-6472-5(3))* Candlewick Pr.

—Everybody Bonjours! Kimmelman, Leslie. 40p. (J). (gr. -1-2). 2015. pap. 7.99 *(978-0-553-50782-9(6)*, Dragonfly Bks.); 2008. (ENG.). 16.99 *(978-0-375-84443-0(0)*, Knopf Bks. for Young Readers) Random Hse. Children's Bks.

—The First Rule of Little Brothers. Davis, Jill. 2008. (ENG.). 40p. (J). (gr. -1-2). 16.99 *(978-0-375-84046-3(X)*, Knopf Bks. for Young Readers) Random Hse. Children's Bks.

—The Louvre. Candlewick Press Staff. 2014. (Panorama Pops Ser.). (ENG.). 64p. (J). (gr. k-4). 8.99 *(978-0-7636-7506-6(7))* Candlewick Pr.

—Venice: a 3D Keepsake Cityscape. Candlewick Press Staff. 2014. (Panorama Pops Ser.). (ENG.). 20p. (J). (gr. k-4). 8.99 *(978-0-7636-7186-0(X))* Candlewick Pr.

McMenemy, Sarah. Paris: A 3D Keepsake Cityscape. McMenemy, Sarah. 2012. (Panorama Pops Ser.). (ENG.). 20p. (J). (gr. k-12). 8.99 *(978-0-7636-5894-6(4))* Candlewick Pr.

—Washington D. C. A 3D Keepsake Cityscape. McMenemy, Sarah. 2012. (Panorama Pops Ser.). (ENG.). 20p. (J). (gr. k-12). 8.99 *(978-0-7636-5935-6(5))* Candlewick Pr.

McMillan, Stephanie. Mischief in the Forest: A Yarn Yarn. Jensen, Derrick. 2010. (Flashpoint Press Ser.). (ENG.). 40p. (J). (gr. -1-k). pap. 14.95 *(978-1-60486-081-8(2))* PM Pr.

McMilleon, Jessica. Prosiaczek: A Little Pig. Czarnecki, Janina. 2017. (POL.). 26p. (J). pap. 9.13 *(978-0-9888517-1-9(7))* Czarnecki, Janina.

McMillian, Jr Marvin & Ocasio, Carlos. Hey, It Could Happen! Bernart, Patrick. 2019. (ENG.). 116p. (J). (gr. k-4). pap. 23.95 ***(978-1-63132-077-4(7))*** Advanced Publishing LLC.

McMorris, Kelley. D-Day: Battle on the Beach. Messner, Kate. 2018. (Ranger in Time Ser.: 7). (ENG.). 160p. (J). (gr. 2-5). pap. 5.99 *(978-1-338-13390-5(X))* Scholastic, Inc.

—Danger in Ancient Rome. Messner, Kate. 2015. (Ranger in Time Ser.: 2). (ENG.). 160p. (J). (gr. 2-5). pap. 5.99 *(978-0-545-63917-0(4)*, Scholastic Pr.) Scholastic, Inc.

—The Dead House. Johnson, Allen, Jr. 2014. (Blackwater Novels Ser.: Vol. 2). (ENG.). 212p. (J). (gr. 4-7). 14.99 *(978-1-933725-34-5(6))* Premium Pr. America.

—Disaster on the Titanic. Messner, Kate. 2019. (Ranger in Time Ser.: 9). (ENG.). 144p. (J). (gr. 2-5). pap. 5.99 *(978-1-338-13398-1(5))*; lib. bdg. 17.99 *(978-1-338-13399-8(3))* Scholastic, Inc. (Scholastic Pr.).

—Escape from the Great Earthquake. Messner, Kate. 2017. (Ranger in Time Ser.: 6). (ENG.). 160p. (J). (gr. 2-5). pap. 5.99 *(978-0-545-90983-9(X))* Scholastic, Inc.

—Escape from the Twin Towers. Messner, Kate. 2020. (Ranger in Time Ser.: 11). (ENG.). 144p. (J). (gr. 2-5). pap. 5.99 *(978-1-338-53794-9(6))* Scholastic, Inc.

—Hurricane Katrina Rescue. Messner, Kate. 2018. (Ranger in Time Ser.: 8). (ENG.). 160p. (J). (gr. 2-5). pap. 5.99 *(978-1-338-13395-0(0))*; lib. bdg. 25.99 *(978-1-338-13396-7(9))* Scholastic, Inc. (Scholastic Pr.).

—Land of Fire & Ice. Messner, Kate. 2017. (Ranger in Time Ser.: 5). (ENG.). 160p. (J). (gr. 2-5). pap. 5.99 *(978-0-545-90978-5(3))* Scholastic, Inc.

—Long Road to Freedom. Messner, Kate. 2015. (Ranger in Time Ser.: 3). (ENG.). 160p. (J). (gr. 2-5). pap. 5.99 *(978-0-545-63920-0(4))* Scholastic, Inc.

—The March on Washington. Bader, Bonnie. 2018. (American Girl: Real Stories from My Time Ser.). (ENG.). 128p. (J). (gr. 2-5). pap. 5.99 *(978-1-338-19301-5(5))* Scholastic, Inc.

—My Brother's Story. Johnson, Allen, Jr. 2014. (Blackwater Novels Ser.: Vol. 1). (ENG.). 191p. (J). (gr. 4-7). 14.99 *(978-1-933725-37-6(0))* Premium Pr. America.

—Night of Soldiers & Spies. Messner, Kate. 2019. (Ranger in Time Ser.: 10). (ENG.). 160p. (J). (gr. 2-5). pap. 5.99 *(978-1-338-13401-8(9))*; lib. bdg. 17.99 *(978-1-338-13402-5(7))* Scholastic, Inc. (Scholastic Pr.).

—Pearl Harbor. Swanson, Jennifer. 2018. (American Girl: Real Stories from My Time Ser.: 4). (ENG.). 112p. (J). (gr. 2-5). pap. 5.99 *(978-1-338-14894-7(X))* Scholastic, Inc.

—Pearl Harbor. Swanson, Jennifer & Larson, Kirby. 2018. 106p. (J). *(978-1-5444-0721-0(1))* Scholastic, Inc.

—Race to the South Pole. Messner, Kate. 2016. (Ranger in Time Ser.: 4). (ENG.). 160p. (J). (gr. 2-5). pap. 5.99 *(978-0-545-63925-5(5))* Scholastic, Inc.

—Rescue on the Oregon Trail. Messner, Kate. 2015. (Ranger in Time Ser.: 1). (ENG.). 144p. (J). (gr. 2-5). pap. 5.99 *(978-0-545-63914-9(X)*, Scholastic Pr.) Scholastic, Inc.

—The Titanic. Berne, Emma Carlson. 2017. (Real Stories from My Time Ser.: 2). (ENG.). 112p. (J). (gr. 2-5). pap. 5.99 *(978-1-338-19306-0(6))* Scholastic, Inc.

—The Underground Railroad (American Girl: Real Stories from My Time) Bader, Bonnie & Porter, Connie. 2017. (American Girl: Real Stories from My Time Ser.: 1). (ENG.). 112p. (J). (gr. 3-7). pap. 5.99 *(978-1-338-14892-3(3))* Scholastic, Inc.

—The Wishner's Curse. Campbell, Camille S. 2019. (Wishner Prophecy Ser.: Vol. 1). (ENG.). 116p. (J). pap. 5.99 *(978-1-7338672-2-1(8))* Hom, Jonathan.

McMullan, Jim. As Warm As the Sun. McMullan, Kate. 2019. (ENG.). 32p. (J). (gr. -1-2). 18.99 *(978-0-8234-4327-7(2)*, Neal Porter Bks) Holiday Hse., Inc.

—Hogwash! Wilson, Karma. 2011. 40p. (J). (gr. -1-3). 18.99 *(978-0-316-98840-7(5))* Little, Brown Bks. for Young Readers.

—I Stink! McMullan, Kate. 2006. (ENG.). 40p. (J). (gr. -1-3). reprint ed. pap. 7.99 *(978-0-06-443836-0(8))* HarperCollins Pubs.

—I Stink! Board Book. McMullan, Kate. 2005. (ENG.). 34p. (J). (gr. -1-k). bds. 7.99 *(978-0-06-074592-9(4)*, HarperFestival) HarperCollins Pubs.

—I'm Bad! McMullan, Kate. 2008. (ENG.). 40p. (J). (gr. -1-3). 16.99 *(978-0-06-122971-8(7))* HarperCollins Pubs.

—I'm Big! McMullan, Kate. 2010. (ENG.). 40p. (J). (gr. -1-3). 16.99 *(978-0-06-122974-9(1))* HarperCollins Pubs.

—I'm Brave! McMullan, Kate. 2014. (ENG.). 40p. (J). (gr. -1-3). 16.99 *(978-0-06-220318-2(5)*, Balzer & Bray) HarperCollins Pubs.

—I'm Cool! McMullan, Kate. 2015. (ENG.). 40p. (J). (gr. -1-3). 17.99 *(978-0-06-230629-6(4))* HarperCollins Pubs.

—I'm Dirty! McMullan, Kate. (ENG.). 40p. (J). (gr. -1-3). 2015. pap. 7.99 *(978-0-06-009295-5(5))*; 2006. 16.99 *(978-0-06-009293-1(9))* HarperCollins Pubs.

—I'm Dirty! Board Book. McMullan, Kate. 2015. (ENG.). 34p. (J). (gr. -1 — 1). bds. 7.99 *(978-0-06-234318-5(1))* HarperCollins Pubs.

—I'm Fast! McMullan, Kate. 2012. (ENG.). 40p. (J). (gr. -1-3). 16.99 *(978-0-06-192085-1(1))*; lib. bdg. 17.89 *(978-0-06-192086-8(X))* HarperCollins Pubs.

—I'm Mighty! McMullan, Kate. 2003. (ENG.). 40p. (J). (gr. -1-3). 17.99 *(978-0-06-009290-0(4))* HarperCollins Pubs.

—I'm Smart! McMullan, Kate. 2017. (ENG.). 40p. (J). (gr. -1-3). 17.99 *(978-0-06-244923-8(0))* HarperCollins Pubs.

—I'm Tough! McMullan, Kate. 2018. (ENG.). 40p. (J). (gr. -1-3). 17.99 *(978-0-06-244925-2(7)*, Balzer & Bray) HarperCollins Pubs.

McMullen, Nigel. Beauty & the Beast. Tyrrell, Melissa. 2005. (Fairytale Friends Ser.). 12p. (J). bds. 5.95 *(978-1-58117-153-2(6)*, Intervisual/Piggy Toes) Bendon, Inc.

—The Gingerbread Man. Tyrrell, Melissa. 2005. (Fairytale Friends Ser.: Vol. 8). 12p. (J). (gr. -1-k). bds. 5.95 *(978-1-58117-154-9(4)*, Intervisual/Piggy Toes) Bendon, Inc.

—Hansel & Gretel. Tyrrell, Melissa. 2005. (Fairytale Friends Ser.). 12p. (J). bds. 5.95 *(978-1-58117-152-5(8)*, Intervisual/Piggy Toes) Bendon, Inc.

—No Te Preocupes, Guille. Morton, Christine. (Buenas Noches Ser.). (SPA.). 26p. (J). (gr. k-3). 8.95 *(978-958-04-5088-7(9))* Norma S.A. COL. Dist: Distribuidora Norma, Inc.

—Pinocchio. Tyrrell, Melissa. 2005. (Fairytale Friends Ser.: Vol. 7). 12p. (J). (gr. -1-k). bds. 5.95 *(978-1-58117-151-8(X)*, Intervisual/Piggy Toes) Bendon, Inc.

McMullen, Nigel. Let's Dance, Grandma! McMullen, Nigel. 2014. (ENG.). 32p. (J). (gr. -1-3). 16.99 *(978-0-06-050747-3(0))* HarperCollins Pubs.

McMullen, T. C. Princess Annado Tandy's Versery Rhymes. Ruble, Kam. l.t. ed. 2007. 88p. (J). per. *(978-0-9779680-4-6(9))* Global Authors Pubns.

McMullin, Marcus. The Big Bend Guide. Parent, Laurence, photos by. Kimball, Allan. 2008. (ENG.). 104p. (YA). pap. 5.95 *(978-1-892588-20-3(X))* Great Texas Line Pr.

McMunn, Hugh. Beyond the Evergreens: A Story of a Boy, His Dog, & Their Final Adventure. Zark. Gafni, Gabriella, ed. 2019. (ENG.). 54p. (J). (gr. k-6). 18.99 ***(978-0-578-62223-1(8))*** Zark.

McMurray, Becky. Percy Vere: The Little Pony Who Never Gave Up. Donnor-Broom, Louise & Donnor-Broom, Charlotte. 2019. (ENG.). 22p. (J). pap. ***(978-1-78324-139-2(X))*** Wordzworth Publishing.

McMurry, Marena. Don't Even Think about It. Booth, Chrissie. 2011. 24p. pap. 24.95 *(978-1-4560-8289-5(2))* America Star Bks.

McNallly, Emma R. Harold Huxley & the Mysterious Island. McNally, Emma R. Writing and Editorial Services, Jmd, ed. 2017. (Adventures of Harold Huxley Ser.: Vol. 6). (ENG.). (J). (gr. k-2). pap. *(978-0-9930806-7-8(7))* R McNally, Emma.

—The Puffin Pirates. McNally, Emma R. Writing and Editorial Services, Jmd, ed. 2017. (Harold Huxley's Rhyming Picture Bks.: Vol. 6). (ENG.). (J). (gr. k-2). pap. *(978-0-9930806-6-1(9))* R McNally, Emma.

McNally, Bruce. Moose's Loose Tooth. Clarke, Jacqueline A. 2003. (J). *(978-0-439-41183-7(1))* Scholastic, Inc.

McNally, Emma R. The Confused Kangaroo. McNally, Emma R. Jmd Editorial and Writing Services, ed. 2014. (ENG.). (J). pap. *(978-0-9930005-2-2(5))* R McNally, Emma.

McNally, Nicholas. The Wolf & the Shield: An Adventure with Saint Patrick. Smith, Sherry. 2016. 118p. (J). pap. *(978-0-8198-8356-8(5))* Pauline Bks. & Media.

McNamara-Gordon, Sallie. How the Mockingbird Found His Tune. Salad, Grandma. 2017. (ENG.). 38p. (J). pap. 11.99 *(978-1-945620-35-5(8))* Hear My Heart Publishing.

McNaught, Harry. Howdy Doody's Lucky Trip. Kean, Edward. 2011. 30p. 35.95 *(978-1-258-02772-8(0))* Literary Licensing, LLC.

McNaughton, Colin. Dracula's Tomb. McNaughton, Colin. 2009. (ENG.). 24p. (J). (gr. k-4). 14.99 *(978-0-7636-4488-8(9))* Candlewick Pr.

—Gôl! McNaughton, Colin. Williams, Dylan, tr. from ENG. 2005.Tr. of Goal!. (WEL.). 30p. *(978-0-948930-79-9(9))* Cymdeithas Lyfrau Ceredigion.

McNaughton, Tina. Snowball: The Baby Bigfoot. Symes, Ruth. 2016. (Secret Animal Society Ser.). (ENG.). 176p. (J). (gr. k-3). pap. 8.99 *(978-1-84812-463-9(5))* Bonnier Publishing GBR. Dist: Independent Pubs. Group.

—What a Wonderful World! Chiew, Suzanne. 2013. (ENG.). 32p. (J). (gr. -1-2). 16.95 *(978-1-58925-129-8(6))* Tiger Tales.

McNeal, Drema & Teets, Ashley. Jake Learns All 8 Parts of Speech. 2010. (J). *(978-0-929915-55-5(0))* Headline Bks., Inc.

McNee, Ian. Illustrated Stories for Boys. Sims, Lesley & Stowell, Louie. 2007. (Usborne Illustrated Stories Ser.). 352p. (J). 19.99 *(978-0-7945-1420-4(0)*, Usborne) EDC Publishing.

—The Roman Soldier's Handbook: Everything a Beginner Soldier Needs to Know. Sims, Lesley. 2006. (English Heritage Ser.). 80p. (J). (gr. 4-7). 12.99 *(978-0-7945-0837-1(5)*, Usborne) EDC Publishing.

—The Story of Exploration. Claybourne, Anna. 2010. (Science Stories Ser.). 103p. (YA). (gr. 3-18). pap. 10.99 *(978-0-7945-2400-5(1)*, Usborne) EDC Publishing.

—Titanic. Claybourne, Anna & Daynes, Katie. 2006. (Usborne Young Reading Ser.). 64p. (J). (gr. 3-7). 8.99 *(978-0-7945-1269-9(0)*, Usborne) EDC Publishing.

—Treasure Island. 2006. 158p. (J). (gr. 5-9). per. 4.99 *(978-0-7945-1230-9(5)*, Usborne) EDC Publishing.

—True Stories of Gangsters. Brook, Henry. 2004. (True Adventure Stories Ser.). 144p. (J). pap. 4.95 *(978-0-7945-0722-0(0)*, Usborne) EDC Publishing.

—True Stories of the Blitz. Brook, Henry. 2006. (True Adventure Stories Ser.). 160p. (J). (gr. 4-7). per. 4.99 *(978-0-7945-1245-3(3)*, Usborne) EDC Publishing.

—Tutankhamun. Harvey, Gill. 2006. (Usborne Young Reading Ser.). 64p. (J). (gr. 3-7). 8.99 *(978-0-7945-1271-2(2)*, Usborne) EDC Publishing.

—The Usborne Official Pirate's Handbook. Taplin, Sam. 2007. (Usborne Official Handbooks Ser.). 80p. (J). (gr. -1-3). 12.99 *(978-0-7945-1463-1(4)*, Usborne) EDC Publishing.

McNee, Ian, jt. illus. see Mayer, Uwe.

McNeely, Tom. Isis & the Seven Scorpions, 1 vol. 2012. (Egyptian Myths Ser.). (ENG.). 32p. (J). (gr. 3-5). pap. 8.95 *(978-1-4048-7241-7(8))*; lib. bdg. 29.32 *(978-1-4048-7150-2(0))* Capstone. (Picture Window Bks.).

McNeely, William. Jumpy the Frog Learns the Meaning of Love, 1 vol. Ross, Margaret Clark. 2010. 20p. pap. 24.95 *(978-1-4489-8370-4(3))* PublishAmerica, Inc.

McNeil, Carla Speed, et al. Pinkie Pie & Applejack, 1 vol. De Campi, Alex. 2016. (My Little Pony: Friends Forever Ser.). (ENG.). 24p. (J). (gr. 1-8). 27.07 *(978-1-61479-508-7(8)*, 21414, Graphic Novels) Spotlight.

McNeill, Jim. Dropping in on Andy Warhol. Stephens, Pamela Geiger. 2006. (J). 15.95 *(978-1-56290-433-3(7))* Crystal Productions.

—Dropping in on Grandma Moses. Stephens, Pamela. 2008. 32p. (J). 15.95 *(978-1-56290-598-9(8))* Crystal Productions.

—Dropping in on Grant Wood. Stephens, Pamela Greiger. 2005. (J). 15.95 *(978-1-56290-348-0(9))* Crystal Productions.

—Dropping in on Impressionists. Stephens, Pamela Geiger. 2009. (ENG.). 32p. (J). 15.95 *(978-1-56290-633-7(X))* Crystal Productions.

—Dropping in on Matisse. Stephens, Pamela Geiger. 2004. 32p. (J). 15.95 *(978-1-56290-322-0(5))* Crystal Productions.

—Dropping in on Picasso. Stephens, Pamela Geiger. 2004. 32p. (J). 15.95 *(978-1-56290-325-1(X))* Crystal Productions.

—Dropping in on Renaissance Artists. Geiger Stephens, Pamela. 2010. 32p. (J). 15.95 *(978-1-56290-658-0(5))* Crystal Productions.

—Dropping in on Romare Bearden. Stephens, Pamela Geiger. 2007. (ENG.). 32p. (J). 15.95 *(978-1-56290-539-2(2))* Crystal Productions.

McNeill, Sharlene. Smiley Discovers Rain. Pinette, Carol. 2019. (ENG.). 32p. (J). pap. ***(978-1-987982-38-1(X))*** Artistic Warrior Publishing.

—Smiley Goes to School. Pinette, Carol. 2020. (ENG.). 34p. (J). pap. ***(978-1-987982-42-8(8))*** Artistic Warrior Publishing.

McNeill, Sharlene. Smiley's Birthday. Pinette, Carol. 2018. (ENG.). 40p. (J). pap. *(978-1-987982-32-9(0))* Artistic Warrior Publishing.

—Smiley's Town. Pinette, Carol. 2019. (ENG.). 48p. (J). pap. *(978-1-987982-34-3(7))* Artistic Warrior Publishing.

McNevin, Dale. Crosby & Me, 1 vol. MacDonald, Hugh. ed. 2010. (ENG.). 32p. (J). (gr. 1-3). pap. 9.95 *(978-1-894838-50-4(5)*, 21f231df-192e-463c-a8c9-9916c67b62f0) Acorn Pr., The CAN. Dist: Baker & Taylor Publisher Services (BTPS).

—Everything That Shines. Weale, David. ed. (ENG.). 24p. pap. 6.95 *(978-0-9698606-8-6(4))* Acorn Pr., The CAN. Dist: Goose Lane Editions.

—Marty the Mailbox. Stretch, Ian. 2009. 24p. pap. 10.95 *(978-1-4251-8435-3(9))* Trafford Publishing.

—Three Tall Trees. Weale, David. ed. 2004. (ENG.). 24p. pap. 6.95 *(978-1-894838-13-9(0))* Acorn Pr., The CAN. Dist: Univ. of Toronto Pr.

McNicholas, Shelagh. Ballet Stars. Holub, Joan. 2012. (Step into Reading Ser.). 24p. (J). (gr. -1-1). pap. 4.99 *(978-0-375-86909-9(3)*, Random Hse. Bks. for Young Readers) Random Hse. Children's Bks.

—Dear Daddy, I Love You. Allison, Catherine. 2014. (ENG.). (J). (gr. -1-3). *(978-1-74363-284-0(3))* Hinkler Bks. Pty, Ltd.

—Los Mejores Amigos. Anderson, Rachael. 2003. (SPA.). 120p. (J). (gr. 3-5). 9.95 *(978-84-204-4377-5(8))* Ediciones Alfaguara ESP. Dist: Santillana USA Publishing Co., Inc.

—Soo's Boo-Boos: She's Got 10! Balsley, Tilda. 2013. (ENG.). 32p. (J). (gr. -1-2). 12.95 *(978-1-58925-118-2(0))* Tiger Tales.

—Tea Time with Sophia Grace & Rosie. Brownlee, Sophia Grace & McClelland, Rosie. 2013. (J). (ENG.). 40p. (gr. -1-k). 17.99 *(978-0-545-50214-6(4))*; pap. *(978-0-545-58534-7(1))* Scholastic, Inc. (Orchard Bks.).

McNicholas, Shelagh & Cascio, Maria Cristina Lo. Little Princess Treasury. Davidson, Susanna & Daynes, Katie. 2006. (English Heritage Ser.). 96p. (J). 7.99 *(978-0-7945-1442-6(1)*, Usborne) EDC Publishing.

McNicholas, Shelagh, jt. illus. see Cascio, Maria Cristina Lo.

McNicholas, Shelagh, jt. illus. see Guicciardini, Desideria.

McNicolas, Shelagh. I Love Ponies. Aspley, Brenda. 2013. 20p. (J). (gr. -1-k). 7.99 *(978-1-84322-565-2(4)*, Armadillo) Anness Publishing GBR. Dist: National Bk. Network.

McNiven, Steve, et al. Coming Home, Vol. 4. Kesel, Barbara. 2003. (Meridian Traveler Ser.: Vol. 4). 160p. (YA). (gr. 6-18). pap. 9.95 *(978-1-59314-004-5(5))* CrossGeneration Comics, Inc.

—Going to Ground, Vol. 2. Kesel, Barbara. 2003. (Meridian Traveler Ser.: Vol. 2). 192p. (YA). (gr. 7-18). pap. 9.95 *(978-1-931484-69-5(4))* CrossGeneration Comics, Inc.

—Marvel Knights Fantastic Four by Aguirre-Sacasa, Mcniven & Muniz: the Complete Collection Vol. 1. 2019. (ENG.). 424p. (YA). (gr. 8-17). pap. 39.99 *(978-1-302-91632-9(7))* Marvel Worldwide, Inc.

—Meridian, Vol. 6. Kesel, Barbara. 2003. (Meridian Ser.: Vol. 6). 160p. (YA). pap. 15.95 *(978-1-931484-95-4(3))* CrossGeneration Comics, Inc.

—Minister of Cadador, Vol. 5. Kesel, Barbara. (Meridian Traveler Ser.: Vol. 5). 160p. 2004. (YA). pap. 9.95 *(978-1-59314-050-2(9))*; 2003. (gr. 7-18). pap. 7.95 *(978-1-931484-70-1(8))* CrossGeneration Comics, Inc.

McNiven, Steve. New Avengers - Volume 2: Sentry, Vol. 2. 2006. (ENG.). 152p. (J). (gr. 4-17). 14.99 *(978-0-7851-1672-1(9))* Marvel Worldwide, Inc.

—Return of Wolverine. 2019. (ENG.). 160p. (gr. 10-17). 17.99 *(978-1-302-91198-0(8))* Marvel Worldwide, Inc.

McNiven, Steve, et al. Taking the Skies, Vol. 3. Kesel, Barbara. 2003. (Meridian Traveler Ser.: Vol. 3). 160p. (YA). (gr. 6-18). pap. 9.95 *(978-1-931484-84-8(8))* CrossGeneration Comics, Inc.

McPartland, Dorothy. Wishing Stars. McPartland, Dorothy. 2004. 34p. (J). bds. 15.95 *(978-0-9755374-0-4(7))* Little Light Pr.

McPhail, David. The Adventures of Anatole. Willard, Nancy. 2018. 320p. (J). (gr. k-4). pap. 12.99 *(978-1-68137-292-1(4)*, NYRB Kids) New York Review of Bks., Inc., The.

—All the Awake Animals Are Almost Asleep. Dragonwagon, Crescent. 2016. 32p. (J). (gr. -1 — 1). bds. 7.99 *(978-0-316-33627-7(0))* Little, Brown Bks. for Young Readers.

—Animal Stackers. Belle, Jennifer. 2005. (ENG.). 40p. (gr. k-4). 15.99 *(978-0-7868-1834-1(4))* Hyperion Pr.

—Bunny's First Spring, 1 vol. Lloyd-Jones, Sally. 2015. (ENG.). 32p. (J). 16.99 *(978-0-310-73386-7(3))* Zonderkidz.

—La Colcha de Retazos, Level 3. Avery, Kristin. Flor Ada, Alma, tr. 2003. (Dejame Leer Ser.). (SPA.). 16p. (J). (gr. -1-3). 6.50 *(978-0-673-36303-9(1)*, Good Year Bks.) Celebration Pr.

—Grandma Loves You Because You're You. Baker, Liza. 2018. (ENG.). 20p. (J). (gr. -1 — 1). bds. 8.99 *(978-1-338-27143-0(1)*, Cartwheel Bks.) Scholastic, Inc.

—Hooked. Greenwald, Tommy. 2018. (ENG.). 32p. (J). 16.99 *(978-1-59643-996-2(3)*, 9781596439962) Roaring Brook Pr.

—I Love You Because You're You. Baker, Liza. (ENG.). (J). (gr. -1-k). 2008. 24p. bds. 8.99 *(978-0-545-02931-5(7)*, Cartwheel Bks.); 2006. audio compact disk 9.99 *(978-0-439-89558-3(8))* Scholastic, Inc.

—I Love You Because You're You (a StoryPlay Book) Baker, Liza. 2016. (StoryPlay Ser.). (ENG.). 32p. (J). (gr. -1 — 1). 5.99 *(978-0-545-94527-1(5)*, Cartwheel Bks.) Scholastic, Inc.

—If You Were My Bunny. McMullan, Kate. 2017. (StoryPlay Ser.). (ENG.). 32p. (J). (gr. -1-k). 5.99 *(978-1-338-23219-6(3))* Scholastic, Inc.

—Just Clowning Around: Two Stories. MacDonald, Steven. 2003. (Green Light Readers Level 1 Ser.). (ENG.). 24p. (J). (gr. -1-3). pap. 3.95 *(978-0-15-204856-3(1)*, 1194664) Houghton Mifflin Harcourt Publishing Co.

—Just Clowning Around: Two Stories. MacDonald, Steven. ed. 2003. (Green Light Readers Level 1 Ser.). 20p. (gr. -1-3). lib. bdg. 13.50 *(978-0-613-66362-5(4))* Turtleback.

—A Place for Nicholas. Floyd, Lucy. 2005. (Green Light Readers Level 2 Ser.). (J). (ENG.). 24p. (gr. -1-3). pap. 4.99 *(978-0-15-205149-5(X)*, 1195539); 20p. (gr. k-2). 16.19 *(978-0-15-205150-1(3))* Houghton Mifflin Harcourt Publishing Co.

—A Place for Nicholas. Floyd, Lucy. 2005. (Green Light Readers Level 2 Ser.). 18p. (gr. k-2). 13.95 *(978-0-7569-5243-3(3))* Perfection Learning Corp.

—The Tale of Peter Rabbit. Potter, Beatrix. 2014. (ENG.). 28p. (J). (gr. -1 — 1). bds. 6.99 *(978-0-545-65096-0(8)*, Cartwheel Bks.) Scholastic, Inc.

—When I Was King. Ashman, Linda. 2008. 32p. (J). (gr. -1-3). 17.89 *(978-0-06-029052-8(8))* HarperCollins Pubs.

—When Papa Comes Home Tonight. Spinelli, Eileen. 2009. (ENG.). 32p. (J). (gr. -1-k). 16.99 *(978-1-4169-1028-2(X)*, Simon & Schuster Bks. For Young Readers) Simon & Schuster Bks. For Young Readers.

McPhail, David. Andrew Draws. McPhail, David. 2014. (ENG.). 32p. (J). (gr. -1-3). 16.95 *(978-0-8234-3063-5(4))* Holiday Hse., Inc.

—Baby Pig Pig Talks. McPhail, David. 2014. 14p. (J). (— 1). bds. 6.95 *(978-1-58089-597-2(2))* Charlesbridge Publishing, Inc.

—Baby Pig Pig Walks. McPhail, David. 2014. 14p. (J). (— 1). bds. 6.95 *(978-1-58089-596-5(4))* Charlesbridge Publishing, Inc.

—Beatrix Potter & Her Paint Box. McPhail, David. 2015. (ENG.). 40p. (J). (gr. -1-3). 17.99 *(978-0-8050-9170-0(X)*, 9780805091700, Holt, Henry & Co. Bks. For Young Readers) Holt, Henry & Co.

—Big Brown Bear's up & down Day. McPhail, David. 2005. 42p. (J). (gr. -1-3). reprint ed. 16.00 *(978-0-7567-8542-0(1))* DIANE Publishing Co.

—Boy, Bird, & Dog. McPhail, David. (I Like to Read Ser.). (ENG.). 24p. (J). (gr. -1-3). 2012. pap. 6.99 *(978-0-8234-2639-3(4))*; 2011. 14.95 *(978-0-8234-2346-0(8))* Holiday Hse., Inc.

—Crash! the Cat. McPhail, David. 2016. (ENG.). 32p. (J). (gr. -1-k). 16.95 *(978-0-8234-3649-1(7))* Holiday Hse., Inc.

—My Mother Goose: A Collection of Favorite Rhymes, Songs, & Concepts. McPhail, David. 2013. (ENG.). 96p. (J). (gr. -1-k). 19.99 *(978-1-59643-526-1(7)*, 900060692) Roaring Brook Pr.

—Pig Pig Meets the Lion. McPhail, David. 2012. pap. 15.95 *(978-1-60734-080-5(1))*; 32p. (J). (gr. -1-3). 15.95 *(978-1-58089-358-9(9))* Charlesbridge Publishing, Inc.

—Pig Pig Returns. McPhail, David. 2011. 32p. (J). (gr. -1-3). 15.95 *(978-1-58089-356-5(2))* Charlesbridge Publishing, Inc.

—The Searcher & Old Tree. McPhail, David. 2011. 32p. (J). (gr. -1-2). pap. 7.95 *(978-1-58089-224-7(8))* Charlesbridge Publishing, Inc.

—Sisters. McPhail, David. 2003. (ENG.). 32p. (J). (gr. -1-3). 9.95 *(978-0-15-204659-0(3)*, 1194040) Houghton Mifflin Harcourt Publishing Co.

—The Teddy Bear. McPhail, David. 2005. (ENG.). 32p. (J). (gr. -1-1). reprint ed. pap. 8.99 *(978-0-8050-7882-4(7)*, 900030909) Square Fish.

—Weezer Changes the World. McPhail, David. 2009. (ENG.). 40p. (J). (gr. -1-2). 15.99 *(978-1-4169-9000-0(3)*, Beach Lane Bks.) Beach Lane Bks.

McPherson, Heath. Bible Stories for Toddlers from the New Testament: Connecting Christ Throughout God's Story. B&H Editorial Staff, ed. 2019. (One Big Story Ser.). (ENG.). 44p. (J). (— 1). bds. 9.99 *(978-1-5359-4781-7(0)*, 005812827, B&H Kids) B&H Publishing Group.

—Bible Stories for Toddlers from the Old Testament. B&H Editorial Staff, ed. 2018. (One Big Story Ser.). (ENG.). 44p. (J). (— 1). bds. 9.99 *(978-1-5359-4152-5(9)*, 005811544, B&H Kids) B&H Publishing Group.

—The Big Picture Interactive Bible Stories for Toddlers New Testament: Connecting Christ Throughout God's Story. B&H Editorial Staff, ed. 2014. (Big Picture Interactive / the Gospel Project Ser.). (ENG.). 44p. (J). (— 1). bds. 9.99 *(978-1-4336-8429-6(2)*, 005670784, B&H Kids) B&H Publishing Group.

—Brave Queen Esther/David & the Giant Flip-Over Book. B&H Kids Editorial Staff. 2016. (One Big Story Ser.). (ENG.). 32p. (J). (gr. -1-3). pap. 3.99 *(978-1-4336-4329-3(4)*, 005786147, B&H Kids) B&H Publishing Group.

—Epic: The Story That Changed the World. B&H Kids Editorial Staff. 2019. (One Big Story Ser.). (ENG.). 320p. (J). (gr. 3-7). 16.99 *(978-1-5359-3812-9(9)*, 005810873, B&H Kids) B&H Publishing Group.

—Epic Devotions: 52 Weeks in the Story That Changed the World. Armstrong, Aaron. 2019. (One Big Story Ser.). (ENG.). 224p. (J). (gr. 3-7). 16.99 *(978-1-4336-4933-2(0)*, 005791142, B&H Kids) B&H Publishing Group.

—In the Beginning/the Great Flood Flip-Over Book. B&H Kids Editorial Staff. 2016. (One Big Story Ser.). (ENG.). 32p. (J). (gr. -1-3). pap. 3.99 *(978-1-4336-4328-6(6)*, 005786146, B&H Kids) B&H Publishing Group.

—It's All about Jesus Bible Storybook (padded) 100 Bible Stories. B&H Kids Editorial Staff. 2016. (One Big Story Ser.). (ENG.). 320p. (J). (gr. k-5). 16.99 *(978-1-4336-9165-2(5)*, 006103095, B&H Kids) B&H Publishing Group.

—Jesus' Miracles/Finding the Lost, Flip-Over Book. B&H Kids Editorial Staff. 2016. (One Big Story Ser.). (ENG.). 32p. (J). (gr. -1-3). pap. 3.99 *(978-1-4336-4332-3(4)*, 005786150, B&H Kids) B&H Publishing Group.

—Mighty Miracles/Joseph the Dreamer Flip-Over Book. B&H Kids Editorial Staff. 2016. (One Big Story Ser.). (ENG.). 32p. (J). (gr. -1-3). pap. 3.99 *(978-1-4336-4330-9(8)*, 005786148, B&H Kids) B&H Publishing Group.

—One Big Story 52-Week Bible Story Devotional. B&H Editorial Staff, ed. 2018. (One Big Story Ser.). (ENG.). 224p. (J). (gr. 1-5). 16.99 *(978-1-5359-3497-8(2)*, 005809997, B&H Kids) B&H Publishing Group.

—One Big Story Bible Stories in 5 Minutes (padded) Connecting Christ Throughout God's Story. B&H Kids Editorial Staff, ed. 2018. (One Big Story Ser.). (ENG.). 192p. (J). (gr. -1-3). 12.99 *(978-1-5359-4796-1(9)*, 005812849, B&H Kids) B&H Publishing Group.

—Timmy & Tammy's Train of Thought. Chin, Oliver. 2007. (ENG.). 36p. (J). (gr. -1-3). 15.95 *(978-1-59702-008-4(7))* Immedium.

M

McPherson, Melinda. Taber Is Beautiful. DeGrasse, Samantha. 2011. 28p. pap. 12.56 *(978-1-4269-5825-0(0))* Trafford Publishing.

McPhillips, Robert. The Bard & the Beast. Quinn, Jordan. 2015. (Kingdom of Wrenly Ser.: 9). (ENG.). 128p. (J). (gr. k-4). pap. 5.99 *(978-1-4814-4396-8(8),* Little Simon) Little Simon.

McPhillips, Robert. Den of Wolves. Quinn, Jordan. 2020. (Kingdom of Wrenly Ser.: 15). (ENG.). 128p. (J). (gr. k-4). 17.99 ***(978-1-5344-6526-8(X))***; pap. 5.99 ***(978-1-5344-6525-1(1))*** Little Simon. (Little Simon).

McPhillips, Robert. The False Fairy. Quinn, Jordan. 2016. (Kingdom of Wrenly Ser.: 11). (ENG.). 128p. (J). (gr. k-4). pap. 5.99 *(978-1-4814-8586-9(5),* Little Simon) Little Simon.

—A Ghost in the Castle. Quinn, Jordan. 2019. (Kingdom of Wrenly Ser.: 14). (ENG.). 128p. (J). (gr. k-4). 16.99 *(978-1-5344-4511-6(0))*; pap. 5.99 *(978-1-5344-4510-9(2))* Little Simon. (Little Simon).

—The Kingdom of Wrenly 3 Books In 1! The Lost Stone; the Scarlet Dragon; Sea Monster! Quinn, Jordan. 2017. (Kingdom of Wrenly Ser.). (ENG.). 368p. (J). (gr. k-4). pap. 8.99 *(978-1-5344-0934-7(3),* Little Simon) Little Simon.

—The Kingdom of Wrenly Collection #3: The Bard & the Beast; the Pegasus Quest; the False Fairy; the Sorcerer's Shadow. Quinn, Jordan. ed. 2017. (Kingdom of Wrenly Ser.). (ENG.). 512p. (J). (gr. k-4). pap. 23.99 *(978-1-5344-0918-7(1),* Little Simon) Little Simon.

—Let the Games Begin! Quinn, Jordan. 2015. (Kingdom of Wrenly Ser.: 7). (ENG.). 128p. (J). (gr. k-4). pap. 5.99 *(978-1-4814-2379-3(7),* Little Simon) Little Simon.

—The Lost Stone. Quinn, Jordan. 2014. (Kingdom of Wrenly Ser.: 1). (ENG.). 128p. (J). (gr. k-4). pap. 5.99 *(978-1-4424-9690-3(8),* Little Simon) Little Simon.

—The Lost Stone. Quinn, Jordan. 2014. (Kingdom of Wrenly Ser.: Vol. 1). (ENG.). (J). (gr. k-4). lib. bdg. 16.60 *(978-1-62765-847-8(5))* Perfection Learning Corp.

—The Pegasus Quest. Quinn, Jordan. 2016. (Kingdom of Wrenly Ser.: 10). (ENG.). 128p. (J). (gr. k-4). pap. 5.99 *(978-1-4814-5870-2(1),* Little Simon) Little Simon.

—The Scarlet Dragon. Quinn, Jordan. 2014. (Kingdom of Wrenly Ser.: 2). (ENG.). 128p. (J). (gr. k-4). pap. 5.99 *(978-1-4424-9693-4(2),* Little Simon) Little Simon.

—The Scarlet Dragon. Quinn, Jordan. 2014. (Kingdom of Wrenly Ser.: Vol. 2). (ENG.). (J). (gr. k-4). lib. bdg. 16.60 *(978-1-62765-839-3(4))* Perfection Learning Corp.

—Sea Monster! Quinn, Jordan. 2014. (Kingdom of Wrenly Ser.: 3). (ENG.). 128p. (J). (gr. k-4). pap. 5.99 *(978-1-4814-0072-5(X),* Little Simon) Little Simon.

—The Secret World of Mermaids. Quinn, Jordan. 2015. (Kingdom of Wrenly Ser.: 8). (ENG.). 128p. (J). (gr. k-4). pap. 5.99 *(978-1-4814-3122-4(6),* Little Simon) Little Simon.

—The Sorcerer's Shadow. Quinn, Jordan. 2017. (Kingdom of Wrenly Ser.: 12). (ENG.). 128p. (J). (gr. k-4). 16.99 *(978-1-5344-0000-9(1))*; pap. 5.99 *(978-1-4814-9999-6(8))* Little Simon. (Little Simon).

—The Thirteenth Knight. Quinn, Jordan. 2018. (Kingdom of Wrenly Ser.: 13). (ENG.). 128p. (J). (gr. k-4). 16.99 *(978-1-5344-1275-0(1))*; pap. 5.99 *(978-1-5344-1274-3(3))* Little Simon. (Little Simon).

—The Witch's Curse. Quinn, Jordan. 2014. (Kingdom of Wrenly Ser.: 4). (ENG.). 128p. (J). (gr. k-4). pap. 5.99 *(978-1-4814-0075-6(4),* Little Simon) Little Simon.

McQuane, Antonia. Muinjij Becomes a Man. Joe, Saqamaw Mi'sel. 2012. (ENG.). 64p. pap. *(978-1-55081-167-4(3))* Breakwater Bks., Ltd.

McQuarrie, Ralph. Star Wars the Adventures of Luke Skywalker, Jedi Knight. DiTerlizzi, Tony. 2014. (ENG.). 64p. (J). (gr. 1-3). 19.99 *(978-1-4847-0668-8(4))* Disney Pr.

McQue, Ian. Night Flights: A Mortal Engines Collection. Reeve, Philip. 2018. (Mortal Engines Ser.). (ENG.). 208p. (YA). (gr. 7-7). pap. 12.99 *(978-1-338-28970-1(5),* Scholastic Pr.) Scholastic, Inc.

McQueen, Lucinda. Please Say Please, Grumpy Bunny! Fontes, Justine. 2007. (J). *(978-0-439-02012-1(3))* Scholastic, Inc.

—Turn the Key: Who Do You See? Merberg, Julie. 2011. (ENG.). 12p. (J). (gr. -1). bds. 11.99 *(978-1-935703-11-2(0))* Downtown Bookworks.

—Turn the Key: Around Town: Look & See! Merberg, Julie. 2012. (ENG.). 12p. (J). (gr. -1 — 1). bds. 11.99 *(978-1-935703-44-0(7))* Downtown Bookworks.

McQueen, Lucinda. The Little Red Hen. McQueen, Lucinda. abr. ed. 2007. (ENG.). (J). (gr. -1-3). 18.99 *(978-0-545-00511-1(6))* Scholastic, Inc.

McQueen, Stacey Dressen. How Dalia Put a Big Yellow Comforter Inside a Tiny Blue Box: And Other Wonders of Tzedakah. Heller, Linda. 2011. (ENG.). 32p. (J). (gr. -1-2). 16.99 *(978-1-58246-378-0(6),* Tricycle Pr.) Random Hse. Children's Bks.

McQueen, Todd. Bob & Rob & Corn on the Cob. McQueen, Todd. 2014. 32p. (J). (gr. -1-k). 16.95 *(978-1-62873-591-8(0),* Sky Pony Pr.) Skyhorse Publishing Co., Inc.

McQuillan, David. The Legend of Lumpus & Ogols. Mcintyre, Mel. 2009. 28p. pap. 10.95 *(978-1-935137-96-2(4))* Guardian Angel Publishing, Inc.

McQuillan, Mary. A Bed of Your Own. Kelly, Mij. 2011. 32p. (J). (gr. -1-1). pap. 8.99 *(978-0-7641-4768-5(4),* B.E.S. Publishing) Peterson's.

McQuitty, LaVonia Corbin. Henrietta Hippo Learns to Dance. Ralls, Ken. 2nd ed. 2013. 24p. (J). 15.00 *(978-0-9884125-3-8(5))* Scribe's Closet Pubns., The.

—I'm Glad God Made Me... Me. Ware, Richard. 2013. 32p. (J). 17.00 *(978-0-9884125-4-5(3))* Scribe's Closet Pubns., The.

—Jesus Does Good Things. White, Susan K. 2013. 24p. (J). 15.00 *(978-0-9832570-6-6(X))* Scribe's Closet Pubns., The.

—Tinky Turtle Finds the Word. Oliver, Sheila. 2011. (ENG.). 16p. (J). 6.00 *(978-0-9801269-4-5(0))* Scribe's Closet Pubns., The.

Mcrae, Scott, jt. illus. see Staton, Joe.

McSherry, Drew. The Wild Buck (Book 1 of the Huckleberry Hill Adventure Series) Carlson, Maxine. 2017. (ENG.). 46p. (J). pap. 6.93 *(978-0-692-89191-9(9))* Huckleberry Hill Adventure LLC.

McSwain, Ray. The Legend of Caribou Boy, 1 vol. Blondin, John & Blondin, George. Sundberg, Mary Rose, tr. ed. 2009. (ENG & DGR.). 40p. (J). (gr. 1-3). pap. 19.95 *(978-1-894778-71-8(5))* Theytus Bks., Ltd. CAN. Dist: Orca Bk. Pubs. USA.

McSweeney, Ben. The Rithmatist. Sanderson, Brandon. 2014. (ENG.). 384p. (YA). (gr. 7). pap. 10.99 *(978-0-7653-3844-0(0),* 900126287, Tor Teen) Doherty, Tom Assocs., LLC.

McSweeney, Kelsey. My Mommy's Not a Peanut. Griffin, Khristine. 2017. (ENG.). 42p. (J). 24.99 *(978-1-5434-6840-3(3))*; pap. 17.99 *(978-1-5434-6839-7(X))* Xlibris Corp.

McTaggart, Dave. Ladies & Gentlemen... the Penguins! Davis, Ivor. 2018. (ENG.). 32p. (J). 17.99 *(978-0-9903710-5-2(0))*; pap. 9.99 *(978-0-9903710-6-9(9))* Cockney Kid Publishing.

McTeigue, Jane, jt. illus. see Miralles, Jose.

McVey, Alex. Sam & Luke Discover Thanksgiving. Little, Paul D. 2017. (ENG.). (J). pap. 12.99 *(978-0-9814748-8-5(8))* King's Way Pr.

McWeeney, Tom. The Changing Tides: The Imperium Saga: Fall of the Imperium Trilogy, 3 vols., Vol. 2. Bowyer, Clifford B. 2005. (Imperium Saga: 2). (ENG.). 547p. (YA). 27.95 *(978-0-9744354-5-9(7),* BK0005) Silver Leaf Bks., LLC.

—The Siege of Zoldex: The Imperium Saga: Fall of the Imperium Trilogy, 3 vols., Vol. 3. Bowyer, Clifford B. 2007. (Imperium Saga: 3). (ENG.). 556p. (YA). 29.95 *(978-0-9744354-6-6(5),* BK0009) Silver Leaf Bks., LLC.

McWherter, Seth. I Should Have Been a Bear. Mcwherter, Barbara. 2011. 24p. pap. 24.95 *(978-1-4626-3532-0(6))* America Star Bks.

McWherter, Shelley. Oliver & His Mountain Climbing Adventures. Mcwherter, Barbara. 2012. 34p. 24.95 *(978-1-4626-7601-9(4))* America Star Bks.

McWilliam, Howard. The Adventures of Huckleberry Finn. Twain, Mark. 2010. (Calico Illustrated Classics Ser.: No. 1). (ENG.). 112p. (J). (gr. 2-5). 29.93 *(978-1-60270-702-3(2),* 3957, Calico Chapter Bks.) ABDO Publishing Co.

—Are You My Monster? Noll, Amanda. 2019. (I Need My Monster Ser.). (ENG.). 26p. (J). bds. 8.99 *(978-1-947277-32-8(4))* Flashlight Pr.

—David Copperfield, 1 vol. Dickens, Charles. 2010. (Calico Illustrated Classics Ser.). (ENG.). 112p. (J). (gr. 2-5). 29.93 *(978-1-60270-745-0(6),* 3991, Calico Chapter Bks.) ABDO Publishing Co.

—Dinosaur Christmas. Pallotta, Jerry. (J). (gr. k-2). 2013. (ENG.). 32p. 12.99 *(978-0-545-43360-0(6))*; 2011. *(978-0-545-24963-8(5))* Scholastic, Inc.

—Don't Read This!, 1 vol. Enderle, Dotti. 2009. (Ghost Detectors Ser.: No. 1). (ENG.). 80p. (J). (gr. 2-5). 29.93 *(978-1-60270-695-8(6),* 8810, Calico Chapter Bks.) ABDO Publishing Co.

—Draw!, 1 vol. Enderle, Dotti. 2009. (Ghost Detectors Ser.: No. 1). (ENG.). 80p. (J). (gr. 2-5). 29.93 *(978-1-60270-694-1(8),* 8808, Calico Chapter Bks.) ABDO Publishing Co.

—Elbow Grease. Cena, John. (Elbow Grease Ser.). (J). 2019. (ENG.). 34p. (— 1). bds. 8.99 *(978-1-5247-7356-4(5))*; 2018. 40p. (gr. -1-2). 17.99 *(978-1-5247-7350-2(6))*; 2018. (ENG.). 40p. (gr. -1-2). lib. bdg. 20.99 *(978-1-5247-7351-9(4))* Random Hse. Children's Bks. (Random Hse. Bks. for Young Readers).

—Elbow Grease vs. Motozilla. Cena, John. 2019. (Elbow Grease Ser.). (ENG.). 40p. (J). (gr. -1-2). 17.99 *(978-1-5247-7353-3(0))*; lib. bdg. 20.99 *(978-1-5247-7354-0(9))* Random Hse. Children's Bks. (Random Hse. Bks. for Young Readers).

—Ghost Detectors Volume 1: Let the Specter-Detecting Begin, Books 1-3. Enderle, Dotti. 2013. (Ghost Detectors Ser.: 1). (ENG.). 192p. (gr. 2-7). pap. 8.95 *(978-1-938063-28-2(7),* Mighty Media Junior Readers) Mighty Media Pr.

—Grow a Ghost!, 1 vol. Enderle, Dotti. 2015. (Ghost Detectors Ser.). (ENG.). 80p. (J). (gr. 2-5). 29.93 *(978-1-62402-100-8(X),* 18142, Calico Chapter Bks.) ABDO Publishing Co.

—Hey, That's My Monster! Noll, Amanda. 2016. (I Need My Monster Ser.). 32p. (J). (gr. k-2). 17.95 *(978-1-936261-37-6(5))* Flashlight Pr.

—How I Met My Monster. Noll, Amanda. 2019. (I Need My Monster Ser.). (ENG.). 32p. (J). (gr. k-2). 17.95 *(978-1-947277-09-0(X))* Flashlight Pr.

—Hush up & Hibernate, 1 vol. Markle, Sandra. 2018. (Hush Up Ser.: 1). (ENG.). 36p. (J). (gr. -1-3). 16.95 *(978-1-943978-36-6(0),* f3e7a2c2-df2e-461f-bd8b-c9f67ce99e31, Persnickety Pr.) WunderMill, Inc.

—Hush up & Migrate, 1 vol. Markle, Sandra. 2020. (Hush Up Ser.: 2). (ENG.). (J). 16.95 *(978-1-943978-42-7(5),* f81f9714-c5c3-4f89-a4f9-53c02081169d, Persnickety Pr.) WunderMill, Inc.

—I Dare You! Enderle, Dotti. 2009. (Ghost Detectors Ser.: No. 1). (ENG.). 80p. (J). (gr. 2-5). 29.93 *(978-1-60270-693-4(X),* 8806, Calico Chapter Bks.) ABDO Publishing Co.

—I Love My Dragon. Moore, Jodi. 2019. (When a Dragon Moves In Ser.). (ENG.). 24p. (J). bds. 7.99 *(978-1-947277-30-4(8))* Flashlight Pr.

—I Need My Monster. Noll, Amanda. 2009. (I Need My Monster Ser.). 32p. (J). (gr. k-3). 16.95 *(978-0-9799746-2-5(3))* Flashlight Pr.

—I'm Gonna Get You!, 1 vol. Enderle, Dotti. 2009. (Ghost Detectors Ser.: No. 1). (ENG.). 80p. (J). (gr. 2-5). 29.93 *(978-1-60270-691-0(3),* 8802, Calico Chapter Bks.) ABDO Publishing Co.

—It Creeps!, 1 vol. Enderle, Dotti. 2009. (Ghost Detectors Ser.: No. 1). (ENG.). 80p. (J). (gr. 2-5). 29.93 *(978-1-60270-690-3(5),* 8800, Calico Chapter Bks.) ABDO Publishing Co.

—King Arthur & the Knights of the Round Table, 1 vol. Pyle, Howard. 2010. (Calico Illustrated Classics Ser.: No. 1). (ENG.). 112p. (J). (gr. 2-5). 29.93 *(978-1-60270-707-8(3),* 3967, Calico Chapter Bks.) ABDO Publishing Co.

—The Legend of Sleepy Hollow & Rip Van Winkle, 1 vol. Irving, Washington. 2010. (Calico Illustrated Classics Ser.). (ENG.). 112p. (J). (gr. 2-5). 29.93 *(978-1-60270-747-4(2),* 3995, Calico Chapter Bks.) ABDO Publishing Co.

—Oliver Twist, 1 vol. Dickens, Charles. 2011. (Calico Illustrated Classics Ser.: No. 3). (ENG.). 112p. (J). (gr. 2-5). 29.93 *(978-1-61641-106-0(6),* 4019, Calico Chapter Bks.) ABDO Publishing Co.

—Shmelf the Hanukkah Elf. Wolfe, Greg. 2016. 32p. (J). 17.99 *(978-1-61963-521-0(6),* 900139020, Bloomsbury USA Childrens) Bloomsbury Publishing USA.

—Spaced Out!, 1 vol. Enderle, Dotti. 2015. (Ghost Detectors Ser.: 18). (ENG.). 80p. (J). (gr. 2-5). 29.93 *(978-1-62402-101-5(8),* 18144, Calico Chapter Bks.) ABDO Publishing Co.

—T. Rex Teeth? And Other Dinosaur Parts. Markle, Sandra. 2018. (What If You Had... ? Ser.). (ENG.). 32p. (J). (gr. -1-3). pap. 4.99 *(978-1-338-27139-3(3))* Scholastic, Inc.

—Tell No One!, 1 vol. Enderle, Dotti. 2009. (Ghost Detectors Ser.: No. 1). (ENG.). 80p. (J). (gr. 2-5). 29.93 *(978-1-60270-692-7(1),* 8804, Calico Chapter Bks.) ABDO Publishing Co.

—What I Saw in the Teachers' Lounge. Pallotta, Jerry. 2012. (J). *(978-0-545-38472-8(9))* Scholastic, Inc.

—What If You Had an Animal Nose? Markle, Sandra. 2016. (What If You Had... ? Ser.). (ENG.). 32p. (J). (gr. -1-3). pap. 4.99 *(978-0-545-85922-6(0))* Scholastic, Inc.

—What If You Had an Animal Nose!? Markle, Sandra. 2017. 32p. (J). *(978-1-338-20647-0(8))* Scholastic, Inc.

—What If You Had an Animal Tail!? Markle, Sandra. 2018. (What If You Had... ? Ser.). (ENG.). 32p. (J). (gr. -1-3). pap. 4.99 *(978-1-338-20878-8(0))* Scholastic, Inc.

—What If You Had Animal Ears? Markle, Sandra. 2016. (What If You Had... ? Ser.). (ENG.). 32p. (J). (gr. -1-3). pap. 4.99 *(978-0-545-85926-4(3),* Scholastic Nonfiction) Scholastic, Inc.

—What If You Had Animal Eyes? Markle, Sandra. 2017. (What If You Had... ? Ser.). (ENG.). 32p. (J). (gr. -1-3). pap. 4.99 *(978-1-338-10108-9(0))*; lib. bdg. 19.99 *(978-1-338-20645-6(1))* Scholastic, Inc.

—What If You Had Animal Feet? Markle, Sandra. 2015. (ENG.). 32p. (J). (gr. k-3). pap. 4.99 *(978-0-545-73312-0(X),* Scholastic Paperbacks) Scholastic, Inc.

—What If You Had Animal Hair? Markle, Sandra. 2014. (What If You Had... ? Ser.). (ENG.). 32p. (J). (gr. k-3). pap. 3.99 *(978-0-545-63085-6(1),* Scholastic Paperbacks) Scholastic, Inc.

—What If You Had Animal Teeth? Markle, Sandra. 2013. (ENG.). 32p. (J). (gr. -1-3). pap. 4.99 *(978-0-545-48438-1(3),* Scholastic Paperbacks) Scholastic, Inc.

—What If You Had Animal Teeth!? Markle, Sandra. 2013. 32p. (J). *(978-0-545-56727-5(0))* Scholastic, Inc.

—When a Dragon Moves In. Moore, Jodi. 2011. (When a Dragon Moves In Ser.). (ENG.). 32p. (J). (gr. k-2). 16.95 *(978-0-9799746-7-0(4))* Flashlight Pr.

—When a Dragon Moves in Again. Moore, Jodi. 2015. (When a Dragon Moves In Ser.). (ENG.). 32p. (J). (gr. k-2). 17.95 *(978-1-936261-35-2(9))* Flashlight Pr.

McWilliam, Howard, jt. illus. see Mullarkey, Lisa.

McWilliams, Scott P. The Magical Apple Tree. McWilliams, Scott P. 2019. (ENG.). 26p. (J). pap. 9.99 *(978-1-5004-2880-8(9))* CreateSpace Independent Publishing Platform.

McWryat, Aine. Larp. Weiman, Tracy. 2017. (ENG.). 258p. (J). pap. *(978-90-826624-3-6(4))* Red Admiral Pr.

Meacham, Mike. Right Where You Belong: An Adoption Story. Meacham, Ashlie. 2018. (ENG.). 36p. (J). 23.95 *(978-1-64003-760-1(8))* Covenant Bks.

Meachen Rau, Dana, et al. All about Me: My Book by Me - My Pinkie Finger - My Special Space. Meachen Rau, Dana & Franco-Feeney, Betsy. 2006. (ENG.). 93p. (J). (gr. k-2). pap. 9.95 *(978-0-531-16924-7(3),* Children's Pr.) Scholastic Library Publishing.

Meade, Gregory S. I Just Might! E.C., Nanci. 2007. 20p. per. 9.95 *(978-1-59858-548-3(7))* Dog Ear Publishing, LLC.

Meade, Heather. Worburt the Worrywart. Gaither, Kerri. 2019. (ENG.). 44p. (J). pap. 12.95 *(978-1-7988-8992-3(7))* Independently Published.

Meade, Holly. And Then Comes Halloween. Brenner, Tom. 2011. (Holiday Books: Halloween Ser.). 32p. (J). (gr. -1-2). 21.19 *(978-0-7636-3659-3(2))*; pap. 6.99 *(978-0-7636-5299-9(7))* Candlewick Pr.

—Hush! A Thai Lullaby. Ho, Mingfong. ed. 2004. (J). (gr. -1-1). spiral bd. *(978-0-616-07255-4(4))* Canadian National Institute for the Blind/Institut National Canadien pour les Aveugles.

—In the Sea. Elliott, David. 2014. (ENG.). (J). (gr. -1-2). lib. bdg. 17.60 *(978-1-62765-427-2(5))* Perfection Learning Corp.

—In the Wild. Elliott, David. 2013. 32p. (J). (gr. -1-3). pap. 6.99 *(978-0-7636-6337-7(9))* Candlewick Pr.

—Naamah & the Ark at Night. Bartoletti, Susan Campbell. 2011. 32p. (J). (gr. -1-3). 16.99 *(978-0-7636-4242-6(8))* Candlewick Pr.

—On the Farm. Elliott, David. 32p. (J). (gr. -1-2). 2012. pap. 6.99 *(978-0-7636-5591-4(0))*; 2008. 16.99 *(978-0-7636-3322-6(4))* Candlewick Pr.

—Rata-Pata-Scata-Fata: A Caribbean Story, 1 vol. Gershator, Phillis. 2005. (ENG.). 32p. (J). (gr. -1-3). 5.95 *(978-1-932065-95-4(4))*; 15.95 *(978-1-932065-94-7(6))* Star Bright Bks., Inc.

—That's What Friends Are For. Heide, Florence Parry. 2007. 40p. pap. 6.99 *(978-0-7636-3283-0(X))* Candlewick Pr.

—That's What Friends Are For. Heide, Florence Parry & Clief, Sylvia Van. 2007. 30p. (gr. -1-3). 17.00 *(978-0-7569-8126-6(3))* Perfection Learning Corp.

—Virginnie's Hat. Chaconas, Dori. 2007. (ENG.). 32p. (J). (gr. -1-1). 16.99 *(978-0-7636-2397-5(0))* Candlewick Pr.

Meade, Holly. If I Never Forever Endeavor. Meade, Holly. 2011. 32p. (J). (gr. -1-3). 18.99 *(978-0-7636-4071-2(9))* Candlewick Pr.

—John Willy & Freddy Mcgee, 0 vols. Meade, Holly. unabr. ed. 2003. (ENG.). 32p. (J). (gr. -1-k). pap. 9.99 *(978-0-7614-5143-3(9),* 9780761451433, Two Lions) Amazon Publishing.

Meade, Sarah. ABCs for Little Yogis: Bhakti Yoga Flash Cards. Nonino, Lauren. 2014. (ENG.). 26p. (J). (gr. -1). 16.95 *(978-1-60887-340-1(4))* Mandala Publishing.

Meadow, Amy. Benny's Pets. Whimsy. 2005. 32p. (J). 15.95 *(978-0-9702675-0-4(9))* World of Whimsy Productions, LLC.

Meadows, Cynthia. The Adventures of Stop-Sign Sam. Robbins, Matt. 2019. (ENG.). 26p. (J). (gr. -1-1). pap. 9.99 ***(978-1-61254-403-8(7))*** Brown Books Publishing Group.

—Little Copper Penny. Barker, Stephenie. 2019. (ENG.). 34p. (J). (gr. -1-3). pap. 11.99 ***(978-1-61254-395-6(2))*** Brown Books Publishing Group.

—Little Quinn the Inquisitor: The Water Cycle. Gouge, Bianca. 2019. (ENG.). 26p. (J). pap. 9.99 ***(978-1-61254-384-0(7))*** Brown Books Publishing Group.

Meadows, Cynthia. When Mommy & Daddy Say No, They Still Love You. Ennis, Nancy. 2014. (ENG.). 24p. (J). 14.95 net. *(978-1-61254-198-3(4))* Brown Books Publishing Group.

Meadows, Sarah. Hello Hokie Bird! Aryal, Aimee Sutter. 2003. (J). 18.95 *(978-0-9743442-0-1(6))* Mascot Bks., Inc.

Meaker, Michael, jt. illus. see Barlowe, Wayne D.

Meane, Jinarta. Fairy Princess ABC - Letter Tracing Workbook: Over 120 Pages - Uppercase & Lowercase Letters - 26 Fairy Coloring Pages. Workbooks, Little Learner. 2019. (Little Learner Workbooks Ser.: Vol. 7). (ENG.). 130p. (J). pap. 7.99 ***(978-1-7103-4458-5(X))*** Independently Published.

Mebberson, Amy. Disney First Tales the Lion King: We Are (Not) Lost. Eden, Marie. 2017. (Disney First Tales Ser.). (ENG.). 64p. (J). (gr. 1-3). 10.99 *(978-1-4847-9955-0(0))* Disney Pr.

—Monsters, Inc: Laugh Factory. Benjamin, Paul. 2011. (Kaboom! Graphic Novels Ser.). (ENG.). 112p. (J). (gr. 4-7). 26.19 *(978-1-60886-508-6(8))* Boom! Studios.

—Muppet Peter Pan. Randolph, Grace & Barks, Carl. 2010. (Muppet Show Ser.). (ENG.). 112p. (J). 24.99 *(978-1-60886-531-4(2))* Boom! Studios.

—Muppet Peter Pan. Randolph, Grace. 2010. (Muppet Show Ser.). (ENG.). 112p. (J). pap. 9.99 *(978-1-60886-507-9(X))* Boom! Studios.

—Muppet Sherlock Holmes. Storck, Patrick. 2011. (Muppet Show Ser.). 128p. pap. 9.99 *(978-1-60886-613-7(0))* Boom! Studios.

Mebberson, Amy, et al. My Little Pony: Friendship Is Magic. Cook, Katie & Nuhfer, Heather. 2015. (My Little Pony: Friendship Is Magic Ser.). (ENG.). 24p. (J). (gr. 2-5). lib. bdg. 27.07 *(978-1-61479-382-3(4),* 18213);6. lib. bdg. 27.07 *(978-1-61479-381-6(6),* 18212) Spotlight. (Graphic Novels).

—My Little Pony: Friendship Is Magic: Vol. 15. Nuhfer, Heather. 2018. (My Little Pony: Friendship Is Magic Ser.). (ENG.). 24p. (J). (gr. 2-8). lib. bdg. 27.07 *(978-1-5321-4231-4(5),* 31108, Graphic Novels) Spotlight.

—My Little Pony: Friendship Is Magic: Vol. 16. Nuhfer, Heather. 2018. (My Little Pony: Friendship Is Magic Ser.). (ENG.). 24p. (J). (gr. 2-8). lib. bdg. 27.07 *(978-1-5321-4232-1(3),* 31109, Graphic Novels) Spotlight.

Mebberson, Amy. My Little Pony: Friendship Is Magic Volume 2, 2 Nuhfer, Heather. 2013. (My Little Pony Ser.: 2). 104p. (J). (gr. 4-7). pap. 17.99 *(978-1-61377-760-2(4),* 9781613777602) Idea & Design Works, LLC.

—Pony Tales, Vol. 2. Anderson, Ted et al. 2014. (MLP Pony Tales Ser.: 2). 104p. pap. 17.99 *(978-1-61377-873-9(2),* 9781613778739) Idea & Design Works, LLC.

Mebberson, Amy, et al. Twilight Sparkle & Shining Armor, 1 vol. Anderson, Rob. 2016. (My Little Pony: Friends Forever Ser.). (ENG.). 24p. (J). (gr. 1-8). 27.07 *(978-1-61479-512-4(6),* 21418, Graphic Novels) Spotlight.

Mebberson, Amy. Volume 1: the Baby Berrykin Baking Challenge Part 1. Ball, Georgia. 2017. (Strawberry Shortcake Ser.). (ENG.). 24p. (J). (gr. 2-8). lib. bdg. 27.07 *(978-1-5321-4029-7(0),* 25461, Graphic Novels) Spotlight.

—Volume 2: the Baby Berrykin Baking Challenge Part 2. Ball, Georgia. 2017. (Strawberry Shortcake Ser.). (ENG.). 24p. (J). (gr. 2-8). lib. bdg. 27.07 *(978-1-5321-4030-3(4),* 25462, Graphic Novels) Spotlight.

Mebberson, Amy. Disney Princess: Follow Your Heart. Mebberson, Amy. 2020. (ENG.). 104p. (J). (gr. 3-7). pap. 10.99 *(978-1-5067-1671-8(7),* Dark Horse Books) Dark Horse Comics.

—Disney Princess: Friends, Family, Fantastic. Mebberson, Amy. 2020. (ENG.). 104p. (J). (gr. 3-7). pap. 10.99 *(978-1-5067-1670-1(9),* Dark Horse Books) Dark Horse Comics.

Mebberson, Amy & Baldari, Nicoletta. Volume 4: the Cane Critique. Ball, Georgia & Gudsnuk, Kristen. 2017. (Strawberry Shortcake Ser.). (ENG.). 24p. (J). (gr. 2-8). lib. bdg. 27.07 *(978-1-5321-4032-7(0),* 25464, Graphic Novels) Spotlight.

Mebberson, Amy & Pena, Nico. Volume 3: the Stuff Dreams Are Made Of. Ball, Georgia & Gudsnuk, Kristen. 2017. (Strawberry Shortcake Ser.). (ENG.). 24p. (J). (gr. 2-8). lib. bdg. 27.07 *(978-1-5321-4031-0(2),* 25463, Graphic Novels) Spotlight.

Mebberson, Amy & Rosa, Don. Monsters, Inc: Laugh Factory. Benjamin, Paul & Rosa, Don. 2010. (ENG.). 112p. (J). 24.99 *(978-1-60886-533-8(9))* Boom! Studios.

Mebberson, Amy & Uyetake, Neil. My Little Pony: Friendship Is Magic. Cook, Katie & Nuhfer, Heather. 2015. (My Little Pony: Friendship Is Magic Ser.). (ENG.). 24p. (J). (gr. 2-5). lib. bdg. 27.07 *(978-1-61479-383-0(2),* 18214, Graphic Novels) Spotlight.

Mebberson, Amy, jt. illus. see Hickey, Brenda.

Mebberson, Amy, jt. illus. see Langridge, Roger.

Mecham, Ann M. The Best Little Discombobulated Angel. Kear, Kathleen. 2016. (ENG.). (J). pap. 9.99 *(978-1-4984-9333-8(5))* Salem Author Services.

Mecham, Janeal A. Christmas Gifts. Mecham, Janeal A. l.t. unabr. ed. 2003. 32p. (J). (gr. k-3). 12.95 *(978-1-932280-16-6(2)*, 80162) Granite Publishing & Distribution.

Meconis, Dylan. The Fifth Musketeer. Fontes, Justine & Fontes, Ron. 2012. (Twisted Journeys Ser.: 19). (ENG.). 112p. (J). (gr. 4-7). pap. 45.32 *(978-0-7613-9289-7(0))*; lib. bdg. 27.93 *(978-0-7613-4594-7(9))* Lerner Publishing Group. (Graphic Universe™).

Meconis, Dylan. Queen of the Sea. Meconis, Dylan. 400p. (J). (gr. 5-9). 2020. pap. 14.99 ***(978-1-5362-1517-5(1))***; 2019. 24.99 *(978-1-5362-0498-8(6))* Candlewick Pr.

Meconni, Beppe. El Pulpo Campanero. Brignole, Giancarla, tr. (Fabulas De Familia Ser.). (SPA.). 32p. *(978-970-20-0262-8(1))* Castillo, Ediciones, S. A. de C. V.

Medaglia, Mike. Can I Tell You about Sensory Processing Difficulties? A Guide for Friends, Family & Professionals. Allen, Sue. 2015. (Can I Tell You About... ? Ser.).Tr. of 56. (ENG.). 56p. pap. 14.95 *(978-1-84905-640-3(4)*, 693804) Kingsley, Jessica Pubs. GBR. Dist: Hachette UK Distribution.

Meddaugh, Susan. The Best Halloween of All. Wojciechowski, Susan. 2012. 24p. (J). (gr. -1-3). pap. 3.99 *(978-0-7636-6008-6(6))* Candlewick Pr.

—In the Haunted House. Bunting, Eve. 2013. (ENG.). 16p. (J). (gr. -1-3). 6.99 *(978-0-544-06670-0(7)*, 1535018) Houghton Mifflin Harcourt Publishing Co.

—A Perfect Father's Day. Bunting, Eve. 2016. (ENG.). 40p. (J). (gr. -1-3). 8.99 *(978-0-544-70900-3(4)*, 1628911, HMH Books For Young Readers) Houghton Mifflin Harcourt Publishing Co.

Medeiros, Giovana. Britannica Kids: Look at Her Go! Women Athletes Who Played to Win. Broderick, Kathy. 2020. (ENG.). 20p. (J). bds. *(978-1-5037-5278-8(X)*, 39904481-f1f9-4752-b10c-d1f4281a8b06, p i kids) Phoenix International Publications, Inc.

—Fantastical Fairies Matching Game. Chronicle Books Staff. 2015. (ENG.). 36p. (J). (gr. -1-1). 14.99 *(978-1-4521-3083-5(3))* Chronicle Bks. LLC.

—Running on Sunshine: How Does Solar Energy Work? DeCristofano, Carolyn Cinami. 2018. (Let's-Read-And-Find-Out Science 2 Ser.). (ENG.). 40p. (J). (gr. -1-3). 17.99 *(978-0-06-247311-0(5))*; pap. 6.99 *(978-0-06-247310-3(7))* HarperCollins Pubs.

Medeiros, Vânia. De Como Meninas Guerreiras Contaram Heroínas. Lyra, Luciana. 2011. (POR.). 173p. (J). *(978-85-60676-35-4(X))* Confraria Do Vento.

Medhurst, David. Don't Forget to Feed the Fish. Tarrington, Lindsay. 2018. (ENG.). 30p. (J). pap. 11.62 *(978-1-7904-4487-8(X))* Independently Published.

Media, Mindstir. My Daddy Might Be a Wizard. Hebert, J. J. 2019. (ENG.). 24p. (J). pap. 14.99 ***(978-1-7342210-0-8(3))*** Mindstir Media.

Medina, Andre. Meet the Monsters. 2015. (Hotel Transylvania 2 Ser.). (ENG.). 16p. (J). (gr. -1-3). pap. 5.99 *(978-1-4814-4802-4(1)*, Simon Spotlight) Simon Spotlight.

Medina, Erika. Margot & the Moon Landing. Fitzpatrick, A. C. 2020. 40p. (J). (gr. -1-2). 18.95 *(978-1-77321-360-6(1))* Annick Pr., Ltd. CAN. Dist: Publishers Group West (PGW).

Medina, Hector. El Libro de Los Maravillosos Automatas de Juguete. Rendon, Gilberto. rev. ed. 2006. (SPA & ENG.). 96p. (YA). (gr. 7-10). pap. 12.95 *(978-968-5920-87-2(7))* Castillo, Ediciones, S. A. de C. V. MEX. Dist: Macmillan.

Medina, Jose. Thank You, Crow. Medina, Jose. Minkowitz, Michael. 2018. (ENG.). 40p. (J). 16.95 *(978-0-9987999-8-8(X))* Penny Candy Bks., LLC.

Medina, Juana. I'm a Baked Potato! Primavera, Elise. 2019. (ENG.). 32p. (J). (gr. -1-k). 16.99 *(978-1-4521-5592-0(5))* Chronicle Bks. LLC.

—Lena's Shoes Are Nervous: A First-Day-of-School Dilemma. Calabrese, Keith. 2018. (ENG.). 40p. (J). (gr. -1-3). 17.99 *(978-1-5344-0894-4(0))* Simon & Schuster Children's Publishing.

Medina, Juana. Juana & Lucas. Medina, Juana. 96p. (J). (gr. k-3). 2019. pap. 7.99 *(978-1-5362-0639-5(3))*; 2016. 14.99 *(978-0-7636-7208-9(4))* Candlewick Pr.

—Juana & Lucas: Big Problemas. Medina, Juana. 2019. 96p. (J). (gr. k-3). 14.99 *(978-1-5362-0131-4(6))* Candlewick Pr.

Medina, Lan. Black Panther & the Agents of Wakanda Vol. 1: Eye of the Storm, Vol. 1. 2020. 112p. (YA). (gr. 4-17). pap. 17.99 *(978-1-302-92008-1(1))* Marvel Worldwide, Inc.

Medina, Paco. U. S. Avengers Vol. 1: American Intelligence Mechanics. 2017. (ENG.). 136p. (YA). (gr. 8-17). pap. 17.99 *(978-1-302-90641-2(0))* Marvel Worldwide, Inc.

—U. S. Avengers Vol. 2: Cannonball Run. 2018. (ENG.). 136p. (YA). (gr. 8-17). pap. 17.99 *(978-1-302-90642-9(9))* Marvel Worldwide, Inc.

Medina, Paco & Izaakse, Sean. Avengers: No Road Home. 2019. (ENG.). 256p. (YA). pap. 29.99 *(978-1-302-91485-1(5))* Marvel Worldwide, Inc.

Medina, Paco & Perez, Ramon. Marvel 2-In-One Vol. 2: Next of Kin. 2019. (Marvel 2-In-One - 2017 Ser.: 2). (ENG.). 160p. (J). (gr. 4-17). pap. 17.99 *(978-1-302-91491-2(X))* Marvel Worldwide, Inc.

Medina, Victor. Great Ports of the World: From New York to Hong Kong. Berchtig, Frauke. 2018. (ENG.). 40p. (J). (gr. -1-3). 14.95 *(978-3-7913-7355-3(2))* Prestel Verlag GmbH & Co KG. DEU. Dist: Penguin Random Hse. LLC.

MEE (Minoru Tachikawa). Hyper Police, Vol. 3. MEE (Minoru Tachikawa). rev. ed. 2005. 192p. pap. 9.99 *(978-1-59532-296-8(5)*, Tokyopop Adult) TOKYOPOP, Inc.

Meehan, Martin. White Plains. Perkin, Rebecca. 2017. (ENG.). 388p. (YA). (gr. 7-12). pap. *(978-0-9957984-2-7(7))* Perkin, Rebecca.

Meek, Ct. Finding Shapes & Lines with K. Meek, Ct. 2018. (ENG.). 32p. (J). pap. 6.39 *(978-1-7313-7884-2(X))* Independently Published.

Meeks, Arone Raymond. Enora & the Black Crane. Meeks, Arone Raymond. 2nd ed. 2010. (ENG.). 36p. (J). (gr. k-2). pap. 16.95 *(978-1-921248-02-3(5))* Magabala Bks. AUS. Dist: Independent Pubs. Group.

Meens, Estelle. Boss No More. 2014. 32p. (J). *(978-1-4338-1641-3(5)*, Magination Pr.) American Psychological Assn.

—Mom's Busy Days. Raucy, Elise. 2018. 32p. (J). *(978-1-4338-2820-1(0)*, Magination Pr.) American Psychological Assn.

Meesukhon, Patcharee & Yeesman, Vinit. All about Thailand: Stories, Songs & Crafts for Kids. Russell, Elaine. 2016. 64p. (J). (gr. 3-6). 14.95 *(978-0-8048-4427-7(5))* Tuttle Publishing.

Meeuwissen, Tony. Remarkable Animals (mini Edition) Mix & Match to Create 100 Crazy Creatures. rev. ed. 2016. (ENG.). 24p. (J). (gr. -1-k). 9.99 *(978-1-84780-762-5(3)*, Frances Lincoln Children's Bks.) Quarto Publishing Group UK GBR. Dist: Hachette Bk. Group.

Megahan, John & Rose, Melanie. W Is for Waves: An Ocean Alphabet. Smith, Marie & Smith, Roland. 2008. (ENG.). 32p. (J). (gr. k-6). 17.95 *(978-1-58536-254-7(9))* Sleeping Bear Pr.

Megale, Marina. Kids to the Rescue! First Aid Techniques for Kids. Boelts, Maribeth & Boelts, Darwin. rev. ed. 2003. (ENG.). 72p. (J). (gr. -1-7). pap. 9.95 *(978-1-884734-78-6(2))* Parenting Pr., Inc.

Megan, Egan. The Bedtimeasnaurus. Bayliss, Mike. 2017. (ENG.). 32p. (J). pap. *(978-1-9998572-0-2(8))* Bespoke Bk. Publishing.

Meganck, Margaux. The Marvelous Mustard Seed. Levine, Amy-Jill & Eisenberg Sasso, Sandy. 2018. (ENG.). 48p. (J). (gr. -1-3). 16.00 *(978-0-664-26275-4(9)*, 664262759, Flyaway Bks.) Westminster John Knox Pr.

—¿Quién Cuenta? 100 Ovejas, 10 Monedas y 2 Hijos. Levine, Amy-Jill & Eisenberg Sasso, Sandy. 2018. (ENG.). 40p. (J). (gr. -1-3). pap. 10.00 *(978-0-664-26406-2(9))* Westminster John Knox Pr.

—Who Counts? (Korean Edition) 100 Sheep, 10 Coins, & 2 Sons. Levine, Amy-Jill & Sasso, Sandy Eisenberg. 2019. (KOR.). 40p. (J). (gr. -1-2). pap. 10.00 *(978-1-947888-17-3(X)*, Flyaway Bks.) Westminster John Knox Pr.

Meganck, Margaux 0. Who Counts? 100 Sheep, 10 Coins, & 2 Sons. Levine, Amy-Jill & Sasso, Sandy Eisenberg. 2017. (ENG.). 40p. (J). (gr. -1-2). 16.00 *(978-0-664-26274-7(0))* Westminster John Knox Pr.

Meganck, Robert. Amphibian Acrobats, 1 vol. Bulion, Leslie. 2020. (ENG.). 60p. (J). (gr. 3-7). 15.99 *(978-1-68263-098-3(6))*; pap. 7.99 *(978-1-68263-184-3(2))* Peachtree Publishing Co. Inc.

—Leaf Litter Critters. Bulion, Leslie. (ENG.). 48p. (J). (gr. 3-7). 2020. pap. 7.99 *(978-1-68263-183-6(4))*; 2018. 14.95 *(978-1-56145-950-6(X))* Peachtree Publishing Co. Inc.

—Superlative Birds. Bulion, Leslie. (ENG.). 56p. (J). (gr. 3-7). 2020. pap. 7.99 *(978-1-68263-185-0(0))*; 2019. 15.95 *(978-1-56145-951-3(8))* Peachtree Publishing Co. Inc.

Meganck, Robert & Communication Design (Firm) Staff. Around the World with the Percussion Family!, 1 vol. Shaskan, Trisha Speed. 2010. (Musical Families Ser.). (ENG.). 24p. (J). (gr. k-3). lib. bdg. 25.99 *(978-1-4048-6044-5(4)*, Picture Window Bks.) Capstone.

—The Keyboard Family Takes Center Stage!, 1 vol. Shaskan, Trisha Speed. 2010. (Musical Families Ser.). (ENG.). 24p. (J). (gr. k-3). lib. bdg. 25.99 *(978-1-4048-6045-2(2)*, Picture Window Bks.) Capstone.

—Opening Night with the Woodwind Family!, 1 vol. Shaskan, Trisha Speed. 2010. (Musical Families Ser.). (ENG.). 24p. (J). (gr. k-3). lib. bdg. 25.99 *(978-1-4048-6042-1(8)*, Picture Window Bks.) Capstone.

—The String Family in Harmony!, 1 vol. Shaskan, Trisha Speed. 2010. (Musical Families Ser.). (ENG.). 24p. (J). (gr. k-3). lib. bdg. 25.99 *(978-1-4048-6043-8(6)*, Picture Window Bks.) Capstone.

Megenhardt, Bill. Grandma Spoils Me. Wright, Mary H. l.t. ed. 2005. 32p. (J). lib. bdg. 16.95 *(978-0-9645493-4-0(4))* Bluebonnets, Boots & Bks. Pr.

—Skoot Smells Something Funny: An Urban Animal Tale. Durbin, Kay Perry. 2019. (ENG.). 36p. (J). *(978-1-5255-4555-9(8))*; pap. *(978-1-5255-4556-6(6))* FriesenPress.

—Who Is Santa? And How Did He Get to the North Pole? Bigalow, Stephen W. 2013. (ENG.). 144p. (J). (gr. 4-7). 19.95 *(978-0-9773757-3-8(0))* Profit Publishing.

Meguerditchian, Laura. Hilary & the Tadpole. Green, Stella. 2016. (ENG.). (J). pap. *(978-0-9937118-1-7(2))* Green, Stella Mary.

Mehan, Abby. Together in Heaven. Petit, Karen. 2020. (ENG.). 58p. (J). 24.99 ***(978-1-64786-586-3(7))*** Primedia eLaunch LLC.

Mehee, Loic. Cat & Mouse Come to My House! Husar, Stephane. 2015. (Av2 Fiction Readalong 2016 Ser.). (ENG.). (J). lib. bdg. 34.28 *(978-1-4896-3804-5(0)*, AV2 by Weigl) Weigl Pubs., Inc.

—Cat & Mouse Eat Good Food! Husar, Stephane. 2015. (Av2 Fiction Readalong 2016 Ser.). (ENG.). (J). lib. bdg. 34.28 *(978-1-4896-3807-6(5)*, AV2 by Weigl) Weigl Pubs., Inc.

—Cat & Mouse Feelings. Husar, Stephane. 2015. (Av2 Fiction Readalong 2016 Ser.). (ENG.). (J). lib. bdg. 34.28 *(978-1-4896-3810-6(5)*, AV2 by Weigl) Weigl Pubs., Inc.

—Cat & Mouse Learn the Colors! Husar, Stephane. 2015. (Av2 Fiction Readalong 2016 Ser.). (ENG.). (J). lib. bdg. 34.28 *(978-1-4896-3813-7(X)*, AV2 by Weigl) Weigl Pubs., Inc.

—Cat & Mouse Let's Go Shopping! Husar, Stephane. 2015. (Av2 Fiction Readalong 2016 Ser.). (ENG.). (J). lib. bdg. 34.28 *(978-1-4896-3816-8(4)*, AV2 by Weigl) Weigl Pubs., Inc.

—Cat & Mouse Meet the Animals! Husar, Stephane. 2015. (Av2 Fiction Readalong 2016 Ser.). (ENG.). (J). lib. bdg. 34.28 *(978-1-4896-3819-9(9)*, AV2 by Weigl) Weigl Pubs., Inc.

Méhée, Loïc. Dinosaurs. Amiot, Romain. 2017. (ENG.). 32p. (J). 12.99 *(978-1-4413-2474-0(7)*, 993b8c32-b56d-4ab5-a26e-28e02dfd336c) Peter Pauper Pr. Inc.

Mehlen, Erik. Did Dinosaurs Have Dentists?, 1 vol. O'Donnell, Patrick. 2018. (ENG.). 32p. (J). (gr. -1-3). 14.99 *(978-0-7643-5602-5(X)*, 9906) Schiffer Publishing, Ltd.

—Do Penguins Have Pediatricians?, 1 vol. O'Donnell, Patrick. 2019. (ENG.). 32p. pap. 9.99 *(978-0-7643-5878-4(2)*, 20583); (J). 14.99 *(978-0-7643-5777-0(8)*, 16331) Schiffer Publishing, Ltd.

Mehlhorn, Alyssa. The Family Tree. Cowell, Julie. 2019. (King Street Club Ser.: Vol. 11). (ENG.). 116p. (J). pap. 8.99 ***(978-1-6994-6226-3(7))*** Independently Published.

—Leaping Heap of Trouble! Cowell, Julie. 2020. (King Street Club Ser.: Vol. 12). (ENG.). 112p. (J). pap. 8.99 ***(978-1-6737-9304-8(5))*** Independently Published.

Mehrlich, Cynthia. Splugworth Saves the Day, 1 vol. Mehrlich Iii, Ferdinand Paul. 2009. 43p. pap. 24.95 *(978-1-60836-765-8(7))* America Star Bks.

Meier, Kerry L. Adam's Grouchy Day. Muench-Williams, Heather. l.t. ed. 2005. (HRL Big Book Ser.). (J). (gr. -1-k). pap. 10.95 *(978-1-57332-320-8(9))*; pap. 10.95 *(978-1-57332-321-5(7))* Carson-Dellosa Publishing, LLC. (HighReach Learning, Incorporated).

—Caillou's Family & Friends. Jarrell, Pamela R. l.t. ed. 2005. (HRL Board Book Ser.). (J). (gr. k-18). pap. 10.95 *(978-1-57332-327-7(6)*, HighReach Learning, Incorporated) Carson-Dellosa Publishing, LLC.

—Caillou Visits the Farmer's Market. Vonthron, Satanta C. l.t. ed. 2005. (HRL Board Book Ser.). (J). (gr. -1-k). pap. 10.95 *(978-1-57332-310-9(1)*, HighReach Learning, Incorporated) Carson-Dellosa Publishing, LLC.

—If You Go into the Forest. Howard-Parham, Pam. l.t. ed. 2005. (HRL Board Book Ser.). (J). (gr. -1-k). pap. 10.95 *(978-1-57332-324-6(1)*, HighReach Learning, Incorporated) Carson-Dellosa Publishing, LLC.

Meier, Paul. Big Church. Pope, Amy. 2004. (J). bds. 9.99 *(978-1-4183-0008-1(X))* Christ Inspired, Inc.

—Crazy Old Lou. Parra, Jen. 2005. (J). bds. 9.99 *(978-1-4183-0063-0(2))* Christ Inspired, Inc.

—The Isle of Nam. Hansen, Eric. 2004. (J). bds. 9.99 *(978-1-4183-0016-6(0))* Christ Inspired, Inc.

—Princess Shannon & the Yellow Moon. Parra, Jen. 2004. (J). bds. 9.99 *(978-1-4183-0012-8(8))* Christ Inspired, Inc.

—The Ten Commandments. Alsbrooks, Stephanie. 2005. (J). bds. 9.99 *(978-1-4183-0064-7(0))* Christ Inspired, Inc.

Meier, Ty. Children of the Sea. Ruby, Anne. 2007. (YA). per. *(978-0-9787881-0-0(9))* Seachild.

Meierhofer, Brian. The Big Rescue: The Greenwood Forest Series, 1 vol. Knoch, Frank. 2010. 32p. pap. 24.95 *(978-1-4489-6158-0(0))* PublishAmerica, Inc.

Meijer, Marja. Anna's Tight Squeeze. De Smet, Marian. 2003. Orig. Title: Op Slot. 32p. (J). pap. 5.95 *(978-1-58925-378-0(7))* Tiger Tales.

—Benny Learns to Swim. Koppens, Judith. 2020. (Sam & Benny Ser.). 32p. (J). (gr. -1). 9.95 *(978-1-60537-516-8(0))*; 17.95 *(978-1-60537-497-0(0))* Clavis Publishing.

—A Book for Benny. Koppens, Judith. 2017. (Sam & Benny Ser.). (ENG.). 32p. (J). (gr. -1 — 1). 17.95 *(978-1-60537-352-2(4))* Clavis Publishing.

—A Book for Benny. Koppens, Judith. 2017. (Sam & Benny Ser.). 32p. (J). (gr. -1-2). pap. 9.95 *(978-1-60537-393-5(1))* Clavis ROM. Dist: Publishers Group West (PGW).

Meilichson, Alex. Bubbie & Zadie Come to My House: A Story of Hanukkah. Bloom, Daniel Halevi. 2006. (ENG.). 32p. (J). (gr. -1-3). 16.95 *(978-0-7570-0298-4(6))* Square One Pubs.

Meilihove, Jenny. When I Look Up. DeLange, Ellen. 2019. (ENG.). 32p. (J). 17.95 *(978-1-60537-431-4(8))*; 9.95 *(978-1-60537-475-8(X))* Clavis Publishing.

Meinke, Jeanne, jt. illus. see Meinke, Peter.

Meinke, Peter & Meinke, Jeanne. The Elf Poem, or, Nine Not Very Golden Rules for Children Who Like to Write Poetry. 2015. 104p. (J). pap. *(978-1-59732-129-7(X))* Univ. of Tampa Pr.

Meirink, Tineke. Traveling by Airplane. Winters, Pierre. 2012. (Want to Know Ser.). (ENG.). 30p. (J). (gr. -1-k). 16.95 *(978-1-60537-137-5(8))* Clavis Publishing.

Meisel, Paul. Brendan & Belinda & the Slam Dunk! Rockwell, Anne. 2007. (Good Sports Ser.). 40p. (J). (gr. -1-1). 15.99 *(978-0-06-028443-5(9))* HarperCollins Pubs.

—The Cool Crazy Crickets Club. Elliott, David. 2010. 48p. (J). (gr. 1-4). 5.99 *(978-0-7636-4659-2(8))* Candlewick Pr.

—The Cool Crazy Crickets to the Rescue. Elliott, David. 2010. 48p. (J). (gr. 1-4). 5.99 *(978-0-7636-4658-5(X))* Candlewick Pr.

—Dear Baby: Letters from Your Big Brother. Sullivan, Sarah. 2005. (ENG.). 40p. (J). (gr. k-3). 14.99 *(978-0-7636-2126-1(9))* Candlewick Pr.

—Forces Make Things Move. Bradley, Kimberly Brubaker. 2005. (Let's Read-And-Find-Out Science Stage 2 Ser.). (ENG.). 32p. (J). (gr. 1-3). lib. bdg. 18.69 *(978-0-06-028907-2(4))* HarperCollins Pubs.

—Forces Make Things Move. Bradley, Kimberly. 2005. (Let's-Read-And-Find-Out Science 2 Ser.). (ENG.). 40p. (J). (gr. -1-3). pap. 5.99 *(978-0-06-445214-4(X))* HarperCollins Pubs.

—Go Away, Dog. Nodset, Joan L. 2003. (My First I Can Read Ser.). (ENG.). 32p. (J). (gr. -1-3). pap. 4.99 *(978-0-06-444231-2(4)*, HarperCollins) HarperCollins Pubs. Ltd. GBR. Dist: HarperCollins Pubs.

—Go Away, Dog. Nodset, Joan L. ed. 2003. (My First I Can Read Ser.). 32p. (J). (gr. -1-k). lib. bdg. 13.55 *(978-0-613-13602-0(0))* Turtleback.

—Harriet's Had Enough! Guest, Elissa Haden. 2009. 32p. (J). (gr. -1-2). 15.99 *(978-0-7636-3454-4(9))* Candlewick Pr.

—How to Talk to Your Cat. George, Jean Craighead. 2003. (ENG.). 40p. (J). (gr. 1-4). pap. 7.99 *(978-0-06-000622-8(6))* HarperCollins Pubs.

—Katie Catz Makes a Splash. Rockwell, Anne. 2003. (Good Sports Ser.). 40p. (J). (gr. -1-1). 15.99 *(978-0-06-028441-1(2))* HarperCollins Pubs.

—A Kid's Guide to the Green New Deal: How to Save the Planet. Goodman, Billy. 2019. (Camelot World Ser.: Vol. 1). (ENG.). 84p. (J). (gr. 3-6). pap. 9.95 *(978-1-59687-862-4(2)*, ipicturebooks) ibooks, Inc.

—The Leprechaun under the Bed. Bateman, Teresa. 32p. (J). (gr. -1-3). 2019. pap. 7.99 *(978-0-8234-4181-5(4))*; 2012. (ENG.). 17.95 *(978-0-8234-2221-0(6))* Holiday Hse., Inc.

—Light Is All Around Us. Pfeffer, Wendy. (Let's-Read-And-Find-Out Science 2 Ser.). (ENG.). 40p. (J). (gr. -1-3). 2015. pap. 6.99 *(978-0-06-238190-3(3))*; 2014. 17.99 *(978-0-06-029121-1(4))* HarperCollins Pubs.

—Light Is All Around Us. Pfeffer, Wendy. 2014. (Let's-Read-And-Find-Out Science: Stage 2 Ser.). (ENG.). (J). (gr. -1-3). lib. bdg. 16.60 *(978-1-62765-367-1(8))* Perfection Learning Corp.

—The Little Red Hen & the Passover Matzah. Kimmelman, Leslie. 2011. (ENG.). 32p. (J). (gr. -1-3). pap. 8.99 *(978-0-8234-2327-9(1))* Holiday Hse., Inc.

—Looking for Leprechauns. Keenan, Sheila. 2005. (J). *(978-0-439-68057-8(3))* Scholastic, Inc.

—Mr. Ouchy's First Day. Hennessy, B. G. 2007. (J). (gr. k-3). 27.95 incl. audio *(978-0-8045-6946-0(0))*; 29.95 incl. audio compact disk *(978-0-8045-4160-2(4))* Spoken Arts, Inc.

—Run for Your Life! Predators & Prey on the African Savanna. Schaefer, Lola M. 2016. (ENG.). 32p. (J). (gr. -1-3). 16.95 *(978-0-8234-3555-5(5))* Holiday Hse., Inc.

—Scat, Cat! Capucilli, Alyssa Satin. 2010. (My First I Can Read Ser.). (ENG.). 32p. (J). (gr. -1 — 1). 16.99 *(978-0-06-117754-5(7))*; pap. 4.99 *(978-0-06-117756-9(3))* HarperCollins Pubs.

—The Schmutzy Family. Rosenberg, Madelyn. 2018. 32p. (J). (gr. -1-3). pap. 8.99 *(978-0-8234-4241-6(1))* Holiday Hse., Inc.

—Stinky Spike & the Royal Rescue. Meisel, Peter. (Read & Bloom Ser.). 80p. (J). 2018. pap. 6.99 *(978-1-61963-886-0(X)*, 900150927, Bloomsbury Children's Bks.); 2017. (ENG.). 9.99 *(978-1-61963-883-9(5)*, 9781619638839, Bloomsbury USA Childrens) Bloomsbury Publishing USA.

—Stinky Spike the Pirate Dog. Meisel, Peter. 2017. (ENG.). 80p. (J). 9.99 *(978-1-61963-778-8(2)*, 900148819, Bloomsbury USA Childrens) Bloomsbury Publishing USA.

—Things That Go. Highlights for Children, Highlights for & Jordan, Karen. 2015. (Highlights(TM) Find It Board Bks.). (ENG.). 14p. (J). (— 1). bds. 7.99 *(978-1-62979-414-3(7)*, Highlights) Boyds Mills Pr.

—The Three Bears' Christmas. Duval, Kathy. 2007. (J). *(978-0-545-05421-8(4))* Scholastic, Inc.

—Trick or Treat? Martin, Bill, Jr. & Sampson, Michael. 2005. (ENG.). 32p. (J). (gr. -1-3). reprint ed. 7.99 *(978-1-4169-0262-1(7)*, Aladdin) Simon & Schuster Children's Publishing.

—Vampire Baby. Bennett, Kelly. 2013. 32p. (J). (gr. -1-3). 15.99 *(978-0-7636-4691-2(1))* Candlewick Pr.

—We All Sing with the Same Voice. Miller, J. Philip & Greene, Sheppard M. 2005. (ENG.). 40p. (J). (gr. -1-2). reprint ed. pap. 7.99 *(978-0-06-073900-3(2))* HarperCollins Pubs.

—What Happens to Our Trash? Ward, D. J. 2012. (Let's-Read-And-Find-Out Science 2 Ser.). (ENG.). 40p. (J). (gr. -1-3). 16.99 *(978-0-06-168756-3(1))*; pap. 5.99 *(978-0-06-168755-6(3)*, Collins) HarperCollins Pubs.

—What Is the World Made Of? All about Solids, Liquids, & Gases. Zoehfeld, Kathleen Weidner. 2015. (Let's-Read-And-Find-Out Science 2 Ser.). (ENG.). 32p. (J). (gr. -1-3). pap. 6.99 *(978-0-06-238195-8(4))* HarperCollins Pubs.

—What's So Bad about Gasoline? Fossil Fuels & What They Do. Rockwell, Anne. 2009. (Let's-Read-And-Find-Out Science 2 Ser.). (ENG.). 40p. (J). (gr. -1-3). pap. 5.99 *(978-0-06-157527-3(5)*, Collins) HarperCollins Pubs.

—What's the Matter in Mr. Whiskers' Room? Ross, Michael Elsohn. 2007. (ENG.). 48p. (J). (gr. 1-4). pap. 7.99 *(978-0-7636-3566-4(9))* Candlewick Pr.

—Why Are the Ice Caps Melting? The Dangers of Global Warming. Rockwell, Anne. 2006. (Let's-Read-And-Find-Out Science 2 Ser.). (ENG.). 40p. (J). (gr. k-4). pap. 5.99 *(978-0-06-054671-7(9)*, Collins) HarperCollins Pubs.

Meisel, Paul. See Me Dig. Meisel, Paul. 2013. (I Like to Read Ser.). (ENG.). 24p. (J). (gr. -1-3). 14.95 *(978-0-8234-2743-7(9))* Holiday Hse., Inc.

—See Me Run. Meisel, Paul. (I Like to Read Ser.). (ENG.). 24p. (J). (gr. -1-3). 2012. pap. 7.99 *(978-0-8234-2638-6(6))*; 2011. 14.95 *(978-0-8234-2349-1(2))* Holiday Hse., Inc.

Meisel, Paul, jt. illus. see Wilkin, Eloise.

Meissner, Amy. The Misadventures of Seldovia Sam. Springer, Susan Woodward. 2018. (ENG.). (J). (gr. 1-3). 262p. 27.99 *(978-1-5132-6167-6(3))*; 258p. pap. 14.99 *(978-1-5132-6166-9(5))* West Margin Pr. (Alaska Northwest Bks.).

—Sam's Ride, 1 vol. Citra, Becky. 2009. (Orca Echoes Ser.). (ENG.). 64p. (J). (gr. 1-3). pap. 6.95 *(978-1-55469-160-9(5))* Orca Bk. Pubs. USA.

—Saving Sammy, 1 vol. Walters, Eric. 2014. (Orca Echoes Ser.). (ENG.). 64p. (J). (gr. 1-3). pap. 6.95 *(978-1-4598-0499-9(6))* Orca Bk. Pubs. USA.

—Sea Dog. Gaetz, Dayle Campbell. 2006. 62p. (J). lib. bdg. 20.00 *(978-1-4242-1249-1(9))* Fitzgerald Bks.

—Sea Dog, 1 vol. Gaetz, Dayle Campbell. 2006. (Orca Echoes Ser.). (ENG.). 64p. (J). (gr. 1-3). per. 6.95 *(978-1-55143-406-3(7))* Orca Bk. Pubs. USA.

—Seeing Orange, 1 vol. Cassidy, Sara. 2012. (Orca Echoes Ser.). (ENG.). 64p. (J). (gr. 1-3). pap. 6.95 *(978-1-55469-991-9(6))* Orca Bk. Pubs. USA.

—Seldovia Sam & the Very Large Clam. Springer, Susan Woodward. 2003. (Misadventures of Seldovia Sam Ser.: 1). (ENG.). 64p. (J). (gr. -1-4). pap. 6.95 *(978-0-88240-570-4(5)*, Alaska Northwest Bks.) West Margin Pr.

—Seldovia Sam & Wildfire Escape. Springer, Susan Woodward. 2005. (Misadventures of Seldovia Sam Ser.: Bk. 3). (ENG.). 64p. (J). (gr. -1-4). per. 6.95

M

(978-0-88240-601-5(9), Alaska Northwest Bks.) West Margin Pr.

—The Wrong Bus, 1 vol. Peterson, Lois. 2012. (Orca Echoes Ser.). (ENG.). 64p. (J). (gr. 1-3). pap. 6.95 *(978-1-55469-869-1(3))* Orca Bk. Pubs. USA.

Meister, Charles, jt. illus. see Landau, Helena Von.

Meister, Charles E. Our Little Crusader Cousin of Long Ago. Stein, Evaleen. 2007. 136p. per. 8.95 *(978-1-59915-243-1(6))* Yesterday's Classics.

Meister, Michael. Le Monstrueux Livre des Monstres Suisses. Darling, Jeanne. Olsen, Dag, tr. 2018. (FRE.). 72p. (J). 38.00 *(978-3-03869-026-9(0))* Bergli Bks. CHE. Dist: ISD.

—Swisstory: The Untold, Bloody, & Absolutely Real History of Switzerland. Delarue-Theurer, Laurie. 2019. (ENG.). 270p. (J). pap. 25.00 *(978-3-03869-082-5(1))* Bergli Bks. CHE. Dist: ISD.

Meitin, Ryan J. Monsters Are People Too! Meitin, Sharon T. 2019. (ENG.). 24p. (J). pap. 10.00 *(978-1-7171-7702-5(6))* CreateSpace Independent Publishing Platform.

Mejía, Estella. The Legend of the Colombian Mermaid. Balletta, Janet. 2013. 36p. (J). pap. 14.95 *(978-0-9856762-9-2(9))* WRB Pub.

Mejia, Estella. La Leyenda de Roberto Cofresi un Heroe de Puerto Rico. Balletta, Janet. Morris, Ana, tr. 2016. (SPA.). (J). (gr. k-6). pap. 14.95 *(978-0-9909040-8-3(3))* WRB Pub.

Mejias, John & Mejias, John. The Hungry Brothers. 2009. (ENG.). 32p. (J). (gr. -1-2). 15.95 *(978-0-9798841-1-5(X))* 4N Publishing LLC.

Mejias, John, jt. illus. see Mejias, John.

Mejías, Mónica. Aprendiendo a Leer con Mili y Molo: Learn How to Read in Spanish. Mejías, Mónica. 2004.Tr. of Lernen Sie Spanish Lesen, Impara a leggere in Spagnolo, Aprenda a ler Espanhol, Apprenez à lire L'espagnol. 40p. (J). audio compact disk 12.00 *(978-0-9753799-0-5(9))* Ediciones Alas, Inc.

Mekis, Pete. Tommy Books: Faith, 10 vols. Brown, Mark. l.t. ed. 2005. 24p. (J). 12.99 *(978-0-9762690-0-7(7))* Tommy Bks. Pubng.

—Tommy Books: Kings, 10 vols. Brown, Mark. l.t. ed. 2005. 24p. (J). 12.99 *(978-0-9762690-4-5(X))* Tommy Bks. Pubng.

—Tommy Books Vol. 2: Love, 10 vols. Brown, Mark. l.t. ed. 2005. 24p. (J). 12.99 *(978-0-9762690-1-4(5))* Tommy Bks. Pubng.

—Tommy Books Vol. 3: Too Busy, 10 vols. Brown, Mark. l.t. ed. 2005. 24p. (J). 12.99 *(978-0-9762690-2-1(3))* Tommy Bks. Pubng.

—Tommy Books Vol. 4: Praise, 10 vols. Brown, Mark. l.t. ed. 2005. 20p. (J). 12.99 *(978-0-9762690-3-8(1))* Tommy Bks. Pubng.

Melanson, Luc. Book of Big Brothers, 1 vol. Fagan, Cary. 2010. (ENG.). 32p. (J). (gr. -1-2). 17.95 *(978-0-88899-977-1(1))* Groundwood Bks. CAN. Dist: Publishers Group West (PGW).

—How to Become a Perfect Princess in Five Days. Dube, Pierrette. 2009. (Rainy Day Readers Ser.). 32p. (J). (gr. -1-3). 25.60 *(978-1-60754-376-3(1))* Windmill Bks.

—Redheaded Robbie's Christmas Story. Luttrel, Bill. 2003. (ENG.). 32p. (J). (gr. k-6). 16.95 *(978-1-58536-136-6(4))* Sleeping Bear Pr.

—Rosario's Fig Tree, 1 vol. Wahl, Charis. 2015. (ENG.). 32p. (J). (gr. -1-2). 18.95 *(978-1-55498-341-4(X))* Groundwood Bks. CAN. Dist: Publishers Group West (PGW).

Melanson, Matt. Against All Odds. Kropp, Paul. 2012. (HIP Sr Ser.). (ENG.). 87p. (J). (gr. 7-12). 26.19 *(978-1-897039-06-9(9))* High Interest Publishing (HIP) CAN. Dist: Children's Plus, Inc.

—The Kid Is Lost. Kropp, Paul. 2004. (HIP Sr Ser.). (ENG.). 88p. (J). (gr. 7-12). 26.19 *(978-1-897039-04-5(2))* High Interest Publishing (HIP) CAN. Dist: Children's Plus, Inc.

—Our Plane Is Down. Paton, Doug. 2004. (New Series Canada). 90p. (J). pap. *(978-1-897039-03-8(4))* High Interest Publishing (HIP).

—Student Narc. Kropp, Paul. 2004. (HIP Sr Ser.). (ENG.). 94p. (J). (gr. 7-12). 26.19 *(978-1-897039-05-2(0))* High Interest Publishing (HIP) CAN. Dist: Children's Plus, Inc.

Melaranci, Elisabetta, et al. Race for the Stars. Weinberg, Jennifer et al. 2017. 24p. (J). *(978-1-5182-2673-1(6))* Random Hse., Inc.

Melaranci, Elisabetta, et al. Tangled. Ferrari, Alessandro. 2020. (Disney Princesses Ser.). (ENG.). 52p. (J). (gr. 2-6). lib. bdg. 28.50 ***(978-1-5321-4569-8(1)***, 35216, Graphic Novels) Spotlight.

Melaranci, Elisabetta & Merli, Anna. Monsters, Inc. Bazaldua, Charles. 2020. (Disney & Pixar Movies Ser.). (ENG.). 48p. (J). (gr. 2-6). lib. bdg. 28.50 ***(978-1-5321-4553-7(5)***, 35200, Graphic Novels) Spotlight.

Melaranci, Elisabetta & Usai, Luca. The Princess & the Frog. Macchetto, Augusto. 2020. (Disney Princesses Ser.). (ENG.). 52p. (J). (gr. 2-6). lib. bdg. 28.50 ***(978-1-5321-4566-7(7)***, 35213, Graphic Novels) Spotlight.

Melaranci, Elisabetta, jt. illus. see Disney Storybook Art Team.

Melaranci, Elisabetta, jt. illus. see Liu, Chun.

Melaranci, Elisabetta, jt. illus. see Priori, Giulia.

Melby, Walker. Creepers Crashed My Party: Redstone Junior High #2. Stevens, Cara J. 2018. (Redstone Junior High Ser.: 2). (ENG.). 192p. (J). (gr. 3-7). pap. 11.99 *(978-1-5107-3262-9(4)*, Sky Pony Pr.) Skyhorse Publishing Co., Inc.

—Dragons Never Die: Redstone Junior High #3. Stevens, Cara J. 2018. (Redstone Junior High Ser.: 3). (ENG.). 192p. (J). (gr. 3-7). pap. 11.99 *(978-1-5107-3797-6(9)*, Sky Pony Pr.) Skyhorse Publishing Co., Inc.

—Saving Xenos: An Unofficial Graphic Novel for Minecrafters, #6. Stevens, Cara J. 2018. (Unofficial Graphic Novel for Minecrafter Ser.). (ENG.). 192p. (J). (gr. 3-7). pap. 11.99 *(978-1-5107-2719-9(1)*, Sky Pony Pr.) Skyhorse Publishing Co., Inc.

—When Endermen Attack: Redstone Junior High #4. Stevens, Cara J. 2018. (Redstone Junior High Ser.: 4). (ENG.). 192p. (J). (gr. 3-7). pap. 11.99 *(978-1-5107-3798-3(7)*, Sky Pony Pr.) Skyhorse Publishing Co., Inc.

Melcher, Mary. Puppies Count. 2010. (J). *(978-1-58865-596-7(2))* Kidsbooks, LLC.

Melcher, Michele. Elvis: A Graphic Novel. Collins, Terry. (American Graphic Ser.). (ENG.). 32p. (gr. 3-4). 2011. pap. 47.70 *(978-1-4296-6434-9(7)*, Capstone Pr.); 2010. (J). lib. bdg. 31.32 *(978-1-4296-5476-0(7))* Capstone.

Melchishua, Tewodross. Shango's Son. Winmilawe. 2012. 20p. pap. 9.95 *(978-0-9839318-0-5(1))* Gazing In Publishing.

Meldrum, Ned, photos by. Big Balloon, 1 vol. Dale, Jay. 2012. (Engage Literacy Yellow Ser.). (ENG., 32p. (gr. k-2). pap. 5.99 *(978-1-4296-8962-5(5)*, Capstone Pr.) Capstone.

—Circus Tricks, 1 vol. Giulieri, Anne. 2012. (Engage Literacy Green Ser.). (ENG., 32p. (gr. k-2). pap. 5.99 *(978-1-4296-9006-5(2)*, Capstone Pr.) Capstone.

—Cooking Pancakes, 1 vol. Giulieri, Anne. 2012. (Engage Literacy Red Ser.). (ENG., 32p. (gr. k-2). pap. 5.99 *(978-1-4296-8950-2(1)*, Capstone Pr.) Capstone.

—The Environment Park, 1 vol. Dale, Jay. 2012. (Engage Literacy Green Ser.). (ENG., 32p. (gr. k-2). pap. 5.99 *(978-1-4296-8997-7(8)*, Capstone Pr.) Capstone.

—Make a Secret Playhouse, 1 vol. Giulieri, Anne. 2012. (Engage Literacy Green Ser.). (ENG., 32p. (gr. k-2). pap. 5.99 *(978-1-4296-9001-0(1)*, Capstone Pr.) Capstone.

—My Big Sandwich, 1 vol. Dale, Jay. 2012. (Engage Literacy Red Ser.). (ENG., 32p. (gr. k-2). pap. 5.99 *(978-1-4296-8834-5(3)*, Capstone Pr.) Capstone.

—My Dinosaurs, 1 vol. Giulieri, Anne. 2012. (Engage Literacy Red Ser.). (ENG., 32p. (gr. k-2). pap. 5.99 *(978-1-4296-8938-0(2)*, Capstone Pr.) Capstone.

—My Rock Pool, 1 vol. Giulieri, Anne. 2012. (Engage Literacy Green Ser.). (ENG., 32p. (gr. k-2). pap. 5.99 *(978-1-4296-9013-3(5)*, Capstone Pr.) Capstone.

Melendez, Abigail. Lulu Bakes: #1 a Lovely Discovery. Melendez, Iris R. 2019. (Lulu Bakes Ser.: Vol. 1). (ENG.). 44p. (J). pap. 15.00 ***(978-1-0916-1209-9(9))*** Independently Published.

Melendez, Angela. El Primer día de Clases. Mira, Katish. 2018. (SPA.). 38p. (J). (gr. k-3). *(978-958-48-3871-1(7))* Restrepo, Ana.

Melendez, Nef. Suzy Has a Secret. Leuthner, Carolina & Deborah, Nichols H. 2016. (Edgeceus Kiddies Ser.: Vol. 1). (ENG.). (J). pap. 16.99 *(978-0-9996501-1-0(4))* Edge, Inc.

Meler, Kerry L. Caillou's Castle. Williams, Heather L. l.t. ed. 2005. (HRL Board Book Ser.). (J). (gr. -1-1). pap. 10.95 *(978-1-57332-291-1(1)*, HighReach Learning, Incorporated) Carson-Dellosa Publishing, LLC.

—Planting a Seed. Jarrell, Pamela R. l.t. ed. 2006. 12p. (J). (gr. -1-k). pap. 10.95 *(978-1-57332-350-5(0)*, HighReach Learning, Incorporated) Carson-Dellosa Publishing, LLC.

—Pretend. Mullican, Judy. l.t. ed. 2005. (HRL Board Book Ser.). 10p. (J). (gr. -1-1). pap. 10.95 *(978-1-57332-283-6(0)*, HighReach Learning, Incorporated) Carson-Dellosa Publishing, LLC.

Melhuish, Eva. Christmas Magic. Stainton, Sue. 2007. 32p. (J). (gr. -1-1). lib. bdg. 16.89 *(978-0-06-078572-7(1)*, Tegen, Katherine Bks) HarperCollins Pubs.

Melinda, Sheffler. Cuddles the Chocolate Cow & Friends. Edmond, Wally. 2006. 39p. (J). 14.95 *(978-1-59879-108-2(7))*; per. 9.99 *(978-1-59879-125-9(7))* Lifevest Publishing, Inc.

Melinda, Shoals. The Spritelees: A Christmas Tale about Kindness. 2006. 32p. (J). 16.00 *(978-0-9773460-0-4(5))* Spritelee Enterprises.

Mellin, Jeanne. Annie: The Mysterious Morgan Horse. Feld, Ellen F. 2007. 206p. (J). per. 9.95 *(978-0-9709002-9-6(5))* Willow Bend Publishing.

—Blackjack: Dreaming of a Morgan Horse, 4 vols. Feld, Ellen F. 3rd rev. ed. 2007. (ENG.). 238p. (J). (gr. 4-6). per. 9.95 *(978-0-9709002-8-9(7))* Willow Bend Publishing.

—Rimfire: The Barrel Racing Morgan Horse. Feld, Ellen F. 2009. (ENG.). 206p. (J). pap. 9.95 *(978-0-9709002-1-0(X))* Willow Bend Publishing.

—Robin: The Lovable Morgan Horse, 4 vols. Feld, Ellen F. 2005. (ENG.). 204p. (J). (gr. 4-6). per. 9.95 *(978-0-9709002-5-8(2))* Willow Bend Publishing.

Melling, David. First Arabic Words. Morris, Neil. 2009. (First Words Ser.). (ENG.). 48p. (YA). (gr. 3-18). pap. 12.95 *(978-0-19-911135-0(9))* Oxford Univ. Pr., Inc.

—First Italian Words. 2009. (First Words Ser.). 48p. (J). (gr. 3-18). pap. 12.95 *(978-0-19-911100-8(6))* Oxford Univ. Pr., Inc.

—The Flying Diggers. Whybrow, Ian. 2009. (J). *(978-1-4351-6500-7(4))* Barnes & Noble, Inc.

—Jerry's Trousers. Boswall, Nigel. 2003. (ENG.). 26p. (J). pap. 4.99 *(978-0-333-68359-0(5))* Macmillan Pubs., Ltd. GBR. Dist: Trafalgar Square Publishing.

Melling, David. D Is for Duck. Melling, David. 2017. 32p. (J). 12.99 *(978-1-61067-580-2(0))* Kane Miller.

—Dont Worry Douglas. Melling, David. 2011. (ENG.). 32p. 12.95 *(978-1-58925-106-9(7))* Tiger Tales.

—Hugless Douglas & the Big Sleepover. Melling, David. 2019. (ENG.). 32p. (J). (gr. 1-3). 17.99 *(978-1-68412-376-6(3)*, Silver Dolphin Bks.) Printers Row Publishing Group.

—Hugless Dougless. Melling, David. 2010. (ENG.). 32p. (J). (gr. -1-2). 15.95 *(978-1-58925-098-7(2))* Tiger Tales.

—Splish, Splash, Splosh! Melling, David. 2013. (ENG.). 22p. (J). (gr. -1). bds. 8.95 *(978-1-58925-643-9(3))* Tiger Tales.

Melling, David. Cold Enough for Snow. Melling, David, tr. McKay, Hilary. 2003. (Pudding Bag School Ser.: Bk. 2). (ENG.). 144p. (J). pap. *(978-0-340-87750-0(2)*, Hodder Children's Books) Hachette Children's Group.

Mello, Beatriz. Miles Away in the Caribbean. Marshall, Yolanda T. 2019. (ENG.). 38p. (J). (gr. k-6). *(978-1-9991155-1-7(1))* Gamalma Pr.

Mello, Eduardo, et al. Marvel: 8-Book Library & Electronic Reader. Houlihan, Brian. 2019. (Me Reader Ser.). (ENG.). 192p. (J). *(978-1-5037-4805-7(7)*, 3444a09d-e43c-46c0-b936-940441251238, p i kids) Phoenix International Publications, Inc.

Mello, Eugenia. Dr. Wangari Maathai Plants a Forest. Rebel Girls. 2020. (Good Night Stories for Rebel Girls Chapter Book Ser.). (ENG.). 128p. (J). (gr. 2-5). 12.99 *(978-1-7333292-1-7(8)*, Rebel Girls) Timbuktu Labs, inc.

Mello, Roger. Charcoal Boys. Mello, Roger. Hahn, Daniel, tr. 2019. (ENG.). 46p. (J). (gr. k-3). 20.00 *(978-1-939810-19-9(1)*, Elsewhere Editions) Steerforth Pr.

—You Can't Be Too Careful! Mello, Roger. Hahn, Daniel, tr. 2017. (ENG.). 36p. (J). (gr. k-3). 18.00 *(978-0-914671-64-0(2)*, Elsewhere Editions) Steerforth Pr.

Mellors, Zoe. The Song Garden. Weber, Vicky. 2020. (ENG.). 36p. (J). 18.99 ***(978-1-7342129-6-9(9))*** Trunk Up Bks.

—The Song Garden. Weber, Vicky. 2020. (ENG.). 36p. (J). pap. 12.99 ***(978-1-7342129-7-6(7))*** Trunk Up Bks.

Melmon, Deborah. Adventures at Hound Hotel. Swanson Sateren, Shelley. 2016. (Adventures at Hound Hotel Ser.). (ENG.). 72p. (J). (gr. 1-3). lib. bdg., lib. bdg., lib. bdg. 202.56 *(978-1-5158-0078-1(4)*, Picture Window Bks.) Capstone.

—Adventures at Tabby Towers, 4 vols. Swanson Sateren, Shelley. 2017. (Adventures at Tabby Towers Ser.). (ENG.). 72p. (J). (gr. 1-4). 101.28 *(978-1-5158-1565-5(X)*, 26990); pap., pap., pap. 19.80 *(978-1-5158-1566-2(8)*, 26991) Capstone. (Picture Window Bks.).

—Adventures of Hound Hotel Collection. Swanson Sateren, Shelley. ed. 2017. (Adventures at Hound Hotel Ser.). (ENG.). 272p. (J). 9.99 *(978-1-5158-1891-5(8)*, 136489, Picture Window Bks.) Capstone.

—Albert Adds Up! May, Eleanor. 2014. (Mouse Math ® Ser.). 32p. (J). (gr. -1-1). 22.60 *(978-1-57565-744-8(9))* Astra Publishing Hse.

—Albert Doubles the Fun. May, Eleanor. 2017. (Mouse Math ® Ser.). (ENG.). 32p. (J). (gr. -1-1). 22.65 *(978-1-57565-834-6(8))* Astra Publishing Hse.

—Albert Doubles the Fun: Adding Doubles. May, Eleanor. ed. 2017. (Mouse Math ® Ser.). (ENG.). 32p. (gr. -1-1). E-Book 34.65 *(978-1-57565-836-0(4))* Astra Publishing Hse.

—Albert Helps Out: Counting Money. May, Eleanor. 2017. (Mouse Math ® Ser.). (ENG.). 32p. (J). (gr. -1-1). 7.95 *(978-1-57565-860-5(7))* Astra Publishing Hse.

—Albert Helps Out: Counting Money. May, Eleanor. 2017. (Mouse Math ® Ser.). (ENG.). 32p. (gr. -1-1). (J). lib. bdg. 22.65 *(978-1-57565-857-5(7))*; E-Book 34.65 *(978-1-57565-863-6(1))* Astra Publishing Hse.

—Albert Is Not Scared. May, Eleanor. 2013. (Mouse Math Ser.). (ENG.). 32p. (J). (gr. -1-1). lib. bdg. 22.60 *(978-1-57565-628-1(0))* Astra Publishing Hse.

—Albert Is NOT Scared: Direction Words. May, Eleanor. 2013. (Mouse Math ® Ser.). (ENG.). 32p. (J). (gr. -1-1). pap. 7.95 *(978-1-57565-629-8(9)*, 9781575656298); E-Book 34.65 *(978-1-57565-630-4(2))* Astra Publishing Hse.

—Albert Keeps Score. Skinner, Daphne. 2012. (Mouse Math Ser.). (ENG.). 32p. (J). (gr. -1-1). lib. bdg. 22.60 *(978-1-57565-449-2(0))* Astra Publishing Hse.

—Albert Keeps Score: Comparing Numbers. May, Eleanor. 2012. (Mouse Math ® Ser.). (ENG.). 32p. (J). (gr. -1-1). 7.95 *(978-1-57565-444-7(X)*, 9781575654447) Astra Publishing Hse.

—Albert Starts School. May, Eleanor. 2015. (Mouse Math ® Ser.). (ENG.). 32p. (J). (gr. -1-1). 22.65 *(978-1-57565-741-7(4))* Astra Publishing Hse.

—Albert the Muffin-Maker. May, Eleanor. 2014. (Mouse Math Ser.). 32p. (J). (gr. -1-1). lib. bdg. 22.60 *(978-1-57565-631-1(0))* Astra Publishing Hse.

—Albert's Amazing Snail. May, Eleanor. 2012. (Mouse Math Ser.). (ENG.). 32p. (J). (gr. -1-1). 22.60 *(978-1-57565-448-5(2))* Astra Publishing Hse.

—Albert's Amazing Snail: Position Words. May, Eleanor. 2012. (Mouse Math ® Ser.). (ENG.). 32p. (J). (gr. -1-1). pap. 7.95 *(978-1-57565-442-3(3)*, 9781575654423) Astra Publishing Hse.

—Albert's BIGGER Than Big Idea: Comparing Sizes: Big/Small. May, Eleanor. 2013. (Mouse Math ® Ser.). (ENG.). 32p. (J). (gr. -1-1). pap. 7.95 *(978-1-57565-522-2(5)*, 9781575655222) Astra Publishing Hse.

—Baby Wants Mama, 0 vols. Loewen, Nancy. 2013. (ENG.). 24p. (J). (gr. -1-k). 14.99 *(978-1-4778-1651-6(8)*, 9781477816516, Two Lions) Amazon Publishing.

—A Beach for Albert. May, Eleanor. 2013. (Mouse Math Ser.). 32p. (gr. -1-1). lib. bdg. 22.60 *(978-1-57565-530-7(6))* Astra Publishing Hse.

—A Beach for Albert: Capacity. May, Eleanor. 2013. (Mouse Math ® Ser.). (ENG.). 32p. (J). (gr. -1-1). pap. 7.95 *(978-1-57565-531-4(4)*, 9781575655314) Astra Publishing Hse.

—Boxing Bootsie. Swanson Sateren, Shelley. 2017. (Adventures at Tabby Towers Ser.). (ENG.). 72p. (J). (gr. 1-4). pap. 4.95 *(978-1-5158-1551-8(X)*, 136119); lib. bdg. 25.32 *(978-1-5158-1547-1(1)*, 136114) Capstone. (Picture Window Bks.).

—Bravo, Albert! Houran, Lori Haskins. 2017. (Mouse Math ® Ser.). (ENG.). 32p. (J). (gr. -1-1). lib. bdg. 22.65 *(978-1-57565-856-8(9))* Astra Publishing Hse.

—Bravo, Albert! Patterns. Houran, Lori Haskins. 2017. (Mouse Math ® Ser.). (ENG.). 32p. (J). (gr. -1-1). 7.95 *(978-1-57565-859-9(3))* Astra Publishing Hse.

—Bravo, Albert! Patterns. Houran, Lori Haskins. ed. 2017. (Mouse Math ® Ser.). (ENG.). 32p. (gr. -1-1). E-Book 34.65 *(978-1-57565-862-9(3))* Astra Publishing Hse.

—Chicken Soup, Chicken Soup. Mayer, Pamela. 2016. (ENG.). 32p. (J). (gr. -1-3). 17.99 *(978-1-4677-8934-9(8)*, 9781467789349, Kar-Ben Publishing) Lerner Publishing Group.

—Cool Crosby. Swanson Sateren, Shelley. 2016. (Adventures at Hound Hotel Ser.). (ENG.). 72p. (J). (gr. 1-3). lib. bdg. 25.32 *(978-1-5158-0066-8(0)*, Picture Window Bks.) Capstone.

—Count off, Squeak Scouts! Driscoll, Laura. 2013. (Mouse Math Ser.). 32p. (J). (gr. -1-1). 22.60 *(978-1-57565-524-6(1))* Astra Publishing Hse.

—Count off, Squeak Scouts! Number Sequence. Driscoll, Laura. 2013. (Mouse Math ® Ser.). (ENG.). 32p. (J). (gr. -1-1). pap. 7.95 *(978-1-57565-525-3(X)*, 9781575655253) Astra Publishing Hse.

—Disappearing Darcy. Swanson Sateren, Shelley. 2017. (Adventures at Tabby Towers Ser.). (ENG.). 72p. (J). (gr. 1-4). pap. 4.95 *(978-1-5158-1550-1(1)*, 136118); lib. bdg. 25.32 *(978-1-5158-1546-4(3)*, 136113) Capstone. (Picture Window Bks.).

—Drooling Dudley. Swanson Sateren, Shelley. 2016. (Adventures at Hound Hotel Ser.). (ENG.). 72p. (J). (gr. 1-3). lib. bdg. 25.32 *(978-1-5158-0220-4(5)*, Picture Window Bks.) Capstone.

—Fearless Freddie. Sateren, Shelley Swanson. 2015. (Adventures at Hound Hotel Ser.). (ENG.). 72p. (J). (gr. 1-3). lib. bdg. 25.32 *(978-1-4795-5898-8(2)*, Picture Window Bks.) Capstone.

—Fishing Frankie. Swanson Sateren, Shelley. 2017. (Adventures at Tabby Towers Ser.). (ENG.). 72p. (J). (gr. 1-4). pap. 4.95 *(978-1-5158-1552-5(8)*, 136120); lib. bdg. 25.32 *(978-1-5158-1548-8(X)*, 136115) Capstone. (Picture Window Bks.).

—Give up, Gecko!, 0 vols. MacDonald, Margaret Read. unabr. ed. 2013. (ENG.). 32p. (J). (gr. k-3). 16.99 *(978-1-4778-1635-6(6)*, 9781477816356, Two Lions) Amazon Publishing.

—Growling Gracie. Sateren, Shelley Swanson. 2015. (Adventures at Hound Hotel Ser.). (ENG.). 72p. (J). (gr. 1-3). lib. bdg. 25.32 *(978-1-4795-5899-5(0)*, Picture Window Bks.) Capstone.

—Homesick Herbie. Sateren, Shelley Swanson. 2015. (Adventures at Hound Hotel Ser.). (ENG.). 72p. (J). (gr. 1-3). lib. bdg. 25.32 *(978-1-4795-5897-1(4)*, Picture Window Bks.) Capstone.

—Hooray for Feet!, Vol. Hunt, Connie. 2008. (ENG.). (J). *(978-1-58728-699-5(8)*, Two-Can Publishing) T&N Children's Publishing.

—Hooray for Hands!, Vol. Hunt, Connie. 2008. (ENG.). (J). *(978-1-58728-700-8(5)*, Two-Can Publishing) T&N Children's Publishing.

—Leaping Lizzie. Swanson Sateren, Shelley. 2017. (Adventures at Tabby Towers Ser.). (ENG.). 72p. (J). (gr. 1-4). pap. 4.95 *(978-1-5158-1549-5(8)*, 136117); lib. bdg. 25.32 *(978-1-5158-1545-7(5)*, 136112) Capstone. (Picture Window Bks.).

—Make a Wish, Albert! Houran, Lori Haskins. 2015. (Mouse Math ® Ser.). (ENG.). 32p. (J). (gr. -1-1). lib. bdg. 22.65 *(978-1-57565-797-4(X))* Astra Publishing Hse.

—Mice on Ice. May, Eleanor. 2013. (Mouse Math Ser.). 32p. (J). (gr. -1-1). 22.60 *(978-1-57565-527-7(6))* Astra Publishing Hse.

—Mice on Ice: 2-D Shapes. May, Eleanor. 2013. (Mouse Math ® Ser.). (ENG.). 32p. (J). (gr. -1-1). pap. 7.95 *(978-1-57565-528-4(4)*, 9781575655284) Astra Publishing Hse.

—Mighty Murphy. Swanson Sateren, Shelley. 2016. (Adventures at Hound Hotel Ser.). (ENG.). 72p. (J). (gr. 1-3). lib. bdg. 25.32 *(978-1-5158-0067-5(9)*, Picture Window Bks.) Capstone.

—Mitzvah Pizza. Scheerger, Sarah Lynn. 2019. (ENG.). 32p. (J). (gr. k-4). 17.99 *(978-1-5415-2170-4(6)*, Kar-Ben Publishing) Lerner Publishing Group.

—The Mousier the Merrier. May, Eleanor. 2012. (Mouse Math Ser.). (ENG.). 32p. (J). (gr. -1-1). 22.60 *(978-1-57565-447-8(4))* Astra Publishing Hse.

—The Mousier the Merrier! Counting. May, Eleanor. 2012. (Mouse Math ® Ser.). (ENG.). 32p. (J). (gr. -1-1). pap. 7.95 *(978-1-57565-440-9(7)*, 9781575654409) Astra Publishing Hse.

—A Mousy Mess. Driscoll, Laura. 2014. (Mouse Math ® Ser.). 32p. (J). (gr. -1-1). 22.60 *(978-1-57565-646-5(9))* Astra Publishing Hse.

—Mudball Molly. Sateren, Shelley Swanson. 2015. (Adventures at Hound Hotel Ser.). (ENG.). 72p. (J). (gr. 1-3). lib. bdg. 25.32 *(978-1-4795-5900-8(8)*, Picture Window Bks.) Capstone.

—On the Farm. Ring, Susan. 2008. (ENG.). 10p. (J). (gr. 3-17). 12.99 *(978-1-58476-729-9(4))* Innovative Kids.

—One Good Deed. Fields, Terri. ed. 2015. (ENG.). 24p. (J). (gr. -1-3). E-Book 23.99 *(978-1-4677-8841-0(4))*; Vol. pap. 7.99 *(978-1-4677-3479-0(9)*, 9781467734790) Lerner Publishing Group. (Kar-Ben Publishing).

—Puppy Parade. Abramson, Jill & O'Connor, Jane. 2013. (Penguin Young Readers, Level 2 Ser.). (ENG.). 32p. (J). (gr. 1-2). 14.99 *(978-0-448-46574-6(4))*; pap. 4.99 *(978-0-448-45676-8(1))* Penguin Young Readers Group. (Penguin Young Readers).

—The Right Place for Albert. Skinner, Daphne. 2012. (Mouse Math Ser.). (ENG.). 32p. (J). (gr. -1-1). lib. bdg. 22.60 *(978-1-57565-446-1(6))* Astra Publishing Hse.

—The Right Place for Albert: One-To-One Correspondence. Skinner, Daphne. 2012. (Mouse Math ® Ser.). (ENG.). 32p. (J). (gr. -1-1). 7.95 *(978-1-57565-438-6(5)*, 9781575654386) Astra Publishing Hse.

—Speak up, Tommy! Dembar Greene, Jacqueline. 2012. (ENG.). 32p. (J). (gr. -1-3). lib. bdg. 7.99 *(978-0-7613-7497-8(3)*, 9780761374978, Kar-Ben Publishing) Lerner Publishing Group.

—Stand Beautiful - Picture Book, 1 vol. Howard, Chloe. 2018. (ENG.). 32p. (J). 16.99 *(978-0-310-76495-3(5))* Zonderkidz.

—Stinky Stanley. Swanson Sateren, Shelley. 2016. (Adventures at Hound Hotel Ser.). (ENG.). 72p. (J). (gr. 1-3). lib. bdg. 25.32 *(978-1-5158-0221-1(3)*, Picture Window Bks.) Capstone.

—'Twas the Night Before Christmas: A Highlights Hidden Pictures® Storybook. Moore, Clement Clarke. 2019. (Highlights Hidden Pictures Storybooks Ser.). (ENG.). 32p. (J). (gr. -1-3). 12.99 *(978-1-68437-649-0(1)*, Highlights) Boyds Mills Pr.

—Where's Albert? Counting & Skip Counting. May, Eleanor. 2017. (Mouse Math ® Ser.). (ENG.). 32p. (J). (gr. -1-1). 7.95 *(978-1-57565-858-2(5))* Astra Publishing Hse.

—Where's Albert? Counting & Skip Counting. May, Eleanor. 2017. (Mouse Math ® Ser.). (ENG.). 32p. (J). (gr. -1-1). lib. bdg. 22.65 *(978-1-57565-855-1(0))* Astra Publishing Hse.

—Where's Albert? Counting & Skip Counting. May, Eleanor. ed. 2017. (Mouse Math ® Ser.). (ENG.). 32p. (J). (gr. -1-1). E-Book 34.65 *(978-1-57565-861-2(5))* Astra Publishing Hse.

Melmon, Deborah, jt. illus. see Dussling, Deborah.

Melnychuck, Karen & Melnychuck, Sofia. Art Saguaros. Melnychuck, Karen & Melnychuck, Sofia. 2016. (ENG.). 24p. (J). pap. 9.99 *(978-0-9859171-5-9(6),* PinkPowerful Bks.) PinkPowerful LLC.

Melnychuck, Sofia, jt. illus. see Melnychuck, Karen.

Melnychuk, Monika. Centsibility: The Planet Girl Guide to Money. Roderick, Stacey & Warwick, Ellen. 2008. (Planet Girl Ser.). (ENG.). 80p. (J). (gr. 5-9). 12.95 *(978-1-55453-208-7(6))* Kids Can Pr., Ltd. CAN. Dist: Hachette Bk. Group.

Melnyczuk, Peter. The Dragon Charmer. Hill, Douglas. 2005. 151p. (J). (gr. -1-k). pap. 4.95 *(978-1-903015-36-0(7))* Barn Owl Bks, London GBR. Dist: Independent Pubs. Group.

Melnyk, Olha. Elizabeth Dances Pow-Wow. McArthur, Elaine. 2019. (ENG.). 28p. (J). pap. 16.00 ***(978-1-6950-1384-1(0))*** Independently Published.

Melo, Esperança. JoJo the Giant. Barclay, Jane. 2012. (ENG.). 32p. (J). (gr. -1-1). 17.95 *(978-0-88776-976-4(4),* Tundra Bks.) Tundra Bks. CAN. Dist: Penguin Random Hse. LLC.

—Love You More, 1 vol. Musgrave, Susan. 2014. (ENG.). 24p. (J). (gr. -1 — 1). bds. 9.95 *(978-1-4598-0240-7(3))* Orca Bk. Pubs. USA.

—Merci Mister Dash! Kulling, Monica. 2011. (ENG.). 32p. (J). (gr. -1-2). 17.95 *(978-0-88776-964-1(0),* Tundra Bks.) Tundra Bks. CAN. Dist: Penguin Random Hse. LLC.

—Mister Dash & the Cupcake Calamity. Kulling, Monica. 2013. (ENG.). 32p. (J). (gr. -1-2). 17.95 *(978-1-77049-396-4(4),* Tundra Bks.) Tundra Bks. CAN. Dist: Penguin Random Hse. LLC.

—More Blueberries!, 1 vol. Musgrave, Susan. 2017. (ENG.). 28p. (J). (gr. -1 — 1). 6.95 *(978-1-4598-1505-6(X))* Orca Bk. Pubs. USA.

Melo, Esperanca, jt. illus. see Slavin, Bill.

Melrose, Katie. My America, the Beautiful. Bates, Katharine Lee. 2018. (ENG.). 20p. (J). (gr. k-3). bds. 12.99 *(978-1-64170-019-1(X),* 550019) Familius LLC.

Melton, Beverly Marie. Milo & the Mustang. Hayes, Alycin. 2015. (ENG.). (J). pap. *(978-0-9730320-3-1(0))* Echo Hill Productions.

Melton, Eric. The House at the Bend of Contently Creek. Tuck, Helen. 2003. 107p. (J). pap. 11.95 *(978-0-7414-1682-7(4))* Infinity Publishing.

Melton, Jo Lynn. Juanita Maria Sophia Bug Diva: Lived down South in the West. Blake-Brekke, Carri. 2004. (Mrs. B'S Story Time-. . with A Twist! Ser.). 20p. (J). pap. 11.95 incl. audio compact disk *(978-0-9720549-3-5(6))* Mom's Pride Enterprises.

Melton, Jodi. Billy Bully Bug: Learns a Lesson in Hawaii. Blake-Brekke, Carri. 2003. (Mrs. B's Story Time... With a Twist! Ser.). 20p. (J). pap. 11.95 incl. audio compact disk *(978-0-9720549-2-8(8))* Mom's Pride Enterprises.

Melville, Jacqui, photos by. Little Kitchen: 40 Delicious & Simple Things That Children Can Really Make. Parrini, Sabrina. 2010. 128p. pap. *(978-1-74066-743-2(3))* Hardie Grant Bks. AUS. Dist: Independent Pubs. Group.

Melvin, Alice. Grandma's House. 2015. (ENG.). 32p. (J). (gr. -1-3). 19.95 *(978-1-84976-222-9(8))* Tate Publishing, Ltd. GBR. Dist: Hachette Bk. Group.

Melvin, Anita. Too Many Choices. Salyers, Rita. 2004. (J). per. 9.95 *(978-0-9763423-0-4(8))* The Publishing Place LLC.

Melvin, Anita. What to do with Boogers. Melvin, Anita. 2004. 14p. (J). per. 9.95 *(978-0-9760129-8-6(7))* The Publishing Place LLC.

Melvin, Anita Flannery. An Internet Adventure with Safari Sam. Fuzy, Jim. 2004. 24p. (J). per. 14.95 *(978-0-9760129-7-9(9))* The Publishing Place LLC.

Melvin, James. Color with the Wright Brothers: See How They Made History. Tate, Suzanne. 2003. (Suzanne Tate's History Ser.). 32p. (J). pap. 2.95 *(978-1-878405-41-8(1))* Nags Head Art, Inc.

—Danny & Daisy: A Tale of a Dolphin Duo. Tate, Suzanne. 2004. (Suzanne Tate's Nature Ser.: No. 13). 32p. (J). per. 10.95 *(978-1-878405-44-9(6))* Nags Head Art, Inc.

—Flyer: A Tale of the Wright Dog. Tate, Suzanne. 2003. (Suzanne Tate's History Ser.). (J). pap. 4.95 *(978-1-878405-42-5(X))* Nags Head Art, Inc.

—Great Sharky Shark: A Tale of a Big Hunter. Tate, Suzanne. 2004. (Suzanne Tate's Nature Ser.: No. 20). 32p. (J). per. 10.95 *(978-1-878405-46-3(2))* Nags Head Art, Inc.

—Johnny Longlegs: A Tale of Big Birds. Tate, Suzanne. 2005. (Suzanne Tate's Nature Ser.: No. 28). 28p. (J). pap. 4.95 *(978-1-878405-50-0(0))* Nags Head Art, Inc.

—Katie K. Whale: A Whale of a Tale. Tate, Suzanne. 2004. (Suzanne Tate's Nature Ser.: No. 17). 32p. (J). per. 10.95 *(978-1-878405-47-0(0))* Nags Head Art, Inc.

—Rosie Ray: A Tale of Watery Wings. Tate, Suzanne. 2003. (Suzanne Tate's Nature Ser.: No. 25). 28p. (J). (gr. -1-3). pap. 4.95 *(978-1-878405-40-1(3))* Nags Head Art, Inc.

—Sandy Seal: A Tale of Sea Dogs. Tate, Suzanne. l.t. ed. 2004. (Suzanne Tate's Nature Ser.: No. 27). 28p. (J). pap. 4.95 *(978-1-878405-49-4(7))* Nags Head Art, Inc.

—Skippy Scallop: A Tale of Bright Blue Eyes. Tate, Suzanne. 2003. (Suzanne Tate's Nature Ser.: No. 26). 28p. (J). pap. 4.95 *(978-1-878405-43-2(8))* Nags Head Art, Inc.

—Tammy Turtle: A Tale of Saving Sea Turtles. Tate, Suzanne. 2004. (Suzanne Tate's Nature Ser.: No. 11). 32p. (J). per. 10.95 *(978-1-878405-45-6(4))* Nags Head Art, Inc.

—Teena Tortoise: A Tale of a Little Giant. Tate, Suzanne. 2012. 32p. (J). pap. 4.95 *(978-1-878405-60-9(8))* Nags Head Art, Inc.

Memarzadeh, Sudabeh. Brush Barry Brush. Valderrama, Linda N. 2011. 32p. (J). pap. 11.95 *(978-0-578-06605-9(X))* Shirley's Girl Pubns.

Mena, Jessica, jt. illus. see Design, Chelms.

Mena, Pato. La Gran Fiesta de Los Olores. Mena, Pato. 2019. (ENG.). 48p. (J). 16.95 *(978-84-17123-97-0(0))* NubeOcho Ediciones ESP. Dist: Consortium Bk. Sales & Distribution.

—Wonder Mole's Scent Costume Party. Mena, Pato. 2019. (ENG.). 48p. (J). 16.95 *(978-84-17123-98-7(9))* NubeOcho Ediciones ESP. Dist: Consortium Bk. Sales & Distribution.

Mena, Virginia. El niño Que Vive Junto Al Mar. Tome, Angeles. 2017. (SPA.). 32p. (J). (gr. k-3). *(978-1-910650-09-7(9))* Liberum Vox Bks. Ltd.

Menard, Adrienne. The Ghoul in Our School. Menard, Michele Rose. 2013. 36p. pap. 11.95 *(978-0-9887969-9-7(6))* Four Menards, The.

Menard, Christine. For the Love of Hockey. Fevrier, Sean. 2018. (Storytime 2017 Ser.: Vol. 2). (ENG.). 22p. (J). (gr. k-3). pap. 9.99 *(978-1-55323-788-4(9),* ExamWise) Total Recall Learning, Inc.

Menard, John C. The Bees & the Bears. Menard, James. 2008. 36p. pap. 16.99 *(978-1-4389-2150-1(0))* AuthorHouse.

Menard, Michael. I Can Read Now! Easy Sight Words for Developing Young Readers. Fernstedt, David. 2018. (ENG.). 104p. (J). (gr. -1-2). 14.99 *(978-1-63158-360-5(3),* Racehorse Publishing) Skyhorse Publishing Co., Inc.

Menchin, Scott. Bounce. Cronin, Doreen. 2007. (ENG.). 40p. (J). (gr. -1-3). 18.99 *(978-1-4169-1627-7(X),* Atheneum Bks. for Young Readers) Simon & Schuster Children's Publishing.

—Rescue Bunnies. Cronin, Doreen. 2010. (ENG.). 32p. (J). (gr. -1-3). 16.99 *(978-0-06-112871-4(6))* HarperCollins Pubs.

—Song of Middle C. Mcghee, Alison. 2009. (ENG.). 32p. (J). (gr. k-3). 16.99 *(978-0-7636-3013-3(6))* Candlewick Pr.

—Stretch. Cronin, Doreen. 2009. (ENG.). 40p. (J). (gr. -1-3). 18.99 *(978-1-4169-5341-8(8),* Atheneum Bks. for Young Readers) Simon & Schuster Children's Publishing.

—Wiggle. Cronin, Doreen. 2005. (ENG.). 40p. (J). (gr. -1-3). 18.99 *(978-0-689-86375-2(6),* Atheneum Bks. for Young Readers) Simon & Schuster Children's Publishing.

Menchin, Scott. Harry Goes to Dog School. Menchin, Scott. 2012. (ENG.). 32p. (J). (gr. -1-3). 16.99 *(978-0-06-195801-4(8))* HarperCollins Pubs.

—Taking a Bath with the Dog & Other Things That Make Me Happy. Menchin, Scott. 2013. 40p. (J). (gr. -1-3). 7.99 *(978-0-7636-6335-3(2))* Candlewick Pr.

—What If Everything Had Legs? Menchin, Scott. 2011. (ENG.). 32p. (J). (gr. -1-3). 15.99 *(978-0-7636-4220-4(7))* Candlewick Pr.

Menchin, Scott & Lewin, Betsy. Wiggle, 1 vol. Cronin, Doreen. 2006. (Doreen Cronin: Click-Clack & More Ser.). (ENG.). 36p. (J). (gr. k-3). lib. bdg. 27.07 *(978-1-59961-093-1(0),* 5421, Picture Bk.) Spotlight.

Menci, R. The Frontier Boys in the Saddle. Roosevelt, Wyn. 2014. (ENG.). (J). pap. 12.95 *(978-1-4794-1634-9(7))* Wildside Pr., LLC.

Menck, Kevin. Stories That End with a Prayer. Elkins, Stephen. 32p. (J). (gr. k-8). 12.98 *(978-1-56919-003-6(8))* Wonder Workshop.

Mendel, Zhanna. The Pajama Zoo Parade: The Funniest Bedtime ABC Book. Green, Agnes. 2018. (Funniest ABC Bks.: Vol. 2). (ENG.). 44p. (J). (gr. -1-3). 19.99 ***(978-1-5323-7795-2(9))*** Independent Pub.

Mendel, Zhanna. The Perfect Potty Zoo: The Funniest ABC Book. Green, Agnes. l.t. ed. 2018. (Funniest ABC Bks.: Vol. 1). (ENG.). 42p. (J). 19.99 *(978-1-5323-7794-5(0))* April Tale Bks.

Mendelson, Harvey, photos by. Divine Kosher Cuisine: Catering to Family & Friends. Routenburg, Rise' & Wasser, Barbara. Keen, Annette, ed. 2006. 382p. 32.99 *(978-0-9770172-0-1(6))* Congregation Agudat Achim.

Mendenhall, Cheryl. The Frog in the Pond. Mara, Wil. 2007. (Rookie Reader Skill Set Ser.). (ENG.). 32p. (J). (gr. -1-3). 19.50 *(978-0-531-17541-5(3),* Children's Pr.) Scholastic Library Publishing.

—God's Creation. Dalmatian Press Staff. 2004. (ENG.). 24p. (J). 2.99 *(978-1-4037-0962-2(9),* Spirit Pr.) Bendon, Inc.

—Joseph & His Coat of Many Colors. 2004. (ENG.). 24p. (J). 2.99 *(978-1-4037-0966-0(1),* Spirit Pr.) Bendon, Inc.

—Moses Baby in the Bulrushes. 2004. (ENG.). 24p. (J). 2.99 *(978-1-4037-0963-9(7),* Spirit Pr.) Bendon, Inc.

—Moses Parting the Red Sea. 2004. (ENG.). 24p. (J). 2.99 *(978-1-4037-0964-6(5),* Spirit Pr.) Bendon, Inc.

Mendez, Simon. Asi Nace un Arbol. Llewellyn, Claire. 2004. (Colección Así Nace... / Starting Life Collection Ser.). (SPA.). 24p. (gr. k-6). pap. 14.95 *(978-1-59437-449-4(X))* Santillana USA Publishing Co., Inc.

—Asi Nace un Pato. Llewellyn, Claire. 2004. (Colección Así Nace... / Starting Life Collection Ser.). (SPA.). 24p. (gr. k-6). pap. 14.95 *(978-1-59437-448-7(1))* Santillana USA Publishing Co., Inc.

—Asi Nace una Mariposa. Llewellyn, Claire. Giraldo, Maria Cristina, tr. 2003. (Colección Así Nace... / Starting Life Collection Ser.). (SPA.). 24p. (gr. k-6). pap. 14.95 *(978-1-59437-788-4(X))* Santillana USA Publishing Co., Inc.

—Asi Nace una Rana. Llewellyn, Claire. 2003. (Colección Así Nace... / Starting Life Collection Ser.). (SPA.). 24p. (gr. k-6). pap. 14.95 *(978-1-59437-789-1(8))* Santillana USA Publishing Co., Inc.

—Creatures of the Rain Forest. Rake, Matthew. 2015. (Real-Life Monsters Ser.). (ENG.). 32p. (J). (gr. 3-6). lib. bdg. 27.99 *(978-1-4677-6363-9(2),* 9781467763639, Hungry Tomato ®) Lerner Publishing Group.

—Creepy, Crawly Creatures. Rake, Matthew. 2015. (Real-Life Monsters Ser.). (ENG.). 32p. (J). (gr. 3-6). lib. bdg. 27.99 *(978-1-4677-6362-2(4),* 9781467763622, Hungry Tomato ®) Lerner Publishing Group.

—If Prehistoric Beasts Were Alive Today. Rake, Matthew. 2019. (ENG.). 96p. (J). (gr. 2-6). 19.99 *(978-1-913077-13-6(6),* e67c7add-d9f5-4328-b00a-cfd69feb31f8, Beetle Bks.) Hungry Tomato Ltd. GBR. Dist: Baker & Taylor Publisher Services (BTPS).

—Ladybug. Lewellyn, Claire. 2004. (Starting Life Ser.). (ENG.). 24p. (J). (gr. k-3). 16.95 *(978-1-55971-892-9(7))* Cooper Square Publishing Llc.

—Mama, Why? Wilson, Karma. 2011. (ENG.). 40p. (J). (gr. -1-2). 16.99 *(978-1-4169-4205-4(X),* McElderry, Margaret K. Bks.) McElderry, Margaret K. Bks.

—Muddypaws. Butterfield, Moira. 2010. (Picture Books Ser.). (J). (gr. -1-k). bds. *(978-1-4075-8757-8(9))* Parragon, Inc.

—Myths & Monsters: Secrets Revealed. Edwards, Katie. 2004. 29p. (J). pap. 6.95 *(978-1-57091-582-6(2))* Charlesbridge Publishing, Inc.

—One Winter's Night. Freedman, Claire. ed. 2009. (J). lib. bdg. *(978-1-84895-013-9(6),* Scholastic) Scholastic, Inc.

—Prehistoric Ancestors of Modern Animals. Rake, Matthew. 2017. (If Extinct Beasts Came to Life Ser.). (ENG.). 32p. (J). (gr. 3-6). 7.99 *(978-1-5124-1159-1(0),* 9781512411591); E-Book 42.65 *(978-1-5124-0906-2(5));* E-Book 42.65 *(978-1-5124-3608-2(9),* 9781512436082); E-Book 4.99 *(978-1-5124-3609-9(7),* 9781512436099) Lerner Publishing Group. (Hungry Tomato ®).

—Prehistoric Giants. Rake, Matthew. 2017. (If Extinct Beasts Came to Life Ser.). (ENG.). 32p. (J). (gr. 3-6). 27.99 *(978-1-5124-0635-1(X),* 9781512406351); E-Book 4.99 *(978-1-5124-3612-9(7),* 9781512436129); E-Book 42.65 *(978-1-5124-3611-2(9),* 9781512436112); E-Book 42.65 *(978-1-5124-0912-3(X))* Lerner Publishing Group. (Hungry Tomato ®).

—Prehistoric Predators. Rake, Matthew. 2017. (If Extinct Beasts Came to Life Ser.). (ENG.). 32p. (J). (gr. 3-6). 27.99 *(978-1-5124-0633-7(3),* 9781512406337); E-Book 4.99 *(978-1-5124-3615-0(1),* 9781512436150); E-Book 42.65 *(978-1-5124-0907-9(3));* E-Book 42.65 *(978-1-5124-3614-3(3),* 9781512436143) Lerner Publishing Group. (Hungry Tomato ®).

—Prehistoric Sea Beasts. Rake, Matthew. 2017. (If Extinct Beasts Came to Life Ser.). (ENG.). 32p. (J). (gr. 3-6). 7.99 *(978-1-5124-1158-4(2),* 9781512411584); E-Book 4.99 *(978-1-5124-3618-1(6),* 9781512436181); E-Book 42.65 *(978-1-5124-0909-3(X));* E-Book 42.65 *(978-1-5124-3617-4(8),* 9781512436174) Lerner Publishing Group. (Hungry Tomato ®).

—Real Life Monsters: Amazing Monster-Like Animals of the Rainforest, Desert. Rake, Matthew. 2019. (ENG.). 96p. (J). (gr. 2-6). 19.99 *(978-1-913077-12-9(8),* f9f68b9e-f044-49e4-9259-205da889c746, Beetle Bks.) Hungry Tomato Ltd. GBR. Dist: Baker & Taylor Publisher Services (BTPS).

—Scaly, Slippery Creatures. Rake, Matthew. 2015. (Real-Life Monsters Ser.). (ENG.). 32p. (J). (gr. 3-6). pap. 7.99 *(978-1-4677-7645-5(9),* 9781467776455, Hungry Tomato ®) Lerner Publishing Group.

—The Snow Bear. Webb, Holly. 2019. (Winter Journeys Ser.). (ENG.). 192p. (J). (gr. 1-4). 6.99 *(978-1-68010-446-2(2));* lib. bdg. 22.99 *(978-1-68010-168-3(4))* Tiger Tales.

Mendez, Simon. Duck. Mendez, Simon, tr. Llewellyn, Claire. 2004. (Starting Life Ser.). (ENG.). 24p. (J). (gr. k-3). 16.95 *(978-1-55971-878-3(1))* Cooper Square Publishing Llc.

—Tree. Mendez, Simon, tr. Llewellyn, Claire. 2004. (Starting Life Ser.). (ENG.). 24p. (J). (gr. k-3). 16.95 *(978-1-55971-879-0(X))* Cooper Square Publishing Llc.

Mendez, Simon & Artful Doodlers, Artful. The Reindeer Girl. Webb, Holly. 2020. (Winter Journeys Ser.). (ENG.). 192p. (J). (gr. 1-4). pap. 6.99 ***(978-1-68010-474-5(8))***; lib. bdg. 17.99 ***(978-1-68010-221-5(4))*** Tiger Tales.

Mendez, Simon & Warnes, Tim. My Little Box of Christmas Stories: One Winter's Night/Hurry, Santa!/a Magical Christmas/the Gift of Christmas/the Special Christmas Tree/the Christmas Bear. Freedman, Claire et al. 2013. (ENG.). (J). (gr. -1-1). pap. 8.95 *(978-1-58925-443-5(0))* Tiger Tales.

Mendicino, Valentina. Dinosaur Rhyme Time. Gayford, Cecily. 2014. (ENG.). 32p. (J). 13.00 *(978-0-571-30833-0(3),* Faber & Faber Children's Bks.) Faber & Faber, Inc.

Mendonca, Angela. Nursery Rhymes Island Style. Mendonca, Angela. 2013. 24p. pap. 9.99 *(978-0-9843125-6-6(0))* Wealth of Wisdom LLC, A.

Mendoza, Abraham. Sam the Ant - Glow in the Dark: Brillando en la Oscuridad. Feldman, Enrique C. & Feldman, Sam Sierra. 2016. (Sam the Ant Ser.: Vol. 2). (ENG.). (J). (gr. k-3). pap. 13.99 *(978-0-9974877-2-5(0))* Feldman, Enrique C.

—Sam the Ant - Mirrors: Espejos: Mirros: Espejos. Feldman, Enrique C. & Sierra-Feldman, Sam. 2018. (Sam the Ant Ser.: Vol. 4). (ENG.). 42p. (J). (gr. k-4). pap. 13.99 *(978-0-9974877-6-3(3))* Feldman, Enrique C.

Mendoza, Abraham. Sam the Ant - Tunnels: T�neles. Feldman, Enrique C. & Sierra-Feldman, Sam. 2019. (Sam the Ant Ser.: Vol. 5). (ENG.). 42p. (J). (gr. k-4). pap. 13.99 ***(978-0-9974877-8-7(X))*** Feldman, Enrique C.

Mendoza, Carlos. Down under in Australia. Hulin, Pamela. 2007. 20p. per. 24.95 *(978-1-4241-8929-8(2))* America Star Bks.

Mendoza, Fredy. Lola the Ladybug. Brinson, Sarah M. 2018. (Lola the Ladybug Ser.). (ENG.). 36p. (J). (gr. k-5). 24.95 *(978-0-9906301-2-8(9))* GB Pr.

Mendoza, George. Colors of the Wind: The Story of Blind Artist & Champion Runner George Mendoza. Powers, J. L. 2014. (J). 18.95 *(978-1-930900-73-8(2))* Purple Hse. Pr.

Mendoza, Megan Elizabeth. Tony Loved to Learn. Riddle, Sharon Kay & Sanders, Nancy/Ida. 2007. 32p. (J). pap. 15.00 *(978-0-9761583-6-3(1))* Olive Leaf Pubns.

Mendoza, Mendoza. Insane Jane. Hunchar, Zach. 2017. (Insane Jane Ser.). (ENG.). 128p. (YA). pap. 19.99 *(978-1-948216-75-3(2))* TidalWave.

Mendoza, Molly. Freedom, We Sing. León, Amyra. 2020. 40p. (J). (gr. -1-2). 16.95 *(978-1-912497-32-4(8))* Flying Eye Bks. GBR. Dist: Penguin Random Hse. LLC.

Menéndez, Margarita. Acertijos, Chistes y Canciones: Chupachus. Menéndez, Margarita, tr. Fuertes, Gloria. 2003. (SPA.). 121p. *(978-84-305-7803-0(X),* SU5202) Susaeta Ediciones, S.A. ESP. Dist: Lectorum Pubns., Inc.

Meng, Shi. Chinese New Year Wishes: Chinese Spring & Lantern Festival Celebration. Lin, Jillian. 2019. (Fun Festivals Ser.: Vol. 2). (ENG.). 34p. (J). pap. 10.99 *(978-1-7930-9778-1(X))* Independently Published.

Mengert, Hollie. Holly Jolly Santa Songs. Berry-Byrd, Holly. Cottage Door Press, ed. 2020. (5-Button Early Bird Song Book Ser.). (ENG.). 10p. (J). (gr. -1-k). bds. 14.99 ***(978-1-68052-984-5(6),*** 1006110) Cottage Door Pr.

Mengert, Hollie. Luis & Tabitha. Campisi, Stephanie. 2018. (ENG.). 32p. (J). (gr. 3-5). 16.99 *(978-1-64170-040-5(8),* 550040) Familius LLC.

—Sparkleton #1: the Magic Day. Glass, Calliope. 2020. (HarperChapters Ser.). 96p. (J). (gr. 1-5). 15.99 *(978-0-06-294792-5(3));* (ENG.). pap. 5.99 *(978-0-06-294791-8(5))* HarperCollins Pubs. Ltd. GBR. (HarperCollins). Dist: HarperCollins Pubs.

—Sparkleton #2: the Glitter Parade. Glass, Calliope. 2020. (HarperChapters Ser.). 96p. (J). (gr. 1-5). 15.99 *(978-0-06-294795-6(8));* (ENG.). pap. 5.99 *(978-0-06-294794-9(X))* HarperCollins Pubs. Ltd. GBR. (HarperCollins). Dist: HarperCollins Pubs.

—Unicorn (and Horse) Miles, David W. 2018. (ENG.). 48p. (J). 16.99 *(978-1-945547-76-8(6),* 554776) Familius LLC.

—Winner Takes All! (DC Super Hero Girls) David, Erica. 2019. (ENG.). 144p. (J). (gr. 1-4). 6.99 *(978-1-9848-9453-3(6));* 12.99 *(978-1-9848-9454-0(4))* Random Hse. Children's Bks. (Random Hse. Bks. for Young Readers).

Menichini, M. M. The Orphans' Plight: An African Adventure. Botha, Maretha. Perkins, Karen, ed. 2016. (ENG.). (J). pap. *(978-1-910115-60-2(6))* LionheArt Publishing Hse.

Menix, Cinda & McGuire, Bryan. Tenbrook Farms. Menix, Cinda. 2007. 67p. (J). (gr. 4-7). per. 23.99 *(978-1-59879-338-3(1))* Lifevest Publishing, Inc.

Menking, Amanda & Fisher, Sean. The Happy Dragon, 1 vol. Bucher, Heatherly & Menking, Amanda. 2006. 32p. (J). *(978-0-9790920-1-5(9))* MoonRattles.

Menley, Claire. Jungle Jeep. Randall, Ronne. Cottage Door Press & Parragon Books, eds. 2020. (ENG.). 10p. (J). (gr. -1-k). bds. 8.99 ***(978-1-68052-862-6(9),*** 2003170, Parragon Books) Cottage Door Pr.

—Tractor Trouble. Randall, Ronne. Cottage Door Press & Parragon Books, eds. 2020. (ENG.). 10p. (J). (gr. -1-k). bds. 8.99 ***(978-1-68052-863-3(7),*** 2003180, Parragon Books) Cottage Door Pr.

Mensah, Enoch Yaw. Dear Kweku. Andoh, Franka Maria. 2019. (Stories for Paul Ser.: Vol. 3). (ENG.). 34p. (J). pap. 15.99 ***(978-1-6984-7431-1(8))*** Independently Published.

Menten, Ted, jt. illus. see Denslow, W. W.

Mentis, Anastassios, photos by. Fiesta Latina: Fabulous Food for Sizzling Parties. Palomino, Rafael. 2006. (ENG., 144p. (gr. 8-17). 19.95 *(978-0-8118-4410-9(2))* Chronicle Bks. LLC.

Menton3. The X-Files: JFK Disclosure. Tipton, Denton J. 2018. (ENG.). 72p. 14.99 *(978-1-68405-254-7(8))* Idea & Design Works, LLC.

Menzel, Peter, photos by. What the World Eats. Menzel, Peter. D'Aluisio, Faith. 2008. 160p. (J). (gr. 1-4). 22.99 *(978-1-58246-246-2(1),* Tricycle Pr.) Random Hse. Children's Bks.

Meppem, William, photos by. The Glorious Soups & Stews of Italy. Marchetti, Domenica. 2006. (ENG., 168p. (gr. 8-17). pap. 19.95 *(978-0-8118-4817-6(5))* Chronicle Bks. LLC.

Mercado, Jorge. Chicken Little. Sommer, Carl. 2014. (Sommer-Time Story Classics Ser.). (ENG.). 32p. (J). (gr. k-4). 16.95 *(978-1-57537-076-7(X))* Advance Publishing, Inc.

—Divide to Conquer. Sommer, Carl & Aesop, Aesop. 2009. (Quest for Success Ser.). (ENG.). 40p. (YA). pap. 4.95 *(978-1-57537-275-4(4));* lib. bdg. 12.95 *(978-1-57537-250-1(9))* Advance Publishing, Inc.

—Divide to Conquer(Divide y Venceras) Sommer, Carl & Aesop, Aesop. ed. 2009. (Quest for Success Bilingual Ser.). (ENG & SPA.). 72p. (YA). lib. bdg. 14.95 *(978-1-57537-225-9(8))* Advance Publishing, Inc.

—The Lion & the Mouse. Sommer, Carl. 2014. (Sommer-Time Story Classics Ser.). (ENG.). 32p. (J). (gr. k-4). 16.95 *(978-1-57537-082-8(4))* Advance Publishing, Inc.

—The Lion & the Three Bulls. Sommer, Carl. 2014. (Sommer-Time Story Classics Ser.). (ENG.). 32p. (J). (gr. k-4). 16.95 *(978-1-57537-083-5(2))* Advance Publishing, Inc.

—The Tiny Giant. Sommer, Carl & Aesop, Aesop. 2009. (Quest for Success Ser.). (ENG.). 40p. (YA). pap. 4.95 *(978-1-57537-286-0(X));* lib. bdg. 12.95 *(978-1-57537-261-7(4))* Advance Publishing, Inc.

—Tiny Giant(La Gigante Pequeña) Sommer, Carl & Aesop, Aesop. ed. 2009. (Quest for Success Bilingual Ser.). (ENG & SPA.). 72p. (YA). lib. bdg. 14.95 *(978-1-57537-236-5(3))* Advance Publishing, Inc.

Merced, Eric, jt. illus. see Wong, Scott.

Merced, Zuleika, photos by. Mujer de Medio Siglo... Atesorndo Vivencias. Merced, Zuleika. l.t. ed. 2003. 100p. (YA). pap. *(978-1-931481-42-7(3))* LIArt-Literature & Art.

mercedes cecilia & mercedes cecilia. Kusikiy A Child from Taquile, Peru. mercedes cecilia. 2011. (J). pap. 24.99 *(978-0-9844079-9-6(5))* Keepers of Wisdom and Peace Bks.

mercedes cecilia, jt. illus. see mercedes cecilia.

Mercer, Lynn. PC Polly to the Rescue. Allan, Jayne. 2003. (ENG.). 32p. (J). (gr. 1-18). pap. 10.95 *(978-0-9535413-8-6(X))* iynx publishing GBR. Dist: Dufour Editions, Inc.

Mercer, Matthew. The Monster Run. Butterworth, MyLinda. Day, Linda S., ed. l.t. ed. 2004. 32p. (J). (gr. -1-3). 14.95 *(978-1-890905-23-1(2),* Day to Day Bks.) Day to Day Enterprises.

Mercer, Michael. From the Dust #1: The Last King of Judah. 2012. (ENG.). 110p. (J). pap. 14.99 *(978-0-9859884-1-8(X))* Spider Comics.

Mercer, Sarah-Jayne. Kol Hakavod: Way to Go! Kiffel-Alcheh, Jamie. 2019. (ENG.). 24p. (J). (gr. -1-1). 17.99 *(978-1-5415-2211-4(7),* 9781541522114); Vol. pap. 7.99 *(978-1-5415-3835-1(8),* 9781541538351) Lerner Publishing Group. (Kar-Ben Publishing).

Merchant, Donna. Goblins Will Be Seen: When It's Time for Halloween. Donnell, Frances. Hebert, Catherine, ed. 2005. 38p. (J). 16.95 *(978-0-9770893-0-7(4))* 2 Donn Bks.

Merchant, J'Aaron. Your Own Kind of Beautiful! Frazier, Tamara Pray. 2019. (Walking with Grace Ser.: Vol. 1). (ENG.). 36p. (J). (gr. k-6). pap. 13.95 ***(978-0-578-48848-6(5))*** Julian's Legacy.

Merchant, Jon. ELPHA! Happy to Be Me! Mercer, Gwen. 2020. (Elpha Ser.). (ENG.). 28p. (J). ***(978-1-5255-6562-5(1))*** FriesenPress.

Mercier, J. Colors. 2019. (ENG.). 12p. (J). bds. 9.99 *(978-2-7338-6733-4(4))* Auzou, Philippe Editions FRA. Dist: Consortium Bk. Sales & Distribution.

Meredith. The Guardian's Guide to Complete Dragon Care. Hunt, Bill. 2017. (Garson the Dragon Ser.: Vol. 4). (ENG.). 162p. (J). (gr. 3-6). pap. 10.99 *(978-1-68160-243-1(1))* Crimson Cloak Publishing.

—The Substitute Santa. MacGregor, Cynthia. 2016. (ENG.). (J). pap. 9.50 *(978-1-68160-203-5(2))* Crimson Cloak Publishing.

Meredith, Sam. Follow That Dinosaur! Taylor, Georgie. 2020. (Trace the Trails Ser.). (ENG.). 10p. (J). (-k). bds. 8.99 *(978-1-78958-418-9(3))* Top That! Publishing PLC GBR. Dist: Independent Pubs. Group.

—Follow That Tractor! Taylor, Georgie. 2020. (Trace the Trails Ser.). (ENG.). 10p. (J). (-k). bds. 8.99 *(978-1-78958-427-1(2))* Top That! Publishing PLC GBR. Dist: Independent Pubs. Group.

—Follow That Unicorn! Taylor, Georgie. 2020. (Trace the Trails Ser.). (ENG.). 10p. (J). (-k). bds. 8.99 *(978-1-78958-419-6(1))* Top That! Publishing PLC GBR. Dist: Independent Pubs. Group.

Meredith, Samantha. Flip & Find Builders: A Guess Who/where Flap Book about Builders. 2016. (Flip & Find Ser.). (ENG.). 10p. (J). (— 1). bds. 7.99 *(978-1-4472-7714-9(7))* Pan Macmillan GBR. Dist: Independent Pubs. Group.

—I Love You Every Day. Cottage Door Press. Cottage Door Press, ed. 2018. (Finger Puppet Board Book Ser.). (ENG.). 12p. (J). (gr. -1 — 1). bds. 6.99 *(978-1-68052-485-7(2)*, 2000790) Cottage Door Pr.

—I Spy Bible: A Picture Puzzle Bible for the Very Young. Stone, Julia. ed. 2019. (ENG.). 32p. (J). (gr. -1-k). 8.99 *(978-0-7459-7832-1(0))* Lion Hudson PLC GBR. Dist: Independent Pubs. Group.

—I Spy Bible Sticker Book. Stone, Julia. ed. 2018. (ENG.). 24p. (J). (gr. -1-k). pap. 5.99 *(978-0-7459-7729-4(4))* Lion Hudson PLC GBR. Dist: Independent Pubs. Group.

—Lots to Spot: Farm. Walden, Libby. 2018. (ENG.). 12p. (J). (gr. -1 — 1). bds. 7.99 *(978-1-68412-170-0(1)*, Silver Dolphin Bks.) Printers Row Publishing Group.

—Spooky, Spooky Little Bat. VonFeder, Rosa. Cottage Door Press, ed. 2019. (Finger Puppet Board Book Ser.). (ENG.). 12p. (J). (gr. -1 — 1). bds. 6.99 *(978-1-68052-680-6(4)*, 2002820) Cottage Door Pr.

—Ten Little Farm Friends. Litton, Jonathan. 2020. (ENG.). 26p. (J). (-k). pap. 4.99 *(978-1-68010-464-6(0))* Tiger Tales.

—Trick or Treat Little Pumpkin. VonFeder, Rosa. Cottage Door Press, ed. 2019. (Children's Interactive Finger Puppet Board Book Ser.). (ENG.). 12p. (J). (gr. -1 — 1). bds. 6.99 *(978-1-68052-679-0(0)*, 2002810) Cottage Door Pr.

—50 Things to Do on Vacation. Clarke, Catriona. 2007. (Activity Cards Ser.). 50p. (J). (gr. 4-7). 9.99 *(978-0-7945-1704-5(8)*, Usborne) EDC Publishing.

Meredith, Samantha & Wyk, Hanri van. Weddings Sticker Color Book. ed. 2011. (First Sticker Coloring Bks). 20p. (J). pap. 5.99 *(978-0-7945-3108-9(3)*, Usborne) EDC Publishing.

Meredith, Samantha, jt. illus. see Goodings, Christina.

Merer, Laura. Fuzzy Ducky's Birthday: A Touch-and-Feel Pop-up Book. 2005. 10p. (J). 8.95 *(978-1-58117-324-6(5)*, Intervisual/Piggy Toes) Bendon, Inc.

Merer, Laura. Let's Go to the Library. Grazulis, Rebecca. 2020. (ENG.). 18p. (J). bds. ***(978-1-64269-252-5(2)***, 5628d7a0-92cf-499a-9c57-d54e53ad9328, Sequoia Publishing & Media LLC) Phoenix International Publications, Inc.

Merer, Laura. My Five Senses. 2010. (My World Ser.). (ENG.). 24p. (J). (gr. -1-1). pap. 8.15 *(978-1-61533-029-4(1))* Windmill Bks.

—My Senses/Mis Sentidos. Rosa-Mendoza, Gladys. 2007. (English Spanish Foundations Ser.). (ENG & SPA.). 20p. (J). (gr. -1-k). bds. 6.95 *(978-1-931398-21-3(6))* Me+Mi Publishing.

Meret, Sasha. Walking the Bible: An Illustrated Journey for Kids Through the Greatest Stories Ever Told. Meret, Sasha, tr. Feiler, Bruce. ed. 2004. 112p. (J). (gr. 2-7). 16.99 *(978-0-06-051117-3(6))* HarperCollins Pubs.

Merino, Jose Luis. Puss in Boots/el Gato con Botas. 2004. (Bilingual Fairy Tales Ser.: BILI). (ENG.). 32p. (J). (gr. -1-7). pap. 6.99 *(978-0-8118-3924-2(9)*, Chronicle Bks.) Chronicle Bks. LLC.

Merkel, Joe F. Evil Comes in Pairs. Egan, Kate. 2009. (Spider-Man Ser.). 64p. (J). (gr. 2-5). pap. 4.99 *(978-0-06-162625-8(2)*, HarperFestival) HarperCollins Pubs.

Merkel, Joe F. & Sazaklis, John. Surf's Up. Rao, Lisa. 2007. (Surf's Up Ser.). 32p. (J). (gr. -1-2). 4.99 *(978-0-06-115335-8(4)*, Harper Entertainment) HarperCollins Pubs.

Merker, Gerold, photos by. Zonata: The California Mountain Kingsnake. Mulks, Mitchell. 2004. 64p. pap. 15.95 *(978-0-9760770-0-8(0))* LM Digital.

Merkin, Richard. Leagues Apart: The Men & Times of the Negro Baseball Leagues. Ritter, Lawrence S. 2004. 35p. (J). (gr. k-4). reprint ed. pap. 12.00 *(978-0-7567-7714-2(3))* DIANE Publishing Co.

Merli, Anna. Lilo & Stitch. Ehrbar, Greg. 2020. (Disney Classics Ser.). (ENG.). 48p. (J). (gr. 2-6). lib. bdg. 28.50 ***(978-1-5321-4539-1(X)***, 35186, Graphic Novels) Spotlight.

Merli, Anna. Sweeties #2: Summer/Coco. Grisseaux, Veronique & Cassidy, Cathy. 2019. (Sweeties Ser.: 2). (ENG.). 96p. (J). 14.99 *(978-1-62991-838-9(5)*, 900181003) Papercutz.

—Sweeties #2: Summer/Coco. Grisseaux, Veronique. 2019. (Sweeties Ser.: 2). (ENG.). 96p. (J). pap. 9.99 *(978-1-62991-837-2(7)*, 900181004) Papercutz.

Merli, Anna, jt. illus. see Melaranci, Elisabetta.

Merli, Luca, jt. illus. see Celoni, Fabio.

Merlino, Elena. The Twelve Parables. 2017. (ENG.). (J). (gr. k-3). pap. *(978-0-9951731-3-2(3))* Baeiena Bks.

Merola, Caroline. Toni Biscotti's Magic Trick. Merola, Caroline. Cummins, Sarah, tr. 2006. (Formac First Novels Ser.: 60). (ENG.). 64p. (J). (gr. 2-5). 14.95 *(978-0-88780-719-0(4)*, 719); 4.95 *(978-0-88780-715-2(1)*, 715) Formac Publishing Co., Ltd. CAN. Dist: Formac Lorimer Bks. Ltd.

—La Trahison de Laurent Lareau. Merola, Caroline. 2003. (Premier Roman Ser.). (FRE.). 64p. (J). (gr. 1-4). pap. *(978-2-89021-645-7(4))* Diffusion du livre Mirabel (DLM).

Merola, Caroline. Jesus: A Story of Love. Merola, Caroline, tr. Dumont, C. & Lacoursiere, Suzanne. 2003. 32p. (J). mass mkt. 5.95 *(978-0-8198-3977-0(9)*, 332-153) Pauline Bks. & Media.

Merola, Marcelo & Nichx. The Chameleon Chronicles, Vol. 1. Leiter, Andrew S. 2005. (YA). per. 21.95 *(978-0-9767076-0-8(8))* Empowered Entertainment.

Merrell, David. Absolutely Lucy #4: Lucy on the Ball. Cooper, Ilene. 2011. (Lucy Ser.: 4). 112p. (J). (gr. 1-4). 5.99 *(978-0-375-85559-7(9)*, Random Hse. Bks. for Young Readers) Random Hse. Children's Bks.

—Absolutely Lucy #5: Lucy's Tricks & Treats. Cooper, Ilene. 2012. (Lucy Ser.: 5). 112p. (J). (gr. 1-4). 5.99 *(978-0-375-86997-6(2)*, Random Hse. Bks. for Young Readers) Random Hse. Children's Bks.

—Absolutely Lucy #6: Thanks to Lucy. Cooper, Ilene. 2013. (Lucy Ser.: 6). 112p. (J). (gr. 1-4). 4.99 *(978-0-375-86998-3(0)*, Random Hse. Bks. for Young Readers) Random Hse. Children's Bks.

—The Fortress of the Treasure Queen. Abbott, Tony. 2004. (Secrets of Droon Ser.: No. 23). 115p. (J). lib. bdg. 15.38 *(978-1-4242-0312-3(0))* Fitzgerald Bks.

—The Isle of Mists, 22. Abbott, Tony. 2004. (Secrets of Droon Ser.: 22). (ENG.). 128p. (J). (gr. 2-4). 16.19 *(978-0-439-56048-1(9))* Scholastic, Inc.

—Look at Lucy! Cooper, Ilene. 2009. (Lucy Ser.: 3). (ENG.). 112p. (J). (gr. 1-4). 4.99 *(978-0-375-85558-0(0)*, Random Hse. Bks. for Young Readers) Random Hse. Children's Bks.

—Lucy on the Ball, 4. Cooper, Ilene. 2011. (Absolutely Lucy Ser.). (ENG.). 112p. (J). (gr. 2-4). lib. bdg. 17.44 *(978-0-375-95559-4(3))* Random House Publishing Group.

—The Riddle of Zorfendorf Castle. Abbott, Tony. 2005. (Secrets of Droon Ser.: No. 25). 124p. (J). lib. bdg. 15.38 *(978-1-4242-0310-9(4))* Fitzgerald Bks.

—The Riddle of Zorfendorf Castle, 25. Abbott, Tony. 2005. (Secrets of Droon Ser.: 25). (ENG.). 124p. (J). (gr. 2-4). 16.19 *(978-0-439-67173-6(6))* Scholastic, Inc.

Merrell, David & Jessell, Tim. In the Shadow of Goll, 28. Abbott, Tony. 2006. (Secrets of Droon Ser.: 28). (ENG.). 123p. (J). (gr. 2-4). 16.19 *(978-0-439-67176-7(0))* Scholastic, Inc.

—The Tower of the Elf King, 9. Abbott, Tony. 2010. (Secrets of Droon Ser.: 9). (ENG.). 100p. (J). (gr. 2-4). 16.19 *(978-0-439-20772-0(X))* Scholastic, Inc.

—Wizard or Witch? Abbott, Tony. 2004. (Secrets of Droon Ser.: 2). (ENG.). 161p. (J). (gr. 2-4). 18.69 *(978-0-439-56049-8(7))* Scholastic, Inc.

Merrell, Vernon R. Wilbur's Great Adventure. Hilderbrandt, Sandra June. 2011. 32p. (J). 19.95 *(978-1-59649-587-6(1))* Whispering Pine Pr. International, Inc.

—Wilbur's Great Adventure. Hilderbrandt, Sandra June. Whispering Pine Press International, Inc. Staff, ed. 2011. (ENG.). 32p. (J). per. 12.95 *(978-1-59434-312-4(8))* Whispering Pine Pr. International, Inc.

Merrifield, Monarca. Inch Worm Inch Worm. Kayaalp, Suzan. 2013. 20p. pap. 12.95 *(978-1-62838-072-9(1))* Page Publishing Inc.

Merrifield, Teagan Trif. And You Can Love Me: A Story for Everyone Who Loves Someone with Autism Spectrum Disorder (Asd) Lee, Sherry Quan & Gaylor, Kyra. 2019. (ENG.). 40p. (J). (gr. k-2). 26.95 *(978-1-61599-425-0(4))* Loving Healing Pr., Inc.

Merrifield, Teagan Trif & Gaylor, Kyra. And You Can Love Me: A Story for Everyone Who Loves Someone with Autism Spectrum Disorder (Asd) Lee, Sherry Quan. 2019. (ENG.). 40p. (J). (gr. -1-3). pap. 15.95 *(978-1-61599-424-3(6))* Loving Healing Pr., Inc.

Merrill, Christine Herman. There's an Owl in the Shower. George, Jean Craighead. 2019. (ENG.). 144p. (J). (gr. 3-7). pap. 6.99 *(978-0-06-440682-6(2)*, HarperCollins) HarperCollins Pubs. Ltd. GBR. Dist: HarperCollins Pubs.

Merrill, Frank T. Boy Scouts in the White Mountains: the Story of a Long Hike. Eaton, Walter Prichard. 2006. (ENG.). 316p. per. 30.95 *(978-1-4286-4117-4(3))* Kessinger Publishing, LLC.

—Honor Bright (Illustrated Edition) Richards, Laura E. 2016. (ENG.). (J). pap. *(978-1-4068-7992-6(4))* Echo Library.

Merriman, Christi. The Wish: Johnny's Story. Bernal, Sandra Marie. 2011. 48p. pap. 24.95 *(978-1-4560-4934-8(8))* America Star Bks.

Merriman, Rachel. The Story of Me: A Girl's Journal. 2008. (ENG.). 144p. (J). (gr. 4-7). *(978-1-84597-624-8(X)*, CICO Books) Ryland Peters & Small.

Merrino, Gemma. The Sheep Who Hatched an Egg. Merino, Gemma. 2017. (ENG.). 32p. (J). (gr. -1-3). 16.99 *(978-0-8075-7338-9(8)*, 807573388) Whitman, Albert & Co.

Merris, Laura. Lost in Wildcat Cove. Cook, Sandra. Freeman, Ryan P., ed. 2016. (Critters of Wildcat Cove Ser.: Vol. 1). (ENG.). 28p. (J). pap. 14.99 *(978-1-0937-2808-8(6))* Independently Published.

—Sammy the Short Tailed Squrriel. Miller, Bruce. Freeman, Ryan P., ed. 2018. (ENG.). 28p. (J). pap. 14.99 *(978-1-0952-8557-2(2))* Independently Published.

Merrison, Stacy. Paddle Tail. LeGrand, Hank, 3rd. I.t. ed. 2004. 63p. (J). per. 7.95 *(978-1-59466-020-7(4)*, Growing Years) Port Town Publishing.

Merrit, Kory. Poptrópica: El Misterio del Mapa. Chabert, Jack. 2017. (SPA.). 120p. (J). (gr. 2-4). pap. 11.95 *(978-607-735-911-1(4))* Editorial Oceano de Mexico MEX. Dist: Independent Pubs. Group.

—Poptrópica 2. la Expedición Perdida. Chabert, Jack & Krpata, Mitch. 2017. (SPA.). 120p. (J). (gr. 2-4). pap. 11.95 *(978-607-527-022-7(1))* Editorial Oceano de Mexico MEX. Dist: Independent Pubs. Group.

Merritt, Kate. Indestructibles: Baby Babble. 2012. (Indestructibles Ser.). (ENG.). 12p. (J). (gr. k — 1). pap. 5.95 *(978-0-7611-6880-5(X)*, 16880) Workman Publishing Co., Inc.

—Indestructibles: Baby Faces: Chew Proof · Rip Proof · Nontoxic · 100% Washable (Book for Babies, Newborn Books, Safe to Chew) 2012. (Indestructibles Ser.). (ENG.). 12p. (J). (gr. k — 1). pap. 5.95 *(978-0-7611-6881-2(8)*, 16881) Workman Publishing Co., Inc.

—Indestructibles: Baby Night-Night. 2014. (Indestructibles Ser.). (ENG.). 12p. (J). pap. 5.95 *(978-0-7611-8182-8(2)*, 18182) Workman Publishing Co., Inc.

—Indestructibles: Baby Peekaboo. 2014. (Indestructibles Ser.). (ENG.). 12p. (J). pap. 5.95 *(978-0-7611-8181-1(4)*, 18181) Workman Publishing Co., Inc.

—Indestructibles: Beach Baby. 2016. (Indestructibles Ser.). (ENG.). 12p. (J). pap. 5.95 *(978-0-7611-8732-5(4)*, 18732) Workman Publishing Co., Inc.

Merritt, Kimberly. Running the Race of Life. Finch, Debbie Southard. Services, Christian Editing, ed. 2019. (ENG.). 32p. (J). pap. 10.00 *(978-1-0725-5750-0(9))* Independently Published.

—Thank You, God ... for Dirt & Worms Journal Coloring Book. Carter, Christy. Services, Christian Editing, ed. 2018. (ENG.). 64p. (J). pap. 10.00 *(978-1-7904-5532-4(4))* Independently Published.

—Watch the Light to Find God's Will. Finch, Debbie Southard. Services, Christian Editing, ed. 2019. (ENG.). 38p. (J). pap. 10.00 *(978-1-7908-7094-3(1))* Independently Published.

Merritt, Kory. The End of Time (Poptropica Book 4) Krpata, Mitch. 2017. (ENG.). 112p. (J). (gr. 1-4). 9.99 *(978-1-4197-2557-9(2)*, Amulet Bks.) Abrams, Inc.

—The Lost Expedition. Krpata, Mitch. ed. 2016. (Poptropica Graphic Novels Ser.: 2). (J). lib. bdg. 20.80 *(978-0-606-39019-4(7))* Turtleback.

—Poptrópica 3. la Sociedad Secreta. Krpata, Mitch. 2018. (SPA.). 120p. (J). (gr. 2-4). pap. 11.95 *(978-607-527-112-5(0))* Editorial Oceano de Mexico MEX. Dist: Independent Pubs. Group.

—Poptropica: Book 2: The Lost Expedition. Krpata, Mitch. 2016. (ENG.). 112p. (J). (gr. 1-4). 9.95 *(978-1-4197-2129-8(1)*, Amulet Bks.) Abrams, Inc.

—Poptropica: Book 3: The Secret Society. Krpata, Mitch. 2017. (ENG.). 112p. (J). (gr. 1-4). 9.95 *(978-1-4197-2311-7(1)*, Amulet Bks.) Abrams, Inc.

Merritt, Richard. Dino. Garnett, Jaye. Cottage Door Press, ed. 2020. (Peek-A-Flap Children's Interactive Lift-a-Flap Board Book Ser.). (ENG.). 12p. (J). (gr. -1-2). bds. 8.99 ***(978-1-64638-042-8(8)***, 1006180) Cottage Door Pr.

Merritt, Richard. Dinosaurs. Crowe, Carmen. Cottage Door Press, ed. 2019. (Early Bird Sound Books 5 Button Ser.). (ENG.). 12p. (J). (gr. -1-2). bds. 14.99 *(978-1-68052-639-4(1)*, 1004320) Cottage Door Pr.

—Flip-Flap Friends: Mermicorns. 2019. (ENG.). 12p. (J). (gr. -1-k). bds. 6.99 *(978-1-68412-957-7(5)*, Silver Dolphin Bks.) Printers Row Publishing Group.

—Peek & Play Rhymes: Old MacDonald Had a Farm. 2018. (Peek & Play Rhymes Ser.). (ENG.). 14p. (J). (— 1). bds. 7.99 *(978-1-68412-304-9(6)*, Silver Dolphin Bks.) Printers Row Publishing Group.

—Peek & Play Rhymes: the Wheels on the Bus. 2018. (Peek & Play Rhymes Ser.). (ENG.). 14p. (J). (— 1). bds. 7.99 *(978-1-68412-303-2(8)*, Silver Dolphin Bks.) Printers Row Publishing Group.

Merritt, Richard. When I Grow up: I Want to Be# Lloyd, Rosamund. 2020. (ENG.). 12p. (J). (-k). bds. 9.99 ***(978-1-68010-613-8(9))*** Tiger Tales.

—When I Grow up: I Want to Drive# Lloyd, Rosamund. 2020. (ENG.). 12p. (J). (-k). bds. 9.99 ***(978-1-68010-612-1(0))*** Tiger Tales.

Merry, Alex. Jasper & the Magpie: Enjoying Special Interests Together. Mayfield, Dan. 2014. (ENG.). 36p. (J). 15.95 *(978-1-84905-579-6(3)*, 694471) Kingsley, Jessica Pubs. GBR. Dist: Hachette UK Distribution.

—Why Johnny Doesn't Flap: NT Is OK. Morton, Clay & Morton, Gail. 2015. (ENG.). 32p. (J). 16.95 *(978-1-84905-721-9(4)*, 693892) Kingsley, Jessica Pubs. GBR. Dist: Hachette UK Distribution.

Merryweather, Jack. Kit Carson. Beals, Frank Lee. 2011. 194p. 42.95 *(978-1-258-08971-9(8))* Literary Licensing, LLC.

Mertins, Lisa. Jimmy Finds His Voice. Doti, James. 2013. (J). 14.95 *(978-1-935204-47-3(5))* Salem Author Services.

Merveille, David. Juke Box. Merveille, David. 2008. (ENG.). 48p. (J). (gr. 4-7). 9.99 *(978-1-933605-72-2(3))* Kane Miller.

Merwin, Decie. Schoolroom in the Parlor. Caudill, Rebecca. I.t. ed. 2005. (ENG.). 145p. (J). (gr. 2-3). pap. 11.95 *(978-1-883937-82-9(5))* Ignatius Pr.

—Up & down the River. Caudill, Rebecca. 2005. 143p. (J). (gr. -1-17). pap. 11.95 *(978-1-883937-81-2(7))* Bethlehem Bks.

Meschenmoser, Sebastian. The Wind in the Willows. Grahame, Kenneth. 2017. (ENG.). 220p. (J). (gr. -1-3). 30.00 *(978-0-7358-4295-3(7))* North-South Bks., Inc.

Meschenmoser, Sebastian. Waiting for Winter. Meschenmoser, Sebastian. 2015. (ENG.). 58p. (J). (gr. k-3). 10.99 *(978-1-61067-435-5(9))* Kane Miller.

Meschini, Leonardo. How to Draw Amazing Animals, 1 vol. McCurry, Kristen. 2013. (Smithsonian Drawing Bks.). (ENG.). 64p. (gr. 3-6). pap. 7.19 *(978-1-62065-726-3(0)*, Capstone Pr.); pap. 41.70 *(978-1-62065-727-0(9))* Capstone.

—The Prince & the Sphinx, 1 vol. 2012. (Egyptian Myths Ser.). (ENG.). 32p. (J). (gr. 3-5). pap. 8.95 *(978-1-4048-7242-4(6))*; lib. bdg. 29.32 *(978-1-4048-7149-6(7))* Capstone. (Picture Window Bks.).

Meserve, Jessica. Daisy Dawson & the Big Freeze. Voake, Steve. 2011. (Daisy Dawson Ser.). (ENG.). 96p. (J). (gr. 1-4). pap. 5.99 *(978-0-7636-5627-0(5))* Candlewick Pr.

—Daisy Dawson & the Secret Pond. Voake, Steve. (Daisy Dawson Ser.: 2). (ENG.). 96p. (J). (gr. 1-4). 2010. pap. 5.99 *(978-0-7636-4730-8(6))*; 2. 2009. 18.69 *(978-0-7636-4009-5(3))* Candlewick Pr.

—Daisy Dawson at the Beach. Voake, Steve. (Daisy Dawson Ser.: 4). (ENG.). 96p. (J). (gr. 1-4). 2012. pap. 5.99 *(978-0-7636-5946-2(0))*; 2011. 14.99 *(978-0-7636-5306-4(3))* Candlewick Pr.

—Daisy Dawson Is on Her Way! Voake, Steve. 2009. (Daisy Dawson Ser.: 1). (ENG.). 112p. (J). (gr. 1-4). pap. 5.99 *(978-0-7636-4294-5(0))* Candlewick Pr.

—Daisy Dawson on the Farm. Voake, Steve. 2012. (Daisy Dawson Ser.: 5). (ENG.). 96p. (J). (gr. 1-4). 14.99 *(978-0-7636-5882-3(0))* Candlewick Pr.

—Daisy Dawson on the Farm. Voake, Steve. 2013. (Daisy Dawson Ser.). (ENG.). 96p. (J). (gr. 1-4). pap. 5.99 *(978-0-7636-6340-7(9))* Candlewick Pr.

Meserve, Jessica. Un d�a Muy Ocupado. Schaefer, Lola M. 2018. (Buenas Noches Ser.). (SPA.). 40p. (J). pap. ***(978-958-8860-53-4(9))*** Norma Ediciones, S.A.

Meserve, Jessica. Dibujemos Juntos. Thebo, Mimi. rev. ed. 2006. (Castillo de la Lectura Blanca Ser.). (ENG.). 64p. (J). (gr. k-2). pap. 6.95 *(978-970-20-0849-1(2))* Castillo, Ediciones, S. A. de C. V. MEX. Dist: Macmillan.

—Lucky Me, Lucy Mcgee. Amato, Mary. 2020. (Lucy Mcgee Ser.: 3). 176p. (J). (gr. 2-5). 15.99 *(978-0-8234-4364-2(7))*; pap. 7.99 *(978-0-8234-4525-7(9))* Holiday Hse., Inc.

—Misty. Dencer, Christine. 2015. (Stanley & Me Ser.: 1). (ENG.). 34p. (J). 12.95 *(978-1-927018-59-0(5))* Simply Read Bks. CAN. Dist: Ingram Publisher Services.

—News from Me, Lucy Mcgee. Amato, Mary. (Lucy Mcgee Ser.). 144p. (J). (gr. 2-5). 2020. pap. 7.99 *(978-0-8234-4439-7(2))*; 2018. 15.99 *(978-0-8234-3871-6(6))* Holiday Hse., Inc.

—One Special Day: A Story for Big Brothers & Sisters. Schaefer, Lola. 2012. 40p. (J). (gr. -1-k). 16.99 *(978-1-4231-3760-3(4))* Hyperion Pr.

Meserve, Jessica. One Special Day: A Story for Big Brothers & Sisters. Schaefer, Lola M. 2018. 32p. (J). bds. 7.99 ***(978-1-4847-8842-4(7))*** Little, Brown Bks. for Young Readers.

Meserve, Jessica. Sing with Me, Lucy Mcgee. Amato, Mary. (Lucy Mcgee Ser.: 2). (J). (gr. 2-5). 2020. 144p. pap. 7.99 *(978-0-8234-4545-5(3))*; 2019. 176p. 15.99 *(978-0-8234-3876-1(7))* Holiday Hse., Inc.

Meserve, Jessica. Bedtime Without Arthur. Meserve, Jessica. 2010. (ENG.). 32p. (J). (gr. -1-3). 16.95 *(978-0-7613-5497-0(2)*, 9780761354970) Lerner Publishing Group.

Meserve, Jessica & Jones, Noah Z. Magic at the Bed & Biscuit. Carris, Joan Davenport. 2011. 128p. (J). (gr. 1-4). 15.99 *(978-0-7636-4306-5(8))* Candlewick Pr.

Meshon, Aaron. Tomorrow Is Waiting. Frank, Kiley. 2019. 32p. (J). (gr. -1-2). 16.99 *(978-1-101-99437-5(1)*, Dial Bks) Penguin Young Readers Group.

Meshon, Aaron. Delivery. Meshon, Aaron. 2017. (ENG.). 48p. (J). (gr. -1-3). 17.99 *(978-1-4814-4175-9(2))* Simon & Schuster Children's Publishing.

—Now That I'm Here. Meshon, Aaron. 2018. (ENG.). 40p. (J). (-k). 16.99 *(978-0-7352-2936-5(8)*, Dial Bks) Penguin Young Readers Group.

—Take Me Out to the Yakyu. Meshon, Aaron. 2013. (ENG.). 40p. (J). (gr. -1-3). 18.99 *(978-1-4424-4177-4(1)*, Atheneum Bks. for Young Readers) Simon & Schuster Children's Publishing.

—Tools Rule! Meshon, Aaron. 2014. (ENG.). 40p. (J). (gr. -1-3). 18.99 *(978-1-4424-9601-9(0)*, Atheneum Bks. for Young Readers) Simon & Schuster Children's Publishing.

Meskin, Mike, photos by. Ollie & Moon in New York City. Kredensor, Diane. 2017. (Pictureback(R) Ser.). 32p. (J). (gr. -1-2). pap. 5.99 *(978-1-5247-1574-8(3)*, Random Hse. Bks. for Young Readers) Random Hse. Children's Bks.

Mesquita, Camila. Elecciones Que Brillan. Camossa, Silvia. 2004. 64p. pap. 8.95 *(978-85-7416-193-8(4))* Callis Editora Ltda BRA. Dist: Independent Pubs. Group.

—Frida Kahlo. Lenero, Carmen. 2004. (Niñez de...Ser.). 24p. pap. 6.95 *(978-85-7416-216-4(7))* Callis Editora Ltda BRA. Dist: Independent Pubs. Group.

Messenger, Norman. An Artist's Alphabet. Messenger, Norman. 2016. (ENG.). 48p. (J). (gr. k-12). 17.99 *(978-0-7636-8123-4(7))* Candlewick Pr.

Messer, Celia. All Across Ohio: A Bird's Eye View with Worthington Cardinal, 7 bks. Gray, Susan. 2003. 24p. (J). 7.95 *(978-0-9742862-0-4(6))* Two's Company.

—Plain & Simple: A Bird's Eye View with Worthington Cardinal, 7 bks. Gray, Susan. 2003. 24p. (J). 7.95 *(978-0-9742862-4-2(9))* Two's Company.

—A River Ride: A Bird's Eye View with Worthington Cardinal, 7 bks. Gray, Susan. 2003. 24p. (J). 7.95 *(978-0-9742862-3-5(0))* Two's Company.

—Wagon-O! A Bird's Eye View with Worthington Cardinal, 7 bks. Gray, Susan. 2003. 24p. (J). 7.95 *(978-0-9742862-2-8(2))* Two's Company.

—We Can Fly! A Bird's Eye View with Worthington Cardinal, 7 bks. Gray, Susan. 2003. 24p. (J). 7.95 *(978-0-9742862-1-1(4))* Two's Company.

Messer, Celia, jt. illus. see Gray, Susan.

Messer, Claire. It's a Field Trip, Busy Bus! Shaffer, Jody Jensen. 2019. (Busy Bus Ser.). (ENG.). 40p. (J). (gr. -1-3). 17.99 *(978-1-5344-4081-4(X)*, Beach Lane Bks.) Beach Lane Bks.

—It's Your First Day of School, Busy Bus! Shaffer, Jody Jensen. 2018. (Busy Bus Ser.). (ENG.). 32p. (J). (gr. -1-3). 18.99 *(978-1-4814-9467-0(8)*, Beach Lane Bks.) Beach Lane Bks.

Messer, Claire. Grumpy Pants. Messer, Claire. 2016. (ENG.). 32p. (J). (gr. -1-3). 16.99 *(978-0-8075-3075-7(1)*, 807530751) Whitman, Albert & Co.

—Lazybones. Messer, Claire. 2018. (ENG.). 32p. (J). (gr. -1-k). 16.99 *(978-0-8075-4402-0(7),* 807544027) Whitman, Albert & Co.

Messer, Corey. Cat, Cat, Feral Cat. Wolf, Clarissa. 2009. 28p. pap. 9.99 *(978-1-935105-26-8(4))* Avid Readers Publishing Group.

Messer, Dawn. Where Is Little Fairy Pippuff? Siwiec, Carrie. 2017. (ENG.). 37p. (J). 28.95 *(978-1-4787-9486-8(0));* pap. 19.95 *(978-1-4787-9343-4(0))* Outskirts Pr., Inc.

Messer, Florence I. My Daily Prayer Journal: For Boys. Ether, Judy. 2019. (ENG.). 108p. (J). pap. 5.95 ***(978-1-7132-5795-0(5))*** Independently Published.

Messer, Jennifer K. Hoosier Heart. Messer, Luke. 2006. 32p. (J). 16.95 *(978-0-9786799-1-0(1))* Eva Publishing, LLC.

Messersmith, Patrick. Martín de León: Tejano Empresario. Alter, Judy. 2007. (Stars of Texas Ser.: 4). (ENG.). 72p. (J). (gr. 4-7). 14.95 *(978-1-933337-08-1(7))* State Hse. Pr.

—Mirabeau B. Lamar: Second President of Texas. Alter, Judy. 2005. (Stars of Texas Ser.: 2). (ENG.). 72p. (J). (gr. 4-7). 17.95 *(978-1-880510-97-1(9))* State Hse. Pr.

—Miriam Ma Ferguson: First Woman Governor of Texas. Alter, Judy. 2006. (Stars of Texas Ser.: 3). (ENG.). 72p. (J). (gr. 4-7). 17.95 *(978-1-933337-01-2(X))* State Hse. Pr.

Messick, Christianna. The Greatest Gift: A Fairy Tale about Following Your Dreams. Schisler, Amy. 2017. (ENG.). (J). pap. 11.99 *(978-0-692-83640-8(3))* Schisler, Amy MacWilliams.

Messimer, Maria. Paisley the Pear. Messimer, Maria. 2019. (ENG.). 34p. (J). pap. 12.00 *(978-0-578-54307-9(9))* Messimer, Maria S.

Messina, Chiara. La Fantastica Storia Di Tempo: Le Stagioni. D'Amato, Giuseppina. 2020. (Favole Dentro la Borsa Ser.: Vol. 1). (ITA.). 44p. (J). pap. 15.21 ***(978-1-0892-0514-2(7))*** Independently Published.

Messina, David, et al. Best of Klingons. Tipton, Scott et al. 2013. (Star Trek Ser.). 234p. pap. 24.99 *(978-1-61377-725-1(6),* 9781613777251) Idea & Design Works, LLC.

Messina, Lilli. Alice the Armadillo: A Tale of Self Discovery. Law, Felicia. 2010. (Animal Fair Values Ser.). 32p. (J). (gr. -1-3). pap. 10.55 *(978-1-60754-809-6(7));* lib. bdg. 25.60 *(978-1-60754-805-8(4))* Windmill Bks.

—Florence the Flamingo: A Tale of Pride. Law, Felicia. 2010. (Animal Fair Values Ser.). (ENG.). 32p. (J). (gr. -1-3). pap. 10.55 *(978-1-60754-907-9(7));* lib. bdg. 25.60 *(978-1-60754-901-7(8))* Windmill Bks.

—Limpopo the Lion: A Tale of Laziness & Lethargy. Law, Felicia. 2010. (Animal Fair Values Ser.). 32p. (J). (gr. -1-3). pap. 10.55 *(978-1-60754-808-9(9));* lib. bdg. 25.60 *(978-1-60754-804-1(6))* Windmill Bks.

—Zanzibar the Zebra: A Tale of Individuality. Law, Felicia. 2010. (Animal Fair Values Ser.). 32p. (J). (gr. -1-3). pap. 10.55 *(978-1-60754-807-2(0));* lib. bdg. 25.60 *(978-1-60754-803-4(8))* Windmill Bks.

Messina, Linda. FirstFires. Lightner, Laura. 2008. 27p. (J). 31.99 *(978-1-4363-4542-2(1))* Xlibris Corp.

Messing, Dave. How Different Is Good: Nick the Wise Old Cat. Sicks, Linda. 2010. (Importance of Friendship Ser.). (ENG.). 40p. (J). 18.95 *(978-1-936193-04-2(3))* Nick The Cat, LLC.

—Monty the Menace: Understanding Differences. Baum, Lonna. 2012. (ENG.). 32p. (J). 16.95 *(978-0-9839373-0-2(3))* Baum & Baum, LLC.

—Monty the Menace: Understanding Differences: Vision. Baum, Lonna. 2019. (ENG.). 36p. (J). 22.00 *(978-1-64446-003-0(3));* pap. 14.00 *(978-1-64446-004-7(1))* Rowe Publishing.

—Nick the Wise Old Cat: How I Found My Family. Sicks, Linda. 2010. (ENG.). 40p. (J). 18.95 *(978-1-936193-00-4(0))* Nick The Cat, LLC.

—Nick the Wise Old Cat How I Found My Family. Sicks, Linda. 2009. 32p. (J). 17.95 *(978-1-934878-63-7(4))* Mascot Bks., Inc.

—Nick's Holiday Celebration. Sicks, Linda. 2010. (Importance of Family Ser.). 40p. (J). 18.95 *(978-1-936193-05-9(1))* Nick The Cat, LLC.

Messing, David. As-Tu Rempli un Seau Aujourd'hui? Un Guide du Bonheur Quotidien Pour Enfants. McCloud, Carol. 2012. (ENG & FRE.). 32p. (J). pap. 9.95 *(978-1-933916-92-7(3),* Ferne Pr.) Nelson Publishing & Marketing.

—Fill a Bucket: A Guide to Daily Happiness for Young Children. McCloud, Carol & Martin, Katherine. 2018. 24p. (J). (gr. -1 — 1). 9.95 *(978-0-9960999-8-1(0))* Bucket Fillers, Inc.

—Have You Filled a Bucket Today? A Guide to Daily Happiness for Kids. McCloud, Carol. 10th ed. 2015. 31p. (J). (gr. -1-4). pap. 9.95 *(978-0-9960999-3-6(X))* Bucket Fillers, Inc.

—Have You Filled a Bucket Today? A Guide to Daily Happiness for Kids. McCloud, Carol. (ENG.). 32p. (J). 2007. 17.95 *(978-1-933916-16-3(8));* 2006. (gr. -1-3). pap. 9.95 *(978-0-9785075-1-0(7),* Ferne Pr.) Nelson Publishing & Marketing.

—Myrtle the Hurdler: And Her Pink & Purple Polka-Dotted Girdle. Dillon-Butler, Marybeth. 2005. (ENG.). 32p. (J). (gr. -1-2). pap. 11.95 *(978-0-9785075-9-6(2),* Ferne Pr.) Nelson Publishing & Marketing.

Messner, Dennis. Moopy el Monstruo Subterráneo/Moopy the Underground Monster. Meister, Cari. Heck, Claudia M., tr. 2012. (Los Amigos Monstruos/Monster Friends Ser.). (ENG.). 32p. (J). (gr. 2-3). lib. bdg. 22.65 *(978-1-4342-3785-9(0),* Stone Arch Bks.) Capstone.

—Moopy on the Beach, 1 vol. Meister, Cari. 2010. (Monster Friends Ser.). (ENG.). 32p. (J). (gr. 2-3). pap. 6.25 *(978-1-4342-2304-3(3));* lib. bdg. 22.65 *(978-1-4342-1874-2(0))* Capstone. (Stone Arch Bks.).

—Moopy the Underground Monster, 1 vol. Meister, Cari. 2009. (Monster Friends Ser.). (ENG.). 32p. (J). (gr. 2-3). 22.65 *(978-1-4342-1630-4(6));* pap. 6.25 *(978-1-4342-1745-5(0))* Capstone. (Stone Arch Bks.).

—Ora - El Monstruo Marino. Meister, Cari. Heck, Claudia M., tr. 2012. (Los Amigos Monstruos/Monster Friends Ser.).Tr. of Ora - The Sea Monster. (ENG.). 32p. (J). (gr. 2-3). lib. bdg. 22.65 *(978-1-4342-3784-2(2),* Stone Arch Bks.) Capstone.

—Ora - The Sea Monster. Meister, Cari. 2009. (Monster Friends Ser.). (ENG.). 32p. (J). (gr. 2-3). pap. 6.25 *(978-1-4342-1746-2(9),* Stone Arch Bks.) Capstone.

—Ora at the Monster Contest, 1 vol. Meister, Cari. 2010. (Monster Friends Ser.). (ENG.). 32p. (J). (gr. 2-3). pap. 6.25 *(978-1-4342-2305-0(1));* lib. bdg. 22.65 *(978-1-4342-1875-9(9))* Capstone. (Stone Arch Bks.).

—Ora the Sea Monster. Meister, Cari. 2009. (Monster Friends Ser.). (ENG.). 32p. (J). (gr. 2-3). 22.65 *(978-1-4342-1631-1(4),* Stone Arch Bks.) Capstone.

—Snorp: The City Monster. Meister, Cari. 2009. (Monster Friends Ser.). (ENG.). 32p. (J). (gr. 2-3). 22.65 *(978-1-4342-1632-8(2));* pap. 6.25 *(978-1-4342-1747-9(7))* Capstone. (Stone Arch Bks.).

—Snorp on the Slopes, 1 vol. Meister, Cari. 2010. (Monster Friends Ser.). (ENG.). 32p. (J). (gr. 2-3). pap. 6.25 *(978-1-4342-2306-7(X));* lib. bdg. 22.65 *(978-1-4342-1873-5(2))* Capstone. (Stone Arch Bks.).

—Three Claws in the City, 1 vol. Meister, Cari. 2010. (Monster Friends Ser.). (ENG.). 32p. (J). (gr. 2-3). pap. 6.25 *(978-1-4342-2307-4(8));* lib. bdg. 22.65 *(978-1-4342-1872-8(4))* Capstone. (Stone Arch Bks.).

—Three Claws the Mountain Monster. Meister, Cari. 2009. (Monster Friends Ser.). (ENG.). 32p. (J). (gr. 2-3). 22.65 *(978-1-4342-1633-5(0));* pap. 6.25 *(978-1-4342-1748-6(5))* Capstone. (Stone Arch Bks.).

Mesturini, C. Astronaut. Caviezel, Giovanni. 2012. (Little People Shape Bks.). (ENG.). 10p. (J). (gr. -1-2). bds. 8.99 *(978-0-7641-6573-3(9),* B.E.S. Publishing) Peterson's.

—Ballerina. Caviezel, Giovanni. 2011. (Mini People Shape Bks.). (ENG.). 10p. (J). (gr. -1-1). bds. 5.99 *(978-0-7641-6436-1(8),* B.E.S. Publishing) Peterson's.

—Builder. Caviezel, Giovanni. 2011. (Mini People Shape Bks.). (ENG.). 10p. (J). (gr. -1-1). bds. 5.99 *(978-0-7641-6437-8(6),* B.E.S. Publishing) Peterson's.

—Cowboy. Caviezel, Giovanni. 2009. (Little People Shape Bks.). (ENG.). 12p. (J). (gr. -1-2). bds. 10.99 *(978-0-7641-6191-9(1),* B.E.S. Publishing) Peterson's.

—Fireman's Safety Hints. Caviezel, Giovanni. 2012. (Little People Shape Bks.). (ENG.). 10p. (J). (gr. k-2). bds. 8.99 *(978-0-7641-6594-8(1),* B.E.S. Publishing) Peterson's.

—Pirates! Caviezel, Giovanni. 2011. (Mini People Shape Bks.). (ENG.). 10p. (J). (gr. -1-1). bds. 5.99 *(978-0-7641-6441-5(4),* B.E.S. Publishing) Peterson's.

Mesturini, Cristina. Fairy. Caviezel, Giovanni. 2009. (Mini People Shape Bks.). (ENG.). 12p. (J). (gr. -1-1). bds. 5.99 *(978-0-7641-6218-3(7),* B.E.S. Publishing) Peterson's.

—La Liebre y la Tortuga. Mantegazza, Giovanna. 2019. (SPA.). 8p. (J). (gr. -1-1). 5.95 *(978-84-414-0362-8(7))* Editorial Edaf, S.L. ESP. Dist: Spanish Pubs., LLC.

—Little Elf. Caviezel, Giovanni. 2012. (Mini People Shape Bks.). (ENG.). 10p. (J). (gr. -1-2). bds. 4.99 *(978-0-7641-6577-1(1),* B.E.S. Publishing) Peterson's.

—My Own Human Body. Caviezel, Giovanni. 2012. (Little People Shape Bks.). (ENG.). 10p. (J). (gr. k-1). bds. 8.99 *(978-0-7641-6570-2(4),* B.E.S. Publishing) Peterson's.

—Princess. Caviezel, Giovanni. 2009. (Mini People Shape Bks.). (ENG.). 12p. (J). (gr. -1-1). bds. 5.99 *(978-0-7641-6219-0(5),* B.E.S. Publishing) Peterson's.

Metallinou, Renia. Now I'm a Bird. Ganz-Schmitt, Sue. 2020. (ENG.). 32p. (J). (gr. -1-3). 16.99 ***(978-0-8075-2329-2(1),*** 0807523291) Whitman, Albert & Co.

Metayer, Annabelle. Roxbury Park Dog Club #1: Mission Impawsible. Maple, Daphne. 2016. (Roxbury Park Dog Club Ser.: 1). (ENG.). 224p. (J). (gr. 3-7). pap. 6.99 *(978-0-06-232767-3(4))* HarperCollins Pubs.

—Roxbury Park Dog Club #2: When the Going Gets Ruff. Maple, Daphne. 2016. (Roxbury Park Dog Club Ser.: 2). (ENG.). 224p. (J). (gr. 3-7). pap. 6.99 *(978-0-06-232769-7(0))* HarperCollins Pubs.

—Roxbury Park Dog Club #3: Top Dog. Maple, Daphne. 2016. (Roxbury Park Dog Club Ser.: 3). (ENG.). 224p. (J). (gr. 3-7). pap. 6.99 *(978-0-06-232771-0(2))* HarperCollins Pubs.

—Roxbury Park Dog Club #4: All Paws on Deck. Maple, Daphne. 2016. (Roxbury Park Dog Club Ser.: 4). (ENG.). 224p. (J). (gr. 3-7). pap. 6.99 *(978-0-06-232773-4(9))* HarperCollins Pubs.

—Roxbury Park Dog Club #5: a New Leash on Life. Maple, Daphne. 2017. (Roxbury Park Dog Club Ser.: 5). (ENG.). 224p. (J). (gr. 3-7). pap. 6.99 *(978-0-06-237100-3(2))* HarperCollins Pubs.

—Roxbury Park Dog Club #6: a Bone to Pick. Maple, Daphne. 2017. (Roxbury Park Dog Club Ser.: 6). (ENG.). 208p. (J). (gr. 3-7). pap. 6.99 *(978-0-06-237102-7(9))* HarperCollins Pubs.

Metcalf, Kristin. Emily Waits for Her Family. Zelaya, Carol. 2007. (Emily the Chickadee Ser.). 32p. (J). (gr. 2-3). 14.95 *(978-0-9796265-0-0(1))* Richlee Publishing.

Metcalf, Paula. Have You Seen My Blankie? Rowland, Lucy. 2019. (ENG.). 32p. (J). (-k). 16.99 *(978-1-5362-0819-1(1),* Nosy Crow) Candlewick Pr.

—My Picture Encyclopedia. Phillips, Sarah. 2007. 64p. (J). (gr. k-2). *(978-1-84610-445-9(9))* Make Believe Ideas.

—Nothing Can Frighten a Bear. Dale, Elizabeth. 2018. (ENG.). 32p. (J). (gr. -1-2). 15.99 *(978-0-7636-9627-6(7),* Nosy Crow) Candlewick Pr.

—Run, Run! Lane, Alex. 2014. (Traditional Tales Ser.). (ENG.). 12p. (J). (gr. -1-k). pap. 5.95 *(978-1-62521-600-7(9),* Capstone Classroom) Capstone.

Metola, Patricia. Hansel y Gretel (Colorín Colorado/That Is the End of the Story) Maestro, Pepe. 2009. (SPA.). 14p. (J). *(978-84-263-7179-9(5))* Vives, Luis Editorial (Edelvives).

Metrano, Dylan. Every Day Birds. VanDerwater, Amy Ludwig. 2016. (ENG.). 32p. (J). (gr. -1-k). 17.99 *(978-0-545-69980-8(0),* Orchard Bks.) Scholastic, Inc.

Mets, Marilyn. Good-Bye Tonsils! Hatkoff, Craig & Hatkoff, Juliana Lee. 2004. (ENG.). 32p. (J). (gr. k-3). pap. 7.99 *(978-0-14-240133-0(1),* Puffin Books) Penguin Young Readers Group.

Mets, Marilyn & Ledwon, Peter. Waiting for the Sun, 1 vol. Lohans, Alison. 2006. (ENG.). 32p. (J). (gr. k-3). per. 6.95 *(978-0-88995-358-1(9),* 58896360-c81f-4818-80ac-51128ad8241b) Red Deer Pr. CAN. Dist: Firefly Bks., Ltd.

Mettler, Joe. Don't eat your Broccoli! Morris, Lynn. 2007. 32p. (J). per. 6.95 *(978-0-9755548-2-1(4))* Log Cabin Bks.

Mettler, Renè. The Jungle. 2012. (ENG.). 36p. (J). (gr. -1-k). spiral bd. 13.99 *(978-1-85103-399-7(8))* Moonlight Publishing, Ltd. GBR. Dist: Independent Pubs. Group.

Mettler, René. Birds. Mettler, René. 2012. (My First Discoveries Ser.: 15). (ENG.). 36p. (J). (gr. -1-k). spiral bd. 13.99 *(978-1-85103-397-3(1))* Moonlight Publishing, Ltd. GBR. Dist: Independent Pubs. Group.

—The Egg. Mettler, René. Mathews, Sarah. 2012. (ENG.). 34p. (J). (gr. -1-k). 13.99 *(978-1-85103-380-5(7))* Moonlight Publishing, Ltd. GBR. Dist: Independent Pubs. Group.

—Jungle. Mettler, René. First Discovery Staff. 2006. (ENG.). 36p. (J). (gr. k-3). spiral bd. 11.99 *(978-1-85103-183-2(9))* Moonlight Publishing, Ltd. GBR. Dist: Independent Pubs. Group.

—Woods & Forests. Mettler, René. Fuhr, Ute & Sautai, Raoul. Stanley-Baker, Penelope, tr. 2013. (ENG.). 36p. (J). (gr. -1-k). spiral bd. 13.99 *(978-1-85103-421-5(8))* Moonlight Publishing, Ltd. GBR. Dist: Independent Pubs. Group.

Metu, jt. illus. see Lakes, Lofton.

Metzgar, Linda. The Dolphin, the Sea, & Princess Annemarie. Corriere, Michael F. 2017. (ENG.). (J). pap. *(978-1-4602-8474-2(7))* FriesenPress.

Metzger, Jan. Slick 'n Slide. Lambert, Joyce. 2008. 36p. 9.95 *(978-0-9801146-0-7(8))* Lamweg Publishing.

Metzger, Steve & Antonini, Gabriele. Huggapotamus. 2011. (J). *(978-0-545-34352-7(6))* Scholastic, Inc.

Metzger, Wolfgang. Los Bomberos. Caballero, D., tr. 2006. (Junior (Silver Dolphin) Ser.). (SPA.). 16p. (J). (gr. 5). 9.95 *(978-970-718-344-5(6))* Readerlink Distribution Services, LLC.

Meugniot, Will. The Boy Who Cried Wolf. Aesop, Aesop. 2010. (Short Tales Fables Ser.). (ENG.). 32p. (J). (gr. 1-4). 27.07 *(978-1-60270-552-4(6),* 13405, Short Tales) Magic Wagon.

—Pandora. Reed, Gary. 2008. (Short Tales Greek Myths Ser.). (ENG.). 32p. (J). (gr. 3-6). 27.07 *(978-1-60270-138-0(5),* 13441, Short Tales) Magic Wagon.

Meurer, Caleb. And the Winner Is... Miglis, Jenny. ed. 2005. (SpongeBob SquarePants Ser.: 4). 22p. (J). lib. bdg. 15.00 *(978-1-59054-824-0(8))* Fitzgerald Bks.

—And the Winner Is... Miglis, Jenny. 2004. (SpongeBob SquarePants Ser.). (ENG.). 24p. (J). pap. 3.99 *(978-0-689-86327-1(6),* Simon Spotlight/Nickelodeon) Simon Spotlight/Nickelodeon.

—Star Wars: a New Hope (Star Wars) Smith, Geof. 2015. (Little Golden Book Ser.). (ENG.). 24p. (J). (-k). 4.99 *(978-0-7364-3538-3(7),* Golden Bks.) Random Hse. Children's Bks.

—Star Wars: the Force Awakens (Star Wars) Golden Books. 2016. (Little Golden Book Ser.). (ENG.). 24p. (J). (-k). 4.99 *(978-0-7364-3491-1(7),* Golden Bks.) Random Hse. Children's Bks.

—Triceratops for Lunch. Golden Books Staff. 2010. (Little Golden Book Ser.). (ENG.). 24p. (J). (gr. -1-2). 4.99 *(978-0-375-86151-2(3),* Golden Bks.) Random Hse. Children's Bks.

Meurer, Caleb & Rose, Micky. A New Hope (Star Wars) Smith, Geof. 2017. (Big Golden Book Ser.). (ENG.). 48p. (J). (gr. -1-2). 10.99 *(978-0-7364-3692-2(8),* Golden Bks.) Random Hse. Children's Bks.

Meurer, Caleb, jt. illus. see Golden Books.

Mew, Matt. Fruits & Veggies Making Faces. Russ-Ayon, Angela Y. 2016. (ENG.). 32p. (J). pap. 11.95 ***(978-0-9799612-3-6(8))*** Russ Invision.

Mey. Ana y la Maldicion de Las Pecas, Vol. 1. Schuff, Nicolás & Fraticelli, Damin. 2013. (Coleccion Heroinas Ser.).Tr. of Ana & the Cursed Freckles. (SPA.). 96p. (J). (gr. 4-7). pap. 10.95 *(978-987-1710-84-3(4))* Ediciones Urano S. A. ESP. Dist: Spanish Pubs., LLC.

Meyer, Alex Eben. Creature vs. Teacher. Fuller, T. Nat. 2018. (ENG.). 16p. (J). (gr. -1 — 1). bds. 7.99 *(978-1-4197-3155-6(6),* Abrams Appleseed) Abrams, Inc.

—Hero vs. Villain: A Book of Opposites. Fuller, T. Nat. 2018. (ENG.). 16p. (J). (gr. -1 — 1). bds. 7.99 *(978-1-4197-2825-9(3),* Abrams Appleseed) Abrams, Inc.

Meyer, Alison. Berc's Inner Voice. Ragan, Lyn. 2013. 24p. pap. 14.95 *(978-0-9860205-3-7(2))* HourGlass Publishing.

Meyer, Alyssa Rae. The Boy Who Found His Colors. Meyer, Alyssa Rae. 2018. (ENG.). 42p. (J). (gr. k-3). 19.99 *(978-1-948365-67-3(7))* Orange Hat Publishing.

Meyer, Ashley M. Forget the Vet. Lynn, Elizabeth B. 2012. 32p. 24.95 *(978-1-936688-21-0(2))* AKA:yoLa.

Meyer, Chloe. The Butterfly & the Bee. Hurth, Barbi. 2008. 32p. pap. 24.95 *(978-1-60610-226-8(5))* America Star Bks.

Meyer-Hullmann, Kerstin. Das Grundschulwoerterbuch. (Duden Ser.). (GER.). 224p. (J). *(978-3-411-06061-0(1))* Bibliographisches Institut & F. A. Brockhaus AG DEU. Dist: International Bk. Import Service, Inc.

—Rechtschreibtraining fuer die 3. Klasse. (Duden-Lernminuten Ser.). (GER.). 44p. (J). wbk. ed. *(978-3-411-70801-7(8))* Bibliographisches Institut & F. A. Brockhaus AG DEU. Dist: International Bk. Import Service, Inc.

—Rechtschreibtraining fuer die 3. und 4. Klasse. (Duden-Lernminuten Ser.). (GER.). 44p. (J). wbk. ed. *(978-3-411-70811-6(5))* Bibliographisches Institut & F. A. Brockhaus AG DEU. Dist: International Bk. Import Service, Inc.

Meyer, Jane G. & Gannon, Ned. The Woman & the Wheat. Meyer, Jane G. & Gannon, Ned. 2009. 32p. (J). 18.00 *(978-0-88141-059-4(4))* St. Vladimir's Seminary Pr.

Meyer, Jean. Helen Keller, Girl of Courage. Sabin, Francene & Mattern, Joanne. 2006. 56p. (J). *(978-0-439-66043-3(2))* Scholastic, Inc.

Meyer, Jeff. You've Got a Friend. Eareckson Tada, Joni. 2004. 31p. (gr. -1-3). 14.99 *(978-1-58134-060-0(5))* Crossway.

Meyer, Jennifer. A Little Owl. Wren, Rosalee. Cottage Door Press, ed. 2019. (ENG.). 10p. (J). (gr. -1-k). bds. 4.99 *(978-1-68052-631-8(6),* 1004241) Cottage Door Pr.

—A Mother's Prayer. Burton, Linda K. 2018. (J). 17.99 *(978-1-62972-471-3(8))* Deseret Bk. Co.

Meyer, Jennifer L. Lily to the Rescue. Cameron, W. Bruce. 2020. (Lily to the Rescue! Ser.: 1). (ENG.). 128p. (J). 15.99 *(978-1-250-23434-6(4),* 900210053); pap. 5.99 *(978-1-250-23435-3(2),* 900210054) Doherty, Tom Assocs., LLC. (Starscape).

—Lily to the Rescue: Dog Dog Goose. Cameron, W. Bruce. 2020. (Lily to the Rescue! Ser.: 4). (ENG.). 144p. (J). 15.99 *(978-1-250-23451-3(4),* 900210087); pap. 5.99 *(978-1-250-23452-0(2),* 900210088) Doherty, Tom Assocs., LLC. (Starscape).

—Lily to the Rescue: the Not-So-Stinky Skunk. Cameron, W. Bruce. 2020. (Lily to the Rescue! Ser.: 3). (ENG.). 144p. (J). 15.99 *(978-1-250-23447-6(6),* 900210084); pap. 5.99 *(978-1-250-23448-3(4),* 900210085) Doherty, Tom Assocs., LLC. (Starscape).

—Lily to the Rescue: Two Little Piggies. Cameron, W. Bruce. 2020. (Lily to the Rescue! Ser.: 2). (ENG.). 128p. (J). 15.99 *(978-1-250-23444-5(1),* 900210069); pap. 5.99 *(978-1-250-23445-2(X),* 900210070) Doherty, Tom Assocs., LLC. (Starscape).

—Saving Emma the Pig. Chester, John. 2019. (Biggest Little Farm Ser.). (ENG.). 40p. (J). 17.99 *(978-1-250-18779-6(6),* 900191877) Feiwel & Friends.

—Star Wars Adventures: Chewbacca & the Slavers of the Shadowlands. Cerasi, Chris. 2013. (Star Wars Digests Ser.). (ENG.). 80p. (J). (gr. 3-8). lib. bdg. 29.93 *(978-1-61479-057-0(4),* 13760, Graphic Novels) Spotlight.

—Who Gives a Hoot?: Calpurnia Tate, Girl Vet. Kelly, Jacqueline. 2018. (Calpurnia Tate, Girl Vet Ser.: 3). (ENG.). 128p. (J). pap. 6.99 *(978-1-250-14339-6(X),* 900161290) Square Fish.

Meyer, Jennifer L., jt. illus. see White, Teagan.

Meyer, Karen. Halfback Attack. Christopher, Matt. ed. 2005. (Sports Classics II Ser.). 104p. (J). lib. bdg. 15.00 *(978-1-59054-752-6(7))* Fitzgerald Bks.

Meyer, Ken, Jr. Lucky Lionel. 2009. (J). *(978-1-60108-020-2(4))* Red Cygnet Pr.

Meyer, Kerry. Nursery Rhymes Touchy-Feely Board Book. Watt, Fiona. 2010. (Luxury Touchy-Feely Board Bks). 10p. (J). bds. 15.99 *(978-0-7945-2662-7(4),* Usborne) EDC Publishing.

Meyer, Megan. The Great Adventures of Larriot the Liger. Meyer, Megan. 2010. (ENG.). 30p. 16.95 *(978-0-9830359-0-9(3))* Brosen Bks.

Meyer, Naama. Siddurchik: Prayer Book for Young Children. 2006. 32p. 12.95 *(978-965-229-328-2(8))* Gefen Publishing Hse., Ltd ISR. Dist: Gefen Bks.

Meyer, Nancy. Between Two Rivers: Stories from the Red Hills to the Gulf. Cerulean, Susan I. et al, eds. 2004. 352p. (YA). per. 21.95 *(978-0-9759339-0-9(6))* Red Hills Writers Project.

Meyer, Sarah. Detective Stephy Wephy Holmes in the Missing Cake. Rader, Josh. 2007. 36p. (J). (gr. -1-3). per. 14.99 *(978-1-59879-399-4(3))* Lifevest Publishing, Inc.

Meyer, Susan. Gorilla Dawn. Lewis, Gill. (ENG.). (J). (gr. 4-9). 2018. 448p. pap. 8.99 *(978-1-4814-8658-3(6));* 2017. 432p. 16.99 *(978-1-4814-8657-6(8),* Atheneum/Caitlyn Dlouhy Books) Simon & Schuster Children's Publishing.

—Scarlet Ibis. Lewis, Gill. (ENG.). (J). (gr. 4-9). 2019. 304p. pap. 8.99 *(978-1-4814-4942-7(7));* 2018. 288p. 17.99 *(978-1-4814-4941-0(9))* Simon & Schuster Children's Publishing. (Atheneum/Caitlyn Dlouhy Books).

Meyer, Therese. La Petite Ballerine et Ses Amis les Cygnes (The Little Ballerina & Her Friends the Swans) Meyer, Therese. 2004. (FRE.). 52p. *(978-0-9750325-1-0(8))* Baby Swan.

Meyerhoff, Jill. How Many Are Here? Goldish, Meish. l.t. ed. 2005. (Sadlier Phonics Reading Program). 8p. (gr. -1-1). 23.00 net. *(978-0-8215-7344-0(6))* Sadlier, William H. Inc.

Meyers, Haily. All Aboard California, 1 vol. Meyers, Haily. Meyers, Kevin. 2015. 22p. (J). bds. 9.99 *(978-1-4236-4080-6(2))* Gibbs Smith, Publisher.

—All Aboard! New York, 1 vol. Meyers, Haily. Meyers, Kevin. 2015. 22p. (J). bds. 9.99 *(978-1-4236-4074-5(8))* Gibbs Smith, Publisher.

—All Aboard Paris, 1 vol. Meyers, Haily. Meyers, Kevin. 2015. 22p. (J). bds. 9.99 *(978-1-4236-4077-6(2),* 1394332) Gibbs Smith, Publisher.

Meyers, Jeff. Jason's First Day. Busic, Valerie. OI Foundation, ed. l.t. ed. 2004. 48p. per. 8.50 *(978-0-9642189-4-9(1))* Osteogenesis Imperfecta Foundation.

Meyers, Jonboy. The Terrible Threat of the Living Brain! Lee, Stan. 2006. (Spider-Man Ser.: No. 1). (ENG.). 24p. (J). (gr. 2-6). 27.07 *(978-1-59961-008-5(6),* 13603, Marvel Age) Spotlight.

—Two for One. Dezago, Todd. 2010. (Spider-Man Ser.: No. 4). (ENG.). 24p. (J). (gr. 2-6). lib. bdg. 27.07 *(978-1-59961-779-4(X),* 13639, Marvel Age) Spotlight.

Meyers, Mark. The All-Star Joker. Kelly, David A. 2012. (Ballpark Mysteries Ser.: 5). (ENG.). 112p. (J). (gr. 1-4). 5.99 *(978-0-375-86884-9(4),* Random Hse. Bks. for Young Readers) Random Hse. Children's Bks.

—The All-Star Joker. Kelly, David A. ed. 2012. (Ballpark Mysteries Ser.: Bk. 5). lib. bdg. 14.75 *(978-0-606-26401-3(9))* Turtleback.

—The Astro Outlaw. Kelly, David A. 2012. (Ballpark Mysteries Ser.: 4). (ENG.). 112p. (J). (gr. 1-4). pap. 5.99 *(978-0-375-86883-2(6),* Random Hse. Bks. for Young Readers) Random Hse. Children's Bks.

—Ballpark Mysteries #10: the Rookie Blue Jay. Kelly, David A. 2015. (Ballpark Mysteries Ser.: 10). (ENG.). 112p. (J). (gr. 1-4). 5.99 *(978-0-385-37875-8(0),* Random Hse. Bks. for Young Readers) Random Hse. Children's Bks.

—Ballpark Mysteries #14: the Cardinals Caper. Kelly, David A. 2018. (Ballpark Mysteries Ser.: 14). (ENG.). 112p. (J). (gr. 1-4). 5.99 *(978-1-5247-6751-8(4));* lib. bdg. 12.99 *(978-1-5247-6752-5(2))* Random Hse. Children's Bks. (Random Hse. Bks. for Young Readers).

—Ballpark Mysteries #16: the Colorado Curveball. Kelly, David A. 2020. (Ballpark Mysteries Ser.: 16). (ENG.). 112p. (J).

M

(gr. 1-4). lib. bdg. 12.99 *(978-0-525-57899-4(4)*, Random Hse. Bks. for Young Readers) Random Hse. Children's Bks.
—Ballpark Mysteries #3: the L. A. Dodger. Kelly, David A. 2011. (Ballpark Mysteries Ser.: 3). (ENG.). 112p. (J). (gr. 1-4). 5.99 *(978-0-375-86885-6(2)*, Random Hse. Bks. for Young Readers) Random Hse. Children's Bks.
—Ballpark Mysteries #6: the Wrigley Riddle. Kelly, David A. 2013. (Ballpark Mysteries Ser.: 6). (ENG.). 112p. (J). (gr. 1-4). pap. 5.99 *(978-0-307-97776-2(5)*, Random Hse. Bks. for Young Readers) Random Hse. Children's Bks.
—Ballpark Mysteries #7: the San Francisco Splash. Kelly, David A. 2013. (Ballpark Mysteries Ser.: 7). (ENG.). 112p. (J). (gr. 1-4). pap. 5.99 *(978-0-307-97779-3(X)*, Random Hse. Bks. for Young Readers) Random Hse. Children's Bks.
—Ballpark Mysteries #8: the Missing Marlin. Kelly, David A. 2014. (Ballpark Mysteries Ser.: 8). (ENG.). 112p. (J). (gr. 1-4). 5.99 *(978-0-307-97782-3(X)*, Random Hse. Bks. for Young Readers) Random Hse. Children's Bks.
—Ballpark Mysteries Super Special #3: Subway Series Surprise. Kelly, David A. 2018. (Ballpark Mysteries Ser.: 3). (ENG.). 128p. (J). (gr. 1-4). 5.99 *(978-0-525-57892-5(7))*; lib. bdg. 12.99 *(978-0-525-57893-2(5))* Random Hse. Children's Bks. (Random Hse. Bks. for Young Readers).
—Ballpark Mysteries Super Special #4: the World Series Kids. Kelly, David A. 2019. (Ballpark Mysteries Ser.). (ENG.). 128p. (J). (gr. 1-4). pap. 5.99 *(978-0-525-57895-6(1)*, Random Hse. Bks. for Young Readers) Random Hse. Children's Bks.
—The Baltimore Bandit. Kelly, David A. 2019. (Ballpark Mysteries Ser.: 15). (ENG.). 112p. (J). (gr. 1-4). 12.99 *(978-1-5247-6755-6(7)*, Random Hse. Bks. for Young Readers) Random Hse. Children's Bks.
—Baltimore Bandit. Kelly, David A. 2019. (Ballpark Mysteries Ser.: 15). (ENG.). 112p. (J). (gr. 1-4). pap. 5.99 *(978-1-5247-6754-9(9)*, Random Hse. Bks. for Young Readers) Random Hse. Children's Bks.
—The Capital Catch. Kelly, David A. 2017. (Ballpark Mysteries Ser.: 13). (ENG.). 112p. (J). (gr. 1-4). 5.99 *(978-0-399-55189-5(1)*, Random Hse. Bks. for Young Readers) Random Hse. Children's Bks.
—Christmas in Cooperstown. Kelly, David A. 2017. (Ballpark Mysteries Ser.: 2). (ENG.). 144p. (J). (gr. 1-4). 5.99 *(978-0-399-55192-5(1))*; lib. bdg. 12.99 *(978-0-399-55193-2(X))* Random Hse. Children's Bks. (Random Hse. Bks. for Young Readers).
—The Fenway Foul-Up. Kelly, David A. 2011. (Ballpark Mysteries Ser.: 1). (ENG.). 112p. (J). (gr. 1-4). pap. 5.99 *(978-0-375-86703-3(1)*, Random Hse. Bks. for Young Readers) Random Hse. Children's Bks.
—Goldilocks Meets Desidero. Spetzler, Carl. 2011. 36p. pap. 16.86 *(978-1-4634-2684-2(4))* AuthorHouse.
—The Philly Fake. Kelly, David A. 2014. (Ballpark Mysteries Ser.: 9). (ENG.). 112p. (J). (gr. 1-4). 5.99 *(978-0-307-97785-4(4)*, Random Hse. Bks. for Young Readers) Random Hse. Children's Bks.
—The Pinstripe Ghost. Kelly, David A. 2011. (Ballpark Mysteries Ser.: 2). (ENG.). 112p. (J). (gr. 1-4). 5.99 *(978-0-375-86704-0(X)*, Random Hse. Bks. for Young Readers) Random Hse. Children's Bks.
—The Rangers Rustlers. Kelly, David A. 2016. (Ballpark Mysteries Ser.: 12). (ENG.). 112p. (J). (gr. 1-4). pap. 5.99 *(978-0-385-37881-9(5)*, Random Hse. Bks. for Young Readers) Random Hse. Children's Bks.
—The Tiger Troubles. Kelly, David A. 2015. (Ballpark Mysteries Ser.: 11). (ENG.). 112p. (J). (gr. 1-4). pap. 5.99 *(978-0-385-37878-9(5)*, Random Hse. Bks. for Young Readers) Random Hse. Children's Bks.
—Victricia Malicia: Book-Loving Buccaneer. Clickard, Carrie. 2012. (ENG.). 32p. (J). (gr. 2-4). 16.95 *(978-1-936261-12-3(X))* Flashlight Pr.
—The World Series Curse. Kelly, David A. 2016. (Ballpark Mysteries Ser.: 1). (ENG.). 144p. (J). (gr. 1-4). 5.99 *(978-0-385-37884-0(X)*, Random Hse. Bks. for Young Readers) Random Hse. Children's Bks.

Meyers, Nancy. King & Kayla & the Case of Found Fred. Butler, Dori Hillestad. 2019. (King & Kayla Ser.). (ENG.). 48p. (J). (gr. 2-4). 14.95 *(978-1-68263-052-5(8))* Peachtree Publishing Co. Inc.
—King & Kayla & the Case of the Lost Tooth, 1 vol. Butler, Dori Hillestad. 2018. (King & Kayla Ser.). (ENG.). 48p. (J). (gr. 2-4). pap. 6.99 *(978-1-68263-018-1(8))*; 14.95 *(978-1-56145-880-6(5))* Peachtree Publishing Co. Inc.
—King & Kayla & the Case of the Missing Dog Treats, 1 vol. Butler, Dori Hillestad. (King & Kayla Ser.). (ENG.). 48p. (J). (gr. 2-4). 2018. pap. 6.99 *(978-1-68263-015-0(3))*; 2017. 14.95 *(978-1-56145-877-6(5))* Peachtree Publishing Co. Inc.
—King & Kayla & the Case of the Mysterious Mouse. Butler, Dori Hillestad. (King & Kayla Ser.). (ENG.). 48p. (J). (gr. 2-4). 2018. pap. 6.99 *(978-1-68263-017-4(X))*; 2017. 14.95 *(978-1-56145-879-0(1))* Peachtree Publishing Co. Inc.
—King & Kayla & the Case of the Secret Code, 1 vol. Butler, Dori Hillestad. (King & Kayla Ser.). (ENG.). 48p. (J). (gr. 2-4). 2018. pap. 6.95 *(978-1-68263-016-7(1))*; 2017. 14.95 *(978-1-56145-878-3(3))* Peachtree Publishing Co. Inc.
—King & Kayla & the Case of the Unhappy Neighbor. Butler, Dori Hillestad. 2020. (King & Kayla Ser.). (ENG.). 48p. (J). (gr. 2-4). 14.99 *(978-1-68263-055-6(2))* Peachtree Publishing Co. Inc.
—Operation: Oddball. Bankert, Lisa. 2007. 100p. per. 5.99 *(978-0-9795364-0-3(5))* Chowder Bay Bks.
—Planet Patrol: A Kids' Action Guide to Earth Care. Lorbiecki, Marybeth. 2005. (ENG.). 48p. (J). (gr. 4-7). 15.95 *(978-1-58728-514-1(2))* Cooper Square Publishing Llc.

Meyers, Nancy. Doodles Shapes. Meyers, Nancy. 2012. (Doodles Ser.). (ENG.). 64p. (J). (gr. k-5). pap. 7.95 *(978-1-61608-668-8(8)*, 608668, Sky Pony Pr.) Skyhorse Publishing Co., Inc.
—Doodles Time. Meyers, Nancy. 2012. (Doodles Ser.). (ENG.). 64p. (J). (gr. k-5). pap. 7.95 *(978-1-61608-670-1(X)*, 608670, Sky Pony Pr.) Skyhorse Publishing Co., Inc.

Meyers, Sarah. Sandy's Dream. Rader, Jared. 2007. 16p. (J). (gr. -1-3). 10.99 *(978-1-59879-398-7(5))* Lifevest Publishing, Inc.

Meyers, Stephanie. Larry Bendeco Johannes Von Sloop. Larry, V. & Mark, K. 2014. (ENG.). 32p. (J). (gr. k-5). 7.99 *(978-1-4867-0000-4(4))* Flowerpot Children's Pr. Inc. CAN. Dist: Cardinal Pubs. Group.

Meynell, Louis. The Little Colonel's House Party. Johnston, Annie Fellows. 2007. 176p. per. *(978-1-4065-3514-3(1))* Dodo Pr.

Meza, Erica. The Tree House. Lindeen, Mary. 2015. (Early Rising Readers Ser.). (J). (gr. -1-k). 5.83 *(978-1-4788-1712-3(7))* Newmark Learning LLC.

Meza, Erika. Adriana's Angels, Vol. Goring, Ruth. 2017. (ENG.). (J). 16.99 *(978-1-5064-1832-2(5)*, Sparkhouse Family) Augsburg Fortress, Pubs.
—Apple Picking Day! Ransom, Candice. 2016. (Step into Reading Ser.). 32p. (J). (gr. -1-1). pap. 4.99 *(978-0-553-53858-8(6)*, Random Hse. Bks. for Young Readers) Random Hse. Children's Bks.
—The Big Rain, 1 vol. McDonald, Kirsten. 2015. (Carlos & Carmen Ser.). (ENG.). 32p. (J). (gr. k-3). 28.50 *(978-1-62402-137-4(9)*, 19071, Calico Chapter Bks) Magic Wagon.
—Carlos & Carmen, 4 vols. McDonald, Kirsten. 2015. (Carlos & Carmen Ser.: 4). 32p. (J). (gr. k-3). lib. bdg. 108.28 *(978-1-62402-136-7(0)*, 19069, Calico Chapter Bks) Magic Wagon.
—Carlos & Carmen Set 2, 4 vols. McDonald, Kirsten. 2016. (Carlos & Carmen Ser.). (ENG.). 32p. (J). (gr. -1-3). 108.28 *(978-1-62402-141-1(7)*, 21549, Calico Chapter Bks) Magic Wagon.
—Carlos & Carmen Set 2 (Spanish Version) (Set), 4 vols. McDonald, Kirsten. 2018. (Carlos & Carmen (Spanish Version) Ser.). 32p. (J). (gr. -1-3). lib. bdg. 108.28 *(978-1-5321-3320-6(0)*, 28503, Calico Chapter Bks) Magic Wagon.
—La Casita Del árbol. Lindeen, Mary. 2016. (Early Rising Readers Ser.). (SPA.). (J). (gr. -1). 6.67 *(978-1-4788-3708-4(X))* Newmark Learning LLC.
—El Concurso de Disfraces (the Costume Contest) McDonald, Kirsten. 2018. (Carlos & Carmen (Spanish Version) (Calico Kid) Ser.). (SPA.). 32p. (J). (gr. -1-3). lib. bdg. 28.50 *(978-1-5321-3356-5(1)*, 31185, Calico Chapter Bks) Magic Wagon.
—The Costume Contest. McDonald, Kirsten. 2016. (Carlos & Carmen Ser.). (ENG.). 32p. (J). (gr. -1-3). lib. bdg. 28.50 *(978-1-62402-182-4(4)*, 24543, Calico Chapter Bks) Magic Wagon.
—El Error Rico (the Yummy Mistake) McDonald, Kirsten. 2018. (Carlos & Carmen (Spanish Version) (Calico Kid) Ser.). (SPA.). 32p. (J). (gr. -1-3). lib. bdg. 28.50 *(978-1-5321-3324-4(3)*, 28511, Calico Chapter Bks) Magic Wagon.
—Este Es Mi Mural. Lindeen, Mary. 2016. (Early Rising Readers Ser.). (SPA.). 16p. (J). (gr. 1-1). 6.67 *(978-1-4788-4177-7(X))* Newmark Learning LLC.
—El Fin de Semana Arenoso (the Sandy Weekend) McDonald, Kirsten. 2018. (Carlos & Carmen (Spanish Version) (Calico Kid) Ser.). (SPA.). 32p. (J). (gr. -1-3). lib. bdg. 28.50 *(978-1-5321-3321-3(9)*, 28505, Calico Chapter Bks) Magic Wagon.
—Garden Day! Ransom, Candice. 2019. (Step into Reading Ser.). 32p. (J). (gr. -1-1). (ENG.). pap. 4.99 *(978-1-5247-2040-7(2))*; lib. bdg. 12.99 *(978-1-5247-2041-4(0))* Random Hse. Children's Bks. (Random Hse. Bks. for Young Readers).
—The Green Surprise, 1 vol. McDonald, Kirsten. 2015. (Carlos & Carmen Ser.). (ENG.). 32p. (J). (gr. k-3). 28.50 *(978-1-62402-138-1(7)*, 19073, Calico Chapter Bks) Magic Wagon.
—I Put This On. Lindeen, Mary. 2015. (Early Rising Readers Ser.). (J). (gr. -1-k). 5.83 *(978-1-4788-2169-4(8))* Newmark Learning LLC.
—Las Piñatas Perfectas (the Perfect Piñatas) McDonald, Kirsten. 2018. (Carlos & Carmen (Spanish Version) (Calico Kid) Ser.). (SPA.). 32p. (J). (gr. -1-3). lib. bdg. 28.50 *(978-1-5321-3357-2(X)*, 31187, Calico Chapter Bks) Magic Wagon.
—Las Ruedas Tambaleantes (the Wobbly Wheels) McDonald, Kirsten. 2018. (Carlos & Carmen (Spanish Version) (Calico Kid) Ser.). (SPA.). 32p. (J). (gr. -1-3). lib. bdg. 28.50 *(978-1-5321-3323-7(5)*, 28509, Calico Chapter Bks) Magic Wagon.
—Luna & the Lost Shell. Meister, Cari. 2017. (Scholastic Reader, Level 1 Ser.). (ENG.). 32p. (J). (gr. -1-1). pap. 3.99 *(978-1-338-12182-7(0))* Scholastic, Inc.
—The Nighttime Noise, 1 vol. McDonald, Kirsten. 2015. (Carlos & Carmen Ser.). (ENG.). 32p. (J). (gr. k-3). 28.50 *(978-1-62402-139-8(5)*, 19075, Calico Chapter Bks) Magic Wagon.
—La Noche Centelleante (the Sparkly Night) McDonald, Kirsten. 2018. (Carlos & Carmen (Spanish Version) (Calico Kid) Ser.). (SPA.). 32p. (J). (gr. -1-3). lib. bdg. 28.50 *(978-1-5321-3359-6(6)*, 31191, Calico Chapter Bks) Magic Wagon.
—The One-Tire House, 1 vol. McDonald, Kirsten. 2015. (Carlos & Carmen Ser.). (ENG.). 32p. (J). (gr. k-3). 28.50 *(978-1-62402-140-4(9)*, 19077, Calico Chapter Bks) Magic Wagon.
—The Perfect Piñatas. McDonald, Kirsten. 2016. (Carlos & Carmen Ser.). (ENG.). 32p. (J). (gr. -1-3). lib. bdg. 28.50 *(978-1-62402-183-1(2)*, 24545, Calico Chapter Bks) Magic Wagon.
—The Pet Show Problem. McDonald, Kirsten. 2016. (Carlos & Carmen Ser.). (ENG.). 32p. (J). (gr. -1-3). lib. bdg. 28.50 *(978-1-62402-184-8(0)*, 24547, Calico Chapter Bks) Magic Wagon.
—El Problema con el Espectáculo de Mascotas (the Pet Show Problem) McDonald, Kirsten. 2018. (Carlos & Carmen (Spanish Version) (Calico Kid) Ser.). (SPA.). 32p. (J). (gr. -1-3). lib. bdg. 28.50 *(978-1-5321-3358-9(8)*, 31189, Calico Chapter Bks) Magic Wagon.
—Salsa Lullaby. Arena, Jen. 2019. (ENG.). 32p. (J). (gr. -1-2). lib. bdg. 20.99 *(978-0-525-57972-4(9)*, Knopf Bks. for Young Readers) Random Hse. Children's Bks.
—The Sandy Weekend, 1 vol. McDonald, Kirsten. 2016. (Carlos & Carmen Ser.). (ENG.). 32p. (J). (gr. -1-3). 28.50 *(978-1-62402-142-8(5)*, 21551, Calico Chapter Bks) Magic Wagon.
—Snow Day! Ransom, Candice. 2018. (Step into Reading Ser.). 32p. (J). (gr. -1-1). pap. 4.99 *(978-1-5247-2037-7(2))*; lib. bdg. 12.99 *(978-1-5247-2038-4(0))* Random Hse. Children's Bks. (Random Hse. Bks. for Young Readers).
—The Sparkly Night. McDonald, Kirsten. 2016. (Carlos & Carmen Ser.). (ENG.). 32p. (J). (gr. -1-3). lib. bdg. 28.50 *(978-1-62402-185-5(9)*, 24549, Calico Chapter Bks) Magic Wagon.
—El Tiempo de Uncle. McDonald, Kirsten. 2018. (Carlos & Carmen (Spanish Version) (Calico Kid) Ser.). (SPA.). 32p. (J). (gr. -1-3). lib. bdg. 28.50 *(978-1-5321-3322-0(7)*, 28507, Calico Chapter Bks) Magic Wagon.
—Tío Time, 1 vol. McDonald, Kirsten. 2016. (Carlos & Carmen Ser.). (ENG.). 32p. (J). (gr. -1-3). 28.50 *(978-1-62402-143-5(3)*, 21553, Calico Chapter Bks) Magic Wagon.
—The Wobbly Wheels, 1 vol. McDonald, Kirsten. 2016. (Carlos & Carmen Ser.). (ENG.). 32p. (J). (gr. -1-3). 28.50 *(978-1-62402-144-2(1)*, 21555, Calico Chapter Bks) Magic Wagon.
—The Yummy Mistake. McDonald, Kirsten. 2016. (Carlos & Carmen Ser.). (ENG.). 32p. (J). (gr. -1-3). 28.50 *(978-1-62402-145-9(X)*, 21557, Calico Chapter Bks) Magic Wagon.

Meza, Erika. Los Angeles de Adriana (Spanish Edition), Vol. Meza, Erika. Goring, Ruth. 2017. (ENG.). (J). 16.99 *(978-1-5064-2507-8(0)*, Sparkhouse Family) Augsburg Fortress, Pubs.

Meza, Estelí. El Mejor Regalo. Zepeda Sein, Monica Francoise. 2016. (Cuentamelo Otra Vez Ser.). (SPA.). (J). 16.95 *(978-1-68165-269-6(2))* Trialtea USA, LLC.

Meza, Estelí. A Place to Stay: A Shelter Story. Gunti, Erin. 2019. (ENG.). 32p. (J). ***(978-1-78285-824-9(5))***; pap. ***(978-1-78285-825-6(3))*** Barefoot Bks., Inc.

Mhan, Pop & Anindito, Ario. Aero & Sword Master: Origins & Odysseys. 2020. (ENG.). 136p. (YA). (gr. 8-17). pap. 17.99 ***(978-1-302-92261-0(0))*** Marvel Worldwide, Inc.

Mhan, Pop, jt. illus. see Barrionuevo, Al.

Mhasane, Ruchi. Bible Promises for a Little Boy. Joslin, Mary. ed. 2014. (ENG.). 32p. (J). (gr. -1-2). 9.99 *(978-0-7459-6404-1(4))* Lion Hudson PLC GBR. Dist: Independent Pubs. Group.
—Bible Promises for a Little Girl. Joslin, Mary. ed. 2014. (ENG.). 32p. (J). (gr. -1-2). 9.99 *(978-0-7459-6405-8(2))* Lion Hudson PLC GBR. Dist: Independent Pubs. Group.
—The Selkie Girl, 30 vols. Mackay, Janis. 2014. (Traditional Scottish Tales Ser.). (ENG.). 32p. (J). pap. 11.95 *(978-1-78250-130-5(4)*, Kelpies) Floris Bks. GBR. Dist: Consortium Bk. Sales & Distribution.

Miao, Huai-Kuang, Sr. & Miao, Huai-Kuang. The Genesis of It All. Shaw, Luci. 2006. 32p. (J). (gr. -1-3). 17.95 *(978-1-55725-480-1(X))* Paraclete Pr., Inc.

Miao, Huai-Kuang, jt. illus. see Miao, Huai-Kuang, Sr.

Miao, Sang. Out, Out Away from Here. Woodward, Rachel. 2018. 32p. (J). (-k). 16.95 *(978-1-911171-33-1(X))* Flying Eye Bks. GBR. Dist: Penguin Random Hse. LLC.

Micale, Albert. The Long Trail: The Story of Buffalo Bill. Kolars, Frank. 2011. 190p. 42.95 *(978-1-258-05136-5(2))* Literary Licensing, LLC.

Micallef, Bernard & Zammit, Jeanelle. Il-Wied Tad-Dinosawri. Pace, David. 2nd ed. 2019. (MLT.). 134p. (J). pap. *(978-99957-48-95-1(9))* Faraxa Publishing.

Miceli, Monica. Hielito, el Pinguino. Aldovini, Giulia. Brignole, Giancarla, tr. rev. ed. 2007. (Fabulas De Familia Ser.). (SPA & ENG.). 32p. (J). (gr. 4-7). pap. 6.95 *(978-970-20-0259-8(1))* Castillo, Ediciones, S. A. de C. V. MEX. Dist: Macmillan.
—El Rey Perezoso. Mostacchi, Massimo. Brignole, Giancarla, tr. rev. ed. 2006. (Fabulas De Familia Ser.). (SPA & ENG.). 32p. (J). (gr. k-4). pap. 6.95 *(978-970-20-0274-1(5))* Castillo, Ediciones, S. A. de C. V. MEX. Dist: Macmillan.

Mich. Carnet Blanc la Risette. 2016. (Bnf Affiches Ser.). (FRE.). (J). pap. *(978-2-01-116956-3(9))* Hachette Groupe Livre.
—Carnet Ligne la Risette. 2016. (Bnf Affiches Ser.). (FRE.). (J). pap. *(978-2-01-116981-5(X))* Hachette Groupe Livre.

Michael A. Cicchetti. Healthy Fun with Benjamin & Jasmine: ABCs of the Human Body. Sherri L. Berner. 2009. 32p. pap. 12.99 *(978-1-4343-8297-9(4))* AuthorHouse.

Michael, Cavallaro, et al. The Wizard of Oz. Baum, L. Frank. 2005. (ENG.). 176p. (J). (gr. 3-7). 10.99 *(978-0-14-240471-3(3)*, Puffin Books) Penguin Young Readers Group.

Michael, Fitterling. The Elson Readers Teacher's Guide, Vol. 6. Newcomer, Mary Jane et al. 2005. (ENG.). 332p. (J). (gr. -1-12). tchr. ed., per. 22.99 *(978-1-890623-30-2(X))* Lost Classic Bks.

Michael, Joan. Find & Point Birthday. Wallin, Marisa. 2019. (Rookie Toddler Ser.). (ENG.). 12p. (J). (gr. -1 — 1). bds. 6.95 *(978-0-531-12930-2(6)*, Children's Pr.) Scholastic Library Publishing.
—I Love Trucks. Miller, Amanda. 2018. (Rookie Toddler Ser.). (ENG.). 12p. (J). (gr. -1 — 1). bds. 6.95 *(978-0-531-22887-6(8)*, Children's Pr.) Scholastic Library Publishing.
—Let's Make Letters: ABC Kids. Behrens, Janice. 2007. (Let's Find Out Early Learning Bks.). (ENG.). 32p. (J). (gr. -1-3). 18.00 *(978-0-531-14867-9(X)*, Children's Pr.) Scholastic Library Publishing.
—Let's Play a Five Senses Guessing Game. Miller, Amanda. 2007. (Let's Find Out Early Learning Bks.). (ENG.). 24p. (J). (gr. -1-3). 18.00 *(978-0-531-14871-6(8)*, Children's Pr.) Scholastic Library Publishing.
—My Favorite Book of Colors. Behrens, Janice. 2017. (Rookie Toddler Ser.). (ENG.). 12p. (J). (gr. -1 — 1). bds. 6.95 *(978-0-531-22685-8(9)*, Children's Pr.) Scholastic Library Publishing.
—My Favorite Book of Numbers. Behrens, Janice. 2017. (Rookie Toddler Ser.). (ENG.). 12p. (J). (gr. -1 — 1). bds. 6.95 *(978-0-531-22684-1(0)*, Children's Pr.) Scholastic Library Publishing.

Michael, Joan & Larsen, Eric. Let's Talk about Opposites, Morning to Night. Falk, Laine. 2007. (Let's Find Out Early Learning Bks.). (ENG.). 24p. (J). (gr. -1-3). 18.00 *(978-0-531-14872-3(6)*, Children's Pr.) Scholastic Library Publishing.

Michaels, Lisa J. The Inner Light. Porada, Henry. 2013. 32p. pap. 12.99 *(978-1-937260-98-9(4))* Sleepytown Pr.

Michau, Pablo. Milo & Ze. Watson, Mark. 2014. (ENG.). (J). (gr. k-4). *(978-0-9956448-3-0(7))* Watson, Mark Bks.

Michaud, Monique. Book of Dreams - the Ringtail Family. Michaud, Sylvie. 2012. 24p. pap. *(978-0-9782955-8-5(7))* Crafty Canuck, Inc.
—Book of Love - the Ringtail Family. Michaud, Sylvie. 2012. 24p. pap. *(978-1-927471-00-5(1))* Crafty Canuck, Inc.
—Book of Wishes - the Ringtail Family. Michaud, Sylvie. 2012. 24p. pap. *(978-0-9782955-9-2(5))* Crafty Canuck, Inc.

Michaud, Nancy. Heart of Stone. Monnar, Ana. 2007. 24p. (J). per. 11.99 *(978-0-9768035-5-3(0))* Readers Are Leaders U.S.A., Inc.

Michaux, Marie. Petits Moments Littéraires: Édition Spéciale Partir en Livre 2018. Pardossi-Sarno, Beatrice. Livio Editions, ed. 2018. (FRE.). 44p. (J). pap. *(978-2-35455-009-7(X))* Livio Informatique.

Michel, Jean. Blood on the Handle. Montgomery, R. A. 2010. (ENG.). 144p. (J). (gr. 4-8). pap. 6.99 *(978-1-933390-33-8(6))* Chooseco LLC.

Michel, June. Going Places: True Tales from Young Travelers. 2003. 160p. (J). (gr. 4-12). pap. *(978-1-58270-070-0(2))* Beyond Words Publishing, Inc.

Michell, Michael & Ranucci, Claudia. We Wish for a Monster Christmas. Fliess, Sue. 2017. 32p. (J). (gr. -1). 16.95 *(978-1-4549-1894-3(2))* Sterling Publishing Co., Inc.

Michelle, Aliyat & Simsek, Denise Michele. The Isle of the Crocodile. Simsek, Denise Michele. 2019. (ENG.). 54p. (J). pap. 11.50 ***(978-1-0729-7845-9(8))*** Independently Published.

Michelle, Ciappa. The Spider Who Never Gave Up. Flores, Travis. 2004. (J). *(978-0-9759077-0-2(0))* Inclusive Global Inc.

Michelle, Jean & D'Ariggo, Jay. Naba II: A Journey. Michelle, Jean. 2011. 20p. pap. 24.95 *(978-1-4626-4381-3(7))* America Star Bks.

Michelle, Lainy. Mr. All-This-And-That. Gibbs, Andrea. 2018. (ENG.). 30p. (J). (gr. k-2). 19.99 *(978-1-7325932-0-6(5))* Gibbs, Andrea.

Michels-Boyce, Steven. When Jesus Was A Kid Like Me: A Counting Song about Jesus When He Was a Kid Like You & Me. 2005. (J). 15.95 *(978-0-9761477-0-1(X))* SoJam Pr.

Michie, Karena H. J. Magic of the Crystal Caves. Starr, Sarah Jane. 2018. (ENG.). 46p. (J). pap. 20.45 *(978-1-9822-0273-6(4)*, Balboa Pr.) Author Solutions, Inc.

Midbeck, Caroline. A Feeling of Me: Mindfulness for Children. Bjarkvik, Anna. 2019. (Mindfulness for Children Ser.: Vol. 1). (ENG.). 32p. (J). (gr. 1-2). ***(978-91-88375-73-5(0))*** Ehrlin Publishing AB.

Middlemiss, Laura B. The Great Hamstini. Middlemiss, David. 2010. 108p. *(978-1-907211-18-8(7))* Grosvenor Hse. Publishing Ltd.

Middleton, Amy Baird. Charlie: The Brave Little Teddy Bear. Middleton, Amy Baird. 2017. (ENG.). 38p. (J). (gr. k-3). 20.00 *(978-0-9915467-2-5(5)*, Wren's Nest Productions LLC) Struminger, Alexander.

Middleton, Charlotte. Summer Beat. Franco, Betsy. 2011. (ENG.). 36p. (J). (gr. -1-1). 14.99 *(978-1-4424-4339-6(1)*, McElderry, Margaret K. Bks.) McElderry, Margaret K. Bks.

Middleton, Gayle. Color & Iron-Ons Book. Frantz, Jennifer. 2005. (My Little Pony Ser.). 32p. (J). (gr. -1-1). 3.99 *(978-0-06-074441-0(3)*, HarperFestival) HarperCollins Pubs.
—My Little Pony: A Secret Gift. Benjamin, Ruth. 2006. 24p. (J). lib. bdg. 15.00 *(978-1-4242-1536-2(6))* Fitzgerald Bks.
—A Secret Gift/el Regalo Secreto. Benjamin, Ruth. Abboud, Adela, tr. from ENG. 2006. (I Can Read Bks.). (SPA & ENG.). 24p. (J). (gr. k-3). per. 3.99 *(978-0-06-112391-7(9)*, Rayo) HarperCollins Pubs.

Middleton, Gayle & Edwards, Ken. Color & Poster Book. Bak, Jenny. 2006. (My Little Pony Ser.). 32p. (J). (gr. -1-1). 3.99 *(978-0-06-079470-5(4)*, HarperFestival) HarperCollins Pubs.

Middleton, Joshua, et al. Flying Solo. Kesel, Barbara. 2003. (Meridian Traveler Ser.: Vol. 1). 192p. (YA). (gr. 7-18). pap. 9.95 *(978-1-931484-54-1(6))* CrossGeneration Comics, Inc.

Middleton, Mikell. Flitter, Flutter Butterfly. Jarrell, Pamela R. l.t. ed. 2005. (HRL Board Book Ser.). 12p. (J). (gr. -1-1). pap. 10.95 *(978-1-57332-286-7(5)*, HighReach Learning, Incorporated) Carson-Dellosa Publishing, LLC.
—Helping in My Town. Hensley, Sarah M. l.t. ed. 2003. (HRL Big Book Ser.). 8p. (J). (gr. -1-1). pap. 10.95 *(978-1-57332-274-4(1))*; pap. 10.95 *(978-1-57332-275-1(X))* Carson-Dellosa Publishing, LLC. (HighReach Learning, Incorporated).

Middleton, Taquon. Katy, the Cooking Kangaroo. Owens, Carmen. Otis, Michelle, ed. 2013. (J). pap. 12.95 *(978-0-9888644-5-0(2))* Knowledge Power Communications.

Middy Chilman, Thomas. Gooney Bird Greene. Lois, Lowry. 2004. (Gooney Bird Ser.: No. 1). 88p. (gr. 2-5). 16.00 *(978-0-7569-2583-3(5))* Perfection Learning Corp.

Miele, Brianna. Eldy & Ohi. Sexton, Jessa Rose. 2012. 36p. pap. 8.00 *(978-0-9860150-9-0(1))* O'More Publishing.

Miello, Tony, jt. illus. see Reed, Gary.

Mier, Colin. Sam Sorts It Out. Cross, Gillian. 2005. (ENG.). 24p. (J). lib. bdg. 23.65 *(978-1-59646-702-6(9))* Dingles & Co.

Mier, Vanessa. Animal Companions: In Our Hearts, Our Lives, & Our World. Pomerance, Diane. 2004. (YA). per. 9.95 *(978-0-9708500-3-4(4))* Polaire Pubns.

—Animal Companions: Your Friends, Teachers & Guides. Pomerance, Diane. 2003. 9.95 *(978-0-9708500-2-7(6))* Polaire Pubns.

Migachyov, Larisa. Equations in Geometry: How to Make Your Child Successful in Math. Migachyov, Larisa. Migachyov, Dina. 2004. 267p. per. 29.99 *(978-0-9672535-4-1(3))* Quatemion Pr.

Migani, Loretta. Explosion News. Halsey, Jacqueline. 2015. (ENG.). 32p. (J). (gr. -1-4). 16.95 *(978-1-4595-0401-1(1),* 0401) Formac Publishing Co., Ltd. CAN. Dist: Formac Lorimer Bks. Ltd.

Migliardo, Emiliano. Bible Stories Gone Crazy!, 1 vol. Edwards, Josh. ed. 2015. (ENG.). 24p. (J). (gr. -1-k). 10.99 *(978-1-78128-190-1(4),* Candle Bks.) Lion Hudson PLC GBR. Dist: Independent Pubs. Group.

—Bible Stories Gone Even More Crazy! David, Juliet & Edwards, Josh. ed. 2018. (ENG.). 24p. (J). (gr. k-2). 8.99 *(978-1-78128-339-4(7))* Lion Hudson PLC GBR. Dist: Independent Pubs. Group.

Migliari, Paola. I Am a Dump Truck. Page, Josephine. 2007. (ENG.). 4p. (J). (gr. -1 — 1). 4.99 *(978-0-439-91617-2(8),* Cartwheel Bks.) Scholastic, Inc.

—I Am a Fire Truck. Page, Josephine. 2007. (ENG.). 4p. (J). (gr. -1 — 1). 4.99 *(978-0-439-91618-9(6))* Scholastic, Inc.

—I Am a Garbage Truck. Landers, Ace & Cartwheel Editors. Scholastic, Inc. Staff, ed. 2008. (ENG.). 8p. (J). (gr. -1 — 1). 4.99 *(978-0-545-07963-1(2),* Cartwheel Bks.) Scholastic, Inc.

—I Am a Train. Landers, Ace. 2008. (ENG.). 8p. (J). (gr. -1 — 1). bds. 4.99 *(978-0-545-07962-4(4),* Cartwheel Bks.) Scholastic, Inc.

—I Am a Zamboni Machine. 2018. (ENG.). (J). (gr. -1-k). 5.99 *(978-1-338-27773-9(1),* Cartwheel Bks.) Scholastic, Inc.

Miglio, Paige. Bunny Christmas: A Family Celebration. Walton, Rick. 2004. 32p. (J). (ENG.). 15.99 *(978-0-06-008415-8(4));* lib. bdg. 16.89 *(978-0-06-008416-5(2))* HarperCollins Pubs.

—So Many Bunnies Board Book: A Bedtime ABC & Counting Book. Walton, Rick. 2018. (ENG.). 32p. (J). (gr. -1 — 1). bds. 6.99 *(978-0-688-17364-7(0),* HarperFestival) HarperCollins Pubs.

—What Do We Do with the Baby? Walton, Rick. 2008. 32p. (J). (gr. -1-k). lib. bdg. 17.89 *(978-0-06-008420-2(0))* HarperCollins Pubs.

Miglio, Paige. Bear's Baby. Miglio, Paige. Date not set. 32p. (J). (gr. -1-18). 15.99 *(978-0-06-029240-9(7));* pap. 5.99 *(978-0-06-443741-7(8));* lib. bdg. 16.89 *(978-0-06-029241-6(5))* HarperCollins Pubs.

Migliore, Valentina. Le Cerf-Volant de Mon Père. Slater, Veronica D. 2019. (FRE.). 34p. (J). pap. *(978-1-9990247-2-7(9))* Gauvin, Jacques.

—My Father's Kite. Slater, Veronica D. 2019. (ENG.). 34p. (J). pap. *(978-1-9990247-0-3(2))* Gauvin, Jacques.

Mignano, Daniel. Petey the One Lopped Eared Dog, 1 vol. Wingate, Barbara. 2009. 20p. pap. 24.95 *(978-1-60836-931-7(5))* America Star Bks.

Mignard, Phyllis. Draw/Color/Write Journal for Kids: Featuring Ro-Bits. Journals, Everything. 2016. (ENG.). (J). pap. 14.95 *(978-0-9980714-2-8(0))* Everything Journals.

Mignola, Mike. El Ejercito Perdido. Golden, Christopher. 2005. (Hellboy Ser.). (SPA.). 229p. per. 19.95 *(978-1-59497-108-2(0))* Public Square Bks.

Mignola, Mike & Stewart, Dave. Conqueror Worm, Vol. 5. Mignola, Mike & Dark Horse Comics Staff. Allie, Scott, ed. 2nd ed. 2004. (Hellboy Ser.: Vol. 5). (ENG.). 144p. pap. 17.99 *(978-1-59307-092-2(6))* Dark Horse Comics.

Miguel, Maridel Maddie & Watson, Nancy. Stevie Tenderheart Seven Rules: On Becoming a Fantastic Kid. Laible, Steve William. 2019. (ENG.). 40p. (J). pap. 9.95 ***(978-1-62485-044-8(8))*** Kodel Group, LLC, The.

Miguéns, Marta Álvarez. A Tiger Called Tomás. Zolotow, Charlotte. 2018. (ENG.). 40p. (J). (-2). 17.99 *(978-1-4926-0171-5(3))* Sourcebooks, Inc.

Migy. Who Wants to Be a Princess? What It Was Really Like to Be a Medieval Princess. Heos, Bridget. 2017. (ENG.). 32p. (J). 16.99 *(978-0-8050-9769-6(4),* 900118847, Holt, Henry & Co. Bks. For Young Readers) Holt, Henry & Co.

Mihara, Mitsukazu. Mitsukazu Mihara - Haunted House. Mihara, Mitsukazu. 2006. 200p. (gr. 9-18). per. 9.99 *(978-1-59816-321-6(3))* TOKYOPOP, Inc.

Mihara, Mitsukazu. Doll, 6 vols. Mihara, Mitsukazu, creator. rev. ed. 2005. Vol. 4. 192p. pap. 9.99 *(978-1-59532-390-3(2));* Vol. 5. 176p. pap. 9.99 *(978-1-59532-391-0(0))* TOKYOPOP, Inc.

Mihelich, Taj L. Bernie the Bike Builder. Mihelich, Taj L. 2019. (ENG.). 40p. (J). (gr. 1-6). 25.00 *(978-0-578-50129-1(5));* pap. 17.50 *(978-0-578-51600-4(4))* Fairdale Bikes.

Mihran, Turley Joyce. Totally Out There Gd Glacier Natl Park. Love, Donna. 2010. 0096p. (J). pap. 15.00 *(978-0-87842-566-2(7))* Mountain Pr. Publishing Co., Inc.

Mijangos, Amanda. El Sueno de una Alubia. Carrera, Eduardo. 2015. (SPA.). 48p. (J). pap. 10.95 *(978-607-01-2810-3(9))* Santillana USA Publishing Co., Inc.

Mike. Lemon Drop Rain: Poems & Drawings by Mr. Mike. Mike. l.t. ed. 2003. (ENG.). 180p. (J). pap. 14.95 *(978-0-9658365-6-2(8))* Beetle Bug Bks.

—New Pet. Mike. l.t. ed. 2005. (ENG.). 32p. (J). lib. bdg. 14.95 *(978-0-9658365-8-6(4))* Beetle Bug Bks.

Mike, Motz. My Dancing Tap Shoes Color Illustrated Paperback. Nelson, Chesley. 2016. (ENG.). (J). (gr. 2-5). pap. 13.98 *(978-0-692-75287-6(0))* 1948.

Mikec, Larry. Firefly at Stony Brook Farm. Pfeffer, Wendy. 2005. (Smithsonian's Backyard Ser.). (ENG.). 32p. (J). (gr. -1-2). 15.95 *(978-1-59249-282-4(7),* B5026) Soundprints.

—Firefly at Stonybrook Farm. Pfeffer, Wendy. 2004. (Smithsonian's Backyard Ser.). (ENG.). 32p. (J). (gr. -1-2). 8.95 *(978-1-59249-306-7(8),* SC5026); (gr. -1-3). 9.95 *(978-1-59249-308-1(4),* PB5076); (gr. -1-2). 19.95 *(978-1-59249-307-4(6),* BC5026); (gr. 2-2). 4.99 *(978-1-59249-283-1(5),* B5076) Soundprints.

Mikecz, Melanie. What Is a Flamingo? Swift, Ginger. Cottage Door Press, ed. 2020. (ENG.). 12p. (J). (gr. -1 — 1). bds. 7.99 *(978-1-68052-636-3(7),* 1004290) Cottage Door Pr.

—What Is a Narwhal? Swift, Ginger. Cottage Door Press, ed. 2019. (ENG.). 12p. (J). (gr. -1 — 1). bds. 7.99 *(978-1-68052-635-6(9),* 1004280) Cottage Door Pr.

Mikhail, Jess. Batter Splatter! Morgan, Ruth. 2005. (ENG.). 24p. (J). lib. bdg. 23.65 *(978-1-59646-704-0(5))* Dingles & Co.

—Florentine & Pig. Katzler, Eva. 2012. (ENG.). 32p. (J). 17.89 *(978-1-59990-949-3(9),* 9781599909493); (gr. -1-6). 16.99 *(978-1-59990-847-2(6),* 9781599908472) Bloomsbury Publishing USA. (Bloomsbury USA Childrens).

—Mouse with No Name. Morgan, Michaela. 2004. (ENG.). 24p. (J). lib. bdg. 23.65 *(978-1-59646-682-1(0))* Dingles & Co.

—Ten Little Eggs: A Celebration of Family, 1 vol. Zondervan Staff. 2020. (ENG.). 32p. (J). 17.99 *(978-0-310-76881-4(0))* Zonderkidz.

Mikhail, Jessica. Eleanore Won't Share. Gassman, Julie A. 2010. (Little Boost Ser.). (ENG.). 32p. (J). (gr. -1-1). lib. bdg. 23.99 *(978-1-4048-6358-3(3),* Picture Window Bks.) Capstone.

Mikhails, Jess. Nat's Naughty Nits. Andreae, Giles. 2018. 32p. (J). (gr. -1-k). pap. 9.99 *(978-1-4083-3024-1(5),* Orchard Bks.) Hachette Children's Group GBR. Dist: Hachette Bk. Group.

Miki. Treasure Box. Juliana, M. et al, eds. 2nd l.t. rev. ed. 2009. (Treasure Box Ser.: 1). (ENG.). 32p. (J). (gr. k-2). Vol. 1. 6.95 *(978-0-89555-551-9(4),* 1341); Vol. 2. 6.95 *(978-0-89555-552-6(2),* 1342) TAN Bks.

Mikimoto, Haruhiku. Ecole du Ciel, Vol. 2. Mikimoto, Haruhiku, creator. 2nd rev. ed. 2006. pap. 14.99 *(978-1-59532-852-6(1),* Tokyopop Adult) TOKYOPOP, Inc.

Mikki. The Calabash Tales. Abrams, Penny. 2011. 66p. 28.00 *(978-1-4349-1169-8(1))* Dorrance Publishing Co., Inc.

Mikle, Toby. The Adventures of Joshua: Spencer Spine & the Back Attack. Butler, Tiffany T. 2018. (Adventures of Joshua Ser.). (ENG.). 32p. (J). (gr. 3-5). 21.99 *(978-1-7322956-9-8(7))* Testimony Pubs., LLC.

—The Cookie That Saved My Family. Freund, William C. 2011. (J). *(978-0-9846346-7-5(3))* Adibooks.com.

—My Family Forest. Voiles, Alison. 2010. 28p. pap. 13.99 *(978-1-4389-1682-8(5))* AuthorHouse.

—Procrastimonsters! They're Everywhere. Hull, Claudia. 2012. 44p. pap. 15.95 *(978-1-257-64007-2(0))* Shalako Pr.

—Sammy's Midnight Hunger. Chaudhary, Shahida. 2012. 38p. pap. 14.50 *(978-1-61897-255-2(3),* Strategic Bk. Publishing) Strategic Book Publishing & Rights Agency (SBPRA).

—Skippy the Dog in the Band. Palumbo, Mary Lou. 2009. 48p. pap. 19.49 *(978-1-4389-9218-1(1))* AuthorHouse.

—Sleepytown Beagles Penny's 4th of July. Glass, Timothy. 2006. 24p. (J). per. 15.95 *(978-1-888461-10-7(1));* 16.95 *(978-1-888461-11-4(X))* Islewest Publishing.

Mikle, Toby, jt. illus. see Jones, Branson.

Mikler, Lisa M. Divine Providence: A Child's History of the United States. Smith, Ruth J. 2005. 224p. (J). per. 19.95 net. *(978-0-9705618-5-5(7))* Bradford Pr., Inc.

—Liberty & Justice for All: A Child's History of the United States of America. Smith, Ruth J. 2003. 208p. (J). per. 19.95 *(978-0-9705618-3-1(0))* Bradford Pr., Inc.

Miko, Szilvia. Shirley the Unicorn: Sometimes the Best of Friends Are the Ones Who Are Unseen. the Ones Who Don't Expect Any Praise but Are Always There When You Need Them Most. This Is the Story of One Such Friend. de Silva, Ramesh & Gomes, Dinusha. 2019. (Shirley's Adventures Ser.: Vol. 1). (ENG.). 26p. (J). pap. 9.90 ***(978-1-6709-0904-6(2))*** Independently Published.

Miksch, Alison, photos by. Mastering the Grill: The Owner's Manual for Outdoor Cooking. Schloss, Andrew & Joachim, David. 2007. (ENG., 416p. (gr. 8-17). pap. 24.95 *(978-0-8118-4964-7(3))* Chronicle Bks. LLC.

—Quick & Easy Thai: 70 Everyday Recipes. McDermott, Nancie. 2003. (ENG., 168p. (gr. 8-17). pap. 18.95 *(978-0-8118-3731-6(9))* Chronicle Bks. LLC.

Milacic, Bianca. A Christmas Carol. Dickens, Charles. 2018. (ENG.). 36p. (J). (gr. k-2). 19.99 *(978-1-948131-26-1(9))* Whaler, Norman / Beneath Another Sky Bks.

—Un Villancico Navideño (Spanish Edition of a Christmas Carol) Dickens, Charles. 2018. (SPA.). 36p. (J). (gr. k-2). 19.99 *(978-1-948131-29-2(3))* Whaler, Norman / Beneath Another Sky Bks.

Milagrito, El. La saga de los jugadores de Pelota. Rendon, Gilberto. rev. ed. 2003. (Castillo de la Lectura Roja Ser.). (SPA & ENG.). 240p. (J). pap. 8.95 *(978-970-20-0335-9(0))* Castillo, Ediciones, S. A. de C. V. MEX. Dist: Macmillan.

Milam, C. J. Micah & the Magic Helment: The Helmet & the Dragon. Parrish, Kat. 2011. (ENG.). 32p. (J). (gr. k-7). pap. 8.95 *(978-0-938467-29-8(8),* Headline Kids) Headline Bks., Inc.

Milani, Alice. Marie Curie: A Life of Discovery. Milani, Alice. 2019. 208p. (YA). (gr. 9-12). (ENG.). pap. 14.99 *(978-1-5415-7286-7(6),* 9781541572867); lib. bdg. 33.32 *(978-1-5415-2817-8(4),* 9781541528178) Lerner Publishing Group. (Graphic Universe™).

Milano, Jacque. Stay-at-Home Hank: The Little Hummingbird That Couldn't Fly. Milano, Jacque. l.t. ed. 2003. 30p. (J). 9.95 *(978-0-9728432-0-1(5))* Milano, Jacque & Assocs.

Milano, Nicolas. Alex & the Elephant: An Adventurous Story about Listening to Your Parents. Wingo, Kelly. Collings, Erick, ed. 2019. (Adventures of Alex Ser.: Vol. 1). (ENG.). 28p. (J). pap. 14.99 *(978-1-7296-2891-1(5))* CreateSpace Independent Publishing Platform.

—Gavin & Chloe Wish for Snow: The First Book in the Cousin Adventure Series. MS Wood. 2017. (ENG.). (J). 29.99 *(978-1-5462-1087-0(3));* pap. 16.99 *(978-1-5462-1089-4(X))* AuthorHouse.

Mildenberger, Vivien. All in a Drop: How Antony Van Leeuwenhoek Discovered an Invisible World. Alexander, Lori. 2019. (ENG.). 96p. (J). (gr. 3-7). 17.99 *(978-1-328-88420-6(1),* 1698170, HMH Books For Young Readers) Houghton Mifflin Harcourt Publishing Co.

—Judah Touro Didn't Want to Be Famous. Ades, Audrey. 2020. (ENG.). 32p. (J). (gr. k-3). 17.99 *(978-1-5415-4561-8(3),* Kar-Ben Publishing) Lerner Publishing Group.

—Think Smart, Be Fearless: A Biography of Bill Gates. Mentyka, Sharon. 2019. (Growing to Greatness Ser.). 48p. (J). (gr. k-4). 18.99 *(978-1-63217-176-4(7),* Little Bigfoot) Sasquatch Bks.

Mildred, Adele. Sign Here: A Treasury of Forms for Dreams, Fairies, Friends, Pets, Secrets, & Other Miscellany. Djanogly, Gabrielle. 2018. (ENG.). 48p. (J). (gr. 1-4). pap. 14.95 *(978-3-7913-7297-6(1))* Prestel Verlag GmbH & Co KG. DEU. Dist: Penguin Random Hse. LLC.

Milelli, Pascal. The Art Room, 1 vol. Griek, Susan Vande. 2019. (ENG.). 24p. (J). (gr. k-2). 9.95 *(978-1-77306-239-6(5))* Groundwood Bks. CAN. Dist: Publishers Group West (PGW).

—Go Home Bay, 1 vol. Griek, Susan Vande. 2016. (ENG.). 32p. (J). (gr. k-4). 18.95 *(978-1-55498-701-6(6))* Groundwood Bks. CAN. Dist: Publishers Group West (PGW).

—Seal Song, 1 vol. Spalding, Andrea. 2011. (ENG.). 32p. (J). (gr. -1-k). 19.95 *(978-1-55469-242-2(3))* Orca Bk. Pubs. USA.

—Waiting for the Owl's Call. Whelan, Gloria. 2009. (Tales of the World Ser.). (ENG.). 32p. (J). (gr. 1-4). 19.99 *(978-1-58536-418-3(5),* 202153) Sleeping Bear Pr.

Miles, David. Bernida: A Michigan Sailing Legend. Declercq, Al et al. 2014. (ENG.). 32p. (J). (gr. 1-4). 16.99 *(978-1-58536-904-1(7),* 203553) Sleeping Bear Pr.

—Brave Queen Esther, 1 vol. 2015. (I Can Read! / Adventure Bible Ser.). (ENG.). 32p. (J). pap. 4.99 *(978-0-310-74666-9(3))* Zonderkidz.

—Cop's Night Before Christmas, 1 vol. Harrison, Michael. 2010. (Night Before Christmas Ser.). (ENG.). 32p. (J). (gr. k-3). 16.99 *(978-1-58980-800-3(2),* Pelican Publishing) Arcadia Publishing.

—Elijah, God's Mighty Prophet, 1 vol. 2016. (I Can Read! / Adventure Bible Ser.). (ENG.). 32p. (J). pap. 4.99 *(978-0-310-75081-9(4))* Zonderkidz.

—Facing the Blazing Furnace, 1 vol. 2015. (I Can Read! / Adventure Bible Ser.). (ENG.). 32p. (J). pap. 4.99 *(978-0-310-75093-2(8))* Zonderkidz.

—God's Great Creation, 1 vol. Zondervan Staff. 2014. (I Can Read! / Adventure Bible Ser.). (ENG.). 32p. (J). pap. 4.99 *(978-0-310-73238-9(7))* Zondervan.

—The Good Samaritan, 1 vol. Zondervan Staff. 2015. (I Can Read! / Adventure Bible Ser.). (ENG.). 32p. (J). pap. 4.99 *(978-0-310-74662-1(0))* Zonderkidz.

—Great Stories of the Bible, 1 vol. 2016. (I Can Read! / Adventure Bible Ser.). (ENG.). 192p. (J). 11.99 *(978-0-310-75099-4(7))* Zonderkidz.

—Heroes of the Bible Treasury, 1 vol. 2016. (I Can Read! / Adventure Bible Ser.). (ENG.). 192p. (J). 11.99 *(978-0-310-75096-3(2))* Zonderkidz.

—Joseph the Dreamer, 1 vol. 2015. (I Can Read! / Adventure Bible Ser.). 32p. (J). (ENG.). pap. 4.99 *(978-0-310-75084-0(9));* *(978-1-5182-0994-9(7))* Zonderkidz.

—Lit for Little Hands: the Secret Garden. Jorden, Brooke. 2019. (Lit for Little Hands Ser.: 4). (ENG.). 16p. (J). bds. 12.99 *(978-1-64170-105-1(6),* 550105) Familius LLC.

—Marty's Mission: An Apollo 11 Story. Young, Judy. 2019. (Tales of Young Americans Ser.). (ENG.). 32p. (J). (gr. 1-4). 17.99 *(978-1-5341-1014-4(3),* 204648) Sleeping Bear Pr.

—Mommy's Favorite Smell. Eastman, Brock & Eastman, Elsie. 2019. (ENG.). 32p. (J). (gr. -1-2). 16.99 *(978-0-7369-7476-9(8),* 6974769) Harvest Hse. Pubs.

—Moses Leads the People, 1 vol. Zondervan Staff. 2014. (I Can Read! / Adventure Bible Ser.). (ENG.). 32p. (J). pap. 4.99 *(978-0-310-73236-5(0))* Zondervan.

—Noah's Voyage, 1 vol. Zondervan Bibles Staff. 2015. (I Can Read! / Adventure Bible Ser.). (ENG.). 32p. (J). pap. 4.99 *(978-0-310-74683-6(3))* Zonderkidz.

—Paul Meets Jesus, 1 vol. 2016. (I Can Read! / Adventure Bible Ser.). (ENG.). 32p. (J). pap. 4.99 *(978-0-310-75076-5(8))* Zonderkidz.

—Ruth & Naomi, 1 vol. Zondervan, A. 2015. (I Can Read! / Adventure Bible Ser.). (ENG.). 32p. (J). pap. 4.99 *(978-0-310-74650-8(7))* Zonderkidz.

—Wild about the Bible Sticker & Activity Book, 1 vol. 2016. (Adventure Bible Ser.). (ENG.). 32p. (J). pap. 6.99 *(978-0-310-75405-3(4))* Zonderkidz.

Miles, David W. Color Blocked. Sorenson, Ashley. 2017. (ENG.). 40p. (J). 16.99 *(978-1-944822-82-8(8),* 552282) Familius LLC.

—Let's Count Texas: Numbers & Colors in the Lone Star State. Madson, Trish. 2017. (ENG.). 20p. (J). bds. 12.99 *(978-1-942934-79-0(3),* 553479) Familius LLC.

—Lit for Little Hands: Alice's Adventures in Wonderland. Carroll, Lewis. 2018. (Lit for Little Hands Ser.: 2). (ENG.). 16p. (J). bds. 12.99 *(978-1-945547-68-3(5),* 554768) Familius LLC.

—Mommy Loves Me. Miles, Stephanie. 2018. (ENG.). 10p. (J). bds. 12.99 *(978-1-945547-94-2(4),* 554794) Familius LLC.

—The Very Cold, Freezing, No-Number Day. Sorenson, Ashley. 2016. (ENG.). 32p. (J). 16.95 *(978-1-942934-34-9(3),* 553434) Familius LLC.

—W Is for Washington: An Evergreen State ABC Primer. Madson, Trish & Madson, Trish. 2016. (ENG.). 20p. (J). bds. 12.95 *(978-1-944822-02-6(X),* 552202) Familius LLC.

Miles, Gail. Naughty Nicky & the Good Ship Oggy. Miles, Colin. 2013. 24p. pap. *(978-1-909202-16-0(9))* Little Acorns Publishing.

Miles, Jacob. Baby the Freeway Bird Goes to Hollywood. Welles, Caryn. 2019. (ENG.). 38p. (J). pap. 11.99 *(978-1-7979-6912-1(9))* Independently Published.

Miles, Peregrine B. The Mucky Yucky Swamp. Smithrud, Norma. 2011. 28p. pap. 24.95 *(978-1-4560-8790-6(8))* America Star Bks.

Milgram, Al, jt. illus. see Smith, Tod G.

Milgrim, David. The Adventures of Otto Collector's Set: See Otto; See Pip Point; Swing, Otto, Swing!; See Santa Nap; Ride, Otto, Ride!; Go, Otto, Go! Milgrim, David. ed. 2017. (Adventures of Otto Ser.). (ENG.). 192p. (J). (gr. -1-k). pap. 17.99 *(978-1-4814-9984-2(X),* Simon Spotlight) Simon Spotlight.

Milgrim, David. Come In, Zip! Milgrim, David. 2020. (Adventures of Zip Ser.). (ENG.). 32p. (J). (gr. -1-k). 17.99 ***(978-1-5344-6564-0(2));*** pap. 4.99 ***(978-1-5344-6563-3(4))*** Simon Spotlight. (Simon Spotlight).

—For Otto. Milgrim, David. 2020. (Adventures of Otto Ser.). (ENG.). 32p. (J). (gr. -1-k). 17.99 ***(978-1-5344-6567-1(7));*** pap. 4.99 ***(978-1-5344-6566-4(9))*** Simon Spotlight. (Simon Spotlight).

Milgrim, David. Go, Otto, Go! Milgrim, David. 2016. (Adventures of Otto Ser.). (ENG.). 32p. (J). (gr. -1-k). pap. 4.99 *(978-1-4814-6723-0(9),* Simon Spotlight) Simon Spotlight.

—Look Out! a Storm! Milgrim, David. 2019. (Adventures of Otto Ser.). (ENG.). 32p. (J). (gr. -1-k). 17.99 *(978-1-5344-4197-2(2));* pap. 4.99 *(978-1-5344-4196-5(4))* Simon Spotlight. (Simon Spotlight).

—Moo Bird. Milgrim, David. 2015. (Scholastic Reader, Level 1 Ser.). (ENG.). 32p. (J). (gr. -1-1). pap. 3.99 *(978-0-545-82502-3(4))* Scholastic, Inc.

—Moo Dog. Milgrim, David. 2016. (Scholastic Reader, Level 1 Ser.). (ENG.). 32p. (J). (gr. -1-1). pap. 3.99 *(978-0-545-82503-0(2))* Scholastic, Inc.

—My Friend Lucky. Milgrim, David. 2017. (Ready-To-Reads Ser.). (ENG.). 32p. (J). (gr. -1-k). pap. 4.99 *(978-1-4814-8901-0(1),* Simon Spotlight) Simon Spotlight.

—My Friend Lucky: A Love Story. Milgrim, David. 2010. (ENG.). 32p. (J). (gr. -1-2). 13.99 *(978-1-4424-2937-6(2),* Atheneum Bks. for Young Readers) Simon & Schuster Children's Publishing.

—Poof! a Bot! Ready-To-Read Ready-to-Go! Milgrim, David. 2019. (Adventures of Zip Ser.). (ENG.). 32p. (J). (gr. -1-k). pap. 4.99 *(978-1-5344-1102-9(X))* Simon & Schuster, Inc.

—Ride, Otto, Ride! Milgrim, David. 2016. (Adventures of Otto Ser.). (ENG.). 32p. (J). (gr. -1-k). pap. 3.99 *(978-1-4814-6793-3(X),* Simon Spotlight) Simon Spotlight.

—See Otto. Milgrim, David. 2016. (Adventures of Otto Ser.). (ENG.). 32p. (J). (gr. -1-k). pap. 4.99 *(978-1-4814-6796-4(4),* Simon Spotlight) Simon Spotlight.

—See Pip Flap: Ready-To-Read Pre-Level 1. Milgrim, David. 2018. (Adventures of Otto Ser.). (ENG.). 32p. (J). (gr. -1-k). 17.99 *(978-1-5344-1636-9(6));* pap. 4.99 *(978-1-5344-1635-2(8))* Simon Spotlight. (Simon Spotlight).

—See Pip Point. Milgrim, David. 2016. (Adventures of Otto Ser.). (ENG.). 32p. (J). (gr. -1-k). pap. 3.99 *(978-1-4814-6784-1(0),* Simon Spotlight) Simon Spotlight.

—See Santa Nap. Milgrim, David. 2016. (Adventures of Otto Ser.). (ENG.). 32p. (J). (gr. -1-k). pap. 3.99 *(978-1-4814-6787-2(5),* Simon Spotlight) Simon Spotlight.

—See Zip Zap. Milgrim, David. 2018. (Adventures of Zip Ser.). (ENG.). 32p. (J). (gr. -1-k). 17.99 *(978-1-5344-1100-5(3));* pap. 4.99 *(978-1-5344-1099-2(6))* Simon Spotlight. (Simon Spotlight).

—Swing Otto Swing! Milgrim, David. 2005. (Ready-to-Read Ser.). (J). (gr. -1-k). 11.65 *(978-0-7569-6497-9(0))* Perfection Learning Corp.

Milgrom, Al, et al. John Brown's Raid on Harpers Ferry. Glaser, Jason. 2005. (Graphic History Ser.). (ENG.). 32p. (J). (gr. 3-9). 31.32 *(978-0-7368-4369-0(8),* Capstone Pr.) Capstone.

Milgrom, Al & Smith, Tod G. Decoding Genes with Max Axiom, Super Scientist: 4D an Augmented Reading Science Experience. Keyser, Amber J. 2019. (Graphic Science 4D Ser.). (ENG.). 32p. (J). (gr. 3-9). pap. 7.95 *(978-1-5435-7545-3(5),* 141077); lib. bdg. 34.65 *(978-1-5435-7247-6(2),* 140588) Capstone.

—The Earth-Shaking Facts about Earthquakes with Max Axiom, Super Scientist: 4D an Augmented Reading Science Experience. Krohn, Katherine. 2019. (Graphic Science 4D Ser.). (ENG.). 32p. (J). (gr. 3-9). pap. 7.95 *(978-1-5435-6004-6(0),* 140065); lib. bdg. 34.65 *(978-1-5435-5871-5(2),* 139795) Capstone.

—Investigating the Scientific Method with Max Axiom, Super Scientist: 4D an Augmented Reading Science Experience. Lemke, Donald B. 2019. (Graphic Science 4D Ser.). (ENG.). 32p. (J). (gr. 3-9). pap. 7.95 *(978-1-5435-6003-9(2),* 140064); lib. bdg. 34.65 *(978-1-5435-5870-8(4),* 139794) Capstone.

—Steve Jobs, Steve Wozniak, & the Personal Computer, 1 vol. Lemke, Donald B. 2006. (Inventions & Discovery Ser.). (ENG.). 32p. (gr. 3-9). (J). pap. 8.10 *(978-0-7368-9650-4(3));* pap. 47.70 *(978-0-7368-9762-4(3))* Capstone. (Capstone Pr.).

Milgrom, Al, jt. illus. see Martin, Cynthia.

Milgrom, Al, jt. illus. see Smith, Tod G.

Milian, Tomaso. Friends (Mostly) Joosse, Barbara M. 2010. (ENG.). 32p. (J). (gr. -1-3). 16.99 *(978-0-06-088221-1(2),* Greenwillow Bks.) HarperCollins Pubs.

Milicevic, Adam. Hamster Cheeks. Delittle, Cathy. 2007. 32p. (J). 14.95 *(978-1-892633-14-9(0))* Delittle Storyteller Co.

Miline, Bill, photos by. Big Bagel, Little Bagel. Shulman, Mark. 2006. 10p. (J). (gr. k-4). reprint ed. 6.00 *(978-1-4223-5709-5(0))* DIANE Publishing Co.

—I'll Take a Dozen! Shulman, Mark. 2006. 12p. (J). (gr. k-4). reprint ed. 6.00 *(978-1-4223-5725-5(2))* DIANE Publishing Co.

—My Square Breakfast. Shulman, Mark. 2006. 10p. (J). (gr. k-4). reprint ed. 6.00 *(978-1-4223-5710-1(4))* DIANE Publishing Co.

—There's No Blue on a Bagel. Shulman, Mark. 2006. 12p. (J). (gr. k-4). reprint ed. 6.00 *(978-1-4223-5711-8(2))* DIANE Publishing Co.

Militello, Joy. What Was My Mother Thinking? Hodkin, Faith. 2013. (J). 22.95 *(978-1-933420-02-8(2))* Ravenwood Studios.

Milkau, Liz. Princess Backwards, 1 vol. Gray, Jane. 2003. (ENG.). 24p. (J). (gr. 1-3). 15.95 (978-1-896764-64-1(9)) Second Story Pr. CAN. Dist: Orca Bk. Pubs. USA.

Millan, Blanca. Child's Play. Peralta, Ramiro Jose. Jon Brokenbrow, Jon Brokenbrow, tr. 2020. 28p. (J). (gr. -1-3). 16.95 (978-84-16733-76-7(7)) Cuento de Luz SL ESP. Dist: Publishers Group West (PGW).

—Juego de niños. Peralta, Ramiro Jose. 2020. (SPA.). 28p. (J). (gr. -1-3). 16.95 (978-84-16733-75-0(9)) Cuento de Luz SL ESP. Dist: Publishers Group West (PGW).

Millar, H. R. The Enchanted Castle. Nesbit, E. 2019. (ENG.). 256p. (YA). (gr. 7-12). pap. **(978-1-5287-1304-7(4))** Read Bks.

Millar, H. R. Five Children & It. Nesbit, E. l.t. ed. 2007. (ENG.). 198p. pap. 21.99 (978-1-4346-7587-3(4)) Creative Media Partners, LLC.

—Five Children & It. Nesbit, E. 2007. (ENG.). 204p. per. (978-1-4065-3077-3(8)) Dodo Pr.

—The House of Arden (Illustrated Edition) Nesbit, E. 2018. (ENG.). 196p. (J). pap. (978-1-4068-2024-9(5)) Echo Library.

—The Wonderful Garden (Illustrated Edition) Nesbit, E. 2016. (ENG.). (J). pap. (978-1-4068-8026-7(4)) Echo Library.

Millar, H. R., jt. illus. see Fell, H. Granville.

Millar, H. R., jt. illus. see Nesbit, E.

Millar, H. R., jt. illus. see Pape, Frank.

Millard, Kerry. Nim's Island. Orr, Wendy. ed. 2008. (Nim Ser.). (ENG.). 128p. (J). (gr. 3-7). 6.99 (978-0-385-73606-0(1), Yearling) Random Hse. Children's Bks.

—The Web. Hilton, Nette. 2013. (ENG.). 80p. (J). (gr. 2-4). 18.69 (978-1-61067-087-6(6)) Kane Miller.

Milledge, Sas. The Lost Carnival: a Dick Grayson Graphic Novel. Moreci, Michael. 2020. 208p. (YA). (gr. 7-9). pap. 16.99 (978-1-4012-9102-0(3)) DC Comics.

Milleker, Melody. A Big Tub of Water. Krenek-Oliver, Tamara. 2019. (ENG.). 28p. (J). pap. (978-1-78830-258-6(3)) Olympia Publishers.

Miller, Alexandra. The Beastie Book: An Alphabestiary. Harter, Penny. 2009. (ENG.). 56p. (J). 21.95 (978-1-934860-05-2(0)) Shenanigan Bks.

—Wisteria's Show & Tell Spectacular: Older Than the Dinosaurs. Grigsby, Susan. 2012. (J). (978-1-934860-12-0(3)) Shenanigan Bks.

Miller, Allan, jt. illus. see Miller, Christopher.

Miller, Amanda. Polka-Dot Village. White, Betty. 2019. (ENG.). 32p. (J). (gr. 2-2). 14.95 (978-1-944903-48-0(8), Roundtree Pr.) Cameron + Co.

—The Soaky-Croaky, Slippy-Drippy, Sloshy-Galoshy Day. White, Betty. 2019. (ENG.). 32p. (J). (gr. 2-2). 14.95 (978-1-944903-49-7(6), Roundtree Pr.) Cameron + Co.

Miller, Andy J. So Many Sounds. McCanna, Tim. 2018. (ENG.). 24p. (J). (gr. -1-k). 12.99 (978-1-4197-3156-3(4), Abrams Appleseed) Abrams, Inc.

Miller, Antonia, et al. Art Projects. Allman, Howard, photos by. Watt, Fiona. 2005. 96p. (J). (gr. 5-9). 7.99 (978-0-7945-1111-1(2), Usborne) EDC Publishing.

Miller, Antonia. Art Skills. Watt, Fiona. 2004. (Art Ideas Ser.). (ENG.). 96p. (J). pap. 18.95 (978-0-7945-0351-2(9)) EDC Publishing.

—Drawing, Doodling & Coloring Fashion. Watt, Fiona. ed. 2013. (Activity Bks). 128p. (J). pap. 13.99 (978-0-7945-3336-6(1), Usborne) EDC Publishing.

Miller, Antonia, et al. The Usborne Complete Book of Art Ideas. Watt, Fiona. 2006. (Art Ideas Ser.). 288p. (J). pap. 19.99 (978-0-7945-1439-6(1), Usborne) EDC Publishing.

Miller, Antonia & Figg, Non. Art Projects. Allman, Howard, photos by. Watt, Fiona. 2003. (Art Ideas Ser.). (ENG.). 96p. (J). (gr. 5-9). 18.95 (978-0-7945-0657-5(7), Usborne) EDC Publishing.

Miller, Antonia, jt. illus. see Baggott, Stella.

Miller-Bandas, Jamie. General Wolf & Sergeant Wilcox: A Scottales Book. Schweppe, Scott C. Pauley, Christopher D., ed. 2018. (ENG.). 56p. (J). pap. 6.00 (978-1-7322560-2-6(0)) Horn, Jonathan.

Miller, Beverly Annette. The Adventures of Topsy & Sunshine. Kincaid, Vanda. 2018. (ENG.). 36p. (J). (gr. 1-6). pap. 14.95 (978-1-947589-04-9(0)) Waldenhouse Pubs., Inc.

Miller, Bob. Finn the Foolish Fish: Trouble with Bubbles, Set. Paul, Sherry. (See How I Read Ser.). 32p. (Orig.). (J). (gr. -1-2). pap. 14.10 (978-0-675-01084-9(5)) CPI Publishing, Inc.

Miller, Bryan. I Love to Leap! Rundstrom, Teressa. 2004. 35p. (J). per. (978-1-932062-42-7(4)) Hability Solution Services, Inc.

Miller, Bryan & Marshall, H. Keene. Cherry the Sheep Finds Her Sheep Sound. Rundstrom, Teressa. 2004. 25p. (J). per. (978-1-932062-40-3(8)) Hability Solution Services, Inc.

Miller, Caroline. Beyond the River, 1 vol. Miller, Alex. 2011. (ENG.). 64p. 16.99 (978-0-7643-3741-3(6), 9780764337413, Schiffer Publishing Ltd) Schiffer Publishing, Ltd.

Miller, Christopher & Miller, Allan. The Legend of Gid the Kid & the Black Bean Bandits, 2 bks., Bk.1. Miller, Christopher & Miller, Allan. 2007. (Heroes of Promise Ser.). (ENG.). 32p. (J). (gr. 1-5). 12.99 (978-1-59317-202-2(8)) Warner Pr., Inc.

—The Legend of Ten-Gallon Sam & the Perilous Mine, 2 bks., Bk.2. Miller, Christopher & Miller, Allan. 2007. (Heroes of Promise Ser.). (ENG.). 32p. (J). (gr. -1-5). 12.99 (978-1-59317-225-1(7)) Warner Pr., Inc.

Miller, David Humphreys. Indian Friends & Foes: A Baker's Dozen Portraits from Pocahontas to Geronimo. Heiderstadt, Dorothy. 2011. 144p. 40.95 (978-1-258-08676-3(X)) Literary Licensing, LLC.

Miller, Dawn Ellen. Keri. McGee, Pamela M. 2012. 20p. pap. 24.95 (978-1-4626-8593-6(5)) America Star Bks.

—Keri: Dandelions. McGee, Pamela M. 2012. 24p. pap. 24.95 (978-1-4626-9977-3(4)) America Star Bks.

—Keri: The Wedding. McGee, Pamela M. 2013. 20p. pap. 24.95 (978-1-63004-171-7(8)) America Star Bks.

Miller, Ed. Me & My Amazing Body. Sweeney, Joan. 2018. 32p. (J). (gr. -1-2). 12.99 (978-1-5247-7359-5(X), Knopf Bks. for Young Readers); (ENG.). pap. 7.99 (978-1-5247-7362-5(X), Dragonfly Bks.) Random Hse. Children's Bks.

Miller, Edward. Button Your Buttons: It's a Snowy Day! Houran, Lori. Cottage Door Press, ed. 2020. (ENG.). 34p. (J). (gr. -1-2). 9.99 **(978-1-68052-954-8(4)**, 1005970) Cottage Door Pr.

Miller, Edward. Circles. Adler, David A. (ENG.). 32p. (J). (gr. 1-4). 2017. 7.99 (978-0-8234-3883-9(X)); 2016. 17.95 (978-0-8234-3642-2(X)) Holiday Hse., Inc.

—A Drop of Blood. Showers, Paul. 2004. (Let's-Read-And-Find-Out Science 2 Ser.). 32p. (J). (ENG.). (gr. -1-3). pap. 5.99 (978-0-06-009110-1(X), Collins); (gr. k-4). 15.99 (978-0-06-009108-8(8)); (gr. k-4). lib. bdg. 16.89 (978-0-06-009109-5(6)) HarperCollins Pubs.

—Fractions, Decimals, & Percents. Adler, David A. (ENG.). 32p. (J). (gr. 1-4). 2011. pap. 7.99 (978-0-8234-2354-5(9)); 2010. 17.95 (978-0-8234-2199-2(6)) Holiday Hse., Inc.

—Fractions, Decimals, & Percents. Adler, David A. 2010. (J). (978-0-545-25162-4(1)) Scholastic, Inc.

Miller, Edward, III. Fun with Roman Numerals. Adler, David A. 2009. (ENG.). 32p. (J). (gr. 1-4). pap. 7.99 (978-0-8234-2255-5(0)) Holiday Hse., Inc.

Miller, Edward. Gravity Is a Mystery. Branley, Franklyn M. 2007. (Let's-Read-and-Find-Out Science Ser.). 33p. (gr. k-4). 16.00 (978-0-7569-8103-7(4)) Perfection Learning Corp.

—Gravity Is a Mystery. Branley, Franklyn Mansfield. 2nd rev. ed. 2007. (Let's-Read-and-Find-Out Science Ser.). (ENG.). 40p. (J). (gr. k-4). 15.99 (978-0-06-028532-6(X)) HarperCollins Pubs.

—Gravity Is a Mystery. Branley, Franklyn M. 2nd rev. ed. 2007. (Let's-Read-And-Find-Out Science 2 Ser.). (ENG.). 40p. (J). (gr. -1-3). pap. 6.99 (978-0-06-445201-4(8)) HarperCollins Pubs.

—A House for Birdie. Murphy, Stuart J. 2004. (MathStart 1 Ser.). (ENG.). 40p. (J). (gr. -1). pap. 5.99 (978-0-06-052353-4(0)) HarperCollins Pubs.

—Let's Estimate: A Book about Estimating & Rounding Numbers. Adler, David A. 32p. (J). (gr. 1-4). 2018. pap. 7.99 (978-0-8234-4017-7(6)); 2017. (ENG.). 17.95 (978-0-8234-3668-2(3)) Holiday Hse., Inc.

—Millions, Billions, & Trillions: Understanding Big Numbers. Adler, David A. (ENG.). 32p. (J). (gr. 1-4). 2014. 7.99 (978-0-8234-3049-9(9)); 2013. 18.99 (978-0-8234-2403-0(0)) Holiday Hse., Inc.

—Money Madness. Adler, David A. 2009. (ENG.). 32p. (J). (gr. -1-3). pap. 7.99 (978-0-8234-2272-2(0)) Holiday Hse., Inc.

—Money Math: Addition & Subtraction. Adler, David A. 32p. (J). (gr. 1-4). 2019. pap. 7.99 (978-0-8234-4182-2(2)); 2017. (ENG.). 17.95 (978-0-8234-3698-9(5)) Holiday Hse., Inc.

—Monsters Come Out Tonight! Glasser, Frederick. 2019. (ENG.). 18p. (J). (gr. -1-k). bds. 8.99 (978-1-4197-3722-0(8), 1277110, Abrams Appleseed) Abrams, Inc.

—Mystery Math: A First Book of Algebra. Adler, David A. 2012. (ENG.). 32p. (J). (gr. 1-4). pap. 7.99 (978-0-8234-2548-8(7)) Holiday Hse., Inc.

—Perimeter, Area, & Volume: A Monster Book of Dimensions. Adler, David A. 2013. (ENG.). 32p. (J). (gr. 2-5). pap. 8.99 (978-0-8234-2763-5(3)) Holiday Hse., Inc.

—Place Value. Adler, David A. 2017. (ENG.). 32p. (J). (gr. k-3). 8.99 (978-0-8234-3770-2(1)) Holiday Hse., Inc.

—Prices! Prices! Prices! Why They Go up & Down. Adler, David A. (ENG.). 32p. (J). (gr. 1-4). 2016. 7.99 (978-0-8234-3574-6(1)); 2015. 17.99 (978-0-8234-3293-6(9)) Holiday Hse., Inc.

—Squares, Rectangles, & Other Quadrilaterals. Adler, David A. 2018. 32p. (J). (gr. 1-4). 18.99 (978-0-8234-3759-7(0)) Holiday Hse., Inc.

—Squares, Rectangles & Other Quadrilaterals. Adler, David A. 2019. 32p. (J). (gr. 1-4). pap. 8.99 (978-0-8234-4440-3(6)) Holiday Hse., Inc.

—Telling Time. Adler, David A. 2019. 32p. (J). (gr. 1-4). 18.99 (978-0-8234-4092-4(3)) Holiday Hse., Inc.

—Triangles. Adler, David A. 2015. (ENG.). 32p. (J). (gr. 1-4). 7.99 (978-0-8234-3305-6(6)) Holiday Hse., Inc.

—What's the Weather? Cali, Jennifer. 2009. (Rookie Preschool-NEW Ser.). (ENG.). 24p. (J). pap. 6.95 (978-0-531-24585-9(3)) Scholastic Library Publishing.

—Working with Fractions. Adler, David A. (ENG.). 32p. (J). 2009. (gr. 1-4). pap. 8.99 (978-0-8234-2207-4(0)); 2007. (gr. 4-7). 22.44 (978-0-8234-2010-0(8)) Holiday Hse., Inc.

—You Can, Toucan, Math: Word Problem-Solving Fun. Adler, David A. 2006. (ENG.). 32p. (J). (gr. -1-3). 17.95 (978-0-8234-1919-7(3)) Holiday Hse., Inc.

Miller, Frank. Cursed. Wheeler, Thomas. 2019. (ENG.). 416p. (YA). (gr. 9). 24.99 (978-1-5344-2533-0(0), Simon & Schuster Bks. For Young Readers) Simon & Schuster Bks. For Young Readers.

Miller, Frank. Cursed. Wheeler, Thomas. ed. 2020. (ENG.). 416p. (YA). (gr. 9). 19.99 **(978-1-5344-7733-9(0)**, Simon & Schuster Bks. For Young Readers) Simon & Schuster Bks. For Young Readers.

Miller, Frank, et al. New Mutants Epic Collection: Renewal. Mantlo, Bill & Claremont, Chris. 2020. (ENG.). 520p. (J). (gr. 4-17). pap. 39.99 **(978-1-302-92577-2(6))** Marvel Worldwide, Inc.

Miller, Fujiko. Bad Luck Boy. Brin, Susannah. 2003. (Romance Ser.). 60p. (J). pap. 4.95 (978-1-58659-458-9(3)) Artesian Pr.

—The Climb. Brin, Susannah. rev. ed. 2004. (Take Ten Ser.). 61p. (J). (gr. 4-12). pap. 4.95 (978-1-58659-042-0(1)) Artesian Pr.

—Connie's Secret. Epstein, Dwayne. 2003. (Romance Ser.). 58p. (J). pap. 4.95 (978-1-58659-460-2(5)) Artesian Pr.

—Crystal's Chance. Brin, Susannah. 2003. (Romance Ser.). 62p. (J). pap. 4.95 (978-1-58659-459-6(1)) Artesian Pr.

—The Howling House. Schraff, Anne. rev. ed. 2004. (Standing Tall Mysteries Ser.). 51p. (J). (gr. 4-12). pap. 4.95 (978-1-58659-083-3(9)) Artesian Pr.

—Search & Rescue. Brin, Susannah. rev. ed. 2004. (Take Ten Ser.). 62p. (J). (gr. 4-12). pap. 4.95 (978-1-58659-043-7(X)) Artesian Pr.

—To Nicole with Love. West, Casey. 2003. (Romance Ser.). 60p. (J). pap. 4.95 (978-1-58659-188-5(6)) Artesian Pr.

—Tough Guy. Brin, Susannah. rev. ed. 2004. (Take Ten Ser.). 62p. (J). (gr. 4-12). pap. 4.95 (978-1-58659-045-1(6)) Artesian Pr.

Miller, Gina. Spooky Texas Tales. Tingle, Tim & Moore, James W. 2005. x, 85p. (J). pap. (978-0-89672-566-9(9)) Texas Tech Univ. Pr.

—Spooky Texas Tales. Tingle, Tim & Moore, Doc. 2005. (ENG.). 128p. (gr. 4-6). 18.95 (978-0-89672-565-2(0)) Texas Tech Univ. Pr.

Miller, Gloria. Ma Kokum a Téléphoné Aujourd'hui. Loewen, Iris. 2015. (FRE.). 32p. (J). mass mkt. 10.95 (978-1-894717-60-1(0), 7c8e5e7e-dd83-4ada-891e-a2615dee3580) Pemmican Pubns., Inc. CAN. Dist: Firefly Bks., Ltd.

—My Kookum Called Today. Loewen, Iris. 2015. (ENG.). 32p. (J). mass mkt. 10.95 (978-0-921827-36-8(9), 74aa3ead-4716-4871-848b-0305a1605151) Pemmican Pubns., Inc. CAN. Dist: Firefly Bks., Ltd.

Miller, Hartley. Rub It In. Goudie, Cathy a & Goudie, Michael L. M. 2018. (ENG.). 28p. (J). pap. (978-1-5255-0249-1(2)) FriesenPress.

Miller, Heidi. What the World Is Like to Bea Moore: The Treasure. Catanzarite, Lisa. 2009. 56p. pap. 17.26 (978-1-4251-6321-1(1)) Trafford Publishing.

Miller, J. P. The House That Jack Built. Golden Books. 2008. (Little Golden Book Ser.). 32p. (J). (gr. -1-2). 4.99 (978-0-375-83530-8(X), Golden Bks.) Random Hse. Children's Bks.

—I Am a Mouse. Risom, Ole. 2018. (Golden Sturdy Book Ser.). 26p. (J). (gr. k — 1). bds. 7.99 (978-0-375-87491-8(7), Golden Bks.) Random Hse. Children's Bks.

—Jingle Bells. Daly, Kathleen N. 2015. (Little Golden Book Ser.). (ENG.). 24p. (J). (-k). 4.99 (978-0-553-51112-3(2), Golden Bks.) Random Hse. Children's Bks.

—Little Golden Book Nursery Tales. 2017. 80p. (J). (gr. -1-2). 7.99 (978-0-553-53667-6(2), Golden Bks.) Random Hse. Children's Bks.

—The Little Red Hen. Golden Books. 2015. 26p. (J). (-k). bds. 7.99 (978-0-385-39094-1(7), Golden Bks.) Random Hse. Children's Bks.

—The Sweet Smell of Christmas. Scarry, Patricia M. 2003. (ENG.). 36p. (J). (gr. -1-2). 9.99 (978-0-375-82643-6(2), Golden Bks.) Random Hse. Children's Bks.

Miller Jamison, Veronica. A Computer Called Katherine: How Katherine Johnson Helped Put America on the Moon. Slade, Suzanne. 2019. 40p. (J). (gr. -1-3). 18.99 (978-0-316-43517-8(1)) Little Brown & Co.

Miller, Jayna. Too Much Trick or Treat. Miller, Jayna. Thatch, Nancy, ed. 2005. 29p. (J). per. 19.95 (978-0-933849-83-9(4)) landmark Hse., Ltd.

Miller, Jo. Phases of the Moon, 1 vol. Olson, Gillia M. 2006. (Patterns in Nature Ser.). (ENG.). 24p. (gr. k-1). 24.65 (978-0-7368-6340-7(0), Capstone Pr.) Capstone.

Miller, Joanna. The Brass Serpent. Kimmel, Eric A. 2005. 32p. (J). 14.95 (978-1-930143-41-8(9), 3419); pap. 9.95 (978-1-930143-42-5(7), 3427) Simcha Media Group. (Devora Publishing).

Miller, Jonathan, et al. Baby Animals: A Spotting Game (My Bath Book) 2018. 6p. (J). (— 1). 5.99 (978-2-924786-75-8(4), CrackBoom! Bks.) Chouette Publishing CAN. Dist: Publishers Group West (PGW).

—Colors: under the Sea (My Bath Book) 2018. (ENG.). 6p. (J). (— 1). 5.99 (978-2-924786-73-4(8), CrackBoom! Bks.) Chouette Publishing CAN. Dist: Publishers Group West (PGW).

Miller, Jonathan. Farm Animals Fun Box. 2017. (ENG.). 24p. (J). (gr. -1-k). 7.99 (978-2-9815807-2-6(8), CrackBoom! Bks.) Chouette Publishing CAN. Dist: Publishers Group West (PGW).

—When I Grow Up. 2011. 16p. (J). (978-1-58865-637-7(3)) Kidsbooks, LLC.

—Winter, Spring, Summer, Fall. 2010. 16p. (J). (978-1-58865-578-3(4)) Kidsbooks, LLC.

Miller, Jonathan & Dupuis, Karina. Farm Noises. 2017. 6p. (J). (gr. -1 — 1). 5.99 (978-2-924786-15-4(0), CrackBoom! Bks.) Chouette Publishing CAN. Dist: Publishers Group West (PGW).

—Ocean Fun Box: Includes a Storybook & a 2-in-1 Puzzle. Vallières, Nathalie & Guion, Marine. 2018. 24p. (J). (gr. -1). 7.99 (978-2-924786-23-9(1), CrackBoom! Bks.) Chouette Publishing CAN. Dist: Publishers Group West (PGW).

Miller, Josh, jt. illus. see Howard, Philip.

Miller, Jules. Ellie & the Truth about the Tooth Fairy. 2014. (ENG.). 36p. (J). (gr. -1-k). 16.95 (978-1-62873-590-1(2), Sky Pony Pr.) Skyhorse Publishing Co., Inc.

—When Night Became Day. 2015. (ENG.). 32p. (J). (gr. -1-k). 16.95 (978-1-62914-632-4(3), Sky Pony Pr.) Skyhorse Publishing Co., Inc.

Miller, Julia Love. The Other Day I Met a Bear. Feierabend, John M. 2014. (First Steps in Music Ser.). 32p. (J). (gr. -1-k). 16.95 (978-1-62277-076-2(5)) G I A Pubns., Inc.

Miller, Justin. Devil's Canyon: Forensic Geography. McIntosh, Kenneth. 2007. (Crime Scene Club Ser.: Bk. 1). 144p. (YA). (gr. 9-12). 24.95 (978-1-4222-0247-0(X)) Mason Crest.

—The Earth Cries Out: Forensic Chemistry & Environmental Science, 8 vols. McIntosh, Kenneth. 2007. (Crime Scene Club Ser.: Bk. 9). 144p. (YA). (gr. 9-12). lib. bdg. 24.95 (978-1-4222-0254-8(2)) Mason Crest.

—If the Shoe Fits: Footwear Analysis, 7 vols. McIntosh, Kenneth. 2007. (Crime Scene Club Ser.). 144p. (YA). (gr. 9-12). lib. bdg. 24.95 (978-1-4222-0253-1(4)) Mason Crest.

—Poison & Peril: Forensic Toxicology, 4 vols. McIntosh, Kenneth. 2007. (Crime Scene Club Ser.). 144p. (YA). (gr. 9-12). lib. bdg. 24.95 (978-1-4222-0250-0(X)) Mason Crest.

—The Trickster's Image: Forensic Art, 3 vols. McIntosh, Kenneth. 2007. (Crime Scene Club Ser.). 144p. (YA). (gr. 9-12). lib. bdg. 24.95 (978-1-4222-0249-4(6)) Mason Crest.

Miller, Justus. Lost in the Mess. Hancock, Joy. 2019. (ENG.). 38p. (J). pap. 10.99 **(978-1-0890-0351-9(X))** Independently Published.

Miller, Kate. Naughty Bailey, Naughty. Loizzo, Paula. 2017. (ENG.). (J). (gr. -1-2). 9.99 (978-1-943331-83-3(9)) Orange Hat Publishing.

Miller, Kathy M., photos by. Chippy Chipmunk Parties in the Garden. Miller, Kathy M. 2009. (ENG., 40p. (J). (gr. 2-3). 19.95 (978-0-9840893-0-7(6), 9780984089307) Celtic Sunrise.

Miller, Kelly Leigh. I Am a Wolf. Miller, Kelly Leigh. 2019. (ENG.). 32p. (J). (gr. -1-3). 17.99 (978-0-525-55329-8(0), Dial Bks) Penguin Young Readers Group.

Miller, Linzi. The Broken Law. Harris, Tumeka. Sea Breeze Productions & Phelps, Janice, eds. ed. 2006. 32p. (J). 14.95 (978-0-9769366-0-2(7)) Dividion Group, LLC, The.

—The Goody Bag. Harris, Tumeka. Sea Breeze Productions, ed. 2006. 36p. (J). 14.95 (978-0-9769366-2-6(3)) Dividion Group, LLC, The.

—Home Sweet Home. Harris, Tumeka. Sea Breeze Productions, ed. 2006. 36p. (J). 14.95 (978-0-9769366-3-3(1)) Dividion Group, LLC, The.

—Trouble in Paradise. Harris, Tumeka. Sea Breeze Productions & Phelps, Janice, eds. 2006. 36p. (J). 14.95 (978-0-9769366-1-9(5)) Dividion Group, LLC, The.

Miller, Liz. The Gift of Faith. Miller, Liz. 2019. (Abba's Land Ser.: Vol. 1). (ENG.). 38p. (J). pap. 9.25 (978-1-0909-4969-1(3)) Independently Published.

—Heaven Awaits. Miller, Liz. 2018. (ENG.). 30p. (J). 18.99 (978-0-692-10115-5(2)) Miller, Elizabeth.

Miller, Madeline. Year of the Dragon. Foutz, Ian. 2014. (J). (978-1-62086-634-4(X)) Mascot Bks., Inc.

Miller, Margaret, photos by. POP! a Book about Bubbles. Bardley, Kimberly Brubaker. 2015. 40p. pap. 6.00 (978-1-61003-614-6(X)) Center for the Collaborative Classroom.

Miller, Margot. Massimo's Meatballs. Mure, Nancy. 2015. (ENG.). 40p. (J). pap. 9.98 (978-0-7443-2196-8(4)) CamCat Publishing.

Miller, Mark. Jake the Sadder Ladder. German, Lana. 2012. 20p. (-18). pap. 24.95 (978-1-4626-9574-4(4)) America Star Bks.

Miller, Marlene. I Know Where the Freighters Go. Miller, Marlene. 2008. (ENG.). 32p. pap. 9.95 (978-1-933916-29-3(X)) Nelson Publishing & Marketing.

Miller, Mike. Black Tide: Awakening of the Key. Bishop, Debbie. 2004. (ENG.). 208p. pap. 19.99 (978-1-932431-00-1(4)) Left Field,Angel Gate.

Miller, Mike, jt. illus. see Axworthy, Anni.

Miller, Mike S. The Sworn Sword: the Graphic Novel: The Graphic Novel, 0 vols. Martin, George R. R. & Avery, Ben. 2014. (Game of Thrones Ser.: 2). (ENG.). 184p. pap. 14.95 (978-1-4778-4929-3(7), 9781477849293, Jet City Comics) Amazon Publishing.

Miller, Mitchell. 25 Days to Jesus. Waltersdorff, Christy J. 2018. (J). (978-0-87178-258-8(8)) Brethren Pr.

Miller, Nancy. Rockabye Baby Jesus. Tietz, Heather. 2011. 20p. 12.95 (978-0-8091-6760-9(3)) Paulist Pr.

—Yes, Jesus Loves You. Tietz, Heather. 2009. 20p. (J). (gr. k-4). 14.95 (978-0-8091-6743-2(3), Ambassador Bks.) Paulist Pr.

Miller, Nick. Native American Classics, Vol. 24. Smelcer, John E. et al. Pomplun, Tom et al, eds. 2013. Orig. Title: 2013. (ENG.). 144p. (YA). pap. 17.95 (978-0-9825630-6-9(X), 16f1f150-750a-43dd-abec-67b80349a064) Eureka Productions.

Miller, Norbert. Overleaf: The Second Leaf. Miller, Norbert B. 2020. (ENG.). 334p. (J). pap. 14.95 **(978-1-6592-1285-3(5))** Independently Published.

Miller, Paton. Sit! Stay! Sign! Margolis, Alysia. 2007. 32p. (J). (978-1-4257-5919-3(X)) Margolis, Marion.

Miller, Peter, photos by. Vermont People. Miller, Peter. 5th ed. 2003. 144p. 34.95 (978-0-9628064-6-9(3)); pap. 22.95 (978-0-9628064-9-0(8)) Silver Print Pr., Inc.

Miller, Phil, et al. Henry Ford & the Model T, 1 vol. O'Hearn, Michael. 2006. (Inventions & Discovery Ser.). (ENG.). 32p. (J). (gr. 3-9). 31.32 (978-0-7368-6480-0(6), Capstone Pr.) Capstone.

Miller, Phil. Isaac Newton & the Laws of Motion, 1 vol. Gianopoulos, Andrea & Barnett, Charles, III. 2007. (Inventions & Discovery Ser.). (ENG.). 32p. (J). (gr. 3-9). pap. 8.10 (978-0-7368-7899-9(8), 1264949, Capstone Pr.) Capstone.

Miller, Phil, et al. Thomas Edison & the Lightbulb, 1 vol. Welvaert, Scott R. 2006. (Inventions & Discovery Ser.). (ENG.). 32p. (J). (gr. 3-9). 31.32 (978-0-7368-6489-3(X)) Capstone.

Miller, Phil & Barnett, Charles, III. The Triangle Shirtwaist Factory Fire. Gunderson, Jessica Sarah. 2006. (Disasters in History Ser.). (ENG.). 32p. (J). (gr. 3-9). per. 8.10 (978-0-7368-6878-5(X), Capstone Pr.) Capstone.

Miller, Phil & Barnett III, Charles. The Triangle Shirtwaist Factory Fire. Gunderson, Jessica. 2006. (Disasters in History Ser.). (ENG.). 32p. (gr. 3-4). pap. 47.70 (978-0-7368-6999-7(9), Capstone Pr.) Capstone.

Miller, Phil, jt. illus. see Barnett, Charles, III.

Miller, Rachelle. More Than Balloons, 1 vol. Crozier, Lorna. 2017. (ENG.). 26p. (J). (gr. -1 — 1). bds. 9.95 (978-1-4598-1028-0(7)) Orca Bk. Pubs. USA.

Miller, Rebecca. The Littlest Nephite in Nephi & the Brass Plates. Olsen, Bevan Lloyd. 2008. 14p. (J). (gr. 3-7). 15.99 (978-1-59955-087-9(3)) Cedar Fort, Inc./CFI Distribution.

—Teeny Tiny Talks IV: My Eternal Family. Hammari, Kimiko. 2008. 116p. (J). pap. 12.99 (978-1-59955-188-3(8)) Cedar Fort, Inc./CFI Distribution.

Miller, Richard. Along Little Dogie: Harley's Great Adventures. Pogo the Clown. 2005. (J). 12.95 (978-0-9755253-3-3(6)) Chiliric Pubns.

—The Littlest Tiger: Harley's Great Adventures. Pogo the Clown. 2004. (J). 12.95 (978-0-9755253-2-6(8)) Chiliric Pubns.

—Ricki Roars. Clown, Pogo the. 2006. 32p. (J). 12.95 (978-0-9755253-8-8(7)) Chiliric Pubns.

Miller, Richard D. A Brave Little Lion: Harley's Great Adventures. Pogo the Clown. 2005. (J). 12.95 (978-0-9755253-5-7(2)) Chiliric Pubns.

—The Great Blue Sky: Harley's Great Adventures. Pogo the Clown. 2005. (J). 12.95 (978-0-9755253-6-4(0)) Chiliric Pubns.

—A Little Gray Mouse: Harley's Great Adventures. Pogo the Clown. 2005. (J). 12.95 (978-0-9755253-7-1(9)) Chiliric Pubns.

—A Taste of Shrimp: Harley's Great Adventures. Pogo the Clown. 2005. (J). 12.95 (978-0-9755253-4-0(4)) Chiliric Pubns.

Miller, Robert. A Dream Vacation. Haile, Carol J. 2003. 32p. (J). per. 19.95 (978-0-9724699-0-6(7)) Panda Bear Pr.

Miller, Roger, photos by. United States Naval Academy: Annapolis. Foster, Linda. 2006. 168p. 39.95 (978-0-911897-49-4(6)) Image Publishing, Ltd.

Miller, Ron. Worlds Around Us: A Space Voyage. Jackson, Ellen. 2006. (Exceptional Science Title for Intermediate Grades). 37p. (J). (gr. 3-7). lib. bdg. 23.93 (978-0-7613-3405-7(X), Millbrook Pr.) Lerner Publishing Group.

Miller, Ron. Special Effects: An Introduction to Movie Magic. Miller, Ron. 2006. (ENG.). 128p. (gr. 7-12). 26.60 (978-0-7613-2918-3(8)) Lerner Publishing Group.

Miller, Rowen. Nest Quest. McDonald, Rhonda. 2nd ed. 2019. (ENG.). 42p. (J). (gr. k-5). pap. 13.00 **(978-1-0878-0110-0(9))** SDC Publishing, LLC.

Miller, Russell. The Pocket Guide to Spy Stuff, 1 vol. King, Bart. 2018. 216p. (J). pap. 9.99 (978-1-4236-4982-3(6)) Gibbs Smith, Publisher.

Miller, Sara Zieve. The Little Queen. Geddes, Meia. Alexander, Lindsey, ed. 2017. (ENG.). 107p. (YA). pap. 12.50 (978-1-945366-66-6(4)) Poetose Pr.

Miller, Seaerra. Hilda & the Great Parade: Hilda Netflix Tie-In 2. Pearson, Luke & Davies, Stephen. (Hilda Tie-In Ser.: 2). (ENG.). 200p. (J). (gr. 2-5). ed. 2020. pap. 10.99 (978-1-912497-72-0(7)); 2nd ed. 2019. 13.95 (978-1-911171-45-4(3)) Flying Eye Bks. GBR. Dist: Penguin Random Hse. LLC.

—Hilda & the Hidden People: Hilda Netflix Tie-In 1. Pearson, Luke & Davies, Stephen. (Hilda Tie-In Ser.: 1). (ENG.). (J). (gr. 2-5). 2019. 216p. pap. 10.99 (978-1-912497-88-1(3)); 2018. 179p. 13.95 (978-1-911171-44-7(5)) Flying Eye Bks. GBR. Dist: Penguin Random Hse. LLC.

—Hilda & the Nowhere Space: Hilda Netflix Tie-In 3. Pearson, Luke & Davies, Stephen. (Hilda Tie-In Ser.: 3). (ENG.). (J). (gr. 2-5). 2019. 200p. 13.95 (978-1-911171-50-8(X)); 2020. 216p. pap. 10.99 **(978-1-912497-59-1(X))** Flying Eye Bks. GBR. Dist: Penguin Random Hse. LLC.

Miller, Shane. Hawk of the Nile. Green, Robert James. 2012. 222p. 44.95 (978-1-258-25119-2(1)); pap. 29.95 (978-1-258-25551-0(0)) Literary Licensing, LLC.

—Riddles, Riddles, Riddles: Enigmas & Anagrams, Puns & Puzzles, Quizzes & Conundrums! 2014. (ENG.). 256p. (J). (gr. 3-8). pap. 9.99 (978-0-486-78186-0(0)) Dover Pubns., Inc.

Miller, Sharee. Shai & Emmie Star in Break an Egg! Wallis, Quvenzhané & Wallis, Quvenzhané. 2017. (Shai & Emmie Story Ser.: 1). (ENG.). 128p. (J). (gr. 1-5). 15.99 (978-1-4814-5882-5(5), Simon & Schuster Bks. For Young Readers) Simon & Schuster Bks. For Young Readers.

—Shai & Emmie Star in Dancy Pants! Wallis, Quvenzhané. 2018. (Shai & Emmie Story Ser.: 2). (ENG.). 128p. (J). (gr. 1-5). 17.99 (978-1-4814-5885-6(X), Simon & Schuster Bks. For Young Readers) Simon & Schuster Bks. For Young Readers.

—Shai & Emmie Star in to the Rescue! Wallis, Quvenzhané. (Shai & Emmie Story Ser.). (ENG.). 128p. (J). (gr. 1-5). 2019. pap. 6.99 (978-1-4814-5889-4(2)); 2018. 15.99 (978-1-4814-5888-7(4)) Simon & Schuster Bks. For Young Readers. (Simon & Schuster Bks. For Young Readers).

Miller, Steve. Big Box, Little Box: The Forecast Calls for Potential Rain! Nash, Damien K. H. & Nash, Kathy. 2012. 80p. pap. 13.99 (978-0-9846507-1-2(7)) Faith Bks. & MORE.

Miller, Susan. Fast-Draw Freddie. Hamsa, Bobbie. rev. ed. 2003. (Rookie Reader Ser.). (ENG.). 32p. (J). (gr. k-2). pap. 4.95 (978-0-516-27150-7(4), Children's Pr.) Scholastic Library Publishing.

—Step-by-Step. Taylor-Butler, Christine. 2005. (My First Reader Ser.). (ENG.). 32p. (J). (gr. k-1). lib. bdg. 18.50 (978-0-516-24875-2(8), Children's Pr.) Scholastic Library Publishing.

Miller, Tim. Hamstersaurus Rex. O'Donnell, Tom. 2016. (Hamstersaurus Rex Ser.: 1). (ENG.). 272p. (J). (gr. 3-7). 12.99 (978-0-06-237754-8(X)) HarperCollins Pubs.

—Hamstersaurus Rex Gets Crushed. O'Donnell, Tom. 2018. (Hamstersaurus Rex Ser.: 3). (ENG.). 304p. (J). (gr. 3-7). 12.99 (978-0-06-237758-6(2)) HarperCollins Pubs.

—Hamstersaurus Rex vs. Squirrel Kong. O'Donnell, Tom. 2017. (Hamstersaurus Rex Ser.: 2). (ENG.). 304p. (J). (gr. 3-7). 12.99 (978-0-06-237756-2(6)) HarperCollins Pubs.

—Hamstersaurus Rex vs. the Cutepocalypse. O'Donnell, Tom. 2018. (Hamstersaurus Rex Ser.: 4). (ENG.). 368p. (J). (gr. 3-7). 12.99 (978-0-06-237760-9(4)) HarperCollins Pubs.

—Horse Meets Dog. Kalan, Elliott. 2018. (ENG.). 40p. (J). (gr. -1-3). 17.99 (978-0-06-279110-8(9), Balzer & Bray) HarperCollins Pubs.

—Margarash. Riddle, Mark. 2016. 48p. (J). (gr. -1-3). 17.95 (978-1-59270-216-9(3)) Enchanted Lion Bks., LLC.

Miller, Tim. Moo Moo in a Tutu. Miller, Tim. 2017. (Moo Moo & Mr. Quackers Book Ser.). (ENG.). 32p. (J). (gr. -1-3). 17.99 (978-0-06-241440-3(2)) HarperCollins Pubs.

—What's Cooking, Moo Moo? Miller, Tim. 2018. (Moo Moo & Mr. Quackers Book Ser.). (ENG.). 32p. (J). (gr. -1-3). 17.99 (978-0-06-241441-0(0), Balzer & Bray) HarperCollins Pubs.

Miller, Tim J. Snappsy the Alligator & His Best Friend Forever (Probably) Falatko, Julie. 2017. 32p. (J). (gr. -1-3). 16.99 (978-0-425-28865-8(X), Viking Books for Young Readers) Penguin Young Readers Group.

—Snappsy the Alligator (Did Not Ask to Be in This Book) Falatko, Julie. 2016. 40p. (J). (gr. -1-3). 16.99 (978-0-451-46945-8(3), Viking Books for Young Readers) Penguin Young Readers Group.

Miller, Tom, jt. illus. see Fetherston, Catherine.

Miller, Victoria. Dora & the Unicorn King. 2011. (Dora the Explorer Ser.). (ENG.). 24p. (J). pap. 3.99 (978-1-4424-1312-2(3), Simon Spotlight/Nickelodeon) Simon Spotlight/Nickelodeon.

—Dora in Wonderland (Dora the Explorer) Tillworth, Mary. 2014. (Pictureback(R) Ser.). (ENG.). 24p. (J). (gr. -1-2). 3.99 (978-0-385-37119-3(5), Random Hse. Bks. for Young Readers) Random Hse. Children's Bks.

—Dora the Explorer to the Moon. Burroughs, Caleb. 2007. (Play a Tune Tale Ser.). 16p. (J). (gr. -1-3). 12.98 (978-1-4127-8830-4(7)) Publications International, Ltd.

—Dora's Christmas Star (Dora the Explorer) Tillworth, Mary. 2013. (Pictureback(R) Ser.). (ENG.). 16p. (J). (gr. -1-2). 4.99 (978-0-449-81780-3(6), Random Hse. Bks. for Young Readers) Random Hse. Children's Bks.

—Dora's Magic Watering Can. Rao, Lisa. 2008. (Dora the Explorer Ser.). (ENG.). 16p. (J). (gr. -1-1). pap. 4.99 (978-1-4169-4772-1(8), Simon Spotlight/Nickelodeon) Simon Spotlight/Nickelodeon.

—Dora's Perfect Pumpkin. Larsen, Kirsten. 2007. (Dora the Explorer Ser.). (ENG.). 24p. (J). (gr. -1-3). pap. 3.99 (978-1-4169-3438-7(3), Simon Spotlight/Nickelodeon) Simon Spotlight/Nickelodeon.

—Dora's Sleepover. Bergen, Lara Rice & Bergen, Lara. 2006. (Dora the Explorer Ser.: 12). (ENG.). 24p. (J). (gr. -1-1). pap. 3.99 (978-1-4169-1508-9(7), Simon Spotlight/Nickelodeon) Simon Spotlight/Nickelodeon.

—Flowers for Mami Unicorn! 2010. (Dora the Explorer Ser.). (ENG.). 24p. (J). (gr. -1-2). pap. 3.99 (978-1-4169-9064-2(X), Simon Spotlight/Nickelodeon) Simon Spotlight/Nickelodeon.

—I Love My Abuela! Ricci, Christine. 2009. (Dora the Explorer Ser.: 28). (ENG.). 24p. (J). pap. 3.99 (978-1-4169-6866-5(0), Simon Spotlight/Nickelodeon) Simon Spotlight/Nickelodeon.

—Lemonade with a Twist. Banks, Steven. 2004. (Fairly Oddparents Ser.). 32p. (J). (gr. k-2). 11.65 (978-0-7569-1990-0(8)) Perfection Learning Corp.

—Rainbow Adventure. Golden Books Staff. 2010. (ENG.). 96p. (J). (gr. -1-2). pap. 3.99 (978-0-375-86350-9(8), Golden Bks.) Random Hse. Children's Bks.

—Rainbow Rescue! (Dora the Explorer) Golden Books. 2014. (Color Plus Chunky Crayons Ser.). (ENG.). 48p. (J). (gr. -1-2). pap. 3.99 (978-0-385-37436-1(4), Golden Bks.) Random Hse. Children's Bks.

—Save the Unicorn King! Golden Books Staff. 2011. (ENG.). 48p. (J). (gr. -1-2). pap. 3.99 (978-0-375-87391-1(0), Golden Bks.) Random Hse. Children's Bks.

—Super Babies! 2006. (Dora the Explorer Ser.: 18). (ENG.). 24p. (J). (gr. -1-3). pap. 3.99 (978-1-4169-1485-3(4), Simon Spotlight/Nickelodeon) Simon Spotlight/Nickelodeon.

—Súper Bebés! Inches, Alison. 2006. (Dora la Exploradora Ser.). (SPA.). 24p. (J). (gr. -1-3). pap. 3.99 (978-1-4169-2461-6(2), Libros Para Ninos) Libros Para Ninos.

—Welcome to Wonderland! (Dora the Explorer) Golden Books. 2014. (ENG.). 48p. (J). (gr. -1-2). pap. 3.99 (978-0-449-81760-5(1), Golden Bks.) Random Hse. Children's Bks.

Miller, Victoria, jt. illus. see Aikins, Dave.

Miller, Victoria, jt. illus. see Mangano, Tom.

Miller, Woody. Meet the Howlers! Sayre, April Pulley. 2010. 32p. (J). (gr. -1-2). pap. 7.95 (978-1-57091-734-9(5)); (gr. k-3). 22.44 (978-1-57091-733-2(7)) Charlesbridge Publishing, Inc.

—Tefilat Haderech: The Traveler's Prayer. 2012. (ENG.). 32p. (J). 17.95 (978-0-939144-69-3(7)) EKS Publishing Co.

—Tefilat Haderech: The Traveler's Prayer. 2012. (ENG.). 32p. (J). pap. 10.95 (978-0-939144-68-6(9)) EKS Publishing Co.

—Zishe the Strongman. Rubinstein, Robert E. 2010. (Kar-Ben Favorites Ser.). (ENG.). 32p. (J). (gr. k-3). lib. bdg. 17.95 (978-0-7613-3958-8(2), Kar-Ben Publishing) Lerner Publishing Group.

Millet, Claude & Millet, Denise. La Biblia: Los Grandes Relatos del Antiguo y del Nuevo Testamento. Marchon, Blandine. 4th ed.Tr. of Bible: Favorite Stories from the Old & New Testament. (SPA.). 158p. (J). (gr. 3-5). 25.56 (978-84-263-3249-3(8)) Vives, Luis Editorial (Edelvives) ESP. Dist: Lectorum Pubns., Inc.

Millet, Denise, jt. illus. see Millet, Claude.

Millet, Esao & Millet, Jocelyn. The Boy's Book of Adventure: The Little Guidebook for Smart & Resourceful Boys. Lecreux, Michele & Gallais, Celia. 2013. 128p. (J). (gr. 3-7). 14.99 (978-0-7641-6611-2(5), B.E.S. Publishing) Peterson's.

—The Girl's Book of Adventure: The Little Guidebook for Smart & Resourceful Girls. Lecreux, Michele & Gallais, Celia. 2013. 128p. (J). (gr. 3-7). 14.99 (978-0-7641-6610-5(7), B.E.S. Publishing) Peterson's.

Millet, Jason. Beyond Escape! Montgomery, R. A. 2006. (Choose Your Own Adventure Ser.: 15). (ENG.). 144p. (J). (gr. 4-8). per. 6.99 (978-1-933390-15-4(8), CHCL15) Chooseco LLC.

—Escape. Montgomery, R. A. 2006. (Choose Your Own Adventure Ser.: No. 8). (ENG.). 144p. (J). (gr. 4-8). per. 6.99 (978-1-933390-08-6(5), CHCL08) Chooseco LLC.

—Freedom Songs: A Tale of the Underground Railroad, 1 vol. Robbins, Trina. 2008. (Historical Fiction Ser.). (ENG.). 56p. (J). (gr. 3-6). pap. 6.25 (978-1-4342-0495-0(2), Stone Arch Bks.) Capstone.

—Indian Trail. Montgomery, R. A. 2007. (Choose Your Own Adventure - Dragonlarks Ser.). (ENG.). 80p. (J). (gr. 2-7). pap. 7.99 (978-1-933390-53-6(0)) Chooseco LLC.

—Lost on the Amazon. Montgomery, R. A. 2006. (Choose Your Own Adventure Ser.: No. 9). (ENG.). 144p. (J). (gr. 4-8). per. 6.99 (978-1-933390-09-3(3), CHCL09) Chooseco LLC.

—Prisoner of the Ant People. Montgomery, R. A. 2006. (Choose Your Own Adventure Ser.: No. 10). (ENG.). 144p. (J). (gr. 4-8). per. 6.99 (978-1-933390-10-9(7), CHCL10) Chooseco LLC.

—Punishment: Earth. Montgomery, R. A. 2010. (ENG.). 144p. (J). (gr. 4-8). pap. 6.99 (978-1-933390-36-9(0)) Chooseco LLC.

—War with the Evil Power Master. Montgomery, R. A. 2006. (Choose Your Own Adventure Ser.: No. 12). (ENG.). 144p. (J). (gr. 4-8). per. 6.99 (978-1-933390-12-3(3), CHCL12) Chooseco LLC.

Millet, Jason, jt. illus. see Lim, Ron.

Millet, Jocelyn, jt. illus. see Millet, Esao.

Millett, Melanie. Teeny Tiny Talks: Junior Primary: I Will Follow God's Plan for Me, Vol. 1. Millett, Melanie. 2004. (J). per. 12.95 (978-1-55517-778-2(6), Cedar Fort, Inc.) Cedar Fort, Inc./CFI Distribution.

Milley, Nicole. Hermie & Me under the Spaghetti Tree. Briceland, Donna. 2019. (ENG.). 30p. (J). (gr. k-2). 19.95 **(978-1-7326830-6-8(9))** Primedia eLaunch LLC.

Millican, JoAnn. Ballad of Koko-Ma. Millican, Jacob. 2003. (J). (978-1-59404-014-6(1)) Peanut Butter Publishing.

Millidge, Hattie. The Big Catch of Fish: A Read Aloud Bible Story Book for Kids - the Easter Story, Retold for Beginners. the New Testament Story of Jesus, from the Shores of Galilee to the Cross & Resurrection. Carter, Jennifer. 2019. (Inspirational Bedtime Bible Stories for Children Ser.: Vol. 2). (ENG.). 80p. (J). pap. (978-1-908567-17-8(1)) Hope Bks., Ltd.

Milligen, Emma. Rocket the Rescue Dog. Caitlin, Jessica. 2020. (ENG.). 40p. (J). **(978-1-5255-6877-0(9))**; pap. **(978-1-5255-6878-7(7))** FriesenPress.

Millingen, Stephen & Blake, Edward. History Quick Reads, No. 4. Oakden, David. 2018. (History Quick Reads Ser.). (ENG.). 64p. (J). pap. 9.99 **(978-1-871173-26-0(4))** BookLife Publishing Ltd. GBR. Dist: Independent Pubs. Group.

Million, Liz. Elephant Rides Again. Harrison, Paul. 2009. (Get Ready (Windmill Books) Ser.). 32p. (J). (gr. k-2). lib. bdg. 25.60 (978-1-60754-259-9(5)) Windmill Bks.

—Not so Silly Sausage. Gurney, Stella. 2011. 32p. pap. (978-1-84089-707-4(4)) Zero to Ten, Ltd.

Millis, Lokken. El Flamingo Felipe. Millis, Lokken. Conway, Jill Ker. 2009. (ENG.). 32p. (J). (gr. -1-3). pap. 9.95 (978-1-55591-714-2(3)) Fulcrum Publishing.

Mills. Understanding Jason. Osborn. 2009. 24p. pap. 11.49 (978-1-4389-4403-6(9)) AuthorHouse.

Mills, Beth. Ella Mckeen, Kickball Queen. Mills, Beth. 2019. (ENG.). 32p. (J). (gr. k-3). lib. bdg. 17.99 (978-1-5415-2897-0(2), Carolrhoda Bks.) Lerner Publishing Group.

Mills, Christopher. Freddy Flamingo & the Kindertown Five. Gershenson, Harold P. 2005. 27p. (J). (978-1-58987-070-3(0)) Kindermusik International.

—The Kindertown Fire Brigade. Gershenson, Harold P. 2006. (J). (978-1-58987-019-2(0)) Kindermusik International.

—Noodles from Scratch. Gershenson, Harold P. 2006. (J). (978-1-58987-007-9(7)) Kindermusik International.

Mills, Cindy. Cass Railroad Fun Book. 2007. 32p. (J). pap. 2.95 (978-0-929915-74-6(7)) Headline Bks., Inc.

Mills, Faythe. The Captain's Hat. Mercier, Deborah. 2007. 32p. (J). 17.99 (978-0-9799410-0-9(8)) Minnewaska Pr.

Mills, Jasmine. Am I Black or Am I White? Whaler, Norman. 2018. (ENG.). 30p. (J). (gr. k-2). 19.99 (978-1-948131-08-7(0)) Whaler, Norman / Beneath Another Sky Bks.

—Auntie's Lullaby. Senat, Stacey. 2018. (ENG.). 22p. (J). 16.99 (978-0-692-17262-9(9)) Bee Instinctive.

—Blueberry Lu. Goff, Lisa. 2018. (ENG.). 40p. (J). pap. 13.95 (978-1-64096-207-1(7)) Newman Springs Publishing, Inc.

—Blueberry Lu Learns to Cook. Goff, Lisa. 2019. (ENG.). 34p. (J). pap. 12.95 (978-1-64096-928-5(4)) Newman Springs Publishing, Inc.

—Home: Casa. Scott, Sandra Elaine. 2018. (ENG.). 52p. (J). (gr. k-2). 22.00 (978-0-9969049-2-6(1)) Vision Your Dreams.

Mills, Jasmine. The Magical Day Activity Book. Scott, Sandra Elaine. 2019. (ENG.). 18p. (J). (gr. k-3). pap. 8.00 **(978-0-9969049-3-3(X))** Vision Your Dreams.

Mills, Jasmine. Puerto Rico: Its Own Land! Guerrero, Elsie. 2019. (ENG.). 34p. (J). (gr. k-6). 19.99 (978-1-7327573-3-2(X)) Elsie Publishing Co.

—Sneaky the Hairy Mountain Monster: A Christmas Holiday. Fleagane, Norma. 2018. (ENG.). 46p. (J). 21.95 (978-1-64299-597-8(5)) Christian Faith Publishing.

—Three Little Monsters & the Ghost of Wisdom Woods. Snape, Jessica. 2016. (Three Little Monsters Ser.: Vol. 1). (ENG.). (J). (gr. 3-6). pap. (978-0-9956087-0-2(9)) Doe, Jessica Snape.

—Three Little Monsters In: Gruesome Gets a Toothache. Snape, Jessica. 2016. (Three Little Monsters Ser.: Vol. 2). (ENG.). (J). (gr. 3-5). pap. (978-0-9956087-2-6(5)) Doe, Jessica Snape.

Mills, Jasmine. �Soy Negra o Soy Blanca? Whaler, Norman. Hoskins, Seraphine B., tr. 2019. (SPA.). 32p. (J). (gr. k-2). 19.99 **(978-1-948131-44-5(7))** Whaler, Norman / Beneath Another Sky Bks.

Mills, Lori. Meet Toado & Friends. Mills, Linda Sue. l.t. ed. 2008. (ENG.). 30p. (J). 20.99 (978-1-59879-246-1(6), Lifevest) Lifevest Publishing, Inc.

—Meet Toado & Friends. Brooks, Linda Sue. l.t. ed. 2008. (Toado & Friends Ser.). (ENG.). 30p. (J). (gr. -1-3). per. 11.99 (978-1-59879-314-7(4), Lifevest) Lifevest Publishing, Inc.

Mills, Meredith. Herbie's Happy Birthday! Jackson, Donte & Phillips, Athena. 2018. (Herbie Vore the Dinosaur Ser.: Vol. 1). (ENG.). 54p. (J). pap. 9.95 (978-0-578-41493-5(7)) Wicked Stepsister Productions.

Mills, Meredith E. Carnie Vore Helps with Chores. Phillips, Athena Z. 2019. (Carnie Vore Ser.: Vol. 1). (ENG.). 28p. (J). (gr. k-2). 18.99 (978-1-7331879-1-6(X)); pap. 8.99 (978-1-7331879-0-9(1)) Wicked Stepsister Productions.

—Herbie's Happy Birthday! Phillips, Athena Z. 2018. (Herbie Vore the Dinosaur Ser.: Vol. 1). (ENG.). 54p. (J). (gr. k-2). 19.95 (978-0-692-10358-6(9)) Wicked Stepsister Productions.

Mills, Tom. What Am I? Illinois. Lewis, Anne Margaret. 2011. (ENG.). 24p. (J). (gr. -1 — 1). bds. 9.99 (978-0-8075-8960-1(8), 807589608) Whitman, Albert & Co.

Millsap, Lonnie. The Cow-Pie Chronicles. Butler, James L. 2013. (ENG.). 192p. (J). (gr. 2-4). pap. 9.95 (978-1-938778-32-2(4)) Publishing Syndicate LLC.

Millward, Gwen. How Do You Hug a Porcupine? Isop, Laurie. 2011. (ENG.). 32p. (J). (gr. -1-1). 16.99 (978-1-4424-1291-0(7), Simon & Schuster Bks. For Young Readers) Simon & Schuster Bks. For Young Readers.

—The Snuggle Sandwich. Doyle, Malachy. 2013. 32p. (J). (gr. -1-k). pap. 9.99 (978-1-84939-420-8(2)) Andersen Pr. GBR. Dist: Independent Pubs. Group.

—Stories from Bug Garden. Moser, Lisa. 2016. 32p. (J). (gr. -1-3). 16.99 (978-0-7636-6534-0(7)) Candlewick Pr.

Millward, Hayley. Emerson Learns about Surgery. May, Erica. 2013. (ENG.). (J). (gr. -1-3). 14.95 (978-1-62086-279-7(4)) Mascot Bks., Inc.

Milne, Alex & Ruffolo, Rob. Mix & Match. Roe, David & Reader's Digest Editors. 2007. (ENG.). 12p. (J). (gr. -1-1). bds. 14.99 (978-0-7944-1286-9(6)) Reader's Digest Assn., Inc., The.

Milne, Alex & Salgado, Jimbo. Transformers: IDW Collection Phase Two Volume 3, 3. Roberts, James et al. 2016. (IDW Collection Phase Two Ser.: 3). (ENG.). 332p. 49.99 (978-1-63140-540-2(3), 9781631405402) Idea & Design Works, LLC.

Milne, April dela Noche. The Blue Road: A Fable of Migration. 2019. (ENG.). 128p. (J). pap. 18.95 (978-1-55152-777-2(4)) Arsenal Pulp Pr. CAN. Dist: Consortium Bk. Sales & Distribution.

Milne, David. I Spy with My Little Eye: Baseball. Herzog, Brad. 2011. (I Spy with My Little Eye Ser.). (ENG.). 32p. (J). (gr. 1-4). 15.99 (978-1-58536-496-1(7), 202195) Sleeping Bear Pr.

Milne, David, photos by. I Spy with My Little Eye - Hockey. Napier, Matt. 2008. (ENG., 32p. (J). (gr. k-6). 13.95 (978-1-58536-365-0(0)) Sleeping Bear Pr.

Milne, Jessica. Jeremy & the Enchanted Theater. Citra, Becky. 2004. 64p. (J). lib. bdg. 20.00 (978-1-4242-1258-3(8)) Fitzgerald Bks.

—Jeremy & the Enchanted Theater, 1 vol. Citra, Becky. 2004. (Orca Echoes Ser.). (ENG.). 64p. (J). (gr. 1-3). pap. 6.95 (978-1-55143-322-6(2)) Orca Bk. Pubs. USA.

—Jeremy & the Fantastic Flying Machine, 1 vol. Citra, Becky. 2008. (Orca Echoes Ser.). (ENG.). 64p. (J). (gr. 1-3). pap. 6.95 (978-1-55143-950-1(6)) Orca Bk. Pubs. USA.

—Jeremy & the Golden Fleece, 1 vol. Citra, Becky. 2007. (Orca Echoes Ser.). (ENG.). 64p. (J). (gr. 1-3). per. 6.95 (978-1-55143-657-9(4)) Orca Bk. Pubs. USA.

Milne, Terry. Anxious Charlie to the Rescue. Milne, Terry. 2019. (ENG.). 32p. (J). (gr. -1-1). 16.99 (978-1-5362-0916-7(3)) Candlewick Pr.

Milne, Veronika. The Pink Purse. Pehar, Julie. 2016. (ENG.). (J). pap. (978-1-4602-9887-9(X)) FriesenPress.

Milner, Charlotte. B Is for Bee. Milner, Charlotte. 2020. (ENG.). 16p. (J). (— 1). bds. 7.99 (978-1-4654-9053-7(1), DK Children) Dorling Kindersley Publishing, Inc.

—The Bat Book. Milner, Charlotte. 2020. (ENG.). 48p. (J). (gr. k-3). 15.99 (978-1-4654-9049-0(3), DK Children) Dorling Kindersley Publishing, Inc.

—Peek & Seek. Milner, Charlotte. Dorling Kindersley Publishing Staff. 2018. (ENG.). 18p. (J). (gr. -1-1). bds. 12.99 (978-1-4654-6865-9(X), DK Children) Dorling Kindersley Publishing, Inc.

—The Sea Book. Milner, Charlotte. 2019. (ENG.). 48p. (J). (gr. k-3). 15.99 (978-1-4654-7882-5(5), DK Children) Dorling Kindersley Publishing, Inc.

Milner, Elizabeth B. Canoe Trip. Beasley, David R. 2006. 129p. (YA). per. 15.00 (978-0-915317-21-9(4)) Davus Publishing.

Milner, Fran & Brewer, Trish. Astrology for Regular People. Pluto Project Staff & Semkiw, Walter. 2007. (For Regular People Ser.). (ENG.). 198p. pap. 24.95 (978-0-9662982-7-7(6)) Pluto Project.

Milner, Kate. Overheard in a Tower Block: Poems. Coelho, Joseph. 2017. (ENG.). 112p. (J). (gr. 3-7). pap. 10.99 (978-1-910959-58-9(8)) Otter-Barry Bks. GBR. Dist: Independent Pubs. Group.

Milord, Susan. Pebble: A Story about Belonging. Milord, Susan. 2007. (ENG.). 32p. (J). (gr. -1-2). 15.99 (978-0-06-085807-0(9)) HarperCollins Pubs.

Milosevic, Tamara. The Wash Cloth & the Turtle. Knight, Deidre Denise. 2013. 36p. 17.95 (978-0-9893091-2-7(6)) Cube Marketing.

Milstrey, Dawn Bourdeau. I Can Sleep Alone. Mahr, Frank J. 2013. 34p. pap. 6.99 (978-1-4575-1895-9(3)) Dog Ear Publishing, LLC.

Miltenberger, Dave & Miltenberger, Jeri. Bessie's Little Mouse Day Care. Johnson, Gerald J. J. 2012. 32p. pap. 24.95 (978-1-62709-430-6(X)) America Star Bks.

Miltenberger, Dave, jt. illus. see Miltenberger, Jeri.

Miltenberger, Dave & Jeri. Officer Buck MacDuck. Johnson, Gerald J. J. 2013. 24p. pap. 24.95 (978-1-62709-429-0(6)) America Star Bks.

Miltenberger, Jeri & Miltenberger, Dave. Buffy Bunny. Johnson, Gerald J. J. 2011. 32p. pap. 24.95 (978-1-4512-5292-7(7)) America Star Bks.

—Miss Spinny, the Spider. Johnson, Gerald Jj. 2012. 24p. 24.95 (978-1-4626-6488-7(1)) America Star Bks.

—Misty's Christmas Present, 1 vol. Johnson, Gerald J. J. 2010. 32p. 24.95 (978-1-4512-1330-0(1)) PublishAmerica, Inc.

Miltenberger, Jeri, jt. illus. see Miltenberger, Dave.

M

Miltenberger, Jeri and Dave. Betty, the Chubby Butterfly. Johnson, Gerald J. J. 2011. 24p. pap. 24.95 (978-1-4489-3990-9(9)) America Star Bks.

Milton, Stephanie. More Adventures with the Bury Road Girls: Stories from the Bruce Peninsula. Jansen, Donna. 2018. (ENG.). 122p. (J). (gr. 2-5). pap. (978-1-4866-1750-0(6)) Word Alive Pr.

Milway, Alex. Pigsticks & Harold & the Incredible Journey. Milway, Alex. (Candlewick Sparks Ser.). 84p. (J). (gr. k-4). 2015. pap. 4.99 (978-0-7636-8105-0(9)); 2014. (ENG.). 12.99 (978-0-7636-6615-6(7)) Candlewick Pr.

—Pigsticks & Harold & the Pirate Treasure. Milway, Alex. (Candlewick Sparks Ser.). (ENG.). 64p. (J). (gr. k-4). 2018. pap. 5.99 (978-0-7636-9960-4(8)); 2016. 12.99 (978-0-7636-8157-9(1)) Candlewick Pr.

—Pigsticks & Harold & the Tuptown Thief. Milway, Alex. (Candlewick Sparks Ser.). (ENG.). 80p. (J). (gr. k-4). 2017. pap. 4.99 (978-0-7636-9400-5(2)); 2015. 12.99 (978-0-7636-7809-8(0)) Candlewick Pr.

—Pigsticks & Harold & the Tuptown Thief. Milway, Alex. ed. 2017. (Pigsticks & Harold Ser.). (ENG.). (J). (gr. k-4). lib. bdg. 13.55 (978-0-606-39840-4(6)) Turtleback.

—Pigsticks & Harold Lost in Time! Milway, Alex. 2017. (Pigsticks & Harold Ser.). (ENG.). 64p. (J). (gr. k-4). 12.99 (978-0-7636-8186-9(5)) Candlewick Pr.

—Terror of the Deep: Armed, Dangerous & Covered in Fur! Milway, Alex. 2013. (ENG.). 256p. (J). pap. 5.99 (978-1-61067-075-3(2)) Kane Miller.

Miminoshvili, Ana. Adelita, a Sea Turtle's Journey. Goebel, Jenny. 2020. (ENG.). 32p. (J). (gr. -1-3). 16.99 (978-0-8075-8114-8(3), 0807581143) Whitman, Albert & Co.

Mims, Ashley. The Emperor's New Clothes. Namm, Diane. 2014. (Silver Penny Stories Ser.). (ENG.). 48p. (J). (gr. -1-1). 4.95 (978-1-4027-8428-6(7)) Sterling Publishing Co., Inc.

—The Little Mermaid. McFadden, Deanna & Andersen, Hans. 2013. (Silver Penny Stories Ser.). 48p. (J). (gr. -1-1). 4.95 (978-1-4027-8336-4(1)) Sterling Publishing Co., Inc.

Mims, Ashley & Sansom, Fiona. Rapunzel. McFadden, Deanna. 2012. (Silver Penny Stories Ser.). 48p. (J). (gr. -1-1). 4.95 (978-1-4027-8338-8(8)) Sterling Publishing Co., Inc.

Min, Eun-Jeong. Un Río de Piedras de Lava Rojas y Calientes / a River of Red, Hot Lava Stones. So, Hyeon. 2018. (SPA.). 32p. (J). (gr. 3-7). pap. 18.99 (978-1-949061-26-0(4), Altea) Penguin Random House Grupo Editorial ESP. Dist: Penguin Random Hse. LLC.

Min, Ken. Ah-Choo! Koehler, Lana & Adams, Gloria. 2016. (ENG.). 40p. (J). (gr. k-2). 14.95 (978-1-4549-1415-0(7)) Sterling Publishing Co., Inc.

—Hot, Hot Roti for Dada-Ji. Zia, F. 2011. (ENG.). 32p. (J). (gr. k-5). 17.95 (978-1-60060-443-0(9)) Lee & Low Bks., Inc.

—Love Is Love. Genhart, Michael. 2018. 32p. (J). (gr. -1-3). 18.99 (978-1-939775-13-9(2)) March 4th, Inc.

—What Does It Mean to Be an Entrepreneur? Dryden, Emma D. & DiOrio, Rana. 2016. (What Does It Mean to Be... ? Ser.: 0). 36p. (J). (gr. -1-3). 17.95 (978-1-939775-12-2(4), Little Pickle Pr.) Sourcebooks, Inc.

Min Lin, Jia. Dexter the Very Good Goat, 1 vol. Malone, Jean. 2016. (ENG.). 32p. (J). (gr. -1-3). 14.99 (978-0-7643-5051-1(X), 6834) Schiffer Publishing, Ltd.

Minagawa, Ryoji. Project Arms. Nanatsuki, Kyoichi. (Project Arms Ser.). (ENG.). Vol. 10. 2005. 216p. pap. 9.99 (978-1-4215-0073-7(6)); Vol. 12. 2006. 208p. pap. 9.99 (978-1-4215-0386-8(7)) Viz Media.

MinaLima. Bigfoot Is Missing! Lewis, J. Patrick et al. 2015. (ENG.). 40p. (J). (gr. 2-5). 17.99 (978-1-4521-1895-6(7)) Chronicle Bks. LLC.

Minalima Ltd., Minalima. Peter Pan (Illustrated with Interactive Elements) Barrie, J. M. 2015. (ENG.). 256p. 27.99 (978-0-06-236222-3(4), Harper Design) HarperCollins Pubs.

Minch, Edwin & Minch, Jason. Caminos de Baja California: Geologia y Biologica Para Su Viaje. Minch, John & Minch, Edwin, photos by. Minch, Jason, photos by. Minch, John & Ledesma Vazquez, Jorge. Ledesma Vazquez, Jorge, tr. 2003. (SPA.). 192p. per. 23.95 (978-0-9631090-2-6(2)) Minch, John Publishing.

Minch, Jason, jt. illus. see Minch, Edwin.

Minckler, Kathleen L. Bobo, Chen Odasye A / Bobo, the Sneaky Dog: Mancy's Haitian Folktale Collection. Lauture, Mireille B. 2010. 28p. pap. 12.49 (978-1-4520-6173-3(4)) AuthorHouse.

—Mancy's Haitian Folktale Collection: Father Misery. Lauture, Mireille B. 2011. 24p. pap. 12.50 (978-1-4634-3682-7(3)) AuthorHouse.

Mind Wave Inc. Strawberry Moshi's Activity Book. Mind Wave Inc. 2012. (MoshiMoshiKawaii Ser.). (ENG.). 28p. (J). (gr. -1-2). pap. 4.99 (978-0-7636-6236-3(4)) Candlewick Pr.

—Strawberry Princess Moshi's Activity Book. Mind Wave Inc. 2012. (MoshiMoshiKawaii Ser.). (ENG.). 28p. (J). (gr. -1-2). pap., act. bk. ed. 4.99 (978-0-7636-6237-0(2)) Candlewick Pr.

Mindy Liang, ミンディ･リア;. Terry Treetop & the Little Bear テリー･ツリートップとちいさなくま; Bilingual Japanese - English バイリンガル 英語 － 日本語 Carmi Tali, タリ･カーミ;. Sarah Ikeya, いけや咲良;, tr. 2019. (JPN.). 42p. (J). pap. (978-965-200-020-0(5)) Valcal Software Ltd.

Mindy Liang, ミンディ･リア;. Terry Treetop & the Little Bear テリー･ツリートップとちいさなくま; Bilingual Japanese - English バイリンガル 英語 － 日本語 Tali Carmi, タリ･カーミ;. Sarah Ikeya, いけや咲良;, tr. 2020. (JPN.). 42p. (J). (gr. k-3). (978-965-575-050-8(7)) Valcal Software Ltd.

Mineev, V. Chto Byvalo I Drugie Rasskazy. Zhitkov, Boris. 2017. (RUS.). 124p. (J). (978-5-389-09223-5(6)) RosmYn-Press, Izdatel'stvo.

Mineker, Vivian. The Road Not Taken. Frost, Robert. 2019. (ENG.). 32p. (J). (gr. 3). 17.99 (978-1-64170-107-5(2), 550107) Familius LLC.

Minekura, Kazuya. Saiyuki, 9 vols., Vol. 8. Minekura, Kazuya, creator. rev. ed. 2005. 192p. pap. 9.99 (978-1-59532-433-7(X)) TOKYOPOP, Inc.

Miner, Deb. I get Around. Miner, Deb. 2007. (ENG.). 32p. (J). bds. 11.00 (978-0-9794262-0-9(0)) do be you.

Miner, Julia. The Lighthouse Santa. Hunter, Sara Hoagland. 2011. (ENG.). 36p. (J). (gr. -1-3). 17.95 (978-1-61168-006-5(9)) Univ. Pr. of New England.

—The Unbreakable Code. Hunter, Sara Hoagland. 2007. (ENG.). 32p. (J). (gr. 1-3). per. 7.95 (978-0-87358-917-8(3)) Cooper Square Publishing Llc.

Minervini, Giuseppe. Jasmine Wants to Be: Jasmine Wants to Be. Boston, Heath James. 2017. (Jasmine Wants To... Ser.: Vol. 1). (ENG.). 52p. (J). pap. 14.95 (978-1-9815-0037-6(5)) CreateSpace Independent Publishing Platform.

Ming, Choo Hill. Space Aliens in Our School. Cowley, Joy. 2004. (ENG.). 8p. (J). (gr. 1-1). pap. 4.67 (978-1-56270-755-2(8), Dominie Elementary) Savvas Learning Co.

Mingming. Neon Genesis Evangelion Vol. 2: Campus Apocalypse, 4 vols. Mingming. 2011. (Neon Genesis Evangelion: Campus Apocalypse Ser.: 2). (ENG.). 117p. pap. 10.99 (978-1-59582-661-9(0)) Dark Horse Comics.

Mingo, Norman & Ernst, Clara. Alice Faye Paper Dolls: Glamorous Movie Star Paper Dolls & Costumes. Mingo, Norman. 2007. 8p. pap. 12.00 (978-0-9795053-0-0(5)) Paper Studio Pr.

—Bette Davis Paper Dolls. Mingo, Norman. Taliadoros, Jenny, ed. 2007. (ENG.). 16p. pap. 12.00 (978-0-9790668-2-5(4)) Paper Studio Pr.

—Navy Scouts Paper Dolls. Mingo, Norman. Taliadoros, Jenny, ed. 2007. (ENG.). 16p. pap. 12.00 (978-0-9790668-3-2(2)) Paper Studio Pr.

—Rita Hayworth Paper Dolls. Mingo, Norman. Taliadoros, Jenny, ed. 2006. 16p. pap. 12.00 (978-0-9790668-0-1(8)) Paper Studio Pr.

Mingo, Norman & Ernt, Clara. Deanna Durbin Paper Dolls. Mingo, Norman. 2007. 16p. pap. 12.00 (978-0-9790668-5-6(9)) Paper Studio Pr.

Mingus, Cathi. Fashion Disaster. Santopolo, Jill. 2016. (Sparkle Spa Ser.: 9). (ENG.). 96p. (J). (gr. 2-5). 16.99 (978-1-4814-6392-8(6), Simon & Schuster/Paula Wiseman Bks.) Simon & Schuster/Paula Wiseman Bks.

—Glam Opening! Santopolo, Jill. 2017. (Sparkle Spa Ser.: 10). (ENG.). 112p. (J). (gr. 2-5). pap. 5.99 (978-1-4814-6395-9(0), Aladdin) Simon & Schuster Children's Publishing.

—Leading Ladies. Kimmel, Elizabeth Cody. 2012. (Forever Four Ser.: 2). 224p. (J). (gr. 3-7). pap. 6.99 (978-0-448-45549-5(8), Grosset & Dunlap) Penguin Young Readers Group.

—Picture Perfect #5: All Together Now. Simmons, Cari & Burns, Laura J. 2016. (Picture Perfect Ser.: 5). (ENG.). 192p. (J). (gr. 3-7). pap. 6.99 (978-0-06-233676-7(2)) HarperCollins Pubs.

—Sami's Sleepaway Summer. Meyerhoff, Jenny. 2012. (ENG.). 128p. (J). (gr. 2-5). 18.69 (978-0-545-36267-2(9)) Scholastic, Inc.

—#1 Forever Four. Kimmel, Elizabeth Cody. 2012. (Forever Four Ser.: 1). (ENG.). 224p. (J). (gr. 3-7). pap. 6.99 (978-0-448-45548-8(X), Grosset & Dunlap) Penguin Young Readers Group.

Minguzzi, Roberto. Poppy Veut Préparer un Gâteau. Stevens, Hazel. 2018. (FRE.). 20p. (J). (gr. k-2). pap. (978-1-911424-35-2(1)) Black Wolf Edition & Publishing Ltd.

Mini Pois Etc. Maks & Mila on a Special Journey. Bakker, Merel. 2013. 54p. (978-2-9700865-0-5(6)) Mila Publishing, Merel Bakker.

Minick, Mike. Doc, Willie, & the Pack: Secrets, Gifts, Family: (a Hickory Doc's Tale) Harkey, Linda. 2019. (ENG.). 52p. (J). 28.95 (978-1-4808-8049-8(3)); pap. 20.95 (978-1-4808-8048-1(5)) Archway Publishing.

—Doc's Dog Days: A Hickory Doc's Activity Book. Harkey, Linda. 2019. (ENG.). 38p. (J). pap. 9.99 (978-1-7023-1667-5(X)) Independently Published.

Minifie, Mary Hampson. The Book on the Mysteries of Purification for Children: Book Three from the Ihya Ulum Al-Din. Ghazzali. 2017. 112p. (J). (978-1-941610-33-6(1)) Fons Vitae of Kentucky, Inc.

MiniKim, et al. Even for a Dreamer Like Me. Mariolle, Mathieu. 2010. (Nola's Worlds Ser.: 3). (ENG.). 128p. (J). (gr. 6-9). 30.60 (978-0-7613-6505-1(2)) Lerner Publishing Group.

—Ferrets & Ferreting Out. Mariolle, Mathieu. 2010. (Nola's Worlds Ser.: 2). (ENG.). 136p. (J). (gr. 6-9). 30.60 (978-0-7613-6504-4(4)) Lerner Publishing Group.

Minina, Tatiana. Charlie & Chocolate's Furry Forgiveness. Hicks, J. Suthern. Bryan, Diane, ed. 2018. (ENG.). 30p. (J). pap. 9.99 (978-0-9970778-1-0(6)) Shophar So Good.

Minina, Tatiana. Feel Brave Teaching Guide, 1 vol. McDonald, Avril. 2016. (ENG.). 64p. (C). 39.95 (978-1-78583-016-7(3)) Crown Hse. Publishing LLC.

Minina, Tatiana. The Grand Wolf, 1 vol. McDonald, Avril. 2016. (ENG.). 32p. (C). pap. 12.95 (978-1-78583-019-8(8)) Crown Hse. Publishing LLC.

Minina, Tatiana. The Wolf & the Baby Dragon, 1 vol. McDonald, Avril. 2016. (ENG.). 32p. (C). pap. 12.95 (978-1-78583-021-1(X)) Crown Hse. Publishing LLC.

—The Wolf & the Shadow Monster, 1 vol. McDonald, Avril. 2016. (ENG.). 32p. (C). pap. 12.95 (978-1-78583-018-1(X)) Crown Hse. Publishing LLC.

Minina, Tatiana. The Wolf Is Not Invited, 1 vol. McDonald, Avril. 2016. (ENG.). 32p. (C). pap. 12.95 (978-1-78583-017-4(1)) Crown Hse. Publishing LLC.

Minina, Tatiana. The Wolf's Colourful Coat, 1 vol. McDonald, Avril. 2016. (ENG.). 32p. (C). pap. 12.95 (978-1-78583-020-4(1)) Crown Hse. Publishing LLC.

Minister, Peter. The Rise of Mammals. Rake, Matthew. 2015. (Prehistoric Field Guides). (ENG.). 32p. (J). (gr. 3-6). lib. bdg. 27.99 (978-1-4677-6351-6(9), 9781467763516, Hungry Tomato ®) Lerner Publishing Group.

Minko, Alyssa. Before the Sun Wakes Up. Bindas, Rachael. 2018. (ENG.). 20p. (J). 19.99 (978-0-692-09217-0(X)) Minko, Alyssa.

Minnerly, Denise Bennett. Molly Meets Mona & Friends: A Magical Day in the Museum. 2004. (ENG.). 40p. (J). 17.95 (978-1-56290-324-4(1)) Crystal Productions.

Minnich, Matt. Sunburn: Bridging School to Home - C. Prokopchak, Ann. l.t. ed. 2003. (ENG.). 8p. (gr. k-1). pap. 7.95 (978-1-57874-014-7(2), Kaeden Bks.) Kaeden Corp.

Minns, Karen M. C. Patterns in Arithmetic: Parent/Teacher Guide & Student Workbook: Book 1. Glenn, Suki & Carpenter, Susan. 2004. 305p. (YA). spiral bd. 45.00 (978-0-9729248-2-5(5)) Pattern Pr.

—Patterns in Arithmetic 2: Parent/Teacher Guide: Book 2. Glenn, Suki & Carpenter, Susan. 2005. 260p. (gr. 2-18). spiral bd. 22.00 (978-0-9729248-3-2(3)) Pattern Pr.

Minns, Karen Marie Christa. Patterns in Arithmetic 2: Student Workbook: Book 2. Glenn, Suki & Carpenter, Susan. 2005. (ENG.). 269p. (gr. 2-18). spiral bd. (978-0-9729248-5-6(X)) Pattern Pr.

Minor, Marcin. The Lost Star. Wechterowicz, Przemyslaw. ed. 2019. 40p. (J). (gr. k). 16.95 (978-1-912537-84-6(2), Scribblers) Book Hse. GBR. Dist: Sterling Publishing Co., Inc.

Minor, Rebecca P. Dusty's Adventures: The Beginning. Akers, T. J. 2018. (Dusty's Adventures: Ser.: Vol. 1). (ENG.). 354p. (J). (gr. 4-6). pap. 14.99 (978-0-692-13912-7(5)) Peterson, Mark.

Minor, Sarah. Pillow Talk: Loving affirmations to encourage & guide your Children. 2008. (ENG.). 96p. (YA). 16.95 (978-0-9816942-0-7(9)) Beck Global Publishing.

Minor, Wendell. Abe Lincoln Remembers. Turner, Ann. 2003. (ENG.). 32p. (J). (gr. 1-4). pap. 7.99 (978-0-06-051107-4(9)) HarperCollins Pubs.

—Abraham Lincoln Comes Home. Burleigh, Robert. 2014. (ENG.). (J). (gr. 1-4). lib. bdg. 17.60 (978-1-62765-373-2(2)) Perfection Learning Corp.

—Abraham Lincoln Comes Home. Burleigh, Robert. 2009. (J). (gr. 3-5). 27.95 incl. audio (978-0-8045-6977-4(0)) Spoken Arts, Inc.

—Abraham Lincoln Comes Home. Burleigh, Robert. 2014. (ENG.). 40p. (J). (gr. 1-4). 7.99 (978-1-250-03989-7(4), 900123692) Square Fish.

—America the Beautiful. Bates, Katherine Lee. 2006. (J). (gr. -1-3). pap. incl. audio (978-1-59112-953-0(2)); pap. 39.95 incl. audio compact disk (978-1-59112-957-8(5)) Live Oak Media.

—Ben's Revolution: Benjamin Russell & the Battle of Bunker Hill. Philbrick, Nathaniel. 2017. 64p. (J). (gr. 2-4). 17.99 (978-0-399-16674-7(2), Nancy Paulsen Books) Penguin Young Readers Group.

—The Buffalo Are Back. George, Jean Craighead. 2010. (ENG.). 32p. (J). (gr. k-3). 17.99 (978-0-525-42215-0(3), Dutton Books for Young Readers) Penguin Young Readers Group.

—Cat, What Is That? Johnston, Tony. 2008. (ENG.). 32p. (J). pap. 9.95 (978-1-56792-351-3(8)) Godine, David R. Pub.

—Crowbar, the Smartest Bird in the World. George, Jean Craighead. 2015. (J). (978-0-06-000257-2(3)) HarperCollins Pubs.

—The Eagles Are Back. George, Jean Craighead. 2013. (ENG.). 32p. (J). (gr. 1-3). 17.99 (978-0-8037-3771-6(8), Dial Bks) Penguin Young Readers Group.

—Edward Hopper Paints His World. Burleigh, Robert. 2014. (ENG.). 40p. (J). (gr. k-4). 17.99 (978-0-8050-8752-9(4), 900049744, Holt, Henry & Co. Bks. For Young Readers) Holt, Henry & Co.

—Galapagos George. George, Jean Craighead. 2014. (ENG.). 40p. (J). (gr. k-3). 15.99 (978-0-06-028793-1(4)) HarperCollins Pubs.

—Galapagos Picture Book. George, Jean Craighead. Date not set. 32p. (J). (gr. k-3). 5.99 (978-0-06-443648-9(9)) HarperCollins Pubs.

—Ghost Ship. Clark, Mary Higgins. 2007. (ENG.). 40p. (J). (gr. 1-5). 19.99 (978-1-4169-3514-8(2), Simon & Schuster/Paula Wiseman Bks.) Simon & Schuster/Paula Wiseman Bks.

—Heartland. Siebert, Diane. 2015. (ENG.). 32p. (J). (gr. -1-3). 17.95 (978-1-56792-535-7(9)) Godine, David R. Pub.

—Hi, I'm Norman: The Story of American Illustrator Norman Rockwell. Burleigh, Robert. 2019. (ENG.). 48p. (J). (gr. -1-3). 18.99 (978-1-4424-9670-5(3), Simon & Schuster Bks. For Young Readers) Simon & Schuster Bks. For Young Readers.

—How to Be a Bigger Bunny. Minor, Florence. 2017. (ENG.). 32p. (J). (gr. -1-3). 14.99 (978-0-06-235255-2(5), Tegen, Katherine Bks) HarperCollins Pubs.

—If You Were a Panda Bear. Minor, Florence. 2013. (ENG.). 32p. (J). (gr. -1-3). 17.99 (978-0-06-195090-2(4), Tegen, Katherine Bks) HarperCollins Pubs.

—If You Were a Penguin. Minor, Florence F. 2009. 32p. (J). (gr. -1-2). lib. bdg. 18.89 (978-0-06-113098-4(2)) HarperCollins Pubs.

—If You Were a Penguin. Minor, Florence. 2008. (ENG.). 32p. (J). (gr. -1-2). 17.99 (978-0-06-113097-7(4), Tegen, Katherine Bks) HarperCollins Pubs.

—Into the Woods: John James Audubon Lives His Dream. Burleigh, Robert. 2011. (ENG.). 40p. (J). (gr. 1-4). pap. 19.99 (978-1-4424-5337-1(0), Atheneum Bks. for Young Readers) Simon & Schuster Children's Publishing.

—Jack London & the Klondike Gold Rush. Lourie, Peter. 2017. (ENG.). 208p. (J). 18.99 (978-0-8050-9757-3(0), 900118483, Holt, Henry & Co. Bks. For Young Readers) Holt, Henry & Co.

—Julie. George, Jean Craighead. 2019. (Julie of the Wolves Ser.: 2). (ENG.). 256p. (J). (gr. 3-7). pap. 7.99 (978-0-06-288431-2(X), Tegen, Katherine Bks) HarperCollins Pubs.

—The Last Polar Bear. George, Jean Craighead. (ENG.). 32p. (J). (gr. -1-2). 2014. pap. 7.99 (978-0-06-124069-0(9), Tegen, Katherine Bks); 2009. 16.99 (978-0-06-124067-6(2)) HarperCollins Pubs.

—The Last Train. Titcomb, Gordon. 2010. (ENG.). 32p. (J). (gr. -1-3). 19.99 (978-1-59643-164-5(4), 9781596431645) Roaring Brook Pr.

—Look to the Stars. Aldrin, Buzz. 2009. (ENG.). 40p. (J). (gr. 1-3). 18.99 (978-0-399-24721-7(1), G.P. Putnam's Sons Books for Young Readers) Penguin Young Readers Group.

—Luck: The Story of a Sandhill Crane. George, Jean Craighead. 2006. (Outdoor Adventures Ser.). 32p. (J). (gr. -1-3). (ENG.). 16.99 (978-0-06-008201-7(1), Geringer, Laura Book); 18.89 (978-0-06-008202-4(X)) HarperCollins Pubs.

—Luck: The Story of a Sandhill Crane. George, Jean Craighead. 2008. (J). (gr. k-4). 28.95 incl. audio compact disk (978-1-4301-0332-5(9)) Live Oak Media.

—A Lucky Thing: Poems & Paintings. Schertle, Alice. 2006. 28p. (J). (gr. 4-8). reprint ed. 17.00 (978-1-4223-5417-9(2)) DIANE Publishing Co.

—The Magic of Letters. Johnston, Tony. 2019. 32p. (J). (gr. -1-3). 18.99 (978-0-8234-4159-4(8), Neal Porter Bks) Holiday Hse., Inc.

—The Magical Christmas Horse. Clark, Mary Higgins. 2011. (ENG.). 40p. (J). (gr. -1-3). 19.99 (978-1-4169-9478-7(5), Simon & Schuster/Paula Wiseman Bks.) Simon & Schuster/Paula Wiseman Bks.

—Nibble Nibble. Brown, Margaret Wise. 2007. (ENG.). 32p. (J). (gr. -1-3). 17.99 (978-0-06-059208-0(7)) HarperCollins Pubs.

—Night Flight: Amelia Earhart Crosses the Atlantic. Burleigh, Robert. 2011. (ENG.). 40p. (J). (gr. -1-3). 18.99 (978-1-4169-6733-0(8), Simon & Schuster/Paula Wiseman Bks.) Simon & Schuster/Paula Wiseman Bks.

—Night Train, Night Train. Burleigh, Robert. 2018. 32p. (J). (-k). lib. bdg. 16.99 (978-1-58089-717-4(7)) Charlesbridge Publishing, Inc.

—Pumpkin Heads. 2019. (J). lib. bdg. (978-1-58089-935-2(8)) Charlesbridge Publishing, Inc.

—Rachel: The Story of Rachel Carson. Ehrlich, Amy. 2008. (ENG.). 32p. (J). (gr. -1-3). pap. 7.99 (978-0-15-206324-5(2), 1198942) Houghton Mifflin Harcourt Publishing Co.

—Reaching for the Moon. Aldrin, Buzz. (ENG.). 40p. (J). (gr. 1-4). 2008. 7.99 (978-0-06-055447-7(9), Collins); 2005. 17.99 (978-0-06-055445-3(2)) HarperCollins Pubs.

—Reaching for the Moon. Aldrin, Buzz. unabr. ed. 2005. (Picture Book Readalong Ser.). (gr. k-4). 28.95 incl. audio compact disk (978-1-59519-582-1(3)) Live Oak Media.

—The Seashore Book. Zolotow, Charlotte. 2004. (Reading Rainbow Bks.). (gr. -1-3). 17.00 (978-0-7569-4234-2(9)) Perfection Learning Corp.

—Sequoia. Johnston, Tony. 2014. (ENG.). 40p. (J). (gr. -1-3). 18.99 (978-1-59643-727-2(8), 900076125) Roaring Brook Pr.

—Shaker Hearts. Turner, Ann Warren. 2006. 35p. (J). (gr. 4-8). pap. 11.00 (978-1-4223-5856-6(9)) DIANE Publishing Co.

—Sitting Bull Remembers. Turner, Ann Warren. 2007. (ENG.). 32p. (J). (gr. 1-4). 16.99 (978-0-06-051399-3(3)) HarperCollins Pubs.

—Snowboard Twist. George, Jean Craighead. 2004. (Outdoor Adventures Ser.). (ENG.). 32p. (J). 15.99 (978-0-06-050595-0(8)) HarperCollins Pubs.

—Southwest Sunrise. Grimes, Nikki. 2020. (ENG.). 40p. (J). 18.99 (978-1-5476-0082-3(9), 900197954, Bloomsbury Children's Bks.) Bloomsbury Publishing USA.

—This Is the Earth. Shore, Diane Z. & Alexander, Jessica. 2016. (ENG.). 40p. (J). (gr. -1-3). 17.99 (978-0-06-055526-9(2)) HarperCollins Pubs.

—Tiny Bird: A Hummingbird's Amazing Journey. Burleigh, Robert. 2020. (ENG.). 40p. (J). 18.99 (978-1-62779-369-8(0), 900148125, Holt, Henry & Co. Bks. For Young Readers) Holt, Henry & Co.

—Trapped! (1 Hardcover/1 CD) A Whale's Rescue. Burleigh, Robert. 2017. (ENG.). (J). (gr. -1-1). 29.95 (978-1-4301-2684-3(1)) Live Oak Media.

—Trapped! a Whale's Rescue. Burleigh, Robert. 2018. (ENG.). 32p. (J). (gr. -1-1). pap. 8.99 (978-1-58089-559-0(X)) Charlesbridge Publishing, Inc.

—Wild Orca: The Oldest, Wisest Whale in the World. Peterson, Brenda. 2018. (ENG.). 40p. (J). 17.99 (978-1-250-11069-5(6), 900169711, Holt, Henry & Co. Bks. For Young Readers) Holt, Henry & Co.

—Willa: The Story of Willa Cather, an American Writer. Ehrlich, Amy. 2016. (ENG.). 72p. (J). (gr. 2-5). 16.99 (978-0-689-86573-2(2), Simon & Schuster Bks. For Young Readers) Simon & Schuster Bks. For Young Readers.

—The Wolves Are Back. George, Jean Craighead. 2008. (J). (gr. 1-4). 25.95 incl. audio (978-1-4301-0591-6(7)) Live Oak Media.

—The Wolves Are Back. George, Jean Craighead. 2008. (ENG.). 32p. (J). (gr. -1-3). 17.99 (978-0-525-47947-5(3), Dutton Books for Young Readers) Penguin Young Readers Group.

Minor, Wendell. America the Beautiful. Minor, Wendell. Bates, Katharine Lee. 2020. 48p. (J). (gr. -1-2). 18.99 (978-1-62354-121-7(2)) Charlesbridge Publishing, Inc.

—Christmas Tree! Minor, Wendell. Minor, Florence. 2005. (ENG.). 40p. (J). (gr. -1-3). 16.99 (978-0-06-056034-8(7), Tegen, Katherine Bks) HarperCollins Pubs.

—Daylight Starlight Wildlife. Minor, Wendell. Airgood, Ellen. 2015. 32p. (J). (gr. -1-k). 17.99 *(978-0-399-24662-3(2)*, Nancy Paulsen Books) Penguin Young Readers Group.
—How Big Could Your Pumpkin Grow? Minor, Wendell. 32p. (J). 2019. (ENG.). (— 1). bds. 7.99 *(978-0-593-10821-5(3))*; 2013. (gr. -1-k). 16.99 *(978-0-399-24684-5(3))* Penguin Young Readers Group. (Nancy Paulsen Books).
—My Farm Friends. Minor, Wendell. 2013. (ENG.). 26p. (J). (gr. -1-k). bds. 7.99 *(978-0-399-25799-5(3)*, Nancy Paulsen Books) Penguin Young Readers Group.
Minter, Daniel. Ellen's Broom. Lyons, Kelly Starling. 2012. (ENG.). 32p. (J). (gr. k-3). 17.99 *(978-0-399-25003-3(4)*, G.P. Putnam's Sons Books for Young Readers) Penguin Young Readers Group.
—Going down Home with Daddy. Lyons, Kelly Starling. 2019. (ENG.). 32p. (J). (gr. k-3). 17.99 *(978-1-56145-938-4(0))* Peachtree Publishing Co. Inc.
—So Tall Within: Sojourner Truth's Long Walk Toward Freedom. Schmidt, Gary D. 2018. (ENG.). 48p. (J). 18.99 *(978-1-62672-872-1(0)*, 900176273) Roaring Brook Pr.
—Step Right Up: How Doc & Jim Key Taught the World about Kindness, 1 vol. Bowman, Donna Janell. 2016. (ENG.). 48p. (J). (gr. 2-8). 19.95 *(978-1-62014-148-9(5))* Lee & Low Bks., Inc.
—The Women Who Caught the Babies: A Story of African American Midwives. Greenfield, Eloise. 2019. (ENG.). 32p. (J). (gr. 3-6). 17.95 *(978-0-9977720-7-4(7)*, Alazar Pr.) Royal Swan Enterprises, Inc.
Minter, Daniel & Ely, Donald. Cay & Adlee Find Their Voice. Quaglia, Russell J. & Quaglia, Cali. 2017. 48p. (J). pap. 15.95 *(978-1-4166-2505-6(4))* Association for Supervision & Curriculum Development.
Minter, Katie. The Little Baby Sequoia. French, Heidi M. 2019. (ENG.). 32p. (J). pap. 7.99 ***(978-1-7102-8192-7(8))*** Independently Published.
Minto, Monica. Notty Nectar. Koivisto, Ron. 2018. (ENG.). 138p. (J). pap. 13.49 *(978-1-5456-4481-2(0))* Salem Author Services.
Mintzi, Vali. The Girl with a Brave Heart. Jahanforuz, Rita. 2013. 40p. (J). (gr. k-5). 16.99 *(978-1-84686-929-7(3))* Barefoot Bks., Inc.
—Long Summer Nights. Appelfeld, Aharon. Green, Jeffrey, tr. 2019. 160p. (J). (gr. 5-9). 18.95 *(978-1-60980-898-3(3)*, Triangle Square) Seven Stories Pr.
—Signs in the Well. Smith, Shoham. 2019. (ENG.). 32p. (J). 22.95 *(978-1-78438-377-0(5))* Greenhill Bks. GBR. Dist: Casemate Pubs. & Bk. Distributors, LLC.
Mion, Francie. Carrie's Flight. Wickstrom, Lois. 2019. (Grandma's Closet Ser.: Vol. 1). (ENG.). 28p. (J). pap. 12.00 *(978-1-0908-2822-4(5))* Independently Published.
Mion, Francie. Loretta's Caterpillar Large Print Edition. Wickstrom, Lois. 2019. (Loretta's Insects Ser.: Vol. 4). (ENG.). 80p. (J). pap. 16.99 ***(978-1-7101-8954-4(1))*** Independently Published.
Mioroney, Tracy. A Child's Book of Parables. Froeb, Lori. 2003. 32p. (J). 15.99 *(978-0-7847-1278-8(6)*, 04344) Standard Publishing.
Miracola, Jeff. Welcome to Monster Isle. Chin, Oliver. 2008. (ENG.). 36p. (J). (gr. -1-3). 15.95 *(978-1-59702-016-9(8))* Immedium.
Miralles, Ana. Waluk. Ruiz, Emilio. ed. 2013. (ENG.). 56p. (J). (gr. 2-5). E-Book 39.99 *(978-1-4677-2057-1(7)*, 9781467720571, Graphic Universe™) Lerner Publishing Group.
Miralles, Jose & McTeigue, Jane. Christmas Star: A Light-up Shadow-Box Book. 2005. 10p. (J). (gr. k-4). reprint ed. 10.00 *(978-0-7567-9559-7(1))* DIANE Publishing Co.
Miralles, Joseph. Pride & Prejudice. Austen, Jane. 2005. (Great Illustrated Classics Ser.). 236p. (gr. 3-8). 21.35 *(978-1-59679-249-4(3))* Spotlight.
Miramon, Sabrina. Beauty & the Beast: An Interactive Fairy Tale Adventure. Doeden, Matt. 2018. (You Choose: Fractured Fairy Tales Ser.). (ENG.). 112p. (J). (gr. 3-7). lib. bdg. 32.65 *(978-1-5435-3007-0(9)*, 138604, Capstone Pr.) Capstone.
—Hansel & Gretel: An Interactive Fairy Tale Adventure. Doeden, Matt. 2017. (You Choose: Fractured Fairy Tales Ser.). (ENG.). 112p. (J). (gr. 3-7). pap. 6.95 *(978-1-5157-6952-1(6)*, 135424); lib. bdg. 32.65 *(978-1-5157-6944-6(5)*, 135418) Capstone. (Capstone Pr.).
—Snow White & the Seven Dwarfs: An Interactive Fairy Tale Adventure. Gunderson, Jessica. 2017. (You Choose: Fractured Fairy Tales Ser.). (ENG.). 112p. (J). (gr. 3-7). pap. 6.95 *(978-1-5157-6951-4(8)*, 135423); lib. bdg. 32.65 *(978-1-5157-6943-9(7)*, 135417) Capstone. (Capstone Pr.).
Miranda, Francisco. What Is My Song? Linn, Dennis et al. 2005. 32p. (J). 16.95 *(978-0-8091-6722-7(0)*, 6722-0) Paulist Pr.
Miranda, Pedro. A Collection of Street Games. Eckdahl, Judith & Eckdahl, Kathryn. O'Regan, Lucy, ed. 2005. 42p. pupil's gde. ed. 13.95 *(978-0-9767200-3-0(0))* Lesen Pub.
Miray, Yalcinkaya. Atlas the Rabbit. Caparti, Ebru. 2019. (ENG.). 40p. (J). (gr. k-2). 17.99 *(978-0-578-47635-3(5))* Caparti, Ebru.
Mireault, Bernie. The Devil Inside. Wagner, Matt. 2004. (Grendel Ser.). (ENG.). 88p. pap. 12.95 *(978-1-56971-604-5(8))* Dark Horse Comics.
Mireault, Bernie, et al. Fallout: J. Robert Oppenheimer, Leo Szilard, & the Political Science of the Atomic Bomb. Ottaviani, Jim & Lieber, Steve. 2013. (ENG.). 240p. (YA). pap. 24.95 *(978-0-9660106-3-3(9)*, 5f9237a5-22aa-4275-86dd-6f315a49c018) G T Labs.
Mirhady, Irandought. Thorn-Bush Boy: Pesare Tigh. Mirhady, Irandought. 2004. Orig. Title: Pesare Tigh. (PEO.). 63p. (YA). per. 9.95 *(978-0-9760323-0-4(9))* Mirhady, Farhad.
Mirocha, Paul. Amazing Armadillos. Mckerley, Jennifer. 2009. (Step into Reading Ser.). 48p. (J). (gr. k-3). pap. 4.99 *(978-0-375-84352-5(3)*, Random Hse. Bks. for Young Readers) Random Hse. Children's Bks.
—The Bee Tree. Cohn, Diana & Buchmann, Stephen. 2007. (ENG.). 40p. (J). (gr. 4-6). 17.95 *(978-0-938317-98-2(9))* Cinco Puntos Pr.
—Hungry Plants. Batten, Mary. 2004. (Step into Reading: Step 4 Ser.). (ENG.). 48p. (J). (gr. 1-3). lib. bdg. 16.19 *(978-0-375-92533-7(3))* Random House Publishing Group.
—Hungry Plants. Batten, Mary. 2004. (Step into Reading Ser.). 48p. (J). (gr. 2-4). pap. 4.99 *(978-0-375-82533-0(9)*, Random Hse. Bks. for Young Readers) Random Hse. Children's Bks.
—Mr Goethes Garden, 1 vol. Cohn, Diana. 2003. (ENG.). 32p. (J). 17.95 *(978-0-88010-521-7(6))* SteinerBooks, Inc.
—Platypus! Clarke, Ginjer L. 2004. (Step into Reading Ser.). 32p. (J). (gr. -1-1). pap. 3.99 *(978-0-375-82417-3(0)*, Random Hse. Bks. for Young Readers) Random Hse. Children's Bks.
Mirocha, Paul & Nicholson, Trudy. The North Atlantic Coast: A Literary Field Guide. St. Antoine, Sara, ed. 2004. (Stories from Where We Live Ser.). (ENG.). 288p. (J). pap., instr.'s gde. ed. 10.95 *(978-1-57131-643-1(4))* Milkweed Editions.
Mirocha, Paul, jt. illus. see Nicholson, Trudy.
Mirocha, Stephanie. I Wanna Be a Dinosaur! Haugen, Matt & Haugen, Marty. 2015. (ENG.). 32p. (J). (— 1). 16.95 *(978-1-57999-999-5(9))* G I A Pubns., Inc.
—My Little Book of Manatees, Vol. Marston, Hope Irvin. 2007. 32p. (J). (gr. k-5). pap. 7.95 *(978-0-89317-065-3(8)*, Windward Publishing) Finney Co., Inc.
Miroglio, Brian. Mummy, 1 vol. Stoker, Bram. 2007. (Graphic Horror Ser.). (ENG.). 32p. (J). (gr. 3-6). 29.93 *(978-1-60270-061-1(3)*, 9076, Graphic Planet - Fiction) Magic Wagon.
Mironiuc, Andreea. A Garden of Flowers: A Story about Alzheimer's. Mendez Ma, Marta Schmidt. 2019. (ENG.). 38p. (J). pap. 10.50 *(978-1-7276-7747-8(1))* CreateSpace Independent Publishing Platform.
—Mi Hermano Es Especial, Mi Hermano Tiene el Síndrome de Down: Un Cuento Acerca de Aceptación. Mendez Ma, Marta Schmidt. Urquijo, J. I., tr. 2018. (SPA.). 38p. (J). pap. 10.50 *(978-1-7275-9744-8(3))* CreateSpace Independent Publishing Platform.
—My Brother Is Special My Brother Has down Syndrome: A Story about Acceptance. Schmidt-Mendez Ma, Marta. 2018. (ENG.). 38p. (J). pap. 10.50 *(978-1-7210-7763-2(4))* CreateSpace Independent Publishing Platform.
Mirtalipova, Dinara. EtchArt: Forgotten Jungle. Wood, A. J. & Jolley, Mike. 2018. (Etchart Ser.). (ENG.). 20p. (J). (gr. 2-5). 14.99 *(978-1-78603-141-9(8)*, 302829, Wide Eyed Editions) Quarto Publishing Group UK GBR. Dist: Hachette Bk. Group.
—Etchart: Hidden Forest: Reveal the Wonders of the Wild in 9 Amazing Etchart Scenes. Wood, A. J. & Jolley, Mike. ed. 2017. (Etchart Ser.). (ENG.). 20p. (J). (gr. 2-5). 14.99 *(978-1-78603-048-1(9)*, 300631, Wide Eyed Editions) Quarto Publishing Group UK GBR. Dist: Hachette Bk. Group.
—Etchart: Secret Sea. Wood, A. J. & Jolley, Mike. 2017. (Etchart Ser.). (ENG.). 20p. (J). (gr. 2-5). 14.99 *(978-1-78603-049-8(7)*, 300638, Wide Eyed Editions) Quarto Publishing Group UK GBR. Dist: Hachette Bk. Group.
—Leila in Saffron. Guidroz, Rukhsanna. 2019. (ENG.). 32p. (J). (gr. -1-3). 17.99 *(978-1-5344-2564-4(0)*, Salaam Reads) Simon & Schuster Bks. For Young Readers.
—The Princess & the Pea. Perkins, Chloe. 2017. (Once upon a World Ser.). (ENG.). 24p. (J). (gr. -1 — 1). bds. 8.99 *(978-1-5344-0019-1(2)*, Little Simon) Little Simon.
Mirza, Yunzila. Wash Your Hands: Health Promotion for Children. Alam-Mirza, Farah. 2020. (Health Promotion Ser.: Vol. 1). (ENG.). 40p. (J). pap. 9.13 ***(978-1-7295-8142-1(0))*** CreateSpace Independent Publishing Platform.
Mish. Softly Comes the Rain. Mish. 2005. 64p. (YA). per. 5.95 *(978-0-9766597-4-7(3))* Augusta Win Publishing.
Misirlou, Ilaeira. Elias Zapple's Rhymes from the Cabbage Patch. Zapple, Elias. 2018. (ENG.). 84p. (J). (gr. 4-6). pap. *(978-1-912704-11-8(0))* Heads or Tales Pr.
—Elias Zapple's Rhymes from the Cabbage Patch: American-English Edition. Zapple, Elias. 2018. (ENG.). 84p. (J). (gr. 4-6). pap. *(978-1-912704-10-1(2))* Heads or Tales Pr.
—Jellybean the Dragon. Zapple, Elias. 2018. (Jellybean the Dragon Stories American-English Ser.: Vol. 1). (ENG.). 82p. (J). (gr. 4-6). pap. *(978-1-912704-14-9(5))*; pap. *(978-1-912704-15-6(3))* Heads or Tales Pr.
Miskimins, Jason. The Bug in the Jug Wants a Hug. Cleary, Brian P. 2009. (Sounds Like Reading ® Ser.: 1). (ENG.). (gr. -1-2). pap. 39.62 *(978-0-7613-4700-2(3))* Lerner Publishing Group.
—The Clown in the Gown Drives the Car with the Star. Cleary, Brian P. 2009. (Sounds Like Reading ® Ser.: 8). (ENG.). (gr. -1-2). pap. 39.62 *(978-0-7613-4707-1(0))* Lerner Publishing Group.
—The Frail Snail on the Trail. Cleary, Brian P. 2009. (Sounds Like Reading ® Ser.: 4). (ENG.). (gr. -1-2). pap. 39.62 *(978-0-7613-4703-3(8))* Lerner Publishing Group.
—The Nice Mice in the Rice. Cleary, Brian P. 2009. (Sounds Like Reading ® Ser.: 3). (ENG.). (gr. -1-2). pap. 39.62 *(978-0-7613-4702-6(X))* Lerner Publishing Group.
—The Peaches on the Beaches. Cleary, Brian P. 2009. (Sounds Like Reading ® Ser.: 7). (ENG.). (gr. -1-2). pap. 39.62 *(978-0-7613-4706-4(2))* Lerner Publishing Group.
—Stop, Drop, & Flop in the Slop. Cleary, Brian P. 2009. (Sounds Like Reading ® Ser.: 2). (ENG.). (gr. -1-2). pap. 39.62 *(978-0-7613-4701-9(1))* Lerner Publishing Group.
—The Thing on the Wing Can Sing. Cleary, Brian P. 2009. (Sounds Like Reading ® Ser.: 5). (ENG.). (gr. -1-2). pap. 39.62 *(978-0-7613-4704-0(6))* Lerner Publishing Group.
—The Thing on the Wing Can Sing: Short Vowel Sounds & Consonant Digraphs. Cleary, Brian P. & Maday, Alice M. 2009. (Sounds Like Reading ® Ser.: 5). (ENG.). 32p. (J). (gr. -1-2). lib. bdg. 23.99 *(978-0-8225-7639-6(2)*, Millbrook Pr.) Lerner Publishing Group.
—Whose Shoes Would You Choose. Cleary, Brian P. 2009. (Sounds Like Reading ® Ser.: 6). (ENG.). (gr. -1-2). pap. 39.62 *(978-0-7613-4705-7(4))* Lerner Publishing Group.
—Whose Shoes Would You Choose? A Long Vowel Sounds Book with Consonant Digraphs. Cleary, Brian P. & Maday, Alice M. 2009. (Sounds Like Reading ® Ser.: 6). (ENG.). 32p. (J). (gr. -1-2). lib. bdg. 23.99 *(978-0-8225-7640-2(6)*, Millbrook Pr.) Lerner Publishing Group.
Missey, Erica. The Dog Who Remembered Tomorrow. Kesselman, Eric. 2019. (Animalosophy Ser.: Vol. 5). (ENG.). 32p. (J). pap. 9.99 ***(978-1-7130-1338-9(X))*** Independently Published.
Missey, Erica. The Pooch Chronicles. Schoen, Clint. 2018. (ENG.). 80p. (J). pap. 13.99 *(978-1-947239-11-1(2))* Best Publishing Co.
MissPaty. May's Wild Walk, No. 1. Sacks, Nathan & Paty, Miss. 2017. (Whiskers Sisters Ser.: 1). 40p. (J). (gr. k-3). 26.65 *(978-1-5124-2527-7(3)*, 9781512425277, Graphic Universe™) Lerner Publishing Group.
Misstigri. Princesses of World. Goyer, Katell. 2009. 3p. (J). (gr. -1-3). 17.99 *(978-0-8437-1445-6(X))* Hammond World Atlas Corp.
Mistry, Nilesh. A Calendar of Festivals: Celebrations from Around the World. Gilchrist, Cherry & Cann, Helen. 2005. 80p. (J). pap. 12.99 *(978-1-84148-970-4(0))* Barefoot Bks., Inc.
—Don't Bully Me. Robert, Na'ima bint. 2004. (POL, ENG & KUR.). 24p. (J). pap. *(978-1-84444-558-5(5))* Mantra Lingua.
—Fabulous Story of Fashion. Daynes, Katie. 2006. (Young Reading Series 2 Gift Bks.). 64p. (J). (gr. 2-5). 8.99 *(978-0-7945-1263-7(1)*, Usborne) EDC Publishing.
—Marie Antoinette. Daynes, Katie. 2005. 64p. (J). 8.95 *(978-0-7945-1049-7(3)*, Usborne) EDC Publishing.
—Nico's Octopus. Pitcher, Caroline. 2003. (ENG.). 32p. (J). (gr. k-3). 15.95 *(978-1-56656-483-0(2)*, Crocodile Bks.) Interlink Publishing Group, Inc.
—The Revealing Story of Underwear. Daynes, Katie. 2006. (Young Reading Series 2 Gift Bks.). 64p. (J). (gr. 2-5). 8.99 *(978-0-7945-1352-8(2)*, Usborne) EDC Publishing.
—Stories from the Silk Road. Gilchrist, Cherry. 2005. (ENG.). 80p. (J). pap. 12.99 *(978-1-84148-804-2(6))* Barefoot Bks., Inc.
—The Story of Divaali. Verma, Jatinder. 2007. 40p. (J). (gr. -1-3). pap. 7.99 *(978-1-84686-131-4(4))* Barefoot Bks., Inc.
—The Swirling Hijaab. Robert, Na'ima Bint. 2004. 24p. (J). *(978-1-85269-910-9(8))*; (ARA & ENG.). pap. *(978-1-85269-119-6(0))*; (URD & ENG.). pap. *(978-1-85269-143-1(3))*; (BEN & ENG.). pap. *(978-1-85269-160-8(3))*; (PER & ENG.). pap. *(978-1-85269-163-9(8))*; (GER & ENG.). pap. *(978-1-85269-165-3(4))*; (ITA & ENG.). pap. *(978-1-85269-167-7(0))*; (PAN & ENG.). pap. *(978-1-85269-178-3(6))*; (POR & ENG.). pap. *(978-1-85269-179-0(4))*; (SER & ENG.). pap. *(978-1-85269-180-6(8))*; (SOM & ENG.). pap. *(978-1-85269-181-3(6))*; (SPA & ENG.). pap. *(978-1-85269-182-0(4))*; (TAM & ENG.). pap. *(978-1-85269-188-2(3))*; (TUR & ENG.). pap. *(978-1-85269-189-9(1))*; (CZE & ENG.). pap. *(978-1-85269-629-0(X))* Mantra Lingua.
—The Swirling Hijaab: Le Foulard Qui Tourbillonne. Robert, Naima Bint, tr. 2004. (FRE & ENG.). 24p. (J). pap. *(978-1-85269-164-6(6))* Mantra Lingua.
—The Swirling Hijaab: Percja Valezuese. Robert, Na'ima Bint, tr. 2004. (ALB & ENG.). 24p. (J). pap. *(978-1-85269-105-9(0))* Mantra Lingua.
Mistry, Nilesh, jt. illus. see Mayo, Diana.
Mistry, Poonam. You're Safe with Me. Soundar, Chitra. 2018. 32p. (J). (gr. -1-2). 17.99 *(978-1-911373-29-2(3))* Lantana Publishing GBR. Dist: Lerner Publishing Group.
—You're Snug with Me. Soundar, Chitra. 2018. 40p. (J). (gr. k-2). 17.99 *(978-1-911373-47-6(1))* Lantana Publishing GBR. Dist: Lerner Publishing Group.
—You're Strong with Me. Soundar, Chitra. 2019. 40p. (J). (gr. k-2). 17.99 *(978-1-911373-75-9(7))* Lantana Publishing GBR. Dist: Lerner Publishing Group.
Mitcham, Naomi. Le Roi de Glace / Mkumiey Eleke'wit / the Ice King. Gallant, Corinne. Mitcham, Allison, tr. 2012. (FRE.). 26p. (J). pap. *(978-2-923518-64-0(0))* Bouton d'or Acadie.
Mitcham, Sherry. The Adventures of Snap. Daba, Levidia. 2018. (ENG.). 28p. (J). 22.99 *(978-1-5456-5336-4(4))*; pap. 12.49 *(978-1-5456-5335-7(6))* Salem Author Services.
Mitchell, Anne. How to Grow a Hippo! Schantz, Becky. 2014. (ENG.). (J). (gr. -1-3). 14.95 *(978-1-62086-609-2(9))* Mascot Bks., Inc.
Mitchell, Anthony W. The Adventures of Sammy the Squirrel: Buying Shoes. Terrell, Andrea M. 2008. (ENG.). 28p. pap. 13.99 *(978-1-4343-5608-6(6))* AuthorHouse.
Mitchell, Carrie. Feed Me! A Hungry Goat's Journey. Mitchell, Carrie. 2019. (ENG.). 44p. (J). (gr. k-4). 17.99 *(978-0-9997737-1-0(2))* Nordikgirl.
Mitchell, David. A Present for Paul. Ashley, Bernard. 2004. 28p. (J). *(978-1-85269-359-6(2))*; *(978-1-85269-360-2(6))* Mantra Lingua.
Mitchell, Derrick Lee. Miyah & Koala's First Day. Mitchell, Derrick Lee. Howard, Assuanta. 2012. 30p. 18.00 *(978-1-934947-69-2(5))* Asta Publications, LLC.
Mitchell, Gail A., photos by. Learning English the Cultural Way. Mitchell, Gail A. 2004. 40p. (J). per. 20.00 *(978-0-9653308-9-3(3))* Africana Homestead Legacy Pubs., Inc.
Mitchell, Ged. The Snowman's Coat & Other Science Questions, 4 vols. Naylor, Brenda & Naylor, Stuart. (ENG.). 32p. (J). pap. *(978-0-340-75755-0(8))* Hodder & Stoughton.
Mitchell, Hazel. Animally. Parrish Sutton, Lynn. 2016. (ENG.). 30p. (J). 11.99 *(978-1-61067-345-7(X))* Kane Miller.
—Borrowing Bunnies: A Surprising True Tale of Fostering Rabbits. Lord, Cynthia. 2019. (ENG.). 40p. (J). 17.99 *(978-0-374-30841-4(1)*, 900186026, Farrar, Straus & Giroux (BYR)) Farrar, Straus & Giroux.
—Cassie & Mr. Ant. Powell, Glenda. 2008. 30p. (J). (gr. -1-3). per. 7.95 *(978-0-9779445-6-9(5))* Zoe Life Publishing.
—Do Fairies Bring the Spring, Vol. Walsh, Liza Gardner. 2019. (ENG.). 22p. (J). (gr. -1-12). bds. 8.95 *(978-1-60893-660-1(0))* Down East Bks.
—Double-Crossed at Cactus Flats: An Up2 U Western Adventure, 1 vol. Wallace, Rich. 2013. (Up2U Adventures Ser.). (ENG.). 80p. (J). (gr. 2-5). lib. bdg. 29.93 *(978-1-61641-966-0(0)*, 15215, Calico Chapter Bks.) ABDO Publishing Co.
—F Is for Feelings. Millar, Goldie & Berger, Lisa A. 2014. (ENG.). 40p. (J). (gr. -1-3). 15.99 *(978-1-57542-475-0(4))* Free Spirit Publishing, Inc.
—Fairies 1, 2, 3. Walsh, Liza Gardner. 2017. (ENG.). 24p. (J). (gr. -1 — 1). bds. 7.95 *(978-1-60893-951-0(0))* Down East Bks.
—The Fall Fairy Gathering. Walsh, Liza Gardner. 2020. (ENG.). 32p. (J). (gr. -1-3). 17.95 *(978-1-60893-592-5(2))* Down East Bks.
—Hidden New Jersey. Barth, Linda J. 2012. 32p. (J). (gr. 1-4). 17.95 *(978-1-934133-23-1(X))*; pap. 8.95 *(978-1-934133-40-8(X))* Charlesbridge Publishing, Inc. (Mackinac Island Press, Inc.).
—How Do Fairies Have Fun in the Sun?, Vol. Walsh, Liza Gardner. 2019. (ENG.). 22p. (J). (gr. -1 — 1). bds. 8.95 *(978-1-60893-661-8(9))* Down East Bks.
—Imani's Moon. Brown-Wood, Janay. 2014. (ENG.). 32p. (J). (gr. 1-4). pap. 7.95 *(978-1-934133-58-3(2)*, Mackinac Island Press, Inc.) Charlesbridge Publishing, Inc.
—Imani's Moon (1 Hardcover/1 CD) Brown-Wood, Janay. 2015. (ENG.). (J). (gr. 1-4). audio compact disk 32.95 *(978-1-4301-1900-5(4))* Live Oak Media.
—Imani's Moon (4 Paperback/1 CD) Brown-Wood, Janay. 2015. (ENG.). (J). (gr. 1-4). audio compact disk 44.95 *(978-1-4301-1901-2(2))* Live Oak Media.
—Kenya's Art. Trice, Linda. 2016. 32p. (J). (gr. -1-3). 16.95 *(978-1-57091-848-3(1))* Charlesbridge Publishing, Inc.
—Luke's 1st Haircut. Marek, Catherine. ed. 2007. (ENG.). 32p. (J). (gr. -1-3). per. *(978-0-9748251-5-1(8))* Zoe Life Publishing.
—One Word Pearl. Groeneweg, Nicole. 2013. 32p. (J). (gr. k-3). 17.95 *(978-1-934133-53-8(1))*; pap. 7.95 *(978-1-934133-54-5(X))* Charlesbridge Publishing, Inc.
—Sara's 1st Haircut, Marek, Catherine. l.t. ed. 2007. (ENG.). 32p. (J). (gr. -1-3). per. *(978-0-9748251-3-7(1))* Zoe Life Publishing.
—Tickles the Bear Goes on a Cruise, 1 bk. Pighin, Marcel. 2006. 48p. (J). per. 10.49 *(978-0-9776679-7-0(9))* MP2ME Enterprise.
—Too Many Freckles! Gomez, Sally. 2008. (ENG.). 32p. pap. *(978-1-934363-32-4(4))* Zoe Life Publishing.
—Why Am I Here? A Story about Becoming The-Best-Version-Of-Yourself! Kelly, Matthew. 2009. 60p. 17.99 *(978-0-9841318-0-8(9)*, Little Sparrow) Blue Sparrow Bks.
Mitchell, Hazel. Toby. Mitchell, Hazel. 2016. 40p. (J). (gr. -1-1). 16.99 *(978-0-7636-8093-0(1))* Candlewick Pr.
Mitchell, Hazle. The Naughty Grandmother. Bradley, Judy. 2012. (J). *(978-0-615-57032-7(1))* Bradley, Judy & Assocs., LLC.
Mitchell, Hetty. Martin Luther King Jr. Day, 2nd Edition. Lowery, Linda. rev. ed. 2003. (On My Own Holidays Ser.). (ENG.). 56p. (J). (gr. 2-4). pap. 7.99 *(978-1-57505-709-5(3)*, First Avenue Editions) Lerner Publishing Group.
Mitchell, Jana Christy, jt. illus. see Christy, Jana.
Mitchell, Jason. Kids under$Tanding Money. Norwood, R. Edward. 2009. (ENG.). 46p. (YA). pap. 19.95 *(978-1-4389-4053-3(X))* AuthorHouse.
Mitchell, Jerica Webster. In the Presence of a King. Webster, Angela. 2012. (ENG.). 66p. pap. 28.99 *(978-1-4685-5442-7(5))* AuthorHouse.
Mitchell, Jim. Great Explorers: Christopher Columbus & Neil Armstrong: Band 09/Gold (Collins Big Cat) Guillain, Charlotte. 2015. (Collins Big Cat Ser.). (ENG.). 24p. (J). (gr. 2-2). pap. 9.99 *(978-0-00-759119-0(5))* HarperCollins Pubs. Ltd. GBR. Dist: Independent Pubs. Group.
Mitchell, Jon. Rowan the Red Squirrel, 30 vols. Rickards, Lynne. 2018. (ENG.). 32p. (J). 11.95 *(978-1-78250-477-1(X)*, Kelpies) Floris Bks. GBR. Dist: Consortium Bk. Sales & Distribution.
—Skye the Puffling: A Baby Puffin's Adventure, 30 vols. Rickards, Lynne. 2016. (ENG.). 32p. (J). pap. 11.95 *(978-1-78250-255-5(6)*, Kelpies) Floris Bks. GBR. Dist: Consortium Bk. Sales & Distribution.
—Skye the Puffling: A Wee Puffin Board Book, 30 vols. Rickards, Lynne. 2018. (ENG.). 14p. (J). 9.95 *(978-1-78250-487-0(7)*, Kelpies) Floris Bks. GBR. Dist: Consortium Bk. Sales & Distribution.
Mitchell Jr., Leonard. Stray's Great Adventure. Alexander, Troas James. 2010. 40p. pap. 15.95 *(978-1-60844-200-3(4))* Dog Ear Publishing, LLC.
Mitchell, Judith. A Dragon in the Family. Koller, Jackie French. 2018. (Dragonling Ser.: 2). (ENG.). 96p. (J). (gr. 2-5). 16.99 *(978-1-5344-0065-8(6))*; pap. 5.99 *(978-1-5344-0064-1(8))* Simon & Schuster Children's Publishing. (Aladdin).
—Dragon Quest. Koller, Jackie French. 2018. (Dragonling Ser.: 3). (ENG.). 128p. (J). (gr. 2-5). 16.99 *(978-1-5344-0068-9(0))*; pap. 5.99 *(978-1-5344-0067-2(2))* Simon & Schuster Children's Publishing. (Aladdin).
—Dragon Trouble. Koller, Jackie French. 2019. (Dragonling Ser.: 5). (ENG.). 128p. (J). (gr. 2-5). 16.99 *(978-1-5344-0074-0(5))*; pap. 5.99 *(978-1-5344-0073-3(7))* Simon & Schuster Children's Publishing. (Aladdin).
—The Dragonling. Koller, Jackie French. 2018. (Dragonling Ser.: 1). (ENG.). 80p. (J). (gr. 2-5). 16.99 *(978-1-5344-0062-7(1))*; pap. 5.99 *(978-1-5344-0061-0(3))* Simon & Schuster Children's Publishing. (Aladdin).
—The Dragonling 4 Books In 1! The Dragonling; a Dragon in the Family; Dragon Quest; Dragons of Krad. Koller, Jackie French. 2019. (Dragonling Ser.). (ENG.). 368p. (J). (gr. 1-4). 14.99 *(978-1-5344-5395-1(4)*, Aladdin) Simon & Schuster Children's Publishing.

M

Mitchell, Judith. The Dragonling Complete Collection: The Dragonling; a Dragon in the Family; Dragon Quest; Dragons of Krad; Dragon Trouble; Dragons & Kings. Koller, Jackie French. ed. 2020. (Dragonling Ser.). (ENG.). 672p. (J). (gr. 2-5). pap. 35.99 ***(978-1-5344-5996-0(0)***, Aladdin) Simon & Schuster Children's Publishing.

—Dragons & Kings. Koller, Jackie French. 2020. (Dragonling Ser.: 6). (ENG.). 112p. (J). (gr. 2-5). 17.99 ***(978-1-5344-0077-1(X))***; pap. 5.99 ***(978-1-5344-0076-4(1))*** Simon & Schuster Children's Publishing. (Aladdin).

Mitchell, Judith. Dragons of Krad. Koller, Jackie French. 2019. (Dragonling Ser.: 4). (ENG.). 128p. (J). (gr. 2-5). 16.99 *(978-1-5344-0071-9(0))*; pap. 5.99 *(978-1-5344-0070-2(2))* Simon & Schuster Children's Publishing. (Aladdin).

Mitchell, Laura. The Creatures #3, 1 vol. O'Neill, Corey. 2016. (Gladiator Island Ser.). (ENG.). 216p. (J). (gr. 6-12). lib. bdg. 28.56 *(978-1-68076-269-3(9)*, 21507, Epic Edge) EPIC Pr.

—The Main Event #2, 1 vol. O'Neill, Corey. 2016. (Gladiator Island Ser.). (ENG.). 216p. (YA). (gr. 6-12). lib. bdg. 28.56 *(978-1-68076-268-6(0)*, 21505, Epic Edge) EPIC Pr.

—The Revolt #6, 1 vol. O'Neill, Corey. 2016. (Gladiator Island Ser.). (ENG.). 216p. (YA). (gr. 6-12). lib. bdg. 28.56 *(978-1-68076-272-3(9)*, 21513, Epic Edge) EPIC Pr.

—The Triangle #4, 1 vol. O'Neill, Corey. 2016. (Gladiator Island Ser.). (ENG.). 216p. (J). (gr. 6-12). lib. bdg. 28.56 *(978-1-68076-270-9(2)*, 21509, Epic Edge) EPIC Pr.

—The War Design #5, 1 vol. O'Neill, Corey. 2016. (Gladiator Island Ser.). (ENG.). 216p. (YA). (gr. 6-12). lib. bdg. 28.56 *(978-1-68076-271-6(0)*, 21511, Epic Edge) EPIC Pr.

Mitchell, Lori. Holly Bloom's Garden. Ashman, Sarah & Parent, Nancy. (ENG.). 32p. (J). (gr. k-3). 2008. pap. 7.95 *(978-0-9799746-0-1(7))*; 2004. 15.95 *(978-0-9729225-0-0(4))* Flashlight Pr.

Mitchell, Lori. Marfan Syndrome A-Z. Mitchell, Lori, compiled by. 2007. 36p. (J). pap. *(978-0-918335-14-2(0))* National Marfan Foundation, The.

Mitchell, Mark. Raising la Belle. Mitchell, Mark. (Professor Wigglestix & the Weather Ser.). 112p. 10.95 *(978-1-57168-703-6(3))* Eakin Pr.

Mitchell, Mary. Lily & Flinge & the Piece of Kibble. Mitchell, Steve. 2019. (ENG.). 52p. (J). pap. *(978-1-9994730-0-6(0))* Mitchell, Mary.

Mitchell, Mary Ames. Henry's Big Kaboom: Henry Knox Claims the Artillery from Fort Ticonderoga, 1775-1776. a Ballad. Mitchell, Mary Ames. 2017. (ENG.). (J). 22.99 *(978-0-9991505-0-4(2))*; pap. 12.99 *(978-0-9850530-9-3(7))* Peach Plum Pr.

Mitchell, Melanie. All Aboard Noah's Ark: A Touch & Feel Book. Price, Olivia. 2008. (ENG.). 12p. (J). (gr. -1). 12.95 *(978-1-58117-778-7(X)*, Intervisual/Piggy Toes) Bendon, Inc.

—Are You Ticklish? McKendry, Sam. 2006. (ENG.). 12p. (J). (gr. -1-18). bds. 10.95 *(978-1-58117-376-5(8)*, Intervisual/Piggy Toes) Bendon, Inc.

—Are You Ticklish? McKendry, Sam. ed. 2008. (ENG.). 12p. (J). bds. 5.95 *(978-1-58117-706-0(2)*, Intervisual/Piggy Toes) Bendon, Inc.

—Are You Ticklish? A Touch & Tickle Book. McKendry, Sam. 2007. 15.95 *(978-1-58117-571-4(X)*, Intervisual/Piggy Toes) Bendon, Inc.

—Are You Ticklish?/Tienes Cosquillas? McKendry, Sam. 2005. (ENG.). 12p. (gr. -1-k). 10.95 *(978-1-58117-472-4(1)*, Intervisual/Piggy Toes) Bendon, Inc.

—Bible Stories: A Touch & Feel Book. Price, Olivia. 2008. (ENG.). 12p. (J). (gr. -1). 12.95 *(978-1-58117-802-9(6)*, Intervisual/Piggy Toes) Bendon, Inc.

—The Biggest Thing in the World. Steven, Kenneth C. ed. 2013. (ENG.). 32p. (J). (gr. -1-k). 6.99 *(978-0-7459-6402-7(8))* Lion Hudson PLC GBR. Dist: Independent Pubs. Group.

—Christmas Story, 1 vol. Tebbs, Victoria. 2009. (See & Say! Ser.). 24p. (J). 6.99 *(978-0-8254-7884-0(7)*, Lion Children's) Lion Hudson PLC GBR. Dist: Kregel Pubns.

—Curious Kitties: A Color Book. McKendry, Sam. 2007. (ENG.). 14p. (J). (gr. -1-3). bds. 5.95 *(978-1-58117-554-7(X)*, Intervisual/Piggy Toes) Bendon, Inc.

—Curious Kitties: A Colors Book. McKendry, Sam. 2005. (ENG.). 16p. (J). bds. 9.95 *(978-1-58117-417-5(9)*, Intervisual/Piggy Toes) Bendon, Inc.

—Deep in the Jungle. 2011. (ENG.). 6p. (J). (gr. -1-k). 14.95 *(978-1-61524-471-3(9)*, Intervisual/Piggy Toes) Bendon, Inc.

—God's Winter Wonderland. Nolan, Allia Zobel. 2006. 10p. (J). bds. 8.99 *(978-0-8254-5526-1(X))* Kregel Pubns.

—Good Morning. 2008. (ENG.). 10p. (J). bds. 5.95 *(978-1-58117-708-4(9)*, Intervisual/Piggy Toes) Bendon, Inc.

—Good Morning, Good Night! 2007. (Touch & Feel Ser.). 13p. 15.95 *(978-1-58117-572-1(8)*, Intervisual/Piggy Toes) Bendon, Inc.

—Good Morning, Good Night! Imperato, Teresa. 2006. (ENG.). 12p. (J). (gr. -1-18). 9.95 *(978-1-58117-279-9(6)*, Intervisual/Piggy Toes) Bendon, Inc.

—Good Morning, Good Night! A Touch & Feel Bedtime Book. 2006. 12p. (J). (gr. -1-k). 12.95 *(978-1-58117-461-8(6)*, Intervisual/Piggy Toes) Bendon, Inc.

—Good Morning, Good Night Bilingual: Buenos Dias! Buenas Noches! 2005. (ENG & SPA.). 12p. (J). 9.95 *(978-1-58117-389-5(X)*, Intervisual/Piggy Toes) Bendon, Inc.

—Good Night. 2008. (ENG.). 6p. (J). bds. 5.95 *(978-1-58117-709-1(7)*, Intervisual/Piggy Toes) Bendon, Inc.

—I Love My Mum. Piper, Sophie. ed. 2011. (ENG.). 32p. (J). (gr. -1-k). 8.99 *(978-0-7459-6906-0(2))* Lion Hudson PLC GBR. Dist: Independent Pubs. Group.

—Little Bunny's Bible, 1 vol. Zondervan Staff & Lyons, P. J. 2015. (ENG.). 16p. (J). bds. 15.99 *(978-0-310-74444-3(X))* Zonderkidz.

—Little Chick's Bible, 1 vol. Zondervan Staff & Lyons, P. J. 2015. (ENG.). 16p. (J). bds. 15.99 *(978-0-310-74780-2(5))* Zonderkidz.

—Molly Mouse Is Shy: A Story of Shyness. Gibbs, Lynne. 2009. (Let's Grow Together Ser.). 32p. (J). (gr. -1-2). pap. 10.55 *(978-1-60754-761-7(9))*; lib. bdg. 25.60 *(978-1-60754-756-3(2))* Windmill Bks.

—My Little Bible Board Book, 1 vol. Goodings, Christina. ed. 2007. (ENG.). 40p. (J). (— 1). bds. 9.99 *(978-0-7459-6046-3(4))* Lion Hudson PLC GBR. Dist: Independent Pubs. Group.

—My Little Prayer Board Book. Goodings, Christina. ed. 2008. (ENG.). 40p. (J). bds. 9.99 *(978-0-7459-6104-0(5))* Lion Hudson PLC GBR. Dist: Independent Pubs. Group.

—Noah's Ark Story, 1 vol. Tebbs, Victoria. 2009. (See & Say! Ser.). 24p. (J). 6.99 *(978-0-8254-7885-7(5)*, Lion Children's) Lion Hudson PLC GBR. Dist: Kregel Pubns.

—Teddy Bear Says Goodnight. Senior, Suzy & Senior, Suzanne. ed. 2014. (Teddy Bear Says Ser.). (ENG.). 12p. (J). (— 1). bds. 7.99 *(978-0-7459-6436-2(2))* Lion Hudson PLC GBR. Dist: Independent Pubs. Group.

—Three Craws: A Lift-The-Flap Scottish Rhyme, 30 vols. 2018. (ENG.). 12p. (J). 9.95 *(978-1-78250-511-2(3)*, Kelpies) Floris Bks. GBR. Dist: Consortium Bk. Sales & Distribution.

—Time to Share: A Story of Sharing. Gibbs, Lynne. 2009. (Let's Grow Together Ser.). 32p. (J). (gr. -1-2). lib. bdg. 25.60 *(978-1-60754-757-0(0))* Windmill Bks.

—Wake up Little Ones. 2009. (ENG.). 12p. 10.95 *(978-1-58117-927-9(8)*, Intervisual/Piggy Toes) Bendon, Inc.

—Who Do You Love? 2008. (ENG.). 6p. (J). bds. 5.95 *(978-1-58117-707-7(0)*, Intervisual/Piggy Toes) Bendon, Inc.

—Who Do You Love? A Touch & Feel Book. Wang, Margaret. 2007. (gr. -1-k). 15.95 *(978-1-58117-570-7(1)*, Intervisual/Piggy Toes) Bendon, Inc.

Mitchell, Nanci. Anna & Her Mommy. Champion, Gina. 2005. 36p. (J). (gr. k-6). pap. 10.00 *(978-1-884363-20-7(2))* Odenwald Pr.

Mitchell, Peter. Freaking Out: Real-Life Stories about Anxiety. Wells, Polly. 2013. (ENG.). 136p. (YA). (gr. 7-12). pap. 12.95 *(978-1-55451-544-8(0)*, 9781554515448) Annick Pr., Ltd. CAN. Dist: Publishers Group West (PGW).

Mitchell, Rhonda. Daddy Calls Me Man. Johnson, Angela. 2014. 32p. pap. 7.00 *(978-1-61003-309-1(4))* Center for the Collaborative Classroom.

Mitchell, Steven. Amazing Stories from Times Past: Devotions for Children & Families. Farenhorst, Christine. 2005. 142p. (J). (gr. 2-7). per. 8.99 *(978-0-87552-823-6(6))* P & R Publishing.

Mitchell, Susan. Claire & the Unicorn Happy Ever After. Hennessy, B. G. 2006. (ENG.). 32p. (J). (gr. -1-3). 18.99 *(978-1-4169-0815-9(3)*, Simon & Schuster Bks. For Young Readers) Simon & Schuster Bks. For Young Readers.

—Hugs for Baby! Zobel-Nolan, Allia. 2008. (Lift-the-Flap Hear-the-Sound Ser.). 10p. (J). (gr. -1). 12.95 *(978-1-932915-64-8(8))* Sandvik Innovations, LLC.

—The Little Christmas Elf. Smith, Nikki Shannon. 2011. (Little Golden Book Ser.). 24p. (J). (gr. -1-k). 4.99 *(978-0-375-87348-5(1)*, Golden Bks.) Random Hse. Children's Bks.

—My Dad & Me. Capucilli, Alyssa Satin. 2009. (ENG.). 16p. (J). (gr. -1-1). 7.99 *(978-1-4169-5828-4(2)*, Little Simon) Little Simon.

—My Mom & Me. Capucilli, Alyssa Satin. 2009. (ENG.). 16p. (J). (gr. -1-1). 7.99 *(978-1-4169-5829-1(0)*, Little Simon) Little Simon.

—Nana's Bible Stories. Simpson, Roberta. 2007. (ENG.). 96p. (J). (gr. -1-3). 16.99 *(978-1-4003-1187-3(X))* Nelson, Thomas Inc.

—Paula Deen's Cookbook for the Lunch-Box Set. Deen, Paula. 2009. (ENG.). 192p. (J). (gr. 2-7). spiral bd. 21.99 *(978-1-4169-8268-5(X)*, Simon & Schuster Bks. For Young Readers) Simon & Schuster Bks. For Young Readers.

—Paula Deen's My First Cookbook. Deen, Paula. 2008. (ENG.). 176p. (J). (gr. -1-3). spiral bd. 21.99 *(978-1-4169-5033-2(8)*, Simon & Schuster Bks. For Young Readers) Simon & Schuster Bks. For Young Readers.

—Pumpkin Baby. Yolen, Jane. 2009. (ENG.). 32p. (J). (gr. -1). *(978-1-55470-141-4(4))* Me to We.

—Too Many Fairies: A Celtic Tale, 0 vols. MacDonald, Margaret Read. 2010. (ENG.). 32p. (J). (gr. -1-3). 17.99 *(978-0-7614-5604-9(X)*, 9780761456049, Two Lions) Amazon Publishing.

—Whoosh! A Watery World of Wonderful Creatures, 0 vols. Baillie, Marilyn. 2014. (ENG.). 32p. (J). (gr. -1-2). 16.95 *(978-1-926973-98-2(4)*, Owlkids) Owlkids Bks. Inc. CAN. Dist: Publishers Group West (PGW).

Mitchell, Susan K. Mitchell. Regeneration: Regrowing Heads, Tails, & Legs, 1 vol. Hurt, Avery Elizabeth. 2019. (Animal Defense! Ser.). (ENG.). 48p. (gr. 3-4). pap. 11.70 *(978-1-9785-0817-0(4))* Enslow Publishing, LLC.

Mitchell, Susanne. Liputto: Stories of Gnomes & Trolls, 1 vol. Streit, Jakob. Mitchell, David, ed. Kuettel, Nina J., tr. 2nd rev. ed. 2016. (ENG.). 60p. (J). reprint ed. pap. 16.00 *(978-1-888365-26-9(9))* Waldorf Publications.

Mitchell, Susanne Althea. Liputto: Stories of Gnomes & Trolls, 1 vol. Streit, Jakob. Kuettel, Nina, tr. 2nd rev. ed. 2016. (ENG.). 60p. (J). pap. 16.00 *(978-1-936367-95-5(5))* Waldorf Publications.

Mitchell, Suzanne. Calvin's Giant Jumps. Mitchell, Marvin. 2003. 32p. 15.95 *(978-0-9727639-0-5(2))* Beachwalker Pr.

Mitchell, Tina. Crazy Colours. Lovell, Brandy. 2011. 42p. pap. *(978-0-9867761-0-6(6))* Bing Long Bks.

Mitchell, Tracy. The Great Divide: A Mathematical Marathon. Dodds, Dayle Ann. 2005. 32p. (J). (gr. k-4). reprint ed. pap. 7.99 *(978-0-7636-1592-5(7))* Candlewick Pr.

Mitchum, Lynn Tyner. Happy Being Me. Mitchum, Lynn Tyner. 2006. (J). bds. 21.95 *(978-0-9745191-0-4(3))* Lynn Tyner Mitchum & James Rogers.

Mithuna, R. Michael. El Nacimiento: El Papel de una Doula = Being Born: The Doula's Role. Mithuna, R. Michael. Hernandez, Jewel. 2009. (SPA & ENG.). (J). pap. *(978-1-890772-91-8(7))* Hohm Pr.

Mithuna, Shukyu Linn. Nos Gusta Amamantar / We Like to Nurse. Martin, Chia. 2nd alt. ed. 2016. (Family & World Health Ser.). (ENG.). 28p. (J). 12.95 *(978-1-942493-12-9(6))* Hohm Pr.

Mitra, Annie. The Christmas Witch, an Italian Legend: Level 3. Oppenheim, Joanne. 2020. (Bank Street Readt-To-Read Ser.). (ENG.). 50p. (J). pap. 11.95 ***(978-1-876966-72-0(6))*** ibooks, Inc.

Mitrea, Silvia. Peripetiile Ratonului Nasturica: - Bantu, Eli. 2014. (RUM.). 558p. (J). pap. *(978-606-8601-13-7(7))* Sukhu, Karim.

Mitsein, Rebekah & Baughman, Lee. The Great Rift Valley Lakes: In English & Tigrinya. Ready Set Go Books. 2019. (ENG.). 36p. (J). pap. 11.99 *(978-1-0793-8715-5(3))* Independently Published.

Mitsein, Rebekah, jt. illus. see Students from Clark College Continuing E.

Mitsopoulos, Dimitris. The Moon Saga: How Dancing Turtle Captured the Moon. Tobias, Harris. 2019. (ENG.). 34p. (J). pap. 14.99 *(978-1-950454-57-0(6))* Pen It! Pubns., LLC.

Mitsui Brown, Janet. Oshogatsu with Obaachan. 2005. (J). *(978-1-879965-24-9(0))* Polychrome Publishing Corp.

Mitsui-Kids, jt. illus. see Shogakukan.

Mittal, Shiekha. The Why & What of Epilepsy: A Book for Children & Teens. Karia, Roopal. 2008. 17p. pap. 24.95 *(978-1-60610-951-9(0))* America Star Bks.

Mittan, J. Barry, jt. photos by see Adeff, Jay.

Mitten, Christopher, et al. Man-Thing by R. L. Stine. 2017. (ENG.). 112p. (YA). (gr. 8-17). pap. 15.99 *(978-1-302-90200-1(8))* Marvel Worldwide, Inc.

Mitter, Kathryn. Cones, 1 vol. Hamilton, Laura. 2012. (Everyday 3-D Shapes Ser.). (ENG.). 24p. (J). (gr. -1-2). lib. bdg. 27.07 *(978-1-61641-872-4(9)*, 6867, Looking Glass Library) Magic Wagon.

—Cubes, 1 vol. Hamilton, Laura. 2012. (Everyday 3-D Shapes Ser.). (ENG.). 24p. (J). (gr. -1-2). lib. bdg. 27.07 *(978-1-61641-873-1(7)*, 6869, Looking Glass Library) Magic Wagon.

—Cylinders, 1 vol. Hamilton, Laura. 2012. (Everyday 3-D Shapes Ser.). (ENG.). 24p. (J). (gr. -1-2). lib. bdg. 27.07 *(978-1-61641-874-8(5)*, 6871, Looking Glass Library) Magic Wagon.

—Duck for Turkey Day. Jules, Jacqueline. 2017. (ENG.). 32p. (J). (gr. -1-3). pap. 7.99 *(978-0-8075-1735-2(6)*, 807517356) Whitman, Albert & Co.

—Eloise Has a Lesson. 2005. (Eloise Ser.). (ENG.). 32p. (J). (gr. -1-1). pap. 4.99 *(978-0-689-87367-6(0)*, Simon Spotlight) Simon Spotlight.

—Maple Syrup from the Sugarhouse. Knowlton, Laurie Lazzaro. 2017. (ENG.). 32p. (J). (gr. k-2). 16.99 *(978-0-8075-7943-5(2)*, 807579432) Whitman, Albert & Co.

—Prisms, 1 vol. Hamilton, Laura. 2012. (Everyday 3-D Shapes Ser.). (ENG.). 24p. (J). (gr. -1-2). lib. bdg. 27.07 *(978-1-61641-875-5(3)*, 6873, Looking Glass Library) Magic Wagon.

—Pyramids, 1 vol. Hamilton, Laura. 2012. (Everyday 3-D Shapes Ser.). (ENG.). 24p. (J). (gr. -1-2). lib. bdg. 27.07 *(978-1-61641-876-2(1)*, 6875, Looking Glass Library) Magic Wagon.

—Spheres, 1 vol. Hamilton, Laura. 2012. (Everyday 3-D Shapes Ser.). (ENG.). 24p. (J). (gr. -1-2). lib. bdg. 27.07 *(978-1-61641-877-9(X)*, 6877, Looking Glass Library) Magic Wagon.

—Things I See at Baptism. Stiegemeyer, Julie. 2007. 20p. (J). (gr. -1-3). bds. 5.49 *(978-0-7586-1246-5(X))* Concordia Publishing Hse.

—Things I See at Christmas. Stiegemeyer, Julie. 2005. 16p. (J). (gr. -1-17). bds. 5.49 *(978-0-7586-0809-3(8))* Concordia Publishing Hse.

—What Does This Mean? Bergt, Carolyn. 16p. (gr. -1-k). 20.00 *(978-0-570-05545-7(8)*, 54-0077) Concordia Publishing Hse.

Mitter, Kathy. Here Is the Church. Stohs, Anita. 2009. 32p. (J). (gr. -1). 8.99 *(978-0-7586-1633-3(3))* Concordia Publishing Hse.

—Things I Hear in Church. Stiegemeyer, Julie. 2003. 20p. (J). bds. 5.49 *(978-0-7586-0125-4(5))* Concordia Publishing Hse.

—Things I See at Easter. Stiegemeyer, Julie. 2005. 20p. (J). bds. 5.49 *(978-0-7586-0797-3(0))* Concordia Publishing Hse.

—Things I See in Church. Stiegemeyer, Julie. 2003. 20p. (J). bds. 5.49 *(978-0-7586-0357-9(6))* Concordia Publishing Hse.

—When Jesus Was Born. Hartman, Sara. 2007. 16p. (J). (gr. k-4). 1.99 *(978-0-7586-1281-6(8))* Concordia Publishing Hse.

Miura, Taro. The Big Princess. Miura, Taro. 2015. (ENG.). 40p. (J). (-k). 14.99 *(978-0-7636-7459-5(1))* Candlewick Pr.

—Bum, Bum. Miura, Taro. 2016. (ENG.). 24p. (J). (— 1). bds. 8.99 *(978-0-7636-8784-7(7))* Candlewick Pr.

—There, There. Miura, Taro. 2016. (ENG.). 22p. (J). (— 1). bds. 8.99 *(978-0-7636-8785-4(5))* Candlewick Pr.

—The Tiny King. Miura, Taro. 2013. (ENG.). 32p. (J). (-k). 14.99 *(978-0-7636-6687-3(4))* Candlewick Pr.

Miyabe, Miyuki. The Book of Heroes. Miyabe, Miyuki. 2011. (Book of Heroes Ser.: 1). (ENG.). 350p. pap. 14.99 *(978-1-4215-4083-2(5))* Viz Media.

Miyabi, Haruka. Lafcadio Hearn's Japanese Ghost Stories. Wilson, Sean Michael. 2007. 144p. (YA). per. *(978-0-9788804-3-9(9))* Demented Dragon.

Miyake, Yoshi. Abigail Adams: Young Patriot. Sabin, Francene & Macken, JoAnn Early. 2007. 55p. (J). pap. *(978-0-439-88003-9(3))* Scholastic, Inc.

—All about Pets. Kain, Kathleen. 2004. (Treasure Tree Ser.). 32p. (J). *(978-0-7166-1626-9(2))* World Bk., Inc.

—Baby Jesus Visits the Temple. Maas, Alice E. 2004. (ENG.). 16p. (J). 1.99 *(978-0-570-07575-2(0))* Concordia Publishing Hse.

—Nicodemus & Jesus. Schkade, Jonathan. 2014. (Arch Bks.). (ENG.). 16p. (J). (gr. k-4). pap. 2.49 *(978-0-7586-4606-4(2))* Concordia Publishing Hse.

—The Ten Commandments. Miller, Claire. 2004. (Arch Bks.). 16p. (J). 1.99 *(978-0-7586-0672-3(9))* Concordia Publishing Hse.

Miyake, Yoski. Jesus, My Good Shepherd. Rottmann, Erik. 2005. (ENG.). 16p. (J). 1.99 *(978-0-7586-0725-6(3))* Concordia Publishing Hse.

Miyakoshi, Akiko. I Dream of a Journey. Miyakoshi, Akiko. 2020. (ENG.). 32p. (J). (gr. -1-3). 16.99 *(978-1-5253-0478-1(X))* Kids Can Pr., Ltd. CAN. Dist: Hachette Bk. Group.

—The Tea Party in the Woods. Miyakoshi, Akiko. 2015. (ENG.). 32p. (J). (gr. -1-2). 16.99 *(978-1-77138-107-9(8))* Kids Can Pr., Ltd. CAN. Dist: Hachette Bk. Group.

—The Way Home in the Night. Miyakoshi, Akiko. 2017. (ENG.). 32p. (J). (gr. -1-2). 16.95 *(978-1-77138-663-0(0))* Kids Can Pr., Ltd. CAN. Dist: Hachette Bk. Group.

Miyakoshi, Wason. Seikai Trilogy Vol. 3: Banner of the Stars II, 3 vols. Morioka, Hiroyuki. rev. ed. 2004. 248p. pap. 9.99 *(978-1-59182-859-4(7))* TOKYOPOP, Inc.

Miyares, Daniel. The Boy Who Dreamed of Infinity: a Tale of the Genius Ramanujan. Alznauer, Amy. 2020. 48p. (J). (gr. k-4). 17.99 *(978-0-7636-9048-9(1))* Candlewick Pr.

—A Chip off the Old Block. Shaffer, Jody Jensen. 2018. 32p. (J). (gr. k-3). 17.99 *(978-0-399-17388-2(9)*, Nancy Paulsen Books) Penguin Young Readers Group.

—Come Next Season. Norman, Kim. 2019. (ENG.). 40p. (J). 17.99 *(978-0-374-30598-7(6)*, 900173047, Farrar, Straus & Giroux (BYR)) Farrar, Straus & Giroux.

—Little Fox in the Snow. London, Jonathan. 2018. 40p. (J). (gr. -1-3). 16.99 *(978-0-7636-8814-1(2))* Candlewick Pr.

—Papi's Bodega. Chambers, Veronica & Clampet, Jason. 2013. (J). *(978-1-4231-0125-3(1))* Disney Pr.

—Surf's Up. Alexander, Kwame. (ENG.). (J). (— 1). 2018. 24p. bds. 7.95 *(978-0-7358-4313-4(9))*; 2016. 32p. 17.95 *(978-0-7358-4220-5(5))* North-South Bks., Inc.

—That Is My Dream! A Picture Book of Langston Hughes's Dream Variation. Hughes, Langston. 2017. (ENG.). 32p. (J). (gr. -1-3). 17.99 *(978-0-399-55017-1(8))*; lib. bdg. 20.99 *(978-0-399-55018-8(6))* Random Hse. Children's Bks. (Schwartz & Wade Bks.).

—Waking up Is Hard to Do. Sedaka, Neil et al. 2010. 26p. (J). (gr. k-4). 19.99 *(978-1-936140-13-8(6))* Charlesbridge Publishing, Inc.

Miyares, Daniel. Bring Me a Rock! Miyares, Daniel. 2016. (ENG.). 40p. (J). (gr. -1-3). 18.99 *(978-1-4814-4602-0(9)*, Simon & Schuster Bks. For Young Readers) Simon & Schuster Bks. For Young Readers.

—Float. Miyares, Daniel. 2015. (ENG.). 48p. (J). (gr. -1-3). 17.99 *(978-1-4814-1524-8(7)*, Simon & Schuster Bks. For Young Readers) Simon & Schuster Bks. For Young Readers.

—Pardon Me! Miyares, Daniel. 2014. (ENG.). 40p. (J). (gr. -1-3). 19.99 *(978-1-4424-8997-4(9)*, Simon & Schuster Bks. For Young Readers) Simon & Schuster Bks. For Young Readers.

—That Neighbor Kid. Miyares, Daniel. 2017. (ENG.). 32p. (J). (gr. -1-3). 17.99 *(978-1-4814-4979-3(6)*, Simon & Schuster Bks. For Young Readers) Simon & Schuster Bks. For Young Readers.

Miyazawa, Takeshi, et al. Cloak & Dagger: Runaways & Reversals. 2018. (ENG.). 368p. (YA). (gr. 8-17). pap. 34.99 *(978-1-302-91058-7(2))* Marvel Worldwide, Inc.

Miyazawa, Takeshi. Ghost-Spider Vol. 1: Dogs Days Are Over. 2020. (ENG.). 112p. (YA). (gr. 4-17). pap. 15.99 *(978-1-302-92012-8(X))* Marvel Worldwide, Inc.

—Ms. Marvel Vol. 7, Vol. 7. 2017. 136p. (YA). (gr. 8-17). pap. 17.99 *(978-1-302-90305-3(5))* Marvel Worldwide, Inc.

Miyazawa, Takeshi, et al. Runaways Vol. 5: Escape to New York. 2017. (ENG.). 168p. (YA). (gr. 8-17). pap. 14.99 *(978-1-302-90870-6(7))* Marvel Worldwide, Inc.

Miyazawa, Takeshi. Spider-Gwen: Ghost-Spider Vol. 2: Impossible Year. 2019. (ENG.). 112p. (YA). (gr. 4-17). pap. 17.99 *(978-1-302-91477-6(4))* Marvel Worldwide, Inc.

—Spider-Man Loves Mary Jane: the Real Thing. 2019. (ENG.). 272p. (J). (gr. 4-7). pap. 12.99 *(978-1-302-91873-6(7))* Marvel Worldwide, Inc.

Miyazawa, Takeshi & de Landro, Valentin. Spider-Man Loves Mary Jane: the Unexpected Thing. 2019. (ENG.). 256p. (J). (gr. 4-7). pap. 12.99 *(978-1-302-91978-8(4))* Marvel Worldwide, Inc.

Mizieliński, Alexandra & Mizieliński, Daniel. Impossible Inventions: Ideas That Shouldn't Work. Mycielska, Małgorzata. 2018. (ENG.). 128p. (J). (gr. k-5). 23.99 *(978-1-77657-170-3(3))* Gecko Pr. NZL. Dist: Lerner Publishing Group.

Mizieliński, Daniel, jt. illus. see Mizieliński, Alexandra.

Mizsenko, Ingrid. La Abuela. Härtling, Peter. 2003. (SPA.). 103p. (J). (gr. 5-8). pap. 9.95 *(978-968-19-0730-3(2))* Santillana USA Publishing Co., Inc.

Mizumura, Kazue. A Pair of Red Clogs. Matsuno, Masako. 2019. (ENG.). 32p. (J). (gr. k-3). pap. 13.95 *(978-1-948959-06-3(2))* Purple Hse. Pr.

Mizuno, Junko. Junko Mizuno's Hansel & Gretel. Mizuno, Junko. 2003. (Junko Mizuno Ser.). (ENG.). 144p. pap. 15.95 *(978-1-56931-869-0(7))* Viz Media.

—Junko Mizuno's Princess Mermaid. Mizuno, Junko. 2003. (Junko Mizuno Ser.). (ENG.). 144p. pap. 15.95 *(978-1-59116-117-2(7))* Viz Media.

Mizuno, Junko & Ishibash, Toshiharu. Collector File 003. Mizuno, Junko & Anzai, Yuko. 2003. (ENG.). 48p. pap. 9.95 *(978-1-56931-983-3(9))* Viz Media.

Mizuto, Aqua & Mizuto, Aqua. Yume Kira Dream Shoppe, Vol. 1. Mizuto, Aqua & Mizuto, Aqua. 2007. (Yume Kira Dream Shoppe Ser.: 1). (ENG.). 200p. (YA). (gr. 8-18). pap. 8.99 *(978-1-4215-1173-8(8))* Viz Media.

Mizuto, Aqua, jt. illus. see Mizuto, Aqua.

MJ Illustrations. Count on the Easter Pups! (PAW Patrol) Random House. 2018. (ENG.). 22p. (J). (— 1). bds. 6.99 *(978-1-5247-6872-0(3)*, Random Hse. Bks. for Young Readers) Random Hse. Children's Bks.

—Dora Goes to School/Dora Va a la Escuela (Dora the Explorer) Random House. 2014. (Pictureback(R) Ser.). (ENG.). 24p. (J). (gr. -1-2). 3.99 *(978-0-385-37496-5(8)*, Random Hse. Bks. for Young Readers) Random Hse. Children's Bks.

—Gold Rush Pups! (PAW Patrol) Random House. 2017. (Pictureback(R) Ser.). (ENG.). 16p. (J). (gr. -1-2). pap. 5.99 *(978-1-5247-1684-4(7)*, Random Hse. Bks. for Young Readers) Random Hse. Children's Bks.

MJ Illustrations. Grumpy America: a Paper Doll Book (Grumpy Cat) Random House. 2020. 32p. (J). (gr. -1-2). pap. 8.99 ***(978-1-9848-5135-2(7)***, Random Hse. Bks. for Young Readers) Random Hse. Children's Bks.

MJ Illustrations. Haunted House Party! (Bubble Guppies) Random House. 2015. (ENG.). 64p. (J). (gr. -1-2). pap. 4.99 *(978-0-385-38407-0(6)*, Golden Bks.) Random Hse. Children's Bks.

—Hide-And-Go-Swim! (Bubble Guppies) Random House. 2014. (ENG.). 12p. (J). (— 1). bds. 5.99 *(978-0-385-38515-2(3)*, Random Hse. Bks. for Young Readers) Random Hse. Children's Bks.

—High-Flying Skye (PAW Patrol) Random House. 2016. (ENG.). 24p. (J). (gr. -1-2). pap. 6.99 *(978-1-101-93686-3(X)*, Random Hse. Bks. for Young Readers) Random Hse. Children's Bks.

—It's Time for Ballet! (Bubble Guppies) Tillworth, Mary. 2015. (ENG.). 16p. (J). (gr. -1-2). 5.99 *(978-0-553-52117-7(9)*, Random Hse. Bks. for Young Readers) Random Hse. Children's Bks.

—Mighty Twins! (PAW Patrol) Huntley, Tex. (Step into Reading Ser.). (ENG.). 24p. (J). (gr. -1-1). 2020. 12.99 *(978-0-593-12135-1(X))*; 2019. 5.99 ***(978-0-593-12134-4(1))*** Random Hse. Children's Bks. (Random Hse. Bks. for Young Readers).

MJ Illustrations. One Magical Night (Butterbean's Cafe) Webster, Christy. 2020. (Pictureback(R) Ser.). (ENG.). 24p. (J). (gr. -1-2). 5.99 ***(978-0-593-12279-2(8)***, Random Hse. Bks. for Young Readers) Random Hse. Children's Bks.

—Ready, Race, Rescue! (PAW Patrol) James, Hollis. 2019. (Pictureback(R) Ser.). (ENG.). 24p. (J). (gr. -1-1). 5.99 ***(978-0-593-12133-7(3)***, Random Hse. Bks. for Young Readers) Random Hse. Children's Bks.

MJ Illustrations. Shape Patrol! (Paw Patrol) Random House. 2016. (ENG.). 24p. (J). (— 1). bds. 6.99 *(978-1-101-93695-5(9)*, Random Hse. Bks. for Young Readers) Random Hse. Children's Bks.

—Track That Monkey! (PAW Patrol) Neumann, Casey. 2019. (Pictureback(R) Ser.). (ENG.). 24p. (J). (gr. -1-2). 5.99 *(978-0-525-64748-5(1)*, Random Hse. Bks. for Young Readers) Random Hse. Children's Bks.

—A Very Puppy Christmas! (PAW Patrol) Golden Books. 2016. (ENG.). 32p. (J). (gr. -1-2). pap. 5.99 *(978-0-399-55356-1(8)*, Golden Bks.) Random Hse. Children's Bks.

MJ Illustrations, jt. illus. see Moore, Harry.

MJ Illustrations Staff. Grumpy Cat: Puzzles, Games & More - 100% Not Fun! Chlebowski, Rachel & Random House Staff. 2019. 48p. (J). (gr. -1-2). pap. 5.99 *(978-1-9848-5130-7(6)*, Random Hse. Bks. for Young Readers) Random Hse. Children's Bks.

—Here Comes Bubble Bunny! (Bubble Guppies) Golden Books Staff. 2014. (ENG.). 48p. (J). (gr. -1-2). pap. 3.99 *(978-0-385-37497-2(6)*, Golden Bks.) Random Hse. Children's Bks.

MJ Illustrations Staff, jt. illus. see Jackson, Mike.

MJ Illustrations Staff, jt. illus. see Mcgee, Warner.

MJ Illustrations Staff, jt. illus. see Random House Beginners Books Staff.

Mkhoiani, Nina. Jack. Whaler, Norman. 2018. (ENG.). 32p. (J). (gr. 1-2). 19.99 *(978-1-948131-15-5(3))* Whaler, Norman / Beneath Another Sky Bks.

Mkhoiani, Nina. The Pig Magician. Alexandrov, John V. 2019. (Axdorian Fairy Tales Ser.: Vol. 1). (ENG.). 80p. (J). pap. 16.00 ***(978-1-6985-9301-2(5))*** Independently Published.

Mkwa Tsun, Zaawaazit. The Dream Catcher Pool. Chartrand, Jane. 2015. (ENG.). 32p. (J). mass mkt. 9.95 *(978-1-894717-26-7(0)*, 87c4af37-26a0-426c-8a4f-918e7aefb772) Pemmican Pubns., Inc. CAN. Dist: Firefly Bks., Ltd.

MM, Shanith. Super-Sonic Submarine. Lake, Angie. ed. 2016. (Danny Dingle's Fantastic Finds Ser.). (ENG.). (J). pap. *(978-1-78226-260-2(1))* Sweet Cherry Publishing.

MMStudios & Allman, Howard, photos by. Big & Little: A Book about Opposites. 2007. (Usborne Look & Say Ser.). 18p. (J). (gr. -1-3). bds. 14.99 *(978-0-7945-1884-4(2)*, Usborne) EDC Publishing.

Mo, Xiangyi. Access Asia: Primary Teaching & Learning Units. Glascodine, Carolyn, ed. 2003. 192p. pap. 35.95 *(978-1-86366-345-8(2))* Education Services Australia Ltd. AUS. Dist: Cheng & Tsui Co.

Moates, Carol Meetze. A Light to Keep. Silcox, Diane. 2013. 30p. pap. 14.95 *(978-1-938101-36-6(7))* Indigo Sea Pr., LLC.

Mobley, Qin. Zana the Brave. Mason, L. K. Matthews, Monique N., ed. 2019. (ENG.). 38p. (J). pap. 14.99 *(978-1-7918-4029-7(9))* Independently Published.

Mochizuki, Chiemi. The Promise. Mochizuki, Chiemi. Randle, Walt R., ed. 2003. 38p. (J). (gr. 3-6). 16.99 *(978-0-9720691-0-6(0))* Berkeley Major Publishing.

Mock, Rebecca. Compass South. Larson, Hope. 2016. (Four Points Ser.: 1). (ENG.). 224p. (J). 18.99 *(978-0-374-30043-2(7)*, 900132565, Farrar, Straus & Giroux (BYR)) Farrar, Straus & Giroux.

—Knife's Edge: A Graphic Novel (Four Points, Book 2) Larson, Hope. 2017. (Four Points Ser.: 2). (ENG.). 224p. (J). 19.99 *(978-0-374-30044-9(5)*, 900132566, Farrar, Straus & Giroux (BYR)) Farrar, Straus & Giroux.

—Knife's Edge: A Graphic Novel (Four Points, Book 2) Larson, Hope. 2018. (Four Points Ser.: 2). (ENG.). 224p. (J). pap. 12.99 *(978-1-250-15846-8(X)*, 900185491) Square Fish.

Mockford, Caroline. Cleo & Caspar. Blackstone, Stella. 2013. 24p. (J). pap. 6.99 *(978-1-78285-053-3(8))* Barefoot Bks., Inc.

—Cleo in the Snow. Blackstone, Stella. 2013. 24p. (J). pap. 6.99 *(978-1-78285-055-7(4))*; bds. 6.99 *(978-1-78285-054-0(6))* Barefoot Bks., Inc.

—Cleo on the Move. Blackstone, Stella. 2013. 24p. (J). bds. 6.99 *(978-1-78285-056-4(2))*; (gr. -1-k). pap. 6.99 *(978-1-78285-057-1(0))* Barefoot Bks., Inc.

—Cleo the Cat. Blackstone, Stella. 2013. 24p. (J). (gr. -1-k). pap. 6.99 *(978-1-78285-051-9(1))* Barefoot Bks., Inc.

—Cleo the Cat. (J). 12.99 *(978-1-84148-458-7(X))* Barefoot Bks., Inc.

—Cleo's Color Book. Blackstone, Stella. (J). 2010. 32p. pap. 6.99 *(978-1-84686-440-7(2))*; 2006. 0032p. 15.99 *(978-1-905236-30-5(1))* Barefoot Bks., Inc.

—Cleo's Counting Book. Blackstone, Stella. 2003. (Cleo the Cat Ser.). (ENG.). 24p. (J). (gr. -1-3). 15.99 *(978-1-84148-207-1(2))* Barefoot Bks., Inc.

—Come Here, Cleo! Blackstone, Stella. 2013. 24p. (J). (gr. -1-k). pap. 6.99 *(978-1-84148-330-6(3))* Barefoot Bks., Inc.

—The Elephants' Ears. Chamber, Catherine. 2004. 32p. (J). pap. 6.99 *(978-1-84148-249-1(8))* Barefoot Bks., Inc.

—Elephants' Ears. Chambers, Catherine. 2016. (ENG.). 32p. (J). (gr. -1-2). pap. 8.99 *(978-1-78285-282-7(4))* Barefoot Bks., Inc.

—Talk with Me! Blackstone, Stella. 2009. (ENG.). 14p. (J). (gr. -1). 7.99 *(978-1-84686-180-2(2))* Barefoot Bks., Inc.

—Walk with Me! Blackstone, Stella. 2009. (ENG.). 14p. (J). (gr. -1). bds. 7.99 *(978-1-84686-179-6(9))* Barefoot Bks., Inc.

Mockford, Caroline. Cleo's Color Book. Mockford, Caroline. Blackstone, Stella. 2007. (Cleo Ser.). 24p. (J). (gr. -1-k). bds. 6.99 *(978-1-84686-060-7(1))* Barefoot Bks., Inc.

—What's This? A Seed's Story. Mockford, Caroline. 2007. (ENG.). 32p. (J). (gr. -1-2). pap. 7.99 *(978-1-84686-071-3(7))* Barefoot Bks., Inc.

Mockler, Sean. Alex Has Had Enough! Johnson Mockler, Nicole. 2011. 64p. pap. *(978-1-77067-334-2(2))* FriesenPress.

Modak, Tejas. Rescue by Design: Madhubani Art. Raghbeer, Anjali. 2012. (Art Tales from India Ser.). (ENG.). 24p. (J). 14.95 *(978-81-8328-194-2(X))* Wisdom Tree IND. Dist: SCB Distributors.

Modéré, Armelle. Solamente un Poco de Gripe. Modéré, Armelle. Dufresne, Didier & Modere, Armelle-dufresnedidier. Vinent, Julia, tr. 2003. (SPA.). 32p. (J). (gr. k-2). 15.99 *(978-84-8470-123-1(9))* Corimbo, Editorial S.L. ESP. Dist: Lectorum Pubns., Inc.

Modeste, Caroline. My First 1000 Words. 2016. (ENG.). 64p. (J). (gr. -1 — 1). 19.95 *(978-1-77085-797-1(4)*, e5273533-78f5-4600-ba87-a0b0542668e6) Firefly Bks., Ltd.

Modica, Cathy, photos by. Niik & Bling: The Friendship Begins. Modica, Cathy. Van Eyck, Laura. l.t. ed. 2005. 40p. (J). 19.95 *(978-0-9762466-0-2(0))* Wholesome Puppy Tales.

Modugno, Tina. Clarence the Clam. Lambert, Susan Dodd. 2013. 28p. pap. 6.95 *(978-0-9883893-5-9(5))* Borgo Publishing.

Moebius. Silver Surfer: Parable 30th Anniversary Edition. 2020. (ENG.). 88p. (YA). (gr. 8-17). pap. 14.99 ***(978-1-302-92370-9(6))*** Marvel Worldwide, Inc.

Moeckel, Christine. Dick the Duck. Moeckel, Christine. l.t. ed. 2004. 31p. (J). spiral bd. 9.98 *(978-0-9720350-2-6(8))* Duckpond Publishing, Inc.

Moeller, Bill, photos by. Crazy Horse: A Photographic Biography. Moeller, Bill. Moeller, Jan et al. rev. ed. 168p. (J). (gr. 4). pap. *(978-0-87842-424-5(5)*, 648) Mountain Pr. Publishing Co., Inc.

Moeller mé illuminé, Jo. La Hormiguita ¿ A Folktale about the Perseverant Little Ant. 2005. (SPA.). (J). *(978-0-9644678-4-2(4))* Bilingual Pubns.

Moeller, Richard. Grandpa Lolo's Navajo Saddle Blanket: La Tilma de Abuelito Lolo. Moeller, Richard, photos by. García, Nasario. 2012. (J). *(978-0-8263-5078-7(X))*; (ENG & SPA.). 72p. pap. 19.95 *(978-0-8263-5079-4(8))* Univ. of New Mexico Pr.

Moen Cabanting, Ruth. 1-2-3 Waikiki Trolley. BeachHouse Publishing. 2005. (ENG.). 20p. (J). (gr. -1-1). bds. 8.95 *(978-1-933067-06-3(3))* Beachhouse Publishing, LLC.

Moen, Ruth. Lio the Carousel Horse. Wing, Carol. 2010. (ENG.). 32p. (J). (gr. -1-2). 14.95 *(978-1-933067-37-7(3))* Beachhouse Publishing, LLC.

—S Went Surfing in Hawai'i. Gillespie, Jane. 2013. (ENG.). 32p. (J). (gr. -1-1). 12.95 *(978-1-933067-50-6(0))* Beachhouse Publishing, LLC.

Moen, Tyler. Daddy Is That the Best You Got? Seelen, Christopher. 2005. 36p. (J). pap. 8.99 *(978-0-9776385-0-5(2)*, Cotton Candy Pr.) Unveiled Media, LLC.

Moerbeek, Kees. Goldilocks. 2006. (Roly Poly Box Bks.). 24p. (J). spiral bd. *(978-1-84643-017-6(8))* Child's Play International Ltd.

—Make 24 Paper Planes: Includes Awesome Launcher Kit! Golding, Elizabeth. 2015. (ENG.). 24p. (J). (gr. 2-6). pap. 11.99 *(978-1-4380-0640-6(3)*, B.E.S. Publishing) Peterson's.

—Raggedy Ann & Andy & the Camel with the Wrinkled Knees. Gruelle, Johnny. collector's ed. 2003. (Raggedy Ann Ser.). (ENG.). 14p. (J). (gr. -1-2). 32.99 *(978-0-689-85775-1(6)*, Little Simon) Little Simon.

Moerbeek, Kees. Cinderella. Moerbeek, Kees. 2006. (Roly Poly Box Bks.). 24p. (J). spiral bd. *(978-1-84643-019-0(4))* Child's Play International Ltd.

—Cinderella: My Secret Scrapbook Diary. Moerbeek, Kees. 2011. (My Secret Scrapbook Diary Ser.). 10p. (J). *(978-1-84643-450-1(5))* Child's Play International Ltd.

—Jack & the Beanstalk: My Secret Scrapbook Diary. Moerbeek, Kees. 2011. (My Secret Scrapbook Diary Ser.). 10p. (J). *(978-1-84643-449-5(1))* Child's Play International Ltd.

—Little Red Riding Hood: My Secret Scrapbook Diary. Moerbeek, Kees. 2011. (My Secret Scrapbook Diary Ser.). 10p. (J). *(978-1-84643-447-1(5))* Child's Play International Ltd.

Moerbeek, Kees. Jungle. Moerbeek, Kees, des. 2008. (Roly Poly Box Bks.). 24p. (J). (gr. -1-1). spiral bd. *(978-1-84643-243-9(X))* Child's Play International Ltd.

—Snow. Moerbeek, Kees, des. 2008. (Roly Poly Box Bks.). 24p. (J). (gr. -1-1). spiral bd. *(978-1-84643-244-6(8))* Child's Play International Ltd.

Moerman, Cilla. Plastic Fantastic: Echte Helden in Een Wereld Die Schreeuwt Om Hulp. Veldhuijzen, Lorena. 2018. (DUT.). 48p. (J). (gr. 3-6). pap. 11.99 *(978-1-7322434-3-9(3))* Charbonneau, Bradley.

—Plastic Fantastic: Real Heroes in a World That Wants to Be Saved. Veldhuijzen, Lorena. Charbonneau, Saskia, tr. 2018. (ENG.). 50p. (J). (gr. 3-6). pap. 11.99 *(978-1-7322434-2-2(5))* Charbonneau, Bradley.

Moerner, John. Don't Play with Your Food!, Rock, Brian. 2005. 32p. (J). 14.99 *(978-0-9754411-0-7(8))* First Light Publishing.

Mofett, Patricia. The Beast Beneath the Stairs: 10th Anniversary Edition. Dahl, Michael. 10th ed. 2017. (Library of Doom Ser.). (ENG.). 48p. (J). (gr. 4-8). pap. 6.25 *(978-1-4965-5536-6(8)*, 136560); lib. bdg. 23.99 *(978-1-4965-5530-4(9)*, 136554) Capstone. (Stone Arch Bks.).

Moffat, Ross. Cow Story. Arkangel, Brian. 2009. 24p. pap. 24.95 *(978-1-60703-272-4(4))* America Star Bks.

Moffatt, Angelyca. We Stand up for What's Right. El-Tayyab, Hassan & Caravas, Audra. 2020. (ENG.). 36p. (J). pap. 15.00 ***(978-1-7337025-8-4(X))*** Poetic Matrix Pr.

Moffatt, Etta. Fionn MacCool et le Saumon de la Sagesse: Un Conte Traditionnel Au Sujet d'un Héros Gaélique Présenté Comme une Histoire Gestuelle Pour les Enfants à Lire à Haute Voix. Roberts, Terri M. Close, Melany, tr. 2019. (FRE.). 24p. (J). (gr. k-3). pap. *(978-1-988747-40-8(6))* Bradan Pr.

Moffatt, Jacob. The Hedgehog in the Fog: An Autumn Tale. Hough, Kellyn. 2020. (ENG.). 30p. (J). ***(978-0-2288-2307-0(2))***; pap. ***(978-0-2288-2306-3(4))*** Tellwell Talent.

Moffatt, Judith. Slide & Discover: It's Time! 2005. (Slide & Discover Ser.). 8p. (J). bds. 7.95 *(978-1-58117-247-8(8)*, Intervisual/Piggy Toes) Bendon, Inc.

—Slide & Discover: What's My Job? 2005. (Slide & Discover Ser.). 8p. (J). bds. 7.95 *(978-1-58117-248-5(6)*, Intervisual/Piggy Toes) Bendon, Inc.

Moffet, Patricia. Ghosts vs. Witches: Tussle of the Tricksters. O'Hearn, Michael. 2011. (Monster Wars Ser.). (ENG.). 32p. (gr. 3-4). pap. 47.70 *(978-1-4296-7262-7(5)*, Capstone Pr.) Capstone.

Moffet, Patricia, et al. Monster Wars. O'Hearn, Michael. 2011. (Monster Wars Ser.). (ENG.). 32p. (gr. 3-4). pap. 190.80 *(978-1-4296-7270-2(6)*, Capstone Pr.) Capstone.

Moffet, Patricia. Zombies vs. Mummies: Clash of the Living Dead. O'Hearn, Michael. 2011. (Monster Wars Ser.). (ENG.). 32p. (gr. 3-4). pap. 47.70 *(978-1-4296-7268-9(4))*; (J). lib. bdg. 28.65 *(978-1-4296-6520-9(3))* Capstone. (Capstone Pr.).

Moffett, Patricia. La Bestia de Las Escaleras. Dahl, Michael. 2019. (Biblioteca Maldita Ser.). (SPA.). 40p. (J). (gr. 4-8). lib. bdg. 23.99 *(978-1-4965-8537-0(2)*, 141286, Stone Arch Bks.) Capstone.

—The Black Dragon. Sedgwick, Julian. (Mysterium Ser.). (ENG.). 352p. (J). (gr. 4-8). 2018. pap. 9.99 *(978-1-5415-1489-8(0)*, 9781541514898); 2016. E-Book 29.32 *(978-1-4677-9555-5(0))* Lerner Publishing Group. (Carolrhoda Bks.).

—The Palace of Memory. Sedgwick, Julian. (Mysterium Ser.). (ENG.). 352p. (J). (gr. 4-8). 2019. pap. 9.99 *(978-1-5415-5456-6(6))*; 2017. E-Book 29.32 *(978-1-5124-2690-8(3))*; No. 2. 2017. 18.99 *(978-1-4677-7568-7(1)*, 9781467775687) Lerner Publishing Group. (Carolrhoda Bks.).

—The Wheel of Life & Death. Sedgwick, Julian. (Mysterium Ser.). (ENG.). 344p. (J). (gr. 4-8). 2020. pap. 9.99 *(978-1-5415-8685-7(9))*; No. 3. 2018. 18.99 *(978-1-4677-7569-4(X)*, 9781467775694) Lerner Publishing Group. (Carolrhoda Bks.).

Mogensen, Jan. El Hijo del Elefante. Kipling, Rudyard. (Barril Sin Fondo Ser.).Tr. of Elephant's Child. (SPA.). (J). (gr. 3-5). pap. 8.76 *(978-968-6465-06-8(5))* Casa de Estudios de Literatura y Talleres Artisticos Amaquemecan A.C. MEX. Dist: Lectorum Pubns., Inc.

Mogensen, Jan & Schroeder, Binnette. Crocodile, Crocodile. Kipling, Rudyard. 2003. Orig. Title: Krokodil, Krokodil. pap. 7.95 *(978-1-56656-512-7(X))* Interlink Publishing Group, Inc.

Mogorrón, Guillermo. The Hunt for Hidden Treasure: A Mystery about Rocks. Beauregard, Lynda. 2012. (Summer Camp Science Mysteries Ser.: 3). (ENG.). 48p. (gr. 3-6). pap. 39.62 *(978-0-7613-9270-5(X)*, Graphic Universe™) Lerner Publishing Group.

—The Hunt for Hidden Treasure No. 3: A Mystery about Rocks. Beauregard, Lynda. 2012. (Summer Camp Science Mysteries Ser.: 3). (ENG.). 48p. (J). (gr. 3-6). lib. bdg. 29.32 *(978-0-7613-5690-5(8)*, 9780761356905, Graphic Universe™) Lerner Publishing Group.

Mogorrón, Guillermo & Mogorrón, Guillermo. The Hunt for Hidden Treasure No. 3: A Mystery about Rocks. Beauregard, Lynda. 2012. (Summer Camp Science Mysteries Ser.: 3). (ENG.). 48p. (J). (gr. 3-6). pap. 6.95 *(978-0-7613-8545-5(2)*, 9780761385455, Graphic Universe™) Lerner Publishing Group.

Mogorrón, Guillermo, jt. illus. see Mogorrón, Guillermo.

Mogyorosi, Nicole. Three Dogs Go Walking. Post, Grace. 2009. 32p. pap. 24.95 *(978-1-61546-147-9(7))* America Star Bks.

Mohamed, Lina, et al. Ear Tubes... Ear Tubes... a to Zeeeee... 2020. (Ready for a Happy Dream Ser.: Vol. 1). (ENG.). 36p. (J). pap. 10.00 ***(978-1-6514-9303-8(0))*** Independently Published.

Mohamed, Sultan. The Story of Coffee. Mohamed, Sultan, tr. 2003. (ENG & AMH.). 24p. (J). (gr. 4-5). 15.99 *(978-0-9605670-9-6(7))* Ananse Pr.

Mohammed, Munir D. Wherever I Go. Copp, Mary Wagley. 2020. (ENG.). 32p. (J). (gr. 1-4). 17.99 *(978-1-5344-1919-3(5))* Simon & Schuster Children's Publishing.

Mohanamani, Imodraj. Not Opposites. Ragsdale, Linda. 2017. (ENG.). 24p. (J). (gr. -1-3). *(978-1-4867-1255-7(X))* Flowerpot Children's Pr. Inc.

—Words. Ragsdale, Linda. 2017. (ENG.). 24p. (J). (gr. -1-3). *(978-1-4867-1254-0(1))* Flowerpot Children's Pr. Inc.

Moharram, Hend. Mili & the Dragonfly: Responding with Empathy. Mohan, Divya. 2019. (Gift a Value Ser.: Vol. 1). (ENG.). 26p. (J). (gr. k-2). *(978-0-6485321-0-1(0))*; pap. *(978-0-6485321-1-8(9))* Value Buds, The.

—Mom's Chair. Berry, Deirdre. 2018. (ENG.). 26p. (J). pap. 9.25 *(978-1-7905-9330-9(1))* Independently Published.

Mohler, Jeremy. Stories of Survival & Revenge: From Inuit Folklore, 1 vol. Qitsualik-Tinsley, Rachel & Qitsualik-Tinsley, Sean. 2015. (ENG.). 88p. (J). (gr. 7). pap. 12.95 *(978-1-77227-001-3(6))* Inhabit Media Inc. CAN. Dist: Consortium Bk. Sales & Distribution.

Mohney, Lynn. Daddy's Cloud. Robbins, Lisa. 2016. (ENG.). (J). pap. 11.99 *(978-1-945620-08-9(0))* Hear My Heart Publishing.

—The Many Names of Penelope Jane. Camper, Penney. 2016. (ENG.). (J). pap. 11.99 *(978-1-945620-15-7(3))* Hear My Heart Publishing.

—An Oyster Tale: God's Love Never Ends. Dee, Terry. 2018. (ENG.). 28p. (J). 19.99 *(978-1-945620-54-6(4))*; pap. 11.99 *(978-1-945620-51-5(X))* Hear My Heart Publishing.

—Patch. McCroskey, Selena. 2017. (ENG.). 32p. (J). 22.00 *(978-1-945620-40-9(4))*; pap. 11.99 *(978-1-945620-31-7(5))* Hear My Heart Publishing.

Mohnhaupt, Adrianne. Lost & Found in Tijuana: The Unexpected Adventure. Mohnhaupt, Adrianne. 2018. (ENG.). 40p. (J). pap. 9.99 *(978-1-7291-3858-8(6))* Independently Published.

Mohrbacher, Peter. The Three Furies. Kingsley, Kaza. (Erec Rex Ser.: 4). (ENG.). 576p. (J). (gr. 5-9). 2011. pap. 9.99 *(978-1-4169-7991-3(3))*; 2010. 17.99 *(978-1-4169-7990-6(5))* Simon & Schuster Bks. For Young Readers. (Simon & Schuster Bks. For Young Readers).

Moignot, Daniel. Animals Underground. Delafosse, Claude. Gibson, Sarah, tr. 2012. (ENG.). 36p. (J). (gr. -1-k). spiral bd. 13.99 *(978-1-85103-408-6(0))* Moonlight Publishing, Ltd. GBR. Dist: Independent Pubs. Group.

—Atlas of the Earth. 2012. (ENG.). 36p. (J). (gr. -1-k). spiral bd. 14.99 *(978-1-85103-406-2(4))* Moonlight Publishing, Ltd. GBR. Dist: Independent Pubs. Group.

Moisan, Elizabeth. The Lobsters' Night Before Christmas, 1 vol. Laurie, Christina. 2019. (ENG.). 32p. (J). 16.99 *(978-0-7643-5826-5(X)*, 16236) Schiffer Publishing, Ltd.

Moise, Nahomie. Big E, Meet Zeke, Your New Brother. Fichthorn, Ashley. 2011. 36p. pap. 24.95 *(978-1-4560-6941-4(1))* America Star Bks.

Moises, Yesenia. Honeysmoke: A Story of Finding Your Color. Fields, Monique. 2019. (ENG.). 32p. (J). 17.99 *(978-1-250-11582-9(5)*, 900171765) Imprint IND. Dist: Macmillan.

Mojica, Victor Ramon. Little Miss HISTORY Travels to Hyde Park, Home of FRANKLIN D. ROOSEVELT: Presidential Library & Museum. Mojica, Barbara Ann. 2019. (Little Miss History Travels To Ser.: Vol. 10). (ENG.). 52p. (J). (gr. 3-6). 21.95 ***(978-0-9989154-5-6(9))*** eugenus STUDIOS, LLC.

Mojica, Victor Ramon. Little Miss History Travels to Mount Rushmore. Mojica, Barbara Ann. 2012. 36p. pap. 13.95 *(978-0-9885030-0-7(X))* eugenus STUDIOS.

—Little Miss History Travels to the North Pole. Mojica, Barbara Ann. 2018. (ENG.). 40p. (J). 20.95 *(978-0-9989154-4-9(0))*; (Little Miss History Travels To Ser.: Vol. 9). pap. 10.95 *(978-0-9989154-2-5(4))* eugenus STUDIOS, LLC.

Mojica, Victor Ramon. Little Miss HISTORY Travels to TOMBSTONE ARIZONA. Mojica, Barbara Ann. 2020. (Little Miss History Travels To Ser.: Vol. 11). (ENG.). 48p. (J). (gr. k-6). 19.95 ***(978-0-9989154-9-4(1))*** eugenus STUDIOS, LLC.

Mojica, Victor Ramon. Captain Crossbones in the Treasure Hunt. Mojica, Victor Ramon. 2017. (ENG.). 34p. (J). (gr. k-6). pap. 10.50 *(978-0-692-05160-3(0))* eugenus STUDIOS, LLC.

Mojonnier, James. My Uncle Keith Died. Loehr, Carol Ann. 2009. (ENG.). 26p. pap. 12.00 *(978-1-4251-0262-3(X))* Trafford Publishing.

Mok, Carmen. Cone Cat. Howden, Sarah. 2020. (ENG.). 32p. (J). (gr. k-4). 17.95 ***(978-1-77147-361-3(4))*** Owlkids Bks. Inc. CAN. Dist: Publishers Group West (PGW).

Mok, Carmen. Grandmother's Visit. Quan, Betty. 2018. (ENG.). 32p. E-Book *(978-1-55498-955-3(8))* Groundwood Bks.

—Grandmother's Visit, 1 vol. Quan, Betty. 2018. (ENG.). 32p. (gr. k-2). 17.95 *(978-1-55498-954-6(X))* Groundwood Bks. CAN. Dist: Publishers Group West (PGW).

—A Stopwatch from Grampa. Garbutt, Loretta. 2020. (ENG.). 32p. (J). (gr. -1-2). 17.99 *(978-1-5253-0144-5(6))* Kids Can Pr., Ltd. CAN. Dist: Hachette Bk. Group.

—Violet Shrink, 1 vol. Baldacchino, Christine. 2020. 32p. (J). (gr. -1-2). 17.95 *(978-1-77306-205-1(0))* Groundwood Bks. CAN. Dist: Publishers Group West (PGW).

Mokona. Okimono Kimono. Mokona. Clamp Staff. 2010. (ENG.). 128p. pap. 12.99 *(978-1-59582-456-1(1))* Dark Horse Comics.

Mokry, Shannon L. La Elafantita Rosadita. Mokry, Shannon L. Hornor, Katie, tr. 2nd ed. 2019.Tr. of Little Pink Elephant. (SPA.). 20p. (J). 15.99 ***(978-1-951521-07-3(2))*** Sillygeese Publishing, LLC.

—The Little Donkey. Mokry, Shannon L. 2020. (ENG.). 40p. (J). 15.95 ***(978-1-951521-31-8(5))***; pap. 9.95 ***(978-1-951521-28-8(5))*** Sillygeese Publishing, LLC.

Mokry, Shannon L. The Little Pink Elephant. Mokry, Shannon L. 2019. (ENG.). (J). 24p. pap. 9.99 *(978-0-9987112-8-7(4))*; 22p. 14.99 ***(978-1-951521-05-9(6))*** Sillygeese Publishing, LLC.

—The Little Purple Porcupine. Mokry, Shannon L. 2019. (ENG.). 24p. (J). pap. 9.99 (978-0-9987112-3-2(3)); 16.99 (978-1-951521-06-6(4)) Sillygeese Publishing, LLC.

Mokry, Shannon L. The Little Yellow Llama. Mokry, Shannon L. 2019. (ENG.). (J). 38p. 16.95 (978-1-951521-09-7(9)); 40p. pap. 9.95 (978-1-951521-08-0(0)) Sillygeese Publishing, LLC.

—Take a Walk on the Beach. Mokry, Shannon L. 2020. (Take a Walk Ser.: Vol. 1). (ENG.). 22p. (J). 16.95 (978-1-951521-12-7(9)); pap. 9.95 (978-1-951521-13-4(7)) Sillygeese Publishing, LLC.

—Take a Walk on the Beach: Dyslexic Edition. Mokry, Shannon L. 2020. (Take a Walk Ser.: Vol. 1). (ENG.). 22p. (J). 16.95 (978-1-951521-14-1(5)); pap. 9.95 (978-1-951521-15-8(3)) Sillygeese Publishing, LLC.

Mokrzycki, Olivia. Wesley Raccoon: The Old Man in the Houseboat. Porter, Michelle. 2019. (ENG.). 24p. (J). (978-0-2288-2020-8(0)); pap. (978-0-2288-2019-2(7)) Tellwell Talent.

Mola, Maria. Bedtime Prayers Praying Hands. Swift, Ginger. Cottage Door Press, ed. 2020. (Little Sunbeams Ser.). (ENG.). 10p. (J). (gr. -1-1). bds. 4.99 (978-1-68052-814-5(9), 1005270) Cottage Door Pr.

—Jeremy's Dreidel. Gellman, Ellie B. rev. ed. 2012. (ENG.). 32p. (J). (gr. k-3). lib. bdg. 17.95 (978-0-7613-7507-4(4), 9780761375074, Kar-Ben Publishing) Lerner Publishing Group.

—Jeremy's Dreidel, Vol. Gellman, Ellie B. rev. ed. 2012. (ENG.). 32p. (J). (gr. k-3). 7.95 (978-0-7613-7508-1(2), 9780761375081, Kar-Ben Publishing) Lerner Publishing Group.

—Jesus Loves Me Praying Hands. Swift, Ginger. Cottage Door Press, ed. 2020. (Little Sunbeams Ser.). (ENG.). 10p. (J). (gr. -1-1). bds. 4.99 (978-1-68052-802-2(5), 1005150) Cottage Door Pr.

—Koala Challah. Gehl, Laura. 2017. (ENG.). 24p. (J). (gr. -1-1). 17.99 (978-1-5124-2087-6(5), 9781512420876); Vol. pap. 7.99 (978-1-5124-2088-3(3), 9781512420883) Lerner Publishing Group. (Kar-Ben Publishing).

—Maya Papaya & Amigos Play Dress-Up. Elya, Susan Middleton. 2018. 32p. (J). (gr. -1-2). lib. bdg. 16.99 (978-1-58089-803-4(3)) Charlesbridge Publishing, Inc.

—Sparkle Boy, 1 vol. Newman, Lesléa. 2017. (ENG.). 32p. (J). (gr. k-3). 18.95 (978-1-62014-285-1(6), 717cbddb-59b7-4048-98f2-73acd3183f2a) Lee & Low Bks., Inc.

Molan, Chris. Cleopatra, the Queen of Kings. MacDonald, Fiona. 2006. (DK Discoveries Ser.). (ENG.). 48p. (J). (gr. 3-6). 21.19 (978-0-7894-7761-3(0)) Dorling Kindersley Publishing, Inc.

—Explore the Bible Book by Book, 1 vol. Martin, Peter. ed. 2018. (ENG.). 160p. (J). 19.99 (978-0-7459-7705-8(7), Lion Children's) Lion Hudson PLC GBR. Dist: Kregel Pubns.

Molina, Adrian H., jt. illus. see RH Disney Staff.

Molina, Claudio. The Brain Storm. Ragsdale, Linda. 2019. (ENG.). 32p. (J). (gr. k-2). 17.99 (978-1-4867-1787-3(X), 5f8674c3-66b0-47aa-806f-c232e9a01e10); 16.99 (978-1-4867-1556-5(7), 3879188d-73c1-4c1d-b804-fe6e7d84e946) Flowerpot Pr.

Molina, Jorge. Man Out of Time. Waid, Mark. 2011. (Captain America Ser.). (ENG.). 24p. (J). (gr. 4-8). Pt. 1. lib. bdg. 27.07 (978-1-59961-936-1(9), 4104); Pt. 2. lib. bdg. 27.07 (978-1-59961-937-8(7), 4105); Pt. 3. lib. bdg. 27.07 (978-1-59961-938-5(5), 4106); Pt. 4. lib. bdg. 27.07 (978-1-59961-939-2(3), 4107); Pt. 5. lib. bdg. 27.07 (978-1-59961-940-8(7), 4108) Spotlight. (Marvel Age).

—X-Men Blue Vol. 3: Cross-Time Capers. 2018. (ENG.). 136p. (YA). (gr. 8-17). pap. 15.99 (978-1-302-90978-9(9)) Marvel Worldwide, Inc.

Molina, Jorge & Lopez, Julian. X-Men Blue Vol. 1: Strangest, Vol. 1. 2017. (ENG.). 144p. (YA). (gr. 8-17). pap. 15.99 (978-1-302-90728-0(X)) Marvel Worldwide, Inc.

Molinari, Carlo. Baseball: A Nonfiction Companion to Magic Tree House #29: a Big Day for Baseball. Osborne, Mary Pope & Boyce, Natalie Pope. 2017. (Magic Tree House (R) Fact Tracker Ser.: 37). (ENG.). 128p. (J). (gr. 2-5). 6.99 (978-1-101-93642-9(8)); lib. bdg. 12.99 (978-1-101-93643-6(6)) Random Hse. Children's Bks. (Random Hse. Bks. for Young Readers).

—China: Land of the Emperor's Great Wall: A Nonfiction Companion to Magic Tree House #14: Day of the Dragon King. Osborne, Mary Pope & Boyce, Natalie Pope. 2014. (Magic Tree House (R) Fact Tracker Ser.: 31). (ENG.). 128p. (J). (gr. 2-5). pap. 6.99 (978-0-385-38635-7(4), Random Hse. Bks. for Young Readers) Random Hse. Children's Bks.

—Dogsledding & Extreme Sports: A Nonfiction Companion to Magic Tree House Merlin Mission #26: Balto of the Blue Dawn. Osborne, Mary Pope & Boyce, Natalie Pope. 2016. (Magic Tree House (R) Fact Tracker Ser.: 34). 128p. (J). (gr. 2-5). 6.99 (978-0-385-38644-9(3), Random Hse. Bks. for Young Readers) Random Hse. Children's Bks.

—Dragons & Mythical Creatures: A Nonfiction Companion to Magic Tree House Merlin Mission #27: Night of the Ninth Dragon. Boyce, Natalie Pope & Osborne, Mary Pope. 2016. (Magic Tree House (R) Fact Tracker Ser.: 35). (ENG.). 128p. (J). (gr. 2-5). 6.99 (978-1-101-93636-8(3), Random Hse. Bks. for Young Readers) Random Hse. Children's Bks.

—Mary Walker Wears the Pants: The True Story of the Doctor, Reformer, & Civil War Hero. Harness, Cheryl. 2013. (ENG.). 32p. (J). (gr. 1-3). 16.99 (978-0-8075-4990-2(8), 807549908) Whitman, Albert & Co.

—Nanabozho & the Maple Trees: A Tale from Canada. Bioletti, Lucy. 2016. 24p. (J). pap. 9.95 (978-1-927244-64-7(1)) Flying Start Bks. NZL. Dist: Flying Start Bks.

—Sharks & Other Predators. Osborne, Mary Pope & Boyce, Natalie Pope. 2015. (Magic Tree House (R) Fact Tracker Ser.: 32). (ENG.). 128p. (J). (gr. 2-5). 12.99 (978-0-385-38642-5(7), Random Hse. Bks. for Young Readers) Random Hse. Children's Bks.

—True Stories of the Civil War, 1 vol. Yomtov, Nelson. 2012. (Stories of War Ser.). (ENG.). 32p. (J). (gr. 3-9). pap. 8.10 (978-1-4296-9340-0(1)); lib. bdg. 31.32 (978-1-4296-8624-2(3)) Capstone. (Capstone Pr.).

—True Stories of the Civil War. Yomtov, Nel. 2012. (Stories of War Ser.). (ENG.). 32p. (gr. 3-4). pap. 47.70 (978-1-4296-9341-7(X), Capstone Pr.) Capstone.

—Vikings: Magic Tree House Fact Tracker. Osborne, Mary Pope & Boyce, Natalie Pope. 2015. (Magic Tree House (R) Fact Tracker Ser.: 33). 128p. (J). (gr. 2-5). 6.99 (978-0-385-38638-8(9), Random Hse. Bks. for Young Readers) Random Hse. Children's Bks.

—Wild West: A Nonfiction Companion to Magic Tree House #10: Ghost Town at Sundown. Osborne, Mary Pope & Boyce, Natalie Pope. 2018. (Magic Tree House (R) Fact Tracker Ser.: 38). 128p. (J). (gr. 2-5). 6.99 (978-1-101-93645-0(2)); (ENG.). lib. bdg. 12.99 (978-1-101-93646-7(0)) Random Hse. Children's Bks. (Random Hse. Bks. for Young Readers).

—World War II: A Nonfiction Companion to Magic Tree House Super Edition #1: World at War 1944. Osborne, Mary Pope & Boyce, Natalie Pope. 2017. (Magic Tree House (R) Fact Tracker Ser.: 36). 128p. (J). (gr. 4-7). 6.99 (978-1-101-93639-9(8), Random Hse. Bks. for Young Readers) Random Hse. Children's Bks.

Molinari, Fernando. The Eye in the Graveyard: 10th Anniversary Edition. Dahl, Michael. 10th ed. 2017. (Library of Doom Ser.). (ENG.). 48p. (J). (gr. 4-8). pap. 6.25 (978-1-4965-5534-2(1), 136558); lib. bdg. 23.99 (978-1-4965-5528-1(7), 136552) Capstone. (Stone Arch Bks.).

—Isabel Allende: Memories for a Story: Isabel Allende: Recuerdos para un Cuento. Benatar, Raquel. Petersen, Patricia, tr. 2003. (SPA & ENG.). 32p. 16.95 (978-1-55885-379-9(0), Piñata Books) Arte Publico Pr.

—El Ojo Del Cementerio. Dahl, Michael. 2019. (Biblioteca Maldita Ser.). (SPA.). 40p. (J). (gr. 4-8). lib. bdg. 23.99 (978-1-4965-8535-6(6), 141284, Stone Arch Bks.) Capstone.

Molinari, Francesca. Annie's Famous Ginger Soup. Molinari, Francesca. 2019. (Froumo Group Ser.: Vol. 4). (ENG.). 26p. (J). pap. 9.99 (978-1-7938-1588-0(7)) Independently Published.

—Ducks & Pigs. Molinari, Francesca. 2018. (Froumo Group Ser.: Vol. 1). (ENG.). 30p. (J). pap. 9.99 (978-1-7239-1909-1(8)) Independently Published.

—Ducks & Pigs Coloring Book. Molinari, Francesca. 2018. (Froumo Group Coloring Bks.: Vol. 1). (ENG.). 30p. (J). pap. 5.99 (978-1-7239-4045-3(3)) Independently Published.

—Hugs. Molinari, Francesca. 2018. (Froumo Group Ser.: Vol. 3). (ENG.). 34p. (J). pap. 9.99 (978-1-7909-9160-0(9)) Independently Published.

Moline, Karl, et al. Highway of Horror. Bedard, Tony. 2003. (Route 666 Ser.: Vol. 1). 160p. (YA). (gr. 7-18). pap. 15.95 (978-1-931484-56-5(2)) CrossGeneration Comics, Inc.

—Most Haunted, Vol. 2. Bedard, Tony. 2004. (Route 666 Traveler Ser.: Vol. 2). 160p. (YA). pap. 9.95 (978-1-59314-055-7(X)) CrossGeneration Comics, Inc.

—Route 666, Vol. 2. Bedard, Tony. 2003. (Route 666 Ser.: Vol. 2). 160p. (YA). pap. 15.95 (978-1-931484-92-3(9)) CrossGeneration Comics, Inc.

—Route 666 Traveler: Highway of Horror. Bedard, Tony. 2004. (Route 666 Traveler Ser.). 160p. (YA). pap. 9.95 (978-1-59314-041-0(X)) CrossGeneration Comics, Inc.

Molinet, Michael. Guinevere: The Legend. Carpinello, Cheryl. 2019. (Tales & Legends for Reluctant Readers: Guinevere Ser.: Vol. 3). (ENG.). 178p. (J). (gr. 3-6). pap. (978-1-912513-49-9(8)) Silver Quill Publishing.

Molinet, Michael. Before You Were Born. Molinet, Michael. Molinet, Kelly. 2003. 22p. (J). 12.99 (978-0-9705996-7-4(6)) Practical Christianity Foundation.

—Just Like You. Molinet, Michael. Molinet, Kelly. 2004. 22p. (J). 15.99 (978-1-932587-34-0(9)) Practical Christianity Foundation.

Molitor, Sherrie. The Lucky Nickel. DoNascimento, Nicole. 2014. (ENG & POL.). 20p. (J). pap. 9.99 (978-0-9835120-0-4(0)) Briggs & Schuster.

Molk, Laurel. It's a ... It's a ... It's a Mitzvah. Suneby, Liz & Heiman, Diane. (ENG.). 38p. (J). 2017. pap. 14.99 (978-1-68336-772-7(3)); 2012. 24.99 (978-1-58023-509-9(3), 2b22e42c-0985-4849-8130-5e5cfadcc977) LongHill Partners, Inc. (Jewish Lights Publishing).

—That's a Mitzvah. Heiman, Diane & Suneby, Liz. 2014. (ENG.). 24p. (J). bds. 8.99 (978-1-58023-804-5(1), 111caa34-316a-4f5f-8071-8473379a8103, Jewish Lights Publishing) LongHill Partners, Inc.

—There Might Be Lobsters. Crimi, Carolyn. 2017. 32p. (J). (gr. -1-2). 16.99 (978-0-7636-7542-4(3)) Candlewick Pr.

Moll, Shawn. Heimdall. Worley, Rob M. 2010. (Short Tales Norse Myths Ser.). (ENG.). 32p. (J). (gr. 1-4). 27.07 (978-1-60270-566-1(6), 13461, Short Tales) Magic Wagon.

Mollett, Irene. Groundhog Breakfast, Soft Petals, & a Roof That Don't Leak Too Much, 1 vol. Williamson, Linda. 2009. 23p. pap. 24.95 (978-1-60749-618-2(6)) America Star Bks.

Molloy, Bryan Thomas. Jack: An Ancient Celtic Tradition: How the Jack o'Lantern Came to Be. Molloy, Bryan Thomas. 2018. (ENG.). 32p. (J). pap. 11.99 (978-1-7273-5629-8(2)) CreateSpace Independent Publishing Platform.

Molloy, Sophie. The Cat Did Not Know. McCarthy, Margaret. 2006. (ENG.). 36p. (J). pap. 14.95 (978-1-85390-923-8(8)) Veritas Pubns. IRL. Dist: Casemate Pubs. & Bk. Distributors, LLC.

Molly, Crouch, jt. illus. see Katie, Katzenmeyer.

Molnar, Albert. Field Day. Jones, Melanie Davis. 2011. (ENG.). 40p. (J). (gr. -1-k). pap. 5.95 (978-0-531-26826-1(8)); lib. bdg. 25.00 (978-0-531-27176-6(5)) Scholastic Library Publishing. (Children's Pr.).

Molnar, Albert & McKillip Thornburgh, Rebecca. The School Box: Field Day - 100th Da of School - One Happy Classroom. Davis Jones, Melanie et al. 2004. (Rookie Reader Ser.). (ENG.). 96p. (J). (gr. k-2). pap. 9.95 (978-0-516-24554-6(6), Children's Pr.) Scholastic Library Publishing.

Molony, Meghan. Growing Around: Party Panic. Rozanski, Johnathan Enter. 2016. (ENG.). (J). pap. 12.00 (978-0-9983327-9-6(8)) Rozanski, Johnathan.

Molton, Jennifer R. The Lilac Thief. Molton, Jennifer R. 2018. (ENG.). 28p. (J). pap. 10.95 (978-1-7224-3284-3(5)) CreateSpace Independent Publishing Platform.

Molver, Luke W. Shaka Rising: A Graphic Novel. Molver, Luke W. 2018. (African Graphic Novel Ser.). (ENG.). 96p. (J). (gr. 6). pap. 16.99 (978-1-946498-98-4(X), Story Pr. Africa) Catalyst Bk. Pr.

Momaday, N. Scott. Four Arrows & Magpie: A Kiowa Story. Momaday, N. Scott. 2006. 35p. (J). (gr. -1-3). pap. 9.95 (978-1-930709-63-8(3)) HAWK Publishing Group.

Moments, Ministering, photos by. Anmir, Different? A Journal. Jones, Miracle. 2017. (ENG.). (J). pap. 10.00 (978-1-942022-90-9(5)) Butterfly Typeface, The.

Momin, Azra. Allah Made Everything: The Song Book. Bhika, Zain. 2019. (ENG.). 30p. (J). 11.95 (978-0-86037-770-2(9)) Kube Publishing Ltd. GBR. Dist: Consortium Bk. Sales & Distribution.

Mommaerts, Robb. Cinnamon & the April Shower. Johnson, Amy Crane. 2009. (ENG.). 32p. (J). (gr. -1-3). 16.95 (978-1-934960-54-7(3), Raven Tree Pr.,Csi) Continental Sales, Inc.

—A Home for Pearl Squirrel. Johnson, Amy Crane. 2009. (ENG.). 32p. (J). (gr. -1-3). 16.95 (978-1-934960-58-5(6), Raven Tree Pr.,Csi) Continental Sales, Inc.

—A Home for Pearl Squirrel: Una casa para la ardilla Perla, 4 vols. Crane Johnson, Amy. de la Vega, Eida, tr. rev. ed. 2004. (Solomon Raven Ser.: 1).Tr. of casa para la ardilla Perla. (SPA & ENG.). 32p. (J). (gr. 4-7). 16.95 (978-0-9724973-4-3(X), 626999, Raven Tree Pr.,Csi) Continental Sales, Inc.

Mommaerts, Robb. Klawde: Evil Alien Warlord Cat #1. Marciano, Johnny & Chenoweth, Emily. (Klawde: Evil Alien Warlord Cat Ser.: 1). 224p. (J). (gr. 3-7). 2020. pap. 7.99 (978-0-593-22523-3(6)); 2019. (ENG.). 14.99 (978-1-5247-8720-2(5)) Penguin Young Readers Group. (Penguin Workshop).

—Klawde: Evil Alien Warlord Cat: Enemies #2. Marciano, Johnny & Chenoweth, Emily. (Klawde: Evil Alien Warlord Cat Ser.: 2). 224p. (J). (gr. 3-7). 2020. pap. 7.99 (978-0-593-22524-0(4)); 2019. 14.99 (978-1-5247-8722-6(1)) Penguin Young Readers Group. (Penguin Workshop).

Mommaerts, Robb. Klawde: Evil Alien Warlord Cat: Target: Earth #4. Marciano, Johnny & Chenoweth, Emily. 2020. (Klawde: Evil Alien Warlord Cat Ser.: 4). 224p. (J). (gr. 3-7). 14.99 (978-1-5247-8729-5(9), Penguin Workshop) Penguin Young Readers Group.

—Lewis Cardinal's First Winter. Johnson, Amy Crane. 2009. (ENG.). 32p. (J). (gr. 4-7). 16.95 (978-1-934960-60-8(8), Raven Tree Pr.,Csi) Continental Sales, Inc.

—Mason Moves Away. Johnson, Amy Crane. 2009. (ENG.). 32p. (J). (gr. 4-7). 16.95 (978-1-934960-56-1(X), Raven Tree Pr.,Csi) Continental Sales, Inc.

—Mason Moves Away/Mason se Muda: A Solomon Raven Story: un cuento del cuervo Salomon, 4 vols. Johnson, Amy Crane. de la Vega, Eida, tr. 2004. (Solomon Raven Ser.: 4).Tr. of Mason se Muda. (SPA & ENG.). 32p. (J). (gr. -1-3). 16.95 (978-0-9720192-3-1(5), 626999, Raven Tree Pr.,Csi) Continental Sales, Inc.

—The Spacedog Cometh, 3. Marciano, Johnny & Chenoweth, Emily. 2019. (Klawde: Evil Alien Warlord Cat Ser.: 3). 224p. (J). (gr. 3-7). 14.99 (978-1-5247-8724-0(8), Penguin Workshop) Penguin Young Readers Group.

Momokawa, Haruhiko. The Good Witch of the West, Vol. 6. Ogiwara, Noriko & Noriko, Ogiwara. 2008. (Good Witch of the West Ser.). 208p. (gr. 8-18). pap. 9.99 (978-1-4278-0889-9(9)) TOKYOPOP, Inc.

Momose, Takeaki. Rahxephon. Izubuchi, Yutaka. 2004. (Rahxephon Ser.). (ENG.). (YA). 192p. pap. 9.95 (978-1-59116-407-4(9)); Vol. 2. 200p. pap. 9.95 (978-1-59116-427-2(3)); Vol. 3. 200p. pap. 9.95 (978-1-59116-428-9(1)) Viz Media.

Mon, Brian, et al. The Hunchback of Notre Dame. Steiner, Jeanette. 2020. (Disney Classics Ser.). (ENG.). 48p. (J). (gr. 2-6). lib. bdg. 28.50 (978-1-5321-4537-7(3), 35184, Graphic Novels) Spotlight.

Mona, Larkins. Pablo's Art Adventures: Exploring the Studio. Mona, Larkins. 2004. 27p. (J). 14.99 (978-0-9740841-3-8(1)) K&B Products.

Monaco, Octavia. Klimt & His Cat. Capatti, Bérénice. 2004. (ENG.). 40p. (J). 20.00 (978-0-8028-5282-3(3)) Eerdmans, William B. Publishing Co.

—El Nacimiento de las Estaciones: El Mito de Demetery Persefone. Lossani, Chiara. 2009. (SPA.). (YA). (gr. 5-10). (978-968-5389-62-4(4)) El Naranjo, Ediciones.

—Vincent Van Gogh & the Colors of the Wind. Lossani, Chiara & van Gogh, Vincent. 2011. (ENG.). 40p. (YA). (gr. 2). 19.00 (978-0-8028-5390-5(0), Eerdmans Bks For Young Readers) Eerdmans, William B. Publishing Co.

Monaghan, N. P. The Reel. Miles, Amanda. 2017. (ENG.). 82p. (J). pap. (978-1-9999383-0-7(5)) Miles and Miles Publishing.

Monahan, Leo. The Twelve Days of Christmas. Monahan, Leo. 2007. (ENG.). 24p. (J). 19.95 (978-1-58117-624-7(4), Intervisual/Piggy Toes) Bendon, Inc.

Monahan, Liz. The Swiss Family Robinson. Wyss, Johann David. 2014. 46p. (J). (978-1-4351-5826-9(1)) Barnes & Noble, Inc.

Monahan, Nicole Stremlow. Kitsy B Goes to the Beach. Bushmaker, Carolyn. 2016. (ENG.). (J). pap. 9.99 (978-1-4984-8520-3(0)) Salem Author Services.

—A Loud Whisper. Nagawo, Sheiko. 2017. (ENG.). (J). pap. (978-1-4602-9371-3(1)) FriesenPress.

Moncao, Nathan. Scaredy Cali. Williams, Jessica. 2019. (ENG.). 32p. (J). (gr. k-2). (978-1-7753456-9-5(6)); pap. (978-1-9995397-0-2(2)) All Write Here Publishing.

Monceaux, Morgan. My Heroes, My People: African Americans & Native Americans in Thewest. Monceaux, Morgan. Katcher, Ruth. 2004. 63p. (J). (gr. k-4). reprint ed. 18.00 (978-0-7567-7868-2(9)) DIANE Publishing Co.

Mondal, Argha. Timey & Friends Amya Tells the Truth: Teach the Value of Timey's Driving Principle: Honesty. Gavin, Elnora & El, Auntie. 2019. (Exclusive Level up Limited Edition Ser.: Vol. 1). (ENG.). 40p. (J). pap. 200.00 (978-1-7117-8303-1(X)) Independently Published.

Mondal, Argha. Tommy Two-Toes: Teaches the Jungle about Being Vegetarian. Mason, Dayton & Mason, Darci. 2017. (ENG.). 26p. (J). (978-0-9959983-2-2(9)) Green Bamboo Publishing.

Mondragon, Manny. How Can I Be Special? Chinn, Jacqueline. 2003. (J). pap. 15.95 (978-0-929526-55-3(4)) Double B Pubns.

Mones, Isidre. Bambi's Hide-and-Seek. RH Disney Staff & Posner-Sanchez, Andrea. 2013. (Step into Reading Ser.). (ENG.). 32p. (J). (gr. -1-1). pap. 3.99 (978-0-7364-1347-3(2), RH/Disney) Random Hse. Children's Bks.

—Benjamin Franklin: To the Future, Ben Franklin! Osborne, Mary Pope & Boyce, Natalie Pope. 2019. (Magic Tree House (R) Fact Tracker Ser.: 41). 128p. (J). (gr. 2-5). pap. 6.99 (978-1-9848-9317-8(3), Random Hse. Bks. for Young Readers) Random Hse. Children's Bks.

—Cloudy with a Chance of Meatballs 3: Planet of the Pies. Barrett, Judi. 2013. (ENG.). 32p. (J). (gr. -1-3). 17.99 (978-1-4424-9027-7(6), Atheneum Bks. for Young Readers) Simon & Schuster Children's Publishing.

—Narwhals & Other Whales. Osborne, Mary Pope & Boyce, Natalie Pope. 2020. (Magic Tree House (R) Fact Tracker Ser.: 42). 128p. (J). (gr. 2-5). lib. bdg. 12.99 (978-1-9848-9321-5(1), Random Hse. Bks. for Young Readers) Random Hse. Children's Bks.

—Puppy Mudge Has a Snack. Rylant, Cynthia. 2005. (Puppy Mudge Ser.). (gr. -1-k). 14.00 (978-0-7569-5764-3(8)) Perfection Learning Corp.

—Puppy Mudge Has a Snack. Rylant, Cynthia. (Puppy Mudge Ser.). (ENG.). 32p. (J). (gr. -1-k). 2004. pap. 4.99 (978-0-689-86995-2(9)); 2003. 17.99 (978-0-689-83981-8(2)) Simon Spotlight. (Simon Spotlight).

—Puppy Mudge Loves His Blanket. Rylant, Cynthia. (Puppy Mudge Ser.). (ENG.). 32p. (J). (gr. -1-k). 2005. pap. 4.99 (978-1-4169-0336-9(4)); 2004. 16.99 (978-0-689-83983-2(9)) Simon Spotlight. (Simon Spotlight).

—Puppy Mudge Takes a Bath. Rylant, Cynthia. 2004. (Puppy Mudge Ser.). (ENG.). 32p. (J). (gr. -1-k). pap. 4.99 (978-0-689-86621-0(6), Simon Spotlight) Simon Spotlight.

—Texas: A Nonfiction Companion to Magic Tree House #30 - Hurricane Heroes in Texas. Osborne, Mary Pope & Boyce, Natalie Pope. 2018. (Magic Tree House (R) Fact Tracker Ser.: 39). 128p. (J). (gr. 2-5). 6.99 (978-1-101-93648-1(7), Random Hse. Bks. for Young Readers) Random Hse. Children's Bks.

—Texas: A Nonfiction Companion to Magic Tree House #30: Hurricane Heroes in Texas. Osborne, Mary Pope & Boyce, Natalie Pope. 2018. (Magic Tree House (R) Fact Tracker Ser.: 39). (ENG.). 128p. (J). (gr. 2-5). lib. bdg. 12.99 (978-1-101-93649-8(5), Random Hse. Bks. for Young Readers) Random Hse. Children's Bks.

—Warriors. Osborne, Mary Pope & Boyce, Natalie Pope. 2019. (Magic Tree House (R) Fact Tracker Ser.: 40). 128p. (J). (gr. 2-5). 6.99 (978-1-101-93651-1(7), Random Hse. Bks. for Young Readers) Random Hse. Children's Bks.

—Warriors: A Nonfiction Companion to Magic Tree House #31: Warriors in Winter. Osborne, Mary Pope & Boyce, Natalie Pope. 2019. (Magic Tree House (R) Fact Tracker Ser.: 40). (ENG.). 128p. (J). (gr. 2-5). lib. bdg. 12.99 (978-1-101-93652-8(5), Random Hse. Bks. for Young Readers) Random Hse. Children's Bks.

—Wild West. Osborne, Mary Pope & Boyce, Natalie Pope. 2018. 123p. (J). (978-1-5444-0190-4(6)) Random Hse., Inc.

Mones, Marc. Be Honest, Jess Lap Book. Garcia, Ellen. 2014. (MySELF Ser.). (J). (gr. -1-k). 27.00 (978-1-4788-0508-3(0)) Newmark Learning LLC.

Monés, Marc. Carlos Es Responsable. Garcia, Ellen. 2015. (MySELF Ser.). (SPA.). (J). (gr. -1-k). 4.49 (978-1-4788-1969-1(3)) Newmark Learning LLC.

—Carlos Es Responsable: Lap Book. Garcia, Ellen. 2015. (MySELF Ser.). (SPA.). (J). (gr. -1-k). 29.00 (978-1-4788-2314-8(3)) Newmark Learning LLC.

Mones, Marc. Charlie Is Responsible Lap Book. Garcia, Ellen. 2014. (MySELF Ser.). (J). (gr. -1-k). 27.00 (978-1-4788-0507-6(2)) Newmark Learning LLC.

Monés, Marc. Gracias Por Compartir, Tomás. Giachetti, Julia. 2015. (MySELF Ser.). (SPA.). (J). (gr. -1-k). 4.49 (978-1-4788-1965-3(0)) Newmark Learning LLC.

—Gracias Por Compartir, Tomás: Lap Book. Giachetti, Julia. 2015. (MySELF Ser.). (SPA.). (J). (gr. -1-k). 29.00 (978-1-4788-2310-0(0)) Newmark Learning LLC.

Mones, Marc. I Can Be Kind Lap Book. Williams, Dinah. 2014. (MySELF Ser.). (J). (gr. -1-k). 27.00 (978-1-4788-0504-5(8)) Newmark Learning LLC.

Monés, Marc. I Put My Body In. Corriols, Carmen. 2015. (Early Rising Readers Ser.). (J). (gr. -1-k). 5.83 (978-1-4788-2148-9(5)) Newmark Learning LLC.

Mones, Marc. I Show Respect. Linde, Barbara M. 2014. (J). (gr. -1). 3.99 (978-1-4788-0468-0(8)) Newmark Learning LLC.

—I Show Respect Lap Book. Linde, Barbara M. 2014. (MySELF Ser.). (J). (gr. -1-k). 27.00 (978-1-4788-0505-2(6)) Newmark Learning LLC.

—Muevo Mi Cuerpo. Corriols, Carmen. 2016. (Early Rising Readers Ser.). (SPA.). 16p. (J). (gr. 1-1). 6.67 (978-1-4788-4176-0(1)) Newmark Learning LLC.

Monés, Marc. ¡No Es Justo! Daniel, Claire. 2015. (MySELF Ser.). (SPA.). (J). (gr. -1-k). 4.49 (978-1-4788-1968-4(5)) Newmark Learning LLC.

—¡No Es Justo! Lap Book. Daniel, Claire. 2015. (MySELF Ser.). (SPA.). (J). (gr. -1-k). 29.00 *(978-1-4788-2313-1(5))* Newmark Learning LLC.

—Sé Honesta, Julia. Smith, Molly. 2015. (MySELF Ser.). (SPA.). (J). (gr. -1-k). 4.49 *(978-1-4788-1970-7(7))* Newmark Learning LLC.

—Sé Honesta, Julia: Lap Book. Smith, Molly. 2015. (MySELF Ser.). (SPA.). (J). (gr. -1-k). 29.00 *(978-1-4788-2315-5(1))* Newmark Learning LLC.

Mones, Marc. Thanks for Sharing, Tommy. Giachetti, Julia. 2014. (J). (gr. -1). 3.99 *(978-1-4788-0466-6(1))* Newmark Learning LLC.

—Thanks for Sharing, Tommy Lap Book. Giachetti, Julia. 2014. (MySELF Ser.). (J). (gr. -1-k). 27.00 *(978-1-4788-0503-8(X))* Newmark Learning LLC.

—That's Not Fair! Lap Book. Daniel, Claire. 2014. (MySELF Ser.). (J). (gr. -1-k). 27.00 *(978-1-4788-0506-9(4))* Newmark Learning LLC.

—Time for a Trim. Reed, Jennifer. 2012. (Little Birdie Bks.). (ENG.). 24p. (gr. 1-2). pap. 8.95 *(978-1-61810-319-2(9),* 9781618103192) Rourke Educational Media.

—Vote for Me! Robertson, J. Jean. 2012. (Little Birdie Bks.). (ENG.). 24p. (gr. 1-2). pap. 8.95 *(978-1-61810-316-1(4),* 9781618103161) Rourke Educational Media.

—What Makes You You? Arbuthnott, Gill. 2016. (ENG.). 64p. (J). *(978-0-7787-2239-7(2))* Crabtree Publishing Co.

—What Makes Your Body Work? Arbuthnott, Gill. 2016. (ENG.). 64p. (J). *(978-0-7787-2241-0(4))* Crabtree Publishing Co.

Monés, Marc. Yo Puedo Ser Amable. Pippin, Jessica. 2015. (MySELF Ser.). (SPA.). (J). (gr. -1-k). 4.49 *(978-1-4788-1966-0(9))* Newmark Learning LLC.

—Yo Puedo Ser Amable: Lap Book. Pippin, Jessica. 2015. (MySELF Ser.). (SPA.). (J). (gr. -1-k). 29.00 *(978-1-4788-2311-7(9))* Newmark Learning LLC.

—Yo Soy Respetuosa: Lap Book. Linde, Barbara M. 2015. (MySELF Ser.). (SPA.). (J). (gr. -1-k). 29.00 *(978-1-4788-2312-4(7))* Newmark Learning LLC.

Mones, Marc. Your Guide to Life on Earth. Arbuthnott, Gill. 2016. (ENG.). 64p. (J). lib. bdg. *(978-0-7787-2243-4(0))* Crabtree Publishing Co.

—Your Guide to the Periodic Table. Arbuthnott, Gill. 2016. (ENG.). 64p. (J). lib. bdg. *(978-0-7787-2245-8(7))* Crabtree Publishing Co.

Monescillo, Maria. Many Days, One Shabbat, 0 vols. Manushkin, Fran. 2011. (ENG.). 24p. (J). (gr. -1-3). 12.99 *(978-0-7614-5965-1(0),* 9780761459651, Two Lions) Amazon Publishing.

—The Tallest of Smalls, 1 vol. Lucado, Max. 2009. (ENG.). 32p. (gr. -1-2). 16.99 *(978-1-4003-1514-7(X))* Nelson, Thomas Inc.

Monescillo, Maria. Charlotte Jane Battles Bedtime. Monescillo, Maria. Wolfe, Myra. 2011. (ENG.). 32p. (J). (gr. -1-3). 16.99 *(978-0-15-206150-0(9),* 1198466) Houghton Mifflin Harcourt Publishing Co.

Monesi, Mirella. The Lost Journal. Steele, Phillip. 2011. (ENG.). 40p. (gr. 3). 22.68 *(978-1-84732-640-9(4))* Carlton Bks., Ltd. GBR. Dist: Two Rivers Distribution.

Money, Greg. Princesses Don't Hit. Morrissey, Lynda I. 2012. 24p. pap. *(978-1-77097-976-5(X))* FriesenPress.

—Sophie's Magic Backpack. Morrissey, Lynda I. 2018. (ENG.). 24p. (J). *(978-1-5255-2163-8(2));* pap. *(978-1-5255-2164-5(0))* FriesenPress.

Moneymaker, Janet. Chemistry Pre-Level I. Keller, Rebecca W. 2005. (Real Science-4-Kids Ser.). 79p. (J). (gr. 1-3). 21095.00 *(978-0-9765097-0-7(9))* Gravitas Pubns., Inc.

Moneysmith, David. Mommy Breastfeeds My Baby Brother/ Mama Amamanta A Mi Hermanito. Repkin, Mark. 2011.Tr. of Mama Amamanta A Mi Hermanito. 24p. (J). pap. 9.99 *(978-0-9816538-1-5(2))* Istoria Hse.

Mongeau, Marc. The Bug House Family Restaurant, 1 vol. Brenna, Beverley. 2014. (ENG.). 64p. (J). (gr. 1-3). pap. 12.95 *(978-1-926890-01-2(9))* Tradewind Bks. CAN. Dist: Orca Bk. Pubs. USA.

—Mimi Power & the I-Don't-Know-What, 1 vol. Miles, Victoria. 2013. (ENG.). 224p. (J). (gr. 4-7). pap. 12.95 *(978-1-896580-65-4(3))* Tradewind Bks. CAN. Dist: Orca Bk. Pubs. USA.

—My Daddy's Footsteps. Barcelo, François. 2009. (My First Stories Ser.). 24p. (J). (gr. -1-3). 25.60 *(978-1-60754-359-6(1));* pap. 8.15 *(978-1-60754-360-2(5))* Windmill Bks.

—My Mommy's Hands. Barcelo, François. 2009. (My First Stories Ser.). 24p. (J). (gr. -1-3). 25.60 *(978-1-60754-362-6(1));* pap. 8.15 *(978-1-60754-365-7(6))* Windmill Bks.

—Shake Awakes, 1 vol. Heidbreder, Robert. 2012. (ENG.). 48p. (J). (gr. 1-3). 18.95 *(978-1-896580-71-5(8))* Tradewind Bks. CAN. Dist: Orca Bk. Pubs. USA.

Mongiardo, Massimo. Hamlet, the Algonquin Cat. Martini, Leslie. 2018. (ENG.). 40p. (J). (gr. 3-3). 16.95 *(978-1-944903-47-3(X),* Roundtree Pr.) Cameron + Co.

Mongiovi, Jorge. Bugs & Spiders. Orme, David. 2010. (Fact to Fiction Ser.). 36p. pap. 7.45 *(978-0-7891-7990-6(3))* Perfection Learning Corp.

—Life in Space. Orme, Helen. 2008. (Trailblazers Ser.). (ENG.). 36p. pap. *(978-1-84167-690-6(X))* Ransom Publishing Ltd.

—Lost Animals. Orme, David. 2010. (Fact to Fiction Grafx Ser.). 36p. pap. 7.45 *(978-0-7891-7993-7(8))* Perfection Learning Corp.

Mongtomery Gibson, Jane. Don't Renege! It's Just an Egg! Mongtomery Gibson, Jane. 2005. (J). bds. 8.99 *(978-1-4183-0036-4(5))* Christ Inspired, Inc.

—In Olden Days. Mongtomery Gibson, Jane. 2005. (YA). bds. 8.99 *(978-1-4183-0042-5(X))* Christ Inspired, Inc.

—Jesus' Bread. Mongtomery Gibson, Jane. 2005. (J). bds. 8.99 *(978-1-4183-0028-9(4))* Christ Inspired, Inc.

—My Heart Goes with You. Mongtomery Gibson, Jane. 2005. (J). bds. 8.99 *(978-1-4183-0029-6(2))* Christ Inspired, Inc.

Mongtomgery Gibson, Jane. Angels Long. Mongtomgery Gibson, Jane. 2005. (YA). bds. 8.99 *(978-1-4183-0035-7(7))* Christ Inspired, Inc.

Monica, Brufton. Without Surprise. Maude, Tony. 2013. 60p. pap. *(978-2-917183-29-8(2))* Nigeria Baptist Convention, Pubns. Dept.

Monical, Olivia R. The Forest of Thinks. Monical, Olivia R. 2012. (ENG.). 28p. (J). pap. 10.95 *(978-1-57733-267-1(9),* Papillon Publishing) Blue Dolphin Publishing, Inc.

Monick, Susie. A Boy & His God. Fite, Ramona. 2012. 36p. 22.50 *(978-1-937763-37-4(4))* Published by Westview, Inc.

Moniz, Michael. Wazzyjump. (J). (gr. -1-2). 2017. 40p. 8.99 *(978-1-77229-017-2(3));* 2012. (ENG.). 44p. 16.95 *(978-1-897476-58-1(2))* Simply Read Bks. CAN. Dist: Ingram Publisher Services.

Moniz, Michael. The Cardinal & the Crow. Moniz, Michael. 2015. 235p. (J). 16.95 *(978-1-927018-58-3(7))* Simply Read Bks. CAN. Dist: Ingram Publisher Services.

Monkman, Don. Nanabosho Steals Fire, 1 vol. McLellan, Joseph. 2015. (ENG.). 32p. (J). pap. 10.95 *(978-0-921827-05-4(9),* 914f2a3e-a451-4ee6-ae7a-25e3677ad7fa) Pemmican Pubns., Inc. CAN. Dist: Firefly Bks., Ltd.

Monkman, Kent. A Coyote Columbus Story, 1 vol. King, Thomas. 2007. (ENG.). 32p. (J). (gr. -1-k). pap. 8.95 *(978-0-88899-830-9(9))* Groundwood Bks. CAN. Dist: Publishers Group West (PGW).

Monks, Christian. The Wilkins Family Farm, 1 vol. May, Gary L. 2009. 75p. pap. 19.95 *(978-1-4489-2605-3(X))* America Star Bks.

Monks, Elizabeth. Clare & the Apple Faerie, & the Bad Troll. Roscoe, P. J. 2018. (Adventures of Faerie Folk Ser.: Vol. 3). (ENG.). 36p. (J). (gr. 1-5). pap. 9.99 *(978-1-68160-559-3(7))* Crimson Cloak Publishing.

Monks, Elizabeth. Jack & the Snowdrop Faerie & William Walnut. Roscoe, P. J. 2019. (Adventures of the Faerie Folk Ser.: Vol. 4). (ENG.). 46p. (J). pap. 10.99 ***(978-1-68160-705-4(0))*** Crimson Cloak Publishing.

Monks, Lydia. Aaaarrgghh, Spider! 2004. (ENG.). 32p. (J). pap. *(978-1-4052-1044-7(3))* Egmont Bks., Ltd.

—Christmas with Princess Mirror-Belle. Donaldson, Julia. (Princess Mirror-Belle Ser.). (ENG.). 96p. (J). (gr. k-2). 2018. pap. 8.99 *(978-1-5098-3892-9(9));* 2016. 14.99 *(978-1-5098-1426-8(4))* Pan Macmillan GBR. Dist: Independent Pubs. Group.

—Falling for Rapunzel. Wilcox, Leah. 32p. (J). (gr. -1-3). 2005. (ENG.). pap. 7.99 *(978-0-14-240399-0(7),* Puffin Books); 2003. 16.99 *(978-0-399-23794-2(1),* G.P. Putnam's Sons Books for Young Readers) Penguin Young Readers Group.

—The Flying Horse, 2 Bks in 1. Donaldson, Julia. 2017. (Princess Mirror-Belle Ser.). (ENG.). 192p. (J). (gr. k-2). 8.99 *(978-1-5098-3890-5(2))* Pan Macmillan GBR. Dist: Independent Pubs. Group.

—Frog Hops Off: Twit Twoo Book 2. 2018. (Twit Twoo School Ser.: 2). (ENG.). 32p. (J). (gr. -1-k). pap. 12.99 *(978-1-5098-2845-6(1))* Pan Macmillan GBR. Dist: Independent Pubs. Group.

—Glitter Kitty. Bergman, Mara. 2014. (ENG.). 32p. (J). 8.99 *(978-1-4711-2216-3(6),* Simon & Schuster Children's) Simon & Schuster, Ltd. GBR. Dist: Simon & Schuster, Inc.

—My Big (Strange) Happy Family. McCombie, Karen. 2009. (J). pap. *(978-0-385-73597-1(9),* Yearling) Random Hse. Children's Bks.

—Princess Mirror-Belle & the Magic Shoes (Bind Up 2) Donaldson, Julia. 2017. (Princess Mirror-Belle Ser.). (ENG.). 192p. (J). (gr. k-2). pap. 8.99 *(978-1-5098-3882-0(1))* Pan Macmillan GBR. Dist: Independent Pubs. Group.

—Princess Mirror-Belle Bind Up 1. Donaldson, Julia. 2017. (Princess Mirror-Belle Ser.). (ENG.). 192p. (J). (gr. k-2). pap. 8.99 *(978-1-5098-3872-1(4))* Pan Macmillan GBR. Dist: Independent Pubs. Group.

—Queen Munch & Queen Nibble. Duffy, Carol Ann. 2008. (ENG.). 64p. (J). (gr. -1-3). *(978-1-59692-238-9(9))* MacAdam/Cage Publishing, Inc.

—Queen Munch & Queen Nibble. Duffy, Carol Ann. 2018. (ENG.). 64p. (J). (gr. k-3). 13.99 *(978-1-5098-3091-6(X))* Pan Macmillan GBR. Dist: Independent Pubs. Group.

—The Rhyming Rabbit Sticker Book. Donaldson, Julia. 2017. (ENG.). 24p. (J). (gr. -1-1). pap. 9.99 *(978-1-5098-3925-4(9))* Pan Macmillan GBR. Dist: Independent Pubs. Group.

—Sharing a Shell Sticker Book. Donaldson, Julia. 2018. (ENG.). 24p. (J). (gr. -1-1). pap. 8.99 *(978-1-5098-3924-7(0))* Pan Macmillan GBR. Dist: Independent Pubs. Group.

—Shout, Show & Tell! Agnew, Kate. 2005. (Green Bananas Ser.). (ENG.). 48p. (J). (gr. -1-1). *(978-0-7787-1040-0(8))* Crabtree Publishing Co.

—Shout, Show, & Tell. Agnew, Kate. 2005. (Green Bananas Ser.). (ENG.). 48p. (J). lib. bdg. *(978-0-7787-1024-0(6))* Crabtree Publishing Co.

—Shout, Show & Tell! Agnew, Kate. 2nd ed. 2016. (Reading Ladder Ser.). (ENG.). 48p. (J). (gr. k-2). pap. 7.99 *(978-1-4052-8224-6(X))* Egmont Bks., Ltd. GBR. Dist: Independent Pubs. Group.

—The Skipping-Rope Snake. 2016. (ENG.). 32p. (J). (gr. -1-1). pap. 9.99 *(978-1-5098-3245-3(9))* Pan Macmillan GBR. Dist: Independent Pubs. Group.

—Waking Beauty. Wilcox, Leah. 2011. (ENG.). 32p. (J). (gr. -1-k). pap. 7.99 *(978-0-14-241538-2(3),* Puffin Books) Penguin Young Readers Group.

—What the Ladybug Heard. Donaldson, Julia. 2010. (What the Ladybug Heard Ser.: 2). (ENG.). 32p. (J). (gr. -1-1). 18.99 *(978-0-8050-9028-4(2),* 900059187, Holt, Henry & Co. Bks. For Young Readers) Holt, Henry & Co.

—What the Ladybug Heard at the Zoo. Donaldson, Julia. 2019. (What the Ladybug Heard Ser.). (ENG.). 32p. (J). 17.99 *(978-1-250-15670-9(X),* 900184962, Holt, Henry & Co. Bks. For Young Readers) Holt, Henry & Co.

—What the Ladybug Heard Next. Donaldson, Julia. 2018. (What the Ladybug Heard Ser.: 1). (ENG.). 32p. (J). 17.99 *(978-1-250-15652-5(1),* 900184933, Holt, Henry & Co. Bks. For Young Readers) Holt, Henry & Co.

Monks, Lydia, jt. illus. see Henry, Thomas.

Monlongo, Jorge. All Grown Up? (Rugrats) Carbone, Courtney. 2019. (Little Golden Book Ser.). (ENG.). 24p. (J). (-k). 4.99 *(978-0-525-70767-7(0),* Golden Bks.) Random Hse. Children's Bks.

—Over the Garden Wall: Hollow Town. Lowenthal, Celia. 2019. (Over the Garden Wall Ser.: 1). (ENG.). 144p. (J). pap. 14.99 *(978-1-68415-383-1(2))* Boom! Studios.

—Trick ARRR Treat: A Pirate Halloween. Kimmelman, Leslie. 2017. (ENG.). 32p. (J). (gr. -1-3). pap. 7.99 *(978-0-8075-8066-0(X),* 080758066X) Whitman, Albert & Co.

—Trick Arrr Treat: A Pirate Halloween. Kimmelman, Leslie. 2015. (ENG.). 32p. (J). (gr. -1-3). 16.99 *(978-0-8075-8061-5(9),* 807580619) Whitman, Albert & Co.

Monlongo, Jorge. Hello Kitty: Just Imagine. Monlongo, Jorge. Chabot, Jacob. 2014. 64p. (J). pap. 7.99 *(978-1-4215-7362-5(8))* Viz Media.

Monn, Margaret A. Cause I Live Here. Monn, Margaret A. 2011. 32p. pap. 24.95 *(978-1-4560-7311-4(7))* PublishAmerica, Inc.

Monreal, Violeta. Manuela. Osorio, Marta. 6th ed. (SPA.). 32p. (J). (gr. 1-3). *(978-84-236-2674-8(1))* Edebé ESP. Dist: Lectorum Pubns., Inc.

—Manuela y el Mar. Osorio, Marta. 5th ed. (SPA.). (J). (gr. 1-3). pap. *(978-84-236-3390-6(X))* Edebé ESP. Dist: Lectorum Pubns., Inc.

Monroe, Chris. Burp, Spit & Fart: The Science Behind the Gross Things Babies Do. Garstecki, Julia. 2019. (ENG.). 64p. (J). (gr. 3-7). pap. 17.99 *(978-0-7603-6476-5(1),* Voyageur Pr.) Quarto Publishing Group USA.

—Pick, Spit & Scratch: The Science of Disgusting Habits. Garstecki, Julia. 2018. (ENG.). 64p. (J). (gr. 3-7). 17.99 *(978-0-7603-6178-8(9),* Voyageur Pr.) Quarto Publishing Group USA.

—Sniff, Lick & Scratch: The Science of Disgusting Animal Habits. Garstecki, Julia. 2018. (ENG.). 64p. (J). (gr. 3-7). pap. 17.99 *(978-0-7603-6345-4(5),* Voyageur Pr.) Quarto Publishing Group USA.

—Totally Uncool. Levy, Janice. 2003. (Picture Bks.). 32p. (J). (gr. -1-3). reprint ed. 6.95 *(978-1-57505-555-8(4),* Carolrhoda Bks.) Lerner Publishing Group.

—Trash Mountain. Yolen, Jane. ed. 2015. (ENG.). 184p. (J). (gr. 3-6). E-Book 27.99 *(978-1-4677-7170-2(8),* Carolrhoda Bks.) Lerner Publishing Group.

Monroe, Chris. Bug on a Bike. Monroe, Chris. 2014. (ENG.). 32p. (J). (gr. -1-2). 16.95 *(978-1-4677-2154-7(9),* 9781467721547, Carolrhoda Bks.) Lerner Publishing Group.

—Cookie, the Walker. Monroe, Chris. 2013. (ENG.). 32p. (J). (gr. -1-2). lib. bdg. 16.95 *(978-0-7613-5617-2(7),* 9780761356172, Carolrhoda Bks.) Lerner Publishing Group.

—Monkey with a Tool Belt. Monroe, Chris. 2008. (Monkey with a Tool Belt Ser.). (ENG.). 32p. (J). (gr. -1-2). lib. bdg. 17.99 *(978-0-8225-7631-0(7),* Carolrhoda Bks.) Lerner Publishing Group.

—Monkey with a Tool Belt & the Maniac Muffins. Monroe, Chris. 2016. (Monkey with a Tool Belt Ser.). (ENG.). 32p. (J). (gr. -1-2). 17.99 *(978-1-4677-2155-4(7),* 9781467721554); E-Book 35.99 *(978-1-4677-9562-3(3))* Lerner Publishing Group. (Carolrhoda Bks.).

—Monkey with a Tool Belt & the Noisy Problem. Monroe, Chris. 2009. (Monkey with a Tool Belt Ser.). (ENG.). 32p. (J). (gr. -1-2). 17.99 *(978-0-8225-9247-1(9),* Carolrhoda Bks.) Lerner Publishing Group.

—Monkey with a Tool Belt & the Seaside Shenanigans. Monroe, Chris. 2011. (Monkey with a Tool Belt Ser.). (ENG.). 32p. (J). (gr. -1-2). lib. bdg. 17.99 *(978-0-7613-5616-5(9),* 9780761356165, Carolrhoda Bks.) Lerner Publishing Group.

—Monkey with a Tool Belt & the Silly School Mystery. Monroe, Chris. 2017. (Monkey with a Tool Belt Ser.). (ENG.). 32p. (J). (gr. -1-2). 17.99 *(978-1-5124-3010-3(2),* 9781512430103, Carolrhoda Bks.) Lerner Publishing Group.

Monroe, Chris. Monkey with a Tool Belt Blasts Off! Monroe, Chris. 2020. (Monkey with a Tool Belt Ser.). (ENG.). 32p. (J). (gr. -1-2). 17.99 ***(978-1-5415-7757-2(4),*** Carolrhoda Bks.) Lerner Publishing Group.

Monroe, Dan. Dad, I Wish You Were My Age. Burwick, Josh. 2012. 40p. (J). pap. 14.99 *(978-0-9852146-3-0(5))* AM Ink Publishing.

Monroe, Daniel. Macho Dad. Camacho, Hector, Jr. & Warburton, Dustin. 2014. (ENG.). (J). 19.99 *(978-0-9960374-3-3(8))* Dragonbrush Arts.

—What Do You Do, If You Lose Your Lalaboo? Eleniak, Erika. 2013. 22p. pap. 9.99 *(978-0-9884468-7-8(1))* AM Ink Publishing.

Monroe Donovan, Jane. Winter's Gift. Monroe Donovan, Jane. 2004. (Holiday Ser.). (ENG.). 32p. (J). 16.95 *(978-1-58536-231-8(X))* Sleeping Bear Pr.

Monroe Donovan, Jane & Donovan, Jane Monroe. My Teacher Likes to Say. Brennan-Nelson, Denise. rev. ed. 2004. (ENG.). 32p. (J). (gr. k-6). 15.95 *(978-1-58536-212-7(3))* Sleeping Bear Pr.

Monroe Donovan, Jane, jt. illus. see Monroe, Michael Glenn.

Monroe, Joan Kiddell. The Great Barrier Reef. Patchett, Mary Elwyn. 2011. 210p. 44.95 *(978-1-258-08492-9(9))* Literary Licensing, LLC.

Monroe, Michael Glenn. A Is for Ark: Noah's Journey. Monroe, Colleen. 2004. 38p. (gr. -1-1). pap. 17.95 *(978-0-9754942-0-2(1))* Storytime Pr., Inc.

—Buzzy the Bumblebee. Brennan-Nelson, Denise. 2003. (ENG.). 32p. (J). (gr. 1-4). pap. 6.95 *(978-1-58536-166-3(6),* 202260) Sleeping Bear Pr.

—Grady the Goose. Brennan-Nelson, Denise & Brennan-Nelson, Dense. rev. ed. 2006. (ENG.). 32p. (J). (gr. k-6). 16.95 *(978-1-58536-282-0(4))* Sleeping Bear Pr.

—I Saw It in the Garden. Brennan, Martin. 2006. 32p. (J). (gr. -1-3). 17.95 *(978-1-58726-296-8(7),* Mitten Pr.) Ann Arbor Editions LLC.

—Little Florida. Crane, Carol. 2010. (My Little State Ser.). (ENG.). 22p. (J). 9.95 *(978-1-58536-487-9(8))* Sleeping Bear Pr.

—Little Illinois. Hershenhorn, Esther. 2011. (My Little State Ser.). (ENG.). 22p. (J). 9.95 *(978-1-58536-537-1(8))* Sleeping Bear Pr.

—Little Michigan. Brennan-Nelson, Denise. 2010. (My Little State Ser.). (ENG.). 22p. (J). 9.95 *(978-1-58536-479-4(7))* Sleeping Bear Pr.

—Little Ohio. Schonberg, Marcia. 2011. (My Little State Ser.). (ENG.). 20p. (J). 9.95 *(978-1-58536-527-2(0))* Sleeping Bear Pr.

—Little Texas. Crane, Carol. 2010. (My Little State Ser.). (ENG.). 22p. (J). 9.95 *(978-1-58536-488-6(6))* Sleeping Bear Pr.

—Penny: The Forgotten Coin. Brennan-Nelson, Denise. 2003. (ENG.). 32p. (J). (gr. 1-4). 15.95 *(978-1-58536-128-1(3),* 201990) Sleeping Bear Pr.

—Sleepy Snoozy Cozy Coozy: A Book of Animal Beds. Young, Judy. 2015. (ENG.). 32p. (J). (gr. 1-3). 15.99 *(978-1-58536-908-9(X),* 203808) Sleeping Bear Pr.

—A Wish to Be a Christmas Tree. Monroe, Colleen. 2005. (Holiday Ser.). (ENG.). 32p. (J). (gr. -1-1). 8.99 *(978-1-58536-269-1(7),* 202284) Sleeping Bear Pr.

—The Wonders of Nature Sketchbook: Learn about Nature & How to Draw It. Monroe, Colleen. 2006. 40p. (J). (gr. 4-7). lib. bdg. 15.00 *(978-0-9754942-1-9(X))* Storytime Pr., Inc.

Monroe, Michael Glenn & Monroe Donovan, Jane. Discover Florida, 2 bks. Crane, Carol. 2003. (ENG.). 40p. (J). 27.95 *(978-1-58536-226-4(3))* Sleeping Bear Pr.

Monroe, Michael Glenn & Tsairis, Jeannie Brett. Little South Carolina. Crane, Carol. 2011. (My Little State Ser.). (ENG.). 22p. (J). 9.95 *(978-1-58536-486-2(X))* Sleeping Bear Pr.

Monroe, Patrick. Oops!! Monroe, Cathy. 2018. (Cousin Crusaders Ser.: Vol. 1). (ENG.). 22p. (J). 21.95 *(978-1-64003-765-6(9))* Covenant Bks.

Monroy, Manuel. Caravan to the North: Misael's Long Walk, 1 vol. Argueta, Jorge. Bell, Elizabeth, tr. 2019. (ENG.). 112p. (J). (gr. 4). 16.95 *(978-1-77306-329-4(4))* Groundwood Bks. CAN. Dist: Publishers Group West (PGW).

—Caravana Al Norte: La Larga Caminata de Misael, 1 vol. Argueta, Jorge. 2019. (ENG.). 112p. (J). (gr. 4). 16.95 *(978-1-77306-332-4(4))* Groundwood Bks. CAN. Dist: Publishers Group West (PGW).

—El Dia Que Exploto la Abuela. Aguilera, Flor. 2016. (Serie Azul Ser.). (SPA.). 232p. (J). (gr. 4-7). pap. 12.95 *(978-607-01-3334-3(X))* Santillana USA Publishing Co., Inc.

—La Gitana de las Flores. Lujan, Jorge Elias. 2003. (SPA.). 32p. (J). (gr. k-3). pap. 8.95 *(978-968-19-0748-8(5))* Santillana USA Publishing Co., Inc.

—Una Mascota Inesperada. Chacek, Karen. rev. ed. 2007. (Castillo de la Lectura Blanca Ser.). (ENG.). 48p. (J). pap. 6.95 *(978-970-20-0850-7(6))* Castillo, Ediciones, S. A. de C. V. MEX. Dist: Macmillan.

—Rooster / Gallo, 1 vol. Luján, Jorge. Amado, Elisa, tr. ed. 2016. (SPA.). 24p. (J). 8.95 *(978-1-55498-936-2(1))* Groundwood Bks. CAN. Dist: Publishers Group West (PGW).

—Why Are You Doing That?, 1 vol. Amado, Elisa. 2014. (ENG.). 28p. (J). (gr. -1-2). 16.95 *(978-1-55498-453-4(X))* Groundwood Bks. CAN. Dist: Publishers Group West (PGW).

Monroy Romeral, Ver�nica. Amigas Forever: Parte IV de la Saga Forever. Pariente Nogueras, Nuria. 2019. (Forever Ser.: Vol. 4). (SPA.). 334p. (J). pap. 12.09 ***(978-1-0912-6672-8(7))*** Independently Published.

Monson, Lois, photos by. God Is for Every Day® - Horse Dreams: Teach-a-Child Companion Book/DVD Set. Monson, Lois. 2008. 28p. (J). ring bd. 14.95 *(978-0-9727786-8-8(3))* JoySoul Corp.

Monster, Sfe R. The Other Boy. Hennessey, M. G. 2016. (ENG.). 240p. (J). (gr. 3-7). 16.99 *(978-0-06-242766-3(0))* HarperCollins Pubs.

Monster, Sfé R. The Other Boy. Hennessey, M. G. 2019. (ENG.). 256p. (J). (gr. 3-7). pap. 6.99 *(978-0-06-242767-0(9))* HarperCollins Pubs.

Montag, Maria. I Want to Be a Reader! Powers, Mark. 2017. (ENG.). 14p. (J). (— 1). bds. 7.99 *(978-1-936669-55-4(2))* Blue Manatee Press.

Montagna, Frank. From Head to Toe: The Girls' Life Guide to Taking Care of You. Harrison, Emma. 2004. 124p. (J). *(978-0-439-44983-0(9))* Scholastic, Inc.

Montague, Christine. The Little Monkey & the Crocodile. Sithole, Thelma. 2007. 32p. per. 12.00 *(978-1-59858-204-8(6))* Dog Ear Publishing, LLC.

Montague, Ruth. The Gypsy Chickens Alphabet. Monroe, Judith W. 2006. (J). 7.00 *(978-0-9768370-2-2(1))* Seastory Pr.

Montaini-Klovdahl, Luisa. Why Do I Have To? A Book for Children Who Find Themselves Frustrated by Everyday Rules. Leventhal-Belfer, Laurie. 2008. (ENG.). 80p. (C). pap. 10.95 *(978-1-84310-891-7(7),* 696051) Kingsley, Jessica Pubs. GBR. Dist: Hachette UK Distribution.

Montalbano, Antonella. Natale Di Zucchero e Di Magia. Montalbano, Adriana. 2019. (ITA.). 32p. (J). pap. 8.00 ***(978-1-7124-0529-1(2))*** Independently Published.

Montalto, Luisa. Big Dog Decisions, 1 vol. Jakubowski, Michele. 2014. (Sidney & Sydney Ser.). (ENG.). 128p. (J). (gr. 1-3). 25.32 *(978-1-4795-5226-9(7),* Picture Window Bks.) Capstone.

—Dodgeball, Drama, & Other Dilemmas. Jakubowski, Michele. (Sidney & Sydney Ser.). (ENG.). 128p. (J). (gr. 1-3). 2016. pap. 6.95 *(978-1-4795-6755-3(8));* 2013. 8.95 *(978-1-4795-2116-6(7));* 2013. lib. bdg. 25.32 *(978-1-4048-8061-0(5))* Capstone. (Picture Window Bks.).

—Third Grade Mix-Up. Jakubowski, Michele. (Sidney & Sydney Ser.). (ENG.). 128p. (J). (gr. 1-3). 2015. pap. 7.15 *(978-1-4795-6754-6(X));* 2013. 8.95 *(978-1-4048-8104-4(2));* 2013. lib. bdg. 25.32 *(978-1-4048-8001-6(1))* Capstone. (Picture Window Bks.).

Montalvo-Lagos, Tomás. Guardians of the Galaxy Doodles. Snider, Brandon T. 2017. (Doodle Book Ser.). (ENG.). 128p. (J). (gr. 1-3). pap. 12.99 *(978-1-4847-8767-0(6)*, Marvel Pr.) Disney Publishing Worldwide.

—Spider-Man Doodles. Snider, Brandon T. 2017. (Doodle Book Ser.). (ENG.). 128p. (J). (gr. 1-3). pap. 12.99 *(978-1-4847-8771-7(4)*, Marvel Pr.) Disney Publishing Worldwide.

Montalvo, Rodolfo. The Contagious Colors of Mumpley Middle School. DeWitt, Fowler. 2013. (ENG.). 272p. (J). (gr. 2-5). 16.99 *(978-1-4424-7829-9(2)*, Atheneum Bks. for Young Readers) Simon & Schuster Children's Publishing.

—Dear Dragon: A Pen Pal Tale. Funk, Josh. 2016. 40p. (J). (gr. -1-3). 16.99 *(978-0-451-47230-4(6)*, Viking Books for Young Readers) Penguin Young Readers Group.

Montañà, Marta. El Lobo y Los Siete Cabritos. Bailer, Darice & Domínguez, Madelca. 2007. (SPA & ENG.). 28p. (J). *(978-0-545-02962-9(7))* Scholastic, Inc.

Montana, Petra Rose. Super Silly Cinnamon. Streit, Evie Oliverio. 2019. (ENG.). 23p. (J). pap. 15.95 ***(978-1-9772-1680-9(3))*** Outskirts Pr., Inc.

Montana, Scarlett. Lunch with a Blue Kitty. Montana, Scarlett. 2007. 41p. (J). pap. *(978-0-9796814-0-0(5))* Blue Kitty, The.

Montanari, Donata. Children Around the World. 2004. (Around the World Ser.). (ENG.). 32p. (J). (gr. -1-2). pap. 8.99 *(978-1-55337-684-2(6))* Kids Can Pr., Ltd. CAN. Dist: Hachette Bk. Group.

—Children Around the World. 2004. (Around the World Ser.). (ENG.). 32p. (J). (gr. -1-2). 19.80 *(978-1-5311-7658-7(5))* Perfection Learning Corp.

Montanari, Eva. Princess Matilda. 2007. 24p. (J). (gr. -1-1). *(978-1-84539-276-5(0))* Meadowside Children's Bks.

—Show; Don't Tell! Secrets of Writing. Nobisso, Josephine. 2004. (ENG.). 40p. (J). (gr. 2-6). 28.95 *(978-0-940112-13-1(2))* Gingerbread Hse.

Montano, Andrea. Kai's Pie. Oliver, June a. 2018. (ENG.). 34p. (J). pap. 14.95 *(978-0-692-63587-2(4))* Kai Adventures.

—My Friends the Penguins: Having Fun Together. Aubitz, Katlyn & Aubitz, Ann. 2018. (ENG.). 34p. (J). pap. 12.95 *(978-1-946195-23-4(5))* FuzionPrint.

Montano, Andrea & Aubitz, Ashley. My Friends the Penguins - Make Soup Together. Aubitz, Katlyn. 2020. (ENG.). 30p. (J). pap. 12.95 ***(978-1-946195-68-5(5))*** FuzionPrint.

Montano, Irene. The Little Shepherd, Vol. Jaeger, Elizabeth. 2019. (ENG.). 32p. (J). (gr. -1-k). 16.99 *(978-1-5064-4873-2(9)*, Beaming Books) Augsburg Fortress, Pubs.

—Nighty Night Narwhal, 1 vol. Zondervan Staff. 2020. (ENG.). 18p. (J). bds. 9.99 *(978-0-310-76934-7(5))* Zonderkidz.

Montano, Irene, jt. illus. see Lindsay, Ashling.

Monteagudo, Carly. My Big Sister, My Guardian Angel. Keen, Tammi Croteau & Kirch, Peggy-Lynn. 2018. (ENG.). 32p. (J). pap. 14.95 *(978-1-9852-0074-6(0))* CreateSpace Independent Publishing Platform.

—My Big Sister, My Guardian Angel Coloring Book. Kirch, Peggy-Lynn. Keen, Tammi Croteau, ed. 2018. (ENG.). 26p. (J). pap. 6.95 *(978-1-9853-0098-9(2))* CreateSpace Independent Publishing Platform.

Montecalvo, Janet. A Day without Sugar / un día sin Azúcar. De Anda, Diane. Baeza Ventura, Gabriela, tr. 2012. (SPA & ENG.). (J). 17.95 *(978-1-55885-702-5(8)*, Piñata Books) Arte Publico Pr.

Montel, Anne. A Thousand Billion Things (and Some Sheep) Clement, Loic. 2017. (ENG.). 32p. (J). (gr. -1-2). 17.95 *(978-1-910277-42-3(8)*, Words & Pictures) Quarto Publishing Group UK GBR. Dist: Hachette Bk. Group.

Montenat, Michael. Last Sacrafice. Hart, Joe & Moore, Stuart. 2017. (Dominion Trilogy Ser.). (ENG.). 128p. pap. 14.95 *(978-1-5039-4242-4(2)*, 9781503942424, Jet City Comics) Amazon Publishing.

Montenegro, Evandro. El Bolo & Cupcake vs the Tres Leches Gang. Carvalho, George. 2019. (ENG.). 32p. (J). pap. 9.95 *(978-1-0769-5375-9(1))* Independently Published.

Montero, Barbara Bibas. Barbara's World: A Mom's Labor of Love. Bibas, Susan Mingins. 2019. (ENG.). 28p. (J). pap. 12.95 ***(978-0-578-60331-5(4))*** Barbara Bibas Montero.

Montero Galan, Daniel. It's a Pain to Be a Princess! Gil, Carmen. Brokenbrow, Jon, tr. 2012. 28p. (J). (gr. k-2). 14.95 *(978-84-15241-78-2(X))* Cuento de Luz SL ESP. Dist: Publishers Group West (PGW).

—Que Fastidio Ser Princesa! Gil, Carmen. 2012. (SPA.). 28p. (J). (gr. k-2). 14.95 *(978-84-15241-14-0(3))* Cuento de Luz SL ESP. Dist: Publishers Group West (PGW).

Montero, Jose Perez. The Best of Charles Dickens' Classics. Dickens, Charles & De Graaf, Anne. 2003. 240p. *(978-87-7247-184-6(0))* Scandinavia Publishing Hse.

Montero, José Pérez. Bible Sleuth: New Testament. 2017. (Bible Sleuth Ser.). (ENG.). 32p. (J). 12.99 *(978-1-4964-2243-9(0)*, 20_28917, Tyndale Kids) Tyndale Hse. Pubs.

—Bible Sleuth: Old Testament. 2017. (Bible Sleuth Ser.). (ENG.). 32p. (YA). 12.99 *(978-1-4964-2244-6(9)*, 20_29647, Tyndale Kids) Tyndale Hse. Pubs.

Montero, Jose Perez. Big God, Little Me: An Ask & Learn Storybook Bible, 1 vol. De Graaf, Anne. 2019. 352p. 17.99 *(978-0-8254-4595-8(7))* Kregel Pubns.

—Big God, Little Me Activity Book: Ages 4-7, 1 vol. Jensen, Leyah & Gao, Isabelle. 2020. 232p. (J). pap. 15.99 *(978-0-8254-4642-9(2))* Kregel Pubns.

—Big God, Little Me Activity Book: Ages 7+, 1 vol. Alex, L. M. 2020. 232p. (J). pap. 15.99 *(978-0-8254-4643-6(0))* Kregel Pubns.

—Children's Activity Bible: For Children Ages 4-7, 1 vol. Leyah, Jensen & Gao, Isabelle. 2018. 232p. (J). pap. 15.99 *(978-0-8254-4586-6(8))* Kregel Pubns.

—Children's Activity Bible: For Children Ages 7 & Up, 1 vol. Alex, L. M. 2018. 232p. (J). pap. 15.99 *(978-0-8254-4587-3(6))* Kregel Pubns.

—Gruff Ar Antur Yn y Beibl. Mortensen, Carl Anker. Davies, Aled, tr. from ENG. 2005. (WEL.). 66p. *(978-1-85994-503-2(1))* Cyhoeddiadau'r Gair.

—The Little Children's Bible Storybook. De Graaf, Anne. 2003. 448p. *(978-87-7247-132-7(8))* Scandinavia Publishing Hse.

—Seek & Find in the Bible. 2003. 64p. incl. cd-rom *(978-87-7247-305-5(3))* Scandinavia Publishing Hse.

Montero, Miguel. Mi Libro de Palabras, Oraciones y Cuentos. Ronnholm, Ursula O. Deliz, Osdila O., ed. (SPA.). 100p. (J). (gr. k-6). pap. 7.00 *(978-0-941911-02-3(0))* Two Way Bilingual, Inc.

Montes. My Smelly Ass: Kids Funny Bedtime Story Picture Book. Pong Wong, Lee. 2018. (My Smelly Ass Ser.: Vol. 1). (ENG.). 28p. (J). (gr. k-2). pap. *(978-1-9993483-2-8(X))* Credwell Ltd.

Montes de Oca, Gonzalo. Cuba for Kids: Illustrated History Book/Libro de Historia Ilustrado. Roque-Velasco, Ismael. (SPA & ENG.). (J). (gr. 3-5). 16.00 net. *(978-0-9706319-0-9(1))* Roque-Velasco, Dr. Ismael.

Montes, Keoni. Kimo's Summer Vacation. Germain, Kerry. 2003. 52p. (J). 12.95 *(978-0-9705889-4-4(1))* Island Paradise Publishing.

Montgomerie, Genevieve. Bullying, Change, Friendship & Trust. Vagner, Bohdanka. 2013. 106p. pap. *(978-1-921883-51-4(0)*, MBS Pr.) Pick-a-Woo Woo Pubs.

Montgomery, Annabel. On Wings of the Wind. Bradford, Ruth & Bradford, Larry. 2019. (ENG.). 28p. (J). pap. 21.99 ***(978-1-7960-6334-9(7))*** Xlibris Corp.

Montgomery, Daniel E. The Quantum Realm: Philly the Photon. Montgomery, Mark. Jacobsen, Matthew E., ed. 2017. (ENG.). (J). pap. 6.99 *(978-1-4566-2897-0(6))* eBookit.com.

Montgomery Gibson, Jane. Claire, Claire! Wash Your Hair! Montgomery Gibson, Jane. 2005. (J). bds. 8.99 *(978-1-4183-0044-9(6))* Christ Inspired, Inc.

—Daddy's Valentine. Montgomery Gibson, Jane. 2005. (J). bds. 8.99 *(978-1-4183-0046-3(2))* Christ Inspired, Inc.

—Go Find Christmas. Montgomery Gibson, Jane. 2019. (ENG.). (YA). (gr. 10-11). 8.99 *(978-1-4183-0025-8(X))* Savvas Learning Co.

—God's Little Boy. Montgomery Gibson, Jane. 2005. (YA). bds. 8.99 *(978-1-4183-0034-0(9))* Christ Inspired, Inc.

—God's Little Girl. Montgomery Gibson, Jane. 2005. (YA). bds. 8.99 *(978-1-4183-0045-6(4))* Christ Inspired, Inc.

—Gracie Got Glasses. Montgomery Gibson, Jane. 2005. (J). bds. 8.99 *(978-1-4183-0039-5(X))* Christ Inspired, Inc.

—Hey, You Birds! Montgomery Gibson, Jane. 2004. (J). bds. 8.99 *(978-1-4183-0022-7(5))* Christ Inspired, Inc.

—How Do You Clean a Ballerina? Montgomery Gibson, Jane. 2019. (ENG.). (J). (gr. 10-11). 8.99 *(978-1-4183-0020-3(9))* Savvas Learning Co.

—I Touched Jesus Today. Montgomery Gibson, Jane. 2005. (YA). bds. 8.99 *(978-1-4183-0027-2(6))* Christ Inspired, Inc.

—I'll Tell You in Heaven. Montgomery Gibson, Jane. 2005. (YA). bds. 8.99 *(978-1-4183-0043-2(8))* Christ Inspired, Inc.

—The Inner Soul. Montgomery Gibson, Jane. 2005. (YA). bds. 8.99 *(978-1-4183-0049-4(7))* Christ Inspired, Inc.

—Jake the Fake Snake. Montgomery Gibson, Jane. 2005. (J). bds. 8.99 *(978-1-4183-0026-5(8))* Christ Inspired, Inc.

—Jesus Is! Montgomery Gibson, Jane. 2005. (J). bds. 8.99 *(978-1-4183-0033-3(0))* Christ Inspired, Inc.

—Jesus Loves Me. Montgomery Gibson, Jane. 2005. (J). bds. 8.99 *(978-1-4183-0048-7(9))* Christ Inspired, Inc.

—Jesus Smith or Jones. Montgomery Gibson, Jane. 2005. (YA). bds. 8.99 *(978-1-4183-0031-9(4))* Christ Inspired, Inc.

—The Keeper of Lost & Found. Montgomery Gibson, Jane. 2005. (YA). bds. 8.99 *(978-1-4183-0052-4(7))* Christ Inspired, Inc.

—A Little Bit Gone. Montgomery Gibson, Jane. 2005. (YA). bds. 8.99 *(978-1-4183-0037-1(3))* Christ Inspired, Inc.

—Mabel at the Table. Montgomery Gibson, Jane. 2005. (J). bds. 8.99 *(978-1-4183-0041-8(1))* Christ Inspired, Inc.

—Maggie Makeup. Montgomery Gibson, Jane. 2005. (J). bds. 9.99 *(978-1-4183-0030-2(6))* Christ Inspired, Inc.

—Maker of Prayer. Montgomery Gibson, Jane. 2005. (YA). bds. 8.99 *(978-1-4183-0047-0(0))* Christ Inspired, Inc.

—Mama's Wings. Montgomery Gibson, Jane. 2005. (YA). bds. 8.99 *(978-1-4183-0050-0(0))* Christ Inspired, Inc.

—Measure My Heart. Montgomery Gibson, Jane. 2005. (YA). bds. 8.99 *(978-1-4183-0023-4(3))* Christ Inspired, Inc.

—My Christmas Friend. Montgomery Gibson, Jane. 2005. (YA). bds. 8.99 *(978-1-4183-0066-1(7))* Christ Inspired, Inc.

—Oh Forsooth! I've Lost a Tooth! Montgomery Gibson, Jane. 2005. (J). bds. 8.99 *(978-1-4183-0021-0(7))* Christ Inspired, Inc.

—Pink Potatoes. Montgomery Gibson, Jane. 2005. (J). bds. 8.99 *(978-1-4183-0038-8(1))* Christ Inspired, Inc.

—Shiny Pants. Montgomery Gibson, Jane. 2005. (YA). bds. 8.99 *(978-1-4183-0032-6(2))* Christ Inspired, Inc.

—Sit down, Clown! Montgomery Gibson, Jane. 2005. (J). bds. 8.99 *(978-1-4183-0040-1(3))* Christ Inspired, Inc.

—Through Jesus Eyes. Montgomery Gibson, Jane. 2005. (J). bds. 8.99 *(978-1-4183-0024-1(1))* Christ Inspired, Inc.

Montgomery, Grant & Design, Leslie. The Secret Garden: Mary's Journal. Dey, Sia. 2020. (Secret Garden Movie Ser.). (ENG.). 96p. (J). (gr. 3-7). 9.99 *(978-0-06-297104-3(2)*, HarperCollins) HarperCollins Pubs. Ltd. GBR. Dist: HarperCollins Pubs.

Montgomery-Higham, Amanda. Monkey's Clever Tale. 2003. (Traditional Tales with a Twist Ser.). 32p. (J). (gr. 2-3). *(978-0-85953-051-4(5))* Child's Play International Ltd.

—Our Cat Cuddles. Phinn, Gervase. 2006. (Child's Play Library). 32p. (J). *(978-1-84643-027-5(5))* Child's Play International Ltd.

Montgomery, Lee & Jackson, Ian. The Usborne World of Animals. Davidson, Susanna & Unwin, Mike. 2005. 128p. (J). pap. *(978-0-439-86321-6(X))* Scholastic, Inc.

Montgomery, Lee & Pastor, Terry. Fantastic Press-Out Flying Airplanes: Includes 18 Flying Models. Hawcock, David. 2015. (ENG.). 76p. (J). (gr. 2-4). pap. 14.99 *(978-0-486-80127-8(6))* Dover Pubns., Inc.

Montgomery, Lee, jt. illus. see Gaudenzi, Giacinto.

Montgomery, Lewis B. & Wummer, Amy. The Case of the Poisoned Pig, No. 2. Montgomery, Lewis B. 2009. (Milo & Jazz Mysteries ® Ser.). (ENG.). 96p. (J). (gr. 2-5). 22.65 *(978-1-57565-289-4(7)*, 9781575652894) Astra Publishing Hse.

Montgomery, Margaret. The Adventures of Anna Banana Shoeshine: Anna Banana Takes a Bath. 2006. 40p. (J). *(978-1-930401-49-5(3))* Central Coast Bks./Pr.

Montgomery, Michael G. Darling, Mercy Dog of World War I, 1 vol. Hart, Alison. (Dog Chronicles Ser.: 5). (ENG.). 160p. (J). (gr. 2-5). 2017. pap. 7.95 *(978-1-56145-981-0(X))*; 2013. 12.95 *(978-1-56145-705-2(1))* Peachtree Publishing Co. Inc.

—Finder, Coal Mine Dog. Hart, Alison. (Dog Chronicles Ser.). (ENG.). (J). (gr. 2-5). 2020. 160p. pap. 7.99 *(978-1-68263-163-8(X))*; 2015. 192p. 12.95 *(978-1-56145-860-8(0))* Peachtree Publishing Co. Inc.

—First Dog Fala, 1 vol. Van Steenwyk, Elizabeth. 2008. (ENG.). 32p. (J). (gr. k-3). 16.95 *(978-1-56145-411-2(7))* Peachtree Publishing Co. Inc.

—Leo, Dog of the Sea, 1 vol. Hart, Alison. (Dog Chronicles Ser.). (ENG.). 176p. (J). (gr. 2-5). 2019. pap. 7.95 *(978-1-68263-089-1(7))*; 2017. 12.95 *(978-1-56145-964-3(X))* Peachtree Publishing Co. Inc.

—Murphy, Gold Rush Dog, 1 vol. Hart, Alison. 2018. (Dog Chronicles Ser.). (ENG.). 160p. (J). (gr. 2-5). pap. 7.95 *(978-1-68263-039-6(0))* Peachtree Publishing Co. Inc.

—Murphy, Gold Rush Dog, 1 vol. 2014. (Dog Chronicles Ser.). (ENG.). 32p. (J). (gr. 2-5). 12.95 *(978-1-56145-769-4(8))* Peachtree Publishing Co. Inc.

—Night Rabbits, 1 vol. Posey, Lee. 2007. (ENG.). 32p. (J). (gr. k-3). 7.95 *(978-1-56145-397-9(8))* Peachtree Publishing Co. Inc.

—Santa's Eleven Months Off, 1 vol. Reiss, Mike. 2016. (ENG.). 32p. (J). (gr. -1-3). pap. 7.95 *(978-1-56145-962-9(3))* Peachtree Publishing Co. Inc.

Montgomery, Samantha. The Snoozles. Lujan Ed.D., Nan. 2012. 20p. pap. 24.95 *(978-1-4626-8831-9(4))* America Star Bks.

Montgomery, Shani. Luna. Carpenter, Anjelica L. 2018. (ENG.). 28p. (J). pap. 16.99 *(978-1-7271-9962-8(6))* CreateSpace Independent Publishing Platform.

Montgomery, Tanya. Affirmations for Children. Dymally, R. Ceci. 2004. (ENG.). 54p. pap. 28.50 *(978-1-4120-2463-1(3))* Trafford Publishing.

Montgomery, Violet. 3 Big Steps. Murphy, Eileen. 2008. 25p. pap. 24.95 *(978-1-60563-310-7(0))* America Star Bks.

Montiel, Martin. Lady Mechanika Volume 4: The Clockwork Assassin, vol. 4. Benitez, Joe & Chen, M. M. 2018. (ENG.). 88p. (YA). pap. 9.99 *(978-0-9966030-9-6(3)*, c1b1c335-2305-4eea-82eb-ac1f8aaf25a7) Benitez Productions.

Montijo, Rhode. Attack of the Valley Girls, 6. Trine, Greg. 6th ed. 2008. (Melvin Beederman, Superhero Ser.: 6). (ENG.). 137p. (J). (gr. 2-4). 22.44 *(978-0-8050-8160-2(7)*, Holt, Henry & Co.) Holt, Henry & Co.

—Attack of the Valley Girls. Trine, Greg. 6th ed. 2008. (Melvin Beederman, Superhero Ser.: 6). (ENG.). 144p. (J). (gr. 2-5). pap. 8.99 *(978-0-8050-8161-9(5)*, 900040235) Square Fish.

—Benny Shark Goes to Friend School. Reed, Lynn Rowe. 2017. (ENG.). 32p. (J). (gr. -1-2). 17.99 *(978-1-4778-2803-8(6)*, 9781477828038, Two Lions) Amazon Publishing.

—The Brotherhood of the Traveling Underpants. Trine, Greg. 7th ed. 2009. (Melvin Beederman, Superhero Ser.: 7). (ENG.). 144p. (J). (gr. 2-5). pap. 8.99 *(978-0-8050-8163-3(1)*, 900040237) Square Fish.

—The Curse of the Bologna Sandwich. Trine, Greg. 2006. (Melvin Beederman, Superhero Ser.: 1). (ENG.). 144p. (J). (gr. 2-5). pap. 8.99 *(978-0-8050-7836-7(3)*, 900030183) Square Fish.

—The Fake Cape Caper. Trine, Greg. 5th rev. ed. 2007. (Melvin Beederman, Superhero Ser.: 5). (ENG.). 144p. (J). (gr. 2-5). pap. 8.99 *(978-0-8050-8159-6(3)*, 900040230) Square Fish.

—The Grateful Fred. Trine, Greg. 3rd rev. ed. 2006. (Melvin Beederman, Superhero Ser.: 3). (ENG.). 144p. (J). (gr. 2-5). pap. 8.99 *(978-0-8050-7922-7(X)*, 900031581) Square Fish.

—Invasion from Planet Dork. Trine, Greg. 2010. (Melvin Beederman, Superhero Ser.: 8). (ENG.). 144p. (J). (gr. 2-7). pap. 11.99 *(978-0-8050-8167-1(4)*, 900040241) Square Fish.

—The Revenge of the Mcnasty Brothers. Trine, Greg. 2nd rev. ed. 2006. (Melvin Beederman, Superhero Ser.: 2). (ENG.). 144p. (J). (gr. 2-5). pap. 8.99 *(978-0-8050-7837-4(1)*, 900030184) Square Fish.

—Terror in Tights. Trine, Greg. 4th rev. ed. 2007. (Melvin Beederman, Superhero Ser.: 4). (ENG.). 144p. (J). (gr. 2-5). pap. 8.99 *(978-0-8050-7924-1(6)*, 900031584) Square Fish.

Montijo, Rhode. The Gumazing Gum Girl! Chews Your Destiny. Montijo, Rhode. 2013. (Gumazing Gum Girl! Ser.: 1). (ENG.). 128p. (J). (gr. 1-5). 14.99 *(978-1-4231-5740-3(0))* Hyperion Pr.

Montijo, Rhode. The Gumazing Gum Girl! Chews Your Destiny. Montijo, Rhode. 2017. (Gumazing Gum Girl! Ser.: 1). (ENG.). 128p. (J). (gr. 1-3). pap. 5.99 ***(978-1-4231-5794-6(X))*** Little, Brown Bks. for Young Readers.

Montijo, Rhode. The Gumazing Gum Girl! Gum Luck. Montijo, Rhode. Reynolds, Luke. 2017. (Gumazing Gum Girl! Ser.: 2). (ENG.). 160p. (J). (gr. 1-5). 14.99 *(978-1-4231-6117-2(3))* Hyperion Bks. for Children.

—The Halloween Kid. Montijo, Rhode. 2010. (ENG.). 40p. (J). (gr. -1-3). 15.99 *(978-1-4169-3575-9(4)*, Simon & Schuster Bks. For Young Readers) Simon & Schuster Bks. For Young Readers.

Montileaux, Donald F. The Enchanted Buffalo. Baum, L. Frank. 2010. 40p. (J). (gr. 2-5). 14.95 *(978-0-9822749-3-4(9)*, South Dakota State Historical Society Pr.) South Dakota Historical Society Pr.

Montileaux, Donald F. Muskrat & Skunk / Sinkpe Na Maka: A Lakota Drum Story. Montileaux, Donald F., as told by. 2017. (ENG & DAK.). 32p. (J). 19.95 *(978-1-941813-16-4(X))* South Dakota Historical Society Pr.

Montmeat, Jack. The Memory Tree. Neff, Fred. 2008. 36p. pap. 14.99 *(978-1-59858-854-5(0))* Dog Ear Publishing, LLC.

Montoya, Jeremy. Grandpa Lolo & Trampa: A Story of Surprise & Mystery = Abuelito Lolo y Trampa: Un Cuento de Sorpresa y Misterio. García, Nasario. 2014. (SPA & ENG.). 41p. (J). 9.99 *(978-1-936744-30-5(9))* LPD Pr.

—The Talking Lizard: New Mexico's Magic & Mystery. García, Nasario. 2014. (SPA & ENG.). (J). pap. *(978-1-936744-36-7(8)*, Rio Grande Bks.) LPD Pr.

Montoya, Jerry. Ol' Jimmy Dollar. Randles, Slim. 2018. (ENG.). 52p. (J). (gr. 1-3). pap. 17.95 *(978-1-943681-24-2(4))* Nuevo Bks.

Montoya, Jerry, jt. illus. see Randles, Slim.

Montoya, Manu. Free for You & Me: The First Amendment. Mihaly, Christy. 2020. (ENG.). 32p. (J). (gr. -1-3). 16.99 ***(978-0-8075-2441-1(7)***, 807524417) Whitman, Albert & Co.

Montoya, Manu. What Is a Llama? Cottage Door Press, ed. 2019. (ENG.). 12p. (J). (gr. -1 — 1). bds. 7.99 *(978-1-68052-634-9(0)*, 1004270) Cottage Door Pr.

—What Is a Sloth? Swift, Ginger. Cottage Door Press, ed. 2019. (Chunky Lift-A-Flap Board Book Ser.). (ENG.). 12p. (J). (gr. -1 — 1). bds. 7.99 *(978-1-68052-633-2(2)*, 1004260) Cottage Door Pr.

Montoya, Robin Michelle. Tsa Ch'ayah How the Turtle Got Its Squares: A Traditional Caddo Indian Children's Story. Weller, Sadie Bedoka. Chafe, Wallace, tr. 2005. (ENG.). 42p. (gr. 3-7). per. 16.99 *(978-1-4134-8836-4(6))* Xlibris Corp.

Montross, Doug. The Blackbird's Nest: Saint Kevin of Ireland. Schroedel, Jenny. 2004. 32p. (J). 18.00 *(978-0-88141-258-1(9))* St. Vladimir's Seminary Pr.

Montserrat, Pep. Aladdin & the Magic Lamp/Aladino y la l?mpara Maravillosa. 2006. (Bilingual Fairy Tales Ser.: BILI). (ENG.). 32p. (J). (gr. -1-3). 14.95 *(978-0-8118-5061-2(7))* Chronicle Bks. LLC.

—Aladdin & the Magic Lamp/Aladino y la lámpara Maravillosa. 2006. (Bilingual Fairy Tales Ser.: BILI). (ENG.). 32p. (J). (gr. -1-3). pap. 6.99 *(978-0-8118-5062-9(5))* Chronicle Bks. LLC.

—The Mcelderry Book of Greek Myths. Kimmel, Eric A. 2008. (ENG.). 112p. (J). (gr. 1-5). 21.99 *(978-1-4169-1534-8(6)*, McElderry, Margaret K. Bks.) McElderry, Margaret K. Bks.

—The Musicians of Bremen/Los Musicos de Bremen. Ros, Roser. 2005. (Bilingual Fairy Tales Ser.: BILI). (ENG.). 32p. (J). (gr. -1-3). 6.99 *(978-0-8118-4796-4(9))* Chronicle Bks. LLC.

Moody, Jason. Wendell Has a Cracked Shell. Powers, Emily. 2008. 32p. (gr. -1-18). pap. 14.95 *(978-0-9801357-6-3(1))* Tree of Life Publishing Hse.

Moody, Julie. Fruit of the Spirit - Love. Sama, Kent. 2005. (J). bds. 9.99 *(978-1-4183-0060-9(8))* Christ Inspired, Inc.

—Great White Judgment. Hansen, Eric. 2005. (YA). bds. 9.99 *(978-1-4183-0059-3(4))* Christ Inspired, Inc.

—Shelby's 'Doption Story. Henson, Andora. 2004. (J). bds. 9.99 *(978-1-4183-0013-5(6))* Christ Inspired, Inc.

Moody, Stacy. The Prince of Deep Within. Dalton, Mary. 2019. (ENG.). 66p. (J). pap. 10.00 *(978-1-0976-6261-6(6))* Independently Published.

—Tiny the Tree: A Christmas Story. Dalton, Mary. 2019. (ENG.). 36p. (J). pap. 13.50 *(978-1-0974-9998-4(7))* Independently Published.

Moon, Anna. Danger the Donkey. Parkinson, Jedd K. 2019. (ENG.). 26p. (J). pap. 11.95 ***(978-1-7068-4985-8(0))*** Independently Published.

Moon, Heather B. Lottie Saves the Bees: Imagine a World Without Bees! Moon, Heather B. 2017. (Lottie Lovall International Investigator Ser.: Vol. 1). (ENG.). 160p. (J). pap. *(978-1-9997043-1-5(2))* Reading Holdings.

—Lottie Saves the Dolphins: Imagine a Life of Captivity! Moon, Heather B. 2018. (ENG.). 204p. (J). pap. *(978-1-9997043-4-6(7))* Reading Holdings.

Moon, Heather B. Lottie Saves the Polar Bears: Lottie Lovall International Investigator. Moon, Heather B. 2020. (Lottie Lovall: International Investigator Ser.: Vol. 4). (ENG.). 136p. (J). (gr. 4-6). pap. ***(978-1-9162337-0-6(8))*** Reading Holdings.

Moon, Heather B. Silly Trunk. Moon, Heather B. 2017. (ENG.). 36p. (J). pap. *(978-1-9997043-0-8(4))* Reading Holdings.

—Tillie & the Golden Phantom: A Spooky Halloween Story. Moon, Heather B. 2018. (Tillie's Adventures Ser.: Vol. 1). (ENG.). 134p. (J). (gr. 3-6). pap. *(978-1-9997043-7-7(1))* Reading Holdings.

Moon, Jo. Making Letters. 2006. (Making... Ser.). 14p. (J). (gr. -1-3). bds. 7.95 *(978-1-57791-248-4(9))* Brighter Minds Children's Publishing.

—Making Numbers. 2006. (Making... Ser.). 14p. (J). (gr. -1-3). bds. 7.95 *(978-1-57791-249-1(7))* Brighter Minds Children's Publishing.

—Making Shapes. Butler, Roberta. 2006. (Making... Ser.). 14p. (J). (gr. -1-3). bds. 7.95 *(978-1-57791-250-7(0))* Brighter Minds Children's Publishing.

—Old MacDonald Had a Farm. 2016. (Carousel Bks.). (ENG.). 10p. (J). (gr. -1 — 1). bds. 8.99 *(978-0-7641-6859-8(2)*, B.E.S. Publishing) Peterson's.

—Twinkle, Twinkle Little Star. 2016. (Carousel Bks.). (ENG.). 10p. (J). (gr. -1 — 1). bds. 8.99 *(978-0-7641-6860-4(6)*, B.E.S. Publishing) Peterson's.

—A Whale of a Tail! 2017. (J). *(978-1-62885-287-5(9))* Kidsbooks, LLC.

Moon, Jo. Draw Animals with Simple Shapes. Moon, Jo. 2019. (ENG.). 96p. (J). pap. 9.99 *(978-1-78888-746-5(8)*, 3001da4d-8229-44c4-89ef-4ea02dcc5c2d) Arcturus Publishing GBR. Dist: Baker & Taylor Publisher Services (BTPS).

Moon, Jung Who. Yongbi, the Invincible 1, Vol. 1. Ryu, Ki Woon. 2004. 200p. pap. 9.99 *(978-1-58664-967-8(1)*, CPM Manhwa) Central Park Media Corp.

Moon, K. B. Disgusting Diseases. Moore, J. J. 2018. 156p. (J). pap. 14.99 *(978-1-921024-96-2(8))* New Holland Pubs. Pty, Ltd. AUS. Dist: Independent Pubs. Group.

Moon, Paul, jt. illus. see Boddy, James.

Moon, Poppy. How to be a Bully... NOT! Nass, Marcia. 2011. 56p. (J). pap. 16.95 *(978-1-59850-101-8(1))* Youthlight, Inc.

—Kicky's Friendship Card Game. 2011. (J). 17.95 *(978-1-59850-097-4(X))* Youthlight, Inc.

Mooney, Alyssa. Pet Parade. Velasquez, Maria. 2007. (J). pap. 21.00 *(978-0-15-379895-5(5))* Houghton Mifflin Harcourt School Pubs.

Mooney, Jim, et al. Captain Marvel: Ms. Marvel - a Hero Is Born. 2019. (ENG.). 720p. (J). (gr. 4-17). 100.00 *(978-1-302-91539-1(8))* Marvel Worldwide, Inc.

—Ms. Marvel Epic Collection: This Woman, This Warrior. 2019. (Ms. Marvel Epic Collection: 1). (ENG.). 312p. (J). (gr. 4-17). pap. 34.99 *(978-1-302-91639-8(4))* Marvel Worldwide, Inc.

Mooney, Stephen. The Web of Black Widow. 2020. (ENG.). 112p. (YA). (gr. 8-17). pap. 15.99 *(978-1-302-92007-4(3))* Marvel Worldwide, Inc.

Mooneyham, Chris. Scream Vol. 1: Curse of Carnage. 2020. 112p. (YA). (gr. 8-17). pap. 17.99 ***(978-1-302-92100-2(2))*** Marvel Worldwide, Inc.

Moor, Becka. Cinderella & the Incredible Techno-Slippers. Thomas, Isabel et al. 2015. (Fairy Tales Today Ser.). (ENG.). 24p. (J). (gr. -1-2). 23.99 *(978-1-4795-8616-5(1)*, Picture Window Bks.) Capstone.

—The Royal Wedding Crashers. Beauvais, Clémentine & Beauvais, Clémentine. 2015. 240p. (J). (gr. 1-3). pap. 10.99 *(978-1-4088-5544-7(5)*, 900153467, Bloomsbury Children's Bks.) Bloomsbury Publishing USA.

—The Three Ninja Pigs. Bedford, David. 2016. (ENG.). 32p. (J). pap. 10.99 *(978-1-4711-2191-3(7)*, Simon & Schuster Children's) Simon & Schuster, Ltd. GBR. Dist: Simon & Schuster, Inc.

—Violet & the Hidden Treasure. Whitehorn, Harriet. 2017. (ENG.). 208p. (J). pap. 7.99 *(978-1-4711-1897-5(5)*, Simon & Schuster Children's) Simon & Schuster, Ltd. GBR. Dist: Simon & Schuster, Inc.

—Violet & the Mummy Mystery. Whitehorn, Harriet. 2018. (ENG.). 224p. (J). pap. 7.99 *(978-1-4711-4719-7(3)*, Simon & Schuster Children's) Simon & Schuster, Ltd. GBR. Dist: Simon & Schuster, Inc.

—Violet & the Pearl of the Orient. Whitehorn, Harriet. 2017. (ENG.). 192p. (J). pap. 7.99 *(978-1-4711-1895-1(9)*, Simon & Schuster Children's) Simon & Schuster, Ltd. GBR. Dist: Simon & Schuster, Inc.

—Violet & the Smugglers. Whitehorn, Harriet. (ENG.). 208p. (J). 2018. pap. 7.99 *(978-1-4711-1899-9(1))*; 2016. 13.00 *(978-1-4711-2263-7(8))* Simon & Schuster, Ltd. GBR. (Simon & Schuster Children's). Dist: Simon & Schuster, Inc.

Moor, Becka, jt. illus. see Parker, Paul.

Moor, Beka, et al. A Fish Wish - Lunch for Patch - Squid Twins: BuildUp Unit 4 Lap Book. Lee, Wan et al. 2015. (Build up Core Phonics Ser.). (J). (gr. 1). *(978-1-4900-2603-9(7))* Benchmark Education Co.

Moore, Clement C. & Gorsline, Douglas. The Night Before Christmas. Moore, Clement C., ed. 32p. (J). Random Hse. Children's Bks.

Moore, Clement C. & Winget, Susan. The Night Before Christmas. Moore, Clement C., ed. 2004. 32p. 18.00 *(978-0-7412-1939-8(5))* Lang Graphics, Ltd.

Moore, Cyd. Arbor Day Square, 1 vol. Galbraith, Kathryn O. 2016. (ENG.). 32p. (J). (gr. -1-3). pap. 7.95 *(978-1-56145-922-3(4))* Peachtree Publishing Co. Inc.

—Arbor Day Square, 1 vol. Galbraith, Kathryn O. 2010. (ENG.). 32p. (J). (gr. -1-3). 16.95 *(978-1-56145-517-1(2))* Peachtree Publishing Co. Inc.

—Diary of a Canadian Kid. Sleeping Bear Press. 2012. (Country Journal Ser.). (ENG.). 128p. (J). (gr. 4-8). pap. 11.95 *(978-1-58536-812-9(1)*, 202346) Sleeping Bear Pr.

—Goodnight, Stinky Face. McCourt, Lisa. 2016. (ENG.). 32p. (J). (— 1). bds. 6.99 *(978-0-545-90592-3(3)*, Cartwheel Bks.) Scholastic, Inc.

—Happy Halloween, Stinky Face. McCourt, Lisa. (ENG.). 32p. (J). 2016. (gr. -1-k). 3.99 *(978-1-338-02920-8(7))*; 2011. (gr. k — 1). bds. 6.99 *(978-0-545-28542-1(9)*, Cartwheel Bks.) Scholastic, Inc.

—He's Been a Monster All Day. Brennan-Nelson, Denise. 2013. (ENG.). 32p. (J). (gr. -1-1). 14.99 *(978-1-58536-827-3(X)*, 202363) Sleeping Bear Pr.

—I Love You, Stinky Face. McCourt, Lisa. (ENG.). (J). 2004. 16p. (gr. 3 — 1). bds. 6.99 *(978-0-439-63572-1(1))*; 2003. 32p. (gr. -1-3). pap. 6.99 *(978-0-439-63469-4(5))* Scholastic, Inc.

—I Miss You. McCourt, Lisa. 2014. (Stinky Face Ser.). (ENG.). 32p. (J). (gr. -1 — 1). bds. 6.99 *(978-0-545-74848-3(8)*, Cartwheel Bks.) Scholastic, Inc.

—I Miss You, Stinky Face. McCourt, Lisa. 2009. (Stinky Face Ser.). (ENG.). (J). (gr. -1-3). audio compact disk 9.99 *(978-0-545-13849-9(3))* Scholastic, Inc.

—If You're Happy & You Know It. Raffi. 2007. (Raffi Songs to Read Ser.). 32p. (J). (gr. k — 1). bds. 6.99 *(978-0-375-82919-2(9)*, Knopf Bks. for Young Readers) Random Hse. Children's Bks.

—It's Time for School. McCourt, Lisa. 2017. (Stinky Face Ser.). (ENG.). 32p. (J). (— 1). bds. 6.99 *(978-1-338-13582-4(1)*, Cartwheel Bks.) Scholastic, Inc.

—Merry Christmas, Stinky Face. McCourt, Lisa. (ENG.). 32p. (J). (— 1). 2016. 3.99 *(978-1-338-02919-2(3))*; 2008. bds. 6.99 *(978-0-439-73123-2(2))* Scholastic, Inc. (Cartwheel Bks.).

—Practical Plays: Grades 1-5. Marx, Pamela. 2nd rev. ed. 2007. 170p. (J). (gr. 1-6). per. 17.95 *(978-1-59647-196-2(4))* Good Year Bks.

—Ready for Kindergarten, Stinky Face? McCourt, Lisa. 2010. (Scholastic Reader: Level 1 Ser.). (ENG.). 32p. (J). (gr. -1-1). 16.19 *(978-0-545-11518-6(3))* Scholastic, Inc.

—Thank You, Stinky Face. McCourt, Lisa. 2018. (Stinky Face Ser.). (ENG.). 20p. (J). (gr. -1 — 1). bds. 6.99 *(978-1-338-27020-4(6)*, Cartwheel Bks.) Scholastic, Inc.

—What Do Parents Do (When You're Not Home)?, 1 vol. Ransom, Jeanie Franz. 2007. (ENG.). 496p. (J). (gr. k-3). 16.95 *(978-1-56145-409-9(5))* Peachtree Publishing Co. Inc.

—When It Snows. Nelson, Joanne. 2012. (Discovery Phonics Ser.). (ENG.). 16p. (J). (gr. -1-3). pap. 10.47 *(978-0-8136-1087-0(7))* Modern Curriculum Pr.

—Willow. Brennan-Nelson, Denise & Brennan, Rosemarie. 2008. (ENG.). 32p. (J). (gr. k-6). 16.95 *(978-1-58536-342-1(1))* Sleeping Bear Pr.

—Willow & the Snow Day Dance. Brennan-Nelson, Denise. 2010. (ENG.). 32p. (J). (gr. k-6). lib. bdg. 16.95 *(978-1-58536-522-7(X))* Sleeping Bear Pr.

—Willow & the Wedding. Brennan-Nelson, Denise. 2017. (ENG.). 32p. (J). (gr. k-3). 16.99 *(978-1-58536-966-9(7)*, 204236) Sleeping Bear Pr.

—You Can Do It, Stinky Face! McCourt, Lisa. 2016. (ENG.). 32p. (J). (— 1). bds. 6.99 *(978-0-545-80648-0(8)*, Cartwheel Bks.) Scholastic, Inc.

Moore, Cyd. Merry Christmas: A Storybook Collection. Moore, Cyd. Smath, Jerry et al. 2007. (ENG.). 96p. (J). (gr. -1-k). 8.99 *(978-0-545-01341-3(0)*, Cartwheel Bks.) Scholastic, Inc.

Moore, D., jt. illus. see De Angel, Miguel.

Moore, Danny. Hello Aubie! Aryal, Aimee. 2004. 22p. (J). 19.95 *(978-0-9743442-8-7(1))* Mascot Bks., Inc.

—Hello Big Al! Aryal, Aimee. 2004. 24p. (J). lib. bdg. 19.95 *(978-1-932888-03-4(9))* Mascot Bks., Inc.

—Hello Bully! Aryal, Aimee. 2004. 24p. (J). 19.95 *(978-0-9743442-6-3(5))* Mascot Bks., Inc.

—Hello Buzz! Aryal, Aimee. 2004. 24p. (J). 19.95 *(978-1-932888-27-0(6))* Mascot Bks., Inc.

—Hello, Mr. Met. Staub, Rusty. 2006. 24p. (J). lib. bdg. 17.95 *(978-1-932888-82-9(9))* Mascot Bks., Inc.

—Hello, Wally! Boston Red Sox. Remy, Jerry. 2006. 24p. (J). lib. bdg. 17.95 *(978-1-932888-80-5(2))* Mascot Bks., Inc.

—Let's Go, Yankees! Berra, Yogi. 2006. 24p. (J). 17.95 *(978-1-932888-81-2(0))* Mascot Bks., Inc.

—Wally the Green Monster & His Journey Through Red Sox Nation. Remy, Jerry. 2007. 24p. (J). 14.95 *(978-1-932888-89-8(6))* Mascot Bks., Inc.

Moore, David, jt. illus. see McGeehan, Dan.

Moore, Debra. Fluffy's Story Part 1 Fluffy's Journey. Joyce, Samantha & Joyce, Caroline. 2005. 48p. (J). 16.95 *(978-0-9770898-0-2(0))* Paw Print Publishing.

Moore, Donna Louise. The Elf Child: The Blue Dark. Davidson, Kenneth Michael. 2018. (ENG.). 28p. (J). pap. *(978-0-9958107-2-3(9))* FriesenPress.

Moore, Dwain. The Adventures of Murphy the Mouse. Jones, Brenda. 2007. (J). per. 12.99 *(978-1-59712-069-2(3))* Catawba Publishing Co.

Moore, Eileen, photos by. Arizona Trails for Children: 135 Trails Across Arizona for Children & Adults. Moore, Eileen. 2005. 360p. (YA). (gr. 4-18). pap. 14.99 *(978-0-9672576-0-0(3))* Morten Moore Publishing.

Moore, Elyse. Miss Milli's Adventure: Garden Adventure Series. Cayce, Jw & Guy, K. T. 2011. 26p. pap. 13.95 *(978-1-4575-0002-2(7))* Dog Ear Publishing, LLC.

Moore, Gustav. Earth Cycles. Ross, Michael Elsohn. 2003. (Cycles Ser.). (ENG.). 32p. (J). (gr. 2-4). pap. 7.99 *(978-0-7613-1977-1(8)*, First Avenue Editions) Lerner Publishing Group.

—Everybody's Somebody's Lunch, 1 vol. Mason, Cherie. 2005. (ENG.). 40p. (J). (gr. 3-6). 7.95 *(978-0-88448-200-0(6))* Tilbury Hse. Pubs.

—Life Cycles. Ross, Michael. 2003. 32p. (J). (gr. 2-5). pap. 7.95 *(978-0-7613-1975-7(1)*, First Avenue Editions) Lerner Publishing Group.

—Re-Cycles. Ross, Michael Elsohn. 2003. (Cycles Ser.). (ENG.). 32p. (J). (gr. 2-4). pap. 7.99 *(978-0-7613-1949-8(2)*, First Avenue Editions) Lerner Publishing Group.

—Stone Wall Secrets. Thorson, Robert & Thorson, Kristine. 2010. 40p. (J). (gr. 3-7). 16.95 *(978-0-88448-195-9(6))* Tilbury Hse. Pubs.

Moore, Harry. Behold, No Cavities! A Visit to the Dentist. Willson, Sarah. 2007. (SpongeBob SquarePants Ser.: 15). (ENG.). 24p. (J). (gr. -1-3). pap. 3.99 *(978-1-4169-3566-7(5)*, Simon Spotlight/Nickelodeon) Simon Spotlight/Nickelodeon.

—Bug Parade! (Bubble Guppies) Random House & Pohlmeyer, Krista. 2014. (Pictureback(R) Ser.). (ENG.). 24p. (J). (gr. -1-2). 5.99 *(978-0-385-38517-6(X)*, Random Hse. Bks. for Young Readers) Random Hse. Children's Bks.

—The Case of the Vanished Squirrel. Lewman, David. 2008. (SpongeBob SquarePants Ser.). (ENG.). 16p. (J). (gr. -1-3). pap. 5.99 *(978-1-4169-4939-8(9)*, Simon Spotlight/Nickelodeon) Simon Spotlight/Nickelodeon.

—Disney Paw Patrol: Search with Skye! Skwish, Emily. 2018. (Look & Find Ser.). (ENG.). 24p. (J). *(978-1-5037-4046-4(3)*, 1eb39592-92bc-4470-9d6b-95165c185e42, p i kids) Phoenix International Publications, Inc.

Moore, Harry, Jr. Double Trouble: The Case of the Missing Spatula - The Case of the Vanished Squirrel. Lewman, David. 2010. (SpongeBob SquarePants Ser.). (ENG.). 36p. (J). bds. 10.99 *(978-1-4424-1337-5(9)*, Simon Spotlight/Nickelodeon) Simon Spotlight/Nickelodeon.

Moore, Harry. Just Say Please! Willson, Sarah. 2007. (SpongeBob SquarePants Ser.). (ENG.). 32p. (J). (gr. k-2). pap. 3.99 *(978-1-4169-4129-3(0)*, Simon Spotlight/Nickelodeon) Simon Spotlight/Nickelodeon.

—Nickelodeon PAW Patrol: First Look & Find Book & Giant Puzzle. Skwish, Emily. 2018. (Look & Find Ser.). (ENG.). 16p. (J). bds. *(978-1-5037-4044-0(7)*, d6e6342f-5516-48ce-aa5d-328bafbaa109, p i kids) Phoenix International Publications, Inc.

—Nickelodeon PAW Patrol: Potty Time with the PAW Patrol. Halpern, Rachel. 2020. (Play-A-Sound Ser.). (ENG.). 12p. (J). *(978-1-5037-5236-8(4)*, f3bdc565-6399-4d03-995c-eab00bffec7a, p i kids) Phoenix International Publications, Inc.

—PAW Patrol Big Lift-And-Look Board Book (PAW Patrol) Random House. 2017. (ENG.). 12p. (J). (— 1). bds. 11.99 *(978-1-5247-1722-3(3)*, Random Hse. Bks. for Young Readers) Random Hse. Children's Bks.

—Pick a Dad, Any Dad! Banks, Steven. ed. 2005. (Fairly Odd Parents Ser.: 7). 24p. (J). lib. bdg. 15.00 *(978-1-59054-804-2(3))* Fitzgerald Bks.

—Pup, Pup, & Away! (Paw Patrol) Random House. 2015. (Pictureback(R) Ser.). (ENG.). 24p. (J). (gr. -1-2). 5.99 *(978-0-553-50794-2(X)*, Random Hse. Bks. for Young Readers) Random Hse. Children's Bks.

—The Pups Save Christmas! (Paw Patrol) Golden Books. 2015. (Big Golden Book Ser.). (ENG.). 48p. (J). (gr. -1-2). 9.99 *(978-0-553-52391-1(0)*, Golden Bks.) Random Hse. Children's Bks.

—Rubble's Big Wish. Depken, Kristen L. 2017. 17p. (J). *(978-1-5182-3644-0(8))* Random Hse., Inc.

—Rubble's Big Wish (PAW Patrol) Depken, Kristen L. 2017. (Step into Reading Ser.). (ENG.). 24p. (J). (gr. -1-1). pap. 4.99 *(978-0-399-55884-9(5)*, Random Hse. Bks. for Young Readers) Random Hse. Children's Bks.

—SpongeBob's Slap Shot. Lewman, David. 2008. (SpongeBob SquarePants Ser.). (ENG.). 24p. (J). (gr. -1-3). pap. 3.99 *(978-1-4169-6153-6(4)*, Simon Spotlight/Nickelodeon) Simon Spotlight/Nickelodeon.

Moore, Harry & MJ Illustrations. Nickelodeon PAW Patrol: Ruff-Ruff Rescue Vehicles. PI Kids. 2020. (Play-A-Sound Ser.). (ENG.). 14p. (J). bds. ***(978-1-5037-5225-2(9)***, 5dfdb297-7358-4e5d-b119-30a3a8697815, p i kids) Phoenix International Publications, Inc.

Moore, Harry & Petrossi, Fabrizio. Nickelodeon PAW Patrol. Wagner, Veronica. (Me Reader Ser.). (ENG.). 192p. (J). 2018. *(978-1-5037-4019-8(6)*, c73eeddc-db3a-4e86-9c60-7463f31a4d86); 2017. *(978-1-5037-1693-3(7)*, e805117c-2b67-40ee-a920-a7e4fa114373) Phoenix International Publications, Inc. (p i kids).

—Nickelodeon, Paw Patrol: ABCs My Write-and-Erase Book. Wagner, Veronica & P. I. Kids Staff. 2017. (Play-A-Sound Ser.). (ENG.). 16p. (J). *(978-1-5037-1691-9(0)*, 68b3e02b-d51e-46bb-aa57-9ac03f02908a, p i kids) Phoenix International Publications, Inc.

—Nickelodeon PAW Patrol: Lights Out! 2016. (Play-A-Sound Ser.). (ENG.). 10p. (J). *(978-1-5037-0747-4(4)*, 323f5ad1-5da8-4dca-a2b8-0d9202497749, p i kids) Phoenix International Publications, Inc.

Moore, Harry & Petrossi, Fabrizio. Nickelodeon PAW Patrol: Pups at Play. PI Kids. 2020. (ENG.). 80p. (J). ***(978-1-5037-5458-4(8)***, 18802f95-8d52-4118-aeff-1f885be820f9, p i kids) Phoenix International Publications, Inc.

—Nickelodeon PAW Patrol: Sweet Dreams, Pups! PI Kids. 2020. (Play-A-Song Ser.). (ENG.). 12p. (J). bds. ***(978-1-5037-5242-9(9)***, 71fe10e2-4067-469d-ae81-cc72993b061a, p i kids) Phoenix International Publications, Inc.

Moore, Harry & Trover, Zachary. Nickelodeon: Bubble Guppies. Wagner, Veronica. 2014. (ENG.). 120p. (J). bds. *(978-1-4508-7991-0(8)*, 15218627-cca3-45e5-bbf4-e74ce474cb9b, p i kids) Phoenix International Publications, Inc.

Moore, Harry, jt. illus. see Petrossi, Fabrizio.

Moore, Harry, jt. illus. see Random House Staff.

Moore, Inga. The Secret Garden. Burnett, Frances Hodgson. 2008. 272p. (J). (gr. 1-4). 22.99 *(978-0-7636-3161-1(2))* Candlewick Pr.

—The Secret Garden. Burnett, Frances Hodgson. 2010. (ENG.). 272p. (J). (gr. 1-4). pap. 16.99 *(978-0-7636-4732-2(2))* Candlewick Pr.

—The Wind in the Willows. Grahame, Kenneth. 184p. 2009. pap. 12.99 *(978-0-7606-4211-5(7))*; 2003. (ENG.). (J). 22.99 *(978-0-7636-2242-8(7))* Candlewick Pr.

—The Wind in the Willows. Grahame, Kenneth. 2009. (Candlewick Illustrated Classics Ser.). (ENG.). 184p. (J). (gr. 5-12). pap. 14.99 *(978-0-7636-4211-2(8))* Candlewick Pr.

Moore, Inga. Captain Cat. Moore, Inga. 2013. (ENG.). 48p. (J). (gr. -1-2). 15.99 *(978-0-7636-6151-9(1))* Candlewick Pr.

Moore, Jen. Your Family: A Donor Kid's Story. Kramer, Wendy. 2nd ed. 2018. (Your Family: a Donor Kid's Story Ser.: Vol. 1). (ENG.). 40p. (J). (gr. k-2). pap. 14.95 *(978-0-692-10693-8(6))* Donor Sibling Registry.

Moore, Jennifer. Tu Familia: La Historia de un niño Nacido Por Donante. Kramer, Wendy. Chardon, Estela, tr. 2018. (Your Family: a Donor Kid's Story Ser.: Vol. 2). (SPA.). 40p. (J). pap. 14.95 *(978-0-692-14016-1(6))* Donor Sibling Registry.

Moore, Jo. Sticker Dolly Dressing Parties. Watt, Fiona. ed. 2013. (Sticker Dolly Dressing Ser.). 34p. (J). pap. 8.99 *(978-0-7945-3370-0(1)*, Usborne) EDC Publishing.

Moore, Jo, jt. illus. see Watton, Ross.

Moore, Jonathan. Who Was Alfred Hitchcock? Belviso, Meg et al. 2014. (Who Was? Ser.). 112p. (J). (gr. 3-7). pap. 5.99 *(978-0-448-48237-8(1)*, Penguin Workshop) Penguin Young Readers Group.

—Who Was J. R. R. Tolkien? Belviso, Meg et al. 2015. (Who Was? Ser.). 112p. (J). (gr. 3-7). 5.99 *(978-0-448-48302-3(5)*, Penguin Workshop) Penguin Young Readers Group.

Moore, Jonathan & Harrison, Nancy. Who Was J. R. R. Tolkien? Pollack, Pam & Belviso, Meg. 2015. 105p. (J). *(978-1-4806-8935-0(1))* Baker & Taylor, CATS.

Moore, Kimberly. Arithmetic Village Presents King David Divide. Moore, Kimberly. 2nd ed. 2012. 24p. pap. *(978-0-9845731-9-6(4))* Roxby Media Ltd.

—Arithmetic Village Presents Linus Minus. Moore, Kimberly. 2nd ed. 2012. 24p. pap. *(978-0-9845731-7-2(8))* Roxby Media Ltd.

—Arithmetic Village Presents Tina Times. Moore, Kimberly. 2nd ed. 2012. 24p. pap. *(978-0-9845731-8-9(6))* Roxby Media Ltd.

Moore, Kimberly Ann. Arithmetic Village Presents Polly Plus. Moore, Kimberly Ann. 2nd ed. 2012. 24p. pap. *(978-0-9845731-6-5(X))* Roxby Media Ltd.

Moore, Kristen L. Is God Behind the Big Blue Sky? Moore, Katherine Roberts. 2010. 34p. pap. 13.95 *(978-1-60911-705-4(0)*, Eloquent Bks.) Strategic Book Publishing & Rights Agency (SBPRA).

Moore, Lindsay. A Whale of the Wild. Parry, Rosanne. 2020. (ENG.). 336p. (J). (gr. 3-7). 17.99 ***(978-0-06-299592-6(8)***, Greenwillow Bks.) HarperCollins Pubs.

Moore, Lindsay. Sea Bear: A Journey for Survival. Moore, Lindsay. 2019. (ENG.). 48p. (J). (gr. -1-3). 17.99 *(978-0-06-279128-3(1)*, Greenwillow Bks.) HarperCollins Pubs.

Moore, Lishia. Project Book: Ideas, Tips & Techniques for School Projects. Moore, Lishia, photos by. Warner, Amy, photos by. Warner, Penny. Wagner, Amy, ed. 2007. 80p. pap. 9.98 *(978-1-887436-05-2(7))* Woodland Scenics.

Moore, Margie. Bartholomew's Blessing. Tolan, Stephanie S. 2004. 32p. (J). (gr. -1-3). lib. bdg. 16.89 *(978-0-06-001198-7(X))* HarperCollins Pubs.

—Bear of My Heart. Ryder, Joanne. 2009. (ENG.). 32p. (J). (gr. -1 — 1). bds. 9.99 *(978-1-4169-5472-9(4)*, Little Simon) Little Simon.

—Blue-Ribbon Dad. Raisner Glass, Beth. 2011. (ENG.). 32p. (J). (gr. -1-2). 15.95 *(978-0-8109-9727-1(4)*, Abrams Bks. for Young Readers) Abrams, Inc.

—A Horse's Tale: A Colonial Williamsburg Adventure. Lubner, Susan. 2008. (ENG.). 32p. (J). (gr. -1-1). 17.95 *(978-0-8109-9490-4(9)*, Abrams Bks. for Young Readers) Abrams, Inc.

—It's Your First Day of School, Annie Claire. Carlstrom, Nancy White. 2009. (ENG.). 32p. (J). (gr. -1-2). 16.95 *(978-0-8109-4057-4(4)*, Abrams Bks. for Young Readers) Abrams, Inc.

—Looking for Easter, 1 vol. Chaconas, Dori. 2011. (Holiday Books: Easter Ser.). (ENG.). 32p. (J). (gr. -1-3). 21.19 *(978-0-8075-4749-6(2))* Whitman, Albert & Co.

—Looking for Easter. Chaconas, Dori. 2012. (J). 34.28 *(978-1-61913-120-0(X))* Weigl Pubs., Inc.

—Mice Are Nice. Williams, Rozanne Lanczak. 2005. (Reading for Fluency Ser.). 16p. (J). pap. 3.49 *(978-1-59198-156-5(5)*, 4256) Creative Teaching Pr., Inc.

—Ruby Bakes a Cake. Hill, Susan. 2004. (My First I Can Read Bks.). 32p. (J). (gr. k-3). lib. bdg. 16.89 *(978-0-06-008976-4(8))* HarperCollins Pubs.

—Ruby Bakes a Cake, 1 vol. Hill, Susan. 2010. (I Can Read! / Ruby Raccoon Ser.). (ENG.). 32p. (J). pap. 4.99 *(978-0-310-72022-5(2))* Zonderkidz.

—Ruby's Perfect Day. Hill, Susan. 2006. (I Can Read Bks.). 32p. (J). (gr. -1-3). 15.99 *(978-0-06-008982-5(2))* HarperCollins Pubs.

Moore, Mary. The Faces of Krampus. Moore, Joe. 2017. (ENG.). (YA). (gr. 7-12). pap. 19.95 *(978-0-9992977-0-4(8))* North Pole Pr.

—Ford Macharley, Master Wheelsmith. Moore, Joseph. 2017. (Santa's Elf Ser.: 6). (ENG.). (J). (gr. k-3). pap. 12.50 *(978-0-9992977-1-1(6))* North Pole Pr.

—Keeney Eagleye: Naughty/Nice List Manager. Moore, Joseph. 2016. (Santa's Elf Ser.: Vol. 4). (ENG.). (J). (gr. k-4). pap. 12.50 *(978-0-9787129-4-5(3))* North Pole Pr.

Moore, Megan. Count Your Way Through Afghanistan. Haskins, James & Benson, Kathleen. 2006. (Count Your Way Ser.). 40p. (J). (gr. -1-3). lib. bdg. 19.93 *(978-1-57505-880-1(4)*, Millbrook Pr.) Lerner Publishing Group.

Moore, Michael. Cool Hand Cuke Vol. 5: A Lesson in Giving, 1 vol. Kenney, Cindy. 2006. (Big Idea Books / VeggieTown Values Ser.: Bk. 5). (ENG.). 32p. (J). (gr. -1-3). pap. 3.99 *(978-0-310-70738-7(2))* Zonderkidz.

Moore, Natalia. Animal Poems. 2017. (Poems Just for Me Ser.). 32p. (gr. 7-8). pap. 10.00 *(978-1-4994-8389-5(9)*, Windmill Bks.) Rosen Publishing Group, Inc., The.

—Bundle of Nerves: A Story of Courage. Schuh, Mari C. 2018. (Cloverleaf Books (tm) — Stories with Character Ser.). (ENG.). 24p. (J). (gr. k-2). 25.32 *(978-1-5124-8645-2(0)*, Millbrook Pr.) Lerner Publishing Group.

—Bundle of Nerves: A Story of Courage. Schuh, Mari. 2018. (Cloverleaf Books (tm) — Stories with Character Ser.). (ENG.). 24p. (J). (gr. k-2). pap. 8.99 *(978-1-5415-1066-1(6)*, Millbrook Pr.) Lerner Publishing Group.

—Cheer: A Book to Celebrate Community. Aurora, Uncle Ian. 2020. (ENG.). 32p. (J). (gr. k-2). 16.99 *(978-1-4867-1808-5(6)*, bfcfb176-2f78-48b4-bc85-b0772cd8b85f) Flowerpot Pr.

—Clap. Aurora, Uncle Ian. 2017. (ENG.). 32p. (J). (gr. k-4). *(978-1-4867-1278-6(9))* Flowerpot Children's Pr. Inc.

—Collins Big Cat Phonics for Letters & Sounds - Nap Tap: Band 01A/Pink A. Wells, Alexandra. 2020. (Collins Big Cat Phonics for Letters & Sounds Ser.). (ENG.). 16p. (J). (gr. -1-k). pap. 6.99 *(978-0-00-835755-9(2))* HarperCollins Pubs. Ltd. GBR. Dist: Independent Pubs. Group.

—Grandpa's Cake & Not a Lot in Grandpa's Pot. Treleaven, Lou. 2020. (Early Bird Readers — Red (Early Bird Stories (tm)) Ser.). (ENG.). 32p. (J). (gr. -1-2). pap. 7.99 *(978-1-5415-8733-5(2)*, Lerner Pubns.) Lerner Publishing Group.

Moore, Natalia. How to Get a Daddy to Sleep, 1 vol. Parker, Amy. 2020. 32p. (J). 14.99 ***(978-1-4002-1462-4(9))*** Nelson, Thomas Inc.

—How to Get a Mommy to Sleep, 1 vol. Parker, Amy. 2020. 32p. (J). 14.99 ***(978-1-4002-1461-7(0))*** Nelson, Thomas Inc.

Moore, Natalia. Stomp. Aurora, Uncle Ian. 2019. (ENG.). 32p. (J). (gr. -1-1). 16.99 *(978-1-4867-1554-1(0)*, bc6f1f64-c021-4e2a-a6da-c7e8c00fbdfc) Flowerpot Pr.

—A Very Thankful Prayer, 1 vol. Jensen, Bonnie Rickner. 2017. (ENG.). 24p. (J). bds. 8.99 *(978-0-7180-9883-4(8))* Nelson, Thomas Inc.

Moore, Natalia. The Wolf Who Learned to Be Good. Moore, Natalia. 2017. (ENG.). 32p. (J). (gr. k-2). 16.99 *(978-0-8075-9204-5(8)*, 807592048) Whitman, Albert & Co.

Moore, Nicolette. Kimo's Surfing Lesson. Germain, Kerry. 2007. 48p. (gr. k-5). (J). 12.95 *(978-0-9705889-5-1(X))*; pap. 12.95 *(978-0-9705889-3-7(3))* Island Paradise Publishing.

M

Moore, P. M. The Smallest Forest. Lewis, Regina N. 2013. 60p. pap. 12.95 *(978-1-935083-12-2(0))* CyPress Pubns.
—The Smallest Schoolhouse. Lewis, Regina N. 2007. 56p. (J). pap. 12.95 *(978-0-9776958-3-6(2))* CyPress Pubns.
Moore, Phyllis M. The Smallest Toy Store, A Christmas Story. Lewis, Regina N. 2004. 44p. (J). per. 12.95 *(978-0-9672585-8-4(8))* CyPress Pubns.
Moore, Richard. Disney 365 Days with Winnie the Pooh. Disney & Ferguson, Don. 2019. (ENG.). 352p. (gr. 2-7). 24.99 *(978-1-5067-1469-1(2))* Dark Horse Comics.
Moore, Robert Charles. Little Leona & a Chessie Tale. Sherwood, Jae. 2017. (Little Leona Ser.: Vol. 2). (ENG.). 30p. (J). (gr. k-4). 18.95 *(978-0-692-04621-0(6))* Sherwood, Jae Anne.
—Little Leona of Monsters & Fire. Sherwood, Jae. 2017. (ENG.). (J). pap. 14.95 *(978-1-942914-35-8(0))* Maple Creek Media.
—Little Leona of Monsters & Fire. Sherwood, Jae. 2017. (Little Leona Ser.: Vol. 1). (ENG.). 36p. (J). (gr. k-4). 20.00 *(978-0-692-04564-0(3))* Sherwood, Jae Anne.
Moore, Russell. Phonics Readers - Big Books: Grade 1, Bk. 10. Najimy, Norman. (Phonics Beginning Readers Ser.). (J). (gr. 1-18). 38.01 *(978-0-02-686023-9(6))* SRA/McGraw-Hill.
Moore, Sasha & Tilak, Brian. My Shaking Eyes. Elliott, Sherria L. 2013. 30p. pap. 12.99 *(978-0-9846963-2-1(6))* 4Elliott Publishing, Inc.
Moore, Saxton. Animals of Australia. Parker, Jo. 2020. 14p. (J). (— 1). bds. 8.99 ***(978-0-593-22501-1(5)***, Penguin Workshop) Penguin Young Readers Group.
Moore, Saxton. Care Bears Lullaby: A Night Light Book. Flasterstein, Ran. 2007. 8p. (J). bds. 12.95 incl. audio compact disk *(978-1-57791-303-0(5)*, Little Melody Pr.) Brighter Minds Children's Publishing.
Moore, Saxton & McGee, Warner. Plant a Garden. Sander, Sonia. 2008. (Care Bears Ser.). (ENG.). 24p. (J). (gr. -1-3). pap. 3.99 *(978-0-545-00908-9(1)*, Scholastic) Scholastic, Inc.
Moore, Scott. The Battle of Antietam: The Bloodiest Day of Battle. Hama, Larry. 2007. (Graphic Battles of the Civil War Ser.). (ENG.). 48p. (YA). (gr. 4-7). lib. bdg. 35.45 *(978-1-4042-0775-2(9))* Rosen Publishing Group, Inc., The.
—The Battle of First Bull Run: The Civil War Begins. Hama, Larry. 2007. (Graphic Battles of the Civil War Ser.). (ENG.). 48p. (YA). (gr. 4-7). lib. bdg. 35.45 *(978-1-4042-0776-9(7))* Rosen Publishing Group, Inc., The.
—The Battle of Shiloh: Surprise Attack! Hama, Larry. 2007. (Graphic Battles of the Civil War Ser.). (ENG.). 48p. (J). (gr. 4-7). lib. bdg. 35.45 *(978-1-4042-0779-0(1))* Rosen Publishing Group, Inc., The.
Moore, Sean L. What's up, Bear? A Book about Opposites. Wishinsky, Frieda. 2012. (ENG.). 32p. (J). (gr. -1-2). 16.95 *(978-1-926973-41-8(0)*, Owlkids) Owlkids Bks. Inc. CAN. Dist: Publishers Group West (PGW).
—Where Are You, Bear? A Canadian Alphabet Adventure. Wishinsky, Frieda. 2010. (ENG.). 32p. (J). (gr. -1-2). 17.95 *(978-1-897349-91-5(2)*, Owlkids) Owlkids Bks. Inc. CAN. Dist: Publishers Group West (PGW).
Moore, Sparky. The Lion King. Weiss, Bobbi Jg. 2020. (Disney Classics Ser.). (ENG.). 48p. (J). (gr. 2-6). lib. bdg. 28.50 ***(978-1-5321-4540-7(3)***, 35187, Graphic Novels) Spotlight.
Moore, Stacy. T� No Eres una Nutria: La Historia de C�mo Los ni�os Se Convierten en Aventureros Exploradores de Alimentos. Potock, Melanie. 2020. (SPA.). 34p. (J). pap. 11.99 ***(978-1-6505-2864-9(7))*** Independently Published.
Moore, Steve. King of the Bench: Comeback Kid. Moore, Steve. 2018. (King of the Bench Ser.: 4). (ENG.). 192p. (J). (gr. 3-7). 13.99 *(978-0-06-220336-6(3))* HarperCollins Pubs.
—King of the Bench: Control Freak. Moore, Steve. 2017. (King of the Bench Ser.: 2). (ENG.). 224p. (J). (gr. 3-7). 13.99 *(978-0-06-220332-8(0))* HarperCollins Pubs.
—King of the Bench: Kicking & Screaming. Moore, Steve. 2018. (King of the Bench Ser.: 3). (ENG.). 176p. (J). (gr. 3-7). 13.99 *(978-0-06-220334-2(7))* HarperCollins Pubs.
—King of the Bench: No Fear! Moore, Steve. 2017. (King of the Bench Ser.: 1). (ENG.). 224p. (J). (gr. 3-7). 13.99 *(978-0-06-220330-4(4))* HarperCollins Pubs.
Moore, Tony & Del Mundo, Mike. Thor Vol. 2: Road to War of the Realms. 2019. 120p. (YA). pap. 15.99 *(978-1-302-91290-1(9))* Marvel Worldwide, Inc.
Moore, Tradd. Secret Warriors Vol. 2: If Trouble Must Come. 2018. (ENG.). 120p. (YA). (gr. 8-17). pap. 19.99 *(978-1-302-90693-1(3))* Marvel Worldwide, Inc.
—Silver Surfer: Black Treasury Edition. 2019. 112p. (YA). (gr. 8-17). pap. 29.99 *(978-1-302-91743-2(9))* Marvel Worldwide, Inc.
Moore, Trudy E. Kelly Kapers: Adventures of Kelly & Her Family. Moore, Trudy E. Kinderman, Robert W. 2011. 42p. pap. 23.00 *(978-1-4349-1035-6(0))* Dorrance Publishing Co., Inc.
Moore, Truman, photos by. Complete Charleston: A Guide to the Architecture, History & Gardens of Charleston & the Low Country. Moore, Margaret. 3rd ed. 2005. 304p. (YA). per. 19.95 *(978-0-9660144-2-6(1))* TM Photography, Inc.
Moore, Yvonne Lifferth. Granny Twitcholeen, the Turkey Queen. Moore, Yvonne Lifferth. 2018. (Granny Twitcholeen Ser.: Vol. 3). (ENG.). 26p. (J). pap. 12.00 *(978-1-9732-8935-7(0))* Independently Published.
Moore, Yvonne Lifferth. Granny Twitcholeen's Wacky Quacky Day. Moore, Yvonne Lifferth. 2019. (Granny Twitcholeen Ser.: Vol. 10). (ENG.). 30p. (J). pap. 12.00 ***(978-1-7031-7631-5(6))*** Independently Published.
Moores, Jeff. Good Luck Charlie. Kramer, Jennifer E. 2005. (Rookie Reader Ser.). (ENG.). 32p. (J). (gr. k-2). pap. 4.95 *(978-0-516-25826-3(5)*, Children's Pr.) Scholastic Library Publishing.
Moorhouse, Jess. Do Lions Go Moo? Make Believe Ideas Ltd. 2020. (ENG.). 12p. (J). bds. ***(978-1-78947-361-2(6))*** Make Believe Ideas.
—Don't Feed the Pumpkin. Make Believe Ideas Ltd & Greening, Rosie. 2020. (ENG.). 10p. (J). bds. ***(978-1-78947-686-6(0))*** Make Believe Ideas.
—Have You Met My Pet Dragon? Make Believe Ideas Ltd. 2020. (ENG.). 24p. (J). bds. ***(978-1-78947-424-4(8))*** Make Believe Ideas.
—My Pet Dragon. Make Believe Ideas Ltd & Best, Elanor. 2020. (ENG.). 12p. (J). bds. ***(978-1-78947-422-0(1))*** Make Believe Ideas.
—My Pet Unicorn. Make Believe Ideas Ltd & Best, Elanor. 2020. (ENG.). 12p. (J). bds. ***(978-1-78947-420-6(5))*** Make Believe Ideas.
Moors, Steve. Encounter: Narrative Nonfiction Picture Books. Gassman, Julie. 2016. (Encounter: Narrative Nonfiction Picture Bks.). (ENG.). (gr. 3-4). lib. bdg., lib. bdg., lib. bdg. 140.59 *(978-1-5157-3364-5(5))* Encounter Bks.
—Salvados Por Los Barcos: La Heroica Evacuación Por Mar Del 11 de Septiembre. Gassman, Julie. 2019. (Encuentros: Narrativa de No Ficción Ser.). (SPA.). 32p. (J). (gr. 3-6). lib. bdg. 27.99 *(978-1-5435-8267-3(2)*, 141300) Capstone.
—Saved by the Boats: The Heroic Sea Evacuation of September 11. Gassman, Julie. 2016. (Encounter: Narrative Nonfiction Picture Bks.). (ENG.). 32p. (J). (gr. 3-6). lib. bdg. 27.99 *(978-1-5157-0269-6(3)*, Capstone Pr.) Capstone.
Moors, Steve, jt. illus. see Bock, Janna Rose.
Moose, David. A Soup Opera. Gill, Jim. 2009. (ENG.). 32p. (J). lib. bdg. *(978-0-9815721-0-9(3))* Gill, Jim Music.
Mora, Elsa. The Water & the Wild. Ormsbee, K. E. 2015. (ENG.). 448p. (J). (gr. 3-7). 16.99 *(978-1-4521-1386-9(6))* Chronicle Bks. LLC.
Mora, Francisco X. Delicious Hullabaloo (Pachanga Deliciosa) Mora, Pat. 2010. (J). (gr. -1-2). pap. 18.75 incl. audio compact disk *(978-1-4301-0837-5(1))* Live Oak Media.
Mora, Giovanni. Case of Pen Gone Missing/El Caso de la Pluma Perdida. Saldana, Rene. Villarroel, Carolina, tr. from ENG. 2009. (SPA & ENG.). 80p. (J). (gr. 3-7). pap. 9.95 *(978-1-55885-555-7(6)*, Piñata Books) Arte Publico Pr.
—Rattling Chains & Other Stories for Children/Ruido de Cadenas y Otros Cuentos para Ninos. García, Nasario. 2009. (SPA & ENG.). 160p. (J). (gr. 3-7). pap. 9.95 *(978-1-55885-544-1(0)*, Piñata Books) Arte Publico Pr.
Mora, Julissa. Besties, Sleepovers, & Drama Queens: Questions & Answers about Friends. Loewen, Nancy & Skelley, Paula. 2015. (Girl Talk Ser.). (ENG.). 32p. (J). (gr. 3-9). lib. bdg. 28.65 *(978-1-4914-1859-8(1)*, Capstone Pr.) Capstone.
—Girl Talk. Loewen, Nancy & Skelley, Paula. 2015. (Girl Talk Ser.). (ENG.). 32p. (J). (gr. 3-9). lib. bdg., lib. bdg., lib. bdg. 114.60 *(978-1-4914-1862-8(1)*, Capstone Pr.) Capstone.
—Girl Talk: Questions & Answers about Daily Dramas, Disasters, & Delights. Loewen, Nancy & Skelley, Paula. 2015. (ENG.). 112p. (J). (gr. 3-9). pap. 12.95 *(978-1-62370-218-2(6)*, Capstone Young Readers) Capstone.
—Good Night Martin Luther King Jr. Gamble, Adam & Jasper, Mark. 2020. (Good Night Our World Ser.). 20p. (J). (— 1). bds. 9.95 *(978-1-60219-851-7(9))* Good Night Bks.
—Hello, Garden Bugs: A High-Contrast Book. duopress labs. 2017. (ENG.). 20p. (J). (gr. -1 — 1). bds. 7.95 *(978-1-938093-84-5(4)*, 809384, Duo Pr. Llc (US)) Duo Pr. LLC.
—Lunch Lines, Tryouts, & Making the Grade: Questions & Answers about School. Loewen, Nancy & Skelley, Paula. 2015. (Girl Talk Ser.). (ENG.). 32p. (J). (gr. 3-9). lib. bdg. 28.65 *(978-1-4914-1861-1(3)*, Capstone Pr.) Capstone.
—The Night Before Peepsmas. Posner-Sanchez, Andrea & Posner, Fran. 2017. (Big Golden Book Ser.). 32p. (J). (gr. -1-2). 10.99 *(978-1-5247-6392-3(6)*, Golden Bks.) Random Hse. Children's Bks.
—Siblings, Curfews, & How to Deal: Questions & Answers about Family Life. Loewen, Nancy & Skelley, Paula. 2015. (Girl Talk Ser.). (ENG.). 32p. (J). (gr. 3-9). lib. bdg. 28.65 *(978-1-4914-1858-1(3)*, Capstone Pr.) Capstone.
—Tangles, Growth Spurts, & Being You: Questions & Answers about Growing Up. Loewen, Nancy & Skelley, Paula. 2015. (Girl Talk Ser.). (ENG.). 32p. (J). (gr. 3-9). lib. bdg. 28.65 *(978-1-4914-1860-4(5)*, Capstone Pr.) Capstone.
—When Your Parents Divorce: A Kid-To-Kid Guide to Dealing with Divorce. King, Kimberly. 2017. (ENG.). (J). (gr. 1-5). 21.95 *(978-1-63393-446-7(2))*; pap. 14.95 *(978-1-63393-444-3(6))* kid2kid publishing.
Mora, Liliana. Una Gota de Bondad. Kubiak, Jeff. Tamez, Eugenia, tr. 2019. (SPA.). 34p. (J). pap. 15.99 ***(978-1-970133-58-5(9))*** EduMatch.
Mora, Magdalena. Equality's Call: The Story of Voting Rights in America. Diesen, Deborah. 2020. (ENG.). 48p. (J). (gr. -1-3). 17.99 *(978-1-5344-3958-0(7)*, Beach Lane Bks.) Beach Lane Bks.
Mora, Mauricio. Abra Cadabra, Patas de Cabra: A Spanish, English Story for Young Readers. Drew, Alejandrina. Satcher, David & Ford, Richard, trs. 41p. (J). pap. 15.95 *(978-1-57168-505-6(7))* Eakin Pr.
Mora, Oge. The Oldest Student: How Mary Walker Learned to Read. Hubbard, Rita Lorraine. 2020. (ENG.). 40p. (J). (gr. -1-3). 17.99 *(978-1-5247-6828-7(6))*; lib. bdg. 20.99 *(978-1-5247-6829-4(4))* Random Hse. Children's Bks. (Schwartz & Wade Bks.).
Mora, Pat & López, Rafael. Yum! Mmmm! Que Rico! America's Sproutings. Mora, Pat & López, Rafael. 2008. (SPA & ENG.). (J). (gr. k-6). 7.95 *(978-1-60060-267-2(3))* Lee & Low Bks., Inc.
Mora, Reynaldo. Mommy, Tell Me Why I Am Radiant: Mami, Dime Por Que Soy Radiante? Gonzalez, Sandra & Rodriguez, Julia Rae. 2017. (ENG.). (J). (gr. k-3). 25.00 *(978-0-9989520-1-7(X))*; pap. 15.00 *(978-0-9989520-0-0(1))* Skillful & Soulful Pr.
—Mommy, Tell Me Why I Am Radiant: Mamma, Perché Sono Radiosa? Gonzalez, Sandra & Rodriguez, Julia Rae. 2018. (MUL.). 32p. (J). (gr. k-3). 25.00 *(978-0-9989520-2-4(8))* Skillful & Soulful Pr.
Mora, Roman Garcia. The World of Dinosaurs. 2018. (ENG.). 20p. (J). (gr. 1). 14.95 *(978-88-544-1293-4(7))* White Star ITA. Dist: Sterling Publishing Co., Inc.
Mora Vega, Raquel. We March for You: Messages to Girls from the Women's Marches. MC Donald, Penny. 2018. (ENG.). 46p. (J). (gr. 3-6). 23.00 *(978-0-578-40270-3(X))* Banana Luna Bks.
Morais, Flavio. Voices in First Person: Reflections on Latino Identity. Carlson, Lori Marie, ed. 2008. (ENG.). 96p. (YA). (gr. 7-18). 17.99 *(978-1-4169-0635-3(5)*, Atheneum Bks. for Young Readers) Simon & Schuster Children's Publishing.
Moraja, Melissa Perry. Jake's Adventures - the Secret of the Shark Tooth Crab Claw. Moraja, Melissa Perry. 2012. 118p. pap. *(978-0-9834751-8-7(0))* Roxby Media Ltd.
—Madison & G. A. - a Tale of the Slimy Spitball. Moraja, Melissa Perry. 2012. 94p. pap. *(978-0-9834751-7-0(2))* Roxby Media Ltd.
Moralde, Jhunny. Fishing with Grandpa. John, Jeremy. 2018. (ENG.). 26p. (J). pap. *(978-9980-900-21-0(0))* Library For All Limited.
Morales, Albert. Chieftain's Daughter. Wagner, Alisa Hope. 2019. (Violet Moon Ser.: Vol. 2). (ENG.). 358p. (J). pap. 14.99 ***(978-1-7334333-2-7(5))*** Marked Writers Publishing.
—Spreading Her Wings. Wagner, Alisa Hope. 2019. (Butterfly Princess Ser.: Vol. 1). (ENG.). 30p. (J). pap. 12.99 ***(978-1-7334333-0-3(9))*** Marked Writers Publishing.
Morales, Andrew. Brady O'Brian Saves the Day. Mutrie, Matthew. 2007. 37p. pap. 24.95 *(978-1-4241-9009-6(6))* America Star Bks.
Morales, Eva. The Big, Bad Bully. Canfield, Jack & Laundry, Miriam. 2019. (ENG.). 48p. (J). (gr. 3-6). 12.95 *(978-0-7573-2308-9(1))* Health Communications, Inc.
Morales, Fifi. Welcome to the USA. Bello, Ecrahim, photos by. Nohemi, Esther. Morris, Edwin, ed. I.t. ed. 2003. (YA). pap. *(978-1-931481-87-8(3))* LiArt-Literature & Art.
Morales, Jethro & Jensen, Josh. House of Fear: Attack of the Killer Snowmen & Other Stories. Powell, James. 2019. (ENG.). 144p. (gr. 3-7). pap. 12.99 *(978-1-5067-1132-4(4))* Dark Horse Comics.
Morales, Jose. I-Can't & I-Can! Willow, Bim. 2012. 28p. pap. 8.99 *(978-0-9853574-3-6(6))* Mountan Creek Pubns.
Morales, Judith. Gracias a Johannes. Helguera, Luis Ignacio. 2003. (SPA.). *(978-968-494-086-4(6)*, CI5287) Centro de Informacion y Desarrollo de la Comunicacion y la Literatura MEX. Dist: Lectorum Pubns., Inc.
Morales, Magaly. Chavela's Magic Chicle. Brown, Monica. 2008. (ENG & SPA.). (J). 15.95 *(978-0-87358-918-5(1)*, Luna Rising) Northland Publishing.
—A Piñata in a Pine Tree: A Latino Twelve Days of Christmas. Mora, Pat. 2009. (ENG.). 32p. (J). (gr. -1-3). 17.99 *(978-0-618-84198-1(9)*, 100563) Houghton Mifflin Harcourt Publishing Co.
—¿Qué Puedes Hacer con una Paleta? (What Can You Do with a Paleta Spanish Edition) Tafolla, Carmen. 2009. 32p. (J). (gr. -1-2). 17.99 *(978-1-58246-289-9(5)*, Tricycle Pr.) Random Hse. Children's Bks.
—What Can You Do with a Paleta? Tafolla, Carmen. 2009. 32p. (J). (gr. -1-2). 16.99 *(978-1-58246-221-9(6)*, Tricycle Pr.) Random Hse. Children's Bks.
—�Qu� Puedes Hacer con una Paleta? (What Can You Do with a Paleta Spanish Edition) Tafolla, Carmen. 2014. 32p. (J). (gr. -1-2). 7.99 *(978-0-385-75537-5(6)*, Dragonfly Bks.) Random Hse. Children's Bks.
Morales, Rodolfo. Angel's Kite (La estrella de Angel), 1 vol. Blanco, Alberto. Bellm, Dan, tr. 2014. (ENG & SPA.). 32p. (J). (gr. 1-5). pap. 10.95 *(978-0-89239-156-1(1)*, bd3038f0-43f9-4b5c-b4a1-f6944b53d8b0) Lee & Low Bks., Inc.
Morales, Yuyi. Cosechando Esperanza: La Historia de César Chávez. Krull, Kathleen. Campoy, F. Isabel & Flor Ada, Alma, trs. 2004. (SPA.). 48p. (J). (gr. -1-3). pap. 7.99 *(978-0-15-205169-3(4)*, 1195591) Houghton Mifflin Harcourt Publishing Co.
—Escalera a la Luna. Soetoro-Ng, Maya. 2017. 48p. (J). (gr. k-4). 7.99 *(978-0-7636-9342-8(1))*; (SPA.). 17.99 *(978-0-7636-9341-1(3))* Candlewick Pr.
—Floating on Mama's Song. Lacamara, Laura. 2010. (ENG.). 32p. (J). (gr. -1-2). 16.99 *(978-0-06-084368-7(3)*, Tegen, Katherine Bks) HarperCollins Pubs.
—Harvesting Hope: The Story of Cesar Chavez. Krull, Kathleen. 2003. (ENG.). 48p. (J). (gr. -1-3). 17.99 *(978-0-15-201437-7(3)*, 1189864) Houghton Mifflin Harcourt Publishing Co.
—Ladder to the Moon. Soetoro-Ng, Maya. 48p. (J). (gr. -1-3). 2017. 8.99 *(978-0-7636-9343-5(X))*; 2011. (ENG.). 16.99 *(978-0-7636-4570-0(2))* Candlewick Pr.
—Ladder to the Moon with CD. Soetoro-Ng, Maya. 2012. (ENG.). 48p. (J). (gr. -1-3). 19.99 *(978-0-7636-6006-2(X))* Candlewick Pr.
—My Abuelita. Johnston, Tony. 2009. (ENG.). 32p. (J). (gr. -1-3). 17.99 *(978-0-15-216330-3(1)*, 1200683) Houghton Mifflin Harcourt Publishing Co.
—Sand Sister. White, Amanda. 2004. 32p. (J). 16.99 *(978-1-84148-617-8(5))* Barefoot Bks., Inc.
—Thunder Boy Jr. Alexie, Sherman. 2016. (ENG.). 40p. (J). (gr. -1-3). 18.99 *(978-0-316-01372-7(2))* Little, Brown Bks. for Young Readers.
Morales, Yuyi. Georgia in Hawaii: When Georgia O'Keeffe Painted What She Pleased. Morales, Yuyi. Novesky, Amy. 2012. (ENG.). 40p. (J). (gr. 1-4). 17.99 *(978-0-15-205420-5(0)*, 1196314) Houghton Mifflin Harcourt Publishing Co.
—Just in Case: A Trickster Tale & Spanish Alphabet Book. Morales, Yuyi. 2008. (ENG.). 40p. (J). (gr. -1-3). 18.99 *(978-1-59643-329-8(9)*, 900045825) Roaring Brook Pr.
—Just in Case: A Trickster Tale & Spanish Alphabet Book. Morales, Yuyi. 2018. (ENG.). 40p. (J). pap. 8.99 *(978-1-250-18849-6(0)*, 900192100) Square Fish.
—Niño: Wrestles the World. Morales, Yuyi. 2013. (ENG.). 40p. (J). (gr. -1-3). 18.99 *(978-1-59643-604-6(2)*, 900065749) Roaring Brook Pr.
Morales, Yuyi & O'Meara, Tim. Viva Frida. Morales, Yuyi. 2014. (ENG.). 40p. (J). (gr. -1-3). 18.99 *(978-1-59643-603-9(4)*, 900065746) Roaring Brook Pr.
Moran, Bruce. Boats the Story of Billy Lee Telliot & the Bay Blaster Shootout. Swarbrick, David E. 2018. (Fast Boats (Tm) Ser.: Vol. 1). (ENG.). 80p. (J). (gr. k-6). pap. 12.99 *(978-1-59095-134-7(4)*, ExamWise) Total Recall Learning, Inc.
—Trucks: The Legend of Beverly Joe Breece. Swarbrick, David. 2018. (Fast Truck Ser.: Vol. 1). (ENG.). 46p. (J). (gr. 2-6). pap. 12.99 *(978-1-59095-360-0(6)*, ExamWise) Total Recall Learning, Inc.
—Trucks II the Baytona 300. David, Swarbrick E. 2019. (Fast Trucks Ser.: Vol. 2). (ENG.). 72p. (J). (gr. k-5). pap. 12.99 *(978-1-59095-372-3(X)*, ExamWise) Total Recall Learning, Inc.
Moran, Edna. Miracle Puzzlers. Schlegel, William. 2009. 64p. pap. 10.99 *(978-0-7586-1605-0(8))* Concordia Publishing Hse.
Moran Lavado, Cesar. Aria II: Desaf�o en la Espesura. Moran Lavado, Juan. 2019. (Aria Ser.: Vol. 2). (SPA.). 298p. (J). pap. 15.00 ***(978-1-0755-9007-8(8))*** Independently Published.
Moran, Lyn. I Want That! Claus, Rimana. 2012. 36p. pap. 15.97 *(978-1-61897-838-7(1)*, Strategic Bk. Publishing) Strategic Book Publishing & Rights Agency (SBPRA).
Moran, Michael & Moran, Mike. Do-4U the Robot Experiences Forces & Motion. Weakland, Mark. 2012. (In the Science Lab Ser.). (ENG.). 24p. (J). (gr. k-3). lib. bdg. 27.32 *(978-1-4048-7145-8(4)*, Picture Window Bks.) Capstone.
Moran, Mike. Construction Workers in My Community. Heos, Bridget. 2018. (Meet a Community Helper (Early Bird Stories (tm)) Ser.). (ENG.). 24p. (J). (gr. k-2). 27.99 *(978-1-5415-2018-9(1)*, Lerner Pubns.) Lerner Publishing Group.
—Do-4U the Robot Experiences Forces & Motion. Weakland, Mark. 2012. (In the Science Lab Ser.). (ENG.). 24p. (J). (gr. k-3). pap. 9.95 *(978-1-4048-7239-4(6)*, Picture Window Bks.) Capstone.
—Do Trees Get Hungry? Noticing Plant & Animal Traits. Rustad, Martha E. H. 2015. (Cloverleaf Books (tm) — Nature's Patterns Ser.). (ENG.). 24p. (J). (gr. k-2). pap. 8.99 *(978-1-4677-8605-8(5)*, 9781467786058); lib. bdg. 25.32 *(978-1-4677-8559-4(8)*, 9781467785594) Lerner Publishing Group. (Millbrook Pr.).
—Doctors in My Community. Heos, Bridget. 2018. (Meet a Community Helper (Early Bird Stories (tm)) Ser.). (ENG.). 24p. (J). (gr. k-2). 27.99 *(978-1-5415-2023-3(8)*, Lerner Pubns.) Lerner Publishing Group.
—Ella Earns Her Own Money. Bullard, Lisa. 2013. (Cloverleaf Books (tm) — Money Basics Ser.). (ENG.). 24p. (J). (gr. k-2). pap. 8.99 *(978-1-4677-1511-9(5)*, 9781467715119, Millbrook Pr.) Lerner Publishing Group.
—Friendship on the High Seas. Yolen, Jane. 2019. (School of Fish Ser.). (ENG.). 32p. (J). (gr. -1-1). pap. 4.99 *(978-1-5344-3891-0(2)*, Simon Spotlight) Simon Spotlight.
—Gabriel Gets a Great Deal. Bullard, Lisa. 2013. (Cloverleaf Books (tm) — Money Basics Ser.). (ENG.). 24p. (J). (gr. k-2). pap. 8.99 *(978-1-4677-1512-6(3)*, 9781467715126, Millbrook Pr.) Lerner Publishing Group.
—Give a 'Bot a Bone. Krulik, Nancy & Burwasser, Amanda. 2018. (Project Droid Ser.: 5). 112p. (J). (gr. 1-3). 13.99 *(978-1-5107-2663-5(2))*; pap. 4.99 *(978-1-5107-2655-0(1))* Skyhorse Publishing Co., Inc. (Sky Pony Pr.).
—I'm from Outer Space! Meet an Alien. Bullard, Lisa. 2014. (Monster Buddies Ser.). (ENG.). 24p. (J). (gr. k-2). lib. bdg. 23.99 *(978-0-7613-9193-7(2)*, 9780761391937, Millbrook Pr.) Lerner Publishing Group.
—Let's Meet a Construction Worker. Heos, Bridget. 2013. (Cloverleaf Books (tm) — Community Helpers Ser.). (ENG.). 24p. (J). (gr. k-2). pap. 8.99 *(978-1-4677-0799-2(6)*, 9781467707992); lib. bdg. 25.32 *(978-0-7613-9023-7(5)*, 9780761390237) Lerner Publishing Group. (Millbrook Pr.).
—Let's Meet a Doctor. Heos, Bridget. 2013. (Cloverleaf Books (tm) — Community Helpers Ser.). (ENG.). 24p. (J). (gr. k-2). pap. 8.99 *(978-1-4677-0801-2(1)*, 9781467708012, Millbrook Pr.) Lerner Publishing Group.
—Pain in the Brain. Krulik, Nancy & Burwasser, Amanda. 2017. (Project Droid Ser.). 104p. (J). (gr. 1-4). 13.99 *(978-1-5107-1020-7(5)*, Sky Pony Pr.) Skyhorse Publishing Co., Inc.
—Phone-Y Friends. Krulik, Nancy & Burwasser, Amanda. 2017. (Project Droid Ser.). 104p. (J). (gr. 1-3). 13.99 *(978-1-5107-2662-8(4))*; pap. 4.99 *(978-1-5107-2654-3(3))* Skyhorse Publishing Co., Inc. (Sky Pony Pr.).
—Racing the Waves. Yolen, Jane. 2019. (School of Fish Ser.). (ENG.). 32p. (J). (gr. -1-1). 17.99 *(978-1-5344-5305-0(9))*; pap. 4.99 *(978-1-5344-5304-3(0))* Simon Spotlight. (Simon Spotlight).
Moran, Mike. Rocking the Tide. Yolen, Jane. 2020. (School of Fish Ser.). (ENG.). 32p. (J). (gr. -1-1). 17.99 ***(978-1-5344-5308-1(3)***, Simon Spotlight) Simon Spotlight.
Moran, Mike. School of Fish: Ready-To-Read Level 1. Yolen, Jane. 2019. (School of Fish Ser.). (ENG.). 32p. (J). (gr. -1-1). 17.99 *(978-1-5344-3889-7(0))*; pap. 4.99 *(978-1-5344-3888-0(2))* Simon Spotlight. (Simon Spotlight).
—Science No Fair! Project Droid #1. Krulik, Nancy & Burwasser, Amanda. 2016. (Project Droid Ser.). (ENG.). 112p. (J). (gr. 1-4). 13.99 *(978-1-5107-1018-4(3)*, Sky Pony Pr.) Skyhorse Publishing Co., Inc.
—Soccer Shocker! Project Droid #2. Krulik, Nancy & Burwasser, Amanda. 2016. (Project Droid Ser.). (ENG.). 104p. (J). (gr. 1-4). 13.99 *(978-1-5107-1019-1(1))*; pap. 5.99 *(978-1-5107-1029-0(9))* Skyhorse Publishing Co., Inc. (Sky Pony Pr.).
—Someone's Got a Screw Loose. Krulik, Nancy & Burwasser, Amanda. 2018. (Project Droid Ser.: 6). 112p. (J). (gr. 1-3). (ENG.). 13.99 *(978-1-5107-2664-2(0))*; pap. 4.99 *(978-1-5107-2656-7(X))* Skyhorse Publishing Co., Inc. (Sky Pony Pr.).

—Stealing the Show. Finn, Perdita. 2006. (Time Flyers Ser.: Vol. 1). 109p. (J). pap. *(978-0-439-74433-1(4))* Scholastic, Inc.

Moran, Mike. Testing the Waters. Yolen, Jane. 2020. (School of Fish Ser.). (ENG.). 32p. (J). (gr. -1-1). 17.99 ***(978-1-5344-6626-5(6))***; pap. 4.99 ***(978-1-5344-6625-8(8))*** Simon Spotlight. (Simon Spotlight).

Moran, Mike. To Mars! Bellisario, Gina. 2017. (Cloverleaf Books (tm) — Space Adventures Ser.). (ENG.). 24p. (J). (gr. k-2). 25.32 *(978-1-5124-2539-0(7)*, 9781512425390); E-Book 38.65 *(978-1-5124-3887-1(1)*, 9781512438871); E-Book 4.99 *(978-1-5124-3888-8(X)*, 9781512438888); E-Book 38.65 *(978-1-5124-2832-2(9))* Lerner Publishing Group. (Millbrook Pr.).

—To the Stars! Bellisario, Gina. 2017. (Cloverleaf Books (tm) — Space Adventures Ser.). (ENG.). 24p. (J). (gr. k-2). 25.32 *(978-1-5124-2537-6(0)*, 9781512425376); E-Book 4.99 *(978-1-5124-3897-0(9)*, 9781512438970); E-Book 38.65 *(978-1-5124-3896-3(0)*, 9781512438963); E-Book 38.65 *(978-1-5124-2834-6(5))* Lerner Publishing Group. (Millbrook Pr.).

Moran, Mike, jt. illus. see Moran, Michael.

Moran, Paul. What If... Humans Were Like Animals? Taylor, Marianne. 2012. (ENG.). 128p. 7.99 *(978-1-78055-042-8(1)*, Buster Bks.) O'Mara, Michael Bks., Ltd. GBR. Dist: Littlehampton Bk Services, Ltd.

—Where's the Unicorn? A Magical Search-And-Find Book. Marx, Jonny. 2018. (Remarkable Animals Search Book Ser.: 1). (ENG.). 48p. (J). (gr. 3). pap. 9.95 *(978-1-4549-3166-9(3))* Sterling Publishing Co., Inc.

—Where's the Unicorn Now? A Magical Search-And-Find Book. Schrey, Sophie. 2019. (Remarkable Animals Search Book Ser.: 2). (ENG.). 48p. (J). (gr. 3). pap. 9.95 *(978-1-4549-3404-2(2))* Sterling Publishing Co., Inc.

—World's Greatest Who What Where When Quiz Book for Kids. 2003. 112p. (J). pap. 3.99 *(978-0-603-56100-9(4))* Egmont Bks., Ltd. GBR. Dist: Trafalgar Square Publishing.

Moran, Rosslyn. All the Tales from the Ark, 1 vol. Rowlands, Avril. 2nd ed. 2016. (ENG.). 400p. (J). (gr. 2-4). pap. 9.99 *(978-0-7459-7682-2(4)*, Lion Books) Lion Hudson PLC GBR. Dist: Independent Pubs. Group.

—The Rainbow's End & Other Tales from the Ark. Rowlands, Avril. 128p. (J). pap. 6.95 *(978-0-7459-4073-1(0)*, Lion Books) Lion Hudson PLC GBR. Dist: Trafalgar Square Publishing.

Morandi, Andrea. Bears. Parker, Steve. 2010. (I Love Animals Ser.). (ENG.). 24p. (J). (gr. 1-5). pap. 8.15 *(978-1-61533-232-8(4))*; lib. bdg. 25.60 *(978-1-61533-226-7(X))* Windmill Bks.

—Owls. Parker, Steve. 2010. (I Love Animals Ser.). (ENG.). 24p. (J). (gr. 1-5). lib. bdg. 25.60 *(978-1-61533-229-8(4))* Windmill Bks.

Morandi, Andrea, jt. illus. see Cantucci, Alessandro.

Moranelli, Romina. L' Esercito Degli Spietati. Moranelli, Angelica Elisa. 2018. (Armonia Di Pietragrigia Ser.: Vol. 3). (ITA.). 406p. (J). pap. 14.65 *(978-1-9831-0346-9(2))* Independently Published.

—Il Regno Dell'imperatore Fantasma. Moranelli, Angelica Elisa. 2018. (Armonia Di Pietragrigia Ser.: Vol. 4). (ITA.). 378p. (J). pap. 14.65 *(978-1-9831-0369-8(1))* Independently Published.

Morante, Mireia. She Loves Me All the Same. Gaddis, Alisha. 2019. (ENG.). 28p. (J). (gr. k-3). 16.99 ***(978-1-941015-43-8(3))*** Red Sky Presents.

Morchiladze, Manana. The Dark. Baghdasaryan, Rouzanna. 2007. 32p. (J). (ARA & ENG.). pap. 12.95 *(978-1-60195-086-4(1))*; (POL & ENG.). pap. 12.95 *(978-1-60195-096-3(9))* International Step by Step Assn.

—The Littlest One. Kruk, Halya. 2007. 32p. (J). (POL & ENG.). pap. 14.95 *(978-1-60195-102-1(7))*; (ARA & ENG.). pap. 14.95 *(978-1-60195-090-1(X))* International Step by Step Assn.

Morco, Ysha. Alberto's Allergies: Mediwonderland. Hall, Wendy J. 2018. (ENG.). 32p. (J). pap. 9.99 *(978-1-7905-5632-8(5))* Independently Published.

—Andy's X-Ray: Mediwonderland. Hall, Wendy J. 2017. (ENG.). 32p. (J). pap. 9.99 *(978-1-7932-7227-0(1))* Independently Published.

—Denton's Dentist Visit: Mediwonderland. Hall, Wendy J. 2019. (ENG.). 34p. (J). pap. 9.99 *(978-1-0905-8210-2(2))* Independently Published.

—Hadrian's Headaches: Mediwonderland. Hall, Wendy J. 2019. (ENG.). 34p. (J). pap. 9.99 *(978-1-0914-2585-9(X))* Independently Published.

—Shirley & Shaun's Shots: Mediwonderland. Hall, Wendy J. 2019. (ENG.). 32p. (J). pap. 9.99 *(978-1-7968-7007-7(2))* Independently Published.

Morcos, Annie. Cloudgirl. Gureghian, Sahag. 2016. (ENG.). (J). (gr. k-5). 29.99 *(978-0-9980763-0-0(9))*; pap. 14.99 *(978-0-9980763-2-4(5))* Little Hat Bks.

Mordan, C. B. Guinea Pig Scientists: Bold Self-Experimenters in Science & Medicine. Boring, Mel & Dendy, Leslie. 2014. (ENG.). (J). (gr. 5-12). lib. bdg. 23.60 *(978-1-62765-723-5(1))* Perfection Learning Corp.

—Oh Rats! The Story of Rats & People. Marrin, Albert. 2014. 112p. (J). (gr. 5). pap. 8.99 *(978-0-14-751281-9(6)*, Puffin Books) Penguin Young Readers Group.

—Silent Movie. Avi. 2003. (ENG.). 48p. (J). (gr. -1-3). 19.99 *(978-0-689-84145-3(0)*, Atheneum Bks. for Young Readers) Simon & Schuster Children's Publishing.

Morden, Naphtali & Moss, Stephan. UW Huskies from a to Z. Ascani, Kristi & Stuart, Leinora. 2013. (ENG.). 56p. (J). 21.95 *(978-1-937499-06-8(5))* Green Beanie Bks.

Morden, Richard. Biodiversity of Coral Reefs. Pyers, Greg. 2011. (Biodiversity Ser.). 32p. (gr. 4-4). 29.50 *(978-1-60870-070-7(4))* Cavendish Square Publishing LLC.

—Biodiversity of Rain Forests. Pyers, Greg. 2011. (Biodiversity Ser.). 32p. (gr. 4-4). 29.50 *(978-1-60870-073-8(9))* Cavendish Square Publishing LLC.

—Greenhouse Gases. Jakab, Cheryl. 2011. (Environment in Focus Ser.). 32p. (gr. 4-4). 29.50 *(978-1-60870-091-2(7))* Cavendish Square Publishing LLC.

—In Temperate Zones. Baker, Stuart. 2010. (Climate Change Ser.). 32p. (gr. 4-4). 29.50 *(978-0-7614-4441-1(6))* Cavendish Square Publishing LLC.

—In the Antarctic. Baker, Stuart. 2010. (Climate Change Ser.). 32p. (gr. 4-4). 29.50 *(978-0-7614-4438-1(6))* Cavendish Square Publishing LLC.

More, Dyana. Princess Pirates Book 3: Opal the Monstrous Forest. Lacey, Rose. 2019. (Princess Pirates Ser.). (ENG.). 128p. (J). (gr. 2-4). pap. 4.99 *(978-1-78700-733-8(2))* Willow Tree Bks. GBR. Dist: Independent Pubs. Group.

More Gordon, Domenica. Archie. More Gordon, Domenica. 2012. (ENG.). 48p. (J). (gr. -1-1). 18.89 *(978-1-59990-947-9(2)*, 9781599909479, Bloomsbury USA Childrens) Bloomsbury Publishing USA.

Morea, Marisa. I Am the Boss of This Chair. Crimi, Carolyn. 2018. 32p. (J). (gr. -1-2). 16.95 *(978-1-4549-2322-0(9))* Sterling Publishing Co., Inc.

Moreiro, Enrique S. Pedrín y la Garza. Perera, Hilda & Hilda, Perera. 2005. (SPA.). 36p. (J). (gr. 3-5). 14.99 *(978-84-241-8637-1(0))* Everest Editora ESP. Dist: Lectorum Pubns., Inc.

—El Rey de las Octavas. Romeu, Emma. 2007. (SPA.). 40p. (J). (gr. 3-5). 17.99 *(978-1-933032-26-9(X))* Lectorum Pubns., Inc.

Moreiro, Enrique S. Federico García Lorca. Moreiro, Enrique S. Lázaro, Georgina. 2009. (Cuando los Grandes Eran Pequenos Ser.). (SPA.). 32p. (J). (gr. 4-6). 14.99 *(978-1-933032-39-9(1))* Lectorum Pubns., Inc.

Morejon, Tom. Puddles. Ladd, Debbie. 2006. 32p. (J). pap. 8.95 *(978-0-9727615-4-3(3))* Deb on Air Bks.

Moreland Krass, Melanie. Psalm 1 for Kidz: I'm So Happy I Want to Shout! Trudgian, Sherri. 2013. 32p. (J). *(978-0-9779194-6-8(3))* Little Sprout Publishing Hse.

Moreland, Melanie. Psalm 148: Let all Heaven & Earth Praise the Lord! 2006. 32p. (J). *(978-0-9779194-0-6(4)*, Psalms for Kidz) Little Sprout Publishing Hse.

—Psalm 23: The Lord Is my Shepherd. I am His Lamb. 2007. 32p. (J). 10.00 *(978-0-9779194-1-3(2)*, Psalms for Kidz) Little Sprout Publishing Hse.

Morenilla, Alejandra. The Maker's Guide to Building Robots: A Step-By-Step Guide to Ordering Parts, Using Sensors & Lights, Programming, & More. Laperia, Raúl & Marsal, Andreu. 2019. (ENG.). 208p. (J). (gr. 2-6). 14.99 *(978-1-5107-4428-8(2)*, Sky Pony Pr.) Skyhorse Publishing Co., Inc.

Moreno, Ada. Jill Helps & Sings. Mast, Esta & Hege, Evelyn. 2016. (ENG.). 32p. (J). (gr. -1). 2.95 *(978-0-7399-2541-6(5))* Rod & Staff Pubs., Inc.

Moreno, Chris. Toy Story: The Mysterious Stranger. Jolley, Dan. (Kaboom! Graphic Novels Ser.). (ENG.). 112p. (J). 2011. (gr. 4-7). 26.19 *(978-1-934506-91-2(5))*; 2009. 24.99 *(978-1-60886-523-9(1))* Boom! Studios.

Moreno, Chris & Fotos, Jay. Dracula vs. King Arthur #1. Beranek, Adam & Beranek, Christian. 2005. 40p. 2.95 *(978-0-9752582-2-4(2))* Silent Devil Productions.

Moreno, Jorge Jimenez. Dark of the Moon, Vol. 4. Barber, John. 2012. (Transformers: Dark of the Moon Official Movie Adaptation Ser.). (ENG.). 24p. (J). (gr. 2-6). 27.07 *(978-1-59961-969-9(5)*, 14863, Graphic Novels) Spotlight.

—Official Movie Adaptation. Barber, John. 2012. (Transformers: Dark of the Moon Official Movie Adaptation Ser.). (ENG.). 24p. (J). (gr. 2-6). 27.07 *(978-1-59961-966-8(0)*, 14860); 27.07 *(978-1-59961-967-5(9)*, 14861) Spotlight. (Graphic Novels).

—Official Movie Adaption. Barber, John. 2012. (Transformers: Dark of the Moon Official Movie Adaptation Ser.). (ENG.). 24p. (J). (gr. 2-6). 27.07 *(978-1-59961-968-2(7)*, 14862, Graphic Novels) Spotlight.

Moreno, Juan M. The Boy Who Cried Wolf, Narrated by the Sheepish but Truthful Wolf. Loewen, Nancy. 2018. (Other Side of the Fable Ser.). (ENG.). 24p. (J). (gr. -1-3). lib. bdg. 27.99 *(978-1-5158-2869-3(7)*, 138407, Picture Window Bks.) Capstone.

Moreno, Rene King. Bravo! Guy, Ginger Foglesong. 2010. (ENG.). 32p. (J). (gr. -1-k). 17.99 *(978-0-06-173180-8(3)*, Greenwillow Bks.) HarperCollins Pubs.

—Dias y Dias/Days & Days: Bilingual Spanish-English Children's Book. Guy, Ginger Foglesong. 2019. (ENG & SPA.). 40p. (J). (gr. -1-3). 16.99 *(978-0-06-173182-2(X)*, Greenwillow Bks.) HarperCollins Pubs.

—Fiesta. Guy, Ginger Foglesong. 2007. (ENG & SPA.). (J). (gr. -1-3). lib. bdg. 17.60 *(978-1-68065-377-9(6))* Perfection Learning Corp.

—Fiesta! Bilingual Spanish-English. Guy, Ginger Foglesong. 2007. (ENG.). 32p. (J). (gr. -1-3). 6.99 *(978-0-06-088226-6(3)*, Greenwillow Bks.) HarperCollins Pubs.

—Fiesta! Board Book: Bilingual Spanish-English. Guy, Ginger Foglesong. 2003. (SPA.). 34p. (J). (gr. -1-3). bds. 7.99 *(978-0-06-009263-4(7)*, Greenwillow Bks.) HarperCollins Pubs.

—Papi's Gift. Stanton, Karen. 2007. (ENG.). 32p. (J). (gr. 2-k). 16.95 *(978-1-59078-422-8(7))* Boyds Mills Pr.

—Siesta. Guy, Ginger Foglesong. 2005. (ENG.). 32p. (J). (gr. -1-k). 17.99 *(978-0-06-056061-4(4)*, Greenwillow Bks.) HarperCollins Pubs.

—Siesta Board Book: Bilingual Spanish-English. Guy, Ginger Foglesong. 2009. (SPA.). 34p. (J). (gr. -1 — 1). bds. 7.99 *(978-0-06-168884-3(3)*, Greenwillow Bks.) HarperCollins Pubs.

—Under the Lemon Moon. Fine, Edith H. 2013.Tr. of Bajo la Luna de Limon. (ENG.). 32p. (J). pap. 10.95 *(978-1-58430-051-9(5))* Lee & Low Bks., Inc.

Moreno, Sergio. Cuenta Cuenta. Anaya, Hector. 2nd rev. ed. 2005. (Castillo de la Lectura Verde Ser.). (SPA & ENG.). 184p. (J). (gr. -1-7). pap. 7.95 *(978-970-20-0135-5(8))* Castillo, Ediciones, S. A. de C. V. MEX. Dist: Macmillan.

Morentorn, Alice. Royal Rap: Band 08/Purple (Collins Big Cat) Anholt, Laurence. 2015. (Collins Big Cat Ser.). (ENG.). 24p. (J). (gr. 2-2). pap. 8.99 *(978-0-00-759113-8(6))* HarperCollins Pubs. Ltd. GBR. Dist: Independent Pubs. Group.

Morentorn, Alice A. Calum's Big Break, 44 vols. Scott, Danny. 2016. (Scotland Stars FC Ser.). (ENG.). 152p. (J). pap. 6.95 *(978-1-78250-265-4(3)*, Kelpies) Floris Bks. GBR. Dist: Consortium Bk. Sales & Distribution.

—Calum's Cup Final, 34 vols. Scott, Danny. 2016. (Scotland Stars FC Ser.). (ENG.). 152p. (J). pap. 6.95 *(978-1-78250-282-1(3)*, Kelpies) Floris Bks. GBR. Dist: Consortium Bk. Sales & Distribution.

—Calum's Hard Knock, 36 vols. Scott, Danny. 2016. (Scotland Stars FC Ser.). (ENG.). 152p. (J). pap. 6.95 *(978-1-78250-280-7(7)*, Kelpies) Floris Bks. GBR. Dist: Consortium Bk. Sales & Distribution.

—Calum's New Boots, 44 vols. Scott, Danny. 2016. (Scotland Stars FC Ser.). (ENG.). 152p. (J). pap. 6.95 *(978-1-78250-264-7(5)*, Kelpies) Floris Bks. GBR. Dist: Consortium Bk. Sales & Distribution.

—Calum's New Team, 30 vols. Scott, Danny. 2016. (Scotland Stars FC Ser.). (ENG.). 152p. (J). pap. 6.95 *(978-1-78250-263-0(7)*, Kelpies) Floris Bks. GBR. Dist: Consortium Bk. Sales & Distribution.

—Calum's Tough Match, 36 vols. Scott, Danny. 2016. (Scotland Stars FC Ser.). (ENG.). 152p. (J). pap. 6.95 *(978-1-78250-281-4(5)*, Kelpies) Floris Bks. GBR. Dist: Consortium Bk. Sales & Distribution.

Moreton, Daniel. I Knew Two Who Said Moo: A Counting & Rhyming Book. Barrett, Judi. 2003. (ENG.). 32p. (J). (gr. -1-3). 7.99 *(978-0-689-85935-9(X)*, Atheneum Bks. for Young Readers) Simon & Schuster Children's Publishing.

—Lost! Trimble, Patti & Moran, Alex. 2003. (Green Light Readers Level 1 Ser.). (ENG.). 24p. (J). (gr. -1-3). pap. 4.99 *(978-0-15-204864-8(2)*, 1194688) Houghton Mifflin Harcourt Publishing Co.

—What Day Is It? Moran, Alex & Trimble, Patti. 2003. (Green Light Readers Level 1 Ser.). (ENG.). 24p. (J). (gr. -1-3). pap. 3.95 *(978-0-15-204846-4(4)*, 1194633) Houghton Mifflin Harcourt Publishing Co.

—What Day Is It? Trimble, Patti. ed. 2003. (Green Light Readers Level 1 Ser.). (gr. -1-3). lib. bdg. 13.50 *(978-0-613-66388-5(8))* Turtleback.

—What Day Is It? (¿Qué Día es Hoy?) Moran, Alex. Campoy, F. Isabel & Flor Ada, Alma, trs. 2008. (Green Light Readers Level 1 Ser.). (ENG.). 28p. (J). (gr. -1-3). pap. 4.99 *(978-0-15-206281-1(5)*, 1198827) Houghton Mifflin Harcourt Publishing Co.

Moretti, Danilo. Dawning Star: Operation Quick Launch. Hammock, Lee & Jacobson, Justin. 2005. 208p. pap. 29.95 *(978-0-9763795-0-8(3)*, BDV05001) Blue Devil Games.

Morey, Marey. You're in Charge... with Barnabus the Knight. Morey, Marey. Auzou Publishing Staff. 2019. 52p. (J). bds. 11.95 *(978-2-7338-6739-6(3))* Auzou, Philippe Editions FRA. Dist: Consortium Bk. Sales & Distribution.

—You're in Charge... with Wendy the Witch. Morey, Marey. 2019. 52p. (J). bds. 11.95 *(978-2-7338-6738-9(5))* Auzou, Philippe Editions FRA. Dist: Consortium Bk. Sales & Distribution.

Morgan, Akasha. Dreamer's Powerful Tiger: A New Lucid Dreaming Classic for Children & Parents of the 21st Century. 2018. (ENG.). 90p. (J). (gr. k-6). pap. 29.95 *(978-0-692-10136-0(5))* Dreambridge.

Morgan, Akasha, jt. illus. see Morgan, Angel.

Morgan, Angel & Morgan, Akasha. Dreamer's Powerful Tiger: A New Lucid Dreaming Classic for Children & Parents of the 21st Century. Morgan, Angel. 2018. (ENG.). 90p. (J). (gr. k-6). 39.95 *(978-0-692-10397-5(X))* Dreambridge.

Morgan, Christopher. One, Two, Buckle My Shoe. Everett, Melissa. 2013. (ENG.). 20p. (J). 8.99 *(978-1-77093-523-5(1))* Flowerpot Children's Pr. Inc. CAN. Dist: Cardinal Pubs. Group.

—One, Two, Buckle My Shoe. Everett, Melissa. 2017. (ENG.). 20p. (J). (gr. -1-1). bds. *(978-1-4867-1245-8(2))* Flowerpot Children's Pr. Inc.

Morgan, Dennis W. Pumpkin Head Harvey. Morgan, Dennis W. 2013. 40p. pap. 14.99 *(978-0-9892295-1-7(3))* Dreamstreet Studios, Inc. (A Div. of DSMV Industries, Inc.).

Morgan, Jeffrey. Under & over the Snow. Zygmont, Jeffrey. 2020. (ENG.). 28p. (J). pap. 8.95 ***(978-0-9991163-4-0(7))*** Free People Publishing.

Morgan-Jones, Tom. The Boy Who Biked the World: On the Road to Africa, Vol. Humphreys, Alastair. 2012. (Boy Who Biked the World Ser.: 1). (ENG.). 192p. (J). (gr. 4-7). pap. 9.99 *(978-1-903070-75-8(9))* Eye Bks. GBR. Dist: Independent Pubs. Group.

—The Boy Who Biked the World: Riding the Americas, Vol. Humphreys, Alastair. 2015. (Boy Who Biked the World Ser.: 2). (ENG.). 192p. (J). (gr. 4-7). pap. 9.99 *(978-1-903070-87-1(2))* Eye Bks. GBR. Dist: Independent Pubs. Group.

Morgan, Josh. Cannonball. Cotter, Sacha. 2020. (ENG.). 40p. (J). (-4). 17.99 *(978-1-7282-1756-7(3)*, Sourcebooks Jabberwocky) Sourcebooks, Inc.

Morgan, Mark. Bumper's Garage. Holladay, Geoff. 2019. (Bumper's Garage Ser.: Vol. 1). (ENG.). 32p. (J). (gr. k-6). 19.00 *(978-0-9983352-2-3(3)*, Bk.ify by Sanitaryum) Sanitaryum.

Morgan, Mark & Gallenson, Ann. Town Website Project for Macromedia Dreamweaver MX 2004: Communicating Information & Ideas on the Web, 2 bks. Underwood, Dale & Aho, Kirsti. Dharkar, Anuja & McCain, Malinda, eds. 2003. 39p. spiral bd. 10.00 *(978-0-9742273-8-2(2)*, Macromedia Education) Macromedia, Inc.

Morgan, Mary. When You Wander: A Search-and-Rescue Dog Story. Engle, Margarita. 2013. (ENG.). 32p. (J). (gr. -1-3). 16.99 *(978-0-8050-9312-4(5)*, 9780805093124, Holt, Henry & Co. Bks. For Young Readers) Holt, Henry & Co.

Morgan, Mary. Sleep Tight, Little Mouse. Morgan, Mary. 2015. 32p. (J). (gr. -1-2). bds. 6.99 *(978-0-553-49829-5(0)*, Knopf Bks. for Young Readers) Random Hse. Children's Bks.

Morgan, Nicolette. All about Me: Briana's Neighborhood. 2007. 24p. (J). 15.99 *(978-0-9793904-0-1(0))* It's Me Briana, LLC.

Morgan, Paulina. An ABC of Equality. Ewing, Chana Ginelle. 2019. (ENG.). 52p. (J). (gr. -1-k). bds. ***(978-1-78603-742-8(4))*** Frances Lincoln Childrens Bks.

Morgan, Paulina. What on Earth?: Bees. Quigley, Andrea. 2017. (What on Earth? Ser.). (ENG.). 64p. (J). (gr. 1-4). 14.95 *(978-1-68297-149-9(X))* QEB Publishing Inc.

Morgan, Paulina. What on Earth?: Trees. Warwick, Kevin. 2018. (What on Earth? Ser.). (ENG.). 64p. (J). (gr. 1-4). 12.95 ***(978-1-68297-305-9(0))*** QEB Publishing Inc.

—What on Earth: Robots. Fretland VanVoorst, Jenny. 2018. (What on Earth? Ser.). (ENG.). 64p. (J). (gr. 1-7). 12.95 ***(978-1-68297-345-5(X))*** QEB Publishing Inc.

Morgan, Pierr. The Children's Garden: Growing Food in the City. Schaefer, Carole Lexa. 2017. 32p. (J). (gr. -1-3). 16.99 *(978-1-57061-984-7(0)*, Little Bigfoot) Sasquatch Bks.

Morgan, Richard. Alan & the Animals. Foster, Evelyn. 2011. (Tadpoles Ser.). (ENG.). (J). (gr. -1-3). lib. bdg. 17.55 *(978-1-61383-938-6(3))* Perfection Learning Corp.

—Bella at the Ball. Sykes, Julie. 2014. 119p. (J). pap. *(978-0-545-69221-2(0))* Scholastic, Inc.

—Leo's New Pet. Gowar, Mick. 2008. (Tadpoles Ser.). (ENG.). 24p. (J). (gr. -1-3). pap. *(978-0-7787-3886-2(8))*; lib. bdg. *(978-0-7787-3855-8(8))* Crabtree Publishing Co.

—Thorfinn & the Awful Invasion, 30 vols., Bk. 1. MacPhail, David. 2015. (Thorfinn the Nicest Viking Ser.). (ENG.). 136p. (J). pap. 6.95 *(978-1-78250-158-9(4)*, Kelpies) Floris Bks. GBR. Dist: Consortium Bk. Sales & Distribution.

—Thorfinn & the Dreadful Dragon, 30 vols. MacPhail, David. 2019. (Thorfinn the Nicest Viking Ser.). (ENG.). 136p. (J). pap. 6.95 *(978-1-78250-565-5(2)*, Kelpies) Floris Bks. GBR. Dist: Consortium Bk. Sales & Distribution.

—Thorfinn & the Putrid Potion, 28 vols. MacPhail, David. 2020. (Thorfinn the Nicest Viking Ser.). (ENG.). 128p. (J). pap. 8.95 *(978-1-78250-637-9(3)*, Kelpies) Floris Bks. GBR. Dist: Consortium Bk. Sales & Distribution.

—Thorfinn & the Raging Raiders, 30 vols. MacPhail, David. 2016. (Thorfinn the Nicest Viking Ser.). (ENG.). 136p. (J). pap. 6.95 *(978-1-78250-233-3(5)*, Kelpies) Floris Bks. GBR. Dist: Consortium Bk. Sales & Distribution.

—Thorfinn & the Terrible Treasure, 30 vols. MacPhail, David. 2016. (Thorfinn the Nicest Viking Ser.). (ENG.). 136p. (J). pap. 6.95 *(978-1-78250-235-7(1)*, Kelpies) Floris Bks. GBR. Dist: Consortium Bk. Sales & Distribution.

—Thorfinn the Nicest Viking & the Disgusting Feast, 32 vols. MacPhail, David. 2016. (Thorfinn the Nicest Viking Ser.). (ENG.). 136p. (J). pap. 6.95 *(978-1-78250-231-9(9)*, Kelpies) Floris Bks. GBR. Dist: Consortium Bk. Sales & Distribution.

—Thorfinn the Nicest Viking & the Gruesome Games, 30 vols. MacPhail, David. 2015. (Thorfinn the Nicest Viking Ser.). (ENG.). 136p. (J). 8.95 *(978-1-78250-159-6(2)*, Kelpies) Floris Bks. GBR. Dist: Consortium Bk. Sales & Distribution.

—Thorfinn the Nicest Viking & the Rotten Scots, 32 vols. MacPhail, David. 2016. (Thorfinn the Nicest Viking Ser.). (ENG.). 136p. (J). pap. 8.95 *(978-1-78250-229-6(7)*, Kelpies) Floris Bks. GBR. Dist: Consortium Bk. Sales & Distribution.

—The Wheels on the Bus - The Boat on the Waves. 2013. (ENG.). 24p. (J). *(978-0-7787-1148-3(X))* Crabtree Publishing Co.

—The Wheels on the Bus; The Boat on the Waves. 2013. (ENG.). 24p. (J). pap. *(978-0-7787-1152-0(8))* Crabtree Publishing Co.

Morgan, Richard & Fennell, Tracy. Oliver Twist. Dickens, Charles. 2008. 48p. (J). (gr. 4-7). pap. 10.00 *(978-1-4190-5075-6(3))* Steck-Vaughn.

Morgan, Rick. An Illustrated Timeline of Inventions & Inventors, 1 vol. Spengler, Kremena T. 2011. (Visual Timelines in History Ser.). (ENG.). 32p. (J). (gr. 2-4). pap. 7.49 *(978-1-4048-7017-8(2))*; (gr. 3-4). pap. 41.70 *(978-1-4048-7021-5(0))* Capstone. (Picture Window Bks.).

—An Illustrated Timeline of U. S. States, 1 vol. Wooster, Patricia. 2011. (Visual Timelines in History Ser.). (ENG.). 32p. (J). (gr. 2-4). pap. 7.49 *(978-1-4048-7020-8(2)*, Picture Window Bks.) Capstone.

—Rookie Racer. Pruett, Scott et al. 2005. (J). *(978-0-9670600-2-6(8))* Word Weaver Bks., Inc.

Morgan, Sally. Dreamers. Kwaymullina, Ezekiel. 2020. 32p. (J). 12.95 ***(978-1-922089-84-7(2))*** Fremantle Pr. AUS. Dist: Independent Pubs. Group.

Morgan, Tom & Mounts, Paul. Godzilla Saves America: A Monster Showdown in 3-D! Cerasini, Marc. 2006. 20p. (J). (gr. k-4). reprint ed. 12.00 *(978-1-4223-5409-4(1))* DIANE Publishing Co.

Morgan, Trish. A Lab's Tale. Malpass, Suzanne M. 2012. 38p. (J). 12.95 *(978-1-937406-68-4(7))* Mascot Bks., Inc.

Morgan, Vincent. Big Boy. Banks, Robin Washington. 2011. 20p. pap. 24.95 *(978-1-4560-7068-7(1))* PublishAmerica, Inc.

Morgand, Virginie. What Do Grown-Ups Do All Day? Morgand, Virginie. 2016. (ENG.). 64p. (J). 24.99 *(978-1-84780-809-7(3)*, 314987, Wide Eyed Editions) Quarto Publishing Group UK GBR. Dist: Hachette UK Distribution.

Morgin, W. J. & W., E. Sowing Beside All Waters: A Tale of the World in the Church. Leslie, Emma. 2007. 300p. 24.95 *(978-1-934671-06-1(1))*; per. 14.95 *(978-1-934671-07-8(X))* Salem Ridge Press LLC.

Mori, Midori & Revels, Robert. Neem el Media Nino. Shah, Idries. Wirkala, Rita, tr. 2007. 32p. (J). 18.00 *(978-1-883536-96-1(0))*; pap. 7.99 *(978-1-883536-97-8(9))* I S H K. (Hoopoe Bks.).

—Neem the Half-Boy. Shah, Idries. 2007. (ENG.). 32p. (J). (gr. 2). pap. 9.99 *(978-1-883536-95-4(2)*, Hoopoe Bks.) I S H K.

—Neem the Half-Boy: English-Dari Edition. Shah, Idries. 2017. (Hoopoe Teaching-Stories Ser.). (ENG.). (J). (gr. k-6). pap. 9.99 *(978-1-946270-15-3(6)*, Hoopoe Bks.) I S H K.

—Neem the Half-Boy: English-Pashto Edition. Shah, Idries. 2017. (Hoopoe Teaching-Stories Ser.). (ENG & PUS.). (J).

M

(gr. 2-6). pap. 9.99 *(978-1-944493-60-8(3)*, Hoopoe Bks.) I S H K.

—Neem the Half-Boy: English-Urdu Bilingual Edition. Shah, Idries. 2016. (URD & ENG.). (J). (gr. k-6). pap. 9.99 *(978-1-942698-77-7(1)*, Hoopoe Bks.) I S H K.

Mori, Midori & Revels, Robert. Nim le Demi-Gar�on: French-Arabic Edition. Shah, Idries. 2018. (Hoopoe Teaching-Stories Ser.). (FRE.). 40p. (J). (gr. 3-6). pap. 9.99 ***(978-1-949358-49-0(6)***, Hoopoe Bks.) I S H K.

Mori, Paula & Vela, David. El Motín Del Miño: La Aventura de Tita y Tito. Marzo, José. 2016. (SPA.). 38p. (J). pap. *(978-84-944688-9-6(8))* ACVF Editorial.

Morice, Dave. A Visit from St. Alphabet. Morice, Dave. 2005. (ENG.). 24p. (Orig.). (J). (gr. -1-3). 9.95 *(978-1-56689-179-0(5))* Coffee Hse. Pr.

Moricuchi, Mique. Little Mouse Deer & the Crocodile. Hughes, Mónica. 2004. 24p. (J). lib. bdg. 23.65 *(978-1-59646-684-5(7))* Dingles & Co.

Morikawa, Julie. Hana's Cube Adventure. Morikawa, Julie. 2016. (ENG.). 42p. (J). pap. ***(978-4-902422-17-7(4))*** Forest River Pr.

Morimoto, Sango. Taro & the Magic Pencil, 1. Morimoto, Sango. 2010. (Adventures of Taro Ser.). (ENG.). 104p. (J). (gr. 1-5). 22.44 *(978-1-4215-3524-1(6))* Viz Media.

Morin, Leane. The Carpet Boy's Gift, 1 vol. Shea, Pegi Deitz & Deitz Shea, Pegi. 2005. (ENG.). 40p. (J). (gr. 3-6). 16.95 *(978-0-88448-248-2(0))* Tilbury Hse. Pubs.

Morin, Mauricio Gomez. Harvey Angel y la Nina Fantasma. Hendry, Diana. Alban, Rafael Segovia, tr. 2003. (la Orilla Del Viento Ser.). (SPA.). 166p. (J). reprint ed. pap., pap. 7.50 *(978-968-16-6723-8(9))* Fondo de Cultura Economica USA.

Morin, Paul. The Ghost Dance, 1 vol. McLerran, Alice. 2018. (ENG.). 32p. (J). (gr. 4-6). 14.95 *(978-1-55455-407-2(1)*, c543ca13-9825-4db3-ab83-737bd8528db7) Fitzhenry & Whiteside, Ltd. CAN. Dist: Firefly Bks., Ltd.

—Mr. Hiroshi's Garden, 1 vol. Trottier, Maxine. 2006. (ENG.). 32p. (J). (gr. 1-3). 9.95 *(978-1-55005-152-0(0)*, ad264dda-9f84-4452-a2fc-f86ba8e7f358) Trifolium Bks., Inc. CAN. Dist: Firefly Bks., Ltd.

—The Vision Seeker, 1 vol. Freeman, Yusuf, photos by. Whetung, James. 2011. (ENG.). 32p. (J). (gr. 2-3). pap. 9.95 *(978-1-55455-194-1(3)*, f41c752f-006d-4983-b81a-d43038a4ef00) Fitzhenry & Whiteside, Ltd. CAN. Dist: Firefly Bks., Ltd.

—When God Made the Dakotas. Kessler, Tim. 2006. 32p. (J). (gr. k). 17.00 *(978-0-8028-5275-5(0)*, Eerdmans Bks For Young Readers) Eerdmans, William B. Publishing Co.

Morin, Paul. Animal Dreaming, 1 vol. Morin, Paul. 2019. (ENG.). 32p. (J). (gr. 1-4). 9.95 *(978-0-7737-3062-5(1)*, 06acd772-9da4-4819-b341-8863c8d38544) Trifolium Bks., Inc. CAN. Dist: Firefly Bks., Ltd.

Morin, Paul, jt. illus. see Collier, John.

Morinaga, Ai. Duck Prince: Transformation, 6 bks, Bk. 1. Morinaga, Ai. Pannone, Frank, ed. Jackson, Laura & Kobayashi, Yoko, trs. from JPN. 2004. Orig. Title: Ahiruno Oujisama 1. 176p. pap. 9.99 *(978-1-58664-931-9(0)*, CMX 65201G, CPM Manga) Central Park Media Corp.

Morino, Sakana. Becoming a Dragon. Morino, Sakana. 2014. (J). 8.95 *(978-1-935523-67-3(8))* World Tribune Pr.

Moritsu, Wakako. O Holy Night: The First Christmas. Yamamoto, Makoto. 2005. 24p. (J). (gr. -1-3). per. 16.95 *(978-0-8198-5440-7(9))* Pauline Bks. & Media.

Moritz, Bea. Chicken Little. 2017. (5 Minute Storytime Ser.). (ENG.). 32p. (J). (gr. k-3). 6.99 *(978-1-4867-1276-2(2)*, 0da006d7-d326-473b-b4a5-7144fd86a65c) Flowerpot Pr.

Moriuchi, Mique. Fresh Delicious. Latham, Irene. 2016. (ENG.). 40p. (J). (gr. -1-3). 16.95 *(978-1-62979-103-6(2)*, Wordsong) Boyds Mills Pr.

—Goodnight Prayers. Piper, Sophie. ed. 2008. (ENG.). 64p. (J). (gr. -1-k). 7.99 *(978-0-7459-6065-4(0))* Lion Hudson PLC GBR. Dist: Independent Pubs. Group.

—I'll See You in the Morning. Jolley, Mike. 2008. (ENG.). (J). (gr. -1 — 1). bds. 6.99 *(978-0-8118-6543-2(6))* Chronicle Bks. LLC.

—Mix & Match Animals: Over 20 Different Animal Combinations! 2007. (ENG.). 10p. (gr. -1). 10.95 *(978-1-58117-603-2(1)*, Intervisual/Piggy Toes) Bendon, Inc.

Moriya, Kwanchai. Birds from Head to Tail. Roderick, Stacey. 2018. (Head to Tail Ser.). (ENG.). 36p. (J). (gr. -1-2). 16.99 *(978-1-77138-925-9(7))* Kids Can Pr., Ltd. CAN. Dist: Hachette Bk. Group.

—Bugs from Head to Tail. Roderick, Stacey. 2017. (Head to Tail Ser.). (ENG.). 36p. (J). (gr. -1-2). 16.99 *(978-1-77138-729-3(7))* Kids Can Pr., Ltd. CAN. Dist: Hachette Bk. Group.

—Dinosaurs from Head to Tail. Roderick, Stacey. 2015. (Head to Tail Ser.). (ENG.). 36p. (J). (gr. -1-2). 16.95 *(978-1-77138-044-7(6))* Kids Can Pr., Ltd. CAN. Dist: Hachette Bk. Group.

—Ocean Animals from Head to Tail. Roderick, Stacey. 2016. (Head to Tail Ser.). (ENG.). 36p. (J). (gr. -1-2). 16.95 *(978-1-77138-345-5(3))* Kids Can Pr., Ltd. CAN. Dist: Hachette Bk. Group.

Morley, Amanda, et al. Fact & Fiction 1: Reece to the Rescue; Here Comes a Thunderstorm; Garden Giant; A Sunflower Life Cycle; Mugs Indoors & Outdoors; Cats Are Hunters; Beach Days; Oceans All Around Us, 8 bks., Set. McCarrier, Andrea et al. 2006. (ENG.). 16p. (J). pap. 120.00 *(978-1-893986-25-1(X))* Keep Bks.

Morley, Farah. The Spider & the Doves: The Story of the Hijra. 2012. (ENG.). 30p. (J). (gr. -1-2). 8.95 *(978-0-86037-449-7(1))* Kube Publishing Ltd. GBR. Dist: Consortium Bk. Sales & Distribution.

Morley, Taia. Anna's Table. Bunting, Eve. 2003. (ENG.). 32p. (J). (gr. 3-6). 16.95 *(978-1-55971-841-7(2))* Cooper Square Publishing Llc.

—Ho Ho Homework. Larsen, Mylisa. 2019. (ENG.). 32p. (J). (gr. -1-3). 17.99 *(978-0-06-279688-2(7))* HarperCollins Pubs.

—Hurricane Watch. Stewart, Melissa. 2015. (Let's-Read-And-Find-Out Science 2 Ser.). (ENG.). 40p. (J). (gr. -1-3). pap. 6.99 *(978-0-06-232775-8(5))* HarperCollins Pubs.

—Looking Good! How to Get Stylin' with Your Friends. Hurley, Jo. 2007. 64p. (J). *(978-0-439-02013-8(1))* Scholastic, Inc.

—My New Big-Kid Bed. Bertram, Debbie. 2017. 32p. (J). (gr. -1-2). 16.99 *(978-1-101-93731-0(9)*, Random Hse. Bks. for Young Readers) Random Hse. Children's Bks.

—Slumber-ific! Great Sleepover Ideas for You & Your Friends. Hurley, Jo. 2007. 63p. (J). *(978-0-439-02015-2(8))* Scholastic, Inc.

—The Sun & the Moon. DeCristofano, Carolyn Cinami. 2016. (Let's-Read-And-Find-Out Science 1 Ser.). (ENG.). 40p. (J). (gr. -1-3). pap. 6.99 *(978-0-06-233803-7(X))* HarperCollins Pubs.

—Thump Goes the Rabbit: How Animals Communicate. Hodgkins, Fran. 2020. (Let's-Read-And-Find-Out Science 1 Ser.). (ENG.). 40p. (J). (gr. -1-3). 17.99 *(978-0-06-249101-5(6))*; pap. 6.99 *(978-0-06-249097-1(4))* HarperCollins Pubs. Ltd. GBR. (HarperCollins). Dist: HarperCollins Pubs.

—Wake up, Color Pup. 2019. (ENG.). 32p. (J). (gr. -1-2). 17.99 *(978-0-399-55945-7(0))*; lib. bdg. 20.99 *(978-0-399-55946-4(9))* Random Hse. Children's Bks. (Random Hse. Bks. for Young Readers).

Morling, Donovan. The Disaster Caster. Carter, Grant Matthew. 2012. 38p. pap. 16.00 *(978-1-4349-8432-6(X)*, RoseDog Bks.) Dorrance Publishing Co., Inc.

Moro, Robin, et al. Read Aloud Spooky Stories. 2006. 320p. (J). (gr. 4-7). 15.98 *(978-0-7853-6338-5(6)*, 7159100) Publications International, Ltd.

Moroney, Christopher. Animal Alphabet (Sesame Street) Random House. 2005. (ENG.). 20p. (J). (gr. k — 1). bds. 7.99 *(978-0-375-83228-4(9)*, Random Hse. Bks. for Young Readers) Random Hse. Children's Bks.

—Busy as a Bee! Tillworth, Mary. 2012. (Write-On/Wipe-off Activity Book Ser.). (ENG.). 12p. (J). (gr. k — 1). bds. 9.99 *(978-0-307-93011-8(4)*, Golden Bks.) Random Hse. Children's Bks.

—The Cat in the Hat: Cooking with the Cat (Dr. Seuss) Worth, Bonnie. 2003. (Step into Reading Ser.). (ENG.). 32p. (J). (gr. -1-1). pap. 4.99 *(978-0-375-82494-4(4)*, 53560581, Random Hse. Bks. for Young Readers) Random Hse. Children's Bks.

—Elmo's Little Dreidel (Sesame Street) Kleinberg, Naomi. 2011. (ENG.). 12p. (J). (gr. k — 1). bds. 5.99 *(978-0-375-87396-6(1)*, Random Hse. Bks. for Young Readers) Random Hse. Children's Bks.

—Elmo's Monster Mash. Kleinberg, Naomi. 2010. (ENG.). 12p. (J). (gr. k — 1). 4.99 *(978-0-375-85804-8(0)*, Random Hse. Bks. for Young Readers) Random Hse. Children's Bks.

—Happy Holi-Doodles! Golden Books. 2012. (ENG.). 128p. (J). (gr. -1-2). pap. 5.99 *(978-0-307-93198-6(6)*, Golden Bks.) Random Hse. Children's Bks.

—In Elmo's Easter Parade (Sesame Street) Kleinberg, Naomi. 2009. (ENG.). 12p. (J). (gr. k — 1). bds. 4.99 *(978-0-375-84480-5(5)*, Random Hse. Bks. for Young Readers) Random Hse. Children's Bks.

—King Cecil the Sea Horse (Dr. Seuss/Cat in the Hat) Rabe, Tish. 2013. (Little Golden Book Ser.). (ENG.). 24p. (J). (-k). 3.99 *(978-0-449-81010-1(0)*, Golden Bks.) Random Hse. Children's Bks.

—My Fuzzy Valentine (Sesame Street) Kleinberg, Naomi. 2005. (ENG.). 12p. (J). (gr. k — 1). bds. 5.99 *(978-0-375-83392-2(7)*, Random Hse. Bks. for Young Readers) Random Hse. Children's Bks.

—Naptime/Cuddles (Sesame Street) Kleinberg, Naomi. 2017. (ENG.). 24p. (J). (— 1). bds. 8.99 *(978-1-5247-1636-3(7)*, Random Hse. Bks. for Young Readers) Random Hse. Children's Bks.

—P Is for Potty! (Sesame Street) Kleinberg, Naomi. 2014. (Lift-The-Flap Ser.). (ENG.). 12p. (J). (— 1). bds. 5.99 *(978-0-385-38369-1(X)*, Random Hse. Bks. for Young Readers) Random Hse. Children's Bks.

—Sesame Beginnings: Potty Time! (Sesame Street) Sawyer, Parker K. 2006. (Sesame Beginnings Ser.). (ENG.). 12p. (J). (gr. k — 1). bds. 5.99 *(978-0-375-83695-4(0)*, Random Hse. Bks. for Young Readers) Random Hse. Children's Bks.

—So Big! (Sesame Street) Hays, Anna Jane. 2003. (Sesame Beginnings Ser.: Vol. 2). (ENG.). 14p. (J). (gr. k — 1). bds. 7.99 *(978-0-375-81537-9(6)*, Random Hse. Bks. for Young Readers) Random Hse. Children's Bks.

—1, 2, 3 Count with Me (Sesame Street) Kleinberg, Naomi. 2005. (ENG.). 20p. (J). (gr. k — 1). bds. 7.99 *(978-0-375-83227-7(0)*, Random Hse. Bks. for Young Readers) Random Hse. Children's Bks.

Moroney, Trace. Lift the Flap Bible. Jones, Sally Lloyd. 2011. (Lift-The-Flap Ser.). (ENG.). 20p. (J). (gr. -1-k). bds. 10.99 *(978-0-7944-2278-3(0)*, Reader's Digest Children's Bks.) Studio Fun International.

—Lift the Flap Nativity. Zobel-Nolan, Allia. 2015. (Lift-The-Flap Ser.). (ENG.). 20p. (J). (gr. -1-k). 10.99 *(978-0-7944-3527-1(0)*, Reader's Digest Children's Bks.) Studio Fun International.

—My Bible Story Collection. Nolan, Allia Zobel. 2004. 96p. (J). 14.99 *(978-0-8254-5515-5(4))* Kregel Pubns.

—My First Book of Nursery Rhymes: Jigsaw Book. (My First Book Ser.). 12p. (J). *(978-1-74124-628-5(8))* Five Mile Australia.

—My First Book of Nursery Songs: Jigsaw Book. (My First Book Ser.). 12p. (J). *(978-1-74124-630-8(X))* Five Mile Australia.

—Stories Jesus Told. Littleton, Mark. 2004. 20p. (J). bds. 10.99 *(978-0-8254-5519-3(7))* Kregel Pubns.

—The Story of Noah's Ark. Nolan, Allia Zobel. 2006. 24p. (J). pap. 3.99 *(978-0-8254-5532-2(4))* Kregel Pubns.

Moroney, Trace. Bathtime: Baxter Bear Chubby. Moroney, Trace. 2008. (Baxter Bear Collection). 10p. (J). (gr. -1-1). bds. *(978-1-86463-175-3(9))* Brimax Books Ltd.

—Bedtime: The Baxter Bear Collection. Moroney, Trace. 2008. (Baxter Bear Collection). 10p. (gr. -1-1). bds. 5.99 *(978-1-86463-176-0(7))* Gardner Pubns.

—Dinnertime: Baxter Bear Chubby. Moroney, Trace. 2008. 10p. (J). (gr. -1-1). bds. 5.99 *(978-1-86463-174-6(0))* Gardner Pubns.

—Playtime. Moroney, Trace. 2008. (Baxter Bear Collection). 10p. (gr. -1-1). bds. 5.99 *(978-1-86463-177-7(5))* Gardner Pubns.

Moroney, Tracey. A Child's Book of Miracles & Wonders. Tuck, Mildred. 2006. 28p. (J). (gr. -1-3). 15.99 *(978-0-7847-1437-9(1)*, 04076) Standard Publishing.

—Little Fox's Surprise. 2015. (J). *(978-0-545-84956-2(X))* Scholastic, Inc.

—A Snowman for Little Bear. 2016. (J). *(978-0-545-84958-6(6))* Scholastic, Inc.

Morosan, Andra. Harold Angel. McWood, Allison. 2018. (ENG.). 28p. (J). pap. *(978-1-9994377-2-5(1))* Annelid Pr.

Morozov, Yuri. The Three Little Pigs Halloween Adventure. Cartoon, Surprise. Saroyan, Isabella, ed. 2018. (ENG.). 42p. (J). pap. 11.99 *(978-1-7293-9949-1(5))* Independently Published.

Morozova, Anastasia. Rose-Pie. Sexton, Jessa Rose. 2011. 20p. pap. 6.00 *(978-0-9846244-0-9(6))* O'More Publishing.

Morphew, Betsy. Imagine That! Duvall, Rhea. 2017. (ENG.). 28p. (J). (gr. k-4). 14.99 *(978-1-946171-14-6(X))* Kids At Heart Publishing, LLC.

Morphew, Betsy. Tissie's Travels: Charleston, South Carolina. Judy, Sandy. 2019. (Tissie's Travels Ser.: Vol. 2). (ENG.). 38p. (J). (gr. k-5). 17.99 ***(978-1-946171-37-5(9))*** Kids At Heart Publishing, LLC.

Morphew, Betsy. Tissie's Travels: New York City. Judy, Sandy. 2018. (Tissie's Travels New York City Ser.: Vol. 1). (ENG.). 32p. (J). (gr. k-2). 17.99 *(978-1-946171-20-7(4))* Kids At Heart Publishing, LLC.

Morraes, Leeron. Abc's of Food: Alphabet Book & Workbook. Education, Beansprout & Grant, Miss. 2019. (ENG.). 58p. (J). 17.99 *(978-1-950471-04-1(7))* BeanSprout Bks.

—Scooter, Lima Bean, & the Magical Candy Factory. Grant, Tahlonna. 2019. (Adventures of Scooter & Lima Bean Ser.: Vol. 1). (ENG.). 50p. (J). pap. 16.99 *(978-1-950471-01-0(2))*; 19.99 *(978-1-950471-00-3(4))* BeanSprout Bks.

—UFO Book for Kids. Chapple, Netali. 2018. (ENG.). 50p. (J). pap. 16.99 *(978-0-692-09482-2(2))* BeanSprout Bks.

Morrell, Cris. Basura No, Gracias! Pittar, Gill & Gill, Pittar. Rioja, Alberto Jimenez, tr. 2003. (Milly Molly Ser.). (SPA.). 24p. (J). pap. *(978-84-241-8695-1(8))* Everest Editora ESP. Dist: Lectorum Pubns., Inc.

—Las Ciruelas de Isa Bela. Pittar, Gill & Gill, Pittar. Rioja, Alberto Jimenez, tr. 2003. (Milly Molly Ser.). (SPA.). 24p. (J). pap. *(978-84-241-8687-6(7))* Everest Editora ESP. Dist: Lectorum Pubns., Inc.

—Milly & Molly's Monday. Pittar, Gill. 2nd rev. ed. 2003. 27p. *(978-1-877297-06-9(2))* Milly Molly Bks.

—Milly, Molly & Beaky. Pittar, Gill. 2005. 28p. (gr. -1). pap. *(978-1-86972-048-3(2))* Milly Molly Bks.

—Milly, Molly & the Ferryman. Pittar, Gill. 2004. 28p. pap. *(978-1-86972-004-9(0))* Milly Molly Bks.

—Milly, Molly & the Picnic. Pittar, Gill. 2005. 28p. (gr. -1). pap. *(978-1-86972-045-2(8))* Milly Molly Bks.

—Milly, Molly & the Runaway Bean. Pittar, Gill. 2005. 28p. (J). (gr. -1). pap. *(978-1-86972-049-0(0))* Milly Molly Bks.

—De Quien es Este Sombrero? Pittar, Gill & Gill, Pittar. Rioja, Alberto Jimenez, tr. 2003. (Milly Molly Ser.). (SPA.). 24p. (J). pap. *(978-84-241-8679-1(6))* Everest Editora ESP. Dist: Lectorum Pubns., Inc.

Morrill, Leslie. The Celery Stalks at Midnight, 3. Howe, James. 2006. (Bunnicula & Friends Ser.). (ENG.). 144p. (J). (gr. 3-7). pap. 7.99 *(978-1-4169-2814-0(6))* Simon & Schuster, Inc.

—Nighty-Nightmare. Howe, James. 2007. (Bunnicula & Friends Ser.). (ENG.). 144p. (J). (gr. 3-7). pap. 7.99 *(978-1-4169-3966-5(0)*, Atheneum Bks. for Young Readers) Simon & Schuster Children's Publishing.

—Totally Disgusting! Wallace, Bill. 2008. (ENG.). 144p. (J). (gr. 3-7). pap. 5.99 *(978-1-4169-5805-5(3)*, Simon & Schuster/Paula Wiseman Bks.) Simon & Schuster/Paula Wiseman Bks.

Morris. The Bluefeet Are Coming! 2014. (Lucky Luke Ser.: 43). (ENG.). 48p. pap. 11.95 *(978-1-84918-173-0(X))* CineBook GBR. Dist: National Bk. Network.

—The Daily Star. Léturgie, Jean & Fauche, Xavier. 2013. (Lucky Luke Ser.: 41). (ENG.). 48p. pap. 11.95 *(978-1-84918-160-0(8))* CineBook GBR. Dist: National Bk. Network.

—The Daltons Always on the Run. Goscinny, René. 2012. (Lucky Luke Ser.: 34). (ENG.). 48p. (J). (gr. 3-12). pap. 11.95 *(978-1-84918-119-8(5))* CineBook GBR. Dist: National Bk. Network.

—Daltons in the Blizzard. Goscinny, René. 2009. (Lucky Luke Ser.: 15). (ENG.). 48p. (J). (gr. 3-17). pap. 11.95 *(978-1-905460-76-2(7))* CineBook GBR. Dist: National Bk. Network.

—The Dashing White Cowboy. Goscinny, René. 2009. (Lucky Luke Ser.: 14). (ENG.). 46p. (J). (gr. -1-17). pap. 11.95 *(978-1-905460-66-3(X))* CineBook GBR. Dist: National Bk. Network.

—Doc Doxey's Elixir. 2013. (Lucky Luke Ser.: 38). (ENG.). 48p. pap. 11.95 *(978-1-84918-141-9(1))* CineBook GBR. Dist: National Bk. Network.

—Lucky Luke Versus Joss Jamon. Goscinny, René. 27th ed. 2011. (Lucky Luke Ser.: 27). (ENG.). 48p. (gr. 3-17). pap. 11.95 *(978-1-84918-071-9(7))* CineBook GBR. Dist: National Bk. Network.

—Lucky Luke Versus Pat Poker. 2014. (Lucky Luke Ser.: 44). (ENG.). 48p. pap. 11.95 *(978-1-84918-179-2(9))* CineBook GBR. Dist: National Bk. Network.

—Phil Wire. 2013. (Lucky Luke Ser.: 40). (ENG.). 48p. pap. 11.95 *(978-1-84918-155-6(1))* CineBook GBR. Dist: National Bk. Network.

Morris, Alexander. Abc's of Health & Safety. Abramovitz, Melissa. 2012. 16p. pap. 9.95 *(978-1-61633-276-1(X))* Guardian Angel Publishing, Inc.

—Bearly Learning about Water. Esparza-Vela, Mary. 2012. 16p. pap. 9.95 *(978-1-61633-288-4(3))* Guardian Angel Publishing, Inc.

—Frankie's Perfect Home. McClure, Beverly Stowe. 2011. 16p. pap. 9.95 *(978-1-61633-162-7(3))* Guardian Angel Publishing, Inc.

—Juggerum. Kennedy, J. Aday. 2012. 16p. pap. 9.95 *(978-1-61633-348-5(0))* Guardian Angel Publishing, Inc.

—My Brother the Frog. McNamee, Kevin. 2011. 24p. 19.95 *(978-1-61633-167-2(4))*; pap. 10.95 *(978-1-61633-159-7(3))* Guardian Angel Publishing, Inc.

—The Water Cycle: Water Play Series Book 1. Calvani, Mayra. 2012. 20p. pap. 10.95 *(978-1-61633-237-2(9))* Guardian Angel Publishing, Inc.

Morris, Alfred. A Cure for the Daltons, Vol. 23. Goscinny, René. 2010. (Lucky Luke Ser.: 23). (ENG.). 48p. (J). (gr. 3-17). pap. 11.95 *(978-1-84918-034-4(2))* CineBook GBR. Dist: National Bk. Network.

—Jesse James. Goscinny, René. 2007. (Lucky Luke Ser.: 4). (ENG.). 48p. (J). (gr. 4-7). per. 11.95 *(978-1-905460-14-4(7))* CineBook GBR. Dist: National Bk. Network.

—The Judge. 2010. (Lucky Luke Ser.: 24). (ENG.). 46p. (J). (gr. 3-17). pap. 11.95 *(978-1-84918-045-0(8))* CineBook GBR. Dist: National Bk. Network.

—The Tenderfoot. Goscinny, René. 2008. (Lucky Luke Ser.: 13). (ENG.). 48p. (J). (gr. -1-17). pap. 11.95 *(978-1-905460-65-6(1))* CineBook GBR. Dist: National Bk. Network.

—Western Circus. Goscinny, René. 2008. (Lucky Luke Ser.: 11). (ENG.). 48p. pap. 11.95 *(978-1-905460-55-7(4))* CineBook GBR. Dist: National Bk. Network.

Morris, Don. Luna & the Big Blur: A Story for Children Who Wear Glasses. Day, Shirley. 2008. 32p. (J). (gr. -1-3). 14.95 *(978-1-4338-0398-7(4))*; pap. 9.95 *(978-1-4338-0399-4(2))* American Psychological Assn. (Magination Pr.).

Morris, Douglas. Here I Am Look at Me! Morris, Deborah K. 2010. 36p. pap. 13.95 *(978-1-60911-739-9(5)*, Eloquent Bks.) Strategic Book Publishing & Rights Agency (SBPRA).

Morris, Garvin. Dump Dog. Morris, Garvin. (J). 2008. 32p. pap. 6.95 *(978-1-60108-022-6(0))*; 2007. 40p. (gr. -1-2). 15.95 *(978-1-60108-012-7(3))* Red Cygnet Pr.

Morris, Hannah. The Hyena & the Seven Little Kids. Bloch, Carole. 2012. (Best Loved Tales for Africa Ser.). 32p. (J). (gr. k-2). pap. 9.95 *(978-1-77009-820-6(8))* Jacana Media ZAF. Dist: Independent Pubs. Group.

Morris, J. E. Fish Are Not Afraid of Doctors. Morris, J. E. (Maud the Koala Ser.). 32p. (J). (gr. -1-3). 2019. (ENG.). 4.99 *(978-0-593-09596-6(0))*; 2018. 8.99 *(978-1-5247-8443-0(5))* Penguin Young Readers Group. (Penguin Workshop).

—Flubby Is Not a Good Pet! Morris, J. E. (Flubby Ser.). 32p. (J). 2020. (ENG.). (gr. k-1). 4.99 *(978-1-5247-9078-3(8))*; 2019. (gr. -1-3). 9.99 *(978-1-5247-8776-9(0))* Penguin Young Readers Group. (Penguin Workshop).

—Flubby Will Not Play with That. Morris, J. E. (Flubby Ser.). 32p. (J). 2020. (ENG.). (gr. k-1). 4.99 *(978-1-5247-9083-7(4))*; 2019. (gr. -1-3). 9.99 *(978-1-5247-8778-3(7))* Penguin Young Readers Group. (Penguin Workshop).

—Meet Maud the Koala. Morris, J. E. 2020. (Maud the Koala Ser.). (ENG.). 64p. (J). (gr. -1-3). pap. 9.99 *(978-0-593-09436-5(0)*, Penguin Workshop) Penguin Young Readers Group.

—Much Too Much Birthday. Morris, J. E. 2018. (Maud the Koala Ser.). 32p. (J). (gr. -1-3). 8.99 *(978-1-5247-8446-1(X)*, Penguin Workshop) Penguin Young Readers Group.

Morris, Jackie. The Greatest Gift: The Story of the Other Wise Man. Summers, Susan. 2011. 30p. (J). 16.99 *(978-1-84686-578-7(6))* Barefoot Bks., Inc.

—Mariana & the Merchild. Pitcher, Caroline. 2004. 32p. (J). (gr. -1-7). 17.00 *(978-0-8028-5204-5(1))* Eerdmans, William B. Publishing Co.

—Mariana & the Merchild: A Folk Tale from Chile. Pitcher, Caroline. 2006. 24p. (J). (gr. k-4). reprint ed. 17.00 *(978-1-4223-5136-9(X))* DIANE Publishing Co.

—Starlight Sailor. Mayhew, James. (ENG.). 24p. (J). (gr. -1-2). 2018. 7.99 *(978-1-84686-750-7(9))*; 2009. 16.99 *(978-1-84686-185-7(3))* Barefoot Bks., Inc.

Morris, Jackie. Classic Poems. Morris, Jackie. 2018. (ENG.). 128p. (J). (gr. -1-12). 19.99 *(978-1-78285-427-2(4))* Barefoot Bks., Inc.

—Y Tu Dragón, ¿Cómo Es? Morris, Jackie. 2010. (SPA.). 28p. (J). (gr. k-2). 14.95 *(978-84-92595-21-1(3))* Thule Ediciones, S. L. ESP. Dist: Independent Pubs. Group.

Morris, James R. Ranger Trails: Jobs of Adventure in America's Parks. Yanuchi, Lori & Yanuchi, Jeff. 2005. 64p. (J). per. 12.95 *(978-0-9670177-2-3(6))* Ridge Rock Pr.

Morris, Jean. The Wagon Train. Goscinny, René. 2008. (Lucky Luke Ser.: 9). (ENG.). 48p. pap. 11.95 *(978-1-905460-40-3(6))* CineBook GBR. Dist: National Bk. Network.

Morris, Jeanne L. Jody's Travelbooks for Kids Vol. I: Frankenmuth, Michigan. Arrathoon, Leigh A. & Davio, John. 48p. (J). (gr. 2-6). pap. 4.95 *(978-0-9648564-7-9(6))* Archus Pr., LLC.

—Jody's Travelbooks for Kids Vol. II: Holland, Michigan. Arrathoon, Leigh A. & Davio, John. 48p. (J). (gr. 2-6). pap. 4.95 *(978-0-9648564-8-6(4))* Archus Pr., LLC.

—Jody's Travelbooks for Kids Vol. III: Mackinaw, Michigan. Arrathoon, Leigh A. & Davio, John. 48p. (J). (gr. 2-6). pap. 4.95 *(978-0-9648564-9-3(2))* Archus Pr., LLC.

Morris, Jennifer & Morris, Jennifer E. If a Monkey Jumps onto Your School Bus. Cochran, Jean M. 2008. (ENG.). 32p. (J). (gr. -1-k). 16.95 *(978-0-9792035-2-7(X))* Pleasant St. Pr.

Morris, Jennifer E. It's Halloween Night! O'Connell, Jennifer. 2012. (ENG.). 32p. (J). (gr. -1-k). pap. 6.99 *(978-0-545-40283-5(2)*, Cartwheel Bks.) Scholastic, Inc.

Morris, Jennifer E. The Lemonade Hurricane: A Story of Mindfulness & Meditation. Morelli, Licia. 2020. (ENG.). 32p. (J). (gr. -1-3). pap. 9.95 ***(978-0-88448-877-4(2)***, 884877) Tilbury Hse. Pubs.

Morris, Jennifer E. Little Red Rolls Away. Whalen, Linda. 2017. (ENG.). 32p. (J). (gr. k-2). 16.99 *(978-1-58536-987-4(X)*, 204227) Sleeping Bear Pr.

—Most People: (are Good People), 1 vol. Leannah, Michael. 2017. (ENG.). 32p. (J). (gr. -1-2). 16.95 *(978-0-88448-554-4(4)*, 884554) Tilbury Hse. Pubs.

—On a Dark, Dark Night. Cochran, Jean M. 2009. (ENG.). 32p. (J). (gr. k-2). 16.95 *(978-1-935025-00-9(7))* Pleasant St. Pr.

Morris, Jennifer E. May I Please Have a Cookie? Morris, Jennifer E. (Scholastic Reader, Level 1 Ser.). (ENG.). (J). 2015. 30p. (— 1). bds. 6.99 *(978-0-545-81502-4(9))*; 2005. 32p. (gr. -1-3). per. 4.99 *(978-0-439-73819-4(9))* Scholastic, Inc. (Cartwheel Bks.).

—Please Write Back! Morris, Jennifer E. 2010. (Scholastic Reader Level 1 Ser.). (ENG.). 32p. (J). (gr. -1-3). pap. 3.99 *(978-0-545-11506-3(X)*, Cartwheel Bks.) Scholastic, Inc.

Morris, Jennifer E., jt. illus. see Morris, Jennifer.

Morris, Jessica. Treasure Delight: A Sweet Story about the Joy in Sharing. Lynn, Deidre. 2013. 36p. pap. 12.95 *(978-0-9893181-0-5(9))* LoveLight Media.

Morris, Jordynn. Amelia the Fart Detector. Sumpter, Anthony. 2020. (ENG.). 18p. (J). (gr. 2-3). pap. 9.95 ***(978-1-949290-42-4(5))*** Bedazzled Ink Publishing Co.

—Rebel the Superhero. Sumpter, Anthony. 2020. (ENG.). 18p. (J). (gr. 2-4). pap. 9.95 ***(978-1-949290-39-4(5))*** Bedazzled Ink Publishing Co.

Morris, Julie, jt. illus. see Nieto-Phillips, John M.

Morris, Keisha. Bitty Brown Babe, Vol. LeFalle, Deborah. 2019. (ENG.). 24p. (J). (gr. -1 — 1). 7.99 *(978-1-5064-4853-4(4)*, Beaming Books) Augsburg Fortress, Pubs.

Morris, Kiran. Lies Your Parents Tell You. O'Neil, Dave. 2005. 160p. pap. *(978-0-7344-0292-9(9)*, Lothian Children's Bks.) Hachette Australia.

Morris, Lillie. Wally the Whale Learns How to Be a Winner. Riner, Sherry. 2004. 43p. pap. 24.95 *(978-1-4137-3129-3(5))* PublishAmerica, Inc.

Morris, Michael. Puzzle Cards Letters. gif. ed. 2005. 16p. (J). 9.99 *(978-1-57791-188-3(1))* Brighter Minds Children's Publishing.

—Puzzle Cards Numbers. gif. ed. 2005. 16p. (J). 9.99 *(978-1-57791-187-6(3))* Brighter Minds Children's Publishing.

—Sad Sam & the Magic Cookies. Quest, Stacy. Wertheimer, Beverly & Ronsley, Jill, eds. 2006. (ENG.). (J). 16.95 *(978-1-932367-01-0(2))* BookBound Publishing.

Morris, Phoebe. Hero of the Sea: Sir Peter Blake's Mighty Ocean Quests. Hill, David. 2018. (David Hill Kiwi Legends Ser.). (ENG.). 32p. (J). (gr. k-2). 21.99 *(978-0-14-377165-4(5))* Penguin Group New Zealand, Ltd. NZL. Dist: Independent Pubs. Group.

—Sky High: Jean Batten's Incredible Flying Adventures. Hill, David Morris. 2017. 32p. (J). (gr. k-2). 24.99 *(978-0-14-377036-7(5))* Penguin Group New Zealand, Ltd. NZL. Dist: Independent Pubs. Group.

—Speed King: Burt Munro, the World's Fastest Indian. Hill, David. 2016. 32p. (J). 17.99 *(978-0-14-350722-2(2))* Penguin Group New Zealand, Ltd. NZL. Dist: Independent Pubs. Group.

Morris Publishing Company Staff. The Bounty Hunter, Vol. 26. Goscinny, René. 2011. (Lucky Luke Ser.: 26). (ENG.). 48p. pap. 11.95 *(978-1-84918-059-7(8))* CineBook GBR. Dist: National Bk. Network.

—The Escort, Vol. 18. Goscinny, René. 2009. (Lucky Luke Ser.: 18). (ENG.). 46p. (J). (gr. 4-7). pap. 11.95 *(978-1-905460-98-4(8))* CineBook GBR. Dist: National Bk. Network.

—Fingers. Banda, Lo Hartog Van. 2013. (Lucky Luke Ser.: 37). (ENG.). 48p. (J). (gr. 3-12). pap. 11.95 *(978-1-84918-138-9(1))* CineBook GBR. Dist: National Bk. Network.

—The Rivals of Painful Gulch. Goscinny, René. 2009. (Lucky Luke Ser.: 12). (ENG.). 48p. pap. 11.95 *(978-1-905460-60-1(0))* CineBook GBR. Dist: National Bk. Network.

—Seven Stories, Vol. 50. Goscinny, René. 2015. (Lucky Luke Ser.: 50). (ENG.). 48p. pap. 11.95 *(978-1-84918-226-3(4))* CineBook GBR. Dist: National Bk. Network.

—The Stagecoach. Goscinny, René. 2011. (Lucky Luke Ser.: 25). (ENG.). 48p. (J). (gr. 3-17). pap. 11.95 *(978-1-84918-052-8(0))* CineBook GBR. Dist: National Bk. Network.

Morris, Rebecca. There's Glory Underneath My Skin. Morris, Rebecca. 2018. (ENG.). 24p. (J). pap. *(978-0-6399841-9-3(3))* Seraph Creative.

Morris, Robin C. Sometimes I Worry Too Much: A Book to Help Children Who Worry When They Don't Need To. Huebner, Dawn. Schader, Karen, ed. 2003. (J). per. 17.95 *(978-1-58815-060-8(7)*, 63814) Childswork/Childsplay.

Morris, Samuel L. Gwynepe Slew the Dragon Almost. Diggs, Linda. Hanna, Ellen & Steier, John, eds. 2004. 49p. (J). (gr. k-6). 17.99 *(978-0-9754126-0-2(4))* Willie & Willie.

Morris, Sandra. Hoppity Hop, 6 pack. Holden, Pam. 2009. (Red Rocket Readers Ser.). 16p. (gr. -1-1). pap. *(978-1-877363-19-1(7)*, Red Rocket Readers) Flying Start Bks.

Morris, Sandra. Welcome to New Zealand: a Nature Journal. Morris, Sandra. 2015. (ENG.). 48p. (J). (gr. 3-7). 16.99 *(978-0-7636-7477-9(X))* Candlewick Pr.

Morris, Shelley. Who Lives in the Jungle? Glithero, Chris. 2017. (ENG.). 30p. (J). pap. *(978-1-9998439-0-8(8))* Glithero, Chris.

Morris, Siân. Syniad Da lawn! Dafydd, Myrddin ap. 2005. (WEL.). 196p. pap. *(978-0-86381-641-3(X))* Gwasg Carreg Gwalch.

Morris, Susan. Elijah Helps the Widow. Thoreson-Snipes, Nanette. 2004. (ENG.). 16p. (J). 1.99 *(978-0-570-07574-5(2))* Concordia Publishing Hse.

—Elizabeth's Christmas Story. Dede, Vivian Hughes. 2004. 16p. (J). 1.99 *(978-0-7586-0478-1(5))* Concordia Publishing Hse.

—The Parable of the Talents. Dreyer, Nicole E. 2007. 16p. (J). (gr. k-4). 1.99 *(978-0-7586-1282-3(6))* Concordia Publishing Hse.

Morris, Suzanne. A Trapezoid Is Not a Dinosaur! Morris, Suzanne. 2019. 32p. (J). (gr. k-3). pap. 7.99 *(978-1-58089-580-4(8))* Charlesbridge Publishing, Inc.

Morris, Ting. Barbed Wire on the Prairie. Goscinny, René & Spear, Luke. Spear, Luke, tr. 2007. (Lucky Luke Ser.: 7). (ENG.). 48p. (J). (gr. 4-7). pap. 11.95 *(978-1-905460-24-3(4))* CineBook GBR. Dist: National Bk. Network.

—Tortillas for the Daltons. Goscinny, René. Spear, Luke, tr. 2008. (Lucky Luke Ser.: 10). (ENG.). 48p. pap. 11.95 *(978-1-905460-49-6(X))* CineBook GBR. Dist: National Bk. Network.

Morris, Tony. Children's Guide to the Bible. Willoughby, Robert. 2003. 128p. 9.99 *(978-1-85999-072-8(X))* Scripture Union GBR. Dist: Gabriel Resources.

—David & Goliath. Frank, Penny. 2nd rev. ed. (ENG.). 24p. pap. 2.99 *(978-0-7459-4111-0(7)*, Lion Books) Lion Hudson PLC GBR. Dist: Trafalgar Square Publishing.

—Let My People Go! Frank, Penny. 2nd rev. ed. (ENG.). 24p. pap. 2.99 *(978-0-7459-4108-0(7)*, Lion Books) Lion Hudson PLC GBR. Dist: Trafalgar Square Publishing.

—The Princess & the Baby. Frank, Penny. 2nd rev. ed. (ENG.). 24p. pap. 2.99 *(978-0-7459-4107-3(9)*, Lion Books) Lion Hudson PLC GBR. Dist: Trafalgar Square Publishing.

—The Story of the Good Samaritan. Frank, Penny. rev. ed. (ENG.). 24p. pap. 2.99 *(978-0-7459-4119-6(2)*, Lion Books) Lion Hudson PLC GBR. Dist: Trafalgar Square Publishing.

Morrison, Bill. The Beatles Yellow Submarine. 2018. 112p. 29.99 *(978-1-78586-394-3(0))* Titan Bks. Ltd. GBR. Dist: Penguin Random Hse. LLC.

Morrison, Cameron & Morrison, Connor. Why Bears Don't Live in Humble, 1 vol. Morrison, Maria. 2010. 26p. pap. 24.95 *(978-1-4489-9748-0(8))* PublishAmerica, Inc.

Morrison, Cathy. Animalogy: Animal Analogies, 1 vol. Berkes, Marianne Collins. 2011. (ENG.). 32p. (J). (gr. -1-3). 16.95 *(978-1-60718-127-9(4)*, 9781607181279); pap. 8.95 *(978-1-60718-137-8(1))* Arbordale Publishing.

—Baby on Board: How Animals Carry Their Young, 1 vol. Berkes, Marianne. 2017. (ENG.). 32p. (J). (gr. 8-3). 16.95 *(978-1-58469-592-9(7)*, Dawn Pubns.) Sourcebooks, Inc.

—Daisylocks, 1 vol. Berkes, Marianne. 2014. (ENG.). 32p. (J). (gr. -1-3). pap. 9.95 *(978-1-62855-215-7(8))* Arbordale Publishing.

—Dino Tracks, 1 vol. Rhonda Lucas Donald, Rhonda Lucas. 2013. (ENG.). 32p. (J). (gr. 1-4). 17.95 *(978-1-60718-619-9(5))* Arbordale Publishing.

—Dino Tracks, 1 vol. Donald, Rhonda Lucas. 2013. (ENG.). 32p. (J). (gr. 1-4). pap. 9.95 *(978-1-60718-631-1(4))* Arbordale Publishing.

—Dino Treasures, 1 vol. Donald, Rhonda Lucas. 2015. (ENG.). 32p. (J). (gr. 1-4). 17.95 *(978-1-62855-450-2(9))* Arbordale Publishing.

—Evening Song. Zimelman, Nathan. 2003. (Books for Young Learners). (ENG.). 12p. (J). 5.75 net. *(978-1-57274-536-0(3)*, 2741, Bks. for Young Learners) Owen, Richard C. Pubs., Inc.

—If You Love Honey. Sullivan, Martha. 2015. (ENG.). 32p. (J). (gr. k-4). 16.95 *(978-1-58469-533-2(1)*, Dawn Pubns.) Sourcebooks, Inc.

—La Naturaleza Recicla¿lo Haces Tú?, 1 vol. Lord, Michelle. 2013. (ENG & SPA.). 32p. (J). (gr. -1-4). 17.95 *(978-1-60718-711-0(6))* Arbordale Publishing.

—Nature Recycles: How about You?, 1 vol. Lord, Michelle. 2013. (ENG.). 32p. (J). (gr. -1-4). 17.95 *(978-1-60718-615-1(2))*; pap. 9.95 *(978-1-60718-627-4(6))* Arbordale Publishing.

—Over on the Farm. Berkes, Marianne Collins. 2016. (ENG.). 32p. (J). (gr. -1-2). 16.95 *(978-1-58469-548-6(X)*, Dawn Pubns.) Sourcebooks, Inc.

—Pitter & Patter, 1 vol. Sullivan, Martha. 2015. (ENG.). 32p. (J). (gr. k-4). pap. 8.95 *(978-1-58469-509-7(9)*, Dawn Pubns.) Sourcebooks, Inc.

—The Prairie That Nature Built, 1 vol. 2014. (ENG.). 32p. (J). (gr. k-4). pap. 8.95 *(978-1-58469-492-2(0)*, Dawn Pubns.) Sourcebooks, Inc.

—Saint Thomas Aquinas: Missionary of Truth. Trouvé, Marianne Lorraine. 2015. 137p. (J). pap. 8.95 *(978-0-8198-9026-9(X))* Pauline Bks. & Media.

—This Land Is Your Land, 1 vol. Ciocchi, Catherine. 2015. (ENG.). 32p. (J). (gr. 1-4). 17.95 *(978-1-62855-557-8(2))* Arbordale Publishing.

—Three Little Beavers, 1 vol. Diehl, Jean Heilprin. 2012. (ENG.). 32p. (J). (gr. -1-3). 17.95 *(978-1-60718-524-6(5))*; pap. 9.95 *(978-1-60718-533-8(4))* Arbordale Publishing.

Morrison, Cathy. The Tiny Giant. Ciletti, Barbara. 2020. (ENG.). 32p. (J). (gr. -1-3). 16.99 ***(978-0-7643-6029-9(9)***, 17470) Schiffer Publishing, Ltd.

Morrison, Cathy. The Tortoise & Hare's Amazing Race, 1 vol. Berkes, Marianne. 2015. (ENG & SPA.). 32p. (J). (gr. k-3). 17.95 *(978-1-62855-635-3(8))* Arbordale Publishing.

—What's This Tail Saying?, 1 vol. Combs, Carolyn. 2020. 32p. (J). (gr. -1-3). pap. 16.95 *(978-1-58469-661-2(3)*, Dawn Pubns.) Sourcebooks, Inc.

—Wild Ones: Observing City Critters. Malnor, Carol L. 2016. (ENG.). 32p. (J). (gr. k-4). 16.95 *(978-1-58469-553-0(6)*, Dawn Pubns.) Sourcebooks, Inc.

Morrison, Cathy. Esta Tierra, Es Tu País. Morrison, Cathy. Ciocchi, Catherine. 2015. (ENG & SPA.). 32p. (J). (gr. 1-4). pap. 11.95 *(978-1-62855-575-2(0))* Arbordale Publishing.

—La Plantita Margarita, 1 vol. Morrison, Cathy. Berkes, Marianne Collins & Toth, Rosalyna. 2014. (SPA.). 32p. (J). (gr. -1-3). pap. 11.95 *(978-1-62855-224-9(7))* Arbordale Publishing.

—Si una Momia Pudiera Hablar... Morrison, Cathy. Donald, Rhonda Lucas. de la Torre, Alejandra, tr. from ENG. 2019. (SPA.). (J). pap. 11.95 *(978-1-60718-748-6(5))* Arbordale Publishing.

Morrison, Cathy, jt. illus. see Maydak, Michael S.

Morrison, Connor, jt. illus. see Morrison, Cameron.

Morrison, Frank. The Adventures of Wrong Man & Power Girl! London, C. Alexander. 2018. 32p. (J). (gr. -1-2). 17.99 *(978-0-399-54893-2(9)*, Philomel Bks.) Penguin Young Readers Group.

—Ballerina Dreams: from Orphan to Dancer (Step into Reading, Step 4) DePrince, Michaela & Deprince, Elaine. 2014. (Step into Reading Ser.). (ENG.). 48p. (J). (gr. 2-4). 4.99 *(978-0-385-75515-3(5)*, Random Hse. Bks. for Young Readers) Random Hse. Children's Bks.

—Clayton Byrd Goes Underground. Williams-Garcia, Rita. (ENG.). 176p. (J). (gr. 3-7). 2018. pap. 7.99 *(978-0-06-221593-2(0)*, Amistad); 2017. 16.99 *(978-0-06-221591-8(4)*, Amistad); 2017. E-Book *(978-0-06-221594-9(9)*, Quill Tree Books) HarperCollins Pubs.

—George Crum & the Saratoga Chip, 1 vol. Taylor, Gaylia. 2006. (ENG.). 32p. (J). (gr. 1-5). 16.95 *(978-1-58430-255-1(0))* Lee & Low Bks., Inc.

—How Sweet the Sound: The Story of Amazing Grace. Weatherford, Carole Boston. 2018. (ENG.). 48p. (J). (gr. -1-3). 17.99 *(978-1-4814-7206-7(2))* Simon & Schuster Children's Publishing.

—I Got the Christmas Spirit. Schofield-Morrison, Connie. 2018. (J). *(978-1-68119-529-2(1))* Bloomsbury Pr.

—I Got the Christmas Spirit. Schofield-Morrison, Connie. 2018. 32p. (J). 16.99 *(978-1-68119-528-5(3)*, 900176377, Bloomsbury Children's Bks.) Bloomsbury Publishing USA.

—I Got the Rhythm. Schofield-Morrison, Connie. 2014. 32p. (J). (gr. -1-1). 17.99 *(978-1-61963-178-6(4)*, 900123805, Bloomsbury USA Childrens) Bloomsbury Publishing USA.

—I Got the School Spirit. Schofield-Morrison, Connie. 2020. (ENG.). 32p. (J). 17.99 *(978-1-5476-0261-2(9)*, 900208429, Bloomsbury Children's Bks.) Bloomsbury Publishing USA.

—Keena Ford & the Secret Journal Mix-Up. Thomson, Melissa. 2011. (Keena Ford Ser.: 3). 128p. (J). (gr. 1-3). 5.99 *(978-0-14-241937-3(0)*, Puffin Books) Penguin Young Readers Group.

—Let the Children March. Clark-Robinson, Monica. 2018. (ENG.). 40p. (J). (gr. 1-4). 17.99 *(978-0-544-70452-7(5)*, 1628273, HMH Books For Young Readers) Houghton Mifflin Harcourt Publishing Co.

—Little Melba & Her Big Trombone, 1 vol. Russell-Brown, Katheryn. 2014. (ENG.). 40p. (J). (gr. 1-5). 18.95 *(978-1-60060-898-8(1)*, a825d490-9ae4-47c3-a11e-cdb3c5e2f861) Lee & Low Bks., Inc.

—Long Shot: Never Too Small to Dream Big. Paul, Chris. 2009. (ENG.). 32p. (J). (gr. -1-3). 19.99 *(978-1-4169-5079-0(6)*, Simon & Schuster Bks. For Young Readers) Simon & Schuster Bks. For Young Readers.

—Mango Delight. Hyman, Fracaswell. 2018. (Mango Delight Ser.: 1). 224p. (J). (gr. 4-8). pap. 6.95 *(978-1-4549-2962-8(6))* Sterling Publishing Co., Inc.

—March Forward, Girl: From Young Warrior to Little Rock Nine. Beals, Melba Patillo. 2018. (ENG.). 224p. (J). (gr. 5-7). 16.99 *(978-1-328-88212-7(8)*, 1697888, HMH Books For Young Readers) Houghton Mifflin Harcourt Publishing Co.

—Muhammad Ali: A Champion Is Born. Barretta, Gene. 2017. (ENG.). 40p. (J). (gr. -1-3). 17.99 *(978-0-06-243016-8(5)*, Tegen, Katherine Bks) HarperCollins Pubs.

—Out of the Ballpark. Rodriguez, Alex. 2012. (ENG.). 32p. (J). (gr. -1-3). pap. 7.99 *(978-0-06-115196-5(3))* HarperCollins Pubs.

—Play, Louis, Play! The True Story of a Boy & His Horn. Weinstein, Muriel Harris. 2013. 112p. (J). (gr. 2-4). pap. 7.99 *(978-1-59990-994-3(4)*, 900097535, Bloomsbury USA Childrens) Bloomsbury Publishing USA.

—Quacky Baseball. Abrahams, Peter. 2011. (ENG.). 32p. (J). (gr. -1-3). 16.99 *(978-0-06-122978-7(4))* HarperCollins Pubs.

—Queen of the Scene. Queen Latifah. 2006. 32p. (J). (gr. -1-3). 17.89 incl. audio compact disk *(978-0-06-077857-6(1)*, Geringer, Laura Book) HarperCollins Pubs.

—The Quickest Kid in Clarksville. Miller, Pat Zietlow. 2016. (ENG.). 40p. (J). (gr. k-3). 16.99 *(978-1-4521-2936-5(3))* Chronicle Bks. LLC.

Morrison, Frank. Respect: Aretha Franklin, the Queen of Soul. Weatherford, Carole Boston. 2020. (ENG.). 48p. (J). (gr. -1-3). 18.99 ***(978-1-5344-5228-2(1)***, Atheneum Bks. for Young Readers) Simon & Schuster Children's Publishing.

Morrison, Frank. The Roots of Rap: 16 Bars on the 4 Pillars of Hip-Hop. Boston Weatherford, Carole. 2019. (ENG.). 48p. (J). (gr. -1-3). 18.99 *(978-1-4998-0411-9(3))* Little Bee Books Inc.

—The Secret Garden of George Washington Carver. Barretta, Gene. 2020. (ENG.). 40p. (J). (gr. -1-3). 18.99 *(978-0-06-243015-1(7)*, Tegen, Katherine Bks) HarperCollins Pubs.

—Shoebox Sam, 1 vol. Barrett, Mary Brigid. 2011. (ENG.). 32p. (J). 15.99 *(978-0-310-71549-8(0))* Zonderkidz.

—Stars in the Shadows: The Negro League All-Star Game Of 1934. Smith Jr., Charles R. 2012. (ENG.). 112p. (J). (gr. 3-7). 14.99 *(978-0-689-86638-8(0)*, Atheneum Bks. for Young Readers) Simon & Schuster Children's Publishing.

Morrison, Frank. Starstruck: The Cosmic Journey of Neil DeGrasse Tyson. Krull, Kathleen & Brewer, Paul. 48p. (J). (gr. -1-3). 2020. pap. 7.99 ***(978-0-399-55027-0(5)***, Dragonfly Bks.); 2018. 17.99 *(978-0-399-55024-9(0)*, Crown Books For Young Readers); 2018. (ENG.). lib. bdg. 20.99 *(978-0-399-55025-6(9)*, Crown Books For Young Readers) Random Hse. Children's Bks.

Morrison, Frank. Sweet Music in Harlem. Taylor, Debbie A. 2014. 32p. pap. 9.00 *(978-1-61003-220-9(9))* Center for the Collaborative Classroom.

Morrison, Frank. World of Reading for the Love of Soccer! Level 2. Pelé. 2020. (World of Reading Ser.). 32p. (J). (gr. -1-3). 14.99 ***(978-1-368-05629-8(6))***; pap. 4.99 ***(978-1-368-05633-5(4))*** Hyperion Bks. for Children.

—World of Reading Por Amor Al Fútbol: Level 2. Pelé. 2020. (World of Reading Ser.). 32p. (J). (gr. -1-3). 14.99 ***(978-1-368-05630-4(X))***; pap. 4.99 ***(978-1-368-05634-2(2))*** Hyperion Bks. for Children.

Morrison, Jeff. Tony Stewart. Carney, Larry. PC Treasures Staff, ed. 2009. (Nascar Drivers Coloring/Sticker Book Ser.). (ENG.). 96p. (J). pap. 6.95 *(978-1-60072-166-3(4))* PC Treasures, Inc.

Morrison, Jeff, jt. illus. see Houghton, Chris.

Morrison, Nancy. Land of the Angels, 1 vol. Sylvester, Sr. 2009. 32p. pap. 24.95 *(978-1-60836-888-4(2))* America Star Bks.

—Talking Memories. Sylvester, Sr. 2011. 36p. pap. 24.95 *(978-1-4489-4967-0(X))* America Star Bks.

Morrison, Stacey. The Adventures of Chewy the Chihuahua & Her Sidekick Cupcake. Smith, Jay. 2019. (ENG.). 50p. (J). 24.95 *(978-1-64471-027-2(7))*; pap. 14.95 *(978-1-64471-026-5(9))* Covenant Bks.

Morrison, Taylor. The Buffalo Nickel. Morrison, Taylor. 2006. 32p. (J). (gr. 4-8). reprint ed. 16.00 *(978-1-4223-5858-0(5))* DIANE Publishing Co.

Morrison, Tyler. Goofus & Other Silly Poems, 1 vol. Wilson, Murray. 2010. 28p. pap. 24.95 *(978-1-4489-6288-4(9))* PublishAmerica, Inc.

Morrissey, Dean. The Crimson Comet. Morrissey, Dean. Krensky, Stephen. 2006. 32p. (J). (gr. k-4). 17.89 *(978-0-06-008070-9(1))* HarperCollins Pubs.

—The Monster Trap. Morrissey, Dean. Krensky, Stephen. 2004. 40p. (J). lib. bdg. 17.89 *(978-0-06-052499-9(5))* HarperCollins Pubs.

—The Wizard Mouse. Morrissey, Dean. Krensky, Stephen. 2011. (ENG.). 32p. (J). (gr. k-4). 16.99 *(978-0-06-008066-2(3))* HarperCollins Pubs.

Morrissey, Kay, jt. photos by see Carrillo, Azalea.

Morrissey, Kay, jt. photos by see Ramírez, Antonio.

Morrissey, Leah. Daddies. Morrissey, Laci. 2018. (ENG.). 20p. (J). 21.95 *(978-1-64003-198-2(7))*; pap. 11.95 *(978-1-64300-282-8(1))* Covenant Bks.

Morrow-Cribbs, Briony. Wicked Bugs (Young Readers Edition) The Meanest, Deadliest, Grossest Bugs on Earth. Stewart, Amy. 2017. (ENG.). 192p. (J). (gr. 3-7). 19.95 *(978-1-61620-755-7(8)*, 73755); pap. 12.95 *(978-1-61620-699-4(3)*, 73699) Algonquin Bks. of Chapel Hill.

Morrow, E. Moose Shoes. Petersen, Jean. 2007. 52p. per. 24.95 *(978-1-4241-8399-9(5))* America Star Bks.

Morrow, George. The Marvellous Land of Snergs. Wyke-Smith, E. A. 2006. (Dover Children's Classics Ser.). (ENG.). 224p. (gr. 3-12). per. 11.95 *(978-0-486-45255-5(7))* Dover Pubns., Inc.

Morrow, Glenn, jt. illus. see Frankfeldt, Gwen.

Morrow, Gray. Carl Ben Eielson: Young Alaskan Pilot. Myers, Hortense & Burnett, Ruth. 2011. 200p. 44.95 *(978-1-258-01949-5(3))* Literary Licensing, LLC.

Morrow, J. T. The Constellation Cassiopeia: The Story of the Queen. Owings, Lisa. 2013. (Constellations Ser.). (ENG.). 32p. (J). (gr. 2-5). 14.21 *(978-1-62323-484-3(0)*, 206252) Child's World, Inc., The.

—The Constellation Draco: The Story of the Dragon. Zee, Amy Van. 2013. (Constellations Ser.). (ENG.). 32p. (J). (gr. 2-5). 14.21 *(978-1-62323-485-0(9)*, 206253) Child's World, Inc., The.

—The Constellation Hercules: The Story of the Hero. York, M. J. 2013. (Constellations Ser.). (ENG.). 32p. (J). (gr. 2-5). 14.21 *(978-1-62323-486-7(7)*, 206254) Child's World, Inc., The.

—The Constellation Scorpius: The Story of the Scorpion. Ringstad, Arnold. 2013. (Constellations Ser.). (ENG.). 32p. (J). (gr. 2-5). 14.21 *(978-1-62323-488-1(3)*, 206251) Child's World, Inc., The.

—The Constellation Taurus: The Story of the Bull. Ringstad, Arnold. 2013. (Constellations Ser.). (ENG.). 32p. (J). (gr. 2-5). 14.21 *(978-1-62323-483-6(2)*, 206256) Child's World, Inc., The.

—The Constellation Ursa Major: The Story of the Big Bear. Owings, Lisa. 2013. (Constellations Ser.). (ENG.). 32p. (J). (gr. 2-5). 14.21 *(978-1-62323-489-8(1)*, 206257) Child's World, Inc., The.

—The Constellation Ursa Minor: The Story of the Little Bear. Owings, Lisa. 2013. (Constellations Ser.). (ENG.). 32p. (J). (gr. 2-5). 14.21 *(978-1-62323-490-4(5)*, 206258) Child's World, Inc., The.

—Edgar Degas. Cernak, Linda. 2014. (World's Greatest Artists Ser.). (ENG.). 24p. (J). (gr. 2-5). 28.50 *(978-1-62687-349-0(6)*, 207189) Child's World, Inc., The.

—Llama Llama Loves to Read. Dewdney, Anna & Duncan, Reed. 2018. (Llama Llama Ser.). (ENG.). 40p. (J). (-k). 18.99 *(978-0-670-01397-5(8)*, Viking Books for Young Readers) Penguin Young Readers Group.

—Mary Cassatt. Cernak, Linda. 2014. (World's Greatest Artists Ser.). (ENG.). 24p. (J). (gr. 2-5). 28.50 *(978-1-62687-350-6(X)*, 207190) Child's World, Inc., The.

—Michelangelo. Bailer, Darice. 2014. (World's Greatest Artists Ser.). (ENG.). 24p. (J). (gr. 2-5). 28.50 *(978-1-62687-352-0(6)*, 207192) Child's World, Inc., The.

—Rembrandt. Bailer, Darice. 2014. (World's Greatest Artists Ser.). (ENG.). 24p. (J). (gr. 2-5). 28.50 *(978-1-62687-354-4(2)*, 207194) Child's World, Inc., The.

—Vincent Van Gogh. Cernak, Linda. 2014. (World's Greatest Artists Ser.). (ENG.). 24p. (J). (gr. 2-5). 28.50 *(978-1-62687-355-1(0)*, 207195) Child's World, Inc., The.

Morrow, J. T., jt. illus. see Rohrbach, Sophie.

Morrow, Jaime-Lynn. Had a Little Rooster. Feierabend, John. 2019. (First Steps in Music Ser.). (ENG.). 32p. (J). (gr. -1-k). 17.95 *(978-1-62277-359-6(4))* G I A Pubns., Inc.

Morrow, Jason. One Can Never Have Too Many Cats!! Lashley, Beverly. 2006. (J). *(978-0-9786835-0-4(1))* Two Tired Teachers Connection, Inc., The.

Morrow, Jt, jt. illus. see Rohrbach, Sophie.

Morrow, Nicole. Lions Can't Eat Spaghetti. Ramos, Bethany. 2016. (ENG.). (J). (gr. k-2). 21.99 *(978-1-940310-47-3(4))* 4RV Pub.

Mors, Nynne. Earth to Kids. Kelly, Peta. 2020. (ENG.). 36p. (J). ***(978-0-6487624-8-5(3))***; pap. ***(978-0-6487624-9-2(1))*** Serenity Press.

Morse, Dorothy Bayley. Boy of the Pyramids: A Mystery of Ancient Egypt. Jones, Ruth Fosdick. 2011. 150p. 40.95 *(978-1-258-06798-4(6))* Literary Licensing, LLC.

Morse, Joe. Go Show the World: A Celebration of Indigenous Heroes. Kinew, Wab. 2018. (ENG.). 40p. (J). (gr. k-4). 17.99 *(978-0-7352-6292-8(6)*, Tundra Bks.) Tundra Bks. CAN. Dist: Penguin Random Hse. LLC.

—Hoop Genius: How a Desperate Teacher & a Rowdy Gym Class Invented Basketball. Coy, John. 2013. (ENG.). 32p.

M

(J). (gr. 2-5). lib. bdg. 17.99 (978-0-7613-6617-1(2), 9780761366171, Carolrhoda Bks.) Lerner Publishing Group.

—Play Ball, Jackie! Krensky, Stephen. 2011. (Single Titles Ser.). (ENG.). 32p. (J). (gr. 2-5). lib. bdg. 16.95 (978-0-8225-9030-9(1), Millbrook Pr.) Lerner Publishing Group.

Morse, Michelle. Captain Courage & the Fear-Squishing Shoes. Marshall, Stacey A. 2012. 16p. pap. 9.95 (978-1-61633-319-5(7)) Guardian Angel Publishing, Inc.

—Captain Courage & the World's Most Shocking Secret Book 2. Marshall, Stacey A. 2013. 24p. 19.95 (978-1-61633-431-4(2)) Guardian Angel Publishing, Inc.

—Emily, the Brave. McDuke, Doc. 2010. 20p. pap. 10.95 (978-1-61633-065-1(1)) Guardian Angel Publishing, Inc.

Morse, Nessa Neilson. Lights of Imani. St. James, Leah. 2013. 28p. pap. 9.99 (978-0-9853123-6-7(X)) Allen, Edward Publishing, LLC.

Morse, Patti. Tales of Zoftic. MacVicar, Andrea. 2007. 58p. (J). per. 16.95 (978-0-9798395-0-4(5)) Inspiration Pr. Inc.

Morse, Scott. Dugout: the Zombie Steals Home. Morse, Scott. 2019. (ENG.). 256p. (J). (gr. 3-7). pap. 12.99 (978-1-338-18809-7(7), Graphix) Scholastic, Inc.

—Magic Pickle. Morse, Scott. 2008. (Magic Pickle Ser.). (ENG.). 112p. (J). (gr. 2-5). pap. 9.99 (978-0-439-87995-8(7), Graphix) Scholastic, Inc.

Morse, Tony. Armful of Memories. Honigsberg, Peter Jan. 2004. 32p. 17.95 (978-1-57143-089-2(X)) RDR Bks.

—Pillow of Dreams. Honigsberg, Peter Jan. 2004. 32p. (gr. k-4). 17.95 (978-1-57143-076-2(8)) RDR Bks.

Morstad, Julie. Bloom: a Story of Fashion Designer Elsa Schiaparelli. Maclear, Kyo. 2018. (ENG.). 40p. (J). (gr. -1-3). 17.99 (978-0-06-244761-6(0)) HarperCollins Pubs.

—The Dress & the Girl. Andros, Camille. 2018. (ENG.). 40p. (J). (gr. -1-3). 17.99 (978-1-4197-3161-7(0), Abrams Bks. for Young Readers) Abrams, Inc.

Morstad, Julie. Girl on a Motorcycle. Novesky, Amy. 2020. 48p. (J). (gr. k-4). 17.99 **(978-0-593-11629-6(1)**, Viking Books for Young Readers) Penguin Young Readers Group.

Morstad, Julie. House of Dreams: The Life of L. M. Montgomery. Rosenberg, Liz. 2018. 352p. (J). (gr. 5-9). 17.99 (978-0-7636-6057-4(4)) Candlewick Pr.

—House of Dreams: the Life of L. M. Montgomery. Rosenberg, Liz. 2020. 352p. (J). (gr. 5-9). pap. 9.99 (978-1-5362-1314-0(4)) Candlewick Pr.

—It Began with a Page: How Gyo Fujikawa Drew the Way. Maclear, Kyo. 2019. (ENG.). 48p. (J). (gr. -1-3). 17.99 (978-0-06-244762-3(9)) HarperCollins Pubs.

—Julia, Child. Maclear, Kyo. (ENG.). 32p. (J). (gr. -1-2). 2018. pap. 7.99 (978-0-7352-6401-4(5)); 2014. 17.99 (978-1-77049-449-7(9)) Tundra Bks. CAN. (Tundra Bks.). Dist: Penguin Random Hse. LLC.

—Singing Away the Dark. Woodward, Caroline. 2017. 44p. (J). (gr. -1-3). 16.95 (978-1-77229-019-6(X)) Simply Read Bks. CAN. Dist: Ingram Publisher Services.

—Swan: The Life & Dance of Anna Pavlova. Snyder, Laurel. 2015. (ENG.). 52p. (J). (gr. 1-4). 17.99 (978-1-4521-1890-1(6)) Chronicle Bks. LLC.

—The Swing. Stevenson, Robert Louis. 2012. 16p. (J). 8.95 (978-1-897476-48-2(5)) Simply Read Bks. CAN. Dist: Ingram Publisher Services.

—This Is Sadie. O'Leary, Sara. (ENG.). (J). 2018. 30p. (— 1). bds. 7.99 (978-0-7352-6324-6(8)); 2015. 32p. (gr. -1-2). 17.99 (978-1-77049-532-6(0)) Tundra Bks. CAN. (Tundra Bks.). Dist: Penguin Random Hse. LLC.

—When I Was Small. O'Leary, Sara. 2012. (ENG.). 32p. (J). (gr. -1-3). 16.95 (978-1-897476-38-3(8)) Simply Read Bks. CAN. Dist: Ingram Publisher Services.

—When You Were Small. O'Leary, Sara. 2006. 32p. (J). (gr. -1-3). 16.95 (978-1-894965-36-1(1)) Simply Read Bks. CAN. Dist: Ingram Publisher Services.

—When You Were Small. O'Leary, Sara. 2017. 40p. (J). (gr. -1-3). 8.99 (978-1-77229-008-0(4)) Simply Read Bks. CAN. Dist: Ingram Publisher Services.

—Where You Came From. O'Leary, Sara. 2008. (ENG.). 32p. (J). (gr. -1-3). 16.95 (978-1-894965-46-0(9)) Simply Read Bks. CAN. Dist: Ingram Publisher Services.

—Zingy. O'Leary, Sara & Opal, Paola. 2013. (Simply Small Ser.: 10). (ENG.). 24p. (J). (gr. k — 1). bds. 7.95 (978-1-897476-75-8(2)) Simply Read Bks. CAN. Dist: Ingram Publisher Services.

Morstad, Julie. How To. Morstad, Julie. 2013. 36p. (J). (gr. -1-3). 16.95 (978-1-897476-57-4(4)) Simply Read Bks. CAN. Dist: Ingram Publisher Services.

Mortensen, Carl. Flea & Gang & the Tube Dogs. Mortensen, Carl. 2009. 16p. pap. 11.95 (978-1-4251-8657-9(2)) Trafford Publishing.

Mortensen, Lyn. Effie May & Her Outrageous Hats. Mortensen, Lyn. 2006. (J). per. (978-0-9767570-1-6(X)) Wild daisy art.

—My Favorite Flower Is the Daisy... & other Silly Poems. Mortensen, Lyn. 2005. 48p. (J). per. (978-0-9767570-0-9(1)) Wild daisy art.

Mortimer, Alexander. Pick-a-WooWoo - KC the Conscious Camel: A furry jaunt to peace & Contentment. McRae, Suzanne. 12th ed. 2010. 32p. pap. (978-0-9806520-3-1(0)) Pick-a-Woo Woo Pubs.

Mortimer, Anne. The Chocolate Cat. Stainton, Sue. 2007. 32p. (J). (gr. -1-3). 17.89 (978-0-06-057246-4(9)) HarperCollins Pubs.

—The Lighthouse Cat. Stainton, Sue. 2004. (ENG.). 32p. (J). (gr. -1-2). 16.99 (978-0-06-009604-5(7), Tegen, Katherine Bks) HarperCollins Pubs.

—The Owl & the Pussycat. Lear, Edward. 2006. (ENG.). 32p. (J). (gr. -1-4). 16.99 (978-0-06-027228-9(7), Tegen, Katherine Bks) HarperCollins Pubs.

—A Pussycat's Christmas. Brown, Margaret Wise. 2009. (ENG.). 32p. (J). (gr. k-4). 9.99 (978-0-06-186978-5(3), Tegen, Katherine Bks) HarperCollins Pubs.

—Sneakers, the Seaside Cat. Brown, Margaret Wise. 2005. (ENG.). 32p. (J). (gr. -1-3). pap. 7.99 (978-0-06-443622-9(5)) HarperCollins Pubs.

Mortimer, Anne. Bunny's Easter Egg. Mortimer, Anne. 2010. (ENG.). 32p. (J). (gr. -1-2). 12.99 (978-0-06-136664-2(1), Tegen, Katherine Bks) HarperCollins Pubs.

—Christmas Mouse. Mortimer, Anne. 2013. (ENG.). 24p. (J). (gr. -1-3). 12.99 (978-0-06-208928-1(5), Tegen, Katherine Bks) HarperCollins Pubs.

—Pumpkin Cat. Mortimer, Anne. 2011. (ENG.). 24p. (J). (gr. -1-2). 14.99 (978-0-06-187485-7(X), Tegen, Katherine Bks) HarperCollins Pubs.

Mortimer, Lauren. What Was the Boston Tea Party? Krull, Kathleen & Who HQ. 2013. (What Was? Ser.). (ENG.). 112p. (J). (gr. 3-7). pap. 5.99 (978-0-448-46288-2(5), Penguin Workshop) Penguin Young Readers Group.

—What Was the First Thanksgiving? Holub, Joan & Who HQ. 2013. (What Was? Ser.). (ENG.). 112p. (J). (gr. 3-7). pap. 5.99 (978-0-448-46463-3(2), Penguin Workshop) Penguin Young Readers Group.

—What Was the Underground Railroad? McDonough, Yona Zeldis & Who HQ. 2013. (What Was? Ser.). (ENG.). 112p. (J). (gr. 3-7). 5.99 (978-0-448-46712-2(7), Penguin Workshop) Penguin Young Readers Group.

Mortimer, Mitch. Ideas. Spiegel, Al. 2003. 32p. (J). lib. bdg. 13.99 (978-0-9743553-0-6(5)) Crazy Man Press, LLC.

—Kit & Kaboodle Go Camping. Portice, Michelle. 2020. (Highlights Puzzle Readers Ser.). 32p. (J). (gr. -1-2). 16.99 (978-1-68437-987-3(3)); pap. 4.99 (978-1-68437-935-4(0)) Boyds Mills Pr. (Highlights).

—Kit & Kaboodle Take the Train. Portice, Michelle. 2020. (Highlights Puzzle Readers Ser.). 32p. (J). (gr. -1-2). 16.99 (978-1-68437-986-6(5)); pap. 4.99 (978-1-68437-934-7(2)) Boyds Mills Pr. (Highlights).

Mortlock, Olivia & Mortlock, Samantha. Trevor's Got a Toothache. Mortlock, Michael. 2019. (Seven Lions Ser.: Vol. 2). (ENG.). 76p. (J). (gr. k-6). pap. (978-981-14-0365-1(1)) Mortlock, Michael.

—What's Different about Trevor: A Seven Lions Story. Mortlock, Michael. 2017. (Seven Lions Ser.: Vol. 1). (ENG.). 64p. (J). (gr. k-6). (978-981-11-5702-8(2)); pap. (978-981-11-4348-9(X)) Mortlock, Michael.

Mortlock, Samantha, jt. illus. see Mortlock, Olivia.

Morton, Annette. Once upon a Star. Sherwood, Laura. 2019. (ENG.). 26p. (J). pap. 10.00 (978-1-0996-6343-7(1)) Independently Published.

Morton, Ken. The Gingerbread Man (Floor Book) My First Reading Book. Brown, Janet. 2013. (ENG.). 24p. (J). (gr. -1-2). pap. 6.99 (978-1-84322-900-1(5), Armadillo) Anness Publishing GBR. Dist: National Bk. Network.

—Goldilocks & the Three Bears (Floor Book) My First Reading Book. Brown, Janet. 2013. (ENG.). 24p. (J). (gr. -1-2). pap. 6.99 (978-1-84322-901-8(3), Armadillo) Anness Publishing GBR. Dist: National Bk. Network.

—Jack & the Beanstalk: My First Reading Book. Brown, Janet. 2015. (ENG.). 24p. pap. 6.99 (978-1-86147-474-2(1), Armadillo) Anness Publishing GBR. Dist: National Bk. Network.

—Pinocchio: My First Reading Book. Brown, Janet. 2015. (ENG.). 24p. pap. 6.99 (978-1-86147-475-9(X), Armadillo) Anness Publishing GBR. Dist: National Bk. Network.

—Puss in Boots. Brown, Janet. 2012. 24p. (J). (gr. -1-12). 5.99 (978-1-84322-848-6(3)) Anness Publishing GBR. Dist: National Bk. Network.

—Puss in Boots (Floor Book) My First Reading Book. Brown, Janet. 2013. (ENG.). 24p. (J). (gr. -1-2). pap. 6.99 (978-1-84322-902-5(1), Armadillo) Anness Publishing GBR. Dist: National Bk. Network.

—Red Riding Hood (Floor Book) My First Reading Book. Brown, Janet. 2015. (ENG.). 24p. (J). (gr. -1-1). pap. 6.99 (978-1-86147-399-8(0), Armadillo) Anness Publishing GBR. Dist: National Bk. Network.

—Snow White & the Seven Dwarves. Brown, Janet. 2012. 24p. (J). (gr. -1-12). 5.99 (978-1-84322-850-9(5)) Anness Publishing GBR. Dist: National Bk. Network.

—Snow White & the Seven Dwarves (Floor Book) My First Reading Book. Brown, Janet. 2013. (ENG.). 30p. (J). (gr. -1-2). pap. 6.99 (978-1-84322-903-2(X), Armadillo) Anness Publishing GBR. Dist: National Bk. Network.

—The Three Billy Goats Gruff: My First Reading Book. 2013. (ENG.). 24p. 5.99 (978-1-84322-832-5(7), Armadillo) Anness Publishing GBR. Dist: National Bk. Network.

—The Three Billy Goats Gruff (Floor Book) Brown, Janet. 2015. (ENG.). 24p. (J). (gr. -1-1). pap. 6.99 (978-1-86147-397-4(4), Armadillo) Anness Publishing GBR. Dist: National Bk. Network.

—Three Little Pigs (Floor Book) My First Reading Book. Brown, Janet. 2015. (ENG.). 24p. (J). (gr. -1-1). pap. 6.99 (978-1-86147-396-7(6), Armadillo) Anness Publishing GBR. Dist: National Bk. Network.

—The Ugly Duckling. Brown, Janet. 2012. 24p. (J). (gr. -1-12). 5.99 (978-1-84322-851-6(3)) Anness Publishing GBR. Dist: National Bk. Network.

—The Ugly Duckling (Floor Book) My First Reading Book. Brown, Janet. 2015. (ENG.). 24p. (J). (gr. -1-1). pap. 6.99 (978-1-86147-398-1(2), Armadillo) Anness Publishing GBR. Dist: National Bk. Network.

—Witches, Wizards & Magicians. Baxter, Nicola. 2012. 80p. (J). (gr. k-4). pap. 9.99 (978-1-84322-807-3(6)) Anness Publishing GBR. Dist: National Bk. Network.

Morton, Lisa. The Girl & the Mirror. Monnar, Alberto. Weiner, Linda, ed. 2008. per. 14.99 (978-0-9768035-8-4(5)) Readers Are Leaders U.S.A., Inc.

Morton, Robert, et al. Why Do Tigers Have Stripes? Unwin, Mike. 2006. (Usborne Starting Point Science Ser.). 22p. (J). (gr. 1-4). pap. 4.99 (978-0-7945-1408-2(1), Usborne) EDC Publishing.

Morton, Robert. Why Do Tigers Have Stripes? Unwin, Mike. 2006. (Usborne Starting Point Science Ser.). 22p. (J). (gr. 1). lib. bdg. 12.99 (978-1-58086-939-3(4), Usborne) EDC Publishing.

Morton, Vivian. Power Reading: Nail-Biters! 2. Cole, Bob. 2005. 94p. (J). (gr. 6-18). vinyl bd. 89.95 (978-1-883186-25-8(0), PPNB2) National Reading Styles Institute, Inc.

Morton, Wendy S. Flipper & Dipper in the Royal Wedding. Morton, Wendy S. 2018. (ENG.). 34p. (J). pap. 9.95 (978-0-9704379-5-2(1), Social Motion Publishing) Social Motion Publishing.

Moruno, Sonia. Children of Aramar. Jos. 2019. 48p. (J). (gr. 4-7). pap. 9.99 (978-1-68405-502-9(4)) Idea & Design Works, LLC.

Moscal, Manuela. The Unseen Paths of the Forest: 13 Tales about Love & Friendship. Panaitescu, Simona. 2012. (ENG.). 263p. pap. 14.95 (978-1-4327-7908-5(7)) Outskirts Pr., Inc.

Moscato, Diego. Plant Life: Flower Power: The Story of How Plants Are Pollinated. Heneghan, Judith. 2019. (Plant Life Ser.). 32p. (J). (gr. -1-3). pap. 9.99 (978-1-5263-0764-4(2)); (ENG.). (gr. k-3). 13.99 **(978-0-7502-8769-2(1))** Hachette Children's Group GBR. (Wayland). Dist: Hachette Bk. Group.

—Plant Life: Living Leaf: The Story of How Plants Grow & Survive. Heneghan, Judith. 2019. (Plant Life Ser.). 32p. (J). (gr. k-3). pap. 9.99 (978-1-5263-0723-1(5), Wayland) Hachette Children's Group GBR. Dist: Hachette Bk. Group.

—Plant Life: Roots & Shoots. Heneghan, Judith. 2019. (Plant Life Ser.). 32p. (J). (gr. -1-3). pap. 9.99 (978-1-5263-0722-4(7)); (ENG.). (gr. k-3). 13.99 **(978-0-7502-8767-8(5))** Hachette Children's Group GBR. (Wayland). Dist: Hachette Bk. Group.

—Plant Life: Seed Safari: The Story of How Plants Scatter Their Seeds. Heneghan, Judith. 2019. (Plant Life Ser.). 32p. (J). (gr. k-3). pap. 9.99 (978-1-5263-0724-8(3), Wayland) Hachette Children's Group GBR. Dist: Hachette Bk. Group.

Mosedale, Julian. Bungleman: Band 13/Topaz (Collins Big Cat) Strong, Jeremy. 2007. (Collins Big Cat Ser.). (ENG.). 32p. (J). (gr. 2-3). pap. 10.99 (978-0-00-723083-9(4)) HarperCollins Pubs. Ltd. GBR. Dist: Independent Pubs. Group.

—Collins Big Cat Phonics for Letters & Sounds - Wow Cow!: Band 02B/Red B, Bd. 2B. Coe, Catherine. 2018. (Collins Big Cat Phonics Ser.). (ENG.). 16p. (J). (gr. -1-k). pap. 6.99 (978-0-00-825149-9(5)) HarperCollins Pubs. Ltd. GBR. Dist: Independent Pubs. Group.

—Leopard & His Spots Red Band. Harper, Kathryn. 2016. (Cambridge Reading Adventures Ser.). (ENG.). 16p. pap. 7.37 (978-1-316-50308-9(9)) Cambridge Univ. Pr.

—The Mean Monkey Blue Band. DelaHaye, Rachel. 2017. (Cambridge Reading Adventures Ser.). (ENG.). 16p. pap. 5.62 (978-1-108-43971-8(3)) Cambridge Univ. Pr.

—Mojo & Weeza & the New Hat: Band 04/Blue (Collins Big Cat) Taylor, Sean. 2007. (Collins Big Cat Ser.). (ENG.). 16p. (J). (gr. -1-1). pap. 7.99 (978-0-00-718662-4(2)) HarperCollins Pubs. Ltd. GBR. Dist: Independent Pubs. Group.

—Our Head Teacher Is a Super-Villain: Band 10/White (Collins Big Cat) Donbavand, Tommy. 2015. (Collins Big Cat Ser.). (ENG.). 32p. (J). (gr. 2-2). pap. 8.95 (978-0-00-759122-0(5)) HarperCollins Pubs. Ltd. GBR. Dist: Independent Pubs. Group.

Moseley, Dudley. Pop-Up Bible Adventures, 2. Dowley, Tim. 2007. 12p. (J). (gr. k-2). 11.99 (978-0-8254-7328-9(4), Candle Bks.) Lion Hudson PLC GBR. Dist: Kregel Pubns.

Moseley, Rachel. Jordan & the Dreadful Golem. Goldman, Karen. 2013. (ENG.). 224p. (J). (gr. 4-7). 15.95 (978-0-9838685-2-1(2)) Penlight Pubns.

Moseng, Elisabeth. Higgledy Piggledy the Hen Who Loved to Dance. Simon, Francesca. 2016. (ENG.). 32p. (J). 17.99 (978-0-00-813946-9(6), HarperCollins Children's Bks.) HarperCollins Pubs. Ltd. GBR. Dist: HarperCollins Pubs.

—Soccer Beat. Brug, Sandra Gilbert. 2012. (ENG.). 32p. (J). (gr. -1-1). 16.99 (978-1-4424-8610-2(4), McElderry, Margaret K. Bks.) McElderry, Margaret K. Bks.

Moser, Barry. The Blessing of the Beasts. Pochocki, Ethel. 2014. (ENG.). 40p. (J). (gr. -1). pap. 19.99 (978-1-61261-582-0(1)) Paraclete Pr., Inc.

—The Call of the Wild. London, Jack. 2011. (ENG.). 144p. (J). (gr. 4-9). pap. 8.99 (978-1-4424-3411-0(2), Simon & Schuster Bks. For Young Readers) Simon & Schuster Bks. For Young Readers.

—Cat Talk. Charest, Emily MacLachlan & MacLachlan, Patricia. 2013. (ENG.). 32p. (J). (gr. -1-3). 17.99 (978-0-06-027978-3(8)); lib. bdg. 18.89 (978-0-06-027979-0(6)) HarperCollins Pubs. (Tegen, Katherine Bks).

—The Cheshire Cheese Cat: A Dickens of a Tale, 1 vol. Deedy, Carmen Agra & Wright, Randall. 2011. (ENG.). 256p. (J). 16.95 (978-1-56145-595-9(4)) Peachtree Publishing Co. Inc.

—Earthquack! Palatini, Margie. 2005. (ENG.). 32p. (J). (gr. -1-3). 7.99 (978-1-4169-0260-7(0), Simon & Schuster Bks. For Young Readers) Simon & Schuster Bks. For Young Readers.

—Franklin & Winston: A Christmas That Changed the World. Wood, Douglas. 2011. 40p. (J). (gr. 1-4). 16.99 (978-0-7636-3383-7(6)) Candlewick Pr.

—I Can Make a Difference: A Treasury to Inspire Our Children. Edelman, Marian Wright. 2005. (ENG.). 112p. (J). (gr. 3-7). 21.99 (978-0-06-028051-2(4), Amistad) HarperCollins Pubs.

—Jack London's Dog. Wales, Dirk. 2008. 64p. (YA). (gr. 5-9). 17.95 (978-0-9632459-3-9(7)) Great Plains Pr.

—Lousy Rotten Stinkin' Grapes. Palatini, Margie. 2009. (ENG.). 32p. (J). (gr. -1-3). 17.99 (978-0-689-80246-1(3), Simon & Schuster Bks. For Young Readers) Simon & Schuster Bks. For Young Readers.

—The Mushroom Man, 1 vol. Pochocki, Ethel. 2006. (ENG.). 32p. (J). (gr. 2-6). reprint ed. 7.95 (978-0-88448-278-9(2), 884278) Tilbury Hse. Pubs.

—One Small Garden. Nichol, Barbara. 2004. (ENG.). 56p. (J). (gr. 3-7). pap. 9.95 (978-0-88776-687-9(0), Tundra Bks.) Tundra Bks. CAN. Dist: Penguin Random Hse. LLC.

—Pilgrim's Progress. Schmidt, Gary D. 2008. (ENG.). 189p. (J). (gr. 4-18). 16.50 (978-0-8028-5346-2(3)) Eerdmans, William B. Publishing Co.

—The Pomegranate Witch. Doyen, Denise. 2013. (J). (978-0-375-87057-6(1)); lib. bdg. (978-0-375-97057-3(6)) Random Hse., Inc.

—The Three Silly Billies. Palatini, Margie. 2005. (ENG.). 32p. (J). (gr. -1-3). 19.99 (978-0-689-85862-8(0), Simon & Schuster Bks. For Young Readers) Simon & Schuster Bks. For Young Readers.

Moser, Barry & Moser, Cara. Sit, Truman! Harper, Dan. 2004. (ENG.). 32p. (J). (gr. -1-3). reprint ed. pap. 6.99 (978-0-15-205068-9(X), 1195307) Houghton Mifflin Harcourt Publishing Co.

Moser, Cara, jt. illus. see Moser, Barry.

Moser, Chris & Moser, Liz. The Discoveries of Shuggs, A Curious Cat. Moser, Chris & Moser, Liz. 2011. (J). pap. 10.95 (978-0-9842881-9-9(8)) Capital City Bks. LLC.

Moser, Liz, jt. illus. see Moser, Chris.

Moses, Grandma. The Night Before Christmas. 2007. (ENG.). 32p. (J). (gr. k-4). 17.95 (978-0-7893-1568-7(8)) Universe Publishing.

Moses, Will. Raining Cats & Dogs: A Collection of Irresistible Idioms & Illustrations to Tickle the Funny Bones. Moses, Will. 2008. 40p. (J). (gr. k-3). 17.99 (978-0-399-24233-5(3), Philomel Bks.) Penguin Young Readers Group.

Mosher, Scott, jt. illus. see Tucker, Lewis R.

Mosler, Robin. My Dog Monkey. Taylor, Jon. 2018. (My Dog Monkey Ser.: Vol. 1). (ENG.). 26p. (J). (gr. k-3). pap. 9.99 (978-0-692-07792-4(8)) Mighty Publishing, LLC.

—Try Ceratops: If at First Try Doesn't Succeed, Will Try Try Again? Cooper, Kristen. 2016. (Dinomightysaurs Ser.: Vol. 4). (ENG.). (J). (gr. k-3). pap. 9.99 (978-0-9966739-9-0(7)) Mighty Publishing, LLC.

Mosley, Bonita K. Pebbles Wants a Friend. Viner, Callie Lee. 2017. (Pebbles the Counting Pup Ser.: Vol. 2). (ENG.). (J). (gr. k-1). pap. 9.95 (978-0-9986572-0-2(4)) Counting Pup Pr.

—Pebbles Wants a Friend. Viner, Callie. 2018. (Pebbles the Counting Pup Ser.: Vol. 2). (ENG.). 28p. (J). (gr. k-1). 17.99 (978-0-9986572-2-6(0)) Counting Pup Pr.

Mosqueda, Olga. An Amazing Snowman. Hicks, Barbara Jean. 2020. (ENG.). 32p. (J). (gr. -1-k). bds. 7.99 **(978-1-368-06390-6(X))** Disney Pr.

Mosqueda, Olga. Frozen: Olaf Gives Thanks. 2018. (ENG.). 24p. (J). (gr. 1-3). 10.99 (978-1-368-02320-7(7)) Disney Pr.

Mosqueda, Olga T. & Tucker, Marianne. Learn to Draw Plus Disney Winnie the Pooh. 2012. (J). (978-1-936309-68-9(8)) Quarto Publishing Group USA.

Mosquera, Maria Jose. David Travels to the Past. Martinez De Antonana, Gonzalo. Publisher, Saure, ed. 2016. (ENG.). (YA). (gr. 9-12). (978-84-16197-69-9(5)) Saure, Jean-Francois Editor.

Mosquito, Angel. Hombres Lobo y Estados de la Materia. Slingerland, Janet. 2019. (Ciencias Monstruosas Ser.). (SPA.). 32p. (J). (gr. 3-9). lib. bdg. 31.32 (978-1-5435-8263-5(X), 141273) Capstone.

—Werewolves & States of Matter, 1 vol. Slingerland, Janet. 2011. (Monster Science Ser.). (ENG.). 32p. (gr. 3-9). (J). pap. 8.10 (978-1-4296-7333-4(8)); pap. 47.70 (978-1-4296-7334-1(6)); (J). lib. bdg. 31.32 (978-1-4296-6578-0(5)) Capstone. (Capstone Pr.).

Moss, Chris, jt. illus. see Edwards, Mark.

Moss, Drew. Terrible Lizard. Bunn, Cullen. 2015. (ENG.). 136p. pap. 19.99 (978-1-62010-236-7(6), 9781620102367, Lion Forge) Oni Pr., Inc.

Moss, Jennifer & Moss, Jessica. Shandy & Orion: Two Happy Guinea Pigs. Rocus, Kathy. 2019. (ENG.). 46p. (J). (gr. k-6). 16.99 (978-1-948288-12-5(5)); pap. 9.99 (978-1-948288-10-1(9)) BLACK LACQUER Pr. & MARKETING INC.

Moss, Jessica, jt. illus. see Moss, Jennifer.

Moss, Maria. Moonbeam's Arctic Adventure. Holbom, Molly Janet & Williams, David Morgan. 2019. (ENG.). 48p. (J). 11.00 (978-1-78461-618-2(4)) Y Lolfa GBR. Dist: Casemate Pubs. & Bk. Distributors, LLC.

Moss, Marissa. Alien Eraser Reveals the Secret of Evolution. Moss, Marissa. 2009. 56p. (J). (gr. 3-7). 15.99 (978-0-7636-3579-4(0)); pap. 6.99 (978-0-7636-4419-2(6)) Candlewick Pr.

—The All-New Amelia. Moss, Marissa. (ENG.). (J). 2013. 5.99 (978-1-4169-1289-7(4)); 2007. 40p. (gr. 2-5). 14.99 (978-1-4169-0908-8(7)) Simon & Schuster/Paula Wiseman Bks. (Simon & Schuster/Paula Wiseman Bks.).

—Amelia Tells All. Moss, Marissa. 2007. (Amelia Ser.). (ENG.). 64p. (J). (gr. 2-5). 9.99 (978-1-4169-0918-7(4), Simon & Schuster/Paula Wiseman Bks.) Simon & Schuster/Paula Wiseman Bks.

—Amelia Writes Again. Moss, Marissa. (Amelia Ser.). (ENG.). (J). (gr. 2-5). 2012. 32p. pap. 7.99 (978-1-4169-1285-9(1)); 2006. 40p. 12.99 (978-1-4169-0904-0(4)) Simon & Schuster/Paula Wiseman Bks. (Simon & Schuster/Paula Wiseman Bks.).

—Amelia's 5th-Grade Notebook. Moss, Marissa. 2006. (Amelia Ser.). (ENG.). (J). 5.99 (978-1-4169-1292-7(4)); 40p. (gr. 2-5). 14.99 (978-1-4169-0912-5(5)) Simon & Schuster/Paula Wiseman Bks. (Simon & Schuster/Paula Wiseman Bks.).

—Amelia's 6th-Grade Notebook. Moss, Marissa. 2005. (Amelia Ser.). (ENG.). 80p. (J). (gr. 4-7). 12.99 (978-0-689-87040-8(X), Simon & Schuster/Paula Wiseman Bks.) Simon & Schuster/Paula Wiseman Bks.

—Amelia's 7th-Grade Notebook. Moss, Marissa. 2007. (Amelia Ser.). (ENG.). 80p. (J). (gr. 5-8). 14.99 (978-1-4169-3661-9(0), Simon & Schuster/Paula Wiseman Bks.) Simon & Schuster/Paula Wiseman Bks.

—Amelia's Are-We-There-Yet Longest Ever Car Trip. Moss, Marissa. (Amelia Ser.). (ENG.). 40p. (J). (gr. 2-5). 2012. pap. 7.99 (978-1-4169-1287-3(8)); 2006. 14.99 (978-1-4169-0906-4(0)) Simon & Schuster/Paula Wiseman Bks. (Simon & Schuster/Paula Wiseman Bks.).

—Amelia's Back-to-School Survival Guide: Vote 4 Amelia - Amelia's Guide to Babysitting. Moss, Marissa. 2012. (Amelia Ser.). (ENG.). 160p. (J). (gr. 5-8). 12.99 (978-1-4424-4349-5(9), Simon & Schuster/Paula Wiseman Bks.) Simon & Schuster/Paula Wiseman Bks.

—Amelia's BFF. Moss, Marissa. 2011. (Amelia Ser.). (ENG.). 64p. (J). (gr. 5-8). 9.99 *(978-1-4424-0376-5(4),* Simon & Schuster/Paula Wiseman Bks.) Simon & Schuster/Paula Wiseman Bks.

—Amelia's Book of Notes & Note Passing. Moss, Marissa. 2006. (Amelia Ser.). (ENG.). 80p. (J). (gr. 4-7). 14.99 *(978-0-689-87446-8(4),* Simon & Schuster/Paula Wiseman Bks.) Simon & Schuster/Paula Wiseman Bks.

—Amelia's Boredom Survival Guide. Moss, Marissa. 2006. (Amelia Ser.). (ENG.). 64p. (J). (gr. 2-5). 12.99 *(978-1-4169-0916-3(8))* Simon & Schuster, Inc.

—Amelia's Boredom Survival Guide. Moss, Marissa. 2013. (Amelia Ser.). (ENG.). 64p. (J). (gr. 2-5). pap. 6.99 *(978-1-4424-8369-9(5),* Simon & Schuster/Paula Wiseman Bks.) Simon & Schuster/Paula Wiseman Bks.

—Amelia's Boy Survival Guide. Moss, Marissa. 2012. (Amelia Ser.). (ENG.). 80p. (J). (gr. 4-8). 9.99 *(978-1-4424-4084-5(8),* Simon & Schuster/Paula Wiseman Bks.) Simon & Schuster/Paula Wiseman Bks.

—Amelia's Bully Survival Guide. Moss, Marissa. 2006. (Amelia Ser.). (ENG.). 40p. (J). (gr. 2-5). 14.99 *(978-1-4169-0907-1(9),* Simon & Schuster/Paula Wiseman Bks.) Simon & Schuster/Paula Wiseman Bks.

—Amelia's Cross-My-Heart, Hope-To-Die Guide to the Real, True You! Moss, Marissa. 2010. (Amelia Ser.). (ENG.). 64p. (J). (gr. 5-8). 9.99 *(978-1-4169-8710-9(X),* Simon & Schuster/Paula Wiseman Bks.) Simon & Schuster/Paula Wiseman Bks.

—Amelia's Family Ties. Moss, Marissa. 2013. (Amelia Ser.). (ENG.). (J). 5.99 *(978-1-4169-1293-4(2),* Simon & Schuster/Paula Wiseman Bks.) Simon & Schuster/Paula Wiseman Bks.

—Amelia's Guide to Babysitting. Moss, Marissa. 2008. (Amelia Ser.). (ENG.). 80p. (J). (gr. 5-8). 14.99 *(978-1-4169-5051-6(6),* Simon & Schuster/Paula Wiseman Bks.) Simon & Schuster/Paula Wiseman Bks.

—Amelia's Guide to Gossip: The Good, the Bad, & the Ugly. Moss, Marissa. 2006. (Amelia Ser.). (ENG.). 80p. (J). (gr. 5-8). 9.95 *(978-1-4169-1475-4(7),* Simon & Schuster/Paula Wiseman Bks.) Simon & Schuster/Paula Wiseman Bks.

—Amelia's Itchy-Twitchy, Lovey-Dovey Summer at Camp Mosquito. Moss, Marissa. 2008. (Amelia Ser.). (ENG.). 80p. (J). (gr. 5-8). 12.99 *(978-1-4169-4722-6(1),* Simon & Schuster/Paula Wiseman Bks.) Simon & Schuster/Paula Wiseman Bks.

—Amelia's Longest, Biggest, Most-Fights-Ever Family Reunion. Moss, Marissa. 2006. (Amelia Ser.). (ENG.). 80p. (J). (gr. 4-7). 12.99 *(978-0-689-87447-5(2),* Simon & Schuster/Paula Wiseman Bks.) Simon & Schuster/Paula Wiseman Bks.

—Amelia's Middle School Survival Guide: Amelia's Most Unforgettable Embarrassing Moments, Amelia's Guide to Gossip. Moss, Marissa. 2009. (Amelia Ser.). (ENG.). 160p. (J). (gr. 5-8). 14.99 *(978-1-4169-7987-6(5),* Simon & Schuster/Paula Wiseman Bks.) Simon & Schuster/Paula Wiseman Bks.

—Amelia's Most Unforgettable Embarrassing Moments. Moss, Marissa. 2005. (Amelia Ser.). (ENG.). 80p. (J). (gr. 4-7). 14.99 *(978-0-689-87041-5(8),* Simon & Schuster/Paula Wiseman Bks.) Simon & Schuster/Paula Wiseman Bks.

—Amelia's Must-Keep Resolutions for the Best Year Ever! Moss, Marissa. 2006. (Amelia Ser.). (ENG.). 40p. (J). (gr. 4-7). 14.99 *(978-1-4169-3361-8(1),* Simon & Schuster/Paula Wiseman Bks.) Simon & Schuster/Paula Wiseman Bks.

—Amelia's Notebook. Moss, Marissa. 2006. (Amelia Ser.). (ENG.). (J). 5.99 *(978-1-4169-1286-6(X));* 40p. (gr. 2-5). 14.99 *(978-1-4169-0905-7(2))* Simon & Schuster/Paula Wiseman Bks. (Simon & Schuster/Paula Wiseman Bks.).

—Amelia's School Survival Guide. Moss, Marissa. 2006. (Amelia Ser.). (ENG.). 64p. (J). (gr. 2-5). 14.99 *(978-1-4169-0915-6(X),* Simon & Schuster/Paula Wiseman Bks.) Simon & Schuster/Paula Wiseman Bks.

—Amelia's Science Fair Disaster. Moss, Marissa. 2008. (Amelia Ser.). (ENG.). 80p. (J). (gr. 5-8). 12.99 *(978-1-4169-6494-0(0),* Simon & Schuster/Paula Wiseman Bks.) Simon & Schuster/Paula Wiseman Bks.

—Amelia's Summer Survival Guide: Amelia's Longest, Biggest, Most-Fights-Ever Family Reunion; Amelia's Itchy-Twitchy, Lovey-Dovey Summer at Camp Mosquito. Moss, Marissa. 2011. (Amelia Ser.). (ENG.). 160p. (J). (gr. 5-8). 12.99 *(978-1-4424-2331-2(5),* Simon & Schuster/Paula Wiseman Bks.) Simon & Schuster/Paula Wiseman Bks.

—Bully Survival Guide. Moss, Marissa. 2012. (Amelia Ser.). (ENG.). 40p. (J). (gr. 2-5). pap. 6.99 *(978-1-4169-1288-0(6),* Simon & Schuster/Paula Wiseman Bks.) Simon & Schuster/Paula Wiseman Bks.

—The Fake Friend! Moss, Marissa. 2012. (Daphne's Diary of Daily Disasters Ser.). (ENG.). 96p. (J). (gr. 2-5). 9.99 *(978-1-4424-4014-2(7));* pap. 5.99 *(978-1-4424-4015-9(5))* Simon & Schuster/Paula Wiseman Bks. (Simon & Schuster/Paula Wiseman Bks.).

—Friendship Survival Guide: And Trying to Be the Best BFF Amelia. Moss, Marissa. 2013. (Amelia Ser.). (ENG.). 144p. (J). (gr. 5-8). 12.99 *(978-1-4424-8304-0(0),* Simon & Schuster/Paula Wiseman Bks.) Simon & Schuster/Paula Wiseman Bks.

—The Name Game! Moss, Marissa. 2011. (Daphne's Diary of Daily Disasters Ser.). (ENG.). 80p. (J). (gr. 2-5). pap. 5.99 *(978-1-4424-1738-0(2));* lib. bdg. 9.99 *(978-1-4424-2676-4(4))* Simon & Schuster/Paula Wiseman Bks. (Simon & Schuster/Paula Wiseman Bks.).

—The Vampire Dare! Moss, Marissa. 2011. (Daphne's Diary of Daily Disasters Ser.). (ENG.). 80p. (J). (gr. 2-5). pap. 5.99 *(978-1-4424-1737-3(4));* lib. bdg. 9.99 *(978-1-4424-2677-1(2))* Simon & Schuster/Paula Wiseman Bks. (Simon & Schuster/Paula Wiseman Bks.).

—Vote 4 Amelia. Moss, Marissa. 2007. (Amelia Ser.). (ENG.). 80p. (J). (gr. 4-7). 14.99 *(978-1-4169-2789-1(1),* Simon & Schuster/Paula Wiseman Bks.) Simon & Schuster/Paula Wiseman Bks.

Moss, P. Buckley. Reuben & the Balloon. Good, Merle. rev. ed. 2016. (ENG.). 32p. (J). (gr. -1-3). 16.99 *(978-1-68099-149-9(3),* Good Bks.) Skyhorse Publishing Co., Inc.

—Reuben & the Blizzard. Good, Merle. rev. ed. 2016. (ENG.). 32p. (J). (gr. -1-3). 16.99 *(978-1-68099-147-5(7),* Good Bks.) Skyhorse Publishing Co., Inc.

—Reuben & the Fire. Good, Merle. rev. ed. 2016. (ENG.). 32p. (J). (gr. -1-3). 16.99 *(978-1-68099-153-6(1),* Good Bks.) Skyhorse Publishing Co., Inc.

—Reuben & the Quilt. Good, Merle. rev. ed. 2016. (ENG.). 32p. (J). (gr. -1-3). 16.99 *(978-1-68099-151-2(5),* Good Bks.) Skyhorse Publishing Co., Inc.

Moss, Rachel. African: A Children's Picture Book. Tosh, Peter. 2020. (LyricPop Ser.). 32p. (J). 16.95 *(978-1-61775-799-0(3))* Akashic Bks.

—I Am a Promise. Fraser Pryce, Shelly Ann. 2020. (ENG.). 24p. (J). 15.95 *(978-1-61775-764-8(0))* Akashic Bks.

—The Secret Ingredient: The Search for Love. Jackson, Pd. 2019. (ENG.). 32p. (J). (gr. k-3). *(978-0-578-44090-3(3))* ISeeYou Media I.G.

Moss, Stephan, jt. illus. see Morden, Naphtali.

Mossiano, Sage. My New Mommy. Mossiano, Lilly. 2012. 28p. pap. 24.95 *(978-1-4626-8898-2(5))* PublishAmerica, Inc.

Most, Andee. I Am Special: Jesus Is Our Friend. Plum, Joan Ensor & Plum, Paul S. 5th ed. 2007. 112p. (J). (gr. k-1). per. 11.95 *(978-1-59276-296-5(4))* Our Sunday Visitor, Publishing Div.

Mostert, Mauritz. How the Zebra Got His Stripes. Mostert, Mauritz. Mostert, Cari, ed. 2018. (ENG.). 44p. (YA). (gr. 8-12). pap. *(978-0-620-80172-0(7))* Mostert, Mauritz.

Mostmand, Reza. The Spirit Within Club. Sabati, Sahar. 2019. (ENG.). 208p. (J). pap. 14.95 ***(978-0-85398-555-6(3))*** Ronald, George Pub., Ltd.

Mostmand, Reza. Spirit Within Club 2. Sabati, Sahar. 2019. (Spirit Within Club Ser.: Vol. 2). (ENG.). 326p. (J). pap. 13.99 *(978-1-393-15484-6(0))* Draft2Digital.

Mostov, Alexander. Go, Bikes, Go! Boswell, Addie. 2019. (In Motion Ser.). 22p. (J). (— 1). bds. 9.99 *(978-1-63217-220-4(8),* Little Bigfoot) Sasquatch Bks.

—Go, Boats, Go! Boswell, Addie. 2020. (In Motion Ser.). 22p. (J). (— 1). bds. 9.99 *(978-1-63217-268-6(2),* Little Bigfoot) Sasquatch Bks.

Mostov, Alexander. Let's Save Our Planet: Forests: Uncover the Facts. Be Inspired. Make a Difference. Jess French, Jess. 2020. (Let's Save Our Planet Ser.). (ENG.). 64p. (J). (gr. 3-5). 19.99 ***(978-1-78240-952-6(1))*** Ivy Pr., The GBR. Dist: Hachette Bk. Group.

—The Secret Life of Spies: Uncover True Stories of Secrecy & Espionage Inspired by 20 Real-Life Spies. Noble, Michael. 2020. (ENG.). 48p. (J). (gr. 2-5). ***(978-0-7112-4756-7(0),*** Wide Eyed Editions) Quarto Publishing Group UK.

Mostowska, Beata. The King & the Cockerel. Morrell, Sarah. 2018. (ENG.). 40p. (J). pap. *(978-1-912765-06-5(3))* Blue Falcon Publishing.

Mostyn, David. Amazing Magic Tricks. 2014. (ENG.). 128p. (J). (gr. 2). 9.99 *(978-0-486-78034-4(1))* Dover Pubns., Inc.

—Close-Up Magic. Lane, Mike. 2012. (Miraculous Magic Tricks Ser.). (ENG.). 32p. (J). (gr. 3-6). pap. 11.75 *(978-1-4488-6737-0(1));* lib. bdg. 29.50 *(978-1-61533-515-2(3))* Windmill Bks.

—Comedy Magic, 1. Canavan, Thomas. 2014. (Miraculous Magic Tricks Ser.). (ENG.). 32p. (J). (gr. 3-6). 27.50 *(978-1-4777-9061-8(6),* Windmill Bks.) Rosen Publishing Group, Inc., The.

—Don't Take Your Elephant to School: An Alphabet of Poems. Turner, Steve. ed. 2006. (ENG.). 96p. (J). (gr. 2-4). pap. 8.99 *(978-0-7459-6020-3(0))* Lion Hudson PLC GBR. Dist: Independent Pubs. Group.

—Hairy Mole's Adventures on the High Seas. Owen, Christopher. 2007. (Hairy Mole the Pirate Ser.). (ENG.). 80p. (J). per. *(978-1-84167-563-3(6))* Ransom Publishing Ltd.

—I'm Not Wearing That! Clarke, Jane. 2005. (ENG.). 24p. (J). lib. bdg. 23.65 *(978-1-59646-716-3(9))* Dingles & Co.

—Magical Escapes, 1. Canavan, Thomas. 2014. (Miraculous Magic Tricks Ser.). (ENG.). 32p. (J). (gr. 3-6). 27.50 *(978-1-4777-9057-1(8),* Windmill Bks.) Rosen Publishing Group, Inc., The.

—Magical Illusions, 1. Canavan, Thomas. 2014. (Miraculous Magic Tricks Ser.). (ENG.). 32p. (J). (gr. 3-6). 27.50 *(978-1-4777-9049-6(7),* Windmill Bks.) Rosen Publishing Group, Inc., The.

—Mental Magic, 1. Canavan, Thomas. 2014. (Miraculous Magic Tricks Ser.). (ENG.). 32p. (J). (gr. 3-6). 27.50 *(978-1-4777-9065-6(9),* Windmill Bks.) Rosen Publishing Group, Inc., The.

—Mind Magic. Lane, Mike. 2012. (Miraculous Magic Tricks Ser.). 32p. (J). (gr. 3-6). pap. 11.75 *(978-1-4488-6735-6(5));* lib. bdg. 29.50 *(978-1-61533-514-5(5))* Windmill Bks.

—Number Magic, 1. Canavan, Thomas. 2014. (Miraculous Magic Tricks Ser.). (ENG.). 32p. (J). (gr. 3-6). 27.50 *(978-1-4777-9069-4(1),* Windmill Bks.) Rosen Publishing Group, Inc., The.

—Spring-Heeled Jack. Pullman, Philip. 2004. (ENG.). 112p. (J). (gr. 3-7). per. 6.99 *(978-0-440-41881-8(X),* Yearling) Random Hse. Children's Bks.

—Table Magic, 1. Canavan, Thomas. 2014. (Miraculous Magic Tricks Ser.). (ENG.). 32p. (J). (gr. 3-6). 27.50 *(978-1-4777-9053-3(5),* Windmill Bks.) Rosen Publishing Group, Inc., The.

—Toad Swims for his Life! Atkins, Jill. 2004. (ENG.). 24p. (J). lib. bdg. 23.65 *(978-1-59646-712-5(6))* Dingles & Co.

Mostyn, David, jt. illus. see Charbonnel, Olivier.

Mostyn, David, jt. illus. see Spoor, Mike.

Mosz, Gosia. Hanukkah Moon. Da Costa, Deborah. 2007. (Hanukkah Ser.). 32p. (J). (gr. -1-3). 17.95 *(978-1-58013-244-2(8),* Kar-Ben Publishing) Lerner Publishing Group.

Motano, Yong, et al. Werewolf by Night: the Complete Collection Vol. 3. 2018. (ENG.). 464p. (YA). (gr. 8-17). pap. 39.99 *(978-1-302-91158-4(9))* Marvel Worldwide, Inc.

Motley, Chris and Jim Young. Pollywogs & Other Friends. Hardy, Ed & Young, Jim. 2007. 28p. per. 24.95 *(978-1-4137-2834-7(0))* America Star Bks.

Motley, T. The Golden Ass of Lucius Apuleius. Usher, M. D. 2011. (ENG.). 85p. (J). 17.95 *(978-1-56792-418-3(2))* Godine, David R. Pub.

Motoyama, Keiko. Bears, Bears, Everywhere. Milios, Rita. rev. ed. 2003. (Rookie Reader Ser.). (ENG.). 32p. (J). (gr. k-2). pap. 4.95 *(978-0-516-27830-8(4),* Children's Pr.) Scholastic Library Publishing.

—I Can Tell the Truth. Burch, Regina G. & Donovan Guntly, Jenette. 2004. (Doing the Right Thing Ser.). 16p. (J). (gr. -1-2). lib. bdg. 21.00 *(978-0-8368-4249-4(9),* Gareth Stevens Learning Library) Stevens, Gareth Publishing LLLP.

—Lost Puppy, Found Puppy. Williams, Rozanne Lanczak. 2006. (Learn to Write Ser.). 16p. (J). (gr. k-2). pap. 3.49 *(978-1-59198-296-8(0),* 6190) Creative Teaching Pr., Inc.

—Lost Puppy, Found Puppy. Williams, Rozanne Lanczak. Maio, Barbara, ed. 2006. (J). per. 8.99 *(978-1-59198-347-7(9))* Creative Teaching Pr., Inc.

—Peter's Easter Story. Dreyer, Nicole E. 2004. (Arch Bks.). (ENG.). 16p. (J). 1.99 *(978-0-7586-0477-4(7))* Concordia Publishing Hse.

—The Prince & the Potty. Lewison, Wendy Cheyette. 2006. (ENG.). 40p. (J). (gr. -1-3). 16.99 *(978-0-689-87808-4(7),* Simon & Schuster Bks. For Young Readers) Simon & Schuster Bks. For Young Readers.

Mottahedeh Bos, Elaheh. Bahá'í Prayers for Children. 2018. (ENG.). 15p. (J). (gr. -1-k). bds. 9.95 *(978-1-61851-123-2(8))* Baha'i Publishing.

—Bahá'í Readings for Children: Selections from the Words of Bahá'u'lláh And 'Abdu'l-Bahá. 2018. (ENG.). 15p. (J). (gr. -1-k). bds. 9.95 *(978-1-61851-124-9(6))* Baha'i Publishing.

—Divine Springtime: Selections from the Hidden Words of Bahá'u'lláh. 2018. (ENG.). 15p. (J). (gr. -1-k). bds. 9.95 *(978-1-61851-125-6(4))* Baha'i Publishing.

—I Am a Child. 2019. (Tender Years Ser.). (ENG.). 12p. (J). (— 1). bds. 6.95 *(978-1-61851-136-2(X))* Baha'i Publishing.

Mottahedeh Bos, Elaheh. Like unto a Pearl. 2020. (Tender Years Ser.). (ENG.). 12p. (J). bds. 6.95 ***(978-1-61851-161-4(0))*** Baha'i Publishing.

Mottahedeh Bos, Elaheh. Rose of Love. 2019. (Tender Years Ser.). (ENG.). 12p. (J). (— 1). bds. 6.95 *(978-1-61851-138-6(6))* Baha'i Publishing.

Mottahedeh Bos, Elaheh. This Fresh Plant. 2020. (Tender Years Ser.). (ENG.). 12p. (J). bds. 6.95 ***(978-1-61851-159-1(9))*** Baha'i Publishing.

Mottahedeh Bos, Elaheh. A Tiny Seed. 2019. (Tender Years Ser.). (ENG.). 12p. (J). (— 1). bds. 6.95 *(978-1-61851-137-9(8))* Baha'i Publishing.

Mottahedeh Bos, Elaheh. With Loving Kindness. 2020. (Tender Years Ser.). (ENG.). 12p. (J). bds. 6.95 ***(978-1-61851-160-7(2))*** Baha'i Publishing.

Mottashed, Susie. Who Lives in Your Backyard? Creating a journal that opens your eyes & heart to nature's nearby Wonders. Mottashed, Susie. 2005. 96p. 24.95 *(978-0-9759300-0-7(1))* Sketches From The Heart Publishing.

Motto, Amy. Puppies Need Pockets. Motto, Amy. 2018. (ENG.). 36p. (J). (gr. k-4). 17.95 *(978-0-692-14939-3(2));* pap. 14.95 *(978-0-692-14862-4(0))* Motto, Amy.

Mottram, Dave. Fire Truck Dreams. Chriscoe, Sharon. 2018. 32p. (J). (gr. -1-3). 17.99 *(978-0-7624-6285-8(X),* Running Pr. Kids) Running Pr.

—Melvin the Mouth. Blanc, Katherine & Ebbeler, Jeffrey. 2017. 32p. (J). (gr. -1-3). lib. bdg. 16.99 *(978-1-58089-714-3(2))* Charlesbridge Publishing, Inc.

—The New Kitten. Oates, Joyce Carol. 2019. (ENG.). 32p. (J). (gr. -1-3). 17.99 *(978-0-06-256392-7(0),* HarperCollins) HarperCollins Pubs. Ltd. GBR. Dist: HarperCollins Pubs.

—Oy Vey! Life in a Shoe. Grubman, Bonnie. 2019. *(978-1-68115-556-2(7),* Apples & Honey Pr.); Vol. 2016. (ENG.). (J). *(978-1-68115-515-9(X))* Behrman Hse., Inc.

—Race Car Dreams. Chriscoe, Sharon. 2016. 32p. (J). (gr. -1 — 1). 16.99 *(978-0-7624-5964-3(6),* Running Pr. Kids) Running Pr.

—Willow the Armadillo. Reeder, Marilou. 2020. (ENG.). 32p. (J). (gr. -1-3). 16.99 *(978-1-4197-4105-0(5),* Abrams Bks. for Young Readers) Abrams, Inc.

—Wordy Birdy. Sauer, Tammi. 32p. (J). (gr. -1-2). 2019. pap. 7.99 *(978-0-593-11898-6(7),* Dragonfly Bks.); 2018. 16.99 *(978-1-5247-1929-6(3),* Doubleday Bks. for Young Readers); 2018. (ENG.). lib. bdg. 19.99 *(978-1-5247-1930-2(7),* Doubleday Bks. for Young Readers) Random Hse. Children's Bks.

—Wordy Birdy Meets Mr. Cougarpants. Sauer, Tammi. (ENG.). 32p. (J). (gr. -1-2). 2020. pap. 7.99 ***(978-0-593-30343-6(1),*** Dragonfly Bks.); 2019. 19.99 *(978-1-5247-1931-9(5),* Doubleday Bks. for Young Readers) Random Hse. Children's Bks.

Mottram, David. Basil & the Big Cheese Cook-Off. Hapka, Cathy. 2018. (Great Mouse Detective Ser.: 6). (ENG.). 96p. (J). (gr. 1-4). 16.99 *(978-1-5344-1860-8(1),* Aladdin) Simon & Schuster Children's Publishing.

—Basil & the Big Cheese Cook-Off. Hapka, Cathy. 2018. (Great Mouse Detective Ser.: 6). (ENG.). 96p. (J). (gr. 1-4). pap. 5.99 *(978-1-5344-1859-2(8),* Aladdin) Simon & Schuster Children's Publishing.

—Basil & the Royal Dare. Hapka, Cathy. 2019. (Great Mouse Detective Ser.: 7). (ENG.). 96p. (J). (gr. 1-4). 16.99 *(978-1-5344-1863-9(6));* pap. 5.99 *(978-1-5344-1862-2(8))* Simon & Schuster Children's Publishing. (Aladdin).

Mottram, David. The Great Pet Heist. Ecton, Emily. 2020. (ENG.). 256p. (J). (gr. 3-7). 17.99 ***(978-1-5344-5536-8(1),*** Atheneum Bks. for Young Readers) Simon & Schuster Children's Publishing.

—Horace & Bunwinkle. Gardner, P. J. 2020. 208p. (J). (gr. 3-7). 16.99 ***(978-0-06-294654-6(4),*** Balzer & Bray) HarperCollins Pubs.

Mottram, David. Mighty Tug. Capucilli, Alyssa Satin. 2020. (Classic Board Bks.). (ENG.). 36p. (J). (gr. -1-k). bds. 7.99 ***(978-1-5344-6444-5(1),*** Little Simon) Little Simon.

Mottram, David. Mighty Tug. Capucilli, Alyssa Satin. 2018. (ENG.). 40p. (J). (gr. -1-3). 17.99 *(978-1-4814-7681-2(5),* Simon & Schuster/Paula Wiseman Bks.) Simon & Schuster/Paula Wiseman Bks.

Mottram, David, jt. illus. see Galdone, Paul.

Motuelle, Bérengère. Colors. 2012. (J). *(978-1-4351-5501-5(7))* Barnes & Noble, Inc.

—Numbers. 2012. (J). *(978-1-4351-5502-2(5))* Barnes & Noble, Inc.

—Opposites. 2014. *(978-1-4351-5503-9(3))* Barnes & Noble, Inc.

Motum, Markus. Curiosity: The Story of a Mars Rover. Motum, Markus. 2018. (ENG.). 56p. (J). (gr. 3-7). 22.99 *(978-0-7636-9504-0(1))* Candlewick Pr.

Motyashok, Iryna. Sideline Ink: (book Two) Rehak, Jay C. 2018. (Sideline Ser.: Vol. 2). (ENG.). 346p. (J). pap. 12.99 *(978-0-9992905-4-5(1))* Sideline Ink Publishing.

Motz, Mike. At the Park with Tommy & Scales. Little, Celeste. 2012. 26p. (J). (-18). 12.95 *(978-1-60131-139-9(7),* Castlebridge Bks.) Big Tent Bks.

—The Buffalo & the Bunny. Hatton, Robert. 2016. (ENG.). (J). 19.99 *(978-0-692-79740-2(8))* Hatton, Robert.

—Laila Saves the Day. Dart, Julie. 2017. (ENG.). (J). 19.99 *(978-0-692-84334-5(5))* Dart Publishing.

—Mommy's Coming Home from Treatment. Crosson, Denise D. 2009. (ENG.). 44p. (J). (gr. -1-3). pap. 14.95 *(978-0-9799869-4-9(X))* Central Recovery Pr.

—Mommy's Gone to Treatment. Crosson, Denise D. 2008. (ENG.). 44p. (J). (gr. k-3). pap. 14.95 *(978-0-9799869-1-8(5))* Central Recovery Pr.

—The Old Cookie Jar. Snow, Susie. 2012. 34p. pap. 19.99 *(978-1-61996-595-9(X))* Salem Author Services.

—Scales. Little, Celeste. 2012. 24p. (J). 12.95 *(978-1-60131-116-0(8))* Big Tent Bks.

—The Smiling Burro. Esparza-Vela, Mary. 2012. 16p. pap. 9.95 *(978-1-61633-323-2(5))* Guardian Angel Publishing, Inc.

—Thank You God for Onions. Tennsiwood, Mark. 2006. (J). 14.95 *(978-1-60131-003-3(X))* Big Tent Bks.

Motz, Mike. Timid Tumy Tinkers with French. Coleman, Laura E. 2020. (ENG.). 28p. (J). pap. 11.99 ***(978-1-7951-9654-3(8))*** Independently Published.

Motz, Mike. The Treasure of Trust: The Hidden Treasures of My Kingdom Pals, Page, Julie & Adams, Sabrina. McTeer, Rhonda, ed. 2005. 72p. (J). (gr. 4-7). 14.95 *(978-0-9748251-0-6(7),* 825106) Zoe Life Publishing.

—Wendell Learns a Lesson. Kranz, Steve. 2017. (ENG.). (J). 18.99 *(978-0-9983495-0-3(X))* Golfing Bee, LLC.

—You Can't Take the Dinosaur Home. Esparza- Vela, Mary. 2013. 16p. pap. 9.95 *(978-1-61633-364-5(2))* Guardian Angel Publishing, Inc.

Motzko, Juliana. Happy Hanukkah, Little Dreidel. Puffinton, Brick. Cottage Door Press, ed. 2020. (Children's Interactive Finger Puppet Board Book Ser.). (ENG.). 12p. (J). (gr. -1 — 1). bds. 6.99 ***(978-1-64638-056-5(8),*** 1006290) Cottage Door Pr.

Motzko, Juliana. Pencil's Perfect Picture. McKay, Jodi. 2019. (ENG.). 32p. (J). (gr. -1-k). 16.99 *(978-0-8075-6476-9(1),* 807564761) Whitman, Albert & Co.

Mouchet, Klutt, jt. illus. see Schmitz, Cecile.

Mould, Chris. A Boy Called Christmas. Haig, Matt. (ENG.). (J). (gr. 3-7). 2018. 256p. 7.99 *(978-0-399-55268-7(5),* Yearling); 2016. 240p. 16.99 *(978-0-399-55265-6(0),* Knopf Bks. for Young Readers) Random Hse. Children's Bks.

—Captain Beastlie's Pirate Party. Coats, Lucy. 2014. (ENG.). 32p. (J). (gr. -1-2). 15.99 *(978-0-7636-7399-4(4),* Nosy Crow) Candlewick Pr.

—Father Christmas & Me. Haig, Matt. (ENG.). (J). 2019. 304p. 14.00 *(978-1-78689-072-6(0));* 2018. 288p. 17.00 *(978-1-78689-068-9(2),* 4684) Canongate Bks. GBR. Dist: Publishers Group West (PGW).

—The Girl Who Saved Christmas. Haig, Matt. (ENG.). 320p. (J). (gr. 3-7). 2018. 7.99 *(978-1-5247-0047-8(9),* Yearling); 2017. 16.99 *(978-1-5247-0044-7(4),* Knopf Bks. for Young Readers) Random Hse. Children's Bks.

—Machines in Motion: The Amazing History of Transportation. Jackson, Tom. 2020. 64p. (J). *(978-1-5476-0338-1(0))* Bloomsbury Pr.

—The Prince & the Pee. Gormley, Greg. 2018. (ENG.). 32p. (J). (gr. -1-2). 16.99 *(978-0-7636-9916-1(0),* Nosy Crow) Candlewick Pr.

—Sandwich that Jack Made. Graham, Elspeth. 2004. (ENG.). 24p. (J). lib. bdg. 23.65 *(978-1-59646-698-2(7))* Dingles & Co.

—School Trip. Hawes, Alison. 2004. (ENG.). 24p. (J). lib. bdg. 23.65 *(978-1-59646-694-4(4))* Dingles & Co.

—Spangles Mcnasty & the Diamond Skull. Webb, Steve. 2018. (Spangles Mcnasty Ser.). 192p. (J). (gr. 2-4). pap. 11.99 *(978-1-78344-638-4(2))* Andersen Pr. GBR. Dist: Independent Pubs. Group.

Mould, Chris. The Great Cheese Robbery. Mould, Chris. 2018. (Pocket Pirates Ser.: 1). (ENG.). 160p. (J). (gr. 1-4). 17.99 *(978-1-4814-9115-0(6));* pap. 6.99 *(978-1-4814-9114-3(8))* Simon & Schuster Children's Publishing. (Aladdin).

—The Great Drain Escape. Mould, Chris. 2018. (Pocket Pirates Ser.: 2). (ENG.). 144p. (J). (gr. 1-4). 17.99 *(978-1-4814-9118-1(0));* pap. 6.99 *(978-1-4814-9117-4(2))* Simon & Schuster Children's Publishing. (Aladdin).

—The Great Flytrap Disaster. Mould, Chris. 2019. (Pocket Pirates Ser.: 3). (ENG.). 144p. (J). (gr. 1-4). 17.99 *(978-1-4814-9121-1(0));* pap. 6.99 *(978-1-4814-9120-4(2))* Simon & Schuster Children's Publishing. (Aladdin).

—The Great Treasure Hunt. Mould, Chris. 2019. (Pocket Pirates Ser.: 4). (ENG.). 160p. (J). (gr. 1-4). 17.99 *(978-1-4814-9124-2(5));* pap. 6.99

M

(978-1-4814-9123-5(7)) Simon & Schuster Children's Publishing. (Aladdin).
—Pocket Pirates Collection Books 1-4: The Great Cheese Robbery; the Great Drain Escape; the Great Flytrap Disaster; the Great Treasure Hunt. Mould, Chris. ed. 2019. (Pocket Pirates Ser.). (ENG.). 608p. (J). (gr. 1-4). pap. 27.99 *(978-1-5344-5116-2(1),* Aladdin) Simon & Schuster Children's Publishing.
Moulder, Bob. Daily Life in Ancient & Modern Athens. Kotapish, Dawn. 2005. (Cities Through Time Ser.). 64p. (gr. 5-12). 25.26 *(978-0-8225-3216-3(6))* Lerner Publishing Group.
—Hit It!, 1 vol. Hardcastle, Michael. 2006. (Graphic Quest Ser.). (ENG.). 88p. (J). (gr. 3-8). per. 6.95 *(978-1-59889-164-5(2),* Stone Arch Bks.) Capstone.
—The Loch Ness Monster & Other Lake Mysteries. Jeffrey, Gary. 2006. (Graphic Mysteries Ser.). (ENG.). 48p. (gr. 5-8). pap. 14.05 *(978-1-4042-0807-0(0))* Rosen Publishing Group, Inc., The.
Moulder, Bob, jt. illus. see Spender, Nik.
Moulton, Joy. Starrats III: Reunion. Moulton, Joy. Menth, Joe, ed. 2018. (Starrats Ser.: Vol. 3). (ENG.). 40p. (J). pap. 14.99 *(978-1-7296-2927-7(X))* CreateSpace Independent Publishing Platform.
Mouly, Françoise, jt. illus. see Spiegelman, Art.
Mount, Arthur. Picnic on a Cloud. Icanberry, Mark. 2010. (Look, Learn & Do Ser.). 48p. (J). (gr. -1-3). pap. 7.95 *(978-1-893327-02-3(7))* Look, Learn & Do Pubns.
Mounter, Paddy. Agent Arthur's Island Adventures. Sims, Lesley. 2003. (Puzzle Adventures Ser.). 48p. (J). (gr. 3). lib. bdg. 12.95 *(978-1-58086-463-3(5))* EDC Publishing.
—Aladdin & His Magical Lamp. 2004. (1001 Things to Spot Ser.). 48p. (J). (gr. 1). lib. bdg. 14.95 *(978-1-58086-558-6(5),* Usborne) EDC Publishing.
—Ali Baba & the Forty Thieves. 2004. (Young Reading Ser.: Vol. 1). 48p. (J). (gr. 2-18). lib. bdg. 13.95 *(978-1-58086-642-2(5),* Usborne) EDC Publishing.
—Jack & the Beanstalk. Daynes, Katie. 2006. 48p. (J). 8.99 *(978-0-7945-1238-5(0),* Usborne) EDC Publishing.
Mountford, Karl. A Cinderella Atlas. Peattie, Cindy. 2017. (Text Connections Guided Close Reading Ser.). (J). (gr. 1). *(978-1-4900-1819-5(0))* Benchmark Education Co.
Mountford, Karl James. Last Stop on the Reindeer Express. Powell-Tuck, Maudie. 2018. (ENG.). 32p. (J). (gr. -1-2). 17.99 *(978-1-5247-7166-9(X),* Doubleday Bks. for Young Readers) Random Hse. Children's Bks.
—Maurice the Unbeastly. Dixon, Amy. 2017. 32p. (J). (gr. -1). 16.95 *(978-1-4549-1953-7(1))* Sterling Publishing Co., Inc.
—Peril in Paris. Woodfine, Katherine. 2019. (Taylor & Rose Secret Agents Ser.: 1). (ENG.). 336p. (J). (gr. 4-6). pap. 10.99 *(978-1-4052-8704-3(7))* Egmont Bks., Ltd. GBR. Dist: Independent Pubs. Group.
—The Space Train. Powell-Tuck, Maudie. 2019. (ENG.). 32p. (J). (gr. -1-2). 17.99 *(978-1-68010-158-4(7))* Tiger Tales.
—The Uncommoners #2: The Shadows of Doom. Bell, Jennifer. 2019. (Uncommoners Ser.: 2). (ENG.). 336p. (J). (gr. 3-7). 16.99 *(978-0-553-49847-9(9),* Crown Books For Young Readers) Random Hse. Children's Bks.
Mountford, Katie. The Notre Dame Spirit. Lenhart, Kristin & Passamani, Julia. 2012. 30p. (J). 19.95 *(978-0-9859377-0-6(X))* Corby Books.
Mounts, Paul, jt. illus. see Morgan, Tom.
Mouraviova, Yulia. Tales of the Little Hedgehogs: Fairy Plays. Haupt, Wolfgang & Bland, Janice. 2009. (J). *(978-0-88734-978-2(1))* Players Pr., Inc.
Mourning, Tuesday. Art Queen. Peschke, Marci. 2018. (Kylie Jean Ser.). (ENG.). 112p. (J). (gr. 1-3). 8.95 *(978-1-5158-2935-5(9),* 138474); lib. bdg. 22.65 *(978-1-5158-2927-0(8),* 138470) Capstone. (Picture Window Bks.).
—Back on the Beam, 1 vol. Maddox, Jake. 2009. (Jake Maddox Girl Sports Stories Ser.). (ENG.). 72p. (J). (gr. 3-6). 25.32 *(978-1-4342-1211-5(4),* Stone Arch Bks.) Capstone.
—Ballet Bullies, 1 vol. Maddox, Jake & Berne, Emma Carlson. 2009. (Jake Maddox Girl Sports Stories Ser.). (ENG.). 72p. (J). (gr. 3-6). 25.32 *(978-1-4342-1604-5(7),* Stone Arch Bks.) Capstone.
—Blueberry Queen, 1 vol. Peschke, Marci. 2011. (Kylie Jean Ser.). (ENG.). 112p. (J). (gr. 1-3). pap. 4.95 *(978-1-4048-6615-7(9));* lib. bdg. 22.65 *(978-1-4048-6756-7(2))* Capstone. (Picture Window Bks.).
—Breakfast Recipe Queen. Green, Gail & Peschke, Marci. 2018. (Kylie Jean Recipe Queen Ser.). (ENG.). 32p. (J). (gr. 1-3). lib. bdg. 27.99 *(978-1-5158-2850-1(6),* 138399, Picture Window Bks.) Capstone.
—Cheer Challenge. Maddox, Jake. 2008. (Jake Maddox Girl Sports Stories Ser.). (ENG.). 72p. (J). (gr. 3-6). lib. bdg. 25.32 *(978-1-4342-0468-4(5));* per. 5.95 *(978-1-4342-0518-6(5))* Capstone. (Stone Arch Bks.).
—Cooking Queen. Peschke, Marci. 2017. (Kylie Jean Ser.). (ENG.). 112p. (J). (gr. 1-3). lib. bdg. 22.65 *(978-1-4795-9899-1(2),* 135431, Picture Window Bks.) Capstone.
—Cupcake Queen. Peschke, Marci. (Kylie Jean Ser.). (ENG.). 112p. (J). (gr. 1-3). 2015. pap. 4.95 *(978-1-4795-6753-9(1));* 2013. 8.95 *(978-1-4048-8102-0(6));* 2013. lib. bdg. 22.65 *(978-1-4048-7580-7(8))* Capstone. (Picture Window Bks.).
—Dancing Queen, 1 vol. Peschke, Marci. 2012. (Kylie Jean Ser.). (ENG.). 112p. (J). (gr. 1-3). pap. 4.95 *(978-1-4048-7209-7(4));* lib. bdg. 22.65 *(978-1-4048-6798-7(8))* Capstone. (Picture Window Bks.).
—Dinner Recipe Queen. Green, Gail & Peschke, Marci. 2018. (Kylie Jean Recipe Queen Ser.). (ENG.). 32p. (J). (gr. 1-3). lib. bdg. 27.99 *(978-1-5158-2849-5(2),* 138398, Picture Window Bks.) Capstone.
—Double or Nothing with the Two & Only Kelly Twins. Hurwitz, Johanna. 80p. (J). (gr. 1-4). 2019. pap. 4.99 *(978-1-5362-0372-1(6));* 2017. 14.99 *(978-0-7636-8808-0(8))* Candlewick Pr.
—Drama Queen, 1 vol. Peschke, Marci. 2011. (Kylie Jean Ser.). (ENG.). 112p. (J). (gr. 1-3). lib. bdg. 22.65 *(978-1-4048-6757-4(0),* Picture Window Bks.) Capstone.
—Drama Queen, 1 vol. Peschke, Marci. 2011. (Kylie Jean Ser.). (ENG.). 112p. (J). (gr. 1-3). pap. 4.95 *(978-1-4048-6616-4(7),* Picture Window Bks.) Capstone.
—Ellie, Engineer. Pearce, Jackson. 2018. 192p. (J). 15.99 *(978-1-68119-519-3(4),* 900175872, Bloomsbury USA Childrens) Bloomsbury Publishing USA.
—Fashion Queen. Peschke, Marci. 2015. (Kylie Jean Ser.). (ENG.). 112p. (J). (gr. 1-3). 8.95 *(978-1-4795-5881-0(8),* Picture Window Bks.) Capstone.
—Field Hockey Firsts, 1 vol. Maddox, Jake. 2009. (Jake Maddox Girl Sports Stories Ser.). (ENG.). 72p. (J). (gr. 3-6). 25.32 *(978-1-4342-1606-9(3),* Stone Arch Bks.) Capstone.
—Fishing Queen. Peschke, Marci. 2017. (Kylie Jean Ser.). (ENG.). 112p. (J). (gr. 1-3). lib. bdg. 22.65 *(978-1-4795-9900-4(X),* 135433, Picture Window Bks.) Capstone.
—Football Queen, 1 vol. Peschke, Marci. 2012. (Kylie Jean Ser.). (ENG.). 112p. (J). (gr. 1-3). pap. 4.95 *(978-1-4048-7210-3(8));* lib. bdg. 22.65 *(978-1-4048-6799-4(6))* Capstone. (Picture Window Bks.).
—Full Court Dreams. Maddox, Jake. 2008. (Jake Maddox Girl Sports Stories Ser.). (ENG.). 72p. (J). (gr. 3-6). lib. bdg. 25.32 *(978-1-4342-0469-1(3));* per. 5.95 *(978-1-4342-0519-3(3))* Capstone. (Stone Arch Bks.).
—Green Queen, 1 vol. Peschke, Marci. 2014. (Kylie Jean Ser.). (ENG.). 112p. (J). (gr. 1-3). 22.65 *(978-1-4795-2351-1(8),* Picture Window Bks.) Capstone.
—Gymnastics Queen. Peschke, Marci. 2016. (Kylie Jean Ser.). (ENG.). 112p. (J). (gr. 1-3). lib. bdg. 22.65 *(978-1-5158-0052-1(0),* Picture Window Bks.) Capstone.
—Half-Pipe Prize, 1 vol. Maddox, Jake. 2009. (Jake Maddox Girl Sports Stories Ser.). (ENG.). 72p. (J). (gr. 3-6). 25.32 *(978-1-4342-1607-6(1),* Stone Arch Bks.) Capstone.
—Hoop Doctor, 1 vol. Maddox, Jake & Berne, Emma Carlson. 2009. (Jake Maddox Girl Sports Stories Ser.). (ENG.). 72p. (J). (gr. 3-6). 25.32 *(978-1-4342-1605-2(5),* Stone Arch Bks.) Capstone.
—Hoop Queen, 1 vol. Peschke, Marci. 2011. (Kylie Jean Ser.). (ENG.). 112p. (J). (gr. 1-3). lib. bdg. 22.65 *(978-1-4048-5962-3(4),* Picture Window Bks.) Capstone.
—Hoop Queen, 1 vol. Peschke, Marci. 2011. (Kylie Jean Ser.). (ENG.). 112p. (J). (gr. 1-3). pap. 4.95 *(978-1-4048-6617-1(5),* Picture Window Bks.) Capstone.
—Horseback Hopes, 1 vol. Maddox, Jake. 2009. (Jake Maddox Girl Sports Stories Ser.). (ENG.). 72p. (J). (gr. 3-6). 25.32 *(978-1-4342-1214-6(9),* Stone Arch Bks.) Capstone.
—Icky, Sticky, Hairy Scary Bible Stories: 60 Poems for Kids. Schkade, Jonathan. 2010. 125p. (J). pap. 14.99 *(978-0-7586-2671-4(1))* Concordia Publishing Hse.
—Jump Serve. Maddox, Jake. 2008. (Jake Maddox Girl Sports Stories Ser.). (ENG.). 72p. (J). (gr. 3-6). lib. bdg. 25.32 *(978-1-4342-0470-7(7));* per. 5.95 *(978-1-4342-0520-9(7))* Capstone. (Stone Arch Bks.).
—Kylie Jean Collection. Peschke, Marci. ed. 2017. (Kylie Jean Ser.). (ENG.). 304p. (J). 9.99 *(978-1-5158-1892-2(6),* 136491, Picture Window Bks.) Capstone.
—Kylie Jean Craft Queen, 1 vol. Ventura, Marne et al. 2014. (Kylie Jean Craft Queen Ser.). (ENG.). 112p. (J). (gr. 1-3). pap. 9.95 *(978-1-4795-2971-1(0),* Picture Window Bks.) Capstone.
—Kylie Jean Party Craft Queen, 1 vol. Ventura, Marne & Peschke, Marci. 2014. (Kylie Jean Craft Queen Ser.). (ENG.). 32p. (J). (gr. 1-3). lib. bdg. 27.32 *(978-1-4795-2191-3(4),* Picture Window Bks.) Capstone.
—Kylie Jean Pirate Craft Queen, 1 vol. Meinking, Mary & Peschke, Marci. 2014. (Kylie Jean Craft Queen Ser.). (ENG.). 32p. (J). (gr. 1-3). lib. bdg. 27.32 *(978-1-4795-2192-0(2),* Picture Window Bks.) Capstone.
—Kylie Jean Rodeo Craft Queen, 1 vol. Meinking, Mary & Peschke, Marci. 2014. (Kylie Jean Craft Queen Ser.). (ENG.). 32p. (J). (gr. 1-3). lib. bdg. 27.32 *(978-1-4795-2190-6(6),* Picture Window Bks.) Capstone.
—Kylie Jean Summer Camp Craft Queen, 1 vol. Ventura, Marne & Peschke, Marci. 2014. (Kylie Jean Craft Queen Ser.). (ENG.). 32p. (J). (gr. 1-3). lib. bdg. 27.32 *(978-1-4795-2193-7(0),* Picture Window Bks.) Capstone.
—Lunch Recipe Queen. Green, Gail & Peschke, Marci. 2018. (Kylie Jean Recipe Queen Ser.). (ENG.). 32p. (J). (gr. 1-3). lib. bdg. 27.99 *(978-1-5158-2848-8(4),* 138397, Picture Window Bks.) Capstone.
—Over the Net, 1 vol. Maddox, Jake. 2009. (Jake Maddox Girl Sports Stories Ser.). (ENG.). 72p. (J). (gr. 3-6). 25.32 *(978-1-4342-1213-9(0),* Stone Arch Bks.) Capstone.
—Party Queen, 1 vol. Peschke, Marci. 2013. (Kylie Jean Ser.). (ENG.). 112p. (J). (gr. 1-3). lib. bdg. 22.65 *(978-1-4048-7582-1(4),* Picture Window Bks.) Capstone.
—Pirate Queen. Peschke, Marci. (Kylie Jean Ser.). (ENG.). 112p. (J). (gr. 1-3). 2015. pap. 4.95 *(978-1-4795-8020-0(1));* 2013. 8.95 *(978-1-4048-8103-7(4));* 2013. lib. bdg. 22.65 *(978-1-4048-7581-4(6))* Capstone. (Picture Window Bks.).
—Princess Peepers Picks a Pet. Calvert, Pam. 2015. (ENG.). (J). (gr. k-4). lib. bdg. 20.60 *(978-1-62765-602-3(2))* Perfection Learning Corp.
—Robot Queen. Peschke, Marci. 2018. (Kylie Jean Ser.). (ENG.). 112p. (J). (gr. 1-3). 8.95 *(978-1-5158-2934-8(0),* 138473); lib. bdg. 22.65 *(978-1-5158-2926-3(X),* 138469) Capstone. (Picture Window Bks.).
—Rodeo Queen, 1 vol. Peschke, Marci. 2011. (Kylie Jean Ser.). (ENG.). 112p. (J). (gr. 1-3). pap. 4.95 *(978-1-4048-6618-8(3));* lib. bdg. 22.65 *(978-1-4048-5961-6(6))* Capstone. (Picture Window Bks.).
—Running Rivals. Maddox, Jake. 2008. (Jake Maddox Girl Sports Stories Ser.). (ENG.). 72p. (J). (gr. 3-6). 25.32 *(978-1-4342-0778-4(1),* Stone Arch Bks.) Capstone.
—Singing Queen, 1 vol. Peschke, Marci. 2012. (Kylie Jean Ser.). (ENG.). 112p. (J). (gr. 1-3). pap. 4.95 *(978-1-4048-7211-0(6));* lib. bdg. 22.65 *(978-1-4048-6800-7(3))* Capstone. (Picture Window Bks.).
—Skater's Secret, 1 vol. Maddox, Jake. 2009. (Jake Maddox Girl Sports Stories Ser.). (ENG.). 72p. (J). (gr. 3-6). 25.32 *(978-1-4342-1212-2(2),* Stone Arch Bks.) Capstone.
—Soccer Queen. Peschke, Marci. 2015. (Kylie Jean Ser.). (ENG.). 112p. (J). (gr. 1-3). 22.65 *(978-1-4795-5882-7(6),* Picture Window Bks.) Capstone.
—Soccer Spirit. Maddox, Jake. 2008. (Jake Maddox Girl Sports Stories Ser.). (ENG.). 72p. (J). (gr. 3-6). 25.32 *(978-1-4342-0780-7(3),* Stone Arch Bks.) Capstone.
—Spelling Queen, 1 vol. Peschke, Marci. 2012. (Kylie Jean Ser.). (ENG.). 112p. (J). (gr. 1-3). pap. 4.95 *(978-1-4048-7212-7(4));* lib. bdg. 22.65 *(978-1-4048-6801-4(1))* Capstone. (Picture Window Bks.).
—Stolen Bases. Maddox, Jake. 2008. (Jake Maddox Girl Sports Stories Ser.). (ENG.). 72p. (J). (gr. 3-6). 25.32 *(978-1-4342-0779-1(X),* Stone Arch Bks.) Capstone.
—Storm Surfer, 1 vol. Maddox, Jake. 2008. (Jake Maddox Girl Sports Stories Ser.). (ENG.). 72p. (J). (gr. 3-6). lib. bdg. 25.32 *(978-1-4342-0471-4(5));* per. 5.95 *(978-1-4342-0521-6(5))* Capstone. (Stone Arch Bks.).
—Summer Camp Queen, 1 vol. Peschke, Marci. 2013. (Kylie Jean Ser.). (ENG.). 112p. (J). (gr. 1-3). lib. bdg. 22.65 *(978-1-4048-7583-8(2),* Picture Window Bks.) Capstone.
—Tennis Trouble. Maddox, Jake. 2008. (Jake Maddox Girl Sports Stories Ser.). (ENG.). 72p. (J). (gr. 3-6). 25.32 *(978-1-4342-0781-4(1),* Stone Arch Bks.) Capstone.
—Treat Recipe Queen. Green, Gail & Peschke, Marci. 2018. (Kylie Jean Recipe Queen Ser.). (ENG.). 32p. (J). (gr. 1-3). lib. bdg. 27.99 *(978-1-5158-2847-1(6),* 138396, Picture Window Bks.) Capstone.
—The Two & Only Kelly Twins. Hurwitz, Johanna. 96p. (J). (gr. 1-4). 2018. pap. 4.99 *(978-1-5362-0050-8(6));* 2013. 14.99 *(978-0-7636-5602-7(X))* Candlewick Pr.
—Vacation Queen. Peschke, M. 2016. (Kylie Jean Ser.). (ENG.). 112p. (J). (gr. 1-3). 8.95 *(978-1-5158-0059-0(8),* Picture Window Bks.) Capstone.
—Vacation Queen. Peschke, Marci. 2016. (Kylie Jean Ser.). (ENG.). 112p. (J). (gr. 1-3). lib. bdg. 22.65 *(978-1-5158-0058-3(X),* Picture Window Bks.) Capstone.
—Valentine Queen, 1 vol. Peschke, Marci. 2014. (Kylie Jean Ser.). (ENG.). 112p. (J). (gr. 1-3). 22.65 *(978-1-4795-2352-8(6),* Picture Window Bks.) Capstone.
Mourrain, Sébastian. The Tiny Tale of Little Pea. Cali, Davide. 2017. (ENG.). 40p. (J). (gr. -1-2). 17.99 *(978-1-77138-843-6(9))* Kids Can Pr., Ltd. CAN. Dist: Hachette Bk. Group.
Moursund, Gry. Snake in the Grass. Sande, Hans. Vetleseter, Tonje, tr. from NOR. 2008. 40p. (J). (gr. -1-1). 16.95 *(978-0-9815761-0-7(9))* Mackenzie Smiles, LLC.
Moussa, Karen M. The Secret of the Sand. Valeska, John & Fripp, Jean. Fripp, Jean, ed. 2003. (Dolphin Watch Ser.). 32p. (J). (gr. k-5). pap. 5.99 *(978-0-9701008-2-5(5))* Bicast, Inc.
Moutafis, Greg. Hero Corps: The Rookie. Becker, Jason Earl. 2005. (YA). per. 7.95 *(978-0-9765125-0-9(5))* Baby Shark Productions.
Moutarde & Blanchin, Matthieu. Half & Half-Voyage into Space. Kemoun, Hubert Ben & Grenier, Christian. 2008. (J). 48p. pap. 4.99 *(978-1-60115-210-7(8));* (ENG.). 45p. 17.44 *(978-1-60115-209-1(4))* Treasure Bay, Inc.
Moutte-Baur, Pascale. Duck Is Stuck. Mouhssin, Zoubida. 2018. (ENG.). 32p. (J). 17.95 *(978-1-60537-415-4(6));* 9.95 *(978-1-60537-429-1(6))* Clavis Publishing.
Movshina, Marina. Angels Do That. Cox, Tracey M. 2012. 16p. pap. 9.95 *(978-1-61633-299-0(9))* Guardian Angel Publishing, Inc.
—Buster Bear & Uncle B. Kennedy, J. Aday. 2012. 20p. pap. 10.95 *(978-1-61633-235-8(2))* Guardian Angel Publishing, Inc.
Movshina, Marina. Free As a Butterfly. Fenimore, Jan. l.t. ed. 2020. (ENG.). 20p. (J). (gr. k-5). pap. 10.95 ***(978-1-951545-09-3(5))*** Guardian Angel Publishing, Inc.
Movshina, Marina. Golden Daffodils. Maher, Liam. 2010. 20p. pap. 10.95 *(978-1-61633-073-6(2))* Guardian Angel Publishing, Inc.
—If I Could Be Anything. McNamee, Kevin. 2009. 16p. pap. 9.95 *(978-1-61633-011-8(2))* Guardian Angel Publishing, Inc.
—Just for Today. McNamee, Kevin. 2012. 16p. pap. 9.95 *(978-1-61633-314-0(6))* Guardian Angel Publishing, Inc.
—Kitty Kerplunking: Preposition Fun. Reeg, Cynthia. 2006. 24p. (J). E-Book 9.95 incl. cd-rom *(978-1-933090-27-6(8))* Guardian Angel Publishing, Inc.
—Macaroni & Cheese for Thanksgiving. Malandrinos, Cheryl C. l.t. ed. 2016. (ENG.). (J). (gr. k-3). pap. 9.95 *(978-1-61633-811-4(3))* Guardian Angel Publishing, Inc.
—My Grandma's Kitchen Rules. Kirk, Bill. 2009. 24p. pap. 10.95 *(978-1-935137-88-7(3))* Guardian Angel Publishing, Inc.
—Romeo's Rescue. Reed, Emma & Reed, Jennifer. 2012. 24p. pap. 10.95 *(978-1-61633-247-1(6))* Guardian Angel Publishing, Inc.
—Too Many Kitties. Clineff, Jeff. 2007. 22p. (J). E-Book 9.95 incl. cd-rom *(978-1-933090-45-0(6))* Guardian Angel Publishing, Inc.
—Too Many Kitties. Clineff, Jeff. 2007. (ESK.). 24p. (J). 9.95 *(978-1-933090-10-8(3))* Guardian Angel Publishing, Inc.
Movshsina, Marina. DandyLion. Douglas, Carol J. l.t. ed. 2019. (ENG.). 16p. (J). (gr. k-3). pap. 9.95 ***(978-1-61633-997-5(7))*** Guardian Angel Publishing, Inc.
Mowatt, Ken N. The First Fry Bread: A Gitxsan Story. Smith, M. Jane. Wheeler, Jordan, ed. 2012. 32p. pap. *(978-1-4602-0226-5(0))* FriesenPress.
Mowery, Linda Williams & Murphy, Emmy Lou. The Bible Is the Best Book. Why? Gunderson, Vivian D. 36p. (J). (gr. 4-8). pap., wbk. ed. 2.00 *(978-0-915374-00-7(5))* Rapids Christian Pr., Inc.
Moxham, Barbara. Hello Goodbye Little Island. Boukarim, Leila. 2018. (ENG.). 40p. 10.00 *(978-981-4794-43-5(0))* Marshall Cavendish International (Asia) Private Ltd. SGP. Dist: National Bk. Network.
—A Warm Christmas. Boukarim, Leila. 2019. (ENG.). 40p. (J). (gr. k-4). 10.00 *(978-981-4828-29-1(7))* Marshall Cavendish International (Asia) Private Ltd. SGP. Dist: National Bk. Network.
Moxley, Sheila. The Arabian Nights: Sixteen Stories from Sheherazade. 2019. 160p. (J). (gr. -1-12). 16.00 *(978-1-86147-864-1(X),* Armadillo) Anness Publishing GBR. Dist: National Bk. Network.
—El Baile del Elefante: Recuerdos de la India. Heine, Theresa. 2005. (SPA.). 44p. (gr. 2-3). 22.99 *(978-84-8452-356-7(X))* Fundacion Intermon ESP. Dist: Lectorum Pubns., Inc.
—Diary of a Princess: A Tale from Marco Polo's Travels. Maisner, Heather. 2006. 26p. (gr. k-4). reprint ed. pap. 8.00 *(978-1-4223-5302-8(8))* DIANE Publishing Co.
—Elephant Dance: A Journey to India. Heine, Theresa. 2006. (ENG.). 40p. (J). (gr. -1-2). 8.99 *(978-1-905236-79-4(4))* Barefoot Bks., Inc.
—Elephant Dance: Memories of India. Heine, Teresa & Heine, Theresa. 2004. 40p. (J). 16.99 *(978-1-84148-917-9(4))* Barefoot Bks., Inc.
—Practical Happiness: Simple Techniques for Bringing Positivity, Joy & Balance into Everyday Life. Davies, Kim. 2019. 128p. (J). (gr. -1-12). 15.00 *(978-0-7548-3463-2(8),* Armadillo) Anness Publishing GBR. Dist: National Bk. Network.
—Stone Girl Bone Girl: The Story of Mary Anning of Lyme Regis. Anholt, Laurence. 2006. (ENG.). 32p. (J). (gr. k-3). pap. 8.99 *(978-1-84507-700-6(8),* 315159, Frances Lincoln Children's Bks.) Quarto Publishing Group UK GBR. Dist: Hachette Bk. Group.
Moxley, Sheila. Grandpa's Garden. Moxley, Sheila. Fry, Stella. 2012. 40p. (J). (gr. -1-2). pap. 8.99 *(978-1-84686-809-2(2))* Barefoot Bks., Inc.
Moxley, Sheila. Come to the Great World: Poems from Around the Globe. Moxley, Sheila, tr. Cooling, Wendy, ed. 2004. (ENG.). 48p. (J). (gr. k-3). tchr. ed. 17.95 *(978-0-8234-1822-0(7))* Holiday Hse., Inc.
Moxley, Sheila, jt. illus. see Jago.
Moy, Philip, jt. illus. see McKenny, Stewart.
Moya, Patricia. Parade of Lights. Sharpe, Gerald. 2007. (What Lies Beneath the Bed Ser.). 487p. (J). per. 11.00 *(978-1-933894-01-0(6))* IJN Publishing, Inc.
—Tommy's Tales. Sharpe, Gerald. 2006. (Tommy's Tales Ser.). 300p. (J). per. 7.00 *(978-1-933894-00-3(8))* IJN Publishing, Inc.
Moyer, Aubrie. Are You the Babe of Bethlehem. Haws, Dona. 2018. (ENG.). 32p. (J). (gr. k-3). 14.99 *(978-1-4621-2273-8(6))* Cedar Fort, Inc./CFI Distribution.
Moyer, Barry. The Planet of Trash: An Environmental Fable. Poppel, George. 2016. (Pandamonium Bks.). (ENG.). (J). (gr. k-5). pap. 12.95 *(978-0-9973316-3-9(1))* Inprint Bks.
Moyer, Brett, jt. illus. see Stauffer, Lori.
Moyer, J. Ben & Elvis: The Miracle of a Stormy Christmas. Page, J. & Rainier, S. T. 2012. 28p. pap. 8.99 *(978-0-9829669-4-5(6))* Elv Enterprises.
Moyer, Tom. The Adventures of Drew & Ellie: The Daring Rescue. Noland, Charles. 2nd ed. 2006. 92p. (J). per. 7.95 *(978-0-9789297-2-5(1))* TMD Enterprises.
Moyers, William. Three Together: Story of the Wright Brothers & Their Sister. Mills, Lois. 2011. 160p. 41.95 *(978-1-258-05968-2(1))* Literary Licensing, LLC.
—Wild Stallion. Murphy, Bud. 2011. 176p. 42.95 *(978-1-258-05633-9(X))* Literary Licensing, LLC.
Moyle, David C. The Adventures of Tommy the Texan & Captain Billy: A Return to Blue Skies. Moyle, William. O'Connor, Laura E., ed. 2019. (ENG.). 166p. (J). pap. 13.99 ***(978-1-4808-8280-5(1))*** Archway Publishing.
Moyle, Eunice. ABC Dance! An Animal Alphabet. Moyle, Sabrina. 2020. (Hello!Lucky Ser.). (ENG.). 26p. (J). (— 1). bds. 7.95 *(978-1-5235-0746-7(2),* 100746) Workman Publishing Co., Inc.
—Christmas Is Awesome! (a Hello!Lucky Book) Hello!Lucky & Moyle, Sabrina. 2019. (Hello!Lucky Book Ser.). (ENG.). 24p. (J). (gr. -1 — 1). bds. 7.99 *(978-1-4197-3427-4(X),* 1265610, Abrams Appleseed) Abrams, Inc.
—Good Night, Baboon! A Bedtime Counting Book. Moyle, Sabrina. 2020. (Hello!Lucky Ser.). (ENG.). 22p. (J). (— 1). bds. 7.95 *(978-1-5235-0747-4(0),* 100747) Workman Publishing Co., Inc.
Moyle, Eunice. I Believe in You. Moyle, Sabrina. 2020. (Hello!Lucky Ser.). (ENG.). 32p. (J). (gr. -1-3). 12.95 ***(978-1-5235-0748-1(9),*** 100748) Workman Publishing Co., Inc.
Moyle, Eunice. My Mom Is Magical. Moyle, Sabrina. 2018. (Hello!Lucky Book Ser.). (ENG.). 24p. (J). (gr. -1 — 1). bds. 7.99 *(978-1-4197-2962-1(4),* 1212110, Abrams Appleseed) Abrams, Inc.
Moyle, Eunice & Hello!Lucky. My Dad Is Amazing. Moyle, Sabrina. 2018. (Hello!Lucky Book Ser.). (ENG.). 24p. (J). (gr. -1 — 1). bds. 7.99 *(978-1-4197-2961-4(6),* 1212010) Abrams, Inc.
Moyler, Alan. The Curies & Radium. Rubin, Elizabeth. 2011. 122p. 40.95 *(978-1-258-09479-9(7))* Literary Licensing, LLC.
Mozi, Jennifer. The Adventures of Mr. Chicken Butt. Bidelman, Jeff. 2013. (ENG.). (J). 14.95 *(978-1-62086-354-1(5))* Mascot Bks., Inc.
Moziak, Rose Mary Casciano, jt. illus. see Casciano, Christie.
Mozley, Peggy. Alphascripts: The ABC's of the Bible. Wimbrey, Crystal M. 2006. 56p. 14.95 *(978-1-933285-63-4(X))* Brown Books Publishing Group.
Mozz. In Search of the Holey Whale: The Top Secret Riddles & Left-Handed Scribbles of Mozz. Mozz. 2008. 176p. (J). (gr. 3-6). lib. bdg. 17.95 *(978-0-9726130-3-3(X))* Goofy Guru Publishing.
Mpagazehe, Joshua N. The Clocks' Holiday. Mpagazehe, Belinda Derr Illustrated by J. 2016. (ENG.). (J). pap. 19.99 *(978-1-4984-8773-3(4))* Salem Author Services.
Mrozek, Elizabeth. The Fifth Chair. Mrozek, Elizabeth. 2013. 38p. 19.95 *(978-1-935766-80-3(5))* Windy City Pubs.

Mroziewicz, Elsa. Peek-A-Who? Mroziewicz, Elsa. 2018. (ENG.). 22p. (J). (gr. -1-k). bds. 11.99 *(978-988-8341-57-3(X)*, Minedition) Neugebauer, Michael (Publishing) Limited HKG. Dist: Penguin Random Hse. LLC.

—Peek-A-Who Too? Mroziewicz, Elsa. 2019. (ENG.). 22p. (J). (gr. -1-k). bds. 11.99 *(978-988-8341-81-8(2)*, Minedition) Neugebauer, Michael (Publishing) Limited HKG. Dist: Penguin Random Hse. LLC.

Mshindu. Fun with Letters. Taylor, Maxwell. Date not set. (Fun with Ser.: Vol. 3). (J). (gr. -1-1). pap. 3.95 *(978-1-881316-42-8(4))* A & B Distributors & Pubs. Group.

Mucha-Sullivan, Emily V., jt. illus. see Mucha-Sullivan, Kalie A.

Mucha-Sullivan, Kalie A. & Mucha-Sullivan, Emily V. My Favorite Time of Year. Mucha Aydlott, Julie A. l.t. ed. 2004. 22p. (J). 5.95 *(978-0-9746093-2-4(3))* JA Pubns., Ltd.

Muckle, Christine. The Adventures of Annika. Saunders, Vivien. 2013. 42p. pap. *(978-1-909730-02-1(5))* Abbotsley Publishing.

Mudzongo, Marvin. The Other Side. Nwaogwugwu, Naysa Simone. 2019. (ENG.). 74p. (J). (gr. 3-6). pap. ***(978-1-912551-76-7(4))*** Conscious Dreams Publishing.

Muehlenhardt, Amy Bailey. Beauty & the Beast, 1 vol. Jones, Christianne C. 2013. (My First Classic Story Ser.). (ENG.). 32p. (J). (gr. k-3). pap. 7.10 *(978-1-4795-1851-7(4)*, Picture Window Bks.) Capstone.

—I Drive a Fire Engine, 1 vol. Bridges, Sarah. 2006. (Working Wheels Ser.). (ENG.). 24p. (J). (gr. -1-2). 27.32 *(978-1-4048-1606-0(2)*, Picture Window Bks.) Capstone.

—I Drive a Freight Train, 1 vol. Bridges, Sarah. 2006. (Working Wheels Ser.). (ENG.). 24p. (J). (gr. -1-2). 27.32 *(978-1-4048-1607-7(0)*, Picture Window Bks.) Capstone.

—Johnny Appleseed, 1 vol. Blair, Eric. 2011. (My First Classic Story Ser.).Tr. of Johnny Appleseed. (ENG.). 32p. (J). (gr. k-3). pap. 7.10 *(978-1-4048-7367-4(8)*, Picture Window Bks.) Capstone.

—Johnny Appleseed, 1 vol. Blair, Eric. Robledo, Sol, tr. 2006. (Read-It! Readers en Español: Cuentos Exagerados Ser.).Tr. of Johnny Appleseed. (SPA.). 32p. (J). (gr. k-3). 21.32 *(978-1-4048-1655-8(0)*, Picture Window Bks.) Capstone.

—Kids Talk about Bullying, 1 vol. Finn, Carrie. 2006. (Kids Talk Jr Ser.). (ENG.). 32p. (J). (gr. -1-2). lib. bdg. 27.32 *(978-1-4048-2315-0(8)*, Picture Window Bks.) Capstone.

—Kids Talk about Fairness, 1 vol. Finn, Carrie. 2006. (Kids Talk Jr Ser.). (ENG.). 32p. (J). (gr. -1-2). lib. bdg. 27.32 *(978-1-4048-2316-7(6)*, Picture Window Bks.) Capstone.

—Rapunzel: A Retelling of the Grimms' Fairy Tale, 1 vol. Jones, Christianne C. 2013. (My First Classic Story Ser.). (ENG.). 32p. (J). (gr. k-3). pap. 7.10 *(978-1-4795-1852-4(2)*, Picture Window Bks.) Capstone.

—Whose Hat Is This? A Look at Hats Workers Wear - Hard, Tall, & Shiny, 1 vol. Cooper, Sharon Katz. 2006. (Whose Is It?: Community Workers Ser.). (ENG.). 24p. (J). (gr. -1-2). lib. bdg. 27.32 *(978-1-4048-1600-8(3)*, Picture Window Bks.) Capstone.

Muehlenhardt, Amy Bailey. Beginner's Guide to Drawing: Animals, Bugs, Dinosaurs, & Other Cool Stuff! Muehlenhardt, Amy Bailey. 2010. (Sketch It! Ser.). (ENG.). 144p. (J). (gr. k-4). pap. 14.95 *(978-1-4048-6166-4(1)*, Picture Window Bks.) Capstone.

—Drawing & Learning about Cars: Using Shapes & Lines, 1 vol. Muehlenhardt, Amy Bailey. 2004. (Sketch It! Ser.). (ENG.). 24p. (J). (gr. k-4). 27.32 *(978-1-4048-0269-8(X)*, Picture Window Bks.) Capstone.

—Drawing & Learning about Faces: Using Shapes & Lines. Muehlenhardt, Amy Bailey. 2004. (Sketch It! Ser.). (ENG.). 24p. (J). (gr. k-4). 27.32 *(978-1-4048-0271-1(1)*, 1229557, Picture Window Bks.) Capstone.

—Drawing & Learning about Fashion: Using Shapes & Lines, 1 vol. Muehlenhardt, Amy Bailey. 2005. (Sketch It! Ser.). (ENG.). 24p. (J). (gr. k-4). lib. bdg. 27.32 *(978-1-4048-1191-1(5)*, 1243855, Picture Window Bks.) Capstone.

Mueller, Janet. A Star from Grandma. Mueller, Janet. 2004. (J). pap. 8.96 *(978-0-9746932-3-1(5))* Stella Bks, Inc.

Mueller, Lisa. The King Who Left His Kingdom: El Rey Que Dejó Su Reino. Altman, Deanna. 2018. (ENG.). 34p. (J). (gr. k-3). pap. 12.95 *(978-1-5069-0613-3(3))* First Edition Design eBook Publishing.

Mueller, Mike, photos by. Pickup Trucks. Zuehlke, Jeffrey. 2007. (Motor Mania Ser.). (ENG., 48p. (J). (gr. 4-7). lib. bdg. 26.60 *(978-0-8225-6564-2(1))* Lerner Publishing Group.

Mueller, Miranda. Gardening with Grandma. Brunsvold, Eric. 2010. 24p. pap. 9.95 *(978-0-615-38944-8(9))* Specialized Printing, LLC.

—Mishka: An Adoption Tale. 2007. 32p. (J). 16.95 *(978-1-933084-01-5(4))* DRT Pr.

Mueller, Nicholes. The Prairie Sea. Yaremko, Leslie. 2018. (ENG.). 40p. (J). pap. *(978-1-5255-0977-3(2))* FriesenPress.

Mueller, Olivia Chin. I Am a Kitten. Risom, Ole. 2018. (Golden Sturdy Book Ser.). 26p. (J). (-k). bds. 7.99 *(978-1-5247-6729-7(8)*, Golden Bks.) Random Hse. Children's Bks.

—I Am a Puppy. Risom, Ole. 2018. 26p. (J). (-k). bds. 7.99 *(978-1-5247-7218-5(6)*, Golden Bks.) Random Hse. Children's Bks.

—Mirabel's Missing Valentines. Lawler, Janet. 2018. 32p. (J). (gr. -1-2). 16.95 *(978-1-4549-2739-6(9))* Sterling Publishing Co., Inc.

—Princess Puffybottom ... & Darryl. Nielsen, Susin. 2019. (ENG.). 32p. (J). (gr. -1-2). 17.99 *(978-1-101-91925-5(6)*, Tundra Bks.) Tundra Bks. CAN. Dist: Penguin Random Hse. LLC.

—Royal Rescues #1: the Naughty Kitten. Harrison, Paula. 2020. (Royal Rescues Ser.). (ENG.). 112p. (J). 15.99 *(978-1-250-26488-6(X)*, 900221926); pap. 5.99 *(978-1-250-25923-3(1)*, 900221008) Feiwel & Friends.

—Royal Rescues #2: the Lost Puppy. Harrison, Paula. 2020. (Royal Rescues Ser.). (ENG.). 112p. (J). 15.99 *(978-1-250-26490-9(1)*, 900221928); pap. 5.99 *(978-1-250-25925-7(8)*, 900221011) Feiwel & Friends.

—Walk with Me. Brown, Margaret Wise. 2019. (Margaret Wise Brown Classics Ser.). (ENG.). 32p. (J). (gr. -1-k). 12.99 *(978-1-68412-748-1(3)*, Silver Dolphin Bks.) Printers Row Publishing Group.

Mueller, Pete. Black Out!: Animals That Live in the Dark: Animals That Live in the Dark. Clarke, Ginjer L. 2008. (Penguin Young Readers, Level 3 Ser.). (ENG.). 48p. (J). (gr. 1-3). mass mkt. 4.99 *(978-0-448-44824-4(6)*, Penguin Young Readers) Penguin Young Readers Group.

—Bug Out! The World's Creepiest, Crawliest Critters. Clarke, Ginjer L. 2007. (Penguin Young Readers, Level 3 Ser.). (ENG.). 48p. (J). (gr. 1-3). pap. 4.99 *(978-0-448-44543-4(3)*, Penguin Young Readers) Penguin Young Readers Group.

—Bug Out! The World's Creepiest, Crawliest Critters. Clarke, Ginjer L. 2007. (All Aboard Science Reader Ser.). (gr. -1-3). 14.00 *(978-0-7569-8168-6(9))* Perfection Learning Corp.

—Fake Out! Animals That Play Tricks. Clarke, Ginjer L. 2007. (Penguin Young Readers, Level 3 Ser.). (ENG.). 48p. (J). (gr. 1-3). pap. 4.99 *(978-0-448-44656-1(1)*, Penguin Young Readers) Penguin Young Readers Group.

—Fake Out! Animals That Play Tricks. Clarke, Ginjer L. 2007. (All Aboard Science Reader Ser.). 48p. (gr. 1-3). 14.00 *(978-0-7569-8170-9(0))* Perfection Learning Corp.

—Far Out! Animals That Do Amazing Things. Clarke, Ginjer L. 2009. (Penguin Young Readers, Level 3 Ser.). (ENG.). 48p. (J). (gr. 1-3). 4.99 *(978-0-448-44826-8(2)*, Penguin Young Readers) Penguin Young Readers Group.

—Freak Out! Animals Beyond Your Wildest Imagination. Clarke, Ginjer L. 2007. (All Aboard Science Reader Ser.). 48p. (gr. 1-3). 14.00 *(978-0-7569-8173-0(5))* Perfection Learning Corp.

—Gross Out! Animals That Do Disgusting Things. Clarke, Ginjer L. 2007. (All Aboard Science Reader Ser.). 46p. (gr. 1-3). 14.00 *(978-0-7569-8172-3(7))* Perfection Learning Corp.

—Honeybees. Milton, Joyce. 2003. (Penguin Young Readers, Level 3 Ser.). 48p. (J). (gr. 1-3). pap. 4.99 *(978-0-448-42846-8(6)*, Penguin Young Readers) Penguin Young Readers Group.

—Maxed Out! Gigantic Creatures from the Past. Clarke, Ginjer L. 2010. (Penguin Young Readers, Level 3 Ser.). (ENG.). 48p. (J). (gr. 1-3). mass mkt. 4.99 *(978-0-448-44827-5(0)*, Penguin Young Readers) Penguin Young Readers Group.

—Watch Out! The World's Most Dangerous Creatures. Clarke, Ginjer L. 2012. (Penguin Young Readers, Level 3 Ser.). (ENG.). 48p. (J). (gr. 1-3). pap. 4.99 *(978-0-448-45108-4(5)*, Penguin Young Readers) Penguin Young Readers Group.

Mueller, Peter. Pets: Step-by-Step Insructions for 23 Favorite Animals. Walter Foster Creative Team. 2011. (Learn to Draw Ser.). 32p. (J). (gr. 1-4). 28.50 *(978-1-936309-17-7(3))* Quarto Publishing Group USA.

Muellner, Nancy. The Hustle & Bustle of Poor Mrs. Tustle. Berggren, Joyce D. 2010. 32p. pap. 12.95 *(978-0-9819860-5-0(6))* Amber Skye Publishing LLC.

Mueting, Brian R. With All You've Got. Lill, Abigail C. K. 2019. (ENG.). 28p. (J). pap. 11.95 ***(978-0-578-58026-5(8))*** Horn, Jonathan.

Mugambi, Christina Nkirote. Maybe the Truth about Santa. Powell Zalewski, Amy. 2005. 32p. (J). (gr. -1-3). 15.00 *(978-0-9773608-1-9(4))* Shiny Red Ball Publishing.

Mugisha, Joseph. Hattie Mae's Halloween. Wargel, Claudine. 2015. (ENG.) (J). (gr. 2-5). pap. 9.99 *(978-0-692-75888-5(7))* Brush Creek Publishing.

Mugnaini, Joe, jt. illus. see Bradbury, Ray.

Mugnaini, Joseph. The Halloween Tree. Bradbury, Ray. ed. 2007. (ENG.). 160p. (J). (gr. 3-7). reprint ed. 15.99 *(978-0-394-82409-3(1)*, Knopf Bks. for Young Readers) Random Hse. Children's Bks.

Muhammad, Mecca. Family, I Love You! Muhammad, Mecca. 2019. (ENG.). 36p. (J). pap. 10.00 *(978-1-0996-5565-4(X))* Independently Published.

Muhle, Raafat. La Prière Pour les Jeunes. Muhammad Salama, Salama. 2016. (FRE.). 26p. (J). pap. 11.00 *(978-1-0713-7818-2(X))* Independently Published.

Mühle, Jörg. Be at the Ark by Eight. Hub, Ulrich. 2012. (ENG.). 68p. (J). 12.00 *(978-0-8028-5410-0(9)*, Eerdmans Bks For Young Readers) Eerdmans, William B. Publishing Co.

—Becoming the Wolf. Hub, Ulrich & Ragg-Kirkby, Helena. 2012. (ENG.). 64p. (J). 12.00 *(978-0-8028-5409-4(5)*, Eerdmans Bks For Young Readers) Eerdmans, William B. Publishing Co.

Muhle, Jorg. See Inside Pirate Ships. Jones, Rob Lloyd. 2007. (See Inside Board Bks). 15p. (J). (gr. -1-3). bds. 12.99 *(978-0-7945-1601-7(7)*, Usborne) EDC Publishing.

Muhle, Jorg. Bathtime for Little Rabbit. Muhle, Jorg. 2017. (Little Rabbit Ser.). (ENG.). 20p. (J). (gr. -1 — 1). bds. 9.99 *(978-1-77657-137-6(1))* Gecko Pr. NZL. Dist: Lerner Publishing Group.

—Poor Little Rabbit. Muhle, Jorg. 2018. (Little Rabbit Ser.). (ENG.). 20p. (J). (gr. -1 — 1). bds. 9.99 *(978-1-77657-177-2(0))* Gecko Pr. NZL. Dist: Lerner Publishing Group.

—Tickle My Ears. Muhle, Jorg. 2016. (Little Rabbit Ser.). (ENG.). 20p. (J). (gr. -1 — 1). bds. 9.99 *(978-1-77657-076-8(6)*, 9781776570768) Gecko Pr. NZL. Dist: Lerner Publishing Group.

—Two for Me, One for You. Muhle, Jorg. 2019. (ENG.). 32p. (J). (gr. -1-2). 17.99 *(978-1-77657-239-7(4))* Gecko Pr. NZL. Dist: Lerner Publishing Group.

Muhlmeister, Karl. Geschichten Für Kinder und Auch Für Solche, Welche Die Kinder Lieb Haben: Heimatlos + Moni + Heidi + Rosenresli + Was Die Großmutter Gelehrt Hat und Mehr (Vollständige Ausgabe Mit Illustrationen) Spyri, Johanna. 2017. (GER.). 696p. (J). pap. *(978-80-268-5646-7(5))* E-Artnow.

Muhn, Gu-seon. Mango Trees: Philippines. Kim, Tae-yeon. 2015. (Global Kids Storybooks Ser.). (ENG.). 32p. (J). (gr. 1-4). pap. 8.99 *(978-1-925233-46-9(4)*, Big and SMALL) ChoiceMaker Pty. Ltd., The AUS. Dist: Lerner Publishing Group.

—Mango Trees: Philippines. Kim, Tae-yeon. Cowley, Joy, ed. 2015. (Global Kids Storybooks Ser.). (ENG.). 32p. (gr. 1-4). 26.65 *(978-1-925246-07-0(8))*; 26.65 *(978-1-925246-33-9(7))*; 7.99 *(978-1-925246-59-9(0))* ChoiceMaker Pty. Ltd., The AUS. (Big and SMALL). Dist: Lerner Publishing Group.

Muhr, Jason & Broccardo, Andrea. Doctor Strange/Punisher: Magic Bullets. 2017. (ENG.). 128p. (YA). (gr. 8-17). pap. 15.99 *(978-1-302-90718-1(2))* Marvel Worldwide, Inc.

Muir, Coll. Are You a Cat? Muir, Coll. 2020. 32p. (J). (gr. -1-3). 17.99 *(978-0-06-286594-6(3)*, HarperCollins) HarperCollins Pubs. Ltd. GBR. Dist: HarperCollins Pubs.

—Can Cat & Bird Be Friends? Muir, Coll. 2019. (ENG.). 32p. (J). (gr. -1-3). 17.99 *(978-0-06-286593-9(5))* HarperCollins Pubs.

Muir, Toobz & Cassels, Allison. Thanks, You're Awesome! a Little Person's Guide to Creating Good Vibes in the World. Harrison, Jill. 2017. (ENG.). 34p. (J). pap. 11.99 *(978-0-9968660-7-1(8))* Buddha Baby Bks.

Muirhead, Deborah. Freedom Business: Including a Narrative of the Life & Adventures of Venture, a Native of Africa. Nelson, Marilyn. 2008. (ENG.). 72p. (YA). (gr. 1-4). 18.95 *(978-1-932425-57-4(8)*, Front Street) Boyds Mills Pr.

Muise, Doris. Wild Woman Alphabet, 1 vol. 2017. (ENG.). 72p. (J). (gr. 1-3). 24.95 ***(978-1-926886-48-0(8))*** Theytus Bks., Ltd. CAN. Dist: Orca Bk. Pubs. USA.

Mukherjee, Aiswarya & S., Bijan. My Family! ABCs with Keesha. 2011. (J). pap. 2.99 *(978-0-9767273-9-2(0))* Dodi Pr.

Mukherjee, Aniruddha. Siddhartha Gautama: The Life of the Buddha - Based on Original Sources. Seth, Shantum. adapted ed. 2014. (ENG.). 64p. pap. 6.95 *(978-1-906230-61-6(7))* Real Reads Ltd. GBR. Dist: Casemate Pubs. & Bk. Distributors, LLC.

Mukhida, Zul & Card, Vanessa. Buddhist Vihara. Ganeri, Anita. 2004. 32p. pap. *(978-0-7136-5498-1(8)*, A&C Black) Bloomsbury Publishing Plc.

Muki, Gon. Peter & Paul Had Hope. Firman, Hayley. 2019. (ENG.). 34p. (J). pap. ***(978-0-646-80534-4(7))*** Lambie Nguyen Co. Ltd., The.

Mukthavaram, Vasantha. Aesop's Fables: Eternal Leaf Art. Mukthavaram, Vasantha. 2011. (ENG.). (J). 19.99 *(978-0-615-46456-5(4))* Vikasam.

Muktirina, Aprilia. The Abc's of Shakespeare. Bahney, Kelly. 2018. (ENG.). 34p. (J). pap. 10.99 *(978-0-9894685-5-8(0))* Little Owl Publishing.

Mukuc, Lucy. What Am I? Hillert, Margaret. 2016. (BeginningtoRead Ser.). (ENG.). 32p. (J). (gr. -1-2). pap. 11.94 *(978-1-60357-982-7(6))*; (gr. 3-2). 22.60 *(978-1-59953-820-4(2))* Norwood Hse. Pr.

Mulara, Nadia. Cora & the Cola Bottle: Understanding Emotions. Saher, Janan. 2020. (Care & Share Collection: Vol. 1). (ENG.). 48p. (J). pap. 16.98 ***(978-1-7091-3907-9(2))*** Independently Published.

Mulazzani, Simona. Animal Supermarket. Zoboli, Giovanna & Watkinson, Laura. 2015. (ENG.). 26p. (J). 16.00 *(978-0-8028-5448-3(6)*, Eerdmans Bks For Young Readers) Eerdmans, William B. Publishing Co.

—The Big Book of Slumber. Zoboli, Giovanna. 2014. (ENG.). 26p. (J). 16.00 *(978-0-8028-5439-1(7)*, Eerdmans Bks For Young Readers) Eerdmans, William B. Publishing Co.

—The Home Builders. Bajaj, Varsha. 2019. 32p. (J). (-k). 17.99 *(978-0-399-16685-3(8)*, Nancy Paulsen Books) Penguin Young Readers Group.

—I Wish I Had... Zoboli, Giovanna & Mathews, Leslie. 2013. (ENG.). 26p. (J). 16.00 *(978-0-8028-5415-5(X)*, Eerdmans Bks For Young Readers) Eerdmans, William B. Publishing Co.

Mulazzani, Simona. The Right Place. Masini, Beatrice. 2020. (J). ***(978-1-78285-981-9(0))***; (ENG.). pap. ***(978-1-78285-982-6(9))*** Barefoot Bks., Inc.

Mulazzani, Simona. Tree of Wonder. Messner, Kate. 2015. (ENG.). 36p. (J). (gr. k-3). 16.99 *(978-1-4521-1248-0(7))* Chronicle Bks. LLC.

Mulder, Irene. Het Geheim Van de Oude Kist. Mulder, Martijn. 2017. (De Avonturen Van Tommy & Anouk Ser.: Vol. 1). (DUT.). (J). (gr. 3-6). *(978-90-819674-2-6(8))* Stichting Historisch Egmond.

Muldoon, Eilidh. Amazing Maps Activity Book. Muldoon, Eilidh. 2019. (ENG.). 96p. (J). pap. 9.99 *(978-1-78888-213-2(X)*, e515579b-ee71-42bd-bc57-8a0f4e96a349) Arcturus Publishing GBR. Dist: Baker & Taylor Publisher Services (BTPS).

—World Explorer Maze Book. Muldoon, Eilidh. 2019. (ENG.). 96p. (J). pap. 9.99 *(978-1-78950-633-4(6)*, 494cc49d-d7a7-423f-8183-ec785925158a) Arcturus Publishing GBR. Dist: Baker & Taylor Publisher Services (BTPS).

Muldoon, Melissa. Mouse & the Storm. Quayle, Susan. 2017. (ENG.). 56p. 15.95 *(978-1-84819-344-4(0)*, 696462, Singing Dragon) Kingsley, Jessica Pubs. GBR. Dist: Hachette UK Distribution.

—Mouse's Best Day Ever: Children's Reflexology to Soothe Sore Teeth & Tums. Quayle, Susan. 2016. (ENG.). 44p. 16.95 *(978-1-84819-315-4(7)*, 696042, Singing Dragon) Kingsley, Jessica Pubs. GBR. Dist: Hachette UK Distribution.

Mulford, Aja. That's Not Your Mommy Anymore: A Zombie Tale. Mogk, Matt. 2011. (ENG.). 32p. pap. 10.00 *(978-1-56975-926-4(X))* Ulysses Pr.

Mulholland, Bailey. Grandpa Isn't Grandpa Anymore. Durben, Toni. 2006. (J). lib. bdg. *(978-1-933556-33-8(1))* Publishers' Graphics, L.L.C.

Mulholland, Tian. Octicorn Party! Diller, Kevin & Lowe, Justin. 2020. (ENG.). 48p. (J). (gr. -1-3). 17.99 *(978-0-06-238794-3(4)*, Balzer & Bray) HarperCollins Pubs.

Mulkey Young, Kim. Under Three Flags: Exploring Early St. Louis History. Hoessle, Maureen. 2004. (J). pap. 14.95 *(978-1-891442-28-5(7))* Virginia Publishing Corp.

Mullaly, Glen. I Shrank My Teacher. Coville, Bruce. 2020. (Sixth-Grade Alien Ser.: 2). (ENG.). 176p. (J). (gr. 3-7). 17.99 ***(978-1-5344-6480-3(8))***; pap. 6.99 ***(978-1-5344-6479-7(4))*** Simon & Schuster Children's Publishing. (Aladdin).

—Lunch Swap Disaster. Coville, Bruce. 2020. (Sixth-Grade Alien Ser.: 4). (ENG.). 176p. (J). (gr. 3-7). 17.99 ***(978-1-5344-6486-5(7))***; pap. 6.99 ***(978-1-5344-6485-8(9))*** Simon & Schuster Children's Publishing. (Aladdin).

—Missing — One Brain! Coville, Bruce. 2020. (Sixth-Grade Alien Ser.: 3). (ENG.). 160p. (J). (gr. 3-7). 17.99 ***(978-1-5344-6484-1(0))***; pap. 6.99 ***(978-1-5344-6482-7(4))*** Simon & Schuster Children's Publishing. (Aladdin).

—Sixth-Grade Alien. Coville, Bruce. 2020. (Sixth-Grade Alien Ser.: 1). (ENG.). 192p. (J). (gr. 3-7). 17.99 ***(978-1-5344-6467-4(0))***; pap. 6.99 ***(978-1-5344-6466-7(2))*** Simon & Schuster Children's Publishing. (Aladdin).

—Sixth-Grade Alien Out-Of-This-World Collection: Sixth-Grade Alien; I Shrank My Teacher; Missing — One Brain!; Lunch Swap Disaster. Coville, Bruce. ed. 2020. (Sixth-Grade Alien Ser.). (ENG.). 704p. (J). (gr. 3-7). pap. 27.99 ***(978-1-5344-6488-9(3)***, Aladdin) Simon & Schuster Children's Publishing.

Mullan, G. E. Canticle: Biblical Songs Illuminated. Shea, John. 2009. (J). 29.95 *(978-1-58459-427-7(6))* World Library Pubns.

Mullan, Michael. Karl & Carolina Uncover the Parts of a Book, 1 vol. Donovan, Sandy. 2010. (In the Library). (ENG.). 24p. (J). (gr. k-4). lib. bdg. 27.32 *(978-1-4048-5760-5(5)*, Picture Window Bks.) Capstone.

Mullani, Stephanie. The Snowflake Snatcher. Garner, Jennifer. 2018. (Cozy Cottage Stories Ser.: Vol. 2). (ENG.). 46p. (J). (gr. k-3). 19.99 *(978-1-941420-44-7(3))* Tru Publishing.

Mullany, Hilary. Sula's Little One. Carlini, Denise L. 2018. (Nature's Resilience Ser.: Vol. 1). (ENG.). 32p. (J). pap. 9.99 *(978-1-7327733-0-1(0))* Horn, Jonathan.

Mullarkey, Lisa & McWilliam, Howard. Tom Sawyer, 1 vol. Twain, Mark. 2010. (Calico Illustrated Classics Ser.: No. 1). (ENG.). 112p. (J). (gr. 2-5). 29.93 *(978-1-60270-704-7(9)*, 3961, Calico Chapter Bks.) ABDO Publishing Co.

Mullen, Amy. The Colors of Ancient Egypt. 2016. 24p. (J). bds. 10.95 *(978-0-7649-7541-7(2)*, POMEGRANATE KIDS) Pomegranate Communications, Inc.

—My First Lift-The-Flap Animal Book. duopress labs. 2018. (ENG.). 20p. (J). (gr. -1-1). bds. 9.95 *(978-1-946064-95-0(5)*, 806495) Duo Pr. LLC.

Mullen, Amy. Annabel & Cat. Mullen, Amy. 2017. (ENG.). 32p. (J). (gr. -1-1). pap. 9.99 *(978-1-5324-0180-0(9))* Xist Publishing.

—Annabel & Cat / Annabel y Gato. Mullen, Amy. 2018. (Xist Kids Bilingual Spanish English Ser.). (ENG & SPA.). 32p. (J). (gr. -1-3). pap. 9.99 *(978-1-5324-0621-8(5))* Xist Publishing.

—Annabel on the Go / Annabel Siempre en Movimiento. Mullen, Amy. 2018. (Xist Kids Bilingual Spanish English Ser.). (ENG & SPA.). 32p. (J). (gr. -1-3). pap. 9.99 *(978-1-5324-0086-5(1))* Xist Publishing.

—Annabel Siempre en Movimiento. Mullen, Amy. 2018. (Xist Kids Spanish Bks.). (SPA.). 32p. (J). (gr. -1-3). pap. 9.99 *(978-1-5324-0108-4(6))* Xist Publishing.

—Annabel y Gato. Mullen, Amy. 2018. (Xist Kids Spanish Bks.). (SPA.). 32p. (J). (gr. -1-3). pap. 9.99 *(978-1-5324-0699-7(1))* Xist Publishing.

—Tongue Twisters. Mullen, Amy. 2018. (ENG.). 32p. (J). (gr. -1-3). pap. 9.99 *(978-1-5324-0824-3(2))* Xist Publishing.

Mullen, Tina. 1, 2, 3 Team! Gardner, Susie. 2016. 32p. (J). 16.00 *(978-0-88146-590-7(9))* Mercer Univ. Pr.

Mullens, Tanya. The Black Fire Chronicles: Guardians 1 - Dorothy the Dreamer. Rigby, Kim. 2019. (Black Fire Chronicles Kids Fantasy Book Ser.: Vol. 4). (ENG.). 204p. (J). pap. 8.19 ***(978-1-7130-8301-6(9))*** Independently Published.

Muller, Cristina. Claudia y Daniel. Strepponi, Blanca. 2004. (SPA.). 28p. (J). pap. 7.99 *(978-980-257-268-7(3))* Ekare, Ediciones VEN. Dist: Lectorum Pubns., Inc.

Muller, Daniel. Knights of the Castle. Linke, Uwe. 2008. 24p. (J). (gr. -1-3). bds. 11.95 *(978-0-7358-2201-6(8))* North-South Bks., Inc.

—Two Birthdays. Thorup, Bryce. 2005. (J). 18.95 *(978-0-9765964-0-0(7))* Round Tower Pr.

Muller, Helene. Mary's Little Donkey, 30 vols. Sehlin, Gunhild. 2016. (ENG.). 32p. (J). 17.95 *(978-1-78250-294-4(7))* Floris Bks. GBR. Dist: Consortium Bk. Sales & Distribution.

—The Snow Girl, 40 vols. Giraud, Robert. 2014. Orig. Title: La Fille de Neige. (ENG.). 32p. (J). 17.95 *(978-1-78250-132-9(0))* Floris Bks. GBR. Dist: Consortium Bk. Sales & Distribution.

Müller, Hildegard. The Cowboy. Maccarone, Grace. 2015. (I Like to Read Ser.). (ENG.). 24p. (J). (gr. -1-3). 14.95 *(978-0-8234-3202-8(5))* Holiday Hse., Inc.

Müller, Hildegard. The Cowboy. Müller, Hildegard. 2015. (I Like to Read Ser.). (ENG.). 24p. (J). (gr. -1-3). 7.99 *(978-0-8234-3316-2(1))* Holiday Hse., Inc.

Muller, Ruth. Doctor Matthews' Family Christmas. Thorup, Bryce. 2005. (J). 18.95 *(978-0-9765964-1-7(5))* Round Tower Pr.

Mullerova, Lucie. Un Loro en Mi Granja. Bruno, Pep. 2009. (SPA.). 32p. (J). (gr. 1-3). *(978-84-263-7341-0(0))* Vives, Luis Editorial (Edelvives).

Müllerová, Lucie. Ojos de Lobo. Sobrino, Javier. 2018. (Baby Thule Ser.). (SPA.). 30p. (J). (— 1). 12.00 *(978-84-16817-03-0(0))* Thule Ediciones, S. L. ESP. Dist: Independent Pubs. Group.

—¡Tachán, Tachán! Sobrino, Javier. 2018. (Baby Thule Ser.). (SPA.). 30p. (J). (— 1). 12.00 *(978-84-16817-02-3(2))*

Thule Ediciones, S. L. ESP. Dist: Independent Pubs. Group.

Mulles, Jessica. Hopeful Henry: Linda Mason's. Mason, Linda C. Mason, Nona, ed. 2017. (Spirit of Truth Storybook Ser.: Vol. 8). (ENG.). 40p. (J). pap. 9.75 *(978-1-5356-0886-2(2))* Lulu Pr., Inc.

—Jumping Josey: Book # 10. Mason, Linda C. Mason, Nona J., ed. 2018. (Spirit of Truth Storybook Ser.: Vol. 10). (ENG.). 36p. (J). pap. 9.75 *(978-1-5356-1560-0(5))* Lulu Pr., Inc.

—Spirit of Truth Storybooks A-F: Editor's Edition #1 Full Color Mini. Mason, Linda C. Mason, Nona J., ed. 2019. (Spirit of Truth Storybooks 1-6 Ser.: Vol. 1). (ENG.). 138p. (J). pap. 26.75 *(978-1-7990-7954-5(6))* Independently Published.

—Ungrateful Ursula Second Edition: Book # 21. Mason, Linda C. Mason, Nona J., ed. 2018. (Spirit of Truth Storybook Series from a Through Z Ser.: Vol. 21). (ENG.). 54p. (J). pap. 11.95 *(978-1-7249-1749-2(8))* CreateSpace Independent Publishing Platform.

—Valiant Vivica - Zealous Zeporah Book 6: A Spirit of Truth Coloring Book #6. Mason, Linda. 2019. (Spirit of Truth Coloring Book Ser.: Vol. 6). (ENG.). 136p. (J). pap. 7.45 *(978-1-0714-0736-3(8))* Independently Published.

—Within My Reach: An in Hgp Book # 3. Mason, Linda C. Mason, Nona J., ed. 2018. (In His Grace Project Ser.: Vol. 3). (ENG.). 182p. (J). pap. 9.95 *(978-1-5323-7136-3(5))* Independent Pub.

—X-Con Xavier Second Edition: Book # 24. Mason, Linda C. Mason, Nona J., ed. 2018. (Spirit of Truth Storybook Series from a Through Z Ser.: Vol. 24). (ENG.). 44p. (J). pap. 10.75 *(978-1-7249-1781-2(1))* CreateSpace Independent Publishing Platform.

—Yearning Yolanda Second Edition: Book # 25. Mason, Linda C. Mason, Nona J., ed. 2018. (Spirit of Truth Storybook Series from A-Z Ser.: Vol. 25). (ENG.). 50p. (J). pap. 11.75 *(978-1-7249-1793-5(5))* CreateSpace Independent Publishing Platform.

Mullett, Viv. The Case of the Cat with the Missing Ear: From the Notebooks of Edward R. Smithfield D. V. M. Emerson, Scott. 2011. (Adventures of Samuel Blackthorne Ser.: 1). (ENG.). 240p. (J). (gr. 3-7). pap. 11.99 *(978-0-689-87615-8(7)*, Simon & Schuster Bks. For Young Readers) Simon & Schuster Bks. For Young Readers.

Mulligan, Todd. The Story Behind Santa Sacks. Moore, Brian L. 2004. 32p. *(978-0-9732651-0-1(8))* Hills-n-Hollows Publishing.

Mullin, John E. ABC'z. Mullin, John E. 2019. (ENG.). 58p. (J). (gr. k-1). 17.99 *(978-1-7321442-2-4(2))* JM Studio.

Mullock, Emily. Wenda the Wacky Wiggler. Aslan, Christopher. 2016. (ENG.). 34p. (J). pap. *(978-0-9921654-1-3(5))* Aslan Studios Inc.

Mulock, Julian. Bees. Hodge, Deborah. 2004. (Denver Museum of Nature & Science Bks.). (ENG.). 32p. (J). (gr. k-3). 5.95 *(978-1-55337-656-9(0))* Kids Can Pr., Ltd. CAN. Dist: Hachette Bk. Group.

Mulryan, Doreen. Halloween. Morey, Allan. 2017. (Holidays in Rhythm & Rhyme Ser.). (ENG.). 24p. (J). (gr. -1-3). lib. bdg. 33.99 incl. audio compact disk *(978-1-68410-031-6(3)*, 31519) Cantata Learning.

Mulryan, Doreen, jt. illus. see Marts, Doreen.

Mulvaney, Cynthia. A Party in the Mountains: The Story of Kasha & Katuwe. Shaffer, Gayle. 2018. (ENG.). 26p. (J). pap. 9.50 *(978-1-7907-0480-4(4))* Independently Published.

Mulyasari, Winda. The Goat on a Boat: If You Are Shy Give It a Try - Coloring Book. Kendal, Mary Lee. 2018. (ENG.). 26p. (J). pap. 5.99 *(978-1-7909-7470-2(4))* Independently Published.

—A Pig in a Wig: An Anti Bullying Coloring Book for Kids. Kendal, Mary Lee. 2018. (ENG.). 28p. (J). pap. 5.99 *(978-1-7904-9171-1(1))* Independently Published.

Mulyasari, Winda. Rolling Through Life with Mommy. Grzyb, TaLisha. 2019. (ENG.). 28p. (J). (gr. k-2). 17.99 ***(978-0-578-55018-3(0))*** Rolling Through Life With TaLisha.

Mulyasari, Winda. What Christmas Means to Me at the Angel Oak Tree - Coloring Book: A Story of Family, Friends, Giving & Love. Kendal, Mary Lee. 2018. (ENG.). 40p. (J). pap. 5.99 *(978-1-7902-9633-0(1))* Independently Published.

—Why Can't I Have a Cell Phone Yet? Coloring Book. Kendal, Mary Lee. 2018. (ENG.). 34p. (J). pap. 5.99 *(978-1-7909-6676-9(0))* Independently Published.

Mumper-Drumm, Heidrun. A Web of Good Manners - Grown-up Manners for Young People. Hillings, Phyllis & Hillings, Pamela. (J). 19.95 *(978-0-9725364-1-7(8))* Perrin & Kabel Publishing.

Munasinghe, Gayanjali. Love the Skin You're In. Hardrick, Joseline J. 2020. (ENG.). 40p. (J). pap. 12.99 ***(978-1-6737-1797-6(7))*** Independently Published.

Muncaster, Harriet. Happy Halloween, Witch's Cat! Muncaster, Harriet. 2015. (ENG.). 32p. (J). (gr. -1-3). 15.99 *(978-0-06-222916-8(8))* HarperCollins Pubs.

—I Am a Witch's Cat. Muncaster, Harriet. 2014. (ENG.). 32p. (J). (gr. -1-3). 15.99 *(978-0-06-222914-4(1))* HarperCollins Pubs.

Mundie, Ken. Two Fires in the Night: The Third Part of the Crazy Horse Chronicles. Jepperson, Richard. 2003. viii, 56p. (YA). (gr. 7-12). 16.95 *(978-0-9672012-2-1(5))* String of Beads Pubns.

Mundt, A. M. Le Ballon Est Condamne. Eyton, Christopher. Daigneault, Patricia, tr. 2017. (FRE.). (J). pap. *(978-0-9938273-2-7(2))* Syniad Hse.

Mundy, Jen. Lily's Little Life Lessons: Lily's Laces. Coniglio, Rebecca Perlman. 2013. (ENG.). 24p. (J). (gr. -1-3). 14.95 *(978-1-62086-408-1(8))* Mascot Bks., Inc.

—Mommy, Mommy! Is This for Me? Connolly, Megan B. 2013. (ENG.). (J). 14.95 *(978-1-62086-356-5(1))* Mascot Bks., Inc.

—N Is for Nepal. Adhikary, Anita. 2011. (J). 14.95 *(978-1-936319-52-7(7))* Mascot Bks., Inc.

Munger, Nancy, et al. Best-Loved Christmas Stories. Olive, Teresa et al. 2014. (ENG.). 102p. (J). 9.99 *(978-0-7586-4661-3(5))* Concordia Publishing Hse.

Munger, Nancy. Bethlehem Town: Where Jesus Was Born. Hoffman, Patricia. 2003. 32p. (J). 9.49 *(978-0-7586-0412-5(2))* Concordia Publishing Hse.

—David & Goliath: A Story about Trusting in God: Based on 1 Samuel 17:1/50. Pingry, Patricia A. 2005. (Children of the Bible Ser.). (ENG.). 23p. (J). bds. 6.95 *(978-0-8249-6570-9(1)*, Ideal Pubns.) Worthy Publishing.

—God Said & Moses Led. Holder, Jennifer. 2014. (Happy Day Ser.). (ENG.). 16p. (J). pap. 2.49 *(978-1-4143-9483-1(7)*, 4608473) Tyndale Hse. Pubs.

—Jesus in the Temple: Based on Luke 2:40/52. Pingry, Patricia A. 2008. (ENG.). 26p. (J). bds. 6.95 *(978-0-8249-6569-3(8)*, Ideal Pubns.) Worthy Publishing.

—Little Visits for Toddlers. Simon, Mary Manz. 3rd ed. 2006. (Little Visits Ser.). Orig. Title: Little Visits 1-2-3. 275p. (J). (gr. -1-3). per. 13.49 *(978-0-7586-0845-1(4))* Concordia Publishing Hse.

—My Story of Jesus. Holder, Jennifer. 2014. (Happy Day Ser.). (ENG.). 16p. (J). pap. 2.49 *(978-1-4143-9325-4(3)*, 4608315) Tyndale Hse. Pubs.

—The Parable of the Lily, 1 vol. Higgs, Liz Curtis. 10th anniv. ed. 2007. (Parable Ser.). (ENG.). 32p. (gr. -1-2). 7.99 *(978-1-4003-0844-6(5))* Nelson, Thomas Inc.

—La Parabola del Lirio. Higgs, Liz Curtis. 2005.Tr. of Parable of the Lily. 32p. (J). (gr. -1-3). pap. 5.99 *(978-0-8254-1327-8(3))* Kregel Pubns.

—The Sunflower Parable, 1 vol. Higgs, Liz Curtis. 10th anniv. ed. 2007. (Parable Ser.). (ENG.). 32p. (gr. -1-2). 7.99 *(978-1-4003-0845-3(3))* Nelson, Thomas Inc.

—Why I Trust You, God. Adams, Michelle Medlock. 2006. 20p. (J). (gr. -1). bds. 5.49 *(978-0-7586-0913-7(2))* Concordia Publishing Hse.

Municio-Planas, Jordi, et al. Disney Princess: Dream Big, Princess. 2017. (Me Reader Ser.). (ENG.). 192p. (J). *(978-1-5037-1695-7(3)*, 2df1114f-9a53-4a55-89c7-d3030e0b8dca, p i kids) Phoenix International Publications, Inc.

Muniz, Bere. Strange Boarders. Terrell, Brandon. 2018. (Jake Maddox Graphic Novels Ser.). (ENG.). 72p. (J). (gr. 3-8). pap. 6.95 *(978-1-4965-6050-6(7)*, 137431, Stone Arch Bks.) Capstone.

—Strange Boarders. Maddox, Jake. 2018. (Jake Maddox Graphic Novels Ser.). (ENG.). 72p. (J). (gr. 3-8). lib. bdg. 26.65 *(978-1-4965-6046-9(9)*, 137427, Stone Arch Bks.) Capstone.

Muñiz, Bere. Vuelta Al Juego. Maddox, Jake. 2019. (Jake Maddox Novelas Gráficas Ser.). (SPA.). 72p. (J). (gr. 3-8). pap. 6.95 *(978-1-4965-8587-5(9)*, 141328); lib. bdg. 26.65 *(978-1-4965-8574-5(7)*, 141311) Capstone. (Stone Arch Bks.).

Muniz, Berenice. Basketball Camp Champ. Maddox, Jake. 2020. (Jake Maddox Graphic Novels Ser.). (ENG.). 72p. (J). (gr. 3-8). pap. 6.95 *(978-1-4965-8454-0(6)*, 140979); lib. bdg. 26.65 *(978-1-4965-8375-8(2)*, 140674) Capstone. (Stone Arch Bks.).

—Comeback Catcher. Maddox, Jake. 2017. (Jake Maddox Graphic Novels Ser.). (ENG.). 72p. (J). (gr. 3-8). lib. bdg. 26.65 *(978-1-4965-3700-3(9)*, Stone Arch Bks.) Capstone.

—Half-Pipe Panic. Maddox, Jake. 2018. (Jake Maddox Graphic Novels Ser.). (ENG.). 72p. (J). (gr. 3-8). lib. bdg. 26.65 *(978-1-4965-6044-5(2)*, 137425, Stone Arch Bks.) Capstone.

—Johnny Slimeseed & the Freaky Forest: A Graphic Novel. Peters, Stephanie True. 2019. (Far Out Folktales Ser.). (ENG.). 40p. (J). (gr. 3-6). lib. bdg. 25.32 *(978-1-4965-7843-3(0)*, 139309, Stone Arch Bks.) Capstone.

—Pánico en la Pista. Maddox, Jake. 2020. (Jake Maddox Novelas Gráficas Ser.).Tr. of Half-Pipe Panic. (SPA.). 72p. (J). (gr. 3-8). pap. 6.95 *(978-1-4965-9312-2(X)*, 142342); lib. bdg. 26.65 *(978-1-4965-9177-7(1)*, 142085) Capstone. (Stone Arch Bks.).

—Skaters Feroces. Maddox, Jake. 2020. (Jake Maddox Novelas Gráficas Ser.).Tr. of Strange Boarders. (SPA.). 72p. (J). (gr. 3-8). pap. 6.95 *(978-1-4965-9314-6(6)*, 142344); lib. bdg. 26.65 *(978-1-4965-9179-1(8)*, 142088) Capstone. (Stone Arch Bks.).

Muniz, Berenice. A Taste for Victory. Maddox, Jake. 2020. (Jake Maddox Graphic Novels Ser.). (ENG.). 72p. (J). (gr. 3-6). pap. 6.95 ***(978-1-4965-9924-7(1)***, 201335); lib. bdg. 26.65 ***(978-1-4965-9714-4(1)***, 199337) Capstone. (Stone Arch Bks.).

Muniz, Jim. Divine Time, Vol. 3. Aguirre-Sacasa, Roberto. 2005. (Marvel Knights 4 Ser.). 144p. (YA). pap. 14.99 *(978-0-7851-1678-3(8))* Marvel Worldwide, Inc.

Muñoz, Claudio. !Bravo, Rosina! Thomas, Maria Jose & Thomas, María José. 2005. (SPA.). 48p. (J). (gr. -1-5). 10.40 *(978-980-257-242-7(X)*, EK33833) Ekare, Ediciones VEN. Dist: Lectorum Pubns., Inc.

—Captain & Matey Set Sail. Laurence, Daniel. 2003. (I Can Read Bks.). 64p. (gr. 1-3). 15.00 *(978-0-7569-1402-8(7))* Perfection Learning Corp.

—Just Another Morning. Ashman, Linda. 2004. (ENG.). 32p. (J). (gr. -1-3). 15.99 *(978-0-06-029053-5(6))* HarperCollins Pubs.

Munoz, Claudio. Tia Isa Quiere un Carro. Medina, Meg. 2012.Tr. of Tia Isa Wants a Car. (SPA.). 32p. (J). (gr. -1-2). pap. 6.99 *(978-0-7636-5751-2(4))* Candlewick Pr.

Muñoz, Claudio. Tia Isa Wants a Car. Medina, Meg. 2011. 32p. (J). (gr. -1-2). 16.99 *(978-0-7636-4156-6(1))* Candlewick Pr.

Munoz, Claudio. Tia Isa Wants a Car. Medina, Meg. 2016. 32p. (J). (gr. -1-2). 6.99 *(978-0-7636-5752-9(2))* Candlewick Pr.

Muñoz, Isabel. Adventures to School: Real-Life Journeys of Students from Around the World. Paul, Miranda & Paul, Baptiste. 2018. (ENG.). 40p. (J). (gr. -1-3). 17.99 *(978-1-4998-0665-6(5))* Little Bee Books Inc.

Munoz, Isabel. Albert Einstein. 2019. (Genius Ser.). (ENG.). 42p. (J). (gr. 1). 9.95 *(978-88-544-1337-5(2))* White Star ITA. Dist: Sterling Publishing Co., Inc.

Muñoz, Isabel. Alice in Wonderland. Carroll, Lewis. 2018. (Seek & Find Classics Ser.). (ENG.). 48p. (J). (gr. 2). 9.99 *(978-1-4998-0684-7(1)*, BuzzPop) Little Bee Books Inc.

Munoz, Isabel. Amazing Women: Sticker Scenes. Egmont Publishing UK. 2020. (ENG.). 32p. (J). (gr. k-2). pap. 9.99 ***(978-1-4052-9468-3(X)***, Red Shed) Egmont Bks., Ltd. GBR. Dist: Independent Pubs. Group.

Munoz, Isabel. Buttercup the Bigfoot. Rees, Douglas. 2020. (ENG.). 40p. (J). 18.99 *(978-1-250-20934-4(X)*, 900203221, Holt, Henry & Co. Bks. For Young Readers) Holt, Henry & Co.

—Ella Fitzgerald. 2020. (Genius Ser.). (ENG.). 42p. (J). (gr. 1). 9.95 *(978-88-544-1622-2(3))* White Star ITA. Dist: Sterling Publishing Co., Inc.

—Frida Kahlo. 2019. (Genius Ser.). (ENG.). 42p. (J). (gr. 1). 9.95 *(978-88-544-1360-3(7))* White Star ITA. Dist: Sterling Publishing Co., Inc.

Muñoz, Isabel. It's Not Fair! A Book about Having Enough, Vol. Rivadeneira, Caryn. 2018. (ENG.). 32p. (J). 14.99 *(978-1-5064-4680-6(9)*, Beaming Books) Augsburg Fortress, Pubs.

Munoz, Isabel. Leonardo Da Vinci. 2019. (Genius Ser.). (ENG.). 42p. (J). (gr. 1). 9.95 *(978-88-544-1332-0(1))* White Star ITA. Dist: Sterling Publishing Co., Inc.

—Louis Pasteur. 2020. (Genius Ser.). (ENG.). 42p. (J). (gr. 1). 9.95 *(978-88-544-1621-5(5))* White Star ITA. Dist: Sterling Publishing Co., Inc.

—Marie Curie. 2019. (Genius Ser.). (ENG.). 42p. (J). (gr. 1). 9.95 *(978-88-544-1361-0(5))* White Star ITA. Dist: Sterling Publishing Co., Inc.

—The Milkmaid & Her Pail. Hoena, Blake. 2018. (Classic Fables in Rhythm & Rhyme Ser.). (ENG.). 24p. (C). (gr. k-2). lib. bdg. 33.99 *(978-1-68410-387-4(8)*, 140367) Cantata Learning.

—Stephen Hawking. 2019. (Genius Ser.). (ENG.). 42p. (J). (gr. 1). 9.95 *(978-88-544-1362-7(3))* White Star ITA. Dist: Sterling Publishing Co., Inc.

—Wolfgang Amadeus Mozart. 2019. (Genius Ser.). (ENG.). 42p. (J). (gr. 1). 9.95 *(978-88-544-1336-8(4))* White Star ITA. Dist: Sterling Publishing Co., Inc.

Muñoz, Isabel, jt. illus. see Wright, Louise.

Munoz, Julian. Arbor Street Buddies: Carnival Days, Campout, the Great July 4th Block Party. Frenes, Genevieve. Collins, Lorna, ed. 2020. (Arbor Street Buddies Ser.: Vol. 1). (ENG.). 64p. (J). pap. 14.99 ***(978-1-7207-5145-8(5))*** CreateSpace Independent Publishing Platform.

Munoz, Lera. Leia & Theo Play Hide & Seek. Egger, Daniel. 2019. (ENG.). 26p. (J). pap. ***(978-3-9504270-1-1(5))*** Egger, Daniel.

—Mari e T�o Brincam de Esconde-Esconde. Egger, Daniel. 2019. (POR.). 26p. (J). pap. ***(978-3-9504270-8-0(2))*** Egger, Daniel.

—Mari e Teo Giocano a Nascondino. Egger, Daniel. 2019. (ITA.). 22p. (J). ***(978-3-9504270-6-6(6))*** Egger, Daniel.

—Mari y Teo Juegan Al Escondite. Egger, Daniel. Pereira, Eliana, ed. 2019. (SPA.). 26p. (J). ***(978-3-9504270-3-5(1))*** Egger, Daniel.

—レイアとテオの Egger, Daniel. 2019. (JPN.). 22p. (J). pap. ***(978-3-9504270-4-2(X))*** Egger, Daniel.

—莱娅与西奥玩捉$ Egger, Daniel. 2019. (CHI.). 22p. (J). pap. ***(978-3-9504270-9-7(0))*** Egger, Daniel.

Munoz, Olga M. Opposites Are Fun. Milne, Barbara L. W. I.t. ed. 2005. 40p. (J). 19.95 *(978-0-9708796-0-8(1)*, TLConcepts, Inc.) Tender Learning Concepts.

Munoz, Rie. Goodbye, My Island. Rogers, Jean. 2015. (ENG.). 96p. (YA). (gr. 7-9). 21.99 *(978-1-943328-15-4(3)*, Alaska Northwest Bks.) West Margin Pr.

Muñoz, William. Call of the Osprey. Patent, Dorothy Hinshaw. 2020. (Scientists in the Field Ser.). (ENG.). 80p. (J). (gr. 5-7). pap. 9.99 *(978-0-358-10547-3(1)*, 1748671, HMH Books For Young Readers) Houghton Mifflin Harcourt Publishing Co.

Munoz, William. Dog on Board: The True Story of Eclipse, the Bus-Riding Dog. Patent, Dorothy Hinshaw & Young, Jeffrey. 2016. 40p. (J). (gr. -1-3). 16.99 *(978-0-399-54988-5(9)*, Crown Books For Young Readers) Random Hse. Children's Bks.

Muñoz, William. The Call of the Osprey. Muñoz, William, photos by. Patent, Dorothy Hinshaw. 2015. (Scientists in the Field Ser.). (ENG.). 80p. (J). (gr. 5-7). 18.99 *(978-0-544-23268-6(2)*, 1564093, HMH Books For Young Readers) Houghton Mifflin Harcourt Publishing Co.

—Life in a Desert. Muñoz, William, photos by. Patent, Dorothy Hinshaw. 2003. (Ecosystems in Action Ser.). (ENG.). 72p. (gr. 5-9). 26.60 *(978-0-8225-2140-2(7))* Lerner Publishing Group.

Munoz, William, photos by. Homesteading: Settling America's Heartland. Patent, Dorothy Hinshaw. 2013. 48p. (J). pap. 12.00 *(978-0-87842-605-8(1))* Mountain Pr. Publishing Co., Inc.

Muñoz, William, photos by. The Lewis & Clark Trail: Then & Now. Patent, Dorothy Hinshaw. 2006. 60p. (J). (gr. 4-8). reprint ed. 20.00 *(978-1-4223-5732-3(5))* DIANE Publishing Co.

Munoz, William, photos by. Made for Each Other: Why Dogs & People Are Perfect Partners. Patent, Dorothy Hinshaw. 2018. 64p. (J). (gr. 1-4). 17.99 *(978-1-101-93104-2(3)*, Crown Books For Young Readers) Random Hse. Children's Bks.

—Made for Each Other: Why Dogs & People Are Perfect Partners. Patent, Dorothy Hinshaw. 2018. (ENG., 64p. (J). (gr. 1-4). lib. bdg. 20.99 *(978-1-101-93105-9(1)*, Crown Books For Young Readers) Random Hse. Children's Bks.

Munro, Roxie. Crocodiles, Camels & Dugout Canoes: Eight Adventurous Episodes. Zaunders, Bo. 2006. 48p. (J). (gr. 4-8). reprint ed. 17.00 *(978-1-4223-5397-4(4))* DIANE Publishing Co.

—The Great Bridge-Building Contest. Zaunders, Bo. 2006. 30p. (J). (gr. 4-8). reprint ed. 17.00 *(978-1-4223-5239-7(0))* DIANE Publishing Co.

Munro, Roxie. Busy Builders, 0 vols. Munro, Roxie. 2012. (ENG.). 40p. (J). (gr. 1-6). 17.99 *(978-0-7614-6105-0(1)*, 9780761461050, Two Lions) Amazon Publishing.

—The Inside-Outside Book of New York City. Munro, Roxie. 2005. 44p. (J). (gr. 4-8). reprint ed. 16.00 *(978-0-7567-9455-2(2))* DIANE Publishing Co.

Munroe, Norman, photos by. Louisbourg: A Living History Colourguide. Biagi, Susan & Young de Biagi, Susan. 2006. (Illustrated Site Guide Ser.). (ENG., 72p. pap. 10.95 *(978-0-88780-362-8(8))* Formac Publishing Co., Ltd. CAN. Dist: Casemate Pubs. & Bk. Distributors, LLC.

Munsawami, Jennifer. The Third Eye. Maldonado, L. A. Barselow, Todd, ed. 2019. (ENG.). 222p. (J). pap. 9.99 ***(978-1-6990-1862-0(6))*** Independently Published.

Munsawmi, Jennifer. Angelic. Maldonado, L. A. Scholl, Genevieve, ed. 2019. (ENG.). 232p. (J). pap. 9.99 *(978-1-5331-1618-5(0))* CreateSpace Independent Publishing Platform.

Munsinger, Lynn. Batter up Wombat. Lester, Helen. ed. 2006. (ENG.). 32p. (J). (gr. k-3). 24.80 *(978-1-4287-0160-1(5)*, Follettbound) Follett School Solutions.

—Beatrice Doesn't Want To. Numeroff, Laura. 2008. 32p. (J). (gr. -1-2). pap. 7.99 *(978-0-7636-3843-6(9))* Candlewick Pr.

—Bunny Tails. Brenner, Barbara et al. 2005. 32p. 15.95 *(978-0-689-03925-6(5)*, Milk & Cookies) Ibooks, Inc.

—Dinosaurs in Disguise. Krensky, Stephen. 2016. (ENG.). 32p. (J). (gr. -1-3). 17.99 *(978-0-544-47271-6(3)*, 1601680, HMH Books For Young Readers) Houghton Mifflin Harcourt Publishing Co.

—Happy Birdday, Tacky! Lester, Helen. 2017. (Tacky the Penguin Ser.). (ENG.). 32p. (J). (gr. -1-3). pap. 7.99 *(978-1-328-74057-1(9)*, 1677031, HMH Books For Young Readers) Houghton Mifflin Harcourt Publishing Co.

—Hooway for Wodney Wat, 1 vol. Lester, Helen. 2011. (ENG.). 32p. (J). (gr. -1-3). 10.99 *(978-0-547-55217-0(3)*, 1450662) Houghton Mifflin Harcourt Publishing Co.

—Howliday Inn. Howe, James. 2006. 195p. (gr. 3-7). 16.00 *(978-0-7569-6807-6(0))* Perfection Learning Corp.

—Howliday Inn. Howe, James. 2nd ed. 2006. (Bunnicula & Friends Ser.). (ENG.). 224p. (J). (gr. 3-7). pap. 7.99 *(978-1-4169-2815-7(4)*, Atheneum Bks. for Young Readers) Simon & Schuster Children's Publishing.

—Hunter's Best Friend at School. Elliott, Laura Malone. 2005. (gr. -1-2). 17.00 *(978-0-7569-5786-5(9))* Perfection Learning Corp.

—Hunter's Best Friend at School. Elliott, Laura Malone. 2005. (ENG.). 32p. (J). (gr. -1-2). reprint ed. pap. 7.99 *(978-0-06-075319-1(6)*, Tegen, Katherine Bks) HarperCollins Pubs.

—Hurty Feelings. Lester, Helen. 2007. (Laugh-Along Lessons Ser.). (ENG.). 32p. (J). (gr. -1-3). 7.99 *(978-0-618-84062-5(1)*, 439864) Houghton Mifflin Harcourt Publishing Co.

—The Jellybeans & the Big Book Bonanza. Evans, Nate & Numeroff, Laura. 2010. (ENG.). 32p. (J). (gr. -1-3). 17.95 *(978-0-8109-8412-7(1)*, Abrams Bks. for Young Readers) Abrams, Inc.

—The Jellybeans & the Big Dance. Evans, Nate & Numeroff, Laura. 2008. (ENG.). 32p. (J). (gr. -1-1). 17.95 *(978-0-8109-9352-5(X)*, Abrams Bks. for Young Readers) Abrams, Inc.

—The Jellybeans Love to Dance. Evans, Nate & Numeroff, Laura. 2013. (ENG.). 24p. (J). (gr. -1 — 1). bds. 7.95 *(978-1-4197-0622-6(5)*, Abrams Appleseed) Abrams, Inc.

—Listen Buddy. Lester, Helen. 2008. (Laugh-Along Lessons Ser.). (ENG.). 32p. (gr. -1-3). pap. 7.99 *(978-0-395-85402-0(4)*, 489854) Perfection Learning Corp.

—Listen, Buddy. Lester, Helen. 2013. (Laugh-Along Lessons Ser.). (ENG.). 32p. (J). (gr. -1-3). 8.99 *(978-0-544-00322-4(5)*, 1526364) Houghton Mifflin Harcourt Publishing Co.

—The Loch Mess Monster. Lester, Helen. 2014. (ENG.). 32p. (J). (gr. -1-3). 16.99 *(978-0-544-09990-6(7)*, 1539514, HMH Books For Young Readers) Houghton Mifflin Harcourt Publishing Co.

—Me First. Lester, Helen. 2013. (Laugh-Along Lessons Ser.). (ENG.). 32p. (J). (gr. -1-3). 8.99 *(978-0-544-00321-7(7)*, 1526363) Houghton Mifflin Harcourt Publishing Co.

—Miss Nelson Is Missing! Lester, Helen. 2015. 32p. pap. 7.00 *(978-1-61003-507-1(0))* Center for the Collaborative Classroom.

—La Mochila de Lin, Level 2. Lester, Helen. Flor Ada, Alma, tr. from ENG. 3rd ed. 2003. (Dejame Leer Ser.).Tr. of Lin's Backpack. (SPA.). 8p. (J). (gr. -1-1). 6.50 *(978-0-673-36291-9(4)*, Good Year Bks.) Celebration Pr.

—One Monkey Too Many. Koller, Jackie French. 2003. (ENG.). 32p. (J). (gr. -1-3). pap. 7.99 *(978-0-15-204764-1(6)*, 1194373) Houghton Mifflin Harcourt Publishing Co.

—A Porcupine Named Fluffy. Lester, Helen. 2013. (Laugh-Along Lessons Ser.). (ENG.). 32p. (J). (gr. -1-3). 8.99 *(978-0-544-00319-4(5)*, 1526352) Houghton Mifflin Harcourt Publishing Co.

—The Sheep in Wolf's Clothing. Lester, Helen. 2014. (Laugh-Along Lessons Ser.). (ENG.). 32p. (J). (gr. -1-3). 8.99 *(978-0-544-23300-3(X)*, 1563484, HMH Books For Young Readers) Houghton Mifflin Harcourt Publishing Co.

—A String of Hearts. Elliott, Laura Malone. 2010. (ENG.). 32p. (J). (gr. -1-2). 16.99 *(978-0-06-000085-1(6)*, Tegen, Katherine Bks) HarperCollins Pubs.

—Tacky & the Haunted Igloo. Lester, Helen. 2015. (Tacky the Penguin Ser.). (ENG.). 32p. (J). 17.99 *(978-0-544-33994-1(0)*, 1584695, HMH Books For Young Readers) Houghton Mifflin Harcourt Publishing Co.

—Tacky & the Winter Games. Lester, Helen. 2007. (Tacky the Penguin Ser.). (ENG.). 32p. (J). (gr. -1-3). 7.99 *(978-0-618-95674-6(3)*, 1021437) Houghton Mifflin Harcourt Publishing Co.

—Tacky in Trouble. Lester, Helen. 2005. (Tacky the Penguin Ser.). (ENG.). 32p. (J). (gr. -1-3). 7.99 *(978-0-618-38008-4(6)*, 489857) Houghton Mifflin Harcourt Publishing Co.

—Tacky the Penguin. Lester, Helen. (Tacky the Penguin Ser.). (ENG.). 32p. (J). (gr. -1-3). 2008. bds. 7.99 *(978-0-547-13344-7(8)*, 1048740); 2006. 10.99

(978-0-618-73754-3(5), 489199) Houghton Mifflin Harcourt Publishing Co.

—Tackylocks & the Three Bears. Lester, Helen. 2004. (Tacky the Penguin Ser.). (ENG.). 32p. (J). (gr. -1-3). pap. 7.99 *(978-0-618-43953-9(6)*, 439862, HMH Books For Young Readers) Houghton Mifflin Harcourt Publishing Co.

—The Teeny Tiny Ghost & the Monster, Vol. 3. Winters, Kay. 2004. (ENG.). 32p. (J). (gr. -1-3). 14.99 *(978-0-06-028884-6(1))* HarperCollins Pubs.

—Thanksgiving Day Thanks. Elliott, Laura Malone. 2013. (ENG.). 32p. (J). (gr. -1-3). 17.99 *(978-0-06-000236-7(0))* HarperCollins Pubs.

—What Aunts Do Best / What Uncles Do Best. Numeroff, Laura Joffe. 2004. (ENG.). 32p. (J). (gr. -1-3). 17.99 *(978-0-689-84825-4(0)*, Simon & Schuster Bks. For Young Readers) Simon & Schuster Bks. For Young Readers.

—What Brothers Do Best: (Big Brother Books for Kids, Brotherhood Books for Kids, Sibling Books for Kids) Numeroff, Laura. 2012. (ENG.). 20p. (J). (gr. -1 — 1). bds. 7.99 *(978-1-4521-1073-8(5))* Chronicle Bks. LLC.

Munsinger, Lynn. What Grandmas Do Best/What Grandpas Do Best. Numeroff, Laura Joffe. 2010. (CHI.). 36p. (J). (gr. -1-2). ***(978-986-211-136-9(4))*** Hsaio Lu Publishing Co., Ltd.

Munsinger, Lynn. What Sisters Do Best: (Big Sister Books for Kids, Sisterhood Books for Kids, Sibling Books for Kids) Numeroff, Laura. 2012. (ENG.). 20p. (J). (gr. -1 — 1). bds. 7.99 *(978-1-4521-1074-5(3))* Chronicle Bks. LLC.

—Wodney Wat's Wobot. Lester, Helen. 2011. (ENG.). 32p. (J). (gr. -1-3). 16.99 *(978-0-547-36756-9(2)*, 1422687) Houghton Mifflin Harcourt Publishing Co.

Munsinger, Lynn. Nighty-Night, Cooper. Munsinger, Lynn. Numeroff, Laura Joffe. 2013. (ENG.). 32p. (J). (gr. -1-3). 17.99 *(978-0-547-40205-5(8)*, 1427979) Houghton Mifflin Harcourt Publishing Co.

Munsinger, Lynn, jt. illus. see Lester, Helen.

Munson, Kayla. Night Night. 2013. (ENG.). 34p. (J). pap. 12.95 *(978-0-9821956-3-5(X))* Fleur De Lis Publishing, LLC.

Muntada, Anna Clariana. My First Color by Numbers & Shapes: Over 50 Fantastic Puzzles. Butterfield, Moira. 2018. (My First Activity Bks.). (ENG.). 64p. (J). (gr. -1-2). pap. 5.99 *(978-1-4380-1143-1(1)*, B.E.S. Publishing) Peterson's.

Munte Vidal, Marta. KUKU AND MWEWE: A SWAHILI FOLKTALE. Munte Vidal, Marta. Brokenbrow, Jon, tr. 2013. (ENG.). 30p. (J). (gr. -1-k). 16.95 *(978-84-15619-97-0(9))* Cuento de Luz SL ESP. Dist: Publishers Group West (PGW).

Munz, Casey "Naanaage Binesik". Sshtaa taa Haa! Oh No! 2004. (OJI & ENG.). 16p. (J). per. *(978-0-9758801-0-4(1))* Bay Mills Indian Community.

Muraida, Thelma. Cecilia & Miguel Are Best Friends. Bertrand, Diane Gonzales. Ventura, Gabriela Baeza, tr. 2014.Tr. of Cecilia y Miguel Son Mejores Amigos. (SPA & ENG.). 32p. (J). 17.95 *(978-1-55885-794-0(X))* Arte Publico Pr.

—Clara & the Curandera / Clara y la Curandera. Brown, Monica & Ventura, Gabriela Baeza. 2011. (J). 16.95 *(978-1-55885-700-1(1)*, Piñata Books) Arte Publico Pr.

—My Big Sister / Mi Hermana Mayor. Caraballo, Samuel. 2012. (ENG & SPA.). (J). (gr. 3-8). 16.95 *(978-1-55885-750-6(8)*, Piñata Books) Arte Publico Pr.

Muraida, Thelma. The Place Where You Live / el Lugar Donde Vives. Muraida, Thelma. Luna, James & Ventura, Gabriela Baeza. 2015. (SPA & ENG.). 32p. (J). (gr. k-3). 17.95 *(978-1-55885-813-8(X))* Arte Publico Pr.

Murakami, Jon. Geckos Go to Bed. BeachHouse Publishing. 2008. (ENG.). 24p. (J). (gr. -1-k). bds. 8.95 *(978-1-933067-26-1(8))* Beachhouse Publishing, LLC.

—Geckos Make a Rainbow. BeachHouse Publishing. 2010. (ENG.). 28p. (J). (gr. -1-1). bds. 8.95 *(978-1-933067-38-4(1))* Beachhouse Publishing, LLC.

Murakami, Maki. Gravitation, Vol. 12. Yoshimoto, Ray, tr. from JPN. rev. ed. 2005. 192p. pap. 9.99 *(978-1-59532-415-3(1))* TOKYOPOP, Inc.

Murakami, Maki. Gravitation, 12 vols. Murakami, Maki. rev. ed. Vol. 3. 2003. 192p. (gr. 8-18). pap. 9.99 *(978-1-59182-335-3(8))*; Vol. 4. 2004. 208p. (gr. 8-18). pap. 9.99 *(978-1-59182-336-0(6))*; Vol. 5. 2004. 208p. (gr. 8-18). pap. 9.99 *(978-1-59182-337-7(4))*; Vol. 10. 2005. 216p. pap. 9.99 *(978-1-59182-342-1(0))*; Vol. 11. 2005. 176p. pap. 9.99 *(978-1-59532-414-6(3))* TOKYOPOP, Inc.

Murakami, Yasanuri & Kimura, Ken. 999 Frogs & a Little Brother. 2015. (ENG.). 40p. (J). 17.95 *(978-0-7358-4202-1(7))* North-South Bks., Inc.

Muraki, Yasushi. Mom Loves Little Jumbo: Hello, I Am Jumbo. Muraki, Yasushi. 2019. (ENG.). 22p. (J). (gr. -1-k). bds. 9.99 *(978-988-8341-78-8(2)*, Minedition) Neugebauer, Michael (Publishing) Limited HKG. Dist: Penguin Random Hse. LLC.

Murali, Lekha. The Thirsty Crow & the Crow & the Fox: Children's Folk Tales from India. Murali, Lekha. 2nd ed. 2018. (ENG.). 26p. (J). (gr. k-1). 22.00 *(978-0-692-13010-0(1)*, Lekha Murali) Lekha Vippu.

—The Thirsty Crow & the Crow & the Fox: Children's Folk Tales from India. Murali, Lekha. 2nd ed. 2018. (ENG.). 26p. (J). (gr. k-1). pap. 12.00 *(978-1-7327053-0-2(5)*, Lekha Murali) Lekha Vippu.

Murariu, Lorraine. Peter Rabbit & My Tulips. Gulino, ViTina Corso. 2012. 26p. (J). pap. 9.95 *(978-1-61863-275-3(2))* Bookstand Publishing.

Murase, Sho. High School Musical Mystery II: The Lost Verse, 21. Petrucha, Stefan & Kinney, Sarah. 2010. (Nancy Drew Girl Detective Graphic Novels Ser.: 21). (ENG.). 96p. (J). (gr. 4-6). 22.44 *(978-1-59707-196-3(X))* Papercutz.

—Vampire Slayer, 2. Petrucha, Stefan & Kinney, Sarah. 2011. (Nancy Drew the New Case Files Graphic Novels Ser.: 2). (ENG.). 64p. (J). (gr. 5-8). 21.19 *(978-1-59707-234-2(6)*, 900073804) Papercutz.

—Writ in Stone, 2. Petrucha, Stefan. 2nd rev. ed. 2005. (Nancy Drew Girl Detective Graphic Novels Ser.: 2). (ENG.). 96p. (J). (gr. 4-6). 22.44 *(978-1-59707-006-5(8)*, 9781597070065) Papercutz.

Murata, Yusuke. Eyeshield 21, Vol. 1. Inagaki, Riichiro. 2005. (Eyeshield 21 Ser.: 1). (ENG.). 208p. (gr. 11-17). pap. 9.99 *(978-1-59116-752-5(3))* Viz Media.

—Eyeshield 21, Vol. 2. Inagaki, Riichiro. 2005. (Eyeshield 21 Ser.: 2). (ENG.). 208p. pap. 9.99 *(978-1-59116-809-6(0))* Viz Media.

—Eyeshield 21, Vol. 3. Inagaki, Riichiro. 2005. (Eyeshield 21 Ser.: 3). (ENG.). 200p. pap. 9.99 *(978-1-59116-874-4(0))* Viz Media.

—Eyeshield 21, Vol. 4. Inagaki, Riichiro. 2005. (Eyeshield 21 Ser.: 4). (ENG.). 200p. pap. 9.99 *(978-1-4215-0074-4(4))* Viz Media.

—Eyeshield 21, Vol. 5, Vol. 5. Inagaki, Riichiro. 2005. (Eyeshield 21 Ser.: 5). (ENG.). 200p. pap. 9.99 *(978-1-4215-0113-0(9))* Viz Media.

—Eyeshield 21, Vol. 6. Inagaki, Riichiro. 2006. (Eyeshield 21 Ser.: 6). (ENG.). 200p. pap. 9.99 *(978-1-4215-0274-8(7))* Viz Media.

—Eyeshield 21, Vol. 7, Vol. 7. Inagaki, Riichiro. 2006. (Eyeshield 21 Ser.: 7). (ENG.). 208p. pap. 9.99 *(978-1-4215-0405-6(7))* Viz Media.

Muravski, Marie. Claws of Rage: A Beastly Crimes Book (#3) Starobinets, Anna. Bugaeva, Jane, tr. 2019. (ENG.). 176p. (gr. 2-6). 16.99 *(978-0-486-82952-4(9)*, 829529) Dover Pubns., Inc.

—The Plucker: A Beastly Crimes Book (#4) Starobinets, Anna. Bugaeva, Jane, tr. 2019. (ENG.). 304p. (gr. 2-6). 16.99 *(978-0-486-82953-1(7)*, 829537) Dover Pubns., Inc.

Murawski, Darlyne A., photos by. Spiders & Their Webs. Murawski, Darlyne A. 2007. 31p. (J). reprint ed. 17.00 *(978-1-4223-6813-8(0))* DIANE Publishing Co.

Murawski, Kevin. Harold's Birthday Surprise: Harold & the Purple Crayon. Marsoli, Lisa Ann. 2005. 10p. (J). 6.95 *(978-1-58117-261-4(3)*, Intervisual/Piggy Toes) Bendon, Inc.

Murch, Frank. Jed Smith: Trail Blazer of the West. Latham, Frank. McHugh, Michael J., ed. 2003. 121p. pap. 6.95 *(978-1-930367-86-9(4))* Christian Liberty Pr.

Murchison, Leon, et al. Struggle for Freedom & Henry Box Brown: A Read along Book. Johnston, Brenda A. & Pruitt, Pamela. McCluskey, John A., ed. (Read-Along Bk.). 22p. (J). (gr. 2-4). reprint ed. pap. 4.00 incl. audio *(978-0-913678-16-9(3))* New Day Pr.

Murdocca, Sal. Abe Lincoln at Last! Osborne, Mary Pope. 2013. (Magic Tree House Merlin Missions Ser.: No. 19). (ENG.). (J). (gr. 2-5). lib. bdg. 15.60 *(978-1-62765-816-4(5))* Perfection Learning Corp.

—Abe Lincoln at Last! Osborne, Mary Pope. 2013. (Magic Tree House (R) Merlin Mission Ser.: 19). 144p. (J). (gr. 2-5). 5.99 *(978-0-375-86797-2(X)*, Random Hse. Bks. for Young Readers) Random Hse. Children's Bks.

—Abraham Lincoln: A Nonfiction Companion to Magic Tree House Merlin Mission #19: Abe Lincoln at Last. Osborne, Mary Pope & Boyce, Natalie Pope. 2011. (Magic Tree House (R) Fact Tracker Ser.: 25). 128p. (J). (gr. 2-5). 6.99 *(978-0-375-87024-8(5)*, Random Hse. Bks. for Young Readers) Random Hse. Children's Bks.

—Amazing Animals! Magic Tree House Fact Tracker Boxed Set: Dolphins & Sharks; Polar Bears & the Arctic; Penguins & Antarctica; Pandas & Other Endangered Species, 4 vols. Osborne, Mary Pope & Boyce, Natalie Pope. 2018. (Magic Tree House (R) Fact Tracker Ser.). 128p. (J). (gr. 2-5). 27.96 *(978-0-525-64538-2(1)*, Random Hse. Bks. for Young Readers) Random Hse. Children's Bks.

—American Revolution: A Nonfiction Companion to Magic Tree House #22: Revolutionary War on Wednesday. Osborne, Mary Pope & Boyce, Natalie Pope. 2004. (Magic Tree House (R) Fact Tracker Ser.: 11). 128p. (J). (gr. 2-5). pap. 6.99 *(978-0-375-82379-4(4)*, Random Hse. Bks. for Young Readers) Random Hse. Children's Bks.

—Ancient Rome & Pompeii: Magic Tree House Fact Tracker. Osborne, Mary Pope & Boyce, Natalie Pope. 2006. (Magic Tree House (R) Fact Tracker Ser.: 14). 128p. (J). (gr. 2-5). 6.99 *(978-0-375-83220-8(3)*, Random Hse. Bks. for Young Readers) Random Hse. Children's Bks.

—Animal Games & Puzzles. Osborne, Mary Pope & Boyce, Natalie Pope. 2015. (Magic Tree House (R) Ser.). 266p. (J). (gr. 2-5). 6.99 *(978-0-553-50840-6(7)*, Random Hse. Bks. for Young Readers) Random Hse. Children's Bks.

—Balto of the Blue Dawn. Osborne, Mary Pope. 128p. (J). (gr. 2-5). 2017. (Magic Tree House (R) Merlin Mission Ser.: 26). 5.99 *(978-0-553-51088-1(6))*; 2016. (Magic Tree House Merlin Missions Ser.: No. 26). 13.99 *(978-0-553-51085-0(1))* Random Hse. Children's Bks. (Random Hse. Bks. for Young Readers).

—Barcos Vikingos Al Amanecer. Osborne, Mary Pope. Brovelli, Marcela, tr. from ENG. 2007. (Casa del Arbol Ser.: 15). (SPA.). 73p. (J). per. 6.99 *(978-1-933032-21-4(9))* Lectorum Pubns., Inc.

—A Big Day for Baseball. Osborne, Mary Pope. 2017. (Magic Tree House (R) Ser.: 29). (ENG.). 96p. (J). (gr. 1-4). lib. bdg. 16.99 *(978-1-5247-1309-6(0)*, Random Hse. Bks. for Young Readers) Random Hse. Children's Bks.

—Blizzard of the Blue Moon. Osborne, Mary Pope. 2007. (Magic Tree House Merlin Missions Ser.: No. 8). (ENG.). (J). (gr. 1-4). lib. bdg. 15.60 *(978-1-62765-890-4(4))* Perfection Learning Corp.

—Blizzard of the Blue Moon. Osborne, Mary Pope. 2007. (Magic Tree House (R) Merlin Mission Ser.: 8). 144p. (J). (gr. 2-5). 5.99 *(978-0-375-83038-9(3)*, Random Hse. Bks. for Young Readers) Random Hse. Children's Bks.

—Carnival at Candlelight. Osborne, Mary Pope & PLC Editors Staff. 2006. (Magic Tree House Merlin Missions Ser.: No. 5). 105p. (gr. 2-6). 15.00 *(978-0-7569-6690-4(6))* Perfection Learning Corp.

—Carnival at Candlelight, Vol. 5. Osborne, Mary Pope. 2006. (Magic Tree House (R) Merlin Mission Ser.: 5). 144p. (J). (gr. 2-5). 5.99 *(978-0-375-83034-1(0)*, Random Hse. Bks. for Young Readers) Random Hse. Children's Bks.

—The Case of the Dirty Clue. Stanley, George Edward. 2005. (Ready-for-Chapters Ser.). (J). lib. bdg. 15.00 *(978-1-59054-898-1(1))* Fitzgerald Bks.

—Christmas in Camelot. Osborne, Mary Pope. 2009. (Magic Tree House (R) Merlin Mission Ser.: 1). (ENG.). 144p. (J). (gr. 2-5). 5.99 *(978-0-375-85812-3(1)*, Random Hse. Bks. for Young Readers) Random Hse. Children's Bks.

—A Crazy Day with Cobras. Osborne, Mary Pope. (Magic Tree House (R) Merlin Mission Ser.: 17). 128p. (J). (gr. 2-5). 2012. 5.99 *(978-0-375-86795-8(3))*; 2011. (ENG.). 12.99 *(978-0-375-86823-8(2))* Random Hse. Children's Bks. (Random Hse. Bks. for Young Readers).

—Dancing Granny, 1 vol. Winthrop, Elizabeth. 2003. (ENG.). 32p. (J). 16.95 *(978-0-7614-5141-9(2))* Marshall Cavendish Corp.

—Danger in the Darkest Hour. Osborne, Mary Pope. 2015. (Stepping Stone Book Ser.: No. 1). 192p. (J). (gr. 2-5). 14.99 *(978-0-553-49772-4(3)*, Random Hse. Bks. for Young Readers) Random Hse. Children's Bks.

—Dark Day in the Deep Sea. Osborne, Mary Pope. 2009. (Magic Tree House (R) Merlin Mission Ser.: 11). 144p. (J). (gr. 2-5). 5.99 *(978-0-375-83732-6(9)*, Random Hse. Bks. for Young Readers) Random Hse. Children's Bks.

—Dinosaurs: A Nonfiction Companion to Dinosaurs Before Dark. Osborne, Will & Osborne, Mary Pope. 2004. (Magic Tree House Research Guides: No. 1). 119p. 16.00 *(978-0-7569-2209-2(7))* Perfection Learning Corp.

—Dog Heroes: Magic Tree House Fact Tracker. Osborne, Mary Pope & Boyce, Natalie Pope. 2011. (Magic Tree House (R) Fact Tracker Ser.: 24). 128p. (J). (gr. 2-5). 6.99 *(978-0-375-86012-6(6)*, Random Hse. Bks. for Young Readers) Random Hse. Children's Bks.

—Dogs in the Dead of Night, Bk. 18. Osborne, Mary Pope. 2013. (Magic Tree House (R) Merlin Mission Ser.: 18). 144p. (J). (gr. 2-5). 5.99 *(978-0-375-86796-5(1)*, Random Hse. Bks. for Young Readers) Random Hse. Children's Bks.

—Dolphins & Sharks: A Nonfiction Companion to Magic Tree House #9: Dolphins at Daybreak. Osborne, Mary Pope & Boyce, Natalie Pope. 2003. (Magic Tree House (R) Fact Tracker Ser.: 9). 128p. (J). (gr. 2-5). 6.99 *(978-0-375-82377-0(8)*, Random Hse. Bks. for Young Readers) Random Hse. Children's Bks.

—Dragon of the Red Dawn. Osborne, Mary Pope. 2008. (Magic Tree House (R) Merlin Mission Ser.: 9). 144p. (J). (gr. 2-5). 5.99 *(978-0-375-83728-9(0)*, Random Hse. Bks. for Young Readers) Random Hse. Children's Bks.

—Eve of the Emperor Penguin. Osborne, Mary Pope. (Magic Tree House (R) Merlin Mission Ser.: 12). (J). (gr. 2-5). 2009. (ENG.). 144p. 5.99 *(978-0-375-83734-0(5))*; 2008. 128p. 11.99 *(978-0-375-83733-3(7))* Random Hse. Children's Bks. (Random Hse. Bks. for Young Readers).

—The Fun Starts Here! Four Favorite Chapter Books in One. Osborne, Mary Pope et al. 2018. (ENG.). 336p. (J). (gr. 1-4). 8.99 *(978-1-9848-3059-3(7)*, Random Hse. Bks. for Young Readers) Random Hse. Children's Bks.

—Games & Puzzles from the Tree House: Over 200 Challenges! Osborne, Mary Pope & Boyce, Natalie Pope. 2010. (Magic Tree House (R) Ser.). 256p. (J). (gr. 1-4). act. bk. ed. 6.99 *(978-0-375-86216-8(1)*, Random Hse. Bks. for Young Readers) Random Hse. Children's Bks.

—A Ghost Tale for Christmas Time. Osborne, Mary Pope. 2012. (Magic Tree House (R) Merlin Mission Ser.: 16). (ENG.). 144p. (J). (gr. 2-5). pap. 5.99 *(978-0-375-85653-2(6)*, Random Hse. Bks. for Young Readers) Random Hse. Children's Bks.

—Ghosts: A Nonfiction Companion to Magic Tree House Merlin Mission #14: a Good Night for Ghosts. Osborne, Mary Pope & Boyce, Natalie Pope. 2009. (Magic Tree House (R) Fact Tracker Ser.: 20). 128p. (J). (gr. 2-5). 6.99 *(978-0-375-84666-3(2)*, Random Hse. Bks. for Young Readers) Random Hse. Children's Bks.

—A Good Night for Ghosts. Osborne, Mary Pope. 2009. (Magic Tree House Merlin Missions Ser.: No. 14). 112p. (J). Non-ISBN Publisher.

—A Good Night for Ghosts. Osborne, Mary Pope. 2011. (Magic Tree House (R) Merlin Mission Ser.: 14). 144p. (J). (gr. 2-5). 5.99 *(978-0-375-85649-5(8)*, Random Hse. Bks. for Young Readers) Random Hse. Children's Bks.

—Grover's Own Alphabet (Sesame Street) Golden Books. 2019. (Little Golden Book Ser.). (ENG.). 24p. (J). (-k). 4.99 *(978-1-9848-4793-5(7)*, Golden Bks.) Random Hse. Children's Bks.

—Haunted Castle on Hallows Eve. Osborne, Mary Pope. 2010. (Magic Tree House Merlin Missions Ser.: No. 2). (ENG.). (J). (gr. 1-4). lib. bdg. 15.60 *(978-1-62765-792-1(4))* Perfection Learning Corp.

—Haunted Castle on Hallows Eve. Osborne, Mary Pope. 2010. (Magic Tree House (R) Merlin Mission Ser.: 2). 144p. (J). (gr. 2-5). pap. 5.99 *(978-0-375-86090-4(8)*, Random Hse. Bks. for Young Readers) Random Hse. Children's Bks.

—Heroes for All Times: Magic Tree House Fact Tracker. Osborne, Mary Pope & Boyce, Natalie Pope. 2014. (Magic Tree House (R) Fact Tracker Ser.: 28). 128p. (J). (gr. 2-5). 6.99 *(978-0-375-87027-9(X)*, Random Hse. Bks. for Young Readers) Random Hse. Children's Bks.

—High Tide in Hawaii. Osborne, Mary Pope. 2003. (Magic Tree House (R) Ser.: 28). 96p. (J). (gr. 1-4). pap. 5.99 *(978-0-375-80616-2(4)*, Random Hse. Bks. for Young Readers) Random Hse. Children's Bks.

—High Time for Heroes. Osborne, Mary Pope. 128p. (J). (gr. 2-5). 2016. (Magic Tree House (R) Merlin Mission Ser.: 23). 5.99 *(978-0-307-98052-6(9))*; 2014. (Magic Tree House (R) Merlin Mission Ser.: 51). (ENG.). lib. bdg. 15.99 *(978-0-307-98050-2(2))*; 2014. (Magic Tree House Merlin Missions Ser.: No. 23). 13.99 *(978-0-307-98049-6(9))* Random Hse. Children's Bks. (Random Hse. Bks. for Young Readers).

—La Hora de Los Juegos Olimpicos. Osborne, Mary Pope. Brovelli, Marcela, tr. 2007. (Casa del Arbol Ser.: 16).Tr. of Hour of the Olympics Games. (ENG & SPA.). 68p. (J). per. 6.99 *(978-1-933032-22-1(7))* Lectorum Pubns., Inc.

—Horse Heroes: Magic Tree House Fact Tracker. Osborne, Mary Pope & Boyce, Natalie Pope. 2013. (Magic Tree House (R) Fact Tracker Ser.: 27). 128p. (J). (gr. 2-5). 6.99 *(978-0-375-87026-2(1)*, Random Hse. Bks. for Young Readers) Random Hse. Children's Bks.

—Hurry up, Houdini! Osborne, Mary Pope. 2015. (Magic Tree House (R) Merlin Mission Ser.: 22). (ENG.). 144p. (J). (gr. 2-5). 5.99 *(978-0-307-98048-9(0)*, Random Hse. Bks. for Young Readers) Random Hse. Children's Bks.

—Leonardo Da Vinci: A Nonfiction Companion to Magic Tree House Merlin Mission #10: Monday with a Mad Genius. Osborne, Mary Pope & Boyce, Natalie Pope. 2009. (Magic Tree House (R) Fact Tracker Ser.: 19). 128p. (J). (gr. 2-5). 6.99 *(978-0-375-84665-6(4)*, Random Hse. Bks. for Young Readers) Random Hse. Children's Bks.

—Leprechaun in Late Winter. Osborne, Mary Pope. 2012. (Magic Tree House (R) Merlin Mission Ser.: 15). 144p. (J). (gr. 2-5). 5.99 *(978-0-375-85651-8(X)*, Random Hse. Bks. for Young Readers) Random Hse. Children's Bks.

—Leprechaun in Late Winter: Magic Tree House. Osborne, Mary Pope. 2010. (Magic Tree House (R) Merlin Mission Ser.: No. 15). 128p. (J). (gr. 2-5). 12.99 *(978-0-375-85650-1(1)*, Random Hse. Bks. for Young Readers) Random Hse. Children's Bks.

—Leprechauns & Irish Folklore: A Nonfiction Companion to Magic Tree House Merlin Mission #15: Leprechaun in Late Winter. Osborne, Mary Pope & Boyce, Natalie Pope. 2010. (Magic Tree House (R) Fact Tracker Ser.: 21). 128p. (J). (gr. 2-5). 6.99 *(978-0-375-86009-6(6)*, Random Hse. Bks. for Young Readers) Random Hse. Children's Bks.

—Magic Tree House Books 13-16 Boxed Set, 4 vols. Osborne, Mary Pope. 2008. (Magic Tree House (R) Ser.: Nos. 13-16). 96p. (J). (gr. k-3). 23.96 *(978-0-375-84661-8(1)*, Random Hse. Bks. for Young Readers) Random Hse. Children's Bks.

—Magic Tree House Books 17-20 Boxed Set: The Mystery of the Enchanted Dog, 4 vols., Bks. 17-20. Osborne, Mary Pope. 2009. (Magic Tree House (R) Ser.). 96p. (J). (gr. 1-4). 23.96 *(978-0-375-85811-6(3)*, Random Hse. Bks. for Young Readers) Random Hse. Children's Bks.

—Magic Tree House Books 21-24 Boxed Set: American History Quartet, 4 vols. Osborne, Mary Pope. 2014. (Magic Tree House (R) Ser.). 96p. (J). (gr. 1-4). 23.96 *(978-0-385-38957-0(4)*, Random Hse. Bks. for Young Readers) Random Hse. Children's Bks.

Murdocca, Sal. Magic Tree House Box of Puzzles, Games, & Activities (3 Book Set), 3 vols. Osborne, Mary Pope & Boyce, Natalie Pope. 2020. (Magic Tree House (R) Ser.). 640p. (J). (gr. 1-4). 19.97 ***(978-0-593-37311-8(1)***, Random Hse. Bks. for Young Readers) Random Hse. Children's Bks.

Murdocca, Sal. Magic Tree House Incredible Fact Book. Osborne, Mary Pope & Boyce, Natalie Pope. 2016. (Magic Tree House (R) Ser.). 144p. (J). (gr. 2-5). 16.99 *(978-0-399-55117-8(4)*, Random Hse. Bks. for Young Readers) Random Hse. Children's Bks.

—Magic Tree House Survival Guide. Osborne, Mary Pope & Boyce, Natalie Pope. 2014. (Magic Tree House (R) Ser.). (ENG.). 144p. (J). (gr. 2-5). 13.99 *(978-0-553-49737-3(5)*, Random Hse. Bks. for Young Readers) Random Hse. Children's Bks.

—Magic Tree House Volumes 9-12 Boxed Set, 4 vols. Osborne, Mary Pope. 2003. (Magic Tree House (R) Ser.: Nos. 9-12). 96p. (J). (gr. 1-4). 23.96 *(978-0-375-82553-8(3)*, Random Hse. Bks. for Young Readers) Random Hse. Children's Bks.

—Monday with a Mad Genius. Osborne, Mary Pope. (Magic Tree House (R) Merlin Mission Ser.: 10). (J). (gr. 2-5). 2009. 144p. 5.99 *(978-0-375-83730-2(2))*; 2007. 128p. 11.99 *(978-0-375-83729-6(9))* Random Hse. Children's Bks. (Random Hse. Bks. for Young Readers).

—Moonlight on the Magic Flute, Bk. 13. Osborne, Mary Pope. 2010. (Magic Tree House (R) Merlin Mission Ser.: 13). 144p. (J). (gr. 2-5). pap. 5.99 *(978-0-375-85647-1(1)*, Random Hse. Bks. for Young Readers) Random Hse. Children's Bks.

—Night of the New Magicians. Osborne, Mary Pope. 2007. (Magic Tree House (R) Merlin Mission Ser.: 7). 144p. (J). (gr. 2-5). 5.99 *(978-0-375-83036-5(7)*, Random Hse. Bks. for Young Readers) Random Hse. Children's Bks.

—Night of the Ninth Dragon. Osborne, Mary Pope. (Magic Tree House (R) Merlin Mission Ser.: 27). 144p. (J). (gr. 2-5). 2018. 5.99 *(978-0-553-51092-8(4))*; 2016. 13.99 *(978-0-553-51089-8(4))* Random Hse. Children's Bks. (Random Hse. Bks. for Young Readers).

—Ninjas & Samurai: A Nonfiction Companion to Magic Tree House #5: Night of the Ninjas. Osborne, Mary Pope & Boyce, Natalie Pope. 2014. (Magic Tree House (R) Fact Tracker Ser.: 30). (ENG.). 128p. (J). (gr. 2-5). 6.99 *(978-0-385-38632-6(X)*, Random Hse. Bks. for Young Readers) Random Hse. Children's Bks.

—Pandas & Other Endangered Species: A Nonfiction Companion to Magic Tree House Merlin Mission #20: a Perfect Time for Pandas. Osborne, Mary Pope & Boyce, Natalie Pope. 2012. (Magic Tree House (R) Fact Tracker Ser.: 26). 128p. (J). (gr. 2-5). 6.99 *(978-0-375-87025-5(3)*, Random Hse. Bks. for Young Readers) Random Hse. Children's Bks.

—Penguins & Antarctica. Osborne, Mary Pope & Boyce, Natalie Pope. 2008. (Magic Tree House (R) Fact Tracker Ser.: 18). 128p. (J). (gr. 2-5). 6.99 *(978-0-375-84664-9(6)*, Random Hse. Bks. for Young Readers) Random Hse. Children's Bks.

—A Perfect Time for Pandas, Bk. 20. Osborne, Mary Pope. 2014. (Magic Tree House (R) Merlin Mission Ser.: 20). 128p. (J). (gr. 2-5). pap. 5.99 *(978-0-375-86798-9(8)*, Random Hse. Bks. for Young Readers) Random Hse. Children's Bks.

—Pilgrims: A Nonfiction Companion to Magic Tree House #27: Thanksgiving on Thursday. Osborne, Mary Pope & Boyce, Natalie Pope. 2005. (Magic Tree House (R) Fact Tracker Ser.: 13). 128p. (J). (gr. 2-5). 6.99 *(978-0-375-83219-2(X)*, Random Hse. Bks. for Young Readers) Random Hse. Children's Bks.

—Polar Bears & the Arctic: A Nonfiction Companion to Magic Tree House #12: Polar Bears Past Bedtime. Osborne, Mary Pope & Boyce, Natalie Pope. 2007. (Magic Tree House (R) Fact Tracker Ser.: 16). 128p. (J). (gr. 2-5). 6.99

M

(978-0-375-83222-2(X), Random Hse. Bks. for Young Readers) Random Hse. Children's Bks.
—Sabertooths & the Ice Age: A Nonfiction Companion to Sunset of the Sabertooth. Osborne, Mary Pope & Boyce, Natalie Pope. 2005. (Magic Tree House (R) Fact Tracker Ser.: 12). 128p. (J). (gr. 2-5). 6.99 *(978-0-375-82380-0(8)*, Random Hse. Bks. for Young Readers) Random Hse. Children's Bks.
—Sea Monsters: A Nonfiction Companion to Dark Day in the Deep Sea. Osborne, Mary Pope & Boyce, Natalie Pope. 2008. (Magic Tree House Research Guides: No. 17). 121p. (J). (gr. 1-5). 12.65 *(978-0-7569-8809-8(8))* Perfection Learning Corp.
—Sea Monsters: A Nonfiction Companion to Magic Tree House Merlin Mission #11: Dark Day in the Deep Sea. Osborne, Mary Pope & Boyce, Natalie Pope. 2008. (Magic Tree House (R) Fact Tracker Ser.: 17). 128p. (J). (gr. 2-5). 6.99 *(978-0-375-84663-2(8)*, Random Hse. Bks. for Young Readers) Random Hse. Children's Bks.
—Season of the Sandstorms, Bk. 6. Osborne, Mary Pope. 2006. (Magic Tree House (R) Merlin Mission Ser.: 6). 144p. (J). (gr. 2-5). 5.99 *(978-0-375-83032-7(4)*, Random Hse. Bks. for Young Readers) Random Hse. Children's Bks.
—The Secret of the Green Skin. Stanley, George Edward. ed. 2005. (Third-Grade Detectives Ser.: Bk. 6). 62p. (J). lib. bdg. 15.00 *(978-1-59054-916-2(3))* Fitzgerald Bks.
—Shadow of the Shark. Osborne, Mary Pope. 2017. (Magic Tree House (R) Merlin Mission Ser.: 25). 144p. (J). (gr. 2-5). 5.99 *(978-0-553-51084-3(3)*, Random Hse. Bks. for Young Readers) Random Hse. Children's Bks.
—Snakes & Other Reptiles: Magic Tree House Research Guide. Osborne, Mary Pope & Boyce, Natalie Pope. 2011. (Magic Tree House (R) Fact Tracker Ser.: 23). 128p. (J). (gr. 2-5). 6.99 *(978-0-375-86011-9(8)*, Random Hse. Bks. for Young Readers) Random Hse. Children's Bks.
—Soccer: Soccer on Sunday. Osborne, Mary Pope & Boyce, Natalie Pope. 2014. (Magic Tree House (R) Fact Tracker Ser.: 29). 128p. (J). (gr. 2-5). 6.99 *(978-0-385-38629-6(X)*, Random Hse. Bks. for Young Readers) Random Hse. Children's Bks.
—Soccer on Sunday. Osborne, Mary Pope. 2016. (Magic Tree House (R) Merlin Mission Ser.: 24). (ENG.). 144p. (J). (gr. 2-5). 5.99 *(978-0-307-98056-4(1)*, Random Hse. Bks. for Young Readers) Random Hse. Children's Bks.
—Spain. Parker, Lewis K. 2003. (Discovering Cultures Ser.). 48p. (gr. 3-4). 29.50 *(978-0-7614-1520-6(3))* Cavendish Square Publishing LLC.
—Stallion by Starlight. Osborne, Mary Pope. 2014. (Magic Tree House (R) Merlin Mission Ser.: 21). 128p. (J). (gr. 2-5). pap. 5.99 *(978-0-307-98044-1(8)*, Random Hse. Bks. for Young Readers) Random Hse. Children's Bks.
—Summer of the Sea Serpent, Bk. 3. Osborne, Mary Pope. 2011. (Magic Tree House (R) Merlin Mission Ser.: 3). 144p. (J). (gr. 2-5). 5.99 *(978-0-375-86491-9(1)*, Random Hse. Bks. for Young Readers) Random Hse. Children's Bks.
—Tsunamis & Other Natural Disasters: A Nonfiction Companion to Magic Tree House #28: High Tide in Hawaii. Osborne, Mary Pope & Boyce, Natalie Pope. 2007. (Magic Tree House (R) Fact Tracker Ser.: 15). 128p. (J). (gr. 2-5). 6.99 *(978-0-375-83221-5(1)*, Random Hse. Bks. for Young Readers) Random Hse. Children's Bks.
—Vacaciones Al Pie de un Volcan. Osborne, Mary Pope. Brovelli, Marcela, tr. from ENG. 2007. (Casa del Arbol Ser.: 13).Tr. of Vacation under the Volcano. (SPA.). 74p. (J). per. 6.99 *(978-1-933032-19-1(7))* Lectorum Pubns., Inc.
—Winter of the Ice Wizard. Osborne, Mary Pope. 2011. (Magic Tree House Merlin Missions Ser.: No. 4). (ENG.). (J). (gr. 1-4). lib. bdg. 15.60 *(978-1-62765-950-5(1))* Perfection Learning Corp.
—Winter of the Ice Wizard. Osborne, Mary Pope. (Magic Tree House (R) Merlin Mission Ser.: 4). (J). (gr. 2-5). 2011. 144p. 5.99 *(978-0-375-87395-9(3))*; 2004. 128p. 11.95 *(978-0-375-82736-5(6))* Random Hse. Children's Bks. (Random Hse. Bks. for Young Readers).
—World at War 1944. Osborne, Mary Pope. 2017. (Magic Tree House Super Edition Ser.: 1). (ENG.). 208p. (J). (gr. 2-5). 6.99 *(978-0-553-50885-7(7)*, Random Hse. Bks. for Young Readers) Random Hse. Children's Bks.
Murdocca, Sal. Buenos Días, Gorilas. Murdocca, Sal. Osborne, Mary Pope & Brovelli, Marcela. 2014. (SPA.). 88p. (J). (gr. 2-4). pap. 6.99 *(978-1-933032-93-1(6))* Lectorum Pubns., Inc.
—Búfalos Antes Del Desayuno. Murdocca, Sal. Osborne, Mary Pope & Brovelli, Marcela. 2008. (Casa del Arbol Ser.: 18).Tr. of Buffalo Before Breakfast. (SPA.). (J). (gr. 2-4). pap. 6.99 *(978-1-933032-48-1(0))* Lectorum Pubns., Inc.
—Carnaval a Media Luz. Murdocca, Sal. Osborne, Mary Pope & Brovelli, Marcela. 2016. (SPA.). 113p. (J). (gr. 2-4). pap. 6.99 *(978-1-63245-643-4(5))* Lectorum Pubns., Inc.
—Día Negro en el Fondo Del Mar. Murdocca, Sal. Osborne, Mary Pope & Brovelli, Marcela. 2018. (SPA.). 118p. (J). (gr. 2-4). pap. 6.99 *(978-1-63245-682-3(6))* Lectorum Pubns., Inc.
—El Dragon Del Amanecer Rojo. Murdocca, Sal. Osborne, Mary Pope & Brovelli, Marcela. 2018. (SPA.). 132p. (J). (gr. 2-4). pap. 6.99 *(978-1-63245-680-9(X))* Lectorum Pubns., Inc.
—Esta Noche en el Titanic. Murdocca, Sal. Osborne, Mary Pope. 2008. (Casa del Arbol Ser.: 17).Tr. of Tonight on the Titanic. (SPA.). (J). (gr. 2-4). pap. 6.99 *(978-1-933032-47-4(2))* Lectorum Pubns., Inc.
—La Estación de Las Tormentas de Arena. Murdocca, Sal. Osborne, Mary Pope & Brovelli, Marcela. 2016. (SPA.). 107p. (J). (gr. 2-4). pap. 5.99 *(978-1-63245-644-1(3))* Lectorum Pubns., Inc.
—Jueves de Acción de Gracias. Murdocca, Sal. Osborne, Mary Pope & Brovelli, Marcela. 2014. (SPA.). 88p. (J). (gr. 2-4). pap. 6.99 *(978-1-933032-94-8(4))* Lectorum Pubns., Inc.
—Un Lunes con un Genio Loco. Murdocca, Sal. Osborne, Mary Pope & Brovelli, Marcela. 2018. (SPA.). 132p. (J). (gr. 2-4). pap. 6.99 *(978-1-63245-681-6(8))* Lectorum Pubns., Inc.
—Maremoto en Hawái. Murdocca, Sal. Osborne, Mary Pope & Brovelli, Marcela. 2014. (SPA.). 88p. (J). (gr. 2-4). pap. 6.99 *(978-1-933032-95-5(2))* Lectorum Pubns., Inc.
—Miedo Escénico en una Noche de Verano. Murdocca, Sal. Osborne, Mary Pope & Brovelli, Marcela. 2014. (SPA.). 86p. (J). (gr. 2-4). pap. 6.99 *(978-1-933032-92-4(8))* Lectorum Pubns., Inc.
—La Noche de Los Nuevos Magos. Murdocca, Sal. Osborne, Mary Pope & Brovelli, Marcela. 2016. (SPA.). 111p. (J). (gr. 2-4). pap. 6.99 *(978-1-63245-645-8(1))* Lectorum Pubns., Inc.
—Perros Salvajes a la Hora de la Cena. Murdocca, Sal. Osborne, Mary Pope & Brovelli, Marcela. 2008. (Casa del Arbol Ser.: 20).Tr. of Dingoes at Dinnertime. (SPA.). (J). (gr. 2-4). pap. 6.99 *(978-1-933032-50-4(2))* Lectorum Pubns., Inc.
—El Regalo Del Pingüino Emperador. Murdocca, Sal. Osborne, Mary Pope & Brovelli, Marcela. 2018. (SPA.). 118p. (J). (gr. 2-4). pap. 6.99 *(978-1-63245-683-0(4))* Lectorum Pubns., Inc.
—Tigres Al Anochecer. Murdocca, Sal. Osborne, Mary Pope & Brovelli, Marcela. 2008. (Casa del Arbol Ser.: 19).Tr. of Tigers at Twilight. (SPA.). (J). (gr. 2-4). pap. 6.99 *(978-1-933032-49-8(9))* Lectorum Pubns., Inc.
—Tormenta de Nieve en Luna Azul. Murdocca, Sal. Osborne, Mary Pope & Brovelli, Marcela. 2016. (SPA.). (J). (gr. 2-4). pap. 6.99 *(978-1-63245-646-5(X))* Lectorum Pubns., Inc.
Murdocca, Sal. Ancient Greece & the Olympics: Magic Tree House Fact Tracker. Murdocca, Sal, tr. Osborne, Mary Pope & Boyce, Natalie Pope. 2004. (Magic Tree House (R) Fact Tracker Ser.: 10). 128p. (J). (gr. 2-5). pap. 6.99 *(978-0-375-82378-7(6)*, Random Hse. Bks. for Young Readers) Random Hse. Children's Bks.
Murdocca, Sal & Ford, A. G. A Big Day for Baseball. Osborne, Mary Pope. 2017. (Magic Tree House (R) Ser.: 29). 80p. (J). (gr. 1-4). 13.99 *(978-1-5247-1308-9(2)*, Random Hse. Bks. for Young Readers) Random Hse. Children's Bks.
Murdocca, Sal & Vilela, Luiz. Magic Tricks from the Tree House: A Fun Companion to Magic Tree House Merlin Mission #22: Hurry up, Houdini! Osborne, Mary Pope & Boyce, Natalie Pope. 2013. (Magic Tree House (R) Ser.). (ENG.). 128p. (J). (gr. 2-5). 5.99 *(978-0-449-81790-2(3)*, Random Hse. Bks. for Young Readers) Random Hse. Children's Bks.
Murdocca, Salvatore. The Case of the Bank-Robbing Bandit. Stanley, George E. 2004. (Third-Grade Detectives Ser.: 9). (ENG.). 80p. (J). (gr. 1-4). pap. 5.99 *(978-0-689-86489-6(2)*, Aladdin) Simon & Schuster Children's Publishing.
—The Case of the Dirty Clue. Stanley, George E. 2003. (Third-Grade Detectives Ser.: 7). (ENG.). 80p. (J). (gr. 1-4). pap. 5.99 *(978-0-689-86357-8(8)*, Simon & Schuster/Paula Wiseman Bks.) Simon & Schuster/Paula Wiseman Bks.
—The Mystery of the Stolen Statue, 10. Stanley, George E. 2004. (Third-Grade Detectives Ser.: 10). (ENG.). 80p. (J). (gr. 1-4). pap. 5.99 *(978-0-689-86491-9(4))* Simon & Schuster, Inc.
—The Riddle of the Stolen Sand. Stanley, George E. 2003. (Third-Grade Detectives Ser.: 5). (ENG.). 64p. (J). (gr. 1-4). pap. 5.99 *(978-0-689-85376-0(9)*, Aladdin) Simon & Schuster Children's Publishing.
—The Secret of the Green Skin. Stanley, George E. 2003. (Third-Grade Detectives Ser.: 6). (ENG.). 64p. (J). (gr. 1-4). pap. 5.99 *(978-0-689-85378-4(5)*, Aladdin) Simon & Schuster Children's Publishing.
—The Secret of the Wooden Witness, 8. Stanley, George E. 2004. (Third-Grade Detectives Ser.: 8). (ENG.). 80p. (J). (gr. 1-4). pap. 5.99 *(978-0-689-86487-2(6))* Simon & Schuster, Inc.
Murdocca, Salvatore. Third-Grade Detectives Mystery Masters Collection: The Clue of the Left-Handed Envelope; the Puzzle of the Pretty Pink Handkerchief; the Mystery of the Hairy Tomatoes; the Cobweb Confession; the Riddle of the Stolen Sand; the Secret of the Green Skin; the Case of the Dirty Clue; Etc. Stanley, George E. ed. 2020. (Third-Grade Detectives Ser.). (ENG.). 736p. (J). (gr. 1-4). pap. 59.99 ***(978-1-5344-6152-9(3)***, Aladdin) Simon & Schuster Children's Publishing.
Murfield, Anna. Adventures in the Weeping Willow Tree. Goebel, Kelly. 2013. 26p. pap. 9.99 *(978-1-937165-49-9(3))* Orange Hat Publishing.
—Growing up Cranberry. Gray, Shannon. 2012. 24p. pap. 9.50 *(978-1-937165-27-7(2))* Orange Hat Publishing.
—The Perfect Puppy. Marquardt, Michelle. 2013. 24p. pap. 9.99 *(978-1-937165-65-9(5))* Orange Hat Publishing.
Murfield, Anna. The Sea Glass Treasure. Peters, Shelly. 2020. (ENG.). 40p. (J). 19.99 ***(978-1-64538-108-2(0))***; pap. 12.99 ***(978-1-64538-109-9(9))*** Orange Hat Publishing.
Murfield, Anna. Sharlene & Her Animal Friends. Merline, Sharlene. Rongner, Bridget, ed. 2012. 106p. pap. 8.99 *(978-1-937165-09-3(4))* Orange Hat Publishing.
Murfin, Teresa. Back-To-School Rules. Friedman, Laurie. 2011. (ENG.). 32p. (J). (gr. k-3). lib. bdg. 17.99 *(978-0-7613-6070-4(0)*, Carolrhoda Bks.) Lerner Publishing Group.
—Birthday Rules. Friedman, Laurie. 2015. (ENG.). 32p. (J). (gr. k-3). lib. bdg. 16.99 *(978-0-7613-6071-1(9)*, 9780761360711, Carolrhoda Bks.) Lerner Publishing Group.
—Birthday Rules. Friedman, Laurie. ed. 2015. (ENG.). 32p. (J). (gr. k-3). E-Book 27.99 *(978-1-4677-6177-2(X)*, Carolrhoda Bks.) Lerner Publishing Group.
—I'm Not Afraid of This Haunted House. Friedman, Laurie. 2005. 32p. (J). (gr. k-3). 16.95 *(978-1-57505-751-4(4)*, Carolrhoda Bks.) Lerner Publishing Group.
—Naughty Toes. Bonwill, Ann. 2011. (ENG.). 32p. 15.95 *(978-1-58925-103-8(2))*; pap. 7.95 *(978-1-58925-430-5(9))* Tiger Tales.
—Oh, Jack! Vogler, Sara & Burchett, Jan. 2014. (Traditional Tales Ser.). (ENG.). 24p. (J). (gr. k-1). pap. 6.95 *(978-1-62521-592-5(4)*, Capstone Classroom) Capstone.
Murguia, Bethanie. Princess! Fairy! Ballerina! Murguia, Bethanie. 2016. (ENG.). 40p. (J). (gr. -1-k). 17.99 *(978-0-545-73240-6(9))* Scholastic, Inc.
Murguia, Bethanie Deeney. Violet & Victor Write the Best-Ever Bookworm Book. Kuipers, Alice. 2014. 48p. (J). (gr. -1-3). 17.00 *(978-0-316-21200-7(8))* Little, Brown Bks. for Young Readers.
Murguia, Bethanie Deeney. The Best Parts of Christmas. Murguia, Bethanie Deeney. 2015. 32p. (J). (gr. -1-2). 14.99 *(978-0-7636-7556-1(3))* Candlewick Pr.
—Buglette, the Messy Sleeper. Murguia, Bethanie Deeney. 2011. (ENG.). 32p. (J). (gr. -1-2). 15.99 *(978-1-58246-375-9(1)*, Tricycle Pr.) Random Hse. Children's Bks.
—Do You Believe in Unicorns? Murguia, Bethanie Deeney. 2018. 32p. (J). (gr. -1-2). 14.99 *(978-0-7636-9468-5(1))* Candlewick Pr.
—The Favorite Book. Murguia, Bethanie Deeney. 2019. (ENG.). 32p. (J). (gr. -1-2). 16.99 *(978-1-5362-0446-9(3))* Candlewick Pr.
—I Feel Five! Murguia, Bethanie Deeney. 2014. 32p. (J). (gr. -1-3). 14.99 *(978-0-7636-6291-2(7))* Candlewick Pr.
—Zoe's Room (No Sisters Allowed) Murguia, Bethanie Deeney. 2013. (ENG.). 40p. (J). (gr. -1-k). 16.99 *(978-0-545-45781-1(5)*, Levine, Arthur A. Bks.) Scholastic, Inc.
Murguia, Jose J. Uarhiri sapirhatiecheri Jukambekua: La velacion de los Angelitos. Andrade, Mary J., photos by. Andrade, Mary J. 2005. Orig. Title: The Vigil of the Little Angels. 40p. (J). (gr. 3-6). pap. 9.95 *(978-0-9665876-8-5(5))* La Oferta Publishing Co.
Murillo, Abbi. The Twelve o'Clock Cookies. Lewis-Marchell, Duranda. 2019. (ENG.). 26p. (J). pap. 10.00 ***(978-1-6926-0703-6(0))*** Independently Published.
Murkey, Lee. My Day at School: A Bullying Awareness Book. Wooten, Chandra & Crowder, Liz, eds. 2019. (ENG.). 28p. (J). pap. 12.00 ***(978-0-578-52851-9(7))*** SpeakToChange Enterprise.
Murnan, Jared. Animals Are Miracles. Guemann, Steven a. 2017. (ENG.). 50p. (J). pap. 10.99 *(978-0-9909120-4-0(3))* Guemann, Steven.
Muro, Jenny. The Little Pig. Waterbury, Matthew. 2013. 16p. pap. 24.95 *(978-1-4512-2919-6(4))* America Star Bks.
Muronaka, Michael & Kaylor, Emiko. Adventures in Japanese. Peterson, Hiromi & Omizo, Naomi. 2004. (JPN & ENG.). Vol. 2. (gr. 7-10). pap., tchr. ed., ldr.'s hndbk. ed. 59.95 *(978-0-88727-322-3(X))*; Vol. 2. 210p. (gr. 7-10). pap., wbk. ed. 19.95 *(978-0-88727-321-6(1))*; Vol. 3. (gr. 9-11). pap., tchr. ed., ldr.'s hndbk. ed. 59.95 *(978-0-88727-398-8(X))* Cheng & Tsui Co.
—Adventures in Japanese Level 1, 4 vols. Peterson, Hiromi & Omizo, Naomi. 2nd ed. 2005. pap., stu. ed., wbk. ed. 24.95 *(978-0-88727-450-3(1))* Cheng & Tsui Co.
Murphey, Christina. Slug Slime. Murphey, John M. 2017. (ENG.). (J). 19.95 *(978-1-945375-07-1(8))* Bk. Cravers Publishing, LLC.
Murphy, Aileen. The Bravest Girl in School. Gaynor, Kate. 2013. 20p. pap. *(978-0-9555787-4-8(4))* Special Stories Publishing.
Murphy, Al. Bathroom Boogie. Foges, Clare. 2018. (ENG.). 32p. (J). 16.95 *(978-0-571-34045-3(8)*, Faber & Faber Children's Bks.) Faber & Faber, Inc.
—Kitchen Disco. Foges, Clare. 2017. (ENG.). 32p. (J). (-k). pap. 9.95 *(978-0-571-30788-3(4))* Faber & Faber, Inc.
Murphy, Andrea. Wilkinson Tales: A Collection of Adventure Short Stories for Young People. Wilkinson, Richard Fergus. 2010. 88p. pap. 27.49 *(978-1-4490-5489-2(7))* AuthorHouse.
Murphy, Betsy. A Christmas Problem for Samuel James. Yaun, Ellen R. 59p. (J). (gr. 2-5). pap. 5.95 *(978-0-9673970-1-6(4))* Blue Chip Publishing.
Murphy, Bob. Two-B & the Rock 'n' Roll Band. Set. Paul, Sherry. (See How I Read Ser.). 32p. (Orig.). (J). (gr. -1-2). pap. 14.10 *(978-0-675-01082-5(9))* CPI Publishing, Inc.
Murphy, Brendán. Ready for School, Murphy? [8x8 with Stickers]. Murphy, Brendán. 2017. 40p. (J). (gr. -1-3). pap. 5.99 ***(978-1-368-00299-8(4))*** Little, Brown Bks. for Young Readers.
Murphy, Charles R. Chickadees At Night. Smith, Bill O. 2012. 32p. *(978-0-615-56972-7(2))* Smith, Bill O.
Murphy, Chris. Mango's Revenge. Logue, Stephanie. 2006. (J). pap. *(978-1-59336-769-5(4))* Mondo Publishing.
Murphy, Claire. Meet Nellie Melba. Brian, Janeen. 2016. 32p. (J). (gr. k-2). 22.99 *(978-0-14-378029-8(8))* Random Hse. Australia AUS. Dist: Independent Pubs. Group.
—Meet... Nellie Melba. Brian, Janeen. 2017. 36p. (J). (gr. 2). 15.99 *(978-0-14-378031-1(X))* Random Hse. Australia AUS. Dist: Independent Pubs. Group.
Murphy, D. L. The Warrior Princess. Murphy, D. L. 2019. (ENG.). 46p. (J). (gr. k-4). 24.99 *(978-1-7329658-0-5(3))* Murphy, D. L.
Murphy, David. Sir Mike. Black, Robyn Hood. 2006. (Rookie Reader Skill Set Ser.). (ENG.). 32p. (J). (gr. k-2). per. 4.95 *(978-0-516-25020-5(5)*, Children's Pr.) Scholastic Library Publishing.
Murphy, Dennis. From the Farm to You Coloring Book. Triplett, Annette. Vale, Joe, ed. 2012. 28p. (J). *(978-0-933842-34-2(1))* Univ. of Missouri, Extension.
Murphy, Emmy Lou, jt. illus. see Mowery, Linda Williams.
Murphy, Fredrick. Batboy's Crazy Day. Poole, Catherine Cheyenne. 2008. 24p. pap. 8.95 *(978-1-935105-18-3(3))* Avid Readers Publishing Group.
Murphy, Gabi. Daddy Loves Me. Wren, Georgina. 2020. (5-Minute Stories Padded Board B Ser.). (ENG.). 22p. (J). (— 1). bds. 9.99 ***(978-1-78958-627-5(5))*** Top That! Publishing PLC GBR. Dist: Independent Pubs. Group.
—Mommy Loves Me. Wren, Georgina. 2020. (5-Minute Stories Patt Padded Board B Ser.). (ENG.). 22p. (J). bds. 9.99 ***(978-1-78958-628-2(3))*** Top That! Publishing PLC GBR. Dist: Independent Pubs. Group.
—Sleepy Time Colors: a Lift-The-Flap Book, 1 vol. Gruelle, Deb. 2020. 20p. (J). bds. 8.99 ***(978-0-310-77076-3(9))*** Zonderkidz.
Murphy, Gabi. Ten Little Night Stars, 1 vol. Gruelle, Deb. 2018. (ENG.). 22p. (J). bds. 9.99 *(978-0-310-76212-6(X))* Zonderkidz.
Murphy, Gabrielle. Biblia Descubre y Aprende. Castells, Elisenda. 2020. (SPA.). 32p. (J). 12.95 *(978-0-8294-4966-2(3))* Loyola Pr.
—Seek & Find Bible. Castells, Elisenda. 2020. (ENG.). 32p. (J). 12.95 *(978-0-8294-4955-6(8))* Loyola Pr.
Murphy, Hugh. The Book about Nothing. Bender, Mike. 2018. (ENG.). 40p. (J). (gr. -1-2). 17.99 *(978-0-399-55109-3(3))*; lib. bdg. 20.99 *(978-0-399-55110-9(7))* Random Hse. Children's Bks. (Crown Books For Young Readers).
Murphy, Ivan. Gadzooks: The Christmas Goose, 1 vol. McGrath, Jennifer. ed. 2010. (ENG.). 32p. (J). (gr. -1-k). 19.95 *(978-1-55109-794-7(X)*, 271de8c9-f8b9-40d4-b8b3-d29261247496) Nimbus Publishing, Ltd. CAN. Dist: Baker & Taylor Publisher Services (BTPS).
Murphy, Janet. Critterstory. LeClair, Niki. 2018. (ENG.). 64p. (J). 19.75 *(978-1-59152-225-6(0)*, Sweetgrass Bks.) Farcountry Pr.
Murphy, Jill. A Bad Spell for the Worst Witch. Murphy, Jill. 2014. (Worst Witch Ser.: 2). (ENG.). 128p. (J). (gr. 3-7). pap. 6.99 *(978-0-7636-7252-2(1))* Candlewick Pr.
Murphy, Jill. First Prize for the Worst Witch. Murphy, Jill. 2020. (Worst Witch Ser.). (ENG.). 192p. (J). (gr. 3-7). 14.99 ***(978-1-5362-1101-6(X))*** Candlewick Pr.
Murphy, Jill. Five Minutes' Peace. Murphy, Jill. 2012. (ENG.). 24p. (J). (gr. -1 — 1). bds. 8.99 *(978-0-399-25707-0(1)*, G.P. Putnam's Sons Books for Young Readers) Penguin Young Readers Group.
—Meltdown! Murphy, Jill. 2016. (ENG.). 40p. (J). (gr. -1-2). 15.99 *(978-0-7636-8926-1(2))* Candlewick Pr.
—Mr. Large in Charge. Murphy, Jill. 2007. (Large Family Ser.). (ENG.). 40p. (J). (gr. -1-3). 16.99 *(978-0-7636-3504-6(9))* Candlewick Pr.
—Mr. Large in Charge. Murphy, Jill. 2018. (Large Family Ser.). (ENG.). 40p. (J). (gr. -1-3). 7.99 *(978-0-7636-9973-4(X))* Candlewick Pr.
—On the Way Home. Murphy, Jill. 2nd rev. ed. 2007. (ENG.). 36p. (J). (gr. k-2). pap. 11.95 *(978-0-230-01584-5(0))* Pan Macmillan GBR. Dist: Independent Pubs. Group.
—The Worst Witch & the Wishing Star. Murphy, Jill. 2015. (Worst Witch Ser.: 7). (ENG.). 208p. (J). (gr. 3-7). 14.99 *(978-0-7636-7000-9(6))* Candlewick Pr.
—The Worst Witch Saves the Day. Murphy, Jill. 2014. (Worst Witch Ser.: 5). (ENG.). 160p. (J). (gr. 3-7). pap. 6.99 *(978-0-7636-7255-3(6))* Candlewick Pr.
—The Worst Witch to the Rescue. Murphy, Jill. (Worst Witch Ser.: 6). (ENG.). 176p. (J). (gr. 3-7). 2015. pap. 5.99 *(978-0-7636-7862-3(7))*; 2014. 14.99 *(978-0-7636-6999-7(7))* Candlewick Pr.
Murphy, Jobi. In Search of the Time & Space Machine: Max Remy Superspy 1. Abela, Deborah. 2005. (Spy Force Ser.). 256p. (Orig.). (J). 14.95 *(978-1-74051-765-2(2)*, Simon & Schuster Bks. For Young Readers) Simon & Schuster Bks. For Young Readers.
—Muddled-Up Farm, 1 vol. Dumbleton, Mike. 2013. (ENG.). 32p. (J). 16.99 *(978-1-59572-630-8(6))*; pap. 6.99 *(978-1-59572-631-5(4))* Star Bright Bks., Inc.
Murphy, Kelly. Alex & the Amazing Time Machine. Cohen, Rich. 2013. (ENG.). (J). (gr. 3-7). lib. bdg. 17.60 *(978-1-68065-146-1(3))* Perfection Learning Corp.
—Alex & the Amazing Time Machine. Cohen, Rich. 2013. (ENG.). 176p. (J). (gr. 3-7). pap. 14.99 *(978-1-250-02729-0(2)*, 900098301) Square Fish.
—Anton & Cecil, Book 2: Cats on Track. Martin, Lisa & Martin, Valerie. (Anton & Cecil Ser.: 2). (ENG.). 272p. (J). (gr. 3-7). 2016. pap. 6.95 *(978-1-61620-638-3(1)*, 73638); 2015. 16.95 *(978-1-61620-419-8(2)*, 73419) Algonquin Bks. of Chapel Hill.
—Anton & Cecil, Book 3: Cats Aloft. Martin, Lisa & Martin, Valerie. 2016. (Anton & Cecil Ser.: 3). (ENG.). 272p. (J). (gr. 3-7). 16.95 *(978-1-61620-459-4(1)*, 73459) Algonquin Bks. of Chapel Hill.
—The Basilisk's Lair. LaFevers, R. L. 2011. (Nathaniel Fludd, Beastologist Ser.: 2). (ENG.). 160p. (J). (gr. 1-4). pap. 6.99 *(978-0-547-54957-6(1)*, 1450109) Houghton Mifflin Harcourt Publishing Co.
—Behind the Bookcase. Steensland, Mark. 2013. 288p. (J). (gr. 3-7). 6.99 *(978-0-385-74072-2(7)*, Yearling) Random Hse. Children's Bks.
—Brand-New Baby Blues. Appelt, Kathi. 2009. (ENG.). 32p. (J). (gr. -1-1). 16.99 *(978-0-06-053233-8(5))* HarperCollins Pubs.
—The Case of the Counterfeit Criminals (the Wollstonecraft Detective Agency, Book 3) Stratford, Jordan. 2017. (Wollstonecraft Detective Agency Ser.). (ENG.). 208p. (J). (gr. 3-7). 16.99 *(978-0-385-75448-4(5)*, Knopf Bks. for Young Readers) Random Hse. Children's Bks.
—The Case of the Girl in Grey (the Wollstonecraft Detective Agency, Book 2) Stratford, Jordan. 2016. (Wollstonecraft Detective Agency Ser.: 2). (ENG.). 224p. (J). (gr. 3-7). 16.99 *(978-0-385-75444-6(2)*, Knopf Bks. for Young Readers) Random Hse. Children's Bks.
—The Case of the Perilous Palace (the Wollstonecraft Detective Agency, Book 4) Stratford, Jordan. 2018. (Wollstonecraft Detective Agency Ser.: 4). 224p. (J). (gr. 3-7). 16.99 *(978-0-553-53644-7(3)*, Knopf Bks. for Young Readers) Random Hse. Children's Bks.
—Creepy Monsters, Sleepy Monsters. Yolen, Jane. 2013. (ENG.). 32p. (J). (gr. -1-2). 7.99 *(978-0-7636-6283-7(6))* Candlewick Pr.
—The Door by the Staircase. Marsh, Katherine. 2017. (ENG.). 288p. (J). (gr. 3-7). pap. 7.99 *(978-1-4231-3785-6(X))* Hyperion Bks. for Children.
—Face Bug. Siskind, Fred, photos by. Lewis, J. Patrick. 2013. (ENG.). 36p. (J). (gr. 1-4). 16.95 *(978-1-59078-925-4(3)*, Wordsong) Boyds Mills Pr.
—A Festival of Ghosts. Alexander, William. 2018. (ENG.). 272p. (J). (gr. 3-7). 17.99 *(978-1-4814-6918-0(5)*, McElderry, Margaret K. Bks.) McElderry, Margaret K. Bks.

—Fiona's Luck. Bateman, Teresa. 32p. (J). (gr. -1-3). 2009. pap. 7.95 *(978-1-57091-643-4(8))*; 2007. (ENG.). 22.44 *(978-1-57091-651-9(9))* Charlesbridge Publishing, Inc.

—Flight of the Phoenix Bk. 1. LaFevers, R. L. 2010. (Nathaniel Fludd, Beastologist Ser.: 1). (ENG.). 144p. (J). (gr. 1-4). pap. 6.99 *(978-0-547-40845-3(5)*, 1428742) Houghton Mifflin Harcourt Publishing Co.

—James to the Rescue. Broach, Elise. 2015. (Masterpiece Adventures Ser.: 2). (ENG.). 112p. (J). (gr. 1-4). 15.99 *(978-1-62779-316-2(X)*, 900146226, Holt, Henry & Co. Bks. For Young Readers) Holt, Henry & Co.

—Loony Little: The Ice Cap Is Melting. Aston, Dianna Hutts. 2020. 32p. (J). (gr. -1-3). lib. bdg. 16.99 *(978-1-62354-117-0(4))* Charlesbridge Publishing, Inc.

—Marvin & James Save the Day & Elaine Helps! Broach, Elise. 2019. (Masterpiece Adventures Ser.: 4). (ENG.). 112p. (J). 15.99 *(978-1-250-18607-2(2)*, 900191475, Holt, Henry & Co. Bks. For Young Readers) Holt, Henry & Co.

—Marvin & James Save the Day & Elaine Helps! Broach, Elise. 2020. (Masterpiece Adventures Ser.: 4). (ENG.). 112p. (J). pap. 5.99 *(978-1-250-23321-9(6)*, 900191476) Square Fish.

—Masterpiece. Broach, Elise. 2010. (Masterpiece Adventures Ser.). (ENG.). 320p. (J). (gr. 4-6). pap. 8.99 *(978-0-312-60870-5(5)*, 900065170) Square Fish.

—The Miniature World of Marvin & James. Broach, Elise. 2014. (Masterpiece Adventures Ser.: 1). (ENG.). 112p. (J). (gr. 1-4). 15.99 *(978-0-8050-9190-8(4)*, 900065718, Holt, Henry & Co. Bks. For Young Readers) Holt, Henry & Co.

—A Properly Unhaunted Place. Alexander, William. 2017. (ENG.). 192p. (J). (gr. 3-7). 16.99 *(978-1-4814-6915-9(0)*, McElderry, Margaret K. Bks.) McElderry, Margaret K. Bks.

—Romping Monsters, Stomping Monsters. Yolen, Jane. 2013. (ENG.). 32p. (J). (gr. -1-2). 14.99 *(978-0-7636-5727-7(1))* Candlewick Pr.

—The Slowest Book Ever. Sayre, April Pulley. 2016. (ENG.). 176p. (J). (gr. 3-7). 16.95 *(978-1-62091-783-1(1))* Boyds Mills Pr.

—A Trip to the Country for Marvin & James. Broach, Elise. 2020. (Masterpiece Adventures Ser.: 5). (ENG.). 112p. (J). 16.99 *(978-1-250-18609-6(9)*, 900191478, Holt, Henry & Co. Bks. For Young Readers) Holt, Henry & Co.

—Trouble at School for Marvin & James. Broach, Elise. 2017. (Masterpiece Adventures Ser.: 3). (ENG.). 112p. (J). 15.99 *(978-1-62779-318-6(6)*, 900146231, Holt, Henry & Co. Bks. For Young Readers) Holt, Henry & Co.

—Trouble at School for Marvin & James. Broach, Elise. 2018. (Masterpiece Adventures Ser.: 3). (ENG.). 112p. (J). pap. 5.99 *(978-1-250-18338-5(3)*, 900190818) Square Fish.

—The Unicorn's Tale. LaFevers, R. L. 2012. (Nathaniel Fludd, Beastologist Ser.: 4). (ENG.). 160p. (J). (gr. 1-4). pap. 6.99 *(978-0-547-85079-5(4)*, 1501039) Houghton Mifflin Harcourt Publishing Co.

—The Wyverns' Treasure. LaFevers, R. L. 2012. (Nathaniel Fludd, Beastologist Ser.: 3). (ENG.). 160p. (J). (gr. 1-4). pap. 6.99 *(978-0-547-85823-4(X)*, 1502147) Houghton Mifflin Harcourt Publishing Co.

Murphy, Kelly & Revoy, Antoine. Haunted Houses. San Souci, Robert D. 2012. (Are You Scared Yet? Ser.). (ENG.). 304p. (J). (gr. 4-7). pap. 16.99 *(978-0-312-55136-0(3)*, 900074422) Square Fish.

Murphy, Liz. Poodles Don't Play Tennis. Rizzuto, Katherine. 2013. (ENG.). 32p. (J). 19.99 *(978-1-938501-06-7(3))* Turn the Page Publishing.

Murphy, Mary. Are You My Mommy? Murphy, Mary. 2015. (ENG.). 16p. (J). (gr. -1 — 1). bds. 7.99 *(978-0-7636-7372-7(2))* Candlewick Pr.

—Good Night Like This. Murphy, Mary. 2016. (ENG.). 32p. (J). (gr. -1-k). 12.99 *(978-0-7636-7970-5(4))* Candlewick Pr.

—How Kind! Murphy, Mary. 2004. (ENG.). 24p. (J). (gr. k-k). bds. 6.99 *(978-0-7636-2307-4(5))* Candlewick Pr.

—I Kissed the Baby! Murphy, Mary. 2004. (ENG.). 24p. (J). (— 1). bds. 6.99 *(978-0-7636-2443-9(8))* Candlewick Pr.

—Mouse Is Small. Murphy, Mary. 2017. (ENG.). 14p. (J). (— 1). bds. 7.99 *(978-0-7636-9059-5(7))* Candlewick Pr.

—Only a Tree Knows How to Be a Tree. Murphy, Mary. 2020. (ENG.). 32p. (J). (gr. -1-2). 16.99 *(978-1-5362-1470-3(1))* Candlewick Pr.

—Picken: Mix & Match the Farm Animals! Murphy, Mary. 2019. (ENG.). 12p. (J). (— 1). bds. 8.99 *(978-0-7636-9730-3(3))* Candlewick Pr.

—Quick Duck! Murphy, Mary. 2013. (ENG.). 16p. (J). (— 1). bds. 6.99 *(978-0-7636-6022-2(1))* Candlewick Pr.

—Say Hello Like This. Murphy, Mary. 2014. (ENG.). 32p. (J). (-k). 12.99 *(978-0-7636-6951-5(2))* Candlewick Pr.

Murphy, Matt. Man of the Atom, Vol. 2. Newman, Paul S. 2005. (ENG.). 200p. 49.95 *(978-1-59307-327-5(5))* Dark Horse Comics.

Murphy, Patrick J. Las Armas de Fuego. Reiter, David P. Rosales-Martinez, Guadalupe, tr. from ENG. 2010.Tr. of Real Guns. (SPA.). 32p. (YA). *(978-1-921479-44-1(2))* Interactive Pubns. Pty, Ltd.

Murphy, Phil. Powerpuff Girls: the Time Tie. Mancini, Haley & Goldman, Jake. 2018. (Powerpuff Girls Ser.). (ENG.). 80p. (J). (gr. 4-7). 12.99 *(978-1-68405-100-7(2))* Idea & Design Works, LLC.

Murphy, Philip. Powerpuff Girls: the Bureau of Bad. Mancini, Haley & Goldman, Jake. 2018. (Powerpuff Girls Ser.). (ENG.). 72p. (J). (gr. 2-5). 12.99 *(978-1-68405-247-9(5))* Idea & Design Works, LLC.

Murphy, Scott. Overboard, 1 vol. Brezenoff, Steve. 2012. (Return to Titanic Ser.). (ENG.). 112p. (J). (gr. 3-6). pap. 6.95 *(978-1-4342-3912-9(8))*; lib. bdg. 25.32 *(978-1-4342-3302-8(2))* Capstone. (Stone Arch Bks.).

—Stowaways, 1 vol. Brezenoff, Steve. 2012. (Return to Titanic Ser.). (ENG.). 112p. (J). (gr. 3-6). lib. bdg. 25.32 *(978-1-4342-3300-4(6)*, Stone Arch Bks.) Capstone.

—Time Voyage, 1 vol. Brezenoff, Steve. 2012. (Return to Titanic Ser.). (ENG.). 112p. (J). (gr. 3-6). pap. 6.95 *(978-1-4342-3909-9(8))*; lib. bdg. 25.32 *(978-1-4342-3299-1(9))* Capstone. (Stone Arch Bks.).

—An Unsinkable Ship, 1 vol. Brezenoff, Steve. 2012. (Return to Titanic Ser.). (ENG.). 112p. (J). (gr. 3-6). lib. bdg. 25.32 *(978-1-4342-3301-1(4)*, Stone Arch Bks.) Capstone.

Murphy, Stef. You're the Hero: Pirate Adventure. Murray, Lily. 2020. (Let's Tell a Story Ser.). (ENG.). 32p. (J). pap. 14.99 ***(978-1-78240-940-3(8)***, 327276, Ivy Kids) Ivy Group, The GBR. Dist: Hachette UK Distribution.

Murphy, Stuart J. & Bjorkman, Steve. Coyotes All Around. Murphy, Stuart J. 2003. (Mathstart: Level 2 (HarperCollins Paperback) Ser.). (ENG.). (J). (gr. 1). lib. bdg. 16.60 *(978-1-62765-799-0(1))* Perfection Learning Corp.

Murphy, Stuart J. & Martin, Pedro. Hamster Champs. Murphy, Stuart J. 2005. (Mathstart: Level 3 (HarperCollins Paperback) Ser.). (ENG.). (J). (gr. 2). lib. bdg. 16.60 *(978-1-62765-926-0(9))* Perfection Learning Corp.

Murphy, Terri. Arch Books: The Centurion at the Cross. Bohnet, Eric C. 2007. (Arch Bks.). (J). 1.99 *(978-0-7586-1260-1(5))* Concordia Publishing Hse.

—Dance Y'all, Dance. Bennett, Kelly. 2010. (ENG.). 32p. (J). (gr. k-2). 17.95 *(978-1-933979-65-6(8))* Night Heron Media.

Murphy, Terri. Hazel Grove. Booth, Leslie Barnard. 2020. (ENG.). 28p. (J). pap. ***(978-1-922374-97-4(0))*** Library For All Limited.

—Milo & Button Take Flight. Kruck, Carrie. 2020. (ENG.). 20p. (J). pap. ***(978-1-922331-98-4(8))*** Library For All Limited.

Murphy, Terri. My School. 2010. (My World Ser.). (ENG.). 24p. (J). (gr. -1-1). pap. 8.15 *(978-1-61533-039-3(9))*; lib. bdg. 25.60 *(978-1-60754-953-6(0))* Windmill Bks.

—My School/Mi Escuela. Rosa-Mendoza, Gladys. 2007. (English Spanish Foundations Ser.). (ENG & SPA.). (J). (gr. -1-k). bds. 6.95 *(978-1-931398-23-7(2))* Me+Mi Publishing.

—One Day I Went Rambling. Bennett, Kelly. 2012. (ENG.). 24p. (J). (gr. k-2). pap. 17.95 *(978-1-936474-06-6(9))* Night Heron Media.

—The Ten Plagues. Hartman, Sara. 2006. 16p. (J). 1.99 *(978-0-7586-0875-8(6))* Concordia Publishing Hse.

Murphy, Tom. A Boy & His Bunny. Bryan, Sean. 2011. (ENG.). 32p. (J). (gr. -1-k). 14.95 *(978-1-61145-023-1(3)*, 611023, Arcade Publishing) Skyhorse Publishing Co., Inc.

—A Girl & Her Gator. Bryan, Sean. 2011. (ENG.). 32p. (J). (gr. -1-k). 14.95 *(978-1-61145-032-3(2)*, 611032, Arcade Publishing) Skyhorse Publishing Co., Inc.

—The Juggling Pug. Bryan, Sean. 32p. (J). 2014. (-k). 12.95 *(978-1-62873-596-3(1))*; 2011. (gr. -1-k). 12.95 *(978-1-61608-329-8(8)*, 608329) Skyhorse Publishing Co., Inc. (Sky Pony Pr.).

Murr, Bob. How to Beat Granddad at Checkers. Cardie, John P. 2007. 62p. per. 15.95 *(978-1-59879-390-1(X))* Lifevest Publishing, Inc.

Murrah, Brayden. The Flower of Her Youth: Every Great Woman Was Once a Young Girl, to Some She Did Nothing, to Others She Changed Their World. Murrah, Emma-Grace. Elise, Sony, ed. 2018. (ENG.). 340p. (J). pap. 12.25 *(978-1-7321239-0-8(X))* Murrah, Emma-Grace.

Murray, Alison. Fairy Felicity's Moonlight Adventure. Murray, Alison. 2016. (ENG.). 24p. (J). (gr. -1-2). 15.99 *(978-0-7636-8945-2(9)*, Nosy Crow) Candlewick Pr.

—Hare & Tortoise. Murray, Alison. 2016. (ENG.). 32p. (J). (-k). 16.99 *(978-0-7636-8721-2(9))* Candlewick Pr.

—Hickory Dickory Dog. Murray, Alison. 2014. (ENG.). 32p. (J). (-k). 16.99 *(978-0-7636-6826-6(5))* Candlewick Pr.

—The House That Zack Built. Murray, Alison. 2016. (ENG.). 32p. (J). (-k). 16.99 *(978-0-7636-7844-9(9))* Candlewick Pr.

Murray, Carol. Cooking with Ginger: Ginger Gets Lost Book I. Keenan, Penny. 2005. (J). per. 19.95 *(978-1-932604-23-8(5))* Tennessee Valley Publishing.

Murray, Dale Edwin. The Queer Eye Guide: How to Love Yourself the Fab Five Way. Penguin Workshop, Penguin. 2020. (ENG.). 128p. (YA). (gr. 7). 14.99 *(978-0-593-09459-4(X)*, Penguin Workshop) Penguin Young Readers Group.

Murray, Ian. Super Structures. Graham, Ian. 2018. (ENG.). 48p. (J). (gr. 2-5). 24.95 ***(978-0-7603-6340-9(4))*** QEB Publishing Inc.

Murray, Jake. What Is the Story of Wonder Woman? Who HQ & Korte, Steve. 2019. (What Is the Story Of? Ser.). 112p. (J). (gr. 3-7). 6.99 *(978-1-5247-8827-8(9))*; 15.99 *(978-1-5247-8828-5(7))* Penguin Young Readers Group. (Penguin Workshop).

—What Was Stonewall? Medina, Nico & Who HQ. 2019. (What Was? Ser.). 112p. (J). (gr. 3-7). 5.99 *(978-1-5247-8600-7(4))*; lib. bdg. 15.99 *(978-1-5247-8602-1(0))* Penguin Young Readers Group. (Penguin Workshop).

—What Were the Roaring Twenties? Mortlock, Michele & Who HQ. 2018. (What Was? Ser.). 112p. (J). (gr. 3-7). 5.99 *(978-1-5247-8638-0(1))*; lib. bdg. 15.99 *(978-1-5247-8639-7(X))* Penguin Young Readers Group. (Penguin Workshop).

—Who Is R. L. Stine? Payne, M. D. & Who HQ. 2019. (Who Was? Ser.). 112p. (J). (gr. 3-7). 5.99 *(978-0-399-53959-6(X))*; 15.99 *(978-0-399-53960-2(3))* Penguin Young Readers Group. (Penguin Workshop).

—Who Is Ruth Bader Ginsburg? Demuth, Patricia Brennan & Who HQ. 2019. (Who Was? Ser.). 112p. (J). (gr. 3-7). 5.99 *(978-1-5247-9353-1(1))*; (ENG.). 15.99 *(978-1-5247-9354-8(X))* Penguin Young Readers Group. (Penguin Workshop).

—Who Was Andrew Jackson? Yacka, Douglas & Who HQ. 2017. (Who Was? Ser.). 112p. (J). (gr. 3-7). 5.99 *(978-0-399-53990-9(5)*, Penguin Workshop) Penguin Young Readers Group.

—Who Was Booker T. Washington? Buckley, James & Who HQ. 2018. (Who Was? Ser.). 112p. (J). (gr. 3-7). 5.99 *(978-0-448-48851-6(5)*, Penguin Workshop) Penguin Young Readers Group.

Murray, Jake. Who Was Celia Cruz? Pollack, Pam et al. 2020. (Who Was? Ser.). 112p. (J). (gr. 3-7). 5.99 ***(978-0-448-48869-1(8))***; 15.99 ***(978-1-5247-9213-8(6))*** Penguin Young Readers Group. (Penguin Workshop).

Murray, Jake. Who Was Henry VIII? Labrecque, Ellen & Who HQ. 2018. (Who Was? Ser.). (ENG.). 112p. (J). (gr. 3-7). 5.99 *(978-0-448-48854-7(X)*, Penguin Workshop) Penguin Young Readers Group.

—Who Were the Tuskegee Airmen? Smith, Sherri L. & Who HQ. 2018. (Who Was? Ser.). (ENG.). 112p. (J). (gr. 3-7). 5.99 *(978-0-399-54194-0(2))*; lib. bdg. 15.99 *(978-1-5247-8674-8(8))* Penguin Young Readers Group. (Penguin Workshop).

Murray, James. Tilda Pinkerton's Magical Hats. Shelton, Angela. 2013. 196p. pap. 11.99 *(978-0-9859443-7-7(4))* Quiet Owl Bks.

Murray, Joelle. Libby Loves Science. Derting, Kimberly. 2020. (Loves Science Ser.). 40p. (J). (gr. -1-3). 17.99 *(978-0-06-294604-1(8)*, Greenwillow Bks.) HarperCollins Pubs.

Murray, Laura. Amazing Alabama: A Coloring Book Journey Through Our 67 Counties. 2017. (ENG.). 80p. (J). pap. 9.95 *(978-1-58838-339-6(3)*, NewSouth Bks.) NewSouth, Inc.

Murray, Patricia. Make It & Pray It. Murray, Patricia. gif. ed. 2005. 110p. (J). (gr. 3-7). 22.00 *(978-0-88489-895-5(4))* Saint Mary's Press of Minnesota.

—Make It & Pray It: The Rosary Kit for Young People, 10 pack. Murray, Patricia. 2005. 63p. (J). (gr. -1-7). 58.75 *(978-0-88489-870-2(9))* Saint Mary's Press of Minnesota.

Murray, Paula. Pupazzo's Colorful World. Keylock, Joanna Murray. Pelayo, Ruben, tr. 2006.Tr. of colorido mundo de Pupazzo. (J). 10.00 *(978-1-889289-62-5(0))* Ye Olde Font Shoppe.

Murray, Rhett E. The Aaronic Priesthood: Seven Principles That Will Make This Power a Part of Your Daily Life. Daybell, Chad. 2003. 100p. (YA). pap. 8.95 *(978-1-55517-717-1(4)*, 77174) Cedar Fort, Inc./CFI Distribution.

Murray, Sheryl. Hand in Hand. Capucilli, Alyssa Satin. 2020. (New Books for Newborns Ser.). (ENG.). 16p. (J). (— 1). bds. 7.99 *(978-1-5344-4172-9(7)*, Little Simon) Little Simon.

Murray, Steven. Arguing: Word by Word, 1 vol. Slavens, Elaine. 2016. (Lorimer Deal with It Ser.). (ENG.). 32p. (J). (gr. 4-9). 24.95 *(978-1-55277-498-4(8)*, d7af59e9-a311-4aca-af4e-3a4b0ead221e) James Lorimer & Co. Ltd., Pubs. CAN. Dist: Lerner Publishing Group.

—Authority: Deal with It Before It Deals with You, 1 vol. Aikins, Anne Marie. 2016. (Lorimer Deal with It Ser.). (ENG.). 32p. (J). (gr. 4-9). 12.95 *(978-1-55028-869-8(5)*, a9fb8b28-adf1-465b-b976-54c657bd3e28) James Lorimer & Co. Ltd., Pubs. CAN. Dist: Lerner Publishing Group.

—Competition: From Start to Finish, 1 vol. Messier, Mireille. 2016. (Lorimer Deal with It Ser.). (ENG.). 32p. (J). (gr. 4-9). 12.95 *(978-1-55028-832-2(6)*, 94f0b9c5-60a2-4f51-b9c0-f66a556a5287) James Lorimer & Co. Ltd., Pubs. CAN. Dist: Lerner Publishing Group.

—Fighting: Without Coming to Blows, 1 vol. Slavens, Elaine. 2nd ed. 2016. (Lorimer Deal with It Ser.). (ENG.). 32p. (J). (gr. 4-9). 24.95 *(978-1-55277-501-1(1)*, 501) James Lorimer & Co. Ltd., Pubs. CAN. Dist: Lerner Publishing Group.

—Fighting: Without Coming to Blows, 1 vol. Slavens, Elaine & James Lorimer and Company Ltd. Staff. 2nd ed. 2010. (Lorimer Deal with It Ser.). (ENG.). 32p. (J). (gr. 4-8). pap. 12.95 *(978-1-55277-517-2(8)*, 9781552775172) James Lorimer & Co. Ltd., Pubs. CAN. Dist: Orca Bk. Pubs. USA.

—Girlness: Body & Soul, 1 vol. Peters, Diane. 2005. (Lorimer Deal with It Ser.). (ENG.). 32p. (J). (gr. 4-6). pap. 12.95 *(978-1-55028-891-9(1)*, 891) James Lorimer & Co. Ltd., Pubs. CAN. Dist: Formac Lorimer Bks. Ltd.

—Girlness: Deal with It Body & Soul. Peters, Diane. 2017. (Lorimer Deal with It Ser.). (ENG.). 32p. (J). (gr. 4-9). lib. bdg. 22.65 *(978-1-4594-1186-9(2)*, f89faafe-3773-4e82-8ad9-e27681f497a4) James Lorimer & Co. Ltd., Pubs. CAN. Dist: Lerner Publishing Group.

—Guyness: Body & Soul, 1 vol. Pitt, Steve. 2005. (Lorimer Deal with It Ser.). (ENG.). 32p. (J). (gr. 4-6). pap. 12.95 *(978-1-55028-892-6(X)*, 892) James Lorimer & Co. Ltd., Pubs. CAN. Dist: Formac Lorimer Bks. Ltd.

—Guyness: Deal with It Body & Soul. Pitt, Steve. 2017. (Lorimer Deal with It Ser.). (ENG.). 32p. (J). (gr. 4-9). lib. bdg. 22.65 *(978-1-4594-1187-6(0)*, 05f1373f-5f6c-4e28-aeb2-02cb60b566db) James Lorimer & Co. Ltd., Pubs. CAN. Dist: Lerner Publishing Group.

—Misconduct: Deal with It Without Bending the Rules, 1 vol. Aikins, Anne Marie. 2016. (Lorimer Deal with It Ser.). (ENG.). 32p. (J). (gr. 4-9). 12.95 *(978-1-55028-871-1(7)*, 82ec5b95-d7dc-4b72-bd3a-6bcab3e2ea59) James Lorimer & Co. Ltd., Pubs. CAN. Dist: Lerner Publishing Group.

—Racism: Deal with It Before It Gets under Your Skin, 1 vol. Aikins, Anne Marie. (Lorimer Deal with It Ser.). (ENG.). 32p. (J). (gr. 4-9). 2016. 24.95 *(978-1-55277-495-3(3)*, 76491fb1-3549-4243-a90c-5b0f156c9598); 2004. 12.95 *(978-1-55028-844-5(X)*, 844) James Lorimer & Co. Ltd., Pubs. CAN. Dist: Lerner Publishing Group.

Murrell, Diane. Friends Learn about Tobin. Murrell, Diane. 2007. (ENG.). 29p. (J). (gr. -1-3). 16.95 *(978-1-932565-41-6(8))* Future Horizons, Inc.

—Oliver Onion: The Onion Who Learns to Accept & Be Himself. Murrell, Diane. 2004. 40p. (J). (gr. -1-4). 16.95 *(978-1-931282-64-2(1))* Autism Asperger Publishing Co.

Murrish, Layne Keeton. Bubbles & Billy Sandwalker. Mogavera, Cyndie Lepori & Richards, Courtland William. 2nd ed. 2012. 106p. pap. 19.95 *(978-0-9856754-0-0(3))* IAMPress.

Murrow, Ethan. The Whale. Murrow, Vita. 2016. (ENG.). 32p. (J). (gr. -1-3). 17.99 *(978-0-7636-7965-1(8)*, Templar) Candlewick Pr.

Murrow, Ethan & Murrow, Vita. Zero Local: Next Stop: Kindness. Murrow, Ethan & Murrow, Vita. 2020. 40p. (J). (gr. -1-3). 17.99 *(978-0-7636-9747-1(8))* Candlewick Pr.

Murrow, Vita, jt. illus. see Murrow, Ethan.

Murry, Paul. Mickey Mouse Timeless Tales, Vol. 1. Wright, Bill et al. 2016. (MICKEY MOUSE Timeless Tales Ser.: 1). 260p. (J). 29.99 *(978-1-63140-580-8(2)*, 9781631405808) Idea & Design Works, LLC.

Murtas, Sara. The Birds of Glick. MacDonald, Erik. 2018. (ENG.). 52p. (J). (gr. 3-6). 19.95 *(978-0-692-13687-4(8))* EGM Pr.

—The Birds of Glick. MacDonald, Erik. 2018. (ENG.). 52p. (J). pap. 14.95 *(978-1-7199-9136-0(7))* Independently Published.

Musacchia, Vince. Scooby-Doo! The Case of the Disappearing Scooby Snacks. 2005. (Media Favorites!! Ser.). 22p. (J). 9.95 *(978-1-58117-214-0(1)*, Intervisual/Piggy Toes) Bendon, Inc.

Muscarello, James. Bad Rats. Drachman, Eric. 2008. (ENG.). 32p. (J). (gr. -1-3). 18.95 incl. lp *(978-0-9703809-4-4(1))* Kidwick Bks.

—Ellison the Elephant. Drachman, Eric. 2005. (ENG.). 32p. (J). (gr. -1-2). 18.95 incl. audio compact disk *(978-0-9703809-1-3(7))* Kidwick Bks.

—A Frog Thing. Drachman, Eric. 2006. (ENG.). 32p. (J). (gr. -1-2). 18.95 incl. audio compact disk *(978-0-9703809-3-7(3))* Kidwick Bks.

—Leo the Lightning Bug. Drachman, Eric. l.t. ed. 2005. (ENG.). 32p. (J). (gr. -1-2). 18.95 incl. audio compact disk *(978-0-9703809-0-6(9))* Kidwick Bks.

Muschinske, Emily. Fingerprint Critters: Turning Your Prints into Fun Art. 2006. 48p. (J). pap. *(978-0-439-81338-9(7))* Scholastic, Inc.

—Let's Draw a Bear with Squares. Campbell, Kathy Kuhtz. 2004. (Let's Draw with Shapes Ser.). 24p. (J). (gr. k-1). lib. bdg. 24.60 *(978-1-4042-2501-5(3)*, PowerKids Pr.) Rosen Publishing Group, Inc., The.

—Let's Draw a Bird with Shapes. Randolph, Joanne. 2005. (Let's Draw with Shapes Ser.). 24p. (J). (gr. k-1). lib. bdg. 24.60 *(978-1-4042-2792-7(X)*, PowerKids Pr.) Rosen Publishing Group, Inc., The.

—Let's Draw a Butterfly with Circles. Randolph, Joanne. 2005. (Let's Draw with Shapes Ser.). 24p. (J). (gr. k-1). lib. bdg. 22.60 *(978-1-4042-2500-8(5)*, PowerKids Pr.) Rosen Publishing Group, Inc., The.

—Let's Draw a Butterfly with Circles: Vamos a Dibujar una Mariposa Usando Circulos. Randolph, Joanne. 2004. (Let's Draw with Shapes / Vamos a dibujar con figuras Ser.). (ENG & SPA.). 24p. (J). (gr. -1-1). lib. bdg. 24.60 *(978-1-4042-7500-3(2))* Rosen Publishing Group, Inc., The.

—Let's Draw a Dinosaur with Shapes. Randolph, Joanne. 2005. (Let's Draw with Shapes Ser.). 24p. (J). (gr. k-1). lib. bdg. 24.60 *(978-1-4042-2793-4(8)*, PowerKids Pr.) Rosen Publishing Group, Inc., The.

—Let's Draw a Fire Truck with Shapes. Randolph, Joanne. 2005. (Let's Draw with Shapes Ser.). 24p. (J). (gr. k-1). lib. bdg. 24.60 *(978-1-4042-2794-1(6)*, PowerKids Pr.) Rosen Publishing Group, Inc., The.

—Let's Draw a Fire Truck with Shapes: Vamos a Dibujar un Camion de Bomberos Usando Figuras. Randolph, Joanne. 2005. (Let's Draw with Shapes / Vamos a Dibujar con Figuras Ser.). (ENG & SPA.). (J). 22.60 *(978-1-4042-7556-0(8)*, PowerKids Pr.) Rosen Publishing Group, Inc., The.

—Let's Draw a House with Shapes. Randolph, Joanne. 2005. (Let's Draw with Shapes Ser.). 24p. (J). (gr. k-1). lib. bdg. 24.60 *(978-1-4042-2795-8(4)*, PowerKids Pr.) Rosen Publishing Group, Inc., The.

—Let's Draw a House with Shapes: Vamos a Dibujar una Casa Usando Figuras. Randolph, Joanne. 2005. (Let's Draw with Shapes / Vamos a dibujar con figuras Ser.). (ENG & SPA.). (J). 24.60 *(978-1-4042-7558-4(4))* Rosen Publishing Group, Inc., The.

—Let's Draw a School Bus with Shapes. Randolph, Joanne. 2005. (Let's Draw with Shapes Ser.). 24p. (J). (gr. k-1). lib. bdg. 24.60 *(978-1-4042-2791-0(1)*, PowerKids Pr.) Rosen Publishing Group, Inc., The.

—Let's Draw a School Bus with Shapes: Vamos a Dibujar un Autobus Escolar Usando Figuras. Randolph, Joanne. 2005. (Let's Draw with Shapes / Vamos a Dibujar con Figuras Ser.). (ENG & SPA.). (J). 22.60 *(978-1-4042-7557-7(6)*, PowerKids Pr.) Rosen Publishing Group, Inc., The.

—Let's Draw a Truck with Shapes. Randolph, Joanne. 2005. (Let's Draw with Shapes Ser.). 24p. (J). (gr. k-1). lib. bdg. 24.60 *(978-1-4042-2796-5(2)*, PowerKids Pr.) Rosen Publishing Group, Inc., The.

—Let's Draw a Truck with Shapes: Vamos a Dibujar un Camion Usando Figuras. Randolph, Joanne. 2005. (Let's Draw with Shapes / Vamos a Dibujar con Figuras Ser.). (ENG & SPA.). (J). 22.60 *(978-1-4042-7554-6(1)*, PowerKids Pr.) Rosen Publishing Group, Inc., The.

Muschinske, Emily. Let's Draw a Frog with Ovals: Vamos a Dibujar una Rana Usando Ovalos. Muschinske, Emily, tr. Campbell, Kathy Kuhtz. 2004. (Let's Draw with Shapes / Vamos a dibujar con figuras Ser.). (ENG & SPA.). 24p. (J). (gr. -1-1). lib. bdg. 24.60 *(978-1-4042-7503-4(7))* Rosen Publishing Group, Inc., The.

—Let's Draw a Horse with Rectangles. Muschinske, Emily, tr. Randolph, Joanne. 2004. (Let's Draw with Shapes Ser.). 24p. (gr. -1-1). 24.60 *(978-1-4042-2502-2(1)*, PowerKids Pr.) Rosen Publishing Group, Inc., The.

Musheno, Erica. Krumbuckets. Mohr, L. C. 2007. (ENG.). 144p. (J). (gr. 2-7). 13.95 *(978-0-9769417-6-7(7))* Blooming Tree Pr.

Musofi, Lufthi. The Curious Robot. Klein, David. 2020. (ENG.). 28p. (J). pap. 14.99 ***(978-1-6723-5191-1(X))*** Independently Published.

Muss, Angela. Little Bear's Sparkly Christmas. Stone, Julia. ed. 2013. (ENG.). 6p. (J). (gr. -1-k). bds. 7.99 *(978-0-7459-6262-7(9))* Lion Hudson PLC GBR. Dist: Independent Pubs. Group.

Musselman, Annie Marie, photos by. Lobos: A Wolf Family Returns to the Wild. Peterson, Brenda. 2018. 32p. (J). (gr. k-4). 17.99 *(978-1-63217-084-2(1)*, Little Bigfoot) Sasquatch Bks.

Musselwhite, Helen. A Walk Through the Woods. Greig, Louise. 2018. (ENG.). 20p. (J). (gr. k). 19.95 *(978-1-4549-2988-8(X))* Sterling Publishing Co., Inc.

Mussenbrock, Anne. The Christmas Surprise. Meyer, Brigit. 2004. 10p. (J). bds. 5.99 *(978-1-59384-061-7(6))* Parklane Publishing.

—Merry Christmas, Little Bear. Meyer, Brigit. 2004. 10p. (J). bds. 5.99 *(978-1-59384-062-4(4))* Parklane Publishing.
Musso, Florencia. Little Miss Kitty. Carkhuff, Annette. 2019. (ENG.). 146p. (J). pap. 26.95 ***(978-1-64559-144-3(1))*** Covenant Bks.
Mustooch, Chloe Bluebird. Siha Tooskin Knows the Best Medicine. Bearhead, Charlene & Bearhead, Wilson. 2020. (Siha Tooskin Knows Ser.: 6). (ENG.). 24p. (J). (gr. 3-6). pap. *(978-1-55379-840-8(6)*, HighWater Pr.) Portage & Main Pr.
—Siha Tooskin Knows the Catcher of Dreams. Bearhead, Charlene & Bearhead, Wilson. 2020. (Siha Tooskin Knows Ser.: 4). (ENG.). 32p. (J). (gr. 3-6). pap. *(978-1-55379-832-3(5)*, HighWater Pr.) Portage & Main Pr.
—Siha Tooskin Knows the Gifts of His People. Bearhead, Charlene & Bearhead, Wilson. 2020. (Siha Tooskin Knows Ser.: 1). (ENG.). 24p. (J). (gr. 3-6). pap. *(978-1-55379-834-7(1)*, HighWater Pr.) Portage & Main Pr.
—Siha Tooskin Knows the Love of the Dance. Bearhead, Charlene & Bearhead, Wilson. 2020. (Siha Tooskin Knows Ser.: 8). (ENG.). 40p. (J). (gr. 3-6). *(978-1-55379-852-1(X)*, HighWater Pr.) Portage & Main Pr.
—Siha Tooskin Knows the Nature of Life. Bearhead, Charlene & Bearhead, Wilson. 2020. (Siha Tooskin Knows Ser.: 5). (ENG.). 40p. (J). (gr. 3-6). *(978-1-55379-843-9(0)*, HighWater Pr.) Portage & Main Pr.
—Siha Tooskin Knows the Offering of Tobacco. Bearhead, Charlene & Bearhead, Wilson. 2020. (Siha Tooskin Knows Ser.: 7). (ENG.). 24p. (J). (gr. 3-6). *(978-1-55379-846-0(5)*, HighWater Pr.) Portage & Main Pr.
—Siha Tooskin Knows the Sacred Eagle Feather. Bearhead, Charlene & Bearhead, Wilson. 2020. (Siha Tooskin Knows Ser.: 2). (ENG.). 32p. (J). (gr. 3-6). *(978-1-55379-849-1(X)*, HighWater Pr.) Portage & Main Pr.
—Siha Tooskin Knows the Strength of His Hair. Bearhead, Charlene & Bearhead, Wilson. 2020. (Siha Tooskin Knows Ser.: 3). (ENG.). 24p. (J). (gr. 3-6). *(978-1-55379-837-8(6)*, HighWater Pr.) Portage & Main Pr.
Mustooche, Chloe "Bluebird". Sunflower's Story, 1 vol. Paul, Sunflower. 2020. (Finding Wakâ Ser.). (ENG.). 52p. (J). pap. 10.95 ***(978-1-926696-84-3(0)***, f88499da-72d9-4505-834f-10233c3008de) Eschia Bks. CAN. Dist: Lone Pine Publishing USA.
Mustooche, Chloe "Bluebird". Jaysen's Story, 1 vol. Flett-Paul, Jaysen. 2020. (Finding Wakâ Ser.). (ENG.). 36p. (J). pap. 9.95 ***(978-1-926696-82-9(4)***, 65088179-dab9-412a-bfbc-3acb821ad3b3) Eschia Bks. CAN. Dist: Lone Pine Publishing USA.
Muszynski, Eva. Brer Rabbit down the Well. Stowell, Louie. 2010. (First Reading Level 2 Ser.). 32p. (J). 6.99 *(978-0-7945-2674-0(8)*, Usborne) EDC Publishing.
Muszynski, Maria. Quarantine: Keep Out! Cowan, Trudy. 2018. (ENG.). 40p. (J). *(978-1-5255-2160-7(8))*; pap. *(978-1-5255-2161-4(6))* FriesenPress.
Muth, Jon J. Blowin' in the Wind. Dylan, Bob. 2011. 28p. (J). (gr. k-3). 17.95 *(978-1-4027-8002-8(8))* Sterling Publishing Co., Inc.
—The Christmas Magic. Thompson, Lauren. 2009. (ENG.). 40p. (J). (gr. -1-2). 17.99 *(978-0-439-77497-0(7)*, Scholastic Pr.) Scholastic, Inc.
—City Dog, Country Frog. Willems, Mo. 2010. (ENG.). 64p. (J). (gr. -1-k). 17.99 *(978-1-4231-0300-4(9))* Hyperion Pr.
—A Family of Poems: My Favorite Poetry for Children. Kennedy, Caroline. 2005. (ENG.). 144p. (J). (gr. 5-9). 21.99 *(978-0-7868-5111-9(2))* Hyperion Pr.
—I Will Hold You 'Til You Sleep. Zuckerman, Linda. 2006. (J). *(978-0-439-43421-8(1)*, Levine, Arthur A. Bks.) Scholastic, Inc.
—Mr. George Baker. Hest, Amy. 2007. (ENG.). 32p. (J). (gr. k-3). 6.99 *(978-0-7636-3308-0(9))* Candlewick Pr.
—No Dogs Allowed! Manzano, Sonia. 2004. (ENG.). 32p. (J). (gr. -1-2). 17.99 *(978-0-689-83088-4(2)*, Atheneum Bks. for Young Readers) Simon & Schuster Children's Publishing.
—No Dogs Allowed! Manzano, Sonia. 2005. (J). 27.95 incl. audio *(978-0-8045-6927-9(4)*, SAC6927); 29.95 incl. audio compact disk *(978-0-8045-4101-5(9)*, SACD4101) Spoken Arts, Inc.
—Old Turtle & the Broken Truth. Wood, Douglas. 2003. (ENG.). 64p. (J). (gr. -1-3). 17.99 *(978-0-439-32109-9(3))* Scholastic, Inc.
Muth, Jon J. Poems to Learn by Heart. Kennedy, Caroline & Kennedy, Caroline. 2013. 192p. (J). (gr. 5-9). 21.99 ***(978-1-4231-0805-4(1))*** Little, Brown Bks. for Young Readers.
Muth, Jon J. Poems to Learn by Heart. Kennedy, Caroline & Sampson, Ana. 2014. (ENG.). 224p. 22.95 *(978-1-78243-145-9(4))* O'Mara, Michael Bks., Ltd. GBR. Dist: Independent Pubs. Group.
—Poems to Share. Kennedy, Caroline. 2008. 32p. 17.99 *(978-1-4231-1658-5(5))* Hyperion Pr.
Muth, Jon J. Addy's Cup of Sugar. Muth, Jon J. 2010. 40p. (J). (gr. -1-3). 17.99 *(978-0-439-63430-4(X)*, Scholastic Pr.) Scholastic, Inc.
—Mama Lion Wins the Race. Muth, Jon J. 2017. 40p. (J). (gr. -1-k). 17.99 *(978-0-545-85282-1(X)*, Scholastic Pr.) Scholastic, Inc.
—Stone Soup. Muth, Jon J. (ENG.). (J). (gr. -1-3). 2011. audio compact disk 10.99 *(978-0-545-35394-6(7))*; 2003. 32p. 18.99 *(978-0-439-33909-4(X)*, Scholastic Pr.) Scholastic, Inc.
—Zen Happiness. Muth, Jon J. 2019. (ENG.). 32p. (J). (gr. k-2). 8.99 *(978-1-338-34602-2(4)*, Scholastic Pr.) Scholastic, Inc.
—Zen Shorts. Muth, Jon J. 2005. (ENG.). 40p. (J). (gr. -1-3). 17.99 *(978-0-439-33911-7(1))* Scholastic, Inc.
—Zen Socks. Muth, Jon J. 2015. 40p. (J). (gr. -1-3). 17.99 *(978-0-545-16669-0(1)*, Scholastic Pr.) Scholastic, Inc.
—Zen Ties. Muth, Jon J. 2008. (ENG.). 40p. (J). (gr. -1-3). 17.99 *(978-0-439-63425-0(3)*, Scholastic Pr.) Scholastic, Inc.
Muths, Tohn. Princess Dessabelle Makes a Friend. Dzidrums, Christine. 2011. 32p. (J). pap. 9.99 *(978-0-9826435-6-3(X))*; 17.99 *(978-0-9826435-7-0(8))* Creative Media Publishing.
Muths, Tohn Fayette. Princess Dessabelle: Tennis Star. Dzidrums, Christine. 2013. 50p. pap. 10.99 *(978-1-938438-34-9(5))* Creative Media Publishing.
Mutti, Andrea, et al. G. I. JOE: the IDW Collection Volume 1, Vol. 1. Hama, Larry & Dixon, Chuck. 2013. (Gi Joe Idw Collection: 1). (ENG.). 352p. 49.99 *(978-1-61377-549-3(0)*, 9781613775493) Idea & Design Works, LLC.
Mutz, Steve. The Big Adventures of Little Church Mouse. Bushnell, Steven G. 2017. (ENG.). (J). pap. 24.99 *(978-1-4984-9776-3(4))* Salem Author Services.
Muzzio, Denise. Geraldine & the Most Spectacular Science Project, 1 vol. Regwan, Sol. 2020. (Gizmo Girl Ser.: 1). (ENG.). 32p. (J). (gr. -1-3). 16.99 *(978-0-7643-5898-2(7)*, 17457) Schiffer Publishing, Ltd.
Muzzio, Denise. Geraldine & the Space Bees. Regwan, Sol. 2020. (Gizmo Girl Ser.: 2). (ENG.). 32p. (J). (gr. -1-3). 16.99 ***(978-0-7643-5994-1(0)***, 18556) Schiffer Publishing, Ltd.
Muzzucchelli, David. Daredevil: Born Again. 2010. 248p. (YA). (gr. 8-17). pap. 19.99 *(978-0-7851-3481-7(6))* Marvel Worldwide, Inc.
My Wolf Dog. A Peek into the Secret Little Ones of Turtle Back Island. Avignone, June. 2004. 40p. (J). pap. *(978-0-9654628-2-2(X))* Mill Street Forward, The.
Myagmardorj, Enkhtungalag. The Doll That Flew Away. Batkhuu, Kh. 2007. 32p. (J). (POL & ENG.). pap. 12.95 *(978-1-60195-098-7(5))*; (ARA & ENG.). pap. 12.95 *(978-1-60195-092-5(6))* International Step by Step Assn.
Mycek-Wodecki, Anna. How Would It Feel? Goddard, Mary Beth. 2005. (ENG.). 32p. (J). (gr. -1-6). 15.95 *(978-1-59143-050-6(X)*, Bear Cub Bks.) Bear & Co.
Mycek-Wodecki, Anna. The Bilingual Dog. Mycek-Wodecki, Anna. Abt, Diana, tr. 2008. (Minutka Ser.). (ENG.). 48p. (J). (gr. -1-k). 9.95 *(978-1-84059-509-3(4))* Milet Publishing.
—The Bilingual Dog/Iki Dilli Kopek. Mycek-Wodecki, Anna. Erdogan, Fatih, tr. 2008. (Minutka Ser.). (ENG.). 48p. (J). (gr. -1-k). 9.95 *(978-1-84059-510-9(8))* Milet Publishing.
—Minutka: The Bilingual Dog & Friends. Mycek-Wodecki, Anna. ed. 2009. (Minutka Ser.). (ENG.). 48p. (J). (gr. k—1). 9.95 *(978-1-84059-527-7(2))* Milet Publishing.
Myer, Ed. Deadly Dinosaurs. George, Joshua. 2019. (Lift-The-flap History Ser.). (ENG.). 10p. (J). (gr. -1-k). 9.99 *(978-1-78700-982-0(3))* Top That! Publishing PLC GBR. Dist: Independent Pubs. Group.
—Dinosaurs. George, Joshua. 2016. (Sticker History Ser.). (ENG.). 38p. (J). (gr. k-6). pap. 8.99 *(978-1-78445-859-1(7))* Top That! Publishing PLC GBR. Dist: Independent Pubs. Group.
—Famous Explorers. George, Joshua. 2019. (Lift-The-flap History Ser.). (ENG.). 10p. (J). (gr. k-2). 9.99 *(978-1-78700-996-7(3))* Top That! Publishing PLC GBR. Dist: Independent Pubs. Group.
—Firefighters in My Community. Bellisario, Gina. 2018. (Meet a Community Helper (Early Bird Stories (tm)) Ser.). (ENG.). 24p. (J). (gr. k-2). 27.99 *(978-1-5415-2019-6(X)*, Lerner Pubns.) Lerner Publishing Group.
—Go Wild! Bible Stories for Little Ones, 1 vol. Zondervan & Bowman, Crystal. 2018. (ENG.). 32p. (J). bds. 9.99 *(978-0-310-76169-3(7))* Zonderkidz.
—Go Wild! Prayers for Little Ones, 1 vol. Zondervan et al. 2018. (ENG.). 30p. (J). bds. 9.99 *(978-0-310-76143-3(3))* Zonderkidz.
—Ice Age. George, Joshua. 2016. (Sticker History Ser.). (ENG.). 38p. (J). (gr. 2-6). pap. 8.99 *(978-1-78445-860-7(0))* Top That! Publishing PLC GBR. Dist: Independent Pubs. Group.
—In the Big City. Suen, Anastasia. 2012. (Little Birdie Bks.). (ENG.). 24p. (gr. k-1). pap. 8.95 *(978-1-61810-302-4(4)*, 9781618103024) Rourke Educational Media.
—In the Doghouse. Steinkraus, Kyla. 2012. (Little Birdie Bks.). (ENG.). 24p. (gr. 2-3). pap. 8.95 *(978-1-61810-332-1(6)*, 9781618103321) Rourke Educational Media.
—Johnny Appleseed. Suen, Anastasia. 2012. (Little Birdie Bks.). (ENG.). 24p. (gr. k-1). pap. 8.95 *(978-1-61810-301-7(6)*, 9781618103017) Rourke Educational Media.
—Let's Meet a Firefighter. Bellisario, Gina. 2013. (Cloverleaf Books (tm) — Community Helpers Ser.). (ENG.). 24p. (J). (gr. k-2). pap. 8.99 *(978-1-4677-0802-9(X)*, 9781467708029); lib. bdg. 25.32 *(978-0-7613-9025-1(1)*, 9780761390251) Lerner Publishing Group. (Millbrook Pr.).
—Let's Meet a Librarian. Bellisario, Gina. 2013. (Cloverleaf Books (tm) — Community Helpers Ser.). (ENG.). 24p. (J). (gr. k-2). pap. 8.99 *(978-1-4677-0803-6(8)*, 9781467708036, Millbrook Pr.) Lerner Publishing Group.
—Librarians in My Community. Bellisario, Gina. 2018. (Meet a Community Helper (Early Bird Stories (tm)) Ser.). (ENG.). 24p. (J). (gr. k-2). pap. 7.99 *(978-1-5415-2708-9(9))*; lib. bdg. 27.99 *(978-1-5415-2021-9(1)*, Lerner Pubns.) Lerner Publishing Group.
—Little Red Riding Hood. Selleck, Richelle. 2012. (Little Birdie Bks.). (ENG.). 24p. (gr. 2-3). pap. 8.95 *(978-1-61810-324-6(5)*, 9781618103246) Rourke Educational Media.
—Money down the Drain. Steinkraus, Kyla. 2012. (Little Birdie Bks.). (ENG.). 24p. (gr. 2-3). pap. 8.95 *(978-1-61810-329-1(6)*, 9781618103291) Rourke Educational Media.
—We're Going on a Dinosaur Dig. Suen, Anastasia. 2012. (Little Birdie Bks.). (ENG.). 24p. (gr. k-1). pap. 8.95 *(978-1-61810-299-7(0)*, 9781618102997) Rourke Educational Media.
—Zoom! & Come Back, Mack! Jinks, Jenny. 2020. (Early Bird Readers — Red (Early Bird Stories (tm)) Ser.). (ENG.). 32p. (J). (gr. -1-2). pap. 7.99 *(978-1-5415-8732-8(4)*, Lerner Pubns.) Lerner Publishing Group.
Myer, Ed & Beach, Bryan. The Science of Spacecraft: The Cosmic Truth about Rockets, Satellites, & Probes. Woolf, Alex. 2019. (Science of Engineering Ser.). (ENG.). 32p. (J). (gr. 3-3). lib. bdg. 29.00 *(978-0-531-13197-8(1)*, Watts, Franklin) Scholastic Library Publishing.
Myers, Alishea. The Adventures of Brady Bean: Operation: Canine Caper. Wafer, C. K. 2008. (J). pap. 5.95 *(978-0-9797580-1-0(7))* CK Bks.
—The Adventures of Brady Bean: Operation: Georgie Porgie. Wafer, C. K. & Wafer, C. K. 2007. (J). pap. 5.95 *(978-0-9797580-0-3(9))* CK Bks.
Myers, Anna. I Love My Name. Grant, Linda Ahdieh. 2020. (ENG.). 40p. (J). (gr. k-2). 12.95 ***(978-1-61851-156-0(4))*** Baha'i Publishing.
Myers, Bernice & Myers, Lou. Sailing on a Very Fine Day. Ives, Burl. 2011. 32p. pap. 35.95 *(978-1-258-04002-4(6))* Literary Licensing, LLC.
Myers, Christopher. Autobiography of My Dead Brother. Myers, Walter Dean. 2006. (ENG.). 224p. (YA). (gr. 9). pap. 9.99 *(978-0-06-058293-7(6)*, Amistad) HarperCollins Pubs.
—Firebird. Copeland, Misty. 2014. 40p. (J). (gr. k-3). 17.99 *(978-0-399-16615-0(7)*, G.P. Putnam's Sons Books for Young Readers) Penguin Young Readers Group.
—Jazz. Myers, Walter Dean. 2008. (ENG.). 48p. (J). (gr. 3-7). pap. 12.99 *(978-0-8234-2173-2(2))* Holiday Hse., Inc.
—Lies & Other Tall Tales. Hurston, Zora Neale & Thomas, Joyce Carol. 2015. (ENG.). 40p. (J). (gr. -1-3). pap. 7.99 *(978-0-06-000657-0(9))* HarperCollins Pubs.
—Looking Like Me. Myers, Walter Dean. 2009. (ENG.). 32p. (J). (gr. k-3). 18.99 *(978-1-60684-001-6(0)*, 9781606840016, Carolrhoda Bks.) Lerner Publishing Group.
—We Are America: A Tribute from the Heart. Myers, Walter Dean. (ENG.). 40p. (J). (gr. 1-5). 2015. pap. 6.99 *(978-0-06-052310-7(7))*; 2011. 16.99 *(978-0-06-052308-4(5))* HarperCollins Pubs. (Collins).
Myers, Christopher. H. O. R. S. E. Myers, Christopher. 2012. (ENG.). 32p. (J). (gr. -1-6). 19.99 *(978-1-60684-218-8(8)*, 9781606842188, Carolrhoda Bks.) Lerner Publishing Group.
—Jazz. Myers, Christopher. Myers, Walter Dean. 2006. (ENG.). 48p. (J). (gr. 3-7). 18.95 *(978-0-8234-1545-8(7))* Holiday Hse., Inc.
Myers, Christopher & Kaa Illustration. Nighttime Symphony. Timbaland & Myers, Christopher. 2019. (ENG.). 32p. (J). (gr. -1-3). 17.99 *(978-1-4424-1208-8(9)*, Atheneum Bks. for Young Readers) Simon & Schuster Children's Publishing.
Myers, Christopher A. Monster. Myers, Walter Dean. ed. 2004. (National Book Award Finalist Ser.). 281p. (YA). (gr. 7-12). lib. bdg. 20.85 *(978-0-613-35985-6(2))* Turtleback.
Myers, Courtney. If You Were a Bandicoot. Wheeler, Ty. 2020. (ENG.). 28p. (J). pap. 12.99 ***(978-1-947773-74-5(7)***, Yawn Publishing LLC) Yawn's Bks. & More, Inc.
Myers, Doug. Seeing the Sky: 100 Projects, Activities & Explorations in Astronomy. Schaaf, Fred. 2012. (Dover Children's Science Bks.). (ENG.). 224p. (C). (gr. 8). pap. 14.95 *(978-0-486-48888-2(8))* Dover Pubns., Inc.
Myers, Garret. Don't Be a Bully. Brown, Joel. 2017. (Zoom-Boom Book Ser.: 4). (ENG.). (J). (gr. k-2). 17.99 *(978-1-946683-00-7(0))* Rapier Publishing Co., LLC.
Myers, Garrett. Delia & Friends Coloring & Activity Book. Johnson-Myers, Sharon. 2019. (ENG.). 26p. (J). (gr. k-5). pap. 9.99 *(978-1-942871-17-0(1))* Hope of Vision Publishing.
—Don't Be a Bully. Brown, Joel. 2017. (Zoom-Boom the Scarecrow & Friends Ser.: 4). (ENG.). (J). (gr. k-3). pap. 12.95 *(978-1-946683-06-9(X))* Rapier Publishing Co., LLC.
Myers, Garrett. Eli Makes Room. Torrence, Jaala. 2019. (ENG.). 22p. (J). (gr. k-2). 16.95 ***(978-1-946683-28-1(0))*** Rapier Publishing Co., LLC.
—Eli Meets Someone New. Torrence, Jaala. 2019. (ENG.). 20p. (J). (gr. k-2). pap. 12.95 ***(978-1-946683-32-8(9))***; 16.95 ***(978-1-946683-29-8(9))*** Rapier Publishing Co., LLC.
Myers, Garrett. Eye on the Cross. Daniels, LaTonya. 2016. (Best Break Ever Ser.: 1). (ENG.). (J). (gr. 2-4). 17.99 *(978-0-9977029-8-9(2))* Rapier Publishing Co., LLC.
—Fire! with Matchell the Crow. Brown, Joel. 2017. (Zoom-Boom Book Ser.: 5). (ENG.). (J). (gr. k-3). 17.99 *(978-1-946683-01-4(9))*; pap. 12.95 *(978-1-946683-07-6(8))* Rapier Publishing Co., LLC.
—The Money ($$$) Tree with Anthony Ant. Brown, Joel. 2017. (Zoom-Boom the Scarecrow & Friends Ser.: 6). (ENG.). (J). (gr. 1-3). pap. 12.95 *(978-1-946683-08-3(6))*; 17.99 *(978-1-946683-02-1(7))* Rapier Publishing Co., LLC.
—Tall Tales with Lyman the Liar, & Zoom-Boom. Brown, Joel. 2018. (Zoom-Boom the Scarecrow & Friends Ser.: 8). (ENG.). 30p. (J). (gr. k-3). pap. 12.95 *(978-1-946683-21-2(3))*; 17.99 *(978-1-946683-13-7(2))* Rapier Publishing Co., LLC.
—The Water Cycle: Wyatt the Water Drop. Phillips, Zack (Z J.). 2019. (ENG.). 18p. (J). (gr. k-2). 16.95 *(978-1-946683-23-6(X))* Rapier Publishing Co., LLC.
—Water Worries with Graham Quackers, & Zoom-Boom. Brown, Joel. 2018. (Zoom-Boom the Scarecrow & Friends Ser.: 9). (ENG.). 30p. (J). (gr. k-3). pap. 12.95 *(978-1-946683-22-9(1))*; 17.99 *(978-1-946683-14-4(0))* Rapier Publishing Co., LLC.
Myers, Garrett. Eli Makes Room. Myers, Garrett. Torrence, Jaala. 2019. (ENG.). 22p. (J). (gr. k-2). pap. 12.95 ***(978-1-946683-30-4(2))*** Rapier Publishing Co., LLC.
Myers, Glenn. Solomon Builds the Temple: 1 Kings 5:1-8:66. 2005. (Little Learner Bible Story Books). 16p. (J). pap. 2.29 *(978-0-7586-0944-1(2))* Concordia Publishing Hse.
—Stephen Stands Strong. Stiegemeyer, Julie. 2004. (ENG.). 16p. (J). 1.99 *(978-0-570-07576-9(9))* Concordia Publishing Hse.
Myers, Kevin. EDGE: Tommy Donbavand's Funny Shorts: Dinner Ladies of Doooooom! Donbavand, Tommy. ed. 2018. (EDGE: Tommy Donbavand's Funny Shorts Ser.). 64p. (J). (gr. 2-4). 12.99 *(978-1-4451-5385-8(8)*, Franklin Watts) Hachette Children's Group GBR. Dist: Hachette Bk. Group.
Myers, Kristen. Piper's Great Adventures. Lowry, Mark & Bolton, Martha. 2005. (ENG.). 124p. pap. 15.99 *(978-1-58229-474-2(7)*, Howard Bks.) Howard Bks.
Myers, Lawrence E. Glow-In-The-Dark Zombie Science. Hall, Kirsten. 2009. 32p. (J). pap. *(978-0-545-22626-4(0))* Scholastic, Inc.
—Night Sky. Salzano, Tammi J. 2009. 48p. (J). pap. *(978-0-545-13832-1(9))* Scholastic, Inc.
—Space. Dakota, Heather. 2008. 64p. (J). pap. *(978-0-545-08503-8(9))* Scholastic, Inc.
Myers, Lindsay. Pug & Dot: A Day to Remember. Lowe, Stuart. 2018. (My Favorite Stories Ser.). (ENG.). 20p. (J). *(978-1-5255-3353-2(3))*; pap. *(978-1-5255-3354-9(1))* FriesenPress.
Myers, Lou, jt. illus. see Myers, Bernice.
Myers, Marie Honre. Little Duck. Barrows, Marjorie. 2011. 50p. 35.95 *(978-1-258-08897-2(5))* Literary Licensing, LLC.
Myers, Mary A. Frankie in the Farmyard. Jessee, Anne K. 2017. (Frankie Files Ser.). (ENG.). 36p. (J). 16.99 ***(978-1-936354-63-4(2))*** Tremendous Life Bks.
Myers, Matt. Danger Goes Berserk. Barnett, Mac. 2013. (Brixton Brothers Ser.: 4). (ENG.). 256p. (J). (gr. 3-7). pap. 8.99 *(978-1-4424-3978-8(5)*, Simon & Schuster Bks. For Young Readers) Simon & Schuster Bks. For Young Readers.
—A Dog Named Doug. Wilson, Karma. 2018. (ENG.). 40p. (J). (gr. -1-3). 17.99 *(978-1-4424-4931-2(4)*, McElderry, Margaret K. Bks.) McElderry, Margaret K. Bks.
—The Infamous Ratsos. LaReau, Kara. (Infamous Ratsos Ser.). (J). (gr. k-3). 2017. 96p. 14.99 *(978-0-7636-7637-7(3))*; 2017. 64p. pap. 4.99 *(978-0-7636-9875-1(X))*; 2016. 64p. 14.99 *(978-0-7636-7636-0(5))* Candlewick Pr.
—The Infamous Ratsos Are Not Afraid. LaReau, Kara. 2018. (Infamous Ratsos Ser.). 96p. (J). (gr. k-3). pap. 5.99 *(978-1-5362-0368-4(8))* Candlewick Pr.
—The Infamous Ratsos Camp Out. LaReau, Kara. 2020. (Infamous Ratsos Ser.). 80p. (J). (gr. k-3). 14.99 *(978-1-5362-0006-5(9))* Candlewick Pr.
—The Infamous Ratsos: Project Fluffy. LaReau, Kara. (Infamous Ratsos Ser.). 96p. (J). (gr. k-3). 2020. pap. 5.99 *(978-1-5362-0880-1(9))*; 2018. 14.99 *(978-1-5362-0005-8(0))* Candlewick Pr.
—The Most Terrible of All. Van, Muon Thi. 2019. (ENG.). 40p. (J). (gr. -1-3). 17.99 *(978-1-5344-1716-8(8)*, McElderry, Margaret K. Bks.) McElderry, Margaret K. Bks.
—Pirate's Perfect Pet. Ferry, Beth. 2016. (ENG.). 32p. (J). (gr. -1-3). 16.99 *(978-0-7636-7288-1(2))* Candlewick Pr.
—Scarecrow Magic. Masessa, Ed. 2015. (ENG.). 32p. (J). (gr. -1-k). 16.99 *(978-0-545-69109-3(5))* Scholastic, Inc.
—Tiny & the Big Dig. Rinker, Sherri Duskey. 2018. (ENG.). 32p. (J). (gr. -1-k). 16.99 *(978-0-545-90429-2(3)*, Scholastic Pr.) Scholastic, Inc.
Myers, Matt, jt. illus. see Rex, Adam.
Myers, Matthew. Bartholomew Biddle & the Very Big Wind. Ross, Gary. 2012. (ENG.). 96p. (J). (gr. 1-4). 17.99 *(978-0-7636-4920-3(1))* Candlewick Pr.
—Battle Bunny. Scieszka, Jon & Barnett, Mac. 2013. (ENG.). 32p. (J). (gr. k-4). 15.99 *(978-1-4424-4673-1(0)*, Simon & Schuster Bks. For Young Readers) Simon & Schuster Bks. For Young Readers.
—Clink. DiPucchio, Kelly. 2011. (ENG.). 32p. (J). (gr. -1-2). 16.99 *(978-0-06-192928-1(X))* HarperCollins Pubs.
—Cock-a-Doodle-Doo-Bop. Black, Michael Ian. 2015. (ENG.). 40p. (J). (gr. -1-3). 17.99 *(978-1-4424-9510-4(3)*, Simon & Schuster Bks. For Young Readers) Simon & Schuster Bks. For Young Readers.
—Danger Goes Berserk. Barnett, Mac. 2012. (Brixton Brothers Ser.: 4). (ENG.). 256p. (J). (gr. 3-7). 17.99 *(978-1-4424-3977-1(7)*, Simon & Schuster Bks. For Young Readers) Simon & Schuster Bks. For Young Readers.
—A Is for Musk Ox. Cabatingan, Erin. 2012. (Musk Ox Ser.: 1). (ENG.). 40p. (J). (gr. k-2). 18.99 *(978-1-59643-676-3(X)*, 900071112) Roaring Brook Pr.
—What James Said. Rosenberg, Liz. 2015. (ENG.). 32p. (J). (gr. k-3). 17.99 *(978-1-59643-908-5(4)*, 900120638) Roaring Brook Pr.
—The World According to Musk Ox. Cabatingan, Erin. 2014. (Musk Ox Ser.: 3). (ENG.). 40p. (J). (gr. k-2). 17.99 *(978-1-59643-799-9(5)*, 9781596437999) Roaring Brook Pr.
Myers, Megan Marie. Together. Heinz, Derek. 2017. (ENG.). (J). pap. 10.95 *(978-0-578-19115-7(6))* Heinz, Derek.
Myers, Nate. The Barn Quilt: A Christmas Story. Michels, Patti. 2019. (ENG.). 26p. (J). 22.99 ***(978-1-68314-983-5(1))***; pap. 12.99 ***(978-1-68314-982-8(3))*** Redemption Pr.
Myers, Nneka. Dancing Queen #4. Starling Lyons, Kelly. 2019. (Jada Jones Ser.: 4). 96p. (J). (gr. 1-3). (ENG.). 6.99 *(978-1-5247-9058-5(3))*; 15.99 *(978-1-5247-9059-2(1))* Penguin Young Readers Group. (Penguin Workshop).
—I Love King Dad! (Nella the Princess Knight) Random House. 2017. (Step into Reading Ser.). (ENG.). 24p. (J). (gr. -1-1). pap. 4.99 *(978-1-5247-6889-8(8))*; lib. bdg. 12.99 *(978-1-5247-6890-4(1))* Random Hse. Children's Bks. (Random Hse. Bks. for Young Readers).
—The Share Fair (Nella the Princess Knight) Finnegan, Delphine. 2019. (Step into Reading Ser.). (ENG.). 24p. (J). (gr. -1-1). 4.99 *(978-0-525-64731-7(7))*; 12.99 *(978-0-525-64732-4(5))* Random Hse. Children's Bks. (Random Hse. Bks. for Young Readers).
—Sing Your Song! (Nella the Princess Knight) Depken, Kristen L. 2017. (Step into Reading Ser.). (ENG.). 24p. (J). (gr. -1-1). pap. 4.99 *(978-1-5247-6505-7(8))*; lib. bdg. 12.99 *(978-1-5247-6506-4(6))* Random Hse. Children's Bks. (Random Hse. Bks. for Young Readers).

—Who Did It First? 50 Politicians, Activists, & Entrepreneurs Who Revolutionized the World. Leslie, Jay. Hart, Alex, ed. 2020. (Who Did It First? Ser.: 2). (ENG.). 128p. (J). 18.99 *(978-1-250-21172-9(7)*, 900203647, Holt, Henry & Co. Bks. For Young Readers) Holt, Henry & Co.

Myers, Nneka & Brantley-Newton, Vanessa. Sleepover Scientist #3. Lyons, Kelly Starling. 2019. (Jada Jones Ser.: 3). 96p. (J). (gr. 1-3). lib. bdg. 15.99 *(978-1-5247-9056-1(7)*, Penguin Workshop) Penguin Young Readers Group.

—Sleepover Scientist #3. Starling Lyons, Kelly. 2019. (Jada Jones Ser.: 3). 96p. (J). (gr. 1-3). 6.99 *(978-1-5247-9055-4(9)*, Penguin Workshop) Penguin Young Readers Group.

Myers, Nneka, jt. illus. see Random House.

Myers, Robbie. Brinley Discovers Santa: A Bold Introduction to the Meaning Behind Santa Claus. Smith, Brooke. 2018. (ENG.). 44p. (J). pap. 11.48 *(978-1-7918-7365-3(0))* Independently Published.

Myers, Robbie. Brinley Discovers Santa: A Bold Introduction to the Meaning Behind Santa Claus. Smith, Brooke. 2nd ed. 2015. (ENG.). 44p. (J). 21.95 ***(978-0-578-43645-6(0))*** Wonder Storm Productions, LLC.

Myers, Shari. Rising above Global Warming. DeFrancesco, B. J. 2007. 46p. (J). per. 19.95 *(978-0-9801555-0-1(9))* Argus Enterprises International, Inc.

—The Wild Adventures of a Curious Princess. McGhee, Heather. 2008. (J). per. 9.99 *(978-0-9788985-9-5(1))* W & B Pubs.

Myers, Shelly. Colorful Vern. Savage, Jerelyn E. 2005. (ENG.). 34p. per. 20.25 *(978-1-4208-6449-6(1))* AuthorHouse.

Myers, Shirley. Mother Hen & Her Ten. Hege, Lynnita Rae. 2015. (ENG.). 164p. (J). (gr. -1). 13.50 *(978-0-7399-2499-0(0))* Rod & Staff Pubs., Inc.

Myers, V. G. Mind-Boggling Word Puzzles. Gardner, Martin. 2010. (Dover Children's Activity Bks.). (ENG.). 96p. (J). (gr. 3-5). pap. 4.99 *(978-0-486-47496-0(8))* Dover Pubns., Inc.

Mykalevych, Viktoriia. Teddy Bear's Birthday Bash. Taylor, Courtney. 2019. (ENG.). 36p. (J). *(978-1-5255-4084-4(X))*; pap. *(978-1-5255-4085-1(8))* FriesenPress.

Mykhalevych, Viktoriia. Jobear. Valente, Sarah Hawkes & Hawkes Jr, George W. 2018. (ENG.). 44p. (J). pap. 12.95 *(978-1-948384-03-2(5))* Whatever is Lovely Pubns.

—Today I'm a Monster. Green, Agnes. I.t. ed. 2018. (ENG.). 34p. (J). (gr. k-1). 19.99 *(978-1-5323-7793-8(2))* April Tale Bks.

Myler, Terry. Back up the Beanstalk. Keilty, Derek. 2003. (Chimps Ser.: 5). (ENG.). 64p. (J). pap. 10.95 *(978-1-901737-45-5(4))* Anvil Bks., Ltd. IRL. Dist: Dufour Editions, Inc.

—Cookie & Curley. Mulligan, Frank. 2003. (Chimps Ser.: 2). (ENG.). 64p. (J). (gr. k-18). pap. 9.95 *(978-1-901737-38-7(1))* Anvil Bks., Ltd. IRL. Dist: Dufour Editions, Inc.

—A Fresh Start. Regan, Peter. 2004. (Shannon Harps Ser.: 03). (ENG.). 112p. (J). per. 10.95 *(978-1-901737-49-3(7))* Anvil Bks., Ltd. IRL. Dist: Dufour Editions, Inc.

—The Return of the Big Bad Wolf. Farrell, Liam. 2004. (ENG.). 64p. (J). pap. 10.95 *(978-1-901737-48-6(9))* Anvil Bks., Ltd. IRL. Dist: Dufour Editions, Inc.

—Riverside: The Curse. Regan, Peter. 2004. (Riverside Ser.). (ENG.). 127p. (J). pap. 11.95 *(978-1-901737-46-2(2))* Anvil Bks., Ltd. IRL. Dist: Dufour Editions, Inc.

—Shannon Harps. Regan, Peter. 2003. (Shannon Harps Ser.: 01). (ENG.). 128p. (J). (gr. 3-18). pap. 10.95 *(978-1-901737-41-7(1))* Anvil Bks., Ltd. IRL. Dist: Dufour Editions, Inc.

—Something New, Vol. 2. Regan, Peter. 2004. (Shannon Harps Ser.: 02). (ENG.). 112p. (J). pap. 10.95 *(978-1-901737-52-3(7))* Anvil Bks., Ltd. IRL. Dist: Dufour Editions, Inc.

—Two Mad Dogs. Harrison, Cora. 2003. (Chimps Ser.: 4). (ENG.). 64p. (J). pap. 10.95 *(978-1-901737-44-8(6))* Anvil Bks., Ltd. IRL. Dist: Dufour Editions, Inc.

—Where's Jacko? Hickey, Tony. 2006. (ENG.). 64p. (J). pap. 10.95 *(978-1-901737-47-9(0))* Anvil Bks., Ltd. IRL. Dist: Dufour Editions, Inc.

Myles, Marlena. Powwow Day. Sorell, Traci. 2020. (J). lib. bdg. *(978-1-58089-948-2(X))* Charlesbridge Publishing, Inc.

—Thanku: Poems of Gratitude. Paul, Miranda. 2019. (ENG.). 40p. (J). (gr. 1-4). lib. bdg. 19.99 *(978-1-5415-2363-0(6)*, Millbrook Pr.) Lerner Publishing Group.

Mytinger, Liz. Pet Portraits Locked Diary. Mudpuppy. 2017. (ENG.). 192p. (J). (gr. -1-7). 10.99 *(978-0-7353-5211-7(9))* Mudpuppy Pr.

—Read & Ride: Magical Horses. 2019. (ENG.). 5p. (J). (gr. -1 — 1). bds. 15.99 *(978-1-4521-6547-9(5))* Chronicle Bks. LLC.

M©zi¬res, Jean-Claude. Valerian Vol. 2: The Complete Collection. 2017. (Valerian & Laureline Ser.: Volume 2). (ENG.). 172p. 29.99 *(978-1-84918-356-7(2))* CineBook GBR. Dist: National Bk. Network.

N

N Gallerie Studios. The Island Hunters - Book III: The Legend of Brown Eyed James. Walford, N. E. 2016. 180p. (J). 26.99 *(978-0-9818347-6-4(0))* N Gallerie Pr. LLC.

N Gallerie Studios. The Island Hunters Book II: Trail of the Tomb Robbers, vols. 2, vol. 2. N Gallerie Studios, . 2nd ed. 2016.Tr. of Los Cazadores de la Isla. (ENG.). 130p. (J). 14.99 *(978-0-9818347-7-1(9))* N Gallerie Pr. LLC.

—The Island Hunters Book III: The Legend of Brown Eyed James, vols. 2, vol. 2. N Gallerie Studios, . 2nd ed. 2016.Tr. of Los Cazadores de la Isla. (ENG.). 196p. (J). 16.99 *(978-0-9818347-8-8(7))* N Gallerie Pr. LLC.

N, Ninekyu. The Good Big Sister's Checklist. Sparrow, Johanna. Pendley, Heather, ed. 2020. (Little Miss Maple Ser.: Vol. 3). (ENG.). 24p. (J). pap. 14.99 ***(978-1-6579-9584-0(4))*** Independently Published.

Na, Il Sung. The Dreamer. 2018. (ENG.). 52p. (J). (gr. -1-k). 16.99 *(978-1-4521-5608-8(5))* Chronicle Bks. LLC.

—The Opposite Zoo. 2016. 24p. (J). (-k). 16.99 *(978-0-553-51127-7(0)*, Knopf Bks. for Young Readers) Random Hse. Children's Bks.

—Welcome Home, Bear: A Book of Animal Habitats. 2015. (ENG.). 32p. (J). (— 1). lib. bdg. 19.99 *(978-0-385-75376-0(4)*, Knopf Bks. for Young Readers) Random Hse. Children's Bks.

Naalchigar, Jennifer. Once upon an Apple Cake: A Rosh Hashanah Story. Rubinstein, Elana. 2019. (J). *(978-1-68115-549-4(4)*, Apples & Honey Pr.) Behrman Hse., Inc.

Naba, Dajana. Crowder Pea, Don't Bite! Jones, Angela & Jones, Sourou. 2010. 16p. pap. 9.99 *(978-1-60911-735-1(2)*, Eloquent Bks.) Strategic Book Publishing & Rights Agency (SBPRA).

Nabaum, Alexander. Look Both Ways: A Tale Told in Ten Blocks. Reynolds, Jason. 2019. (ENG.). 208p. (J). (gr. 5-9). 17.99 *(978-1-4814-3828-5(X)*, Atheneum/Caitlyn Dlouhy Books) Simon & Schuster Children's Publishing.

Nacaytuna, Dwight. Good Girl, Ginger! Cook, Karyn. 2019. (ENG.). 28p. (J). pap. 17.49 ***(978-1-7960-6452-0(1))*** Xlibris Corp.

NaCaytuna, Dwight. I See a Bee! Baby's First Sentences. McCarthy, Maren. 2018. (ENG.). 26p. (J). pap. 15.99 *(978-1-9845-3708-9(3))* Xlibris Corp.

Nachbauer, Amanda. Cats Everywhere. Hueging, Heather. 2016. (ENG.). (J). *(978-1-4602-9479-6(3))*; pap. *(978-1-4602-9480-2(7))* FriesenPress.

Nadaskay, Lori. Baseball Billy. Johnson, Sandi. Johnson, Britt, ed. I.t. ed. 2003. 12p. (J). (gr. k-5). spiral bd. 5.99 *(978-1-929063-30-7(X)*, 320) Moons & Stars Publishing For Children.

Nadeau, Gail. The Golden Dress: A Fairy Tale. Barkat, L. L. 2018. (ENG.). 48p. (J). pap. 12.95 *(978-1-943120-20-8(X))* T.S. Poetry Pr.

Nadeau, Janice. All about Grandmas. Schotter, Roni. 2012. 32p. (J). (gr. -1-k). 16.99 *(978-0-8037-3714-3(9)*, Dial Bks) Penguin Young Readers Group.

—Harvey: How I Became Invisible, 1 vol. Bouchard, Herve. Mixter, Helen, tr. 2017. (ENG.). 168p. (J). (gr. 4). pap. 14.95 *(978-1-77306-005-7(8))* Groundwood Bks. CAN. Dist: Publishers Group West (PGW).

—My Best Friend. Tibo, Gilles. 2019. (ENG.). 52p. (J). (gr. k-4). 16.95 *(978-1-77229-022-6(X))* Simply Read Bks. CAN. Dist: Ingram Publisher Services.

—The Tooth Mouse. Hood, Susan. 2012. (ENG.). 32p. (J). (gr. -1-2). 16.95 *(978-1-55453-565-1(4))* Kids Can Pr., Ltd. CAN. Dist: Hachette Bk. Group.

Nadel, Carolina. Daddy's Home. Nadel, Carolina. 2012. 32p. 19.95 *(978-0-9792761-4-9(4))* Mookind Pr.

Nadel, Ileana. A New Family for Dominick. Alarie, Shirley. 2016. (ENG.). (J). pap. 11.00 *(978-0-9968087-4-3(4))* Alarie, Shirley.

Nadler, Anna. Turbo & Tuxedo. Hoffman, Don & Palmer, Priscilla. 2016. (ENG.). 32p. (J). (gr. -1-k). pap. 3.99 *(978-1-943154-04-3(X))* Peek-A-Boo Publishing.

Naenix, Robin. Jessie's Walk. Brewer, Dottie A. 2004. 20p. (J). 4.95 *(978-0-9707945-7-4(6))* Billion $ Baby Pubns.

—Saul the Pelican. Brewer, Dottie A. 2004. 30p. (J). 4.95 *(978-0-9707945-9-8(2))* Billion $ Baby Pubns.

Nafeeza, Hassan. My Yoga Workbook: A Winter Yoga Journey. Hocheiser, Lara E. 2016. (My Yoga Workbook: Seasons Ser.: Vol. 1). (ENG.). (J). (gr. k-6). pap. 14.83 *(978-1-68418-148-3(8))* Primedia eLaunch LLC.

Nagai, Tomohiro. Full Metal Panic - Overload!, Vol. 5. Gatou, Shouji. 2006. (Full Metal Panic: Overload! Ser.). 200p. (YA). pap. 9.99 *(978-1-4139-0342-3(8))* ADV Manga.

Nagar, Sachin. Kama: Victory in Death. Hoskin, Rik. 2017. (Campfire Graphic Novels Ser.: 14). (ENG.). 160p. (YA). (gr. 7). pap. 14.99 *(978-93-81182-30-7(2)*, Campfire) Steerforth Pr.

—Mother Teresa: Saint of the Slums: Campfire Biography-Heroes Line. Helfand, Lewis. 2013. (Campfire Graphic Novels Ser.). (ENG.). 88p. (YA). (gr. 5). pap. 11.99 *(978-93-80028-70-5(9)*, Campfire) Steerforth Pr.

—Photo Booth. Helfand, Lewis. 2011. (Campfire Graphic Novels Ser.: 3). (ENG.). 80p. (YA). (gr. 3-7). pap. 9.99 *(978-93-80028-65-1(2)*, Campfire) Steerforth Pr.

—Sundarkaand: Triumph of Hanuman. Tulsidas. 2013. (Campfire Graphic Novels Ser.: 10). (ENG.). 72p. (YA). (gr. 5-12). pap. 9.99 *(978-93-80741-70-3(7)*, Campfire) Steerforth Pr.

—The Treasured Thief. Foley, Ryan. 2012. (Campfire Graphic Novels Ser.: 7). (ENG.). 64p. (YA). (gr. 3-7). pap. 9.99 *(978-93-80741-11-6(1)*, Campfire) Steerforth Pr.

Nagar, Sachin, jt. illus. see Tayal, Amit.

Nagara, Innosanto. A Is for Activist. Nagara, Innosanto. 2012. (ENG.). 28p. bds. 15.00 *(978-0-9883448-9-1(0))* Kupu Kupu Pr.

—M Is for Movement. Nagara, Innosanto. 2019. 96p. (J). (gr. 3-7). 19.95 *(978-1-60980-935-5(1)*, Triangle Square) Seven Stories Pr.

Nagaraju, Harsha. Deep Sea Creatures. Yelagalawadi, Jyoti. 2004. 32p. (J). 14.99 *(978-0-9725901-2-9(9))* Lekha Pubs., LLC.

—Laugh with Dinosaurs. Yelagalawadi, Jyoti. 2004. 32p. (J). 14.99 *(978-0-9725901-1-2(0))* Lekha Pubs., LLC.

Nagatomo, Hiroko. My Dad's Hat: Otousan No Boushi. Amano, Yuichi. 2020. (ENG.). 26p. (YA). 21.68 ***(978-1-0983-1126-1(4))*** BookBaby.

Naggi, Elena, jt. illus. see Shimabukuro, Denise.

Nagulakonda, Rajesh. Buddha: an Enlightened Life. Moore, Keiron. 2017. (Campfire Graphic Novels Ser.). (ENG.). 160p. (YA). (gr. 7). pap. 16.99 *(978-93-81182-29-1(9)*, Campfire) Steerforth Pr.

—Ganesha: Ravana & the Magic Stone. Dutta, Sourav. 2016. (Campfire Graphic Novels Ser.). (ENG.). 24p. (J). (gr. -1-2). pap. 5.99 *(978-93-81182-24-6(8)*, Campfire) Steerforth Pr.

—Krishna - The Defender of Dharma. Taneja, Sweta. 2013. (Campfire Graphic Novels Ser.: 8). (ENG.). 152p. (YA). (gr. 5-12). pap. 14.99 *(978-93-80741-12-3(X)*, Campfire) Steerforth Pr.

—The Time Machine: New Edition. Wells, H. G. 2020. (Campfire Graphic Novels Ser.). (ENG.). 72p. (J). (gr. 5-12). pap. 12.99 *(978-93-81182-77-2(9)*, Campfire) Steerforth Pr.

Nagy, Ian. How to Write Your Life Story. Fletcher, Ralph. 2007. 112p. (J). (gr. 3-7). 15.99 *(978-0-06-050770-1(5))* HarperCollins Pubs.

Nagy, Krisztina. Fuzzy Bear Goes to School. Bentley, Dawn. 2005. (Fuzzy Bear Ser.). 10p. (J). 10.95 *(978-1-58117-124-2(2)*, Intervisual/Piggy Toes) Bendon, Inc.

—Fuzzy Bear's Bedtime. Bentley, Dawn. 2005. (Fuzzy Bear Ser.). 10p. (J). (gr. -1-k). act. bk. ed. 10.95 *(978-1-58117-055-9(6)*, Intervisual/Piggy Toes) Bendon, Inc.

Nagy, Krisztina Kallai. The Lion Storyteller Awesome Book of Stories. Hartman, Bob. ed. 2016. (ENG.). 256p. (J). (gr. k-2). pap. 12.99 *(978-0-7459-7636-5(0))* Lion Hudson PLC GBR. Dist: Independent Pubs. Group.

—The Lion Storyteller Bible, 4 vols. Hartman, Bob. ed. 2013. (ENG.). 160p. (J). (gr. k-2). audio compact disk 22.99 *(978-0-7459-6433-1(8))* Lion Hudson PLC GBR. Dist: Independent Pubs. Group.

—The Lion Storyteller Book of Parables, 1 vol. Hartman, Bob. ed. 2015. (ENG.). 64p. (J). (gr. k-4). 14.99 *(978-0-7459-6446-1(X))* Lion Hudson PLC GBR. Dist: Independent Pubs. Group.

—The Lion Storyteller Christmas Book. Hartman, Bob. ed. 2012. (ENG.). 128p. (J). (gr. k-2). pap. 16.99 *(978-0-7459-6379-2(X))* Lion Hudson PLC GBR. Dist: Independent Pubs. Group.

—Mi Primera Biblia / the Lion Storyteller Bible. Hartman, Bob. 2018. (SPA.). 160p. (J). (gr. k-4). 15.95 *(978-1-945540-53-0(2))* Penguin Random House Grupo Editorial ESP. Dist: Penguin Random Hse. LLC.

Nagy, Krisztina Kallai. My Advent Calendar Christmas Book. Nagy, Krisztina Kallai. Jackson, Antonia. ed. 2013. (ENG.). 32p. (J). (-2). 9.99 *(978-0-7459-6392-1(7))* Lion Hudson PLC GBR. Dist: Independent Pubs. Group.

Nagy, Robert. Talisman of Zandria, 1. Norris, Christine. 2005. 187p. (YA). pap. 14.95 *(978-1-885093-44-8(6)*, LBF/Hadrosaur) Hadrosaur Pr.

Nahab, Katie. Warriors for God: Fighting Evil with Weapons of Faith. RoggenKamp, Kirsten. 2018. 208p. (J). pap. *(978-0-8163-6315-5(3))* Pacific Pr. Publishing Assn.

Nahomni Mani, Jean M. Legend of Timpanogos Mountain: A Native American Legend. Nahomni Mani, Jean M. 2019. (ENG.). 32p. (J). pap. 14.95 *(978-0-692-65514-6(X))* Dakota Legends.

Naidoo, Melvyn. The King's Test. Adebowale, Diamond. 2020. (ENG.). 48p. (J). pap. ***(978-1-928348-95-5(5))*** Verity Pubs.

Naidoo, Melvyn. Thabo en Die Klein Drakie (Afrikaans) Olivier, Malie. 2019. (AFR.). 42p. (J). pap. *(978-1-928348-38-2(6))* Verity Pubs.

Naidu, Lavanya. Prankenstein: The Book of Crazy Mischief. Bond, Ruskin & Pinto, Jerry, eds. 2017. (ENG.). 154p. (YA). (gr. 7-12). pap. *(978-93-87164-44-4(6))* Speaking Tiger Publishing.

Naifeh, Ted. Kin. Black, Holly. 2008. (Good Neighbors Ser.: 1). (ENG.). 128p. (J). (gr. 4-7). 16.99 *(978-0-439-85562-4(4)*, Graphix) Scholastic, Inc.

—Kind. Black, Holly. 2011. (Good Neighbors Ser.: 3). 128p. (YA). (gr. 7-7). pap. 12.99 *(978-0-439-85567-9(5)*, Graphix) Scholastic, Inc.

Naifeh, Ted & Wucinich, Warren. Courtney Crumrin Vol. 3: The Twilight Kingdom, Vol. 3. Naifeh, Ted. 2018. (Courtney Crumrin Ser.: 3). (ENG.). 144p. (J). pap. 12.99 *(978-1-62010-518-4(7)*, Lion Forge) Oni Pr., Inc.

—Courtney Crumrin Vol. 6: The Final Spell. Naifeh, Ted. 2020. (Courtney Crumrin Ser.: 6). (ENG.). 144p. (J). pap. 12.99 *(978-1-62010-683-9(3)*, Lion Forge) Oni Pr., Inc.

Naifeh, Ted, jt. illus. see Roman, Dave.

Naik, Neha, jt. illus. see Boldrin, Elisa.

Naim, Justice. My Gracie. Gangemi, Nikki. 2018. (ENG.). 28p. (J). (gr. 2-5). pap. 9.95 *(978-0-692-05033-0(7))* Mindful Matters LLC.

Nair, Kanika. Farmer Falgu Goes Kite Flying. Soundar, Chitra. 2019. (Farmer Falgu Ser.). (ENG.). 32p. (J). 12.95 *(978-81-8190-386-0(2))* Karadi Tales Co. Pvt. Ltd. IND. Dist: Consortium Bk. Sales & Distribution.

Najm, Fauzia & Art, Zephyr. Amber's Special Birthday Wish & Other Stories. Farrugia, Diane. 2019. (ENG.). 50p. (J). pap. ***(978-1-913289-71-3(0))*** Terence, Michael Publishing.

Nakai, Ryan. The Adventures of Young Starbury: Practice Makes Perfect. Marbury, Stephon & Dean, Marshall. 2007. 36p. (J). 12.99 *(978-0-9798250-0-2(8))* Godspeed Pr.

Nakasone, Shaun. Ethan the Ending Eater. Ladd, Debbie. 2008. 64p. (J). 17.95 *(978-0-9727615-2-9(7))* Deb on Air Bks.

—Nurse Robin's Hats. Ladd, Debbie. 2006. 52p. (J). 16.95 *(978-0-9727615-3-6(5))* Deb on Air Bks.

Nakata, Hiroe. Baby Builders. Guest, Elissa Haden. 2020. 32p. (J). (-k). 17.99 *(978-0-525-55270-3(7)*, Dial Bks) Penguin Young Readers Group.

—Baby Shoes (padded Board Book) Slater, Dashka. 2019. 26p. (J). 9.99 *(978-1-5476-0115-8(9)*, 900199135, Bloomsbury Children's Bks.) Bloomsbury Publishing USA.

—Baby's Blessings. Newman, Lesléa. 2019. (ENG.). 12p. (J). (gr. -1 — 1). bds. 5.99 *(978-1-5415-2214-5(1)*, Kar-Ben Publishing) Lerner Publishing Group.

—Clover Kitty Goes to Kittygarten. Salas, Laura Purdie. 2020. (ENG.). 40p. (J). (gr. -1-1). 17.99 *(978-1-5420-4246-8(1)*, 9781542042468, Two Lions) Amazon Publishing.

—I Love Fall! A Touch-And-Feel Board Book. Inches, Alison et al. 2009. (ENG.). 12p. (J). (gr. -1-1). bds. 6.99 *(978-1-4169-3609-1(2)*, Little Simon) Little Simon.

—One More Hug. Alexander, Megan. 2019. (ENG.). 40p. (J). (gr. -1-3). 17.99 *(978-1-5344-2971-0(9)*, Aladdin) Simon & Schuster Children's Publishing.

—Snow Happy! Hubbell, Patricia. 2010. (ENG.). 32p. (J). (gr. -1-2). 15.99 *(978-1-58246-329-2(8)*, Tricycle Pr.) Random Hse. Children's Bks.

—Tell Me My Story, Mama. Lund, Deborah S. 2004. 40p. (J). lib. bdg. 16.89 *(978-0-06-028877-8(9))* HarperCollins Pubs.

—This Is the Way a Baby Rides. Meyers, Susan. 2005. (ENG.). 32p. (J). (gr. -1-1). 15.95 *(978-0-8109-5763-3(9)*, Abrams Bks. for Young Readers) Abrams, Inc.

—Two Is for Twins. Lewison, Wendy Cheyette. 2011. (ENG.). 28p. (J). (gr. -1 — 1). bds. 7.99 *(978-0-670-01310-4(2)*, Viking Books for Young Readers) Penguin Young Readers Group.

Nakatsuka, Nako. A Is for Atom: ABCs for Aspiring Chemists. McMahon, Heidi. 2017. (ENG.). (J). pap. 14.99 *(978-0-692-95226-9(8))* PawlingPr.

Nakayama, David. Is He Man or Monster Or-Is He Both? Benjamin, Paul. 2008. (Hulk Ser.: No. 2). (ENG.). 24p. (J). (gr. 2-6). 27.07 *(978-1-59961-547-9(9)*, 9675, Marvel Age) Spotlight.

Nakayama, David, et al. Marvel Vault of Heroes: Hulk: Biggest & Best. Benjamin, Paul. 2019. 288p. (J). (gr. 4-7). pap. 17.99 *(978-1-68405-661-3(6))* Idea & Design Works, LLC.

Nakayama, David. Mayhem! Benjamin, Paul. 2008. (Hulk Ser.: No. 2). (ENG.). 24p. (J). (gr. 2-6). 27.07 *(978-1-59961-548-6(7)*, 9676, Marvel Age) Spotlight.

—Radioactive. Benjamin, Paul. 2008. (Hulk Ser.: No. 2). (ENG.). 24p. (J). (gr. 2-6). 27.07 *(978-1-59961-549-3(5)*, 9677, Marvel Age) Spotlight.

Nakhla, Jacklyn. A Rox Tail: The Adventures of Samurai Dog & Ninja Cat. Nakhla, Randy. 2019. (Rox Tail Ser.: Vol. 1). (ENG.). 34p. (J). pap. 9.99 ***(978-1-6976-6421-8(0))*** Independently Published.

Nam, Doan. Gordon & Li Li Count in Mandarin. McSween, Michele. 2010. 32p. 9.99 *(978-0-9820881-3-5(2))* McWong Ink.

—Gordon & Li Li Learn Animals in Mandarin. McSween, Michele. 2010. 32p. 9.99 *(978-0-9820881-2-8(4))* McWong Ink.

Nam, InSong. Pepper Miss Pepperoni Finds Someone to Love Her. Stapler, Jodi. 2018. (ENG.). 66p. (J). pap. 16.99 *(978-1-948256-08-7(8))* Willow Moon Publishing.

—Pepper Miss Pepperoni Finds Someone to Love Her. Stapler, Jodi. 2018. (ENG.). 66p. (J). pap. 13.99 *(978-1-948256-16-2(9))* Willow Moon Publishing.

Nam, Lorraine. Look up with Me: Neil DeGrasse Tyson: a Life among the Stars. Berne, Jennifer. 2020. 40p. (J). (gr. -1-3). pap. 8.99 ***(978-0-06-284495-8(4)***, Tegen, Katherine Bks) HarperCollins Pubs.

Namiki. Let's Make a Scribble Drawing: Adventures with Irodorikuma. Frost, Steve. 2018. (ENG.). 32p. (J). pap. *(978-0-9877096-2-2(3))* Broken Wing Media.

Nanatsuki, Kyoichi. The Gallows Bell. Nanatsuki, Kyoichi. Minagawa, Ryoji. 2005. (Project Arms Ser.: Vol. 8). (ENG.). 216p. pap. 9.99 *(978-1-59116-732-7(9))* Viz Media.

—Project Arms, Vol. 13. Nanatsuki, Kyoichi. 2006. (Project Arms Ser.). (ENG.). 208p. pap. 9.99 *(978-1-4215-0502-2(9))* Viz Media.

Nance, Dan. The Story of the H. L. Hunley & Queenie's Coin. Hawk, Frank. 2004. (ENG.). 40p. (J). (gr. k-6). 16.95 *(978-1-58536-218-9(2))* Sleeping Bear Pr.

Nancy, Elizabeth. The Mission to Save Goodness Garden. Scott, Debora. 2016. (ENG.). (J). pap. 7.99 *(978-0-9972797-0-2(2))* Wisehearted Warrior Enterprises.

Nancy Raj. Malli. Jeeva Raghunath & Nayar, Deeya. 2005. (HIN & ENG.). 16p. (J). *(978-81-8146-089-9(8))* Tulika Pubs.

Nancy, Scheibe. Kamer's Quest for Blue Lupine. Dickens, Sara Jo. 2014. (J). 18.95 *(978-1-59298-923-2(3))* Beaver's Pond Pr., Inc.

Nancy, Van Buren. Flash & Fancy - Book Two: Saving the River: More Otter Adventures on the Waccamaw River. Christine Thomas, Doran & Tom, Doran. 2016. (ENG.). (J). (gr. 2-6). pap. 14.95 *(978-1-941069-61-5(4))* ProsePress.

Nanitsos, Florance. It All Began... with a Seed. Nanitsos, Ilina. 2019. (ENG.). 26p. (J). pap. 9.99 *(978-1-5471-8184-1(2))* CreateSpace Independent Publishing Platform.

Nanny Fanny. Touch the Stars: A Children's Book. Fanny, Nanny. 2013. 32p. pap. 12.99 *(978-1-61204-275-6(9)*, Strategic Bk. Publishing) Strategic Book Publishing & Rights Agency (SBPRA).

Nanten, Yutaka. Cowboy Bebop VI. ed. 2005. 192p. pap. 9.99 *(978-1-59816-038-3(9))* TOKYOPOP, Inc.

Naomi, Greaves. Imagine. Sharp, Jennifer. 2019. (ENG.). 24p. (J). (gr. k-4). pap. ***(978-0-6482202-6-8(5))*** Daisy Lane Publishing.

Naoshi. Ice Cream Work. Naoshi. 2015. (ENG.). 40p. (J). 14.99 *(978-0-9834917-3-6(9))* Overcup Pr.

Nap, Dug & Sweet, Melissa. Weather! A Book about Pink Snow, Fighting Kites, Lightning Rods, Rains of Frogs, Typhoons, Tornadoes, & Ice Balls from Space. Rupp, Rebecca. 2003. (ENG.). 144p. (J). (gr. 3-8). pap. 14.95 *(978-1-58017-420-6(5)*, 67420) Storey Publishing, LLC.

Napier, Barb. A Foxy Christmas. Krause, Hannah Sue. Krause, Jeremiah, ed. 2018. (ENG.). 28p. (J). pap. 9.99 *(978-1-7290-5481-9(1))* Independently Published.

Napier, Louise S. Kate's Fan. Ballard, Elizabeth Silance. 2008. 48p. (J). pap. 18.95 *(978-0-9706823-3-8(6))* Righter Publishing Co., Inc.

Napoletano, Marissa. Over in the Meadow. Feierabend, John M. 2016. (First Steps in Music Ser.). 32p. (J). (gr. k-2). 16.95 *(978-1-62277-178-3(8))* G I A Pubns., Inc.

Napoli, Elena. Creepy Customers. Cooper, Brigitte Henry. 2018. (Odd Jobs Ser.). (ENG.). 48p. (J). (gr. 3-7). lib. bdg. 29.93 *(978-1-5321-3188-2(7)*, 28481, Spellbound) Magic Wagon.

—Odd Jobs (Set), 4 vols. Cooper, Brigitte Henry. 2018. (Odd Jobs Ser.). 48p. (J). (gr. 3-7). lib. bdg. 114.00

(978-1-5321-3187-5(9), 28479, Spellbound) Magic Wagon.

—Peculiar Packages. Cooper, Brigitte Henry. 2018. (Odd Jobs Ser.). (ENG.). 48p. (J). (gr. 3-7). lib. bdg. 29.93 *(978-1-5321-3189-9(5)*, 28483, Spellbound) Magic Wagon.

—Spooky Spots. Cooper, Brigitte Henry. 2018. (Odd Jobs Ser.). (ENG.). 48p. (J). (gr. 3-7). lib. bdg. 29.93 *(978-1-5321-3190-5(9)*, 28485, Spellbound) Magic Wagon.

—Terrifying Tales. Cooper, Brigitte Henry. 2018. (Odd Jobs Ser.). (ENG.). 48p. (J). (gr. 3-7). lib. bdg. 29.93 *(978-1-5321-3191-2(7)*, 28487, Spellbound) Magic Wagon.

Napp, Daniel. Stories of Dragon & Bear. Suchocki, Marjorie Hewitt & Framm, Catherine, trs. 2019. (ENG.). 102p. (J). pap. 8.50 *(978-1-0769-6167-9(3))* Independently Published.

Naranjo, Santiago. The Word No: Picture Book. Espinosa, Ana María & Daydreams. 2020. (ENG.). 34p. (J). pap. 9.99 ***(978-1-9793-7965-6(3))*** CreateSpace Independent Publishing Platform.

Narayanan, P. Marlu: The Mango Lunchkin. Ravula, S. S. 2019. (ENG.). 44p. (J). 24.99 *(978-1-7960-2233-9(0))*; pap. 17.49 *(978-1-7960-2234-6(9))* Xlibris Corp.

Narciso, Massimiliano, et al. Disney Frozen & Frozen 2: the Story of the Movies in Comics. Ferrari, Alessandro. 2020. (ENG.). 120p. (J). (gr. 3-7). 14.99 ***(978-1-5067-1738-8(1)***, Dark Horse Books) Dark Horse Comics.

Narciso, Massimiliano. Frozen. Ferrari, Alessandro. 2020. (Disney Princesses Ser.). (ENG.). 52p. (J). (gr. 2-6). lib. bdg. 28.50 ***(978-1-5321-4561-2(6)***, 35208, Graphic Novels) Spotlight.

Narciso, Massimiliano & KAWAII CREATIVE STUDIO. Disney the Nightmare Before Christmas: the Story of the Movie in Comics. Ferrari, Alessandro. 2020. (ENG.). 56p. (J). (gr. 3-7). 10.99 ***(978-1-5067-1742-5(X)***, Dark Horse Books) Dark Horse Comics.

Nardandrea, Swannee. Funny, Dust & Honey & the Giant Carrot. Stroud, David Wayne. l.t. ed. 2005. 32p. (J). 17.95 *(978-0-9762835-2-2(2))* Shooting Star Publishing.

Nardi, Tisa. Princess the Pygmy Goat. Carmen, Indigo. 2009. 24p. pap. 24.95 *(978-1-60703-824-5(2))* America Star Bks.

Nardone, Cailey J. Scoodles Escapes! Plettner, Edith D. 2019. (Scoodles Escapes! Scoodles the Pup Ser.: Vol. 4). (ENG.). 36p. (J). pap. 10.00 *(978-1-9876-5553-7(2))* CreateSpace Independent Publishing Platform.

—Scoodles Goes to Church. Plettner, Edith D. 2019. (Scoodles Goes to Church Scoodles the Pup Ser.: Vol. 6). (ENG.). 46p. (J). pap. 10.00 *(978-1-9876-5568-1(0))* CreateSpace Independent Publishing Platform.

—Scoodles Says Don't Go. Plettner, Edith D. 2019. (Scoodles Says Don't Go Scoodles the Pup Ser.: Vol. 5). (ENG.). 42p. (J). pap. 10.00 *(978-1-9876-5559-9(1))* CreateSpace Independent Publishing Platform.

—Scoodles Says Hello. Plettner, Edith D. 2019. (Scoodles Says Hello Scoodles the Pup Ser.: Vol. 1). (ENG.). 40p. (J). pap. 10.00 *(978-1-9877-8918-8(0))* CreateSpace Independent Publishing Platform.

—Scoodles Uncaged. Plettner, Edith D. 2019. (Scoodles Uncaged Scoodles the Pup Ser.: Vol. 3). (ENG.). 42p. (J). pap. 10.00 *(978-1-9876-5550-6(8))* CreateSpace Independent Publishing Platform.

Narváez, Nicole. We Wish You a Poopy Christmas: Fudgy the Poopman's Collection of Christmas Classics Made Crappy. Miller, Bonnie. 2018. (Illustrated Bathroom Bks.). (ENG.). 64p. 14.95 *(978-1-61243-843-6(1))* Ulysses Pr.

Nascimbene, Yan. The Creative Collection of American Short Stories. Various Authors, Chronicle. 2010. (ENG.). 272p. (J). (gr. 4-7). 28.95 *(978-1-56846-202-8(6)*, Creative Editions) Creative Co., The.

—Crouching Tiger. Compestine, Ying Chang. 40p. (J). (gr. 1-4). 2019. 6.99 *(978-1-5362-0560-2(5))*; 2011. 16.99 *(978-0-7636-4642-4(3))* Candlewick Pr.

—E Is for Eiffel Tower: A France Alphabet. Wilbur, Helen L. 2010. (Discover the World Ser.). (ENG.). 40p. (J). (gr. 1-3). 17.95 *(978-1-58536-505-0(X)*, 202199) Sleeping Bear Pr.

—Eight Dolphins of Katrina: A True Tale of Survival. Coleman, Janet Wyman. (ENG.). 40p. (J). (gr. 1-4). 2017. pap. 8.99 *(978-0-544-93261-6(7)*, 1657976, HMH Books For Young Readers); 2013. lib. bdg. 17.99 *(978-0-547-71923-8(X)*, 1481836) Houghton Mifflin Harcourt Publishing Co.

—First Grade Jitters. Quackenbush, Robert. 2010. (ENG.). 32p. (J). (gr. k-2). 16.99 *(978-0-06-077632-9(3))* HarperCollins Pubs.

—Yuki & the One Thousand Carriers. Whelan, Gloria. 2008. (Tales of the World Ser.). (ENG.). 40p. (J). (gr. 1-4). 17.95 *(978-1-58536-352-0(9)*, 202139) Sleeping Bear Pr.

Nascimbeni, Barbara. Images of God. Delval, Marie-Hélène. 2010. (ENG.). 96p. (J). (gr. -1-3). 16.50 *(978-0-8028-5391-2(9)*, Eerdmans Bks For Young Readers) Eerdmans, William B. Publishing Co.

—Little Miss Muffet. (Classic Books with Holes Big Book Ser.). (J). 2014. 16p. spiral bd. *(978-1-84643-668-0(0))*; 2012. 14p. spiral bd. *(978-1-84643-511-9(0))*; 2012. 16p. pap. *(978-1-84643-500-3(5))* Child's Play International Ltd.

—Our Father. Oberthür, Rainer. 2016. (ENG.). 58p. (J). 16.00 *(978-0-8028-5468-1(0)*, Eerdmans Bks For Young Readers) Eerdmans, William B. Publishing Co.

—Samuel, lo Siento. Turpin, Nick. 2006. (Lectores Relampago / Lightning Readers: Level P Ser.). (SPA.). 32p. (J). (gr. -1-k). 16.19 *(978-0-7696-4216-1(0))* School Specialty, Incorporated.

—Undersea Adventure. Harrison, Paul. 2011. 32p. pap. *(978-1-84089-638-1(8))* Zero to Ten, Ltd.

Nash, Doug. Who'd Be a Fly? Griffiths, Neil. 2015. (ENG.). 24p. (J). pap. 9.99 *(978-0-9545353-5-3(9)*, Red Robin Bks.) Corner To Learn Ltd. GBR. Dist: Parkwest Pubns., Inc.

Nash, Gisele. The Wise Man's Last Wish: A Christmas Tale. Alexander, Marilee. 2012. (ENG.). 23p. (J). 23.95 *(978-1-4327-8307-5(6))*; pap. 14.95 *(978-1-4327-8040-1(9))* Outskirts Pr., Inc.

Nash, Joshua. Moose N' Me. Loggins, Kenny. 2013. 32p. (J). (gr. -1-3). 14.95 *(978-0-578-07552-5(0))* Charlesbridge Publishing, Inc.

Nash, Kelli. Jemma's Got the Travel Bug, 1 vol. Glick, Susan. 2010. (ENG.). 32p. (J). (gr. -1-3). 14.99 *(978-0-7643-3632-4(0)*, 9780764336324) Schiffer Publishing, Ltd.

—Olly Explores 7 Wonders of the Chesapeake Bay, 1 vol. Allen, Elaine Ann. 2015. (ENG.). 32p. (J). (gr. -1-3). 16.99 *(978-0-7643-4938-6(4)*, 6693) Schiffer Publishing, Ltd.

—Olly the Oyster Cleans the Bay, 1 vol. Allen, Elaine Ann. 2009. (ENG.). 30p. (J). 13.95 *(978-0-87033-603-4(7)*, 9780870336034, Cornell Maritime Pr./Tidewater Pubs.) Schiffer Publishing, Ltd.

—Olly's Treasure, 1 vol. Allen, Elaine Ann. 2011. (ENG.). 40p. (J). (gr. -1-3). 16.99 *(978-0-7643-3772-7(6)*, 9780764337727, Schiffer Publishing Ltd) Schiffer Publishing, Ltd.

Nash, Mike, et al. Drawing. 2012. (Drawing Ser.). (ENG.). 48p. (J). (gr. 5-9). lib. bdg., lib. bdg., lib. bdg. 163.25 *(978-1-4296-8229-9(9))* Capstone.

—How to Draw the Coolest, Most Creative Tattoo Art, 1 vol. 2012. (Drawing Ser.). (ENG.). 48p. (J). (gr. 5-9). lib. bdg. 32.65 *(978-1-4296-7539-0(X))* Capstone.

—How to Draw the Meanest, Most Terrifying Monsters, 1 vol. 2012. (Drawing Ser.). (ENG.). 48p. (J). (gr. 5-9). lib. bdg. 32.65 *(978-1-4296-7538-3(1))* Capstone.

Nash, Scott. Betsy Red Hoodie. Levine, Gail Carson. 2010. (ENG.). 40p. (J). (gr. -1-3). 17.99 *(978-0-06-146870-4(3))* HarperCollins Pubs.

—Betsy Who Cried Wolf. Levine, Gail Carson. 2005. (ENG.). 40p. (J). (gr. -1-3). reprint ed. pap. 7.99 *(978-0-06-443640-3(3))* HarperCollins Pubs.

—The Bugliest Bug. Shields, Carol Diggory. 2005. (ENG.). 32p. (J). (gr. -1-3). pap. 7.99 *(978-0-7636-2293-0(1))* Candlewick Pr.

—Catch That Baby! Coffelt, Nancy. 2011. (ENG.). 40p. (J). (gr. -1-3). 16.99 *(978-1-4169-9148-9(4)*, Aladdin) Simon & Schuster Children's Publishing.

—Flat Stanley (picture Book Edition) Brown, Jeff. 2006. (Flat Stanley Ser.). (ENG.). 40p. (J). (gr. -1-3). 17.99 *(978-0-06-112904-9(6))* HarperCollins Pubs.

—Hooper Humperdink... ? Not Him! Seuss. 2006. (Bright & Early Books(R) Ser.). (ENG.). 48p. (J). (gr. -1-k). 9.99 *(978-0-679-88129-2(8)*, Random Hse. Bks. for Young Readers) Random Hse. Children's Bks.

—I'm Afraid Your Teddy Is in the Principal's Office. Dunn, Jancee. 2020. 40p. (J). (gr. -1-2). 16.99 *(978-1-5362-0198-7(7))* Candlewick Pr.

—I'm Afraid Your Teddy Is in Trouble Today. Dunn, Jancee. 2017. (ENG.). 40p. (J). (gr. -1-2). 15.99 *(978-0-7636-7537-0(7))* Candlewick Pr.

—My Beastly Brother. Leuck, Laura. 2003. 32p. (J). (gr. -1-1). 16.89 *(978-0-06-029548-6(1))* HarperCollins Pubs.

—My Creature Teacher. Leuck, Laura. 2004. (ENG.). 32p. (J). (gr. -1-1). 15.99 *(978-0-06-029694-0(1))* HarperCollins Pubs.

—Saturday Night at the Dinosaur Stomp. Shields, Carol Diggory. 2008. (ENG.). 32p. (J). (gr. -1-3). pap. 7.99 *(978-0-7636-3887-0(0))* Candlewick Pr.

—Solomon Snow & the Silver Spoon. Umansky, Kaye. 2007. (ENG.). 304p. (J). (gr. 2-5). 12.99 *(978-0-7636-3218-2(X))* Candlewick Pr.

—Solomon Snow & the Stolen Jewel. Umansky, Kaye. 2007. (ENG.). 256p. (J). (gr. 2-5). 12.99 *(978-0-7636-2793-5(3))* Candlewick Pr.

—Stanley in Space. Brown, Jeff. ed. 2009. (Flat Stanley Ser.: 3). (J). (gr. k-3). lib. bdg. 14.75 *(978-0-613-66735-7(2))* Turtleback.

—Uh-Oh, Baby! Coffelt, Nancy. 2013. (ENG.). 40p. (J). (gr. -1-3). 16.99 *(978-1-4169-9149-6(2)*, Simon & Schuster/Paula Wiseman Bks.) Simon & Schuster/Paula Wiseman Bks.

Nash, Scott. The High-Skies Adventures of Blue Jay the Pirate. Nash, Scott. 2012. (ENG.). 368p. (J). (gr. 4-7). 17.99 *(978-0-7636-3264-9(3))* Candlewick Pr.

—Shrunken Treasures: Literary Classics, Short, Sweet & Silly. Nash, Scott. 2016. 40p. (J). (gr. k-3). 15.99 *(978-0-7636-6972-0(5))* Candlewick Pr.

—Tuff Fluff: The Case of Duckie's Missing Brain. Nash, Scott. 2004. (J). 101.94 *(978-0-7636-2503-0(5))*; (ENG.). 40p. (gr. 1-4). 17.99 *(978-0-7636-1882-7(9))* Candlewick Pr.

Nashton, Nashon. Marshall Island Legends & Stories. Kelin, Daniel. 2003. 160p. 22.95 *(978-1-57306-141-4(7))*; 272p. pap. 9.95 *(978-1-57306-140-7(9))* Bess Pr., Inc.

Nasif, Iwan. Dragons: Riders of Berk Collection Volume 3. Furman, Simon. 2016. (Dragons: Riders of Berk Ser.: 3). (ENG.). 112p. (J). (gr. 1-4). pap. 12.99 *(978-1-78585-177-3(2))* Titan Bks. Ltd. GBR. Dist: Penguin Random Hse. LLC.

Nasmith, Ted. Auld Lang Syne: The Story of Scotland's Most Famous Poet, Robert Burns, 1 vol. Findon, Joanne. 2004. (ENG.). 32p. (J). (gr. 3-5). pap. 8.95 *(978-1-55005-121-6(0)*, dcbfd975-1386-4ed0-80e0-0209ae6a1d12) Trifolium Bks., Inc. CAN. Dist: Firefly Bks., Ltd.

Nasner, Alyssa & Wood, Steven. 2000 Stickers Christmas Activity Book: Frosty, Festive, & Fun! Gippetti, Rachel. Parragon Books, ed. ed. 2020. (2000 Sticker Activity Bks.). (ENG.). 48p. (J). (gr. -1-3). 6.99 ***(978-1-68052-879-4(3)***, 2003340, Parragon Books) Cottage Door Pr.

Nasrin, Irana. Alba-Alba's Birthday Party: World of Cats. Skrypnyk-Hamagea, Anastasia & Hamagea Theophilus, Suzana. 2019. (ENG.). 30p. (J). pap. 9.99 *(978-1-0931-1325-9(1))* Independently Published.

Nassner, Alyssa. All Shook Up! Crozon, Alain. 2015. (ENG.). 12p. (J). (gr. -1 — 1). bds. 10.99 *(978-1-4521-4013-1(8))* Chronicle Bks. LLC.

—Busy Baby Friends. Gillingham, Sara. 2015. (ENG.). 10p. (J). (gr. -1 — 1). bds. 9.99 *(978-1-4521-4188-6(6))* Chronicle Bks. LLC.

—Lullaby & Kisses Sweet: Poems to Love with Your Baby. Hopkins, Lee Bennett. 2015. (ENG.). 44p. (J). (gr. -1-1). bds. 15.95 *(978-1-4197-1037-7(0))* Abrams, Inc.

—Montessori: Letter Work. George, Bobby & George, June. 2012. (ENG.). 24p. (J). (gr. -1-k). bds. 10.99 *(978-1-4197-0411-6(7)*, Abrams Appleseed) Abrams, Inc.

—Montessori: Number Work. George, Bobby & George, June. 2012. (ENG.). 24p. (J). (gr. -1-k). bds. 10.99 *(978-1-4197-0412-3(5)*, Abrams Appleseed) Abrams, Inc.

—Secretos de la Costa: Shine-A-light. Brown, Carron. 2019.Tr. of Secrets of the Seashore. (SPA.). (J). 12.99 *(978-1-61067-912-1(1))* Kane Miller.

Nast, Thomas. Fat Boy (HC) 2011. (American Antiquarian Society Ser.). (ENG.). 24p. (gr. 1). 24.95 *(978-1-4290-9736-9(1))* Applewood Bks.

Nast, Thos., jt. illus. see Willcox Smith, Jessie.

Nastanlieva, Vanya. The Bear Who Couldn't Sleep. Nastro, Caroline. (ENG.). 32p. (J). 2018. (gr. -1-2). pap. 9.95 *(978-0-7358-4333-2(3))*; 2016. 17.95 *(978-0-7358-4268-7(X))* North-South Bks., Inc.

—The Bear Who Couldn't Sleep (Spanish) Nastro, Caroline. 2018. (SPA.). 32p. (J). (gr. -1-2). pap. 9.95 *(978-0-7358-4334-9(1))* North-South Bks., Inc.

—I Am Goose! Rohner, Dorothia. 2020. (ENG.). 32p. (J). (gr. -1-3). 17.99 *(978-1-328-84159-9(6)*, 1691734, Clarion Bks.) Houghton Mifflin Harcourt Trade & Reference Pubs.

—The Island & the Bear, 50 vols. Greig, Louise. 2017. (ENG.). 24p. (J). 11.95 *(978-1-78250-368-2(4)*, Kelpies) Floris Bks. GBR. Dist: Consortium Bk. Sales & Distribution.

Nastanlieva, Vanya. The New Arrival. Nastanlieva, Vanya. 2013. (ENG.). 32p. (J). (gr. -1-3). 16.95 *(978-1-927018-13-2(7))* Simply Read Bks. CAN. Dist: Ingram Publisher Services.

Nastari, Nadine. Mr. TLC (Three-Legged Cat) 2007. 36p. (J). spiral bd. 14.95 *(978-0-9798387-5-0(4))* Nastari, Nadine.

Nasu, Yukie. Here is Greenwood, 1. Nasu, Yukie. Smith, Joe. 2004. (ENG.). 208p. (YA). pap. 9.99 *(978-1-59116-604-7(7))* Viz Media.

—Here Is Greenwood. Nasu, Yukie. 2005. (Here Is Greenwood Ser.). (ENG.). (YA). Vol. 2. 216p. pap. 9.99 *(978-1-59116-605-4(5))*; Vol. 3. 200p. pap. 9.99 *(978-1-59116-606-1(3))* Viz Media.

Natale, Vince. Passion & Poison: Tales of Shape-Shifters, Ghosts, & Spirited Women, 0 vols. Del Negro, Janice M. 2013. (ENG.). 64p. (J). (gr. 5-7). pap. 9.99 *(978-1-4778-1685-1(2)*, 9781477816851, Skyscape) Amazon Publishing.

Natalini, Sandro & Baruzzi, Agnese. The True Story of Goldilocks. Natalini, Sandro & Baruzzi, Agnese. 2009. (ENG.). 18p. (J). (gr. -1-3). 14.99 *(978-0-7636-4475-8(7)*, Templar) Candlewick Pr.

Natchev, Alexi. Rock-A-Bye Farm. Hamm, Diane Johnston. 2008. (ENG.). 32p. (J). (gr. -1 — 1). bds. 7.99 *(978-1-4169-3621-3(1)*, Little Simon) Little Simon.

—The Tale of Urso Brunov: Little Father of All Bears. Jacques, Brian. 2003. (ENG.). 48p. (J). (gr. -1-1). 21.19 *(978-0-399-23762-1(3))* Penguin Young Readers Group.

Natelli, Kenny. Jimmy the Gnome Won't Leave His Home, 1 vol. Welch, Eric. 2009. 17p. pap. 24.95 *(978-1-60836-679-8(0))* America Star Bks.

Nath, Vann & Pouriseth, Phal. Sinat & the Instrument of the Heart: A Story of Cambodia. pierSath, Chath. 2010. (Make Friends Around the World Ser.). (ENG.). 32p. (J). (gr. k-3). 9.95 *(978-1-60727-117-8(6))*; 9.95 *(978-1-60727-098-0(6))*; 9.95 *(978-1-60727-116-1(8))*; 19.95 *(978-1-60727-097-3(8))*; 16.95 *(978-1-60727-087-4(0))*; pap. 6.95 *(978-1-60727-088-1(9))* Soundprints.

Nathan, Cheryl. Glaciers: Nature's Icy Caps. Harrison, David L. 2006. (Earth Works). (ENG.). 32p. (J). (gr. k-2). 15.95 *(978-1-59078-372-6(7))* Boyds Mills Pr.

—The Kissing Skunks. Deak, Gloria. 2006. 40p. (J). (gr. -1). 16.95 *(978-1-932065-46-6(6))* Star Bright Bks., Inc.

—Let's Visit Israel, Vol. Groner, Judye & Wikler, Madeline. 2004. (ENG.). 12p. (J). (gr. -1 — 1). bds. 5.95 *(978-1-58013-087-5(9)*, Kar-Ben Publishing) Lerner Publishing Group.

—My Brother Needs a Boa, 1 vol. Weston, Anne. 2005. (ENG.). 32p. (J). (gr. -1-3). 15.95 *(978-1-932065-96-1(2))* Star Bright Bks., Inc.

—Oceans: The Vast, Mysterious Deep. Harrison, David L. 2003. (Earth Works). (ENG.). 32p. (J). (gr. k-2). 15.95 *(978-1-59078-018-3(3))* Boyds Mills Pr.

Nathan, James. Bug Team Alpha, 4 vols. Sutton, Laurie S. 2017. (Bug Team Alpha Ser.). (ENG.). 112p. (J). (gr. 3-6). 103.96 *(978-1-4965-5199-3(0)*, 27024, Stone Arch Bks.) Capstone.

—Can You Survive a Global Blackout? An Interactive Doomsday Adventure. Doeden, Matt. 2015. (You Choose: Doomsday Ser.). (ENG.). 112p. (J). (gr. 3-7). lib. bdg. 32.65 *(978-1-4914-5850-1(X)*, Capstone Pr.) Capstone.

—Can You Survive a Zombie Apocalypse? Wacholtz, Anthony. 2015. (You Choose: Doomsday Ser.). (ENG.). 112p. (J). (gr. 3-7). pap. 6.95 *(978-1-4914-5925-6(5)*, Capstone Pr.) Capstone.

—Can You Survive in a Dystopia? An Interactive Doomsday Adventure. Wacholtz, Anthony. 2016. (You Choose: Doomsday Ser.). (ENG.). 112p. (J). (gr. 3-7). lib. bdg. 32.65 *(978-1-4914-8110-3(2)*, Capstone Pr.) Capstone.

—The Dig. Sutton, Laurie S. 2017. (Bug Team Alpha Ser.). (ENG.). 112p. (J). (gr. 3-6). lib. bdg. 25.99 *(978-1-4965-5183-2(4)*, 136186, Stone Arch Bks.) Capstone.

—The Draco. Sutton, Laurie S. 2017. (Bug Team Alpha Ser.). (ENG.). 112p. (J). (gr. 3-6). lib. bdg. 25.99 *(978-1-4965-5186-3(9)*, 136189, Stone Arch Bks.) Capstone.

—Invisible Enemy. Sutton, Laurie S. 2017. (Bug Team Alpha Ser.). (ENG.). 112p. (J). (gr. 3-6). lib. bdg. 25.99 *(978-1-4965-5184-9(2)*, 136187, Stone Arch Bks.) Capstone.

—Jason, the Argonauts, & the Golden Fleece: An Interactive Mythological Adventure. Hoena, Blake. 2016. (You Choose: Ancient Greek Myths Ser.). (ENG.). 112p. (J). (gr. 3-7). lib. bdg. 32.65 *(978-1-4914-8113-4(7)*, Capstone Pr.) Capstone.

—Stranded. Sutton, Laurie S. 2017. (Bug Team Alpha Ser.). (ENG.). 112p. (J). (gr. 3-6). lib. bdg. 25.99 *(978-1-4965-5185-6(0)*, 136188, Stone Arch Bks.) Capstone.

Nathan, Paula. Alexandra's ABC Book: African American Girl with Black Hair. Burke, John & Kase, Chad. 2019. (ENG.). 30p. (J). pap. 12.95 *(978-1-0955-9647-0(0))* Independently Published.

—Jennifer's ABC Book. Kase, Chad. 2018. (ENG.). 30p. (J). pap. 12.95 *(978-1-7929-2600-6(6))* Independently Published.

—Muhammad's ABC Book. Burke, John & Kase, Chad. 2018. (ENG.). 30p. (J). pap. 12.95 *(978-1-9833-3721-5(8))* Independently Published.

Nation, Tate. My Purple Kisses. Hahn, Blair. 2011. (My Purple Toes Ser.). 26p. (J). bds. 10.99 *(978-0-9844556-7-6(1))* My Purple Toes, LLC.

—My Purple Toes. Hahn, Blair. 2010. 24p. (J). 10.99 *(978-0-9844556-4-5(7))* My Purple Toes, LLC.

Natsumoto, Masato. Lost War Chronicles, Vol. 2. rev. ed. 2006. (Mobile Suit Gundam Ser.). 160p. pap. 9.99 *(978-1-59816-214-1(4)*, Tokyopop Kids) TOKYOPOP, Inc.

—Mobile Suit Gundam Lost War Chronicles, 2 vols., Vol. 1. Chiba, Tomohiro & Games, Incbandai. 2006. (Mobile Suit Gundam Ser.). 144p. (gr. 8-12). pap. 9.99 *(978-1-59816-213-4(6)*, Tokyopop Kids) TOKYOPOP, Inc.

Natti, Susanna. Beany & the Dreaded Wedding. Wojciechowski, Susan. 2005. (Beany Adventures Ser.). 121p. (J). 13.65 *(978-0-7569-6498-6(9))* Perfection Learning Corp.

—Beany & the Magic Crystal. Wojciechowski, Susan. 2005. (Beany Adventures Ser.). 87p. (J). lib. bdg. 13.65 *(978-0-7569-5836-7(9))* Perfection Learning Corp.

—Beany Goes to Camp. Wojciechowski, Susan. 2005. (Beany Adventures Ser.). 104p. (J). (gr. 4-7). 13.65 *(978-0-7569-6499-3(7))* Perfection Learning Corp.

—Beany (Not Beanhead) Wojciechowski, Susan. 2005. (Beany Adventures Ser.). 68p. (J). lib. bdg. 12.65 *(978-0-7569-5835-0(0))* Perfection Learning Corp.

—Cam Jansen & the Catnapping Mystery. Adler, David A. 2005. (Cam Jansen Ser.). 58p. (gr. 2-5). 14.00 *(978-0-7569-5045-3(7))* Perfection Learning Corp.

—Cam Jansen & the Secret Service Mystery #26. Adler, David A. 2008. (Cam Jansen Ser.: 26). (ENG.). 64p. (J). (gr. 2-5). 4.99 *(978-0-14-241074-5(8)*, Puffin Books) Penguin Young Readers Group.

—Cam Jansen: Cam Jansen & the Valentine Baby Mystery #25. Adler, David A. 25th ed. 2006. (Cam Jansen Ser.: 25). (ENG.). 80p. (J). (gr. 2-5). 4.99 *(978-0-14-240694-6(5)*, Puffin Books) Penguin Young Readers Group.

—Cam Jansen: the Barking Treasure Mystery #19. Adler, David A. 2005. (Cam Jansen Ser.: 19). (ENG.). 64p. (J). (gr. 2-5). 4.99 *(978-0-14-240319-8(9)*, Puffin Books) Penguin Young Readers Group.

—Cam Jansen: the Birthday Mystery #20. Adler, David A. 2005. (Cam Jansen Ser.: 20). (ENG.). 64p. (J). (gr. 2-5). 4.99 *(978-0-14-240354-9(7)*, Puffin Books) Penguin Young Readers Group.

—Cam Jansen: the Catnapping Mystery #18, 18 vols. Adler, David A. 2005. (Cam Jansen Ser.: 18). (ENG.). 64p. (J). (gr. 2-5). 4.99 *(978-0-14-240289-4(3)*, Puffin Books) Penguin Young Readers Group.

—Cam Jansen: the Chocolate Fudge Mystery #14, 14 vols. Adler, David A. 2004. (Cam Jansen Ser.: 14). (ENG.). 64p. (J). (gr. 2-5). 4.99 *(978-0-14-240211-5(7)*, Puffin Books) Penguin Young Readers Group.

—Cam Jansen: the First Day of School Mystery #22, 22 vols. Adler, David A. 2005. (Cam Jansen Ser.: 22). (ENG.). 64p. (J). (gr. 2-5). 4.99 *(978-0-14-240326-6(1)*, Puffin Books) Penguin Young Readers Group.

—Cam Jansen: the Mystery at the Haunted House #13, 13 vols. Adler, David A. 2004. (Cam Jansen Ser.: 13). (ENG.). 64p. (J). (gr. 2-5). 4.99 *(978-0-14-240210-8(9)*, Puffin Books) Penguin Young Readers Group.

—Cam Jansen: the Mystery of Flight 54 #12, 12 vols. Adler, David A. 2004. (Cam Jansen Ser.: 12). (ENG.). 64p. (J). (gr. 2-5). 4.99 *(978-0-14-240179-8(X)*, Puffin Books) Penguin Young Readers Group.

—Cam Jansen: the Mystery of the Carnival Prize #9, 9 vols. Adler, David A. 2004. (Cam Jansen Ser.: 9). (ENG.). 64p. (J). (gr. 2-5). 4.99 *(978-0-14-240018-0(1)*, Puffin Books) Penguin Young Readers Group.

—Cam Jansen: the Mystery of the Circus Clown #7, 7 vols. Adler, David A. 2004. (Cam Jansen Ser.: 7). (ENG.). 64p. (J). (gr. 2-5). 4.99 *(978-0-14-240016-6(5)*, Puffin Books) Penguin Young Readers Group.

—Cam Jansen: the Mystery of the Gold Coins #5, 5 vols. Adler, David A. 2004. (Cam Jansen Ser.: 5). (ENG.). 64p. (J). (gr. 2-5). 4.99 *(978-0-14-240014-2(9)*, Puffin Books) Penguin Young Readers Group.

—Cam Jansen: the Mystery of the Stolen Corn Popper #11, 11 vols. Adler, David A. 2004. (Cam Jansen Ser.: 11). (ENG.). 64p. (J). (gr. 2-5). 4.99 *(978-0-14-240178-1(1)*, Puffin Books) Penguin Young Readers Group.

—Cam Jansen: the Mystery of the Stolen Diamonds #1. Adler, David A. 2004. (Cam Jansen Ser.: 1). (ENG.). 64p. (J). (gr. 2-5). pap. 4.99 *(978-0-14-240010-4(6)*, Puffin Books) Penguin Young Readers Group.

—Cam Jansen: the Mystery of the U. F. O. #2, 2 vols. Adler, David A. 2004. (Cam Jansen Ser.: 2). (ENG.). 64p. (J). (gr. 2-5). 4.99 *(978-0-14-240011-1(4)*, Puffin Books) Penguin Young Readers Group.

—Cam Jansen: the Scary Snake Mystery #17. Adler, David A. 2005. (Cam Jansen Ser.: 17). (ENG.). 64p. (J). (gr. 2-5). 4.99 *(978-0-14-240288-7(5)*, Puffin Books) Penguin Young Readers Group.

—Cam Jansen: the School Play Mystery #21. Adler, David A. 2005. (Cam Jansen Ser.: 21). (ENG.). 64p. (J). (gr. 2-5). 4.99 *(978-0-14-240355-6(5)*, Puffin Books) Penguin Young Readers Group.

—Cam Jansen: the Snowy Day Mystery #24, 24 vols. Adler, David A. 2005. (Cam Jansen Ser.: 24). (ENG.). 64p. (J). (gr. 2-5). 4.99 *(978-0-14-240417-1(9)*, Puffin Books) Penguin Young Readers Group.

—Cam Jansen: the Triceratops Pops Mystery #15, 15 vols. Adler, David A. 2004. (Cam Jansen Ser.: 15). (ENG.). 64p. (J). (gr. 2-5). 4.99 *(978-0-14-240206-1(0),* Puffin Books) Penguin Young Readers Group.
—The Ghostly Mystery, Vol. 16. Adler, David A. 2005. (Cam Jansen Ser.: 16). (ENG.). 64p. (J). (gr. 2-5). 4.99 *(978-0-14-240287-0(7),* Puffin Books) Penguin Young Readers Group.
—Midnight Moon. Watson, Clyde. 2006. (ENG.). 24p. (J). (gr. -1-k). *(978-1-59692-162-7(5))* MacAdam/Cage Publishing, Inc.
—The Mystery of Flight 427: Inside a Crash Investigation. Adler, David A. 2004. (Cam Jansen Ser.: No. 12). 56p. (J). pap. *(978-0-439-13384-5(X),* Puffin) Penguin Publishing Group.
—The Mystery of the Monkey House. Adler, David A. 2004. (Cam Jansen Ser.: 10). (ENG.). 64p. (J). (gr. 2-5). 4.99 *(978-0-14-240019-7(X),* Puffin Books) Penguin Young Readers Group.
—The Mystery of the Monster Movie, 8 vols. Adler, David A. 2004. (Cam Jansen Ser.: 8). (ENG.). 64p. (J). (gr. 2-5). 4.99 *(978-0-14-240017-3(3),* Puffin Books) Penguin Young Readers Group.
—The Mystery of the Television Dog, 4 vols. Adler, David A. 2004. (Cam Jansen Ser.: 4). (ENG.). 64p. (J). (gr. 2-5). 4.99 *(978-0-14-240013-5(0),* Puffin Books) Penguin Young Readers Group.
—The Secret Service Mystery. Adler, David A. 2008. (Cam Jansen Ser.: Bk. 26). 57p. (J). (gr. 2-5). 11.65 *(978-0-7569-8917-0(5))* Perfection Learning Corp.
—The Tennis Trophy Mystery. Adler, David A. 2005. (Cam Jansen Ser.: 23). (ENG.). 64p. (J). (gr. 2-5). 4.99 *(978-0-14-240290-0(7),* Puffin Books) Penguin Young Readers Group.
—Young Cam Jansen & the 100th Day of School Mystery, 15 vols. Adler, David A. 2010. (Young Cam Jansen Ser.: 15). (ENG.). 32p. (J). (gr. 1-3). mass mkt. 4.99 *(978-0-14-241685-3(1),* Penguin Young Readers) Penguin Young Readers Group.
—Young Cam Jansen & the Circus Mystery. Adler, David A. 2013. (Young Cam Jansen Ser.: 17). (ENG.). 32p. (J). (gr. 1-3). pap. 4.99 *(978-0-448-46614-9(7),* Penguin Young Readers) Penguin Young Readers Group.
—Young Cam Jansen & the Double Beach Mystery. Adler, David A. 2003. (Young Cam Jansen Ser.: 8). (ENG.). 32p. (J). (gr. 1-3). mass mkt. 4.99 *(978-0-14-250079-8(8),* Penguin Young Readers) Penguin Young Readers Group.
—Young Cam Jansen & the Double Beach Mystery. Adler, David A. ed. 2003. (Young Cam Jansen — Penguin Young Readers Level 3 Ser.: 8). 30p. (gr. -1-3). lib. bdg. 13.55 *(978-0-613-67477-5(4))* Turtleback.
—Young Cam Jansen & the Goldfish Mystery. Adler, David A. 2014. (Young Cam Jansen Ser.: 19). (ENG.). 32p. (J). (gr. 1-3). pap. 4.99 *(978-0-14-242224-3(X),* Penguin Young Readers) Penguin Young Readers Group.
—Young Cam Jansen & the Knock, Knock Mystery. Adler, David A. 2015. (Young Cam Jansen Ser.: 20). (ENG.). 32p. (J). (gr. 1-3). pap. 4.99 *(978-0-14-242225-0(8),* Penguin Young Readers) Penguin Young Readers Group.
—Young Cam Jansen & the Lions' Lunch Mystery, No. 13. Adler, David A. 2008. (Young Cam Jansen Ser.: 13). (ENG.). 32p. (J). (gr. 1-3). mass mkt. 4.99 *(978-0-14-241176-6(0),* Penguin Young Readers) Penguin Young Readers Group.
—Young Cam Jansen & the Magic Bird Mystery. Adler, David A. 2013. (Young Cam Jansen Ser.: 18). (ENG.). 32p. (J). (gr. 1-3). pap. 4.99 *(978-0-448-46613-2(9),* Penguin Young Readers) Penguin Young Readers Group.
—Young Cam Jansen & the Molly Shoe Mystery, No. 14. Adler, David A. 2009. (Young Cam Jansen Ser.: 14). (ENG.). 32p. (J). (gr. 1-3). mass mkt. 4.99 *(978-0-14-241402-6(6),* Penguin Young Readers) Penguin Young Readers Group.
—Young Cam Jansen & the New Girl Mystery. Adler, David A. 2005. (Young Cam Jansen Ser.: 10). (ENG.). 32p. (J). (gr. 1-3). mass mkt. 4.99 *(978-0-14-240353-2(9),* Penguin Young Readers) Penguin Young Readers Group.
—Young Cam Jansen & the New Girl Mystery. Adler, David A. 2005. (Young Cam Jansen Ser.: Bk. 10). 32p. (gr. k-2). 14.00 *(978-0-7569-5522-9(X))* Perfection Learning Corp.
—Young Cam Jansen & the Speedy Car Mystery, 16 vols. Adler, David A. 2011. (Young Cam Jansen Ser.: 16). (ENG.). 32p. (J). (gr. 1-3). mass mkt. 4.99 *(978-0-14-241868-0(4),* Penguin Young Readers) Penguin Young Readers Group.
—Young Cam Jansen & the Spotted Cat Mystery, No. 12. Adler, David A. 2007. (Young Cam Jansen Ser.: 12). (ENG.). 32p. (J). (gr. 1-3). pap. 4.99 *(978-0-14-241012-7(8),* Penguin Young Readers) Penguin Young Readers Group.
—Young Cam Jansen & the Spotted Cat Mystery. Adler, David A. 2007. (Young Cam Jansen (prebound) Ser.). 31p. (gr. -1-3). 14.00 *(978-0-7569-8155-6(7))* Perfection Learning Corp.
—Young Cam Jansen & the Substitute Mystery, No. 11. Adler, David A. 2006. (Young Cam Jansen Ser.: 11). (ENG.). 32p. (J). (gr. 1-3). mass mkt. 4.99 *(978-0-14-240660-1(0),* Penguin Young Readers) Penguin Young Readers Group.
—Young Cam Jansen & the Zoo Note Mystery. Adler, David A. 2013. (Puffin Young Readers, L3 Ser.). (ENG.). 31p. (J). (gr. -1-3). pap. 3.99 *(978-0-448-46633-0(3),* Puffin) Penguin Publishing Group.
—Young Cam Jansen & the Zoo Note Mystery. Adler, David A. 2004. (Young Cam Jansen Ser.: 9). (ENG.). 32p. (J). (gr. 1-3). mass mkt. 4.99 *(978-0-14-240204-7(4),* Penguin Young Readers) Penguin Young Readers Group.
Nauck, Todd, et al. Death of Wolverine Companion. 2019. (ENG.). 512p. (gr. 10-17). pap. 39.99 *(978-1-302-91610-7(6))* Marvel Worldwide, Inc.
Nauck, Todd. Inauguration Day. Wells, Zeb. 2010. (Spider-Man Ser.: No. 4). (ENG.). 24p. (J). (gr. 2-6). 27.07 *(978-1-59961-777-0(3),* 13637, Marvel Age) Spotlight.
Nauck, Todd & Di Vito, Andrea. Avengers Assemble: Living Legends. 2019. 112p. (YA). (gr. 7-17). pap. 9.99 *(978-1-302-91638-1(6))* Marvel Worldwide, Inc.
Naughton, Terry. Alexander the Great Rocks the World. Shecter, Vicky Alvear. 2006. 128p. (J). (gr. 5-7). lib. bdg. 18.95 *(978-1-58196-045-7(X),* Darby Creek) Lerner Publishing Group.
—My Personal Panther. Cesak, Jerry. 2012. (J). *(978-0-578-10507-9(1))* Canyon Hawk Bks.
Nault, S. &R. Mr Scruffpot's Pony. Nault, Susan. 2013. 30p. pap. *(978-0-9870744-1-6(5))* Kingdom Pr.
Nausley, Kathy. The Gift. Sheets, Judy. 2005. 40p. (J). lib. bdg. 24.00 *(978-0-9726451-2-6(8))* Sheets, Judy.
—The Snow Angels' Christmas. Michaels, M. J. 2016. (ENG.). 24p. (J). (gr. -1-1). 14.95 *(978-1-63322-124-6(5),* Seagrass) Quarto Publishing Group USA.
Nautilus Studio, Nautilus. The Planet of Bamalias: Book 23. Gonnard, Christel et al. ed. 2015. (Little Prince Ser.: 23). (ENG.). 48p. (J). (gr. 4-8). E-Book 39.99 *(978-1-4677-6198-7(2),* Graphic Universe™) Lerner Publishing Group.
—The Planet of the Snake: Book 24. Magnat, Julien. ed. 2015. (Little Prince Ser.: 24). (ENG.). 48p. (J). (gr. 4-8). E-Book 39.99 *(978-1-4677-6199-4(0),* Graphic Universe™) Lerner Publishing Group.
Nava, Francisco. La Vaca Roja. Lujan, Jorge Elias. 2003. (SPA.). 27p. (J). (gr. k-3). pap. 7.95 *(978-968-19-0629-0(2))* Santillana USA Publishing Co., Inc.
Navarra, Nino. Ooze Control. Random House Staff. 2013. (Pictureback Ser.). (ENG.). 16p. (J). (gr. -1-2). pap. 4.99 *(978-0-307-98229-2(7),* Random Hse. Bks. for Young Readers) Random Hse. Children's Bks.
Navarrete, Cecilia J. Sacred Seeds: A Girl, Her Abuelos, & the Heart of Northern New Mexico. Jaramillo, Mari-Luci. 2019. (ENG.). (J). (gr. 5-6). 236p. 24.95 ***(978-1-939604-34-7(6));*** 238p. pap. 14.95 ***(978-1-939604-35-4(4))*** Barranca Pr.
Navarrete, Vicente. The New Kid, Bk. 2. Williamson, Joshua & Navarrete, Vinny. 2013. (Sketch Monsters Ser.: 2). (ENG.). 40p. (J). 12.99 *(978-1-62010-012-7(6),* 9781620100127, Lion Forge) Oni Pr., Inc.
—Sketch Monsters Book 1: Escape of the Scribbles: Escape of the Scribbles. Williamson, Joshua. 2011. (Sketch Monsters Ser.: 1). (ENG.). 40p. (J). 12.99 *(978-1-934964-69-9(7),* 9781934964699, Lion Forge) Oni Pr., Inc.
Navarro, Claudia. Dance Like a Leaf. Irving, A. J. 2020. (ENG.). 32p. (J). pap. ***(978-1-64686-058-6(6))*** Barefoot Bks., Inc.
Navarro, Claudia. La Frontera. Alva, Alfredo & Mills, Deborah. 2018. (SPA & ENG.). 48p. (J). (gr. k-4). 17.99 *(978-1-78285-388-6(X));* pap. 9.99 *(978-1-78285-392-3(8))* Barefoot Bks., Inc.
—Kayapo, Jibaros y Cashinahuas. Navarrete, Federico. 2014. (SPA.). 76p. (J). (gr. 4-7). pap. 11.95 *(978-607-8237-50-0(0))* Nostra Ediciones MEX. Dist: Independent Pubs. Group.
—Musica de Todo el Mundo. Mansilla Sepulveda, Elena Beatriz. 2016. (Cuentamelo Otra Vez Ser.). (ENG & SPA.). (J). 16.95 *(978-1-68165-271-9(4))* Trialtea USA, LLC.
—Quiero Ser un Héroe. Basich, Ninah. 2019. (SPA.). 48p. (J). (gr. k-2). pap. 10.00 *(978-607-8469-59-8(2))* Nostra Ediciones MEX. Dist: Independent Pubs. Group.
Navarro, Don Emidio. O Chapéu Mágico: As Aventuras Da Bruxinha Hippie, Volume 1. Sonderegger, Ueli. Lisboa, Leo Bryan, tr. 2016. (As Aventuras Da Bruxinha Hippie Ser.: Vol. 1). (POR.). 24p. (J). (gr. k-4). *(978-85-92973-08-7(2));* pap. *(978-85-92973-07-0(4))* Pitanga.
Navarro, Marcos. Wilderness: Jungle, Rain Forest, Jungle, Rain Forest, Tundra, Taiga, Savanna & Desert. Cassany, Mia. 2019. (ENG.). 48p. (J). (gr. 1-4). 19.95 *(978-3-7913-7372-0(2))* Prestel Verlag GmbH & Co KG. DEU. Dist: Penguin Random Hse. LLC.
Navarro Sanchez, May. A Hole Between Worlds. Perez Sempere, Beatriz. 2019. (ENG.). 124p. (J). pap. 6.00 *(978-1-0722-8503-8(7))* Independently Published.
Navas, David. Metallica: The Unauthorized Biography. Romero, Soledad. 2020. (Band Bios Ser.). 40p. (J). (-3). 14.99 *(978-1-7282-1088-9(7))* Sourcebooks, Inc.
Navas, Tamera. Aldon the Sloth. Sammons, Teresa. 2019. (ENG.). 32p. (J). pap. 12.95 *(978-1-64096-584-3(X))* Newman Springs Publishing, Inc.
Nayberg, Yevgenia. Drop by Drop: A Story of Rabbi Akiva. Jules, Jacqueline. 2017. (ENG.). 32p. (J). (gr. -1-2). 9.99 *(978-1-5124-2090-6(5),* 9781512420906, Kar-Ben Publishing) Lerner Publishing Group.
—Numbers in Motion: Sophie Kowalevski, Queen of Mathematics. Wallmark, Laurie. 2020. (ENG.). 32p. (J). (gr. 3-6). 18.99 *(978-1-939547-63-7(6))* Creston Bks.
—The Wren & the Sparrow. Lewis, J. Patrick. ed. 2015. (ENG.). 32p. (J). (gr. 3-6). E-Book 27.99 *(978-1-4677-6210-6(5),* Kar-Ben Publishing) Lerner Publishing Group.
Nayberg, Yevgenia. Anya's Secret Society. Nayberg, Yevgenia. 2019. 32p. (J). (gr. -1-3). lib. bdg. 17.99 *(978-1-58089-830-0(0))* Charlesbridge Publishing, Inc.
Nayler, Sarah. Flash Harriet & the Loch Ness Monster: Band 13/Topaz (Collins Big Cat) Wallace, Karen. 2007. (Collins Big Cat Ser.). (ENG.). 32p. (J). (gr. 2-4). pap. 9.99 *(978-0-00-723082-2(6))* HarperCollins Pubs. Ltd. GBR. Dist: Independent Pubs. Group.
—What's So Special about Dickens? Rosen, Michael. 2018. (ENG.). 160p. (J). (gr. 3-7). pap. 7.99 *(978-0-7636-9993-2(4));* 14.99 *(978-0-7636-9992-5(6))* Candlewick Pr.
—What's So Special about Shakespeare? Rosen, Michael. 2018. (ENG.). 160p. (J). (gr. 3-7). pap. 6.99 *(978-0-7636-9995-6(0));* 14.99 *(978-0-7636-9994-9(2))* Candlewick Pr.
Nazar, Alexandria. Little Blue Planet. Riggs, Jon & Evanoff, Corrine R. 2014. 24p. (J). (-5). 16.95 *(978-1-939621-07-8(0))* ORO Editions.
Nazareth, Carla. Nuestros Derechos. Carvalho, Maria Joao & João, Carvalho Maria. 2003. (SPA.). 48p. (J). (gr. k-2). pap. 8.50 *(978-84-241-8335-6(5))* Everest Editora ESP. Dist: Lectorum Pubns., Inc.
Nazario, Rafael. Mr. Blue Butterfly. Kennedy, Kirk. 2013. (ENG.). (J). (gr. -1-3). 14.95 *(978-1-62086-256-8(5))* Mascot Bks., Inc.
Nazarova, Jenny. Myself Today. Giesbrecht, Karen. 2018. (ENG.). 44p. (J). (gr. k-3). pap. *(978-0-9951983-5-7(7))* Mill Lake Bks.
Nazif, Iwan. Dragon Down, Vol. 1. Titan Comics Staff & Furman, Simon. 2014. (Riders of Berk Ser.). (ENG.). 64p. (J). (gr. 3-7). pap. 6.99 *(978-1-78276-076-4(8))* Titan Bks. Ltd. GBR. Dist: Penguin Random Hse. LLC.
Nazif, Iwan & Lawrence, Jack. Dragons: Defenders of Berk Volume 1. Furman, Simon. 2016. (FBI Profiler Novel Ser.: 1). 112p. (J). (gr. 1-4). pap. 12.99 *(978-1-78585-678-5(2))* Titan Bks. Ltd. GBR. Dist: Penguin Random Hse. LLC.
Nazran, Govinder. Aladdin. 2017. 24p. pap. 7.99 *(978-1-86147-819-1(4));* 2014. (ENG.). 48p. (J). (gr. 2-5). pap. 7.99 *(978-1-84322-790-8(8))* Anness Publishing GBR. (Armadillo). Dist: National Bk. Network.
Ndlovu, Busisiwe. The Hare & the Tortoise. Adebowale, Diamond. 2019. (ENG.). 54p. (J). pap. *(978-1-928348-83-2(1))* Verity Pubs.
—Jessie Die Kameelperd Soek Werk. Olivier, Malie. 2019. (AFR.). 48p. (J). pap. *(978-1-928348-50-4(5))* Verity Pubs.
—Ryno Die Klein Renoster. Olivier, Malie. 2019. (AFR.). 44p. (J). pap. *(978-1-928348-63-4(7))* Verity Pubs.
Neal, Alicia. The Cracks in the Sidewalk: Poems for Kids. Chisholm, Gordon. 2019. (ENG.). 64p. (J). *(978-1-5255-4468-2(3));* pap. *(978-1-5255-4469-9(1))* FriesenPress.
Neal, Amee S. Aliera Wants to Be a Monkey. Rowe, Janet. 2018. (ENG.). 26p. (J). pap. 12.95 *(978-1-64300-941-4(9))* Covenant Bks.
Neal, Bill. A Little Piece of Ground. Laird, Elizabeth. 2006. (ENG.). 240p. (J). (gr. 4-6). pap. 12.99 *(978-1-931859-38-7(8))* Haymarket Bks.
Neal, Charity. Beautiful... Just the Way You Are. Gaines, Alan J. L. 2020. (ENG.). 278p. (YA). (gr. 7-12). pap. 25.00 ***(978-1-5136-5536-9(1))*** Gaines, Alan.
Neal, Christopher Silas. From Tree to Sea. Thomas, Shelley Moore. 2019. (ENG.). 32p. (J). (gr. -1-3). 17.99 *(978-1-4814-9531-8(3),* Simon & Schuster/Paula Wiseman Bks.) Simon & Schuster/Paula Wiseman Bks.
—Go to Sleep, Little Farm. Ray, Mary Lyn. (ENG.). (J). 2018. 38p. (— 1). bds. 12.99 *(978-1-328-77004-2(4),* 1681070); 2015. 38p. (— 1). bds. 8.99 *(978-0-544-57916-3(X),* 1613308); 2014. 40p. (gr. -1-3). 16.99 *(978-0-544-15014-0(7),* 1548158) Houghton Mifflin Harcourt Publishing Co. (HMH Books For Young Readers).
—How Do I Love Thee? Adams, Jennifer. 2018. (ENG.). 32p. (J). (gr. -1-3). 17.99 *(978-0-06-239444-6(4),* Balzer & Bray) HarperCollins Pubs.
Neal, Christopher Silas. Hurry Up! A Book about Slowing Down. Dopirak, Kate. 2020. (ENG.). 40p. (J). (gr. -1-3). 17.99 ***(978-1-5344-2497-5(0),*** Beach Lane Bks.) Beach Lane Bks.
Neal, Christopher Silas. Lifetime: The Amazing Numbers in Animal Lives. Schaefer, Lola M. 2013. (ENG.). 40p. (J). (gr. -1-3). 17.99 *(978-1-4521-0714-1(9))* Chronicle Bks. LLC.
—Lifetime: The Amazing Numbers in Animal Lives. Schaefer, Lola M. 2016. (ENG.). 40p. (J). (gr. k-3). 8.99 *(978-1-4521-5210-3(1))* Chronicle Bks. LLC.
—Over & under the Pond: (Environment & Ecology Books for Kids, Nature Books, Children's Oceanography Books, Animal Books for Kids) Messner, Kate. 2017. (ENG.). 48p. (J). 17.99 *(978-1-4521-4542-6(3))* Chronicle Bks. LLC.
—Over & under the Rainforest. Messner, Kate. 2020. (ENG.). 48p. (J). (gr. k-3). 18.99 *(978-1-4521-6940-8(3))* Chronicle Bks. LLC.
—Over & under the Snow. Messner, Kate. (ENG.). 44p. (J). 2014. (gr. k-3). 7.99 *(978-1-4521-3646-2(7));* 2011. (gr. -1-3). 17.99 *(978-0-8118-6784-9(6))* Chronicle Bks. LLC.
—Prairie Boy: Frank Lloyd Wright Turns the Heartland into a Home. Rosenstock, Barb. 2019. (ENG.). 32p. (J). (gr. 2-5). 17.99 *(978-1-62979-440-2(6),* Calkins Creek) Boyds Mills Pr.
—Up in the Garden & down in the Dirt: (Nature Book for Kids, Gardening & Vegetable Planting, Outdoor Nature Book) Messner, Kate. 2017. (ENG.). 56p. (J). pap. 7.99 *(978-1-4521-6136-5(4))* Chronicle Bks. LLC.
Neal, Christopher Silas. Everyone. Neal, Christopher Silas. 2016. (ENG.). 32p. (J). (gr. -1-1). 15.99 *(978-0-7636-7683-4(7))* Candlewick Pr.
—I Won't Eat That. Neal, Christopher Silas. 2017. 40p. (J). (gr. -1-1). 15.99 *(978-0-7636-7909-5(7))* Candlewick Pr.
Neal, Jill Faith. Aunt Linda's Shape Book. Dudley, Linda S. 2007. (ENG.). 32p. per. 24.95 *(978-1-4241-8618-1(8))* America Star Bks.
Neal, Lindsay, jt. illus. see Lutz, Patrick.
Neal, Penelope. Moose with Loose Poops. Cowan, Charlotte. 2008. (Dr. Hippo Ser.). (ENG.). 32p. (J). (gr. -1-2). 17.95 *(978-0-9753516-5-9(6))* Hippocratic Pr., The.
Neal, Susan Goodwin. The Adventures of Squeek & Smithers: Going to the Beach. Goodwin, Margaret Hobkirk. 2019. (Adventures of Squeek & Smithers Ser.: Vol. 4). (ENG.). 30p. (J). pap. 12.50 ***(978-1-7040-2767-8(5))*** Independently Published.
Neal, Tony. Alphabet Adventure. Broderick, Kathy. 2020. (What Do You See? Ser.). (ENG.). 20p. (J). bds. *(978-1-5037-5228-3(3),* 7a7ba67a-7c3e-436c-b6d3-fb212c20b45e, p i kids) Phoenix International Publications, Inc.
—Colors of Love. Gallo, Tina. 2018. (Crayola Ser.). (ENG.). 26p. (J). (gr. -1-k). bds. 8.99 *(978-1-5344-1113-5(5),* Simon Spotlight) Simon Spotlight.
—Drawing a Bridge. Spinner, Caia. 2018. (Crayola Ser.). (ENG.). 26p. (J). (gr. -1-k). bds. 8.99 *(978-1-5344-1738-0(9),* Simon Spotlight) Simon Spotlight.
—I Dream in Color. Finnegan, Delphine. 2019. (Crayola Ser.). (ENG.). 26p. (J). (gr. -1-k). bds. 8.99 *(978-1-5344-3211-6(6),* Simon Spotlight) Simon Spotlight.
—It's Impossible! Corderoy, Tracey. 2020. (ENG.). 32p. (J). (gr. -1-2). 17.99 *(978-1-68010-191-1(9))* Tiger Tales.
—Not yet a Yeti. Treleaven, Lou. 2019. (ENG.). 32p. (J). (gr. -1-3). 17.99 *(978-1-84886-414-6(0))* Maverick Arts Publishing GBR. Dist: Lerner Publishing Group.
—Sneaky Beak. Corderoy, Tracey. 2019. (ENG.). 32p. (J). (gr. -1-2). 17.99 *(978-1-68010-175-1(7))* Tiger Tales.
—24 Bk Carry Case Now I Know My ABCs. Brooke, Susan Rich. 2018. (ENG.). (J). pap. 7.98 *(978-1-5037-2728-1(9))* Phoenix International Publications, Inc.
Nealon, Eve, jt. illus. see Espinola, Nicole.
Neate, Andy. Hewitch. Deveze, Winky. 2006. (J). *(978-0-9787174-0-7(6))* Love Bug Bks.
Neave, Thai, photos by. The Playbook: 52 Rules to Aim, Shoot, & Score in This Game Called Life. Alexander, Kwame. 2017. (ENG.). 176p. (J). (gr. 5-7). 16.99 *(978-0-544-57097-9(9),* 1612556, HMH Books For Young Readers) Houghton Mifflin Harcourt Publishing Co.
—The Playbook: 52 Rules to Aim, Shoot, & Score in This Game Called Life. Alexander, Kwame. ed. 2017. (ENG., (J). (gr. 5-7). lib. bdg. 26.95 *(978-0-606-39814-5(7))* Turtleback.
Nebres, Rudy, et al. Deadly Hands of Kung Fu Omnibus Vol. 2. 2017. (ENG.). 1000p. (YA). (gr. 12-17). 125.00 *(978-1-302-90134-9(6))* Marvel Worldwide, Inc.
Necsulescu, Diana. Abby Invents Unbreakable Crayons. Simon, Arlyne. 2018. (ENG.). 40p. (J). (gr. 1-3). 17.99 *(978-1-7321975-1-0(2))* Agnes, Bella Bks.
Necsulescu, Diana. Abby Invents Unbreakable Crayons. Simon, Arlyne. 2018. (ENG.). 40p. (J). pap. 12.99 ***(978-1-7321975-0-3(4))*** Agnes, Bella Bks.
Nedelcu, Ovi. Cowboy Car. Ransom, Jeanie Franz. 2017. (ENG.). 40p. (J). (gr. -1-2). 17.99 *(978-1-5039-5097-9(2),* 9781503950979, Two Lions) Amazon Publishing.
—DreamWorks Shrek. Golden Books. 2017. (Little Golden Book Ser.). (ENG.). 24p. (J). (-k). 4.99 *(978-1-5247-6770-9(0),* Golden Bks.) Random Hse. Children's Bks.
—Puss in Boots. Golden Books. 2017. (Little Golden Book Ser.). 24p. (J). (-k). 4.99 *(978-1-5247-6766-2(2),* Golden Bks.) Random Hse. Children's Bks.
Nedved, Cindy. Broken Christmas Toys. Mayberry, Lynn M. 2017. (ENG.). (J). 18.95 *(978-0-9993410-2-5(2))* Synchrony Hse. Publishing.
Nedved, Cindy. Charlie Goes to the Doctor. Thomas-Newman, Anne. 2019. (Charlie & Mr. Bunny Ser.: Vol. 2). (ENG.). 40p. (J). (gr. k-6). 19.95 ***(978-1-945338-63-2(6))*** United Writers Pr.
Needham, James M. Many Biomes, One Earth. Collard, Sneed B., III. 2009. (ENG.). 32p. (J). (gr. k-3). pap. 7.95 *(978-1-57091-632-8(2))* Charlesbridge Publishing, Inc.
Needham, Sam. The Quest for the Enchanted Sword: An Unofficial Graphic Novel for Minecrafters. Stevens, Cara J. 2020. (Unofficial Battle Station Prime Ser.: 3). 192p. (J). (gr. 2-6). pap. 11.99 *(978-1-5107-4725-8(7),* Sky Pony Pr.) Skyhorse Publishing Co., Inc.
—The Spirit in the Stone: An Unofficial Graphic Novel for Minecrafters. Stevens, Cara J. 2020. (Unofficial Battle Station Prime Ser.: 4). 192p. (J). (gr. 2-6). pap. 11.99 *(978-1-5107-4730-2(3),* Sky Pony Pr.) Skyhorse Publishing Co., Inc.
Neel, Julien. Lou! Neel, Julien. 2012. (Lou! Ser.). 48p. (J). (gr. 4-8). lib. bdg. 55.86 *(978-0-7613-8903-3(2),* Graphic Universe™) Lerner Publishing Group.
—Lou! 6Pack Set. Neel, Julien. 2012. (Lou! Ser.). 48p. (J). (gr. 4-8). pap. 102.03 *(978-0-7613-9288-0(2),* Graphic Universe™) Lerner Publishing Group.
—Lou! Single Copy Set. Neel, Julien. 2012. (Lou! Ser.). 48p. (J). (gr. 4-8). pap. 17.01 *(978-0-7613-9287-3(4),* Graphic Universe™) Lerner Publishing Group.
—Secret Diary. Neel, Julien. 2012. (Lou! Ser.). 48p. (J). (gr. 4-8). pap. 51.02 *(978-0-7613-9285-9(8));* (ENG.). (gr. 6-9). pap. 8.95 *(978-0-7613-8868-5(0))* Lerner Publishing Group. (Graphic Universe™).
—Summertime Blues. Neel, Julien. 2012. (Lou! Ser.). 48p. (J). (gr. 4-8). pap. 51.02 *(978-0-7613-9286-6(6),* Graphic Universe™) Lerner Publishing Group.
Neel, Kate. Lucy & the Fox. Deboe, Meg C. 2020. (ENG.). 36p. (J). pap. 11.99 ***(978-1-6551-1356-7(9))*** Independently Published.
Neel, Preston. Margaret Strong, Toy Collector. Appleton-Smith, Laura & Blackaby, Susan. 2014. (Book to Remember Ser.). (ENG.). 22p. (J). pap. 8.95 *(978-1-60541-152-1(3),* Books To Remember) Flyleaf Publishing.
—Oh My, It Must Be the Sky! Appleton-Smith, Laura. 2004. (Book to Remember Ser.). (ENG.). 52p. pap. 8.95 *(978-1-929262-21-2(3),* Books To Remember) Flyleaf Publishing.
—Queen Bee Needs to Be Free. Appleton-Smith, Laura. 2005. (Book to Remember Ser.). (ENG.). 35p. pap. 8.95 *(978-1-929262-43-4(4),* Books To Remember) Flyleaf Publishing.
Neely, Keith. Play Ball Like the Hall of Famers: The Inside Scoop from 19 Baseball Greats, 1 vol. Krasner, Steve. 2005. (ENG.). 208p. (J). (gr. 5-9). pap. 14.95 *(978-1-56145-339-9(0))* Peachtree Publishing Co. Inc.
—St. Jude: A Friend in Hard Times. Aquilina, Michael, III. 2004. 76p. (J). 14.95 *(978-0-8198-7075-9(7),* 332-371) Pauline Bks. & Media.
Neely, Keith R. Something Is Wrong at My House: A Book about Parents' Fighting. Davis, Diane. 2010.Tr. of Algo anda mal en mi Casa. (ENG.). 32p. (J). (gr. -1-3). pap. 9.95 *(978-1-884734-65-6(0))* Parenting Pr., Inc.
Neely, Scott. Animal Doodles with Scooby-Doo! Bird, Benjamin. 2017. (Scooby-Doodles! Ser.). (ENG.). 32p. (J). (gr. 3-9). lib. bdg. 28.65 *(978-1-5157-3405-5(6),* Capstone Pr.) Capstone.
—The Case of the Cheese Thief, 1 vol. Bright, J. E. 2014. (You Choose Stories: Scooby-Doo Ser.). (ENG.). 112p. (J). (gr. 2-6). pap. 6.95 *(978-1-4342-7927-9(8),* Stone Arch Bks.) Capstone.

N

—The Case of the Clown Carnival. Sutton, Laurie S. 2017. (You Choose Stories: Scooby-Doo Ser.). (ENG.). 112p. (J). (gr. 2-6). lib. bdg. 32.65 (978-1-4965-4333-2(5), Stone Arch Bks.) Capstone.

—The Case of the Fright Flight. Steele, Michael Anthony. 2016. (You Choose Stories: Scooby-Doo Ser.). (ENG.). 112p. (J). (gr. 2-6). lib. bdg. 32.65 (978-1-4965-2662-5(7), Stone Arch Bks.) Capstone.

—The Curse of Atlantis. Sutton, Laurie S. 2015. (You Choose Stories: Scooby-Doo Ser.). (ENG.). 112p. (J). (gr. 2-6). lib. bdg. 32.65 (978-1-4965-0477-7(1), Stone Arch Bks.) Capstone.

—Curse of the Stage Fright. Korte, Steve. 2016. (Scooby-Doo Comic Chapter Bks.). (ENG.). 88p. (J). (gr. 3-7). pap. 5.95 (978-1-4965-3587-0(1)); lib. bdg. 27.32 (978-1-4965-3583-2(9)) Capstone. (Stone Arch Bks.).

—Food Doodles with Scooby-Doo! Bird, Benjamin. 2017. (Scooby-Doodles! Ser.). (ENG.). 32p. (J). (gr. 3-9). lib. bdg. 28.65 (978-1-5157-3407-9(2), Capstone Pr.) Capstone.

—The Fright at Zombie Farm. Sutton, Laurie S. 2015. (You Choose Stories: Scooby-Doo Ser.). (ENG.). 112p. (J). (gr. 2-6). lib. bdg. 32.65 (978-1-4342-9713-6(6), Stone Arch Bks.) Capstone.

—The Ghost of the Bermuda Triangle, 1 vol. Sutton, Laurie S. 2014. (You Choose Stories: Scooby-Doo Ser.). (ENG.). 112p. (J). (gr. 2-6). 32.65 (978-1-4342-9126-4(X), Stone Arch Bks.) Capstone.

—The House on Spooky Street. Sutton, Laurie S. 2015. (You Choose Stories: Scooby-Doo Ser.). (ENG.). 112p. (J). (gr. 2-6). lib. bdg. 32.65 (978-1-4342-9714-3(4), Stone Arch Bks.) Capstone.

—Legend of the Gator Man. Sutton, Laurie S. 2016. (Scooby-Doo Comic Chapter Bks.). (ENG.). 88p. (J). (gr. 3-7). pap. 5.95 (978-1-4965-3588-7(X)); lib. bdg. 27.32 (978-1-4965-3584-9(7)) Capstone. (Stone Arch Bks.).

—Monster Doodles with Scooby-Doo! Bird, Benjamin. 2017. (Scooby-Doodles! Ser.). (ENG.). 32p. (J). (gr. 3-9). lib. bdg. 28.65 (978-1-5157-3406-2(4), Capstone Pr.) Capstone.

—The Mystery of the Aztec Tomb, 1 vol. Sutton, Laurie S. 2014. (You Choose Stories: Scooby-Doo Ser.). (ENG.). 112p. (J). (gr. 2-6). 32.65 (978-1-4342-9127-1(8), Stone Arch Bks.) Capstone.

—The Mystery of the Mayhem Mansion. Manning, Matthew K. 2016. (You Choose Stories: Scooby-Doo Ser.). (ENG.). 112p. (J). (gr. 2-6). lib. bdg. 32.65 (978-1-4965-2661-8(9), Stone Arch Bks.) Capstone.

—The Mystery of the Maze Monster, 1 vol. Sazaklis, John. 2014. (You Choose Stories: Scooby-Doo Ser.). (ENG.). 112p. (J). (gr. 2-6). pap. 6.95 (978-1-4342-7928-6(6), Stone Arch Bks.) Capstone.

—Mystery of the Mist Monster. Manning, Matthew K. 2016. (Scooby-Doo Comic Chapter Bks.). (ENG.). 88p. (J). (gr. 3-7). pap. 5.95 (978-1-4965-3590-0(1)); lib. bdg. 27.32 (978-1-4965-3586-3(3)) Capstone. (Stone Arch Bks.).

—The Salem Witch Showdown. Manning, Matthew K. 2017. (You Choose Stories: Scooby-Doo Ser.). (ENG.). 112p. (J). (gr. 2-6). lib. bdg. 32.65 (978-1-4965-4334-9(3), Stone Arch Bks.) Capstone.

—Scooby-Doo! a Time Mystery: The Case of the Spinning Spook. Adamson, Heather & Adamson, Thomas K. 2017. (Solve It with Scooby-Doo!: Math Ser.). (ENG.). 24p. (J). (gr. k-2). lib. bdg. 28.65 (978-1-5157-7910-0(6), 136025, Capstone Pr.) Capstone.

—Scooby-Doo! an Estimation Mystery: The Case of the Greedy Ghost. Adamson, Heather & Adamson, Thomas K. 2017. (Solve It with Scooby-Doo!: Math Ser.). (ENG.). 24p. (J). (gr. k-2). lib. bdg. 28.65 (978-1-5157-7905-6(X), 136020, Capstone Pr.) Capstone.

—Scooby-Doo Comic Chapter Books. 2016. (Scooby-Doo Comic Chapter Bks.). (ENG.). 88p. (J). (gr. 3-7). pap., pap., pap. 23.80 (978-1-4965-3604-4(5)) Capstone.

—Scooby-Doo Comic Chapter Books. Korte, Steve et al. 2016. (Scooby-Doo Comic Chapter Bks.). (ENG.). 88p. (J). (gr. 3-7). lib. bdg., lib. bdg., lib. bdg. 109.28 (978-1-4965-3603-7(7)) Capstone.

—The Secret of the Flying Saucer. Sutton, Laurie S. 2015. (You Choose Stories: Scooby-Doo Ser.). (ENG.). 112p. (J). (gr. 2-6). lib. bdg. 32.65 (978-1-4965-0478-4(X), Stone Arch Bks.) Capstone.

—Secret of the Haunted Cave. Manning, Matthew K. 2016. (Scooby-Doo Comic Chapter Bks.). (ENG.). 88p. (J). (gr. 3-7). pap. 5.95 (978-1-4965-3589-4(8)); lib. bdg. 27.32 (978-1-4965-3585-6(5)) Capstone. (Stone Arch Bks.).

—The Secret of the Sea Creature, 1 vol. Sutton, Laurie S. 2014. (You Choose Stories: Scooby-Doo Ser.). (ENG.). 112p. (J). (gr. 2-6). pap. 6.95 (978-1-4342-7925-5(1), Stone Arch Bks.) Capstone.

—Solve It with Scooby-Doo!: Math. Adamson, Thomas K. and Heather. 2017. (Solve It with Scooby-Doo!: Math Ser.). (ENG.). 24p. (J). (gr. k-2). 171.90 (978-1-5157-7924-7(6), 26952, Capstone Pr.) Capstone.

—The Terror of the Bigfoot Beast, 1 vol. Sutton, Laurie S. 2014. (You Choose Stories: Scooby-Doo Ser.). (ENG.). 112p. (J). (gr. 2-6). pap. 6.95 (978-1-4342-7926-2(X), Stone Arch Bks.) Capstone.

—Vehicle Doodles with Scooby-Doo! Bird, Benjamin. 2017. (Scooby-Doodles! Ser.). (ENG.). 32p. (J). (gr. 3-9). lib. bdg. 28.65 (978-1-5157-3408-6(0), Capstone Pr.) Capstone.

—You Choose Stories: Scooby-Doo. Manning, Matthew K. & Sutton, Laurie S. 2017. (You Choose Stories: Scooby-Doo Ser.). (ENG.). 112p. (J). (gr. 2-6). 457.10 (978-1-4965-4341-7(6), 25802, Stone Arch Bks.) Capstone.

Neely, Scott & Pope, Robert. Scooby-Doo in Terror Is Afoot! Cunningham, Scott. 2010. (Scooby-Doo Graphic Novels Ser.: No. 1). (ENG.). 24p. (J). (gr. 2-6). 27.07 (978-1-59961-698-8(X), 566, Graphic Novels) Spotlight.

Nefcy, Daron, et al. Star vs. the Forces of Evil the Magic Book of Spells. Nefcy, Daron et al. 2018. (ENG.). 256p. (J). (gr. 3-7). 19.99 (978-1-368-02050-3(X)) Disney Pr.

Neff, Henry H. The Hound of Rowan, 1. Neff, Henry H. 2007. (Tapestry Ser.: Bk. 1). (ENG.). 432p. (J). (gr. 4-6). lib. bdg. 24.94 (978-0-375-93894-8(X)) Random House Publishing Group.

—The Maelstrom: Book Four of the Tapestry, Bk. 4. Neff, Henry H. 2013. (Tapestry Ser.: 4). (ENG.). 480p. (J). (gr. 3-7). 8.99 (978-0-375-87148-1(9), Yearling) Random Hse. Children's Bks.

Negley, Keith. The Boy & the Wild Blue Girl. Negley, Keith. 2020. (ENG.). 40p. (J). (gr. -1-3). 17.99 (978-0-06-284680-8(9), Balzer & Bray) HarperCollins Pubs.

—Mary Wears What She Wants. Negley, Keith. 2019. (ENG.). 48p. (J). (gr. -1-3). 17.99 (978-0-06-284679-2(5), Balzer & Bray) HarperCollins Pubs.

Negrin, Fabian. El Milagro de la Primera Flora de Nochebuena: Un Cuento Mexicano Sobre la Navidad. Oppenheim, Joanne F. 2003. (SPA & ENG.). 32p. (J). 16.99 (978-1-84148-308-5(7)) Barefoot Bks., Inc.

—The Miracle of the First Poinsettia. Oppenheim, Joanne F. 2003. (ENG.). 32p. (J). 16.99 (978-1-84148-245-3(5)) Barefoot Bks., Inc.

—Miracle of the First Poinsettia. Oppenheim, Joanne F. 32p. pap. 8.99 (978-1-84148-364-1(8)) Barefoot Bks., Inc.

—The Riverbank. Darwin, Charles. 2010. (ENG.). 32p. (J). (gr. 1-3). 17.95 (978-1-56846-207-3(7), Creative Editions) Creative Co., The.

—Wizard Tales. 2003. 96p. 19.95 (978-1-55285-558-4(9)) Whitecap Bks., Ltd. CAN. Dist: Graphic Arts Ctr. Publishing Co.

Negrin, Fabin. The Story of Captain Nemo. Eggers, Dave. 2019. (Save the Story Ser.: 2). (ENG.). 104p. (J). (gr. 3-7). pap. 12.95 (978-1-78269-208-9(8), Pushkin Children's Bks.) Steerforth Pr.

Nehrebecki, Jr Robert. The Crayons in Rainbow Land. Cappelli, Susan V. 2017. (ENG.). 58p. (J). pap. 13.95 (978-1-64003-296-5(7)) Covenant Bks.

Neibert, Alissa. Count Your Way Through South Africa. Haskins, Jim & Benson, Kathleen. 2006. (Count Your Way Ser.). (ENG.). 24p. (gr. 2-5). lib. bdg. 19.93 (978-1-57505-883-2(9), Millbrook Pr.) Lerner Publishing Group.

Neidigh, Sherry. Bailey & the Beagle Brigade. Heit Schwaeber, Barbie. 2011. (ENG.). 32p. (J). 6.95 (978-1-60727-218-2(0)) Soundprints.

—Count down to Fall, 1 vol. Hawk, Fran. 2009. (ENG.). 32p. (J). (gr. -1-3). 16.95 (978-1-934359-94-5(7)) Arbordale Publishing.

—Deep in the Desert, 1 vol. Donald, Rhonda Lucas. 2011. (ENG.). 32p. (J). (gr. -1-3). 16.95 (978-1-60718-125-5(8)); pap. 8.95 (978-1-60718-135-4(5), 9781607181354) Arbordale Publishing.

—Falcons. Lynch, Wayne. 2005. (Our Wild World Ser.). (ENG.). 48p. (J). (gr. 2-5). 10.95 (978-1-55971-911-7(7)) Cooper Square Publishing Llc.

—Falcons. Lynch, Wayne, photos by. Lynch, Wayne. 2005. (Our Wild World Ser.). (ENG.). 48p. (J). (gr. 2-5). pap. 7.95 (978-1-55971-912-4(5)) Cooper Square Publishing Llc.

—Une Journée Dans un Milieu Humide Boisé: (a Day in a Forested Wetland in French) Kurtz, Kevin. Troff, Sophie, tr. 2019. (FRE.). 32p. (J). 11.95 (978-1-64351-593-9(4)) Arbordale Publishing.

—Vultures. Lynch, Wayne, photos by. Lynch, Wayne. 2005. (Our Wild World Ser.). (ENG.). 48p. (J). (gr. 2-5). pap. 7.95 (978-1-55971-918-6(4)) Cooper Square Publishing Llc.

Neidigh, Sherry. Un Día en el Bosque Del Humedal. Neidigh, Sherry. Kurtz, Kevin. 2018. (SPA.). 32p. (J). (gr. 2-3). pap. 9.95 (978-1-62855-914-9(4), 9781628559149) Arbordale Publishing.

Neidy, Zoe. Blip. Marie, Natalie. 2018. (Storytime 2017 Ser.: Vol. 1). (ENG.). 22p. (J). (gr. k-3). pap. 9.99 (978-1-55323-786-0(2), ExamWise) Total Recall Learning, Inc.

Neighbor, Douglas. My Grandpa Tom & Me, 1 vol. Godell, Rick. 2009. 29p. pap. 24.95 (978-1-61546-026-7(8)) America Star Bks.

Neilan, Andrew. Mars in the Outback. Neilan, Flynn & Neilan, Marley. 2019. (ENG.). 26p. (J). pap. 9.90 **(978-1-6944-3543-9(1))** Independently Published.

Neilan, Eujin Kim. Fly Free. Thong, Roseanne. 2010. (ENG.). 32p. (J). (gr. -1-3). 17.99 (978-1-59078-550-8(9)) Boyds Mills Pr.

—Imagine a Dragon. Pringle, Laurence. 2008. (ENG.). 32p. (J). (gr. 2-k). 16.95 (978-1-56397-328-4(6)) Boyds Mills Pr.

—Rabbit & the Dragon King: Based on a Korean Folk Tale. San Souci, Daniel. 2006. (ENG.). 32p. (J). (gr. 1-k). pap. 9.95 (978-1-59078-418-1(9)) Boyds Mills Pr.

Neill, John R. Dorothy & the Wizard in Oz. Baum, L. Frank. 2019. (ENG.). 172p. (J). pap. 10.00 **(978-1-6935-5757-6(6))** Independently Published.

Neill, John R. Little Wizard Stories of Oz. Baum, L. Frank. 2011. (Dover Children's Classics Ser.). (ENG.). 160p. (J). (gr. 3-5). pap. 14.99 (978-0-486-47644-5(8)) Dover Pubns., Inc.

—The Silver Princess in Oz. Thompson, Ruth Plumly & Baum, L. Frank. 2011. 248p. 46.95 (978-1-258-01166-6(2)) Literary Licensing, LLC.

—A Wonderful Welcome to Oz: The Marvelous Land of Oz, Ozma of Oz, & the Emerald City of Oz, Vol. Baum, L. Frank. Maguire, Gregory, ed. 2006. (Modern Library Classics Ser.). 624p. per. 17.00 (978-0-8129-7494-2(8), Modern Library) Random House Publishing Group.

Neill, John R., jt. illus. see Baum, L. Frank.

Neilson, Ginger. Gunter the Underwater Elephant. Neilson, Ginger. 2011. 32p. pap. 15.99 (978-0-9832740-2-5(9)) 4RV Pub.

Neilson, Heidi. Play, Said the Earth to Air. Lewis, Richard. 2013. (ENG.). 44p. (J). (gr. -1). pap. 12.00 (978-1-929299-12-6(5)) Touchstone Ctr. Pubns.

Neira, Muyi. Los Siete Mejores Cuentos Rabes. Escobar, Melba. 2004. (SPA.). (J). (gr. 3-5). (978-958-04-7212-4(2)) Norma S.A.

Neis, Karen. El Frankenstein de la Caja de Manzanas: Una Historia Posiblemente Verdadera de Los orígenes Del Monstruo. Viglione, Julia Douthwaite. Dela Cruz, Jeremy Llanes, tr. 2019. (SPA.). 36p. (J). (gr. 3-6). 24.99 (978-0-9984432-4-9(7)) Honey Girl Bks.

—Le Frankenstein du Cageot à Pommes: Ou Comment le Monstre Est Né, de Source (presque) Sûre. Viglione, Julia Douthwaite. Jauneau, Vincent, tr. 2019. (Honey Girl Bks.). (FRE.). 36p. (J). (gr. 3-6). 24.99 (978-0-9984432-3-2(9)) Honey Girl Bks.

—The Frankenstein of the Apple Crate: A Possibly True Story of the Monster's Origins. Viglione, Julia Douthwaite. 2nd ed. 2018. (Honey Girl Bks.: Vol. 1). (ENG.). 36p. (J). (gr. 4-6). 24.99 (978-0-9984432-9-4(8)) Honey Girl Bks.

Neitz, Erica. Shapesville. Mills, Andy & Osborn, Becky. 2003. (ENG.). 32p. (J). 15.95 (978-0-936077-47-5(6)); pap. 15.99 (978-0-936077-44-4(1)) Turner Publishing Co. (Gurze Bks).

Nelissen, Marieke. Yokki & the Parno Gry. Quarmby, Katharine & O'Neill, Richard. 2017. (Child's Play Library). (ENG.). 32p. (J). (978-1-84643-927-8(2)) Child's Play International Ltd.

Nelligan, Kevin, jt. illus. see Ocello, Salvatore.

Nellis, Philip. Themes to Remember, 3, Vol. 1. Persons, Marjorie Kiel. 2007. 124p. (J). lib. bdg. 31.95 incl. audio compact disk (978-0-9794947-0-3(2)) Classical Magic, Inc.

—Themes to Remember Teacher's Guide Vol. 2: A Theme Recognition Based Method for Teaching Music Appreciation, 2 vols. Persons, Marjorie Kiel. 2003. 128p. tchr. ed. 24.95 (978-0-9675997-4-8(1)) Classical Magic, Inc.

Nellis, Philip & Johnson, George Ann. Antonin Dvorak from the New World with Lyrics. Persons, Marjorie Kiel. 2004. 80p. (J). lib. bdg. 31.95 (978-0-9675997-6-2(8)) Classical Magic, Inc.

—Classical Karaoke for Kids. Persons, Marjorie Kiel. 2003. 128p. (J). lib. bdg. 31.95 (978-0-9675997-2-4(5)) Classical Magic, Inc.

—Themes to Remember, Volume 2, Vol. 2. Persons, Marjorie Kiel. rev. ed. 2004. 128p. (J). lib. bdg. 31.95 (978-0-9675997-5-5(X)) Classical Magic, Inc.

Nelms, Humphrey. We Can Stop the Lion: In English & Afaan Oromo. Ready Set Go Books. Gemeda, Ahmed Dedo, tr. 2019. (ENG.). 32p. (J). pap. 9.99 **(978-1-7034-6476-4(1))** Independently Published.

Nelms, Kate. See What a Seal Can Do. Butterworth, Chris. 2013. (ENG.). 32p. (J). (gr. k-4). 14.99 (978-0-7636-6574-6(6)) Candlewick Pr.

—See What a Seal Can Do. Butterworth, Christine. 2015. (Read & Wonder Ser.). (ENG.). 32p. (J). (gr. -1-3). 7.99 (978-0-7636-7649-0(7)) Candlewick Pr.

—See What a Seal Can Do. Butterworth, Christine. 2015. (Read & Wonder Ser.). (ENG.). (J). (gr. -1-3). lib. bdg. 17.60 (978-1-62765-776-1(2)) Perfection Learning Corp.

Nelson, Andy. The Impressionists Coloring Book. Nelson, Andy. 2nd ed. 2004. 96p. (Orig.). (J). (gr. 1-6). pap. 8.95 (978-0-929636-26-9(0)) Syren Bk. Co.

Nelson, Anndria. School Rules! Williams, Shannon. 2010. 36p. pap. 16.99 (978-1-4520-3924-4(0)) AuthorHouse.

Nelson, Annika. Dominga's Wonderful Year/El Año Maravilloso del Domingo. Yonikus, Sandi. 2005. (SPA & ENG.). 32p. (J). 16.95 (978-0-8146-2876-8(1)) Liturgical Pr.

Nelson, Annika & Diaz, David. Canto Familiar. Soto, Gary. 2007. (ENG.). 96p. (J). (gr. 3-7). pap. 7.95 (978-0-15-205885-2(0), 1197669) Houghton Mifflin Harcourt Publishing Co.

Nelson, Annika M. Colors of Me. Barnes, Brynne. 2011. (ENG.). 28p. (J). (gr. 1-4). 15.95 (978-1-58536-541-8(6), 202219) Sleeping Bear Pr.

Nelson, Casey. The Boy Who Ate America. Jones, Nathan Smith. 2007. 32p. (J). (gr. -1-3). 16.95 (978-1-59038-814-3(3), Shadow Mountain) Shadow Mountain Publishing.

—Exploring the Pioneer Trail: A Flashlight Discovery Book. Gibby, Shauna. 2019. (J). 16.99 (978-1-62972-575-8(7)) Deseret Bk. Co.

—Heroic Stories from the Book of Mormon: A Flashlight Discovery Book. Gibby, Shauna. 2017. (J). 16.99 (978-1-62972-319-8(3)) Deseret Bk. Co.

—My First Book of Temples. Buck, Deanna Draper;. 2012. 28p. (J). bds. 15.99 (978-1-60907-158-5(1)) Deseret Bk. Co.

Nelson, Christine. Heavenites Angels to Zebras Board Book with Audio CD. Collison, Shauna. 2007. 26p. (J). 15.95 (978-0-9792510-0-9(1)) Revelation Products LLC.

—Heavenites Learning to Count on God Board Book with audio CD. Collisin, Shauna. 2007. 22p. (J). 15.95 (978-0-9792510-1-6(X)) Revelation Products LLC.

Nelson, Craig. I'll Be with You Always. Eareckson Tada, Joni. 2004. 32p. (gr. 8-12). 14.99 (978-1-58134-000-6(1)) Crossway.

Nelson, Darrel. Adams A to Z. Pearson, Jaci Conrad. 2011. 51p. (J). (978-0-9793584-3-2(4)) TDG Communications, Inc.

Nelson, Don. How the World Began. Heal, Edith. 2012. 112p. 39.95 (978-1-258-23527-7(7)); pap. 24.95 (978-1-258-24549-8(3)) Literary Licensing, LLC.

Nelson, Douglas, jt. illus. see Nelson, Ray.

Nelson, Emist. Atlantis Motherland. Collins, Robert, photos by. Flying Eagle & Whispering Wind. 2004. 168p. (YA). 39.00 (978-0-9719580-0-5(9)) COSMIC VORTEX.

Nelson, Gail M. Go Eat, Pete. Nelson, Gail M. Nelson, Katie M. 2013. 32p. pap. 9.99 (978-1-936499-05-2(3)) Jewel Publishing LLC.

Nelson, Holly. Believe & You're There at the Miracles of Jesus. Johnson, Alice W. & Warner, Allison H. 2009. 96p. (J). pap. 8.95 (978-1-59038-722-1(8)) Deseret Bk. Co.

—Believe & You're There When the Stone Was Rolled Away. Johnson, Alice W. & Warner, Allison H. 2009. 96p. (J). pap. 8.95 (978-1-59038-723-8(6)) Deseret Bk. Co.

—Believe & You're There When the White Dove Descended. Johnson, Alice W. & Warner, Allison H. 2009. 96p. (J). pap. 8.95 (978-1-59038-721-4(X)) Deseret Bk. Co.

Nelson, Jane E. God Makes It Right: Three Stories for Children Based on Favorite Bible Verses. Murphy, Elspeth Campbell. 72p. (J). (978-1-55513-109-8(3)) Cook, David C.

Nelson, Jim. The Curse of King Tut's Mummy. Zoehfeld, Kathleen Weidner. 2007. (Totally True Adventures Ser.). (ENG.). 112p. (J). (gr. 2-5). per. 5.99 (978-0-375-83862-0(7), Random Hse. Bks. for Young Readers) Random Hse. Children's Bks.

—Finding the First T. Rex. Zoehfeld, Kathleen Weidner. 2008. (Totally True Adventures Ser.). (ENG.). 112p. (J). (gr. 2-5). 5.99 (978-0-375-84662-5(X), Random Hse. Bks. for Young Readers) Random Hse. Children's Bks.

—The Gnawer of Rocks, 1 vol. Flaherty, Louise. 2017. (ENG.). 56p. (J). (gr. 7). 22.95 (978-1-77227-165-2(9)) Inhabit Media Inc. CAN. Dist: Consortium Bk. Sales & Distribution.

—Looking for Bigfoot. Worth, Bonnie. 2010. (Step into Reading Ser.). 48p. (J). (gr. 2-4). pap. 4.99 (978-0-375-86331-8(1), Random Hse. Bks. for Young Readers) Random Hse. Children's Bks.

Nelson, Joe. Princess Lydi & the Baby Brother. Webb, Genie. 2017. (ENG.). (J). (gr. -1-3). 18.95 (978-0-692-86133-2(5)) Webb, Genie.

Nelson, Judy. Desert Tails. Reasoner, Charles. 2011. (Tail Spin Bks.). (ENG.). 14p. (J). (gr. -1). 9.99 (978-1-934650-93-6(5)) Just For Kids Pr., LLC.

—Ocean Tails. Reasoner, Charles. 2011. (Tail Spin Bks.). (ENG.). 14p. (J). (gr. -1-3). bds. 9.99 (978-1-934650-92-9(7)) Just For Kids Pr., LLC.

—Whose Ears? Kenna, Kara. 2011. (Whose Whose Bks.). (ENG.). 10p. (gr. -1-k). bds. 9.99 (978-1-935498-52-0(5)) Just For Kids Pr., LLC.

—Whose Eyes? Kenna, Kara. 2011. (Whose Whose Bks.). (ENG.). 10p. (gr. -1-k). bds. 9.99 (978-1-935498-51-3(7)) Just For Kids Pr., LLC.

—Whose Feet? Kenna, Kara. 2011. (Whose Whose Bks.). (ENG.). 12p. (J). (gr. -1). bds. 9.99 (978-1-935498-53-7(3)) Just For Kids Pr., LLC.

Nelson, Judy A. Whose Nose? Kenna, Kara. 2011. (Whose Whose Bks.). (ENG.). 10p. (gr. -1-k). bds. 9.99 (978-1-935498-54-4(1)) Just For Kids Pr., LLC.

Nelson, Kadir. Abe's Honest Words. Rappaport, Doreen. 2009. (J). (gr. 2-4). 27.95 incl. audio (978-0-8045-6984-2(3)) Spoken Arts, Inc.

—Abe's Honest Words: The Life of Abraham Lincoln. Rappaport, Doreen. 2016. (Big Words Book Ser.: 5). (ENG.). 48p. (J). (gr. -1-3). pap. 8.99 (978-1-4847-4958-6(8)) Hyperion Bks. for Children.

—Abe's Honest Words: The Life of Abraham Lincoln. Rappaport, Doreen. 2008. (Big Words Book Ser.: 5). (ENG.). 48p. (J). (gr. 3-7). 16.99 (978-1-4231-0408-7(0)) Hyperion Pr.

—All God's Critters. Staines, Bill. 2009. (ENG.). 36p. (J). (gr. k-3). 19.99 (978-0-689-86959-4(2), Simon & Schuster Bks. For Young Readers) Simon & Schuster Bks. For Young Readers.

—Basket Ball. 2019. (J). (978-1-4847-7181-5(8)) Disney Publishing Worldwide.

—Big Jabe. Nolen, Jerdine. 2003. (ENG.). 32p. (J). (gr. k-5). pap. 7.99 (978-0-06-054061-6(3), Amistad) HarperCollins Pubs.

—Big Jabe. Nolen, Jerdine. 2004. (gr. 1). 17.00 (978-0-7569-3184-1(3)) Perfection Learning Corp.

—Blue Sky White Stars. Naberhaus, Sarvinder. 2017. (ENG.). 40p. (J). (gr. -1-3). 17.99 (978-0-8037-3700-6(9), Dial Bks) Penguin Young Readers Group.

—Blue Sky White Stars Bilingual Edition. Naberhaus, Sarvinder. 2019. 40p. (J). (gr. -1-3). pap. 8.99 (978-0-451-48164-1(X), Puffin Books) Penguin Young Readers Group.

—Coretta Scott. Shange, Ntozake. (ENG.). 32p. (J). (gr. -1-4). 2011. pap. 7.99 (978-0-06-125366-9(9)); 2009. 17.99 (978-0-06-125364-5(2)) HarperCollins Pubs. (Tegen, Katherine Bks).

—Dancing in the Wings. Allen, Debbie. 2003. (ENG.). 32p. (J). (gr. -1-3). 7.99 (978-0-14-250141-2(7), Puffin Books) Penguin Young Readers Group.

—Dancing in the Wings. Allen, Debbie. 2003. (J). (gr. -1-3). 14.65 (978-0-7569-7022-2(9)) Perfection Learning Corp.

—Ellington Was Not a Street. Shange, Ntozake. 2004. (ENG.). 40p. (J). (gr. k-6). 19.99 (978-0-689-82884-3(5), Simon & Schuster Bks. For Young Readers) Simon & Schuster Bks. For Young Readers.

—Ellington Was Not a Street. Shange, Ntozake. 2005. (J). 29.95 (978-0-439-77582-3(5), WHCD672) Weston Woods Studios, Inc.

—Henry's Freedom Box: A True Story from the Underground Railroad. Levine, Ellen. 2007. (ENG.). 40p. (J). (gr. -1-3). 17.99 (978-0-439-77733-9(X), Scholastic Pr.) Scholastic, Inc.

—Henry's Freedom Box: A True Story from the Underground Railroad. Levine, Ellen. 2011. (J). (gr. 2-5). 29.95 (978-0-545-13455-2(2)) Weston Woods Studios, Inc.

—Hewitt Anderson's Great Big Life. Nolen, Jerdine. (ENG.). 40p. (J). (gr. k-3). 2013. 8.99 (978-1-4424-6035-5(0)); 2005. 18.99 (978-0-689-86866-5(9)) Simon & Schuster/Paula Wiseman Bks. (Simon & Schuster/Paula Wiseman Bks.).

—I Have a Dream (Book & CD), 1 vol. King, Martin Luther, Jr. & King, Martin Luther. 2012. (ENG.). 40p. (J). (gr. -1-3). 18.99 (978-0-375-85887-1(3), Schwartz & Wade Bks.) Random Hse. Children's Bks.

—Mama Miti: Wangari Maathai & the Trees of Kenya. Napoli, Donna Jo. 2010. (ENG.). 40p. (J). (gr. -1-3). 19.99 (978-1-4169-3505-6(3), Simon & Schuster/Paula Wiseman Bks.) Simon & Schuster/Paula Wiseman Bks.

—Michael's Golden Rules. Jordan, Deloris. 2007. (ENG.). 32p. (J). (gr. 1-5). 18.99 (978-0-689-87016-3(7), Simon & Schuster/Paula Wiseman Bks.) Simon & Schuster/Paula Wiseman Bks.

—Miles Morales: Spider-Man. Reynolds, Jason. (Marvel YA Novel Ser.). (ENG.). 272p. (YA). (gr. 7-17). 2018. pap. 9.99 (978-1-4847-8850-9(8)); 2017. 17.99

(978-1-4847-8748-9(X)) Disney Publishing Worldwide. (Marvel Pr.).

—Moses: When Harriet Tubman Led Her People to Freedom. Weatherford, Carole Boston. 2006. (ENG.). 48p. (J). (gr. 1-3). 15.99 (978-0-7868-5175-1(9), Jump at the Sun) Hyperion Bks. for Children.

—A Nation's Hope: the Story of Boxing Legend Joe Louis: The Story of Boxing Legend Joe Louis. de la Peña, Matt. 2013. 40p. (J). (gr. 1-3). 8.99 (978-0-14-751061-7(9), Puffin Books) Penguin Young Readers Group.

—Please, Baby, Please. Lee, Spike & Lee, Tonya Lewis. 2007. (Classic Board Bks.). (ENG.). 32p. (J). (gr. -1-k). bds. 8.99 (978-1-4169-4911-4(9), Little Simon) Little Simon.

—Please, Baby, Please. Lee, Spike & Lee, Tonya Lewis. 2006. (ENG.). 38p. (J). (gr. -1-3). reprint ed. 7.99 (978-0-689-83457-8(8), Simon & Schuster Bks. For Young Readers) Simon & Schuster Bks. For Young Readers.

—Please, Puppy, Please. Lee, Tonya Lewis & Lee, Spike. 2005. (ENG.). 32p. (J). (gr. -1-3). 18.99 (978-0-689-86804-7(9), Simon & Schuster Bks. For Young Readers) Simon & Schuster Bks. For Young Readers.

—Salt in His Shoes: Michael Jordan in Pursuit of a Dream. Jordan, Deloris & Jordan, Roslyn M. 2003. (ENG.). 32p. (J). (gr. -1-3). pap. 8.99 (978-0-689-83419-6(5), Simon & Schuster Bks. For Young Readers) Simon & Schuster Bks. For Young Readers.

—Salt in His Shoes: Michael Jordan in Pursuit of a Dream. Jordan, Deloris & Jordan, Roslyn M. ed. 2003. lib. bdg. 18.40 (978-0-613-89001-4(9)) Turtleback.

—A Strong Right Arm: The Story of Mamie Peanut Johnson. Green, Michelle Y. 2004. (ENG.). 128p. (J). (gr. 3-7). 6.99 (978-0-14-240072-2(6), Puffin Books) Penguin Young Readers Group.

—Testing the Ice: A True Story about Jackie Robinson. Robinson, Sharon. 2009. (ENG.). 40p. (J). (gr. 2-5). 18.99 (978-0-545-05251-1(3), Scholastic Pr.) Scholastic, Inc.

—Thunder Rose. Nolen, Jerdine. 2007. (ENG.). 32p. (J). (gr. k-3). pap. 7.99 (978-0-15-206006-0(5), 1198036, HMH Books For Young Readers) Houghton Mifflin Harcourt Publishing Co.

—Thunder Rose. Nolen, Jerdine. 2007. (gr. k-3). 17.00 (978-0-7569-8199-0(9)) Perfection Learning Corp.

—The Undefeated. Alexander, Kwame. 2019. (ENG.). 40p. (J). (gr. 1-4). 17.99 (978-1-328-78096-6(1), 1682408, Versify) Houghton Mifflin Harcourt Publishing Co.

—The Village That Vanished. 2004. 40p. (J). (gr. k-3). reprint ed. pap. 7.99 (978-0-14-240190-3(0), Puffin Books) Penguin Young Readers Group.

Nelson, Kadir. Baby Bear. Nelson, Kadir. 2014. (ENG.). 40p. (J). (gr. -1-3). 17.99 (978-0-06-224172-6(9), Balzer & Bray) HarperCollins Pubs.

—Baby Bear Board Book. Nelson, Kadir. 2019. (ENG.). 36p. (J). (gr. -1 — 1). bds. 7.99 (978-0-06-293157-3(1), Balzer & Bray) HarperCollins Pubs.

—Change Has Come: An Artist Celebrates Our American Spirit. Nelson, Kadir. Obama, Barack. 2009. (ENG.). 64p. (J). (gr. 1). 12.99 (978-1-4169-8955-4(2), Simon & Schuster Bks. For Young Readers) Simon & Schuster Bks. For Young Readers.

—Heart & Soul: The Story of America & African Americans. Nelson, Kadir. (ENG.). (J). (gr. 1-5). 2013. 112p. pap. 9.99 (978-0-06-173079-5(3)); 2011. 108p. 21.99 (978-0-06-173074-0(2)); 2011. 108p. lib. bdg. 20.89 (978-0-06-173076-4(9)) HarperCollins Pubs.

—He's Got the Whole World in His Hands. Nelson, Kadir. 2005. (ENG.). 32p. (J). (gr. -1-3). 17.99 (978-0-8037-2850-9(6), Dial Bks) Penguin Young Readers Group.

—He's Got the Whole World in His Hands. Nelson, Kadir. unabr. ed. 2006. (J). (gr. -1-2). 29.95 (978-0-439-90581-7(8)) Weston Woods Studios, Inc.

—If You Plant a Seed. Nelson, Kadir. 2015. (ENG.). 32p. (J). (gr. -1-3). 18.99 (978-0-06-229889-8(5), Balzer & Bray) HarperCollins Pubs.

—If You Plant a Seed Board Book. Nelson, Kadir. 2020. (ENG.). 32p. (J). (gr. -1 — 1). bds. 7.99 (978-0-06-293203-7(9), Balzer & Bray) HarperCollins Pubs.

—Nelson Mandela. Nelson, Kadir. (ENG.). 40p. (J). (gr. -1-3). 2019. pap. 6.99 (978-0-06-178377-7(3)); 2013. 17.99 (978-0-06-178374-6(9)); 2013. lib. bdg. 18.89 (978-0-06-178376-0(5)) HarperCollins Pubs. (Tegen, Katherine Bks).

—We Are the Ship: The Story of Negro League Baseball. Nelson, Kadir. 2008. 96p. (J). (gr. 3-7). 19.99 (978-0-7868-0832-8(2), Jump at the Sun) Hyperion Bks. for Children.

Nelson, Mary Beth. Elmo's World: First Flap-Book Library (Sesame Street) Balls!; Puppies!; Babies!; Food! Random House. 2008. (Sesame Street(R) Elmos World(TM) Ser.). (ENG.). 12p. (J). (— 1). bds. 9.99 (978-0-375-84512-3(7), Random Hse. Bks. for Young Readers) Random Hse. Children's Bks.

—Elmo's World: Love! (Sesame Street) McMahon, Kara. 2004. (Sesame Street(R) Elmos World(TM) Ser.). (ENG.). 12p. (J). (— 1). bds. 4.99 (978-0-375-82843-0(5), Random Hse. Bks. for Young Readers) Random Hse. Children's Bks.

—We're Amazing 1,2,3! a Story about Friendship & Autism (Sesame Street) Kimmelman, Leslie. 2017. (Big Golden Book Ser.). (ENG.). 32p. (J). (gr. -1-2). 10.99 (978-1-5247-6621-4(6), Golden Bks.) Random Hse. Children's Bks.

Nelson, Mary Beth & Linn, Laurent. Elmo's Big Word Book/el Libro Grande de Palabras de Elmo. Barrett, John E., photos by. 2006. (Elmo's Big Word Book/el Libro Grande de Palabras de Elmo Ser.). (SPA, MUL & ANG.). 12p. (J). (gr. -1 — 1). bds. 8.95 (978-0-87358-906-2(8)) Cooper Square Publishing Llc.

Nelson, Marybeth. Dream: With Sesame Street. Sesame Workshop & Hill, Susanna Leonard. (Sesame Street Scribbles Ser.). (ENG.). (J). (-3). 2020. 40p. 17.99 (978-1-7282-1050-6(X)); 2019. 32p. 12.99 (978-1-4926-9500-4(9), Sourcebooks Jabberwocky) Sourcebooks, Inc.

Nelson, Marybeth. Sweet Dreams: A Goodnight Lullaby. Sesame Workshop. 2020. (Sesame Street Scribbles Ser.). (ENG.). 40p. (J). (-3). 10.99 **(978-1-7282-2920-1(0))** Sourcebooks, Inc.

Nelson, Marybeth, jt. illus. see Weiss, Ellen.

Nelson, Megan. Hey Guys: A Story about Going to Day Camp. Freedman, Sharon. 2004. (ENG.). 39p. 24.95 (978-1-4137-2422-6(1)) PublishAmerica, Inc.

Nelson, Michelle L. A Secret or a Surprise? Nelson, Michelle L. 2017. (ENG.). (J). (978-1-5255-1972-7(7)); pap. (978-1-5255-0771-7(0)) FriesenPress.

Nelson, Michiyo. My First 100 Words. Scholastic. 2008. (ENG.). 32p. (J). (gr. -1-3). pap. 7.99 (978-0-545-05657-1(8), Cartwheel Bks.) Scholastic, Inc.

—Sign Language: My First 100 Words. Scholastic Book Editors. 2008. 32p. (gr. -1-3). 17.00 (978-0-7569-8911-8(6)) Perfection Learning Corp.

Nelson, Natalie. How Emily Saved the Bridge, 1 vol. Wishinsky, Frieda. 2019. (ENG.). 32p. (J). (gr. 2-5). 19.95 (978-1-77306-104-7(6)) Groundwood Bks. CAN. Dist: Publishers Group West (PGW).

—A Storytelling of Ravens, 1 vol. Lukoff, Kyle. 2018. (ENG.). 32p. (J). (gr. k-4). 18.95 (978-1-55498-912-6(4)) Groundwood Bks. CAN. Dist: Publishers Group West (PGW).

—Uncle Holland, 1 vol. Lawson, JonArno. 2017. (ENG.). 32p. (J). (gr. -1-2). 17.95 (978-1-55498-929-4(9)) Groundwood Bks. CAN. Dist: Publishers Group West (PGW).

Nelson, Nicola. Super Ollie Outsmarts Overwhelm. Dibb, Carolyn. 2017. (ENG.). (J). pap. (978-1-5255-1302-2(8)) FriesenPress.

Nelson, Ray & Nelson, Douglas. Greetings from America: Postcards from Donovan Willoughby. Nelson, Ray & Nelson, Douglas. Tronslin, Andrea, ed. 2nd ed. 48p. (J). (gr. k-5). 14.95 (978-1-56977-409-0(9)) Flying Rhinoceros, Inc.

Nelson, Robin. Paper Zoo / Zoologico de Papel: An Adventure to South Africa / una Aventura a Sudafrica. Woods, Leslie. 2018. (ENG.). 42p. (J). pap. 12.95 (978-0-9994985-1-4(7)) Leaning Rock Pr.

Nelson, Robin T. Jeremiah the Donkey & the Day of Palms: An Adventure to Jerusalem. Hammons, Pastor. 2018. (Biblical Adventures for Children Ser.: 1). (ENG.). 38p. (J). (gr. -1-2). 16.95 (978-0-9998744-0-0(3)) Leaning Rock Pr.

—The Message of Monteverde / el Mensaje de Monteverde: An Adventure to Costa Rica's Cloud Forest / una Aventura Al Bosque Nuboso de Costa Rica. Woods, Leslie a. 2018. (Colibri Children's Adventures Ser.: Vol. 4). (ENG.). 42p. (J). (gr. k-4). 17.95 (978-0-9998744-3-1(8)); pap. 12.95 (978-0-9998744-4-8(6)) Leaning Rock Pr.

Nelson, Robin T. The Magic Fishbowl: An Adventure under the Sea. Nelson, Robin T. 2nd ed. 2020. (Colibri Ser.: Vol. 3). (ENG.). 38p. (J). 17.95 **(978-1-950323-31-9(5))**; pap. 12.95 **(978-1-950323-30-2(7))** Leaning Rock Pr.

Nelson, Robin T. The Magic Fishbowl / la Pecera Magica: An Adventure under the Sea / una Aventura Bajo el Mar. Nelson, Robin T. Woods, Leslie a. 2018. (ENG.). 42p. (J). (gr. k-4). pap. 12.95 (978-0-9994985-7-6(6)) Leaning Rock Pr.

—The Magic Fishbowl / la Pecera Magica: An Adventure under the Sea / una Aventura Bajo el Mar. Nelson, Robin T. Woods, Leslie a, tr. 2018. (Colibri Children's Adventures Ser.: Vol. 1). (ENG.). 42p. (J). (gr. k-4). 17.95 (978-0-9994985-6-9(8)) Leaning Rock Pr.

Nelson, Robin T. La Pecera Mágica: Una Aventura Bajo el Mar: Spanish Classroom Version. Nelson, Robin T. 2nd ed. 2020. (Colibri Ser.: Vol. 4). (SPA.). 38p. (J). pap. 6.95 **(978-1-950323-28-9(5))** Leaning Rock Pr.

Nelson, S. D. Crazy Horse's Vision. Bruchac, Joseph. 2006. (gr. 1-4). 20.45 (978-0-7569-6691-1(4)) Perfection Learning Corp.

—Dance in a Buffalo Skull. Zitkala-Sa. 2007. (Prairie Tales Ser.). 40p. (J). (gr. -1-2). 14.95 (978-0-9777955-2-9(7), South Dakota State Historical Society Pr.) South Dakota Historical Society Pr.

—Greet the Dawn: The Lakota Way. 2012. 48p. (J). 18.95 (978-0-9845041-6-9(8), South Dakota State Historical Society Pr.) South Dakota Historical Society Pr.

Nelson, S. D. Jim Thorpe's Bright Path, 1 vol. Nelson, S. D., tr. Bruchac, Joseph. 2004. (ENG.). 40p. (J). (gr. 1-4). 17.95 (978-1-58430-166-0(X)) Lee & Low Bks., Inc.

Nelson, S. M. The Big Stink. Nelson, S. M. Ward, Nancy. 2019. (Little Virtue Ponds Ser.: Vol. 2). (ENG.). 42p. (J). (gr. k-2). pap. 14.99 (978-1-948123-12-9(6)) Brainiac Bloomers, LLC.

—We're Going to Dinner & You're My Ride: What Are We Riding In? Nelson, S. M. Nelson, L. A., ed. 2018. (ENG.). 40p. (J). (gr. k-2). 24.99 (978-1-948123-04-4(5)) Brainiac Bloomers, LLC.

Nelson, S. M. & Ward, Nancy. The Big Stink. Nelson, S. M. 2019. (Little Virtue Ponds Ser.: Vol. 2). (ENG.). 42p. (J). (gr. k-2). 24.99 (978-1-948123-13-6(4)) Brainiac Bloomers, LLC.

—Uptop Christmas. Nelson, S. M. 2018. (ENG.). 42p. (J). (gr. k-2). 24.99 (978-1-948123-10-5(X)); pap. 14.99 (978-1-948123-09-9(6)) Brainiac Bloomers, LLC.

—We're Going Traveling & You're My Ride Volume 1: What Are We Riding In? Nelson, S. M. 2018. (ENG.). 40p. (J). (gr. k-2). pap. 14.99 (978-1-948123-01-3(0)) Brainiac Bloomers, LLC.

Nelson, Sarah. Alphabeasties. Werner, Sharon et al. 2010. (ENG.). 26p. (J). (gr. k-12). 15.99 (978-1-60905-003-0(7)) Blue Apple Bks.

Nelson-Schmidt, Michelle. Bob Is a Unicorn. Nelson-Schmidt, Michelle. 2014. (ENG.). 28p. (J). 14.99 (978-1-61067-155-2(4)) Kane Miller.

—José Juan y el Monstruo Ysi. Nelson-Schmidt, Michelle. 2019.Tr. of Jonathan James & the Whatif Monster. (SPA.). (J). pap. 6.99 (978-1-61067-924-4(5)) Kane Miller.

Nelson, Scott. Patch the Porcupine & the Bike Shop Job. Nelson, Scott. 2004. 28p. (J). 14.95 (978-0-9745715-3-9(9)) KRBY Creations, LLC.

Nelson, Shannon. Ryan's Vitiligo. May, Cynthia. 2003. (J). pap. 8.95 (978-0-615-12578-7(6)) May, Cynthia D.

Nelson, Will, et al. Alphabet of Bears. Schwaeber, Barbie Heit. 2011. (Alphabet Bks.). (ENG.). 40p. (J). (gr. -1-3). 17.95 (978-1-60727-668-5(2)) Soundprints.

—Alphabet of Bears. Schwaeber, Barbie Heit. 2007. (Alphabet Of... Ser.). (ENG.). 40p. (J). 15.95 (978-1-59249-689-1(X)) Soundprints.

Nelson, Will. Black Bear Cub at Sweet Berry Trail. Galvin, Laura Gates. 2008. (ENG.). 32p. (J). (gr. k-2). 6.95 (978-1-59249-775-1(6)); pap. 8.95 (978-1-59249-777-5(2)); 19.95 (978-1-59249-776-8(4)); 16.95 (978-1-59249-773-7(X)); pap. 6.95 (978-1-59249-774-4(8)) Soundprints.

—Panda Bear Cub. Moody-Luther, Jacqueline. 2006. (ENG.). 32p. (J). pap. 3.95 (978-1-59249-585-6(0)) Soundprints.

Nelson, William. Then & Now Stories. Stonesifer, Gertrude. 2003. (ENG.). 112p. (J). 21.95 (978-1-878044-86-0(9)) Mayhaven Publishing, Inc.

Nelvana, et al. Ranger Rob at Big Sky Park (Little Detectives) 2018. 14p. (J). (gr. -1-1). bds. 9.99 (978-2-924786-45-1(2), CrackBoom! Bks.) Chouette Publishing CAN. Dist: Publishers Group West (PGW).

Nelvana Ltd. & Legdani, Sanaa. Ranger Rob: My Essential Ranger Guide: A Carry along Book. 2018. (ENG.). 24p. (J). (gr. -1-1). bds. 7.99 (978-2-924786-61-1(4), CrackBoom! Bks.) Chouette Publishing CAN. Dist: Publishers Group West (PGW).

Nelvana Ltd. & Yuichi, Kimura. Max & Ruby: Bunny Adventures: A Look & Find Book. 2019. (ENG.). 14p. (J). (gr. -1). bds. 9.99 (978-2-89802-066-7(4), CrackBoom! Bks.) Chouette Publishing CAN. Dist: Publishers Group West (PGW).

Nelvana Ltd. Staff. Ranger Rob: Bug Hunt: My Cave Light Adventure Book. 2018. 14p. (J). (gr. -1-k). 12.99 (978-2-924786-53-6(3), CrackBoom! Bks.) Chouette Publishing CAN. Dist: Publishers Group West (PGW).

Nelvana Ltd., Staff. Ranger Rob: My Yeti Friend Gift Set: Book with 2 Stories & Stomper Plush. Delporte, Corinne. 2018. (ENG.). 48p. (J). (gr. -1). 19.99 (978-2-924786-80-2(0), CrackBoom! Bks.) Chouette Publishing CAN. Dist: Publishers Group West (PGW).

Nelvana Ltd. Staff & Dupuis, Karina. Ranger Rob: a Campfire Story. Chouette Publishing Staff, tr. 2018. (ENG.). 24p. (J). (gr. -1-1). 3.99 (978-2-924786-43-7(6), CrackBoom! Bks.) Chouette Publishing CAN. Dist: Publishers Group West (PGW).

Nelvana Ltd., Staff & Dupuis, Karina. Ranger Rob: My First Sticker Book. 2019. (Ranger Rob Ser.). (ENG.). 64p. (J). (gr. -1). bds. 9.99 (978-2-924786-91-8(6), CrackBoom! Bks.) Chouette Publishing CAN. Dist: Publishers Group West (PGW).

Nelvana Ltd. Staff & Dupuis, Karina. Ranger Rob: Nature Quest. 2018. (ENG.). 24p. (J). (gr. -1-1). 3.99 (978-2-924786-41-3(X), CrackBoom! Bks.) Chouette Publishing CAN. Dist: Publishers Group West (PGW).

—Read with Ranger Rob: My Pet Ranger (Level 2: Apprentice Ranger) 2019. (Ranger Rob Ser.). (ENG.). 32p. (J). (gr. -1). 3.99 (978-2-89802-007-0(9), CrackBoom! Bks.) Chouette Publishing CAN. Dist: Publishers Group West (PGW).

—Read with Ranger Rob: Scent Trail (Level 1: Budding Ranger) 2019. (Ranger Rob Ser.). (ENG.). 32p. (J). (gr. -1). 3.99 (978-2-89802-005-6(2), CrackBoom! Bks.) Chouette Publishing CAN. Dist: Publishers Group West (PGW).

Nelvana Ltd., Staff & Yuichi, Kimura. Max & Ruby: Bunny Christmas: Lift-The-Flap Book. 2019. (Max & Ruby Ser.). 10p. (J). (gr. -1). bds. 7.99 (978-2-89802-070-4(2), CrackBoom! Bks.) Chouette Publishing CAN. Dist: Publishers Group West (PGW).

—Max & Ruby: Max's Nightlight: A Bedtime Book. 2019. (Max & Ruby Ser.). (ENG.). 14p. (J). (gr. -1). 12.99 (978-2-89802-059-9(1), CrackBoom! Bks.) Chouette Publishing CAN. Dist: Publishers Group West (PGW).

—Max & Ruby Play Hide-And-Seek: Lift-The-Flap Book. 2019. (Max & Ruby Ser.). 10p. (J). (gr. -1). bds. 7.99 (978-2-89802-071-1(0), CrackBoom! Bks.) Chouette Publishing CAN. Dist: Publishers Group West (PGW).

Nemett, Barry & Nemett, Laini. Adam's Crayons. Leopold, Nikia Speliakos Clark. 2011. (J). (978-0-9817519-1-7(1)) Galileo Pr.

Nemett, Laini, jt. illus. see Nemett, Barry.

Neo, Anngee. Do Gallery Sitters Sit All Day? Things People Really Do in a Museum. How, Ryan. 2018. (ENG.). 36p. pap. 15.00 (978-981-11-4514-8(8)) National Gallery Singapore SGP. Dist: Pennsylvania State Univ. Pr.

Neogi, Joyeeta. Andre, Kid Aviator. Alston, Shenek. 2019. (ENG.). 26p. (J). 18.00 **(978-1-7321464-3-3(8))**; pap. 13.00 **(978-1-7321464-2-6(X))** Shenek.

Neogi, Joyeeta. Anna, Kid Engineer. Alston, Shenek. 2018. (ENG.). 30p. (J). pap. 12.00 (978-1-7321464-1-9(1)) Shenek.

—Bumble Bee, How Did You Get Your Stripes? Smith, Alexis D. 2018. (ENG.). 36p. (J). pap. 19.95 (978-1-7260-9397-2(2)) CreateSpace Independent Publishing Platform.

—Mummy's Gorgeous Hair. Williams, Vivienne. 2013. 26p. pap. (978-0-9576680-9-6(0)) Williams, Vivienne.

Neonakis, Alexandria. Birdhouse Builder. Cobb, Amy. 2017. (Libby Wimbley Ser.). (ENG.). 32p. (J). (gr. -1-3). lib. bdg. 28.50 (978-1-5321-3023-6(6), 25524, Calico Chapter Bks) Magic Wagon.

—Bug Rescuer. Cobb, Amy. 2017. (Libby Wimbley Ser.). (ENG.). 32p. (J). (gr. -1-3). lib. bdg. 28.50 (978-1-5321-3024-3(4), 25526, Calico Chapter Bks) Magic Wagon.

—Constructora de Casitas para Pájaros (Birdhouse Builder) Cobb, Amy. 2018. (Libby Wimbley Ser.). (SPA.). 32p. (J). (gr. -1-3). lib. bdg. 28.50 (978-1-5321-3471-5(1), 31195, Calico Chapter Bks) Magic Wagon.

—Cow Girl. Cobb, Amy. 2018. (Libby Wimbley Ser.). (ENG.). 32p. (J). (gr. -1-3). lib. bdg. 28.50 (978-1-5321-3253-7(0), 31135, Calico Chapter Bks) Magic Wagon.

—Entrenadora de Cabras (Goat Trainer) Cobb, Amy. 2018. (Libby Wimbley Ser.). (SPA.). 32p. (J). (gr. -1-3). lib. bdg. 28.50 (978-1-5321-3473-9(8), 31199, Calico Chapter Bks) Magic Wagon.

—Goat Trainer. Cobb, Amy. 2017. (Libby Wimbley Ser.). (ENG.). 32p. (J). (gr. -1-3). lib. bdg. 28.50 (978-1-5321-3025-0(2), 25528, Calico Chapter Bks) Magic Wagon.

—Instructora de Gallos (Rooster Instructor) Cobb, Amy. 2018. (Libby Wimbley Ser.). (SPA.). 32p. (J). (gr. -1-3). lib. bdg. 28.50 (978-1-5321-3474-6(6), 31201, Calico Chapter Bks) Magic Wagon.

—Juniper Kai - Super Spy. Gehl, Laura. 2019. 32p. (J). (gr. -1-3). 17.99 (978-1-5420-4332-8(8), 9781542043328, Two Lions) Amazon Publishing.

—Mother Hen. Cobb, Amy. 2018. (Libby Wimbley Ser.). (ENG.). 32p. (J). (gr. -1-3). lib. bdg. 28.50 (978-1-5321-3254-4(9), 31137, Calico Chapter Bks) Magic Wagon.

—Rescatadora de Bichos (Bug Rescuer) Cobb, Amy. 2018. (Libby Wimbley Ser.). (SPA.). 32p. (J). (gr. -1-3). lib. bdg. 28.50 (978-1-5321-3472-2(X), 31197, Calico Chapter Bks) Magic Wagon.

—Rooster Instructor. Cobb, Amy. 2017. (Libby Wimbley Ser.). (ENG.). 32p. (J). (gr. -1-3). lib. bdg. 28.50 (978-1-5321-3026-7(0), 25530, Calico Chapter Bks) Magic Wagon.

—Sweetest Kulu, 1 vol. Kalluk, Celina. 2018. (ENG.). 36p. (J). (gr. -1 — 1). 10.95 (978-1-77227-183-6(7)) Inhabit Media Inc. CAN. Dist: Consortium Bk. Sales & Distribution.

—Sweetest Kulu 5th Anniversary Limited Edition, 1 vol. Kalluk, Celina. 2019. (ENG.). 32p. (J). 17.95 (978-1-77227-260-4(4)) Inhabit Media Inc. CAN. Dist: Consortium Bk. Sales & Distribution.

—This Is MY Room! (No Tigers Allowed) Jacobson, Jennifer Richard. 2019. (ENG.). 48p. (J). (gr. -1-3). 17.99 (978-1-5344-0211-9(X), Simon & Schuster Bks. For Young Readers) Simon & Schuster Bks. For Young Readers.

—Tour Guide. Cobb, Amy. 2018. (Libby Wimbley Ser.). (ENG.). 32p. (J). (gr. -1-3). lib. bdg. 28.50 (978-1-5321-3255-1(7), 31139, Calico Chapter Bks) Magic Wagon.

—Worm Wrangler. Cobb, Amy. 2018. (Libby Wimbley Ser.). (ENG.). 32p. (J). (gr. -1-3). lib. bdg. 28.50 (978-1-5321-3256-8(5), 31141, Calico Chapter Bks) Magic Wagon.

NeonSeon. Life of Shouty: Food & Fitness, bk. 2. NeonSeon. 2011. (Life of Shouty Ser.: 2). (ENG.). 32p. (J). 14.95 (978-0-9842069-1-9(4)) RIXKIN.

—Life of Shouty: Good Habits, bk. 1. NeonSeon. 2010. (Life of Shouty Ser.: No. 1). (ENG.). 32p. (J). (gr. 3-18). 14.95 (978-0-9842069-0-2(6)) RIXKIN.

Nepomniachi, Leonid. El Monstruo Graciopeo. Dayan, Linda Marcos. (Barril Sin Fondo Ser.). (SPA.). (J). (gr. 3-5). pap. (978-968-6465-60-0(X)) Casa de Estudios de Literatura y Talleres Artisticos Amaquemecan A.C. MEX. Dist: Lectorum Pubns., Inc.

Nepomniatchi, Leonid. Los Artistas de Las Plumas: The Feather Artists. Barrera, Norma Anabel. rev. ed. 2006. (Otra Escalera Ser.). (SPA & ENG.). 36p. (J). (gr. 2-4). pap. 9.95 (978-968-5920-53-7(2)) Castillo, Ediciones, S. A. de C. V. MEX. Dist: Macmillan.

Neradova, M. The Seasons. 2019. (My First Interactive Board Book Ser.). (ENG.). 12p. (J). bds. 9.99 (978-2-7338-6735-8(0)) Auzou, Philippe Editions FRA. Dist: Consortium Bk. Sales & Distribution.

Neradova, Maria. Hello Farm! Crowe, Carmen. Cottage Door Press, ed. 2019. (Lift-A-Sound Board Book Ser.). (ENG.). 12p. (J). (gr. -1-k). bds. 12.99 (978-1-68052-528-1(X), 1004110) Cottage Door Pr.

—Rainy Day Activity Fun & Games: Drawing, Searching, Numbers, More! Dot to Dot, Mazes, Puzzles Galore! Golding, Elizabeth. 2016. (What Shall I Do? Bks.). (ENG.). 64p. (J). (gr. -1-2). bds. 8.99 (978-0-7641-6863-5(0), B.E.S. Publishing) Peterson's.

—Sunny Day Activity Fun & Games: Drawing, Searching, Numbers, More! Dot to Dot, Mazes, Puzzles Galore! Golding, Elizabeth. 2016. (What Shall I Do? Bks.). (ENG.). 64p. (J). (gr. -1-2). bds. 8.99 (978-0-7641-6864-2(9), B.E.S. Publishing) Peterson's.

Nerlove, Miriam. Dot, Stripe, Squiggle. 2018. (ENG.). 28p. (J). (gr. -1-1). 9.99 (978-1-56846-325-4(1), Creative Editions) Creative Co., The.

—Greenhorn. Olswanger, Anna. 2012. (ENG.). (J). E-Book 9.99 (978-1-60306-159-9(2)); 48p. 17.95 (978-1-58838-235-1(4)) NewSouth, Inc. (NewSouth Bks.).

—I Am Polar Bear. Lewis, J. Patrick. 2019. 32p. (J). (gr. 1-3). 18.99 (978-1-56846-332-2(4), Creative Editions) Creative Co., The.

—Spot, Spike, Spiral. Tuttle, Sarah Grace. 2019. (ENG.). 28p. (J). (gr. -1-k). bds. 8.99 (978-1-56846-333-9(2), Creative Editions) Creative Co., The.

Nerob, Rojene. The Adventures of Robyn & Calico: The Case of the Missing Eggs. T Long, Cheryl. 2019. (Adventures of Robyn & Calico Ser.: Vol. 2). (ENG.). 26p. (J). pap. 9.50 (978-1-0759-3536-7(9)) Independently Published.

Nesbit, E. & Millar, H. R. Five Children & It. Nesbit, E. 2004. 240p. (gr. 12-18). 14.00 (978-0-14-303915-0(6), Penguin Classics) Penguin Publishing Group.

Nesme, Alexis. L' Anniversaire. Berkane, Nadia. 2011. (Bebe Koala Ser.: Vol. 2266542). (FRE.). (J). (978-2-01-226654-4(1)) Hachette Jeunesse.

—Le Jardin. Berkane, Nadia. 2011. (Bebe Koala Ser.: Vol. 2266534). (FRE.). (J). (978-2-01-226653-7(3)) Hachette Jeunesse.

—A la Garderie. Berkane, Nadia. 2007. (Bebe Koala Ser.: Vol. 2247773). (FRE.). (J). (978-2-01-224777-2(6)) Hachette Jeunesse.

—A la Mer ! Berkane, Nadia. 2009. (Bebe Koala Ser.: Vol. 2260131). (FRE.). (J). (978-2-01-226013-9(6)) Hachette Jeunesse.

N

Nesser, Stephen. Child of Wonder. Haugen, Marty. 2018. (ENG.). 32p. (J). (gr. k-2). 16.95 *(978-1-62277-285-8(7))* G I A Pubns., Inc.

Nesterova, Natalia. Ein Schmetterling Ohne Flügel. Powers, David M. F. Vail, Sue, tr. 2013. 42p. pap. 9.99 *(978-0-9860373-3-7(8))* Pants On Fire Pr.

Nestler, David. The Art of Dave Nestler. 2003. 48p. (YA). (gr. 12-18). pap. *(978-0-86562-065-0(2))* Anabas Marketing, Ltd.

Netflix. Over the Moon: the Novelization. Shang, Wendy Wan-Long. 2020. (Over the Moon Ser.). (ENG.). 208p. (J). (gr. 3-7). 10.99 ***(978-0-06-300243-2(4)***, HarperCollins) HarperCollins Pubs. Ltd. GBR. Dist: HarperCollins Pubs.

Netflix. Go! Go! Cory Carson: Cory's First Day of School. Netflix. 2020. (My First I Can Read Ser.). 32p. (J). (gr. -1-3). pap. 4.99 ***(978-0-06-300223-4(X)***, HarperCollins) HarperCollins Pubs. Ltd. GBR. Dist: HarperCollins Pubs.

—Go! Go! Cory Carson: Meet Cory Carson Board Book. Netflix. 2020. (Go! Go! Cory Carson Ser.). 18p. (J). (gr. -1 — 1). bds. 8.99 ***(978-0-06-300222-7(1)***, HarperFestival) HarperCollins Pubs.

Nethercot, Michelle. Room 23 & the Lock down Drill. Wolf, Szanne & Grace, Guy. 2017. (ENG.). (J). (gr. k-5). pap. 12.95 *(978-1-936449-90-3(0))* Hugo House Publishers, Ltd.

Nettrour, Autumn. Imagynairs of Jemmidar. Nettrour, Nelani. 2003. 78p. pap. 11.95 *(978-1-929381-99-9(9)*, Third Millennium Publishing) Sci Fi-Arizona, Inc.

—Nunkey's Adventures, Bk. 1. Nettrour, Nelani. 2003. 70p. (J). pap. 11.95 *(978-1-929381-17-3(4)*, Third Millennium Publishing) Sci Fi-Arizona, Inc.

Nettrour, Heather. All about Krammer: Dogtails 2. Nettrour, Nelani A. 2005. 100p. pap. 11.95 *(978-1-932657-30-2(4))* Third Millennium Pubns.

—Banshees Bk. 2: Dragon Lands. Nettrour, Nelani. l.t. ed. 2003. 114p. (J). pap. 11.95 *(978-1-932657-03-6(7))* Third Millennium Pubns.

—The Dragon Lands Bk. 1: The Ripple. Nettrour, Nelani. 2003. 100p. pap. 11.95 *(978-1-929381-46-3(8)*, Third Millennium Publishing) Sci Fi-Arizona, Inc.

—Jodi & the Seasons. Nettrour, Nelani. l.t. ed. 2004. 88p. pap. 11.95 *(978-1-932657-16-6(9))* Third Millennium Pubns.

—Jodi's Bugs. Nettrour, Nelani. l.t. ed. 2003. 66p. (J). pap. 11.95 *(978-1-932657-04-3(5))* Third Millennium Pubns.

—Meeshu's Keep Bk. 1: Dragon Guardians. Nettrour, Nelani. 2005. 113p. pap. 14.95 *(978-1-932657-37-1(1))* Third Millennium Pubns.

Neu, Debra. ABC Literacy Storytimes: Storytimes to Promote Literacy & Learning. Lohnes, Marilyn. 2008. 251p. pap. 19.95 *(978-1-60213-023-4(X)*, Upstart Bks.) Highsmith Inc.

Neubecker, Robert. I Got Two Dogs. Lithgow, John. 2008. (ENG.). 32p. (J). (gr. -1-1). 19.99 *(978-1-4169-5881-9(9)*, Simon & Schuster Bks. For Young Readers) Simon & Schuster Bks. For Young Readers.

—I Won a What? Vernick, Audrey. 2016. 40p. (J). (gr. -1-2). 17.99 *(978-0-553-50993-9(4)*, Knopf Bks. for Young Readers) Random Hse. Children's Bks.

—Just Like Rube Goldberg: The Incredible True Story of the Man Behind the Machines. Aronson, Sarah. 2019. (ENG.). 48p. (J). (gr. -1-3). 17.99 *(978-1-4814-7668-3(8)*, Beach Lane Bks.) Beach Lane Bks.

—Keith Haring: The Boy Who Just Kept Drawing. Haring, Kay. 2017. 40p. (J). (gr. k-3). 17.99 *(978-0-525-42819-0(4)*, Dial Bks) Penguin Young Readers Group.

—King Louie's Shoes. Steinberg, D. J. 2017. (ENG.). 48p. (J). (gr. -1-3). 17.99 *(978-1-4814-2657-2(5)*, Beach Lane Bks.) Beach Lane Bks.

—Monsters on Machines. Lund, Deb. 2017. (ENG.). 40p. (J). (gr. -1-3). pap. 6.99 *(978-0-544-92783-4(4)*, 1657204, HMH Books For Young Readers) Houghton Mifflin Harcourt Publishing Co.

—Monsters on Machines. Lund, Deb. ed. 2017. (ENG.). (J). (gr. -1-3). lib. bdg. 17.20 *(978-0-606-39815-2(5))* Turtleback.

—The President's Stuck in the Bathtub: Poems about the Presidents. Katz, Susan. 2012. (ENG.). 64p. (J). (gr. 1-4). 18.99 *(978-0-547-18221-6(X)*, 1055967) Houghton Mifflin Harcourt Publishing Co.

—The Problem with Not Being Scared of Kids. Richards, Dan. 2015. (ENG.). 32p. (J). (gr. -1-3). 16.95 *(978-1-62979-102-9(4))* Boyds Mills Pr.

—The Problem with Not Being Scared of Monsters. Richards, Dan. 2014. (ENG.). 32p. (J). (gr. -1-3). 15.95 *(978-1-62091-024-5(1))* Boyds Mills Pr.

—Shiver Me Timbers! Pirate Poems & Paintings. Florian, Douglas. 2012. (ENG.). 32p. (J). (gr. 1-5). 16.99 *(978-1-4424-1321-4(2)*, Beach Lane Bks.) Beach Lane Bks.

—Sophie Peterman Tells the Truth! Weeks, Sarah. 2009. (ENG.). 32p. (J). (gr. -1-3). 19.99 *(978-1-4169-8686-7(3)*, Beach Lane Bks.) Beach Lane Bks.

—Space Boy & His Dog. Regan, Dian Curtis. 2015. (Space Boy Ser.). (ENG.). 32p. (J). (gr. -1-2). 16.95 *(978-1-59078-955-1(5))* Boyds Mills Pr.

—Space Boy & the Snow Monster. Regan, Dian. 2017. (Space Boy Ser.). (ENG.). 32p. (J). (gr. -1-2). 17.95 *(978-1-59078-957-5(1))* Boyds Mills Pr.

—Space Boy & the Space Pirate. Regan, Dian Curtis. 2016. (Space Boy Ser.). (ENG.). 40p. (J). (gr. -1-2). 16.95 *(978-1-59078-956-8(3))* Boyds Mills Pr.

—Tick Tock Clock. Cuyler, Margery. 2012. (My First I Can Read Ser.). (ENG.). 32p. (J). (gr. -1 — 1). 16.99 *(978-0-06-136309-2(X))*; pap. 4.99 *(978-0-06-136311-5(1))* HarperCollins Pubs.

Neubecker, Robert. Fall Is for School. Neubecker, Robert. 2017. (ENG.). 32p. (J). (gr. -1-k). 17.99 *(978-1-4847-3254-0(5))* Disney Pr.

—Linus the Vegetarian T. Rex. Neubecker, Robert. 2013. (ENG.). 40p. (J). (gr. -1-3). 17.99 *(978-1-4169-8512-9(3)*, Beach Lane Bks.) Beach Lane Bks.

—Too Many Monsters! A Halloween Counting Book. Neubecker, Robert. 2010. (ENG.). 26p. (J). (gr. -1-k). bds. 7.99 *(978-1-4424-0172-3(9)*, Little Simon) Little Simon.

Neuburger, Jenny. Andre' Angel in a Poodle Suit. Danner, Pamela. 2003. 32p. (J). per. *(978-0-9728429-0-7(X)*, 4290X) Poodle Suit Publishing.

Neuburger, Jenny, jt. illus. see Mailey, Maria C.

Neuendorf, Silvio. No Quiero Verte Mas! Abedí, Isabel & Neuendorf, Abedi -. 2003. (SPA.). 196p. (J). (gr. -1-3). 17.99 *(978-84-261-3303-8(7))* Juventud, Editorial ESP. Dist: Lectorum Pubns., Inc.

Neufeld, Juliana. House of Robots. Patterson, James & Grabenstein, Chris. (House of Robots Ser.: 1). (ENG.). (J). (gr. 3-7). 2015. 336p. pap. 8.99 *(978-0-316-34679-5(9))*; 2014. 352p. 13.99 *(978-0-316-40591-1(4))* Little Brown & Co. (Jimmy Patterson).

—House of Robots: Robot Revolution. Patterson, James. 2017. (House of Robots Ser.: 3). (ENG.). 336p. (J). (gr. 3-7). 13.99 *(978-0-316-34958-1(5)*, Jimmy Patterson) Little Brown & Co.

—House of Robots: Robots Go Wild! Patterson, James & Grabenstein, Chris. 2015. (House of Robots Ser.: 2). (ENG.). 336p. (J). (gr. 3-7). 13.99 *(978-0-316-28479-0(3)*, Jimmy Patterson) Little Brown & Co.

—Treasure Hunters. Patterson, James & Grabenstein, Chris. (Treasure Hunters Ser.: 1). (ENG.). 480p. (J). (gr. 3-7). 2015. pap. 7.99 *(978-0-316-20757-7(8))*; 2013. 14.99 *(978-0-316-20756-0(X))* Little Brown & Co. (Jimmy Patterson).

—Treasure Hunters. Patterson, James et al. 2013. 451p. (J). *(978-0-316-24262-2(4))* Little Brown & Co.

—Treasure Hunters: All-American Adventure. Patterson, James & Grabenstein, Chris. 2019. (Treasure Hunters Ser.: 6). (ENG.). 368p. (J). (gr. 3-7). 14.99 *(978-0-316-41743-3(2)*, Jimmy Patterson) Little Brown & Co.

—Treasure Hunters: Danger down the Nile. Patterson, James & Grabenstein, Chris. (Treasure Hunters Ser.: 2). (ENG.). 480p. (J). (gr. 3-7). 2018. pap. 7.99 *(978-0-316-51510-8(8))*; 2014. 14.99 *(978-0-316-37086-8(X))* Little Brown & Co. (Jimmy Patterson).

—Treasure Hunters: Peril at the Top of the World. Patterson, James & Grabenstein, Chris. 2016. (Treasure Hunters Ser.: 4). (ENG.). 384p. (J). (gr. 3-7). 14.99 *(978-0-316-34693-1(4)*, Jimmy Patterson) Little Brown & Co.

—Treasure Hunters: Quest for the City of Gold. Patterson, James. 2018. (Treasure Hunters Ser.: 5). (ENG.). 384p. (J). (gr. 3-7). 14.99 *(978-0-316-34955-0(0)*, Jimmy Patterson) Little Brown & Co.

—Treasure Hunters: Secret of the Forbidden City. Patterson, James & Grabenstein, Chris. 2015. (Treasure Hunters Ser.: 3). (ENG.). 448p. (J). (gr. 3-7). 14.99 *(978-0-316-28480-6(7)*, Jimmy Patterson) Little Brown & Co.

Neufeld, Juliana. Treasure Hunters: the Plunder down Under. Patterson, James & Grabenstein, Chris. 2020. (Treasure Hunters Ser.: 7). (ENG.). 336p. (J). (gr. 3-7). 14.99 ***(978-0-316-42058-7(1)***, Jimmy Patterson) Little Brown & Co.

Neuhaus, Julia. I Am Ivan Crocodile! Gouichoux, René. 2015. (ENG.). 36p. (J). (gr. k-3). 16.99 *(978-0-9806711-3-1(2))* Berbay Publishing AUS. Dist: Independent Pubs. Group.

Neuman, Richard. It's Time to Combine. Gabel, Stacey. 2009. 24p. pap. 13.95 *(978-1-60844-121-1(0))* Dog Ear Publishing, LLC.

—The New Blue Tractor. Gabel, Stacey. 2007. 24p. per. 13.95 *(978-1-59858-424-0(3))* Dog Ear Publishing, LLC.

Neumann, Brian S. Bo Bear Meets Cody Cub. Neumann, Kamy Lynn. 2020. (Bo Bear Bks.: Vol. 2). (ENG.). 28p. (J). pap. 12.99 ***(978-1-64826-247-0(3))*** Independently Published.

Neusca, Guy, Jr. & Porter, Lynda C. Tofu Ling & the Angel: Seeds of Corruptions. Beasley, Jonathan & Porter, Rosanna I. 2009. (ENG.). (YA). pap. 16.00 *(978-0-615-31157-9(1))* Hero Builder Comics.

Nevarez, Lisa. Dodger the Dragon, 1 vol. McMillin, Jack. 2009. pap. 24.95 *(978-1-60703-930-3(3))* PublishAmerica, Inc.

Nevarez, Lisa D. The Water Dog. McMillin, Jack D. 2011. 24p. pap. 24.95 *(978-1-4626-0544-6(3))* America Star Bks.

Neverov, Leah. My CC ABCs, Cycle 3. Bortins, Robert. 2017. 26p. (J). bds. 10.99 *(978-0-9972442-5-0(9))* Classical Conversations, Inc.

Neves, Amanda. Christmas Coloring Book for Kids Ages 4-8: Fun & Learning Coloring Pages for Preschool, Kindergarten, & School-Age Children with Beautiful Christmas Holiday Designs (Large Print Activity Books for Kids) Reid, Olivia. l.t. ed. 2019. (ENG.). 110p. (J). pap. 6.99 ***(978-1-7096-3016-3(7))*** Independently Published.

—My Natural Hair Dictionary. Gray, Aundia. 2019. (ENG.). 66p. (J). (gr. k-6). 25.00 ***(978-1-7332492-0-1(6))*** Tree Top Bks.

Neves, Amanda. Sue Marie Goes on a Field Trip: Short Story with Pictures for Kids, Bedtime Storybook for Preschool Children, Children's Stories with Moral Lessons. Cooper, Amby. 2019. (Vol Ser.: Vol. 2). (ENG.). 30p. (J). pap. 9.99 *(978-1-0994-4126-4(9))* Independently Published.

Neves, Amanda. Thanksgiving Coloring Book for Kids Ages 3-5: Fun & Relaxing Thanksgiving Holiday Coloring Pages for Toddlers & Preschool Children with Beautiful Autumn Designs (Large Print Activity Books for Kids) Reid, Olivia. l.t. ed. 2019. (ENG.). 110p. (J). pap. 6.99 ***(978-1-7024-5086-7(4))*** Independently Published.

Neves, Diogenes. New Mutants by Zeb Wells: the Complete Collection. 2018. (ENG.). 496p. (YA). (gr. 8-17). pap. 39.99 *(978-1-302-91016-7(7))* Marvel Worldwide, Inc.

Neves, Diogenes & Walker, Cory. Masters of the Universe: He-Man's Icons of Evil. Kirkman, Robert. 2004. (Masters of the Universe Ser.). 160p. (YA). pap. 9.95 *(978-1-59314-040-3(1))* CrossGeneration Comics, Inc.

Neves, Nik & Camargo, Nina de. Capitals. Jerven, Taraneh Ghajar. 2018. (ENG.). 64p. (J). (gr. 2-5). 21.99 *(978-1-4998-0696-0(5))* Little Bee Books Inc.

Neveu, Fred. Caillou's Dinosaur Day. Vonthron, Satanta C. l.t. ed. 2004. (HRL Board Book Ser.). (J). (gr. -1-1). pap. 10.95 *(978-1-57332-288-1(1)*, HighReach Learning, Incorporated) Carson-Dellosa Publishing, LLC.

—The Dinosaur Surprise. Howard-Parham, Pam. l.t. ed. 2004. (HRL Little Book Ser.). (J). (gr. -1-1). pap. 10.95 *(978-1-57332-294-2(6))*; pap. 10.95 *(978-1-57332-293-5(8))* Carson-Dellosa Publishing, LLC. (HighReach Learning, Incorporated).

Nevins, Daniel. With a Mighty Hand: The Story in the Torah. Ehrlich, Amy. 2013. 224p. (J). (gr. k-12). 29.99 *(978-0-7636-4395-9(5))* Candlewick Pr.

New, Mathew. Billy Johnson & His Duck Are Explorers. New, Mathew. 2020. (ENG.). 144p. (J). (gr. 3-5). lib. bdg. 15.99 ***(978-1-68446-150-9(2)***, 142001, Capstone Editions) Capstone.

New Seasons. Brain Games - Sticker by Number - Christmas. Publications International Ltd. & Brain Games. 2020. (Brain Games - Sticker by Number Ser.). (ENG.). 52p. (J). spiral bd. 8.98 ***(978-1-64558-426-1(7)***, 5795400) Publications International, Ltd.

Newbatt, David. The Very Old Donkey. Hedley Burton, Michael. 2018. (ENG.). 20p. (J). pap. *(978-0-946206-72-8(4))* Wynestones Pr.

Newberry, Clare Turlay. Marshmallow. Newberry, Clare Turlay. 2008. (ENG.). 32p. (J). (gr. -1-1). 16.99 *(978-0-06-072486-3(2))* HarperCollins Pubs.

Newberry, Loretta. Sundancer. Marlow, Herb. 2004. 56p. (J). lib. bdg. 21.95 *(978-1-893595-39-2(0))*; per. 14.95 *(978-1-893595-41-5(2))* Four Seasons Bks., Inc.

Newbigging, Martha. Archers, Alchemists, & 98 Other Medieval Jobs You Might Have Loved or Loathed. Galloway, Priscilla. 5th ed. 2003. (Jobs in History Ser.). (ENG.). 96p. (J). (gr. 4-7). pap. 16.95 *(978-1-55037-810-8(4)*, 9781550378108) Annick Pr., Ltd. CAN. Dist: Publishers Group West (PGW).

Newbold, Greg. If Da Vinci Painted a Dinosaur, 1 vol. Newbold, Amy. 2018. (ENG.). 40p. (J). (gr. 1-5). 17.95 *(978-0-88448-667-1(2)*, 884667) Tilbury Hse. Pubs.

—If Picasso Painted a Snowman, 1 vol. Newbold, Amy. 2017. (ENG.). 36p. (J). (gr. 1-6). 17.95 *(978-0-88448-593-3(5)*, 884593) Tilbury Hse. Pubs.

Newborne, David / F. The Lion That Finally Roared: Inspirational Story of Purpose & Destiny. Chidebelu-Eze / Dove Publishing, Chibueze Obi. 2008. 80p. (J). 17.99 *(978-0-9766578-5-9(6))*; pap. 11.99 *(978-0-9766578-6-6(4))* Dove Publishing, Inc.

—The Tales of Tortoise: Inspirational Stories of Wisdom. Chidebelu-Eze/Dove Publishing, Chibueze / Obi. 2005. (ENG.). 76p. (J). 16.00 *(978-0-9766578-0-4(5))* Dove Publishing, Inc.

Newcomb, Kristene. Festus & His New Job. Balmer, Fred. 2004. 26p. (J). per. 7.00 *(978-0-9760790-1-9(1))* Folsom Fallies Pr.

—Festus & the Hole in the Fence Gang. Balmer, Fred. 2005. 33p. (J). per. 7.00 *(978-0-9760790-3-3(8))* Folsom Fallies Pr.

—Festus & the Missing Bag of Feed. Balmer, Fred. 2004. 26p. (J). per. 7.00 *(978-0-9760790-0-2(3))* Folsom Fallies Pr.

—Festus & the Monster. Balmer, Fred. 2004. 27p. (J). per. 6.95 *(978-0-9760790-2-6(X))* Folsom Fallies Pr.

—Festus & the Stranger. Balmer, Fred. Miller, Callie, ed. 2007. 30p. (J). per. 7.00 *(978-0-9760790-4-0(6))* Folsom Fallies Pr.

Newcomb, Kristene. Molly Q's Trash Travels Through the Water Cycle. Newcomb, Kristene. Paschall, Patricia, ed. 2007. 32p. (J). per. 8.00 *(978-0-9760790-9-5(7))* Folsom Fallies Pr.

Newell, Brian. The Bird Lady. Jones, Angela. 2009. 16p. pap. 7.31 *(978-1-4251-8612-8(2))* Trafford Publishing.

Newell, Claudia. Design It! The Ordinary Things You Use Every Day & the Not-So-Ordinary Ways They Came to Be. Arato, Rona. 2010. 72p. (J). (gr. 4-7). pap. 20.95 *(978-0-88776-846-0(6)*, Tundra Bks.) Tundra Bks. CAN. Dist: Penguin Random Hse. LLC.

Newell, Keith. Cars. Brooks, Felicity. 2008. (Usborne Lift & Look Ser.). 12p. (J). (gr. -1-3). bds. 9.99 *(978-0-7945-1958-2(X)*, Usborne) EDC Publishing.

—Construction Sites. Brooks, Felicity. 2010. (Lift & Look Board Bks.). 12p. (J). bds. 9.99 *(978-0-7945-2728-0(0)*, Usborne) EDC Publishing.

Newell, Keith, jt. illus. see Van Wyk, Hanri.

Newell, Lennette. Welcome to the World. Wyatt, Valerie. 2011. (ENG.). 24p. (J). (gr. -1 — 1). 14.95 *(978-1-55453-593-4(X))* Kids Can Pr., Ltd. CAN. Dist: Hachette Bk. Group.

Newell, Luke, jt. illus. see Hanson, Eric Wolfe.

Newell, Peter. The Caterpillar & Alice: 2020 Daily Calendar with Goal Setting Section & Habit Tracking Pages, 6 X9. Journals, Paper Trail. 2019. (ENG.). 438p. (J). pap. 15.95 ***(978-1-7084-9802-3(8))*** Independently Published.

—The Caterpillar & Alice: 2020 Weekly Calendar with Goal Setting Section & Habit Tracking Pages, 6 X9. Journals, Paper Trail. 2019. (ENG.). 124p. (J). pap. 8.50 ***(978-1-6881-8967-6(X))*** Independently Published.

—The Runaway Equator (Illustrated Edition) Bell, Lilian. 2020. (ENG.). 72p. (J). pap. ***(978-1-84702-122-9(0))*** Echo Library.

Newell, Peter. 2019 Weekly Planner: Alice in Wonderland Calendar with Goal-Setting Section, 8. 5 X11. Roman's, Minnie and. 2018. (ENG.). 92p. (J). pap. 8.95 *(978-1-7315-2119-4(7))* Independently Published.

Newell, Peter. The Hole Book: Original Edition Of 1908. Newell, Peter. 2016. (ENG.). (J). (gr. 2-6). pap. *(978-3-95940-232-3(5))* Henkea.

—The Hole Book: The Original Edition Of 1908. Newell, Peter. 2016. (ENG.). (J). (gr. 2-6). pap. *(978-3-95940-231-6(7))* Henkea.

—Peter Newell's Pictures & Rhymes: The Original Edition Of 1903. Newell, Peter. 2016. (ENG.). (J). pap. *(978-3-95940-230-9(9))* Henkea.

Newey, Gail. The Barefoot Book of Faeries. Batt, Tanya Robyn. (ENG.). 64p. (J). 2009. 19.99 *(978-1-84686-317-2(1))*; 2008. (gr. -1-3). 15.99 *(978-1-84686-163-5(2))* Barefoot Bks., Inc.

—Barefoot Book of Faeries. Batt, Tanya Robyn & Barefoot Books. 2015. 64p. (J). (gr. k-5). 16.99 *(978-1-78285-225-4(5))* Barefoot Bks., Inc.

—Faerie Stickers. 15.00 *(978-1-84148-177-7(7))* Barefoot Bks., Inc.

—My Mama Hung the World for Me. Katz, Susan B. 2009. (J). *(978-1-84686-269-4(8))* Barefoot Bks., Inc.

Newfeld, Frank. Alligator Pie Classic Edition. Lee, Dennis. 2012. (ENG.). 64p. (J). 15.99 *(978-1-4434-1151-6(5))* HarperCollins Pubs.

Newfeld, Frank & Hilb, Nora. Alligator Pie. Lee, Dennis. rev. ed. 2008. (ENG.). 16p. (J). (gr. k-k). bds. *(978-1-55263-674-9(7))* Me to We.

Newhouse, Judy. Hey Ranger! Kids Ask Questions about Rocky Mountain National Park. Justesen, Kim Williams. 2005. (Hey Ranger! Ser.). (ENG.). 48p. (J). (gr. -1-12). pap. 9.95 *(978-0-7627-3848-9(0)*, Falcon Guides) Globe Pequot Pr., The.

Newhouse, Maxwell. Emily Carr: At the Edge of the World. Bogart, Jo Ellen. 2003. 40p. (J). (gr. 5-18). 22.95 *(978-0-88776-640-4(4)*, Tundra Bks.) Tundra Bks. CAN. Dist: Penguin Random Hse. LLC.

Newkirk, Errol Q. Arrione's Daddies!, 1 vol. Edison-Clark, Gina. 2010. 24p. pap. 24.95 *(978-1-4489-6511-3(X))* PublishAmerica, Inc.

—I Just Want My Daddy! Edison-Clark, Gina. 2008. 13p. pap. 24.95 *(978-1-60672-026-4(0))* America Star Bks.

Newland, G. F. The Bathysphere Boys: The Depth-Defying Diving of Messrs. Beebe & Barton, 1 vol. Enik, Ted. 2019. (Unhinged History Ser.: 2). (ENG.). 48p. (J). (gr. -1-3). 16.99 *(978-0-7643-5793-0(X)*, 8964) Schiffer Publishing, Ltd.

Newland, g. f. Sticks 'N Stones 'N Dinosaur Bones. Enik, Ted. 2013. 42p. pap. 12.99 *(978-1-939322-10-4(3))* Pixel Mouse Hse.

Newland, G. F. Sticks 'n' Stones 'n' Dinosaur Bones: Being a Whimsical Take on a (pre)Historical Event, 1 vol. Enik, Ted. 2017. (Unhinged History Ser.: 1). (ENG.). 48p. (J). (gr. -1-3). 16.99 *(978-0-7643-5394-9(2)*, 7730) Schiffer Publishing, Ltd.

Newland, Gillian. Big & Small, Room for All. Bogart, Jo Ellen. 2017. (ENG.). 32p. (J). (— 1). bds. 7.99 *(978-0-14-319893-2(9)*, Tundra Bks.) Tundra Bks. CAN. Dist: Penguin Random Hse. LLC.

—I Am Not a Number, 1 vol. Dupuis, Jenny Kay & Kacer, Kathy. 2016. (ENG.). 32p. (J). (gr. 1-3). 18.95 *(978-1-927583-94-4(2))* Second Story Pr. CAN. Dist: Orca Bk. Pubs. USA.

—I Am Not a Number / Gaawin Ndoo-Gindaaswisii. Dupuis, Jenny Kay & Kacer, Kathy. Sawyer, Muriel & McLeod, Geraldine, trs. ed. 2019. (ENG & OJI.). 32p. (J). (gr. 4-7). pap. 14.95 *(978-1-77260-099-5(7))* Second Story Pr. CAN. Dist: Orca Bk. Pubs. USA.

—The Magician of Auschwitz, 1 vol. Kacer, Kathy. 2014. (ENG.). 32p. (J). (gr. 1-3). 18.95 *(978-1-927583-46-3(2))* Second Story Pr. CAN. Dist: Orca Bk. Pubs. USA.

Newland, Gillian & Second Story Press Staff. A Chanukah Noel: A True Story, 1 vol. Jennings, Sharon. 2010. (ENG.). 24p. (J). (gr. 1-3). 15.95 *(978-1-897187-74-6(2))* Second Story Pr. CAN. Dist: Orca Bk. Pubs. USA.

Newland, Jane. Festivals & Celebrations. Lawrence, Sandra. 2017. (ENG.). (J). 72p. (gr. 1-4). 12.99 *(978-1-944530-10-5(X))*; 64p. *(978-1-84857-595-0(5))* Tiger Tales. (360 Degrees).

—Look! Bugs! Calmenson, Stephanie. 2018. (Look! Ser.). (ENG.). 24p. (J). (gr. -1-1). 8.99 *(978-1-4998-0543-7(8))* Little Bee Books Inc.

—The Secret Garden, 1 vol. Wakeham, Kate. 2018. 28p. (J). 12.99 *(978-1-4236-4923-6(0))* Gibbs Smith, Publisher.

Newlun, Shawn. The Sleep Fairy. Peterson, Janie & Peterson, Macy. 2003. (ENG.). 32p. (J). (gr. -1-5). 16.95 *(978-0-9714405-0-6(9))* Behave'n Kids Pr.

Newman, Barbara Johansen. Barnyard Purim. Terwilliger, Kelly. 2012. (ENG.). 32p. (J). (gr. k-3). lib. bdg. 7.99 *(978-0-7613-4513-8(2)*, 9780761345138); Vol. pap. 7.95 *(978-0-7613-4514-5(0))* Lerner Publishing Group. (Kar-Ben Publishing).

—Bones & the Apple Pie Mystery. Adler, David A. 2014. (Penguin Young Readers: Level 3 Ser.). (ENG.). (J). (gr. 1-3). lib. bdg. 14.60 *(978-1-62765-704-4(5))* Perfection Learning Corp.

—Bones & the Big Yellow Mystery. Adler, David A. 2008. (Puffin Easy-to-Read Ser.). 32p. (gr. k-3). 14.00 *(978-0-7569-8914-9(0))* Perfection Learning Corp.

—Bones & the Birthday Mystery, No. 5. Adler, David A. 2009. (Bones Ser.: 5). (ENG.). 32p. (J). (gr. 1-3). mass mkt. 4.99 *(978-0-14-241432-3(8)*, Penguin Young Readers) Penguin Young Readers Group.

—Bones & the Cupcake Mystery, No. 3. Adler, David A. 2008. (Bones Ser.: 3). (ENG.). 32p. (J). (gr. 1-3). mass mkt. 4.99 *(978-0-14-241147-6(7)*, Penguin Young Readers) Penguin Young Readers Group.

—Bones & the Dinosaur Mystery. Adler, David A. 2005. (Jeffrey Bones Mystery Ser.: No. 4). 32p. (J). *(978-0-670-05970-6(6)*, Viking Adult) Penguin Publishing Group.

—Bones & the Dinosaur Mystery, No. 4. Adler, David A. 2009. (Bones Ser.: 4). (ENG.). 32p. (J). (gr. 1-3). mass mkt. 4.99 *(978-0-14-241341-8(0)*, Penguin Young Readers) Penguin Young Readers Group.

—Bones & the Dog Gone Mystery, No. 2. Adler, David A. 2008. (Bones Ser.: 2). (ENG.). 32p. (J). (gr. 1-3). mass mkt. 4.99 *(978-0-14-241043-1(8)*, Penguin Young Readers) Penguin Young Readers Group.

—Bones & the Dog Gone Mystery. Adler, David A. 2008. (Puffin Easy-to-Read Ser.: Bk. 2). 32p. (gr. k-3). 14.00 *(978-0-7569-8916-3(7))* Perfection Learning Corp.

—Bones & the Math Test Mystery. Adler, David A. 2010. (Bones Ser.: 6). (ENG.). 32p. (J). (gr. 1-3). mass mkt. 4.99 *(978-0-14-241519-1(7)*, Penguin Young Readers) Penguin Young Readers Group.

—Bones & the Roller Coaster Mystery, 7 vols. Adler, David A. 2010. (Bones Ser.: 7). (ENG.). 32p. (J). (gr. 1-3). mass mkt. 3.99 *(978-0-14-241687-7(8)*, Penguin Young Readers) Penguin Young Readers Group.

—The Case of the Barfy Birthday. Torrey, Michele. 2009. (Doyle & Fossey, Science Detectives Ser.: 4). 96p. (J). pap. 6.95 *(978-1-4027-4964-3(3))* Sterling Publishing Co., Inc.

—The Case of the Crooked Carnival. Torrey, Michele. 2010. (Doyle & Fossey, Science Detectives Ser.). 96p. (J). (gr. 4-7). pap. 6.95 *(978-1-4027-4965-0(1))* Sterling Publishing Co., Inc.

—The Case of the Graveyard Ghost. Torrey, Michele. 2009. (Doyle & Fossey, Science Detectives Ser.: 3). 96p. (J). pap. 6.95 *(978-1-4027-4963-6(5))* Sterling Publishing Co., Inc.

—The Case of the Terrible T. Rex, 6. Torrey, Michele. 2010. (Doyle & Fossey, Science Detectives Ser.). (ENG.). 96p. (J). (gr. 4-6). 21.19 *(978-1-4027-4966-7(X))* Sterling Publishing Co., Inc.

—Shoo! Scat!, 1 vol. Grambling, Lois G. 2004. (ENG.). 32p. (J). 16.95 *(978-0-7614-5167-9(6))* Marshall Cavendish Corp.

Newman, Barbara Johansen, jt. illus. see Torrey, Michele.

Newman, Ben. Astro Kittens: Cosmic Machines. Walliman, Dominic. 2019. 20p. (J). (— 1). bds. 8.99 *(978-1-912497-28-7(X))* Flying Eye Bks. GBR. Dist: Penguin Random Hse. LLC.

—Astro Kittens: into the Unknown. Walliman, Dominic. 2019. 20p. (J). (— 1). bds. 8.99 *(978-1-912497-27-0(1))* Flying Eye Bks. GBR. Dist: Penguin Random Hse. LLC.

—Professor Astro Cat's Atomic Adventure. Walliman, Dominic. 2016. (Professor Astro Cat Ser.). 56p. (J). (gr. 2-5). 24.00 *(978-1-909263-60-4(5))* Flying Eye Bks. GBR. Dist: Penguin Random Hse. LLC.

—Professor Astro Cat's Deep Sea Voyage. Walliman, Dominic. 2020. (ENG.). 64p. (J). (gr. 2-5). 19.95 *(978-1-912497-89-8(1))* Flying Eye Bks. GBR. Dist: Penguin Random Hse. LLC.

—Professor Astro Cat's Frontiers of Space. Walliman, Dominic. 2nd ed. 2013. (Professor Astro Cat Ser.). 64p. (J). (gr. 2-5). 19.95 *(978-1-909263-07-9(9))* Flying Eye Bks. GBR. Dist: Penguin Random Hse. LLC.

—Professor Astro Cat's Human Body Odyssey. Walliman, Dominic. 2018. (ENG.). 64p. (J). (gr. 2-5). 24.00 *(978-1-911171-91-1(7))* Flying Eye Bks. GBR. Dist: Penguin Random Hse. LLC.

—Professor Astro Cat's Solar System. Walliman, Dominic. 2017. (Professor Astro Cat Ser.). 32p. (J). (gr. k-2). 13.99 *(978-1-911171-37-9(2))* Flying Eye Bks. GBR. Dist: Penguin Random Hse. LLC.

—Professor Astro Cat's Space Rockets. Walliman, Dominic. 2018. (ENG.). 32p. (J). (gr. k-2). 13.99 *(978-1-911171-94-2(1))* Flying Eye Bks. GBR. Dist: Penguin Random Hse. LLC.

—Professor Astro Cat's Stargazing. Walliman, Dominic. 2019. (ENG.). 32p. (J). (gr. k-2). 13.99 *(978-1-912497-83-6(2))* Flying Eye Bks. GBR. Dist: Penguin Random Hse. LLC.

—Zoom! Matching Game Book: 4 Activities In 1! Babin, Stephanie. 2019. (Matching Game Bks.: 2). (ENG.). 12p. (J). (gr. -1-k). bds. 14.99 *(978-2-408-01283-0(X))* Éditions Tourbillon FRA. Dist: Hachette Bk. Group.

Newman, Dale. KidGlovz. Hunt, Julie. 2017. (ENG.). 288p. (J). (gr. 3-7). 19.99 *(978-1-74237-852-7(8))* Allen & Unwin AUS. Dist: Independent Pubs. Group.

Newman Gray, James & Joseph, John. Dear Santa & Miracle on 34th Street Picture Book Gift Set: Christmas Books for Kids. Valentine Davies Estate et al. 2020. (ENG.). (J). (-3). 19.99 ***(978-1-7282-4060-2(3))*** Sourcebooks, Inc.

Newman, Heather. And Sometimes Y. Schultz, Leslie & Braulick, J. J. M. 2013. 302p. pap. 12.99 *(978-1-937848-07-1(8))* Do Life Right, Inc.

Newman, James. Tales from Christmas Wood. Senior, Suzy. 2016. (ENG.). 32p. (J). (gr. k-4). 16.99 *(978-0-7459-7666-2(2)*, Lion Children's) Lion Hudson PLC GBR. Dist: Independent Pubs. Group.

Newman, Jeff. Can One Balloon Make an Elephant Fly? Richards, Dan. 2016. (ENG.). 40p. (J). (gr. -1-3). 17.99 *(978-1-4424-5215-2(3))* Simon & Schuster Bks. For Young Readers.

—Phoebe & Digger. Springstubb, Tricia. 32p. (J). (gr. -1-2). 2016. 7.99 *(978-0-7636-8894-3(0))*; 2013. (ENG.). 16.99 *(978-0-7636-5281-4(4))* Candlewick Pr.

Newman, Jeff. The Boys. Newman, Jeff. 2010. (ENG.). 40p. (J). (gr. -1-2). 19.99 *(978-1-4169-5012-7(5)*, Simon & Schuster Bks. For Young Readers) Simon & Schuster Bks. For Young Readers.

—Hand Book. Newman, Jeff. 2011. (ENG.). 40p. (J). (gr. -1-3). 15.99 *(978-1-4169-5013-4(3)*, Simon & Schuster Bks. For Young Readers) Simon & Schuster Bks. For Young Readers.

Newman, Langley. Black History Playing Card Deck: With 52 Portraits of Distinguished Black Americans. Holt, Deloris L. (History Channel Ser.). 120p. pap. 12.00 *(978-1-57281-422-6(5)*, HCBH55) U.S. Games Systems, Inc.

Newman, M. S. Amanda. The Moon Keeper. Morningstar, Bonny L. 2016. (ENG.). (J). pap. *(978-0-9951567-1-5(9))* Morningstar Publishing.

Newman, Mark. Polar Bears. Newman, Mark. 2010. (ENG.). 32p. (J). (gr. -1-3). 16.99 *(978-0-8050-8999-8(3)*, 9780805089998, Holt, Henry & Co. Bks. For Young Readers) Holt, Henry & Co.

Newman, Sara Luise. Milo the Littlest Barn Owl. Newman, Sara Luise. 2016. (ENG.). (J). pap. 10.99 *(978-0-9971552-0-4(5))* cottage in the woods Pr.

Newmann, Ed. Marvin Monster's Big Date. 2007. (ENG.). 32p. (J). (gr. -1-3). 6.95 *(978-0-9792371-4-0(9))* Keene Publishing.

—Marvin Monster's Teacher Jitters. 2006. (ENG.). 48p. (J). (gr. 4-7). per. 6.95 *(978-0-9766805-3-6(X))* Keene Publishing.

Newnham, Jack. Whispering in the Wind. Marshall, Alan. 2019. (ENG.). 240p. (J). 7.95 *(978-1-925773-06-4(X))* Text Publishing Co. AUS. Dist: Consortium Bk. Sales & Distribution.

Newsom, Carol. The Emperor's New Clothes: A Country Storybook. Gill, Vince. 2006. 30p. (J). (gr. 4-8). reprint ed. 17.00 *(978-1-4223-5729-3(5))* DIANE Publishing Co.

—Five Little Ducks. Schiller, Pam. 2014. 19p. (J). *(978-1-60128-879-0(4))* Frog Street Pr.

—Give My Regards to Broadway. Cohan, George M. & Schwaeber, Barbie. 2008. (American Favorites Ser.). (ENG.). 32p. (J). (gr. -1-3). 8.95 *(978-1-59249-727-0(6))*; 14.95 *(978-1-59249-726-3(8))* Soundprints.

Newsom, Sarah. Born on Broadway. Beene, Alex. 2017. (ENG.). 42p. (J). (gr. k-3). 19.99 *(978-0-9990090-2-4(8))* Hilliard Pr.

Newsom, Tom. The First Noel. 2006. 14p. (J). (gr. k-4). reprint ed. 8.00 *(978-1-4223-5413-1(X))* DIANE Publishing Co.

—My First Night Before Christmas. Moore, Clement C. 2008. (ENG.). 12p. (J). 9.95 *(978-1-58117-808-1(5)*, Intervisual/Piggy Toes) Bendon, Inc.

—The Mystery of the Cupboard. Banks, Lynne Reid. 2004. (Indian in the Cupboard Ser.: No. 4). (ENG.). 256p. (J). (gr. 4-18). pap. 7.99 *(978-0-380-72013-2(2)*, HarperCollins) HarperCollins Pubs. Ltd. GBR. Dist: HarperCollins Pubs.

—The Night Before Christmas. Moore, Clement C. 2007. (ENG.). 18p. (J). (gr. -1-3). 19.95 *(978-1-4037-2947-7(6)*, Intervisual/Piggy Toes) Bendon, Inc.

—The Night Before Christmas. Moore, Clement C. 2012. (J). *(978-1-4508-5375-0(7))* Publications International, Ltd.

—Our Family Christmas Album: A Book about Us! 2008. (ENG.). 24p. (J). 12.95 *(978-1-58117-795-4(X)*, Intervisual/Piggy Toes) Bendon, Inc.

—Our Night Before Christmas: Memory Book - A Book about Us! 2008. (ENG.). 24p. (YA). (gr. 2-18). 12.95 *(978-1-58117-796-1(8)*, Intervisual/Piggy Toes) Bendon, Inc.

Newsome, Andy. The Gift of the Gold Coin. Bauld, Jane S. Carpenter, Christina D., ed. Date not set. 32p. (J). (gr. -1-5). 15.95 *(978-1-886440-03-6(4))* Portunus Publishing Co.

Newsome, Toby. Gogo's List. Dery, Portia. 2019. (ENG.). 32p. (J). pap. 8.95 *(978-1-4314-2850-2(7))* Jacana Media ZAF. Dist: Independent Pubs. Group.

Newson, Karl. Puss in Boots. Pirotta, Saviour. 2017. (Once upon a Time ... Ser.). (ENG.). 24p. (J). (gr. -1-k). lib. bdg. 19.99 *(978-1-68297-171-0(6))* QEB Publishing Inc.

—Superchimp. Paley-Phillips, Giles. 2016. (J). *(978-1-4351-6574-8(8))* Barnes & Noble, Inc.

Newton, Bev. A Boy in a Box. Belliveau, B. A. 2018. (ENG.). 26p. (J). pap. *(978-1-926898-97-1(4))* Pine Lake Bks.

—Walter Wind. Daulby, Joan. 2018. (Walter Wind Ser.: Vol. 1). (ENG.). 26p. (J). pap. *(978-1-926898-98-8(2))* Pine Lake Bks.

—Walter Wind & Red Hat. Daulby, Joan. 2018. (Walter Wind Ser.: Vol. 5). (ENG.). 34p. (J). pap. *(978-1-989322-02-4(6))* Pine Lake Bks.

—Walter Wind & the Turbine. Daulby, Joan. 2018. (Walter Wind Ser.: Vol. 2). (ENG.). 28p. (J). pap. *(978-1-989322-00-0(X))* Pine Lake Bks.

—Walter Wind & Trash Recycled. Daulby, Joan. 2018. (Walter Wind Ser.: Vol. 3). (ENG.). 26p. (J). pap. *(978-1-926898-99-5(0))* Pine Lake Bks.

—Walter Wind Rescues Santa. Daulby, Joan. 2018. (Walter Wind Ser.: Vol. 4). (ENG.). 28p. (J). pap. *(978-1-989322-01-7(8))* Pine Lake Bks.

Newton, Jill. Crash Bang Donkey! 2015. 32p. (J). *(978-1-4896-3858-8(X))* Weigl Pubs., Inc.

—Daniel & the Beast of Babylon. McGough, Roger. 2004. (ENG.). 32p. (J). (gr. k-2). pap. 11.00 *(978-0-7459-4753-2(0))* Lion Hudson PLC GBR. Dist: Independent Pubs. Group.

—Keeping up with Cheetah. Camp, Lindsay. 2004. 28p. (J). (gr. -1-2). *(978-1-85269-150-9(6))* Mantra Lingua.

—Larry & Rita. Michalak, Jamie. 2007. (Brand New Readers Ser.). (ENG.). 48p. (J). (gr. -1-3). 14.99 *(978-0-7636-2963-2(4))* Candlewick Pr.

—Monkey's Noisy Jungle. Ziefert, Harriet. 2007. bds. 7.95 *(978-1-59354-598-7(3))* Blue Apple Bks.

—Old MacNoah Had an Ark. Lloyd-Jones, Sally. 2008. (HarperBlessings Ser.). 32p. (J). (gr. -1-2). 17.89 *(978-0-06-055718-8(4))* HarperCollins Pubs.

Newton, Jill. Don't Wake Mr Bear! Newton, Jill. 2011. (ENG.). 32p. (J). (gr. -1). 17.99 *(978-1-4052-4965-2(X))* Egmont Bks., Ltd. GBR. Dist: Independent Pubs. Group.

Newton, Joy. The Very Berry Counting Book. Pallotta, Jerry. 2017. (Jerry Pallotta's Counting Bks.). 10p. (J). (— 1). bds. 6.99 *(978-1-58089-784-6(3))* Charlesbridge Publishing, Inc.

Newton, Keit. Your Very Own Robot Goes Cuckoo Bananas! Montgomery, R. A. 2009. (ENG.). 80p. (J). (gr. 2). pap. 7.99 *(978-1-933390-39-0(5))* Chooseco LLC.

Newton, Keith. Always Picked Last. Montgomery, R. A. 2009. 64p. (J). (gr. 2). pap. 7.99 *(978-1-933390-38-3(7))* Chooseco LLC.

—Caravan. Montgomery, R. A. 2007. (Choose Your Own Adventure - Dragonlarks Ser.). (ENG.). 80p. (J). (gr. 3-7). pap. 7.99 *(978-1-933390-54-3(9))* Chooseco LLC.

—Dragon Day. Montgomery, Anson. 2010. (ENG.). 80p. (J). (gr. 2-3). pap. 7.99 *(978-1-933390-61-1(1))* Chooseco LLC.

—Fire! Montgomery, R. A. 2015. (ENG.). 80p. (Orig.). (J). (gr. 2). pap. 7.99 *(978-1-937133-49-8(4))* Chooseco LLC.

—Ghost Island. Gilligan, Shannon. 2008. (Dragonlarks Ser.). (ENG.). 80p. (J). (gr. 3-3). pap. 7.99 *(978-1-933390-57-4(3))* Chooseco LLC.

—Gus vs. the Robot King. Montgomery, R. A. 2014. (ENG.). 80p. (J). (gr. 3). pap. 7.99 *(978-1-937133-44-3(3))* Chooseco LLC.

—The Haunted House. Montgomery, R. A. 2007. (Choose Your Own Adventure Ser.). (ENG.). 80p. (J). (gr. 2-7). pap. 7.99 *(978-1-933390-51-2(4))* Chooseco LLC.

—The Lake Monster Mystery. Gilligan, Shannon. 2009. (Dragonlarks Ser.). (ENG.). 80p. (J). (gr. 2-3). pap. 7.99 *(978-1-933390-60-4(3))* Chooseco LLC.

—Lost Dog! Montgomery, R. A. 2010. (Dragonlarks Ser.). (ENG.). 80p. (J). (gr. 2-3). pap. 7.99 *(978-1-933390-00-0(X))* Chooseco LLC.

—Monsters of the Deep. Montgomery, R. A. 2010. (ENG.). 80p. (J). pap. 7.99 *(978-1-933390-37-6(9))* Chooseco LLC.

—Return to Haunted House. Montgomery, R. A. 2009. (ENG.). 80p. (J). (gr. 2). pap. 7.99 *(978-1-933390-40-6(9))* Chooseco LLC.

—Sand Castle. Montgomery, R. A. 2013. (ENG.). 80p. (J). (gr. 3-3). pap. 7.99 *(978-1-933390-59-8(X))* Chooseco LLC.

—Search for the Dragon Queen. Montgomery, Anson. 2010. (ENG.). 80p. (J). (gr. 2-3). pap. 7.99 *(978-1-933390-56-7(5))* Chooseco LLC.

—Space Pup. Montgomery, R. A. 2014. (ENG.). 80p. (J). (gr. 2). pap. 7.99 *(978-1-937133-43-6(5))* Chooseco LLC.

—Your Grandparents Are Zombies! Montgomery, Anson. 2010. (ENG.). 80p. (J). (gr. 2). pap. 7.99 *(978-1-933390-90-1(5))* Chooseco LLC.

—Your Purrr-Fect Birthday. Montgomery, R. A. 2007. (Dragonlarks Ser.). (ENG.). 80p. (J). (gr. 3-3). per. 7.99 *(978-1-933390-55-0(7))* Chooseco LLC.

—Your Very Own Robot. Montgomery, R. A. 2007. (Choose Your Own Adventure Ser.). (ENG.). 80p. (J). (gr. 2-7). pap. 7.99 *(978-1-933390-52-9(2))* Chooseco LLC.

Newton, Kimberly. Earl's Big Adventure in Costa Rica. Haidar, Hanna. Hutcheson, Meredith, ed. 2007. 22p. (J). per. 7.99 *(978-0-9800975-0-4(9))* Old Silver Pr.

—Earl's Big Adventure in Costa Rica. Haidar, Hanna. 2nd ed. 2012. 22p. (J). *(978-0-9800975-2-8(5))* Old Silver Pr.

—Earl's Big Adventure in Japan. Haidar, Hanna. 2012. 26p. (J). *(978-0-9800975-1-1(7))* Old Silver Pr.

Newton, Pilar. No Descanso Para Sparky. Arruzza, Rick. 2004. (SPA.). 24p. (J). mass mkt. 7.95 *(978-0-9744509-3-3(6))* Three Spots Productions.

—No Rest for Sparky. Arruzza, Rick. 2004. 24p. (J). mass mkt. 7.95 *(978-0-9744509-2-6(8))* Three Spots Productions.

—El Paseo de Sparky. Arruzza, Rick. 2003. (SPA.). 24p. mass mkt. 7.95 *(978-0-9744509-1-9(X))* Three Spots Productions.

—Sparky's Walk. Arruzza, Rick. 2003. 24p. (J). mass mkt. 7.95 *(978-0-9744509-0-2(1))* Three Spots Productions.

Newton, Vanessa. One Love: (Multicultural Childrens Book, Mixed Race Childrens Book, Bob Marley Book for Kids, Music Books for Kids) Marley, Cedella. 2011. (ENG.). 32p. (J). (gr. -1-1). 16.99 *(978-1-4521-0224-5(4))* Chronicle Bks. LLC.

—Think Big. Garton Scanlon, Liz. 2012. 32p. (J). (gr. -1-6). 16.99 *(978-1-59990-611-9(2)*, 900073399, Bloomsbury USA Childrens) Bloomsbury Publishing USA.

Newton, Vanessa & Brantley Newton, Vanessa. The Plans I Have for You, 1 vol. Parker, Amy. 2015. (ENG.). 32p. (J). 16.99 *(978-0-310-72410-0(4))* Zonderkidz.

Newton, Vanessa Brantley. Brand New School, Brave New Ruby. Barnes, Derrick D. 2008. (Ruby & the Booker Boys Ser.: 1). (ENG.). 144p. (J). (gr. 2-5). pap. 5.99 *(978-0-545-01760-2(2)*, Scholastic Paperbacks) Scholastic, Inc.

—Ruby Flips for Attention. Barnes, Derrick D. 2009. (Ruby & the Booker Boys Ser.: 4). (ENG.). 144p. (J). (gr. 2-5). pap. 5.99 *(978-0-545-01763-3(7)*, Scholastic Paperbacks) Scholastic, Inc.

—The Slumber Party Payback, 3. Barnes, Derrick D. 2008. (Ruby & the Booker Boys Ser.: 3). (ENG.). 176p. (J). (gr. 2-5). pap. 5.99 *(978-0-545-01762-6(9))* Scholastic, Inc.

—Trivia Queen. Barnes, Derrick D. 2008. (Ruby & the Booker Boys Ser.: 2). (ENG.). 144p. (J). (gr. 2-5). pap. 5.99 *(978-0-545-01761-9(0))* Scholastic, Inc.

Nex, Anthony, photos by. Little Feet Love. 2009. 12p. 7.95 *(978-1-58117-881-4(6)*, Intervisual/Piggy Toes) Bendon, Inc.

—Little Hands Love. 2009. (ENG., 12p. (J). 8.95 *(978-1-58117-851-7(4)*, Intervisual/Piggy Toes) Bendon, Inc.

—My Little Pony Bracelets for Besties! Speregen, Devra Newberger. 2018. (ENG., 56p. (J). 16.99 *(978-1-948206-05-1(6)*, Curiosity Bks.) Curiosity Ink Media, LLC.

—My Little Pony Get Ponified Hair! Sparkly Styles Inspired by Equestria. Speregen, Devra Newberger. 2018. (ENG., 56p. (J). spiral bd. 16.99 *(978-1-948206-02-0(1)*, Curiosity Bks.) Curiosity Ink Media, LLC.

Neyret, Aurélie. Bedtime Is Canceled. Meng, Cece. 2016. (ENG.). 32p. (J). (gr. -1-3). 7.99 *(978-0-544-66837-9(5)*, 1625436, HMH Books For Young Readers) Houghton Mifflin Harcourt Publishing Co.

—Cici's Journal. Chamblain, Joris. 2017. (Cici's Journal Ser.). (ENG.). 160p. (J). 17.99 *(978-1-62672-248-4(X)*, 900146951, First Second Bks.) Roaring Brook Pr.

Nez, John. Amazing Autumn. Marino Walters, Jennifer. 2016. (Seasons Ser.). (ENG.). 24p. (J). (gr. -1-1). lib. bdg. 25.32 *(978-1-63440-045-9(3)*, Rocking Chair Kids) Red Chair Pr.

—Bubble Trouble. Gabriel, Nat. 2004. 32p. (J). lib. bdg. 20.00 *(978-1-4242-1085-5(2))* Fitzgerald Bks.

—Bubble Trouble. Gabriel, Nat. 2004. (Science Solves It Ser.). 32p. (gr. -1-3). 15.00 *(978-0-7569-4286-1(1))* Perfection Learning Corp.

—Bubble Trouble: Bubbles. Gabriel, Nat. 2006. (Science Solves It! ® Ser.). (ENG.). 32p. (J). (gr. k-2). pap. 5.95 *(978-1-57565-133-0(5))* Astra Publishing Hse.

—The Creeping Tide: Tides. Herman, Gail. 2006. (Science Solves It! ® Ser.). (ENG.). 32p. (J). (gr. k-2). pap. 5.95 *(978-1-57565-128-6(9))* Astra Publishing Hse.

—The Dragon Painter. 2006. (First Reading Level 4 Ser.). 48p. (J). (gr. 1-4). 8.99 *(978-0-7945-1275-0(5)*, Usborne) EDC Publishing.

—Gotcha! Magnets. Dussling, Jennifer. 2006. (Science Solves It! ® Ser.). (ENG.). 32p. (J). (gr. 1-3). pap. 5.95 *(978-1-57565-124-8(6))* Astra Publishing Hse.

—New Dog in Town: Neighborhoods. Herman, Gail. 2006. (Social Studies Connects ® Ser.). (ENG.). 32p. (J). (gr. k-2). pap. 5.95 *(978-1-57565-165-1(3))* Astra Publishing Hse.

—No Money? No Problem! Bartering. Haskins, Lori. 2006. (Social Studies Connects ® Ser.). (ENG.). 32p. (J). (gr. k-2). pap. 5.95 *(978-1-57565-141-5(6))* Astra Publishing Hse.

—Pet Peeves: Free Enterprise. Willson, Sarah. 2006. (Social Studies Connects ® Ser.). (ENG.). 32p. (J). (gr. 1-3). pap. 5.95 *(978-1-57565-149-1(1))* Astra Publishing Hse.

—Surprising Spring. Marino Walters, Jennifer. 2016. (Seasons Ser.). (ENG.). 24p. (J). (gr. -1-1). lib. bdg. 25.32 *(978-1-63440-047-3(X)*, Rocking Chair Kids) Red Chair Pr.

—Sweet Summer. Marino Walters, Jennifer. 2016. (Seasons Ser.). (ENG.). 24p. (J). (gr. -1-1). lib. bdg. 25.32 *(978-1-63440-048-0(8)*, Rocking Chair Kids) Red Chair Pr.

—Tightwad Tod: Using Money. Skinner, Daphne. 2006. (Math Matters ® Ser.). (ENG.). 32p. (J). (gr. k-3). pap. 5.95 *(978-1-57565-109-5(2))* Astra Publishing Hse.

—Tod el Apretado: Math Matters en Espanol. Skinner, Daphne. 2005. (SPA.). 32p. (J). pap. 5.95 *(978-1-57565-155-2(6))* Astra Publishing Hse.

—A Twin Is to Hug. Ashburn, Boni. 2019. (ENG.). 32p. (J). (gr. -1-1). 14.99 *(978-1-4197-3158-7(0)*, Abrams Bks. for Young Readers) Abrams, Inc.

—Wonderful Winter. Marino Walters, Jennifer. 2016. (Seasons Ser.). (ENG.). 24p. (J). (gr. -1-1). lib. bdg. 25.32 *(978-1-63440-046-6(1)*, 1408798, Rocking Chair Kids) Red Chair Pr.

Nez, John Abbott. Daisy Diaz Shakes up Camp: Trade & Interdependence. Harkrader, Lisa. 2009. (Social Studies Connects ® Ser.). (ENG.). 32p. (J). (gr. 1-3). pap. 5.95 *(978-1-57565-292-4(7))* Astra Publishing Hse.

—Dancing Clock. Metzger, Steve. 2011. (ENG.). 32p. 12.95 *(978-1-58925-100-7(8))*; (J). pap. 7.95 *(978-1-58925-429-9(5))* Tiger Tales.

Nez, John Abbott. The Twelve Days of Christmas in Washington. Nez, John Abbott. 2011. (Twelve Days of Christmas in America Ser.). 40p. (J). (gr. k-3). 12.95 *(978-1-4027-7068-5(5))* Sterling Publishing Co., Inc.

Nez, Jon. Mouse's Christmas Cookie, 0 vols. Thomas, Patricia. 2013. (ENG.). 24p. (J). (gr. -1-2). 14.99 *(978-1-4778-4704-6(9)*, 9781477847046, Two Lions) Amazon Publishing.

Ng-Benitez, Shirley. Baxter & Danny Stand up to Bullying. Foley, James M. 2018. 32p. (J). *(978-1-4338-2818-8(9))* American Psychological Assn.

—Baxter Turns down His Buzz: A Story for Little Kids about ADHD. Foley, James M. 2016. 32p. (J). 15.95 *(978-1-4338-2268-1(7)*, Magination Pr.) American Psychological Assn.

—Buddy Bench, 1 vol. Hooks, Gwendolyn. 2019. (Confetti Kids Ser.: 8). (ENG.). 32p. (J). (gr. k-2). pap. 9.95 *(978-1-62014-572-2(3)*, e98b9f07-2d33-4e29-ac6b-06864377d280) Lee & Low Bks., Inc.

—Danny & the Blue Cloud: Coping with Childhood Depression. Foley, James. 2016. 32p. (J). *(978-1-4338-2103-5(6)*, Magination Pr.) American Psychological Assn.

—A Feel Better Book for Little Tears. Brochmann, Holly & Bowen, Leah. 2019. 31p. (J). *(978-1-4338-3031-0(0)*, Magination Pr.) American Psychological Assn.

—A Feel Better Book for Little Tempers. Brochmann, Holly & Bowen, Leah. 2018. 32p. (J). *(978-1-4338-2817-1(0))* American Psychological Assn.

—A Feel Better Book for Little Worriers. Brochmann, Holly & Bowen, Leah. 2017. 32p. (J). 15.95 *(978-1-4338-2718-1(2)*, Magination Pr.) American Psychological Assn.

—The Garden. Hooks, Gwendolyn. 2018. (Confetti Kids Ser.). (ENG.). 32p. (J). pap. 5.95 *(978-1-62014-566-1(9))* Lee & Low Bks., Inc.

—How Do You Say Good Night? Jin, Cindy. 2019. (ENG.). 26p. (J). (gr. -1 — 1). bds. 7.99 *(978-1-5344-3159-1(4)*, Little Simon) Little Simon.

—How Do You Say I Love You? Eliot, Hannah. 2017. (ENG, JPN, POR, HIN & SPA.). 26p. (J). (gr. -1 — 1). bds. 7.99 *(978-1-5344-0012-2(5)*, Little Simon) Little Simon.

—I'M Not a Scaredy-Cat: A Prayer for When You Wish You Were Brave, 1 vol. Lucado, Max. 2017. (ENG.). (J). 32p. 17.99 *(978-0-7180-7491-3(2))*; 22p. bds. 9.99 *(978-0-7180-7492-0(0))* Nelson, Thomas Inc.

—Lily's New Home. Yoo, Paula. 2016. (Confetti Kids Ser.). (ENG.). 32p. (J). (gr. -1-3). 14.95 *(978-1-62014-249-3(X))* Lee & Low Bks., Inc.

—Mindful Day. Hopkinson, Deborah. 2020. (ENG.). 32p. (J). 17.99 *(978-1-68364-279-4(1)*, 900220936) Sounds True, Inc.

—The Perfect Gift, 1 vol. Yoo, Paula. 2018. (Confetti Kids Ser.). (ENG.). 32p. (J). (gr. k-2). pap. 7.95 *(978-1-62014-568-5(5)*, 661be99b-fc05-446c-99f3-4054bd94d0d7) Lee & Low Bks., Inc.

—Project Popcorn: Mean/Median/Mode. Driscoll, Laura. 2017. (Math Matters ® Ser.). (ENG.). 32p. (J). (gr. k-3). 5.95 *(978-1-57565-865-0(8))*; E-Book 23.99 *(978-1-57565-868-1(2))* Astra Publishing Hse.

—The Space Rock Mystery: Rocks & Minerals. Lukidis, Lydia. 2018. (Science Solves It! ® Ser.). (ENG.). 32p. (J). (gr. 1-3). pap. 5.95 *(978-1-63592-005-5(1))* Astra Publishing Hse.

—Want to Play? Yoo, Paula. 2016. (Confetti Kids Ser.). (ENG.). 32p. (J). (gr. k-2). 14.95 *(978-1-62014-250-9(3))* Lee & Low Bks., Inc.

Ng, Drew. Falling Star. Cutting, Robert. 2007. 48p. (J). lib. bdg. 23.08 *(978-1-4242-1625-3(7))* Fitzgerald Bks.

—Marco Polo & the Roc. Boyd, David. 2007. 48p. (J). lib. bdg. 23.08 *(978-1-4242-1621-5(4))* Fitzgerald Bks.

—Pearl Harbor. Boyd, David. 2007. 48p. (J). lib. bdg. 23.08 *(978-1-4242-1640-6(0))* Fitzgerald Bks.

Ng, Henry W. Rocket & Rover/All about Rockets. Skwish, Emily. 2019. (ENG.). 24p. (J). bds. *(978-1-5037-4820-0(0)*, f692e217-12d5-4d59-ba9d-c14316924468, p i kids) Phoenix International Publications, Inc.

Ng, James. The Secret of Ashona. Kingsley, Kaza. (Erec Rex Ser.: 5). (ENG.). 528p. (J). (gr. 5-9). 2013. pap. 8.99 *(978-1-4169-7993-7(X))*; 2012. 16.99 *(978-1-4169-7992-0(1))* Simon & Schuster Bks. For Young Readers. (Simon & Schuster Bks. For Young Readers).

Ng, Leandro. Passage 2: HIV/AIDS — First Love. Roman, Annette. 2005. (1 World Manga Ser.: Vol. 2). (ENG.). 40p. (J). pap. 3.99 *(978-0-8213-6406-2(5))* World Bank Pubns.
—1 World Manga. Roman, Annette. (1 World Manga Ser.: Vol. 3). (ENG.). 2006. 40p. pap. 3.99 *(978-1-4215-0366-0(2))*; Vol. 1. 2005. 40p. pap. 3.99 *(978-1-4215-0364-6(6))*; Vol. 2. 2005. 40p. pap. 3.99 *(978-1-4215-0365-3(4))*; Vol. 5. 2007. 240p. pap. 3.99 *(978-1-4215-1169-6(X))* Viz Media.
Ng, Leandro & Wong, Walden. One World Manga, Vols. 1-6. Roman, Annette. 2007. (1 World Manga Ser.). (ENG.). 240p. (gr. 1). pap. 9.99 *(978-1-4215-1584-7(9))* Viz Media.
Ng, Neiko. Hop, Hop Bunny. Seresin, Lynn & Schwartz, Betty Ann. 2015. (Follow-Along Book Ser.). (ENG.). 10p. (J). (gr. -1 — 1). bds. 9.99 *(978-1-4521-2464-3(7))* Chronicle Bks. LLC.
—My First Search & Find: Dinosaurs. Editors of Silver Dolphin Books. 2019. (My First Search & Find Ser.). (ENG.). 14p. (J). (gr. -1-k). bds. 9.99 *(978-1-68412-597-5(9))*, Silver Dolphin Bks.) Printers Row Publishing Group.
—My First Search & Find: Things That Go. Editors of Silver Dolphin Books. 2019. (My First Search & Find Ser.). (ENG.). 14p. (J). (gr. -1-k). bds. 9.99 *(978-1-68412-598-2(7))*, Silver Dolphin Bks.) Printers Row Publishing Group.
—Run, Run Piglet. Schwartz, Betty Ann & Seresin, Lynn. 2015. (Follow-Along Book Ser.). (ENG.). 10p. (J). (gr. -1 — 1). bds. 9.99 *(978-1-4521-2467-4(1))* Chronicle Bks. LLC.
Ng, Robyn. I Had a Favorite Hat. Ashburn, Boni. 2015. (ENG.). 32p. (J). (gr. -1-3). 16.95 *(978-1-4197-1462-7(7))*, Abrams Bks. for Young Readers) Abrams, Inc.
Ng, Simon. Tales from Gold Mountain, 1 vol. Yee, Paul. 2011. (ENG.). 64p. (J). (gr. 1-5). pap. 14.95 *(978-1-55498-125-0(5))* Groundwood Bks. CAN. Dist: Publishers Group West (PGW).
Ng, Vivian. Adventure Time with Fionna & Cake Original Graphic Novel: Party Bash Blues. Sheridan, Kate. 2019. (Adventure Time Ser.). (ENG.). 96p. (J). pap. 9.99 *(978-1-68415-400-5(6))* Boom! Studios.
Ngai, Victo. Dazzle Ships: World War I & the Art of Confusion. Barton, Chris. 2017. (ENG.). 36p. (J). (gr. 2-5). lib. bdg. 19.99 *(978-1-5124-1014-3(4)*, 9781512410143, Millbrook Pr.) Lerner Publishing Group.
—Unfolding Journeys - Following the Great Wall, 1 vol. Ross, Stewart & Lonely Planet Kids. 2017. (Unfolding Journeys Ser.). (ENG.). 16p. (J). (gr. 4-7). 17.99 *(978-1-78657-198-4(6)*, 5414) Lonely Planet Global Ltd. IRL. Dist: Hachette Bk. Group.
Ngo, Jean. Five Stars Means I Get It! Ngo, Alita. 2007. (ENG.). 46p. pap. 17.99 *(978-1-4257-4733-6(7))* Xlibris Corp.
Ngo, Mai. Zora, the Water Dog. Lowney, Amanda. 2019. (1 Ser.: Vol. 1). (ENG.). 30p. (J). pap. 14.99 *(978-0-578-47290-4(2))* Amanda Lowney Bks. LLC.
—Zora, the Water Dog. Lowney, Amanda. 2019. (ENG.). 30p. (J). 19.99 *(978-0-578-47451-9(4))* Amanda Lowney Bks. LLC.
Ngo, Raven. Alyssa. Kitson, Keri a. Mason, Jeanne, ed. 2019. (Estrel Ser.: Vol. 2). (ENG.). 76p. (J). pap. *(978-976-95857-0-6(X))* Kitson, Keri.
Nguyen, Albert. Artemisia of Caria. Bridges, Shirin Yim & Yim Bridges, Shirin. 2010. (Thinking Girl's Treasury of Real Princesses Ser.). (ENG.). 24p. (J). (gr. 3-8). 18.95 *(978-0-9845098-1-2(X))* Goosebottom Bks. LLC.
—Isabella of Castile. Bridges, Shirin Yim. 2010. (Thinking Girl's Treasury of Real Princesses Ser.). (ENG.). 24p. (J). (gr. 3-8). 18.95 *(978-0-9845098-4-3(4))* Goosebottom Bks. LLC.
—Nur Jahan of India. Bridges, Shirin Yim & Yim Bridges, Shirin. 2010. (Thinking Girl's Treasury of Real Princesses Ser.). 24p. (J). (gr. 3-8). 18.95 *(978-0-9845098-5-0(2))* Goosebottom Bks. LLC.
—Qutlugh Terkan Khatun of Kirman. Bridges, Shirin Yim & Yim Bridges, Shirin. 2010. (Thinking Girl's Treasury of Real Princesses Ser.). (ENG.). 24p. (J). (gr. 3-8). 18.95 *(978-0-9845098-3-6(6))* Goosebottom Bks. LLC.
—Sacajawea of the Shoshone. Yim, Natasha. 2012. (Thinking Girl's Treasury of Real Princesses Ser.). (ENG.). 32p. (J). (gr. 3-8). 18.95 *(978-0-9845098-6-7(0))* Goosebottom Bks. LLC.
Nguyen, Ann. The Ocean, Sea & Me. Whyte, Cara. 2019. (ENG.). 34p. (J). ***(978-0-6485891-2-9(9))*** Serenity Press.
Nguyen, Bich. The Tet Pole/Su Tich Cay Neu Ngay Tet: The Story of Tet Festival. Tran, Quoc. Smith, William, tr. from VIE. 2006. (ENG & VIE.). 32p. (J). (gr. 1-4). 16.95 *(978-0-9701654-5-9(5))* East West Discovery Pr.
Nguyen, Diem. A Gnome Who Liked Reading. Dovich, Galina. 2019. (ENG.). 34p. (J). pap. 10.49 ***(978-1-7125-8683-9(1))*** Independently Published.
Nguyen, Dong & Nguyen, Hop Thi. My First Book of Vietnamese Words: An ABC Rhyming Book of Vietnamese Language & Culture. Tran, Phuoc Thi Minh. 2017. 32p. (J). (gr. -1-3). 10.95 *(978-0-8048-4907-4(2))* Tuttle Publishing.
Nguyen, Duke, jt. illus. see Kuon, Vuthy.
Nguyen, Dustin. Batman Tales: Once upon a Crime. Fridolfs, Derek. 2020. 192p. (J). (gr. 3-7). pap. 9.99 *(978-1-4012-8340-7(3))* DC Comics.
—Christmas & New Year's Eve, 1 vol. Stone Arch Books. 2014. (Batman: Li'l Gotham Ser.). (ENG.). 32p. (J). (gr. 1-5). 22.60 *(978-1-4342-9217-9(7)*, Stone Arch Bks.) Capstone.
—Descender 2: La Máquina Lunar. Lemire, Jeff. 2018. (SPA.). 120p. (J). (gr. 4-7). pap. 12.95 *(978-607-527-111-8(2))* Editorial Oceano de Mexico MEX. Dist: Independent Pubs. Group.
Nguyen, Dustin. Descender IV. Mecánica Orbital. Lemire, Jeff. 2020. (Descender Ser.). (SPA.). 120p. (YA). (gr. 7). pap. 12.95 ***(978-607-557-068-6(3))*** Editorial Oceano de Mexico MEX. Dist: Independent Pubs. Group.
Nguyen, Dustin. Detention of Doom (DC Comics: Secret Hero Society #3) Fridolfs, Derek. 2017. (DC Comics: Secret Hero Society Ser.: 3). (ENG.). 176p. (J). (gr. 3-7). 12.99 *(978-1-338-03312-0(3))* Scholastic, Inc.
—Finders Creepers (Half Past Peculiar Book 1) Fridolfs, Derek. 2020. (ENG.). 224p. (J). (gr. 3-7). 14.99 *(978-1-338-25446-4(4))* Scholastic, Inc.
—Fort Solitude (DC Comics: Secret Hero Society #2) Fridolfs, Derek. 2016. (DC Comics: Secret Hero Society Ser.: 2). (ENG.). 176p. (J). (gr. 3-7). 12.99 *(978-0-545-87684-1(2))* Scholastic, Inc.
—Halloween & Thanksgiving, 1 vol. Stone Arch Books. 2014. (Batman: Li'l Gotham Ser.). (ENG.). 32p. (J). (gr. 1-5). 22.60 *(978-1-4342-9208-7(8))*, Stone Arch Bks.) Capstone.
—Sandwich Day & Our Family Album. Kane, Bob. 2015. (Batman: Li'l Gotham Ser.). (ENG.). 32p. (J). (gr. 1-5). lib. bdg. 22.60 *(978-1-4342-9737-2(3)*, Stone Arch Bks.) Capstone.
—Secret Hero Society- Study Hall of Justice. Fridolfs, Derek. 2016. 176p. (J). pap. *(978-1-76027-653-9(7))* Scholastic, Inc.
—Valentine's Day & the Lunar New Year, 1 vol. Stone Arch Books. 2014. (Batman: Li'l Gotham Ser.). (ENG.). 32p. (J). (gr. 1-5). 22.60 *(978-1-4342-9218-6(5)*, Stone Arch Bks.) Capstone.
Nguyen, Eric. Quicksilver: No Surrender. 2018. (Quicksilver: No Surrender (2018) Ser.: 1). (ENG.). 112p. (YA). (gr. 8-17). pap. 15.99 *(978-1-302-91295-6(X))* Marvel Worldwide, Inc.
Nguyen, Hop Thi, jt. illus. see Nguyen, Dong.
Nguyen, Mai K. Pilu of the Woods. Nguyen, Mai K. 2019. (Pilu of the Woods Ser.). (ENG.). 160p. (J). (gr. 4-6). 17.99 *(978-1-62010-551-1(9)*, Lion Forge) Oni Pr., Inc.
Nguyen-Ng, Linh. Daddy's Little Wordlings. Nguyen-Ng, Linh. 2019. (ENG.). 42p. (J). (gr. k-3). 18.99 *(978-1-7323275-2-8(1))* Prose & Concepts.
—Mommy's Little Wordlings. Nguyen-Ng, Linh. 2019. (ENG.). 42p. (J). (gr. k-3). 18.99 *(978-1-7323275-0-4(5))*; 10.99 *(978-1-7323275-1-1(3))* Prose & Concepts.
Nguyen, Nghia Cuong. H Is for Hanoi. Rush, Elizabeth. 2013. (Alphabetical World Ser.). (ENG & VIE.). 48p. (gr. k-4). 12.95 *(978-1-934159-42-2(5))* ThingsAsian Pr.
Nguyen, Sang. The Adventures of Derby & Charlie - Derby & Charlie Go Fishing: The Magic of Attitude. Twede, Shane K. 2019. (Adventures of Derby & Charlie Ser.: Vol. 2). (ENG.). 24p. (J). (gr. k-6). 21.95 *(978-0-578-50961-7(X))* Kory Industries.
—Christine the Clairvoyant. Blom, Tracy. 2018. (ENG.). 28p. (J). 19.99 *(978-0-578-40953-5(4))*; pap. 14.99 *(978-0-578-41236-8(5))* Blom Pubns.
Nguyen, Sang. The Little Pharaoh: Book 2. Blom, Tracy. 2019. (ENG.). 32p. (J). 16.99 ***(978-1-7336349-4-6(0))*** Blom Pubns.
Nguyen, Shishi. Birds of the World: 250 of Earth's Most Majestic Creatures. Della Pietà, Cesare. 2020. 192p. (J). (gr. 1-5). 24.99 ***(978-0-7624-9810-9(2)**, Black Dog & Leventhal Pubs. Inc.) Running Pr.
Nguyen, Tao. Mighty Mite: A New Beginning. Nguyen, Tao. 2006. (J). 14.95 *(978-0-9776282-1-6(3))* Amazing Factory, The.
Nguyen, Taohuu. Mighty Mite 2: Zoo Gone Wild. Nguyen, Taohuu. 2007. (J). 14.95 *(978-0-9788469-2-3(3))* Amazing Factory, The.
—Mighty Mite 3: Good Mites, Bad Mites. Nguyen, Taohuu. 2007. (J). 14.95 *(978-0-9790302-3-9(4))* Amazing Factory, The.
Nguyen Thi, Tuyet My. L' Ile Paradis. Pollack, Barry. 2019. (FRE.). 44p. (J). pap. 9.99 *(978-1-7932-5209-8(2))* Independently Published.
—Paradise Isle. Pollack, Barry. 2019. (ENG.). 44p. (J). pap. 9.99 *(978-1-7930-7921-3(8))* Independently Published.
Nguyen, Vincent. Buzz. Spinelli, Eileen. 2010. (ENG.). 32p. (J). (gr. -1-3). 17.99 *(978-1-4169-4925-1(9))*, Simon & Schuster Bks. For Young Readers) Simon & Schuster Bks. For Young Readers.
—The Crabfish. 2010. (First Steps in Music Ser.). 24p. (J). (gr. -1-k). 16.95 *(978-1-57999-772-4(4))* G I A Pubns., Inc.
—The Dragon & the Turtle. Paul, Donita K. & Denmark, Evangeline. 2010. (ENG.). 40p. (J). (gr. k-12). 11.99 *(978-0-307-44644-2(1)*, WaterBrook Pr.) Crown Publishing Group, The.
—The Dragon & the Turtle Go on Safari. Paul, Donita K. & Denmark, Evangeline. 2011. (ENG.). 40p. (J). (gr. k-12). 11.99 *(978-0-307-44645-9(X)*, WaterBrook Pr.) Crown Publishing Group, The.
—Gorilla Garage, 0 vols. Shulman, Mark. 2013. (ENG.). 42p. (J). (gr. -1-3). pap. 9.99 *(978-1-4778-1663-9(1)*, 9781477816639, Two Lions) Amazon Publishing.
—Jungle Bullies, 0 vols. Kroll, Steven. 2006. (ENG.). 34p. (J). (gr. -1-2). pap. 7.99 *(978-0-7614-5620-9(1)*, 9780761456209, Two Lions) Amazon Publishing.
—The Polar Bears' Home: A Story about Global Warming. Bergen, Lara. 2008. (Little Green Bks.). (ENG.). 24p. (J). (gr. -1-1). pap. 4.99 *(978-1-4169-6787-3(7)*, Little Simon) Little Simon.
—The Truly Terribly Horrible Sweater... That Grandma Knit. Macomber, Debbie & Carney, Mary Lou. 2009. (ENG.). 32p. (J). (gr. -1-2). 16.99 *(978-0-06-165093-2(5))* HarperCollins Pubs.
—Whoosh Went the Wind!, 0 vols. Derby, Sally. 2013. (ENG.). 32p. (J). (gr. k-3). pap. 9.99 *(978-1-4778-1677-6(1)*, 9781477816776, Two Lions) Amazon Publishing.
Nguyen, Vivian. A Little Goes a Long Way. Monaghan, Ashley Mills. 2013. (ENG.). 48p. (J). 24.99 *(978-0-692-38179-3(1))* Reading Tree Pr.
Nhem, Sopaul. Half Spoon of Rice: A Survival Story of the Cambodian Holocaust. Smith, Icy. 2009. (J). (gr. 2-7). 19.95 *(978-0-9821675-8-8(X))* East West Discovery Pr.
Nicely, Darthy. Where Is Grandmother? Lampkin, Laveta M. 2011. 36p. pap. 24.95 *(978-1-4626-1579-7(1))* America Star Bks.
Nicholai, Rachel, et al. Bird Adventures. Nicholai, Rachel et al. 2006. (Adventure Story Collection Ser.). 28p. (J). (gr. 2-6). pap. 10.00 *(978-1-58084-246-4(1))* Lower Kuskokwim Schl. District.
Nicholas, Corasue. The Tag-a-long Trio: Zak, Lizze & Ben Too! Malokas, Ann. 2007. (J). 15.95 *(978-0-9708415-8-2(2))* Guilty Mom Pr.
Nicholas, Frank. Wildcat, the Seminole: The Florida War. Clark, Electa. 2011. 194p. 42.95 *(978-1-258-06128-9(7))* Literary Licensing, LLC.
Nicholas, Jacob. When My Nose Runs, Where Does It Go? Rogala, Jennifer. 2006. 36p. per. 11.95 *(978-1-58939-866-5(1))* Virtualbookworm.com Publishing, Inc.
Nicholas, Jamar. The Grosse Adventures Vol. 3: Trouble at Twilight Cave, 1 vol. Auerbach, Annie. 2008. (Tokyopop Ser.). (ENG.). 96p. (J). (gr. 2-6). 28.50 *(978-1-59961-562-2(2)*, 14806, Graphic Novels) Spotlight.
Nicholas, Kristin. Kids Knitting: Projects for Kids of All Ages. Hartlove, Chris, photos by. Falick, Melanie. 2003. (ENG.). 128p. (J). pap. 18.95 *(978-1-57965-241-8(7)*, 85241) Artisan.
Nicholas, Mark. The Story of Tantrum O'Furrily. Cowell, Cressida. 2018. 32p. (J). (gr. -1-k). pap. 9.99 *(978-1-4449-3381-9(7))* Hachette Children's Group GBR. Dist: Hachette Bk. Group.
Nicholls, Calvin. The World Before This One: A Novel Told in Legend. Martin, Rafe. 2005. (ENG.). 208p. (J). (gr. 3-7). per. 6.99 *(978-0-590-37980-9(1)*, Levine, Arthur A. Bks.) Scholastic, Inc.
Nicholls, Emma, jt. illus. see Wallis, Diz.
Nicholls, Paul. Candle Pop-Up Bible Atlas, 1 vol. Dowley, Tim & David, Juliet. ed. 2014. (ENG.). 12p. (J). (gr. k-2). 16.99 *(978-1-78128-100-0(9)*, Candle Bks.) Lion Hudson PLC GBR. Dist: Kregel Pubns.
—I Want to Be A... Pirate. 2014. (J). *(978-1-4351-5500-8(9))* Barnes & Noble, Inc.
—My World: My Busy Day. Wang, Adria. 2005. 10p. (J). 4.95 *(978-1-58117-251-5(6)*, Intervisual/Piggy Toes) Bendon, Inc.
—My World: My Family. Wang, Adria. 2005. (My World Bks.). 10p. (J). 4.95 *(978-1-58117-252-2(4)*, Intervisual/Piggy Toes) Bendon, Inc.
—My World: My Outdoors. Wang, Adria. 2005. (My World Bks.). 10p. (J). 4.95 *(978-1-58117-249-2(4)*, Intervisual/Piggy Toes) Bendon, Inc.
—My World: My Playtimes Toys. Wang, Adria. 2005. 10p. (J). 4.95 *(978-1-58117-250-8(8)*, Intervisual/Piggy Toes) Bendon, Inc.
—Please Stop, Sara! Pink a Band. Harper, Kathryn. 2016. (Cambridge Reading Adventures Ser.). (ENG.). 16p. pap. 7.37 *(978-1-316-50313-3(5))* Cambridge Univ. Pr.
—Quack! Fitzpatrick, Joe. 2018. (ENG.). 20p. (J). (gr. -1-1). bds. 12.99 *(978-1-4867-1385-1(8)*, 4031f83e-beaa-406d-8a6d-742bcb6723fa) Flowerpot Pr.
—The Smart Hat. Jones, Cath. 2019. (Early Bird Readers — Blue (Early Bird Stories (tm)) Ser.). (ENG.). 32p. (J). (gr. -1-2). pap. 7.99 *(978-1-5415-4614-1(8))* Lerner Publishing Group.
—Twinkle, Star of the Week. Holub, Joan. 2012. (J). *(978-1-61913-137-8(4))* Weigl Pubs., Inc.
Nichols, Chris. King for a Day. Goss, Leon. 2005. (J). pap. *(978-1-933156-09-5(0))*; per. 16.99 *(978-1-933156-01-9(5))* GSVQ Publishing. (VisionQuest Kids).
Nichols, Clayton. Faith Found New, 1. Showell, Isaiah, Sr. 2004. 82p. (YA). per. 15.00 incl. audio compact disk *(978-0-9754489-0-8(0))* Divine Intertwine Publishing.
Nichols, Dave. Help Your Buddy Learn English, Bk. 1. Claire, Elizabeth. l.t. ed. 2003. 64p. 15.00 *(978-0-937630-04-4(7))* Eardley Pubns.
Nichols, Garry, jt. illus. see Yesh, Jeff.
Nichols, Jon, jt. illus. see Nichols, Tucker.
Nichols, Kevin. Wisp the Wayfinder. Hauser, J. M. 2016. (ENG.). (J). pap. 6.99 *(978-1-943183-60-9(0))* Dragon Scale Publishing.
Nichols, Lori. Go Sleep in Your Own Bed. Fleming, Candace. 2017. 40p. (J). (gr. -1-2). 17.99 *(978-0-375-86648-7(5)*, Schwartz & Wade Bks.) Random Hse. Children's Bks.
—No, No, Kitten! Thomas, Shelley Moore. 2015. (ENG.). 40p. (J). (gr. -1-2). 16.95 *(978-1-62091-631-5(2))* Boyds Mills Pr.
—Shine, Baby, Shine. Staub, Leslie. 2020. (ENG.). 32p. (J). (-k). 17.99 *(978-1-59078-931-5(8))* Boyds Mills Pr.
—This Orq. (He #1!) Elliott, David. 2016. (ENG.). 40p. (J). (gr. -1-2). 16.95 *(978-1-62979-336-8(1))* Boyds Mills Pr.
—This Orq. (He Cave Boy.) Elliott, David. 2014. (ENG.). 40p. (J). (gr. -1-2). 15.95 *(978-1-62091-521-9(9))* Boyds Mills Pr.
—This Orq. (He Say UGH!) Elliott, David. 2015. (ENG.). 40p. (J). (gr. -1-2). 16.95 *(978-1-62091-789-3(0))* Boyds Mills Pr.
Nichols, Lori. Maple. Nichols, Lori. 32p. (J). 2019. (— 1). bds. 8.99 *(978-1-9848-1298-8(X))*; 2014. (gr. -1-k). 17.99 *(978-0-399-16085-1(X))* Penguin Young Readers Group. (Nancy Paulsen Books).
—Maple & Willow Together. Nichols, Lori. 2014. (ENG.). 32p. (J). (gr. -1-k). 16.99 *(978-0-399-16283-1(6)*, Nancy Paulsen Books) Penguin Young Readers Group.
—Maple & Willow's Christmas Tree. Nichols, Lori. 2016. 32p. (J). (-k). 16.99 *(978-0-399-16756-0(0)*, Nancy Paulsen Books) Penguin Young Readers Group.
Nichols, Lydia. The ABCs of Halloween: An Alphabet Book. 2019. 26p. (J). (gr. -1 — 1). 8.99 *(978-0-7624-6656-6(1)*, Running Pr. Kids) Running Pr.
—Halloween Trick or Treat: A Colors Book. 2018. 22p. (J). (gr. -1 — 1). 8.99 *(978-0-7624-9316-6(X)*, Running Pr. Kids) Running Pr.
—I Thought I Saw a Bear. Templar Books. 2019. (ENG.). 10p. (J). (— 1). bds. 7.99 *(978-1-5362-0573-2(7)*, Templar) Candlewick Pr.
—I Thought I Saw a Dinosaur! Templar Books. 2018. (ENG.). 10p. (J). (— 1). bds. 7.99 *(978-0-7636-9945-1(4)*, Templar) Candlewick Pr.
—I Thought I Saw a Lion! Templar Books. 2018. (ENG.). 10p. (J). (— 1). bds. 7.99 *(978-0-7636-9946-8(2)*, Templar) Candlewick Pr.
—I Thought I Saw a Monkey! The Templar Company LTD. 2020. (I Thought I Saw Ser.). (ENG.). 10p. (J). (— 1). bds. 8.99 *(978-1-5362-1015-6(3)*, Templar) Candlewick Pr.
—I Thought I Saw a Penguin! The Templar Company LTD. 2020. (I Thought I Saw Ser.). (ENG.). 10p. (J). (— 1). bds. 8.99 *(978-1-5362-0997-6(X)*, Templar) Candlewick Pr.
—I Thought I Saw an Elephant. Templar Books. 2019. (ENG.). 10p. (J). (— 1). bds. 7.99 *(978-1-5362-0574-9(5)*, Templar) Candlewick Pr.
Nichols, Paul. Pirate Sticker Book. Watt, Fiona. ed. 2011. (Sticker Activity Books Ser.). 24p. (J). pap. 8.99 *(978-0-7945-2915-4(1)*, Usborne) EDC Publishing.
Nichols, Sandy. Alligator Pie Brd Bk. Lee, Dennis. 2014. (ENG.). 13p. (J). bds. 10.50 *(978-1-4434-1161-5(2))* HarperCollins Pubs.
—The Bagel King. Larsen, Andrew. 2018. (ENG.). 32p. (J). (gr. -1-2). 16.99 *(978-1-77138-574-9(X))* Kids Can Pr., Ltd. CAN. Dist: Hachette Bk. Group.
—Tallulah Plays the Tuba. Stone, Tiffany. 2019. (ENG.). 32p. (J). (gr. k-2). 18.95 *(978-1-77321-307-1(5))* Annick Pr., Ltd. CAN. Dist: Publishers Group West (PGW).
Nichols, Tucker. This Bridge Will Not Be Gray. Eggers, Dave. rev. ed. 2018. (ENG.). 112p. (J). (gr. k-3). 19.99 *(978-1-4521-6280-5(8))* Chronicle Bks. LLC.
Nichols, Tucker & Nichols, Jon. Crabtree. 2013. 32p. (J). (gr. -1-3). 17.95 *(978-1-936365-82-1(0)*, 22a1a80e-8061-4397-b174-0c5b6a87312c) McSweeney's Publishing.
Nicholson, Aislinn. Donkey Oatie's Early Days. Rath, Tom H. 2016. (Donkey Oatie Ser.: Vol. 7). (ENG.). 23p. (J). pap. *(978-1-987852-08-0(7))* Wood Islands Prints.
Nicholson, Dorinda Makanaōnalani, photos by. The School the Aztec Eagles Built, 1 vol. Nicholson, Dorinda Makanaōnalani. 2016. (ENG., 48p. (J). 18.95 *(978-1-60060-440-9(4))* Lee & Low Bks., Inc.
Nicholson, Kat & Cardy, Jason. A Midsummer Night's Dream. Shakespeare, William. Bryant, Clive, ed. 2012. (ENG.). 144p. (gr. 6). lib. bdg. 24.95 *(978-1-907127-44-1(5))* Classical Comics GBR. Dist: Publishers Group West (PGW).
Nicholson, Melissa. Prissy & Pop: Big Day Out. Nicholson, Melissa. 2016. (ENG.). 32p. (J). (gr. -1-3). 17.99 *(978-0-06-243995-6(2))* HarperCollins Pubs.
—Prissy & Pop Deck the Halls. Nicholson, Melissa. 2016. (ENG.). 32p. (J). (gr. -1-3). 17.99 *(978-0-06-243996-3(0))* HarperCollins Pubs.
Nicholson, Trudy. Alligator Crossing. Douglas, Marjory Stoneman & Milkweed Editions Staff. 2003. (ENG.). 192p. (J). (gr. 3-8). pap. 7.95 *(978-1-57131-644-8(2))* Milkweed Editions.
Nicholson, Trudy & Mirocha, Paul. The South Atlantic Coast & Piedmont: A Literary Field Guide. Milkweed Editions Staff. St. Antoine, Sara, ed. 2006. (Stories from Where We Live Ser.). (ENG.). 256p. (J). (gr. 4-7). per. 10.95 *(978-1-57131-664-6(7))* Milkweed Editions.
Nicholson, Trudy, jt. illus. see Mirocha, Paul.
Nicholson, William. The Velveteen Collection Set: The Velveteen Principles & the Velveteen Rabbit, 2 vols. Williams, Margery & Raiten-D'Antonio, Toni. 2005. (ENG.). 296p. (gr. -1-3). 19.95 *(978-0-7573-0347-0(1))* Health Communications, Inc.
—The Velveteen Rabbit. Williams, Margery. 2011. (Dover Children's Classics Ser.). (ENG.). 48p. (J). (gr. k-5). pap. 9.99 *(978-0-486-48606-2(0))* Dover Pubns., Inc.
—The Velveteen Rabbit. Williams, Margery. ed. 2014. (ENG.). 48p. (J). (gr. -1-k). pap. 9.99 *(978-1-4052-1054-6(0))* Egmont Bks., Ltd. GBR. Dist: Independent Pubs. Group.
—The Velveteen Rabbit. Williams, Margery. 44p. (J). (gr. 2-3). pap. 3.50 *(978-0-8072-1346-9(2)*, Listening Library) Random Hse. Audio Publishing Group.
—The Velveteen Rabbit. Williams, Margery. 2014. 48p. (J). (gr. -1-2). 19.99 *(978-0-385-37566-5(2)*, Doubleday Bks. for Young Readers) Random Hse. Children's Bks.
—The Velveteen Rabbit: The Original 1922 Edition in Full Color. Williams, Margery. 2017. (ENG.). 44p. (J). 12.95 *(978-1-947844-20-9(2))* Athanatos Publishing Group.
—The Velveteen Rabbit Book & Charm. Williams, Margery. 2006. 40p. (J). (gr. -1-3). pap. 4.99 *(978-0-06-076067-0(2)*, HarperFestival) HarperCollins Pubs.
—The Velveteen Rabbit, or, How Toys Become Real. Bianco, Margery Williams. 2015. iii, 27p. (J). pap. *(978-1-4677-9307-0(8)*, First Avenue Editions) Lerner Publishing Group.
Nicholson, William S. The Velveteen Rabbit. Williams, Margery. 2017. (ENG.). 48p. (J). (gr. k-3). 12.99 *(978-1-944686-46-8(0)*, Racehorse Publishing) Skyhorse Publishing Co., Inc.
Nichx, jt. illus. see Merola, Marcelo.
Nick, Christopher. Dust Storm. McKellips, Jane. 2016. 48p. (J). 16.95 *(978-1-938923-25-8(1))* Oklahoma Heritage Assn.
Nick, Watson. Friendly Ness Goes Fishing: You'll Never Guess What Clever Ness Catches! Tarrant, Marcus Adrian. 2019. (ENG.). 28p. (J). pap. *(978-0-6484718-2-0(9))* M A Tarrant Nominees Pty Ltd.
—The Ness Monsters Learn First Aid: Guess Who Ends up Looking Like a Mummy! Tarrant, Marcus Adrian. 2019. (ENG.). 28p. (J). pap. *(978-0-6484718-4-4(5))* M A Tarrant Nominees Pty Ltd.
Nickel, Adam. No One Likes a Fart. Blake, Zoe Foster. 2020. (ENG.). 32p. (J). (gr. -1-2). 9.99 *(978-1-5247-9189-6(X)*, Penguin Workshop) Penguin Young Readers Group.
Nickell, Jillian. Insect Superpowers: 18 Real Bugs That Smash, Zap, Hypnotize, Sting, & Devour! (Insect Book for Kids, Book about Bugs for Kids) Messner, Kate. 2019. (ENG.). 80p. (J). (gr. 3-7). 17.99 *(978-1-4521-3910-4(5))* Chronicle Bks. LLC.
Nicki Greenberg. Aussie Kids: Meet Taj at the Lighthouse. Beneba Clarke, Maxine. 2020. (Aussie Kids Ser.). 64p. (J). (gr. 1-3). 12.99 ***(978-1-76089-452-8(4)**, Puffin)* Penguin Random Hse. AUS. Dist: Independent Pubs. Group.
Nicklaus, Carol. ¿Adonde Vamos? Dentro y Fuera de tu mente. Carlson, Dale. Guix, Joan Carles, tr. from ENG. 2004.Tr. of In & Out of your Mind. Where are we Going?. (SPA.). 64p. *(978-84-9754-117-6(0)*, 88303) Ediciones Oniro S.A.

—Are You Human, or What? Carlson, Dale Bick & Carlson, Hannah. 2008. (ENG.). 143p. (J). (gr. 7-18). pap. 14.95 *(978-1-884158-33-9(1))* Bick Publishing Hse.

—Elmo's ABC Book (Sesame Street) November, Deborah. 2007. (Big Bird's Favorites Board Bks.). (ENG.). 24p. (J). (gr. k — 1). bds. 4.99 *(978-0-375-84037-1(0)*, Random Hse. Bks. for Young Readers) Random Hse. Children's Bks.

—I Am a Book. Hayward, Linda. (Silly Millies Ser.). 32p. (J). (gr. k-2). 2005. pap. 4.99 *(978-0-7613-1826-2(7)*, First Avenue Editions); 2004. lib. bdg. 17.90 *(978-0-7613-2905-3(6)*, Millbrook Pr.) Lerner Publishing Group.

—I Am a Pencil. Hayward, Linda. 2003. (Silly Millies Ser.). 32p. lib. bdg. 17.90 *(978-0-7613-2904-6(8)*, Millbrook Pr.) Lerner Publishing Group.

—The Mountain of Truth. Carlson, Dale Bick. 2nd ed. 2005. (ENG.). 169p. (gr. 8-12). reprint ed. pap. 14.95 *(978-1-884158-30-8(7))* Bick Publishing Hse.

—Talk: Teen Art of Communication. Carlson, Dale Bick. Khalmar, Kishore, ed. 2006. (ENG.). 154p. (gr. 7-18). pap. 14.95 *(978-1-884158-32-2(3))* Bick Publishing Hse.

—The Teen Brain Book: Who & What Are You? Carlson, Dale. Teasdale, Nancy, ed. 2004. (ENG.). 230p. (gr. 7-12). pap. 14.95 *(978-1-884158-29-2(3))* Bick Publishing Hse.

—Who Said What? Philosophy Quotes for Teens. Carlson, Dale. 2003. (ENG.). 224p. (gr. 7-12). pap. 14.95 *(978-1-884158-28-5(5))* Bick Publishing Hse.

Nicklaus, Carol, jt. illus. see Carlson, Al.

Nickle, Jackie. Foreververse: A Fairy Tale. Farina, Anthony. Grayson, Sharilyn S., ed. 2016. (ENG.). (YA). pap. 15.99 *(978-1-68419-338-7(9))*; (gr. 7-12). 27.99 *(978-1-68419-337-0(0))* Gold 5 Publishing.

Nickle, John. The Brixen Witch. DeKeyser, Stacy. (ENG.). 208p. (J). (gr. 3-7). 2013. pap. 6.99 *(978-1-4424-3329-8(9))*; 2012. 15.99 *(978-1-4424-3328-1(0))* McElderry, Margaret K. Bks. (McElderry, Margaret K. Bks.).

—Hans My Hedgehog: A Tale from the Brothers Grimm. Grimm, Jacob & Grimm, Wilhelm K. 2012. (ENG.). 40p. (J). (gr. k-3). 16.99 *(978-1-4169-1533-1(8)*, Atheneum Bks. for Young Readers) Simon & Schuster Children's Publishing.

—Never Take a Shark to the Dentist: (and Other Things Not to Do) Barrett, Judi. 2008. (ENG.). 34p. (J). (gr. -1-3). 19.99 *(978-1-4169-0724-4(6)*, Atheneum Bks. for Young Readers) Simon & Schuster Children's Publishing.

—Who Pushed Humpty Dumpty? And Other Notorious Nursery Tale Mysteries. Levinthal, David. 2012. 40p. (J). (gr. -1-3). 17.99 *(978-0-375-84195-8(4)*, Schwartz & Wade Bks.) Random Hse. Children's Bks.

Nickolls, Leo. The Dollhouse Murders (35th Anniversary Edition) Wright, Betty Ren. 35th ed. 2019. (ENG.). 160p. (J). (gr. 3-7). pap. 8.99 *(978-0-8234-3984-3(4))* Holiday Hse., Inc.

Nico. Les Contes de Big et Bang. Fayet Charra, Corinne. 2018. (Contes des Deux Comtés Ser.). (FRE.). 176p. (J). pap. *(978-2-490647-01-9(6))* Les Lutins de Kelach.

Nicol, Brock. Le Chandail Orange de Phyllis. Webstad, Phyllis. Payette, Marie-Christine, tr. from ENG. 2020. Orig. Title: Phyllis's Orange Shirt. (FRE.). 28p. (J). (gr. -1-k). 11.95 ***(978-1-989122-48-8(5))*** Medicine Wheel Education CAN. Dist: Orca Bk. Pubs. USA.

Nicol, Brock. Little Sam's Secret Place. Walters Iii, Harry C. 2012. 44p. 24.95 *(978-1-937763-41-1(2))*; pap. 14.95 *(978-1-937763-40-4(4))* Published by Westview, Inc.

—Make a Change, 1 vol. 2017. (ENG.). 32p. (J). (gr. -1-3). 16.99 *(978-1-4556-2275-7(3)*, Pelican Publishing) Arcadia Publishing.

Nicola, Christos, jt. photos by see Taylor, Peter Lane.

Nicolas, Otero. How Chile Came to New Mexico. Anaya, Rudolfo A. Nasario, Garcia, tr. from ENG. 2014. (SPA & ENG.). 48p. (J). (gr. -1-3). 24.95 *(978-1-936744-20-6(1)*, Rio Grande Bks.) LPD Pr.

—How Chile Came to New Mexico = Como Llego el Chile a Nuevo Mexico. Anaya, Rudolfo A. Nasario, Garcia, tr. 2018. (ENG.). 48p. (J). (gr. 1-3). pap. 17.95 *(978-1-943681-26-6(0))* Nuevo Bks.

Nicolet, Stéphane. The Refuge. Guen, Sandra. Hahn, Daniel, tr. 2020. (ENG.). 36p. (J). (gr. k-3). 17.99 *(978-1-5420-2050-3(6)*, 9781542020503, AmazonCrossing) Amazon Publishing.

Nicolle, Ethan. Ollie Possum. 2018. (J). pap. *(978-1-947644-48-9(3))* Canon Pr.

Nicolle, Ethan. I Named My Toys Alex. Nicolle, Ethan. 2019. (ENG.). 66p. (J). pap. 8.99 ***(978-1-7024-4196-4(2))*** Independently Published.

Nicolson, Cynthia Pratt & Slavin, Bill. The Jumbo Book of Space. Nicolson, Cynthia Pratt & Bourgeois, Paulette. 2007. (Jumbo Bks.). 208p. (J). 17.95 *(978-1-55453-020-5(2))* Kids Can Pr., Ltd. CAN. Dist: Hachette Bk. Group.

Nicolucci, Andrea, et al. Robin Hood. Corteggiani, François. 2020. (Disney Classics Ser.). (ENG.). 48p. (J). (gr. 2-6). lib. bdg. 28.50 ***(978-1-5321-4541-4(1)***, 35190, Graphic Novels) Spotlight.

Nidenoff, Michele. Sleeping Dragons All Around, 1 vol. Fitch, Sheree. ed. 2010. (ENG.). 32p. (J). (gr. 1-3). pap. 12.95 *(978-1-55109-772-5(9)*, 5cb2a369-c97f-45da-9860-07c0df50a9e6) Nimbus Publishing, Ltd. CAN. Dist: Baker & Taylor Publisher Services (BTPS).

Nidhom Mtd. What It Means to Be Me. Boykin, Dee. 2019. (What It Means to Be Me Ser.: Vol. 1). (ENG.). 64p. (J). (gr. 1-4). 19.95 ***(978-0-578-56077-9(1))*** DBW KIDS Publishing.

Niebuhr, Marvin. The Adventures of Marcos the Wise. Niebuhr, Marvin. Hausman, Gerald. 2014. (ENG.). 48p. (J). (gr. 3-6). 18.99 *(978-1-5154-3911-0(9))* Wilder Pubns., Corp.

Niednagel, David & Marco, Harvey. Your Key to Sports Success: Using Your Unique Brain Type to Maximize Athletic Performance. Niednagel, Jonathan P. 8th rev. ed. 2005. 408p. (Orig.). pap. 24.95 *(978-0-916309-01-5(0))* Cerebral Press International.

Nielander, Amy. The Ladybug Race. Nielander, Amy. 2015. (ENG.). 40p. (J). 19.95 *(978-0-7649-7187-7(5)*, POMEGRANATE KIDS) Pomegranate Communications, Inc.

Nieländer, Peter. La Bicicleta Robada. Preller, James. 5th ed. 2007. (Nino Puzle Ser.). (SPA.). 78p. (J). (gr. -1-3). 13.95 *(978-84-263-5272-9(3))* Vives, Luis Editorial (Edelvives) ESP. Dist: Ediciones Urano S. A.

—El Hamster Desaparecido. Preller, James. 5th ed. 2007. (Nino Puzle Ser.). (SPA.). 78p. (J). (gr. -1-3). 13.95 *(978-84-263-5269-9(3))* Vives, Luis Editorial (Edelvives) ESP. Dist: Ediciones Urano S. A.

Nielsen, Caleb. Home Is Where the Heart Is: A Grandmother's Tale of Value of a Happy Home. Boychuck, Debbie. 2020. (ENG.). 34p. (J). pap. 9.99 ***(978-1-6950-1967-6(9))*** Independently Published.

Nielsen, Chris. Once upon an ABC. Masson, Sophie. 2017. (ENG.). 32p. (J). (gr. -1-k). 17.99 *(978-1-76012-843-2(0))* Little Hare Bks. AUS. Dist: Independent Pubs. Group.

Nielsen, Gwyn English & Colby, Devon English. Serendipity & the Dream Catcher. Nielsen, Gwyn English. 2003. 176p. (gr. 3-7). pap. 5.95 *(978-0-9660726-2-4(6))* C.G.S. Pr.

Nielsen, Janet Marie. A Song for Me: A Muslim Holiday Story. Abdelsalam, Lisa. 2006. 34p. (J). *(978-0-9755975-1-4(5))* Abdelsalam Corp.

Nielsen, Kay. The Twelve Dancing Princesses & Other Fairy Tales. Quiller-Couch, Arthur Thomas. 2012. (Calla Editions Ser.). (ENG.). 208p. (gr. 4). 40.00 *(978-1-60660-025-2(7))* Dover Pubns., Inc.

Nielsen, Lee. Claws & Effect. Kientz, Chris & Hockensmith, Steve. 2016. (Secret Smithsonian Adventures Ser.: 2). 64p. (gr. 4-7). pap. 10.95 *(978-1-58834-567-7(X)*, Smithsonian Bks.) Smithsonian Institution Scholarly Pr.

—It's Treason, by George! Kientz, Chris & Hockensmith, Steve. 2017. (Secret Smithsonian Adventures Ser.: 3). 64p. (gr. 3-7). pap. 10.95 *(978-1-58834-586-8(6)*, Smithsonian Bks.) Smithsonian Institution Scholarly Pr.

—The Wrong Wrights. Kientz, Chris & Hockensmith, Steve. 2016. (Secret Smithsonian Adventures Ser.: 1). 64p. (gr. 4-7). 10.95 *(978-1-58834-541-7(6)*, Smithsonian Bks.) Smithsonian Institution Scholarly Pr.

Nielsen, Ric, jt. illus. see Madaras, Diana.

Nielson, Doug, jt. illus. see Storey, Linda.

Nielson, Ginger. The Adventures of Cali. Lallouz, Michele. 2007. 32p. (J). pap. 9.95 *(978-0-9793004-0-0(1))* Cali Publishing.

—Carla's Cloud Catastrophe. Reinke, Beth Bence. 2011. 28p. pap. 14.99 *(978-0-9828346-0-2(8))* 4RV Pub.

—Count 1, 2, 3 with Me. Arnold, Connie. 2013. 24p. pap. 12.99 *(978-1-940310-12-1(1))* 4RV Pub.

—Daniel & the Harmonica. Dubreuil, Robert. Eisenstadter, Dave, ed. 2010. 48p. (J). (gr. 1-7). 16.95 *(978-0-88045-088-1(6))* Stemmer Hse. Pubs.

—A Dinner Date for Dilly. Jones, Rena. 2012. 28p. pap. 14.99 *(978-0-9852661-2-7(0))* 4RV Pub.

—I Like Pink. Zabel, Vivian. 2013. 28p. pap. 12.99 *(978-0-9889617-1-5(7))* 4RV Pub.

—Journey Through Flowerland. Garteiz, John. 2018. (ENG.). 34p. (J). (gr. k-5). 19.99 *(978-0-578-40228-4(9))* Garteiz, John.

—A New Friend for Dilly. Jones, Rene'. 2011. 32p. pap. 14.99 *(978-0-9826423-0-6(X))* 4RV Pub.

—Pony Strings & Critter Things. Jones, Rena. 2012. 28p. pap. 14.99 *(978-0-9838018-0-1(0))* 4RV Pub.

Nielson, Ginger. Blink: Can You Keep a Secret? Nielson, Ginger. 2019. (ENG.). 34p. (J). (gr. k-5). 22.95 *(978-0-578-53427-5(4))* Ginger Nielson - Children's Bk. Illustration.

—Forest Friends: A Book for Coloring & Learning. Nielson, Ginger. 2019. (ENG.). 60p. (J). (gr. k-6). pap. 18.95 *(978-0-578-50225-0(9))* Ginger Nielson - Children's Bk. Illustration.

—Gunther's Journey: Where the Blueberry Sea Meets the Lemonade Sky. Nielson, Ginger. 2019. (ENG.). 76p. (J). 21.95 *(978-0-9913093-9-9(1))*; pap. 19.95 *(978-0-578-44108-5(X))* Ginger Nielson - Children's Bk. Illustration.

—Willow, an Elephant's Tale. Nielson, Ginger. 2012. 32p. pap. 11.65 *(978-0-9852661-1-0(2))* 4RV Pub.

Nielson, Ginger a. Wake up Ponte Vedra. Small, Brian C. 2019. (ENG.). 34p. (J). (gr. k-3). 24.95 *(978-0-578-45676-8(1))* Small Group, LLC, The.

Nielson, Ginger a. Gunther's Excellent Adventure: Gunther Remembers to Help His Friends. Nielson, Ginger a. 2018. (ENG.). 42p. (J). (gr. k-3). 19.95 *(978-0-578-41662-5(X))* Ginger Nielson - Children's Bk. Illustration.

Nielson, Ginger a. Lenoxx: (the Last Dragon?) Nielson, Ginger a. 2019. (ENG.). 40p. (J). (gr. k-3). 23.95 ***(978-0-578-51323-2(4))*** Ginger Nielson - Children's Bk. Illustration.

Nielson, Sam. Neversink. Wolverton, Barry. (ENG.). (J). (gr. 3-7). 2013. 320p. pap. 6.99 *(978-0-06-202793-1(X))*; 2012. 304p. 16.99 *(978-0-06-202791-7(3))* HarperCollins Pubs. (Waldon Pond Pr.).

—Neversink. Wolverton, Barry. 2012. xiii, 287p. (J). *(978-0-06-202792-4(1))* Longman Publishing.

—The Zoo at the Edge of the World. Gale, Eric Kahn. (ENG.). 240p. (J). (gr. 3-7). 2015. pap. 6.99 *(978-0-06-212517-0(6))*; 2014. 16.99 *(978-0-06-212516-3(8))* HarperCollins Pubs. (Balzer & Bray).

Niemann, Christoph. The Boy with Two Belly Buttons. Dubner, Stephen J. 2007. 32p. (J). (gr. -1-1). 17.89 *(978-0-06-113403-6(1))* HarperCollins Pubs.

—One Minute till Bedtime: 60-Second Poems to Send You off to Sleep. Nesbitt, Kenn, ed. 2016. 176p. (J). (gr. -1-3). 19.99 *(978-0-316-34121-9(5))* Little, Brown Bks. for Young Readers.

Niemann, Christoph. The Pet Dragon: A Story about Adventure, Friendship, & Chinese Characters. Niemann, Christoph. 2008. (ENG.). 40p. (J). (gr. -1-3). 16.99 *(978-0-06-157776-5(6)*, Greenwillow Bks.) HarperCollins Pubs.

—Subway. Niemann, Christoph. 2010. (ENG.). 40p. (J). (gr. -1-k). 16.99 *(978-0-06-157779-6(0)*, Greenwillow Bks.) HarperCollins Pubs.

—That's How! Niemann, Christoph. 2011. (ENG.). 32p. (J). (gr. -1-k). 16.99 *(978-0-06-201963-9(5)*, Greenwillow Bks.) HarperCollins Pubs.

—Words Limited Edition. Niemann, Christoph. ltd. ed. 2016. (ENG.). 352p. (J). (gr. -1 — 1). 175.00 *(978-0-06-266276-7(7)*, Greenwillow Bks.) HarperCollins Pubs.

Nieminen, Lotta. Walk This World. Broom, Jenny. 2013. (ENG.). 24p. (J). (gr. k-3). 18.99 *(978-0-7636-6895-2(8)*, Big Picture Press) Candlewick Pr.

Nieminen, Virpi. Lars - Den Lille Vandraren: Swedish Edition of Leo, the Little Wanderer. Pere, Tuula. Nikolowski-Bogomoloff, Angelika, tr. 2018. (SWE.). 46p. (J). (gr. k-6). *(978-952-357-026-9(9))*; pap. *(978-952-325-089-5(2))* Wickwick oy.

—Lauri - Pikku Matkamies: Finnish Edition of Leo, the Little Wanderer. Pere, Tuula. 2018. (FIN.). 46p. (J). (gr. k-6). *(978-952-357-025-2(0))*; pap. *(978-952-325-082-6(5))* Wickwick oy.

—Leo, the Little Wanderer. Pere, Tuula. Korman, Susan, ed. 2018. (ENG.). 46p. (J). (gr. k-6). *(978-952-357-024-5(2))*; pap. *(978-952-325-081-9(7))* Wickwick oy.

Nieto, Gina L. My Angel & Me. Nieto, Nancy. 2003. 19p. (J). *(978-1-932046-04-5(6))* Pastime Pr.

Nieto Guridi, Raul. No Water No Bread. Amavisca, Luis. 2017. (ENG.). 40p. (J). (gr. -1-3). 15.95 *(978-84-945971-3-8(2))* NubeOcho Ediciones ESP. Dist: Consortium Bk. Sales & Distribution.

Nieto Guridi, Raúl. Relaxations: Big Tools for Little Warriors. Duch, Mamen. 2018. (J). *(978-1-4338-2904-8(5)*, Magination Pr.) American Psychological Assn.

Nieto Guridi, Raul. Sin Agua y Sin Pan. Amavisca, Luis. 2017. (SPA.). 40p. (J). (gr. -1-3). 15.95 *(978-84-946333-7-9(6))* NubeOcho Ediciones ESP. Dist: Consortium Bk. Sales & Distribution.

Nieto-Phillips, John M. & Morris, Julie. Telma, la Hormiguita. Nieto-Phillips, John M. & Morris, Julie. 2006. (ENG & SPA.). 29p. (J). *(978-0-9772852-3-5(5))*; pap. *(978-0-9772852-2-8(7))* Lectura Bks.

Nievelstein, Ralf. The Secret of the Twelfth Continent. Michaelis, Antonia. Hosmer-Dillard, Mollie, tr. 2013. 288p. (J). (gr. 2-7). 14.95 *(978-1-62087-539-1(X)*, 620539, Sky Pony Pr.) Skyhorse Publishing Co., Inc.

Night & Day Studios. Peekaboo Barn Farm Day. Night & Day Studios. 2017. (Peekaboo Ser.). (ENG.). 20p. (J). (— 1). bds. 7.99 *(978-0-7636-7566-0(0)*, Candlewick Entertainment) Candlewick Pr.

Nighthawk, Tori. Don't Judge a Bird by Its Feathers. Nighthawk, Tori. 2013. (ENG.). 60p. (J). (gr. -1-3). 17.99 *(978-0-9858811-9-1(4))* Stone, Anne Publishing.

Nightingale, Jenny. Think Green! Getz, Jeanine Behr. 2008. (ENG.). 32p. (J). 15.50 *(978-0-9797362-0-9(X))* Kids Think Big LLC.

Nightow, Yasuhiro. Trigun Maximum - Bottom of the Dark Vol. 4, 13 vols., Vol. 4. Nightow, Yasuhiro. Horse, Dark. 2005. (ENG.). 208p. pap. 9.99 *(978-1-59307-314-5(3))* Dark Horse Comics.

Nihei, Tsutomu. Wolverine Legends Vol. 5: Snikt! Nihei, Tsutomu. 2003. (Wolverine Legends Ser.). 120p. (YA). (gr. 7-18). pap. 13.99 *(978-0-7851-1239-6(1))* Marvel Worldwide, Inc.

Nihoff, Tim. I Fooled You: Ten Stories of Tricks, Jokes & Switcheroos. Hurwitz, Johanna, ed. 2010. (ENG.). 192p. (J). (gr. 4-7). 16.99 *(978-0-7636-3789-7(0))* Candlewick Pr.

—Otter Everywhere: Brand New Readers. Webster, Christine. 2007. (Brand New Readers Ser.). (ENG.). 48p. (J). (gr. -1-3). pap. 5.99 *(978-0-7636-2922-9(7))* Candlewick Pr.

—Teddy Bear Addition. McGrath, Barbara Barbieri. 2014. (McGrath Math Ser.). 32p. (J). (gr. -1-3). pap. 7.95 *(978-1-58089-425-8(9))* Charlesbridge Publishing, Inc.

—Teddy Bear Counting. McGrath, Barbara Barbieri. 2010. (McGrath Math Ser.). 32p. (J). (gr. -1-2). pap. 7.95 *(978-1-58089-216-2(7))* Charlesbridge Publishing, Inc.

—Teddy Bear Math. McGrath, Barbara Barbieri. 2011. (McGrath Math Ser.). 32p. (J). (gr. k-3). 16.95 *(978-1-58089-283-4(3))*; pap. 7.95 *(978-1-58089-284-1(1))* Charlesbridge Publishing, Inc.

—Teddy Bear Patterns. McGrath, Barbara Barbieri. 2013. (McGrath Math Ser.: 4). 32p. (J). (gr. -1-1). lib. bdg. 22.44 *(978-1-58089-422-7(4))*; pap. 7.95 *(978-1-58089-423-4(2))* Charlesbridge Publishing, Inc.

—Teddy Bear Subtraction. McGrath, Barbara Barbieri. 2016. (McGrath Math Ser.). 32p. (J). (gr. -1-3). pap. 7.95 *(978-1-58089-427-2(5))*; lib. bdg. 17.95 *(978-1-58089-426-5(7))* Charlesbridge Publishing, Inc.

—Teddy Bear, Teddy Bear, School Day Math. McGrath, Barbara Barbieri. 2012. (McGrath Math Ser.). 3). 32p. (J). (gr. -1-1). 22.44 *(978-1-58089-420-3(8))*; pap. 7.95 *(978-1-58089-421-0(6))* Charlesbridge Publishing, Inc.

Nijland, Stern, jt. illus. see Haan, Linda de.

Nijs, Anouk. Mila Has Two Beds. Koppens, Judith. 2020. (Mila Ser.). (ENG.). 24p. (J). 14.95 *(978-1-60537-535-9(7))* Clavis Publishing.

Nikiel, Laura. If I Had a Cat. O'Neill, Juliana. 2018. (Reading Stars Ser.). (ENG.). 26p. (J). (gr. -1-3). pap. 9.99 *(978-1-5324-0760-4(2))* Xist Publishing.

—If I Had a Cat / Si Tuviera un Gato. O'Neill, Juliana. 2018. (Xist Kids Bilingual Spanish English Ser.). (ENG & SPA.). 32p. (J). (gr. -1-3). pap. 9.99 *(978-1-5324-0663-8(0))* Xist Publishing.

—If I Had a Dog. O'Neill, Juliana. 2018. (Reading Stars Ser.). (ENG.). 26p. (J). (gr. -1-3). pap. 9.99 *(978-1-5324-0762-8(9))* Xist Publishing.

—If I Had a Dog / Si Tuviera un Perro. O'Neill, Juliana. 2018. (Xist Kids Bilingual Spanish English Ser.). (ENG & SPA.). 32p. (J). (gr. -1-3). pap. 9.99 *(978-1-5324-0665-2(7))* Xist Publishing.

—Si Tuviera un Gato. O'Neill, Juliana. 2018. (Xist Kids Spanish Bks.). (SPA.). 32p. (J). (gr. -1-3). pap. 9.99 *(978-1-5324-0731-4(9))* Xist Publishing.

—Si Tuviera un Perro. O'Neill, Juliana. 2018. (Xist Kids Spanish Bks.). (SPA.). 32p. (J). (gr. -1-3). pap. 9.99 *(978-1-5324-0733-8(5))* Xist Publishing.

Nikiel, Laura Gibbons. Egermeier's ABC Bible Storybook: Favorite Stories Adapted for Young Children. Egermeier, Elsie E. Rhodes, Karen, ed. 2006. (ENG.). 56p. (gr. -1-k). 12.99 *(978-1-59317-156-8(0))* Warner Pr., Inc.

—Egermeier's ABC Bible Storybook: Favorite Stories Adapted for Young Children. Egermeier, Elsie. Rhodes, Karen, ed. 2007. (ENG.). 56p. (J). (gr. -1-5). 14.99 incl. audio compact disk *(978-1-59317-198-8(6))* Warner Pr., Inc.

—In Jesse's Shoes: Appreciating Kids with Special Needs. Lewis, Beverly. 2007. (ENG.). 32p. (J). (gr. -1-4). 11.99 *(978-0-7642-0313-8(4))* Bethany Hse. Pubs.

Nikirk Butcher, Kathy. Princess Pricilla Persimmon & Prince Padishah the Plucky. Finley, M. Elaine. 2019. (ENG.). 54p. (J). 21.99 *(978-1-950034-28-4(3))* Yorkshire Publishing Group.

Niko. Les Contes de Chrysanthème. Calviac, Audrey. 2019. (Contes des Deux Comtés Ser.). (FRE.). 260p. (J). pap. *(978-2-490647-00-2(8))* Les Lutins de Kelach.

—Les Contes de L'Arc-En-Ciel. Aprahamian, Pathilia. 2019. (Contes des 2 Comtés Ser.). (FRE.). 158p. (J). pap. *(978-2-490647-03-3(2))* Les Lutins de Kelach.

Niko & Chabarb. Les Contes Hors-S�rie. Mest Tom. 2019. (Contes des Deux Comt�s Ser.: Vol. 6). (FRE.). 168p. (J). pap. ***(978-2-490647-08-8(3))*** Les Lutins de Kelach.

Nikola, Pavlovic. Scoot to Bed. Irving, Andreja. 2019. (Ai Ser.: Vol. 1). (ENG.). 44p. (J). (gr. k-2). pap. *(978-1-9994057-0-0(6))* Shadow Skyland Pr.

N

Niland, Deborah. This Little Piggy Went Dancing. Wild, Margaret. 2014. (ENG.). 24p. (J). (-k). 15.99 *(978-1-74331-511-8(2))* Allen & Unwin AUS. Dist: Independent Pubs. Group.

Niland, Deborah. Annie's Chair. Niland, Deborah. 2005. 32p. (J). *(978-0-670-04249-4(8))* Penguin Random Hse.

Niles, Kim. Westie the Dog. Anjou, Colette. 2005. 28p. (J). (gr. -1-3). per. 15.95 *(978-0-9748933-6-5(6))* E & E Publishing.

Nilesh, Misty. The Seven Wise Princesses: A Medieval Persian Epic. Tarnowska, Wafa'. 2008. (ENG.). 96p. (J). (gr. 5-9). 19.99 *(978-1-84686-250-2(7))* Barefoot Bks., Inc.

Nille, Peggy. The Dreaming Giant: A Children's Book Inspired by Wassily Kandinsky. Massenot, Véronique. 2017. (Children's Books Inspired by Famous Artworks Ser.). (ENG.). 32p. (J). (gr. -1-3). 14.95 *(978-3-7913-7279-2(3))* Prestel Verlag GmbH & Co KG. DEU. Dist: Penguin Random Hse. LLC.

—The Drummer Boy. Min, SooHyeon. 2014. (MySELF Bookshelf Ser.). (ENG.). 32p. (J). (gr. k-2). pap. 11.94 *(978-1-60357-696-3(7))*; lib. bdg. 25.27 *(978-1-59953-661-3(7))* Norwood Hse. Pr.

—Hidden in the Jungle: A Search & Find Book. 2018. 10p. (J). *(978-1-4413-2653-9(7))* Peter Pauper Pr. Inc.

Nilsen, Anna. The Amazeing Voyage of Charles Darwin. Nilsen, Anna. 2003. 32p. (Orig.). pap., act. bk. ed. *(978-1-877003-28-8(X))* Little Hare Bks. AUS. Dist: HarperCollins Pubs. Australia.

—Robotics: Maths, Games & Puzzles. Nilsen, Anna. 2004. 32p. pap., act. bk. ed. *(978-1-877003-61-5(1))* Little Hare Bks. AUS. Dist: HarperCollins Pubs. Australia.

Nilsen, Mary Ylvisaker, photos by. The Blessing of Feelings. Nilsen, Erika. 2007. 32p. (J). 10.95 *(978-0-9627147-4-0(7))* Zion Publishing.

Nilssen, Jens R. The Boys from Vangen: Vangsgutane. Halse, Leif. Huntrods, Alexander Knud, tr. 2009. (ENG & NNO.). 176p. (J). 19.95 *(978-0-9760541-5-3(9))* Astri My Astri Publishing.

Nilsson, Al. The Tennessee Tater. Nilsson, Al. 2003. (YA). per. *(978-0-9741294-9-5(6)*, MSP) Main St Publishing, Inc.

Nilsson, Troy, 2nd. Hiroshima Stones: The Shadow Stones of Hiroshima. Nilsson, Troy, 2nd. 2003. 248p. (YA). pap. 9.95 *(978-0-9724771-0-9(1)*, Nilsson, Troy) Nilsson Media.

—Hiroshima Stones: The Shadow Stones of Hiroshima - a Story of Love & War. Nilsson, Troy, 2nd. collector's aut. ed. 2003. Orig. Title: Hiroshima Stones. 248p. (YA). 24.95 *(978-0-9724771-1-6(X)*, Nilsson, Troy) Nilsson Media.

Nin, Xuahan. A Most Unlikely Hero, Volume 4. Varnell, Brandon. 2018. (Most Unlikely Hero Ser.: Vol. 4). (ENG.). 288p. (YA). (gr. 7-12). pap. 13.00 *(978-0-9978028-7-0(1))* Kitsune Inc.

—A Most Unlikely Hero, Volume 5. Varnell, Brandon. 2019. (Most Unlikely Hero Ser.: Vol. 5). (ENG.). 304p. (YA). (gr. 7-12). pap. 13.00 *(978-0-9989942-0-8(0))* Kitsune Inc.

Nina, Berghausen. Jamison! a Shark Returns. Consie, Berghausen. 2018. (ENG.). 42p. (J). pap. 14.99 *(978-0-9988773-5-8(2))* Richer Life, LLC.

Ninaltowski, Eric. Confession, 1 vol., 3. Miller, Mike S. 2008. (Hand of the Morning Star Ser.). (ENG.). 160p. (YA). (gr. 8-11). 21.19 *(978-0-310-71371-5(4))* Zondervan.

—Emergence, 1 vol., 4. Burner, Brett A. & Rogers, Bud. 2008. (Hand of the Morning Star Ser.). (ENG.). 160p. (YA). (gr. 8-11). 21.19 *(978-0-310-71372-2(2))* Zondervan.

Nineell, K. As Sure As a Goose Goes Barefoot: It Can Have So Much Fun. Hammit, James. Amato, Jody, ed. 2019. (ENG.). 24p. (J). pap. 10.99 ***(978-1-6787-1869-5(6))*** Independently Published.

Ninekyu, L. Murray: The Nicest Monster You Could Have. Parker, Anita. Pendley, Heather, ed. 2019. (ENG.). 36p. (J). pap. 11.99 ***(978-1-6764-1298-4(0))*** Independently Published.

Ninekyu, N. Ida's Sweet Southern Jelly & Jam. Sparrow, Johanna. Amato, Jody, ed. 2019. (ENG.). 24p. (J). pap. 11.00 ***(978-1-6790-9519-1(6))*** Independently Published.

Nippert, Brenda & Nippert, George. An Alphabet of Catholic Saints, bks. 13000. Nippert, Brenda & Nippert, George. 3rd ed. 2006. (ENG.). 64p. (J). pap. 11.95 *(978-0-9787035-1-6(0))* Joseph's Heartprint.

—An Alphabet of Mary, bks. 3000. Nippert, Brenda & Nippert, George. 2012. (ENG.). 64p. (J). pap. 12.95 *(978-0-9787035-0-9(2))* Joseph's Heartprint.

Nippert, George, jt. illus. see Nippert, Brenda.

Nirattisai, Preston. Welcome Aboard the Disneyland Railroad! The Complete Disneyland Railroad Reference Guide. DeGaetano, Steve. 2004. 318p. 64.95 *(978-0-9758584-0-0(8))* Steam Passages Pubns.

Nisenson, Samuel. Great Moments in Catholic History. Curran, Rev Edward Lodge. 2017. (ENG.). (J). pap. 16.95 *(978-0-9976647-7-5(0))* Hillside Education.

Nishii. The Adventures of the Big Dog & the Little Dog: They First Meet! Johnsen, Erin L. 2013. 32p. pap. 24.95 *(978-1-4626-2346-4(8))* America Star Bks.

Nishimori, Hiroyuki. Cheeky Angel. Nishimori, Hiroyuki. Yamazaki, Joe, tr. from JPN. (Cheeky Angel Ser.: Vol. 7). (ENG.). (YA). 2005. 184p. pap. 9.95 *(978-1-59116-839-3(2))*; 2004. 200p. pap. 9.95 *(978-1-59116-620-7(9))* Viz Media.

—Cheeky Angel. Nishimori, Hiroyuki. (Cheeky Angel Ser.). (ENG.). 3. 2004. 200p. (YA). pap. 9.95 *(978-1-59116-503-3(2))*; Vol. 2. 2004. 200p. (YA). pap. 9.95 *(978-1-59116-467-8(2))*; Vol. 5. 2005. 200p. (YA). pap. 9.95 *(978-1-59116-631-3(4))*; Vol. 6. 2005. 192p. (YA). pap. 9.95 *(978-1-59116-774-7(4))*; Vol. 8. 2005. 192p. pap. 9.99 *(978-1-59116-979-6(8))*; Vol. 9. 2005. 192p. pap. 9.99 *(978-1-4215-0069-0(8))*; Vol. 11. 2006. 194p. pap. 9.99 *(978-1-4215-0317-2(4))*; Vol. 12. 2006. 208p. pap. 9.99 *(978-1-4215-0446-9(4))*; Vol. 13. 2006. 208p. pap. 9.99 *(978-1-4215-0447-6(2))* Viz Media.

Nishio, Kimiyo, jt. illus. see Fall, Brandon.

Nishiyama, Akira. Wonderful Houses Around the World. 2004. 48p. (J). pap. 12.95 *(978-0-936070-34-6(X))* Shelter Pubns., Inc.

Nister, Ernest. Merry Magic-Go-Round: An Antique Book of Changing Pictures. 2005. 14p. (J). (gr. k-4). reprint ed. 19.00 *(978-0-7567-9156-8(1))* DIANE Publishing Co.

Niswandee, Chris. Mothers Hold Their Children's Hands for Short While but Their Hearts Forever: Gifts for Mother, Journal Lined Notebook to Write in 6x 9 100 Blank Journal Page. Publishing, Mom. 2019. (ENG.). 102p. (J). pap. 5.99 *(978-1-7982-0966-0(7))* Independently Published.

Nitzsche, Shane. Constellations Activity Book, 1 vol. Jacobson, Ryan. 2012. (Color & Learn Ser.). 64p. (J). (gr. k-5). pap. 6.95 *(978-1-59193-325-0(0)*, Adventure Pubns.) AdventureKEEN.

—The Ghost of J. Stokely. Temple, Bob. 2008. (Shade Bks.). (ENG.). 80p. (J). (gr. 5-9). 25.32 *(978-1-4342-0796-8(X)*, Stone Arch Bks.) Capstone.

—Great Smoky Mountains Activity Book, 1 vol. Ellis, Paula. 2015. (Color & Learn Ser.). (ENG.). 64p. (J). (gr. k-5). pap. 6.95 *(978-1-59193-455-4(9)*, Adventure Pubns.) AdventureKEEN.

—Minnesota Activity Book, 1 vol. Ellis, Paula. 2013. (Color & Learn Ser.). (ENG.). 64p. (J). (gr. k-5). pap. 6.95 *(978-1-59193-377-9(3)*, Adventure Pubns.) AdventureKEEN.

—Texas Activity Book, 1 vol. Ellis, Paula. 2012. (Color & Learn Ser.). (ENG.). 64p. (J). (gr. k-5). pap. 6.95 *(978-1-59193-376-2(5)*, Adventure Pubns.) AdventureKEEN.

—Yellowstone & Grand Teton Activity Book. Ellis, Paula. 2011. (Color & Learn Ser.). (ENG.). 64p. (J). (gr. 3-7). pap. 5.95 *(978-1-59193-356-4(0)*, Adventure Pubns.) AdventureKEEN.

—Yosemite Activity Book, 1 vol. Ellis, Paula. 2013. (Color & Learn Ser.). 64p. (J). (gr. 2-3). pap. 5.95 *(978-1-59193-299-4(8)*, Adventure Pubns.) AdventureKEEN.

Nitzsche, Shane & Christenson, Anna. Great Lakes Activity Book, 1 vol. Ellis, Paula. 2015. (Color & Learn Ser.). (ENG.). 64p. (J). (gr. 3-7). pap. 6.95 *(978-1-59193-526-1(1)*, Adventure Pubns.) AdventureKEEN.

Nivola, Claire A. Emma's Poem: The Voice of the Statue of Liberty. Glaser, Linda. (ENG.). 32p. (J). (gr. -1-3). 2013. pap. 7.99 *(978-0-544-10508-9(7)*, 1540808); 2010. 17.99 *(978-0-547-17184-5(6)*, 1054295) Houghton Mifflin Harcourt Publishing Co.

—The Flag Maker: A Story of the Star-Spangled Banner. Bartoletti, Susan Campbell. 2007. (ENG.). 32p. (J). (gr. 3-7). 7.99 *(978-0-618-80911-0(2)*, 481243) Houghton Mifflin Harcourt Publishing Co.

—The Secret Kingdom: Nek Chand, a Changing India, & a Hidden World of Art. Rosenstock, Barb. 2018. 48p. (J). (gr. 2-5). 17.99 *(978-0-7636-7475-5(3))* Candlewick Pr.

—The Silent Witness: A True Story of the Civil War. Friedman, Robin. 2008. (ENG.). 32p. (J). (gr. -1-3). pap. 7.99 *(978-0-547-01436-4(8)*, 1030951) Houghton Mifflin Harcourt Publishing Co.

Nivola, Claire A. Life in the Ocean: The Story of Oceanographer Sylvia Earle, 1 vol. Nivola, Claire A. 2012. (ENG.). 32p. (J). (gr. -1-3). 18.99 *(978-0-374-38068-7(6)*, 900068269, Farrar, Straus & Giroux (BYR)) Farrar, Straus & Giroux.

—Planting the Trees of Kenya: The Story of Wangari Maathai. Nivola, Claire A. 2008. (ENG.). 32p. (J). (gr. k-3). 18.99 *(978-0-374-39918-4(2)*, 900042039, Farrar, Straus & Giroux (BYR)) Farrar, Straus & Giroux.

Niwano, Makoto. Deltora Quest 1. Rodda, Emily. 2011. (Deltora Quest Ser.: 1). (ENG.). 208p. (gr. 8-12). pap. 10.99 *(978-1-935429-28-9(0))* Kodansha America, Inc.

—Deltora Quest 2. Rodda, Emily. 2011. (Deltora Quest Ser.: 2). (ENG.). 208p. (gr. 8-12). pap. 10.99 *(978-1-935429-29-6(9))* Kodansha America, Inc.

—Deltora Quest 3. Rodda, Emily. 2011. (Deltora Quest Ser.: 3). (ENG.). 208p. (J). (gr. 8-12). pap. 10.99 *(978-1-935429-30-2(2))* Kodansha America, Inc.

—Deltora Quest 4. Rodda, Emily. 2012. (Deltora Quest Ser.: 4). (ENG.). 192p. (gr. 8-12). pap. 10.99 *(978-1-935429-31-9(0))* Kodansha America, Inc.

—Deltora Quest 5. Rodda, Emily. 2012. (Deltora Quest Ser.: 5). (ENG.). 192p. (J). (gr. 8-12). pap. 10.99 *(978-1-61262-011-4(6))* Kodansha America, Inc.

—Deltora Quest 6. Rodda, Emily. 2012. (Deltora Quest Ser.: 6). (ENG.). 176p. (gr. 8-12). pap. 10.99 *(978-1-61262-012-1(4))* Kodansha America, Inc.

—Deltora Quest 7. Rodda, Emily. 2012. (Deltora Quest Ser.: 7). (ENG.). 192p. (gr. 8-12). pap. 10.99 *(978-1-61262-013-8(2))* Kodansha America, Inc.

—Deltora Quest 8. Rodda, Emily. 2012. (Deltora Quest Ser.: 8). (ENG.). 176p. (J). (gr. 8-12). pap. 10.99 *(978-1-61262-014-5(0))* Kodansha America, Inc.

—Deltora Quest 9. Rodda, Emily. 2012. (Deltora Quest Ser.: 9). (ENG.). 176p. (J). (gr. 8-12). pap. 10.99 *(978-1-61262-015-2(9))* Kodansha America, Inc.

Nix, Pamela, jt. illus. see Paulson, Arlie.

Nix, Rob. Siuluk: The Last Tuniq, 1 vol. Sammurtok, Nadia. 2018. (ENG.). 28p. (J). (gr. k-2). 10.95 *(978-1-77227-178-2(0))* Inhabit Media Inc. CAN. Dist: Consortium Bk. Sales & Distribution.

Nixey, Troy. Mary Scary. Cosby, Andrew. 2007. (ENG.). 56p. (gr. 7). pap. 9.95 *(978-1-59307-730-3(0))* Dark Horse Comics.

Nixon, John. Stitches. Morrison, Kevin. 2003. 32p. (J). 12.95 *(978-1-929039-15-9(8))* Ambassador Bks., Inc.

Nixon, Tom. Sled Dog Wisdom: Humorous & Heartwarming Tales from Alaska's Mushers. 2006. (ENG.). 64p. 4.95 *(978-0-9745014-5-1(X))* Epicenter Pr., Inc.

Niyavarani, Baharah. Hilhili Va Mah Pishuni. Arab Amiri, Nasim. 2017. (PER.). (J). *(978-964-337-899-8(3))* Ketab-e Neyestan.

Niyonzima, Isabelle. Water, Water, Why Do You Hide? Warugaba, Christine. 2017. (ENG.). 28p. (J). pap. *(978-99977-771-3-3(1))* FURAHA Pubs. Ltd.

Nizar, 'iffah. Thank You Allah for My Sight. Nawawi, Huda. 2018. (ENG.). 28p. (J). pap. 9.49 *(978-1-7219-9929-3(9))* CreateSpace Independent Publishing Platform.

Nkomo, Khaya. Sunset Hike: A Children's Hiking Book, to Motivate Children to Step Outside & Explore Nature. Dowd, Dineo. 2019. (ENG.). 26p. (J). (gr. k-3). 21.00 ***(978-1-0878-5152-5(1))*** dineo dowd.

No New Art Needed. DuckTales: Living Mummies! / Tunnel of Terror! Geron, Eric. 2018. (ENG.). 48p. (J). (gr. 1-3). pap. 5.99 *(978-1-368-00572-2(1))* Disney Pr.

—Girl Meets World Follow Your Heart. Disney Book Group. 2015. (Girl Meets World Junior Novel Ser.). (ENG.). 128p. (J). (gr. 3-7). pap. 5.99 *(978-1-4847-2812-3(2))* Disney Pr.

—Girl Meets World Friend Power. Disney Book Group. 2016. (Girl Meets World Junior Novel Ser.). (ENG.). 128p. (J). (gr. 3-7). pap. 5.99 *(978-1-4847-6715-3(2))* Disney Pr.

—Girl Meets World Let's Do This! Disney Book Group. 2016. (Girl Meets World Junior Novel Ser.). (ENG.). 128p. (J). (gr. 3-7). pap. 5.99 *(978-1-4847-2813-0(0))* Disney Pr.

No New Art Needed & Disney Storybook Art Team. Gravity Falls Once upon a Swine. Disney Book Group. 2014. (Gravity Falls Chapter Book Ser.: 2). (ENG.). 112p. (J). (gr. 1-3). pap. 4.99 *(978-1-4847-1140-8(8))* Disney Pr.

No New Art Needed, jt. illus. see Disney Storybook Art Team.

No, Yi-Jung. Visitor. No, Yi-Jung, creator. 2005. 192p. (YA). pap. 9.99 *(978-1-59532-342-2(2))* TOKYOPOP, Inc.

Noad, Jordan. Isabella & the Merry Mouse House: A Christmas Story Coloring Book. Pachek, Mary C. 2009. 34p. pap. 14.49 *(978-1-4389-8467-4(7))* AuthorHouse.

Noah, Ian & Logan, Stephanie. Mike's Math Club Presents the Monstrously Fun Fraction Book. Noah, Ian & Logan, Stephanie. Milken-Noah, Joni et al, eds. 2003. 382p. pap. 24.95 *(978-0-9646425-1-5(4))* Milken Family Foundation.

Noakes, Polly. Dare to Dream Big. Gutierrez, Lorna. 2020. (ENG.). 40p. (J). (-3). 10.99 *(978-1-4926-9485-4(1))*; 17.99 *(978-1-4926-9716-9(8))* Sourcebooks, Inc. (Sourcebooks Jabberwocky).

Noakes, Polly. Hide & Seek. Noakes, Polly. 2019. (Child's Play Library). 32p. (J). *(978-1-78628-182-1(1))*; pap. *(978-1-78628-181-4(3))* Child's Play International Ltd.

—The Very Long Sleep. Noakes, Polly. 2018. (Child's Play Library). 32p. (J). pap. *(978-1-78628-128-9(7))*; *(978-1-78628-127-2(9))* Child's Play International Ltd.

Noakes, Polly, jt. illus. see Cumming, Hannah.

Nobati, Eugenia. ¡A la Busqueda del Tesoro! White, Amy. Kratky, Lada J., tr. 2009. (Colección Fácil de Leer Ser.). (SPA.). 16p. (gr. k-2). pap. 5.99 *(978-1-60396-418-0(5))* Ediciones Alfaguara ESP. Dist: Santillana USA Publishing Co., Inc.

—Bat's Big Game. Aesop, Aesop. 2012. (J). 34.28 *(978-1-61913-131-6(5))* Weigl Pubs., Inc.

—Eek, You Reek! Poems about Animals That Stink, Stank, Stunk. Yolen, Jane & Stemple, Heidi E. Y. 2019. (ENG.). 32p. (J). (gr. 2-5). 19.99 *(978-1-5124-8201-0(3)*, Millbrook Pr.) Lerner Publishing Group.

Nobati, Eugenia. The Incredible Shrinking Horror. Terrell, Brandon. 2020. (Michael Dahl Presents: Mysteries Ser.). (ENG.). 72p. (J). (gr. 3-5). pap. 5.95 ***(978-1-4965-9887-5(3)***, 201248); lib. bdg. 25.32 ***(978-1-4965-9708-3(7)***, 199330) Capstone. (Stone Arch Bks.).

—The Witch in the Wardrobe. Collins, Ailynn. 2020. (Michael Dahl Presents: Mysteries Ser.). (ENG.). 72p. (J). (gr. 3-5). pap. 5.95 ***(978-1-4965-9888-2(1)***, 201250); lib. bdg. 25.32 ***(978-1-4965-9707-6(9)***, 199329) Capstone. (Stone Arch Bks.).

Nobens, C. A. Bashful Ball Pythons, 1 vol. Doudna, Kelly. 2013. (Unusual Pets Ser.). (ENG.). 24p. (J). (gr. -1-3). 27.07 *(978-1-61783-397-7(5)*, 15197, SandCastle) ABDO Publishing Co.

—Beetle Mania, 1 vol. Hanson, Anders. 2006. (Critter Chronicles Ser.). (ENG.). 24p. (J). (gr. k-3). lib. bdg. 27.07 *(978-1-59928-432-3(4)*, 4964, SandCastle) ABDO Publishing Co.

—The Best Thing about Christmas. Tangvald, Christine Harder. 2014. (Faith That Sticks Bks.). (ENG.). 27p. (J). pap. 3.99 *(978-1-4964-0087-1(9)*, 4611762) Tyndale Hse. Pubs.

—Brilliant Birds, 1 vol. Salzmann, Mary Elizabeth. 2007. (Perfect Pets Ser.). (ENG.). 24p. (J). (gr. k-3). lib. bdg. 27.07 *(978-1-59928-744-7(7)*, 12586, SandCastle) ABDO Publishing Co.

—El Caracol de la Tortuga. Salzmann, Mary Elizabeth. 2006. (Cuentos de Animales Ser.). (SPA.). 24p. (J). (gr. k-3). lib. bdg. 27.07 *(978-1-59928-657-0(2)*, 5018, SandCastle) ABDO Publishing Co.

—Cheeky Chinchillas, 1 vol. Doudna, Kelly. 2013. (Unusual Pets Ser.). (ENG.). 24p. (J). (gr. -1-3). 27.07 *(978-1-61783-398-4(3)*, 15199, SandCastle) ABDO Publishing Co.

—Dandy Dogs, 1 vol. Salzmann, Mary Elizabeth. 2007. (Perfect Pets Ser.). (ENG.). 24p. (J). (gr. k-3). lib. bdg. 27.07 *(978-1-59928-746-1(3)*, 12590, SandCastle) ABDO Publishing Co.

—Elephant Trunks. Kompelien, Tracy. 2006. (Fact & Fiction Ser.). 24p. (J). pap. 48.42 *(978-1-59679-936-3(6))* ABDO Publishing Co.

—Frisky Ferrets, 1 vol. Doudna, Kelly. Craig, Diane, ed. 2007. (Perfect Pets Ser.). (ENG.). 24p. (J). (gr. k-3). lib. bdg. 27.07 *(978-1-59928-748-5(X)*, 12594, SandCastle) ABDO Publishing Co.

—God Made You Special. Holder, Jennifer. (Happy Day Ser.). (ENG.). (J). 2015. 16p. pap. 2.49 *(978-1-4964-1110-5(2)*, 4612785, Happy Day); 2014. 24p. pap. 3.99 *(978-1-4964-0086-4(0)*, 4611761) Tyndale Hse. Pubs.

—Goofy Guinea Pigs, 1 vol. Salzmann, Mary Elizabeth. Craig, Diane, ed. 2007. (Perfect Pets Ser.). (ENG.). 24p. (J). (gr. k-3). lib. bdg. 27.07 *(978-1-59928-749-2(8)*, 12596, SandCastle) ABDO Publishing Co.

—Hilarious Hedgehogs, 1 vol. Doudna, Kelly. 2013. (Unusual Pets Ser.). (ENG.). 24p. (J). (gr. -1-3). 27.07 *(978-1-61783-399-1(1)*, 15201, SandCastle) ABDO Publishing Co.

—Horse Shoes. Tuminelly, Nancy. 2006. (Fact & Fiction Ser.). 24p. (J). pap. 48.42 *(978-1-59679-944-8(7))* ABDO Publishing Co.

—Humming Hummingbird, 1 vol. Salzmann, Mary Elizabeth. 2006. (Critter Chronicles Ser.). (ENG.). 24p. (J). (gr. k-3). lib. bdg. 27.07 *(978-1-59928-442-2(1)*, 4974, SandCastle) ABDO Publishing Co.

—I Can Pray! Stortz, Diane & Holder, Jennifer. 2014. (Faith That Sticks Bks.). (ENG.). 24p. (J). pap. 3.99 *(978-1-4964-0085-7(2)*, 4611760) Tyndale Hse. Pubs.

—Iguana Mama, 1 vol. Hanson, Anders. 2006. (Critter Chronicles Ser.). (ENG.). 24p. (J). (gr. k-3). lib. bdg. 27.07 *(978-1-59928-444-6(8)*, 4976, SandCastle) ABDO Publishing Co.

—Kangaroo Boxers. Hanson, Anders. 2006. (Fact & Fiction Ser.). 24p. (J). pap. 48.42 *(978-1-59679-946-2(3))* ABDO Publishing Co.

—Lion Manes. Kompelien, Tracy. 2006. (Fact & Fiction Ser.). 24p. (J). pap. 48.42 *(978-1-59679-950-9(1))* ABDO Publishing Co.

—Magnificent Macaws, 1 vol. Kuskowski, Alex. 2013. (Unusual Pets Ser.). (ENG.). 24p. (J). (gr. -1-3). 27.07 *(978-1-61783-400-4(9)*, 15203, SandCastle) ABDO Publishing Co.

—Octopus's Garden, 1 vol. Kompelien, Tracy. 2006. (Critter Chronicles Ser.). (ENG.). 24p. (J). (gr. k-3). lib. bdg. 27.07 *(978-1-59928-456-9(1)*, 4988, SandCastle) ABDO Publishing Co.

—Los Pantaloncillos Del Canguro. Hanson, Anders. 2006. (Cuentos de Animales Ser.). (SPA.). 24p. (J). (gr. k-3). lib. bdg. 27.07 *(978-1-59928-655-6(6)*, 5016, SandCastle) ABDO Publishing Co.

—Pelican's Pouch, 1 vol. Scheunemann, Pam. 2006. (Critter Chronicles Ser.). (ENG.). 24p. (J). (gr. k-3). lib. bdg. 27.07 *(978-1-59928-462-0(6)*, 4994, SandCastle) ABDO Publishing Co.

—Pig Pens. Scheunemann, Pam. 2006. (Fact & Fiction Ser.). 24p. (J). pap. 48.42 *(978-1-59679-960-8(9))* ABDO Publishing Co.

—Presidential Seal, 1 vol. Salzmann, Mary Elizabeth. 2006. (Critter Chronicles Ser.). (ENG.). 24p. (J). (gr. k-3). lib. bdg. 27.07 *(978-1-59928-464-4(2)*, 4996, SandCastle) ABDO Publishing Co.

—Rabbit Ears. Doudna, Kelly. 2006. (Fact & Fiction Ser.). 24p. (J). pap. 48.42 *(978-1-59679-962-2(5))* ABDO Publishing Co.

—Rhino Horns. Hanson, Anders. 2006. (Fact & Fiction Ser.). 24p. (J). pap. 48.42 *(978-1-59679-964-6(1))* ABDO Publishing Co.

—Sea Horse Races, 1 vol. Salzmann, Mary Elizabeth. 2006. (Critter Chronicles Ser.). (ENG.). 24p. (J). (gr. k-3). lib. bdg. 27.07 *(978-1-59928-468-2(5)*, 5000, SandCastle) ABDO Publishing Co.

—Snake Charmer, 1 vol. Doudna, Kelly. 2006. (Critter Chronicles Ser.). (ENG.). 24p. (J). (gr. k-3). lib. bdg. 27.07 *(978-1-59928-470-5(7)*, 5002, SandCastle) ABDO Publishing Co.

—Special Memories. Williams, Rozanne Lanczak. Maio, Barbara, ed. 2006. (J). per. 8.99 *(978-1-59198-360-6(6))* Creative Teaching Pr., Inc.

—Spelling Bee, 1 vol. Scheunemann, Pam. 2006. (Critter Chronicles Ser.). (ENG.). 24p. (J). (gr. k-3). lib. bdg. 27.07 *(978-1-59928-472-9(3)*, 5004, SandCastle) ABDO Publishing Co.

—Tricky Tarantulas, 1 vol. Kuskowski, Alex. 2013. (Unusual Pets Ser.). (ENG.). 24p. (J). (gr. -1-3). 27.07 *(978-1-61783-402-8(5)*, 15207, SandCastle) ABDO Publishing Co.

—La Tuba Del Rinoceronte. Hanson, Anders. 2006. (Realidad y Ficción Ser.). (SPA.). 24p. (J). 48.42 *(978-1-59928-666-2(1))* ABDO Publishing Co.

—La Tuba del Rinoceronte. Hanson, Anders. 2006. (Cuentos de Animales Ser.). (SPA.). 24p. (J). (gr. k-3). lib. bdg. 27.07 *(978-1-59928-665-5(3)*, 5024, SandCastle) ABDO Publishing Co.

—Turtle Shells. Salzmann, Mary Elizabeth. 2006. (Fact & Fiction Ser.). 24p. (J). pap. 48.42 *(978-1-59679-970-7(6))* ABDO Publishing Co.

—Whale Tale, 1 vol. Hanson, Anders. 2006. (Critter Chronicles Ser.). (ENG.). 24p. (J). (gr. k-3). lib. bdg. 27.07 *(978-1-59928-476-7(6)*, 5008, SandCastle) ABDO Publishing Co.

—Los Zapatos de la Potranca. Tuminelly, Nancy. 2006. (Cuentos de Animales Ser.). 24p. (J). (gr. k-3). lib. bdg. 25.65 *(978-1-59928-677-8(7)*, 5034, SandCastle) ABDO Publishing Co.

—Zebra Stripes. Kompelien, Tracy. 2006. (Fact & Fiction Ser.). 24p. (J). pap. 48.42 *(978-1-59679-972-1(2))* ABDO Publishing Co.

Nobens, Cheryl. Colores - Colors. 2006. (ENG & SPA.). (J). bds. 5.99 *(978-1-934113-03-5(4))* Little Cubans, LLC.

—How to Make a Friend. Williams, Rozanne Lanczak. 2005. (Reading for Fluency Ser.). 16p. (J). pap. 3.49 *(978-1-59198-155-8(7)*, 4255) Creative Teaching Pr., Inc.

Nobens, Cheryl A. Elephant Trunks, 1 vol. Kompelien, Tracy. 2006. (Animal Tales Ser.). (ENG.). 24p. (J). (gr. k-3). lib. bdg. 27.07 *(978-1-59679-935-6(8)*, 2731, SandCastle) ABDO Publishing Co.

—Horse Shoes, 1 vol. Tuminelly, Nancy. 2006. (Animal Tales Ser.). (ENG.). 24p. (J). (gr. k-3). lib. bdg. 27.07 *(978-1-59679-943-1(9)*, 2739, SandCastle) ABDO Publishing Co.

—Kangaroo Boxers, 1 vol. Hanson, Anders. 2006. (Animal Tales Ser.). (ENG.). 24p. (J). (gr. k-3). lib. bdg. 27.07 *(978-1-59679-945-5(5)*, 2741, SandCastle) ABDO Publishing Co.

—Pig Pens, 1 vol. Scheunemann, Pam. 2006. (Animal Tales Ser.). (ENG.). 24p. (J). (gr. k-3). lib. bdg. 27.07 *(978-1-59679-959-2(5)*, 2755, SandCastle) ABDO Publishing Co.

—Rabbit Ears, 1 vol. Doudna, Kelly. 2006. (Animal Tales Ser.). (ENG.). 24p. (J). (gr. k-3). lib. bdg. 27.07 *(978-1-59679-961-5(7)*, 2757, SandCastle) ABDO Publishing Co.

—Rhino Horns, 1 vol. Hanson, Anders. 2006. (Animal Tales Ser.). (ENG.). 24p. (J). (gr. k-3). lib. bdg. 27.07 *(978-1-59679-963-9(3)*, 2759, SandCastle) ABDO Publishing Co.

—Turtle Shells, 1 vol. Salzmann, Mary Elizabeth. 2006. (Animal Tales Ser.). (ENG.). 24p. (J). (gr. k-3). lib. bdg. 27.07 *(978-1-59679-969-1(2)*, 2765, SandCastle) ABDO Publishing Co.

—Zebra Stripes, 1 vol. Kompelien, Tracy. 2006. (Animal Tales Ser.). (ENG.). 24p. (J). (gr. k-3). lib. bdg. 27.07 *(978-1-59679-971-4(4)*, 2767, SandCastle) ABDO Publishing Co.

Noble, Amy. Creepy Chicago: A Ghosthunter's Tales of the City's Scariest Sites. Bielski, Ursula. 2003. (ENG.). 136p. (J). (gr. 3-7). pap. 7.95 *(978-1-933272-28-3(7))* Thunder Bay Pr.

Noble, Edwin & Grieve, Walter G. The Natural History Story Book. Talbot, Ethel. 2008. 336p. pap. 13.95 *(978-1-59915-295-0(9))* Yesterday's Classics.

Noble, Lisa. I Was a Teen Ghoul. Warpeha, Katherine. 2017. (ENG.). 214p. (YA). (gr. 8-10). pap. 15.95 *(978-1-63492-715-4(X))* Booklocker.com, Inc.

Noble, Lisa Meredith Shah. Bella Bella Cinderella. Miller, Connie Madrid. 2019. (ENG.). 30p. (J). pap. 10.99 *(978-1-7229-0664-1(2))* CreateSpace Independent Publishing Platform.

Noble, Marty. A First Book of Irish Songs & Celtic Dances: For the Beginning Pianist with Downloadable MP3s. Bergerac, ed. 2015. (ENG.). 48p. pap. 7.95 *(978-0-486-40405-9(6))* Dover Pubns., Inc.

Noble, Penny. Jerboth Weaves a Song. Brown, Linda Kayse. 2007. (ENG.). 20p. (J). pap. 9.95 *(978-0-9769742-0-8(7))* Bay Villager, The.

Noble, Roger. Bedtime Baby, 1 vol. Baker, Jaime. 2010. 16p. pap. 24.95 *(978-1-4489-6234-1(X))* PublishAmerica, Inc.

Noble, Sheilagh. Let's Look at Eyes. Sideri, Simona. 2003. (Let's Look at Ser.). 24p. (J). *(978-1-84089-146-1(7))* Zero to Ten, Ltd.

—Let's Look at Mouths. Sideri, Simona. 2003. (Let's Look at Ser.). 24p. (J). *(978-1-84089-147-8(5))* Zero to Ten, Ltd.

Noble, Stuart, jt. illus. see Grant, Sophia.

Noble, Trinka Hakes. Apple Tree Christmas. Noble, Trinka Hakes. 2005. (Holiday Ser.). (ENG.). 32p. (J). (gr. -1-3). 16.95 *(978-1-58536-270-7(0))* Sleeping Bear Pr.

Nocete, Charlo. Kaytee, Queen of the Pirates. Whisnant, Tony. 2012. (ENG.). 26p. (J). pap. 21.99 ***(978-1-4691-4079-7(9))*** Xlibris Corp.

Nodel, Norman. The Ox-Bow Incident. Graham, Lorenz B. & Clark, Walter Van Tilburg. 2016. (Classics Illustrated Ser.). 48p. pap. 9.95 *(978-1-906814-69-4(4))* Classic Comic Store, Ltd. GBR. Dist: Casemate Pubs. & Bk. Distributors, LLC.

—Yossi & Laibel Learn to Help. Rosenfeld, Dina. 2012. 14p. (J). 6.95 *(978-1-929628-62-9(5))* Hachai Publishing.

Noé. The Eagle & the Chickens. Sommer, Carl. 2016. (J). *(978-1-57537-945-6(7))* Advance Publishing, Inc.

—The Great Deception. Sommer, Carl. 2009. (Quest for Success Ser.). (ENG.). 40p. (YA). pap. 4.95 *(978-1-57537-279-2(7))*; lib. bdg. 12.95 *(978-1-57537-254-9(1))* Advance Publishing, Inc.

—The Great Deception(El Gran Engaño) Sommer, Carl. ed. 2009. (Quest for Success Bilingual Ser.). (ENG & SPA.). 72p. (YA). lib. bdg. 14.95 *(978-1-57537-228-0(2))* Advance Publishing, Inc.

—The Sonics on Tour: The Respiratory System. Reif, Cheryl. 2012. (J). lib. bdg. *(978-1-57537-900-5(7))* Advance Publishing, Inc.

Noé, Ignacio. The Ant & the Grasshopper. Sommer, Carl. 2016. (ENG.). 32p. (J). (gr. k-4). lib. bdg. 16.95 *(978-1-57537-925-8(2)*, Another Sommer-Time Story) Advance Publishing, Inc.

Noe, Ignacio. The Country Mouse & the City Mouse. Sommer, Carl. 2014. (Sommer-Time Story Classics Ser.). (ENG.). 32p. (J). (gr. k-4). 16.95 *(978-1-57537-080-4(8))* Advance Publishing, Inc.

Noé, Ignacio. The Donkey, Fox, & the Lion. Sommer, Carl. 2016. (ENG.). 32p. (J). (gr. k-4). lib. bdg. 16.95 *(978-1-57537-926-5(0)*, Another Sommer-Time Story) Advance Publishing, Inc.

Noe, Ignacio. The Emperor's New Clothes. Sommer, Carl. 2014. (Sommer-Time Story Classics Ser.). (ENG.). 32p. (J). (gr. k-4). 16.95 *(978-1-57537-081-1(6))* Advance Publishing, Inc.

—The Little Red Hen. Sommer, Carl. 2014. (Sommer-Time Story Classics Ser.). (ENG.). 32p. (J). (gr. k-4). 16.95 *(978-1-57537-084-2(0))* Advance Publishing, Inc.

—Little Red Riding Hood. Sommer, Carl. 2014. (Sommer-Time Story Classics Ser.). (ENG.). 32p. (J). (gr. k-4). 16.95 *(978-1-57537-077-4(8))* Advance Publishing, Inc.

Noel, E. Of Bullfrogs & Snapdragons. Geiger, A. R. Swoboda, Beth, ed. 2019. (ENG.). 88p. (J). pap. 7.00 ***(978-1-6985-7505-6(X))*** Independently Published.

Noel, Green. God Made Me: The Safe Touch Coloring Book. Beth, Robinson. 2007. 20p. (J). pap. 3.99 *(978-0-9799092-0-7(1))* Robinson, Beth.

Noel III, jt. illus. see Rio, Adam del.

Noeth, Chris, et al. Zombielicious!, 3. Bilgrey, Marc et al. 3rd ed. 2008. (Tales from the Crypt Ser.: 3). (ENG.). 112p. (J). (gr. 5-12). 22.44 *(978-1-59707-091-1(2)*, 9781597070911) Papercutz.

Noguchi, Jamie. School for Extraterrestrial Girls #1: Girl on Fire. Whitley, Jeremy. 2020. (School for Extraterrestrial Girls Ser.: 1). (ENG.). 132p. (J). 19.99 *(978-1-5458-0492-6(3)*, 900219695); pap. 12.99 *(978-1-5458-0493-3(1)*, 900219696) Papercutz.

Noh, Mi Young. Threads of Time, 11 vols., Vol. 6. Noh, Mi Young. 6th rev. ed. 2006. (Threads of Time Ser.). 192p. per. 9.99 *(978-1-59532-037-7(7))* TOKYOPOP, Inc.

Noh, Mikyo. David Attenborough. Sanchez Vegara, Maria Isabel. ed. 2020. (Little People, BIG DREAMS Ser.: 34). (ENG.). 32p. (J). (gr. -1-2). 14.99 ***(978-0-7112-4563-1(0)***, 328344, Frances Lincoln Children's Bks.) Quarto Publishing Group UK GBR. Dist: Hachette UK Distribution.

Noh, Seong-bin. Where Are You, Sun Bear? Malaysia. Choi, Eun-Mi. Cowley, Joy, ed. 2015. (Global Kids Storybooks Ser.). (ENG.). 32p. (J). (gr. 1-4). 26.65 *(978-1-925246-02-5(7))*; 26.65 *(978-1-925246-28-5(0))*; 7.99 *(978-1-925246-54-4(X))* ChoiceMaker Pty. Ltd., The AUS. (Big and SMALL). Dist: Lerner Publishing Group.

—Where Are You, Sun Bear? Malaysia. Choi, Eun-Mi. 2015. (Global Kids Storybooks Ser.). (ENG.). 32p. (J). (gr. 1-4). pap. 8.99 *(978-1-925233-45-2(6)*, Big and SMALL) ChoiceMaker Pty. Ltd., The AUS. Dist: Lerner Publishing Group.

Noiset, Michele. The Alphabet. Rosa-Mendoza, Gladys. Cifuentes, Carolina, ed. 2004. (English-Spanish Foundations Ser.).Tr. of El Alfabeto. (ENG & SPA.). 32p. (J). bds. 6.95 *(978-0-9679748-0-4(1))* Me+Mi Publishing.

—Colors & Shapes. Rosa-Mendoza, Gladys. Cifuentes, Carolina, ed. 2004. (English-Spanish Foundations Ser.).Tr. of Los Colores y las Figuras. (ENG & SPA.). 20p. (J). bds. 6.95 *(978-0-9679748-3-5(6))* Me+Mi Publishing.

—English-Spanish Foundations Series: The Alphabet; Numbers; Colors & Shapes. Rosa-Mendoza, Gladys. Cifuentes, Carolina, ed. 2004. (Spanish Foundations Ser.). (ENG & SPA.). (J). bds. 19.95 *(978-0-9679748-1-1(X))* Me+Mi Publishing.

—Numbers. Rosa-Mendoza, Gladys. Cifuentes, Carolina, ed. 2004. (English-Spanish Foundations Ser.).Tr. of Los Numeros. (ENG & SPA.). 20p. (J). bds. 6.95 *(978-0-9679748-2-8(8))* Me+Mi Publishing.

—We Read Phonics-Bugs on the Bus. Orshoski, Paul. 2010. 32p. (J). 9.95 *(978-1-60115-325-8(2))*; pap. 4.99 *(978-1-60115-326-5(0))* Treasure Bay, Inc.

Noj, Nahta. The Lion & the Mouse: Turn-And-Tell Tales. Broom, Jenny. 2014. (ENG.). 32p. (J). (gr. -1-2). 14.99 *(978-0-7636-6619-4(X)*, Templar) Candlewick Pr.

—The Tortoise & the Hare. Ritchie, Alison. 2015. (ENG.). 32p. (J). (-k). 15.99 *(978-0-7636-7601-8(2)*, Templar) Candlewick Pr.

Nojiri, Housuke. Rocket Girls: The Last Planet (Novel-Paperback) Nojiri, Housuke. 2011. (ENG.). 250p. pap. 13.99 *(978-1-4215-3765-8(6))* Viz Media.

Nolan, Alan. Cliffs of Moher & the Burren: My Ireland Activity Book. Mac a'Bháird, Natasha. 2015. (ENG.). 24p. (J). pap. 12.00 *(978-1-84717-770-4(0))* O'Brien Pr., Ltd., The IRL. Dist: Casemate Pubs. & Bk. Distributors, LLC.

—Dublin: My Ireland Activity Book. Mac a'Bháird, Natasha. 2017. (ENG.). 24p. (J). pap. 10.00 *(978-1-84717-892-3(8))* O'Brien Pr., Ltd., The IRL. Dist: Casemate Pubs. & Bk. Distributors, LLC.

Nolan, Amanda M. Emily: Dream Believe Achieve. Symington, Martha M. 2008. 36p. pap. *(978-1-897435-21-2(5))* Agio Publishing Hse.

Nolan, Dennis. An Ellis Island Christmas. Leighton, Maxinne Rhea. 2018. 32p. (J). (gr. k-3). pap. 7.99 *(978-0-451-48133-7(X)*, Puffin Books) Penguin Young Readers Group.

—Thunder Horse. Bunting, Eve. 2017. (ENG.). 32p. (J). 17.99 *(978-1-62672-443-3(1)*, 9781626724433) Roaring Brook Pr.

—William Shakespeare's a Midsummer Night's Dream. Coville, Bruce. 2003. 48p. (J). (gr. k-3). pap. 7.99 *(978-0-14-250168-9(9)*, Puffin Books) Penguin Young Readers Group.

Nolan, Dennis. Hunters of the Great Forest. Nolan, Dennis. 2014. (ENG.). 40p. (J). (gr. -1-2). 17.99 *(978-1-59643-896-5(7)*, 900120128) Roaring Brook Pr.

—Sea of Dreams. Nolan, Dennis. 2011. (ENG.). 40p. (J). (gr. -1-2). 18.99 *(978-1-59643-470-7(8)*, 900055552) Roaring Brook Pr.

Nolan, Graham. The Bunker. Van Lente, Fred. 2010. (Iron Man Ser.: No. 3). (ENG.). 24p. (J). (gr. 2-6). lib. bdg. 27.07 *(978-1-59961-771-8(4)*, 10035, Marvel Age) Spotlight.

—Web of Lies. Van Lente, Fred. 2010. (Iron Man Ser.: No. 3). (ENG.). 24p. (J). (gr. 2-6). lib. bdg. 27.07 *(978-1-59961-774-9(9)*, 10038, Marvel Age) Spotlight.

Nolan, Graham & Cordeiro, James. Ghost of a Chance. Van Lente, Fred. 2009. (Iron Man Ser.: No. 2). (ENG.). 24p. (J). (gr. 2-6). lib. bdg. 27.07 *(978-1-59961-590-5(8)*, 10031, Marvel Age) Spotlight.

Noll, Cheryl Kirk. The Black Regiment of the American Revolution. Brennan, Linda. 2005. 32p. (J). (gr. 4-7). per. 8.95 *(978-1-931659-18-5(4))* Moon Mountain Publishing, Inc.

—Bokuden & the Bully. Krensky, Stephen. 2008. (On My Own Folklore Ser.). (ENG.). 48p. (J). (gr. 2-4). lib. bdg. 25.26 *(978-0-8225-7547-4(7)*, Millbrook Pr.) Lerner Publishing Group.

—Bokuden & the Bully: [a Japanese Folktale]. Krensky, Stephen. 2009. (On My Own Folklore Ser.). (ENG.). 48p. (J). (gr. 2-4). pap. 7.99 *(978-1-58013-847-5(0)*, First Avenue Editions) Lerner Publishing Group.

Nolte, Larry. Flowers: Read Well Level K Unit 9 Storybook. Gunn, Barbara & Dunn, Richard. 2004. (Read Well Level K Ser.). 20p. (J). *(978-1-57035-680-3(7))* Cambium Education, Inc.

—Mi Perrito, Level 1. Greene, Inez. Flor Ada, Alma, tr. 3rd ed. 2003. (Dejame Leer Ser.). (SPA.). 8p. (J). (gr. -1-k). 6.50 *(978-0-673-36289-6(2)*, Good Year Bks.) Celebration Pr.

—Monkey Business: Read Well Level K Unit 3 Storybook. Sprick, Marilyn. 2003. (Read Well Level K Ser.). 20p. (J). *(978-1-57035-675-9(0))* Cambium Education, Inc.

Nolting, Mia. The Cat King of Havana. Crosshill, Tom. 2016. (ENG.). 368p. (YA). (gr. 8). 17.99 *(978-0-06-242283-5(9)*, Tegen, Katherine Bks) HarperCollins Pubs.

Nomoco. The Great Realization. Roberts (Tomfoolery), Tomos. 2020. (ENG.). 32p. (J). (gr. -1-3). 18.99 ***(978-0-06-306636-6(X)***, HarperCollins) HarperCollins Pubs. Ltd. GBR. Dist: HarperCollins Pubs.

Non Identifie. Carnet Blanc Ligue Maritime Bordeaux. 2016. (Bnf Monuments Ser.). (FRE.). (J). pap. *(978-2-01-116969-3(0))* Hachette Groupe Livre.

—Carnet Blanc Skieur. 2016. (Bnf Sports Ser.). (FRE.). (J). pap. *(978-2-01-116947-1(X))*; pap. *(978-2-01-116972-3(0))* Hachette Groupe Livre.

—Carnet Ligne Ligue Maritime Bordeaux. 2016. (Bnf Monuments Ser.). (FRE.). (J). pap. *(978-2-01-116944-0(5))* Hachette Groupe Livre.

Nonato, Paul. Christmas Coloring Book for Teens & Adults: Christmas Holiday Coloring Pages for Relaxation Featuring Beautiful & Festive Christmas Scenes & Ornaments (Large Print Holiday Activity Books) Reid, Olivia. 2019. (ENG.). 110p. (J). pap. 6.99 ***(978-1-7096-5061-1(3))*** Independently Published.

—Food Coloring Book for Kids Ages 3-5: Fun & Learning Coloring Pages for Toddlers & Preschoolers (Large Print Children's Activity Book) Reid, Olivia. l.t. ed. 2019. (ENG.). 108p. (J). pap. 6.99 ***(978-1-6980-0319-1(6))*** Independently Published.

Nonato, Paul. Funny Jokes about Animals: 100 Jokes for Kids of All Ages, Funny Jokes for Children, Joke Book with Illustrations. Cooper, Amby. 2019. (ENG.). 26p. (J). pap. 9.99 *(978-1-0956-2376-3(1))* Independently Published.

Noon, Connie & Zraick, Robert. Dinosaurs & Donuts. Moor-Doucette, Saba. 2013. 28p. pap. 10.95 *(978-0-578-13447-5(0))* Gratitude Works.

Noon, Steve. A Child Through Time: The Book of Children's History. Wilkinson, Phil. 2017. (ENG.). 128p. (J). (gr. 3-7). 21.99 *(978-1-4654-4493-6(9)*, DK Children) Dorling Kindersley Publishing, Inc.

—A City Through Time. Steele, Philip & Dorling Kindersley Publishing Staff. 2013. (ENG.). 48p. (J). (gr. 2-5). 17.99 *(978-1-4654-0249-3(7)*, DK Children) Dorling Kindersley Publishing, Inc.

—Story of the Titanic. DK. 2012. (ENG.). 48p. (J). (gr. 3-7). 17.99 *(978-0-7566-9171-4(0)*, DK Children) Dorling Kindersley Publishing, Inc.

—A Street Through Time: A 12,000 Year Journey along the Same Street. 2020. (ENG.). 32p. (J). (gr. 2-4). 17.99 *(978-1-4654-9063-6(9)*, DK Children) Dorling Kindersley Publishing, Inc.

Noonan, Julia. Baby Bat's Lullaby. Mitchard, Jacquelyn. 2004. 32p. (J). (gr. -1-1). lib. bdg. 16.89 *(978-0-06-050761-9(6))* HarperCollins Pubs.

—Over the Rainbow. Harburg, E. Y. & Arlen, Harold. 2004. 24p. (J). (gr. 4-8). reprint ed. 16.00 *(978-0-7567-7340-3(7))* DIANE Publishing Co.

—Over the Rainbow. Harburg, E. Y. Date not set. 32p. (J). 5.99 *(978-0-06-443677-9(2))* HarperCollins Pubs.

—Sweetwater. Yep, Laurence. 2004. 191p. (J). pap. 5.99 *(978-0-06-056029-4(0))* HarperCollins Pubs.

—You're Just What I Need. Krauss, Ruth. 2019. (ENG.). 40p. (J). (gr. -1-3). 16.99 *(978-0-06-243181-3(1))* HarperCollins Pubs.

—You're Just What I Need Board Book. Krauss, Ruth. 2018. (Growing Tree Ser.). (ENG.). 36p. (J). (gr. -1 — 1). bds. 7.99 *(978-0-694-01304-3(8)*, HarperFestival) HarperCollins Pubs.

Noone, Cathleen L. Among the Buildings That Touch the Sky: Philadelphia. Kelly, Elaine A. & Carl, Jean R. 2009. *(978-0-578-06873-2(7))* Kelly, Elaine A.

Norberg, Ken. Angel George Series James Needs a Miracle. Lynn, Debbie. 2006. (J). 15.95 *(978-0-9771318-9-1(0))* Hope Harvest Publishing.

Norberg, Tora Marie. Nordic Fairy Tales: An Adventure Game. 2019. (ENG.). 20p. 24.95 ***(978-1-58423-708-2(2)***, f71db45d-3985-411c-b3af-9bda2ad0df6c, Gingko Pr.) Gingko Pr., Inc.

Norbu, Tenzing. Shantideva: How to Wake up a Hero. Townsend, Dominique. 2015. (ENG.). 64p. (J). 22.95 *(978-1-61429-058-2(X))* Wisdom Pubns.

Norcross, David. Dylan Discovers His Brain ! Almarode, John. 2010. 28p. pap. 12.99 *(978-1-4490-5491-5(9))* AuthorHouse.

Norcross, Harry. The Nature of Study Skills: Hardworking Helen K Honeybee Study Skills 3. Cali, Charlene C. 56p. (J). (gr. 8-9). 14.95 *(978-1-57543-101-7(7))* MAR*CO Products, Inc.

Nord, Cary, et al. Conan Chronicles Epic Collection: Out of the Darksome Hills. 2019. (Conan Chronicles Epic Collection: 1). (ENG.). 496p. (YA). (gr. 8-17). pap. 39.99 *(978-1-302-91590-2(8))* Marvel Worldwide, Inc.

—Conan Chronicles Epic Collection: the Heart of Yag-Kosha. 2019. (ENG.). 504p. (YA). (gr. 8-17). pap. 39.99 *(978-1-302-91591-9(6))* Marvel Worldwide, Inc.

Nord, Mary. ABC Talking Book Adventures. McTaggart, Stephen & McTaggart, Debra. (Talking Book Adventures Ser.). 12p. (J). (gr. -1-18). 16.95 *(978-0-9627001-2-5(6))* Futech Educational Products, Inc.

—Bookee Presents 1, 2, 3 Count with Me. McTaggart, Stephen & McTaggart, Debra. (Talking Book Adventures Ser.). 14p. (J). (gr. -1-18). 16.95 *(978-0-9627001-3-2(4))* Futech Educational Products, Inc.

—Bookee Presents Colors, Shapes & Sounds. Kidd, Ron. (Talking Book Adventures Ser.). 12p. (J). (gr. -1-18). 16.95 *(978-0-9627001-1-8(8))* Futech Educational Products, Inc.

—Bookee's Sounds Around. McTaggart, Stephen & McTaggart, Debra. (Talking Book Adventures Ser.). 12p. (J). (gr. -1-18). 16.95 *(978-0-9627001-0-1(X))* Futech Educational Products, Inc.

Nordeen, Craig. Go Grandma Go! Becker, Dorothy C. 2016. (ENG.). (J). pap. 7.95 *(978-0-692-81633-2(X))* Blondvic Enterprises.

Nordeen, Sandra, jt. illus. see Bradley, Katie.

Nordenstrom, Michael. Hina & the Sea of Stars. Nordenstrom, Michael, adapted by. 2003. 32p. 10.95 *(978-1-57306-167-4(0))* Bess Pr., Inc.

Nordheim, Astrid. Brave: A My Invisible Powers Story. Assheton, Deb. 2018. (ENG.). 32p. (J). pap. *(978-0-6483127-0-3(4))* Deb A.

Nordli, Ernest. Roy Rogers on the Double-R Ranch. Beecher, Elizabeth. 2011. 78p. 37.95 *(978-1-258-03590-7(1))* Literary Licensing, LLC.

Nordqvist, Sven. Findus Plants Meatballs, 23 vols. Nordqvist, Sven. Large, Nathan, tr. 2013. (ENG.). 28p. (J). (gr. -1-3). *(978-1-907359-29-3(X))* Hawthorn Pr.

—Pancakes for Findus, 25 vols. Nordqvist, Sven. 2008. (Findus & Pettson Ser.). (ENG.). 28p. (J). *(978-1-903458-79-2(X))* Hawthorn Pr.

Nordstrom, Kevin. Luda & Chairsy: Making Friends. Gogolushko, Luda. 2019. (ENG.). 32p. (J). (gr. k-5). 21.99 *(978-0-9861927-6-0(7))* INCLUDAS Publishing.

Noreika, Robert. Marsh Morning. Berkes, Marianne. 2003. 32p. lib. bdg. 22.90 *(978-0-7613-2568-0(9))*; (J). 14.95 *(978-0-7613-1936-8(0))* Lerner Publishing Group. (Millbrook Pr.).

—Marsh Music. Berkes, Marianne. 2011. (ENG.). 32p. (J). (gr. k-3). pap. 9.99 *(978-0-7613-7461-9(2)*, Millbrook Pr.) Lerner Publishing Group.

—Seashells by the Seashore. Berkes, Marianne Collins. 2004. (Sharing Nature with Children Book Ser.). 32p. (J). (gr. -1-5). 16.95 *(978-1-58469-035-1(6))* Dawn Pubns.

—Through Sophie's Eyes. Gibson, Catherine. 2009. (ENG.). 32p. (J). 15.95 *(978-0-578-00980-3(3))* For Children With Love Pubns.

Norell, Aaron. Urban Legends: Strange Stories Behind Modern Myths, 1 vol., Vol. 1. Mott, A. S. rev. ed. 2004. (Ghost Stories Ser.: 45). (ENG.). 232p. (gr. 4). pap. 12.95 *(978-1-894877-41-1(1)*, 32415cc3-a2ce-43a0-95f2-af6dc93189a0, Ghost Hse. Bks.) Lone Pine Publishing USA.

—Werewolves & Shapeshifters, 1 vol., Vol. 1. Zenko, Darren. rev. ed. 2004. (Ghost Stories Ser.: 47). (ENG.). 216p. (gr. 4). pap. 12.95 *(978-1-894877-53-4(5)*, d33b2f32-85e9-4e53-baae-14b9298deea1, Ghost Hse. Bks.) Lone Pine Publishing USA.

Norgren, David & Norgren, Elias. The Ender Eye Prophecy: An Unofficial Graphic Novel for Minecrafters, #3. Stevens, Cara J. 2016. (Unofficial Graphic Novel for Minecrafter Ser.: 3). 192p. (J). (gr. 2-7). pap. 11.99 *(978-1-5107-1483-0(9)*, Sky Pony Pr.) Skyhorse Publishing Co., Inc.

Norgren, Elias, jt. illus. see Norgren, David.

Norhelm, Karen. Clarabelle the Cat Loses Her Hair. Theis, Patricia & Theis, Matthew. 2008. 24p. pap. 12.95 *(978-1-59858-865-1(6))* Dog Ear Publishing, LLC.

Norie, Rooney. Gracie's Hill. Knights, Nancy. 2007. 28p. per. 7.95 *(978-1-58275-192-4(7))* Black Forest Pr.

Noriega, Fernando. Poemas para la Paz. Torices, Jose Gonzalez et al. 2004.Tr. of Poems for Peace. (SPA.). 68p. (J). (gr. 2-3). 14.99 *(978-84-241-8726-2(1))* Everest Editora ESP. Dist: Lectorum Pubns., Inc.

Norling, Beth. The Simple Things. Condon, Bill. 2015. (ENG.). 168p. (J). (gr. 3-5). 9.99 *(978-1-74331-724-2(7))* Allen & Unwin AUS. Dist: Independent Pubs. Group.

Norling, Beth. The Stone Baby. Norling, Beth. 2004. 32p. (J). (gr. k-2). *(978-0-7344-0353-7(4)*, Lothian Children's Bks.) Hachette Australia.

Norman, Floyd. A Kiss Goodnight. Sherman, Richard M. 2017. (ENG.). 48p. 19.99 *(978-1-4847-8228-6(3)*, Disney Editions) Disney Pr.

Norman, Justin & Starkings, Richard. Solstice. Seagle, Steven T. 2005. per. 12.95 *(978-0-9766761-1-9(7))* Active Images.

Norman, Vera Stone. Guide Book for Language, Grade Three: Shepherd-Parkman Language Series. Parkman, Mary Rosetta. 2011. 236p. 46.95 *(978-1-258-08037-2(0))* Literary Licensing, LLC.

Normand, Hal. Souvenirs from Space: The Oscar E. Monnig Meteorite Gallery. Alter, Judy. 2007. (ENG.). 24p. (J). (gr. 4-7). pap. 4.95 *(978-0-87565-346-4(4))* Texas Christian Univ. Pr.

Normand, Jean-Pierre. Odyssey, 1 vol. Czerneda, Julie E., ed. 2004. (Wonder Zone Ser.). (ENG.). 130p. (J). (gr. 4-7). pap. 9.95 *(978-1-55244-080-3(X)*, 2520cb1b-a57f-44c1-922e-e52d426cf3a2) Fitzhenry & Whiteside, Ltd. CAN. Dist: Firefly Bks., Ltd.

—Polaris: A Celebration of Polar Science, 1 vol. Czerneda, Julie E., ed. 2007. (Wonder Zone Ser.). (ENG.). 174p. (YA). (gr. 5-8). per. 6.95 *(978-0-88995-372-7(4)*, 1799d92e-49c0-4d3c-a827-0b7c9fbf0639) Red Deer Pr. CAN. Dist: Firefly Bks., Ltd.

Norona, Bill, jt. illus. see Alley, Ashleigh.

Norridge-Austen, Terry. Hilmy the Hippo Becomes a Hero. Norridge-Austen, Terry, tr. Norridge, Rae. 2007. (ENG.). 25p. 7.95 *(978-0-86037-343-6(5))* Kube Publishing Ltd. GBR. Dist: Consortium Bk. Sales & Distribution.

Norridge, Terry. Hilmy the Hippo Learns about Creation. Norridge, Rae. 2007. (ENG.). 29p. 7.95 *(978-0-86037-313-1(4))* Kube Publishing Ltd. GBR. Dist: Consortium Bk. Sales & Distribution.

Norris, Aaron, jt. illus. see Jones, Penny.

Norris, Cameron, jt. illus. see Kalina, Lacey.

Norris, Judy-Jo Harris. The CBARCs of Cannon Bay: Storm Clouds over Cannon Bay, 5 bks, Bk.3. Norris, David A. 2012. 128p. (YA). pap. 16.95 *(978-1-937493-30-1(X))* Dancing Moon Pr.

Norstrand, Torstein. Seven Wonders Book 2: Lost in Babylon. Lerangis, Peter. (Seven Wonders Ser.: 2). (ENG.). (J). (gr. 3-7). 2014. 400p. pap. 7.99 *(978-0-06-207044-9(4))*; 2013. 384p. 17.99 *(978-0-06-207043-2(6))* HarperCollins Pubs.

—Seven Wonders Book 3: the Tomb of Shadows. Lerangis, Peter. (Seven Wonders Ser.: 3). (ENG.). (J). (gr. 3-7). 2015. 368p. pap. 7.99 *(978-0-06-207047-0(9))*; 2014. 352p. 17.99 *(978-0-06-207046-3(0))* HarperCollins Pubs.

—Seven Wonders Book 4: the Curse of the King. Lerangis, Peter. (Seven Wonders Ser.: 4). (ENG.). 320p. (J). (gr. 3-7). 2016. pap. 7.99 *(978-0-06-207050-0(9))*; 2015. 17.99 *(978-0-06-207049-4(5))* HarperCollins Pubs.

—Seven Wonders Book 5: the Legend of the Rift. Lerangis, Peter. 2016. (Seven Wonders Ser.: 5). (ENG.). 448p. (J). (gr. 3-7). 17.99 *(978-0-06-207052-4(5))* HarperCollins Pubs.

Norstrand, Torstein & Reagan, Mike. Seven Wonders Book 1: the Colossus Rises, Bk. 1. Lerangis, Peter. 2013. (Seven Wonders Ser.: 1). (ENG.). 384p. (J). (gr. 3-7). pap. 7.99 *(978-0-06-207041-8(X))* HarperCollins Pubs.

Norstrand, Torstein, jt. illus. see Reagan, Mike.

North, Ryan. Dinosaur Comics. North, Ryan. 2005. 112p. 14.99 *(978-0-7560-0518-4(3))* Teacher's Discovery.

Northcott, Ed. Degrassi the Next Generation Extra Credit Suddenly, Last Summer. Torres, J. 2nd ed. 2006. (Degrassi the Next Generation Ser.). (ENG.). 128p. (J). pap. *(978-1-55168-320-1(2))* Fenn, H. B. & Co., Ltd.

Northcutt, Leslie L., jt. illus. see Taylor, David W., Jr.

Northfield, Gary. Sleeping Beauty — 100 Years Later. North, Laura. 2014. (Tadpoles: Fairytale Twists Ser.). (ENG.). 32p. (J). (gr. 1-2). *(978-0-7787-0444-7(0))*; pap. *(978-0-7787-0479-9(3))* Crabtree Publishing Co.

Northfield, Gary. Derek the Sheep. Northfield, Gary. 2009. 64p. (J). (gr. k-2). 16.95 *(978-0-7475-9424-6(4))* Bloomsbury Publishing Plc GBR. Dist: Independent Pubs. Group.

—Gary's Garden. Northfield, Gary. 2016. (ENG.). 64p. (J). (gr. 2-5). pap. 7.99 *(978-0-545-86183-0(7))* Scholastic, Inc.

—Julius Zebra: Rumble with the Romans! Northfield, Gary. 2016. (Julius Zebra Ser.: 1). (ENG.). 288p. (J). (gr. 2-5). 15.99 *(978-0-7636-7853-1(8))* Candlewick Pr.

—Julius Zebra: Battle with the Britons! Northfield, Gary. (Julius Zebra Ser.: 2). (ENG.). 288p. (J). (gr. 2-5). 2019. pap. 7.99 *(978-1-5362-0636-4(9))*; 2018. 15.99 *(978-0-7636-7854-8(6))* Candlewick Pr.

—Julius Zebra: Rumble with the Romans! Northfield, Gary. 2018. (Julius Zebra Ser.: 1). (ENG.). 288p. (J). (gr. 2-5). pap. 7.99 *(978-0-7636-9846-1(6))* Candlewick Pr.

Northrup, Jodie. A Mole's Tale. Northrup, Dawn. 2019. (ENG.). 36p. (J). 23.95 *(978-1-64300-791-5(2))*; pap. 13.95 *(978-1-64300-790-8(4))* Covenant Bks.

Nortman, Simon. Heloise Helps! Capadona, Cassie. 2018. (ENG.). 44p. (J). pap. 14.95 *(978-1-59594-622-5(5)*, Wingspan Pr.) WingSpan Publishing.

Norton, Allyssa. Momma, Buy Me a China Doll. Feierabend, John M. 2017. (First Steps in Music Ser.). (ENG.). 32p. (J). (— 1). 17.95 *(978-1-62277-226-1(1))* G I A Pubns., Inc.

Norton, Carolyn. A Kid's Multicultural Math Adventure: Amazing Activities to Explore Math's Global Roots! McCallum, Ann. 2004. (Williamson Multicultural Kids Can! Book Ser.). 128p. (J). pap. 14.95 *(978-1-885593-92-4(9)*, Ideal Pubns.) Worthy Publishing.

Norton, Dorothy S. Ice Age Mammals of North America: A Guide to the Big, the Hairy, & the Bizarre, 1 vol., Vol. 1. Lange, Ian. rev. ed. (ENG.). 224p. (J). (gr. 4). pap. *(978-0-87842-403-0(2)*, 329) Mountain Pr. Publishing Co., Inc.

Norton, Ellie. Celeste & Her Nest. Friedman, Joyce Miriam. 2018. (ENG.). 40p. (J). pap. 8.99 *(978-0-578-41520-8(8))* Joyce Miriam Friedman.

Norton, Jen. Paddy & the Wolves: A Coloring Book about St. Patrick When He Was a Boy. Nagel, Steve. 2019. (ENG.). 44p. (J). pap. 8.95 *(978-1-68192-523-3(0))* Our Sunday Visitor, Publishing Div.

Norton, Jeremy. The Crystal Caverns. Charman, Katrina. 2017. (Last Firehawk Ser.: 2). (ENG.). 96p. (J). (gr. 1-3). 15.99 *(978-1-338-12252-7(5))* Scholastic, Inc.

—The Ember Stone. Charman, Katrina. 2017. (Last Firehawk Ser.: 1). (ENG.). 96p. (J). (gr. 1-3). pap. 4.99 *(978-1-338-12213-8(4))* Scholastic, Inc.

—Lullaby Lake. Charman, Katrina. 2018. (Last Firehawk Ser.: 4). (ENG.). 96p. (J). (gr. 1-3). pap. 4.99 *(978-1-338-12267-1(3))*; lib. bdg. 24.99 *(978-1-338-12271-8(1))* Scholastic, Inc.

—The Shadowlands. Charman, Katrina. 2019. (Last Firehawk Ser.: 5). (ENG.). 96p. (J). (gr. 1-3). pap. 4.99 *(978-1-338-30711-5(8))* Scholastic, Inc.

—The Tale of Oliver Esro. McFarland, Myndie. 2017. (ENG.). 104p. (J). (gr. 3-5). pap. 12.95 *(978-0-9908136-6-8(5))* Warren Publishing, Inc.

—The Whispering Oak. Charman, Katrina. 2018. (Last Firehawk Ser.: 3). (ENG.). 96p. (J). (gr. 1-3). pap. 4.99 *(978-1-338-12255-8(X))* Scholastic, Inc.

Norton, Mike. Doom with a View! McKeever, Sean & Lee, Stan. 2007. (Spider-Man Ser.: No. 2). (ENG.). 24p. (J). (gr. 2-6). lib. bdg. 27.07 *(978-1-59961-208-9(9)*, 13620, Marvel Age) Spotlight.

—Haunted, 1 vol. Baltazar, Art & Aureliani, Franco. 2012. (Young Justice Ser.). (ENG.). 32p. (J). (gr. 3-6). lib. bdg. 22.60 *(978-1-4342-4553-3(5)*, Stone Arch Bks.) Capstone.

—Make Mine Mysterio! Lee, Stan. 2007. (Spider-Man Ser.: No. 2). (ENG.). 24p. (J). (gr. 2-6). lib. bdg. 27.07 *(978-1-59961-211-9(9)*, 13623, Marvel Age) Spotlight.

—Mega Man 5: Rock of Ages. Flynn, Ian. 2013. (Mega Man Ser.: 5). (ENG.). 104p. (J). (gr. 4-7). pap. 11.99 *(978-1-936975-48-8(3))* Archie Comic Pubns., Inc.

N

Norton, Mike & Alphona, Adrian. Runaways Vol. 7: Live Fast. 2017. 152p. (YA). (gr. 8-17). pap. 14.99 *(978-1-302-90872-0(3))* Marvel Worldwide, Inc.

Noruzi, Charlotte. Necessary Noise: Stories about Our Families as They Really Are. Cart, Michael. 2003. 256p. (J). (gr. 12-18). lib. bdg. 16.89 *(978-0-06-027500-6(6))* HarperCollins Pubs.

—Necessary Noise: Stories about Our Families As They Really Are. Cart, Michael. 2006. (ENG.). 256p. (YA). (gr. 8-12). reprint ed. pap. 9.99 *(978-0-06-051437-2(X),* HarperTeen) HarperCollins Pubs.

Noschese, Kip. The Little Penguin. Gates, Margo. 2019. (Let's Look at Animal Habitats (Pull Ahead Readers — Fiction) Ser.). (ENG.). 16p. (J). (gr. -1-1). pap. 6.99 *(978-1-5415-7308-6(0),* 9781541573086, Lerner Pubns.) Lerner Publishing Group.

—Making Tea. Gates, Margo. 2019. (Science All Around Me (Pull Ahead Readers — Fiction) Ser.). (ENG.). 16p. (J). (gr. -1-1). 22.65 *(978-1-5415-5856-4(1),* 9781541558564, Lerner Pubns.) Lerner Publishing Group.

Not, Sara. Fairy's First Day of School. Heos, Bridget. 2018. (ENG.). 32p. (J). (gr. -1-3). 17.99 *(978-1-328-71559-3(0),* 1674034, Clarion Bks.) Houghton Mifflin Harcourt Trade & Reference Pubs.

—Like Magic. Vickers, Elaine. (ENG.). (J). (gr. 3-7). 2017. 288p. pap. 7.99 *(978-0-06-241432-8(1));* 2016. 272p. 16.99 *(978-0-06-241431-1(3))* HarperCollins Pubs.

—No Tooting at Tea. Heim, Alastair. 2017. (ENG.). 40p. (J). (gr. -1-3). 16.99 *(978-0-544-77474-2(4),* 1637141, Clarion Bks.) Houghton Mifflin Harcourt Trade & Reference Pubs.

—Paper Chains. Vickers, Elaine. 2017. (ENG.). 304p. (J). (gr. 3-7). 16.99 *(978-0-06-241434-2(8))* HarperCollins Pubs.

Notaert, Amandine. On the Farm. 2018. (My First Interactive Board Book Ser.). (ENG.). 10p. (J). bds. 9.99 *(978-2-7338-5913-1(7))* Auzou, Philippe Editions FRA. Dist: Consortium Bk. Sales & Distribution.

Noto, Phil. Black Squadron: Volume 1. Soule, Charles. 2017. (Star Wars: Poe Dameron Ser.). (ENG.). 24p. (YA). (gr. 6-12). lib. bdg. 27.07 *(978-1-5321-4134-8(3),* 27007, Graphic Novels) Spotlight.

—Black Squadron: Volume 2. Soule, Charles. 2017. (Star Wars: Poe Dameron Ser.). (ENG.). 24p. (YA). (gr. 6-12). lib. bdg. 27.07 *(978-1-5321-4135-5(1),* 27008, Graphic Novels) Spotlight.

—Black Squadron: Volume 3. Soule, Charles. 2017. (Star Wars: Poe Dameron Ser.). (ENG.). 24p. (YA). (gr. 6-12). lib. bdg. 27.07 *(978-1-5321-4136-2(X),* 27009, Graphic Novels) Spotlight.

—Daredevil: Back in Black Vol. 8: The Death of Daredevil. 2019. (Daredevil: Back in Black Ser.: 8). (ENG.). 168p. (YA). (gr. 8-17). pap. 19.99 *(978-1-302-91452-3(9))* Marvel Worldwide, Inc.

—Inhumans: Once & Future Kings. 2018. (ENG.). 112p. (YA). (gr. 8-17). pap. 15.99 *(978-1-302-90940-6(1))* Marvel Worldwide, Inc.

—Journey to Star Wars: the Force Awakens Lost Stars. Gray, Claudia. 2015. (ENG.). 560p. (YA). (gr. 7-12). 17.99 *(978-1-4847-2498-9(4),* Disney Lucasfilm Press) Disney Publishing Worldwide.

—Journey to Star Wars: the Force Awakens Smuggler's Run: A Han Solo Adventure. Rucka, Greg. 2015. (ENG.). 192p. (J). (gr. 5-9). 12.99 *(978-1-4847-2495-8(X),* Disney Lucasfilm Press) Disney Publishing Worldwide.

—Journey to Star Wars: the Force Awakens the Weapon of a Jedi: A Luke Skywalker Adventure. Fry, Jason. 2015. (ENG.). 192p. (J). (gr. 5-9). 12.99 *(978-1-4847-2496-5(8),* Disney Lucasfilm Press) Disney Publishing Worldwide.

—Journey to Star Wars: the Rise of Skywalker Spark of the Resistance. Ireland, Justina. 2019. (ENG.). 224p. (J). (gr. 3-7). 16.99 *(978-1-368-05081-4(6),* Disney Lucasfilm Press) Disney Publishing Worldwide.

—Lockdown: Volume 1. Soule, Charles. 2017. (Star Wars: Poe Dameron Ser.). (ENG.). 24p. (YA). (gr. 6-12). lib. bdg. 27.07 *(978-1-5321-4137-9(8),* 27010, Graphic Novels) Spotlight.

—Lockdown: Volume 2. Soule, Charles. 2017. (Star Wars: Poe Dameron Ser.). (ENG.). 24p. (YA). (gr. 6-12). lib. bdg. 27.07 *(978-1-5321-4138-6(6),* 27011, Graphic Novels) Spotlight.

—Lockdown: Volume 3. Soule, Charles. 2017. (Star Wars: Poe Dameron Ser.). (ENG.). 24p. (YA). (gr. 6-12). lib. bdg. 27.07 *(978-1-5321-4139-3(4),* 27012, Graphic Novels) Spotlight.

—Star Wars: Before the Awakening. LucasFilm Press Staff. 2015. E-Book *(978-1-4847-3550-3(1))* Disney Publishing Worldwide.

—Star Wars the Force Awakens: Before the Awakening. Rucka, Greg. 2015. (ENG.). 224p. (J). (gr. 3-7). 12.99 *(978-1-4847-2822-2(X))* Disney Pr.

—Star Wars: the Last Jedi Cobalt Squadron. Wein, Elizabeth. 2017. (ENG.). 256p. (J). (gr. 3-7). 16.99 *(978-1-368-00837-2(2),* Disney Lucasfilm Press) Disney Publishing Worldwide.

—Star Wars Vol. 13: Rogues & Rebels. 2020. (ENG.). 120p. (YA). (gr. 4-17). pap. 17.99 *(978-1-302-92168-2(1))* Marvel Worldwide, Inc.

Noto, Phil & Del Mundo, Mike. Avengers: Unleashed Vol. 2: Secret Empire. 2017. (ENG.). 136p. (YA). (gr. 8-17). pap. 15.99 *(978-1-302-90612-2(7))* Marvel Worldwide, Inc.

Nouf, Feras. My Bonus Mom! Taking the Step Out of Stepmom. Butcher, Tami. 2011. (ENG.). 54p. (J). (gr. -1-3). 16.95 *(978-1-58985-081-1(5),* Story Monsters Pr.) Story Monsters LLC.

Nouhen, Élodie. The Magic Doll: A Children's Book Inspired by African Art. Yabouza, Adrienne. 2020. (Children's Books Inspired by Famous Artworks Ser.). (ENG.). 32p. (J). (gr. -1-3). 14.95 ***(978-3-7913-7446-8(X))*** Prestel Verlag GmbH & Co KG. DEU. Dist: Penguin Random Hse. LLC.

Nouhen, Elodie. Songs From the Baobab. 2011. (ENG.). 52p. (J). (gr. -1-k). 16.95 *(978-2-923163-79-6(6))* La Montagne Secrete CAN. Dist: Independent Pubs. Group.

Nourigat, Natalie. Debt Dangers: A Book in the Series Marvels of Money ... for Kids. Nourigat, Paul. 2012. (Marvels of Money for Kids Ser.: 4). (ENG.). 38p. (J). lib. bdg. 12.29 *(978-1-936872-03-9(X))* FarBeyond Publishing LLC.

—Earning Excitement: a book in the series Marvels of Money ... for Kids. Nourigat, Paul. 2014. (Marvels of Money for Kids Ser.: 1). 38p. (J). pap. 9.29 *(978-1-936872-21-3(8))* FarBeyond Publishing LLC.

—Earning Excitement: A Book in the Series Marvels of Money ... for Kids. Nourigat, Paul. l.t. ed. 2012. (Marvels of Money for Kids Ser.: 1). (ENG.). 38p. (J). 12.29 *(978-1-936872-01-5(3))* FarBeyond Publishing LLC.

—Giving Greatness: A Book in the Series Marvels of Money ... for Kids. Nourigat, Paul. 2012. (Marvels of Money for Kids Ser.: 3). (ENG.). 38p. (J). lib. bdg. 12.29 *(978-1-936872-04-6(8))* FarBeyond Publishing LLC.

—Spending Success: A Book in the Series Marvels of Money ... for Kids. Nourigat, Paul. 2014. (Marvels of Money for Kids Ser.: 2). 38p. (J). pap. *(978-1-936872-22-0(6))* FarBeyond Publishing LLC.

—Terrific Tools for Money: A Book in the Series Marvels of Money ... for Kids. Nourigat, Paul. 2012. (Marvels of Money for Kids Ser.: 5). (ENG.). 38p. (J). lib. bdg. 12.89 *(978-1-936872-05-3(6))* FarBeyond Publishing LLC.

Nourigat, Natalie Marie. Wrapped up in You: Book 6, No. 6. Jolley, Dan. 2012. (My Boyfriend Is a Monster Ser.: 6). (ENG.). 128p. (YA). (gr. 7-12). pap. 9.95 *(978-0-8225-9425-3(0),* 9780822594253, Graphic Universe™) Lerner Publishing Group.

Novak, Matt. No Zombies Allowed. Novak, Matt. 2014. (ENG.). 32p. (J). (gr. -1-1). 16.99 *(978-1-4814-2540-7(4),* Atheneum Bks. for Young Readers) Simon & Schuster Children's Publishing.

—A Wish for You. Novak, Matt. 2010. 32p. (J). 16.99 *(978-0-06-155202-1(5),* Greenwillow Bks.) HarperCollins Pubs.

Novak, Steven. A Caring Deed for Becky. Widgen, Susan. 2012. 36p. pap. 8.99 *(978-1-60820-579-0(7))* MLR Pr., LLC.

Novi, Nathalie. Songs in the Shade of the Olive Tree. Favret, Hafida & Lerasle, Magdeleine. 2012. (ENG.). 52p. (J). (gr. -1-k). 16.95 *(978-2-923163-84-0(2))* La Montagne Secrete CAN. Dist: Independent Pubs. Group.

Novicky Martinez, Joyce. The Ball That Wouldn't Bounce. Novicky Martinez, Joyce. 2018. (ENG.). 28p. (J). (gr. k-3). pap. 10.00 *(978-0-9817244-8-5(5))* Dyeing Arts.

Novoa, Teresa. Azul. (Cocorolos Ser.). (SPA.). 12p. (J). (gr. -1-k). bds. 7.95 *(978-84-294-6923-3(0))* Santillana USA Publishing Co., Inc.

—Rojo. (Cocorolos Ser.). (SPA.). 12p. (J). (gr. -1-k). bds. 7.95 *(978-84-294-6921-9(4))* Santillana USA Publishing Co., Inc.

Novy & Waltch. Knights Club: the Message of Destiny: The Comic Book You Can Play. Shuky. 2019. (Comic Quests Ser.: 4). 184p. (J). (gr. 3-7). pap. 9.99 *(978-1-68369-065-8(6))* Quirk Bks.

Novy, jt. illus. see Waltch.

Novytska, Iryna. Name That Animal. Tye, Noah. 2018. (ENG.). 32p. (J). pap. 16.99 *(978-1-5320-5732-8(6))* iUniverse, Inc.

Nowak, Carolyn & Sotuyo, Ayme. Lumberjanes: to the Max Vol. 5. Leyh, Kat. 2019. (Lumberjanes Ser.). (ENG.). 256p. (YA). (gr. 4-7). 39.99 *(978-1-68415-312-1(3))* Boom! Studios.

Nowak, Cheri. The Horseshoe. Nelson, Suzanne. 2012. (J). 14.95 *(978-1-937406-49-3(0))* Mascot Bks., Inc.

Nowakoski, Marcin & Lovero, Ernesto. Battles of World War II: Bridges Edition. Burgan, Michael. 2015. (Prime Plus Ser.). (YA). (gr. 6-8). pap. *(978-1-4900-1953-6(7))* Benchmark Education Co.

—Battles of World War II: Bridges Edition Set of 6 with Common Core Indicators. Burgan, Michael. 2015. (Prime Plus Ser.). (YA). (gr. 6-8). 69.00 net. *(978-1-4900-2049-5(7))* Benchmark Education Co.

Nowakowski, Marcin. The Night Before Christmas. Moore, Clement C. 2019. (J). bds. 9.99 *(978-1-950416-16-5(X))* Little Hippo Bks.

Nowakowski, Voytek. Flight of the Outcasts, 1 vol., 2. McGrath, Alister. 2012. (Aedyn Chronicles Ser.). (ENG.). 176p. (J). (gr. 4-7). 16.95 *(978-0-310-71813-0(9))* Zondervan.

Nowicka, Agata. First Generation: 36 Trailblazing Immigrants & Refugees Who Make America Great. Neil Wallace, Sandra & Wallace, Rich. 2018. 96p. (J). (gr. 3-7). 18.99 *(978-0-316-51524-5(8))* Little, Brown Bks. for Young Readers.

Nowlan, Kevin, et al. Doctor Strange Vol. 2. 2018. (Doctor Strange (2015) HC Ser.: 2). (ENG.). 272p. (YA). (gr. 8-17). 34.99 *(978-1-302-90937-3(0))* Marvel Worldwide, Inc.

Nowowiejska, Kasia. Cheep Cheep Pop-Up Fun. Litton, Jonathan. 2015. (Little Snappers Ser.). (ENG.). 10p. (J). (-k). bds. 9.99 *(978-1-58925-549-4(6))* Tiger Tales.

—Dinosaurs: A Busy Sticker Activity Book. Stansbie, Stephanie. 2016. (Little Snappers Ser.). (ENG.). 96p. (J). (gr. -1-2). 9.99 *(978-1-58925-319-3(1))* Tiger Tales.

—Farm Fun: A Busy Sticker Activity Book. Stansbie, Stephanie. 2016. (Little Snappers Ser.). (ENG.). 96p. (J). (gr. -1-2). 9.99 *(978-1-58925-318-6(3))* Tiger Tales.

—Hoot Hoot Pop-Up Fun. Edwards, Nicola. 2018. (Little Snappers Ser.). (ENG.). 10p. (J). (gr. -1-k). bds. 9.99 *(978-1-68010-542-1(6))* Tiger Tales.

—Little Duckling's Easter Prayers, 1 vol. Zondervan Staff. 2020. 30p. (J). bds. 9.99 *(978-0-310-76835-7(7))* Zonderkidz.

—Peek-Through Forest. Litton, Jonathan. 2015. (Little Snappers Ser.). (ENG.). 12p. (J). (gr. -1-k). bds. 9.99 *(978-1-68010-508-7(6))* Tiger Tales.

—Peek-Through Jungle. Litton, Jonathan. 2015. (Little Snappers Ser.). (ENG.). 12p. (J). (gr. -1-k). bds. 9.99 *(978-1-68010-504-9(3))* Tiger Tales.

—Phones Keep Us Connected. Zoehfeld, Kathleen Weidner. 2017. (Let's-Read-And-Find-Out Science 2 Ser.). (ENG.). 40p. (J). (gr. -1-3). pap. 6.99 *(978-0-06-238667-0(0))* HarperCollins Pubs.

—Ready to Be Responsible. Simon, Jenne. 2016. 32p. (J). *(978-1-338-03338-0(7))* Scholastic, Inc.

—A Roar of Respect. Simon, Jenne. 2016. 32p. (J). pap. *(978-1-338-03341-0(7))* Scholastic, Inc.

—Snip Snap Pop-Up Fun. Litton, Jonthan. 2015. (Little Snappers Ser.). (ENG.). 10p. (J). (-k). bds. 9.99 *(978-1-58925-548-7(8))* Tiger Tales.

—Splish Splash Pop-Up Fun. Litton, Jonathan. 2016. (Little Snappers Ser.). (ENG.). 10p. (J). (gr. -1-k). bds. 9.99 *(978-1-58925-259-2(4))* Tiger Tales.

—To Dad, with Love. 2018. (Special Delivery Bks.). (ENG.). 8p. (J). (— 1). bds. 6.49 *(978-1-68412-269-1(4),* Silver Dolphin Bks.) Printers Row Publishing Group.

—Zoo. Garnett, Jaye. Cottage Door Press, ed. 2019. (SPA.). 12p. (J). (gr. -1-1). bds. 8.99 *(978-1-68052-844-2(0),* 1001190-SLA) Cottage Door Pr.

—Zoo: Chunky Peek a Flap Board Book. Garnett, Jaye. Cottage Door Press, ed. 2016. (Peek a Flap Ser.). (ENG.). 12p. (J). (gr. -1-1). bds. 8.99 *(978-1-68052-126-9(8),* 1001190) Cottage Door Pr.

Nowowiejska, Kasia & Steuerwald, Joy. Peek a Flap Zoo & Moo 2 Pack: Chunky Peek a Flap Board Book 2 Pack. Garnett, Jaye. Cottage Door Press, ed. 2016. (Peek a Flap Ser.). (ENG.). (J). (gr. -1-k). bds. 17.98 *(978-1-68052-170-2(5),* 9000520) Cottage Door Pr.

Noy, Violeta. The Right One for Roderic. Noy, Violeta. 2019. (ENG.). 40p. (J). (gr. k-2). 16.99 *(978-1-5362-0572-5(9),* Templar) Candlewick Pr.

Noyes, Deborah. African Acrostics: A Word in Edgeways. Noyes, Deborah, photos by. Harley, Avis. 2012. 40p. (J). (gr. 2-5). 21.19 *(978-0-7636-3621-0(5))* Candlewick Pr.

—African Acrostics: A Word in Edgeways. Noyes, Deborah, photos by. Harley, Avis. ed. 2012. lib. bdg. 18.40 *(978-0-606-23808-3(5))* Turtleback.

Noyes, Deborah, photos by. African Acrostics: A Word in Edgeways. Harley, Avis. 2012. 40p. (J). (gr. 3-7). pap. 7.99 *(978-0-7636-5818-2(9))* Candlewick Pr.

Noyes, Diana. The Tickle Bug. Noyes, Diana. l.t. ed. 2005. 20p. (J). per. 9.99 *(978-1-59879-080-1(3))* Lifevest Publishing, Inc.

Noyes, Eli. From Wibbleton to Wobbleton: Adventures with the Elements of Music & Movement. Harding, James. 2014. (Pentatonic Press Integrated Learning Ser.: 3). (ENG.). 201p. pap. 32.00 *(978-0-9773712-5-9(5))* Pentatonic Pr.

Noyes, Leighton. Alone in the Arctic. Bailey, Gerry. 2014. (Science to the Rescue Ser.). (ENG.). 32p. (J). (gr. 4-4). *(978-0-7787-0428-7(9))* Crabtree Publishing Co.

—Bubbles in the Bathroom. Martineau, Susan. 2011. (Everyday Science Experiments Ser.). (ENG.). 24p. (J). (gr. 3-6). pap. 10.60 *(978-1-61533-409-4(2));* lib. bdg. 28.25 *(978-1-61533-371-4(1))* Windmill Bks.

—Bugs in the Garden. Martineau, Susan. 2011. (Everyday Science Experiments Ser.). (ENG.). 24p. (J). (gr. 3-6). pap. 10.60 *(978-1-61533-408-7(4));* lib. bdg. 28.25 *(978-1-61533-370-7(3))* Windmill Bks.

—Caught in the Rapids. Law, Felicia & Bailey, Gerry. 2015. (Science to the Rescue Ser.). (ENG.). 32p. (J). (gr. 4-4). *(978-0-7787-1674-7(0))* Crabtree Publishing Co.

—Dry in the Desert. Bailey, Gerry. 2014. (Science to the Rescue Ser.). (ENG.). 32p. (J). (gr. 4-4). *(978-0-7787-0429-4(7))* Crabtree Publishing Co.

—Escape from the Volcano. Law, Felicia & Bailey, Gerry. 2015. (Science to the Rescue Ser.). (ENG.). 32p. (J). (gr. 4-4). *(978-0-7787-1675-4(9))* Crabtree Publishing Co.

—Fizz in the Kitchen. Martineau, Susan. 2011. (Everyday Science Experiments Ser.). (ENG.). 24p. (J). (gr. 3-6). pap. 10.60 *(978-1-61533-411-7(4),* 1328714); lib. bdg. 28.25 *(978-1-61533-373-8(8),* 1328714) Windmill Bks.

—Julius Caesar's Sandals. Bailey, Gerry & Foster, Karen. 2008. (Stories of Great People Ser.). (ENG.). 40p. (J). (gr. 3-6). pap. *(978-0-7787-3717-9(9));* lib. bdg. *(978-0-7787-3695-0(4))* Crabtree Publishing Co.

—Lost in the Cave. Law, Felicia & Bailey, Gerry. 2015. (Science to the Rescue Ser.). (ENG.). 32p. (J). (gr. 4-4). *(978-0-7787-1677-8(5))* Crabtree Publishing Co.

—Shadows in the Bedroom. Martineau, Susan. 2011. (Everyday Science Experiments Ser.). (ENG.). 24p. (J). (gr. 3-6). pap. 10.60 *(978-1-61533-410-0(6));* lib. bdg. 28.25 *(978-1-61533-372-1(X))* Windmill Bks.

—Stranded on an Island. Bailey, Gerry. 2014. (Science to the Rescue Ser.). (ENG.). 32p. (J). (gr. 4-4). *(978-0-7787-0430-0(0))* Crabtree Publishing Co.

—Swept Away by the Storm. Bailey, Gerry. 2014. (Science to the Rescue Ser.). (ENG.). 32p. (J). (gr. 4-4). *(978-0-7787-0431-7(9))* Crabtree Publishing Co.

—Tangled in the Rainforest. Bailey, Gerry. 2014. (Science to the Rescue Ser.). (ENG.). 32p. (J). (gr. 4-4). *(978-0-7787-0432-4(7))* Crabtree Publishing Co.

—Trapped on the Rock. Bailey, Gerry. 2014. (Science to the Rescue Ser.). (ENG.). 32p. (J). (gr. 4-4). *(978-0-7787-0433-1(5))* Crabtree Publishing Co.

—Trouble in Space. Law, Felicia & Bailey, Gerry. 2015. (Science to the Rescue Ser.). (ENG.). 32p. (J). (gr. 4-4). *(978-0-7787-1676-1(7))* Crabtree Publishing Co.

Noyes, Leighton & Radford, Karen. Galileo's Telescope. Bailey, Gerry & Foster, Karen. 2008. (Stories of Great People Ser.). (ENG.). 40p. (J). (gr. 3-6). lib. bdg. *(978-0-7787-3694-3(6));* pap. *(978-0-7787-3716-2(0))* Crabtree Publishing Co.

—Mozart's Wig. Bailey, Gerry & Foster, Karen. 2008. (Stories of Great People Ser.). (ENG.). 40p. (J). (gr. 3-6). lib. bdg. *(978-0-7787-3696-7(2))* Crabtree Publishing Co.

—Queen Victoria's Diamond. Bailey, Gerry & Foster, Karen. 2008. (Stories of Great People Ser.). (ENG.). 40p. (J). (gr. 3-6). lib. bdg. *(978-0-7787-3697-4(0));* pap. *(978-0-7787-3719-3(5))* Crabtree Publishing Co.

Noyes, Leighton, jt. illus. see Radford, Karen.

Noze, Patrick. Dassi's World. Nicolas, Hadascha. 2020. (ENG.). 32p. (J). 22.95 ***(978-1-948877-50-3(3))*** Watersprings Media Hse.

Nsorma, Ammar. I Am a Boy of Color. Singh, Deanna. 2016. (ENG.). (J). (gr. k-6). 19.99 *(978-1-943331-21-5(9))* Orange Hat Publishing.

Nugent, Cynthia. The Emerald Curse, 1 vol. Rose, Simon. 384th ed. 2006. (ENG.). 96p. (J). (gr. 4-7). per. 7.95 *(978-1-896580-90-6(4))* Tradewind Bks. CAN. Dist: Orca Bk. Pubs. USA.

—I Want to Go to the Moon. Saunders, Tom. 2012. 32p. (J). (gr. -1-2). 16.95 *(978-1-897476-56-7(6))* Simply Read Bks. CAN. Dist: Ingram Publisher Services.

—Kiddo, 1 vol. 2019. (ENG.). 148p. (J). (gr. 4-7). pap. 10.95 *(978-1-896580-66-1(1))* Tradewind Bks. CAN. Dist: Orca Bk. Pubs. USA.

—A Time to Be Brave. Stuchner, Joan Betty. 2014. (Stepping Stone Book(TM) Ser.). (ENG.). 112p. (J). (gr. 2-5). 4.99 *(978-0-385-39205-1(2),* Random Hse. Bks. for Young Readers) Random Hse. Children's Bks.

Nugent, Suzanne. Cup of Death. Gilligan, Shannon. 2007. (Choose Your Own Adventure Ser.). (ENG.). 144p. (J). (gr. 4-8). per. 7.99 *(978-1-933390-70-3(0))* Chooseco LLC.

—Inca Gold: Choose Your Own Adventure #20. Becket, Jim. 2007. (Choose Your Own Adventure Ser.: 20). (ENG.). 144p. (J). (gr. 4-8). per. 7.99 *(978-1-933390-20-8(4),* CHCL20) Chooseco LLC.

—Secret of the Ninja. Leibold, Jay. 2006. (Choose Your Own Adventure Ser.: 16). (ENG.). 144p. (J). (gr. 4-8). per. 7.99 *(978-1-933390-16-1(6))* Chooseco LLC.

Nugent, Suzanne & Donploypetch, Jintanan. Search for the Mountain Gorillas. Wallace, Jim. 2008. (Choose Your Own Adventure Ser.: 25). (ENG.). 144p. (J). (gr. 4-8). pap. 7.99 *(978-1-933390-25-3(5))* Chooseco LLC.

Nugraha. What Makes My Dad Special? Selbherr, C. 2019. (ENG.). 34p. (J). (gr. k-4). *(978-3-947677-09-2(X))* Selbherr. , Charlotte Harlescott Bks.

Nugraha, Rizky. Diary of a Minecraft Herobrine: Minecraft Herobrine Books. Herobrine, Lord. 2018. (Minecraft Herobrine Adventures Ser.: Vol. 1). (ENG.). 208p. (J). pap. 9.95 *(978-1-927558-70-6(0))* Birch Tree Publishing.

—Diary of Farty Philip. Birch, Kiri a. 2017. (ENG.). (J). pap. 8.00 *(978-1-927558-61-4(1))* Birch Tree Publishing.

—Diary of Steve the Minecraft Zombie. Kid, Zombie. 2017. (ENG.). 62p. (J). pap. 8.00 *(978-1-927558-66-9(2))* Birch Tree Publishing.

—Herobrine's Army Battle of the Great Sea Zombies. Herobrine, Lord. 2017. (ENG.). (J). pap. 13.00 *(978-1-927558-63-8(8))* Birch Tree Publishing.

Nugroho, Wahyu. Floating Away: A Book to Help Children Understand Addiction. Bauman, Andrew J. 2019. (ENG.). 38p. (J). pap. 9.49 ***(978-1-0725-4472-2(5))*** Independently Published.

Nugumanova, Aigul. Papa Said Don't Say Fat, Say Big! Okeyo, Joseph Odundo. 2018. (ENG.). 62p. (J). pap. 12.99 *(978-1-7904-8745-5(5))* Independently Published.

Numberman, Neil. Flip & Fin: Super Sharks to the Rescue! Gill, Timothy. 2016. (ENG.). 32p. (J). (gr. -1-3). 15.99 *(978-0-06-224301-0(2),* Greenwillow Bks.) HarperCollins Pubs.

—Flip & Fin: We Rule the School! Gill, Timothy. 2014. (ENG.). 32p. (J). (gr. -1-3). 14.99 *(978-0-06-224300-3(4),* Greenwillow Bks.) HarperCollins Pubs.

Numberman, Neil, jt. illus. see Weaver, Brian M.

Nunez, Jose Luis. Cuando Mi Mama Me Lee/When My Mama Reads to Me. Elkus, Julie. Fagin, Cristina, tr. from ENG. 2005. (SPA & ENG.). 24p. (J). (gr. -1-3). 8.95 *(978-1-933197-06-7(4))* Orange Frazer Pr.

Núñez, Pablo. El Guardian de la Luna. Núñez, Pablo, tr. Sierra i Fabra, Jordi. (SPA.). 80p. 15.95 *(978-84-207-6282-1(2))* Grupo Anaya, S.A. ESP. Dist: Distribooks, Inc.

Nuñez, Ruddy. El Mejor Regalo del Mundo; The Best Gift of All: La Leyenda de la Vieja Belen; The Legend of La Vieja Belen. Alvarez, Julia. Espaillat, Rhina P., tr. 2009. (Bilingual Bks). (SPA & ENG.). 32p. (gr. 3-5). 14.99 *(978-1-60396-325-1(1))* Santillana USA Publishing Co., Inc.

Nunn, Duane. I Am Brave, I Am Bold. Fenwick, James. 2019. (ENG.). 34p. (J). pap. 9.99 ***(978-1-6864-1390-2(4))*** Independently Published.

—Pepon the Pumpkin. Fenwick, James. 2019. (ENG.). 40p. (J). pap. 9.99 ***(978-1-6978-9348-9(1))*** Independently Published.

Nunn Iba, Patty. Come with Me, Together We'll See the Beauty of ... Hawaii. Fung, Jeannie & Madison. 2016. (ENG.). (J). pap. 12.99 *(978-0-578-18737-2(X))* Kung, Jeannie M.

Nunn, Paul, jt. illus. see Random House Staff.

Nunn, Paul E. Firefighter Gil! (Bubble Guppies) Tillworth, Mary. 2013. (Pictureback(R) Ser.). (ENG.). 24p. (J). (gr. -1-2). 4.99 *(978-0-449-81770-4(9),* Random Hse. Bks. for Young Readers) Random Hse. Children's Bks.

—Planters & Cultivators: With Casey & Friends. Dufek, Holly. 2016. (Casey & Friends Ser.: 4). (ENG.). 32p. (J). (gr. k-3). 14.99 *(978-1-937747-55-8(7))* Octane Pr.

—Uncle Arthur's Art Studio. Forrester, Emma. 2008. (Spiderwick Chronicles). (ENG.). 48p. (J). (gr. 2-7). 10.99 *(978-1-4169-4955-8(0),* Simon Scribbles) Simon Scribbles.

—A Year on the Farm: With Casey & Friends. Dufek, Holly. 2nd ed. 2015. (Casey & Friends Ser.: 1). (ENG.). 32p. (J). (gr. k-3). 14.99 *(978-1-937747-56-5(5))* Octane Pr.

Nunn, Paul E. A Year on the Farm: with Casey & Friends: With Casey & Friends. Dufek, Holly. 2020. (Casey & Friends Ser.: 1). (ENG.). 32p. (J). (gr. k-3). pap. 14.99 ***(978-1-64234-032-7(4))*** Octane Pr.

Nunn, Paul E. & Kasun, Mike. Busy on the Farm: With Casey & Friends, 7 vols. Dufek, Holly. 2017. (Casey & Friends Ser.: 6). (ENG.). 32p. (J). (gr. k-3). 14.99 *(978-1-937747-79-4(4))* Octane Pr.

Nunnally, Carson. How Sparkles Came About: The Adventures of Sparkles. Wellings, Chris R. 2011. 32p. pap. 24.95 *(978-1-4560-4119-9(3))* America Star Bks.

Nuovo, Avalon. Ancient Wonders. Volant, Iris. 2019. (ENG.). 64p. (J). (gr. 2). 19.95 *(978-1-912497-91-1(3))* Flying Eye Bks. GBR. Dist: Penguin Random Hse. LLC.

Nuovo, Avalon. Ancient Wonders (Literati Edition) Volant, Iris. 2019. (ENG.). 64p. (J). (gr. 2). 19.95 ***(978-1-83874-025-2(2))*** Flying Eye Bks. GBR. Dist: Penguin Random Hse. LLC.

Nurullah, Sawsan. Ahlam an Akun Tahyan. Tahir, Samar. 2018. (ARA.). 24p. (J). (978-614-03-2017-8(8)) Dar al saqi.
Nurullah, Seitu. Froggie Sang Tenor. Fogerty, Ramona. 2005. (FRE.). (J). per. 15.00 (978-0-9759889-0-9(5)) Potenial Psychotherapy Counseling & Remedial Service.
Nutt, Robert. Amy's Light. Nutt, Robert. 2010. (ENG.). 44p. (J). (gr. -1-3). 16.95 (978-1-58469-128-0(X)); pap. 8.95 (978-1-58469-129-7(8)) Sourcebooks, Inc. (Dawn Pubns.).
Nuytten, Bobbie. Fingerprint Animals. Nuytten, Bobbie. 2016. (Fun with Fingerprints Ser.). (ENG.). 24p. (J). (gr. -1-2). lib. bdg. 27.32 (978-1-4795-8687-5(0), Picture Window Bks.) Capstone.
—Fingerprint Bugs. Nuytten, Bobbie. 2016. (Fun with Fingerprints Ser.). (ENG.). 24p. (J). (gr. -1-2). lib. bdg. 27.32 (978-1-4795-8684-4(6), Picture Window Bks.) Capstone.
—Fingerprint Characters. Nuytten, Bobbie. 2016. (Fun with Fingerprints Ser.). (ENG.). 24p. (J). (gr. -1-2). lib. bdg. 27.32 (978-1-4795-8685-1(4), Picture Window Bks.) Capstone.
—Fingerprint Vehicles. Nuytten, Bobbie. 2016. (Fun with Fingerprints Ser.). (ENG.). 24p. (J). (gr. -1-2). lib. bdg. 27.32 (978-1-4795-8686-8(2), Picture Window Bks.) Capstone.
Nuyttens, Joseph Pierre. Azalea at Sunset Gap (Illustrated Edition) Peattie, Elia Wilkinson. 2017. (ENG.). (J). pap. (978-1-4068-8543-9(6)) Echo Library.
Nuzzo, Valentina. Carrie Can't Choose a Costume. Hardin, Joy. 2019. (Choosy Carrie Bks.: Vol. 1). (ENG.). 34p. (J). pap. 9.13 (978-1-6962-9203-0(4)) Independently Published.
Nyamor, Eric. The Adventures of Princess Zari. Pope, Cheryl Lynn. 2009. 34p. pap. 12.99 (978-0-9840660-1-8(2)) Second Time Media & Communications.
—Choices: Upper Elementary. Jackson, Sharinese. 2010. 112p. pap. 12.95 (978-0-9840660-3-2(9)) Second Time Media & Communications.
Nye, Barbara. Somewhere a Bell Is Ringing. Nye, Barbara. 2018. 48p. (J). 16.95 (978-0-9987999-2-6(0)) Penny Candy Bks., LLC.
Nye, Penny. My Kindergarten Year. 2003. 41p. (J). spiral bd. 7.00 net. (978-1-890703-33-2(8), Bookmates) Penny Laine Papers, Inc.
Nyeu, Tao. Mamas' Kisses. McMullan, Kate. 2017. 40p. (J). (-k). 16.99 (978-0-525-42832-9(1), Dial Bks) Penguin Young Readers Group.
Nyeusi Mawazo, Kelvin. Black Sun: The Longest Night (Book 01 - Invasion) Nyeusi Mawazo, Kelvin. 2018. (ENG.). 38p. (YA). pap. (978-0-9958185-4-5(1)) Black Sun Comics.
Nyhus, Svein. Angryman. Dahle, Gro. 2019. (ENG.). 48p. (J). (gr. 2-6). 17.95 (978-0-7358-4340-0(6)) North-South Bks., Inc.
—What Does the Fox Say? Løchstøer, Christian et al. 2013. (ENG.). 32p. (J). (gr. -1-3). 17.99 (978-1-4814-2223-9(5), Simon & Schuster Bks. For Young Readers) Simon & Schuster Bks. For Young Readers.
—Why Kings & Queens Don't Wear Crowns. Louise, Martha. Sevig-Fajardo, Mari Elise, tr. from NOR. 2005. Orig. Title: Hvorfor de kongelige ikke har krone på Hodet. 32p. (J). 17.95 (978-1-57534-037-1(2), CSC 100) Skandisk, Inc.
—Why Kings & Queens Don't Wear Crowns (with CD) Märtha Louise, Princess. Sevig-Fajardo, Mari Elise, tr. from NOR. 2006. Orig. Title: Fvorfor de kongelige ikke har krone på Hodet. 32p. (J). 19.95 incl. audio compact disk (978-1-57534-038-8(0), CSC 100C) Skandisk, Inc.
Nyman, Ingrid. Do You Know Pippi Longstocking? Lindgren, Astrid. Dyssegaard, Elisabeth Kallick, tr. 2005. 32p. (J). pap. 4.95 (978-91-29-66203-0(6)) R & S Bks. SWE. Dist: Macmillan.
Nyquist, Eric. Children of the Different. Flynn, Stuart. 2016. (ENG.). (J). pap. (978-0-9543118-6-5(8)) Agape Publications.
Nytra, David. The Secret of the Stone Frog. Nytra, David. 2012. (Leah & Alan Adventures Ser.). (ENG.). 80p. (J). (gr. 2-7). 16.95 (978-1-935179-18-4(7)) TOON Books / RAW Junior, LLC.

O

O' Hare, Michael. The Man Called Electro! Lee, Stan. 2006. (Spider-Man Ser.: No. 1). (ENG.). 24p. (J). (gr. 2-6). 27.07 (978-1-59961-021-4(3), 13616, Marvel Age) Spotlight.
Oakey, James, jt. illus. see Oakey, Tristan.
Oakey, Tristan & Oakey, James. From the Depths of Vispa. Oakey, E. E. 2018. (Gallant Saga Ser.: Vol. 1). (ENG.). 274p. (J). (gr. 4-6). pap. (978-0-9876441-0-7(6)) E E Oakey.
Oanta, Sorina. Where Is Joni? Porter, Gregory L. 2019. (ENG.). 28p. (J). pap. 14.99 (978-1-7970-0802-8(1)) Independently Published.
Oapos, Jem, jt. illus. see Bronte, Jules.
Oatman, M. Scott. He Said Yes: The Story of Father Mychal Judge. Lynch, Kelly Ann. 2007. 32p. (J). (gr. -1-3). 12.95 (978-0-8091-6740-1(9), 6740-1) Paulist Pr.
Oback, Sonia, jt. illus. see Brooks, Mark.
Obata, Claudia. The Lion's Drum: A Retelling of an African Folk Tale. Gregory, Steven. 2007. 32p. (J). 13.95 (978-0-615-15540-1(5)) Words & Music.
Obata, Takeshi. Death Note, Vol. 1, 13 vols. Ohba, Tsugumi. 2005. (Death Note Ser.: 1). (ENG.). 200p. pap. 9.99 (978-1-4215-0168-0(6)) Viz Media.
—Death Note, Vol. 2, 13 vols. Ohba, Tsugumi. 2005. (Death Note Ser.: 2). (ENG.). 200p. pap. 9.99 (978-1-4215-0169-7(4)) Viz Media.
—Death Note, Vol. 3, 13 vols. Ohba, Tsugumi. 2006. (Death Note Ser.: 3). (ENG.). 200p. pap. 9.99 (978-1-4215-0170-3(8)) Viz Media.
—Death Note, Vol. 6, 12 vols. Ohba, Tsugumi. 2006. (Death Note Ser.: 6). (ENG.). 224p. pap. 9.99 (978-1-4215-0627-2(0)) Viz Media.
—Death Note, Vol. 7, 12 vols. Ohba, Tsugumi. 2006. (Death Note Ser.: 7). (ENG.). 216p. pap. 9.99 (978-1-4215-0628-9(9)) Viz Media.
Obenhaus, Grace, et al. The Fire & the Trial. 2019. (Torch in the Empire Ser.: Vol. 1). (ENG.). 218p. (J). pap. 10.00 (978-1-0912-7357-3(X)) Independently Published.
—The Invisible Guide. 2018. (ENG.). 180p. (J). pap. 10.00 (978-1-7260-2902-5(6)) CreateSpace Independent Publishing Platform.
Ober, Jonathan & Willoughby, Yuko. John & Betty Stam: Missionary Martyrs to China. Weitzel, Karen E. 2008. (ENG.). 52p. (J). pap. (978-1-932381-12-2(0), 5190) Bible Visuals International, Inc.
Ober, Jonathan, jt. illus. see Hertzler, Frances B.
Ober, Jules & Coonan, Felicity. The Good Son: A Story from the First World War, Told in Miniature. Ober, Pierre-Jacques. 2019. (ENG.). 104p. (YA). (gr. 9). 22.00 (978-1-5362-0482-7(X)) Candlewick Pr.
Oberdieck, Bernhard & Olafsdottir, Linda. The Princess & the Pea. Cech, John & Namm, Diane. 2015. (Classic Fairy Tale Collection). 32p. (J). (gr. -1-2). pap. 6.95 (978-1-4549-1678-9(8)) Sterling Publishing Co., Inc.
Oberlin, Linda. Eco in the Garden. Oberlin, Linda. 2013. 26p. pap. 10.00 (978-0-9911382-0-3(1)) Little Worm Publishing.
Obraztsova, Darya. The Adventure of Rufus the Unicorn: Short Story with Moral Lesson, Fantasy Book for Kids of All Ages, Story about a Unicorn. Cooper, Amby. 2019. (ENG.). 26p. (J). pap. 9.99 (978-1-0759-2905-2(9)) Independently Published.
Obraztsova, Darya. Boy's Best Friend: A Story about a Boy & His Best Friend, Bedtime Stories for Preschoolers, Children's Dog Story Book, Puppy Lover's Book. Cooper, Amby. 2019. (ENG.). 26p. (J). pap. 9.99 (978-1-6872-7431-1(2)) Independently Published.
Obregón, José María. Cambio Climático: Los Gases de Efecto Invernadero y la Capa de Ozono. Faust, Daniel R. 2009. (Historietas Juveniles: Peligros del medio ambiente Ser.). (SPA.). 24p. (gr. 3-6). (YA). lib. bdg. 27.25 (978-1-4358-8462-5(0)); pap. 10.60 (978-1-4358-8463-2(9)) Rosen Publishing Group, Inc., The.
Obregon, Jose Maria. Mitologia Egipcia: Isis y Osiris. Daning, Tom. 2009. (Historietas Juveniles: Mitologías (Jr. Graphic Mythologies) Ser.). (SPA.). 24p. (J). (gr. 3-6). lib. bdg. 27.25 (978-1-4358-8567-7(8)) Rosen Publishing Group, Inc., The.
—Mitología Africana: Anansi. Herdling, Glenn. 2009. (Historietas Juveniles: Mitologías (Jr. Graphic Mythologies) Ser.). (SPA.). 24p. (J). (gr. 3-6). 27.25 (978-1-4358-8565-3(1)) Rosen Publishing Group, Inc., The.
Obregón, José María. Mitologia Mesoamericana: Quetzalcóatl. Daning, Tom. 2009. (Historietas Juveniles: Mitologías (Jr. Graphic Mythologies) Ser.). (SPA.). 24p. (J). (gr. 3-6). lib. bdg. 27.25 (978-1-4358-8569-1(4)) Rosen Publishing Group, Inc., The.
—Mitologia Romana: Rómulo y Remo. Daning, Tom. 2009. (Historietas Juveniles: Mitologías (Jr. Graphic Mythologies) Ser.). (SPA.). 24p. (J). (gr. 3-6). lib. bdg. 27.25 (978-1-4358-8570-7(8)) Rosen Publishing Group, Inc., The.
Obrero, Rudy. Sweet Dreams, Curious George. Anderson, R. P. 2005. (J). (gr. -1-k). pap. (978-0-618-69493-8(5)) Houghton Mifflin Harcourt Trade & Reference Pubs.
O'Brien, Anne Sibley. Flower Garden. Havill, Juanita. 2015. 32p. pap. 7.00 (978-1-61003-503-3(8)) Center for the Collaborative Classroom.
—Jamaica Tag-Along, 1 vol. Havill, Juanita. 2011. (ENG.). 32p. (J). (gr. -1-3). 10.99 (978-0-547-48105-0(5), 1439408) Houghton Mifflin Harcourt Publishing Co.
—Jamaica's Blue Marker. Havill, Juanita. 2003. (ENG.). 32p. (J). (gr. -1-3). pap. 7.99 (978-0-618-36917-1(1), 487457) Houghton Mifflin Harcourt Publishing Co.
—Jamaica's Blue Marker. Havill, Juanita. 2003. (ENG.). (J). (gr. -1-3). lib. bdg. 17.60 (978-1-68065-099-0(8)) Perfection Learning Corp.
—Jamaica's Find. Havill, Juanita. 2009. (ENG.). 32p. (J). (gr. -1-3). 10.99 (978-0-547-11961-8(5), 1047233) Houghton Mifflin Harcourt Publishing Co.
—Jouanah: A Hmong Cinderella. Coburn, Jewell Reinhart & Lee, Tzexa Cherta. 2014. (ENG.). 32p. (J). pap. 11.95 (978-1-885008-41-1(4), Shen's Bks.) Lee & Low Bks., Inc.
—Talking Walls. Knight, Margy Burns. 2004. 34p. (gr. 3-8). 19.45 (978-0-7569-4256-4(X)) Perfection Learning Corp.
—Talking Walls: Discover Your World, 1 vol. Knight, Margy Burns. 2014. (ENG.). 64p. (J). (gr. 2-7). 18.95 (978-0-88448-356-4(8), 884356) Tilbury Hse. Pubs.
—What Will You Be, Sara Mee? Avraham, Kate Aver. 2010. 32p. (J). (gr. -1-3). pap. 7.95 (978-1-58089-211-7(6)); (gr. k-2). 22.44 (978-1-58089-210-0(8)) Charlesbridge Publishing, Inc.
—Who Belongs Here? Knight, Margy Burns et al. 2nd ed. 2005. 40p. (gr. 3-8). pap., tchr. ed., tchr.'s training gde. ed. 9.95 (978-0-88448-111-9(5)) Tilbury Hse. Pubs.
—Who Belongs Here? An American Story. Knight, Margy Burns. 2004. 32p. 19.45 (978-0-7569-2426-3(X)) Perfection Learning Corp.
O'Brien, Anne Sibley. I'm New Here. O'Brien, Anne Sibley. 2015. 32p. (J). (gr. k-3). lib. bdg. 16.95 (978-1-58089-612-2(X)) Charlesbridge Publishing, Inc.
—The Legend of Hong Kil Dong: The Robin Hood of Korea. O'Brien, Anne Sibley. 2008. 48p. (J). (gr. 4-7). per. 8.95 (978-1-58089-303-9(1)) Charlesbridge Publishing, Inc.
—A Path of Stars. O'Brien, Anne Sibley. 2012. 40p. (J). (gr. k-3). 17.99 (978-1-57091-735-6(3)) Charlesbridge Publishing, Inc.
—Someone New. O'Brien, Anne Sibley. 2018. (ENG.). 32p. (J). (gr. k-3). 16.99 (978-1-58089-831-7(9)) Charlesbridge Publishing, Inc.
O'Brien, Anne Sibley & O'Brien, Perry Edmond. After Gandhi: One Hundred Years of Nonviolent Resistance. O'Brien, Anne Sibley & O'Brien, Perry Edmond. 2009. 192p. (J). (gr. 5-7). 24.95 (978-1-58089-129-5(2)) Charlesbridge Publishing, Inc.
O'Brien, Bob. Joyous Jayden. Medicus, Christine. 2019. (Wingman Ser.: Vol. 1). (ENG.). 34p. (J). (gr. k-6). pap. 12.95 (978-1-941069-92-9(4)) ProsePress.
—Joyous Jayden. Christine, Medicus. 2019. (ENG.). 34p. (J). (gr. k-6). 18.95 (978-1-941069-93-6(2)) ProsePress.
—Joyous Jayden - Coloring - Story Book. Medicus, Christine. 2020. (ENG.). 30p. (J). (gr. k-6). pap. 6.95 (978-1-950768-12-7(0)) ProsePress.
O'Brien, Christine. What's the Matter? Heiss, Renee & Stewart, Gary a. 2016. (Enteletrons(r) Ser.: Vol. 2). (ENG.). (J). (gr. 1-4). pap. 14.95 (978-0-9887813-1-3(X)) Entelechy Education, LLC.
O'Brien, Gregory. The ACB with Honora Lee. De Goldi, Kate. 2017. (ENG.). 128p. (J). (gr. 5). pap. 9.99 (978-1-77049-724-5(2), Tundra Bks.) Tundra Bks. CAN. Dist: Penguin Random Hse. LLC.
O'brien, John. Abe Lincoln: His Wit & Wisdom from A to Z. Schroeder, Alan. 2015. (ENG.). 32p. (J). (gr. 1-4). 17.95 (978-0-8234-2420-7(0)) Holiday Hse., Inc.
—Abe Lincoln: His Wit & Wisdom from A-Z. Schroeder, Alan. 2016. (ENG.). 32p. (J). (gr. 1-4). 7.99 (978-0-8234-3575-3(X)) Holiday Hse., Inc.
O'Brien, John. Air Is All Around You. Branley, Franklyn M. 2006. (Let's-Read-And-Find-Out Science 1 Ser.). (ENG.). 40p. (J). (gr. -1-3). pap. 5.99 (978-0-06-059415-2(2), Collins) HarperCollins Pubs.
—Blockhead: The Life of Fibonacci. D'Agnese, Joseph. 2010. (ENG.). 40p. (J). (gr. 1-4). 18.99 (978-0-8050-6305-9(6), 900018927, Holt, Henry & Co. Bks. For Young Readers) Holt, Henry & Co.
—The Cat in Numberland. Ekeland, Ivar. 2006. 56p. (J). (gr. 3-9). 19.95 (978-0-8126-2744-2(X)) Cricket Bks.
O'brien, John. The Curious Adventures of Jimmy McGee. Estes, Eleanor. 2005. (ENG.). 224p. (J). (gr. 3-7). pap. 10.95 (978-0-15-205517-2(7), 1196590) Houghton Mifflin Harcourt Publishing Co.
O'Brien, John. Eat Your Words. Jones, Charlotte Foltz. 2018. (ENG.). 128p. (J). (gr. 3-7). 12.99 (978-1-5247-6681-8(X), Delacorte Bks. for Young Readers) Random Hse. Children's Bks.
—I Know a Shy Fellow Who Swallowed a Cello. Garriel, Barbara S. (ENG.). 32p. (J). (gr. k-2). 2012. pap. 8.99 (978-1-59078-946-9(6)); 2004. 17.99 (978-1-59078-043-5(4)) Boyds Mills Pr.
—Mistakes That Worked: The World's Familiar Inventions & How They Came to Be. Jones, Charlotte Foltz. 2016. (ENG.). 96p. (J). (gr. 3-7). 12.99 (978-0-399-55202-1(2), Delacorte Bks. for Young Readers) Random Hse. Children's Bks.
—¿Quién Fue Marco Polo? Holub, Joan & Who HQ. 2012. (¿Quién Fue? Ser.). 112p. (J). (gr. 3-7). pap. 7.99 (978-0-448-46174-8(9), Penguin Workshop) Penguin Young Readers Group.
—Revolutionary Rogues: John André & Benedict Arnold. Castrovilla, Selene. 2017. (ENG.). 48p. (J). (gr. 4-7). 17.95 (978-1-62979-341-2(8), Calkins Creek) Boyds Mills Pr.
—Thomas Jefferson Builds a Library. Rosenstock, Barb. 2013. (ENG.). 32p. (J). (gr. 1-4). 17.99 (978-1-59078-932-2(6), Calkins Creek) Boyds Mills Pr.
—Washington D. C. from A-Z. Schroeder, Alan. 2018. (ENG.). 32p. (J). (gr. 1-4). 17.95 (978-0-8234-3678-1(0)) Holiday Hse., Inc.
—Where Is Machu Picchu? Stine, Megan & Who HQ. 2018. (Where Is? Ser.). (ENG.). 112p. (J). (gr. 3-7). 5.99 (978-0-515-15961-5(1), Penguin Workshop) Penguin Young Readers Group.
—Where Is the Colosseum? Who HQ & O'Connor, Jim. 2017. (Where Is? Ser.). (ENG.). 112p. (J). (gr. 3-7). 5.99 (978-0-399-54190-2(X), Penguin Workshop) Penguin Young Readers Group.
—Who Is Barack Obama? Edwards, Roberta & Who HQ. 2009. (Who Was? Ser.). (ENG.). 112p. (J). (gr. 3-7). pap. 5.99 (978-0-448-45330-9(4), Penguin Workshop) Penguin Young Readers Group.
—Who Is Bob Dylan? Who HQ & O'Connor, Jim. 2013. (Who Was? Ser.). 112p. (J). (gr. 3-7). pap. 5.99 (978-0-448-46461-9(6), Penguin Workshop) Penguin Young Readers Group.
—Who Is Jane Goodall? Edwards, Roberta & Who HQ. 2012. (Who Was? Ser.). 112p. (J). (gr. 3-7). 5.99 (978-0-448-46192-2(7), Penguin Workshop) Penguin Young Readers Group.
—Who Is Michelle Obama? Stine, Megan & Who HQ. 2013. (Who Was? Ser.). (ENG.). 112p. (J). (gr. 3-7). 5.99 (978-0-448-47863-0(3), Penguin Workshop) Penguin Young Readers Group.
—Who Was Abigail Adams? Kelley, True & Who HQ. 2014. (Who Was? Ser.). 112p. (J). (gr. 3-7). 5.99 (978-0-448-47890-6(0), Penguin Workshop) Penguin Young Readers Group.
O'brien, John. Who Was Ben Franklin? Fradin, Dennis Brindell. 2003. (Who Was... ? Ser.). 105p. (gr. 4-7). 15.00 (978-0-7569-1589-6(9)) Perfection Learning Corp.
O'Brien, John. Who Was Betsy Ross? Buckley, James, Jr. et al. 2014. (Who Was? Ser.). 112p. (J). (gr. 3-7). 5.99 (978-0-448-48243-9(6), Penguin Workshop) Penguin Young Readers Group.
—Who Was Elvis Presley? Edgers, Geoff & Who HQ. 2007. (Who Was? Ser.). (ENG.). 112p. (J). (gr. 3-7). pap. 5.99 (978-0-448-44642-4(1), Penguin Workshop) Penguin Young Readers Group.
O'brien, John. Who Was Elvis Presley? Edgers, Geoff. 2007. (Who Was... ? Ser.). 105p. (gr. 2-5). 15.00 (978-0-7569-8164-8(6)) Perfection Learning Corp.
O'Brien, John. Who Was Franklin Roosevelt? Frith, Margaret & Who HQ. 2010. (Who Was? Ser.). (ENG.). 112p. (J). (gr. 3-7). pap. 5.99 (978-0-448-45346-0(0), Penguin Workshop) Penguin Young Readers Group.
—Who Was Galileo? Demuth, Patricia Brennan & Who HQ. 2015. (Who Was? Ser.). (ENG.). 112p. (J). (gr. 3-7). 5.99 (978-0-448-47985-9(0), Penguin Workshop) Penguin Young Readers Group.
—Who Was Jackie Robinson? Herman, Gail & Who HQ. 2010. (Who Was? Ser.). (ENG.). 112p. (J). (gr. 3-7). pap. 5.99 (978-0-448-45557-0(9), Penguin Workshop) Penguin Young Readers Group.
O'brien, John. Who Was Jackie Robinson? Herman, Gail. 2010. (Who Was... ? Ser.). (ENG.). (J). (gr. 3-7). lib. bdg. 16.60 (978-1-62765-649-8(9)) Perfection Learning Corp.
O'Brien, John. Who Was Louis Armstrong? McDonough, Yona Zeldis & Who HQ. 2004. (Who Was? Ser.). 112p. (J). (gr. 3-7). pap. 5.99 (978-0-448-43368-4(0), Penguin Workshop) Penguin Young Readers Group.
—Who Was Marco Polo? Holub, Joan & Who HQ. 2007. (Who Was? Ser.). (ENG.). 112p. (J). (gr. 3-7). pap. 5.99 (978-0-448-44540-3(9), Penguin Workshop) Penguin Young Readers Group.
O'brien, John. Who Was Marco Polo? Holub, Joan. 2007. (Who Was... ? Ser.). 105p. (gr. 4-7). 15.00 (978-0-7569-8165-5(4)) Perfection Learning Corp.
O'Brien, John. Who Was Marie Antoinette? Rau, Dana Meachen & Who HQ. 2015. (Who Was? Ser.). 112p. (J). (gr. 3-7). 5.99 (978-0-448-48310-8(6), Penguin Workshop) Penguin Young Readers Group.
O'Brien, John. Who Was Marie Antoinette? Rau, Dana Meachen. 2015. 106p. (J). (978-1-4806-9210-7(7), Grosset & Dunlap) Penguin Publishing Group.
O'Brien, John. Who Was Mark Twain? Prince, April Jones & Who HQ. 2004. (Who Was? Ser.). 112p. (J). (gr. 3-7). pap. 5.99 (978-0-448-43319-6(2), Penguin Workshop) Penguin Young Readers Group.
O'brien, John. Who Was Mark Twain? Prince, April Jones. 2004. (Who Was... ? Ser.). 105p. (gr. 3-7). 16.00 (978-0-7569-4590-9(9)) Perfection Learning Corp.
O'Brien, John. Who Was Paul Revere? Edwards, Roberta & Who HQ. 2011. (Who Was? Ser.). 112p. (J). (gr. 3-7). pap. 5.99 (978-0-448-45715-4(6), Penguin Workshop) Penguin Young Readers Group.
—Who Was Robert E. Lee? Bader, Bonnie & Who HQ. 2014. (Who Was? Ser.). 112p. (J). (gr. 3-7). 5.99 (978-0-448-47909-5(5), Penguin Workshop) Penguin Young Readers Group.
—Who Was Steve Jobs? Pollack, Pam et al. 2012. (Who Was? Ser.). (ENG.). 112p. (J). (gr. 3-7). pap. 5.99 (978-0-448-46211-0(7), Penguin Workshop) Penguin Young Readers Group.
O'brien, John. Who Was Steve Jobs? Pollack, Pam & Belviso, Meg. 2012. (Who Was... ? Ser.). (ENG.). (J). (gr. 3-7). lib. bdg. 16.60 (978-1-62765-913-0(7)) Perfection Learning Corp.
O'Brien, John. Who Was Thomas Alva Edison? Frith, Margaret & Who HQ. 2005. (Who Was? Ser.). (ENG.). 112p. (J). (gr. 3-7). pap. 5.99 (978-0-448-43765-1(1), Penguin Workshop) Penguin Young Readers Group.
O'brien, John. Who Was Thomas Alva Edison? Frith, Margaret. 2005. (Who Was... ? Ser.). 106p. (gr. 3-7). 15.00 (978-0-7569-5830-5(X)) Perfection Learning Corp.
O'Brien, John. Who Was Thomas Jefferson? Fradin, Dennis Brindell & Who HQ. 2003. (Who Was? Ser.). 112p. (J). (gr. 3-7). pap. 5.99 (978-0-448-43145-1(9), Penguin Workshop) Penguin Young Readers Group.
O'brien, John. Who Was William Shakespeare? Mannis, Celeste Davidson & Kramer, Sydelle. 2006. (Who Was... ? Ser.). 105p. (gr. 2-6). 15.00 (978-0-7569-6952-3(2)) Perfection Learning Corp.
O'Brien, John. Who Was William Shakespeare? Mannis, Celeste & Who HQ. 2006. (Who Was? Ser.). 112p. (J). (gr. 3-7). pap. 5.99 (978-0-448-43904-4(2), Penguin Workshop) Penguin Young Readers Group.
—Who Were the Brothers Grimm? Reed, Avery & Who HQ. 2015. (Who Was? Ser.). (ENG.). 112p. (J). (gr. 3-7). 5.99 (978-0-448-48314-6(9), Penguin Workshop) Penguin Young Readers Group.
O'brien, John. Who Were the Brothers Grimm? Reed, Avery. 2015. (Who Was-? Chapters Ser.). (ENG.). 112p. (J). (gr. 4-6). 18.69 (978-1-4844-6177-8(0)) Penguin Publishing Group.
O'Brien, John A. The Twelve Days of Christmas. 2003. (ENG.). 32p. (J). (gr. k-12). pap. 8.95 (978-1-59078-086-2(8)) Boyds Mills Pr.
O'Brien, Josh. Super Heroes Storybook Bible, 1 vol. Syswerda, Jean E. 2018. (ENG.). 224p. (J). 17.99 (978-0-310-75018-5(0)) Zonderkidz.
O'Brien, Laurel. Chester's Field. Riley, Christine. 2004. 296p. (J). per. 17.50 (978-0-9740683-6-7(5)) Authors & Artists Publishers of New York, Inc.
O'Brien, Patrick. Captain Raptor & the Moon Mystery. O'Malley, Kevin. 2005. (Captain Raptor Ser.). (ENG.). 32p. (J). (gr. k-5). 18.99 (978-0-8027-8935-8(8), 900034813, Bloomsbury USA Childrens) Bloomsbury Publishing USA.
O'Brien, Patrick. Captain Raptor & the Doomed World. O'Brien, Patrick. O'Malley, Kevin. 2018. (Captain Raptor Ser.: 3). 32p. (J). (gr. -1-3). lib. bdg. 17.99 (978-1-58089-809-6(2)) Charlesbridge Publishing, Inc.
—Captain Raptor & the Space Pirates. O'Brien, Patrick. O'Malley, Kevin. 2007. (Captain Raptor Ser.). (ENG.). 32p. (J). (gr. k-3). 17.99 (978-0-8027-9571-7(4), 900040057, Bloomsbury USA Childrens) Bloomsbury Publishing USA.
—You Are the First Kid on Mars. O'Brien, Patrick. 2009. 32p. (J). (gr. k-3). 17.99 (978-0-399-24634-0(7), G.P. Putnam's Sons Books for Young Readers) Penguin Young Readers Group.
O'Brien, Perry Edmond, jt. illus. see O'Brien, Anne Sibley.
O'Brien, Renee McMullen. The Amazing Mocha & His Courageous Journey. O'Brien, Renee McMullen. 2009. 28p. pap. 12.95 (978-1-936051-60-1(5)) Peppertree Pr., The.

O

O'Brien, Tony, photos by. Afghan Dreams: Young Voices of Afghanistan. O'Brien, Tony. Sullivan, Michael P. 2008. (ENG., 80p. (J). (gr. 2-10). 19.99 *(978-1-59990-287-6(7)*, 9781599902876, Bloomsbury USA Childrens) Bloomsbury Publishing USA.

Obrist, Jürg. Complex Cases: Three Major Mysteries for You to Solve. Obrist, Jürg. 2006. (Mini-Mysteries for You to Solve Ser.). (ENG.). 96p. (gr. 4-6). 23.93 *(978-0-7613-3419-4(X)*, Millbrook Pr.) Lerner Publishing Group.

Oburkova, Eva. Toby's Travels Through Time: Puzzle Adventures in Dinosaur Days. Oburkova, Eva. 2007. (Toby's Travels Through Time: Puzzle Adventures in Dinosaur Days Ser.). 32p. (gr. k-3). lib. bdg. 29.00 *(978-0-8368-7497-6(8)*, Gareth Stevens Learning Library) Stevens, Gareth Publishing LLLP.

O'Byrne, Chelsea. Hello, Crow. Savage, Candace. 2019. 32p. (J). (gr. -1-3). 17.95 *(978-1-77164-444-0(3)*, Greystone Bks.) Greystone Books Ltd. CAN. Dist: Publishers Group West (PGW).

—Our Corner Store, 1 vol. Heidbreder, Robert. 2020. (ENG.). 64p. (J). (gr. 1-4). 16.95 *(978-1-77306-216-7(6))* Groundwood Bks. CAN. Dist: Publishers Group West (PGW).

O'Byrne, Nicola. Dear Dinosaur: With Real Letters to Read! Strathie, Chae. 2017. (Dear Dinosaur Ser.). (ENG.). 28p. (J). (gr. -1-3). 11.99 *(978-0-7641-6898-7(3)*, B.E.S. Publishing) Peterson's.

—Gorilla Loves Vanilla. Strathie, Chae. 2016. (ENG.). 32p. (J). (gr. -1-k). 11.99 *(978-0-7641-6853-6(3)*, B.E.S. Publishing) Peterson's.

—Love. O'Dare, Helen. 2016. (ENG.). 26p. (J). (gr. -1 — 1). bds. 6.99 *(978-1-62686-677-5(5)*, Silver Dolphin Bks.) Printers Row Publishing Group.

—Open Very Carefully: A Book with Bite. Bromley, Nick. (ENG.). (J). 2017. 30p. (— 1). bds. 8.99 *(978-0-7636-9630-6(7))*; 2013. 32p. (gr. -1-2). 15.99 *(978-0-7636-6163-2(5))* Candlewick Pr. (Nosy Crow).

—T. Rex on Tour: With Real Letters to Read! Strathie, Chae. 2018. (Dear Dinosaur Ser.). (ENG.). 32p. (J). (gr. -1-3). 11.99 *(978-1-4380-5050-8(X)*, B.E.S. Publishing) Peterson's.

O'Byrne, Nicola. Use Your Imagination. O'Byrne, Nicola. 2015. (ENG.). 36p. (J). (gr. -1-2). 15.99 *(978-0-7636-8001-5(X)*, Nosy Crow) Candlewick Pr.

—What's Next Door? O'Byrne, Nicola. 2018. (ENG.). 32p. (J). (gr. -1-2). 15.99 *(978-0-7636-9634-4(X)*, Nosy Crow) Candlewick Pr.

O'Cain, Leeana. Tiny World: Soap! O'Cain, Leeana. Odd Dot. 2020. (Tiny World Ser.: 6). (ENG.). 32p. (J). pap. 14.99 *(978-1-250-20817-0(3)*, 900203026, Odd Dot) St. Martin's Pr.

O'Callaghan, Gemma. Half a Man. Morpurgo, Michael. 2015. (ENG.). 64p. (J). (gr. 5). 16.99 *(978-0-7636-7747-3(7))* Candlewick Pr.

Ocasio, Carlos, jt. illus. see McMillian, Jr Marvin.

Ocegueda, Aleida. Ópatas, Tarahumaras, Yaquis y Seris. Gutiérrez Schott, Lorena. 2013. (SPA.). 88p. (J). (gr. 4-7). pap. 11.95 *(978-607-8237-12-8(8))* Nostra Ediciones MEX. Dist: Independent Pubs. Group.

Ocello, Salvatore & Nelligan, Kevin. Peppy Up: Eat Your Best, Be Your Best! Nelligan, Patty. 2013. 32p. pap. 12.95 *(978-1-939418-41-8(0))* Writer of the Round Table Pr.

Ochoa, Ana. Lupe Lupita, Where Are You?/Lupe Lupita, Donde Estas? Rosa-Mendoza, Gladys. 2005. (English-Spanish Foundations Ser.). (SPA & ENG.). 20p. (J). (gr. -1). bds. 6.95 *(978-1-931398-16-9(X))* Me+Mi Publishing.

—Lupe Lupita, Where Are You?/Lupe Lupita Donde Estas? Rosa-Mendoza, Gladys. 2007. (English Spanish Foundations Ser.). 20p. (gr. -1-k). pap. 19.95 *(978-1-931398-82-4(8))* Me+Mi Publishing.

—Miss Pinkeltink's Purse, 1 vol. Brozo, Patty. 2018. (ENG.). 36p. (J). (gr. 1-4). 17.95 *(978-0-88448-626-8(5)*, 884626) Tilbury Hse. Pubs.

—So Many Me's. Neasi, Barbara J. (Rookie Ready to Learn Ser.). (J). 2011. (ENG.). 40p. pap. 5.95 *(978-0-531-26677-9(X))*; 2011. 40p. (gr. -1-k). lib. bdg. 23.00 *(978-0-531-26372-3(X))*; 2003. 32p. 19.50 *(978-0-516-22883-9(8))* Scholastic Library Publishing. (Children's Pr.).

—Una Vaca Querida. Antillano, Laura. (Literary Encounters Ser.). (SPA.). (J). (gr. 3-5). pap. *(978-968-494-077-2(7)*, CI7709) Centro de Informacion y Desarrollo de la Comunicacion y la Literatura MEX. Dist: Lectorum Pubns., Inc.

Ochoa, Ana. Muchas Veces Yo. Ochoa, Ana. Neasi, Barbara J. 2011. (Rookie Ready to Learn Español Ser.). (SPA.). 40p. (J). pap. 5.95 *(978-0-531-26789-9(X))*; (gr. -1-1). lib. bdg. 23.00 *(978-0-531-26121-7(2))* Scholastic Library Publishing. (Children's Pr.).

Ochoa, Francisco. La Plaza. Deltoro, Antonio. 2004.Tr. of Plaza. (SPA.). (J). (gr. k-2). pap. 11.99 *(978-968-494-045-1(9))* Centro de Informacion y Desarrollo de la Comunicacion y la Literatura MEX. Dist: Lectorum Pubns., Inc.

O'Connell, Caitlin & Rodwell, Timothy. A Baby Elephant in the Wild. O'Connell, Caitlin. 2014. (ENG.). 40p. (J). (gr. -1-3). 17.99 *(978-0-544-14944-1(0)*, 1546119, HMH Books For Young Readers) Houghton Mifflin Harcourt Publishing Co.

O'Connell, Dave. Always Late Nate. Krivitzky, Nathan & Nathan, Krivitzky. 2009. (ENG.). 32p. (J). pap. 10.95 *(978-1-933916-41-5(9))* Nelson Publishing & Marketing.

O'Connell, David. Creature Teacher. Watkins, Sam. 2017. (Creature Teacher Ser.). (ENG.). 176p. (J). (gr. 2-4). pap. 6.95 *(978-1-4965-5681-3(X)*, 136595); pap., pap., pap. 27.80 *(978-1-4965-5682-0(8)*, 27297); 98.60 *(978-1-4965-5701-8(8)*, 27309); lib. bdg. 24.65 *(978-1-4965-5702-5(6)*, 136591) Capstone. (Stone Arch Bks.).

—Creature Teacher Goes Wild. Watkins, Sam. 2017. (Creature Teacher Ser.). (ENG.). 176p. (J). (gr. 2-4). pap. 6.95 *(978-1-4965-5684-4(4)*, 136597); lib. bdg. 24.65 *(978-1-4965-5703-2(4)*, 136592) Capstone. (Stone Arch Bks.).

—Creature Teacher Out to Win. Watkins, Sam. 2017. (Creature Teacher Ser.). (ENG.). 176p. (J). (gr. 2-4). pap. 6.95 *(978-1-4965-5687-5(9)*, 136598); lib. bdg. 24.65 *(978-1-4965-5704-9(2)*, 136594) Capstone. (Stone Arch Bks.).

—Creature Teacher Science Shocker. Watkins, Sam. 2017. (Creature Teacher Ser.). (ENG.). 176p. (J). (gr. 2-4). pap. 6.95 *(978-1-4965-5689-9(5)*, 136596); lib. bdg. 24.65 *(978-1-4965-5705-6(0)*, 136593) Capstone. (Stone Arch Bks.).

—Dave the Unicorn: Team Spirit. Bird, Pip. 2020. (Dave the Unicorn Ser.: 2). (ENG.). 176p. (J). 15.99 *(978-1-250-25636-2(4)*, 900219258); pap. 5.99 ***(978-1-250-76877-3(2)***, 900219259) Imprint IND. Dist: Macmillan.

—Dave the Unicorn: Welcome to Unicorn School. Bird, Pip. 2020. (Dave the Unicorn Ser.: 1). (ENG.). 176p. (J). 15.99 *(978-1-250-25634-8(8)*, 900219254); pap. 5.99 ***(978-1-250-76876-6(4)***, 900219255) Imprint IND. Dist: Macmillan.

O'Connell, David. How Can I Remember All That? Simple Stuff to Improve Your Working Memory. Packiam Alloway, Tracy Packiam. 2019. (ENG.). 64p. 15.95 ***(978-1-78592-633-4(0)***, 697019) Kingsley, Jessica Pubs. GBR. Dist: Hachette UK Distribution.

O'Connell, Jennifer. The Eye of the Whale: A Rescue Story, 1 vol. O'Connell, Jennifer. 2013. (Tilbury House Nature Book Ser.: 0). (ENG.). 32p. (J). (gr. 1-7). 17.95 *(978-0-88448-335-9(5)*, 884335) Tilbury Hse. Pubs.

O'Connell, Jennifer Barrett. A Garden of Whales. Davis, Maggie Steincrohn. 25th ed. 2008. 32p. (J). (gr. -1-2). reprint ed. pap. 7.95 *(978-0-944475-35-5(3)*, 5b780fd6-3810-44ed-9c16-2e3d1b2e19a2) Firefly Bks., Ltd.

O'Connell, Lorraine. Super Soap (Team Umizoomi) Random House Staff. 2013. (Step into Reading Ser.). (ENG.). 24p. (J). (gr. -1-2). pap. 3.99 *(978-0-449-81387-4(8)*, Random Hse. Bks. for Young Readers) Random Hse. Children's Bks.

O'Connell, Lorraine, jt. illus. see Random House Staff.

OConner, Kim. Nika Goes to Camp. Melkonian, Sheyda Mia. 2011. 28p. pap. 14.95 *(978-1-4575-0524-9(X))* Dog Ear Publishing, LLC.

O'Connor, Bailey, jt. illus. see O'Connor, Marcy.

O'Connor, Claire. The Queen's Creek Rug. Hayes, Martha. 2020. (ENG.). 40p. (J). pap. 14.99 ***(978-1-6572-6351-2(7))*** Independently Published.

O'Connor, Deborah. A Garden of Emotions: Cultivating Peace Through Eft Tapping. Yates, Brad. 2018. (ENG.). 34p. (J). (gr. k-6). 19.99 *(978-1-63233-190-8(X))*; pap. 14.99 *(978-1-63233-189-2(6))* Eifrig Publishing.

O'Connor, Fergal. Magical Celtic Tales. Leavy, Una. 2016. (ENG.). 96p. (J). 25.00 *(978-1-84717-546-5(5))* O'Brien Pr., Ltd., The IRL. Dist: Casemate Pubs. & Bk. Distributors, LLC.

O'Connor, George. Captain Awesome & the Easter Egg Bandit. Kirby, Stan. 2015. (Captain Awesome Ser.: 13). (ENG.). 128p. (J). (gr. k-4). pap. 5.99 *(978-1-4814-2558-2(7)*, Little Simon) Little Simon.

—Captain Awesome & the Missing Elephants. Kirby, Stan. 2014. (Captain Awesome Ser.: 10). (ENG.). 128p. (J). (gr. k-4). 17.99 *(978-1-4424-8995-0(2))*; pap. 5.99 *(978-1-4424-8994-3(4))* Little Simon. (Little Simon).

—Captain Awesome & the Mummy's Treasure. Kirby, Stan. 2015. (Captain Awesome Ser.: 15). (ENG.). 128p. (J). (gr. k-4). pap. 5.99 *(978-1-4814-4438-5(7)*, Little Simon) Little Simon.

—Captain Awesome & the New Kid. Kirby, Stan. 2012. (Captain Awesome Ser.: 3). (ENG.). 128p. (J). (gr. k-4). 17.99 *(978-1-4424-4200-9(X))*; pap. 5.99 *(978-1-4424-4199-6(2))* Little Simon. (Little Simon).

—Captain Awesome & the New Kid: #3. Kirby, Stan. 2018. (Captain Awesome Ser.). (ENG.). 120p. (J). (gr. k-4). lib. bdg. 27.07 *(978-1-5321-4201-7(3)*, 28545, Chapter Bks.) Spotlight.

—Captain Awesome & the Trapdoor. Kirby, Stan. 2019. (Captain Awesome Ser.: 21). (ENG.). 128p. (J). (gr. k-4). 16.99 *(978-1-5344-3315-1(5))*; pap. 5.99 *(978-1-5344-3314-4(7))* Little Simon. (Little Simon).

—Captain Awesome & the Ultimate Spelling Bee. Kirby, Stan. 2013. (Captain Awesome Ser.: 7). (ENG.). 128p. (J). (gr. k-4). 17.99 *(978-1-4424-5156-8(4))*; pap. 5.99 *(978-1-4424-5158-2(0))* Little Simon. (Little Simon).

—The Captain Awesome Collection: A MI-TEE Boxed Set: Captain Awesome to the Rescue!; Captain Awesome vs. Nacho Cheese Man; Captain Awesome & the New Kid; Captain Awesome Takes a Dive. Kirby, Stan. ed. 2013. (Captain Awesome Ser.). (ENG.). 512p. (J). (gr. k-2). pap. 23.99 *(978-1-4424-8977-6(4)*, Little Simon) Little Simon.

—Captain Awesome for President. Kirby, Stan. 2018. (Captain Awesome Ser.: 20). (ENG.). 128p. (J). (gr. k-4). 16.99 *(978-1-5344-2084-7(3))*; pap. 5.99 *(978-1-5344-2083-0(5))* Little Simon. (Little Simon).

—Captain Awesome Gets a Hole-In-One. 2014. (Captain Awesome Ser.: 12). (ENG.). 128p. (J). (gr. k-4). pap. 5.99 *(978-1-4814-1431-9(3)*, Little Simon) Little Simon.

—Captain Awesome Gets Crushed. Kirby, Stan. 2013. (Captain Awesome Ser.: 9). (ENG.). 128p. (J). (gr. k-2). pap. 5.99 *(978-1-4424-8212-8(5))*; 16.99 *(978-1-4424-8213-5(3))* Little Simon. (Little Simon).

—Captain Awesome Goes to Superhero Camp. Kirby, Stan. 2015. (Captain Awesome Ser.: 14). (ENG.). 128p. (J). (gr. k-4). pap. 5.99 *(978-1-4814-3153-8(6)*, Little Simon) Little Simon.

—Captain Awesome Has the Best Snow Day Ever? Kirby, Stan. 2016. (Captain Awesome Ser.: 18). (ENG.). 128p. (J). (gr. k-4). 17.99 *(978-1-4814-7816-8(8)*, Little Simon) Little Simon.

—Captain Awesome Meets Super Dude! Super Special. Kirby, Stan. 2016. (Captain Awesome Ser.: 17). (ENG.). 160p. (J). (gr. k-4). pap. 5.99 *(978-1-4814-6695-0(X)*, Little Simon) Little Simon.

—Captain Awesome Saves the Winter Wonderland. Kirby, Stan. 2012. (Captain Awesome Ser.: 6). (ENG.). 128p. (J). (gr. k-4). 16.99 *(978-1-4424-4335-8(9))*; pap. 5.99 *(978-1-4424-4334-1(0))* Little Simon. (Little Simon).

—Captain Awesome Saves the Winter Wonderland: #6. Kirby, Stan. 2018. (Captain Awesome Ser.). (ENG.). 128p. (J). (gr. k-4). lib. bdg. 27.07 *(978-1-5321-4204-8(8)*, 28548, Chapter Bks.) Spotlight.

—Captain Awesome Says the Magic Word. Kirby, Stan. 2020. (Captain Awesome Ser.: 22). (ENG.). 128p. (J). (gr. k-4). 16.99 *(978-1-5344-6090-4(X))*; pap. 5.99 *(978-1-5344-6089-8(6))* Little Simon. (Little Simon).

—Captain Awesome, Soccer Star. Kirby, Stan. 2012. (Captain Awesome Ser.: 5). (ENG.). 128p. (J). (gr. k-4). 17.99 *(978-1-4424-4332-7(4))*; pap. 5.99 *(978-1-4424-4331-0(6))* Little Simon. (Little Simon).

—Captain Awesome, Soccer Star: #5. Kirby, Stan. 2018. (Captain Awesome Ser.). (ENG.). 120p. (J). (gr. k-4). lib. bdg. 27.07 *(978-1-5321-4203-1(X)*, 28547, Chapter Bks.) Spotlight.

—Captain Awesome Takes a Dive. Kirby, Stan. 2012. (Captain Awesome Ser.: 4). (ENG.). 128p. (J). (gr. k-4). 16.99 *(978-1-4424-4203-0(4))*; pap. 5.99 *(978-1-4424-4202-3(6))* Little Simon. (Little Simon).

—Captain Awesome Takes a Dive: #4. Kirby, Stan. 2018. (Captain Awesome Ser.). (ENG.). 128p. (J). (gr. k-4). lib. bdg. 27.07 *(978-1-5321-4202-4(1)*, 28546, Chapter Bks.) Spotlight.

—Captain Awesome Takes Flight. Kirby, Stan. 2017. (Captain Awesome Ser.: 19). (ENG.). 128p. (J). (gr. k-4). pap. 5.99 *(978-1-4814-9441-0(4)*, Little Simon) Little Simon.

—Captain Awesome to the Rescue! Kirby, Stan. 2012. (Captain Awesome Ser.: 1). (ENG.). 128p. (J). (gr. k-2). 17.99 *(978-1-4424-4090-6(2))*; pap. 5.99 *(978-1-4424-3561-2(5))* Little Simon. (Little Simon).

—Captain Awesome to the Rescue! #1. Kirby, Stan. 2018. (Captain Awesome Ser.). (ENG.). 112p. (J). (gr. k-4). lib. bdg. 27.07 *(978-1-5321-4199-7(8)*, 28543, Chapter Bks.) Spotlight.

—Captain Awesome vs. Nacho Cheese Man. Kirby, Stan. 2012. (Captain Awesome Ser.: 2). (ENG.). 128p. (J). (gr. -1-2). 16.99 *(978-1-4424-4091-3(0))*; (gr. k-4). pap. 5.99 *(978-1-4424-3563-6(1))* Little Simon. (Little Simon).

—Captain Awesome vs. Nacho Cheese Man: #2. Kirby, Stan. 2018. (Captain Awesome Ser.). (ENG.). 120p. (J). (gr. k-4). lib. bdg. 27.07 *(978-1-5321-4200-0(5)*, 28544, Chapter Bks.) Spotlight.

—Captain Awesome vs. the Evil Babysitter. Kirby, Stan. 2014. (Captain Awesome Ser.: 11). (ENG.). 128p. (J). (gr. k-4). pap. 5.99 *(978-1-4814-0446-4(6)*, Little Simon) Little Simon.

—Captain Awesome vs. the Sinister Substitute Teacher. Kirby, Stan. 2016. (Captain Awesome Ser.: 16). (ENG.). 128p. (J). (gr. k-4). pap. 5.99 *(978-1-4814-5858-0(2)*, Little Simon) Little Simon.

—Captain Awesome vs. the Spooky, Scary House. Kirby, Stan. 2013. (Captain Awesome Ser.: 8). (ENG.). 128p. (J). (gr. k-2). 16.99 *(978-1-4424-7255-6(3))*; pap. 5.99 *(978-1-4424-7254-9(5))* Little Simon. (Little Simon).

—Mission: Hollywood. Abela, Deborah. 2007. (Spy Force Ser.: 4). (ENG.). 240p. (J). (gr. 3-7). pap. 10.99 *(978-1-4169-3969-6(5)*, Aladdin) Simon & Schuster Children's Publishing.

—Super Turbo 4 Books In 1! Super Turbo Saves the Day!; Super Turbo vs. the Flying Ninja Squirrels; Super Turbo vs. the Pencil Pointer; Super Turbo Protects the World. Kirby, Lee. 2019. (Super Turbo Ser.). (ENG.). 512p. (J). (gr. k-4). 14.99 *(978-1-5344-5635-8(X)*, Little Simon) Little Simon.

—Super Turbo & the Fire-Breathing Dragon. Kirby, Lee. 2017. (Super Turbo Ser.: 5). (ENG.). 128p. (J). (gr. k-4). 16.99 *(978-1-4814-9997-2(1))*; pap. 5.99 *(978-1-4814-9996-5(3))* Little Simon. (Little Simon).

—Super Turbo & the Fountain of Doom. Kirby, Lee. 2019. (Super Turbo Ser.: 9). (ENG.). 128p. (J). (gr. k-4). 16.99 *(978-1-5344-4507-9(2))*; pap. 5.99 *(978-1-5344-4506-2(4))* Little Simon. (Little Simon).

—The Super Turbo Collection: Super Turbo Saves the Day!; Super Turbo vs. the Flying Ninja Squirrels; Super Turbo vs. the Pencil Pointer; Super Turbo Protects the World. Kirby, Lee. 2018. (Super Turbo Ser.). (ENG.). 512p. (J). (gr. k-4). pap. 23.99 *(978-1-5344-1505-8(X)*, Little Simon) Little Simon.

—Super Turbo Gets Caught. Kirby, Lee. 2018. (Super Turbo Ser.: 8). (ENG.). 128p. (J). (gr. k-4). 16.99 *(978-1-5344-2986-4(7))*; pap. 5.99 *(978-1-5344-2985-7(9))* Little Simon. (Little Simon).

—Super Turbo Meets the Cat-Nappers. Kirby, Lee. 2018. (Super Turbo Ser.: 7). (ENG.). 128p. (J). (gr. k-4). 16.99 *(978-1-5344-1185-2(2))*; pap. 5.99 *(978-1-5344-1184-5(4))* Little Simon. (Little Simon).

—Super Turbo Protects the World. Kirby, Lee. 2017. (Super Turbo Ser.: 4). (ENG.). 128p. (J). (gr. k-4). 16.99 *(978-1-4814-9994-1(7))*; pap. 5.99 *(978-1-4814-9993-4(9))* Little Simon. (Little Simon).

—Super Turbo Saves the Day! Kirby, Lee. 2016. (Super Turbo Ser.: 1). (ENG.). 128p. (J). (gr. k-4). 16.99 *(978-1-4814-8885-3(6))*; pap. 5.99 *(978-1-4814-8884-6(8))* Little Simon. (Little Simon).

—Super Turbo vs. the Flying Ninja Squirrels. Lee, Jack et al. 2016. (Super Turbo Ser.: 2). (ENG.). 128p. (J). (gr. k-4). 16.99 *(978-1-4814-8888-4(0)*, Little Simon) Little Simon.

—Super Turbo vs. the Flying Ninja Squirrels. Kirby, Lee. 2016. (Super Turbo Ser.: 2). (ENG.). 128p. (J). (gr. k-4). pap. 5.99 *(978-1-4814-8887-7(2)*, Little Simon) Little Simon.

—Super Turbo vs. the Pencil Pointer. Kirby, Lee. 2017. (Super Turbo Ser.: 3). (ENG.). 128p. (J). (gr. k-4). pap. 5.99 *(978-1-4814-9438-0(4)*, Little Simon) Little Simon.

—Super Turbo vs. Wonder Pig. Kirby, Lee. 2018. (Super Turbo Ser.: 6). (ENG.). 128p. (J). (gr. k-4). 16.99 *(978-1-5344-1182-1(8))*; pap. 5.99 *(978-1-5344-1181-4(X))* Little Simon. (Little Simon).

O'Connor, George. Aphrodite: Goddess of Love. O'Connor, George. 2013. (Olympians Ser.: 6). (ENG.). 80p. (J). (gr. 4-9). 18.99 *(978-1-59643-947-4(5)*, 900123798, First Second Bks.) Roaring Brook Pr.

—Athena Bk. 2: Grey-Eyed Goddess. O'Connor, George. 2010. (Olympians Ser.: 2). (ENG.). 80p. (J). (gr. 4-9). pap. 10.99 *(978-1-59643-432-5(5)*, 900054270, First Second Bks.) Roaring Brook Pr.

—Hades: Lord of the Dead. O'Connor, George. 2012. (Olympians Ser.: 4). (ENG.). 80p. (J). (gr. 4-9). 18.99 *(978-1-59643-761-6(8)*, 900080448); pap. 10.99 *(978-1-59643-434-9(1)*, 900054272) Roaring Brook Pr. (First Second Bks.).

—Hera: The Goddess & Her Glory. O'Connor, George. 2011. (Olympians Ser.: 3). (ENG.). 80p. (J). (gr. 4-9). 18.99 *(978-1-59643-724-1(3)*, 900075971); pap. 10.99 *(978-1-59643-433-2(3)*, 900054271) Roaring Brook Pr. (First Second Bks.).

—If I Had a Raptor. O'Connor, George. 2014. (ENG.). 32p. (J). (gr. -1-2). 15.99 *(978-0-7636-6012-3(4))* Candlewick Pr.

—If I Had a Triceratops. O'Connor, George. 2015. (ENG.). 32p. (J). (gr. -1-2). 15.99 *(978-0-7636-6013-0(2))* Candlewick Pr.

—Kapow! O'Connor, George. 2007. (ENG.). 48p. (J). (gr. -1-3). 12.99 *(978-1-4169-6847-4(4)*, Aladdin) Simon & Schuster Children's Publishing.

—Ker-Splash! O'Connor, George. 2010. (ENG.). 40p. (J). (gr. -1-3). 19.99 *(978-1-4424-2196-7(7)*, Simon & Schuster Bks. For Young Readers) Simon & Schuster Bks. For Young Readers.

—Olympians: Ares: Bringer of War. O'Connor, George. 2015. (Olympians Ser.: 7). (ENG.). 80p. (J). (gr. 4-9). pap. 10.99 *(978-1-62672-013-8(4)*, 900131512, First Second Bks.) Roaring Brook Pr.

—Olympians: Athena Bk. 2: Grey-Eyed Goddess. O'Connor, George. 2010. (Olympians Ser.: 2). (ENG.). 80p. (J). (gr. 4-9). 19.99 *(978-1-59643-649-7(2)*, 900069009, First Second Bks.) Roaring Brook Pr.

—Olympians: Zeus: King of the Gods. O'Connor, George. 2010. (Olympians Ser.: 1). (ENG.). 80p. (J). (gr. 4-9). 18.99 *(978-1-59643-625-1(5)*, 900066747); pap. 10.99 *(978-1-59643-431-8(7)*, 900054269) Roaring Brook Pr. (First Second Bks.).

—Poseidon: Earth Shaker. O'Connor, George. 2013. (Olympians Ser.: 5). (ENG.). 80p. (J). (gr. 4-9). 18.99 *(978-1-59643-828-6(2)*, 900087634); pap. 10.99 *(978-1-59643-738-8(3)*, 900077385) Roaring Brook Pr. (First Second Bks.).

O'Connor, George & Sycamore, Hilary. Journey into Mohawk Country. Bogaert, Harmen Meyndertsz van. 2006. (ENG.). (YA). (gr. 7). lib. bdg. 30.60 *(978-1-61383-839-6(5))* Perfection Learning Corp.

O'Connor, Gr. Santa's Wish. O'Connor, Karen. 2018. (ENG.). 38p. (J). pap. *(978-0-9929385-5-0(4))* Moybella Pr.

O'Connor, Jeff. You & Your Horse: How to Whisper Your Way into Your Horse's Life. Mackall, Dandi Daley. 2009. (ENG.). 160p. (J). (gr. 4-8). pap. 5.99 *(978-1-4169-6449-0(5)*, Aladdin) Simon & Schuster Children's Publishing.

O'Connor, John. The Blue Door, 1 vol. McPhail, David. 2005. (First Flight Level 1 Ser.). (ENG.). 32p. (J). (gr. -1-1). pap. 4.95 *(978-1-55041-917-7(X)*, bdcf204b-55d5-45b9-9e69-bf9ad776a1d9) éditeur, Annika Parance CAN. Dist: Firefly Bks., Ltd.

—The Blue Door, 1 vol. McPhail, David. Ellis, Sarah, ed. 2003. (First Flight Level 2 Ser.). (ENG.). 32p. (J). (gr. -1-1). pap. 4.95 *(978-1-55041-802-6(5)*, e00e64fc-e139-4123-a087-796c57062883) Fitzhenry & Whiteside, Ltd. CAN. Dist: Firefly Bks., Ltd.

O'Connor, Kaitlyn Shea. Shirley Chisholm. Calkhoven, Laurie. 2020. (You Should Meet Ser.). (ENG.). 48p. (J). (gr. 1-3). 17.99 ***(978-1-5344-6558-9(8))***; pap. 4.99 ***(978-1-5344-6557-2(X))*** Simon Spotlight. (Simon Spotlight).

O'Connor, Marcy & O'Connor, Bailey. Little Bee the Size of a Pe. Ceballos, Jacalyn Martin. 2011. 28p. pap. 24.95 *(978-1-4626-3005-9(7))* America Star Bks.

O'Connor, Niamh, jt. illus. see Garvey, Brann.

O'Connor, Shannon. Rags the Recycled Doll. Jackson, Ann. 2004. 49p. 12.95 *(978-1-57197-405-1(9))* Pentland Pr., Inc.

O'Connor, Sophia. Watership Down. 2019. (ENG.). 48p. (J). (gr. -1-2). 17.99 *(978-1-5344-5706-5(2)*, Simon Spotlight) Simon Spotlight.

—Watership down the Coloring Book. 2019. (ENG.). 96p. (J). (gr. -1). 9.99 *(978-1-5344-5708-9(9)*, Simon Spotlight) Simon Spotlight.

O'Connor, Tara. The Agony House. Priest, Cherie. 2018. (ENG.). 272p. (YA). (gr. 7-7). 18.99 *(978-0-545-93429-9(X)*, Levine, Arthur A. Bks.) Scholastic, Inc.

O'Connor, Tim. Being Nice to Others: A Book about Rudeness. Larsen, Carolyn. 2016. (Growing God's Kids Ser.). (ENG.). 32p. (J). pap. 5.99 *(978-0-8010-0957-0(X))* Baker Bks.

—The Journeys of Wobblefoot the Beginning. Cogar, Tubal U. et al. Cogar, Karen S., ed. 2003. (J). pap. 17.50 *(978-0-9747149-0-5(9))* Wobblefoot Ltd.

—Keeping Your Cool: A Book about Anger. Larsen, Carolyn. 2016. (Growing God's Kids Ser.). (ENG.). 32p. (J). pap. 5.99 *(978-0-8010-0912-9(X))* Baker Bks.

—Mi Biblia Pijama. Holmes, Andy. ed. 2008. 33p. (J). (gr. -1). bds. 13.99 *(978-1-4143-1979-7(7)*, 4600969, Tyndale Espanol) Tyndale Hse. Pubs.

—Sharing with Others: A Book about Selfishness. Larsen, Carolyn. 2017. (Growing God's Kids Ser.). (ENG.). 32p. (J). pap. 4.99 *(978-0-8010-0960-0(X))* Baker Bks.

—Telling the Truth: A Book about Lying. Larsen, Carolyn. 2016. (Growing God's Kids Ser.). (ENG.). 32p. (J). pap. 5.99 *(978-0-8010-0926-6(X))* Baker Bks.

—The Word & Song Bible. Elkins, Stephen. 2004. (J). 34.99 incl. audio *(978-0-8054-3012-7(1))*; 34.99 incl. audio compact disk *(978-0-8054-3018-9(0))*; 448p. (gr. -1-5). 19.99 *(978-0-8054-1689-3(7))* B&H Publishing Group.

Oda, Kancho. The Moon Princess, 1 vol. McCarthy, Ralph F. 2013. (Kodansha's Children's Bilingual Classics Ser.: 1). (ENG.). 48p. (J). (gr. k-12). 9.95 *(978-1-56836-527-5(6))* Kodansha International JPN. Dist: Penguin Random Hse. LLC.

Oda, Mayumi. Random Kindness & Senseless Acts of Beauty. Herbert, Anne & Pavel, Margaret Paloma. 2017. (ENG.). 40p. (gr. 2-7). 12.95 *(978-1-61332-023-5(X),* 3254) New Village Pr.

Oda, Takashi. We Are Dolphins. Grooms, Molly. 2004. (ENG.). 32p. (J). (gr. -1-2). pap. 7.95 *(978-1-55971-904-9(4))* Cooper Square Publishing Llc.

Oddi, Sara. The Story of Gulliver. Coe, Jonathan. 2019. (Save the Story Ser.: 3). (ENG.). 96p. (J). (gr. 3-7). pap. 12.95 *(978-1-78269-207-2(X),* Pushkin Children's Bks.) Steerforth Pr.

Ode, Eric. Paulina & the Pirate's Hat, 1 vol. Ode, Eric. 2018. (ENG.). 32p. (J). (gr. k-3). 16.99 *(978-1-4556-2351-8(2),* Pelican Publishing) Arcadia Publishing.

Odell, Catherine Lazar. I'm Done! McLellan, Gretchen Brandenburg. 2018. 40p. (J). (gr. -1-1). 17.99 *(978-0-8234-3705-4(1))* Holiday Hse., Inc.

Odermatt, Brian. The Wonders of Waldorf Chemistry: Notes from a Teacher's Notebook, 1 vol. Mitchell, David. 2004. (ENG.). 250p. (gr. 7-9). per. 22.00 *(978-1-888365-16-0(1))* Waldorf Publications.

Odjick, Jay. Bear for Breakfast. Munsch, Robert. 2020. (ENG.). 32p. (J). (gr. -1-3). pap. 7.99 *(978-1-4431-7055-0(0))* Scholastic Canada, Ltd. CAN. Dist: Publishers Group West (PGW).

Odjick, Jay. Bear for Breakfast / Makwa Kidji Kijebà Wisiniyàn. Munsch, Robert. 2020. (ENG.). 32p. (J). (gr. -1-3). pap. 7.99 ***(978-1-4431-7511-1(0))*** Scholastic Canada, Ltd. CAN. Dist: Publishers Group West (PGW).

Odjick, Jay & Odjick, Jay. Bear for Breakfast. Munsch, Robert. 2020. (ENG.). 32p. (J). (gr. -1-3). 19.99 ***(978-1-4431-7054-3(2),*** North Winds Pr) Scholastic Canada, Ltd. CAN. Dist: Publishers Group West (PGW).

Odjick, Jay, jt. illus. see Odjick, Jay.

Odom, Kelly. It's Not Easy Being a Purple Goose. Parrish, Edith E. 2011. 44p. pap. 24.95 *(978-1-4626-4207-6(1))* America Star Bks.

—Sarah the Purple Goose Gets Lost. Parrish, Edith. 2011. 34p. 23.95 *(978-1-60844-930-9(0))* Dog Ear Publishing, LLC.

Odone, Jamison. Alice's Adventures in Wonderland. Odone, Jamison. 2010. (Stickfiguratively Speaking Ser.). (ENG.). 192p. (gr. 2-3). 14.95 *(978-1-935557-61-6(0))* PublishingWorks.

O'Donnell, Aileen. All about Ben: Helping Children with Attachment Issues to Understand Their Feelings. O'Donnell, Aileen. Markham, Dorothy. 2018. (ENG.). 40p. (C). pap. 13.95 *(978-1-78592-499-6(0),* 696838) Kingsley, Jessica Pubs. GBR. Dist: Hachette UK Distribution.

O'Donnell, Allison. On the Backs of the Enslaved. Amendola, Cherylanne. 2019. (ENG.). 36p. (J). pap. 9.99 ***(978-1-7040-0732-8(1))*** Independently Published.

Odriozola, Elena. Marte y Las Princesas Voladores. Baranda, María. 2007. (la Orilla del Viento Ser.). (SPA.). 35p. (J). pap. *(978-968-16-8141-8(X))* Fondo de Cultura Economica.

Odriozola, Elena. The Story Blanket. Wolff, Ferida & Savitz, Harriet May. 2020. (ENG.). 32p. (J). (gr. -1-3). 8.99 ***(978-1-68263-219-2(9))*** Peachtree Publishing Co. Inc.

Odriozola, Elena. What I Do with Vegetable Glue. Chandler, Susan. 2012. (ENG.). 24p. (J). (gr. k-3). 16.95 *(978-1-61608-661-9(0),* 608661, Sky Pony Pr.) Skyhorse Publishing Co., Inc.

Odynski, Tay. A Tale of Two Brothers: A Rhyming Story about Making Healthy Choices. Andrejcin, Brittany. 2017. (ENG.). (J). (gr. -1-3). *(978-0-9958790-0-3(1))* Andrejcin, Brittany.

Oe, Patricia Daly. Blue Mouse, Yellow Mouse. Oe, Patricia Daly. 2007. (R. I. C. Story Chest Ser.). 20p. (J). (gr. -1-k). 11.95 incl. audio compact disk *(978-1-74126-439-5(1))* R.I.C. Pubns. AUS. Dist: SCB Distributors.

—Where Are My Stripes? Oe, Patricia Daly. 2007. (R. I. C. Story Chest Ser.). 20p. (J). (gr. -1-k). 11.95 incl. audio compact disk *(978-1-74126-438-8(3))* R.I.C. Pubns. AUS. Dist: SCB Distributors.

Oehlers, Adam. The Errand. LaFleur, Leo. 2017. 44p. (J). (gr. 1-5). 16.95 *(978-1-77229-024-0(6))* Simply Read Bks. CAN. Dist: Ingram Publisher Services.

Oehlert, Mark. Bella & Hippo in Mystery of the Black Forest. Taylor, Patricia. 2017. (ENG.). 82p. (J). (gr. 3-5). pap. 20.95 *(978-0-9985254-2-6(1))* Independent Pub.

Oehm, Kent. Appalachian Christmas ABCs. Hall, Francie. 2010. (ENG.). 53p. (J). 16.95 *(978-1-57072-328-5(1))* Overmountain Pr.

Oelofsen, Vian. Mom & Dad Don't Live Together Anymore. Stinson, Kathy. 3rd rev. ed. 2007. (ENG.). 24p. (J). (gr. -1-2). pap. 6.95 *(978-1-55451-093-1(7),* 9781554510931) Annick Pr., Ltd. CAN. Dist: Publishers Group West (PGW).

—That Dog! Hay, Sam. 2011. (My Phonics Readers: Level 2 Ser.). 24p. (J). (gr. -1-1). 24.25 *(978-1-84898-510-0(X))* Sea-To-Sea Pubns.

Oelrich, Deborah, photos by. Amazing Creatures. 2009. 48p. pap. 19.00 *(978-1-4343-6713-6(4))* AuthorHouse.

Oeltjenbruns, Joni. Christmas Around the World. Kelley, Emily. rev. ed. 2004. (On My Own Holidays Ser.). 48p. (J). (gr. 2-4). lib. bdg. 25.26 *(978-0-87614-915-7(8))* Lerner Publishing Group.

—Christmas Around the World, 2nd Edition. Kelley, Emily. rev. ed. 2003. (On My Own Holidays Ser.). (ENG.). 48p. (J). (gr. 2-4). pap. 7.99 *(978-1-57505-580-0(5),* First Avenue Editions) Lerner Publishing Group.

—La Navidad Alrededor del Mundo. Kelley, Emily. 2005. (Yo Solo Festividades Ser.). (SPA.). 48p. (J). (gr. 2-4). per. 5.95 *(978-0-8225-3117-3(8))* Lerner Publishing Group.

—La Navidad Alrededor del Mundo. Kelley, Emily. Translations.com Staff, tr. 2005. (Yo Solo - Festividades (on My Own - Holidays) Ser.). (SPA & ENG.). 48p. (gr. 2-4). lib. bdg. 25.26 *(978-0-8225-3116-6(X))* Lerner Publishing Group.

—Not Enough Beds! A Christmas Alphabet Book. Bullard, Lisa. 2004. (Picture Bks.). 32p. (J). (gr. -1-3). 15.95 *(978-1-57505-356-1(X),* Carolrhoda Bks.); per. 6.95 *(978-1-57505-797-2(2))* Lerner Publishing Group.

—Trick-or-Treat on Milton Street. Bullard, Lisa. (Carolrhoda Picture Books Ser.). 32p. (J). 2004. (gr. k-4). pap. 6.95 *(978-1-57505-793-4(X));* 2003. (gr. -1-3). 15.95 *(978-1-57505-158-1(3),* Carolrhoda Bks.) Lerner Publishing Group.

—5 Cheesy Stories: About Friendship, Bravery, Bullying, & More, 1 vol. Clairmont, Patsy. 2007. (Tails from the Pantry Ser.). (ENG.). 144p. (gr. -1-2). 15.99 *(978-1-4003-1042-5(3))* Nelson, Thomas Inc.

Oelze, Don. The First Flute, 1 vol. Bouchard, David. 2015. (ENG.). 32p. (J). (gr. 2-5). 24.95 *(978-0-88995-475-5(5),* fbf40340-7b10-41f0-9dfe-b1f89a5d295a) Trifolium Bks., Inc. CAN. Dist: Firefly Bks., Ltd.

Oeming, Michael Avon. Powers Vol. 4: Supergroup. Bendis, Brian Michael. 2003. 176p. (YA). (gr. 8-18). 29.95 *(978-1-58240-290-1(6))* Image Comics.

—Takio. Bendis, Brian Michael. 2019. 216p. (J). (gr. 2). pap. 16.99 *(978-1-4012-9063-4(9),* Jinxworld) DC Comics.

Oertel, Jennifer. Boo! Hall, Jacque. 2018. (ENG.). 26p. (J). (gr. k-3). 18.99 *(978-1-63132-054-5(8))* Advanced Publishing LLC.

Oesch, Brian. Our Presidents Rock!, 1 vol. Turner, Juliette. 2014. (ENG.). 320p. (J). pap. 16.99 *(978-0-310-73095-8(3))* Zonderkidz.

Ofer, Avi. Bear & Fred: A World War II Story. Argaman, Iris. Appel, Annette, tr. 2020. (ENG.). 48p. (J). (gr. 1-4). 17.99 *(978-1-5420-1821-0(8),* 9781542018210, AmazonCrossing) Amazon Publishing.

—A Concert in the Sand. Shem-Tov, Tami & Sandbank, Rachella. 2017. (ENG.). 32p. (J). (gr. -1-3). 17.99 *(978-1-5124-0099-1(8),* 9781512400991, Kar-Ben Publishing) Lerner Publishing Group.

—A Queen in Jerusalem. Shem-Tov, Tami & Sandbank, Rachella. 2018. (ENG.). 32p. (J). (gr. -1-2). 17.99 *(978-1-5124-4441-4(3),* Kar-Ben Publishing) Lerner Publishing Group.

O'Ferrall, Zoe More. Queer, There, & Everywhere: 23 People Who Changed the World. Prager, Sarah. (ENG.). 272p. (YA). (gr. 8). 2018. pap. 10.99 *(978-0-06-247432-2(4));* 2017. 17.99 *(978-0-06-247431-5(6))* HarperCollins Pubs. Ltd. GBR. (HarperCollins). Dist: HarperCollins Pubs.

Offermann, Andrea. The Boneshaker. Milford, Kate. 2011. (ENG.). 384p. (J). (gr. 5-7). pap. 7.99 *(978-0-547-55004-6(9),* 1450216) Houghton Mifflin Harcourt Publishing Co.

—The Broken Lands. Milford, Kate. 2015. (ENG.). 464p. (J). (gr. 5-7). pap. 8.99 *(978-0-544-43942-9(2),* 1596841, HMH Books For Young Readers) Houghton Mifflin Harcourt Publishing Co.

—The Midnight Zoo. Hartnett, Sonya. 2018. (ENG.). 224p. (J). (gr. 5-9). pap. 7.99 *(978-0-7636-6462-6(6))* Candlewick Pr.

—Some Snow Is... Yeomans, Ellen. 2019. (ENG.). 32p. (J). (gr. -1-3). 16.99 *(978-0-399-54754-6(1),* G.P. Putnam's Sons Books for Young Readers) Penguin Young Readers Group.

—The Thickety #3: Well of Witches. White, J. A. 2017. (Thickety Ser.: 3). (ENG.). 528p. (J). (gr. 5). pap. 7.99 *(978-0-06-225731-4(5),* Tegen, Katherine Bks) HarperCollins Pubs.

—The Thickety #4: the Last Spell. White, J. A. (Thickety Ser.: 4). (ENG.). (J). (gr. 5). 2019. 528p. pap. 8.99 *(978-0-06-238140-8(7));* 2017. 512p. 16.99 *(978-0-06-238139-2(3))* HarperCollins Pubs. (Tegen, Katherine Bks).

—The Thickety: a Path Begins. White, J. A. 2014. (Thickety Ser.: 1). (ENG.). 496p. (J). (gr. 5-7). 16.99 *(978-0-06-225724-6(2),* Tegen, Katherine Bks) HarperCollins Pubs.

—Well of Witches. White, J. A. 2016. (Thickety Ser.: 3). (ENG.). 512p. (J). (gr. 5). 16.99 *(978-0-06-225732-1(3),* Tegen, Katherine Bks) HarperCollins Pubs.

—The Whispering Trees. White, J. A. 2015. (Thickety Ser.: 2). (ENG.). 528p. (J). (gr. 5). 16.99 *(978-0-06-225729-1(3),* Tegen, Katherine Bks) HarperCollins Pubs.

—Yvain: The Knight of the Lion. Anderson, M. T. 2017. 144p. (J). (gr. 7). 19.99 *(978-0-7636-5939-4(8))* Candlewick Pr.

Officer, Robyn. Sariah McDuff: Primary Program Diva. Setzer, Lee Ann. 2004. 61p. (J). pap. 4.95 *(978-1-55517-786-7(7))* Cedar Fort, Inc./CFI Distribution.

Official Roblox, Official. Roblox Ultimate Guide Collection: Top Adventure Games, Top Role-Playing Games, Top Battle Games. Official Roblox, Official. 2020. (ENG.). 288p. (J). (gr. 3). 29.99 ***(978-0-06-302333-8(4),*** HarperCollins) HarperCollins Pubs. Ltd. GBR. Dist: HarperCollins Pubs.

Offir, Amit. How to Draw Pirates: Drawing Easily for Beginners. Offir, Amit. 2019. (How to Draw Cartoon Characters - Black & White Ser.: Vol. 1). (ENG.). 36p. (J). pap. 7.49 *(978-1-7985-6214-7(6))* Independently Published.

Offner, Naomi. Purple Puppy. Faith, Susan. 2005. 32p. (J). 19.95 *(978-0-9707793-0-4(5))* Purple People, Inc.

Offord, Roszella. Adriann Takes a Stand. Roberson, Melondy. 2017. (ENG.). 36p. (J). (gr. -1-3). pap. 12.00 *(978-1-59755-442-8(1),* Advantage BibleStudy) Advantage Bks.

Oftedal, Kristin. Big Bear, Little Brother. Norac, Carl. 2012. (ENG.). 32p. (J). (gr. -1-1). pap. 26.19 *(978-0-230-01684-2(7),* Macmillan Children's Bks.) Pan Macmillan GBR. Dist: Children's Plus, Inc.

Ogasawara, Tomofumi. Mobile Suit Gundam Seed, Vol. 1. Goto, Liu & Yatate, Hajime. 2005. (Mobile Suit Gundam Seed (Novels) Ser.). 272p. pap. 7.99 *(978-1-59532-881-6(5),* Tokyopop Kids) TOKYOPOP, Inc.

—Mobile Suit Gundam WING, 10: Glory of the Losers. Sumizawa, Katsuyuki. 2019. (ENG.). 13p. (YA). (gr. 8-12). pap. 12.95 *(978-1-947194-27-4(5),* Vertical Comics) Vertical, Inc.

—Mobile Suit Gundam WING, 8: Glory of the Losers. Sumizawa, Katsuyuki. 2018. (ENG.). 13p. (YA). (gr. 8-12). pap. 12.95 *(978-1-947194-16-8(X),* Vertical Comics) Vertical, Inc.

—Mobile Suit Gundam WING, 9: Glory of the Losers. Sumizawa, Katsuyuki. 2018. (ENG.). 13p. (YA). (gr. 8-12). pap. 12.95 *(978-1-947194-22-9(4),* Vertical Comics) Vertical, Inc.

Ogata, Michael. New Friend for Nai'a. 2009. (J). *(978-1-56647-912-7(6))* Mutual Publishing LLC.

Ogawa, Grace. Angeldevil V: Tales, Tools, Pawns & Fools. Ogawa, Grace. 2010. 228p. (YA). pap. 12.00 *(978-0-9769275-8-7(6))* Eltsar Pr.

Ogawa, Suharu. Piece It Together Family Puzzle: Catstronauts. 2020. (ENG.). 100p. (J). (gr. -1-k). 14.99 ***(978-1-4521-7463-1(6))*** Chronicle Bks. LLC.

Ogawa, Suharu. Why Don't Cars Run on Apple Juice? Real Science Questions from Real Kids. Vermond, Kira. 2019. 88p. (J). (gr. 2-6). 16.95 *(978-1-77321-302-6(4))* Annick Pr., Ltd. CAN. Dist: Publishers Group West (PGW).

Ogawa, Yayoi. Tramps Like Us. Ogawa, Yayoi. 2005. 192p. Vol. 4. rev. ed. pap. 14.99 *(978-1-59532-142-8(X));* Vol. 6. 6th rev. ed. pap. 14.99 *(978-1-59532-144-2(6))* TOKYOPOP, Inc. (Tokyopop Adult).

Ogden, Betina. Pal Saves the Day. Herman, R. A. 2004. (Pal the Pony Ser.). 32p. (J). pap. *(978-0-439-64985-8(4));* pap. *(978-0-439-57746-5(2))* Scholastic, Inc.

—A Stocking for Jesus. Arruda, Suzanne M. 2005. (J). pap. 7.95 *(978-0-8198-7076-6(5),* 332-372) Pauline Bks. & Media.

Ogden, Bill. The Dog That Called the Signals. Christopher, Matt. 2010. (Matt Christopher Sports Readers Ser.). 48p. (J). (gr. 1-3). lib. bdg. 23.93 *(978-1-59953-349-0(9))* Norwood Hse. Pr.

—The Dog That Stole the Football Plays. Christopher, Matt. 2010. (Matt Christopher Sports Readers Ser.). 48p. (J). (gr. 1-3). lib. bdg. 23.93 *(978-1-59953-350-6(2))* Norwood Hse. Pr.

Oge-E, Eugene. Carnet Blanc Biere de L'Eclair. 2016. (Bnf Affiches Ser.). (FRE.). (J). pap. *(978-2-01-116961-7(5))* Hachette Groupe Livre.

—Carnet Ligne Biere de L'Eclair. 2016. (Bnf Affiches Ser.). (FRE.). (J). pap. *(978-2-01-116938-9(0))* Hachette Groupe Livre.

Oge, Eugene. Carnet Blanc a Qui Dois-Je Mon Chic ? 2016. (Bnf Affiches Ser.). (FRE.). (J). pap. *(978-2-01-116955-6(0))* Hachette Groupe Livre.

—Carnet Ligne a Qui Dois-Je Mon Chic ? 2016. (Bnf Affiches Ser.). (FRE.). (J). pap. *(978-2-01-116980-8(1))* Hachette Groupe Livre.

Ogene, Chuma C. I Wish for Snow. Perkins, Nicole D. 2005. (J). per. 19.95 *(978-0-9755566-0-3(6))* Azreal Publishing Co.

Ogilvie, Sara. The Detective Dog. Donaldson, Julia. 2018. (ENG.). 32p. (J). 17.99 *(978-1-250-15676-1(9),* 900185100, Holt, Henry & Co. Bks. For Young Readers) Holt, Henry & Co.

—Dogs Don't Do Ballet. Kemp, Anna. 2010. (ENG.). 32p. (J). (gr. -1-3). 18.99 *(978-1-4169-9839-6(X),* Simon & Schuster Bks. For Young Readers) Simon & Schuster Bks. For Young Readers.

—Dogs Don't Do Ballet. Kemp, Anna. 2010. (ENG.). 32p. pap. *(978-1-84738-474-4(9))* Simon & Schuster, Ltd.

—How the Bear Lost His Tail. Price, Susan. 2014. (Traditional Tales Ser.). (ENG.). 24p. (J). (gr. 1-2). pap. 6.95 *(978-1-62521-568-0(1),* Capstone Classroom) Capstone.

—Izzy Gizmo, 1 vol. Jones, Pip. 2018. (ENG.). 32p. (J). (gr. -1-3). 17.99 *(978-1-68263-021-1(8))* Peachtree Publishing Co. Inc.

—Izzy Gizmo & the Invention Convention. Jones, Pip. 2020. (ENG.). 32p. (J). (gr. -1-3). 17.99 *(978-1-68263-164-5(8))* Peachtree Publishing Co. Inc.

—Meet the Parents. Bently, Peter. 2014. (ENG.). 32p. (J). (gr. -1-3). 17.99 *(978-1-4814-1483-8(6),* Simon & Schuster/Paula Wiseman Bks.) Simon & Schuster/Paula Wiseman Bks.

—Once upon a Wish. Sparkes, Amy. 2017. (ENG.). 32p. (J). (gr. -1-k). pap. 9.99 *(978-1-84941-661-0(3),* Red Fox) Random House Children's Books GBR. Dist: Independent Pubs. Group.

—Rhinos Don't Eat Pancakes. Kemp, Anna. 2015. (ENG.). 32p. (J). (gr. -1-3). 17.99 *(978-1-4814-3845-2(X),* Simon & Schuster/Paula Wiseman Bks.) Simon & Schuster/Paula Wiseman Bks.

—The Wildest Cowboy. Jennings, Garth. ed. 2017. (ENG.). 32p. (J). (gr. -1-k). 19.99 *(978-0-230-76923-6(3))* Pan Macmillan GBR. Dist: Independent Pubs. Group.

Ogilvie, Sara, jt. illus. see Henry, Thomas.

Ogilvie, Shane. The Institute of Fantastical Inventions II: Magnetic Attraction. Leys, Dave. 2019. 264p. (J). (gr. 4-7). pap. 9.99 *(978-1-76079-134-6(2))* New Holland Pubs. Pty. Ltd. AUS. Dist: Independent Pubs. Group.

—Powman 2: Discover the Strength Within. Tabain, Dave & Worland, Nadia. 2020. (Powman Ser.). 128p. (J). (gr. 2-4). pap. 9.99 *(978-1-76079-146-9(6))* New Holland Pubs. Pty. Ltd. AUS. Dist: Independent Pubs. Group.

Ogiwara, Noriko. Mirror Sword & Shadow Prince. Ogiwara, Noriko. 2011. (ENG.). 500p. 21.99 *(978-1-4215-3725-2(7))* Viz Media.

Ogle, Nancy Gray. Looking at Wild Cats. Hodge, Deborah. 2008. (Kids Can Read Ser.). (ENG.). 32p. (J). (gr. k-1). pap. 3.95 *(978-1-55453-285-8(X))* Kids Can Pr., Ltd. CAN. Dist: Hachette Bk. Group.

—Otters. Mason, Adrienne. 2003. (Kids Can Press Wildlife Ser.). (ENG.). 32p. (J). (gr. k-5). 11.99 *(978-1-55337-407-7(X))* Kids Can Pr., Ltd. CAN. Dist: Hachette Bk. Group.

—Owls. Mason, Adrienne. 2004. (Kids Can Press Wildlife Ser.). (ENG.). 32p. (J). (gr. k-5). 7.95 *(978-1-55337-624-8(2))* Kids Can Pr., Ltd. CAN. Dist: Hachette Bk. Group.

—Skunks. Mason, Adrienne. 2006. (Kids Can Press Wildlife Ser.). (ENG.). 32p. (J). (gr. k-5). 11.99 *(978-1-55337-734-4(6))* Kids Can Pr., Ltd. CAN. Dist: Hachette Bk. Group.

Oglesby, Maria. Stand Up! The Courage to Care. April, Elyse & Ryan, Regina Sara. 2016. (Family & World Health Ser.). (ENG.). 32p. (J). pap. 9.95 *(978-1-942493-17-4(7))* Hohm Pr.

Ogmios. Megan & Riley Share the Joy of Christmas. Keeney, Kenneth. 2018. (ENG.). 32p. (J). 19.99 *(978-0-9979274-5-0(3));* pap. 10.99 *(978-0-9979274-4-3(5))* Farmer's Daughter Pr.

Ogo, Luis S. Illuminating the Legacy: A Coloring & Activity Book of the CNMI's History. Sanchez, John Joseph P. 2006. 106p. (J). (gr. 4-5). pap. *(978-1-878453-89-1(0))* Univ. of Guam, Micronesian Area Research Ctr.

Ogorek, Elchanan. As Bs CS Oh My! Ogorek, Elchanan. 2016. (ENG.). (J). 13.00 *(978-0-692-76640-8(5))* Ogorek, Elchanan.

O'Grady, Laurie. Day to Day. David, Sophia. 2018. (ENG.). 22p. (J). (gr. k-6). 24.95 *(978-0-692-15777-0(8))* Lily The Reindeer.

Oh, Charlotte. First Look at Insects. Gates Galvin, Laura. 2011. (ENG.). 16p. (J). *(978-1-60727-223-6(7))* Soundprints.

Oh, Daniella. The 3 Trees. 2008. Orig. Title: Les 3 Arbres. 32p. (J). (gr. -1-1). 8.95 *(978-0-8198-7426-9(4))* Pauline Bks. & Media.

Oh, Jiwon. Mr. Monkey's Classroom. Oh, Jiwon. 2005. 32p. (J). (gr. -1-2). lib. bdg. 15.89 *(978-0-06-055722-5(2))* HarperCollins Pubs.

Oh, Joowon. Our Favorite Day. Oh, Joowon. 2019. (ENG.). 32p. (J). (gr. -1-2). 16.99 *(978-1-5362-0357-8(2))* Candlewick Pr.

Oh, Lee. Where the Winds Meet: Mongolia. Joo, Mi-hwa. Cowley, Joy, ed. 2015. (Global Kids Storybooks Ser.). (ENG.). 32p. (gr. 1-4). 26.65 *(978-1-925246-03-2(5));* 26.65 *(978-1-925246-29-2(9));* 7.99 *(978-1-925246-55-1(8))* ChoiceMaker Pty. Ltd., The AUS. (Big and SMALL). Dist: Lerner Publishing Group.

Oh, Mo, jt. illus. see Timmons, Anne.

Oh Rhe Bar Ghun. Peigenz, 8 vols., Vol. 1. Oh Rhe Bar Ghun. 2004. (Peigenz Ser.: Vol. 1). 192p. (YA). per. 9.95 *(978-1-59697-021-2(9))* Infinity Studios LLC.

Oh, Seung-min. Good Friends: Symbiotic Relationships. Jang, Ki-hwa & Kim, In-sook. Cowley, Joy, ed. 2015. (Science Storybooks Ser.). (ENG.). 32p. (gr. k-3). 26.65 *(978-1-925246-20-9(5));* 7.99 *(978-1-925246-72-8(8))* ChoiceMaker Pty. Ltd., The AUS. (Big and SMALL). Dist: Lerner Publishing Group.

—Good Friends: Symbiotic Relationships. Jang, Ki-hwa. Cowley, Joy, ed. 2015. (Science Storybooks Ser.). (ENG.). 32p. (J). (gr. k-4). 10.00 *(978-1-925233-58-2(8),* Big and SMALL) ChoiceMaker Pty. Ltd., The AUS. Dist: Lerner Publishing Group.

—Good Friends: Symbiotic Relationships. Jang, Ki-hwa & Kim, In-sook. Cowley, Joy, ed. 2015. (Science Storybooks Ser.). (ENG.). 32p. (gr. k-3). 26.65 *(978-1-925246-46-9(9),* Big and SMALL) ChoiceMaker Pty. Ltd., The AUS. Dist: Lerner Publishing Group.

Oh!, Gramma. White Cow Blue Cow. Oh!, Gramma. 2015. (ENG.). 30p. (J). pap. 10.00 ***(978-1-7309-6584-5(9))*** Independently Published.

O'Hagan, Katie. What I Think about When I'm Running. Levenson, Eleanor. 2018. (Picture Books Troika Ser.). (ENG.). 32p. (J). (gr. -1-k). pap. 9.99 *(978-1-909991-17-0(1))* Troika Bks. GBR. Dist: Independent Pubs. Group.

O'Hara, Catherine, jt. illus. see de Sève, Peter.

O'Hara, Cynthia, jt. illus. see Amory, Deanna.

O'Hara, Lauren. Madame Badobedah. Dahl, Sophie. 2020. (ENG.). 56p. (J). (gr. k-3). 18.99 *(978-1-5362-1022-4(6))* Candlewick Pr.

O'Hara, Melanie Marie. Blazing Wyoming Bonnets: Twenty-Five Women Who Helped Forge Our State. Mead, Carol. 2019. (ENG.). 56p. (J). pap. 12.95 ***(978-1-7045-8727-1(1))*** Independently Published.

O'Hare, Michael. Fashion Victims! Van Lente, Fred. Paniccia, Mark, ed. 2007. (Spider-Man Ser.: No. 3). (ENG.). 24p. (J). (gr. 2-6). lib. bdg. 27.07 *(978-1-59961-395-6(6),* 13633, Marvel Age) Spotlight.

O'hehir, Trisha. The Toothpaste Secret. O'hehir, Trisha. 2003. 56p. (J). (gr. 2-6). 9.95 *(978-0-9659236-1-3(4))* Perio Reports.

O'Herron, Mary. A Letter from Marty: Grandma & Grandpa's Cat. O'Herron, Mary. 2004. 32p. (J). (gr. -1-1). pap. 8.95 *(978-0-9664732-4-7(8))* Countinghouse Pr., Inc.

Ohi, Debbie Ridpath. Freckle Juice. Blume, Judy. 2014. (ENG.). (J). (gr. 1-5). lib. bdg. 16.60 *(978-1-62765-552-1(2))* Perfection Learning Corp.

—Freckle Juice. Blume, Judy. 2014. (ENG.). 64p. (J). (gr. 1-5). pap. 5.99 *(978-1-4814-1102-8(0),* Atheneum Bks. for Young Readers) Simon & Schuster Children's Publishing.

Ohi, Debbie Ridpath. Gurple & Preen: A Broken Crayon Cosmic Adventure. Park, Linda Sue. 2020. (ENG.). 48p. (J). (gr. -1-3). 17.99 ***(978-1-5344-3141-6(1))*** Simon & Schuster.

Ohi, Debbie Ridpath. I'm Bored. Black, Michael Ian. 2012. (I'm Bks.). (ENG.). 40p. (J). (gr. -1-3). 17.99 *(978-1-4424-1403-7(0),* Simon & Schuster Bks. For Young Readers) Simon & Schuster Bks. For Young Readers.

—I'm Sad. Black, Michael Ian. 2018. (I'm Bks.). (ENG.). 40p. (J). (gr. -1-3). 17.99 *(978-1-4814-7627-0(0),* Simon & Schuster Bks. For Young Readers) Simon & Schuster Bks. For Young Readers.

—I'm Worried. Black, Michael Ian. 2019. (I'm Bks.). (ENG.). 40p. (J). (gr. -1-3). 17.99 *(978-1-5344-1586-7(6),* Simon & Schuster Bks. For Young Readers) Simon & Schuster Bks. For Young Readers.

—Mitzi Tulane, Preschool Detective in the Secret Ingredient. McLaughlin, Lauren. 2017. (J). (-k). 32p. 17.99 *(978-0-449-81916-6(7));* (ENG.). 40p. lib. bdg. 20.99 *(978-0-375-97177-8(7))* Random Hse. Children's Bks. (Random Hse. Bks. for Young Readers).

—Naked! Black, Michael Ian. 2014. (ENG.). 40p. (J). (gr. -1-3). 18.99 *(978-1-4424-6738-5(X),* Simon & Schuster Bks. For Young Readers) Simon & Schuster Bks. For Young Readers.

—The One in the Middle Is the Green Kangaroo. Blume, Judy. 2014. (ENG.). (J). (gr. 1-5). lib. bdg. 16.60 *(978-1-62765-590-3(5))* Perfection Learning Corp.

—The One in the Middle Is the Green Kangaroo. Blume, Judy. 2014. (ENG.). 48p. (J). (gr. 1-5). pap. 5.99 *(978-1-4814-1131-8(4)*, Atheneum Bks. for Young Readers) Simon & Schuster Children's Publishing.

—The Pain & the Great One. Blume, Judy. 2014. (ENG.). 48p. (J). (gr. 1-5). pap. 5.99 *(978-1-4814-1145-5(4)*, Atheneum Bks. for Young Readers) Simon & Schuster Children's Publishing.

—Ruby Rose, Big Bravos. Sanders, Rob. 2017. (ENG.). 40p. (J). (gr. -1-3). 15.99 *(978-0-06-223571-8(0))* HarperCollins Pubs.

—Ruby Rose: off to School She Goes. Sanders, Rob. 2016. (ENG.). 32p. (J). (gr. -1-3). 15.99 *(978-0-06-223569-5(9))* HarperCollins Pubs.

—Sea Monkey & Bob. Reynolds, Aaron. 2017. (ENG.). 40p. (J). (gr. -1-3). 17.99 *(978-1-4814-0676-5(0)*, Simon & Schuster Bks. For Young Readers) Simon & Schuster Bks. For Young Readers.

Ohi, Debbie Ridpath. Sam & Eva. Ohi, Debbie Ridpath. 2017. (ENG.). 40p. (J). (gr. -1-3). 17.99 *(978-1-4814-1628-3(6)*, Simon & Schuster Bks. For Young Readers) Simon & Schuster Bks. For Young Readers.

—Where Are My Books? Ohi, Debbie Ridpath. (ENG.). 40p. (J). (gr. -1-3). 2019. 7.99 *(978-1-5344-5320-3(2))*; 2015. 17.99 *(978-1-4424-6741-5(X))* Simon & Schuster Bks. For Young Readers. (Simon & Schuster Bks. For Young Readers).

Ohi, Ruth. Into My Mother's Arms. Jennings, Sharon. 2003. (ENG.). 32p. (J). (gr. -1-3). pap. 6.95 *(978-1-55041-800-2(9)*, c32454d3-2f82-4539-8cd0-2c09b02a3fab) Fitzhenry & Whiteside, Ltd. CAN. Dist: Firefly Bks., Ltd.

—Naomi's Road, 1 vol. Kogawa, Joy. 2005. (ENG.). 120p. (Orig.). (J). (gr. 3-6). pap. 9.95 *(978-1-55005-115-5(6)*, 621bd9bf-b3c3-40d5-8bb9-93d96227d8c6) Fitzhenry & Whiteside, Ltd. CAN. Dist: Firefly Bks., Ltd.

—Naomi's Tree, 1 vol. Kogawa, Joy. 2011. (ENG.). 32p. (J). (gr. 4-6). pap. 9.95 *(978-1-55455-184-2(6)*, f862ef7e-47dc-47dc-be11-165b1858bc27) Trifolium Bks., Inc. CAN. Dist: Firefly Bks., Ltd.

—No Monsters Here, 1 vol. Jennings, Sharon. 2006. (ENG.). 24p. (J). (gr. -1-k). pap. 7.95 *(978-1-55041-789-0(4)*, d353d85b-81e0-45ff-841d-064ed711334e) éditeur, Annika Parance CAN. Dist: Firefly Bks., Ltd.

Ohi, Ruth. Fox & Squirrel. Ohi, Ruth. 2013. (ENG.). 32p. (gr. -1-2). *(978-1-4431-1914-6(8))* Scholastic Canada, Ltd.

—Shh! My Brother's Napping. Ohi, Ruth. 2017. 28p. (J). 11.99 *(978-1-61067-552-9(5))* Kane Miller.

Ohi, Ruth, jt. illus. see Krykorka, Vladyana.

Ohkami, Mineko. Dragon Knights, 17 vols., Vol. 7. Ohkami, Mineko. Yoshida, Agnes, tr. from JPN. rev. ed. 2003. (Graphic Novel-Manga Ser.). 208p. (gr. 8-18). pap. 9.99 *(978-1-59182-111-3(8))* TOKYOPOP, Inc.

—Dragon Knights, 17 vols. Ohkami, Mineko. rev. ed. 2003. (Graphic Novel-Manga Ser.). 192p. Vol. 10. pap. 9.99 *(978-1-59182-114-4(2))*; Vol. 11. pap. 9.99 *(978-1-59182-115-1(0))* TOKYOPOP, Inc.

—Dragon Knights, 17 vols., Vol. 12. Ohkami, Mineko. Nakamura, Yuki, tr. from JPN. rev. ed. 2004. (Graphic Novel-Manga Ser.). 200p. pap. 9.99 *(978-1-59182-440-4(0))* TOKYOPOP, Inc.

—Dragon Knights. Ohkami, Mineko. Vol. 18. rev. ed. 2005. 208p. pap. 9.99 *(978-1-59182-961-4(5))*; Vol. 21. 21st rev. ed. 2005. 192p. pap. 9.99 *(978-1-59532-634-8(0))*; Vol. 22. 22nd rev. ed. 2006. 200p. per. 9.99 *(978-1-59532-635-5(9))*; Vol. 24. 24th rev. ed. 2007. 208p. per. 9.99 *(978-1-59816-797-9(9))* TOKYOPOP, Inc.

Ohkami, Mineko. Dragon Knights, Vol. 19. Ohkami, Mineko, creator. 19th rev. ed. 2005. 192p. pap. 9.99 *(978-1-59182-962-1(3))* TOKYOPOP, Inc.

OHora, Zachariah. Bikes for Sale (Story Books for Kids, Books about Friendship, Preschool Picture Books) Higgins, Carter. 2019. (ENG.). 40p. (J). (gr. -1-k). 16.99 *(978-1-4521-5932-4(7))* Chronicle Bks. LLC.

—Horrible Bear! Dyckman, Ame. 2016. (ENG.). 40p. (J). (gr. -1-3). 17.99 *(978-0-316-28283-3(9))* Little Brown & Co.

—If Your Monster Won't Go to Bed. Vega, Denise. 2017. 40p. (J). (gr. -1-2). 17.99 *(978-0-553-49655-0(7)*, Knopf Bks. for Young Readers) Random Hse. Children's Bks.

—The Pet Project: Cute & Cuddly Vicious Verses. Wheeler, Lisa. 2013. (ENG.). 40p. (J). (gr. -1-3). 16.99 *(978-1-4169-7595-3(0)*, Atheneum Bks. for Young Readers) Simon & Schuster Children's Publishing.

—Read the Book, Lemmings! Dyckman, Ame. 2017. (ENG.). 40p. (J). (gr. -1-3). 17.99 *(978-0-316-34348-0(X))* Little Brown & Co.

—Tyrannosaurus Wrecks! Bardhan-Quallen, Sudipta. 2014. (ENG.). 32p. (J). (gr. -1-3). 14.95 *(978-1-4197-1035-3(4)*, Abrams Bks. for Young Readers) Abrams, Inc.

—Tyrannosaurus Wrecks! A Preschool Story. Bardhan-Quallen, Sudipta. 2018. (ENG.). 32p. (J). (gr. -1 — 1). pap. 7.99 *(978-1-4197-3322-2(2)*, Abrams Appleseed) Abrams, Inc.

—Who Wet My Pants? Shea, Bob. 2019. 40p. (J). (gr. -1-3). 17.99 *(978-0-316-52521-3(9))* Little Brown & Co.

—Wolfie the Bunny. Dyckman, Ame. 2015. (ENG.). 40p. (J). (gr. -1-3). 18.99 *(978-0-316-22614-1(9))* Little, Brown Bks. for Young Readers.

OHora, Zachariah. No Fits, Nilson! OHora, Zachariah. 2013. 32p. (J). (gr. -1-k). 17.99 *(978-0-8037-3852-2(8)*, Dial Bks) Penguin Young Readers Group.

—Stop Snoring, Bernard! OHora, Zachariah. 2012. (ENG.). 32p. (J). (gr. -1-2). pap. 8.99 *(978-1-250-00717-9(8)*, 9781250007179) Square Fish.

Ohtsuka, Tommy, et al. Flesh for the Beast. Komada, Yoshihiro et al. Pannone, Frank, ed. 2004. 132p. pap. 9.99 *(978-1-58655-556-6(1)*, SSNOV-0419) Media Blasters, Inc.

Oien, Jennifer. Tessie the Toad. Grandma Poo Poo. 2008. 28p. pap. 24.95 *(978-1-60610-325-8(3))* America Star Bks.

Ojala, Eiko. All Year Round. Katz, Susan B. 2016. (ENG.). 32p. (J). (gr. -1-1). 17.99 *(978-0-545-74100-2(9)*, Orchard Bks.) Scholastic, Inc.

—Her Right Foot. Eggers, Dave. 2017. (ENG.). 104p. (J). (gr. k-3). 19.99 *(978-1-4521-6281-2(6))* Chronicle Bks. LLC.

Ojeda, Carlos. As Long As We Can Smile. Perks, Joseph M. 2018. (ENG.). 34p. (J). pap. *(978-1-5272-2002-7(8))* Perks, Joseph.

Ok, SeoJeong. Oh That Snow! Kim, JeongHo. 2014. (MySELF Bookshelf Ser.). (ENG.). 32p. (J). (gr. k-2). pap. 11.94 *(978-1-60357-697-0(5))*; lib. bdg. 25.27 *(978-1-59953-662-0(5))* Norwood Hse. Pr.

Okabe, Akiko. Die Geheimnisvolle Blume. Pouatcha, Pearly. Schroer, P., tr. 2018. (GER.). 66p. (J). (gr. 3-6). pap. 14.99 *(978-0-578-40010-5(3))* PloohFX Investments.

—La Fleur Mystique. Pouatcha, Pearly. Fedor, Ashley, ed. 2018. (Cristaux Manquants Ser.). (FRE.). 68p. (J). (gr. 3-6). pap. 14.99 *(978-0-692-19825-4(3))* PloohFX Investments.

Okada, Chiaki. For All the Stars Across the Sky. Newson, Karl. 2019. (ENG.). 32p. (J). (gr. -1-2). 15.99 *(978-1-5362-0542-8(7))* Candlewick Pr.

Okamoto, Alan. Kingdom of Nu - TJ's Tale: TJ's Tale. Okamoto, Rod. 2006. (J). per. 19.95 *(978-0-9764116-0-4(1))* Nutrishare Publishing.

—Max Goes to Mars: A Science Adventure with Max the Dog. Bennett, Jeffrey. 2015. (Science Adventures with Max the Dog Ser.). (ENG.). 32p. (J). (gr. 2-4). 15.00 *(978-1-937548-44-5(9))* Big Kid Science.

—Max Goes to the Moon: A Science Adventure with Max the Dog. Bennett, Jeffrey. 2nd ed. 2012. (Science Adventures with Max the Dog Ser.). 32p. (J). (gr. 2-4). 15.00 *(978-1-937548-20-9(1))* Big Kid Science.

O'Kane, George & McEntee, Bill. Hook Em's Colorful Campus Tour - University of Texas A-Z: Forty Acres (A-Z) 2004. (J). 9.99 *(978-1-933069-01-2(5))* Odd Duck Ink, Inc.

O'Kane, George & Weikert, Dana. Baldwin's Colorful Campus Tour - Boston College A-Z. 2004. (J). 9.99 *(978-1-933069-00-5(7))* Odd Duck Ink, Inc.

Oke, Rachel, jt. illus. see Haynes, Jason.

O'Keefe, Laurie. Gopher to the Rescue! A Volcano Recovery Story, 1 vol. Jennings, Terry Catasús. 2012. (ENG.). 32p. (J). (gr. -1-4). 17.95 *(978-1-60718-131-6(2))*; pap. 9.95 *(978-1-60718-141-5(X))* Arbordale Publishing.

OKeefe, Raven. If Your Possum Go Daylight. Lofficier, Randy. 2009. (ENG.). 60p. (J). pap. 12.95 *(978-1-934543-78-8(0))* HollywoodComics.com, LLC.

O'Keeffe, Alejandro. Queen Dog. Heos, Bridget. 2017. 40p. (J). (gr. -1-k). 16.99 ***(978-1-4847-2852-9(1))*** Little, Brown Bks. for Young Readers.

O'Keeffe, Alejandro. Rumpelstiltskin. Nadin, Joanna. 2014. (Traditional Tales Ser.). (ENG.). 32p. (J). (gr. 1-2). pap. 7.95 *(978-1-62521-598-7(3)*, Capstone Classroom) Capstone.

Oketch, Alphonce Omondi. Rfaud Tastes Wisdom. Carlson, Martin D. 2013. 36p. pap. 11.00 *(978-0-9848791-2-0(9))* BoCook Publishing.

O'Kif. I'm Taller Than You! Benjamin, A. H. 2008. (Tadpoles Ser.). (ENG.). 24p. (J). (gr. -1-3). lib. bdg. *(978-0-7787-3854-1(X))* Crabtree Publishing Co.

—No Somos Irrompibles (12 Cuentos de Chicos Enamorados) 2003. (SPA.). 143p. (J). (gr. 8-12). pap. 9.95 *(978-950-511-243-2(2))* Santillana USA Publishing Co., Inc.

—La Tarea Segun Natacha. Pescetti, Luis Mariá. 2003. (Coleccion Derechos Del Nino Ser.). (SPA.). 32p. (J). (gr. 3-5). pap. 7.95 *(978-84-204-5836-6(8))* Santillana USA Publishing Co., Inc.

O'Kif, Alejandro. Beauty & the Beast (Tales to Grow By) A Story about Trust. 2020. (Tales to Grow By Ser.). (ENG.). 32p. (J). (gr. k-1). pap. 6.95 *(978-0-531-24621-4(3))*; lib. bdg. 26.00 *(978-0-531-23187-6(9))* Scholastic Library Publishing. (Children's Pr.).

Oklejak, Marianna. Boom! Boom! Boom! Wechterowicz, Przemystaw. ed. 2019. 32p. (J). (gr. -1-k). 16.95 *(978-1-912537-95-2(8)*, Scribblers) Book Hse. GBR. Dist: Sterling Publishing Co., Inc.

Okonji, Azuka. Malaik: A Poetry Collection for Children & Those Who Love Them. Chukwumerije, Dikeogu. 2012. 60p. pap. *(978-0-9557940-9-4(9))* Afriscope Publishing.

Oksner, Judith. Barking: The Dogs with the Barking Genes. Milton, Edith. 2017. (ENG.). 56p. pap. 16.00 *(978-0-87233-244-7(6))* Bauhan Publishing LLC.

—Snowball: The Dancing Cockatoo. Montgomery, Sy. 2013. (ENG.). 64p. (J). pap. 15.00 *(978-0-87233-156-3(3))* Bauhan Publishing LLC.

Okstad, Ella. The Big Country Fair. Jones, Pip. 2018. (Squishy Mcfluff Ser.). (ENG.). 80p. (J). pap. 8.95 *(978-0-571-32070-7(8))* Faber & Faber, Inc.

—Five Children & It. Nesbit, E. 2017. (Alma Junior Classics Ser.). (ENG.). 160p. (J). pap. 9.99 *(978-1-84749-636-2(9)*, 351528) Alma Classics GBR. Dist: Bloomsbury Publishing Plc.

—Halloween Good Night. Grabill, Rebecca. 2017. (ENG.). 32p. (J). (gr. -1-3). 17.99 *(978-1-4814-5061-4(1))* Simon & Schuster Children's Publishing.

—Meets Mad Nana Dot. Jones, Pip. 2018. (Squishy Mcfluff Ser.). (ENG.). 80p. (J). pap. 8.95 *(978-0-571-30254-3(8)*, Faber & Faber Children's Bks.) Faber & Faber, Inc.

—Princess Kitty. Metzger, Steve. 2017. (ENG.). 32p. (J). (gr. -1-3). 17.99 *(978-0-06-230662-3(6))* HarperCollins Pubs.

—The Psammead Trilogy, 3 vols. Nesbit, E. 2019. 1p. (J). 31.99 *(978-0-7145-4912-5(6)*, 442878) Alma Classics GBR. Dist: Bloomsbury Publishing Plc.

—Seaside Rescue! Jones, Pip. 2018. (Squishy Mcfluff Ser.). (ENG.). 80p. (J). pap. 8.95 *(978-0-571-32068-4(6))* Faber & Faber, Inc.

—Sophie Johnson, Unicorn Expert. Hood, Morag. 2018. (Sophie Johnson, Unicorn Expert Ser.). (ENG.). 32p. (J). (gr. -1-3). 17.99 *(978-1-5344-3161-4(6)*, Aladdin) Simon & Schuster Children's Publishing.

—Squishy McFluff: Supermarket Sweep! Jones, Pip. 2017. (Squishy Mcfluff Ser.). (ENG.). 80p. (J). (gr. k-2). pap. 8.95 *(978-0-571-30252-9(1)*, Faber & Faber Children's Bks.) Faber & Faber, Inc.

—Squishy McFluff: Tea with the Queen. Jones, Pip. 2019. (Squishy Mcfluff Ser.). (ENG.). 32p. (J). 16.95 *(978-0-571-33727-9(9))* Faber & Faber, Inc.

—The Story of the Amulet. Nesbit, E. 2019. (Alma Junior Classics Ser.). 320p. (J). pap. 11.00 *(978-1-84749-790-1(X)*, 441048) Alma Classics GBR. Dist: Bloomsbury Publishing Plc.

—Tiny Tantrum. Crowe, Caroline. 2017. (ENG.). 32p. (J). (gr. -1-2). 16.99 *(978-1-68010-072-3(6))* Tiger Tales.

Okum, David. Napoleon's Last Stand. Boyd, David. 2007. 48p. (J). lib. bdg. 23.08 *(978-1-4242-1639-0(7))* Fitzgerald Bks.

—Rebel Prince. Downey, Glen. 2007. 48p. (J). lib. bdg. 23.08 *(978-1-4242-1642-0(7))* Fitzgerald Bks.

Olafsdottir, Linda. The Enormous Turnip. Olmstead, Kathleen. 2013. (J). *(978-1-4027-8344-9(2))* Sterling Publishing Co., Inc.

—The Sorcerer's Apprentice. Olmstead, Kathleen. 2015. (J). *(978-1-4027-8350-0(7))* Sterling Publishing Co., Inc.

Olafsdottir, Linda, jt. illus. see Oberdieck, Bernhard.

Olafsdottir, Linda, jt. illus. see Zilber, Denis.

Olah, Tina. Lester's Great Adventure. Dobson, Julie M. 2018. (ENG.). 48p. (J). *(978-1-5255-1876-8(3))*; pap. *(978-1-5255-1877-5(1))* FriesenPress.

Olan, Agnieszka. The Forgotten Birthday. Lenington, Paula. 2011. 28p. pap. 24.95 *(978-1-4560-2711-7(5))* America Star Bks.

Olberg, Henry. The Magical Tooth Fairies: A Surprise in Mexico. 2012. (J). *(978-0-86715-568-6(X))* Edition Q, Inc.

Olbey, Arpad. Crab Campaign: An Invasive Species Tracker's Journal. Watson, J. A. 2019. (Science Squad Set 2 (Set Of 2) Ser.). (ENG.). 192p. (J). 28.50 *(978-1-63163-295-2(7)*, 1631632957, Jolly Fish Pr.) North Star Editions.

—Hatchling Hero: A Sea Turtle Defender's Journal. Watson, J. A. 2018. (Science Squad Ser.). (ENG.). 192p. (J). 28.50 *(978-1-63163-160-3(8)*, 1631631608); pap. 9.99 *(978-1-63163-161-0(6)*, 1631631616) North Star Editions. (Jolly Fish Pr.).

—Monarch Mystery: A Butterfly Researcher's Journal. Watson, J. A. 2018. (Science Squad Ser.). (ENG.). 192p. (J). pap. 9.99 *(978-1-63163-184-9(5)*, 1631631845, Jolly Fish Pr.) North Star Editions.

—Nocturnal Symphony: A Bat Detector's Journal. Watson, J. A. 2019. (Science Squad Set 2 (Set Of 2) Ser.). (ENG.). 192p. (J). 28.50 *(978-1-63163-299-0(X)*, 163163299X, Jolly Fish Pr.) North Star Editions.

—Pigeon Problems: An Urban Bird Researcher's Journal. Watson, J. A. 2018. (Science Squad Ser.). (ENG.). 192p. (J). pap. 9.99 *(978-1-63163-188-7(8)*, 1631631888, Jolly Fish Pr.) North Star Editions.

—Runway ZomBee: A Zombie Bee Hunter's Journal. Watson, J. A. 2018. (Science Squad Ser.). (ENG.). 192p. (J). 28.50 *(978-1-63163-164-1(0)*, 1631631640); pap. 9.99 *(978-1-63163-165-8(9)*, 1631631659) North Star Editions. (Jolly Fish Pr.).

—Science Squad Set 2 (Set Of 2) Watson, J. A. 2019. (Science Squad Set 2 (Set Of 2) Ser.). (ENG.). 384p. (J). pap. 19.98 *(978-1-63163-292-1(2)*, 1631632922); lib. bdg. 57.00 *(978-1-63163-291-4(4)*, 1631632914) North Star Editions. (Jolly Fish Pr.).

—Tamerlane & the Boy 4 Voyagers. Bradman, Tom and Tony. 2017. (Cambridge Reading Adventures Ser.). (ENG.). 40p. pap. 8.99 *(978-1-108-41087-8(1))* Cambridge Univ. Pr.

Oldfield, Rachel. I Like the Snow. Nelson, Sarah. 2020. (ENG.). (J). pap. ***(978-1-64686-097-5(7))*** Barefoot Bks., Inc.

—I Like the Sun. Nelson, Sarah. 2020. (ENG.). (J). pap. ***(978-1-64686-101-9(9))*** Barefoot Bks., Inc.

—I Like the Wind. Nelson, Sarah. 2020. (ENG.). (J). pap. ***(978-1-64686-095-1(0))*** Barefoot Bks., Inc.

Oldfield, Rachel. Outdoor Opposites. Williams, Brenda. 2015. 32p. (J). (gr. -1-2). 9.99 *(978-1-78285-095-3(3))* Barefoot Bks., Inc.

—Up, up, Up! Reed, Susan. 2010. 24p. (J). (gr. -1-2). 16.99 *(978-1-84686-369-1(4))* Barefoot Bks., Inc.

Oldham, Cindi. Marianne's Secret Cousins. Williams, Annie Morris. 2005. (Family History Adventures for Young Readers Ser.: 2). 240p. (J). per. 10.00 *(978-0-9645272-8-7(6))* Field Stone Pubs.

Oldham, Marion. Carrots, Just a Little Boy. Molesworth, Mary Louisa. 2004. reprint ed. pap. 22.95 *(978-1-4179-3800-1(5))* Kessinger Publishing, LLC.

Oldland, Nicholas. Big Bear Hug. Oldland, Nicholas. (Life in the Wild Ser.). (ENG.). 32p. (J). (gr. -1-2). 2020. bds. 9.99 *(978-1-5253-0379-1(1))*; 2014. 7.99 *(978-1-77138-151-2(5))*; 2009. 16.95 *(978-1-55453-464-7(X))* Kids Can Pr., Ltd. CAN. Dist: Hachette Bk. Group.

—The Busy Beaver. Oldland, Nicholas. 2011. (Life in the Wild Ser.). (ENG.). 32p. (J). (gr. -1-2). 16.95 *(978-1-55453-749-5(5))* Kids Can Pr., Ltd. CAN. Dist: Hachette Bk. Group.

—Dinosaur Countdown. Oldland, Nicholas. 2012. (ENG.). 24p. (J). (gr. -1-1). 15.95 *(978-1-55453-834-8(3))* Kids Can Pr., Ltd. CAN. Dist: Hachette Bk. Group.

Oldland, Nicholas. Hockey in the Wild. Oldland, Nicholas. 2020. (Life in the Wild Ser.). (ENG.). 32p. (J). (gr. -1-2). 16.99 ***(978-1-5253-0241-1(8))*** Kids Can Pr., Ltd. CAN. Dist: Hachette Bk. Group.

Oldland, Nicholas. Making the Moose Out of Life. Oldland, Nicholas. (Life in the Wild Ser.). (ENG.). 32p. (J). (gr. -1-2). 2015. pap. 7.95 *(978-1-55453-627-6(8))*; 2010. 16.95 *(978-1-55453-580-4(8))* Kids Can Pr., Ltd. CAN. Dist: Hachette Bk. Group.

—One Wild Christmas. Oldland, Nicholas. 2019. (Life in the Wild Ser.). (ENG.). 32p. (J). (gr. -1-2). 16.99 *(978-1-5253-0203-9(5))* Kids Can Pr., Ltd. CAN. Dist: Hachette Bk. Group.

Oldroyd, Mark. John Henry. Krensky, Stephen. 2007. (On My Own Folklore Ser.). (ENG.). 48p. (J). (gr. 2-4). per. 7.99 *(978-0-8225-6477-5(7)*, First Avenue Editions) Lerner Publishing Group.

—John Henry. Krensky, Stephen. 2006. (On My Own Folklore Ser.). (ENG.). 48p. (J). (gr. 2-4). lib. bdg. 25.26 *(978-1-57505-887-0(1)*, Millbrook Pr.) Lerner Publishing Group.

—Leif Eriksson. Knudsen, Shannon. 2005. (On My Own Biography Ser.). (ENG.). 48p. (gr. 2-4). (J). pap. 7.99 *(978-1-57505-828-3(6)*, First Avenue Editions); lib. bdg. 25.26 *(978-1-57505-649-4(6)*, Carolrhoda Bks.) Lerner Publishing Group.

—Sarah Emma Edmonds Was a Great Pretender: The True Story of a Civil War Spy. Jones, Carrie. 2011. (ENG.). 32p. (J). (gr. 2-5). 17.95 *(978-0-7613-5399-7(2)*, 9780761353997, Carolrhoda Bks.) Lerner Publishing Group.

—Stowaway!: Band 14/Ruby (Collins Big Cat) Jarman, Julia. 2007. (Collins Big Cat Ser.). (ENG.). 48p. (J). (gr. 3-4). pap. 11.99 *(978-0-00-723088-4(5))* HarperCollins Pubs. Ltd. GBR. Dist: Independent Pubs. Group.

Olds, Irene. How Do the Children Pray? Denis, Toni. 2010. 16p. 10.99 *(978-1-4490-5164-8(2))* AuthorHouse.

Olea, Francisco. Life Without Nico. Maturana, Andrea. 2016. (ENG.). 40p. (J). (gr. -1-2). 16.95 *(978-1-77138-611-1(8))* Kids Can Pr., Ltd. CAN. Dist: Hachette Bk. Group.

O'Leary Brown, Erin. El Cuento Dorado, un Libro de Aventura, la Historia de Goldentail. Hoffmann, Dana Marie. 2004. (SPA.). 42p. (J). 9.95 *(978-0-9753106-1-8(5))* Hoffmann Partnership, The.

—The Golden Tale: A Goldentail Adventure Story Book. Hoffmann, Dana. 2004. (ENG.). 44p. (J). 19.95 *(978-0-9753106-0-1(7))* Hoffmann Partnership, The.

—The Golden Tale, A Goldentail Adventure Story Book. Hoffmann, Dana Marie. 2004. 42p. (J). 9.95 *(978-0-9753106-3-2(1))* Hoffmann Partnership, The.

—Here Little Teacup! up! Up! Hoffmann, Catherine E. & Hoffmann, Dana Marie. 2005. 16p. (J). 6.95 *(978-0-9753106-2-5(3))* Hoffmann Partnership, The.

—In My Backyard. Curry, Don L. 2011. (Rookie Ready to Learn — Animals Ser.). 32p. (J). (gr. -1-k). lib. bdg. 25.00 *(978-0-531-26416-4(5))*; pap. 5.95 *(978-0-531-26697-7(4))* Scholastic Library Publishing. (Children's Pr.).

O'Leary Brown, Erin. En Mi Patio. O'Leary Brown, Erin. Curry, Don L. 2011. (Rookie Ready to Learn Español Ser.). (SPA.). 32p. (J). lib. bdg. 23.00 *(978-0-531-26116-3(6)*, Children's Pr.) Scholastic Library Publishing.

O'Leary, Chris. The Leaf Man. Miranda, Patricia J. 2019. (ENG.). 32p. (J). (gr. -1-k). 16.99 *(978-0-8075-4416-7(7)*, 807544167) Whitman, Albert & Co.

O'Leary, John. Goldilocks: A Pop-Up Book. O'Leary, John. 2015. (ENG.). 16p. (J). (gr. -1-k). 19.99 *(978-1-85707-888-6(8))* Tango Bks. GBR. Dist: Independent Pubs. Group.

Oleynikov, Igor. Mahalia Mouse Goes to College: Book & CD. Lithgow, John. 2007. (ENG.). 40p. (J). (gr. -1-3). 19.99 *(978-1-4169-2715-0(8)*, Simon & Schuster Bks. For Young Readers) Simon & Schuster Bks. For Young Readers.

—The Nightingale. Andersen, Hans. 2007.Tr. of Nattergalen. (ENG.). 40p. (J). (gr. k). lib. bdg. 16.50 *(978-1-933327-31-0(6))*; (gr. 1). 15.95 *(978-1-933327-30-3(8))* Purple Bear Bks., Inc.

—Tiny Bear's Bible, 1 vol. Lloyd-Jones, Sally. 2015. (ENG.). 22p. (J). bds. 16.99 *(978-0-310-74787-1(2))* Zonderkidz.

—Tiny Bear's Bible, 1 vol. Lloyd-Jones, Sally. (Furry Bible Stories Ser.). (ENG.). 22p. (J). (gr. -1-k). 2009. pap. 14.99 *(978-0-310-71818-5(X))*; 2007. bds. 14.99 *(978-0-310-71082-0(0))* Zonderkidz.

—Who Came First. Dargaw, Kate. 2008. 32p. 15.95 *(978-1-933327-45-7(6))* Purple Bear Bks., Inc.

Olien, Jessica. Hamsters Don't Fight Fires! Root, Andrew. 2017. (ENG.). 40p. (J). (gr. -1-3). 17.99 *(978-0-06-245294-8(0))* HarperCollins Pubs.

Olien, Jessica. Adrift: An Odd Couple of Polar Bears. Olien, Jessica. 2017. (ENG.). 40p. (J). (gr. -1-3). 17.99 *(978-0-06-245177-4(4))* HarperCollins Pubs.

—The Blobfish Book. Olien, Jessica. 2016. (ENG.). 40p. (J). (gr. -1-3). 17.99 *(978-0-06-239415-6(0))* HarperCollins Pubs.

—Right Now. Olien, Jessica. 2018. (ENG.). 40p. (J). (gr. -1-3). 17.99 *(978-0-06-256828-1(0)*, Balzer & Bray) HarperCollins Pubs.

—Shark Detective! Olien, Jessica. 2015. (ENG.). 32p. (J). (gr. -1-3). 17.99 *(978-0-06-235714-4(X))* HarperCollins Pubs.

—When a Tiger Comes to Dinner. Olien, Jessica. 2019. (ENG.). 32p. (J). (gr. -1-3). 17.99 *(978-0-06-256829-8(9)*, Balzer & Bray) HarperCollins Pubs.

Oliphant, Manelle. At the Beach, 1 vol. Spurr, Elizabeth. 2013. (ENG.). 22p. (J). (gr. -1 — 1). bds. 6.95 *(978-1-56145-583-6(0))* Peachtree Publishing Co. Inc.

—In the Garden, 1 vol. Spurr, Elizabeth. 2012. (ENG.). 22p. (J). bds. 6.95 *(978-1-56145-581-2(4))* Peachtree Publishing Co. Inc.

—In the Rain, 1 vol. Spurr, Elizabeth. 2018. (In the Weather Ser.). (ENG.). 22p. (J). (gr. -1-1). bds. 6.95 *(978-1-56145-853-0(8))* Peachtree Publishing Co. Inc.

—In the Snow, 1 vol. Spurr, Elizabeth. 2017. (In the Weather Ser.). (ENG.). 22p. (J). (gr. -1 — 1). bds. 6.95 *(978-1-56145-855-4(4))* Peachtree Publishing Co. Inc.

—In the Wind, 1 vol. Spurr, Elizabeth. 2016. (In the Weather Ser.). (ENG.). 22p. (J). (gr. -1-k). bds. 6.95 *(978-1-56145-854-7(6))* Peachtree Publishing Co. Inc.

—In the Woods, 1 vol. Spurr, Elizabeth. 2012. (ENG.). 22p. (J). bds. 6.95 *(978-1-56145-582-9(2))* Peachtree Publishing Co. Inc.

Oliva, Octavio. My Ducky Buddy. Smith, Michael & Wang, Emily. 2011. (CHI & ENG.). 23p. (J). *(978-0-9821675-7-1(1))* East West Discovery Pr.

—My Ducky Buddy. Smith, Michael. 2011. 23p. (J). *(978-0-9821675-4-0(7))* East West Discovery Pr.

—My Ducky Buddy. Smith, Michael. 2015. (ARA & ENG.). 23p. (J). *(978-0-9913454-3-4(6))* East West Discovery Pr.

—My Ducky Buddy/Mi Amigo el Pato. Smith, Michael. 2011. (ENG & SPA.). 24p. (J). (gr. -1-3). 12.95 *(978-0-9821675-5-7(5))* East West Discovery Pr.

—Relativity. Smith, Michael. 2011. 30p. (J). *(978-0-9799339-8-1(6))* East West Discovery Pr.

Oliva, Octavio. Grasshopper Buddy. Oliva, Octavio. Smith, Michael. 2012. (SPA & ENG.). (J). *(978-0-9856237-0-8(5))* East West Discovery Pr.

—Relativity: Relatividad. Oliva, Octavio. Smith, Michael. 2011. (SPA & ENG.). (J). *(978-0-9832278-3-0(7))* East West Discovery Pr.

Olive, Phyllis Carol. The Gift of the Holy Ghost. Olive, Phyllis Carol. unabr. ed. 2003. 25p. (J). (gr. k-4). 12.95 *(978-1-932280-08-1(1)*, 80081) Granite Publishing & Distribution.

Oliveira, Jô. JK, o Lobo-Guará. Roscoe, Alessandra Pontes. 2010. (POR.). 29p. (J). *(978-85-06-06063-6(X))* Companhia Melhoramentos de Sao Paulo Industrias de Papel.

Oliver, Alison. The Adventures of Huckleberry Finn: A Camping Primer, 1 vol. Adams, Jennifer. ed. 2014. 22p. (J). (gr. k-1). bds. 9.99 *(978-1-4236-3622-9(8))* Gibbs Smith, Publisher.

—Alice in Wonderland: A Colors Primer, 1 vol. Adams, Jennifer. 2012. 22p. (J). (gr. k-1). bds. 9.99 *(978-1-4236-2477-6(7))* Gibbs Smith, Publisher.

—Alice in Wonderland Playset: A Babylit® Color Primer Board Book & Playset, 1 vol. Adams, Jennifer. ed. 2014. (J). (gr. k-1). 19.99 *(978-1-4236-3644-1(9))* Gibbs Smith, Publisher.

—Anna Karenina: A Babylit Fashion Primer, 1 vol. Adams, Jennifer. 2013. 22p. (J). (gr. k-1). bds. 9.99 *(978-1-4236-3483-6(7))* Gibbs Smith, Publisher.

—Arabian Nights Aladdin & the Wonderful Lamp, 1 vol. Adams, Jennifer. 2017. 22p. (J). bds. 9.99 *(978-1-4236-4592-4(8))* Gibbs Smith, Publisher.

—Around the World in 80 Days: A BabyLit Transportation Primer, 1 vol. Adams, Jennifer. 2018. 22p. (J). bds. 9.99 *(978-1-4236-4746-1(7))* Gibbs Smith, Publisher.

—BabyLit ABCs: an Alphabet Primer, 1 vol. Adams, Jennifer. 2017. 32p. (J). bds. 9.99 *(978-1-4236-4805-5(6))* Gibbs Smith, Publisher.

—The Bear's Garden. Colleen, Marcie. 2020. (ENG.). 40p. (J). 18.99 *(978-1-250-31481-9(X)*, 900199580) Imprint IND. Dist: Macmillan.

—Cat Tote, 1 vol. 2012. (ENG.). 20.00 *(978-1-4236-3153-8(6))* Gibbs Smith, Publisher.

—A Christmas Carol: A Babylit Colors Primer, 1 vol. Adams, Jennifer. 2012. 22p. (J). (gr. k-1). bds. 9.99 *(978-1-4236-2575-9(7))* Gibbs Smith, Publisher.

—Don Quixote: A Spanish Language Primer, 1 vol. Adams, Jennifer. 2015. 22p. (J). (gr. k-1). bds. 9.99 *(978-1-4236-3875-9(1))* Gibbs Smith, Publisher.

—Dracula, 1 vol. Adams, Jennifer. 2012. 22p. (J). (gr. k-1). bds. 9.99 *(978-1-4236-2480-6(7))* Gibbs Smith, Publisher.

—Frankenstein: An Anatomy Primer, 1 vol. Adams, Jennifer. 2014. 22p. (J). (gr. k-1). bds. 9.99 *(978-1-4236-3741-7(0))* Gibbs Smith, Publisher.

—Jabberwocky: A Nonsense Primer, 1 vol. Adams, Jennifer. 2013. 22p. (J). (gr. k-1). bds. 9.99 *(978-1-4236-3408-9(X))* Gibbs Smith, Publisher.

—Jane Eyre: A Counting Primer, 1 vol. Adams, Jennifer. 2012. 22p. (J). (gr. k-1). bds. 9.99 *(978-1-4236-2474-5(2))* Gibbs Smith, Publisher.

—The Jungle Book: An Animal Primer, 1 vol. Adams, Jennifer. 2014. 22p. (J). (gr. k-1). bds. 9.99 *(978-1-4236-3548-2(5))* Gibbs Smith, Publisher.

—A Midsummer Night's Dream: A Babylit Fairies Primer, 1 vol. Adams, Jennifer. 2016. 22p. (J). bds. 9.99 *(978-1-4236-4181-0(7))* Gibbs Smith, Publisher.

—Moby-Dick, 1 vol. Adams, Jennifer. 2013. (BabyLit Ser.). 22p. (J). (gr. k-1). bds. 9.99 *(978-1-4236-3204-7(4))* Gibbs Smith, Publisher.

—Moby-Dick: Board Book & Playset, 1 vol. Adams, Jennifer. 2015. 22p. (J). 19.99 *(978-1-4236-3871-1(9))* Gibbs Smith, Publisher.

—Peter Pan: A BabyLit Adventures Primer, 1 vol. Adams, Jennifer. 2018. 22p. (J). bds. 9.99 *(978-1-4236-4860-4(9))* Gibbs Smith, Publisher.

—Pride & Prejudice: A Counting Primer, 1 vol. Adams, Jennifer. 2011. (ENG.). 22p. (J). (gr. k-1). bds. 9.99 *(978-1-4236-2202-4(2))* Gibbs Smith, Publisher.

—Pride & Prejudice: Counting Primer Book & Playset, 1 vol. Adams, Jennifer. 2013. 22p. (J). (gr. k-1). 19.99 *(978-1-4236-3515-4(9))* Gibbs Smith, Publisher.

—Romeo & Juliet: A Babylit Counting Primer, 1 vol. Adams, Jennifer. 2011. 22p. (J). (gr. k-1). bds. 9.99 *(978-1-4236-2205-5(7))* Gibbs Smith, Publisher.

—The Secret Garden: A Flowers Primer, 1 vol. Adams, Jennifer. 2015. 22p. (J). (gr. k-1). bds. 9.99 *(978-1-4236-3872-8(7)*, 1386748) Gibbs Smith, Publisher.

—Sense & Sensibility: An Opposites Primer, 1 vol. Adams, Jennifer. 2013. 22p. (J). (gr. k-1). bds. 9.99 *(978-1-4236-3170-5(6))* Gibbs Smith, Publisher.

—Sherlock Homes in the Hound of the Baskervilles: A Babylit® Sounds Primer, 1 vol. Adams, Jennifer. 2013. 22p. (J). (gr. k-1). bds. 9.99 *(978-1-4236-3411-9(X))* Gibbs Smith, Publisher.

—The Wonderful Wizard of Oz, 1 vol. Adams, Jennifer. 2014. 22p. (J). (gr. k-1). bds. 9.99 *(978-1-4236-3718-9(6))* Gibbs Smith, Publisher.

—Wuthering Heights: A Weather Primer, 1 vol. Adams, Jennifer. 2013. 22p. (J). (gr. k-1). bds. 9.99 *(978-1-4236-3173-6(0))* Gibbs Smith, Publisher.

Oliver, Angel. The Adventures of Little Sprout. Rowland, Dawn. 2010. 32p. 12.99 *(978-1-4490-7725-9(0))* AuthorHouse.

Oliver, Juan, jt. illus. see Bautista, Juan.

Oliver, Juan Bautista Juan. How the Camel Got Its Hump - 6 Pack: Set of 6 with Common Core Teacher Materials. 2015. (Classic Tales Ser.). (J). (gr. k-1). 39.00 *(978-1-5125-8345-8(6))* Benchmark Education Co.

—Las Preguntas de Diego. Daniel, Claire. 2015. (MySELF Ser.). (SPA.). (J). (gr. -1-k). 4.49 *(978-1-4788-1981-3(2))* Newmark Learning LLC.

—Las Preguntas de Diego: Lap Book. Daniel, Claire. 2015. (MySELF Ser.). (SPA.). (J). (gr. -1-k). 29.00 *(978-1-4788-2326-1(7))* Newmark Learning LLC.

—Manos a la Obra. Sparks, Stacey. 2015. (MySELF Ser.). (SPA.). (J). (gr. -1-k). 4.49 *(978-1-4788-1980-6(4))* Newmark Learning LLC.

—Manos a la Obra: Lap Book. Sparks, Stacey. 2015. (MySELF Ser.). (SPA.). (J). (gr. -1-k). 29.00 *(978-1-4788-2325-4(9))* Newmark Learning LLC.

—¡No Te des Por Vencida! Giachetti, Julia. 2015. (MySELF Ser.). (SPA.). (J). (gr. -1-k). 4.49 *(978-1-4788-1979-0(0))* Newmark Learning LLC.

—¡No Te des Por Vencida! Lap Book. Giachetti, Julia. 2015. (MySELF Ser.). (SPA.). (J). (gr. -1-k). 29.00 *(978-1-4788-2324-7(0))* Newmark Learning LLC.

—La Sorpresa. Koons, Linda. 2016. (Early Rising Readers Ser.). (SPA.). 16p. (J). (gr. 1-1). 6.67 *(978-1-4788-4191-3(5))* Newmark Learning LLC.

—¡Soy una Estrella! Pippin, Jessica. 2015. (MySELF Ser.). (SPA.). (J). (gr. -1-k). 4.49 *(978-1-4788-1978-3(2))* Newmark Learning LLC.

—¡Soy una Estrella! Lap Book. Pippin, Jessica. 2015. (MySELF Ser.). (SPA.). (J). (gr. -1-k). 29.00 *(978-1-4788-2323-0(2))* Newmark Learning LLC.

—El Tiempo. Schmauss, Judy Kentor. 2016. (Early Rising Readers Ser.). (SPA.). 16p. (J). (gr. 1-1). 6.67 *(978-1-4788-4202-6(4))* Newmark Learning LLC.

—Who Will Bell the Cat? - 6 Pack: Set of 6 with Common Core Teacher Materials. 2015. (Classic Tales Ser.). (J). (gr. k-1). 39.00 *(978-1-5125-8373-1(1))* Benchmark Education Co.

—Yo Puedo Hacer un Plan. Garcia, Ellen. 2015. (MySELF Ser.). (SPA.). (J). (gr. -1-k). 4.49 *(978-1-4788-1977-6(4))* Newmark Learning LLC.

—Yo Puedo Hacer un Plan: Lap Book. Garcia, Ellen. 2015. (MySELF Ser.). (SPA.). (J). (gr. -1-k). 29.00 *(978-1-4788-2322-3(4))* Newmark Learning LLC.

—Yo Voy a Encontrar la Manera. Linde, Barbara M. 2015. (MySELF Ser.). (SPA.). (J). (gr. -1-k). 4.49 *(978-1-4788-1982-0(0))* Newmark Learning LLC.

—Yo Voy a Encontrar la Manera: Lap Book. Linde, Barbara M. 2015. (MySELF Ser.). (SPA.). (J). (gr. -1-k). 29.00 *(978-1-4788-2327-8(5))* Newmark Learning LLC.

Oliver, Juanbjuan. The King Who Thought He Was Clever: a Folk Tale from Russia: Band 14/Ruby (Collins Big Cat) Bradman, Tony. 2017. (Collins Big Cat Tales Ser.). (ENG.). 48p. (J). (gr. 3-4). pap. 10.99 *(978-0-00-817940-3(9))* HarperCollins Pubs. Ltd. GBR. Dist: Independent Pubs. Group.

—The Prince & the Three Oranges a Fairy Tale from Mexico. 2017. (Text Connections Guided Close Reading Ser.). (J). (gr. 1). *(978-1-4900-1822-5(0))* Benchmark Education Co.

—Sang Kancil & Crocodile Orange Band. Carrington, Jim. 2016. (Cambridge Reading Adventures Ser.). (ENG.). 16p. pap. 7.37 *(978-1-107-57604-9(0))* Cambridge Univ. Pr.

—Sang Kancil & the Farmer Gold Band. Carrington, Jim. 2017. (Cambridge Reading Adventures Ser.). (ENG.). 24p. pap. 6.74 *(978-1-108-40574-4(6))* Cambridge Univ. Pr.

—Sang Kancil & the Tiger. Carrington, Jim. 2016. (Cambridge Reading Adventures Ser.). (ENG.). 16p. pap. 7.37 *(978-1-107-55092-6(0))* Cambridge Univ. Pr.

oliver, juanbjuan & Eskandari, Elmira. School Bus Safety. Coyle, Becky. 2018. (School Safety Ser.). (ENG.). 32p. (J). (gr. k-2). 12.99 *(978-1-4867-1430-8(7)*, 89b3d726-b096-4478-a42d-b4032a2ba971) Flowerpot Pr.

Oliver, Julia. My Bedtime Angel. Darens, Cat. 2010. 18p. (J). (gr. -1-k). 7.95 *(978-0-8091-6745-6(X)*, Ambassador Bks.) Paulist Pr.

—My Morning Angel. Darens, Cat. 2010. 18p. (J). (gr. -1-k). 7.95 *(978-0-8091-6753-1(0)*, Ambassador Bks.) Paulist Pr.

Oliver, Liana. Buntley's Wing Kit. Adams, Paul Robert. 2012. 34p. pap. *(978-0-9871712-6-9(7))* Fastnet Bks.

Oliver, Maria Fernanda. Retablillo de Navidad. Nazoa, Aquiles.Tr. of Christmas Nativity. (SPA.). (J). (gr. 3-5). 10.95 *(978-980-257-067-6(2))* Ekare, Ediciones VEN. Dist: Lectorum Pubns., Inc.

Oliver, Mark. Are You Sleeping? Harris, Brooke. 2010. (Rising Readers Ser.). (J). 3.49 *(978-1-60719-685-3(9))* Newmark Learning LLC.

—Bear Went over the Mountain. Fuerst, Jeffrey B. 2010. (Rising Readers Ser.). (J). 3.49 *(978-1-60719-686-0(7))* Newmark Learning LLC.

—Monsters Unleashed. Kloepfer, John. (Monsters Unleashed Ser.: 1). (ENG.). (J). (gr. 3-7). 2018. 224p. pap. 6.99 *(978-0-06-229031-1(2))*; 2017. 208p. 16.99 *(978-0-06-229030-4(4))* HarperCollins Pubs.

—Monsters Unleashed #2: Bugging Out. Kloepfer, John. 2018. (Monsters Unleashed Ser.: 2). (ENG.). (J). (gr. 3-7). 192p. pap. 6.99 *(978-0-06-242754-0(7))*; 176p. 16.99 *(978-0-06-242753-3(9))* HarperCollins Pubs.

—Speak up, Spike. Ewart, Franzeska G. 2005. (Yellow Go Bananas Ser.). (ENG.). 48p. (J). (gr. 3-4). *(978-0-7787-2744-6(0))*; lib. bdg. *(978-0-7787-2722-4(X))* Crabtree Publishing Co.

Oliver, Narelle. The Best Beak in Boonaroo Bay. Oliver, Narelle. 48p. (YA). pap. *(978-0-85091-671-3(2)*, Lothian Children's Bks.) Hachette Australia.

—Sand Swimmers: The Secret Life of Australia's Desert Wilderness. Oliver, Narelle. 2015. (ENG.). 40p. (J). (gr. 2-5). 16.99 *(978-0-7636-6761-0(7))* Candlewick Pr.

—Tide Pool Secrets. Oliver, Narelle. 2017. (ENG.). 32p. (J). (gr. -1-2). 18.99 *(978-0-7636-9159-2(3))* Candlewick Pr.

—Twilight Hunt, 1 vol. Oliver, Narelle. 2007. (Seek-and-Find Bks.). (ENG.). 32p. (J). (gr. 3-7). 16.95 *(978-1-59572-107-5(X))* Star Bright Bks., Inc.

Oliver, Stephen, photos by. Tamanos. 2005. (Coleccion Primeras Imagenes).Tr. of My First Look at Sizes. (SPA., (J). (gr. -1-18). pap. 7.95 *(978-950-11-0907-8(0)*, SGM9070) Sigmar ARG. Dist: Continental Bk. Co., Inc.

Oliver, Tony. Frogs Sing Songs. Winer, Yvonne. 2003. 32p. (J). pap. 6.95 *(978-1-57091-549-9(0))*; (gr. -1-4). 16.95 *(978-1-57091-548-2(2))* Charlesbridge Publishing, Inc.

Olivera, Fernando. The Woman Who Outshone the Sun (la mujer que brillaba aun mas que el Sol) Zubizarreta, Rosalma et al. 2014. (ENG & SPA.). 32p. (J). (gr. -1 — 1). pap. 10.95 *(978-0-89239-126-4(X))* Lee & Low Bks., Inc.

Olivera, Ramon. ABCs on Wheels. Olivera, Ramon. 2016. (ENG.). 40p. (J). (gr. -1-k). 19.99 *(978-1-4814-3244-3(3)*, Little Simon) Little Simon.

—ABCs on Wings. Olivera, Ramon. (Classic Board Bks.). (ENG.). (J). (gr. -1-k). 2020. 36p. bds. 7.99 ***(978-1-5344-6191-8(4))***; 2015. 40p. 17.99 *(978-1-4814-3242-9(7))* Little Simon. (Little Simon).

Olivetti, Ariel, et al. Cable: the Last Hope. 2018. (ENG.). 464p. (YA). (gr. 8-17). pap. 39.99 *(978-1-302-91216-1(X))* Marvel Worldwide, Inc.

Olivetti, Ariel. Phazer: A Man Lost in Alternative Universes. Nicieza, Mariano. 2008. 48p. (YA). per. 14.95 *(978-0-9740212-7-0(X))* Cedar Grove Bks.

Olivetti, Ariel, et al. Thor: Heaven & Earth. Brooks, Mark. 2012. (ENG.). 112p. (YA). (gr. 8-17). pap. 14.99 *(978-0-7851-4833-3(7))* Marvel Worldwide, Inc.

Olivier-Argyle, Daniel. Alfie & Reid: A Fine Partnership Indeed. Thornton, Stephen. 2019. (ENG.). 20p. (J). *(978-1-4602-6169-9(0))*; pap. *(978-1-4602-6170-5(4))* FriesenPress.

Oller, Erika. Cats, Cats, Cats! Newman, Lesléa. 2004. (ENG.). 32p. (J). (gr. -1-3). reprint ed. 8.99 *(978-0-689-86697-5(6)*, Simon & Schuster Bks. For Young Readers) Simon & Schuster Bks. For Young Readers.

—Dogs, Dogs, Dogs! Newman, Lesléa & Newman, Lesléa. 2011. (ENG.). 30p. (J). (gr. -1-3). pap. 16.99 *(978-1-4424-5228-2(5)*, Simon & Schuster Bks. For Young Readers) Simon & Schuster Bks. For Young Readers.

Ollerenshaw, Sue. Practical Guide to Teaching Reading Skills at All Levels: With Examples in French, German & Spanish. Ollerenshaw, Jenny. 2003. (ENG.). 36p. pap., tchr. ed. 11.80 *(978-0-9532440-6-5(7))* Advance Materials Ltd. GBR. Dist: Cambridge Univ. Pr.

Olliffe, Pat, jt. illus. see Frenz, Ron.

Olliver, Linda. Exemplary Evidence: Scientists & Their Data. Fries-Gaither, Jessica. 2019. (ENG.). 32p. (J). pap. 14.95 *(978-1-68140-361-8(7))* National Science Teachers Assn.

Ollweiler, D. R. The Strange Wish. Ollweiler, Angela Messina. 2010. 112p. pap. 10.95 *(978-1-60844-274-8(8))* Dog Ear Publishing, LLC.

Olmanson, Shaina, photos by. Coco Idea Lab. Olmanson, Shaina. 2019. (Disney STEAM Projects Ser.). (ENG., 32p. (J). (gr. 2-5). 29.32 *(978-1-5415-5479-5(5)*, 9781541554795); pap. 8.99 *(978-1-5415-7402-1(8)*, 9781541574021) Lerner Publishing Group. (Lerner Pubns.).

—Lion King Idea Lab. Olmanson, Shaina. 2019. (Disney STEAM Projects Ser.). (ENG., 32p. (J). (gr. 2-5). 29.32 *(978-1-5415-5485-6(X)*, 9781541554856, Lerner Pubns.) Lerner Publishing Group.

—The Lion King Idea Lab. Olmanson, Shaina. 2019. (Disney STEAM Projects Ser.). (ENG., 32p. (J). (gr. 2-5). pap. 8.99 *(978-1-5415-7404-5(4)*, 9781541574045, Lerner Pubns.) Lerner Publishing Group.

Olmos, Roger. Las Trenzas del Abuelo. Figueras, Nuria. 2003. (Llibros para Soñar Ser.). (SPA.). 32p. *(978-84-8464-180-3(5))* Kalandraka Editora, S.L. ESP. Dist: Lectorum Pubns., Inc.

Olofsdotter, Marie. A Picture Book of Cesar Chavez. Adler, David A. & Adler, Michael S. (Picture Book Biography Ser.). 32p. (J). (gr. -1-3). 2018. pap. 7.99 *(978-0-8234-4058-0(3))*; 2011. (ENG.). pap. 7.99 *(978-0-8234-2383-5(2))* Holiday Hse., Inc.

Olortegui, Diego. X-23 Vol. 2: X-Assassin, Vol. 2. 2019. (ENG.). 136p. (YA). (gr. 8-17). pap. 17.99 *(978-1-302-91686-2(6))* Marvel Worldwide, Inc.

Olrun, Prudy, jt. illus. see Amos, Muriel.

Olsen, Christian. Make the World a Better Place! My Sharing Time, Talent & Treasure Activity Book. Flikkema, Elizabeth. 2006. 47p. 19.95 *(978-0-9774155-0-2(3))* Learning to Give.

—Thickened Flied Lice: A Limerick in Six Chapters. Robidoux, Annette & Sommerfeldt, Jim. 2004. (ENG.). 26p. pap. 12.99 *(978-1-4134-6260-9(X))* Xlibris Corp.

Olsen, Greg. I Am a Child of God. 2004. (J). 17.95 *(978-1-57734-933-4(4))* Covenant Communications, Inc.

Olsen, Lucas & Guardino, Sabrina. Wait a Minute! I Matter! Gomez, Allison M. 2018. (ENG.). 26p. (J). pap. 9.99 *(978-1-7266-7447-8(9))* Independently Published.

Olson, Cindy. A ferret in a Garret. Hoffman, Peter. 2008. 36p. (J). 24.99 *(978-0-9790247-6-4(5))* Artpacks.

Olson, Ed. Christ & the Church Vol. 42: New Testament Volume 42 Revelation Part 1. Greiner, Ruth B. 2010. 36p. (J). pap. *(978-1-932381-29-0(5)*, 1042) Bible Visuals International, Inc.

—Clopper & the Lost Boy, 1 vol. King, Emily. 2009. 32p. (J). 12.99 *(978-0-8254-2946-0(3))* Kregel Pubns.

—Clopper & the Night Travelers. King, Emily. 2007. 32p. (J). (gr. -1-3). 12.99 *(978-0-8254-3066-4(6))* Kregel Pubns.

—Clopper the Christmas Donkey, 1 vol. King, Emily. 2003. 32p. (J). 12.99 *(978-0-8254-3069-5(0))* Kregel Pubns.

—The Little Man in the Map: With Clues to Remember All 50 States. Martonyi, E. Andrew. 2007. (ENG.). 64p. (gr. -1-3). 19.95 *(978-0-9785100-4-6(6))* Schoolside Pr.

Olson, Ed & Willoughby, Yuko. Ly Huy's Escape: A Story of Vietnam. Carvin, Rose-Mae. Neal, Sharon & Mayer, Kristin, eds. 2010. (ENG.). 40p. (J). spiral bd. *(978-1-932381-13-9(9)*, 5275) Bible Visuals International, Inc.

Olson, Ed, jt. illus. see Hertzler, Frances H..

Olson, Ed, jt. illus. see Hertzler, Frances.

Olson, Ed, jt. illus. see Mayer, Melody.

Olson, Johan, jt. illus. see Olson, John.

Olson, John & Olson, Johan. Los Cuentos de la Casa del Arbol. Munoz, Norma. rev. ed. 2005. (Castillo de la Lectura Blanca Ser.). (SPA & ENG.). 72p. (J). (gr. -1-3). pap. 6.95 *(978-970-20-0124-9(2))* Castillo, Ediciones, S. A. de C. V. MEX. Dist: Macmillan.

Olson, Julie. Already Asleep. 2006. (ENG.). 32p. (J). (gr. -1-3). 12.95 *(978-0-9766805-6-7(4))* Keene Publishing.

—Herd of Cows! Flock of Sheep! Walton, Rick. 2011. (ENG.). 36p. (gr. 2-3). pap. 7.99 *(978-1-4236-2090-7(9))* Gibbs Smith, Publisher.

—Hip, Hip, Hooray! for Annie Mcrae, 1 vol. Wilcox, Brad. 2019. (ENG.). 32p. (J). pap. 7.99 *(978-1-4236-5235-9(5))* Gibbs Smith, Publisher.

—The Kickball Kids, 1 vol. Meister, Cari. 2009. (My First Graphic Novel Ser.). (ENG.). 32p. (J). (gr. k-2). pap. 6.25 *(978-1-4342-1410-2(9))*; lib. bdg. 24.65 *(978-1-4342-1294-8(7))* Capstone. (Stone Arch Bks.).

—The Opposites of My Jewish Year, Vol. Dion, L. N. 2005. (Very First Board Bks.). (ENG.). 12p. (J). (gr. -1 — 1). bds. 5.95 *(978-1-58013-113-1(1)*, Kar-Ben Publishing) Lerner Publishing Group.

—The Princess Twins & the Birthday Party, 1 vol. Hodgson, Mona. 2016. (I Can Read! / Princess Twins Ser.). (ENG.). 32p. (J). pap. 4.99 *(978-0-310-75067-3(9))* Zonderkidz.

—The Princess Twins & the Puppy, 1 vol. Hodgson, Mona. 2015. (I Can Read! / Princess Twins Ser.). (ENG.). 32p. (J). pap. 4.99 *(978-0-310-75064-2(4))* Zonderkidz.

—The Princess Twins & the Tea Party, 1 vol. Hodgson, Mona. 2016. (I Can Read! / Princess Twins Ser.). (ENG.). 32p. (J). pap. 4.99 *(978-0-310-75038-3(5))* Zonderkidz.

—The Princess Twins Collection, 1 vol. Hodgson, Mona. 2017. (I Can Read! / Princess Twins Ser.). (ENG.). 128p. (J). 12.99 *(978-0-310-75319-3(8))* Zonderkidz.

—The Princess Twins Play in the Garden, 1 vol. Hodgson, Mona. 2015. (I Can Read! / Princess Twins Ser.). (ENG.). 32p. (J). pap. 4.99 *(978-0-310-75050-5(4))* Zonderkidz.

—Purple. Hickman, Kirt. 2012. 32p. pap. 15.99 *(978-0-9796330-8-9(7))* Quillrunner Publishing LLC.

Olson, Kyle. Dust Flowers. Olson, Lisa Gammon. 2018. (Tales from American Herstory Ser.: Vol. 1). (ENG.). (J). (gr. k-5). pap. 9.99 *(978-1-63233-076-5(8))* Elfrig Publishing.

Olson, Robert, photos by. Alaska - Hints of Paradise: Photographs & Essays by Robert Olson. Olson, Robert. 2004. 160p. 39.95 *(978-0-9749570-0-5(3))* Visions Of Nature.

Olson, Ryan. I Lost My Sock. Jakary, Lin. 2008. 40p. (J). (gr. -1-3). 16.99 *(978-1-934867-01-3(2))* Wocto Publishing.

Olson, Stan. Johnny Appleseed. Kunstler, James Howard. 2005. (Rabbit Ears-A Classic Tale Ser.). 36p. (J). (gr. k-5). 25.65 *(978-1-59197-765-0(7))* Spotlight.

Olson, Tom. The Tale of the Not-So-Perfect Christmas Tree. Cruikshank, Fran. 2005. 17p. (J). 9.95 *(978-1-59971-055-6(2))* Aardvark Global Publishing.

Olson, Zechariah. Hearts at War. Winblad, Rob. Winblad, Kimberly, ed. 2nd ed. 2019. (Two Month Novel Challenge Ser.: Vol. 2). (ENG.). 122p. (YA). (gr. 7-12). pap. 20.00 *(978-0-578-50969-3(5))* S.C. TreeHouse LLC.

Olszewska, Agata. Vinnie & Vicki - the Vibrant Viruses! McMahon, Maryann. 2019. (ENG.). 32p. (J). (gr. k-3). pap. 11.99 ***(978-1-7320725-3-4(1))*** Maryann.

Olten, Manuela. Mama, I Can't Sleep. Raab, Brigitte. 2012. 32p. (J). (gr. -1-k). 16.95 *(978-1-61608-965-8(2)*, 608965, Sky Pony Pr.) Skyhorse Publishing Co., Inc.

—Mom, There's a Bear at the Door. Lipan, Sabine. 2016. (ENG.). 34p. (J). 16.00 *(978-0-8028-5460-5(5)*, Eerdmans Bks For Young Readers) Eerdmans, William B. Publishing Co.

Omac, Meg. Steven Universe Orignal Graphic Novel: Ultimate Dough-Down: Ultimate Dough-Down. Perper, Talya. 2018. (Steven Universe Ser.). (ENG.). 144p. (J). (gr. 4-7). pap. 14.99 *(978-1-68415-281-0(X))* Boom! Studios.

O'Malley, Jason. Christmas at the Zoo 10th Anniversary Edition: A Pop-Up Wonderland. White, George. 2017. (ENG.). 7p. (J). 19.95 *(978-1-62348-459-0(6))* Jumping Jack Pr.

—Halloween at the Zoo 10th Anniversary Edition. White, George. 2017. (ENG.). 7p. (J). 19.99 *(978-1-62348-457-6(X))* Jumping Jack Pr.

O'Malley, Kathleen. A Fishy Story. Zimelman, Nathan. 2003. (Books for Young Learners). (ENG.). 16p. (J). pap. 5.75 *(978-1-57274-538-4(X)*, 2453, Bks. for Young Learners) Owen, Richard C. Pubs., Inc.

—Five-Minute Mini-Mysteries. Smith, Stan. 2003. 96p. pap. 7.95 *(978-1-4027-0031-6(8))* Sterling Publishing Co., Inc.

O'Malley, Kathy. How Fox Became Red. Hamilton, Martha & Weiss, Mitch. 2005. (ENG.). 12p. (J). 5.75 *(978-1-57274-717-3(X)*, 2749, Bks. for Young Learners) Owen, Richard C. Pubs., Inc.

—Lazy Days of Summer. Young, Judy. rev. ed. 2007. (ENG.). 32p. (J). (gr. k-6). 15.95 *(978-1-58536-241-7(7))* Sleeping Bear Pr.

—Murphy's Three Homes: A Story for Children in Foster Care. Gilman, Jan Levinson. 2008. 32p. (J). (gr. -1-2). 14.95 *(978-1-4338-0384-0(4))*; pap. 9.95 *(978-1-4338-0385-7(2))* American Psychological Assn. (Magination Pr.).

—Prairie Numbers: An Illinois Number Book. Wargin, Kathy-jo. 2006. (Count Your Way Across the U. S. A. Ser.). (ENG.). 40p. (J). (gr. -1-3). 17.95 *(978-1-58536-180-9(1))* Sleeping Bear Pr.

O'Malley, Kevin. The Birthday Pet, 0 vols. Javernick, Ellen. 2012. (ENG.). 34p. (J). (gr. 1-3). pap. 7.99 *(978-0-7614-6238-5(4)*, 9780761462385, Two Lions) Amazon Publishing.

—Caught! Nabbing History's Most Wanted. Bragg, Georgia. 2019. 224p. (J). (gr. 5-9). 18.99 *(978-1-5247-6741-9(7))*; (ENG.). lib. bdg. 21.99 *(978-1-5247-6742-6(5))* Random Hse. Children's Bks. (Crown Books For Young Readers).

—How They Choked: Failures, Flops, & Flaws of the Awfully Famous. Bragg, Georgia. 2016. (ENG.). 208p. (J). pap. 10.99 *(978-1-68119-216-1(0)*, 900164097, Bloomsbury USA Childrens) Bloomsbury Publishing USA.

—How They Croaked: The Awful Ends of the Awfully Famous. Bragg, Georgia. 2012. (ENG.). 192p. (J). (gr. 5-14). pap. 14.99 *(978-0-8027-2794-7(8)*, 900081242, Bloomsbury USA Childrens) Bloomsbury Publishing USA.

—If Beaver Had a Fever, 0 vols. Ketteman, Helen. 2011. (ENG.). 32p. (J). (gr. -1-3). 16.99 *(978-0-7614-5951-4(0)*, 9780761459514, Two Lions) Amazon Publishing.

—King of the Kooties, 1 vol. Dadey, Debbie. 2006. (ENG.). 86p. (J). (gr. 4-7). 7.95 *(978-1-55455-030-2(0)*,

585e7e81-7bad-40d8-bbd5-97533b734b97) Fitzhenry & Whiteside, Ltd. CAN. Dist: Firefly Bks., Ltd.
—The Planets in Our Solar System. Branley, Franklyn M. 2015. (Let's-Read-And-Find-Out Science 2 Ser.). (ENG.). 32p. (J). (gr. -1-3). pap. 6.99 *(978-0-06-238194-1(6))* HarperCollins Pubs.
—Slugs in Love, 0 vols. Pearson, Susan. 2012. (ENG.). 34p. (J). (gr. -1-3). pap. 7.99 *(978-0-7614-6248-4(1),* 9780761462484, Two Lions) Amazon Publishing.
—Someday Is Not a Day of the Week. Brennan-Nelson, Denise. 2005. (ENG.). 32p. (J). (gr. 1-4). 15.95 *(978-1-58536-243-1(3),* 202066) Sleeping Bear Pr.
—Something Rotten: A Fresh Look at Roadkill. Montgomery, Heather L. (ENG.). 176p. (J). 2019. pap. 12.99 *(978-1-5476-0250-6(3),* 900208152); 2018. 16.99 *(978-1-68119-900-9(9),* 900191668) Bloomsbury Publishing USA. (Bloomsbury Children's Bks.).
—Spies, Lies, & Disguise: The Daring Tricks & Deeds That Won World War II. Swanson, Jennifer. 2019. (ENG.). 144p. (J). 21.99 *(978-1-68119-779-1(0),* 900186286, Bloomsbury Children's Bks.) Bloomsbury Publishing USA.
—Testing Miss Malarkey. Finchler, Judy. 2003. (Miss Malarkey Ser.). (ENG.). 32p. (J). (gr. k-4). pap. 7.99 *(978-0-8027-7624-2(8),* 900033137, Bloomsbury USA Childrens) Bloomsbury Publishing USA.
—Twelve Days: A Christmas Countdown. Snell, Gordon. 2005. 30p. (J). (gr. -1-2). reprint ed. 16.00 *(978-0-7567-9403-3(X))* DIANE Publishing Co.
O'Malley, Kevin. Congratulations, Miss Malarkey! O'Malley, Kevin. Finchler, Judy. 2011. (Miss Malarkey Ser.). (ENG.). 32p. (J). (gr. k-2). 21.19 *(978-0-8027-9836-7(5),* 9780802798367) Walker & Co.
—Gimme Cracked Corn & I Will Share. O'Malley, Kevin. 2007. (ENG.). 32p. (J). (gr. k-2). 22.44 *(978-0-8027-9684-4(2),* 9780802796844) Walker & Co.
—Grandfather Duck, Vol. O'Malley, Kevin. 2018. (ENG.). 32p. (J). (gr. -1-3). 15.95 *(978-1-63076-335-0(7))* Muddy Boots Pr.
—Lucky Leaf. O'Malley, Kevin. 2007. (ENG.). 32p. (J). (gr. -1-2). 8.99 *(978-0-8027-9647-9(8),* 9780802796479, Bloomsbury USA Childrens) Bloomsbury Publishing USA.
—Miss Malarkey Leaves No Reader Behind. O'Malley, Kevin. Finchler, Judy. 2010. (Miss Malarkey Ser.). (ENG.). 32p. (J). (gr. k-3). pap. 7.99 *(978-0-8027-2098-6(6),* 900066992, Bloomsbury USA Childrens) Bloomsbury Publishing USA.
—Miss Malarkey's Field Trip. O'Malley, Kevin. Finchler, Judy. 2004. (Miss Malarkey Ser.). (ENG.). 32p. (J). (gr. k-2). 21.19 *(978-0-8027-8913-6(7),* 9780802789136) Walker & Co.
O'Mara Holeman, Chelsea. Awesome Minds: Comic Book Creators. Arbona, Alejandro. 2019. (Awesome Minds Ser.). (ENG.). 140p. (J). (gr. 3-7). 14.95 *(978-1-947458-77-2(9),* 805877, Duo Pr. Llc (US)) Duo Pr. LLC.
—Awesome Minds: Video Game Creators. Arbona, Alejandro. 2018. (Awesome Minds Ser.). (ENG.). 156p. (J). (gr. 3-7). 14.95 *(978-1-947458-22-2(1),* 805822, Duo Pr. Llc (US)) Duo Pr. LLC.
Omary, Oussama. Brain Games Soduko & Word Search 2 In 1: It Includes All Levels, Very Easy to Ultra Extreme,109 Puzzles, 16 Grids in the Page, Mini Book of Sudoku to Keep Him Always with You or with Your Kids, Best Brain Game for Kids. Creation, Puzzle. 2019. (ENG.). 40p. (J). pap. 5.99 ***(978-1-6501-9176-8(6))*** Independently Published.
—My Recipe Book: Blank Recipe Book Journal to Write Your Favorite Recipes & Meals. Books, Recipe. 2019. (ENG.). 132p. (J). pap. 6.03 ***(978-1-6776-2827-8(8))*** Independently Published.
Omary, Rachel. Animals in Dari. l.t. ed. 2003. 4p. (J). spiral bd. 10.95 *(978-0-9740535-3-0(8))* Knight Publishing.
—Animals in Farsi. l.t. ed. 2003. 4p. (J). spiral bd. 10.95 *(978-0-9740535-4-7(6))* Knight Publishing.
—Animals in Pashto. l.t. ed. 2003. 4p. (J). spiral bd. 10.95 *(978-0-9740535-5-4(4))* Knight Publishing.
—Shapes & Colors in Dari. 2004. 5p. (J). spiral bd. 14.95 *(978-0-9740535-7-8(0))* Knight Publishing.
—Shapes & Colors in Farsi. l.t. ed. 2004. 5p. (J). spiral bd. 14.95 *(978-0-9740535-6-1(2))* Knight Publishing.
—Shapes & Colors in Pashto. l.t. ed. 2004. 5p. (J). spiral bd. 14.95 *(978-0-9740535-8-5(9))* Knight Publishing.
O'Meara, Tim, jt. illus. see Morales, Yuyi.
Omishi, Ray. Sorcerer Hunters Vol. 2: Authentic Relaunch. rev. ed. 2005. 192p. pap. 9.99 *(978-1-59532-495-5(X))* TOKYOPOP, Inc.
—Sorcerer Hunters Authentic Relaunch. 2005. Vol. 1. 208p. pap. 9.99 *(978-1-59532-494-8(1));* Vol. 3. 192p. pap. 9.99 *(978-1-59532-496-2(8))* TOKYOPOP, Inc.
Omiunu, Irene. Philly & Friends: Who Do I See in the Mirror? Aghoghovbia Aladewolu, Vese. 2019. (ENG.). 32p. (J). *(978-1-9993498-0-6(6))* Philly & Belle Publishing.
Omoto, Garrett. Kai the 'Opihi Gets the Point. Omoto, Gail. 2006. 32p. (J). 16.95 *(978-1-933835-05-1(2))* Partners in Development Foundation.
—Ke Kino - The Body. 2006. Orig. Title: Ke Kino. (HAW.). 16p. (J). 8.95 *(978-1-933835-02-0(8))* Partners in Development Foundation.
—Na Waihooluu. 2006.Tr. of Colors. (HAW & ENG.). 16p. (J). 8.95 *(978-1-933835-00-6(1))* Partners in Development Foundation.
—Pili the 'Iwa Bird Shares the Letter B: Book #1 in the Gift of Reading Series. Hu, Lorna. 2013. (J). pap. 9.95 *(978-1-933835-28-0(1))* Partners in Development Foundation.
—Pili the 'Iwa Bird Shares the Letter P: Book #2 in the Gift of Reading Series. 2013. (Gift of Reading Ser.: Bk. 2). (J). *(978-1-933835-27-3(3))* Partners in Development Foundation.
—Tutu Books Preschool Library, 3 bks. 2006. (ENG & HAW.). 48p. (YA). 29.95 *(978-1-933835-04-4(4))* Partners in Development Foundation.
—'Umi Keiki Li'i Li'i - Ten Little Children. 2006. Orig. Title: 'Umi Keiki Li'i Li'i. (HAW.). 16p. (J). 8.95 *(978-1-933835-01-3(X))* Partners in Development Foundation.
ón, Raúl. Alicia Alonso: Prima Ballerina. Bernier-Grand, Carmen. 2019. (ENG.). 64p. (J). (gr. 4-8). pap. 9.99 *(978-1-4778-1074-3(9),* 9781477810743, Two Lions) Amazon Publishing.
—Already a Butterfly: A Meditation Story. Alvarez, Julia. 2020. (ENG.). 40p. (J). 18.99 *(978-1-62779-932-4(X),* 900163027, Holt, Henry & Co. Bks. For Young Readers) Holt, Henry & Co.
—Angela's Christmas. McCourt, Frank. 2019. (ENG.). 32p. (J). (gr. -1-3). 17.99 *(978-1-5344-6122-2(1),* Simon & Schuster/Paula Wiseman Bks.) Simon & Schuster/Paula Wiseman Bks.
ón, Raul. Annie & Helen. Hopkinson, Deborah. 2020. 48p. (J). (gr. -1-3). pap. 7.99 ***(978-1-9848-5192-5(6),*** Dragonfly Bks.) Random Hse. Children's Bks.
ón, Raúl. Any Small Goodness. Johnston, Tony. 2003. (ENG.). 128p. (J). (gr. 2-5). pap. 6.99 *(978-0-439-23384-2(4))* Scholastic, Inc.
ón, Raul. As Good As Anybody: Martin Luther King, Jr. , & Abraham Joshua Heschel's Amazing March Toward Freedom. Michelson, Richard. 2013. (ENG.). 40p. (J). (gr. 1-4). 7.99 *(978-0-385-75387-6(X),* Dragonfly Bks.) Random Hse. Children's Bks.
ón, Raúl. Baseball Is ... Borden, Louise. 2014. (ENG.). 48p. (J). (gr. 2-5). 17.99 *(978-1-4169-5502-3(X),* McElderry, Margaret K. Bks.) McElderry, Margaret K. Bks.
ón, Raul. Child of the Civil Rights Movement. Shelton, Paula Young. 2013. 48p. (J). (gr. -1-3). 7.99 *(978-0-385-37606-8(5),* Dragonfly Bks.) Random Hse. Children's Bks.
—Child of the Universe. Jayawardhana, Ray. 2020. (ENG.). 40p. (J). (gr. -1-2). 17.99 *(978-1-5247-1754-4(1));* lib. bdg. 20.99 *(978-1-5247-1755-1(X))* Random Hse. Children's Bks.
ón, Raúl. Counting the Stars: The Story of Katherine Johnson, NASA Mathematician. Cline-Ransome, Lesa. 2019. (ENG.). 32p. (J). (gr. -1-3). 17.99 *(978-1-5344-0475-5(9),* Simon & Schuster Bks. For Young Readers) Simon & Schuster Bks. For Young Readers.
ón, Raul. Dona Flor: A Tall Tale about a Giant Woman with a Great Big Heart. Mora, Pat. (ENG.). (J). (gr. -1-2). 2010. 32p. pap. 7.99 *(978-0-375-86144-4(0),* Dragonfly Bks.); 2005. 40p. 16.99 *(978-0-375-82337-4(9),* Knopf Bks. for Young Readers) Random Hse. Children's Bks.
—Fearless Flyer: Ruth Law & Her Flying Machine. Lang, Heather. 2016. (ENG.). 40p. (J). (gr. k-3). 16.95 *(978-1-62091-650-6(9),* Calkins Creek) Boyds Mills Pr.
—Hillary. Winter, Jonah. 2016. 40p. (J). (gr. -1-3). 17.99 *(978-0-553-53388-0(6),* Schwartz & Wade Bks.) Random Hse. Children's Bks.
ón, Raúl. Jose! Born to Dance: The Story of Jose Limon. Reich, Susanna. 2005. (ENG.). 32p. (J). (gr. k-3). 18.99 *(978-0-689-86576-3(7),* Simon & Schuster/Paula Wiseman Bks.) Simon & Schuster/Paula Wiseman Bks.
ón, Raul. Leontyne Price: Voice of a Century. Weatherford, Carole Boston. 2014. 40p. (J). (gr. k-4). 17.99 *(978-0-375-85606-8(4),* Knopf Bks. for Young Readers) Random Hse. Children's Bks.
ón, Raúl. Look Up! Henrietta Leavitt, Pioneering Woman Astronomer. Burleigh, Robert. 2013. (ENG.). 32p. (J). (gr. -1-3). 18.99 *(978-1-4169-5819-2(3),* Simon & Schuster Bks. For Young Readers) Simon & Schuster/Paula Wiseman Bks.
—Miguel y Su Valiente Caballero: El Joven Cervantes Sueña a Don Quijote, 1 vol. Engle, Margarita. 2018. (ENG.). 32p. (J). (gr. 3-7). 18.95 *(978-1-68263-019-8(6))* Peachtree Publishing Co. Inc.
—Miguel's Brave Knight: Young Cervantes & His Dream of Don Quixote, 1 vol. Engle, Margarita. 2017. (ENG.). 32p. (J). (gr. 3-6). 17.95 *(978-1-56145-856-1(2))* Peachtree Publishing Co. Inc.
ón, Raul. The Night Library. Zeltser, David. 2019. (ENG.). 40p. (J). (gr. -1-2). 17.99 *(978-1-5247-1798-8(3));* 20.99 *(978-1-5247-1799-5(1))* Random Hse. Children's Bks. (Random Hse. Bks. for Young Readers).
ón, Raúl. Play Ball! Posada, Jorge. 2010. (ENG.). 32p. (J). (gr. 1-5). 6.99 *(978-1-4169-9825-9(X),* Simon & Schuster/Paula Wiseman Bks.) Simon & Schuster/Paula Wiseman Bks.
ón, Raul. Portraits of Hispanic American Heroes. Herrera, Juan Felipe. 2014. (ENG.). 96p. (J). (gr. 3-7). 19.99 *(978-0-8037-3809-6(9),* Dial Bks) Penguin Young Readers Group.
ón, Raúl. Draw! ón, Raúl. 2014. (ENG.). 40p. (J). (gr. -1-3). 17.99 *(978-1-4424-9492-3(1),* Simon & Schuster/Paula Wiseman Bks.) Simon & Schuster/Paula Wiseman Bks.
Ondrasík, Pavel. Barney the Piglet-Following the Nose (with Coloring Book & Pencil) Ondrasíková, Taťána. 2019. (ENG.). 40p. (J). 12.99 ***(978-1-912268-02-3(7),*** ea86058e-e8bc-48a9-a199-0862038e3b8c) Design Media Publishing Ltd. HKG. Dist: Baker & Taylor Publisher Services (BTPS).
O'Neal, Kerry. I Wish I Could Fly/I Can Fly! The Lonely Caterpillar BOOK I & the Lonely Butterfly BOOK II. O'Neal, Kerry. l.t. ed. 2006. 60p. (J). 29.99 *(978-1-59879-197-6(4))* Lifevest Publishing, Inc.
O'Neal, Taylor. Serve It to Me, Too! O'Neal, Briah. 2019. (o'Neal Sisters Tennis Adventures Ser.: Vol. 3). (ENG.). 30p. (J). pap. 12.99 ***(978-1-6934-3553-9(5))*** Independently Published.
O'Neal-Thorpe, Rochelle. Gabe & the Bike: Riding the Minuteman Trail. O'Neal-Thorpe, Rochelle. 2010. 30p. (J). pap. 12.95 *(978-0-9823906-8-9(8))* Wiggles Pr.
—Gabe & the Park & his Big Toy Box: The Adventures of Gabe Series. O'Neal-Thorpe, Rochelle. 2010. 38p. (J). pap. 10.95 *(978-0-9823906-9-6(6))* Wiggles Pr.
O'Neil, Kristy. The Terrible Timing of Terry Tortoise. Gunn, Sharyn. 2017. (ENG.). (J). *(978-1-925681-16-1(5));* pap. *(978-1-925681-12-3(2))* Vivid Publishing.
O'Neil, Sharron. Who Lives in the Sea?/Qui'n Vive en el Mar? Rosa-Mendoza, Gladys. 2007. (English Spanish Foundations Ser.). (ENG & SPA.). 20p. (J). (gr. -1-k). bds. 6.95 *(978-1-931398-24-4(0))* Me+Mi Publishing.
O'Neill, Agatha. Arty et les Insectes - Insect Workbook: Bilingual English / French. Davis, Mandie. Davis, Badger, ed. 2019. (ENG.). 34p. (J). pap. *(978-1-9164839-5-8(X))* Davis, Mandie.
O'Neill, Catharine. Benjy: A Ferocious Fairy Tale. O'Connor, Edwin. 2006. 96p. (J). reprint ed. pap. 12.00 *(978-1-4223-5421-6(0))* DIANE Publishing Co.
O'Neill, Catharine. Annie & Simon. O'Neill, Catharine. 2008. (ENG.). 64p. (J). (gr. k-4). 15.99 *(978-0-7636-2688-4(0))* Candlewick Pr.
—Annie & Simon: The Sneeze & Other Stories. O'Neill, Catharine. 2013. 64p. (J). (gr. k-4). 15.99 *(978-0-7636-4921-0(X))* Candlewick Pr.
—Annie & Simon: Banana Muffins & Other Stories. O'Neill, Catharine. 2017. 64p. (J). (gr. k-3). 15.99 *(978-0-7636-7498-4(2))* Candlewick Pr.
O'Neill, Dave. The Boston Balloonies. Shankman, Ed. (Shankman & O'Neill Ser.). (gr. -1-3). 2012. (ENG.). 40p. pap. 12.95 *(978-1-933212-66-1(7));* 2008. 36p. (J). 14.95 *(978-1-933212-76-0(4))* Applewood Bks. (Commonwealth Editions).
—The Bourbon Street Band Is Back. Shankman, Ed. 2011. (Shankman & O'Neill Ser.). (ENG.). 32p. (gr. -1-3). 14.95 *(978-1-933212-79-1(9),* Commonwealth Editions) Applewood Bks.
—Champ & Me by the Maple Tree: A Vermont Tale. Shankman, Ed. 2010. (Shankman & O'Neill Ser.). (ENG.). 32p. (gr. -1-3). 14.95 *(978-0-9819430-5-3(5),* Commonwealth Editions) Applewood Bks.
—The Cods of Cape Cod. Shankman, Ed. 2009. (Shankman & O'Neill Ser.). (ENG.). 32p. (gr. -1-3). 14.95 *(978-1-933212-78-4(0),* Commonwealth Editions) Applewood Bks.
—I Met a Moose in Maine One Day. Shankman, Ed. 2008. (Shankman & O'Neill Ser.). (ENG.). 32p. (J). (gr. -1-3). 14.95 *(978-1-933212-77-7(2),* Commonwealth Editions) Applewood Bks.
—Monkey See, Zebra Do: A Zoo Party. Shankman, Ed. 2020. (Shankman & O'Neill Ser.). (ENG.). 32p. (J). 14.95 *(978-1-64194-108-2(1),* Commonwealth Editions) Applewood Bks.
—My Grandma Lives in Florida. Shankman, Ed. 2013. (Shankman & O'Neill Ser.). (ENG.). 32p. (J). (gr. -1-3). 14.95 *(978-1-933212-35-7(7),* Commonwealth Editions) Applewood Bks.
—Where's the Bathroom? Shankman, Ed. 2017. (Shankman & O'Neill Ser.). (ENG.). 32p. (J). 14.95 *(978-1-938700-40-8(6),* Commonwealth Editions) Applewood Bks.
—A Whimsical Washington Night: The Adventures of a DC Duo. Shankman, Ed. 2018. (Shankman & O'Neill Ser.). (ENG.). 32p. (J). 14.95 *(978-1-64194-000-9(X),* Commonwealth Editions) Applewood Bks.
O'Neill, Ewa. Violet's Special ACT. Jackson, Amber L. 2017. (ENG.). (J). (gr. k-2). 18.99 *(978-0-692-84096-2(6))* Jackson, Amber.
O'Neill, Ewa. Wimfiddle Finds His Voice. Jackson, Amber. 2019. (ENG.). 40p. (J). (gr. k-4). 21.99 ***(978-0-578-60073-4(0))*** Jackson, Amber.
O'Neill, Gemma. Monty's Magnificent Mane. O'Neill, Gemma. 2015. (ENG.). 40p. (J). (gr. -1-2). 15.99 *(978-0-7636-7593-6(8),* Templar) Candlewick Pr.
—Oh Dear, Geoffrey! O'Neill, Gemma. 2014. (ENG.). 32p. (J). (gr. -1-2). 15.99 *(978-0-7636-6659-0(9),* Templar) Candlewick Pr.
O'Neill, Jacquie. Figure Skating. 2010. (Sticker Stories Ser.). (ENG.). 16p. (J). (gr. -1-k). pap. 5.99 *(978-0-448-45343-9(6),* Grosset & Dunlap) Penguin Publishing Group.
O'Neill, Katie. Crystal Cadets Vol. 1. Toole, Anne. 2016. (ENG.). 128p. (J). pap. 12.99 *(978-1-941302-16-3(5),* 7e636ac5-2ec6-4bab-be53-c19c34c9ab48, Lion Forge) Oni Pr., Inc.
O'Neill, Katie. For Unicorn Lovers Only: History, Mythology, Facts, & More. Gwynne, Penelope. 2020. (ENG.). 176p. (J). 16.99 ***(978-1-250-75939-9(0),*** 900226703) Feiwel & Friends.
O'Neill, Katie. Aquicorn Cove. O'Neill, Katie. 2018. (ENG.). 96p. (J). (gr. 4-6). 12.99 *(978-1-62010-529-0(2),* Lion Forge) Oni Pr., Inc.
—Dewdrop. O'Neill, Katie. 2020. (Dewdrop Ser.). (ENG.). 40p. (J). (gr. k-3). 16.99 *(978-1-62010-689-1(2),* Lion Forge) Oni Pr., Inc.
—Princess Princess Ever After. O'Neill, Katie. 2020. (ENG.). 80p. (J). pap. 9.99 *(978-1-62010-714-0(7),* Lion Forge) Oni Pr., Inc.
O'Neill, Katie. The Tea Dragon Society. O'Neill, Katie. 2020. (Tea Dragon Society Ser.). (ENG.). 72p. (J). pap. 9.99 ***(978-1-62010-737-9(6),*** Lion Forge) Oni Pr., Inc.
O'Neill, Kelly. Collins Big Cat Phonics for Letters & Sounds - Lee & the Box: Band 02B/Red B. Casey, Catherine. 2020. (Collins Big Cat Phonics for Letters & Sounds Ser.). (ENG.). 16p. (J). (gr. -1-k). pap. 6.99 *(978-0-00-835768-9(4))* HarperCollins Pubs. Ltd. GBR. Dist: Independent Pubs. Group.
O'Neill, Lauren. Blazing a Trail: Irish Women Who Changed the World. Webb, Sarah. 2018. (ENG.). 64p. 25.00 *(978-1-78849-004-7(5))* O'Brien Pr., Ltd., The IRL. Dist: Casemate Pubs. & Bk. Distributors, LLC.
O'Neill, Martin. Playlist: The Rebels & Revolutionaries of Sound. Rhodes, James. 2019. (ENG.). 72p. (J). (gr. 7). 29.99 *(978-1-5362-1214-3(8))* Candlewick Pr.
O'Neill-McGrath, Michael. Jesus A to Z. O'Neill-McGrath, Michael. 2007. 32p. 16.99 *(978-1-58459-332-4(6))* World Library Pubns.
O'Neill, Michael Patrick, photos by. Ocean Magic. O'Neill, Michael Patrick, . 2008. 48p. (J). (gr. 1-4). 19.95 *(978-0-9728653-5-7(7))* Batfish Bks.
—Shark Encounters. O'Neill, Michael Patrick, . 2008. 48p. (J). (gr. 1-4). 19.95 *(978-0-9728653-4-0(9))* Batfish Bks.
O'Neill, Michael Patrick, photos by. Fishy Friends: A Journey Through the Coral Kingdom. O'Neill, Michael Patrick. 2003. 64p. (J). 19.95 *(978-0-9728653-0-2(6))* Batfish Bks.
—Let's Explore Coral Reefs. O'Neill, Michael Patrick. 2006. 32p. (J). 15.95 *(978-0-9728653-3-3(0))* Batfish Bks.
—Let's Explore Sea Turtles. O'Neill, Michael Patrick. 2006. 32p. (J). 15.95 *(978-0-9728653-2-6(2))* Batfish Bks.
—Let's Explore Sharks. O'Neill, Michael Patrick. 2006. 32p. (J). 15.95 *(978-0-9728653-1-9(4))* Batfish Bks.
O'Neill, Philomena. Dance Me, Daddy, 1 vol. Morgan, Cindy. 2009. (ENG.). 32p. (J). (gr. -1-2). 16.99 *(978-0-310-71762-1(0))* Zonderkidz.
—Equal Shmequal. Kroll, Virginia. 2005. (Charlesbridge Math Adventures Ser.). (ENG.). 32p. (J). (gr. k-3). per. 7.95 *(978-1-57091-892-6(9))* Charlesbridge Publishing, Inc.
—Little Shrew Caboose. Stolberg, Tina. 2009. (ENG.). 32p. (J). (gr. k-2). 16.95 *(978-0-9792035-7-2(0))* Pleasant St. Pr.
—The Thanksgiving Bowl, 1 vol. Kroll, Virginia. 2007. (ENG.). 32p. (J). (gr. k-3). 16.99 *(978-1-58980-365-7(5),* Pelican Publishing) Arcadia Publishing.
—Toads & Tessellations. Morrisette, Sharon. 2012. (Charlesbridge Math Adventures Ser.). 32p. (J). (gr. 2-5). 16.95 *(978-1-58089-354-1(6));* pap. 7.95 *(978-1-58089-355-8(4))* Charlesbridge Publishing, Inc.
O'Neill, Rachael. I Won't Do That Today: A Story of Stubbornness. Davies, Gill. 2009. (Let's Grow Together Ser.). 32p. (J). (gr. -1-2). pap. 10.55 *(978-1-60754-765-5(1));* lib. bdg. 25.60 *(978-1-60754-758-7(9))* Windmill Bks.
—My First Library: With Nine Colorful Books. (J). *(978-1-85479-804-6(9))* O'Mara, Michael Bks., Ltd.
—A Special Wish: A Story of Confidence. Davies, Gill. 2009. (Let's Grow Together Ser.). 32p. (J). (gr. -1-2). pap. 10.55 *(978-1-60754-769-3(4));* lib. bdg. 25.60 *(978-1-60754-760-0(0))* Windmill Bks.
O'Neill, Rachael. Do You Want a Hug, Honey Bunny? O'Neill, Rachael. 2008. (Tiger Tales Ser.). 12p. (J). (gr. -1-k). 8.95 *(978-1-58925-829-7(0))* Tiger Tales.
O'Neill, Sean, et al. Adventures in Science. Yomtov, Nel. 2012. (Adventures in Science Ser.). (ENG.). 32p. (gr. 3-4). pap. 190.80 *(978-1-4296-8470-5(4),* Capstone Pr.) Capstone.
O'Neill, Sean. Complex Vowels. Blevins, Wiley. 2019. (Sound It Out (LOOK! Books (tm)) Ser.). (ENG.). 32p. (J). (gr. -1-3). pap. 6.99 *(978-1-63440-353-5(3));* lib. bdg. 25.32 *(978-1-63440-341-2(X))* Red Chair Pr.
—Consonants. Blevins, Wiley. 2019. (Sound It Out (LOOK! Books (tm)) Ser.). (ENG.). 32p. (J). (gr. -1-3). pap. 6.99 *(978-1-63440-348-1(7));* lib. bdg. 25.32 *(978-1-63440-336-8(3))* Red Chair Pr.
—Digraphs & Blends. Blevins, Wiley. 2019. (Sound It Out (LOOK! Books (tm)) Ser.). (ENG.). 32p. (J). (gr. -1-3). pap. 6.99 *(978-1-63440-350-4(9));* lib. bdg. 25.32 *(978-1-63440-338-2(X))* Red Chair Pr.
—Long Vowels. Blevins, Wiley. 2019. (Sound It Out (LOOK! Books (tm)) Ser.). (ENG.). 32p. (J). (gr. -1-3). pap. 6.99 *(978-1-63440-351-1(7));* lib. bdg. 25.32 *(978-1-63440-339-9(8))* Red Chair Pr.
—More Consonants. Blevins, Wiley. 2019. (Sound It Out (LOOK! Books (tm)) Ser.). (ENG.). 32p. (J). (gr. -1-3). pap. 6.99 *(978-1-63440-349-8(5));* lib. bdg. 25.32 *(978-1-63440-337-5(1))* Red Chair Pr.
—Short Vowels. Blevins, Wiley. 2019. (Sound It Out (LOOK! Books (tm)) Ser.). (ENG.). 32p. (J). (gr. -1-3). pap. 6.99 *(978-1-63440-352-8(5));* lib. bdg. 25.32 *(978-1-63440-340-5(1))* Red Chair Pr.
—When Volcanoes Erupt!, 1 vol. Yomtov, Nelson. 2012. (Adventures in Science Ser.). (ENG.). 32p. (J). (gr. 3-9). pap. 8.10 *(978-1-4296-7990-9(5));* lib. bdg. 31.32 *(978-1-4296-7547-5(0))* Capstone.
—When Volcanoes Erupt! Yomtov, Nel. 2012. (Adventures in Science Ser.). (ENG.). 32p. (gr. 3-4). pap. 47.70 *(978-1-4296-8468-2(2),* Capstone Pr.) Capstone.
—Will & Wendy Build a Website with Digital Tools. Bailer, Darice. 2014. (Writing Builders Ser.). (ENG.). 32p. (J). (gr. 2-4). pap. 11.94 *(978-1-60357-558-4(8));* lib. bdg. 25.27 *(978-1-59953-584-5(X))* Norwood Hse. Pr.
O'Neill, Sean. Rocket Robinson & the Pharaoh's Fortune. O'Neill, Sean. 2018. (ENG.). 248p. (J). (gr. 5-9). pap. 14.99 *(978-1-5067-0618-4(5))* Dark Horse Comics.
—Rocket Robinson & the Secret of the Saint. O'Neill, Sean. 2018. (ENG.). 248p. (J). (gr. 5-9). pap. 14.99 *(978-1-5067-0679-5(7))* Dark Horse Comics.
O'Neill, Sean. 50 Things You Didn't Know about Ancient Egypt. O'Neill, Sean. 2020. (50 Things You Didn't Know About Ser.). (ENG.). 32p. (J). (gr. 2-5). pap. 8.99 ***(978-1-63440-798-4(9));*** lib. bdg. 27.99 *(978-1-63440-792-2(X))* Red Chair Pr.
—50 Things You Didn't Know about Ancient Greece. O'Neill, Sean. 2020. (50 Things You Didn't Know About Ser.). (ENG.). 32p. (J). (gr. 2-5). pap. 8.99 ***(978-1-63440-799-1(7));*** lib. bdg. 27.99 *(978-1-63440-793-9(8))* Red Chair Pr.
—50 Things You Didn't Know about Ancient Rome. O'Neill, Sean. 2020. (50 Things You Didn't Know About Ser.). (ENG.). 32p. (J). (gr. 2-5). pap. 8.99 ***(978-1-63440-800-4(4));*** lib. bdg. 27.99 *(978-1-63440-794-6(6))* Red Chair Pr.
—50 Things You Didn't Know about Colonial America. O'Neill, Sean. 2020. (50 Things You Didn't Know About Ser.). (ENG.). 32p. (J). (gr. 2-5). pap. 8.99 ***(978-1-63440-802-8(0));*** lib. bdg. 27.99 *(978-1-63440-796-0(2))* Red Chair Pr.
—50 Things You Didn't Know about the Middle Ages. O'Neill, Sean. 2020. (50 Things You Didn't Know About Ser.). (ENG.). 32p. (J). (gr. 2-5). pap. 8.99 ***(978-1-63440-801-1(2));*** lib. bdg. 27.99 *(978-1-63440-795-3(4))* Red Chair Pr.
O'Neill, Sean. 50 Things You Didn't Know about the Old West. O'Neill, Sean. 2020. (50 Things You Didn't Know About Ser.). (ENG.). 32p. (J). (gr. 2-5). pap. 8.99 ***(978-1-63440-803-5(9));*** lib. bdg. 27.99 *(978-1-63440-797-7(0))* Red Chair Pr.

O'Neill, Todd. Mary Cohen's Tuneful Introduction to 2nd Finger Spacing: Easy Well-Known Pieces for Violin. Cohen, Mary. 2003. (Faber Edition Ser.). (ENG.). 24p. pap. 11.95 *(978-0-571-51806-7(0))* Faber & Faber, Ltd. GBR. Dist: Alfred Publishing Co., Inc.

Ong, Cristina. I Knew You Could! A Book for All the Stops in Your Life. Dorfman, Craig. 2003. (Little Engine That Could Ser.). 32p. (J). (gr. -1-2). 11.99 *(978-0-448-43148-2(3),* Grosset & Dunlap) Penguin Young Readers Group.

—I'm a Good Friend! Parker, David. 2004. (J). pap. *(978-0-439-62807-5(5))* Scholastic, Inc.

Ong, Cristina. The Little Engine That Could: Choo Choo Charlie Saves the Carnival. Ong, Cristina, tr. Bryant, Megan E. 2004. (Little Engine That Could Ser.). (ENG.). 32p. (J). (gr. -1-1). 16.19 *(978-0-448-43513-8(6))* Penguin Young Readers Group.

Ong, Olivia. Whitebeard. Etheridge, M. C. D. 2018. (Adventures of Whitebeard Ser.: Vol. 1). (ENG.). 222p. (J). (gr. 2-6). pap. *(978-0-6483590-0-5(X))* Flash Knight.

Ong, Wilson. Mommy Promises. Steigemeyer, Julie. 2008. 32p. pap. 7.49 *(978-0-7586-1479-7(9))* Concordia Publishing Hse.

—Paper Son: Lee's Journey to America. James, Helen Foster & Loh, Virginia Shin-Mui. 2013. (Tales of Young Americans Ser.). (ENG.). 32p. (J). (gr. 1-4). 16.99 *(978-1-58536-833-4(4),* 202366) Sleeping Bear Pr.

—T Is for Tutu: A Ballet Alphabet. Rodriguez, Sonia & Browning, Kurt. 2011. (ENG.). 32p. (J). (gr. k-5). 16.95 *(978-1-58536-312-4(X))* Sleeping Bear Pr.

Ongaro, Isabella. The Day I Ran Away. Niner, Holly L. 2017. (ENG.). 32p. (J). (gr. k-2). 17.95 *(978-1-936261-89-5(8))* Flashlight Pr.

Onishi, Satoru. Who's Hiding? Onishi, Satoru. 2018. (ENG.). 36p. (J). (gr. -1-1). 16.99 *(978-1-877467-12-7(X))* Gecko Pr. NZL. Dist: Lerner Publishing Group.

Ono, Kenji. The Year of the Monkey: Tales from the Chinese Zodiac. Chin, Oliver. 2015. (Tales from the Chinese Zodiac Ser.: 11). (ENG.). 36p. (J). (gr. -1). 15.95 *(978-1-59702-118-0(0))* Immedium.

Ono, Toshihiro. Seikai Trilogy: Banner of the Stars: The Shape of Bonds, 3 vols., Vol. 2. Morioka, Hiroyuki. rev. ed. 2004. (Seikai Trilogy). 200p. pap. 9.99 *(978-1-59182-858-7(9))* TOKYOPOP, Inc.

Onoda, Yuta. La Niña Que Bebió la Luna. Barnhill, Kelly. 2018.Tr. of Girl Who Drank the Moon. (SPA.). 424p. pap. 17.95 *(978-1-64101-210-2(2),* Loqueleo) Santillana USA Publishing Co., Inc.

—Wild Wings. Lewis, Gill. (ENG.). 304p. (J). (gr. 3-7). 2012. pap. 8.99 *(978-1-4424-1446-4(4));* 2011. 21.99 *(978-1-4424-1445-7(6))* Simon & Schuster Children's Publishing. (Atheneum Bks. for Young Readers).

Onque, Sulaiman. It's in the Book: Good Ol' Friends, 9. 3rd ed. 2005. (ENG.). 60p. (J). per. *(978-0-9763841-2-0(4))* Anointed Pubs.

Onque, Suliman & de Almeida, Melissa. The Adventures of Jae & Gia: Growing Pains. Dotson, C. J. 2019. (Adventures of Jae & Gia Ser.: Vol. 2). (ENG.). 130p. (J). pap. 15.95 *(978-1-7194-1686-3(9))* CreateSpace Independent Publishing Platform.

Opal, Paola. Bitsy. 2012. (Simply Small Ser.). (ENG.). 76p. (J). (gr. k — 1). bds. 7.95 *(978-1-897476-65-9(5))* Simply Read Bks. CAN. Dist: Ingram Publisher Services.

—Dotty. 2010. (Simply Small Ser.). (ENG.). 24p. (J). (gr. -1 — 1). bds. 7.95 *(978-1-897476-54-3(X))* Simply Read Bks. CAN. Dist: Ingram Publisher Services.

—Ollie. 2010. (ENG.). 24p. (J). (gr. -1 — 1). bds. 7.95 *(978-1-897476-12-3(4))* Simply Read Bks. CAN. Dist: Ingram Publisher Services.

—Perry. 2010. (ENG.). 24p. (J). (gr. -1-3). bds. 7.95 *(978-1-897476-47-5(7))* Simply Read Bks. CAN. Dist: Ingram Publisher Services.

—Rokko. 2012. (ENG.). 24p. (J). (gr. -1-3). bds. 7.95 *(978-1-897476-59-8(0))* Simply Read Bks. CAN. Dist: Ingram Publisher Services.

—Saffy & Ollie. 2012. 24p. (J). (gr. -1 — 1). bds. 7.95 *(978-1-897476-69-7(8))* Simply Read Bks. CAN. Dist: Ingram Publisher Services.

—Saffy Looks for Rain. 2009. (ENG.). 24p. (J). (gr. k — 1). bds. 7.95 *(978-1-897476-03-1(5))* Simply Read Bks. CAN. Dist: Ingram Publisher Services.

—Stinky Skunk Mel. Winters, Kari-Lynn. 2014. (ENG.). 32p. (J). (gr. -1-3). 15.95 *(978-1-897476-83-3(3))* Simply Read Bks. CAN. Dist: Ingram Publisher Services.

—Totty. 2009. (Simply Small Ser.). (ENG.). 24p. (J). (gr. -1 — 1). bds. 7.95 *(978-1-897476-06-2(X))* Simply Read Bks. CAN. Dist: Ingram Publisher Services.

—Zingy. 2020. (Simply Small Ser.: 10). (ENG.). 24p. (J). (gr. -1 — 1). bds. 6.95 *(978-1-77229-039-4(4))* Simply Read Bks. CAN. Dist: Ingram Publisher Services.

Opatz, Shane. Behind the Zoo: Find Out What the Animals Eat & Do at Irvine Park Zoo, Chippewa Falls, Wisconsin. Opatz, Shane, photos by. Holtz, Monica Stauber. 2011. (J). *(978-0-9837617-1-6(X))* Holtz Creative Enterprises.

Opie, David. Border Breakdown: The Fall of the Berlin Wall. Smith, Molly. 32p. (J). (gr. 1-6). 2010. (ENG.). 9.95 *(978-1-60727-126-0(5));* 2010. (ENG.). 19.95 *(978-1-60727-125-3(7));* 2010. (ENG.). 16.95 *(978-1-60727-123-9(0));* 2010. (ENG.). pap. 6.95 *(978-1-60727-124-6(9));* 2009. (ENG.). 17.95 *(978-1-60727-112-3(5));* 2009. 17.95 incl. audio *(978-1-60727-102-4(8));* 2009. pap. 9.95 incl. audio *(978-1-60727-103-1(6))* Soundprints.

—Dozer's Run: A True Story of a Dog & His Race. Levy, Debbie & Panza, Rosana. 2014. (ENG.). 32p. (J). (gr. 1-4). 16.99 *(978-1-58536-896-9(2),* 203665) Sleeping Bear Pr.

—Monkey & the Engineer. 2007. 24p. (J). 14.95 *(978-0-9793972-6-4(X))* JD Publishing.

Oppenheimer, Nancy. Tali's Jerusalem Scrapbook. Rouss, Sylvia A. 2003. 32p. (J). (gr. 1-4). 14.95 *(978-1-930143-68-5(0));* pap. 9.95 *(978-1-930143-69-2(9))* Simcha Media Group. (Pitspopany Pr.).

Opsahl, Gail Kohler. Talking with My Treehouse Friends about Cancer: An Activity Book for Children of Parents with Cancer. Van Dernoot, Peter R. & van Dernoot, Peter R. 2007. (ENG.). 24p. (J). (gr. 1-7). pap. 12.95 *(978-1-55591-630-5(9))* Fulcrum Publishing.

Oquendo, Lisa. Abecedario. 2006. (SPA.). bds. 5.99 *(978-1-934113-04-2(2))* Little Cubans, LLC.

—Números - Numbers. 2006. (ENG & SPA.). (J). bds. 5.99 *(978-1-934113-01-1(8))* Little Cubans, LLC.

Or, Elbert & Beaton, Jill. Lola: A Ghost Story. Torres, J. 2020. (Lola Ser.). (ENG.). 120p. (J). (gr. 3-6). pap. 12.99 *(978-1-62010-691-4(4),* Lion Forge) Oni Pr., Inc.

Ora, Vania & Mangiarotti, Adriana. My Colors. Kone, Kevin D. 2018. (ENG.). 56p. (J). (gr. 2-6). pap. 19.99 *(978-0-9997562-0-1(6))* kevindkone.

Oral, Feridun. Aunt Fanny's Star. Weineger, Brigitte. 2017. (ENG.). 36p. (J). (gr. -1-k). 18.99 *(978-988-8341-30-6(8),* Minedition) Neugebauer, Michael (Publishing) Limited HKG. Dist: Penguin Random Hse. LLC.

—The Hat Who Was Left Behind. Lamour-Crochet, Céline. 2020. 32p. (J). (gr. -1-k). 17.99 *(978-988-8341-77-1(4),* Minedition) Neugebauer, Michael (Publishing) Limited HKG. Dist: Penguin Random Hse. LLC.

—The Message of the Birds. Westerlund, Kate. 2017. (Minedition Minibooks Ser.). (ENG.). 32p. (J). (gr. k-2). 9.99 *(978-988-8341-51-1(0),* Minedition) Neugebauer, Michael (Publishing) Limited HKG. Dist: Penguin Random Hse. LLC.

—A Whisper in the Snow. Westerlund, Kate. 2018. (ENG.). 32p. (J). (gr. k-2). 17.99 *(978-988-8341-52-8(9),* Minedition) Neugebauer, Michael (Publishing) Limited HKG. Dist: Penguin Random Hse. LLC.

Oral, Feridun. A Friend in Winter. Oral, Feridun. 2019. (ENG.). 32p. (J). (-k). 17.99 *(978-988-8341-87-0(1),* Minedition) Neugebauer, Michael (Publishing) Limited HKG. Dist: Penguin Random Hse. LLC.

—When the Moon Came Down. Oral, Feridun. 2019. (ENG.). 32p. (J). (gr. -1-k). 17.99 *(978-988-8341-76-4(6),* Minedition) Neugebauer, Michael (Publishing) Limited HKG. Dist: Penguin Random Hse. LLC.

Orazzini, Francesco. Circus Dogs Roscoe & Rolly. Pere, Tuula. Korman, Susan, ed. 2018. (ENG.). 40p. (J). (gr. k-4). pap. *(978-952-7107-63-8(6))* Wickwick oy.

—Cirkushundarna Rufus Och Ruffe: Swedish Edition of Circus Dogs Roscoe & Rolly. Pere, Tuula. Nikolowski-Bogomoloff, Angelika, tr. 2018. (SWE.). 40p. (J). (gr. k-4). pap. *(978-952-7107-65-2(2))* Wickwick oy.

—Sirkuskoirat Roope Ja Rops: Finnish Edition of Circus Dogs Roscoe & Rolly. Pere, Tuula. 2018. (FIN.). 40p. (J). (gr. k-4). pap. *(978-952-7107-64-5(4))* Wickwick oy.

Orazzini, Francesco. Τα Σκυλιά του Τσίρκου Ρόσκο και Ρόλι Greek Edition of Circus Dogs Roscoe & Rolly. Pere, Tuula. Papakosta, Irene, tr. 2018. (GRE.). 40p. (J). ***(978-952-7107-88-1(1))***; pap. *(978-952-7107-87-4(3))* Wickwick oy.

Orazzini, Francesco. Цирковые собаки Роско и Ролли Russian Edition of Circus Dogs Roscoe & Rolly. Pere, Tuula. Lutska, Yulia, tr. 2018. (RUS.). 40p. (J). ***(978-952-7107-90-4(3))***; pap. *(978-952-7107-89-8(X))* Wickwick oy.

Orbaan, Albert. Thunder Rolling: The Story of Chief Joseph. Miller, Helen Markley. 2011. 190p. 42.95 *(978-1-258-06189-0(9))* Literary Licensing, LLC.

Orback, Craig. Benjamin Banneker: Pioneering Scientist. Wadsworth, Ginger. 2003. (On My Own Biography Ser.). (ENG.). 48p. (J). (gr. 2-4). per. 7.99 *(978-0-87614-104-5(1),* First Avenue Editions) Lerner Publishing Group.

—Benjamin Banneker: Pioneering Scientist. Wadsworth, Ginger. 2006. (On My Own Biographies Ser.). 47p. (gr. 2-5). 17.00 *(978-0-7569-6705-5(8))* Perfection Learning Corp.

—Born to Draw Comics: The Story of Charles Schulz & the Creation of Peanuts. Wadsworth, Ginger. 2019. (ENG.). 40p. (J). 18.99 *(978-1-250-17373-7(6),* 900189051, Holt, Henry & Co. Bks. For Young Readers) Holt, Henry & Co.

—Boys Camp: Nate's Story. Jazynka, Kitson. 2015. (ENG.). 144p. (J). (gr. 1-5). pap. 9.95 *(978-1-62914-806-9(7),* Sky Pony Pr.) Skyhorse Publishing Co., Inc.

—Boys Camp: Zack's Story. Dokey, Cameron. 2015. (ENG.). 128p. (J). (gr. 1-5). pap. 9.95 *(978-1-62914-805-2(9),* Sky Pony Pr.) Skyhorse Publishing Co., Inc.

—Boys Camp: Zee's Story. Jazynka, Kitson & Tripp, Valerie. 2015. 144p. (J). (gr. 1-5). 14.99 *(978-1-62914-754-3(0),* Sky Pony Pr.) Skyhorse Publishing Co., Inc.

—Bronco Charlie & the Pony Express. Brill, Marlene Targ. 2004. (On My Own History Ser.). (ENG.). 48p. (gr. 2-4). (J). pap. 7.99 *(978-1-57505-618-0(6),* First Avenue Editions); lib. bdg. 25.26 *(978-1-57505-587-9(2))* Lerner Publishing Group.

—Bronco Charlie y el Pony Express. Brill, Marlene Targ. 2005. (Yo Solo Historia Ser.). (SPA.). 46p. (J). (gr. 2-5). per. 6.95 *(978-0-8225-3093-0(7))* Lerner Publishing Group.

—Clara Morgan & the Oregon Trail Journey. Figley, Marthy Rhodes. 2011. (History Speaks: Picture Books Plus Reader's Theater Ser.). 48p. pap. 56.72 *(978-0-7613-7631-6(3))* Lerner Publishing Group.

—Clara Morgan & the Oregon Trail Journey. Figley, Marthy Rhodes & Figley, Marty Rhodes. 2011. (History Speaks: Picture Books Plus Reader's Theater Ser.). (ENG.). 48p. (gr. 2-4). pap. 9.95 *(978-0-7613-7115-1(X))* Lerner Publishing Group.

—The Flyer Flew! The Invention of the Airplane. Hill, Lee Sullivan. 2006. (On My Own Science Ser.). 48p. (J). (gr. 3-7). per. 6.95 *(978-1-57505-855-9(3));* (gr. k-3). lib. bdg. 25.26 *(978-1-57505-758-3(1),* Millbrook Pr.) Lerner Publishing Group.

Orback, Craig. Gifts from the Enemy. Ludwig, Trudy. 2019. (ENG.). 34p. (J). (gr. 3-6). pap. 12.95 ***(978-0-578-55326-9(0))*** Ludwig Creative, Inc.

Orback, Craig. Hot Pursuit: Murder in Mississippi. Deutsch, Stacia & Cohon, Rhody. 2010. (ENG.). 40p. (J). (gr. 3-5). pap. 7.95 *(978-0-7613-3956-4(6),* 9780761339564, Kar-Ben Publishing) Lerner Publishing Group.

—John Adams Speaks for Freedom. Hopkinson, Deborah. ed. 2005. 32p. (J). lib. bdg. 15.00 *(978-1-59054-992-6(9))* Fitzgerald Bks.

—John Adams Speaks for Freedom. Hopkinson, Deborah. 2005. (Ready-To-read SOFA Ser.). (ENG.). 32p. (J). (gr. 1-3). pap. 4.99 *(978-0-689-86907-5(X),* Simon Spotlight) Simon Spotlight.

—John Greenwood's Journey to Bunker Hill. Figley, Marty Rhodes. 2010. (History Speaks: Picture Books Plus Reader's Theater Ser.). (ENG.). 48p. (gr. 2-4). pap. 9.95 *(978-0-7613-6134-3(0))* Lerner Publishing Group.

—Keeping the Promise: A Torah's Journey. Lehman-Wilzig, Tami. 2004. 32p. (J). (gr. 1-5). 16.95 *(978-1-58013-117-9(4),* Kar-Ben Publishing) Lerner Publishing Group.

—Nate's Story, Bk. 2. Jazynka, Kitson. 2013. 144p. (J). (gr. 2-5). 14.95 *(978-1-62087-981-8(6),* 620981, Sky Pony Pr.) Skyhorse Publishing Co., Inc.

—Nature's Paintbox: A Seasonal Gallery of Art & Verse. Thomas, Patricia. 2007. (Millbrook Picture Books Ser.). (ENG.). 32p. (J). (gr. 2-4). lib. bdg. 16.95 *(978-0-8225-6807-0(1),* Millbrook Pr.) Lerner Publishing Group.

—Paul Bunyan. Krensky, Stephen. 2007. (On My Own Folklore Ser.). (ENG.). 48p. (J). (gr. 2-4). per. 7.99 *(978-0-8225-6479-9(3),* First Avenue Editions) Lerner Publishing Group.

—Paul Bunyan. 2006. (On My Own Folklore Ser.). 48p. (J). (gr. -1-3). lib. bdg. 25.26 *(978-1-57505-888-7(X),* Millbrook Pr.) Lerner Publishing Group.

—Prisoner for Liberty. Figley, Marty Rhodes. (On My Own History Ser.). (ENG.). 48p. (gr. 2-4). 2009. (J). pap. 7.99 *(978-0-8225-9022-4(0),* First Avenue Editions); 2008. lib. bdg. 25.26 *(978-0-8225-7280-0(X),* Millbrook Pr.) Lerner Publishing Group.

—Survival in the Snow. Wadsworth, Ginger. 2011. 48p. (J). pap. 6.95 *(978-0-7613-3941-0(8),* First Avenue Editions) Lerner Publishing Group.

—An Uncommon Revolutionary: A Story about Thomas Paine. Waxman, Laura Hamilton. 2003. (Creative Minds Biography Ser.). (J). pap. 5.95 *(978-1-57505-608-1(9),* Carolrhoda Bks.) Lerner Publishing Group.

—Washington Is Burning. Figley, Marty Rhodes. (On My Own History Ser.). 48p. (J). (gr. 2-4). 2007. (ENG.). per. 7.99 *(978-0-8225-6050-0(X),* First Avenue Editions); 2006. lib. bdg. 25.26 *(978-1-57505-875-7(8))* Lerner Publishing Group.

—Zack's Story, Bk. 1. Dokey, Cameron. 2013. 128p. (J). (gr. 2-5). 14.95 *(978-1-62087-528-5(4),* 620528, Sky Pony Pr.) Skyhorse Publishing Co., Inc.

Orban, Jani. Avalanche! Johnson, Terry Lynn. 2018. (Survivor Diaries). (ENG.). 112p. (J). (gr. 3-7). pap. 6.99 *(978-1-328-51906-1(6),* 1720632); 9.99 *(978-0-544-97039-7(X),* 1662544) Houghton Mifflin Harcourt Publishing Co. (HMH Books For Young Readers).

—Dust Storm! Johnson, Terry Lynn. 2018. (Survivor Diaries). (ENG.). 128p. (J). (gr. 3-7). 9.99 *(978-0-544-97098-4(5),* 1662531); pap. 5.99 *(978-1-328-52929-9(0),* 1722007) Houghton Mifflin Harcourt Publishing Co. (HMH Books For Young Readers).

—Lost! Johnson, Terry Lynn. 2018. (Survivor Diaries). (ENG.). 112p. (J). (gr. 3-7). 9.99 *(978-0-544-97118-9(3),* 1662530); pap. 5.99 *(978-1-328-51907-8(4),* 1720643) Houghton Mifflin Harcourt Publishing Co. (HMH Books For Young Readers).

—Overboard! Johnson, Terry Lynn. 2018. (Survivor Diaries). (ENG.). 112p. (J). (gr. 3-7). pap. 5.99 *(978-1-328-51905-4(8),* 1720631, HMH Books For Young Readers) Houghton Mifflin Harcourt Publishing Co.

Orban, Jani, jt. illus. see Ukropina, Jovan.

Orban, Paul. Father of the American Navy: John Barry. Anderson, Floyd. 2011. 188p. 42.95 *(978-1-258-07454-8(0))* Literary Licensing, LLC.

Orbe, Alex. Pickled Watermelon. Schachter, Esty. 2018. (ENG.). 144p. (J). (gr. 4-7). 17.99 *(978-1-5415-4233-4(9),* Kar-Ben Publishing) Lerner Publishing Group.

Orbie. The Little Pig, the Bicycle, & the Moon. Dubé, Pierrette. 2018. (ENG.). 40p. (J). (gr. -1-3). 17.99 *(978-1-5344-1472-3(X),* McElderry, Margaret K. Bks.) McElderry, Margaret K. Bks.

Orchard, Eric. Bluenose Adventure. Halsey, Jacqueline. 2013. (ENG.). 32p. (J). (gr. -1-3). 16.95 *(978-1-4595-0280-2(9),* 0280) Formac Publishing Co., Ltd. CAN. Dist: Formac Lorimer Bks. Ltd.

—If I Were a Zombie, 1 vol. Inglis, Kate. (ENG.). 32p. (J). 2016. (gr. 1-3). 19.95 *(978-1-77108-356-0(5),* 61daa8c8-285d-4ddf-9e42-0dc2604817e3); 2nd ed. 2020. pap. 9.95 ***(978-1-77108-880-0(X),*** 093335cb-0b16-429e-a837-867650f8059f) Nimbus Publishing, Ltd. CAN. Dist: Baker & Taylor Publisher Services (BTPS).

—The Terrible, Horrible, Smelly Pirate, 1 vol. Muller, Carrie & Halsey, Jacqueline. ed. 2008. (ENG.). 32p. (J). (gr. -1-k). pap. 11.95 *(978-1-55109-655-1(2),* 51fc9f01-2b8f-4dc9-b6ea-9aedb23560d6) Nimbus Publishing, Ltd. CAN. Dist: Baker & Taylor Publisher Services (BTPS).

Orchard, Fleur. The Adventures of Cyril Squirrel- SOS Superhero. Fisher, Cat & Fisher, Stu. 2017. (ENG.). (J). pap. *(978-0-9956127-4-7(9))* Snufflesnout Hse. Bks.

—Doug the Slug. Fisher, Cat & Fisher, Stu. 2018. (ENG.). 26p. (J). pap. *(978-0-9956127-5-4(7))* Snufflesnout Hse. Bks.

Orciari, Emanuela. The Story of King Lear. Mazzucco, Melania G. Jewiss, Virginia, tr. 2016. (Save the Story Ser.). (ENG.). 104p. (J). (gr. 3-7). 19.95 *(978-1-78269-020-7(4),* Pushkin Children's Bks.) Steerforth Pr.

Ord, G. W. Tommy Smith's Animals. Selous, Edmund. 2009. 166p. pap. 9.95 *(978-1-59915-376-6(9))* Yesterday's Classics.

—Tommy Smith's Animals (Illustrated Edition) Selous, Edmund. 2016. (ENG.). (J). pap. *(978-1-4068-7888-2(X))* Echo Library.

Ord, Mandy. Chalk Boy. Wild, Margaret. 2019. (ENG.). 32p. (J). (gr. k-2). 16.99 *(978-1-76063-068-3(3))* Allen & Unwin AUS. Dist: Independent Pubs. Group.

Ordas, Emi. Christmas Sticker Activities. Tiger Tales. 2014. (My First Ser.). (ENG.). 40p. (J). (gr. -1-2). 6.99 *(978-1-58925-307-0(8))* Tiger Tales.

—Halloween Sticker Activities. Tiger Tales. 2014. (My First Ser.). (ENG.). 40p. (J). (gr. -1-2). 6.99 *(978-1-58925-306-3(X))* Tiger Tales.

—Sticker Dressing Extreme Sports. Gillespie, Lisa Jane. 2014. (Usborne Activities Ser.). (ENG.). 24p. (J). (gr. -1-3). 8.99 *(978-0-7945-3164-5(4),* Usborne) EDC Publishing.

—Sticker Dressing Warriors. Gillespie, L. ed. 2013. (Sticker Dressing Ser.). 34p. (J). pap. 8.99 *(978-0-7945-3353-3(1),* Usborne) EDC Publishing.

Ordaz, Francisco. The Very First Christmas. Maier, Paul L. (J). 2004. 20p. (gr. -1-k). bds. 7.49 *(978-0-7586-0689-1(3));* 2003. 32p. (gr. 1-5). 7.49 *(978-0-7586-0616-7(8))* Concordia Publishing Hse.

—The Very First Easter. Maier, Paul L. (J). 2005. 20p. bds. 7.49 *(978-0-7586-0717-1(2));* 2004. 32p. pap. 7.49 *(978-0-7586-0627-3(3));* 2004. 32p. 13.49 *(978-0-570-07053-5(8))* Concordia Publishing Hse.

Ordaz, Frank. Be Careful, Kangaroo! Langeland, Deirdre. 2005. (Soundprints' Read-and-Discover Ser.). (ENG.). 48p. (J). (gr. -1-1). 12.95 *(978-1-59249-146-9(4),* PS2010) Soundprints.

—The Titanic Game. Warner, Michael N. 2018. (ENG.). 208p. (J). pap. 11.95 *(978-0-9744446-2-8(6))* All About Kids Publishing.

—Waves of Grace. Doherty, Patrick. 2007. (ENG.). 160p. (YA). (gr. 9-12). pap. 11.95 *(978-0-9744446-6-6(9))* All About Kids Publishing.

Ordóñez, María Antonia. Beba y la Isla Nena: Beba & the Little Island. Landrón, Rafael & Landrón, José Rafael. 2010. (SPA & ENG.). 32p. (J). *(978-1-934370-05-6(3),* Campanita Bks.) Editorial Campana.

Ordóñez, Miguel. Everything Is Mama. Fallon, Jimmy. 2019. (ENG.). 32p. (J). bds. 7.99 *(978-1-250-12583-5(9),* 900174972) Feiwel & Friends.

Ordonez, Miguel. Going to the Volcano. Stanton, Andy. 2020. 32p. (J). (gr. -1-k). pap. 10.99 *(978-1-4449-3345-1(0))* Hachette Children's Group GBR. Dist: Hachette Bk. Group.

Ordóñez, Miguel. Jimmy Fallon's MAMA & DADA. Fallon, Jimmy. 2018. (ENG.). (J). 33.98 *(978-1-250-29784-6(2),* 900196047) Feiwel & Friends.

—This Is Baby. Fallon, Jimmy. 2019. (ENG.). 40p. (J). 16.99 *(978-1-250-24560-1(5),* 900212610) Feiwel & Friends.

—The Three Billy Goats Buenos. Elya, Susan Middleton. 2020. 32p. (J). (gr. -1-3). 16.99 *(978-0-399-54739-3(8),* G.P. Putnam's Sons Books for Young Readers) Penguin Young Readers Group.

Ordóñez, Miguel & Ordóñez, Miguel. Everything Is Mama. Fallon, Jimmy. 2017. (ENG.). 40p. (J). 16.99 *(978-1-250-12584-2(7),* 900174971) Feiwel & Friends.

—Your Baby's First Word Will Be DADA. Fallon, Jimmy. 2015. (ENG.). (J). (gr. -1 — 1). 40p. 16.99 *(978-1-250-00934-0(0),* 900083991); 34p. bds. 7.99 *(978-1-250-07181-1(X),* 900149794) Feiwel & Friends.

Ordóñez, Miguel, jt. illus. see Ordóñez, Miguel.

O'Reilly, John, jt. illus. see Teo, Ali.

O'Reilly, Zoe, jt. illus. see Clarke, Gail.

Orellana, Nery. Before She Gets Her Period: Talking with Your Daughter about Menstruation. Gillooly, Jessica B. 2003. 163p. (J). pap. 13.95 *(978-0-9622036-9-5(6))* Perspective Publishing, Inc.

Oren, Rony. The Animated Menorah: Travels on a Space Dreidel. Sidon, Ephraim. 2007. (Animated Holydays Ser.). 48p. 17.95 *(978-965-7108-80-2(2),* Lambda) Urim Pubns. ISR. Dist: Coronet Bks.

Origin Communications. Princess Amara & the Magic Fruit. 2007. 23p. (J). 15.99 *(978-0-9800538-0-7(3))* Ufodike, Ekwutosi.

Origlio, Peter. Charlie & Albert. 2007. 22p. (J). pap. 12.95 *(978-0-9801329-0-8(8))* Charlie & Albert.

Oriol, Elsa. The Patchwork Torah. Ofanansky, Allison Maile. 2014. (ENG.). 32p. (J). (gr. -1-5). 17.95 *(978-1-4677-0426-7(1),* 9781467704267); Vol. 7.95 *(978-1-4677-0427-4(X),* 9781467704274) Lerner Publishing Group. (Kar-Ben Publishing).

Orkrania, Alexia. I'm Just a Little Cow. Reasoner, Charles. 2014. (ENG.). 12p. (J). (gr. -1). *(978-1-78244-588-3(9))* Top That! Publishing PLC.

—I'm Just a Little Horse. Rose, Eilidh. 2014. (ENG.). 12p. (gr. -1). *(978-1-78244-589-0(7))* Top That! Publishing PLC.

—123 Dreams. Graham, Oakley. 2014. (ENG.). 12p. (J). (gr. -1-k). 7.99 *(978-1-78244-534-0(X))* Top That! Publishing PLC GBR. Dist: Independent Pubs. Group.

Orkrania, Alexia & Fisher, Henry. When I Dream Of 123. Graham, Oakley. 2018. (Picture Storybooks Ser.). (ENG.). 26p. (J). (gr. -1-1). bds. 8.99 *(978-1-78700-257-9(8))* Top That! Publishing PLC GBR. Dist: Independent Pubs. Group.

Orlandi, Lorenzo. Look Inside the Time of Jesus. Rock, Lois. ed. 2016. (ENG.). 8p. (J). (gr. k-2). 12.99 *(978-0-7459-6398-3(6))* Lion Hudson PLC GBR. Dist: Independent Pubs. Group.

Orlando, jt. illus. see Gribel, Christiane.

Orlando, Jade. I Can Code: And/or. Fang, Vicky. 2020. (I Can Code Ser.). 22p. (J). bds. 8.99 ***(978-1-7282-0959-3(5))*** Sourcebooks, Inc.

—I Can Code: If/Then. Fang, Vicky. 2020. (I Can Code Ser.). 22p. (J). bds. 8.99 ***(978-1-7282-0957-9(9))*** Sourcebooks, Inc.

O

Orman, Roscoe. Ricky & Mobo. 2007. (J). 14.95 *(978-1-59299-255-3(2))* Inkwater Pr.

Orme, Harinani. Kili & the Singing Snails. Crowl, Janice. 2011. (J). 16.95 *(978-1-58178-104-5(0))* Bishop Museum Pr.

—Pulelehua & Mamaki. Crowl, Janice. 2009. 36p. (J). 14.95 *(978-1-58178-090-1(7),* Kamahoi Pr.) Bishop Museum Pr.

Ormerod, Jan. Adios, Ratoncito. Harris, Robie H. Rioja, Alberto Jimenez, tr. (SPA.). (J). (gr. k-2). 16.00 *(978-1-930332-34-8(3),* LC8567) Lectorum Pubns., Inc.

—The Buffalo Storm. Applegate, Katherine. 2014. (ENG.). 32p. (J). (gr. -1-3). pap. 7.99 *(978-0-544-33921-7(5),* 1584492, HMH Books For Young Readers) Houghton Mifflin Harcourt Publishing Co.

—Goodbye Mousie. Harris, Robie H. 2004. (ENG.). 32p. (J). (gr. -1-3). reprint ed. 16.99 *(978-0-689-87134-4(1),* Aladdin) Simon & Schuster Children's Publishing.

—I Am Not Going to School Today! Harris, Robie H. 2003. (ENG.). 32p. (J). (gr. -1-3). 19.99 *(978-0-689-83913-9(8),* McElderry, Margaret K. Bks.) McElderry, Margaret K. Bks.

—Mama's Day. Ashman, Linda. 2011. (ENG.). 32p. (J). (gr. -1-1). pap. 16.99 *(978-1-4424-5233-6(1),* Simon & Schuster Bks. For Young Readers) Simon & Schuster Bks. For Young Readers.

—May I Pet Your Dog? The How-to Guide for Kids Meeting Dogs (and Dogs Meeting Kids) Calmenson, Stephanie. 2007. (ENG.). 32p. (J). (gr. -1-3). 13.99 *(978-0-618-51034-4(6),* 100806, Clarion Bks.) Houghton Mifflin Harcourt Trade & Reference Pubs.

Ormerod, Jan. Lizzie Nonsense. Ormerod, Jan. 2004. 40p. (J). *(978-1-877003-59-2(X))* Little Hare Bks. AUS. Dist: HarperCollins Pubs. Australia.

—Lizzie Nonsense. Ormerod, Jan. 2013. (ENG.). 32p. (J). (gr. -1-1). 11.99 *(978-1-74297-678-5(6))* Little Hare Bks. AUS. Dist: Independent Pubs. Group.

Ormes, Jane. Animal Families: Farm. Nosy Crow. 2019. (Animal Families Ser.). (ENG.). 14p. (J). (— 1). bds. 9.99 *(978-1-5362-0830-6(2),* Nosy Crow) Candlewick Pr.

—Animal Families: Forest. Nosy Crow. 2020. (Animal Families Ser.). (ENG.). 14p. (J). (— 1). bds. 9.99 *(978-1-5362-1198-6(2),* Nosy Crow) Candlewick Pr.

—Animal Families: Jungle. Nosy Crow. 2019. (Animal Families Ser.). (ENG.). 14p. (J). (— 1). bds. 9.99 *(978-1-5362-0831-3(0),* Nosy Crow) Candlewick Pr.

—Animal Families: Safari. Nosy Crow. 2020. (Animal Families Ser.). (ENG.). 14p. (J). (— 1). bds. 9.99 *(978-1-5362-1199-3(0),* Nosy Crow) Candlewick Pr.

—Little Honeybee. Haworth, Katie. 2016. (ENG.). 14p. (J). (gr. -1-2). bds. 14.99 *(978-0-7636-8531-7(3),* Big Picture Press) Candlewick Pr.

Ormsby, Lawrence. A Pika's Tail: A Children's Story about Mountain Wildlife. Plumb, Sally. Milligan, Sharlene, ed. 2012. (ENG.). 40p. (J). (gr. -1-5). pap. 9.95 *(978-0-931895-25-8(1))* Grand Teton Assn.

Ornia-Blanco, Miguel. Cold Feet, 1 vol. Dahl, Michael. 2010. (Monster Street Ser.). (ENG.). 32p. (J). (gr. 1-3). lib. bdg. 23.99 *(978-1-4048-6070-4(3),* Picture Window Bks.) Capstone.

—Two Heads Are Better Than One, 1 vol. Dahl, Michael. 2010. (Monster Street Ser.). (ENG.). 32p. (J). (gr. 1-3). lib. bdg. 23.99 *(978-1-4048-6067-4(3),* Picture Window Bks.) Capstone.

Ornoff, Theresa. Logan's Journey. Heath, Kathy & Martin, Karla. 2007. 32p. (J). (gr. -1-3). lib. bdg. 17.95 *(978-1-933982-02-1(0))* Bumble Bee Publishing.

Oronoz, Alan. Agradecer Es lo Maximo! Alva, C. 2017. (SPA.). (J). (gr. k-4). *(978-1-988071-77-0(1))* Hasmark Services Publishing.

—Being Grateful Rocks! Alva, C. (ENG.). (J). (gr. k-4). 2018. 38p. pap. *(978-1-988071-84-8(4));* 2017. *(978-1-988071-57-2(7))* Hasmark Services Publishing.

O'Rourke, Page Eastburn. Grandma's Button Box: Sorting. Williams Aber, Linda. 2006. (Math Matters ® Ser.). (ENG.). 32p. (J). (gr. k-2). pap. 5.95 *(978-1-57565-110-1(6))* Astra Publishing Hse.

—Henry Keeps Score: Comparing. Skinner, Daphne. 2006. (Math Matters ® Ser.). (ENG.). 32p. (J). (gr. k-2). pap. 5.95 *(978-1-57565-102-6(5))* Astra Publishing Hse.

—Henry Lleva la Cuenta (Henry Keeps Score) Comparing. Skinner, Daphne. 2007. (Math Matters en Español Ser.). (SPA.). 32p. (J). (gr. k-2). pap. 5.95 *(978-1-57565-250-4(1))* Astra Publishing Hse.

—¿Qué Sigue, Nina? (What's Next, Nina?) Patterns. Kassirer, Sue. 2006. (Math Matters en Español Ser.). (SPA.). 32p. (J). (gr. k-2). pap. 5.95 *(978-1-57565-152-1(1))* Astra Publishing Hse.

—Slow down, Sara! Friction. Driscoll, Laura. 2006. (Science Solves It! ® Ser.). (ENG.). 32p. (J). (gr. 1-3). pap. 5.95 *(978-1-57565-125-5(4))* Astra Publishing Hse.

—What Homework? Plant Structure. Hayward, Linda. 2006. (Science Solves It! ® Ser.). (ENG.). 32p. (J). (gr. k-2). pap. 5.95 *(978-1-57565-116-3(5))* Astra Publishing Hse.

—What's Next, Nina? Patterns. Kassirer, Sue. 2006. (Math Matters ® Ser.). (ENG.). 32p. (J). (gr. k-2). pap. 5.95 *(978-1-57565-106-4(8))* Astra Publishing Hse.

—Where's Harley? Ordinal Numbers. Felton, Carol & Felton, Amanda. 2006. (Math Matters ® Ser.). (ENG.). 32p. (J). (gr. k-2). pap. 5.95 *(978-1-57565-132-3(7))* Astra Publishing Hse.

O'Rourke, Ryan. Alphabet Boats. Vamos, Samantha R. 2018. 32p. (J). (gr. -1-2). lib. bdg. 14.99 *(978-1-58089-731-0(2))* Charlesbridge Publishing, Inc.

—Alphabet Trains. Vamos, Samantha R. 2015. 32p. (J). (gr. -1-2). lib. bdg. 14.95 *(978-1-58089-592-7(1))* Charlesbridge Publishing, Inc.

—Eight Days Gone. McReynolds, Linda. 2012. 40p. (J). (gr. k-2). 22.44 *(978-1-58089-364-0(3))* Charlesbridge Publishing, Inc.

—Mouseling's Words. Crum, Shutta. 2017. (ENG.). 32p. (J). (gr. -1-3). 16.99 *(978-0-544-30216-7(8),* 1575894, Clarion Bks.) Houghton Mifflin Harcourt Trade & Reference Pubs.

—Night Night, Curiosity. Sayres, Brianna Caplan. 2020. 32p. (J). (gr. -1-2). lib. bdg. 16.99 *(978-1-58089-893-5(9))* Charlesbridge Publishing, Inc.

—One Big Rain: Poems for Every Season. Gray, Rita. ed. 2014. 32p. (J). (gr. 2-5). pap. 7.95 *(978-1-57091-717-2(5))* Charlesbridge Publishing, Inc.

—Read! Read! Read! Vanderwater, Amy Ludwig. 2017. (ENG.). 32p. (J). (gr. k-4). 17.99 *(978-1-59078-975-9(X),* Wordsong) Boyds Mills Pr.

—Struttin' with Some Barbecue: Lil Harden Armstrong Becomes the First Lady of Jazz. Vamos, Samantha R. et al. 2018. (ENG.). 96p. (J). (gr. 4-7). 18.99 *(978-1-58089-740-2(1))* Charlesbridge Publishing, Inc.

—Up! up! up! Skyscraper. Suen, Anastasia. 2017. 32p. (J). (gr. -1-2). lib. bdg. 16.99 *(978-1-58089-710-5(X))* Charlesbridge Publishing, Inc.

—Write! Write! Write! Vanderwater, Amy Ludwig. 2020. (ENG.). 32p. (J). (gr. k-4). 17.99 *(978-1-68437-362-8(X),* Wordsong) Boyds Mills Pr.

O'Rourke, Ryan. Bella Lost & Found. O'Rourke, Ryan. 2014. (ENG.). 40p. (J). (gr. -1-3). 17.99 *(978-0-06-221861-2(1))* HarperCollins Pubs.

—Bella up, up, & Away. O'Rourke, Ryan. 2016. (ENG.). 40p. (J). (gr. -1-3). 17.99 *(978-0-06-221863-6(8))* HarperCollins Pubs.

Oroz, Joyce. Sammy the Dump Truck / Sammy el Camion Volquete (English & Spanish Edition) Weitzel, Nancy. Mlawer, Teresa, tr. 2016. (ENG.). (J). pap. 14.99 *(978-0-9979788-8-9(0))* Mindstir Media.

Orpinas, Jean-Paul. The Age of Bronze, 1 vol. Kidd, Rob. 2008. (Pirates of the Caribbean, Jack Sparrow Ser.: Bk. 5). (ENG.). 144p. (J). (gr. 3-6). 27.07 *(978-1-59961-527-1(4),* 12654, Chapter Bks.) Spotlight.

—The Coming Storm, 1 vol. Kidd, Rob. 2008. (Pirates of the Caribbean, Jack Sparrow Ser.: Bk. 1). (ENG.). 144p. (J). (gr. 3-6). 27.07 *(978-1-59961-523-3(1),* 12650, Chapter Bks.) Spotlight.

—Jack Sparrow: The Siren Song. Kidd, Rob. 2006. 122p. (J). lib. bdg. 16.00 *(978-1-4242-1571-3(4))* Fitzgerald Bks.

Orpinas, Jean-Paul, et al. Kingdom of Color (Disney Tangled) Lagonegro, Melissa. 2010. (Step into Reading Ser.). (ENG.). 32p. (J). (gr. k-3). pap. 4.99 *(978-0-7364-2687-9(6),* RH/Disney) Random Hse. Children's Bks.

—Outside My Window (Disney Tangled) Lagonegro, Melissa. 2010. (Step into Reading Ser.). (ENG.). 32p. (J). (gr. k-3). pap. 4.99 *(978-0-7364-2688-6(4),* RH/Disney) Random Hse. Children's Bks.

Orpinas, Jean-Paul. The Pirate Chase, 1 vol. Kidd, Rob. 2008. (Pirates of the Caribbean, Jack Sparrow Ser.: Bk. 3). (ENG.). 128p. (J). (gr. 3-6). 27.07 *(978-1-59961-525-7(8),* 12652, Chapter Bks.) Spotlight.

—Silver, 1 vol. Kidd, Rob. 2008. (Pirates of the Caribbean, Jack Sparrow Ser.: Bk. 6). (ENG.). 128p. (J). (gr. 3-6). 27.07 *(978-1-59961-528-8(2),* 12655, Chapter Bks.) Spotlight.

—The Siren Song, 1 vol. Kidd, Rob. 2008. (Pirates of the Caribbean, Jack Sparrow Ser.: Bk. 2). (ENG.). 128p. (J). (gr. 3-6). 27.07 *(978-1-59961-524-0(X),* 12651, Chapter Bks.) Spotlight.

—The Sword of Cortes, 1 vol. Kidd, Rob. 2008. (Pirates of the Caribbean, Jack Sparrow Ser.: Bk. 4). (ENG.). 128p. (J). (gr. 3-6). 27.07 *(978-1-59961-526-4(6),* 12653, Chapter Bks.) Spotlight.

—The Timekeeper, 1 vol. Kidd, Rob. 2008. (Pirates of the Caribbean, Jack Sparrow Ser.: Bk. 8). (ENG.). 128p. (J). (gr. 3-6). 27.07 *(978-1-59961-530-1(4),* 12657, Chapter Bks.) Spotlight.

Orpinas, Jean-Paul & Tilley, Scott. Cars (Disney/Pixar Cars) 2006. (Little Golden Book Ser.). (ENG.). 24p. (J). (gr. -1-2). 4.99 *(978-0-7364-2347-2(8),* Golden/Disney) Random Hse. Children's Bks.

Orpinas, Jean-Paul, jt. illus. see Tilley, Scott.

Orr, Katherine. Discover Hawaii's Volcanoes: Birth by Fire. Cook, Mauliola. rev. ed. 2010. (ENG.). 44p. pap. *(978-1-59700-849-5(4))* Island Heritage Publishing.

Orr, Katherine. Master Dao & the Energy of Life. Orr, Katherine. 2nd ed. 2020. (ENG.). 38p. (J). (gr. k-5). pap. 10.99 ***(978-0-578-67655-5(9))*** Dragongate Publishing.

Orrelle, Yael Kimhi. Engineer Arielle & the Israel Independence Day Surprise, Vol. Cohen, Deborah Bodin. 2017. (ENG.). 32p. (J). (gr. k-3). pap. 7.99 *(978-1-5124-2095-1(6),* 9781512420951, Kar-Ben Publishing) Lerner Publishing Group.

Orsini, Cheryl. The Fairy Dancers. Prior, Natalie Jane. 2020. 48p. 12.99 *(978-0-7333-3357-6(5))* ABC Bks. AUS. Dist: HarperCollins Pubs.

Orsini, Janice. Packy the Pack Rat. Moller, Tommie. 2019. (ENG.). 44p. (J). (gr. k-6). pap. 15.00 *(978-0-578-44895-4(5))* ABCS OF GOD.

Orsolini, Laura. Lulu the Shy Piglet. Jeong, SoYun. rev. ed. 2014. (MySELF Bookshelf Ser.). (ENG.). 32p. (J). (gr. k-2). pap. 11.94 *(978-1-60357-654-3(1));* lib. bdg. 25.27 *(978-1-59953-645-3(5))* Norwood Hse. Pr.

Ortac, Feride. Sharp Kids Activity. Ortac, Arda. 2009. 80p. Bk. 1. pap. 9.00 *(978-1-60743-151-0(3));* Bk. 02. pap. 9.00 *(978-1-60743-152-7(1))* Independent Pub.

Ortakales, Denise. Good Morning, Garden. Brenner, Barbara. 2004. (ENG.). 32p. (J). (gr. -1-k). 15.95 *(978-1-55971-888-2(9))* Cooper Square Publishing Llc.

Ortega, Damian. Alegre Roger y el Tesoro Submarino. French, Vivian. Solana, Maria T., tr. 2006. (la Orilla Del Viento Ser.). (SPA.). 125p. (J). pap. 7.50 *(978-968-16-6837-2(5),* 163) Fondo de Cultura Economica USA.

Ortega, David. I Am Special. Lisi, Charlotte. 2006. 16p. (J). 9.99 *(978-1-4120-8911-1(5))* Trafford Publishing.

Ortega, James. Snowflakes in June. Ortiz, Andrea. 2013. 36p. 14.00 *(978-0-9884237-9-4(0))* CLF Publishing.

Ortega, Jose. Agua Agua Agua, Level 2. Mora, Pat. Flor Ada, Alma, tr. 3rd ed. 2003. (Dejame Leer Ser.). (SPA.). 16p. (J). (gr. -1-1). 6.50 *(978-0-673-36292-6(2),* Good Year Bks.) Celebration Pr.

—Fiesta. McConnie Zapater, Beatriz. 2005. (Multicultural Celebrations Ser.). 32p. (J). 4.95 *(978-1-59373-009-3(8))* Bunker Hill Publishing, Inc.

Ortega, Macarena. The Turtle's Shell. Campos, Paula. 2008.Tr. of tortuga Golosa. (J). pap. 14.95 *(978-0-9801147-5-1(6))* Jorge Pinto Bks.

Ortega, Mirelle. Book 1: Escaping the Fire. Smith, Emma Bland. 2019. (Gavin Mcnally's Year Off Ser.). (ENG.). 48p. (J). (gr. 3-7). lib. bdg. 29.93 *(978-1-5321-3506-4(8),* 31931, Spellbound) Magic Wagon.

—Book 2: Weathering the Blizzard. Smith, Emma Bland. 2019. (Gavin Mcnally's Year Off Ser.). (ENG.). 48p. (J). (gr. 3-7). lib. bdg. 29.93 *(978-1-5321-3507-1(6),* 31933, Spellbound) Magic Wagon.

—Book 3: Saving the Alligators. Smith, Emma Bland. 2019. (Gavin Mcnally's Year Off Ser.). (ENG.). 48p. (J). (gr. 3-7). lib. bdg. 29.93 *(978-1-5321-3508-8(4),* 31935, Spellbound) Magic Wagon.

—Book 4: Hunting the Treasure. Smith, Emma Bland. 2019. (Gavin Mcnally's Year Off Ser.). (ENG.). 48p. (J). (gr. 3-7). lib. bdg. 29.93 *(978-1-5321-3509-5(2),* 31937, Spellbound) Magic Wagon.

—Gavin Mcnally's Year Off (Set), 4 vols. Smith, Emma Bland. 2019. (Gavin Mcnally's Year Off Ser.). 48p. (J). (gr. 3-7). lib. bdg. 114.00 *(978-1-5321-3505-7(X),* 31929, Spellbound) Magic Wagon.

—Love Sugar Magic: a Dash of Trouble. Meriano, Anna. (Love Sugar Magic Ser.: 1). (ENG.). (J). (gr. 3-7). 2019. 336p. pap. 7.99 *(978-0-06-249847-2(9));* 2018. 320p. 16.99 *(978-0-06-249846-5(0))* HarperCollins Pubs. (Waldon Pond Pr.).

—Love Sugar Magic: a Mixture of Mischief. Meriano, Anna. 2020. (Love Sugar Magic Ser.: 3). (ENG.). 304p. (J). (gr. 3-7). 16.99 *(978-0-06-291590-0(8),* Waldon Pond Pr.) HarperCollins Pubs.

—Love Sugar Magic: a Sprinkle of Spirits. Meriano, Anna. (Love Sugar Magic Ser.: 2). (ENG.). (J). (gr. 3-7). 2020. 336p. pap. 7.99 *(978-0-06-249852-6(5));* 2019. 320p. 16.99 *(978-0-06-249849-6(5))* HarperCollins Pubs. (Waldon Pond Pr.).

—Pepe & the Parade: A Celebration of Hispanic Heritage. Kyle, Tracey. 2019. (ENG.). 32p. (J). (gr. -1-3). 16.99 *(978-1-4998-0666-3(3))* Little Bee Books Inc.

Ortega, Nathalie. Collins Big Cat Phonics for Letters & Sounds - Mess on the Rocks: Band 01B/Pink B, Bd. 1B. Clarke, Zoe. 2018. (Collins Big Cat Ser.). (ENG.). 16p. (J). pap. 7.99 *(978-0-00-823019-7(6))* HarperCollins Pubs. Ltd. GBR. Dist: Independent Pubs. Group.

Ortiz, Abimael. Arturo & the Hidden Treasure. Felicie-Soto, Ada. 2015. (ENG.). 32p. (J). (gr. 1-5). lib. bdg. 27.59 *(978-1-4994-1863-7(9),* PowerKids Pr.) Rosen Publishing Group, Inc., The.

Ortiz, Ada. Does It Really Rain Cats & Dogs? Whaley, Michelle Marie. 2008. 36p. pap. 24.95 *(978-1-60563-233-9(3))* America Star Bks.

Ortiz Bello, Frank Joseph. Mi Raton Bufon. Terron Tamez, Irma Ilia. 2018. (SPA.). 34p. (J). pap. 11.99 *(978-1-881741-74-9(5))* Ediciones Eleos.

Ortiz, Edgar. Phillip Flies Home. Fortson, Dorris. l.t. ed. 2016. (ENG.). (J). (gr. k-4). pap. 10.95 *(978-1-61633-791-9(5))* Guardian Angel Publishing, Inc.

Ortiz, Edgar. Roy the Little Red Tractor. Fortson, Dorris. l.t. ed. 2019. (ENG.). 24p. (J). (gr. k-3). pap. 10.95 ***(978-1-61633-994-4(2))*** Guardian Angel Publishing, Inc.

Ortiz, Jhon. The One Great Gnome. Dinardo, Jeff. 2020. (ENG.). 128p. (J). (gr. 2-5). 12.99 ***(978-1-947159-59-4(3),*** One Elm Books) Red Chair Pr.

Ortiz, Lydia. Little Feminist 500 Piece Family Puzzle. Galison. 2017. (ENG.). (J). (gr. 3-7). 13.99 *(978-0-7353-5382-4(4))* Mudpuppy Pr.

—Little Feminist Board Book Set. Mudpuppy. 2017. (ENG.). (J). (gr. -1-k). bds. 14.99 *(978-0-7353-5381-7(6),* Mudpuppy) Galison.

—Little Feminist Playing Cards. Galison. 2017. (ENG.). (J). (gr. -1-7). 12.99 *(978-0-7353-5383-1(2))* Mudpuppy Pr.

—Opposites with Frank Lloyd Wright. Mudpuppy. 2018. (ENG.). 30p. (J). (gr. -1-k). bds. 12.99 *(978-0-7353-5408-1(1),* Mudpuppy) Galison.

Ortiz, Lydia, jt. illus. see Rafanan, Patrick.

Ortiz, Miguel. Mi Vida con Las Estrellas. Chimal, Carlos. 2015. (Serie Azul Ser.).Tr. of My Life with the Stars. (SPA.). 200p. (J). pap. 10.95 *(978-1-64101-169-3(6))* Santillana USA Publishing Co., Inc.

Ortiz, Monica. La Vaca Estela y Su Viaje a Bogota. Rodriguez, Silvia. Atuesta, Ana Maria, ed. 2020. (SPA.). 38p. (J). pap. 12.99 ***(978-1-6769-5150-6(4))*** Independently Published.

Ortiz Montanez, Nivea. The Gang & the Biggest Book in the World. Quinones, Juan Carlos. 2004. (Purple Ser.). 48p. (J). *(978-1-57581-438-4(2))* Ediciones Santillana, Inc.

—The Lost Sock. Iturrondo, Angeles Molina & Iguina, Adriana. 2004. (Green Ser.). 24p. (J). *(978-1-57581-434-6(X))* Ediciones Santillana, Inc.

—La Pandilla Bajo el Arbol. Quinones, Juan Carlos. 2004. (Purple Ser.). (SPA.). 44p. (J). (gr. 3-5). pap. 5.95 *(978-1-57581-439-1(0))* Santillana USA Publishing Co., Inc.

Ortiz, Nivea. The Little Mermaid. Eliot, Hannah. 2018. (Once upon a World Ser.). (ENG.). 24p. (J). (gr. -1 — 1). bds. 8.99 *(978-1-5344-3575-9(1),* Little Simon) Little Simon.

Ortiz, Nivea. Sopa de Hortalizas. Molina, Angeles. 2004. (SPA & ENG.). (J). *(978-0-8477-0131-5(X))* Univ. of Puerto Rico Pr.

Ortiz, Oscar. The Poet Upstairs. Cofer, Judith Ortiz. 2012. (J). (gr. 5-9). 16.95 *(978-1-55885-704-9(4),* Piñata Books) Arte Publico Pr.

—La Poeta Del Piso de Arriba. Cofer, Judith Ortiz. Baeza Ventura, Gabriela, tr. from ENG. 2014. (SPA.). (J). 17.95 *(978-1-55885-788-9(5),* Piñata Books) Arte Publico Pr.

Ortiz, Phillip. Barkley the Bear Belongs: Overcoming an Orphan Heart. Russell, Reba. 2017. (ENG.). 42p. (J). (gr. k-3). 18.99 *(978-0-9974913-4-0(5));* (Adventures of Kingdom Forest Ser.: Vol. 2). pap. 12.99 *(978-0-9974913-2-6(9))* Kingdom Door Publishing LLC.

Ortner, Nick & Polizzi, Michelle. My Magic Breath: Finding Calm Through Mindful Breathing. Ortner, Nick & Taylor, Alison. 2018. (ENG.). 32p. (J). (gr. -1-3). 17.99 *(978-0-06-268776-0(X),* HarperCollins) HarperCollins Pubs. Ltd. GBR. Dist: HarperCollins Pubs.

Ortu, Davide. Bedtime on the Farm Red Band. Eeles, Alex. 2016. (Cambridge Reading Adventures Ser.). (ENG.). 16p. pap. 7.37 *(978-1-316-50081-1(0))* Cambridge Univ. Pr.

—The Boy Who Said No Yellow Band. Eeles, Alex. 2017. (Cambridge Reading Adventures Ser.). (ENG.). 16p. pap. 5.62 *(978-1-108-40077-0(9))* Cambridge Univ. Pr.

—Cinderella. Askew, Amanda. 2018. (Once upon a Time ... Ser.). (ENG.). 24p. (J). (gr. -1-k). lib. bdg. 19.99 *(978-1-68297-297-7(6))* QEB Publishing Inc.

—Collins Big Cat Phonics for Letters & Sounds - up in a Rocket: Band 02A/Red A, Bd. 2A. Atkins, Jill. 2018. (Collins Big Cat Phonics Ser.). (ENG.). 16p. (J). (gr. -1-k). pap. 6.99 *(978-0-00-825145-1(2))* HarperCollins Pubs. Ltd. GBR. Dist: Independent Pubs. Group.

Orum-Nielsen, Pernille. Butterfly Battle! (DC Super Hero Girls) Carbone, Courtney. 2018. (Step into Reading Ser.). (ENG.). 32p. (J). (gr. -1-1). lib. bdg. 12.99 *(978-1-5247-6918-5(5),* Random Hse. Bks. for Young Readers) Random Hse. Children's Bks.

—Trouble in Space! Carbone, Courtney. 2017. (Step into Reading Ser.). (ENG.). 32p. (J). (gr. k-3). lib. bdg. 12.99 *(978-1-5247-6607-8(0),* Random Hse. Bks. for Young Readers) Random Hse. Children's Bks.

Ørum, Pernille. Butterfly Battle! Carbone, Courtney. 2018. 29p. (J). *(978-1-5444-0226-0(0))* Random Hse., Inc.

Orum, Pernille. Butterfly Battle! (DC Super Hero Girls) Carbone, Courtney. 2018. (Step into Reading Ser.). (ENG.). 32p. (J). (gr. -1-1). pap. 4.99 *(978-1-5247-6917-8(7),* Random Hse. Bks. for Young Readers) Random Hse. Children's Bks.

Ørum, Pernille. Showdown in Space! Carbone, Courtney. 2017. 32p. (J). *(978-1-5182-5211-2(7))* Random Hse., Inc.

Orum, Pernille. Showdown in Space! (DC Super Hero Girls) Carbone, Courtney. 2017. (Step into Reading Ser.). (ENG.). 32p. (J). (gr. k-3). pap. 4.99 *(978-1-5247-6606-1(2),* Random Hse. Bks. for Young Readers) Random Hse. Children's Bks.

Orum, Pernille. Three Big Bullies! (DC Super Heroes: Wonder Woman) Webster, Christy. 2020. (Step into Reading Ser.). (ENG.). 32p. (J). (gr. -1-1). 5.99 ***(978-0-593-12212-9(7));*** 14.99 ***(978-0-593-12213-6(5))*** Random Hse. Children's Bks. (Random Hse. Bks. for Young Readers).

—Wonder Woman (DC Super Heroes: Wonder Woman) Hitchcock, Laura. 2020. (Little Golden Book Ser.). (ENG.). 24p. (J). (-k). 4.99 ***(978-1-9848-9503-5(6),*** Golden Bks.) Random Hse. Children's Bks.

Ory, Lucie. Mission Canari. Ferre, Gil. 2017. (FRE.). (J). pap. *(978-2-930821-48-1(5))* Plannum.

Osada, Ryuta. Manga Shakespeare: Othello. Shakespeare, William. 2009. (Manga Shakespeare Ser.). (ENG.). 208p. (YA). (gr. 7-11). pap. 14.99 *(978-0-8109-8350-2(8),* Amulet Bks.) Abrams, Inc.

Osadchuk, Keit. When I Was Big. Kaplan, Debbie. 2010. (J). pap. *(978-1-57043-318-4(6))* Eckankar.

Osban, Rodger. Maria & the Stars of Nazca (Maria y las Estrellas de Nazca) Jepson-Gilbert, Anita. Casis, Carmen A., tr. 2004.Tr. of Maria y las Estrellas de Nazca. (SPA & ENG.). 32p. (J). pap. incl. audio compact disk *(978-0-9749745-0-7(1))* TAE Nazca Resources.

—Maria & the Stars of Nazca (Maria y las Estrellas de Nazca), without audio CD. Jepson-Gilbert, Anita. 2004.Tr. of Maria y las Estrellas de Nazca. (ENG & SPA.). pap. 14.95 *(978-0-9749745-1-4(X))* TAE Nazca Resources.

Osbert, Shabamukama. Better Together. Logan, L. M. 2018. (Adventures at Camp Pootie-Cho Ser.: Vol. 1). (ENG.). 28p. (J). pap. 10.95 *(978-1-945408-33-5(2))* Village Tales Publishing.

—Games & Puzzles Activity Book. Lewis, Ophelia S. 2018. (ENG.). 120p. (J). pap. 12.00 *(978-1-945408-39-7(1))* Village Tales Publishing.

Osbert, Shabamukama. Good Manners ABCs: Activity Book. Lewis, Ophelia S. 2019. (Adventures at Camp Pootie-Cho Ser.: Vol. 3). (ENG.). 74p. (J). (gr. k-6). pap. 12.00 ***(978-1-945408-54-0(5))*** Village Tales Publishing.

Osbert, Shabamukama. Keeping Secrets. Lewis, Ophelia S. 2018. (Ian & Applecat Ser.: Vol. 101). (ENG.). 46p. (J). pap. 10.95 *(978-1-945408-34-2(0))* Village Tales Publishing.

Osbert, Shabamukama. Sapo for President. Lewis, Ophelia S. 2020. (Adventures at Camp Pootie-Cho Ser.: Vol. 4). (ENG.). 38p. (J). (gr. 1-6). pap. 10.95 ***(978-1-945408-57-1(X))*** Village Tales Publishing.

Osborn, Eliza. Abstract Blue Journal. Press, Inkbleed. 2020. (ENG.). 162p. (J). pap. 8.99 ***(978-1-6618-0640-8(6))*** Independently Published.

Osborn, Jim. Manners Made Easy. Moore, June Hines. 2004. 96p. pap., tchr. ed., stu. ed. 9.99 *(978-0-8054-3770-6(3))* B&H Publishing Group.

Osborn, Kathy. A Horse in the House & Other Strange but True Animal Stories. Ablow, Gail. 2007. (ENG.). 40p. (J). (gr. 1-4). 17.99 *(978-0-7636-2838-3(7))* Candlewick Pr.

Osborn, Tonia Benington. Learning Magick. Kyrja. 2016. (Rupert's Tales Ser.: 6). (ENG.). 56p. (J). (gr. -1-3). 16.99 *(978-0-7643-4973-7(2),* 6754) Schiffer Publishing, Ltd.

—Rupert's Tales: Rupert Helps Clean Up, 1 vol. Kyrja. 2013. (ENG.). 64p. (J). (gr. -1-3). 19.99 *(978-0-7643-4284-4(3),* 4882) Schiffer Publishing, Ltd.

Osborn, Tonia Bennington. Rupert's Tales: A Book of Bedtime Stories, 1 vol. Kyrja. 2014. (ENG.). 64p. (J). (gr. -1-3). 19.99 *(978-0-7643-4694-1(6),* 5110) Schiffer Publishing, Ltd.

—Rupert's Tales: Making More Magick, 1 vol. Kyrja. 2016. (ENG.). 56p. (J). (gr. -1-3). 16.99 *(978-0-7643-5124-2(9),* 7401) Schiffer Publishing, Ltd.

—Rupert's Tales: The Wheel of the Year - Samhain, Yule, Imbolc, & Ostara, 1 vol. Kyrja. 2012. (ENG.). 64p. 19.99 *(978-0-7643-3987-5(7),* 4366) Schiffer Publishing, Ltd.

—Rupert's Tales: The Wheel of the Year Activity Book, 1 vol. Kyrja. 2012. (ENG.). 40p. pap. 9.99 *(978-0-7643-4020-8(4),* 4367) Schiffer Publishing, Ltd.

Osborn, Traci. Trinity Tales of Tresia: A Perfectly Magnificent Cane (Book III) McPhail, J. A. 2018. (ENG.). 320p. (J). (gr. 3-6). 22.00 *(978-1-64446-000-9(9));* pap. 14.95 *(978-1-64446-001-6(7))* Rowe Publishing.

Osborne, Amber. Puffy Buffy Jones Jones Osborne Dadoot Da Do. Osborne, Amber. Osborne, Dwight. ed. 2006. (J). pap. 11.99 *(978-0-9786431-0-2(0))* AAO Publishing.

Osborne, Graham. Build Your Own Steam Locomotive: A Complete, Easy-to-Assemble Model. Farrington, Karen & Constable, Nick. 2004. 34p. (J). (gr. 4-8). reprint ed. pap. 17.00 *(978-0-7567-8261-0(9))* DIANE Publishing Co.

Osborne, Richard. Animal Stories: Young Readers. Thomas, David, ed. 2011. 190p. 42.95 *(978-1-258-10206-7(4))* Literary Licensing, LLC.

—Teenage Animal Stories. Carter, Russell Gordon. 2011. 252p. 46.95 *(978-1-258-09864-3(4))* Literary Licensing, LLC.

—Teenage Horse Stories. Thomas, David, ed. 2011. 252p. 46.95 *(978-1-258-09866-7(0))* Literary Licensing, LLC.

Oseid, Kelsey. The Animal World: The Amazing Connections & Diversity Found in the Animal Family Tree. Howard, Jules. 2018. (ENG.). 80p. (J). (gr. 2-5). 23.99 *(978-1-4998-0632-8(9))* Little Bee Books Inc.

—Iris & Ian Learn about Interjections. Bailer, Darice. 2014. (Language Builders Ser.). (ENG.). 32p. (J). (gr. 2-4). pap. 11.94 *(978-1-60357-707-6(6))*; lib. bdg. 25.27 *(978-1-59953-672-9(2))* Norwood Hse. Pr.

—Whose Poop Is That? Lunde, Darrin. 2017. 32p. (J). (gr. -1-2). lib. bdg. 16.99 *(978-1-57091-798-1(1))* Charlesbridge Publishing, Inc.

Oseman, Alice. Heartstopper (Heartstopper #1) Oseman, Alice. 2020. (Heartstopper Ser.: 1). (ENG.). 288p. (YA). (gr. 7-7). 24.99 *(978-1-338-61744-3(3))*; pap. 14.99 *(978-1-338-61743-6(5))* Scholastic, Inc. (Graphix).

Osenchakov, Yuri. Snyder: The Pig's Tale. Nilsen, Morten. 2007. 116p. 24.95 *(978-0-9774906-0-8(2))* Counterbalance Bks.

O'Shaughnessy, Nancy. Where Do the Bubbles Go? Macaluso, Jennifer. 2006. (ENG.). 40p. (J). (gr. -1-3). pap. 21.99 *(978-1-4259-3929-8(5))* AuthorHouse.

O'Shea, Bonnie. Henrietta the Farmer & the Long, Long, Long, Long Vacation! Winter, Christopher. 2012. 32p. pap. 13.95 *(978-1-60594-856-0(X))* Aeon Publishing Inc.

O'Shea, Ellen Margaret. Piper & the Red Boat Coloring Book. O'Shea, Ellen Margaret. 2018. (ENG.). 36p. (J). (gr. k-3). pap. 9.95 *(978-1-7321023-1-6(7))* O'Shea, Ellen Storyteller.

Oshida, Tim. The Society's Traitor. Finnish, V. K. 2012. (The Discoveries of Arthur Grey ser.: 1). (ENG.). 298p. (J). (gr. 4-8). 27.99 *(978-0-9852202-0-4(1))* Panama Hat Publishing, Ltd.

—The Society's Traitor. 2nd ed. 2015. (The Discoveries of Arthur Grey ser.: 1). (ENG.). 304p. (J). (gr. 4-8). 27.99 *(978-1-943317-00-4(3))* Panama Hat Publishing, Ltd.

Oshii, Mamoru, jt. illus. see Katsura, Masakazu.

Osker, Denise. All White Dogs Love Mud. Davis, Dayna. 14p. (J). (gr. 1-5). pap. *(978-0-9660350-1-8(1))* Suzalooz Pr.

Osley, Joseph. Alessa: The Girl Who Would Be Sneeze. Rhodes, Daniel. Rhodes, Reese, ed. 2019. (ENG.). 130p. (J). pap. 6.00 ***(978-1-7074-2702-4(X))*** Independently Published.

Oslizlo, Roksana. Bears Can't Play Soccer. Thompson, Beth. 2019. (ENG.). 26p. (J). (gr. k-3). *(978-1-9164680-5-4(5))* Aireborough Pr.

—Blythe & Rosie Poo's Hot Air Balloon Adventure. Dortch, Stephanie. 2018. (ENG.). 26p. (J). pap. 9.99 *(978-1-7239-9320-6(4))* Independently Published.

Osmond, Jack. A Fishy Adventure. Osmond, Joanne H. 2013. 152p. pap. 12.99 *(978-1-933334-26-4(6))* Vision Tree, Ltd., The.

Osnaya, Ricardo. Ali Baba & the Forty Thieves, 1 vol. Manning, Matthew K. 2010. (Classic Fiction Ser.). (ENG.). 72p. (J). (gr. 5-9). 27.99 *(978-1-4342-1988-6(7))*, Stone Arch Bks.) Capstone.

Osorio, Sergio. Ajedrez Infantil: Diviertete Con el Juego Mas Inteligente! Kidder, Harvey. 2005.Tr. of Chess for Children. (SPA.). 128p. (YA). (gr. 2). pap. *(978-968-403-315-3(X))* Selector, S.A. de C.V.

—El Arca de Noé. Fernandez, Francisco. 2005. (Historia de la Biblia Ser.). (SPA.). 64p. (J). pap. 4.70 *(978-970-643-872-0(6))* Selector, S.A. de C.V. MEX. Dist: Spanish Pubs., LLC.

—La Creacion. Fernandez, Francisco. 2005. (Historia de la Biblia Ser.). (SPA.). 64p. (J). pap. 4.70 *(978-970-643-871-3(8))* Selector, S.A. de C.V. MEX. Dist: Spanish Pubs., LLC.

—Jonas. Fernandez, Francisco. 2005. (Historia de la Biblia Ser.). (SPA.). 64p. (J). pap. 4.70 *(978-970-643-876-8(9))* Selector, S.A. de C.V. MEX. Dist: Spanish Pubs., LLC.

—Los Milagros de Jesus. Fernandez, Francisco. 2005. (Historia de la Biblia Ser.). (SPA.). 64p. (J). pap. 4.70 *(978-970-643-882-9(3))* Selector, S.A. de C.V. MEX. Dist: Spanish Pubs., LLC.

—Moises. Fernandez, Francisco. 2005. (Historia de la Biblia Ser.). (SPA.). 64p. (J). pap. 4.70 *(978-970-643-875-1(0))* Selector, S.A. de C.V. MEX. Dist: Spanish Pubs., LLC.

Osorno, Laura. Invitacion a la Fiesta del Gran Gorila. Baena, Gloria. 2003. (SPA.). 32p. (J). 8.95 *(978-958-04-7072-4(3))* Norma S.A. COL. Dist: Distribuidora Norma, Inc.

Ospital, Geneveive. The Story of the Infinipede. Kamke, Bridget. 2003. (J). 19.95 *(978-0-9744306-0-7(9))* You Can Do It! Productions.

Ossio, Fico, et al. Dive, Dive, Dive! Part 1. Marz, Ron & Rodriguez, David A. 2017. (Skylanders: SuperChargers Ser.). (ENG.). 24p. (J). (gr. 1-5). lib. bdg. 27.07 *(978-1-5321-4036-5(3))*, 25441, Graphic Novels) Spotlight.

—Dive, Dive, Dive! Part 2. Marz, Ron & Rodriguez, David A. 2017. (Skylanders: SuperChargers Ser.). (ENG.). 24p. (J). (gr. 1-5). lib. bdg. 27.07 *(978-1-5321-4037-2(1))*, 25442, Graphic Novels) Spotlight.

—The Kaos Trap: Welcome to Skylander Academy. Marz, Ron & Rodriguez, David A. 2015. (Skylanders Set 1 Ser.). (ENG.). 24p. (J). (gr. 1-5). lib. bdg. 27.07 *(978-1-61479-388-5(3))*, 18219, Graphic Novels) Spotlight.

Ossio, Fico. Marvel Action: Spider-Man: a New Beginning (Book One) Dawson, Delilah S. 2019. (Marvel Action: Spider-Man Ser.: 1). 80p. (J). (gr. 4-7). pap. 9.99 *(978-1-68405-514-2(8))* Idea & Design Works, LLC.

—Marvel Action: Spider-Man: Bad Luck (Book Three) Dawson, Delilah S. 2020. (Marvel Action: Spider-Man Ser.: 3). 80p. (J). (gr. 4-7). pap. 9.99 *(978-1-68405-562-3(8))* Idea & Design Works, LLC.

Ossio, Fico, et al. Return of the Dragon King Part 3: Reach for the Sky. Marz, Ron & Rodriguez, David A. 2018. (Skylanders Ser.). (ENG.). 24p. (J). (gr. 1-5). lib. bdg. 27.07 *(978-1-5321-4248-2(X))*, 28576, Graphic Novels) Spotlight.

—Secret Agent Secrets Part 1. Marz, Ron & Rodriguez, David A. 2017. (Skylanders: SuperChargers Ser.). (ENG.). 24p. (J). (gr. 1-5). lib. bdg. 27.07 *(978-1-5321-4039-6(8))*, 25444, Graphic Novels) Spotlight.

—Secret Agent Secrets Part 2. Marz, Ron & Rodriguez, David A. 2017. (Skylanders: SuperChargers Ser.). (ENG.). 24p. (J). (gr. 1-5). lib. bdg. 27.07 *(978-1-5321-4040-2(1))*, 25445, Graphic Novels) Spotlight.

—Secret Agent Secrets Part 3. Marz, Ron & Rodriguez, David A. 2017. (Skylanders: SuperChargers Ser.). (ENG.). 24p. (J). (gr. 1-5). lib. bdg. 27.07 *(978-1-5321-4041-9(X))*, 25446, Graphic Novels) Spotlight.

Ossio, Fico & Cruz, David Garcia. Return of the Dragon King Part 1: All's Fairy in Love & War. Marz, Ron & Rodriguez, David A. 2018. (Skylanders Ser.). (ENG.). 24p. (J). (gr. 1-5). lib. bdg. 27.07 *(978-1-5321-4246-8(3))*, 28574, Graphic Novels) Spotlight.

—Return of the Dragon King Part 2: The Menace of Malefor. Marz, Ron & Rodriguez, David A. 2018. (Skylanders Ser.). (ENG.). 24p. (J). (gr. 1-5). lib. bdg. 27.07 *(978-1-5321-4247-5(1))*, 28575, Graphic Novels) Spotlight.

Osterhold, Jared. For the Love of Bubbles. Banks, Steven et al. 2006. (SpongeBob SquarePants Ser.: 12). (ENG.). 64p. (J). pap. 4.99 *(978-1-4169-1633-8(4))*, Simon Spotlight/Nickelodeon) Simon Spotlight/Nickelodeon.

—How to Draw Incredible Ocean Animals, 1 vol. McCurry, Kristen. 2013. (Smithsonian Drawing Bks.). (ENG.). 64p. (gr. 3-6). (J). pap. 7.19 *(978-1-62065-728-7(7))*, Capstone Pr.); pap. 41.70 *(978-1-62065-729-4(5))*; (J). lib. bdg. 34.65 *(978-1-4296-9940-2(X))*, Capstone Pr.) Capstone.

—The Magic Nutcracker. Hillert, Margaret. 2016. (BeginningtoRead Ser.). (ENG.). 32p. (J). (gr. -1-2). pap. 11.94 *(978-1-60357-943-8(5))*; (gr. 1-2). 22.60 *(978-1-59953-802-0(4))* Norwood Hse. Pr.

—Olivia Leaps! Shaw, Natalie. 2010. (Olivia TV Ser.). (ENG.). 12p. (J). bds. 8.99 *(978-1-84738-612-0(1))* Simon & Schuster Children's Publishing.

Osterhold, Jared & Johnson, Shane L. Olivia & Her Great Adventures. Falconer, Ian et al. 2012. (J). *(978-1-4351-4316-6(7))*, Simon Spotlight) Simon Spotlight.

Ostermeyer, Tim, photos by. Titus & Tiana: Lesson for Baby Tigers. 2011. 18.95 *(978-0-9794228-6-7(8))* Ostermeyer Photography.

Ostertag, Molly Knox. The Hidden Witch. Ostertag, Molly Knox. 2018. (ENG.). 208p. (J). (gr. 3-7). 24.99 *(978-1-338-25376-4(X))*; pap. 12.99 *(978-1-338-25375-7(1))* Scholastic, Inc. (Graphix).

Ostin, Joyce, photos by. Hollywood Moms. 2005. 112p. (YA). reprint ed. 30.00 *(978-0-7567-9363-0(7))* DIANE Publishing Co.

Ostrom, Bob. April. Kelley, K. C. 2014. (Twelve Magic Months Ser.). (ENG.). 24p. (J). (gr. k-3). 14.21 *(978-1-62687-362-9(3))*, 207202) Child's World, Inc., The.

—August. Kelley, K. C. 2014. (Twelve Magic Months Ser.). (ENG.). 24p. (J). (gr. k-3). 14.21 *(978-1-62687-363-6(1))*, 207203) Child's World, Inc., The.

—Baseball Jokes. Rosenberg, Pam. 2014. (Laughing Matters Ser.). (ENG.). 24p. (J). (gr. 1-4). 27.07 *(978-1-62323-993-0(1))*, 206782) Child's World, Inc., The.

—Bug Jokes. Rosenberg, Pam. 2014. (Laughing Matters Ser.). (ENG.). 24p. (J). (gr. 1-4). 27.07 *(978-1-62323-994-7(X))*, 206783) Child's World, Inc., The.

—A Bully-Free Bus, 1 vol. Hall, Pamela. 2012. (World Free of Bullying Ser.). (ENG.). 24p. (J). (gr. -1-4). 27.07 *(978-1-61641-844-1(3))*, 15481, Looking Glass Library) Magic Wagon.

—A Bully-Free Party, 1 vol. Hall, Pamela. 2012. (World Free of Bullying Ser.). (ENG.). 24p. (J). (gr. -1-4). 27.07 *(978-1-61641-845-8(1))*, 15483, Looking Glass Library) Magic Wagon.

—A Bully-Free Playground, 1 vol. Hall, Pamela. 2012. (World Free of Bullying Ser.). (ENG.). 24p. (J). (gr. -1-4). 27.07 *(978-1-61641-846-5(X))*, 15485, Looking Glass Library) Magic Wagon.

—A Bully-Free School, 1 vol. Hall, Pamela. 2012. (World Free of Bullying Ser.). (ENG.). 24p. (J). (gr. -1-4). 27.07 *(978-1-61641-847-2(8))*, 15487, Looking Glass Library) Magic Wagon.

—December. Kelley, K. C. 2014. (Twelve Magic Months Ser.). (ENG.). 24p. (J). (gr. k-3). 14.21 *(978-1-62687-364-3(X))*, 207204) Child's World, Inc., The.

—Dinosaur Jokes. Rosenberg, Pam. 2014. (Laughing Matters Ser.). (ENG.). 24p. (J). (gr. 1-4). 27.07 *(978-1-62323-995-4(8))*, 206784) Child's World, Inc., The.

—Dinosaurs Then & Wow! Shulman, Mark. 2005. (Storytime Stickers Ser.). 16p. (J). (gr. k-2). pap. 5.95 *(978-1-4027-1805-2(5))* Sterling Publishing Co., Inc.

—February. Kelley, K. C. 2014. (Twelve Magic Months Ser.). (ENG.). 24p. (J). (gr. k-3). 14.21 *(978-1-62687-365-0(8))*, 207205) Child's World, Inc., The.

—Friends till the End! ed. 2005. (Teenage Mutant Ninja Turtles Ser.: No. 3). 24p. (J). lib. bdg. 15.00 *(978-1-59054-833-2(7))* Fitzgerald Bks.

—Gross-Out Jokes. Rosenberg, Pam. 2014. (Laughing Matters Ser.). (ENG.). 24p. (J). (gr. 1-4). 27.07 *(978-1-62323-996-1(6))*, 206785) Child's World, Inc., The.

—How a Library Works. StJohn, Amanda. 2012. (Library Skills Ser.). (ENG.). 24p. (J). (gr. -1-2). 14.21 *(978-1-61473-247-1(7))*, 204949) Child's World, Inc., The.

—How an e-Book Works. StJohn, Amanda. 2012. (Library Skills Ser.). (ENG.). 24p. (J). (gr. -1-2). 14.21 *(978-1-61473-248-8(5))*, 204950) Child's World, Inc., The.

—How to Check Out a Book. StJohn, Amanda. 2012. (Library Skills Ser.). (ENG.). 24p. (J). (gr. -1-2). 14.21 *(978-1-61473-249-5(3))*, 204951) Child's World, Inc., The.

—How to Find a Book. StJohn, Amanda. 2012. (Library Skills Ser.). (ENG.). 24p. (J). (gr. -1-2). 14.21 *(978-1-61473-250-1(7))*, 204952) Child's World, Inc., The.

—How to Find Information Online. StJohn, Amanda. 2012. (Library Skills Ser.). (ENG.). 24p. (J). (gr. -1-2). 14.21 *(978-1-61473-251-8(5))*, 204953) Child's World, Inc., The.

—How to Treat a Book. StJohn, Amanda. 2012. (Library Skills Ser.). (ENG.). 24p. (J). (gr. -1-2). 14.21 *(978-1-61473-252-5(3))*, 204954) Child's World, Inc., The.

—I Like Potatoes. Scelsa, Greg. Faulkner, Stacey, ed. 2006. (J). pap. 2.99 *(978-1-59198-316-3(9))* Creative Teaching Pr., Inc.

—January. Kelley, K. C. 2014. (Twelve Magic Months Ser.). (ENG.). 24p. (J). (gr. k-3). 14.21 *(978-1-62687-366-7(6))*, 207206) Child's World, Inc., The.

—Javier's Hummingbird: Solids/Liquids/Gases. Driscoll, Laura. 2018. (Science Solves It! ® Ser.). (ENG.). 32p. (J). (gr. k-2). pap. 5.95 *(978-1-63592-007-9(8))* Astra Publishing Hse.

—July. Kelley, K. C. 2014. (Twelve Magic Months Ser.). (ENG.). 24p. (J). (gr. k-3). 14.21 *(978-1-62687-367-4(4))*, 207207) Child's World, Inc., The.

—June. Kelley, K. C. 2014. (Twelve Magic Months Ser.). (ENG.). 24p. (J). (gr. k-3). 14.21 *(978-1-62687-368-1(2))*, 207208) Child's World, Inc., The.

—Making a Bully-Free World, 1 vol. Hall, Pamela. 2012. (World Free of Bullying Ser.). (ENG.). 24p. (J). (gr. -1-4). 27.07 *(978-1-61641-848-9(6))*, 15489, Looking Glass Library) Magic Wagon.

—March. Kelley, K. C. 2014. (Twelve Magic Months Ser.). (ENG.). 24p. (J). (gr. k-3). 14.21 *(978-1-62687-369-8(0))*, 207209) Child's World, Inc., The.

—May. Kelley, K. C. 2014. (Twelve Magic Months Ser.). (ENG.). 24p. (J). (gr. k-3). 14.21 *(978-1-62687-370-4(4))*, 207210) Child's World, Inc., The.

—Monster Jokes. Rosenberg, Pam. 2014. (Laughing Matters Ser.). (ENG.). 24p. (J). (gr. 1-4). 27.07 *(978-1-62323-998-5(2))*, 206787) Child's World, Inc., The.

—November. Kelley, K. C. 2014. (Twelve Magic Months Ser.). (ENG.). 24p. (J). (gr. k-3). 14.21 *(978-1-62687-371-1(2))*, 207211) Child's World, Inc., The.

—October. Kelley, K. C. 2014. (Twelve Magic Months Ser.). (ENG.). 24p. (J). (gr. k-3). 14.21 *(978-1-62687-372-8(0))*, 207212) Child's World, Inc., The.

—Santa's Little Helpers (Team Umizoomi) Random House. 2013. (Pictureback(R) Ser.). (ENG.). 16p. (J). (gr. -1-2). 4.99 *(978-0-449-81881-7(0))*, Random Hse. Bks. for Young Readers) Random Hse. Children's Bks.

—Save the Kitten!/Buster's Big Day (Team Umizoomi) Random House. 2014. (Pictureback(R) Ser.). (ENG.). 32p. (J). (gr. -1-2). 4.99 *(978-0-385-37520-7(4))*, Random Hse. Bks. for Young Readers) Random Hse. Children's Bks.

—School Jokes. Rosenberg, Pam. 2014. (Laughing Matters Ser.). (ENG.). 24p. (J). (gr. 1-4). 27.07 *(978-1-62323-999-2(0))*, 206788) Child's World, Inc., The.

—The Secret. Murphy, Steve & Murphy, Sonia. 2004. (Teenage Mutant Ninja Turtles Ser.). 32p. (J). (gr. k-2). 11.65 *(978-0-7569-5401-7(0))* Perfection Learning Corp.

—September. Kelley, K. C. 2014. (Twelve Magic Months Ser.). (ENG.). 24p. (J). (gr. k-3). 14.21 *(978-1-62687-373-5(9))*, 207213) Child's World, Inc., The.

—Staying Bully-Free Online, 1 vol. Hall, Pamela. 2012. (World Free of Bullying Ser.). (ENG.). 24p. (J). (gr. -1-4). 27.07 *(978-1-61641-849-6(4))*, 15491, Looking Glass Library) Magic Wagon.

—Step-by-Step Experiments with Electricity. Hagler, Gina. 2012. (Step-By-Step Experiments Ser.). (ENG.). 32p. (J). (gr. 1-4). lib. bdg. 29.93 *(978-1-60973-338-4(X))*, 201230) Child's World, Inc., The.

—Step-by-Step Experiments with Insects. Marsico, Katie. 2012. (Step-By-Step Experiments Ser.). (ENG.). 32p. (J). (gr. 1-4). lib. bdg. 29.93 *(978-1-60973-339-1(8))*, 201231) Child's World, Inc., The.

—Step-by-Step Experiments with Life Cycles. Marsico, Katie. 2012. (Step-By-Step Experiments Ser.). (ENG.). 32p. (J). (gr. 1-4). lib. bdg. 29.93 *(978-1-60973-587-6(0))*, 201232) Child's World, Inc., The.

—Step-by-Step Experiments with Light & Vision. Jacobson, Ryan. 2012. (Step-By-Step Experiments Ser.). (ENG.). 32p. (J). (gr. 1-4). lib. bdg. 29.93 *(978-1-60973-588-3(9))*, 201233) Child's World, Inc., The.

—Step-by-Step Experiments with Soils. Hagler, Gina. 2012. (Step-By-Step Experiments Ser.). (ENG.). 32p. (J). (gr. 1-4). lib. bdg. 29.93 *(978-1-60973-592-0(7))*, 201238) Child's World, Inc., The.

—Step-by-Step Experiments with Sound. Hagler, Gina. 2012. (Step-By-Step Experiments Ser.). (ENG.). 32p. (J). (gr. 1-4). lib. bdg. 29.93 *(978-1-60973-593-7(5))*, 201239) Child's World, Inc., The.

—Step-by-Step Experiments with Taste & Digestion. Marsico, Katie. 2012. (Step-By-Step Experiments Ser.). (ENG.). 32p. (J). (gr. 1-4). lib. bdg. 29.93 *(978-1-60973-614-9(1))*, 201240) Child's World, Inc., The.

—Step-by-Step Experiments with the Water Cycle. Duke, Shirley. 2012. (Step-By-Step Experiments Ser.). (ENG.). 32p. (J). (gr. 1-4). lib. bdg. 29.93 *(978-1-60973-615-6(X))*, 201241) Child's World, Inc., The.

—Tongue Twisters. Rosenberg, Pam. 2014. (Laughing Matters Ser.). (ENG.). 24p. (J). (gr. 1-4). 27.07 *(978-1-62687-000-0(4))*, 206789) Child's World, Inc., The.

—Wrinkles. Miller, Pam. 2005. (Rookie Readers Ser.). (ENG.). 32p. (J). (gr. k-2). lib. bdg. 19.50 *(978-0-516-24860-8(X))*, Children's Pr.) Scholastic Library Publishing.

—Wrinkles. Miller, Pam. 2006. (Rookie Reader Skill Set Ser.). (ENG.). 32p. (J). (gr. k-2). per. 4.95 *(978-0-516-25021-2(3))*, Children's Pr.) Scholastic Library Publishing.

Ostrove, Karen. Fins & Scales: A Kosher Tale. Ostrove, Karen. Miller, Deborah U. 2004. (Israel Ser.). 32p. (J). (gr. 1-3). pap. 4.95 *(978-0-929371-25-2(9))*, Kar-Ben Publishing) Lerner Publishing Group.

Ostrovsky, Alexsandr. Birthday: Companies-Products-Services. Ostrovsky, Alexsandr. (Childrens Ser.). (Orig.). (J). pap. 14.95 *(978-0-934393-17-1(6))* Rector Pr., Ltd.

—Clouds: Companies-Products-Services. Ostrovsky, Alexsandr. (Childrens Ser.). (Orig.). (J). pap. 14.95 *(978-0-934393-20-1(6))* Rector Pr., Ltd.

—Paper Kite. Ostrovsky, Alexsandr. (Childrens Ser.). (Orig.). (J). pap. 14.95 *(978-0-934393-18-8(4))* Rector Pr., Ltd.

Ostrowski, Justin. Sky, the Blue Bunny. Vezeau, Sheila. 2012. 16p. pap. 24.95 *(978-1-4626-7533-3(6))* America Star Bks.

O'Such, Holly. Aunt Ruby, Do I Look Like God? 2004. (J). lib. bdg. 9.95 *(978-0-9745122-0-4(6))* Urban Advocacy.

O'Sullivan, Tom & Bacon, Paul. Shirley Temple's Fairyland: The Wild Swans; Beauty & the Beast; Rumpelstiltskin; the Sleeping Beauty. 2011. 62p. 36.95 *(978-1-258-04207-3(X))* Literary Licensing, LLC.

Osuna Cabral, Erick. Impecables S�per H�roes Extra-Ordinarios: El Poder Del Trabajo en Equipo. Francis, Ryan & Chandler, Chaucey. 2019. (Impecables S�per H�roes Extra-Ordinarios Ser.: Vol. 2). (SPA.). 70p. (J). pap. 15.99 ***(978-0-9983570-7-2(3))*** Two Sees Inc.

Osuna, Rosa. Grandparents. Heras, Chema. 2020. 36p. (J). (gr. -1-3). 17.95 ***(978-1-77164-566-9(0))***, Greystone Bks.) Greystone Books Ltd. CAN. Dist: Publishers Group West (PGW).

Osuna, Rosa. No es Facil, Pequena Ardilla. 2004.Tr. of It's Not Easy, Little Squirrel. (SPA.). (J). 15.99 *(978-84-8464-202-2(X))* Kalandraka Editora, S.L. ESP. Dist: Lectorum Pubns., Inc.

Oswald, Ash. Mind Games, 3. Larry, H. I. 2008. (Zac Power Ser.: 3). (ENG.). 91p. (J). (gr. 2-4). 16.19 *(978-0-312-34657-7(3))*, 900042758, Feiwel & Friends) Feiwel & Friends.

—The Secret Club, 1. Perry, Chrissie. 2007. (Go Girl! Ser.: 7). (ENG.). 87p. (Orig.). (J). (gr. 1-3). 16.19 *(978-0-312-34652-2(2))*, 900042754, Feiwel & Friends) Feiwel & Friends.

—Sleep-Over!, 5. McAuley, Rowan. 2008. (Go Girl! Ser.: 2). (ENG.). 85p. (J). (gr. 1-3). 16.19 *(978-0-312-34641-6(7))*, 9780312346416, Feiwel & Friends) Feiwel & Friends.

—The Worst Gymnast, 2. Kalkipsakis, Thalia. 2007. (Go Girl! Ser.: 5). (ENG.). 86p. (Orig.). (J). (gr. 1-3). 16.19 *(978-0-312-34642-3(5))*, 9780312346423, Feiwel & Friends) Feiwel & Friends.

—Zac Power #1: Poison Island: 24 Hours to Save the World ... & Walk the Dog. Larry, H. I. 2008. (Zac Power Ser.: 1). (ENG.). 96p. (J). (gr. 3-6). pap. 5.99 *(978-0-312-34659-1(X))*, 900042759) Square Fish.

—Zac Power #2: Deep Waters: 24 Hours to Save the World ... & Finish His Homework, 2. Larry, H. I. 2008. (Zac Power Ser.: 2). (ENG.). 96p. (J). (gr. 2-4). pap. 6.99 *(978-0-312-34655-3(7))*, 900042756) Square Fish.

—Zac Power #4: Frozen Fear: 24 Hours to Save the World ... & Get Home for Dinner. Larry, H. I. 2008. (Zac Power Ser.: 4). (ENG.). 96p. (J). (gr. 3-6). pap. 7.99 *(978-0-312-34656-0(5))*, 900042757) Square Fish.

Oswald, Bonnie. The Creation. Brady, Janeen. 2008. (J). 16.99 *(978-1-59955-139-5(X))* Cedar Fort, Inc./CFI Distribution.

Oswald, Pete. All about Animals! A Lift-The-Flap Book of Fun Facts. Eliot, Hannah. 2018. (Did You Know? Ser.). (ENG.). 24p. (J). (gr. -1-k). bds. 7.99 *(978-1-5344-1135-7(6))*, Little Simon) Little Simon.

—The Bad Seed. John, Jory. 2017. (ENG.). 40p. (J). (gr. -1-3). 18.99 *(978-0-06-246776-8(X))*, HarperCollins) HarperCollins Pubs. Ltd. GBR. Dist: HarperCollins Pubs.

—Chickens Don't Fly: And Other Fun Facts. DiSiena, Laura Lyn & Eliot, Hannah. 2014. (Did You Know? Ser.). (ENG.). 32p. (J). (gr. -1-3). 17.99 *(978-1-4424-9353-7(4))*; pap. 7.99 *(978-1-4424-9326-1(7))* Little Simon. (Little Simon).

—The Cool Bean. John, Jory. 2019. (ENG.). 40p. (J). (gr. -1-3). 18.99 *(978-0-06-295452-7(0))*, HarperCollins) HarperCollins Pubs. Ltd. GBR. Dist: HarperCollins Pubs.

—Eat Your Rocks, Croc!: Dr. Glider's Advice for Troubled Animals. Keating, Jess. 2020. (ENG.). 40p. (J). (gr. -1-3). 17.99 *(978-1-338-23988-1(0))*, Orchard Bks.) Scholastic, Inc.

—The Good Egg. John, Jory. 2019. (ENG.). 40p. (J). (gr. -1-3). 18.99 *(978-0-06-286600-4(1))*, HarperCollins) HarperCollins Pubs. Ltd. GBR. Dist: HarperCollins Pubs.

—The Good Egg Presents: the Great Eggscape! John, Jory. 2020. (ENG.). 32p. (J). (gr. -1-3). 10.99 *(978-0-06-297567-6(6))*, HarperCollins) HarperCollins Pubs. Ltd. GBR. Dist: HarperCollins Pubs.

—Hippos Can't Swim: And Other Fun Facts. DiSiena, Laura Lyn & Eliot, Hannah. 2014. (Did You Know? Ser.). (ENG.). 32p. (J). (gr. -1-3). pap. 7.99 *(978-1-4424-9324-7(0))*, Little Simon) Little Simon.

—Rainbows Never End: And Other Fun Facts. DiSiena, Laura Lyn & Eliot, Hannah. 2014. (Did You Know? Ser.). (ENG.). 32p. (J). (gr. -1-3). 17.99 *(978-1-4814-0277-4(3))*; pap. 7.99 *(978-1-4814-0275-0(7))* Little Simon. (Little Simon).

—The Sad Little Fact. Winter, Jonah. 2019. 40p. (J). (gr. -1-2). 17.99 *(978-0-525-58179-6(0))*, Schwartz & Wade Bks.) Random Hse. Children's Bks.

—That's What Dinosaurs Do. John, Jory. 2019. (ENG.). 32p. (J). (gr. -1-3). 17.99 *(978-0-06-234319-2(X))* HarperCollins Pubs.

Oswald, Pete. Hike. Oswald, Pete. 2020. (ENG.). 40p. (J). (gr. -1-3). 17.99 *(978-1-5362-0157-4(X))* Candlewick Pr.

Oswald, Pete & Spurgeon, Aaron. Did You Know? Hippos Can't Swim; Chickens Don't Fly; Rainbows Never End; Trains Can Float. DiSiena, Laura Lyn & Eliot, Hannah. ed. 2014. (Did You Know? Ser.). (ENG.). 128p. (J). (gr. -1-3). pap. 23.99 *(978-1-4814-3032-6(7))*, Little Simon) Little Simon.

—Saturn Could Sail: And Other Fun Facts. DiSiena, Laura Lyn & Eliot, Hannah. 2014. (Did You Know? Ser.). (ENG.). 32p. (J). (gr. -1-3). 17.99 *(978-1-4814-1429-6(1))*; pap. 6.99 *(978-1-4814-1428-9(3))* Little Simon. (Little Simon).

—Trains Can Float: And Other Fun Facts. DiSiena, Laura Lyn & Eliot, Hannah. 2014. (Did You Know? Ser.). (ENG.).

32p. (J). (gr. -1-3). 17.99 *(978-1-4814-0281-1(1)*, Little Simon) Little Simon.

Oswald, Pete & Thompson, Justin K. Mingo the Flamingo. Oswald, Pete & Thompson, Justin K. 2017. (ENG.). 40p. (J). (gr. -1-3). 17.99 *(978-0-06-239198-8(4))* HarperCollins Pubs.

Ot, Elli. Iris y el Gato Negro. Ot, Elli. Brignole, Giancarla, tr. rev. ed. 2007. (Fabulas De Familia Ser.). 32p. (J). (gr. k-4). pap. 6.95 *(978-970-20-0275-8(3))* Castillo, Ediciones, S. A. de C. V. MEX. Dist: Macmillan.

Ota, Yuko. Detective Frankenstein. Johnson, Alaya Dawn. 2011. (Twisted Journeys Ser.: 17). (ENG.). 112p. (J). (gr. 4-7). pap. 45.32 *(978-0-7613-7613-2(5)*, Graphic Universe™) Lerner Publishing Group.

—The Secret Ghost: A Mystery with Distance & Measurement, 3 vols. 2009. (Manga Math Mysteries Ser.: No. 3). 48p. (J). (gr. 2-5). 29.27 *(978-0-7613-3855-0(1))* Lerner Publishing Group.

Ota, Yuko & Helmer, Der-shing. The Kung Fu Puzzle: A Mystery with Time & Temperature. Thielbar, Melinda. 2009. (Manga Math Mysteries Ser.: No. 4). 48p. (J). (gr. 2-5). 29.27 *(978-0-7613-3856-7(X))* Lerner Publishing Group.

Ota, Yuko Geneviev. Detective Frankenstein. Johnson, Alaya Dawn. 2011. (Twisted Journeys ® Ser.: 17). (ENG.). 112p. (J). (gr. 4-7). lib. bdg. 27.99 *(978-0-8225-8942-6(7)*, Graphic Universe™) Lerner Publishing Group.

—The Secret Ghost No. 3: A Mystery with Distance & Measurement. Thielbar, Melinda. 2010. (Manga Math Mysteries Ser.: 3). (ENG.). 48p. (J). (gr. 3-5). pap. 6.95 *(978-0-7613-5245-7(7)*, 9780761352457, Graphic Universe™) Lerner Publishing Group.

Ota, Yuko Geneviev & Xian Nu Studio. A Match Made in Heaven: Book 8, No. 8. Robbins, Trina. 2013. (My Boyfriend Is a Monster Ser.: 8). (ENG.). 128p. (YA). (gr. 7-12). pap. 9.95 *(978-1-4677-0732-9(5)*, 9781467707329, Graphic Universe™) Lerner Publishing Group.

Ota, Yuko Geneviev, jt. illus. see Xian Nu Studio Staff.

Otéro, Nicolas. How Hollyhocks Came to New Mexico. Anaya, Rudolfo. Garcia, Nasario, tr. from ENG. 2012. (SPA & ENG.). 48p. (J). 24.95 *(978-1-936744-12-1(0)*, Rio Grande Bks.) LPD Pr.

Otero, Nicolas. How Hollyhocks Came to New Mexico. Anaya, Rudolfo. Garcia, Nasario, tr. 2018. (ENG.). 48p. (J). (gr. 1-3). pap. 17.95 *(978-1-943681-22-8(8))* Nuevo Bks.

Otero, Sole. All-American Girl Style: Fun Fashions You Can Sketch, 1 vol. Bolte, Mari. 2013. (Drawing Fun Fashions Ser.). (ENG.). 32p. (J). (gr. 3-9). lib. bdg. 28.65 *(978-1-62065-039-4(8))* Capstone.

—Patrick & Paula Learn about Prepositions. Atwood, Megan. 2014. (Language Builders Ser.). (ENG.). 32p. (J). (gr. 2-4). pap. 11.94 *(978-1-60357-708-3(4))*; lib. bdg. 25.27 *(978-1-59953-673-6(0))* Norwood Hse. Pr.

—The People Could Fly: An African-American Folktale. Malaspina, Ann. 2013. (Folktales from Around the World Ser.). (ENG.). 24p. (J). (gr. k-3). 28.50 *(978-1-62323-617-5(7)*, 206385) Child's World, Inc., The.

—The Tale of Little Red Riding Hood. Bradman, Tony. 2014. (Traditional Tales Ser.). (ENG.). 32p. (J). (gr. 1-2). pap. 7.95 *(978-1-62521-580-2(0)*, Capstone Classroom) Capstone.

Otey Little, Mimi. Yoshiko & the Foreigner. Otey Little, Mimi. 2004. 31p. (J). (gr. 4-8). reprint ed. 16.00 *(978-0-7567-7510-0(8))* DIANE Publishing Co.

Otis, Chad. Cuddle Monkey. Hellman, Blake Liliane. 2020. (ENG.). 40p. (J). (gr. -1-3). 17.99 *(978-1-5344-3117-1(9)*, Atheneum Bks. for Young Readers) Simon & Schuster Children's Publishing.

O'Toole, Jeanette. Animals. Filipek, Nina. 2009. (Bright Basics Ser.). 12p. (J). (gr. -1-k). bds. 11.40 *(978-1-60754-688-7(4))* Windmill Bks.

—Cinderella. Filipek, Nina. 2009. (Fairy Tale Firsts Ser.). 12p. (J). (gr. -1-k). bds. 11.40 *(978-1-60754-691-7(4))* Windmill Bks.

—Colors. Filipek, Nina. 2009. (Bright Basics Ser.). 12p. (J). (gr. -1-k). bds. 11.40 *(978-1-60754-687-0(6))* Windmill Bks.

—Counting. Filipek, Nina. 2009. (Bright Basics Ser.). 12p. (J). (gr. -1-k). bds. 11.40 *(978-1-60754-686-3(8))* Windmill Bks.

—The Gingerbread Man. Filipek, Nina. 2009. (Fairy Tale Firsts Ser.). 12p. (J). (gr. -1-k). bds. 11.40 *(978-1-60754-694-8(9))* Windmill Bks.

—Goldilocks & the Three Bears. Filipek, Nina. 2009. (Fairy Tale Firsts Ser.). 12p. (J). (gr. -1-k). bds. 11.40 *(978-1-60754-689-4(2))* Windmill Bks.

—The Three Little Pigs. Filipek, Nina. 2009. (Fairy Tale Firsts Ser.). 12p. (J). (gr. -1-k). bds. 11.40 *(978-1-60754-693-1(0))* Windmill Bks.

—The Ugly Duckling. Filipek, Nina & Andersen, Hans. 2009. (Fairy Tale Firsts Ser.). 12p. (J). (gr. -1-k). bds. 11.40 *(978-1-60754-692-4(2))* Windmill Bks.

—Words. Filipek, Nina. 2009. (Bright Basics Ser.). 12p. (J). (gr. -1-k). bds. 11.40 *(978-1-60754-685-6(X))* Windmill Bks.

O'Toole, Jeanette, jt. illus. see Canals, Sonia.

O'Toole, Julianne. The Smelly Shoe. Giangregorio, Kimberly A. 2012. 24p. pap. 24.95 *(978-1-4626-9387-0(3))* America Star Bks.

O'Toole, Shannon. Unusual Pattern. Cole, David. 2019. (Math Kids Ser.: 3). (ENG.). 120p. (J). (gr. 3-6). pap. 11.95 *(978-1-988761-37-4(9))* Common Deer Pr. CAN. Dist: National Bk. Network.

O'Toole, Shannon, photos by. Stop Reading This Book! Fernandez, Caroline. 2019. (ENG., 36p. (J). (gr. k-3). pap. 10.95 *(978-1-988761-41-1(7))* Common Deer Pr. CAN. Dist: National Bk. Network.

Otoshi, Kathryn. Maneki Neko: The Tale of the Beckoning Cat. Lendroth, Susan. 2010. (J). *(978-1-885008-39-8(2)*, Shen's Bks.) Lee & Low Bks., Inc.

—Marcello: The Movie Mouse. Hockinson, Liz. 2005. (ENG.). 40p. (J). (gr. k). 16.95 *(978-0-9723946-2-8(1))* KO Kids Bks.

Otoshi, Kathryn. What Emily Saw. Otoshi, Kathryn. 2004. (ENG.). 36p. (J). (gr. -1-12). 16.95 *(978-0-9723946-0-4(5))* KO Kids Bks.

Otoshi, Kathryn & Ciccarelli, Gary. Bedtime Safari. Friden, Chris. 2007. (J). *(978-0-9758785-3-8(0))* Haydenburri Lane.

Ott, Candace. Together Bears. Nguyen Lay, Ngoc. 2017. (ENG.). 10p. (J). bds. 12.95 *(978-0-692-03261-9(4)*, 9780692032619) Skybox Event Productions.

Ott, Margot Janet. Invincible. Romansky, Sally Rosenberg. 2006. (J). pap. 8.95 *(978-0-9723729-4-7(6))* Imagination Stage, Inc.

Ott, Steve, jt. illus. see Wedgeworth, Frederick.

Ott, Thomas. We Have Always Lived in the Castle: (Penguin Classics Deluxe Edition) Jackson, Shirley. deluxe ed. 2006. (Penguin Classics Deluxe Edition Ser.). (ENG.). 160p. (gr. 12-18). 17.00 *(978-0-14-303997-6(0)*, Penguin Classics) Penguin Publishing Group.

Ottinger, Jon. My Little Red Lunchbox Book. Pugliano-Martin, Carol. 2004. (Sparkle Shape Bks.). 10p. (J). (gr. -1-18). bds. 6.99 *(978-1-57151-716-6(2))* Playhouse Publishing.

Ottley, Matt. Me & My Dad. Morgan, Sally & Kwaymullina, Ezekiel. 2012. (ENG.). 24p. (J). (gr. -1-k). pap. 14.99 *(978-1-921714-45-0(X))* Little Hare Bks. AUS. Dist: Independent Pubs. Group.

—Parachute. Parker, Danny. 2016. (ENG.). 32p. (J). 16.00 *(978-0-8028-5469-8(9)*, Eerdmans Bks For Young Readers) Eerdmans, William B. Publishing Co.

—Sarah & the Steep Slope. Parker, Danny. 2019. (ENG.). 32p. (J). (gr. -1-k). pap. 11.99 *(978-1-76050-373-4(8))* Little Hare Bks. AUS. Dist: Independent Pubs. Group.

—Suri's Wall. Estela, Lucy. 2018. 32p. (J). (gr. 1-5). 13.99 *(978-0-14-350596-9(3)*, Puffin) Penguin Random Hse. AUS. Dist: Independent Pubs. Group.

—Teacup. Young, Rebecca. 2016. (ENG.). 40p. (J). (gr. -1-3). 17.99 *(978-0-7352-2777-4(2)*, Dial Bks) Penguin Young Readers Group.

—Tree: A Little Story about Big Things. Parker, Danny. 2014. (ENG.). 32p. (J). (gr. -1-k). 19.99 *(978-1-921714-41-2(7))* Little Hare Bks. AUS. Dist: Independent Pubs. Group.

Ottley, Ryan. Amazing Spider-Man by Nick Spencer Vol. 1: Back to Basics, Vol. 1. 2018. (Amazing Spider-Man (2018) Ser.: 1). 152p. (J). (gr. 4-17). pap. 15.99 *(978-1-302-91231-4(3))* Marvel Worldwide, Inc.

—Amazing Spider-Man by Nick Spencer Vol. 3: Lifetime Achievement. 2019. 112p. (YA). pap. 15.99 *(978-1-302-91433-2(2))* Marvel Worldwide, Inc.

—Amazing Spider-Man by Nick Spencer Vol. 5: Behind the Scenes. 2019. (Amazing Spider-Man by Nick Spencer Ser.: 5). 156p. (YA). (gr. 4-17). pap. 19.99 *(978-1-302-91435-6(9))* Marvel Worldwide, Inc.

—Amazing Spider-Man by Nick Spencer Vol. 6: Absolute Carnage. 2020. (Amazing Spider-Man by Nick Spencer Ser.: 6). 112p. (gr. 10-17). pap. 17.99 *(978-1-302-91727-2(7))* Marvel Worldwide, Inc.

—Amazing Spider-Man: Hunted (Vol. 4) TPB. 2019. (ENG.). 272p. (YA). (gr. 4-17). pap. 39.99 *(978-1-302-91434-9(0))* Marvel Worldwide, Inc.

Ottley, Ryan & Coello, Iban. Amazing Spider-Man by Nick Spencer Vol. 8: Threats & Menaces. 2020. (ENG.). 160p. (J). (gr. 4-17). pap. 17.99 ***(978-1-302-92023-4(5))*** Marvel Worldwide, Inc.

Ouachtok, Yassine. Coloring Fish: Coloring Book for Kids Ages 4-8 - Great Gift for Boys & Girls. Books, Perfect Coloring. 2020. (ENG.). 32p. (J). pap. 5.99 ***(978-1-6562-3759-0(8))*** Independently Published.

Ouano, Kevin. Birthday Grandpa & Me. Engelbrecht, Becca. 2016. (ENG.). 26p. (J). pap. 9.99 *(978-1-7903-1487-4(9))* Independently Published.

Oudinot, Wanda & Baum, Kipley, photos by. Colors of a City: Philadelphia. Sedlacek, Jan Gill. 2012. 46p. (J). pap. 14.00 *(978-0-9836878-7-0(0))* Aperture Pr., LLC.

Ouellet, Joanne. The Memory Stone, 1 vol. MacDonald, Anne Louise. 2003. (ENG.). 24p. (J). (gr. -1-3). 7.95 *(978-1-55109-442-7(8)*, 8941c539-6a2b-4c29-a836-d68b665bb29f) Nimbus Publishing, Ltd. CAN. Dist: Baker & Taylor Publisher Services (BTPS).

Ouellette, Michelle. The Case of the Stolen Crown. Harrison, Paula. 2017. 129p. (J). *(978-1-338-20498-8(X))* Scholastic, Inc.

Ouellette, Troy David. Giant Declan & Snugglight's Christmas. Ouellette, Troy David. 2019. (Giant Declan Ser.: Vol. 3). (ENG.). 54p. (J). (gr. k-3). pap. ***(978-1-9995534-1-8(1))*** Rushing River Bks.

Oughton, Taylor. I Love My Brother. Galvin, Laura Gates. 2008. (ENG.). 16p. (J). (gr. -1-k). bds. 6.95 *(978-1-59249-866-6(3))* Soundprints.

Oughton, Taylor, et al. I Love My Sister. Galvin, Laura Gates. 2011. (I Love My... Ser.). (ENG.). 16p. (J). (gr. -1-k). 6.95 *(978-1-60727-311-0(X))* Soundprints.

Oughton, Taylor. Loon at Northwood Lake. Ring, Elizabeth. 2005. (Smith Sonian's Backyard Ser.). 32p. (J). (gr. -1-3). (ENG.). 6.95 *(978-1-59249-482-8(X)*, S5017); pap. 8.95 incl. audio *(978-1-59249-491-0(9)*, SC5013) Soundprints.

—Mallard Duck at Meadow View Pond. Pfeffer, Wendy. (Smithsonian's Backyard Ser.). (ENG.). 32p. (J). (gr. -1-2). 2005. 19.95 *(978-1-56899-958-6(5)*, BC5021); 2005. pap. 4.95 *(978-1-56899-957-9(7)*, B5071); 2003. 9.95 *(978-1-56899-961-6(5)*, PB5071); 2003. 8.95 *(978-1-59249-063-9(8)*, SC5021) Soundprints.

—Mallard Duck at Mountain View Pond. Pfeffer, Wendy. 2005. (Smithsonian's Backyard Ser.). (ENG.). 32p. (J). (gr. -1-2). 15.95 *(978-1-56899-956-2(9)*, B5021) Soundprints.

Ouimet, David. Dare to Be Scared: Thirteen Stories to Chill & Thrill. San Souci, Robert D. 2003. (Dare to Be Scared Ser.). (ENG.). 144p. (J). (gr. 3-7). 17.95 *(978-0-8126-2688-9(5))* Cricket Bks.

—Dare to Be Scared 4: Thirteen More Tales of Terror. San Souci, Robert D. 2009. (Dare to Be Scared Ser.: 4). (ENG.). 229p. (J). (gr. 2-9). 17.95 *(978-0-8126-2754-1(7))* Cricket Bks.

—Double-Dare to Be Scared: Another Thirteen Chilling Tales. San Souci, Robert D. 2004. (Dare to Be Scared Ser.). 144p. (J). 17.95 *(978-0-8126-2716-9(4))* Cricket Bks.

—Triple-Dare to Be Scared: Thirteen Further Freaky Tales. San Souci, Robert D. 2007. (Dare to Be Scared Ser.). (ENG.). 240p. (J). (gr. 2-9). 16.95 *(978-0-8126-2749-7(0))* Cricket Bks.

Oum, Siya, jt. illus. see Henderson, Erica.

Ouren, Todd. The Capitol Building, 1 vol. Stille, Darlene R. 2008. (Our Nation's Pride Ser.). (ENG.). 32p. (J). (gr. k-4). 28.50 *(978-1-60270-112-0(1)*, 11966, Looking Glass Library) Magic Wagon.

—Do Polar Bears Snooze in Hollow Trees? A Book about Animal Hibernation. Salas, Laura Purdie. 2006. (Animals All Around Ser.). (ENG.). 24p. (J). (gr. -1-2). lib. bdg. 27.32 *(978-1-4048-2231-3(3)*, Picture Window Bks.) Capstone.

—Dog-Faced Bats, 1 vol. Britton, Tamara L. 2010. (Bats Ser.). 24p. (J). (gr. 3-6). 27.07 *(978-1-61613-390-0(2)*, 3413, Checkerboard Library) ABDO Publishing Co.

—Downhill Fun: A Counting Book about Winter, 1 vol. Dahl, Michael. 2004. (Know Your Numbers Ser.). (ENG.). 24p. (J). (gr. -1-2). per. 8.95 *(978-1-4048-1092-1(7)*, Picture Window Bks.) Capstone.

—Fisherman Bats, 1 vol. Britton, Tamara L. 2010. (Bats Ser.). 24p. (J). (gr. 3-6). 27.07 *(978-1-61613-391-7(0)*, 3415, Checkerboard Library) ABDO Publishing Co.

—Flying Fox Bats, 1 vol. Britton, Tamara L. 2010. (Bats Ser.). 24p. (J). (gr. 3-6). 27.07 *(978-1-61613-392-4(9)*, 3417, Checkerboard Library) ABDO Publishing Co.

—The Frog Prince: A Retelling of the Grimm's Fairy Tale, 1 vol. Blair, Eric. 2013. (My First Classic Story Ser.). (ENG.). 32p. (J). (gr. k-3). pap. 7.10 *(978-1-4795-1853-1(0)*, Picture Window Bks.) Capstone.

—From the Garden: A Counting Book about Growing Food, 1 vol. Dahl, Michael. 2004. (Know Your Numbers Ser.). (ENG.). 24p. (J). (gr. -1-2). per. 8.95 *(978-1-4048-1116-4(8)*, Picture Window Bks.) Capstone.

—Un Gran Edificio: Un Libro para Contar Sobre Construcción. Dahl, Michael. 2010. (Apréndete Tus Números/Know Your Numbers Ser.).Tr. of One Big Building - A Counting Book about Construction. (ENG.). 24p. (J). (gr. -1-2). lib. bdg. 27.32 *(978-1-4048-6294-4(3)*, Picture Window Bks.) Capstone.

—Huevos y Patas: Cuenta de Dos en Dos. Dahl, Michael. 2010. (Apréndete Tus Números/Know Your Numbers Ser.).Tr. of Eggs & Legs/Counting by Twos. (ENG.). 24p. (J). (gr. -1-2). lib. bdg. 27.32 *(978-1-4048-6296-8(X)*, Picture Window Bks.) Capstone.

—I Am a Sea Horse: The Life of a Dwarf Sea Horse, 1 vol. Shaskan, Trisha Speed. 2008. (I Live in the Ocean Ser.). (ENG.). 24p. (J). (gr. -1-2). lib. bdg. 27.32 *(978-1-4048-4728-6(6)*, Picture Window Bks.) Capstone.

—I Am an Octopus: The Life of a Common Octopus, 1 vol. Shaskan, Trisha Speed. 2008. (I Live in the Ocean Ser.). (ENG.). 24p. (J). (gr. -1-2). lib. bdg. 27.32 *(978-1-4048-4729-3(4)*, Picture Window Bks.) Capstone.

—In the Goose Pen, 1 vol. Stockland, Patricia M. 2009. (Barnyard Buddies Ser.). (ENG.). 24p. (J). (gr. -1-3). 27.07 *(978-1-60270-643-9(3)*, 3403, Looking Glass Library) Magic Wagon.

—In the Llama Yard, 1 vol. Stockland, Patricia M. 2009. (Barnyard Buddies Ser.). (ENG.). 24p. (J). (gr. -1-3). 27.07 *(978-1-60270-644-6(1)*, 3405, Looking Glass Library) Magic Wagon.

—In the Rabbit Hutch, 1 vol. Stockland, Patricia M. 2009. (Barnyard Buddies Ser.). (ENG.). 24p. (J). (gr. -1-3). 27.07 *(978-1-60270-645-3(X)*, 3407, Looking Glass Library) Magic Wagon.

—¡Montones de Mariquitas! Cuenta de Cinco en Cinco. Dahl, Michael. 2010. (Apréndete Tus Números/Know Your Numbers Ser.).Tr. of Lots of Ladybugs! - Counting by Fives. (ENG.). 24p. (J). (gr. -1-2). lib. bdg. 27.32 *(978-1-4048-6297-5(8)*, Picture Window Bks.) Capstone.

—The National Anthem, 1 vol. Hall, M. C. 2008. (Our Nation's Pride Ser.). (ENG.). 32p. (J). (gr. k-4). 28.50 *(978-1-60270-113-7(X)*, 11968, Looking Glass Library) Magic Wagon.

—One Big Building: A Counting Book about Construction, 1 vol. Dahl, Michael. 2004. (Know Your Numbers Ser.). (ENG.). 24p. (J). (gr. -1-2). per. 8.95 *(978-1-4048-1120-1(6)*, Picture Window Bks.) Capstone.

—The Pledge of Allegiance, 1 vol. Doering Tourville, Amanda. 2008. (Our Nation's Pride Ser.). (ENG.). 32p. (J). (gr. k-4). 28.50 *(978-1-60270-114-4(8)*, 11970, Looking Glass Library) Magic Wagon.

—Puss in Boots: A Retelling of the Grimm's Fairy Tale, 1 vol. Blair, Eric. 2011. (My First Classic Story Ser.). (ENG.). 32p. (J). (gr. k-3). pap. 7.10 *(978-1-4048-7359-9(7)*, Picture Window Bks.) Capstone.

—Sand, Leaf, or Coral Reef: A Book about Animal Habitats. Stockland, Patricia M. 2005. (Animal Wise Ser.). (ENG.). 24p. (J). (gr. k-2). 27.32 *(978-1-4048-0932-1(5)*, Picture Window Bks.) Capstone.

—Sleeping Beauty: A Retelling of the Grimm's Fairy Tale, 1 vol. Blair, Eric. 2011. (My First Classic Story Ser.). (ENG.). 32p. (J). (gr. k-3). pap. 7.10 *(978-1-4048-7360-5(0)*, Picture Window Bks.) Capstone.

—Sleeping Beauty: A Retelling of the Grimm's Fairy Tale, 1 vol. Blair, Eric et al. 2010. (My First Classic Story Ser.). (ENG.). 32p. (J). (gr. k-3). lib. bdg. 22.65 *(978-1-4048-6080-3(0)*, Picture Window Bks.) Capstone.

—Spear-Nosed Bats, 1 vol. Britton, Tamara L. 2010. (Bats Ser.). 24p. (J). (gr. 3-6). 27.07 *(978-1-61613-393-1(7)*, 3419, Checkerboard Library) ABDO Publishing Co.

—The Star-Spangled Banner: America's National Anthem & Its History, 1 vol. 2003. (Patriotic Songs Ser.). (ENG.). 24p. (J). (gr. -1-4). 27.32 *(978-1-4048-0175-2(8)*, Picture Window Bks.) Capstone.

—The Statue of Liberty, 1 vol. Stille, Darlene R. 2008. (Our Nation's Pride Ser.). (ENG.). 32p. (J). (gr. k-4). 28.50 *(978-1-60270-115-1(6)*, 11972, Looking Glass Library) Magic Wagon.

—Stripes, Spots, or Diamonds: A Book about Animal Patterns. Stockland, Patricia M. 2005. (Animal Wise Ser.). (ENG.). 24p. (J). (gr. k-2). 27.32 *(978-1-4048-0934-5(1)*, Picture Window Bks.) Capstone.

—Tom Thumb: A Retelling of the Grimm's Fairy Tale, 1 vol. Blair, Eric. 2013. (My First Classic Story Ser.). (ENG.). 32p. (J). (gr. k-3). pap. 7.10 *(978-1-4795-1847-0(6)*, Picture Window Bks.) Capstone.

—The United States Flag, 1 vol. Doering Tourville, Amanda. 2008. (Our Nation's Pride Ser.). (ENG.). 32p. (J). (gr. k-4). 28.50 *(978-1-60270-116-8(4)*, 11974, Looking Glass Library) Magic Wagon.

—Vampire Bats, 1 vol. Britton, Tamara L. 2010. (Bats Ser.). 24p. (J). (gr. 3-6). 27.07 *(978-1-61613-394-8(5)*, 3421, Checkerboard Library) ABDO Publishing Co.

—Veteran's Day, 1 vol. Tourville, Amanda Doering. 2008. (Our Nation's Pride Ser.). (ENG.). 32p. (J). (gr. k-4). 28.50 *(978-1-60270-117-5(2)*, 11976, Looking Glass Library) Magic Wagon.

—Wrinkle-Faced Bats, 1 vol. Britton, Tamara L. 2010. (Bats Ser.). 24p. (J). (gr. 3-6). 27.07 *(978-1-61613-395-5(3)*, 3423, Checkerboard Library) ABDO Publishing Co.

Ouren, Todd, jt. illus. see Lyles, Christopher.

Ouseley, Deryk. Do Fish Fart? Answers to Kids' Questions about Lakes. Thomas, Keltie. 2016. (ENG.). 48p. (J). (gr. 3-7). pap. 9.95 *(978-1-77085-727-8(3)*, 93c939c1-f1d0-400b-b972-b0035b9c7b02) Firefly Bks., Ltd.

Ousley, Clayton Gerard, photos by. Charley Finds A Family. Duchene-Marshall, Michele A. Marshall, Alan David, ed. l.t. ed. 2004. Orig. Title: Charley finds a Home. 20p. (J). spiral bd. 10.00 *(978-0-9761675-2-5(2))* Storybook Acres.

—Shirley's Red Satin Shoes. Duchene-Marshall, Michele A. Marshall, Alan David, ed. l.t. ed. 2003. 17p. (J). spiral bd. 10.00 *(978-0-9761675-1-8(4))* Storybook Acres.

Outohak, Diana. Lulu Learns about Reporting: Ending the Tattle Battle. Golden, Pam. 2007. 28p. (J). pap. 18.95 *(978-0-9659650-8-8(2))* Roedway Pr.

Ovakimyan, Liza. Johnathan & Geneva the Adventures of Zeallionaire Kid's. Perry, Melanie Denise. Neal, Albert, ed. 2013. 34p. pap. 11.99 *(978-0-9911077-1-1(3))* Sankofa Pr.

—Jonathan y Geneva Las Aventuras de Los Zeallionaire Kids. Perry, Melanie Denise. Neal, Albert, ed. 2013. 34p. pap. 11.99 *(978-0-9911077-0-4(5))* Sankofa Pr.

Ovani, Germano. The Monkey King. 2007. (Young Reading Series 1 Gift Bks). 47p. (J). (gr. -1-3). 8.99 *(978-0-7945-1593-5(2)*, Usborne) EDC Publishing.

Over, John, jt. illus. see Yerrill, Gail.

Overbee, Kara. Princess Aubree's Grand Adventures: The Enchanted Land. Overbee, Kara. Overbee, Aubree. 2018. (ENG.). 38p. (J). pap. 12.99 *(978-1-7278-0052-4(4))* CreateSpace Independent Publishing Platform.

Overett, A. M. Amelia & the Magic Jungle. Overett, A. M. 2018. (ENG.). 198p. (J). pap. 9.95 *(978-1-64373-221-3(8))*; (gr. 1-6). pap. 26.95 *(978-1-64373-220-6(X))*; (gr. 1-6). pap. 11.95 *(978-1-64373-222-0(6))* LPC.

Overley, Kristen V., jt. illus. see Manwiller, S. A.

Overton, Kim. Sip, Pick, & Pack... How Pollinators Help Plants Make Seeds. Cheney, Polly. 2016. (ENG.). 27p. (J). 16.99 *(978-1-939710-55-0(3))* Orange Frazer Pr.

Overwater, Georgien. Enormous Turnip. Daynes, Katie. 2006. (First Reading Level 3 Ser.). 48p. (J). (gr. 1-4). 8.99 *(978-0-7945-1376-4(X)*, Usborne) EDC Publishing.

—The Three Little Pigs. 2007. (Usborne First Reading: Level 3 Ser.). 48p. (J). 8.99 *(978-0-7945-1598-0(3)*, Usborne) EDC Publishing.

Ovocheva, Zhanna. Animal Alphabet. George, Joshua. 2019. (Animal Friends Padded Board Bks.). (ENG.). 30p. (J). (— 1). bds. 9.99 *(978-1-78958-164-5(8))* Top That! Publishing PLC GBR. Dist: Independent Pubs. Group.

—Animal Counting. George, Joshua. 2019. (Animal Friends Padded Board Bks.). (ENG.). 30p. (J). (— 1). bds. 9.99 *(978-1-78958-165-2(6))* Top That! Publishing PLC GBR. Dist: Independent Pubs. Group.

—Goodnight Bear. George, Joshua. 2018. (Torchlight Bks.). (ENG.). 10p. (J). bds. 7.99 *(978-1-78700-611-9(5))* Top That! Publishing PLC GBR. Dist: Independent Pubs. Group.

—Goodnight Lion. George, Joshua. 2018. (Torchlight Bks.). (ENG.). 10p. (J). bds. 7.99 *(978-1-78700-612-6(3))* Top That! Publishing PLC GBR. Dist: Independent Pubs. Group.

—Hello, Cat! Linn, Susie. 2019. (Touch & Trace Ser.). (ENG.). 10p. (J). 7.99 *(978-1-78700-617-1(4))* Top That! Publishing PLC GBR. Dist: Independent Pubs. Group.

—Hello, Dog! Linn, Susie. 2019. (Touch & Trace Ser.). (ENG.). 10p. (J). 7.99 *(978-1-78700-618-8(2))* Top That! Publishing PLC GBR. Dist: Independent Pubs. Group.

Ovocheva, Zhanna. Look & See ABC. Lily, Amber. 2020. (Animal Friends Concept Board Bks.). (ENG.). 28p. (J). (— 1). bds. 9.99 ***(978-1-78958-496-7(5))*** Top That! Publishing PLC GBR. Dist: Independent Pubs. Group.

Ovresat, Laura. Bath Time. Gerver, Jane E. 2004. (My First Reader Ser.). 31p. (J). 18.50 *(978-0-516-24677-2(1)*, Children's Pr.) Scholastic Library Publishing.

—Did You See Chip? Yee, Wong Herbert. 2004. (Green Light Readers Level 2 Ser.). (ENG.). 24p. (J). (gr. -1-3). pap. 3.95 *(978-0-15-205096-2(5)*, 1195388) Houghton Mifflin Harcourt Publishing Co.

—Guess Who Ocean Friends. Shepherd, Jodie. 2007. (Guess Who Ser.). (ENG.). 12p. (J). (gr. -1-k). bds. 8.99 *(978-0-7944-1122-0(3)*, Reader's Digest Children's Bks.) Studio Fun International.

—The Picnic. Williams, David K. & Williams, David. 2006. (Green Light Readers Level 1 Ser.). (ENG.). 24p. (J). (gr. -1-3). pap. 4.99 *(978-0-15-205782-4(X)*, 1197377) Houghton Mifflin Harcourt Publishing Co.

—The Picnic. Williams, David K. 2006. (Green Light Readers Level 1 Ser.). (gr. -1-1). 13.95 *(978-0-7569-7209-7(4))* Perfection Learning Corp.

—Tick Tock. Williams, David K. & Williams, David. 2006. (Green Light Readers Level 1 Ser.). (ENG.). 24p. (J). (gr. -1-3). pap. 4.99 *(978-0-15-205605-6(X)*, 1196859) Houghton Mifflin Harcourt Publishing Co.

Owen, Elizabeth. Lilly in the Middle, 1 vol. Bellingham, Brenda. 2003. (Formac First Novels Ser.: 25). (ENG.). 64p. (J). (gr. 1-5). 4.95 *(978-0-88780-589-9(2)*, 589); 14.95 *(978-0-88780-590-5(6)*, 590) Formac Publishing Co., Ltd. CAN. Dist: Formac Lorimer Bks. Ltd.

Owen, Erich. Beast Academy Guide 3B. Batterson, Jason. 2012. 104p. (J). pap. 15.00 *(978-1-934124-42-0(7))* AoPS Inc.
—Beast Academy Guide 3C. Batterson, Jason. 2012. 112p. pap. 15.00 *(978-1-934124-44-4(3))* AoPS Inc.
Owen, Erich. Fruit Ninja. 2018. 78p. (J). ***(978-1-5490-7114-0(9))*** Andrews McMeel Publishing.
Owen, Erich. Fruit Ninja: Frenzy Force. Halfbrick Studios Staff. 2018. (ENG.). 80p. (J). pap. 9.99 *(978-1-4494-8097-4(7))* Andrews McMeel Publishing.
—Fruit Ninja: Frenzy Force. Studios, Halfbrick. 2018. (ENG.). 82p. (J). (gr. 2-6). 26.99 *(978-1-4494-9740-8(3))* Andrews McMeel Publishing.
—Mail Order Ninja, 1 vol., Vol. 1. Elder, Joshua. 2008. (Tokyopop Ser.). (ENG.). 96p. (J). (gr. 2-6). 28.50 *(978-1-59961-568-4(1)*, 14810, Graphic Novels) Spotlight.
—Mail Order Ninja Vol. 2: Timmy Strikes Back, 1 vol. Elder, Joshua. 2008. (Tokyopop Ser.). (ENG.). 104p. (J). (gr. 2-6). 28.50 *(978-1-59961-569-1(X)*, 14811, Graphic Novels) Spotlight.
Owen, James A. The Dragon's Apprentice. Owen, James A. (Chronicles of the Imaginarium Geographica Ser.: 5). (ENG.). (YA). (gr. 7). 2012. 400p. pap. 12.99 *(978-1-4169-5898-7(3))*; 2010. 384p. 17.99 *(978-1-4169-5897-0(5))* Simon & Schuster Bks. For Young Readers. (Simon & Schuster Bks. For Young Readers).
—The Dragons of Winter. Owen, James A. (Chronicles of the Imaginarium Geographica Ser.: 6). (ENG.). (YA). (gr. 7). 2013. 416p. pap. 12.99 *(978-1-4424-1224-8(0))*; 2012. 400p. 17.99 *(978-1-4424-1223-1(2))* Simon & Schuster Bks. For Young Readers. (Simon & Schuster Bks. For Young Readers).
—The First Dragon. Owen, James A. (Chronicles of the Imaginarium Geographica Ser.: 7). (ENG.). 304p. (YA). (gr. 7). 2014. pap. 13.99 *(978-1-4424-1227-9(5))*; 2013. 17.99 *(978-1-4424-1226-2(7))* Simon & Schuster Bks. For Young Readers. (Simon & Schuster Bks. For Young Readers).
—Here, There Be Dragons. Owen, James A. (Chronicles of the Imaginarium Geographica Ser.: 1). (ENG.). (YA). (gr. 7-12). 2007. 352p. pap. 12.99 *(978-1-4169-1228-6(2))*; 2006. 336p. 24.99 *(978-1-4169-1227-9(4))* Simon & Schuster Bks. For Young Readers. (Simon & Schuster Bks. For Young Readers).
—The Indigo King. Owen, James A. 2010. (Chronicles of the Imaginarium Geographica Ser.: 3). (ENG.). 400p. (YA). (gr. 7). pap. 13.99 *(978-1-4169-5108-7(3)*, Simon & Schuster Bks. For Young Readers) Simon & Schuster Bks. For Young Readers.
—The Indigo King, 3. Owen, James A. 2008. (Chronicles of the Imaginarium Geographica Ser.: 3). (ENG.). 384p. (YA). (gr. 7-12). 17.99 *(978-1-4169-5107-0(5))* Simon & Schuster, Inc.
—Lost Treasures of the Pirates of the Caribbean. Owen, James A. Owen, Jeremy. 2011. (ENG.). 32p. (J). (gr. 3-7). pap. 16.99 *(978-1-4424-3093-8(1)*, Simon & Schuster Bks. For Young Readers) Simon & Schuster Bks. For Young Readers.
—The Search for the Red Dragon. Owen, James A. 2008. (Chronicles of the Imaginarium Geographica Ser.: 2). (ENG.). (YA). (gr. 7). 400p. pap. 13.99 *(978-1-4169-4851-3(1))*; 384p. 17.99 *(978-1-4169-4850-6(3))* Simon & Schuster Bks. For Young Readers. (Simon & Schuster Bks. For Young Readers).
—The Shadow Dragons. Owen, James A. 2009. (Chronicles of the Imaginarium Geographica Ser.: 4). (ENG.). 432p. (YA). (gr. 7-18). 21.99 *(978-1-4169-5879-6(7)*, Simon & Schuster Bks. For Young Readers) Simon & Schuster Bks. For Young Readers.
Owen, Ken & Owen, Siân. Golwg Gyntaf Ar Bethau Byw. Wadsworth, Pamela. 2005. (WEL.). 24p. pap. *(978-1-85596-250-7(0))* Dref Wen.
—Gwahanol Blanhigion AC Anifeiliaid. Wadsworth, Pamela. 2005. (WEL.). 24p. pap. *(978-1-85596-223-1(3))* Dref Wen.
Owen, R. Emmett. The Go Ahead Boys & Simon's Mine. Kay, Ross. 2007. 184p. per. *(978-1-4065-1857-3(3))* Dodo Pr.
Owen, Ramon. Shadi, the Shadow Who Wanted to Be Free. Cyr, Joe. 2010. 40p. pap. 14.95 *(978-1-936343-08-9(8))* Peppertree Pr., The.
—Two Happy Stories. Cyr, Joe. 2007. 36p. per. 12.95 *(978-1-934246-73-3(5))* Peppertree Pr., The.
Owen, Rob. Spy Boy, Cheyenne, & Ninety-Six Crayons: A "Mardi Gras" Indian's Story, 1 vol. Owen, Rob. 2013. (ENG.). 32p. (J). (gr. k-3). 16.99 *(978-1-4556-1799-9(7)*, Pelican Publishing) Arcadia Publishing.
Owen, Ruth. Xtreme! Woods, Mark. 2010. (Top Score Maths Ser.). 32p. pap. *(978-0-237-54282-5(X))* Evans Brothers, Ltd.
Owen, Siân, jt. illus. see Owen, Ken.
Owens, Alana. A Living Mascot. Edwards, Rhonda S. 2013. (ENG.). 38p. (J). pap. 9.99 *(978-0-7443-2013-8(5))* CamCat Publishing.
Owens, Mary Beth. A Penny for a Hundred. Pochocki, Ethel. 2005. 31p. (J). (gr. 2-5). pap. 9.95 *(978-1-883937-52-2(3))* Bethlehem Bks.
—Saints & Heroes. Pochocki, Ethel. 2012. (ENG.). 258p. pap. 15.95 *(978-1-932350-51-7(9))* Ignatius Pr.
Owens, Mary Beth. The Caribou Alphabet: A Tilbury House Nature Book, 1 vol. Owens, Mary Beth. exp. ed. 2015. (Tilbury House Nature Book Ser.: 0). (ENG.). 36p. (J). (gr. -1-3). pap. 9.95 *(978-0-88448-446-2(7)*, 884446) Tilbury Hse. Pubs.
Owens, Sky. Amir's First Haircut: The Ongoing Saga of Life's Lessons Through the Eyes of a Young Boy. Syndreamz, Hope. 2019. (ENG.). 78p. (J). pap. 21.95 *(978-0-9964684-7-3(1))* Dumplinz Bk. Publishing.
Owenson, Meg. Epiphany. Sridhar, Priya. 2019. (Powered Ser.). (ENG.). 112p. (J). (gr. 3-6). lib. bdg. 26.65 *(978-1-4965-7884-6(8)*, 139560, Stone Arch Bks.) Capstone.
—Jars of Hope: How One Woman Helped Save 2,500 Children During the Holocaust. Roy, Jennifer. 2015. (Encounter: Narrative Nonfiction Picture Bks.). (ENG.). 32p. (J). (gr. 1-5). lib. bdg. 27.99 *(978-1-4914-6072-6(5)*, Capstone Young Readers) Capstone.
—Novice. Sridhar, Priya. 2019. (Powered Ser.). (ENG.). 112p. (J). (gr. 3-6). lib. bdg. 26.65 *(978-1-4965-7886-0(4)*, 139562, Stone Arch Bks.) Capstone.
—Sabotage. Sridhar, Priya. 2019. (Powered Ser.). (ENG.). 112p. (J). (gr. 3-6). lib. bdg. 26.65 *(978-1-4965-7887-7(2)*, 139564, Stone Arch Bks.) Capstone.
—Stolen. Sridhar, Priya. 2019. (Powered Ser.). (ENG.). 112p. (J). (gr. 3-6). lib. bdg. 26.65 *(978-1-4965-7885-3(6)*, 139561, Stone Arch Bks.) Capstone.
Owings, Rae. Max & Friends. Surman, Susan. 150p. (J). (gr. k-3). 9.99 *(978-0-88092-452-8(7))* Royal Fireworks Publishing Co.
Owsley, Anthony. Crazy Concoctions: A Mad Scientist's Guide to Messy Mixtures. Brown, Jordan D. 2012. 80p. (J). (gr. 3-7). 14.95 *(978-1-936140-51-0(9))* Charlesbridge Publishing, Inc.
—Ouch! The Weird & Wild Ways Your Body Deals with Agonizing Aches, Ferocious Fevers, Lousy Lumps, Crummy Colds, Bothersome Bites, Breaks, Bruises & Burns & Makes Them Feel Better! Rhatigan, Joe. 2015. 80p. (J). (gr. 4-7). pap. 9.95 *(978-1-62354-053-1(4))* Charlesbridge Publishing, Inc.
—Science Stunts: Fun Feats of Physics. Brown, Jordan D. 2016. 80p. (J). (gr. 3-7). 16.95 *(978-1-62354-064-7(X))* Charlesbridge Publishing, Inc.
—The Totally Hilarious All about America Activity Book. Rhatigan, Joe. 2016. (All You Need Is a Pencil Ser.: 3). 144p. (J). (gr. 2-5). pap. 7.95 *(978-1-62354-076-0(3))* Charlesbridge Publishing, Inc.
—The Ultimate Activity Book for Mad Scientists. Rhatigan, Joe. 2017. (Just a Pencil Gets You Many Days of Fun Ser.). (ENG.). 144p. (J). (gr. 3-9). pap., act. bk. ed. 7.95 *(978-1-63322-163-5(6)*, Moondance) Quarto Publishing Group USA.
—The Ultimate Brain Bender Activity Book. Rhatigan, Joe. 2017. (Just a Pencil Gets You Many Days of Fun Ser.). (ENG.). 144p. (J). (gr. 2-8). pap., act. bk. ed. 9.99 *(978-1-63322-162-8(8)*, 224366, Moondance) Quarto Publishing Group USA.
—Weird Quizzes, Wacky Games, & Disturbing Doodles. Rhatigan, Joe. 2016. (All You Need Is a Pencil Ser.: 4). 144p. (J). (gr. 2-5). pap. 7.95 *(978-1-62354-077-7(1))* Charlesbridge Publishing, Inc.
Oxelstrand, Sofia. The Lost Mitten. Morley, J. S. 2018. (Hiding Behind the Couch Ser.). (ENG.). 42p. (J). *(978-1-78645-208-5(1))* Beaten Track Publishing.
Oxenbury, Helen. Alice Through the Looking-Glass. Carroll, Lewis. 2009. (ENG.). 208p. (J). (gr. 3-7). pap. 14.99 *(978-0-7636-4262-4(2))* Candlewick Pr.
—Alice's Adventures in Wonderland. Carroll, Lewis. 2003. (ENG.). 208p. (J). (gr. 3-7). pap. 16.99 *(978-0-7636-2049-3(1))* Candlewick Pr.
—Big Momma Makes the World. Root, Phyllis. 2007. (ENG.). 48p. (J). (gr. -1-3). pap. 7.99 *(978-0-7636-2600-6(7))* Candlewick Pr.
—Captain Jack & the Pirates. Bently, Peter. 2016. (ENG.). 32p. (J). (-k). 17.99 *(978-0-525-42950-0(6)*, Dial Bks) Penguin Young Readers Group.
—Charley's First Night. Hest, Amy. 2012. (ENG.). 32p. (J). (gr. -1-2). 15.99 *(978-0-7636-4055-2(7))* Candlewick Pr.
—El Desayuno de Tomas. Cutler, Ivor. (SPA.). 30p. (J). (gr. k-3). pap. 6.95 *(978-1-56014-629-2(X))* Santillana USA Publishing Co., Inc.
—Diez Deditos de Las Manos y Diez Deditos de Los Pies / Ten Little Fingers & Ten Little Toes Bilingual Board Book. Fox, Mem. 2012. (ENG.). 38p. (J). (gr. k — 1). bds. 8.99 *(978-0-547-87006-9(X)*, 1504629) Houghton Mifflin Harcourt Publishing Co.
—Farmer Duck. Waddell, Martin. 2008. (Candlewick Storybook Animations Ser.). (ENG.). 40p. (J). (gr. -1-k). 14.99 *(978-0-7636-3512-1(X))* Candlewick Pr.
—The Giant Jumperee. Donaldson, Julia. 2017. (ENG.). 32p. (J). (-k). 17.99 *(978-0-7352-2797-2(7)*, Dial Bks) Penguin Young Readers Group.
—La Gran Mamá Hace el Mundo. Root, Phyllis. 2004. (SPA.). (J). 23.99 *(978-84-88342-48-5(9))* S.A. Kokinos ESP. Dist: Lectorum Pubns., Inc.
—The Growing Story. Krauss, Ruth. 2007. (ENG.). 40p. (J). (gr. -1-3). 16.99 *(978-0-06-024716-4(9))* HarperCollins Pubs.
—King Jack & the Dragon. Bently, Peter. 2011. (ENG.). 32p. (J). (gr. -1-k). 17.99 *(978-0-8037-3698-6(3)*, Dial Bks) Penguin Young Readers Group.
—Red Riding Hood. Potter, Beatrix. 2019. (ENG.). 48p. (J). (gr. -1-2). 20.00 *(978-0-241-37534-1(7)*, Warne) Penguin Young Readers Group.
—So Much! Cooke, Trish. 2008. (ENG.). 48p. (J). (gr. -1-2). pap. 6.99 *(978-0-7636-4091-0(3))* Candlewick Pr.
—So Much! Cooke, Trish. ed. 2008. (J). (gr. -1-1). lib. bdg. 17.20 *(978-0-613-08774-2(7))* Turtleback.
—Ten Little Fingers & Ten Little Toes. Fox, Mem. (ENG.). (J). 2018. 40p. (— 1). 26.99 *(978-1-328-85225-0(3)*, 1694584, HMH Books For Young Readers); 2010. 38p. (gr. k — 1). bds. 8.99 *(978-0-547-36620-3(5)*, 1422523); 2008. 40p. (gr. -1 — 1). 17.99 *(978-0-15-206057-2(X)*, 1198193) Houghton Mifflin Harcourt Publishing Co.
—Ten Little Fingers & Ten Little Toes Lap Board Book. Fox, Mem. 2011. (ENG.). 38p. (J). (gr. k — 1). bds. 12.99 *(978-0-547-58103-3(3)*, 1459676) Houghton Mifflin Harcourt Publishing Co.
—There's Going to Be a Baby. Burningham, John. 48p. (J). 2014. (ENG.). (-k). 8.99 *(978-0-7636-7265-2(3))*; 2010. *(978-0-7445-4996-6(5))*; 2010. (ENG.). (gr. -1-k). 16.99 *(978-0-7636-4907-4(4))* Candlewick Pr.
—The Three Little Wolves & the Big Bad Pig. Trivizas, Eugene. 2015. 32p. pap. 8.00 *(978-1-61003-621-4(2))* Center for the Collaborative Classroom.
—The Three Little Wolves & the Big Bad Pig. Trivizas, Eugene. 2004. (ENG.). 16p. (J). 24.95 *(978-1-4052-0669-3(1))* Egmont Bks., Ltd. GBR. Dist: Trafalgar Square Publishing.
—The Three Little Wolves & the Big Bad Pig: A Pop-up Storybook. Trivizas, Eugene. 2006. 16p. (J). (gr. k-4). reprint ed. 27.00 *(978-0-7567-9913-7(9))* DIANE Publishing Co.
—Time Now to Dream. Knapman, Timothy. 2017. (ENG.). 32p. (J). (gr. -1-2). 16.99 *(978-0-7636-9078-6(3))* Candlewick Pr.
—Los Tres Lobitos y el Cochino Feroz. Trivizas, Eugene. 2003. (SPA.). 32p. (J). (gr. k-3). pap. 12.99 *(978-980-257-246-5(2)*, EK1366) Ekare, Ediciones VEN. Dist: Kane Miller, Lectorum Pubns., Inc.
—Vamos a Caca de Um Urso. Rosen, Michael. 2004. Orig. Title: We're Going on a Bear Hunt. (ENG & POR.). 33p. (J). pap. *(978-1-85269-715-0(6))* Mantra Lingua.
—We're Going on a Bear Hunt. Rosen, Michael. 2014. (We're Going on a Bear Hunt Ser.). (ENG.). 22p. (J). (gr. -1-2). 19.99 *(978-0-7636-7073-3(1))* Candlewick Pr.
—We're Going on a Bear Hunt. 2004. 33p. (J). *(978-1-85269-719-8(9))*; (GUJ.). *(978-1-85269-713-6(X))*; (ENG & ARA.). pap. *(978-1-85269-707-5(5))* Mantra Lingua.
—We're Going on a Bear Hunt. Rosen, Michael. 2004. (J). 32p. *(978-1-85269-720-4(2))*; 32p. *(978-1-85269-718-1(0))*; (ENG.). 32p. *(978-1-85269-716-7(4))*; 32p. *(978-1-85269-711-2(3))*; 32p. *(978-1-85269-710-5(5))*; 32p. *(978-1-85269-706-8(7))*; (ENG & BEN.). 33p. pap. *(978-1-85269-708-2(3))*; (ENG & PAN.). 33p. pap. *(978-1-85269-714-3(8))*; (ENG & URD.). 33p. pap. *(978-1-85269-721-1(0))*; (ENG & FRE.). 33p. pap. *(978-1-85269-712-9(1))* Mantra Lingua.
—We're Going on a Bear Hunt. Rosen, Michael. 2003. (ENG.). 36p. (J). (gr. -1-3). pap. 7.99 *(978-0-689-85349-4(1)*, McElderry, Margaret K. Bks.) McElderry, Margaret K. Bks.
—We're Going on a Bear Hunt. Rosen, Michael. 2007. (ENG.). (gr. -1-k). 18.00 *(978-0-7569-7866-2(1))* Perfection Learning Corp.
—We're Going on a Bear Hunt. Rosen, Michael. ed. 2003. (gr. k-3). 18.40 *(978-0-613-61665-2(0))* Turtleback.
—We're Going on a Bear Hunt: 30th Anniversary Edition. Rosen, Michael. ed. 2019. (ENG.). 36p. (J). (gr. -1-k). bds. 9.99 *(978-1-5344-5420-0(9)*, Little Simon) Little Simon.
—We're Going on a Bear Hunt: 30th Anniversary Edition. Rosen, Michael. ed. 2019. (ENG.). 40p. (J). (gr. -1-3). 9.99 *(978-1-5344-5642-6(2)*, McElderry, Margaret K. Bks.) McElderry, Margaret K. Bks.
—We're Going on a Bear Hunt: A Celebratory Pop-Up Edition. Rosen, Michael. 2007. (ENG.). 30p. (J). (gr. -1). 29.99 *(978-1-4169-3665-7(3)*, Little Simon) Little Simon.
—We're Going on a Bear Hunt: Anniversary Edition of a Modern Classic. Rosen, Michael. ed. 2009. (Classic Board Bks.). (ENG.). 36p. (J). (gr. -1-k). bds. 9.99 *(978-1-4169-8712-3(6)*, Little Simon) Little Simon.
—We're Going on a Bear Hunt: Anniversary Edition of a Modern Classic. Rosen, Michael. ed. 2009. (ENG.). 40p. (J). (gr. -1-3). 18.99 *(978-1-4169-8711-6(8)*, McElderry, Margaret K. Bks.) McElderry, Margaret K. Bks.
—We're Going on a Bear Hunt: Sound Book. Rosen, Michael. 2014. (We're Going on a Bear Hunt Ser.). (ENG.). 40p. (J). (gr. -1-2). 19.99 *(978-0-7636-7702-2(7))* Candlewick Pr.
—We're Going on a Bear Hunt: Changing Picture Book. Rosen, Michael. 2018. (ENG.). 20p. (J). (gr. -1-2). 18.99 *(978-0-7636-9601-6(3)*, Candlewick Entertainment) Candlewick Pr.
—We're Going on a Bear Hunt: Snow Globe Edition. Rosen, Michael. 2017. (ENG.). 24p. (J). (-k). 16.99 *(978-1-5362-0029-4(8))* Candlewick Pr.
—We're Going on a Bear Hunt Sound Book. Rosen, Michael. 2020. (ENG.). 18p. (J). (-k). bds. 9.99 *(978-1-5362-1261-7(X))* Candlewick Pr.
—When Charley Met Grampa. Hest, Amy. 2013. (ENG.). 40p. (J). (gr. -1-2). 15.99 *(978-0-7636-5314-9(4))* Candlewick Pr.
Oxenbury, Helen. Baby Love Set: All Fall down - Clap Hands - Say Goodnight - Tickle, Tickle. Oxenbury, Helen. gif. ed. 2009. (ENG.). 40p. (J). (gr. -1 — 1). bds. 9.99 *(978-1-4169-9546-3(3)*, Little Simon) Little Simon.
—It's My Birthday. Oxenbury, Helen. 2010. 24p. (J). (gr. -1-k). bds. 9.99 *(978-0-7636-4970-8(8))* Candlewick Pr.
—Pig Tale. Oxenbury, Helen. 2010. (ENG.). 32p. (J). (gr. -1-1). 16.99 *(978-1-4424-2153-0(3)*, McElderry, Margaret K. Bks.) McElderry, Margaret K. Bks.
—Vamos a Cazar un Oso. Oxenbury, Helen. Rosen, Michael & Rosen, Michael. 2005. (SPA.). 36p. (gr. 2-1). 25.99 *(978-980-257-107-9(5)*, EK5539) Ekare, Ediciones VEN. Dist: Lectorum Pubns., Inc.
Oxenbury, Helen, jt. illus. see Rosen, Michael.
Oxfam Staff. W Is for World Big Book: A Round-the-World ABC. Cave, Kathryn. 2004. 32p. (J). pap. *(978-1-84507-026-7(7)*, White Lion Publishing) Quarto Publishing Group UK.
Oxford Bible Staff. Abraham Lincoln, 1 vol. Raum, Elizabeth. 2012. (American Biographies Ser.). (ENG.). 48p. (gr. 4-6). lib. bdg. 33.32 *(978-1-4329-6453-5(4)*, Heinemann) Capstone.
—George Washington, 1 vol. Rand, Casey. 2012. (American Biographies Ser.). (ENG.). 48p. (gr. 4-6). lib. bdg. 33.32 *(978-1-4329-6452-8(6)*, Heinemann) Capstone.
Oxley, Jennifer. The Big Island Race (Clifford) Rusu, Meredith. 2020. (Clifford Ser.). (ENG.). 24p. (J). (gr. -1-k). pap. 4.99 *(978-1-338-54194-6(3))* Scholastic, Inc.
—Melia & Jo. Aronson, Billy. 2018. (ENG.). 48p. (J). (gr. -1-3). 17.99 *(978-1-328-91626-6(X)*, 1701986, HMH Books For Young Readers) Houghton Mifflin Harcourt Publishing Co.
Oxley, Jennifer, jt. illus. see Kanemoto, Dan.
Oxton, Alex, jt. illus. see Pigott, Louise.
Oyama, Misuzu. Rue de la Nuit: Labyrinth. 2010. (ENG.). 40p. (gr. 1). 25.95 *(978-1-935557-02-9(5))* PublishingWorks.
Oz, Robin. The Fight: Level 2. Boegehold, Betty D. 2020. (ENG.). 34p. (J). pap. 9.95 ***(978-1-876965-78-5(9))*** ibooks, Inc.
Ozaki, Kaori. Immortal Rain. Ozaki, Kaori, creator. rev. ed. 2005. Vol. 5. 216p. pap. 9.99 *(978-1-59182-991-1(7))*; Vol. 6. 192p. pap. 9.99 *(978-1-59532-799-4(1))* TOKYOPOP, Inc.
Ozama, Marcel & Dzama, Marcel. Bed, Bed, Bed. Might Be Giants Staff et al. 2003. (ENG.). 48p. (gr. -1-5). 16.95 *(978-0-7432-5024-5(9))* Simon & Schuster.
Ozcan, Pervin. Have You Seen This Fish? Ball, Erin. 2019. (ENG.). (J). (gr. -1-3). 34p. 21.00 *(978-1-7337375-0-0(2))*; 36p. 11.00 *(978-1-7337375-1-7(0))* Writing Times Publishing.
Ozdemir, Kelly G. Wishes That Smell Like Cinnamon - Christmas Book & Gift for Kids. Ozdemir, Kelly G. 2018. (ENG.). 34p. (J). pap. 9.45 *(978-1-7310-4289-7(2))* Independently Published.
Ozdemir, Oktay. Harold's Non-Swimmer Swimsuit. Ozdemir, Kelly G. 2018. (ENG.). 26p. (J). pap. 9.65 *(978-1-7241-0124-2(2))* Independently Published.
Ozoude, Marie & Tognoni Miller, Christine. The Adventures of Alex & Dante. Ozoude, Alexander. 2019. (ENG.). 26p. (J). pap. 9.13 ***(978-1-7081-7621-1(7))*** Independently Published.
—The Places I've Been. Ozoude, Marie. 2020. (ENG.). 42p. (J). pap. 9.13 ***(978-1-6546-5300-2(4))*** Independently Published.
Ozzy. The Leprechaun. Smyth, Jimmy. 2013. 32p. pap. *(978-0-9569314-1-2(3))* Smith, Jimmy.

P

P, N. Alphabet Country: A Read-Together ABC Game. P, N. 2012. (ENG.). 26p. (J). spiral bd. 9.00 *(978-0-615-59362-3(3))* Easy Reach Corp.
P, N. Down on the Ranch: A Counting Book, 1. P, N., text. 2011. 24p. (J). spiral bd. 9.00 *(978-0-615-50973-0(8))* Easy Reach Corp.
P�rez, Ram�n K. Cyclist BikeList: The Book for Every Rider. Robinson, Laura. 2010. (ENG.). 64p. (J). (gr. 4-7). pap. 17.95 *(978-0-88776-784-5(2)*, Tundra Bks.) Tundra Bks. CAN. Dist: Penguin Random Hse. LLC.
P�rez, Soraya Bartolom�. Dogs Want to Be Loved Dyslexic Edition: Dyslexic Font. English, Patrick. 2020. (ENG.). 20p. (J). (gr. k-6). 15.99 ***(978-1-64372-540-6(8))***; pap. 11.99 ***(978-1-64372-541-3(6))*** MacLaren-Cochrane Publishing, Inc.
—The Twelve o'clock Cats Dyslexic Edition: Dyslexic Font. English, Patrick. 2020. (ENG.). 20p. (J). (gr. k-6). 15.99 ***(978-1-64372-542-0(4))*** MacLaren-Cochrane Publishing, Inc.
PA Illustrator. Annabelle Discovers the Missing Lunch Money. Hauf, Kyle. 2011. 36p. pap. 24.95 *(978-1-4560-3656-0(4))* America Star Bks.
—Hooray! We're Making Memories Today! Gittens, Sandra L. 2011. 48p. pap. 24.95 *(978-1-4560-0914-4(1))* America Star Bks.
Paarmann, Lesley, photos by. Please Let Me Help: I Need Validation. Paarmann, Al. unabr. ed. 2003. 150p. (YA). pap. 12.95 *(978-0-9715963-1-3(X))* Paarmann, Al International.
Paavo, Rebecca E. Beauty & the Beast: An Illustrated Fairy Tale Classic. Fichter, Brittany. 2018. (Illustrated Fairy Tale Classics Ser.: Vol. 1). (ENG.). 40p. (J). 18.99 *(978-1-949710-02-1(5))* Fichter, Brittany.
Pabalinas Jr, Rosendo. The Bag. Spelman, Emma. 2019. (ENG.). 20p. (J). pap. *(978-1-925932-02-7(8))* Library For All Limited.
Pabalinas, Rosendo. Baby Is Crying. Sadler, Rachelle. 2019. (ENG.). 26p. (J). pap. *(978-1-925932-19-5(2))* Library For All Limited.
Pacala, Michelle. Boopie Goes to Dreamlandia. Schmidt, Matt. 2019. (ENG.). 30p. (J). pap. 9.99 *(978-1-0963-2774-5(0))* Independently Published.
Pace, Alycia. Christmas Angels. Castor, Rachelle. 2018. (ENG.). 32p. (J). (gr. k-3). 14.99 *(978-1-4621-2263-9(9))* Cedar Fort, Inc./CFI Distribution.
—The Drummer Boy. Schmidt, Calie. 2019. (ENG.). 32p. (J). 15.99 *(978-1-4621-3586-8(2))* Cedar Fort, Inc./CFI Distribution.
Pace, Brittany Lee Ann. Walter S. (Spy) Pigeon, 1 vol. Collier, Kathy Lynn. 2009. 20p. pap. 24.95 *(978-1-60813-543-1(8))* America Star Bks.
Pace, Christine. Kipper Finds a Home: A White Squirrel Parable Volume 1. Guess, Catherine Ritch. 2005. (ENG.). 32p. (J). (gr. -1-7). pap. 13.95 *(978-1-933341-00-2(9))* CRM.
Pace, Julie. Leah's Pride. Daniel, Lashawn L. 2008. (ENG.). 24p. (J). pap. 11.49 ***(978-1-4251-1527-2(6))*** Trafford Publishing.
Pace, Sara. Count Candy Corn. Brugger, Ruth L. 2013. (ENG.). 32p. pap. 13.99 *(978-1-4808-0190-5(9))* Archway Publishing.
Pacheco, Alma Rosa & Pacheco, Guadalupe. Felicia y Odicia. Palacios, Maria Eugenia Blanco & Blanco, Maria. rev. ed. 2005. (Castillo de la Lectura Blanca Ser.). (SPA & ENG.). 56p. (J). (gr. -1-3). pap. 6.95 *(978-970-20-0125-6(0))* Castillo, Ediciones, S. A. de C. V. MEX. Dist: Macmillan.
—Que Te Pasa, Calabaza! Ortiz, Orlando & Ortiz, Orlando. rev. ed. 2007. (Castillo de la Lectura Blanca Ser.). (SPA & ENG.). 72p. (J). (gr. k-2). pap. 6.95 *(978-970-20-0172-0(2))* Castillo, Ediciones, S. A. de C. V. MEX. Dist: Macmillan.
Pacheco, Alma Rosa, jt. illus. see Pacheco, Luis Gabriel.
Pacheco, Carlos. Cable Vol. 1: Conquest. 2017. (ENG.). 112p. (YA). (gr. 8-17). pap. 15.99 *(978-1-302-90482-1(5))* Marvel Worldwide, Inc.

P

—The Life of Captain Marvel. 2019. (Life of Captain Marvel Ser.: 1). 120p. (YA). (gr. 8-17). pap. 15.99 (978-1-302-91253-6(4)) Marvel Worldwide, Inc.

—The Life of Captain Marvel Marvel Select Edition. 2020. (ENG.). 120p. (YA). (gr. 8-17). 24.99 (978-1-302-92122-4(3)) Marvel Worldwide, Inc.

Pacheco, Carlos, et al. Starjammers. 2019. (ENG.). 256p. (YA). (gr. -1-17). pap. 29.99 (978-1-302-91869-9(9)) Marvel Worldwide, Inc.

Pacheco, Carlos & Jacinto, K. I. M. Uncanny Inhumans Vol. 2. 2017. (ENG.). 264p. (YA). (gr. 8-17). 34.99 (978-1-302-90845-4(6)) Marvel Worldwide, Inc.

Pacheco, Gabriel. Las Aventuras de Pinocho. Collodi, Carlo. Garrido, Felipe, tr. 2016. (SPA.). 240p. (YA). (gr. 7). pap. 18.00 (978-607-8469-21-5(5)) Nostra Ediciones MEX. Dist: Independent Pubs. Group.

—El Papalote y el Nopal. Petterson, Aline. 2003. (SPA.). 34p. (J). (gr. 3-5). 15.95 (978-968-19-0750-1(7)) Santillana USA Publishing Co., Inc.

—Peter Pan y Wendy. Barrie, J. M. Garrido, Felipe, tr. 2018.Tr. of Peter Pan & Wendy. (SPA.). 240p. (J). (gr. 4-7). pap. 19.00 (978-607-8469-40-6(1)) Nostra Ediciones MEX. Dist: Independent Pubs. Group.

—Tchaikovsky's Swan Lake. Lee, Ji-yeong. 2016. (Music Storybooks Ser.). (ENG.). 44p. (J). (gr. 3-5). pap. 9.99 (978-1-925247-11-4(2), Big and SMALL) ChoiceMaker Pty. Ltd., The AUS. Dist: Lerner Publishing Group.

Pacheco, Guadalupe, jt. illus. see Pacheco, Alma Rosa.

Pacheco, Jorge M. Harry & Hannah: The American Adventure. Herrington, Chris. 2003. (Adventures of Harry & Hannah Ser.). (ENG.). 72p. (J). (gr. 1-5). 15.00 (978-0-9722343-0-6(6)) Herrington Teddy Bears.

Pacheco, Kaila. Karate Testing for My Dad Coloring Book: From the Authors of Karate Testing for My Dad. McGriff, Robert. 2019. (ENG.). 24p. (J). pap. 9.95 (978-1-9772-0660-2(3)) Outskirts Pr., Inc.

Pacheco, Luis Gabriel & Pacheco, Alma Rosa. Juegos Recreativos para Ninos. 2003. (SPA.). 182p. (J). pap. (978-970-651-625-1(5)) Editorial Oceano De Mexico, S.A. DE C.V.

Pacheco, Luis Gabriel, jt. illus. see Alvarado, Dalia.

Pacheco Marcos, Guadalupe. Un Superh�roe en el Tejado y Otros Cuentos. Perez, Luis Bernardo. 2019. (Torre Azul Ser.). (SPA.). 128p. (J). pap. (978-607-722-130-2(9)) Norma Ediciones, S.A.

Pacheco, Robert. Trade on the Taos Mountain Trail. Martinez Martinez, Deborah. 2010. (ENG.). 48p. (J). pap. 15.00 (978-0-9823445-0-7(3)) Vanishing Horizons.

Pacific, Lin. Christopher Cat's Marvelous Kids, Bell & Miro: They Love Art & Music. Pacific, Lin. 2016. (Christopher Cat's Marvelous Family Ser.: Vol. 6). (ENG.). 36p. (J). pap. 9.99 (978-1-5375-9770-6(1)) CreateSpace Independent Publishing Platform.

—Christopher Cat's Marvelous Kids, Bell & Miro: They Love Art & Music. Pacific, Lin. 2020. (Marvelous Christopher Cat Ser.: Vol. 6). (ENG.). 36p. (J). pap. 14.99 (978-1-6552-2927-5(3)) Independently Published.

Pacifico, Phyllis. This Morning Maxwelton Got up on the Wrong Side. Slosberg, Susie. 2017. (Childrens Idioms Ser.: Vol. 1). (ENG.). 32p. (J). (gr. k-6). (978-0-9964913-3-4(3)) SPPS.

Paciocco, Nelida. Outside My Window. Sykes, Bonnie. 2019. (ENG.). 38p. (J). pap. 12.00 (978-1-7956-2265-3(2)) Independently Published.

Packer, Emily. Dramatizando la Gallinita Roja: Un Cuento para Contar y Actuar. Thistle, Louise. l.t. ed. 2003.Tr. of Dramatizing the Little Red Hen. (SPA.). 32p. (J). (gr. k-2). pap. 10.00 (978-0-9644186-4-6(9)) Literature Dramatization Pr.

—Dramatizing the Little Red Hen. Thistle, Louise. Landes, William-Alan, ed. l.t. ed. 2003. 32p. (J). (gr. k-2). pap. 10.00 (978-0-9644186-5-3(7)) Literature Dramatization Pr.

Packer, Neil. Book. Agard, John. 2015. 144p. (J). (gr. 5). 15.99 (978-0-7636-7236-2(X)) Candlewick Pr.

—The Iliad. Cross, Gillian. 2015. (ENG.). 160p. (J). (gr. 3-7). 19.99 (978-0-7636-7832-6(5)) Candlewick Pr.

—The Iliad/the Odyssey Boxed Set. Cross, Gillian. 2017. 338p. (J). (gr. 3-7). 39.98 (978-0-7636-9813-3(X)) Candlewick Pr.

—The Odyssey. Cross, Gillian. 2012. (ENG.). 178p. (J). (gr. 3-7). 19.99 (978-0-7636-4791-9(8)) Candlewick Pr.

—The Silk Roads: A New History of the World - Illustrated Edition. Frankopan, Peter. 2018. (ENG.). 128p. (J). 24.99 (978-1-5476-0021-2(7), 900195170, Bloomsbury Children's Bks.) Bloomsbury Publishing USA.

Pacovska, Kveta. Mr. Hollyberry's Christmas Gift. Westerlund, Kate. 2018. (ENG.). 32p. (J). (gr. -1-k). 17.99 (978-988-8341-62-7(6), Minedition) Neugebauer, Michael (Publishing) Limited HKG. Dist: Penguin Random Hse. LLC.

Pacovskà, Kveta. Flying. Pacovskà, Kveta. 2005.Tr. of Turme. 39p. (J). reprint ed. 20.00 (978-0-7567-8532-1(4)) DIANE Publishing Co.

Pacovska, Kveta. The Take It-Take It-Lady. Pacovska, Kveta. 2018. (ENG.). 64p. (J). (gr. 2-4). 39.99 (978-988-8341-65-8(0), Minedition) Neugebauer, Michael (Publishing) Limited HKG. Dist: Penguin Random Hse. LLC.

Pacuma, J. S. Pan & Pam: Kiar & the Catnips. Lijesta, E. M. 2018. (Beginner Readers Ser.: Vol. 2). (ENG.). 32p. (J). pap. 9.74 (978-1-7290-2560-4(9)) Independently Published.

Padavick, Nate. Know Your State Activity Book Washington, 1 vol. Hansen Moench, Megan. 2015. (ENG.). 272p. (J). pap. 14.99 (978-1-4236-4059-2(4)) Gibbs Smith, Publisher.

Padilla, Agustin. Rage of the Dinobots. Johnson, Mike & Scott, Mairghread. 2013. (Transformers Ser.). 104p. pap. 17.99 (978-1-61377-606-3(3), 9781613776063) Idea & Design Works, LLC.

—A Real American Hero, Vol. 1. Hama, Larry. 2011. (G. I. Joe Ser.). 152p. pap. 19.99 (978-1-60010-864-8(4), 9781600108648) Idea & Design Works, LLC.

Padilla, Ariel. The Argon Deception, 1 vol. Krueger, Jim. 2008. (Z Graphic Novels / Tomo Ser.). (ENG.). 160p. (J). (gr. 4-7). pap. 6.99 (978-0-310-71303-6(X)) Zondervan.

—The Battle for Argon Falls, 1 vol. Krueger, Jim. 2012. (Z Graphic Novels / Tomo Ser.). (ENG.). 160p. (J). pap. 6.99 (978-0-310-71307-4(2)) Zondervan.

—Betrayal of Trust, 1 vol., 7. Krueger, Jim & Zondervan Staff. 2009. (Tomo Ser.). (ENG.). 160p. (J). (gr. 4-6). 21.19 (978-0-310-71306-7(4)) Zondervan.

—Child of Destiny, 1 vol. Krueger, Jim. 2008. (Z Graphic Novels / Tomo Ser.). (ENG.). 160p. (J). (gr. 4-7). pap. 6.99 (978-0-310-71302-9(1)) Zondervan.

—I Was an Eighth-Grade Ninja, 1 vol. Simmons, Andrew & Averdonz, N. R. 2007. (Z Graphic Novels / Tomo Ser.). (ENG.). 160p. (J). (gr. 3-7). pap. 6.99 (978-0-310-71300-5(5)) Zondervan.

—My Double-Edged Life, 1 vol. Kreuger, Jim & Averdonz, N. R. 2007. (Z Graphic Novels / Tomo Ser.). (ENG.). 160p. (J). (gr. 3-7). pap. 6.99 (978-0-310-71301-2(3)) Zondervan.

—Secret Alliance, 1 vol. Krueger, Jim. 2008. (Z Graphic Novels / Tomo Ser.). (ENG.). 160p. (J). pap. 6.99 (978-0-310-71304-3(8)) Zondervan.

—Truth Revealed, 1 vol., 6. Rogers, Bud et al. 2009. (Tomo Ser.). (ENG.). 160p. (J). (gr. 4-6). 21.19 (978-0-310-71305-0(6)) Zondervan.

Padilla, Eren Star. Smiling at the Rain. Padilla, Felix M. 32p. (J). (gr. 3-18). 16.00 (978-0-9710860-4-3(4)) Libros, Encouraging Cultural Literacy.

Padilla, Joe. The Ramones: The Unauthorized Biography. 2020. (Band Bios Ser.). 40p. (J). (-3). 14.99 (978-1-7282-1097-1(6)) Sourcebooks, Inc.

Padilla, Joseph N. From the Magical Island of Jo-Pa Comes the Story of Dragon Dee & the Fireman. 2016. (ENG.). (J). 22.99 (978-1-4984-7756-7(9)); pap. 11.99 (978-1-4984-7755-0(0)) Salem Author Services.

Padilla, Teofilo. The Adventures of Cowboy Bob: Total Eclipse of the Sun. Batchelor, Pat. 2019. (Adventures of Cowboy Bob Ser.: Vol. 1). (ENG.). 28p. (J). 14.97 (978-0-578-49904-8(5)) Engineering Search Partners.

Padmos, Steffie. Builders. Ollivier, Reina & Claes, Karel. 2020. (Super Animals Ser.). (ENG.). 60p. (J). (gr. k). 19.95 (978-1-60537-578-6(0)) Clavis Publishing.

Padovano, Chris. The Best of America. Philp, J. R. 2018. (Best Of Ser.: Vol. 6). (ENG.). 42p. (J). pap. 10.99 (978-1-7198-6560-9(4)) Independently Published.

—The Butterfly Princess. Newton, Chelle. 2012. 44p. pap. 11.99 (978-1-61286-129-6(6)) Avid Readers Publishing Group.

—Gold Old Gets a Little Help from His Friends. Carothers, Nina. Nilsen, Richard J., ed. 2013. 32p. pap. 12.97 (978-1-937376-29-1(X)) All Star Pr.

—Pink Ink's Purpose. Carothers, Nina. Nilsen, Richard J., ed. 2013. 36p. pap. 12.97 (978-1-937376-26-0(5)) All Star Pr.

—Red Ed & the True Meaning of Christmas. Carothers, Nina. Nilsen, Richard J., ed. 2013. 32p. pap. 12.97 (978-1-937376-27-7(3)) All Star Pr.

—The Wonderful World of Color Olors. Carothers, Nina. Nilsen, Richard J., ed. 2013. 36p. pap. 12.97 (978-1-937376-28-4(1)) All Star Pr.

Padrón, Alicia. Bathtime Mathtime. McKellar, Danica. 2018. 20p. (J). (-k). bds. 8.99 (978-1-101-93394-7(1), Crown Books For Young Readers) Random Hse. Children's Bks.

—Bathtime Mathtime: Shapes. McKellar, Danica. 2019. 20p. (J). (— 1). bds. 8.99 (978-1-101-93396-1(8), Crown Books For Young Readers) Random Hse. Children's Bks.

Padron, Alicia. The Birthday Bears. Huven, Kim. 2010. 10p. bds. 10.95 (978-1-60747-774-7(2), Pickwick Pr.) Phoenix Bks., Inc.

—Brush, Brush, Brush! 2010. (Rookie Toddler Ser.). (ENG.). 12p. (J). (gr. -1 — 1). bds. 6.95 (978-0-531-25236-9(1), Children's Pr.) Scholastic Library Publishing.

Padrón, Alicia. Goodnight, Numbers. McKellar, Danica. (ENG.). (J). (-k). 2018. 30p. bds. 8.99 (978-1-101-93381-7(X)); 2017. 32p. 16.99 (978-1-101-93378-7(X)) Random Hse. Children's Bks. (Crown Books For Young Readers).

Padron, Alicia. I Love You All Year Round. Shubuck, Sheila. 2008. (ENG.). 16p. (J). (gr. -1). 10.95 (978-1-58117-786-2(0), Intervisual/Piggy Toes) Bendon, Inc.

—Wash, Wash, Wash! Chanko, Pamela. 2018. (Rookie Toddler Ser.). (ENG.). 12p. (J). (gr. -1 — 1). bds. 6.95 (978-0-531-22893-7(2), Children's Pr.) Scholastic Library Publishing.

Padron, Angela. My Body Belongs to Me: A Book about Body Safety. Starishevsky, Jill. 2014. (ENG.). 32p. (J). (gr. -1-3). 12.99 (978-1-57542-461-3(4)) Free Spirit Publishing, Inc.

Padron, Aya. My First Book of Chinese Words: An ABC Rhyming Book. Wu, Faye-Lynn. 2013. 32p. (J). (gr. -1-3). 12.95 (978-0-8048-4367-6(8)) Tuttle Publishing.

—My First Book of Chinese Words: An ABC Rhyming Book of Chinese Language & Culture. Wu, Faye-Lynn. 2017. 32p. (J). (gr. -1-3). 10.95 (978-0-8048-4941-8(2)) Tuttle Publishing.

—My First Book of Japanese Words: An ABC Rhyming Book. Brown, Michelle Haney. 2013. (ENG.). 32p. (J). (gr. -1-3). 12.95 (978-4-8053-1201-8(7)) Tuttle Publishing.

—My First Book of Japanese Words: An ABC Rhyming Book of Japanese Language & Culture. Brown, Michelle Haney. 2017. 32p. (J). (gr. -1-3). 10.95 (978-0-8048-4953-1(6)) Tuttle Publishing.

—My First Book of Korean Words: An ABC Rhyming Book of Korean Language & Culture. Park, Kyubyong & Amen, Henry J. 2017. 32p. (J). (gr. -1-3). 10.95 (978-0-8048-4940-1(4)) Tuttle Publishing.

Padua, Rochelle. I Can, You Can, Toucan! Mayfield, Sue. 2005. (Green Bananas Ser.). (ENG.). 48p. (J). (gr. k-2). pap. 5.99 (978-1-4052-1793-4(6)) Egmont Bks., Ltd. GBR. Dist: Independent Pubs. Group.

Padula, Lily. The Defiant. Quint, M. 2015. 256p. (J). (gr. 2-7). 18.99 (978-1-936365-54-8(5), a2d9a85f-56ac-44e0-9136-0bea11095324) McSweeney's Publishing.

Padur, Simone. 3 on a Moonbeam. Sandilands, Joyce. 2004. 64p. (978-0-9734383-1-4(2)) Whitlands Publishing, Ltd.

Paes, Rob. Mighty Machines. 2003. 12p. (J). (gr. k-3). 20.00 (978-0-7567-6652-8(4)) DIANE Publishing Co.

Pagan, Daniel. I Wonder Why It's a Dragonfly. Burns, Rowland. 2018. (ENG.). 28p. (J). pap. (978-0-6482480-0-2(3)) Flaming Ads & Voices.

—To Be or Not to Be a Bee. Burns, Rowland. 2019. (ENG.). 30p. (J). pap. (978-0-6482480-1-9(1)) Flaming Ads & Voices.

Paganelli, Elisa. Breath by Breath: A Mindfulness Guide to Feeling Calm. Christelis, Paul. 2018. (Everyday Mindfulness Ser.). (ENG.). 32p. (J). (gr. k-4). 12.99 (978-1-63198-331-3(8)) Free Spirit Publishing, Inc.

—Exploring Emotions: A Mindfulness Guide to Understanding Feelings. Christelis, Paul. 2018. (Everyday Mindfulness Ser.). (ENG.). 32p. (J). (gr. k-4). 12.99 (978-1-63198-332-0(6)) Free Spirit Publishing, Inc.

—Get Outdoors: A Mindfulness Guide to Noticing Nature. Christelis, Paul. 2018. (Everyday Mindfulness Ser.). (ENG.). 32p. (J). (gr. k-4). 12.99 (978-1-63198-333-7(4)) Free Spirit Publishing, Inc.

—Good Night. Lennon, John & McCartney, Paul. 2018. (J). (978-1-4926-4979-3(1)) Sourcebooks, Inc.

—The Highland Falcon Thief: Adventures on Trains #1. Leonard, M. G. & Sedgman, Sam. 2020. (Adventures on Trains Ser.: 1). (ENG.). 256p. (J). 16.99 (978-1-250-22289-3(3), 900208104) Feiwel & Friends.

Paganelli, Elisa. How to Build an Orchestra. Auld, Mary. 2020. (ENG.). 48p. (J). 18.95 (978-1-62371-871-8(6), Crocodile Bks.) Interlink Publishing Group, Inc.

Paganelli, Elisa. Mars' First Friends: Come on over, Rovers! Hill, Susanna Leonard. 2020. 40p. (J). (-3). 17.99 (978-1-7282-0518-2(2)) Sourcebooks, Inc.

—The Moon's First Friends: How the Moon Met the Astronauts from Apollo 11. Hill, Susanna Leonard. 2019. 40p. (J). (-3). 17.99 (978-1-4926-5680-7(1), Sourcebooks Jabberwocky) Sourcebooks, Inc.

Paganelli, Elisa. Moon's First Friends: One Giant Leap for Friendship. Hill, Susanna Leonard. 2020. 32p. (J). (-3). 8.99 (978-1-7282-2308-7(3)) Sourcebooks, Inc.

Paganelli, Elisa. Sleep Easy: A Mindfulness Guide to Getting a Good Night's Sleep. Christelis, Paul. 2018. (Everyday Mindfulness Ser.). (ENG.). 32p. (J). (gr. k-4). 12.99 (978-1-63198-334-4(2)) Free Spirit Publishing, Inc.

Paganelli, Elisa. Space Stories for Kids: The Moon, Mars, & Friendship Picture Books for Kids. Hill, Susanna Leonard. 2020. (ENG.). (J). (-3). 35.98 (978-1-7282-4062-6(X)) Sourcebooks, Inc.

—What about Neko? (Lerner Edition) A Story of Divorce. Loewen, Nancy. 2020. (Helping Hand Ser.). (ENG.). 24p. (J). (gr. k-2). lib. bdg. 27.99 (978-0-7112-5103-8(7)) QEB Publishing Inc.

Pagano, A. I Was There. Guglielmi, R. 2018. (ENG.). 40p. (J). (978-1-5255-2194-2(2)); pap. (978-1-5255-2195-9(0)) FriesenPress.

Pagano, Kiera. Electoral College What? Fernandez, Dana. 2020. (ENG.). 32p. (YA). 26.99 (978-1-6632-0790-6(9)); pap. 16.99 (978-1-6632-0788-3(7)) iUniverse, Inc.

Pagay, Jeff. Mele da Mynah's Noisy 'Ohana. Geshell, Carmen. 2004. 24p. 10.95 (978-1-57306-225-1(1)) Bess Pr., Inc.

—The Surf Rats of Waikiki Beach. Geshell, Carmen. 2004. 24p. 10.95 (978-1-57306-226-8(X)) Bess Pr., Inc.

—Waltah Melon: Local-Kine Hero. Geshell, Carmen. 2004. 24p. (J). 10.95 (978-1-57306-205-3(7)) Bess Pr., Inc.

Page. Don't Be Afraid of the Storm. Caban, Connie. 2011. 32p. pap. 12.95 (978-1-936343-97-3(5)) Peppertree Pr., The.

Page, Debbie. Chickadee - the Traveler, 11 vols. Keaster, Diane W. l.t. ed. 2004. (ZC Horses: Vol. 8). (ENG.). 80p. (J). per. 7.95 (978-0-9721496-7-9(8)) ZC Horses Series of Children's Bks.

Page, Debbie, et al. Darby - the Cow Dog, 9 vols. Keaster, Diane W. l.t. ed. 2005. (ZC Horses: 9). (ENG.). 68p. (J). per. 7.95 (978-0-9721496-8-6(6)) ZC Horses Series of Children's Bks.

Page, Debbie. Goldie - the Wise, 25 vols. Keaster, Diane W. l.t. ed. 2004. (ZC Horses: 7). (ENG.). 87p. (J). per. 7.95 (978-0-9721496-6-2(X)) ZC Horses Series of Children's Bks.

—Leroy - the Stallion, 25 vols. Keaster, Diane W. l.t. ed. 2003. (ZC Horses: 6). (ENG.). 79p. (J). per. 7.95 (978-0-9721496-5-5(1)) ZC Horses Series of Children's Bks.

—Tawny-The Beauty. Keaster, Diane. 2013. 70p. pap. 7.95 (978-0-9791719-2-5(X)) ZC Horses Series of Children's Bks.

Page, Joy. Olivia's Wonderful Day. Best, Bonnie. 2017. (ENG.). 38p. (J). 23.95 (978-1-64114-398-1(3)) Christian Faith Publishing.

Page, Mark. No Boys Allowed! Scholastic, Inc. Staff & Taylor-Butler, Christine. 2004. (Just for You Ser.). (ENG.). 32p. (gr. k-3). pap. 3.99 (978-0-439-56856-2(0)) Scholastic, Inc.

—The Two Tyrones. Hudson, Wade. 2004. 32p. (J). lib. bdg. 15.00 (978-1-4242-0239-3(6)) Fitzgerald Bks.

—The Two Tyrones. Hudson, Wade. 2004. (Just for You Ser.). (ENG.). 32p. (gr. k-3). pap. 3.99 (978-0-439-56866-1(8)) Scholastic, Inc.

Page, Philip. Romeo & Juliet. Page, Philip, ed. Petit, Marilyn, ed. 2005. (Picture This! Shakespeare Ser.). (ENG.). 58p. (gr. 5-8). 22.44 (978-0-7641-3144-8(3), B.E.S. Publishing) Peterson's.

Page, Robin. Octopuses One to Ten. Jackson, Ellen. 2016. (ENG.). 32p. (J). (gr. -1-3). 17.99 (978-1-4814-3182-8(X), Beach Lane Bks.) Beach Lane Bks.

—Who Eats Orange? White, Dianne. 2018. (ENG.). 32p. (J). (-3). 17.99 (978-1-5344-0408-3(2), Beach Lane Bks.) Beach Lane Bks.

Page, Robin. A Chicken Followed Me Home! Questions & Answers about a Familiar Fowl. Page, Robin. 2015. (ENG.). 40p. (J). (gr. k-5). 17.99 (978-1-4814-1028-1(8), Beach Lane Bks.) Beach Lane Bks.

—Seeds Move! Page, Robin. 2019. (ENG.). 32p. (J). (gr. -1-3). 17.99 (978-1-5344-0915-6(7), Beach Lane Bks.) Beach Lane Bks.

Page, Steve. Downward Mule. Hammond, Jenna. 2017. (ENG.). (J). (gr. k-4). 17.99 (978-1-365-44567-5(4)); pap. 13.99 (978-1-365-44564-4(X)) Lulu Pr., Inc.

—Downward Mule Dyslexic Font. Hammond, Jenna. 2017. (ENG.). (J). (gr. k-6). pap. 13.99 (978-1-365-44566-8(6)) Lulu Pr., Inc.

Page, Steve. Jersey's Spots. Lotz, Sally. 2019. (ENG.). 30p. (J). (gr. k-3). 17.99 (978-1-64372-300-6(6)); pap. 13.99 (978-1-64372-299-3(9)) MacLaren-Cochrane Publishing, Inc. (Huskies Pub).

—Jersey's Spots: Dyslexic Font. Lotz, Sally. 2019. (ENG.). 30p. (J). (gr. k-6). 19.99 (978-1-64372-055-5(4)); pap. 15.99 (978-1-64372-301-3(4)) MacLaren-Cochrane Publishing, Inc.

Page, Steve. The Pencil Eater. Corrigan, Stacey. ed. 2019. (Pencil Eater Ser.). (ENG.). 32p. (J). (gr. k-6). 17.99 (978-1-64372-132-3(1)); 13.99 (978-1-64372-200-9(X)) MacLaren-Cochrane Publishing, Inc. (Huskies Pub).

Page, Terry. The Fathers of the Friendly Forest. Page, Terry. 24p. (J). (gr. 2-6). pap. 4.00 (978-1-887864-69-5(5)); lib. bdg. 7.00 (978-1-887864-38-1(5)) Boo Bks., Inc.

—The Fathers of the Friendly Forest Coloring Book. Page, Terry. 32p. (J). (gr. -1-5). pap. 3.00 (978-1-887864-39-8(3)) Boo Bks., Inc.

—The Saddest Centaur. Page, Terry. 24p. (J). (gr. 2-6). pap. 4.00 (978-1-887864-68-8(7)); lib. bdg. 7.00 (978-1-887864-36-7(9)) Boo Bks., Inc.

—The Saddest Centaur Coloring Book. Page, Terry. 32p. (J). (gr. -1-5). pap. 3.00 (978-1-887864-37-4(7)) Boo Bks., Inc.

Page, Tyler. The Bark in Space: Book 5, No. 5. Robbins, Trina. 2013. (Chicagoland Detective Agency Ser.: 5). (ENG.). 64p. (J). (gr. 4-8). pap. 6.95 (978-1-4677-0725-1(2), 9781467707251, Graphic Universe™) Lerner Publishing Group.

—The Drained Brains Caper: Book 1, No. 1. Robbins, Trina. 2010. (Chicagoland Detective Agency Ser.: 1). (ENG.). 64p. (J). (gr. 4-8). pap. 6.95 (978-0-7613-5635-6(5), 9780761356356, Graphic Universe™) Lerner Publishing Group.

—Night of the Living Dogs. Robbins, Trina. 2012. (Chicagoland Detective Agency Ser.). 64p. (J). (gr. 4-8). pap. 39.62 (978-0-7613-9313-9(7), Graphic Universe™) Lerner Publishing Group.

—Night of the Living Dogs: Book 3, Bk. 3. Robbins, Trina. 2012. (Chicagoland Detective Agency Ser.: 3). (ENG.). 64p. (J). (gr. 4-8). pap. 6.95 (978-0-7613-5637-0(1), 9780761356370, Graphic Universe™) Lerner Publishing Group.

Page, Tyler, jt. illus. see Doerrfeld, Cori.

Paget, Walter Stanley & Sperling, Tom. The Life & Adventures of Robinson Crusoe. Defoe, Daniel. 2019. (Illustrated Classic Ser.). (ENG.). 352p. (J). (gr. 5-5). 12.99 (978-1-68412-793-1(9), Canterbury Classics) Printers Row Publishing Group.

Paglia, Rhonda & Galaska, Taylor. The Little Lambs & the Very Special Mission. Paglia, Rhonda. 2013. 44p. pap. 12.95 (978-0-9899141-1-6(9)) Angels Landing.

Pagnoni, Roberta. Humpty Dumpty's Nursery Rhymes. 2010. (ENG.). 10p. (J). (gr. -1-k). bds. 7.99 (978-0-7641-6278-7(0), B.E.S. Publishing) Peterson's.

—It's Easter Time. 2010. (ENG.). 10p. (J). (gr. -1-k). bds. 6.99 (978-0-7641-6334-0(5), B.E.S. Publishing) Peterson's.

Pagnoni, Roberta, et al. My Ballet Bag. Ravera, Giuseppe. 2015. 8p. (J). (gr. -1-k). bds. 6.99 (978-0-7641-6786-7(3), B.E.S. Publishing) Peterson's.

Pagnoni, Roberta. Santa's Sleigh. Auerbach, Annie. 2017. (ENG.). 12p. (J). (gr. -1-k). bds. 5.99 (978-1-4380-5000-3(3), B.E.S. Publishing) Peterson's.

Pagnoni, Roberta & Rigo, Laura. The Christmas Stocking. Caviezel, Giovanni & Lorini, Andrea. 2018. (Mini People Shape Bks.). (ENG.). 10p. (J). (gr. -1-k). bds. 4.99 (978-1-4380-5058-4(5), B.E.S. Publishing) Peterson's.

—My Kitten Bag. Auerbach, Annie. 2018. (My Bag Ser.). 10p. (J). (gr. -1-k). bds. 6.99 (978-1-4380-5028-7(3), B.E.S. Publishing) Peterson's.

—My Princess Bag. 2016. 8p. (J). (gr. -1-k). bds. 6.99 (978-0-7641-6841-3(X), B.E.S. Publishing) Peterson's.

—My Puppy Bag. Auerbach, Annie. 2018. (My Bag Ser.). 10p. (J). (gr. -1-k). bds. 6.99 (978-1-4380-5029-4(1), B.E.S. Publishing) Peterson's.

—The Nutcracker. Barron's Editorial Staff. 2015. (Little People Shape Bks.). (ENG.). 10p. (J). (gr. -1 — 1). bds. 7.99 (978-0-7641-6796-6(0), B.E.S. Publishing) Peterson's.

—The Nutcracker. Caviezel, Giovanni & Lorini, Andrea. 2018. (Mini People Shape Bks.). (ENG.). 10p. (J). (gr. -1-k). bds. 4.99 (978-1-4380-5057-7(7), B.E.S. Publishing) Peterson's.

Pagona, Aurora. The Magical Purple-Blue Frog, 1 vol. De Jesus, Opal. 2010. 16p. pap. 24.95 (978-1-4489-5925-9(X)) PublishAmerica, Inc.

Pagulayan, Carlo. The Master of Sound. Parker, Jeff. 2007. (Fantastic Four Ser.: No. 2). (ENG.). 24p. (J). (gr. 2-6). lib. bdg. 27.07 (978-1-59961-391-8(3), 7229, Marvel Age) Spotlight.

Pahetti, Antonio. Big: A Little Story about Respect & Self-Esteem. Blum, Ingo. 2018. (ENG.). 40p. (J). (gr. k-3). (978-3-947410-89-7(1)) Blum, Ingo Planet-Oh Concepts.

—Our Wonderful Colorful Highway: 2 in 1 Picture Book + Coloring Book. Blum, Ingo. 2018. (ENG.). 60p. (J). (gr. k-4). pap. (978-3-947410-56-9(5)) Blum, Ingo Planet-Oh Concepts.

—Where Is My Little Crocodile? - Coloring Book. Blum, Ingo. 2018. (Where Is... ? - Coloring Bks.: Vol. 1). (ENG.). 42p. (J). (gr. k-3). pap. (978-3-947410-21-7(2)) Blum, Ingo Planet-Oh Concepts.

—Where Is My Little Dog? - Coloring Book. Blum, Ingo. 2018. (Where Is... ? - Coloring Bks.: Vol. 4). (ENG.). 42p. (J). (gr. k-3). pap. (978-3-947410-43-9(3)) Blum, Ingo Planet-Oh Concepts.

—Where Is My Little Dragon? - Coloring Book. Blum, Ingo. 2018. (Where Is... ? - Coloring Bks.: Vol. 2). (ENG.). 42p. (J). (gr. k-3). pap. (978-3-947410-23-1(9)) Blum, Ingo Planet-Oh Concepts.

—Where Is My Little Elephant? - Coloring Book. Blum, Ingo. 2018. (Where Is... ? - Coloring Bks.: Vol. 3). (ENG.). 42p. (J). (gr. k-3). pap. (978-3-947410-25-5(5)) Blum, Ingo Planet-Oh Concepts.

Paidge, Emma. Nutsi Veut Attraper la Lune. Paidge, Emma. 2017. (FRE.). (J). pap. *(978-2-9559553-0-7(2))* Paidge, Emma.

Paige, Coren. Vonny B & Me. Green, DeWana. 2019. (ENG.). 20p. (J). 27.99 *(978-1-64516-236-0(2))* Courageous Me.

Paillier, Jeremy. Dragon Dancer. Chng, Joyce. 2018. (ENG.). 32p. (J). (gr. -1-2). 17.99 *(978-1-911373-26-1(9))* Lantana Publishing GBR. Dist: Lerner Publishing Group.

Paillot, Jim. The Amazing Turkey Rescue. Metzger, Steve. 2007. (J). *(978-0-545-01420-5(4))* Scholastic, Inc.

—Bedtime Math: a Fun Excuse to Stay up Late. Overdeck, Laura. 2013. (Bedtime Math Ser.). (ENG.). 96p. (J). (gr. -1-2). 16.99 *(978-1-250-03585-1(6),* 900121845) Feiwel & Friends.

—Bedtime Math: the Truth Comes Out. Overdeck, Laura. 2015. (Bedtime Math Ser.). (ENG.). 96p. (J). (gr. -1-2). 16.99 *(978-1-250-04775-5(7),* 900132482) Feiwel & Friends.

—Bedtime Math: This Time It's Personal: This Time It's Personal. Overdeck, Laura. 2014. (Bedtime Math Ser.). (ENG.). 96p. (J). (gr. -1-2). 16.99 *(978-1-250-04096-1(5),* 900125483) Feiwel & Friends.

—The Big Crunch. Blevins, Wiley. 2017. (Funny Bone Books (tm) First Chapters — Ick & Crud Ser.). (ENG.). 32p. (J). (gr. k-2). lib. bdg. 19.99 *(978-1-63440-206-4(5),* 9781634402064) Red Chair Pr.

—The Big Crunch (Book 4), Bk. 4. Blevins, Wiley. 2017. (Funny Bone Books (tm) First Chapters — Ick & Crud Ser.). (ENG.). 32p. (J). (gr. k-2). pap. 4.99 *(978-1-63440-207-1(3))* Red Chair Pr.

—The Big Snow (Book 7) Blevins, Wiley. 2019. (Funny Bone Books (tm) First Chapters — Ick & Crud Ser.). (ENG.). 32p. (J). (gr. k-2). pap. 4.99 *(978-1-63440-267-5(7));* lib. bdg. 19.99 *(978-1-63440-263-7(4))* Red Chair Pr.

—Dogs, Cats, & Dung Beetles. Gutman, Dan. 2018. 186p. (J). *(978-1-5490-6850-8(4))* HarperCollins Pubs.

—Dr. Carbles Is Losing His Marbles! Gutman, Dan. 2007. (My Weird School Ser.: No. 19). 112p. (J). (gr. 2-5). lib. bdg. 15.89 *(978-0-06-123478-1(8))* HarperCollins Pubs.

—Dr. Carbles Is Losing His Marbles! Gutman, Dan. 2007. (My Weird School Ser.: No. 19). 99p. (J). (gr. 2-5). 11.65 *(978-0-7569-8810-4(1))* Perfection Learning Corp.

—First Day of School (Book 5) Blevins, Wiley. 2019. (Funny Bone Books (tm) First Chapters — Ick & Crud Ser.). (ENG.). 32p. (J). (gr. k-2). pap. 4.99 *(978-1-63440-265-1(0));* lib. bdg. 19.99 *(978-1-63440-261-3(8))* Red Chair Pr.

—Going to the Vet. Blevins, Wiley. 2017. (Funny Bone Books (tm) First Chapters — Ick & Crud Ser.). (ENG.). 32p. (J). (gr. k-2). lib. bdg. 19.99 *(978-1-63440-187-6(5),* 9781634401876) Red Chair Pr.

—Going to the Vet (Book 3) Blevins, Wiley. 2017. (Funny Bone Books (tm) First Chapters — Ick & Crud Ser.). (ENG.). 32p. (J). (gr. k-2). pap. 4.99 *(978-1-63440-190-6(5))* Red Chair Pr.

—The Great Turkey Race. Metzger, Steve. 2006. (J). *(978-0-439-85930-1(1))* Scholastic, Inc.

—Happy Halloween (Book 6) Blevins, Wiley. 2019. (Funny Bone Books (tm) First Chapters — Ick & Crud Ser.). (ENG.). 32p. (J). (gr. k-2). pap. 4.99 *(978-1-63440-266-8(9));* lib. bdg. 19.99 *(978-1-63440-262-0(6))* Red Chair Pr.

—Ick's Bleh Day, Bk. 1. Blevins, Wiley. 2017. (Funny Bone Books (tm) First Chapters — Ick & Crud Ser.). (ENG.). 32p. (J). (gr. k-2). lib. bdg. 19.99 *(978-1-63440-185-2(9))* Red Chair Pr.

—Ick's Bleh Day (Book 1), Bk. 1. Blevins, Wiley. 2017. (Funny Bone Books (tm) First Chapters — Ick & Crud Ser.). (ENG.). 32p. (J). (gr. k-2). pap. 4.99 *(978-1-63440-188-3(3),* 9781634401883) Red Chair Pr.

—Miss Kraft Is Daft! Gutman, Dan. ed. 2012. (My Weirder School Ser.: 7). (J). lib. bdg. 14.75 *(978-0-606-27125-7(2))* Turtleback.

—Miss Newman Isn't Human! Gutman, Dan. 2018. 105p. (J). *(978-1-5182-5371-3(7))* Harper & Row Ltd.

—Miss Suki Is Kooky! Gutman, Dan. ed. 2007. (My Weird School Ser.: 17). (J). 14.75 *(978-1-4177-7430-2(4))* Turtleback.

—Mom, There's a Dinosaur in Beeson's Lake. Trueit, Trudi. 2011. (Secrets of a Lab Rat Ser.). (ENG.). 160p. (J). (gr. 3-7). pap. 6.99 *(978-1-4169-6112-3(7),* Aladdin) Simon & Schuster Children's Publishing.

—Mom, There's a Dinosaur in Beeson's Lake, 2. Trueit, Trudi. 2010. (Secrets of a Lab Rat Ser.). (ENG.). 160p. (J). (gr. 3-7). 14.99 *(978-1-4169-7593-9(4))* Simon & Schuster, Inc.

—Mr. Cooper Is Super! Gutman, Dan. ed. 2015. (My Weirdest School Ser.: 1). (J). lib. bdg. 14.75 *(978-0-606-36482-9(X))* Turtleback.

—Mr. Hynde Is Out of His Mind! Gutman, Dan. 2005. (My Weird School Ser.: No. 6). 112p. (J). (gr. 2-5). lib. bdg. 15.89 *(978-0-06-074521-9(5))* HarperCollins Pubs.

—Mr. Macky Is Wacky! Gutman, Dan. ed. 2006. (My Weird School Ser.: 15). (J). lib. bdg. 14.75 *(978-1-4177-7429-6(0))* Turtleback.

—Mrs. Meyer Is on Fire! Gutman, Dan. 2016. 105p. (J). *(978-1-4806-9926-7(8))* Harper & Row Ltd.

—Mrs. Yonkers Is Bonkers! Gutman, Dan. ed. 2007. (My Weird School Ser.: 18). (J). 14.75 *(978-1-4177-8222-2(6))* Turtleback.

—Ms. Coco Is Loco! Gutman, Dan. ed. 2007. (My Weird School Ser.: 16). (J). 14.75 *(978-1-4177-7428-9(2))* Turtleback.

—Ms. Cuddy Is Nutty! Gutman, Dan. 2015. 106p. (J). *(978-1-4242-6518-3(5))* Harper & Row Ltd.

—Ms. Joni Is a Phony! Gutman, Dan. 2017. 105p. (J). *(978-1-5182-3403-3(8))* Harper & Row Ltd.

—My Weird School: Talent Show Mix-Up. Gutman, Dan. ed. 2016. (My Weird School - I Can Read Ser.). (ENG.). 32p. (J). (gr. -1-3). 13.55 *(978-0-606-39276-1(9))* Turtleback.

—My Weird School #1: Miss Daisy Is Crazy! Gutman, Dan. 2004. (My Weird School Ser.: 1). (ENG.). 96p. (J). (gr. 1-5). pap. 4.99 *(978-0-06-050700-8(4))* HarperCollins Pubs.

—My Weird School #10: Mr. Docker Is off His Rocker! Gutman, Dan. 2006. (My Weird School Ser.: 10). (ENG.). 112p. (J). (gr. 1-5). pap. 4.99 *(978-0-06-082227-9(9))* HarperCollins Pubs.

—My Weird School #11: Mrs. Kormel Is Not Normal! Gutman, Dan. 2006. (My Weird School Ser.: 11). (ENG.). 96p. (J). (gr. 1-5). pap. 4.99 *(978-0-06-082229-3(5))* HarperCollins Pubs.

—My Weird School #12: Ms. Todd Is Odd! Gutman, Dan. 2006. (My Weird School Ser.: 12). (ENG.). 112p. (J). (gr. 1-5). pap. 4.99 *(978-0-06-082231-6(7))* HarperCollins Pubs.

—My Weird School #13: Mrs. Patty Is Batty! Gutman, Dan. 2006. (My Weird School Ser.: 13). (ENG.). 112p. (J). (gr. 1-5). pap. 4.99 *(978-0-06-085380-8(8))* HarperCollins Pubs.

—My Weird School #14: Miss Holly Is Too Jolly! Gutman, Dan. 2006. (My Weird School Ser.: 14). (ENG.). 112p. (J). (gr. 1-5). pap. 4.99 *(978-0-06-085382-2(4))* HarperCollins Pubs.

—My Weird School #15: Mr. Macky Is Wacky! Gutman, Dan. 2006. (My Weird School Ser.: 15). (ENG.). 112p. (J). (gr. 1-5). pap. 4.99 *(978-0-06-114151-5(8))* HarperCollins Pubs.

—My Weird School #16: Ms. Coco Is Loco! Gutman, Dan. 2007. (My Weird School Ser.: 16). (ENG.). 112p. (J). (gr. 1-5). pap. 4.99 *(978-0-06-114153-9(4))* HarperCollins Pubs.

—My Weird School #17: Miss Suki Is Kooky! Gutman, Dan. 2007. (My Weird School Ser.: 17). (ENG.). 112p. (J). (gr. 1-5). pap. 4.99 *(978-0-06-123473-6(7))* HarperCollins Pubs.

—My Weird School #18: Mrs. Yonkers Is Bonkers! Gutman, Dan. 2007. (My Weird School Ser.: 18). (ENG.). 112p. (J). (gr. 1-5). pap. 4.99 *(978-0-06-123475-0(3))* HarperCollins Pubs.

—My Weird School #19: Dr. Carbles Is Losing His Marbles! Gutman, Dan. 2007. (My Weird School Ser.: 19). (ENG.). 112p. (J). (gr. 1-5). pap. 4.99 *(978-0-06-123477-4(X))* HarperCollins Pubs.

—My Weird School #2: Mr. Klutz Is Nuts!, No. 2. Gutman, Dan. 2004. (My Weird School Ser.: 2). (ENG.). 112p. (J). (gr. 1-5). pap. 4.99 *(978-0-06-050702-2(0))* HarperCollins Pubs.

—My Weird School #20: Mr. Louie Is Screwy! Gutman, Dan. 2007. (My Weird School Ser.: 20). (ENG.). 112p. (J). (gr. 1-5). pap. 4.99 *(978-0-06-123479-8(6))* HarperCollins Pubs.

—My Weird School #21: Ms. Krup Cracks Me Up! Gutman, Dan. 2008. (My Weird School Ser.: 21). (ENG.). 112p. (J). (gr. 1-5). pap. 4.99 *(978-0-06-134605-7(5))* HarperCollins Pubs.

—My Weird School #3: Mrs. Roopy Is Loopy! Gutman, Dan. 2004. (My Weird School Ser.: 3). (ENG.). 96p. (J). (gr. 1-5). pap. 4.99 *(978-0-06-050704-6(7))* HarperCollins Pubs.

—My Weird School 4 Books In 1! Books 1-4, 4 bks. in 1. Gutman, Dan. 2016. (My Weird School Ser.). (ENG.). 384p. (J). (gr. 1-5). 14.99 *(978-0-06-249668-3(9))* HarperCollins Pubs.

—My Weird School #4: Ms. Hannah Is Bananas! Gutman, Dan. 2004. (My Weird School Ser.: 4). (ENG.). 96p. (J). (gr. 1-5). pap. 4.99 *(978-0-06-050706-0(3))* HarperCollins Pubs.

—My Weird School #5: Miss Small Is off the Wall! Gutman, Dan. 2005. (My Weird School Ser.: 5). (ENG.). 112p. (J). (gr. 1-5). pap. 4.99 *(978-0-06-074518-9(5))* HarperCollins Pubs.

—My Weird School #6: Mr. Hynde Is Out of His Mind! Gutman, Dan. 2005. (My Weird School Ser.: 6). (ENG.). 112p. (J). (gr. 1-5). pap. 4.99 *(978-0-06-074520-2(7))* HarperCollins Pubs.

—My Weird School #7: Mrs. Cooney Is Loony! Gutman, Dan. 2005. (My Weird School Ser.: 7). (ENG.). 112p. (J). (gr. 1-5). pap. 4.99 *(978-0-06-074522-6(3))* HarperCollins Pubs.

—My Weird School #8: Ms. Lagrange Is Strange! Gutman, Dan. 2005. (My Weird School Ser.: 8). (ENG.). 112p. (J). (gr. 1-5). pap. 4.99 *(978-0-06-082223-1(6))* HarperCollins Pubs.

—My Weird School #9: Miss Lazar Is Bizarre! Gutman, Dan. 2005. (My Weird School Ser.: 9). (ENG.). 96p. (J). (gr. 1-5). pap. 4.99 *(978-0-06-082225-5(2))* HarperCollins Pubs.

—My Weird School Back to School 3-Book Box Set: Back to School, Weird Kids Rule!, Miss Child Has Gone Wild!, & Ms. Krup Cracks Me Up! Gutman, Dan. 2019. (My Weird School Ser.). (ENG.). 368p. (J). (gr. -1-1). pap. 15.97 *(978-0-06-293777-3(4))* HarperCollins Pubs.

—My Weird School: Class Pet Mess! Gutman, Dan. 2017. (I Can Read Level 2 Ser.). (ENG.). 32p. (J). (gr. -1-3). pap. 4.99 *(978-0-06-236746-4(3))* HarperCollins Pubs.

—My Weird School Collection: Books 1 To 4, Bks. 1-4. Gutman, Dan. 2010. (My Weird School Ser.). (ENG.). (J). (gr. 1-5). pap. 16.99 *(978-0-06-189489-3(3),* HarperCollins) HarperCollins Pubs. Ltd. GBR. Dist: HarperCollins Pubs.

—My Weird School Daze! Gutman, Dan. 2007. (J). *(978-1-4287-4814-9(8))* HarperCollins Pubs.

—My Weird School Daze #1: Mrs. Dole Is Out of Control! Gutman, Dan. 2008. (My Weird School Daze Ser.: 1). (ENG.). 112p. (J). (gr. 1-5). pap. 4.99 *(978-0-06-134607-1(1))* HarperCollins Pubs.

—My Weird School Daze #10: Miss Mary Is Scary! Gutman, Dan. 2010. (My Weird School Daze Ser.: 10). (ENG.). 112p. (J). (gr. 1-5). pap. 4.99 *(978-0-06-170397-3(4));* lib. bdg. 15.89 *(978-0-06-170398-0(2))* HarperCollins Pubs.

—My Weird School Daze #11: Mr. Tony Is Full of Baloney! Gutman, Dan. 2010. (My Weird School Daze Ser.: 11). (ENG.). 112p. (J). (gr. 1-5). pap. 4.99 *(978-0-06-170399-7(0));* lib. bdg. 15.89 *(978-0-06-170400-0(8))* HarperCollins Pubs.

—My Weird School Daze 12-Book Box Set: Books 1-12, 12 vols. Gutman, Dan. 2013. (My Weird School Daze Ser.). (ENG.). 500p. (J). (gr. 1-5). pap. 58.88 *(978-0-06-228891-2(1))* HarperCollins Pubs.

—My Weird School Daze #12: Ms. Leakey Is Freaky! Gutman, Dan. 2011. (My Weird School Daze Ser.: 12). (ENG.). 112p. (J). (gr. 1-5). lib. bdg. 15.89 *(978-0-06-170403-1(2))* HarperCollins Pubs.

—My Weird School Daze #12: Ms. Leakey Is Freaky! No. 12. Gutman, Dan. 2011. (My Weird School Daze Ser.: 12). (ENG.). 112p. (J). (gr. 1-5). pap. 4.99 *(978-0-06-170402-4(4))* HarperCollins Pubs.

—My Weird School Daze #2: Mr. Sunny Is Funny!, No. 2. Gutman, Dan. 2008. (My Weird School Daze Ser.: 2). (ENG.). 112p. (J). (gr. 1-5). lib. bdg. 15.89 *(978-0-06-134610-1(1))* HarperCollins Pubs.

—My Weird School Daze #2: Mr. Sunny Is Funny! Gutman, Dan. 2008. (My Weird School Daze Ser.: 2). (ENG.). 112p. (J). (gr. 1-5). pap. 4.99 *(978-0-06-134609-5(8),* HarperCollins) HarperCollins Pubs. Ltd. GBR. Dist: HarperCollins Pubs.

—My Weird School Daze #3: Mr. Granite Is from Another Planet!, No. 3. Gutman, Dan. 2008. (My Weird School Daze Ser.: 3). (ENG.). 112p. (J). (gr. 1-5). pap. 4.99 *(978-0-06-134611-8(X))* HarperCollins Pubs.

—My Weird School Daze #4: Coach Hyatt Is a Riot! Gutman, Dan. 2008. (My Weird School Daze Ser.: 4). (ENG.). 112p. (J). (gr. 1-5). lib. bdg. 15.89 *(978-0-06-155408-7(1));* 4th ed. pap. 4.99 *(978-0-06-155406-3(5))* HarperCollins Pubs.

—My Weird School Daze #5: Officer Spence Makes No Sense! Gutman, Dan. 2009. (My Weird School Daze Ser.: 5). (ENG.). 112p. (J). (gr. 1-5). pap. 4.99 *(978-0-06-155409-4(X));* lib. bdg. 15.89 *(978-0-06-155410-0(3))* HarperCollins Pubs.

—My Weird School Daze #6: Mrs. Jafee Is Daffy! Gutman, Dan. 2009. (My Weird School Daze Ser.: 6). (ENG.). 128p. (J). (gr. 1-5). pap. 4.99 *(978-0-06-155411-7(1))* HarperCollins Pubs.

—My Weird School Daze #7: Dr. Brad Has Gone Mad! Gutman, Dan. 2009. (My Weird School Daze Ser.: 7). (ENG.). 112p. (J). (gr. 1-5). pap. 4.99 *(978-0-06-155412-4(X))* HarperCollins Pubs.

—My Weird School Daze #8: Miss Laney Is Zany! Gutman, Dan. 2010. (My Weird School Daze Ser.: 8). (ENG.). 112p. (J). (gr. 1-5). pap. 4.99 *(978-0-06-155415-5(4));* lib. bdg. 15.89 *(978-0-06-155417-9(0))* HarperCollins Pubs.

—My Weird School Daze #9: Mrs. Lizzy Is Dizzy! Gutman, Dan. 2010. (My Weird School Daze Ser.: 9). (ENG.). 112p. (J). (gr. 1-5). pap. 4.99 *(978-0-06-155416-2(2));* lib. bdg. 15.89 *(978-0-06-155418-6(9))* HarperCollins Pubs.

—My Weird School Fast Facts. Gutman, Dan. 2017. (My Weird School Fast Facts Ser.). (ENG.). 176p. (J). (gr. 2-4). 18.69 *(978-1-5364-1224-6(4))* HarperCollins Pubs.

—My Weird School Fast Facts: Dinosaurs, Dodos, & Woolly Mammoths. Gutman, Dan. 2018. (My Weird School Fast Facts Ser.: 6). (ENG.). 208p. (J). (gr. 1-5). pap. 5.99 *(978-0-06-267309-1(2));* lib. bdg. 16.89 *(978-0-06-267310-7(6))* HarperCollins Pubs.

—My Weird School Fast Facts: Dogs, Cats, & Dung Beetles. Gutman, Dan. 2018. (My Weird School Fast Facts Ser.: 5). (ENG.). 192p. (J). (gr. 1-5). pap. 5.99 *(978-0-06-267306-0(8));* lib. bdg. 16.89 *(978-0-06-267307-7(6))* HarperCollins Pubs.

—My Weird School Fast Facts: Explorers, Presidents, & Toilets. Gutman, Dan. 2017. (My Weird School Fast Facts Ser.). (ENG.). 192p. (J). (gr. 1-5). pap. 5.99 *(978-0-06-230623-4(5))* HarperCollins Pubs.

—My Weird School Fast Facts: Geography. Gutman, Dan. 2016. (My Weird School Fast Facts Ser.). (ENG.). 176p. (J). (gr. 1-5). pap. 5.99 *(978-0-06-230620-3(0))* HarperCollins Pubs.

—My Weird School Fast Facts: Mummies, Myths, & Mysteries. Gutman, Dan. 2019. (My Weird School Fast Facts Ser.: 7). (ENG.). 192p. (J). (gr. 1-5). pap. 5.99 *(978-0-06-267312-1(2));* lib. bdg. 16.89 *(978-0-06-267313-8(0))* HarperCollins Pubs.

—My Weird School Fast Facts: Pizza, Peanut Butter, & Pickles. Gutman, Dan. 2019. (My Weird School Fast Facts Ser.: 8). (ENG.). 208p. (J). (gr. 1-5). pap. 5.99 *(978-0-06-267315-2(7));* lib. bdg. 16.89 *(978-0-06-267316-9(5))* HarperCollins Pubs.

—My Weird School Fast Facts: Space, Humans, & Farts. Gutman, Dan. 2017. (My Weird School Fast Facts Ser.). (ENG.). 192p. (J). (gr. 1-5). pap. 5.99 *(978-0-06-230626-5(X))* HarperCollins Pubs.

—My Weird School Fast Facts: Sports. Gutman, Dan. 2016. (My Weird School Fast Facts Ser.). (ENG.). 176p. (J). (gr. 1-5). pap. 5.99 *(978-0-06-230617-3(0))* HarperCollins Pubs.

—My Weird School Goes to the Museum. Gutman, Dan. 2016. 30p. (J). *(978-1-5182-2157-6(2))* Harper & Row Ltd.

—My Weird School Goes to the Museum. Gutman, Dan. 2016. (I Can Read Level 2 Ser.). (ENG.). 32p. (J). (gr. -1-3). pap. 4.99 *(978-0-06-236742-6(0))* HarperCollins Pubs.

—My Weird School: Jokes, Games, & Puzzles. Gutman, Dan. 2018. (My Weird School Ser.). (ENG.). 192p. (J). (gr. 1-5). pap. 5.99 *(978-0-06-279687-5(9))* HarperCollins Pubs.

—My Weird School Special: Back to School, Weird Kids Rule! Gutman, Dan. 2014. (My Weird School Special Ser.). (ENG.). 144p. (J). (gr. 1-5). pap. 5.99 *(978-0-06-220685-5(0));* lib. bdg. 16.89 *(978-0-06-220686-2(9))* HarperCollins Pubs.

—My Weird School Special: Bummer in the Summer! Gutman, Dan. 2019. (My Weird School Special Ser.: 6). (ENG.). 144p. (J). (gr. 1-5). lib. bdg. 16.89 *(978-0-06-279682-0(8))* HarperCollins Pubs.

—My Weird School Special: Bummer in the Summer! Gutman, Dan. 2019. (My Weird School Special Ser.). (ENG.). 144p. (J). (gr. 1-5). pap. 5.99 *(978-0-06-279681-3(X),* HarperCollins) HarperCollins Pubs. Ltd. GBR. Dist: HarperCollins Pubs.

—My Weird School Special: Bunny Double, We're in Trouble! Gutman, Dan. 2014. (My Weird School Special Ser.). (ENG.). 144p. (J). (gr. 1-5). pap. 5.99 *(978-0-06-228400-6(2));* lib. bdg. 16.89 *(978-0-06-228401-3(0))* HarperCollins Pubs.

—My Weird School Special: Deck the Halls, We're off the Walls! Gutman, Dan. 2013. (My Weird School Special Ser.). (ENG.). 144p. (J). (gr. 1-5). pap. 5.99 *(978-0-06-220682-4(6));* lib. bdg. 16.89 *(978-0-06-220683-1(4))* HarperCollins Pubs.

—My Weird School Special: It's Halloween, I'm Turning Green! Gutman, Dan. 2013. (My Weird School Special Ser.). (ENG.). 144p. (J). (gr. 1-5). pap. 5.99 *(978-0-06-220679-4(6));* lib. bdg. 16.89 *(978-0-06-220680-0(X))* HarperCollins Pubs.

—My Weird School Special: Oh, Valentine, We've Lost Our Minds! Gutman, Dan. 2014. (My Weird School Special Ser.). (ENG.). 144p. (J). (gr. 1-5). pap. 5.99 *(978-0-06-228403-7(7))* HarperCollins Pubs.

—My Weird School Special: We're Red, Weird, & Blue! What Can We Do? Gutman, Dan. 2020. (My Weird School Special Ser.: 7). (ENG.). 144p. (J). (gr. 1-5). pap. 5.99 *(978-0-06-279684-4(4));* lib. bdg. 16.89 *(978-0-06-279685-1(2))* HarperCollins Pubs. Ltd. GBR. (HarperCollins). Dist: HarperCollins Pubs.

—My Weird School Summer Reading 3-Book Box Set: Bummer in the Summer!, Mr. Sunny Is Funny!, & Miss Blake Is a Flake! Gutman, Dan. 2020. (My Weird School Ser.). (ENG.). 368p. (J). (gr. 1-5). pap. 15.97 *(978-0-06-293779-7(0),* HarperCollins) HarperCollins Pubs. Ltd. GBR. Dist: HarperCollins Pubs.

—My Weird School: Teamwork Trouble. Gutman, Dan. 2018. (I Can Read Level 2 Ser.). (ENG.). 32p. (J). (gr. -1-3). 16.99 *(978-0-06-236750-1(1));* pap. 4.99 *(978-0-06-236749-5(8))* HarperCollins Pubs.

—My Weird Writing Tips. Gutman, Dan. 2013. (My Weird School Ser.). (ENG.). 160p. (J). (gr. 3-7). 16.99 *(978-0-06-209107-9(7));* pap. 6.99 *(978-0-06-209106-2(9))* HarperCollins Pubs.

—My Weirder-Est School #1: Dr. Snow Has Got to Go! Gutman, Dan. 2019. (My Weirder-Est School Ser.: 1). (ENG.). 112p. (J). (gr. 1-5). pap. 4.99 *(978-0-06-269101-9(5));* lib. bdg. 16.89 *(978-0-06-269102-6(3))* HarperCollins Pubs.

—My Weirder-Est School #2: Miss Porter Is Out of Order! Gutman, Dan. 2019. (My Weirder-Est School Ser.: 2). (ENG.). 112p. (J). (gr. 1-5). pap. 4.99 *(978-0-06-269104-0(X));* lib. bdg. 16.89 *(978-0-06-269105-7(8))* HarperCollins Pubs.

—My Weirder-Est School #3: Dr. Floss Is the Boss! Gutman, Dan. 2019. (My Weirder-Est School Ser.: 3). (ENG.). 112p. (J). (gr. 1-5). pap. 4.99 *(978-0-06-269107-1(4));* lib. bdg. 16.89 *(978-0-06-269108-8(2))* HarperCollins Pubs.

—My Weirder-Est School 4-Book Box Set: Dr. Snow Has Got to Go!, Miss Porter Is Out of Order!, Dr. Floss Is the Boss!, Miss Blake Is a Flake! Gutman, Dan. 2020. (My Weirder-Est School Ser.). 448p. (J). (gr. 1-5). pap. 19.96 *(978-0-06-298023-6(8),* HarperCollins) HarperCollins Pubs. Ltd. GBR. Dist: HarperCollins Pubs.

—My Weirder-Est School #4: Miss Blake Is a Flake! Gutman, Dan. 2020. (My Weirder-Est School Ser.: 4). (ENG.). 112p. (J). (gr. 1-5). pap. 4.99 *(978-0-06-269110-1(4));* lib. bdg. 16.89 *(978-0-06-269111-8(2))* HarperCollins Pubs. Ltd. GBR. (HarperCollins). Dist: HarperCollins Pubs.

—My Weirder-Est School #5: Mr. Marty Loves a Party! Gutman, Dan. 2020. (My Weirder-Est School Ser.: 5). 112p. (J). (gr. 1-5). pap. 4.99 *(978-0-06-269113-2(9));* (ENG.). lib. bdg. 16.89 *(978-0-06-269114-9(7))* HarperCollins Pubs. Ltd. GBR. (HarperCollins). Dist: HarperCollins Pubs.

—My Weirder School #1: Miss Child Has Gone Wild! Gutman, Dan. 2011. (My Weirder School Ser.: 1). (ENG.). 112p. (J). (gr. 1-5). pap. 4.99 *(978-0-06-196916-4(8));* lib. bdg. 15.89 *(978-0-06-196917-1(6))* HarperCollins Pubs.

—My Weirder School #10: Mr. Jack Is a Maniac! Gutman, Dan. 2014. (My Weirder School Ser.: 10). (ENG.). 112p. (J). (gr. 1-5). pap. 4.99 *(978-0-06-219841-9(6));* lib. bdg. 15.89 *(978-0-06-219842-6(4))* HarperCollins Pubs.

—My Weirder School #11: Miss Klute Is a Hoot! Gutman, Dan. 2014. (My Weirder School Ser.: 11). (ENG.). 112p. (J). (gr. 1-5). 15.89 *(978-0-06-219845-7(9));* pap. 4.99 *(978-0-06-219844-0(0))* HarperCollins Pubs.

—My Weirder School #12: Mrs. Lane Is a Pain! Gutman, Dan. 2014. (My Weirder School Ser.: 12). (ENG.). 112p. (J). (gr. 1-5). pap. 4.99 *(978-0-06-219847-1(5));* lib. bdg. 15.89 *(978-0-06-219848-8(3))* HarperCollins Pubs.

—My Weirder School #2: Mr. Harrison Is Embarrassin'! 2. Gutman, Dan. 2011. (My Weirder School Ser.: 2). (ENG.). 112p. (J). (gr. 1-5). pap. 4.99 *(978-0-06-196918-8(4));* lib. bdg. 15.89 *(978-0-06-196919-5(2))* HarperCollins Pubs.

—My Weirder School #3: Mrs. Lilly Is Silly! Gutman, Dan. 2011. (My Weirder School Ser.: 3). (ENG.). 112p. (J). (gr. 1-5). pap. 4.99 *(978-0-06-196920-1(6))* HarperCollins Pubs.

—My Weirder School #4: Mr. Burke Is Berserk! Gutman, Dan. 2012. (My Weirder School Ser.: 4). (ENG.). 112p. (J). (gr. 1-5). pap. 4.99 *(978-0-06-196922-5(2));* lib. bdg. 15.89 *(978-0-06-196923-2(0))* HarperCollins Pubs.

—My Weirder School #5: Ms. Beard Is Weird! Gutman, Dan. 2012. (My Weirder School Ser.: 5). (ENG.). 112p. (J). (gr. 1-5). pap. 4.99 *(978-0-06-204209-5(2))* HarperCollins Pubs.

—My Weirder School #6: Mayor Hubble Is in Trouble! Gutman, Dan. 2012. (My Weirder School Ser.: 6). (ENG.). 112p. (J). (gr. 1-5). pap. 4.99 *(978-0-06-204212-5(2));* lib. bdg. 15.89 *(978-0-06-204213-2(0))* HarperCollins Pubs.

—My Weirder School #7: Miss Kraft Is Daft! Gutman, Dan. 2012. (My Weirder School Ser.: 7). (ENG.). 112p. (J). (gr. 1-5). lib. bdg. 15.89 *(978-0-06-204216-3(5));*7. pap. 4.99 *(978-0-06-204215-6(7))* HarperCollins Pubs.

—My Weirder School #8: Dr. Nicholas Is Ridiculous! Gutman, Dan. 2013. (My Weirder School Ser.: 8). (ENG.). 112p. (J). (gr. 1-5). 15.89 *(978-0-06-204219-4(X));* pap. 4.99 *(978-0-06-204218-7(1))* HarperCollins Pubs.

—My Weirder School #9: Ms. Sue Has No Clue! Gutman, Dan. 2013. (My Weirder School Ser.: 9). (ENG.). 112p. (J). (gr. 1-5). pap. 4.99 *(978-0-06-219838-9(6));* lib. bdg. 15.89 *(978-0-06-219839-6(4))* HarperCollins Pubs.

P

—My Weirdest School #1: Mr. Cooper Is Super! Gutman, Dan. 2015. (My Weirdest School Ser.: 1). (ENG.). 112p. (J). (gr. 1-5). pap. 4.99 *(978-0-06-228421-1(5))* HarperCollins Pubs.

—My Weirdest School #10: Miss Newman Isn't Human! Gutman, Dan. 2018. (My Weirdest School Ser.: 10). (ENG.). 112p. (J). (gr. 1-5). pap. 4.99 *(978-0-06-242939-1(6))*; lib. bdg. 16.89 *(978-0-06-242940-7(X))* HarperCollins Pubs.

—My Weirdest School #11: Mr. Will Needs to Chill! Gutman, Dan. 2018. (My Weirdest School Ser.: 11). (ENG.). 112p. (J). (gr. 1-5). pap. 4.99 *(978-0-06-242942-1(6))*; lib. bdg. 16.89 *(978-0-06-242943-8(4))* HarperCollins Pubs.

—My Weirdest School #12: Ms. Hall Is a Goofball! Gutman, Dan. 2018. (My Weirdest School Ser.: 12). (ENG.). 112p. (J). (gr. 1-5). pap. 4.99 *(978-0-06-242945-2(0))*; lib. bdg. 16.89 *(978-0-06-242946-9(9))* HarperCollins Pubs.

—My Weirdest School #2: Ms. Cuddy Is Nutty! Gutman, Dan. 2015. (My Weirdest School Ser.: 2). (ENG.). 112p. (J). (gr. 1-5). pap. 4.99 *(978-0-06-228424-2(X))*; lib. bdg. 15.89 *(978-0-06-228425-9(8))* HarperCollins Pubs.

—My Weirdest School #3: Miss Brown Is Upside Down! Gutman, Dan. 2015. (My Weirdest School Ser.: 3). (ENG.). 112p. (J). (gr. 1-5). pap. 4.99 *(978-0-06-228427-3(4))* HarperCollins Pubs.

—My Weirdest School #4: Mrs. Meyer Is on Fire! Gutman, Dan. 2016. (My Weirdest School Ser.: 4). (ENG.). 112p. (J). (gr. 1-5). pap. 4.99 *(978-0-06-228430-3(4))* HarperCollins Pubs.

—My Weirdest School #5: Miss Daisy Is Still Crazy! Gutman, Dan. 2016. (My Weirdest School Ser.: 5). (ENG.). 112p. (J). (gr. 1-5). lib. bdg. 15.89 *(978-0-06-228433-4(9))* HarperCollins Pubs.

—My Weirdest School #6: Mr. Nick Is a Lunatic! Gutman, Dan. 2016. (My Weirdest School Ser.: 6). (ENG.). 112p. (J). (gr. 1-5). pap. 4.99 *(978-0-06-228436-5(3))* HarperCollins Pubs.

—My Weirdest School #7: Ms. Joni Is a Phony! Gutman, Dan. 2017. (My Weirdest School Ser.: 7). (ENG.). 112p. (J). (gr. 1-5). pap. 4.99 *(978-0-06-242929-2(9))* HarperCollins Pubs.

—My Weirdest School #8: Mrs. Master Is a Disaster! Gutman, Dan. 2017. (My Weirdest School Ser.: 8). (ENG.). 112p. (J). (gr. 1-5). pap. 4.99 *(978-0-06-242933-9(7))* HarperCollins Pubs.

—My Weirdest School #9: Miss Tracy Is Spacey! Gutman, Dan. 2017. (My Weirdest School Ser.: 9). (ENG.). 112p. (J). (gr. 1-5). pap. 4.99 *(978-0-06-242936-0(1))*; lib. bdg. 16.89 *(978-0-06-242937-7(X))* HarperCollins Pubs.

—Mystery in the Barn, Bk. 2. Blevins, Wiley. 2017. (Funny Bone Books (tm) First Chapters — Ick & Crud Ser.). (ENG.). 32p. (J). (gr. k-2). lib. bdg. 19.99 *(978-1-63440-186-9(7))* Red Chair Pr.

—Mystery in the Barn (Book 2), Bk. 2. Blevins, Wiley. 2017. (Funny Bone Books (tm) First Chapters — Ick & Crud Ser.). (ENG.). 32p. (J). (gr. k-2). pap. 4.99 *(978-1-63440-189-0(1)*, 9781634401890) Red Chair Pr.

—No Girls Allowed (Dogs Okay) Trueit, Trudi. 2010. (Secrets of a Lab Rat Ser.). (ENG.). 144p. (J). (gr. 3-7). pap. 5.99 *(978-1-4169-6111-6(9)*, Aladdin) Simon & Schuster Children's Publishing.

—No Girls Allowed (Dogs Okay) Trueit, Trudi. 2009. (Secrets of a Lab Rat Ser.). (ENG.). 128p. (J). (gr. 3-7). 14.99 *(978-1-4169-7592-2(6)*, Simon & Schuster/Paula Wiseman Bks.) Simon & Schuster/Paula Wiseman Bks.

—Scab for Treasurer? Trueit, Trudi. 2011. (Secrets of a Lab Rat Ser.). (ENG.). 160p. (J). (gr. 3-7). pap. 5.99 *(978-1-4169-6113-0(5)*, Aladdin) Simon & Schuster Children's Publishing.

—Scab for Treasurer?, 3. Trueit, Trudi. 2011. (Secrets of a Lab Rat Ser.). (ENG.). 160p. (J). (gr. 4-6). 17.44 *(978-1-4169-7594-6(2))* Simon & Schuster, Inc.

—Talent Show Mix-Up. Gutman, Dan. 2016. (I Can Read Book: Level 2 Ser.). (ENG.). 32p. (J). (gr. k-2). 17.44 *(978-1-4844-9320-5(6))* HarperCollins Pubs.

—Teamwork Trouble. Gutman, Dan. 2018. 30p. (J). *(978-1-5444-0102-7(7))* Harper & Row Ltd.

—They're There on Their Vacation. Cleary, Brian P. ed. 2015. (ENG.). 32p. (J). (gr. 2-5). E-Book 39.99 *(978-1-4677-8847-2(3)*, Millbrook Pr.) Lerner Publishing Group.

—The Turkey Train. Metzger, Steve. 2013. (ENG.). 32p. (J). (gr. -1-k). 6.99 *(978-0-545-49229-4(7)*, Cartwheel Bks.) Scholastic, Inc.

—Who Did It? (Book 8) Blevins, Wiley. 2019. (Funny Bone Books (tm) First Chapters — Ick & Crud Ser.). (ENG.). 32p. (J). (gr. k-2). pap. 4.99 *(978-1-63440-268-2(5))*; lib. bdg. 19.99 *(978-1-63440-264-4(2))* Red Chair Pr.

—101 Ways to Gross Out Your Friends. Huffman, Julie. 2017. (101 Ser.). (ENG.). 144p. (J). (gr. 3-5). 33.32 *(978-1-942875-16-1(9)*, Walter Foster Jr) Quarto Publishing Group USA.

Paine, Colin. Big George & the Winter King. Pringle, Eric. 2004. 208p. (J). pap. 12.99 *(978-0-7475-6341-9(1))* Bloomsbury Publishing Plc GBR. Dist: Independent Pubs. Group.

Paint, Rana Digi. Peanut Butter & Jelly for Lunch! Minor, Makeia. 2019. (ENG.). 26p. (J). pap. 12.99 ***(978-1-0957-0695-4(0))*** Independently Published.

Painted Daisies Inc. Staff. Shermit's Adventure to Sprinkle Island. Painted Daisies Inc. Staff. Borgatti, Katherine. 2010. (ENG.). 32p. (J). 15.95 *(978-0-615-34491-1(7))* Painted Daisies Inc.

Painter, Andrew, jt. illus. see Brecon, Connah.

Pais, Goncalo. The Boy Who Saved the Earth. Ramos, Laura. Pitacas, Iris, ed. 2019. (ENG.). 144p. (J). pap. 14.00 ***(978-1-0869-9162-8(1))*** Independently Published.

Paj, Eduardo. What If an Alligator Ate an Avalanche. Macalino, Damien. 2013. 32p. pap. 10.00 *(978-0-9836303-8-8(0))* Crystal Mosaic Bks.

Paj, Edurdo. The Dragon Who Lost His Fire. Rensburg, Gerrit Van. 2019. (ENG.). 32p. (J). pap. 9.13 *(978-1-0710-8272-0(8))* Independently Published.

Pajot, Lauren. Machine Gun Inventors: A Military History Coloring Book. Segel, Robert G. 2016. 16p. 4.95 *(978-0-9823918-2-2(X))* Chipotle Publishing, LLC.

Pak, Amy. History Through the Ages - America's History: Historical Timeline Figures (Explorers to 21st Century) Pak, Amy. 2003. (J). pap. 29.95 *(978-0-9720265-2-9(5))* Home Schl. in the Woods.

—History Through the Ages - Napoleon to Now: Historical Timeline Figures (1750 AD - Present) Pak, Amy. 2003. (J). pap. 19.95 *(978-0-9720265-3-6(3))* Home Schl. in the Woods.

Pak, Kenard. Cat Wishes. Brill, Calista. 2018. (ENG.). 40p. (J). (gr. -1-3). 17.99 *(978-0-544-61055-2(5)*, 1617393, HMH Books For Young Readers) Houghton Mifflin Harcourt Publishing Co.

—Flowers Are Calling. Gray, Rita. 2015. (ENG.). 32p. (J). (gr. -1-3). 17.99 *(978-0-544-34012-1(4)*, 1584710, HMH Books For Young Readers) Houghton Mifflin Harcourt Publishing Co.

—The Fog. MacLear, Kyo. 2017. (ENG.). 48p. (J). (gr. -1-3). 16.99 *(978-1-77049-492-3(8)*, Tundra Bks.) Tundra Bks. CAN. Dist: Penguin Random Hse. LLC.

—Have You Heard the Nesting Bird? Gray, Rita. 2014. (ENG.). 32p. (J). (gr. -1-3). 16.99 *(978-0-544-10580-5(X)*, 1540827, HMH Books For Young Readers) Houghton Mifflin Harcourt Publishing Co.

—The Hundred-Year Barn. MacLachlan, Patricia. 2019. (ENG.). 48p. (J). (gr. -1-3). 17.99 *(978-0-06-268773-9(5)*, Tegen, Katherine Bks) HarperCollins Pubs.

—I Wonder. Holt, Kari Anne. 2019. (ENG.). 40p. (J). (gr. -1-2). 17.99 *(978-1-5247-1422-2(4))*; lib. bdg. 20.99 *(978-1-5247-1423-9(2))* Random Hse. Children's Bks. (Random Hse. Bks. for Young Readers).

—On the Horizon. Lowry, Lois. 2020. (ENG.). 80p. (J). (gr. 5-7). 16.99 *(978-0-358-12940-0(0)*, 1752988, HMH Books For Young Readers) Houghton Mifflin Harcourt Publishing Co.

—When the World Is Dreaming. Gray, Rita. 2016. (ENG.). 32p. (J). (gr. -1-3). 17.99 *(978-0-544-58262-0(4)*, 1613704, HMH Books For Young Readers) Houghton Mifflin Harcourt Publishing Co.

Pak, Kenard. Goodbye Autumn, Hello Winter. Pak, Kenard. 2017. (ENG.). 32p. (J). 17.99 *(978-1-62779-416-9(6)*, 900149958, Holt, Henry & Co. Bks. For Young Readers) Holt, Henry & Co.

—Goodbye Summer, Hello Autumn. Pak, Kenard. 2016. (ENG.). 32p. (J). 17.99 *(978-1-62779-415-2(8)*, 900149957, Holt, Henry & Co. Bks. For Young Readers) Holt, Henry & Co.

—Goodbye Winter, Hello Spring. Pak, Kenard. 2020. (ENG.). 32p. (J). 17.99 *(978-1-250-15172-8(4)*, 900183396, Holt, Henry & Co. Bks. For Young Readers) Holt, Henry & Co.

Pak, Mi-Son. The Seven Brothers & the Big Dipper/Heungbu, Nolbu & the Magic Gourds. 2008. (Korean Folk Tales for Children Ser.: Vol. 4). (ENG.). 44p. (J). (gr. 2-5). lib. bdg. 14.50 *(978-0-930878-74-0(4))* Hollym International Corp.

Pak, Mi-Son & Kim, Yon-Kyong. The Greedy Princess/the Rabbit & the Tiger, vols. 10, vol. 7. 2008. (Korean Folk Tales for Children Ser.: 7). (ENG.). 44p. (J). (gr. k-5). lib. bdg. 18.50 *(978-0-930878-90-0(6))* Hollym International Corp.

Pakarnyk, Alan. My Mom Is So Unusual, 1 vol. Loewen, Iris. 2015. (ENG.). 32p. (J). pap. 7.95 *(978-0-919143-37-1(7)*, f4e06253-2f7e-44f1-92df-1b390d7510ec) Pemmican Pubns., Inc. CAN. Dist: Firefly Bks., Ltd.

Pal, Pamela. My King. Pal, Sunita. 2019. (ENG.). 32p. (J). pap. 9.99 ***(978-1-7072-6330-1(2))*** Independently Published.

Palacios G., Sara Helena. De Aqui para Alla. Segovia, Silvia. rev. ed. 2007. (Castillo de la Lectura Blanca Ser.). (SPA & ENG.). 56p. (J). (gr. k-2). pap. 6.95 *(978-970-20-0197-3(8))* Castillo, Ediciones, S. A. de C. V. MEX. Dist: Macmillan.

Palacios, John. Readers' Theater: Scripts for Young Readers. Stewart, Kelly, ed. 2009. 16p. (J). pap. 16.95 *(978-1-60184-146-9(9))*; pap. 16.95 *(978-1-60184-148-3(5))*; pap. 16.95 *(978-1-60184-150-6(7))*; pap. 16.95 *(978-1-60184-152-0(3))*; pap. 16.95 *(978-1-60184-154-4(X))*; pap. 16.95 *(978-1-60184-160-5(4))*; pap. 16.95 *(978-1-60184-166-7(3))* Primary Concepts, Inc.

—Readers' Theater: Scripts for Young Readers: How the Tiger Got Its Stripes. 2009. 16p. (J). pap. 16.95 *(978-1-60184-162-9(0))* Primary Concepts, Inc.

—Readers' Theater: Scripts for Young Readers: the Monkey & the Crocodile. Stewart, Kelly, ed. 2009. 16p. (J). pap. 16.95 *(978-1-60184-164-3(7))* Primary Concepts, Inc.

—Readers' Theater: Scripts for Young Readers: the Peach Boy. Stewart, Kelly, ed. 2009. 16p. (J). pap. 16.95 *(978-1-60184-156-8(6))* Primary Concepts, Inc.

—Readers' Theater: Scripts for Young Readers: the Spear Throwing Contest. Stewart, Kelly, ed. 2009. 16p. (J). pap. 16.95 *(978-1-60184-158-2(2))* Primary Concepts, Inc.

Palacios, Sara. Agnes & Clarabelle Celebrate! Griffin, Adele & Sheinmel, Courtney. (Agnes & Clarabelle Ser.). 80p. (J). 2018. pap. 6.99 *(978-1-68119-090-7(7)*, 900158410, Bloomsbury Children's Bks.); 2017. 9.99 *(978-1-61963-217-2(9)*, 900126618, Bloomsbury USA Childrens) Bloomsbury Publishing USA.

—Between Us & Abuela: A Family Story from the Border. Perkins, Mitali. 2019. (ENG.). 40p. (J). 17.99 *(978-0-374-30373-0(8)*, 900157191, Farrar, Straus & Giroux (BYR)) Farrar, Straus & Giroux.

Palacios, Sara. Facing Fear. Williams, Karen Lynn. 2021. (ENG.). 44p. (J). ***(978-0-8028-5490-2(7)***, Eerdmans Bks For Young Readers) Eerdmans, William B. Publishing Co.

Palacios, Sara. The Flying Girl: How Aida de Acosta Learned to Soar. Engle, Margarita. 2018. (ENG.). 40p. (J). (gr. -1-3). 17.99 *(978-1-4814-4502-3(2))* Simon & Schuster Children's Publishing.

—How to Code a Rollercoaster. Funk, Josh. 2019. 44p. (J). (gr. -1-3). 17.99 *(978-0-425-29203-7(7)*, Viking Books for Young Readers) Penguin Young Readers Group.

—How to Code a Sandcastle. Funk, Josh. 2018. 44p. (J). (gr. -1-3). 17.99 *(978-0-425-29198-6(7)*, Viking Books for Young Readers) Penguin Young Readers Group.

Palacios, Sara, et al. I Am Sam - I See - I See Nat: StartUp Unit 2 Lap Book. Bennett, Liza & Ling, Lei. 2015. (Start up Core Phonics Ser.). (J). (gr. k). *(978-1-4900-2591-9(X))* Benchmark Education Co.

Palacios, Sara. Lola Knows a Lot. McCarthy, Jenna. 2016. (ENG.). 32p. (J). (gr. -1-3). 17.99 *(978-0-06-225017-9(5))* HarperCollins Pubs.

—Lola's Rules for Friendship. McCarthy, Jenna. 2017. (ENG.). 32p. (J). (gr. -1-3). 17.99 *(978-0-06-225018-6(3)*, Balzer & Bray) HarperCollins Pubs.

—Marisol McDonald & the Clash Bash/Marisol Mcdonald y la Fiesta Sin Igual. Brown, Monica. 2013. (Marisol Mcdonald Ser.). (ENG & SPA.). 40p. (J). 18.95 *(978-0-89239-273-5(8))* Lee & Low Bks., Inc.

—Marisol Mcdonald & the Monster: Marisol Mcdonald y el Monstruo. Brown, Monica. 2016. (Marisol Mcdonald Ser.). (ENG & SPA.). 32p. (J). (gr. k-3). 18.95 *(978-0-89239-326-8(2))* Lee & Low Bks., Inc.

—Marisol Mcdonald Doesn't Match / Marisol Mcdonald no Combina, 1 vol. Brown, Monica. 2013. (Marisol Mcdonald Ser.). (SPA & ENG.). 32p. (J). (gr. k-3). 18.95 *(978-0-89239-235-3(5)*, 48b81954-61ed-4125-bf3d-2ed3eb020f92) Lee & Low Bks., Inc.

—One Big Family. Harshman, Marc. 2016. (ENG.). 40p. (J). 17.00 *(978-0-8028-5388-2(9)*, Eerdmans Bks For Young Readers) Eerdmans, William B. Publishing Co.

—The Princess & the Frogs. Bartles, Veronica. 2016. (ENG.). 40p. (J). (gr. -1-3). 17.99 *(978-0-06-236591-0(6))* HarperCollins Pubs.

Palacios, Sara. Thanksgiving, Here I Come! Steinberg, D. J. 2020. (Here I Come! Ser.). 32p. (J). (gr. -1-1). pap. 5.99 ***(978-0-593-09422-8(0)***, Grosset & Dunlap) Penguin Young Readers Group.

Palacios, Sara. A Way with Wild Things. Theule, Larissa. 2020. 32p. (J). 17.99 *(978-1-68119-039-6(7)*, 900156508, Bloomsbury Children's Bks.) Bloomsbury Publishing USA.

—Win, Win, Win! - I Am Lin - Jim & Jan: StartUp Unit 7 Lap Book. Hassan, Miriam et al. 2015. (Start up Core Phonics Ser.). (J). (gr. k). *(978-1-4900-2596-4(0))* Benchmark Education Co.

Palacios, Sara & Battuz, Christine. Fran Grabs It - Stop! It's a Frog! - the Best Nest: BuildUp Unit 3 Lap Book. Akers, Martin et al. 2015. (Build up Core Phonics Ser.). (J). (gr. 1). *(978-1-4900-2602-2(9))* Benchmark Education Co.

Palacios, Sara, jt. illus. see Kahn, Sara.

Palacios, Sara Helena. Conoce a Gabriela Mistral: Get to Know Gabriela Mistral. Leon, Georgina Lazaro. 2014. (Personajes Del Mundo Hispnico Ser.). (ENG & SPA.). 32p. (J). (gr. -1-3). 15.95 *(978-1-61435-351-5(4)*, Alfaguara) Santillana USA Publishing Co., Inc.

Palacios, Sarah. Mi Gatito. Schmauss, Judy Kentor. 2016. (Early Rising Readers Ser.). (SPA.). 16p. (J). (gr. 1-1). 6.67 *(978-1-4788-3724-4(1))* Newmark Learning LLC.

—My Little Cat. Schmauss, Judy Kentor. 2015. (Early Rising Readers Ser.). (J). (gr. -1-k). 5.83 *(978-1-4788-1702-4(X))* Newmark Learning LLC.

Palacios, William & Jacome, Nelson. Romeo y Julieta. Shakespeare, William. 2017.Tr. of Romeo & Juliet. (SPA.). 126p. (J). pap. *(978-9978-18-208-6(X))* Radmandi Editorial, Compania Ltd.

Palacious, John. Readers' Theater Paul Bunyan: Scripts for Young Readers. 2009. 16p. (J). pap. *(978-1-60184-144-5(2))* Primary Concepts, Inc.

Paladino, Lance. George Washington Carver. Carter, Andy & Saller, Carol. 2006. (Yo Solo Biografías Ser.). 48p. (J). (gr. 2-5). lib. bdg. 23.93 *(978-0-8225-6258-0(8)*, Ediciones Lerner) Lerner Publishing Group.

Palagonia, Peter. Matzah & Miracles: A Passover Musical & Chapter Book. Akselrad, January & Young, Jennifer. 2012. (ENG.). 88p. (J). 15.00 *(978-0-9822134-8-3(4))* See The Wish.

Palatini, Margie. Geek Chic: the Zoey Zone. Palatini, Margie. (Zoey Zone Ser.). (ENG.). 192p. (J). (gr. 3-6). 2010. pap. 6.99 *(978-0-06-113900-0(9))*; 2008. 10.99 *(978-0-06-113898-0(3)*, Tegen, Katherine Bks) HarperCollins Pubs.

—Hogg, Hogg, & Hog. Palatini, Margie. 2011. (ENG.). 32p. (J). (gr. -1-3). 15.99 *(978-1-4424-0322-2(5)*, Simon & Schuster Bks. For Young Readers) Simon & Schuster Bks. For Young Readers.

Palecek, Josef. Hans Christian Andersen Fairy Tale Collection. Andersen, Hans Christian. 2019. (ENG.). 176p. (J). (gr. -1-2). 25.00 *(978-0-7358-4380-6(5))* North-South Bks., Inc.

Palen, Debbie. How Not to Babysit Your Brother. Hapka, Cathy & Titlebaum, Ellen. 2005. (Step into Reading Ser.). 48p. (J). (gr. 2-4). pap. 4.99 *(978-0-375-82856-0(7)*, Random Hse. Bks. for Young Readers) Random Hse. Children's Bks.

—How Not to Run for Class President. Hapka, Catherine A. & Vandenberg, Ellen. 2016. (Step into Reading Ser.). 48p. (J). (gr. k-3). 3.99 *(978-1-101-93362-6(3)*, Random Hse. Bks. for Young Readers) Random Hse. Children's Bks.

—How Not to Start Third Grade. Hapka, Cathy & Titlebaum, Ellen. 2007. (Step into Reading Ser.). 48p. (J). (gr. 2-4). pap. 4.99 *(978-0-375-83904-7(6)*, Random Hse. Bks. for Young Readers) Random Hse. Children's Bks.

—How to Deal with Bullies Superhero-Style: Response to Bullying. Blevins, Wiley. 2015. (Funny Bone Readers (tm) — Dealing with Bullies Ser.). (ENG.). 24p. (J). (gr. k-2). lib. bdg. 19.99 *(978-1-63440-009-1(7)*, 1392167) Red Chair Pr.

—How to Start Kindergarten. Hapka, Catherine A. et al. 2018. (Step into Reading Ser.). 32p. (J). (gr. -1-1). pap. 4.99 *(978-1-5247-1551-9(4))*; (ENG.). lib. bdg. 12.99 *(978-1-5247-1552-6(2))* Random Hse. Children's Bks. (Random Hse. Bks. for Young Readers).

—In the Garden. Greenburg, J. C. 2003. (Andrew Lost Ser.: 4). (ENG.). 96p. (J). (gr. 1-4). 4.99 *(978-0-375-81280-4(6)*, Random Hse. Bks. for Young Readers) Random Hse. Children's Bks.

—The Period Book: A Girl's Guide to Growing Up. Gravelle, Karen & Gravelle, Jennifer. 2017. 176p. (J). pap. 13.99 *(978-1-61963-662-0(X)*, 900144913, Bloomsbury USA Childrens) Bloomsbury Publishing USA.

—Roosevelt Banks, Good-Kid-In-Training. Calkhoven, Laurie. 2020. (ENG.). 128p. (J). (gr. 2-5). pap. 7.99 *(978-1-947159-19-8(4))*; 14.99 *(978-1-947159-18-1(6))* Red Chair Pr. (One Elm Books).

—The Ultimate Girls' Guide to Science: From Backyard Experiments to Winning the Nobel Prize. Hoyt, Beth Caldwell & Ritter, Erica. 2004. 128p. (J). (gr. 4-12). pap. *(978-1-58270-092-2(3))* Beyond Words Publishing, Inc.

Paley, Joan. The Emperor Lays an Egg. Guiberson, Brenda Z. Schonhorst, Elizabeth, ed. rev. ed. 2004. (ENG.). 32p. (J). (gr. -1-3). pap. 8.99 *(978-0-8050-7636-3(0)*, 900024495) Square Fish.

—The Secret Life of the Woolly Bear Caterpillar. Pringle, Laurence. 2014. (Secret Life Ser.). (ENG.). 32p. (J). (gr. k-2). 16.95 *(978-1-62091-000-9(4))* Boyds Mills Pr.

—Star of the Sea: A Day in the Life of a Starfish. Halfmann, Janet. 2011. (ENG.). 32p. (J). (gr. k-2). 17.99 *(978-0-8050-9073-4(8)*, 900061332, Holt, Henry & Co. Bks. For Young Readers) Holt, Henry & Co.

Palin, Nicki. Flip the Flaps: Planet Earth. Goldsmith, Mike. 2012. (Flip the Flaps Ser.). (ENG.). 32p. (J). (gr. -1-1). pap. 6.99 *(978-0-7534-6860-9(3)*, 900084474, Kingfisher) Roaring Brook Pr.

Palin, Tim. Circles & Crescents: A Song about Drawing with Shapes. Hoena, Blake. 2017. (Sing & Draw! Ser.). (ENG.). 24p. (J). (gr. 1-3). lib. bdg. 33.99 incl. audio compact disk *(978-1-68410-015-6(1)*, 31580) Cantata Learning.

—The Crow & the Pitcher. Berne, Emma Carlson. 2019. (Classic Fables in Rhythm & Rhyme Ser.). (ENG.). 24p. (J). (gr. -1-2). lib. bdg. 33.99 *(978-1-68410-330-0(4)*, 140250) Cantata Learning.

—The Days of the Week. Berne, Emma Carlson. 2019. (Patterns of Time Ser.). (ENG.). 24p. (J). (gr. -1-2). pap. 7.95 *(978-1-68410-435-2(1)*, 141229) Cantata Learning.

—Monster Party: A Song about Drawing with Numbers. Hoena, Blake. 2017. (Sing & Draw! Ser.). (ENG.). 24p. (J). (gr. 1-3). lib. bdg. 33.99 incl. audio compact disk *(978-1-68410-041-5(0)*, 31581) Cantata Learning.

—The Months of the Year. Berne, Emma Carlson. 2019. (Patterns of Time Ser.). (ENG.). 24p. (J). (gr. -1-2). pap. 7.95 *(978-1-68410-436-9(X)*, 141231); lib. bdg. 33.99 *(978-1-68410-409-3(2)*, 141219) Cantata Learning.

Palin, Tim. Patterns of Time. Berne, Emma Carlson. 2019. (Patterns of Time Ser.). (ENG.). (J). (gr. -1-2). pap., pap. 31.80 ***(978-1-5158-7781-3(7)***, 203171); 135.96 *(978-1-68410-414-7(9)*, 29714) Cantata Learning.

Palin, Tim. Rectangles & Triangles: A Song about Drawing with Shapes. Hoena, Blake. 2017. (Sing & Draw! Ser.). (ENG.). 24p. (J). (gr. 1-3). lib. bdg. 33.99 incl. audio compact disk *(978-1-68410-047-7(X)*, 31582) Cantata Learning.

—The Seasons of the Year. Berne, Emma Carlson. 2019. (Patterns of Time Ser.). (ENG.). 24p. (J). (gr. -1-2). 33.99 *(978-1-68410-410-9(6)*, 141220) Cantata Learning.

—Smarts! Everybody's Got Them! Armstrong, Thomas. 2019. (ENG.). 44p. (J). pap. 14.99 *(978-1-63198-366-5(0))* Free Spirit Publishing, Inc.

—Superhero Playbook: Lessons in Life from Your Favorite Superheroes. Lotowycz, Randall. 2019. (ENG.). 136p. (J). (gr. 1-4). 11.95 *(978-1-947458-76-5(0)*, 805876, Duo Pr. Llc (US)) Duo Pr. LLC.

—Telling Time. Berne, Emma Carlson. 2019. (Patterns of Time Ser.). (ENG.). 24p. (J). (gr. -1-2). pap. 7.95 *(978-1-68410-438-3(6)*, 141233) Cantata Learning.

—The Tortoise & the Hare. Hoena, Blake. 2018. (Classic Fables in Rhythm & Rhyme Ser.). (ENG.). 24p. (C). (gr. k-2). 33.99 *(978-1-68410-309-6(6)*, 140703); lib. bdg. 33.99 incl. audio compact disk *(978-1-68410-134-4(4)*, 31836) Cantata Learning.

Pallace, Chris. Skallywaggs Card Game: The Mix-n-match Pirate Game. 2005. (YA). *(978-0-9768848-0-4(1))* Bent Castle Workshops.

Pallace, Chris, jt. illus. see Serwacki, Kevin.

Pallmer, Elisa. The Llamacorn Is Kind, 1 vol. Coombs, Kate. 2019. 32p. (J). (gr. -1-3). 16.99 *(978-1-4236-5262-5(2))* Gibbs Smith, Publisher.

Palmer, Bailey. Dragons Are Meant to Fly. Klaman, Kevin, ed. 2019. (World of Lizards, Squirrels, & Men Ser.: Vol. 1). (ENG.). 120p. (J). pap. 7.49 *(978-1-0958-9064-6(6))* Independently Published.

Palmer, Bailey. Humans Are People Too. Klaman, Kevin, ed. 2020. (World of Lizards, Squirrels, & Men Ser.: Vol. 2). (ENG.). 126p. (J). pap. 7.49 ***(978-1-6961-3677-8(6))*** Independently Published.

Palmer, Barbara A. A Clue Book for Boo-Boo. 2012. 32p. (J). *(978-0-9728228-3-1(6))* Palmer, Barbara A.

—The Journey of Cattail. 2012. 26p. (J). *(978-0-9728228-4-8(4))* Palmer, Barbara A.

Palmer, Barbara A. Finding Fido the Feline: Flip Book with American Sign Language. Palmer, Barbara A. 2004. (J). bds. 11.99 *(978-0-9728228-1-7(X))* Palmer, Barbara A.

—The Journey of Cattail. Palmer, Barbara A. 2004. 26p. (J). 16.95 *(978-0-9728228-0-0(1))* Palmer, Barbara A.

Palmer, Charly. My Rainy Day Rocket Ship. Sheppard, Markette. 2020. (ENG.). 32p. (J). (gr. -1-3). 17.99 *(978-1-5344-6177-2(9)*, Simon & Schuster Bks. For Young Readers) Simon & Schuster Bks. For Young Readers.

Palmer, Charly. A Plan for the People. McDivitt, Lindsay. 2021. (ENG.). 48p. (J). ***(978-0-8028-5502-2(4)***, Eerdmans Bks For Young Readers) Eerdmans, William B. Publishing Co.

—There's a Dragon in My Closet. Taylor, Dorothea. 2020. (ENG.). 32p. (J). (gr. -1-3). 17.99 ***(978-1-5344-7646-2(6))*** Simon & Schuster, Inc.

Palmer, Gary. H Is for Hook: A Fishing Alphabet. Young, Judy. 2008. (Sports Alphabet Ser.). (ENG.). 40p. (J). (gr. 1-4). 17.95 *(978-1-58536-347-6(2)*, 202305) Sleeping Bear Pr.

—H Is for Hook: A Fishing Alphabet. Young, Judy. 2015. (Av2 Fiction Readalong 2016 Ser.). (ENG.). (J). (gr. 1-4). lib.

bdg. 34.28 *(978-1-4896-3747-5(8),* AV2 by Weigl) Weigl Pubs., Inc.
—Handkerchief Quilt. Crane, Carol. 2010. (ENG.). 32p. (J). (gr. k-3). 15.95 *(978-1-58536-344-5(8))* Sleeping Bear Pr.
—Net Numbers: A South Carolina Numbers Book. Crane, Carol. 2006. (Count Your Way Across the U. S. A. Ser.). (ENG.). 40p. (J). (gr. -1-3). 17.95 *(978-1-58536-202-8(6))* Sleeping Bear Pr.
—T Is for Tar Heel: A North Carolina Alphabet. Crane, Carol. 2003. (Discover America State by State Ser.). (ENG.). 40p. (J). 17.95 *(978-1-58536-082-6(1))* Sleeping Bear Pr.
—Wright Numbers: A North Carolina Number Book. Crane, Carol. 2005. (America by the Numbers Ser.). (ENG.). 40p. (J). (gr. 1-3). 19.99 *(978-1-58536-196-0(8),* 202038) Sleeping Bear Pr.
Palmer, James. The Little Red Hen: Classic Tales Series. Smith, Carrie. 2011. (Classic Tales Ser.). (J). *(978-1-936258-66-6(8))* Benchmark Education Co.
—El Patito Feo. Strom, Laura Layton. 2016. (Jump into Genre Ser.). (SPA.). (J). (gr. 3). 5.25 *(978-1-4788-3623-0(7))* Newmark Learning LLC.
—Pinocchio & Peter Pan: Selections from Two Classic Children's Novels. Collodi, Carlo et al. 2014. (Text Connections Ser.). (J). (gr. 3). *(978-1-4509-9648-8(5))* Benchmark Education Co.
—Pinocchio & Peter Pan - Selections from Two Classic Children's Novels: Set Of 6. Collodi, Carlo & Barrie, J. M. 2014. (Text Connections Ser.). (J). (gr. 3). 49.00 net. *(978-1-4900-0124-1(7))* Benchmark Education Co.
Palmer, Jan. Raggedy Ann & Rags. Gruelle, Johnny. 2010. (Raggedy Ann Ser.). (ENG.). 40p. (J). (gr. -1-2). 19.99 *(978-1-4424-2198-1(3),* Simon & Schuster Bks. For Young Readers) Simon & Schuster Bks. For Young Readers.
Palmer, Judd. Driftwood Ellesmere. Davidge, James. 2010. (ENG.). 206p. (J). (gr. 8-12). 7.95 *(978-1-896209-81-4(5))* Bayeux Arts, Inc. CAN. Dist: Chicago Distribution Ctr.
Palmer, Kate S. Baseball Fun. Geddes, Diana E. Kaeden Corp. Staff, ed. 2003. (ENG.). 12p. (gr. k-2). pap. 7.95 *(978-1-879835-72-6(X),* Kaeden Bks.) Kaeden Corp.
—Day at the Races: World of Discovery II. Bauer, Roger. l.t. ed. 2006. (ENG.). 8p. (gr. k-2). pap. 7.95 *(978-1-879835-48-1(7),* Kaeden Bks.) Kaeden Corp.
—Hockey Practice. Geddes, Diana E. 2005. (ENG.). 12p. (gr. k-2). pap. 7.95 *(978-1-57874-001-7(0),* Kaeden Bks.) Kaeden Corp.
—Let's Play Basketball. Geddes, Diana E. Kaeden Corp. Staff, ed. 2005. (ENG.). 16p. (gr. k-1). pap. 7.95 *(978-1-879835-55-9(X),* Kaeden Bks.) Kaeden Corp.
Palmer, Kate Salley. My Brother Wants to Be Like Me. Mader, Jan. l.t. ed. 2005. (ENG.). 16p. (gr. k-2). pap. 7.95 *(978-1-879835-27-6(4),* Kaeden Bks.) Kaeden Corp.
Palmer, Kate Salley. Almost Invisible Blk Patriots. Palmer, Kate Salley. 2008. (ENG.). 56p. (J). pap. 11.95 *(978-0-9667114-6-2(7))* Warbranch Pr., Inc.
Palmer, Kimmy. Olivia's Tree, 1 vol. Flatley, Paula Chorman. 2010. 16p. pap. 24.95 *(978-1-4489-5870-2(9))* America Star Bks.
Palmer, Ruth. Alice Ray & the Salem Witch Trials. Knudsen, Shannon. 2011. (History Speaks: Picture Books Plus Reader's Theater Ser.). 48p. pap. 56.72 *(978-0-7613-7629-3(1));* (ENG.). (gr. 2-4). pap. 9.95 *(978-0-7613-7114-4(1))* Lerner Publishing Group.
—Good Night Central Park. Gamble, Adam & Jasper, Mark. 2013. (Good Night Our World Ser.). (ENG.). 20p. (J). (— 1). bds. 9.95 *(978-1-60219-082-5(8))* Good Night Bks.
—Good Night New Mexico. Gamble, Adam & Jasper, Mark. 2014. (Good Night Our World Ser.). (ENG.). 20p. (J). (— 1). bds. 9.95 *(978-1-60219-088-7(7))* Good Night Bks.
—Good Night Pittsburgh. Jasper, Mark. 2012. (Good Night Our World Ser.). (ENG.). 20p. (J). (gr. k — 1). bds. 9.95 *(978-1-60219-073-3(9))* Good Night Bks.
—Good Night Twin Cities. Gamble, Adam & Jasper, Mark. 2015. (Good Night Our World Ser.). (ENG.). 20p. (J). (— 1). bds. 9.95 *(978-1-60219-232-4(4))* Good Night Bks.
—I Hate Everyone. Kelly, Mij. 2003. 32p. (YA). *(978-1-85602-362-7(1),* Pavilion Children's Books) Pavilion Bks.
—Peter Rabbit & the Pumpkin Patch. Potter, Beatrix. 2013. (Peter Rabbit Ser.). (ENG.). 32p. (J). (gr. -1-2). pap. 4.99 *(978-0-7232-7124-6(0),* Warne) Penguin Young Readers Group.
Palmer, Ruth & Veno, Joe. Good Night Austin. Gamble, Adam & Jasper, Mark. 2015. (Good Night Our World Ser.). (ENG.). 20p. (J). (— 1). bds. 9.95 *(978-1-60219-233-1(2))* Good Night Bks.
Palmer, Scott. The Lord's Supper... Let's Get Ready! Donahue, Laurie & Phillips, Paul. 2005. 96p. per. 10.99 *(978-0-9718306-6-0(5))* LifeSong Pubs.
Palmer, Tom, et al. Star Wars Legends Epic Collection: the Original Marvel Years Vol. 4. 2019. (ENG.). 464p. (YA). (gr. 4-17). pap. 39.99 *(978-1-302-91849-1(4))* Marvel Worldwide, Inc.
Palmer, Troy Locker. A Dog Named Saturday: Coloring Book. Henry, Dutch. 2019. (ENG.). 60p. (J). pap. 9.99 ***(978-1-6890-2629-1(4))*** Independently Published.
Palmisciano, Diane. A Case for Jenny Archer. Conford, Ellen. 2nd ed. 2006. (ENG.). 64p. (J). (gr. 1-4). per. 8.99 *(978-0-316-01486-1(9))* Little, Brown Bks. for Young Readers.
—Fair Is Fair! Bar Graphs. Dussling, Jennifer. 2006. (Math Matters ® Ser.). (ENG.). 32p. (J). (gr. k-3). pap. 5.95 *(978-1-57565-131-6(9))* Astra Publishing Hse.
—Follow That Clue! Walker, Nan. 2009. (Social Studies Connects ® Ser.). (ENG.). (gr. k-2). pap. 33.92 *(978-0-7613-4805-4(0))* Lerner Publishing Group.
—Follow That Clue! Community Helpers. Walker, Nan. 2008. (Social Studies Connects ® Ser.). (ENG.). 32p. (J). (gr. k-2). pap. 5.95 *(978-1-57565-274-0(9))* Astra Publishing Hse.
—The Garden Monster. Giff, Patricia Reilly. 2013. (J). *(978-0-545-24460-2(9),* Orchard Bks.) Scholastic, Inc.
—Gifts from the Heart, Vol. Osteen, Victoria. 2010. (ENG.). 32p. (J). (gr. -1-2). 19.99 *(978-1-4169-5551-1(8),* Little Simon Inspirations) Little Simon Inspirations.
—¡lo Justo Es Justo! (Fair Is Fair!) Bar Graphs. Dussling, Jennifer. 2008. (Math Matters en Español Ser.). (SPA.). 32p. (J). (gr. 1-3). pap. 5.95 *(978-1-57565-269-6(2))* Astra Publishing Hse.
—Mac & Cheese, Pleeeeze! Mental Math. May, Eleanor. 2008. (Math Matters ® Ser.). (ENG.). 32p. (J). (gr. k-3). pap. 5.95 *(978-1-57565-260-3(9))* Astra Publishing Hse.
—Monster Bug. Hayward, Linda. 2004. 32p. (J). lib. bdg. 20.00 *(978-1-4242-1097-8(6))* Fitzgerald Bks.
—Monster Bug. Hayward, Linda. 2004. (Science Solves It Ser.). 32p. (gr. -1-3). 15.00 *(978-0-7569-4313-4(2))* Perfection Learning Corp.
—Monster Bug: Shadows. Hayward, Linda. 2006. (Science Solves It! ® Ser.). (ENG.). 32p. (J). (gr. k-2). pap. 5.95 *(978-1-57565-135-4(1))* Astra Publishing Hse.
—The Sneaky Snow Fox. Giff, Patricia Reilly. 2012. (Fiercely & Friends Ser.). (ENG.). 40p. (J). (gr. k-2). 22.99 *(978-0-545-43378-5(9),* Orchard Bks.) Scholastic, Inc.
—Unexpected Treasures. Osteen, Victoria. 2009. (ENG.). 32p. (J). (gr. -1-3). 19.99 *(978-1-4169-5550-4(X),* Little Simon Inspirations) Little Simon Inspirations.
Palmore, Iyende, jt. illus. see Breckenridge, Trula.
Palmquist, Eric. Rasmus & the Vagabond. Lindgren, Astrid. Bothmer, Gerry, tr. 2014. 180p. pap. 9.95 *(978-0-87486-597-4(2))* Plough Publishing Hse.
Palmtag, Nele. If My Moon Was Your Sun: With CD Audiobook & Music. Steinhöfel, Andreas. 2017. (ENG.). 80p. (gr. 8-12). 19.00 *(978-0-87486-079-5(2))* Plough Publishing Hse.
Palo, Jefte, et al. Taskmaster: the Right Price. 2020. (ENG.). 216p. (YA). (gr. 8-17). pap. 24.99 *(978-1-302-92132-3(0))* Marvel Worldwide, Inc.
Palomares, Franz. Angelica's Hope: A Story for Young People & Their Parents about the Need to Talk about Things That No One Talks About. Nelson, Annabelle. 2003. (SPA.). *(978-0-9656732-9-7(4))* WHEEL Council, Inc., The.
—Ricardo's Pain: A Story for Young People & Their Parents about Staying Strong, Finding Courage & Overcoming Adversity. Nelson, Annabelle. 2003. (SPA.). *(978-0-9656732-8-0(6))* WHEEL Council, Inc., The.
Palomino, Juan. Maria the Monarch. Aridjis, Homero. Aridjis, Eva, tr. 2017. (Young Eco Fiction Ser.: 1). (ENG.). 64p. (J). (gr. 2-7). 19.95 *(978-1-942134-34-3(7));* pap. 12.99 *(978-1-942134-33-6(9))* Mandel Vilar Pr.
Palomo, Gabriela M. The Fabulous Feats of Mr. B: Mr. B's First Day. Weinberg, Bruce P. 2018. (Fabulous Feats of Mr. B Ser.: Vol. 1). (ENG.). 30p. (J). pap. 9.99 *(978-0-9994692-6-2(6))* Mad Hatter Publishing, Inc.
Palomo, Gabriela M. The Fabulous Feats of Mr. B: Opposite Day. Weinberg, Bruce P. 2019. (ENG.). 30p. (J). pap. 9.99 ***(978-1-7332346-8-9(3))*** Mindstir Media.
Palone, Terry & Permane, Terry, photos by. Thomas & the Treasure. Hooke, R. Schuyler. 2008. (Thomas & Friends Ser.). (ENG., 24p. (J). (gr. -1-2). pap. 3.99 *(978-0-375-84287-0(X),* Random Hse. Bks. for Young Readers) Random Hse. Children's Bks.
Palumbo, Debi. Santa, NASA y el Hombre en la Luna. Kaplan, Richard et al.Tr. of Santa, NASA & the Man in the Moon. (SPA.). (Orig.). (J). (gr. -1-5). pap. 14.95 *(978-0-9649608-1-7(8))* Batyah Productions, Inc.
Palumbo, S. Violette. Filo y Los Supersacros. Mishriky, Mireille. 2016. (SPA.). (J). pap. *(978-0-9952459-3-8(2))* Mishriky., Mireille.
—Philo & the Patience Superholy. Mishriky, Mireille. (ENG.). (J). (gr. 2-6). 2017. (Philo & the Superholies Ser.: Vol. 2). *(978-0-9952459-7-6(5));* 2016. pap. *(978-0-9952459-1-4(6))* Mishriky., Mireille.
—Philo et les SuperDons. Mishriky, Mireille. 2018. (FRE.). 32p. (J). (gr. 2-6). pap. *(978-0-9952459-9-0(1))* Mishriky., Mireille.
—Philo, Rose & the Joy Superholy. Mishriky, Mireille. 2018. (Philo & the Superholies Ser.: Vol. 3). (ENG.). 30p. (J). (gr. 2-6). pap. *(978-1-7753852-0-2(5))* Mishriky., Mireille.
—Philo, Rose et le Superdon Joie. Mishriky, Mireille. 2018. (FRE.). 30p. (J). (gr. 2-6). pap. *(978-1-7753852-3-3(X))* Mishriky., Mireille.
Palumbo, Violette S. Philo & the Superholies. Mishriky, Mireille. 2017. (Philo & the Superholies Ser.: Vol. 1). (ENG.). (J). (gr. 2-6). *(978-0-9952459-8-3(3))* Mishriky., Mireille.
Paluseka, Julia. Sparkles Visits the Farm. Wellings, Chris. 2011. 36p. pap. 24.95 *(978-1-4560-4102-1(9))* America Star Bks.
Pamintuan, Angelo. The Untold Story of Dinosaur School. Chase, Poppy. 2018. (ENG.). 38p. (J). (gr. k-2). pap. ***(978-1-9996577-8-9(0))*** Little Goblins' Bks.
Pamintuan, Macky. Alien in My Pocket #1: Blast Off! Ball, Nate. 2014. (Alien in My Pocket Ser.: 1). (ENG.). 160p. (J). (gr. 1-5). pap. 4.99 *(978-0-06-221623-6(6))* HarperCollins Pubs.
—Alien in My Pocket #2: the Science Unfair. Ball, Nate. 2014. (Alien in My Pocket Ser.: 2). (ENG.). 144p. (J). (gr. 1-5). pap. 4.99 *(978-0-06-221625-0(2))* HarperCollins Pubs.
—Alien in My Pocket #3: Radio Active. Ball, Nate. 2014. (Alien in My Pocket Ser.: 3). (ENG.). 144p. (J). (gr. 1-5). 15.99 *(978-0-06-231493-2(9));* pap. 4.99 *(978-0-06-221627-4(9))* HarperCollins Pubs.
—Alien in My Pocket #4: on Impact! Ball, Nate. 2014. (Alien in My Pocket Ser.: 4). (ENG.). 128p. (J). (gr. 1-5). pap. 4.99 *(978-0-06-221629-8(5))* HarperCollins Pubs.
—Alien in My Pocket #5: Ohm vs. Amp. Ball, Nate. 2015. (Alien in My Pocket Ser.: 5). (ENG.). 144p. (J). (gr. 1-5). 15.99 *(978-0-06-231489-5(0))* HarperCollins Pubs.
—Alien in My Pocket #6: Forces of Nature. Ball, Nate. 2015. (Alien in My Pocket Ser.: 6). (ENG.). 144p. (J). (gr. 1-5). pap. 4.99 *(978-0-06-221633-5(3))* HarperCollins Pubs.
—Alien in My Pocket #7: Telescope Troubles. Ball, Nate. 2016. (Alien in My Pocket Ser.: 7). (ENG.). 144p. (J). (gr. 1-5). pap. 4.99 *(978-0-06-237088-4(X))* HarperCollins Pubs.
—Alien in My Pocket #8: Space Invaders. Ball, Nate. 2016. (Alien in My Pocket Ser.: 8). (ENG.). 144p. (J). (gr. 1-5). pap. 4.99 *(978-0-06-237091-4(X))* HarperCollins Pubs.
—April Fool's Day. Keene, Carolyn. 2009. (Nancy Drew & the Clue Crew Ser.: 19). (ENG.). 96p. (J). (gr. 1-4). pap. 5.99 *(978-1-4169-7518-2(7),* Aladdin) Simon & Schuster Children's Publishing.
—Babysitting Bandit. Keene, Carolyn. 2009. (Nancy Drew & the Clue Crew Ser.: 23). (ENG.). 96p. (J). (gr. 1-4). pap. 5.99 *(978-1-4169-7813-8(5),* Aladdin) Simon & Schuster Children's Publishing.
—Bedtime at the Swamp. Crow, Kristyn. 2008. (ENG.). 32p. (J). (gr. -1-1). 16.99 *(978-0-06-083951-2(1))* HarperCollins Pubs.
—Believe - Coloring Book: Think, Act, & Be Like Jesus, 1 vol. Zondervan Staff. 2015. (ENG.). 64p. (J). pap. 6.99 *(978-0-310-75222-6(1))* Zonderkidz.
—Buggy Breakout. Keene, Carolyn. 2010. (Nancy Drew & the Clue Crew Ser.: 25). (ENG.). 96p. (J). (gr. 1-4). pap. 5.99 *(978-1-4169-7814-5(3),* Aladdin) Simon & Schuster Children's Publishing.
—Camp Creepy. Keene, Carolyn. 2010. (Nancy Drew & the Clue Crew Ser.: 26). (ENG.). 96p. (J). (gr. 1-4). pap. 5.99 *(978-1-4169-9438-1(6),* Aladdin) Simon & Schuster Children's Publishing.
—Cape Mermaid Mystery. Keene, Carolyn. 2012. (Nancy Drew & the Clue Crew Ser.: 32). (ENG.). 96p. (J). (gr. 1-4). pap. 5.99 *(978-1-4424-4625-0(0),* Aladdin) Simon & Schuster Children's Publishing.
—Case of the Sneaky Snowman. Keene, Carolyn. 5th ed. 2006. (Nancy Drew & the Clue Crew Ser.: 5). (ENG.). 96p. (J). (gr. 1-4). pap. 5.99 *(978-1-4169-1254-5(1),* Aladdin) Simon & Schuster Children's Publishing.
—Cat Burglar Caper. Keene, Carolyn. 2010. (Nancy Drew & the Clue Crew Ser.: 27). (ENG.). 96p. (J). (gr. 1-4). pap. 5.99 *(978-1-4169-9436-7(X),* Aladdin) Simon & Schuster Children's Publishing.
—Chick-Napped! Keene, Carolyn. 13th ed. 2008. (Nancy Drew & the Clue Crew Ser.: 13). (ENG.). 96p. (J). (gr. 1-4). pap. 5.99 *(978-1-4169-5522-1(4),* Aladdin) Simon & Schuster Children's Publishing.
—Chick-Napped!, 1 vol. Keene, Carolyn. 2009. (Nancy Drew & the Clue Crew Ser.). (ENG.). 96p. (J). (gr. 2-4). 27.07 *(978-1-59961-641-4(6),* 11727, Chapter Bks.) Spotlight.
—The Cinderella Ballet Mystery. Keene, Carolyn. 4th ed. 2006. (Nancy Drew & the Clue Crew Ser.: 4). (ENG.). 96p. (J). (gr. 1-4). pap. 5.99 *(978-1-4169-1256-9(8),* Aladdin) Simon & Schuster Children's Publishing.
—The Circus Scare. Keene, Carolyn. 2009. (Nancy Drew & the Clue Crew Ser.). (ENG.). 96p. (J). (gr. 2-4). 27.07 *(978-1-59961-642-1(4),* 11728, Chapter Bks.) Spotlight.
—Cooking Camp Disaster. Keene, Carolyn. 2013. (Nancy Drew & the Clue Crew Ser.: 35). (ENG.). 96p. (J). (gr. 1-4). pap. 5.99 *(978-1-4169-9466-4(1),* Aladdin) Simon & Schuster Children's Publishing.
—Cupcake Chaos, 34. Keene, Carolyn. 2013. (Nancy Drew & the Clue Crew Ser.: 34). (ENG.). 96p. (J). (gr. 1-4). pap. 5.99 *(978-1-4424-5351-7(6),* Aladdin) Simon & Schuster Children's Publishing.
—Dance Off. Keene, Carolyn. 2011. (Nancy Drew & the Clue Crew Ser.: 30). (ENG.). 96p. (J). (gr. 1-4). pap. 5.99 *(978-1-4169-9459-6(9),* Aladdin) Simon & Schuster Children's Publishing.
—Designed for Disaster. Keene, Carolyn. 2011. (Nancy Drew & the Clue Crew Ser.: 29). (ENG.). 96p. (J). (gr. 1-4). pap. 5.99 *(978-1-4169-9439-8(4),* Aladdin) Simon & Schuster Children's Publishing.
—Double Take. Keene, Carolyn. 2009. (Nancy Drew & the Clue Crew Ser.: 21). (ENG.). 112p. (J). (gr. 1-4). pap. 5.99 *(978-1-4169-7812-1(7),* Aladdin) Simon & Schuster Children's Publishing.
—Dude, Where's My Spaceship? Greenburg, Dan. 2006. (Weird Planet Ser.: 1). (ENG.). 96p. (J). (gr. 1-4). 3.99 *(978-0-375-83344-1(7),* Random Hse. Bks. for Young Readers) Random Hse. Children's Bks.
—Earth Day Escapade. Keene, Carolyn. 2009. (Nancy Drew & the Clue Crew Ser.: 18). (ENG.). 96p. (J). (gr. 1-4). pap. 5.99 *(978-1-4169-7218-1(8),* Aladdin) Simon & Schuster Children's Publishing.
—The Fashion Disaster. Keene, Carolyn. 6th ed. 2007. (Nancy Drew & the Clue Crew Ser.: 6). (ENG.). 96p. (J). (gr. 1-4). pap. 5.99 *(978-1-4169-3485-1(5),* Aladdin) Simon & Schuster Children's Publishing.
—The Fashion Disaster. Keene, Carolyn. 2009. (Nancy Drew & the Clue Crew Ser.). (ENG.). 96p. (J). (gr. 2-4). 27.07 *(978-1-59961-643-8(2),* 11729, Chapter Bks.) Spotlight.
—Flat Stanley 4 Books in 1! Flat Stanley, His Original Adventure; Stanley, Flat Again!; Stanley in Space; Stanley & the Magic Lamp. Brown, Jeff. 2016. (Flat Stanley Ser.). (ENG.). 416p. (J). (gr. 1-5). 16.99 *(978-0-06-249670-6(0))* HarperCollins Pubs.
—Flat Stanley & the Bees. Brown, Jeff. 2019. (I Can Read Level 2 Ser.). (ENG.). 32p. (J). (gr. -1-3). 16.99 *(978-0-06-236601-6(7));* pap. 4.99 *(978-0-06-236600-9(9))* HarperCollins Pubs.
—Flat Stanley & the Firehouse. Brown, Jeff. 2011. (I Can Read Level 2 Ser.). (ENG.). 32p. (J). (gr. -1-3). 16.99 *(978-0-06-143006-0(4));* pap. 4.99 *(978-0-06-143009-1(9))* HarperCollins Pubs.
—Flat Stanley & the Firehouse. Houran, Lori Haskins. 2013. 32p. (J). *(978-1-4351-5055-3(4))* Barnes & Noble, Inc.
—Flat Stanley & the Haunted House. Brown, Jeff. 2010. (I Can Read Level 2 Ser.). (ENG.). 32p. (J). (gr. -1-3). 16.99 *(978-0-06-143004-6(8));* pap. 4.99 *(978-0-06-143005-3(6))* HarperCollins Pubs.
—Flat Stanley & the Lost Treasure. Brown, Jeff. 2016. (I Can Read Level 2 Ser.). (ENG.). 32p. (J). (gr. -1-3). pap. 4.99 *(978-0-06-236595-8(9))* HarperCollins Pubs.
—Flat Stanley & the Missing Pumpkins. Brown, Jeff. 2017. (I Can Read Level 2 Ser.). (ENG.). 32p. (J). (gr. -1-3). 16.99 *(978-0-06-236598-9(3));* pap. 4.99 *(978-0-06-236594-1(0))* HarperCollins Pubs.
—Flat Stanley & the Very Big Cookie. Brown, Jeff. 2015. (I Can Read Level 2 Ser.). (ENG.). 32p. (J). (gr. -1-3). 16.99 *(978-0-06-218979-0(4));* pap. 4.99 *(978-0-06-218978-3(6))* HarperCollins Pubs.
—Flat Stanley at Bat. Brown, Jeff. 2012. (I Can Read Level 2 Ser.). (ENG.). 32p. (J). (gr. k-3). 16.99 *(978-0-06-143010-7(2));* pap. 4.99 *(978-0-06-143012-1(9))* HarperCollins Pubs.
—The Flat Stanley Collection Box Set: Flat Stanley, Invisible Stanley, Stanley in Space, & Stanley, Flat Again!, Set. Brown, Jeff. 2013. (Flat Stanley Ser.). (ENG.). 400p. (J). (gr. 1-5). pap. 14.99 *(978-0-06-180247-8(6),* HarperCollins) HarperCollins Pubs. Ltd. GBR. Dist: HarperCollins Pubs.
—Flat Stanley Goes Camping. Brown, Jeff. 2013. (I Can Read Level 2 Ser.). (ENG.). 32p. (J). (gr. -1-3). 16.99 *(978-0-06-143013-8(7));* pap. 4.99 *(978-0-06-143015-2(3))* HarperCollins Pubs.
—Flat Stanley: His Original Adventure! Brown, Jeff. 40th anniv. ed. 2013. (Flat Stanley Ser.). (ENG.). 96p. (J). (gr. 1-5). pap. 4.99 *(978-0-06-009791-2(4),* HarperCollins) HarperCollins Pubs. Ltd. GBR. Dist: HarperCollins Pubs.
—Flat Stanley: on Ice. Brown, Jeff. 2015. (I Can Read Level 2 Ser.). (ENG.). 32p. (J). (gr. -1-3). pap. 4.99 *(978-0-06-218981-3(6))* HarperCollins Pubs.
—Flat Stanley on Ice. Houran, Lori Haskins. 2015. 29p. (J). *(978-1-4242-6418-6(9))* HarperCollins Pubs.
—Flat Stanley: Show-And-Tell, Flat Stanley! Brown, Jeff. 2014. (I Can Read Level 2 Ser.). (ENG.). 32p. (J). (gr. -1-3). 16.99 *(978-0-06-218976-9(X));* pap. 4.99 *(978-0-06-218975-2(1))* HarperCollins Pubs.
—Flat Stanley's Worldwide Adventures #1: the Mount Rushmore Calamity. Brown, Jeff. 2009. (Flat Stanley's Worldwide Adventures Ser.: 1). (ENG.). 96p. (J). (gr. 2-5). 15.99 *(978-0-06-142991-0(0));* pap. 4.99 *(978-0-06-142990-3(2))* HarperCollins Pubs.
—Flat Stanley's Worldwide Adventures #10: Showdown at the Alamo. Brown, Jeff. 2013. (Flat Stanley's Worldwide Adventures Ser.: 10). (ENG.). 112p. (J). (gr. 1-5). 15.99 *(978-0-06-218988-2(3));* pap. 4.99 *(978-0-06-218987-5(5))* HarperCollins Pubs.
—Flat Stanley's Worldwide Adventures #11: Framed in France. Brown, Jeff. 2014. (Flat Stanley's Worldwide Adventures Ser.: 11). (ENG.). 128p. (J). (gr. 1-5). 15.99 *(978-0-06-218985-1(9));* pap. 4.99 *(978-0-06-218984-4(0))* HarperCollins Pubs.
—Flat Stanley's Worldwide Adventures #12: Escape to California. Brown, Jeff. 2014. (Flat Stanley's Worldwide Adventures Ser.: 12). (ENG.). 128p. (J). (gr. 1-5). pap. 4.99 *(978-0-06-218990-5(5))* HarperCollins Pubs.
—Flat Stanley's Worldwide Adventures #13: the Midnight Ride of Flat Revere. Brown, Jeff. 2016. (Flat Stanley's Worldwide Adventures Ser.: 13). (ENG.). 144p. (J). (gr. 1-5). pap. 4.99 *(978-0-06-236603-0(3))* HarperCollins Pubs.
—Flat Stanley's Worldwide Adventures #14: on a Mission for Her Majesty. Brown, Jeff. 2017. (Flat Stanley's Worldwide Adventures Ser.: 14). (ENG.). 128p. (J). (gr. 1-5). 15.99 *(978-0-06-236607-8(6));* pap. 4.99 *(978-0-06-236606-1(8))* HarperCollins Pubs.
—Flat Stanley's Worldwide Adventures #15: Lost in New York. Brown, Jeff. 2018. (Flat Stanley's Worldwide Adventures Ser.: 15). (ENG.). 128p. (J). (gr. 1-5). 15.99 *(978-0-06-236610-8(6));* pap. 4.99 *(978-0-06-236609-2(2))* HarperCollins Pubs.
—Flat Stanley's Worldwide Adventures #2: the Great Egyptian Grave Robbery. Brown, Jeff. 2009. (Flat Stanley's Worldwide Adventures Ser.: 2). (ENG.). 96p. (J). (gr. 2-5). pap. 4.99 *(978-0-06-142992-7(9))* HarperCollins Pubs.
—Flat Stanley's Worldwide Adventures #2: the Great Egyptian Grave Robbery No. 2. Brown, Jeff. 2009. (Flat Stanley's Worldwide Adventures Ser.: 2). (ENG.). 96p. (J). (gr. 2-5). 15.99 *(978-0-06-142993-4(7))* HarperCollins Pubs.
—Flat Stanley's Worldwide Adventures #4: the Intrepid Canadian Expedition. Brown, Jeff. 2009. (Flat Stanley's Worldwide Adventures Ser.: 4). (ENG.). 112p. (J). (gr. 2-5). 15.99 *(978-0-06-142997-2(X))* HarperCollins Pubs.
—Flat Stanley's Worldwide Adventures #4: the Intrepid Canadian Expedition Vol. 4. Brown, Jeff. 2009. (Flat Stanley's Worldwide Adventures Ser.: 4). (ENG.). 112p. (J). (gr. 2-5). pap. 4.99 *(978-0-06-142996-5(1))* HarperCollins Pubs.
—Flat Stanley's Worldwide Adventures #5: the Amazing Mexican Secret. Brown, Jeff. 2010. (Flat Stanley's Worldwide Adventures Ser.: 5). (ENG.). 112p. (J). (gr. 2-5). pap. 4.99 *(978-0-06-142998-9(8));*No. 5. 15.99 *(978-0-06-142999-6(6))* HarperCollins Pubs.
—Flat Stanley's Worldwide Adventures #6: the African Safari Discovery. Brown, Jeff. 2010. (Flat Stanley's Worldwide Adventures Ser.: 6). (ENG.). 112p. (J). (gr. 2-5). pap. 4.99 *(978-0-06-143000-8(5));*No. 6. 15.99 *(978-0-06-143001-5(3))* HarperCollins Pubs.
—Flat Stanley's Worldwide Adventures #7: the Flying Chinese Wonders. Brown, Jeff. 2011. (Flat Stanley's Worldwide Adventures Ser.: 7). (ENG.). 96p. (J). (gr. 1-5). 15.99 *(978-0-06-143003-9(X));* pap. 4.99 *(978-0-06-143002-2(1))* HarperCollins Pubs.
—Flat Stanley's Worldwide Adventures #8: the Australian Boomerang Bonanza. Brown, Jeff. 2011. (Flat Stanley's Worldwide Adventures Ser.: 8). (ENG.). 112p. (J). (gr. 2-5). 15.99 *(978-0-06-157435-1(X))* HarperCollins Pubs.
—Flat Stanley's Worldwide Adventures #8: the Australian Boomerang Bonanza No. 8. Brown, Jeff. 2011. (Flat Stanley's Worldwide Adventures Ser.: 8). (ENG.). 112p. (J). (gr. 2-5). pap. 4.99 *(978-0-06-143018-3(8))* HarperCollins Pubs.
—Flat Stanley's Worldwide Adventures #9: the US Capital Commotion. Brown, Jeff. 2011. (Flat Stanley's Worldwide Adventures Ser.: 9). (ENG.). 112p. (J). (gr. 2-5). 15.99 *(978-0-06-157436-8(8));* pap. 4.99 *(978-0-06-143019-0(6))* HarperCollins Pubs.
—The Flower Show Fiasco. Keene, Carolyn. 2014. (Nancy Drew & the Clue Crew Ser.: 37). (ENG.). 96p. (J). (gr. 1-4). pap. 5.99 *(978-1-4424-8668-3(6),* Aladdin) Simon & Schuster Children's Publishing.
—Grand Old Flag. Nussbaum, Ben. 2006. (American Favorites Ser.). (ENG.). 32p. (J). (gr. -1-3). 14.95 *(978-1-59249-572-6(9));* 9.85 *(978-1-59249-593-1(1))* Soundprints.
—The Halloween Hoax. Keene, Carolyn. 9th ed. 2007. (Nancy Drew & the Clue Crew Ser.: 9). (ENG.). 96p. (J). (gr. 1-4).

P

pap. 5.99 *(978-1-4169-3664-0(5)*, Aladdin) Simon & Schuster Children's Publishing.

—The Halloween Hoax. Keene, Carolyn. 2009. (Nancy Drew & the Clue Crew Ser.). (ENG.). 96p. (J). (gr. 2-4). 27.07 *(978-1-59961-644-5(0)*, 11730, Chapter Bks.) Spotlight.

—I Saw an Ant on the Railroad Track. Prince, Joshua. 2006. 24p. (J). (gr. -1-k). 14.95 *(978-1-4027-2183-0(8)*, 1252268) Sterling Publishing Co., Inc.

—Invisible Stanley. Brown, Jeff. 2009. (Flat Stanley Ser.). (ENG.). 112p. (J). (gr. 2-5). pap. 4.99 *(978-0-06-009792-9(2)*, HarperCollins) HarperCollins Pubs. Ltd. GBR. Dist: HarperCollins Pubs.

—Kisses for Kindergarten. Crouse, Livingstone. 2017. (ENG.). 40p. (J). (gr. -1 — 1). 17.99 *(978-1-62686-703-1(8)*, Silver Dolphin Bks.) Printers Row Publishing Group.

—Lights, Camera ... Cats! Keene, Carolyn. 8th ed. 2007. (Nancy Drew & the Clue Crew Ser.: 8). (ENG.). 96p. (J). (gr. 1-4). pap. 5.99 *(978-1-4169-3957-3(1)*, Aladdin) Simon & Schuster Children's Publishing.

—Lights, Camera... Cats!, 1 vol. Keene, Carolyn. 2009. (Nancy Drew & the Clue Crew Ser.). (ENG.). 96p. (J). (gr. 2-4). 27.07 *(978-1-59961-645-2(9)*, 11731, Chapter Bks.) Spotlight.

—The Make-A-Pet Mystery. Keene, Carolyn. 2012. (Nancy Drew & the Clue Crew Ser.: 31). (ENG.). 96p. (J). (gr. 1-4). pap. 6.99 *(978-1-4169-9464-0(5)*, Aladdin) Simon & Schuster Children's Publishing.

—Mall Madness. Keene, Carolyn. 15th ed. 2008. (Nancy Drew & the Clue Crew Ser.: 15). (ENG.). 96p. (J). (gr. 1-4). pap. 5.99 *(978-1-4169-5900-7(9)*, Aladdin) Simon & Schuster Children's Publishing.

—Mall Madness, 1 vol. Keene, Carolyn. 2009. (Nancy Drew & the Clue Crew Ser.). (ENG.). 96p. (J). (gr. 2-4). 27.07 *(978-1-59961-646-9(7)*, 11732, Chapter Bks.) Spotlight.

—Max & Maddy & the Bursting Balloons Mystery. McCall Smith, Alexander. 2008. (Max & Maddy Ser.). (ENG.). 70p. (J). (gr. 3-6). 17.44 *(978-1-59990-035-3(1)*, 9781599900353) Bloomsbury Publishing USA.

—Max & Maddy & the Chocolate Money Mystery. McCall Smith, Alexander. 2008. (Max & Maddy Ser.). (ENG.). 72p. (J). (gr. 3-6). 17.44 *(978-1-59990-036-0(X)*, 9781599900360) Bloomsbury Publishing USA.

—The Midnight Ride of Flat Revere. Egan, Kate. 2016. 134p. (J). *(978-1-5182-2203-0(X))* Harper & Row Ltd.

—The Midnight Ride of Flat Revere. Brown, Jeff. ed. 2016. (Flat Stanley's Worldwide Adventures Ser.: 13). (ENG.). 112p. (J). (gr. 1-5). 14.75 *(978-0-606-39266-2(1))* Turtleback.

—A Musical Mess. Keene, Carolyn. 2014. (Nancy Drew & the Clue Crew Ser.: 38). (ENG.). 96p. (J). (gr. 1-4). pap. 5.99 *(978-1-4424-9512-8(X)*, Aladdin) Simon & Schuster Children's Publishing.

—Nancy Drew & the Clue Crew - 4 Titles, 3 vols. ABDO Publishing Company Staff & Keene, Carolyn. 2007. (Nancy Drew & the Clue Crew Ser.). (ENG.). 96p. (J). (gr. 2-4). lib. bdg. 81.21 *(978-1-59961-344-4(1)*, 11720, Chapter Bks.) Spotlight.

—The Nancy Drew & the Clue Crew Collection: Sleepover Sleuths; Scream for Ice Cream; Pony Problems; the Cinderella Ballet Mystery; Case of the Sneaky Snowman. Keene, Carolyn. ed. 2014. (Nancy Drew & the Clue Crew Ser.). (ENG.). 480p. (J). (gr. 1-4). pap. 29.99 *(978-1-4814-1472-2(0)*, Aladdin) Simon & Schuster Children's Publishing.

—The Night Before Baseball at the Park by the Bay. Schnell, David. 2013. (ENG.). 32p. 0.00 *(978-0-9891043-0-2(3))* Prospect Palo Alto Publishing.

—Pirates Coming Through, 24 vols., Vol. 4257. Williams, Rozanne Lanczak. 2005. (Reading for Fluency Ser.). 16p. (J). pap. 3.49 *(978-1-59198-157-2(3)*, 4257) Creative Teaching Pr., Inc.

—Pony Problems. Keene, Carolyn. 3rd ed. 2006. (Nancy Drew & the Clue Crew Ser.: 3). (ENG.). 96p. (J). (gr. 1-4). pap. 5.99 *(978-1-4169-1815-8(9)*, Aladdin) Simon & Schuster Children's Publishing.

—Pony Problems, 1 vol. Keene, Carolyn. 2007. (Nancy Drew & the Clue Crew Ser.). (ENG.). 80p. (J). (gr. 2-4). 27.07 *(978-1-59961-346-8(8)*, 11722, Chapter Bks.) Spotlight.

—Princess Mix-Up Mystery, No. 24. Keene, Carolyn. 2009. (Nancy Drew & the Clue Crew Ser.: 24). (ENG.). 96p. (J). (gr. 1-4). pap. 5.99 *(978-1-4169-7811-4(9)*, Aladdin) Simon & Schuster Children's Publishing.

—The Pumpkin Patch Puzzle. Keene, Carolyn. 2012. (Nancy Drew & the Clue Crew Ser.: 33). (ENG.). 112p. (J). (gr. 1-4). pap. 5.99 *(978-1-4169-9465-7(3)*, Aladdin) Simon & Schuster Children's Publishing.

—Scream for Ice Cream. Keene, Carolyn. 2nd ed. 2006. (Nancy Drew & the Clue Crew Ser.: 2). (ENG.). 96p. (J). (gr. 1-4). pap. 5.99 *(978-1-4169-1253-8(3)*, Aladdin) Simon & Schuster Children's Publishing.

—Scream for Ice Cream, 1 vol. Keene, Carolyn. 2007. (Nancy Drew & the Clue Crew Ser.). (ENG.). 89p. (J). (gr. 2-4). 27.07 *(978-1-59961-347-5(6)*, 11723, Chapter Bks.) Spotlight.

—The Secret of the Scarecrow. Keene, Carolyn. 2013. (Nancy Drew & the Clue Crew Ser.: 36). (ENG.). 96p. (J). (gr. 1-4). pap. 4.99 *(978-1-4424-5353-1(2)*, Aladdin) Simon & Schuster Children's Publishing.

—Ski School Sneak. Keene, Carolyn. 11th ed. 2007. (Nancy Drew & the Clue Crew Ser.: 11). (ENG.). 96p. (J). (gr. 1-4). pap. 5.99 *(978-1-4169-4936-7(4)*, Aladdin) Simon & Schuster Children's Publishing.

—Ski School Sneak, 1 vol. Keene, Carolyn. 2009. (Nancy Drew & the Clue Crew Ser.). (ENG.). 96p. (J). (gr. 2-4). 27.07 *(978-1-59961-647-6(5)*, 11733, Chapter Bks.) Spotlight.

—Sleepover Sleuths, 1. Keene, Carolyn. 2006. (Nancy Drew & the Clue Crew Ser.: 1). (ENG.). 96p. (J). (gr. 1-4). pap. 5.99 *(978-1-4169-1255-2(X))* Simon & Schuster, Inc.

—Sleepover Sleuths, 1 vol. Keene, Carolyn. 2007. (Nancy Drew & the Clue Crew Ser.). (ENG.). 81p. (J). (gr. 2-4). 27.07 *(978-1-59961-348-2(4)*, 11724, Chapter Bks.) Spotlight.

—Stanley & the Magic Lamp. Brown, Jeff. 2009. (Flat Stanley Ser.). (ENG.). 128p. (J). (gr. 2-5). pap. 4.99 *(978-0-06-009793-6(0)*, HarperCollins) HarperCollins Pubs. Ltd. GBR. Dist: HarperCollins Pubs.

—Stanley, Flat Again! Brown, Jeff. 2009. (Flat Stanley Ser.). (ENG.). 96p. (J). (gr. 2-5). pap. 4.99 *(978-0-06-442173-7(2)*, HarperCollins) HarperCollins Pubs. Ltd. GBR. Dist: HarperCollins Pubs.

—Stanley in Space. Brown, Jeff. 2009. (Flat Stanley Ser.). (ENG.). 128p. (J). (gr. 2-5). pap. 4.99 *(978-0-06-442174-4(0)*, HarperCollins) HarperCollins Pubs. Ltd. GBR. Dist: HarperCollins Pubs.

—Stanley's Christmas Adventure. Brown, Jeff. 2010. (Flat Stanley Ser.). (ENG.). 96p. (J). (gr. 2-5). pap. 4.99 *(978-0-06-442175-1(9)*, HarperCollins) HarperCollins Pubs. Ltd. GBR. Dist: HarperCollins Pubs.

—Thanksgiving Thief. Keene, Carolyn. 2008. (Nancy Drew & the Clue Crew Ser.: 16). (ENG.). 96p. (J). (gr. 1-4). pap. 5.99 *(978-1-4169-6777-4(X)*, Aladdin) Simon & Schuster Children's Publishing.

—Thanksgiving Thief, 1 vol. Keene, Carolyn. 2009. (Nancy Drew & the Clue Crew Ser.). (ENG.). 96p. (J). (gr. 2-4). 27.07 *(978-1-59961-648-3(3)*, 11734, Chapter Bks.) Spotlight.

—Ticket Trouble, 10. Keene, Carolyn. 10th ed. 2007. (Nancy Drew & the Clue Crew Ser.: 10). (ENG.). 96p. (J). (gr. 1-4). pap. 5.99 *(978-1-4169-4733-2(7))* Simon & Schuster, Inc.

—Ticket Trouble, 1 vol. Keene, Carolyn. 2009. (Nancy Drew & the Clue Crew Ser.). (ENG.). 96p. (J). (gr. 2-4). 27.07 *(978-1-59961-649-0(1)*, 11735, Chapter Bks.) Spotlight.

—Time Thief. Keene, Carolyn. 2011. (Nancy Drew & the Clue Crew Ser.: 28). (ENG.). 96p. (J). (gr. 1-4). pap. 5.99 *(978-1-4169-9458-9(0)*, Aladdin) Simon & Schuster Children's Publishing.

—Treasure Trouble. Keene, Carolyn. 2009. (Nancy Drew & the Clue Crew Ser.: 20). (ENG.). 112p. (J). (gr. 1-4). pap. 5.99 *(978-1-4169-7809-1(7)*, Aladdin) Simon & Schuster Children's Publishing.

—Unicorn Uproar. Keene, Carolyn. 2009. (Nancy Drew & the Clue Crew Ser.: 22). (ENG.). 96p. (J). (gr. 1-4). pap. 5.99 *(978-1-4169-7810-7(0)*, Aladdin) Simon & Schuster Children's Publishing.

—Valentine's Day Secret. Keene, Carolyn. 12th ed. 2007. (Nancy Drew & the Clue Crew Ser.: 12). (ENG.). 96p. (J). (gr. 1-4). pap. 5.99 *(978-1-4169-4944-2(5)*, Aladdin) Simon & Schuster Children's Publishing.

—Valentine's Day Secret, 1 vol. Keene, Carolyn. 2009. (Nancy Drew & the Clue Crew Ser.). (ENG.). 96p. (J). (gr. 2-4). 27.07 *(978-1-59961-650-6(5)*, 11736, Chapter Bks.) Spotlight.

—Wedding Day Disaster. Keene, Carolyn. 2008. (Nancy Drew & the Clue Crew Ser.: 17). (ENG.). 96p. (J). (gr. 1-4). pap. 5.99 *(978-1-4169-6778-1(8)*, Aladdin) Simon & Schuster Children's Publishing.

—The Zoo Crew. Keene, Carolyn. 14th ed. 2008. (Nancy Drew & the Clue Crew Ser.: 14). (ENG.). 96p. (J). (gr. 1-4). pap. 5.99 *(978-1-4169-5899-4(1)*, Aladdin) Simon & Schuster Children's Publishing.

—The Zoo Crew. Keene, Carolyn. 2009. (Nancy Drew & the Clue Crew Ser.). (ENG.). 96p. (J). (gr. 2-4). 27.07 *(978-1-59961-651-3(3)*, 11737, Chapter Bks.) Spotlight.

—Zoo Zoom! Ryan, Candace. 2015. 32p. (J). (gr. -1-1). 16.99 *(978-1-61963-357-5(4)*, 900134207, Bloomsbury USA Childrens) Bloomsbury Publishing USA.

Pamintuan, Macky & Wang, Qi. Grand Old Flag. Schwaeber, Barbie. Nussbaum, Ben, ed. 2006. (Smithsonian American Favorites Ser.). (ENG.). 32p. (J). (gr. -1-3). 9.85 *(978-1-59249-650-1(4))* Soundprints.

Pamment, Katie. Can't-Dance-Cameron: A Scottish Capercaillie Story, 50 vols. Dodd, Emily. 2014. (ENG.). 24p. (J). 11.95 *(978-1-78250-095-7(2)*, Kelpies) Floris Bks. GBR. Dist: Consortium Bk. Sales & Distribution.

—The Prince & the Pauper. Twain, Mark. 2008. (Young Reading Series 2 Gift Books Ser.). 63p. (J). 8.99 *(978-0-7945-1818-9(4)*, Usborne) EDC Publishing.

Pan, Hsinping. Be Kind: You Can Make the World a Happier Place! 125 Kind Things to Say & Do. Shulman, Naomi. 2019. (ENG.). 80p. (J). 12.95 *(978-1-63586-154-9(3)*, 626154) Storey Publishing, LLC.

—Big Words for Little Geniuses. Patterson, James & Patterson, Susan. 2017. (Big Words for Little Geniuses Ser.: 1). (ENG.). 32p. (J). (gr. -1-1). 17.99 *(978-0-316-50293-1(6)*, Jimmy Patterson) Little Brown & Co.

—Bigger Words for Little Geniuses. Patterson, Susan & Patterson, James. 2019. (ENG.). 32p. (J). (gr. -1-1). 17.99 *(978-0-316-53445-1(5)*, Jimmy Patterson) Little Brown & Co.

—Cuddly Critters for Little Geniuses. Patterson, Susan & Patterson, James. (ENG.). 32p. (J). (gr. -1 — 1). 2019. bds. 8.99 *(978-0-316-48715-3(5))*; 2018. (Big Words for Little Geniuses Ser.: 2). 17.99 *(978-0-316-48628-6(0))* Little Brown & Co. (Jimmy Patterson).

—The Cutest Thing Ever. Ignatow, Amy. 2019. (ENG.). 32p. (J). (gr. -1-k). 16.99 *(978-1-4197-3357-4(5)*, Abrams Appleseed) Abrams, Inc.

Pan, Hui-Mei. El Cochinito en mi Bolsillo, 1 vol. Pan, Hui-Mei. Vernescu, Maritza, tr. from ENG. 2004.Tr. of Piggy in My Pocket. (SPA.). 32p. (J). bds. 5.95 *(978-1-932065-04-6(0)*, 1-718-784-9112) Star Bright Bks., Inc.

—Piggy in My Pocket (Spanish/English), 1 vol. Pan, Hui-Mei. del Risco, Elda, tr. 2004. (ENG & SPA.). 32p. (J). bds. 5.95 *(978-1-932065-11-4(3))* Star Bright Bks., Inc.

—¿Qué hay en la bolsa de Abuelita? Pan, Hui-Mei. 2004.Tr. of What's in Grandma's Grocery Bag?. (SPA.). 16p. (J). bds. 6.25 *(978-1-932065-05-3(9))* Star Bright Bks., Inc.

Pană, Andra. Three Little Froglets. McWood, Allison. 2020. (ENG.). 30p. (J). pap. ***(978-1-7771360-7-9(5))*** Annelid Pr.

Pana, Andra. Douglas the Pinecone's Christmas Crunch. McWood, Allison. 2019. (ENG.). 30p. (J). pap. ***(978-1-9992475-6-0(6))*** Annelid Pr.

Panaccione, Nancy. Emma's Very Busy Week. Dakota, Heather. 2009. 31p. (J). *(978-0-545-17227-1(6))* Scholastic, Inc.

Panagarry, Rachelle. The Catacombs of Chaos: A Lottie Lipton Adventure. Metcalf, Dan. 2017. (Adventures of Lottie Lipton Ser.). (ENG.). 80p. (J). (gr. 2-5). pap. 6.99 *(978-1-5124-8185-3(8)*, 9781512481853); lib. bdg. 25.32 *(978-1-5124-8183-9(1))* Lerner Publishing Group. (Darby Creek).

—The Curse of the Cairo Cat: A Lottie Lipton Adventure. Metcalf, Dan. 2017. (Adventures of Lottie Lipton Ser.). (ENG.). 80p. (J). (gr. 2-5). pap. 6.99 *(978-1-5124-8186-0(6))*; lib. bdg. 25.32 *(978-1-5124-8179-2(3)*, 9781512481792) Lerner Publishing Group. (Darby Creek).

—The Eagle of Rome: A Lottie Lipton Adventure. Metcalf, Dan. 2017. (Adventures of Lottie Lipton Ser.). (ENG.). 80p. (J). (gr. 2-5). pap. 6.99 *(978-1-5124-8187-7(4))*; lib. bdg. 25.32 *(978-1-5124-8184-6(X)*, 9781512481846) Lerner Publishing Group. (Darby Creek).

—The Egyptian Enchantment: A Lottie Lipton Adventure. Metcalf, Dan. 2017. (Adventures of Lottie Lipton Ser.). (ENG.). 96p. (J). (gr. 2-5). pap. 6.99 *(978-1-5124-8188-4(2)*, 9781512481884); lib. bdg. 25.32 *(978-1-5124-8182-2(3))* Lerner Publishing Group. (Darby Creek).

—The Scroll of Alexandria: A Lottie Lipton Adventure. Metcalf, Dan. 2017. (Adventures of Lottie Lipton Ser.). (ENG.). 80p. (J). (gr. 2-5). pap. 6.99 *(978-1-5124-8189-1(0))*; 25.32 *(978-1-5124-8181-5(5)*, 9781512481815) Lerner Publishing Group. (Darby Creek).

—The Secrets of the Stone: A Lottie Lipton Adventure. Metcalf, Dan. 2017. (Adventures of Lottie Lipton Ser.). (ENG.). 80p. (J). (gr. 2-5). pap. 6.99 *(978-1-5124-8190-7(4)*, 9781512481907); 25.32 *(978-1-5124-8180-8(7))* Lerner Publishing Group. (Darby Creek).

Pancheshnaya, Dasha. Silent As a Stone: Mother Maria of Paris & the Trash Can Rescue. Forest, Jim. 2007. (ENG.). 32p. (J). 18.00 *(978-0-88141-314-4(3))* St. Vladimir's Seminary Pr.

Panchyshyn, Roksolana. Avulias Taskurapu: Finnish Edition of the Caring Crab. Pere, Tuula. 2018. (Colin the Crab Ser.: Vol. 1). (FIN.). 54p. (J). (gr. k-4). pap. *(978-952-7107-49-2(0))* Wickwick oy.

—The Caring Crab. Pere, Tuula. Korman, Susan, ed. 2018. (Colin the Crab Ser.: Vol. 1). (ENG.). 54p. (J). (gr. k-4). pap. *(978-952-7107-48-5(2))* Wickwick oy.

—Colin the Crab Falls in Love. Pere, Tuula. Korman, Susan, ed. 2018. (Colin the Crab Ser.: Vol. 3). (ENG.). 50p. (J). (gr. k-4). pap. *(978-952-7107-54-6(7))* Wickwick oy.

—Colin the Crab Finds a Treasure. Pere, Tuula. Korman, Susan, ed. 2018. (Colin the Crab Ser.: Vol. 2). (ENG.). 48p. (J). (gr. k-4). pap. *(978-952-7107-51-5(2))* Wickwick oy.

—Colin the Crab Gets Married. Pere, Tuula. Korman, Susan, ed. 2nd ed. 2019. (Colin the Crab Ser.: Vol. 4). (ENG.). 48p. (J). (gr. k-4). *(978-952-357-082-5(X))*; pap. *(978-952-357-081-8(1))* Wickwick oy.

—Den Hjälpsamma Krabban: Swedish Edition of the Caring Crab. Pere, Tuula. Torstensson, Elisabeth, tr. 2018. (Colin the Crab Ser.: Vol. 1). (SWE.). 54p. (J). (gr. k-4). pap. *(978-952-7107-50-8(4))* Wickwick oy.

—Isbjörnarnas Resa: Swedish Edition of the Polar Bears' Journey. Pere, Tuula. Nikolowski-Bogomoloff, Angelika, tr. 2018. (SWE.). 40p. (J). (gr. k-4). pap. *(978-952-7107-38-6(5))* Wickwick oy.

—Jääkarhujen Matka: Finnish Edition of the Polar Bears' Journey. Pere, Tuula. 2018. (FIN.). 40p. (J). (gr. k-4). pap. *(978-952-7107-37-9(7))* Wickwick oy.

—Kaj Krabba Blir Förälskad: Swedish Edition of Colin the Crab Falls in Love. Pere, Tuula. Torstensson, Elisabeth, tr. 2018. (Colin the Crab Ser.: Vol. 3). (SWE.). 50p. (J). (gr. k-4). pap. *(978-952-7107-56-0(3))* Wickwick oy.

—Kaj Krabba Finner en Skatt: Swedish Edition of Colin the Crab Finds a Treasure. Pere, Tuula. Torstensson, Elisabeth, tr. 2018. (Colin the Crab Ser.: Vol. 2). (SWE.). 48p. (J). (gr. k-4). pap. *(978-952-7107-53-9(9))* Wickwick oy.

—Kaj Krabba Gifter Sig: Swedish Edition of Colin the Crab Gets Married. Pere, Tuula. Torstensson, Elisabeth, tr. 2nd ed. 2019. (Kaj Krabba Ser.: Vol. 4). (SWE.). 48p. (J). (gr. k-4). *(978-952-357-086-3(2))*; pap. *(978-952-357-085-6(4))* Wickwick oy.

—The Lost Narwhal. McGee, Tori. 2019. (ENG.). 38p. (J). (gr. -1-2). 10.95 *(978-1-7339196-0-9(0))*; 17.95 *(978-1-7339196-1-6(9))* Rowboat Pr.

—The Polar Bears' Journey. Pere, Tuula. Korman, Susan, ed. 2018. (ENG.). 40p. (J). (gr. k-4). pap. *(978-952-7107-36-2(9))* Wickwick oy.

—Sloths Don't Run. McGee, Tori. 2018. (ENG.). 30p. (J). (gr. -1-3). 17.95 *(978-0-578-42401-9(0))* Rowboat Pr.

—Timo Taskurapu Ja Suuri Juhla: Finnish Edition of Colin the Crab Gets Married. Pere, Tuula. 2nd ed. 2019. (Timo Taskurapu Ser.: Vol. 4). (FIN.). 48p. (J). (gr. k-4). *(978-952-357-084-9(6))*; pap. *(978-952-357-083-2(8))* Wickwick oy.

—Timo Taskurapu Rakastuu: Finnish Edition of Colin the Crab Falls in Love. Pere, Tuula. 2018. (Colin the Crab Ser.: Vol. 3). (FIN.). 50p. (J). (gr. k-4). pap. *(978-952-7107-55-3(5))* Wickwick oy.

—Timo Taskuravun Aarre: Finnish Edition of Colin the Crab Finds a Treasure. Pere, Tuula. 2018. (Colin the Crab Ser.: Vol. 2). (FIN.). 48p. (J). (gr. k-4). pap. *(978-952-7107-52-2(0))* Wickwick oy.

—Ο; Καλόκαρδος; Κάβουρας ; Greek Edition of the Caring Crab. Pere, Tuula. Papakosta, Irene, tr. 2018. (Colin the Crab Ser.: Vol. 1). (GRE.). 54p. (J). (gr. k-4). pap. *(978-952-7107-85-0(7))*; ***(978-952-7107-86-7(5))*** Wickwick oy.

Panders, Wendy. Hey There, Earth Dweller! Dive into This World We Call Earth. Ter Horst, Marc. Watkinson, Laura, tr. 2019. (ENG.). 184p. (J). (gr. 3-7). 19.99 *(978-1-58270-656-6(5))* Aladdin/Beyond Words.

Pandu, Lingtang. Honey & the Bee. Brigger, Laura. 2020. (ENG.). 32p. (J). 14.95 ***(978-0-9963482-4-9(7))*** Galway Pr.

Pandya, Yamini. Nyagrodha. Kalpish Ratna. 2006. 287p. (J). *(978-0-670-04969-1(7)*, Puffin) Penguin Publishing Group.

Panelli, Leigha. Noah's Adventures with Grandma Jill & Grandpa Al: Grandma Jill & Grandpa Al Visit Three Year Old Noah & Spend Time with Him in the City. York, Albert. Meyer, Jill, ed. 2019. (ENG.). 28p. (J). pap. 9.99 ***(978-1-7126-3081-5(4))*** Independently Published.

Pang, Alex. Military Vehicles. Gilpin, Daniel. 2011. (Machines Close-Up Ser.). 32p. (gr. 4-4). 29.50 *(978-1-60870-109-4(3))* Cavendish Square Publishing LLC.

—Modern Military Aircraft. Gilpin, Daniel. 2011. (Machines Close-Up Ser.). 32p. (gr. 4-4). 29.50 *(978-1-60870-108-7(5))* Cavendish Square Publishing LLC.

—Modern Warships & Submarines. Gilpin, Daniel & West, David. 2011. (Machines Close-Up Ser.). 32p. (gr. 4-4). 29.50 *(978-1-60870-110-0(7))* Cavendish Square Publishing LLC.

—Record Breakers. Gilpin, Daniel. 2011. (Machines Close-Up Ser.). 32p. (gr. 4-4). 29.50 *(978-1-60870-113-1(1))* Cavendish Square Publishing LLC.

—Rescue Vehicles. Gilpin, Daniel. 2011. (Machines Close-Up Ser.). 32p. (gr. 4-4). 29.50 *(978-1-60870-111-7(5))* Cavendish Square Publishing LLC.

—Spacecraft. Gilpin, Daniel. 2011. (Machines Close-Up Ser.). 32p. (gr. 4-4). 29.50 *(978-1-60870-112-4(3))* Cavendish Square Publishing LLC.

—Speed Machines. Parker, Steve. 2010. (How It Works Ser.). 40p. (J). (gr. 3-18). lib. bdg. 19.95 *(978-1-4222-1800-6(7)*, 1317938) Mason Crest.

Pang, Alex, jt. illus. see Fox, Christyan.

Pang, Bonnie. Mvp: Most Valuable Puppy. Greenberg, Mike & Greenberg, Stacy Steponate. 2018. (ENG.). 32p. (J). (gr. -1-3). 17.99 *(978-1-4814-8931-7(3)*, Aladdin) Simon & Schuster Children's Publishing.

Pang, Bonnie. Prehistoric Deep Sea. Feldman, Thea. Cottage Door Press, ed. 2020. (Smithsonian Kids Deluxe Activity Book Ser.). (ENG.). 12p. (J). (gr. -1-1). bds. 12.99 ***(978-1-68052-946-3(3)***, 1005890) Cottage Door Pr.

Pang, Bonnie. Wild Bios: Amelia Harehart. Acampora, Courtney & Fischer, Maggie. 2019. (Wild Bios Ser.). (ENG.). 16p. (J). (— 1). bds. 7.99 *(978-1-68412-654-5(1)*, Silver Dolphin Bks.) Printers Row Publishing Group.

—Yao Bai & the Egg Pirates. Myers, Tim J. 2019. (ENG.). 32p. (J). (gr. 1-4). 16.99 *(978-1-5132-6144-7(4)*, West Margin Pr.) West Margin Pr.

Pang, YaWen Ariel. P Is for Pumpkin: God's Harvest Alphabet, 1 vol. Wargin, Kathy-jo. 2008. (ENG.). 40p. (J). (gr. -1-3). 15.99 *(978-0-310-71180-3(0))* Zonderkidz.

Pangbourne, Daniel. Learn with Me 123. Pangbourne, Daniel, photos by. Bulloch, Ivan & James, Diane. 2007. (ENG.). 46p. (J). (gr. -1 — 1). pap. 6.95 *(978-1-58728-622-3(X))* Cooper Square Publishing Llc.

Pangbourne, Daniel, photos by. Learn with Me ABC. Bulloch, Ivan & James, Diane. 2007. (ENG., 45p. (J). (gr. -1-3). pap. 6.95 *(978-1-58728-599-8(1))* Cooper Square Publishing Llc.

Pangburn, Shane. The Unbelievable Oliver & the Four Jokers. Bosch, Pseudonymous. (Unbelievable Oliver Ser.: 1). 192p. (J). (gr. 2-4). 2020. 7.99 *(978-0-525-55233-8(2)*, Puffin Books); 2019. 15.99 *(978-0-525-55232-1(4)*, Dial Bks) Penguin Young Readers Group.

—The Unbelievable Oliver & the Sawed-in-Half Dads. Bosch, Pseudonymous. 2020. (Unbelievable Oliver Ser.: 2). 208p. (J). (gr. 2-4). 7.99 *(978-0-525-55236-9(7)*, Puffin Books); 16.99 *(978-0-525-55235-2(9)*, Dial Bks) Penguin Young Readers Group.

Panju, Sakeena. Where Is My Imam? Kermalli, Shelina. 2017. (ENG.). 28p. (J). pap. ***(978-1-908110-42-8(2))*** Sunlight Pubns.

Pankey, Jill. Splash Tails. McBeth, Mary G. & Stokes, Fraye. 2018. (ENG.). 28p. (J). (gr. k-3). 20.00 *(978-0-692-06328-6(5))*; pap. 12.00 *(978-0-692-06303-3(X))* McBeth, Mary.

Pankhurst, Kate. Big Red Balloon. Fine, Anne. 2013. (Blue Bananas Ser.). (ENG.). 48p. (J). (gr. k-2). pap. 5.99 *(978-1-4052-5433-5(5))* Egmont Bks., Ltd. GBR. Dist: Independent Pubs. Group.

—Big Red Balloon. Fine, Anne. 2nd ed. 2016. (Reading Ladder Ser.). (ENG.). 48p. (J). (gr. k-2). 7.99 *(978-1-4052-8212-3(6))* Egmont Bks., Ltd. GBR. Dist: Independent Pubs. Group.

—A Friend in Need! Jarman, Julia. 2015. (Friends Ser.: 2). 96p. (J). (gr. 2-4). 11.99 *(978-1-84939-576-2(4))* Andersen Pr. GBR. Dist: Independent Pubs. Group.

—Make Friends Break Friends. Jarman, Julia. 2015. (Friends Ser.: 1). 96p. (J). (gr. 2-4). pap. 6.99 *(978-1-84939-509-0(8))* Andersen Pr. GBR. Dist: Independent Pubs. Group.

—New Friend Old Friends. Jarman, Julia. 2015. (Friends Ser.: 3). 112p. (J). (gr. 2-4). 6.99 *(978-1-78344-004-7(X))* Andersen Pr. GBR. Dist: Independent Pubs. Group.

—The Three Billy Goats Gruff. Tiger Tales. adapted ed. 2015. (My First Fairy Tales Ser.). (ENG.). 32p. (J). (gr. -1-2). 7.99 *(978-1-58925-459-6(7))* Tiger Tales.

Pankratz, Justin. Blue Monkey. 2003. (J). 5.95 *(978-0-9742637-0-0(2))* Pankratz Creations.

—Humpty Dumpty, Back Together Again? Summers, Sherri Pankratz. 2003. 32p. (J). 8.95 *(978-0-9742637-1-7(0))* Pankratz Creations.

Pannell, Nick. Daddy Keeps Us Free. Mann, Scott. 2011. 36p. pap. 24.95 *(978-1-4560-6075-6(9))* America Star Bks.

Panosian, Dan. The Amazing Spider-Man: the Spider-Man Secret! Behling, Steve. 2017. (ENG.). 48p. (J). (gr. 1-3). 10.99 *(978-1-4847-4928-9(6)*, Marvel Pr.) Disney Publishing Worldwide.

—Doom in a Box. Sudduth, Brent & Meredith Books Staff. 2008. 22p. (J). pap. 3.99 *(978-0-696-23956-4(6))* Meredith Bks.

—Grodd's Army. West, Tracey. 2010. (Batman: the Brave & the Bold Ser.). (ENG.). 64p. (J). (gr. 1-3). pap. 4.99 *(978-0-448-45384-2(3)*, Grosset & Dunlap) Penguin Publishing Group.
—Night of the Mummy. West, Tracey. 2010. (Batman: the Brave & the Bold Ser.). (ENG.). 64p. (J). (gr. 3-7). pap. 4.99 *(978-0-448-45339-2(8)*, Grosset & Dunlap) Penguin Publishing Group.
Panse, Sonal. Just Too Little. Miller, Judith J. 2013. 16p. pap. 9.95 *(978-1-61633-413-0(4))* Guardian Angel Publishing, Inc.
—Rescue Dog. Duncan, Al. 2005. (J). per. 10.00 *(978-0-9754298-6-0(8)*, Ithaca Pr.) Authors & Artists Publishers of New York, Inc.
Panske, Andy, jt. illus. see Goeddaeus, Donna.
Pantazis, Pete, jt. illus. see Di Vito, Andrea.
Pantazis, Peter, jt. illus. see Di Vito, Andrea.
Pantic, Dunja. Mom, Mac & Cheese, Please! Olin, Marilyn. 2013. 28p. (J). (gr. -1-k). 16.95 *(978-1-62087-995-5(6)*, 620995, Sky Pony Pr.) Skyhorse Publishing Co., Inc.
Pantoja, Maria Kristina. The Hundred-Dollar Robber: A Mystery with Money. Thielbar, Melinda. 2009. (Manga Math Mysteries Ser.: 2). (ENG.). 48p. (gr. 3-5). 29.27 *(978-0-7613-3854-3(3))* Lerner Publishing Group.
Pantoja, Maria Kristina Sb. The Ancient Formula No. 5: A Mystery with Fractions. Thielbar, Melinda. 2011. (Manga Math Mysteries Ser.: 5). (ENG.). 48p. (J). (gr. 3-5). pap. 6.95 *(978-0-7613-8134-1(1)*, 9780761381341, Graphic Universe™) Lerner Publishing Group.
—The Hundred-Dollar Robber: A Mystery with Money. Thielbar, Melinda. 2010. (Manga Math Mysteries Ser.: 2). (ENG.). 48p. (J). (gr. 3-5). pap. 6.95 *(978-0-7613-5243-3(0)*, 9780761352433, Graphic Universe™) Lerner Publishing Group.
—The Lost Key: A Mystery with Whole Numbers. Thielbar, Melinda. 2010. (Manga Math Mysteries Ser.: 1). (ENG.). 48p. (J). (gr. 3-5). pap. 6.95 *(978-0-7613-5244-0(9)*, 9780761352440, Graphic Universe™) Lerner Publishing Group.
Pantoja, Tintin. #5 the Ancient Formula: A Mystery with Fractions. Thielbar, Melinda. 2011. (Manga Math Mysteries Set II Ser.). pap. 39.62 *(978-0-7613-8362-8(X)*, Graphic Universe™) Lerner Publishing Group.
Pantoja, Tintin & Amante, Mike. Unplugged & Unpopular. Heagerty, Mat. 2019. (ENG.). 144p. (J). (gr. 5-8). pap. 12.99 *(978-1-62010-669-3(8)*, Lion Forge) Oni Pr., Inc.
Pantoja, Tintin, jt. illus. see Amante, Mike.
Pants, Pencil. Discombobulate. Pants, Marti. 2019. (Big Words for Little Nerds Ser.: Vol. 10). (ENG.). 48p. (J). pap. 10.50 *(978-1-7257-4465-3(1))* CreateSpace Independent Publishing Platform.
Paoletti, Laura. The Story of Antigone. Smith, Ali. 2019. (Save the Story Ser.: 1). (ENG.). 100p. (J). (gr. 3-7). pap. 12.95 *(978-1-78269-089-4(1)*, Pushkin Children's Bks.) Steerforth Pr.
Paolini, Alison. Carina & Her Care Partner Gramma. Hall, Kirk. 2013. 26p. 19.95 *(978-1-61314-158-8(0))*; pap. 15.95 *(978-1-61314-171-7(8))* Innovo Publishing, LLC.
—Carson & His Shaky Paws Grampa. Hall, Kirk. 2011. 24p. (J). pap. 15.95 *(978-1-61314-009-3(6))*; lib. bdg. 19.95 *(978-1-936076-91-8(8))* Innovo Publishing, LLC.
Paolo, Domeniconi. Colors of Nature. Riggs, Kate. 2017. (ENG.). 14p. (J). (gr. -1 — 1). bds. 8.99 *(978-1-56846-299-8(9)*, Creative Education) Creative Co., The.
Papademetriou, Lisa & Swaab, Neil. Middle School Box Set. Patterson, James et al. 2017. (Middle School Ser.). (ENG.). 1184p. (J). (gr. 3-7). 49.95 *(978-0-316-47651-5(X)*, Jimmy Patterson) Little Brown & Co.
Papadopulosová, Niké. The Big Book of Snow & Ice. Sekaninová, Štepánka. ed. 2017. (ENG.). 24p. (J). (gr. 2). 14.95 *(978-1-912006-83-0(9))* Book Hse. GBR. Dist: Sterling Publishing Co., Inc.
Papaleo, Antonio. The Kite Who Was Scared of Heights. Williams, Simon. 2013. 38p. pap. *(978-1-910053-36-2(8))* Legend Pr.
Papalia, Roberta. Home Ice Rivals. Maddox, Jake. 2020. (Jake Maddox Graphic Novels Ser.). (ENG.). 72p. (J). (gr. 3-6). pap. 6.95 ***(978-1-4965-9921-6(7)***, 201332); lib. bdg. 26.65 ***(978-1-4965-9710-6(9)***, 199332) Capstone. (Stone Arch Bks.).
Paparone, Pam. Flip, Float, Fly: Seeds on the Move. Macken, JoAnn Early. 2008. (ENG.). 32p. (J). (gr. 1-4). 17.95 *(978-0-8234-2043-8(4))* Holiday Hse., Inc.
—Flip, Float, Fly: Seeds on the Move. Macken, JoAnn Early. 2016. (ENG.). 32p. (J). (gr. 1-4). 8.99 *(978-0-8234-3758-0(2))* Holiday Hse., Inc.
—Where Do Chicks Come From? Sklansky, Amy E. 2005. (Let's-Read-and-Find-Out-Science Ser.). 40p. (J). (gr. -1-1). (ENG.). 15.99 *(978-0-06-028892-1(2))*; lib. bdg. 16.89 *(978-0-06-028893-8(0))*; (ENG.). pap. 6.99 *(978-0-06-445212-0(3))* HarperCollins Pubs.
Paparone, Pamela. A Big Surprise. Butler, Kristi T. 2005. (Green Light Readers Level 1 Ser.). (ENG.). 24p. (J). (gr. -1-3). pap. 4.99 *(978-0-15-205141-9(4)*, 1195515) Houghton Mifflin Harcourt Publishing Co.
—The Greatest Invention: The Story of Walter Hunt. Polette, Nancy. 2008. (ENG.). 32p. (J). *(978-0-15-205824-1(9))* Harcourt Trade Pubs.
—The Little School Bus. Roth, Carol. 32p. (J). 2012. (ENG.). (gr. -1-1). 22.44 *(978-0-7358-1646-6(8))*; 2004. (gr. k-1). pap. 8.95 *(978-0-7358-1905-4(X))* North-South Bks., Inc.
—Nobody Owns the Sky. Lindbergh, Reeve. 2004. 32p. (J). *(978-1-85269-342-8(8))*; *(978-1-85269-343-5(6))*; *(978-1-85269-344-2(4))*; *(978-1-85269-345-9(2))*; *(978-1-85269-347-3(9))* Mantra Lingua.
—Ten Dirty Pigs/Ten Clean Pigs: An Upside-Down, Turn-Around Bathtime Counting Book. Roth, Carol. 2008. 22p. (J). (gr. -1-k). bds. 7.95 *(978-0-7358-2213-9(1))* North-South Bks., Inc.
Papastathopoulos, Giorgos. Color Me Pretty (Indonesia) Pearson, Marti Whiting-. 2019. (ENG.). 48p. (J). pap. 10.35 *(978-1-0959-9776-5(9))* Independently Published.
—Where Are Your Manners. Pearson, Marti Whiting-. 2019. (ENG.). 50p. (J). pap. 10.53 *(978-1-0927-4470-6(3))* Independently Published.
Pape, Catherine. Can I Tell You about Being Jewish? A Helpful Introduction for Everyone. Cooper, Howard. 2019. (Can I Tell You About... ? Ser.). (ENG.). 88p. 14.95 ***(978-1-78592-491-0(5)***, 696828) Kingsley, Jessica Pubs. GBR. Dist: Hachette UK Distribution.
Pape, Catherine Noel. Psalms for My Day: A Child's Praise Devotional. MacKenzie, Carine & Motyer, Alec. rev. ed. 2019. (ENG.). 96p. (J). 17.99 *(978-1-5271-0181-4(9)*, 4adf867f-bfa8-489c-8cbd-118be6873637, CF4Kids) Christian Focus Pubns. GBR. Dist: Baker & Taylor Publisher Services (BTPS).
Pape, Frank & Millar, H. R. The Diamond Fairy Book: From the Many Countries. Vairous. 2019. (ENG.). 262p. (J). (gr. k-4). ***(978-605-7748-64-5(6))***; pap. *(978-605-7876-44-7(X))* Uhrayoglu, Murat E Kitap Projesi.
Pape, Frank C. The Russian Story Book. Wilson, Richard. 2019. (ENG.). 278p. (J). (gr. k-4). ***(978-605-7748-84-3(0))***; pap. *(978-605-7876-84-3(9))* Uhrayoglu, Murat E Kitap Projesi.
Pape, Jane. Adventures of the Six Cousins. Blyton, Enid. 2013. 330p. (J). 16.50 *(978-1-84135-589-4(5))* Award Pubns. Ltd. GBR. Dist: Parkwest Pubns., Inc.
Pape, Wendy Fehrle. Tea & Cookie. LeBlanc, Ellen Lieb. 2005. (J). bds. *(978-0-9773010-0-3(1))* Talmage Publishing.
Papeo, Maria Eugenia & Saumell, Marina. Why Is My Name Sam? Canady, Mary Monica. 2008. 24p. pap. 24.95 *(978-1-60474-028-8(0))* America Star Bks.
Paperman, Ross. The Black Velvet Jacket. Litwin, Suzanne Reisler. 2016. (ENG.). 40p. (J). pap. *(978-1-939288-43-1(6))* Suzie I.N.K.
Papetti, Marina. I Mostri Delle Ragazze Riot. Piccoli, Anaïs. 2019. (ITA.). 152p. (J). pap. 6.66 ***(978-1-0791-9647-4(1))*** Independently Published.
Papi, Liza. Carnavalia! African-Brazilian Folklore & Crafts. Papi, Liza. 2004. 48p. (J). (gr. k-4). reprint ed. 20.00 *(978-0-7567-7760-9(7))* DIANE Publishing Co.
Papierowska, Marta. Wiara Malego Powstanca. Speer, Wendell. 2019. (POL.). 106p. (J). (gr. 3-6). pap. 6.99 ***(978-0-9983113-2-6(4))*** Magic Space.
Papillion, Allison. Penelope Pencil: A Story of Writing Imagination. Ibrahim, Benita & Ibrahim, Joshua. 2018. (ENG.). 28p. (J). 11.99 *(978-1-945464-98-0(4))* Heritage Pr. Pubns., LLC.
Papish, Adam. Sissy's Christmas Program. Seglie, Susan & Schiefelbein, Janis. Zagorski, Astrid, tr. 2003. (ENG & SPA.). (J). 4.95 *(978-0-9747243-1-7(9))* Seglie, Susan M.
Papish, Ram & Papish, Ram. The Little Fox: An Alaska Adventure. Papish, Ram. 2nd ed. 2008. (ENG.). 38p. (gr. 3-7). 15.95 *(978-1-889963-87-7(9))* Univ. of Alaska Pr.
Papish, Ram, jt. illus. see Papish, Ram.
Paplinksie, Cecilia. Color Me Happy. Harris, Sally M. 2009. 24p. pap. 10.95 *(978-1-935137-75-7(1))* Guardian Angel Publishing, Inc.
Papoulas, Ted. The Sound of All Things, 1 vol. Uhlberg, Myron. 2016. (ENG.). 36p. (J). (gr. 1-5). 17.95 *(978-1-56145-833-2(3))* Peachtree Publishing Co. Inc.
Papp, Kathy, jt. illus. see Papp, Robert.
Papp, Lisa. My Mom's Wedding. Bunting, Eve. 2006. (ENG.). 32p. (J). (gr. k-6). 16.95 *(978-1-58536-288-2(3))* Sleeping Bear Pr.
—One for All: A Pennsylvania Number Book. Noble, Trinka Hakes. 2005. (Count Your Way Across the USA Ser.). (ENG.). 40p. (J). (gr. k-5). 16.95 *(978-1-58536-200-4(X))* Sleeping Bear Pr.
Papp, Lisa. Madeline Finn & the Library Dog. Papp, Lisa. (ENG.). 32p. (J). (gr. -1-3). 2020. pap. 8.99 *(978-1-68263-059-4(5))*; 2016. 17.95 *(978-1-56145-910-0(0))* Peachtree Publishing Co. Inc.
—Madeline Finn & the Shelter Dog. Papp, Lisa. 2019. (ENG.). 32p. (J). (gr. -1-3). 17.95 *(978-1-68263-075-4(7))* Peachtree Publishing Co. Inc.
Papp, Lisa. Madeline Finn & the Therapy Dog. Papp, Lisa. 2020. (ENG.). 32p. (J). (gr. -1-3). 17.99 ***(978-1-68263-149-2(4))*** Peachtree Publishing Co. Inc.
Papp, Lisa & Papp, Robert. The Town That Fooled the British: A War of 1812 Story. Papp, Lisa & Papp, Robert. 2011. (Tales of Young Americans Ser.). (ENG.). 32p. (J). (gr. 1-4). 16.95 *(978-1-58536-484-8(3)*, 202192) Sleeping Bear Pr.
Papp, Lisa, jt. illus. see Papp, Robert.
Papp, Robert. The Amazing Mystery Show. 2010. (Boxcar Children Mysteries Ser.: 123). (ENG.). 128p. (J). (gr. 1-5). pap. 6.99 *(978-0-8075-0315-7(0)*, 807503150);No. 123. 14.99 *(978-0-8075-0314-0(2)*, 807503142) Whitman, Albert & Co.
—Anna Maria's Gift. Shefelman, Janice Jordan. 2010. (Stepping Stones Chapter Book: History Ser.). (ENG.). 112p. (J). (gr. 1-4). lib. bdg. 17.44 *(978-0-375-95881-6(9))* Random House Publishing Group.
—Anna Maria's Gift: Stepping Stone Book(TM) Ser.). 112p. (J). (gr. 2-5). pap. 4.99 *(978-0-375-85882-6(2)*, Random Hse. Bks. for Young Readers) Random Hse. Children's Bks.
—The Battles. Papp, Lisa & Noble, Trinka Hakes. 2013. (American Adventures Ser.). (ENG.). (J). (gr. 3-6). lib. bdg. 21.10 *(978-1-62765-944-4(7))* Perfection Learning Corp.
—The Battles. Papp, Lisa & Noble, Trinka Hakes. 2013. (American Adventures Ser.). (ENG.). 88p. (J). (gr. 2-4). pap. 24.94 *(978-1-58536-861-7(X)*, 202368) Sleeping Bear Pr.
—Best Friends Forever? Medearis, Angela Shelf. 2004. 124p. (J). *(978-0-439-52330-1(3))* Scholastic, Inc.
—The Box That Watch Found. 2007. (Boxcar Children Mysteries Ser.: 113). (ENG.). 128p. (J). (gr. 1-5). lib. bdg. 14.99 *(978-0-8075-5568-2(1)*, 807555681); per. 5.99 *(978-0-8075-5569-9(X)*, 080755569X) Whitman, Albert & Co.
—The Clue in the Recycling Bin. 2011. (Boxcar Children Mysteries Ser.: 126). (ENG.). 128p. (J). (gr. 1-5). pap. 6.99 *(978-0-8075-1209-8(5)*, 807512095) Whitman, Albert & Co.
—The Clue in the Recycling Bin. 2011. (Boxcar Children Mysteries Ser.: 126). (ENG.). 128p. (J). (gr. 1-5). lib. bdg. 14.99 *(978-0-8075-1208-1(7)*, 807512087) Whitman, Albert & Co.
—The Creature in Ogopogo Lake. 2006. (Boxcar Children Mysteries Ser.: 108). (ENG.). 128p. (J). (gr. 1-5). per. 6.99 *(978-0-8075-1337-8(7)*, 807513377) Whitman, Albert & Co.
—The Cupcake Caper. 2010. (Boxcar Children Mysteries Ser.: 125). (ENG.). 128p. (J). (gr. 1-5). 14.99 *(978-0-8075-1373-6(3)*, 807513733);No. 125. pap. 5.99 *(978-0-8075-1374-3(1)*, 807513741) Whitman, Albert & Co.
—Encyclopedia Brown & the Case of the Jumping Frogs. Sobol, Donald J. 2005. (Encyclopedia Brown Ser.). 69p. (J). (gr. 3-7). 13.15 *(978-0-7569-5100-9(3))* Perfection Learning Corp.
—The Game Store Mystery. 2005. (Boxcar Children Mysteries Ser.: 104). (ENG.). 144p. (J). (gr. 1-5). per. 6.99 *(978-0-8075-2739-9(4)*, 807527394) Whitman, Albert & Co.
—The Ghost in the First Row, Vol. 112. 2007. (Boxcar Children Mysteries Ser.: 112). (ENG.). 128p. (J). (gr. 1-5). per. 5.99 *(978-0-8075-5567-5(3)*, 807555673) Whitman, Albert & Co.
—The Ghost of the Chattering Bones. 2007. (Boxcar Children Ser.). 120p. 15.00 *(978-0-7569-7611-8(1))* Perfection Learning Corp.
—The Ghost of the Chattering Bones. 2005. (Boxcar Children Mysteries Ser.: 102). (ENG.). 128p. (J). (gr. 1-5). pap. 5.99 *(978-0-8075-0874-9(8)*, 807508748) Whitman, Albert & Co.
—The Giant Yo-Yo Mystery. 2006. (Boxcar Children Mysteries Ser.: 107). (ENG.). 128p. (J). (gr. 1-5). per. 5.99 *(978-0-8075-0879-4(9)*, 807508799) Whitman, Albert & Co.
—The Great Detective Race. 2008. (Boxcar Children Mysteries Ser.: 115). (ENG.). 128p. (J). (gr. 1-5). 14.99 *(978-0-8075-5573-6(8)*, 807555738) Whitman, Albert & Co.
—The Great Detective Race. 2008. (Boxcar Children Mysteries Ser.: 115). (ENG.). 128p. (J). (gr. 1-5). pap. 5.99 *(978-0-8075-5574-3(6)*, 807555746) Whitman, Albert & Co.
—The Great Turkey Heist. 2011. (Boxcar Children Mysteries Ser.: 129). (ENG.). (J). (gr. 1-5). 144p. 6.99 *(978-0-8075-3051-1(4)*, 807530514); 128p. lib. bdg. 14.99 *(978-0-8075-3050-4(6)*, 807530506) Whitman, Albert & Co.
—A Horse Named Dragon. 2008. (Boxcar Children Mysteries Ser.: 114). (ENG.). 128p. (J). (gr. 1-5). lib. bdg. 14.99 *(978-0-8075-5571-2(1)*, 807555711); per. 5.99 *(978-0-8075-5572-9(X)*, 080755572X) Whitman, Albert & Co.
—Lanie, Bk. 1. Kurtz, Jane. Hirsch, Jennifer, ed. 2010. (American Girl: Lanie Ser.). (ENG.). 112p. (J). (gr. 2-4). pap. 21.19 *(978-1-59369-682-5(5))* American Girl Publishing, Inc.
—Lanie's Real Adventures. Kurtz, Jane. 2010. (American Girl Today Ser.). (ENG.). 112p. (YA). (gr. 3-18). 12.95 *(978-1-59369-685-6(X))* American Girl Publishing, Inc.
—The Last Brother: A Civil War Tale. Noble, Trinka Hakes. 2006. (Tales of Young Americans Ser.). (ENG.). 48p. (J). (gr. 1-4). 17.95 *(978-1-58536-253-0(0)*, 202069) Sleeping Bear Pr.
—M Is for Meow: A Cat Alphabet. Wilbur, Helen L. rev. ed. 2006. (ENG.). 40p. (J). (gr. 1-4). 19.99 *(978-1-58536-304-9(9)*, 202109) Sleeping Bear Pr.
—Monkey Trouble. 2011. (Boxcar Children Mysteries Ser.: 127). (ENG.). 128p. (J). (gr. 1-5). pap. 5.99 *(978-0-8075-5240-7(2)*, 807552402) Whitman, Albert & Co.
—Monkey Trouble. 2011. (Boxcar Children Mysteries Ser.: 127). (ENG.). 128p. (J). (gr. 1-5). lib. bdg. 14.99 *(978-0-8075-5239-1(9)*, 807552399) Whitman, Albert & Co.
—The Mystery of the Orphan Train. 2005. (Boxcar Children Mysteries Ser.: 105). (ENG.). 128p. (J). (gr. 1-5). lib. bdg. 14.99 *(978-0-8075-5558-3(4)*, 807555584); per. 6.99 *(978-0-8075-5559-0(2)*, 807555592) Whitman, Albert & Co.
—The Pumpkin Head Mystery, No. 124. 2010. (Boxcar Children Mysteries Ser.: 124). (ENG.). 128p. (J). (gr. 1-5). pap. 5.99 *(978-0-8075-6669-5(1)*, 807566691) Whitman, Albert & Co.
—Quake! Disaster in San Francisco 1906, 1 vol. Karwoski, Gail Langer. 2004. (ENG.). 192p. (J). (gr. 3-7). 15.95 *(978-1-56145-310-8(2))* Peachtree Publishing Co. Inc.
—The Rock 'n' Roll Mystery. 2006. (Boxcar Children Mysteries Ser.: 109). (ENG.). 128p. (J). (gr. 1-5). lib. bdg. 14.99 *(978-0-8075-7089-0(3)*, 807570893); per. 5.99 *(978-0-8075-7090-6(7)*, 807570907) Whitman, Albert & Co.
—The Scarlet Stockings Spy. Noble, Trinka Hakes. 2004. (Tales of Young Americans Ser.). (ENG.). 48p. (J). (gr. 1-4). 16.95 *(978-1-58536-230-1(1)*, 202055) Sleeping Bear Pr.
—The Seattle Puzzle. 2007. (Boxcar Children Mysteries Ser.: 111). (ENG.). 128p. (J). (gr. 1-5). lib. bdg. 14.99 *(978-0-8075-5560-6(6)*, 807555606); per. 5.99 *(978-0-8075-5561-3(4)*, 807555614) Whitman, Albert & Co.
—The Secret of the Mask. 2007. (Boxcar Children Mysteries Ser.: 110). (ENG.). 128p. (J). (gr. 1-5). lib. bdg. 14.99 *(978-0-8075-5564-4(9)*, 807555649); per. 5.99 *(978-0-8075-5565-1(7)*, 807555657) Whitman, Albert & Co.
—Spooktacular Special. 2013. (Boxcar Children Mysteries Ser.). (ENG.). 400p. (J). (gr. 1-5). 9.99 *(978-0-8075-7605-2(0)*, 807576050) Whitman, Albert & Co.
—The Spy Game. 2009. (Boxcar Children Mysteries Ser.: 118). (ENG.). 128p. (J). (gr. 1-5). pap. 5.99 *(978-0-8075-7604-5(2)*, 807576042) Whitman, Albert & Co.
—The Spy in the Bleachers. 2010. (Boxcar Children Mysteries Ser.: 122). (ENG.). 128p. (J). (gr. 1-5). 14.99 *(978-0-8075-7606-9(9)*, 807576069);No. 122. pap. 6.99 *(978-0-8075-7607-6(7)*, 807576077) Whitman, Albert & Co.
—The Sword of the Silver Knight. 2005. (Boxcar Children Mysteries Ser.: 103). (ENG.). 128p. (J). (gr. 1-5). per. 6.99 *(978-0-8075-0876-3(4)*, 807508764) Whitman, Albert & Co.
—Titanicat. Crisp, Marty. 2008. (ENG.). 40p. (J). (gr. k-6). 17.95 *(978-1-58536-355-1(3))* Sleeping Bear Pr.
—The Zombie Project. 2011. (Boxcar Children Mysteries Ser.: 128). (ENG.). 128p. (J). (gr. 1-5). 6.99 *(978-0-8075-9493-3(8)*, 807594938); lib. bdg. 14.99 *(978-0-8075-9492-6(X)*, 080759492X) Whitman, Albert & Co.
Papp, Robert & Papp, Kathy. The Pumpkin Head Mystery. 2010. (Boxcar Children Mysteries Ser.: 124). (ENG.). 128p. (J). (gr. 1-5). 14.99 *(978-0-8075-6668-8(3)*, 807566683) Whitman, Albert & Co.
Papp, Robert & Papp, Lisa. P Is for Princess: A Royal Alphabet. Layne, Deborah & Layne, Steven. rev. ed. 2007. (ENG.). 40p. (J). (gr. k-6). 17.95 *(978-1-58536-306-3(5))* Sleeping Bear Pr.
Papp, Robert, jt. illus. see Papp, Lisa.
Papp, Robert L. The Dog-Gone Mystery. 2009. (Boxcar Children Mysteries Ser.: 119). (ENG.). 128p. (J). (gr. 1-5). pap. 6.99 *(978-0-8075-1657-7(0)*, 807516570) Whitman, Albert & Co.
—The Spy Game. 2009. (Boxcar Children Mysteries Ser.: 118). (ENG.). 128p. (J). (gr. 1-5). 14.99 *(978-0-8075-7603-8(4)*, 807576034) Whitman, Albert & Co.
—Superstar Watch. 2009. (Boxcar Children Mysteries Ser.: 121). (ENG.). 128p. (J). (gr. 1-5). pap. 6.99 *(978-0-8075-7668-7(9)*, 807576689); lib. bdg. 14.99 *(978-0-8075-7667-0(0)*, 807576670) Whitman, Albert & Co.
—The Vampire Mystery. 2009. (Boxcar Children Mysteries Ser.: 120). (ENG.). 128p. (J). (gr. 1-5). pap. 6.99 *(978-0-8075-8461-3(4)*, 807584614) Whitman, Albert & Co.
Paprocki, Greg. A Is for Atom: A Midcentury Alphabet, 1 vol. 2016. 32p. (J). bds. 9.99 *(978-1-4236-4426-2(3))* Gibbs Smith, Publisher.
—Baby Loves Political Science: Democracy! Spiro, Ruth. 2020. (Baby Loves Science Ser.). 20p. (J). (— 1). bds. 8.99 *(978-1-62354-227-6(8))* Charlesbridge Publishing, Inc.
—C Is for Castle: A Medieval Primer, 1 vol. 2016. 32p. (J). bds. 9.99 *(978-1-4236-4281-7(3))* Gibbs Smith, Publisher.
—D Is for Dreidel: A Hanukkah Alphabet, 1 vol. 2018. 32p. (J). bds. 9.99 *(978-1-4236-5038-6(7))* Gibbs Smith, Publisher.
—G Is for Go-Go: A Sixties Alphabet, 1 vol. 2017. (ENG.). 32p. (J). bds. 9.99 *(978-1-4236-4667-9(3))* Gibbs Smith, Publisher.
—J Is for Jazz: A Roaring Twenties Alphabet, 1 vol. 2017. (ENG.). 32p. (J). bds. 9.99 *(978-1-4236-4604-4(5))* Gibbs Smith, Publisher.
—Little Leonardo's Fascinating World of Engineering, 1 vol. Cooper, Bob. 2018. 24p. (J). 12.99 *(978-1-4236-4957-1(5))* Gibbs Smith, Publisher.
—Little Leonardo's Fascinating World of Math, 1 vol. Cooper, Bob. 2018. 24p. (J). bds. 12.99 *(978-1-4236-4936-6(2))* Gibbs Smith, Publisher.
—Little Leonardo's Fascinating World of Science, 1 vol. Cooper, Bob. 2018. 24p. (J). 12.99 *(978-1-4236-4874-1(9))* Gibbs Smith, Publisher.
—Little Leonardo's Fascinating World of Technology, 1 vol. Cooper, Bob. 2018. 24p. (J). 12.99 *(978-1-4236-4956-4(7))* Gibbs Smith, Publisher.
—Little Leonardo's Fascinating World of the Arts, 1 vol. Cooper, Bob. 2018. 24p. (J). bds. 12.99 *(978-1-4236-4873-4(0))* Gibbs Smith, Publisher.
—M Is for Monocle - Victorian Alphabet, 1 vol. 2016. 32p. (J). bds. 9.99 *(978-1-4236-4284-8(8))* Gibbs Smith, Publisher.
—Makerlab Robots, 1 vol. King, Bart. 2019. 32p. (J). 12.99 *(978-1-4236-5116-1(2))* Gibbs Smith, Publisher.
—Makerlab Space, 1 vol. King, Bart. 2019. 32p. (J). 12.99 *(978-1-4236-5115-4(4))* Gibbs Smith, Publisher.
—Math-Terpieces: The Art of Problem-Solving. Tang, Greg. 2003. (ENG.). 32p. (J). (gr. 2-5). 18.99 *(978-0-439-44388-3(1))* Scholastic, Inc.
—R Is for Railway: An Industrial Revolution Alphabet, 1 vol. 2016. 32p. bds. 9.99 *(978-1-4236-4423-1(9))* Gibbs Smith, Publisher.
—S Is for Sabertooth: a Stone Age Alphabet, 1 vol. 2016. 32p. (J). bds. 9.99 *(978-1-4236-4420-0(4))* Gibbs Smith, Publisher.
—S Is for School: A Classroom Alphabet, 1 vol. 2018. (BabyLit Ser.). 32p. (J). bds. 9.99 *(978-1-4236-4958-8(3))* Gibbs Smith, Publisher.
—Storyland: the Marvelous Mccrittersons — Road Trip to Grandma's: A Story Coloring Book. Paprocki, Beth. 2015. (ENG.). 32p. (J). (gr. k-5). pap. 3.99 *(978-0-486-79383-2(4))* Dover Pubns., Inc.
—Wild West Alphabet, 1 vol. 2016. (ENG.). 32p. (J). bds. 9.99 *(978-1-4236-4251-0(1))* Gibbs Smith, Publisher.
Paprocki, Greg, jt. illus. see Anderson, Derek.
Papson, Kylie. The Magnificent Journey of Roopert the Scribe & the Great Princess Paasha. Robinson, Beatriz M. 2018. (ENG.). 66p. (J). 33.99 *(978-1-68314-837-1(1))*; pap. 23.99 *(978-1-68314-695-7(6))* Redemption Pr.
Paquette, Denise. Lilybella et le Don des Fées. Lavallee, Jeannie. 2013. (FRE.). 94p. (J). pap. *(978-2-349-72292-8(9))* Editions La Grande Maree.
Paquette, John R. The Little Purple Mardi Gras Bead, 1 vol. Rowley, Julie P. 2016. (ENG.). 32p. pap. 8.99 *(978-1-4556-2344-0(X)*, Pelican Publishing) Arcadia Publishing.
Paquette Jr., Edward D. Kammy the Chameleon Goes to School. Paquette, Heather. 2012. 24p. pap. 24.95 *(978-1-62709-765-9(1))* America Star Bks.

P

Paquin, Pauline. Carry Me Mama, 1 vol. Devine, Monica. 2005. (ENG.). 32p. (J). (gr. k-2). pap. 9.95 *(978-1-55005-150-6(4),* dca77f29-5bf9-48bf-bb03-2b9b837a2c79) Fitzhenry & Whiteside, Ltd. CAN. Dist: Firefly Bks., Ltd.

Paradero, Shannen Marie. The Adventures of Princess Jordan 1: Forest Magic — Believe! Asbroek, Karen. 2017. (ENG.). 24p. (J). pap. 20.69 *(978-1-5434-0578-1(9));* 34.49 *(978-1-5434-0579-8(7))* Xlibris Corp.

—The Adventures of Princess Jordan 2: Green Grass Romp. Asbroek, Karen. 2017. (ENG.). 24p. pap. 20.69 *(978-1-5434-0581-1(9))* Xlibris Corp.

—The Adventures of Princess Jordan 3: Cloud Hopping. Asbroek, Karen. 2017. (ENG.). 24p. pap. 20.69 *(978-1-5434-0583-5(5))* Xlibris Corp.

Paradero, Shannen Marie. Maks & Mama. Sanchez, Tawny. 2020. (ENG.). 34p. (J). pap. 14.99 ***(978-1-6641-2167-6(6))*** Xlibris Corp.

Paradis & Legdani, Sanaa. Texas Monsters. Paradis. 2017. (ENG.). 22p. (gr. -1). bds. 9.99 *(978-2-924734-07-0(X))* City Monsters Bks. CAN. Dist: Publishers Group West (PGW).

Paradisi, Eros. Saint George & the Dragon. del Rosso, Chiara. 2019. (ENG.). 34p. (J). pap. 9.90 *(978-1-0917-6506-1(5))* Independently Published.

Parajes, Danilo. Priscilla & the Sandman. Roseberg, Anders. 2016. (ENG.). (J). pap. *(978-957-43-3967-9(X))* Rui xing tu shu gu fen you xian gong si.

Paramonova, Lea. Princess Charming. Wildsmith, Sarah. 2013. 32p. pap. 14.99 *(978-1-62380-970-6(3),* Harmony Ink Pr.) Dreamspinner Pr.

Paramore, Leslie. Anything's Possible: Anything Goes! The Sparkler Princess. Paramore, Scott, ed. 2018. (Imagination Ser.: Vol. 1). (ENG.). 50p. (J). (gr. k-2). pap. 9.95 *(978-0-692-15585-1(6))* Heart-centered Productions.

—Anything's Possible. Anything Goes! The Sparkler Princess. Paramore, Scott, ed. 2017. (Imagination Ser.: Vol. 1). (ENG.). 50p. (J). (gr. k-2). 14.95 *(978-0-692-15583-7(X))* Heart-centered Productions.

Parasca, Alma. The Heart-Seed. Fourneau, Sacha. 2018. (ENG.). 26p. (J). pap. 10.49 *(978-1-7309-0287-1(1))* Independently Published.

Paraschiv, Doina. Christopher's Adventures: A Prayer on Angel Wings. Parr, Susan Sherwood. 2004. (ENG.). 16p. 10.95 *(978-0-9728590-3-5(9),* Kid-E Bks.) Word Productions LLC.

—Christopher's Adventures: Chris Visits the Hospital, Vol. 2. Parr, Susan Sherwood. 2nd alt. ed. 2013. (ENG.). 24p. (J). pap. 8.95 *(978-0-9827998-8-8(8),* Kid-E Bks.) Word Productions LLC.

Paraschiv, Doina. Safety Safari. Wilhoite, Joellen. 2015. (ENG.). 40p. (J). pap. 9.95 ***(978-1-938905-55-1(5),*** Joey Bks.) Acclaim Pr., Inc.

Paraskevas, Michael. Peter Pepper's Pet Spectacular. Paraskevas, Betty. 2007. 32p. (J). (gr. 2-6). pap. 14.95 *(978-1-60095-257-9(7))* Carson-Dellosa Publishing, LLC.

—Poetry for Kids: Robert Frost. Frost, Robert. Parini, Jay, ed. 2017. (Poetry for Kids Ser.). (ENG.). 48p. (J). (gr. 3-8). 16.95 *(978-1-63322-220-5(9),* Moondance) Quarto Publishing Group USA.

Parathian, Hannah. Peppy - a Long Way from Home. Hevesi, Rachel. 2008. 48p. pap. *(978-1-906210-76-2(4))* Grosvenor Hse. Publishing Ltd.

Parchow, Marc, et al. Challenging Dot-To-Dot: 68 Timed Puzzles to Test Your Skill. Poitier, Anton. 2016. (Challlenging... Bks.). (ENG.). 96p. (J). (gr. 3-7). pap. 7.99 *(978-1-4380-0932-2(1),* B.E.S. Publishing) Peterson's.

—Incredible Dot to Dot: Over 75 Timed Puzzles to Test Your Skills. 2017. (Challenging... Bks.). (ENG.). 96p. (J). (gr. 3-7). pap. 7.99 *(978-1-4380-1085-4(0),* B.E.S. Publishing) Peterson's.

Parchow, Marc, jt. illus. see Lombardo, Giulia.

Parchow, Marc, jt. illus. see Mallet, Lisa.

Parcus, Stephanie. Jupiter Storm. gif. ltd. ed. 2017. 256p. (J). (gr. 3-6). pap. 14.99 *(978-1-943169-31-3(4))* Plum Street Press.

—Leah & Rhea: Spell: Book 1. Helms, Melissa Hines. 2018. (ENG.). 140p. (J). pap. 7.99 *(978-0-9969893-1-2(5))* Helmshines.

Parda, Piotr. Graduation Day. Parda, Piotr. 2017. (ENG.). 52p. (J). (gr. k-2). 18.99 *(978-0-9913866-7-3(1))* Ripple Grove Pr.

Pardi, Charlotte. Cry, Heart, but Never Break. Ringtved, Glenn. Moulthrop, Robert, tr. 2016. 32p. (J). (gr. -1-3). 16.95 *(978-1-59270-187-2(6))* Enchanted Lion Bks., LLC.

Pardo DeLange, Alex. Esteban de Luna, Baby Rescuer / Esteban de Luna, ¡rescatador de Bebés! Mercado-López, Larissa. 2017. (ENG & SPA.). 32p. (J). (gr. k-3). 17.95 *(978-1-55885-847-3(4),* Piñata Books) Arte Publico Pr.

—Pepita & the Bully: Pepita y la Peleonera. Lachtman, Ofelia Dumas. Baeza Ventura, Gabriela, tr. 2011. (SPA & ENG.). 32p. (J). (gr. -1-3). 16.95 *(978-1-55885-689-9(7),* Piñata Books) Arte Publico Pr.

Paredes, Donna. Cassandra & the Night Sky. Jackson, Amy. 2017. (ENG.). 32p. (J). 18.95 *(978-1-942945-40-6(X),* 49eca96b-cf91-4cdf-8f3c-fc62e05db54b) Night Heron Media.

Paredes, Rub. Los Mundos de Julia. Paredes, Alberto Rodriguez. 2018. (SPA.). 28p. (J). pap. 10.25 *(978-1-7908-4881-2(4))* Independently Published.

Parekh, Rikin. The Beekeeper. Morgan, Bernard. Emecz, Steve, ed. 2007. 28p. per. *(978-1-904312-26-0(8))* MX Publishing, Ltd.

—Pszczelarz. Morgan, Bernard P. Juraszek, Barbara, tr. 2008. 28p. pap. *(978-1-904312-44-4(6))* MX Publishing, Ltd.

Parel, Gerald. Iron Man: Invincible Origins. 2019. (ENG.). 144p. (gr. 10-17). pap. 15.99 *(978-0-7851-6671-9(8))* Marvel Worldwide, Inc.

Parent, Dan. Archie Meets Glee. Aguirre-Sacasa, Roberto. 2013. (Archie & Friends All-Stars Ser.: 20). (ENG.). 112p. (J). (gr. 5). pap. 12.99 *(978-1-936975-45-7(9))* Archie Comic Pubns., Inc.

Parent, Lauren. I'm Different but I'm Special. Parent, Lauren. l.t. ed. 2006. 21p. (J). (gr. -1-3). per. 10.99 *(978-1-59879-259-1(8))* Lifevest Publishing, Inc.

Parent, Samuel & Sampar. Do You Know Owls?, 1 vol. Quintin, Michel & Bergeron, Alain M. Dollison, Pamela D., tr. 2019. (Do You Know? Ser.). (ENG.). 64p. (J). (gr. 2-4). 9.95 *(978-1-55455-352-5(0),* 9a06904f-5aee-4afd-ab26-c220b289bf08) Fitzhenry & Whiteside, Ltd. CAN. Dist: Firefly Bks., Ltd.

—Do You Know Piranhas?, 1 vol. Quintin, Michel & Bergeron, Alain M. Dollison, Pamela D., tr. 2019. (Do You Know? Ser.). (ENG.). 64p. (J). (gr. 2-4). 9.95 *(978-1-55455-353-2(9),* 11a38aae-79fd-469b-9280-298588e90f11) Fitzhenry & Whiteside, Ltd. CAN. Dist: Firefly Bks., Ltd.

Parett, Lisa. The Girls' Life Guide to Being a Style Superstar! Lundsten, Apryl. 2004. 124p. (J). *(978-0-439-44984-7(7))* Scholastic, Inc.

—The Girls' Life Guide to Being the Best You! White, Kelly. 2003. 124p. (J). *(978-0-439-44978-6(2))* Scholastic, Inc.

Paris, Pat. Jesus Walks Away. Carolyn, Berg. 2003. (Arch Bks.). 16p. (J). 2.49 *(978-0-7586-0504-7(8))* Concordia Publishing Hse.

—A Meal for Many: My Gift for Jesus. Rottmann, Erik. 2003. (Arch Bks.). (ENG.). 16p. (J). (gr. k-4). 1.99 *(978-0-7586-0377-7(0))* Concordia Publishing Hse.

Parish, Shannon. The Best Belcher. Medlyn, Lynda Lee & Staudenmier, Kelley Anne. 2008. (ENG.). 32p. (J). (gr. k-2). lib. bdg. *(978-0-9793738-0-0(8))* Window Box Pr. LLC.

—The Monster Solution. Zimet, Sara Goodman. 2005. 32p. (J). 16.95 *(978-0-9645159-1-8(1),* 1245168) Discovery Pr. Pubns., Inc.

Parish, Steve. Clown Fish Finds a Friend. Johnson, Rebecca. 2005. (Animal Storybooks Ser.). 24p. (gr. k-3). lib. bdg. 23.00 *(978-0-8368-5969-0(3),* Gareth Stevens Learning Library) Stevens, Gareth Publishing LLLP.

—The Kangaroos' Great Escape. 2005. (Animal Storybooks Ser.). 24p. (gr. k-3). lib. bdg. 23.00 *(978-0-8368-5971-3(5),* Gareth Stevens Learning Library) Stevens, Gareth Publishing LLLP.

—Little Dolphin's Big Leap. Johnson, Rebecca. 2005. (Animal Storybooks Ser.). 24p. (gr. k-3). lib. bdg. 23.00 *(978-0-8368-5973-7(1),* Gareth Stevens Learning Library) Stevens, Gareth Publishing LLLP.

—The Proud Pelican's Secret. Johnson, Rebecca. 2005. (Animal Storybooks Ser.). 24p. (gr. k-3). lib. bdg. 23.00 *(978-0-8368-5974-4(X),* Gareth Stevens Learning Library) Stevens, Gareth Publishing LLLP.

—Sea Turtle's Clever Plan. Johnson, Rebecca. 2005. (Animal Storybooks Ser.). 24p. (gr. k-3). lib. bdg. 23.00 *(978-0-8368-5975-1(8),* Gareth Stevens Learning Library) Stevens, Gareth Publishing LLLP.

—Tree Frog Hears a Sound. Johnson, Rebecca. 2005. (Animal Storybooks Ser.). 24p. (gr. k-3). lib. bdg. 23.00 *(978-0-8368-5976-8(6),* Gareth Stevens Learning Library) Stevens, Gareth Publishing LLLP.

Parisi, Andrea & Krysinski, Grzegorz. Chaos at the Castle. Millici, Nate. 2016. 29p. (J). *(978-1-4844-8620-7(X))* Disney Publishing Worldwide.

—Finn & Poe Team Up! Millici, Nate. 2016. (World of Reading: Level 1 Ser.). (ENG.). 32p. (J). (gr. -1-1). 16.19 *(978-1-4844-8261-2(1))* Disney Pr.

—Star Wars: Finn & Poe Team Up! Millici, Nate. 2017. (World of Reading Level 1 Ser.). (ENG.). 32p. (J). (gr. -1-3). 27.07 *(978-1-5321-4054-9(1),* 25426) Spotlight.

—Star Wars: Chaos at the Castle. Millici, Nate. 2019. (World of Reading Level 1 Ser.). (ENG.). 32p. (J). (gr. -1-3). lib. bdg. 27.07 *(978-1-5321-4406-6(7),* 33811) Spotlight.

Parisi, Anthony. Monster for President. Pollock, Hal. 2008. 28p. 14.95 *(978-0-9816554-1-3(6))* Esquire Publishing, Inc.

Parisi, Mark. Marty Pants #1: Do Not Open! Parisi, Mark. 2017. (Marty Pants Ser.: 1). (ENG.). 256p. (J). (gr. 3-7). 12.99 *(978-0-06-242776-2(8))* HarperCollins Pubs.

—Marty Pants #2: Keep Your Paws Off! Parisi, Mark. 2018. (Marty Pants Ser.: 2). (ENG.). 256p. (J). (gr. 3-7). 12.99 *(978-0-06-242778-6(4))* HarperCollins Pubs.

—Marty Pants #3: How to Defeat a Wizard. Parisi, Mark. 2018. (Marty Pants Ser.: 3). (ENG.). 256p. (J). (gr. 3-7). 12.99 *(978-0-06-242780-9(6))* HarperCollins Pubs.

Parisot, Felicite. Bou. Perry, Caroline. 2019. (FRE.). 34p. (J). pap. 12.00 ***(978-1-7330378-0-8(2))*** Hom, Jonathan.

Park, Andy. The Fairies of Bladderwhack Pond. Bishop, Debbie. 2003. (Fairies of Bladderwhack Pond Ser.: Vol. 1). (ENG.). 152p. (J). (gr. 4-9). 19.99 *(978-1-932431-01-8(2))* Left Field,Angel Gate.

Park, Clare, photos by. Yoga for Kids. Lark, Liz. 2005. 127p. (J). reprint ed. pap. 20.00 *(978-0-7567-9410-1(2))* DIANE Publishing Co.

Park, Darcie. S Is for Silver: A Nevada Alphabet. Coerr, Eleanor. 2004. (State Ser.). (ENG.). 40p. (J). 17.95 *(978-1-58536-117-5(8))* Sleeping Bear Pr.

Park, Hye-Jin. Chronicles of the Cursed Sword, 10 vols. Yuy, Beub-Ryong. 2003.Tr. of Pa Keum Gee. 176p. (gr. 8-18). Vol. 1. pap. 9.99 *(978-1-59182-254-7(8));* Vol. 2. pap. 9.99 *(978-1-59182-255-4(6));* Vol. 3. pap. 9.99 *(978-1-59182-256-1(4))* TOKYOPOP, Inc.

Park, Hyeondo. Under His Spell, 4 vols., No. 4. Croall, Marie P. 2011. (My Boyfriend Is a Monster Ser.: 4). (ENG.). 128p. (YA). (gr. 7-12). 29.32 *(978-0-7613-5602-8(9),* 9780761356028, Graphic Universe™) Lerner Publishing Group.

—Veda: Assembly Required. Teer, Samuel. 2015. (ENG.). 144p. (J). (gr. 7). pap. 14.99 *(978-1-61655-497-2(5))* Dark Horse Comics.

Park, Janie Jaehyun. Count Your Way Through Zimbabwe. Haskins, Jim & Benson, Kathleen. 2006. (Count Your Way Ser.). (ENG.). 24p. (gr. 2-5). lib. bdg. 19.93 *(978-1-57505-885-6(5),* Millbrook Pr.) Lerner Publishing Group.

Park, Julie. Deedee's Easter Surprise. Kinnear, Kay. 2003. 25p. (J). pap. 9.99 *(978-0-7459-4443-2(4),* Lion Books) Lion Hudson PLC GBR. Dist: Trafalgar Square Publishing.

Park, Jung-a, jt. illus. see Gwangjo.

Park, Junghwa. While Grandpa Naps. Danis, Naomi. 2019. (ENG.). 32p. (J). (gr. -1-2). 17.99 *(978-1-57687-909-2(7),* powerHouse Bks.) powerHse. Bks.

Park, Kathy. Clara's Red Balloon. Lee, Jc. 2011. 40p. pap. 24.95 *(978-1-4560-2491-8(4))* America Star Bks.

Park, Keun. The Three Pig Sisters. Kim, Cecil. 2014. (MySELF Bookshelf Ser.). (ENG.). 32p. (J). (gr. k-2). pap. 11.94 *(978-1-60357-689-5(4));* lib. bdg. 25.27 *(978-1-59953-654-5(4))* Norwood Hse. Pr.

Park, Laura. Abner & Ian Get Right-Side Up. Eggers, Dave. 2019. 256p. (J). (gr. -1-3). 18.99 *(978-0-316-48586-9(1),* LB Kids) Little, Brown Bks. for Young Readers.

—From Hero to Zero. Patterson, James & Tebbetts, Christopher. 2017. 268p. (J). pap. *(978-0-316-35756-2(1))* Little Brown & Co.

—I Even Funnier: A Middle School Story. Patterson, James & Grabenstein, Chris. (I Funny Ser.: 2). (ENG.). 368p. (J). (gr. 3-7). 2017. pap. 8.99 *(978-0-316-20695-2(4));* 2013. 13.99 *(978-0-316-20697-6(0))* Little Brown & Co. (Jimmy Patterson).

—I Funny: A Middle School Story. Patterson, James & Grabenstein, Chris. (I Funny Ser.: 1). (ENG.). 320p. (J). (gr. 3-7). 2015. pap. 8.99 *(978-0-316-20692-1(X));* 2013. 13.99 *(978-0-316-32200-3(8))* Little Brown & Co. (Jimmy Patterson).

—I Funny: A Middle School Story. Grabenstein, Chris. Patterson, James, ed. 2012. 303p. (J). 11.99 *(978-0-316-22638-7(6),* 1351607) Little Brown & Co.

—I Funny: A Middle School Story. Grabenstein, Chris & Patterson, James. 2012. (I Funny Ser.: 1). (ENG.). 320p. (J). (gr. 3-7). 29.00 *(978-0-316-20693-8(8),* Jimmy Patterson) Little Brown & Co.

—I Funny TV: A Middle School Story. Patterson, James & Grabenstein, Chris. 2015. (I Funny Ser.: 4). (ENG.). 336p. (J). (gr. 3-7). 13.99 *(978-0-316-30109-1(4),* Jimmy Patterson) Little Brown & Co.

—I Totally Funniest: A Middle School Story. Patterson, James & Grabenstein, Chris. 2015. (J). 320p. *(978-0-316-26161-6(0));* (I Funny Ser.: 3). (ENG.). 336p. (gr. 3-7). 13.99 *(978-0-316-40593-5(0),* Jimmy Patterson) Little Brown & Co.

—Middle School: from Hero to Zero. Patterson, James & Tebbetts, Chris. 2018. (Middle School Ser.: 10). (ENG.). 288p. (J). (gr. 3-7). 13.99 *(978-0-316-34690-0(X))* Little Brown & Co.

—Middle School: Get Me Out of Here! Patterson, James & Tebbetts, Chris. (Middle School Ser.: 2). (ENG.). 288p. (J). (gr. 3-7). 2018. pap. 8.99 *(978-0-316-20669-3(5));* 2014. 13.99 *(978-0-316-32201-0(6),* Jimmy Patterson); 2012. 28.00 *(978-0-316-20671-6(7),* Jimmy Patterson) Little Brown & Co.

—Middle School: How I Survived Bullies, Broccoli, & Snake Hill. Patterson, James & Tebbetts, Chris. 2017. (Middle School Ser.: 4). (ENG.). 336p. (J). (gr. 3-7). 13.99 *(978-0-316-50513-0(7),* Jimmy Patterson) Little Brown & Co.

—Middle School: Just My Rotten Luck. Patterson, James & Tebbetts, Chris. 2015. (Middle School Ser.: 7). (ENG.). 320p. (J). (gr. 3-7). 13.99 *(978-0-316-28477-6(7),* Jimmy Patterson) Little Brown & Co.

—Middle School: Save Rafe! Patterson, James & Tebbetts, Chris. 2014. (Middle School Ser.: 6). (ENG.). 288p. (J). (gr. 3-7). 13.99 *(978-0-316-32212-6(1),* Jimmy Patterson) Little Brown & Co.

—Middle School, the Worst Years of My Life. Patterson, James & Tebbetts, Chris. (Middle School Ser.: 1). (ENG.). (J). (gr. 3-7). 2014. 320p. 13.99 *(978-0-316-32202-7(4));* 2012. 336p. pap. 8.00 *(978-0-316-10169-1(9));* 2011. 288p. 28.00 *(978-0-316-10187-5(7))* Little Brown & Co. (Jimmy Patterson).

—Middle School, the Worst Years of My Life. Tebbetts, Chris & Patterson, James. ed. 2016. (Middle School Ser.: 1). (ENG.). 320p. (J). (gr. 3-7). pap. 7.99 *(978-0-316-27691-7(X),* Jimmy Patterson) Little Brown & Co.

—Save Rafe! Patterson, James & Tebbetts, Christopher. 2014. 269p. (J). *(978-0-316-28629-9(X))* Little Brown & Co.

—Unstoppable: (Family Read-Aloud Book, Silly Book about Cooperation) Rex, Adam. 2020. (ENG.). 56p. (J). (gr. k-3). 16.99 *(978-1-4521-6504-2(1))* Chronicle Bks. LLC.

—The Worst Years of My Life. Patterson, James & Tebbetts, Chris. 2013. (Middle School Ser.: Bk. 1). (ENG.). (J). (gr. 3-7). pap. 0.01 *(978-0-316-25251-5(4))* Little Brown & Co.

—The Worst Years of My Life. Patterson, James & Tebbetts, Chris. ed. 2012. (Middle School Ser.: 1). (J). lib. bdg. 18.45 *(978-0-606-26164-7(8))* Turtleback.

Park-MacNeil, Chrissie. So Imagine Me: Nature Riddles in Poetry, 1 vol. Davies, Lynn. 2020. (ENG.). 32p. (J). 7.95 ***(978-1-77108-867-1(2),*** 8e1a8369-0c7d-4576-a071-6f9c26713b26) Nimbus Publishing, Ltd. CAN. Dist: Baker & Taylor Publisher Services (BTPS).

Park, Meg. Anna, Banana, & Friends — A Four-Book Paperback Collection! Anna, Banana, & the Friendship Split; Anna, Banana, & the Monkey in the Middle; Anna, Banana, & the Big-Mouth Bet; Anna, Banana, & the Puppy Parade. Rissi, Anica Mrose. ed. 2017. (Anna, Banana Ser.). (ENG.). 544p. (J). (gr. 1-5). pap. 23.99 *(978-1-5344-1153-1(4),* Simon & Schuster Bks. For Young Readers) Simon & Schuster Bks. For Young Readers.

—Anna, Banana, & the Big-Mouth Bet. Rissi, Anica Mrose. 2016. (Anna, Banana Ser.: 3). (ENG.). 128p. (J). (gr. 1-5). pap. 6.99 *(978-1-4814-1612-2(X),* Simon & Schuster Bks. For Young Readers) Simon & Schuster Bks. For Young Readers.

—Anna, Banana, & the Friendship Split. Rissi, Anica Mrose. 2015. (Anna, Banana Ser.: 1). (ENG.). 128p. (J). (gr. 1-5). 16.99 *(978-1-4814-1605-4(7),* Simon & Schuster Bks. For Young Readers) Simon & Schuster Bks. For Young Readers.

—Anna, Banana, & the Little Lost Kitten. Rissi, Anica Mrose. 2017. (Anna, Banana Ser.: 5). (ENG.). 144p. (J). (gr. 1-5). 16.99 *(978-1-4814-8669-9(1));* pap. 6.99 *(978-1-4814-8670-5(5))* Simon & Schuster Bks. For Young Readers. (Simon & Schuster Bks. For Young Readers).

—Anna, Banana, & the Monkey in the Middle. Rissi, Anica Mrose. 2015. (Anna, Banana Ser.: 2). (ENG.). 128p. (J). (gr. 1-5). 15.99 *(978-1-4814-1608-5(1),* Simon & Schuster Bks. For Young Readers) Simon & Schuster Bks. For Young Readers.

—Anna, Banana, & the Puppy Parade. Rissi, Anica Mrose. 2017. (Anna, Banana Ser.: 4). (ENG.). 144p. (J). (gr. 1-5). pap. 5.99 *(978-1-4814-1615-3(4),* Simon & Schuster Bks. For Young Readers) Simon & Schuster Bks. For Young Readers.

—Anna, Banana, & the Recipe for Disaster. Rissi, Anica Mrose. 2018. (Anna, Banana Ser.: 6). (ENG.). 128p. (J). (gr. 1-5). 16.99 *(978-1-4814-8672-9(1));* pap. 5.99 *(978-1-4814-8673-6(X))* Simon & Schuster Bks. For Young Readers. (Simon & Schuster Bks. For Young Readers).

—Beauty & the Beast. Rylant, Cynthia. 2017. 40p. (J). (gr. -1-k). 16.99 *(978-1-4231-1981-4(9))* Disney Pr.

Park, Mi-Ok. Booyoung & Sea Turtle's Adventure: God's Creatures' Adventures Series 1. Roh, Grace S. 2013. 52p. pap. 17.50 *(978-1-62212-718-4(8),* Strategic Bk. Publishing) Strategic Book Publishing & Rights Agency (SBPRA).

Park, Min-Seo. Blazin' Barrels. Park, Min-Seo. 192p. rev. ed. 2005. (Blazin' Barrels Ser.: Vol. 3). per. 9.99 *(978-1-59532-560-0(3));* Vol. 2. 2nd rev. ed. 2005. pap. 9.99 *(978-1-59532-559-4(X));* Vol. 4. 4th rev. ed. 2006. (Blazin' Barrels Ser.). per. 9.99 *(978-1-59532-561-7(1))* TOKYOPOP, Inc.

Park, Molly. Suee & the Shadow. Ly, Ginger. 2017. (ENG.). 240p. (J). (gr. 4-7). 21.99 *(978-1-4197-2563-0(7));* pap. 12.99 *(978-1-4197-2564-7(5))* Abrams, Inc. (Amulet Bks.).

—Suee & the Shadow (Scholastic Paperback Edition) Ly, Ginger. 2017. (ENG.). 240p. (J). (gr. 4-7). pap. 12.99 *(978-1-4197-3011-5(8),* Amulet Bks.) Abrams, Inc.

Park, Sang-Sun. Les Bijoux, 6 vols. Jo, Eun-Ha. 2004. 200p. Vol. 4. 4th rev. ed. pap. 14.99 *(978-1-59182-693-4(4));* Vol. 5. 5th rev. ed. pap. 14.99 *(978-1-59182-694-1(2))* TOKYOPOP, Inc. (Tokyopop Adult).

Park, Scott. Star Wars Battle Cries: Creatures vs. Aliens: Sounds from the Showdown. Hidalgo, Pablo. 2019. (ENG.). 24p. (J). (gr. 1-3). 21.99 *(978-0-7603-6404-8(4),* 13750) becker&mayer! books.

Park, Seung-bum. Mother to the Poor: The Life of Blessed Teresa of Calcutta. Ko, Jung-wook. 2008. Orig. Title: Mongdangyeonpili Doen Mother Teresa. (KOR.). 140p. (J). (gr. 3-5). pap. 14.95 *(978-0-8198-4863-5(8))* Pauline Bks. & Media.

Park, Soyoo H. Look What We've Brought You from Korea: Crafts, Games, Recipes, Stories & Other Cultural Activities from Korean-Americans. Shalant, Phyllis. (J). (gr. 2-18). pap. 7.95 *(978-0-382-24994-5(1))* Silver, Burdett & Ginn, Inc.

Park, Su-jeong. The Salamander's Trial: A Wetland Story. Yang, Dae-seung. 2020. (Green Earth Tales Ser.). (ENG.). 32p. (J). (gr. k-4). pap. 8.99 ***(978-1-925235-57-9(2));*** lib. bdg. 27.99 ***(978-1-925235-61-6(0))*** ChoiceMaker Pty. Ltd., The AUS. (Big and SMALL). Dist: Lerner Publishing Group.

Park, Sun. El Hogar. Schmauss, Judy Kentor. 2016. (Early Rising Readers Ser.). (SPA.). 16p. (J). (gr. 1-1). 6.67 *(978-1-4788-4193-7(1))* Newmark Learning LLC.

Park, Sung-Woo. Peigenz, 8 vols. Oh Rhe Bar Ghun. (Peigenz Ser.: Vol. 2). (YA). Vol. 2. 2004. 192p. per. 9.95 *(978-1-59697-022-9(7));* Vol. 3. 2004. 176p. per. 9.95 *(978-1-59697-023-6(5));* Vol. 4. 2005. 176p. per. 9.95 *(978-1-59697-024-3(3));* Vol. 5. 2005. 176p. per. 9.95 *(978-1-59697-025-0(1));* Vol. 6. 2006. 176p. per. 9.95 *(978-1-59697-026-7(X));* Vol. 7. 2006. 176p. per. 9.95 *(978-1-59697-027-4(8));* Vol. 8. 2006. 192p. per. 9.95 *(978-1-59697-028-1(6))* Infinity Studios LLC.

—Zero, 10 vols. Ihm, Dar-Young. (Zero Ser.: Vol. 5). (YA). Vol. 5. 2007. 204p. per. 9.95 *(978-1-59697-035-9(9));* Vol. 6. 2007. 204p. per. 9.95 *(978-1-59697-036-6(7));* Vol. 7. 2007. 204p. per. 9.95 *(978-1-59697-037-3(5));* Vol. 8. 2008. 204p. per. 9.95 *(978-1-59697-038-0(3));* Vol. 9. 2008. 204p. per. 9.95 *(978-1-59697-039-7(1));* Vol. 10. 2008. 230p. per. 9.95 *(978-1-59697-040-3(5))* Infinity Studios LLC.

Park, Sung-Woo. Now. Park, Sung-Woo. 2006. (NOW Ser.: Vol. 5). 217p. Vol. 5. (YA). per. 9.95 *(978-1-59697-185-1(1));* Vol. 7. (YA). per. 9.95 *(978-1-59697-187-5(8));* Vol. 8. (YA). per. 9.95 *(978-1-59697-188-2(6));* Vol. 9. per. 9.95 *(978-1-59697-189-9(4))* Infinity Studios LLC.

Park, Trip. Ant, Ant, Ant! An Insect Chant. Sayre, April Pulley. 2005. (American City Ser.). (ENG.). 32p. (J). (gr. k-3). 15.95 *(978-1-55971-922-3(2))* Cooper Square Publishing Llc.

—Battle of the Dum Diddys, 12. Stine, R. L. 2011. (Rotten School Ser.: No. 12). (ENG.). 128p. (J). (gr. 2-6). 27.07 *(978-1-59961-836-4(2),* 13139, Chapter Bks.) Spotlight.

—The Big Blueberry Barf-Off! Stine, R. L. 2005. (Rotten School Ser.: No. 1). 128p. (J). (ENG.). 6.99 *(978-0-06-078586-4(1));* lib. bdg. 14.89 *(978-0-06-078587-1(X))* HarperCollins Pubs.

—The Big Blueberry Barf-Off! Stine, R. L. 2011. (Rotten School Ser.: No. 1). (ENG.). 128p. (J). (gr. 2-6). 27.07 *(978-1-59961-825-8(7),* 13128, Chapter Bks.) Spotlight.

—Calling All Birdbrains. Stine, R. L. 2007. (Rotten School Ser.: No. 15). (ENG.). 128p. (J). (gr. 3-7). 6.99 *(978-0-06-123275-6(0))* HarperCollins Pubs.

—Dudes, the School Is Haunted! Stine, R. L. 2011. (Rotten School Ser.: No. 7). (ENG.). 128p. (J). (gr. 2-6). 27.07 *(978-1-59961-831-9(1),* 13134, Chapter Bks.) Spotlight.

—The Good, the Bad & the Very Slimy. Stine, R. L. 2011. (Rotten School Ser.: No. 3). (ENG.). 128p. (J). (gr. 2-6). 27.07 *(978-1-59961-827-2(3),* 13130, Chapter Bks.) Spotlight.

—The Great Smelling Bee, 2. Stine, R. L. 2011. (Rotten School Ser.: No. 2). (ENG.). 128p. (J). (gr. 2-6). 27.07 *(978-1-59961-826-5(5),* 13129, Chapter Bks.) Spotlight.

—The Heinie Prize. Stine, R. L. 2006. (Rotten School Ser.: No. 6). 128p. (J). pap. 4.99 *(978-0-06-078816-2(X)*, Harper Trophy) HarperCollins Pubs.
—The Heinie Prize, 1 vol. Stine, R. L. 2011. (Rotten School Ser.: No. 6). (ENG.). 128p. (J). (gr. 2-6). 27.07 *(978-1-59961-830-2(3))*, 13133, Chapter Bks.) Spotlight.
—Lose, Team, Lose!, 4. Stine, R. L. 2011. (Rotten School Ser.: No. 4). (ENG.). 128p. (J). (gr. 2-6). 27.07 *(978-1-59961-828-9(1))*, 13131, Chapter Bks.) Spotlight.
—Night of the Creepy Things. Stine, R. L. (Rotten School Ser.: Bk. 14). 4.99 *(978-0-06-123274-9(2))* HarperCollins Pubs.
—Party Poopers. Stine, R. L. (Rotten School Ser.: Bk. 9). 4.99 *(978-0-06-078826-1(7))* HarperCollins Pubs.
—Party Poopers. Stine, R. L. 2011. (Rotten School Ser.: No. 9). (ENG.). 128p. (J). (gr. 2-6). 27.07 *(978-1-59961-833-3(8))*, 13136, Chapter Bks.) Spotlight.
—Punk'd & Skunked, 1 vol. Stine, R. L. 2011. (Rotten School Ser.: No. 11). (ENG.). 128p. (J). (gr. 2-6). 27.07 *(978-1-59961-835-7(4))*, 13138, Chapter Bks.) Spotlight.
—Rotten School - Dudes, the School Is Haunted! Stine, R. L. 2009. (Rotten School Ser.: No. 7). 128p. (J). pap. 4.99 *(978-0-06-078820-9(8))*, Harper Trophy) HarperCollins Pubs.
—Rotten School #1: the Big Blueberry Barf-Off! Stine, R. L. 2008. (Rotten School Ser.: 1). (ENG.). 128p. (J). (gr. 3-7). pap. 5.99 *(978-0-06-078588-8(8))* HarperCollins Pubs.
—Rotten School #11: Punk'd & Skunked. Stine, R. L. 2007. (Rotten School Ser.: 11). (ENG.). 128p. (J). (gr. 3-7). 6.99 *(978-0-06-078830-8(5))* HarperCollins Pubs.
—Rotten School #12: Battle of the Dum Diddys. Stine, R. L. 4.99 *(978-0-06-078835-3(6))* HarperCollins Pubs.
—Rotten School #15: Calling All Birdbrains. Stine, R. L. 4.99 *(978-0-06-123277-0(7))* HarperCollins Pubs.
—Rotten School #16: Dumb Clucks. Stine, R. L. 4.99 *(978-0-06-123280-0(7))* HarperCollins Pubs.
—Rotten School #2: the Great Smelling Bee. Stine, R. L. 2008. (Rotten School Ser.: 2). (ENG.). 128p. (J). (gr. 3-7). pap. 5.99 *(978-0-06-078591-8(8))* HarperCollins Pubs.
—Rotten School #3: the Good, the Bad & the Very Slimy. Stine, R. L. 2008. (Rotten School Ser.: 3). (ENG.). 128p. (J). (gr. 3-7). pap. 5.99 *(978-0-06-078594-9(2))* HarperCollins Pubs.
—Rotten School #4: Lose, Team, Lose! Stine, R. L. 2008. (Rotten School Ser.: 4). (ENG.). 128p. (J). (gr. 3-7). pap. 5.99 *(978-0-06-078810-0(0))* HarperCollins Pubs.
—Rotten School #5: Shake, Rattle, & Hurl! Stine, R. L. 2008. (Rotten School Ser.: 5). (ENG.). 128p. (J). (gr. 3-7). pap. 6.99 *(978-0-06-078813-1(5))* HarperCollins Pubs.
—The Rottenest Angel. Stine, R. L. (Rotten School Ser.: Bk. 10). 4.99 *(978-0-06-078829-2(1))* HarperCollins Pubs.
—The Rottenest Angel, Set. Stine, R. L. 2011. (Rotten School Ser.: No. 10). (ENG.). 128p. (J). (gr. 2-6). 27.07 *(978-1-59961-834-0(6))*, 13137, Chapter Bks.) Spotlight.
—Shake, Rattle, & Hurl! Stine, R. L. 2006. (Rotten School Ser.: No. 5). (ENG.). 128p. (J). (gr. 3-7). 6.99 *(978-0-06-078811-7(9))* HarperCollins Pubs.
—Shake, Rattle, & Hurl! Stine, R. L. 2011. (Rotten School Ser.: No. 5). (ENG.). 128p. (J). (gr. 2-6). 27.07 *(978-1-59961-829-6(X))*, 13132, Chapter Bks.) Spotlight.
—The Teacher from Heck. Stine, R. L. 2009. (Rotten School Ser.: No. 8). 128p. (J). pap. 4.99 *(978-0-06-078823-0(2))*, Harper Trophy) HarperCollins Pubs.
—The Teacher from Heck. Stine, R. L. 2011. (Rotten School Ser.: No. 8). (ENG.). 128p. (J). (gr. 2-6). 27.07 *(978-1-59961-832-6(X))*, 13135, Chapter Bks.) Spotlight.
—Trout, Trout, Trout: (A Fish Chant) Sayre, April Pulley. 2007. (American City Ser.). (ENG.). 32p. (J). (gr. k-3). pap. 8.95 *(978-1-55971-979-7(6))* Cooper Square Publishing Llc.
Park, Yeong Jin. What Lives in the Sea? Marine Life. Borin & Rin, Bo. Cowley, Joy, ed. 2015. (Science Storybooks Ser.). (ENG.). 32p. (J). (gr. k-4). 10.00 *(978-1-925233-63-6(4))*, Big and SMALL) ChoiceMaker Pty. Ltd., The AUS. Dist: Lerner Publishing Group.
Park, Yeong-jin. What Lives in the Sea? Marine Life. Gam Do, Rin Bo. Cowley, Joy, ed. 2015. (Science Storybooks Ser.). (ENG.). 32p. (gr. k-3). 7.99 *(978-1-925246-77-3(9))*, Big and SMALL) ChoiceMaker Pty. Ltd., The AUS. Dist: Lerner Publishing Group.
—What Lives in the Sea? Marine Life. Gam Do, Rin Bo. Cowley, Joy, ed. 2015. (Science Storybooks Ser.). (ENG.). 32p. (gr. k-3). 26.65 *(978-1-925246-51-3(5))*, Big and SMALL) ChoiceMaker Pty. Ltd., The AUS. Dist: Lerner Publishing Group.
—What Lives in the Sea? Marine Life. Gam Do, Rin Bo. Cowley, Joy, ed. 2015. (Science Storybooks Ser.). (ENG.). 32p. (gr. k-3). 26.65 *(978-1-925246-25-4(6))*, Big and SMALL) ChoiceMaker Pty. Ltd., The AUS. Dist: Lerner Publishing Group.
Parker, Al. Jane's Blanket. Miller, Arthur. 2017. (ENG.). 64p. (J). (gr. -1-3). 24.95 *(978-3-89955-786-2(7))* Die Gestalten Verlag DEU. Dist: Ingram Publisher Services.
Parker, Andy. House that Jack Built. Goodhart, Pippa. 2004. (ENG.). 24p. (J). lib. bdg. 23.65 *(978-1-59646-700-2(2))* Dingles & Co.
—Mekanimals Clockwork Safari. 2004. 8p. (J). bds. 12.95 *(978-1-59223-145-4(4))*, Silver Dolphin Bks.) Readerlink Distribution Services, LLC.
—Mekanimals Cyber Bugs. 2004. 8p. (J). bds. 12.95 *(978-1-59223-146-1(2))*, Silver Dolphin Bks.) Readerlink Distribution Services, LLC.
Parker, Ant. Amazing Airplanes. Mitton, Tony. 2005. (Amazing Machines Ser.). (ENG.). (J). (gr. -1-k). lib. bdg. 15.60 *(978-1-68065-291-8(5))* Perfection Learning Corp.
—Amazing Airplanes. Mitton, Tony. 2016. (Amazing Machines Ser.). (ENG.). 24p. (J). pap., act. bk. ed. 5.99 *(978-0-7534-7255-2(4))*, 900156294, Kingfisher) Roaring Brook Pr.
—Amazing Airplanes Sound Book: A Very Noisy Book. 2017. (Amazing Machines Ser.). (ENG.). 24p. (J). 15.99 *(978-0-7534-7328-3(3))*, 9780753473283, Kingfisher) Roaring Brook Pr.
Parker, Ant. Amazing Animals: Forest Adventure. Mitton, Tony. 2020. (Amazing Animals Ser.). (ENG.). 20p. (J). bds. 6.99 ***(978-0-7534-7628-4(2)***, 900226419, Kingfisher) Roaring Brook Pr.
Parker, Ant. Amazing Machines First Concepts: Colors. 2015. (ENG.). 12p. (J). (gr. -1-1). bds. 5.99 *(978-0-7534-7233-0(3))*, 9780753472330, Kingfisher) Roaring Brook Pr.
—Amazing Machines First Concepts: Opposites. 2015. (ENG.). 12p. (J). (gr. -1-1). bds. 5.99 *(978-0-7534-7234-7(1))*, 9780753472347, Kingfisher) Roaring Brook Pr.
—Amazing Machines First Concepts: Sounds. 2015. (ENG.). 12p. (J). (gr. -1-1). bds. 5.99 *(978-0-7534-7232-3(5))*, 9780753472323, Kingfisher) Roaring Brook Pr.
—Amazing Machines: First Numbers. Mitton, Tony. 2018. (Amazing Machines Ser.). (ENG.). 22p. (J). bds. 9.99 *(978-0-7534-7440-2(9))*, 900192346, Kingfisher) Roaring Brook Pr.
—Amazing Machines: First Words. Mitton, Tony. 2018. (Amazing Machines Ser.). (ENG.). 22p. (J). bds. 9.99 *(978-0-7534-7439-6(5))*, 900192345, Kingfisher) Roaring Brook Pr.
—Amazing Machines Flashing Fire Engines Activity Book. Mitton, Tony. 2016. (Amazing Machines Ser.). (ENG.). 24p. (J). pap., act. bk. ed. 4.99 *(978-0-7534-7256-9(2))*, 900156246, Kingfisher) Roaring Brook Pr.
—Amazing Machines: Rescue Vehicles. Mitton, Tony. 2020. (Amazing Machines Ser.). (ENG.). 72p. (J). pap. 12.99 *(978-0-7534-7573-7(1))*, 900219374, Kingfisher) Roaring Brook Pr.
—Awesome Ambulances. Mitton, Tony. 2019. (Amazing Machines Ser.). (ENG.). 20p. (J). bds. 6.99 *(978-0-7534-7494-5(8))*, 900198572, Kingfisher) Roaring Brook Pr.
—Busy Boats. Mitton, Tony. 2005. (Amazing Machines Ser.). (ENG.). (J). (gr. -1-k). lib. bdg. 15.60 *(978-1-68065-286-4(9))* Perfection Learning Corp.
—Charlie Chick Counting. Denchfield, Nick. 2018. (Charlie Chick Ser.). (ENG.). 8p. (J). (gr. -1-k). bds. 7.99 *(978-1-5098-8136-9(0))* Pan Macmillan GBR. Dist: Independent Pubs. Group.
—Charlie Chick Finds an Egg. Denchfield, Nick & Denchdfield, Nick. 2017. (Charlie Chick Ser.: 5). (ENG.). 16p. (J). (gr. -1-k). 11.99 *(978-1-5098-2883-8(4))*, Campbell Bks.) Pan Macmillan GBR. Dist: Independent Pubs. Group.
—Charlie Chick Goes on Holiday. Denchfield, Nick. 2018. (Charlie Chick Ser.). (ENG.). 16p. (J). (gr. -1-k). 12.99 *(978-1-5098-6675-5(2))* Pan Macmillan GBR. Dist: Independent Pubs. Group.
—Charlie Chick Wants to Play. Denchfield, Nick. 2017. (Charlie Chick Ser.: 6). (ENG.). 10p. (J). (-k). bds. 9.99 *(978-1-5098-2900-2(8))* Pan Macmillan GBR. Dist: Independent Pubs. Group.
—Forest Adventure. Mitton, Tony. 2015. (Amazing Animals Ser.). (ENG.). 24p. (J). (gr. -1-1). pap. 4.99 *(978-0-7534-7229-3(5))*, 900149034, Kingfisher) Roaring Brook Pr.
—High-Flying Helicopters. Mitton, Tony. (Amazing Machines Ser.). (ENG.). (J). 2018. 20p. bds. 6.99 *(978-0-7534-7418-1(2))*, 900187137); 2016. 24p. 9.99 *(978-0-7534-7290-3(2))*, 9780753472903) Roaring Brook Pr. (Kingfisher).
—Marvelous Motorcycles. Mitton, Tony. (Amazing Machines Ser.). (ENG.). (J). 2018. 20p. bds. 6.99 *(978-0-7534-7419-8(0))*, 900187154); 2016. 24p. 9.99 *(978-0-7534-7292-7(9))*, 9780753472927) Roaring Brook Pr. (Kingfisher).
—My Amazing Machines Cool Cars Activity Book. Mitton, Tony. 2017. (Amazing Machines Ser.). (ENG.). 24p. (J). pap. 5.99 *(978-0-7534-7296-5(1))*, 9780753472965, Kingfisher) Roaring Brook Pr.
—My Amazing Machines Roaring Rockets. Mitton, Tony. 2016. (Amazing Machines Ser.). (ENG.). 24p. (J). pap., act. bk. ed. 5.99 *(978-0-7534-7257-6(0))*, 900156295, Kingfisher) Roaring Brook Pr.
—My Amazing Machines Terrific Trains Activity Book. Mitton, Tony. 2017. (Amazing Machines Ser.). (ENG.). 24p. (J). pap. 5.99 *(978-0-7534-7295-8(3))*, 9780753472958, Kingfisher) Roaring Brook Pr.
—Patrolling Police Cars. Mitton, Tony. 2019. (Amazing Machines Ser.). (ENG.). 20p. (J). bds. 6.99 *(978-0-7534-7495-2(6))*, 900198573, Kingfisher) Roaring Brook Pr.
—Sherman Swaps Shells. Clarke, Jane. 2003. (Flying Foxes Ser.). (ENG.). 48p. (J). lib. bdg. *(978-0-7787-1485-9(3))* Crabtree Publishing Co.
—Tough Trucks. Mitton, Tony. 2016. (Amazing Machines Ser.). (ENG.). 24p. (J). pap., act. bk. ed. 4.99 *(978-0-7534-7254-5(6))*, 9780753472545, Kingfisher) Roaring Brook Pr.
—Who Jumps? Lewis, Edwina. 2003. (Who... Ser.). 16p. (YA). *(978-1-85602-447-1(4))*, Pavilion Children's Books) Pavilion Bks.
—Who Plays? Lewis, Edwina. 2003. (Who... Ser.). 16p. (J). *(978-1-85602-469-3(5))*, Pavilion Children's Books) Pavilion Bks.
—Who Swims? Lewis, Edwina. 2003. (Who... Ser.). 16p. (YA). *(978-1-85602-448-8(2))*, Pavilion Children's Books) Pavilion Bks.
Parker, Aura. Twig. Parker, Aura. 2018. (ENG.). 32p. (J). (gr. -1-3). 17.99 *(978-1-5344-2468-5(7))*, Simon & Schuster Bks. For Young Readers) Simon & Schuster Bks. For Young Readers.
Parker, Buzz, jt. illus. see Reger, Rob.
Parker, Curtis. DreddieLocks & the Three Slugs. Hyde, Margaret E. 2003. 36p. (J). lib. bdg. 16.95 *(978-1-888108-07-1(X))* Budding Artists, Inc.
—Dreddielocks & the Three Slugs, 1 vol. Hyde, Margaret 2003. (ENG.). 36p. (J). (gr. k-3). 17.99 *(978-1-58980-231-5(4))*, Pelican Publishing) Arcadia Publishing.
Parker, David. Csi Expert! Forensic Science for Kids. Schulz, Karen K. 2008. (ENG.). 160p. (gr. 5-8). pap. 19.95 *(978-1-59363-312-7(2))* Prufrock Pr.
Parker, Edward, photos by. Istanbul. Bowden, Rob. 2007. (Global Cities Ser.). 61p. (gr. 5-8). lib. bdg. 30.00 *(978-0-7910-8850-0(2))*, Chelsea Hse.) Facts On File, Inc.
—Rio de Janeiro. Scoones, Simon. 2006. (Global Cities Ser.). 61p. (gr. 5-8). 30.00 *(978-0-7910-8857-9(X))*, Chelsea Hse.) Facts On File, Inc.
Parker, Edward, photos by. Mexico City. Parker, Edward. 2006. (Global Cities Ser.). 61p. (gr. 5-8). 30.00 *(978-0-7910-8854-8(5))*, Chelsea Hse.) Facts On File, Inc.
Parker, Eric. Yucky Riddles. Helmer, Marilyn. 2003. (Level 3 — Riddle Bks.). (ENG.). (J). (gr. 1-3). lib. bdg. 14.55 *(978-0-7569-3071-4(5))* Perfection Learning Corp.
—Yummy Riddles. Helmer, Marilyn. 2003. (Kids Can Read! Ser.). (ENG.). (J). (gr. 1-3). lib. bdg. 14.55 *(978-0-7569-3072-1(3))* Perfection Learning Corp.
Parker, Gretel. Pinwheel Days, 1 vol. Tarlow, Ellen. 2007. (ENG.). 32p. (J). (gr. -1-3). pap. 6.95 *(978-1-59572-059-7(6))* Star Bright Bks., Inc.
Parker, Jack. Ernie the Ermine. Patterson, Horace. 2007. 28p. per. 7.99 *(978-1-58942-374-9(7))* R.H. Boyd Publishing Corp.
Parker, Jake. Apple ABC. McNamara, Margaret. 2012. (J). *(978-0-439-72809-6(6))* Scholastic, Inc.
—The Astonishing Secret of Awesome Man. Chabon, Michael. 2011. (ENG.). 40p. (J). (gr. -1-3). 17.99 *(978-0-06-191462-1(2))* HarperCollins Pubs.
Parker, Jake. The Astonishing Secret of Awesome Man. Chabon, Michael. 2020. (ENG.). 40p. (J). (gr. -1-3). pap. 7.99 ***(978-0-06-191464-5(9)***, HarperCollins) HarperCollins Pubs. Ltd. GBR. Dist: HarperCollins Pubs.
—Awesome Man: the Mystery Intruder. Chabon, Michael. 2020. (ENG.). 40p. (J). (gr. -1-3). 18.99 ***(978-0-06-287509-9(4)***, HarperCollins) HarperCollins Pubs. Ltd. GBR. Dist: HarperCollins Pubs.
Parker, Jake. The Girl Who Wouldn't Brush Her Hair. Bernheimer, Kate. 2013. 40p. (J). (gr. -1-3). 17.99 *(978-0-375-86878-8(X))*, Schwartz & Wade Bks.) Random Hse. Children's Bks.
—Goldilocks for Dinner: A Funny Book about Manners. Montanari, Susan. 2019. 40p. (J). (gr. -1-3). 17.99 *(978-0-399-55235-9(9))*, Schwartz & Wade Bks.) Random Hse. Children's Bks.
—The Little Snowplow. Koehler, Lora. (J). 2018. 30p. (— 1). bds. 8.99 *(978-1-5362-0340-0(8))*; 2015. 32p. (gr. -1-2). 15.99 *(978-0-7636-7074-0(X))* Candlewick Pr.
—The Little Snowplow Wishes for Snow. Koehler, Lora. 2019. 40p. (J). (gr. -1-2). 16.99 *(978-1-5362-0117-8(0))* Candlewick Pr.
—The Tooth Fairy Wars. Coombs, Kate. 2014. (ENG.). 40p. (J). (gr. -1-3). 17.99 *(978-1-4169-7915-9(8))* Simon & Schuster Children's Publishing.
—Who's the Grossest of Them All? Montanari, Susan McElroy. 2016. 40p. (J). (gr. -1-3). 17.99 *(978-0-553-51190-1(4))*, Schwartz & Wade Bks.) Random Hse. Children's Bks.
—The 12 Sleighs of Christmas. Rinker, Sherri Duskey. 2017. (ENG.). 40p. (J). (gr. -1-k). 16.99 *(978-1-4521-4514-3(8))* Chronicle Bks. LLC.
Parker, Laurie. It Really Said Christmas. Parker, Laurie. 2005. (J). pap. 17.95 *(978-0-9772096-0-6(1))* Wild Hare Publishing.
—It Really Said Christmas. Parker, Laurie. 2003. (J). *(978-0-9729615-0-9(X))* Parker, Laurie.
Parker, Nancy Winslow. Who Will I Be? A Halloween Rebus Story. Neitzel, Shirley. 2005. 32p. (J). lib. bdg. 13.89 *(978-0-06-056068-3(1))* HarperCollins Pubs.
Parker, Natalie. Australia's Endangered Animals. Adam, Luisa. 2016. (ENG.). 244p. (J). (gr. k-2). pap. *(978-1-925386-86-8(4))*, Brolly Bks.) Borghesi & Adam Pubs. Pty Ltd.
—Marshall Mouse's Mornings - Marshall Mouse's Nights. Adam, Luisa. 2016. (Marshall Mouse Ser.). (ENG.). 16p. (J). (— 1). bds. *(978-1-925386-14-1(7))*, Brolly Bks.) Borghesi & Adam Pubs. Pty Ltd.
—When Marshall Mouse Is Happy - When Marshall Mouse Is Sad. Adam, Luisa. 2016. (Marshall Mouse Ser.). (ENG.). 16p. (J). (gr. -1-k). bds. *(978-1-925386-15-8(5))*, Brolly Bks.) Borghesi & Adam Pubs. Pty Ltd.
—When Marshall Mouse Is Hot - When Marshall Mouse Is Cold. Adam, Luisa. 2016. (Marshall Mouse Ser.). (ENG.). 16p. (J). (— 1). bds. *(978-1-925386-13-4(9))*, Brolly Bks.) Borghesi & Adam Pubs. Pty Ltd.
Parker, Paul & Moor, Becka. Snakes. MacLaine, James. 2014. (Usborne Beginners Ser.). (ENG.). 32p. (J). (gr. 1-4). 4.99 *(978-0-7945-2686-3(1))*, Usborne) EDC Publishing.
Parker-Rees, Guy. Be Brave, Little Penguin. Andreae, Giles. 2017. (ENG.). 32p. (J). (gr. -1-k). 16.99 *(978-1-338-15039-1(1))*, Orchard Bks.) Scholastic, Inc.
—Diggory Digger & the Dinosaurs. Bently, Peter. 2013. (ENG.). 32p. (J). (gr. -1-k). pap. 10.99 *(978-1-4052-6118-0(8))* Egmont Bks., Ltd. GBR. Dist: Independent Pubs. Group.
—Dinosaurumpus! Mitton, Tony. 2014. (ENG.). 30p. (J). (gr. -1-k). bds. 6.99 *(978-0-545-69480-3(9))*, Cartwheel Bks.) Scholastic, Inc.
—Dinosaurumpus! (a StoryPlay Book) Mitton, Tony. 2016. (ENG.). 40p. (J). (gr. -1-k). 5.99 *(978-1-338-11536-9(7))*, Cartwheel Bks.) Scholastic, Inc.
—Down by the Cool of the Pool (a StoryPlay Book) Mitton, Tony. 2017. (StoryPlay Ser.). (ENG.). 32p. (J). (gr. -1-k). 5.99 *(978-1-338-15841-0(4))*, Cartwheel Bks.) Scholastic, Inc.
—Giraffes Can't Dance. Andreae, Giles. (J). (gr. -1-3). 2012. (ENG.). 32p. bds. 6.99 *(978-0-545-39255-6(1))*, Cartwheel Bks.); 2008. (ENG.). 10.99 *(978-0-545-09738-3(X))*; 2007. 24.95 incl. audio *(978-0-439-02733-5(0))* Scholastic, Inc.
—Giraffes Can't Dance. Andreae, Giles. unabr. ed. 2011. (J). (gr. -1-1). 29.95 *(978-0-439-02734-2(9))* Weston Woods Studios, Inc.
—Giraffes Can't Dance: Number Rumba. Andreae, Giles. 2014. (ENG.). 12p. (J). (gr. -1 — 1). bds. 7.99 *(978-0-545-63996-5(4))*, Cartwheel Bks.) Scholastic, Inc.
—Never Ask a Dinosaur to Dinner. Edwards, Gareth. 2015. (ENG.). 32p. (J). (gr. -1-k). 17.99 *(978-0-545-81296-2(8))*, Scholastic Pr.) Scholastic, Inc.
—Three Grumpy Trucks. Tarpley, Todd. 2018. (ENG.). 40p. (J). (gr. -1-3). 17.99 *(978-0-316-34122-6(3))* Little Brown & Co.
Parker, Rick. Breaking Down, 2. Petrucha, Stefan. 2011. (Papercutz Slices Ser.: 2). (ENG.). 64p. (J). (gr. 6-8). 21.19 *(978-1-59707-245-8(1))*, 900073819) Papercutz.
—My Name Is Orange - Secret Agent Orange!, 1. Salicrup, Jim et al. 2013. (Annoying Orange Graphic Novels Ser.). (ENG.). 64p. (J). (gr. 4-7). 18.69 *(978-1-59707-362-2(8))*, 9781597073622) Papercutz.
Parker, Robert Andrew. Across the Blue Pacific: A World War II Story. Borden, Louise W. 2015. (ENG.). 48p. (J). (gr. -1-3). 7.99 *(978-0-544-55552-5(X))*, 1610459, HMH Books For Young Readers) Houghton Mifflin Harcourt Publishing Co.
—Action Jackson. Greenberg, Jan & Jordan, Sandra. 2007. (ENG.). 32p. (J). (gr. 1-5). pap. 8.99 *(978-0-312-36751-0(1))*, 900042355) Square Fish.
—Action Jackson. Jordan, Sandra & Greenberg, Jan. pap. incl. audio *(978-1-59112-961-5(3))*; pap. incl. audio compact disk *(978-1-59112-965-3(6))* Live Oak Media.
—The Impossible Major Rogers. Gauch, Patricia Lee. 2008. (J). *(978-1-59078-334-4(4))* Boyds Mills Pr.
—The Magician's Visit: A Passover Tale. Peretz, I. L. & Goldin, Barbara Diamond. 2006. 28p. (J). (gr. 4-8). reprint ed. 15.00 *(978-1-4223-5408-7(3))*; pap. 5.00 *(978-1-4223-5400-1(8))* DIANE Publishing Co.
—Who Was Albert Einstein? Brallier, Jess M. 2003. (Who Was... ? Ser.). 105p. (gr. 4-7). 15.00 *(978-0-7569-1586-5(4))* Perfection Learning Corp.
Parker, Robert Andrew. Piano Starts Here: The Young Art Tatum. Parker, Robert Andrew. 2016. (ENG.). 40p. (J). (gr. -1-3). 7.99 *(978-0-553-53392-7(4))*, Dragonfly Bks.) Random Hse. Children's Bks.
Parker, Ron. Voices from the Wild: An Animal Sensagoria, 1 vol. Bouchard, David. 2014. (ENG.). 72p. (J). (gr. 5-8). 24.95 *(978-1-55455-295-5(8))*, 9a2f69e5-c4c7-4174-8862-ff2058bde07d) Trifolium Bks., Inc. CAN. Dist: Firefly Bks., Ltd.
Parker-Thomas, Feronia. How the Crayons Saved the Rainbow. Sweeney, Monica. 2016. 32p. (J). (gr. -1-k). 16.99 *(978-1-5107-0583-8(X))*, Sky Pony Pr.) Skyhorse Publishing Co., Inc.
—How the Crayons Saved the Unicorn. Sweeney, Monica. 2019. 32p. (J). (-1). 16.99 *(978-1-5107-4819-4(9))*, Sky Pony Pr.) Skyhorse Publishing Co., Inc.
—Mind Your Manners. Edwards, Nicola. 2019. (J). 12.99 *(978-1-61067-811-7(7))* Kane Miller.
—Polonius the Pit Pony. O'Neill, Richard. 2018. (Child's Play Library). 32p. (J). *(978-1-78628-186-9(4))*; pap. *(978-1-78628-185-2(6))* Child's Play International Ltd.
Parker, Zac. We Like to Nurse Too. Young, Mary. 2009. (ENG.). 32p. (J). (gr. -1). pap. 9.95 *(978-1-890772-98-7(4))* Hohm Pr.
Parker, Zachary. Nos Gusta Vivir Verde: We Like to Live Green. Young, Mary. 2010. (SPA.). 32p. pap. 10.95 *(978-1-935387-01-5(4))* Kalindi Pr.
Parkerson, Hannah. Where Did My Stars Go? Wendt, K. 2019. (ENG.). 26p. (J). pap. 9.95 *(978-1-7322968-2-4(0))* Ladybug Writings.
Parkes, Elizabeth. Mommy's Going to the Hospital. Leon, Josie. 2017. (ENG.). (J). pap. 9.99 *(978-0-9994628-6-7(5))* Homecooked Entertainment.
Parkin, Marie. Mummy What Is a Shop? Schraider, Hannah-Marie. 2018. (ENG.). 26p. (J). pap. 9.99 *(978-1-7315-1878-1(1))* Independently Published.
Parkins, David. The Adventures of Old Bo Bear. Schertle, Alice. 2005. (J). 16.95 *(978-978-081-183-9(4))* Chronicle Bks. LLC.
—Ben's Robot, 1 vol. Stevenson, Robin. 2010. (Orca Echoes Ser.). (ENG.). 64p. (J). (gr. 1-3). pap. 6.95 *(978-1-55469-153-1(2))* Orca Bk. Pubs. USA.
—Brigadier: Gentle Hero. Andrekson, Judy. 2009. (True Horse Stories Ser.). 96p. (J). (gr. 4-7). pap. 7.95 *(978-0-88776-904-7(7))*, Tundra Bks.) Tundra Bks. CAN. Dist: Penguin Random Hse. LLC.
—Captain Pepper's Pets. Grindley, Sally. 2004. 48p. (J). pap. *(978-0-7534-1042-4(7))*, Kingfisher) Roaring Brook Pr.
—Don't Eat That! Charles, Veronika Martenova. 2008. (Easy-To-Read Spooky Tales Ser.). (ENG.). 56p. (J). (gr. k-3). pap. 5.99 *(978-0-88776-857-6(1))*, Tundra Bks.) Tundra Bks. CAN. Dist: Penguin Random Hse. LLC.
—Don't Enter the House! Charles, Veronika Martenova. 2008. (Easy-To-Read Spooky Tales Ser.). 56p. (J). (gr. k-3). pap. 5.99 *(978-0-88776-856-9(3))*, Tundra Bks.) Tundra Bks. CAN. Dist: Penguin Random Hse. LLC.
—Don't Forget! Charles, Veronika Martenova. 2008. (Easy-To-Read Spooky Tales Ser.). 56p. (J). (gr. k-3). pap. 5.95 *(978-0-88776-859-0(8))*, Tundra Bks.) Tundra Bks. CAN. Dist: Penguin Random Hse. LLC.
—Don't Go in There! Charles, Veronika Martenova. 2007. (Easy-To-Read Spooky Tales Ser.). 56p. (J). (gr. k-3). pap. 5.99 *(978-0-88776-781-4(8))*, Tundra Bks.) Tundra Bks. CAN. Dist: Penguin Random Hse. LLC.
—Don't Go into the Forest! Charles, Veronika Martenova. 2007. (Easy-To-Read Spooky Tales Ser.). 56p. (J). (gr. k-3). pap. 5.95 *(978-0-88776-778-4(8))*, Tundra Bks.) Tundra Bks. CAN. Dist: Penguin Random Hse. LLC.
—Don't Go near the Water! Charles, Veronika Martenova. 2007. (Easy-To-Read Spooky Tales Ser.). 56p. (J). (gr. k-3). pap. 5.99 *(978-0-88776-780-7(X))*, Tundra Bks.) Tundra Bks. CAN. Dist: Penguin Random Hse. LLC.
—Don't Open the Door! Charles, Veronika Martenova. 2007. (Easy-To-Read Spooky Tales Ser.). 56p. (J). (gr. k-3). pap. 6.99 *(978-0-88776-779-1(6))*, Tundra Bks.) Tundra Bks. CAN. Dist: Penguin Random Hse. LLC.
—Don't Talk to Strangers! Charles, Veronika Martenova. 2008. (Easy-To-Read Spooky Tales Ser.). (ENG.). 56p. (J). (gr. k-3). pap. 5.99 *(978-0-88776-847-7(4))*, Tundra Bks.) Tundra Bks. CAN. Dist: Penguin Random Hse. LLC.
—Don't Touch That! Charles, Veronika Martenova. 2008. (Easy-To-Read Spooky Tales Ser.). 56p. (J). (gr. k-3). pap. 5.95 *(978-0-88776-858-3(X))*, Tundra Bks.) Tundra Bks. CAN. Dist: Penguin Random Hse. LLC.

P

—Don't Walk Alone at Night! Charles, Veronika Martenova. 2007. (Easy-To-Read Spooky Tales Ser.). (ENG.). 56p. (J). (gr. k-3). pap. 5.99 *(978-0-88776-782-1(6)*, Tundra Bks.) Tundra Bks. CAN. Dist: Penguin Random Hse. LLC.

—Egyptian Diary: The Journal of Nakht. Platt, Richard. 2014. (ENG.). 128p. (J). (gr. 4-7). pap. 6.99 *(978-0-7636-7054-2(5))* Candlewick Pr.

—Fosta: Marathon Master. Andrekson, Judy. 2008. (True Horse Stories Ser.). 104p. (J). (gr. 4-7). pap. 7.95 *(978-0-88776-838-5(5)*, Tundra Bks.) Tundra Bks. CAN. Dist: Penguin Random Hse. LLC.

—Gilgamesh the Hero. McCaughrean, Geraldine. 2003. (ENG.). 96p. (J). (gr. 6-9). 20.00 *(978-0-8028-5262-5(9))* Eerdmans, William B. Publishing Co.

—Going Up! Kulling, Monica. 2014. (Great Idea (Tundra Books) Ser.). (ENG.). (J). (gr. k-3). lib. bdg. 18.60 *(978-1-62765-720-4(7))* Perfection Learning Corp.

—Going Up! Elisha Otis's Trip to the Top. Kulling, Monica. 2014. (Great Idea Ser.: 4). (ENG.). 32p. (J). (gr. k-3). pap. 7.99 *(978-1-77049-516-6(9)*, Tundra Bks.) Tundra Bks. CAN. Dist: Penguin Random Hse. LLC.

—Gunner: Hurricane Horse. Andrekson, Judy. 2010. (True Horse Stories Ser.). 104p. (J). (gr. 4-6). 22.44 *(978-0-88776-905-4(5)*, Tundra Bks.) Tundra Bks. CAN. Dist: Children's Plus, Inc.

—I Always, Always Get My Way. Krasnesky, Thad. 2009. (ENG.). 32p. (J). (gr. k-2). 16.95 *(978-0-9799746-4-9(X))* Flashlight Pr.

—I'm a Truck Driver. London, Jonathan. (ENG.). (J). 2018. 24p. bds. 7.99 *(978-1-250-17506-9(2)*, 900189297); 2010. 32p. (gr. -1-2). 15.99 *(978-0-8050-7989-0(0)*, 9780805079890) Holt, Henry & Co. (Holt, Henry & Co. Bks. For Young Readers).

—In the Bag! Margaret Knight Wraps It Up. Kulling, Monica. (Great Idea Ser.: 3). 32p. (J). (gr. k-3). 2013. (ENG.). pap. 7.95 *(978-1-77049-515-9(0))*; 2011. 17.95 *(978-1-77049-239-4(9))* Tundra Bks. CAN. (Tundra Bks.). Dist: Penguin Random Hse. LLC.

—It's Not about the Apple! Charles, Veronika Martenova. 2010. (Easy-To-Read Wonder Tales Ser.). 64p. (J). (gr. k-3). pap. 5.95 *(978-0-88776-955-9(1)*, Tundra Bks.) Tundra Bks. CAN. Dist: Penguin Random Hse. LLC.

—It's Not about the Ball! Charles, Veronika Martenova. 2013. (Easy-To-Read Wonder Tales Ser.). (ENG.). 64p. (J). (gr. k-3). pap. 5.95 *(978-1-77049-330-8(1)*, Tundra Bks.) Tundra Bks. CAN. Dist: Penguin Random Hse. LLC.

—It's Not about the Beanstalk! Charles, Veronika Martenova. 2013. (Easy-To-Read Wonder Tales Ser.: 10). (ENG.). 64p. (J). (gr. k-3). pap. 5.95 *(978-1-77049-327-8(1)*, Tundra Bks.) Tundra Bks. CAN. Dist: Penguin Random Hse. LLC.

—It's Not about the Crumbs! Charles, Veronika Martenova. 2010. (Easy-To-Read Wonder Tales Ser.). 64p. (J). (gr. k-3). pap. 5.99 *(978-0-88776-953-5(5)*, Tundra Bks.) Tundra Bks. CAN. Dist: Penguin Random Hse. LLC.

—It's Not about the Diamonds! Charles, Veronika Martenova. 2013. (Easy-To-Read Wonder Tales Ser.). (ENG.). 64p. (J). (gr. k-2). pap. 18.69 *(978-1-77049-328-5(X)*, Tundra Bks.) Tundra Bks. CAN. Dist: Children's Plus, Inc.

—It's Not about the Hunter! Easy-To-Read Wonder Tales. Charles, Veronika Martenova. 2010. (Easy-To-Read Wonder Tales Ser.: 1). (ENG.). 56p. (J). (gr. k-3). pap. 5.95 *(978-0-88776-948-1(9)*, Tundra Bks.) Tundra Bks. CAN. Dist: Penguin Random Hse. LLC.

—It's Not about the Pumpkin! Charles, Veronika Martenova. 2010. (Easy-To-Read Wonder Tales Ser.). 64p. (J). (gr. k-3). pap. 5.95 *(978-0-88776-949-8(7)*, Tundra Bks.) Tundra Bks. CAN. Dist: Penguin Random Hse. LLC.

—It's Not about the Rose! Charles, Veronika Martenova. 2010. (Easy-To-Read Wonder Tales Ser.). 64p. (J). (gr. k-3). pap. 5.95 *(978-0-88776-954-2(3)*, Tundra Bks.) Tundra Bks. CAN. Dist: Penguin Random Hse. LLC.

—It's Not about the Straw! Charles, Veronika Martenova. 2013. (Easy-To-Read Wonder Tales Ser.). (ENG.). 64p. (J). (gr. k-3). pap. 5.95 *(978-1-77049-326-1(3)*, Tundra Bks.) Tundra Bks. CAN. Dist: Penguin Random Hse. LLC.

—It's Not about the Tiny Girl! Charles, Veronika Martenova. 2013. (Easy-To-Read Wonder Tales Ser.). (ENG.). 64p. (J). (gr. k-2). pap. 18.69 *(978-1-77049-329-2(8)*, Tundra Bks.) Tundra Bks. CAN. Dist: Children's Plus, Inc.

—JB Andrew: Mustang Magic. Andrekson, Judy. 2008. (True Horse Stories Ser.). 88p. (J). (gr. 4-7). pap. 7.95 *(978-0-88776-837-8(7)*, Tundra Bks.) Tundra Bks. CAN. Dist: Penguin Random Hse. LLC.

—Little Squire: The Jumping Pony. Andrekson, Judy. 2007. (True Horse Stories Ser.). 80p. (J). (gr. 4-7). pap. 7.99 *(978-0-88776-770-8(2)*, Tundra Bks.) Tundra Bks. CAN. Dist: Penguin Random Hse. LLC.

—Miskeen: The Dancing Horse. Andrekson, Judy. 2007. (True Horse Stories Ser.). 96p. (J). (gr. 4-7). pap. 7.99 *(978-0-88776-771-5(0)*, Tundra Bks.) Tundra Bks. CAN. Dist: Penguin Random Hse. LLC.

—Prince for a Princess, 1 vol. Walters, Eric. 2012. (Orca Echoes Ser.). (ENG.). 64p. (J). (gr. 1-3). pap. 6.95 *(978-1-4598-0200-1(4))* Orca Bk. Pubs. USA.

—Roman Diary: The Journal of Iliona, a Young Slave. Platt, Richard. 2014. (ENG.). 128p. (J). (gr. 4-7). pap. 6.99 *(978-0-7636-7053-5(7))* Candlewick Pr.

—Roman Diary: The Journal of Iliona of Mytilini, Who Was Captured & Sold As a Slave in Rome, AD 107. Platt, Richard. 2009. (ENG.). 64p. (J). (gr. 3-7). 18.99 *(978-0-7636-3480-3(8))* Candlewick Pr.

—Ruckus, 1 vol. Elmquist, Laurie. 2019. (Orca Echoes Ser.). (ENG.). 96p. (J). (gr. 1-3). pap. 7.95 *(978-1-4598-1795-1(8))* Orca Bk. Pubs. USA.

—Shhhhh! Everybody's Sleeping. Markes, Julie. 32p. (J). (gr. -1-1). 2005. lib. bdg. 16.89 *(978-0-06-053791-3(4))*; 2004. (ENG.). 16.99 *(978-0-06-053790-6(6))* HarperCollins Pubs.

—Skye Above, 1 vol. Walters, Eric. 2014. (Orca Echoes Ser.). (ENG.). 64p. (J). (gr. 1-3). pap. 6.95 *(978-1-4598-0701-3(4))* Orca Bk. Pubs. USA.

—Spic-and-Span! Lillian Gilbreth's Wonder Kitchen. Kulling, Monica. 2016. (Great Idea Ser.: 6). (ENG.). 32p. (J). (gr. k-3). pap. 6.99 *(978-1-101-91843-2(8)*, Tundra Bks.) Tundra Bks. CAN. Dist: Penguin Random Hse. LLC.

—That Cat Can't Stay. Krasnesky, Thad. 2010. (ENG.). 32p. (J). (gr. k-2). 16.95 *(978-0-9799746-5-6(8))* Flashlight Pr.

—To the Rescue! Garrett Morgan Underground. Kulling, Monica. (Great Idea Ser.: 7). (ENG.). 32p. (J). (gr. k-3). 2017. pap. 6.99 *(978-1-101-91882-1(9))*; 2016. pap. 17.99 *(978-1-77049-520-3(7))* Tundra Bks. CAN. (Tundra Bks.). Dist: Penguin Random Hse. LLC.

—The Water Horse. King-Smith, Dick. 2007. (ENG.). 128p. (J). (gr. 1-4). 7.99 *(978-0-375-84231-3(4)*, Yearling) Random Hse. Children's Bks.

—When the Worst Happens: Extraordinary Stories of Survival. Lloyd Kyi, Tanya. 2014. (ENG.). 128p. (J). (gr. 5-8). pap. 14.95 *(978-1-55451-682-7(X)*, 9781554516827) Annick Pr., Ltd. CAN. Dist: Publishers Group West (PGW).

—Where's Burgess?, 1 vol. Elmquist, Laurie. 2018. (Orca Echoes Ser.). (ENG.). 96p. (J). (gr. 1-3). pap. 6.95 *(978-1-4598-1478-3(9))* Orca Bk. Pubs. USA.

Parkinson, Cheryl. Santa's Stormy Christmas Eve. Parkinson, Cheryl, tr. MacLennan, David. 2004. 32p. 7.95 *(978-0-9731960-0-9(9))* Full Satchel Pr. CAN. Dist: Gatewood Pr.

Parkinson, David. Aunt Nancy & the Bothersome Visitors. Root, Phyllis. 2007. (ENG.). 64p. (J). (gr. 2-5). 16.99 *(978-0-7636-3074-4(8))* Candlewick Pr.

Parkinson, Kate. Grace. Parkinson, Kate. 2015. (I Like to Read Ser.). (ENG.). 24p. (J). (gr. -1-3). 14.95 *(978-0-8234-3207-3(6))* Holiday Hse., Inc.

Parkinson, Kathy. When I Care about Others. Spelman, Cornelia Maude. 2013. (AV2 Fiction Readalong Ser.). (ENG.). (J). (gr. -1-3). 32.71 *(978-1-62127-907-5(3)*, AV2 by Weigl) Weigl Pubs., Inc.

—When I Feel Good about Myself. Spelman, Cornelia Maude. 2003. (Way I Feel Bks.). (ENG.). 24p. (J). (gr. -1-3). pap. 6.99 *(978-0-8075-8901-4(2)*, 807589012) Whitman, Albert & Co.

—When I Feel Jealous. Spelman, Cornelia Maude. 2003. (Way I Feel Bks.). (ENG.). 24p. (J). (gr. -1-3). 6.99 *(978-0-8075-8902-1(0)*, 807589020) Whitman, Albert & Co.

—When I Feel Scared. Spelman, Cornelia Maude. 2010. (Way I Feel Ser.). (ENG.). 16p. (J). (gr. -1 — 1). bds. 7.99 *(978-0-8075-8905-2(5)*, 0807589055) Whitman, Albert & Co.

—When I Feel Scared. Spelman, Cornelia. 2012. (J). *(978-1-61913-141-5(2))* Weigl Pubs., Inc.

—When I Feel Worried. Maude Spelman, Cornelia & Spelman, Cornelia Maude. 2014. (Way I Feel Bks.). (ENG.). 24p. (J). (gr. -1-3). pap. 6.99 *(978-0-8075-8895-6(4)*, 807588954) Whitman, Albert & Co.

—When I Miss You. Spelman, Cornelia Maude. 2004. (Way I Feel Bks.). (ENG.). 24p. (J). (gr. -1-3). pap. 6.99 *(978-0-8075-8903-8(9)*, 807589039) Whitman, Albert & Co.

Parks, Paul, jt. illus. see Damerum, Kanako.

Parks, Phil. Basement of the Undead, 1 vol. Strange, Jason. 2011. (Jason Strange Ser.). (ENG.). 72p. (J). (gr. 3-6). pap. 6.25 *(978-1-4342-3433-9(9))*; lib. bdg. 25.32 *(978-1-4342-3234-2(4))* Capstone. (Stone Arch Bks.).

—Blazing Courage. Halls, Kelly Milner. ed. 2015. (Animal Rescues Ser.: 1). (ENG.). 96p. (J). (gr. 4-8). E-Book 6.99 *(978-1-4677-8990-5(9)*, 9781467789905, Darby Creek) Lerner Publishing Group.

—Every Day's a Holiday: Amusing Rhymes for Happy Times. Koontz, Dean. 2003. 144p. (J). 18.89 *(978-0-06-008585-8(1))* HarperCollins Pubs.

—Faceless Friend, 1 vol. Strange, Jason. 2011. (Jason Strange Ser.). (ENG.). 72p. (J). (gr. 3-6). pap. 6.25 *(978-1-4342-3431-5(2))*; lib. bdg. 25.32 *(978-1-4342-3232-8(8))* Capstone. (Stone Arch Bks.).

—The Mothman's Shadow, 1 vol. Strange, Jason. 2011. (Jason Strange Ser.). (ENG.). 72p. (J). (gr. 3-6). pap. 6.25 *(978-1-4342-3093-5(7)*, Stone Arch Bks.) Capstone.

—Realm of Ghosts, 1 vol. Strange, Jason. 2011. (Jason Strange Ser.). (ENG.). 72p. (J). (gr. 3-6). pap. 6.25 *(978-1-4342-3096-6(1))*; 25.32 *(978-1-4342-2962-5(9))* Capstone. (Stone Arch Bks.).

—Robot Santa: The Further Adventures of Santa's Twin. Koontz, Dean. 2004. (Santa's Twin Ser.: Bk. 2). 72p. (J). 20.89 *(978-0-06-050944-6(9))* HarperCollins Pubs.

—Santa's Twin. Koontz, Dean. 2004. (Santa's Twin Ser.: Bk. 1). (ENG.). 64p. pap. 12.95 *(978-0-06-057223-5(X)*, William Morrow Paperbacks) HarperCollins Pubs.

—To Wake the Dead, 1 vol. Strange, Jason. 2011. (Jason Strange Ser.). (ENG.). 72p. (J). (gr. 3-6). pap. 6.25 *(978-1-4342-3094-2(5))*; 25.32 *(978-1-4342-2963-2(7))* Capstone. (Stone Arch Bks.).

—Zombie Winter, 1 vol. Strange, Jason. 2011. (Jason Strange Ser.). (ENG.). 72p. (J). (gr. 3-6). pap. 6.25 *(978-1-4342-3095-9(3)*, Stone Arch Bks.) Capstone.

Parks, Phil & Dal Lago, Alberto. Full Moon Horror, 1 vol. Strange, Jason. 2011. (Jason Strange Ser.). (ENG.). 72p. (J). (gr. 3-6). pap. 6.25 *(978-1-4342-3434-6(7))*; lib. bdg. 25.32 *(978-1-4342-3235-9(2))* Capstone. (Stone Arch Bks.).

—Text 4 Revenge, 1 vol. Strange, Jason. 2011. (Jason Strange Ser.). (ENG.). 72p. (J). (gr. 3-6). pap. 6.25 *(978-1-4342-3432-2(0))*; lib. bdg. 25.32 *(978-1-4342-3233-5(6))* Capstone. (Stone Arch Bks.).

Parks, Phil, jt. illus. see Soleiman, Serg.

Parlagreco, Aurora M., jt. illus. see Rogers, Jacqueline.

Parlin, Tim. Milton Hershey. Sutcliffe, Jane. 2003. (History Maker Biographies Ser.). (ENG.). 48p. (gr. 3-6). 27.93 *(978-0-8225-0247-0(X)*, Lerner Pubns.) Lerner Publishing Group.

Parlin, Tim. Chief Joseph. Parlin, Tim, tr. Sutcliffe, Jane. 2004. (History Maker Bios Ser.). 48p. (J). (gr. 3-5). lib. bdg. 26.60 *(978-0-8225-0696-6(3))* Lerner Publishing Group.

—Geronimo. Parlin, Tim, tr. Welch, Catherine A. 2004. (History Maker Bios Ser.). 47p. (J). 26.60 *(978-0-8225-0698-0(X)*, Carolrhoda Bks.) Lerner Publishing Group.

—Sitting Bull. Parlin, Tim, tr. Aller, Susan Bivin. 2004. (History Maker Bios Ser.). 47p. (J). 26.60 *(978-0-8225-0700-0(5)*, Carolrhoda Bks.) Lerner Publishing Group.

Parlingayan, Nikka. Don't Fall Franny: A Children's Book about Fall Safety. Part of the Stop the Slip Series. Etherton, Veronica & Disch, Thom. 2020. (Stop the Slip Ser.: Vol. 2). (ENG.). 40p. (J). pap. 12.99 ***(978-1-6998-9868-0(5))*** Independently Published.

Parmar, Tavisha. The Class Photograph. 2005. (J). *(978-81-902492-1-8(5))* Vivera Bks.

Parme, Fabrice. Caesar, Who's He? Surget, Alain & Yeardley, Glynne. 2014. 95p. (J). *(978-1-4351-5328-8(6))* Barnes & Noble, Inc.

—Cleopatra Must Be Saved! Surget, Alain & Yeardley, Glynne. 2014. 95p. (J). *(978-1-4351-5329-5(4))* Barnes & Noble, Inc.

—Danger at the Circus! Surget, Alain & Yeardley, Glynne. 2014. 95p. (J). *(978-1-4351-5334-9(0))* Barnes & Noble, Inc.

—Prisoners in the Pyramid. Surget, Alain & Yeardley, Glynne. 2014. 94p. (J). *(978-1-4351-5326-4(X))* Barnes & Noble, Inc.

Parmelee, George. Gerald Giraffe's Garage. Berresford, J. R. 2013. (ENG.). 32p. (J). (gr. -1-3). 11.95 *(978-0-9860321-0-3(7))* Tuscarora Publishing Company.

Parn, Priit. The Gothamites. Raud, Eno. Cullen, Adam, tr. 2019. (ENG.). 44p. (J). (gr. k-3). 18.00 *(978-1-939810-28-1(0)*, Elsewhere Editions) Steerforth Pr.

Parnelli, Martina. Saint Clare & Her Cat. Jackson, Dessi. 2019. (ENG.). 38p. (J). pap. 10.99 ***(978-0-9976747-3-6(3))*** Silver Fire Publishing.

Parod, Claire Armstrong. I'm a Pretty Little Black Girl! Bynum, Betty K. 2013. (I'm a Girl! Collection: 1). (ENG.). 36p. (J). (gr. k-7). 16.95 *(978-0-615-78551-6(4))* Workhouse Road Productions.

Paroline, Michelle. Tricky Fox Tales: Book 3, No. 3. Schweizer, Chris. 2011. (Tricky Journeys (tm) Ser.: 3). (ENG.). 64p. (J). (gr. 2-4). pap. 6.95 *(978-0-7613-7861-7(8)*, 9780761378617, Graphic Universe™) Lerner Publishing Group.

Paroline, Michelle, jt. illus. see Paroline, Shelli.

Paroline, Shelli. Adventure Time, Vol. 1. North, Ryan & Lamb, Branden. 2012. (Adventure Time Ser.). (ENG.). 128p. (J). (gr. 4-7). pap. 14.99 *(978-1-60886-280-1(1))* Boom! Studios.

—Muppet Snow White. Snider, Jesse Blaze. 2010. (Muppet Show Ser.). 112p. (J). (gr. 3-6). pap. 9.99 *(978-1-60886-574-1(6))* Boom! Studios.

Paroline, Shelli & Lamb, Braden. Adventure Time, Vol. 2. North, Ryan. 2013. (Adventure Time Ser.: 1). (ENG.). 128p. (J). (gr. 4). 34.99 *(978-1-60886-321-1(2))* Boom! Studios.

—Adventure Time Vol. 2. North, Ryan. 2013. (Adventure Time Ser.). (ENG.). 112p. (J). (gr. 4-7). pap. 14.99 *(978-1-60886-323-5(9))* Boom! Studios.

—Adventure Time Vol. 3. North, Ryan. 2013. (Adventure Time Ser.). (ENG.). 112p. (J). (gr. 4-7). pap. 14.99 *(978-1-60886-317-4(4))* Boom! Studios.

—Adventure Time Vol. 3 Mathematical Edition. 2014. (Adventure Time Ser.: 3). (ENG.). 128p. (J). (gr. 4). 34.99 *(978-1-60886-347-1(6))* Boom! Studios.

Paroline, Shelli & Paroline, Michelle. Tricky Fox Tales. Schweizer, Chris. 2011. (Tricky Journeys Ser.: 3). (ENG.). (J). (gr. 2-4). pap. 39.62 *(978-0-7613-8627-8(0))* Lerner Publishing Group.

Paroline, Shelli, jt. illus. see Lamb, Braden.

Parpan, Justin. Gwango's Lonesome Trail. 2006. 32p. (J). (gr. -1-3). 15.95 *(978-1-60108-004-2(2))* Red Cygnet Pr.

Parr, Todd. The Family Book. Parr, Todd. 2019. (Todd Parr Picture Bks.). (ENG.). 32p. (J). (gr. -1-2). 27.07 *(978-1-5321-4370-0(2)*, 31820, Picture Bk.) Spotlight.

—The Feelings Book. Parr, Todd. 2019. (Todd Parr Picture Bks.). (ENG.). 32p. (J). (gr. -1-2). 27.07 *(978-1-5321-4371-7(0)*, 31821, Picture Bk.) Spotlight.

—The Goodbye Book. Parr, Todd. 2015. 32p. (J). (gr. -1-1). 17.99 *(978-0-316-40497-6(7))* Little, Brown Bks. for Young Readers.

—The Goodbye Book. Parr, Todd. 2019. (Todd Parr Picture Bks.). (ENG.). 32p. (J). (gr. -1-2). 27.07 *(978-1-5321-4372-4(9)*, 31822, Picture Bk.) Spotlight.

—El Gran Libro de la Amistad. Parr, Todd. Morell, Ivonne Bonsfill, tr. 2010. (Mundo de Todd Ser.). (SPA.). 10p. (J). 17.95 *(978-84-92691-19-7(0))* Roca Editorial ESP. Dist: Spanish Pubs., LLC.

—The I'm Not Scared Book. Parr, Todd. 2019. (Todd Parr Picture Bks.). (ENG.). 32p. (J). (gr. -1-2). 27.07 *(978-1-5321-4373-1(7)*, 31823, Picture Bk.) Spotlight.

—It's Okay to Be Different. Parr, Todd. 2019. (Todd Parr Picture Bks.). (ENG.). 32p. (J). (gr. -1-2). 27.07 *(978-1-5321-4374-8(5)*, 31824, Picture Bk.) Spotlight.

—It's Okay to Make Mistakes. Parr, Todd. 2019. (Todd Parr Picture Bks.). (ENG.). 32p. (J). (gr. -1-2). 27.07 *(978-1-5321-4375-5(3)*, 31825, Picture Bk.) Spotlight.

—Love the World. Parr, Todd. 2019. (Todd Parr Picture Bks.). (ENG.). 32p. (J). (gr. -1-2). 27.07 *(978-1-5321-4376-2(1)*, 31826, Picture Bk.) Spotlight.

—The Peace Book. Parr, Todd. 2019. (Todd Parr Picture Bks.). (ENG.). 32p. (J). (gr. -1-2). 27.07 *(978-1-5321-4377-9(X)*, 31827, Picture Bk.) Spotlight.

—The Thankful Book. Parr, Todd. 2019. (Todd Parr Picture Bks.). (ENG.). 32p. (J). (gr. -1-2). 27.07 *(978-1-5321-4378-6(8)*, 31828, Picture Bk.) Spotlight.

—Todd Parr Picture Books (Set), 9 vols. Parr, Todd. 2019. (Todd Parr Picture Bks.). (ENG.). 32p. (J). (gr. -1-2). 243.63 *(978-1-5321-4369-4(9)*, 31819, Picture Bk.) Spotlight.

Parra, John. Frida Kahlo & Her Animalitos. Brown, Monica. 2017. (ENG.). 40p. (J). (gr. -1-3). 17.95 *(978-0-7358-4269-4(8))* North-South Bks., Inc.

—Frida Kahlo y Sus Animalitos. Brown, Monica. 2017. (SPA.). 40p. (J). (gr. -1-3). 17.95 *(978-0-7358-4292-2(2))* North-South Bks., Inc.

—Green Is a Chile Pepper: A Book of Colors. Thong, Roseanne Greenfield. (ENG.). 40p. (J). (gr. -1-k). 2016. 7.99 *(978-1-4521-5645-3(X))*; 2014. 16.99 *(978-1-4521-0203-0(1))* Chronicle Bks. LLC.

—Hey, Wall: A Story of Art & Community. Verde, Susan. 2018. (ENG.). 40p. (J). (gr. -1-3). 17.99 *(978-1-4814-5313-4(0)*, Simon & Schuster/Paula Wiseman Bks.) Simon & Schuster/Paula Wiseman Bks.

—Little Libraries, Big Heroes. Paul, Miranda. 2019. (ENG.). 40p. (J). (gr. -1-3). 17.99 *(978-0-544-80027-4(3)*, 1640324, Clarion Bks.) Houghton Mifflin Harcourt Trade & Reference Pubs.

—Marvelous Cornelius: Hurricane Katrina & the Spirit of New Orleans. Bildner, Phil. 2015. (ENG.). 44p. (J). (gr. k-3). 16.99 *(978-1-4521-2578-7(3))* Chronicle Bks. LLC.

—One Is a Piñata: a Book of Numbers (Learn to Count Books, Numbers Books for Kids, Preschool Numbers Book) Thong, Roseanne Greenfield. 2019. (ENG.). 40p. (J). (gr. -1-k). 16.99 *(978-1-4521-5584-5(4))* Chronicle Bks. LLC.

Parra, John. Oye, Muro (Hey, Wall) Un Cuento de Arte y Comunidad. Verde, Susan. Romay, Alexis, tr. 2020. (SPA.). 40p. (J). (gr. -1-3). 17.99 ***(978-1-5344-6845-0(5))***; 7.99 ***(978-1-5344-6846-7(3))*** Simon & Schuster/Paula Wiseman Bks. (Simon & Schuster/Paula Wiseman Bks.).

Parra, John. P Is for Pinata. Johnston, Tony. 2008. (Discover the World Ser.). (ENG.). 40p. (J). (gr. 1-5). 17.95 *(978-1-58536-144-1(5))* Sleeping Bear Pr.

—The Power of Her Pen: The Story of Groundbreaking Journalist Ethel L. Payne. Cline-Ransome, Lesa. 2020. (ENG.). 48p. (J). (gr. -1-3). 17.99 *(978-1-4814-6289-1(X)*, Simon & Schuster Bks. For Young Readers) Simon & Schuster Bks. For Young Readers.

—Round Is a Tortilla: A Book of Shapes. Thong, Roseanne Greenfield. 2013. (ENG.). 40p. (J). (gr. -1-k). 16.99 *(978-1-4521-0616-8(9))* Chronicle Bks. LLC.

—Round Is a Tortilla: A Book of Shapes. Thong, Roseanne. 2015. (ENG.). 40p. (J). (gr. -1-k). 7.99 *(978-1-4521-4568-6(7))* Chronicle Bks. LLC.

—Waiting for the Biblioburro. Brown, Monica. 2011. (ENG.). 32p. (J). (gr. k-3). 17.99 *(978-1-58246-353-7(0)*, Tricycle Pr.) Random Hse. Children's Bks.

Parra, Lola, jt. illus. see Cos, Manrique.

Parra, Rocio. Globito Manual. Reyes, Carlos Jose. 2004. (Primer Acto: Teatro Infantil y Juvenil Ser.). (SPA.). 30p. (J). (gr. -1-7). pap. *(978-958-30-0317-2(4))* Panamericana Editorial.

—Lucy Es Pecosa. Arciniegas, Triunfo. 2004. (Primer Acto: Teatro Infantil y Juvenil Ser.). (SPA.). 43p. (J). (gr. -1-7). pap. *(978-958-30-0316-5(6))* Panamericana Editorial.

—Siriko y la Flauta. Rodriguez, Julia. 2004. (Primer Acto: Teatro Infantil y Juvenil Ser.). (SPA.). 28p. (J). (gr. 4-7). pap. *(978-958-30-0315-8(8))* Panamericana Editorial.

Parramon's Editorial Team Staff, photos by. Metal. Parramon's Editorial Team Staff. Parramon's Editorial Team. 2004. (Let's Create! Ser.). 32p. (gr. 1-4). lib. bdg. 27.00 *(978-0-8368-4016-2(X)*, Gareth Stevens Learning Library) Stevens, Gareth Publishing LLLP.

—Papier-Mâché. Parramon's Editorial Team Staff. 2004. (Let's Create! Ser.). 32p. (gr. 1-4). lib. bdg. 27.00 *(978-0-8368-4017-9(8)*, Gareth Stevens Learning Library) Stevens, Gareth Publishing LLLP.

—Recyclables. Parramon's Editorial Team Staff. 2004. (Let's Create! Ser.). 32p. (gr. 1-4). lib. bdg. 27.00 *(978-0-8368-4018-6(6)*, Gareth Stevens Learning Library) Stevens, Gareth Publishing LLLP.

—Stones & "Stuff" Parramon's Editorial Team Staff. 2004. (Let's Create! Ser.). 32p. (gr. 1-4). lib. bdg. 27.00 *(978-0-8368-4019-3(4)*, Gareth Stevens Learning Library) Stevens, Gareth Publishing LLLP.

Parrilli, Sara. The Kingdom of Beautiful Colours: a Picture Book for Children, 17 vols. Wyatt, Isabel. 2019. (ENG.). 32p. (J). 19.95 *(978-1-78250-597-6(0))* Floris Bks. GBR. Dist: Consortium Bk. Sales & Distribution.

—Through the Rainbow: A Waldorf Birthday Story for Children, 15 vols. Harvey-Zahra, Lou. 2018. (ENG.). 32p. (J). 19.95 *(978-1-78250-507-5(5))* Floris Bks. GBR. Dist: Consortium Bk. Sales & Distribution.

Parris, Kitty. If I Were a Monkey. Batchler, Daria. 2005. 24p. (J). bds. 12.95 *(978-0-9746959-2-1(0))* Falcon Publishing LTD.

Parrish, Beth. Secrets of the Toad: Reflection. (patty Page), Trisha. 2020. (ENG.). 100p. (J). pap. 7.99 ***(978-1-64237-887-0(9))*** Gatekeeper Pr.

Parrish, Emma. Buzzy Bee: A Slide-And-Seek Book. Little Bee Books. 2017. (Slide-And-Seek Ser.). (ENG.). 10p. (J). (gr. -1-k). bds. 8.99 *(978-1-4998-0469-0(5))* Little Bee Books Inc.

Parrish, Fayrene. Pancho Saves the Day: Shipmates Learning Adventures Venture. Parrish, Fayrene. 2010. 42p. (J). 15.95 *(978-0-9826717-8-8(4))* Parrish, Fayrene.

Parrish, Kirk. El Rey Midas y el Toque de Oro. Strom, Laura Layton. 2016. (Jump into Genre Ser.). (SPA.). (J). (gr. 3). 5.25 *(978-1-4788-3624-7(5))* Newmark Learning LLC.

Parrish, Maria, et al. Little Bird Greetings: Whooo Loves Baby, Bless Child, Little Boys: Keepsake Greeting Card Board Book 3 Pack. Birdsong, Minnie. 2015. (Little Bird Greetings Ser.). (ENG.). 16p. (J). (gr. -1-k). bds., bds., bds. 20.97 *(978-1-68052-247-1(7)*, 9000810) Cottage Door Pr.

Parrish, Maria. Whooo Loves Baby: Keepsake Greeting Card Board Book. Birdsong, Minnie. ed. 2017. (Little Bird Greetings Ser.). (ENG.). 8p. (J). (gr. -1-k). bds. 6.99 *(978-1-68052-212-9(4)*, 1000441) Cottage Door Pr.

Parrish, Maxfield. The Arabian Nights: Their Best-Known Tales. Wiggin, Kate Douglas & Smith, Nora A. 2019. (Scribner Classics Ser.). (ENG.). 384p. (J). (gr. 3-7). 29.99 *(978-1-5344-3018-1(0)*, Atheneum Bks. for Young Readers) Simon & Schuster Children's Publishing.

—The Knave of Hearts. Saunders, Louise. 2008. (Calla Editions Ser.). (ENG.). 40p. (gr. 3). 30.00 *(978-1-60660-001-6(X))* Dover Pubns., Inc.

Parrott, Aaron. The Christmas Flash Couldn't Even. Martindale, Kari Ann. 2017. (ENG.). (J). (gr. k-3). pap. 10.95 *(978-0-9994504-1-3(7))* karilogue.

Parrott, Heather. Dale the Uniclyde: An adventure in Friendship. von Rosenberg, Byron. 2007. 22p. (J). 11.95 *(978-0-9759858-6-1(8))* Red Mountain Creations.

Parry, Alan. The Kregel Pictorial Guide to the Tabernacle, 1 vol. Dowley, Tim. 2003. (Kregel Pictorial Guide Ser.). 32p. pap. 11.99 *(978-0-8254-2468-7(2))* Kregel Pubns.

Parry, Jo. Alphabet Farm. Top That Publishing Staff, ed. 2007. (Magnetic - Alphabet Ser.). 10p. (J). (gr. -1). bds. *(978-1-84666-272-0(9)*, Tide Mill Pr.) Top That! Publishing PLC.

—Alphabet Farm (large Version) Top That!. 2007. 10p. (J). (gr. -1). *(978-1-84666-553-0(1)*, Tide Mill Pr.) Top That! Publishing PLC.

—Amazing Bible Stories. David, Juliet. ed. 2019. (ENG.). 16p. (J). (gr. -1-k). 16.99 *(978-1-78128-288-5(9))* Lion Hudson PLC GBR. Dist: Independent Pubs. Group.

—Beetle Bugs Party: A Counting Book. Depisco, Dorothea. 2005. 10p. (J). (gr. -1-3). 10.95 *(978-1-58117-415-1(2)*, Intervisual/Piggy Toes) Bendon, Inc.

—Bluebird's Nest. DePrisco, Dorothea. 2006. (ENG.). 16p. (J). 9.95 *(978-1-58117-390-1(3)*, Intervisual/Piggy Toes) Bendon, Inc.

—Bluebird's Nest. DePrisco, Dorothea. 2006. (ENG.). 14p. (gr. -1-k). 5.95 *(978-1-58117-504-2(3)*, Intervisual/Piggy Toes) Bendon, Inc.

—Bright Night, 1 vol. Grover, Lorie Ann. 2017. (ENG.). 16p. (J). bds. 8.99 *(978-0-310-75736-8(3))* Zonderkidz.

—Candle Bible for Kids, 1 vol. David, Juliet. 2018. 400p. (J). 16.99 *(978-0-8254-5557-5(X))* Kregel Pubns.

—Candle Prayers for Kids, 1 vol. Freedman, Claire. ed. 2014. (ENG.). 128p. (J). 12.99 *(978-1-78128-102-4(5)*, Candle Bks.) Lion Hudson PLC GBR. Dist: Kregel Pubns.

—The Christmas Story, 1 vol. David, Juliet. 2009. (Candle Read & Play Ser.). 12p. (J). bds. 11.99 *(978-0-8254-7400-2(0)*, Candle Bks.) Lion Hudson PLC GBR. Dist: Kregel Pubns.

—Color Safari (large Version) Top That!. 2007. 10p. (J). (gr. -1). *(978-1-84666-554-7(X)*, Tide Mill Pr.) Top That! Publishing PLC.

—Daddy Loves You So Much, 1 vol. Thomas Nelson Publishing Staff. 2015. (ENG.). 20p. (J). bds. 9.99 *(978-0-529-12335-0(5))* Nelson, Thomas Inc.

—Fantastic Bible Stories. David, Juliet. ed. 2019. (ENG.). 18p. (J). (gr. -1-k). 16.99 *(978-1-78128-289-2(7))* Lion Hudson PLC GBR. Dist: Independent Pubs. Group.

—Favourite Fairy Tales: Picture Fairy Tales for Little Ones. Baxter, Nicola. 2016. (ENG.). 16p. (J). (gr. -1-12). bds. 10.99 *(978-1-84322-625-3(1)*, Armadillo) Anness Publishing GBR. Dist: National Bk. Network.

—The Great Flood, 1 vol. David, Juliet. 2014. 12p. (J). bds. 3.99 *(978-1-85985-991-9(7)*, Candle Bks.) Lion Hudson PLC GBR. Dist: Kregel Pubns.

—Jungle Numbers. Top That Publishing Staff, ed. 2007. (Magnetic - Numbers Ser.). 10p. (J). (gr. -1). bds. *(978-1-84666-163-1(3)*, Tide Mill Pr.) Top That! Publishing PLC.

—Jungle Numbers (large Version) Top That!. 2007. 10p. (J). (gr. -1). *(978-1-84666-552-3(3)*, Tide Mill Pr.) Top That! Publishing PLC.

—Magnetic Color Safari. Ranson, Erin. 2007. 10p. (J). (gr. -1-3). *(978-1-84666-361-1(X)*, Tide Mill Pr.) Top That! Publishing PLC.

—Magnetic Playtime Shapes. Ranson, Erin. 2007. (Magnetic Playtime Shapes Ser.). 10p. (J). (gr. -1-3). *(978-1-84666-363-5(6)*, Tide Mill Pr.) Top That! Publishing PLC.

—The Midnight Visitors, 1 vol. David, Juliet. 2015. 32p. (J). 14.99 *(978-1-78128-233-5(1)*, Candle Bks.); (ENG.). (gr. -1-k). pap. 7.99 *(978-1-78128-196-3(3))* Lion Hudson PLC GBR. Dist: Kregel Pubns., Independent Pubs. Group.

—Mommy Loves You So Much, 1 vol. Thomas Nelson Publishing Staff. 2015. (ENG.). 20p. (J). bds. 9.99 *(978-0-529-12338-1(X))* Nelson, Thomas Inc.

—My First Fairy Tales: Eight Exciting Picture Stories for Little Ones. Baxter, Nicola. 2013. (ENG.). 16p. (J). (gr. -1-2). bds. 13.99 *(978-1-84322-991-9(9)*, Armadillo) Anness Publishing GBR. Dist: National Bk. Network.

—Playtime Shapes (large Version) Top That!. 2007. 10p. (J). (gr. -1). *(978-1-84666-555-4(8)*, Tide Mill Pr.) Top That! Publishing PLC.

—Ten Christmas Lights: Count the Lights from One to Ten! Imperato, Teresa. 2005. (ENG.). 20p. (J). 10.95 *(978-1-58117-321-5(0)*, Intervisual/Piggy Toes) Bendon, Inc.

—Traditional Fairy Tales: Eight Exciting Picture Stories for Little Ones. Baxter, Nicola & Francis, Jan. 2013. 16p. (J). (gr. -1-2). 13.99 *(978-1-84322-992-6(7)*, Armadillo) Anness Publishing GBR. Dist: National Bk. Network.

Parry, Jo. Sleep, Little Pup. Parry, Jo. 2017. (Story Corner Ser.). (ENG.). 24p. (J). (gr. -1-k). lib. bdg. 19.99 *(978-1-68297-183-3(X))* QEB Publishing Inc.

Parry, Launie. The 5,000 Friends of Veronica Veetch. Hanson, Jean. 2017. (ENG.). 32p. (J). 17.95 *(978-1-934649-27-5(9))* Bailiwick Pr.

Parry, Linda. The Bible Made Easy: A Pop-Up, Pull-Out, Interactive Bible Adventure. Parry, Alan. (J). 14.99 *(978-1-85608-399-7(3))* Hunt, John Publishing Ltd. GBR. Dist: O. M. Literature.

Parsley, Elise. The Magic Word. Barnett, Mac. 2016. (ENG.). 40p. (J). (gr. -1-3). 17.99 *(978-0-06-235484-6(1))* HarperCollins Pubs.

Parsloe, Alismarie. Wesley's World. Brown, Kathy. 2011. 36p. pap. 24.95 *(978-1-4489-8461-9(0))* America Star Bks.

Parsons, Arielle, jt. illus. see Stanley, Christopher Heath.

Parsons, Garry. Are You the Pirate Captain? Jones, Gareth P. 2016. (ENG.). 32p. (J). (gr. -1-3). 16.95 *(978-1-5124-0427-2(6)*, 9781512404272); E-Book 27.99 *(978-1-5124-0446-3(2))* Lerner Publishing Group.

—Digging for Dinosaurs. Waite, Judy. 2003. (Flying Foxes Ser.). (ENG.). 48p. (J). lib. bdg. *(978-0-7787-1483-5(7))* Crabtree Publishing Co.

—The Dinosaur That Pooped a Planet! Fletcher, Tom & Poynter, Dougie. 2017. (Dinosaur That Ser.). (ENG.). 32p. (J). (gr. -1-3). 15.99 *(978-1-4814-9866-1(5)*, Aladdin) Simon & Schuster Children's Publishing.

—The Dinosaur That Pooped Christmas! Fletcher, Tom & Poynter, Dougie. 2019. (Dinosaur That Ser.). (ENG.). 32p. (J). (gr. -1-3). 17.99 *(978-1-4814-9872-2(X)*, Aladdin) Simon & Schuster Children's Publishing.

—The Dinosaur That Pooped the Bed! Fletcher, Tom & Poynter, Dougie. 2018. (Dinosaur That Ser.). (ENG.). 32p. (J). (gr. -1-3). 15.99 *(978-1-4814-9870-8(3)*, Aladdin) Simon & Schuster Children's Publishing.

—The Dinosaur That Pooped the Past! Fletcher, Tom & Poynter, Dougie. 2018. (Dinosaur That Ser.). (ENG.). 32p. (J). (gr. -1-3). 15.99 *(978-1-4814-9868-5(1)*, Aladdin) Simon & Schuster Children's Publishing.

—The Dinosaurs Are Having a Party! Jones, Gareth P. ed. 2015. (ENG.). 32p. (J). (gr. -1-3). E-Book 27.99 *(978-1-4677-6317-2(9))* Lerner Publishing Group.

—The Dragonsitter in the Land of the Dragons. Lacey, Josh. 2019. (Dragonsitter Ser.: 10). 80p. (J). (gr. 2-4). 8.99 *(978-1-78344-800-5(8))* Penguin Random Hse. AUS. Dist: Independent Pubs. Group.

—The Dragonsitter: Trick or Treat? Lacey, Josh. 2017. (Dragonsitter Ser.). (ENG.). 80p. (J). (gr. 1-5). 15.99 *(978-0-316-55582-1(7))*; pap. 8.99 *(978-0-316-55584-5(3))* Little, Brown Bks. for Young Readers.

—The Dragonsitter's Island. Lacey, Josh. 2016. (Dragonsitter Ser.: 4). (ENG.). 96p. (J). (gr. 1-5). pap. 8.99 *(978-0-316-29908-4(1))* Little, Brown Bks. for Young Readers.

—The Dragonsitter's Surprise. Lacey, Josh. 2019. (Dragonsitter Ser.: 9). 80p. (J). (gr. 2-4). 8.99 *(978-1-78344-623-0(4))* Penguin Random Hse. AUS. Dist: Independent Pubs. Group.

—The Football Ghosts. Doyle, Malachy. 2nd ed. 2016. (Reading Ladder Ser.). (ENG.). 48p. (J). (gr. k-2). pap. 7.99 *(978-1-4052-8243-7(6))* Egmont Bks., Ltd. GBR. Dist: Independent Pubs. Group.

—The Four Franks. Mayfield, Sue. 2005. (Blue Go Bananas Ser.). (ENG.). 48p. (J). (gr. 1-2). *(978-0-7787-2651-7(7))* Crabtree Publishing Co.

—G. E. M. Clarke, Jane. 2008. (ENG.). 32p. (J). (gr. -1-k). pap. 9.95 *(978-0-09-948012-9(3)*, Red Fox) Random House Children's Books GBR. Dist: Independent Pubs. Group.

—George & the Big Bang. Hawking, Lucy & Hawking, Stephen. 2012. (George's Secret Key Ser.). (ENG.). 336p. (J). (gr. 3-7). 22.99 *(978-1-4424-4005-0(8)*, Simon & Schuster Bks. For Young Readers) Simon & Schuster Bks. For Young Readers.

—George & the Big Bang. Hawking, Stephen & Hawking, Lucy. 2013. (George's Secret Key Ser.). (ENG.). 304p. (J). (gr. 3-7). pap. 12.99 *(978-1-4424-4006-7(6)*, Simon & Schuster Bks. For Young Readers) Simon & Schuster Bks. For Young Readers.

—George & the Blue Moon. Hawking, Stephen & Hawking, Lucy. (George's Secret Key Ser.). (ENG.). 336p. (J). (gr. 3-7). 2018. pap. 10.99 *(978-1-4814-6631-8(3))*; 2017. 22.99 *(978-1-4814-6630-1(5))* Simon & Schuster Bks. For Young Readers. (Simon & Schuster Bks. For Young Readers).

—George & the Ship of Time. Hawking, Lucy. 2019. (George's Secret Key Ser.). (ENG.). 416p. (J). (gr. 3-7). 18.99 *(978-1-5344-3730-2(4)*, Simon & Schuster Bks. For Young Readers) Simon & Schuster Bks. For Young Readers.

—George & the Unbreakable Code. Hawking, Lucy & Hawking, Stephen. 2017. (George's Secret Key Ser.). (ENG.). 368p. (J). (gr. 3-7). pap. 12.99 *(978-1-4814-6628-8(3)*, Simon & Schuster Bks. For Young Readers) Simon & Schuster Bks. For Young Readers.

—George & the Unbreakable Code. Hawking, Stephen & Hawking, Lucy. 2016. (George's Secret Key Ser.). (ENG.). 352p. (J). (gr. 3-7). 19.99 *(978-1-4814-6627-1(5)*, Simon & Schuster Bks. For Young Readers) Simon & Schuster Bks. For Young Readers.

—George's Cosmic Treasure Hunt. Hawking, Stephen & Hawking, Lucy. 2009. (George's Secret Key Ser.). (ENG.). 320p. (J). (gr. 3-7). 19.99 *(978-1-4169-8671-3(5)*, Simon & Schuster Bks. For Young Readers) Simon & Schuster Bks. For Young Readers.

—George's Cosmic Treasure Hunt. Hawking, Lucy & Hawking, Stephen. 2011. (George's Secret Key Ser.). (ENG.). 352p. (J). (gr. 3-7). pap. 12.99 *(978-1-4424-2175-2(4)*, Simon & Schuster Bks. For Young Readers) Simon & Schuster Bks. For Young Readers.

—George's Secret Key Complete Hardcover Collection: George's Secret Key to the Universe; George's Cosmic Treasure Hunt; George & the Big Bang; George & the Unbreakable Code; George & the Blue Moon; George & the Ship of Time. Hawking, Lucy & Hawking, Stephen. ed. 2019. (George's Secret Key Ser.). (ENG.). 2064p. (J). (gr. 3-7). 123.99 *(978-1-5344-5136-0(6)*, Simon & Schuster Bks. For Young Readers) Simon & Schuster Bks. For Young Readers.

Parsons, Garry. George's Secret Key Complete Paperback Collection: George's Secret Key to the Universe; George's Cosmic Treasure Hunt; George & the Big Bang; George & the Unbreakable Code; George & the Blue Moon; George & the Ship of Time. Hawking, Lucy & Hawking, Stephen. ed. 2020. (George's Secret Key Ser.). (ENG.). 2096p. (J). (gr. 3-7). pap. 74.99 ***(978-1-5344-5137-7(4)**,* Simon & Schuster Bks. For Young Readers) Simon & Schuster Bks. For Young Readers.

Parsons, Garry. George's Secret Key to the Universe. Hawking, Stephen & Hawking, Lucy. (George's Secret Key Ser.). (ENG.). (J). (gr. 3-7). 2009. 336p. pap. 12.99 *(978-1-4169-8584-6(0))*; 2007. 304p. 22.99 *(978-1-4169-5462-0(7))* Simon & Schuster Bks. For Young Readers. (Simon & Schuster Bks. For Young Readers).

—George's Secret Key to the Universe. Hawking, Stephen & Hawking, Lucy. l.t. ed. 2008. (Literacy Bridge Middle Reader Ser.). 359p. (J). (gr. 3-7). 24.95 *(978-1-4104-0638-5(5))* Thorndike Pr.

—Happy Easter, Tooth Fairy! Bently, Peter. 2019. (Tooth Fairy Ser.). 32p. (J). (gr. -1-1). pap. 9.99 *(978-1-4449-3390-1(6))* Hachette Children's Group GBR. Dist: Hachette Bk. Group.

—Molly's Magic Wardrobe: the Mermaid Mission. Guillain, Adam & Guillain, Charlotte. 2019. (Molly's Magic Wardrobe Ser.: 2). (ENG.). 32p. (J). (gr. -1-k). pap. 9.99 *(978-1-4052-8537-7(0))* Egmont Bks., Ltd. GBR. Dist: Independent Pubs. Group.

—Movie Maker: The Ultimate Guide to Making Films. Grabham, Tim et al. 2010. (ENG.). 48p. (J). (gr. 3-7). 19.99 *(978-0-7636-4949-4(X))* Candlewick Pr.

—That Naughty Meerkat! Whybrow, Ian. 2016. (ENG.). 32p. (J). 17.99 *(978-0-00-813945-2(8)*, HarperCollins Children's Bks.) HarperCollins Pubs. Ltd. GBR. Dist: HarperCollins Pubs.

—The Tooth Fairy's Christmas. Bently, Peter. 2014. (J). *(978-1-4351-5739-2(7))* Barnes & Noble, Inc.

—Wrong Kind of Bark. Donaldson, Julia. 2004. (Red Bananas Ser.). (ENG.). 48p. (J). (gr. k-2). pap. 5.99 *(978-1-4052-1062-1(1))* Egmont Bks., Ltd. GBR. Dist: Independent Pubs. Group.

—The Wrong Kind of Bark. Donaldson, Julia. 2005. (Red Bananas Ser.). (ENG.). 48p. (J). lib. bdg. *(978-0-7787-1073-8(4))*; (gr. 1-3). *(978-0-7787-1089-9(0))* Crabtree Publishing Co.

Parsons, Garry. Krong! Parsons, Garry. 2006. 32p. (J). (gr. -1-3). 15.95 *(978-1-58925-061-1(3))* Tiger Tales.

Parsons, Garry, jt. illus. see Sharratt, Nick.

Parsons, Gary. Would You Believe It? Agnew, Kate. (ENG.). 128p. (J). pap. 7.50 *(978-1-4052-0520-7(2))* Egmont Bks., Ltd. GBR. Dist: Trafalgar Square Publishing.

Parsons, Jackie & Larranaga, Ana Martin. Three Little Duckies. Jugran, Jan. 2006. (ENG.). 6p. (J). (gr. -1 — 1). 14.99 *(978-1-58476-352-9(3)*, IKIDS) Innovative Kids.

Parsons, Sally. Madeline Island ABC Book. Henry, Marcia Kierland. 2008. (ENG.). 52p. (J). (gr. -1-4). pap. 18.95 *(978-1-4243-3753-8(4))* Univ. of Wisconsin Pr.

—Madeline Island ABC Coloring Book. Henry, Marcia. 2008. (ENG.). 32p. (J). (gr. k-6). pap. 6.95 *(978-0-9817723-0-1(7))* Univ. of Wisconsin Pr.

Partington, Deborah. Collins Big Cat Phonics for Letters & Sounds - I Spy Fairytales: Band 00/Lilac. Raby, Charlotte & Guille-Marrett, Emily. 2018. (Collins Big Cat Phonics Ser.). (ENG.). 16p. (J). pap. 6.99 *(978-0-00-825125-3(8))* HarperCollins Pubs. Ltd. GBR. Dist: Independent Pubs. Group.

—Meet Rue. Burns, Hazlette H. 2018. (Adventures of Rue, Pooters & Cali Ser.: Vol. 1). (ENG.). 22p. (J). (gr. k-2). pap. 5.99 *(978-0-692-10725-6(8))* Burns, Hazlette H.

Partis, Joanne. Bella's Butterfly Ball. Nilsen, Anna. 2012. (ENG.). 20p. (J). (gr. -1-k). pap. 10.99 *(978-1-84365-194-9(7)*, Pavilion Children's Books) Pavilion Bks. GBR. Dist: Penguin Random Hse. LLC.

—Bella's Midsummer Secret. Nilsen, Anna. 2005. (ENG.). 18p. (J). (gr. -1-k). pap. 9.99 *(978-1-84458-338-6(4)*, Pavilion Children's Books) Pavilion Bks. GBR. Dist: Penguin Random Hse. LLC.

Partis, Joanne. Oh, No, Bear! Partis, Joanne. 2019. (ENG.). 32p. (J). (gr. -1-2). 17.99 *(978-1-68010-174-4(9))* Tiger Tales.

—Stripe. Partis, Joanne. (Carolrhoda Picture Books Ser.). 32p. (J). 2004. pap. 6.95 *(978-1-57505-667-8(4))*; 2003. (gr. -1-3). 14.95 *(978-1-57505-450-6(7))* Lerner Publishing Group.

Parton, Daron. Dinosaur Disco. Kelly, Deborah. 2016. 32p. (J). (gr. -1-k). 16.99 *(978-0-85798-136-3(6))* Random Hse. Australia AUS. Dist: Independent Pubs. Group.

—Where Is My Butt? Budge, Donald. (J). (gr. -1-2). 2019. 26p. bds. 7.95 *(978-1-4549-3447-9(6))*; 2016. 32p. 14.95 *(978-1-4549-1697-0(4))* Sterling Publishing Co., Inc.

Parton, Paua. Room 17 Where History Comes Alive! Book I-Indians. Parton, Paula. 2007. 128p. 19.95 *(978-0-9794815-2-9(X))* Bellissima Publishing, LLC.

Parton, Paula. China Dahl. Parton, Paula. l.t. ed. 2018. (ENG.). 32p. (J). (gr. k-6). pap. 12.60 *(978-1-61477-347-4(5))* Bellissima Publishing, LLC.

—I Always Wondered. Parton, Paula. 2009. 44p. pap. 11.95 *(978-1-935118-48-0(X))* Bellissima Publishing, LLC.

—Room 17 - Where History Comes Alive - Missions. Parton, Paula. 2010. 126p. pap. 8.95 *(978-1-935630-19-7(9))* Bellissima Publishing, LLC.

—Room 17 Where History Comes Alive Book I — Indians. Parton, Paula. 2007. 128p. per. 8.95 *(978-0-9794815-0-5(3))* Bellissima Publishing, LLC.

—We Love Christmas! Parton, Paula. 2009. 30p. pap. 11.95 *(978-1-935118-84-8(6))* Bellissima Publishing, LLC.

Partridge, Magda. Tales of Crinkley Wood. White, Dave & White, Barbi. 2018. (ENG.). 30p. (J). (gr. 1-5). pap. 10.99 *(978-1-68160-569-2(4))* Crimson Cloak Publishing.

Parts, Art, jt. illus. see Grabas, Peter.

Paruit, Marie. Little Box of Emotions: Matching & Memory Cards, 1 vol. Nielman, Louison. 2020. (ENG.). 32p. (J). (gr. -1-3). 19.99 *(978-0-7643-5897-5(9)*, 18531) Schiffer Publishing, Ltd.

Parvensky Barwell, Catherine A. Tommi Goes Camping, 4 vols. Parvensky Barwell, Catherine A. Barwell, Matthew W. et al, eds. 2006. 40p. (J). 14.95 *(978-0-9774409-3-1(1)*, TL004) ILT Publishing.

Pasamar, Concha. The Kite of Dreams. Lopez Avila, Pilar & Merlan, Paula. 2020. 27p. (J). (gr. -1-3). 16.95 *(978-84-16733-68-2(6))* Cuento de Luz SL ESP. Dist: Publishers Group West (PGW).

Paschkis, Julie. Albert the Fix-It Man, 1 vol. Lord, Janet. (ENG.). 32p. (J). 2015. (gr. 1-3). pap. 7.95 *(978-1-56145-830-1(9))*; 2008. (gr. k-3). 15.95 *(978-1-56145-433-4(8))* Peachtree Publishing Co. Inc.

—Albert the Fix-It Man. Lord, Janet. 2015. (ENG.). (J). (gr. -1-2). lib. bdg. 18.55 *(978-1-62765-698-6(7))* Perfection Learning Corp.

Paschkis, Julie. Eek! A Noisy Journey from a to Z. Larios, Julie. 2020. (ENG.). 32p. (J). (gr. -1-1). 16.99 ***(978-1-68263-169-0(9))*** Peachtree Publishing Co. Inc.

Paschkis, Julie. Fat Cat: A Danish Folktale. MacDonald, Margaret Read. 2005. (ENG.). 32p. (J). (gr. -1-2). pap. 8.95 *(978-0-87483-765-0(0))* August Hse. Pubs., Inc.

—Fearsome Giant, Fearless Child: A Worldwide Jack & the Beanstalk Story. Fleischman, Paul. 2019. (Worldwide Stories Ser.). (ENG.). 40p. (J). 17.99 *(978-1-250-15177-3(5)*, 900183401, Holt, Henry & Co. Bks. For Young Readers) Holt, Henry & Co.

—Glass Slipper, Gold Sandal: a Worldwide Cinderella: A Worldwide Cinderella. Fleischman, Paul. 2007. (Worldwide Stories Ser.). (ENG.). 32p. (J). (gr. k-5). 18.99 *(978-0-8050-7953-1(X)*, 900031915, Holt, Henry & Co. Bks. For Young Readers) Holt, Henry & Co.

—The Great Smelly, Slobbery, Small-Tooth Dog: A Folktale from Great Britain. 2007. (ENG.). 32p. (J). (gr. -1-3). 16.95 *(978-0-87483-808-4(8))* August Hse. Pubs., Inc.

—Head, Body, Legs: A Story from Liberia. Paye, Won-Ldy & Lippert, Margaret H. 2006. (gr. -1-3). lib. bdg. 18.00 *(978-0-7569-6925-7(5))* Perfection Learning Corp.

—Head, Body, Legs: A Story from Liberia. Paye, Won-Ldy & Lippert, Margaret H. 2005. (ENG.). 32p. (J). (gr. -1-3). pap. 9.99 *(978-0-8050-7890-9(8)*, 900031146) Square Fish.

—Here Comes Grandma! Lord, Janet. rev. ed. 2005. (ENG.). 32p. (J). (gr. -1-k). 17.99 *(978-0-8050-7666-0(2)*, 900030219, Holt, Henry & Co. Bks. For Young Readers) Holt, Henry & Co.

—Knock on Wood: Poems about Superstitions. Wong, Janet S. 2003. (ENG.). 40p. (J). (gr. 2-5). 19.99 *(978-0-689-85512-2(5)*, McElderry, Margaret K. Bks.) McElderry, Margaret K. Bks.

—Mrs. Chicken & the Hungry Crocodile. Paye, Won-Ldy & Lippert, Margaret H. 2014. (ENG.). (J). (gr. -1-2). lib. bdg. 17.60 *(978-1-62765-429-6(1))* Perfection Learning Corp.

—Mrs. Chicken & the Hungry Crocodile. Paye, Won-Ldy & Lippert, Margaret H. 2014. (ENG.). 32p. (J). (gr. -1-2). pap. 7.99 *(978-1-250-04673-4(4)*, 900131760) Square Fish.

—Night of the Moon: A Muslim Holiday Story. Khan, Hena. 2018. (ENG.). 36p. (J). (gr. -1-k). pap. 7.99 *(978-1-4521-6896-8(2))* Chronicle Bks. LLC.

—Pablo Neruda: Poet of the People. Brown, Monica. 2011. (ENG.). 300p. (J). (gr. 1-4). 17.99 *(978-0-8050-9198-4(X)*, 900065887, Holt, Henry & Co. Bks. For Young Readers) Holt, Henry & Co.

—Summer Birds: The Butterflies of Maria Merian. Engle, Margarita. 2010. (ENG.). 32p. (J). (gr. k-3). 18.99 *(978-0-8050-8937-0(3)*, 900055290, Holt, Henry & Co. Bks. For Young Readers) Holt, Henry & Co.

—Through Georgia's Eyes. Rodriguez, Rachel Victoria. rev. ed. 2006. (ENG.). 32p. (J). (gr. k-3). 18.99 *(978-0-8050-7740-7(5)*, 900031594, Holt, Henry & Co. Bks. For Young Readers) Holt, Henry & Co.

—Twist: Yoga Poems. Wong, Janet S. 2007. (ENG.). 40p. (J). (gr. 2-5). 19.99 *(978-0-689-87394-2(8)*, McElderry, Margaret K. Bks.) McElderry, Margaret K. Bks.

—Where Is Catkin?, 1 vol. Lord, Janet. (ENG.). 32p. (J). (gr. -1-1). 2013. 7.95 *(978-1-56145-684-0(5))*; 2010. 16.95 *(978-1-56145-523-2(7))* Peachtree Publishing Co. Inc.

Paschkis, Julie. Flutter & Hum / Aleteo y Zumbido: Animal Poems / Poemas de Animales. Paschkis, Julie. 2015. (ENG.). 32p. (J). (gr. -1-3). 18.99 *(978-1-62779-103-8(5)*, 900135316, Holt, Henry & Co. Bks. For Young Readers) Holt, Henry & Co.

—Kalinka & Grakkle, 1 vol. Paschkis, Julie. 2018. (ENG.). 32p. (J). (gr. -1-3). 17.95 *(978-1-68263-030-3(7))* Peachtree Publishing Co. Inc.

—Magic Spell. Paschkis, Julie. 2017. (ENG.). 32p. (J). (gr. -1-3). 17.99 *(978-1-4814-2210-9(3)*, Simon & Schuster Bks. For Young Readers) Simon & Schuster Bks. For Young Readers.

—Mooshka, a Quilt Story, 1 vol. Paschkis, Julie. 2012. (ENG.). 32p. (J). 16.95 *(978-1-56145-620-8(9))* Peachtree Publishing Co. Inc.

—P. Zonka Lays an Egg, 1 vol. Paschkis, Julie. 2015. (ENG.). 32p. (J). (gr. 1-3). 16.95 *(978-1-56145-819-6(8))* Peachtree Publishing Co. Inc.

—Vivid: Poems & Notes about Color. Paschkis, Julie. 2018. (ENG.). 32p. (J). 17.99 *(978-1-250-12229-2(5)*, 900173588, Holt, Henry & Co. Bks. For Young Readers) Holt, Henry & Co.

Pascoe, Jed. Performance Poems. Moses, Brian, ed. 2013. (ENG.). 80p. pap. 16.50 *(978-1-85741-087-7(4))* Southgate Pubs. GBR. Dist: Parkwest Pubns., Inc.

—Rip-Roaring Round Book. Kempton, Clive & Atkin, Alan. 2013. (ENG.). 112p. pap. 21.50 *(978-1-85741-062-4(9))* Southgate Pubs. GBR. Dist: Parkwest Pubns., Inc.

Pascoe, Pete. A Pig Called Pete. Bowater, Alan. 2009. (Pig Called Pete Ser.). 32p. (J). (gr. -1-2). 25.60 *(978-1-60754-558-3(6))*; pap. 10.55 *(978-1-60754-559-0(4))* Windmill Bks.

—A Pig Called Pete Meets a Cat Called Kitty. Bowater, Alan. 2009. (Pig Called Pete Ser.). 32p. (J). (gr. -1-2). 25.60 *(978-1-60754-561-3(6))*; pap. 10.55 *(978-1-60754-562-0(4))* Windmill Bks.

—A Pig Called Pete Meets a Cow Called Carlotta. Bowater, Alan. 2009. (Pig Called Pete Ser.). 32p. (J). (gr. -1-2). 25.60 *(978-1-60754-567-5(5))*; pap. 10.55 *(978-1-60754-568-2(3))* Windmill Bks.

—A Pig Called Pete Meets a Dog Called Doug. Bowater, Alan. 2009. (Pig Called Pete Ser.). 32p. (J). (gr. -1-2). 25.60 *(978-1-60754-564-4(0))*; pap. 10.55 *(978-1-60754-565-1(9))* Windmill Bks.

—A Pig Called Pete Meets a Sheep Called Sean. Bowater, Alan. 2009. (Pig Called Pete Ser.). 32p. (J). (gr. -1-2). 25.60 *(978-1-60754-570-5(5))*; pap. 10.55 *(978-1-60754-571-2(3))* Windmill Bks.

Pascuzzo, Phil. No Ordinary Apple: A Story about Eating Mindfully. Marlowe, Sara. 2013. (ENG.). 36p. (J). (gr. -1-3). 16.95 *(978-1-61429-076-6(8))* Wisdom Pubns.

Pasek, Joanna. Alphapoetical Soup: An a-Z Collection of Poetic Forms. Deats, Dorie. 2019. (ENG.). 68p. (J). pap. 15.00 *(978-1-7326064-2-5(0))* Deats, Dorie.

—Christmas with Snowman Paul. Lapid, Yossi. 2018. (Snowman Paul Ser.: Vol. 7). (ENG.). 42p. (J). (gr. k-2). 24.99 *(978-1-949091-60-1(0))* Lapid, Yosef.

—Loving Granna Rose. Deats, Dorie. 2018. (ENG.). 36p. (J). pap. 12.00 *(978-1-7326064-0-1(4))* Deats, Dorie.

P

—Mo's Little Giant. Deats, Dorie. 2018. (ENG.). 38p. (J). pap. 12.00 *(978-1-7326064-1-8(2))* Deats, Dorie.

—Mother's Day with Snowman Paul. Lapid, Yossi. 2018. (Snowman Paul Ser.: Vol. 9). (ENG.). 38p. (J). (gr. k-2). 22.99 *(978-0-9993361-8-2(5))*; pap. 9.99 *(978-0-9993361-9-9(3))* Lapid, Yosef.

—My Snowman, Paul. Laipid, Yossi. 2018. (Snowman Paul Ser.: Vol. 1). (ENG.). 42p. (J). (gr. k-2). 24.99 *(978-1-949091-09-0(0))* Lapid, Yosef.

—Rainbow Pals. Sanchez, Shayla. 2017. (ENG.). (J). (gr. k-1). pap. 4.99 *(978-0-9993636-1-4(1))* Sanchez, Shayla.

—Snowman Paul at the Winter Olympics. Lapid, Yossi. 2018. (Snowman Paul Ser.: Vol. 2). (ENG.). 46p. (J). (gr. k-2). 24.99 *(978-1-949091-02-1(3))* Lapid, Yosef.

—Snowman Paul Returns to the Winter Olympics. Lapid, Yossi. 2018. (Snowman Paul Ser.: Vol. 8). (ENG.). 42p. (J). (gr. k-2). 24.99 *(978-1-949091-00-7(7))* Lapid, Yosef.

—Snowman Paul Saves Kate's Birthday. Lapid, Yossi. 2018. (Snowman Paul Ser.: Vol. 3). (ENG.). 52p. (J). (gr. k-2). 24.99 *(978-1-949091-03-8(1))* Lapid, Yosef.

—Tha Amazing Snowman Duel. Lapid, Yossi. 2018. (Snowman Paul Ser.: Vol. 5). (ENG.). 50p. (J). (gr. k-2). 24.99 *(978-1-949091-05-2(8))* Lapid, Yosef.

—Yara's Tawari Tree. Lapid, Yossi. 2019. (Yara's Rainforest Ser.: Vol. 1). (ENG.). 44p. (J). (gr. k-2). pap. 9.99 *(978-0-9973899-5-1(8))* Lapid, Yosef.

Pasishnychenko, Oksana. Twinkle, Twinkle, Little Star. Everett, Melissa. 2013. 20p. (J). (gr. -1-3). bds. 8.99 *(978-1-77093-534-1(7))* Flowerpot Children's Pr. Inc. CAN. Dist: Cardinal Pubs. Group.

Paskey Gill, Jacqueline. Sailing Away to Nod. Spalding, Brenda M. 2017. (ENG.). (J). (gr. 2-3). 20.95 *(978-0-692-97652-4(3))* Spalding, Brenda.

Pasqualotto, Chiara. All Eyes on Alexandra. Levine, Anna. 2018. (ENG.). 32p. (J). (gr. -1-2). lib. bdg. 17.99 *(978-1-5124-4439-1(1))*; Vol. pap. 7.99 *(978-1-5124-4440-7(5))* Lerner Publishing Group. (Kar-Ben Publishing).

—The Suitcase: A Story to Learn How to Give. Meyer, Jane G. 2017. (ENG.). (J). (gr. -1). pap. 16.99 *(978-1-61261-776-3(X))* Paraclete Pr., Inc.

Pasquariello, Karen. The Story of the Second Bus Driver. Morosco, Larissa. 2019. (ENG.). 42p. (J). pap. 12.00 ***(978-1-0804-2134-3(3))*** Independently Published.

Passarella, Jennie. U.S. Presidents & Their Animal Friends. Autrey, Jacquelyn & Yeager, Alice. 2004. 32p. (J). *(978-1-59421-005-1(5))* Seacoast Publishing, Inc.

Passchier, Anne. Go Vote, Baby! Lambert, Nancy. 2020. 14p. (J). (gr. -1 — 1). bds. 9.99 *(978-0-06-297119-7(0),* HarperFestival) HarperCollins Pubs.

—Maddy. Pitman, Gayle E. 2020. (J). *(978-1-4338-3044-0(2),* Magination Pr.) American Psychological Assn.

—The Pumpkin Is Missing! (novelty Board Book) Houghton Mifflin Harcourt, Houghton Mifflin. 2020. (ENG.). 16p. (J). (— 1). bds. 8.99 *(978-0-358-17543-8(7),* 1758557, HMH Books For Young Readers) Houghton Mifflin Harcourt Publishing Co.

—Rainbow: A First Book of Pride. Genhart, Michael. 2019. 24p. (J). *(978-1-4338-3087-7(6),* Magination Pr.) American Psychological Assn.

—Santa's Cookie Is Missing! Gryta, Thomas. 2019. (ENG.). 16p. (J). (— 1). bds. 8.99 *(978-0-358-04054-5(X),* 1740928, HMH Books For Young Readers) Houghton Mifflin Harcourt Publishing Co.

—She'll Be Coming 'Round the Mountain. (Classic Books with Holes 8x8 Ser.). (ENG.). (J). 2019. 16p. pap. *(978-1-78628-211-8(9))*; 2019. 14p. bds. *(978-1-78628-216-3(X))*; 2018. 16p. *(978-1-78628-232-3(1))*; 2018. 16p. *(978-1-78628-228-6(3))*; 2018. 16p. pap. *(978-1-78628-141-8(4))* Child's Play International Ltd.

Passman, Emily. Dancing With My Mother. Bissex, Rachel. 2003. 14p. (J). spiral bd. 10.00 *(978-0-9742516-0-8(7))* Minimal Pr., The.

Passwater, Yvonne. One. Henderson, Donna. 2018. (ENG.). 34p. (J). pap. 9.25 *(978-1-5335-2468-3(8))* CreateSpace Independent Publishing Platform.

Pastars, Chris. Washington Farm-Toons Coloring & Activity Book. O'Neil, Patrick. 2nd ed. 2003. (J). *(978-0-9742610-0-3(9))* Applied Database Technology, Inc.

Pastel, Elyse & Pastel, Elyse. Tutu Twins. Bergen, Lara. 2008. (ENG.). 24p. (J). (gr. k-17). per. 3.99 *(978-1-58476-615-5(8))* Innovative Kids.

Pastel, Elyse, jt. illus. see Pastel, Elyse.

Pastis, Stephan. Mistakes Were Made. Pastis, Stephan. 2013. 304p. (J). (gr. 3-7). (Timmy Failure Ser.: No. 1). 14.99 *(978-0-7636-6050-5(7))*; (ENG.). 100.00 *(978-0-7636-6689-7(0))* Candlewick Pr.

—Now Look What You've Done. Pastis, Stephan. 2014. (Timmy Failure Ser.: No. 2). 288p. (J). (gr. 3-7). 15.99 *(978-0-7636-6051-2(5))* Candlewick Pr.

—Timmy Failure: Mistakes Were Made. Pastis, Stephan. 2015. (Timmy Failure Ser.: 1). (ENG.). 320p. (J). (gr. 3-7). pap. 7.99 *(978-0-7636-6927-0(X))* Candlewick Pr.

—Timmy Failure: It's the End When I Say It's the End. Pastis, Stephan. 2018. (Timmy Failure Ser.: 7). (ENG.). 352p. (J). (gr. 3-7). 14.99 *(978-1-5362-0240-3(1))* Candlewick Pr.

—Timmy Failure It's the End When I Say It's the End. Pastis, Stephan. 2019. (Timmy Failure Ser.). (ENG.). 352p. (J). (gr. 3-7). pap. 7.99 *(978-1-5362-0910-5(4))* Candlewick Pr.

—Timmy Failure: Now Look What Mistakes Were Made. Pastis, Stephan. 2017. (Timmy Failure Ser.). (ENG.). 592p. (J). (gr. 3-7). pap. 12.99 *(978-0-7636-9760-0(5))* Candlewick Pr.

—Timmy Failure: Now Look What You've Done. Pastis, Stephan. 2016. (Timmy Failure Ser.: 2). (ENG.). 304p. (J). (gr. 3-7). pap. 7.99 *(978-0-7636-8014-5(1))* Candlewick Pr.

—Timmy Failure: Sanitized for Your Protection. Pastis, Stephan. (Timmy Failure Ser.). (ENG.). 288p. (J). (gr. 3-7). 2019. pap. 7.99 *(978-1-5362-0876-4(0))*; 2015. 15.99 *(978-0-7636-8092-3(3))* Candlewick Pr.

—Timmy Failure: the Book You're Not Supposed to Have. Pastis, Stephan. (Timmy Failure Ser.). (ENG.). 304p. (J). (gr. 3-7). 2019. pap. 7.99 *(978-1-5362-0908-2(2))*; 2016. 15.99 *(978-0-7636-9004-5(X))* Candlewick Pr.

—Timmy Failure: the Cat Stole My Pants. Pastis, Stephan. (Timmy Failure Ser.). (ENG.). 288p. (J). (gr. 3-7). 2019. pap. 7.99 *(978-1-5362-0909-9(0))*; 2017. 14.99 *(978-0-7636-9733-4(8))* Candlewick Pr.

—Timmy Failure: the Maximum Greatness Collection. Pastis, Stephan. 2019. (Timmy Failure Ser.). (ENG.). 4p. (J). (gr. 3-7). pap. 54.99 *(978-1-5362-0911-2(2))* Candlewick Pr.

—Timmy Failure: the Movie. Pastis, Stephan. 2020. (Timmy Failure Ser.). (ENG.). (J). (gr. 3-7). pap. 7.99 *(978-1-5362-0907-5(4),* Candlewick Entertainment) Candlewick Pr.

—Timmy Failure: We Meet Again. Pastis, Stephan. 2016. (Timmy Failure Ser.: 3). (ENG.). 288p. (J). (gr. 3-7). pap. 7.99 *(978-0-7636-9106-6(2))* Candlewick Pr.

Pastor, Terry & Haggerty, Tim. The Solar System Internet Referenced. Bone, Emily. 2010. (Beginner's Science Ser.). 32p. (J). (gr. 1). 4.99 *(978-0-7945-2812-6(0),* Usborne) EDC Publishing.

Pastor, Terry, jt. illus. see Montgomery, Lee.

Pastore, Vicki. The Apostles' Creed. 2007. 32p. (J). (gr. -1-3). per. 7.95 *(978-0-8091-6738-8(7),* 6738-8) Paulist Pr.

Pastrana, Beatriz. Nana's Rocking Railroad. Fraser, Melissa a. 2020. (ENG.). 44p. (J). pap. 12.99 ***(978-1-6741-1995-3(X))*** Independently Published.

Pastrovicchio, Alessandro & Kawaii Studio. Star Wars: Original Trilogy Graphic Novel. Ferrari, Alessandro. 2016. (ENG.). 208p. (J). (gr. 3-7). 19.99 *(978-1-4847-3784-2(9),* Disney Lucasfilm Press) Disney Publishing Worldwide.

Pastrovicchio, Lorenzo. Mouse Magic. Ambrosio, Stefano. 2010. (ENG.). 112p. (J). 24.99 *(978-1-60886-550-5(9))*; Vol. 1. pap. 9.99 *(978-1-60886-541-3(X))* Boom! Studios.

—Why, Mommy!!, 1 vol. Alvarez, Miguel et al. 2009. 17p. pap. 24.95 *(978-1-60749-429-4(9))* America Star Bks.

Pastrovicchio, Lorenzo & Magic Eye Studios. Wizards of Mickey - Grand Tournament, Vol. 2. Ambrosio, Stefano. 2010. (Wizards of Mickey Ser.). (ENG.). 128p. (J). (gr. 3-6). pap. 9.99 *(978-1-60886-564-2(9))* Boom! Studios.

Patachitra, Studio & Majumder, Ankur. Grady the Grasshopper Graduates. Peterson, M. S. Natasha C. 2018. (ENG.). 28p. (J). pap. *(978-0-9952330-4-1(7))* Peterson, Natasha.

Patagonia School. Lillie's Treasures/Los tesoros de Lili. Chesne, Sabrina. Capasso, Diana, tr. 2004. (ENG & SPA.). 32p. per. 15.00 *(978-0-9630310-9-0(0))* Will Hall Bks.

Patch, Michael. Tales of the Lush Green Woods. Patch, Lisa. 2012. 42p. 16.50 *(978-0-9852501-5-7(1))* Inkwell Books LLC.

—Who Is in That Shell? Amdahl Elco, Anita & Weikert Stelmach, Katherine. 2012. 130p. (J). pap. 13.50 *(978-0-9883568-0-1(5))* Inkwell Books LLC.

Patch, Sebastion. Thimble the Fairy's Acorns & Tea. Thimble The Fairy. 2011. (ENG.). 48p. (J). 8.99 *(978-0-9827304-0-9(3))* Eleve Publishing.

Patch, Sophia. The Case of the Stolen Bikes. Dunbar, L. J. 2019. (Two-Inch Detective Finch's Tasty Mysteries Ser.: Vol. 1). (ENG.). 108p. (J). pap. 8.99 ***(978-1-0820-7881-1(6))*** Independently Published.

Patcha, El. Tiny World: Embroidery! Patcha, El. Odd Dot. 2019. (Tiny World Ser.: 1). (ENG.). 32p. (J). pap. 14.99 *(978-1-250-20383-0(X),* 900200602, Odd Dot) St. Martin's Pr.

Pate, Jeremy. Piedy Makes a Friend. Sutton, Jake. McRady, Tonja, ed. 2020. (ENG.). 24p. (J). pap. 9.95 ***(978-1-7326661-6-0(4))*** Kaio Pubns., Inc.

Pate, Rodney. Joe Louis, My Champion, 1 vol. Pate, Rodney, tr. Miller, William. 2004. (ENG.). 32p. (J). 16.95 *(978-1-58430-161-5(9))* Lee & Low Bks., Inc.

Pate, Rodney S. Jackie Robinson. Walker, Sally M. 2005. (Yo Solo Biografías Ser.). (SPA.). 48p. (J). (gr. 2-4). per. 5.95 *(978-0-8225-3127-2(5))* Lerner Publishing Group.

—Jackie Robinson. Walker, Sally M. Translations.com Staff, tr. 2005. (Yo Solo: Biografías (on My Own Biographies) Ser.). (SPA & ENG.). 48p. (gr. 2-4). lib. bdg. 25.26 *(978-0-8225-3126-5(7),* Ediciones Lerner) Lerner Publishing Group.

—Joe Louis, My Champion. Miller, William. 2004. (ENG.). 32p. (J). pap. 10.95 *(978-1-60060-426-3(9))* Lee & Low Bks., Inc.

—A Lesson for Martin Luther King Jr. Patrick, Denise Lewis. 2003. (Ready-To-read COFA Ser.). (ENG.). 32p. (J). (gr. k-2). pap. 4.99 *(978-0-689-85397-5(1),* Simon Spotlight) Simon Spotlight.

Patel, Kalpna. Alis the Aviator. Metcalfe-Chenail, Danielle. 2019. (ENG.). 40p. (J). (gr. -1-2). 17.99 *(978-1-101-91905-7(1),* Tundra Bks.) Tundra Bks. CAN. Dist: Penguin Random Hse. LLC.

Patel, Krina. The Curiosity Box: Animals. Riley, Peter. ed. 2019. (Curiosity Box Ser.). 32p. (J). (gr. 1-3). pap. 10.99 *(978-1-4451-4639-3(8),* Franklin Watts) Hachette Children's Group GBR. Dist: Hachette Bk. Group.

—The Curiosity Box: Human Body. Riley, Peter. ed. 2019. (Curiosity Box Ser.). 32p. (J). (gr. 1-3). pap. 10.99 *(978-1-4451-4648-5(7),* Franklin Watts) Hachette Children's Group GBR. Dist: Hachette Bk. Group.

—The Curiosity Box: Plants. Riley, Peter. ed. 2019. (Curiosity Box Ser.). 32p. (J). (gr. 1-3). pap. 10.99 *(978-1-4451-4636-2(3),* Franklin Watts) Hachette Children's Group GBR. Dist: Hachette Bk. Group.

—The Curiosity Box: the Seashore. Riley, Peter. ed. 2019. (Curiosity Box Ser.). 32p. (J). (gr. 1-3). pap. 10.99 *(978-1-4451-4632-4(0),* Franklin Watts) Hachette Children's Group GBR. Dist: Hachette Bk. Group.

Patenaude, Brian. Firefly Fred. Porter, Todd. 2004. (ENG.). 36p. (J). (gr. -1-3). 19.95 *(978-1-932278-00-2(1))* Mayhaven Publishing, Inc.

Paterson, Alex. Belly Laugh Fart Jokes for Kids: 350 Hilarious Fart Jokes. Sky Pony Press. 2018. (ENG.). 128p. (J). (gr. k-7). 9.99 *(978-1-5107-3361-9(2),* Sky Pony Pr.) Skyhorse Publishing Co., Inc.

—Collins Big Cat Phonics for Letters & Sounds - the Best Vest Quest: Band 03/Yellow, Bd. 3. Hemming, Alice. 2018. (Collins Big Cat Phonics Ser.). (ENG.). 16p. (J). pap. 6.99 *(978-0-00-825156-7(8))* HarperCollins Pubs. Ltd. GBR. Dist: Independent Pubs. Group.

—Gus the Famous Football Cat. Palmer, Tom. 2018. (Reading Ladder Ser.). (ENG.). 48p. (J). (gr. -1-k). pap. 8.99 *(978-1-4052-9094-4(3))* Egmont Bks., Ltd. GBR. Dist: Independent Pubs. Group.

—What Pirates Really Do. Joyce, Melanie. 2016. (ENG.). 32p. (J). (gr. -1-3). 16.99 *(978-1-4998-0257-3(9))* Little Bee Books Inc.

Paterson, Alys. The Shape of My Heart. Sperring, Mark. 32p. (J). 2015. (gr. -1-1). bds. 7.99 *(978-1-68119-017-4(6),* 900155505); 2012. (ENG.). lib. bdg. 15.89 *(978-1-59990-963-9(4),* 900095689); 2012. (ENG.). (gr. -1-k). 16.99 *(978-1-59990-962-2(6),* 900095688) Bloomsbury Publishing USA. (Bloomsbury USA Childrens).

Paterson, Diane. Love, Lizzie: Letters to a Military Mom. McElroy, Lisa Tucker. 2009. (ENG.). 32p. (J). (gr. -1-3). pap. 6.99 *(978-0-8075-4778-6(6),* 807547786) Whitman, Albert & Co.

Paterson, John. I Am the Rain, 1 vol. Paterson, John. 2018. (ENG.). 32p. (J). (gr. -1-3). 16.95 *(978-1-58469-615-5(X),* Dawn Pubns.) Sourcebooks, Inc.

Paterson, Roz. Sadie & the Snow Globe: A Mermaid Adventure. Paterson, Roz. 2016. (ENG.). 304p. (J). pap. *(978-0-473-22314-4(7))* Shrew Pubns. Ltd.

Paterson, Wendy. A Little Horse Called Pancakes & the Beach. Noakes-Dobson, Candice. 2019. (ENG.). 44p. (J). pap. 7.95 *(978-1-928230-52-6(0))* Jacana Media ZAF. Dist: Independent Pubs. Group.

Patete, Christine. Super Phil & the Missing Mom. Tucker, Mark. 2003. 24p. (J). 4.50 *(978-1-882440-01-6(3))* God's World Pubns. Inc.

—Super Phil & the Sphiddle of the Rinks. Tucker, Mark. 2003. (J). 4.50 *(978-1-882440-02-3(1))* God's World Pubns. Inc.

Pathak, Ashutosh. Amie & the Chawl of Colour. Rao, Chatura. 2004. 100p. pap. *(978-0-14-333592-4(8),* Puffin) Penguin Publishing Group.

Pathak, Varun. Stop That Wagon, Please! The Amazing Dessert Chase. Zorn, Frederick J. 2019. (ENG.). 32p. (J). pap. *(978-1-77143-387-7(6))* CCB Publishing.

Patience, John. I Can Read. Gikow, Louise. 2004. (My First Reader Ser.). 31p. (J). 18.50 *(978-0-516-24678-9(X),* Children's Pr.) Scholastic Library Publishing.

—I Can Read. Gikow, Louise A. 2005. (My First Reader Ser.). (ENG.). 32p. (J). (gr. k-1). pap. 3.95 *(978-0-516-25114-1(7),* Children's Pr.) Scholastic Library Publishing.

Patience, John. Favourite Stories from Fern Hollow. Patience, John. 2019. (Tales from Fern Hollow Ser.). (ENG.). 80p. (J). (gr. k-2). ***(978-1-9161646-5-9(X))*** Talewater Pr.

Patients from East Tennessee Children's Hospital. East Tennessee from a to Z. McMillan, Jenna. 2013. (ENG.). 26p. 20.00 *(978-0-9830954-2-2(6))* Books by Kids LLC.

Patil, Amruta. Am I Your Pet? Wolfe, Carolyn. 2017. (ENG.). (J). (gr. k-6). pap. 15.99 *(978-1-61286-318-4(3))* Avid Readers Publishing Group.

Patkau, Karen. Forest, 1 vol. Gamblin, Kate Moss. 2019. (See to Learn Ser.: 1). (ENG.). 24p. (J). (gr. k-2). 16.95 *(978-1-55498-879-2(9))* Groundwood Bks. CAN. Dist: Publishers Group West (PGW).

—A Good Trade. Fullerton, Alma. 2020. 32p. (J). (gr. k-3). 14.95 *(978-1-77278-118-2(5))*; (ENG.). 18.95 *(978-1-77278-117-5(7))* Pajama Pr. CAN. Dist: Ingram Publisher Services.

—One Hungry Heron, 1 vol. Beck, Carolyn. 2014. (ENG.). 32p. (J). (gr. -1-1). 19.95 *(978-1-55455-361-7(X),* 71030349-b390-4191-b8b4-32780674c684) Fitzhenry & Whiteside, Ltd. CAN. Dist: Firefly Bks., Ltd.

—One Watermelon Seed, 1 vol. Lottridge, Celia. 2012. (ENG.). 32p. (J). (gr. -1-2). pap. 9.95 *(978-1-55455-222-1(2),* d276c15e-f25b-4ba7-b74a-2d2b24d1dfa3) Fitzhenry & Whiteside, Ltd. CAN. Dist: Firefly Bks., Ltd.

Patkau, Karen. Creatures Yesterday & Today. Patkau, Karen. (ENG.). 32p. (J). (gr. 1-4). 2012. pap. 8.95 *(978-1-77049-310-0(7))*; 2008. 18.95 *(978-0-88776-833-0(4))* Tundra Bks. CAN. (Tundra Bks.). Dist: Penguin Random Hse. LLC.

—Triceratops Stomp. Patkau, Karen. 2019. (ENG.). 32p. (J). (gr. -1-1). 17.95 *(978-1-77278-079-6(0))* Pajama Pr. CAN. Dist: Ingram Publisher Services.

Patlan, Alyssa A. The Magical City of Northopolis; a Christmas Story. Banda, Rey A. 2012. 50p. (-18). pap. 16.95 *(978-0-615-69125-1(0))* Northopolis.

Patouille, Pati. Children & Toddler Coloring Book Ages 1-3 & 2-4: 35+ Fun & Easy Coloring Pages, a Relaxing Childrens Book. Sila, Zuno. Karuna, Metta, ed. 2019. (Children's Activity Books for Kids Ages 1-3, 2-4, Boys, Girls, Toddlers Coloring Books, Early Childh Ser.: Vol. 1). (ENG.). 82p. (J). pap. 5.99 *(978-1-0951-1592-3(8))* Independently Published.

—LIBRI INTERATTIVI per BAMBINI 3 a 6 ANNI, Volume 2: Più Di 35 Disegni Da Colorare. Arteterapia: un Libro per Esprimere le Tue Emozioni e la Tua Creatività. Sila, Zuno. 2019. (Libri per Bambini, Libri Da Colorare Bambini 3,4,5,6 Anni, Librone Da Disegnare, Libri Interattivi P Ser.: Vol. 2). (ITA.). 82p. (J). pap. 5.99 *(978-1-0702-5838-6(5))* Independently Published.

—LIBRO DA COLORARE per BAMBINI, 2-5 ANNI, Volume 2:] Di 35 Disegni Da Colorare. un Libro per Sviluppare il Gioco e la Creatività. Sila, Zuno. 2019. (Libri per Bambini, Libri Da Colorare Bambini 2,3,4,5 Anni, Librone Da Disegnare, Libri Interattivi P Ser.: Vol. 2). (ITA.). 86p. (J). pap. 5.99 *(978-1-0702-5576-7(9))* Independently Published.

—Libro Da Colorare per Bambini Da 2 a 5 Anni, Volume 1: + Di 35 Pagine Di Disegni Da Colorar. un Libro per Sviluppare il Gioco e la Creatività. Sila, Zuno. 2019. (Libri per Bambini, Libri Da Colorare Bambini 2,3,4,5 Anni, Librone Da Disegnare, Libri Interattivi P Ser.: Vol. 1). (ITA.). 82p. (J). pap. 5.99 *(978-1-0702-5360-2(X))* Independently Published.

—Libro Infantiles para Colorear: Un Libro de Arte Terapia para Relajarse y Desarrollar Su Creatividad. Sila, Zuno. Karuna, Metta, ed. 2019. (Libros para Colorear, Edad 2-5, Infantil, Manualidades y Juegos, Libros de Actividades, Aprendizaje Ser.: Vol. 1). (J). (SPA.). 82p. pap. 5.99 *(978-1-0953-0090-9(3))*; (FRE.). 86p. pap. 5.99 *(978-1-0953-1318-3(5))* Independently Published.

—LIBRONE DA DISEGNARE BAMBINI 3 a 6 ANNI, Volume 1: + Di 35 Disegni Da Colorare. Arteterapia: un Libro per Esprimere le Tue Emozioni e la Tua Creatività. Sila, Zuno. 2019. (Libri per Bambini, Libri Da Colorare Bambini 3,4,5,6 Anni, Librone Da Disegnare, Libri Interattivi P Ser.: Vol. 1). (ITA.). 82p. (J). pap. 5.99 *(978-1-0702-5685-6(4))* Independently Published.

Patradol Kitcharoen. Pandi's Adventures in Afric. Alfred Sole. 2012. 86p. pap. 23.97 *(978-1-61897-493-8(9),* Strategic Bk. Publishing) Strategic Book Publishing & Rights Agency (SBPRA).

Patricelli, Leslie. Mini Myths: Be Careful, Icarus! Holub, Joan. 2015. (ENG.). 22p. (J). (gr. -1 — 1). bds. 6.95 *(978-1-4197-1677-5(8))* Abrams, Inc.

—Mini Myths: Brush Your Hair, Medusa! Holub, Joan. 2015. (Mini Myths Ser.). (ENG.). 24p. (J). (gr. -1 — 1). bds. 6.95 *(978-1-4197-0953-1(4))* Abrams, Inc.

—Mini Myths: Don't Get Lost, Odysseus! Holub, Joan. 2016. (Mini Myths Ser.). (ENG.). 24p. (J). (gr. -1 — 1). bds. 6.95 *(978-1-4197-1897-7(5),* Abrams Appleseed) Abrams, Inc.

—Mini Myths: Good Job, Athena! Holub, Joan. 2016. (Mini Myths Ser.). (ENG.). 24p. (J). (gr. -1 — 1). bds. 6.95 *(978-1-4197-1898-4(3),* Abrams Appleseed) Abrams, Inc.

—Mini Myths: Make a Wish, Midas! Holub, Joan. 2015. (Mini Myths Ser.). (ENG.). 24p. (J). (gr. -1 — 1). bds. 6.95 *(978-1-4197-0952-4(6))* Abrams, Inc.

—Mini Myths: Please Share, Aphrodite! Holub, Joan. 2015. (ENG.). 22p. (J). (gr. -1 — 1). bds. 6.95 *(978-1-4197-1678-2(6))* Abrams, Inc.

Patricelli, Leslie. Baby Happy Baby Sad. Patricelli, Leslie. 2008. (Leslie Patricelli Board Bks.). (ENG.). 24p. (J). (— 1). bds. 7.99 *(978-0-7636-3245-8(7))* Candlewick Pr.

—Baby Happy Baby Sad/Bebé Feliz Bebé Triste. Patricelli, Leslie. 2018. (Leslie Patricelli Board Bks.). 24p. (J). (— 1). bds. 7.99 *(978-1-5362-0348-6(3))* Candlewick Pr.

—Best Buds under Frogs. Patricelli, Leslie. 2018. 288p. (J). (gr. 2-5). 15.99 *(978-0-7636-5104-6(4))* Candlewick Pr.

Patricelli, Leslie. Big Kid Bed. Patricelli, Leslie. (J). (— 1). 2020. (ENG.). 24p. 5.99 ***(978-1-5362-1600-4(3))***; 2018. 26p. bds. 7.99 *(978-0-7636-7934-7(8))* Candlewick Pr.

Patricelli, Leslie. Big Little. Patricelli, Leslie. 2003. (Leslie Patricelli Board Bks.). 24p. (J). (— 1). bds. 7.99 *(978-0-7636-1951-0(5))* Candlewick Pr.

—Big Little / Grande Pequeño. Patricelli, Leslie. 2018. (Leslie Patricelli Board Bks.). 24p. (J). (— 1). bds. 7.99 *(978-0-7636-9966-6(7))* Candlewick Pr.

—Bigger! Bigger! Patricelli, Leslie. 2018. (ENG.). 32p. (J). (-k). 15.99 *(978-0-7636-7930-9(5))* Candlewick Pr.

—Binky. Patricelli, Leslie. 2005. (Leslie Patricelli Board Bks.). (ENG.). 24p. (J). (— 1). bds. 7.99 *(978-0-7636-2364-7(4))* Candlewick Pr.

—The Birthday Box. Patricelli, Leslie. 2009. (Leslie Patricelli Board Bks.). 26p. (J). (gr. k — 1). bds. 7.99 *(978-0-7636-4449-9(8))* Candlewick Pr.

—Blankie. Patricelli, Leslie. 2005. (Leslie Patricelli Board Bks.). (ENG.). 24p. (J). (— 1). bds. 7.99 *(978-0-7636-2363-0(6))* Candlewick Pr.

—Blankie/Mantita. Patricelli, Leslie. 2016. (Leslie Patricelli Board Bks.). 24p. (J). (— 1). bds. 7.99 *(978-0-7636-8897-4(5))* Candlewick Pr.

—Boo! Patricelli, Leslie. 2015. (Leslie Patricelli Board Bks.). 26p. (J). (— 1). bds. 7.99 *(978-0-7636-6320-9(4))* Candlewick Pr.

—Boo! / ¡Bu! Patricelli, Leslie. 2017. (Leslie Patricelli Board Bks.). 26p. (J). (— 1). bds. 7.99 *(978-0-7636-9314-5(6))* Candlewick Pr.

Patricelli, Leslie. Doggie Gets Scared. Patricelli, Leslie. 2020. (Leslie Patricelli Board Bks.). (ENG.). 26p. (J). (— 1). bds. 7.99 ***(978-1-5362-0379-0(3))*** Candlewick Pr.

Patricelli, Leslie. Fa la La. Patricelli, Leslie. 2012. (Leslie Patricelli Board Bks.). (ENG.). 26p. (J). (gr. k — 1). bds. 7.99 *(978-0-7636-3247-2(3))* Candlewick Pr.

—Fa la La/Tra-La-la. Patricelli, Leslie. 2017. (Leslie Patricelli Board Bks.). 26p. (J). (— 1). bds. 6.99 *(978-0-7636-9524-8(6))* Candlewick Pr.

—Faster! Faster! Patricelli, Leslie. (Leslie Patricelli Board Bks.). (J). (-k). 2013. 30p. bds. 7.99 *(978-0-7636-6222-6(4))*; 2012. 32p. 15.99 *(978-0-7636-5473-3(6))* Candlewick Pr.

—Faster! Faster!/Mas Rapido! Mas Rapido! Patricelli, Leslie. 2013. (Leslie Patricelli Board Bks.). 30p. (J). (-k). bds. 7.99 *(978-0-7636-6611-8(4))* Candlewick Pr.

—Grande Pequeño. Patricelli, Leslie. Rozarena, P., tr. 2003. (SPA.). 25p. (J). (gr. -1-k). bds. 7.95 *(978-970-29-0988-0(0))* Santillana USA Publishing Co., Inc.

—Hair. Patricelli, Leslie. 2017. (Leslie Patricelli Board Bks.). 26p. (J). (— 1). bds. 6.99 *(978-0-7636-7931-6(3))* Candlewick Pr.

—Higher! Higher! Patricelli, Leslie. 2010. (Leslie Patricelli Board Bks.). (ENG.). 30p. (J). (-k). bds. 7.99 *(978-0-7636-4433-8(1))* Candlewick Pr.

—Hop! Hop! Patricelli, Leslie. 2015. (Leslie Patricelli Board Bks.). (ENG.). 26p. (J). (— 1). bds. 7.99 *(978-0-7636-6319-3(0))* Candlewick Pr.

—Hop! Hop!/¡Salto! ¡Salto! Patricelli, Leslie. 2018. (Leslie Patricelli Board Bks.). 26p. (J). (— 1). bds. 7.99 *(978-0-7636-9525-5(4))* Candlewick Pr.

—Huggy Kissy. Patricelli, Leslie. (Leslie Patricelli Board Bks.). (ENG.). 26p. (J). (— 1). 2019. bds. 9.99 *(978-1-5362-1135-1(4))*; 2012. bds. 7.99 *(978-0-7636-3246-5(5))* Candlewick Pr.

—Huggy Kissy/Abrazos y Besitos. Patricelli, Leslie. 2016. (Leslie Patricelli Board Bks.). 26p. (J). (— 1). bds. 7.99 *(978-0-7636-8896-7(7))* Candlewick Pr.

Patricelli, Leslie. Mad, Mad, MAD. Patricelli, Leslie. 2020. (Leslie Patricelli Board Bks.). (ENG.). 26p. (J). (— 1). bds. 7.99 ***(978-1-5362-0380-6(7))*** Candlewick Pr.

Patricelli, Leslie. Nighty-Night. Patricelli, Leslie. 2017. (Leslie Patricelli Board Bks.). (ENG.). 26p. (J). (— 1). bds. 7.99 *(978-0-7636-7932-3(1))* Candlewick Pr.

—No No Yes Yes. Patricelli, Leslie. 2008. (Leslie Patricelli Board Bks.). (ENG.). 24p. (J). (— 1). bds. 7.99 *(978-0-7636-3244-1(9))* Candlewick Pr.

—No No Yes Yes/No No Sí Sí. Patricelli, Leslie. 2018. (Leslie Patricelli Board Bks.). 24p. (J). (— 1). bds. 6.99 *(978-1-5362-0349-3(1))* Candlewick Pr.

—The Patterson Puppies & the Midnight Monster Party. Patricelli, Leslie. 2010. (Patterson Puppies Ser.). 32p. (J). (gr. -1-k). 14.99 *(978-0-7636-3243-4(0))* Candlewick Pr.

—The Patterson Puppies & the Rainy Day. Patricelli, Leslie. 2009. (Patterson Puppies Ser.). (ENG.). 40p. (J). (gr. -1-k). 14.99 *(978-0-7636-3242-7(2))* Candlewick Pr.

—Potty. Patricelli, Leslie. 2010. (Leslie Patricelli Board Bks.). (ENG.). 28p. (J). (gr. k — 1). bds. 7.99 *(978-0-7636-4476-5(5))* Candlewick Pr.

—Potty/Bacinica. Patricelli, Leslie. 2016. (Leslie Patricelli Board Bks.). (J). (— 1). bds. 7.99 *(978-0-7636-8777-9(4))* Candlewick Pr.

—Quiet Loud. Patricelli, Leslie. 2003. (Leslie Patricelli Board Bks.). (ENG.). 24p. (J). (gr. k — 1). bds. 7.99 *(978-0-7636-1952-7(3))* Candlewick Pr.

—Quiet Loud / Silencioso Ruidoso. Patricelli, Leslie. 2018. (Leslie Patricelli Board Bks.). 24p. (J). (— 1). bds. 7.99 *(978-0-7636-9976-5(4))* Candlewick Pr.

—Silencio Ruido. Patricelli, Leslie. Rozarena, P., tr. 2003. (SPA.). 25p. (J). (gr. -1-k). bds. 7.95 *(978-970-29-0987-3(2))* Santillana USA Publishing Co., Inc.

—Tickle. Patricelli, Leslie. 2014. (Leslie Patricelli Board Bks.). (ENG.). 26p. (J). (— 1). bds. 7.99 *(978-0-7636-6322-3(0))* Candlewick Pr.

—Toot. Patricelli, Leslie. 2014. (Leslie Patricelli Board Bks.). (ENG.). 24p. (J). (— 1). bds. 7.99 *(978-0-7636-6321-6(2))* Candlewick Pr.

Patricelli, Leslie. Tooth. Patricelli, Leslie. (J). (— 1). 2020. (ENG.). 24p. 5.99 ***(978-1-5362-1601-1(1))***; 2018. 26p. bds. 7.99 *(978-0-7636-7933-0(X))* Candlewick Pr.

Patricelli, Leslie. Tubby. Patricelli, Leslie. 2010. (Leslie Patricelli Board Bks.). (ENG.). 28p. (J). (— 1). bds. 7.99 *(978-0-7636-4567-0(2))* Candlewick Pr.

—Tubby/Bañito. Patricelli, Leslie. 2017. (Leslie Patricelli Board Bks.). 28p. (J). (— 1). bds. 7.99 *(978-0-7636-9316-9(2))* Candlewick Pr.

—Yummy Yucky. Patricelli, Leslie. 2003. (Leslie Patricelli Board Bks.). (ENG.). 24p. (J). (gr. k — 1). bds. 7.99 *(978-0-7636-1950-3(7))* Candlewick Pr.

—Yummy Yucky/¡Ñam! ¡Puaj! Patricelli, Leslie. 2016. (Leslie Patricelli Board Bks.). (J). (— 1). bds. 7.99 *(978-0-7636-8776-2(6))* Candlewick Pr.

Patrick, Alex. Never-Ending Activity Book: a Leap of Leopards. Fischer, Maggie. 2018. (ENG.). 30p. (J). (gr. -1-k). 14.99 *(978-1-68412-322-3(4)*, Silver Dolphin Bks.) Printers Row Publishing Group.

Patrick, Hawkins. Tommy Turner's Tremendous Travels. Seegar, Ali. 2016. (ENG.). 192p. (J). pap. *(978-99959-965-0-5(2))* Kingsbury, A.K.

Patrick, Jean L. S. & Faricy, Patrick. Face to Face with Mount Rushmore. Patrick, Jean L. S. 2008. (J). *(978-0-9798823-1-9(1))* Mount Rushmore Bookstores.

Patrick, Scot. Pink Milk Sea Coloring Book. Frances, Dee. Date not set. 32p. (J). pap. 3.00 *(978-1-885519-26-9(5))* DDDD Pubns.

Patrick, Tom. Hurray for Snow! Tyrell, Melissa. enl. ed. 2005. (ENG.). 10p. (J). (gr. -1-3). 4.95 *(978-1-58117-118-1(8)*, Intervisual/Piggy Toes) Bendon, Inc.

PatrickGeorge. A Filth of Starlings: A Compilation of Bird & Aquatic Animal Group Names. PatrickGeorge. 2011. 48p. (J). (gr. 2). pap. 12.99 *(978-0-9562558-1-5(7))* PatrickGeorge GBR. Dist: Independent Pubs. Group.

Patrissi, Elisa. The Owl Who Couldn't Growl. Brooke, Susan Rich. 2020. (ENG.). 40p. (J). *(978-1-5037-5244-3(5)*, 3eef17da-d667-4e7b-a7d9-17ed3fb8e534, p i kids) Phoenix International Publications, Inc.

Patrizzi, Barbara. O Is for Oystercatcher: A Book of Seaside ABCs. Patrizzi, Barbara. 2003. 55p. 15.95 *(978-1-59322-008-2(1))* Down The Shore Publishing Corp.

Patsy, Seager. Bartholomew. Kempers, Elizabeth. 2019. (ENG.). 32p. (J). (gr. k-6). pap. ***(978-0-6485076-0-4(2))*** Sweetfields Publishing.

Pattenden, Marc. C Is for Cat. DK. 2020. (ENG.). 16p. (J). (— 1). bds. 7.99 ***(978-0-7440-2416-6(1)***, DK Children) Dorling Kindersley Publishing, Inc.

Patterson, Annie. Too Hot? Too Cold? Keeping Body Temperature Just Right. Arnold, Caroline. 2013. 32p. (J). (gr. 1-3). (ENG.). 22.44 *(978-1-58089-276-6(0))*; pap. 7.95 *(978-1-58089-277-3(9))* Charlesbridge Publishing, Inc.

—Turtle, Turtle, Watch Out! Sayre, April Pulley. 2010. 32p. (J). (gr. k-3). pap. 7.95 *(978-1-58089-149-3(7))* Charlesbridge Publishing, Inc.

—Whale Snow. Edwardson, Debby Dahl. 2004. 32p. (J). (gr. -1-3). pap. 7.95 *(978-1-57091-394-5(3))* Charlesbridge Publishing, Inc.

Patterson, Bill. Rudolph's Night Off. Black, Baxter A. 2011. (ENG.). 32p. (J). (gr. -1-3). 19.95 *(978-0-939343-54-6(1))* Coyote Cowboy Co.

Patterson, Christina. ABC Animal Adventure: Polymer Clay Sculpture by Christina Patterson. Patterson, Christina. 2019. (ENG.). 30p. (J). pap. 14.99 *(978-1-0928-1984-8(3))* Independently Published.

Patterson, Kelsey. Manny the Mindful Manatee. Powers, Ray. 2019. (Manny the Mindful Manatee Ser.: Vol. 1). (ENG.). 48p. (J). pap. 10.99 *(978-1-0973-4660-8(9))* Independently Published.

—Wylie's Wishes: Andy's Story. Wylie. 2019. (Child's Journey Through Trauma Ser.: Vol. 1). (ENG.). 40p. (J). pap. 11.99 *(978-1-0936-3152-4(X))* Independently Published.

Patterson, Lacey. Katarina's Sleeping Adventure. Ulsrud, Al. 2019. (ENG.). 36p. (J). 24.99 *(978-1-7960-1648-2(9))*; pap. 17.49 *(978-1-7960-1647-5(0))* Xlibris Corp.

Patterson, Nancy. May the Magnificent Lighthouse. Patterson, Nancy. 2012. 24p. 18.95 *(978-0-615-61021-4(8))* Bayberry Cottage Gallery.

Patterson, Priscilla. The Always Tree. Anderson, Donna. 2019. (ENG.). 30p. (J). pap. 12.99 ***(978-1-7338162-3-6(2))*** Climb Your Moutain Publishing.

—Rufus Rides a Catfish: (and Other Fables from the Farmstead) Roegiers, Charles B. 2020. (ENG.). 294p. (YA). (gr. 7-12). pap. 36.95 ***(978-1-7321976-7-1(9))*** Jujapa Pr.

Patterson, Robin. 101 Cool Pool Games for Children: Fun & Fitness for Swimmers of All Levels. Rodomista, Kim. 2006. (SmartFun Activity Bks.). (ENG.). 160p. (gr. -1). per. 15.99 *(978-0-89793-483-1(0)*, Hunter Hse.) Turner Publishing Co.

Patterson, Traci a. Unami the Unicorn: A Story of Enchantment & Healing. Patterson, Traci a. 2019. (ENG.). 22p. (J). (gr. 1-6). 24.99 ***(978-0-578-58123-1(X))*** Traci A Patterson.

Patterson, Victoria. The Fairy First Day. Matheis, Mickie. 2019. (ENG.). 32p. (J). (gr. -1-2). 9.99 *(978-1-9848-9258-4(4)*, Random Hse. Bks. for Young Readers) Random Hse. Children's Bks.

Patteson, Nelda. Adina de Zavala: "Angel of the Alamo" Her Life Story Presented Through the Clothes She Wore. Patteson, Nelda. 2003. (Women of Texas Ser.: Vol. 3). Orig. Title: Angel of the Alamo. 32p. (J). (gr. 4-8). pap. 14.95 *(978-0-9629001-2-9(5))* Smiley Co.

Patti, Sheila. Ollie Ollie Ox in Free. Ferguson, Linda. 2004. 189p. (YA). per. *(978-0-9755288-0-8(7))* Ferguson, Linda.

Patton, Julia. Are You Listening, Jack? Garcia, Ellen. 2014. (J). (gr. -1). 3.99 *(978-1-4788-0472-7(6))* Newmark Learning LLC.

—Are You Listening, Jack? Lap Book. Garcia, Ellen. 2014. (MySELF Ser.). (J). (gr. -1-k). 27.00 *(978-1-4788-0509-0(9))* Newmark Learning LLC.

—Be Patient, Maddie Lap Book. Garcia, Ellen. 2014. (MySELF Ser.). (J). (gr. -1-k). 27.00 *(978-1-4788-0512-0(9))* Newmark Learning LLC.

—Clean up, Everybody Lap Book. Sparks, Stacey. 2014. (MySELF Ser.). (J). (gr. -1-k). 27.00 *(978-1-4788-0514-4(5))* Newmark Learning LLC.

—Espero Mi Turno. Linde, Barbara M. 2015. (MySELF Ser.). (SPA.). (J). (gr. -1-k). 4.49 *(978-1-4788-1975-2(8))* Newmark Learning LLC.

—Espero Mi Turno: Lap Book. Linde, Barbara M. 2015. (MySELF Ser.). (SPA.). (J). (gr. -1-k). 29.00 *(978-1-4788-2320-9(8))* Newmark Learning LLC.

—From Apple Trees to Cider, Please! Chernesky, Felicia Sanzari. 2015. (ENG.). 32p. (J). (gr. -1-3). 16.99 *(978-0-8075-6513-1(X)*, 080756513X) Whitman, Albert & Co.

—I Can Follow the Rules. Williams, Dinah. 2014. (J). (gr. -1). 3.99 *(978-1-4788-0473-4(4))* Newmark Learning LLC.

—I Can Follow the Rules Lap Book. Williams, Dinah. 2014. (MySELF Ser.). (J). (gr. -1-k). 27.00 *(978-1-4788-0510-6(2))* Newmark Learning LLC.

—I Can Stay Calm. Daniel, Claire. 2014. (J). (gr. -1). 3.99 *(978-1-4788-0474-1(2))* Newmark Learning LLC.

—I Can Stay Calm Lap Book. Daniel, Claire. 2014. (MySELF Ser.). (J). (gr. -1-k). 27.00 *(978-1-4788-0511-3(0))* Newmark Learning LLC.

—I Take Turns. Linde, Barbara M. 2014. (J). (gr. -1). 3.99 *(978-1-4788-0476-5(9))* Newmark Learning LLC.

—I Take Turns Lap Book. Linde, Barbara M. 2014. (MySELF Ser.). (J). (gr. -1-k). 27.00 *(978-1-4788-0513-7(7))* Newmark Learning LLC.

—¿Me Escuchas, Juan? Garcia, Ellen. 2015. (MySELF Ser.). (SPA.). (J). (gr. -1-k). 4.49 *(978-1-4788-1971-4(5))* Newmark Learning LLC.

—¿Me Escuchas, Juan? Lap Book. Garcia, Ellen. 2015. (MySELF Ser.). (SPA.). (J). (gr. -1-k). 29.00 *(978-1-4788-2316-2(X))* Newmark Learning LLC.

—Mind-Boggling Numbers. Rosen, Michael J. 2016. (ENG.). 32p. (J). (gr. 2-5). 19.99 *(978-1-4677-3489-9(6)*, 9781467734899); E-Book 30.65 *(978-1-5124-1108-9(6))* Lerner Publishing Group. (Millbrook Pr.).

—My Friends: Set Of 6. Parkes, Brenda. 2014. (Shared Reading Foundations Ser.). (J). (gr. 1). 36.00 net. *(978-1-4900-0027-5(5))* Benchmark Education Co.

—My Friends Book Set. Parkes, Brenda. 2014. (Shared Reading Foundations Ser.). (J). (gr. 1). 72.00 net. *(978-1-4509-9997-7(2))* Benchmark Education Co.

—Paciencia, María. Smith, Molly. 2015. (MySELF Ser.). (SPA.). (J). (gr. -1-k). 4.49 *(978-1-4788-1974-5(X))* Newmark Learning LLC.

—Paciencia, María: Lap Book. Smith, Molly. 2015. (MySELF Ser.). (SPA.). (J). (gr. -1-k). 29.00 *(978-1-4788-2319-3(4))* Newmark Learning LLC.

—PB&J Hooray! Your Sandwich's Amazing Journey from Farm to Table. Nolan, Janet. 2014. (ENG.). 32p. (J). (gr. -1-3). 16.99 *(978-0-8075-6397-7(8)*, 807563978) Whitman, Albert & Co.

—The Shoemaker & the Elves. Parkes, Brenda. 2015. (Shared Reading Classics Ser.). (J). (gr. k-1). *(978-1-4900-2110-2(8))* Benchmark Education Co.

—The Shoemaker & the Elves: Big Book Edition. Parkes, Brenda. 2015. (Shared Reading Classics Ser.). (J). (gr. k-1). *(978-1-4900-2106-5(X))* Benchmark Education Co.

—Snail Mail. Berger, Samantha. 2018. (ENG.). 32p. (J). (gr. -1-3). 17.99 *(978-0-7624-6251-3(5)*, Running Pr. Kids) Running Pr.

—Stinker. Zeltser, David. 2017. (ENG.). 32p. (J). (gr. -1-3). 17.99 *(978-1-5124-1792-0(0)*, 9781512417920, Carolrhoda Bks.) Lerner Publishing Group.

—Strawberry Girl: Set Of 6. Parkes, Brenda. 2014. (Shared Reading Foundations Ser.). (J). (gr. 1). 36.00 net. *(978-1-4900-0052-7(6))* Benchmark Education Co.

—Strawberry Girl Book Set. Parkes, Brenda. 2014. (Shared Reading Foundations Ser.). (J). (gr. 1). 72.00 net. *(978-1-4900-0022-0(4))* Benchmark Education Co.

—Vamos a Limpiar. Sparks, Stacey. 2015. (MySELF Ser.). (SPA.). (J). (gr. -1-k). 4.49 *(978-1-4788-1976-9(6))* Newmark Learning LLC.

—Vamos a Limpiar: Lap Book. Sparks, Stacey. 2015. (MySELF Ser.). (SPA.). (J). (gr. -1-k). 29.00 *(978-1-4788-2321-6(6))* Newmark Learning LLC.

—Yo Puedo Mantener la Calma. Daniel, Claire. 2015. (MySELF Ser.). (SPA.). (J). (gr. -1-k). 4.49 *(978-1-4788-1973-8(1))* Newmark Learning LLC.

—Yo Puedo Mantener la Calma: Lap Book. Daniel, Claire. 2015. (MySELF Ser.). (SPA.). (J). (gr. -1-k). 29.00 *(978-1-4788-2318-6(6))* Newmark Learning LLC.

—Yo Puedo Seguir Las Reglas. Smith, Molly. 2015. (MySELF Ser.). (SPA.). (J). (gr. -1-k). 4.49 *(978-1-4788-1972-1(3))* Newmark Learning LLC.

—Yo Puedo Seguir Las Reglas: Lap Book. Smith, Molly. 2015. (MySELF Ser.). (SPA.). (J). (gr. -1-k). 29.00 *(978-1-4788-2317-9(8))* Newmark Learning LLC.

Patton, Julia. Drat That Fat Cat! Patton, Julia. 2016. (ENG.). 32p. (J). (gr. -1-3). 16.99 *(978-0-8075-1713-0(5)*, 807517135) Whitman, Albert & Co.

Patton, Julia & Jones, Damien. Get Set! Piano - My First Piano Book. Marshall, Karen. 2020. (Get Set! Ser.). (ENG.). 64p. (J). (gr. 2-4). pap. 13.99 *(978-0-00-835323-0(9))* HarperCollins Pubs. Ltd. GBR. Dist: Independent Pubs. Group.

—Get Set! Piano - My First Piano Pieces, Puzzles & Activities. Marshall, Karen. 2020. (Get Set! Ser.). (ENG.). 32p. (J). (gr. 2-4). pap. 11.99 *(978-0-00-835324-7(7))* HarperCollins Pubs. Ltd. GBR. Dist: Independent Pubs. Group.

Patton, Kaela, jt. illus. see Patton, Melanie.

Patton, Lucia. Surprise on Wheels. Friskey, Margaret. 2004. reprint ed. pap. 15.95 *(978-1-4191-1496-0(4))* Kessinger Publishing, LLC.

Patton, Melanie & Patton, Kaela. Kindergarten Equestrian Activity Book. Patton, Melanie. 2018. (Equestrian-4-Kids Ser.). (ENG.). 74p. (J). pap. 15.98 *(978-1-7200-1434-8(5))* Independently Published.

—Pre-K Equestrian Activity Book. Patton, Melanie. 2018. (Equestrian-4-Kids Ser.). (ENG.). 70p. (J). pap. 15.88 *(978-1-7200-1336-5(5))* Independently Published.

Patton, Scott. Stories Told under the Sycamore Tree: Bible Plant Object Lessons. Patton, Scott, tr. Hahn, Samuel J. 2003. 191p. (J). pap. 19.95 *(978-0-7880-1972-2(4))* CSS Publishing Co.

Pattullo, Alice. Goddesses & Heroines: Women of Myth & Legend. Gresham-Knight, Xanthe. 2020. (ENG.). 128p. (J). (gr. 4-7). 19.95 ***(978-0-500-65191-9(4)***, 565191) Thames & Hudson.

Patzelt, Kasie. Land of Pink. Sanders, Roy E. 2007. (Not So Far Ago Ser.). 37p. (J). (gr. -1-3). 19.99 *(978-1-59879-327-7(6))* Lifevest Publishing, Inc.

—Twiggle. Staton, Debbie. 2007. (J). (gr. -1-3). 17.99 *(978-1-59879-362-8(4))*; 26p. per. 12.99 *(978-1-59879-199-0(0))* Lifevest Publishing, Inc.

Paul, Corky. First Day: Band 06/Orange (Collins Big Cat) Gray, Kes. 2007. (Collins Big Cat Ser.). (ENG.). 24p. (J). (gr. 1-2). pap. 8.99 *(978-0-00-718666-2(5))* HarperCollins Pubs. Ltd. GBR. Dist: Independent Pubs. Group.

Paul de Quay, John. Ready, Aim, Launch! Make Your Own Small Launchers. Ives, Rob. 2016. (Tabletop Wars Ser.). (ENG.). 32p. (J). (gr. 3-6). lib. bdg. 27.99 *(978-1-5124-0636-8(8)*, 9781512406368, Hungry Tomato ®) Lerner Publishing Group.

—Stickmen's Guide to Aircraft. Farndon, John. ed. 2016. (Stickmen's Guides to How Everything Works). (ENG.). 32p. (J). (gr. 3-6). E-Book 42.65 *(978-1-4677-9592-0(5))*; E-Book 42.65 *(978-1-5124-0690-0(2)*, 9781512406900) Lerner Publishing Group. (Hungry Tomato ®).

—Stickmen's Guide to Gigantic Machines. Farndon, John. ed. 2016. (Stickmen's Guides to How Everything Works). (ENG.). 32p. (J). (gr. 3-6). E-Book 42.65 *(978-1-4677-9596-8(8)*, Hungry Tomato ®) Lerner Publishing Group.

—Stickmen's Guide to Trains & Automobiles. Farndon, John. ed. 2016. (Stickmen's Guides to How Everything Works). (ENG.). 32p. (J). (gr. 3-6). E-Book 42.65 *(978-1-4677-9590-6(9)*, Hungry Tomato ®) Lerner Publishing Group.

—Stickmen's Guide to Watercraft. Farndon, John. ed. 2016. (Stickmen's Guides to How Everything Works). (ENG.). 32p. (J). (gr. 3-6). E-Book 42.65 *(978-1-5124-0699-3(6)*, 9781512406993); E-Book 42.65 *(978-1-4677-9594-4(1))* Lerner Publishing Group. (Hungry Tomato ®).

—Surprise the Enemy: Make Your Own Traps & Triggers. Ives, Rob. 2016. (Tabletop Wars Ser.). (ENG.). 32p. (J). (gr. 3-6). lib. bdg. 27.99 *(978-1-5124-0637-5(6)*, 9781512406375, Hungry Tomato ®) Lerner Publishing Group.

Paul, John. Stickmen's Guide to How Things Work: Discover How Planes, Trains, Automobiles & Other Great Machines Work. Farndon, John. 2020. (Stickmen's Guides: 1). (ENG.). 96p. (J). (gr. 2-6). 19.99 *(978-1-913077-16-7(0)*, d5602510-b49e-4462-b99f-983ea94a9661, Beetle Bks.) Hungry Tomato Ltd. GBR. Dist: Baker & Taylor Publisher Services (BTPS).

Paul Jr, Robert. Noel Goes to College. Lewis, Loukisha & Hinton, Noel. 2019. (ENG.). 38p. (J). pap. 14.00 ***(978-1-7221-3483-9(6))*** CreateSpace Independent Publishing Platform.

Paul, Kate. The Adventures of Jake & George: Jake Gets a New Brother. Swift, K. Marie. 2010. 26p. pap. 11.75 *(978-1-60693-863-8(0)*, Eloquent Bks.) Strategic Book Publishing & Rights Agency (SBPRA).

Paul, Korky. Collins Big Cat Phonics for Letters & Sounds - Jake & Jen in the Tomb of Ice: Band 07/Turquoise, Bd. 7. Bradford, Chris. 2018. (Collins Big Cat Phonics Ser.). (ENG.). 24p. (J). (gr. 1-2). pap. 6.99 *(978-0-00-825178-9(9))* HarperCollins Pubs. Ltd. GBR. Dist: Independent Pubs. Group.

—Get That Ball! Corbalis, Judy. 2018. 32p. (J). (-k). 19.99 *(978-1-78344-169-3(0))* Andersen Pr. GBR. Dist: Independent Pubs. Group.

—Get That Ball! Corbalis, Judy. 2019. 32p. (J). (gr. -1-k). pap. 13.99 *(978-1-78344-756-5(7))* Penguin Random Hse. AUS. Dist: Independent Pubs. Group.

—Pa Jinglebob - The Fastest Knitter in the West. Arrigan, Mary. 2005. (Red Bananas Ser.). (ENG.). 48p. (J). lib. bdg. *(978-0-7787-1072-1(6))* Crabtree Publishing Co.

—The Very Noisy House. Rhodes, Julie. 2014. (ENG.). 32p. (J). (gr. -1-k). 17.99 *(978-1-84507-983-3(3)*, Frances Lincoln Children's Bks.) Quarto Publishing Group UK GBR. Dist: Hachette Bk. Group.

—Where's Dad? Dyches, Richard W. Hudson, Edward K., ed. 2016. (ENG.). (J). (gr. k-6). pap. 8.95 *(978-0-9829203-0-5(X))* Children Left Behind.

—Winnie's Big Bad Robot. Thomas, Valerie. 2015. (ENG.). 32p. *(978-0-19-273874-5(7))* Oxford Univ. Pr.

Paul, Leonard. Long Powwow Nights, 1 vol. Bouchard, David & Aleekuk, Pam. 2009. (ENG.). 32p. (J). (gr. 2-5). 24.95 *(978-0-88995-427-4(5)*, 8aa564d9-7d92-4565-9de0-d06259b30d69) Trifolium Bks., Inc. CAN. Dist: Firefly Bks., Ltd.

Paul, Leonard. Long Powwow Nights. Bouchard, David & Aleekuk, Pam. 2020. (ENG.). 32p. (J). (gr. 3-7). pap. 16.95 ***(978-0-88995-607-0(3)***, 555c87ea-71b6-45cd-9bf9-a4a922e9e18e) Red Deer Pr. CAN. Dist: Firefly Bks., Ltd.

Paul, Leonard & Stevens, Art. Gathering, 1 vol. Meuse, Theresa. 2018. (ENG.). 32p. (J). (gr. 1-3). 22.95 *(978-1-77108-466-6(9)*, 7dba527e-cda8-40f3-a30d-49ba92ae60f7) Nimbus Publishing, Ltd. CAN. Dist: Baker & Taylor Publisher Services (BTPS).

Paul, Linda. Jess & James, the Time Travel Paper Dolls. Paul, Linda. 2018. (ENG.). 40p. (J). (gr. 2-6). pap. 12.99 *(978-1-68160-591-3(0))* Crimson Cloak Publishing.

—Linda's Masks. Paul, Linda. 2018. (ENG.). 48p. (J). (gr. 1-6). pap. 14.99 *(978-1-68160-590-6(2))* Crimson Cloak Publishing.

Paul Reising. Beyond All Imagination: The First Souvenir. Leigh-Anna Tehan. 2009. 44p. pap. 18.49 *(978-1-4389-6452-2(8))* AuthorHouse.

Paul, Ruth. Cookie Boo. Paul, Ruth. 2020. (ENG.). 32p. (J). (gr. -1-3). 10.99 ***(978-0-06-286956-2(6)***, HarperCollins) HarperCollins Pubs. Ltd. GBR. Dist: HarperCollins Pubs.

Paul, Ruth. Hedgehog's Magic Tricks. Paul, Ruth. 2013. (ENG.). 32p. (J). (gr. -1-2). 12.99 *(978-0-7636-6385-8(9))* Candlewick Pr.

—Red Panda's Candy Apples. Paul, Ruth. 2014. (ENG.). 32p. (J). (gr. -1-2). 14.99 *(978-0-7636-6758-0(7))* Candlewick Pr.

Paule, Renee. The Frightened Little Flower Bud. Paule, Renee. Hewitt, G. R. 2017. (ENG.). (J). pap. *(978-0-9935098-3-4(5))*; pap. *(978-0-9935098-4-1(3))* RPG Publishing.

Paulin, Sian. That's Me. Leonard, Donna Marie. (ENG.). 42p. (J). (gr. k-6). 2019. pap. 14.99 *(978-0-578-53544-9(0))*; 2018. 22.99 *(978-0-692-19340-2(5))* Rosemary Publishing.

Pauling, Galen T. Q. T. Pie Meets Smart E. Sanders, Stephanie. l.t. ed. 2003. (Q.T. Pie Ser.). 36p. (J). mass mkt. 4.99 *(978-0-9670875-4-2(6)*, 313-533-7383) SanPaul Group, LLC, The.

Paull, Grace. The Bounces of Cynthiann' Lampman, Evelyn Sibley. 2018. (ENG.). 270p. (J). (gr. 3-6). pap. 11.99 *(978-1-4794-3717-7(4))* Wildside Pr., LLC.

—Forgotten Island. Coatsworth, Elizabeth Jane. 2011. 74p. 36.95 *(978-1-258-07461-6(3))* Literary Licensing, LLC.

Paulsen, Bree. Twelve Terribly Active Princesses Who Were Not Exactly Dancing. Dobbs, Michael Ann. 2017. (ENG.). 36p. (J). (gr. k-3). pap. 9.99 *(978-1-5324-0198-5(1))* Xist Publishing.

Paulsen, Haley. Incy's Adventure Begins. Crescitelli, Mike & Crescitelli, John. 2018. (ENG.). 134p. (J). pap. 8.99 *(978-1-947678-10-1(8))* Glass Onion Publishing.

Paulsen, Ruth Wright. La Tortilleria. Paulsen, Gary. Andujar, Gloria Dearagon, tr. from ENG. 2006.Tr. of Tortilla Factory. 27p. (J). (gr. k-4). reprint ed. 16.00 *(978-1-4223-5319-6(2))* DIANE Publishing Co.

Paulson, Arlie & Nix, Pamela. Tummel the Tumbleweed. Nix, Pamela. Barnes, Trisha, ed. 2011. 26p. (J). pap. 7.99 *(978-0-9815914-9-0(3))* River Canyon Pr.

Paultyn, Tony, jt. illus. see Brown, Robert.

Pauwels, Jess. Cowhide-And-Seek. Dillard, Sheri. 2019. 32p. (J). (gr. -1-3). 17.99 *(978-0-7624-9184-1(1)*, Running Pr. Kids) Running Pr.

—Pirate Chicken: All Hens on Deck. Yanish, Brian. 2019. 32p. (J). (-3). 17.99 *(978-1-4926-6520-5(7)*, Sourcebooks Jabberwocky) Sourcebooks, Inc.

—Whobert Whover, Owl Detective. Jason June, Jason. 2017. (ENG.). 40p. (J). (gr. -1-1). 17.99 *(978-1-4814-6271-6(7)*, McElderry, Margaret K. Bks.) McElderry, Margaret K. Bks.

Pavey, Peter. One Dragon's Dream. Pavey, Peter. 2009. (ENG.). 40p. (J). (gr. -1-2). 17.99 *(978-0-7636-4470-3(6))* Candlewick Pr.

Pavlet, Terry. Zelda's Zombie Zoo. Reed, Gary. 2020. (ENG.). 52p. (J). pap. 9.99 ***(978-1-63529-845-1(8))*** Caliber Comics.

Pavlic, Dusan. Explore: How to Explore Everything, Everywhere. Ganeri, Anita. 2020. (Buster Know-How Ser.). (ENG.). 128p. (J). (gr. 4-6). pap. 16.99 *(978-1-78055-508-9(3)*, Buster Bks.) O'Mara, Michael Bks., Ltd. GBR. Dist: Independent Pubs. Group.

—Time Travel: How to Be the Best Time Traveller Ever. Stride, Lottie. 2020. (Buster Know-How Ser.). (ENG.). 128p. (J). (gr. 4-6). pap. 16.99 *(978-1-78055-507-2(5)*, Buster Bks.) O'Mara, Michael Bks., Ltd. GBR. Dist: Independent Pubs. Group.

Pavlova, Vera. A Child's Bedtime Companion. Henry, Sandy. 2005. 26p. (J). (gr. -1-2). per. 12.95 *(978-1-929039-31-9(X))* Ambassador Bks., Inc.

—Daddy's Good Cookin' Johnson, Vincent L. 2006. 32p. (J). 16.95 *(978-0-9657033-3-8(9))* Marzetta Bks.

Pavlova, Xenia. Best Friends Forever. 2016. (ENG.). 26p. (J). bds. 8.99 *(978-1-78557-061-2(7))* Igloo Bks. GBR. Dist: Simon & Schuster, Inc.

Pavlović, Milan. Kabungo, 1 vol. Rolli, Anna. 2016. (ENG.). 176p. (J). (gr. 1-5). 14.95 *(978-1-55498-804-4(7))* Groundwood Bks. CAN. Dist: Publishers Group West (PGW).

P

—Seamus's Short Story, 1 vol. Hartt-Sussman, Heather. 2017. (ENG.). 32p. (J). (gr. k-2). 16.95 *(978-1-55498-793-1(8))* Groundwood Bks. CAN. Dist: Publishers Group West (PGW).

—The Snuggly, 1 vol. Huser, Glen. 2018. (ENG.). 32p. (J). (gr. k-2). 16.95 *(978-1-55498-901-0(9))* Groundwood Bks. CAN. Dist: Publishers Group West (PGW).

—Son of Happy, 1 vol. Fagan, Cary. 2020. (ENG.). 44p. (J). (gr. 1-4). 18.95 *(978-1-77306-178-8(X))* Groundwood Bks. CAN. Dist: Publishers Group West (PGW).

Pavlovi?, Milan. The Boy Who Invented the Popsicle: The Cool Science Behind Frank Epperson's Famous Frozen Treat. Renaud, Anne. 2019. (ENG.). 40p. (J). (gr. -1-3). 16.99 *(978-1-5253-0028-8(8))* Kids Can Pr., Ltd. CAN. Dist: Hachette Bk. Group.

Pavlovic, Milan. Danny, Who Fell in a Hole, 1 vol. Fagan, Cary. 2013. (ENG.). 96p. (J). 14.95 *(978-1-55498-311-7(8))* Groundwood Bks. CAN. Dist: Publishers Group West (PGW).

Pavlovic, Milan. Terry Fox & Me. Leatherdale, Mary Beth. 2020. (ENG.). 32p. (J). (gr. -1-3). 17.99 ***(978-0-7352-6768-8(5)***, Tundra Bks.) Tundra Bks. CAN. Dist: Penguin Random Hse. LLC.

Pavon, David, et al. Blue Boat, Green Frog, Red Barn, Yellow Bee 4 Pack: Chunky Lift a Flap Board Book 4 Pack. Swift, Ginger. Cottage Door Press, ed. 2016. (Lift a Flap Ser.). (ENG.). 48p. (J). (gr. -1-k). bds. 31.96 *(978-1-68052-139-9(X)*, 9000310) Cottage Door Pr.

Pavon, David. Little Red Barn: Chunky Lift a Flap Board Book. Swift, Ginger. Cottage Door Press, ed. 2015. (Lift a Flap Ser.). (ENG.). 12p. (J). (gr. -1-k). bds. 7.99 *(978-1-68052-055-2(5)*, 1000560) Cottage Door Pr.

Pavon, David & Persico, Zoe. Little Red Barn & Little Blue Boat 2 Pack: Chunky Lift a Flap Board Book 2 Pack. Swift, Ginger. Cottage Door Press, ed. 2016. (Lift a Flap Ser.). (ENG.). 12p. (J). (gr. -1-k). bds. 15.98 *(978-1-68052-163-4(2)*, 9000450) Cottage Door Pr.

Pavska, Kseniya. Le Livre d'Apprentissage du Pot Pour la Famille Dinosaure. Monson, Ezra. Vernay, Manon, tr. 2018. (FRE.). 30p. (J). pap. 10.13 *(978-1-7250-2233-1(8))* CreateSpace Independent Publishing Platform.

Pawelak, Lydia, photos by. The Ballet Book: The Young Performer's Guide to Classical Dance. Bowes, Deborah & Kain, Karen. 2nd rev. ed. 2018. (ENG., 144p. (J). (gr. 3-9). pap. 19.95 *(978-0-2281-0066-9(6)*, 67633443-134c-4e74-a842-fcee8df1965b) Firefly Bks., Ltd.

Pawlak, Paweł. Oscar Seeks a Friend. Pawlak, Paweł. 2019. 40p. (J). (gr. k-2). 17.99 *(978-1-911373-79-7(X))* Lantana Publishing GBR. Dist: Lerner Publishing Group.

Pawlak, Pawel. Excuse Me... Are You a Witch? Horn, Emily. 2004. (ENG.). 32p. (J). (gr. -1-2). pap. 7.95 *(978-1-58089-103-5(9))* Charlesbridge Publishing, Inc.

Pawlitza, Marius. The Accursed Inheritance of Henrietta Achilles: Book 1. Hörnig, Haiko. 2020. (House Divided Ser.). 96p. (gr. 7-12). (J). lib. bdg. 29.32 *(978-1-5415-7243-0(2))*; (ENG.). (YA). pap. 9.99 *(978-1-5415-8692-5(1))* Lerner Publishing Group. (Graphic Universe™).

Paws, Inc., Inc. A Garfield ® Guide to Online Etiquette: Be Kind Online. Nickel, Scott et al. 2020. (Garfield's ® Guide to Digital Citizenship Ser.). (ENG.). 32p. (J). (gr. 2-5). lib. bdg. 27.99 *(978-1-5415-7280-5(7)*, Lerner Pubns.) Lerner Publishing Group.

—A Garfield ® Guide to Online Friends: Not the Same As Real Friends! Nickel, Scott et al. 2020. (Garfield's ® Guide to Digital Citizenship Ser.). (ENG.). 32p. (J). (gr. 2-5). lib. bdg. 27.99 *(978-1-5415-7277-5(7)*, Lerner Pubns.) Lerner Publishing Group.

—A Garfield ® Guide to Posting Online: Pause Before You Post. Nickel, Scott et al. 2020. (Garfield's ® Guide to Digital Citizenship Ser.). (ENG.). 32p. (J). (gr. 2-5). lib. bdg. 27.99 *(978-1-5415-7279-9(3)*, Lerner Pubns.) Lerner Publishing Group.

—A Garfield ® Guide to Safe Downloading: Downloading Disaster! Nickel, Scott et al. 2020. (Garfield's ® Guide to Digital Citizenship Ser.). (ENG.). 32p. (J). (gr. 2-5). lib. bdg. 27.99 *(978-1-5415-7278-2(5)*, Lerner Pubns.) Lerner Publishing Group.

Pax, H. H. Metta's Bedtime Stories. World Peace, Metta & McBride, Heddrick. 2013. 36p. pap. 12.95 *(978-0-615-70075-5(6))* McBride, Heddrick.

Pax, Hh. Grandma & Me on the Run. Graziano II, Anthony John. 2019. (ENG.). 38p. (J). pap. 13.00 ***(978-1-0955-7251-1(2))*** Independently Published.

Pax, Hh. Madison's World: A Bad Hair Day Daddy to the Rescue. McIntyre, Madison G. 2019. (Madison's World Ser.: Vol. 2). (ENG.). 36p. (J). pap. 9.99 *(978-1-7932-0307-6(5))* Independently Published.

Paxton, Cameron L. Arthur, the Talking Goat. Cromwell, Daisy. 2007. 52p. (J). pap. 18.99 *(978-0-9800675-1-4(0))* Mirror Publishing.

Payne, C. F. Brave Harriet. Moss, Marissa. 2015. 32p. pap. 8.00 *(978-1-61003-492-0(9))* Center for the Collaborative Classroom.

—Bunnicula in a Box: Bunnicula; Howliday Inn; the Celery Stalks at Midnight; Nighty-Nightmare; Return to Howliday Inn; Bunnicula Strikes Again; Bunnicula Meets Edgar Allan Crow. Howe, James. ed. 2013. (Bunnicula & Friends Ser.). (ENG.). 1136p. (J). (gr. 3-7). pap. 55.99 *(978-1-4424-8521-1(3)*, Atheneum Bks. for Young Readers) Simon & Schuster Children's Publishing.

—Casey at the Bat: A Ballad of the Republic Sung in the Year 1888. Thayer, Ernest L. 2003. (ENG.). 40p. (J). (gr. -1-3). 19.99 *(978-0-689-85494-1(3)*, Simon & Schuster Bks. For Young Readers) Simon & Schuster Bks. For Young Readers.

—Hide-And-Squeak. Frederick, Heather Vogel. 2011. (ENG.). 32p. (J). (gr. -1-1). 16.99 *(978-0-689-85570-2(2)*, Simon & Schuster Bks. For Young Readers) Simon & Schuster Bks. For Young Readers.

—The Legend of the Curse of the Bambino. Shaughnessy, Dan. 2005. (ENG.). 32p. (J). (gr. k-3). 16.95 *(978-0-689-87235-8(6)*, Simon & Schuster/Paula Wiseman Bks.) Simon & Schuster/Paula Wiseman Bks.

—Lineup for Yesterday. Nash, Ogden. 2011. (ENG.). 56p. (J). (gr. 1-3). 24.99 *(978-1-56846-212-7(3)*, Creative Editions) Creative Co., The.

—Lineup for Yesterday ABC Baseball Cards. Nash, Ogden. 2013. (ENG.). (J). (gr. 1-3). 12.99 *(978-1-56846-249-3(2)*, Creative Editions) Creative Co., The.

—Micawber. Lithgow, John. 2005. (ENG.). 40p. (J). (gr. -1-3). reprint ed. 9.99 *(978-0-689-83542-1(6)*, Simon & Schuster Bks. For Young Readers) Simon & Schuster Bks. For Young Readers.

—Mickey Mantle: the Commerce Comet. Winter, Jonah. 2017. 40p. (J). (gr. -1-3). 17.99 *(978-1-101-93352-7(6)*, Schwartz & Wade Bks.) Random Hse. Children's Bks.

—Mighty Jackie: The Strike-Out Queen. Moss, Marissa. 2004. (ENG.). 32p. (J). (gr. k-3). 18.99 *(978-0-689-86329-5(2)*, Simon & Schuster/Paula Wiseman Bks.) Simon & Schuster/Paula Wiseman Bks.

—Miss Mary Reporting: The True Story of Sportswriter Mary Garber. Macy, Sue. 2016. (ENG.). 40p. (J). (gr. k-3). 18.99 *(978-1-4814-0120-3(3)*, Simon & Schuster Bks. For Young Readers) Simon & Schuster Bks. For Young Readers.

—Mousetronaut: Based on a (Partially) True Story. Kelly, Mark. 2012. (ENG.). 40p. (J). (gr. -1-3). 19.99 *(978-1-4424-5824-6(0)*, Simon & Schuster/Paula Wiseman Bks.) Simon & Schuster/Paula Wiseman Bks.

—Mousetronaut Goes to Mars. Kelly, Mark. 2013. (ENG.). 40p. (J). (gr. -1-3). 19.99 *(978-1-4424-8426-9(8)*, Simon & Schuster/Paula Wiseman Bks.) Simon & Schuster/Paula Wiseman Bks.

—Pop's Bridge. Bunting, Eve. 2006. (ENG.). 32p. (J). (gr. -1-3). 17.99 *(978-0-15-204773-3(5)*, 1194402) Houghton Mifflin Harcourt Publishing Co.

—The Remarkable Farkle Mcbride. Lithgow, John. 2003. (ENG.). 40p. (J). (gr. -1-3). pap. 8.99 *(978-0-689-83541-4(8)*, Simon & Schuster Bks. For Young Readers) Simon & Schuster Bks. For Young Readers.

—Shoeless Joe & Black Betsy. Bildner, Phil. 2006. (ENG.). 40p. (J). (gr. k-3). reprint ed. 8.99 *(978-0-689-87437-6(5)*, Simon & Schuster Bks. For Young Readers) Simon & Schuster Bks. For Young Readers.

—The Shot Heard 'Round the World. Bildner, Phil. 2010. (ENG.). 32p. (J). (gr. k-3). 16.99 *(978-1-4424-2195-0(9)*, Simon & Schuster Bks. For Young Readers) Simon & Schuster Bks. For Young Readers.

—To Dare Mighty Things: The Life of Theodore Roosevelt. Rappaport, Doreen. 2013. (Big Words Book Ser.: 7). 48p. (J). (gr. 1-3). 17.99 *(978-1-4231-2488-7(X))* Hyperion Pr.

—What to Do with a String. Yolen, Jane. 2019. 32p. (J). (gr. 1-3). 18.99 *(978-1-56846-322-3(7)*, Creative Editions) Creative Co., The.

Payne, Emerald M. Brown Eyes: Ojos Marrones. Payne, Yadira V. Payne, Yadira V., ed. 2004. (MUL.). (J). pap. 12.50 *(978-0-9747350-1-6(9))* Payne, Yadira V. Publishing.

Payne, Emily 'Madge'. The Rucklestone. Payne, Emily 'Madge'. 2016. (ENG.). (J). pap. *(978-0-9933792-2-2(2))* Elephant Stamp Publishing Ltd.

Payne, Glenn. The Amazing Discovery! An Austin & Justin Story. Arnold, Jim. 2018. (ENG.). 26p. (J). pap. 10.00 *(978-1-7200-7789-3(4))* Independently Published.

—Austin & Justin Find a Rainbow. Arnold, Jim. 2018. (Austin & Justin Stories Ser.: Vol. 3). (ENG.). 26p. (J). pap. 10.00 *(978-1-7241-4237-5(2))* Independently Published.

Payne, Henry. The Ear Book. Perkins, Al. (Bright & Early Board Books(TM) Ser.). (J). (— 1). 2008. (ENG.). 24p. bds. 4.99 *(978-0-375-84279-5(9))*; 2007. 36p. 9.99 *(978-0-375-84251-1(9))* Random Hse. Children's Bks. (Random Hse. Bks. for Young Readers).

Payne, Katie. Guess Who's the Latter-Day Prophet. Carter, Molly. 2019. (ENG.). 32p. (J). 15.99 *(978-1-4621-2320-9(1))* Cedar Fort, Inc./CFI Distribution.

Payne, Kay. Beth's Fella. Strong, Frances Dinkins. 2006. 112p. (J). pap. 9.95 *(978-0-9720267-6-5(2))* Learning Abilities Bks.

Payne, Kevin. Forest: Touch & Feel. Colombe, Rose. Cottage Door Press, ed. 2019. (Lamaze Activity Bks.). (ENG.). 10p. (J). (gr. -1-k). bds. 9.99 *(978-1-68052-737-7(1)*, 1004580) Cottage Door Pr.

Payne, Mark. Hilhairyass Poems: By a Six Year Old Adult. Lebachen, Medyhne. 2012. 76p. (YA). *(978-0-9872816-4-7(X))* Heart Space Pubns.

Payne, Rachel & Song, Danielle. Miss Spellin' Helen. Payne, Jody. 2012. 148p. pap. 6.99 *(978-0-9846687-0-0(5))* Absalon Pr.

Payne, Sally. Mother Goose's Classic Nursery Rhymes. Brooks, Susie. 2020. (ENG.). 148p. (J). (— 1). 17.99 *(978-1-68412-673-6(8)*, Silver Dolphin Bks.) Printers Row Publishing Group.

Payne, Yadira V. ¡Viva los Colores! Payne, Yadira V. 2004. (MUL.). (J). pap. 12.50 *(978-0-9747350-0-9(0))* Payne, Yadira V. Publishing.

Payol, Faythe. Drake & Daphne Make a Discovery. 2020. (ENG.). 34p. (J). 21.99 ***(978-1-952894-96-1(4))*** Pen It! Pubns., LLC.

—It's Dark in the Ark. Vajko Srch, Ren�e. 2020. (ENG.). 26p. (J). 18.99 ***(978-1-952011-64-1(7))*** Pen It! Pubns., LLC.

Peabody, Rob. Achy Ali. Hersey, Jodi. 2011. pap. 5.00 *(978-1-4276-5272-0(4))* Aardvark Global Publishing.

Peach-Pit Press Staff. DearS, Vol. 2. Peach-pit. rev. ed. 2005. 208p. pap. 9.99 *(978-1-59532-309-5(0)*, Tokyopop Adult) TOKYOPOP, Inc.

—DearS, Vol. 3. rev. ed. 2005. (DearS Ser.). 208p. pap. 9.99 *(978-1-59532-310-1(4)*, Tokyopop Adult) TOKYOPOP, Inc.

Peach-Pit Press Staff. DearS, Vol. 5. Peach-Pit Press Staff. rev. ed. 2006. (DearS Ser.). 192p. pap. 9.99 *(978-1-59532-797-0(5)*, Tokyopop Adult) TOKYOPOP, Inc.

Peacock, Ausa M. As My Heart Awakes: A Waldorf Reader for Early Third Grade. Pittis, Arthur M. Mitchell, David S., ed. 2005. (J). bds. 10.00 *(978-1-888365-62-7(5))* Waldorf Publications.

—Fee Fi Fo Fum: A Waldorf Reader for Late Second Grade. Pittis, Arthur M. Mitchell, David S., ed. 2005. (J). bds. 10.00 *(978-1-888365-63-4(3))* Waldorf Publications.

—Sun So Hot I Froze to Death: A Waldorf Reader for Advanced Fourth Grade. Pittis, Arthur M. Mitchell, David S., ed. 2005. (ENG.). (J). bds. 12.00 *(978-1-888365-65-8(X))* Waldorf Publications.

—When I Hear My Heart Wonder: A Waldorf Reader for Late Third Grade. Pittis, Arthur M. Mitchell, David S., ed. 2005. (J). bds. 10.00 *(978-1-888365-66-5(8))* Waldorf Publications.

Peacock, Bessie Merle. Benny the Beetle, 1 vol. Peacock-Williams, Carol A. & Williams, Christy Jo. 2010. 28p. 24.95 *(978-1-4489-8373-5(8))* PublishAmerica, Inc.

Peacock, Phyllis Hornung. Pythagoras & the Ratios: A Math Adventure. Ellis, Julie. 2010. (Charlesbridge Math Adventures Ser.). 32p. (J). (gr. 2-5). pap. 7.95 *(978-1-57091-776-9(0))*; (ENG.). (gr. k-3). 22.44 *(978-1-57091-775-2(2))* Charlesbridge Publishing, Inc.

Peacock, Ralph. Wulf the Saxon: A Story of the Norman Conquest. Henty, George. 2010. (Dover Children's Classics Ser.). (ENG.). 352p. (YA). (gr. 3-8). pap. 8.95 *(978-0-486-47595-0(6))* Dover Pubns., Inc.

Peacock, Robert M., photos by. Southern Cocktails: Dixie Drinks, Party Potions, & Classic Libations. Gee, Denise. 2007. (ENG., 120p. (gr. 8-17). 14.95 *(978-0-8118-5243-2(1))* Chronicle Bks. LLC.

Peacock, Sarah. Cleo the Snappy Crocodile Activity Book for Children Who Are Afraid to Get Close: A Therapeutic Story with Creative Activities about Trust, Anger & Relationships for Children Aged 5-10. Treisman, Karen. 2019. (Therapeutic Treasures Collection). (ENG.). 160p. (C). 26.95 ***(978-1-78592-551-1(2)***, 696894) Kingsley, Jessica Pubs. GBR. Dist: Hachette UK Distribution.

Peacock, Sarah. Frog's Breathtaking Speech: How Children (And Frogs) Can Use the Breath to Deal with Anxiety, Anger & Tension. Chissick, Michael. 2012. (ENG.). 48p. (J). 19.95 *(978-1-84819-091-7(3)*, 694212, Singing Dragon) Kingsley, Jessica Pubs. GBR. Dist: Hachette UK Distribution.

—Seahorse's Magical Sun Sequences: How All Children (And Sea Creatures) Can Use Yoga to Feel Positive, Confident & Completely Included. Chissick, Michael. 2015. (ENG.). 48p. (J). 19.95 *(978-1-84819-283-6(5)*, 693880, Singing Dragon) Kingsley, Jessica Pubs. GBR. Dist: Hachette UK Distribution.

—Sitting on a Chicken: The Best (Ever) 52 Yoga Games to Teach in Schools. Chissick, Michael. 2016. (ENG.). 112p. pap. 24.95 *(978-1-84819-325-3(4)*, 696301, Singing Dragon) Kingsley, Jessica Pubs. GBR. Dist: Hachette UK Distribution.

Peake, Mervyn. The Hunting of the Snark. Carroll, Lewis. 2004. 64p. *(978-0-413-74380-0(2))* Methuen Publishing Ltd.

Peaks, Jaiya. The Wishing Stone #3: Mesmerizing Mermaids. Hoopes, Lorana. 2018. (Wishing Stone Ser.: Vol. 3). (ENG.). 66p. (J). pap. 7.99 *(978-1-7238-5714-0(9))* Independently Published.

Pearce, Arline June. Sunrise the Barnegat Pony. Pearce, Arline June. 2011. (ENG.). 26p. pap. 15.99 *(978-1-4628-8601-2(9))* Xlibris Corp.

Pearce, Carl. Attention, Girls! A Guide to Learn All about Your AD/HD. Quinn, Patricia O. 2009. 112p. (J). (gr. 4-7). 16.95 *(978-1-4338-0447-2(6))*; pap. 12.95 *(978-1-4338-0448-9(4))* American Psychological Assn. (Magination Pr.).

—John Deere's Powerful Idea: The Perfect Plow. Collins, Terry. 2015. (Story Behind the Name Ser.). (ENG.). 32p. (J). (gr. 2-4). lib. bdg. 29.32 *(978-1-4795-7138-3(5)*, Picture Window Bks.) Capstone.

—The Silence Seeker. Morley, Ben. 2009. (ENG.). 32p. (J). (gr. k-2). pap. 14.99 *(978-1-84853-003-4(X))* Transworld Publishers Ltd. GBR. Dist: Independent Pubs. Group.

Pearce, Carl, jt. illus. see Chesworth, Michael.

Pearce, Gillian M. Growing up Pagan: A Workbook for Wiccan Families, 1 vol. Hill, Raine. 2009. (ENG.). 64p. pap., wbk. ed. 19.99 *(978-0-7643-3143-5(4)*, 9780764331435) Schiffer Publishing, Ltd.

Pearce, Shane. Unbearably Bored. Evans, Hannah. 2017. (ENG.). (J). 18.95 *(978-0-9985496-0-6(6))*; pap. 12.95 *(978-0-9985496-1-3(4))* Open Suitcase.

Pearcey, Dawn. Escape Plans. Posesorski, Sherie. 2005. 272p. (J). (gr. 5). 8.95 *(978-1-55050-177-3(1))* Coteau Bks. CAN. Dist: Fitzhenry & Whiteside, Ltd.

Pearl, Debi & Pearl, Michael. Listen to My Dream. Pearl, Debi. 2009. (ENG.). 40p. pap. 6.95 *(978-0-9819737-1-5(X))* No Greater Joy Ministries, Inc.

Pearl, Michael, jt. illus. see Pearl, Debi.

Pearlman, Esther, jt. illus. see Pearlman, Larry.

Pearlman, Larry & Pearlman, Esther. Cute Li'l Donkeys: (Raisin' & Grazin') 2014. (J). *(978-0-935047-81-3(6))* Americas Group, The.

Pearn, Kayley. Even Cows Wear Moo Moos. Hackett, J. J. 2013. 24p. (J). pap. 14.95 *(978-0-9897242-1-0(2)*, Over the Rainbow) Pearn & Assocs. Inc.

Pearn, Kris. Project Superhero. Zehr, E. Paul. 2014. (ENG.). 224p. (J). (gr. 2-7). 13.95 *(978-1-77041-180-7(1)*, 9781770411807) ECW Pr. CAN. Dist: Baker & Taylor Publisher Services (BTPS).

Pearse, Alfred. A Tale of the Western Plains. Henty, George. 2006. (Dover Children's Classics Ser.). (ENG.). 352p. (YA). (gr. 3-8). pap. 8.95 *(978-0-486-45261-6(1))* Dover Pubns., Inc.

Pearse, Asha. The Adventures of Tom Sawyer. 2017. (ENG.). 32p. (J). (gr. -1-3). *(978-1-4867-1271-7(1))* Flowerpot Children's Pr. Inc.

—Alice in Wonderland. 2017. (ENG.). 32p. (J). (gr. -1-3). *(978-1-4867-1270-0(3))* Flowerpot Children's Pr. Inc.

—A Sailor Went to Sea, Sea, Sea. Everett, Melissa. 2017. (ENG.). 20p. (J). (gr. -1-2). bds. *(978-1-4867-1243-4(6))* Flowerpot Children's Pr. Inc.

—Wizard of Oz. 2017. (ENG.). 32p. (J). (gr. 1-5). *(978-1-4867-1269-4(X))* Flowerpot Children's Pr. Inc.

—Wizard of Oz. 2017. (10 Minute Classics Ser.). (ENG.). 32p. (J). (gr. 1-4). 16.99 *(978-1-4867-1221-2(5)*, 2a834f32-24f6-43e5-9453-9e2085c24675) Flowerpot Pr.

—Wizard of Oz. 2014. (ENG.). 16p. (J). (gr. -1-4). 7.99 *(978-1-4867-0009-7(8))* Flowerpot Children's Pr. Inc. CAN. Dist: Cardinal Pubs. Group.

—Yo Veo un Arbol. Koons, Linda. 2016. (Early Rising Readers Ser.). (SPA.). 16p. (J). (gr. 1-1). 6.67 *(978-1-4788-4208-8(3))* Newmark Learning LLC.

Pearse, Stephen. Native Trees of British Columbia. Pearse, Stephen, tr. Halter, Reese & Turner, Nancy J. rev. ed. 2003. 96p. pap. *(978-0-9684143-3-0(8))* Global Forest Pr. CAN. Dist: Lone Pine Publishing.

Pearson, Catherine. Dragonfly. Bissonette, Aim�e M. 2020. (Imagine This! Ser.). 32p. (J). (gr. -1-3). 17.99 ***(978-0-8075-5821-8(4)***, 0807558214) Whitman, Albert & Co.

Pearson, Colin. Military Jets up Close, 01 vols., 1. Jackson, Robert. 2016. (Military Technology: Top Secret Clearance Ser.). (ENG.). 224p. (YA). 43.60 *(978-1-5081-7080-8(0)*, Rosen Young Adult) Rosen Publishing Group, Inc., The.

—Modern Warships up Close, 01 vols., 1. Dougherty, Martin J. 2016. (Military Technology: Top Secret Clearance Ser.). (ENG.). 224p. (YA). 43.60 *(978-1-5081-7084-6(3)*, Rosen Young Adult) Rosen Publishing Group, Inc., The.

—Tanks of World War II up Close, 01 vols., 1. Dougherty, Martin J. 2016. (Military Technology: Top Secret Clearance Ser.). (ENG.). 224p. (YA). 43.60 *(978-1-5081-7086-0(X)*, Rosen Young Adult) Rosen Publishing Group, Inc., The.

—Warplanes of World War II up Close, 01 vols., 1. Jackson, Robert. 2016. (Military Technology: Top Secret Clearance Ser.). (ENG.). 224p. (YA). 43.60 *(978-1-5081-7078-5(9)*, Rosen Young Adult) Rosen Publishing Group, Inc., The.

Pearson, David, jt. illus. see Custard, P. T.

Pearson, Derek. Tulsi the Tiger: & Stories of His Jungle Friends. Chet Trivedy. 2019. (ENG.). 50p. (J). *(978-1-912576-36-4(8))*; pap. *(978-1-912576-37-1(6))* Boughton, George Publishing.

Pearson, Larry Leroy. The Three Little Jayhawks. Sanner, Jennifer Jackson, ed. 2006. 40p. (J). per. 20.00 *(978-0-9742918-1-9(1))* Kansas Alumni Assoc.

Pearson, Luke. Adventure Time: Finn. Pope, Paul et al. 2019. (Adventure Time Ser.). (ENG.). 208p. (J). (gr. 4-7). pap. 9.99 *(978-1-68415-293-3(3))* Boom! Studios.

Pearson, Maria. Animal Stencil Cards. 2008. (Stencil Cards Ser.). 16p. (J). 9.99 *(978-0-7945-1961-2(X)*, Usborne) EDC Publishing.

—Spooky Stencil Cards. 2008. (Stencil Cards Ser.). 16p. (J). 9.99 *(978-0-7945-2415-9(X)*, Usborne) EDC Publishing.

Pearson, Maria, jt. illus. see Field, Mandy.

Pearson, Randell. The Emancipation of Grandpa Sandy Wills. Wills, Cheryl. 2016. (ENG.). 48p. (J). pap. 18.63 *(978-1-61717-886-3(1))* Sussman Sales Co.

Pearson, Scott. Batjack. Neville, Ann. 2013. (ENG.). 184p. (J). pap. *(978-0-9941227-1-1(3))* CreateBooks Ltd.

Pearson, Tracey Campbell. Elephant's Story. Pearson, Tracey Campbell. 2013. (ENG.). 40p. (J). (gr. -1-3). 17.99 *(978-0-374-39913-9(1)*, 9780374399139, Farrar, Straus & Giroux (BYR)) Farrar, Straus & Giroux.

Pearson, Victoria, photos by. Four Seasons Pasta: A Year of Inspired Recipes in the Italian Tradition. Fletcher, Janet. 2004. (ENG., 132p. (gr. 8-17). pap. 19.95 *(978-0-8118-3908-2(7))* Chronicle Bks. LLC.

Pease, Pamela. Design Dossier: Architecture. Pease, Pamela. 2011. (Design Dossiers Ser.). (ENG.). 96p. (J). (gr. 4-7). 24.00 *(978-0-9777905-3-1(3))* Paintbox Pr.

Pease, Tristyn. Noah's Little Lamb, 1 vol. Jelsma, Amber. 2010. 32p. pap. 24.95 *(978-1-4489-6068-2(1))* PublishAmerica, Inc.

Peat, Fern Bisel. A Child's Garden of Verses: A Collection of Scriptures, Prayers & Poems. Stevenson, Robert Louis. 2011. (Dover Read & Listen Ser.). (ENG.). 96p. (J). (gr. 3-8). pap. 14.99 incl. audio compact disk *(978-0-486-48369-6(X))* Dover Pubns., Inc.

—The Sugar-Plum Tree & Other Verses: Includes a Read-and-Listen. Field, Eugene. 2010. (Dover Read & Listen Ser.). (ENG.). 80p. (J). (gr. 1-5). pap. 14.99 *(978-0-486-47675-9(8))* Dover Pubns., Inc.

—A Treasury of Bedtime Stories: Classic Tales for Children. Clinton, Althea L. & Madsen, Eleanor. 2017. (Children's Classic Collections). (ENG.). 96p. (J). (gr. -1-3). 12.99 *(978-1-944686-07-9(X)*, Racehorse Publishing) Skyhorse Publishing Co., Inc.

Peattie, Gary. Christmas Time in the Mountains. Luton, Mildred. 2003. 44p. (Orig.). (gr. 1-6). pap. 6.95 *(978-0-87516-434-2(X))* DeVorss & Co.

Peavler, Amy & Peavler, Jan. The King the Queen & the Princess. Peavler, Amy & Peavler, Jan. 2006. 40p. (J). per. *(978-0-9787672-2-8(5))* Lotus Petal Publishing.

Peavler, Jan, jt. illus. see Peavler, Amy.

Peck, Beth. Just Like Josh Gibson. Johnson, Angela. 2007. (J). 14.65 *(978-0-7569-8088-7(7))* Perfection Learning Corp.

—Just Like Josh Gibson. Johnson, Angela. (ENG.). 32p. (J). 2004. (gr. -1-2). 19.99 *(978-0-689-82628-3(1))*; 2007. (gr. k-2). reprint ed. 7.99 *(978-1-4169-2728-0(X))* Simon & Schuster Bks. For Young Readers. (Simon & Schuster Bks. For Young Readers).

—Matthew & Tillie. Jones, Rebecca C. 2015. 32p. pap. 7.00 *(978-1-61003-532-3(1))* Center for the Collaborative Classroom.

—Megan's Year: An Irish Traveler's Story. Whelan, Gloria. 2011. (Tales of the World Ser.). (ENG.). 32p. (gr. k-5). lib. bdg. 16.95 *(978-1-58536-449-7(5))* Sleeping Bear Pr.

—Music for the End of Time. Bryant, Jen. 2005. 32p. (J). (gr. 4-5). 17.00 *(978-0-8028-5229-8(7))* Eerdmans, William B. Publishing Co.

Peck, Bill. Kiernan's Jam. Moore, Nancy Delano. 2006. (J). 10.00 *(978-0-9785775-0-6(7))* Moore, Hullihen.

Peck, Everett. Mose the Fireman: The Legendary Firefighter. Metaxas, Eric. 2004. (Rabbit Ears-A Classic Tale Ser.). (ENG.). 40p. (J). (gr. 2-6). 28.50 *(978-1-59197-766-7(5)*, 12924, Picture Bk.) Spotlight.

Peck, Kama. Abrea Ansus. Hauser, Sheri. aut. ed. 2005. 26p. (YA). per. *(978-0-9766718-7-9(5))* Glorybound Publishing.
—Ba Ba Verde La. Hauser, Sheri. Schaefer, Rita, tr. 2019. (Gbk Ser.: Vol. 2). (ENG.). 30p. (J). pap. 9.95 *(978-1-0803-2554-2(9))* Independently Published.
Peck, Kama. Frog Fray Fun. Hauser, Sheri. 2019. (Hop a Log Ser.: Vol. 4). (ENG.). 32p. (J). pap. 9.95 ***(978-1-0872-3738-1(6))*** Independently Published.
—Jack the Cat Was Very Fat. Golding, Penny. 2019. (ENG.). 30p. (J). pap. 9.95 ***(978-1-6763-4759-0(3))***; pap. 9.95 ***(978-1-7129-9525-9(1))*** Independently Published.
Peck, Kama. Tomasena: Moving from Doubt to Faith. Hauser, Sheri. aut. ed. 2005. 304p. (YA). 39.50 *(978-0-9766718-3-1(2))* Glorybound Publishing.
Peck, Kama. Wiggly Water. Hauser, Sheri. 2019. (Hop-A-Log Ser.: Vol. 9). (ENG.). 36p. (J). pap. 9.95 ***(978-1-7059-2547-8(2))*** Independently Published.
Peck, Lillian Hoban. The Little Brute Family. Hoban, Russell. 2004. (Sunburst Bks.). 17.00 *(978-0-7569-3301-2(3))* Perfection Learning Corp.
Pedersen, Emma. Life Cycles of Caribou. Ittusardjuat, Monica. ed. 2020. (ENG.). 26p. (J). bds. 12.95 ***(978-1-77227-280-2(9))*** Inhabit Media Inc. CAN. Dist: Consortium Bk. Sales & Distribution.
—Looking for Friends (English) 2018. (Mia & the Monsters Ser.). (ENG.). 12p. (gr. 1-1). pap. 7.95 ***(978-0-2287-0157-6(0))*** Inhabit Education CAN. Dist: Consortium Bk. Sales & Distribution.
—Please Don't Change My Diaper! Holden, Sarabeth. 2020. 28p. (J). 16.95 ***(978-1-77227-273-4(6))*** Inhabit Media Inc. CAN. Dist: Consortium Bk. Sales & Distribution.
Pedersen, Emma. Queenie Quail Can't Keep Up. Whittingham, Jane. 2019. (ENG.). 32p. (J). (gr. k-2). 18.95 *(978-1-77278-067-3(7))* Pajama Pr. CAN. Dist: Ingram Publisher Services.
Pedersen, Emma. What Can Ataata Fix? (Inuktitut/English) Sammurtok, Nadia. ed. 2020. (ENG.). 40p. (J). 18.95 ***(978-0-2287-0492-8(8))*** Inhabit Education CAN. Dist: Consortium Bk. Sales & Distribution.
Pedersen, Janet. Bath Time, 1 vol. Spinelli, Eileen. 2003. (ENG.). 32p. (J). 14.95 *(978-0-7614-5117-4(X))* Marshall Cavendish Corp.
—Jake Drake, Bully Buster. Clements, Andrew. 2007. (Jake Drake Ser.: Bk. 1). (ENG.). 80p. (J). (gr. 2-5). pap. 5.99 *(978-1-4169-3933-7(4)*, Atheneum Bks. for Young Readers) Simon & Schuster Children's Publishing.
—Jake Drake, Class Clown. Clements, Andrew. 2007. (Jake Drake Ser.: Bk. 4). (ENG.). 96p. (J). (gr. 2-5). pap. 5.99 *(978-1-4169-4912-1(7)*, Atheneum Bks. for Young Readers) Simon & Schuster Children's Publishing.
—Jake Drake, Know-It-All. Clements, Andrew. 2007. (Jake Drake Ser.: Bk. 2). (ENG.). 112p. (J). (gr. 2-5). pap. 5.99 *(978-1-4169-3931-3(8)*, Atheneum Bks. for Young Readers) Simon & Schuster Children's Publishing.
—Jake Drake, Teacher's Pet. Clements, Andrew. 2007. (Jake Drake Ser.: 3). (ENG.). 96p. (J). (gr. 2-5). pap. 5.99 *(978-1-4169-3932-0(6)*, Atheneum Bks. for Young Readers) Simon & Schuster Children's Publishing.
Pedersen, Janet, jt. illus. see Frazee, Marla.
Pedersen, Judy. Seedfolks. Fleischman, Paul. 2004. (Joanna Cotler Bks.). (ENG.). 112p. (YA). (gr. 8-18). pap. 8.99 *(978-0-06-447207-4(8)*, HarperTeen) HarperCollins Pubs.
—Seedfolks. Fleischman, Paul. ed. 2004. (Joanna Colter Bks.). 102p. (YA). (gr. 5-9). 19.65 *(978-0-613-18276-8(6))* Turtleback.
Pedersen, Kelly. Finding Love on Summer Hill. Pedersen, Kelly. 2016. (ENG.). 38p. (J). pap. 9.95 *(978-1-63047-860-5(1))* Morgan James Publishing.
Pedersen, Robert H. Seeds of Awareness: A Journey Towards Self Realization. Pedersen, Robert H., photos by. 2003. 96p. 24.95 *(978-0-9744163-0-4(4))* Awareness Pubns.
Pedersen, Vilhelm. The Stories of Hans Christian Andersen: A New Translation from the Danish. Andersen, Hans et al. Frank, Diana Crone & Frank, Jeffrey Crone, eds. 2005. (ENG.). 304p. per. 27.95 *(978-0-8223-3693-8(6))* Duke Univ. Pr.
Pedersen, Vilhelm, jt. illus. see Fröhlich, Lorenz.
Pederson, Gunda. Susie Sunflower. Harris, Mary Beth. 2010. 24p. 16.49 *(978-1-4520-5171-0(2))* AuthorHouse.
Pederson, Judy. Gifts from the Sea. Kinsey, Natalie. 2005. 128p. (J). (gr. 3-7). 5.99 *(978-0-440-41970-9(0)*, Yearling) Random Hse. Children's Bks.
Pedigo, Kim Tran. Having Fun with Kandai the Elephant. Pedigo, Kim Tran. 2012. 36p. pap. 12.95 *(978-1-61244-105-4(X))* Halo Publishing International.
Pedlar, Elaine. A Shelter in Our Car. Gunning, Monica. 2013. (ENG.). 32p. (J). pap. 10.95 *(978-0-89239-308-4(4)*, Children's Book Press) Lee & Low Bks., Inc.
Pedlar, Elaine & Tonel. Birthday in the Barrio. Dole, Mayra L. 2004.Tr. of Cumpleaños en el Barrio. (ENG & SPA.). 32p. (J). 16.95 *(978-0-89239-194-3(4))* Lee & Low Bks., Inc.
Pedler, Caroline. Badger & the Big Adventure. Chiew, Suzanne. 2019. (ENG.). 32p. (J). (gr. -1-2). 17.99 *(978-1-68010-149-2(8))* Tiger Tales.
—Bedtime for Little Bears. Bedford, David. 2018. (ENG.). 16p. (J). (— 1). bds. 8.99 *(978-1-5107-3620-7(4)*, Sky Pony Pr.) Skyhorse Publishing Co., Inc.
—A Cuddle for Little Duck. Freedman, Claire. 2009. (ENG.). 20p. (J). (gr. -1-k). 8.99 *(978-0-545-07797-2(4)*, Cartwheel Bks.) Scholastic, Inc.
—A Friend for Bear. Smallman, Steve. 2020. (ENG.). 32p. (J). (gr. -1-2). 17.99 *(978-1-68010-188-1(9))* Tiger Tales.
—Friends to the Rescue. Chiew, Suzanne. 2016. (ENG.). 32p. (J). (gr. -1-2). 16.99 *(978-1-68010-007-5(6))* Tiger Tales.
—I Can't Sleep! Hart, Owen. 2017. (ENG.). 32p. (J). (gr. -1-2). 16.99 *(978-1-68010-066-2(1))* Tiger Tales.
—Imagining Things & Other Poems. Steven, Kenneth. ed. 2005. (ENG.). 96p. (J). (gr. 2-4). pap. 9.99 *(978-0-7459-4907-9(X)*, Lion Books) Lion Hudson PLC GBR. Dist: Independent Pubs. Group.
—It's Potty Time! Corderoy, Tracey. 2014. (ENG.). 22p. (J). (gr. -1-k). bds. 8.99 *(978-1-58925-574-6(7))* Tiger Tales.
—Little Bear & the Butterflies. Quinn, Susan. 2014. 24p. (J). *(978-1-4351-5922-8(5))* Barnes & Noble, Inc.
—A Mouse So Small. McAllister, Angela. 2015. (ENG.). 32p. (J). (gr. -1-2). 16.99 *(978-1-58925-194-6(6))* Tiger Tales.
—A Night Night Prayer, 1 vol. Parker, Amy. (Night Night Ser.). (ENG.). (J). 2015. 24p. pap. 3.99 *(978-0-7180-3652-2(2))*; 2014. 20p. bds. 9.99 *(978-1-4003-2431-6(9))* Nelson, Thomas Inc.
—The Perfect Present. Jones, Stella J. 2016. (ENG.). 32p. (J). (gr. -1-2). 16.99 *(978-1-68010-036-5(X))* Tiger Tales.
—That's What Friends Are For. Chiew, Suzanne. 2017. (ENG.). 32p. (J). (gr. -1-2). 16.99 *(978-1-68010-040-2(8))* Tiger Tales.
—When Grandma Saved Christmas. Hubery, Julia. 2014. (ENG.). 32p. (J). (gr. -1-2). 16.99 *(978-1-58925-164-9(4))* Tiger Tales.
—You & Me Always: A Loveable Tale about Two Best Friends. Moss, Stephanie. 2016. (ENG.). 26p. (J). bds. 8.95 *(978-1-78557-826-7(X))* Igloo Bks. GBR. Dist: Simon & Schuster, Inc.
Pedler, Caroline & Massey, Jane. My Little Box of Bedtime Stories: Can't You Sleep, Puppy?/Time to Sleep, Little Bear!/What Are You Doing in My Bed?/Sleep Tight, Giner Kitten/Good Night, Emily!/Don't Be Afraid, Little Ones. Warnes, Tim et al. 2013. (ENG.). (J). (gr. -1-1). pap. 8.95 *(978-1-58925-442-8(2))* Tiger Tales.
Peebles, Jay. What's a Grandpa? Webb, Dirk. 2018. (ENG.). 30p. (J). pap. 10.00 *(978-1-5440-4942-7(0))* CreateSpace Independent Publishing Platform.
Peecock, Simon & McKissock, Charmaine. An Amazing Storytelling Cat. Williams, Jan. 2013. 120p. pap. *(978-0-9568148-6-9(7))* Swift Publishing.
Peek, Jeannette. My Daddy Is A Fire Fighter: My Daddy Is A Fireman. Beckler, Bruce. l.t. ed. 2004. 16p. (J). 5.59 *(978-0-9745210-8-6(X))* Myers Publishing Co.
—My Mommy Is A Nurse. Beckler, Bruce. l.t. ed. 2004. 20p. (J). 5.59 *(978-0-9745210-9-1(4))* Myers Publishing Co.
Peeler, Dan. Dragons Far & Near: Story Book. Peeler, Dan. Rose, Charles. 2017. (Dragons of Romania Ser.). (ENG.). (J). (gr. k-2). 18.50 *(978-1-946182-98-2(2))* Texas Bk. Pubs. Assn.
Peeler, Rochelle. The Disability Gang Meets F. D. R. Wood, Zach. 2019. (Disability Gang Ser.: Vol. 5). (ENG.). 32p. (J). pap. 15.00 *(978-1-7954-6311-9(2))* Independently Published.
Peeples, Brent. Major X. 2019. (ENG.). 144p. (YA). (gr. 8-17). pap. 24.99 *(978-1-302-91741-8(2))* Marvel Worldwide, Inc.
Peer, Kate. Let's Take a Walk in the Rain. Johnson, Kathy. 2012. 28p. pap. 13.54 *(978-1-4669-3252-4(X))* Trafford Publishing.
Peer, Nancy. Mermaid Tears: A Magical Sea Tale. Lasaracina, Barbara. 2010. 28p. pap. 11.99 *(978-1-60844-451-9(1))* Dog Ear Publishing, LLC.
Peet, Bill. The Caboose Who Got Loose, 1 vol. Peet, Bill. 2008. (ENG.). 48p. (J). (gr. -1-3). 10.99 *(978-0-618-95979-2(3)*, 1021923) Houghton Mifflin Harcourt Publishing Co.
Peet, Sam. Stupendous Science. Beattie, Rob. 2017. (STEAM Activities Ser.). (ENG.). 96p. (J). (gr. 2-4). pap. 12.95 *(978-1-68297-257-1(7))* QEB Publishing Inc.
Pegher, Jonathan. My Little Warrior. Marie, Janet. 2018. (ENG.). 38p. (J). pap. 17.95 *(978-1-64191-281-5(2))* Christian Faith Publishing.
Peguero, Phillip. Neecie & the Sparkling Spring. Barrett, Anna Pearl. Weston, Eunice Guy, ed. 2004. (Neecie Bks.: Vol. 5). 70p. (J). (gr. 1-6). 7.95 *(978-0-9661330-5-9(6))* Over the Rainbow Productions.
Peguy, Laurence. The Abominable Snowman. Montgomery, R. A. 2006. (Choose Your Own Adventure Ser.). (ENG.). 144p. (J). (gr. 4-8). per. 7.99 *(978-1-933390-01-7(8)*, CHCL01) Chooseco LLC.
—Smoke Jumpers. Montgomery, R. A. 2009. (Choose Your Own Adventure Ser.: 29). (ENG.). 144p. (J). (gr. 4-8). pap. 7.99 *(978-1-933390-29-1(8))* Chooseco LLC.
Peilong, Liang. I Have a Zoo: A Story Told in English & Chinese. Mao, Xiao. 2019. 42p. (J). (gr. -1-3). 16.95 *(978-1-60220-457-7(8))* Shanghai Translation Publishing Hse. CHN. Dist: Publishers Group West (PGW).
Peinador, Angeles. Ay, Luna, Luna, Lunita... Canetti, Yanitzia James et al. 2006. (Coleccion Rascacielos Ser.). (SPA.). 32p. (J). (gr. 2-3). 14.99 *(978-84-241-8774-3(1))* Everest Editora ESP. Dist: Lectorum Pubns., Inc.
—Timbuktu 2 Wayfarers. Harper, Kathryn. 2017. (Cambridge Reading Adventures Ser.). (ENG.). 24p. (J). pap. 6.74 *(978-1-108-41085-4(5))* Cambridge Univ. Pr.
Peintre, Marc-Etienne. The Colors of History: How Colors Shaped the World. Gifford, Clive. 2018. (ENG.). 64p. (J). (gr. 3-7). 16.95 ***(978-1-68297-340-0(9))*** QEB Publishing Inc.
Peintre, Marc-Etienne. Ultimate Book of Airplanes & Airports. Bordet-Petillon, Sophie. 2017. (Ultimate Book Ser.: 5). (ENG.). 18p. (J). (gr. k-3). 21.99 Editions Tourbillon FRA. Dist: Hachette Bk. Group.
—Ultimate Spotlight: Astronauts. Dussausois, Sophie. 2019. (Ultimate Spotlight Ser.: 3). (ENG.). 14p. (J). (gr. k-3). 16.99 Editions Tourbillon FRA. Dist: Hachette Bk. Group.
Peipei. Daisy Zebra. Ankhbara, Hetheru & Henry, Rawl, eds. 2019. (ENG.). 34p. (J). pap. 33.00 *(978-1-0790-6505-3(9))* Independently Published.
—Dogs Are People, Too. Levi, Anika. Foxx, Maya, ed. 2019. (ENG.). 34p. (J). pap. 12.99 *(978-1-0783-9751-3(1))* Independently Published.
—Kiya & the Honey Bee. Ankhbara, Hetheru & Henry, Rawl, eds. 2019. (ENG.). 30p. (J). pap. 12.99 *(978-1-0816-2071-4(4))* Independently Published.
—Kiya's Apple Tree. Ankhbara, Hetheru & Foxx, Maya. 2019. (ENG.). 52p. (J). pap. 12.99 *(978-1-0783-9199-3(8))* Independently Published.
—Once Again I's Kwanzaa Time. Ankhbara, Hetheru & Henry, Rawl. 2018. (ENG.). 60p. (J). pap. 14.00 *(978-1-0714-7400-6(6))* Independently Published.
—Things That I LOVE. Henry, Rawl, ed. 2019. (ENG.). 28p. (J). pap. 12.99 *(978-1-0775-8779-3(1))* Independently Published.
—Things That I LOVE. Henry, Rawl & Ankhbara, Hetheru, eds. 2019. (ENG.). 26p. (J). pap. 12.99 *(978-1-0790-3405-9(6))* Independently Published.
Peirce, Lincoln. Big Nate Flips Out. 2013. 216p. (J). *(978-0-06-224637-0(2))* Harper & Row Ltd.
—Max & the Midknights. 2019. (J). pap. *(978-1-101-93111-0(6))* Bantam Doubleday Dell Large Print Group, Inc.
Peirce, Lincoln. Big Nate: The Crowd Goes Wild! Peirce, Lincoln. 2014. (Big Nate Ser.: 9). (ENG.). 224p. (J). 9.99 *(978-1-4494-3634-6(X))* Andrews McMeel Publishing.
—Big Nate Blasts Off. Peirce, Lincoln. 2016. (Big Nate Ser.: 8). (ENG.). 224p. (J). (gr. 3-7). 13.99 *(978-0-06-211111-1(6)*, Balzer & Bray) HarperCollins Pubs.
—Big Nate Boredom Buster. Peirce, Lincoln. 2014. (Big Nate Activity Book Ser.: 1). (ENG.). 224p. (J). (gr. 3-7). pap. 7.99 *(978-0-06-233800-6(5))* HarperCollins Pubs.
—Big Nate Boredom Buster: Super Scribbles, Cool Comix, & Lots of Laughs. Peirce, Lincoln. 2011. (Big Nate Activity Book Ser.: 1). (ENG.). 224p. (J). (gr. 3-7). 10.99 *(978-0-06-206094-5(7))* HarperCollins Pubs.
—Big Nate Doodlepalooza. Peirce, Lincoln. (Big Nate Activity Book Ser.: 3). (ENG.). 224p. (J). (gr. 3-7). 2016. pap. 6.99 *(978-0-06-234952-1(X))*; 2013. 10.99 *(978-0-06-211114-2(0))* HarperCollins Pubs.
—Big Nate Flips Out. Peirce, Lincoln. 2013. (ENG.). 224p. (J). (gr. 3-7). lib. bdg. 14.89 *(978-0-06-199664-1(5))*; (Big Nate Ser.: 5). 13.99 *(978-0-06-199663-4(7))* HarperCollins Pubs.
—Big Nate Fun Blaster: Cheezy Doodles, Crazy Comix, & Loads of Laughs! Peirce, Lincoln. 2012. (Big Nate Activity Book Ser.: 2). (ENG.). 224p. (J). (gr. 3-7). 10.99 *(978-0-06-209045-4(3))* HarperCollins Pubs.
—Big Nate: Fun Blaster: Cheezy Doodles, Crazy Comix, & Loads of Laughs! Peirce, Lincoln. 2015. (Big Nate Activity Book Ser.: 2). (ENG.). 224p. (J). (gr. 3-7). pap. 7.99 *(978-0-06-234951-4(1))* HarperCollins Pubs.
—Big Nate: Genius Mode. Peirce, Lincoln. 2013. (Big Nate Comix Ser.: 3). (ENG.). 224p. (J). (gr. 3-7). pap. 9.99 *(978-0-06-208698-3(7))* HarperCollins Pubs.
—Big Nate Goes for Broke. Peirce, Lincoln. (Big Nate Ser.: 4). (ENG.). 224p. (J). (gr. 3-7). 2016. pap. 7.99 *(978-0-06-236753-2(6))*; 2012. 13.99 *(978-0-06-199661-0(0))*; 2012. lib. bdg. 14.89 *(978-0-06-199662-7(9))* HarperCollins Pubs.
—Big Nate: Here Goes Nothing. Peirce, Lincoln. 2012. (Big Nate Comix Ser.: 2). (ENG.). 224p. (J). (gr. 3-7). pap. 9.99 *(978-0-06-208696-9(0))* HarperCollins Pubs.
—Big Nate: in a Class by Himself. Peirce, Lincoln. (Big Nate Ser.: 1). (ENG.). 224p. (J). (gr. 3-7). 2015. pap. 7.99 *(978-0-06-228359-7(6))*; 2010. 13.99 *(978-0-06-194434-5(3))* HarperCollins Pubs.
—Big Nate: in a Class by Himself. Peirce, Lincoln. 2010. (Big Nate Ser.: 1). (ENG.). 224p. (J). (gr. 3-7). lib. bdg. 14.89 *(978-0-06-194435-2(1)*, HarperCollins) HarperCollins Pubs. Ltd. GBR. Dist: HarperCollins Pubs.
—Big Nate: in a Class by Himself Special Edition: Includes 16 Extra Pages of Fun! Peirce, Lincoln. ed. 2012. (Big Nate Ser.: 1). (ENG.). 240p. (J). (gr. 3-7). 12.99 *(978-0-06-220773-9(3))* HarperCollins Pubs.
—Big Nate: in the Zone. Peirce, Lincoln. 2014. (Big Nate Ser.: 6). (ENG.). 224p. (J). (gr. 3-7). 13.99 *(978-0-06-199665-8(3)*, HarperCollins); lib. bdg. 14.89 *(978-0-06-199666-5(1))* HarperCollins Pubs.
—Big Nate Laugh-O-Rama. Peirce, Lincoln. 2014. (Big Nate Activity Book Ser.: 4). (ENG.). 224p. (J). (gr. 3-7). pap. 6.99 *(978-0-06-211116-6(7))* HarperCollins Pubs.
—Big Nate Lives It Up. Peirce, Lincoln. 2015. (Big Nate Ser.: 7). (ENG.). 224p. (J). (gr. 3-7). lib. bdg. 14.89 *(978-0-06-211109-8(4)*, Balzer & Bray) HarperCollins Pubs.
—Big Nate Makes the Grade. Peirce, Lincoln. Harper, Chuck et al. 2012. (Big Nate Ser.: 4). (ENG.). 224p. (J). 11.99 *(978-1-4494-2566-1(6))* Andrews McMeel Publishing.
—Big Nate: Mr. Popularity. Peirce, Lincoln. 2014. (Big Nate Comix Ser.: 4). (ENG.). 224p. (J). (gr. 3-7). pap. 9.99 *(978-0-06-208700-3(2))* HarperCollins Pubs.
—Big Nate on a Roll. Peirce, Lincoln. (Big Nate Ser.: 3). (ENG.). 224p. (J). (gr. 3-7). 2015. pap. 7.99 *(978-0-06-228357-3(X))*; 2011. 13.99 *(978-0-06-194438-3(6))*; 2011. lib. bdg. 14.89 *(978-0-06-194439-0(4))* HarperCollins Pubs.
—Big Nate Strikes Again. Peirce, Lincoln. (Big Nate Ser.: 2). (ENG.). 224p. (J). (gr. 3-7). 2015. pap. 7.99 *(978-0-06-228358-0(8))*; 2010. 13.99 *(978-0-06-194436-9(X))*; 2010. lib. bdg. 14.89 *(978-0-06-194437-6(8))* HarperCollins Pubs.
—Big Nate Super Scribbler. Peirce, Lincoln. 2015. (Big Nate Activity Book Ser.: 5). (ENG.). 224p. (J). (gr. 3-7). pap. 6.99 *(978-0-06-234922-4(8))* HarperCollins Pubs.
—Big Nate Triple Play Box Set: Big Nate: in a Class by Himself, Big Nate Strikes Again, Big Nate on a Roll. Peirce, Lincoln. 2013. (Big Nate Ser.). (ENG.). (J). (gr. 3-7). pap. 16.99 *(978-0-06-228360-3(X))* HarperCollins Pubs.
—Big Nate: What Could Possibly Go Wrong? Peirce, Lincoln. 2012. (Big Nate Comix Ser.: 1). (ENG.). 224p. (J). (gr. 3-7). pap. 9.99 *(978-0-06-208694-5(4))* HarperCollins Pubs.
—Game On! Peirce, Lincoln. 2013. (Big Nate Ser.: 6). (ENG.). 224p. (J). pap. 9.99 *(978-1-4494-2777-1(4))* Andrews McMeel Publishing.
Peirsman, Madeline. Whose Eyes Are These? Gobert-Martin, Virginie. 2017. (ENG.). 64p. (J). (gr. -1-k). 17.95 *(978-1-84976-506-0(5))* Tate Publishing, Ltd. GBR. Dist: Hachette Bk. Group.
Peisner, Laura. The Hopeful Prince. Peisner, Laura. Jackson, Page. 2017. (J). (gr. k-3). pap. 9.95 *(978-0-9969878-1-3(9))* Nearaway Far Pubns.
Peixoto, Andrea. Engelberta Finds Her Feet. Montano, Josie. 2018. (ENG.). 28p. (J). (gr. k-6). 17.99 *(978-1-365-86178-9(3))* Lulu Pr., Inc.
Peixoto Emmerick, Andrea. Engelberta Finds Her Feet. Montano, Josie. 2018. (ENG.). 28p. (J). (gr. k-6). pap. 13.99 *(978-1-365-86180-2(5))* Lulu Pr., Inc.
—Engelberta Finds Her Feet Dyslexic Edition: Dyslexic Font. Montano, Josie. ed. 2018. (ENG.). 30p. (J). (gr. k-6). 21.99 *(978-1-64372-082-1(1))*; pap. 15.99 *(978-1-64372-083-8(X))* MacLaren-Cochrane Publishing, Inc.
Pelaez, Ricardo. El Almohadon de Plumas. Quiroga, Horacio. 2014. (SPA.). 22p. (J). pap. 10.99 *(978-958-59289-5-4(7))* Santillana USA Publishing Co., Inc.
—Corre con Caballos. Burks, Brian. Vinos, Maria, tr. 2003. (la Orilla Del Viento Ser.). (SPA.). 96p. (J). per. 7.50 *(978-968-16-7057-3(4)*, 168) Fondo de Cultura Economica USA.
—En un Martes Trece... Otero, Armando Leiero. 2006. (SPA & ENG.). 36p. (J). (gr. -1-3). pap. 9.95 *(978-968-5920-55-1(9))* Castillo, Ediciones, S. A. de C. V. MEX. Dist: Macmillan.
Pelaez, Ricardo. El ni�o Que Corr�a con el Viento. Trevizo, Elman. 2018. (Torre Azul Ser.). (SPA.). 64p. (J). pap. ***(978-607-13-0459-9(8))*** Norma Ediciones, S.A.
Pelaez, Ricardo. Sonidos, Olores y Colores - la Comunicacion en el Mundo Animal. Ruiz, Maria Emilia Beyer. rev. ed. 2006. (Otra Escalera Ser.). (SPA & ENG.). 36p. (J). (gr. 4). pap. 9.95 *(978-968-5920-79-7(6))* Castillo, Ediciones, S. A. de C. V. MEX. Dist: Macmillan.
Pelayo, Alex. I Want to Be Philberta. Pavon, Mar. Brokenbrow, Jon, tr. 2013. (ENG.). 32p. (J). (gr. k-2). 16.95 *(978-84-15619-73-4(1))* Cuento de Luz SL ESP. Dist: Publishers Group West (PGW).
Pelham, David. Here Comes Santa: A Mini Holiday Pop-Up. Pelham, David. ed. 2008. (ENG.). 18p. (J). 11.99 *(978-1-4169-5440-8(6)*, Little Simon) Little Simon.
—Sam's Hamburger. Pelham, David. 2018. (ENG.). 22p. (J). (gr. -1-2). 12.99 *(978-0-7636-9836-2(9))* Candlewick Pr.
—Sam's Sandwich. Pelham, David. 2015. (ENG.). 24p. (J). (gr. -1-2). 11.99 *(978-0-7636-7808-1(2))* Candlewick Pr.
Peli, Peli. Candida. Silvera, Elvia. 2005. (SPA.). (J). (gr. 2-3). pap. 7.95 *(978-980-257-281-6(0))* Ekare, Ediciones VEN. Dist: Iaconi, Mariuccia Bk. Imports.
Pelicano, Christopher J. Credo: I Believe. Ellis, Colette. Avakoff, Caroline, ed. 2009. (Faith & Life Ser.). 121p. (J). pap. 7.95 *(978-0-89870-898-1(2))* Ignatius Pr.
Pelicano, Megan. With Just an Empty Shoebox. Pelicano, Matt. 2019. (ENG.). 24p. (J). (gr. k-2). pap. 9.95 *(978-0-578-52314-9(0))* April Fool Publishing.
Pelikhovich, Julia. Blair, Where Is Your Hair? Depalma, Stephanie Ann. 2020. (ENG.). 32p. (J). pap. 12.99 ***(978-1-6619-8957-6(8))*** Independently Published.
Pelikhovick, Julia. Paul & Bubu Tau's Christmas Tree. Evari, Caroline. 2019. (ENG.). 22p. (J). pap. *(978-1-925986-56-3(X))* Library For All Limited.
Pellaton, Karen E. The Official M&M's® Brand History of Chocolate. 2004. 32p. (J). (gr. 1-9). pap. 6.95 *(978-1-57091-449-2(4))* Charlesbridge Publishing, Inc.
—The Official M&M's® Brand History of the Calendar. Brimner, Larry Dane. 2004. 32p. (YA). 16.95 *(978-1-57091-431-7(1))*; pap. 6.95 *(978-1-57091-432-4(X))* Charlesbridge Publishing, Inc.
Pellé, Serge. Orbital Vol. 1: Scars. Runberg, Sylvain. Saincatin, Jerome, tr. 2009. (Orbital Ser.: 1). (ENG.). 47p. pap. 11.95 *(978-1-905460-89-2(9))* CineBook GBR. Dist: National Bk. Network.
—Orbital 2: Ruptures. Runberg, Sylivain. Saincatin, Jerome, tr. 2009. (Orbital Ser.: 2). (ENG.). 55p. pap. 13.95 *(978-1-905460-95-3(3))* CineBook GBR. Dist: National Bk. Network.
—Orbital 3: Nomads, Vol. 3. Runberg, Sylvain. 2011. (Orbital Ser.: 3). (ENG.). 56p. pap. 13.95 *(978-1-84918-080-1(6))* CineBook GBR. Dist: National Bk. Network.
Pelle, Serge. Orbital Vol. 5: Justice. Runberg, Sylvain. 2014. (Orbital Ser.: 5). (ENG.). 56p. pap. 13.95 *(978-1-84918-172-3(1))* CineBook GBR. Dist: National Bk. Network.
Pelleg, Tirtsa. I Wish I Were a King. Krohn, Genendel. 50p. 13.95 *(978-1-58330-590-4(4))* Feldheim Pubs.
—The Miracle of the Rock & other Stories: Timeless Tales from the Lives of Our Sages. Krohn, Genendel. 2003. 56p. (J). 14.99 *(978-1-58330-650-5(1))* Feldheim Pubs.
—Who Is the Builder? Krohn, Genendel. 32p. 13.99 *(978-1-58330-515-7(7))* Feldheim Pubs.
Pellegata, Donna. The Harp Mouse Chooses Her Home: The Adventure Begins. 2008. 24p. (J). pap. 6.95 *(978-0-9742174-1-3(7))* Heart & Harp LLC.
Pellegrini, Will. Peppy's Shadow. Trimble, Marcia. 2003. 32p. (J). (gr. -1-3). 15.95 *(978-1-891577-70-3(0))*; pap. 7.95 *(978-1-891577-71-0(9))* Images Pr.
Pellegrino, Rich. Real-World Dragons, 1 vol. Doeden, Matt. 2013. (World of Dragons Ser.). (ENG.). 32p. (J). (gr. 3-9). lib. bdg. 27.32 *(978-1-62065-146-9(7)*, Capstone Pr.) Capstone.
Pellegrino, Rich, jt. illus. see Mayer, Jonathan.
Pellegrino, Richard. The Battle of the Olympians & the Titans, 1 vol. 2011. (Greek Myths Ser.). (ENG.). 32p. (J). (gr. 3-5). lib. bdg. 29.32 *(978-1-4048-6667-6(1)*, Picture Window Bks.) Capstone.
—Stowaway Monster. Dahl, Michael. (Dragonblood Ser.). (ENG.). 40p. (J). (gr. 4-8). 2010. pap. 6.25 *(978-1-4342-2312-8(4))*; 2009. 23.99 *(978-1-4342-1259-7(9))* Capstone. (Stone Arch Bks.).
—Terror Beach. Dahl, Michael. (Dragonblood Ser.). (ENG.). 40p. (J). (gr. 4-8). 2010. pap. 6.25 *(978-1-4342-2313-5(2))*; 2009. 23.99 *(978-1-4342-1263-4(7))* Capstone. (Stone Arch Bks.).
Pellejero, Ruben. The Adventures of Dieter Lumpen. Zentner, Jorge. 2016. 264p. pap. 49.99 *(978-1-63140-606-5(X)*, 9781631406065) Idea & Design Works, LLC.
Pellerin, Kate. The Silver Tree. Cushnie-Mansour, Mary M. Jamieson, Bethany, ed. 2018. (ENG.). 192p. (J). pap. ***(978-1-927899-85-4(0))*** Cavern of Dreams Publishing Hse.
Pellerinn, Kate. My Sister's a Superhero. Morrison, Amanda. 2019. (ENG.). 62p. (J). pap. *(978-1-989027-08-0(3))* Cavern of Dreams Publishing Hse.
PellerinUndo, Joel Ray. Prince Alexander. Davison, Gail. 2016. (ENG.). 28p. (J). pap. 28.22 *(978-1-5245-1787-8(9))* Xlibris Corp.

P

Pelletier, Gilles. The Sugaring off Party. London, Jonathan. 2006. (ENG.). 32p. (J). (gr. 1-3). 9.95 (978-1-55041-470-7(4), ab11eac7-d260-46b2-8c96-ba9667b9e76c) Fitzhenry & Whiteside, Ltd. CAN. Dist: Firefly Bks., Ltd.

Pelletier, Ninon. Le Silence Se Glisse Près de Toi, 1 vol. Hughes, Alison. 2019. (FRE.). 32p. (J). (gr. -1 — 1). 19.95 (978-1-4598-2208-5(0)) Orca Bk. Pubs. USA.

—The Silence Slips In, 1 vol. Hughes, Alison. 2019. (ENG.). 32p. (J). (gr. -1-k). 19.95 (978-1-4598-1706-7(0)) Orca Bk. Pubs. USA.

Pelletier, Paul, et al. Baptism of Fire, Vol. 2. Bedard, Tony. 2003. (Negation Ser.: Vol. 2). 160p. (YA). pap. 12.95 (978-1-931484-59-6(7)) CrossGeneration Comics, Inc.

Pelletier, Paul, et al. Guardians of the Galaxy: Somebody's Got to Do It Marvel Select Edition. 2020. (ENG.). 296p. (YA). (gr. 8-17). 24.99 (978-1-302-92342-6(0)) Marvel Worldwide, Inc.

Pelletier, Paul, et al. Negation, Vol. 3. Bedard, Tony. 2003. (Negation Ser.: Vol. 3). 160p. (YA). pap. 15.95 (978-1-931484-90-9(2)) CrossGeneration Comics, Inc.

—Shock & Awe, Vol. 3. Bedard, Tony. 2004. (Negation Ser.: Vol. 4). 160p. (YA). pap. 15.95 (978-1-59314-046-5(0)) CrossGeneration Comics, Inc.

Pelliccioni, Sanna. Saga Och Den Magiska Stenen: Swedish Edition of Stella & the Magic Stone. Pere, Tuula. Nikolowski-Bogomoloff, Angelika, tr. 2018. (Saga Ser.: Vol. 1). (SWE.). 36p. (J). (gr. k-4). (978-952-7107-96-6(2)); pap. (978-952-7107-93-5(8)) Wickwick oy.

—Sanni Ja Taikakivi: Finnish Edition of Stella & the Magic Stone. Pere, Tuula. 2018. (Sanni Ser.: Vol. 1). (FIN.). 36p. (J). (gr. k-4). (978-952-7107-95-9(4)); pap. (978-952-7107-92-8(X)) Wickwick oy.

—Stella & the Magic Stone. Pere, Tuula. Korman, Susan, ed. 2018. (Stella Ser.: Vol. 1). (ENG.). 36p. (J). (gr. k-4). (978-952-7107-94-2(6)); pap. (978-952-7107-91-1(1)) Wickwick oy.

Pellizzari, Barbara, et al. The Royal Ball. Stilton, Thea & Schaffer, Andrea. 2017. 108p. (J). (978-1-338-18275-0(7)) Scholastic, Inc.

—Thea Stilton & the Madagascar Madness, 24. Clement, Emily. 2016. (Thea Stilton Ser.). (ENG.). 176p. (J). (gr. 2-4). 24.94 (978-1-4844-9901-6(8)) Scholastic, Inc.

Pellizzari, Barbara & Balleello, Chiara. Thea Stilton & the Hollywood Hoax. Clement, Emily. 2015. 159p. (J). (978-1-5182-1175-1(5)) Scholastic, Inc.

Pellizzari, Barbara & Castelli, Francesco. The Friendship Recipe. Stilton, Thea & Pizzelli, Anna. 2017. 128p. (J). (978-1-338-18274-3(9)) Scholastic, Inc.

Pelobello, Genesis Ray. Alali the Flying Mermaid. Hall, Betty. 2017. (ENG.). 46p. (YA). 41.99 (978-1-5434-7599-9(X)) Xlibris Corp.

Pels, Winslow Pinney. Hansel y Cretel. Cross, Ruth Belov. 2003. (SPA.). pap. (978-0-439-19894-3(1), SO30113) Scholastic GBR. Dist: Lectorum Pubns., Inc.

Peltier, Sylvia M. Nanny & I. Peltier, Sylvia M. 2003. 32p. (YA). (gr. -1-18). 16.95 (978-0-9724394-0-4(4)) Sylables.

Pelton, Agnes. When I Was a Little Girl (Illustrated Edition) Gale, Zona. 2019. (ENG.). 176p. (J). pap. (978-1-4068-9869-9(4)) Echo Library.

Pelton, Bonnie L. Bryanna Global Warrior: Attack of the Alaska Aerial Wolf Hunters, 1 vol. Ball Sr., Frank J. 2009. 23p. pap. 24.95 (978-1-61582-587-5(8)) America Star Bks.

—Planet Earth Past, Present, Future: Bryanna Global Warrior Book 3, 1 vol. Ball Sr., Frank J. 2010. 34p. pap. 24.95 (978-1-4489-8321-6(5)) PublishAmerica, Inc.

Pelton, Jonathan. The Elephant Moo. Pelton, Joy. 2017. (ENG.). 24p. (J). 21.95 (978-1-64003-361-0(0)) Covenant Bks.

Peluso, Beth A. The Charcoal Forest: How Fire Helps Animals & Plants. Peluso, Beth A. 2007. 56p. (J). (gr. -1-3). pap. 12.00 (978-0-87842-532-7(2)) Mountain Pr. Publishing Co., Inc.

Peluso, Martina. Collins Big Cat Phonics for Letters & Sounds - Jump on, Jump off!: Band 04/Blue, Bd. 4. Crebbin, June. 2018. (Collins Big Cat Phonics Ser.). (ENG.). 16p. (J). (gr. k-1). pap. 7.99 (978-0-00-825160-4(6)) HarperCollins Pubs. Ltd. GBR. Dist: Independent Pubs. Group.

—Dara's Clever Trap: A Story from Cambodia. Flanagan, Liz et al. 2014. (Princess Stories Ser.). 48p. (J). (gr. 1-5). pap. 8.99 (978-1-78285-103-5(8)) Barefoot Bks., Inc.

—George & the Dragon: Band 13/Topaz (Collins Big Cat) Pirotta, Saviour. 2015. (Collins Big Cat Ser.). (ENG.). 32p. (J). (gr. 2-3). pap. 9.99 (978-0-00-812776-3(X)) HarperCollins Pubs. Ltd. GBR. Dist: Independent Pubs. Group.

—Heidi. Spyri, Johanna & Ladybird Books Staff. 2015. (Ladybird Classics Ser.). 72p. (J). (gr. k-3). 10.99 (978-1-4093-1357-1(3)) Penguin Bks., Ltd. GBR. Dist: Independent Pubs. Group.

—Las camisetas no somos servilletas. Zafrilla, Marta. 2019. (SPA.). 28p. (J). 16.95 (978-84-16733-49-1(X)) Cuento de Luz SL ESP. Dist: Publishers Group West (PGW).

—Let's Celebrate! Special Days Around the World. DePalma, Kate. 2019. (ENG.). 40p. (J). (978-1-78285-833-1(4)); pap. (978-1-78285-834-8(2)) Barefoot Bks., Inc.

—Og's Ark. Marks, Allison & Marks, Wayne. 2016. (ENG.). 32p. (J). (gr. -1-3). 17.99 (978-1-4677-6149-9(4), 9781467761499, Kar-Ben Publishing) Lerner Publishing Group.

—The Princess of the Springs. Finch, Mary & Barefoot Books. 2014. (Princess Stories Ser.). 48p. (J). (gr. 1-5). pap. 8.99 (978-1-78285-101-1(1)) Barefoot Bks., Inc.

—T-Shirts Aren&Rsquo; T Napkins. Marta Zafrilla, Marta. Brokenbrow, Jon, tr. 2019. (ENG.). 28p. (J). 16.95 (978-84-16733-50-7(3)) Cuento de Luz SL ESP. Dist: Publishers Group West (PGW).

—A Visit with Moon & Sun: A Tale from the Inuit. Brereton, Libby. 2016. 24p. (J). pap. 9.95 (978-1-927244-60-9(9)) Flying Start Bks. NZL. Dist: Flying Start Bks.

—A Visit with Moon & Sun (Big Book Edition) A Tale from the Inuit. Brereton, Libby. 2016. 24p. (J). pap. (978-1-927244-70-8(6)) Flying Start Bks.

Pena, Amado M., Jr. Amadito & Spider Woman. Goldman, Lisa Bear. 2003. 32p. (J). 15.95 (978-1-885772-30-5(0)) Kiva Publishing, Inc.

Peña, Karla. Big News! Siegal, Ida. 2015. (Emma Is on the Air Ser.: 1). (ENG.). 128p. (J). (gr. 2-5). pap. 5.99 (978-0-545-68692-1(X), Scholastic Paperbacks) Scholastic, Inc.

—Party Drama! (Emma Is on the Air #2) Siegal, Ida. 2015. (Emma Is on the Air Ser.: 2). (ENG.). 128p. (J). (gr. 2-5). pap. 4.99 (978-0-545-68695-2(4), Scholastic Paperbacks) Scholastic, Inc.

Pena, Nico. Hanazuki: Full of Treasures. 2018. 72p. (J). (gr. 4-7). 12.99 (978-1-68405-102-1(9)) Idea & Design Works, LLC.

Pena, Nico, jt. illus. see Mebberson, Amy.

Peña, Zeke. Epic Athletes: Stephen Curry. Wetzel, Dan. 2019. (Epic Athletes Ser.: 1). (ENG.). 160p. (J). 16.99 (978-1-250-29576-7(9), 900195180, Holt, Henry & Co. Bks. For Young Readers) Holt, Henry & Co.

—Epic Athletes: Stephen Curry. Wetzel, Dan. 2020. (Epic Athletes Ser.: 1). (ENG.). 176p. (J). pap. 7.99 (978-1-250-25062-9(5), 900195181) Square Fish.

—Mi Papi Tiene una Moto. Quintero, Isabel. 2019. (SPA.). 40p. (J). (gr. -1-3). 17.99 (978-0-525-55494-3(7), Kokila) Penguin Young Readers Group.

—My Papi Has a Motorcycle. Quintero, Isabel. 2019. (ENG.). 40p. (J). (gr. -1-3). 17.99 (978-0-525-55341-0(X), Kokila) Penguin Young Readers Group.

—Photographic: The Life of Graciela Iturbide. Quintero, Isabel. 2018. (ENG.). 96p. (J). (gr. 7-17). 19.95 (978-1-947440-00-5(4)) Getty Pubns.

—Photographic: The Life of Graciela Iturbide. Quintero, Isabel & Iturbide, Graciela. 2017. (J). (978-1-60606-557-0(2), J. Paul Getty Museum) Getty Pubns.

Penashue, Mary Ann. Nutaui's Cap, 1 vol. Bartel, Bob. 2019. (ENG.). 68p. (J). (gr. 4-7). 19.95 (978-1-927917-24-4(7)) Running the Goat, Bks. & Broadsides CAN. Dist: Orca Bk. Pubs. USA.

Pence, Karen. Marlon Bundo's Best Christmas Ever. Pence, Charlotte. 2019. (ENG.). 40p. (J). 18.99 (978-1-62157-870-3(4), Regnery Kids) Regnery Publishing, Inc., An Eagle Publishing Co.

—Marlon Bundo's Day in the Life of the Vice President. Pence, Charlotte. 2018. (ENG.). 40p. (J). (gr. -1-3). 18.99 (978-1-62157-776-8(7), Regnery Kids) Regnery Publishing, Inc., An Eagle Publishing Co.

Pender, John. Gorgeous George & His Stupid Stinky Stories: New! Reid, Stuart. 2017. (Gorgeous George Ser.: Vol. 6). (ENG.). 162p. (J). (gr. 2-3). pap. (978-1-910614-08-2(4)) Gorgeous Garage Publishing Ltd.

—Gorgeous George & the Jumbo Jobby Juicer: 2017 Edition. Reid, Stuart. 2nd ed. 2017. (Gorgeous George Ser.: Vol. 5). (ENG.). 154p. (J). (gr. 2-3). pap. (978-1-910614-06-8(8)) Gorgeous Garage Publishing Ltd.

—Gorgeous George & the Timewarp Trouser Trumpets. Reid, Stuart. 2018. (Gorgeous George Ser.: Vol. 7). (ENG.). 162p. (J). pap. (978-1-910614-11-2(4)) Gorgeous Garage Publishing Ltd.

—Gorgeous George & the Unidentified Unsinkable Underpants Part 1: 2017 Edition. Reid, Stuart. 3rd ed. 2017. (Gorgeous George Ser.: Vol. 3). (ENG.). 122p. (J). (gr. 2-3). pap. (978-1-910614-07-5(6)) Gorgeous Garage Publishing Ltd.

—Gorgeous George & the Unidentified Unsinkable Underpants Part 2: 2017 Edition. Reid, Stuart. 2nd ed. 2017. (Gorgeous George Ser.: Vol. 4). (ENG.). 122p. (J). (gr. 2-3). pap. (978-1-910614-01-3(7)) Gorgeous Garage Publishing Ltd.

—Gorgeous George & the Zigzag Zit-Faced Zombies: New 2017 Edition. Reid, Stuart. 3rd ed. 2017. (Gorgeous George Ser.: Vol. 2). (ENG.). 162p. (J). (gr. 2-3). pap. (978-1-910614-04-4(1)) Gorgeous Garage Publishing Ltd.

—Grandpa Jock & the Incredible Iron-Bru-Man Incident. Reid, Stuart. 2019. (Gorgeous George Ser.: Vol. 8). (ENG.). 162p. (J). (gr. 3-6). pap. (978-1-910614-12-9(2)) Gorgeous Garage Publishing Ltd.

Pender, Rachel. Well... What's All That Drilling About? Stone, Andrew & Bryan, Jessica. 2007. 40p. (J). 7.95 (978-0-9641186-3-8(7)) American Ground Water Trust.

Pendergrass, Mark D. May I See the King? Daubenspeck, Julie & Daubenspeck, Vince. 2009. (ENG.). 32p. (gr. k). 14.95 (978-1-59700-797-9(8)) Island Heritage Publishing.

Penfield, James. Dinosaurs & Other Prehistoric Animals, 1 vol. Baltzer, Rochelle. 2015. (I Like to Draw! Ser.). 32p. (J). (gr. 2-5). 28.50 (978-1-62402-081-0(X), 17057, Looking Glass Library) Magic Wagon.

—Dogs & Cats, 1 vol. Baltzer, Rochelle. 2015. (I Like to Draw! Ser.). 32p. (J). (gr. 2-5). 28.50 (978-1-62402-080-3(1), 17055, Looking Glass Library) Magic Wagon.

—Monsters & Other Mythical Creatures, 1 vol. Baltzer, Rochelle. 2015. (I Like to Draw! Ser.). 32p. (J). (gr. 2-5). 28.50 (978-1-62402-083-4(6), 17061, Looking Glass Library) Magic Wagon.

—Pirates on the High Seas, 1 vol. Baltzer, Rochelle. 2015. (I Like to Draw! Ser.). 32p. (J). (gr. 2-5). 28.50 (978-1-62402-084-1(4), 17063, Looking Glass Library) Magic Wagon.

—A Royal Court in Its Kingdom, 1 vol. Baltzer, Rochelle. 2015. (I Like to Draw! Ser.). 32p. (J). (gr. 2-5). 28.50 (978-1-62402-085-8(2), 17065, Looking Glass Library) Magic Wagon.

Penfield, Shiloh. The Bravest Knight Who Ever Lived, 1 vol. Errico, Daniel. 2019. (ENG.). 40p. (J). (gr. -1-3). 16.99 (978-0-7643-5690-2(9), 16250) Schiffer Publishing, Ltd.

—Max's Box: Letting Go of Negative Feelings, 1 vol. Wray, Brian. 2019. (ENG.). 32p. (J). 16.99 (978-0-7643-5804-3(9), 8942); pap. 9.99 (978-0-7643-5879-1(0), 20584) Schiffer Publishing, Ltd.

—Unraveling Rose, 1 vol. Wray, Brian. 2017. (ENG.). 32p. (J). (gr. -1-3). 16.99 (978-0-7643-5393-2(4), 8940) Schiffer Publishing, Ltd.

Peng, Cathy. The Adventure Begins: First Day at Detinu International School. Munnerlyn, Jen. 2006. (ENG.). 34p. pap. 17.95 (978-1-4120-7723-1(0)) Trafford Publishing.

—Yo-Yo & Yeou-Cheng Ma, Finding Their Way: Amazing Asian Americans. Louie, Ai-Ling. 2012. (Biographies of Amazing Asian Americans Ser.: 2). (ENG.). 48p. (J). pap. 16.99 (978-0-9787465-0-6(3)) Dragoneagle Pr.

Peng, Chao. Band of Brothers. Dong Chen, Wei. 2013. (Monkey King Ser.: 18). (ENG.). 176p. (gr. 6-12). pap. 9.99 (978-89-94208-63-3(1)) JR Comics KOR. Dist: Lerner Publishing Group.

—The Dual. Dong Chen, Wei. 2013. (Monkey King Ser.: 14). (ENG.). 176p. (gr. 6-12). pap. 9.99 (978-89-94208-59-6(3)) JR Comics KOR. Dist: Lerner Publishing Group.

—Expulsion of Sun Wu. Dong Chen, Wei. 2013. (Monkey King Ser.: 7). (ENG.). 176p. (YA). (gr. 6-12). pap. 9.99 (978-89-94208-51-0(8)) Lerner Publishing Group.

—The Expulsion of Sun Wu Kong. Chen, Wei Dong. 2013. (Monkey King Ser.: 7). 176p. (YA). (gr. 6-12). lib. bdg. 29.27 (978-89-94208-75-6(5)) Lerner Publishing Group.

—Fanning the Flames. Dong Chen, Wei. 2013. (Monkey King Ser.: 15). (ENG.). 176p. (gr. 6-12). pap. 9.99 (978-89-94208-60-2(7)) JR Comics KOR. Dist: Lerner Publishing Group.

—Fight to the Death. Chen, Wei Dong. 2013. (Monkey King Ser.: 11). 176p. (YA). (gr. 6-12). lib. bdg. 29.27 (978-89-94208-79-4(8)) Lerner Publishing Group.

—Golden Temple. Dong Chen, Wei. 2013. (Monkey King Ser.: 16). (ENG.). 176p. (gr. 6-12). pap. 9.99 (978-89-94208-61-9(5)) JR Comics KOR. Dist: Lerner Publishing Group.

—The Lost Children. Chen, Wei Dong. 2013. (Monkey King Ser.: 12). 176p. (YA). (gr. 6-12). lib. bdg. 29.27 (978-89-94208-80-0(1)) Lerner Publishing Group.

—Monkey King: Birth of the Stone Monkey. Chen, Wei Dong. 2012. (Monkey King Ser.: 1). (ENG.). 176p. (gr. 5-8). lib. bdg. 29.27 (978-89-94208-69-5(0)) JR Comics KOR. Dist: Lerner Publishing Group.

—Monkey King: Enemies & a New Friend. Chen, Wei Dong. 2012. (Monkey King Ser.: 4). (ENG.). 176p. (gr. 5-8). lib. bdg. 29.27 (978-89-94208-72-5(0)) JR Comics KOR. Dist: Lerner Publishing Group.

—Monkey King: Journey to the West. Chen, Wei Dong. 2012. (Monkey King Ser.: 3). (ENG.). 176p. (gr. 5-8). lib. bdg. 29.27 (978-89-94208-71-8(2)) JR Comics KOR. Dist: Lerner Publishing Group.

—Monkey King: The Bane of Heaven. Chen, Wei Dong. 2012. (Monkey King Ser.: 2). (ENG.). 176p. (gr. 5-8). lib. bdg. 29.27 (978-89-94208-70-1(4)) JR Comics KOR. Dist: Lerner Publishing Group.

—Monkey King: The Sacred Tree. Chen, Wei Dong. 2012. (Monkey King Ser.: 6). (ENG.). 176p. (gr. 5-8). lib. bdg. 29.27 (978-89-94208-74-9(7)) JR Comics KOR. Dist: Lerner Publishing Group.

—Monkey King: Three Trials. Chen, Wei Dong. 2012. (Monkey King Ser.: 5). (ENG.). 176p. (gr. 5-8). lib. bdg. 29.27 (978-89-94208-73-2(9)) JR Comics KOR. Dist: Lerner Publishing Group.

—The Realm of the Infant King. Chen, Wei Dong. 2013. (Monkey King Ser.: 10). 176p. (YA). (gr. 6-12). lib. bdg. 29.27 (978-89-94208-78-7(X)) Lerner Publishing Group.

—The Seven Sisters. Dong Chen, Wei. 2013. (Monkey King Ser.: 17). (ENG.). 176p. (gr. 6-12). pap. 9.99 (978-89-94208-62-6(3)) JR Comics KOR. Dist: Lerner Publishing Group.

—The Stolen Kingdom. Chen, Wei Dong. 2013. (Monkey King Ser.: 9). 176p. (YA). (gr. 6-12). lib. bdg. 29.27 (978-89-94208-77-0(1)) Lerner Publishing Group.

—Treasures of the Mountain Kings. Chen, Wei Dong. 2013. (Monkey King Ser.: 8). 176p. (YA). (gr. 6-12). lib. bdg. 29.27 (978-89-94208-76-3(3)) Lerner Publishing Group.

—Treasures of the Mountain Kings. Dong Chen, Wei. 2013. (Monkey King Ser.: 8). (ENG.). 176p. (YA). (gr. 6-12). pap. 9.99 (978-89-94208-52-7(6)) Lerner Publishing Group.

—Trust & Temptation. Dong Chen, Wei. 2013. (Monkey King Ser.: 13). (ENG.). 176p. (gr. 6-12). pap. 9.99 (978-89-94208-58-9(5)) JR Comics KOR. Dist: Lerner Publishing Group.

Penguin, Izy. Grandma Bendy. Penguin, Izy. 2019. (Early Bird Readers — Green (Early Bird Stories (tm)) Ser.). (ENG.). 32p. (J). (gr. k-3). 27.99 (978-1-5415-4205-1(3), 9781541542051); pap. 7.99 (978-1-5415-7407-6(9), 9781541574076) Lerner Publishing Group. (Lerner Pubns.).

Penhale, Douglas. Why Seals Blow Their Noses: Canadian Wildlife in Fact & Fiction, 1 vol. Swanson, Diane. (ENG.). 80p. (J). pap. 12.95 (978-1-55110-038-8(X)) Whitecap Bks., Ltd. CAN. Dist: Graphic Arts Ctr. Publishing Co.

Peniche, Fernando. Forgetting Flynn. Marz, Ron & Rodriguez, David A. 2015. (Skylanders Set 1 Ser.). (ENG.). 24p. (J). (gr. 1-5). lib. bdg. 27.07 (978-1-61479-385-4(9), 18216, Graphic Novels) Spotlight.

Penk, Kathryn. Little Tree's Mightiest Deed. Edgren, Elizabeth. 2009. 36p. pap. 12.95 (978-1-59858-825-5(7)) Dog Ear Publishing, LLC.

Penley, Maegan. Le Mouse Caper. Seigle, Marilyn. 2020. (ENG.). 32p. (J). (gr. k-3). 21.95 (978-1-951565-10-7(X), Belle Isle Bks.) Brandylane Pubs., Inc.

Penn, Audrey, et al. The Kissing Hand. 2010. 23.05 (978-0-7569-9299-6(0)) Natl Bk. Network.

Penn, Karen V. The Doll at the Christmas Bazaar: Christmas Miracles. O'Neal-Thorpe, Rochelle. 2010. 32p. (J). pap. 9.95 (978-0-9823906-2-7(9)) Wiggles Pr.

Penn, Rocky. Sabra & the Amazon City. Billingslea, S. C. 2019. (Arkrames Ser.). (ENG.). 294p. (J). (978-1-5255-5472-8(7)); pap. (978-1-5255-5473-5(5)) FriesenPress.

Pennell, Lauren. The Phantom Stallion. Pennell, Kathleen. 2003. (Pony Investigators Ser.: Vol. 4). 118p. (J). (gr. 3-7). pap. 5.95 (978-1-930353-73-2(1)) Masthof Pr.

Pennell, Rhett. Armor Division. Alexander, Cameron. 2018. (Dark Corps Ser.: Vol. 7). (ENG.). 172p. (J). (gr. 3-6). pap. 7.99 (978-1-7321056-6-9(9), Bickering Owls Publishing) Maracle, Derek.

Pennell, Rhett. Dark Ops. Alexander, Cameron. 2020. (Dark Corps Ser.: Vol. 12). (ENG.). 226p. (J). (gr. 1-6). pap. 7.99 (978-1-950594-13-9(0), Bickering Owls Publishing) Maracle, Derek.

Pennell, Rhett. Desert Troop. Alexander, Cameron. 2019. (Dark Corps Ser.: Vol. 8). (ENG.). 164p. (J). (gr. 1-6). pap. 7.99 (978-1-7321056-8-3(5), Bickering Owls Publishing) Maracle, Derek.

Pennell, Rhett. Final Eclipse. Alexander, Cameron. 2020. (Dark Corps Ser.: Vol. 13). (ENG.). 362p. (J). pap. 14.99 (978-1-950594-15-3(7), Bickering Owls Publishing) Maracle, Derek.

—Winter Watch. Alexander, Cameron. 2019. (Dark Corps Ser.: Vol. 11). (ENG.). 200p. (J). (gr. 1-6). pap. 7.99 (978-1-950594-05-4(X), Bickering Owls Publishing) Maracle, Derek.

Pennell, Rhett / R. Look Left, Look Right, Look Left Again. Pate, Ginger. 2013. 28p. (J). 8.50 (978-1-880851-30-2(X)) Greene Bark Pr., Inc.

Penner, Fred, jt. illus. see Harter, Debbie.

Penner, Stephen. Professor Barrister's Dinosaur Mysteries #1: The Case of the Truncated Troodon. Penner, Stephen. 2010. 44p. pap. 19.25 (978-1-60888-005-8(2)) Nimble Bks. LLC.

—Professor Barrister's Dinosaur Mysteries #4: The Case of the Colorful Caudipteryx. Penner, Stephen. 2011. 62p. pap. 14.99 (978-1-60888-111-6(3)) Nimble Bks. LLC.

Penney, Ian. A Noteworthy Tale. Mutchnick, Brenda & Casden, Ron. 2004. 30p. (J). (gr. k-4). reprint ed. 19.00 (978-0-7567-7654-1(6)) DIANE Publishing Co.

Pennington, Beverly A. Jonathan's Discovery. Pennington, Beverly A. 2006. 29p. (J). (gr. -1-3). pap. 12.95 (978-1-56167-920-1(8)) American Literary Pr.

Pennington, Craig. Grandma's Christmas Tree. Sinke, Grandma Janet Mary. l.t. ed. 2004. (Grandma Janet Mary Ser.). 50p. (J). (978-0-9742732-1-1(X)) My Grandma & Me Pubs.

—Grandma's Treasure Chest. Grandma Janet Mary. l.t. ed. 2005. (Grandma Janet Mary Ser.). 50p. (J). 16.95 (978-0-9742732-3-5(6)) My Grandma & Me Pubs.

—Grandpa's Fishin' Friend. Grandma Janet Mary. 2nd ed. 2007. (Grandma Janet Mary Ser.). 28p. (J). 16.95 (978-0-9742732-7-3(9)) My Grandma & Me Pubs.

—I Wanna Go to Grandma's House. Sinke, Grandma Janet Mary. 2003. (Grandma Janet Mary Ser.). 50p. (J). (978-0-9742732-0-4(1)) My Grandma & Me Pubs.

—I Wanna Go to Grandma's House & Grandma's Treasure Chest, 2, Set. Sinke, Janet Mary. 2006. 80p. (J). (978-0-9742732-6-6(0)) My Grandma & Me Pubs.

—Priscilla Mcdoodlenut Doodle Mcmae Asks, Why? Sinke, Janet Mary. 2007. 40p. (J). 17.95 (978-0-9742732-8-0(7)) My Grandma & Me Pubs.

Pennington, Jack & Tank, Daniel. Joseph. Brand, Ruth. 2004. 87p. (J). 19.99 (978-0-8280-1854-8(5), 104-522) Review & Herald Publishing Assn.

—Joseph. 2004. 87p. (J). pap. (978-0-8280-1855-5(3)) Review & Herald Publishing Assn.

Pennington, Kelly. With My Little Box of Crayons. Wooten, Laura. 2008. 50p. pap. 18.95 (978-1-4251-7103-2(6)) Trafford Publishing.

Pennington, Mark. How the World Was Made: A Cherokee Creation Myth. Yasuda, Anita. 2012. (Short Tales Native American Myths Ser.). (ENG.). 32p. (J). (gr. 3-6). lib. bdg. 27.07 (978-1-61641-881-6(8), 13449, Short Tales) Magic Wagon.

—Sky Woman & the Big Turtle: An Iroquois Creation Myth. Yasuda, Anita. 2012. (Short Tales Native American Myths Ser.). (ENG.). 32p. (J). (gr. 3-6). lib. bdg. 27.07 (978-1-61641-882-3(6), 13451, Short Tales) Magic Wagon.

—The Tortoise & the Hare. Aesop, Aesop. 2010. (Short Tales Fables Ser.). (ENG.). 32p. (J). (gr. 1-4). 27.07 (978-1-60270-555-5(0), 13411, Short Tales) Magic Wagon.

—The Warrior Twins: A Navajo Hero Myth. Yasuda, Anita. 2012. (Short Tales Native American Myths Ser.). (ENG.). 32p. (J). (gr. 3-6). lib. bdg. 27.07 (978-1-61641-884-7(2), 13455, Short Tales) Magic Wagon.

Pennington, Mark & Villarrubia, Jose. Cut Here, 3 vols., Vol. 1. Carey, Mike & Fern, Jim. rev. ed. 2007. (ENG.). 128p. pap. 9.99 (978-1-4012-1341-1(3), Vertigo) DC Comics.

Pennington, Mark, jt. illus. see Sears, Bart.

Pennino, Mario del, et al. Halloween Spooktacular. Chabot, Jacob et al. 2019. (Marvel Super Hero Adventures Graphic Novels Ser.). (ENG.). 24p. (J). (gr. 1-5). lib. bdg. 27.07 (978-1-5321-4447-9(4), 33852, Marvel Age) Spotlight.

—Spider-Man: Across the Spider-Verse. Kibblesmith, Daniel et al. 2019. (Marvel Super Hero Adventures Graphic Novels Ser.). (ENG.). 24p. (J). (gr. 1-5). lib. bdg. 27.07 (978-1-5321-4453-0(9), 33858, Marvel Age) Spotlight.

—Spider-Man: Spider-Sense of Adventure. Ryan, Sean et al. 2019. (Marvel Super Hero Adventures Graphic Novels Ser.). (ENG.). 24p. (J). (gr. 1-5). lib. bdg. 27.07 (978-1-5321-4454-7(7), 33859, Marvel Age) Spotlight.

—Spider-Man: Web Designers. Fisch, Sholly & Templeton, Ty. 2019. (Marvel Super Hero Adventures Graphic Novels Ser.). (ENG.). 24p. (J). (gr. 1-5). lib. bdg. 27.07 (978-1-5321-4455-4(5), 33860, Marvel Age) Spotlight.

—Spider-Man: Web of Intrigue! Fisch, Sholly et al. 2019. (Marvel Super Hero Adventures Graphic Novels Ser.). (ENG.). 24p. (J). (gr. 1-5). lib. bdg. 27.07 (978-1-5321-4456-1(3), 33861, Marvel Age) Spotlight.

Penny, Agnes M. The Story of Our Lady of Victory. Penny, Agnes M. 2008. 24p. (J). 4.50 (978-0-9788687-2-7(2)) Requiem Pr.

Penny, Indie. Ven a la Huerta de Manzanas. Lindeen, Mary. 2016. (Early Rising Readers Ser.). (SPA.). 16p. (J). (gr. 1-1). 6.67 (978-1-4788-4214-9(8)) Newmark Learning LLC.

Penny, Mara. Hank & Gertie: A Pioneer Hansel & Gretel Story. Kimmel, Eric A. 2018. (ENG.). 32p. (J). (gr. 1-3). 16.99 (978-1-5132-6122-5(3), West Winds Pr.) West Margin Pr.

—Like a Girl. Degman, Lori. 2019. 40p. (J). (gr. -1-3). 16.95 (978-1-4549-3302-1(X)) Sterling Publishing Co., Inc.

 The check digit for ISBN-10 appears in parentheses after the full ISBN-13

Pennypacker, Mona, jt. illus. see Hill, Vicki Trego.

Pensee, Charles. Carnet Blanc Compagnie des Paquebots. 2016. (Bnf Monuments Ser.). (FRE.). (J). pap. *(978-2-01-116962-4(3))* Hachette Groupe Livre.

—Carnet Ligne Compagnie des Paquebots. 2016. (Bnf Monuments Ser.). (FRE.). (J). pap. *(978-2-01-116939-6(9))* Hachette Groupe Livre.

Pentangelo, Manuela. A Day with My Dad. Waite, Lance. 2008. 24p. (J). (gr. -1-3). 17.99 *(978-1-60131-015-6(3),* Parents Publishing Group) Big Tent Bks.

Pentney, Ryan. Cyclops Tells All: The Way Eye See It. Loewen, Nancy. 2014. (Other Side of the Myth Ser.). (ENG.). 32p. (J). (gr. -1-3). pap. 6.95 *(978-1-4795-2937-7(0),* Picture Window Bks.) Capstone.

—Cyclops Tells All: The Way EYE See It, 1 vol. Loewen, Nancy. 2014. (Other Side of the Myth Ser.). (ENG.). 32p. (J). (gr. -1-3). lib. bdg. 27.99 *(978-1-4795-2180-7(9),* Picture Window Bks.) Capstone.

—An Emperor's Guide. Chambers, Catherine. 2017. (How-To Guides for Fiendish Rulers Ser.). (ENG.). 32p. (J). (gr. 3-6). 7.99 *(978-1-5124-3071-4(4),* 9781512430714, Hungry Tomato ®); lib. bdg. 27.99 *(978-1-5124-1551-3(0),* 9781512415513, Hungry Tomato ®); E-Book 39.99 *(978-1-5124-2707-3(1));* E-Book 42.65 *(978-1-5124-3620-4(8),* 9781512436204, Hungry Tomato ®); E-Book 4.99 *(978-1-5124-3621-1(6),* 9781512436211, Hungry Tomato ®) Lerner Publishing Group.

—A King's Guide. Chambers, Catherine. 2017. (How-To Guides for Fiendish Rulers Ser.). (ENG.). 32p. (J). (gr. 3-6). lib. bdg. 27.99 *(978-1-5124-1550-6(2),* 9781512415506); E-Book 42.65 *(978-1-5124-2706-6(3));* E-Book 42.65 *(978-1-5124-3623-5(2),* 9781512436235); E-Book 4.99 *(978-1-5124-3624-2(0),* 9781512436242) Lerner Publishing Group. (Hungry Tomato ®).

—Pandora Tells All: Not the Curious Kind, 1 vol. Loewen, Nancy. 2014. (Other Side of the Myth Ser.). (ENG.). 32p. (J). (gr. -1-3). pap. 6.95 *(978-1-4795-2938-4(9),* Picture Window Bks.) Capstone.

—A Pharaoh's Guide. Chambers, Catherine. 2017. (How-To Guides for Fiendish Rulers Ser.). (ENG.). 32p. (J). (gr. 3-6). 27.99 *(978-1-5124-1549-0(9),* 9781512415490); E-Book 42.65 *(978-1-5124-2705-9(5));* E-Book 4.99 *(978-1-5124-3627-3(5),* 9781512436273); E-Book 42.65 *(978-1-5124-3626-6(7),* 9781512436266) Lerner Publishing Group. (Hungry Tomato ®).

—A Shogun's Guide. Chambers, Catherine. 2017. (How-To Guides for Fiendish Rulers Ser.). (ENG.). 32p. (J). (gr. 3-6). 27.99 *(978-1-5124-1552-0(9),* 9781512415520, Hungry Tomato ®); E-Book 39.99 *(978-1-5124-2708-0(X));* E-Book 42.65 *(978-1-5124-3629-7(1),* 9781512436297, Hungry Tomato ®); E-Book 4.99 *(978-1-5124-3630-3(5),* 9781512436303, Hungry Tomato ®) Lerner Publishing Group.

Penyas, Ana. Mexique: A Refugee Story from the Spanish Civil War. Ferrada, María José. 2020. (ENG.). 40p. (J). ***(978-0-8028-5545-9(8),*** Eerdmans Bks For Young Readers) Eerdmans, William B. Publishing Co.

Penzel, Karen. Beatrix the Bunny: Helps Buddy Make Friends: a Story for Those Who Struggle to Socialize. Russell, Hilary. 2019. (Beatrix the Bunny Ser.: Vol. 2). (ENG.). 40p. (J). 13.95 ***(978-0-578-51195-5(9))*** Russell, Hilary.

—Beatrix the Bunny: Learns to Be Focused & Kind. Russell, Hilary. 2019. (Beatrix the Bunny Ser.: Vol. 1). (ENG.). 38p. (J). 13.95 ***(978-0-578-50353-0(0))*** Russell, Hilary.

Peoples, Alan. James the Circus Boy. 2013. 80p. pap. 11.99 *(978-1-62839-474-0(9))* Salem Author Services.

Peoples, LaToya. Christmas with Papa & Momuski. Nash, Carol. 2017. (Train up a Child Ser.: Vol. 1). (ENG.). 42p. (J). 16.95 *(978-0-692-98200-6(0))* Kingdom Builders Pubn.

Peoples-Riley, Daria. Gloria Takes a Stand: How Gloria Steinem Listened, Wrote, & Changed the World. Rinker, Jessica M. 2019. (ENG.). 48p. (J). 17.99 *(978-1-68119-676-3(X),* 900180274, Bloomsbury Children's Bks.) Bloomsbury Publishing USA.

Peoples-Riley, Daria. I Got Next. Peoples-Riley, Daria. 2019. (ENG.). 40p. (J). (gr. -1-3). 17.99 *(978-0-06-265777-0(1),* Greenwillow Bks.) HarperCollins Pubs.

—This Is It. Peoples-Riley, Daria. 2018. (ENG.). 40p. (J). (gr. -1-3). 17.99 *(978-0-06-265776-3(3),* Greenwillow Bks.) HarperCollins Pubs.

Pépin, Émilie. The Major Eights 1: Battle of the Bands. Reed, Melody. 2018. (Major Eights Ser.: 1). (ENG.). 112p. (J). (gr. k-3). 16.99 *(978-1-4998-0565-9(9));* pap. 5.99 *(978-1-4998-0564-2(0))* Little Bee Books Inc.

—The Major Eights 2: Scarlet's Big Break. Reed, Melody. 2018. (Major Eights Ser.: 2). (ENG.). 112p. (J). (gr. k-3). 16.99 *(978-1-4998-0568-0(3));* pap. 5.99 *(978-1-4998-0567-3(5))* Little Bee Books Inc.

—The Major Eights 3: the Goo Disaster! Reed, Melody. 2018. (Major Eights Ser.: 3). (ENG.). 112p. (J). (gr. k-3). 16.99 *(978-1-4998-0587-1(X));* pap. 5.99 *(978-1-4998-0586-4(1))* Little Bee Books Inc.

—The Major Eights 4: Starstruck. Reed, Melody. 2018. (Major Eights Ser.: 4). (ENG.). 112p. (J). (gr. k-3). 16.99 *(978-1-4998-0590-1(X));* pap. 5.99 *(978-1-4998-0589-5(6))* Little Bee Books Inc.

—The Major Eights 5: the New Bandmate. Reed, Melody. 2018. (Major Eights Ser.: 5). (ENG.). 112p. (J). (gr. k-3). 16.99 *(978-1-4998-0760-8(0));* pap. 5.99 *(978-1-4998-0759-2(7))* Little Bee Books Inc.

Pepis, Aaron, photos by. What You Will See Inside a Mosque. Khan, Aisha Karen. (What You Will See Inside ... Ser.). 32p. (J). 2008. (ENG., pap. 12.99 *(978-1-59473-257-7(4),* d2b4dd04-7153-4578-9b67-5e3f490a9776); 2003. (gr. 1-5). 16.95 *(978-1-893361-60-7(8))* LongHill Partners, Inc. (Skylight Paths Publishing).

—What You Will See Inside a Mosque. Khan, Aisha Karen. 2003. 32p. *(978-2-89507-398-7(8))* Novalis Publishing.

Pepper, Charlotte. Feelings. Colombe, Rose. Cottage Door Press, ed. 2020. (Lamaze Mirror & Me Children's Interactive Mirrored Board Book Ser.). (ENG.). 10p. (J). (gr. -1 — 1). bds. 8.99 ***(978-1-68052-789-6(4),*** 1005120) Cottage Door Pr.

—My First Learn-To-Draw: Baby Animals. 2020. (ENG.). 56p. (J). (-1). pap. 12.99 ***(978-1-7282-2370-4(9))*** Sourcebooks, Inc.

—My First Learn-To-Draw: Farm Animals. 2020. (ENG.). 56p. (J). (-1). pap. 12.99 ***(978-1-7282-2371-1(7))*** Sourcebooks, Inc.

—My First Learn-To-Draw: Things That Go. 2020. (ENG.). 56p. (J). (-1). pap. 12.99 ***(978-1-7282-2372-8(5))*** Sourcebooks, Inc.

Pepper, Charlotte. Through the Animal Kingdom: Discover Amazing Animals & Their Remarkable Homes. Harvey, Derek. 2019. (Through The... Ser.). (ENG.). 96p. (J). (gr. -1-3). 14.99 *(978-1-4654-8149-8(4),* DK Children) Dorling Kindersley Publishing, Inc.

Peralta, Germán. Age of X-Man: Prisoner X. 2019. (ENG.). 112p. (YA). (gr. 8-17). pap. 15.99 *(978-1-302-91579-7(7))* Marvel Worldwide, Inc.

Peralta, German. Cable Vol. 3: Past Fears. 2018. (Cable (2017) Ser.: 3). (ENG.). 112p. (YA). (gr. 8-17). pap. 15.99 *(978-1-302-91196-6(1))* Marvel Worldwide, Inc.

—Strikeforce Vol. 1: Trust Me. 2020. 112p. (YA). (gr. 8-17). pap. 15.99 *(978-1-302-92009-8(X))* Marvel Worldwide, Inc.

Perard, Victor. Pete Cow Puncher a Story of the Texas Plains. Ames, Joseph B. 2005. reprint ed. pap. 31.95 *(978-0-7661-9421-2(3))* Kessinger Publishing, LLC.

Peratrovich, Roy A., Jr. Little Whale: A Story of the Last Tlingit War Canoe. Peratrovich, Roy A., Jr. 2016. (ENG.). 64p. pap. 16.95 *(978-1-60223-295-2(4))* Univ. of Alaska Pr.

Perciopelo. Susana Worrywart & the Magical Teddy Bear Balloon. Burke, Ellinor Rozecki. 2003. 32p. (J). 17.99 *(978-0-9741586-3-1(1))* Comfort Tales, LLC.

—Susana Worrywart & the Magical Teddy Bear Balloon: With CD for Relaxation. Burke, Ellinor Rozecki. 2003. 32p. (J). 27.00 incl. audio compact disk *(978-0-9741586-0-0(7))* Comfort Tales, LLC.

Percival, Tom. And He's the Good Guy. Landy, Derek. 2007. (Skulduggery Pleasant Ser.: 1). (ENG.). 400p. (J). (gr. 5-7). 17.99 *(978-0-06-123115-5(0))* HarperCollins Pubs.

—Curses for Sale, 1 vol. Brezenoff, Steve. 2012. (Ravens Pass Ser.). (ENG.). 96p. (J). (gr. 3-6). pap. 6.15 *(978-1-4342-4209-9(9));* lib. bdg. 25.32 *(978-1-4342-3763-7(X))* Capstone. (Stone Arch Bks.).

—Monster & Me, 1 vol. Marsh, Robert. 2009. (Monster & Me Ser.). (ENG.). 40p. (J). (gr. 2-5). lib. bdg. 23.99 *(978-1-4342-1589-5(X),* Stone Arch Bks.) Capstone.

—Monster in the Outfield, 1 vol. Marsh, Robert. 2009. (Monster & Me Ser.). (ENG.). 40p. (J). (gr. 2-5). lib. bdg. 23.99 *(978-1-4342-1590-1(3),* Stone Arch Bks.) Capstone.

—Monster Moneymaker, 1 vol. Marsh, Robert. 2010. (Monster & Me Ser.). (ENG.). 40p. (J). (gr. 2-5). lib. bdg. 23.99 *(978-1-4342-1891-9(0),* Stone Arch Bks.) Capstone.

—New in Town, 1 vol. Brezenoff, Steve. 2012. (Ravens Pass Ser.). (ENG.). 96p. (J). (gr. 3-6). pap. 6.15 *(978-1-4342-4210-5(2));* lib. bdg. 25.32 *(978-1-4342-3793-4(1))* Capstone. (Stone Arch Bks.).

—Scepter of the Ancients. Landy, Derek. (Skulduggery Pleasant Ser.: Bk. 1). (ENG.). 416p. (J). 2009. pap. 3.99 *(978-0-06-173155-6(2),* Harper Trophy); 2008. (gr. 5). pap. 7.99 *(978-0-06-123117-9(7))* HarperCollins Pubs.

—The Sleeper, 1 vol. Brezenoff, Steve. 2012. (Ravens Pass Ser.). (ENG.). 96p. (J). (gr. 3-6). pap. 6.15 *(978-1-4342-4211-2(0));* lib. bdg. 25.32 *(978-1-4342-3792-7(3))* Capstone. (Stone Arch Bks.).

—Witch Mayor, 1 vol. Brezenoff, Steve. 2012. (Ravens Pass Ser.). (ENG.). 96p. (J). (gr. 3-6). pap. 6.15 *(978-1-4342-4212-9(9));* lib. bdg. 25.32 *(978-1-4342-3791-0(5))* Capstone. (Stone Arch Bks.).

—50 Things to Do Before You're 11 3/4: an Outdoor Adventure Handbook. Nosy Crow. 2018. (ENG.). 96p. (J). (gr. 3-7). pap. 9.99 *(978-0-7636-9337-4(5),* Nosy Crow) Candlewick Pr.

Percival, Tom Robert James. Monster & Me: The Complete Comics Collection. Marsh, Robert. ed. 2020. (Stone Arch Graphic Novels Ser.). (ENG.). 144p. (J). (gr. 3-6). pap. 8.95 *(978-1-4965-9319-1(7),* 142349); lib. bdg. 27.99 *(978-1-4965-8730-5(8),* 141608) Capstone. (Stone Arch Bks.).

Percy, Sally. Donde Dormiras Pequena Liebre? Cain, Sheridan. (SPA.). (J). (gr. k-2). pap. 16.95 *(978-84-488-0869-3(X),* BS3556) Beascoa, Ediciones S.A. ESP. Dist: Lectorum Pubns., Inc.

Perdomo, Juliana. Rainbow Colors. words&pictures. 2020. (ENG.). 16p. (J). (gr. -1-k). bds. 12.99 ***(978-0-7112-5037-6(5),*** Words & Pictures) Quarto Publishing Group UK GBR. Dist: Hachette Bk. Group.

—What Is Baby Going to Do? Knowles, Laura. 2020. (Flap Flap Ser.). (ENG.). 14p. (J). (gr. -1 — 1). bds. 9.99 ***(978-0-7112-5059-8(6),*** Words & Pictures) Quarto Publishing Group UK GBR. Dist: Hachette Bk. Group.

Perdziak, Jeffrey. Treasures. Klaiber, Sarah. 2016. (ENG.). (J). (gr. k-4). 15.95 *(978-0-9960839-5-9(2))* Kevin W W Blackley Bks., LLC.

Perdziak, Jeffrey Scott. Olivia the Bully. Everett, Engelic. 2017. (ENG.). (J). (gr. k-2). pap. 14.95 *(978-0-9977740-1-6(0))* People Ink Pr.

Pereira, Diego Jourdan. Classics to Color: the Tale of Peter Rabbit. Potter, Beatrix. 2018. (ENG.). 80p. (J). (gr. -1-5). pap. 8.99 *(978-1-63158-170-0(8),* Racehorse Publishing) Skyhorse Publishing Co., Inc.

—Sesame Street at the Airport: Activity Book. Sky Pony Press. 2020. (Sesame Street's Elmo on the Move Ser.). (ENG.). 68p. (J). (-k). pap. 6.99 *(978-1-5107-4931-3(4),* Sky Pony Pr.) Skyhorse Publishing Co., Inc.

—Sesame Street at the Farm: Activity Book. Sky Pony Press. 2020. (Sesame Street's Elmo on the Move Ser.). (ENG.). 68p. (J). (-k). pap. 6.99 *(978-1-5107-4932-0(2),* Sky Pony Pr.) Skyhorse Publishing Co., Inc.

Pereira, Kristin L. Noah's Birds. Massop, Kimberley. 2017. (ENG.). 36p. (J). pap. 8.95 *(978-1-68350-025-4(3))* Morgan James Publishing.

Perera, Maria. What Can You See? at Night. Ware, Kate. 2020. (ENG.). 12p. (J). (-k). bds. 9.99 ***(978-1-68010-615-2(5))*** Tiger Tales.

—What Can You See? on the Farm. Ware, Kate. 2020. (ENG.). 12p. (J). (-k). bds. 9.99 ***(978-1-68010-614-5(7))*** Tiger Tales.

Perera, Rajni. The Boy & the Bindi. Shraya, Vivek. 2016. 32p. (J). (gr. -1-3). 17.95 *(978-1-55152-668-3(9))* Arsenal Pulp Pr. CAN. Dist: Consortium Bk. Sales & Distribution.

Perera, Vasana. The Beast. Perera, Jude. 2016. (ENG.). (YA). (gr. 7-12). pap. *(978-0-9944015-4-0(X))* Aly's Bks.

Perez, Alfred. Silver Soldiers (A. K. A. God's Silver Soldiers) Backed by Tales of Nazareth: The Boyhood of Jesus. Dunn, Rebecca. rev. ed. 2016. (1 Ser.: 1). (ENG.). 48p. (J). 4.00 *(978-1-888092-31-8(9),* 705f8c4f-85d2-4926-b56d-5aecc319bf61) Nordskog Publishing, Inc.

Pérez, Carmen. A Cat Is Chasing Me Through This Book!, 1 vol. Bird, Benjamin. 2014. (Tom & Jerry Ser.). (ENG.). 32p. (J). (gr. -1-2). 22.65 *(978-1-4795-5229-0(1),* Picture Window Bks.) Capstone.

—Don't Give This Book a Bowl of Milk!, 1 vol. Bird, Benjamin. 2014. (Tom & Jerry Ser.). (ENG.). 32p. (J). (gr. -1-2). 22.65 *(978-1-4795-5230-6(5),* Picture Window Bks.) Capstone.

—This Book Is Not a Piece of Cheese!, 1 vol. Bird, Benjamin. 2014. (Tom & Jerry Ser.). (ENG.). 32p. (J). (gr. -1-2). 22.65 *(978-1-4795-5231-3(3),* Picture Window Bks.) Capstone.

Pérez-Cuadrado, Esther. The Tractor Pink a Band. Hawes, Alison. 2017. (Cambridge Reading Adventures Ser.). (ENG.). 16p. pap. 7.37 *(978-1-108-40069-5(8))* Cambridge Univ. Pr.

Pérez, Daniel, et al. The Seven Voyages of Sinbad, 1 vol. Powell, Martin. 2010. (Classic Fiction Ser.). (ENG.). 72p. (J). (gr. 5-9). 27.99 *(978-1-4342-1987-9(9));* pap. 7.15 *(978-1-4342-2775-1(8))* Capstone. (Stone Arch Bks.).

Pérez, Daniel & Ferran, Daniel. Macbeth, 1 vol. Shakespeare, William. 2011. (Shakespeare Graphics Ser.). (ENG.). 88p. (J). (gr. 5-9). pap. 7.15 *(978-1-4342-3447-6(9),* Stone Arch Bks.) Capstone.

Perez, Debi. It's Blue Like You! A Story about Loyalty. Pantelides, Sherry. 2007. 32p. (J). 12.99 *(978-0-9771076-1-2(2))* Lacey Productions.

—It's Red Like Me! A Story about the Blood of Jesus. Pantelides, Sherry. 2007. (J). lib. bdg. 12.99 *(978-0-9771076-0-5(4))* Lacey Productions.

—Make A Choice to Rejoice! A Story about Being Cheerful. Pantelides, Sherry. 2007. 32p. (J). 12.99 *(978-0-9771076-2-9(0))* Lacey Productions.

Perez, Dorothy Thompson. Cómo Participar en la Liturgia: Un Libro de Para los Ninos Anglicanos-Episcopales. Kitch, Anne E. Martell, Oswald Perez, tr. 2008. (ENG.). 48p. pap. *(978-0-8192-2331-9(X),* edefa50a-b589-4222-b291-f96aa5d45d3d, Morehouse Publishing) Church Publishing, Inc.

—What We Do in Advent: An Anglican Kids' Activity Book. Kitch, Anne E. 2006. 48p. (gr. -1-2). pap. *(978-0-8192-2195-7(3),* 171cd8f5-565a-45e1-a5d8-87f153067df1, Morehouse Publishing) Church Publishing, Inc.

—What We Do in Church: An Anglican Child's Activity Book. Kitch, Anne E. 2004. 48p. pap. *(978-0-8192-2105-6(8),* e4a75c07-f9c3-4a14-a65c-6fbe0bed347c, Morehouse Publishing) Church Publishing, Inc.

—What We Do in Lent: A Child's Activity Book. Kitch, Anne E. 2007. (ENG.). 48p. pap. *(978-0-8192-2278-7(X),* 1ced57e3-eb23-4bcd-8d16-139996b90359, Morehouse Publishing) Church Publishing, Inc.

Perez, Esther Ido. Let's Go Camping & Discover Our Nature. Yerushalmi, Miriam. 2007. 28p. (J). (gr. 2-4). 16.50 *(978-0-911643-38-1(9))* Aura Printing, Inc.

—Let's Go Camping & Discover Our Nature. Yerushalmi, Miriam. 2017. (ENG.). 30p. (J). (gr. 2-4). 22.00 *(978-1-934152-56-0(0))* Sane.

Perez, Esther Ito. Carrying a Tune in Tzefat. Yerushalmi, Miriam. 2019. (ENG.). 46p. (J). 20.00 *(978-0-578-44234-1(5))* Sane.

—Carrying a Tune in Tzefat (Yiddish) Yerushalmi, Miriam. 2019. (YID.). 46p. (J). 20.00 *(978-0-578-45117-6(4))* Sane.

—Let's Go Camping & Discover Our Nature (Yiddish) Yerushalmi, Miriam. 2017. (YID.). 32p. (J). (gr. 2-4). 20.00 *(978-1-934152-51-5(X))* Sane.

—Let's Go to Eretz Yisrael. Yerushalmi, Miriam. 2017. (ENG.). 46p. (J). 20.00 *(978-1-934152-44-7(7))* Sane.

—Let's Go to Eretz Yisrael (Yiddish) Yerushalmi, Miriam. Werdiger, Chaim, tr. 2017. (YID.). 42p. (J). 20.00 *(978-1-934152-57-7(9))* Sane.

Perez-Fessenden, Lourdes. Daddy & I. Perez-Fessenden, Lourdes. 2012. 34p. pap. *(978-0-9840862-3-8(4))* Roxby Media Ltd.

Perez, George, et al. Infinity by Starlin & Hickman Omnibus. 2019. (ENG.). 848p. (YA). (gr. 8-17). 125.00 *(978-1-302-91565-0(7))* Marvel Worldwide, Inc.

—Radiant, Vol. 2. Kesel, Barbara. 2004. (Solus Ser.: Vol. 2). 160p. (YA). pap. 15.95 *(978-1-59314-057-1(6))* CrossGeneration Comics, Inc.

—Solus. Kesel, Barbara. 2003. (Solus Ser.: Vol. 1). 160p. (YA). pap. 15.95 *(978-1-931484-97-8(X))* CrossGeneration Comics, Inc.

Perez, George, et al. X-Men Epic Collection: Proteus. 2020. (ENG.). 432p. (J). (gr. 4-17). pap. 39.99 ***(978-1-302-92252-8(1))*** Marvel Worldwide, Inc.

Perez, George & Lim, Ron. Infinity Gauntlet: Deluxe Edition. 2019. (ENG.). 304p. (J). (gr. 4-17). pap. 34.99 *(978-1-302-91595-7(9))* Marvel Worldwide, Inc.

Perez, George & Lim, Ron. Infinity Gauntlet Marvel Select Edition. 2020. 256p. (YA). (gr. 8-17). 29.99 ***(978-1-302-92350-1(1))*** Marvel Worldwide, Inc.

Perez, Gerry. Hello CavMan! Aryal, Aimee. 2004. 24p. (J). 19.95 *(978-0-9743442-3-2(0))* Mascot Bks., Inc.

—Hello Joe Bruin! Aryal, Aimee. 2004. 24p. (J). 19.95 *(978-1-932888-15-7(2))* Mascot Bks., Inc.

—Hello, Ralphie! Aryal, Aimee. 2007. 24p. (J). lib. bdg. 14.95 *(978-1-932888-34-8(9))* Mascot Bks., Inc.

—Hello Tommy Trojan! Aryal, Aimee. 2004. 24p. (J). 19.95 *(978-1-932888-08-9(X))* Mascot Bks., Inc.

Pérez, Javier Serrano. The Shadow Mother, 1 vol. Virgo, Seán. 2014. (ENG.). 64p. (J). (gr. 6). 21.95 *(978-0-88899-971-9(2))* Groundwood Bks. CAN. Dist: Publishers Group West (PGW).

Perez, Joel. A (Very Brief) History of Systemic Racism: a Glimpse into Oppression, Inequity, & Inequality of Black People in the United States of America. Valentine, Chris. 2020. (ENG.). 42p. (YA). pap. 16.99 ***(978-1-6655-0008-1(5))*** AuthorHouse.

Perez, Jose Rubert. The Dragon Kings. Orenshein, Jesse. 2019. (ENG.). 36p. (J). pap. 9.99 ***(978-1-0865-7996-3(8))*** Independently Published.

Perez, Jose S. The Banjoman/El Hombre del Banjo. Perez, Jose S. Norman, Tyler. 2004. (ENG & SPA.). 32p. (J). 12.95 *(978-1-57072-292-9(7))* Overmountain Pr.

Pérez, Laura. Secrets of the Witch: An Initiation into Our History & Our Wisdom. Légère, Julie & Whyte, Elsa. 2020. (ENG.). 80p. (J). (gr. 4-9). 22.99 ***(978-0-7112-5799-3(X),*** Wide Eyed Editions) Quarto Publishing Group UK GBR. Dist: Hachette Bk. Group.

Perez, Linda. Una Dulce Princesa Azteca: Princesas, Estrellas y Dioses. Montalvo, María Luisa. Apodaca, Victor Manuel, ed. 2019. (SPA.). 102p. (J). pap. 19.99 ***(978-1-6981-3095-8(3))*** Independently Published.

Pérez, Magdalena. Tweet! José Ferrada, María. 2020. (ENG.). 28p. (J). bds. ***(978-1-64686-092-0(6))*** Barefoot Bks., Inc.

Perez, Maureen T. Caring - Companion Book. Cesena, Denise. l.t. ed. 2003. 12p. (J). 2.00 *(978-0-9740418-7-2(4))* Night Light Pubns., LLC.

Perez, Maureen T. Caring. Perez, Maureen T. Cesena, Denise. l.t. ed. 2003. 28p. (J). 10.00 *(978-0-9740418-6-5(6))* Night Light Pubns., LLC.

Perez, Maureen T. & Cesena, Denise. Friendliness. Perez, Maureen T. l.t. ed. 2003. 28p. (J). 10.00 *(978-0-9740418-0-3(7))* Night Light Pubns., LLC.

—Friendliness - Companion Book. Perez, Maureen T. l.t. ed. 2003. 12p. (J). 2.00 *(978-0-9740418-1-0(5))* Night Light Pubns., LLC.

Perez, Maureen T., jt. illus. see Cesena, Denise.

Perez-Moliere, Mamie. Los Tres Naufragos. Barsy, Kalman. 2004. (Orange Ser.). (SPA.). 40p. (J). (gr. 3-5). pap. 5.95 *(978-1-57581-469-8(2))* Santillana USA Publishing Co., Inc.

—La Niña y la Estrella. Leon, Georgina Lazaro. 2003. (Yellow Ser.). (SPA.). 31p. (gr. k-3). pap. 7.95 *(978-1-57581-436-0(6))* Santillana USA Publishing Co., Inc.

Pérez, Moni. A Day at the Museum Blue Band. Sagner, Sibel et al. 2016. (Cambridge Reading Adventures Ser.). (ENG.). 16p. pap. 7.37 *(978-1-316-50320-1(8))* Cambridge Univ. Pr.

Perez, Moni. Don't Give up yet! White Band. Kubuitsile, Lauri. 2017. (Cambridge Reading Adventures Ser.). (ENG.). 24p. pap. 6.74 *(978-1-108-40078-7(7))* Cambridge Univ. Pr.

Pérez, Moni. For Today, for Tomorrow. Kubuitsile, Lauri. 2016. (Cambridge Reading Adventures Ser.). (ENG.). 16p. pap. 7.37 *(978-1-107-55081-0(5))* Cambridge Univ. Pr.

—Hide & Seek Green Band. Rickards, Lynne. 2016. (Cambridge Reading Adventures Ser.). (ENG.). 16p. pap. 7.37 *(978-1-107-57599-8(0))* Cambridge Univ. Pr.

—Late for School Yellow Band. Llewellyn, Claire. 2016. (Cambridge Reading Adventures Ser.). (ENG.). 16p. pap. 7.37 *(978-1-107-57679-7(2))* Cambridge Univ. Pr.

Perez, Moni. Leila's Game 1 Pathfinders. Breakwell, Spike & Millar, Colin. 2017. (Cambridge Reading Adventures Ser.). (ENG.). 32p. pap. 7.87 *(978-1-108-40820-2(6))* Cambridge Univ. Pr.

Pérez, Moni. Omar Can Help Red Band. Rickards, Lynne. 2016. (Cambridge Reading Adventures Ser.). (ENG.). 16p. pap. 7.37 *(978-1-107-57572-1(9))* Cambridge Univ. Pr.

—Omar in Trouble Orange Band. Pritchard, Gabby. 2016. (Cambridge Reading Adventures Ser.). (ENG.). 16p. pap. 7.37 *(978-1-316-50329-4(1))* Cambridge Univ. Pr.

—Omar's First Day at School Pink B Band. Fakhouri, Shoua. 2016. (Cambridge Reading Adventures Ser.). (ENG.). 16p. pap. 7.37 *(978-1-316-60811-1(5))* Cambridge Univ. Pr.

Perez, Moni. The Show & Tell Day Blue Band. Sagner, Sibel. 2017. (Cambridge Reading Adventures Ser.). (ENG.). 16p. pap. 5.62 *(978-1-108-40191-3(0))* Cambridge Univ. Pr.

—Sorry Isn't Good Enough Purple Band. Kubuitsile, Lauri. 2017. (Cambridge Reading Adventures Ser.). (ENG.). 24p. pap. 6.74 *(978-1-108-40081-7(7))* Cambridge Univ. Pr.

Pérez, Moni. Tefo & the Lucky Football Boots Gold Band. Kubuitsile, Lauri. 2016. (Cambridge Reading Adventures Ser.). (ENG.). 24p. pap. 8.08 *(978-1-107-55141-1(2))* Cambridge Univ. Pr.

Perez Montero, Jose. Historias de la Biblia para Leer en 5 Minutos / the Little Childrens Bible StoryBook. Graaf, Anne De. 2020. (SPA.). 352p. (J). (gr. -1-2). 15.95 *(978-1-949061-91-8(4))* Penguin Random House Grupo Editorial ESP. Dist: Penguin Random Hse. LLC.

Perez, Nomar. All Day Long, God Loves Me. Keefer, Mikal. 2017. (Best of Li'l Buddies Ser.). (ENG.). 16p. (J). bds. 6.99 *(978-1-4707-4859-3(2))* Group Publishing, Inc.

—Baby's First Nativity. Little Bee Books. 2019. (ENG.). 16p. (J). (— 1). bds. 6.99 *(978-1-4998-0959-6(X))* Little Bee Books Inc.

—Everywhere I Go, God Is with Me. Keefer, Mikal. 2017. (Best of Li'l Buddies Ser.). (ENG.). 16p. (J). bds. 6.99 *(978-1-4707-4857-9(6))* Group Publishing, Inc.

—Never Fear, God Is Near. Keefer, Mikal. 2018. (Best of Li'l Buddies Ser.). (ENG.). 16p. bds. 6.99 *(978-1-4707-5036-7(8))* Group Publishing, Inc.

P

Perez, Pere. War of the Realms: Uncanny X-Men. 2019. (ENG.). 112p. (YA). (gr. 8-17). pap. 15.99 (978-1-302-91919-1(9)) Marvel Worldwide, Inc.

Pérez, Ramón. The Country of Wolves, 1 vol. 2014. (ENG.). 88p. (YA). (gr. 7-8). pap. 19.95 (978-1-927095-35-5(2)) Inhabit Media Inc. CAN. Dist: Consortium Bk. Sales & Distribution.

Perez, Ramon. Tale of Sand. Henson, Jim & Juhl, Jerry. Christy, Stephen & Robinson, Chris, eds. 2011. (ENG.). 120p. (YA). (gr. 2). 29.95 (978-1-936393-09-1(3)) Boom Entertainment, Inc.

Pérez, Ramón & Pérez, Ramón. Max Finder Mystery Collected Casebook Volume 4, Vol. 4. Battle, Craig. 2010. (Max Finder Mystery Collected Casebook Ser.: 4). (ENG.). 96p. (J). (gr. 3-6). pap. 9.95 (978-1-897349-80-9(7)) Owlkids Bks. Inc. CAN. Dist: Publishers Group West (PGW).

—Max Finder Mystery Collected Casebook Volume 5, Vol. 5. Battle, Craig. 2011. (Max Finder Mystery Collected Casebook Ser.: 5). (ENG.). 96p. (J). (gr. 3-6). pap. 9.95 (978-1-926818-12-2(1)) Owlkids Bks. Inc. CAN. Dist: Publishers Group West (PGW).

—Max Finder Mystery Collected Casebook Volume 6, Vol. 6. Battle, Craig. 2012. (Max Finder Mystery Collected Casebook Ser.: 6). (ENG.). 96p. (J). (gr. 3-6). pap. 9.95 (978-1-926973-21-0(6), Owlkids) Owlkids Bks. Inc. CAN. Dist: Publishers Group West (PGW).

Perez, Ramon, jt. illus. see Medina, Paco.

Pérez, Ramón, jt. illus. see Pérez, Ramón.

Pérez, Ramón K. Slaves of the Republic: Slave Traders of Zygerria. Gilroy, Henry. 2010. (Star Wars: Clone Wars Ser.: No. 1). (ENG.). 24p. (J). (gr. 6-12). 27.07 (978-1-59961-711-4(0), 13792, Graphic Novels) Spotlight.

Perez, Robert. Batter's Up! Tilley, E. S. 2019. (ENG.). 42p. (J). pap. 9.50 **(978-1-6791-0867-9(0))** Independently Published.

Perez, Sara. Is a Spider an Insect? Ikids Staff & Schimel, Lawrence. 2009. (ENG.). 22p. (J). (gr. -1-1). 9.99 (978-1-58476-820-3(7), IKIDS) Innovative Kids.

—What's in the Egg? Ikids Staff & Schimel, Lawrence. 2009. (ENG.). 22p. (J). (gr. -1-1). 9.99 (978-1-58476-821-0(5), IKIDS) Innovative Kids.

Pérez, Sara Rojo. The Ant & the Grasshopper: A Retelling of Aesop's Fable, 1 vol. White, Mark & Aesop Enterprise Inc. Staff. 2011. (My First Classic Story Ser.). (ENG.). 24p. (J). (gr. k-3). lib. bdg. 22.65 (978-1-4048-6505-1(5), Picture Window Bks.) Capstone.

—The Ant & the Grasshopper: A Retelling of Aesop's Fable, 1 vol. White, Mark. 2011. (My First Classic Story Ser.). (ENG.). 24p. (J). (gr. k-3). pap. 7.10 (978-1-4048-7363-6(5), Picture Window Bks.) Capstone.

—The Fox & the Grapes: A Retelling of Aesop's Fable, 1 vol. White, Mark. 2013. (My First Classic Story Ser.). (ENG.). 24p. (J). (gr. k-3). pap. 7.10 (978-1-4795-1856-2(5), Picture Window Bks.) Capstone.

—The Fox & the Grapes: A Retelling of Aesop's Fable, 1 vol. White, Mark & Aesop Enterprise Inc. Staff. 2011. (My First Classic Story Ser.). (ENG.). 24p. (J). (gr. k-3). lib. bdg. 22.65 (978-1-4048-6508-2(X), Picture Window Bks.) Capstone.

—The Fox & the Grapes: A Retelling of Aesop's Fable. White, Mark. 2008. (Read-It! Readers: Fables Ser.). (ENG.). 24p. (J). (gr. k-3). per. 3.95 (978-1-4048-0467-8(6), Picture Window Bks.) Capstone.

—El Leon y el Raton: Versión de la Fábula de Esopo. White, Mark. Abello, Patricia, tr. 2006. (Read-It! Readers en Español: Fábulas Ser.).Tr. of Lion & the Mouse - A Retelling of Aesop's Fable. (SPA.). 24p. (J). (gr. k-3). 21.32 (978-1-4048-1623-7(2), Picture Window Bks.) Capstone.

—The Lion & the Mouse: A Retelling of Aesop's Fable, 1 vol. White, Mark. 2010. (My First Classic Story Ser.). (ENG.). 24p. (J). (gr. k-3). pap. 7.10 (978-1-4048-7365-0(1), Picture Window Bks.) Capstone.

—The Lion & the Mouse: A Retelling of Aesop's Fable, 1 vol. White, Mark & Aesop Enterprise Inc. Staff. 2010. (My First Classic Story Ser.). (ENG.). 24p. (J). (gr. k-3). lib. bdg. 22.65 (978-1-4048-6525-9(X), Picture Window Bks.) Capstone.

—Why Do We Recycle? Science Made Simple! Ikids Staff. 2009. (ENG.). 22p. (J). (gr. -1-1). 9.99 (978-1-58476-935-4(1)) Innovative Kids.

—Why Does the Wind Blow? Science Made Simple! Ikids Staff. 2009. (ENG.). 20p. (J). (gr. -1-1). 9.99 (978-1-58476-934-7(3)) Innovative Kids.

—The Wolf in Sheep's Clothing: A Retelling of Aesop's Fable, 1 vol. White, Mark. 2013. (My First Classic Story Ser.). (ENG.). 24p. (J). (gr. k-3). pap. 7.10 (978-1-4795-1857-9(3), Picture Window Bks.) Capstone.

—The Wolf in Sheep's Clothing: A Retelling of Aesop's Fable, 1 vol. White, Mark & Aesop Enterprise Inc. Staff. 2011. (My First Classic Story Ser.). (ENG.). 24p. (J). (gr. k-3). lib. bdg. 22.65 (978-1-4048-6509-9(8), Picture Window Bks.) Capstone.

Perez, Stephanie. Brotherhood of the Rainbow Dragon. Perez, Freddie. 2020. (ENG.). 310p. (J). pap. 15.00 **(978-1-6582-7974-1(3))** Independently Published.

Perez, Stephanie. Odd Hollow & the Ghosts. Perez, Stephanie. Perez, Roseann. 2019. (Odd Hollow Ser.: Vol. 1). (ENG.). 104p. (J). pap. 10.00 **(978-1-6992-9073-6(3))** Independently Published.

Perez-Torres, Juliana. George, Candy, & the Raccoon. Gilbert, George. 2008. 40p. pap. 16.99 (978-1-4389-2848-7(3)) AuthorHouse.

Perez, Vanessa. I Love You More Than the Universe. Castagnola LCSW, Lisa. 2018. (ENG.). 26p. (J). pap. 12.45 (978-1-9822-1765-5(0), Balboa Pr.) Author Solutions, Inc.

Perica. El Baúl de Mi Mundo: Un Libro Sobre Los Tamaños. Cinetto, Liliana. 2008. (Baúl / Treasure Chest Collection). (SPA.). 16p. (J). (gr. -1-1). pap. 6.99 (978-1-63113-901-7(0)) Santillana USA Publishing Co., Inc.

Perin, Pauline. The Bully of Glendale Pond. Smith, Clyde R. 2012. 24p. (-18). pap. 24.95 (978-1-4626-7795-5(9)) America Star Bks.

Peringer, Stephen Mercer. Jordan's Hair. Spruill, Edward L. & Spruill, Sonya. 2005. 16p. (J). (gr. -1-3). 8.00 (978-0-8170-1484-1(5)) Judson Pr.

Perissinotto, Giada & Priori, Giulia. Sunny's Royal Ball (Sunny Day) Carbone, Courtney. 2018. (Little Golden Book Ser.). (ENG.). 24p. (J). (-k). 4.99 (978-1-5247-6855-3(3), Golden Bks.) Random Hse. Children's Bks.

Perkins, Amanda. Savage Days. Martin, Leitha. 2018. (ENG.). 174p. (J). pap. 8.90 (978-1-7202-8626-4(4)) Independently Published.

Perkins, Bill. The Copernicus Legacy: the Forbidden Stone. Abbott, Tony. 2014. (Copernicus Legacy Ser.: 1). (ENG.). 432p. (J). (gr. 3-7). 16.99 (978-0-06-219447-3(X), Tegen, Katherine Bks) HarperCollins Pubs.

Perkins, Chelsea. Have You Ever Seen a Wild Bird Dance? Yost, B. L. 2008. 16p. pap. 24.95 (978-1-60703-127-7(2)) America Star Bks.

Perkins, Grant. Bayani & the Nine Daughters of the Moon. McIntire, Travis. 2020. (Bayani Ser.). (ENG.). 72p. (J). pap. 14.99 **(978-1-63529-842-0(3))** Caliber Comics.

Perkins, Justin. Sammy's New Look. Jackson, Lajuana D. 2017. (ENG.). 42p. (J). pap. 9.99 (978-0-692-96952-6(7)) Power of One , LLC.

Perkins, Ken. Does God Love Michael's Two Daddies. Butt, Sheila K. 2007. (ENG.). 16p. (J). pap. 7.95 (978-0-932859-94-5(1)) Apologetics Pr., Inc.

Perkins, Lori L., jt. illus. see Perkins, William C.

Perkins, Lucy. The American Twins of the Revolution. Perkins, Lucy. 2007. 232p. per. 12.95 (978-0-9776786-7-9(9)) Salem Ridge Press LLC.

Perkins, Lucy Fitch. The American Twins of the Revolution. Perkins, Lucy Fitch. 2008. 240p. 22.95 (978-1-934671-19-1(3)) Salem Ridge Press LLC.

Perkins, Lynne Rae. Seed by Seed: The Legend & Legacy of John Appleseed Anniversary. Codell, Esmé Raji. 2012. (ENG.). 32p. (J). (gr. -1-3). 17.89 (978-0-06-145516-2(4), Greenwillow Bks.) HarperCollins Pubs.

—Seed by Seed: The Legend & Legacy of John Appleseed Chapman. Codell, Esmé Raji. 2012. (ENG.). 32p. (J). (gr. -1-3). 16.99 (978-0-06-145515-5(6), Greenwillow Bks.) HarperCollins Pubs.

Perkins, Lynne Rae. The Cardboard Piano. Perkins, Lynne Rae. 2008. (ENG.). 32p. (J). (gr. -1-2). 17.99 (978-0-06-154265-7(2), Greenwillow Bks.) HarperCollins Pubs.

—Frank & Lucky Get Schooled. Perkins, Lynne Rae. 2016. (ENG.). 32p. (J). (gr. -1-3). 17.99 (978-0-06-237345-8(5), Greenwillow Bks.) HarperCollins Pubs.

—Nuts to You. Perkins, Lynne Rae. 2014. (ENG.). 272p. (J). (gr. 3-7). 16.99 (978-0-06-009275-7(0), Greenwillow Bks.) HarperCollins Pubs.

—Pictures from Our Vacation. Perkins, Lynne Rae. 2007. 32p. (J). (gr. k-3). 17.89 (978-0-06-085098-2(1)); (ENG.). 17.99 (978-0-06-085097-5(3)) HarperCollins Pubs. (Greenwillow Bks.).

—Secret Sisters of the Salty Sea. Perkins, Lynne Rae. (ENG.). (J). (gr. 3-7). 2019. 256p. pap. 6.99 (978-0-06-249967-7(X)); 2018. 240p. 16.99 (978-0-06-249966-0(1)) HarperCollins Pubs. (Greenwillow Bks.).

—Snow Music. Perkins, Lynne Rae. 2003. 40p. (J). lib. bdg. 16.89 (978-0-06-623958-3(3)); (ENG.). (gr. -1-3). 16.99 (978-0-06-623956-9(7), Greenwillow Bks.) HarperCollins Pubs.

—Wintercake. Perkins, Lynne Rae. 2019. (ENG.). 48p. (J). (gr. 1-5). 17.99 (978-0-06-289487-8(0), Greenwillow Bks.) HarperCollins Pubs.

Perkins, Mair. Boris the Lost Badger. Hainsworth, B. R. 2012. 42p. pap. (978-1-78148-585-9(2)) Grosvenor Hse. Publishing Ltd.

Perkins, Mike. Iron Fist Vol. 1: The Trial of the Seven Masters. 2017. (ENG.). 112p. (YA). (gr. 8-17). pap. 15.99 (978-1-302-90776-1(X)) Marvel Worldwide, Inc.

—Iron Fist Vol. 2: Sabertooth - Round 2. 2018. (ENG.). 160p. (YA). (gr. 8-17). pap. 17.99 (978-1-302-90777-8(8)) Marvel Worldwide, Inc.

Perkins, Mike, et al. Thor: the Trial of Thor. 2017. (ENG.). 288p. (YA). (gr. 8-17). pap. 29.99 (978-1-302-90795-2(6)) Marvel Worldwide, Inc.

Perkins, Mike, jt. illus. see Guice, Butch.

Perkins, Nancy. Ben of the Island: The Iceboats & the Phantom Ship. Kerr, Terilyn. 2020. (ENG.). 36p. (J). pap. **(978-1-987852-26-4(5))** Wood Islands Prints.

Perkins, Nancy. Mother Goose Coloring Book. Greenaway, Kate. 2013. (Dover Coloring Bks.). (ENG.). 48p. (J). (gr. -1-8). pap. 4.99 (978-0-486-22883-9(5)) Dover Pubns., Inc.

Perkins, Nicole & Frisk, Maria. I Believe God Will: Book of Devotion & Prayer for Children. Perkins, Nicole. 2008. 32p. (J). 7.00 (978-0-9755566-1-0(4)) Azreal Publishing Co.

Perkins, R. Earth Whispers. 32p. (J). (gr. 3-18). 16.00 (978-0-9710860-2-9(8)) Libros, Encouraging Cultural Literacy.

Perkins, Rodney R., jt. illus. see VanDerTuuk-Perkins, Jennifer E.

Perkins, Ruth. Dozens & Dozens of Cousins & Cousins. Young, Elizabeth L. 2012. 30p. 20.95 (978-1-61633-353-9(7)); pap. 12.95 (978-1-61633-352-2(9)) Guardian Angel Publishing, Inc.

Perkins, Sarah. Talulla Bear Goes Exploring: A Mindful Tale of Discovery. Robbins, Heather Roan. 2017. (ENG.). 32p. (J). 16.95 (978-1-78249-471-3(5), 1782494715, Cico Kidz) Ryland Peters & Small GBR. Dist: Simon & Schuster, Inc.

Perkins, Terrell D. I Know When the Rainbow Comes. Perkins, Miss Quinn. 2013. 28p. pap. 9.95 (978-0-9851628-0-1(5)) Soulful Storytellers, Inc.

Perkins, William C. & Perkins, Lori L. What Makes Honey? Perkins, Myrna. 32p. (Orig.). (J). (gr. -1-3). pap. 3.95 (978-0-937729-03-8(5)) Markins Enterprises.

Perks, Anne-Marie. The Silkie. Horn, Sandra. 2017. (ENG.). 46p. (J). pap. (978-1-909568-11-2(2)) Clucket Pr., The.

Perks, Brad, photos by. Inspirational Harvest & Hope: Brad Perks California Vineyards. Perks, Brad. 2008. 128p. (YA). 24.95 (978-0-9788442-1-9(1)) Perks, Brad Lightscapes Photo Gallery.

Perla, Brian. NiNi Spergelini: Guitar-ific! Spergel, Heather. 2013. (NiNi Spergelini Ser.: 1). (ENG.). 32p. (J). 18.99 (978-0-9832148-5-4(9)) Turn the Page Publishing.

Perla, Fabio. The Mermaid the Girl & the Gondola. Ayachi, Janette. Turoni, Monica, ed. 2016. (ENG.). 73p. (J). (gr. 3-6). (978-1-911424-16-1(5)) Black Wolf Edition & Publishing Ltd.

Perlin, Don, et al. Defenders Epic Collection: the End of All Songs. 2019. (ENG.). 488p. (YA). (gr. 4-17). pap. 39.99 (978-1-302-92070-8(7)) Marvel Worldwide, Inc.

Perlman, Janet. The Delicious Bug. Perlman, Janet. 32p. (J). (gr. -1-2). 2013. (ENG.). 7.95 (978-1-77138-034-8(9)); 2009. 16.95 (978-1-55337-996-6(9)) Kids Can Pr., Ltd. CAN. Dist: Hachette Bk. Group.

Perlow, Janet. Show Dog. 2007. 40p. (J). pap. 14.95 incl. audio compact disk (978-0-9795049-0-7(2)) Kidz Entertainment, Inc.

—Show Dog Coloring Book. 2007. 40p. (J). pap. 4.95 (978-0-9795049-1-4(0)) Kidz Entertainment, Inc.

Permane, Terry, jt. photos by see Palone, Terry.

Perna, Debi. A Great Round Wonder: My Book of the World. Tanaka, Shelley. (J). 4.99 (978-1-55054-213-4(3), Da Capo Pr. Inc.) Hachette Bks.

Pernisco, Atilio. Grandma's Pear Tree. Santillan, Suzanne. 2010. (ENG.). 32p. (J). (gr. 4-7). 16.95 (978-1-934960-82-0(9), Raven Tree Pr.,Csi) Continental Sales, Inc.

Peróls, Sylvaine. Atlas de los animales en peligro. 2nd ed. (Coleccion Mundo Maravilloso). (SPA.). 36p. (J). (gr. 2-4). (978-84-348-5730-8(8), SM0429) SM Ediciones.

Pérols, Sylvaine. El Raton y Otros Roedores. Pérols, Sylvaine. Millet, Claude et al. Jeunesse, Gallimard & Delafosse, Claude, trs. (Coleccion Mundo Maravilloso). (SPA.). 40p. (J). (gr. 2-4). (978-84-348-3727-0(7), SM5471) SM Ediciones ESP. Dist: Lectorum Pubns., Inc.

Perras, Marielle. Bravery is like Love. Chalifoux, Lisa M. 2009. 24p. pap. 10.99 (978-1-4269-0942-9(X)) Trafford Publishing.

Perrault, Charles, jt. illus. see Clarke, Harry.

Perreault, Guillaume. Rock Mammoth. Payette, Eveline. Simon, Karen, tr. from FRE. 2020. (ENG.). 48p. (J). (gr. 4-7). pap. 12.95 **(978-1-4598-2426-3(1))** Orca Bk. Pubs. USA.

Perreault, Guillaume. Sleep, Sheep! Sparrow, Kerry. 2018. (ENG.). 32p. (J). (gr. -1-2). 16.99 (978-1-77138-796-5(3)) Kids Can Pr., Ltd. CAN. Dist: Hachette Bk. Group.

Perret, Delphine. The Pointless Leopard: What Good Are Kids Anyway? Gutman, Colas. Seegmuller, Stephanie, tr. 2014. (ENG.). 40p. (J). (gr. 2-4). pap. 9.99 (978-1-78269-040-5(9), Pushkin Press) Steerforth Pr.

Perret, Delphine. A Bear Named Bjorn: Six Bear Stories. Perret, Delphine. 2020. (ENG.). 64p. (J). (gr. k-3). 17.99 (978-1-77657-269-4(6)) Gecko Pr. NZL. Dist: Lerner Publishing Group.

—Pedro & George. Perret, Delphine. 2015. (ENG.). 32p. (J). (gr. -1-3). 17.99 (978-1-4814-2925-2(6)) Simon & Schuster Children's Publishing.

Perrett, Lisa. Keeker & the Pony Camp Catastrophe: Book 5 in the Sneaky Pony Series, Bk. 5. Higginson, Hadley. 2007. (Keeker & the Sneaky Pony Ser.: KEEK). (ENG.). 56p. (J). (gr. k-3). per. 4.99 (978-0-8118-5597-6(X)) Chronicle Bks. LLC.

—Sugar & Spice. Wax, Wendy. 2007. (ENG.). 24p. (J). (gr. 1-4). per. 3.99 (978-1-58476-614-8(X), IKIDS) Innovative Kids.

—Sugar & Spice - Fashion Girls. Innovative Kids Staff. 2006. (ENG.). 10p. (J). (gr. -1-1). 19.99 (978-1-58476-487-8(2), IKIDS) Innovative Kids.

—Wacky Things about Humans Body: Weird & Amazing Facts about Our Bodies! Rhatigan, Joe. 2019. (Wacky Things Ser.). (ENG.). 32p. (J). (gr. 3-5). lib. bdg. 27.99 (978-1-942875-72-7(X), Walter Foster Jr) Quarto Publishing Group USA.

—Wacky Things Humans Do: Weird & Amazing Facts about Our Bodies! Rhatigan, Joe. 2019. (Wacky Things Ser.). (ENG.). 32p. (J). (gr. 3-5). lib. bdg. 27.99 (978-1-942875-71-0(1), Walter Foster Jr) Quarto Publishing Group USA.

—You've Got Spirit! Cheers, Chants, Tips, & Tricks Every Cheerleader Needs to Know. Hunt, Sara R. ed. 2015. (ENG.). 48p. (J). (gr. 3-6). E-Book 53.32 (978-1-4677-5991-5(0), 9781467759915, Lerner Digital) Lerner Publishing Group.

—50 Wacky Things Humans Do: Weird & Amazing Facts about the Human Body! Walter Foster Jr. Creative Team. 2017. (Wacky Ser.). (ENG.). 112p. (J). (gr. 2-6). 16.95 (978-1-63322-396-7(5), Walter Foster Jr) Quarto Publishing Group USA.

Perri, Anthony F. Repo Elf. Sims, Tom. 2008. (ENG.). 104p. (J). 12.95 (978-0-9787213-4-3(9), Cambridge House Pr.) Sterling & Ross Pubs.

Perrigot, Susan. The Adventures of Billie & Pillie. Evans, Christopher J. 2019. (ENG.). 82p. (J). (gr. k-6). pap. 9.95 (978-1-946540-91-1(9)) Strategic Book Publishing & Rights Agency (SBPRA).

Perrin, Clotilde. The House of Madame M. Perrin, Clotilde. 2020. (ENG.). 10p. (J). (gr. k-3). 21.99 (978-1-77657-274-8(2)) Gecko Pr. NZL. Dist: Lerner Publishing Group.

—Inside the Villains. Perrin, Clotilde. 2018. (ENG.). 12p. (J). (gr. k-3). 21.99 (978-1-77657-198-7(3)) Gecko Pr. NZL. Dist: Lerner Publishing Group.

Perrin, Martine. What Do You See? Perrin, Martine. 2011. (ENG.). 16p. (J). (gr. -1-1). bds. 8.99 (978-0-8075-6712-8(4), 807567124) Whitman, Albert & Co.

Perrin, Renaud. Sagesses et Malices du Touareg Qui Avait Oublié Son Chameau. Siccardi, Jean. 2003. (A. M. Sag Malice Ser.). (FRE.). 171p. (J). (978-2-226-11966-7(3)) Albin-Michel, Editions.

Perrine, Doug, photos by. Sharks: Biggest! Littlest! Markle, Sandra. 2011. (Biggest! Littlest! Ser.). (ENG., 32p. (J). (gr. k-2). pap. 10.95 (978-1-59078-867-7(7)) Boyds Mills Pr.

Perrini, Angela. What's in Your Mind Today? Bladen, Louise. 2020. (ENG.). 32p. (J). (gr. -1-3). 17.99 (978-1-5064-6377-3(0), Beaming Books) Augsburg Fortress, Pubs.

Perritt, Jordona. Cowgirls Dream. Johnson, Sandi. Date not set. (Kooky Kountry Ser.). (J). (gr. -1-6). 8.99 (978-1-929063-56-7(3)) Moons & Stars Publishing For Children.

Perron, Debra. Imagination Goodnight. Burlinson, J. 2005. 24p. (J). 14.95 (978-1-59879-068-9(4)) Lifevest Publishing, Inc.

Perroud, Benoit. Dinosaurs & Other Prehistoric Creatures: 45 Magnetic Pieces. Laboucarie, Sandra. 2017. (Magnetology Ser.: 4). (ENG.). 12p. (J). (gr. -1-k). 21.99 Éditions Tourbillon FRA. Dist: Hachette Bk. Group.

Perruzzi, Diane. Over in My City: San Francisco. Tong, Anthony. 2018. (ENG.). 38p. (J). pap. 9.99 **(978-0-9981412-0-6(8))** Otto PD.

Perry, Adam. The Magicians of Elephant County. Perry, Adam. 2018. (ENG.). 384p. (J). (gr. 3-7). 16.99 (978-0-06-279535-9(X)) HarperCollins Pubs.

Perry, Aumi. Wyoming Trail Ride. Bean, Margo Cronbaugh. l.t. ed. 2017. (ENG.). (J). (gr. k-4). 19.95 (978-1-61633-900-5(4)) Guardian Angel Publishing, Inc.

Perry, Aumi Kauffman. Brutus the Bull. Bean, Margo Cronbaugh. 2013. 24p. 19.95 (978-1-61633-373-7(1)); pap. 11.95 (978-1-61633-374-4(X)) Guardian Angel Publishing, Inc.

—Buffaloed Badger. Bean, Margo Cronbaugh. 2012. 24p. 19.95 (978-1-61633-239-6(5)); pap. 11.95 (978-1-61633-240-2(9)) Guardian Angel Publishing, Inc.

—Midnight the Kitten. Bean, Margo Cronbaugh. l.t. ed. 2016. (ENG.). (J). (gr. k-3). 19.95 (978-1-61633-797-1(4)); pap. 11.95 (978-1-61633-800-8(8)) Guardian Angel Publishing, Inc.

—Vivacious Aunt Violet. Bean, Margo Cronbaugh. l.t. ed. 2019. (ENG.). 24p. (J). (gr. k-4). 19.95 (978-1-61633-973-9(X)); pap. 11.95 (978-1-61633-974-6(8)) Guardian Angel Publishing, Inc.

—Wyoming Trail Ride. Bean, Margo Cronbaugh. l.t. ed. 2017. (ENG.). (J). (gr. k-4). pap. 11.95 (978-1-61633-901-2(2)) Guardian Angel Publishing, Inc.

Perry, Charles, photos by. The Legend of Scarface. Perry, Charles. 2005. (ENG., 12p. (J). 5.75 (978-1-57274-752-4(8), 2764, Bks. for Young Learners) Owen, Richard C. Pubs., Inc.

Perry, Curtis. Always Remember You Are Loved: When a Child Seeks Guidance on Cyber & Peer Bullying. Washington, Angel D. 2012. 40p. pap. 9.95 (978-0-9860041-1-7(1)) Angel's Diary.

Perry, Diana Torri. Clumsy Claudia & the Gentle Forest Friends, 1 vol. Perry, Brad Lee. 2010. 56p. pap. 16.95 (978-1-4489-4633-4(6)) America Star Bks.

Perry, Fred. Cymbeline: Graphic Novel, 1 vol. Shakespeare, William. 2010. (Graphic Shakespeare Ser.). (ENG.). 48p. (J). (gr. 5-10). 31.35 (978-1-60270-763-4(4), 9160, Graphic Planet - Fiction) Magic Wagon.

—Julius Caesar: Graphic Novel, 1 vol. Shakespeare, William. 2010. (Graphic Shakespeare Ser.). (ENG.). 48p. (J). (gr. 5-10). 31.35 (978-1-60270-765-8(0), 9164, Graphic Planet - Fiction) Magic Wagon.

Perry, Gala. A Girl's Guide to Growing up - Booklet, 10 per packet. Smith, Liz. 2005. (J). 63.95 (978-1-55942-207-9(6)) Witcher Productions.

Perry, Gina. It's Great Being a Dad. Bar-El, Dan. 2017. (ENG.). 32p. (J). (gr. -1-3). 16.99 (978-1-77049-605-7(X), Tundra Bks.) Tundra Bks. CAN. Dist: Penguin Random Hse. LLC.

Perry, Jennifer A. TJ & the Good Luck Cricket. Szish, Jill Henry. 2007. 32p. per. 24.95 (978-1-4241-8502-3(5)) America Star Bks.

Perry, Kathy J. Feebs to the Rescue. Perry, Kathy J. Bruno, Elizabeth, ed. 2018. (Bandana Acres Ser.: 1). (ENG.). 50p. (J). (gr. 1-3). pap. 11.00 (978-0-9981291-7-4(8), Chickadee Words) Chickadee Words, LLC.

—Feebs to the Rescue: Night of the Coon. Perry, Kathy J. Bruno, Elizabeth, ed. 2018. (Bandana Acres Ser.: 1). (ENG.). 50p. (J). (gr. 1-3). 18.00 (978-0-9981291-2-9(7), Chickadee Words) Chickadee Words, LLC.

Perry, Lee Ann. Why, Daddy, Why Are There Stars in the Sky? Freeman, Chip. 2012. 20p. (-18). pap. 11.95 (978-1-937770-23-5(0), SPC Bks.) RPJ & Co., Inc.

Perry, Margie. Birdie School Days: The First Day of School. Perrine, David L. 2005. (J). pap. 15.00 (978-0-8059-6699-2(4)) Dorrance Publishing Co., Inc.

Perry, Marie. A Gift for Sadia. Perry, Marie. l.t. ed. 2005. 32p. (J). lib. bdg. 15.95 (978-0-9755675-1-7(9)) Buttonweed Pr., L.L.C.

Perry, Marie/Fritz. Cecil's New Year's Eve Tail. Perry, Marie/Fritz. 2007. 32p. (J). lib. bdg. (978-0-9755675-2-4(7)) Buttonweed Pr., L.L.C.

Perry, Matt, jt. illus. see Unalp, Janet.

Perry, Mike. Libra: Decisions, Decisions. Tea, Michelle. 2019. (Astro Pals Ser.). (ENG.). 56p. (J). 18.95 (978-1-948340-14-4(3)) Dottir Pr.

—Scorpio: Berry Intense. Tea, Michelle. 2019. (Astro Pals Ser.). (ENG.). 56p. (J). 18.95 (978-1-948340-15-1(1)) Dottir Pr.

—Z Goes First. Lamb, Sean. 2018. (ENG.). 32p. (J). 17.99 (978-1-250-12395-4(X), 900174333) Imprint IND. Dist: Macmillan.

Perry, Rex. All Things Bright & Beautiful. 2004. 24p. (J). lib. bdg. 8.00 (978-1-4242-0638-4(3)) Fitzgerald Bks.

—Over the River & Through the Woods. 2004. 24p. (J). lib. bdg. 8.00 (978-1-4242-0640-7(5)) Fitzgerald Bks.

—'Twas the Night Before Christmas. 2004. 24p. (J). lib. bdg. 8.00 (978-1-4242-0641-4(3)) Fitzgerald Bks.

Perry, Rex. Coco's Girls. Perry, Rex. 2008. (ENG.). 36p. (YA). per. 12.95 (978-0-9740212-1-8(0)) Cedar Grove Bks.

Perry, Trudy. Wee Willie Winkie III. Wiedmeyer, Nancy. 2018. (ENG.). 32p. (J). 15.99 (978-0-9996085-6-2(8)) Mindstir Media.

Perry-Warnes, Ned. A Story for Christmas. Clare, Elisabeth. 2017. (ENG.). (J). pap. *(978-1-912192-79-3(9))* Mirador Publishing.

Persiani, Tony. The Day-Glo Brothers: The True Story of Bob & Joe Switzer's Bright Ideas & Brand-New Colors. Barton, Chris. 2009. 44p. (J). (gr. 2-5). 19.95 *(978-1-57091-673-1(X))* Charlesbridge Publishing, Inc.

Persico, Zoe. Aleca Zamm Is a Wonder. Rue, Ginger. 2017. (Aleca Zamm Ser.: 1). (ENG.). 160p. (J). (gr. 2-5). 16.99 *(978-1-4814-7061-2(2)*, Aladdin) Simon & Schuster Children's Publishing.

—Fluttershy's Ferocious Friend! (My Little Pony) May, Tallulah. 2019. (Little Golden Book Ser.). (ENG.). 24p. (J). (-k). 4.99 *(978-1-5247-6976-5(2)*, Golden Bks.) Random Hse. Children's Bks.

—Jack & the Beanstalk: Small Padded Board Book. Crowe, Carmen. 2017. (Little Bird Stories Ser.). (ENG.). 12p. (J). (gr. -1-k). bds. 6.99 *(978-1-68052-152-8(7)*, 1001460) Cottage Door Pr.

—Little Blue Boat: Chunky Lift a Flap Board Book. Swift, Ginger. Cottage Door Press, ed. 2016. (Lift a Flap Ser.). (ENG.). 12p. (J). (gr. -1-k). bds. 7.99 *(978-1-68052-077-4(6)*, 1000800) Cottage Door Pr.

—Me & My Cat. Dahl, Michael. 2016. (Me & My Pet Ser.). (ENG.). 24p. (J). (gr. -1-k). lib. bdg. 22.65 *(978-1-5158-0239-6(6)*, Picture Window Bks.) Capstone.

—Me & My Cat. Dahl, Michael. 2016. (Me & My Pet Ser.). (ENG.). 24p. (J). (gr. -1-k). 6.95 *(978-1-62370-794-1(3)*, Capstone Young Readers) Capstone.

—Me & My Dog. Dahl, Michael. 2016. (Me & My Pet Ser.). (ENG.). 24p. (J). (gr. -1-k). 6.95 *(978-1-62370-793-4(5)*, Capstone Young Readers); lib. bdg. 22.65 *(978-1-5158-0238-9(8)*, Picture Window Bks.) Capstone.

—Mermaids Fast Asleep. Riding, Robin. 2019. (ENG.). 32p. (J). 17.99 *(978-1-250-07635-9(8)*, 900152143) Feiwel & Friends.

—My Adopted Family. Harrington, Claudia. 2017. (My Family Set 2 Ser.). 32p. (J). (gr. -1-4). lib. bdg. 28.50 *(978-1-5321-3016-8(3)*, 25534, Looking Glass Library) Magic Wagon.

—My Blended Family. Harrington, Claudia. 2017. (My Family Set 2 Ser.). 32p. (J). (gr. -1-4). lib. bdg. 28.50 *(978-1-5321-3017-5(1)*, 25536, Looking Glass Library) Magic Wagon.

—My First-Generation Family. Harrington, Claudia. 2017. (My Family Set 2 Ser.). 32p. (J). (gr. -1-4). lib. bdg. 28.50 *(978-1-5321-3018-2(X)*, 25538, Looking Glass Library) Magic Wagon.

—My Grandparents, 1 vol. Harrington, Claudia. 2015. (My Family Ser.). 32p. (J). (gr. -1-3). 28.50 *(978-1-62402-105-3(0)*, 18152, Looking Glass Library) Magic Wagon.

—My Military Mom, 1 vol. Harrington, Claudia. 2015. (My Family Ser.). 32p. (J). (gr. -1-3). 28.50 *(978-1-62402-106-0(9)*, 18154, Looking Glass Library) Magic Wagon.

—My Mom & Dad, 1 vol. Harrington, Claudia. 2015. (My Family Ser.). 32p. (J). (gr. -1-3). 28.50 *(978-1-62402-107-7(7)*, 18156, Looking Glass Library) Magic Wagon.

—My Single Dad. Harrington, Claudia. 2017. (My Family Set 2 Ser.). 32p. (J). (gr. -1-4). lib. bdg. 28.50 *(978-1-5321-3019-9(8)*, 25540, Looking Glass Library) Magic Wagon.

—My Single Mom. Harrington, Claudia. 2017. (My Family Set 2 Ser.). 32p. (J). (gr. -1-4). lib. bdg. 28.50 *(978-1-5321-3020-5(1)*, 25542, Looking Glass Library) Magic Wagon.

—My Special Needs Family. Harrington, Claudia. 2017. (My Family Set 2 Ser.). 32p. (J). (gr. -1-4). lib. bdg. 28.50 *(978-1-5321-3021-2(X)*, 25544, Looking Glass Library) Magic Wagon.

—My Two Dads, 1 vol. Harrington, Claudia. 2015. (My Family Ser.). 32p. (J). (gr. -1-3). 28.50 *(978-1-62402-108-4(5)*, 18158, Looking Glass Library) Magic Wagon.

—My Two Homes, 1 vol. Harrington, Claudia. 2015. (My Family Ser.). 32p. (J). (gr. -1-3). 28.50 *(978-1-62402-109-1(3)*, 18160, Looking Glass Library) Magic Wagon.

—My Two Moms, 1 vol. Harrington, Claudia. 2015. (My Family Ser.). 32p. (J). (gr. -1-3). 28.50 *(978-1-62402-110-7(7)*, 18162, Looking Glass Library) Magic Wagon.

—Pinkie Pie Big Baking Bonanza! May, Tallulah. 2018. (J). *(978-1-5444-0210-9(4)*, Golden Bks.) Random Hse. Children's Bks.

—Rainbow Dash: Reading Rainboom! May, Tallulah. 2018. (J). *(978-1-5444-0924-5(9)*, Golden Bks.) Random Hse. Children's Bks.

—Summer Color! Murray, Diana. 2018. 40p. (J). (gr. -1-3). 17.99 *(978-0-316-37094-3(0))* Little, Brown Bks. for Young Readers.

Persico, Zoe. The Whatifs. Kilgore, Emily. 2020. (ENG.). 40p. (J). (gr. -1-3). 17.99 ***(978-1-4998-1029-5(6))*** Little Bee Books Inc.

Persico, Zoe. Wild Bios: Neil Armswan. Acampora, Courtney & Fischer, Maggie. 2019. (Wild Bios Ser.). (ENG.). 16p. (J). (— 1). bds. 7.99 *(978-1-68412-714-6(9)*, Silver Dolphin Bks.) Printers Row Publishing Group.

Persico, Zoe & Persico, Zoe. You Be Mommy. Clark, Karla. 2020. (ENG.). 208p. (J). 17.99 *(978-1-250-22538-2(8)*, 900208515) Feiwel & Friends.

Persico, Zoe, jt. illus. see Golden Books.

Persico, Zoe, jt. illus. see Pavon, David.

Persico, Zoe, jt. illus. see Persico, Zoe.

Person, Elizabeth. To Live on an Island. Smith, Emma Bland. 2019. 32p. (J). (gr. -1-1). 17.99 *(978-1-61067-181-8(3)*, Little Bigfoot) Sasquatch Bks.

Pertile, Paula. The Gingerbread Man. 2010. (J). *(978-1-60617-141-7(0))* Teaching Strategies, LLC.

—Number One Puppy. Wilson, Zachary. 2011. (Rookie Ready to Learn Ser.). 40p. (J). pap. 5.95 *(978-0-531-26748-6(2))*; (gr. -1-k). lib. bdg. 23.00 *(978-0-531-26448-5(3))* Scholastic Library Publishing. (Children's Pr.).

Perucca, Nancy Call. Multiplication Camp. Perucca, Nancy Call. Evans, Renee Call. 2004. (J). pap. 29.95 *(978-0-9748074-0-9(0))* Nancy's Artworks.

—Sea Notes on the Keyboard: The Fast & Fun Way to Learn the Notes on the Keyboard! Perucca, Nancy Call. Evans, Renee Call. 2004. 32p. (J). pap. 9.95 *(978-0-9748074-1-6(9))* Nancy's Artworks.

Perunko, Linda. My Grandma Is an Angel Now. Havens, Sarita. 2008. 12p. pap. 24.95 *(978-1-60672-350-0(2))* America Star Bks.

Peruzzo, Nicolas. Safari Dreams. Peruzzo, Nicolas. 2012. 26p. pap. 9.99 *(978-1-61225-162-2(5))* Mirror Publishing.

Pervan, Ivo & Bemporad, Alex, photos by. Fate Did Not Let Me Go: A Mother's Farewell Letter, 1 vol. Ollendorff, Valli. 2003. (ENG., 48p. 5.95 *(978-1-58980-153-0(9)*, Pelican Publishing) Arcadia Publishing.

Peschel, Georgia. A Real Meal Table Fable. Chen, Sam. 2007. 60p. (J). *(978-0-9800764-0-0(4))* Uncle Jim's Publishing.

Pesenti, Antonia. Summer Time. Bell, Hilary. 2020. 44p. (J). 24.99 ***(978-1-74223-607-0(3)***, NewSouth) NewSouth Publishing AUS. Dist: Independent Pubs. Group.

Peskimo. A Box of Blocks. Franceschelli, Christopher. 2017. (ENG.). 290p. (J). (gr. -1 — 1). bds. 50.00 *(978-1-4197-2818-1(0)*, Abrams Appleseed) Abrams, Inc.

—Buildablock. Franceschelli, Christopher. 2017. (Alphablock Ser.). (ENG.). 90p. (J). (gr. -1 — 1). bds. 16.95 *(978-1-4197-2569-2(6)*, Abrams Appleseed) Abrams, Inc.

—Cityblock. Franceschelli, Christopher. 2016. (ENG.). 96p. (J). (gr. -1-k). bds. 16.95 *(978-1-4197-2189-2(5)*, Abrams Appleseed) Abrams, Inc.

—Dinoblock. Franceschelli, Christopher. 2015. (ENG.). 96p. (J). (gr. -1 — 1). bds. 16.95 *(978-1-4197-1674-4(3))* Abrams, Inc.

—Disney Block: Magical Moments for Fans of Every Age. Abrams Appleseed. 2020. (Abrams Block Book Ser.). (ENG.). 102p. (J). bds. 16.99 *(978-1-4197-4057-2(1)*, 1300910, Abrams Appleseed) Abrams, Inc.

—Farmblock. Franceschelli, Christopher. 2019. (ENG.). 92p. (J). (gr. -1 — 1). bds. 16.99 *(978-1-4197-3825-8(9)*, 1286510, Abrams Appleseed) Abrams, Inc.

—Marvel Alphablock: The Marvel Cinematic Universe from a to Z. 2019. (ENG.). 104p. (J). 16.99 *(978-1-4197-3588-2(8)*, Abrams Appleseed) Abrams, Inc.

—Star Wars Block: Over 100 Words Every Fan Should Know. Lucasfilm LTD. 2018. (ENG.). 104p. (J). (gr. -1-k). bds. 16.99 *(978-1-4197-2831-0(8)*, Abrams Appleseed) Abrams, Inc.

Pessarrodona, Marina. Leave It to Me! O'Sullivan, Jill Korey. 2018. (ENG.). 34p. (J). (gr. k-4). pap. 9.99 *(978-1-63233-112-0(8))* Eifrig Publishing.

Petelinsek, Kathleen. Actions/Las Acciones. Berendes, Mary. 2008. (WordBooks/Libros de Palabras Ser.). (SPA & ENG.). 24p. (J). (gr. k-3). 25.64 *(978-1-59296-987-6(9)*, 201085) Child's World, Inc., The.

—Adjectives. Gregory, Josh. 2013. (Explorer Junior Library: the Parts of Speech Ser.). (ENG.). 24p. (J). (gr. 1-4). 25.64 *(978-1-62431-180-2(6)*, 203040); pap. 12.79 *(978-1-62431-312-7(4)*, 203042) Cherry Lake Publishing.

—Adverbs. Gregory, Josh. 2013. (Explorer Junior Library: the Parts of Speech Ser.). (ENG.). 24p. (J). (gr. 1-4). 25.64 *(978-1-62431-183-3(0)*, 203052); pap. 12.79 *(978-1-62431-315-8(9)*, 203054) Cherry Lake Publishing.

—Animals. Thornborough, Kathy. 2014. (Talking Hands Ser.). (ENG.). 24p. (J). (gr. k-3). 25.64 *(978-1-62687-314-8(3)*, 207154) Child's World, Inc., The.

—Beauty & the Beast. Higgins, Nadia. 2013. (Fairy Tale Collection). (ENG.). 24p. (J). (gr. k-3). 28.50 *(978-1-62323-607-6(X)*, 206374) Child's World, Inc., The.

—Being Respectful Online. Truesdell, Ann. 2013. (Explorer Junior Library: Information Explorer Junior Ser.). (ENG.). 24p. (J). (gr. 1-4). 28.50 *(978-1-62431-131-4(8)*, 202844); pap. 12.79 *(978-1-62431-263-2(2)*, 202846) Cherry Lake Publishing.

—Ben's Hen. Alinas, Marv. 2018. (Rhyming Word Families Ser.). (ENG.). 24p. (J). (gr. -1-2). lib. bdg. 27.07 *(978-1-5038-2352-5(0)*, 212185) Child's World, Inc., The.

—The Best Log in the Bog. Alinas, Marv. 2018. (Rhyming Word Families Ser.). (ENG.). 24p. (J). (gr. -1-2). lib. bdg. 27.07 *(978-1-5038-2356-3(3)*, 212191) Child's World, Inc., The.

—The Blob on Bob. Alinas, Marv. 2018. (Rhyming Word Families Ser.). (ENG.). 24p. (J). (gr. -1-2). lib. bdg. 27.07 *(978-1-5038-2355-6(5)*, 212192) Child's World, Inc., The.

—The Bug on the Rug. Alinas, Marv. 2018. (Rhyming Word Families Ser.). (ENG.). 24p. (J). (gr. -1-2). lib. bdg. 27.07 *(978-1-5038-2358-7(X)*, 212193) Child's World, Inc., The.

—Chap's Cap. Alinas, Marv. 2019. (Rhyming Word Families Ser.). (ENG.). 24p. (J). (gr. -1-2). lib. bdg. 27.07 *(978-1-5038-2762-2(3)*, 212659) Child's World, Inc., The.

—Choose It! Finding the Right Research Topic. Coleman, Kelly. 2015. (Explorer Junior Library: Information Explorer Junior Ser.). (ENG.). 24p. (J). (gr. 1-4). 29.93 *(978-1-63188-862-5(5)*, 206028) Cherry Lake Publishing.

—Cinderella. Higgins, Nadia. 2013. (Fairy Tale Collection). (ENG.). 24p. (J). (gr. k-3). 28.50 *(978-1-62323-608-3(8)*, 206375) Child's World, Inc., The.

—Cinquain Poems. Simons, Lisa M. Bolt. 2015. (Poetry Party Ser.). (ENG.). 24p. (J). (gr. 2-5). 27.07 *(978-1-63143-693-2(7)*, 208528) Child's World, Inc., The.

—Clothes/la Ropa. Berendes, Mary. 2008. (WordBooks/Libros de Palabras Ser.). (SPA & ENG.). 24p. (J). (gr. k-3). 25.64 *(978-1-59296-989-0(5)*, 201089) Child's World, Inc., The.

—Colors & Shapes. Thornborough, Kathy. 2014. (Talking Hands Ser.). (ENG.). 24p. (J). (gr. k-3). 25.64 *(978-1-62687-315-5(1)*, 207155) Child's World, Inc., The.

—Concrete Poems. Pearson, Yvonne. 2015. (Poetry Party Ser.). (ENG.). 24p. (J). (gr. 2-5). 27.07 *(978-1-63143-694-9(5)*, 208529) Child's World, Inc., The.

—Conjunctions. Marsico, Katie. 2013. (Explorer Junior Library: the Parts of Speech Ser.). (ENG.). 24p. (J). (gr. 1-4). 25.64 *(978-1-62431-181-9(4)*, 203044); pap. 12.79 *(978-1-62431-313-4(2)*, 203046) Cherry Lake Publishing.

—A Crab in the Cab. Alinas, Marv. 2018. (Rhyming Word Families Ser.). (ENG.). 24p. (J). (gr. -1-2). lib. bdg. 27.07 *(978-1-5038-2348-8(2)*, 212183) Child's World, Inc., The.

—Crafting with Duct Tape. Rau, Dana Meachen. 2013. (How-To Library). (ENG.). 32p. (J). (gr. 3-6). 28.50 *(978-1-62431-147-5(4)*, 202908); pap. 14.21 *(978-1-62431-279-3(9)*, 202910) Cherry Lake Publishing.

—Crafting with Recyclables. Rau, Dana Meachen. 2013. (How-To Library). (ENG.). 32p. (J). (gr. 3-6). 28.50 *(978-1-62431-146-8(6)*, 202904); pap. 14.21 *(978-1-62431-278-6(0)*, 202906) Cherry Lake Publishing.

—Crafting with Recyclables: Even More Projects. Rau, Dana Meachen. 2016. (How-To Library). (ENG.). 32p. (J). (gr. 3-6). lib. bdg. 29.93 *(978-1-63471-419-8(9)*, 208455) Cherry Lake Publishing.

—Creating Digital Brochures. Newman, Heather. 2013. (Explorer Library: Information Explorer Ser.). (ENG.). 32p. (J). (gr. 4-8). 28.50 *(978-1-62431-128-4(8)*, 202832); pap. 14.21 *(978-1-62431-260-1(8)*, 202834) Cherry Lake Publishing.

—Creating Halloween Crafts. Rau, Dana Meachen. 2013. (How-To Library). (ENG.). 32p. (J). (gr. 3-6). 28.50 *(978-1-62431-149-9(0)*, 202916); pap. 14.21 *(978-1-62431-281-6(0)*, 202918) Cherry Lake Publishing.

—Creating Thanksgiving Crafts. Rau, Dana Meachen. 2013. (How-To Library). (ENG.). 32p. (J). (gr. 3-6). 28.50 *(978-1-62431-148-2(2)*, 202912); pap. 14.21 *(978-1-62431-280-9(2)*, 202914) Cherry Lake Publishing.

—Creating Winter Crafts. Rau, Dana Meachen. 2013. (How-To Library). (ENG.). 32p. (J). (gr. 3-6). 28.50 *(978-1-62431-150-5(4)*, 202920); pap. 14.21 *(978-1-62431-282-3(9)*, 202922) Cherry Lake Publishing.

—A Cub in the Tub. Alinas, Marv. 2018. (Rhyming Word Families Ser.). (ENG.). 24p. (J). (gr. -1-2). lib. bdg. 27.07 *(978-1-5038-2357-0(1)*, 212184) Child's World, Inc., The.

—Days & Times. Thornborough, Kathy. 2014. (Talking Hands Ser.). (ENG.). 24p. (J). (gr. k-3). 25.64 *(978-1-62687-316-2(X)*, 207156) Child's World, Inc., The.

—Days & Times (Los Días y Las Horas) Berendes, Mary. 2008. (WordBooks/Libros de Palabras Ser.). (ENG.). 24p. (J). (gr. k-3). 25.64 *(978-1-59296-990-6(9)*, 201090) Child's World, Inc., The.

—Feelings/Las Emociones. Berendes, Mary. 2007. (WordBooks/Libros de Palabras Ser.). (SPA & ENG.). 24p. (J). (gr. k-3). 25.64 *(978-1-59296-797-1(3)*, 201091) Child's World, Inc., The.

—The Fisherman & His Wife. Felix, Rebecca. 2013. (Fairy Tale Collection). (ENG.). 24p. (J). (gr. k-3). 28.50 *(978-1-62323-611-3(8)*, 206378) Child's World, Inc., The.

—Folding Origami. Rau, Dana Meachen. 2013. (How-To Library). (ENG.). 32p. (J). (gr. 3-6). 28.50 *(978-1-62431-145-1(8)*, 202900); pap. 14.21 *(978-1-62431-277-9(2)*, 202902) Cherry Lake Publishing.

—Food. Thornborough, Kathy. 2014. (Talking Hands Ser.). (ENG.). 24p. (J). (gr. k-3). 25.64 *(978-1-62687-319-3(4)*, 207159) Child's World, Inc., The.

—Food/la Comida. Berendes, Mary. 2007. (WordBooks/Libros de Palabras Ser.). (SPA & ENG.). 24p. (J). (gr. k-3). 25.64 *(978-1-59296-798-8(1)*, 201092) Child's World, Inc., The.

—Fun in the Sun. Alinas, Marv. 2018. (Rhyming Word Families Ser.). (ENG.). 24p. (J). (gr. -1-2). lib. bdg. 27.07 *(978-1-5038-2359-4(8)*, 212186) Child's World, Inc., The.

—Haikus. Simons, Lisa M. Bolt. 2015. (Poetry Party Ser.). (ENG.). 24p. (J). (gr. 2-5). 27.07 *(978-1-63143-695-6(3)*, 208531) Child's World, Inc., The.

—Hansel & Gretel. Higgins, Nadia. 2013. (Fairy Tale Collection). (ENG.). 24p. (J). (gr. k-3). 28.50 *(978-1-62323-609-0(6)*, 206376) Child's World, Inc., The.

—Having Fun with Felting. Rau, Dana Meachen. 2015. (How-To Library). (ENG.). 32p. (J). (gr. 3-6). pap. 14.21 *(978-1-63362-398-9(X)*, 206901) Cherry Lake Publishing.

—Having Fun with Hair Feathering. Rau, Dana Meachen. 2015. (How-To Library). (ENG.). 32p. (J). (gr. 3-6). 29.93 *(978-1-63362-371-2(8)*, 206904) Cherry Lake Publishing.

—House/la Casa. Berendes, Mary. 2008. (WordBooks/Libros de Palabras Ser.). (SPA & ENG.). 24p. (J). (gr. k-3). 25.64 *(978-1-59296-992-0(5)*, 201094) Child's World, Inc., The.

—How to Handle Cyberbullies. Truesdell, Ann. 2013. (Explorer Library: Information Explorer Ser.). (ENG.). 32p. (J). (gr. 4-8). 28.50 *(978-1-62431-127-7(X)*, 202828); pap. 14.21 *(978-1-62431-259-5(4)*, 202830) Cherry Lake Publishing.

—How to Write a Comic Book. Yomtov, Nelson. 2013. (Explorer Junior Library: How to Write Ser.). (ENG.). 24p. (J). (gr. 1-4). lib. bdg. 25.64 *(978-1-62431-187-1(3)*, 203072) Cherry Lake Publishing.

—How to Write a Comic Book. Yomtov, Nel. 2013. (Explorer Junior Library: How to Write Ser.). (ENG.). 24p. (J). (gr. 1-4). pap. 12.79 *(978-1-62431-319-6(1)*, 203074) Cherry Lake Publishing.

—How to Write a Fractured Fairy Tale. Yomtov, Nel. 2013. (Explorer Junior Library: How to Write Ser.). (ENG.). 24p. (J). (gr. 1-4). 25.64 *(978-1-62431-186-4(5)*, 203068); pap. 12.79 *(978-1-62431-318-9(3)*, 203070) Cherry Lake Publishing.

—How to Write a Lab Report. Yomtov, Nel. 2013. (Explorer Junior Library: How to Write Ser.). (ENG.). 24p. (J). (gr. 1-4). 25.64 *(978-1-62431-185-7(7)*, 203064); pap. 12.79 *(978-1-62431-317-2(5)*, 203066) Cherry Lake Publishing.

—How to Write a Memoir. Yomtov, Nel. 2013. (Explorer Junior Library: How to Write Ser.). (ENG.). 24p. (J). (gr. 1-4). 25.64 *(978-1-62431-188-8(1)*, 203076); pap. 12.79 *(978-1-62431-320-2(5)*, 203078) Cherry Lake Publishing.

—Interjections. Marsico, Katie. 2013. (Explorer Junior Library: the Parts of Speech Ser.). (ENG.). 24p. (J). (gr. 1-4). 25.64 *(978-1-62431-184-0(9)*, 203056); pap. 12.79 *(978-1-62431-316-5(7)*, 203058) Cherry Lake Publishing.

—Kip & Pip's Trip. Alinas, Marv. 2019. (Rhyming Word Families Ser.). (ENG.). 24p. (J). (gr. -1-2). lib. bdg. 27.07 *(978-1-5038-2765-3(8)*, 212660) Child's World, Inc., The.

—Kit's Banana Split. Alinas, Marv. 2018. (Rhyming Word Families Ser.). (ENG.). 24p. (J). (gr. -1-2). lib. bdg. 27.07 *(978-1-5038-2354-9(7)*, 212187) Child's World, Inc., The.

—Learn Arabic Words. York, M. J. 2020. (Foreign Language Basics Ser.). (ENG & ARA.). 24p. (J). (gr. 2-5). lib. bdg. 28.50 *(978-1-5038-3579-5(0)*, 213389) Child's World, Inc., The.

—Learn German Words. York, M. J. 2014. (Foreign Language Basics Ser.). (ENG.). 24p. (J). (gr. 2-5). 27.07 *(978-1-62687-375-9(5)*, 207122) Child's World, Inc., The.

—Learn Hindi Words. York, M. J. 2020. (Foreign Language Basics Ser.). (ENG & HIN.). 24p. (J). (gr. 2-5). lib. bdg. 28.50 *(978-1-5038-3584-9(7)*, 213392) Child's World, Inc., The.

—Learn Japanese Words. York, M. J. 2014. (Foreign Language Basics Ser.). (ENG.). 24p. (J). (gr. 2-5). 27.07 *(978-1-62687-376-6(3)*, 207123) Child's World, Inc., The.

—Learn Korean Words. York, M. J. 2020. (Foreign Language Basics Ser.). (ENG & KOR.). 24p. (J). (gr. 2-5). lib. bdg. 28.50 *(978-1-5038-3581-8(2)*, 213394) Child's World, Inc., The.

—Learn Portuguese Words. York, M. J. 2020. (Foreign Language Basics Ser.). (ENG & POR.). 24p. (J). (gr. 2-5). lib. bdg. 28.50 *(978-1-5038-3583-2(9)*, 213396) Child's World, Inc., The.

—Learn Russian Words. York, M. J. 2014. (Foreign Language Basics Ser.). (ENG.). 24p. (J). (gr. 2-5). 27.07 *(978-1-62687-378-0(X)*, 207125) Child's World, Inc., The.

—Learn Tagalog Words. York, M. J. 2020. (Foreign Language Basics Ser.). (ENG & TGL.). 24p. (J). (gr. 2-5). lib. bdg. 28.50 *(978-1-5038-3582-5(0)*, 213399) Child's World, Inc., The.

—Learn Vietnamese Words. York, M. J. 2020. (Foreign Language Basics Ser.). (ENG & VIE.). 24p. (J). (gr. 2-5). lib. bdg. 28.50 *(978-1-5038-3580-1(4)*, 213400) Child's World, Inc., The.

—Learning & Sharing with a Wiki. Fontichiaro, Kristin & Truesdell, Ann. 2013. (Explorer Junior Library: Information Explorer Junior Ser.). (ENG.). 24p. (J). (gr. 1-4). 28.50 *(978-1-62431-132-1(6)*, 202848); pap. 12.79 *(978-1-62431-264-9(0)*, 202850) Cherry Lake Publishing.

—Learning to Crochet. Rau, Dana Meachen. 2016. (How-To Library). (ENG.). 32p. (J). (gr. 3-6). lib. bdg. 29.93 *(978-1-63471-418-1(0)*, 208451) Cherry Lake Publishing.

—Limericks. Pearson, Yvonne. 2015. (Poetry Party Ser.). (ENG.). 24p. (J). (gr. 2-5). 27.07 *(978-1-63143-696-3(1)*, 208532) Child's World, Inc., The.

—The Little Mermaid. Felix, Rebecca. 2013. (Fairy Tale Collection). (ENG.). 24p. (J). (gr. k-3). 28.50 *(978-1-62323-612-0(6)*, 206379) Child's World, Inc., The.

—Little Red Riding Hood. Higgins, Nadia. 2013. (Fairy Tale Collection). (ENG.). 24p. (J). (gr. k-3). 28.50 *(978-1-62323-610-6(X)*, 206377) Child's World, Inc., The.

—Making Knot Projects. Rau, Dana Meachen. 2016. (How-To Library). (ENG.). 32p. (J). (gr. 3-6). 29.93 *(978-1-63471-420-4(2)*, 208459) Cherry Lake Publishing.

—Las Máquinas. Berendes, Mary. 2007. (WordBooks/Libros de Palabras Ser.).Tr. of Machines. (ENG.). 24p. (J). (gr. k-3). 25.64 *(978-1-59296-799-5(X)*, 201095) Child's World, Inc., The.

—Measuring Length. Bailer, Darice. 2014. (Explorer Junior Library: Math Explorer Junior Ser.). (ENG.). 24p. (J). (gr. 1-4). 28.50 *(978-1-62431-647-0(6)*, 203100) Cherry Lake Publishing.

—Measuring Temperature. Bailer, Darice. 2014. (Explorer Junior Library: Math Explorer Junior Ser.). (ENG.). 24p. (J). (gr. 1-4). 28.50 *(978-1-62431-648-7(4)*, 203104) Cherry Lake Publishing.

—Measuring Time with a Calendar. Bailer, Darice. 2014. (Explorer Junior Library: Math Explorer Junior Ser.). (ENG.). 24p. (J). (gr. 1-4). 28.50 *(978-1-62431-649-4(2)*, 203108) Cherry Lake Publishing.

—Measuring Time with a Calendar. Bailer, Darice. 2014. (Measuring Mania Ser.). (ENG.). 24p. (J). (gr. 1-4). 19.75 *(978-1-5311-8582-4(7))* Perfection Learning Corp.

—Measuring Time with a Clock. Reinke, Beth Bence. 2014. (Explorer Junior Library: Math Explorer Junior Ser.). (ENG.). 24p. (J). (gr. 1-4). 28.50 *(978-1-62431-650-0(6)*, 203112) Cherry Lake Publishing.

—Measuring Time with a Clock. Reinke, Beth Bence. 2014. (Measuring Mania Ser.). (ENG.). 24p. (J). (gr. 1-4). 19.75 *(978-1-5311-8581-7(9))* Perfection Learning Corp.

—Measuring Volume. Reinke, Beth Bence. 2014. (Explorer Junior Library: Math Explorer Junior Ser.). (ENG.). 24p. (J). (gr. 1-4). 28.50 *(978-1-62431-651-7(4)*, 203116) Cherry Lake Publishing.

—Measuring Weight. Reinke, Beth Bence. 2014. (Explorer Junior Library: Math Explorer Junior Ser.). (ENG.). 24p. (J). (gr. 1-4). 28.50 *(978-1-62431-652-4(2)*, 203120) Cherry Lake Publishing.

—My Big Wig. Alinas, Marv. 2018. (Rhyming Word Families Ser.). (ENG.). 24p. (J). (gr. -1-2). lib. bdg. 27.07 *(978-1-5038-2353-2(9)*, 212188) Child's World, Inc., The.

—My Tin Bin. Alinas, Marv. 2019. (Rhyming Word Families Ser.). (ENG.). 24p. (J). (gr. -1-2). lib. bdg. 27.07 *(978-1-5038-2764-6(X)*, 212662) Child's World, Inc., The.

—Nan & Jan's Plan. Alinas, Marv. 2019. (Rhyming Word Families Ser.). (ENG.). 24p. (J). (gr. -1-2). lib. bdg. 27.07 *(978-1-5038-2761-5(5)*, 212663) Child's World, Inc., The.

—Narrative Poems. Pearson, Yvonne. 2015. (Poetry Party Ser.). (ENG.). 24p. (J). (gr. 2-5). 27.07 *(978-1-63143-699-4(6)*, 208534) Child's World, Inc., The.

—Ned, Ted, & the Red Shed. Alinas, Marv. 2018. (Rhyming Word Families Ser.). (ENG.). 24p. (J). (gr. -1-2). lib. bdg. 27.07 *(978-1-5038-2351-8(2)*, 212189) Child's World, Inc., The.

—Neighborhood/el Barrio. Berendes, Mary. 2008. (WordBooks/Libros de Palabras Ser.). (SPA & ENG.). 24p. (J). (gr. k-3). 25.64 *(978-1-59296-993-7(3)*, 201096) Child's World, Inc., The.

—Nouns. Gregory, Josh. 2013. (Explorer Junior Library: the Parts of Speech Ser.). (ENG.). 24p. (J). (gr. 1-4). 25.64 *(978-1-62431-177-2(6)*, 203028); pap. 12.79 *(978-1-62431-309-7(4)*, 203030) Cherry Lake Publishing.

—The Nut near the Hut. Alinas, Marv. 2019. (Rhyming Word Families Ser.). (ENG.). 24p. (J). (gr. -1-2). lib. bdg. 27.07 *(978-1-5038-2767-7(4)*, 212665) Child's World, Inc., The.

—People/Las Personas. Berendes, Mary. 2007. (WordBooks/Libros de Palabras Ser.). (SPA & ENG.).

P

24p. (J). (gr. k-3). 25.64 *(978-1-59296-800-8(7)*, 201097) Child's World, Inc., The.

—Pop's Mop Shop. Alinas, Marv. 2019. (Rhyming Word Families Ser.). (ENG.). 24p. (J). (gr. -1-2). lib. bdg. 27.07 *(978-1-5038-2766-0(6)*, 212661) Child's World, Inc., The.

—Prepositions. Marsico, Katie. 2013. (Explorer Junior Library: the Parts of Speech Ser.). (ENG.). 24p. (J). (gr. 1-4). 25.64 *(978-1-62431-182-6(2)*, 203048); pap. 12.79 *(978-1-62431-314-1(0)*, 203050) Cherry Lake Publishing.

—Pronouns. Marsico, Katie. 2013. (Explorer Junior Library: the Parts of Speech Ser.). (ENG.). 24p. (J). (gr. 1-4). 25.64 *(978-1-62431-178-9(4)*, 203032); pap. 12.79 *(978-1-62431-310-3(8)*, 203034) Cherry Lake Publishing.

—Prose Poems. Pearson, Yvonne. 2015. (Poetry Party Ser.). (ENG.). 24p. (J). (gr. 2-5). 27.07 *(978-1-63143-697-0(X)*, 208530) Child's World, Inc., The.

—The Rag Bag. Alinas, Marv. 2018. (Rhyming Word Families Ser.). (ENG.). 24p. (J). (gr. -1-2). lib. bdg. 27.07 *(978-1-5038-2349-5(0)*, 212194) Child's World, Inc., The.

—Reading & Learning from Informational Text. Hamer, Jennifer L. 2013. (Explorer Junior Library: Information Explorer Junior Ser.). (ENG.). 24p. (J). (gr. 1-4). 28.50 *(978-1-62431-134-5(2)*, 202856); pap. 12.79 *(978-1-62431-266-3(7)*, 202858) Cherry Lake Publishing.

—Review It! Helping Peers Create Their Best Work. Fontichiaro, Kristin. 2015. (Explorer Junior Library: Information Explorer Junior Ser.). (ENG.). 24p. (J). (gr. 1-4). 29.93 *(978-1-63188-865-6(X)*, 206040) Cherry Lake Publishing.

—Rhyming Poems. Simons, Lisa M. Bolt. 2015. (Poetry Party Ser.). (ENG.). 24p. (J). (gr. 2-5). 27.07 *(978-1-63143-698-7(8)*, 208533) Child's World, Inc., The.

—School. Thornborough, Kathy. 2014. (Talking Hands Ser.). (ENG.). 24p. (J). (gr. k-3). 25.64 *(978-1-62687-322-3(4)*, 207162) Child's World, Inc., The.

—School/la Escuela. Berendes, Mary. 2008. (WordBooks/Libros de Palabras Ser.). (SPA & ENG.). 24p. (J). (gr. k-3). 25.64 *(978-1-59296-994-4(1)*, 201098) Child's World, Inc., The.

—Seasons. Thornborough, Kathy. 2014. (Talking Hands Ser.). (ENG.). 24p. (J). (gr. k-3). 25.64 *(978-1-62687-323-0(2)*, 207163) Child's World, Inc., The.

—Sharing Jam & Ham. Alinas, Marv. 2018. (Rhyming Word Families Ser.). (ENG.). 24p. (J). (gr. -1-2). lib. bdg. 27.07 *(978-1-5038-2350-1(4)*, 212190) Child's World, Inc., The.

—Speak up! Giving an Oral Presentation. McHugh, Jeff. 2015. (Explorer Junior Library: Information Explorer Junior Ser.). (ENG.). 24p. (J). (gr. 1-4). 29.93 *(978-1-63188-864-9(1)*, 206036) Cherry Lake Publishing.

—Sports & Games/Los Deportes y Los Juegos. Berendes, Mary. 2007. (WordBooks/Libros de Palabras Ser.). (SPA & ENG.). 24p. (J). (gr. k-3). 25.64 *(978-1-59296-802-2(3)*, 201099) Child's World, Inc., The.

—Starting Your Own Blog. Truesdell, Ann & Fontichiaro, Kristin. 2013. (Explorer Junior Library: Information Explorer Junior Ser.). (ENG.). 24p. (J). (gr. 1-4). 28.50 *(978-1-62431-133-8(4)*, 202852); pap. 12.79 *(978-1-62431-265-6(9)*, 202854) Cherry Lake Publishing.

—Tad's Dad. Alinas, Marv. 2019. (Rhyming Word Families Ser.). (ENG.). 24p. (J). (gr. -1-2). lib. bdg. 27.07 *(978-1-5038-2760-8(7)*, 212664) Child's World, Inc., The.

—Understanding & Creating Infographics. Fontichiaro, Kristin. 2013. (Explorer Library: Information Explorer Ser.). (ENG.). 32p. (J). (gr. 4-8). 28.50 *(978-1-62431-126-0(1)*, 202824); pap. 14.21 *(978-1-62431-258-8(6)*, 202826) Cherry Lake Publishing.

—Using Digital Maps. Matteson, Adrienne. 2013. (Explorer Library: Information Explorer Ser.). (ENG.). 32p. (J). (gr. 4-8). 28.50 *(978-1-62431-129-1(6)*, 202836); pap. 14.21 *(978-1-62431-261-8(6)*, 202838) Cherry Lake Publishing.

—Verbs. Gregory, Josh. 2013. (Explorer Junior Library: the Parts of Speech Ser.). (ENG.). 24p. (J). (gr. 1-4). 25.64 *(978-1-62431-179-6(2)*, 203036); pap. 12.79 *(978-1-62431-311-0(6)*, 203038) Cherry Lake Publishing.

—Watch It! Researching with Videos. Fontichiaro, Kristin. 2015. (Explorer Junior Library: Information Explorer Junior Ser.). (ENG.). 24p. (J). (gr. 1-4). 29.93 *(978-1-63188-863-2(3)*, 206032) Cherry Lake Publishing.

—Weather. Thornborough, Kathy. 2014. (Talking Hands Ser.). (ENG.). 24p. (J). (gr. k-3). 25.64 *(978-1-62687-324-7(0)*, 207164) Child's World, Inc., The.

—Work. Thornborough, Kathy. 2014. (Talking Hands Ser.). (ENG.). 24p. (J). (gr. k-3). 25.64 *(978-1-62687-325-4(9)*, 207165) Child's World, Inc., The.

—You Bet! Alinas, Marv. 2019. (Rhyming Word Families Ser.). (ENG.). 24p. (J). (gr. -1-2). lib. bdg. 27.07 *(978-1-5038-2763-9(1)*, 212666) Child's World, Inc., The.

Petelinsek, Kathleen. Crafting with Duct Tape: Even More Projects. Petelinsek, Kathleen. 2015. (How-To Library). (ENG.). 32p. (J). (gr. 3-6). 29.93 *(978-1-63362-374-3(2)*, 206916) Cherry Lake Publishing.

—Crafting with Tissue Paper. Petelinsek, Kathleen. 2014. (How-To Library). (ENG.). 32p. (J). (gr. 3-6). 28.50 *(978-1-63137-779-2(5)*, 205359) Cherry Lake Publishing.

—Learning to Make Books. Petelinsek, Kathleen. 2015. (How-To Library). (ENG.). 32p. (J). (gr. 3-6). 29.93 *(978-1-63362-372-9(6)*, 206908) Cherry Lake Publishing.

—Learning to Sew. Petelinsek, Kathleen. 2014. (How-To Library). (ENG.). 32p. (J). (gr. 3-6). 28.50 *(978-1-63137-780-8(9)*, 205363) Cherry Lake Publishing.

—Little Jack Horner. Petelinsek, Kathleen. 2011. (Favorite Mother Goose Rhymes Ser.). (ENG.). 16p. (J). (gr. -1-2). lib. bdg. 14.21 *(978-1-60954-280-1(0)*, 200232) Child's World, Inc., The.

—Making Clay Bead Crafts. Petelinsek, Kathleen. 2014. (How-To Library). (ENG.). 32p. (J). (gr. 3-6). 28.50 *(978-1-63137-777-8(9)*, 205351) Cherry Lake Publishing.

—Making Jewelry with Rubber Bands. Petelinsek, Kathleen. 2014. (How-To Library). (ENG.). 32p. (J). (gr. 3-6). 28.50 *(978-1-63137-781-5(7)*, 205367) Cherry Lake Publishing.

—Making Sock Puppets. Petelinsek, Kathleen. 2014. (How-To Library). (ENG.). 32p. (J). (gr. 3-6). 28.50 *(978-1-63137-782-2(5)*, 205371) Cherry Lake Publishing.

—Modeling Clay Creations. Petelinsek, Kathleen. 2014. (How-To Library). (ENG.). 32p. (J). (gr. 3-6). 28.50 *(978-1-63137-783-9(3)*, 205375) Cherry Lake Publishing.

—Pipe Cleaner Crafts. Petelinsek, Kathleen. 2014. (How-To Library). (ENG.). 32p. (J). (gr. 3-6). lib. bdg. 28.50 *(978-1-63137-784-6(1)*, 205379) Cherry Lake Publishing.

Peten, Chantal. A Day at the Museum. Ducatteau, Florence. 2013. (Want to Know Ser.). (ENG.). 32p. (J). (gr. k-2). 16.95 *(978-1-60537-142-9(4))* Clavis Publishing.

Peter Carnavas. My Dad Snores. Williamson, John & Carnavas, Peter. 2019. (ENG.). 32p. (J). (gr. k). 18.99 ***(978-0-14-379379-3(9)***, Puffin) Penguin Random Hse. AUS. Dist: Independent Pubs. Group.

Peter-Henderson, Jeannine. That One Girl. Peter, Joyce. 2019. (ENG.). 50p. (YA). pap. 23.05 *(978-1-5434-9266-8(5))* Xlibris Corp.

Peter, Joshua. Where Is Beau? Grinnell, Suzanne. 2008. 24p. pap. 12.99 *(978-1-59858-612-1(2))* Dog Ear Publishing, LLC.

Peters, Andy & Hewett, Angela. My First 1000 Words. Giles, Sophie & Davis, Kate. 2014. (ENG.). 125p. 17.50 *(978-1-84135-642-6(5))* Award Pubns. Ltd. GBR. Dist: Parkwest Pubns., Inc.

Peters, Darcy. Little Rumely Man. Silcox, Beth Douglass. 2012. 36p. pap. 12.99 *(978-0-9832514-2-2(8))* Gypsy Heart Pr.

Peters, Elf. Meet Baby Crumbles. Shields, Cynthia. 2019. (ENG.). 28p. (J). pap. 10.99 ***(978-1-6760-4993-7(2))*** Independently Published.

Peters, Gabe. Jake! Don't Shake! Mulcahy, Kylie. 2017. (ENG.). 36p. (J). pap. *(978-0-646-97904-5(3))* Mulcahy, Kylie.

Peters, Kathryn. A Pet for Elizabeth Rose. Peters, Kathryn. l.t. ed. 2005. 42p. (J). 8.99 *(978-0-9752647-9-9(6))* Proton Arts.

Peters, Laura. Warm Toes. Mazzitelli, Donna. 2016. (ENG.). (J). (gr. k-3). pap. 10.00 *(978-1-939919-41-0(X))* Merry Dissonance Pr.

Peters, Liam. Bewitched in Oz, 1 vol. Burns, Laura J. 2014. (Bewitched in Oz Ser.). (ENG.). 256p. (J). (gr. 4-8). 12.95 *(978-1-62370-129-1(5)*, Capstone Young Readers); lib. bdg. 30.65 *(978-1-4342-9207-0(X)*, Stone Arch Bks.) Capstone.

Peters, Ramona. Strawberry Thanksgiving. Jennings, Paulla. 2005. (Multicultural Celebrations Ser.). 32p. (J). 4.95 *(978-1-59373-010-9(1))* Bunker Hill Publishing, Inc.

Peters, Rob. Bye, Bye Boogeyman. Davies, Donna M. Bailin-Rembar, Jill, ed. 2013. 32p. pap. 9.95 *(978-0-9853082-5-4(7))* HallowStyle, LLC.

—Eartha Gets Well. Falk, Kristi & Falk, Daniel. 2012. (ENG.). 30p. (J). 24.95 *(978-1-937084-27-1(2)*, BQB Publishing) Boutique of Quality Books Publishing Co., Inc.

Peters, Rob. Francis Frames the Future: With the Wisdom of the Past. Bergles, Matt. 2019. (ENG.). 48p. (J). pap. 10.00 ***(978-1-939919-59-5(2))*** Merry Dissonance Pr.

Peters, Rob. Jessica & Madison: Being Beautiful. Taylor, Derrick & Garnett, Kaila. 2012. 38p. pap. 8.00 *(978-1-62050-492-5(8))*; 14.95 *(978-1-61364-734-9(4))* DTaylor Bks.

—Kansas City Chiefs ABCs And 1-2-3s. 2015. (ENG.). 26p. (J). bds. 18.95 *(978-0-9961944-0-2(1))* Ascend Bks., LLC.

—Night of the Candy Creepers. Davies, Donna. 2013. 32p. pap. 9.95 *(978-0-9853082-1-6(4))* HallowStyle, LLC.

—Pete's Big Paws - Hardcover. Richter, Cindy. 2012. 32p. 15.99 *(978-0-9849732-0-0(6))* Coast View Publishing.

Peters, Robert. Da Goodie Monsta: Chase Dem Nightmares Away. Peters, Robert. 2009. 28p. (YA). lib. bdg. *(978-0-9823906-7-2(X))* Wiggles Pr.

Peterschmidt, Betsy. Blackbird Fly. Kelly, Erin Entrada. (ENG.). (J). (gr. 3-7). 2016. 320p. pap. 7.99 *(978-0-06-223862-7(0))*; 2015. 304p. 16.99 *(978-0-06-223861-0(2))* HarperCollins Pubs. (Greenwillow Bks.).

—Buyer Beware, 1 vol. Rogers, Kelly. 2016. (Rm. 201 Ser.). (ENG.). 48p. (J). (gr. 3-7). lib. bdg. 29.93 *(978-1-62402-167-1(0)*, 21581, Spellbound) Magic Wagon.

—The House Sitters, 1 vol. Rogers, Kelly. 2016. (Rm. 201 Ser.). (ENG.). 48p. (J). (gr. 3-7). lib. bdg. 29.93 *(978-1-62402-168-8(9)*, 21583, Spellbound) Magic Wagon.

—The Key, 1 vol. Rogers, Kelly. 2016. (Rm. 201 Ser.). (ENG.). 48p. (J). (gr. 3-7). lib. bdg. 29.93 *(978-1-62402-169-5(7)*, 21585, Spellbound) Magic Wagon.

—Rm. 201, 4 vols. Rogers, Kelly & ABDO Publishing Company Staff. 2016. (Rm. 201 Ser.). 48p. (J). (gr. 3-7). lib. bdg. 114.00 *(978-1-62402-166-4(2)*, 21579, Spellbound) Magic Wagon.

—Study Group. Rogers, Kelly. 2016. (Rm. 201 Ser.). (ENG.). 48p. (J). (gr. 3-7). lib. bdg. 29.93 *(978-1-62402-170-1(0)*, 21587, Spellbound) Magic Wagon.

Petersen, Alyssa. Katherine Johnson. Feldman, Thea. 2017. (You Should Meet Ser.). (J). (ENG.). 48p. (gr. 1-3). 17.99 *(978-1-5344-0341-3(8))*; (ENG.). 48p. (gr. 1-3). pap. 4.99 *(978-1-5344-0340-6(X))*; 47p. *(978-1-5182-5284-6(2))* Simon Spotlight. (Simon Spotlight).

—Kids Who Are Changing the World. Higginson, Sheila Sweeny. 2019. (You Should Meet Ser.). (ENG.). 48p. (J). (gr. 1-3). 17.99 *(978-1-5344-3215-4(9))*; pap. 4.99 *(978-1-5344-3214-7(0))* Simon Spotlight. (Simon Spotlight).

—Lin-Manuel Miranda. Calkhoven, Laurie. 2018. (You Should Meet Ser.). (ENG.). 48p. (J). (gr. 1-3). 17.99 *(978-1-5344-2242-1(0))*; pap. 4.99 *(978-1-5344-2241-4(2))* Simon Spotlight. (Simon Spotlight).

—Women Who Launched the Computer Age. Calkhoven, Laurie. 2016. (You Should Meet Ser.). (ENG.). 48p. (J). (gr. 1-3). pap. 4.99 *(978-1-4814-7046-9(9)*, Simon Spotlight) Simon Spotlight.

Petersen, Darla & Shields, Erik P. There's a Monster under the Captain's Bed!!! Erik's Monster. Aunt Darla. Date not set. 32p. 16.00 *(978-0-9658926-1-2(1))* Poet Tree Pubns.

Petersen, David. Snowy Valentine. Petersen, David. 2011. (ENG.). 32p. (J). (gr. -1-3). 14.99 *(978-0-06-146378-5(7))* HarperCollins Pubs.

—Winter 1152, Vol. 2. Petersen, David. Illidge, Joseph Phillip, ed. 2009. (Mouse Guard Ser.: 2). (ENG.). 192p. (J). (gr. 8-12). 24.95 *(978-1-932386-74-5(2))* Boom Entertainment, Inc.

Petersen, David, jt. illus. see Villavert, Armand, Jr.

Petersen, Jeff. Burn, Christmas! Burn!! Gage, Brian. 2004. (ENG.). 40p. 17.95 *(978-1-932360-55-4(7)*, Soft Skull Pr.) Counterpoint Pr.

Petersen, Marty. Frieda Tails Coloring Book Volume 2: Frieda & the Big Brown Bear & the Church I. Baltz, Kimberly. 2017. (ENG.). 30p. (J). pap. 6.99 *(978-0-9989256-2-2(4))* Exodus 35:31 Artistry LLC.

Petersen, Sheli. Gigi & the Birthday Ring. Fernandez, Giselle. 2005. (J). *(978-1-56492-358-5(4))* Laredo Publishing Co., Inc.

Petersen, Susan S. Hanging with the Hangers. Reilly, Peter J. Erickson, Donna J., ed. 2013. (ENG.). (J). pap. 10.95 *(978-1-62776-841-2(6))* Independent Pub.

Petersen, William. Amigos de Jesús 2009: A Bilingual Catechetical Program. un Programa Catequético BilingüE. Advent 2008 - November 2009. Aguinaco, Carmen F. 2008.Tr. of Friends of Jesus 2009. (ENG & SPA.). 408p. (J). pap. 99.00 *(978-0-89570-503-7(6))* Claretian Pubns.

Petersham, Maud & Petersham, Miska. A Child's Own Book of Verse, Book One (Yesterday's Classics) Skinner, Ada & Wickes, Frances. 2006. (J). pap. 8.95 *(978-1-59915-051-2(4))* Yesterday's Classics.

—A Child's Own Book of Verse, Book Three (Yesterday's Classics) Skinner, Ada & Wickes, Frances. 2006. (J). pap. 8.95 *(978-1-59915-053-6(0))* Yesterday's Classics.

—A Child's Own Book of Verse, Book Two (Yesterday's Classics) Skinner, Ada & Wickes, Frances. 2006. (J). pap. 8.95 *(978-1-59915-052-9(2))* Yesterday's Classics.

—Rootabaga Stories. Sandburg, Carl. 2003. (ENG.). 192p. (J). (gr. 3-7). pap. 7.99 *(978-0-15-204714-6(X)*, 1194205) Houghton Mifflin Harcourt Publishing Co.

Petersham, Miska, jt. illus. see Petersham, Maud.

Peterson, Barbara. Greek & Latin Roots: Teaching Vocabulary to Improve Reading Comprehension. Callella, Trisha. Rous, Sheri, ed. 2004. 144p. pap. 16.99 *(978-0-88160-381-1(3)*, LW-438) Creative Teaching Pr., Inc.

—I Have, Who Has? Language Arts Grades 1-2. Callella, Trisha. Taylor, Jennifer, ed. 2007. (J). per. 19.99 *(978-1-59198-429-0(7))* Creative Teaching Pr., Inc.

—Prefixes & Suffixes: Teaching Vocabulary to Improve Reading Comprehension. Callella, Trisha. Williams, Carolea & Rous, Sheri, eds. 2004. 144p. pap. 16.99 *(978-0-88160-380-4(5)*, LW-437) Creative Teaching Pr., Inc.

Peterson, Ben. John Henry, 1 vol. Jones, Christianne C. 2013. (My First Classic Story Ser.).Tr. of John Henry. (ENG.). 32p. (J). (gr. k-3). pap. 7.10 *(978-1-4795-1861-6(1)*, Picture Window Bks.) Capstone.

—John Henry, 1 vol. Jones, Christianne C. Robledo, Sol, tr. 2008. (Read-It! Readers en Español: Cuentos Exagerados Ser.).Tr. of John Henry. (SPA.). 32p. (J). (gr. k-3). per. 3.95 *(978-1-4048-2174-3(0)*, Picture Window Bks.) Capstone.

—El Ninito de Jengibre, 1 vol. Blair, Eric. Abello, Patricia, tr. 2006. (Read-It! Readers en Español: Cuentos Folclóricos Ser.).Tr. of Gingerbread Man. (SPA.). 32p. (J). (gr. k-3). 21.32 *(978-1-4048-1647-3(X)*, Picture Window Bks.) Capstone.

Peterson, Bishop. Problem at the Park. Peterson, Manley. 2019. (ENG.). 34p. (J). pap. 9.99 *(978-1-7934-1293-5(6))* Independently Published.

Peterson, Brandon. Chimera. Marz, Ron. 2003. 160p. (YA). pap. 15.95 *(978-1-931484-96-1(1))* CrossGeneration Comics, Inc.

Peterson, Brandon, et al. Mystic Traveler: The Demon Queen, Vol. 2. Marz, Ron. 2004. (Mystic Traveler Ser.). 160p. (YA). pap. 9.95 *(978-1-59314-037-3(1))* CrossGeneration Comics, Inc.

—X-Men Milestones: Fatal Attractions. 2019. (ENG.). 504p. (YA). (gr. 4-17). pap. 44.99 *(978-1-302-91972-6(5))* Marvel Worldwide, Inc.

—X-Men Milestones: X-Cutioner's Song. 2019. (ENG.). 368p. (YA). (gr. 4-17). pap. 34.99 *(978-1-302-91973-3(3))* Marvel Worldwide, Inc.

Peterson, Carol. Jump into Science: Themed Science Fairs, 1 vol. Peterson, Carol. 2007. 152p. (gr. 3-7). per. 35.00 *(978-1-59158-413-1(2)*, TIP4132, Libraries Unlimited) ABC-CLIO, LLC.

Peterson, Carol A. Pony Pointers: How to Safely Care for Your Horse or Pony. Bennett, Kathy. 2004. 48p. (J). per. 7.99 *(978-0-9763209-0-6(8))* Trail Trotters Bk. Ranch.

Peterson, Dawn. Amasa Walker's Spendid Garment, Vol. Chetkowski, Emily. 2003. (ENG.). 48p. (J). (gr. 5-8). reprint ed. pap. 9.95 *(978-0-911469-21-9(4))* Hood, Alan C. & Co., Inc.

—Children's Tea & Etiquette: Brewing Good Manners in Young Minds. Johnson, Dorothea et al. 2014. (ENG.). 40p. (J). (gr. 2-5). 19.95 *(978-0-9663478-9-0(7))* Benjamin Pr.

—Mabel Takes the Ferry, 1 vol. Chetkowski, Emily. 2nd ed. 2012. (ENG.). 32p. (J). pap. 12.95 *(978-1-934031-99-5(2)*, 1605551a-ac66-4d15-9be5-079d9c0202b2) Islandport Pr., Inc.

Peterson, Elise. How Mamas Love Their Babies. Fitzgerald, Juniper. 2018. (ENG.). 36p. (J). (gr. -1-3). 16.95 *(978-1-936932-00-9(8))* Feminist Pr. at The City Univ. of New York.

Peterson, Elise R. The Nightlife of Jacuzzi Gaskett. Purnell, Brontez. 2019. (ENG.). 48p. (J). 18.95 *(978-1-948340-02-1(X))* Dottir Pr.

Peterson, Gary. Gray Wolf's Search, 1 vol. Swanson, Bruce. 2018. (ENG.). 24p. (J). (gr. 1-3). 18.95 *(978-0-9779183-1-7(9))* Second Story Pr. CAN. Dist: Orca Bk. Pubs. USA.

Peterson, Hollyn. Grandma's Wings. Kozich, Jennifer. 2017. (ENG.). 22p. (J). (gr. 2-6). pap. 9.99 *(978-1-943331-96-3(0))* Orange Hat Publishing.

Peterson, Ingela. Ellie & Pinky's Pop-Up Shapes. 2003. (First Concepts Ser.). 10p. (J). 7.95 *(978-1-58117-184-6(6)*, Intervisual/Piggy Toes) Bendon, Inc.

Peterson, Joel & Rogers, Jacqueline. The Littles & the Surprise Thanksgiving Guests. 2004. (Littles First Readers Ser.). 105p. (J). *(978-0-439-68704-1(7))* Scholastic, Inc.

Peterson, Justine. The Feast. Mitchell, N. Kerry. 2019. (ENG.). 32p. (J). pap. 9.99 ***(978-1-9874-3559-7(1))*** CreateSpace Independent Publishing Platform.

Peterson, Kathleen. Girls Who Choose God. Krishna, McArthur & Spalding, Bethany Brady. 2014. (J). 17.99 *(978-1-60907-882-9(9)*, Ensign Peak) Shadow Mountain Publishing.

—Girls Who Choose God: Stories of Strong Women from the Book of Mormon. Krishna, McArthur & Spalding, Bethany Brady. 2015. (J). 18.99 *(978-1-62972-101-9(8))* Deseret Bk. Co.

—Iwalani's Tree. Hale, Constance. 2016. (ENG.). 32p. (J). (gr. k-3). 14.95 *(978-1-933067-80-3(2))* Beachhouse Publishing, LLC.

—Moon Mangoes. Shapiro, Lindy. 2011. (ENG.). 36p. (J). (gr. -1-2). 14.95 *(978-1-933067-42-1(X))* Beachhouse Publishing, LLC.

—Pele & Poliahu: A Tale of Fire & Ice. Collins, Malia. 2018. (ENG.). 24p. (J). (gr. k-4). 12.95 *(978-1-949000-03-0(6))* Beachhouse Publishing, LLC.

Peterson, Kay. Cats vs. Robots #1: This Is War. Stohl, Margaret & Peterson, Lewis. (ENG.). (J). (gr. 3-7). 2019. 336p. pap. 6.99 *(978-0-06-266571-3(5))*; 2018. 320p. 16.99 *(978-0-06-266570-6(7))* HarperCollins Pubs. (Tegen, Katherine Bks).

—Cats vs. Robots #2: Now with Fleas! Stohl, Margaret & Peterson, Lewis. (ENG.). 352p. (J). (gr. 3-7). 2020. pap. 7.99 ***(978-0-06-266574-4(X))***; 2019. 16.99 *(978-0-06-266573-7(1))* HarperCollins Pubs. (Tegen, Katherine Bks).

Peterson, Lennie. When You Have to Say Goodbye: Loving & Letting Go of Your Pet. Mansfield, Monica. 2011. (ENG.). 32p. (J). (gr. k). 9.95 *(978-0-9831032-1-9(6)*, BeanPole Bks.) Harren Communications, LLC.

Peterson, Lynn Ihsen. Twice a Hero: Polish American Heroes of the American Revolutuion. Wales, Dirk. 2007. 31p. (J). (gr. 4-9). 18.95 incl. audio compact disk *(978-0-9632459-4-6(5))* Great Plains Pr.

Peterson, Mary. Dig In! Jenson-Elliott, Cindy. 2016. (ENG.). 40p. (J). (gr. -1-3). 17.99 *(978-1-4424-1261-3(5)*, Beach Lane Bks.) Beach Lane Bks.

—No Time to Nap. Madison, Mike. 2007. (J). (gr. -1-3). *(978-1-59714-046-1(5))* Heyday.

—Ocean Soup: Tide-Pool Poems. Swinburne, Stephen R. 32p. (J). (gr. k-3). 2009. (ENG.). 22.44 *(978-1-58089-200-1(0))*; 2010. pap. 7.95 *(978-1-58089-201-8(9))* Charlesbridge Publishing, Inc.

—Twinkle, Twinkle, Little Car. Dopirak, Kate. 2018. (ENG.). 40p. (J). (gr. -1-3). 17.99 *(978-1-4814-8803-7(1)*, Beach Lane Bks.) Beach Lane Bks.

—Wiggle & Waggle. Arnold, Caroline. 2009. 48p. (J). (gr. k-3). pap. 5.95 *(978-1-58089-307-7(4))* Charlesbridge Publishing, Inc.

Peterson, Mary. Piggies in the Pumpkin Patch. Peterson, Mary. Rofé, Jennifer. 2010. 28p. (J). (gr. -1-2). pap. 7.99 *(978-1-57091-461-4(3))* Charlesbridge Publishing, Inc.

—Snail Finds a Home. Peterson, Mary. 2020. (Pix Ser.). (ENG.). 64p. (J). (gr. 1-4). 15.99 *(978-1-5344-3185-0(3)*, Aladdin) Simon & Schuster Children's Publishing.

—Snail Has Lunch. Peterson, Mary. 2016. (Pix Ser.). (ENG.). 64p. (J). (gr. 1-4). 12.99 *(978-1-4814-5302-8(5)*, Aladdin) Simon & Schuster Children's Publishing.

Peterson, Mary. Snail's Silly Adventures: Snail Has Lunch; Snail Finds a Home. Peterson, Mary. 2020. (ENG.). 128p. (J). (gr. 1-4). 19.99 ***(978-1-5344-6345-5(3))***; pap. 7.99 ***(978-1-5344-6344-8(5))*** Simon & Schuster Children's Publishing. (Aladdin).

Peterson, Mary Joseph. Basic Prayers in My Pocket. 2009. 32p. (J). pap. 1.95 *(978-0-8198-1173-8(4))* Pauline Bks. & Media.

—My First Book about Jesus. Tebo, Mary Elizabeth. 2008. 64p. (J). (gr. 1-3). pap. 7.95 *(978-0-8198-4865-9(4))* Pauline Bks. & Media.

—Saint Clare of Assisi: A Light for the World. Trouvé, Marianne Lorraine. 2009. (J). pap. 7.95 *(978-0-8198-7122-0(2))* Pauline Bks. & Media.

Peterson, Melanie. Explorers of the Word: Episode 1: the Creation. Burshek, Edward & Burshek, Tonja. 2007. (ENG.). 76p. per. 19.95 *(978-1-4241-6691-6(8))* America Star Bks.

Peterson, Rick. Beaky's Guide to Caring for Your Bird, 1 vol. Thomas, Isabel. 2014. (Pets' Guides). (ENG.). 32p. (J). (gr. 1-3). pap. 7.99 *(978-1-4846-0266-9(8))*; 27.99 *(978-1-4846-0259-1(5))* Capstone. (Heinemann).

—Bunny's Guide to Caring for Your Rabbit, 1 vol. Ganeri, Anita. 2013. (Pets' Guides). (ENG.). 32p. (J). (gr. 1-3). pap. 7.99 *(978-1-4329-7142-7(5))*; lib. bdg. 27.99 *(978-1-4329-7135-9(2))* Capstone. (Heinemann).

—The Chicken & the Worm. McBrier, Page. 2008. 36p. (J). *(978-0-9798439-2-1(8))* Heifer Project International.

—Chirp, Chirp! Crickets in Your Backyard. Loewen, Nancy. 2005. (Backyard Bugs Ser.). (ENG.). 24p. (J). (gr. -1-3). lib. bdg. 27.32 *(978-1-4048-1141-6(9)*, Picture Window Bks.) Capstone.

—Garden Wigglers: Earthworms in Your Backyard. Loewen, Nancy. 2005. (Backyard Bugs Ser.). (ENG.). 24p. (J). (gr. -1-3). lib. bdg. 27.32 *(978-1-4048-1144-7(3)*, Picture Window Bks.) Capstone.

—Giggle's Guide to Caring for Your Gerbils, 1 vol. Thomas, Isabel. 2014. (Pets' Guides). (ENG.). 32p. (J). (gr. 1-3). pap. 7.99 *(978-1-4846-0267-6(6))*; 27.99 *(978-1-4846-0260-7(9))* Capstone. (Heinemann).

—Goldie's Guide to Caring for Your Goldfish, 1 vol. Ganeri, Anita. 2013. (Pets' Guides). (ENG.). 32p. (J). (gr. 1-3). pap. 7.99 *(978-1-4329-7139-7(5))*; lib. bdg. 27.99 *(978-1-4329-7132-8(8))* Capstone. (Heinemann).

—Gordon's Guide to Caring for Your Guinea Pigs, 1 vol. Thomas, Isabel. 2014. (Pets' Guides). (ENG.). 32p. (J).

(gr. 1-3). pap. 7.99 *(978-1-4846-0268-3(4))*; 27.99 *(978-1-4846-0261-4(7))* Capstone. (Heinemann).

—Henrietta's Guide to Caring for Your Chickens, 1 vol. Thomas, Isabel. 2014. (Pets' Guides). (ENG.). 32p. (J). (gr. 1-3). pap. 7.99 *(978-1-4846-0269-0(2))*; 27.99 *(978-1-4846-0262-1(5))* Capstone. (Heinemann).

—Kitty's Guide to Caring for Your Cat, 1 vol. Ganeri, Anita. 2013. (Pets' Guides). (ENG.). 32p. (J). (gr. 1-3). pap. 7.99 *(978-1-4329-7137-3(9))*; lib. bdg. 27.99 *(978-1-4329-7130-4(1))* Capstone. (Heinemann).

—Look! [Scholastic]: A Book about Sight. Meachen Rau, Dana. 2010. (Amazing Body: the Five Senses Ser.). 24p. pap. 0.56 *(978-1-4048-4390-5(6)*, Picture Window Bks.) Capstone.

—Ruff's Guide to Caring for Your Dog, 1 vol. Ganeri, Anita. 2013. (Pets' Guides). (ENG.). 32p. (J). (gr. 1-3). pap. 7.99 *(978-1-4329-7138-0(7))*; lib. bdg. 27.99 *(978-1-4329-7131-1(X))* Capstone. (Heinemann).

—Shhhh... [Scholastic]: A Book about Hearing. Meachen Rau, Dana. 2010. (Amazing Body: the Five Senses Ser.). 24p. pap. 0.56 *(978-1-4048-6541-9(1)*, Picture Window Bks.) Capstone.

—Slinky's Guide to Caring for Your Snake, 1 vol. Thomas, Isabel. 2014. (Pets' Guides). (ENG.). 32p. (J). (gr. 1-3). pap. 7.99 *(978-1-4846-0270-6(6))*; 27.99 *(978-1-4846-0263-8(3))* Capstone. (Heinemann).

—Sniff, Sniff [Scholastic]: A Book about Smell. Meachen Rau, Dana. 2010. (Amazing Body: the Five Senses Ser.). 24p. pap. 0.56 *(978-1-4048-6542-6(X)*, Picture Window Bks.) Capstone.

—Soft & Smooth, Rough & Bumpy [Scholastic]: A Book about Touch. Meachen Rau, Dana. 2010. (Amazing Body: the Five Senses Ser.). 24p. pap. 0.56 *(978-1-4048-6544-0(6)*, Picture Window Bks.) Capstone.

—Squeak's Guide to Caring for Your Pet Rats or Mice, 1 vol. Thomas, Isabel. 2014. (Pets' Guides). (ENG.). 32p. (J). (gr. 1-3). pap. 7.99 *(978-1-4846-0271-3(4))*; 27.99 *(978-1-4846-0264-5(1))* Capstone. (Heinemann).

—Winnie's Guide to Caring for Your Horse or Pony, 1 vol. Ganeri, Anita. 2013. (Pets' Guides). (ENG.). 32p. (J). (gr. 1-3). pap. 7.99 *(978-1-4329-7141-0(7))*; lib. bdg. 27.99 *(978-1-4329-7134-2(4))* Capstone. (Heinemann).

—Yum! [Scholastic]: A Book about Taste. Meachen Rau, Dana. 2010. (Amazing Body: the Five Senses Ser.). 24p. pap. 0.56 *(978-1-4048-6543-3(8)*, Picture Window Bks.) Capstone.

Peterson, Roger Tory & Savage, Virginia. Wildflowers. Tenenbaum, Frances & Peterson, Roger Tory. 2013. (Peterson Field Guide Color-In Bks.). (ENG.). 64p. (J). 8.95 *(978-0-544-02697-1(7)*, 1529291) Houghton Mifflin Harcourt Publishing Co.

Peterson, Russell. Saint Brigid & the Cows. Betz, Eva K. 2013. (ENG.). 48p. (J). (gr. k-3). 12.95 *(978-1-930873-95-7(6)*, Neumann Pr.) TAN Bks.

Peterson, Sara & Lindstrom, Brita. The Clock & the Mouse: A Teaching Rhyme about Time. Turley, Sandy. 2006. 32p. (J). lib. bdg. 26.95 *(978-0-9778548-0-6(9))* Helps4Teachers.

Peterson, Scott, photos by. Pizza: More Than 60 Recipes for Delicious Homemade Pizza. Morgan, Diane & Gemignani, Tony. 2005. (ENG., 168p. (gr. 8-17). per. 18.95 *(978-0-8118-4554-0(0))* Chronicle Bks. LLC.

Peterson-Shea, Julie. Echoes of Kansas Past. Boeve, Eunice. 2012. 176p. pap. 10.99 *(978-0-9851196-9-0(1))* Rowe Publishing.

Peterson, Stacy. Babies Love Christmas: Chunky Lift a Flap Board Book. Berry Byrd, Holly. Cottage Door Press, ed. 2016. (Chunky Lift a Flap Board Book Ser.). (ENG.). 12p. (J). (gr. -1-k). bds. 7.99 *(978-1-68052-116-0(0)*, 1001091) Cottage Door Pr.

—Babies Love Halloween: Chunky Lift a Flap Board Book. VonFeder, Rosa. Cottage Door Press, ed. 2016. (Babies Love Children's Interactive Chunky Lift-A-Flap Board Book Ser.). (ENG.). 12p. (J). (gr. -1-k). bds. 7.99 *(978-1-68052-115-3(2)*, 1001081) Cottage Door Pr.

Peterson, Stacy. Bedtime Stories Treasury (Book & 6 Downloadable Apps!) Little Grasshopper Books. 2020. (Treasury Ser.). (ENG.). 160p. (J). (gr. -1-k). 7.98 ***(978-1-64030-983-8(7)**, 6114900, Little Grasshopper Bks.) Publications International, Ltd.

—Bible Stories Treasury (Book & 6 Downloadable Apps! - Stories, Songs, & Poems) Little Grasshopper Books. 2020. (Treasury Ser.). (ENG.). 160p. (J). (gr. -1-k). 7.98 ***(978-1-64030-985-2(3)**, 6115000, Little Grasshopper Bks.) Publications International, Ltd.

—Fairy Tales Treasury (Book & 6 Downloadable Apps!) Little Grasshopper Books. 2020. (Treasury Ser.). (ENG.). 160p. (J). (gr. -1-k). 7.98 ***(978-1-64030-986-9(1)**, 6115100, Little Grasshopper Bks.) Publications International, Ltd.

—Goldilocks & the Three Bears (Book & Downloadable App!) Little Grasshopper Books. 2020. (ENG.). 24p. (J). (gr. -1-k). bds. 5.98 ***(978-1-64030-973-9(X)**, 6112300, Little Grasshopper Bks.) Publications International, Ltd.

—Jack & the Beanstalk (Book & Downloadable App!) Little Grasshopper Books. 2020. (ENG.). 24p. (J). (gr. -1-k). bds. 5.98 ***(978-1-64030-988-3(8)**, 6115200, Little Grasshopper Bks.) Publications International, Ltd.

—The Little Red Hen (Book & Downloadable App!) Little Grasshopper Books. 2020. (ENG.). 24p. (J). (gr. -1-k). bds. 5.98 ***(978-1-64030-955-5(1)**, 6110400, Little Grasshopper Bks.) Publications International, Ltd.

Peterson, Stacy. Mindful Me: Mindfulness & Meditation for Kids. Stewart, Whitney. 2018. (ENG.). 160p. (J). (gr. 3-7). 16.99 *(978-0-8075-5144-8(9)*, 807551449) Whitman, Albert & Co.

—Mindful Me Activity Book. Stewart, Whitney. 2018. (ENG.). 96p. (J). (gr. 4-7). pap. 9.99 *(978-0-8075-5146-2(5)*, 807551465) Whitman, Albert & Co.

Peterson, Stacy. Mother Goose Rhymes (Book & Downloadable App!) Little Grasshopper Books. 2020. (ENG.). 24p. (J). (gr. -1-k). bds. 5.98 ***(978-1-64030-971-5(3)**, 6112100, Little Grasshopper Bks.) Publications International, Ltd.

Peterson, Stacy. My Family Vacation: A Book about Me! Sund, Mike. 2008. (ENG.). 24p. (YA). (gr. 2-18). 12.95 *(978-1-58117-792-3(5)*, Intervisual/Piggy Toes) Bendon, Inc.

Peterson, Stacy. Peter Rabbit (Book & Downloadable App!) Little Grasshopper Books. 2020. (ENG.). 24p. (J). (gr. -1-k). bds. 5.98 ***(978-1-64030-972-2(1)**, 6112200, Little Grasshopper Bks.) Publications International, Ltd.

—The Ugly Duckling (Book & Downloadable App!) Little Grasshopper Books. 2020. (ENG.). 24p. (J). (gr. -1-k). bds. 5.98 ***(978-1-64030-974-6(8)**, 6112400, Little Grasshopper Bks.) Publications International, Ltd.

Peterson, Stacy & Maberry, Maranda. My Pod: Libro de Cuentos y Reproductor Personal de Musica. Miller, Sara. 2007. (SPA.). 38p. (J). (gr. -1-3). *(978-970-718-495-4(7)*, Silver Dolphin en Español) Advanced Marketing, S. de R. L. de C. V.

Petete, Christine. Super Phil. Tucker, Mark. 2003. (J). 4.50 *(978-1-882440-00-9(5))* God's World Pubns. Inc.

Pethkar, Sanket. The Night Monster. Mishra, Sushree. 2018. (ENG.). 30p. (J). 13.95 *(978-81-8190-331-0(5))* Karadi Tales Co. Pvt. Ltd. IND. Dist: Consortium Bk. Sales & Distribution.

Petipas, Jim. The Cows Go Moo! Udderly Crazy Activity & Coloring Book. Petipas, Jim. 2019. (ENG.). 74p. (J). (gr. k-3). pap. 6.99 *(978-0-9976078-0-2(7))* Boardwalk Bks.

Petit, Cory, jt. illus. see Camagni, Jacopo.

Petiti, Lauren. I Read a Book. Walsh, Susan E. 2019. (Solving Problems Through Literacy Ser.: Vol. 1). (ENG.). 34p. (J). pap. 10.00 ***(978-1-6956-4138-9(8))*** Independently Published.

Petitt, Tiffany. The Adventures of T. J. & Dodge. Thompson, Cheryl. 2017. (ENG.). (J). 20.99 *(978-1-4984-9182-2(0))*; pap. 9.99 *(978-1-4984-9181-5(2))* Salem Author Services.

Petitt, Tiffany. Wallie the Whale: Learns to Make Friends. McManus, Amy Leanne. 2019. (ENG.). 24p. (J). pap. 19.99 ***(978-1-5456-8173-2(2))*** Salem Author Services.

Petney, Ryan. Bigfoot. Chambers, Catherine. 2015. (Autobiographies You Never Thought You'd Read! Ser.). (ENG.). 32p. (J). (gr. 3-5). 30.65 *(978-1-4109-7961-2(X)*, Raintree) Capstone.

Petosa-Sigel, Kristi. HOKU the Stargazer: The Exciting Pirate Adventure! Crowe, Ellie & Fry, Juliet. 2009. (ENG.). 28p. (J). *(978-1-59700-601-9(7))* Island Heritage Publishing.

Petra, Romina. The Magical Dreamcatcher: The Power of Believing in Your Inner Light. Angheluta, Alexandra C. 2019. (Magical Affirmations Ser.: Vol. 3). (ENG.). 38p. (J). pap. 10.00 ***(978-1-9860-5220-7(6))*** CreateSpace Independent Publishing Platform.

Petre, Emily. Fishing with Uncle Nathan: Step 4. Martin, Mary S. 2016. (Stepping Forward Ser.). (ENG.). 63p. (J). (gr. -1). 3.95 *(978-0-7399-2524-9(5))* Rod & Staff Pubs., Inc.

Petričić, Dusan. When Apples Grew Noses & White Horses Flew: Tales of Ti-Jean, 1 vol. Andrews, Jan. 2011. (ENG.). 72p. (J). (gr. 1-5). 16.95 *(978-0-88899-952-8(6))* Groundwood Bks. CAN. Dist: Publishers Group West (PGW).

Petri?i?, Duÿan. My Family Tree & Me. Petri?i?, Duÿan. 2015. (ENG.). 24p. (J). (gr. -1-2). 16.95 *(978-1-77138-049-2(7))* Kids Can Pr., Ltd. CAN. Dist: Hachette Bk. Group.

Petricic, Dusan. Bagels from Benny. Davis, Aubrey. 2005. (ENG.). 32p. (J). (gr. -1-3). 7.95 *(978-1-55337-749-8(4))* Kids Can Pr., Ltd. CAN. Dist: Hachette Bk. Group.

—The Dance of the Violin. Stinson, Kathy. 2017. (ENG.). 32p. (J). (gr. k-3). 18.95 *(978-1-55451-900-2(4))* Annick Pr., Ltd. CAN. Dist: Publishers Group West (PGW).

—In the Tree House. Larsen, Andrew. (ENG.). 32p. (J). (gr. -1-2). 2018. pap. 7.99 *(978-1-5253-0017-2(2))*; 2013. 16.95 *(978-1-55453-635-1(9))* Kids Can Pr., Ltd. CAN. Dist: Hachette Bk. Group.

—InvisiBill. Fergus, Maureen. 2015. (ENG.). 44p. (J). (gr. k-4). 17.99 *(978-1-77049-613-2(0)*, Tundra Bks.) Tundra Bks. CAN. Dist: Penguin Random Hse. LLC.

—Jacob Two-Two & the Dinosaur. Richler, Mordecai. 2009. (Jacob Two-Two Ser.). (ENG.). 104p. (J). (gr. 4-7). 10.95 *(978-0-88776-926-9(8))* Tundra Bks. CAN. Dist: Random Hse., Inc.

—Jacob Two-Two Meets the Hooded Fang. Richler, Mordecai. 2009. (Jacob Two-Two Ser.). (ENG.). 96p. (J). (gr. 4-7). 10.99 *(978-0-88776-925-2(X)*, Tundra Bks.) Tundra Bks. CAN. Dist: Penguin Random Hse. LLC.

—Jacob Two-Two on the High Seas. Fagan, Cary. 2009. (Jacob Two-Two Ser.). 112p. (J). (gr. 4-7). 10.95 *(978-0-88776-895-8(4)*, Tundra Bks.) Tundra Bks. CAN. Dist: Penguin Random Hse. LLC.

—Jacob Two-Two's First Spy Case. Richler, Mordecai. 2009. (Jacob Two-Two Ser.). (ENG.). 168p. (J). (gr. 4-7). 10.95 *(978-0-88776-927-6(6))* Tundra Bks. CAN. Dist: Random Hse., Inc.

—The Man with the Violin. Stinson, Kathy. (ENG.). 36p. (J). (gr. k-3). 2016. pap. 9.95 *(978-1-55451-564-6(5))*; 5th ed. 2013. 19.95 *(978-1-55451-565-3(3)*, 9781554515653) Annick Pr., Ltd. CAN. Dist: Publishers Group West (PGW).

—Mattland. Hutchins, Hazel & Herbert, Gail. 3rd ed. 2008. (ENG.). 32p. (J). (gr. -1-2). pap. 8.95 *(978-1-55451-120-4(8)*, 9781554511204) Annick Pr., Ltd. CAN. Dist: Publishers Group West (PGW).

—Mr. Zinger's Hat. Fagan, Cary. 2012. (ENG.). 32p. (J). (gr. -1-1). 17.95 *(978-1-77049-253-0(4)*, Tundra Bks.) Tundra Bks. CAN. Dist: Penguin Random Hse. LLC.

—Mud Puddle. Munsch, Robert. 2012. (ENG.). 26p. (J). (gr. -1 — 1). bds. 7.99 *(978-1-55451-754-1(0)*, 9781554517541) Annick Pr., Ltd. CAN. Dist: Publishers Group West (PGW).

—My New Shirt. Fagan, Cary. 2007. 32p. (J). (gr. -1-1). 18.95 *(978-0-88776-715-9(X)*, Tundra Bks.) Tundra Bks. CAN. Dist: Penguin Random Hse. LLC.

—Ned Mouse Breaks Away, 1 vol. Wynne-Jones, Tim. 2003. (ENG.). 68p. (J). (gr. 3-18). 14.95 *(978-0-88899-474-5(5))* Groundwood Bks. CAN. Dist: Publishers Group West (PGW).

—On Tumbledown Hill, 1 vol. Wynne-Jones, Tim. 2008. (ENG.). 32p. (J). (gr. k-3). pap. 5.95 *(978-0-88995-409-0(7)*, b535b8c2-8843-44c4-a062-fb6fcb6cb8f6) Red Deer Pr. CAN. Dist: Firefly Bks., Ltd.

—The Queen's Feet, 1 vol. Ellis, Sarah. 2008. (ENG.). 32p. (J). (gr. -1-1). 6.95 *(978-0-88995-414-4(3)*, 6d5ffdf0-d1b7-4b2b-892a-aebc7db21c23) Trifolium Bks., Inc. CAN. Dist: Firefly Bks., Ltd.

—Zoomberry Board Book. Lee, Dennis. 2016. (ENG.). 26p. (J). bds. 10.50 *(978-1-4434-1166-0(3))* HarperCollins Pubs.

Petrie, H. D., photos by. All God's Creatures; Jesus Loves Me. ed. 2005. 32p. (J). spiral bd. *(978-0-9774115-0-4(8))* AGC Outreach Ministry.

Petrik, Mike. Bad Brows. Eaton, Jason Carter. 2020. (ENG.). 40p. (J). (gr. -1-2). 16.99 *(978-1-4197-2537-1(8)*, Abrams Bks. for Young Readers) Abrams, Inc.

—Good Sports Don't Give Up. Rumsch, BreAnn. 2019. (Good Sports Ser.). (ENG.). 24p. (J). (gr. -1-2). pap. 7.95 *(978-1-68410-427-7(0)*, 141221); lib. bdg. 33.99 *(978-1-68410-400-0(9)*, 141210) Cantata Learning.

—Good Sports Play Fair. Rumsch, BreAnn & Mallman, Mark. 2019. (Good Sports Ser.). (ENG.). 24p. (J). (gr. -1-2). pap. 7.95 *(978-1-68410-428-4(9)*, 141223) Cantata Learning.

—Good Sports Use Teamwork. Rumsch, BreAnn. 2019. (Good Sports Ser.). (ENG.). 24p. (J). (gr. -1-2). 33.99 *(978-1-68410-402-4(5)*, 141212) Cantata Learning.

—Good Sports, Win or Lose. Rumsch, BreAnn. 2019. (Good Sports Ser.). (ENG.). 24p. (J). (gr. -1-2). pap. 7.95 *(978-1-68410-430-7(0)*, 141225) Cantata Learning.

Petrlik, Andrea. Addition. Lambert, Nat. 2020. (I Can Do It! Ser.). (ENG.). 12p. (J). (gr. k-2). 9.99 *(978-1-78958-470-7(1))* Top That! Publishing PLC GBR. Dist: Independent Pubs. Group.

—All Aboard the Yellow School Bus: Follow the Bus Through the Pages on a Counting Adventure! Cabral, Jeane. Top That Publishing Staff, ed. 2008. (Story Book Ser.). 20p. (J). (gr. -1). *(978-1-84666-543-1(4)*, Tide Mill Pr.) Top That! Publishing PLC.

—Chatterbox Turtle. Rider, Cynthia. 2004. (ENG.). 24p. (J). lib. bdg. 23.65 *(978-1-59646-696-8(0))* Dingles & Co.

—Hansel & Gretel. (Flip-Up Fairy Tales Ser.). 24p. (J). 2007. (gr. -1-2). *(978-1-84643-090-9(9))*; 2006. (gr. 1-2). *(978-1-904550-73-0(8))* Child's Play International Ltd.

—Shoo, Fly! 2008. (J). *(978-0-545-03046-5(3))* Scholastic, Inc.

—The Story of Noah's Ark. Ranson, Erin. 2007. (Interactive Magnetic Book Ser.). 10p. (J). (gr. -1). *(978-1-84666-359-8(8)*, Tide Mill Pr.) Top That! Publishing PLC.

Petroff, Kathryn. A Daddy's Love Through a Girl's Eye. Williams, Joyce. 2012. 58p. pap. 9.99 *(978-0-9852729-3-7(7))* Faith Bks. & MORE.

Petrone, Valeria. Big Boy Underpants. Manushkin, Fran. 2016. 24p. (J). (— 1). bds. 7.99 *(978-0-553-53861-8(6)*, Random Hse. Bks. for Young Readers) Random Hse. Children's Bks.

—Big Girl Panties. Manushkin, Fran. 2012. 24p. (J). (gr. k — 1). bds. 7.99 *(978-0-307-93152-8(8)*, Robin Corey Bks.) Random Hse. Children's Bks.

—Colors All Around: A Turn & Pop Book. Imperato, Teresa. 2005. (Turn & Pop Book Ser.). 10p. (J). bds. 5.95 *(978-1-58117-277-5(X)*, Intervisual/Piggy Toes) Bendon, Inc.

—Dos en el Zoológico: Un Libro para Contar. Smith, Danna. 2011.Tr. of Two at the Zoo - A Counting Book. (ENG.). 30p. (J). (gr. k — 1). bds. 5.99 *(978-0-547-58137-8(8)*, 1459824) Houghton Mifflin Harcourt Publishing Co.

—Double the Ducks. Murphy, Stuart J. 2003. (MathStart Ser.). 40p. (J). 15.99 *(978-0-06-028922-5(8))* HarperCollins Pubs.

—Fish & Frog: Brand New Readers. Knudsen, Michelle. 2005. (Brand New Readers Ser.). (ENG.). 8p. (J). (gr. -1-3). pap. 5.99 *(978-0-7636-2457-6(8))* Candlewick Pr.

—Fish & Frog Big Book: Brand New Readers. Knudsen, Michelle. 2010. (Brand New Readers Ser.). 48p. (J). (gr. -1-3). pap. 24.99 *(978-0-7636-4810-7(8))* Candlewick Pr.

—How Many Ducks in a Row? A Turn & Pop Book. Imperato, Teresa. 2005. 10p. (J). bds. 5.95 *(978-1-58117-278-2(8)*, Intervisual/Piggy Toes) Bendon, Inc.

—Lasso the Moon. Holland, Trish. 2005. (Little Golden Book Ser.). 32p. (J). (gr. -1-2). 4.99 *(978-0-375-83289-5(0)*, Golden Bks.) Random Hse. Children's Bks.

—Plumply, Dumply Pumpkin. Serfozo, Mary. 2006. (Classic Board Bks.). (ENG.). 28p. (J). (gr. -1-1). bds. 7.99 *(978-0-689-86277-9(6)*, Little Simon) Little Simon.

—Potty Animals: What to Know When You've Gotta Go! Vestergaard, Hope. 2010. 32p. (J). (gr. -1-1). 14.95 *(978-1-4027-5996-3(7))* Sterling Publishing Co., Inc.

—The Pup Speaks Up. Hays, Anna Jane. 2003. (Step into Reading Ser.). 32p. (gr. -1-1). 14.00 *(978-0-7569-1696-1(8))* Perfection Learning Corp.

—The Pup Speaks Up. Hays, Anna Jane. 2003. (Step into Reading Ser.). (ENG.). 32p. (J). (gr. -1-1). pap. 4.99 *(978-0-375-81232-3(6)*, Random Hse. Bks. for Young Readers) Random Hse. Children's Bks.

—Red Truck. Hamilton, Kersten. 2012. 24p. (J). (gr. -1-k). bds. 7.99 *(978-0-670-01467-5(2)*, Viking Books for Young Readers) Penguin Young Readers Group.

—Way Far Away on a Wild Safari. Peck, Jan. 2006. (ENG.). 32p. (J). (gr. -1-3). 19.99 *(978-1-4169-0072-6(1)*, Simon & Schuster Bks. For Young Readers) Simon & Schuster Bks. For Young Readers.

—Way up High in a Tall Green Tree. Peck, Jan. 2005. (ENG.). 32p. (J). (gr. -1-3). 18.99 *(978-1-4169-0071-9(3)*, Simon & Schuster Bks. For Young Readers) Simon & Schuster Bks. For Young Readers.

Petrone, Valeria. Blue Boat. Petrone, Valeria. Hamilton, Kersten. 2016. (ENG.). 26p. (J). (-k). bds. 7.99 *(978-1-101-99853-3(9)*, Viking Books for Young Readers) Penguin Young Readers Group.

—Yellow Copter. Petrone, Valeria. Hamilton, Kersten. 2016. 26p. (J). (-k). bds. 7.99 *(978-1-101-99796-3(6)*, Viking Books for Young Readers) Penguin Young Readers Group.

Petropouleas, Niko. From a Street Kid: Stephen Lungu's Incredible Life Journey. Cope Bowley, Tonia. 2012. 192p. pap. *(978-1-78003-380-8(X))* Pen Pr. Pubs., Ltd.

Petrosino, Tamara. Cat Show. Harvey, Jayne. 2003. (Penguin Young Readers, Level 2 Ser.). (ENG.). 32p. (J). (gr. 1-2). mass mkt. 3.99 *(978-0-448-43112-3(2)*, Penguin Young Readers) Penguin Young Readers Group.

Petrossi, Fabrizio. Adventures with Grandpa! Huntley, Tex. 2018. (J). *(978-1-5444-0086-0(1)*, Golden Bks.) Random Hse. Children's Bks.

—Adventures with Grandpa! (PAW Patrol) Golden Books. 2018. (Little Golden Book Ser.). (ENG.). 24p. (J). (-k). 4.99 *(978-1-5247-6874-4(X)*, Golden Bks.) Random Hse. Children's Bks.

—All-Star Pups! (Paw Patrol) Tillworth, Mary. 2016. (Little Golden Book Ser.). (ENG.). 24p. (J). (-k). 4.99 *(978-1-101-93685-6(1)*, Golden Bks.) Random Hse. Children's Bks.

Petrossi, Fabrizio. Bubble Trouble (Corn & Peg) Vitale, Brooke. 2020. (Pictureback(R) Ser.). (ENG.). 24p. (J). (gr. -1-k). 5.99 ***(978-0-593-12420-8(0)**, Random Hse. Bks. for Young Readers) Random Hse. Children's Bks.

Petrossi, Fabrizio. Chase Is on the Case! (Paw Patrol) Random House. 2014. (Step into Reading Ser.). (ENG.). 24p. (J). (gr. -1-1). 4.99 *(978-0-385-38447-6(5)*, Random Hse. Bks. for Young Readers) Random Hse. Children's Bks.

—Disney Mickey Mouse: Let's Explore Outdoors. Fischer, Maggie. 2019. (Carry along Play Book Ser.). (ENG.). 14p. (J). (gr. -1-k). 14.99 *(978-0-7944-4233-0(1)*, Studio Fun International) Printers Row Publishing Group.

—Disney Puppy Dog Pals: When Pugs Fly. 2018. (ENG.). 10p. (J). (gr. -1-k). bds. 9.99 *(978-0-7944-4129-6(7)*, Reader's Digest Children's Bks.) Studio Fun International.

—Fry Cook Freak-Out! (SpongeBob SquarePants) Golden Books. 2014. (ENG.). 48p. (J). (gr. -1-2). pap. 3.99 *(978-0-385-37430-9(5)*, Golden Bks.) Random Hse. Children's Bks.

—The Itty-Bitty Kitty Rescue (Paw Patrol) Golden Books. 2014. (Little Golden Book Ser.). (ENG.). 24p. (J). (-k). 4.99 *(978-0-553-50884-0(9)*, Golden Bks.) Random Hse. Children's Bks.

—Jurassic Bark! (PAW Patrol) James, Hollis. 2017. (Little Golden Book Ser.). (ENG.). 24p. (J). (-k). 4.99 *(978-0-399-55880-1(2)*, Golden Bks.) Random Hse. Children's Bks.

Petrossi, Fabrizio. Nickeldeon PAW Patrol: Little First Look & Find Book & Puzzle. PI Kids. 2020. (Look & Find Ser.). (ENG.). 16p. (J). bds., bds. ***(978-1-5037-5589-5(4)**, 4d149c29-74c4-48b0-8f96-b34a4b61a9b1, p i kids) Phoenix International Publications, Inc.

Petrossi, Fabrizio, et al. Nickelodeon. Editors of PI Kids. 2020. (Look & Find Ser.). (ENG.). 72p. (J). *(978-1-5037-5318-1(2)*, d924ec6a-f888-4695-90fc-c290754ed2d0, p i kids) Phoenix International Publications, Inc.

Petrossi, Fabrizio. Nickelodeon PAW Patrol. Wage, Erin Rose. 2019. (Me Reader Jr Ser.). (ENG.). 80p. (J). *(978-1-5037-5000-5(0)*, 13a3ae73-4e32-47b3-84d4-62f30416d1a5, p i kids) Phoenix International Publications, Inc.

Petrossi, Fabrizio. Nickelodeon PAW Patrol. PI Kids. 2020. (Look & Find Ser.). (ENG.). 18p. (J). ***(978-1-5037-5467-6(7)**, 905e5a1f-36eb-4d23-919d-ab8cca95749f, p i kids) Phoenix International Publications, Inc.

Petrossi, Fabrizio. Nickelodeon PAW Patrol: Best Friends. Wage, Erin Rose. 2015. (Look & Find Ser.). (ENG.). 20p. (J). *(978-1-5037-0288-2(X)*, e4c5c265-0e36-43ab-bbe8-0c4bfa576239, p i kids) Phoenix International Publications, Inc.

—Nickelodeon PAW Patrol: Count down to Christmas. Skwish, Emily. 2016. (Play-A-Song Ser.). (ENG.). 12p. (J). bds. *(978-1-5037-1425-0(X)*, f2bbab77-3170-4a05-b641-e2aa478bafe5, p i kids) Phoenix International Publications, Inc.

—Nickelodeon PAW Patrol: I'm Ready to Read: Chase. Broderick, Kathy. 2019. (Play-A-Sound Ser.). (ENG.). 24p. (J). *(978-1-5037-4699-2(2)*, e151de80-bd3f-4dd1-ab11-d65373e0679a, p i kids) Phoenix International Publications, Inc.

—Nickelodeon: Paw Patrol: PAWsome Adventures. Wage, Erin Rose. 2019. (Look & Find Ser.). (ENG.). 16p. (J). *(978-1-5037-4763-0(8)*, a1cbb10a-482a-4a09-82a4-123feda27e90, p i kids) Phoenix International Publications, Inc.

—Nickelodeon PAW Patrol: PUPtastic Halloween. Skwish, Emily. 2016. (Play-A-Sound Ser.). (ENG.). 12p. (J). bds. *(978-1-5037-1110-5(2)*, bb24aac6-a8b2-4687-ae8b-ebc67704d08f, p i kids) Phoenix International Publications, Inc.

—Nickelodeon PAW Patrol: School Time Adventure. Behling, Steve. 2018. (ENG.). 10p. (J). (gr. -1-k). bds. 9.99 *(978-0-7944-4020-6(7)*, Reader's Digest Children's Bks.) Studio Fun International.

—PAW Patrol. Wage, Erin Rose. (Me Reader Jr Ser.). (ENG.). 80p. (J). 2019. *(978-1-5037-4630-5(5)*, 3157d412-c538-41fb-8456-91bb3e318d89); 2016. *(978-1-5037-1016-0(5)*, 14fe8f46-222d-4d8a-8216-915480cb756e) Phoenix International Publications, Inc. (p i kids).

—Pirate Pups! Ziegler-Sullivan, Ursula. 2016. (J). *(978-1-4806-9717-1(6)*, Golden Bks.) Random Hse. Children's Bks.

—Pirate Pups! (Paw Patrol) Golden Books. 2016. (Little Golden Book Ser.). (ENG.). 24p. (J). (gr. -1-k). 4.99 *(978-0-553-53888-5(8)*, Golden Bks.) Random Hse. Children's Bks.

—Puppy Birthday to You! (Paw Patrol) Golden Books. 2015. (Little Golden Book Ser.). (ENG.). 24p. (J). (-k). 4.99 *(978-0-553-52277-8(9)*, Golden Bks.) Random Hse. Children's Bks.

—Save the School Bus! (PAW Patrol) Matheis, Mickie. 2017. (Little Golden Book Ser.). (ENG.). 24p. (J). (-k). 4.99

P

(978-1-5247-1665-3(0), Golden Bks.) Random Hse. Children's Bks.

Petrossi, Fabrizio & Moore, Harry. Nickelodeon PAW Patrol. Harmening, Derek. 2018. (Look & Find Ser.). (ENG.). 14p. (J). *(978-1-5037-3493-7(5)*, 0fcc2289-2d6e-443f-91c7-9a1f575e4cf4, p i kids) Phoenix International Publications, Inc.

—Nickelodeon PAW Patrol: Read & Play with the PAW Patrol. p i kids. 2018. (ENG.). 104p. (J). *(978-1-5037-3981-9(3)*, 6cc5b858-3521-4203-925e-aa5853511159, p i kids) Phoenix International Publications, Inc.

—Nickelodeon PAW Patrol: To the Lookout! Harmening, Derek. 2020. (Look & Find Ser.). (ENG.). 14p. (J). *(978-1-5037-5264-1(X)*, 8c40b4f8-7cbd-48c0-90ed-7fe45416cb19, p i kids) Phoenix International Publications, Inc.

—Nickelodeon PAW Patrol: Up & Down. Skwish, Emily. 2019. (Take-A-Look Ser.). (ENG.). 20p. (J). *(978-1-5037-4673-2(9)*, c191722b-5537-45e3-b715-951a84b4da5c, p i kids) Phoenix International Publications, Inc.

Petrossi, Fabrizio, jt. illus. see Moore, Harry.

Petrossi, Fabrizio, jt. illus. see Random House Disney Staff.

Petrov, Anton. Jesus lo Hizo por Mi. Mackall, Dandi Daley. 2008. (SPA.). 28p. (J). (gr. -1). pap. 7.99 *(978-0-7586-1585-5(X))* Concordia Publishing Hse.

—The Lighthouse Boy: A Story about Courage. Schneider, Richard H. 2007. (ENG.). 32p. (J). (gr. -1-3). pap. 8.99 *(978-0-8249-5557-1(9)*, Ideal Pubns.) Worthy Publishing.

—Moving Day for Sam: A Story about Change. Kennedy, Pamela. 2007. 32p. (J). (gr. -1-3). 8.99 *(978-0-8249-5558-8(7)*, Ideal Pubns.) Worthy Publishing.

Petrova, Valeria. God Thought of It First. Keener, Joan N. 2006. 28p. (J). 14.99 *(978-0-7847-1432-4(0)*, 04016) Standard Publishing.

Petrovich, Eduard. Disney Frozen: Reunion Road (Graphic Novel) Caramagna, Joe. 2019. (ENG.). 72p. (J). (gr. 3-7). pap. 10.99 *(978-1-5067-1270-3(3))* Dark Horse Comics.

Petrovich, Eduard, et al. Tangled: the Series - Hair & Now. Cook, Katie. 2019. (Tangled Ser.). (ENG.). 112p. (J). (gr. 4-7). pap. 9.99 *(978-1-68405-555-5(5))* Idea & Design Works, LLC.

—Tangled: the Series - Hair-Raising Adventures. Cook, Katie. 2019. (Tangled Ser.). (ENG.). 80p. (J). (gr. 4-7). pap. 9.99 *(978-1-68405-500-5(8))* Idea & Design Works, LLC.

Petru, Suzin. Autumn's Indigo. Costanza, Francine. 2012. 30p. 24.95 *(978-1-4626-6523-5(3))* America Star Bks.

Petruccelli, Jessica, jt. illus. see Fennell, Kristen.

Petruccio, Stephen & Petruccio, Stephen. Dolphin's Rescue. Halfmann, Janet. (Smithsonian Oceanic Collection Ser.). (ENG.). 32p. (J). (gr. -1-2). 8.95 *(978-1-59249-429-3(3)*, SC4028) Soundprints.

Petruccio, Stephen, jt. illus. see Petruccio, Stephen.

Petruccio, Steven. La Galletita. Petruccio, Steven. Hillert, Margaret & Del Risco, Eida. 2018. (BeginningtoRead Ser.).Tr. of Little Cookie. (SPA.). 32p. (J). (gr. -1-2). lib. bdg. 22.60 *(978-1-59953-954-6(3))* Norwood Hse. Pr.

Petruccio, Steven James, et al. Alphabet of Ocean Animals. Galvin, Laura Gates. 2009. (ENG.). 40p. 9.95 *(978-1-60727-024-9(2))* Soundprints.

—Alphabet of Ocean Animals. Galvin, Laura Gates. 2007. (ENG.). 40p. (J). (gr. k-2). 15.95 *(978-1-59249-690-7(3))* Soundprints.

Petruccio, Steven James. The Boy Who Touched the Stars/ el Niño Que Alcanzó Las Estrellas: El Niño Que Alcanzó Las Estrellas. Hernández, José M. & Ventura, Gabriela Baeza. 2019. (ENG & SPA.). 32p. (J). (gr. 1-3). 17.95 *(978-1-55885-882-4(2))* Arte Publico Pr.

—Dolphin's First Day: The Story of a Bottlenose Dolphin. Zoehfeld, Kathleen Weidner. (Smithsonian Oceanic Collection). (J). 2009. 24.95 incl. audio compact disk *(978-1-59249-666-2(0))*; 2003. (ENG.). 32p. (gr. -1-3). pap. 6.95 *(978-1-59249-056-1(5)*, S4001) Soundprints.

—Dolphin's Rescue: The Story of a Pacific White-Sided Dolphin. Halfmann, Janet. (Smithsonian Oceanic Collection Ser.). (ENG.). 32p. (J). 2011. (gr. -1-3). 19.95 *(978-1-60727-646-3(1))*; 2011. (gr. -1-3). 8.95 *(978-1-60727-647-0(X))*; 2005. (gr. -1-3). 19.95 *(978-1-59249-430-9(7)*, BC4028); 2005. (gr. -1-3). 4.95 *(978-1-59249-427-9(7)*, B4078); 2005. (gr. -1-3). pap. 6.95 *(978-1-59249-428-6(5)*, S4028); 2005. (gr. 1-3). 15.95 *(978-1-59249-426-2(9)*, B4028) Soundprints.

—La Galletita. Hillert, Margaret. 2018. (BeginningtoRead Ser.).Tr. of Little Cookie. (SPA.). 32p. (J). (gr. -1-2). pap. 11.94 *(978-1-68404-238-8(0))* Norwood Hse. Pr.

—Great White Shark: Ruler of the Sea. Zoehfeld, Kathleen Weidner. (Smithsonian Oceanic Collection). (J). 2009. 24.95 incl. audio compact disk *(978-1-59249-664-8(4))*; 2005. (ENG.). 32p. (gr. -1-2). per. 6.95 *(978-1-59249-196-4(0)*, S4006) Soundprints.

—The Little Cookie. Hillert, Margaret. 2016. (BeginningtoRead Ser.). (ENG.). 32p. (J). (-2). lib. bdg. 22.60 *(978-1-59953-782-5(6))*; (gr. -1-2). pap. 11.94 *(978-1-60357-908-7(7))* Norwood Hse. Pr.

—Manatee Winter. Zoehfeld, Kathleen Weidner. 2005. (ENG.). 32p. (J). (gr. -1-2). 8.95 *(978-1-59249-072-1(7)*, SC4003) Soundprints.

—Narwhal: The Unicorn of the Sea. Halfmann, Janet. 2008. (ENG.). 32p. (J). (gr. -1-2). 19.95 *(978-1-59249-872-7(8))* Soundprints.

—Narwhal: Unicorn of the Sea. Halfmann, Janet. 2008. (ENG.). 32p. (J). (gr. -1-2). 16.95 *(978-1-59249-868-0(X))*; 4.95 *(978-1-59249-869-7(8))*; pap. 6.95 *(978-1-59249-870-3(1))*; pap. 9.95 *(978-1-59249-871-0(X))* Soundprints.

—Puffer's Surprise. Winkelman, Barbara Gaines. (Smithsonian Oceanic Collection Ser.). (ENG.). 32p. (J). (gr. -1-3). 2011. 19.95 *(978-1-60727-658-6(5))*; 2011. 8.95 *(978-1-60727-659-3(3))*; 2005. 15.95 *(978-1-59249-032-5(8)*, B4024); 2003. 19.95 *(978-1-59249-035-6(2)*, BC4024); 2003. 4.95 *(978-1-59249-033-2(6)*, B4074); 2003. 8.95 *(978-1-59249-062-2(X)*, SC4024); 2003. 9.95 *(978-1-59249-038-7(7)*, PB4074); 2003. 6.95 *(978-1-59249-034-9(4)*, S4024) Soundprints.

—Seahorse Reef: A Story of the South Pacific. Walker, Sally M. 2005. (ENG.). 32p. (J). (gr. -1-2). pap. 6.95 *(978-1-56899-938-8(0)*, S4020); (Smithsonian Oceanic Collection: No. 20). 15.95 *(978-1-56899-869-5(4)*, B4020) Soundprints.

Petruccio, Steven James, jt. illus. see Jack Pullan.

Petruccioli, Rita. Amazing Artists & Designers. Amson-Bradshaw, Georgia. 2018. (Brilliant Women Ser.). (ENG.). 48p. (J). (gr. 4-7). pap. 9.99 *(978-1-4380-1217-9(9)*, B.E.S. Publishing) Peterson's.

—Heroic Leaders & Activists. Amson-Bradshaw, Georgia. 2018. (Brilliant Women Ser.). (ENG.). 48p. (J). (gr. 4-7). pap. 9.99 *(978-1-4380-1218-6(7)*, B.E.S. Publishing) Peterson's.

—Incredible Sporting Champions. Amson-Bradshaw, Georgia. 2018. (Brilliant Women Ser.). (ENG.). 48p. (J). (gr. 4-7). pap. 9.99 *(978-1-4380-1219-3(5)*, B.E.S. Publishing) Peterson's.

—Pioneers of Science & Technology. Amson-Bradshaw, Georgia. 2018. (Brilliant Women Ser.). (ENG.). 48p. (J). (gr. 4-7). pap. 9.99 *(978-1-4380-1220-9(9)*, B.E.S. Publishing) Peterson's.

Petrulis, Sarah. AIDS in the Endzone. Albright, Kendra S. & Gavigan, Karen W., eds. 2014. (Young Palmetto Bks.). (ENG.). 40p. pap. 12.99 *(978-1-61117-424-3(4))* Univ. of South Carolina Pr.

Petrus, Hugo, et al. High Treason. Dumas, Alexandre. 2009. (Man in the Iron Mask Ser.: Vol. 2). (ENG.). 24p. (J). (gr. 6-12). 27.07 *(978-1-59961-595-0(9)*, 11315) ABDO Publishing Co.

Petrus, Hugo. The Pack. Van Lente, Fred. 2013. (Wolverine: First Class Ser.). (ENG.). 24p. (J). (gr. 2-6). lib. bdg. 27.07 *(978-1-61479-179-9(1)*, 15327, Marvel Age) Spotlight.

Petrus, Hugo, et al. The Three Musketeers. Dumas, Alexandre & Thomas, Roy. 2009. (Man in the Iron Mask Ser.: Vol. 1). (ENG.). 24p. (J). (gr. 6-12). 27.07 *(978-1-59961-594-3(0)*, 11314) ABDO Publishing Co.

Petrusek, Brett. El Lobo y los Siete Cabritos. Blair, Eric. Abello, Patricia, tr. 2006. (Read-It! Readers en Español: Cuentos de Hadas Ser.). (SPA.). 32p. (J). (gr. k-3). 21.32 *(978-1-4048-1645-9(3)*, Picture Window Bks.) Capstone.

Petsch, Maggie, photos by. Dora the A-Dora-ble Duck. Petsch, Maggie, text. 2004. (J). per. 9.95 *(978-0-9715860-4-8(7))* From the Asylum Bks. & Pr.

Pett, Mark. This Is My Book! 2016. (ENG.). 40p. (J). (gr. -1-2). 19.99 *(978-1-101-93790-7(4)*, Knopf Bks. for Young Readers) Random Hse. Children's Bks.

—The Very Last Castle. Jonker, Travis. 2018. (ENG.). 40p. (J). (gr. -1-3). 16.99 *(978-1-4197-2574-6(2)*, Abrams Bks. for Young Readers) Abrams, Inc.

Pett, Mark. The Boy & the Airplane. Pett, Mark. 2013. (ENG.). 40p. (J). (gr. -1). 17.99 *(978-1-4424-5123-0(8)*, Simon & Schuster Bks. For Young Readers) Simon & Schuster Bks. For Young Readers.

—The Girl & the Bicycle. Pett, Mark. 2014. (ENG.). 40p. (J). (gr. -1). 18.99 *(978-1-4424-8319-4(9)*, Simon & Schuster Bks. For Young Readers) Simon & Schuster Bks. For Young Readers.

—The Girl Who Never Made Mistakes. Pett, Mark. Rubinstein, Gary. 2011. 32p. (J). (gr. k-3). 16.99 *(978-1-4022-5544-1(6)*, Sourcebooks Jabberwocky) Sourcebooks, Inc.

—Lizard from the Park. Pett, Mark. 2015. (ENG.). 40p. (J). (gr. -1-3). 18.99 *(978-1-4424-8321-7(0)*, Simon & Schuster Bks. For Young Readers) Simon & Schuster Bks. For Young Readers.

Pettapiece, Lauren. TinkerActive Workbooks: 1st Grade Science. Butler, Megan Hewes & Odd Dot. 2019. (TinkerActive Workbooks Ser.: 5). (ENG.). 128p. (J). pap. 12.99 *(978-1-250-30725-5(2)*, 900197988, Odd Dot) St. Martin's Pr.

Pettikas-Barnes, Judy & Clark, Yvonne. The Legend of the Great Alow: The Four Black Holes. Clark, Justin. 2019. (Legend of the Great Alow Ser.: Vol. 1). (ENG.). 48p. (J). pap. 6.99 *(978-1-0974-9869-7(7))* Independently Published.

Pettingill, Charla. One to Ten NYC. Puck. 2013. (ENG.). 22p. (J). (— 1). bds. 9.95 *(978-1-938093-19-7(4)*, 809319) Duo Pr. LLC.

Petty, Colin. The Three Little Pigs: A Tale about Working Hard. 2006. (J). 6.99 *(978-1-59939-016-1(7))* Cornerstone Pr.

Petty, William Kevin. Steamduck Learns to Fly! Bush, Emilie P. 2012. 36p. pap. 11.95 *(978-0-9849028-1-1(3))* Coal City Stories.

Peyo. The Smurfs #1: The Purple Smurfs, No. 1. Delporte, Yvan. 2010. (Smurfs Graphic Novels Ser.: 1). (ENG.). 56p. (J). (gr. 2-5). 12.99 *(978-1-59707-207-6(9)*, 900070209) Papercutz.

—The Smurfs #2: The Smurfs & the Magic Flute. Delporte, Yvan. 2010. (Smurfs Graphic Novels Ser.: 3). (ENG.). 64p. (J). (gr. 2-5). 10.99 *(978-1-59707-209-0(5)*, 900070211) Papercutz.

—The Smurfs & the Magic Flute. Delporte, Yvan. 2010. (Smurfs Graphic Novels Ser.: 2). (ENG.). 56p. (J). (gr. 2-5). pap. 5.99 *(978-1-59707-208-3(7)*, 9781597072083) Papercutz.

Peyo. The Snow Giant. Peyo. 2011. (Ready-To-Read Level 2 Ser.). (ENG.). 32p. (J). (gr. k-2). 16.19 *(978-1-4424-3610-7(7)*, Simon Spotlight) Simon & Schuster Children's Publishing.

Peyrat, Jerome. On My Mountain. Aubineau, Francois. 2020. (ENG.). 32p. (J). (gr. -1-k). 19.95 *(978-1-4598-2232-0(3))* Orca Bk. Pubs. USA.

Peyrols, Sylvaine, et al. Volcanoes. Peyrols, Sylvaine et al. Stanley-Baker, Penelope, tr. 2013. (My First Discoveries Ser.). (ENG.). 36p. (J). (-k). spiral bd. 13.99 *(978-1-85103-420-8(X))* Moonlight Publishing, Ltd. GBR. Dist: Independent Pubs. Group.

Peyrols, Sylvaine. The Body. Peyrols, Sylvaine. 2012. (ENG.). 36p. (J). (gr. -1-k). spiral bd. 14.99 *(978-1-85103-396-6(3))* Moonlight Publishing, Ltd. GBR. Dist: Independent Pubs. Group.

—Crocodile. Peyrols, Sylvaine. 2012. (ENG.). 34p. (J). (gr. k-3). spiral bd. 11.99 *(978-1-85103-317-1(3))* Moonlight Publishing, Ltd. GBR. Dist: Independent Pubs. Group.

—Farm Animals. Peyrols, Sylvaine. Mathews, Sarah. 2012. (ENG.). 36p. (J). (gr. -1-k). spiral bd. 13.99 *(978-1-85103-381-2(5))* Moonlight Publishing, Ltd. GBR. Dist: Independent Pubs. Group.

—The Human Body. Peyrols, Sylvaine. Jeunesse, Gallimard. 2007. (First Discovery Book Ser.). (ENG.). 24p. (J). (gr. -1-k). pap. 5.99 *(978-0-439-91088-0(9))* Scholastic, Inc.

—Ladybugs & Other Insects. Peyrols, Sylvaine. Jeunesse, Gallimard. 2007. (First Discovery Book Ser.). (ENG.). 24p. (J). (gr. -1-k). pap. 5.99 *(978-0-439-91086-6(2))* Scholastic, Inc.

Pez. Los Grendelines. Bornemann, Elsa. 2003.Tr. of Grendelines. (SPA.). 70p. (J). (gr. 3-5). pap. 11.95 *(978-950-511-244-9(0))* Alfaguara S.A. de Ediciones ARG. Dist: Santillana USA Publishing Co., Inc.

—¡Silencio, Niños! y Otros Cuentos. Wolf, Ema. 2019. (Torre de Papel Ser.).Tr. of Be Quiet Children & Other Stories. (SPA.). 112p. (J). (gr. 4-6). pap. 15.99 *(978-958-04-3927-1(3)*, Norma) Norma S.A. COL. Dist: Distribuidora Norma, Inc.

Pezzali, Walter & Sfar, Joann. Sardine in Outer Space 5. Guibert, Emmanuel. 5th ed. 2008. (Sardine in Outer Space Ser.: 5). (ENG.). 112p. (J). (gr. 1-5). pap. 17.99 *(978-1-59643-380-9(9)*, 9781596433809, First Second Bks.) Roaring Brook Pr.

Pezzali, Walter, jt. illus. see Sfar, Joann.

Pfeifenberger, Nina. Sandy Sunday: Ruby & Fini's First Adventure. Doskar, Julia. 2019. (ENG.). 32p. (J). pap. ***(978-1-78623-645-6(1))*** Grosvenor Hse. Publishing Ltd.

Pfeiffer, Ellie. Exactly Right for Me. Rohlfing, Karen. Bakken, Dawn E., ed. 2019. (ENG.). 28p. (J). pap. 12.00 ***(978-1-0893-9627-7(9))*** Independently Published.

Pfeiffer, Judith. Paula's Pickle Picnic. Underwood, Barbara J. 2006. (ENG.). 20p. (gr. 1-3). pap. 8.95 *(978-1-57874-293-6(5)*, Kaeden Bks.) Kaeden Corp.

—Paula's Pickle Picnic (6 Pack) Underwood, Barbara J. 2006. (ENG.). 20p. (gr. 1-3). pap. *(978-1-57874-294-3(3)*, Kaeden Bks.) Kaeden Corp.

—We Didn't Know. 2012. 8p. (J). *(978-0-7367-2742-6(6))* Zaner-Bloser, Inc.

—Zippers. Boland, Janice. 2003. (Books for Young Learners). (ENG.). 8p. (J). pap. 15.00 *(978-1-57274-700-5(5)*, BB2220, Bks. for Young Learners) Owen, Richard C. Pubs., Inc.

Pfeiffer, Stephanie. NSI: Nature Science Investigator: Nature Science Investigator is a Natural Inquirer Publication. Forest Service (U.S.), ed. 2017. (ENG.). 24p. (J). pap. 4.00 *(978-0-16-093869-6(4)*, Forest Service) United States Government Printing Office.

Pfister, Marcus. What a Day... A Story in Emoji. Pfister, Marcus. 2018. (ENG.). 32p. (J). (gr. -1-k). 17.99 *(978-988-8341-23-8(5)*, Minedition) Neugebauer, Michael (Publishing) Limited HKG. Dist: Penguin Random Hse. LLC.

Pfisterer Clark, Pem. An Elephant Story for Alex. McKown, Martha. 2009. 24p. pap. 11.99 *(978-1-4389-4435-7(7))* AuthorHouse.

Pfleegor, Gina. I Like Gum. Tango-Hampton, Doreen. 2007. (ENG.). 32p. (J). (gr. -1-3). 15.95 *(978-0-9726614-2-3(5))* Shenanigan Bks.

—What If There Is a Fire?, 1 vol. Guard, Anara. 2011. (Danger Zone Ser.). (ENG.). 24p. (J). (gr. k-2). lib. bdg. 26.65 *(978-1-4048-6685-0(X)*, Picture Window Bks.) Capstone.

Pfloog, Jan. What Can an Animal Do? Lowery, Lawrence F. 2012. (I Wonder Why Ser.). (ENG.). 40p. (J). (gr. k-3). pap. 11.95 *(978-1-936959-45-7(3))* National Science Teachers Assn.

Pflueger, Maura McArdle. Hello Albert! F. Aryal, Aimee. 2004. 24p. (J). 19.95 *(978-1-932888-12-6(8))* Mascot Bks., Inc.

Pham, Khoi, et al. Doctor Strange: Mystery of the Dark Magic. Snider, Brandon T. 2018. (Mighty Marvel Chapter Bks.). (ENG.). 128p. (J). (gr. 2-7). lib. bdg. 27.07 *(978-1-5321-4215-4(3)*, 28552, Chapter Bks.) Spotlight.

—Mighty Avengers by Dan Slott: the Complete Collection. 2019. (ENG.). 424p. (YA). (gr. 8-17). pap. 39.99 *(978-1-302-91566-7(5))* Marvel Worldwide, Inc.

Pham, Khoi & Sotomayor, Chris. Ant-Man: Zombie Repellent. Wyatt, Chris 'Doc'. 2016. (Mighty Marvel Chapter Bks.). (ENG.). 128p. (J). (gr. 2-7). lib. bdg. 27.07 *(978-1-61479-479-0(0)*, 21392) Spotlight.

—Iron Man: Invasion of the Space Phantoms. Behling, Steve. 2018. (Mighty Marvel Chapter Bks.). (ENG.). 128p. (J). (gr. 2-7). lib. bdg. 27.07 *(978-1-5321-4217-8(X)*, 28554, Chapter Bks.) Spotlight.

Pham, Khoi, jt. illus. see Huat, Tan Eng.

Pham, Leuyen. Akimbo & the Elephants. McCall Smith, Alexander. 2005. (Akimbo Ser.). (ENG.). 68p. (J). (gr. 3-6). 17.44 *(978-1-58234-686-1(0)*, 9781582346861) Bloomsbury Publishing USA.

—All Fall Down. Barrett, Mary Brigid. 2014. 16p. (J). (-k). bds. 7.99 *(978-0-7636-4430-7(7))* Candlewick Pr.

—Alvin Ho: Allergic to Babies, Burglars, & Other Bumps in the Night. Look, Lenore. 2014. (Alvin Ho Ser.: 5). 192p. (J). (gr. 1-4). 6.99 *(978-0-385-38600-5(1)*, Yearling) Random Hse. Children's Bks.

—Alvin Ho: Allergic to Birthday Parties, Science Projects, & Other Man-Made Catastrophes. Look, Lenore. 2011. (Alvin Ho Ser.: 3). 192p. (J). (gr. 1-4). 6.99 *(978-0-375-87369-0(4)*, Yearling) Random Hse. Children's Bks.

—Alvin Ho: Allergic to Camping, Hiking, & Other Natural Disasters. Look, Lenore. 2010. (Alvin Ho Ser.: 2). 192p. (J). (gr. 1-4). 6.99 *(978-0-375-85750-8(8)*, Yearling) Random Hse. Children's Bks.

—Alvin Ho: Allergic to Dead Bodies, Funerals, & Other Fatal Circumstances. Look, Lenore. 2012. (Alvin Ho Ser.: 4). 208p. (J). (gr. 1-4). 6.99 *(978-0-307-97695-6(5)*, Yearling) Random Hse. Children's Bks.

—Alvin Ho: Allergic to Girls, School, & Other Scary Things. Look, Lenore. 2009. (Alvin Ho Ser.: 1). (ENG.). 192p. (J). (gr. 1-4). 6.99 *(978-0-375-84930-5(0)*, Yearling) Random Hse. Children's Bks.

—Alvin Ho: Allergic to the Great Wall, the Forbidden Palace, & Other Tourist Attractions. Look, Lenore. (Alvin Ho Ser.: 6). 176p. (J). (gr. 1-4). 2015. 6.99 *(978-0-553-52055-2(5))*; 2014. 15.99 *(978-0-385-36972-5(7))* Random Hse. Children's Bks. (Schwartz & Wade Bks.).

—Any Which Wall. Snyder, Laurel. 256p. (J). 2010. (gr. 3-7). pap. 7.99 *(978-0-375-85561-0(0))*; 2009. (ENG.). (gr. 6-8). lib. bdg. 21.19 *(978-0-375-95560-0(7))* Random Hse. Children's Bks. (Yearling).

—Bear Came Along. Morris, Richard T. 2019. 40p. (J). (gr. -1-3). 17.99 *(978-0-316-46447-5(3))* Little Brown & Co.

—The Becket List: A Blackberry Farm Story. Griffin, Adele. 2019. (ENG.). 208p. (gr. 2-6). 16.95 *(978-1-61620-790-8(6)*, 73790) Algonquin Bks. of Chapel Hill.

—Bedtime for Mommy. Rosenthal, Amy Krouse. 2010. (ENG.). 32p. (J). (gr. -1-k). 17.99 *(978-1-59990-341-5(5)*, 900055542, Bloomsbury USA Childrens) Bloomsbury Publishing USA.

—Before I Was Your Mother. Lasky, Kathryn. 2007. 32p. (J). (gr. k-2). 18.69 *(978-0-15-201464-3(0))* Houghton Mifflin Harcourt Publishing Co.

—Best Friends. Hale, Shannon. 2019. (Real Friends Ser.: 2). (ENG.). 256p. (J). 21.99 *(978-1-250-31745-2(2)*, 900199984); pap. 12.99 *(978-1-250-31746-9(0)*, 900199985) Roaring Brook Pr. (First Second Bks.).

—Best Friends Forever. Moore, Julianne. 2016. (Step into Reading Ser.). (ENG.). 32p. (J). (gr. -1-1). pap. 3.99 *(978-0-385-39197-9(8)*, Random Hse. Bks. for Young Readers) Random Hse. Children's Bks.

—Best Friends in the Universe. Watson, Stephanie. 2018. (ENG.). 40p. (J). (gr. -1-3). 17.99 *(978-0-545-65988-8(4)*, Orchard Bks.) Scholastic, Inc.

—Bo at Ballard Creek. Hill, Kirkpatrick. 2014. (ENG.). 304p. (J). (gr. 3-7). pap. 7.99 *(978-1-250-04425-9(1)*, 900128317) Square Fish.

—Boy of Mine. Asim, Jabari. 2010. 32p. (J). (gr. -1 — 1). 7.99 *(978-0-316-73577-3(9))* Little, Brown Bks. for Young Readers.

—The Boy Who Loved Math: The Improbable Life of Paul Erdos. Heiligman, Deborah. 2013. (ENG.). 48p. (J). (gr. -1-2). 19.99 *(978-1-59643-307-6(8)*, 900045300) Roaring Brook Pr.

—Fallingwater: The Building of Frank Lloyd Wright's Masterpiece. Harshman, Marc & Smucker, Anna Egan. 2017. (ENG.). 40p. (J). 18.99 *(978-1-59643-718-0(9)*, 9781596437180) Roaring Brook Pr.

—Freckleface Strawberry. Moore, Julianne. 2007. (Freckleface Strawberry Ser.). (ENG.). 40p. (J). (gr. -1-3). 17.99 *(978-1-59990-107-7(2)*, 900044746, Bloomsbury USA Childrens) Bloomsbury Publishing USA.

—Freckleface Strawberry: Monster Time! Moore, Julianne. 2017. (Step into Reading Ser.). 32p. (J). (gr. -1-1). pap. 3.99 *(978-0-385-39200-6(1)*, Random Hse. Bks. for Young Readers) Random Hse. Children's Bks.

—Freckleface Strawberry & the Really Big Voice. Moore, Julianne. 2016. (ENG.). 40p. (J). (gr. -1-2). 19.99 *(978-0-375-97370-3(2)*, Doubleday Bks. for Young Readers) Random Hse. Children's Bks.

—Freckleface Strawberry: Best Friends Forever: Best Friends Forever. Moore, Julianne. 2011. (Freckleface Strawberry Ser.). (ENG.). 40p. (J). (gr. -1-8). 16.99 *(978-1-59990-551-8(5)*, 900069347, Bloomsbury USA Childrens) Bloomsbury Publishing USA.

—Girl of Mine. Asim, Jabari. 2010. (ENG.). 20p. (J). (gr. -1 — 1). bds. 7.99 *(978-0-316-73578-0(7))* Little, Brown Bks. for Young Readers.

—God's Dream. Tutu, Desmond & Abrams, Douglas Carlton. 2008. (ENG.). 40p. (J). (gr. k-12). 17.99 *(978-0-7636-3388-2(7))* Candlewick Pr.

—God's Dream. Abrams, Douglas Carlton & Tutu, Desmond. 2010. 32p. (J). (— 1). bds. 7.99 *(978-0-7636-4742-1(X))* Candlewick Pr.

—Grace for President. DiPucchio, Kelly. 2012. (Grace Ser.: 1). 40p. (J). (gr. -1-3). 17.99 *(978-1-4231-3999-7(2))* Hyperion Pr.

—Hats off to You! Beaumont, Karen. 2017. (ENG.). 40p. (J). (gr. -1-3). 16.99 *(978-0-545-47423-8(X)*, Scholastic Pr.) Scholastic, Inc.

—Hillary Rodham Clinton: Some Girls Are Born to Lead. Markel, Michelle. 2016. (ENG.). 40p. (J). (gr. -1-3). 17.99 *(978-0-06-238122-4(9))* HarperCollins Pubs.

—Isabella for Real. Palatini, Margie. (ENG.). 208p. (J). (gr. 5-7). 2018. pap. 6.99 *(978-1-328-90014-2(2)*, 1700045); 2016. 16.99 *(978-0-544-14846-8(0)*, 1547590) Houghton Mifflin Harcourt Publishing Co. (HMH Books For Young Readers).

Pham, Leuyen. Love Is Powerful. Brewer, Heather Dean. 2020. (ENG.). 32p. (J). (gr. k-3). 16.99 ***(978-1-5362-0199-4(5))*** Candlewick Pr.

Pham, Leuyen. Monster Makeovers. DiPucchio, Kelly. 2006. (J). *(978-0-7868-5181-2(3))* Hyperion Bks. for Children.

—My Chocolate Year: A Novel with 12 Recipes. Herman, Charlotte. 2008. (ENG.). 176p. (J). (gr. 3-7). 15.99 *(978-1-4169-3341-0(7)*, Simon & Schuster Bks. For Young Readers) Simon & Schuster Bks. For Young Readers.

—Pat-a-Cake. Barrett, Mary Brigid. 2014. 16p. (J). (-k). bds. 6.99 *(978-0-7636-4358-4(0))* Candlewick Pr.

—The Princess in Black. Hale, Shannon & Hale, Dean. (Princess in Black Ser.: 1). 96p. (J). (gr. k-3). 2015. pap. 6.99 *(978-0-7636-7888-3(0))*; 2014. 14.99 *(978-0-7636-6510-4(X))* Candlewick Pr.

—The Princess in Black: #1. Hale, Shannon & Hale, Dean. 2018. (Princess in Black Ser.). (ENG.). 96p. (J). (gr. k-3). lib. bdg. 27.07 *(978-1-5321-4219-2(6)*, 28556, Chapter Bks.) Spotlight.

Pham, Leuyen. The Princess in Black & the Bathtime Battle. Hale, Shannon & Hale, Dean. (Princess in Black Ser.). (ENG.). 96p. (J). (gr. k-3). 2020. pap. 6.99 ***(978-1-5362-1575-5(9))***; 2019. 14.99 *(978-1-5362-0221-2(5))* Candlewick Pr.

Pham, Leuyen. The Princess in Black & the Hungry Bunny Horde. Hale, Shannon & Hale, Dean. 2016. (Princess in Black Ser.: 3). 96p. (J). (gr. k-3). pap. 6.99 *(978-0-7636-9089-2(9))*; 14.99 *(978-0-7636-6513-5(4))* Candlewick Pr.

—The Princess in Black & the Hungry Bunny Horde. Hale, Shannon & Hale, Dean. ed. 2016. (Princess in Black Ser.: 3). (ENG.). 85p. (J). (gr. k-3). 17.20 *(978-0-606-39109-2(6))* Turtleback.

—The Princess in Black & the Hungry Bunny Horde: #3. Hale, Shannon & Hale, Dean. 2018. (Princess in Black Ser.). (ENG.). 96p. (J). (gr. k-3). lib. bdg. 27.07 *(978-1-5321-4221-5(8)*, 28558, Chapter Bks.) Spotlight.

—The Princess in Black & the Mysterious Playdate. Hale, Shannon & Hale, Dean. (Princess in Black Ser.: 5). 96p. (J). (gr. k-3). 2018. pap. 6.99 *(978-1-5362-0051-5(4))*; 2017. 14.99 *(978-0-7636-8826-4(6))* Candlewick Pr.

—The Princess in Black & the Mysterious Playdate. Hale, Shannon & Hale, Dean. 2018. (Princess in Black Ser.). (ENG.). 96p. (J). (gr. k-3). lib. bdg. 27.07 *(978-1-5321-4223-9(4)*, 28560, Chapter Bks.) Spotlight.

—The Princess in Black & the Perfect Princess Party. Hale, Shannon & Hale, Dean. (Princess in Black Ser.: 2). (J). (gr. k-3). 2016. 96p. pap. 6.99 *(978-0-7636-8758-8(8))*; 2015. 96p. 14.99 *(978-0-7636-6511-1(8))*; 2015. 87p. ***(978-1-338-11281-8(3))*** Candlewick Pr.

—The Princess in Black & the Perfect Princess Party. Hale, Shannon & Hale, Dean. 2018. (Princess in Black Ser.). (ENG.). 96p. (J). (gr. k-3). lib. bdg. 27.07 *(978-1-5321-4220-8(X)*, 28557, Chapter Bks.) Spotlight.

—The Princess in Black & the Science Fair Scare. Hale, Shannon & Hale, Dean. (Princess in Black Ser.: 6). 96p. (J). (gr. k-3). 2019. pap. 6.99 *(978-1-5362-0686-9(5))*; 2018. 14.99 *(978-0-7636-8827-1(4))* Candlewick Pr.

—The Princess in Black Takes a Vacation. Hale, Shannon & Hale, Dean. 2016. (Princess in Black Ser.). (J). (gr. k-3). 96p. 14.99 *(978-0-7636-6512-8(6))*; 87p. *(978-1-5182-4386-8(X))* Candlewick Pr.

—The Princess in Black Takes a Vacation: #4. Hale, Shannon & Hale, Dean. 2018. (Princess in Black Ser.). (ENG.). 96p. (J). (gr. k-3). lib. bdg. 27.07 *(978-1-5321-4222-2(6)*, 28559, Chapter Bks.) Spotlight.

—The Princess in Black: Three Monster-Battling Adventures. Hale, Shannon & Hale, Dean. 2019. (Princess in Black Ser.). (J). (gr. k-3). pap. 20.97 *(978-1-5362-0953-2(8))* Candlewick Pr.

—The Princess in Black: Three Smashing Adventures. Hale, Shannon & Hale, Dean. 2017. (Princess in Black Ser.). (J). (gr. k-3). pap. 20.97 *(978-0-7636-9777-8(X))* Candlewick Pr.

—Real Friends. Hale, Shannon. 2017. (Real Friends Ser.: 1). (ENG.). 224p. (J). 21.99 *(978-1-62672-416-7(4)*, 900156399); pap. 12.99 *(978-1-62672-785-4(6)*, 900171908) Roaring Brook Pr. (First Second Bks.).

—Sheep 101. Morris, Richard T. 2018. 48p. (J). (gr. -1-3). 17.99 *(978-0-316-21359-2(4))* Little Brown & Co.

—Shoe-la-La! Beaumont, Karen. 2011. (ENG.). 40p. (J). (gr. -1-3). 16.99 *(978-0-545-06705-8(7)*, Scholastic Pr.) Scholastic, Inc.

—A Stick Is an Excellent Thing: Poems Celebrating Outdoor Play. Singer, Marilyn. 2012. (ENG.). 40p. (J). (gr. -1-3). 18.99 *(978-0-547-12493-3(7)*, 1047756) Houghton Mifflin Harcourt Publishing Co.

—Stop That Yawn! Levis, Caron. 2018. (ENG.). 48p. (J). (gr. -1-3). 17.99 *(978-1-4814-4179-7(5)*, Atheneum Bks. for Young Readers) Simon & Schuster Children's Publishing.

—Twenty-One Elephants. Bildner, Phil. 2004. (ENG.). 40p. (J). (gr. -1-3). 19.99 *(978-0-689-87011-8(6)*, Simon & Schuster Bks. For Young Readers) Simon & Schuster Bks. For Young Readers.

—Vampirina at the Beach. Pace, Anne Marie. 2017. (Vampirina Ser.: 3). (ENG.). 40p. (J). (gr. -1-k). 16.99 *(978-1-4847-7342-0(X))* Disney Pr.

—Vampirina Ballerina. Pace, Anne Marie. 2012. (Vampirina Ser.: 1). (ENG.). 40p. (J). (gr. -1-k). 16.99 *(978-1-4231-5753-3(2))* Hyperion Pr.

—Vampirina Ballerina Hosts a Sleepover. Pace, Anne Marie. 2013. (Vampirina Ser.: 2). (ENG.). 40p. (J). (gr. -1-k). 16.99 *(978-1-4231-7570-4(0))* Hyperion Pr.

—Vampirina in the Snow (a Vampirina Ballerina Book) Pace, Anne Marie. 2018. (Vampirina Ser.: 4). (ENG.). 40p. (J). (gr. -1-k). 17.99 *(978-1-368-02318-4(5))* Hyperion Bks. for Children.

—Whose Knees Are These? Asim, Jabari. ed. 2019. 22p. (J). (gr. -1 — 1). 7.99 *(978-0-316-45429-2(X))* Little, Brown Bks. for Young Readers.

—Whose Toes Are Those? Asim, Jabari. ed. 2019. 22p. (J). (gr. -1 — 1). 7.99 *(978-0-316-45432-2(X))* Little, Brown Bks. for Young Readers.

Pham, Leuyen. All the Things I Love about You. Pham, Leuyen. 2010. (ENG.). 40p. (J). (gr. -1-3). 14.99 *(978-0-06-199029-8(9))* HarperCollins Pubs.

—The Bear Who Wasn't There. Pham, Leuyen. 2016. (ENG.). 40p. (J). 16.99 *(978-1-59643-970-2(X)*, 900126977) Roaring Brook Pr.

—Big Sister Little Sister. Pham, Leuyen. 2005. (ENG.). 40p. (J). (gr. -1-k). 15.99 *(978-0-7868-5182-9(1))* Hyperion Pr.

—A Piece of Cake. Pham, Leuyen. 2014. (ENG.). 40p. (J). (gr. -1-3). 16.99 *(978-0-06-199264-3(X))* HarperCollins Pubs.

—Shoe-la-La! A Storyplay Book. Pham, Leuyen. Beaumont, Karen. 2016. (ENG.). 40p. (J). (gr. -1-k). 5.99 *(978-1-338-11555-0(3)*, Cartwheel Bks.) Scholastic, Inc.

Pham, Leuyen, jt. illus. see Shed, Greg.

Pham, Leuyen, jt. illus. see Willems, Mo.

Pham, Xuan. The Turtle Who Couldn't Swim. Petersen, Pat. 2012. 28p. 24.95 *(978-1-4626-8615-5(X))*; pap. 24.95 *(978-1-4626-4847-4(9))* America Star Bks.

Phan, An. Sled Dog Dachshund. Atkins, Laura. 2016. (ENG.). 32p. (J). (gr. k-2). 14.99 *(978-0-9965454-3-3(3))* Minted Prose, LLC.

Phan, Henry, et al. When Watute Wants Some Water. Sarja, Jennifer. 2005. 36p. (J). (gr. -1-3). 20.00 *(978-0-9773451-0-6(6))* Youth Inkwell Publishing.

Phan, Tom M. The Adventures of Tom the Rabbit: Into the Fox's Lair. Phan, Tom M. 2019. (Adventures of Tom the Rabbit Ser.: Vol. 1). (ENG.). 38p. (J). (gr. k-6). 25.99 *(978-0-578-47706-0(8))* Phan, Tom.

Pharis, Davis. Eugene Fishing & Wishing: The Reasoning of a Creative Mouse. Lynn C, Skinner. 2017. (ENG.). (J). (gr. k-4). pap. 11.99 *(978-0-9991679-3-9(6))* Skinner, Lynn C.

Phatak, Bhakti. Basava & the Dots of Fire. Chadha, Radhika. 2005. 24p. (J). *(978-81-8146-165-0(7))* Tulika Pubs.

Phelan, Jennifer. Bobby Orr & the Hand-Me-down Skates. Kootstra, Kara & Orr, Bobby. 2020. (ENG.). 40p. (J). (gr. -1-3). 17.99 ***(978-0-7352-6532-5(1)***, Tundra Bks.) Tundra Bks. CAN. Dist: Penguin Random Hse. LLC.

Phelan, Jennifer. Hey, Boy. Strouse, Benjamin. 2014. (ENG.). 40p. (J). pap. 7.95 *(978-1-4575-3341-9(3))* Dog Ear Publishing, LLC.

—Hey, Boy. Strouse, Benjamin. 2017. (ENG.). 48p. (J). (gr. -1-3). 15.99 *(978-1-4814-7101-5(5)*, McElderry, Margaret K. Bks.) McElderry, Margaret K. Bks.

—The Log Driver's Waltz. Hemsworth, Wade. 2018. (ENG.). 40p. (J). (gr. -1). 17.99 *(978-1-5011-6195-7(4))* Simon & Schuster.

Phelan, Matt. Always. Stott, Ann. 2008. (ENG.). 32p. (J). (gr. k-k). 15.99 *(978-0-7636-3232-8(5))* Candlewick Pr.

—Big George: How a Shy Boy Became President Washington. Rockwell, Anne. 2015. (ENG.). 48p. (J). (gr. 1-4). pap. 8.99 *(978-0-544-58246-0(2)*, 1613675, HMH Books For Young Readers) Houghton Mifflin Harcourt Publishing Co.

—A Box Full of Kittens. Manzano, Sonia. 2007. (ENG.). 40p. (J). (gr. -1-3). 17.99 *(978-0-689-83089-1(0)*, Atheneum Bks. for Young Readers) Simon & Schuster Children's Publishing.

—Flora's Very Windy Day. Birdsall, Jeanne. 2013. (ENG.). 32p. (J). (gr. -1-3). pap. 7.99 *(978-0-547-99485-7(0)*, 1525240) Houghton Mifflin Harcourt Publishing Co.

—The Higher Power of Lucky. Patron, Susan. (ENG.). (J). (gr. 4-6). 2008. 160p. pap. 7.99 *(978-1-4169-7557-1(8)*, Atheneum Bks. for Young Readers); 2006. 144p. 18.99 *(978-1-4169-0194-5(9)*, Atheneum/Richard Jackson Bks.) Simon & Schuster Children's Publishing.

—If Wendell Had a Walrus. Mortensen, Lori. 2018. (ENG.). 32p. (J). 17.99 *(978-1-62779-602-6(9)*, 900156503, Holt, Henry & Co. Bks. For Young Readers) Holt, Henry & Co.

—I'll Be There. Stott, Ann. 2011. (ENG.). 32p. (J). (gr. -1-2). 14.99 *(978-0-7636-4711-7(X))* Candlewick Pr.

—A Kite for Moon, 1 vol. Yolen, Jane & Stemple, Heidi E. Y. 2019. (ENG.). 32p. (J). 17.99 *(978-0-310-75642-2(1))* Zonderkidz.

—Little Robot Alone. Maclachlan, Patricia & Charest, Emily MacLachlan. 2018. (ENG.). 40p. (J). (gr. -1-3). 17.99 *(978-0-544-44280-1(6)*, 1597246, HMH Books For Young Readers) Houghton Mifflin Harcourt Publishing Co.

—Lucky Breaks. Patron, Susan. (ENG.). (J). (gr. 3-7). 2010. 208p. pap. 8.99 *(978-1-4169-9772-6(5))*; 2009. 192p. 16.99 *(978-1-4169-3998-6(9))* Simon & Schuster Children's Publishing. (Atheneum Bks. for Young Readers).

—Marilyn's Monster. Knudsen, Michelle. 40p. (J). (gr. -1-3). 2017. 6.99 *(978-0-7636-9301-5(4))*; 2015. (ENG.). 16.99 *(978-0-7636-6011-6(6))* Candlewick Pr.

—Marilyn's Monster. Knudsen, Michelle. ed. 2017. (ENG.). (J). (gr. -1-3). lib. bdg. 17.20 *(978-0-606-39844-2(9))* Turtleback.

—Miss Emily. Muten, Burleigh. 2014. 144p. (J). (gr. 2-5). 15.99 *(978-0-7636-5734-5(4))* Candlewick Pr.

—The New Girl... & Me. Robbins, Jacqui. 2006. (ENG.). 32p. (J). (gr. -1-2). 19.99 *(978-0-689-86468-1(X)*, Atheneum/Richard Jackson Bks.) Simon & Schuster Children's Publishing.

—The Seven Wonders of Sassafras Springs. Birney, Betty G. 2007. 210p. 17.00 *(978-0-7569-8075-7(5))* Perfection Learning Corp.

—The Seven Wonders of Sassafras Springs. Birney, Betty G. 2007. (ENG.). 224p. (J). (gr. 3-7). pap. 7.99 *(978-1-4169-3489-9(8)*, Atheneum Bks. for Young Readers) Simon & Schuster Children's Publishing.

—Spilling Ink: a Young Writer's Handbook. Potter, Ellen & Mazer, Anne. 2010. (ENG.). 288p. (YA). (gr. 4-9). pap., instr.'s hndbk. ed. 11.99 *(978-1-59643-628-2(X)*, 900067993) Square Fish.

—Two of a Kind. Robbins, Jacqui. 2009. (ENG.). 32p. (J). (gr. -1-2). 18.99 *(978-1-4169-2437-1(X)*, Atheneum Bks. for Young Readers) Simon & Schuster Children's Publishing.

—Very Hairy Bear. Schertle, Alice. ed. 2012. lib. bdg. 17.20 *(978-0-606-26605-5(4))* Turtleback.

—Xander's Panda Party. Park, Linda Sue. (ENG.). 40p. (J). (gr. -1-3). 2017. pap. 7.99 *(978-1-328-74058-8(7)*, 1677033, HMH Books For Young Readers); 2013. 16.99 *(978-0-547-55865-3(1)*, 1453620) Houghton Mifflin Harcourt Publishing Co.

—You Are My Friend: The Story of Mister Rogers & His Neighborhood. Reid, Aimee. 2019. (ENG.). 40p. (J). (gr. k-3). 17.99 *(978-1-4197-3617-9(5)*, Abrams Bks. for Young Readers) Abrams, Inc.

Phelan, Matt. Around the World. Phelan, Matt. (ENG.). 240p. (J). (gr. 4-7). 2014. pap. 12.99 *(978-0-7636-6925-6(3))*; 2011. 24.99 *(978-0-7636-3619-7(3))* Candlewick Pr.

—Around the World. Phelan, Matt. 2014. (ENG.). (J). (gr. 4-7). lib. bdg. 23.60 *(978-1-62765-459-3(3))* Perfection Learning Corp.

—Bluffton. Phelan, Matt. 2013. (ENG.). 240p. (J). (gr. 4-7). 22.99 *(978-0-7636-5079-7(X))* Candlewick Pr.

—Bluffton: My Summers with Buster. Phelan, Matt. 2017. (ENG.). 232p. (J). (gr. 4-7). pap. 12.99 *(978-0-7636-8706-9(5))* Candlewick Pr.

—Bluffton: My Summers with Buster. Phelan, Matt. ed. 2017. (ENG.). (J). (gr. 4-7). lib. bdg. 24.50 *(978-0-606-39837-4(6))* Turtleback.

—Druthers. Phelan, Matt. 2014. 32p. (J). (-k). 15.99 *(978-0-7636-5955-4(X))* Candlewick Pr.

—Knights vs. Dinosaurs. Phelan, Matt. (ENG.). (J). (gr. 3-7). 2019. 176p. pap. 6.99 *(978-0-06-268624-4(0))*; 2018. 160p. 16.99 *(978-0-06-268623-7(2))* HarperCollins Pubs. (Greenwillow Bks.).

—Knights vs. Monsters. Phelan, Matt. (ENG.). (J). (gr. 3-7). 2020. 192p. pap. 7.99 *(978-0-06-268627-5(5))*; 2019. 176p. 16.99 *(978-0-06-268626-8(7))* HarperCollins Pubs. (Greenwillow Bks.).

Phelan, Matt. Knights vs. the End (of Everything) Phelan, Matt. 2020. (ENG.). 192p. (J). (gr. 3-7). pap. 7.99 ***(978-0-06-291098-1(1))***; 16.99 *(978-0-06-291097-4(3))* HarperCollins Pubs. (Greenwillow Bks.).

Phelan, Matt. Pignic. Phelan, Matt. 2018. (ENG.). 32p. (J). (gr. -1-3). 17.99 *(978-0-06-244339-7(9)*, Greenwillow Bks.) HarperCollins Pubs.

—Snow White: A Graphic Novel. Phelan, Matt. 216p. (J). (gr. 5). 2018. pap. 14.99 *(978-1-5362-0055-3(7))*; 2016. 19.99 *(978-0-7636-7233-1(5))* Candlewick Pr.

Phelan, Matt, jt. illus. see Trueman, Matthew.

Phelan, Michele-lee. Mythic Oracle: Wisdom of the Ancient Greek Pantheon. Mellado, Carisa. 2012. (ENG.). 160p. (YA). (gr. 7). pap. 24.99 *(978-1-58270-325-1(6))* Simon Pulse/Beyond Words.

Phelan, Nicky. I'm Proud to Be Me: Poems for Children & Their Parents. Fitzmaurice, Gabriel. 2005. (ENG.). 96p. (J). pap. 12.95 *(978-1-85635-474-5(1))* Mercier Pr., Ltd., The IRL. Dist: Dufour Editions, Inc.

—Penny in Space. O'Hely, Eileen. 2009. (ENG.). 225p. (J). pap. 14.95 *(978-1-85635-571-1(3))* Mercier Pr., Ltd., The IRL. Dist: Dufour Editions, Inc.

—Penny on Safari. O'Hely, Eileen. 2010. (ENG.). 192p. (J). pap. 15.95 *(978-1-85635-572-8(1))* Mercier Pr., Ltd., The IRL. Dist: Dufour Editions, Inc.

—Penny the Pencil. O'Hely, Eileen. 2005. (ENG.). 200p. (J). pap. 13.00 *(978-1-85635-475-2(X))* Mercier Pr., Ltd., The IRL. Dist: Dufour Editions, Inc.

—Splat: And Other Great Poems. Fitzmaurice, Gabriel & Macdonald, Stella. 2012. (ENG.). 96p. (J). pap. 13.95 *(978-1-85635-953-5(0))* Mercier Pr., Ltd., The IRL. Dist: Dufour Editions, Inc.

Phelipon, Laure. Kimberly et la Bête de Feu. O'Neil, Jane. 2018. (Kimberly Ser.: Vol. 4). (FRE.). 114p. (J). pap. *(978-2-924263-16-7(6))* Éditions de la Corde raide.

Phelps Williams, Janice. Still Her Spirit Sings: One Dog's Love, Lessons, Life & Legacy. 2010. 32p. (J). (gr. k-2). 16.95 *(978-0-9760220-1-5(X))* Kidzpoetz Publishing.

Phil. Me & You & the Red Canoe, 1 vol. Pendziwol, Jean E. 2017. (ENG.). 32p. (J). (gr. k). 18.95 *(978-1-55498-847-1(0))* Groundwood Bks. CAN. Dist: Publishers Group West (PGW).

Phil Brannan & Sunni Brannan. Juanita's Flowers. Sally Spencer. 2009. 32p. pap. 14.49 *(978-1-4389-4841-6(7))* AuthorHouse.

Philbrick, Katie, jt. illus. see Stockton, Greta.

Philip Dadd. William Tell Told Again - Illustrated in Color. Wodehouse, Pelham Grenville. 2009. 76p. pap. 14.95 *(978-1-60386-208-0(0)*, Watchmaker Publishing) Wexford College Pr.

Philip, Deg. Mia's Reflections. Marks, Ginger. 2019. (ENG.). 40p. (J). (gr. k-3). pap. 14.99 *(978-1-937801-94-6(2)*, DP Kids Pr.) DocUmeant Publishing.

Philipp, Cathy, et al, photos by. On the Trail Again: Malibu to Santa Barbara, 1. Philipp, Cathy. 2004. 252p. per. *(978-0-9655848-1-4(X))* Philipp, Cathy Publishing.

Philippe, Dupasquier. A Country Far Away. Gray, Nigel. 2012. 32p. pap. *(978-0-9808760-2-4(8))* Vivid Publishing.

Philipponneau, Olivier & Enjary, Raphaële. ONE Very Big Bear. Brière-Haquet, Alice. 2016. (ENG.). 32p. (J). (gr. -1-k). 14.95 *(978-1-4197-2117-5(8)*, Abrams Appleseed) Abrams, Inc.

Philips, Mike. Detective Brother. Johnson, Pete. 2019. 106p. (J). pap. 4.99 *(978-1-61067-744-8(7))* Kane Miller.

—Own Goal. MacPhail, Catherine. 2015. (Collins Big Cat Ser.). (ENG.). 24p. (J). (gr. 2-2). pap. 7.95 *(978-0-00-759114-5(4))* HarperCollins Pubs. Ltd. GBR. Dist: Independent Pubs. Group.

Philips, Sean. Marvel Zombies 2. Kirkman, Robert. 2019. (ENG.). 120p. (YA). (gr. 8-17). pap. 15.99 *(978-1-302-92263-4(7))* Marvel Worldwide, Inc.

Philipson, Patricia, et al. Disney. PI Kids. 2020. (Look & Find Ser.). (ENG.). 72p. (J). ***(978-1-5037-5364-8(6)***, 68f45fe2-626d-4b04-9083-b9deb2d93218, p i kids) Phoenix International Publications, Inc.

Phillip, Ortiz. Courage the Hawk: Overcoming Fear. Russell, Reba. 2017. (ENG.). 42p. (J). (gr. k-3). 18.99 *(978-0-9974913-5-7(3))* Kingdom Door Publishing LLC.

Phillippi, Faith, jt. illus. see Beatty, Connie.

Phillipps, Francis. Jason & the Golden Fleece: A Greek Legend. 2004. (ENG.). 24p. (J). (gr. 3-3). pap. 6.47 net. *(978-0-7685-2126-9(2)*, Dominie Elementary) Savvas Learning Co.

Phillips. Bubbie's Baby. Phillips, . 2006. 28p. (J). 14.99 *(978-0-9774552-0-1(3))* Danza Pubns.

Phillips, Alan, pseud. The Sleepover Surprise. Cushing, Mims. 2010. 24p. pap. 12.95 *(978-1-936343-01-0(0))* Peppertree Pr., The.

Phillips, Andrea, jt. illus. see Phillips, Elizabeth.

Phillips, April. Let's Play Football: In English & Tigrinya. Ready Set Go Books. Dessalegn, Aklilu, tr. 2019. (ENG.). 34p. (J). pap. 11.99 ***(978-1-6892-6656-7(2))*** Independently Published.

Phillips, Craig. The Alchemist War, 1 vol. Seven, John. 2013. (Time-Tripping Faradays Ser.). (ENG.). 160p. (J). (gr. 4-8). 9.95 *(978-1-62370-011-9(6)*, Capstone Young Readers); pap. 5.95 *(978-1-4342-6438-1(6)*, Stone Arch Bks.); lib. bdg. 26.65 *(978-1-4342-6028-4(3)*, Stone Arch Bks.) Capstone.

Phillips, Craig. Alkyoneus & the Warrior Queen. West, Tracey. 2020. (Heroes in Training Ser.: 17). (ENG.). 112p. (J). (gr. 1-4). 17.99 ***(978-1-5344-3295-6(7))***; pap. 5.99 ***(978-1-5344-3294-9(9))*** Simon & Schuster Children's Publishing. (Aladdin).

Phillips, Craig. Apollo & the Battle of the Birds. Holub, Joan & Williams, Suzanne. 2014. (Heroes in Training Ser.: 6). (ENG.). 128p. (J). (gr. 1-4). pap. 5.99 *(978-1-4424-8845-8(X)*, Aladdin) Simon & Schuster Children's Publishing.

—Apollo & the Battle of the Birds. Holub, Joan & Williams, Suzanne. 2014. (Heroes in Training Ser.: 6). (ENG.). 128p. (J). (gr. 1-4). 16.99 *(978-1-4424-8846-5(8)*, Simon & Schuster/Paula Wiseman Bks.) Simon & Schuster/Paula Wiseman Bks.

—Ares & the Spear of Fear. Holub, Joan & Williams, Suzanne. 2014. (Heroes in Training Ser.: 7). (ENG.). 112p. (J). (gr. 1-4). pap. 6.99 *(978-1-4424-8848-9(4)*, Aladdin) Simon & Schuster Children's Publishing.

—Battle Drift. Strasser, Todd. 2006. (DriftX Ser.: 2). (ENG.). 224p. (YA). (gr. 9-12). pap. 10.99 *(978-1-4169-0582-0(0)*, Simon Pulse) Simon Pulse.

—Bogus to Bubbly: An Insider's Guide to the World of Uglies. Westerfeld, Scott. 2008. (Uglies Ser.). (ENG.). 224p. (YA). (gr. 7). pap. 8.99 *(978-1-4169-7436-9(9)*, Simon Pulse) Simon Pulse.

—Chasing Shadows. Avasthi, Swati. 2015. (ENG.). 336p. (YA). (gr. 9). pap. 10.99 *(978-0-375-86343-1(5)*, Ember) Random Hse. Children's Bks.

—Crius & the Night of Fright. Holub, Joan & Williams, Suzanne. 2015. (Heroes in Training Ser.: 9). (ENG.). 96p. (J). (gr. 1-4). pap. 5.99 *(978-1-4814-3506-2(X)*, Aladdin) Simon & Schuster Children's Publishing.

—Dionysus & the Land of Beasts. West, Tracey. 2017. (Heroes in Training Ser.: 14). (ENG.). 112p. (J). (gr. 1-4). 16.99 *(978-1-4814-8835-8(X))*; pap. 5.99 *(978-1-4814-8834-1(1))* Simon & Schuster Children's Publishing. (Aladdin).

—Disguised & Dangerous. Mason, Jane B. & Hines-Stephens, Sarah. 2011. 92p. (J). *(978-0-545-37469-9(3))* Scholastic, Inc.

—The Dragon of Rome, 1 vol. Seven, John. 2013. (Time-Tripping Faradays Ser.). (ENG.). 160p. (J). (gr. 4-8). 9.95 *(978-1-62370-012-6(4)*, Capstone Young Readers); lib. bdg. 26.65 *(978-1-4342-6029-1(1)*, Stone Arch Bks.) Capstone.

—Enemy Rising. West, Tracey. 2010. (Hiro's Quest Ser.: 1). (ENG.). 96p. (J). (gr. 2-5). 4.99 *(978-0-545-16288-3(2)*, Scholastic Paperbacks) Scholastic, Inc.

—Hades & the Helm of Darkness. Holub, Joan & Williams, Suzanne. 2013. (Heroes in Training Ser.: 3). (ENG.). 128p. (J). (gr. 1-4). 15.99 *(978-1-4424-5725-6(2))*; pap. 5.99 *(978-1-4424-5267-1(6))* Simon & Schuster Children's Publishing. (Aladdin).

—Hephaestus & the Island of Terror. Holub, Joan & Williams, Suzanne. 2015. (Heroes in Training Ser.: 10). (ENG.). 128p. (J). (gr. 1-4). pap. 6.99 *(978-1-4814-3509-3(4)*, Aladdin) Simon & Schuster Children's Publishing.

—Hercules & the Nine-Headed Hydra. West, Tracey. 2019. (Heroes in Training Ser.: 16). (ENG.). 112p. (J). (gr. 1-4). 17.99 *(978-1-5344-3292-5(2))*; pap. 5.99 *(978-1-5344-3291-8(4))* Simon & Schuster Children's Publishing. (Aladdin).

—Hermes & the Horse with Wings. West, Tracey. 2017. (Heroes in Training Ser.: 13). (ENG.). 112p. (J). (gr. 1-4). pap. 5.99 *(978-1-4814-8831-0(7)*, Simon & Schuster/Paula Wiseman Bks.) Simon & Schuster/Paula Wiseman Bks.

—Hyperion & the Great Balls of Fire. Holub, Joan & Williams, Suzanne. 2013. (Heroes in Training Ser.: 4). (ENG.). 144p. (J). (gr. 1-4). pap. 6.99 *(978-1-4424-5269-5(2)*, Aladdin) Simon & Schuster Children's Publishing.

—Hyperion & the Great Balls of Fire. Holub, Joan & Williams, Suzanne. 2013. (Heroes in Training Ser.: 4). (ENG.). 144p. (J). (gr. 1-4). 17.99 *(978-1-4424-5803-1(8)*, Simon & Schuster/Paula Wiseman Bks.) Simon & Schuster/Paula Wiseman Bks.

—Let Sleeping Dogs Spy. Mason, Jane B. & Hines-Stephens, Sarah. 2012. 91p. (J). pap. *(978-0-545-37470-5(7))* Scholastic, Inc.

—Perseus & the Monstrous Medusa. Holub, Joan & Williams, Suzanne. 2016. (Heroes in Training Ser.: 12). (ENG.). 128p. (J). (gr. 1-4). 17.99 *(978-1-4814-3516-1(7))*; pap. 5.99 *(978-1-4814-3515-4(9))* Simon & Schuster Children's Publishing. (Aladdin).

—Poseidon & the Sea of Fury. Holub, Joan & Williams, Suzanne. 2012. (Heroes in Training Ser.: 2). (ENG.). 128p. (J). (gr. 1-4). 16.99 *(978-1-4424-5798-0(8))*; pap. 5.99 *(978-1-4424-5265-7(X))* Simon & Schuster Children's Publishing. (Aladdin).

—Sidewayz Glory. Strasser, Todd. 2006. (DriftX Ser.: 3). (ENG.). 208p. (YA). (gr. 9-12). pap. 10.99 *(978-1-4169-0583-7(9)*, Simon Pulse) Simon Pulse.

—Slide or Die. Strasser, Todd. 2006. (DriftX Ser.: 1). (ENG.). 224p. (YA). (gr. 9-18). pap. 10.99 *(978-1-4169-0581-3(2)*, Aladdin) Simon & Schuster Children's Publishing.

—Typhon & the Winds of Destruction. Holub, Joan & Williams, Suzanne. 2013. (Heroes in Training Ser.: 5). (ENG.). 112p. (J). (gr. 1-4). 16.99 *(978-1-4424-8844-1(1))*; pap. 6.99 *(978-1-4424-8842-7(5))* Simon & Schuster Children's Publishing. (Aladdin).

—Uranus & the Bubbles of Trouble. Holub, Joan & Williams, Suzanne. 2015. (Heroes in Training Ser.: 11). (ENG.). 128p. (J). (gr. 1-4). pap. 6.99 *(978-1-4814-3512-3(4)*, Aladdin) Simon & Schuster Children's Publishing.

—Zeus & the Dreadful Dragon. West, Tracey. 2018. (Heroes in Training Ser.: 15). (ENG.). 128p. (J). (gr. 1-4). 16.99 *(978-1-4814-8838-9(4))*; pap. 5.99 *(978-1-4814-8837-2(6))* Simon & Schuster Children's Publishing. (Aladdin).

—Zeus & the Thunderbolt of Doom. Holub, Joan & Williams, Suzanne. 2012. (Heroes in Training Ser.: 1). (ENG.). 112p. (J). (gr. 1-4). 18.99 *(978-1-4424-5787-4(2))*; pap. 6.99 *(978-1-4424-5263-3(3))* Simon & Schuster Children's Publishing. (Aladdin).

—Zeus & the Thunderbolt of Doom/Poseidon & the Sea of Fury: Heroes in Training Flip Book #1-2. Holub, Joan & Williams, Suzanne. 2018. (Heroes in Training Ser.). (ENG.). 240p. (J). (gr. 1-4). pap. 7.99 *(978-1-5344-2858-4(5)*, Aladdin) Simon & Schuster Children's Publishing.

Phillips, Craig. The Adventures of Jack Scratch: The Quest for the Hiss-Paniola. Phillips, Craig. 2018. (Adventures of Jack Scratch Ser.: Vol. 1). (ENG.). 56p. (J). (gr. k-6). 22.00 *(978-0-473-43079-5(7))*; pap. 14.45 *(978-0-473-43001-6(0))* MCA Denver.

P

Pihl, Monique. Professional Bubbleology - the Art of Blowing Bubbles. Maxwell-Stewart, Philip. 2017. (ENG.). 124p. (J). pap. (978-1-5272-0469-0(3)) JWS Europe Ltd.
Pijet, Andre. Rumpelstiltskin. Klioryte, Kristina. 2011. (ENG.). 16p. pap. 12.95 (978-2-89558-410-0(9), 9782895584100) Editions Alexandre Stanke CAN. Dist: Baker & Taylor Publisher Services (BTPS).
Pijoan, Randall. Milagro of the Spanish Bean Pot. Romero-Anderson, Emerita. 2011. (ENG.). 128p. (J). (gr. 4-6). 18.95 (978-0-89672-681-9(9)) Texas Tech Univ. Pr.
Pike, Amanda. Not This Turkey! Steinberg, Jessica. 2016. (ENG.). 32p. (J). (gr. -1-3). 16.99 (978-0-8075-7908-4(4), 807579084) Whitman, Albert & Co.
Pike, Carol, et al. Ten Red Hens - Get up, Meg! - Dan & Ed: StartUp Unit 6 Lap Book. Benjamin, Joseph et al. 2015. (Start up Core Phonics Ser.). (J). (gr. k). (978-1-4900-2595-7(2)) Benchmark Education Co.
Pike, Janene Elise. The Colour Fairies Series Book 9: St Valentine's Day in Fairyland. Jeffrey, Maggie. 2019. (Colour Fairies Ser.: Vol. 9). (ENG.). 36p. (J). pap. 10.00 (978-1-7932-8195-1(5)) Independently Published.
Pikoj, Ed. The True Colors of a Princess Coloring Book: Companion to What Does a Princess Really Look Like? Loewen, Mark. 2019. (Brave Like a Girl Ser.). (ENG.). 40p. (J). (gr. k-2). pap. 8.95 (978-1-945448-36-2(9), BQB Publishing) Boutique of Quality Books Publishing Co., Inc.
Pilatowski, Boris. Diego Rana-Pintor. Cortes, Eunice & Cortes, Laura. 2003. (SPA.). 56p. (J). (gr. 3-5). pap. 13.95 (978-968-19-0604-7(7)) Santillana USA Publishing Co., Inc.
Pileggi, Steve. Four Pals on a Field Trip: An Adventure with Friends Who Are Different. Tucker, Angel. 2013. (Four Pals Ser.). (ENG.). 34p. (J). (gr. -1-3). pap. 8.95 (978-1-62086-487-6(8)) Mascot Bks., Inc.
—Heather & Avery & the Magic Kite. Deubreau, Sharon. l.t. ed. 2006. 23p. (J). per. 11.99 (978-1-59879-143-3(5)) Lifevest Publishing, Inc.
—WHO MOVED MY CHEESE? for Kids. Johnson, Spencer. 2003. (ENG.). 64p. (J). (gr. -1-3). 20.99 (978-0-399-24016-4(0), G.P. Putnam's Sons Books for Young Readers) Penguin Young Readers Group.
Pileggi, Steven. Annoying Alex. Monnar, Alexander. 2008. (J). per. 14.99 (978-0-9768035-9-1(3)) Readers Are Leaders U.S.A., Inc.
Pilgrim, A. W. J. Alfie's Holiday in Monaco. Pocock, Joyce & Downey, Heidi, eds. 2018. (Adventures of Alfie the Talking Bus Ser.: Vol. 2). (ENG.). 26p. (J). pap. (978-1-78926-832-4(X)) Independent Publishing Network.
—The Blue Knights Quest to America. Pocock, Joyce & Downie, Heidi, eds. 2019. (Blue Knights of the Realm Ser.: Vol. 2). (ENG.). 44p. (J). pap. (978-1-78972-117-1(2)) Independent Publishing Network.
Pilgrim, A. W. J. Isley's Invite. Pilgrim, A. W. J. Pocock, Joyce, ed. 2018. (Isley Adventure Chronicles Ser.: Vol. 20). (ENG.). 76p. (J). pap. (978-1-78926-213-1(5)) Independent Publishing Network.
—Sid the Spider Who Lived in a Painting. Pilgrim, A. W. J. Crownson, Jeff, ed. 2018. (ENG.). 42p. (J). pap. (978-1-83853-039-6(8)) Independent Publishing Network.
—Spot the Dog. Pilgrim, A. W. J. Crownson, Jeff, ed. 2018. (ENG.). 30p. (J). pap. (978-1-78808-270-9(2)) Independent Publishing Network.
Pilgrim, Cheryl. Hound Dawg. Vermillion, Patricia. 2015. (ENG.). 40p. 21.95 (978-0-87565-615-1(3)) Texas Christian Univ. Pr.
—The Littlest Voyageur. Preus, Margi. 2020. 176p. (J). (gr. 2-5). 16.99 (978-0-8234-4247-8(0), Margaret Ferguson Books) Holiday Hse., Inc.
Pilkey, Dav. Captain Underpants & the Perilous Plot of Professor Poopypants: The Fourth Epic Novel. Garibaldi, Jose. 2016. 149p. (J). (978-1-5182-1145-4(3), 112964869) Scholastic, Inc.
—Julius. Johnson, Angela. 2015. 32p. pap. 7.00 (978-1-61003-548-4(8)) Center for the Collaborative Classroom.
—One Today. Blanco, Richard. 2015. (ENG.). 40p. (J). (gr. -1-3). 18.00 (978-0-316-37144-5(0)) Little, Brown Bks. for Young Readers.
Pilkey, Dav. The Adventures of Captain Underpants. Pilkey, Dav. 2013. (Captain Underpants Ser.: 1). 144p. (J). (gr. 2-5). 9.99 (978-0-545-49908-8(9)) Scholastic, Inc.
—The Adventures of Ook & Gluk, Kung-Fu Cavemen from the Future. Pilkey, Dav. (Captain Underpants Ser.). (ENG.). 176p. (J). (gr. 2-5). 2011. 5.99 (978-0-545-38577-0(6)); 2010. 9.99 (978-0-545-17530-2(5)) Scholastic, Inc.
—The Adventures of Super Diaper Baby. Pilkey, Dav. 2014. (Captain Underpants Ser.). (ENG.). 144p. (J). (gr. 2-7). 9.99 (978-0-545-66544-5(2)) Scholastic, Inc.
—Las Aventuras de Superbebé Pañal. Pilkey, Dav. 2003. (Captain Underpants Ser.). (SPA.). 128p. (J). (gr. 2-2). mass mkt. 5.99 (978-0-439-55120-5(X), Scholastic en Espanol) Scholastic, Inc.
—Las Aventuras de Uuk y Gluk, Cavernicolas del Futuro y Maestros de Kung Fu. Pilkey, Dav. 2011. (Captain Underpants Ser.). (SPA.). 176p. (J). (gr. 2-2). pap. 5.99 (978-0-545-27916-1(X), Scholastic en Espanol) Scholastic, Inc.
—The Big, Bad Battle of the Bionic Booger Boy: The Night of the Nasty Nostril Nuggets. Pilkey, Dav. 2018. (Captain Underpants Ser.: 6). 176p. (J). (gr. 2-2). 9.99 (978-1-338-27149-2(0)) Scholastic, Inc.
—Brawl of the Wild. Pilkey, Dav. 2018. (Dog Man Ser.: 6). 224p. (J). (gr. 2-2). (ENG.). lib. bdg. 24.99 (978-1-338-29092-9(4)); 9.99 (978-1-338-23657-6(1)) Scholastic, Inc. (Graphix).
—El Capitán Calzoncillos y la Feroz Batalla Contra el Niño Mocobionico: La Parte - La Noche de los Mocos Vivientes. Pilkey, Dav. 2005. (Capitán Calzoncillos Ser.: 6). Orig. Title: Captain Underpants & the Big, Bad Battle of the Bionic Booger Boy: the Night of the Nasty Nostril Nuggets. (SPA.). 176p. (J). (gr. 2-5). mass mkt. 5.99 (978-0-439-66204-8(4), Scholastic en Espanol) Scholastic, Inc.
—El Capitan Calzoncillos y la Feroz Batalla Contra el Nino Mocobionico Pt. 2: La Venganza de los Ridiculos Mocorobots. Pilkey, Dav. Azaola, Miguel, tr. 2005. (Capitán Calzoncillos Ser.: 7). Orig. Title: Captain Underpants & the Big, Bad Battle of the Bionic Booger Boy, Part 2: The Revenge of the Ridiculous Robo-Boogers. (SPA.). 176p. (J). (gr. 2-5). pap. 5.99 (978-0-439-66205-5(2), Scholastic en Espanol) Scholastic, Inc.
—El Capitan Calzoncillos y la Furia de la Supermujer Macroelastica. Pilkey, Dav. Azaola, Miguel, tr. 2003. (Captain Underpants Ser.: 5). (SPA.). 176p. (J). (gr. 2-5). pap. 5.99 (978-0-439-53820-6(3), Scholastic en Espanol) Scholastic, Inc.
—El Capitan Calzoncillos y la Ridicula Historia de los Seres del Inodoro Morado. Pilkey, Dav. 2008. (Capitán Calzoncillos Ser.: 8). (SPA.). 176p. (J). (gr. 2-5). pap. 5.99 (978-0-545-02583-6(4), Scholastic en Espanol) Scholastic, Inc.
—Captain Underpants & the Attack of the Talking Toilets. Pilkey, Dav. 2014. (Captain Underpants Ser.: 2). 160p. (J). (gr. 2-5). 9.99 (978-0-545-59932-0(6)) Scholastic, Inc.
—Captain Underpants & the Big, Bad Battle of the Bionic Booger Boy: The Revenge of the Ridiculous Robo-Boogers. Pilkey, Dav. 2018. (Captain Underpants Ser.: 7). 176p. (J). (gr. 2-2). 9.99 (978-1-338-27150-8(4)) Scholastic, Inc.
—Captain Underpants & the Big, Bad Battle of the Bionic Booger Boy Part 1: The Night of the Nasty Nostril Nuggets. Pilkey, Dav. 2003. (Captain Underpants Ser.: 6). 176p. (J). (gr. 2-5). pap. 5.99 (978-0-439-37610-5(6)) Scholastic, Inc.
—Captain Underpants & the Big, Bad Battle of the Bionic Booger Boy Part 2: The Revenge of the Ridiculous Robo-Boogers. Pilkey, Dav. 2003. (Captain Underpants Ser.: 7). 176p. (J). (gr. 2-5). (ENG.). 18.99 (978-0-439-37611-2(4)); pap. 5.99 (978-0-439-37612-9(2)) Scholastic, Inc.
—Captain Underpants & the Invasion of the Incredibly Naughty Cafeteria Ladies from Outer: And the Invasion of the Incredibly Naughty Cafeteria Ladies from Outer Space (and the Subsequent Assault of the Equally Evil Lunchroom Zombie Nerds) Pilkey, Dav. 2014. (Captain Underpants Ser.: 3). 160p. (J). (gr. 2-5). 9.99 (978-0-545-69470-4(1)) Scholastic, Inc.
—Captain Underpants & the Revolting Revenge of the Radioactive Robo-Boxers. Pilkey, Dav. 2013. (Captain Underpants Ser.: 10). (ENG.). 224p. (J). (gr. 2-5). 9.99 (978-0-545-17536-4(4)) Scholastic, Inc.
—Captain Underpants & the Revolting Revenge of the Radioactive Robo-Boxers: Color Edition (Captain Underpants #10) Color Edition. Pilkey, Dav. 2020. (Captain Underpants Ser.: 10). 224p. (J). (gr. 2-2). 12.99 (978-1-338-34723-4(3)) Scholastic, Inc.
—Captain Underpants & the Sensational Saga of Sir Stinks-a-Lot. Pilkey, Dav. 2015. (Captain Underpants Ser.: 12). (ENG.). 208p. (J). (gr. 2-2). 9.99 (978-0-545-50492-8(9)) Scholastic, Inc.
—Captain Underpants & the Sensational Saga of Sir Stinks-a-Lot. Pilkey, Dav. 2015. (Captain Underpants Ser.: 12). (ENG.). 208p. (J). (gr. 2). lib. bdg. 20.85 (978-0-606-37924-3(X)) Turtleback.
—Captain Underpants & the Tyrannical Retaliation of the Turbo Toilet 2000. Pilkey, Dav. 2014. (Captain Underpants Ser.: 11). (ENG.). 224p. (J). (gr. 2-5). 9.99 (978-0-545-50490-4(2)) Scholastic, Inc.
—Captain Underpants & the Wrath of the Wicked Wedgie Woman. Pilkey, Dav. Garibaldi, Jose. 2018. 165p. (J). (978-1-5444-0229-1(5)) Scholastic, Inc.
—Captain Underpants & the Wrath of the Wicked Wedgie Woman: Color Edition (Captain Underpants #5) Color Edition. Pilkey, Dav. 2nd ed. 2017. (Captain Underpants Ser.: 5). 176p. (J). (gr. 2-2). 9.99 (978-1-338-21623-3(6)) Scholastic, Inc.
—Captain Underpants Color Collection. Pilkey, Dav. 2015. (Captain Underpants Ser.). (ENG.). 160p. (J). (gr. 2-2). 29.97 (978-0-545-87011-5(9)) Scholastic, Inc.
—Dog Breath! The Horrible Trouble with Hally Tosis. Pilkey, Dav. 3rd ed. 2004. (Scholastic Bookshelf Ser.). (ENG.). 32p. (J). (gr. -1-3). pap. 6.99 (978-0-439-59839-2(7), Scholastic Paperbacks) Scholastic, Inc.
—Dog Man. Pilkey, Dav. (Dog Man Ser.: 1). (J). (gr. 2-2). 2019. (ENG.). 240p. 24.99 (978-1-338-61194-6(1)); 2016. 160p. 9.99 (978-0-545-58160-8(5), Graphix) Scholastic, Inc.
—Dog Man - The Epic Collection. Pilkey, Dav. 2017. (Dog Man Ser.). (ENG.). (J). (gr. 2). 29.97 (978-1-338-23064-2(6), Graphix) Scholastic, Inc.
—Dog Man a Tale of Two Kitties. Pilkey, Dav. 2019. (Dog Man Ser.: 3). (ENG.). 256p. (J). (gr. 2-2). 24.99 (978-1-338-61199-1(2)) Scholastic, Inc.
—Dog Man & Cat Kid. Pilkey, Dav. 2017. (Dog Man Ser.: 4). 256p. (J). (gr. 2). 9.99 (978-0-545-93518-0(0)); (ENG.). lib. bdg. 16.99 (978-1-338-23037-6(9)) Scholastic, Inc. (Graphix).
—Dog Man Unleashed. Pilkey, Dav. (Dog Man Ser.: 2). 224p. (J). (gr. 2-2). 2019. (ENG.). 24.99 (978-1-338-61198-4(4)); 2016. 9.99 (978-0-545-93520-3(2), Graphix) Scholastic, Inc.
—Dogzilla. Pilkey, Dav. 2014. 32p. pap. 7.00 (978-1-61003-187-5(3)) Center for the Collaborative Classroom.
—Dragón 1: un Amigo para Dragón: Un Libro de la Serie Acorn. Pilkey, Dav. 2019. (Dragón Ser.: 1). (SPA.). 64p. (J). (gr. k-2). pap. 4.99 (978-1-338-60117-6(2), Scholastic en Espanol) Scholastic, Inc.
—The Dumb Bunnies. Pilkey, Dav. Denim, Sue. 2nd ed. 2005. (Dumb Bunnies Ser.). (ENG.). 32p. (J). (gr. -1-3). pap. 7.99 (978-0-439-66944-3(8)) Scholastic, Inc.
—The Dumb Bunnies' Easter. Pilkey, Dav. 2008. (Dumb Bunnies Ser.). (ENG.). 32p. (J). (gr. -1-3). pap. 6.99 (978-0-545-00880-8(8), Scholastic Paperbacks) Scholastic, Inc.
—Dumb Bunnies' Easter. Pilkey, Dav. 2009. (Dumb Bunnies Ser.). (ENG.). 32p. (J). (gr. -1-3). 16.99 (978-0-545-03946-8(0)) Scholastic, Inc.
—The Dumb Bunnies Go to the Zoo. Pilkey, Dav. 2009. (Dumb Bunnies Ser.). (ENG.). 32p. (J). (gr. -1-3). 16.99 (978-0-545-03937-6(1)) Scholastic, Inc.
—For Whom the Ball Rolls. Pilkey, Dav. 2019. (Dog Man Ser.: 7). 256p. (J). (gr. 2-2). 12.99 (978-1-338-23659-0(8), Graphix) Scholastic, Inc.
—A Friend for Dragon. Pilkey, Dav. 2019. (Dragon Ser.: 1). (ENG.). 64p. (J). (gr. k-2). pap. 4.99 (978-1-338-34105-8(7)) Scholastic, Inc.
Pilkey, Dav. El Gato Gordo de Dragón (Dragon's Fat Cat) Un Libro de la Serie Acorn. Pilkey, Dav. 2020. (Dragón Ser.). (SPA.). 64p. (J). (gr. k-2). pap. 4.99 **(978-1-338-67006-6(9)**, Scholastic en Espanol) Scholastic, Inc.
—Grime & Punishment. Pilkey, Dav. 2020. (Dog Man Ser.: 9). 240p. (J). (gr. 2-2). 12.99 **(978-1-338-53562-4(5))**; (ENG.). 24.99 **(978-1-338-53563-1(3))** Scholastic, Inc. (Graphix).
Pilkey, Dav. The Hallo-Wiener. Pilkey, Dav. 2014. (ENG.). 32p. (J). (gr. -1-k). bds. 6.99 (978-0-545-66136-2(6)) Scholastic, Inc.
—A Historia de Dos Gatitos. Pilkey, Dav. 2018. (Hombre Perro Ser.: 3). (SPA.). 256p. (J). (gr. 2-2). 9.99 (978-1-338-27770-8(7)) Scholastic, Inc.
—Hombre Perro. Pilkey, Dav. 2017. (Hombre Perro Ser.: 1). (SPA.). 240p. (J). (gr. 2-2). 9.99 (978-1-338-11416-4(6), Scholastic en Espanol) Scholastic, Inc.
—Hombre Perro: la Pelea de la Selva. Pilkey, Dav. 2019. (Hombre Perro Ser.: 6). (SPA.). 224p. (J). (gr. 2-2). 12.99 (978-1-338-60129-9(6), Scholastic en Espanol) Scholastic, Inc.
—Hombre Perro Se Desata. Pilkey, Dav. 2017. (Hombre Perro Ser.: 2). (SPA.). 224p. (J). (gr. 2-2). 9.99 (978-1-338-23348-3(3)) Scholastic, Inc.
—Hombre Perro y Supergatito. Pilkey, Dav. 2019. (Hombre Perro Ser.: 4). (SPA.). 256p. (J). (gr. 2-5). 9.99 (978-1-338-33131-8(0), Scholastic en Espanol) Scholastic, Inc.
—The Invasion of the Potty Snatchers. Pilkey, Dav. 2011. (Captain Underpants Ser.: 2). (ENG.). 192p. (J). (gr. 2-5). 9.99 (978-0-545-17532-6(1)) Scholastic, Inc.
—Lord of the Fleas. Pilkey, Dav. 2018. (Dog Man Ser.: 5). 256p. (J). (gr. 2-2). 9.99 (978-0-545-93517-3(2)); (ENG.). lib. bdg. 16.99 (978-1-338-29091-2(6)) Scholastic, Inc. (Graphix).
—The Paperboy. Pilkey, Dav. 2016. 32p. (J). (gr. -1-3). 17.99 (978-0-545-87186-0(7), Orchard Bks.) Scholastic, Inc.
—Perilous Plot of Professor Poopypants. Pilkey, Dav. 2015. (Captain Underpants Ser.: 4). 160p. (J). (gr. 2-2). pap. 9.99 (978-0-545-87187-7(5), 112964869) Scholastic, Inc.
—A Tale of Two Kitties. Pilkey, Dav. 2017. (Dog Man Ser.: 3). 256p. (J). (gr. 2-5). 9.99 (978-0-545-93521-0(0), Graphix) Scholastic, Inc.
—'Twas the Night Before Thanksgiving. Pilkey, Dav. 2004. (Scholastic Bookshelf Ser.). (ENG.). 32p. (J). (gr. -1-k). pap. 6.99 (978-0-439-66937-5(5), Scholastic Paperbacks) Scholastic, Inc.
Pillion, Dean. Those Amazing Engineers. Forbes, Charlotte. 2nd rev. ed. 2005. (Those Amazing... Ser.). (ENG.). 30p. (J). pap. 10.95 (978-0-9772799-0-6(1)) Trilogy Pubns. LLC.
—Those Amazing Scientists. Forbes, Charlotte & Forbes, Charlotte. 2007. 26p. (J). (978-0-9772799-1-3(X)) Trilogy Pubns. LLC.
Pillo, Cary. Do All Bugs Have Wings? And Other Questions Kids Have about Bugs, 1 vol. Slade, Suzanne. 2010. (Kids' Questions Ser.). (ENG.). 24p. (J). (gr. k-2). lib. bdg. 27.32 (978-1-4048-5761-2(3), Picture Window Bks.) Capstone.
—A Fishy Mystery: Venn Diagrams. Harkrader, Lisa. 2017. (Math Matters ® Ser.). (ENG.). 32p. (J). (gr. k-3). 5.95 (978-1-57565-866-7(6)); E-Book 23.99 (978-1-57565-869-8(0)) Astra Publishing Hse.
—Gentle Willow: A Story for Children about Dying. Mills, Joyce C. 2nd ed. 2003. 32p. (J). pap. 9.95 (978-1-59147-072-4(2)); 14.95 (978-1-59147-071-7(4)) American Psychological Assn. (Magination Pr.).
—How Do Tornadoes Form? And Other Questions Kids Have about Weather, 1 vol. Slade, Suzanne. (Kids' Questions Ser.). (ENG.). 24p. (J). (gr. k-2). 2011. pap. 7.49 (978-1-4048-6731-4(7)); 2010. lib. bdg. 27.32 (978-1-4048-6048-3(7)) Capstone. (Picture Window Bks.).
—Let's Go, Snow! May, Eleanor. 2017. (Math Matters ® Ser.). (ENG.). 32p. (J). (gr. k-3). pap. 5.95 (978-1-57565-807-0(0)) Astra Publishing Hse.
—Let's Go, Snow! Temperature Measurement. May, Eleanor. ed. 2017. (Math Matters ® Ser.). (ENG.). 32p. (J). (gr. k-3). E-Book 23.99 (978-1-57565-808-7(9)) Astra Publishing Hse.
—Party Princess. Braver, Vanita. 2005. (Teach Your Children Well Ser.). 24p. (J). (gr. -1). per. 8.95 (978-1-58760-038-8(2), Child & Family Pr.) Child Welfare League of America, Inc.
—Sally Sore Loser: A Story about Winning & Losing. Sileo, Frank J. 2012. 32p. (J). 14.95 (978-1-4338-1189-0(8)); pap. 9.95 (978-1-4338-1190-6(1)) American Psychological Assn. (Magination Pr.).
—Sammy the Elephant & Mr. Camel: A Story to Help Children Overcome Bedwetting. Mills, Joyce C. & Crowley, Richard J. 2nd ed. 2005. 32p. (J). 14.95 (978-1-59147-247-6(4)); pap. 9.95 (978-1-59147-248-3(2)) American Psychological Assn. (Magination Pr.).
—Striped Shirts & Flowered Pants: A Story about Alzheimer's Disease for Young Children. Schnurbush, Barbara. 2006. 32p. (J). (gr. -1-3). 14.95 (978-1-59147-475-3(2)); per. 9.95 (978-1-59147-476-0(0)) American Psychological Assn. (Magination Pr.).
—Werewolf Moon: Phases of the Moon. Hanford, Juliana. 2009. (Science Solves It! ® Ser.). (ENG.). 32p. (J). (gr. 1-3). pap. 5.95 (978-1-57565-291-7(9)) Astra Publishing Hse.
—Where Is My Mommy? Coping When a Parent Leaves (and Doesn't Come Back) Kilgore, Mary & Kilgore, Mitchell. 2010. (ENG.). 32p. (J). (gr. -1-4). pap. 14.99 (978-1-884734-46-5(4)) Parenting Pr., Inc.
—Who Invented Basketball? And Other Questions Kids Have about Sports, 1 vol. Slade, Suzanne. 2011. (Kids' Questions Ser.). (ENG.). 24p. (J). (gr. k-2). pap. 7.49 (978-1-4048-6730-7(9), Picture Window Bks.) Capstone.
—Why Do Dogs Drool? And Other Questions Kids Have about Dogs, 1 vol. Slade, Suzanne. 2010. (Kids' Questions Ser.). (ENG.). 24p. (J). (gr. k-2). lib. bdg. 27.32 (978-1-4048-5762-9(1), Picture Window Bks.) Capstone.
Pillo, Cary. Jenny Is Scared! When Sad Things Happen in the World. Pillo, Cary, tr. Shuman, Carol. 2003. 32p. (J). (gr. k-3). pap. 9.95 (978-1-59147-003-8(X)); 14.95 (978-1-59147-002-1(1)) American Psychological Assn. (Magination Pr.).
Pillot, édéric. The Most Beautiful Images from the Bible: Sharing the Stories with Children. Mrowiec, Katia. 2012. 48p. 19.95 (978-0-8091-6766-1(2)) Paulist Pr.
Pilo, Cary. Rena & Rio Build a Rhyme. Hall, Pamela. 2011. (Poetry Builders Ser.). 32p. (J). (gr. 2-4). lib. bdg. 25.27 (978-1-59953-439-8(X)) Norwood Hse. Pr.
Pilorget, Bruno. The Great Wave: A Children's Book Inspired by Hokusai. Massenot, Véronique. 2011. (Children's Books Inspired by Famous Artworks Ser.). (ENG.). 32p. (J). (gr. -1-3). 14.95 (978-3-7913-7058-3(8)) Prestel Verlag GmbH & Co KG. DEU. Dist: Penguin Random Hse. LLC.
—Journey on the Clouds: A Children's Book Inspired by Marc Chagall. Massenot, Véronique. 2011. (Children's Books Inspired by Famous Artworks Ser.). (ENG.). 32p. (J). (gr. -1-3). 14.95 (978-3-7913-7057-6(X)) Prestel Verlag GmbH & Co KG. DEU. Dist: Penguin Random Hse. LLC.
Pilot Inc. Staff, jt. illus. see Random House.
Pilot Studio. Star Wars Chewie & the Courageous Kid. Lucasfilm Press. 2018. (ENG.). 24p. (J). (gr. 1-3). pap. 4.99 (978-1-368-01631-5(6), Disney Lucasfilm Press) Disney Publishing Worldwide.
—World of Reading Star Wars Use the Force! Level 2. Siglain, Michael. 2015. (World of Reading Ser.). (ENG.). 32p. (J). (gr. 1-3). pap. 3.99 (978-1-4847-0464-6(9)) Disney Pr.
—5-Minute Star Wars Stories Strike Back. Lucasfilm Press. 2017. (ENG.). 192p. (J). (gr. 1-3). 12.99 (978-1-368-00351-3(6), Disney Lucasfilm Press) Disney Publishing Worldwide.
Pilot Studio, jt. illus. see PowerStation Studios.
Pilsworth, Graham. Confederation. Staunton, Ted. 2004. (Dreadful Truth Ser.). (ENG.). 80p. (J). (gr. 3-8). (978-0-88780-630-8(9)) Formac Publishing Co., Ltd.
—The Halifax Citadel. Grant, Vicki. 2003. (Dreadful Truth Ser.). (ENG.). 80p. (J). (gr. 3-8). (978-0-88780-599-8(X)) Formac Publishing Co., Ltd.
Pilutti, Deb. Idea Jar. Lehrhaupt, Adam. 2018. (ENG.). 40p. (J). (gr. -1-3). 18.99 (978-1-4814-5166-6(9), Simon & Schuster/Paula Wiseman Bks.) Simon & Schuster/Paula Wiseman Bks.
—The Twelve Days of Christmas in Michigan. Thoms, Susan Collins. (Twelve Days of Christmas in America Ser.). (J). (-k). 2017. 22p. bds. 7.95 (978-1-4549-2284-1(2)); 2010. 40p. 12.95 (978-1-4027-6351-9(4)) Sterling Publishing Co., Inc.
Pilutti, Deb. Bear & Squirrel Are Friends ... Yes, Really! Pilutti, Deb. 2015. (ENG.). 40p. (J). (gr. -1-3). 17.99 (978-1-4814-2913-9(2), Simon & Schuster Bks. For Young Readers) Simon & Schuster Bks. For Young Readers.
—Old Rock (Is Not Boring) Pilutti, Deb. 2020. (ENG.). 40p. (J). (gr. -1-3). 17.99 (978-0-525-51818-1(5), G.P. Putnam's Sons Books for Young Readers) Penguin Young Readers Group.
—Ten Rules of Being a Superhero. Pilutti, Deb. 2014. (ENG.). 32p. (J). (gr. -1-2). 17.99 (978-0-8050-9759-7(7), 900118487, Holt, Henry & Co. Bks. For Young Readers) Holt, Henry & Co.
Pilz, M. H. The Best Mother's Day Ever: Similarities & Differences. May, Eleanor. 2010. (Social Studies Connects ® Ser.). (ENG.). 32p. (J). (gr. 1-3). pap. 5.95 (978-1-57565-299-3(4)) Astra Publishing Hse.
—A Thousand Theos: Doubling. Houran, Lori Haskins. 2015. (Math Matters ® Ser.). (ENG.). 32p. (J). (gr. k-3). pap. 5.95 (978-1-57565-803-2(8)); E-Book 23.99 (978-1-57565-804-9(6)) Astra Publishing Hse.
—The Yum-Yum House. Walker, Nan. 2009. (Math Matters Complete Set Ser.). 32p. (J). (gr. 3-5). pap. 5.95 (978-1-57565-290-0(0)) Astra Publishing Hse.
Pina, Javier. Captain America: Steve Rogers Vol. 3: Empire Building. 2017. (ENG.). 144p. (YA). (gr. 8-17). pap. 19.99 (978-1-302-90616-0(X)) Marvel Worldwide, Inc.
Pina, Javier & Saiz, Jesus. Doctor Strange by Mark Waid Vol. 2: Remittance. 2019. 136p. (YA). pap. 17.99 (978-1-302-91234-5(8)) Marvel Worldwide, Inc.
Pinchbeck, Neil. Crash, Bang, Yell! 16p. (J). (978-1-85792-366-7(9)) Christian Focus Pubns. GBR. Dist: Riverside.
—The Praying Man. 16p. (J). (978-1-85792-363-6(4)) Christian Focus Pubns. GBR. Dist: Riverside.
—Rescue on the Road. 16p. (J). (978-1-85792-365-0(0)) Christian Focus Pubns. GBR. Dist: Riverside.
Pinchuk, Sofiia. Goosy from Goosenhagen & His Friends: Bedtime Book for Good Night. Wunder, Lola. Ivanov, Leonid, tr. 2019. (ENG.). 46p. (J). pap. 12.00 **(978-1-7132-3135-6(2))** Independently Published.
Pinckney, Jerry. God Bless the Child. Holiday, Billie & Herzog, Arthur, Jr. 2005. 30p. (J). (gr. 4-8). reprint ed. 17.00 (978-0-7567-9650-1(4)) DIANE Publishing Co.
Pincus, Harriet. Tell Me a Mitzi. Segal, Lore. 2017. (ENG.). 40p. (J). 16.95 (978-0-486-81775-0(X)) Dover Pubns., Inc.
—The Wedding Procession of the Rag Doll & the Broom Handle & Who Was in It. Sandburg, Carl. 2017. (ENG.). 32p. 16.95 (978-0-486-81585-5(4)) Dover Pubns., Inc.
Pinder, Andrew. The Boys' Doodle Book: Amazing Pictures to Complete & Create. 2008. (ENG.). 128p. (J). (gr. -1-17). pap. 12.95 (978-0-7624-3506-7(2), Running Pr. Kids) Running Pr.
—Fangs a Lot: Final Notes from a Totally Lame Vampire. Collins, Tim. 2014. (ENG.). 320p. (J). (gr. 5-9). 13.99

(978-1-4814-2134-8(4), Aladdin) Simon & Schuster Children's Publishing.
—The Girls' Doodle Book: Amazing Pictures to Complete & Create. 2008. (ENG.). 128p. (J). (gr. -1-17). pap. 12.95 *(978-0-7624-3505-0(4)*, Running Pr. Kids) Running Pr.
—How Do Astronauts Wee in Space? Mitchell, Chris. 2016. (ENG.). 192p. (J). (gr. 4-7). pap. 8.99 *(978-1-78418-653-1(8))* Blake, John Publishing, Ltd. GBR. Dist: Independent Pubs. Group.
—I Wish I Knew That. Martin, Steve et al. 2017. (Buster Reference Ser.). (ENG.). 128p. (J). (gr. 3-7). pap. 8.99 *(978-1-78055-466-2(4))* O'Mara, Michael Bks., Ltd. GBR. Dist: Independent Pubs. Group.
—Notes from a Hairy-Not-Scary Werewolf. Collins, Tim. 2013. (ENG.). 288p. (J). (gr. 5-9). 12.99 *(978-1-4424-8207-4(9)*, Aladdin) Simon & Schuster Children's Publishing.
—Notes from a Totally Lame Vampire: Because the Undead Have Feelings Too! Collins, Tim. 2010. (ENG.). 336p. (J). (gr. 5-9). 12.99 *(978-1-4424-1183-8(X)*, Aladdin) Simon & Schuster Children's Publishing.
—Off with Their Heads! Oliver, Martin. 2017. (Buster Reference Ser.). (ENG.). 128p. (J). (gr. 3-7). pap. 8.99 *(978-1-78055-465-5(6))* O'Mara, Michael Bks., Ltd. GBR. Dist: Independent Pubs. Group.
—Out of This World: All the Cool Stuff about Space You Want to Know. Gifford, Clive. 2012. (J). *(978-1-60652-571-5(9))* Reader's Digest Assn., Inc., The.
—Prince of Dorkness: More Notes from a Totally Lame Vampire. Collins, Tim. 2011. (ENG.). 336p. (J). (gr. 5-9). 12.99 *(978-1-4424-3388-5(4)*, Aladdin) Simon & Schuster Children's Publishing.

Pindroh, Paula. First Look at Dinosaurs. Galvin, Laura Gates. 2011. (First Look At... (Soundprints) Ser.). (ENG.). 16p. 6.95 *(978-1-60727-285-4(7))* Soundprints.
—First Look at Space. Parisi, Anthony. 2011. (ENG.). 16p. (J). *(978-1-60727-225-0(3)*, Blackbirch Pr., Inc.) Soundprints.

Pine, Hank. Polly Perfect & the Tragic Fart. Richmond, Jacob. 2012. (ENG.). 52p. (J). pap. 9.95 *(978-1-897411-36-0(7))* Bayeux Arts, Inc. CAN. Dist: Chicago Distribution Ctr.

Pineda, Jesus. Sentimientos. Jauregui, Patricia. Jauregui, Reginald, ed. l.t. ed. 2004. (SPA.). 39p. (YA). pap. 19.95 *(978-1-931481-41-0(5))* LiArt-Literature & Art.

Pinelli, Amerigo. Bites, 1 vol. Brezenoff, Steve. 2013. (Ravens Pass Ser.). (ENG.). 96p. (J). (gr. 3-6). pap. 6.15 *(978-1-4342-6217-2(0))*; lib. bdg. 25.32 *(978-1-4342-4617-2(5))* Capstone. (Stone Arch Bks.).
—The Cave at the End of the World 4 Voyagers. Powling, Chris. 2017. (Cambridge Reading Adventures Ser.). (ENG.). 32p. pap. 7.87 *(978-1-108-43979-4(9))* Cambridge Univ. Pr.
—Cheaters, 1 vol. Brezenoff, Steve. 2013. (Ravens Pass Ser.). (ENG.). 96p. (J). (gr. 3-6). lib. bdg. 25.32 *(978-1-4342-4616-5(7)*, Stone Arch Bks.) Capstone.
—Chillax! How Ernie Learns to Chill Out, Relax, & Take Charge of His Anger. Craver, Marcella Marino. 2011. 64p. (J). pap. 9.95 *(978-1-4338-1037-4(9)*, Magination Pr.) American Psychological Assn.
—How to Live Like a Samurai Warrior. Farndon, John. 2016. (How to Live Like ... Ser.). (ENG.). 32p. (J). (gr. 3-6). 27.99 *(978-1-5124-0630-6(9)*, 9781512406306, Hungry Tomato ®) Lerner Publishing Group.
—Lost Island, 1 vol. Brezenoff, Steve. 2013. (Ravens Pass Ser.). (ENG.). 96p. (J). (gr. 3-6). pap. 6.15 *(978-1-4342-6214-1(6))*; lib. bdg. 25.32 *(978-1-4342-4614-1(0))* Capstone. (Stone Arch Bks.).
—Mayflower Girl. McKenzie, Precious. 2016. (History Files Ser.). (ENG.). 96p. (gr. 5-9). 29.93 *(978-1-68191-681-1(9)*, 9781681916811) Rourke Educational Media.
—Mick's Buried Treasure. Jakubowski, Michele. 2016. (Sleuths of Somerville Ser.). (ENG.). 144p. (J). (gr. 4-6). lib. bdg. 25.99 *(978-1-4965-3178-0(7)*, Stone Arch Bks.) Capstone.
—No Place Like Home, 1 vol. Brezenoff, Steve. 2013. (Ravens Pass Ser.). (ENG.). 96p. (J). (gr. 3-6). pap. 6.15 *(978-1-4342-6215-8(4))*; lib. bdg. 25.32 *(978-1-4342-4615-8(9))* Capstone. (Stone Arch Bks.).

Pinelli, Amerigo. Poison Moon. Collins, Ailynn. 2020. (Michael Dahl Presents: Mysteries Ser.). (ENG.). 72p. (J). (gr. 3-5). pap. 5.95 ***(978-1-4965-9885-1(7)***, 201245); lib. bdg. 25.32 ***(978-1-4965-9711-3(7)***, 199333) Capstone. (Stone Arch Bks.).

Pinelli, Amerigo. The Professor's Discovery. Jakubowski, Michele. 2016. (Sleuths of Somerville Ser.). (ENG.). 144p. (J). (gr. 4-6). lib. bdg. 25.99 *(978-1-4965-3177-3(9)*, Stone Arch Bks.) Capstone.
—The Professor's Discovery. Jakubowski, Michele. 2017. (Sleuths of Somerville Ser.). (ENG.). 144p. (J). (gr. 4-6). pap. 6.95 *(978-1-4965-3181-0(7)*, Stone Arch Bks.) Capstone.
—Rockefeller Caper. Rosen, Jonathan. 2016. (History Files Ser.). (ENG.). 96p. (gr. 5-9). 29.93 *(978-1-68191-677-4(0)*, 9781681916774) Rourke Educational Media.
—Secrets in Somerville. Jakubowski, Michele. 2016. (Sleuths of Somerville Ser.). (ENG.). 144p. (J). (gr. 4-6). lib. bdg. 25.99 *(978-1-4965-3175-9(2)*, Stone Arch Bks.) Capstone.
—Shield Up! Craver, Marcella Marino. 2014. 64p. (J). pap. *(978-1-4338-1651-2(2)*, Magination Pr.) American Psychological Assn.
—The Sleuths of Somerville, 4 vols. Jakubowski, Michele. 2016. (Sleuths of Somerville Ser.). (ENG.). 144p. (J). (gr. 4-6). lib. bdg., lib. bdg., lib. bdg. 103.96 *(978-1-4965-3207-7(4)*, Stone Arch Bks.) Capstone.
—Tour of Trouble. Jakubowski, Michele. 2016. (Sleuths of Somerville Ser.). (ENG.). 144p. (J). (gr. 4-6). lib. bdg. 25.99 *(978-1-4965-3176-6(0)*, Stone Arch Bks.) Capstone.
—Tour of Trouble. Jakubowski, Michele. 2017. (Sleuths of Somerville Ser.). (ENG.). 144p. (J). (gr. 4-6). pap. 6.95 *(978-1-4965-3180-3(9)*, Stone Arch Bks.) Capstone.
—Tracking an Assassin! Nickolas Flux & the Assassination of Abraham Lincoln, 1 vol. Yomtov, Nelson. 2014. (Nickolas Flux History Chronicles Ser.). (ENG.). 32p. (J). (gr. 3-9). lib. bdg. 31.32 *(978-1-4914-0252-8(0))* Capstone.

Pinelli, Amerigo. The 30,000-Foot Ghost. Terrell, Brandon. 2020. (Michael Dahl Presents: Mysteries Ser.). (ENG.). 72p. (J). (gr. 3-5). pap. 5.95 ***(978-1-4965-9886-8(5)***, 201246); lib. bdg. 25.32 ***(978-1-4965-9705-2(2)***, 199327) Capstone. (Stone Arch Bks.).

Pinero, Eimi. Four Little Witches, 1 vol. Perkins, T. J. 2015. (ENG.). 40p. (J). 12.99 *(978-0-7643-4943-0(0)*, 6691) Schiffer Publishing, Ltd.

Pinfold, Levi. The Dam. Almond, David. 2018. (ENG.). 32p. (J). (gr. k-4). 17.99 *(978-0-7636-9597-2(1))* Candlewick Pr.
—The Song from Somewhere Else. Harrold, A. F. 2017. (ENG.). 240p. (J). 16.99 *(978-1-68119-401-1(5)*, 900172517, Bloomsbury USA Childrens) Bloomsbury Publishing USA.

Pinfold, Levi. Black Dog. Pinfold, Levi. 2012. (ENG.). 32p. (J). (gr. -1-3). 15.99 *(978-0-7636-6097-0(3)*, Templar) Candlewick Pr.
—The Django. Pinfold, Levi. 2010. (ENG.). 40p. (J). (gr. k-4). 16.99 *(978-0-7636-4788-9(8)*, Templar) Candlewick Pr.

Pinfold, Levi, jt. illus. see Wyatt, David.

Pingk, Rubin. Little Thor Gets Mad. Nguyen, Victoria Watson. 2019. (ENG.). 14p. (J). (— 1). bds. 6.99 *(978-1-5344-5089-9(0)*, Little Simon) Little Simon.

Pingk, Rubin. Samurai Santa: A Very Ninja Christmas. Pingk, Rubin. 2015. (Samurai Holiday Ser.). (ENG.). 40p. (J). (gr. -1-3). 17.99 *(978-1-4814-3057-9(2)*, Simon & Schuster Bks. For Young Readers) Simon & Schuster Bks. For Young Readers.
—Samurai Scarecrow: A Very Ninja Halloween. Pingk, Rubin. 2018. (Samurai Holiday Ser.). (ENG.). 48p. (J). (gr. -1-3). 17.99 *(978-1-4814-3059-3(9)*, Simon & Schuster Bks. For Young Readers) Simon & Schuster Bks. For Young Readers.

Pinilla, Albert. A Bat Colony's Search for a New Home. Klukow, Mary Ellen. 2019. (Animal Habitats at Risk Ser.). (ENG.). 24p. (J). (gr. 1-3). pap. 9.99 *(978-1-68152-486-3(4))* Amicus.
—A Bee's Difficult Search for Food. Klukow, Mary Ellen. 2019. (Animal Habitats at Risk Ser.). (ENG.). 24p. (J). (gr. 1-3). pap. 9.99 *(978-1-68152-489-4(9))* Amicus.
—A Frog's Dangerous Home. Klukow, Mary Ellen. 2019. (Animal Habitats at Risk Ser.). (ENG.). 24p. (J). (gr. 1-3). pap. 9.99 *(978-1-68152-487-0(2))* Amicus.
—From Metal to Bicycles. Meister, Cari. 2020. (J). lib. bdg. *(978-1-68151-695-0(0))* Amicus Publishing.
—From Trees to Paper. Meister, Cari. 2020. (J). lib. bdg. *(978-1-68151-697-4(7)*, Amicus Illustrated) Amicus Publishing.
—From Wax to Crayons. Meister, Cari. 2020. (J). lib. bdg. *(978-1-68151-698-1(5))* Amicus Publishing.
—From Wood to Pencils. Meister, Cari. 2019. (Who Made My Stuff? Ser.). (ENG.). 24p. (J). (gr. 1-3). pap. 9.99 *(978-1-68152-485-6(6))* Amicus.
—A Sparrow's Disappearing Home. Klukow, Mary Ellen. 2019. (Animal Habitats at Risk Ser.). (ENG.). 24p. (J). (gr. 1-3). pap. 9.99 *(978-1-68152-490-0(2))* Amicus.
—A Turtle's Dangerous Journey. Klukow, Mary Ellen. 2019. (Animal Habitats at Risk Ser.). (ENG.). 24p. (J). (gr. 1-3). pap. 9.99 *(978-1-68152-491-7(0))* Amicus.
—A Wild Cat's Shrinking Home. Klukow, Mary Ellen. 2019. (Animal Habitats at Risk Ser.). (ENG.). 24p. (J). (gr. 1-3). pap. 9.99 *(978-1-68152-488-7(0))* Amicus.

Pinillos, Puy. Look! Birds! Calmenson, Stephanie. 2016. (Look! Ser.). (ENG.). 24p. (J). (gr. -1-1). 7.99 *(978-1-4998-0114-9(9))* Little Bee Books Inc.
—Look! Fish! Calmenson, Stephanie. 2016. (Look! Ser.). (ENG.). 24p. (J). (gr. -1-1). 7.99 *(978-1-4998-0166-8(1))* Little Bee Books Inc.
—Look! Flowers! Calmenson, Stephanie. 2016. (Look! Ser.). (ENG.). 24p. (J). (gr. -1-1). 7.99 *(978-1-4998-0115-6(7))* Little Bee Books Inc.
—Purim Chicken. Cuyler, Margery. 2017. (ENG.). 32p. (J). (gr. -1-3). 16.99 *(978-0-8075-3381-9(5)*, 807533815) Whitman, Albert & Co.
—Tiny Whale. George, Joshua. 2018. (Picture Bks.). (ENG.). 32p. (J). (gr. -1-k). 16.99 *(978-1-78700-457-3(0))* Willow Tree Bks. GBR. Dist: Independent Pubs. Group.

Pink, Wazza. My Mindful Walk with Grandma. Mabry, Sheri. 2020. 32p. (J). (gr. -1-3). 16.99 ***(978-0-8075-7072-2(9)***, 807570729) Whitman, Albert & Co.

Pinkfong. Baby Shark: Wash Your Hands! Pinkfong. 2020. (Baby Shark Ser.). (ENG.). 24p. (J). (gr. -1-3). pap. 4.99 ***(978-0-06-305577-3(5)***, HarperCollins) HarperCollins Pubs. Ltd. GBR. Dist: HarperCollins Pubs.

Pinkham, Pamela, jt. illus. see Verhoef, Sharon.

Pinkney, Brian. Boycott Blues: How Rosa Parks Inspired a Nation. Pinkney, Andrea Davis. 2008. (ENG.). 40p. (J). (gr. k-3). 16.99 *(978-0-06-082118-0(3)*, Greenwillow Bks.) HarperCollins Pubs.
—Cut from the Same Cloth: American Women of Myth, Legend, & Tall Tale. San Souci, Robert D. 2005. 140p. 17.00 *(978-0-7569-6284-5(6))* Perfection Learning Corp.
—The Dark-Thirty: Southern Tales of the Supernatural. McKissack, Patricia C. 2004. 122p. (J). (gr. 5-8). reprint ed. pap. 17.00 *(978-0-7567-7601-5(5))* DIANE Publishing Co.
—Duke Ellington: The Piano Prince & His Orchestra. Pinkney, Andrea. 2007. (ENG.). 32p. (J). (gr. 1-3). pap. 6.99 *(978-0-7868-1420-6(9)*, Jump at the Sun) Hyperion Bks. for Children.
—Ella Fitzgerald: The Tale of a Vocal Virtuosa. Pinkney, Andrea. 2007. (ENG.). 32p. (J). (gr. 1-3). pap. 6.99 *(978-0-7868-1416-9(0)*, Jump at the Sun) Hyperion Bks. for Children.
—Hand in Hand: Ten Black Men Who Changed America. Pinkney, Andrea. 2012. (ENG.). 256p. (J). (gr. 3-7). 19.99 *(978-1-4231-4257-7(8))* Hyperion Pr.
—Hip-Hop Lollipop. Montanari, Susan. 2018. 32p. (J). (gr. -1-2). 17.99 *(978-1-101-93482-1(4)*, Schwartz & Wade Bks.) Random Hse. Children's Bks.
—In Your Hands. Weatherford, Carole Boston. 2017. (ENG.). 32p. (J). (gr. -1-3). 17.99 *(978-1-4814-6293-8(8))* Simon & Schuster Children's Publishing.
—Jackie's Bat. Lorbiecki, Marybeth. 2006. (ENG.). 40p. (J). (gr. k-3). 17.99 *(978-0-689-84102-6(7)*, Simon & Schuster Bks. For Young Readers) Simon & Schuster Bks. For Young Readers.
—Let's Clap, Jump, Sing & Shout; Dance, Spin & Turn It Out! Games, Songs, & Stories from an African American Childhood. McKissack, Patricia C. 2017. (ENG.). 184p. (J). (gr. 1-4). 24.99 *(978-0-375-87088-0(1)*, Schwartz & Wade Bks.) Random Hse. Children's Bks.
—Little Diva: Includes a CD with Original Song & Reading by Lachanze. LaChanze. 2010. (ENG.). 32p. (J). (gr. -1-3). 16.99 *(978-0-312-37010-7(5)*, 900044347) Feiwel & Friends.
—Martin Rising: Requiem for a King. Pinkney, Andrea Davis. 2018. (ENG.). 128p. (J). (gr. 4-7). 19.99 *(978-0-545-70253-9(4)*, Scholastic Pr.) Scholastic, Inc.
—Nya's Long Walk: A Step at a Time. Park, Linda Sue. 2019. (ENG.). 32p. (J). (gr. -1-3). 17.99 *(978-1-328-78133-8(X)*, 1685062, Clarion Bks.) Houghton Mifflin Harcourt Trade & Reference Pubs.
—Sit-in: How Four Friends Stood Up by Sitting Down. Pinkney, Andrea Davis. 2011. (J). 37.75 *(978-1-4498-6817-8(7))* Recorded Bks., Inc.
—Sojourner Truth's Step-Stomp Stride. Pinkney, Andrea. 2009. (ENG.). 32p. (J). (gr. 1-3). 16.99 *(978-0-7868-0767-3(9)*, Jump at the Sun) Hyperion Bks. for Children.
—Thumbelina. Andersen, Hans. 2003. 40p. (J). 17.89 *(978-0-688-17477-4(9))* HarperCollins Pubs.
—Where Does the Trail Lead? Albert, Burton. 2008. (ENG.). 40p. (J). (gr. -1-3). 13.99 *(978-1-4169-7138-2(6)*, Aladdin) Simon & Schuster Children's Publishing.

Pinkney, Brian. Max Found Two Sticks. Pinkney, Brian. 2nd ed. 2005. (Stories to Go! Ser.). (ENG.). 40p. (J). 4.99 *(978-1-4169-0310-9(0)*, Simon & Schuster/Paula Wiseman Bks.) Simon & Schuster/Paula Wiseman Bks.
—Puppy Truck. Pinkney, Brian. 2019. (ENG.). 40p. (J). (gr. k-3). 17.99 *(978-1-5344-2687-0(6))* Simon & Schuster Children's Publishing.

Pinkney, Debbie. Panda: Wildlife 3D Puzzle & Book. Toast, Sarah. 2020. (ENG.). (J). ***(978-1-64269-212-9(3)***, 2b06f7f7-6416-4230-b513-15ab7b8c40d5, Sequoia Publishing & Media LLC) Phoenix International Publications, Inc.

Pinkney, J. Brian. Happy Birthday, Martin Luther King. Marzollo, Jean. 2006. (Scholastic Bookshelf Ser.). (ENG.). 32p. (J). (gr. -1-k). per. 6.99 *(978-0-439-78224-1(4)*, Scholastic Paperbacks) Scholastic, Inc.

Pinkney, Jerry. The All-I'll-Ever-Want Christmas Doll. McKissack, Patricia C. 2007. (ENG.). 40p. (J). (gr. -1-3). 17.99 *(978-0-375-83759-3(0)*, Schwartz & Wade Bks.) Random Hse. Children's Bks.
—The Christmas Boot. Wheeler, Lisa. 2016. 32p. (J). (gr. -1-3). 17.99 *(978-0-8037-4134-8(0)*, Dial Bks) Penguin Young Readers Group.
—Las Fabulas de Esopo. 2004.Tr. of Aesop's Fables. (SPA.). (J). pap. 10.99 *(978-84-316-7164-8(5))* Vicens-Vives, Editorial, S.A. ESP. Dist: Lectorum Pubns., Inc.
—God Bless the Child. Holiday, Billie & Herzog, Arthur, Jr. 2008. (ENG.). 40p. (J). (gr. -1-3). per. 7.99 *(978-0-06-443646-5(2))* HarperCollins Pubs.
—God Bless the Child. Holiday, Billie. 2004. 32p. (J). lib. bdg. 17.89 *(978-0-06-029487-8(6)*, Amistad) HarperCollins Pubs.
—Goin' Someplace Special. McKissack, Patricia C. 2008. (ENG.). 40p. (J). (gr. -1-3). 8.99 *(978-1-4169-2735-8(2)*, Aladdin) Simon & Schuster Children's Publishing.
—A Home in the Barn. Brown, Margaret Wise. 2018. (ENG.). 32p. (J). (gr. -1-3). 17.99 *(978-0-06-623787-9(4))* HarperCollins Pubs.
—In Plain Sight. Jackson, Richard. 2016. (ENG.). 40p. (J). 17.99 *(978-1-62672-255-2(2)*, 900147597) Roaring Brook Pr.
—The Moon over Star. Aston, Dianna Hutts. 2008. (ENG.). 32p. (J). (gr. 1-3). 17.99 *(978-0-8037-3107-3(8)*, Dial Bks) Penguin Young Readers Group.

Pinkney, Jerry, et al. Music from Our Lord's Holy Heaven. Pinkney, Gloria Jean. 2005. 48p. (J). (gr. -1-18). lib. bdg. 18.89 incl. audio compact disk *(978-0-06-000769-0(9))* HarperCollins Pubs.

Pinkney, Jerry. A Place to Land: Martin Luther King Jr. & the Speech That Inspired a Nation. Wittenstein, Barry. 2019. (ENG.). 48p. (J). (gr. 2-5). 18.99 *(978-0-8234-4331-4(0)*, Neal Porter Bks) Holiday Hse., Inc.
—Song of the Trees. Taylor, Mildred D. 2003. (ENG.). 80p. (J). (gr. 5-7). 7.99 *(978-0-14-250075-0(5)*, Puffin Books) Penguin Young Readers Group.
—A Starlit Snowfall. Willard, Nancy. 2011. (ENG.). 32p. (J). (gr. -1-3). 6.99 *(978-0-316-18366-6(0))* Little Brown & Co.
—Tales of Uncle Remus (Puffin Modern Classics) The Adventures of Brer Rabbit. Lester, Julius. 2006. (Puffin Modern Classics Ser.). (ENG.). 160p. (J). (gr. 3-7). pap. 7.99 *(978-0-14-240720-2(8)*, Puffin Books) Penguin Young Readers Group.

Pinkney, Jerry. The Little Red Hen. Pinkney, Jerry. 2006. (ENG.). 32p. (J). (gr. -1-3). 17.99 *(978-0-8037-2935-3(9)*, Dial Bks) Penguin Young Readers Group.
—Rikki-Tikki-Tavi. Pinkney, Jerry. Kipling, Rudyard. 2004. (ENG.). 48p. (J). (gr. -1-3). reprint ed. pap. 7.99 *(978-0-06-058785-7(7))* HarperCollins Pubs.
—Three Little Kittens. Pinkney, Jerry. 2010. (ENG.). 40p. (J). (gr. -1-k). 17.99 *(978-0-8037-3533-0(2)*, Dial Bks) Penguin Young Readers Group.

Pinkney, Myles C. Shades of Black: A Celebration of Our Children. Pinkney, Sandra L. 2006. (ENG.). 24p. (J). (gr. -1 — 1). bds. 6.99 *(978-0-439-80251-2(2)*, Cartwheel Bks.) Scholastic, Inc.

Pinkwater, Daniel M. Lizard Music. Pinkwater, Daniel M. 2017. 160p. (J). (gr. 4-7). pap. 9.99 *(978-1-68137-184-9(7)*, NYRB Kids) New York Review of Bks., Inc., The.

Pinkwater, Jill. Dancing Larry, 1 vol. Pinkwater, Daniel M. 2006. (ENG.). 32p. (J). (gr. -1-3). 16.95 *(978-0-7614-5220-1(6))* Marshall Cavendish Corp.
—Sleepover Larry, 0 vols. Pinkwater, Daniel. 2013. (ENG.). 34p. (J). (gr. -1-3). pap. 9.99 *(978-1-4778-4765-7(0)*, 9781477847657, Two Lions) Amazon Publishing.
—Young Larry, 1 vol. Pinkwater, Daniel M. 2005. (ENG.). 32p. (J). pap. 5.95 *(978-0-7614-5177-8(3))* Marshall Cavendish Corp.

Pinna, Amilcar. Generation X Vol. 1: Natural Selection. 2017. (ENG.). 1p. (YA). (gr. 8-17). pap. 17.99 *(978-1-302-90736-5(0))* Marvel Worldwide, Inc.

Pinnock, Nathan. The Sacrament. Bytheway, John. 2013. 18.99 *(978-1-60907-790-7(3))* Deseret Bk. Co.

Pino, Pablo. Crunch & Crack, Oink & Whack! An Onomatopoeia Story. Cleary, Brian P. 2019. (ENG.). 32p. (J). (gr. 2-5). 26.65 *(978-1-4677-8799-4(X)*, Millbrook Pr.) Lerner Publishing Group.
—Dreamboy. Damirón, Anya. 2010. (SPA.). 26p. (J). *(978-9945-421-42-2(5))* Lucia Stories.
—Inventor Boy. Damirón, Anya. 2010. (SPA.). 26p. (J). *(978-9945-00-157-0(4))* Lucia Stories.
—¡Qué Cosas Dice Mi Abuela! Galán, Ana. 2013. (SPA.). 32p. (J). (gr. -1-3). 3.99 *(978-0-545-32863-0(2)*, Scholastic en Espanol) Scholastic, Inc.
—The Night Baafore Christmas. Young, Dawn. 2019. 32p. (J). (gr. -1-3). 17.99 *(978-1-5460-1458-4(6)*, Worthy Kids/Ideals) Worthy Publishing.
—Nino Inventor. Damirón, Anya. 2010. 26p. (J). *(978-9945-00-153-2(1))* Lucia Stories.
—Pacho Nacho. Lopez, Silvia. 2020. (ENG.). 32p. (J). (gr. -1-2). 17.95 *(978-1-68446-098-4(0)*, 141334, Capstone Editions) Capstone.
—What's the Bible All About? Pingry, Patricia A. 2017. (ENG.). 20p. (gr. -1-k). bds. 7.99 *(978-1-945470-29-5(1)*, Museum of the Bible) Worthy Publishing.
—When Walt Disney Rode a Pig. Weakland, Mark. 2017. (Leaders Doing Headstands Ser.). (ENG.). 32p. (J). (gr. 1-4). lib. bdg. 28.65 *(978-1-5158-1576-1(5)*, 136246, Picture Window Bks.) Capstone.

Pintachan. Baby Bowie: A Book about Adjectives. Running Press. 2019. (Baby Rocker Ser.). 26p. (J). (gr. -1 — 1). bds. 9.99 *(978-0-7624-6801-0(7)*, Running Pr. Kids) Running Pr.
—Baby Elvis: A Book about Opposites. Running Press. 2020. (Baby Rocker Ser.). 24p. (J). (gr. -1 — 1). bds. 9.99 *(978-0-7624-6978-9(1)*, Running Pr. Kids) Running Pr.
—Baby KISS: A Book about Colors. Running Press. 2019. (Baby Rocker Ser.). 26p. (J). (gr. -1 — 1). bds. 9.99 *(978-0-7624-6799-0(1)*, Running Pr. Kids) Running Pr.
—Changing Faces: Happy Halloween! Thoms, Nathan. 2018. (ENG.). 18p. (J). (gr. -1 — 1). bds. 7.95 *(978-1-4197-2967-6(5))* Abrams, Inc.

Pinteño, Ismael. Charlotte Bronte: Band 18/Pearl (Collins Big Cat) Castor, Harriet. 2016. (Collins Big Cat Ser.). (ENG.). 80p. (J). (gr. 5-6). pap. 12.99 *(978-0-00-816405-8(3))* HarperCollins Pubs. Ltd. GBR. Dist: Independent Pubs. Group.

Pinter, Laura. Trinkett & the Legend of the Locket. Bello, Stephanie. 2019. (ENG.). 82p. (J). (gr. k-4). 16.99 *(978-1-61984-506-0(7))*; (Trinkett Tales Ser.: Vol. 1). pap. 9.99 *(978-1-61984-507-7(5))* Plum Street Pr.

Pinto, Dan. Hedgehug's Halloween. Sutton, Benn. 2013. (ENG.). 40p. (J). (gr. -1-3). 9.99 *(978-0-06-196104-5(3))* HarperCollins Pubs.

Pinto, Dan. Hedgehug: a Sharp Lesson in Love. Pinto, Dan. 2011. (ENG.). 40p. (J). (gr. -1-2). 9.99 *(978-0-06-196101-4(9))* HarperCollins Pubs.

Pinto, Marcelo, jt. illus. see Lim, Ron.

Pinto, Valentina. Ahsoka & Padmé. Revis, Beth. 2018. (Star Wars: Forces of Destiny Ser.). (ENG.). 24p. (J). (gr. 4-9). lib. bdg. 27.07 *(978-1-5321-4292-5(7)*, 31118, Graphic Novels) Spotlight.

Pinto, Valentina, et al. Strawberry Shortcake Volume 3: Berry Good Life. Dell Lowe, Zena & Ball, Georgia. 2017. (Strawberry Shortcake Ser.: 3). (ENG.). 80p. (J). (gr. 4-7). 12.99 *(978-1-63140-884-7(4))* Idea & Design Works, LLC.

Pinto, Valentina, jt. illus. see Francisco, Tina.

Pinto, Valentina, jt. illus. see Sommariva, Jon.

Pinto, Venantius J. Aani & the Tree Huggers. Atkins, Jeannine. 2013. (ENG.). 28p. (J). (gr. -1-5). pap. 10.95 *(978-1-58430-004-5(3))* Lee & Low Bks., Inc.
—Aani & the Tree Huggers. Powell, Robert et al. Moore, Nancy & Springhouse Publishing Company Staff, eds. 2013. (ENG.). 32p. (J). pap., tchr. ed. 10.95 *(978-1-58000-000-0(2))* Lee & Low Bks., Inc.

Pintor, Ruben. Growing up Yanomamö: Missionary Adventures in the Amazon Rainforest. Dawson, Mike. 2009. (ENG.). 336p. (J). pap. 19.95 *(978-1-60265-009-1(8))* Grace Acres Pr.

Pintozzi, Connie, jt. illus. see Pintozzi, Nick.

Pintozzi, Nick, et al. Bentley & the Great Fire. Pintozzi, Nick. 2004. 16.95 *(978-0-9749465-2-8(4))*; 120p. per. 17.95 *(978-0-9749465-1-1(6))* BentDaiSha, LLC.
—Bentley Finds a Home. Pintozzi, Nick. l.t. ed. 2004. 102p. per. 17.95 *(978-0-9749465-0-4(8))* BentDaiSha, LLC.

Pintozzi, Nick & Pintozzi, Connie. Bentley & the Cactus Rustlers. Pintozzi, Nick. 2006. per. 11.00 *(978-0-9749465-4-2(0))* BentDaiSha, LLC.

Pionessa, Joanne. Fast Phil. Jackson, Kristin. 2019. (ENG.). 36p. (J). (gr. k-3). pap. 7.95 ***(978-1-64713-091-6(3))*** Primedia eLaunch LLC.

Pios, Ronie. The Magical Crystal Island of Morzzagal Where the King & His Three Sons Lived. Gogonya, Carol. 2012. (ENG.). 28p. pap. 32.70 *(978-1-4771-3159-6(0))* Xlibris Corp.

Piotti, Dania. Outsdide with Lil Boo. Bookins, Daddy. 2012. 38p. pap. 13.50 *(978-0-9848019-3-0(6))* Inkwell Books LLC.

Pipe, Jasper. The Adventures of Miss Turtle. Hong, Catherine Thao. 2012. 24p. (J). pap. *(978-0-9873790-0-9(3))* Icky Grass Books.

Piper, Molly. Rosey & Amanda. Piper, Molly. Date not set. (J). (gr. k-6). pap. 7.95 *(978-1-891360-01-5(9))* Little Deer Pr.

P

Piper, Tamara. A Cry for the Ocean. Safieh, Charlotte. 2019. (ENG.). 32p. (J). (gr. k-6). 15.99 ***(978-1-9161776-3-5(8))***; pap. 7.99 ***(978-1-9161776-2-8(X))*** Blue Jay Pr.

Piper, Tamara. I Do Not Like Bugs! Tomlin, Pamela. 2018. (My Truly Most Favorite Fluffy Friend Ser.: Vol. 3). (ENG.). 34p. (J). pap. 9.99 *(978-1-7264-9017-7(3))* CreateSpace Independent Publishing Platform.

Piper, Tom. Animal Rain. Nevis, Lance. Laible MBA, Steve William, ed. 2012. 36p. pap. 10.99 *(978-0-9850142-7-8(X))* Kodel Group, LLC, The.

—The Pollywog Prince. Nevis, Lance. Laible MBA, Steve William, ed. 2012. 46p. pap. 10.99 *(978-0-9850142-8-5(8))* Kodel Group, LLC, The.

—Silly Stew. Nevis, Lance. Laible MBA, Steve William, ed. 2012. 50p. pap. 10.99 *(978-0-9850142-9-2(6))* Kodel Group, LLC, The.

Pippet, Gabriel. Saints & Festivals: A Cycle of the Year for Young People. Salome, Mother Mary. 2018. (ENG.). 264p. (J). (gr. 3-6). pap. 14.95 *(978-1-936639-99-1(8))* St. Augustine Academy Pr.

Pippet, Wilfrid. First Communion Days: And True Stories for First Communicants. Du St Esprit, Sr Julie. 2019. (ENG.). 198p. (J). (gr. k-3). pap. 12.95 *(978-1-64051-074-6(5))* St. Augustine Academy Pr.

Pippin, Barbara. Gramma's Glasses. Guiffre, William. 2008. 32p. (J). (gr. -1-3). pap. 9.95 *(978-1-931650-35-9(7))* Guiffre Bk. Publishing.

—Gramma's Glasses. Guiffre, William A. 2008. 32p. (J). (gr. -1-7). lib. bdg. 17.95 *(978-1-931650-19-9(5))* Guiffre Bk. Publishing.

Pippin, Kristin A. & Pippin, Sheila C. Katrina: Through Mango's Eyes. Pippin, Sheila C. 2007. (J). (gr. -1-5). pap. 12.95 *(978-1-56167-956-0(9))* American Literary Pr.

Pippin-Mathur, Courtney. Maya Was Grumpy. 2013. (J). *(978-0-545-62077-2(5))* Flashlight Pr.

Pippin-Mathur, Courtney. Dragons Rule, Princesses Drool! Pippin-Mathur, Courtney. 2017. (ENG.). 40p. (J). (gr. -1-3). 17.99 *(978-1-4814-6138-2(9))*, Little Simon) Little Simon.

—Maya Was Grumpy. Pippin-Mathur, Courtney. 2013. (ENG.). 32p. (J). (gr. k-2). 16.95 *(978-1-936261-13-0(8))* Flashlight Pr.

Pippin, Sheila C., jt. illus. see Pippin, Kristin A.

Pippins, Andrea. Big Ideas for Young Thinkers: 20 Questions about Life & the Universe. Wilson, Jamia. 2020. (ENG.). 64p. (J). (gr. 5-9). ***(978-0-7112-5835-8(X)***, Wide Eyed Editions) Quarto Publishing Group UK.

—Step into Your Power: 23 Lessons on How to Live Your Best Life. Wilson, Jamia. 2019. (ENG.). 64p. (J). (gr. 4-7). 22.99 ***(978-1-78603-586-8(3)***, Wide Eyed Editions) Quarto Publishing Group UK GBR. Dist: Hachette Bk. Group.

Pippins, Andrea. Young Gifted & Black: Meet 52 Black Heroes from Past & Present. Wilson, Jamia. 2018. (ENG.). 64p. (J). (gr. 2-5). 23.99 *(978-1-78603-158-7(2)*, Wide Eyed Editions) Quarto Publishing Group UK GBR. Dist: Hachette Bk. Group.

Pirie, Lauren & Laurence, Laurence. Ella & the Balloons in the Sky. Appleby, Danny. 2013. (ENG.). 32p. (J). (gr. k-4). 15.95 *(978-1-77049-528-9(2)*, Tundra Bks.) Tundra Bks. CAN. Dist: Penguin Random Hse. LLC.

Pirillo, John. Knight Detective: King Arthur Has Returned; but Not to England. Pirillo, John. 2018. (ENG.). 330p. (J). pap. 15.99 *(978-1-7315-3692-1(5))* Independently Published.

Pirnot, Karen Hutchins. Just Hanging Out, a Collection of Poems for Kids. Klanot, Khaya Dawn. 2008. 48p. pap. 16.95 *(978-0-9814894-5-2(1))* Peppertree Pr., The.

Pirnot, Karen Hutchins. Keeper of the Lullabies, a Book for Grandmothers Who Cherish the World of Children. Pirnot, Karen Hutchins. 2007. 36p. per. 12.95 *(978-1-934246-90-0(5))* Peppertree Pr., The.

—Night Traveler. Pirnot, Karen Hutchins. 2007. 24p. per. 12.95 *(978-1-934246-97-9(2))* Peppertree Pr., The.

Pirolli, Anna. I Hate My Cats (a Love Story) Cali, Davide. 2018. (ENG.). 44p. (J). (gr. k-3). 15.99 *(978-1-4521-6595-0(5))* Chronicle Bks. LLC.

Pisapia, Blasco & Brughera, Pamela. The Dancing Vampire. Pavanello, Roberto. Zeni, Marco, tr. 2012. (Echo & the Bat Pack Ser.). (ENG.). 128p. (J). (gr. 1-3). 25.32 *(978-1-4342-3837-5(7)*, Stone Arch Bks.) Capstone.

—The Midnight Witches, 1 vol. Pavanello, Roberto. Zeni, Marco, tr. 2012. (Echo & the Bat Pack Ser.). (ENG.). 128p. (J). (gr. 1-3). lib. bdg. 25.32 *(978-1-4342-3822-1(9)*, Stone Arch Bks.) Capstone.

Piscopo, Samantha. The Missing Vowel. Cox-Sands, Angela. 2008. 20p. pap. 24.95 *(978-1-60813-028-3(2))* America Star Bks.

Pistorius, Anna. The True Book of Birds We Know. Friskey, Margaret. 2011. 48p. pap. 35.95 *(978-1-258-09819-3(9))* Literary Licensing, LLC.

Pitcairn, Ansel. Portraits of African-American Heroes. Bolden, Tonya. 2005. 96p. (J). (gr. 3-7). pap. 13.99 *(978-0-14-240473-7(X)*, Puffin Books) Penguin Young Readers Group.

Pitcher, Jeff. Hop, Skip & Jump into Reading. Howlett, Bruce et al. 2003. (J). Bk. 1. 9.00 *(978-0-9704183-4-0(5))*; Bk. 2. 9.00 *(978-0-9704183-3-3(7)*, Sound Reading); Bk. 3. 9.00 *(978-0-9704183-8-8(8)*, Sound Reading) Sound Reading Solutions.

Pitilli, Thomas. Gotham High. de la Cruz, Melissa. 2020. 208p. (J). (gr. 11). pap. 16.99 *(978-1-4012-8624-8(0))* DC Comics.

Pitre, Dawn. Beauty's Secret. Gano, Debra. 2008. (Heartlight Girls Ser.). 54p. (J). 17.95 *(978-0-9787689-0-4(6))* Heartlight Girls.

Pitre-Durocher, Sara, jt. illus. see Howell, Corin.

Pitt, Sarah. Animal Friends on the Farm. Reasoner, Charles. 2009. (3D Board Bks.). 12p. (J). (gr. -1-k). bds. 9.99 *(978-1-934650-35-6(8))* Just For Kids Pr., LLC.

—Animals in the Jungle. Reasoner, Charles. 2009. (3D Board Bks.). 12p. (J). (gr. -1-k). bds. 9.99 *(978-1-934650-38-7(2))* Just For Kids Pr., LLC.

—The Busy Christmas Stable, 1 vol. David, Juliet. ed. 2010. (Candle Peek-A-boo Ser.). (ENG.). 8p. (J). (gr. -1 — 1). bds. 11.99 *(978-1-85985-803-5(1)*, Candle Bks.) Lion Hudson PLC GBR. Dist: Kregel Pubns.

—Colors in the Garden. Reasoner, Charles. 2009. (3D Board Bks.). 12p. (J). (gr. -1-k). bds. 9.99 *(978-1-934650-40-0(4))* Just For Kids Pr., LLC.

—First Words at the Park. Reasoner, Charles. 2009. (3D Board Bks.). 12p. (J). (gr. -1-k). bds. 9.99 *(978-1-934650-39-4(0))* Just For Kids Pr., LLC.

—Numbers under the Sea. Reasoner, Charles. 2009. (3D Board Bks.). 12p. (J). (gr. -1-k). bds. 9.99 *(978-1-934650-37-0(4))* Just For Kids Pr., LLC.

Pitt, Sarah. Peek-A-Boo Farm. Rainstorm Publishing. 2018. (ENG.). 20p. (J). bds. 7.99 ***(978-1-989219-83-6(7))*** Rainstorm Pr.

Pitt, Sarah. Shapes at the Beach. Reasoner, Charles. 2009. (3D Board Bks.). 12p. (J). (gr. -1-k). bds. 9.99 *(978-1-934650-36-3(6))* Just For Kids Pr., LLC.

—Tractor Trouble Drive Through Storybook. Reader's Digest Staff. 2011. (Drive-Through Storybooks Ser.). (ENG.). 10p. (J). (gr. -1-1). bds. 12.99 *(978-0-7944-2169-4(5))* Reader's Digest Assn., Inc., The.

Pittenger, Jerry. Benny the Bunny: The True Meaning of Christmas & Easter. Dowell, James "jim" Allen. 2019. (ENG.). 36p. (J). pap. 10.99 ***(978-1-7007-0657-7(8))*** Independently Published.

Pittenger, Jerry. Jesus Loves Me. 2019. (VeggieTales Ser.). 16p. (J). bds. 13.99 *(978-0-8249-1697-8(2)*, Worthy Kids/Ideals) Worthy Publishing.

Pittman, Gail. Anna's Choice. Carter, Catherine. 2005. 24p. (J). (gr. 3-7). 12.95 *(978-1-893062-79-5(1))* Quail Ridge Pr., Inc.

Pittock, Prue. Isla's Family Tree. McKelvey, Katrina. 2020. (ENG.). 32p. (J). (gr. -1-7). 18.99 *(978-1-925820-37-9(8)*, 335023, EK Bks.) Exisle Publishing Pty Ltd. AUS. Dist: Hachette UK Distribution.

Pitz, Henry. Amigo, Circus Horse. Cooper, Page. 2011. 240p. 46.95 *(978-1-258-06394-8(8))* Literary Licensing, LLC.

Pitzer, Marjorie, photos by. Animal Fun for Everyone! Pitzer, Marjorie. 2014. (ENG., 14p. (J). pap. *(978-1-60613-188-6(5))* Woodbine Hse.

Pitzer, Marjorie W., photos by. My up & down & All Around Book. Pitzer, Marjorie W. 2008. (ENG., 16p. (J). (gr. -1-1). pap. 10.95 *(978-1-890627-90-4(9))* Woodbine Hse.

Pitzer, Suzanne. Talking about Divorce & Separation: A Dialogue Between Parent & Child. Grollman, Earl A. 2005. (J). *(978-1-56123-155-3(X))* Centering Corp.

Piu, Amandine. Beware the Monster. Escoffier, Michaël. 2018. (ENG.). 40p. (J). (gr. -1-1). 18.95 *(978-1-77321-022-3(X))* Annick Pr., Ltd. CAN. Dist: Publishers Group West (PGW).

—Beware the Monster. Escoffier, Michaël. 2018. (ENG.). 36p. (J). (gr. -1-1). pap. 9.95 *(978-1-77321-023-0(8))* Annick Pr., Ltd. CAN. Dist: Publishers Group West (PGW).

—Princess Adventures: This Way or That Way? Misslin, Sylvie. 2020. (ENG.). 44p. (J). (gr. -1-3). 14.99 *(978-0-358-05186-2(X)*, 1742179, HMH Books For Young Readers) Houghton Mifflin Harcourt Publishing Co.

Piven, Hanoch. What Presidents Are Made Of. 2012. (ENG.). 40p. (J). (gr. 1-5). 7.99 *(978-1-4424-4433-1(9)*, Atheneum Bks. for Young Readers) Simon & Schuster Children's Publishing.

Piven, Hanoch. Let's Make Faces. Piven, Hanoch. 2013. (ENG.). 40p. (J). (gr. -1-3). 19.99 *(978-1-4169-1532-4(X))* Simon & Schuster Children's Publishing.

—My Best Friend Is As Sharp As a Pencil: & Other Funny Classroom Portraits. Piven, Hanoch. 2010. 40p. (J). (gr. -1-3). 17.99 *(978-0-375-85338-8(3)*, Schwartz & Wade Bks.) Random Hse. Children's Bks.

—My Dog Is As Smelly As Dirty Socks: And Other Funny Family Portraits. Piven, Hanoch. 2012. 40p. (J). (gr. -1-3). pap. 7.99 *(978-0-307-93089-7(0)*, Dragonfly Bks.) Random Hse. Children's Bks.

—What Athletes Are Made Of. Piven, Hanoch. 2015. (ENG.). 40p. (J). (gr. 1-5). 19.99 *(978-1-4814-7508-2(8)*, Atheneum Bks. for Young Readers) Simon & Schuster Children's Publishing.

—What Cats Are Made Of. Piven, Hanoch. 2009. (ENG.). 40p. (J). (gr. -1-3). 16.99 *(978-1-4169-1531-7(1)*, Atheneum Bks. for Young Readers) Simon & Schuster Children's Publishing.

Piworski, Marcin. It's Too Noisy! Rosen, Robert. 2017. (All about Me Ser.). (ENG.). 24p. (gr. -1-2). 29.93 *(978-1-68342-718-6(1)*, 9781683427186) Rourke Educational Media.

—Messy Spaghetti. Lamb, Jenny. 2017. (I Help My Friends Ser.). (ENG.). 24p. (gr. -1-2). 29.93 *(978-1-68342-725-4(4)*, 9781683427254); pap. 8.95 *(978-1-68342-777-3(7)*, 9781683427773) Rourke Educational Media.

—The Perfect Jack-O'-Lantern. Abbott, Victoria. 2017. (My Adventures Ser.). (ENG.). 24p. (gr. -1-2). pap. 8.95 *(978-1-68342-795-7(5)*, 9781683427957) Rourke Educational Media.

—So Many Classes. Wells, Robin. 2017. (School Days Ser.). (ENG.). 24p. (gr. -1-2). pap. 8.95 *(978-1-68342-773-5(4)*, 9781683427735) Rourke Educational Media.

—Where Is My Eraser? Rosen, Robert. 2017. (School Days Ser.). (ENG.). 24p. (gr. -1-2). 29.93 *(978-1-68342-710-0(6)*, 9781683427100) Rourke Educational Media.

Piwowarski, Marcin. All Aboard the Spooky Express! James, Eric. 2017. (Spooky Express Ser.). (ENG.). 32p. (J). (-6). 9.99 *(978-1-4926-5375-2(6)*, Sourcebooks Jabberwocky) Sourcebooks, Inc.

—La Biblia en un Año para Niños. Davies, Rhona. 2007.Tr. of One Year Children's Bible. (SPA.). 352p. (J). (gr. 1-5). 19.99 *(978-1-4143-1500-3(7)*, 4600386, Tyndale Espanol) Tyndale Hse. Pubs.

—Dibs! Gehl, Laura. 2019. (ENG.). 32p. (J). (gr. -1-3). 17.99 *(978-1-5124-6532-7(1)*, Carolrhoda Bks.) Lerner Publishing Group.

—Feet, Legs, Hands. Lindeen, Mary. 2015. (Early Rising Readers Ser.). (J). (gr. -1-k). 5.83 *(978-1-4788-1689-8(9))* Newmark Learning LLC.

—The Giant Turnip: Lap Book Edition. Smith, Carrie. 2016. (My First Reader's Theater Tales Ser.). (J). (gr. k). *(978-1-5021-5505-4(2))* Benchmark Education Co.

—The Giant Turnip: Small Book Edition. Smith, Carrie. 2016. (My First Reader's Theater Tales Ser.). (J). (gr. k). *(978-1-5021-5510-8(9))* Benchmark Education Co.

—Jamila Finds a Friend. Hawes, Alison. 2016. (Cambridge Reading Adventures Ser.). (ENG.). 16p. pap. 7.37 *(978-1-107-54963-0(9))* Cambridge Univ. Pr.

—A Long Car Ride. Lamb, Jenny. 2017. (Family Time Ser.). (ENG.). 24p. (gr. -1-2). pap. 8.95 *(978-1-68342-780-3(7)*, 9781683427803) Rourke Educational Media.

—Numbers in the Classroom. Newman, Constance. 2017. (School Days Ser.). (ENG.). 24p. (gr. -1-2). 29.93 *(978-1-68342-697-4(5)*, 9781683426974) Rourke Educational Media.

—The One Year Children's Bible. Davies, Rhona. 2007. (ENG.). 352p. (J). (gr. 1-5). 19.99 *(978-1-4143-1499-0(X)*, 4600385) Tyndale Hse. Pubs.

—Page-A-Day Children's Bible. Davies, Rhona. 2016. 381p. (J). pap. *(978-0-8198-6032-3(8))* Pauline Bks. & Media.

—The Perfect Jack-O'-Lantern. Abbott, Victoria. 2017. (My Adventures Ser.). (ENG.). 24p. (gr. -1-2). 29.93 *(978-1-68342-743-8(2)*, 9781683427438) Rourke Educational Media.

—Pies, Piernas y Manos. Lindeen, Mary. 2016. (Early Rising Readers Ser.). (SPA.). (J). (gr. -1). 6.67 *(978-1-4788-3711-4(X))* Newmark Learning LLC.

—¿Qué Ves en el Circo? Koons, Linda. 2016. (Early Rising Readers Ser.). (SPA.). (J). (gr. -1). 6.67 *(978-1-4788-3664-3(4))* Newmark Learning LLC.

—The Road to Christmas Day. Godfrey, Jan. 2008. 32p. (J). (gr. -1-1). 14.95 *(978-0-8198-6487-1(0))* Pauline Bks. & Media.

—The Road to Easter Day. Godfrey, Jan. 2009. 32p. (J). (gr. -1-1). 14.95 *(978-0-8198-6486-4(2))* Pauline Bks. & Media.

—See the Circus. Koons, Linda. 2015. (Early Rising Readers Ser.). (J). (gr. -1-k). 5.83 *(978-1-4788-1588-4(4))* Newmark Learning LLC.

—So Many Classes. Wells, Robin. 2017. (School Days Ser.). (ENG.). 24p. (gr. -1-2). 29.93 *(978-1-68342-721-6(1)*, 9781683427216) Rourke Educational Media.

—The Spooky Express Alabama. James, Eric. 2017. (Spooky Express Ser.). (ENG.). 32p. (J). (-6). 9.99 *(978-1-4926-5337-0(3)*, Sourcebooks Jabberwocky) Sourcebooks, Inc.

—The Spooky Express Alaska. James, Eric. 2017. (Spooky Express Ser.). (ENG.). 32p. (J). (-6). 9.99 *(978-1-4926-5338-7(1)*, Sourcebooks Jabberwocky) Sourcebooks, Inc.

—The Spooky Express Albuquerque. James, Eric. 2017. (Spooky Express Ser.). (ENG.). 32p. (J). (-6). 9.99 *(978-1-4926-5339-4(X)*, Sourcebooks Jabberwocky) Sourcebooks, Inc.

—The Spooky Express Arkansas. James, Eric. 2017. (Spooky Express Ser.). (ENG.). 32p. (J). (-6). 9.99 *(978-1-4926-5341-7(1)*, Sourcebooks Jabberwocky) Sourcebooks, Inc.

—The Spooky Express Boston. James, Eric. 2017. (Spooky Express Ser.). (ENG.). 32p. (J). (-6). 9.99 *(978-1-4926-5343-1(8)*, Sourcebooks Jabberwocky) Sourcebooks, Inc.

—The Spooky Express Calgary. James, Eric. 2017. (Spooky Express Ser.). (ENG.). 32p. (J). (-6). 9.99 *(978-1-4926-5345-5(4)*, Sourcebooks Jabberwocky) Sourcebooks, Inc.

—The Spooky Express California. James, Eric. 2017. (Spooky Express Ser.). (ENG.). 32p. (J). (-6). 9.99 *(978-1-4926-5344-8(6)*, Sourcebooks Jabberwocky) Sourcebooks, Inc.

—The Spooky Express Canada. James, Eric. 2017. (Spooky Express Ser.). (ENG.). 32p. (J). (-6). 9.99 *(978-1-4926-5346-2(2)*, Sourcebooks Jabberwocky) Sourcebooks, Inc.

—The Spooky Express Chicago. James, Eric. 2017. (Spooky Express Ser.). (ENG.). 32p. (J). (-6). 9.99 *(978-1-4926-5348-6(9)*, Sourcebooks Jabberwocky) Sourcebooks, Inc.

—The Spooky Express Cincinnati. James, Eric. 2017. (Spooky Express Ser.). (ENG.). 32p. (J). (-6). 9.99 *(978-1-4926-5349-3(7)*, Sourcebooks Jabberwocky) Sourcebooks, Inc.

—The Spooky Express Colorado. James, Eric. 2017. (Spooky Express Ser.). (ENG.). 32p. (J). (-6). 9.99 *(978-1-4926-5350-9(0)*, Sourcebooks Jabberwocky) Sourcebooks, Inc.

—The Spooky Express Connecticut. James, Eric. 2017. (Spooky Express Ser.). (ENG.). 32p. (J). (-6). 9.99 *(978-1-4926-5351-6(9)*, Sourcebooks Jabberwocky) Sourcebooks, Inc.

—The Spooky Express Delaware. James, Eric. 2017. (Spooky Express Ser.). (ENG.). 32p. (J). (-6). 9.99 *(978-1-4926-5352-3(7)*, Sourcebooks Jabberwocky) Sourcebooks, Inc.

—The Spooky Express Edmonton. James, Eric. 2017. (Spooky Express Ser.). (ENG.). 32p. (J). (-6). 9.99 *(978-1-4926-5353-0(5)*, Sourcebooks Jabberwocky) Sourcebooks, Inc.

—The Spooky Express Florida. James, Eric. 2017. (Spooky Express Ser.). (ENG.). 32p. (J). (-6). 9.99 *(978-1-4926-5354-7(3)*, Sourcebooks Jabberwocky) Sourcebooks, Inc.

—The Spooky Express Georgia. James, Eric. 2017. (Spooky Express Ser.). (ENG.). 32p. (J). (-6). 9.99 *(978-1-4926-5355-4(1)*, Sourcebooks Jabberwocky) Sourcebooks, Inc.

—The Spooky Express Hawaii. James, Eric. 2017. (Spooky Express Ser.). (ENG.). 32p. (J). (-6). 9.99 *(978-1-4926-5356-1(X)*, Sourcebooks Jabberwocky) Sourcebooks, Inc.

—The Spooky Express Idaho. James, Eric. 2017. (Spooky Express Ser.). (ENG.). 32p. (J). (-6). 9.99 *(978-1-4926-5357-8(8)*, Sourcebooks Jabberwocky) Sourcebooks, Inc.

—The Spooky Express Illinois. James, Eric. 2017. (Spooky Express Ser.). (ENG.). 32p. (J). (-6). 9.99 *(978-1-4926-5358-5(6)*, Sourcebooks Jabberwocky) Sourcebooks, Inc.

—The Spooky Express Indiana. James, Eric. 2017. (Spooky Express Ser.). (ENG.). 32p. (J). (-6). 9.99 *(978-1-4926-5359-2(4)*, Sourcebooks Jabberwocky) Sourcebooks, Inc.

—The Spooky Express Iowa. James, Eric. 2017. (Spooky Express Ser.). (ENG.). 32p. (J). (-6). 9.99 *(978-1-4926-5360-8(8)*, Sourcebooks Jabberwocky) Sourcebooks, Inc.

—The Spooky Express Kansas. James, Eric. 2017. (Spooky Express Ser.). (ENG.). 32p. (J). (-6). 9.99 *(978-1-4926-5361-5(6)*, Sourcebooks Jabberwocky) Sourcebooks, Inc.

—The Spooky Express Kansas City. James, Eric. 2017. (Spooky Express Ser.). (ENG.). 32p. (J). (-6). 9.99 *(978-1-4926-5362-2(4)*, Sourcebooks Jabberwocky) Sourcebooks, Inc.

—The Spooky Express Kentucky. James, Eric. 2017. (Spooky Express Ser.). (ENG.). 32p. (J). (-6). 9.99 *(978-1-4926-5363-9(2)*, Sourcebooks Jabberwocky) Sourcebooks, Inc.

—The Spooky Express Las Vegas. James, Eric. 2017. (Spooky Express Ser.). (ENG.). 32p. (J). (-6). 9.99 *(978-1-4926-5365-3(9)*, Sourcebooks Jabberwocky) Sourcebooks, Inc.

—The Spooky Express Los Angeles. James, Eric. 2017. (Spooky Express Ser.). (ENG.). 32p. (J). (-6). 9.99 *(978-1-4926-5366-0(7)*, Sourcebooks Jabberwocky) Sourcebooks, Inc.

—The Spooky Express Louisiana. James, Eric. 2017. (Spooky Express Ser.). (ENG.). 32p. (J). (-6). 9.99 *(978-1-4926-5364-6(0)*, Sourcebooks Jabberwocky) Sourcebooks, Inc.

—The Spooky Express Maine. James, Eric. 2017. (Spooky Express Ser.). (ENG.). 32p. (J). (-6). 9.99 *(978-1-4926-5367-7(5)*, Sourcebooks Jabberwocky) Sourcebooks, Inc.

—The Spooky Express Maryland. James, Eric. 2017. (Spooky Express Ser.). (ENG.). 32p. (J). (-6). 9.99 *(978-1-4926-5368-4(3)*, Sourcebooks Jabberwocky) Sourcebooks, Inc.

—The Spooky Express Massachusetts. James, Eric. 2017. (Spooky Express Ser.). (ENG.). 32p. (J). (-6). 9.99 *(978-1-4926-5369-1(1)*, Sourcebooks Jabberwocky) Sourcebooks, Inc.

—The Spooky Express Michigan. James, Eric. 2017. (Spooky Express Ser.). (ENG.). 32p. (J). (-6). 9.99 *(978-1-4926-5370-7(5)*, Sourcebooks Jabberwocky) Sourcebooks, Inc.

—The Spooky Express Minnesota. James, Eric. 2017. (Spooky Express Ser.). (ENG.). 32p. (J). (-6). 9.99 *(978-1-4926-5371-4(3)*, Sourcebooks Jabberwocky) Sourcebooks, Inc.

—The Spooky Express Mississippi. James, Eric. 2017. (Spooky Express Ser.). (ENG.). 32p. (J). (-6). 9.99 *(978-1-4926-5372-1(1)*, Sourcebooks Jabberwocky) Sourcebooks, Inc.

—The Spooky Express Missouri. James, Eric. 2017. (Spooky Express Ser.). (ENG.). 32p. (J). (-6). 9.99 *(978-1-4926-5373-8(X)*, Sourcebooks Jabberwocky) Sourcebooks, Inc.

—The Spooky Express Montana. James, Eric. 2017. (Spooky Express Ser.). (ENG.). 32p. (J). (-6). 9.99 *(978-1-4926-5374-5(8)*, Sourcebooks Jabberwocky) Sourcebooks, Inc.

—The Spooky Express Nebraska. James, Eric. 2017. (Spooky Express Ser.). (ENG.). 32p. (J). (-6). 9.99 *(978-1-4926-5376-9(4)*, Sourcebooks Jabberwocky) Sourcebooks, Inc.

—The Spooky Express Nevada. James, Eric. 2017. (Spooky Express Ser.). (ENG.). 32p. (J). (-6). 9.99 *(978-1-4926-5377-6(2)*, Sourcebooks Jabberwocky) Sourcebooks, Inc.

—The Spooky Express New England. James, Eric. 2017. (Spooky Express Ser.). (ENG.). 32p. (J). (-6). 9.99 *(978-1-4926-5378-3(0)*, Sourcebooks Jabberwocky) Sourcebooks, Inc.

—The Spooky Express New Hampshire. James, Eric. 2017. (Spooky Express Ser.). (ENG.). 32p. (J). (-6). 9.99 *(978-1-4926-5379-0(9)*, Sourcebooks Jabberwocky) Sourcebooks, Inc.

—The Spooky Express New Jersey. James, Eric. 2017. (Spooky Express Ser.). (ENG.). 32p. (J). (-6). 9.99 *(978-1-4926-5380-6(2)*, Sourcebooks Jabberwocky) Sourcebooks, Inc.

—The Spooky Express New Mexico. James, Eric. 2017. (Spooky Express Ser.). (ENG.). 32p. (J). (-6). 9.99 *(978-1-4926-5381-3(0)*, Sourcebooks Jabberwocky) Sourcebooks, Inc.

—The Spooky Express New York. James, Eric. 2017. (Spooky Express Ser.). (ENG.). 32p. (J). (-6). 9.99 *(978-1-4926-5382-0(9)*, Sourcebooks Jabberwocky) Sourcebooks, Inc.

—The Spooky Express New York City. James, Eric. 2017. (Spooky Express Ser.). (ENG.). 32p. (J). (-6). 9.99 *(978-1-4926-5383-7(7)*, Sourcebooks Jabberwocky) Sourcebooks, Inc.

—The Spooky Express Newfoundland. James, Eric. 2017. (Spooky Express Ser.). (ENG.). 32p. (J). (-6). 9.99 *(978-1-4926-5384-4(5)*, Sourcebooks Jabberwocky) Sourcebooks, Inc.

—The Spooky Express North Carolina. James, Eric. 2017. (Spooky Express Ser.). (ENG.). 32p. (J). (-6). 9.99 *(978-1-4926-5385-1(3)*, Sourcebooks Jabberwocky) Sourcebooks, Inc.

—The Spooky Express North Dakota. James, Eric. 2017. (Spooky Express Ser.). (ENG.). 32p. (J). (-6). 9.99 *(978-1-4926-5386-8(1)*, Sourcebooks Jabberwocky) Sourcebooks, Inc.

—The Spooky Express Nova Scotia. James, Eric. 2017. (Spooky Express Ser.). (ENG.). 32p. (J). (-6). 9.99 *(978-1-4926-5387-5(X)*, Sourcebooks Jabberwocky) Sourcebooks, Inc.

—The Spooky Express Ohio. James, Eric. 2017. (Spooky Express Ser.). (ENG.). 32p. (J). (-6). 9.99 *(978-1-4926-5388-2(8)*, Sourcebooks Jabberwocky) Sourcebooks, Inc.

—The Spooky Express Oklahoma. James, Eric. 2017. (Spooky Express Ser.). (ENG.). 32p. (J). (-6). 9.99 *(978-1-4926-5389-9(6)*, Sourcebooks Jabberwocky) Sourcebooks, Inc.

—The Spooky Express Pennsylvania. James, Eric. 2017. (Spooky Express Ser.). (ENG.). 32p. (J). (-6). 9.99 *(978-1-4926-5392-9(6)*, Sourcebooks Jabberwocky) Sourcebooks, Inc.

—The Spooky Express Philadelphia. James, Eric. 2017. (Spooky Express Ser.). (ENG.). 32p. (J). (-6). 9.99 *(978-1-4926-5393-6(4)*, Sourcebooks Jabberwocky) Sourcebooks, Inc.

—The Spooky Express Pittsburgh. James, Eric. 2017. (Spooky Express Ser.). (ENG.). 32p. (J). (-6). 9.99 *(978-1-4926-5394-3(2)*, Sourcebooks Jabberwocky) Sourcebooks, Inc.

—The Spooky Express Rhode Island. James, Eric. 2017. (Spooky Express Ser.). (ENG.). 32p. (J). (-6). 9.99 *(978-1-4926-5396-7(9)*, Sourcebooks Jabberwocky) Sourcebooks, Inc.

—The Spooky Express San Francisco. James, Eric. 2017. (Spooky Express Ser.). (ENG.). 32p. (J). (-6). 9.99 *(978-1-4926-5397-4(7)*, Sourcebooks Jabberwocky) Sourcebooks, Inc.

—The Spooky Express South Carolina. James, Eric. 2017. (Spooky Express Ser.). (ENG.). 32p. (J). (-6). 9.99 *(978-1-4926-5398-1(5)*, Sourcebooks Jabberwocky) Sourcebooks, Inc.

—The Spooky Express South Dakota. James, Eric. 2017. (Spooky Express Ser.). (ENG.). 32p. (J). (-6). 9.99 *(978-1-4926-5399-8(3)*, Sourcebooks Jabberwocky) Sourcebooks, Inc.

—The Spooky Express St. Louis. James, Eric. 2017. (Spooky Express Ser.). (ENG.). 32p. (J). (-6). 9.99 *(978-1-4926-5400-1(0)*, Sourcebooks Jabberwocky) Sourcebooks, Inc.

—The Spooky Express Tennessee. James, Eric. 2017. (Spooky Express Ser.). (ENG.). 32p. (J). (-6). 9.99 *(978-1-4926-5402-5(7)*, Sourcebooks Jabberwocky) Sourcebooks, Inc.

—The Spooky Express Texas. James, Eric. 2017. (Spooky Express Ser.). (ENG.). 32p. (J). (-6). 9.99 *(978-1-4926-5314-1(4)*, Sourcebooks Jabberwocky) Sourcebooks, Inc.

—The Spooky Express Toronto. James, Eric. 2017. (Spooky Express Ser.). (ENG.). 32p. (J). (-6). 9.99 *(978-1-4926-5403-2(5)*, Sourcebooks Jabberwocky) Sourcebooks, Inc.

—The Spooky Express Utah. James, Eric. 2017. (Spooky Express Ser.). (ENG.). 32p. (J). (-6). 9.99 *(978-1-4926-5405-6(1)*, Sourcebooks Jabberwocky) Sourcebooks, Inc.

—The Spooky Express Vancouver. James, Eric. 2017. (Spooky Express Ser.). (ENG.). 32p. (J). (-6). 9.99 *(978-1-4926-5406-3(X)*, Sourcebooks Jabberwocky) Sourcebooks, Inc.

—The Spooky Express Vermont. James, Eric. 2017. (Spooky Express Ser.). (ENG.). 32p. (J). (-6). 9.99 *(978-1-4926-5407-0(8)*, Sourcebooks Jabberwocky) Sourcebooks, Inc.

—The Spooky Express Virginia. James, Eric. 2017. (Spooky Express Ser.). (ENG.). 32p. (J). (-6). 9.99 *(978-1-4926-5408-7(6)*, Sourcebooks Jabberwocky) Sourcebooks, Inc.

—The Spooky Express Washington. James, Eric. 2017. (Spooky Express Ser.). (ENG.). 32p. (J). (-6). 9.99 *(978-1-4926-5409-4(4)*, Sourcebooks Jabberwocky) Sourcebooks, Inc.

—The Spooky Express Washington, D. C. James, Eric. 2017. (Spooky Express Ser.). (ENG.). 32p. (J). (-6). 9.99 *(978-1-4926-5410-0(8)*, Sourcebooks Jabberwocky) Sourcebooks, Inc.

—The Spooky Express West Virginia. James, Eric. 2017. (Spooky Express Ser.). (ENG.). 32p. (J). (-6). 9.99 *(978-1-4926-5411-7(6)*, Sourcebooks Jabberwocky) Sourcebooks, Inc.

—The Spooky Express Wisconsin. James, Eric. 2017. (Spooky Express Ser.). (ENG.). 32p. (J). (-6). 9.99 *(978-1-4926-5412-4(4)*, Sourcebooks Jabberwocky) Sourcebooks, Inc.

—The Spooky Express Wyoming. James, Eric. 2017. (Spooky Express Ser.). (ENG.). 32p. (J). (-6). 9.99 *(978-1-4926-5413-1(2)*, Sourcebooks Jabberwocky) Sourcebooks, Inc.

—Tim's Swim. Grudzina, Rebecca. 2017. (Text Connections Guided Close Reading Ser.). (J). (gr. k). *(978-1-4900-1766-2(6))* Benchmark Education Co.

—Where Do You Want to Travel? Ko, Hannah. 2017. (Field Trip Fun Ser.). (ENG.). 24p. (gr. -1-2). pap. 8.95 *(978-1-68342-794-0(7)*, 9781683427940) Rourke Educational Media.

—Where Is Moggie? Set Of 6. Parkes, Brenda. 2014. (Shared Reading Foundations Ser.). (J). (gr. 1). 36.00 net. *(978-1-4900-0033-6(X))* Benchmark Education Co.

—Where Is Moggie? Book Set. Parkes, Brenda. 2014. (Shared Reading Foundations Ser.). (J). (gr. 1). 72.00 net. *(978-1-4900-0003-9(8))* Benchmark Education Co.

—Who Is Ana Dalt? Cottleston, B. D. 2020. (ENG.). 32p. (J). (gr. k-2). 16.99 *(978-1-4867-1810-8(8)*, 20e1d934-047b-4cc2-95fc-f53039db5d25) Flowerpot Pr.

Piwowarski, Marcin, et al. Why Kittens Hide - Pete Mule's Hat - a Snail in May: BuildUp Unit 6 Lap Book. Cochran, Kate et al. 2015. (Build up Core Phonics Ser.). (J). (gr. 1). *(978-1-4900-2605-3(3))* Benchmark Education Co.

Piwowarski, Marcin. You Belong. Platten, Rachel. 2020. (ENG.). 32p. (J). 17.99 *(978-1-250-24016-3(6)*, 900211484) Feiwel & Friends.

Piwowarski, Marcin & Dunn, Robert. Indiana Books for Kids Gift Set. James, Eric & Smallman, Steve. 2020. (ENG.). (J). (-3). 29.99 ***(978-1-7282-4194-4(4))*** Sourcebooks, Inc.

Piwowarski, Marcin & Marcin, Piwowarski. Five Little Fishes. Hopgood, Sally. 2012. (Five Little Counting Bks.). (ENG.). 10p. (J). (gr. -1). 7.99 *(978-1-84956-659-9(3))* Top That! Publishing PLC GBR. Dist: Independent Pubs. Group.

Piwowarski, Marcin, jt. illus. see Dunn, Robert.

Pixel Mouse House LLC. 1 2 3 Blaze! (Blaze & the Monster Machines) Random House. 2016. (ENG.). 24p. (J). (— 1). bds. 6.99 *(978-1-101-93679-5(7)*, Random Hse. Bks. for Young Readers) Random Hse. Children's Bks.

Pixel Mouse House, Pixel Mouse. Fisher-Price Little People: All Aboard the Bus! Mitter, Matt. 2019. (Fisher Price Lift-The-Flap Ser.). (ENG.). 10p. (J). (gr. -1-k). bds. 9.99 *(978-0-7944-4357-3(5)*, Studio Fun International) Printers Row Publishing Group.

—Fisher-Price Little People: Christmastime Is Here! Mitter, Matt. 2019. (Fisher Price Lift-The-Flap Ser.). (ENG.). 10p. (J). (gr. -1-k). bds. 9.99 *(978-0-7944-4359-7(1)*, Studio Fun International) Printers Row Publishing Group.

—Fisher-Price Little People: Halloween Is Here! Mitter, Matt. 2019. (Fisher Price Lift-The-Flap Ser.). (ENG.). 10p. (J). (gr. -1-k). bds. 9.99 *(978-0-7944-4356-6(7)*, Studio Fun International) Printers Row Publishing Group.

—Fisher-Price Little People: on the Farm. Mitter, Matt. 2019. (Fisher Price Lift-The-Flap Ser.). (ENG.). 10p. (J). (gr. -1-k). bds. 9.99 *(978-0-7944-4358-0(3)*, Studio Fun International) Printers Row Publishing Group.

Pixel Mouse House Staff, jt. illus. see Golden Books.

Pizmoht, Natasa Gruden. See Bee Tee: A Story to Reinforce Positive Thinking in Children. Gaborova, Katarina. 2019. (ENG.). 92p. (J). (gr. 1-6). pap. *(978-1-989048-05-4(6))* Petra Bks.

Pizzolante, Irene. My Feminist ABC. duopress labs. 2018. (ENG.). 20p. (J). (gr. -1-k). bds. 7.95 *(978-1-946064-98-1(X)*, 806498, Duo Pr. Llc (US)) Duo Pr. LLC.

Pizzoli, Greg. Crunch the Shy Dinosaur. Dunlap, Cirocco. 40p. (J). (gr. -1-2). 2020. (ENG.). pap. 7.99 *(978-0-593-17568-2(9)*, Dragonfly Bks.); 2018. 17.99 *(978-0-399-55056-0(9)*, Random Hse. Bks. for Young Readers) Random Hse. Children's Bks.

—Hi, Jack! Barnett, Mac. 2019. (Jack Book Ser.: 1). 80p. (J). (gr. -1-3). 9.99 *(978-0-593-11379-0(9)*, Viking Books for Young Readers) Penguin Young Readers Group.

—I Love You Like a Pig. Barnett, Mac. 2017. (ENG.). 40p. (J). (gr. -1-3). 17.99 *(978-0-06-235483-9(3))* HarperCollins Pubs.

—Jack at Bat. Barnett, Mac. 2020. (Jack Book Ser.: 3). (ENG.). 80p. (J). (gr. -1-3). 9.99 *(978-0-593-11382-0(9)*, Viking Books for Young Readers) Penguin Young Readers Group.

—Jack at the Zoo. Barnett, Mac. 2020. (Jack Book Ser.: 5). (ENG.). 80p. (J). (gr. -1-3). 9.99 *(978-0-593-11391-2(8)*, Viking Books for Young Readers) Penguin Young Readers Group.

—Jack Blasts Off. Barnett, Mac. 2019. (Jack Book Ser.: 2). (ENG.). 80p. (J). (gr. -1-3). 9.99 *(978-0-593-11385-1(3)*, Viking Books for Young Readers) Penguin Young Readers Group.

—Jack Goes West. Barnett, Mac. 2020. (Jack Book Ser.: 4). 80p. (J). (gr. -1-3). 9.99 *(978-0-593-11388-2(8)*, Viking Books for Young Readers) Penguin Young Readers Group.

—Just Itzy. Krumwiede, Lana. 2015. 40p. (J). (-k). 15.99 *(978-0-7636-5811-3(1))* Candlewick Pr.

—London. Adams, Jennifer. 2017. (ENG.). 22p. (J). (gr. -1-k). bds. 9.99 *(978-1-4521-5387-2(6))* Chronicle Bks. LLC.

—New York. Adams, Jennifer. 2017. (ENG.). 22p. (J). (gr. -1-k). bds. 9.99 *(978-1-4521-5388-9(4))* Chronicle Bks. LLC.

—New York City Skyline Playset. Adams, Jennifer. 2017. (ENG.). 8p. (J). (gr. -1-k). 14.99 *(978-1-4521-5389-6(2))* Chronicle Bks. LLC.

—North, South, East, West. Brown, Margaret Wise. 2017. (ENG.). 40p. (J). (gr. -1-3). 17.99 *(978-0-06-026278-5(8))* HarperCollins Pubs.

—Paris. Adams, Jennifer. 2017. (ENG.). 22p. (J). (gr. -1 — 1). bds. 9.99 *(978-1-4521-5390-2(6))* Chronicle Bks. LLC.

—San Francisco. Adams, Jennifer. 2017. (ENG.). 22p. (J). (gr. -1 — 1). bds. 9.99 *(978-1-4521-5391-9(4))* Chronicle Bks. LLC.

—Too Many Jacks. Barnett, Mac. 2020. (Jack Book Ser.: 6). (ENG.). 80p. (J). (gr. -1-3). 9.99 *(978-0-593-11394-3(2)*, Viking Books for Young Readers) Penguin Young Readers Group.

—Two Little Trains. Brown, Margaret Wise. 2020. (ENG.). 40p. (J). (gr. -1-3). 17.99 *(978-0-06-267651-1(2)*, HarperCollins) HarperCollins Pubs. Ltd. GBR. Dist: HarperCollins Pubs.

—What's a Banana? Singer, Marilyn. 2016. (ENG.). 24p. (J). (gr. -1-k). 12.95 *(978-1-4197-2139-7(9)*, Abrams Appleseed) Abrams, Inc.

—What's an Apple? Singer, Marilyn. 2016. (ENG.). 24p. (J). (gr. -1-k). 12.95 *(978-1-4197-2140-3(2)*, Abrams Appleseed) Abrams, Inc.

Pizzoli, Greg. Baloney & Friends. Pizzoli, Greg. 2020. (Baloney & Friends Ser.: 1). 96p. (J). (gr. 1-4). 12.99 ***(978-1-368-05454-6(4))*** Little, Brown Bks. for Young Readers.

Pizzoli, Greg. The Watermelon Seed. Pizzoli, Greg. 2013. 40p. (J). (gr. -1-3). 16.99 *(978-1-4231-7101-0(2))* Disney Pr.

Pizzoli, Greg. The 12 Days of Christmas. Pizzoli, Greg. 2019. (ENG.). 40p. (J). (gr. -1 — 1). bds. 7.99 ***(978-1-368-00300-1(1))*** Little, Brown Bks. for Young Readers.

Place, Francois. Meeting Cezanne. Morpurgo, Michael. 2013. 80p. (J). (gr. 2-5). 15.99 *(978-0-7636-4896-1(5))* Candlewick Pr.

—Toby Alone. De Fombelle, Timothée. Ardizzone, Sarah, tr. 2009. (ENG.). 400p. (J). (gr. 4-6). 24.94 *(978-0-7636-4181-8(2))* Candlewick Pr.

Place, Konohiki. Finding Tir Na Nog: Finding Tir Na Nog: Finding Tir Na Nog. Whyte, S. L. Ronsley, Jill, ed. 2013. (ENG.). 416p. (YA). pap. 12.99 *(978-0-9857523-0-9(0))* Fireglass Publishing.

Placides, Del S. The Safe Place. Vogel-Placides, Joan Katherine. 2013. 58p. 13.99 *(978-0-9888718-3-0(1))* DOMINIONHOUSE Publishing & Design.

Plafkin-Hurwitz, Marsha. Up 2 Snuff: Illustrated Book for Children. Plafkin-Hurwitz, Marsha. 2nd ed. 2010. 32p. (J). pap. *(978-0-578-05270-0(9))* Art as Responsa LLC.

Plage, Stella. Excuses, Excuses!, 1 vol. Rissman, Rebecca. 2013. (Excuses, Excuses! Ser.). (ENG.). 24p. (J). (gr. -1-k). pap. 9.95 *(978-1-4329-7669-9(9)*, Heinemann) Capstone.

Plagens, Frances. Imagine This! Froh, Joanne. 2006. 32p. (J). 19.95 *(978-0-9777640-0-6(1))* Joanne Frances Pr.

Plagerson, Crock. Skippy's Favourite Honey. Rebuck, Anthony. 2016. 42p. (J). 44.35 *(978-1-5144-4613-3(8))*; (ENG.). pap. 28.22 *(978-1-5144-4612-6(X))* Xlibris Corp.

Plain, Ferguson. Eagle Feather - An Honour. Plain, Ferguson. 2015. (ENG.). 24p. (J). (gr. 2-4). pap. 8.95 *(978-0-921827-12-2(1)*, ab1862aa-639a-4ba1-9ad3-75eb3314b49f) Pemmican Pubns., Inc. CAN. Dist: Firefly Bks., Ltd.

Planer, Geoffrey. And Then There Were Three. Seymour, Jane & Keach, James. 2003. (This One & That One Ser.: Vol. 5). (ENG.). 32p. (J). (gr. -1-3). 12.99 *(978-1-932431-09-4(8))* Left Field,Angel Gate.

—Boing! No Bouncing on the Bed. Seymour, Jane & Keach, James. 2003. (This One & That One Ser.: Vol. 1). (ENG.). 32p. (J). (gr. -1-3). 12.99 *(978-1-932431-06-3(3))* Left Field,Angel Gate.

—Fried Pies & Roast Cake. Seymour, Jane & Keach, James. 2003. (This One & That One Ser.: Vol. 5). (ENG.). 32p. (J). (gr. -1-3). 12.99 *(978-1-932431-10-0(1))* Left Field,Angel Gate.

—The Other One: You Make Me Happy. Seymour, Jane & Keach, James. gif. ed. 2003. (This One & That One Ser.). (ENG.). 16p. (J). (gr. -1-3). 5.99 *(978-1-932431-57-5(8))* Left Field,Angel Gate.

—Splat! The Tale of a Colorful Cat. Seymour, Jane & Keach, James. 2003. (This One & That One Ser.: Vol. 2.). (ENG.). 32p. (J). (gr. -1-3). 12.99 *(978-1-932431-07-0(1))* Left Field,Angel Gate.

—Yum! A Tale of Two Cookies. Seymour, Jane & Keach, James. 2nd ed. 2003. (This One & That One Ser.: Vol. 3). (ENG.). 32p. (J). (gr. -1-3). 12.99 *(978-1-932431-08-7(X))* Left Field,Angel Gate.

Planet, Louis, photos by. Carnet Blanc Voilier Peking Sur la Tamise. 2016. (Bnf. Monum. Franc Ser.). (FRE., (J). pap. *(978-2-01-126432-9(4))* Hachette Groupe Livre.

—Carnet Ligne Voilier Peking Sur la Tamise: Librairie Dialogues Brest. 2016. (Bnf Monuments Ser.). (FRE., (J). pap. *(978-2-01-359894-1(7))* Hachette Groupe Livre.

Plant, Andrew. Ancient Animals: Plesiosaur. Thomson, Sarah L. 2017. (Ancient Animals Ser.). 32p. (J). (gr. 1-4). lib. bdg. 12.99 *(978-1-58089-542-2(5))* Charlesbridge Publishing, Inc.

—Living Fossils: Clues to the Past. Arnold, Caroline. 2019. (ENG.). 32p. (J). (gr. -1-2). pap. 7.99 *(978-1-62354-169-9(7))* Charlesbridge Publishing, Inc.

—A Platypus, Probably. Collard, Sneed B., III & Collard, Sneed B. 2005. (ENG.). 32p. (J). (gr. k-3). per. 7.95 *(978-1-57091-584-0(9))* Charlesbridge Publishing, Inc.

—Saber-Toothed Cat. Thomson, Sarah L. 2014. (Ancient Animals Ser.). 32p. (J). (gr. 1-4). pap. 5.95 *(978-1-58089-407-4(0))*; lib. bdg. 12.95 *(978-1-58089-400-5(3))* Charlesbridge Publishing, Inc.

—Terror Birds. Thomson, Sarah L. 2013. (Ancient Animals Ser.). 32p. (J). (gr. 1-4). pap. 5.95 *(978-1-58089-399-2(6))* Charlesbridge Publishing, Inc.

Plante, Beth. Brandy & the Rapids, 1 vol. Finch, Donna. 2009. 36p. pap. 24.95 *(978-1-60749-150-7(8))* America Star Bks.

Plantevin, Guillaume. What's the Difference? 40+ Pairs of the Seemingly Similar. Plantevin, Strack & Strack, Emma. 2018. (ENG.). 124p. (J). (gr. 3-7). 17.99 *(978-1-4521-6101-3(1))* Chronicle Bks. LLC.

Plastilina, Memo. La Fortuna de Bertha. Gutierrez, Lourdes. 2018. (SPA.). 36p. (J). (gr. -1-k). pap. 11.00 *(978-607-8469-41-3(X))* Nostra Ediciones MEX. Dist: Independent Pubs. Group.

Plati, Nuno. Marvel Girl. Fialkov, Joshua Hale. 2011. (X-Men: First Class Ser.: No. 2). (ENG.). 24p. (J). (gr. 2-6). 27.07 *(978-1-59961-950-7(4)*, 15637, Marvel Age) Spotlight.

Platt, Brian. Triplet Tales. Cushion, Hazel. 2006. 32p. pap. *(978-0-9547092-1-1(7))* Accent Pr. Ltd.

Platt, Diana. Flying Colors Fiction: Graffiti, Level Purple, 6 vols. Reilly, Carmel. 2006. (ENG.). (J). (gr. 2). pap. 65.33 *(978-1-4189-1713-5(3))* Rigby Education.

Platt, Greg. Alphie & the Alphabets: A Fun Way to Learn to Read. Sayles, Alayne. 2005. 44p. (J). spiral bd. 79.95 incl. audio compact disk *(978-0-9767506-0-4(0))* Reading Studio Pr.

Platt, Jason. Early Social Skills Stories: Going Potty. Hodson, Sarah E. 2013. (J). *(978-0-7606-1408-2(3))* LinguiSystems, Inc.

Platt, Pierre. Bye-Bye, Katy, Vol. 3. Michaels, David. l.t. ed. 2005. (Sadlier Phonics Reading Program). 8p. (gr. -1-1). 23.00 net. *(978-0-8215-7354-9(3))* Sadlier, William H. Inc.

Platt, Sharai. Goliaths's Secret. Feuer, Bonnie. 2013. (ENG.). 38p. (J). 18.50 *(978-0-9825468-8-8(2))* Connecticut Pr., The.

Playcrib. Six Fingers & the Blue Warrior. Laar-Yond C.T. 2013. 36p. pap. 14.00 *(978-1-62212-177-9(5)*, Strategic Bk. Publishing) Strategic Book Publishing & Rights Agency (SBPRA).

Player, Micah. Around the World Matching Game. 2013. (ENG.). 72p. (J). (gr. -1-1). 14.99 *(978-1-4521-1699-0(7))* Chronicle Bks. LLC.

—Binny for Short. McKay, Hilary. (ENG.). (J). (gr. 3-7). 2014. 288p. pap. 7.99 *(978-1-4424-8276-0(1))*; 2013. 304p. 16.99 *(978-1-4424-8275-3(3))* McElderry, Margaret K. Bks. (McElderry, Margaret K. Bks.).

—Citizen Baby: My Congress. Bryant, Megan E. & Prosterman, Daniel. 2020. (Citizen Baby Ser.). 24p. (J). (— 1). bds. 8.99 *(978-1-5247-9316-6(7)*, Penguin Workshop) Penguin Young Readers Group.

—Citizen Baby: My President. Bryant, Megan E. & Prosterman, Daniel. 2020. (Citizen Baby Ser.). 24p. (J). (— 1). bds. 8.99 *(978-1-5247-9314-2(0)*, Penguin Workshop) Penguin Young Readers Group.

—Citizen Baby: My Supreme Court. Bryant, Megan E. & Prosterman, Daniel. 2020. (Citizen Baby Ser.). 24p. (J). (— 1). bds. 8.99 *(978-1-5247-9318-0(3)*, Penguin Workshop) Penguin Young Readers Group.

—Citizen Baby: My Vote. Bryant, Megan E. & Prosterman, Daniel. 2020. (Citizen Baby Ser.). 24p. (J). (— 1). bds. 8.99 *(978-1-5247-9312-8(4)*, Penguin Workshop) Penguin Young Readers Group.

—Friday Night Wrestlefest. Fox, J. F. 2020. (ENG.). 48p. (J). 17.99 *(978-1-250-21240-5(5)*, 900203724) Roaring Brook Pr.

—Mighty Meg 1: Mighty Meg & the Magical Ring. Griffin, Sammy. 2019. (Mighty Meg Ser.: 1). (ENG.). 112p. (J). (gr. k-3). 17.99 *(978-1-4998-0832-2(1))*; pap. 6.99 *(978-1-4998-0831-5(3))* Little Bee Books Inc.

—Mighty Meg 2: Mighty Meg & the Melting Menace. Griffin, Sammy. 2019. (Mighty Meg Ser.: 2). (ENG.). 112p. (J). (gr. k-3). 17.99 *(978-1-4998-0835-3(6))*; pap. 6.99 *(978-1-4998-0834-6(8))* Little Bee Books Inc.

—Mighty Meg 3: Mighty Meg & the Accidental Nemesis. Griffin, Sammy. 2019. (Mighty Meg Ser.: 3). (ENG.). 112p. (J). (gr. k-3). 17.99 *(978-1-4998-0847-6(X))*; pap. 6.99 *(978-1-4998-0846-9(1))* Little Bee Books Inc.

—Mighty Meg: 4 Books In 1! Griffin, Sammy. 2019. (Mighty Meg Ser.: 1). (ENG.). 416p. (J). (gr. k-3). 14.99 *(978-1-4998-1012-7(1))* Little Bee Books Inc.

—Mighty Meg 4: Mighty Meg & the Super Disguise. Griffin, Sammy. 2019. (Mighty Meg Ser.: 4). (ENG.). 112p. (J). (gr. k-3). 17.99 *(978-1-4998-0850-6(X))*; pap. 6.99 *(978-1-4998-0849-0(6))* Little Bee Books Inc.

—My School, Your School, Our Schools. Berne, Emma Carlson. 2018. (How Are We Alike & Different? Ser.). (ENG.). 24p. (J). (gr. -1-2). pap. 7.95 *(978-1-68410-293-8(6)*, 139064); lib. bdg. 33.99 *(978-1-68410-241-9(3)*, 138445) Cantata Learning.

—Sports Matching Game. 2011. (ENG.). 72p. (J). (gr. -1-3). 14.99 *(978-0-8118-7796-1(5))* Chronicle Bks. LLC.

Playford, Jenn. How to Become an Accidental Genius, 1 vol. Wishinsky, Frieda & MacLeod, Elizabeth. 2019. (ENG.). 128p. (J). (gr. 4-7). 24.95 *(978-1-4598-1676-3(5))* Orca Bk. Pubs. USA.

Plecas, Jennifer. Bug Off! A Story of Fireflies & Friendship. Best, Cari. 2019. (ENG.). 32p. (J). 17.99 *(978-0-374-38062-5(7)*, 900064875, Farrar, Straus & Giroux (BYR)) Farrar, Straus & Giroux.

—Emma's Strange Pet. Little, Jean. (I Can Read Level 3 Ser.). 64p. (J). (gr. k-3). 2004. (ENG.). pap. 4.99 *(978-0-06-444259-6(4))*; 2003. 15.99 *(978-0-06-028350-6(5))* HarperCollins Pubs.

—Get Well, Good Knight. Thomas, Shelley Moore. 2004. (Penguin Young Readers, Level 3 Ser.). (ENG.). 48p. (J). (gr. 1-3). 4.99 *(978-0-14-240050-0(5)*, Penguin Young Readers) Penguin Young Readers Group.

—Get Well, Good Knight. Thomas, Shelley Moore. 2004. (Easy-to-Read Ser.). 44p. (gr. k-3). 14.00 *(978-0-7569-2923-7(7))* Perfection Learning Corp.

—Happy Birthday, Good Knight. Thomas, Shelley Moore. 2014. (Penguin Young Readers, Level 3 Ser.). (ENG.). 48p. (J). (gr. 1-3). pap. 4.99 *(978-0-448-46374-2(1)*, Penguin Young Readers) Penguin Young Readers Group.

—I, Fly: The Buzz about Flies & How Awesome They Are. Heos, Bridget. 2015. (ENG.). 48p. (J). (gr. -1-3). 18.99 *(978-0-8050-9469-5(5)*, 900079177, Holt, Henry & Co. Bks. For Young Readers) Holt, Henry & Co.

—Please Is a Good Word to Say. Joosse, Barbara M. 2007. (J). *(978-1-4287-4649-7(8)*, Philomel) Penguin Publishing Group.

Pledger, Maurice. Noisy Nature: in the Jungle. Martin, Ruth. 2015. (ENG.). 12p. (J). (gr. -1). 16.95 *(978-1-62686-104-6(8)*, Silver Dolphin Bks.) Readerlink Distribution Services, LLC.

—Noisy Nature: in the Ocean. 2015. (Noisy Nature Ser.). (ENG.). 12p. (J). (gr. -1). 16.95 *(978-1-62686-105-3(6)*, Silver Dolphin Bks.) Readerlink Distribution Services, LLC.

—Noisy Nature: on the Farm. Martin, Ruth. 2015. (ENG.). 12p. (J). (gr. -1). 16.95 *(978-1-62686-103-9(X)*, Silver Dolphin Bks.) Readerlink Distribution Services, LLC.

Pleece, Warren. Ancient Cultures of Mesoamerica: Bridges Edition. Sherman, Patrice. 2015. (Prime Plus Ser.). (YA). (gr. 6-8). pap. *(978-1-4900-1937-6(5))* Benchmark Education Co.

—Ancient Cultures of Mesoamerica: Bridges Edition Set of 6 with Common Core Indicators. Sherman, Patrice. 2015. (Prime Plus Ser.). (YA). (gr. 6-8). 69.00 net. *(978-1-4900-2033-4(0))* Benchmark Education Co.

—Ancient Cultures of North America: Bridges Edition. Sherman, Patrice. 2015. (Prime Plus Ser.). (YA). (gr. 6-8). pap. *(978-1-4900-1936-9(7))* Benchmark Education Co.

—Ancient Cultures of North America: Bridges Edition Set of 6 with Common Core Indicators. Sherman, Patrice. 2015. (Prime Plus Ser.). (YA). (gr. 6-8). 69.00 net. *(978-1-4900-2032-7(2))* Benchmark Education Co.

—Ancient Cultures of South America: Bridges Edition. Sherman, Patrice. 2015. (Prime Plus Ser.). (YA). (gr. 6-8). pap. *(978-1-4900-1938-3(3))* Benchmark Education Co.

—Ancient Cultures of South America: Bridges Edition Set of 6 with Common Core Indicators. Sherman, Patrice. 2015. (Prime Plus Ser.). (YA). (gr. 6-8). 69.00 net. *(978-1-4900-2034-1(9))* Benchmark Education Co.

—D-Day: June 6 1944, 1 vol. Biskup, Agnieszka. 2014. (24-Hour History Ser.). (ENG.). 48p. (J). (gr. 3-9). pap. 8.95 *(978-1-4329-9301-6(1)*, Heinemann) Capstone.

Plenzke, Maike. Susan B. Anthony: Her Fight for Equal Rights. Kulling, Monica. 2020. (Step into Reading Ser.). 32p. (J). (gr. -1-1). pap. 4.99 *(978-0-593-11982-2(7)*, Random Hse. Bks. for Young Readers) Random Hse. Children's Bks.

P

Plessix, Michel. The Gates of Dawn. Grahame, Kenneth. Johnson, Joe, tr. 2003. (Wind in the Willows Ser.: Vol. 3). (ENG.). 32p. (gr. 4-7). pap. 15.95 *(978-1-56163-245-9(7))* NBM Publishing Co.

Pletcher, Rory. Mad, Bad Wolf. Pletcher, Cassandra. 2019. (ENG.). 36p. (J). pap. 10.00 ***(978-1-6705-3419-4(7))*** Independently Published.

Ploog, Michael G. L. Frank Baum's the Life & Adventures of Santa Claus. Ploog, Michael G. 2003. 80p. (YA). (gr. 7-12). reprint ed. 25.00 *(978-0-7567-6682-5(6))* DIANE Publishing Co.

Ploog, Mike. The Puppet, the Professor, & the Prophet. Dematteis, J. M. 3rd rev. ed. 2007. 144p. (J). (gr. 4-7). 9.99 *(978-1-4231-0063-8(8))* Hyperion Pr.

—Stardust Kid. DeMatteis, J. M. 2008. (ENG.). 128p. pap. 14.99 *(978-1-934506-04-2(4))* Boom! Studios.

Ploog, Mike, et al. Werewolf by Night: the Complete Collection Vol. 2. 2018. (ENG.). 440p. (YA). (gr. 8-17). pap. 39.99 *(978-1-302-90951-2(7))* Marvel Worldwide, Inc.

Ploss, Skip. If Picasso Were a Fish. Ploss, Skip. 2006. 40p. (gr. k-2). 15.99 *(978-1-4116-9220-6(9))* Lulu Pr., Inc.

Plouffe, Delci J. Extraordinary You: The Life You're Meant to Live. Plouffe, Delci J. 2017. (ENG.). (J). (gr. k-6). pap. 12.99 *(978-0-692-84708-4(1))* Plouffe, Delci.

Plume, Chris Big. Legend of the Loons Necklace. Plume, Christopher Big. 2018. (ENG.). 20p. (J). *(978-1-5255-3092-0(5))*; pap. *(978-1-5255-3093-7(3))* FriesenPress.

Plume, Ilse. Henry & the Huckleberries: A Visit with Mr. Thoreau at Walden Pond. Sanford, Sally. 2017. 32p. (J). (gr. -1-3). 17.99 *(978-1-63226-076-5(X)*, Prospecta Pr.) Easton Studio Pr., LLC.

—Saint Francis & the Wolf. Langton, Jane. 2019. (ENG.). 32p. (J). (gr. -1-3). 17.95 *(978-1-56792-320-9(8))* Godine, David R. Pub.

Plumlee, Buddy. The Ants. McClure, Brian D. 2009. (Brian D. Mcclure Childrens Book Collection). 57p. (J). (gr. -1-3). 16.95 *(978-1-933426-10-5(1))* Universal Flag Publishing.

—The Birds & the Frogs. McClure, Brian D. 2009. (Brian D. Mcclure Childrens Book Collection). 37p. (J). (gr. -1-3). 16.95 *(978-1-933426-13-6(6))* Universal Flag Publishing.

—The Meal. McClure, Brian D. 2009. (Brian D. Mcclure Childrens Book Collection). 59p. (J). (gr. -1-3). 16.95 *(978-1-933426-04-4(7))* Universal Flag Publishing.

—The Up down Day. McClure, Brian D. 2009. (Brian D. Mcclure Childrens Book Collection). 47p. (J). (gr. -1-3). 14.95 *(978-1-933426-07-5(1))* Universal Flag Publishing.

Plumley, Alea. Animals, Vegetables & Minerals from A to Z. O'Donnell, Sallie. l.t. ed. 2005. 60p. pap. 9.95 *(978-0-9764982-5-4(1))* Legacy Publishing Services, Inc.

Plummer, Christy. More Than Food? Broulette, Natalie. 2018. (ENG.). 36p. (J). 17.99 *(978-0-692-15944-6(4))* Plumlette Publishing.

Pluum, Ave. Katrina's New Room. Weinstein, Natalie. 2004. (J). pap. 19.95 *(978-0-9749531-0-6(5))* Images For Presentation.

Plymak, John. A Mess & Andy. Korman, Irv. 2019. (ENG.). 32p. (J). pap. 14.95 ***(978-1-948613-04-0(2))*** Sunny Day Publishing, LLC.

Po, Julia. Could a Deaf Girl Sing? Children's Inspirational Stories; Stories with a Message for Children; Superheroes Children. Manor, Yael. 2020. (ENG.). 30p. (J). pap. 10.90 ***(978-1-64204-632-8(9))*** Primedia eLaunch LLC.

Pocock, Aaron. Bailey Beats the Blah. Tyrrell, Karen. 2013. 34p. pap. *(978-0-9872740-4-5(X))* Digital Future Press.

—The Orange Ray. Blake-Wilson, Pamela. 2010. (Colour Code Ser.: Bk. 2). 266p. pap. *(978-0-9806520-6-2(5))* Pick-a-Woo Woo Pubs.

—Pick-a-WooWoo - Robbie the Butterfly: An enlightening story of Transformation, 16 vols., Vol. 13. Larson, Robert. 2010. 28p. pap. *(978-0-9806520-2-4(2))* Pick-a-Woo Woo Pubs.

—Ready. Set. Discover Logan. Tyrrell, Karen. 2018. (ENG.). 40p. (J). (gr. k-5). pap. *(978-0-9943021-9-9(3))* Digital Future Press.

—The Red Ray. Blake-Wilson, Pamela. 2009. (Colour Code Ser.: Bk. 1). 246p. (J). pap. *(978-0-9806520-0-0(6))* Pick-a-Woo Woo Pubs.

Podesta, Lena. Baby Dragon, Baby Dragon! Marr, Melissa. 2019. 32p. (J). (-k). 17.99 *(978-0-399-17525-1(3)*, Nancy Paulsen Books) Penguin Young Readers Group.

Podgurski, Sharon. I'm Adopted, I'm Special. Rice, Beth. 2008. 32p. pap. 12.95 *(978-0-9817572-0-9(0))* Peppertree Pr., The.

Podwal, Mark H. Mishkan HaNefesh for Youth: A Machzor for Youth & Families. Witman, Melissa Buyer. 2018. (HEB & ENG.). (J). *(978-0-88123-291-2(2))* Central Conference of American Rabbis/CCAR Pr.

Poe, Edgar Allen. Edgar Allan Poe Collection. Poe, Edgar Allen. 2005. (Adventure Classics Ser.). 176p. (J). pap. 6.99 *(978-0-06-075881-3(3)*, HarperFestival) HarperCollins Pubs.

Poer, Nancy Jewel. Mia's Apple Tree. Poer, Nancy Jewel. 2004. 34p. (J). 21.95 *(978-0-9740413-1-5(9))* White Feather Publishing.

Pogány, Willy. The Adventures of Odysseus & the Tale of Troy. Colum, Padraic. 2008. 164p. pap. *(978-1-4068-2730-9(4))* Echo Library.

Pogany, Willy. The Children of Odin. Colum, Padraic. 2019. (ENG.). 166p. (J). (gr. 5-9). pap. 8.99 *(978-1-4209-6159-1(4))* Digireads.com Publishing.

—The Children of Odin: The Book of Northern Myths. Colum, Padraic. 2004. (ENG.). 288p. (J). (gr. 5-9). pap. 10.99 *(978-0-689-86885-6(5)*, Aladdin) Simon & Schuster Children's Publishing.

Pogány, Willy. The Children of Odin: The Book of Northern Myths. Colum, Padraic. 2008. 216p. (gr. 5-9). pap. *(978-1-4065-9868-1(2))* Dodo Pr.

Pogany, Willy. The Children of Odin: The Book of Northern Myths. Colum, Padraic. 2016. (ENG.). (J). pap. 6.95 *(978-1-68422-041-0(6))* Martino Fine Bks.

—The Children of Odin: The Book of Northern Myths. Colum, Padraic. 2019. (ENG.). 288p. (J). (gr. 5-9). 18.99 *(978-1-5344-5038-7(6)*, Aladdin) Simon & Schuster Children's Publishing.

—The Children's Homer: The Adventures of Odysseus & the Tale of Troy. Colum, Padraic. 2004. (ENG.). 256p. (J). (gr. 5-9). pap. 10.99 *(978-0-689-86883-2(9)*, Aladdin) Simon & Schuster Children's Publishing.

—The Children's Homer: The Adventures of Odysseus & the Tale of Troy. Colum, Padraic. 2019. (ENG.). 256p. (J). (gr. 5-9). 18.99 *(978-1-5344-5037-0(8)*, Aladdin) Simon & Schuster Children's Publishing.

Pogány, Willy. The Golden Cockerel: From the Original Russian Fairy Tale of Alexander Pushkin. Pogany, Elaine. 2013. (Dover Children's Classics Ser.). (ENG.). 48p. (J). (gr. 5-8). pap. 14.95 *(978-0-486-49115-8(3))* Dover Pubns., Inc.

Pogany, Willy. The Golden Fleece: And the Heroes Who Lived Before Achilles. Colum, Padraic. 2004. (ENG.). 320p. (J). (gr. 5-9). pap. 10.99 *(978-0-689-86884-9(7)*, Aladdin) Simon & Schuster Children's Publishing.

Pogány, Willy. The Golden Fleece: And the Heroes Who Lived Before Achilles. Colum, Padraic. 2004. 316p. (J). (gr. 5). 17.60 *(978-0-7569-4048-5(6))* Perfection Learning Corp.

Pogany, Willy. The Golden Fleece: And the Heroes Who Lived Before Achilles. Colum, Padraic. 2019. (ENG.). 320p. (J). (gr. 5-9). 18.99 *(978-1-5344-5036-3(X)*, Aladdin) Simon & Schuster Children's Publishing.

Pogány, Willy. The Golden Fleece & the Heroes Who Lived Before Achilles. Colum, Padraic. 2007. 144p. per. 8.99 *(978-1-4209-3040-5(0))* Digireads.com Publishing.

—The Golden Fleece & the Heroes Who Lived Before Achilles. Colum, Padraic. 2010. (Looking Glass Library). (ENG.). 368p. (J). (gr. 3-7). 10.99 *(978-0-375-86709-5(0)*, Random Hse. Bks. for Young Readers) Random Hse. Children's Bks.

Pogany, Willy. The Golden Fleece & the Heroes Who Lived Before Achilles. Colum, Padraic. 2019. (ENG.). 186p. (J). (gr. 5-9). pap. 8.99 *(978-1-4209-6161-4(6))* Digireads.com Publishing.

Pogány, Willy. The King of Ireland's Son. Colum, Padraic. ed. 2009. 308p. pap. 12.95 *(978-1-59915-083-3(2))* Yesterday's Classics.

—The Story of the Golden Fleece. Colum, Padraic. unabr. ed. 2005. (Dover Children's Classics Ser.). (ENG.). 256p. (J). (gr. 3-5). per. 5.95 *(978-0-486-44366-9(3))* Dover Pubns., Inc.

—Tanglewood Tales. Hawthorne, Nathaniel. 2009. 272p. pap. 11.95 *(978-1-59915-091-8(3))* Yesterday's Classics.

—A Treasury of Poems for Children. Edgar, M. G. 2010. (Dover Children's Classics Ser.). (ENG.). 272p. (J). (gr. -1-3). pap. 9.99 *(978-0-486-47376-5(7))* Dover Pubns., Inc.

Pogue, Jamie. The Littlest Easter Bunny (Littlest Series) Dougherty, Brandi. 2020. (Littlest Ser.). (ENG.). 24p. (J). (gr. -1-k). pap. 4.99 *(978-1-338-32912-4(X)*, Cartwheel Bks.) Scholastic, Inc.

—The Littlest Witch. Dougherty, Brandi. 2019. (ENG.). 24p. (J). (gr. -1-k). pap. 4.99 *(978-1-338-32910-0(3)*, Cartwheel Bks.) Scholastic, Inc.

Pogue, Sarah. Library's Most Wanted. Leiloglou, Carolyn. 2020. (ENG.). 32p. (gr. -1-3). 16.99 ***(978-1-4556-2517-8(5)***, Pelican Publishing) Arcadia Publishing.

Poh, Jennie. Basil the Bear Cub. Jones, Janey Louise. 2016. (Superfairies Ser.). (ENG.). 56p. (J). (gr. k-3). lib. bdg. 23.99 *(978-1-4795-8641-7(2)*, Picture Window Bks.) Capstone.

—Clarence's Topsy-Turvy Shabbat. MacLeod, Jennifer Tzivia. 2020. (ENG.). 24p. (J). (gr. -1-2). 17.99 *(978-1-5415-4242-6(8)*, Kar-Ben Publishing) Lerner Publishing Group.

Poh, Jennie. The Copper Queen. Jones, Janey Louise. 2018. (Superfairies Ser.). (ENG.). (J). pap. 41.70 ***(978-1-5158-2433-6(0)***, 27688); 56p. lib. bdg. 23.99 *(978-1-5158-2423-7(3)*, 137399) Capstone. (Picture Window Bks.).

Poh, Jennie. Dancer the Wild Pony. Jones, Janey Louise. 2016. (Superfairies Ser.). (ENG.). 56p. (J). (gr. k-3). lib. bdg. 23.99 *(978-1-4795-8642-4(0)*, Picture Window Bks.) Capstone.

—Elepants. George, Joshua. 2016. (J). *(978-1-4351-6486-4(5))* Barnes & Noble, Inc.

—Farrah the Shy Fawn. Jones, Janey Louise. 2016. (Superfairies Ser.). (ENG.). 56p. (J). (gr. k-3). lib. bdg. 23.99 *(978-1-5158-0432-1(1)*, Picture Window Bks.) Capstone.

—I Love You to the Moon. Woodhouse, Emma. 2014. (ENG.). 22p. (J). (gr. -1). bds. 8.95 *(978-1-58925-642-2(5))* Tiger Tales.

—Little Turtle & the Changing Sea. Davies, Becky. 2020. (ENG.). 32p. (J). (gr. -1-2). 17.99 *(978-1-68010-199-7(4))* Tiger Tales.

Poh, Jennie. Lulu the One & Only. Mawhinney, Lynnette. 2020. 32p. (J). ***(978-1-4338-3159-1(7)***, Magination Pr.) American Psychological Assn.

Poh, Jennie. Martha the Little Mouse. Jones, Janey Louise. 2016. (Superfairies Ser.). (ENG.). 56p. (J). (gr. k-3). lib. bdg. 23.99 *(978-1-4795-8643-1(9)*, Picture Window Bks.) Capstone.

—May I Come In? Arnold, Marsha Diane. 2018. (ENG.). 32p. (J). (gr. k-3). 16.99 *(978-1-58536-394-0(4)*, 204396) Sleeping Bear Pr.

—The Pirate Tree. Orel, Brigita. 2019. 32p. (J). (gr. k-2). 17.99 *(978-1-911373-87-2(0))* Lantana Publishing GBR. Dist: Lerner Publishing Group.

—Porcupine's Pie, Vol. Renauld, Laura. 2018. (ENG.). 32p. (J). 16.99 *(978-1-5064-3180-2(1)*, Beaming Books) Augsburg Fortress, Pubs.

—The Snow Fairy. Jones, Janey Louise. 2018. (Superfairies Ser.). (ENG.). 56p. (J). (gr. k-3). lib. bdg. 23.99 *(978-1-5158-2424-4(1)*, 137400, Picture Window Bks.) Capstone.

—Sonny the Daring Squirrel. Jones, Janey Louise. 2016. (Superfairies Ser.). (ENG.). 56p. (J). (gr. k-3). lib. bdg. 23.99 *(978-1-5158-0433-8(X)*, Picture Window Bks.) Capstone.

—Superfairies: Adventures in Peaseblossom Woods. Jones, Janey Louise. 2017. (ENG.). 192p. (J). (gr. k-3). pap. 6.95 *(978-1-62370-819-1(2)*, Capstone Young Readers) Capstone.

—Superfairies to the Rescue. Jones, Janey Louise. ed. 2018. (ENG.). 192p. (J). (gr. k-3). pap. 6.95 *(978-1-62370-990-7(3)*, 137403, Capstone Young Readers) Capstone.

—The Town Mouse & the Country Mouse. Berne, Emma Carlson. 2019. (Classic Fables in Rhythm & Rhyme Ser.). (ENG.). 24p. (J). (gr. -1-2). lib. bdg. 33.99 *(978-1-68410-335-5(5)*, 140255) Cantata Learning.

—Violet the Velvet Rabbit. Jones, Janey Louise. 2016. (Superfairies Ser.). (ENG.). 56p. (J). (gr. k-3). lib. bdg. 23.99 *(978-1-4795-8644-8(7)*, Picture Window Bks.) Capstone.

Poh, Jennie. Herbie's Big Adventure. Poh, Jennie. (ENG.). (J). (gr. -1-2). 2019. 30p. bds. 7.99 *(978-1-68446-092-2(1)*, 141307, Capstone Editions); 2016. 40p. lib. bdg. 23.32 *(978-1-5158-0234-1(5)*, Picture Window Bks.) Capstone.

Pohl, David. Pawns. Roberts, Willo Davis. 2012. (ENG.). 160p. (J). (gr. 5-9). pap. 8.99 *(978-0-689-83320-5(2)*, Simon & Schuster/Paula Wiseman Bks.) Simon & Schuster/Paula Wiseman Bks.

Pohrt, Tom. The Cats of Roxville Station. George, Jean Craighead. 2009. (ENG.). 192p. (J). (gr. 4-6). 21.19 *(978-0-525-42140-5(8))* Penguin Young Readers Group.

—The Little Gentleman. Pearce, Philippa. 2004. 208p. (J). (gr. 3-18). lib. bdg. 16.89 *(978-0-06-073161-8(3))* HarperCollins Pubs.

—The Walls of Cartagena. Durango, Julia. 2008. (ENG.). 160p. (J). (gr. 3-7). 19.99 *(978-1-4169-4102-6(9)*, Simon & Schuster Bks. For Young Readers) Simon & Schuster Bks. For Young Readers.

—The Wishing Bone, & Other Poems. Mitchell, Stephen. 2003. (ENG.). 56p. (J). (gr. k-12). 16.99 *(978-0-7636-1118-7(2))* Candlewick Pr.

Pohrte, Juliann, jt. illus. see Pohrte, Olivia.

Pohrte, Olivia & Pohrte, Juliann. In the Land of Liviaann. Pohrte, Kathysue & Pohrte, Olivia. Pohrte, Juliann. Pohrte, Kathysue, ed. l.t. ed. 2003. 36p. (J). pap. 17.95 *(978-0-9722296-0-9(4)*, 872493); (gr. -1-6). 12.95 *(978-0-9722296-1-6(2)*, 872493) Pohrte, Dorey Publishing, Inc.

Poilpot, Theophile. Carnet Blanc Chemin de Fer D'Orleans. 2016. (Bnf Monuments Ser.). (FRE.). (J). pap. *(978-2-01-116964-8(X))* Hachette Groupe Livre.

—Carnet Ligne Chemin de Fer D'Orleans. 2016. (Bnf Monuments Ser.). (FRE.). (J). pap. *(978-2-01-116941-9(0))* Hachette Groupe Livre.

Poirier, Nadine. Busy Kids' Colors, Shapes & Sizes. Jaramillo, Gloria. 2008. (Busy Kids Ser.). 36p. (J). (gr. -1-k). bds. 12.99 *(978-2-7641-1677-7(2))* Gardner Pubns.

Poitras, Jim. The Drum Calls Softly, 1 vol. Bouchard, David & Willier, Shelley. 2008. (ENG.). 120p. (J). (gr. 1-2). 24.95 *(978-0-88995-421-2(6)*, fcc48aa9-d9ee-4d79-99b2-d34a50b7cca0) Red Deer Pr. CAN. Dist: Firefly Bks., Ltd.

—Entre Dans la Grande Ronde, 1 vol. Bouchard, David & Willier, Shelley. 4th ed. 2008. (FRE.). 120p. (J). (gr. 4-6). 24.95 *(978-0-88995-424-3(0)*, c34a8b39-e433-4296-b665-fa5867d96037) Red Deer Pr. CAN. Dist: Firefly Bks., Ltd.

Pokoj, Ed. What Does a Princess Really Look Like? Loewen, Mark. 2018. (Brave Like a Girl Ser.). (ENG.). 30p. (J). (gr. k-2). 17.95 *(978-1-945448-17-1(2)*, BQB Publishing) Boutique of Quality Books Publishing Co., Inc.

Polacco, Patricia. When Lightning Comes in a Jar. Polacco, Ernest L. 2007. 40p. (J). (gr. k-3). 7.99 *(978-0-14-240350-1(4)*, Puffin Books) Penguin Young Readers Group.

Polacco, Patricia. An a from Miss Keller. Polacco, Patricia. 2015. (ENG.). 40p. (J). (gr. k-3). 18.99 *(978-0-399-16691-4(2)*, G.P. Putnam's Sons Books for Young Readers) Penguin Young Readers Group.

—The Art of Miss Chew. Polacco, Patricia. 2012. 40p. (J). (gr. k-3). 18.99 *(978-0-399-25703-2(9)*, G.P. Putnam's Sons Books for Young Readers) Penguin Young Readers Group.

—Because of Thursday. Polacco, Patricia. 2016. (ENG.). 40p. (J). (gr. -1-3). 17.99 *(978-1-4814-2140-9(9)*, Simon & Schuster Bks. For Young Readers) Simon & Schuster Bks. For Young Readers.

—The Blessing Cup. Polacco, Patricia. 2013. (ENG.). 48p. (J). (gr. -1-3). 19.99 *(978-1-4424-5047-9(9)*, Simon & Schuster Bks. For Young Readers) Simon & Schuster Bks. For Young Readers.

—The Bravest Man in the World. Polacco, Patricia. 2019. (ENG.). 56p. (J). (gr. -1-3). 17.99 *(978-1-4814-9461-8(9)*, Simon & Schuster Bks. For Young Readers) Simon & Schuster Bks. For Young Readers.

—Bully. Polacco, Patricia. 2012. (ENG.). 48p. (J). (gr. 2-5). 18.99 *(978-0-399-25704-9(7)*, G.P. Putnam's Sons Books for Young Readers) Penguin Young Readers Group.

—Bun Bun Button. Polacco, Patricia. 2011. (ENG.). 40p. (J). (gr. -1-k). 17.99 *(978-0-399-25472-7(2)*, G.P. Putnam's Sons Books for Young Readers) Penguin Young Readers Group.

—Emma Kate. Polacco, Patricia. 2008. 32p. (J). (gr. -1-k). pap. 7.99 *(978-0-14-241196-4(5)*, Puffin Books) Penguin Young Readers Group.

—Fiona's Lace. Polacco, Patricia. 2014. (ENG.). 48p. (J). (gr. -1-3). 17.99 *(978-1-4424-8724-6(0)*, Simon & Schuster/Paula Wiseman Bks.) Simon & Schuster/Paula Wiseman Bks.

—For the Love of Autumn. Polacco, Patricia. 2008. 40p. (J). (gr. 1-4). 18.99 *(978-0-399-24541-1(3)*, Philomel Bks.) Penguin Young Readers Group.

—G Is for Goat. Polacco, Patricia. 2006. (ENG.). 32p. (J). (gr. -1-k). reprint ed. pap. 7.99 *(978-0-14-240550-5(7)*, Puffin Books) Penguin Young Readers Group.

—Gifts of the Heart. Polacco, Patricia. 2013. 40p. (J). (gr. k-3). 18.99 *(978-0-399-16094-3(9)*, G.P. Putnam's Sons Books for Young Readers) Penguin Young Readers Group.

—Ginger & Petunia. Polacco, Patricia. 2007. 40p. (J). (gr. -1-3). 18.99 *(978-0-399-24539-8(1)*, Philomel Bks.) Penguin Young Readers Group.

—The Graves Family. Polacco, Patricia. 2006. 48p. (J). (gr. k-3). reprint ed. pap. 6.99 *(978-0-14-240635-9(X)*, Puffin Books) Penguin Young Readers Group.

—The Graves Family. Polacco, Patricia. 2006. (gr. k-3). 17.00 *(978-0-7569-6715-4(5))* Perfection Learning Corp.

—Holes in the Sky. Polacco, Patricia. 2018. 48p. (J). (gr. 1-4). 18.99 *(978-1-5247-3948-5(0)*, G.P. Putnam's Sons Books for Young Readers) Penguin Young Readers Group.

—In Our Mothers' House. Polacco, Patricia. 2009. (ENG.). 48p. (J). (gr. 1-3). 18.99 *(978-0-399-25076-7(X)*, Philomel Bks.) Penguin Young Readers Group.

—January's Sparrow. Polacco, Patricia. 2009. 96p. (J). (gr. 3-7). 23.99 *(978-0-399-25077-4(8)*, Philomel Bks.) Penguin Young Readers Group.

—John Philip Duck. Polacco, Patricia. 2004. (ENG.). 48p. (J). (gr. k-4). 17.99 *(978-0-399-24262-5(7)*, Philomel Bks.) Penguin Young Readers Group.

—Junkyard Wonders. Polacco, Patricia. 2010. (ENG.). 48p. (J). (gr. 1-4). 18.99 *(978-0-399-25078-1(6)*, Philomel Bks.) Penguin Young Readers Group.

—Just in Time, Abraham Lincoln. Polacco, Patricia. 2011. 48p. (J). (gr. 2-4). 17.99 *(978-0-399-25471-0(4)*, G.P. Putnam's Sons Books for Young Readers) Penguin Young Readers Group.

—The Keeping Quilt: 25th Anniversary Edition. Polacco, Patricia. 25th ed. 2013. (ENG.). 64p. (J). (gr. -1-3). 17.99 *(978-1-4424-8237-1(0)*, Simon & Schuster/Paula Wiseman Bks.) Simon & Schuster/Paula Wiseman Bks.

—The Lemonade Club. Polacco, Patricia. 2007. 48p. (J). (gr. 1-4). 18.99 *(978-0-399-24540-4(5)*, Philomel Bks.) Penguin Young Readers Group.

—The Mermaid's Purse. Polacco, Patricia. 2016. 48p. (J). (gr. k-3). 18.99 *(978-0-399-16692-1(0)*, G.P. Putnam's Sons Books for Young Readers) Penguin Young Readers Group.

—Mommies Say Shhh! Polacco, Patricia. 2007. 32p. (J). (gr. -1 — 1). bds. 7.99 *(978-0-399-24720-0(3)*, Philomel Bks.) Penguin Young Readers Group.

—Mr. Wayne's Masterpiece. Polacco, Patricia. 2014. 40p. (J). (gr. k-3). 18.99 *(978-0-399-16095-0(7)*, G.P. Putnam's Sons Books for Young Readers) Penguin Young Readers Group.

—Oh, Look! Polacco, Patricia. 2004. 32p. (J). (gr. -1-3). 16.99 *(978-0-399-24223-6(6)*, Philomel Bks.) Penguin Young Readers Group.

—An Orange for Frankie. Polacco, Patricia. 2004. 48p. (J). (gr. 1-4). 18.99 *(978-0-399-24302-8(X)*, Philomel Bks.) Penguin Young Readers Group.

—Remembering Vera. Polacco, Patricia. 2017. (ENG.). 32p. (J). (gr. -1-3). 18.99 *(978-1-4814-4227-5(9)*, Simon & Schuster/Paula Wiseman Bks.) Simon & Schuster/Paula Wiseman Bks.

—Rotten Richie & the Ultimate Dare. Polacco, Patricia. 2006. 48p. (J). (gr. k-3). 18.99 *(978-0-399-24531-2(6)*, Philomel Bks.) Penguin Young Readers Group.

—Something about Hensley's. Polacco, Patricia. 2006. 48p. (J). (gr. -1-3). 18.99 *(978-0-399-24538-1(3)*, Philomel Bks.) Penguin Young Readers Group.

—Thank You, Mr. Falker. Polacco, Patricia. 2012. 40p. (J). (gr. k-3). 14.99 *(978-0-399-25762-9(4)*, Philomel Bks.) Penguin Young Readers Group.

—Tucky Jo & Little Heart. Polacco, Patricia. 2015. (ENG.). 48p. (J). (gr. -1-3). 18.99 *(978-1-4814-1584-2(0)*, Simon & Schuster Bks. For Young Readers) Simon & Schuster Bks. For Young Readers.

Polan, Jason. Mermaid in Chelsea Creek. Tea, Michelle. 2013. (ENG.). 240p. (J). (gr. 5-11). 19.95 *(978-1-938073-36-6(3)*, 71096af1-b76f-4def-883b-0ab94f5682da) McSweeney's Publishing.

Poland, James W. Ratdog. Poland, Carol A. & Poland, David W. 2019. (Ratdog Ser.: Vol. 1). (ENG.). 102p. (J). pap. 6.95 ***(978-0-692-17974-1(7))*** DWP.

Polastri, Rosa Elena. El Misterio del Condor. Brignole, Giancarla, tr. (Fabulas De Familia Ser.). (SPA.). 32p. *(978-970-20-0270-3(2))* Castillo, Ediciones, S. A. de C. V.

Polat, Ercan. All about Wudu (Ablution) Gunes, Aysenur. 2017. (Discover Islam Sticker Activity Bks.). (ENG.). 32p. (J). (gr. -1-2). pap., act. bk. ed. 5.95 *(978-0-86037-681-1(8))* Kube Publishing Ltd. GBR. Dist: Consortium Bk. Sales & Distribution.

—Makkah & Madinah Activity Book. Gunes, Aysenur. 2015. (Discover Islam Sticker Activity Bks.). (ENG.). 32p. (J). 5.95 *(978-0-86037-544-9(7))* Kube Publishing Ltd. GBR. Dist: Consortium Bk. Sales & Distribution.

—Mosques of the World Activity Book. Gunes, Aysenur. 2015. (Discover Islam Sticker Activity Bks.). (ENG.). 32p. (J). 5.95 *(978-0-86037-539-5(0))* Kube Publishing Ltd. GBR. Dist: Consortium Bk. Sales & Distribution.

—Prayer & Wudu. Gunes, Aysenur. 2015. (Discover Islam Sticker Activity Bks.). (ENG.). 32p. (J). act. bk. ed. 5.95 *(978-0-86037-610-1(9))* Kube Publishing Ltd. GBR. Dist: Consortium Bk. Sales & Distribution.

—Ramadan & Fasting Activity Book. Gunes, Aysenur. 2016. (Discover Islam Sticker Activity Bks.). (ENG.). 32p. (J). 5.95 *(978-0-86037-615-6(X))* Kube Publishing Ltd. GBR. Dist: Consortium Bk. Sales & Distribution.

Polchlopek, Mary Ann. Little Orly & the Cricket. Lutterbach, Johanna. 2008. 24p. pap. 11.49 *(978-1-4389-0656-0(0))* AuthorHouse.

Polenova, Elena. The Story of Sinko-Filipko & Other Russian Folk Tales. Althaus, Frank. 2020. (ENG.). 64p. 15.00 *(978-1-906257-26-2(2))* Fontanka GBR. Dist: National Bk. Network.

Poley, Lucy. Every Family Is Different: Even Animal Families! O'Connor, Constance & Rojas, Natalia. 2019. (ENG.). 30p. (J). ***(978-1-5255-5787-3(4))***; pap. ***(978-1-5255-5788-0(2))*** FriesenPress.

Polhamus, Bruce, jt. illus. see Speer, Julie.

Polhemus, Coleman. Return to Daemon Hall: Evil Roots. Nance, Andrew. 2011. (ENG.). 256p. (YA). (gr. 7-12). 21.99 *(978-0-8050-8748-2(6)*, 9780805087482, Holt, Henry & Co. Bks. For Young Readers) Holt, Henry & Co.

Polhemus, Coleman. The Crocodile Blues. Polhemus, Coleman. 2007. (ENG.). 48p. (J). (gr. -1-2). 16.99 *(978-0-7636-3543-5(X))* Candlewick Pr.

Poli, Giuseppe. Invisible Jerry. Wallace, Adam. 2018. (ENG.). 32p. (J). (gr. -1-3). 17.99 *(978-1-925335-78-1(X)*, 321972, EK Bks.) Exisle Publishing Pty Ltd. AUS. Dist: Hachette UK Distribution.

Polina, Hrytskova. Balloon Breath. Given, Amanda. 2018. (ENG.). 24p. (J). (gr. k-3). 16.95 *(978-1-7326062-0-3(X))* Govinda Yoga Play.

Poling, Kyle. Can We Ring the Liberty Bell? Rustad, Martha E. H. 2014. (Cloverleaf Books (tm) — Our American Symbols Ser.). (ENG.). 24p. (J). (gr. k-2). pap. 8.99 *(978-1-4677-4467-6(0)*, 9781467744676, Millbrook Pr.) Lerner Publishing Group.

—Can You Sing the Star-Spangled Banner ? Rustad, Martha E. H. 2014. (Cloverleaf Books (tm) — Our American Symbols Ser.). (ENG.). 24p. (J). (gr. k-2). pap. 8.99 *(978-1-4677-4469-0(7)*, 9781467744690, Millbrook Pr.) Lerner Publishing Group.

—The Delicious Dairy Group, 1 vol. Lee, Sally. 2011. (First Graphics: Myplate & Healthy Eating Ser.). (ENG.). 24p. (J). (gr. k-3). lib. bdg. 24.65 *(978-1-4296-6092-1(9))*; (gr. 1-2). pap. 35.70 *(978-1-4296-7165-1(3))* Capstone.

—Easter Bunny's Basket. Karr, Lily. 2011. (ENG.). 10p. (J). (gr. k — 1). bds. 6.99 *(978-0-545-27940-6(2)*, Cartwheel Bks.) Scholastic, Inc.

—The Eco-Neighbor's Guide to a Green Community, 1 vol. Johnson, J. Angelique. 2010. (Point It Out! Tips for Green Living Ser.). (ENG.). 24p. (J). (gr. -1-3). lib. bdg. 27.32 *(978-1-4048-6028-5(2)*, Picture Window Bks.) Capstone.

—The Eco-Shopper's Guide to Buying Green, 1 vol. Johnson, J. Angelique. 2010. (Point It Out! Tips for Green Living Ser.). (ENG.). 24p. (J). (gr. -1-3). lib. bdg. 27.32 *(978-1-4048-6029-2(0)*, Picture Window Bks.) Capstone.

—The Eco-Student's Guide to Being Green at School, 1 vol. Johnson, J. Angelique. 2010. (Point It Out! Tips for Green Living Ser.). (ENG.). 24p. (J). (gr. -1-3). lib. bdg. 27.32 *(978-1-4048-6027-8(4)*, Picture Window Bks.) Capstone.

—The Great Grains Group, 1 vol. Aboff, Marcie. 2011. (First Graphics: Myplate & Healthy Eating Ser.). (ENG.). 24p. (J). (gr. k-3). lib. bdg. 24.65 *(978-1-4296-6088-4(0))*; (gr. 1-2). pap. 35.70 *(978-1-4296-7167-5(X))* Capstone.

—The Incredible Vegetable Group, 1 vol. Aboff, Marcie. 2011. (First Graphics: Myplate & Healthy Eating Ser.). (ENG.). 24p. (J). (gr. k-3). pap. 6.29 *(978-1-4296-7163-7(7))*; (J). (gr. k-3). lib. bdg. 24.65 *(978-1-4296-6089-1(9))*; (gr. 1-2). pap. 35.70 *(978-1-4296-7169-9(6))* Capstone.

—Let's Meet a Dentist. Heos, Bridget. 2013. (Cloverleaf Books (tm) — Community Helpers Ser.). (ENG.). 24p. (J). (gr. k-2). pap. 8.99 *(978-1-4677-0800-5(3)*, 9781467708005, Millbrook Pr.) Lerner Publishing Group.

—Let's Meet a Teacher. Heos, Bridget. 2013. (Cloverleaf Books (tm) — Community Helpers Ser.). (ENG.). 24p. (J). (gr. k-2). pap. 8.99 *(978-1-4677-0805-0(4)*, 9781467708050, Millbrook Pr.) Lerner Publishing Group.

—Spooky Boo: A Halloween Adventure. Karr, Lily. 2011. (ENG.). 12p. (J). (gr. -1 — 1). bds. 6.99 *(978-0-545-29867-4(9)*, Cartwheel Bks.) Scholastic, Inc.

—Teachers in My Community. Heos, Bridget. 2018. (Meet a Community Helper (Early Bird Stories (tm)) Ser.). (ENG.). 24p. (J). (gr. k-2). 27.99 *(978-1-5415-2022-6(X)*, Lerner Pubns.) Lerner Publishing Group.

—Ten Flying Brooms. Oliver, Ilanit. 2015. (ENG.). 24p. (J). (gr. k-2). 16.19 *(978-1-4844-5738-2(2))*; (gr. -1-k). 3.99 *(978-0-545-81336-5(0)*, Cartwheel Bks.) Scholastic, Inc.

—There's a Dinosaur in My Soup! Boniface, William. 2012. (ENG.). 12p. (J). (gr. -1-1). bds. 9.99 *(978-1-4424-4610-6(2)*, Little Simon) Little Simon.

—What Is Inside the Lincoln Memorial? Rustad, Martha E. H. 2014. (Cloverleaf Books (tm) — Our American Symbols Ser.). (ENG.). 24p. (J). (gr. k-2). pap. 8.99 *(978-1-4677-4468-3(9)*, 9781467744683); lib. bdg. 25.32 *(978-1-4677-2135-6(2)*, 9781467721356) Lerner Publishing Group. (Millbrook Pr.).

—Why Are There Stripes on the American Flag? Rustad, Martha E. H. 2014. (Cloverleaf Books (tm) — Our American Symbols Ser.). (ENG.). 24p. (J). (gr. k-2). pap. 8.99 *(978-1-4677-4465-2(4)*, 9781467744652, Millbrook Pr.) Lerner Publishing Group.

—Yummy Bunny Easter Treats! Boniface, William. 2013. (ENG.). 12p. (J). (gr. -1-1). 9.99 *(978-1-4424-5724-9(4)*, Little Simon) Little Simon.

Poling, Kyle & Swift, Gary. First Graphics: Myplate & Healthy Eating. Aboff, Marcie & Lee, Sally. 2011. (First Graphics: Myplate & Healthy Eating Ser.). (ENG.). 24p. (J). (gr. k-3). lib. bdg., lib. bdg., lib. bdg. 123.25 *(978-1-4296-6094-5(5))*; (gr. 1-2). pap. 214.20 *(978-1-4296-7172-9(6))* Capstone.

Polinko, Les. KenKarta: Battle of the Onoxmon. Karevold, Alison. Malone, Susan Mary, ed. 2011. 300p. (J). 25.98 *(978-0-9843166-3-2(9))* Artists' Orchard, LLC, The.

Polinko, Les. The Ganorch under the Porch. Polinko, Les. Donaldson, Connie. 2013. 36p. pap. 9.95 *(978-0-9836682-3-7(X))* Hearthstone Rose.

Polis, Gary A. Scorpion Man: Exploring the World of Scorpions. Pringle, Laurence. 2008. (ENG.). 48p. (J). (gr. 1-3). 11.99 *(978-1-4169-7574-8(8)*, Simon & Schuster/Paula Wiseman Bks.) Simon & Schuster/Paula Wiseman Bks.

Politakos, Pantelis. Niall the High King of Erin: Book II. MacNeill, Lance J. McNeill, Christie, ed. 2018. (Niall Ser.: Vol. 2). (ENG.). 58p. (J). (gr. 3-6). 20.00 *(978-0-692-16251-4(8))* McNeill, Lance.

Polito, Mike. My Special Angel: A Bedtime Story. Donald, Diana. 2005. 33p. (J). (gr. -1-3). incl. audio compact disk *(978-1-894290-01-2(1))* Heart of the Matter Publishing.

Polivka, Rob. A Dream of Flight: Alberto Santos-Dumont's Race Around the Eiffel Tower. Polivka, Rob. Polivka, Jef. 2019. (ENG.). 40p. (J). 18.99 *(978-0-374-30661-8(3)*, 900178015, Farrar, Straus & Giroux (BYR)) Farrar, Straus & Giroux.

Polizzi, Michelle, jt. illus. see Ortner, Nick.

Pollack, Gadi. The Lost Treasure of Tikkun Hamiddos Island. Chait, Baruch. (Good Middos Ser.: Vol. 2). 62p. 25.99 *(978-1-58330-478-5(9))* Feldheim Pubs.

—The Terrifying Trap of the Bad Middos Pirates, 2 vols. Chait, Baruch. (Good Middos Ser.). 96p. 25.99 *(978-1-58330-664-2(1))* Feldheim Pubs.

—Trakht Fun Frier: Herlikhe Mesholim Fun Di Gdoyle Ha-Doyres. 2013. (YID.). 55p. (J). *(978-1-937637-36-1(0))* Kinder Shpiel USA, Inc.

Pollack, Gadi. Purimshpiel. Pollack, Gadi, contrib. by. 19.99 *(978-1-58330-596-6(3))*; (ENG & FRE.). 21.95 *(978-1-58330-601-7(3))*; (ENG & HEB.). *(978-1-58330-611-6(0))* Feldheim Pubs.

Pollack, Gadi & Markovitch, Evegeny. The Miniature Puppet Theater Book. Schreiber, Elisheva. (J). 14.95 *(978-1-58330-617-8(X))* Feldheim Pubs.

Pollak, Barbara. Girl Stuff: A Survival Guide to Growing Up. Blackstone, Margaret & Guest, Elissa Haden. 2006. (ENG.). 181p. (J). (gr. 5-8). 24.94 *(978-0-15-201830-6(1))* Houghton Mifflin Harcourt Publishing Co.

—Heart to Heart with Mallory. Friedman, Laurie. (Mallory Ser.: 6). (ENG.). 160p. (J). (gr. 2-5). 2007. per. 6.99 *(978-0-8225-7133-9(1)*, Darby Creek); 2006. lib. bdg. 15.95 *(978-1-57505-932-7(0)*, Twenty-First Century Bks.) Lerner Publishing Group.

—Honestly, Mallory! Friedman, Laurie. (Mallory Ser.: 8). (ENG.). 160p. (J). (gr. 2-5). 2008. pap. 6.99 *(978-1-58013-840-6(3)*, Darby Creek); 2007. 15.95 *(978-0-8225-6193-4(X)*, Carolrhoda Bks.) Lerner Publishing Group.

—In Business with Mallory. Friedman, Laurie. 2007. (Mallory Ser.: 5). (ENG.). 160p. (J). (gr. 2-5). per. 6.99 *(978-0-8225-6561-1(7)*, Darby Creek) Lerner Publishing Group.

—Mallory on Board. Friedman, Laurie. (Mallory Ser.: 7). (ENG.). 176p. (J). (gr. 2-5). 2008. per. 6.99 *(978-0-8225-9023-1(9)*, Darby Creek); 2007. 15.95 *(978-0-8225-6194-1(8)*, Carolrhoda Bks.) Lerner Publishing Group.

Pollak, Monika. Russell's World: A Story for Kids about Autism. Amenta, Charles A. 2011. 40p. (J). (gr. -1-3). 14.95 *(978-1-4338-0975-0(3))*; pap. 9.95 *(978-1-4338-0976-7(1))* American Psychological Assn. (Magination Pr.).

Pollard, Brian. Heroes of History for Young Readers - George Washington: America's Patriot. Meloche, Renee Taft. 2006. (Heroes of History Ser.). (ENG.). 32p. (J). 8.99 *(978-1-932096-28-6(0))* Emerald Bks.

—Heroes of History for Young Readers - Meriwether Lewis: Journey Aross America. Meloche, Renee Taft. 2006. (Heroes of History Ser.). (ENG.). 32p. (J). (gr. -1-3). 8.99 *(978-1-932096-27-9(2))* Emerald Bks.

Pollard, Bryan. Heroes for Young Readers - Cameron Townsend: Planting God's Word. Meloche, Renee. 2004. (Heroes for Young Readers Ser.). (ENG.). 32p. (J). 8.99 *(978-1-57658-241-1(8))* YWAM Publishing.

—Heroes for Young Readers - Hudson Taylor: Friend of China. Meloche, Renee. 2004. (ENG.). 32p. (J). 8.99 *(978-1-57658-234-3(5))* YWAM Publishing.

—Heroes for Young Readers - Jim Elliot: A Light for God. Meloche, Renee. 2004. (Heroes for Young Readers Ser.). (ENG.). 32p. (J). 8.99 *(978-1-57658-235-0(3))* YWAM Publishing.

—Heroes for Young Readers - Jonathan Goforth: Never Give Up. Meloche, Renee. 2004. (Heroes for Young Readers Ser.). (ENG.). 32p. (J). 8.99 *(978-1-57658-242-8(6))* YWAM Publishing.

—Heroes for Young Readers - Lottie Moon: A Generous Offering. Meloche, Renee. 2004. (Heroes for Young Readers Ser.). (ENG.). 32p. (J). 8.99 *(978-1-57658-243-5(4))* YWAM Publishing.

—Heroes for Young Readers Activity Guide Package Books 1-4: Includes: Activity Guide, Audio CD, & Books 1-4. Meloch, Renee. 2005. (Heroes for Young Readers Ser.). (ENG.). 55.94 incl. audio compact disk *(978-1-57658-375-3(9))* YWAM Publishing.

—Heroes for Young Readers Activity Guide Package Books 13-16: Includes: Activity Guide, Audio CD, & Books 13-16. Meloche, Renee Taft. 2006. (ENG.). 55.94 incl. audio compact disk *(978-1-57658-378-4(3))* YWAM Publishing.

—Heroes for Young Readers Activity Guide Package Books 5-8: Includes: Activity Guide, Audio CD, & Books 5-8. Meloche, Renee Taft. 2005. (Heroes for Young Readers Ser.). (ENG.). 57.94 incl. audio compact disk *(978-1-57658-376-0(7))* YWAM Publishing.

—Heroes for Young Readers Activity Guide Package Books 9-12: Includes: Activity Guide, Audio CD, & Books 9-12. Meloche, Renee Taft. 2005. (Heroes for Young Readers Ser.). (ENG.). 55.94 incl. audio compact disk *(978-1-57658-377-7(5))* YWAM Publishing.

—Heroes of History for Young Readers - Clara Barton: Courage to Serve. Meloche, Renee Taft. 2006. (Heroes of History for Young Readers Ser.). (ENG.). 32p. (J). (gr. -1). 8.99 *(978-1-932096-33-0(7))* Emerald Bks.

—Heroes of History for Young Readers - Daniel Boone: Bravery on the Frontier. Meloche, Renee Taft. 2009. (Heroes of History for Young Readers Ser.). (ENG.). 32p. (J). (gr. 1). 8.99 *(978-1-932096-61-3(2))* Emerald Bks.

—Heroes of History for Young Readers - George Washington Carver: America's Scientist. Meloche, Renee Taft. 2006. (Heroes for Young Readers Ser.). (ENG.). 32p. (J). (gr. 1-4). 8.99 *(978-1-932096-17-0(5))* Emerald Bks.

Pollard, Deborah Hanna. The Legend of Scary Mary: The Journey to Leadership Collection Adventure 2. Smith, I. J. 2004. 96p. (J). 16.95 *(978-0-9727273-1-0(0))* Green Owl, Inc.

—The Musical Fort. Smith, I. J. 2003. 53p. (J). 14.95 *(978-0-9727273-0-3(2))* Green Owl, Inc.

Pollard, Simon, photos by. Insects: Biggest! Littlest! Markle, Sandra. 2011. (Biggest! Littlest! Ser.). (ENG., 32p. (J). (gr. k-2). pap. 10.95 *(978-1-59078-872-1(9))* Boyds Mills Pr.

—Spiders: Biggest! Littlest! Markle, Sandra. 2011. (Biggest! Littlest! Ser.). (ENG., 32p. (J). (gr. k-2). pap. 10.95 *(978-1-59078-875-2(3))* Boyds Mills Pr.

Pollock, Mary Ellen. A Whole Different Animal. Pollock, Jim. 2007. 89p. (J). 17.00 net. *(978-0-9763675-2-9(1))* First Flight Bks.

Polly Jr., Jimmy Wayne. The Mop Heads, 1 vol. Hayes, Angela. 2009. 14p. pap. 24.95 *(978-1-61546-006-9(3))* America Star Bks.

Polseno, Jo. Charles Carroll & the American Revolution. Lomask, Milton. 2011. 188p. 42.95 *(978-1-258-07263-6(7))* Literary Licensing, LLC.

Polsky, Beanie. Tapuchim & Dvash. Cohen, Penny L. 2012. 36p. 24.95 *(978-1-4626-7769-6(X))*; pap. 24.95 *(978-1-4626-6667-6(1))* PublishAmerica, Inc.

Polson, Kristen. Bartholomew: Squire of the Subway. Lester, Carol. 2019. (ENG.). 42p. (J). 24.99 ***(978-1-68314-986-6(6))***; pap. 15.99 ***(978-1-68314-907-1(6))*** Redemption Pr.

Polson, Kristen. Boarding Bunnies. Lewis, Linda. 2018. (ENG.). 22p. (J). pap. 12.99 *(978-1-68314-817-3(7))* Redemption Pr.

—Roo the Kangaroo Cat. Lester, Carol L. 2019. (ENG.). 38p. (J). 24.99 *(978-1-68314-984-2(X))*; pap. 15.99 *(978-1-68314-841-8(X))* Redemption Pr.

polterink. Lumberjanes Original Graphic Novel: the Infernal Compass. Sturges, Lilah. 2018. (Lumberjanes Ser.). (ENG.). 144p. (J). (gr. 4-7). pap. 14.99 *(978-1-68415-252-0(6))* Boom! Studios.

—Lumberjanes Original Graphic Novel: the Shape of Friendship. Sturges, Lilah. 2019. (Lumberjanes Ser.). (ENG.). 144p. (J). pap. 14.99 *(978-1-68415-451-7(0))* Boom! Studios.

Poluzz, Alessandroi. Giant Hunter. Jeffrey, Gary. 2017. (Graphic Prehistoric Animals Ser.). 32p. (gr. 3-7). 31.35 *(978-1-62588-408-4(7)*, Smart Apple Media) Black Rabbit Bks.

—Terminator Pig. Jeffrey, Gary. 2017. (Graphic Prehistoric Animals Ser.). 32p. (gr. 3-7). 31.35 *(978-1-62588-412-1(5)*, Smart Apple Media) Black Rabbit Bks.

Poluzzi, Alessandro. The Black Death. Jeffrey, Gary. 2014. (Graphic Medieval History Ser.). (ENG.). 48p. (J). (gr. 5-5). *(978-0-7787-0400-3(9))*; pap. *(978-0-7787-0406-5(8))* Crabtree Publishing Co.

—Centaurs. Jeffrey, Gary. 2012. (Graphic Mythical Creatures Ser.). (ENG.). 24p. (J). (gr. 3-5). pap. 8.15 *(978-1-4339-6753-5(7))*; lib. bdg. 24.95 *(978-1-4339-6751-1(0))* Stevens, Gareth Publishing LLLP. (Gareth Stevens Learning Library).

—Dawn Horse. West, David. 2017. (Graphic Prehistoric Animals Ser.). 32p. (gr. 3-7). lib. bdg. 31.35 *(978-1-62588-407-7(9))* Black Rabbit Bks.

—Giant Sloth: Graphic Prehistoric Animals. West, David. 2017. (Graphic Prehistoric Animals Ser.). 32p. (gr. 3-7). lib. bdg. 31.35 *(978-1-62588-409-1(5))* Black Rabbit Bks.

—Mega Shark: Graphic Prehistoric Animals. West, David. 2017. (Graphic Prehistoric Animals Ser.). 32p. (gr. 3-7). lib. bdg. 31.35 *(978-1-62588-410-7(9))* Black Rabbit Bks.

—Sabertooth Tiger. West, David. 2017. (Graphic Prehistoric Animals Ser.). 32p. (gr. 3-7). lib. bdg. 31.35 *(978-1-62588-411-4(7))* Black Rabbit Bks.

—Terror Bird. West, David. 2017. (Graphic Prehistoric Animals Ser.). 32p. (gr. 3-7). lib. bdg. 31.35 *(978-1-62588-413-8(3))* Black Rabbit Bks.

—Woolly Mammoth. West, David. 2017. (Graphic Prehistoric Animals Ser.). 32p. (gr. 3-7). lib. bdg. 31.35 *(978-1-62588-414-5(1))* Black Rabbit Bks.

Poluzzi, Allesandro. The Oregon Trail. Jeffrey, Gary. 2012. (Graphic History of the American West Ser.). (ENG.). 24p. (J). (gr. 3-8). pap. 8.15 *(978-1-4339-6745-0(6)*, Gareth Stevens Learning Library); (gr. 4-7). lib. bdg. 24.95 *(978-1-4339-6743-6(X))* Stevens, Gareth Publishing LLLP.

Polyankakul, Polina. The Elf Who Didn't Like Christmas. Best, Jessie L. 2018. (ENG.). 42p. (J). pap. *(978-0-9952015-7-6(9))* Craven Tree Prs.

—Santa's Runaway Elf. Best, Jessie L. Goran, Around86, ed. 2018. (ENG.). 42p. (J). pap. *(978-0-9952015-4-5(4))* Craven Tree Prs.

Polyansky, Nikita. Botero: Paintings & Works on Paper. Bloncourt, Nelson & Botero, Fernando. 2013. (ENG.). 252p. 125.00 *(978-0-9881745-1-1(0))* G Arts LLC.

—Fanny Flies to France. Bloncourt, Nelson. 2019. (Fanny Ser.). (ENG.). 40p. 20.00 *(978-1-943876-49-5(5))* G Arts LLC.

—Fanny the Flying French Bulldog. Bloncourt, Nelson. 2014. (ENG.). 40p. 20.00 *(978-0-9851696-3-3(X))* G Arts LLC.

Polyansky, Nikita. The Sleeping Beauty: A Journey to the Ballet of the Marinsky Theatre. Polyansky, Nikita. Ebong, Ima. 2006. (ENG.). 48p. (J). (gr. 3-17). 20.00 *(978-0-9721152-0-9(X))* G Arts LLC.

Polynkakul, Polina. The Elf Who Didn't Like Christmas. Best, Jessie. Goran, Bdt, ed. 2018. (ENG.). 42p. (J). (gr. k-4). *(978-0-9952015-6-9(0))* Craven Tree Prs.

Pombo, Luis, jt. illus. see Pombo, Luis G.

Pombo, Luis G. & Pombo, Luis. Redondo: O Cuando los Circulos Se Convierten en Esferas. Hernandez, Claudia. 2007. (Otra Escalera Ser.). (ENG.). 36p. (J). (gr. 1-3). pap. 8.95 *(978-970-20-0840-8(9))* Castillo, Ediciones, S. A. de C. V. MEX. Dist: Macmillan.

Pomerantz, Norman. Billy Brahman: The Story of A Calf. Roop, James Q. 2011. 28p. 35.95 *(978-1-258-01757-6(1))* Literary Licensing, LLC.

Pomeroy, John. Un Ninito Los Guiara. Perkins, Greg. 2005. 16p. (J). (gr. 4-7). 8.99 *(978-1-59185-826-3(7)*, Charisma Kids) Charisma Media.

Pomeroy, John. A Little Child Shall Lead Them. Pomeroy, John. 2005. 24p. (J). 9.99 *(978-1-59185-632-0(9)*, Charisma Kids) Charisma Media.

Pomeroy, Shan, jt. illus. see Harrigan, Dayna.

Pommaux, Yvan. All of Us: a Young People's History of the World. Ylla-Somers, Christophe. Lehmann, Anna, tr. 2019. (ENG.). 88p. (J). (gr. 3-6). 29.95 *(978-1-68137-321-8(1)*, NYR Children's Collection) New York Review of Bks., Inc., The.

Pommaux, Yvan. Orpheus in the Underworld, 1 vol. Pommaux, Yvan. Kutner, Richard. 2016. (Toon Graphics Ser.). (ENG.). 56p. (J). (gr. 4-7). lib. bdg. 29.93 *(978-1-61479-500-1(2)*, 21436, Graphic Novels) Spotlight.

Pommier, Maurice. Grandpa's Workshop. Pommier, Maurice. Anderson, Brian, tr. from FRE. 2012.Tr. of Grandpa's Workshop. (ENG.). 48p. (J). 22.00 *(978-0-9850777-2-3(7))* Lost Art Pr. LLC.

Ponce, Carlos. A Pet Is Hard Work! Kelley, Terri. 2018. (ENG.). 24p. (J). pap. 9.99 *(978-1-4922-6264-0(1))* CreateSpace Independent Publishing Platform.

Ponder, Miranda. The Christmas Dragon. Lombardo, Stanley. 2018. (ENG.). 48p. (J). pap. 10.50 *(978-1-7307-5509-5(7))* Independently Published.

—The Raptor Who Ate Roses. Lombardo, Stanley. 2018. (ENG.). 40p. (J). pap. 9.50 *(978-1-7258-1694-7(6))* CreateSpace Independent Publishing Platform.

Pondexter Jr., Billy. Model Behavior: Charlotte. Davis, Nicole A. 2019. (ENG.). 50p. (YA). pap. 23.95 *(978-1-9736-5055-3(X)*, WestBow Pr.) Author Solutions, Inc.

Pongetti, Freda. Why the Chimes Rang. Pongetti, Freda, adapted by. 2007. 18p. (J). 21.00 net. *(978-0-9796625-0-8(8))* GDG Publishing.

Ponguillo Gutierrez, Uwer. Al Caer la Noche: Amores en Tinieblas. Alban Veintimilla, Wilman Ronmel. 2019. (SPA.). 252p. (J). pap. 13.99 ***(978-1-7033-6985-4(8))*** Independently Published.

Ponnay, Brenda. Mi Gato Esta Triste. Streza, Katrina. 2018. (Xist Kids Spanish Bks.). (SPA.). 36p. (J). (gr. -1-3). pap. 9.99 *(978-1-5324-0725-3(4))* Xist Publishing.

—My Cat Is Sad. Streza, Katrina. 2017. (Cat & Dog Readers Ser.). (ENG.). 40p. (J). (gr. -1-2). pap. 9.99 *(978-1-5324-0244-9(9))* Xist Publishing.

—My Cat Is Sad / Mi Gato Esta Triste. Streza, Katrina. 2018. (Xist Kids Bilingual Spanish English Ser.). (ENG & SPA.). 36p. (J). (gr. -1-3). pap. 9.99 *(978-1-5324-0675-1(4))* Xist Publishing.

—My Cat, My Dog. Streza, Katrina. 2015. (Cat & Dog Readers Ser.). (ENG.). 32p. (J). (gr. -1-2). pap. 9.99 *(978-1-62395-453-6(3))* Xist Publishing.

—My Good Dog. Streza, Katrina. 2013. (Cat & Dog Readers Ser.). (ENG.). 40p. (J). (gr. -1-2). pap. 9.99 *(978-1-62395-474-1(6))* Xist Publishing.

—Professor Mcnasty's Collection of Slimes. Bickley, Chris. 2017. (ENG.). 32p. (J). (gr. k-3). pap. 9.99 *(978-1-5324-0535-8(9))* Xist Publishing.

—You Are the Coolest: Positive Puns for Kids. Lee, Calee M. 2020. (Illustrated Jokes Ser.). (ENG.). 28p. (J). (gr. k-3). 12.99 *(978-1-5324-1558-6(3))*; pap. 12.99 *(978-1-5324-1557-9(5))* Xist Publishing.

Ponnay, Brenda. Be Mine. Ponnay, Brenda. 2015. (ENG.). 32p. (J). (gr. -1-3). pap. 9.99 *(978-1-62395-321-8(9))* Xist Publishing.

—Buhito Saca Sus Brios: (Little Hoo Gets the Wiggles Out) Ponnay, Brenda. 2020. (Little Hoo Ser.). (ENG.). 32p. (J). (gr. k-1). pap. 12.99 *(978-1-5324-1348-3(3))* Xist Publishing.

—Buhito Saca Sus Brios: (Little Hoo Gets the Wiggles Out) Ponnay, Brenda. 2020. (Little Hoo Ser.). (ENG.). 32p. (J). (gr. k-1). 12.99 *(978-1-5324-1349-0(1))* Xist Publishing.

Ponnay, Brenda. Code Come. Ponnay, Brenda. 2020. (Cody the Dog Ser.). (SPA.). 8p. (J). (gr. -1-2). pap. 5.99 ***(978-1-5324-2071-9(4))*** Xist Publishing.

—Cody Barks. Ponnay, Brenda. 2020. (Cody the Dog Ser.). (ENG.). 8p. (J). (gr. -1-2). pap. 5.99 ***(978-1-5324-2707-7(7))*** Xist Publishing.

—Cody Barks at Everyone. Ponnay, Brenda. 2020. (Cody the Dog Ser.). (ENG.). 16p. (J). (gr. -1-2). pap. 5.99 ***(978-1-5324-2710-7(7))*** Xist Publishing.

—Cody Come Todo. Ponnay, Brenda. 2020. (Cody the Dog Ser.). (SPA.). 16p. (J). (gr. -1-2). pap. 5.99 ***(978-1-5324-2068-9(4))*** Xist Publishing.

Ponnay, Brenda. Cody Eats. Ponnay, Brenda. 2019. (Cody the Dog Ser.). (ENG.). 8p. (J). (gr. -1-2). pap. 5.99 *(978-1-5324-0943-1(5))* Xist Publishing.

Ponnay, Brenda. Cody Eats / Cody Come. Ponnay, Brenda. 2020. (Cody the Dog Ser.). (ENG.). 8p. (J). (gr. -1-2). pap. 5.99 ***(978-1-5324-2077-1(3))*** Xist Publishing.

Ponnay, Brenda. Cody Eats Everything. Ponnay, Brenda. 2019. (Cody the Dog Ser.). (ENG.). 16p. (J). (gr. -1-2). pap. 5.99 *(978-1-5324-1110-6(3))* Xist Publishing.

Ponnay, Brenda. Cody Eats Everything / Cody Come Todo. Ponnay, Brenda. 2020. (Cody the Dog Ser.). (ENG.). 16p. (J). (gr. -1-2). pap. 5.99 ***(978-1-5324-2074-0(9))*** Xist Publishing.

Ponnay, Brenda. Cody Poops. Ponnay, Brenda. 2019. (Cody the Dog Ser.). (ENG.). 8p. (J). (gr. -1-2). pap. 5.99 *(978-1-5324-1252-3(5))* Xist Publishing.

—Cody Poops Everywhere. Ponnay, Brenda. 2019. (Cody the Dog Ser.). (ENG.). 16p. (J). (gr. -1-2). pap. 5.99 *(978-1-5324-1329-2(7))* Xist Publishing.

—Cody Sheds. Ponnay, Brenda. 2020. (Cody the Dog Ser.). (ENG.). 8p. (J). (gr. k-1). pap. 5.99 *(978-1-5324-1546-3(X))* Xist Publishing.

—Cody Sheds Everywhere. Ponnay, Brenda. 2020. (Cody the Dog Ser.). (ENG.). 16p. (J). (gr. k-1). pap. 5.99 *(978-1-5324-1548-7(6))* Xist Publishing.

—Colores: (Colors) Ponnay, Brenda. Sandoval, Lenny, tr. 2017. (Xist Kids Spanish Bks.). (SPA.). 32p. (J). (gr. -1-3). pap. 9.99 *(978-1-5324-0389-7(5))* Xist Publishing.

—Colors / Colores. Ponnay, Brenda. 2017. (Xist Kids Bilingual Spanish English Ser.). (ENG & SPA.). 28p. (J). (gr. -1-3). pap. 9.99 *(978-1-5324-0313-2(5))* Xist Publishing.

—¡Es la Hora de Alistarse, Conejito! Ponnay, Brenda. Sandoval, Lenny, tr. 2017. (Xist Kids Spanish Bks.). (SPA.). 32p. (J). (gr. -1-1). pap. 9.99 *(978-1-5324-0365-1(8))* Xist Publishing.

—Felices Pascuas Pequeño Buho: (Happy Easter, Little Hoo!) Ponnay, Brenda. 2019. (Little Hoo Ser.). 32p. (J). (gr.

-1-2). (ENG.). 9.99 *(978-1-5324-1139-7(1))*; pap. 9.99 *(978-1-5324-1138-0(3))* Xist Publishing.

—¡feliz Cumpleaños Pequeño Buho! Ponnay, Brenda. 2018. (Little Hoo Ser.). (SPA.). 32p. (J). (gr. -1-3). 9.99 *(978-1-5324-1127-4(8))* Xist Publishing.

—¡Feliz Cumpleaños Pequeño Buho! Ponnay, Brenda. 2018. (Xist Kids Spanish Bks.). (SPA.). 32p. (J). (gr. -1-3). pap. 9.99 *(978-1-5324-0693-5(2))* Xist Publishing.

—Feliz Navidad Buhito: (Merry Christmas, Little Hoo!) Ponnay, Brenda. 2017. (Xist Kids Spanish Bks.). (SPA.). 32p. (J). (gr. -1-3). pap. 9.99 *(978-1-5324-0401-6(8))* Xist Publishing.

—Good Night, Kitty Kitty! Ponnay, Brenda. 2018. (ENG.). 32p. (J). (gr. -1-2). 9.99 *(978-1-5324-1120-5(0))*; pap. 9.99 *(978-1-5324-0826-7(9))* Xist Publishing.

—Happy Birthday, Little Hoo! Ponnay, Brenda. 2017. (Little Hoo Ser.). (ENG.). 32p. (J). (gr. -1-k). pap. 9.99 *(978-1-5324-0190-9(6))*; (gr. k-1). 18.99 *(978-1-5324-1057-4(3))* Xist Publishing.

—Happy Birthday Little Hoo / ¡feliz Cumpleaños Pequeño Buho! Ponnay, Brenda. 2018. (Little Hoo Ser.). (ENG.). 32p. (J). (gr. -1-3). 9.99 *(978-1-5324-1087-1(5))* Xist Publishing.

—Happy Birthday, Little Hoo! (¡Feliz Cumpleaños Pequeño Buho!) Ponnay, Brenda. 2018. (Xist Kids Bilingual Spanish English Ser.). (ENG & SPA.). 32p. (J). (gr. -1-3). pap. 9.99 *(978-1-5324-0637-9(1))* Xist Publishing.

—Happy Easter, Little Hoo! Ponnay, Brenda. 2019. (Little Hoo Ser.). (ENG.). 32p. (J). (gr. -1-2). pap. 9.99 *(978-1-5324-0929-5(X))* Xist Publishing.

—Happy Easter, Little Hoo! / Felices Pascuas Pequeño Buho! Ponnay, Brenda. 2019. (Little Hoo Ser.). 32p. (J). (gr. -1-2). (ENG.). 9.99 *(978-1-5324-1136-6(7))*; pap. 9.99 *(978-1-5324-1135-9(9))* Xist Publishing.

—Hey, Kitty Kitty! Ponnay, Brenda. 2015. (ENG.). 32p. (J). (gr. -1-2). pap. 9.99 *(978-1-62395-405-5(3))* Xist Publishing.

—¡Hora de Comer, Conejito! (Time to Eat, Bunny!) Ponnay, Brenda. 2017. (Xist Kids Spanish Bks.). (SPA.). 32p. (J). (gr. -1-1). pap. 9.99 *(978-1-5324-0367-5(4))* Xist Publishing.

—¡Hora de Dormir, Conejito! Ponnay, Brenda. 2018. (Xist Kids Spanish Bks.). (SPA.). 32p. (J). (gr. -1-3). pap. 9.99 *(978-1-5324-0695-9(9))* Xist Publishing.

—It's Snot Fair: And Other Gross & Disgusting Jokes. Ponnay, Brenda. 2017. (Illustrated Jokes Ser.). (ENG.). 32p. (J). (gr. -1-2). pap. 9.99 *(978-1-5324-0224-1(4))* Xist Publishing.

—Kat Goes. Ponnay, Brenda. 2019. (Kat Can Readers Ser.). (ENG.). 8p. (J). (gr. -1-2). pap. 5.99 *(978-1-5324-1123-6(5))* Xist Publishing.

—Kat Likes. Ponnay, Brenda. 2019. (Kat Can Readers Ser.). (ENG.). 8p. (J). (gr. -1-2). pap. 5.99 *(978-1-5324-1112-0(X))* Xist Publishing.

—Kat Makes. Ponnay, Brenda. 2019. (Kat Can Readers Ser.). (ENG.). 8p. (J). (gr. -1-2). pap. 5.99 *(978-1-5324-1114-4(6))* Xist Publishing.

—Kat Reads. Ponnay, Brenda. 2019. (Kat Can Readers Ser.). (ENG.). 8p. (J). (gr. -1-2). pap. 5.99 *(978-1-5324-1331-5(9))* Xist Publishing.

—Kat Wears. Ponnay, Brenda. 2019. (Kat Can Readers Ser.). (ENG.). 8p. (J). (gr. -1-2). pap. 5.99 *(978-1-5324-0945-5(1))* Xist Publishing.

—Knock Knock, Blub Blub! Fishy Underwater Jokes. Ponnay, Brenda. 2020. (Illustrated Jokes Ser.). (ENG.). 28p. (J). (gr. -1-5). 12.99 *(978-1-5324-1563-0(X))*; pap. 12.99 *(978-1-5324-1544-9(3))* Xist Publishing.

—Knock Knock Boo Who? Ponnay, Brenda. 2017. (Illustrated Jokes Ser.). (ENG.). 32p. (J). (gr. -1-3). pap. 9.99 *(978-1-5324-0226-5(0))* Xist Publishing.

—Knock Knock, Lettuce In! And Other Funny Vegetable Jokes. Ponnay, Brenda. 2019. (Illustrated Jokes Ser.). (ENG.). 26p. (J). (gr. k-6). pap. 9.99 *(978-1-5324-1213-4(4))* Xist Publishing.

—Little Hoo Gets the Wiggles Out. Ponnay, Brenda. 2019. (Little Hoo Ser.). (ENG.). 32p. (J). (gr. -1-2). 9.99 *(978-1-5324-1327-8(0))*; pap. 18.99 *(978-1-5324-1326-1(2))* Xist Publishing.

—Little Hoo Gets the Wiggles Out / Buhito Saca Sus Brios. Ponnay, Brenda. 2020. (Little Hoo Ser.). (ENG.). 32p. (J). (gr. k-1). pap. 12.99 *(978-1-5324-1351-3(3))* Xist Publishing.

—Little Hoo Gets the Wiggles Out / Buhito Saca Sus Bríos. Ponnay, Brenda. 2020. (Little Hoo Ser.). (ENG.). 32p. (J). (gr. k-1). 12.99 *(978-1-5324-1352-0(1))* Xist Publishing.

—Little Hoo Goes Camping. Ponnay, Brenda. 2020. (Little Hoo Ser.). (ENG.). 32p. (J). (gr. k-2). 12.99 *(978-1-5324-1555-5(9))*; pap. 12.99 *(978-1-5324-1554-8(0))* Xist Publishing.

—Little Hoo Goes to School. Ponnay, Brenda. 2018. (Little Hoo Ser.). (ENG.). 32p. (J). (gr. -1-2). 9.99 *(978-1-5324-0934-9(6))*; pap. 9.99 *(978-1-5324-0904-2(4))* Xist Publishing.

—Little Hoo Goes to School / el Pequeño Búho Va a la Escuela. Ponnay, Brenda. 2018. (Xist Kids Bilingual Spanish Ser.). (ENG & SPA.). 32p. (J). (gr. -1-k). pap. 9.99 *(978-1-5324-1055-0(7))* Xist Publishing.

—Little Hoo Goes to School / el Pequeño Búho Va a la Escuela. Ponnay, Brenda. Sandoval, Lenny, tr. 2018. (Little Hoo Ser.). (SPA.). 32p. (J). (gr. -1-k). 9.99 *(978-1-5324-1056-7(5))* Xist Publishing.

—Little Hoo Goes to the Beach. Ponnay, Brenda. 2015. (ENG.). 26p. (J). (gr. k-1). 18.99 *(978-1-5324-1058-1(1))* Xist Publishing.

—Little Hoo Has the Flu. Ponnay, Brenda. 2019. (Little Hoo Ser.). (ENG.). 32p. (J). (gr. -1-2). 9.99 *(978-1-5324-1105-2(7))*; pap. 9.99 *(978-1-5324-0940-0(0))* Xist Publishing.

—Little Hoo Has the Flu / el Pequeño Búho Tiene Gripe. Ponnay, Brenda. 2019. (Little Hoo Ser.). 32p. (J). (gr. -1-2). (ENG.). 9.99 *(978-1-5324-1142-7(1))*; pap. 9.99 *(978-1-5324-1141-0(3))* Xist Publishing.

—Merry Christmas, Little Hoo! Ponnay, Brenda. 2014. (ENG.). 34p. (J). (gr. k-1). 18.99 *(978-1-5324-1059-8(X))* Xist Publishing.

—Merry Christmas, Little Hoo! / Feliz Navidad Buhito. Ponnay, Brenda. Sandoval, Lenny, tr. 2017. (ENG.). (J). 34p. 18.99 *(978-1-5324-1089-5(1))*; 32p. (gr. -1-3). pap. 9.99 *(978-1-5324-0347-7(X))* Xist Publishing.

—Nat Can Code. Ponnay, Brenda. 2020. (Nat Can Readers Ser.). (ENG.). 8p. (J). (gr. k-1). pap. 5.99 *(978-1-5324-1552-4(4))* Xist Publishing.

—Nat Plays Baseball. Ponnay, Brenda. 2020. (Nat Can Readers Ser.). (ENG.). 8p. (J). (gr. k-1). pap. 5.99 *(978-1-5324-1550-0(8))* Xist Publishing.

—Números Secretos Espías de la Agente Secreta Josephine. Ponnay, Brenda. 2017. (Xist Kids Spanish Bks.). (SPA.). 32p. (J). (gr. -1-3). pap. 9.99 *(978-1-5324-0419-1(0))* Xist Publishing.

—El Pequeño Búho Tiene Gripe. Ponnay, Brenda. 2019. (Little Hoo Ser.). 32p. (J). (gr. -1-2). (ENG.). 9.99 *(978-1-5324-1145-8(6))*; pap. 9.99 *(978-1-5324-1144-1(8))* Xist Publishing.

—El Pequeño Búho Va a la Escuela. Ponnay, Brenda. Sandoval, Lenny, tr. 2018. (Little Hoo Ser.). (SPA.). 32p. (J). (gr. -1-2). 9.99 *(978-1-5324-1108-3(1))* Xist Publishing.

—El Pequeño Búho Va a la Escuela: (Little Hoo Goes to School) Ponnay, Brenda. 2018. (Xist Kids Spanish Bks.). (SPA.). 32p. (J). (gr. -1-2). pap. 9.99 *(978-1-5324-1107-6(3))* Xist Publishing.

—El Pequeño Hoo Va a la Playa. Ponnay, Brenda. 2016. (SPA.). 26p. (J). 18.99 *(978-1-5324-1094-9(8))* Xist Publishing.

—¿quién Está Ahí, Pequeño Hoo? Ponnay, Brenda. 2016. (SPA.). 24p. (J). 18.99 *(978-1-5324-1092-5(1))* Xist Publishing.

—¿quién Viene a Cenar, Pequeño Hoo? Ponnay, Brenda. 2016. (SPA.). 28p. (J). 18.99 *(978-1-5324-1093-2(X))* Xist Publishing.

—Secret Agent Josephine in Paris. Ponnay, Brenda. 2013. (ENG.). 32p. (J). (gr. -1-2). pap. 19.99 *(978-1-62395-524-3(6))* Xist Publishing.

—Secret Agent Josephine's Secret Spy Numbers (Números Secretos Espías de la Agente Secreta Josephine) Ponnay, Brenda. Sandoval, Lenny, tr. 2017. (Xist Kids Bilingual Spanish English Ser.). (ENG & SPA.). 32p. (J). (gr. -1-3). pap. 9.99 *(978-1-5324-0349-1(6))* Xist Publishing.

—Time for Bed, Bunny (¡Hora de Dormir, Conejito!) Ponnay, Brenda. 2018. (Xist Kids Bilingual Spanish English Ser.). (ENG & SPA.). 32p. (J). (gr. -1-3). pap. 9.99 *(978-1-5324-0691-1(6))* Xist Publishing.

—Time to Eat, Bunny! Ponnay, Brenda. 2013. (Time for Bunny Ser.). (ENG.). 28p. (J). (gr. -1-k). pap. 9.99 *(978-1-62395-090-3(2))* Xist Publishing.

—Time to Eat, Bunny! / Hora de Comer, Conejito. Ponnay, Brenda. Sandoval, Lenny, tr. 2017. (Xist Kids Bilingual Spanish English Ser.). (ENG & SPA.). 32p. (J). (gr. -1-3). pap. 9.99 *(978-1-5324-0355-2(0))* Xist Publishing.

—Time to Get Ready, Bunny! Ponnay, Brenda. 2013. (Time for Bunny Ser.). (ENG.). 24p. (J). (gr. -1-k). pap. 9.99 *(978-0-9838428-6-6(8))* Xist Publishing.

—Time to Get Ready, Bunny! / Es la Hora de Alistarse, Conejito. Ponnay, Brenda. Sandoval, Lenny, tr. 2017. (Xist Kids Bilingual Spanish English Ser.). (ENG & SPA.). 32p. (J). (gr. -1-3). pap. 9.99 *(978-1-5324-0357-6(7))* Xist Publishing.

—Who's Coming for Dinner, Little Hoo? Ponnay, Brenda. 2014. (ENG.). 30p. (J). (gr. k-1). 18.99 *(978-1-5324-1060-4(3))* Xist Publishing.

—Who's There, Little Hoo? Ponnay, Brenda. 2013. (ENG.). 26p. (J). (gr. k-1). 18.99 *(978-1-5324-1061-1(1))* Xist Publishing.

Pons, Adela. Autumn Babies. Galbraith, Kathryn O. 2018. (Babies in the Park Ser.). (ENG.). 20p. (J). (gr. -1-1). bds. 6.95 *(978-1-68263-066-2(8))* Peachtree Publishing Co. Inc.

—Spring Babies. Galbraith, Kathryn O. 2019. (Babies in the Park Ser.). (ENG.). 20p. (J). (gr. -1-1). bds. 6.95 *(978-1-68263-068-6(4))* Peachtree Publishing Co. Inc.

—Summer Babies, 1 vol. Galbraith, Kathryn O. 2019. (Babies in the Park Ser.). (ENG.). 20p. (J). (gr. -1-1). bds. 6.95 *(978-1-68263-069-3(2))* Peachtree Publishing Co. Inc.

—Winter Babies. Galbraith, Kathryn O. 2018. (Babies in the Park Ser.). (ENG.). 20p. (J). (gr. -1-1). bds. 6.95 *(978-1-68263-067-9(6))* Peachtree Publishing Co. Inc.

Pons, Bernadette. I Love You, Good Night: Lap Edition. Buller, Jon & Schade, Susan. 2013. (ENG.). 28p. (J). (gr. -1 — 1). bds. 12.99 *(978-1-4424-8539-6(6))*, Little Simon) Little Simon.

—Scrubba Dub. Van Laan, Nancy. 2008. (ENG.). 32p. (J). (gr. -1-1). 8.99 *(978-1-4169-7859-6(3))*, Simon & Schuster/Paula Wiseman Bks.) Simon & Schuster/Paula Wiseman Bks.

Ponsor, Justin, jt. illus. see Bianchi, Simone.

Pont, Charles E. Fun with String: A Collection of String Games, Useful Braiding & Weaving, Knot Work & Magic with String & Rope. Leeming, Joseph. 2011. (Dover Children's Activity Bks.). (ENG.). 192p. (J). (gr. 3-8). reprint ed. pap. 12.95 *(978-0-486-23063-4(5))* Dover Pubns., Inc.

Ponte, June. Nifty Thrifty Art Crafts. Miller, Heather. 2007. (Nifty Thrifty Crafts for Kids Ser.). 32p. (gr. 3-3). lib. bdg. 24.94 *(978-0-7660-2780-0(5))*, Enslow Elementary) Enslow Publishing, LLC.

—Nifty Thrifty Sports Crafts. Hollow, Michele C. 2007. (Nifty Thrifty Crafts for Kids Ser.). 32p. (gr. 3-3). lib. bdg. 24.94 *(978-0-7660-2782-4(1))*, Enslow Elementary) Enslow Publishing, LLC.

Ponti, Claude. Pockety: The Tortoise Who Lived As She Pleased. Seyvos, Florence. Provata-Carlone, Mika, tr. 2014. (ENG.). 64p. (J). (gr. 2-4). pap. 9.99 *(978-1-78269-025-2(5))*, Pushkin Children's Bks.) Steerforth Pr.

Ponti, Claude. El Arbol Sin Fin. Ponti, Claude. 2006. (SPA.). 44p. (J). *(978-84-8470-231-3(6))* Corimbo, Editorial S.L.

—Chick & Chickie Play All Day!, 1 vol. Ponti, Claude. 2013. (Toon Bks.). (ENG.). 36p. (J). (gr. -1-1). lib. bdg. 29.93 *(978-1-61479-150-8(3))*, 14842) Spotlight.

—DeZert Isle. Ponti, Claude. Holliday, Mary Martin, tr. 2003. (ENG.). 64p. (J). 16.95 *(978-1-56792-237-0(6))* Godine, David R. Pub.

—Hiznobyuti. Ponti, Claude. Waters, Alyson, tr. 2018. (ENG.). 35p. (J). (gr. k-4). 18.00 *(978-0-914671-90-9(1))*, Elsewhere Editions) Steerforth Pr.

—My Valley. Ponti, Claude. Waters, Alyson, tr. 2017. (ENG.). 42p. (J). (gr. k-4). 24.00 *(978-0-914671-62-6(6))*, Elsewhere Editions) Steerforth Pr.

Ponzio, Jean-Michel. Civilisation, 2 vols. Marazano, Richard. 2010. (Chimpanzee Complex Ser.: 3). (ENG.). 55p. pap. 13.95 *(978-1-84918-043-6(1))* CineBook GBR. Dist: National Bk. Network.

—The Sons of Ares, 2 vols. Marazano, Richard. (Chimpanzee Complex Ser.: 2). (ENG.). 2010. 55p. pap. 13.95 *(978-1-84918-015-3(6))*; 2009. 56p. pap. 13.95 *(978-1-84918-002-3(4))* CineBook GBR. Dist: National Bk. Network.

Pool, Cathy. Second Chance: A Tale of Two Puppies, 1 vol. Masrud, Judy. 2006. 81p. (J). (gr. 1-7). per. 9.95 *(978-0-9774142-0-8(5))*, Birdseed Books for Kids) Birdseed Bks.

Pool, Joyce Oudkerk, photos by. Delicious Dips. Morgan, Diane. 2004. (ENG., 124p. (gr. 8-17). 16.95 *(978-0-8118-4220-4(7))* Chronicle Bks. LLC.

Poole, Helen. ABC Hanukkah Hunt. Balsley, Tilda. ed. 2013. (ENG.). 32p. (J). (gr. -1-2). E-Book 27.99 *(978-1-4677-1637-6(5))*; Vol. 7.95 *(978-1-4677-0421-2(0))*, 9781467704212) Lerner Publishing Group. (Kar-Ben Publishing).

—ABC Passover Hunt. Balsley, Tilda. 2016. (ENG.). 32p. (J). (gr. -1-3). 9.99 *(978-1-4677-7843-5(5))*, 1401803, Kar-Ben Publishing) Lerner Publishing Group.

—Are You Scared, Jacob? Lap Book. Daniel, Claire. 2014. (MySELF Ser.). (J). (gr. -1-k). 27.00 *(978-1-4788-0501-4(3))* Newmark Learning LLC.

—At the Market. Koons, Linda. 2015. (Early Rising Readers Ser.). (J). (gr. -1-k). 5.83 *(978-1-4788-1582-2(5))* Newmark Learning LLC.

—The Birdhouse That Jack Built. Greve, Meg. 2012. (Little Birdie Bks.). (ENG.). 24p. (gr. k-1). pap. 8.95 *(978-1-61810-300-0(8))*, 9781618103000) Rourke Educational Media.

—¡Corre, Ratón, Corre! Canetti, Yanitzia. 2017. (Rising Readers Ser.). (SPA.). (J). (gr. k). 5.83 *(978-1-4788-2720-7(3))* Newmark Learning LLC.

—The Day I Felt Sad. Garcia, Ellen. 2014. (J). (gr. -1). 3.99 *(978-1-4788-0461-1(0))* Newmark Learning LLC.

—The Day I Felt Sad Lap Book. Garcia, Ellen. 2014. (MySELF Ser.). (J). (gr. -1-k). 27.00 *(978-1-4788-0498-7(X))* Newmark Learning LLC.

—El día Que Me Sentí Triste. Smith, Molly. 2015. (MySELF Ser.). (SPA.). (J). (gr. -1-k). 4.49 *(978-1-4788-1960-8(X))* Newmark Learning LLC.

—El día Que Me Sentí Triste: Lap Book. Smith, Molly. 2015. (MySELF Ser.). (SPA.). (J). (gr. -1-k). 29.00 *(978-1-4788-2305-6(4))* Newmark Learning LLC.

—Don't Worry, Mason. Smith, Molly. 2014. (J). (gr. -1). 3.99 *(978-1-4788-0463-5(7))* Newmark Learning LLC.

—Don't Worry, Mason Lap Book. Smith, Molly. 2014. (MySELF Ser.). (J). (gr. -1-k). 27.00 *(978-1-4788-0500-7(5))* Newmark Learning LLC.

—En el Mercado. Koons, Linda. 2016. (Early Rising Readers Ser.). (SPA.). (J). (gr. -1). 6.67 *(978-1-4788-3663-6(6))* Newmark Learning LLC.

—Humpty Dumpty. Greve, Meg. 2012. (Little Birdie Bks.). (ENG.). 24p. (gr. 1-2). pap. 8.95 *(978-1-61810-313-0(X))*, 9781618103130) Rourke Educational Media.

—I Am Growing. Koons, Linda. 2015. (Early Rising Readers Ser.). (J). (gr. -1-k). 5.83 *(978-1-4788-1678-2(3))* Newmark Learning LLC.

—I Was So Mad. Giachetti, Julia. 2014. (J). (gr. -1). 3.99 *(978-1-4788-0462-8(9))* Newmark Learning LLC.

—I Was So Mad Lap Book. Giachetti, Julia. 2014. (MySELF Ser.). (J). (gr. -1-k). 27.00 *(978-1-4788-0499-4(8))* Newmark Learning LLC.

—Itsy Bitsy Spider. Hord, Colleen. 2012. (Little Birdie Bks.). (ENG.). 24p. (gr. 1-2). pap. 8.95 *(978-1-61810-310-9(5))*, 9781618103109) Rourke Educational Media.

—Jealous of Josie. Linde, Barbara M. 2014. (J). (gr. -1). 3.99 *(978-1-4788-0465-9(3))* Newmark Learning LLC.

—Jealous of Josie Lap Book. Linde, Barbara M. 2014. (MySELF Ser.). (J). (gr. -1-k). 27.00 *(978-1-4788-0502-1(1))* Newmark Learning LLC.

—Let's Get Pizza. Greve, Meg. 2012. (Little Birdie Bks.). (ENG.). 24p. (gr. k-1). pap. 8.95 *(978-1-61810-306-2(7))*, 9781618103062); lib. bdg. 29.93 *(978-1-61810-173-0(0))*, 9781618101730) Rourke Educational Media.

—Llamame J. T.! Koons, Linda. 2016. (Early Rising Readers Ser.). (SPA.). 16p. (J). (gr. 1-1). 29.00 *(978-1-4788-3892-0(2))* Newmark Learning LLC.

—Mi día Feliz. Giachetti, Julia. 2015. (MySELF Ser.). (SPA.). (J). (gr. -1-k). 4.49 *(978-1-4788-1959-2(6))* Newmark Learning LLC.

—Mi día Feliz: Lap Book. Giachetti, Julia. 2015. (MySELF Ser.). (SPA.). (J). (gr. -1-k). 29.00 *(978-1-4788-2304-9(6))* Newmark Learning LLC.

—Mi Ensalada. Schmauss, Judy Kentor. 2016. (Early Rising Readers Ser.). (SPA.). 16p. (J). (gr. 1-1). 6.67 *(978-1-4788-3755-8(1))* Newmark Learning LLC.

—Mud Pie Queen. Greve, Meg. 2012. (Little Birdie Bks.). (ENG.). 24p. (gr. k-1). lib. bdg. 29.93 *(978-1-61810-170-9(6))*, 9781618101709) Rourke Educational Media.

—My Happy Day. Giachetti, Julia. 2014. (J). (gr. -1). 3.99 *(978-1-4788-0460-4(2))* Newmark Learning LLC.

—My Happy Day Lap Book. Giachetti, Julia. 2014. (MySELF Ser.). (J). (gr. -1-k). 27.00 *(978-1-4788-0497-0(1))* Newmark Learning LLC.

—My Jolly Red Santa Activity & Sticker Book. Bloomsbury USA. 2015. (ENG.). 32p. (J). (gr. -1-3). pap. 4.99 *(978-1-61963-791-7(X))*, 900148770, Bloomsbury Activity Bks.) Bloomsbury Publishing USA.

—Night-Night Alabama. Sully, Katherine. 2017. (ENG.). 20p. (J). (-1). bds. 9.99 *(978-1-4926-5474-2(4))*, Sourcebooks Jabberwocky) Sourcebooks, Inc.

—Night-Night America. Sully, Katherine. 2017. (Night-Night Ser.). (ENG.). 20p. (J). (-1). bds. 9.99 *(978-1-4926-5019-5(6))*, 9781492650195, Sourcebooks Jabberwocky) Sourcebooks, Inc.

—Night-Night Arizona. Sully, Katherine. 2017. (ENG.). 20p. (J). (-1). bds. 9.99 *(978-1-4926-4771-3(3))*, 9781492647713, Sourcebooks Jabberwocky) Sourcebooks, Inc.

—Night-Night Arkansas. Sully, Katherine. 2017. (ENG.). 20p. (J). (-1). bds. 9.99 *(978-1-4926-5483-4(3))*, Sourcebooks Jabberwocky) Sourcebooks, Inc.

—Night-Night Buffalo. Sully, Katherine. 2017. (Night-Night Ser.). (ENG.). 20p. (J). (-1). bds. 9.99 *(978-1-4926-5492-6(2))*, Sourcebooks Jabberwocky) Sourcebooks, Inc.

—Night-Night Calgary. Sully, Katherine. 2018. (ENG.). 20p. (J). (-1). bds. 9.99 *(978-1-4926-5509-1(0))*, Sourcebooks Jabberwocky) Sourcebooks, Inc.

—Night-Night Canada. Sully, Katherine. 2017. (Night-Night Ser.). (ENG.). 20p. (J). (-1). bds. 9.99 *(978-1-4926-4769-0(1))*, 9781492647690, Sourcebooks Jabberwocky) Sourcebooks, Inc.

—Night-Night Delaware. Sully, Katherine. 2017. (ENG.). 20p. (J). (-1). bds. 9.99 *(978-1-4926-5488-9(4))*, Sourcebooks Jabberwocky) Sourcebooks, Inc.

—Night-Night Idaho. Sully, Katherine. 2017. (ENG.). 20p. (J). (-1). bds. 9.99 *(978-1-4926-5487-2(6))*, Sourcebooks Jabberwocky) Sourcebooks, Inc.

—Night-Night Illinois. Sully, Katherine. 2017. (ENG.). 20p. (J). (-1). bds. 9.99 *(978-1-4926-5472-8(8))*, Sourcebooks Jabberwocky) Sourcebooks, Inc.

—Night-Night Indiana. Sully, Katherine. 2017. (Night-Night Ser.). (ENG.). 20p. (J). (-1). bds. 9.99 *(978-1-4926-4781-2(0))*, 9781492647812, Sourcebooks Jabberwocky) Sourcebooks, Inc.

—Night-Night Iowa. Sully, Katherine. 2017. (Night-Night Ser.). (ENG.). 20p. (J). (-1). bds. 9.99 *(978-1-4926-4770-6(5))*, 9781492647706, Sourcebooks Jabberwocky) Sourcebooks, Inc.

—Night-Night Kansas City. Sully, Katherine. 2017. (ENG.). 20p. (J). (-1). bds. 9.99 *(978-1-4926-5490-2(6))*, Sourcebooks Jabberwocky) Sourcebooks, Inc.

—Night-Night Kentucky. Sully, Katherine. 2017. (ENG.). 20p. (J). (-1). bds. 9.99 *(978-1-4926-4776-8(4))*, 9781492647768, Sourcebooks Jabberwocky) Sourcebooks, Inc.

—Night-Night Los Angeles. Sully, Katherine. 2017. (ENG.). 20p. (J). (-1). bds. 9.99 *(978-1-4926-5491-9(4))*, Sourcebooks Jabberwocky) Sourcebooks, Inc.

—Night-Night Louisiana. Sully, Katherine. 2017. (ENG.). 20p. (J). (-1). bds. 9.99 *(978-1-4926-5471-1(X))*, Sourcebooks Jabberwocky) Sourcebooks, Inc.

—Night-Night Maryland. Sully, Katherine. 2017. (Night-Night Ser.). (ENG.). 20p. (J). (-1). bds. 9.99 *(978-1-4926-4768-3(3))*, 9781492647683, Sourcebooks Jabberwocky) Sourcebooks, Inc.

—Night-Night Massachusetts. Sully, Katherine. 2017. (ENG.). 20p. (J). (-1). bds. 9.99 *(978-1-4926-5485-8(X))*, Sourcebooks Jabberwocky) Sourcebooks, Inc.

—Night-Night Mississippi. Sully, Katherine. 2017. (ENG.). 20p. (J). (-1). bds. 9.99 *(978-1-4926-5477-3(9))*, Sourcebooks Jabberwocky) Sourcebooks, Inc.

—Night-Night Missouri. Sully, Katherine. 2017. (ENG.). 20p. (J). (-1). bds. 9.99 *(978-1-4926-4780-5(2))*, 9781492647805, Sourcebooks Jabberwocky) Sourcebooks, Inc.

—Night-Night Montana. Sully, Katherine. 2017. (ENG.). 20p. (J). (-1). bds. 9.99 *(978-1-4926-5486-5(8))*, Sourcebooks Jabberwocky) Sourcebooks, Inc.

—Night-Night Nebraska. Sully, Katherine. 2017. (ENG.). 20p. (J). (-1). bds. 9.99 *(978-1-4926-5482-7(5))*, Sourcebooks Jabberwocky) Sourcebooks, Inc.

—Night-Night New England. Sully, Katherine. 2017. (ENG.). 20p. (J). (-1). bds. 9.99 *(978-1-4926-4772-0(1))*, 9781492647720, Sourcebooks Jabberwocky) Sourcebooks, Inc.

—Night-Night New York. Sully, Katherine. 2017. (Night-Night Ser.). (ENG.). 20p. (J). (-1). bds. 9.99 *(978-1-4926-5318-9(7))*, Sourcebooks Jabberwocky) Sourcebooks, Inc.

—Night-Night North Carolina. Sully, Katherine. 2017. (Night-Night Ser.). (ENG.). 20p. (J). (-1). bds. 9.99 *(978-1-4926-4778-2(0))*, 9781492647782, Sourcebooks Jabberwocky) Sourcebooks, Inc.

—Night-Night North Dakota. Sully, Katherine. 2017. (ENG.). 20p. (J). (-1). bds. 9.99 *(978-1-4926-5478-0(7))*, Sourcebooks Jabberwocky) Sourcebooks, Inc.

—Night-Night Oklahoma. Sully, Katherine. 2017. (Night-Night Ser.). (ENG.). 20p. (J). (-1). bds. 9.99 *(978-1-4926-5473-5(6))*, Sourcebooks Jabberwocky) Sourcebooks, Inc.

—Night-Night Oregon. Sully, Katherine. 2017. (ENG.). 20p. (J). (-1). bds. 9.99 *(978-1-4926-5484-1(1))*, Sourcebooks Jabberwocky) Sourcebooks, Inc.

—Night-Night Philadelphia. Sully, Katherine. 2017. (ENG.). 20p. (J). (-1). bds. 9.99 *(978-1-4926-4774-4(8))*, 9781492647744, Sourcebooks Jabberwocky) Sourcebooks, Inc.

—Night-Night Pittsburgh. Sully, Katherine. 2017. (Night-Night Ser.). (ENG.). 20p. (J). (-1). bds. 9.99 *(978-1-4926-5479-7(5))*, Sourcebooks Jabberwocky) Sourcebooks, Inc.

—Night-Night San Francisco. Sully, Katherine. 2017. (ENG.). 20p. (J). (-1). bds. 9.99 *(978-1-4926-4765-2(9))*, 9781492647652, Sourcebooks Jabberwocky) Sourcebooks, Inc.

—Night-Night South Carolina. Sully, Katherine. 2017. (ENG.). 20p. (J). (-1). bds. 9.99 *(978-1-4926-4779-9(9))*, 9781492647799, Sourcebooks Jabberwocky) Sourcebooks, Inc.

—Night-Night South Dakota. Sully, Katherine. 2017. (ENG.). 20p. (J). (-1). bds. 9.99 *(978-1-4926-4775-1(6))*,

9781492647751, Sourcebooks Jabberwocky) Sourcebooks, Inc.
—Night-Night St. Louis. Sully, Katherine. 2017. (ENG.). 20p. (J). (-1). bds. 9.99 *(978-1-4926-5480-3(9)*, Sourcebooks Jabberwocky) Sourcebooks, Inc.
—Night-Night Tennessee. Sully, Katherine. 2017. (Night-Night Ser.). (ENG.). 20p. (J). (-1). bds. 9.99 *(978-1-4926-4777-5(2)*, 9781492647775, Sourcebooks Jabberwocky) Sourcebooks, Inc.
—Night-Night Toronto. Sully, Katherine. 2017. (ENG.). 20p. (J). (-1). bds. 9.99 *(978-1-4926-5493-3(0)*, Sourcebooks Jabberwocky) Sourcebooks, Inc.
—Night-Night Utah. Sully, Katherine. 2017. (ENG.). 20p. (J). (-1). bds. 9.99 *(978-1-4926-5476-6(0)*, Sourcebooks Jabberwocky) Sourcebooks, Inc.
—Night-Night Vancouver. Sully, Katherine. 2017. (ENG.). 20p. (J). (-1). bds. 9.99 *(978-1-4926-5494-0(9)*, Sourcebooks Jabberwocky) Sourcebooks, Inc.
—Night-Night Virginia. Sully, Katherine. 2017. (ENG.). 20p. (J). (-1). bds. 9.99 *(978-1-4926-4767-6(5)*, 9781492647676, Sourcebooks Jabberwocky) Sourcebooks, Inc.
—Night-Night Washington. Sully, Katherine. 2017. (Night-Night Ser.). (ENG.). 20p. (J). (-1). bds. 9.99 *(978-1-4926-4766-9(7)*, 9781492647669, Sourcebooks Jabberwocky) Sourcebooks, Inc.
—Night-Night Washington, D. C. Sully, Katherine. 2017. (ENG.). 20p. (J). (-1). bds. 9.99 *(978-1-4926-4773-7(X)*, 9781492647737, Sourcebooks Jabberwocky) Sourcebooks, Inc.
—Night-Night West Virginia. Sully, Katherine. 2017. (ENG.). 20p. (J). (-1). bds. 9.99 *(978-1-4926-5475-9(2)*, Sourcebooks Jabberwocky) Sourcebooks, Inc.
—Night-Night Wyoming. Sully, Katherine. 2017. (ENG.). 20p. (J). (-1). bds. 9.99 *(978-1-4926-5489-6(2)*, Sourcebooks Jabberwocky) Sourcebooks, Inc.
—No Te Preocupes, Mateo. Smith, Molly. 2015. (MySELF Ser.). (SPA.). (J). (gr. -1-k). 4.49 *(978-1-4788-1962-2(6))* Newmark Learning LLC.
—No Te Preocupes, Mateo: Lap Book. Smith, Molly. 2015. (MySELF Ser.). (SPA.). (J). (gr. -1-k). 29.00 *(978-1-4788-2307-0(0))* Newmark Learning LLC.
—Nosotros Tenemos una Bebita. Nunez, Jaclyn. 2016. (Early Rising Readers Ser.). (SPA.). 16p. (J). (gr. 1-1). 6.67 *(978-1-4788-3768-8(3))* Newmark Learning LLC.
—Oh Brodie! Set Of 6. Parkes, Brenda. 2014. (Shared Reading Foundations Ser.). (J). (gr. 1). 36.00 net. *(978-1-4900-0034-3(8))* Benchmark Education Co.
—OH BRODIE! Book Set. Parkes, Brenda. 2014. (Shared Reading Foundations Ser.). (J). (gr. 1). 72.00 net. *(978-1-4900-0004-6(6))* Benchmark Education Co.
—Puddle Pen Christmas, 1 vol. David, Juliet. 2010. (Candle Puddle Pen Ser.). 10p. (J). (gr. -1-k). bds. 12.99 *(978-1-85985-868-4(6)*, Candle Bks.) Lion Hudson PLC GBR. Dist: Kregel Pubns.
—Tengo Envidia de Elsa. Linde, Barbara M. 2015. (MySELF Ser.). (SPA.). (J). (gr. -1-k). 4.49 *(978-1-4788-1964-6(2))* Newmark Learning LLC.
—Tengo Envidia de Elsa: Lap Book. Linde, Barbara M. 2015. (MySELF Ser.). (SPA.). (J). (gr. -1-k). 29.00 *(978-1-4788-2309-4(7))* Newmark Learning LLC.
—¿Tienes Miedo, Jacobo? Daniel, Claire. 2015. (MySELF Ser.). (SPA.). (J). (gr. -1-k). 4.49 *(978-1-4788-1963-9(4))* Newmark Learning LLC.
—¿Tienes Miedo, Jacobo? Lap Book. Daniel, Claire. 2015. (MySELF Ser.). (SPA.). (J). (gr. -1-k). 29.00 *(978-1-4788-2308-7(9))* Newmark Learning LLC.
—Who's Mr. Goldfluss? Hord, Colleen. 2012. (Little Birdie Bks.). (ENG.). 24p. (J). (gr. 1-2). pap. 8.95 *(978-1-61810-318-5(0)*, 9781618103185) Rourke Educational Media.
—Yo Estaba Muy Molesta. Pippin, Jessica. 2015. (MySELF Ser.). (SPA.). (J). (gr. -1-k). 4.49 *(978-1-4788-1961-5(8))* Newmark Learning LLC.
—Yo Estaba Muy Molesta: Lap Book. Pippin, Jessica. 2015. (MySELF Ser.). (SPA.). (J). (gr. -1-k). 29.00 *(978-1-4788-2306-3(2))* Newmark Learning LLC.
—Yo Estoy Creciendo. Koons, Linda. 2016. (Early Rising Readers Ser.). (SPA.). 16p. (J). (gr. 1-1). 6.67 *(978-1-4788-3721-3(7))* Newmark Learning LLC.

Poole, Helen & Dunn, Robert. Minnesota Books for Kids Gift Set. Richmond, Marianne et al. 2020. (ENG.). (J). bds. 20.00 ***(978-1-7282-4197-5(9))*** Sourcebooks, Inc.
Poole, Helen, jt. illus. see Dunn, Robert.
Poole, Helen, jt. illus. see Kolanovic, Dubravka.
Poole, Steven R. Simon the Guide Dog. Reid, Christy. 2012. 38p. 24.95 *(978-1-4626-6052-0(5))* America Star Bks.
Poole, Susie. Animal Tales: Stories Old & New Especially for Reading Aloud. Hartman, Bob. 2003. (ENG.). 120p. (J). (gr. k-4). pap. 13.95 *(978-0-7459-4838-6(3))* Lion Hudson PLC GBR. Dist: Independent Pubs. Group.
—Baby Parade. O'Connell, Rebecca. ed. 2017. (ENG.). 24p. (J). (gr. -1 — 1). bds. 7.99 *(978-0-8075-0515-1(3)*, 807505153) Whitman, Albert & Co.
—Baby Party. O'Connell, Rebecca. 2017. (ENG.). 24p. (J). (gr. -1-3). bds. 7.99 *(978-0-8075-0514-4(5)*, 807505145) Whitman, Albert & Co.
—You Are Very Special. Box, Su. 2003. 32p. (J). pap. 6.95 *(978-0-8198-8807-5(9)*, 332-417) Pauline Bks. & Media.
Poole, Susie. A Christmas Journey. Poole, Susie. 2014. (ENG.). 48p. (gr. -1-3). 12.99 *(978-1-4336-8343-5(1)*, 005617204, B&H Kids) B&H Publishing Group.
Poole, Tracy. Pinta & Polly Go to the Moon, 1 vol. Franklin, Cathy. 2009. 27p. pap. 24.95 *(978-1-60813-861-6(5))* America Star Bks.
Pooler, Paige. Autumn's Secret Gift. Allen, Elise & Stanford, Halle. 2014. (Enchanted Sisters Ser.). 128p. (J). (gr. 2-4). pap. 5.99 *(978-1-61963-254-7(3)*, 9781619632547, Bloomsbury USA Childrens) Bloomsbury Publishing USA.
—Autumn's Secret Gift. Allen, Elise & Stanford, Halle. ed. 2014. (Enchanted Sisters Ser.: 1). (J). lib. bdg. 16.00 *(978-0-606-35519-3(7))* Turtleback.
Pooler, Paige. Bark Park (Bark Park Book 1) Dougherty, Brandi. 2020. (Bark Park Ser.). (ENG.). 96p. (J). 12.99 ***(978-1-5248-6042-4(5))*** Andrews McMeel Publishing.
Pooler, Paige. Cleared for Takeoff. DeVillers, Julia. 2012. (Liberty Porter, First Daughter Ser.: 3). (ENG.). 224p. (J). (gr. 3-7). pap. 7.99 *(978-1-4169-9131-1(X)*, Simon & Schuster/Paula Wiseman Bks.) Simon & Schuster/Paula Wiseman Bks.
—Liberty Porter, First Daughter, 1. DeVillers, Julia. 2009. (Liberty Porter, First Daughter Ser.: 1). (ENG.). 176p. (J). (gr. 4-6). 21.19 *(978-1-4169-9126-7(3)*, Aladdin) Simon & Schuster Children's Publishing.
—Liberty Porter, First Daughter. DeVillers, Julia. 2010. (Liberty Porter, First Daughter Ser.: 1). (ENG.). 192p. (J). (gr. 3-7). pap. 7.99 *(978-1-4169-9127-4(1)*, Simon & Schuster/Paula Wiseman Bks.) Simon & Schuster/Paula Wiseman Bks.
—New Girl in Town, 2. DeVillers, Julia. 2011. (Liberty Porter, First Daughter Ser.: 2). (ENG.). 208p. (J). (gr. 3-6). 18.69 *(978-1-4169-9128-1(X))* Simon & Schuster, Inc.
—New Girl in Town. DeVillers, Julia. 2011. (Liberty Porter, First Daughter Ser.: 2). (ENG.). 224p. (J). (gr. 3-7). pap. 7.99 *(978-1-4169-9129-8(8)*, Simon & Schuster/Paula Wiseman Bks.) Simon & Schuster/Paula Wiseman Bks.
Pooler, Paige. Scouting for Clues (Bark Park Book 1) Dougherty, Brandi. 2020. (Bark Park Ser.). (ENG.). 96p. (J). pap. 6.99 ***(978-1-5248-5824-7(2))*** Andrews McMeel Publishing.
Pooler, Paige. Spring's Sparkle Sleepover. Allen, Elise & Stanford, Halle. 2015. (Enchanted Sisters Ser.). 128p. (J). (gr. 2-4). 15.99 *(978-1-61963-296-7(9)*, 9781619632967); pap. 5.99 *(978-1-61963-269-1(1)*, 9781619632691) Bloomsbury Publishing USA. (Bloomsbury USA Childrens).
—Spring's Sparkle Sleepover. Allen, Elise & Stanford, Halle. ed. 2015. (Enchanted Sisters Ser.: 3). (J). lib. bdg. 16.00 *(978-0-606-36218-4(5))* Turtleback.
—Summer's Friendship Games. Allen, Elise & Stanford, Halle. 2015. (Enchanted Sisters Ser.). 128p. (J). (gr. 2-4). 15.99 *(978-1-61963-271-4(3)*, 9781619632714, Bloomsbury USA Childrens) Bloomsbury Publishing USA.
—Winter's Flurry Adventure. Allen, Elise & Stanford, Halle. ed. 2014. (Enchanted Sisters Ser.: 2). (YA). lib. bdg. 16.00 *(978-0-606-36217-7(7))* Turtleback.
Poon, Janice. Claire & the Bakery Thief. Poon, Janice. 2008. 104p. (J). (gr. 2-5). 15.95 *(978-1-55453-286-5(8))*; pap. 7.95 *(978-1-55453-245-2(0))* Kids Can Pr., Ltd. CAN. Dist: Hachette Bk. Group.
—Claire & the Water Wish. Poon, Janice. 2009. 120p. (J). (gr. 2-5). 7.95 *(978-1-55453-382-4(1))*; (gr. 3-6). 22.44 *(978-1-55453-381-7(3))* Kids Can Pr., Ltd. CAN. Dist: Hachette Bk. Group, Children's Plus, Inc.
Poortvliet, Rien. Boris. Haar, Jaap Ter & Mearns, Martha. 2009. (J). pap. *(978-0-921100-72-0(8))* Inheritance Pubns.
Pop Art Properties Staff. Amazing Story of Cell Phone Technology. Enz, Tammy. 2013. (STEM Adventures Ser.). (ENG.). 32p. (J). (gr. 3-9). 31.32 *(978-1-4765-0137-6(8))*; pap. 8.95 *(978-1-4765-3457-2(8))* Capstone. (Capstone Pr.).
—Amazing Story of Space Travel. Biskup, Agnieszka. 2013. (STEM Adventures Ser.). (ENG.). 32p. (J). (gr. 3-9). 31.32 *(978-1-4765-0124-6(6)*, Capstone Pr.) Capstone.
—Amazing Story of the Combustion Engine. Bolte, Mari. 2013. (STEM Adventures Ser.). (ENG.). 32p. (J). (gr. 3-9). 31.32 *(978-1-4765-3103-8(X)*, Capstone Pr.) Capstone.
—Terrific Tale of Television Technology. Enz, Tammy. 2013. (STEM Adventures Ser.). (ENG.). 32p. (J). (gr. 3-9). 31.32 *(978-1-4765-0138-3(6))*; pap. 8.95 *(978-1-4765-3458-9(6))* Capstone. (Capstone Pr.).
Pop Art Studios. Engineering a Totally Rad Skateboard with Max Axiom, Super Scientist, 1 vol. Enz, Tammy. 2013. (Graphic Science & Engineering in Action Ser.). (ENG.). 32p. (J). (gr. 3-9). pap. 8.10 *(978-1-62065-703-4(1)*, Capstone Pr.) Capstone.
Pop Art Studios Staff. Engineering a Totally Rad Skateboard with Max Axiom, Super Scientist, 1 vol. Enz, Tammy. 2013. (Graphic Science & Engineering in Action Ser.). (ENG.). 32p. (J). (gr. 3-9). lib. bdg. 31.32 *(978-1-4296-9935-8(3)*, Capstone Pr.) Capstone.
—Engineering an Awesome Recycling Center with Max Axiom, Super Scientist, 1 vol. Bethea, Nikole Brooks. 2013. (Graphic Science & Engineering in Action Ser.). (ENG.). 32p. (J). (gr. 3-9). pap. 8.10 *(978-1-62065-699-0(X))*; lib. bdg. 31.32 *(978-1-4296-9934-1(5))* Capstone. (Capstone Pr.).
Popcak, Jacob. Paul & His Friends. Hutto, Rebekah McLeod. 2018. (ENG.). 32p. (J). (gr. -1-2). pap. 15.99 *(978-1-61261-945-3(2))* Paraclete Pr., Inc.
Popcak, Jacob H. Penny Penguin Finds Her Way Home. Damiani, Philip J. 2018. (ENG.). 42p. (J). (gr. k-3). 17.99 *(978-0-9980258-0-3(1))* Philip J. Damiani.
Pope, Kate, jt. illus. see Pope, Liz.
Pope, Kevin. The Exploding Toilet: Modern Urban Legends. 2005. (ENG.). 112p. (J). (gr. -1-9). pap. 7.95 *(978-0-87483-715-5(4)*, 1231866) August Hse. Pubs., Inc.
—Scared Witless: Thirteen Eerie Tales to Tell. Hamilton, Martha & Weise, Mutch. 2015. (ENG.). 64p. (J). (gr. 3-6). pap. 8.95 *(978-1-939160-95-9(2))* August Hse. Pubs., Inc.
Pope, Lauren, jt. illus. see Huber, Becca.
Pope, Liz & Pope, Kate. If I Were a... Ballerina. Hegarty, Pat. 2008. (If I Were A Ser.). 10p. (J). (gr. -1-k). bds. 6.95 *(978-1-58925-834-1(7))* Tiger Tales.
—If I Were a... Firefighter. Hegarty, Pat. 2008. 12p. (J). (gr. -1). bds. 6.95 *(978-1-58925-839-6(8))* Tiger Tales.
—If I Were a... Princess. Hegarty, Pat. 2008. 12p. (J). (gr. -1). bds. 6.95 *(978-1-58925-838-9(X))* Tiger Tales.
—If I Were a... Soccer Star. Hegarty, Pat. 2008. (If I Were A Ser.). 10p. (J). (gr. -1-k). bds. 6.95 *(978-1-58925-835-8(5))* Tiger Tales.
Pope, Liz and Kate. Make & Play Farm Animals. Channing, Margot. ed. 2018. 12p. (J). (gr. -1-k). bds. 8.95 *(978-1-912233-97-7(5)*, Scribblers) Book Hse. GBR. Dist: Sterling Publishing Co., Inc.
Pope, Patricia, jt. illus. see McInturff, Linda.
Pope, Paul. Battling Boy. Pope, Paul. 2013. (Battling Boy Ser.: 1). (ENG.). 208p. (J). (gr. 5-12). pap. 16.99 *(978-1-59643-145-4(8)*, 900034672, First Second Bks.) Roaring Brook Pr.
Pope, Richie. American Graphic. Biskup, Agnieszka & Collins, Terry. 2012. (American Graphic Ser.). (ENG.). 32p. (gr. 3-4). pap. 572.40 *(978-1-4296-9339-4(8))*; (J). pap., pap., pap. 81.00 *(978-1-4296-9338-7(X))* Capstone. (Capstone Pr.).
—Louis Armstrong: Jazz Legend, 1 vol. Collins, Terry. 2012. (American Graphic Ser.). (ENG.). 32p. (gr. 3-9). (J). pap. 8.10 *(978-1-4296-9336-3(3))*; pap. 47.70 *(978-1-4296-9337-0(1))*; (J). lib. bdg. 31.32 *(978-1-4296-8622-8(7))* Capstone. (Capstone Pr.).
Pope, Robert. Christmas Is Here! Schulz, Charles M. 2019. (Peanuts Ser.). (ENG.). 32p. (J). (gr. k-2). 17.99 *(978-1-5344-5056-1(4))*; pap. 4.99 *(978-1-5344-5055-4(6))* Simon Spotlight. (Simon Spotlight).
—Happy Halloween, Charlie Brown! Schulz, Charles M. 2018. (Peanuts Ser.). (ENG.). 16p. (J). (gr. -1-2). 5.99 *(978-1-5344-1641-3(2)*, Simon Spotlight) Simon Spotlight.
—Here Comes the Easter Beagle! Schulz, Charles M. 2018. (Peanuts Ser.). (ENG.). 16p. (J). (gr. -1-2). 5.99 *(978-1-5344-1016-9(3)*, Simon Spotlight) Simon Spotlight.
Pope, Robert. Let's Go to the Library! Schulz, Charles M. 2020. (Peanuts Ser.). (ENG.). 32p. (J). (gr. k-2). 17.99 ***(978-1-5344-6957-0(5))***; pap. 4.99 ***(978-1-5344-6956-3(7))*** Simon Spotlight. (Simon Spotlight).
Pope, Robert. Merry Christmas, Charlie Brown! Schulz, Charles M. 2017. (Peanuts Ser.). (ENG.). 14p. (J). (gr. -1-k). bds. 5.99 *(978-1-5344-0421-2(X)*, Simon Spotlight) Simon Spotlight.
—Nice to Meet You, Franklin! Schulz, Charles M. 2018. (Peanuts Ser.). (ENG.). 24p. (J). (gr. -1-2). pap. 3.99 *(978-1-5344-1702-1(8)*, Simon Spotlight) Simon Spotlight.
—Race for Your Life, Charlie Brown! Schulz, Mark & Cooper, Jason. 2018. (Peanuts Ser.). (ENG.). 96p. (J). (gr. 1-3). pap. 9.99 *(978-1-68415-196-7(1))* Boom! Studios.
—Scooby-Doo in Dead & Let Spy, 1 vol. Simmons, Alex. 2010. (Scooby-Doo Graphic Novels Ser.: No. 1). (ENG.). 24p. (J). (gr. 2-6). 27.07 *(978-1-59961-692-6(0)*, 560, Graphic Novels) Spotlight.
—Scooby-Doo in the Agony of de Feet! Busch, Robbie. 2010. (Scooby-Doo Graphic Novels Ser.: No. 1). (ENG.). 24p. (J). (gr. 2-6). 27.07 *(978-1-59961-690-2(4)*, 558, Graphic Novels) Spotlight.
—Snoopy & Woodstock: Best Friends Forever! Schulz, Charles M. 2018. (Peanuts Ser.). (ENG.). 32p. (J). (gr. k-2). 16.99 *(978-1-5344-0976-7(9))*; pap. 4.99 *(978-1-5344-0975-0(0))* Simon Spotlight. (Simon Spotlight).
—Snoopy, First Beagle on the Moon! Schulz, Charles M. 2019. (Peanuts Ser.). (ENG.). 40p. (J). (gr. k-2). 17.99 *(978-1-5344-4517-8(X))*; pap. 4.99 *(978-1-5344-4516-1(1))* Simon Spotlight. (Simon Spotlight).
Pope, Robert. Snoopy Goes to School. Schulz, Charles M. 2020. (Peanuts Ser.). (ENG.). 24p. (J). (gr. -1-2). pap. 4.99 ***(978-1-5344-6456-8(5)***, Simon Spotlight) Simon Spotlight.
Pope, Robert. Snoopy's Snow Day! Schulz, Charles M. 2019. (Peanuts Ser.). (ENG.). 14p. (J). (gr. -1-2). bds. 6.99 *(978-1-5344-5082-0(3)*, Simon Spotlight) Simon Spotlight.
—You Got a Rock, Charlie Brown! Schulz, Charles. 2015. (Peanuts Ser.). (ENG.). 32p. (J). (gr. k-2). pap. 3.99 *(978-1-4814-3602-1(3)*, Simon Spotlight) Simon Spotlight.
—You Got a Rock, Charlie Brown! Schulz, Charles M. 2017. (Peanuts Ser.). (ENG.). 32p. (J). (gr. k-2). pap. 4.99 *(978-1-5344-0501-1(1)*, Simon Spotlight) Simon Spotlight.
Pope, Robert, jt. illus. see Neely, Scott.
Pope, Robert W. Peanuts Original Graphic Novel: Snoopy: a Beagle of Mars. Schulz, Charles M. & Cooper, Jason. 2020. (Peanuts Ser.). (ENG.). 96p. (J). pap. 9.99 *(978-1-68415-326-8(3))* Boom! Studios.
Popeo, Joanie. Dancing on the Sand: A Story of an Atlantic Blue Crab. Hollenbeck, Kathleen M. (Smithsonian Oceanic Collection). (ENG.). 32p. (J). (gr. -1-2). 2005. per. 6.95 *(978-1-59249-194-0(4)*, S4017); 2004. 15.95 *(978-1-56899-730-8(2)*, B4017) Soundprints.
—Sockeye's Journey Home: The Story of a Pacific Salmon. Winkelman, Barbara Gaines. 2005. (Smithsonian Oceanic Collection: Vol. 19). (ENG.). 32p. (J). (gr. -1-2). 15.95 *(978-1-56899-829-9(5)*, B4019) Soundprints.
—Sockeye's Journey Home: The Story of a Pacific Salmon. Winkelman, Barbara Gaines & Thomas, Peter. 2003. (ENG.). 32p. (J). (gr. -1-3). 9.95 *(978-1-56899-834-3(1)*, PB4069) Soundprints.
Popeson, Pamela. The African Elephant: American Museum of Natural History Book & Diorama. Weiss, Ellen. 2005. 64p. (J). (gr. 4-8). reprint ed. pap. 11.00 *(978-0-7567-8823-0(4))* DIANE Publishing Co.
Popko, Wendy. Hidden Michigan. Lewis, Anne Margaret & Campbell, Janis. 2006. 40p. (J). (gr. 1-4). 12.95 *(978-1-934133-01-9(9)*, Mackinac Island Press, Inc.) Charlesbridge Publishing, Inc.
—How Do I Cure This Cold? Williamson, Greg. 2005. (J). 7.99 *(978-0-9666076-4-2(3))* Peerless Publishing, L.L.C.
—Why Do I Have to Wear Glasses? Williamson, Greg. 2005. (J). 12.99 *(978-0-9666076-5-9(1))* Peerless Publishing, L.L.C.
Popkp, Wendy. Why Do I Have to Wear Glasses? Williamson, Greg. 2005. (J). pap. 7.99 *(978-0-9666076-3-5(5))* Peerless Publishing, L.L.C.
Poplawska, Yolanda. Halifax Harbour 123 (BB) A Counting Book about Halifax Harbour, 1 vol. 2014. (ENG.). 10p. (J). (gr. -1 — 1). bds. 9.95 *(978-1-77108-002-6(7)*, 928654af-a3b3-4571-8c68-1bcf2e162f46) Nimbus Publishing, Ltd. CAN. Dist: Baker & Taylor Publisher Services (BTPS).
Popov, Nikolai. Amazonia: Indigenous Tales from Brazil, 1 vol. Springer, Jane, tr. 2013. (ENG.). 96p. (J). (gr. 4). 24.95 *(978-1-55498-185-4(9))* Groundwood Bks. CAN. Dist: Publishers Group West (PGW).
—The Silly Parade & Other Topsy-Turvy Poems: Russian Folk Nursery Rhymes, Tongue Twisters, & Lullabies. Dwyer, Anne, tr. from RUS. 2017. (ENG.). 48p. (J). (gr. -1-12). 19.95 *(978-0-9845867-6-9(8))* Rovakada, LLC.
Popov, Nikolai. The Great Shoe Parade. Popov, Nikolai. 2018. (ENG.). 40p. (J). (gr. -1-k). 17.99 *(978-988-8341-25-2(1)*, Minedition) Neugebauer, Michael (Publishing) Limited HKG. Dist: Penguin Random Hse. LLC.
Popovic, Danijela. Cara's Best Day! Living with Leber's Congenital Amaurosis. Malda, Sharon O. 2019. (ENG.). 36p. (J). pap. 9.99 *(978-1-0922-7319-0(0))* Independently Published.
—Fleet Week in NYC. Johnson, Robin F. 2018. (ENG.). 26p. (J). pap. 9.99 *(978-1-7217-1269-4(0))* CreateSpace Independent Publishing Platform.
Popovici, Danny. Manjhi Moves a Mountain. Churnin, Nancy. 2017. (ENG.). 32p. (J). (gr. k-5). 17.99 *(978-1-939547-34-7(2))* Creston Bks.
Popp, K. Wendy. One Candle. Bunting, Eve. 2004. (ENG.). 40p. (J). (gr. -1-3). pap. 7.99 *(978-0-06-008560-5(6))* HarperCollins Pubs.
—Where the Sunrise Begins. Wood, Douglas. 2010. (ENG.). 32p. (J). (gr. -1-3). 17.99 *(978-0-689-86172-7(9)*, Simon & Schuster Bks. For Young Readers) Simon & Schuster Bks. For Young Readers.
Poppen, Alex. A Brother-Sister Team. Bitner, Pamela. 2008. 16p. pap. 24.95 *(978-1-60474-583-2(5))* America Star Bks.
Popsicle, Lynnie. Tiny World: Sculpting! Popsicle, Lynnie. Odd Dot. 2019. (Tiny World Ser.: 4). (ENG.). 32p. (J). pap. 14.99 *(978-1-250-20386-1(4)*, 900200609, Odd Dot) St. Martin's Pr.
Populoh, Valeska M. Dinosaur Name Poems/Poemas de Nombres de Dinosaurios. Cunningham, Steven C. Gorospe, Myriam, tr. 2009. (SPA.). 70p. (J). pap. 12.95 *(978-0-9721241-6-4(0))* Three Conditions Pr.
Popwell, Tammy L. Teddy's Pirate Adventure. Stroud, Jacob C. 2018. (Adventures of Teddy Ser.: Vol. 2). (ENG.). 44p. (J). pap. 11.99 *(978-1-7200-8619-2(2))* Independently Published.
Porcellato, Nives. Food. Whittaker, Helen. 2012. (Living Green Ser.). 32p. (gr. 4-4). 29.50 *(978-1-60870-574-0(9))* Cavendish Square Publishing LLC.
—How Big Is Your Shopping Footprint? Mason, Paul. 2010. (Environmental Footprints Ser.). 32p. (gr. 4-4). 29.50 *(978-0-7614-4414-5(9))* Cavendish Square Publishing LLC.
—Waste. Whittaker, Helen. 2012. (Living Green Ser.). 32p. (gr. 4-4). 29.50 *(978-1-60870-577-1(3))* Cavendish Square Publishing LLC.
Porcellino, John. The Next Day. Gilmore, Jason & Peterson, Paul. Jansen, Alex & Poplak, Richard, eds. 2011. (ENG.). 104p. (YA). pap. 16.95 *(978-0-9864884-1-2(0))* Pop Sandbox, Inc. CAN. Dist: Diamond Bk. Distributors.
Porcellino, John. Thoreau at Walden. Porcellino, John. 2018. (Center for Cartoon Studies Presents Ser.). 112p. (J). (gr. 5-9). 17.99 *(978-1-368-02233-0(2))*; pap. 12.99 *(978-1-368-02710-6(5))* Hyperion Bks. for Children.
—Thoreau at Walden. Porcellino, John. 2009. (ENG.). 112p. (J). (gr. 5-18). pap. 9.99 *(978-1-4231-0039-3(5))* Hyperion Pr.
Porcheron, Tammy. Hairy Beary Book Two Bk. 2,Vol. 2: The Great Waterfall, 3 bks. Lewis, Carolyn. DeVince, James, ed. 2003. (Hairy Beary Ser.: 2). 42p. (J). pap. 9.95 *(978-0-9712641-1-3(2))* J M D's Business Services.
Porcheron, Tammy & DeVince, James. The Hairy Beary Adventure Series, 3 bks. Lewis, Carolyn & DeVince, James. 2005. 122p. (J). pap. 24.95 *(978-0-9712641-3-7(9))* J M D's Business Services.
—Hairy Beary Book Three: The Blue Ribbon Hero, 3 bks., Vol. 3. Lewis, Carolyn & DeVince, James. 2003. (Hairy Beary Ser.: 3). 46p. (J). pap. 9.95 *(978-0-9712641-2-0(0))* J M D's Business Services.
Pordd, Giulia. A Testa in Giu' Upside Down. Cozzani, Federica. 2016. (ENG.). (J). (gr. k-3). pap. *(978-88-97551-17-1(3))* Edizioni Lalbero.
Porfirio, Guy. The Day I Could Fly. Loux, Lynn Crosbie. 2003. (ENG.). 32p. (J). (gr. k-3). 15.95 *(978-1-55971-866-0(8))* Cooper Square Publishing Llc.
—Esperanza Means Hope. Harvey, Gwen. 2010. (J). *(978-0-910037-51-8(5))*; pap. *(978-0-910037-52-5(3))* Arizona Historical Society.
—Grandpa's Little One. Crystal, Billy. 2006. 40p. (J). (gr. -1-k). lib. bdg. 17.89 *(978-0-06-078174-3(2))* HarperCollins Pubs.
—Jack & the Beanstalk (Juan y los Frijoles Magicos), Grades Pk-3. Ottolenghi, Carol. ed. 2005. (Keepsake Stories Ser.). (ENG.). 32p. (gr. -1-3). pap. 3.99 *(978-0-7696-3816-4(3)*, 0769638163, Brighter Child) Carson-Dellosa Publishing, LLC.
—Junk Man's Daughter. Levitin, Sonia. rev. ed. 2007. (Tales of Young Americans Ser.). (ENG.). 32p. (J). (gr. 1-4). 17.95 *(978-1-58536-315-5(4)*, 202119) Sleeping Bear Pr.
—The Littlest Angel. Tazewell, Charles. 2004. 32p. (J). 16.95 *(978-0-8249-5473-4(4)*, Ideal Pubns.) Worthy Publishing.
—Sheldon's Adventures in Heaven. Wallace-Lang, Maxine Lois. 2003. 48p. (J). 12.99 *(978-0-8280-1508-0(2))* Review & Herald Publishing Assn.
—The Worst Christmas Ever. Bostrom, Kathleen Long. 2019. (ENG.). 48p. (J). (gr. -1-1). 17.00 *(978-1-947888-09-8(9)*, Flyaway Bks.) Westminster John Knox Pr.
Pornkerd, Vorrarit, et al. The Case of the Silk King. Gilligan, Shannon. 2006. (Choose Your Own Adventure Ser.). (ENG.). 144p. (J). (gr. 4-8). per. 7.99 *(978-1-933390-14-7(X)*, CHCL14) Chooseco LLC.
—Space & Beyond. Montgomery, R. A. 2006. (Choose Your Own Adventure Ser.). (ENG.). 144p. (J). (gr. 4-8). pap. 7.99 *(978-1-933390-03-1(4)*, CHCL03) Chooseco LLC.
Pornkerd, Vorrarit & Yaweera, Sasiprapa. Mystery of the Maya. Montgomery, R. A. 2006. (Choose Your Own Adventure Ser.: No. 5). (ENG.). 144p. (J). (gr. 4-8). per. 6.99 *(978-1-933390-05-5(0)*, CHCL05) Chooseco LLC.

P

Porras, Javier Fernando. Cenicienta. Perrault, Charles. 2003. (Coleccion Letras Pegadas Ser.). (SPA.). 70p. (J). (gr. -1-7). pap. *(978-958-30-0547-3(9))* Panamericana Editorial.

—Historias de Amores y Desvarios en America. 2004. (Literatura Juvenil (Panamericana Editorial) Ser.). (SPA.). 179p. (J). (gr. -1-7). pap. *(978-958-30-0569-5(X),* PV4378) Centro de Informacion y Desarrollo de la Comunicacion y la Literatura MEX. Dist: Lectorum Pubns., Inc.

—The Lazy Bee. Quiroga, Horacio. Leal, Mireya Fonseca, ed. 2003. (Library of Tale Ser.). (SPA.). 12p. (J). (gr. -1-7). pap. *(978-958-30-0988-4(1))* Panamericana Editorial.

Port, Cynthia. Kibble Talk. Port, Cynthia. 2013. 214p. pap. 9.99 *(978-0-9912278-0-8(8))* Port, Cynthia L.

Port, Vanessa. Itty Bitty Yeti. Puffinton, Brick. Cottage Door Press, ed. 2020. (Finger Puppet Board Book Ser.). (ENG.). 12p. (J). (gr. -1 — 1). bds. 6.99 ***(978-1-68052-804-6(1)*** *,* 1005170) Cottage Door Pr.

Portela, Francis. The Pack. Van Lente, Fred. 2013. (Wolverine: First Class Ser.). (ENG.). 24p. (J). (gr. 2-6). lib. bdg. 27.07 *(978-1-61479-178-2(3),* 15326, Marvel Age) Spotlight.

Porter, Cary. Bobbie the Wonder Dog: a True Story. Brown, Tricia. 2016. (ENG.). 32p. (J). (gr. k-3). 16.99 *(978-1-943328-36-9(6),* West Winds Pr.) West Margin Pr.

Porter, David W. Springtime Birds in My Backyard. Yarrish, Karen Kern. 2018. (ENG.). 40p. (J). 29.95 *(978-1-64042-700-6(7));* pap. 15.95 *(978-1-64042-701-3(5),* Swingin' Bridge Bks.) Keystone College Pr.

Porter, Hank & Grant, Bob. Pinocchio. Maris, Merrill de. 2020. (Disney Classics Ser.). (ENG.). 48p. (J). (gr. 2-6). lib. bdg. 28.50 ***(978-1-5321-4543-8(8)*** *,* 35189, Graphic Novels) Spotlight.

Porter, Jane. Brian the Brave. Stewart, Paul. 2019. (ENG.). 32p. (J). (gr. -1-1). 17.00 *(978-1-947888-18-0(8),* Flyaway Bks.) Westminster John Knox Pr.

Porter, Janice Lee. Allen Jay & the Undergound Railroad, 4 bks., Set. Brill, Marlene Targ. 2007. (Readalongs for Beginning Readers Ser.). (J). (gr. 1-3). pap. 37.95 incl. audio *(978-1-59519-947-8(0))* Live Oak Media.

—Allen Jay & the Underground Railroad, 4 bks., Set. 2006. (Readalongs for Beginning Readers Ser.). (J). (gr. 2-5). pap. 39.95 incl. audio compact disk *(978-1-59519-951-5(9))* Live Oak Media.

—Allen Jay y el Ferrocarril Subterraneo. Brill, Marlene Targ. 2007. (Yo Solo - Historia (on My Own - History) Ser.). 48p. (J). (gr. 4-7). per. 6.95 *(978-0-8225-7787-4(9))* Lerner Publishing Group.

—Aunt Clara Brown: Official Pioneer. Lowery, Linda. 2006. (On My Own Biographies Ser.). 48p. 16.95 *(978-0-7569-6699-7(X))* Perfection Learning Corp.

—Bessie Coleman: Daring to Fly. Walker, Sally M. (On My Own Biographies Ser.). 48p. (gr. 2-5). 2005. lib. bdg. 23.93 *(978-0-87614-919-5(0));* 2003. (ENG.). (J). pap. 7.99 *(978-0-87614-103-8(3),* First Avenue Editions) Lerner Publishing Group.

—Blackberry Stew. Monk, Isabell. 2005. 32p. (J). (gr. -1 — 1). lib. bdg. 15.95 *(978-1-57505-605-0(4))* Lerner Publishing Group.

—The Chocolate Tree: A Mayan Folktale. 2008. (On My Own Folklore Ser.). 48p. (J). (gr. 2-4). lib. bdg. 25.26 *(978-0-8225-7545-0(0),* Millbrook Pr.) Lerner Publishing Group.

—The Chocolate Tree: [a Mayan Folktale]. Lowery, Linda & Keep, Richard. 2009. (On My Own Folklore Ser.). (ENG.). 48p. (J). (gr. 2-4). pap. 7.99 *(978-1-58013-851-2(9),* First Avenue Editions) Lerner Publishing Group.

—Colors of China. Zemlicka, Shannon. 2005. (Colors of the World Ser.). 24p. (gr. 3-6). lib. bdg. 19.93 *(978-1-57505-478-0(7))* Lerner Publishing Group.

—Colors of India. Littlefield, Holly. 2003. (Colors of the World Ser.). 24p. (J). (gr. 1-4). 5.95 *(978-1-57505-368-4(3))* Lerner Publishing Group.

—Family. Monk, Isabell. (Carolrhoda Picture Bks.). 32p. (J). 2005. (ENG.). (gr. k-4). per. 10.95 *(978-1-57505-917-4(7));* 2003. (gr. -1-3). 15.95 *(978-1-57505-485-8(X),* Carolrhoda Bks.) Lerner Publishing Group.

—Hope. Monk, Isabell. 2004. (Carolrhoda Picture Books Ser.). 32p. (J). (gr. -1-3). 6.95 *(978-1-57505-792-7(1))* Lerner Publishing Group.

—Jesse Owens. Sutcliffe, Jane. 2006. (On My Own Biographies Ser.). 48p. 17.00 *(978-0-7569-6702-4(3))* Perfection Learning Corp.

—Johnny Appleseed. Swain, Gwenyth. 2003. (On My Own Biographies Ser.). 48p. (J). (gr. 1-3). pap. 6.95 *(978-1-57505-534-3(1))* Lerner Publishing Group.

—Tia Clara Brown: Pionera Oficial. Lowery, Linda. 2005. (Yo Solo Biografias Ser.). (SPA.). 48p. (J). (gr. 2-4). per. 6.95 *(978-0-8225-3129-6(1))* Lerner Publishing Group.

Porter, Lynda C., jt. illus. see Neusca, Guy, Jr.

Porter, Matthew. Calling All Animals. 2010. (ENG.). 28p. (J). (gr. -1 — 1). bds. 8.95 *(978-1-897476-34-5(5))* Simply Read Bks. CAN. Dist: Ingram Publisher Services.

Porter, Matthew. Fox on the Loose! Porter, Matthew. 2014. (ENG.). 20p. (J). (— 1). bds. 9.99 *(978-1-57061-928-1(X),* Little Bigfoot) Sasquatch Bks.

Porter, Steve. I Love Someone with Depression. Bearden, Laura R. 2019. (I Love Someone... Ser.: Vol. 1). (ENG.). 32p. (J). pap. 10.00 ***(978-1-5377-7483-1(2))*** CreateSpace Independent Publishing Platform.

Porter, Sue. McGillycuddy Could! Edwards, Pamela Duncan. 2005. 32p. (J). (gr. -1-1). 14.99 *(978-0-06-029001-6(3))* HarperCollins Pubs.

Porter, Tammy. A Wondrous World of Home. Feather, Tami Flaming. 2012. 24p. pap. 24.95 *(978-1-4626-4544-2(5))* America Star Bks.

Porterfield, Scott. Zangadoo Kangaroo & the Mysterious Boomerang. Lee, Karin. 2012. 94p. pap. 6.99 *(978-0-9847428-2-0(4))* Zangadoo Entertainment.

Portier-Tock, Charlotte. Help! My Feelings Are Too Big! Making Sense of Yourself & the World after a Difficult Start in Life - for Children with Attachment Issues. Aspden, K. L. 2019. (ENG.). 64p. 13.95 ***(978-1-78592-556-6(3)*** *,* 696899) Kingsley, Jessica Pubs. GBR. Dist: Hachette UK Distribution.

Portillo, Josie. The Witch's Glass. Grant, Holly. 2017. (League of Beastly Dreadfuls Ser.: Bk. 3). 305p. (J). pap. *(978-1-101-93369-5(0))* Random Hse., Inc.

Portis, Antoinette. Best Frints at Skrool. Portis, Antoinette. 2018. (Best Frints Ser.). (ENG.). 40p. (J). 17.99 *(978-1-62672-871-4(2),* 900176142) Roaring Brook Pr.

—Froodle. Portis, Antoinette. 2014. (ENG.). 32p. (J). (gr. -1-3). 18.99 *(978-1-59643-922-1(X),* 900121514) Roaring Brook Pr.

—Kindergarten Diary. Portis, Antoinette. 2010. (ENG.). 32p. (J). (gr. -1-3). 12.99 *(978-0-06-145691-6(8))* HarperCollins Pubs.

—Not a Box. Portis, Antoinette. 2006. (ENG.). 32p. (J). (gr. -1 — 1). 15.99 *(978-0-06-112322-1(6));* lib. bdg. 14.89 *(978-0-06-112323-8(4))* HarperCollins Pubs.

—Not a Box Board Book. Portis, Antoinette. 2011. (ENG.). 28p. (J). (gr. -1 — 1). bds. 7.99 *(978-0-06-199442-5(1),* HarperFestival) HarperCollins Pubs.

—Not a Stick. Portis, Antoinette. 2007. (ENG.). 32p. (J). (gr. -1-1). 14.99 *(978-0-06-112325-2(0))* HarperCollins Pubs.

—A Penguin Story. Portis, Antoinette. 2008. (ENG.). 40p. (J). (gr. -1-3). 17.99 *(978-0-06-145688-6(8))* HarperCollins Pubs.

—Princess Super Kitty. Portis, Antoinette. 2011. (ENG.). 40p. (J). (gr. -1-3). 16.99 *(978-0-06-182725-9(8))* HarperCollins Pubs.

Portman, Michelle Eva. Compost, by Gosh! An Adventure with Vermicomposting. Portman, Michelle Eva. l.t. ed. 2003. (ENG.). 42p. (J). 16.95 *(978-0-942256-16-1(6),* Falcon Guides) Globe Pequot Pr., The.

Portnoi, Jeremy. The Animated Jewish Year. Wool, Danny & Yudin, Yefim (Chaim). 2006. 88p. 19.95 *(978-965-7108-79-6(9),* Lambda) Urim Pubns. ISR. Dist: Lambda Pubs., Inc.

Portnoy, Amy. The Magical Ms. Plum. Becker, Bonny. 2011. (ENG.). 112p. (J). (gr. 1-4). 6.99 *(978-0-375-84760-8(X),* Yearling) Random Hse. Children's Bks.

Portolano, Cristina. Incredible Bugs. Farndon, John. 2016. (Animal Bests Ser.). (ENG.). 32p. (J). (gr. 3-6). lib. bdg. 27.99 *(978-1-5124-0640-5(6),* 9781512406405, Hungry Tomato ®) Lerner Publishing Group.

Portwood, Andrew. Escamas de Dragon y Hojas de Sauce. Givens, Terryl L. (SPA.). (J). pap. 7.95 *(978-958-04-4168-7(5))* Norma S.A. COL. Dist: Distribuidora Norma, Inc., Lectorum Pubns., Inc.

Poryes, Michael. The Trouble with Boys, 2 vols., Vol. 2. 2004. (That's So Raven Ser.). 96p. pap. 14.99 *(978-1-59182-807-5(4),* Tokyopop Kids) TOKYOPOP, Inc.

Posada, Mia. Dazzling Dragonflies: A Life Cycle Story. Glaser, Linda. 2008. (Linda Glaser's Classic Creatures Ser.). (ENG.). 32p. (J). (gr. k-3). lib. bdg. 22.60 *(978-0-8225-6753-0(9),* Millbrook Pr.) Lerner Publishing Group.

—Plants Can't Sit Still. Hirsch, Rebecca E. 2016. (ENG.). 32p. (J). (gr. k-4). 19.99 *(978-1-4677-8031-5(6),* 9781467780315); E-Book 30.65 *(978-1-5124-1109-6(4))* Lerner Publishing Group. (Millbrook Pr.).

Posada, Mia. Adivina Qué Está Creciendo Dentro de Este Huevo. Posada, Mia. Translations.com Staff, tr. from ENG. 2008. (SPA.). 32p. (J). (gr. k-3). 16.95 *(978-0-7613-3906-9(X))* Lerner Publishing Group.

—Dandelions: Stars in the Grass. Posada, Mia. 2003. (Picture Bks.). 32p. (J). (gr. -1-3). 15.95 *(978-1-57505-383-7(7))* Lerner Publishing Group.

—Guess What Is Growing Inside This Egg. Posada, Mia. 2007. (ENG.). 32p. (J). (gr. k-3). 17.99 *(978-0-8225-6192-7(1),* Millbrook Pr.) Lerner Publishing Group.

—Summer Green to Autumn Gold: Uncovering Leaves' Hidden Colors. Posada, Mia. 2019. (ENG.). 32p. (J). (gr. k-4). 19.99 *(978-1-5415-2899-4(9),* 9781541528994, Millbrook Pr.) Lerner Publishing Group.

—Who Was Here? Discovering Wild Animal Tracks. Posada, Mia. 2014. (ENG.). 32p. (J). (gr. k-3). 16.95 *(978-1-4677-1871-4(8),* 9781467718714, Millbrook Pr.) Lerner Publishing Group.

Posada, Mia. Robins: Songbirds of Spring. Posada, Mia, tr. 2004. (Carolrhoda Picture Books Ser.). 32p. (J). (gr. k-3). 15.95 *(978-1-57505-615-9(1))* Lerner Publishing Group.

Posen, Mick. Cheetah. Costain, Meredith. 2016. (Wild World Ser.). 00032p. (J). (gr. 1-2). pap. 10.00 *(978-1-4994-8203-4(5),* Windmill Bks.) Rosen Publishing Group, Inc., The.

Posey, Sarah. I Had a Sister. Parker, Joanne. 2019. (Hardcover Ser.). (ENG.). 32p. (J). 14.95 *(978-1-7326049-6-4(7));* pap. 9.95 *(978-1-7326049-3-3(2))* Wyatt Hse. Publishing.

Posner-Sanchez, Andrea. Dog Days. 2016. 22p. (J). *(978-1-5182-3229-9(9))* Random Hse., Inc.

Posner-Sanchez, Andrea, jt. illus. see Cohee, Ron.

Post, Howard. The Magic Boots, 1 vol. Post, Howard. Emerson, Scott. 2019. (ENG.). 32p. (J). (gr. -1-3). reprint ed. ed. pap. 7.99 *(978-0-87905-874-6(9));* 3rd ed. 16.99 *(978-0-87905-603-2(7))* Gibbs Smith, Publisher.

POST, L. E. E. Texas Animals Big & Small. Post, Lee. 2008. 32p. pap. 9.95 *(978-1-934443-33-0(6))* ExpandingBooks.com.

Post, Lee. Alaska! Big & Small: A big book of Alaskan Animals from itsy-bitsy to Gigantic. Post, Lee. 2007. 32p. per. 9.95 *(978-1-934443-94-1(8))* ExpandingBooks.com.

Postgate, Daniel. The Little Red Hen. 2006. (First Reading Level 3 Ser.). 48p. (J). (gr. 1-4). 8.99 *(978-0-7945-1375-7(1),* Usborne) EDC Publishing.

—My Auntie Susan. Bird, Sheila May. 2008. (Tadpoles Ser.). (ENG.). 24p. (J). (gr. -1-3). pap. *(978-0-7787-3889-3(2));* lib. bdg. *(978-0-7787-3858-9(2))* Crabtree Publishing Co.

—Rumpled Stilton Skin. 2015. (Tadpoles: Fairytale Twists Ser.). (ENG.). 32p. (J). (gr. 1-2). *(978-0-7787-1930-4(8))* Crabtree Publishing Co.

—The Ugly Duckling. 2006. (First Reading Level 4 Ser.). 48p. (J). (gr. 1-4). 8.99 *(978-0-7945-1274-3(7),* Usborne) EDC Publishing.

Postgate, Daniel. Esa Inmensa Galaxia. Postgate, Daniel. Poskitt, Kjartan. (SPA.). 158p. (YA). (gr. 5-8). *(978-84-272-2055-3(3))* Molino, Editorial ESP. Dist: Lectorum Pubns., Inc.

—Esas Endiabladas Mates. Postgate, Daniel. Poskitt, Kjartan. (SPA.). 176p. (YA). (gr. 5-8). *(978-84-272-2064-5(2))* Molino, Editorial ESP. Dist: Lectorum Pubns., Inc.

—Esas Insignificantes Fracciones. Postgate, Daniel. Poskitt, Kjartan. (SPA.). 160p. (YA). (gr. 5-8). *(978-84-272-2068-3(5))* Molino, Editorial ESP. Dist: Lectorum Pubns., Inc.

Postgate, Daniel. Esos Extintos Dinosaurios. Postgate, Daniel, tr. Oliver, Martin. 2003. (Coleccion Esa Gran Cultura).Tr. of Dead Dinosaurs. (SPA.). 134p. (YA). 7.96 *(978-84-272-2137-6(1))* Molino, Editorial ESP. Dist: Lectorum Pubns., Inc.

Poston, Valerie Williams. ArbeZ ZebrA Teaches A to Z, 3 vols., Vol. 1. 2007. 33p. (J). spiral bd. 39.99 *(978-0-9779063-0-7(2))* Gain Literacy Skills / Lynette Gain Williams.

Pota, Giovanni, et al. High-Tech Highways & Super Skyways: The Next 100 Years of Transportation. Bethea, Nikole Brooks. 2016. (Our World: the Next 100 Years Ser.). (ENG.). 32p. (J). (gr. 3-9). lib. bdg. 31.32 *(978-1-4914-8266-7(4),* Capstone Pr.) Capstone.

Pota, Giovanni. Our World: the Next 100 Years. Bethea, Nikole Brooks et al. 2016. (Our World: the Next 100 Years Ser.). (ENG.). 32p. (J). (gr. 3-9). lib. bdg., lib. bdg., lib. bdg. 125.28 *(978-1-4914-8272-8(9),* Capstone Pr.) Capstone.

Pota, Giovanni, et al. Power Plays: The Next 100 Years of Energy. Bethea, Nikole Brooks. 2016. (Our World: the Next 100 Years Ser.). (ENG.). 32p. (J). (gr. 3-9). lib. bdg. 31.32 *(978-1-4914-8267-4(2),* Capstone Pr.) Capstone.

Pota, Giovanni & Brown, Alan. Medical Marvels: The Next 100 Years of Medicine. Biskup, Agnieszka. 2016. (Our World: the Next 100 Years Ser.). (ENG.). 32p. (J). (gr. 3-9). lib. bdg. 31.32 *(978-1-4914-8264-3(8),* Capstone Pr.) Capstone.

—Sailing the Solar System: The Next 100 Years of Space Exploration. Yomtov, Nel. 2016. (Our World: the Next 100 Years Ser.). (ENG.). 32p. (J). (gr. 3-9). lib. bdg. 31.32 *(978-1-4914-8265-0(6),* Capstone Pr.) Capstone.

Poteat, Amber. Sammy Explores Columbus, Ohio. Mravetz, Pete. 2019. (ENG.). 24p. (J). pap. 15.99 ***(978-1-7960-5196-4(9))*** Xlibris Corp.

Poteat, Amber. Sammy's Big Adventure: Sammy Explores Columbus, Ohio. Mravetz, Pete. 2019. (Book Ser.: Vol. 4). (ENG.). 24p. (J). pap. 10.50 *(978-1-0987-4216-4(8))* Independently Published.

Pottenkulam, Pooja. Sunshine for Amma. Husain, Zakir & Mishra, Samina. 2004. 16p. (J). *(978-81-89013-41-7(6))* Zubaan.

Potter, Alice. The Fantastic Pineapple. Puffinton, Brick. Cottage Door Press, ed. 2019. (Finger Puppet Board Book Ser.). (ENG.). 12p. (J). (gr. -1 — 1). bds. 6.99 *(978-1-68052-735-3(5),* 1004560) Cottage Door Pr.

Potter, Alice. You Are Magic: a Guided Journal to Unlock the Power of Your Inner Unicorn, Llamacorn, & Narwhal. West, Tracey. 2020. 144p. (J). (gr. 3-7). pap. 12.99 ***(978-0-06-297713-7(X)*** *,* HarperFestival) HarperCollins Pubs.

Potter, Beatrix. The Tale of Peter Rabbit. 2014. (J). pap. *(978-1-4677-5772-0(1),* First Avenue Editions) Lerner Publishing Group.

—The Tale of Peter Rabbit & Other Stories: The Beatrix Potter Collection. 2016. (J). pap. *(978-1-5124-2608-3(3),* First Avenue Editions) Lerner Publishing Group.

Potter, Beatrix. Cecily Parsley's Nursery Rhymes. Potter, Beatrix. 2016. (Beatrix Potter Classics Ser.). (ENG.). 34p. (J). (gr. -1-2). pap. 12.99 *(978-1-5324-0028-5(4))* Xist Publishing.

—Histoire de Pierre Lapin. Potter, Beatrix. 2016. (FRE.). 96p. (J). (gr. -1-2). pap. 12.99 *(978-1-5324-0031-5(4))* Xist Publishing.

—The Peter Rabbit & Friends Treasury. Potter, Beatrix. 2006. 240p. (J). (gr. k-4). reprint ed. 20.00 *(978-1-4223-5452-0(0))* DIANE Publishing Co.

—Peter Rabbit Rainbow Shapes & Colors. Potter, Beatrix. 2006. (Peter Rabbit Seedlings Ser.). (ENG.). 10p. (J). (gr. k-18). bds. 5.99 *(978-0-7232-5722-6(1),* Puffin) Penguin Publishing Group.

—Sgeulachd Bheniamin Coineanach. Potter, Beatrix. MacDonald, James, 1st, tr. from ENG. 2008.Tr. of Tale of Benjamin Bunny. (GAE.). 64p. (J). *(978-0-9552326-4-0(3))* Grace Note Pubns.

—Sgeulachd Pheadair Rabaid. Potter, Beatrix. MacDonald, James, 1st, tr. from ENG. 2008.Tr. of Tale of Peter Rabbit. (GAE.). 84p. *(978-0-9552326-3-3(5))* Grace Note Pubns.

—The Story of a Fierce Bad Rabbit. Potter, Beatrix. 2016. (Beatrix Potter Classics Ser.). (ENG.). 30p. (J). (gr. k-3). pap. 12.99 *(978-1-5324-0030-8(6))* Xist Publishing.

—The Story of Miss Moppet. Potter, Beatrix. 2016. (Beatrix Potter Classics Ser.). (ENG.). 30p. (J). (gr. k-3). pap. 12.99 *(978-1-5324-0026-1(8))* Xist Publishing.

—The Tale of Ginger & Pickles. Potter, Beatrix. 2016. (Beatrix Potter Classics Ser.). (ENG.). 58p. (J). (gr. k-3). pap. 12.99 *(978-1-5324-0027-8(6))* Xist Publishing.

—The Tale of Mr. Jeremy Fisher. Potter, Beatrix. 2016. (Beatrix Potter Classics Ser.). (ENG.). 54p. (J). (gr. k-3). E-Book 12.99 *(978-1-5324-0050-6(0))* Xist Publishing.

—The Tale of Two Bad Mice. Potter, Beatrix. 2016. (Beatrix Potter Classics Ser.). (ENG.). 54p. (J). (gr. k-3). pap. 12.99 *(978-1-5324-0025-4(X))* Xist Publishing.

Potter, Debra. I Am the Music Man. (Classic Books with Holes 8x8 with CD Ser.). (J). 2020. (ENG.). 16p. pap. incl. audio compact disk ***(978-1-78628-481-5(2))*** *;* 2018. (ENG.). 16p. pap. *(978-1-78628-129-6(5));* 2006. 16p. (gr. -1-3). spiral bd. *(978-1-84643-010-7(0));* 2005. 14p. spiral bd. *(978-1-904550-60-0(6));* 2005. 16p. pap. *(978-1-904550-34-1(7))* Child's Play International Ltd.

Potter, Giselle. The Boy Who Loved Words. Schotter, Roni. 2006. (ENG.). 40p. (J). (gr. -1-3). 17.99 *(978-0-375-83601-5(2),* Schwartz & Wade Bks.) Random Hse. Children's Bks.

—The Brave Little Seamstress. Osborne, Mary Pope. 2006. 32p. (gr. -1-3). 17.00 *(978-0-7569-6613-3(2))* Perfection Learning Corp.

—C'mon an' Swing in My Tree! 2005. 14p. (J). bds. 16.95 incl. audio compact disk *(978-0-9763012-0-2(2))* Cow Heard Records.

—The Hare & the Tortoise. Bolt, Ranjit. 2006. (ENG.). 64p. (J). (gr. -1-3). 19.99 *(978-1-905236-54-1(9))* Barefoot Bks., Inc.

—The Honest-To-Goodness Truth. McKissack, Patricia C. 2003. (ENG.). 40p. (J). (gr. -1-3). 8.99 *(978-0-689-85395-1(5),* Aladdin) Simon & Schuster Children's Publishing.

—How to Build a Hug: Temple Grandin & Her Amazing Squeeze Machine. Guglielmo, Amy & Tourville, Jacqueline. 2018. (ENG.). 48p. (J). (gr. -1-3). 18.99 *(978-1-5344-1097-8(X))* Simon & Schuster Children's Publishing.

—Independence Cake: A Revolutionary Confection Inspired by Amelia Simmons, Whose True History Is Unfortunately Unknown. Hopkinson, Deborah. 2017. 44p. (J). (gr. -1-3). 17.99 *(978-0-385-39017-0(3),* Schwartz & Wade Bks.) Random Hse. Children's Bks.

—Kate & the Beanstalk. Osborne, Mary Pope. 2005. (ENG.). 40p. (J). (gr. -1-3). reprint ed. 8.99 *(978-1-4169-0818-0(8),* Aladdin) Simon & Schuster Children's Publishing.

—Mr. Semolina-Semolinus: A Greek Folktale. Manna, Anthony L. & Mitakidou, Christodoula. 2004. (ENG.). 40p. (J). (gr. -1-3). 19.99 *(978-0-689-86698-2(4),* Simon & Schuster/Paula Wiseman Bks.) Simon & Schuster/Paula Wiseman Bks.

—Olive & Pekoe: In Four Short Walks. Davis, Jacky. 2019. (ENG.). 40p. (J). (gr. -1-3). 17.99 *(978-0-06-257310-0(1),* Greenwillow Bks.) HarperCollins Pubs.

—The Orphan: A Cinderella Story from Greece. Manna, Anthony & Mitakidou, Christodoula. 2011. 40p. (J). (gr. -1-3). 17.99 *(978-0-375-86691-3(4),* Schwartz & Wade Bks.) Random Hse. Children's Bks.

—Sleeping Bobby. Osborne, Mary Pope & Osborne, Will. 2005. (ENG.). 40p. (J). (gr. -1-3). 19.99 *(978-0-689-87668-4(8),* Atheneum Bks. for Young Readers) Simon & Schuster Children's Publishing.

—Three Cheers for Catherine the Great! Best, Cari. 2003. (Catherine the Great Ser.). (ENG.). 32p. (J). (gr. -1-3). pap. 8.99 *(978-0-374-47551-2(2),* 900021256) Square Fish.

Potter, Giselle. Tell Me What to Dream About. Potter, Giselle. 2015. 40p. (J). (gr. -1-2). 17.99 *(978-0-385-37423-1(2),* Schwartz & Wade Bks.) Random Hse. Children's Bks.

—This Is My Dollhouse. Potter, Giselle. 2016. 40p. (J). (gr. -1-3). 17.99 *(978-0-553-52153-5(5),* Schwartz & Wade Bks.) Random Hse. Children's Bks.

—The Year I Didn't Go to School. Potter, Giselle. 2015. (ENG.). 40p. (J). (gr. -1-3). 13.99 *(978-1-4814-7995-0(4),* Atheneum Bks. for Young Readers) Simon & Schuster Children's Publishing.

Potter, Heather. Nanna's Button Tin. Wolfer, Dianne. 2018. (ENG.). 32p. (J). (gr. -1-1). 15.99 *(978-0-7636-8096-1(6))* Candlewick Pr.

—Pearl Verses the World. Murphy, Sally. 2011. (ENG.). 80p. (J). (gr. 3-7). 14.99 *(978-0-7636-4821-3(3))* Candlewick Pr.

Potter, Jennifer M. Claude: The True Story of a White Alligator. Smith, Emma Bland. 2020. (ENG.). 32p. (J). (gr. -1-3). 18.99 ***(978-1-63217-269-3(0)*** *,* Little Bigfoot) Sasquatch Bks.

Potter, Jennifer M. A Songbird Dreams of Singing: Poems about Sleeping Animals. Hosford, Kate. 2019. (ENG.). 40p. (J). (gr. -1-3). 19.99 *(978-1-7624-6714-3(2),* Running Pr. Kids) Running Pr.

Potter, Katherine. Always Be Safe. Schulz, Kathy. 2003. (Rookie Reader Skill Set Ser.). (ENG.). (J). (gr. k-2). pap. 4.95 *(978-0-516-26965-8(8),* Children's Pr.) Scholastic Library Publishing.

Potter, Lori. The Little Cat, the Wonderful Witch, & the Clever Mouse. Stuart, Lisa Marie. 2008. 60p. pap. 21.95 *(978-1-59858-691-6(2))* Dog Ear Publishing, LLC.

Potter, Melisande. Pizza for the Queen. Castaldo, Nancy F. 2005. (ENG.). 32p. (J). (gr. -1-3). 16.95 *(978-0-8234-1865-7(0))* Holiday Hse., Inc.

Potter, Melody. Face-To-Face with Big Foot. Fraser, Amy. 2016. (ENG.). (J). pap. 19.95 *(978-0-9981665-2-0(9))* Lexingford Publishing.

Pottie, Marjolein. The Best Bottom. Minne, Brigitte. 2006. (ENG.). 32p. (J). (gr. -1-3). pap. 5.95 *(978-1-59687-387-2(6))* IBks., Inc.

—The Best Bottom. Minne, Brigitte. 2004. 32p. (J). 15.95 *(978-0-689-03595-1(0),* Milk & Cookies) ibooks, Inc.

—Qui?! Nielandt, Dirk. Sarfati, Sonia, tr. from DUT. 2004. (Picture Bks.). (FRE.). 32p. (J). (gr. -1). *(978-2-89021-679-2(9));* pap. *(978-2-89021-678-5(0))* Diffusion du livre Mirabel (DLM).

—Qui Est-Ce Qui... Nielandt, Dirk. Sarfati, Sonia, tr. from DUT. 2004. (Picture Bks.). (FRE.). 32p. (J). (gr. -1). *(978-2-89021-681-5(0));* pap. *(978-2-89021-680-8(2))* Diffusion du livre Mirabel (DLM).

Potts Dawson, Eileen. H Is for Hawkeye. Wagner, Jay. 2003. (J). 16.95 *(978-1-931599-11-5(4),* Trails Bks.) Bower Hse.

Potts, Sam, jt. illus. see Seeley, Scott.

Poulin, Em. Mary's Fairies Coloring Book: Stories about Effy & Her Friends with Pictures to Color. Gagnon, Mary. 2018. (Mary's Fairy Stories Ser.: Vol. 4). (ENG.). 28p. (J). pap. 8.99 *(978-1-7274-9195-1(5))* CreateSpace Independent Publishing Platform.

Poulin, Stephane. La Forêt aux Mille et un Périls, Tome 2. Côté, Denis. 2004. (Roman Jeunesse Ser.). (FRE.). 96p. (J). (gr. 4-7). pap. *(978-2-89021-696-9(9))* Diffusion du livre Mirabel (DLM).

Poupard, et al. Why Are We Here Again? Beka. 2007. (Rugger Boys Ser.: 1). (ENG.). 48p. (J). (gr. 4-7). per. 9.99 *(978-1-905460-33-5(3))* CineBook GBR. Dist: National Bk. Network.

Poupart, Jean-Sébastien. Caillou Leads the Parade. Sulgit, Nicole. 2004. (J). *(978-0-7853-9949-0(6))* Publications International, Ltd.

Pouriseth, Phal, jt. illus. see Nath, Vann.

Pousette, Kelly. Do Not Rake Your Garden in a Party Dress. 2020. (ENG.). 32p. (J). (gr. k-2). 16.95 *(978-1-944903-85-5(2),* Cameron Kids) Cameron + Co.

Pousette, Kelly. If You Were Night. Van, Muon Thi. 2020. (ENG.). 32p. (J). (gr. -1-2). 17.99 ***(978-1-5253-0014-1(8))*** Kids Can Pr., Ltd. CAN. Dist: Hachette Bk. Group.

Pousette, Kelly. Little Things. Dyer, Nick. 2019. (J). *(978-1-4413-2859-5(9))* Peter Pauper Pr. Inc.

—The Very, Very Far North. Bar-el, Dan. 2019. (Very, Very Far North Ser.). (ENG.). 272p. (J). (gr. 3-7). 16.99 *(978-1-5344-3341-0(4))* Simon & Schuster Children's Publishing.

Povenmire, Dan, jt. illus. see Jeff, Marsh.

Povey, Andrea. The Witch Who Liked to Wear Pink. Kane, Gillian. 2013. 24p. pap. 11.50 *(978-1-62516-315-8(0),* Strategic Bk. Publishing) Strategic Book Publishing & Rights Agency (SBPRA).

Powell, Carole Jackson. Hiding in the Dark. Hauser, Sheri. 2019. (ENG.). 30p. (J). pap. 9.95 ***(978-1-6998-4136-5(5))*** Independently Published.

Powell, Claire. At the Heels of History Collection: Filigree's Midnight Ride; Bo-Bo's Cave of Gold; Minsha's Night on Ellis Island. Berkman, Pam & Hearst, Dorothy. ed. 2020. (At the Heels of History Ser.). (ENG.). 592p. (J). (gr. 1-4). pap. 22.99 ***(978-1-5344-7909-8(0),*** McElderry, Margaret K. Bks.) McElderry, Margaret K. Bks.

Powell, Claire. Bo-Bo's Cave of Gold. Berkman, Pam & Hearst, Dorothy. 2020. (At the Heels of History Ser.). (ENG.). 192p. (J). (gr. 1-4). 18.99 *(978-1-5344-3336-6(8));* pap. 7.99 *(978-1-5344-3335-9(X))* McElderry, Margaret K. Bks. (McElderry, Margaret K. Bks.).

—Filigree's Midnight Ride. Berkman, Pam & Hearst, Dorothy. 2019. (At the Heels of History Ser.). (ENG.). 192p. (J). (gr. 1-4). 17.99 *(978-1-5344-3333-5(3));* pap. 6.99 *(978-1-5344-3332-8(5))* McElderry, Margaret K. Bks. (McElderry, Margaret K. Bks.).

Powell, Claire. Minsha's Night on Ellis Island. Berkman, Pam & Hearst, Dorothy. 2020. (At the Heels of History Ser.). (ENG.). 208p. (J). (gr. 1-4). 18.99 ***(978-1-5344-3339-7(2));*** pap. 7.99 ***(978-1-5344-3338-0(4))*** McElderry, Margaret K. Bks. (McElderry, Margaret K. Bks.).

Powell, Claire. Princess Scallywag & the Brave, Brave Knight. Sperring, Mark. 2019. (ENG.). 32p. (J). pap. 6.99 *(978-0-00-832597-8(9),* HarperCollins Children's Bks.) HarperCollins Pubs. Ltd. GBR. Dist: HarperCollins Pubs.

Powell, Consie. Baby Bear Isn't Hungry. Ross, Michael Elsohn. 2006. (ENG.). 26p. (J). (gr. -1-4). 10.95 *(978-1-930238-24-4(X))* Yosemite Conservancy.

—Bird on My Hand (hardcover) Making Friends with Chickadees, 1 vol. Bevis, Mary. 2014. (ENG.). 32p. (J). (gr. 1-2). 17.95 *(978-0-9883508-9-2(0))* Raven Productions, Inc.

—Bird on My Hand (softcover) Making Friends with Chickadees. Bevis, Mary. 2014. (ENG.). 32p. (J). (gr. 1-2). pap. 9.95 *(978-0-9883508-8-5(2))* Raven Productions, Inc.

—Canoeman Joe. Radcliffe, Robin. 2019. (ENG.). 32p. (J). (gr. 3). 17.95 *(978-1-7328540-0-0(9))* Green Writers Pr.

—A Day in the Salt Marsh, 1 vol. Kurtz, Kevin. 2007. (Day in the Habitat Ser.). (ENG.). 32p. (J). (gr. -1-3). 15.95 *(978-0-9768823-5-0(3));* pap. 8.95 *(978-1-934359-19-8(X))* Arbordale Publishing.

—A Day in the Salt Marsh in Chinese. Kurtz, Kevin. Shu, Li, tr. 2019. (CHI.). 32p. (J). (gr. k-3). pap. 11.95 *(978-1-60718-395-2(1))* Arbordale Publishing.

—Nature's Patchwork Quilt. Miche, Mary. 2012. (ENG.). (J). (gr. 2-5). lib. bdg. 20.05 *(978-1-62765-380-0(5))* Perfection Learning Corp.

—Nature's Patchwork Quilt: Understanding Habitats. Miché, Mary. 2012. (ENG.). 32p. (J). (gr. 1-4). 24.94 *(978-1-58469-169-3(7))* Dawn Pubns.

—Nature's Patchwork Quilt: Understanding Habitats, 1 vol. Miché, Mary. 2012. (ENG.). 32p. (J). (gr. k-6). pap. 11.95 *(978-1-58469-170-9(0),* Dawn Pubns.) Sourcebooks, Inc.

—Old Woman Winter. Bevis, Mary. 2010. 32p. (J). (gr. 1-2). pap. 9.95 *(978-0-9819307-6-3(X))* Raven Productions, Inc.

—Who Lives in the Snow?, Vol. Jones, Jennifer Berry. 2012. (ENG.). 32p. (gr. -1-3). pap. 8.95 *(978-1-57098-444-0(1))* Rinehart, Roberts Pubs.

—Wolf Song. Bevis, Mary. 2007. 32p. (gr. 1-2). 18.95 *(978-0-9794202-0-7(2));* pap. 12.95 *(978-0-9794202-1-4(0))* Raven Productions, Inc.

Powell, Consie. Old Dog Cora & the Christmas Tree. Powell, Consie. 2003.Tr. of Ouwe Trouwe Cora en de Kerstboom. 32p. (J). (gr. 1-2). lib. bdg. 14.95 *(978-0-9677057-6-7(2))* Raven Productions, Inc.

—Peregrine's Sky. Powell, Consie. 2009. (ENG.). 32p. (J). pap. 7.95 *(978-1-58369-129-8(4))* Western National Parks Assn.

Powell, Consie, jt. illus. see Bevis, Mary.

Powell, Debbie. Walk This World at Christmastime. Big Picture Press. 2016. (ENG.). 24p. (J). (gr. k-3). 17.99 *(978-0-7636-8921-6(1),* Big Picture Press) Candlewick Pr.

Powell, Debbie. Trucks. Powell, Debbie. 2012. (ENG.). 16p. (J). (gr. -1 — 1). bds. 5.99 *(978-0-7636-5934-9(7))* Candlewick Pr.

Powell, Eric. Adventures of Huckleberry Finn. Twain, Mark. 2012. 276p. 19.99 *(978-1-61377-086-3(3),* 9781613770863) Idea & Design Works, LLC.

Powell, James. The Adventures of Rady Red Comb. Tingwald, Jady Ann. 2005. 33p. (J). (gr. 1-6). 9.00 *(978-0-9706728-1-0(0))* New Millenium Pr., The.

—Orrie's Christmas. Tingwald, July Ann. 2007. 42p. 9.00 *(978-0-9706728-5-8(3))* New Millenium Pr., The.

Powell, Jennifer, photos by. The Colors of Mackinac Island. Powell, Jennifer. 2015. (ENG., 30p. (J). (gr. 1-2). 10.95 *(978-1-933272-49-8(X))* Thunder Bay Pr.

Powell, Luciana Navarro. Babies Come from Airports. Dealey, Erin. 2018. (ENG.). 32p. (J). 12.99 *(978-1-61067-557-4(6))* Kane Miller.

—Colorasaurus. Bryant, Megan E. 2012. (ENG.). 20p. (J). (gr. -1 — 1). bds. 9.99 *(978-1-4521-0814-8(5))* Chronicle Bks. LLC.

—Countasaurus. Bryant, Megan E. 2012. (ENG.). 20p. (J). (gr. -1 — 1). bds. 9.99 *(978-1-4521-0747-9(5))* Chronicle Bks. LLC.

—I Take Care of Myself/Me Se Cuidar! Rosa-Mendoza, Gladys. 2007. (English Spanish Foundations Ser.). (ENG & SPA.). 20p. (J). (gr. -1-k). bds. 6.95 *(978-1-931398-22-0(4))* Me+Mi Publishing.

—Puppies, Puppies, Everywhere! A Back-And-Forth Opposites Book. Schwartz, Betty & Seresin, Lynn. 2015. (J). *(978-1-62370-236-6(4),* Capstone Young Readers) Capstone.

—A Tiny Brown Monkey on the Big Blue Earth. Christie, Tory. 2019. 32p. (J). (gr. 1-3). 17.99 *(978-1-68152-498-6(8))* Amicus.

—Whose Hands Are These? A Community Helper Guessing Book. Paul, Miranda. 2016. (ENG.). 32p. (J). (gr. -1-3). 19.99 *(978-1-4677-5214-5(2),* 9781467752145); E-Book 30.65 *(978-1-4677-9726-9(X));* E-Book 30.65 *(978-1-5124-0738-9(0),* 9781512407389) Lerner Publishing Group. (Millbrook Pr.).

Powell, Mia. Play Like an Animal! Why Critters Splash, Race, Twirl, & Chase. Gianferrari, Maria. 2020. (ENG.). 32p. (J). (gr. k-3). lib. bdg. 19.99 *(978-1-5415-5771-0(9),* Millbrook Pr.) Lerner Publishing Group.

Powell, Nate. March: Book Three. Lewis, John & Aydin, Andrew. 2016. (March Ser.: Vol. 3). (ENG.). 256p. (YA). (gr. 8-11). lib. bdg. 30.80 *(978-1-5311-9480-2(X))* Perfection Learning Corp.

—March: Book Two. Lewis, John & Aydin, Andrew. 2015. (March Ser.: Vol. 2). (ENG.). 192p. (YA). (gr. 8-11). lib. bdg. 30.75 *(978-1-5311-9481-9(8))* Perfection Learning Corp.

—The Year of the Beasts. Castellucci, Cecil. 2012. (ENG.). 192p. (YA). (gr. 7-12). 16.99 *(978-1-59643-686-2(7),* 900071518) Roaring Brook Pr.

—The Year of the Beasts. Castellucci, Cecil. 2014. (ENG.). 208p. (YA). (gr. 7-12). pap. 14.99 *(978-1-250-05076-2(6),* 900134147) Square Fish.

Powell, Nathan. Heroes of Olympus, Book One the Lost Hero: the Graphic Novel (Heroes of Olympus, Book One) Riordan, Rick & Venditti, Robert. 2014. (Heroes of Olympus Ser.: 1). (ENG.). 192p. (J). (gr. 5-9). pap. 12.99 *(978-1-4231-6325-1(7))* Hyperion Bks. for Children.

Powell, Polly. I Howl, I Growl: Southwest Animal Antics. Vaughn, Marcia. 2003. (ENG.). 26p. (J). (gr. -1-k). bds. 7.95 *(978-0-87358-835-5(5))* Cooper Square Publishing Llc.

Powell, Rich. Animal Crackups: 1,001 Beastly Riddles, Jokes, & Tongue Twisters from Highlights. Highlights for Children Editorial Staff. 2015. (Highlights(TM) Laugh Attack! Joke Bks.). (ENG.). 256p. (J). (gr. 1-4). pap. 5.95 *(978-1-62979-426-6(0),* Highlights) Boyds Mills Pr.

Power, Alice. Betsy Bee Wants to Be a Beautician. Delaney, Majella. 2017. (ENG.). (J). pap. *(978-0-9931716-9-7(9))* Carrowmore.

Power, Elle. Goldie Vance: the Hotel Whodunit. Rivera, Lilliam. 2020. 224p. (J). (gr. 3-7). 14.99 *(978-0-316-45664-7(0))* Little, Brown Bks. for Young Readers.

—Goldie Vance Vol. 4. Larson, Hope & Ball, Jackie. 2018. (Goldie Vance Ser.: 4). (ENG.). 112p. (YA). (gr. 4-7). pap. 14.99 *(978-1-68415-140-0(6))* Boom! Studios.

Power, Margaret. The Sea's Secret. Bursztynski, Susan. 2004. iv, 36p. (J). pap. *(978-0-7608-6737-2(2))* Sundance/Newbridge Educational Publishing.

—The Silver Brumby: Including Elyne Mitchell's Ast Brumby Story, 'Wild Echoes Ringing' Mitchell, Elyne. 2003. 232p. *(978-0-207-19862-5(4))* HarperCollins Pubs. Australia.

Powers, Gretchen Ellen, jt. illus. see Gilbert, Anne Yvonne.

Powers, Leon R., photos by. The Forgotten Expedition: The 1907 Baker University Expedition into Idaho & Oregon. Powers, Leon R. 2011. 200p. (YA). pap. 16.95 *(978-0-9800208-1-6(6))* Look-About Bks.

Powers, Mark, et al. Tara's Tiara: Paperback. Powers, Mark & Powers, Megan. 2012. 130p. (J). pap. 14.95 *(978-0-9853817-0-7(1))* Pendentive Pubns.

Powers, Mireille Xioulan, jt. illus. see Colby, J. Z.

Powers, Richard M. Land of the Pharaohs. Cottrell, Leonard. 2012. 130p. 40.95 *(978-1-258-23853-7(5));* pap. 25.95 *(978-1-258-24652-5(X))* Literary Licensing, LLC.

PowerStation Studios & Pilot Studio. Star Wars: 10-Button Sounds: Droids. Harper, Benjamin. 2019. (10-Button Sound Bks.). (ENG.). 10p. (J). (gr. 1-3). bds. 12.99 *(978-0-7944-4380-1(X),* Studio Fun International) Printers Row Publishing Group.

Poxmage, Adrian. Justin Thyme. Oxridge, Panama. 2011. (Tartan of Thyme Ser.). 368p. (YA). 18.99 *(978-0-9562315-9-8(4))* Lerner Publishing Group.

Poydar, Nancy. The Bad-News Report Card. Poydar, Nancy. 2006. (ENG.). 32p. (J). (gr. -1-3). 16.95 *(978-0-8234-1992-0(4))* Holiday Hse., Inc.

—The Biggest Test in the Universe. Poydar, Nancy. 2005. (ENG.). 32p. (J). (gr. -1-3). 16.95 *(978-0-8234-1944-9(4))* Holiday Hse., Inc.

—Busy Bea. Poydar, Nancy. 2013. (ENG.). 32p. (J). (gr. -1-2). 16.99 *(978-1-4814-2161-4(1),* McElderry, Margaret K. Bks.) McElderry, Margaret K. Bks.

—Cool Ali. Poydar, Nancy. 2014. (ENG.). 32p. (J). (gr. -1-2). 16.99 *(978-1-4814-2531-5(5),* McElderry, Margaret K. Bks.) McElderry, Margaret K. Bks.

—The Perfectly Horrible Halloween. Poydar, Nancy. 2005. (ENG.). 32p. (J). (gr. k-3). pap. 6.95 *(978-0-8234-1769-8(7))* Holiday Hse., Inc.

Poynter, Linda. My Invisible Friends. Whitedove, Michelle. l.t. ed. 2005. 30p. (gr. -1-3). spiral bd. 18.95 *(978-0-9714908-4-0(8))* Whitedove Pr.

Pozzo, Adam Dal. The Wiggles Christmas Song & Activity Book. 2006. (ENG.). 44p. per. 10.95 *(978-1-876871-88-8(1),* 14036064) Music Sales Corp.

Prabhat, Sandhya. I Am Brown. Banker, Ashok. 2020. 40p. (J). (gr. k-2). 17.99 *(978-1-911373-94-0(3))* Lantana Publishing GBR. Dist: Lerner Publishing Group.

—Ignore the Trolls. Gershowitz, Jordan. 2019. (ENG.). 32p. (J). (gr. -1-3). 17.99 *(978-1-57687-933-7(X),* powerHouse Bks.) powerHse. Bks.

Prada, Sandra de la. Way Past Mad. Adelman, Hallee. 2020. (Great Big Feelings Ser.). (ENG.). 32p. (J). (gr. -1-3). 16.99 ***(978-0-8075-8685-3(4),*** 807586854) Whitman, Albert & Co.

Prahin, Andrew. Brimsby's Hats. Prahin, Andrew. 2013. (ENG.). 40p. (J). (gr. -1-3). 15.99 *(978-1-4424-8147-3(1),* Simon & Schuster Bks. For Young Readers) Simon & Schuster Bks. For Young Readers.

Prajogo, Agus. Twas the Night Before Bayou Classic. Brew, Andrea. 2017. (ENG.). (J). (gr. -1-3). 14.95 *(978-1-63177-922-0(2))* Mascot Bks., Inc.

Praker, Jon. Trapped in the Bermuda Triangle: Book 5 - Dorp the Scottish Dragon. Brundige, Britt & Durant, Sybrina, eds. 2019. (Dorp the Scottish Dragon Ser.: Vol. 5). (ENG.). 32p. (J). pap. 12.99 ***(978-1-6791-0331-5(8))*** Independently Published.

Praker, Jon. 5 - Dorp the Scottish Dragon: In the Bermuda Triangle, bk. 5. Johnson, Sandi. Brundige, Britt & Durant, Sybrina, eds. 2014. (ENG.). 30p. (J). (gr. -1-6). pap. 12.99 *(978-1-929063-62-8(8),* 161) Moons & Stars Publishing For Children.

Prange, Beckie. Song of the Water Boatman & Other Pond Poems. Sidman, Joyce. 2005. (ENG.). 32p. (J). (gr. -1-3). 17.99 *(978-0-618-13547-9(2),* 595781) Houghton Mifflin Harcourt Publishing Co.

—Ubiquitous: Celebrating Nature's Survivors. Sidman, Joyce. 2010. (ENG.). 40p. (J). (gr. 1-4). 17.99 *(978-0-618-71719-4(6),* 515198) Houghton Mifflin Harcourt Publishing Co.

Prange, Beckie & Bowen, Betsy. One North Star: A Counting Book. Root, Phyllis. 2016. (ENG.). 36p. 16.95 *(978-0-8166-5063-7(2))* Univ. of Minnesota Pr.

Prap, Lila. I Like Black & White. Hicks, Barbara Jean. 2006. 24p. (J). (gr. -1-3). 9.95 *(978-1-58925-056-7(7))* Tiger Tales.

—I Like Colors. Hicks, Barbara Jean. 2006. 24p. (J). (gr. -1-3). 9.95 *(978-1-58925-057-4(5))* Tiger Tales.

Prascak, Maria Desimone. The Day the Chocolate Melted Away. Howard, Uncle Dave. 2019. (Sarris Candy Kindom Chronicles Ser.: Vol. 1). (ENG.). 32p. (J). pap. 11.99 *(978-0-9989598-6-3(3))* Uncle Dave's Bks.

Prasetya, Hendry & Herms, Matt. Mighty Morphin Power Rangers #1. Higgins, Kyle. 2019. (Mighty Morphin Power Rangers Ser.). (ENG.). 24p. (J). (gr. 6-12). lib. bdg. 27.07 *(978-1-5321-4423-3(7),* 33828, Graphic Novels) Spotlight.

—Mighty Morphin Power Rangers #2. Higgins, Kyle. 2019. (Mighty Morphin Power Rangers Ser.). (ENG.). 24p. (J). (gr. 6-12). lib. bdg. 27.07 *(978-1-5321-4424-0(5),* 33829, Graphic Novels) Spotlight.

—Mighty Morphin Power Rangers #3. Higgins, Kyle. 2019. (Mighty Morphin Power Rangers Ser.). (ENG.). 24p. (J). (gr. 6-12). lib. bdg. 27.07 *(978-1-5321-4425-7(3),* 33830, Graphic Novels) Spotlight.

—Mighty Morphin Power Rangers #4. Higgins, Kyle. 2019. (Mighty Morphin Power Rangers Ser.). (ENG.). 24p. (J). (gr. 6-12). lib. bdg. 27.07 *(978-1-5321-4426-4(1),* 33831, Graphic Novels) Spotlight.

—Mighty Morphin Power Rangers #5. Higgins, Kyle. 2019. (Mighty Morphin Power Rangers Ser.). (ENG.). 24p. (J). (gr. 6-12). lib. bdg. 27.07 *(978-1-5321-4427-1(X),* 33832, Graphic Novels) Spotlight.

—Mighty Morphin Power Rangers #7. Higgins, Kyle. 2019. (Mighty Morphin Power Rangers Ser.). (ENG.). 24p. (J). (gr. 6-12). lib. bdg. 27.07 *(978-1-5321-4429-5(6),* 33834, Graphic Novels) Spotlight.

—Mighty Morphin Power Rangers #8. Higgins, Kyle. 2019. (Mighty Morphin Power Rangers Ser.). (ENG.). 24p. (J). (gr. 6-12). lib. bdg. 27.07 *(978-1-5321-4430-1(X),* 33835, Graphic Novels) Spotlight.

—Mighty Morphin Power Rangers #9. Higgins, Kyle. 2019. (Mighty Morphin Power Rangers Ser.). (ENG.). 24p. (J). (gr. 6-12). lib. bdg. 27.07 *(978-1-5321-4431-8(8),* 33836, Graphic Novels) Spotlight.

Prater, Linda. Afikomen Mambo, Vol. Black, Joe. 2011. (ENG.). 24p. (J). (gr. -1 — 1). pap. 8.95 *(978-0-7613-5639-4(8),* 9780761356394, Kar-Ben Publishing) Lerner Publishing Group.

—The Cow That Got Her Wish. Hillert, Margaret. 2016. (BeginningtoRead Ser.). (ENG.). 32p. (J). (gr. -1-2). pap. 11.94 *(978-1-60357-938-4(9));* (gr. 1-2). 22.60 *(978-1-59953-797-9(4))* Norwood Hse. Pr.

—Vivian & Victor Learn about Verbs. Malaspina, Ann. 2014. (Language Builders Ser.). (ENG.). 32p. (J). (gr. 2-4). pap. 11.94 *(978-1-60357-702-1(5));* lib. bdg. 25.27 *(978-1-59953-667-5(6))* Norwood Hse. Pr.

Pratley, Penelope. The Art Garden: Sowing the Seeds of Creativity. Harrison, Penny. 2018. (ENG.). 32p. (J). (gr. -1-3). 17.99 *(978-1-925335-59-0(3),* EK Bks.) Exisle Publishing Pty Ltd. AUS. Dist: Hachette Bk. Group.

—Ella & Mrs Gooseberry: Discovering What Love Looks Like. Conley, Vikki. 2019. (ENG.). 32p. (J). (gr. -1-3). 17.99 *(978-1-925335-25-5(9),* EK Bks.) Exisle Publishing Pty Ltd. AUS. Dist: Hachette Bk. Group.

Prato, Rodica. King Midas & the Golden Touch, 1 vol. Metaxas, Eric. 2007. (Rabbit Ears-A Classic Tale Ser.). (ENG.). 36p. (J). (gr. 2-6). 28.50 *(978-1-59961-309-3(3),* 12962, Picture Bk.) Spotlight.

—Projects about Colonial Life. Broida, Marian. 2005. (Hands-On History Ser.). 48p. (gr. 3-3). lib. bdg. 32.36 *(978-0-7614-1603-6(X))* Cavendish Square Publishing LLC.

—Projects about the Plains Indians. Broida, Marian. 2005. (Hands-On History Ser.). 48p. (gr. 3-3). lib. bdg. 32.36 *(978-0-7614-1601-2(3))* Cavendish Square Publishing LLC.

Pratt, Christen. Oliver's Adventure: Skiing at Mount Snow. Puzzo, Michelle. 2018. (ENG.). 36p. (J). (gr. k-3). 17.95 *(978-0-9994995-0-4(5))* Green Writers Pr.

Pratt, Christine Joy. Sea Queens: Women Pirates Around the World. Yolen, Jane. 112p. (J). (gr. 2-5). 2010. pap. 9.95 *(978-1-58089-132-5(2));* 2008. 18.95 *(978-1-58089-131-8(4))* Charlesbridge Publishing, Inc.

—Sea Queens: Women Pirates Around the World. Yolen, Jane. 2010. (ENG.). (J). (gr. 4-7). lib. bdg. 20.55 *(978-1-61383-072-7(6))* Perfection Learning Corp.

Pratt, Lizz. Jelly Bean Row, 1 vol. Pynn Taylor, Susan. 2011. (ENG.). 32p. (J). (gr. k-5). pap. *(978-1-897174-80-7(2))* Breakwater Bks., Ltd.

Pratt, Ned, photos by. The House of Wooden Santas, 1 vol. Major, Kevin. gif. ed. 2004. (ENG., 96p. (J). 34.95 *(978-0-88995-249-2(3))* Red Deer Pr. CAN. Dist: Fitzhenry & Whiteside, Ltd.

Pratt, Pierre. Albert, the Dog Who Liked to Ride in Taxis. Zarin, Cynthia. 2004. (ENG.). 32p. (J). (gr. -1-3). 18.99 *(978-0-689-84762-2(9),* Atheneum/Richard Jackson Bks.) Simon & Schuster Children's Publishing.

—The Branch. Messier, Mireille. 2016. (ENG.). 32p. (J). (gr. -1-2). 16.95 *(978-1-77138-564-0(2))* Kids Can Pr., Ltd. CAN. Dist: Hachette Bk. Group.

—Doors in the Air, 1 vol. Weale, David. 2012. (ENG.). 32p. (J). (gr. -1-k). 19.95 *(978-1-55469-250-7(4))* Orca Bk. Pubs. USA.

—A Forest in the City, 1 vol. Curtis, Andrea. 2020. (ThinkCities Ser.: 1). (ENG.). 40p. (J). (gr. 3-7). 19.95 *(978-1-77306-142-9(9))* Groundwood Bks. CAN. Dist: Publishers Group West (PGW).

—Le Géant de la Forêt: Un Voyage Musical. Ziskind, Hélio & Duchesne, Christiane. 2014. (FRE & ENG.). 48p. (J). (gr. k-2). 16.95 *(978-2-923163-36-9(2))* La Montagne Secrete CAN. Dist: Independent Pubs. Group.

—Gustave, 1 vol. Simard, Rémy. Tanaka, Shelley, tr. 2014. (ENG.). 64p. (J). (gr. -1-2). 18.95 *(978-1-55498-451-0(3))* Groundwood Bks. CAN. Dist: Publishers Group West (PGW).

—The Ladder. Rasmussen, Halfdan. Nelson, Marilyn, tr. 2006. (ENG.). 62p. (J). (gr. -1-3). 17.99 *(978-0-7636-2282-4(6))* Candlewick Pr.

—No-Matter-What Friend, 1 vol. Winters, Kari-Lynn. 2014. (ENG.). 32p. (J). (gr. 1-3). 16.95 *(978-1-896580-83-8(1))* Tradewind Bks. CAN. Dist: Orca Bk. Pubs. USA.

—One Is a Lot (Except When It's Not) Van, Muon Thi. 2019. (ENG.). 32p. (J). (gr. -1-2). 16.99 *(978-1-5253-0013-4(X))* Kids Can Pr., Ltd. CAN. Dist: Hachette Bk. Group.

—Stop, Thief! Tekavec, Heather. 2014. (ENG.). 32p. (J). (gr. -1-2). 16.95 *(978-1-77138-012-6(8))* Kids Can Pr., Ltd. CAN. Dist: Hachette Bk. Group.

Pratt-Serafini, Kristin Joy. Saguaro Moon: A Desert Journal. 2004. (Sharing Nature with Children Book Ser.). 32p. (YA). 16.95 *(978-1-58469-037-5(2))* Dawn Pubns.

Pratt Serafini, Kristin Joy. A Swim Through the Sea, 1 vol. 2006. (ENG.). 26p. (J). (gr. -1-6). bds. 7.99 *(978-1-58469-080-1(1),* Dawn Pubns.) Sourcebooks, Inc.

Pratt-Serafini, Kristin Joy. A Walk in the Rainforest. Pratt-Serafini, Kristin Joy. 2007. (ENG.). 26p. (J). (gr. -1 — 1). bds. 7.95 *(978-1-58469-088-7(7),* Dawn Pubns.) Sourcebooks, Inc.

Pratt, Susan. Look at Little Lucy, 1 vol. Welty, Carolyn. 2009. 16p. pap. 24.95 *(978-1-60813-444-1(X))* America Star Bks.

Pratt-Thomas, Leslie. Shackles. Wentworth, Marjory. 2009. (ENG.). 36p. (J). 16.99 *(978-0-933101-06-7(6))* Legacy Pubns.

Praught, Alexandria. Marley's Grand Adventures: Book 1: Marley Gets a New Home. Hicks, Kathy & Hicks, Braden. 2018. (Marley's Grand Adventures Ser.: Vol. 1). (ENG.). 28p. (J). 22.95 *(978-1-64114-802-3(0));* pap. 12.95 *(978-1-64114-800-9(4))* Christian Faith Publishing.

Prayan, Animation Studio. The Adventures of Vince the Cat: Vince Discovers the Golden Triangle. Bryant, Heidi. 2nd ed. 2019. (Catnap Stories Ser.: Vol. 2). (ENG.). 58p. (J). (gr. k-5). pap. ***(978-1-9993312-5-2(7))*** Ipsum Agency.

—The Adventures of Vince the Cat: Vince Goes to Paris. Bryant, Heidi. 2nd ed. 2018. (Catnap Stories Ser.: Vol. 1). (ENG.). 58p. (J). (gr. k-5). pap. ***(978-1-9993312-2-1(2))*** Ipsum Agency.

Prebeg, Rick, photos by. Into the Jungle. Prebeg, Rick. 2005. (J). *(978-1-933248-05-9(X))* World Quest Learning.

—Looking for Lions. Prebeg, Rick. 2005. (J). *(978-1-933248-12-7(2))* World Quest Learning.

—Night Cat. Prebeg, Rick. 2005. (J). *(978-1-933248-15-8(7))* World Quest Learning.

—You've Got Cheetah Mail. Prebeg, Rick. 2005. (J). *(978-1-933248-11-0(4))* World Quest Learning.

Prebenna, David. Peekaboo, Elmo! (Sesame Street) Allen, Constance. 2014. (Big Bird's Favorites Board Bks.). (ENG.). 24p. (J). (— 1). bds. 4.99 *(978-0-449-81483-3(1),* Random Hse. Bks. for Young Readers) Random Hse. Children's Bks.

Predic, Ana. Anna Doesn't Listen. Phillips, James L. 2018. (ENG.). 28p. (J). pap. 9.13 *(978-1-7309-1552-9(3))* Independently Published.

Preitano, Manuel. The Oracle Code. Nijkamp, Marieke. 2020. 208p. (YA). (gr. 7-9). pap. 16.99 *(978-1-4012-9066-5(3))* DC Comics.

Premise Entertainment. The Spirit of Lindy. Weeks, Kermit. 2011. (J). 19.95 *(978-0-9790267-1-3(7))* KWIP, Inc.

Premise Entertainment, jt. illus. see Disney Storybook Art Team.

Prendergast, Kate. Dog on a Digger. Prendergast, Kate. 2018. (ENG.). 32p. (J). (gr. -1-1). 16.99 *(978-1-5362-0041-6(7))* Candlewick Pr.

—Sleep: How Nature Gets Its Rest. Prendergast, Kate. 2019. (ENG.). 32p. (J). (gr. k-3). 16.99 *(978-1-5362-0798-9(5))* Candlewick Pr.

Prentice, Priscilla. When You Just Have to Roar! Robertson, Rachel. 2015. (ENG.). 32p. (J). (gr. -1-k). 15.95 *(978-1-60554-362-8(4))* Redleaf Pr.

Prescott, Clara. Bluebell & Snowflake: The Story of an Unlikely Friendship. Tonn, Jessica. 2019. (ENG.). 18p. (J). *(978-1-5255-4387-6(3));* pap. *(978-1-5255-4388-3(1))* FriesenPress.

P

Presley, Loren John. King of Chaos: Shadow's Reign. Tucker, Michael P. 2016. (King of Chaos Ser.: Vol. 2). (ENG.). (YA). (gr. 7-12). pap. 19.95 *(978-0-9978384-3-5(4))* Star Gem Publishing.

Prespentt, Alyssa. La Historia de Snakey. Prespentt, Alyssa, tr. Collazos, James, ed. 2019. (SPA.). 54p. (J). pap. 15.99 *(978-1-7963-3189-9(9))* Independently Published.

Press, Disney Lucasfilm. Daring Adventures: Volume 1. Berne, Emma Carlson. 2019. (Star Wars: Forces of Destiny Chapter Bks.). (ENG.). 128p. (J). (gr. 1-5). lib. bdg. 27.07 *(978-1-5321-4325-0(7)*, 31855, Chapter Bks.) Spotlight.

—Daring Adventures: Volume 2. Berne, Emma Carlson. 2019. (Star Wars: Forces of Destiny Chapter Bks.). (ENG.). 128p. (J). (gr. 1-5). lib. bdg. 27.07 *(978-1-5321-4326-7(5)*, 31856, Chapter Bks.) Spotlight.

—The Leia Chronicles. Berne, Emma Carlson. 2019. (Star Wars: Forces of Destiny Chapter Bks.). (ENG.). 112p. (J). (gr. 1-5). lib. bdg. 27.07 *(978-1-5321-4327-4(3)*, 31857, Chapter Bks.) Spotlight.

—The Rey Chronicles. Berne, Emma Carlson. 2019. (Star Wars: Forces of Destiny Chapter Bks.). (ENG.). 112p. (J). (gr. 1-5). lib. bdg. 27.07 *(978-1-5321-4328-1(1)*, 31858, Chapter Bks.) Spotlight.

Press, Jenny. Bedtime Tales. Baxter, Nicola. 2013. 80p. (J). (gr. -1-k). pap. 9.99 *(978-1-84322-952-0(8))* Anness Publishing GBR. Dist: National Bk. Network.

—Book of Five-Minute Farmyard Tales. Baxter, Nicola. 2013. (ENG.). 80p. (J). (gr. -1-k). pap. 9.99 *(978-1-84322-953-7(6))* Anness Publishing GBR. Dist: National Bk. Network.

—A Book of Five-Minute Kitten Tales: A Treasury of over 35 Bedtime Stories. Baxter, Nicola. 2013. 80p. (J). (gr. -1-12). pap. 9.99 *(978-1-84322-888-2(2))* Anness Publishing GBR. Dist: National Bk. Network.

—A Book of Five-Minute Teddy Bear Tales: A Treasury of over 35 Bedtime Stories. Baxter, Nicola. 2013. (ENG.). 80p. pap. 9.99 *(978-1-84322-889-9(0))* Anness Publishing GBR. Dist: National Bk. Network.

—My Little Treasury of Bedtime Stories. Baxter, Nicola. 2013. (ENG.). 320p. (J). (gr. -1-k). 12.99 *(978-1-84322-729-8(0))* Anness Publishing GBR. Dist: National Bk. Network.

—My Little Treasury of Stories & Rhymes. Baxter, Nicola. 2013. 320p. (J). (gr. -1-k). 12.99 *(978-1-84322-904-9(8))* Anness Publishing GBR. Dist: National Bk. Network.

—My Wonderful Treasury of Five-Minute Stories. Baxter, Nicola. 2012. 256p. (J). (gr. k-4). 18.99 *(978-1-84322-805-9(X))* Anness Publishing GBR. Dist: National Bk. Network.

—Peter Pan. Barrie, J. M. 2013. (Storyteller Book Ser.). (ENG.). 48p. (J). (gr. k-5). pap. 7.99 *(978-1-84322-884-4(X)*, Armadillo) Anness Publishing GBR. Dist: National Bk. Network.

—A Storyteller Book Sleeping Beauty. Young, Lesley. 2013. (ENG.). 48p. (J). (gr. -1-12). pap. 7.99 *(978-1-84322-910-0(2)*, Armadillo) Anness Publishing GBR. Dist: National Bk. Network.

—Tales from the Toy Box. Baxter, Nicola. 2012. 80p. (J). (gr. k-4). pap. 9.99 *(978-1-84322-951-3(X))* Anness Publishing GBR. Dist: National Bk. Network.

Press, Lucasfilm. Star Wars Rebels: Always Bet on Chopper. Ausu, Meredith & Hopps, Kevin. 2017. (World of Reading Level 1 Ser.). (ENG.). 32p. (J). (gr. -1-3). lib. bdg. 27.07 *(978-1-5321-4055-6(X)*, 25427) Spotlight.

—Star Wars Rebels: Ezra & the Pilot. Heddle, Jennifer & Kinberg, Simon. 2017. (World of Reading Level 2 Ser.). (ENG.). 32p. (J). (gr. k-3). lib. bdg. 27.07 *(978-1-5321-4066-2(5)*, 25437) Spotlight.

—Star Wars Rebels: Kanan's Jedi Training. Schaefer, Elizabeth & Murray, Charles. 2017. (World of Reading Level 2 Ser.). (ENG.). 32p. (J). (gr. k-3). lib. bdg. 27.07 *(978-1-5321-4068-6(1)*, 25439) Spotlight.

—Star Wars Rebels: Zeb to the Rescue. Siglain, Michael et al. 2017. (World of Reading Level 1 Ser.). (ENG.). 32p. (J). (gr. -1-3). lib. bdg. 27.07 *(978-1-5321-4056-3(8)*, 25428) Spotlight.

Press, Marvel. Spider-Man: down to a Science! West, Alexandra. 2019. (World of Reading Level 2 Ser.). (ENG.). 32p. (J). (gr. k-3). lib. bdg. 27.07 *(978-1-5321-4411-0(3)*, 33816) Spotlight.

Pressey, Deborah. On My Way to the Market. Pair, Karma A. 2009. 24p. pap. 15.00 *(978-1-4389-6299-3(1))* AuthorHouse.

Pressler, Dave. Back to School with Bigfoot. Berger, Samantha & Brockenbrough, Martha. 2017. (ENG.). 40p. (J). (gr. -1-3). 16.99 *(978-0-545-85973-8(5))* Scholastic, Inc.

Preston, Archie. Thankful, 1 vol. Spinelli, Eileen. (ENG.). (J). 2018. 20p. bds. 8.99 *(978-0-310-76782-4(2))*; 2015. 32p. 16.99 *(978-0-310-00088-4(2))* Zonderkidz.

Preston, Carole. Restless Owl & Other Stories. Littlewood, Graham. 2010. (ENG.). 56p. pap. *(978-1-84748-778-0(5))* Athena Pr.

Preston-Gannon, Frann. Because of an Acorn: (Nature Autumn Books for Children, Picture Books about Acorn Trees) Schaefer, Lola M. & Schaefer, Adam. 2016. (ENG.). 36p. (J). (gr. -1-k). 16.99 *(978-1-4521-1242-8(8))* Chronicle Bks. LLC.

—Busy-Eyed Day. Pace, Anne Marie. 2018. (ENG.). 32p. (J). (-3). 17.99 *(978-1-4814-5903-7(1)*, Beach Lane Bks.) Beach Lane Bks.

—Gator, Gator, Gator! Bernstrom, Daniel. 2018. (ENG.). 40p. (J). (gr. -1-3). 17.99 *(978-0-06-246330-2(6)*, HarperCollins) HarperCollins Pubs. Ltd. GBR. Dist: HarperCollins Pubs.

—One Dark Bird. Scanlon, Liz Garton. 2019. (ENG.). 40p. (J). (-3). 17.99 *(978-1-5344-0443-4(0)*, Beach Lane Bks.) Beach Lane Bks.

—Sing a Song of Seasons: A Nature Poem for Each Day of the Year. Crow, Nosy. Waters, Fiona, ed. 2018. (ENG.). 336p. (J). (gr. k-12). 40.00 *(978-1-5362-0247-2(9)*, Nosy Crow) Candlewick Pr.

Preston-Gannon, Frann. By the Light of the Moon. Preston-Gannon, Frann. 2019. (ENG.). 40p. (J). (gr. -1-2). 16.99 *(978-1-5362-0810-8(8)*, Templar) Candlewick Pr.

—Dandylion Summer. Preston-Gannon, Frann. 2020. (ENG.). 40p. (J). 18.99 *(978-1-250-13339-7(4)*, 900177280, Holt, Henry & Co. Bks. For Young Readers) Holt, Henry & Co.

—Dave's Cave. Preston-Gannon, Frann. 2018. (ENG.). 32p. (J). (gr. -1-2). 15.99 *(978-0-7636-9628-3(5)*, Nosy Crow) Candlewick Pr.

—Dave's Rock. Preston-Gannon, Frann. 2019. (ENG.). 32p. (J). (gr. -1-2). 15.99 *(978-1-5362-0271-7(1)*, Nosy Crow) Candlewick Pr.

Preston, Graham. The Good Wagon. Clark, Paul. 2012. (J). lthr. *(978-1-921633-88-1(3)*, Even Before Publishing) Wombat Bks.

Preston, Lizzie, et al. Draw Your Own Fairy Tale Zendoodles. Huff, Abby. 2017. (Draw Your Own Zendoodles Ser.). (ENG.). 48p. (J). (gr. 4-8). lib. bdg. 31.99 *(978-1-5157-4842-7(1)*, Capstone Pr.) Capstone.

Prettygrafik Design. Merry Christmas: Journal with Positive Affirmations. Miniature Miracles. 2018. (ENG.). 126p. (J). pap. 7.80 *(978-1-7309-4443-7(4))* Independently Published.

Preumayr, Josefina. Alicia Alonso Takes the Stage. Rebel Girls. 2020. (Good Night Stories for Rebel Girls Chapter Book Ser.). (ENG.). 128p. (J). (gr. 2-5). 12.99 ***(978-1-7333292-2-4(6)***, Rebel Girls) Timbuktu Labs, Inc.

Preuss, Sarah Louise. Annie: A Small Ant with Some Big Questions. Diggle, David Mark. 2011. 24p. (J). pap. *(978-0-9871658-2-4(8))* Diggle de Doo Productions Pty, Ltd.

—Bella: Shares Her Sticky Plan. Diggle, David Mark. 2011. 24p. (J). pap. *(978-0-9871658-9-3(5))* Diggle de Doo Productions Pty, Ltd.

—Douglas: Pays the Price for Not Paying Attention. Diggle, David Mark. 2011. 24p. (J). pap. *(978-0-9871658-5-5(2))* Diggle de Doo Productions Pty, Ltd.

—Lilly: The Crazy Little Van. Diggle, David Mark. 2011. 26p. (J). pap. *(978-0-9871658-4-8(4))* Diggle de Doo Productions Pty, Ltd.

—Malana: Learns When Enough Is Enough. Diggle, David Mark. 2011. 24p. (J). pap. *(978-0-9871658-7-9(9))* Diggle de Doo Productions Pty, Ltd.

—Paco: The High-Performance Penguin. Diggle, David Mark. 2011. 24p. (J). pap. *(978-0-9871658-1-7(X))* Diggle de Doo Productions Pty, Ltd.

—Reggie: Learns to Roll with It. Diggle, David Mark. 2011. 24p. (J). pap. *(978-0-9871658-3-1(6))* Diggle de Doo Productions Pty, Ltd.

—Sally: And Her Singing Stage Debut. Diggle, David Mark. 2011. 24p. (J). pap. *(978-0-9871658-6-2(0))* Diggle de Doo Productions Pty, Ltd.

—Samantha: One Finger, One Nose, A Whole Lot of Bugs. Diggle, David Mark. 2011. 24p. (J). pap. *(978-0-9871658-0-0(1))* Diggle de Doo Productions Pty, Ltd.

Prevec, Rose Anne. Toby, the Pet Therapy Dog, Says Be a Buddy Not a Bully. Hammond, Charmaine. 2013. (ENG.). (J). pap. 12.95 *(978-0-9836045-5-6(X)*, Kendahl Hse. Pr.) Youngs, Bettie Bks.

Preveza, Amy. Brinkley Boyd of Weymouth. Hallinan, Annie. 2017. 46p. (J). *(978-0-9971477-4-2(1))* Turnberry Pr.

Previn, Alicia L. The Strange Disappearance of Walter Tortoise. Previn, Alicia L. 2013. 36p. pap. 12.99 *(978-0-9847107-1-3(X))* TortoiseBrand Bks.

Previn, Stacey. Being a Good Citizen: A Book about Citizenship, 1 vol. Small, Mary. 2005. (Way to Be! Ser.). (ENG.). 24p. (J). (gr. k-2). lib. bdg. 27.32 *(978-1-4048-1050-1(1)*, Picture Window Bks.) Capstone.

—Being Considerate. Donahue, Jill Lynn. 2007. (Way to Be! Ser.). (ENG.). 24p. (J). (gr. -1-2). lib. bdg. 27.32 *(978-1-4048-3777-5(9)*, Picture Window Bks.) Capstone.

—Being Respectful: A Book about Respectfulness, 1 vol. Small, Mary. 2005. (Way to Be! Ser.). (ENG.). 24p. (gr. k-2). lib. bdg. 25.99 *(978-1-4048-1053-2(6)*, Picture Window Bks.) Capstone.

—Being Responsible: A Book about Responsibility, 1 vol. Small, Mary. 2005. (Way to Be! Ser.). (ENG.). 24p. (J). (gr. k-2). lib. bdg. 27.32 *(978-1-4048-1052-5(8)*, Picture Window Bks.) Capstone.

—Caring: A Book about Caring, 1 vol. Small, Mary. 2005. (Way to Be! Ser.). (ENG.). 24p. (J). (gr. k-2). lib. bdg. 27.32 *(978-1-4048-1049-5(8)*, Picture Window Bks.) Capstone.

—Ser Honesto. Donahue, Jill Lynn. 2011. (¡Así Debemos Ser!/Way to Be! Ser.).Tr. of Being Honest. (ENG.). 24p. (J). (gr. -1-2). lib. bdg. 27.32 *(978-1-4048-6689-8(2)*, Picture Window Bks.) Capstone.

Prevost, Mikela. Elan, Son of Two Peoples. Hyde, Heidi Smith. 2014. (ENG.). 32p. (J). (gr. k-3). 17.95 *(978-0-7613-9051-0(0)*, 9780761390510, Kar-Ben Publishing) Lerner Publishing Group.

—Trouble Talk. Ludwig, Trudy. 2008. 32p. (J). (gr. 1-4). 17.99 *(978-1-58246-240-0(2)*, Tricycle Pr.) Random Hse. Children's Bks.

Prewett, Maggie. The Grumpy Lighthouse Keeper. Corpus, Terrizita. 2017. 32p. (J). (gr. k-3). pap. 13.99 *(978-1-925360-18-9(0))* Magabala Bks. AUS. Dist: Independent Pubs. Group.

—The Old Frangipani Tree at Flying Fish Point. Saffioti, Trina. 2010. 28p. (J). (gr. 1-7). 18.95 *(978-1-921248-60-3(2))* Magabala Bks. AUS. Dist: Independent Pubs. Group.

Preyzner, Alex. Gospel Truths for the Family. Conrad, Jeremy. 2018. (ENG.). 64p. (J). pap. 13.98 *(978-1-7297-1612-0(1))* CreateSpace Independent Publishing Platform.

Preza, Bruno Gonzalez. Juana Ines. Lazaro, Georgina. 2007. (SPA.). 32p. (J). (gr. 3-5). 14.99 *(978-1-930332-57-7(2))* Lectorum Pubns., Inc.

Prezio, Victor. Teenage Frontier Stories. Furman, A. L., ed. 2011. 256p. 47.95 *(978-1-258-09865-0(2))* Literary Licensing, LLC.

Prezoto, Vanessa. Começo, Meio e Fim. Betto. 2014. (POR.). 30p. (J). *(978-85-62500-68-8(2))* Rocco, Editora, Ltda.

Price, Andy, et al. Applejack & Rarity. Cook, Katie. 2016. (My Little Pony: Friends Forever Ser.). (ENG.). 24p. (J). (gr. 1-8). 27.07 *(978-1-61479-505-6(3)*, 21411, Graphic Novels) Spotlight.

—My Little Pony: Friendship Is Magic. Cook, Katie. 2015. (My Little Pony: Friendship Is Magic Ser.). (ENG.). 24p. (J). (gr. 2-5). lib. bdg. 27.07 *(978-1-61479-376-2(X)*, 18207);4. lib. bdg. 27.07 *(978-1-61479-379-3(4)*, 18210) Spotlight. (Graphic Novels).

Price, Andy. My Little Pony Friendship Is Magic, Pt. 1. Cook, Katie. 2013. (My Little Pony Ser.). 52p. (J). (gr. 4-7). pap. 6.99 *(978-1-61377-628-5(4)*, 9781613776285) Idea & Design Works, LLC.

Price, Andy, et al. My Little Pony: Friendship Is Magic: Vol. 10. Cook, Katie. 2018. (My Little Pony: Friendship Is Magic Ser.). (ENG.). 24p. (J). (gr. 2-8). lib. bdg. 27.07 *(978-1-5321-4226-0(9)*, 31103, Graphic Novels) Spotlight.

—My Little Pony: Friendship Is Magic: Vol. 11. Cook, Katie. 2018. (My Little Pony: Friendship Is Magic Ser.). (ENG.). 24p. (J). (gr. 2-8). lib. bdg. 27.07 *(978-1-5321-4227-7(7)*, 31104, Graphic Novels) Spotlight.

—My Little Pony: Friendship Is Magic: Vol. 12. Cook, Katie. 2018. (My Little Pony: Friendship Is Magic Ser.). (ENG.). 24p. (J). (gr. 2-8). lib. bdg. 27.07 *(978-1-5321-4228-4(5)*, 31105, Graphic Novels) Spotlight.

—My Little Pony: Friendship Is Magic: Vol. 9. Cook, Katie. 2018. (My Little Pony: Friendship Is Magic Ser.). (ENG.). 24p. (J). (gr. 2-8). lib. bdg. 27.07 *(978-1-5321-4225-3(0)*, 31102, Graphic Novels) Spotlight.

Price, Andy. My Little Pony: Friendship Is Magic Volume 1, Vol. 1. Cook, Katie. 2014. (My Little Pony Ser.: 1). (ENG.). 104p. (J). (gr. 4-7). pap. 17.99 *(978-1-61377-605-6(5)*, 9781613776056) Idea & Design Works, LLC.

—My Little Pony: Friendship Is Magic Volume 3, Vol. 3. Cook, Katie. 2014. (My Little Pony Ser.: 3). 104p. (J). (gr. 4-7). pap. 17.99 *(978-1-61377-854-8(6)*, 9781613778548) Idea & Design Works, LLC.

—My Little Pony: Friendship Is Magic Volume 5. Cook, Katie. 2014. (My Little Pony Ser.: 5). 104p. (J). (gr. 4-7). pap. 17.99 *(978-1-63140-105-3(X)*, 9781631401053) Idea & Design Works, LLC.

—My Little Pony: Friendship Is Magic Volume 7, Vol. 7. Cook, Katie. 2015. (My Little Pony Ser.: 7). 104p. (J). (gr. 4-7). pap. 17.99 *(978-1-63140-324-8(9)*, 9781631403248) Idea & Design Works, LLC.

—My Little Pony: Friendship Is Magic Volume 9. Whitley, Jeremy. 2016. (My Little Pony Ser.: 9). 104p. (J). (gr. 4-7). pap. 17.99 *(978-1-63140-556-3(X)*, 9781631405563) Idea & Design Works, LLC.

—My Little Pony: the Movie Prequel. Anderson, Ted. ed. 2017. (MLP the Movie Ser.). 96p. (J). (gr. 4-7). pap. 9.99 *(978-1-68405-107-6(X))* Idea & Design Works, LLC.

—Rarity, 1 vol. Cook, Katie. 2015. (My Little Pony Ser.). (ENG.). 24p. (J). (gr. 1-8). 27.07 *(978-1-61479-335-9(2)*, 17157, Graphic Novels) Spotlight.

Price, Andy & Fleecs, Tony. My Little Pony: Friendship Is Magic Volume 12, Vol. 12. Anderson, Ted et al. 2017. (My Little Pony Ser.: 12). 124p. (J). (gr. 4-7). pap. 19.99 *(978-1-63140-903-5(4))* Idea & Design Works, LLC.

—My Little Pony: Friendship Is Magic Volume 15 Vol. 15. Zahler, Thom et al. 2018. (My Little Pony Ser.: 15). 128p. (J). (gr. 4-7). pap. 17.99 *(978-1-68405-357-5(9))* Idea & Design Works, LLC.

Price, Andy, jt. illus. see Sherron, Kate.

Price, Caleb, jt. illus. see Walker, Trenton.

Price, Carolyn. Vine & Branches, ol. 3. Hakowski, Maryann. 2003. (Resources for Youth Retreats Ser.: Vol. 3). 176p. (J). (gr. 6-7). pap. 24.95 *(978-0-88489-323-3(5))* Saint Mary's Press of Minnesota.

Price, Christine. Frederic Chopin, Son of Poland, Early Years. Wheeler, Opal. 2007. 160p. (J). per. 12.95 *(978-1-933573-11-3(2)*, 4716) Zeezok Publishing, LLC.

—Frederic Chopin, Son of Poland Later Years. Wheeler, Opal. 2007. 160p. (J). per. 12.95 *(978-1-933573-09-0(0)*, 4717) Zeezok Publishing, LLC.

—The Molliwumps. Maiden, Cecil. 2004. 160p. 12.95 *(978-0-9714612-9-1(5))* Green Mansion Pr. LLC.

Price, Christine, jt. illus. see Van Loon, Hendrik Willem.

Price, Dana. What Does Your Daddy Do? Pierce, Heather Vowell. 2010. 32p. pap. 16.49 *(978-1-4520-1723-5(9))* AuthorHouse.

Price, David & Ursell, Martin. Birds & Beasts: Animal songs, games & Activities. Roberts, Sheena. 2006. (Classroom Music Ser.). (ENG.). 80p. (J). (gr. 1-6). *(978-0-7136-5653-4(0)*, A&C Black) Bloomsbury Publishing Plc.

Price, Guy. The Extraordinary, Unordinary Gum Tree. Casey, Karen. 2018. (ENG.). 152p. (J). (gr. 2-5). pap. *(978-0-646-99516-8(2))* Casey, Karen.

Price, Guy J. Gissitback. Parsons, Julie. 2018. (ENG.). 30p. (J). pap. *(978-1-78830-041-4(6))* Olympia Publishers.

Price, Hattie Longstreet. A Little Maid of Newport. Curtis, Alice. 2006. (Little Maid Ser.). 212p. (J). (gr. 4-7). pap. 12.95 *(978-1-55709-339-4(3))* Applewood Bks.

Price, Margaret Evans. The Betty Fairy Book. 2006. (Shape Bks.). (ENG.). 16p. (J). pap. 9.95 *(978-1-59583-092-0(8)*, Green Tiger Pr.) Laughing Elephant.

Price, Margaret Evans, et al. A Christmas Treasury. Dover et al. 2014. (ENG.). 96p. (J). (gr. 1-5). pap. 12.99 *(978-0-486-78184-6(4))* Dover Pubns., Inc.

Price, Margaret Evans. Hansel & Gretel. Grimm, Jacob & Grimm, Wilhelm K. 2005. (Shape Bks.). (ENG.). 16p. (J). (gr. -1-3). 9.95 *(978-1-59583-012-8(X)*, 9781595830128, Green Tiger Pr.) Laughing Elephant.

—Mother Goose: Book of Rhymes. 2007. (Shape Bks.). (ENG.). 16p. (J). (gr. 4-7). pap. 9.95 *(978-1-59583-134-7(7)*, 9781595831347, Green Tiger Pr.) Laughing Elephant.

Price, Margaret Evans. The Night Before Christmas. Moore, Clement C. 2020. (J). 11.88 ***(978-1-64032-233-2(7))***; pap. 3.48 ***(978-1-64032-234-9(5))*** Innovative Eggz LLC. (Puppet Theater Bks.).

Price, Margaret Evans. The Night Before Christmas. Moore, Clement C. 2009. (Dover Children's Classics Ser.). (ENG.). 16p. (J). (gr. k-5). pap. 6.99 *(978-0-486-47369-7(4))* Dover Pubns., Inc.

—The Night Before Christmas. Moore, Clement Clarke. 2004. (Shape Bks.). (ENG.). 16p. (J). (gr. -1-3). pap. 10.95 *(978-1-59583-009-8(X)*, 9781595830098, Green Tiger Pr.) Laughing Elephant.

Price, Margaret Evans. A Child's Book of Myths. Price, Margaret Evans, retold by. 2011. (Dover Read & Listen Ser.). (ENG.). 96p. (J). (gr. 3-8). pap. 14.99 incl. audio compact disk *(978-0-486-48370-2(3))* Dover Pubns., Inc.

Price, Michael, jt. illus. see Adams, Kevin.

Price, Mina. Baker's Magic. Zahler, Diane. 2016. (Middle-Grade Novels Ser.). (ENG.). 336p. (J). (gr. 4-6). lib. bdg. 26.65 *(978-1-4965-2724-0(0)*, Stone Arch Bks.) Capstone.

—Book 1: First Dance. Taddonio, Lea. 2016. (Head over Heels Ser.). (ENG.). 48p. (J). (gr. 3-7). lib. bdg. 29.93 *(978-1-62402-192-3(1)*, 24563, Spellbound) Magic Wagon.

—Book 2: First Date. Taddonio, Lea. 2016. (Head over Heels Ser.). (ENG.). 48p. (J). (gr. 3-7). lib. bdg. 29.93 *(978-1-62402-193-0(X)*, 24565, Spellbound) Magic Wagon.

—Book 3: First Fight. Taddonio, Lea. 2016. (Head over Heels Ser.). (ENG.). 48p. (J). (gr. 3-7). lib. bdg. 29.93 *(978-1-62402-194-7(8)*, 24567, Spellbound) Magic Wagon.

—Book 4: First Kiss. Taddonio, Lea. 2016. (Head over Heels Ser.). (ENG.). 48p. (J). (gr. 3-7). lib. bdg. 29.93 *(978-1-62402-195-4(6)*, 24569, Spellbound) Magic Wagon.

—Curious Mccarthy, 4 vols. Christie, Tory. 2017. (Curious Mccarthy Ser.). (ENG.). (J). (gr. 2-4). 98.60 *(978-1-5158-1664-5(8)*, 27120); pap., pap., pap. 27.80 *(978-1-5158-1665-2(6)*, 27121) Capstone. (Picture Window Bks.).

—Curious Mccarthy's Electric Ideas. Christie, Tory. 2017. (Curious Mccarthy Ser.). (ENG.). 112p. (J). (gr. 2-4). pap. 6.95 *(978-1-5158-1648-5(6)*, 136303); lib. bdg. 25.32 *(978-1-5158-1644-7(3)*, 136299) Capstone. (Picture Window Bks.).

—Curious Mccarthy's Family Chemistry. Christie, Tory. 2017. (Curious Mccarthy Ser.). (ENG.). 112p. (J). (gr. 2-4). pap. 6.95 *(978-1-5158-1649-2(4)*, 136304); lib. bdg. 25.32 *(978-1-5158-1645-4(1)*, 136300) Capstone. (Picture Window Bks.).

—Curious Mccarthy's Not-So-Perfect Pitch. Christie, Tory. 2017. (Curious Mccarthy Ser.). (ENG.). 112p. (J). (gr. 2-4). pap. 6.95 *(978-1-5158-1647-8(8)*, 136302); lib. bdg. 25.32 *(978-1-5158-1643-0(5)*, 136298) Capstone. (Picture Window Bks.).

—Curious Mccarthy's Power of Observation. Christie, Tory. 2017. (Curious Mccarthy Ser.). (ENG.). 112p. (J). (gr. 2-4). pap. 6.95 *(978-1-5158-1650-8(8)*, 136305); lib. bdg. 25.32 *(978-1-5158-1646-1(X)*, 136301) Capstone. (Picture Window Bks.).

—Head over Heels (Set), 4 vols. Taddonio, Lea. 2016. (Head over Heels Ser.). 48p. (J). (gr. 3-7). lib. bdg. 114.00 *(978-1-62402-191-6(3)*, 24561, Spellbound) Magic Wagon.

Price-Mohr, Ruth. Story-Writing-Coding. Price, Colin. 2020. (ENG.). 96p. (J). pap. ***(978-1-8380028-1-7(2))*** Crossbridge Bks.

Price, Nick. Aesop's Fables. 2004. (Young Reading Series Two Ser.). 64p. (J). (gr. 2-18). pap. 5.95 *(978-0-7945-0409-0(4)*, Usborne) EDC Publishing.

—Animal Legends. 2004. 48p. (J). (gr. 2-18). (Young Reading Series One Ser.). pap. 5.95 *(978-0-7945-0408-3(6))*; (Young Reading Ser.: Vol. 1). lib. bdg. 13.95 *(978-1-58086-660-6(3))* EDC Publishing. (Usborne).

—Band of Friends. Morgan, Michaela. 2005. (ENG.). 24p. (J). lib. bdg. 23.65 *(978-1-59646-734-7(7))* Dingles & Co.

—Little Jack Horner. Blane, Francisco. 2010. (Rising Readers Ser.). (J). 3.49 *(978-1-60719-701-0(4))* Newmark Learning LLC.

—Little Jack Horner Eats Pie. Blane, Francisco. 2009. (Reader's Theater Nursery Rhymes & Songs Set B Ser.). 48p. (J). pap. *(978-1-60859-158-9(1))* Benchmark Education Co.

—Magical Animals. 2004. (Young Reading Series One Ser.). 48p. (J). (gr. 2-18). pap. 5.95 *(978-0-7945-0454-0(X)*, Usborne) EDC Publishing.

—The Rose Cottage Tales. Beam, Emily. 2013. (Tumtum & Nutmeg Ser.: 2). (ENG.). 416p. (J). (gr. 3-7). pap. 13.99 *(978-0-316-08598-4(7))* Little, Brown Bks. for Young Readers.

—Tim's Head, Shoulders, Knees, & Toes. Jeffries, Katherine. 2009. (Reader's Theater Nursery Rhymes & Songs Set B Ser.). 48p. (J). pap. *(978-1-60859-169-5(7))* Benchmark Education Co.

—The Wonderful Wizard of Oz. 2009. (ENG.). 12p. (J). 8.95 *(978-1-58117-856-2(5)*, Intervisual/Piggy Toes) Bendon, Inc.

Price, Rebecca. A Lump of Clay. Holliday, Bobby. 2010. 28p. (J). 18.99 *(978-0-9829082-1-1(0))* Lady Hawk Pr.

Price, Ryan. The Raven. Poe, Edgar Allan. 2014. (Visions in Poetry Ser.). (ENG.). 48p. (J). (gr. 5-9). pap. 9.95 *(978-1-55453-459-3(3))* Kids Can Pr., Ltd. CAN. Dist: Hachette Bk. Group.

Price, Susan D. Sing Christmas. Bosley, Judith A. l.t. ed. Date not set. (J). (gr. -1-k). pap. 10.95 *(978-0-930809-26-3(2))* Grand Bks., Inc.

Price, Tom. Champion Sleeper. 2008. 32p. (J). pap. 9.95 *(978-0-9748226-1-7(2))* Murphy's Bone Publishing.

Price, Traer. The Mouse & the Buddha. Price, Kathryn. 2006. (ENG.). 36p. (J). (gr. -1-k). 14.95 *(978-0-9773812-0-3(X))* Little Hse. Pr.

Priceman, Marjorie. The Bake Shop Ghost. Ogburn, Jacqueline K. 2008. (ENG.). 32p. (J). (gr. -1-3). pap. 7.99 *(978-0-547-07677-5(0)*, 1042043) Houghton Mifflin Harcourt Publishing Co.

—The Blue Ribbon Day. Couric, Katie & Couric, Katherine. 2004. 32p. (J). (gr. k-4). lib. bdg. 17.95 *(978-0-385-51292-3(9)*, Doubleday) Knopf Doubleday Publishing Group.

—Cold Snap. Spinelli, Eileen. 40p. (J). (gr. k-3). 2015. 7.99 *(978-0-375-84626-7(3)*, Dragonfly Bks.); 2012. 17.99 *(978-0-375-85700-3(1)*, Knopf Bks. for Young Readers) Random Hse. Children's Bks.

—Follow the Recipe: Poems about Imagination, Celebration, & Cake. Singer, Marilyn. 2020. 48p. (J). (gr. -1-3). 16.99 *(978-0-7352-2790-3(X),* Dial Bks) Penguin Young Readers Group.

—Jazz Age Josephine: Dancer, Singer — Who's That, Who? Why, That's MISS Josephine Baker, to You! Winter, Jonah. 2012. (ENG.). 40p. (J). (gr. -1-3). 17.99 *(978-1-4169-6123-9(2),* Atheneum Bks. for Young Readers) Simon & Schuster Children's Publishing.

Priceman, Marjorie. Julie Andrews' Treasury for All Seasons: Poems & Songs to Celebrate the Year. Andrews, Julie & Hamilton, Emma Walton. 2012. (ENG.). 192p. (J). (gr. -1-3). 21.99 ***(978-0-316-04051-8(7))*** Little, Brown Bks. for Young Readers.

Priceman, Marjorie. Miracle on 133rd Street. Manzano, Sonia. 2015. (ENG.). 48p. (J). (gr. -1-3). 17.99 *(978-0-689-87887-9(7))* Simon & Schuster Children's Publishing.

—The Music of Life: Bartolomeo Cristofori & the Invention of the Piano. Rusch, Elizabeth. 2017. (ENG.). 48p. (J). (gr. -1-3). 18.99 *(978-1-4814-4484-2(0))* Simon & Schuster Children's Publishing.

—The Ride: The Legend of Betsy Dowdy. Griffin, Kitty. 2010. (ENG.). 40p. (J). (gr. -1-3). 17.99 *(978-1-4169-2816-4(2),* Atheneum Bks. for Young Readers) Simon & Schuster Children's Publishing.

—Serefina under the Circumstances. Theroux, Phyllis. 2004. 30p. (J). (gr. k-4). reprint ed. *(978-0-7567-7756-2(9))* DIANE Publishing Co.

—Who Says Women Can't Be Computer Programmers? The Story of Ada Lovelace. Lee Stone, Tanya. 2018. (ENG.). 40p. (J). 18.99 *(978-1-62779-299-8(6),* 9781627792998, Holt, Henry & Co. Bks. For Young Readers) Holt, Henry & Co.

—Zin! Zin! Zin! A Violin. Moss, Lloyd. 2004. (gr. -1-3). 18.00 *(978-0-7569-1919-1(3))* Perfection Learning Corp.

—Zin! Zin! Zin! A Violin. Moss, Lloyd. 2005. (Stories to Go! Ser.). (ENG.). 32p. (J). (gr. -1-3). 4.99 *(978-1-4169-0838-8(2),* Simon & Schuster/Paula Wiseman Bks.) Simon & Schuster/Paula Wiseman Bks.

Priceman, Marjorie. Hot Air: The (Mostly) True Story of the First Hot-Air Balloon Ride. Priceman, Marjorie. 2005. (ENG.). 40p. (J). (gr. -1-3). 18.99 *(978-0-689-82642-9(7),* Atheneum Bks. for Young Readers) Simon & Schuster Children's Publishing.

—How to Make a Cherry Pie & See the U. S. A. Priceman, Marjorie. 2013. 40p. (J). (gr. k-3). 7.99 *(978-0-385-75293-0(8),* Dragonfly Bks.) Random Hse. Children's Bks.

Priddis, C. Michael. A Prophet in Palmyra. Daybell, Chad G. 2004. (Dare to Be True Adventure Ser.: 1). 110p. (YA). pap. 9.95 *(978-1-932898-00-2(X),* 9800X) Spring Creek Bk. Co.

Pride, Matthew. A Star Named Little One (Boy) Dukovich, Amanda J. l.t. ed. 2006. 32p. (J). (gr. -1). 15.99 *(978-1-59879-189-1(3))* Lifevest Publishing, Inc.

—A Star Named Little One (Girl) Dukovich, Amanda J. l.t. ed. 2006. 32p. (J). (gr. -1-k). 15.99 *(978-1-59879-090-0(0))* Lifevest Publishing, Inc.

Priest, Dick. White Ruff: Famous Dog Stories. Balch, Glenn. 2011. 240p. 46.95 *(978-1-258-09962-6(4))* Literary Licensing, LLC.

Priest, Iris Aspinall. Daddy Long Legs. Webster, Jean. Turoni, Monica, ed. 2017. (ENG.). (J). (gr. 4-7). pap. *(978-1-911424-02-4(5))* Black Wolf Edition & Publishing Ltd.

Priest, Saira, photos by. If We Were... Priest, Saira, des. l.t. ed. 2003. 20p. 12.95 *(978-0-9726628-7-1(1))* Niche Publishing & Marketing.

Priester, Jennifer. Mortal Realm Witch: The Magical Adventures of Dww2. Priester, Jennifer. 2016. (Mortal Realm Witch Ser.: Vol. 4). (ENG.). (J). (gr. 3-6). pap. 6.99 *(978-1-938783-08-1(5))* A&M Moonlight Creations.

Priestley, Alice. A Gift for Gita. Gilmore, Rachna. 2004. 24p. (J). *(978-1-85269-403-6(3)); (978-1-85269-407-4(6)); (978-1-85269-408-1(4)); (978-1-85269-409-8(2))* Mantra Lingua.

—Lights for Gita, 1 vol. Gilmore, Rachna. 2016. (Gita Ser.: 1). (ENG.). 24p. (J). (gr. 1-3). pap. 7.95 *(978-0-929005-61-4(9))* Second Story Pr. CAN. Dist: Orca Bk. Pubs. USA.

—Mom & Mum Are Getting Married!, 1 vol. Setterington, Ken. 2004. (ENG.). 24p. (J). (gr. 1-3). 14.95 *(978-1-896764-84-9(3))* Second Story Pr. CAN. Dist: Orca Bk. Pubs. USA.

Priestley, Alice. Mom Marries Mum! Setterington, Ken. 2020. (ENG.). 20p. (J). (gr. -1 — 1). bds. 10.95 ***(978-1-77260-134-3(9))*** Second Story Pr. CAN. Dist: Orca Bk. Pubs. USA.

Priestley, Alice. Roses for Gita. Gilmore, Rachna. 2004. 24p. (J). *(978-1-85269-367-1(3)); (978-1-85269-369-5(X))* Mantra Lingua.

Priestley, Chris. Billy Wizard. Priestley, Chris. 2005. (Young Corgi Ser.). 96p. (J). per. 12.99 *(978-0-552-54689-8(5))* Transworld Publishers Ltd. GBR. Dist: Independent Pubs. Group.

Prieto, Antonio. Rooly & Flora's Reunion: A Story of Cuba. Martinez, Raul. 2006. (ENG.). 32p. (J). pap. 6.95 *(978-1-59249-658-7(X))* Soundprints.

Prigent, Andree. Babak the Beetle. Paranuzzi, Fred. 2016. (ENG.). 32p. (J). 17.95 *(978-0-7358-4251-9(5))* North-South Bks., Inc.

Prigmore, Shane. The All-Purpose SPHDZ Boxed Set: SPHDZ Book #1!; SPHDZ Book #2!; SPHDZ Book #3!; SPHDZ 4 Life!, Set. Scieszka, Jon. ed. 2013. (Spaceheadz Ser.). (ENG.). 864p. (J). (gr. 2-5). pap. 23.99 *(978-1-4424-9858-7(7),* Simon & Schuster Bks. For Young Readers) Simon & Schuster Bks. For Young Readers.

—Planet Kindergarten. Ganz-Schmitt, Sue. 2016. (ENG.). 36p. (J). (gr. -1-k). 7.99 *(978-1-4521-5644-6(1))* Chronicle Bks. LLC.

—Planet Kindergarten. Ganz-Schmitt, Sue. 2014. 37.75 *(978-1-4906-3417-3(7));* 1.25 *(978-1-4906-3415-9(0));* 39.75 *(978-1-4906-3418-0(5))* Recorded Bks., Inc.

—Planet Kindergarten: 100 Days in Orbit. Ganz-Schmitt, Sue. 2016. (ENG.). 36p. (J). (gr. -1-k). 16.99 *(978-1-4521-3776-6(5))* Chronicle Bks. LLC.

—SPHDZ 4 Life! Scieszka, Jon. 2013. (Spaceheadz Ser.: 4). (ENG.). 192p. (J). (gr. 2-5). pap. 5.99 *(978-1-4169-7958-6(1),* Simon & Schuster Bks. For Young Readers) Simon & Schuster Bks. For Young Readers.

—SPHDZ 4 Life!, Bk. 4. Scieszka, Jon. 2013. (Spaceheadz Ser.: 4). (ENG.). 192p. (J). (gr. 2-5). 16.99 *(978-1-4169-7957-9(3),* Simon & Schuster Bks. For Young Readers) Simon & Schuster Bks. For Young Readers.

—SPHDZ Book #1! Scieszka, Jon. 2010. (Spaceheadz Ser.: 1). (ENG.). 176p. (J). (gr. 2-5). 14.99 *(978-1-4169-7951-7(4),* Simon & Schuster Bks. For Young Readers) Simon & Schuster Bks. For Young Readers.

—SPHDZ Book #1! Scieszka, Jon. 2011. (Spaceheadz Ser.: 1). (ENG.). 192p. (J). (gr. 2-5). pap. 7.99 *(978-1-4424-1986-5(5),* Simon & Schuster Bks. For Young Readers) Simon & Schuster Bks. For Young Readers.

—SPHDZ Book #2! Scieszka, Jon. 2010. (Spaceheadz Ser.: 2). (ENG.). 240p. (J). (gr. 2-5). 14.99 *(978-1-4169-7953-1(0),* Simon & Schuster Bks. For Young Readers) Simon & Schuster Bks. For Young Readers.

—SPHDZ Book #2! Scieszka, Jon. 2011. (Spaceheadz Ser.: 2). (ENG.). 256p. (J). (gr. 2-5). pap. 7.99 *(978-1-4169-7954-8(9),* Simon & Schuster Bks. For Young Readers) Simon & Schuster Bks. For Young Readers.

—SPHDZ Book #3! Scieszka, Jon. 2011. (Spaceheadz Ser.: 3). (ENG.). 224p. (J). (gr. 2-5). 15.99 *(978-1-4169-7955-5(7),* Simon & Schuster Bks. For Young Readers) Simon & Schuster Bks. For Young Readers.

—SPHDZ Book #3! Scieszka, Jon. 2012. (Spaceheadz Ser.: 3). (ENG.). 224p. (J). (gr. 2-5). pap. 8.99 *(978-1-4169-7956-2(5),* Simon & Schuster Bks. For Young Readers) Simon & Schuster Bks. For Young Readers.

Primavera, Elise. Fred & Anthony Meet the Heinie Goblins from the Black Lagoon. Fred, Anthony. rev. ed. 2008. 128p. 14.99 *(978-0-7868-3681-9(4))* Hyperion Bks. for Children.

Primavera, Elise. Auntie Claus Gift Edition. Primavera, Elise. 2015. (ENG.). 40p. (J). (gr. -1-3). 17.99 *(978-0-544-53872-6(2),* 1608615, HMH Books For Young Readers) Houghton Mifflin Harcourt Publishing Co.

—Auntie Claus, Home for the Holidays. Primavera, Elise. 2009. (ENG.). 40p. (J). (gr. -1-3). 17.99 *(978-1-4169-5485-9(6),* Simon & Schuster/Paula Wiseman Bks.) Simon & Schuster/Paula Wiseman Bks.

—Fred & Anthony Escape from the Netherworld. Primavera, Elise. Arevamirp, Esile. 2007. (Fred & Anthony Ser.). (ENG.). 122p. (J). (gr. 3-6). 17.44 *(978-0-7868-3678-9(4))* Hyperion Bks. for Children.

—Fred & Anthony Meet the Demented Super-Degerm-O Zombie. Primavera, Elise. Arevamirp, Esile. 2007. (ENG.). 128p. (J). (gr. 2-6). pap. 4.99 *(978-0-7868-3680-2(6))* Hyperion Pr.

—Fred & Anthony Meet the Heinie Goblins from the Black Lagoon. Primavera, Elise. rev. ed. 2008. (ENG.). 128p. (J). (gr. 2-4). pap. 4.99 *(978-0-7868-3682-6(2))* Hyperion Bks. for Children.

—Libby of High Hopes. Primavera, Elise. 2012. (Libby of High Hopes Ser.). (ENG.). 192p. (J). (gr. 2-5). 14.99 *(978-1-4169-5542-9(9),* Simon & Schuster/Paula Wiseman Bks.) Simon & Schuster/Paula Wiseman Bks.

—Marigold Star. Primavera, Elise. 2019. (ENG.). 240p. (J). (gr. 3-7). 16.99 *(978-0-06-056949-5(2))* HarperCollins Canada, Ltd. CAN. Dist: HarperCollins Pubs.

—Marigold Star. Primavera, Elise. 2020. 256p. (J). (gr. 3-7). pap. 7.99 *(978-0-06-056951-8(4),* HarperCollins) HarperCollins Pubs. Ltd. GBR. Dist: HarperCollins Pubs.

—Project Blue Ribbon. Primavera, Elise. 2015. (Libby of High Hopes Ser.). (ENG.). 288p. (J). (gr. 2-5). 16.99 *(978-1-4169-5543-6(7),* Simon & Schuster Bks. For Young Readers) Simon & Schuster Bks. For Young Readers.

—The Secret Order of the Gumm Street Girls. Primavera, Elise. 2008. (ENG.). 464p. (J). (gr. 3-7). pap. 10.99 *(978-0-06-056948-8(4))* HarperCollins Pubs.

Primeau, Chuck. DreamWorks How to Train Your Dragon: the Hidden World: Ready to Fly. Easton, Marilyn. 2019. (Ultra Build It Ser.). (ENG.). 24p. (J). (gr. 1-3). 11.99 *(978-0-7944-4314-6(1),* Studio Fun International) Printers Row Publishing Group.

—Fight This Fire! Steele, Michael Anthony. 2011. (LEGO City Ser.). (ENG.). 24p. (J). (gr. -1-k). pap. 3.99 *(978-0-545-31759-7(2))* Scholastic, Inc.

Primm, Patricia. Tennessee Ocean Frogs. Dudley, Marie Luther. 2008. 24p. pap. 24.95 *(978-1-60474-261-9(5))* America Star Bks.

Primm, Thomas. Tinkum's Dog. Newth, Rebecca. 2005. 32p. (J). 15.00 *(978-0-9630310-7-5(4))* Will Hall Bks.

Primmasone, Bruce. Rufus' Big Scare. Hasan, K. A. 2011. 48p. pap. 24.95 *(978-1-4626-0660-3(1))* America Star Bks.

Prince, Andrea. Lucy & the Halloween Miracle. Morgan, Emily. 2013. 24p. 16.99 *(978-0-9910324-8-8(9))* Mindstir Media.

Prince, Brian. Katie the Cricket. Jonell, Bob. 2009. 12p. pap. 24.95 *(978-1-61546-280-3(5))* America Star Bks.

—Penny the Chinstrap Penguin, 1 vol. Jonell, Bob. 2010. 22p. 24.95 *(978-1-4489-5334-9(0))* PublishAmerica, Inc.

Prince, Liz. Tomboy: A Graphic Memoir. Prince, Liz. 2014. (ENG.). 256p. (YA). (gr. 8-12). pap. 15.99 *(978-1-936976-55-3(2),* Zest Bks.) Lerner Publishing Group.

Princess Marie. Katoufs in Nursery Rhymes: Mother Goose. Kole, Ted & Genet, John, eds. 24p. (J). 50.00 *(978-0-9641381-1-7(5))* Kreative Character Kreations, Inc.

Pringle-Burke, Lesli. Rupert's Tales: Raascal's Bunny Hugs: Friendship Is Magick, Too. Kyrja. 2019. (Friendship Is Magick, Too Ser.: Vol. 4). (ENG.). 26p. (J). (gr. 2-3). pap. 4.95 ***(978-1-64606-715-2(0))*** Mroczka Media.

Pringle-Burke, Lesli. Rupert's Tales: The Nature of Elements, 1 vol. Kyrja. 2017. (ENG.). 72p. (J). (gr. -1-3). 16.99 *(978-0-7643-5387-1(X),* 7672, Red Feather) Schiffer Publishing, Ltd.

Pringle-Burke, Lesli. Rupert's Tales: The Price of Carrots: Friendship Is Magick, Too. Withers, Kyrja. 2019. (Friendship Is Magick, Too Ser.: Vol. 3). (ENG.). 26p. (J). (gr. 2-3). pap. 4.95 ***(978-1-64606-716-9(9))*** Mroczka Media.

—Seeing Through the Storm: Friendship Is Magick, Too. Withers, Kyrja. 2019. (Friendship Is Magick, Too Ser.: Vol. 2). (ENG.). 24p. (J). (gr. 2-3). pap. 4.95 ***(978-1-64606-717-6(7))*** Mroczka Media.

Pringle-Burke, Lesli. What's in a Name? Magick Is Friendship, Too. Withers, Kyrja. 2019. (ENG.). 26p. (J). (gr. 2-3). pap. 4.95 *(978-1-64606-718-3(5))* Mroczka Media.

Pringle, Victoria. Coyote & the Sky: How the Sun, Moon, & Stars Began. Garcia, Emmett. 2006. (ENG.). 32p. (J). (gr. 6-18). 19.95 *(978-0-8263-3730-6(9))* Univ. of New Mexico Pr.

—Sister Rabbit's Tricks. Garcia, Emmett Shkeme. 2013. (ENG.). 40p. (J). pap. 18.95 *(978-0-8263-5268-2(5))* Univ. of New Mexico Pr.

Prinn, Rebecca. A Strong Girls' Guide to Being. Silversides, Lani. 2019. 128p. (J). (gr. 3-7). pap. 12.95 *(978-1-4549-3282-6(1))* Sterling Publishing Co., Inc.

Prior, Natalie Jane. Willow the Wombat. Prior, Natalie Jane. ed. 2015. (ENG.). 24p. (J). (gr. k-2). pap. *(978-1-921756-66-5(7),* Brolly Bks.) Borghesi & Adam Pubs. Pty Ltd.

Priori, Giulia & Melaranci, Elisabetta. Catch That Crook! (DC Super Friends) Hitchcock, Laura. 2018. (Beginner Books(R) Ser.). (ENG.). 48p. (J). (gr. -1-1). 9.99 *(978-0-525-64600-6(0),* Random Hse. Bks. for Young Readers) Random Hse. Children's Bks.

Priori, Giulia, jt. illus. see Perissinotto, Giada.

Priscilla, Louis. Ranch Mystery: Young Readers. Coombs, Charles. 2011. 188p. 42.95 *(978-1-258-09854-4(7))* Literary Licensing, LLC.

Pritchard, Louise. Charlie & Chippo Meet a Ghost. Tossell, David H. 2012. 24p. pap. *(978-1-908773-25-8(1))* Iponymous Publishing, Ltd.

Pritchett and Hull Associates, Inc. Cooper Gets a Cast. Olson, Karen. 2003. (J). 4.50 *(978-0-939838-86-8(9))* Pritchett & Hull Assocs., Inc.

—Cooper Has Diabetes. Olson, Karen. 2003. (ENG.). 34p. (J). 9.95 *(978-0-939838-82-0(6))* Pritchett & Hull Assocs., Inc.

Pritchett, Emily. Oh, Christmas. Beeson, Sam. 2019. (ENG.). 32p. (J). bds. 15.99 *(978-1-4621-2261-5(2))* Cedar Fort, Inc./CFI Distribution.

—The Village of Lights. Stevens, Mitchell. 2018. (ENG.). 32p. (J). (gr. 2-5). 14.99 *(978-1-4621-2275-2(2))* Cedar Fort, Inc./CFI Distribution.

Pritchett, Emily Hurst. The Ride of Molly Tynes: A Tale Passed Down. Barksdale, Mary Alice & Fogelsong, Donna Jessie. 2019. (ENG.). 50p. (J). (gr. 2-6). pap. 14.95 *(978-1-947860-35-3(6),* Belle Isle Bks.) Brandylane Pubs., Inc.

Pritchett, Emily Hurst. A Tree for a Year. Dutton, Ellen. 2020. (ENG.). 50p. (J). (gr. 3-5). 22.95 ***(978-1-947860-69-8(0));*** pap. 12.95 ***(978-1-951565-09-1(6))*** Brandylane Pubs., Inc.

Pritelli, Maria Cristina. Sailing the Unknown. Rosen, Michael J. 2014. (ENG.). 40p. (J). (gr. 1-3). pap. 14.00 *(978-0-89812-976-2(1),* Creative Paperbacks) Creative Co., The.

—Sailing the Unknown: Around the World with Captain Cook. Rosen, Michael J. 2012. (ENG.). 40p. (J). (gr. 1-3). 19.99 *(978-1-56846-216-5(6),* Creative Editions) Creative Co., The.

—See Inside the Second World War. Jones, Rob Lloyd. ed. 2012. (See Inside Board Bks). 16p. (J). ring bd. 13.99 *(978-0-7945-3085-3(0),* Usborne) EDC Publishing.

—A Wish Is a Seed. Young, Jessica. 2020. (ENG.). 32p. (J). (gr. 1-3). 18.99 *(978-1-56846-338-4(3),* Creative Editions) Creative Co., The.

Prittie, Edwin John. Bumper the White Rabbit & His Friends (Illustrated Edition) Walsh, George Ethelbert. 2018. (ENG.). 68p. (J). pap. *(978-1-4068-8915-4(6))* Echo Library.

—Buster the Big Brown Bear (Illustrated Edition) Walsh, George Ethelbert. 2018. (ENG.). 68p. (J). pap. *(978-1-4068-2002-7(4))* Echo Library.

—White Tail the Deer's Adventures (Illustrated Edition) Walsh, George Ethelbert. 2018. (ENG.). 64p. (J). pap. *(978-1-4068-8916-1(4))* Echo Library.

Probert, Tim. Most Valuable Players: A Rip & Red Book. Bildner, Phil. 2018. (Rip & Red Ser.: 4). (ENG.). 240p. (J). 16.99 *(978-0-374-30510-9(2),* 900162697, Farrar, Straus & Giroux (BYR)) Farrar, Straus & Giroux.

—Most Valuable Players: A Rip & Red Book. Bildner, Phil. 2019. (Rip & Red Ser.: 4). (ENG.). 240p. (J). pap. 7.99 *(978-1-250-30853-5(4),* 900162698) Square Fish.

—Pickle: The (Formerly) Anonymous Prank Club of Fountain Point Middle School. Baker, Kimberly. 2012. (ENG.). 240p. (J). (gr. 3-7). 16.99 *(978-1-59643-765-4(0),* 900080659) Roaring Brook Pr.

—Pickle: The (Formerly) Anonymous Prank Club of Fountain Point Middle School. Baker, Kim. 2014. (ENG.). 256p. (J). (gr. 3-7). pap. 7.99 *(978-1-250-04427-3(8),* 900128319) Square Fish.

—Tournament of Champions. Bildner, Phil. 2017. (Rip & Red Ser.: 3). (ENG.). 256p. (J). 16.99 *(978-0-374-30507-9(2),* 900162694, Farrar, Straus & Giroux (BYR)) Farrar, Straus & Giroux.

—Tournament of Champions. Bildner, Phil. 2018. (Rip & Red Ser.: 3). (ENG.). 272p. (J). pap. 7.99 *(978-1-250-15843-7(5),* 900162695) Square Fish.

Probert, Tim. Lightfall: the Girl & the Galdurian. Probert, Tim. 2020. (ENG.). 256p. (J). (gr. 3-7). pap. 12.99 ***(978-0-06-299046-4(2))*** HarperCollins Pubs.

Procenko, Arina. Siti & Cahya. Munir, Gina M. 2020. (ENG.). 54p. (J). pap. 19.95 ***(978-1-0983-1474-3(3))*** BookBaby.

Procter, Bill. It Happened in the Goldfish Bowl. Procter, Diann. 2007. 28p. pap. 24.95 *(978-1-4241-8357-9(X))* America Star Bks.

proctor, brian, jt. illus. see marion, designs.

Proctor, Jon. Book 1: Integrated. Deebs, Tracy. 2017. (Vilified Ser.). (ENG.). 48p. (J). (gr. 3-7). lib. bdg. 29.93 *(978-1-5321-3058-8(9),* 27065, Spellbound) Magic Wagon.

—Book 2: Obstructed. Deebs, Tracy. 2017. (Vilified Ser.). (ENG.). 48p. (J). (gr. 3-7). lib. bdg. 29.93 *(978-1-5321-3059-5(7),* 27066, Spellbound) Magic Wagon.

—Book 3: United. Deebs, Tracy. 2017. (Vilified Ser.). (ENG.). 48p. (J). (gr. 3-7). lib. bdg. 29.93 *(978-1-5321-3060-1(0),* 27067, Spellbound) Magic Wagon.

—Book 4: Vindicated. Deebs, Tracy. 2017. (Vilified Ser.). (ENG.). 48p. (J). (gr. 3-7). lib. bdg. 29.93 *(978-1-5321-3061-8(9),* 27068, Spellbound) Magic Wagon.

—Book 5: Stained. Varley, Dax. 2017. (Demon Slayer Set 2 Ser.). (ENG.). 48p. (J). (gr. 3-7). lib. bdg. 29.93 *(978-1-5321-3006-9(6),* 25558, Spellbound) Magic Wagon.

—Book 6: Pest Control. Varley, Dax. 2017. (Demon Slayer Set 2 Ser.). (ENG.). 48p. (J). (gr. 3-7). lib. bdg. 29.93 *(978-1-5321-3007-6(4),* 25560, Spellbound) Magic Wagon.

—Book 7: Murder of Crows. Varley, Dax. 2017. (Demon Slayer Set 2 Ser.). (ENG.). 48p. (J). (gr. 3-7). lib. bdg. 29.93 *(978-1-5321-3008-3(2),* 25562, Spellbound) Magic Wagon.

—Book 8: Scarlet Portal. Varley, Dax. 2017. (Demon Slayer Set 2 Ser.). (ENG.). 48p. (J). (gr. 3-7). lib. bdg. 29.93 *(978-1-5321-3009-0(0),* 25564, Spellbound) Magic Wagon.

—The Crow. Varley, Dax. 2016. (Demon Slayer Ser.). (ENG.). 48p. (J). (gr. 3-7). lib. bdg. 29.93 *(978-1-62402-160-2(3),* 21567, Spellbound) Magic Wagon.

—Demon Slayer, 4 vols. Varley, Dax & ABDO Publishing Company Staff. 2016. (Demon Slayer Ser.). 48p. (J). (gr. 3-7). lib. bdg. 114.00 *(978-1-62402-156-5(5),* 21559, Spellbound) Magic Wagon.

—Demon Slayer Set 2 (Set), 4 vols. Varley, Dax. 2017. (Demon Slayer Set 2 Ser.). 48p. (J). (gr. 3-7). lib. bdg. 114.00 *(978-1-5321-3005-2(8),* 25556, Spellbound) Magic Wagon.

—The First & Final Voyage: The Sinking of the Titanic, 1 vol. Peters, Stephanie True. 2008. (Historical Fiction Ser.). (ENG.). 56p. (J). (gr. 3-6). pap. 6.25 *(978-1-4342-0494-3(4),* Stone Arch Bks.) Capstone.

—Graveyard Dirt. Varley, Dax. 2016. (Demon Slayer Ser.). (ENG.). 48p. (J). (gr. 3-7). lib. bdg. 29.93 *(978-1-62402-158-9(1),* 21563, Spellbound) Magic Wagon.

—Hideout. Varley, Dax. 2016. (Demon Slayer Ser.). (ENG.). 48p. (J). (gr. 3-7). lib. bdg. 29.93 *(978-1-62402-157-2(3),* 21561, Spellbound) Magic Wagon.

—The Locket. Varley, Dax. 2016. (Demon Slayer Ser.). (ENG.). 48p. (J). (gr. 3-7). lib. bdg. 29.93 *(978-1-62402-159-6(X),* 21565, Spellbound) Magic Wagon.

—True Stories of World War I, 1 vol. Yomtov, Nelson. 2012. (Stories of War Ser.). (ENG.). 32p. (J). (gr. 3-9). pap. 8.10 *(978-1-4296-9344-8(4));* lib. bdg. 31.32 *(978-1-4296-8625-9(1))* Capstone. (Capstone Pr.).

—True Stories of World War I. Yomtov, Nel. 2012. (Stories of War Ser.). (ENG.). 32p. (gr. 3-4). pap. 47.70 *(978-1-4296-9345-5(2),* Capstone Pr.) Capstone.

—Vilified (Set), 4 vols. Deebs, Tracy. 2017. (Vilified Ser.). 48p. (J). (gr. 3-7). lib. bdg. 114.00 *(978-1-5321-3057-1(0),* 27064, Spellbound) Magic Wagon.

Proctor, Peter. Wallie Exercises. Active Spud Press & Ettinger, Steve. 2011. 32p. (J). (gr. -1-3). 15.95 *(978-0-9845388-0-5(1))* Active Spud Pr.

Prodor, Bob. The Duchess Ranch of Old John Ware. Davidge, James. 2010. (ENG.). 104p. pap. 10.95 *(978-1-897411-18-6(9))* Bayeux Arts, Inc. CAN. Dist: Chicago Distribution Ctr.

Producciones, Sunset, jt. illus. see Sunset Producciones.

Proffitt, Hannah. See Me for Me: A Book for Children in Foster Care. Smith, Crystal. 2020. (ENG.). 42p. (J). pap. 9.99 ***(978-1-0976-5720-9(5))*** Independently Published.

Proimos, James. Year of the Jungle. Collins, Suzanne. 2013. 40p. (J). (gr. -1-7). 18.99 *(978-0-545-42516-2(6),* Scholastic Pr.) Scholastic, Inc.

Proimos, James, Jr. Apocalypse Bow Wow. Proimos, James, Jr. Proimos, James, III. 2015. (ENG.). 224p. (J). (gr. 3-6). 13.99 *(978-1-61963-442-8(2),* 9781619634428, Bloomsbury USA Childrens) Bloomsbury Publishing USA.

—Apocalypse Meow Meow. Proimos, James, Jr. 2015. (ENG.). 224p. (J). (gr. 3-6). 15.99 *(978-1-61963-472-5(4),* 900137802, Bloomsbury USA Childrens) Bloomsbury Publishing USA.

—Knuckle & Potty Destroy Happy World. Proimos, James, Jr. 2012. (ENG.). 80p. (J). (gr. 2-5). 12.99 *(978-0-8050-9155-7(6),* 900064073, Holt, Henry & Co. Bks. For Young Readers) Holt, Henry & Co.

Proimos, James. Mac & Cheese: A Friendship Story That Celebrates Being Different. Proimos, James. 2016. (ENG.). 40p. (J). 16.99 *(978-0-8050-9156-4(4),* 9780805091564, Holt, Henry & Co. Bks. For Young Readers) Holt, Henry & Co.

—Todd's TV. Proimos, James. 2010. (ENG.). 40p. (J). (gr. -1-3). 15.99 *(978-0-06-170985-2(9),* Tegen, Katherine Bks) HarperCollins Pubs.

P

—Waddle! Waddle! Proimos, James. 2015. (ENG.). 32p. (J). (gr. -1-3). 17.99 *(978-0-545-41846-1(1)*, Scholastic Pr.) Scholastic, Inc.

Proimos, James, III & Proimos, James, Jr. Apocalypse Bow Wow. Proimos, James, III & Proimos, James, Jr. 2016. (ENG.). 224p. (J). pap. 7.99 *(978-1-68119-088-4(5)*, 900158426, Bloomsbury USA Childrens) Bloomsbury Publishing USA.

Proimos, James, Jr., jt. illus. see Proimos, James, III.

Project Firefly. All of Life Is a School. Weeks, Kermit. 2007. 64p. (J). 19.95 *(978-0-9790267-0-6(9))* KWIP, Inc.

Project Firefly Animation Studios. The Adventures of Lady: The Big Storm. Pearson, Iris & Merrill, Mike. Pearson, Iris, ed. rev. ed. 2007. 34p. (J). 11.99 *(978-0-9789984-2-4(1))* Adventures of Lady LLC, The.

—The Adventures of Lady: The Big Storm Coloring Book. Pearson, Iris & Merrill, Mike. Pearson, Iris, ed. 2007. 34p. (J). pap. 5.49 *(978-0-9789984-3-1(X))* Adventures of Lady LLC, The.

Prole, Helen. Candle Bible for Toddlers, 1 vol. David, Juliet. 2006. (Candle Bible for Toddlers Ser.). 400p. (J). (gr. -1-k). 15.99 *(978-0-8254-7311-1(X)*, Candle Bks.) Lion Hudson PLC GBR. Dist: Kregel Pubns.

Prole, Helen. Candle Bible for Toddlers, 1 vol. David, Juliet. 2020. 400p. (J). 16.99 ***(978-0-8254-4684-9(8))*** Kregel Pubns.

Prole, Helen. Candle Bible for Toddlers, 1 vol. David, Juliet. ed. 2015. (ENG.). 400p. (J). 19.99 incl. audio compact disk *(978-1-78128-201-4(3)*, Candle Bks.) Lion Hudson PLC GBR. Dist: Kregel Pubns.

—Candle Bible for Toddlers Carry along Bible Fun. David, Juliet. 2007. (Candle Bible for Toddlers Ser.). (J). pap. 12.99 *(978-0-8254-7336-4(5)*, Candle Bks.) Lion Hudson PLC GBR. Dist: Kregel Pubns.

—Candle Prayers for Toddlers, 1 vol. David, Juliet. ed. 2010. (Candle Bible for Toddlers Ser.). (ENG.). 128p. (J). (gr. -1-k). 11.99 *(978-1-85985-679-6(9)*, Candle Bks.) Lion Hudson PLC GBR. Dist: Kregel Pubns.

—Candle Prayers for Toddlers & Candle Bible for Toddlers, 2 vols. David, Juliet. 2009. (Candle Bible for Toddlers Ser.). 528p. (J). 24.99 *(978-0-8254-7380-7(2)*, Candle Bks.) Lion Hudson PLC GBR. Dist: Kregel Pubns.

—Follow the Star, 1 vol. David, Juliet. 2005. (Poster Sticker Bks.). 8p. (J). (gr. k-2). pap. 6.99 *(978-0-8254-7304-3(7)*, Candle Bks.) Lion Hudson PLC GBR. Dist: Kregel Pubns.

—Learn & Play: Chalkboard Activities. David, Juliet. 2007. (Candle Bible for Toddlers Ser.). 12p. (J). (gr. -1-k). bds. 11.99 *(978-0-8254-7331-9(4)*, Candle Bks.) Lion Hudson PLC GBR. Dist: Kregel Pubns.

—My First Bible Stories, 1 vol. David, Juliet. ed. 2015. (Candle Bible for Toddlers Ser.). (ENG.). 12p. (J). (gr. -1-k). bds. 16.99 *(978-1-78128-225-0(0)*, Candle Bks.) Lion Hudson PLC GBR. Dist: Kregel Pubns.

—My Friend Jesus, 1 vol. David, Juliet. ed. 2016. (Candle Bible for Toddlers Ser.). (ENG.). 32p. (J). (gr. -1-k). pap. 4.99 *(978-1-78128-280-9(3)*, Candle Bks.) Lion Hudson PLC GBR. Dist: Kregel Pubns.

—My Very First Bible, 1 vol. David, Juliet. 2019. (Candle Bible for Toddlers Ser.). 40p. (J). pap. 4.99 *(978-0-8254-5559-9(6))* Kregel Pubns.

—My Very First Bible & Prayers, 1 vol. David, Juliet & Ayliffe, Alex. ed. 2014. (Candle Bible for Toddlers Ser.). (ENG.). 64p. (J). (gr. -1-k). 9.99 *(978-1-78128-152-9(1)*, Candle Bks.) Lion Hudson PLC GBR. Dist: Kregel Pubns.

—The Nativity Story, 1 vol. David, Juliet. ed. 2015. 12p. (J). (gr. -1-k). bds. 16.99 *(978-1-78128-226-7(9)*, Candle Bks.) Lion Hudson PLC GBR. Dist: Kregel Pubns.

—Noah & His Big Boat: Magnetic Adventures, 1 vol. David, Juliet. ed. 2015. (Candle Bible for Toddlers Ser.). (ENG.). 12p. (J). (gr. -1-k). bds. 16.99 *(978-1-78128-227-4(7)*, Candle Bks.) Lion Hudson PLC GBR. Dist: Kregel Pubns.

—The Story of Christmas, 1 vol. David, Juliet. ed. 2016. (Candle Bible for Toddlers Ser.). (ENG.). 20p. (J). pap. 6.99 *(978-1-78128-309-7(5)*, Candle Bks.) Lion Hudson PLC GBR. Dist: Kregel Pubns.

—The Story of Jesus, 1 vol. David, Juliet. ed. 2016. (Candle Bible for Toddlers Ser.). (ENG.). 20p. (J). pap. 6.99 *(978-1-78128-310-3(9)*, Candle Bks.) Lion Hudson PLC GBR. Dist: Kregel Pubns.

—The Story of Noah, 1 vol. David, Juliet. ed. 2016. (Candle Bible for Toddlers Ser.). (ENG.). 24p. (J). pap. 6.99 *(978-1-78128-308-0(7)*, Candle Bks.) Lion Hudson PLC GBR. Dist: Kregel Pubns.

—The Very First Christmas, 1 vol. David, Juliet. 2007. (Candle Bible for Toddlers Ser.). 24p. (J). (gr. -1-k). act. bk. ed. 6.99 *(978-0-8254-7353-1(5)*, Candle Bks.) Lion Hudson PLC GBR. Dist: Kregel Pubns.

Prom, Shirley. High Plains Heroes: Josiah. Rendall, Jaydine. 2018. (High Plains Heroes Ser.: Vol. 1). (ENG.). 140p. (J). (gr. 3-6). pap. 8.95 *(978-0-9993940-2-1(9))* Windwalker Pr.

Prosek, James. The Day My Mother Left. Prosek, James. 2009. (ENG.). 304p. (J). (gr. 4-7). pap. 7.99 *(978-1-4169-0771-8(8)*, Simon & Schuster Bks. For Young Readers) Simon & Schuster Bks. For Young Readers.

—The Day My Mother Left. Prosek, James. 2007. (ENG.). 290p. (YA). (gr. 7-12). 22.44 *(978-1-4169-0770-1(X))* Simon & Schuster, Inc.

—A Good Day's Fishing. Prosek, James. 2004. (ENG.). 40p. (J). (gr. 1-5). 19.99 *(978-0-689-85327-2(0)*, Simon & Schuster Bks. For Young Readers) Simon & Schuster Bks. For Young Readers.

Prosmitsky, Jenya. Hairy, Scary, Ordinary: What Is an Adjective? Cleary, Brian P. 2006. (Words Are Categorical Ser.). (gr. 2-4). 17.00 *(978-0-7569-6882-3(8))* Perfection Learning Corp.

—To Root, to Toot, to Parachute: What Is a Verb? Cleary, Brian P. 2006. (Words Are Categorical Ser.). (gr. 2-4). 17.00 *(978-0-7569-6884-7(4))* Perfection Learning Corp.

—The Wedding That Saved a Town. Strom, Yale. 2008. (J). (gr. -1). 17.95 *(978-0-8225-7376-0(8)*, Kar-Ben Publishing) Lerner Publishing Group.

Prosofsky, Merle, photos by. The Essential Canadian Christmas Cookbook, 1 vol. Walker, Lovoni. 2nd rev. ed. 2005. (ENG., 160p. pap. 19.95 *(978-1-55105-552-7(X)*, 58ed1ea0-a3e3-4636-9c19-3544e1f0ec68) Lone Pine Publishing USA.

—The Essential Christmas Cookbook, 1 vol., Vol. 1. Walker, Lovoni. rev. ed. 2004. (ENG., 160p. pap. 19.95 *(978-1-55105-446-9(9)*, 0132810c-ff9c-424a-9a1d-626f1e1db4b1) Lone Pine Publishing USA.

Prosofsky, Merle, jt. photos by see Samol, Nanette.

Prosser, Sue. Garden Adventures of Rosie Red. Elson, Clare. 2019. (ENG.). 30p. (J). pap. *(978-1-78830-097-1(1))* Olympia Publishers.

Prothero, Tiffany. Curtains! A High School Musical Mystery. Dahl, Michael. 2008. (Vortex Bks.). (ENG.). 112p. (J). (gr. 5-9). 26.65 *(978-1-4342-0801-9(X)*, Stone Arch Bks.) Capstone.

—The Mummy at Midnight. Brezenoff, Steve. 2008. (Shade Bks.). (ENG.). 80p. (J). (gr. 5-9). 25.32 *(978-1-4342-0797-5(8)*, Stone Arch Bks.) Capstone.

Proud, Amy. Bug Hunt. Koontz, Robin Michal. 2019. 40p. (J). (gr. -1). 16.95 *(978-1-4549-2356-5(3))* Sterling Publishing Co., Inc.

—I Want a Friend. Booth, Anne. ed. 2017. (ENG.). 32p. (J). pap. 8.99 *(978-0-7459-7706-5(5))*; (gr. -1-k). 12.99 *(978-0-7459-7707-2(3))* Lion Hudson PLC GBR. Dist: Independent Pubs. Group.

—Izzy the Very Bad Burglar. 2016. 32p. (J). (gr. -1-k). 16.99 *(978-1-63450-174-3(8)*, Sky Pony Pr.) Skyhorse Publishing Co., Inc.

Prouix, Denis. Little Rina Meets Baby Brother. Loccisano, Rina Fuda. 2011. 48p. pap. 24.95 *(978-1-4512-6299-5(X))* America Star Bks.

—Lucky's Lick. Esparza-Vela, Mary. 2013. 16p. pap. 9.95 *(978-1-61633-406-2(1))* Guardian Angel Publishing, Inc.

—Scotty's Feeder & the Secret Tower. Stein, Clem. 2011. 40p. 16.99 *(978-1-4567-3191-5(2))* AuthorHouse.

Proulx, Denis. The Adventures of Sir Sniffsalot & His Friends. Gould, Terry. 2007. 48p. (gr. -1-3). pap. 15.99 *(978-0-9789057-3-6(3))* Huntington Ludlow Media Group.

—Aunt Ruby's Kisses, 1 vol. Averette, Sonya M. 2009. 35p. pap. 24.95 *(978-1-60749-045-6(5))* America Star Bks.

—Austin & the Bully. Milot, Carryanne. 2012. 40p. pap. *(978-1-77097-970-3(0))* FriesenPress.

—Horace & Giselle. Novinsky, J. L. 2018. (ENG.). 52p. (J). pap. 15.95 *(978-1-64416-867-7(7))* Christian Faith Publishing.

—Pizza Friday Madness. Bell, Shaleena. 2019. (ENG.). 30p. (J). pap. 12.00 *(978-1-0988-6050-9(0))* Independently Published.

—Stuck. M a. 2011. (ENG.). 38p. (J). (gr. 1-5). 15.77 *(978-1-935204-33-6(5))* Salem Author Services.

—Three Wishes from a Leprechaun. Worthen, Rashawn. 2016. (ENG.). (J). pap. 11.99 *(978-0-692-77452-6(1))* Vision & Voice Publishing LLC.

—Where Shall We Go Today? Stephens, Heather. 2018. (ENG.). 36p. (J). *(978-1-5255-3533-8(1))*; pap. *(978-1-5255-3534-5(X))* FriesenPress.

Prout, Louise. Crime Time: Australians Behaving Badly. Bursztynski, Sue. 2009. 208p. (YA). pap. *(978-1-876462-76-5(0))* Ford Street Publishing Pty, Limited.

Provantini, Silvia. The Runaway Pancake. 2006. (First Reading Level 4 Ser.). 48p. (J). (gr. 1-4). 8.99 *(978-0-7945-1276-7(3)*, Usborne) EDC Publishing.

Provencher, Annematie. Susu of the Frufru. Finneron, Karyn A. 2012. 32p. (-18). pap. 9.99 *(978-0-9857362-0-0(8))* Nana's Stories.

Provencher, Jessica. God: A Theological Primer Series. Provencher, Devon. 2020. (Big Theology for Little Hearts Ser.). (ENG.). 22p. (J). bds. 9.99 *(978-1-4335-6523-6(4))* Crossway.

—The Gospel: A Theological Primer Series. Provencher, Devon. 2020. (Big Theology for Little Hearts Ser.). (ENG.). 22p. (J). bds. 9.99 *(978-1-4335-6525-0(0))* Crossway.

—Jesus: A Theological Primer Series. Provencher, Devon. 2020. (Big Theology for Little Hearts Ser.). (ENG.). 22p. (J). bds. 9.99 *(978-1-4335-6524-3(2))* Crossway.

Provensen, Alice. A Day in the Life of Murphy. Provensen, Alice. unabr. rev. ed. 2005. (J). (gr. -1-2). 28.95 incl. audio compact disk *(978-1-59519-538-8(6))* Live Oak Media.

—A Day in the Life of Murphy. Provensen, Alice. 2003. (ENG.). 40p. (J). (gr. -1-3). 17.99 *(978-0-689-84884-1(6)*, Simon & Schuster Bks. For Young Readers) Simon & Schuster Bks. For Young Readers.

—A Day in the Life of Murphy. Provensen, Alice. 2006. (ENG.). 40p. (J). (gr. -1-3). reprint ed. 8.99 *(978-1-4169-1800-4(0)*, Simon & Schuster/Paula Wiseman Bks.) Simon & Schuster/Paula Wiseman Bks.

—The Master Swordsman & the Magic Doorway: Two Legends from Ancient China. Provensen, Alice. 2014. (ENG.). 40p. (J). (gr. k-3). 19.99 *(978-1-4814-2874-3(8)*, Simon & Schuster Bks. For Young Readers) Simon & Schuster Bks. For Young Readers.

—Murphy in the City. Provensen, Alice. 2015. (ENG.). 40p. (J). (gr. -1-3). 17.99 *(978-1-4424-1971-1(7)*, Simon & Schuster Bks. For Young Readers) Simon & Schuster Bks. For Young Readers.

Provensen, Alice & Provensen, Martin. The Color Kittens. Brown, Margaret Wise. 2003. (Little Golden Book Ser.). 32p. (J). (gr. -1-2). 4.99 *(978-0-307-02141-0(6)*, Golden Bks.) Random Hse. Children's Bks.

—The Fuzzy Duckling. Werner Watson, Jane. 2012. (Golden Baby Ser.). 24p. (J). (gr. k — 1). 6.99 *(978-0-307-92966-2(3)*, Golden Bks.) Random Hse. Children's Bks.

Provensen, Alice, jt. illus. see Provensen, Martin.

Provensen, Martin & Provensen, Alice. The Fuzzy Duckling. Werner Watson, Jane. 2015. (Little Golden Book Ser.). 32p. (J). (-k). 4.99 *(978-0-553-52213-6(2)*, Golden Bks.) Random Hse. Children's Bks.

—Katie the Kitten. Jackson, Kathryn. 2018. (Little Golden Book Ser.). 24p. (J). (-k). 4.99 *(978-1-101-93925-3(7)*, Golden Bks.) Random Hse. Children's Bks.

Provensen, Martin, jt. illus. see Provensen, Alice.

Provenzano, Jeannine. Stashi the Rainbow Star: Her Journey Home. Venditti, Stacey Marie. 2008. 52p. pap. 24.95 *(978-1-60474-786-7(2))* America Star Bks.

Prows, Jackie. Quincey's Questions: A French Bulldog Story. Pardew, David. Suggs, Elizabeth, ed. 2020. (ENG.). 32p. (J). 19.00 ***(978-1-7348905-0-1(9))*** Editing Mee.

Prud'homme, Jules. Leo's Midnight Rescue. Leblanc, Louise. 2004. 62p. (J). lib. bdg. 12.00 *(978-1-4242-1217-0(0))* Fitzgerald Bks.

—Leo's Skiing Surprise. Leblanc, Louise. 2007. (Formac First Novels Ser.). (ENG.). 64p. (J). (gr. 2-5). 14.95 *(978-0-88780-738-1(0)*, 738) Formac Publishing Co., Ltd. CAN. Dist: Formac Lorimer Bks. Ltd.

—Leo's Skiing Surprise, 1 vol. Leblanc, Louise. Cummins, Sarah, tr. 2007. (Formac First Novels Ser.). (ENG.). 64p. (J). (gr. 2-5). 4.95 *(978-0-88780-736-7(4)*, 736) Formac Publishing Co., Ltd. CAN. Dist: Formac Lorimer Bks. Ltd.

Prud'homme, Jules & Jules, Prud'homme. Leo's Midnight Rescue, 1 vol. Leblanc, Louise. Cummins, Sarah, tr. 2004. (Formac First Novels Ser.: 53). (ENG.). 64p. (J). (gr. 2-5). 4.95 *(978-0-88780-640-7(6)*, 640); 14.95 *(978-0-88780-641-4(4)*, 641) Formac Publishing Co., Ltd. CAN. Dist: Formac Lorimer Bks. Ltd.

—Leo's Poster Challenge, 1 vol. Leblanc, Louise. Prud'homme, Jules & Cummins, Sarah, trs. 2003. (Formac First Novels Ser.). (ENG.). 64p. (J). (gr. 2-5). 4.95 *(978-0-88780-608-7(2)*, 608); 14.95 *(978-0-88780-609-4(0)*, 609) Formac Publishing Co., Ltd. CAN. Dist: Formac Lorimer Bks. Ltd.

Pruett, Jason. Jesus Worked Miracles. Poelman, Heidi. 2018. (ENG.). 32p. (J). (gr. k-3). 14.99 *(978-1-4621-2277-6(9))* Cedar Fort, Inc./CFI Distribution.

Pruett, Mary. Color the Western Birds: Discover the Great Outdoors. 2010. (Pruett Ser.). (ENG.). 32p. (J). pap. 5.99 *(978-0-87108-957-1(2)*, West Winds Pr.) West Margin Pr.

Pruett, Sasha. Bunny Feet. Pruett, Sasha. 2019. (ENG.). 44p. (J). pap. 9.99 *(978-1-0939-6748-7(X))* Independently Published.

Pruitt, Ginny. All the Muchos in the World: A Special Story about Love. Carson, Diana Pastora. 2006. 32p. (J). pap. 8.95 *(978-0-8198-0779-3(6))* Pauline Bks. & Media.

—One Hundred First Communions. Kelly, Veronica & Goody, Wendy. 2003. (J). (gr. k-5). 14.95 *(978-0-9657218-2-0(5))* WhipperSnapper Bks.

Pruitt, Gwendolyn. The Blake Family Vacation. Ross, Jill. 2010. (ENG.). 130p. (J). (gr. 3-7). pap. 9.95 *(978-1-59825-950-6(4))* Shenanigans Series.

—The Real Nitty-Gritty. Ross, Jill. 2010. (ENG.). 60p. (J). (gr. 3-7). pap. 9.95 *(978-1-59825-949-0(0))* Shenanigans Series.

—What's the Matter, Mr. Ticklebritches? Ross, Jill. 2010. (ENG.). 70p. (J). (gr. 3-7). pap. 9.95 *(978-1-59825-948-3(2))* Shenanigans Series.

Prunier, James. Elephants. 2019. (My First Discoveries Ser.). (ENG.). 36p. (J). (gr. -1-k). spiral bd. 16.99 *(978-1-85103-473-4(0))* Moonlight Publishing, Ltd. GBR. Dist: Independent Pubs. Group.

Prunier, James & Galeron, Henri. Dinosaurs. Jeunesse, Gallimard et al. 2007. (First Discovery Book Ser.). (ENG.). 24p. (J). (gr. -1-k). pap. 5.99 *(978-0-439-91089-7(7))* Scholastic, Inc.

—Dinosaurs. Prunier, James & Matthews, Sarah. 2012. (My First Discoveries Ser.: 3). (ENG.). 36p. (J). (gr. -1-k). spiral bd. 13.99 *(978-1-85103-379-9(3))* Moonlight Publishing, Ltd. GBR. Dist: Independent Pubs. Group.

Prunier, James, jt. illus. see Grant, Donald.

Pry, Rebecca. The Yuckiest Alphabet Book in the World: Everything Icky, Slimy, Messy, & Gooey from a to Z! Novak, Margaret. 2020. (ENG.). 30p. (J). (gr. -1-k). pap. 12.99 ***(978-1-951511-05-0(0))*** Whalen Bk. Works Publishing Co.

Pryce, Adam. Knock, Knock, Monster Who? Monster Jokes for Kids. Rodriguez, Stephanie. 2020. (Illustrated Jokes Ser.). (ENG.). 28p. (J). (gr. 1-6). 12.99 ***(978-1-5324-2964-4(9))***; pap. 12.99 ***(978-1-5324-2963-7(0))*** Xist Publishing.

Pryce, Adam. Meg & Rat & Puff! Puff! Puff! Jones, Cath. 2019. (Early Bird Readers — Pink (Early Bird Stories (tm)) Ser.). (ENG.). 32p. (J). (gr. -1-2). 27.99 *(978-1-5415-4158-0(8)*, Lerner Pubns.) Lerner Publishing Group.

—Monsters Move. O'Neill, Juliana. 2019. (Reading Stars Ser.). (ENG.). 28p. (J). (gr. -1-2). pap. 5.99 *(978-1-5324-0937-0(0))* Xist Publishing.

—Nos Vamos a la Granja. Streza, Nancy. 2017. (Xist Kids Spanish Bks.). (SPA.). 28p. (J). (gr. -1-3). pap. 9.99 *(978-1-5324-0415-3(8))* Xist Publishing.

—Nos Vamos a la Playa. Streza, Nancy. Sandoval, Lenny, tr. 2017. (Xist Kids Spanish Bks.). (SPA.). 28p. (J). (gr. -1-3). pap. 9.99 *(978-1-5324-0417-7(4))* Xist Publishing.

—We're Going to the Beach / Nos Vamos a la Playa. Streza, Nancy. Sandoval, Lenny, tr. 2017. (Xist Kids Bilingual Spanish English Ser.). (ENG & SPA.). 28p. (J). (gr. -1-3). pap. 9.99 *(978-1-5324-0361-3(5))* Xist Publishing.

—We're Going to the Farm / Nos Vamos a la Granja. Streza, Nancy. Sandoval, Lenny, tr. 2017. (Xist Kids Bilingual Spanish English Ser.). (ENG & SPA.). 28p. (J). (gr. -1-3). pap. 9.99 *(978-1-5324-0363-7(1))* Xist Publishing.

Pryke, Julia Linda. Rabbit No-Pants & the Lettuce of Doom. Shone, Lynne Julia & Shone, Kora Isobel, eds. 2019. (Mysteries of Pantaloon Woods Ser.: Vol. 1). (ENG.). 184p. (J). pap. 10.03 *(978-1-0749-1607-7(7))* Independently Published.

Pryor, Frank. The Brightest Star. Tobin, Christine. 2019. (ENG.). 38p. (J). 23.95 ***(978-1-64559-024-8(0))*** Covenant Bks.

Pryor, Jim. Joey Gonzalez, Great American. Robles, Tony. 2008. (ENG.). 48p. (J). (gr. 2-3). 15.95 *(978-0-9767269-3-7(9)*, World Ahead Pr.) WND Bks, Inc.

Pryor, John-Thomas. Midrak Earthshaker. Nanavati, Daniel. 2013. 132p. pap. *(978-1-908867-06-3(X))* FootSteps Pr.

Pryor, Sean. The Catechist's Magic Kit: 80 Simple Tricks for Teaching Catholicism to Kids. Stagnaro, Angelo. 2009. (ENG.). 256p. pap. 29.95 *(978-0-8245-2518-7(3))* Crossroad Publishing Co., The.

Przybylek, Leslie. Big Bear's Arkansas ABCs. Sandage, Charley. 2004. 56p. (J). (gr. k-2). pap. 14.95 *(978-0-9638956-9-1(9))* Archeological Assessments, Inc.

P.S., Ashwathy. One Rainy Day: A Counting Book. Viswanath, Shobha. 2018. (ENG.). 32p. (J). (gr. -1). bds. 12.99 *(978-1-77321-091-9(2))* Annick Pr., Ltd. CAN. Dist: Publishers Group West (PGW).

Psacharopulo, Alessandra. The Firefighter. Goebel, Jenny & dePaola, Tomie. 2015. 32p. (J). (gr. -1-k). bds. 3.99 *(978-0-448-48101-2(4)*, Grosset & Dunlap) Penguin Young Readers Group.

Psacharopulo, Alessandra. Five Minute Fairy Tales. Cottage Door Press, ed. 2020. (ENG.). 192p. (J). (gr. -1-2). 9.99 ***(978-1-68052-861-9(0)****, 2003160)* Cottage Door Pr.

Psacharopulo, Alessandra. Getting Ready for School. 2017. (ENG.). 18p. (J). (gr. -1). bds. 6.95 *(978-88-544-1196-8(5))* White Star ITA. Dist: Sterling Publishing Co., Inc.

—Happy Birthday! 2017. (ENG.). 18p. (J). (gr. -1). bds. 6.95 *(978-88-544-1195-1(7))* White Star ITA. Dist: Sterling Publishing Co., Inc.

—Is It Hanukkah Yet? Barash, Chris. 2015. (Celebrate Jewish Holidays Ser.). (ENG.). 32p. (J). (gr. -1-3). 16.99 *(978-0-8075-3384-0(X)*, 080753384X) Whitman, Albert & Co.

—Is It Passover Yet? Barash, Chris. 2015. (Celebrate Jewish Holidays Ser.). (ENG.). 32p. (J). (gr. -1-3). 16.99 *(978-0-8075-6330-4(7)*, 807563307) Whitman, Albert & Co.

—Is It Purim Yet? Barash, Chris. 2017. (Celebrate Jewish Holidays Ser.). (ENG.). 32p. (J). (gr. -1-3). 16.99 *(978-0-8075-3391-8(2)*, 807533912) Whitman, Albert & Co.

—Is It Rosh Hashanah Yet? Barash, Chris. 2018. (Celebrate Jewish Holidays Ser.). (ENG.). 32p. (J). (gr. -1-k). 16.99 *(978-0-8075-3396-3(3)*, 807533963) Whitman, Albert & Co.

—Is It Sukkot Yet? Barash, Chris. 2016. (Celebrate Jewish Holidays Ser.). (ENG.). 32p. (J). (gr. -1-3). 16.99 *(978-0-8075-3388-8(2)*, 807533882) Whitman, Albert & Co.

—Is It Tu B'Shevat Yet? Barash, Chris. 2019. (Celebrate Jewish Holidays Ser.). (ENG.). 32p. (J). (gr. -1-3). 16.99 *(978-0-8075-6333-5(1)*, 807563331) Whitman, Albert & Co.

—Mom & Dad Go to Work! 2017. (ENG.). 16p. (J). (gr. -1). bds. 6.95 *(978-88-544-1194-4(9))* White Star ITA. Dist: Sterling Publishing Co., Inc.

—Ready, Set, Go! 2017. (ENG.). 18p. (J). (gr. -1). bds. 6.95 *(978-88-544-1193-7(0))* White Star ITA. Dist: Sterling Publishing Co., Inc.

Ptica, Iz. The Forest of Stars. Kassner, Heather. 2020. (ENG.). 288p. (J). 16.99 *(978-1-250-29700-6(1)*, 900195858, Holt, Henry & Co. Bks. For Young Readers) Holt, Henry & Co.

Pu, Dian. The Girl Who Lost Her Country. De Chickera, Amal & Brennan, Deirdre. 2018. (ENG.). 90p. (J). pap. *(978-90-828366-0-8(2))* Institute on Statelessness & Inclusion.

Publishing, Baobab. The Adventures of Meesha: Meesha's First Day at School. Brandon III, Fred Lee. 2018. (ENG.). 52p. (J). pap. 14.99 *(978-1-947045-16-3(4))* Baobab Publishing.

Publishing, Baobab. Akilah & the Red Shoes. Hazziez, Alisha Marie. 2019. (ENG.). 42p. (J). pap. 12.99 ***(978-1-4943-2444-5(X))*** CreateSpace Independent Publishing Platform.

Publishing, Baobab. Created with a Purpose: Even the Smallest. Goldsmith-Tate, Shayla. 2018. (ENG.). 34p. (J). pap. 12.99 *(978-1-947045-12-5(1))* Baobab Publishing.

—Don't Forget Your Crown. Coley, Regina E. 2019. (ENG.). 26p. (J). pap. 14.99 *(978-1-0974-9547-4(7))* Independently Published.

—Emma & the Sea Creatures. Nixon, Tiffany. 2018. (ENG.). 96p. (J). pap. 11.99 *(978-1-7904-0043-0(0))* Independently Published.

—In the Valley of Walnut Hills. Autrey, Matasha Elaine. 2018. (ENG.). 34p. (J). pap. 12.99 *(978-1-947045-14-9(8))* Baobab Publishing.

Publishing, Baobab. Marisol's Hair. Kelvonia, India. 2018. (ENG.). 28p. (J). pap. 12.99 ***(978-1-947045-24-8(5))*** Baobab Publishing.

Publishing Inc, Wild Imagination. Billy the Blue Bear: Tries Fun Creative Things! Publishing Inc, Wild Imagination. Publishing Inc, Wild Imaginati, ed. 2019. (Tries Fun Creative Things! Ser.: Vol. 1). (ENG.). 56p. (J). pap. 11.99 ***(978-1-0885-3827-2(4))*** Independently Published.

Publishing, Jake Stories. Jake Is a Dog Doctor. Labelle, Charles J. 2016. (ENG.). (J). pap. *(978-1-896710-51-8(4))* Storyteller.

—Jake Is a Fisherman. Labelle, Charles J. 2016. (ENG.). (J). pap. *(978-1-896710-58-7(1))* Storyteller.

—Jake Is a Gotchabird Watcher. Labelle, Charles. 2016. (ENG.). (J). pap. *(978-1-896710-49-5(2))* Storyteller.

—Jake Is a Head Bumper. Labelle, Charles J. 2016. (ENG.). (J). pap. *(978-1-896710-53-2(0))* Storyteller.

—Jake Is a Magic Carpet Pilot. Labelle, Charles J. 2016. (ENG.). (J). pap. *(978-1-896710-50-1(6))* Storyteller.

—Jake Is a Missing Glasses Detective. Labelle, Charles J. 2017. (ENG.). (J). pap. *(978-1-896710-57-0(3))* Storyteller.

—Jake Is a Rabbit Tamer. Labelle, Charles J. 2016. (ENG.). (J). pap. *(978-1-896710-59-4(X))* Storyteller.

—Jake Is a Space Pirate Part One. Labelle, Charles J. 2017. (ENG.). (J). pap. *(978-1-896710-60-0(3))* Storyteller.

—Jake Is a Space Pirate Part Three. Labelle, Charles J. 2017. (ENG.). 32p. (J). pap. *(978-1-896710-62-4(X))* Storyteller.

—Jake Is a Space Pirate Part Two. Labelle, Charles J. 2017. (ENG.). (J). pap. *(978-1-896710-61-7(1))* Storyteller.

—Jake Is a Time Changer. Labelle, Charles J. 2016. (ENG.). (J). pap. *(978-1-896710-52-5(2))* Storyteller.

—Shannon's Backyard Give Mother Nature a Rest Book Twenty- Seven. Labelle, Charles J. 2017. (ENG.). (J). pap. *(978-1-896710-70-9(0))* Storyteller.

—Shannon's Backyard Mrs Tiny & Bob Book Twenty-Five. Labelle, Charles J. 2017. (ENG.). (J). pap. *(978-1-896710-68-6(9))* Storyteller.

—Shannon's Backyard Shannon Talks to Mother Nature Book Twenty-Six. Labelle, Charles J. 2017. (ENG.). (J). pap. *(978-1-896710-69-3(7))* Storyteller.

—Shannon's Backyard the Children Part One. Labelle, Charles J. 2017. (ENG.). (J). pap. *(978-1-896710-93-8(X))* Storyteller.

—Shannon's Backyard the Children Part Two. Labelle, Charles J. 2017. (ENG.). (J). pap. *(978-1-896710-94-5(8))* Storyteller.

—Shannon's Backyard the Club Begins Book Twenty-Eight. Labelle, Charles J. 2017. (ENG.). (J). pap. *(978-1-896710-71-6(9))* Storyteller.

—Shannon's Backyard the Horse Book Sixteen: The Horse. Labelle, Charles J. 2016. (ENG.). (J). pap. *(978-1-896710-88-4(3))* Storyteller.

—Shannon's Backyard the Raindrop. Labelle, Charles J. 2016. (ENG.). (J). pap. *(978-1-896710-79-2(4))* Storyteller.

—Shannon's Backyard the Test Book Fifteen: The Test. Labelle, Charles J. 2016. (ENG.). (J). pap. *(978-1-896710-87-7(5))* Storyteller.

—Shannon's Backyard the Tiny Book Nineteen. Labelle, Charles J. 2016. (ENG.). (J). pap. *(978-1-896710-91-4(3))* Storyteller.

Publishing, K&K. Mommy, Do I Have Black Girl Magic? Smith, Ti-Tianna. 2019. (ENG.). 26p. (J). pap. 13.80 ***(978-1-6867-7580-2(6))*** Independently Published.

Puebla, Teo. Dos Plumas de Aguila. Gómez Cerdá, Alfredo et al. 2003. (SPA.). 32p. (gr. 3-5). 14.99 *(978-84-241-8028-7(3))* Everest Editora ESP. Dist: Lectorum Pubns., Inc.

Puente, Evelio. Bacon Goes Boo. Johnson, Olivia. 2019. (ENG.). 40p. (J). ***(978-1-5255-4579-5(5))***; pap. ***(978-1-5255-4580-1(9))*** FriesenPress.

Puerta, Carlos. El Libro de la Selva. Puerta, Carlos, tr. Kipling, Rudyard & Solari, María J.Tr. of Jungle Book. (SPA.). 92p. (J). (gr. 5-8). pap. 12.95 *(978-84-204-5766-6(3))* Santillana USA Publishing Co., Inc.

Pugh, Carson & Goss, Rebecca. Grace, Little & Their Pot Bellied Pigs. Twomey, Patty. 2016. (Grace & Her Little Sister, Little Ser.: Vol. 2). (ENG.). (J). pap. *(978-1-4602-9269-3(3))* FriesenPress.

Pugh, Jonathan. www.Here-I-Am. Stannard, Russell. 2011. (ENG.). 160p. (YA). (gr. 5-8). pap. 9.95 *(978-1-890151-85-0(8))* Templeton Pr.

Pugh, Rob. Down in the Valley. Keeling, Liz. 2018. (ENG.). 16p. (J). pap. *(978-1-78056-013-7(3))* Skoobebooks.

Pugh, Steve, et al. Earth X Trilogy Omnibus: Omega. 2019. (ENG.). 840p. (YA). (gr. 8-17). 100.00 *(978-1-302-91622-0(X))* Marvel Worldwide, Inc.

Puglesi, Cecilia. Anybody's Game: The Story of the First Girl to Play Little League Baseball. Lang, Heather. 2018. (ENG.). 32p. (J). (gr. k-2). 16.99 *(978-0-8075-0379-9(7)*, 807503797) Whitman, Albert & Co.

Puglisi, Adriana. The Pet Store Pet Show, 1 vol. Gallagher, Diana G. 2014. (Pet Friends Forever Ser.). (ENG.). 88p. (J). (gr. 1-3). 25.32 *(978-1-4795-2177-7(9)*, Picture Window Bks.) Capstone.

—Problem Pup, 1 vol. Gallagher, Diana G. 2014. (Pet Friends Forever Ser.). (ENG.). 88p. (J). (gr. 1-3). 25.32 *(978-1-4795-2176-0(0)*, Picture Window Bks.) Capstone.

Puglisi, Adriana, jt. illus. see Juarez, Adriana.

Puig Rosado, Fernando. The Good Little Devil & Other Tales. Gripari, Pierre. Lewis, Sophie, tr. 2014. (ENG.). 300p. (J). (gr. 4-7). 20.00 *(978-1-78269-008-5(5)*, Pushkin Children's Bks.) Steerforth Pr.

Pukac, Michael & Stephen, Marchesi. The Flights of Marceau: Week Three. 2008. (ENG.). 64p. (J). 16.95 *(978-0-9797495-2-0(2))* Majestic Eagle Publishing.

Pulido, Nora. Emma y la Ronda Del Año: Cuentos para Aprender Cada Mes. Ocana, Sylvia. 2018. (SPA.). 58p. (J). pap. 15.76 *(978-1-0915-4590-8(1))* Independently Published.

Pulido, Rene. Costumes of Asia: A Connoisseur's Coloring Book. Heiter, Celeste. 2010. (ENG.). 48p. (J). (gr. k-5). pap. 4.95 *(978-1-934159-20-0(4))* ThingsAsian Pr.

—Fashion Asia: Patterns & Designs of Traditional Cultures. Heiter, Celeste. 2010. (ENG.). 224p. (J). (gr. -1-3). pap. 9.95 *(978-1-934159-19-4(0))* ThingsAsian Pr.

Pullan, Jack. Una Amiga para Querido Dragón. Hillert, Margaret. 2017. (BeginningtoRead Ser.).Tr. of Friend for Dear Dragon. (ENG & SPA.). 32p. (J). (-2). 22.60 *(978-1-59953-828-0(8))*; pap. 11.94 *(978-1-68404-014-8(0))* Norwood Hse. Pr.

—At the Aquarium with Dear Dragon, 10 vols. Conn, Marla. 2019. (Dear Dragon Developing Readers Ser.). (ENG.). 24p. (J). (gr. -1-k). 21.27 *(978-1-68450-997-3(1))* Norwood Hse. Pr.

—At the Police Station with Dear Dragon, 10 vols. Conn, Marla. 2019. (Dear Dragon Developing Readers Ser.). (ENG.). 24p. (J). (gr. -1-k). 21.27 *(978-1-68450-988-1(2))* Norwood Hse. Pr.

—Ayuda para Querido Dragón. Hillert, Margaret. 2017. (BeginningtoRead Ser.). Orig. Title: Help for Dear Dragon. (ENG & SPA.). 32p. (J). (-2). 22.60 *(978-1-59953-832-7(6))*; pap. 11.94 *(978-1-68404-018-6(3))* Norwood Hse. Pr.

—Come to School, Dear Dragon. Hillert, Margaret. 2016. (BeginningtoRead Ser.). (ENG.). 32p. (J). (-2). lib. bdg. 22.60 *(978-1-59953-764-1(8))*; (gr. -1-2). pap. 11.94 *(978-1-60357-877-6(3))* Norwood Hse. Pr.

—Dear Dragon Flies a Kite. Hillert, Margaret. 2014. (BeginningtoRead Ser.). (ENG.). 32p. (J). (gr. k-2). pap. 11.94 *(978-1-60357-709-0(2))*; lib. bdg. 22.60 *(978-1-59953-674-3(9))* Norwood Hse. Pr.

—Dear Dragon Gets a Hole-In-One. Hillert, Margaret. 2015. (BeginningtoRead Ser.). (ENG.). 32p. (J). (gr. k-2). pap. 11.94 *(978-1-60357-790-8(4))*; lib. bdg. 22.60 *(978-1-59953-705-4(2))* Norwood Hse. Pr.

—Dear Dragon Gets a Pet. Hillert, Margaret. 2015. (BeginningtoRead Ser.). (ENG.). 32p. (J). (gr. k-2). pap. 11.94 *(978-1-60357-791-5(2))*; lib. bdg. 22.60 *(978-1-59953-706-1(0))* Norwood Hse. Pr.

—Dear Dragon Goes to Grandpa's Farm. Hillert, Margaret. 2014. (BeginningtoRead Ser.). (ENG.). 32p. (J). (gr. k-2). pap. 11.94 *(978-1-60357-710-6(6))*; lib. bdg. 22.60 *(978-1-59953-675-0(7))* Norwood Hse. Pr.

—Dear Dragon Goes to the Aquarium. Hillert, Margaret. 2014. (BeginningtoRead Ser.). (ENG.). 32p. (J). (gr. k-2). pap. 11.94 *(978-1-60357-712-0(2))*; lib. bdg. 22.60 *(978-1-59953-677-4(3))* Norwood Hse. Pr.

—Dear Dragon Goes to the Beach. Hillert, Margaret. 2015. (BeginningtoRead Ser.). (ENG.). 32p. (J). (gr. k-2). pap. 11.94 *(978-1-60357-789-2(0))*; lib. bdg. 22.60 *(978-1-59953-704-7(4))* Norwood Hse. Pr.

—Dear Dragon Goes to the Police Station. Hillert, Margaret. 2014. (BeginningtoRead Ser.). (ENG.). 32p. (J). (gr. k-2). pap. 11.94 *(978-1-60357-711-3(4))*; lib. bdg. 22.60 *(978-1-59953-676-7(5))* Norwood Hse. Pr.

—Dear Dragon Learns to Read. Hillert, Margaret. 2015. (BeginningtoRead Ser.). (ENG.). 32p. (J). (gr. k-2). pap. 11.94 *(978-1-60357-792-2(0))*; lib. bdg. 22.60 *(978-1-59953-707-8(9))* Norwood Hse. Pr.

—Es Halloween, Querido Dragón. Hillert, Margaret. 2017. (BeginningtoRead Ser.).Tr. of It's Halloween, Dear Dragon. (ENG & SPA.). 32p. (J). (-2). 22.60 *(978-1-59953-836-5(9))*; pap. 11.94 *(978-1-68404-022-3(1))* Norwood Hse. Pr.

—Feliz Cumpleaños, Querido Dragón. Hillert, Margaret. 2017. (BeginningtoRead Ser.).Tr. of Happy Birthday, Dear Dragon. (ENG & SPA.). 32p. (J). (-2). 22.60 *(978-1-59953-830-3(X))*; pap. 11.94 *(978-1-68404-016-2(7))* Norwood Hse. Pr.

—Feliz Navidad, Querido Dragón. Hillert, Margaret. 2017. (BeginningtoRead Ser.).Tr. of Merry Christmas, Dear Dragon. (ENG & SPA.). 32p. (J). (-2). 22.60 *(978-1-59953-838-9(5))*; pap. 11.94 *(978-1-68404-024-7(8))* Norwood Hse. Pr.

—Feliz Pascua, Querido Dragón. Hillert, Margaret. 2017. (BeginningtoRead Ser.).Tr. of Happy Easter, Dear Dragon. (ENG & SPA.). 32p. (J). (-2). 22.60 *(978-1-59953-831-0(8))*; pap. 11.94 *(978-1-68404-017-9(5))* Norwood Hse. Pr.

—A Friend for Dear Dragon. Hillert, Margaret. 2016. (BeginningtoRead Ser.). (ENG.). 32p. (J). (-2). lib. bdg. 22.60 *(978-1-59953-765-8(6))*; (gr. 1-2). pap. 11.94 *(978-1-60357-878-3(1))* Norwood Hse. Pr.

—Go to Sleep, Dear Dragon. Hillert, Margaret. 2016. (BeginningtoRead Ser.). (ENG.). 32p. (J). (-2). lib. bdg. 22.60 *(978-1-59953-766-5(4))*; (gr. -1-2). pap. 11.94 *(978-1-60357-879-0(X))* Norwood Hse. Pr.

—Happy Birthday, Dear Dragon. Hillert, Margaret. 2016. (BeginningtoRead Ser.). (ENG.). 32p. (J). (-2). lib. bdg. 22.60 *(978-1-59953-767-2(2))*; (gr. 1-2). pap. 11.94 *(978-1-60357-880-6(3))* Norwood Hse. Pr.

—Happy Easter, Dear Dragon. Hillert, Margaret. 2016. (BeginningtoRead Ser.). (ENG.). 32p. (J). (-2). lib. bdg. 22.60 *(978-1-59953-768-9(0))*; (gr. 1-2). pap. 11.94 *(978-1-60357-881-3(1))* Norwood Hse. Pr.

—Help for Dear Dragon. Hillert, Margaret. 2016. (BeginningtoRead Ser.). (ENG.). 32p. (J). (-2). lib. bdg. 22.60 *(978-1-59953-769-6(9))* Norwood Hse. Pr.

—I Love You, Dear Dragon. Hillert, Margaret. 2016. (BeginningtoRead Ser.). (ENG.). 32p. (J). (-2). lib. bdg. 22.60 *(978-1-59953-770-2(2))*; (gr. 1-2). pap. 11.94 *(978-1-60357-883-7(8))* Norwood Hse. Pr.

—I Need You, Dear Dragon. Hillert, Margaret. 2016. (BeginningtoRead Ser.). (ENG.). 32p. (J). (-2). lib. bdg. 22.60 *(978-1-59953-771-9(0))*; (gr. -1-2). pap. 11.94 *(978-1-60357-884-4(6))* Norwood Hse. Pr.

—It's Circus Time, Dear Dragon. Hillert, Margaret. 2016. (BeginningtoRead Ser.). (ENG.). 32p. (J). (-2). lib. bdg. 22.60 *(978-1-59953-772-6(9))*; (gr. 1-2). pap. 11.94 *(978-1-60357-885-1(4))* Norwood Hse. Pr.

—It's Halloween, Dear Dragon. Hillert, Margaret. 2016. (BeginningtoRead Ser.). (ENG.). 32p. (J). (-2). lib. bdg. 22.60 *(978-1-59953-773-3(7))*; (gr. -1-2). pap. 11.94 *(978-1-60357-886-8(2))* Norwood Hse. Pr.

—Let's Go, Dear Dragon. Hillert, Margaret. 2016. (BeginningtoRead Ser.). (ENG.). 32p. (J). (-2). lib. bdg. 22.60 *(978-1-59953-774-0(5))* Norwood Hse. Pr.

—Merry Christmas, Dear Dragon. Hillert, Margaret. 2016. (BeginningtoRead Ser.). (ENG.). 32p. (J). (-2). lib. bdg. 22.60 *(978-1-59953-775-7(3))*; (gr. -1-2). pap. 11.94 *(978-1-60357-888-2(9))* Norwood Hse. Pr.

—Te Necesito, Querido Dragón. Hillert, Margaret. 2017. (BeginningtoRead Ser.).Tr. of I Need You, Dear Dragon. (ENG & SPA.). 32p. (J). (-2). 22.60 *(978-1-59953-834-1(2))*; pap. 11.94 *(978-1-68404-020-9(5))* Norwood Hse. Pr.

—Te Quiero, Querido Dragón. Hillert, Margaret. 2017. (BeginningtoRead Ser.).Tr. of I Love You, Dear Dragon. (ENG & SPA.). 32p. (J). (-2). 22.60 *(978-1-59953-833-4(4))*; pap. 11.94 *(978-1-68404-019-3(1))* Norwood Hse. Pr.

—Vamos Al Circo, Querido Dragón. Hillert, Margaret. 2017. (BeginningtoRead Ser.).Tr. of It's Circus Time, Dear Dragon. (ENG & SPA.). 32p. (J). (-2). 22.60 *(978-1-59953-835-8(0))*; pap. 11.94 *(978-1-68404-021-6(3))* Norwood Hse. Pr.

—Vamos, Querido Dragón. Hillert, Margaret. 2017. (BeginningtoRead Ser.).Tr. of Let's Go, Dear Dragon. (ENG & SPA.). 32p. (J). (-2). 22.60 *(978-1-59953-837-2(7))*; pap. 11.94 *(978-1-68404-023-0(X))* Norwood Hse. Pr.

—Ve a Dormir, Querido Dragón. Hillert, Margaret. 2017. (BeginningtoRead Ser.).Tr. of Go to Sleep, Dear Dragon. (ENG & SPA.). 32p. (J). (-2). 22.60 *(978-1-59953-829-7(6))*; pap. 11.94 *(978-1-68404-015-5(9))* Norwood Hse. Pr.

—Ven a la Escuela, Querido Dragón. Hillert, Margaret. 2017. (BeginningtoRead Ser.).Tr. of Come to School, Dear Dragon. (ENG & SPA.). 32p. (J). (-2). 22.60 *(978-1-59953-827-3(X))*; pap. 11.94 *(978-1-68404-013-1(2))* Norwood Hse. Pr.

—We Are Happy, Dear Dragon, 10 vols. Conn, Marla. 2019. (Dear Dragon Developing Readers Ser.). (ENG.). 24p. (J). (gr. -1-k). 21.27 *(978-1-68450-979-9(3))* Norwood Hse. Pr.

—We Are Mad, Dear Dragon, 10 vols. Conn, Marla. 2019. (Dear Dragon Developing Readers Ser.). (ENG.). 24p. (J). (gr. -1-k). 21.27 *(978-1-68450-978-2(5))* Norwood Hse. Pr.

—Who Feels Happy, Dear Dragon? Hillert, Margaret. 2017. (BeginningtoRead Ser.). (ENG.). 32p. (J). (-2). 22.60 *(978-1-59953-824-2(5))*; pap. 11.94 *(978-1-68404-002-5(7))* Norwood Hse. Pr.

—Who Feels Mad, Dear Dragon? Hillert, Margaret. 2017. (BeginningtoRead Ser.). (ENG.). 32p. (J). (-2). 22.60 *(978-1-59953-822-8(9))*; pap. 11.94 *(978-1-68404-000-1(0))* Norwood Hse. Pr.

—Who Feels Sad, Dear Dragon? Hillert, Margaret. 2017. (BeginningtoRead Ser.). (ENG.). 32p. (J). (-2). 22.60 *(978-1-59953-823-5(7))*; pap. 11.94 *(978-1-68404-001-8(9))* Norwood Hse. Pr.

—Who Feels Surprised, Dear Dragon? Hillert, Margaret. 2017. (BeginningtoRead Ser.). (ENG.). 32p. (J). (-2). 22.60 *(978-1-59953-825-9(3))*; pap. 11.94 *(978-1-68404-003-2(5))* Norwood Hse. Pr.

Pullar, Beth. Kitty Stuck. Pullar, Emma. 2018. (Rupert's Reads Ser.: Vol. 1). (ENG.). 34p. (J). pap. *(978-1-9998240-4-4(0))* A Spark in the Sand.

Pullen, Zachary. Alfred Nobel: The Man Behind the Peace Prize. Wargin, Kathy-jo. 2009. (ENG.). 32p. (J). (gr. k-6). 17.95 *(978-1-58536-281-3(6))* Sleeping Bear Pr.

—The Bambino & Me. Hyman, Zachary. 48p. (J). (gr. 1-4). 2015. pap. 7.99 *(978-1-77049-628-6(9))*; 2014. (ENG.). 17.99 *(978-1-77049-627-9(0))* Tundra Bks. CAN. (Tundra Bks.). Dist: Penguin Random Hse. LLC.

—Finn McCool & the Great Fish. Bunting, Eve. 2010. (ENG.). 38p. (J). (gr. k-6). 16.95 *(978-1-58536-366-7(9))* Sleeping Bear Pr.

—Francis & Eddie: The True Story of America's Underdogs. Herzog, Brad. 2013. (ENG.). 32p. (J). (gr. 3-7). 17.95 *(978-0-9849919-2-1(1))* Why Not Bks.

—The Greatest Game Ever Played. Bildner, Phil. 2015. 40p. (J). (gr. k-3). 8.99 *(978-0-14-751451-6(7)*, Puffin Books) Penguin Young Readers Group.

—Hockey Hero. Hyman, Zachary. 2015. 40p. (J). (gr. 1-4). 17.99 *(978-1-77049-630-9(0)*, Tundra Bks.) Tundra Bks. CAN. Dist: Penguin Random Hse. LLC.

—John Appleseed: A Trail of Trees. Winters, Kay. 2007. (J). *(978-1-4263-0101-8(4))* National Geographic Society.

—Lipman Pike: America's First Home Run King. Michelson, Richard. 2011. (ENG.). 32p. (J). (gr. 1-4). 16.95 *(978-1-58536-465-7(7)*, 202186) Sleeping Bear Pr.

—S Is for Story: A Writer's Alphabet. Hershenhorn, Esther. 2009. (ENG.). 40p. (J). (gr. 1-4). 17.95 *(978-1-58536-439-8(8)*, 202167) Sleeping Bear Pr.

—The Toughest Cowboy: Or How the Wild West Was Tamed. Frank, John. 2004. (ENG.). 48p. (J). (gr. 1-3). 19.99 *(978-0-689-83461-5(6)*, Simon & Schuster Bks. For Young Readers) Simon & Schuster Bks. For Young Readers.

Pullen, Zachary. Friday My Radio Flyer Flew. Pullen, Zachary. 2008. (ENG.). 32p. (J). (gr. -1-2). 19.99 *(978-1-4169-3983-2(0)*, Simon & Schuster Bks. For Young Readers) Simon & Schuster Bks. For Young Readers.

—The Toughest Cowboy: Or How the Wild West Was Tamed. Pullen, Zachary. Frank, John. 2008. (ENG.). 48p. (J). (gr. 1-3). 8.99 *(978-0-689-83462-2(4)*, Aladdin) Simon & Schuster Children's Publishing.

Pullenza, Sam. Hey Tree, What Should I Be? Shelton, Josh. 2018. (ENG.). 86p. (J). pap. *(978-1-912551-38-5(1))* Conscious Dreams Publishing.

Pullenza, Sam. Imagine a World. Shelton, Josh. 2019. (ENG.). 68p. (J). (gr. -1-7). pap. ***(978-1-912551-74-3(8))*** Conscious Dreams Publishing.

Pulles, Elizabeth. Dudu's Basket. Stewart, Dianne. 2018. (ENG.). 32p. (J). (gr. k-2). pap. 9.95 *(978-1-4314-2328-6(9))* Jacana Media ZAF. Dist: Independent Pubs. Group.

Pulley, Kelly. Adam & Eve in the Garden, 1 vol. Zondervan Staff. 2008. (I Can Read! / the Beginner's Bible Ser.). (ENG.). 32p. (J). (gr. -1-1). pap. 4.99 *(978-0-310-71552-8(0))* Zonderkidz.

—All Aboard with Noah!, 1 vol. DeVries, Catherine & Zondervan Staff. 2009. (Beginner's Bible Ser.). (ENG.). 12p. (J). bds. 7.99 *(978-0-310-71726-3(4))* Zonderkidz.

—Baby Jesus Is Born, 1 vol. Zondervan Staff. 2009. (I Can Read! / the Beginner's Bible Ser.). (ENG.). 32p. (J). (gr. -1-2). pap. 4.99 *(978-0-310-71780-5(9))* Zonderkidz.

—Baby Moses & the Princess, 1 vol. Zondervan Staff. 2009. (I Can Read! / the Beginner's Bible Ser.). (ENG.). 32p. (J). pap. 4.99 *(978-0-310-71767-6(1))* Zonderkidz.

—The Beginner's Bible: Timeless Children's Stories. 2014. (Beginner's Bible (Zonderkidz) Ser.). (ENG.). (gr. -1-k). 16.97 *(978-0-310-72924-2(6))* Zondervan.

—The Beginner's Bible All about Jesus Sticker & Activity Book, 1 vol. Zondervan Staff. 2015. (Beginner's Bible Ser.). (ENG.). 16p. (J). pap. 3.99 *(978-0-310-74693-5(0))* Zonderkidz.

—The Beginner's Bible Super Heroes of the Bible Sticker & Activity Book, 1 vol. Zondervan Staff. 2015. (Beginner's Bible Ser.). (ENG.). 16p. (J). pap. 4.99 *(978-0-310-74751-2(1))* Zonderkidz.

—La Biblia para Principiantes - Historias Acerca de Jesús, 1 vol. 2017. (Beginner's Bible Ser.). (SPA.). 22p. (J). bds. 9.99 *(978-0-8297-6802-2(5))* Vida Pubs.

—Bridget's Blog. Witherow, Wendy. 2007. 95p. (J). pap. *(978-1-934306-09-3(6))* Mission City Pr., Inc.

—David & the Giant, 1 vol. Zondervan Staff. 2008. (I Can Read! / the Beginner's Bible Ser.). (ENG.). 32p. (J). (gr. -1-1). pap. 4.99 *(978-0-310-71550-4(4))* Zonderkidz.

—En la Granja. Koons, Linda. 2016. (Early Rising Readers Ser.). (SPA.). 16p. (J). (gr. 1-1). 6.67 *(978-1-4788-3745-9(4))* Newmark Learning LLC.

—Flowers. Schmauss, Judy Kentor. 2015. (Early Rising Readers Ser.). (J). (gr. -1-k). 5.83 *(978-1-4788-1602-7(3))* Newmark Learning LLC.

—Jesus & His Friends, 1 vol. Zondervan Staff. ed. 2009. (I Can Read! / the Beginner's Bible / ¡Yo Sé Leer! Ser.). (SPA.). 32p. (J). (gr. -1-2). pap. 4.99 *(978-0-310-71889-5(9))* Zonderkidz.

—Jesus Feeds the People, 1 vol. Zondervan Staff. 2010. (I Can Read! / the Beginner's Bible Ser.). (ENG.). 32p. (J). pap. 4.99 *(978-0-310-71779-9(5))* Zonderkidz.

—Jesus Saves the World, 1 vol. Zondervan Staff. 2008. (I Can Read! / the Beginner's Bible Ser.). (ENG.). 32p. (J). (gr. -1-1). pap. 4.99 *(978-0-310-71553-5(9))* Zonderkidz.

—Joseph & His Brothers, 1 vol. Zondervan Staff. 2009. (I Can Read! / the Beginner's Bible Ser.). (ENG.). 32p. (J). pap. 4.99 *(978-0-310-71731-7(0))* Zonderkidz.

—Las Flores. Schmauss, Judy Kentor. 2016. (Early Rising Readers Ser.). (SPA.). (J). (gr. -1). 6.67 *(978-1-4788-3658-2(X))* Newmark Learning LLC.

—The Lost Son: Based on Luke 15:11-32, 1 vol. Zondervan Staff. 2009. (I Can Read! / the Beginner's Bible Ser.). (ENG.). 32p. (J). pap. 4.99 *(978-0-310-71781-2(7))* Zonderkidz.

—Miranda's Makeover. Witherow, Wendy. 2007. 93p. (J). *(978-1-934306-11-6(8))* Mission City Pr., Inc.

—Moses & the King, 1 vol. Zondervan Bibles Staff. 2009. (I Can Read! / the Beginner's Bible Ser.). (ENG.). 32p. (J). pap. 4.99 *(978-0-310-71800-0(7))* Zonderkidz.

—Queen Esther Helps God's People, 1 vol. Zondervan Staff. 2008. (I Can Read! / the Beginner's Bible Ser.). (ENG.). 32p. (J). pap. 4.99 *(978-0-310-71815-4(5))* Zonderkidz.

—The Story of David. Pingry, Patricia A. 2012. (J). *(978-0-8249-1886-6(X)*, Ideal Pubns.) Worthy Publishing.

—The Very First Christmas, 1 vol. 2008. (Beginner's Bible Ser.). (ENG.). 32p. (J). pap. 47.76 *(978-0-310-71816-1(3))* Zonderkidz.

—The Very First Easter. ed. 2017. (ENG.). 32p. (J). pap. 19.99 *(978-1-78128-361-5(3))* Lion Hudson PLC GBR. Dist: Independent Pubs. Group.

—The Very First Easter, 1 vol. Zondervan Staff. 2009. (Beginner's Bible Ser.). (ENG.). 32p. (J). pap. 47.76 *(978-0-310-71817-8(1))* Zonderkidz.

Pulley, Kelly. Adan y Eva en el Jardin, 1 vol. Pulley, Kelly. Zondervan Staff. ed. 2009. (I Can Read! / the Beginner's Bible / ¡Yo Sé Leer! Ser.).Tr. of Adam & Eve in the Garden. (SPA.). 32p. (J). (gr. -1-2). pap. 4.99 *(978-0-310-71892-5(9))* Zonderkidz.

—The Cycling Wangdoos. Pulley, Kelly. 2011. 32p. (J). (gr. -1-3). 16.95 *(978-0-9820812-1-1(9)*, Frog Legs Ink) Gauthier Pubns. Inc.

—Daniel y los Leones, 1 vol. Pulley, Kelly. Zondervan Staff. ed. 2009. (I Can Read! / Yo Se Leer!: My First the Beginner's Bible Ser.).Tr. of Daniel & the Lions. (SPA.). 32p. (J). (gr. -1-2). 16.19 *(978-0-310-71891-8(0))* Zonderkidz.

—David & the Giant (David y el Gigante), 1 vol. Pulley, Kelly. Zondervan Staff. ed. 2009. (I Can Read! / the Beginner's Bible / ¡Yo Sé Leer! Ser.). (SPA.). 32p. (J). (gr. -1-2). pap. 4.99 *(978-0-310-71890-1(2))* Zonderkidz.

—Jesus Saves the World, 1 vol. Pulley, Kelly. Zondervan Staff. ed. 2009. (I Can Read! / the Beginner's Bible / ¡Yo Sé Leer! Ser.). (SPA.). 32p. (J). (gr. -1-2). pap. 4.99 *(978-0-310-71893-2(7))* Zonderkidz.

—Jonas y el Gran Pez, 1 vol. Pulley, Kelly. Zondervan Staff. ed. 2009. (I Can Read! / Yo Se Leer!: My First the Beginner's Bible Ser.).Tr. of Jonah & the Big Fish. (SPA.). 32p. (J). (gr. -1-2). 16.19 *(978-0-310-71887-1(2))* Zonderkidz.

—Noah & the Ark, 1 vol. Pulley, Kelly. Zondervan Staff. ed. 2009. (I Can Read! / the Beginner's Bible / ¡Yo Sé Leer! Ser.). (SPA.). 32p. (J). pap. 4.99 *(978-0-310-71886-4(4))* Zonderkidz.

—Ten Unusual Features of Lulu McDunn. Pulley, Kelly. 2010. 32p. (J). (gr. -1). 16.95 *(978-0-9820812-7-3(8)*, Frog Legs Ink) Gauthier Pubns. Inc.

Pulsar Studios Staff. Cheer Captain, 1 vol. Maddox, Jake. 2011. (Jake Maddox Girl Sports Stories Ser.). (ENG.). 72p. (J). (gr. 3-6). 25.32 *(978-1-4342-2551-1(8)*, Stone Arch Bks.) Capstone.

—Drive to the Hoop, 1 vol. Maddox, Jake. 2011. (Jake Maddox Girl Sports Stories Ser.). (ENG.). 72p. (J). (gr. 3-6). 25.32 *(978-1-4342-2500-9(3)*, Stone Arch Bks.) Capstone.

—Victory Vault, 1 vol. Maddox, Jake. 2011. (Jake Maddox Girl Sports Stories Ser.). (ENG.). 72p. (J). (gr. 3-6). 25.32 *(978-1-4342-2498-9(8)*, Stone Arch Bks.) Capstone.

Pulsipher, Emily. The Farmer. Strayhorn, Lytrell. 2019. (ENG.). 26p. (J). pap. 15.00 *(978-1-0971-0347-8(1))* Independently Published.

Pulver, Harry, Jr. Eddie the Electron Moves Out. Rooney, Melissa. 2017. (Eddie the Electron Ser.: 2). (ENG.). 27p. (J). (gr. 5-7). pap. 9.99 *(978-1-944995-14-0(5))* Amberjack Publishing Co.

Punniyamurthi, Kavitha. Lucy's Purple Pullover. Punniyamurthi, Kavitha. 2010. 16p. pap. 9.95 *(978-1-61633-075-0(9))* Guardian Angel Publishing, Inc.

Puplampu, Ivan. Mystery of the Hope Diamond. Londa, Jessica. 2019. (Kingston Chronicles Ser.: Vol. 1). (ENG.). 92p. (J). pap. 7.50 ***(978-1-6999-0338-4(7))*** Independently Published.

Purabiya, Ujval. A Mother's Day Adventure. Ruzzene, Joey. 2019. (Joe's Tall Tales Ser.: Vol. 1). (ENG.). 28p. (J). pap. 11.99 ***(978-1-0780-7737-8(1))*** Independently Published.

Purcell, Gordon. George Eastman & the Kodak Camera, 1 vol. Fandel, Jennifer. 2007. (Inventions & Discovery Ser.). (ENG.). 32p. (J). (gr. 3-9). 31.32 *(978-0-7368-6848-8(8)*, Capstone Pr.) Capstone.

—George Eastman & the Kodak Camera, 1 vol. Fandel, Jennifer & Milgrom, Al. 2007. (Inventions & Discovery Ser.). (ENG.). 32p. (J). (gr. 3-9). pap. 8.10 *(978-0-7368-7900-2(5)*, Capstone Pr.) Capstone.

—The Trojan Horse: The Fall of Troy [a Greek Myth]. Fontes, Ron & Fontes, Justine. 2007. (Graphic Myths & Legends Ser.). (ENG.). 48p. (J). (gr. 4-8). per. 9.99

P

(978-0-8225-6484-3(X), 9780822564843, Graphic Universe™) Lerner Publishing Group.

—The Trojan Horse: The Fall of Troy [a Greek Myth]. Fontes, Justine & Fontes, Ron. ed. 2015. (Graphic Myths & Legends Ser.). (ENG.). 48p. (J). (gr. 4-8). E-Book 53.32 *(978-1-4677-5985-4(6)*, 9781467759854, Lerner Digital) Lerner Publishing Group.

Purcell, Gordon & Beatty, Terry. The Creation of the U. S. Constitution, 1 vol. Burgan, Michael & Hoena, Blake A. 2006. (Graphic History Ser.). (ENG.). 32p. (J). (gr. 3-9). 31.32 *(978-0-7368-6491-6(1)*, Capstone Pr.) Capstone.

—The Creation of the U. S. Constitution. Burgan, Michael. 2006. (Graphic History Ser.). (ENG.). 32p. (J). (gr. 3-9). pap. 8.10 *(978-0-7368-9653-5(8)*, Capstone Pr.) Capstone.

—The First Moon Landing, 1 vol. Adamson, Thomas K. 2006. (Graphic History Ser.). (ENG.). 32p. (J). (gr. 3-9). 31.32 *(978-0-7368-6492-3(X))*; per. 8.10 *(978-0-7368-9654-2(6))* Capstone.

—Thomas Jefferson: Great American, 1 vol. Doeden, Matt. 2006. (Graphic Biographies Ser.). (ENG.). 32p. (J). (gr. 3-9). 31.32 *(978-0-7368-5488-7(6)*, Capstone Pr.) Capstone.

Purcell, Gordon & Schulz, Barbara. El Caballo de Troya: La Caida de Troya: un Mito Griego. Fontes, Ron. 2007. (Mitos y leyendas en viñetas (Graphic Myths & Legends) Ser.).Tr. of Trojan Horse. (SPA.). 48p. (J). (gr. 4-7). per. 8.95 *(978-0-8225-7970-0(7)*, Ediciones Lerner) Lerner Publishing Group.

Purcell, Gordon, jt. illus. see Beatty, Terry.

Purchase, Brendan. Alfie & the Mind Virus. Hibbitts, Mark. 2011. (ENG.). 40p. (J). (gr. 4-6). pap. 9.99 *(978-1-907498-60-2(5)*, Book Shaker) Lean Marketing Pr. ESP. Dist: Lightning Source UK, Ltd.

—Alfie & the Seminar. Hibbitts, Mark. 2011. (ENG.). 40p. pap. 9.99 *(978-1-907498-75-6(3)*, Book Shaker) Lean Marketing Pr. ESP. Dist: Lightning Source UK, Ltd.

Purdy, Joanne. It Happened One Night in the Barn. Kormos, Lawrence. 2007. 24p. *(978-1-55452-192-0(0))* Essence Publishing.

Purnama, Adif. Dinosaurs Doing Things: 25 Pictures of Dinosaurs That Are Fun & Easy for Kids to Color. 2019. (ENG.). 52p. (J). pap. 4.99 ***(978-0-9978611-8-1(5))*** Sir Brody Bks.

—Dinosaurs Doing Things, Volume 2: 25 More Pictures of Dinosaurs That Are Fun & Easy for Kids to Color. 2019. (ENG.). 52p. (J). pap. 4.99 ***(978-0-9978611-9-8(3))*** Sir Brody Bks.

Purnawan, Jeff. My Big Brother Troy. Wallace, Danielle. 2019. (My Big Brother Troy Ser.: Vol. 1). (ENG.). 30p. (J). pap. 15.99 ***(978-0-578-44206-8(X))*** Hom, Jonathan.

Purnell, Gerald. Am I a Color Too? Cole, Heidi & Vogl, Nancy. 2005. 32p. (J). (gr. -1-3). 15.95 *(978-0-9740190-5-5(4))* Illumination Arts Publishing Co., Inc.

—God's Promise. Moss, Maureen. 2008. 30p. (J). (gr. -1-3). 15.95 *(978-0-9740190-7-9(0))* Illumination Arts Publishing Co., Inc.

—A Home Run for Bunny. Anderson, Richard. 2013. (ENG.). (J). (gr. -1-3). 16.95 *(978-0-9855417-2-9(5))* Inspire Every Child dba Illumination Arts.

—Pass It On! Burgess, Gloria J. McEwen. 2017. (ENG.). (J). 23.99 *(978-0-9986314-2-4(6))* Two Sylvias Pr.

Purnell, Teresa. The Rainforest Family & Those Terrible Toads. Lamond, Peter. 2011. 92p. pap. 27.25 *(978-1-60976-297-1(5)*, Eloquent Bks.) Strategic Book Publishing & Rights Agency (SBPRA).

Purvis, Leland. Defiance: Resistance Book 2, Bk. 2. Jablonski, Carla. 2011. (Resistance Ser.: 2). (ENG.). 128p. (YA). (gr. 7-12). pap. 18.99 *(978-1-59643-292-5(6)*, 900044632, First Second Bks.) Roaring Brook Pr.

—A House Divided. Poe, Marshall. 2009. (Turning Points Ser.). (ENG.). 128p. (J). (gr. 3-7). pap. 8.99 *(978-1-4169-5057-8(5)*, Simon & Schuster/Paula Wiseman Bks.) Simon & Schuster/Paula Wiseman Bks.

—Resistance: Book 1, Bk. 1. Jablonski, Carla. 2010. (Resistance Ser.: 1). (ENG.). 128p. (YA). (gr. 7-12). pap. 18.99 *(978-1-59643-291-8(8)*, 900044619, First Second Bks.) Roaring Brook Pr.

—Sons of Liberty. Poe, Marshall. 2008. (Turning Points Ser.). (ENG.). 128p. (J). (gr. 3-7). pap. 8.99 *(978-1-4169-5067-7(2))* Simon & Schuster, Inc.

—Victory: Resistance Book 3. Jablonski, Carla. 2012. (Resistance Ser.: 3). (ENG.). 128p. (YA). (gr. 7-3). pap. 18.99 *(978-1-59643-293-2(4)*, 900044633, First Second Bks.) Roaring Brook Pr.

Pushee, Marisa. The Adventures of Miss Chief: Miss Chief Goes to School. Hyde, Noreen. 2007. 28p. per. 9.95 *(978-1-59858-368-7(9))* Dog Ear Publishing, LLC.

Puskarich, Michelle. Bluebonnet's Egg Adventure: A down on the Farm Book. Hill, Lisa. 2016. (ENG.). 12p. (J). 19.99 *(978-1-68314-001-6(X))* Redemption Pr.

Put, Klaartje van der. Little Cat: Finger Puppet Book. Chronicle Books Staff & Image Books Staff. 2014. (Little Finger Puppet Board Bks.). (ENG.). 12p. (J). (gr. -1 — 1). bds. 7.99 *(978-1-4521-2916-7(9))* Chronicle Bks. LLC.

—Little Chick: Finger Puppet Book. Image Books Staff & Chronicle Books Staff. 2015. (ENG.). 12p. (J). (gr. -1 — 1). bds. 6.99 *(978-1-4521-2917-4(7))* Chronicle Bks. LLC.

—Little Chicken. Image Books Staff & Chronicle Books Staff. 2012. (Little Finger Puppet Board Bks.: FING). (ENG.). 12p. (J). (gr. -1 — 1). bds. 6.99 *(978-1-4521-0811-7(0))* Chronicle Bks. LLC.

—Little Dolphin. Image Books Staff & Chronicle Books Staff. 2012. (Little Finger Puppet Board Bks.: FING). (ENG.). 12p. (J). (gr. -1 — 1). bds. 6.99 *(978-1-4521-0816-2(1))* Chronicle Bks. LLC.

—Little Horse - Finger Puppet Book. ImageBooks Staff & Chronicle Books Staff. 2013. (Little Finger Puppet Board Bks.). (ENG.). 12p. (J). (gr. -1 — 1). bds. 7.99 *(978-1-4521-1249-7(5))* Chronicle Bks. LLC.

—Little Monkey - Finger Puppet Book. ImageBooks Staff & Chronicle Books Staff. 2013. (Little Finger Puppet Board Bks.). (ENG.). 12p. (J). (gr. -1 — 1). bds. 6.99 *(978-1-4521-1250-3(9))* Chronicle Bks. LLC.

—Little Moose: Finger Puppet Book. Chronicle Books Staff & ImageBooks Staff. 2015. (ENG.). 12p. (J). (gr. -1 — 1). bds. 7.99 *(978-1-4521-4231-9(9))* Chronicle Bks. LLC.

—Little Pig. Image Books Staff & Chronicle Books Staff. 2012. (Little Finger Puppet Board Bks.). (ENG.). 12p. (J). (gr. -1 — 1). bds. 6.99 *(978-1-4521-0817-9(X))* Chronicle Bks. LLC.

—Little Shark. ImageBooks Staff & Chronicle Books (Firm) Staff. 2013. (Little Finger Puppet Board Bks.). (ENG.). 12p. (J). (gr. -1 — 1). bds. 7.99 *(978-1-4521-1251-0(7))* Chronicle Bks. LLC.

—Little Zebra. ImageBooks Staff & Chronicle Books Staff. 2013. (Little Finger Puppet Board Bks.). (ENG.). 12p. (J). (gr. -1 — 1). bds. 6.99 *(978-1-4521-1252-7(5))* Chronicle Bks. LLC.

Putman, Stanley. Lion-Hearted Quakers. Haines, Marie. 2011. 152p. 41.95 *(978-1-258-03120-6(5))* Literary Licensing, LLC.

Putra, Dede. What Was the Great Depression? Pascal, Janet B. & Who HQ. 2015. (What Was? Ser.). (ENG.). 112p. (J). (gr. 3-7). 5.99 *(978-0-448-48427-3(7)*, Penguin Workshop) Penguin Young Readers Group.

—What Were the Salem Witch Trials? Holub, Joan & Who HQ. 2015. (What Was? Ser.). 112p. (J). (gr. 3-7). 5.99 *(978-0-448-47905-7(2)*, Penguin Workshop) Penguin Young Readers Group.

Putra, Dede. Where Is Chichen Itza? Manzanero, Paula K. & Who HQ. 2020. (Where Is? Ser.). 112p. (J). (gr. 3-7). 5.99 ***(978-0-593-09344-3(5))***; 15.99 ***(978-0-593-09345-0(3))*** Penguin Young Readers Group. (Penguin Workshop).

Putra, Dede. Where Is the Congo? Stine, Megan & Who HQ. 2020. (Where Is? Ser.). 112p. (J). (gr. 3-7). 5.99 *(978-0-593-09321-4(6))*; 15.99 *(978-0-593-09322-1(4))* Penguin Young Readers Group. (Penguin Workshop).

—Where Is the Kremlin? Hopkinson, Deborah & Who HQ. 2019. (Where Is? Ser.). 112p. (J). (gr. 3-7). 5.99 *(978-1-5247-8974-9(7))*; 15.99 *(978-1-5247-8975-6(5))* Penguin Young Readers Group. (Penguin Workshop).

—Where Were the Seven Wonders of the Ancient World? McDonough, Yona Z. & Who HQ. 2020. (Where Is? Ser.). 112p. (J). (gr. 3-7). 15.99 *(978-0-593-09331-3(3))*; (ENG.). 5.99 *(978-0-593-09330-6(5))* Penguin Young Readers Group. (Penguin Workshop).

—Who Is Hillary Clinton? Alexander, Heather & Who HQ. 2016. (Who Was? Ser.). 112p. (J). (gr. 3-7). 15.99 *(978-0-399-54234-3(5)*, Penguin Workshop) Penguin Young Readers Group.

—Who Is Michael Jordan? Anderson, Kirsten & Who HQ. 2019. (Who Was? Ser.). 112p. (J). (gr. 3-7). (ENG.). 5.99 *(978-0-451-53245-9(7))*; lib. bdg. 15.99 *(978-0-451-53247-3(3))* Penguin Young Readers Group. (Penguin Workshop).

—Who Is Oprah Winfrey? Kramer, Barbara & Who HQ. 2019. (Who Was? Ser.). 112p. (J). (gr. 3-7). 5.99 *(978-1-5247-8750-9(7))*; 15.99 *(978-1-5247-8751-6(5))* Penguin Young Readers Group. (Penguin Workshop).

—Who Is Pope Francis? Spinner, Stephanie & Who HQ. 2017. (Who Was? Ser.). 112p. (J). (gr. 3-7). 5.99 *(978-0-451-53336-4(4)*, Penguin Workshop) Penguin Young Readers Group.

—Who Is Sonia Sotomayor? Stine, Megan & Who HQ. 2017. (Who Was? Ser.). (ENG.). 112p. (J). (gr. 3-7). 5.99 *(978-0-399-54192-6(6)*, Penguin Workshop) Penguin Young Readers Group.

—Who Is the Dalai Lama? Rau, Dana Meachen & Who HQ. 2018. (Who Was? Ser.). 112p. (J). (gr. 3-7). 5.99 *(978-1-101-99554-9(8))*; lib. bdg. 15.99 *(978-1-5247-8613-7(6))* Penguin Young Readers Group. (Penguin Workshop).

—Who Was Alexander Hamilton? Pollack, Pam et al. 2017. (Who Was? Ser.). 112p. (J). (gr. 3-7). 5.99 *(978-0-399-54427-9(5)*, Penguin Workshop) Penguin Young Readers Group.

—Who Was Jacques Cousteau? Medina, Nico & Who HQ. 2015. (Who Was? Ser.). (ENG.). 112p. (J). (gr. 3-7). 5.99 *(978-0-448-48234-7(7)*, Penguin Workshop) Penguin Young Readers Group.

—Who Was Julia Child? Edgers, Geoff & Hempel, Carlene. 2015. (Who Was-? Chapters Ser.). (ENG.). 112p. (J). (gr. 4-6). 18.69 *(978-1-4844-6776-3(0))* Penguin Publishing Group.

—Who Was Leif Erikson? Medina, Nico & Who HQ. 2018. (Who Was? Ser.). 112p. (J). (gr. 3-7). 5.99 *(978-0-448-48861-5(2))*; lib. bdg. 15.99 *(978-1-5247-8673-1(X))* Penguin Young Readers Group. (Penguin Workshop).

—Who Was Maya Angelou? Labrecque, Ellen. 2016. (Who Was-? Chapters Ser.). (ENG.). 112p. (J). (gr. 4-6). 18.69 *(978-1-4844-6937-8(2))* Penguin Publishing Group.

—Who Was Mister Rogers? Bailey, Diane & Who HQ. 2019. (Who Was? Ser.). 112p. (J). (gr. 3-7). 5.99 *(978-1-5247-9219-0(5))*; 15.99 *(978-1-5247-9220-6(9))* Penguin Young Readers Group. (Penguin Workshop).

—Who Was Rachel Carson? Fabiny, Sarah & Who HQ. 2014. (Who Was? Ser.). 112p. (J). (gr. 3-7). 5.99 *(978-0-448-47959-0(1)*, Penguin Workshop) Penguin Young Readers Group.

Putra, Dede, jt. illus. see Harrison, Nancy.

Putra, Lio. Argot's Decoration Disaster: A Can You Help Me Find & Learn Book. Lance, B. E. 2019. (ENG.). 52p. (J). pap. 11.99 ***(978-1-6716-8396-9(X))*** Independently Published.

—Argot's Lost Pets: A Can You Help Me Find & Learn Book. Lance, B. E. 2019. (Argot Ser.: Vol. 1). (ENG.). 38p. (J). pap. 9.99 ***(978-1-6940-8660-0(7))*** Independently Published.

Putri, Maria. Scratchie: A Touch-And-Feel Cat-Venture. Putri, Maria. 2019. (ENG.). 24p. (J). (gr. -1-k). bds. 9.99 *(978-1-5344-3765-4(7)*, Little Simon) Little Simon.

Putri, Putut. Bedtime Rhyme. Smith, D. W. 2019. (Stella & Clara Adventures Ser.: Vol. 4). (ENG.). 26p. (J). pap. 10.25 ***(978-1-7092-2511-6(4))*** Independently Published.

Putri, Putut. Being Benjamin. Palavics, Sue. 2016. (Being Benjamin Ser.: Vol. 1). (ENG.). (J). (gr. k-3). 18.99 *(978-0-692-78458-7(6))* Susan Palavics Publishing.

Puttapipat, Niroot. Jingle Bells: A Magical Cut-Paper Edition. Pierpont, James Lord. 2015. (ENG.). 12p. (J). (gr. -1-3). 19.99 *(978-0-7636-7821-0(X))* Candlewick Pr.

Puttapipat, Niroot. The Nutcracker. Puttapipat, Niroot. 2016. (ENG.). 12p. (J). (gr. -1-2). 19.99 *(978-0-7636-8125-8(3))* Candlewick Pr.

Puukila, Johanna. Hi Blue Sky. Cheatham II, Jeffrey Lee. 2019. (ENG.). 26p. (J). pap. 13.99 *(978-1-0926-6098-3(4))* Independently Published.

Puvilland, Alex. Spill Zone. Westerfeld, Scott. 2018. (Spill Zone Ser.: 1). (ENG.). 240p. (YA). pap. 14.99 *(978-1-250-15872-7(9)*, 900185528, First Second Bks.) Roaring Brook Pr.

—Spill Zone Book 1. Westerfeld, Scott. 2017. (Spill Zone Ser.: 1). (ENG.). 224p. (YA). 22.99 *(978-1-59643-936-8(X)*, 900123009, First Second Bks.) Roaring Brook Pr.

—Spill Zone Book 2: The Broken Vow. Westerfeld, Scott. (Spill Zone Ser.: 2). (ENG.). 240p. (YA). 2019. pap. 15.99 *(978-1-250-30942-6(5)*, 900198487); 2018. 22.99 *(978-1-62672-150-0(5)*, 900140522) Roaring Brook Pr. (First Second Bks.).

Puybaret, Eric. Cloud Chaser. Drillon, Anne-Fleur. 2018. (ENG.). 32p. (J). pap. *(978-1-78285-412-8(6))* Barefoot Bks., Ltd.

Puybaret, Éric. The Gospel Told by Animals. Delelis, Bénédicte. 2018. (ENG.). 32p. (J). (gr. k-3). 14.99 *(978-1-62164-248-0(8))* Ignatius Pr.

Puybaret, Eric. How Deep Is the Ocean? Zoehfeld, Kathleen Weidner. 2016. (Let's-Read-And-Find-Out Science 2 Ser.). (ENG.). 40p. (J). (gr. -1-3). pap. 6.99 *(978-0-06-232819-9(0))* HarperCollins Pubs.

—In Search of Happiness. Saumande, Juliette. Weller, Andrew, tr. from FRE. 2010. 32p. (J). (gr. -1-2). 14.99 *(978-0-8416-7141-6(9))* Hammond World Atlas Corp.

Puybaret, Éric. Manfish: The Story of Jacques Cousteau. Berne, Jennifer. 2015. (ENG.). 38p. (J). (gr. k-3). pap. 9.99 *(978-1-4521-4123-7(1))* Chronicle Bks. LLC.

Puybaret, Eric, et al. Mary Stories from the Bible. Grossetête, Charlotte. 2018. (ENG.). 48p. (J). (gr. k-3). 15.99 *(978-1-62164-254-1(2))* Ignatius Pr.

Puybaret, Eric. The Night Before Christmas. Moore, Clement C. 2010. (ENG.). 26p. (J). (gr. k-4). 19.95 *(978-1-936140-06-0(3))* Charlesbridge Publishing, Inc.

—Over the Rainbow. 2010. (ENG.). 26p. (J). (gr. k-4). 19.99 *(978-1-936140-00-8(4))* Charlesbridge Publishing, Inc.

—Puff, the Magic Dragon. Yarrow, Peter & Lipton, Lenny. (J). 2012. 24p. (gr. k — 1). bds. 7.95 *(978-1-4549-0114-3(4))*; 2010. 32p. (gr. k-2). 9.95 *(978-1-4027-7216-0(5))*; 2007. (ENG.). 24p. 16.95 *(978-1-4027-5279-7(2))*; 2007. (ENG.). 24p. 16.95 *(978-1-4027-5219-3(9))*; 2007. 24p. (gr. -1-2). 19.95 *(978-1-4027-4782-3(9))* Sterling Publishing Co., Inc.

—Suite for Human Nature. Lampert, Diane Charlotte. 2016. (ENG.). 48p. (J). (gr. -1). 17.99 *(978-1-4169-5373-9(6)*, Atheneum Bks. for Young Readers) Simon & Schuster Children's Publishing.

—When You Wish upon a Star. Wshington, Ned. 2011. (ENG.). 28p. (J). (gr. k-4). 17.95 *(978-1-936140-35-0(7))* Charlesbridge Publishing, Inc.

Puybaret, Éric & Puybaret, Éric. Manfish: A Story of Jacques Cousteau (Books of Discovery for Creative Kids Contruction Fort Books) Berne, Jennifer. 2008. (ENG.). 40p. (J). (gr. 1-4). 16.99 *(978-0-8118-6063-5(9))* Chronicle Bks. LLC.

Puybaret, Eric, jt. illus. see Marcellino, Fred.

Puybaret, Eric, jt. illus. see Puybaret, Éric.

Pye, Ali. Girls Can Do Anything. Hart, Caryl. 2018. (ENG.). 32p. (J). (gr. -1-2). 12.99 *(978-1-4380-5062-1(3)*, B.E.S. Publishing) Peterson's.

—Mouse's First Night at Moonlight School. Puttock, Simon. 2015. (ENG.). 32p. (J). (gr. -1-2). 16.99 *(978-0-7636-7607-0(1)*, Nosy Crow) Candlewick Pr.

—Something Delicious. Lewis, Jill. 2014. (Little Somethings Ser.: 1). (ENG.). 32p. (J). (gr. -1-k). pap. 9.99 *(978-1-4052-6238-5(9))* Egmont Bks., Ltd. GBR. Dist: Independent Pubs. Group.

—Where Is Fred? Hardy, Edward. 2013. (ENG.). 32p. (J). (gr. -1-1). 26.19 *(978-1-4052-5402-1(5))* Egmont Bks., Ltd. GBR. Dist: Children's Plus, Inc.

—You Can Never Run Out of Love. Docherty, Helen. 2017. (StoryPlay Ser.). (ENG.). 40p. (J). (gr. -1-k). 5.99 *(978-1-338-21543-4(4))* Scholastic, Inc.

Pye, Ali. Copy Cat. Pye, Ali. 2018. (ENG.). 32p. (J). (gr. -1-2). 15.99 *(978-0-7636-9935-2(7)*, Nosy Crow) Candlewick Pr.

Pye, Trevor. Billy Mcbrown. Eggleton, Jill. (Sails Literacy Ser.). 24p. (gr. 1-18). 27.00 *(978-0-7578-6202-1(0))*;Pack. 57.00 *(978-0-7578-8620-1(5))* Rigby Education.

—The Fire. Eggleton, Jill. 2003. (Rigby Sails Early Ser.). (ENG.). 16p. (gr. 1-2). pap. 6.95 *(978-0-7578-8663-8(9))* Houghton Mifflin Harcourt Publishing Co.

—The Ice-Cream Machine. Eggleton, Jill. 2003. (Rigby Sails Early Ser.). (ENG.). 16p. (gr. 1-2). pap. 6.95 *(978-0-7578-8728-4(7))* Houghton Mifflin Harcourt Publishing Co.

—Mickey Maloney's Missing Bag. Eggleton, Jill. 2004. (Rigby Sails Early Ser.). (ENG.). 16p. (gr. 1-2). pap. 6.95 *(978-0-7578-9299-8(X))* Houghton Mifflin Harcourt Publishing Co.

—Stories of the Wild West Gang. Cowley, Joy. 2012. (Gecko Press Titles Ser.). (ENG.). 368p. (gr. -1-1). 16.95 *(978-1-877579-21-9(1))* Gecko Pr. NZL. Dist: Lerner Publishing Group.

Pyers, Kelsey. The Adventures of Granny: Granny Goes to the Zoo. Eberhart, Nancy. 2007. (J). 24p. per. 10.99 *(978-1-59879-372-7(1))*; (gr. -1-3). 13.99 *(978-1-59879-373-4(X))* Lifevest Publishing, Inc.

—Anabelle's Wish. Eberhart, Nancy. 2007. (J). 22p. per. 9.99 *(978-1-59879-370-3(5))*; (gr. -1-3). 13.99 *(978-1-59879-371-0(3))* Lifevest Publishing, Inc.

Pyk, Jan. Joey Goat: Long Vowel O. deRubertis, Barbara. 2006. (Let's Read Together ® Ser.). (ENG.). 32p. (J). (gr. -1-2). pap. 5.95 *(978-1-57565-025-8(8))* Astra Publishing Hse.

Pyke, Jeremy, jt. illus. see Edwards, Mat.

Pyke, Jerry & Quay, John Paul de. Stickmen's Guide to Aircraft. Oxlade, Chris & Farndon, John. 2016. (Stickmen's Guides to How Everything Works). (ENG.). 32p. (J). (gr. 3-6). lib. bdg. 27.99 *(978-1-4677-9359-9(0)*, 9781467793599, Hungry Tomato ®) Lerner Publishing Group.

—Stickmen's Guide to Gigantic Machines. Oxlade, Chris & Farndon, John. 2016. (Stickmen's Guides to How Everything Works). (ENG.). 32p. (J). (gr. 3-6). lib. bdg. 27.99 *(978-1-4677-9361-2(2)*, 9781467793612, Hungry Tomato ®) Lerner Publishing Group.

—Stickmen's Guide to Trains & Automobiles. Oxlade, Chris & Farndon, John. 2016. (Stickmen's Guides to How Everything Works). (ENG.). 32p. (J). (gr. 3-6). lib. bdg. 27.99 *(978-1-4677-9360-5(4)*, 9781467793605, Hungry Tomato ®) Lerner Publishing Group.

—Stickmen's Guide to Watercraft. Oxlade, Chris & Farndon, John. 2016. (Stickmen's Guides to How Everything Works). (ENG.). 32p. (J). (gr. 3-6). lib. bdg. 27.99 *(978-1-4677-9362-9(0)*, 9781467793629, Hungry Tomato ®) Lerner Publishing Group.

Pyle, Chuck. Freddie & Flossie. Hope, Laura Lee. ed. 2005. 32p. (J). lib. bdg. 15.00 *(978-1-59054-999-5(6))* Fitzgerald Bks.

—Freddie & Flossie. Hope, Laura Lee. 2005. (Bobbsey Twins Ser.). (ENG.). 32p. (J). (gr. -1-k). pap. 3.99 *(978-1-4169-0270-6(8)*, Simon Spotlight) Simon Spotlight.

—Freddie & Flossie & Snap. Hope, Laura Lee. 2005. (Bobbsey Twins Ser.). (ENG.). 32p. (J). (gr. -1-k). pap. 13.99 *(978-1-4169-0267-6(8)*, Simon Spotlight) Simon Spotlight.

—Freddie & Flossie & the Train Ride. Hope, Laura Lee. 2005. (Bobbsey Twins Ser.). (ENG.). 32p. (J). (gr. -1-k). pap. 13.99 *(978-1-4169-0269-0(4)*, Simon Spotlight) Simon Spotlight.

—Freddie & Flossie at the Beach. Hope, Laura Lee. 2005. (Bobbsey Twins Ser.). (ENG.). 32p. (J). (gr. -1-k). pap. 13.99 *(978-1-4169-0268-3(6)*, Simon Spotlight) Simon Spotlight.

Pyle, Howard. The Book of Pirates. 2020. (ENG.). 336p. (J). (gr. 3). pap. 16.95 *(978-0-486-84096-3(4)*, 840964) Dover Pubns., Inc.

Pyle, Howard. The Merry Adventures of Robin Hood. Pyle, Howard. ed. 2015. (First Avenue Classics (tm) Ser.). (ENG.). 342p. (YA). (gr. 5-12). E-Book 19.99 *(978-1-4677-5841-3(8)*, First Avenue Editions) Lerner Publishing Group.

—Pepper & Salt & the Wonder Clock, Set. Pyle, Howard. 2006. (Foundations Ser.). (ENG.). 385p. (J). 45.00 *(978-1-933859-14-9(8))* ISI Bks.

Pyle, Howard. The Story of King Arthur & His Knights / Illustrated / 1903 Novel. Pyle, Howard. 2019. (ENG.). 210p. (J). pap. 10.80 ***(978-1-6969-4931-6(9))*** Independently Published.

Pyle, Howard & Boelke, David. Robin Hood Saves Will Stutely - Interpreting a Legend in Three Literary Formats. Pyle, Howard & Boelke, David. 2014. (Text Connections Ser.). (J). (gr. 4). pap. *(978-1-4900-0077-0(1))* Benchmark Education Co.

Pyle, Katharine. In Sunshine Land. Thomas, Edith M. 2019. (ENG.). 164p. (J). pap. 7.95 *(978-1-0714-9028-0(1))* Independently Published.

Pyle, Kevin C. Bad for You: Exposing the War on Fun! Pyle, Kevin C. Cunningham, Scott. 2014. (ENG.). 192p. (YA). (gr. 7). pap. 18.99 *(978-0-8050-9289-9(7)*, 9780805092899, Holt, Henry & Co. Bks. For Young Readers) Holt, Henry & Co.

Pylypchuck, Anna. Chocalin! Calvani, Mayra. 2009. 24p. pap. 10.95 *(978-1-935137-69-6(7))* Guardian Angel Publishing, Inc.

Pym, Christine. Chicken Little. Munton, Gill. 2014. (Traditional Tales Ser.). (ENG.). 16p. (J). (gr. k-1). pap. 6.95 *(978-1-62521-542-0(8)*, Capstone Classroom) Capstone.

—Goat's Coat. Percival, Tom. 2018. (ENG.). 32p. (J). 16.99 *(978-1-68119-901-6(7)*, 900191665, Bloomsbury Children's Bks.) Bloomsbury Publishing USA.

—Toby Is a Big Boy. Peacock, Lou. 2019. (ENG.). 32p. (J). (gr. -1-2). 17.99 *(978-1-9848-4769-0(4))*; lib. bdg. 20.99 *(978-1-9848-4770-6(8))* Random Hse. Children's Bks. (Schwartz & Wade Bks.).

Pym, Christine. Little Mouse's Big Breakfast. Pym, Christine. 2018. (ENG.). 32p. (J). (gr. -1-2). 15.99 *(978-0-7636-9626-9(9)*, Nosy Crow) Candlewick Pr.

Pym, T. Snezhnaya Koroleva - the Snow Queen. Andersen, Hans. 2013. 56p. *(978-1-909115-60-6(6))* Planet, The.

Pynaert, Andrea. Clashmore Mike Comes Home. Guibert, Susan Mullen & O'Shaughnessy, Brendan. 2012. 24p. (J). 19.95 *(978-0-9859377-3-7(4))* Corby Books.

—Clashmore Mike_Dublin to Dome. Guibert, Susan Mullen & O'Shaughnessy, Brendan. 2012. 36p. (J). 19.95 *(978-0-9859377-1-3(8))* Corby Books.

Pysher, Marcie. The Invitation. Pysher, Marcie. 2017. (ENG.). (J). (gr. k-3). 19.95 *(978-0-692-98452-9(6))* Pysher, Brock.

Q

Q, Likit. B Is for Bangkok. Brown, Janet. 2011. (Alphabetical World Ser.). (ENG.). 47p. (J). (gr. k-4). 12.95 *(978-1-934159-26-2(3))* ThingsAsian Pr.

Qadri, Rumaysa Adnan and Zaina. You Never See Me Coming. Syed, Raahem. 2018. (ENG.). 114p. (J). *(978-1-5255-2012-9(1))*; pap. *(978-1-5255-2013-6(X))* FriesenPress.

Qasmi, Shahid Ali. Zoro & the Witch. Greenwell, Alan, ed. Naeem, Rashid, tr. 2016. (Himalayan Tales Ser.: Vol. 2). (ENG.). (J). pap. *(978-0-9935235-1-9(X))* Himalayan Tales Pubns.

Qazi, Insha. Essence of Eid. Riyaz, Najmun. 2020. (ENG.). 38p. (J). (gr. k-6). 17.99 ***(978-1-0878-1486-5(3))*** Indy Pub.

Qi, Nana. Panda. Garnett, Jaye. Cottage Door Press, ed. 2020. (Smithsonian Kids Big Head Board Book Ser.). (ENG.). 12p. (J). (gr. -1-1). bds. 12.99 ***(978-1-68052-803-9(3)***, 1005160) Cottage Door Pr.

Qin, Yinzhi. Bad Dog, Macy! Qin, Wenjun. 2018. 36p. (J). (gr. k-5). 16.95 *(978-1-76036-060-3(0)*, 12bd009a-237e-4840-aba1-4e5699c65dab) Starfish Bay Publishing Pty Ltd. AUS. Dist: Baker & Taylor Publisher Services (BTPS).

Qitsualik-Tinsley, Sean & Bigham, Sean. Tuniit: Mysterious Folk of the Arctic, 1 vol. Qitsualik-Tinsley, Rachel. 2015. (ENG.). 40p. (J). (gr. 2-4). 16.95 *(978-1-927095-76-8(X))* Inhabit Media Inc. CAN. Dist: Consortium Bk. Sales & Distribution.

Qiu, Joseph J. M. Who Is Elton John? Anderson, Kirsten & Who HQ. 2016. (Who Was? Ser.). (ENG.). 112p. (J). (gr. 3-7). pap. 5.99 *(978-0-448-48846-2(9)*, Penguin Workshop) Penguin Young Readers Group.

—Who Was Jacqueline Kennedy? Bader, Bonnie & Who HQ. 2016. (Who Was? Ser.). 112p. (J). (gr. 3-7). lib. bdg. 15.99 *(978-0-399-54242-8(6)*, Penguin Workshop) Penguin Young Readers Group.

—Who Was Jacqueline Kennedy? Bader, Bonnie. ed. 2016. (Who Was... ? Ser.). (ENG.). 112p. (J). (gr. 3-7). 16.00 *(978-0-606-39327-0(7))* Turtleback.

—Who Was Lewis Carroll? Pollack, Pam et al. 2017. (Who Was? Ser.). 112p. (J). (gr. 3-7). 5.99 *(978-0-448-48867-7(1))*; lib. bdg. 15.99 *(978-0-515-15931-8(X))* Penguin Young Readers Group. (Penguin Workshop).

—Who Was Selena? Bisantz, Max et al. 2018. (Who Was? Ser.). (ENG.). 112p. (J). (gr. 3-7). 5.99 *(978-1-101-99549-5(1))*; lib. bdg. 15.99 *(978-1-5247-8675-5(6))* Penguin Young Readers Group. (Penguin Workshop).

—Who Was Selena? Bisantz, Kate & Bisantz, Max. 2018. 108p. (J). *(978-1-5444-0832-3(3)*, Penguin Workshop) Penguin Young Readers Group.

Qiu, Joseph J. M. . Who Was Blackbeard? Buckley, James & Who HQ. 2015. (Who Was? Ser.). 112p. (J). (gr. 3-7). 5.99 *(978-0-448-48308-5(4)*, Penguin Workshop) Penguin Young Readers Group.

Qovaizi, Mo. Riley & the Sleeping Dragon: A Journey Around Beijing. McCartney, Tania Maree. 2008. 32p. (J). pap. *(978-0-9804750-0-5(7))* McCartney, Tania AUS. Dist: Jones, Dennis & Assocs. Pty, Ltd.

Quach, Lam. Baby Chronicles: My Very Own Story: From Pre-Natal to Pre-School. Lebovics, Dania. 2007. 72p. spiral bd. 19.95 *(978-0-9699203-7-3(7)*, aa77e215-f193-4236-aa6b-95ed8ffbe5f4) Kiddy Chronicles Publishing CAN. Dist: Firefly Bks., Ltd.

Quackenbush, Marcia, jt. illus. see Dyrud, Chris Wold.

Quackenbush, Robert. Bicycle to Treachery: A Miss Mallard Mystery. Quackenbush, Robert. 2019. (Quix Ser.). (ENG.). 80p. (J). (gr. k-3). 16.99 *(978-1-5344-1398-6(7))*; pap. 5.99 *(978-1-5344-1397-9(9))* Simon & Schuster Children's Publishing. (Aladdin).

—Cable Car to Catastrophe: A Miss Mallard Mystery. Quackenbush, Robert. 2019. (Quix Ser.). (ENG.). 80p. (J). (gr. k-3). 16.99 *(978-1-5344-1415-0(0))*; pap. 5.99 *(978-1-5344-1414-3(2))* Simon & Schuster Children's Publishing. (Aladdin).

—Dig to Disaster: A Miss Mallard Mystery. Quackenbush, Robert. 2018. (Quix Ser.). (ENG.). 80p. (J). (gr. k-3). 16.99 *(978-1-5344-1313-9(8))*; pap. 5.99 *(978-1-5344-1312-2(X))* Simon & Schuster Children's Publishing. (Aladdin).

—Dogsled to Dread: A Miss Mallard Mystery. Quackenbush, Robert. 2019. (Quix Ser.). (ENG.). 80p. (J). (gr. k-3). 16.99 *(978-1-5344-1421-1(5))*; pap. 5.99 *(978-1-5344-1420-4(7))* Simon & Schuster Children's Publishing. (Aladdin).

—Express Train to Trouble: A Miss Mallard Mystery. Quackenbush, Robert. 2018. (Quix Ser.). (ENG.). 80p. (J). (gr. k-3). 16.99 *(978-1-5344-1403-7(7))*; pap. 5.99 *(978-1-5344-1402-0(9))* Simon & Schuster Children's Publishing. (Aladdin).

—Gondola to Danger: A Miss Mallard Mystery. Quackenbush, Robert. 2019. (Quix Ser.). (ENG.). 80p. (J). (gr. k-3). 16.99 *(978-1-5344-1406-8(1))*; pap. 5.99 *(978-1-5344-1405-1(3))* Simon & Schuster Children's Publishing. (Aladdin).

Quackenbush, Robert. Henry Babysits. Quackenbush, Robert. 2020. (Henry Duck Ser.). (ENG.). 48p. (J). (gr. -1-3). 16.99 ***(978-1-5344-1543-0(2)***, Aladdin) Simon & Schuster Children's Publishing.

Quackenbush, Robert. Henry Goes West. Quackenbush, Robert. 2018. (Henry Duck Ser.). (ENG.). 48p. (J). (gr. -1-3). 16.99 *(978-1-5344-1537-9(8)*, Aladdin) Simon & Schuster Children's Publishing.

—Henry's Awful Mistake. Quackenbush, Robert. 2019. (Henry Duck Ser.). (ENG.). 48p. (J). (gr. -1-3). 16.99 *(978-1-5344-1540-9(8)*, Aladdin) Simon & Schuster Children's Publishing.

—Miss Mallard Mysteries Collection: Texas Trail to Calamity; Dig to Disaster; Stairway to Doom; Express Train to Trouble; Bicycle to Treachery; Gondola to Danger; Surfboard to Peril; Taxi to Intrigue; Cable Car to Catastrophe; Dogsled to Dread. Quackenbush, Robert. ed. 2019. (Quix Ser.). (ENG.). 800p. (J). (gr. k-3). pap. 59.99 *(978-1-5344-6234-2(1)*, Aladdin) Simon & Schuster Children's Publishing.

—Sherlock Chick & the Peekaboo Mystery. Quackenbush, Robert. 2020. (Sherlock Chick Ser.). (ENG.). 48p. (J). (gr. -1-3). 17.99 *(978-1-5344-1531-7(9)*, Aladdin) Simon & Schuster Children's Publishing.

—Sherlock Chick's First Case. Quackenbush, Robert. 2019. (Sherlock Chick Ser.). (ENG.). 48p. (J). (gr. -1-3). 16.99 *(978-1-5344-1521-8(1)*, Aladdin) Simon & Schuster Children's Publishing.

—Stage Door to Terror: A Miss Mallard Mystery. Quackenbush, Robert. 2020. (Quix Ser.). (ENG.). 80p. (J). (gr. k-3). 16.99 *(978-1-5344-1409-9(6))*; pap. 5.99 *(978-1-5344-1408-2(8))* Simon & Schuster Children's Publishing. (Aladdin).

—Stairway to Doom: A Miss Mallard Mystery. Quackenbush, Robert. 2018. (Quix Ser.). (ENG.). 80p. (J). (gr. k-3). 16.99 *(978-1-5344-1316-0(2))*; pap. 5.99 *(978-1-5344-1315-3(4))* Simon & Schuster Children's Publishing. (Aladdin).

—Surfboard to Peril: A Miss Mallard Mystery. Quackenbush, Robert. 2019. (Quix Ser.). (ENG.). 80p. (J). (gr. k-3). 16.99 *(978-1-5344-1418-1(5))*; pap. 5.99 *(978-1-5344-1417-4(7))* Simon & Schuster Children's Publishing. (Aladdin).

—Taxi to Intrigue: A Miss Mallard Mystery. Quackenbush, Robert. 2019. (Quix Ser.). (ENG.). 80p. (J). (gr. k-3). 16.99 *(978-1-5344-1412-9(6))*; pap. 5.99 *(978-1-5344-1411-2(8))* Simon & Schuster Children's Publishing. (Aladdin).

—Texas Trail to Calamity: A Miss Mallard Mystery. Quackenbush, Robert. 2018. (Quix Ser.). (ENG.). 80p. (J). (gr. k-3). 16.99 *(978-1-5344-1310-8(3))*; pap. 5.99 *(978-1-5344-1309-2(X))* Simon & Schuster Children's Publishing. (Aladdin).

Quackenbush, Robert. Henry's Awful Mistake. Quackenbush, Robert, photos by. rev. deluxe ed. 2005. 40p. (J). (gr. k-2). reprint ed. 12.95 *(978-0-9712757-0-6(X))* Quackenbush, Robert Studios.

Quadflieg, Roswitha. La Historia Interminable. Quadflieg, Roswitha, tr. Ende, Michael. Sáenz, Miguel, tr.Tr. of Unendliche Geschichte. (SPA.). 424p. (J). 9.95 *(978-84-204-3226-7(1))* Ediciones Alfaguara ESP. Dist: Santillana USA Publishing Co., Inc.

Qualano, Pascale & Sotomayor, Chris. Guardians of the Galaxy: Gamora's Galactic Showdown. Snider, Brandon T. 2018. (Mighty Marvel Chapter Bks.). (ENG.). 128p. (J). (gr. 2-7). lib. bdg. 27.07 *(978-1-5321-4216-1(1)*, 28553, Chapter Bks.) Spotlight.

Qualano, Pasquale & Sotomayor, Chris. Gamora's Galactic Showdown: Starring Gamora. Snider, Brandon T. 2017. (Marvel Chapter Book Ser.). (ENG.). 128p. (J). (gr. 2-4). 18.69 *(978-1-5364-0786-0(0))* Marvel Worldwide, Inc.

Qualls, Sean. Before John Was a Jazz Giant: A Song of John Coltrane. Weatherford, Carole Boston. 2008. (ENG.). 32p. (J). (gr. k-4). 18.99 *(978-0-8050-7994-4(7)*, 900034598, Holt, Henry & Co. Bks. For Young Readers) Holt, Henry & Co.

—Bird in a Box. Pinkney, Andrea Davis. ed. 2012. (J). lib. bdg. 18.45 *(978-0-606-26157-9(5))* Turtleback.

—Dizzy. Winter, Jonah. 2006. (J). 16.99 *(978-0-439-50736-3(7)*, Levine, Arthur A. Bks.) Scholastic, Inc.

—Emmanuel's Dream: the True Story of Emmanuel Ofosu Yeboah. Thompson, Laurie Ann. 2015. 40p. (J). (gr. -1-3). 17.99 *(978-0-449-81744-5(X)*, Schwartz & Wade Bks.) Random Hse. Children's Bks.

—Freedom Song: The Story of Henry Box Brown. Walker, Sally M. 2012. (ENG.). 40p. (J). (gr. -1-3). 17.99 *(978-0-06-058310-1(X))* HarperCollins Pubs.

—Giant Steps to Change the World. Lee, Spike & Lee, Tonya Lewis. 2011. (ENG.). 40p. (J). (gr. -1). 18.99 *(978-0-689-86815-3(4)*, Simon & Schuster Bks. For Young Readers) Simon & Schuster Bks. For Young Readers.

—Grandad Mandela. Mandela, Zondwa et al. ed. 2018. (ENG.). 40p. (J). (gr. -1-2). 17.99 *(978-1-78603-136-5(1)*, 302120, Frances Lincoln Children's Bks.) Quarto Publishing Group UK GBR. Dist: Hachette Bk. Group.

Qualls, Sean, et al. I Remember: Poems & Pictures of Heritage, 1 vol. Hopkins, Lee Bennett, ed. 2019. (ENG.). 56p. (J). (gr. 3-12). 19.95 *(978-1-62014-311-7(9)*, 27f9a5c4-c005-4db2-8e1f-c32c9f872d36) Lee & Low Bks., Inc.

Qualls, Sean. Jump Back, Paul: The Life & Poems of Paul Laurence Dunbar. Derby, Sally. 2015. 128p. (J). (gr. 4-7). 16.99 *(978-0-7636-6070-3(1))* Candlewick Pr.

—Little Cloud & Lady Wind. Morrison, Toni & Morrison, Slade. 2010. (ENG.). 32p. (J). pap. 7.99 *(978-1-4169-8524-2(7)*, Simon & Schuster Bks. For Young Readers) Simon & Schuster Bks. For Young Readers.

—Little Cloud & Lady Wind. Morrison, Toni & Morrison, Slade. 2010. (ENG.). 32p. (J). (gr. -1-3). 19.99 *(978-1-4169-8523-5(9)*, Simon & Schuster/Paula Wiseman Bks.) Simon & Schuster/Paula Wiseman Bks.

—Lullaby (for a Black Mother) Hughes, Langston. 2013. (ENG.). 32p. (J). (gr. -1-3). 17.99 *(978-0-547-36265-6(X)*, 1421855) Houghton Mifflin Harcourt Publishing Co.

—The Poet Slave of Cuba: A Biography of Juan Francisco Manzano. Engle, Margarita. ed. 2011. (SPA.). 208p. (YA). (gr. 7-12). pap. 10.99 *(978-0-312-65928-8(8)*, 900070514) Square Fish.

—Skit-Scat Raggedy Cat: Ella Fitzgerald. Orgill, Roxane. 2012. (Candlewick Biographies Ser.). 48p. (J). (gr. 3-7). (ENG.). 14.99 *(978-0-7636-6459-6(6))*; pap. 4.99 *(978-0-7636-6458-9(8))* Candlewick Pr.

Qualls, Sean & Alko, Selina. Two Friends: Susan B. Anthony & Frederick Douglass: Susan B. Anthony & Frederick Douglass. Robbins, Dean. 2016. (ENG.). 32p. (J). (gr. -1-3). 17.99 *(978-0-545-39996-8(3)*, Orchard Bks.) Scholastic, Inc.

—Why Am I Me? Britt, Paige. 2017. (ENG.). 40p. (J). (gr. -1-3). 17.99 *(978-1-338-05314-2(0)*, Scholastic Pr.) Scholastic, Inc.

Qualls, Sean, jt. illus. see Alko, Selina.

Qualls, Turbo. The Little Leaf. Shaeffer, Adam. 2013. (ENG.). 36p. (J). (gr. -1-3). pap. 9.99 *(978-1-62395-446-8(0))* Xist Publishing.

—The Queen & the Cats. Lee, Calee M. 2013. (ENG.). 32p. (J). (gr. -1-3). pap. 9.99 *(978-0-9838428-0-4(9))* Xist Publishing.

Quang, Dinh Ngo. Haszie's Christmas Gift & Other Short Stories. Pereira, Mary Delfin. 2019. (ENG.). 102p. (J). pap. 12.00 ***(978-1-7118-7434-0(5))*** Independently Published.

Quang Phuc, Pham. Dear Santa, Love, Washington: An Evergreen State Christmas Celebration — With Real Letters! Everett, Forrest. 2018. (ENG.). 32p. (J). 16.99 *(978-1-64170-039-9(4)*, 550039) Familius LLC.

Quarello, Maurizio. Mister Doctor: Janusz Korczak & the Orphans of the Warsaw Ghetto. Cohen-Janca, Irène & Cohen-Janca, Irène. 68p. (J). 2016. (ENG.). 12.95 *(978-1-55451-861-6(X))*; 2015. (gr. 4-7). 24.95 *(978-1-55451-715-2(X)*, 9781554517152) Annick Pr., Ltd. CAN. Dist: Publishers Group West (PGW).

Quarello, Maurizio A. C. Fly High, John Glenn: The Story of an American Hero. Krull, Kathleen. 2020. (ENG.). 48p. (J). (gr. -1-3). 18.99 *(978-0-06-274714-3(2)*, HarperCollins) HarperCollins Pubs. Ltd. GBR. Dist: HarperCollins Pubs.

—The Frog Prince. Namm, Diane. 2013. (Silver Penny Stories Ser.). 48p. (J). (gr. -1-1). 4.95 *(978-1-4027-8429-3(5))* Sterling Publishing Co., Inc.

—Jack & the Beanstalk. Namm, Diane. 2012. (Silver Penny Stories Ser.). 48p. (J). (gr. -1-1). 4.95 *(978-1-4027-8433-0(3))* Sterling Publishing Co., Inc.

—King Midas. Olmstead, Kathleen. 2014. (Silver Penny Stories Ser.). 48p. (J). (gr. -1-1). 4.95 *(978-1-4027-8346-3(9))* Sterling Publishing Co., Inc.

—Rumpelstiltskin. McFadden, Deanna. 2014. (Silver Penny Stories Ser.). 48p. (J). (gr. -1-1). 4.95 *(978-1-4027-8340-1(X))* Sterling Publishing Co., Inc.

Quast, Colin. Ants in the Drain. Fez. 2006. (ENG.). 50p. pap. 11.50 *(978-1-55369-043-6(5))* Trafford Publishing.

—Brave Jack the Flying Squirrel, Episode #1: The Legend of How Flying Squirrels Came to Be. Fez. 2009. (ENG.). 40p. pap. 21.74 *(978-1-4120-5737-0(X))* Trafford Publishing.

—Granny B. Fez. 2006. (ENG.). 42p. pap. 11.00 *(978-1-55395-754-6(7))* Trafford Publishing.

—Sassy the Amazing Fire Fighting Rescue Dog Episode 3: River Rescue. Fez. 2007. (ENG.). 44p. pap. 24.00 *(978-1-4120-4378-6(6))* Trafford Publishing.

Quateman, India. Daddy Daughter Dinner Dance: A Father's Steps to a Blended Family That Really Works. Quateman, India. Quateman, Bill. 2003. 96p. 17.95 *(978-0-9729866-0-1(X))* Angel Mind.

Quay, Emma. Daddy's Cheeky Monkey. Daddo, Andrew. 2018. 32p. pap. 6.99 *(978-0-7333-3891-5(7))* ABC Bks. AUS. Dist: HarperCollins Pubs.

—Goodnight, Me. Daddo, Andrew. 2007. (ENG.). 32p. (J). (gr. -1-k). 14.99 *(978-1-59990-153-4(6)*, 9781599901534, Bloomsbury USA Childrens) Bloomsbury Publishing USA.

—Topsy & Turvy. D'Ath, Justin. 2020. (Puffin Nibbles Ser.). 80p. (J). (gr. k-2). pap. 9.99 *(978-0-14-130938-5(5)*, Puffin) Penguin Random Hse. AUS. Dist: Independent Pubs. Group.

Quay, John Paul de, jt. illus. see Pyke, Jerry.

Queen, Dana. Runty's Adventure: A Story of Love. Castleton, Chaffee. 2010. (ENG.). 97p. (J). pap. 17.95 *(978-0-578-06109-2(0))* Castleton, Julia J.

Queralt, Carmen. Wild Week. Porcella, Teresa. 2020. (ENG.). (J). bds. ***(978-1-78285-975-8(6))*** Barefoot Bks., Inc.

Querin, Pamela. What Is Heaven Like? Lewis, Beverly. 2006. (ENG.). 32p. (J). (gr. -1-3). 15.99 *(978-0-7642-0184-4(0))* Bethany Hse. Pubs.

Quesada, Joe. The Marvel Art of Joe Quesada - Expanded Edition. 2019. (ENG.). 304p. (YA). (gr. 8-17). 50.00 *(978-1-302-91767-8(6))* Marvel Worldwide, Inc.

—Marvel Portfolio: Joe Quesada. 2020. (ENG.). 12p. (YA). (gr. 8-17). 50.00 *(978-1-302-92133-0(9))* Marvel Worldwide, Inc.

Quesada, Joe, et al. X-Factor Epic Collection: X-Aminations. 2019. (ENG.). 504p. (YA). (gr. 4-17). pap. 39.99 *(978-1-302-92057-9(X))* Marvel Worldwide, Inc.

Quesada, Joe & Kubert, Andy. Wolverine: Origin. 2006. (ENG.). 160p. (J). (gr. 4-17). pap. 14.99 *(978-0-7851-0965-5(X))* Marvel Worldwide, Inc.

Quesada, Maria Fe. Adivina, Adivinanza. Everest. (SPA.). (J). pap. 5.56 *(978-84-241-8037-9(2))* Everest Editora ESP. Dist: Lectorum Pubns., Inc.

Questel, R. R. The Wicked Witch of Fairyland: Part Two. Questel, P. J. 2018. (ENG.). 128p. (J). 25.94 *(978-1-5462-9737-6(5))*; pap. 14.35 *(978-1-5462-9736-9(7))* AuthorHouse.

Quevedo, Enrique. The Dance of Time. Aparici, Irene. Brokenbrow, Jon, tr. 2014. 24p. (gr. k-7). 16.95 *(978-84-16078-08-0(4))* Cuento de Luz SL ESP. Dist: Publishers Group West (PGW).

—Fairground Lights. Nuno, Fran. Brokenbrow, Jon, tr. 2013. (ENG.). 24p. (J). (gr. k-2). 16.95 *(978-84-15784-20-3(1))* Cuento de Luz SL ESP. Dist: Publishers Group West (PGW).

—The Great Magician of the World. Nuno, Fran. Brokenbrow, Jon, tr. 2012. 24p. (J). (gr. k-2). 14.95 *(978-84-15241-11-9(9))* Cuento de Luz SL ESP. Dist: Publishers Group West (PGW).

Qui, Joseph. The Baby King - Arch Books. 2017. (ENG.). (J). pap. 2.99 *(978-0-7586-5736-7(6))* Concordia Publishing Hse.

Quiambao, Nikolai C. It's Nighttime. Quiambao, Maria Eloisa C. 2019. (ENG.). 24p. (J). pap. 21.00 ***(978-1-5437-4799-7(X))*** Partridge Pub.

Quick, Jen Lee. Off*Beat, Vol. 1. 2005. 184p. (YA). (gr. 8-18). pap. 14.99 *(978-1-59816-132-8(6)*, Tokyopop Kids) TOKYOPOP, Inc.

Quiel, Cathy. Angel in My Backpack: Large Print Edition. Grimes, Rich. 2018. (ENG.). 320p. (J). pap. 17.95 *(978-1-7288-3738-3(3))* Independently Published.

Quijas, Evelyn. Little Parakeet, Story & Follow-Up Activities: Periquito, el Cuento y Actividades. Baker, Georgette L. 2018. (ENG.). 40p. (J). pap. 9.95 *(978-1-892306-61-6(1))* Cantemos-bilingual bks. and music.

Quiles, Moses. Ten Steps on Getting the Boogieman Out of Our Room: Diez Pasos para Sacar el Boogie. Quiles, Moses. 2020. (ENG.). 36p. (J). ***(978-0-2288-1453-5(7))***; pap. ***(978-0-2288-1452-8(9))*** Tellwell Talent.

Quiles q's Imaginative Design, Moses. Diez Pasos para Pacar el Boogie. Quiles, Moses. 2020. (SPA.). 36p. (J). ***(978-0-2288-1573-0(8))***; pap. ***(978-0-2288-1572-3(X))*** Tellwell Talent.

Quinn, Courtney. The Little Hospital Book. Dyan, Penelope. 2008. 108p. 19.95 *(978-1-935118-09-1(9))*; pap. 8.95 *(978-1-935118-08-4(0))* Bellissima Publishing, LLC.

—The Warrior Mouse of Forest Hollow. Dyan, Penelope. 2008. 108p. 17.95 *(978-1-935118-00-8(5))* Bellissima Publishing, LLC.

Quinn, Katherine. Pets & Their Famous Humans. Gallo, Ana. 2020. (ENG.). 48p. (J). (gr. 2-5). 17.95 *(978-3-7913-7425-3(7))* Prestel Verlag GmbH & Co KG. DEU. Dist: Penguin Random Hse. LLC.

Quinn, Kitty. The Hummingbird Garden. Schwarz, Evelyn. 2012. (ENG.). 34p. (J). pap. 16.95 *(978-1-4327-9815-4(4))* Outskirts Pr., Inc.

Quinn, Paris. Shadow & Light, Vol. 4. Quinn, Paris. 2003. (ENG.). 48p. (YA). pap. 10.95 *(978-1-56163-327-2(5)*, Amerotica) NBM Publishing Co.

Quinn, Raven. The Ghost, the Buttons, & the Magic of Halloween. Becket. Barselow, Todd, ed. 2015. (ENG.). (J). pap. 11.99 *(978-1-941240-27-4(5))* Becket.

Quinn, Valerie. Hurry Harry! Hurry! Waters, Lilly. 2014. (ENG.). 32p. (J). 14.99 *(978-0-9888610-0-8(3))* Jade Tree Bks.

Quinones, Joe, et al. America Vol. 2: Fast & Fuertona. 2018. 136p. (YA). (gr. 8-17). pap. 17.99 *(978-1-302-90882-9(0))* Marvel Worldwide, Inc.

Quinones, Joe. Peter Parker: the Spectacular Spider-Man Vol. 4: Coming Home. 2018. (Peter Parker: the Spectacular Spider-Man (2017) Ser.: 4). 112p. (J). (gr. 4-17). pap. 19.99 *(978-1-302-91119-5(8))* Marvel Worldwide, Inc.

Quinones, Joe & Reis, Rod. Exiles Vol. 2: The Trial of the Exiles. 2019. (Exiles (2018) Ser.: 2). (ENG.). 136p. (YA). (gr. 8-17). pap. 17.99 *(978-1-302-91166-9(X))* Marvel Worldwide, Inc.

Quinones, Joe, jt. illus. see Henderson, Erica.

Quinones, Mike. Nissa's Mom & Me Activity Book. Walsh, Bb. 2018. (ENG.). 32p. (J). pap. 10.99 *(978-1-7314-8539-7(5))* Independently Published.

Quintana, Donald, photos by. It's Nice to Be a Kit Fox. Woodward, Molly. 2019. (ENG.). 20p. (J). bds. 8.99 *(978-1-59714-401-8(0))* Heyday.

Quintana, Gianna. The Birth Marker. Steber, Bridget. 2019. (ENG.). 24p. (J). 19.95 ***(978-0-578-45211-1(1))*** Bridget Maloy Steber.

Quintanilla, Hazel. The Buddy Bench. Cottleston, B. D. 2019. (ENG.). 32p. (J). (gr. k-2). 16.99 *(978-1-4867-1775-0(6)*, 09f4c6b6-4daf-406c-a2a9-c3cc3f60d117); 7.99 *(978-1-4867-1798-9(5)*, aa3e4de2-a818-4e93-9253-d85bde4c1508) Flowerpot Pr.

—Un Buen Equipo: Un Libro de la Serie Acorn. Burnell, Heather Ayris. 2019. (Unicornio y Yeti Ser.). (SPA.). 64p. (J). (gr. -1-1). pap. 4.99 *(978-1-338-60116-9(4)*, Scholastic en Espanol) Scholastic, Inc.

—Delores Thesaurus. Hutchings, Jessica Lee. 2018. (ENG.). 32p. (J). (gr. 1-4). 16.99 *(978-1-4867-1463-6(3)*, d691203c-57e7-4a8d-986d-80ef93ae7c1c) Flowerpot Pr.

—Ears. Jenkins, Pete. 2017. (I See, I Saw Ser.). (ENG.). 24p. (gr. -1-1). pap. 8.95 *(978-1-68342-194-8(9)*, 9781683421948) Rourke Educational Media.

—Eyes. Jenkins, Pete. 2017. (I See, I Saw Ser.). (ENG.). 24p. (gr. -1-2). 29.93 *(978-1-68342-312-6(7)*, 9781683423126); pap. 8.95 *(978-1-68342-408-6(5)*, 9781683424086) Rourke Educational Media.

—Hair. Jenkins, Pete. 2017. (I See, I Saw Ser.). (ENG.). 24p. (gr. -1-2). 29.93 *(978-1-68342-311-9(9)*, 9781683423119); pap. 8.95 *(978-1-68342-407-9(7)*, 9781683424079) Rourke Educational Media.

—Hands. Jenkins, Pete. 2017. (I See, I Saw Ser.). (ENG.). 24p. (gr. -1-1). pap. 8.95 *(978-1-68342-192-4(2)*, 9781683421924) Rourke Educational Media.

Quintanilla, Hazel. Happy Birthday Abigail. 2020. (Happy Birthday Ser.). (ENG.). 32p. (J). (-3). 7.99 ***(978-1-7282-1143-5(3))*** Sourcebooks, Inc.

—Happy Birthday Addison. 2020. (Happy Birthday Ser.). (ENG.). 32p. (J). (-3). 7.99 ***(978-1-7282-1144-2(1))*** Sourcebooks, Inc.

—Happy Birthday Aiden. 2020. (Happy Birthday Ser.). (ENG.). 32p. (J). (-3). 7.99 ***(978-1-7282-1145-9(X))*** Sourcebooks, Inc.

—Happy Birthday Alexander. 2020. (Happy Birthday Ser.). (ENG.). 32p. (J). (-3). 7.99 ***(978-1-7282-1146-6(8))*** Sourcebooks, Inc.

—Happy Birthday Amelia. 2020. (Happy Birthday Ser.). (ENG.). 32p. (J). (-3). 7.99 ***(978-1-7282-1147-3(6))*** Sourcebooks, Inc.

—Happy Birthday Andrew. 2020. (Happy Birthday Ser.). (ENG.). 32p. (J). (-3). 7.99 ***(978-1-7282-1148-0(4))*** Sourcebooks, Inc.

—Happy Birthday Anna. 2020. (Happy Birthday Ser.). (ENG.). 32p. (J). (-3). 7.99 ***(978-1-7282-1149-7(2))*** Sourcebooks, Inc.

—Happy Birthday Anthony. 2020. (Happy Birthday Ser.). (ENG.). 32p. (J). (-3). 7.99 ***(978-1-7282-1150-3(6))*** Sourcebooks, Inc.

—Happy Birthday Aria. 2020. (Happy Birthday Ser.). (ENG.). 32p. (J). (-3). 7.99 ***(978-1-7282-1151-0(4))*** Sourcebooks, Inc.

—Happy Birthday Aubrey. 2020. (Happy Birthday Ser.). (ENG.). 32p. (J). (-3). 7.99 ***(978-1-7282-1152-7(2))*** Sourcebooks, Inc.

—Happy Birthday Audrey. 2020. (Happy Birthday Ser.). (ENG.). 32p. (J). (-3). 7.99 ***(978-1-7282-1153-4(0))*** Sourcebooks, Inc.

—Happy Birthday Ava. 2020. (Happy Birthday Ser.). (ENG.). 32p. (J). (-3). 7.99 ***(978-1-7282-1154-1(9))*** Sourcebooks, Inc.

—Happy Birthday Avery. 2020. (Happy Birthday Ser.). (ENG.). 32p. (J). (-3). 7.99 ***(978-1-7282-1155-8(7))*** Sourcebooks, Inc.

—Happy Birthday Benjamin. 2020. (Happy Birthday Ser.). (ENG.). 32p. (J). (-3). 7.99 ***(978-1-7282-1156-5(5))*** Sourcebooks, Inc.

—Happy Birthday Brayden. 2020. (Happy Birthday Ser.). (ENG.). 32p. (J). (-3). 7.99 ***(978-1-7282-1157-2(3))*** Sourcebooks, Inc.

—Happy Birthday Brooklyn. 2020. (Happy Birthday Ser.). (ENG.). 32p. (J). (-3). 7.99 ***(978-1-7282-1158-9(1))*** Sourcebooks, Inc.

—Happy Birthday Caleb. 2020. (Happy Birthday Ser.). (ENG.). 32p. (J). (-3). 7.99 ***(978-1-7282-1159-6(X))*** Sourcebooks, Inc.

—Happy Birthday Cameron. 2020. (Happy Birthday Ser.). (ENG.). 32p. (J). (-3). 7.99 ***(978-1-7282-1160-2(3))*** Sourcebooks, Inc.

—Happy Birthday Caroline. 2020. (Happy Birthday Ser.). (ENG.). 32p. (J). (-3). 7.99 ***(978-1-7282-1161-9(1))*** Sourcebooks, Inc.

—Happy Birthday Carter. 2020. (Happy Birthday Ser.). (ENG.). 32p. (J). (-3). 7.99 ***(978-1-7282-1162-6(X))*** Sourcebooks, Inc.

—Happy Birthday Charlotte. 2020. (Happy Birthday Ser.). (ENG.). 32p. (J). (-3). 7.99 ***(978-1-7282-1163-3(8))*** Sourcebooks, Inc.

—Happy Birthday Chloe. 2020. (Happy Birthday Ser.). (ENG.). 32p. (J). (-3). 7.99 ***(978-1-7282-1164-0(6))*** Sourcebooks, Inc.

—Happy Birthday Christopher. 2020. (Happy Birthday Ser.). (ENG.). 32p. (J). (-3). 7.99 ***(978-1-7282-1165-7(4))*** Sourcebooks, Inc.

—Happy Birthday Claire. 2020. (Happy Birthday Ser.). (ENG.). 32p. (J). (-3). 7.99 ***(978-1-7282-1166-4(2))*** Sourcebooks, Inc.

—Happy Birthday Connor. 2020. (Happy Birthday Ser.). (ENG.). 32p. (J). (-3). 7.99 ***(978-1-7282-1167-1(0))*** Sourcebooks, Inc.

—Happy Birthday Daniel. 2020. (Happy Birthday Ser.). (ENG.). 32p. (J). (-3). 7.99 ***(978-1-7282-1168-8(9))*** Sourcebooks, Inc.

—Happy Birthday David. 2020. (Happy Birthday Ser.). (ENG.). 32p. (J). (-3). 7.99 ***(978-1-7282-1169-5(7))*** Sourcebooks, Inc.

—Happy Birthday Dylan. 2020. (Happy Birthday Ser.). (ENG.). 32p. (J). (-3). 7.99 ***(978-1-7282-1170-1(0))*** Sourcebooks, Inc.

—Happy Birthday Elijah. 2020. (Happy Birthday Ser.). (ENG.). 32p. (J). (-3). 7.99 ***(978-1-7282-1171-8(9))*** Sourcebooks, Inc.

—Happy Birthday Elizabeth. 2020. (Happy Birthday Ser.). (ENG.). 32p. (J). (-3). 7.99 ***(978-1-7282-1172-5(7))*** Sourcebooks, Inc.

—Happy Birthday Ella. 2020. (Happy Birthday Ser.). (ENG.). 32p. (J). (-3). 7.99 ***(978-1-7282-1173-2(5))*** Sourcebooks, Inc.

—Happy Birthday Ellie. 2020. (Happy Birthday Ser.). (ENG.). 32p. (J). (-3). 7.99 ***(978-1-7282-1174-9(3))*** Sourcebooks, Inc.

—Happy Birthday Emily. 2020. (Happy Birthday Ser.). (ENG.). 32p. (J). (-3). 7.99 ***(978-1-7282-1175-6(1))*** Sourcebooks, Inc.

—Happy Birthday Emma. 2020. (Happy Birthday Ser.). (ENG.). 32p. (J). (-3). 7.99 ***(978-1-7282-1176-3(X))*** Sourcebooks, Inc.

—Happy Birthday Ethan. 2020. (Happy Birthday Ser.). (ENG.). 32p. (J). (-3). 7.99 ***(978-1-7282-1177-0(8))*** Sourcebooks, Inc.

—Happy Birthday Evelyn. 2020. (Happy Birthday Ser.). (ENG.). 32p. (J). (-3). 7.99 ***(978-1-7282-1178-7(6))*** Sourcebooks, Inc.

—Happy Birthday Gabriel. 2020. (Happy Birthday Ser.). (ENG.). 32p. (J). (-3). 7.99 ***(978-1-7282-1179-4(4))*** Sourcebooks, Inc.

—Happy Birthday Gabriella. 2020. (Happy Birthday Ser.). (ENG.). 32p. (J). (-3). 7.99 ***(978-1-7282-1180-0(8))*** Sourcebooks, Inc.

—Happy Birthday Grace. 2020. (Happy Birthday Ser.). (ENG.). 32p. (J). (-3). 7.99 ***(978-1-7282-1181-7(6))*** Sourcebooks, Inc.

—Happy Birthday Granddaughter. 2020. (Happy Birthday Ser.). (ENG.). 32p. (J). (-3). 7.99 ***(978-1-7282-1182-4(4))*** Sourcebooks, Inc.

—Happy Birthday Grandson. 2020. (Happy Birthday Ser.). (ENG.). 32p. (J). (-3). 7.99 ***(978-1-7282-1183-1(2))*** Sourcebooks, Inc.

—Happy Birthday Grayson. 2020. (Happy Birthday Ser.). (ENG.). 32p. (J). (-3). 7.99 ***(978-1-7282-1184-8(0))*** Sourcebooks, Inc.

—Happy Birthday Hailey. 2020. (Happy Birthday Ser.). (ENG.). 32p. (J). (-3). 7.99 ***(978-1-7282-1185-5(9))*** Sourcebooks, Inc.

—Happy Birthday Hannah. 2020. (Happy Birthday Ser.). (ENG.). 32p. (J). (-3). 7.99 ***(978-1-7282-1186-2(7))*** Sourcebooks, Inc.

—Happy Birthday Harper. 2020. (Happy Birthday Ser.). (ENG.). 32p. (J). (-3). 7.99 ***(978-1-7282-1187-9(5))*** Sourcebooks, Inc.

—Happy Birthday Henry. 2020. (Happy Birthday Ser.). (ENG.). 32p. (J). (-3). 7.99 ***(978-1-7282-1188-6(3))*** Sourcebooks, Inc.

—Happy Birthday Hunter. 2020. (Happy Birthday Ser.). (ENG.). 32p. (J). (-3). 7.99 ***(978-1-7282-1189-3(1))*** Sourcebooks, Inc.

—Happy Birthday Isaac. 2020. (Happy Birthday Ser.). (ENG.). 32p. (J). (-3). 7.99 ***(978-1-7282-1190-9(5))*** Sourcebooks, Inc.

—Happy Birthday Isabella. 2020. (Happy Birthday Ser.). (ENG.). 32p. (J). (-3). 7.99 ***(978-1-7282-1191-6(3))*** Sourcebooks, Inc.

—Happy Birthday Jack. 2020. (Happy Birthday Ser.). (ENG.). 32p. (J). (-3). 7.99 ***(978-1-7282-1192-3(1))*** Sourcebooks, Inc.

—Happy Birthday Jackson. 2020. (Happy Birthday Ser.). (ENG.). 32p. (J). (-3). 7.99 ***(978-1-7282-1193-0(X))*** Sourcebooks, Inc.

—Happy Birthday Jacob. 2020. (Happy Birthday Ser.). (ENG.). 32p. (J). (-3). 7.99 ***(978-1-7282-1194-7(8))*** Sourcebooks, Inc.

—Happy Birthday James. 2020. (Happy Birthday Ser.). (ENG.). 32p. (J). (-3). 7.99 ***(978-1-7282-1195-4(6))*** Sourcebooks, Inc.

—Happy Birthday Jaxon. 2020. (Happy Birthday Ser.). (ENG.). 32p. (J). (-3). 7.99 ***(978-1-7282-1196-1(4))*** Sourcebooks, Inc.

—Happy Birthday Jayden. 2020. (Happy Birthday Ser.). (ENG.). 32p. (J). (-3). 7.99 ***(978-1-7282-1197-8(2))*** Sourcebooks, Inc.

—Happy Birthday John. 2020. (Happy Birthday Ser.). (ENG.). 32p. (J). (-3). 7.99 ***(978-1-7282-1198-5(0))*** Sourcebooks, Inc.

—Happy Birthday Jonathan. 2020. (Happy Birthday Ser.). (ENG.). 32p. (J). (-3). 7.99 ***(978-1-7282-1588-4(9))*** Sourcebooks, Inc.

—Happy Birthday Joseph. 2020. (Happy Birthday Ser.). (ENG.). 32p. (J). (-3). 7.99 ***(978-1-7282-1199-2(9))*** Sourcebooks, Inc.

—Happy Birthday Joshua. 2020. (Happy Birthday Ser.). (ENG.). 32p. (J). (-3). 7.99 ***(978-1-7282-1200-5(6))*** Sourcebooks, Inc.

—Happy Birthday Kennedy. 2020. (Happy Birthday Ser.). (ENG.). 32p. (J). (-3). 7.99 ***(978-1-7282-1202-9(2))*** Sourcebooks, Inc.

—Happy Birthday Landon. 2020. (Happy Birthday Ser.). (ENG.). 32p. (J). (-3). 7.99 ***(978-1-7282-1203-6(0))*** Sourcebooks, Inc.

—Happy Birthday Layla. 2020. (Happy Birthday Ser.). (ENG.). 32p. (J). (-3). 7.99 ***(978-1-7282-1204-3(9))*** Sourcebooks, Inc.

—Happy Birthday Leah. 2020. (Happy Birthday Ser.). (ENG.). 32p. (J). (-3). 7.99 ***(978-1-7282-1205-0(7))*** Sourcebooks, Inc.

—Happy Birthday Levi. 2020. (Happy Birthday Ser.). (ENG.). 32p. (J). (-3). 7.99 ***(978-1-7282-1206-7(5))*** Sourcebooks, Inc.

—Happy Birthday Liam. 2020. (Happy Birthday Ser.). (ENG.). 32p. (J). (-3). 7.99 ***(978-1-7282-1207-4(3))*** Sourcebooks, Inc.

—Happy Birthday Lillian. 2020. (Happy Birthday Ser.). (ENG.). 32p. (J). (-3). 7.99 ***(978-1-7282-1208-1(1))*** Sourcebooks, Inc.

—Happy Birthday Logan. 2020. (Happy Birthday Ser.). (ENG.). 32p. (J). (-3). 7.99 ***(978-1-7282-1209-8(X))*** Sourcebooks, Inc.

—Happy Birthday Lucas. 2020. (Happy Birthday Ser.). (ENG.). 32p. (J). (-3). 7.99 ***(978-1-7282-1210-4(3))*** Sourcebooks, Inc.

—Happy Birthday Lucy. 2020. (Happy Birthday Ser.). (ENG.). 32p. (J). (-3). 7.99 ***(978-1-7282-1211-1(1))*** Sourcebooks, Inc.

—Happy Birthday Luke. 2020. (Happy Birthday Ser.). (ENG.). 32p. (J). (-3). 7.99 ***(978-1-7282-1212-8(X))*** Sourcebooks, Inc.

—Happy Birthday Madelyn. 2020. (Happy Birthday Ser.). (ENG.). 32p. (J). (-3). 7.99 ***(978-1-7282-1213-5(8))*** Sourcebooks, Inc.

—Happy Birthday Madison. 2020. (Happy Birthday Ser.). (ENG.). 32p. (J). (-3). 7.99 ***(978-1-7282-1214-2(6))*** Sourcebooks, Inc.

—Happy Birthday Mason. 2020. (Happy Birthday Ser.). (ENG.). 32p. (J). (-3). 7.99 ***(978-1-7282-1215-9(4))*** Sourcebooks, Inc.

—Happy Birthday Matthew. 2020. (Happy Birthday Ser.). (ENG.). 32p. (J). (-3). 7.99 ***(978-1-7282-1216-6(2))*** Sourcebooks, Inc.

—Happy Birthday Mia. 2020. (Happy Birthday Ser.). (ENG.). 32p. (J). (-3). 7.99 ***(978-1-7282-1217-3(0))*** Sourcebooks, Inc.

—Happy Birthday Michael. 2020. (Happy Birthday Ser.). (ENG.). 32p. (J). (-3). 7.99 ***(978-1-7282-1218-0(9))*** Sourcebooks, Inc.

—Happy Birthday Mila. 2020. (Happy Birthday Ser.). (ENG.). 32p. (J). (-3). 7.99 ***(978-1-7282-1219-7(7))*** Sourcebooks, Inc.

—Happy Birthday Natalie. 2020. (Happy Birthday Ser.). (ENG.). 32p. (J). (-3). 7.99 ***(978-1-7282-1224-1(3))*** Sourcebooks, Inc.

—Happy Birthday Nathan. 2020. (Happy Birthday Ser.). (ENG.). 32p. (J). (-3). 7.99 ***(978-1-7282-1225-8(1))*** Sourcebooks, Inc.

—Happy Birthday Nicholas. 2020. (Happy Birthday Ser.). (ENG.). 32p. (J). (-3). 7.99 ***(978-1-7282-1226-5(X))*** Sourcebooks, Inc.

—Happy Birthday Noah. 2020. (Happy Birthday Ser.). (ENG.). 32p. (J). (-3). 7.99 ***(978-1-7282-1227-2(8))*** Sourcebooks, Inc.

—Happy Birthday Nora. 2020. (Happy Birthday Ser.). (ENG.). 32p. (J). (-3). 7.99 ***(978-1-7282-1228-9(6))*** Sourcebooks, Inc.

—Happy Birthday Oliver. 2020. (Happy Birthday Ser.). (ENG.). 32p. (J). (-3). 7.99 ***(978-1-7282-1229-6(4))*** Sourcebooks, Inc.

—Happy Birthday Olivia. 2020. (Happy Birthday Ser.). (ENG.). 32p. (J). (-3). 7.99 ***(978-1-7282-1230-2(8))*** Sourcebooks, Inc.

—Happy Birthday Owen. 2020. (Happy Birthday Ser.). (ENG.). 32p. (J). (-3). 7.99 ***(978-1-7282-1231-9(6))*** Sourcebooks, Inc.

—Happy Birthday Paisley. 2020. (Happy Birthday Ser.). (ENG.). 32p. (J). (-3). 7.99 ***(978-1-7282-2571-5(X))*** Sourcebooks, Inc.

—Happy Birthday Penelope. 2020. (Happy Birthday Ser.). (ENG.). 32p. (J). (-3). 7.99 ***(978-1-7282-1233-3(2))*** Sourcebooks, Inc.

—Happy Birthday Riley. 2020. (Happy Birthday Ser.). (ENG.). 32p. (J). (-3). 7.99 ***(978-1-7282-1234-0(0))*** Sourcebooks, Inc.

—Happy Birthday Ryan. 2020. (Happy Birthday Ser.). (ENG.). 32p. (J). (-3). 7.99 ***(978-1-7282-1235-7(9))*** Sourcebooks, Inc.

—Happy Birthday Sadie. 2020. (Happy Birthday Ser.). (ENG.). 32p. (J). (-3). 7.99 ***(978-1-7282-1236-4(7))*** Sourcebooks, Inc.

—Happy Birthday Samantha. 2020. (Happy Birthday Ser.). (ENG.). 32p. (J). (-3). 7.99 ***(978-1-7282-1237-1(5))*** Sourcebooks, Inc.

—Happy Birthday Samuel. 2020. (Happy Birthday Ser.). (ENG.). 32p. (J). (-3). 7.99 ***(978-1-7282-1238-8(3))*** Sourcebooks, Inc.

—Happy Birthday Savannah. 2020. (Happy Birthday Ser.). (ENG.). 32p. (J). (-3). 7.99 ***(978-1-7282-1239-5(1))*** Sourcebooks, Inc.

—Happy Birthday Scarlett. 2020. (Happy Birthday Ser.). (ENG.). 32p. (J). (-3). 7.99 ***(978-1-7282-1240-1(5))*** Sourcebooks, Inc.

—Happy Birthday Sebastian. 2020. (Happy Birthday Ser.). (ENG.). 32p. (J). (-3). 7.99 ***(978-1-7282-1241-8(3))*** Sourcebooks, Inc.

—Happy Birthday Sofia. 2020. (Happy Birthday Ser.). (ENG.). 32p. (J). (-3). 7.99 ***(978-1-7282-1589-1(7))*** Sourcebooks, Inc.

—Happy Birthday Sophia. 2020. (Happy Birthday Ser.). (ENG.). 32p. (J). (-3). 7.99 ***(978-1-7282-1242-5(1))*** Sourcebooks, Inc.

—Happy Birthday Stella. 2020. (Happy Birthday Ser.). (ENG.). 32p. (J). (-3). 7.99 ***(978-1-7282-1243-2(X))*** Sourcebooks, Inc.

—Happy Birthday Thomas. 2020. (Happy Birthday Ser.). (ENG.). 32p. (J). (-3). 7.99 ***(978-1-7282-1244-9(8))*** Sourcebooks, Inc.

—Happy Birthday Victoria. 2020. (Happy Birthday Ser.). (ENG.). 32p. (J). (-3). 7.99 ***(978-1-7282-1245-6(6))*** Sourcebooks, Inc.

—Happy Birthday Violet. 2020. (Happy Birthday Ser.). (ENG.). 32p. (J). (-3). 7.99 ***(978-1-7282-1246-3(4))*** Sourcebooks, Inc.

—Happy Birthday William. 2020. (Happy Birthday Ser.). (ENG.). 32p. (J). (-3). 7.99 ***(978-1-7282-1247-0(2))*** Sourcebooks, Inc.

—Happy Birthday Wyatt. 2020. (Happy Birthday Ser.). (ENG.). 32p. (J). (-3). 7.99 ***(978-1-7282-1248-7(0))*** Sourcebooks, Inc.

—Happy Birthday Zoey. 2020. (Happy Birthday Ser.). (ENG.). 32p. (J). (-3). 7.99 ***(978-1-7282-1249-4(9))*** Sourcebooks, Inc.

Quintanilla, Hazel. It's My Birthday! (Dinosaur) 2020. (It's My Birthday Ser.). (ENG.). 32p. (J). (-3). 9.99 *(978-1-7282-2200-4(1))* Sourcebooks, Inc.

—It's My Birthday! (Unicorn) 2020. (It's My Birthday Ser.). (ENG.). 32p. (J). (-3). 9.99 *(978-1-7282-2199-1(4))* Sourcebooks, Inc.

—Nina the Neighborhood Ninja. Panigrahy, Sonia. 2016. (ENG.). (J). (gr. k-2). 19.99 *(978-0-9975956-1-1(2))*; pap. 11.99 *(978-0-9975956-0-4(4))* Panigrahy, Sonia.

—Nose. Jenkins, Pete. 2017. (I See, I Saw Ser.). (ENG.). 24p. (gr. -1-1). pap. 8.95 *(978-1-68342-195-5(7),* 9781683421955) Rourke Educational Media.

—Skin. Jenkins, Pete. 2017. (I See, I Saw Ser.). (ENG.). 24p. (gr. -1-2). 29.93 *(978-1-68342-310-2(0),* 9781683423102); pap. 8.95 *(978-1-68342-406-2(9),* 9781683424062) Rourke Educational Media.

—Sparkly New Friends. Burnell, Heather Ayris. 2019. (Unicorn & Yeti Ser.: 1). (ENG.). 64p. (J). (gr. -1-1). pap. 4.99 *(978-1-338-32901-8(4))* Scholastic, Inc.

—Teeth. Jenkins, Pete. 2017. (I See, I Saw Ser.). (ENG.). 24p. (gr. -1-2). 29.93 *(978-1-68342-313-3(5),* 9781683423133); pap. 8.95 *(978-1-68342-409-3(3),* 9781683424093) Rourke Educational Media.

—Toes. Jenkins, Pete. 2017. (I See, I Saw Ser.). (ENG.). 24p. (gr. -1-1). pap. 8.95 *(978-1-68342-193-1(0),* 9781683421931) Rourke Educational Media.

—Walter the Whale Shark: And His Teeny Tiny Teeth. Crow, Katrine. 2020. (ENG.). 32p. (J). (gr. k-2). 16.99 *(978-1-4867-1809-2(4),* f9047dd8-d074-4968-84e8-dd1ed2901eac) Flowerpot Pr.

Quintero, Jose. Lo Que Si y lo Que No. Murguía, Verónica. rev. ed. 2006. (Otra Escalera Ser.). (SPA & ENG.). 24p. (J). (gr. 2-4). pap. 9.95 *(978-968-5920-56-8(7))* Castillo, Ediciones, S. A. de C. V. MEX. Dist: Macmillan.

Quintero, michelle. Ollie Otter's Special Gift: A Story from Quiet Pond. Reminick, Gerald. 2013. 32p. (J). 10.00 *(978-1-889901-60-2(1),* Palo Alto Bks.) Glencannon Pr.

Quintero, Noel. Green Means Go. Orenshein, Jesse. 2020. (ENG.). 32p. (J). pap. 9.99 ***(978-1-7045-4846-3(2))*** Independently Published.

Quirk, Carol. Sophia's School Worries. Johnson-Siebold, Judith. 2016. (ENG.). (J). pap. 9.95 *(978-1-60571-322-9(8))* Northshire Pr.

Quirk, Carol Hill. Who Will Roar If I Go? Jaeger, Paige. 2018. (If We're Gone Ser.). (ENG.). 40p. (J). (gr. k-2). 18.95 *(978-1-945448-15-7(6),* BQB Publishing) Boutique of Quality Books Publishing Co., Inc.

Quraishi, Ibrahim. The Story of Hurry. Williams, Emma. 2014. 32p. (J). (gr. -1-2). 16.95 *(978-1-60980-589-0(5),* Triangle Square) Seven Stories Pr.

Q2A Staff. Christopher Columbus & the Voyage of 1492. Abnett, Dan. 2007. (Jr. Graphic Biographies Ser.). (ENG.). 24p. (gr. 3-8). pap. 10.60 *(978-1-4042-2143-7(3),* PowerKids Pr.) Rosen Publishing Group, Inc., The.

Q2AMedia Services Private Ltd, Q2AMedia Services. Drawing Appaloosas & Other Handsome Horses, 1 vol. Young, Rae. 2014. (Drawing Horses Ser.). (ENG.). 32p. (J). (gr. 3-9). lib. bdg. 28.65 *(978-1-4765-4001-6(2))* Capstone.

—Drawing Arabians & Other Amazing Horses, 1 vol. Young, Rae. 2014. (Drawing Horses Ser.). (ENG.). 32p. (J). (gr. 3-9). lib. bdg. 28.65 *(978-1-4765-3995-9(2))* Capstone.

—Drawing Barrel Racers & Other Speedy Horses, 1 vol. Young, Rae. 2014. (Drawing Horses Ser.). (ENG.). 32p. (J). (gr. 3-9). lib. bdg. 28.65 *(978-1-4765-3994-2(4))* Capstone.

—Drawing Friesians & Other Beautiful Horses, 1 vol. Young, Rae. 2014. (Drawing Horses Ser.). (ENG.). 32p. (J). (gr. 3-9). lib. bdg. 28.65 *(978-1-4765-3996-6(0))* Capstone.

—Drawing Horses, 1 vol. Young, Rae. 2014. (Drawing Horses Ser.). (ENG.). 32p. (J). (gr. 3-9). lib. bdg., lib. bdg. 171.90 *(978-1-4765-4667-4(3))* Capstone.

—Drawing Mustangs & Other Wild Horses, 1 vol. Young, Rae. 2014. (Drawing Horses Ser.). (ENG.). 32p. (J). (gr. 3-9). lib. bdg. 28.65 *(978-1-4765-4002-3(0))* Capstone.

—Drawing Thoroughbreds & Other Elegant Horses, 1 vol. Young, Rae. 2014. (Drawing Horses Ser.). (ENG.). 32p. (J). (gr. 3-9). lib. bdg. 28.65 *(978-1-4765-3993-5(6))* Capstone.

Q2AMedia Services Private Ltd Staff. The Ultimate Guide to Drawing Horses, 1 vol. Young, Rae. 2013. (Drawing Horses Ser.). (ENG.). 144p. (J). (gr. 3-9). pap. 14.95 *(978-1-4765-3992-8(8),* Capstone Pr.) Capstone.

R

R, Gianna & R, Jordan. A Different Kind of Princess. Gwinnett, Cara. 2019. (ENG.). 32p. (J). pap. 9.99 ***(978-1-0893-6542-6(X))*** Independently Published.

R, Jordan, jt. illus. see R, Gianna.

R Uldal, Anne-Thea. Abenteurer Von Bjerregaard und Lindhardt(Deutsch - Danisch) Eventyrer Af Bjerregaard Og Lindhardt(tysk - Dansk) [Illustriert (in Schwarzwei�) Von: Anne-Th�a R. Uldal]. Bjerregaard, Bjorn. Lindhardt, Claes, tr. 2019. (Einzigartige B�cher Ser.: Vol. 2). (GER.). 64p. (J). pap. 6.00 ***(978-1-6917-9500-0(3))*** Independently Published.

—Als Wir Opa Gegessen Haben und Kuschel und Die Veganen Werte: [Illustriert (in Schwarzwei�) Von: Anne-Th�a R. Uldal]. Bjerregaard, Bjorn. Lindhardt, Claes, tr. 2019. (Einzigartige B�cher Ser.: Vol. 2). (GER.). 62p. (J). pap. 6.00 ***(978-1-6884-9085-7(X))*** Independently Published.

—B. Bjerregaard Og C. Lindhardts Bedste Fort�llinger (Vickey Og Appsene, Dengang Vi Spiste Bedstefar, Nuser Og de Veganske V�rdier) [Med Sk�nne Illustrationer Af Anne-Th�a R. Uldal]. Bjerregaard, Bjorn. Lindhardt, Claes, tr. 2019. (B�meb�ger Til et Unikt Publikum Ser.: Vol. 3). (DAN.). 84p. (J). pap. 8.00 ***(978-1-0770-1116-8(4))*** Independently Published.

R Uldal, Anne-Thea. Nuser Og de Veganske Værdier: [Illusteret (i Sort/hvid) Af Anne-Théa R. Uldal]. Bjerregaard, Bjorn & Lindhardt, Claes. 2019. (Børnebøger Til et Unikt Publikum Ser.: Vol. 2). (DAN.). 32p. (J). pap. 6.00 *(978-1-0745-0976-7(5))* Independently Published.

R. Z. Novit Graphic Design Staff. Alphabet Aa to Zz. Novit, Renee Z. (Kidz & Katz Educational Learning Book Ser.). 16p. (J). (gr. -1). pap. 7.95 *(978-1-883371-00-5(7))* Kidz & Katz Publishing Co.

Ra, Zita. Help! - I've Got an Alarm Bell Going off in My Head! How Panic, Anxiety & Stress Affect Your Body. Aspden, K. L. 2015. (ENG.). 48p. pap. 12.95 *(978-1-84905-704-2(4),* 693933) Kingsley, Jessica Pubs. GBR. Dist: Hachette UK Distribution.

Raab, Ben, et al. Cable & X-Force: Onslaught! 2019. (ENG.). 456p. (J). (gr. 4-17). pap. 39.99 *(978-1-302-91619-0(X))* Marvel Worldwide, Inc.

Raab, Joy. Balboa Park with Ranger Kim. Crooks, Pam. 2018. (ENG.). 38p. (J). (gr. k-3). pap. 14.95 *(978-0-9706219-9-3(X))* Ridgway Park Publishing.

—Toby Came Late. Lyon, Shari. 2015. (ENG.). (J). 19.95 *(978-1-943198-01-6(2))* Southwestern Publishing Hse., Inc.

Raasch, Peg. Reaching Your Goals: The Ultimate Teen Guide, Vol. Courtright, Anne. 2009. (It Happened to Me Ser.: 23). (ENG.). 298p. 58.00 *(978-0-8108-5572-4(0))* Scarecrow Pr., Inc.

Rabei, Carolina. Snow. de la Mare, Walter. 2018. (Four Seasons of Walter de la Mare Ser.). (ENG.). 16p. bds. 7.95 *(978-0-571-33713-2(9),* Faber & Faber Children's Bks.) Faber & Faber, Inc.

Rabei, Carolina. Crunch! Rabei, Carolina. 2016. (Child's Play Library). (ENG.). 36p. (J). pap. *(978-1-84643-732-8(6))*; *(978-1-84643-733-5(4))* Child's Play International Ltd.

Rabei, Caroline. Snow. de la Mare, Walter. 2014. (Four Seasons of Walter de la Mare Ser.). (ENG.). 32p. pap. 9.95 *(978-0-571-30557-5(1),* Faber & Faber Children's Bks.) Faber & Faber, Inc.

Rabenau, Francesca von. Keka en el Museo de Arte de Ponce. Valldejuly, Frances Bragan. 2004. (SPA.). 60p. 21.95 *(978-1-56328-269-0(0))* Editorial Plaza Mayor, Inc.

Rabey, Louise. Dear Baby. Westwood, Courtney. 2019. (ENG.). 36p. (J). pap. 9.99 ***(978-1-7966-6584-0(3))*** Independently Published.

Rabey, Louise. The Magical Teddy Bear. Lacey, Susan. 2019. (ENG.). 50p. (J). pap. *(978-1-78623-453-7(X))* Grosvenor Hse. Publishing Ltd.

Rabideau, Chad J. You're Mine, Walker & All. Parker, Kristina M. 2019. (ENG.). 38p. (J). pap. 11.95 *(978-1-7954-9481-6(6))* Independently Published.

Rabley, Stephen & Ursell, Martin. Red Rock/Roca Roja. Rabley, Stephen. 2009. (Let's Read! Spanish-English Ser.). 32p. (J). (ENG.). (gr. k-3). 17.44 *(978-0-7641-4361-8(1))*; (FRE.). (gr. 3-7). pap. 4.99 *(978-0-7641-4360-1(3))* Peterson's. (B.E.S. Publishing).

Rabon, Elaine Hearn. Dear Marguerite & Me. Dolson, Carol Bland. 2016. (ENG.). (J). (gr. k-3). 18.95 *(978-0-9827614-6-5(5))* Miglior Pr.

—Hattie & the Higgledy-Piggledy Hedge. Dolson, Carol Bland. 2012. (ENG.). 32p. (J). 18.95 *(978-0-9827614-4-1(9),* 9780982761441) Miglior Pr.

—Tim & Sally's Beach Adventure. Thrasher, Grady. 2008. (ENG.). 48p. (J). (gr. -1-3). 18.95 *(978-1-58818-161-9(8))* Hill Street Pr., LLC.

—Tim & Sally's Vegetable Garden. Thrasher, Grady. 2007. (ENG.). 48p. (J). (gr. -1-3). lib. bdg. 18.95 *(978-1-58818-131-2(6))* Hill Street Pr., LLC.

—Tim & Sally's Year in Poems. Thrasher, Grady. 2010. 56p. (J). 18.95 *(978-0-9827614-0-3(6))* Miglior Pr.

Rabou, John. Life of Jesus, 1 vol. Dowley, Tim & Bewley, Robert. 2011. (Candle Discovery Ser.). 16p. (J). (gr. 2-4). 11.99 *(978-1-85985-823-3(6)*, Candle Bks.) Lion Hudson PLC GBR. Dist: Kregel Pubns.

Raboy, Mac. Adam Strange. Binder, Otto & Fox, Gardner. rev. ed. 2006. (Archives Ser.: Vol. 2). (ENG.). 228p. (YA). 49.99 *(978-1-4012-0780-9(4))* DC Comics.

Raboy, Mac. Flash Gordon, Vol. 4. Raboy, Mac. 2004. (ENG.). 256p. pap. 19.95 *(978-1-56971-979-4(9))* Dark Horse Comics.

Rache, Elmer. Uncle Wiggily's Fortune. Garis, Howard R. 2016. (ENG.). (J). pap. 9.99 *(978-1-4794-1740-7(8))* Wildside Pr., LLC.

Rachel, Drapkin. Puffs In: Christmas in Puffville. Joseph, Costa & Christopher, Romero. 2013. 46p. pap. 15.95 *(978-1-62882-016-4(0))* Keith Pubns., LLC.

Rachel Henson. The Angry Thunderstorm. Carol Henson Keesee. 2009. 40p. pap. 20.00 *(978-1-4389-4334-3(2))* AuthorHouse.

Racine, Victoria. The Absolute Truth about Lying. Lopez, Christopher P. 2011. 36p. pap. 24.95 *(978-1-4626-3245-9(9))* America Star Bks.

Rackham, Arthur. Aesop's Fables. Aesop, Aesop. Jones, V. S. Vernon, tr. 2003. (Barnes & Noble Classics Ser.). 304p. pap. 9.95 *(978-1-59308-062-4(X))* Barnes & Noble, Inc.

—Aesop's Fables. Jones, Vernon. 2007. 160p. (J). pap. 5.00 *(978-0-9788914-4-2(9))* Kahley, Glenn.

Rackham, Arthur, et al. Alice's Adventures in Wonderland. 2018. (ENG.). 110p. (J). pap. 6.99 *(978-1-7237-7518-5(5))* Independently Published.

Rackham, Arthur. Beautiful Stories from Shakespeare for Children. Nesbit, E. 2018. 192p. (J). (gr. 3-8). 14.99 *(978-1-63158-274-5(7)*, Racehorse Publishing) Skyhorse Publishing Co., Inc.

—Cinderella Liberator. Solnit, Rebecca. 2019. (ENG.). 32p. 17.95 *(978-1-60846-596-5(9))* Haymarket Bks.

—The Classic Aesop's Fables (Illustrated Edition) Vernon Jones, V. S., tr. 2019. (ENG.). 142p. (J). pap. 9.95 *(978-1-0919-4833-4(X))* Independently Published.

Rackham, Arthur. The Complete Grimm's Fairy Tales: With 23 Full-Page Illustrations by Arthur Rackham. Grimm, Jacob & Grimm, Wilhelm. 2019. (ENG.). 506p. (J). (gr. 3-6). pap. ***(978-1-911405-95-5(0))*** Aziloth Bks.

Rackham, Arthur. Cuentos de Andersen. Andersen, Hans. 2003. (SPA.). 240p. 24.95 *(978-84-261-0273-7(5)*, JV30115) Juventud, Editorial ESP. Dist: Lectorum Pubns., Inc., Distribooks, Inc.

—Cuentos de Grimm. Grimm, Jacob. (Coleccion Cuentos Universales). (SPA.). 144p. (YA). (gr. 4-18). *(978-84-261-1098-5(3)*, JV30116) Juventud, Editorial ESP. Dist: Lectorum Pubns., Inc.

—Fables: Illustrées Par Arthur Rackham. (aesop), Esope. 2019. (Fables D'Esope Ser.: Vol. 1). (FRE.). (J). 132p. pap. 17.04 *(978-1-7980-9919-3(5))*; 140p. pap. 17.04 *(978-1-7980-9994-0(2))* Independently Published.

Rackham, Arthur, et al. Hans Christian Andersen's Fairy Tales: An Illustrated Classic. Andersen, Hans. 2017. (Illustrated Classic Ser.). (ENG.). 260p. (J). 12.99 *(978-1-68412-031-4(4))* Readerlink Distribution Services, LLC.

Rackham, Arthur. Irish Fairy Tales. Stephens, James. 2019. (ENG.). 204p. (J). pap. 37.99 ***(978-1-6975-4362-9(6))*** Independently Published.

Rackham, Arthur. The Night Before Christmas. Moore, Clement C. 2012. 32p. pap. 5.99 *(978-1-61720-437-1(4))* Wilder Pubns., Corp.

—The Night Before Christmas: [illustrated]. Moore, Clement C. (ENG.). (J). (gr. k-7). 2019. 32p. *(978-605-7861-57-3(4))*; 2018. 34p. pap. *(978-605-7566-30-0(0))* Uhrayoglu, Murat E Kitap Projesi.

—Poor Cecco. Bianco, Margery Williams. 2013. (ENG.). 160p. (J). (gr. 3-12). pap. 9.99 *(978-0-486-49226-1(5))* Dover Pubns., Inc.

—The Wind in the Willows. Grahame, Kenneth. 2012. (ENG.). 280p. *(978-1-904919-51-3(0)*, Collector's Library, The) Pan Macmillan.

—The Wind in the Willows: An Illustrated Classic. Grahame, Kenneth. 2017. (Illustrated Classic Ser.). (ENG.). 200p. (J). 12.99 *(978-1-68412-033-8(0)*, Thunder Bay Pr.) Readerlink Distribution Services, LLC.

Rackham, Arthur & Bedford, F. D. The Complete Adventures of Peter Pan Includes: The Little White Bird, Peter Pan in Kensington Gardens(Illustrated) & Peter. Barrie, J. M. 2013. 326p. *(978-1-78139-361-1(3))* Benediction Classics.

Rackham, Arthur, jt. illus. see Bedford, Francis Donkin.

Rackham, Arthur, jt. illus. see Leech, John.

Rackham, Arthur, jt. illus. see Robinson, W. Heath.

Rackham, Jennifer. Kenni & the Roof Slide. Johnson, Mike. 2018. (Kenni & Kiri the Kea Bks.: Vol. 1). (ENG.). 34p. (J). pap. *(978-0-473-42330-8(8))* Lasavia Publishing Ltd.

—Taniwha: Bilingual: English & Te Reo. Johnson, Mike. Rakuraku, Maraea, tr. 2016. (MAO.). (J). pap. *(978-0-473-35413-8(6))* Lasavia Publishing Ltd.

Rackhan, Arthur. Irish Fairy Tales. Stephens, James. 2020. (ENG.). 214p. (J). (gr. k-3). 19.99 ***(978-1-5154-4485-5(6))***; pap. 12.99 ***(978-1-5154-4486-2(4))*** Jorge Pinto Bks. (Illustrated Bks.).

Racklin-Siegel, Alison. Jacob's Travels. 2005. (ENG & HEB.). 32p. (J). per. 10.95 *(978-0-939144-53-2(0))* EKS Publishing Co.

Racklin-Siegel, Carol. Lech Lecha: The Story of Abraham & Rebecca. 2004. (HEB & ENG.). 32p. (J). per. 10.95 *(978-0-939144-49-5(2))* EKS Publishing Co.

—Noah's Ark. 2003. 32p. (J). per. 10.95 *(978-0-939144-42-6(5))* EKS Publishing Co.

Racklyeft, Jess. Ivy Bird. McCartney, Tania. 2020. (ENG.). 32p. (J). 17.95 *(978-1-7331212-1-7(8))* Blue Dot Pubns. LLC.

—See Hear: There's Magic All Around You. What Can You See? What Can You Hear? McCartney, Tania. 2018. (ENG.). 32p. (J). (gr. -1-2). 17.99 *(978-1-925335-67-5(4)*, EK Bks.) Exisle Publishing Pty Ltd. AUS. Dist: Hachette Bk. Group.

—Smile Cry: Happy or Sad, Wailing or Glad - How Do You Feel Today? McCartney, Tania. 2017. (ENG.). 32p. (J). (gr. -1-k). 12.99 *(978-1-925335-37-8(2)*, 317116, EK Bks.) Exisle Publishing Pty Ltd. AUS. Dist: Hachette Bk. Group.

Racz, Michael. The Roman Colosseum: The Story of the World's Most Famous Stadium & Its Deadly Games. Mann, Elizabeth. 2006. (Wonders of the World Book Ser.). (ENG.). 48p. (J). (gr. 4-8). pap. 12.95 *(978-1-931414-17-3(3)*, 7dfff866-9870-4b51-b983-5c628a569a0d) Mikaya Pr.

Raczova, Noemi. Different. Evans, Adriana. 2018. (ENG.). 26p. (J). pap. 11.50 *(978-1-7276-9058-3(3))* CreateSpace Independent Publishing Platform.

Radaviciute, Diana. Tambien Los Insectos Son Perfectos. Blanco, Alberto. 2005.Tr. of Insects Are Perfect, Too. (SPA.). (J). (gr. k-2). pap. 10.95 *(978-968-494-054-3(8))* Centro de Informacion y Desarrollo de la Comunicacion y la Literatura MEX. Dist: Iaconi, Mariuccia Bk. Imports.

Radcliffe, Thomas. When Thomas Edison Fed Someone Worms. Weakland, Mark. (J). 2017. *(978-1-5158-0139-9(X))*; 2016. (ENG.). 32p. (gr. 1-4). lib. bdg. 28.65 *(978-1-4795-9683-6(3))* Capstone. (Picture Window Bks.).

—When Thomas Edison Fed Someone Worms. Weakland, Mark. 2016. (Leaders Doing Headstands Ser.). (ENG.). 32p. (J). (gr. 1-4). pap. 7.95 *(978-1-5158-0135-1(7)*, Picture Window Bks.) Capstone.

Radencich, Michael. Volcanoes: Mountains That Blow Their Tops. Nirgiotis, Nicholas. 2011. (Penguin Young Readers: Level 3 Ser.: Level 2). 48p. (J). (gr. 1-3). 16.19 *(978-0-448-41143-9(1))* Penguin Young Readers Group.

Rader, Laura. The Best Smelling Christmas Book Ever: 9 Scents to Scratch & Sniff! Ziefert, Harriet. 2004. 18p. (J). (gr. k-4). reprint ed. 13.00 *(978-0-7567-7600-8(7))* DIANE Publishing Co.

—Run, Turkey, Run! Mayr, Diane. 2009. (ENG.). 32p. (J). (gr. -1-2). pap. 7.99 *(978-0-8027-8481-0(X)*, 900062746, Bloomsbury USA Childrens) Bloomsbury Publishing USA.

—The Teeny Tiny Woman Level 2. Red. Ziefert, Harriet. 2012. (Penguin Young Readers: Level 2 Ser.). 32p. (J). (gr. k-2). 16.19 *(978-0-14-037625-8(9))* Penguin Young Readers Group.

—What to Expect at Preschool. Murkoff, Heidi. 2003. (What to Expect Kids Ser.). (ENG.). 24p. (J). (gr. -1-k). pap. 3.99 *(978-0-06-052920-8(2))* HarperCollins Pubs.

—What to Expect When Mommy's Having a Baby. Murkoff, Heidi. 2004. (What to Expect Kids Ser.). (ENG.). 24p. (J). (gr. -1-3). pap. 3.99 *(978-0-06-053802-6(3)*, HarperFestival) HarperCollins Pubs.

Rader, Laura. The Twelve Days of Christmas in California. Rader, Laura. 2009. (Twelve Days of Christmas in America Ser.). 40p. (J). (gr. k-3). 12.95 *(978-1-4027-6247-5(X))* Sterling Publishing Co., Inc.

—When Santa Lost His Ho! Ho! Ho! Rader, Laura. 2008. (ENG.). 40p. (J). (gr. -1-3). 14.99 *(978-0-06-114139-3(9))* HarperCollins Pubs.

Rader, Laura & Utt, Mary Ann. A Child's Story of Thanksgiving. 24p. (J). 7.95 *(978-0-8249-5327-0(4)*, Ideal Pubns.) Worthy Publishing.

Radeva, Milena. The Best Summer Guest. Pere, Tuula. Korman, Susan, ed. 2018. (Jonty Ser.: Vol. 1). (ENG.). 44p. (J). (gr. k-4). pap. *(978-952-7107-69-0(5))* Wickwick oy.

—Den Allerbedste Feriegæst: Danish Edition of the Best Summer Guest. Pere, Tuula. Lundbeck, Merete, tr. 2018. (Jonty Ser.: Vol. 1). (DAN.). 44p. (J). (gr. k-4). *(978-952-357-036-8(6))*; pap. *(978-952-325-353-7(0))* Wickwick oy.

—Jonte SOM Sommargäst: Swedish Edition of the Best Summer Guest. Pere, Tuula. Nikolowski-Bogomoloff, Angelika, tr. 2018. (Jonty Ser.: Vol. 1). (SWE.). 44p. (J). (gr. k-4). pap. *(978-952-7107-71-3(7))* Wickwick oy.

—Jonttu Kesävieraana: Finnish Edition of the Best Summer Guest. Pere, Tuula. 2018. (Jonttu Ser.: Vol. 1). (FIN.). 44p. (J). (gr. k-4). pap. *(978-952-7107-70-6(9))* Wickwick oy.

—My Snow Day / Ma Journée de Neige: Babl Children's Books in French & English. Nathaniel, Ally. l.t. ed. 2018. (FRE.). 38p. (J). 14.99 *(978-1-68304-278-5(6))* Babl Books, Incorporated.

—My Snow Day / Meu Dia de Neve: Children's Picture Books in Portuguese. Nathaniel, Ally. 2016. (POR.). (J). (gr. 1-3). 14.99 *(978-1-68304-187-0(9))* Babl Books, Incorporated.

—Runski Punski & the Watermelon Shoes. Yates, K. R. 2019. (Runski Punski Ser.: Vol. 1). (ENG.). 36p. (J). pap. 9.99 *(978-1-9782-8348-0(2))* CreateSpace Independent Publishing Platform.

Radeva, Sabina. Charles Darwin's on the Origin of Species. Radeva, Sabina, adapted by. 2019. (ENG.). 64p. (J). (gr. -1-3). 18.99 *(978-1-9848-9491-5(9)*, Crown Books For Young Readers) Random Hse. Children's Bks.

Radford, Karen & Dreidemy, Joëlle. Storybook Homes. Bailey, Gerry. 2013. (ENG.). 32p. (J). *(978-0-7787-0288-7(X))*; pap. *(978-0-7787-0298-6(7))* Crabtree Publishing Co.

Radford, Karen & Noyes, Leighton. Armstrong's Moon Rock. Bailey, Gerry & Foster, Karen. 2008. (Stories of Great People Ser.). (ENG.). 40p. (J). (gr. 3-8). lib. bdg. *(978-0-7787-3684-4(9))*; (gr. 5-8). pap. *(978-0-7787-3706-3(3))* Crabtree Publishing Co.

—Cleopatra's Coin. Bailey, Gerry & Foster, Karen. 2008. (Stories of Great People Ser.). (ENG.). 40p. (J). (gr. 3-8). pap. *(978-0-7787-3707-0(1))*; lib. bdg. *(978-0-7787-3685-1(7))* Crabtree Publishing Co.

—Columbus's Chart. Bailey, Gerry & Foster, Karen. 2008. (Stories of Great People Ser.). (ENG.). 40p. (J). (gr. 3-8). pap. *(978-0-7787-3708-7(X))*; lib. bdg. *(978-0-7787-3686-8(5))* Crabtree Publishing Co.

—Leonardo's Pallete. Bailey, Gerry & Foster, Karen. 2008. (Stories of Great People Ser.). (ENG.). 40p. (J). (gr. 3-8). lib. bdg. *(978-0-7787-3687-5(3))* Crabtree Publishing Co.

—Marco Polo's Silk Purse. Bailey, Gerry & Foster, Karen. 2008. (Stories of Great People Ser.). (ENG.). 40p. (J). (gr. 3-8). pap. *(978-0-7787-3710-0(1))*; lib. bdg. *(978-0-7787-3688-2(1))* Crabtree Publishing Co.

—Martin Luther King Jr.'s Microphone. Bailey, Gerry & Foster, Karen. 2008. (Stories of Great People Ser.). (ENG.). 40p. (J). (gr. 3-8). pap. *(978-0-7787-3711-7(X))*; lib. bdg. *(978-0-7787-3689-9(X))* Crabtree Publishing Co.

—Mother Teresa's Alms Bowl. Ganeri, Anita. 2008. (Stories of Great People Ser.). (ENG.). 40p. (J). (gr. 3-8). pap. *(978-0-7787-3712-4(8))* Crabtree Publishing Co.

—Shakespeare's Quill. Bailey, Gerry & Foster, Karen. 2008. (Stories of Great People Ser.). (ENG.). 40p. (J). (gr. 3-7). lib. bdg. *(978-0-7787-3691-2(1))*; pap. *(978-0-7787-3713-1(6))* Crabtree Publishing Co.

—Sitting Bull's Tomahawk. Bailey, Gerry & Foster, Karen. 2008. (Stories of Great People Ser.). (ENG.). 40p. (J). (gr. 3-8). pap. *(978-0-7787-3714-8(4))*; lib. bdg. *(978-0-7787-3692-9(X))* Crabtree Publishing Co.

—The Wright Brothers' Glider. Bailey, Gerry & Foster, Karen. 2008. (Stories of Great People Ser.). (ENG.). 40p. (J). (gr. 3-8). pap. *(978-0-7787-3715-5(2))*; lib. bdg. *(978-0-7787-3693-6(8))* Crabtree Publishing Co.

Radford, Karen, jt. illus. see Noyes, Leighton.

Radford, Nick. We Are Music. Stosuy, Brandon. 2018. (ENG.). 32p. (J). (— 1). bds. 8.99 *(978-1-5344-0941-5(6)*, Little Simon) Little Simon.

Radhakrishnan, Santhya S. Octopus! Things You Don't Know. Hobbs, J. T. 2019. (ENG.). 40p. (J). pap. 18.99 *(978-1-5456-7044-6(7)*, Mill City Press, Inc) Salem Author Services.

Raditz, JoAnne. The Mud House Mystery: A Wild Bunch Adventure. Savageau, Tony. 2004. (J). pap. 9.95 *(978-0-9759737-0-7(3))* Blue Mustang Pr.

Radivoeva, Svetla. Malina's Jam: Walt Disney Animation Studios Artist Showcase. Radivoeva, Svetla. 2020. (Artist Showcase Ser.). (ENG.). 48p. (J). (gr. -1-k). 17.99 ***(978-1-368-02458-7(0))*** Disney Pr.

Radjev, Priya. Untangling the Ivy League. Zawel, Marc. Burns, Adam, ed. 2005. (College Prowler: Untangling the Ivy League Ser.). 567p. per. 24.95 *(978-1-59658-500-3(5))* College Prowler, Inc.

Radjou, Anna Nazaretz. A Book for Elie. Trooboff, Rhoda. 2008. (ENG.). 31p. pap. 15.00 *(978-0-9773536-1-3(3))* Tenley Circle Pr.

Radka, Sara. The Decision. Ronan, Amanda. 2015. (My Brother Is a Robot Ser.: 6). (ENG.). 64p. (J). (gr. 3-8). 27.99 *(978-1-62920-509-0(5))* Scobre Pr. Corp.

—The Discovery. Ronan, Amanda. 2015. (My Brother Is a Robot Ser.: 5). (ENG.). 64p. (J). (gr. 3-8). 27.99 *(978-1-62920-506-9(0))* Scobre Pr. Corp.

—The Experiment. Ronan, Amanda. 2015. (My Brother Is a Robot Ser.: 1). (ENG.). 64p. (J). (gr. 3-8). 27.99 *(978-1-62920-494-9(3))* Scobre Pr. Corp.

—The Fight. Ronan, Amanda. 2015. (My Brother Is a Robot Ser.: 4). (ENG.). 64p. (J). (gr. 3-8). 27.99 *(978-1-62920-503-8(6))* Scobre Pr. Corp.

—The Master Plan. Ronan, Amanda. 2015. (My Brother Is a Robot Ser.: 2). (ENG.). 64p. (J). (gr. 3-8). 27.99 *(978-1-62920-497-0(8))* Scobre Pr. Corp.

—The Switch. Ronan, Amanda. 2015. (My Brother Is a Robot Ser.: 3). (ENG.). 64p. (J). (gr. 3-8). 27.99 *(978-1-62920-500-7(1))* Scobre Pr. Corp.

Radmanovic, Ljubica. Color Me Trendy. Radmanovic, Rada. 2010. 68p. pap. 14.99 *(978-1-4520-5795-8(8))* AuthorHouse.

Radtke, Becky. Catholic Corner: Puzzles & Activities: Year C, Ages 5-7. Lucey, Marcia T., ed. 2007. 67p. pap. 14.95 incl. cd-rom *(978-1-58459-362-1(8))* World Library Pubns.

—Four Square: The Personal Writing Coach, Grades 1-3. Burke, Mary F. 2005. 112p. (J). pap. 12.95 *(978-1-57310-446-3(9))* Teaching & Learning Co.

—Hey! There's Science in My Literature! Grades 1-2. Dunn, Justine. 2007. (Rigby Best Teachers Press Ser.). 96p. per. 13.99 *(978-1-4190-2848-9(0))* Houghton Mifflin Harcourt Supplemental Pubs.

—Hey! There's Social Studies in My Literature! Grades 1-2. Dunn, Justine. 2007. (Rigby Best Teachers Press Ser.). 96p. per. 13.99 *(978-1-4190-3400-8(6))* Houghton Mifflin Harcourt Supplemental Pubs.

Radtke, Becky J. Four Square: A Companion to the Four Square Writing Method: Writing in the Content Areas for Grades 1-4. Gould, Judith S. & Gould, Evan Jay. Mitchell, Judy, ed. 2004. 112p. (J). pap. 11.95 *(978-1-57310-421-0(3))* Teaching & Learning Co.

Radtke, Roger. Lucky to Live in Minnesota. Jerome, Kate B. 2017. (Arcadia Kids Ser.). (ENG.). 32p. (J). 16.99 *(978-0-7385-2786-4(6))* Arcadia Publishing.

Radunsky, Vladimir. Advice to Little Girls. Twain, Mark. 2013. (ENG.). 24p. (gr. k). 14.95 *(978-1-59270-129-2(9))* Enchanted Lion Bks., LLC.

—Hip Hop Dog. Raschka, Chris. 2010. (ENG.). 32p. (J). (gr. -1-3). 16.99 *(978-0-06-123963-2(1))* HarperCollins Pubs.

—Mother Goose of Pudding Lane. Raschka, Chris. 2019. 48p. (J). (gr. -1-3). 17.99 *(978-0-7636-7523-3(7))* Candlewick Pr.

—On a Beam of Light: A Story of Albert Einstein. Berne, Jennifer. (ENG.). 56p. (J). 2016. (gr. k-3). pap. 7.99 *(978-1-4521-5211-0(X))*; 2013. (gr. 1-4). 17.99 *(978-0-8118-7235-5(1))* Chronicle Bks. LLC.

Radunsky, Vladimir. What Does Peace Feel Like? Radunsky, Vladimir. 2004. (ENG.). 24p. (J). (gr. -1-3). 17.99 *(978-0-689-86676-0(3)*, Atheneum Bks. for Young Readers) Simon & Schuster Children's Publishing.

Radzinski, Kandy. I Is for Idea: An Inventions Alphabet. Schonberg, Marcia. (Science Alphabet Ser.). (ENG.). 48p. (J). (gr. 1-4). 2006. pap. 7.95 *(978-1-58536-327-8(8)*, 202291); 2005. 16.95 *(978-1-58536-257-8(3)*, 202073) Sleeping Bear Pr.

Radzinski, Kandy. What Cats Want for Christmas. Radzinski, Kandy. rev. ed. 2007. (ENG.). 32p. (J). (gr. k-6). 16.95 *(978-1-58536-340-7(5))* Sleeping Bear Pr.

—What Dogs Want for Christmas. Radzinski, Kandy. 2008. (ENG.). 32p. (J). (gr. k-6). 16.95 *(978-1-58536-363-6(4))* Sleeping Bear Pr.

—Where to Sleep. Radzinski, Kandy. 2009. (ENG.). 32p. (J). (gr. k-6). 15.95 *(978-1-58536-436-7(3))* Sleeping Bear Pr.

Radzinski, Kandy, jt. illus. see Doner, Kim.

Rae, Andrew. The Life & Art of Andy Warhol. Ingram, Catherine. 2016. (Lives of Great Artists Ser.). 00080p. (J). (gr. 8-8). 35.75 *(978-1-4994-6585-3(8))*, Rosen Young Adult) Rosen Publishing Group, Inc., The.

—The Life & Art of Salvador Dali. Ingram, Catherine. 2016. (Lives of Great Artists Ser.). 00080p. (J). (gr. 8-8). 35.75 *(978-1-4994-6580-8(7))* Rosen Publishing Group, Inc., The.

—My Crazy Inventions Sketchbook: 50 Awesome Drawing Activities for Young Inventors. Regan, Lisa. 2015. (ENG.). 128p. (J). (gr. 2-6). pap. 16.99 *(978-1-78067-611-1(5)*, King, Laurence Publishing) Orion Publishing Group, Ltd. GBR. Dist: Hachette Bk. Group.

Rae, John. Reynard the Fox & Other Fables. Larned, W. T. & La Fontaine, Jean de. 2014. (ENG.). 96p. (J). (gr. 3-8). pap. 12.99 *(978-0-486-78197-6(6))* Dover Pubns., Inc.

Rafanan, Patrick & Ortiz, Lydia. Little Artist Board Book Set. Kleinman, Emily & Mudpuppy. 2019. (ENG.). (J). (gr. -1-k). bds. 14.99 *(978-0-7353-5572-9(X)*, Mudpuppy) Galison.

—Little Feminist Picture Book. Mudpuppy & Alpert, Yelena Moroz. 2019. (ENG.). 52p. (J). (gr. -1-5). 16.99 *(978-0-7353-6103-4(7)*, Mudpuppy) Galison.

Raff, Anna. A Big Surprise for Little Card. Harper, Charise Mericle. 2016. (ENG.). 40p. (J). (gr. -1-3). 16.99 *(978-0-7636-7485-4(0))* Candlewick Pr.

—The Day the Universe Exploded My Head: Poems to Take You into Space & Back Again. Wolf, Allan. 2019. 56p. (J). (gr. 3-7). 17.99 *(978-0-7636-8025-1(7))* Candlewick Pr.

—Light Waves. Adler, David A. 2018. 32p. (J). (gr. 1-4). 17.99 *(978-0-8234-3682-8(9))* Holiday Hse., Inc.

—Light Waves. Adler, David A. 2020. 32p. (J). (gr. 1-4). pap. 8.99 *(978-0-8234-4541-7(0))* Holiday Hse., Inc.

—Magnets Push, Magnets Pull. Adler, David A. 32p. (J). (gr. k-3). 2018. pap. 7.99 *(978-0-8234-4018-4(4))*; 2017. (ENG.). 17.99 *(978-0-8234-3669-9(1))* Holiday Hse., Inc.

—Simple Machines: Wheels, Levers, & Pulleys. Adler, David A. (ENG.). 32p. (J). (gr. -1-3). 2016. 8.99 *(978-0-8234-3572-2(5))*; 2015. 17.95 *(978-0-8234-3309-4(9))* Holiday Hse., Inc.

—Solids, Liquids, Gases, & Plasma. Adler, David A. 2019. 32p. (J). (gr. 2-5). 18.99 *(978-0-8234-3962-1(3))* Holiday Hse., Inc.

—Things That Float & Things That Don't. Adler, David A. 2014. (ENG.). 32p. (J). (gr. -1-3). 8.99 *(978-0-8234-3176-2(2))* Holiday Hse., Inc.

—World Rat Day: Poems about Real Holidays You've Never Heard Of. Lewis, J. Patrick. 2013. 40p. (J). (gr. k-3). 17.99 *(978-0-7636-5402-3(7))* Candlewick Pr.

—You Are Not a Cat! Flake, Sharon G. 2016. (ENG.). 40p. (J). (gr. -1-2). 16.95 *(978-1-59078-980-3(6))* Boyds Mills Pr.

—Zora's Zucchini. Pryor, Katherine. 2015. (ENG.). 32p. (J). (gr. -1-5). 16.95 *(978-0-9836615-7-3(X))* READERS to EATERS.

—Zora's Zucchini (1 Paperback/1 CD) Pryor, Katherine. 2016. (ENG.). (J). 19.95 *(978-1-4301-2182-4(3))* Live Oak Media.

—Zora's Zucchini (4 Paperback/1 CD) Pryor, Katherine. 2016. (ENG.). (J). 48.95 *(978-1-4301-2184-8(X))* Live Oak Media.

Raffaella, Ligi. My First Fairyland Book. Davidson, Susanna & Stowell, Louie. ed. 2012. (My First Book Ser.). 16p. (J). ring bd. 6.99 *(978-0-7945-3227-7(6)*, Usborne) EDC Publishing.

Rafferty, Kavel. Food for You. Telesmanic, Shayna. 2018. (ENG.). 64p. (J). (gr. 2-6). 14.95 *(978-1-68297-337-0(9)*, 302566) QEB Publishing Inc.

Rafid, Mostafa. Danny's Adventures. Aleryani, Seba. 2018. (ENG.). 38p. (J). pap. 9.99 *(978-1-7273-7964-8(0))* CreateSpace Independent Publishing Platform.

Raga, Silvia. Billy on the Ball. Harrison, Paul. 2010. 32p. pap. *(978-1-84089-634-3(5))* Zero to Ten, Ltd.

—The Birthday Surprise. Oliver, Jane. 2009. (Get Ready (Windmill Books) Ser.). 32p. (J). (gr. k-2). lib. bdg. 25.60 *(978-1-60754-257-5(9))* Windmill Bks.

—Molly Is New. Turpin, Nick. 2010. 32p. pap. *(978-1-84089-650-3(7))* Zero to Ten, Ltd.

—Mr. Bickle & the Ghost. Gurney, Stella. 2009. (Get Ready (Windmill Books) Ser.). 32p. (J). (gr. k-2). lib. bdg. 25.60 *(978-1-60754-260-5(9))* Windmill Bks.

—My Busy Day. Hibbert, Clare. 2011. (Busy Times Ser.). 24p. (J). (gr. -1-k). lib. bdg. 25.65 *(978-1-60753-101-2(1))* Amicus Publishing.

—My Busy Week. Hibbert, Clare. 2011. (Busy Times Ser.). 24p. (J). (gr. -1-k). lib. bdg. 25.65 *(978-1-60753-102-9(X))* Amicus Publishing.

—My Busy Year. Hibbert, Clare. 2011. (Busy Times Ser.). 24p. (J). (gr. -1-k). lib. bdg. 25.65 *(978-1-60753-103-6(8))* Amicus Publishing.

—Our Busy Lives. Hibbert, Clare. 2011. (Busy Times Ser.). 24p. (J). (gr. -1-k). lib. bdg. 25.65 *(978-1-60753-104-3(6))* Amicus Publishing.

Raga, Sylvia. My Busy Day. Hibbert, Clare. 2011. (Busy Times Ser.). (ENG.). 24p. (J). 19.99 *(978-0-237-54263-4(3))* Evans Brothers, Ltd. GBR. Dist: Independent Pubs. Group.

—Our Busy Lives. Hibbert, Clare. 2011. (Busy Times Ser.). (ENG.). 24p. (J). 19.99 *(978-0-237-54266-5(8))* Evans Brothers, Ltd. GBR. Dist: Independent Pubs. Group.

Ragan, Jewel Coochie. Lost & Found. Ragan, Jewel Coochie. 2012. 46p. pap. 11.11 *(978-0-9853809-1-5(8))* Ragan, Jewel.

Ragel-Dial, Tasha, photos by. Say What?, a Photo Book of Inspirational Bible Verses for Kids - Featuring the Photography of Tasha Ragel-Dial. Ragel-Dial, Tasha. 2013. 24p. 22.95 *(978-1-61493-215-4(8))* Peppertree Pr., The.

Raghuraman, Savitri. Horace Leclaire & His Bottles of Air. Sundaram, Siddhartha & Raghuraman, Renuka S. 2008. 36p. pap. 9.99 *(978-1-935105-03-9(5))* Avid Readers Publishing Group.

Ragland, Teresa. God's Fig Tree. Kile, Joan. 2005. 32p. (J). pap. 7.95 *(978-1-57736-345-3(0))* Providence Hse Pubs.

—God's Fruit Tree. Kile, Joan. 2005. (Musty the Mustard Seed Ser.). 28p. (J). (gr. -1-4). per. 7.95 *(978-1-57736-344-6(2))* Providence Hse Pubs.

R

—God's Mustard Seed: Volume 1, Vol. 1. Kile, Joan. 2005. (Musty the Mustard Seed Ser.). 32p. (J). (gr. -1-3). per. 11.95 *(978-1-57736-342-2(6))* Providence Hse Pubs.
—God's Protecting Angels. Kile, Joan. 2005. (Musty the Mustard Seed Ser.). 28p. (J). (gr. -1-4). per. 7.95 *(978-1-57736-346-0(9))* Providence Hse Pubs.
—God's Rugged Cross. Kile, Joan. 2005. (Musty the Mustard Seed Ser.). 32p. (Orig.). (J). (gr. -1-3). per. 4.95 *(978-1-57736-343-9(4))* Providence Hse Pubs.
Raglin, Tim. The Elephant's Child: From the Just So Stories. Kipling, Rudyard. 2005. (Rabbit Ears-A Classic Tale Ser.). (ENG.). 42p. (J). (gr. 2-6). 28.50 *(978-1-59679-343-9(0),* 12944, Picture Bk.) Spotlight.
—How the Camel Got His Hump, 1 vol. Kipling, Rudyard. 2005. (Rabbit Ears-A Classic Tale Ser.). (ENG.). 28p. (J). (gr. 2-6). 28.50 *(978-1-59197-749-0(5),* 12951, Picture Bk.) Spotlight.
—How the Rhinoceros Got His Skin, 1 vol. Kipling, Rudyard. 2005. (Rabbit Ears-A Classic Tale Ser.). 28p. (J). (gr. 2-6). 28.50 *(978-1-59197-750-6(9),* 12952, Picture Bk.) Spotlight.
—Pecos Bill, 1 vol. Gleeson, Brian. 2004. (Rabbit Ears-A Classic Tale Ser.). (ENG.). 36p. (J). (gr. 2-6). 28.50 *(978-1-59197-768-1(1),* 12926, Picture Bk.) Spotlight.
—The Sheep in Wolf's Clothing. Hartman, Bob. ed. 2014. (ENG.). 32p. (J). (gr. -1). pap. 7.99 *(978-0-7459-6500-0(8),* Lion Children's); (gr. k-2). 12.99 *(978-0-7459-6515-4(6))* Lion Hudson PLC GBR. Dist: Independent Pubs. Group.
—We Both Read Bilingual Edition-The Well-Mannered Monster/el Monstruo Debuenos Modales. Brown, Marcy & Haley, Dennis. ed. 2011. (ENG & SPA.). 44p. (J). pap. 4.99 *(978-1-60115-044-8(X))* Treasure Bay, Inc.
—We Both Read-the Well-Mannered Monster. Brown, Marcy & Haley, Dennis. 2006. (We Both Read Ser.). 40p. (J). (gr. -1-4). 7.99 *(978-1-891327-65-0(8))* Treasure Bay, Inc.
—We Both Read-The Well-Mannered Monster. Brown, Marcy & Haley, Dennis. 2006. (We Both Read Ser.). 44p. (J). (gr. -1-4). pap. 4.99 *(978-1-891327-66-7(6))* Treasure Bay, Inc.
—We Read Phonics-I Want to Be a Cowboy! McKay, Sindy. 2012. 32p. (J). 9.95 *(978-1-60115-351-7(1));* pap. 4.99 *(978-1-60115-352-4(X))* Treasure Bay, Inc.
—The Well-Mannered Monster: Monstruo de Buenos Modales. Brown, Marcy et al. 2010. 41p. (J). *(978-1-60115-043-1(1))* Treasure Bay, Inc.
—The Wolf Who Cried Boy. Hartman, Bob. 2004. (ENG.). 32p. (J). (gr. k-3). pap. 7.99 *(978-0-14-240159-0(5),* Puffin Books) Penguin Young Readers Group.
—The Wolf Who Cried Boy. Hartman, Bob. 2004. (Picture Puffins Ser.). (gr. k-3). 17.00 *(978-0-7569-2950-3(4))* Perfection Learning Corp.
Ragogna, Danielle. The Littlest Inventor. Mathis, Mandi C. 2016. (ENG.). 32p. (J). pap. 11.95 *(978-1-935567-62-2(4))* Sensory Resources.
Ragsdale, Brenda. The Adventures of Little Froggie: And the Little Red Floating Thing. Fondren, Johnny. 2019. (Adventures of Little Froggie Ser.). (ENG.). 28p. (J). 17.99 ***(978-1-951300-90-6(4))*** Liberation's Publishing.
Ragsdale, Brenda. Meet My Mississippi: Expanded Edition. Neely-Dorsey, Patricia. 2018. (ENG.). 76p. (J). (gr. k-6). pap. 21.99 *(978-1-7326934-6-3(3))* Liberation's Publishing.
Ragsdale, Brenda. Prince John & the Unicorn. McCain, Don. 2020. (ENG.). 28p. (J). 19.99 ***(978-1-951300-84-5(X))*** Liberation's Publishing.
—The Queen's New Shoes. McCain, Don. 2019. (ENG.). 28p. (J). 25.00 ***(978-1-951300-85-2(8))*** Liberation's Publishing.
—A Town Called Sadville: They Didn't Know Jesus. Deanes-Henley, Amy. 2019. (ENG.). 50p. (J). 25.00 ***(978-1-951300-97-5(1))*** Liberation's Publishing.
Raham, Gary. Sam & Grim & the Contested Hideout. Biederman, Judy McPherson. 2018. (ENG.). 114p. (J). (gr. 4-6). pap. 7.99 *(978-0-9996944-0-4(5))* Nature Connection.
Rahdiana, Benny. The Seven Days of Creation: Based on Biblical Texts. Mazor, Sarah. 2018. (ENG.). 42p. (J). pap. 12.98 *(978-1-7913-2557-2(2))* Independently Published.
Rahimi, Ilgar. Bihtarin Urdu-Yi Kuhistani. Mastiri, Maryam. 2017. (PER.). 23p. (J). *(978-964-337-845-5(4))* Ketab-e Neyestan.
—Khanah-Yi Dirakhti. Mastiri, Maryam. 2017. (PER.). 23p. (J). *(978-964-337-843-1(8))* Ketab-e Neyestan.
—Tavallud-I Ruzi. Mastiri, Maryam. 2017. (PER.). 23p. (J). *(978-964-337-844-8(6))* Ketab-e Neyestan.
Rahn, Jess. Meet Sneazle. 1. Hollis, Randy. 2004. 20p. (J). 6.95 *(978-0-9758815-0-7(7))* SNZ Publishing.
Rai, Rachel, jt. illus. see Biehn, Curt.
Raible, Alton. The Egypt Game. Snyder, Zilpha Keatley. (ENG.). (J). (gr. 3-7). 2009. 240p. pap. 8.99 *(978-1-4169-9051-2(8));* 2007. 224p. 18.99 *(978-1-4169-6065-2(1))* Simon & Schuster Children's Publishing. (Atheneum Bks. for Young Readers).
—The Egypt Game. Snyder, Zilpha Keatley. ed. 2009. 215p. (gr. 5-9). 19.65 *(978-0-8085-5303-8(8))* Turtleback.
—The Headless Cupid. Snyder, Zilpha Keatley. 2009. (Stanley Family Ser.). (ENG.). 224p. (J). (gr. 3-7). 16.99 *(978-1-4169-9532-6(3),* Atheneum Bks. for Young Readers) Simon & Schuster Children's Publishing.
—The Witches of Worm. Snyder, Zilpha Keatley. 2009. (ENG.). (J). (gr. 3-7). 192p. 19.99 *(978-1-4169-9531-9(5));* 208p. pap. 8.99 *(978-1-4169-9053-6(4))* Simon & Schuster Children's Publishing. (Atheneum Bks. for Young Readers).
Raichert, Lance. Treasury of Values for Children. 2012. 159p. (J). *(978-1-4508-3729-3(8))* Phoenix International Publications, Inc.
Raidt, Gerda. In the New World: A Family in Two Centuries. Holtei, Christa & Woofter, Susi. 2015. (ENG.). 40p. (J). (gr. k-3). lib. bdg. 17.95 *(978-1-58089-630-6(8))* Charlesbridge Publishing, Inc.
Railton, Fanny, jt. illus. see Sanborn, F. C.
Raimbault, Christophe. The Life of Jesus According to Saint Luke. De Mullenheim, Sophie. 2019. (ENG.). 96p. (J). (gr. 2-5). pap. 16.99 *(978-1-62164-267-1(4))* Ignatius Pr.
Raimondi, Pablo. Full Throttle. Reilly, Matthew. 2006. (ENG.). 224p. (J). (gr. 5-9). pap. 10.99 *(978-1-4169-0228-7(7),* Simon & Schuster/Paula Wiseman Bks.) Simon & Schuster/Paula Wiseman Bks.
Raimondi, Pablo, jt. illus. see Hoover, Dave.
Raimundo, Joana. The History of Rock: For Big Fans & Little Punks. Nabais, Rita. 2019. (ENG.). 112p. (J). (gr. 3-6). 19.95 *(978-1-62937-733-9(3))* Triumph Bks.
Rainbow. 44 Cats: Cats Rock! Rainbow. 2020. (I Can Read Level 1 Ser.). (ENG.). 32p. (J). (gr. -1-3). pap. 4.99 ***(978-0-06-300212-8(4),*** HarperCollins) HarperCollins Pubs. Ltd. GBR. Dist: HarperCollins Pubs.
—44 Cats: Meet the Cats. Rainbow. 2020. (44 Cats Ser.). (ENG.). 18p. (J). (gr. -1-k). bds. 8.99 ***(978-0-06-300211-1(6),*** HarperFestival) HarperCollins Pubs.
RainboWindow. Leviticus, I Love You. RainboWindow. l.t. ed. 2009. (RainboWindow Ser.: Vol. 3). (ENG.). 32p. (J). 14.99 *(978-1-931552-03-5(7),* 03-931552) Rocksand, LLC.
Raines, Judith. Andy's Snow Day Play. Bugg, Judy. 2019. (ENG.). 34p. (J). pap. 9.15 ***(978-1-6934-1945-4(9))*** Independently Published.
Raines, Morgan. Grizzer the Goofy Wolf. Raines, Kristy. 2007. (ENG.). 80p. per. 11.95 *(978-1-59594-132-9(0),* Wingspan Pr.) WingSpan Publishing.
Rainey, Merrill. Frog. Frog? Frog! Understanding Sentence Types, 1 vol. Loewen, Nancy. 2013. (Language on the Loose Ser.). (ENG.). 24p. (J). (gr. 2-4). 28.65 *(978-1-4048-8321-5(5));* pap. 7.95 *(978-1-4795-1920-0(0))* Capstone. (Picture Window Bks.).
Rainey, Merrill. Color, Cut, Create Play Sets: Dinosaur World. Rainey, Merrill. Odd Dot. 2020. (Color, Cut, Create Ser.). (ENG.). 176p. (J). pap. 12.99 ***(978-1-250-26263-9(1),*** 900221598, Odd Dot) St. Martin's Pr.
—Color, Cut, Create Play Sets: Horse Ranch. Rainey, Merrill. Odd Dot. 2020. (Color, Cut, Create Ser.). (ENG.). 176p. (J). pap. 12.99 ***(978-1-250-26264-6(X),*** 900221599, Odd Dot) St. Martin's Pr.
Rainier, S. T. Curiosity Strikes: Ben & Elvis Adventures. Rainier, S. T. Page, J. 2011. 28p. (J). pap. 8.99 *(978-0-9829669-3-8(8))* Elv Enterprises.
Rainmaker Entertainment, jt. illus. see Rainmaker Entertainment Staff.
Rainmaker Entertainment Staff & Rainmaker Entertainment. Diamond Castle. Man-Kong, Mary. 2008. (Little Golden Book Ser.). (ENG.). 24p. (J). (gr. -1-2). 3.99 *(978-0-375-87508-3(5),* Golden Bks.) Random Hse. Children's Bks.
Rainville, Roxanne. Cinderella. Mueller, Jenna. 2020. (Fairy Tales As Told by Clementine Ser.). (ENG.). 32p. (J). (gr. -1-4). 28.50 ***(978-1-5321-3807-2(5),*** 35224, Looking Glass Library) Magic Wagon.
—Fairy Tales As Told by Clementine (Set), 6 vols. Mueller, Jenna. 2020. (Fairy Tales As Told by Clementine Ser.). (ENG.). 32p. (J). (gr. -1-4). 171.00 ***(978-1-5321-3806-5(7),*** 35222, Looking Glass Library) Magic Wagon.
—Goldilocks. Mueller, Jenna. 2020. (Fairy Tales As Told by Clementine Ser.). (ENG.). 32p. (J). (gr. -1-4). 28.50 ***(978-1-5321-3808-9(3),*** 35226, Looking Glass Library) Magic Wagon.
—Hansel & Gretel. Mueller, Jenna. 2020. (Fairy Tales As Told by Clementine Ser.). (ENG.). 32p. (J). (gr. -1-4). 28.50 ***(978-1-5321-3809-6(1),*** 35228, Looking Glass Library) Magic Wagon.
Rainville, Roxanne. Hey, Little Baby: Belly Book. Boyle, Jacqueline & Lupone Stonis, Susan. 2018. (Belly Book Ser.). (ENG.). 18p. (J). (gr. -1-k). bds. 9.99 *(978-1-68052-332-4(5),* 1003080) Cottage Door Pr.
Rainville, Roxanne. Jack & the Beanstalk. Mueller, Jenna. 2020. (Fairy Tales As Told by Clementine Ser.). (ENG.). 32p. (J). (gr. -1-4). 28.50 ***(978-1-5321-3810-2(5),*** 35230, Looking Glass Library) Magic Wagon.
—Little Red Riding Hood. Mueller, Jenna. 2020. (Fairy Tales As Told by Clementine Ser.). (ENG.). 32p. (J). (gr. -1-4). 28.50 ***(978-1-5321-3811-9(3),*** 35232, Looking Glass Library) Magic Wagon.
—The Princess & the Pea. Mueller, Jenna. 2020. (Fairy Tales As Told by Clementine Ser.). (ENG.). 32p. (J). (gr. -1-4). 28.50 ***(978-1-5321-3812-6(1),*** 35234, Looking Glass Library) Magic Wagon.
Rainwater, Matt J. & Lattie, Tim. Plants vs. Zombies Volume 7: Battle Extravagonzo. Tobin, Paul. 2017. (ENG.). 80p. (gr. 3-7). 9.99 *(978-1-5067-0189-9(2),* Dark Horse Books) Dark Horse Comics.
Rainwater, Matt J., jt. illus. see Chabot, Jacob.
Rainwater, Matthew J., jt. illus. see Chan, Ron.
Raish, Jason. If You Were a Kid Docking at the International Space Station. Gregory, Josh. 2017. (If You Were a Kid Ser.). (ENG.). 32p. (J). (gr. 2-4). pap. 7.95 *(978-0-531-23947-6(0));* lib. bdg. 26.00 *(978-0-531-23746-5(X))* Scholastic Library Publishing. (Children's Pr.).
—If You Were a Kid in the Wild West. Baptiste, Tracey. 2018. (If You Were a Kid Ser.). (ENG.). 32p. (J). (gr. 2-4). lib. bdg. 26.00 *(978-0-531-23215-6(8),* Children's Pr.) Scholastic Library Publishing.
Raiz, James. Eyes of the Gorgon. Ruka, Greg. rev. ed. 2005. (Wonder Woman Ser.). (ENG.). 144p. (YA). pap. 19.99 *(978-1-4012-0797-7(9))* DC Comics.
Raiz, James, et al. Transformers: Armada Omnibus. Sarracini, Chris & Furman, Simon. 2016. (Transformers Ser.). (ENG.). 416p. pap. 29.99 *(978-1-63140-563-1(2),* 9781631405631) Idea & Design Works, LLC.
Raizk, Leyla Marie. Happy Birthday, Ohio: Celebrating Ohio's Bicentennial 1803-2003, 1. Raizk, Mary Ann. 2003. 32p. (J). pap. 14.95 *(978-1-882203-97-0(6))* Orange Frazer Pr.
Rajagopalan, Ashok. The Runaway Peppercorn. Ramadurai, Suchitra. 2005. 28p. (J). *(978-81-8146-119-3(3))* Tulika Pubs.
Rajak, Juliette. The Ghost Who Was Afraid of Himself. McWood, Allison. 2019. (ENG.). 32p. (J). pap. ***(978-1-9994377-9-4(9))*** Annelid Pr.
Rajak, Juliette. Gladys Squinty Wrecks Christmas. McWood, Allison. 2018. (ENG.). 34p. (J). pap. *(978-1-9994377-1-8(3))* Annelid Pr.
Rajcak, Hélène. Panthera Tigris. Alzial, Sylvain et al. 2019. (ENG.). 32p. (J). *(978-0-8028-5529-9(6),* Eerdmans Bks For Young Readers) Eerdmans, William B. Publishing Co.
—Small & Tall Tales of Extinct Animals. Laverdunt, Damien. 2012. (Gecko Press Titles Ser.). (ENG.). 80p. (gr. -1). 22.95 *(978-1-877579-06-6(8))* Gecko Pr. NZL. Dist: Lerner Publishing Group.
Rajic, Alex. The Alefbet Illuminated. Rajic, Alex. 2010. (ENG.). 56p. 0.00 *(978-0-615-38180-0(4))* Cenozoic Pr.
Rajput, Nadia. Billy the Bear. Hart, Devra. 2019. (ENG.). 26p. (J). 24.99 ***(978-1-7283-4009-8(8));*** pap. 13.99 ***(978-1-7283-4008-1(X))*** AuthorHouse.
Rajvanshi, Ayush. Revenge of the Puppets. D'souza, Nadine. 2013. (ENG.). 32p. (J). (gr. -1). pap. 9.95 *(978-81-8190-197-2(5))* Karadi Tales Co. Pvt, Ltd. IND. Dist: Consortium Bk. Sales & Distribution.
Rakitin, Sarah. Little Hands Create! Art & Activities for Kids Ages 3 to 6. Dall, Mary Doerfler. 2004. (Williamson's Little Hands Book Ser.). (J). pap. 12.95 *(978-1-885593-65-8(1),* Ideal Pubns.) Worthy Publishing.
Rakusin, Sudie. Savannah Blue's Activity Book/Libro de Actividades de Savannah Azul. Sforza, Daniella, ed. Spagnoli, Maria Eugenia, tr. 2005.Tr. of Libro de Actividades de Savannah Azul. (SPA & ENG.). 48p. (J). 10.95 *(978-0-9664805-4-2(6))* Winged Willow Pr.
Rakusin, Sudie. Dear Calla Roo... Love, Savannah Blue No. 2: A Letter about Getting Sick & Feeling Better. Rakusin, Sudie. 2003. 32p. (J). (gr. -1-4). 16.95 *(978-0-9664805-3-5(8))* Winged Willow Pr.
Rallis, Chris. Baby Orca. Batten, Mary. 2016. (ENG.). 32p. (J). (-k). pap. 4.99 *(978-0-448-48839-4(6),* Grosset & Dunlap) Penguin Young Readers Group.
—Owls: Birds of the Night. Sollinger, Emily. 2014. (Penguin Young Readers, Level 3 Ser.). 48p. (J). (gr. 1-3). pap. 4.99 *(978-0-448-48135-7(9),* Penguin Young Readers) Penguin Young Readers Group.
Ralph, Karin. Mayda Saves the Day. Ryan, Mike. 2004. 60p. (J). (gr. 1-5). 14.95 *(978-0-9701319-3-5(3))* Temenos Pr.
Ralston, Peter, photos by. Island Journal: An Annual Publication of the Island Institute, 20. Platt, D. D. & Conkling, Philip, eds. 20th ed. 2003. (Island Journals: 20). 96p. pap. 9.95 *(978-0-942719-33-8(6))* Island Institute.
—Island Journal: An Annual Publication of the Island Institute, Vol. 21. annuals Platt, D. D., ed. 2005. (Island Journals: 21). 96p. pap. 16.95 *(978-0-942719-35-2(2))* Island Institute.
Raluca, Cristina Cirti. Good Girls Do. Hall, Tara. 2013. 36p. pap. 9.99 *(978-1-61286-192-0(X))* Avid Readers Publishing Group.
Rama, Sue. Count Your Way Through Egypt. Haskins, James & Benson, Kathleen. 2006. (Count Your Way Ser.). 24p. (J). (gr. -1-3). lib. bdg. 19.93 *(978-1-57505-882-5(0),* Millbrook Pr.) Lerner Publishing Group.
Rama, Sue. Fantastic Gymnastics. Harley, Diana. 2019. (ENG.). 26p. (J). ***(978-0-646-99759-9(9))*** Harley, Diana.
Rama, Sue. It's Time for Preschool! Codell, Esmé Raji. 2012. (ENG.). 40p. (J). (gr. -1-k). 15.99 *(978-0-06-145518-6(0));* lib. bdg. 16.89 *(978-0-06-145519-3(9))* HarperCollins Pubs. (Greenwillow Bks.).
—Little Ones Talk with God: A Book of Prayers. Wangerin, Walter, Jr. et al. 2006. 56p. 7.49 *(978-0-7586-1132-1(3))* Concordia Publishing Hse.
—Subway Ride. Miller, Heather Lynne. 2011. 32p. (J). (gr. -1-3). pap. 7.95 *(978-1-58089-112-7(8))* Charlesbridge Publishing, Inc.
—Yum! Yuck! A Foldout Book of People Sounds. Park, Linda Sue & Durango, Julia. 2005. 36p. (J). (gr. -1-3). 9.95 *(978-1-57091-659-5(4))* Charlesbridge Publishing, Inc.
Ramachandran, Ganesh, photos by. Shining Lights. Steele, Mariah. 2016. (ENG., 38p. (J). 22.00 *(978-1-941830-22-2(6))* Shanti Arts Publishing.
Ramajo, Fernando, photos by. Postres 2. 2003. (Cocina para Todos Ser.). (SPA., 28p. *(978-958-30-1059-0(6))* Panamericana Editorial.
Ramaswamy, Maya. U Sier Lapalang: A Khasi Tale. 2005. (J). *(978-81-89020-31-6(5))* Katha.
—Walk the Rainforest with Niwupah. Datta, Aparajita & Manjrekar, Nima. 2004. (J). *(978-81-89020-15-6(3))* Katha.
Rambo, Angela. The Story of Rhu the Fairy. Plumier, Lea. 2012. 208p. pap. 11.95 *(978-1-61477-039-8(5))* Bellissima Publishing, LLC.
Ramdas, Jeevaraja. Olivia & Her Magical Jacket. Petrilli, Laura. 2018. (ENG.). 32p. (J). pap. *(978-1-9999606-0-5(2))* Lapet Publishing.
Ramey, Cindy. Where Have All the Fairies Gone? Auxier, Bryan. l.t. ed. 2005. 24p. (J). pap. 7.95 *(978-0-9719144-3-8(5))* Where? Pr., Inc.
Ramey, Penny Lemons. Rosey the Nosey Basset Hound. Ramey, Penny Lemons. 2019. (ENG.). 48p. (J). pap. 11.79 ***(978-1-0861-8967-4(1))*** Independently Published.
Ramirez, Alberto. Uno and the Raptor Pack: The Journey Begins! Blasing, George. 2007. (J). 4.95 *(978-0-9797304-1-2(4))* Raining Popcorn Media.
—Dinosaur George Prehistoric Safari: Raptor Island. Blasing, George. 2007. (J). 4.95 *(978-0-9797304-2-9(2))* Raining Popcorn Media.
Ramírez, Ana. Coco: Miguel & the Grand Harmony. de la Peña, Matt. 2017. (ENG.). 48p. (J). (gr. 1-3). 17.99 *(978-1-4847-8149-4(X),* 119181673) Disney Pr.
Ramírez, Antonio & Morrissey, Kay, photos by. V antología nuevo Milenio: Narración (Cuentos) y Poesía. Kassandra, ed. l.t. ed. 2004. (SPA., 100p. (YA). pap. 12.00 *(978-1-931481-86-1(5))* LiArt-Literature & Art.
Ramirez, Elizandro de los Angeles. Pin Pon. Batres, Ethel. 2010. (SPA.). 16p. (J). (gr. -1-1). pap. incl. audio compact disk *(978-99922-1-351-3(5))* Piedra Santa, Editorial.
Ramirez Gallo, Ricardo. Fairies Love Oreos! Roach, Vicki. 2019. (ENG.). 22p. (J). (gr. k-4). 14.99 *(978-1-63337-270-2(7));* 12.99 *(978-1-63337-271-9(5))* Roland Golf Services.
Ramirez, Gamaliel. The Night We Almost Saw the Three Kings. 32p. (J). (gr. 1-18). 16.00 *(978-0-9710860-8-1(7))* Libros, Encouraging Cultural Literacy.
Ramírez González, Ana. Maybe Tomorrow? Agell, Charlotte. 2019. 40p. (J). (gr. -1-3). 17.99 *(978-1-338-21488-8(8),* Scholastic Pr.) Scholastic, Inc.
Ramirez, Herman. Stories of Mexico's Independence Days & Other Bilingual Children's Fables. Torres, Eliseo & Sawyer, Timothy L. 2005. (ENG & SPA.). 70p. (J). (gr. 3-7). pap. 16.95 *(978-0-8263-3886-0(0))* Univ. of New Mexico Pr.
Ramirez, Jose. Frog & His Friends Save Humanity/la Rana y Sus Amigos Salvan ALA Humanidad. Villaseñor, Victor. Ochoa, Edna, tr. 2005. (ENG & SPA.). 32p. (J). (gr. -1). 16.95 *(978-1-55885-429-1(0),* Piñata Books) Arte Publico Pr.
—Goodnight, Papito Dios/Buenos Noches, Papito Dios. Villasenor, Victor. Villarroel, Carolina, tr. 2007. (SPA & ENG.). 32p. (J). (gr. -1-2). 16.95 *(978-1-55885-467-3(3),* Piñata Books) Arte Publico Pr.
—Quinito's Neighborhood (El Vecindario de Quinito) Cumpiano, Ina. 2005. (ENG & SPA.). 24p. (J). (gr. -1-1). 16.95 *(978-0-89239-209-4(6))* Lee & Low Bks., Inc.
Ramírez, José. Quinito's Neighborhood (El Vecindario de Quinito) Cumpiano, Ina. 2013. (ENG & SPA.). 32p. (J). (gr. -1-3). pap. 10.95 *(978-0-89239-229-2(0))* Lee & Low Bks., Inc.
Ramirez, Jose. When Angels Sing: The Story of Rock Legend Carlos Santana. Mahin, Michael. 2018. (ENG.). 48p. (J). (gr. -1-3). 17.99 *(978-1-5344-0413-7(9))* Simon & Schuster Children's Publishing.
Ramirez, Juanan & Schiti, Valerio. Iron Man: the Ultron Agenda: The Ultron Agenda. 2020. 112p. (YA). (gr. 8-17). pap. 15.99 *(978-1-302-92088-3(X))* Marvel Worldwide, Inc.
Ramirez, Orlando L. Captain Cheech. Marin, Cheech. 2008. 32p. (J). (gr. -1-3). lib. bdg. 17.89 *(978-0-06-113208-7(X))* HarperCollins Pubs.
—Cheech the School Bus Driver. Marin, Cheech. 2007. 32p. (J). (gr. -1-3). lib. bdg. 17.89 *(978-0-06-113202-5(0))* HarperCollins Pubs.
—Cheech y el Autobus Fantasma. Marin, Cheech. Fabiancic, Miriam, tr. 2009. (SPA.). 32p. (J). (gr. -1-3). 17.99 *(978-0-06-113214-8(4),* Rayo) HarperCollins Pubs.
Ramirez, Samuel. Pancho the Green Parrot Lays an Egg, 1 vol. Sanchez, Juanita L. 2009. 24p. pap. 24.95 *(978-1-61546-150-9(7))* America Star Bks.
Ramirez, Stephanie. Gravity Falls Dipper's & Mabel's Guide to Mystery & Nonstop Fun! Houghton, Shane & Renzetti, Rob. 2014. (Guide to Life Ser.). (ENG.). 160p. (J). (gr. 3-7). 12.99 *(978-1-4847-1080-7(0))* Disney Pr.
—Gravity Falls Don't Color This Book! It's Cursed! Cicierega, Emmy. 2017. (ENG.). 64p. pap. 12.99 *(978-1-368-00899-0(2))* Disney Pr.
Ramljak, Marijan. Night-Night, Sleepyhead: A Chock-A-Block Book. McElroy, Jean. 2010. (ENG.). 12p. (J). (gr. -1 — 1). 4.99 *(978-1-4424-0902-6(9),* Little Simon) Little Simon.
Ramlogan, Nitya. A New Life in America. Guerrero, Elsie. 2018. (ENG.). 48p. (J). (gr. k-5). 19.99 *(978-1-7327573-2-5(1))* Elsie Publishing Co.
Ramon, Andy. The Legend of el Patron. Staat, Virginia Parker. 2019. (ENG.). 24p. (J). (gr. 2-6). pap. 12.95 *(978-1-64438-492-3(2))* Booklocker.com, Inc.
Ramon, El Primo. Hedy's Journey: The True Story of a Hungarian Girl Fleeing the Holocaust. Bisson, Michelle. 2017. (Encounter: Narrative Nonfiction Picture Bks.). (ENG.). 40p. (J). (gr. 3-7). 15.95 *(978-1-5157-8222-3(0),* 136168, Capstone Pr.) Capstone.
Ramón, El Primo. Samuel Morse, That's Who! The Story of the Telegraph & Morse Code. Maurer, Tracy Nelson. 2019. (ENG.). 40p. (J). 18.99 *(978-1-62779-130-4(2),* 900136046, Holt, Henry & Co. Bks. For Young Readers) Holt, Henry & Co.
Ramon, Yrgane. Cat & Cat #1: Girl Meets Cat. Cazenove, Christophe & Richez, Herve. 2020. (Cat & Cat Ser.: 1). (ENG.). 96p. (J). 14.99 *(978-1-5458-0427-8(3),* 900211581); pap. 9.99 *(978-1-5458-0428-5(1),* 900211582) Papercutz.
Ramondelli, Livio. Transformers: IDW Collection Phase Two Volume 2. Metzen, Chris et al. 2015. (IDW Collection Phase Two Ser.: 2). (ENG.). 332p. 49.99 *(978-1-63140-364-4(8),* 9781631403644) Idea & Design Works, LLC.
Ramos, Amy Jones. The Treasure Hunt Fish & Miss Bernadette's Wish. Martin, Brenda Damley. 2009. 40p. pap. 14.95 *(978-0-9841074-1-4(X))* Jimsam Inc. Publishing.
Ramos, Beatriz Helena. Ack! Icky, Sticky, Gross Stuff Underground. Rosenberg, Pam. 2007. (Icky, Sticky, Gross-Out Bks.). (ENG.). 24p. (J). (gr. 3-6). 27.07 *(978-1-59296-900-5(3),* 200353) Child's World, Inc., The.
—Eek! Icky, Sticky, Gross Stuff in Your Food. Rosenberg, Pam. 2007. (Icky, Sticky, Gross-Out Bks.). (ENG.). 24p. (J). (gr. 3-6). 27.07 *(978-1-59296-895-4(3),* 200354) Child's World, Inc., The.
—Eew! Icky, Sticky, Gross Stuff in Your Body. Rosenberg, Pam. 2007. (Icky, Sticky, Gross-Out Bks.). (ENG.). 24p. (J). (gr. 3-6). 27.07 *(978-1-59296-894-7(5),* 200355) Child's World, Inc., The.
—Ugh! Icky, Sticky, Gross Stuff in the Hospital. Rosenberg, Pam. 2007. (Icky, Sticky, Gross-Out Bks.). (ENG.). 24p. (J). (gr. 3-6). 27.07 *(978-1-59296-897-8(X),* 200356) Child's World, Inc., The.
—Yecch! Icky, Sticky, Gross Stuff in Your House. Rosenberg, Pam. 2007. (Icky, Sticky, Gross-Out Bks.). (ENG.). 24p. (J). (gr. 3-6). 27.07 *(978-1-59296-898-5(8),* 200357) Child's World, Inc., The.
—Yikes! Icky, Sticky, Gross Stuff Underwater. Rosenberg, Pam. 2007. (Icky, Sticky, Gross-Out Bks.). (ENG.). 24p. (J). (gr. 3-6). 27.07 *(978-1-59296-901-2(1),* 200358) Child's World, Inc., The.
—Yuck! Icky, Sticky, Gross Stuff in Your Garden. Rosenberg, Pam. 2007. (Icky, Sticky, Gross-Out Bks.). (ENG.). 24p. (J). (gr. 3-6). 27.07 *(978-1-59296-896-1(1),* 200359) Child's World, Inc., The.

Ramos, Humberto. Amazing Spider-Man by Nick Spencer Vol. 2: Friends & Foes. 2019. (Amazing Spider-Man by Nick Spencer Ser.: 2). 120p. (J). (gr. 4-17). pap. 15.99 *(978-1-302-91232-1(1))* Marvel Worldwide, Inc.

—Champions: Because the World Still Needs Heroes. 2019. (ENG.). 296p. (J). (gr. 4-7). pap. 12.99 *(978-1-302-91794-4(3))* Marvel Worldwide, Inc.

—Champions Vol. 2: The Freelancer Lifestyle. 2017. (ENG.). 136p. (YA). (gr. 8-17). pap. 19.99 *(978-1-302-90619-1(4))* Marvel Worldwide, Inc.

—Marvel Monograph: the Art of Humberto Ramos - Spider-Man. 2019. 112p. (YA). (gr. -1-17). pap. 19.99 *(978-1-302-91757-9(9))* Marvel Worldwide, Inc.

Ramos, Jose. Animals Talk: Los Animales Hablan. Schiller, Pamela Byrne. 2015. (SPA & ENG.). 15p. (J). *(978-1-63237-038-9(7))* Frog Street Pr.

—Echo & Narcissus. Sanderson, Jeannette & Benchmark Education Co., LLC. 2014. (Text Connections Ser.). (J). (gr. 3). *(978-1-4509-9668-6(X))* Benchmark Education Co.

—Echo & Narcissus: Set Of 6. Sanderson, Jeannette. 2014. (Text Connections Ser.). (J). (gr. 3). 49.00 net. *(978-1-4900-0144-9(1))* Benchmark Education Co.

—Opinions about Odysseus: A Greek Hero. Swain, Cynthia & Benchmark Education Co., LLC. 2014. (Text Connections Ser.). (J). (gr. 3). *(978-1-4509-9669-3(8))* Benchmark Education Co.

—Opinions about Odysseus - a Greek Hero: Set Of 6. Swain, Cynthia. 2014. (Text Connections Ser.). (J). (gr. 3). 49.00 net. *(978-1-4900-0145-6(X))* Benchmark Education Co.

Ramos, Manuel Joao. The Boy Who Did Not Like Television. Zink, Rui. Dreher, Patrick, tr. from POR. 2004. (ENG.). 24p. (J). *(978-1-931561-96-9(6))* MacAdam/Cage Publishing, Inc.

Ramos, Mario. I Am So Clever. Ramos, Mario. 2019. (ENG.). 48p. (J). (gr. k-2). 17.99 *(978-1-77657-248-9(3))* Gecko Pr. NZL. Dist: Lerner Publishing Group.

Ramotar, Alexandra, jt. illus. see Ahmad, Maryam.

Rampley, Leigh. Mommy, Why Am I Sick? Schlimpert, Sherrill. 2016. (ENG.). (J). pap. 9.99 *(978-1-4984-8564-7(2))* Salem Author Services.

Rampley, Leigh, jt. illus. see Huffman, Jared.

Ramsay, M. S. Lydia. The Girl in the Pink Helmet. Denny, M. S. Ange. 2018. (ENG.). 28p. (J). pap. *(978-1-7752444-0-0(7))* Denny, Angie.

Ramsdin-Firth, Bernice & Shandler, Georgette. Return to Lolibran & the Witch's Lair: Black & White Version. Ramsdin-Firth, Bernice. 2017. (ENG.). (J). pap. *(978-0-9878541-7-9(8))* Haresend Publishing.

Ramsey, Ann Louise. Me, the Tree. Ramsey, Ann Louise. 2006. (ENG.). 56p. (J). 19.95 *(978-0-9645663-4-7(6))* Crown Peak Publishing.

Ramsey, Jayne. Boomerang, the Farm Cat. Mustaine Hettinger, Cynthia. 2004. (Electra's Acres Ser.: 4). 32p. (J). per. 14.95 *(978-0-9746330-5-3(4))* Anton Berkshire Publishing.

—Casey the Confused Cow. Mustaine Hettinger, Cynthia. 2003. (Electra's Acres Ser.). 32p. (J). per. 14.95 *(978-0-9746330-1-5(1))* Anton Berkshire Publishing.

—Doc the Pygmy Goat. Mustaine Hettinger, Cynthia. 2003. (Electra's Acres Ser.). 32p. (J). per. 14.95 *(978-0-9746330-0-8(3))* Anton Berkshire Publishing.

—Penelope, the Busy Hen. Mustaine Hettinger, Cynthia. 2004. (Electra's Acres Ser.: Bk. 3). 32p. (J). per. 14.95 *(978-0-9746330-4-6(6))* Anton Berkshire Publishing.

—Travis, the Shetland Sheep. Mustaine Hettinger, Cynthia. 2004. (Electra's Acres Ser.: Bk. 5). 32p. (J). per. 14.95 *(978-0-9746330-6-0(2))* Anton Berkshire Publishing.

Ramsey, L. A. From Plowboy to Mormon Prophet Being a Short History of Joseph Smith for Children. Morton, William A. 2004. reprint ed. pap. 30.95 *(978-1-4179-6860-2(5))* Kessinger Publishing, LLC.

Ramsey, Marcy. Anyone Can Eat Squid!, 0 vols. Naylor, Phyllis Reynolds. 2009. (Simply Sarah Ser.: 1). (ENG.). 80p. (J). (gr. 2-5). pap. 9.99 *(978-0-7614-5540-0(X))*, 9780761455400, Two Lions) Amazon Publishing.

—Cuckoo Feathers, 0 vols. Naylor, Phyllis Reynolds. 2009. (Simply Sarah Ser.: 2). (ENG.). 96p. (J). (gr. 2-5). pap. 7.99 *(978-0-7614-5541-7(8)*, 9780761455417, Two Lions) Amazon Publishing.

—David & His Friend, Jonathan. Dietrich, Julie. 2005. (Arch Bks.). (ENG.). 16p. (J). 1.99 *(978-0-7586-0723-2(7))* Concordia Publishing Hse.

—Eating Enchiladas, 0 vols. Naylor, Phyllis Reynolds. 2011. (Simply Sarah Ser.: 4). (ENG.). 80p. (J). (gr. 1-4). pap. 9.99 *(978-0-7614-5885-2(9)*, 9780761458852, Two Lions) Amazon Publishing.

—Patches & Scratches, 0 vols. Naylor, Phyllis Reynolds. 2010. (Simply Sarah Ser.: 3). (ENG.). 80p. (J). (gr. 2-6). pap. 7.99 *(978-0-7614-5731-2(3)*, 9780761457312, Two Lions) Amazon Publishing.

Ramsey, Marcy Dunn. Beddy Bye in the Bay, 1 vol. Cummings, Priscilla. 2010. (ENG.). 32p. (J). 14.99 *(978-0-7643-3450-4(6)*, 9780764334504) Schiffer Publishing, Ltd.

—Beetle Boddiker, 1 vol. Cummings, Priscilla. 2009. (ENG.). 30p. (J). (gr. -1-3). 13.95 *(978-0-87033-602-7(9)*, 9780870336027, Cornell Maritime Pr./Tidewater Pubs.) Schiffer Publishing, Ltd.

—Counties of Central Maryland, 1 vol. Bunting, Elaine & D'Amario, Patricia. 2009. (ENG.). 160p. (J). 19.95 *(978-0-87033-503-7(0)*, 9780870335037, Cornell Maritime Pr./Tidewater Pubs.) Schiffer Publishing, Ltd.

—Counties of Maryland's Lower Eastern Shore, 1 vol. Bunting, Elaine & D'Amario, Patricia. 2009. (ENG.). 168p. (J). 19.95 *(978-0-87033-555-6(3)*, 9780870335556, Cornell Maritime Pr./Tidewater Pubs.) Schiffer Publishing, Ltd.

—Counties of Northern Maryland, 1 vol. Bunting, Elaine & D'Amario, Patricia. 2010. (ENG.). 176p. (J). (gr. 4-7). 19.95 *(978-0-87033-520-4(0)*, 9780870335204, Cornell Maritime Pr./Tidewater Pubs.) Schiffer Publishing, Ltd.

—Counties of Southern Maryland, 1 vol. Bunting, Elaine & D'Amario, Patricia. 2009. (ENG.). 144p. (J). 19.95 *(978-0-87033-535-8(9)*, 9780870335358, Cornell Maritime Pr./Tidewater Pubs.) Schiffer Publishing, Ltd.

—I Was Born to Be a Sister. Michels-Gualtieri, Akaela S. 2005. (ENG.). 32p. (J). (gr. 4-7). 9.95 incl. lp *(978-1-930775-11-4(3))* Platypus Media, L.L.C.

—I Will Keep Trying! Parker, David. 2005. (J). pap. *(978-0-439-73588-9(2))* Scholastic, Inc.

—It's up to You, Griffin!, 1 vol. Pickford, Susan T. 2009. (ENG.). 32p. (J). (gr. -1-3). 10.95 *(978-0-87033-446-7(8)*, 9780870334467, Cornell Maritime Pr./Tidewater Pubs.) Schiffer Publishing, Ltd.

—Mookey the Monkey Gets over Being Teased. Lonczak, Heather Suzanne. 2006. 32p. (J). (gr. -1-3). 14.95 *(978-1-59147-479-1(5))*; 9.95 *(978-1-59147-480-7(9))* American Psychological Assn. (Magination Pr.).

—Osprey Adventure, 1 vol. Curtis, Jennifer Keats. 2009. (ENG.). 30p. (J). (gr. -1-3). 13.95 *(978-0-87033-593-8(6)*, 9780870335938, Cornell Maritime Pr./Tidewater Pubs.) Schiffer Publishing, Ltd.

—Oyster Moon, 1 vol. Meacham, Margaret. 2009. (ENG.). 112p. (J). (gr. 8-18). pap. 9.95 *(978-0-87033-459-7(X)*, 9780870334597, Cornell Maritime Pr./Tidewater Pubs.) Schiffer Publishing, Ltd.

—Saving Squeak: The Otter Tale, 1 vol. Curtis, Jennifer Keats. 2010. (ENG.). 32p. (J). (gr. -1-3). 14.99 *(978-0-7643-3588-4(X)*, 9780764335884) Schiffer Publishing, Ltd.

—Secret of Belle Meadow, 1 vol. McVicker, Mary. 2009. (ENG.). 152p. (J). per. 9.95 *(978-0-87033-554-9(5)*, 9780870335549, Cornell Maritime Pr./Tidewater Pubs.) Schiffer Publishing, Ltd.

—The World Turned Upside Down: Children of 1776, 1 vol. Jensen, Ann. 2009. (ENG.). 80p. (gr. 3-6). pap. 9.95 *(978-0-87033-534-1(0)*, 3745, Cornell Maritime Pr./Tidewater Pubs.) Schiffer Publishing, Ltd.

Ramsey, Marcy Dunn. Rosie's Posies, 1 vol. Ramsey, Marcy Dunn. 2009. (ENG.). 34p. (J). (gr. -1-3). reprint ed. 14.95 *(978-0-87033-472-6(7)*, 9780870334726, Cornell Maritime Pr./Tidewater Pubs.) Schiffer Publishing, Ltd.

Ramsey, Marshall. The Big Birthday Surprise: Junior Discovers Giving. Ramsey, Dave. 2003. 26p. (J). 7.95 *(978-0-9726323-2-4(8))* Ramsey Pr.

—Careless at the Carnival: Junior Discovers Spending. Ramsey, Dave. 2003. 26p. (J). 7.95 *(978-0-9726323-1-7(X))* Ramsey Pr.

—My Fantastic Fieldtrip: Junior Discovers Saving. Ramsey, Dave. 2003. 26p. (J). 7.95 *(978-0-9726323-3-1(6))* Ramsey Pr.

Ramstad, Ralph L. Dian Fossey & the Mountain Gorillas. Schott, Jane A. 2005. (On My Own Biographies Ser.). 48p. (gr. 2-5). lib. bdg. 23.93 *(978-1-57505-082-9(X))* Lerner Publishing Group.

Ramstein, Anne-Margot & Arégui, Matthias. Inside Outside. Ramstein, Anne-Margot & Arégui, Matthias. 2019. (ENG.). 48p. (J). (gr. -1-3). 18.99 *(978-1-5362-0597-8(4))* Candlewick Pr.

Ran Lee, Hye. El Jardin Secreto. Burnett, Frances Hodgson. 2013.Tr. of Secret Garden. (SPA.). 360p. (J). pap. 21.99 *(978-607-01-3104-2(5))* Santillana USA Publishing Co., Inc.

Ranade, Shilpa. Thukpa for All. Ram, Praba & Preuitt, Sheela. 2019. (ENG.). 48p. (J). 13.95 *(978-81-933889-8-3(4))* Karadi Tales Co. Pvt, Ltd. IND. Dist: Consortium Bk. Sales & Distribution.

Ranchetti, Sebastiano. In the Arctic. Ottina, Laura. 2009. (Learn with Animals Ser.). (ENG.). 24p. (J). (gr. -1-2). pap. 8.15 *(978-1-4339-2088-2(3))*; lib. bdg. 23.00 *(978-1-4339-1911-4(7))* Stevens, Gareth Publishing LLLP. (Weekly Reader Leveled Readers).

—In the Forest. Ottina, Laura. 2009. (Learn with Animals Ser.). (ENG.). 24p. (J). (gr. -1-2). pap. 8.15 *(978-1-4339-2089-9(1))*; lib. bdg. 23.00 *(978-1-4339-1912-1(5))* Stevens, Gareth Publishing LLLP. (Weekly Reader Leveled Readers).

—In the Jungle. Ottina, Laura. 2009. (Learn with Animals Ser.). (ENG.). 24p. (J). (gr. -1-2). pap. 8.15 *(978-1-4339-2090-5(5))*; lib. bdg. 23.00 *(978-1-4339-1913-8(3))* Stevens, Gareth Publishing LLLP. (Weekly Reader Leveled Readers).

—In the Sea. Ottina, Laura. 2009. (Learn with Animals Ser.). (ENG.). 24p. (J). (gr. -1-2). pap. 8.15 *(978-1-4339-2091-2(3))*; lib. bdg. 23.00 *(978-1-4339-1914-5(1))* Stevens, Gareth Publishing LLLP. (Weekly Reader Leveled Readers).

—On the Farm. Ottina, Laura. 2009. (Learn with Animals Ser.). (ENG.). 24p. (J). (gr. -1-2). pap. 8.15 *(978-1-4339-2092-9(1))*; lib. bdg. 23.00 *(978-1-4339-1915-2(X))* Stevens, Gareth Publishing LLLP. (Weekly Reader Leveled Readers).

—On the Savanna. Ottina, Laura. 2009. (Learn with Animals Ser.). (ENG.). 24p. (J). (gr. -1-2). pap. 8.15 *(978-1-4339-2093-6(X))*; lib. bdg. 23.00 *(978-1-4339-1916-9(8))* Stevens, Gareth Publishing LLLP. (Weekly Reader Leveled Readers).

Rand, Colleen. Big Bunny. Rand, Colleen. Rand, Betseygail. 2011. (ENG.). 32p. (J). (gr. -1-2). 14.99 *(978-1-58246-376-6(X)*, Tricycle Pr.) Random Hse. Children's Bks.

Rand, Emily. The House Full of Stuff. 2020. (ENG.). 32p. (J). (gr. -1-17). 16.99 *(978-1-84976-662-3(2))* Tate Publishing, Ltd. GBR. Dist: Hachette Bk. Group.

Rand, Paul. Listen! Listen! Rand, Ann. 2016. (ENG.). 32p. (J). (gr. -1-1). 17.95 *(978-1-61689-494-8(6))* Princeton Architectural Pr.

Rand, Ted. Here Are My Hands. Archambault, John & Martin, Bill, Jr. 2007. (ENG.). 32p. (J). (gr. -1-k). pap. 27.99 *(978-0-8050-8119-0(4)*, 9780805081190, Holt, Henry & Co. Bks. For Young Readers) Holt, Henry & Co.

—If Not for the Cat. Prelutsky, Jack. 2004. (ENG.). 40p. (J). (gr. -1-3). 17.99 *(978-0-06-059677-4(5)*, Greenwillow Bks.) HarperCollins Pubs.

—Mailing May. Tunnell, Michael O. 2015. 32p. pap. 7.00 *(978-1-61003-610-8(7))* Center for the Collaborative Classroom.

—The Night Before Christmas. Moore, Clement C. 2014. 32p. (J). 17.95 *(978-0-7358-4106-2(3))* North-South Bks., Inc.

Rand, Tracy. The World According to August: One Good Friend. Westendorf, Sandra. 2011. *(978-0-9868424-0-5(0))* Purple Birch Publishing.

Randall, Emma. Good Night Octopus: Shaped Board Book down SPEC. Burroughs, Caleb. Cottage Door Press, ed. ed. 2017. (I Can Do It Ser.). (ENG.). 11p. (J). (gr. -1-k). bds. 6.99 *(978-1-68052-239-6(6)*, 1002250) Cottage Door Pr.

—Good Night, Octopus (down Spc'd) An I Can Do It Book. Burroughs, Caleb. 2016. (J). bds. 0.00 *(978-1-68052-104-7(7))* Cottage Door Pr.

—How to Trap a Leprechaun. Fliess, Sue. 2017. (Magical Creatures & Crafts Ser.: 1). 32p. (J). (gr. -1-k). 16.99 *(978-1-5107-0670-5(4)*, Sky Pony Pr.) Skyhorse Publishing Co., Inc.

—Over the River & Through the Wood. 2018. 32p. (J). (gr. -1-2). 16.99 *(978-0-515-15765-9(1)*, Penguin Workshop) Penguin Young Readers Group.

—The Twelve Days of Christmas. 2017. 32p. (J). (gr. -1-2). 16.99 *(978-0-515-15763-5(5)*, Penguin Workshop) Penguin Young Readers Group.

Randall, Emma. A Book of Love. Randall, Emma. 2019. 32p. (J). (gr. -1-2). 16.99 *(978-1-5247-9331-9(0)*, Penguin Workshop) Penguin Young Readers Group.

Randall, Jack. The Old Lady of Wasilla Lake: A Story of the Red-necked Grebes of Wasilla Lake, Alaska. Randall, Jack. Mishler, Clark James, photos by. 2005. 48p. (YA). lib. bdg. 24.95 *(978-1-930580-81-7(9)*, Ulyssian Pubns.) Pine Orchard, Inc.

Randall, Lee Brandt. Chicory & Roux: The Creole Mouse & the Cajun Mouse, 1 vol. St. Pierre, Todd-Michael. 2017. (ENG.). 32p. (J). (gr. k-3). 16.99 *(978-1-4556-2237-5(0)*, Pelican Publishing) Arcadia Publishing.

—Texas State Bird Pageant. Michael, Todd. 2005. 32p. (J). (gr. -1-3). 16.95 *(978-1-893062-75-7(9))* Quail Ridge Pr., Inc.

—Thibodeaux Turtle & Boudreaux Bunny: The Tortoise & the Hare with a Louisiana Twist, 1 vol. St. Pierre, Todd-Michael & Aesop, Aesop. 2019. (ENG.). 32p. (gr. -1-3). 16.99 *(978-1-4556-2450-8(0)*, Pelican Publishing) Arcadia Publishing.

Randall, Ron. Amaterasu: Return of the Sun [a Japanese Myth]. Storrie, Paul D. 2008. (Graphic Myths & Legends Ser.). (ENG.). 48p. (J). (gr. 4-8). per. 9.99 *(978-0-8225-6573-4(0)*, Graphic Universe™) Lerner Publishing Group.

—The Amnesia Countdown. Oirich, Alan. 2003. (Jewish Hero Corps. Ser.: 1). 24p. (J). pap. 3.95 *(978-1-932443-06-6(1)*, JHC1, Shayach Comics) Judaica Pr., Inc., The.

—Beowulf: Monster Slayer. 2007. (Graphic Myths & Legends Ser.). 48p. (J). (gr. 4-8). lib. bdg. 26.60 *(978-0-8225-6757-8(1)*, Graphic Universe™) Lerner Publishing Group.

—Beowulf: Monster Slayer [a British Legend]. Storrie, Paul D. (Graphic Myths & Legends Ser.). (ENG.). 48p. (J). (gr. 4-8). 2008. pap. 9.99 *(978-0-8225-8512-1(X)*, 9780822585121, Graphic Universe™); 2015. E-Book 53.32 *(978-1-4677-5980-9(5)*, 9781467759809, Lerner Digital) Lerner Publishing Group.

—Guan Yu: Blood Brothers to the End [a Chinese Legend]. Jolley, Dan. 2009. (Graphic Myths & Legends Ser.). (ENG.). 48p. (J). (gr. 4-8). pap. 9.99 *(978-1-58013-890-1(X)*, Graphic Universe™) Lerner Publishing Group.

—Thor & Loki: In the Land of Giants [a Norse Myth]. Limke, Jeff. 2007. (Graphic Myths & Legends Ser.). (ENG.). 48p. (J). (gr. 4-8). per. 9.99 *(978-0-8225-6481-2(5)*, 9780822564812, Graphic Universe™) Lerner Publishing Group.

—Thor y Loki: en la Tierra de los Gigantes: Un Mito Escandinavo. Limke, Jeff. 2007. (Mitos y leyendas en viñetas (Graphic Myths & Legends) Ser.). (SPA.). 48p. (J). (gr. 4-7). per. 8.95 *(978-0-8225-7969-4(3)*, Ediciones Lerner) Lerner Publishing Group.

—Tristan & Isolde: The Warrior & the Princess [a British Legend]. Limke, Jeff. 2009. (Graphic Myths & Legends Ser.). (ENG.). 48p. (J). (gr. 4-8). pap. 9.99 *(978-1-58013-889-5(6)*, Graphic Universe™) Lerner Publishing Group.

Randazzo, Tony. Junior Groovies: Things That Fly (Storybook, Fun Facts & Toys) Ikids Staff. 2011. (ENG.). 10p. (J). (gr. -1-1). 15.99 *(978-1-60169-148-4(3))* Innovative Kids.

—Race Cars. Ikids Staff. 2009. (ENG.). 10p. (J). (gr. -1-1). 15.99 *(978-1-58476-939-2(4))* Innovative Kids.

Randles, Slim & Montoya, Jerry. Ol' Jimmy Dollar. 2015. 42p. (J). *(978-1-936744-40-4(6))* LPD Pr.

Randolph, Carolyn. Dinkey the Donkey. Phillips, Rachelle. l.t. ed. 2004. 24p. (J). 7.50 *(978-0-9748591-5-6(X)*, MSP) Main St Publishing, Inc.

Randolph, E. J. Call Me Tony: An American Southwest Illustrated Children's Book. Randolph, E. J. 2019. (ENG.). 56p. (J). pap. 12.99 ***(978-1-6930-4782-4(9))*** Independently Published.

Randolph, Khary. Spidey #8: Blackout! Thompson, Robbie. 2017. (Spidey Ser.). (ENG.). 24p. (J). (gr. 2-8). lib. bdg. 27.07 *(978-1-5321-4156-0(4)*, 27029, Marvel Age) Spotlight.

Randolph, Khary & Silas, Thony. Mosaic Vol. 2: Down Below. 2017. (ENG.). 112p. (YA). (gr. 8-17). pap. 15.99 *(978-1-302-90040-3(4))* Marvel Worldwide, Inc.

Randolph, Khary, jt. illus. see Grant, Keron.

Random House. All about the Trolls. Depken, Kristen L. 2016. (Step into Reading Ser.). (ENG.). 32p. (J). (gr. -1-2). lib. bdg. 12.99 *(978-0-399-55904-4(3)*, Random Hse. Bks. for Young Readers) Random Hse. Children's Bks.

—Animal Crossing Official Sticker Book (Nintendo) Carbone, Courtney. 2019. (ENG.). 64p. (J). (gr. k-4). pap. 12.99 *(978-1-5247-7262-8(3)*, Random Hse. Bks. for Young Readers) Random Hse. Children's Bks.

—Arcade or Bust! (the Loud House) Glass, Amaris. 2018. (Loud House Ser.: 2). (ENG.). 144p. (J). (gr. 3-7). 6.99 *(978-1-5247-7036-5(1))*; lib. bdg. 12.99 *(978-0-525-64507-8(1))* Random Hse. Children's Bks. (Random Hse. Bks. for Young Readers).

—Ash & Pikachu: Alola Region/Team Rocket: Alola Region (Pokémon) Chlebowski, Rachel. 2017. (Pictureback(R) Ser.). (ENG.). 32p. (J). (gr. -1-2). pap. 5.99 *(978-1-5247-7008-2(6)*, Random Hse. Bks. for Young Readers) Random Hse. Children's Bks.

—Awesome Evolutions! (Pokémon) Nestor, C. J. 2019. (Pictureback(R) Ser.). (ENG.). 24p. (J). (gr. -1-2). 5.99 *(978-1-9848-4830-7(5)*, Random Hse. Bks. for Young Readers) Random Hse. Children's Bks.

—Barbie: Fashion Fairytale (Barbie) Man-Kong, Mary. 2010. (Step into Reading Ser.). (ENG.). 32p. (J). (gr. -1-1). pap. 4.99 *(978-0-375-86697-5(3)*, Random Hse. Bks. for Young Readers) Random Hse. Children's Bks.

—Barbie in a Mermaid Tale (Barbie) Webster, Christy. 2010. (Step into Reading Ser.). (ENG.). 32p. (J). (gr. -1-1). pap. 4.99 *(978-0-375-86450-6(4)*, Random Hse. Bks. for Young Readers) Random Hse. Children's Bks.

—Batman 5-Minute Stories (DC Batman) DC Comics. 2019. (ENG.). 160p. (J). (gr. -1-2). 14.99 *(978-0-593-12352-2(2)*, Random Hse. Bks. for Young Readers) Random Hse. Children's Bks.

—Batter up!/¡a Batear!(SpongeBob SquarePants) Lewman, David & Gomez, Yuliana. 2014. (Pictureback(R) Ser.). (ENG.). 24p. (J). (gr. -1-2). 3.99 *(978-0-385-38436-0(X)*, Random Hse. Bks. for Young Readers) Random Hse. Children's Bks.

—Biggie & the Disastrous Dance (DreamWorks Trolls) Lewman, David. 2018. (ENG.). 128p. (J). (gr. 1-4). 6.99 *(978-1-5247-6985-7(1)*, Random Hse. Bks. for Young Readers) Random Hse. Children's Bks.

—Birthday Bonanza! (Rusty Rivets) Matheis, Mickie. 2018. (Pictureback(R) Ser.). (ENG.). 16p. (J). (gr. -1-2). pap. 5.99 *(978-1-5247-6803-4(0)*, Random Hse. Bks. for Young Readers) Random Hse. Children's Bks.

—Birthday Cake Chase! (Blaze & the Monster Machines) Leslie, Tonya. 2018. (Pictureback(R) Ser.). (ENG.). 24p. (J). (gr. -1-2). pap. 5.99 *(978-1-5247-6844-7(8)*, Random Hse. Bks. for Young Readers) Random Hse. Children's Bks.

—Boo Goes There? (Rusty Rivets) Lewman, David. 2018. (Pictureback(R) Ser.). (ENG.). 24p. (J). (gr. -1-2). pap. 6.99 *(978-1-5247-7275-8(5)*, Random Hse. Bks. for Young Readers) Random Hse. Children's Bks.

—Branch & the Cooking Catastrophe (DreamWorks Trolls Chapter Book #2) Lewman, David. 2017. (ENG.). 128p. (J). (gr. 1-4). 6.99 *(978-1-5247-1708-7(8))*; lib. bdg. 12.99 *(978-1-5247-1709-4(6))* Random Hse. Children's Bks. (Random Hse. Bks. for Young Readers).

—Bug Battle! (Teenage Mutant Ninja Turtles) Mangual, Cynthia Ines. 2017. (Step into Reading Ser.). (ENG.). 24p. (J). (gr. -1-1). pap. 4.99 *(978-0-399-55882-5(9)*, Random Hse. Bks. for Young Readers) Random Hse. Children's Bks.

—Bumblebee at Super Hero High (DC Super Hero Girls) Yee, Lisa. 2018. (ENG.). 208p. (J). (gr. 4-7). 13.99 *(978-1-5247-6926-0(6))*; lib. bdg. 16.99 *(978-1-5247-6927-7(4))* Random Hse. Children's Bks. (Random Hse. Bks. for Young Readers).

—Campaign Chaos! (the Loud House) Freilich, Mollie. 2019. (Loud House Ser.). (ENG.). 144p. (J). (gr. 3-7). 12.99 *(978-1-9848-5148-2(9))*; 6.99 *(978-1-5247-7291-8(7))* Random Hse. Children's Bks. (Random Hse. Bks. for Young Readers).

Random House. Catch the Creeper! (Minecraft) Milton, Stephanie. 2020. (ENG.). 48p. (J). (gr. 1-4). 12.99 ***(978-0-593-17312-1(0)***, Random Hse. Bks. for Young Readers) Random Hse. Children's Bks.

Random House. Chase's Loose Tooth! (PAW Patrol) Neumann, Casey. 2018. (Pictureback(R) Ser.). (ENG.). 24p. (J). (gr. -1-2). pap. 6.99 *(978-1-5247-7271-0(2)*, Random Hse. Bks. for Young Readers) Random Hse. Children's Bks.

Random House. Christmas Comes to Paradise Island! (DC Super Heroes: Wonder Woman) Clauss, Lauren. 2020. (ENG.). 32p. (J). (gr. -1-2). 10.99 ***(978-0-593-30647-5(3)***, Random Hse. Bks. for Young Readers) Random Hse. Children's Bks.

Random House. Christmas Peeps (Peeps) Posner-Sanchez, Andrea. 2017. 22p. (J). (gr. -1-2). bds. 6.99 *(978-1-5247-6647-4(X)*, Random Hse. Bks. for Young Readers) Random Hse. Children's Bks.

—Color Fiesta! (Dora & Friends) Tillworth, Mary. 2016. (ENG & SPA.). 24p. (J). (gr. -1 — 1). bds. 6.99 *(978-0-553-53839-7(X)*, Random Hse. Bks. for Young Readers) Random Hse. Children's Bks.

Random House. The Count (Sesame Street Friends) Posner-Sanchez, Andrea. 2020. (ENG.). 26p. (J). (— 1). bds. 7.99 ***(978-0-593-17321-3(X)***, Random Hse. Bks. for Young Readers) Random Hse. Children's Bks.

Random House. Danger: Dinosaurs! (Jurassic World) Carbone, Courtney. 2015. (Step into Reading Ser.). (ENG.). 32p. (J). (gr. -1-1). 4.99 *(978-0-553-53687-4(7)*, Random Hse. Bks. for Young Readers) Random Hse. Children's Bks.

—The DC Super Hero Girls Adventure Collection #1 (DC Super Hero Girls) Wonder Woman at Super Hero High; Supergirl at Super Hero High, 2 vols. Yee, Lisa. 2016. (ENG.). 240p. (J). (gr. 3-7). 27.98 *(978-1-5247-1631-8(6)*, Random Hse. Bks. for Young Readers) Random Hse. Children's Bks.

—Deep Thoughts: How to Live a Bikini Bottom Life (SpongeBob SquarePants) Wygand, Melissa. 2019. (ENG.). 80p. (J). (gr. 5). 9.99 *(978-1-9848-9409-0(9)*, Random Hse. Bks. for Young Readers) Random Hse. Children's Bks.

—Dino Hybrid. Wrecks, Billy. 2016. (Pictureback(R) Ser.). (ENG.). 24p. (J). (gr. -1-2). 5.99 *(978-0-399-55342-4(8)*, Random Hse. Bks. for Young Readers) Random Hse. Children's Bks.

—Dinosaur Rescue! Depken, Kristen L. 2018. (Step into Reading Ser.). (ENG.). 32p. (J). (gr. k-3). lib. bdg. 12.99 *(978-0-525-58079-9(4)*, Random Hse. Bks. for Young Readers) Random Hse. Children's Bks.

—Dinosaur Rescue! (Jurassic World: Fallen Kingdom) Depken, Kristen L. 2018. (Step into Reading Ser.).

(ENG.). 32p. (J). (gr. k-3). pap. 4.99 *(978-0-525-58078-2(6)*, Random Hse. Bks. for Young Readers) Random Hse. Children's Bks.

—Dinosaur Tracker! (Jurassic World: Fallen Kingdom) Chlebowski, Rachel. 2018. (Pictureback(R) Ser.). (ENG.). 24p. (J). (gr. -1-2). pap. 4.99 *(978-0-525-58081-2(6)*, Random Hse. Bks. for Young Readers) Random Hse. Children's Bks.

Random House, et al. Drop the Beat! (DreamWorks Trolls) Lewman, David. 2017. (Step into Reading Ser.). (ENG.). 24p. (J). (gr. -1-1). pap. 4.99 *(978-1-5247-1842-8(4)*, Random Hse. Bks. for Young Readers) Random Hse. Children's Bks.

Random House. Election Connection: the Official Nickelodeon Guide to Electing the President (Nickelodeon) Ring, Susan. 2020. (ENG.). 80p. (J). (gr. 3-7). pap. 8.99 ***(978-0-593-18037-2(2)***, Random Hse. Bks. for Young Readers) Random Hse. Children's Bks.

Random House. Fairytale Collection (Barbie) 2011. (Step into Reading Ser.). (ENG.). 160p. (J). (gr. -1-1). pap. 8.99 *(978-0-375-87255-6(8)*, Random Hse. Bks. for Young Readers) Random Hse. Children's Bks.

—Famous Friends & Foes (Pokémon) Chlebowski, Rachel. 2017. (Pictureback(R) Ser.). 32p. (J). (gr. -1-2). pap. 5.99 *(978-1-5247-7010-5(8)*, Random Hse. Bks. for Young Readers) Random Hse. Children's Bks.

—Favorite First Friends! (Pokémon) Nestor, C. J. 2018. (Pictureback(R) Ser.). (ENG.). 32p. (J). (gr. -1-2). pap. 5.99 *(978-1-5247-7290-1(9)*, Random Hse. Bks. for Young Readers) Random Hse. Children's Bks.

—Fierce Competition! (DC Super Hero Girls) David, Erica. 2020. (ENG.). 144p. (J). (gr. 1-4). 6.99 *(978-1-9848-9456-4(0))*; 12.99 *(978-1-9848-9457-1(9))* Random Hse. Children's Bks. (Random Hse. Bks. for Young Readers).

—Five Puptacular Tales! (PAW Patrol) 2016. (Step into Reading Ser.). (ENG.). 144p. (J). (gr. -1-1). 7.99 *(978-0-399-55300-4(2)*, Random Hse. Bks. for Young Readers) Random Hse. Children's Bks.

—Friend or Foe? (Teenage Mutant Ninja Turtles) Gilbert, Matthew. 2014. (Junior Novel Ser.). (ENG.). 128p. (J). (gr. 3-7). 5.99 *(978-0-385-38505-3(6)*, Random Hse. Bks. for Young Readers) Random Hse. Children's Bks.

—Go, Creature Powers! (Wild Kratts) Kratt, Chris & Kratt, Martin. 2016. (Pictureback(R) Ser.). 24p. (J). (gr. -1-2). 5.99 *(978-1-101-93306-0(2)*, Random Hse. Bks. for Young Readers) Random Hse. Children's Bks.

—Goldie Blox & the Birthday Fail (GoldieBlox) McAnulty, Stacy. 2018. (Stepping Stone Book(TM) Ser.). (ENG.). 144p. (J). (gr. 1-4). 6.99 *(978-1-5247-6805-8(7)*, Random Hse. Bks. for Young Readers) Random Hse. Children's Bks.

—Goldie Blox & the Haunted Hacks (GoldieBlox) McAnulty, Stacy. 2018. (Stepping Stone Book(TM) Ser.). (ENG.). 128p. (J). (gr. 1-4). 6.99 *(978-0-525-57777-5(7)*, Random Hse. Bks. for Young Readers) Random Hse. Children's Bks.

Random House, et al. GoldieBlox Chapter Book #2 (GoldieBlox) Random House. 2017. (Stepping Stone Book(TM) Ser.). (ENG.). 128p. (J). (gr. 1-4). 6.99 *(978-0-399-55636-4(2)*, Random Hse. Bks. for Young Readers) Random Hse. Children's Bks.

Random House. The Great Monkey Show! (Rusty Rivets) Finnegan, Delphine. 2018. (Step into Reading Ser.). (ENG.). 24p. (J). (gr. -1-1). pap. 4.99 *(978-1-5247-7273-4(9))*; lib. bdg. 12.99 *(978-1-5247-7274-1(7))* Random Hse. Children's Bks. (Random Hse. Bks. for Young Readers).

—Greatest Inventions. Castaldo, Nancy F. 2016. (ENG.). 80p. (J). (gr. 2-5). lib. bdg. 12.99 *(978-1-101-93341-1(0)*, Random Hse. Bks. for Young Readers) Random Hse. Children's Bks.

—Green Lantern vs. the Meteor Monster! (DC Super Friends) Wrecks, Billy. 2011. (Pictureback(R) Ser.). (ENG.). 24p. (J). (gr. -1-2). pap. 3.99 *(978-0-375-87297-6(3)*, Random Hse. Bks. for Young Readers) Random Hse. Children's Bks.

Random House. Grover (Sesame Street Friends) Posner-Sanchez, Andrea. 2020. (ENG.). 26p. (J). (— 1). bds. 7.99 ***(978-0-593-17671-9(5)***, Random Hse. Bks. for Young Readers) Random Hse. Children's Bks.

Random House. Guy Diamond & the Rainbow Roundup (DreamWorks Trolls) Lewman, David. 2018. (ENG.). 128p. (J). (gr. 1-4). 6.99 *(978-1-5247-7268-0(2))*; lib. bdg. 12.99 *(978-1-5247-7269-7(0))* Random Hse. Children's Bks. (Random Hse. Bks. for Young Readers).

—Harley Quinn at Super Hero High (DC Super Hero Girls) Yee, Lisa. 2018. (ENG.). 208p. (J). (gr. 3-7). 13.99 *(978-1-5247-6923-9(1))*; lib. bdg. 16.99 *(978-1-5247-6924-6(X))* Random Hse. Children's Bks. (Random Hse. Bks. for Young Readers).

—Here Comes Peter Cottontail. Man-Kong, Mary. 2015. (Pictureback(R) Ser.). 16p. (J). (gr. -1-2). 4.99 *(978-0-553-50821-5(0)*, Random Hse. Bks. for Young Readers) Random Hse. Children's Bks.

—Here We Go! (Nintendo) Foxe, Steve. 2019. (ENG.). 128p. (J). (-k). pap. 7.99 *(978-0-525-64721-8(X)*, Random Hse. Bks. for Young Readers) Random Hse. Children's Bks.

—Hero of the Month! (DC Super Hero Girls) Miller, Mona. 2017. (Pictureback(R) Ser.). (ENG.). 16p. (J). (gr. -1-2). pap. 5.99 *(978-1-5247-6604-7(6)*, Random Hse. Bks. for Young Readers) Random Hse. Children's Bks.

—Hero Story Collection (DC Super Friends) 2012. (Step into Reading Ser.). (ENG.). 160p. (J). (gr. -1-1). pap. 8.99 *(978-0-375-87298-3(1)*, Random Hse. Bks. for Young Readers) Random Hse. Children's Bks.

—Hooray for Easter! (Peter Cottontail) Karl, Linda. 2017. 16p. (J). (-k). bds. 7.99 *(978-0-399-55787-3(3)*, Random Hse. Bks. for Young Readers) Random Hse. Children's Bks.

—Hot Pursuit! (DC Super Friends) Foxe, Steve. 2017. (Pictureback(R) Ser.). (ENG.). 24p. (J). (gr. -1-2). pap. 5.99 *(978-1-5247-1715-5(0)*, Random Hse. Bks. for Young Readers) Random Hse. Children's Bks.

—How to Be a Hero (DC Super Friends) Carbone, Courtney. 2016. (ENG.). 64p. (J). (gr. 1-4). 9.99 *(978-1-101-93958-1(3)*, Random Hse. Bks. for Young Readers) Random Hse. Children's Bks.

—How to Survive in a Stranger Things World (Stranger Things) Gilbert, Matthew J. 2018. (ENG.). 96p. (J). (gr. 7). 12.99 *(978-1-9848-5195-6(0)*, Random Hse. Bks. for Young Readers) Random Hse. Children's Bks.

Random House. In Harmony (DreamWorks Trolls) Man-Kong, Mary. 2020. (ENG.). 14p. (J). (— 1). bds. 12.99 ***(978-0-593-12260-0(7)***, Random Hse. Bks. for Young Readers) Random Hse. Children's Bks.

Random House. Jurassic World: Fallen Kingdom Dinosaur Survival Guide (Jurassic World: Fallen Kingdom) Lewman, David. 2018. (ENG.). 80p. (J). (gr. 1-4). pap. 7.99 *(978-0-525-58083-6(2))*; lib. bdg. 12.99 *(978-0-525-58084-3(0))* Random Hse. Children's Bks. (Random Hse. Bks. for Young Readers).

—Jurassic World: Fallen Kingdom: the Deluxe Junior Novelization (Jurassic World: Fallen Kingdom) Lewman, David. 2018. (ENG.). 144p. (J). (gr. 1-4). 9.99 *(978-0-525-58074-4(3)*, Random Hse. Bks. for Young Readers) Random Hse. Children's Bks.

—Jurassic World: Fallen Kingdom: the Junior Novelization (Jurassic World: Fallen Kingdom) Lewman, David. 2018. (ENG.). 144p. (J). (gr. 1-4). 6.99 *(978-0-525-58076-8(X)*, Random Hse. Bks. for Young Readers) Random Hse. Children's Bks.

—The Legend of Zelda Official Sticker Book (Nintendo) Carbone, Courtney. 2018. (ENG.). 64p. (J). (gr. k-4). pap. 12.99 *(978-1-5247-7007-5(8)*, Random Hse. Bks. for Young Readers) Random Hse. Children's Bks.

—Let Your Peepsonality Shine! (Peeps) Posner-Sanchez, Andrea. 2017. (ENG.). 80p. (J). (gr. 5-12). 9.99 *(978-1-5247-1910-4(2)*, Random Hse. Bks. for Young Readers) Random Hse. Children's Bks.

—Link's Book of Adventure (Nintendo) Foxe, Steve. 2018. (ENG.). 72p. (J). (gr. 2-5). 9.99 *(978-1-5247-7265-9(8)*, Random Hse. Bks. for Young Readers) Random Hse. Children's Bks.

Random House. Lost Bots! (Transformers BotBots) Clauss, Lauren. 2020. (Step into Reading Ser.). (ENG.). 32p. (J). (gr. -1-1). 14.99 ***(978-0-593-17301-5(5))***; 5.99 ***(978-0-593-17300-8(7))*** Random Hse. Children's Bks. (Random Hse. Bks. for Young Readers).

Random House. Mario Time! (Nintendo) Carbone, Courtney. 2018. (ENG.). 72p. (J). (gr. 2-5). 9.99 *(978-1-5247-7264-2(X)*, Random Hse. Bks. for Young Readers) Random Hse. Children's Bks.

Random House. Marvelous Machinery/the Royal Engine (Thomas & Friends) Webster, Christy. 2020. (Pictureback(R) Ser.). (ENG.). 24p. (J). (gr. -1-2). 5.99 ***(978-0-593-12763-6(3)***, Random Hse. Bks. for Young Readers) Random Hse. Children's Bks.

Random House. Mew's Mythical Journey (Pokémon) Nestor, C. J. 2019. (Pictureback(R) Ser.). (ENG.). 16p. (J). (gr. -1-2). 5.99 *(978-0-525-64860-4(7)*, Random Hse. Bks. for Young Readers) Random Hse. Children's Bks.

—Minecraft Official Aquatic Adventure Sticker Book (Minecraft) Milton, Stephanie. 2019. (ENG.). 32p. (J). (gr. 1-4). pap. 9.99 *(978-0-593-12371-3(9)*, Random Hse. Bks. for Young Readers) Random Hse. Children's Bks.

—Minecraft Official Survival Sticker Book (Minecraft) Jelley, Craig & Milton, Stephanie. 2019. (ENG.). 32p. (J). (gr. 1-4). pap. 9.99 *(978-0-593-12278-5(X)*, Random Hse. Bks. for Young Readers) Random Hse. Children's Bks.

—Minecraft Official the Nether & the End Sticker Book (Minecraft) Milton, Stephanie. 2020. (ENG.). 32p. (J). (gr. 1-4). pap. 9.99 *(978-0-593-12469-7(3)*, Random Hse. Bks. for Young Readers) Random Hse. Children's Bks.

—Nickelodeon 5-Minute Adventure Stories (Nickelodeon) James, Hollis. 2019. (ENG.). 160p. (J). (gr. -1-2). 12.99 *(978-0-525-64831-4(3)*, Random Hse. Bks. for Young Readers) Random Hse. Children's Bks.

—Nickelodeon 5-Minute Stories Collection. Tillworth, Mary. 2016. (ENG.). 160p. (J). (gr. -1-2). 12.99 *(978-0-399-55314-1(2)*, Random Hse. Bks. for Young Readers) Random Hse. Children's Bks.

—Ninja Power (Rise of the Teenage Mutant Ninja Turtles 1) Lewman, David. 2018. (ENG.). 128p. (J). (gr. 3-7). lib. bdg. 12.99 *(978-0-525-70765-3(4)*, Random Hse. Bks. for Young Readers) Random Hse. Children's Bks.

—Ninja Power (Rise of the Teenage Mutant Ninja Turtles #1) Lewman, David. 2018. (ENG.). 128p. (J). (gr. 3-7). 6.99 *(978-0-525-64503-0(9)*, Random Hse. Bks. for Young Readers) Random Hse. Children's Bks.

—Ninjas United! (Rise of the Teenage Mutant Ninja Turtles) Lewman, David. 2019. (Pictureback(R) Ser.). (ENG.). 24p. (J). (gr. k-3). 5.99 *(978-0-593-11911-2(8)*, Random Hse. Bks. for Young Readers) Random Hse. Children's Bks.

—Nintendo Splatoon Official Sticker Book (Nintendo) Foxe, Steve. 2018. (ENG.). 64p. (J). (gr. k-4). pap. 12.99 *(978-1-5247-7263-5(1)*, Random Hse. Bks. for Young Readers) Random Hse. Children's Bks.

—One Big Party! (DreamWorks Trolls World Tour) Stephens, Elle. 2020. (Step into Reading Ser.). (ENG.). 24p. (J). (-k). pap. 5.99 *(978-0-593-12244-0(5))*; lib. bdg. 12.99 *(978-0-593-12245-7(3))* Random Hse. Children's Bks. (Random Hse. Bks. for Young Readers).

—Oscar (Sesame Street Friends) Posner-Sanchez, Andrea. 2020. (ENG.). 26p. (J). (— 1). bds. 7.99 *(978-0-593-12249-5(6)*, Random Hse. Bks. for Young Readers) Random Hse. Children's Bks.

—The Park Is Open (Jurassic World) Shealy, Dennis R. 2015. (Pictureback(R) Ser.). (ENG.). 16p. (J). (gr. -1-2). 4.99 *(978-0-553-53692-8(3)*, Random Hse. Bks. for Young Readers) Random Hse. Children's Bks.

—Peep on a Perch (Peeps) Posner-Sanchez, Andrea. 2018. (ENG.). 32p. (J). (gr. -1-2). 24.95 *(978-1-5247-7054-9(X)*, Random Hse. Bks. for Young Readers) Random Hse. Children's Bks.

—Poppy & the Mane Mania (DreamWorks Trolls Chapter Book #1) Lewman, David. 2017. (ENG.). 128p. (J). (gr. 1-4). 6.99 *(978-1-5247-1705-6(3))*; lib. bdg. 12.99 *(978-1-5247-1706-3(1))* Random Hse. Children's Bks. (Random Hse. Bks. for Young Readers).

Random House. Princess Adventure (Barbie) Stephens, Elle. 2020. (Step into Reading Ser.). (ENG.). 32p. (J). (gr. -1-1). pap. 4.99 ***(978-0-593-17861-4(0))***; lib. bdg. 14.99 ***(978-0-593-17862-1(9))*** Random Hse. Children's Bks. (Random Hse. Bks. for Young Readers).

Random House. Pup on the Run (Barbie) Stephens, Elle. 2020. (Step into Reading Ser.). (ENG.). 32p. (J). (-k). pap. 4.99 *(978-0-593-12784-1(6))*; lib. bdg. 14.99 *(978-0-593-12785-8(4))* Random Hse. Children's Bks. (Random Hse. Bks. for Young Readers).

—Riddle Me This! (DC Super Friends) Shealy, Dennis R. 2010. (Pictureback(R) Ser.). (ENG.). 24p. (J). (gr. -1-2). pap. 3.99 *(978-0-375-84747-9(2)*, Random Hse. Bks. for Young Readers) Random Hse. Children's Bks.

—Robot Rumble! (DC Super Hero Girls) Chlebowski, Rachel. 2018. (Pictureback(R) Ser.). (ENG.). 16p. (J). (gr. -1-2). pap. 5.99 *(978-0-525-57775-1(0)*, Random Hse. Bks. for Young Readers) Random Hse. Children's Bks.

—School of Dragons #3: Storm Approaching! (DreamWorks Dragons) Zoehfeld, Kathleen Weidner. 2017. (ENG.). 80p. (J). (gr. 2-5). pap. 7.99 *(978-1-101-93343-5(7)*, Random Hse. Bks. for Young Readers) Random Hse. Children's Bks.

—Secret Life of Pets. Lewman, David. 2016. (ENG.). 144p. (J). (gr. 2-5). 9.99 *(978-0-399-55490-2(4)*, Random Hse. Bks. for Young Readers) Random Hse. Children's Bks.

—Secrets of the City (Rise of the Teenage Mutant Ninja Turtles #2) Lewman, David. 2018. (ENG.). 128p. (J). (gr. 3-7). 6.99 *(978-0-525-64504-7(7))*; lib. bdg. 12.99 *(978-0-525-70766-0(2))* Random Hse. Children's Bks. (Random Hse. Bks. for Young Readers).

—Snow Day! (Frosty the Snowman) Carbone, Courtney. 2014. (Step into Reading Ser.). (ENG.). 32p. (J). (gr. -1-1). 4.99 *(978-0-385-38726-2(1)*, Random Hse. Bks. for Young Readers) Random Hse. Children's Bks.

—Snuggle up, Pups (PAW Patrol) Huntley, Tex. 2020. (ENG.). 26p. (J). (-k). bds. 7.99 *(978-0-593-17560-6(3)*, Random Hse. Bks. for Young Readers) Random Hse. Children's Bks.

—The SpongeBob Movie: Sponge on the Run: the Junior Novelization (SpongeBob SquarePants) Lewman, David. 2020. (ENG.). 144p. (J). (gr. 3-7). 6.99 *(978-0-593-12751-3(X)*, Random Hse. Bks. for Young Readers) Random Hse. Children's Bks.

—Stick with Me! (Sunny Day) Carbone, Courtney. 2018. (Step into Reading Ser.). (ENG.). 24p. (J). (gr. -1-1). pap. 4.99 *(978-0-525-57814-7(5))*; lib. bdg. 12.99 *(978-0-525-57815-4(3))* Random Hse. Children's Bks. (Random Hse. Bks. for Young Readers).

—Super Friends: Going Bananas (DC Super Friends) Harper, Ben. 2009. (Step into Reading Ser.). (ENG.). 32p. (J). (gr. -1-1). pap. 3.99 *(978-0-375-85613-6(7)*, Random Hse. Bks. for Young Readers) Random Hse. Children's Bks.

—Super Hero High Yearbook! (DC Super Hero Girls) Fontana, Shea. 2016. (ENG.). 96p. (J). (gr. 3-7). pap. 9.99 *(978-1-5247-0106-2(8)*, Random Hse. Bks. for Young Readers) Random Hse. Children's Bks.

—Super Mario: Bring on the Bad Guys! (Nintendo) Carbone, Courtney. 2020. (ENG.). 48p. (J). (gr. k-4). pap. 9.99 *(978-1-9848-4972-4(7)*, Random Hse. Bks. for Young Readers) Random Hse. Children's Bks.

—Super Mario Official Sticker Book (Nintendo) Foxe, Steve. 2018. (ENG.). 64p. (J). (gr. k-4). pap. 12.99 *(978-1-5247-7006-8(X)*, Random Hse. Bks. for Young Readers) Random Hse. Children's Bks.

—Supergirl at Super Hero High (DC Super Hero Girls) Yee, Lisa. 2016. (ENG.). 240p. (J). (gr. 3-7). 13.99 *(978-1-101-94062-4(X)*, Random Hse. Bks. for Young Readers) Random Hse. Children's Bks.

—T. Rex: Hunter or Scavenger? (Jurassic World) Holtz, Thomas R. 2003. (Step into Reading Ser.). (ENG.). 48p. (J). (gr. 2-4). pap. 4.99 *(978-0-375-81297-2(0)*, Random Hse. Bks. for Young Readers) Random Hse. Children's Bks.

—Teenage Mutant Ninja Turtles: Out of the Shadows. Lewman, David. 2016. (Deluxe Junior Novel Ser.). (ENG.). 144p. (J). (gr. 3-7). 9.99 *(978-1-101-93919-2(2))*; 6.99 *(978-0-399-55694-4(X))* Random Hse. Children's Bks. (Random Hse. Bks. for Young Readers).

—Thomas' Big Book of Beginner Books (Thomas & Friends) Awdry, W. 2013. (Beginner Books(R) Ser.). (ENG.). 224p. (J). (gr. -1-1). 16.99 *(978-0-449-81643-1(5)*, Random Hse. Bks. for Young Readers) Random Hse. Children's Bks.

Random House, et al. Too Many Cupcakes! (DreamWorks Trolls) Lewman, David. 2018. (Beginner Books(R) Ser.). (ENG.). 48p. (J). (gr. -1-1). 9.99 *(978-0-525-57800-0(5))*; lib. bdg. 12.99 *(978-0-525-57801-7(3))* Random Hse. Children's Bks. (Random Hse. Bks. for Young Readers).

Random House. Trick or Trolls (DreamWorks Trolls) Man-Kong, Mary. 2020. (ENG.). 12p. (J). (— 1). bds. 7.99 ***(978-0-593-12781-0(1)***, Random Hse. Bks. for Young Readers) Random Hse. Children's Bks.

Random House. UmiCar's Big Race/la Gran Carrera de UmiCar (Team Umizoomi) Gomez, Yuliana. 2014. (Pictureback(R) Ser.). (ENG.). 24p. (J). (gr. -1-2). 3.99 *(978-0-385-38437-7(8)*, Random Hse. Bks. for Young Readers) Random Hse. Children's Bks.

—Unhappy Birthday, Grumpy Cat! (Grumpy Cat) Berrios, Frank. 2019. (Step into Reading Ser.). 32p. (J). (gr. -1-1). 12.99 *(978-1-9848-5031-7(8)*, Random Hse. Bks. for Young Readers) Random Hse. Children's Bks.

—Up in the Air!/under the Waves! (PAW Patrol) Tillworth, Mary. 2018. (Step into Reading Ser.). (ENG.). 48p. (J). (gr. -1-2). pap. 5.99 *(978-1-5247-7279-6(8))*; lib. bdg. 12.99 *(978-1-5247-7280-2(1))* Random Hse. Children's Bks. (Random Hse. Bks. for Young Readers).

—Volcano Escape! Zoehfeld, Kathleen Weidner. 2016. (ENG.). 80p. (J). (gr. 2-5). pap. 7.99 *(978-1-101-93337-4(2)*, Random Hse. Bks. for Young Readers) Random Hse. Children's Bks.

—Wally's Best Friends. Depken, Kristen L. 2015. (ENG.). 48p. (J). (-k). bds. 10.99 *(978-0-553-52311-9(2)*, Random Hse. Bks. for Young Readers) Random Hse. Children's Bks.

—We Are the Justice League! (DC Justice League) DC Comics. 2019. (Step into Reading Ser.). (ENG.). 160p. (J). (gr. -1-2). 8.99 *(978-0-593-12356-0(5)*, Random Hse. Bks. for Young Readers) Random Hse. Children's Bks.

—Welcome to the Monster Dome! (Blaze & the Monster Machines) Berrios, Frank. 2017. (ENG.). 16p. (J). (— 1). bds. 7.99 *(978-0-399-55838-2(1)*, Random Hse. Bks. for Young Readers) Random Hse. Children's Bks.

Random House. Wheels on the Road (StoryBots) Emmons, Scott. 2020. (Step into Reading Ser.). (ENG.). 24p. (J). (gr. -1-1). 5.99 ***(978-0-593-18159-1(X))***; 12.99 ***(978-0-593-18161-4(1))*** Random Hse. Children's Bks. (Random Hse. Bks. for Young Readers).

Random House. When Mutants Attack! (Rise of the Teenage Mutant Ninja Turtles. Lewman, David. 2019. (Step into Reading Ser.). (ENG.). 32p. (J). (gr. k-3). 5.99 *(978-0-593-11909-9(6)*, Random Hse. Bks. for Young Readers) Random Hse. Children's Bks.

—When Mutants Attack! (Rise of the Teenage Mutant Ninja Turtles) Lewman, David. 2019. (Step into Reading Ser.). (ENG.). 32p. (J). (gr. k-3). 12.99 *(978-0-593-11910-5(X)*, Random Hse. Bks. for Young Readers) Random Hse. Children's Bks.

—Who Ghost There? Sakas Shropshire, Karla. 2018. (Loud House Ser.: 1). (ENG.). 144p. (J). (gr. 3-7). 6.99 *(978-1-5247-7035-8(3)*, Random Hse. Bks. for Young Readers) Random Hse. Children's Bks.

—Who Ghost There? (the Loud House) Sakas Shropshire, Karla. 2018. (Loud House Ser.: 1). (ENG.). 144p. (J). (gr. 3-7). lib. bdg. 12.99 *(978-0-525-64506-1(3)*, Random Hse. Bks. for Young Readers) Random Hse. Children's Bks.

—Wild Animal Babies! Step into Reading. Kratt, Chris & Kratt, Martin. 2016. (Step into Reading Ser.). 24p. (J). (gr. -1-1). 4.99 *(978-1-101-93171-4(X)*, Random Hse. Bks. for Young Readers) Random Hse. Children's Bks.

—Wild Insects & Spiders! (Wild Kratts) Kratt, Chris & Kratt, Martin. 2016. (Step into Reading Ser.). (ENG.). 24p. (J). (gr. -1-1). 4.99 *(978-1-101-93901-7(X)*, Random Hse. Bks. for Young Readers) Random Hse. Children's Bks.

—Wild Predators (Wild Kratts) Kratt, Chris & Kratt, Martin. 2015. (Step into Reading Ser.). (ENG.). 32p. (J). (gr. -1-1). 4.99 *(978-0-553-52472-7(0)*, Random Hse. Bks. for Young Readers) Random Hse. Children's Bks.

—Wild Reptiles: Snakes, Crocodiles, Lizards, & Turtles! Kratt, Chris & Kratt, Martin. 2015. (Step into Reading Ser.). 32p. (J). (gr. k-4). 4.99 *(978-0-553-50775-1(3)*, Random Hse. Bks. for Young Readers) Random Hse. Children's Bks.

—Wild Tech! (Wild Kratts) Kratt, Chris & Kratt, Martin. 2017. (Pictureback(R) Ser.). (ENG.). 24p. (J). (gr. -1-2). 4.99 *(978-1-101-93904-8(4)*, Random Hse. Bks. for Young Readers) Random Hse. Children's Bks.

—Wild Winter Creatures! (Wild Kratts) Kratt, Chris & Kratt, Martin. 2017. (Step into Reading Ser.). (ENG.). 32p. (J). (gr. -1-1). 4.99 *(978-1-101-93906-2(0))*; lib. bdg. 12.99 *(978-1-101-93907-9(9))* Random Hse. Children's Bks. (Random Hse. Bks. for Young Readers).

—Wonder Woman 5-Minute Stories (DC Wonder Woman) DC Comics. 2019. (ENG.). 160p. (J). (gr. -1-2). 14.99 *(978-0-593-12354-6(9)*, Random Hse. Bks. for Young Readers) Random Hse. Children's Bks.

—Wonder Woman & Her Super Friends! (DC Super Friends) Wrecks, Billy. 2016. (ENG.). 16p. (J). (-k). bds. 7.99 *(978-1-101-93992-5(3)*, Random Hse. Bks. for Young Readers) Random Hse. Children's Bks.

—Wonder Woman at Super Hero High (DC Super Hero Girls) Yee, Lisa. 2016. (ENG.). 240p. (J). (gr. 3-7). 13.99 *(978-1-101-94059-4(X)*, Random Hse. Bks. for Young Readers) Random Hse. Children's Bks.

—5 Wild Creature Adventures! (Wild Kratts) Kratt, Chris & Kratt, Martin. 2017. (Step into Reading Ser.). (ENG.). 160p. (J). (gr. -1-1). 8.99 *(978-1-101-93900-0(1)*, Random Hse. Bks. for Young Readers) Random Hse. Children's Bks.

Random House. The Adventure Bay Treasury (PAW Patrol) Random House. 2017. (ENG.). 30p. (J). (— 1). bds. 11.99 *(978-0-399-55881-8(0)*, Random Hse. Bks. for Young Readers) Random Hse. Children's Bks.

—Adventure Story Collection (Nickelodeon) Random House. 2016. (ENG.). 320p. (J). (gr. -1-2). 15.99 *(978-1-101-93417-3(4)*, Random Hse. Bks. for Young Readers) Random Hse. Children's Bks.

—All about the Troll. Random House. 2016. (Step into Reading Ser.). (ENG.). 32p. (J). (gr. -1-2). pap. 4.99 *(978-0-399-55903-7(5)*, Random Hse. Bks. for Young Readers) Random Hse. Children's Bks.

Random House. The Big Book of Engines (Thomas & Friends) Random House. 2020. (ENG.). 30p. (J). (— 1). bds. 11.99 ***(978-0-593-12761-2(7)***, Random Hse. Bks. for Young Readers) Random Hse. Children's Bks.

Random House. Big Fish, Little Fish: a Book of Opposites (Bubble Guppies) Random House. 2015. (Board Book Ser.). (ENG.). 24p. (J). (-k). bds. 4.99 *(978-0-385-38442-1(4)*, Random Hse. Bks. for Young Readers) Random Hse. Children's Bks.

—A Box Full of Wishes (Shimmer & Shine) 4 Board Books. Random House. 2018. (ENG.). 96p. (J). (— 1). bds. 14.99 *(978-1-5247-7247-5(X)*, Random Hse. Bks. for Young Readers) Random Hse. Children's Bks.

—Chase's Super Sniffer! Random House. 2017. (Scratch-And-Sniff Book Ser.). (ENG.). 24p. (J). (gr. -1-2). 9.99 *(978-0-399-55373-8(8)*, Random Hse. Bks. for Young Readers) Random Hse. Children's Bks.

—Christmas Adventures! (Nickelodeon) Random House. 2018. (ENG.). 96p. (J). (gr. -1-2). 9.99 *(978-0-525-58067-6(0)*, Random Hse. Bks. for Young Readers) Random Hse. Children's Bks.

Random House. Christmas Heroes! (DC Justice League) Random House. 2020. (ENG.). 22p. (J). (-k). bds. 6.99 ***(978-0-593-17846-1(7)***, Random Hse. Bks. for Young Readers) Random Hse. Children's Bks.

Random House. Christmas Heroes! (PAW Patrol) Random House. 2018. (ENG.). 22p. (J). (gr. -1-2). bds. 6.99 *(978-0-525-58185-7(5)*, Random Hse. Bks. for Young Readers) Random Hse. Children's Bks.

—Color Magic (Shimmer & Shine) Random House. 2017. (ENG.). 24p. (J). (— 1). bds. 6.99 *(978-0-399-55789-7(X)*,

Random Hse. Bks. for Young Readers) Random Hse. Children's Bks.

—A Colorful Christmas!/Snow Day! (Frosty the Snowman) Random House. 2017. (Step into Reading Ser.). (ENG.). 48p. (J). (gr. -1-3). pap. 5.99 *(978-1-5247-7037-2(X))*; lib. bdg. 12.99 *(978-1-5247-7038-9(8))* Random Hse. Children's Bks. (Random Hse. Bks. for Young Readers).

—Corn & Peg Step into Reading (Corn & Peg) Random House. 2020. (Step into Reading Ser.). (ENG.). 24p. (J). (gr. -1-1). 12.99 *(978-0-593-12396-6(4))*, Random Hse. Bks. for Young Readers) Random Hse. Children's Bks.

—Country Style! (Sunny Day) Random House. 2019. (Pictureback(R) Ser.). (ENG.). 16p. (J). (gr. -1-2). 5.99 *(978-0-525-64849-9(6))*, Random Hse. Bks. for Young Readers) Random Hse. Children's Bks.

—Dance! Hug! Sing! Random House. Chlebowski, Rachel. 2016. (Pictureback(R) Ser.). (ENG.). 16p. (J). (gr. -1-2). pap. 4.99 *(978-0-399-55897-9(7))*, Random Hse. Bks. for Young Readers) Random Hse. Children's Bks.

—DC Super Friends 5-Minute Story Collection (DC Super Friends) Random House. 2016. (ENG.). 160p. (J). (-k). 12.99 *(978-0-399-55219-9(7))*, Random Hse. Bks. for Young Readers) Random Hse. Children's Bks.

—Do-Gooders Unite! (Corn & Peg) Random House. 2020. (ENG.). 18p. (J). (-k). bds. 8.99 *(978-0-593-17455-5(0))*, Random Hse. Bks. for Young Readers) Random Hse. Children's Bks.

—Dog Days. Random House. Posner-Sanchez, Andrea. ed. 2016. (Step into Reading Level 2 Ser.). (ENG.). 24p. (J). (gr. -1-2). 14.75 *(978-0-606-39356-0(0))* Turtleback.

—Dora's Farm Rescue! (Dora the Explorer) Random House. 2014. (Pictureback(R) Ser.). (ENG.). 24p. (J). (gr. -1-2). 5.99 *(978-0-385-38516-9(1))*, Random Hse. Bks. for Young Readers) Random Hse. Children's Bks.

—DreamWorks: the Official Coloring Book. Random House. 2017. (Adult Coloring Book Ser.). 96p. (J). (gr. k-12). pap. 14.99 *(978-1-5247-6879-9(0))*, Random Hse. Bks. for Young Readers) Random Hse. Children's Bks.

—Duke's Tale. Random House. 2016. (Pictureback(R) Ser.). (ENG.). 24p. (J). (gr. -1-2). 4.99 *(978-0-399-55495-7(5))*, Random Hse. Bks. for Young Readers) Random Hse. Children's Bks.

—Earn Your Wings! (Top Wing) Random House. Tillworth, Mary. 2018. (Pictureback(R) Ser.). (ENG.). 24p. (J). (gr. -1-2). pap. 5.99 *(978-0-525-64580-1(2))*, Random Hse. Bks. for Young Readers) Random Hse. Children's Bks.

—Elmo's World: Dancing! (Sesame Street) Random House. 2018. (Lift-The-Flap Ser.). (ENG.). 12p. (J). (— 1). bds. 7.99 *(978-0-525-57838-3(2))*, Random Hse. Bks. for Young Readers) Random Hse. Children's Bks.

—Elmo's World: Music! (Sesame Street) Random House. 2018. (Lift-The-Flap Ser.). (ENG.). 12p. (J). (— 1). bds. 7.99 *(978-0-525-57839-0(0))*, Random Hse. Bks. for Young Readers) Random Hse. Children's Bks.

—Epic Turtle Tales (Teenage Mutant Ninja Turtles) Random House. 2015. (Pictureback(R) Ser.). (ENG.). 96p. (J). (gr. -1-2). 9.99 *(978-0-553-52471-0(2))*, Random Hse. Bks. for Young Readers) Random Hse. Children's Bks.

—The Evolution of Claire. Random House. Sharpe, Tess. 2018. (ENG.). 400p. (J). (gr. 7). 17.99 *(978-0-525-58072-0(7))*, Random Hse. Bks. for Young Readers) Random Hse. Children's Bks.

—Fabulous Friends! (Shimmer & Shine) Random House. 2017. (ENG.). 48p. (J). (-k). bds. 10.99 *(978-0-399-55790-3(3))*, Random Hse. Bks. for Young Readers) Random Hse. Children's Bks.

—Fairy Friends (Butterbean's Café) Random House. 2019. (ENG.). 18p. (J). (— 1). bds. 8.99 *(978-1-9848-9253-9(3))*, Random Hse. Bks. for Young Readers) Random Hse. Children's Bks.

—Five Fin-Tastic Stories (Bubble Guppies) Random House. 2015. (Step into Reading Ser.). (ENG.). 144p. (J). (gr. -1-1). pap. 7.99 *(978-0-553-52116-0(0))*, Random Hse. Bks. for Young Readers) Random Hse. Children's Bks.

—Five Playtime Tales (Nick, Jr.) Random House. 2015. (Step into Reading Ser.). (ENG.). 160p. (J). (gr. -1-1). 7.99 *(978-0-553-50859-8(8))*, Random Hse. Bks. for Young Readers) Random Hse. Children's Bks.

—Five Undersea Stories (SpongeBob SquarePants) Random House. 2015. (Step into Reading Ser.). (ENG.). 160p. (J). (gr. -1-1). 8.99 *(978-0-553-50860-4(1))*, Random Hse. Bks. for Young Readers) Random Hse. Children's Bks.

—Follow Your Nose! a Scratch-And-Sniff Adventure (Nella the Princess Knight) Random House. 2018. (ENG.). 24p. (J). (gr. -1-2). 9.99 *(978-0-525-57792-8(0))*, Random Hse. Bks. for Young Readers) Random Hse. Children's Bks.

—Goldie Blox Rules the School! Random House. McAnulty, Stacy. 2017. (Stepping Stone Book(TM) Ser.). (ENG.). 128p. (J). (gr. 1-4). 6.99 *(978-0-399-55634-0(6))*, Random Hse. Bks. for Young Readers) Random Hse. Children's Bks.

—Good Night, Adventure Bay! (PAW Patrol) Random House. 2018. (ENG.). 12p. (J). (gr. -1-2). bds. 7.99 *(978-0-525-57774-4(2))*, Random Hse. Bks. for Young Readers) Random Hse. Children's Bks.

—Halloween Adventures! (Nickelodeon) Random House. 2018. (ENG.). 96p. (J). (gr. -1-2). 9.99 *(978-0-525-57785-0(8))*, Random Hse. Bks. for Young Readers) Random Hse. Children's Bks.

—Halloween Heroes! (Paw Patrol) Random House. 2017. (ENG.). 22p. (J). (— 1). bds. 6.99 *(978-1-5247-6622-1(4))*, Random Hse. Bks. for Young Readers) Random Hse. Children's Bks.

—Happy Holidays, Blaze! (Blaze & the Monster Machines) Random House. 2017. (ENG.). 12p. (J). (— 1). bds. 8.99 *(978-1-5247-6383-1(7))*, Random Hse. Bks. for Young Readers) Random Hse. Children's Bks.

—Happy Troll-O-ween! Random House. 2017. (Pictureback(R) Ser.). (ENG.). 16p. (J). (gr. -1-2). pap. 4.99 *(978-1-5247-6958-1(4))*, Random Hse. Bks. for Young Readers) Random Hse. Children's Bks.

—Heart of a Ninja (Teenage Mutant Ninja Turtles) Random House. 2017. (ENG.). 16p. (J). (— 1). bds. 7.99 *(978-1-101-93696-2(7))*, Random Hse. Bks. for Young Readers) Random Hse. Children's Bks.

Random House. Hello, Friends! (Blue's Clues & You) Random House. 2020. (ENG.). 18p. (J). (-k). bds. 8.99 ***(978-0-593-17714-3(2))***, Random Hse. Bks. for Young Readers) Random Hse. Children's Bks.

Random House. Here Comes Frosty! (Frosty the Snowman) Random House. 2015. (Board Book Ser.). (ENG.). 24p. (J). (-k). bds. 4.99 *(978-0-553-52124-5(1))*, Random Hse. Bks. for Young Readers) Random Hse. Children's Bks.

—Here Comes Peter Cottontail. Random House. 2015. (Board Book Ser.). 24p. (J). (-k). bds. 4.99 *(978-0-553-50975-5(6))*, Random Hse. Bks. for Young Readers) Random Hse. Children's Bks.

—The Hero in You! DC SuperHero Girls: My Amazing Adventure Journal. Random House. 2017. 160p. (J). (gr. 2-4). 13.99 *(978-1-5247-1845-9(9))*, Random Hse. Bks. for Young Readers) Random Hse. Children's Bks.

—Holiday Helpers! (PAW Patrol) Random House. 2016. (Pictureback(R) Ser.). (ENG.). 24p. (J). (gr. -1-2). pap. 5.99 *(978-0-399-55874-0(8))*, Random Hse. Bks. for Young Readers) Random Hse. Children's Bks.

—Hooray for Dads! (SpongeBob SquarePants) Random House. 2014. (Pictureback(R) Ser.). (ENG.). 24p. (J). (gr. -1-2). 4.99 *(978-0-385-37607-5(3))*, Random Hse. Bks. for Young Readers) Random Hse. Children's Bks.

—How to Be a Cat/How to Be a Dog (the Secret Life of Pets 2) Random House. 2019. (Pictureback(R) Ser.). (ENG.). 16p. (J). (gr. -1-2). 5.99 *(978-1-9848-4985-4(9))*, Random Hse. Bks. for Young Readers) Random Hse. Children's Bks.

—Hug Day! (DreamWorks Trolls) Random House. 2018. (ENG.). 16p. (J). (— 1). bds. 7.99 *(978-1-9848-4908-3(5))*, Random Hse. Bks. for Young Readers) Random Hse. Children's Bks.

—It's a SpongeBob Christmas! (SpongeBob SquarePants) Random House. 2013. (Pictureback Ser.). (ENG.). 24p. (J). (gr. -1-2). 3.99 *(978-0-385-37856-7(4))*, Random Hse. Bks. for Young Readers) Random Hse. Children's Bks.

—It's Spring! (DreamWorks Trolls) Random House. 2019. (ENG.). 22p. (J). (— 1). bds. 6.99 *(978-1-9848-4894-9(1))*, Random Hse. Bks. for Young Readers) Random Hse. Children's Bks.

—Jingle Pups (PAW Patrol) Random House. 2017. (ENG.). 12p. (J). (— 1). bds. 8.99 *(978-1-5247-6397-8(7))*, Random Hse. Bks. for Young Readers) Random Hse. Children's Bks.

—Jingle Smells!: a Scratch-And-Sniff Adventure (PAW Patrol) Random House. 2018. (ENG.). 24p. (J). (gr. -1-2). 9.99 *(978-0-525-58188-8(X))*, Random Hse. Bks. for Young Readers) Random Hse. Children's Bks.

—Jurassic Park: the Deluxe Novelization (Jurassic Park) Random House. 2018. (ENG.). 96p. (J). (gr. 1-4). 9.99 *(978-0-525-58070-6(0))*, Random Hse. Bks. for Young Readers) Random Hse. Children's Bks.

—The Justice Collection. Random House. 2017. (Pictureback Favorites Ser.). (ENG.). 96p. (J). (gr. -1-2). 9.99 *(978-1-5247-6878-2(2))*, Random Hse. Bks. for Young Readers) Random Hse. Children's Bks.

—The Little Red Rescue Box (PAW Patrol) 4 Board Books. Random House. 2016. (ENG.). 96p. (J). (— 1). bds. 14.99 *(978-0-399-55135-2(2))*, Random Hse. Bks. for Young Readers) Random Hse. Children's Bks.

—Love Is Everywhere! (Sunny Day) Random House. 2018. (ENG.). 22p. (J). (— 1). bds. 6.99 *(978-0-525-64738-6(4))*, Random Hse. Bks. for Young Readers) Random Hse. Children's Bks.

—Magical Pet Friends! (Shimmer & Shine) Random House. 2018. (Pictureback(R) Ser.). (ENG.). 24p. (J). (gr. -1-2). pap. 5.99 *(978-0-525-58014-0(X))*, Random Hse. Bks. for Young Readers) Random Hse. Children's Bks.

—Make It Sparkle! (Shimmer & Shine) Random House. 2016. (ENG.). 12p. (J). (— 1). bds. 8.99 *(978-1-5247-0159-8(9))*, Random Hse. Bks. for Young Readers) Random Hse. Children's Bks.

—Meet the Machines! (Blaze & the Monster Machines) 4 Board Books. Random House. 2016. (ENG.). 48p. (J). (— 1). bds. 10.99 *(978-1-101-93678-8(9))*, Random Hse. Bks. for Young Readers) Random Hse. Children's Bks.

—Meet the Pets. Random House. 2016. (Step into Reading Ser.). (ENG.). 32p. (J). (gr. -1-2). 4.99 *(978-0-399-55483-4(1))*, Random Hse. Bks. for Young Readers) Random Hse. Children's Bks.

—Meet the Pets. Random House. Man-Kong, Mary. 2016. (Step into Reading Ser.). (ENG.). 32p. (J). (gr. -1-2). 12.99 *(978-0-399-55484-1(X))*, Random Hse. Bks. for Young Readers) Random Hse. Children's Bks.

—The Mermaid Park Mystery (Barbie) Random House. 2020. (Step into Reading Ser.). (ENG.). 32p. (J). (-k). pap. 4.99 *(978-0-593-12759-9(5))*; lib. bdg. 12.99 *(978-0-593-12760-5(9))* Random Hse. Children's Bks. (Random Hse. Bks. for Young Readers).

—Merry Christmas, Shimmer & Shine! (Shimmer & Shine) Random House. 2017. (Glitter Board Book Ser.). (ENG.). 12p. (J). (— 1). bds. 8.99 *(978-1-5247-2059-9(3))*, Random Hse. Bks. for Young Readers) Random Hse. Children's Bks.

Random House. Minecraft Official Animals Sticker Book (Minecraft) Random House. 2020. (ENG.). 32p. (J). (gr. 1-4). pap. 9.99 ***(978-0-593-17255-1(8))***, Random Hse. Bks. for Young Readers) Random Hse. Children's Bks.

Random House. Moms Are the Best! (SpongeBob SquarePants) Random House. Wilson, Sarah. 2014. (Step into Reading Ser.). (ENG.). 32p. (J). (gr. -1-1). 3.99 *(978-0-385-37499-6(2))*, Random Hse. Bks. for Young Readers) Random Hse. Children's Bks.

—A Monster Machine Treasury (Blaze & the Monster Machines) Random House. 2016. (ENG.). 30p. (J). (— 1). bds. 11.99 *(978-0-399-55594-7(3))*, Random Hse. Bks. for Young Readers) Random Hse. Children's Bks.

—Monster Machines on the Go! (Blaze & the Monster Machines) 4 Board Books. Random House. 2018. (ENG.). 96p. (J). (-k). bds. 14.99 *(978-0-525-57836-9(6))*, Random Hse. Bks. for Young Readers) Random Hse. Children's Bks.

Random House. Mulan & the Dragon Race/a Song for Cinderella (Disney Princess) Random House. 2020. (Pictureback(R) Ser.). (ENG.). 48p. (J). (gr. -1-2). 6.99 ***(978-0-7364-4120-9(4))***, RH/Disney) Random Hse. Children's Bks.

Random House. The Mutant Files (Teenage Mutant Ninja Turtles) Random House. 2014. (Pictureback(R) Ser.). (ENG.). 24p. (J). (gr. -1-2). 5.99 *(978-0-385-38746-0(6))*, Random Hse. Bks. for Young Readers) Random Hse. Children's Bks.

Random House. My Little Super Hero Word Book (DC Justice League) Random House. 2020. (ENG.). 22p. (J). (— 1). bds. 6.99 ***(978-0-593-12242-6(9))***, Random Hse. Bks. for Young Readers) Random Hse. Children's Bks.

Random House. Nella the Princess Knight Board Book (Nella the Princess Knight) Random House. 2018. (ENG.). 32p. (J). (— 1). bds. 8.99 *(978-0-525-57773-7(4))*, Random Hse. Bks. for Young Readers) Random Hse. Children's Bks.

—Nickelodeon 5-Minute Christmas Stories (Nickelodeon) Random House. 2017. (ENG.). 160p. (J). (gr. -1-2). 12.99 *(978-1-5247-6398-5(5))*, Random Hse. Bks. for Young Readers) Random Hse. Children's Bks.

Random House. Nickelodeon 5-Minute Girl-Power Stories (Nickelodeon) Random House. 2020. (ENG.). 160p. (J). (gr. -1-2). 14.99 ***(978-1-9848-9490-8(0))***, Random Hse. Bks. for Young Readers) Random Hse. Children's Bks.

Random House. Nickelodeon Bedtime Treasury (Nickelodeon) Random House. 2019. (ENG.). 30p. (J). (— 1). bds. 11.99 *(978-1-5247-6842-3(1))*, Random Hse. Bks. for Young Readers) Random Hse. Children's Bks.

—Nickelodeon Pictureback Collection (Nickelodeon) Random House. 2017. (ENG.). 96p. (J). (gr. -1-2). 9.99 *(978-1-5247-0067-6(3))*, Random Hse. Bks. for Young Readers) Random Hse. Children's Bks.

—Off the Leash. Random House. Golden Books Staff. 2019. (ENG.). 48p. (J). (gr. -1-2). pap. 5.99 *(978-1-9848-4981-6(6))*, Golden Bks.) Random Hse. Children's Bks.

—One Paw-Some Christmas: a Magnetic Play Book (PAW Patrol) Random House. 2019. (ENG.). 8p. (J). (gr. -1-2). bds. 12.99 *(978-1-9848-9502-8(8))*, Random Hse. Bks. for Young Readers) Random Hse. Children's Bks.

—Patrol Pals (Paw Patrol) Random House. 2015. (ENG.). 48p. (J). (— 1). bds. 10.99 *(978-0-553-50796-6(6))*, Random Hse. Bks. for Young Readers) Random Hse. Children's Bks.

—PAW Patrol 5-Minute Stories Collection (PAW Patrol) Random House. 2017. (ENG.). 160p. (J). (gr. -1-2). 12.99 *(978-1-5247-6399-2(3))*, Random Hse. Bks. for Young Readers) Random Hse. Children's Bks.

—PAW Patrol Deluxe Step into Reading (PAW Patrol) Random House. 2016. (Step into Reading Ser.). (ENG.). 24p. (J). (gr. -1-1). pap. 4.99 *(978-0-553-52288-4(4))*, Random Hse. Bks. for Young Readers) Random Hse. Children's Bks.

—PAW Patrol on the Roll! (PAW Patrol) Random House. 2016. (Pictureback(R) Ser.). (ENG.). 16p. (J). (gr. -1-2). 4.99 *(978-1-101-93867-6(6))*, Random Hse. Bks. for Young Readers) Random Hse. Children's Bks.

—A Paw Patrol Treasury (PAW Patrol) Random House. 2016. (ENG.). 30p. (J). (— 1). bds. 11.99 *(978-1-101-93957-4(5))*, Random Hse. Bks. for Young Readers) Random Hse. Children's Bks.

—Pawsome Puppy Adventures! Random House. 2016. (ENG.). 96p. (J). (gr. -1-2). 9.99 *(978-1-5247-1438-3(0))*, Random Hse. Bks. for Young Readers) Random Hse. Children's Bks.

—Peter Cottontail: the Great Easter Egg Hunt (Peter Cottontail) Random House. 2016. (Lift-The-Flap Ser.). (ENG.). 12p. (J). (gr. -1-k). bds. 6.99 *(978-1-101-93169-1(8))*, Random Hse. Bks. for Young Readers) Random Hse. Children's Bks.

—Pizza Party! (Teenage Mutant Ninja Turtles) Random House. 2017. (Step into Reading Ser.). (ENG.). 24p. (J). (gr. -1-1). pap. 4.99 *(978-1-5247-6982-6(7))*; lib. bdg. 12.99 *(978-1-5247-6983-3(5))* Random Hse. Children's Bks. (Random Hse. Bks. for Young Readers).

—Pokémon Storybook Treasury (Pokémon) Random House. 2018. (ENG.). 96p. (J). (gr. -1-2). 9.99 *(978-1-5247-7259-8(3))*, Random Hse. Bks. for Young Readers) Random Hse. Children's Bks.

—Poppy & Branch's Big Adventure. Random House. Miller, Mona. 2017. (Step into Reading Ser.). (ENG.). 32p. (J). (gr. -1-2). pap. 4.99 *(978-0-399-55870-2(5))*, Random Hse. Bks. for Young Readers) Random Hse. Children's Bks.

—Poppy Follows Her Nose! Random House. 2017. (ENG.). 24p. (J). (gr. -1-2). 9.99 *(978-1-5247-6642-9(9))*, Random Hse. Bks. for Young Readers) Random Hse. Children's Bks.

—Poppy's Big Day! (DreamWorks Trolls World Tour) Random House. 2020. (Pictureback(R) Ser.). (ENG.). 24p. (J). (gr. -1-2). 5.99 *(978-0-593-12235-8(6))*, Random Hse. Bks. for Young Readers) Random Hse. Children's Bks.

—Pups to the Rescue! (Paw Patrol) Random House. 2014. (Pictureback(R) Ser.). (ENG.). 16p. (J). (gr. -1-2). 3.99 *(978-0-385-38444-5(0))*, Random Hse. Bks. for Young Readers) Random Hse. Children's Bks.

—Queen of Cats (the Secret Life of Pets 2) Random House. 2019. (Step into Reading Ser.). (ENG.). 24p. (J). (gr. -1-1). 12.99 *(978-1-9848-9512-7(5))*; pap. 5.99 *(978-1-9848-9511-0(7))* Random Hse. Children's Bks. (Random Hse. Bks. for Young Readers).

—Racing Colors! (Blaze & the Monster Machines) Random House. 2016. (ENG.). 24p. (J). (gr. -1 — 1). bds. 6.99 *(978-0-553-53892-2(6))*, Random Hse. Bks. for Young Readers) Random Hse. Children's Bks.

—Rise of the Teenage Mutant Ninja Turtles: Official Poster Book (Rise of the Teenage Mutant Ninja Turtles) Random House. 2018. (ENG.). 48p. (J). (gr. 3-7). pap. 8.99 *(978-0-525-64505-4(5))*, Random Hse. Bks. for Young Readers) Random Hse. Children's Bks.

—Saved by the Shell! (Teenage Mutant Ninja Turtles) Random House. 2017. (Pictureback(R) Ser.). (ENG.). 24p. (J). (gr. -1-2). pap. 5.99 *(978-1-5247-6984-0(3))*, Random Hse. Bks. for Young Readers) Random Hse. Children's Bks.

—SCOOB! Those Meddling Kids (Scooby-Doo) Random House. 2020. (Pictureback(R) Ser.). (ENG.). 24p. (J). (gr. -1-2). 5.99 *(978-0-593-17866-9(1))*, Random Hse. Bks. for Young Readers) Random Hse. Children's Bks.

—Seven Ruff-Ruff Rescues! (PAW Patrol) Random House. 2019. (Step into Reading Ser.). (ENG.). 160p. (J). (gr. -1-1). pap. 8.99 *(978-0-525-64797-3(X))*, Random Hse. Bks. for Young Readers) Random Hse. Children's Bks.

—Six Magical Tales! (Shimmer & Shine) Random House. 2018. (Step into Reading Ser.). (ENG.). 144p. (J). (gr. -1-1). pap. 8.99 *(978-1-5247-7278-9(X))*, Random Hse. Bks. for Young Readers) Random Hse. Children's Bks.

—Slime Time! (Nickelodeon) Random House. 2019. (ENG.). 48p. (J). (gr. 1-4). pap. 8.99 *(978-0-593-11965-5(7))*, Random Hse. Bks. for Young Readers) Random Hse. Children's Bks.

—Small Pups, Big Adventures! (PAW Patrol) Random House. 2017. (ENG.). 24p. (J). (— 1). bds. 6.99 *(978-0-399-55879-5(9))*, Random Hse. Bks. for Young Readers) Random Hse. Children's Bks.

—SpongeBob's Slap Shot (SpongeBob SquarePants) Random House. 2014. (Pictureback(R) Ser.). (ENG.). 24p. (J). (gr. -1-2). 3.99 *(978-0-385-37852-9(1))*, Random Hse. Bks. for Young Readers) Random Hse. Children's Bks.

Random House. Super Mario: the Big Coloring Book (Nintendo) Random House. 2020. (ENG.). 48p. (J). (gr. -1-2). pap. 6.99 ***(978-0-593-30777-9(1))***, Random Hse. Bks. for Young Readers) Random Hse. Children's Bks.

Random House. Super Pup Heroes! (PAW Patrol) Random House. 2016. (ENG.). 16p. (J). (— 1). bds. 7.99 *(978-0-399-55313-4(4))*, Random Hse. Bks. for Young Readers) Random Hse. Children's Bks.

—Team Colors (Paw Patrol) Random House. 2015. (Board Book Ser.). (ENG.). 24p. (J). (— 1). bds. 6.99 *(978-0-553-49771-7(5))*, Random Hse. Bks. for Young Readers) Random Hse. Children's Bks.

—Teenage Mutant Ninja Turtles: Out of the Shadows Pictureback. Random House. 2016. (Pictureback(R) Ser.). (ENG.). 16p. (J). (gr. -1-2). 4.99 *(978-1-101-93858-4(7))*, Random Hse. Bks. for Young Readers) Random Hse. Children's Bks.

—Thomas & the Beanstalk. Random House. 2019. (Little Golden Book Ser.). (ENG.). 24p. (J). (-k). 4.99 *(978-0-525-57837-6(4))*, Golden Bks.) Random Hse. Children's Bks.

Random House. Thomas! (Thomas & Friends) Random House. 2020. (ENG.). 26p. (J). (gr. -1 — 1). bds. 9.99 ***(978-0-593-17320-6(1))***, Random Hse. Bks. for Young Readers) Random Hse. Children's Bks.

Random House. Toca Life Pet Playset (Toca Boca) Random House. 2019. (Toca Boca Ser.). (ENG.). 32p. (J). (gr. 1-4). pap. 9.99 *(978-0-525-57803-1(X))*, Random Hse. Bks. for Young Readers) Random Hse. Children's Bks.

—Transformers BotBots Official Sticker Book (Transformers BotBots) Random House. 2019. (ENG.). 48p. (J). (gr. -1-2). pap. 9.99 *(978-0-593-12557-1(6))*, Random Hse. Bks. for Young Readers) Random Hse. Children's Bks.

Random House. Troll-Tastic Tales (DreamWorks Trolls) Random House. 2020. (Step into Reading Ser.). (ENG.). 160p. (J). (gr. -1-1). pap. 7.99 ***(978-0-593-12786-5(2))***, Random Hse. Bks. for Young Readers) Random Hse. Children's Bks.

Random House. Trolls 5-Minute Stories (DreamWorks Trolls) Random House. 2018. (ENG.). 160p. (J). (gr. -1-2). 12.99 *(978-1-5247-7266-6(6))*, Random Hse. Bks. for Young Readers) Random Hse. Children's Bks.

—Trolls Holiday: The Deluxe Junior Novelization. Random House. 2017. (ENG.). 96p. (J). (gr. 3-7). 9.99 *(978-1-5247-1325-6(2))*, Random Hse. Bks. for Young Readers) Random Hse. Children's Bks.

Random House. Trolls Magnetic Play Book (DreamWorks Trolls) Random House. 2020. (ENG.). 8p. (J). (gr. -1-2). 12.99 ***(978-0-593-12262-4(3))***, Random Hse. Bks. for Young Readers) Random Hse. Children's Bks.

Random House. Trolls: the Deluxe Junior Novelization (DreamWorks Trolls) Random House. 2016. (Junior Novel Ser.). (ENG.). 144p. (J). (gr. 2-5). 9.99 *(978-0-399-55909-9(4))*, Random Hse. Bks. for Young Readers) Random Hse. Children's Bks.

—Trolls: the Junior Novelization (DreamWorks Trolls) Random House. 2016. (Junior Novel Ser.). (ENG.). 144p. (J). (gr. 2-5). 6.99 *(978-0-399-55910-5(8))*, Random Hse. Bks. for Young Readers) Random Hse. Children's Bks.

—We Love Monster Machines! (Blaze & the Monster Machines) Random House. 2017. (ENG.). 22p. (J). (-k). bds. 6.99 *(978-1-5247-6888-1(X))*, Random Hse. Bks. for Young Readers) Random Hse. Children's Bks.

Random House & Aikins, Dave. Abraca-Genie! Random House. 2017. (Pictureback(R) Ser.). (ENG.). 24p. (J). (gr. -1-2). pap. 5.99 *(978-1-5247-1784-1(3))*, Random Hse. Bks. for Young Readers) Random Hse. Children's Bks.

—Stripes Roars down the Track! Berrios, Frank. 2017. (Pictureback(R) Ser.). (ENG.). 16p. (J). (gr. -1-2). pap. 4.99 *(978-0-399-55840-5(3))*, Random Hse. Bks. for Young Readers) Random Hse. Children's Bks.

Random House & Batson, Alan. Goldie Blox & the Best! Pet! Ever! (GoldieBlox) McAnulty, Stacy. 2017. (Stepping Stone Book(TM) Ser.). (ENG.). 128p. (J). (gr. 1-4). 6.99 *(978-1-5247-1789-6(4))*; lib. bdg. 12.99 *(978-1-5247-1790-2(8))* Random Hse. Children's Bks. (Random Hse. Bks. for Young Readers).

Random House & Brizuela, Dario. Welcome to Super Hero High! Miller, Mona & Carbone, Courtney. 2017. (Step into Reading Ser.). (ENG.). 32p. (J). (gr. k-3). lib. bdg. 12.99 *(978-1-5247-6612-2(7))*, Random Hse. Bks. for Young Readers) Random Hse. Children's Bks.

Random House & Cartobaleno Staff. The Sweet Smells of Zahramay Falls (Shimmer & Shine) Tillworth, Mary. 2018. (ENG.). 24p. (J). (gr. -1-2). 9.99 *(978-1-5247-7277-2(1))*, Random Hse. Bks. for Young Readers) Random Hse. Children's Bks.

Rankin, Shelly. Amelia & Gabby: More Than Just Sisters. Marino, Lia. 2005. 31p. (J). 18.95 *(978-1-886057-30-2(3))* Warren Publishing, Inc.

Rankine, H. Emma Meets Rosa: Scurrying Through Time. Croucher, Vicki. 2020. (ENG.). 56p. (J). pap. ***(978-1-913460-14-3(2))*** Cloister Hse. Pr., The.

Rankovic, Ana. Gale the Goat: A Cyan Cove Hypnotic Sleep Story. Herda, Kylie. 2019. (Cyan Cove Ser.: Vol. 1). (ENG.). 36p. (J). pap. *(978-0-6484840-0-4(9))* Nexus Hypnotherapy.

—Paige the Penguin: A Cyan Cove Hypnotic Sleep Story. Herda, Kylie. 2019. (Cyan Cove Ser.: Vol. 2). (ENG.). 32p. (J). pap. *(978-0-6484840-1-1(7))* Nexus Hypnotherapy.

Ransome, Arthur. Swallowdale. Ransome, Arthur. 2010. (Swallows & Amazons Ser.). (ENG.). 431p. (J). pap. 15.95 *(978-1-56792-421-3(2))* Godine, David R. Pub.

Ransome, James. Aunt Flossie's Hats (and Crab Cakes Later) Howard, Elizabeth Fitzgerald. 2015. 32p. pap. 8.00 *(978-1-61003-491-3(0))* Center for the Collaborative Classroom.

—Freedom Roads: Searching for the Underground Railroad. Hansen, Joyce & McGowan, Gary. 2003. (ENG.). 166p. (J). (gr. 5-9). 18.95 *(978-0-8126-2673-5(7))* Cricket Bks.

—Germs: Fact & Fiction, Friends & Foes. Cline-Ransome, Lesa. 2017. (ENG.). 40p. (J). 17.99 *(978-0-8050-7915-9(7),* 900031507, Holt, Henry & Co. Bks. For Young Readers) Holt, Henry & Co.

—My Name Is Truth: The Life of Sojourner Truth. Turner, Ann. 2015. (ENG.). 40p. (J). (gr. 1-5). 17.99 *(978-0-06-075898-1(8))*; lib. bdg. 18.89 *(978-0-06-075899-8(6))* HarperCollins Pubs.

—The Nutcracker in Harlem. McMorrow, T. E. 2017. (ENG.). 32p. (J). (gr. -1-3). 17.99 *(978-0-06-117598-5(6))*; lib. bdg. 18.89 *(978-0-06-117599-2(4))* HarperCollins Pubs.

—Sweet Clara & the Freedom Quilt. Hopkinson, Deborah. 2018. (ENG.). 40p. (J). (gr. -1-2). 16.99 *(978-0-679-82311-7(5),* Knopf Bks. for Young Readers) Random Hse. Children's Bks.

—This Is the Dream. Shore, Diane Z. & Alexander, Jessica. 2009. (ENG.). 40p. (J). (gr. k-5). pap. 7.99 *(978-0-06-055521-4(1),* Amistad) HarperCollins Pubs.

—This Is the Dream. Alexander, Jessica & Shore, Diane Z. 2005. (ENG.). 40p. (J). (gr. k-5). 16.99 *(978-0-06-055519-1(X),* Amistad) HarperCollins Pubs.

—This Is the Rope: A Story from the Great Migration. Woodson, Jacqueline. (ENG.). 32p. (J). (gr. k-3). 2017. pap. 8.99 *(978-0-425-28894-8(3),* Puffin Books); 2013. 16.99 *(978-0-399-23986-1(3),* Nancy Paulsen Books) Penguin Young Readers Group.

—Uncle Jed's Barbershop. Mitchell, Margaree King. 2014. 40p. pap. 8.00 *(978-1-61003-368-8(X))* Center for the Collaborative Classroom.

—Visiting Day. Woodson, Jacqueline. 2015. (ENG.). 32p. (J). (gr. k-2). 8.99 *(978-0-14-751608-4(0),* Puffin Books) Penguin Young Readers Group.

—When Grandmama Sings. Mitchell, Margaree King. 2012. (ENG.). 40p. (J). (gr. k-4). 16.99 *(978-0-688-17563-4(5),* Amistad) HarperCollins Pubs.

—Young Pele: Soccer's First Star. Cline-Ransome, Lesa. 2011. (ENG.). 40p. (J). (gr. -1-3). pap. 7.99 *(978-0-375-87156-6(X),* Dragonfly Bks.) Random Hse. Children's Bks.

Ransome, James E. Baby Blessings: A Prayer for the Day You Are Born. Jordan, Deloris. 2010. (ENG.). 32p. (J). (gr. -1-3). 18.99 *(978-1-4169-5362-3(0),* Simon & Schuster/Paula Wiseman Bks.) Simon & Schuster/Paula Wiseman Bks.

—Be a King: Dr. Martin Luther King Jr. 's Dream & You. Weatherford, Carole Boston. 2018. 40p. (J). 17.99 *(978-0-8027-2368-0(3),* 900079719, Bloomsbury USA Childrens) Bloomsbury Publishing USA.

—Before She Was Harriet. Cline-Ransome, Lesa. (ENG.). 32p. (J). (gr. -1-3). 2019. pap. 8.99 *(978-0-8234-4429-8(5))*; 2017. 18.99 *(978-0-8234-2047-6(7))* Holiday Hse., Inc.

—Benny Goodman & Teddy Wilson: Taking the Stage As the First Black-and-White Jazz Band in History. Cline-Ransome, Lesa. 2014. (ENG.). 32p. (J). (gr. 3-7). 16.95 *(978-0-8234-2362-0(X))* Holiday Hse., Inc.

—The Christmas Tugboat: How the Rockefeller Center Christmas Tree Came to New York City. Matteson, George & Ursone, Adele. 2015. (ENG.). 48p. (J). (gr. -1-3). 6.99 *(978-0-544-55548-8(1),* 1610455, HMH Books For Young Readers) Houghton Mifflin Harcourt Publishing Co.

—The Creation (25th Anniversary Edition) Johnson, James Weldon. 2018. (ENG.). 40p. (J). (gr. 1-4). 18.99 *(978-0-8234-4025-2(7))* Holiday Hse., Inc.

—Freedom Bird: A Tale of Hope & Courage. Nolen, Jerdine. 2020. (ENG.). 32p. (J). (gr. k-4). 17.99 *(978-0-689-87167-2(8),* Simon & Schuster/Paula Wiseman Bks.) Simon & Schuster/Paula Wiseman Bks.

—Freedom's School. Cline-Ransome, Lesa. 2015. 32p. (J). (gr. 1-3). 17.99 *(978-1-4231-6103-5(3),* Jump at the Sun) Hyperion Bks. for Children.

—Game Changers: The Story of Venus & Serena Williams. Cline-Ransome, Lesa. 2018. (ENG.). 48p. (J). (gr. -1-3). 17.99 *(978-1-4814-7684-3(X),* Simon & Schuster/Paula Wiseman Bks.) Simon & Schuster/Paula Wiseman Bks.

—Granddaddy's Turn: A Journey to the Ballot Box. Bandy, Michael S. & Stein, Eric. 32p. (J). (gr. 1-4). 2019. 7.99 *(978-1-5362-0561-9(3))*; 2015. 17.99 *(978-0-7636-6593-7(2))* Candlewick Pr.

Ransome, James E. Gridiron: Stories from 100 Years of the National Football League. Bowen, Fred. 2020. (ENG.). 112p. (J). (gr. 3-7). 19.99 ***(978-1-4814-8112-0(6),*** McElderry, Margaret K. Bks.) McElderry, Margaret K. Bks.

Ransome, James E. Helen Keller: The World in Her Heart. Cline-Ransome, Lesa. 2008. 32p. (J). (gr. k-4). lib. bdg. 17.89 *(978-0-06-057075-0(X),* Collins) HarperCollins Pubs.

—It Is the Wind. Wolff, Ferida. Date not set. (ENG.). 32p. (J). (gr. -1-1). pap. 5.99 *(978-0-06-443530-7(X))* HarperCollins Pubs.

—Just a Lucky So & So: The Story of Louis Armstrong. Cline-Ransome, Lesa. 2016. (ENG.). 40p. (J). (gr. 1-4). 16.95 *(978-0-8234-3428-2(1))* Holiday Hse., Inc.

—Light in the Darkness: A Story about How Slaves Learned in Secret. Cline-Ransome, Lesa. 2013. 40p. (J). (gr. 1-3). 16.99 *(978-1-4231-3495-4(8),* Jump at the Sun) Hyperion Bks. for Children.

—Major Taylor, Champion Cyclist. Cline-Ransome, Lesa. 2004. (ENG.). 40p. (J). (gr. 1-5). 19.99 *(978-0-689-83159-1(5),* Atheneum Bks. for Young Readers) Simon & Schuster Children's Publishing.

—Overground Railroad. Cline-Ransome, Lesa. 2020. 48p. (J). (gr. -1-3). 18.99 *(978-0-8234-3873-0(2))* Holiday Hse., Inc.

—Peepers. Bunting, Eve. 2017. (ENG.). 32p. (J). (gr. -1-3). pap. 7.99 *(978-1-328-74047-2(1),* 1677001, HMH Books For Young Readers) Houghton Mifflin Harcourt Publishing Co.

—Satchel Paige. Cline-Ransome, Lesa. 2004. 31p. (J). (gr. k-4). reprint ed. pap. 7.00 *(978-0-7567-7799-9(2))* DIANE Publishing Co.

—Satchel Paige. Cline-Ransome, Lesa. 2003. (ENG.). 40p. (J). (gr. 1-5). 8.99 *(978-0-689-85681-5(4),* Simon & Schuster/Paula Wiseman Bks.) Simon & Schuster/Paula Wiseman Bks.

—Sky Boys: How They Built the Empire State Building. Hopkinson, Deborah. 2012. 48p. (J). (gr. -1-3). pap. 7.99 *(978-0-375-86541-1(1),* Dragonfly Bks.) Random Hse. Children's Bks.

—Sky Boys: How They Built the Empire State Building. Hopkinson, Deborah. ed. 2012. lib. bdg. 18.40 *(978-0-606-23847-2(6))* Turtleback.

—Under the Quilt of Night. Hopkinson, Deborah. 2005. (gr. k-5). 18.00 *(978-0-7569-5077-4(5))* Perfection Learning Corp.

—Under the Quilt of Night. Hopkinson, Deborah. 2005. (ENG.). 40p. (J). (gr. k-5). reprint ed. 7.99 *(978-0-689-87700-1(5),* Aladdin) Simon & Schuster Children's Publishing.

—Under the Quilt of Night. Hopkinson, Deborah. 2005. (ENG.). 40p. (J). (gr. 1-3). 22.44 *(978-0-689-82227-8(8))* Simon & Schuster, Inc.

—What Lincoln Said. Thomson, Sarah L. 2009. 32p. (J). (gr. k-3). lib. bdg. 18.89 *(978-0-06-084820-0(0))* HarperCollins Pubs.

—Words Set Me Free: The Story of Young Frederick Douglass. Cline-Ransome, Lesa. 2011. (ENG.). 32p. (J). (gr. k-4). 18.99 *(978-1-4169-5903-8(3),* Simon & Schuster/Paula Wiseman Bks.) Simon & Schuster/Paula Wiseman Bks.

—Young Pele: Soccer's First Star. Cline-Ransome, Lesa. 2012. (ENG.). 40p. (J). (gr. -1-4). lib. bdg. 22.44 *(978-0-375-93599-2(1),* Dragonfly Bks.) Random Hse. Children's Bks.

Ransome, James E. The Bell Rang. Ransome, James E. 2019. (ENG.). 40p. (J). (gr. -1-3). 17.99 *(978-1-4424-2113-4(4),* Atheneum/Caitlyn Dlouhy Books) Simon & Schuster Children's Publishing.

Ranson, Arthur. X-Factor. Jensen, Jeff. 2003. (X-Men Ser.: Vol. 1). 96p. (YA). pap. 9.99 *(978-0-7851-1016-3(X))* Marvel Worldwide, Inc.

Ranson, Kim & Phillips, Rebekah. Miss Olive Finds Her Furever Friends: The Doggy Diva Diaries. Marie, Susan. 2020. (Doggy Diva Diaries: Vol. 2). (ENG.). 32p. (J). (gr. k-2). 17.99 ***(978-0-578-67286-1(3))*** Doggy Diva Show, Inc., The.

Ranucci, Claudia. ¡Achís! Escrivá, Victoria Pérez. 2010. (Cosas, Cositas y Cacharros Ser.). (SPA.). (J). (gr. k-3). *(978-84-263-7380-9(1))* Vives, Luis Editorial (Edelvives).

—¡Cataplof! Cosas, Cositas Y Cacharros. Escrivá, Victoria Pérez. 2010. (Cosas, Cositas y Cacharros Ser.). (SPA.). (J). (gr. k-3). *(978-84-263-7381-6(X))* Vives, Luis Editorial (Edelvives).

—Don't Wake the Yeti! Freedman, Claire. 2017. (ENG.). 32p. (J). (gr. k-2). 17.99 *(978-0-8075-1690-4(2),* 807516902) Whitman, Albert & Co.

—Fred & the Bedtime Elephants. Crowe, Caroline. 2018. (ENG.). 32p. (J). (gr. -1-k). 17.99 *(978-0-8075-1963-9(4),* 807519634) Whitman, Albert & Co.

—How to Make a Shark Smile: How a Positive Mindset Spreads Happiness. Achor, Shawn & Blankson, Amy. 2020. 40p. (J). (-3). 17.99 *(978-1-4926-9472-4(X),* Little Pickle Pr.) Sourcebooks, Inc.

Ranucci, Claudia. Mootilda's Bad Mood. Rosen Schwartz, Corey & Call, Kirsti. 2020. (ENG.). 32p. (J). (gr. -1-3). 17.99 ***(978-1-4998-1086-8(5))*** Little Bee Books Inc.

Ranucci, Claudia. ¡Splash! Escrivá, Victoria Pérez. 2010. (Cosas, Cositas y Cacharros Ser.). (SPA.). (J). (gr. k-3). *(978-84-263-7379-3(8))* Vives, Luis Editorial (Edelvives).

Ranucci, Claudia, jt. illus. see Michell, Michael.

Rao, Rohitash. Creature Keepers & the Burgled Blizzard-Bristles. Nelson, Peter. 2016. (Creature Keepers Ser.: 3). (ENG.). 336p. (J). (gr. 3-7). 12.99 *(978-0-06-223647-0(4))* HarperCollins Pubs.

—Creature Keepers & the Perilous Pyro-Paws. Nelson, Peter. 2017. (Creature Keepers Ser.: 4). (ENG.). 400p. (J). (gr. 3-7). 12.99 *(978-0-06-223650-0(4))* HarperCollins Pubs.

—Creature Keepers & the Swindled Soil-Soles. Nelson, Peter. 2015. (Creature Keepers Ser.: 2). (ENG.). 384p. (J). (gr. 3-7). 12.99 *(978-0-06-223645-6(8))* HarperCollins Pubs.

—Herbert's Wormhole, 1. Nelson, Peter. 2010. (Herbert's Wormhole Ser.: 1). (ENG.). 304p. (J). (gr. 3-7). pap. 6.99 *(978-0-06-168870-6(3))* HarperCollins Pubs.

—Herbert's Wormhole: AeroStar & the 3 1/2-Point Plan of Vengeance. Nelson, Peter. 2014. (Herbert's Wormhole Ser.: 3). (ENG.). 368p. (J). (gr. 3-7). pap. 6.99 *(978-0-06-201221-0(5))* HarperCollins Pubs.

—Herbert's Wormhole: the Rise & Fall of el Solo Libre. Nelson, Peter. (Herbert's Wormhole Ser.: 2). (ENG.). (J). (gr. 3-7). 2014. 336p. pap. 6.99 *(978-0-06-201219-7(3))*; 2012. 320p. 12.99 *(978-0-06-201218-0(5))* HarperCollins Pubs.

Rappa, Desiree & Brian. Big Red. 2003. (J). 4.95 *(978-0-9722027-0-1(6))* Covered Bridge Bks.

Rappe-Flowers, Hedvig. Spotted Bear: A Rocky Mountain Folktale. Ippisch, Hanneke. Ort, Kathleen, ed. rev. ed. 49p. (J). (gr. 3-4). *(978-0-87842-387-3(7),* 326) Mountain Pr. Publishing Co., Inc.

Rasberry, Lisamarie. Blowing Dandelions with Sea Lions: A Children's Rhyming Poetry Book. Jaqua, Tiffani. 2018. (ENG.). 118p. (J). pap. 9.99 *(978-1-7216-2404-1(X))* CreateSpace Independent Publishing Platform.

Rasch, Heidi M. Indian Boyhood: The True Story of a Sioux Upbringing. Eastman, Charles Alexander. Fitzgerald, Michael Oren, ed. 2016. 40p. (J). (gr. k-3). 17.95 *(978-1-937786-56-4(0),* Wisdom Tales) World Wisdom, Inc.

Rasche, Shelly. Easter ABCs. Anders, Isabel. 2004. 32p. (J). tchr. ed. 9.49 *(978-0-570-07020-7(1),* 56-2040) Concordia Publishing Hse.

Rasche, Shelly S. Write Now! Gould, Judith S. & Burke, Mary F. Mitchell, Judith, ed. 2005. 80p. (J). pap. 6.95 *(978-1-57310-449-4(3))* Teaching & Learning Co.

Raschka, Chris. Another Important Book. Brown, Margaret Wise. 2006. (ENG.). 32p. (J). (gr. -1-k). reprint ed. pap. 7.99 *(978-0-06-443785-1(X))* HarperCollins Pubs.

—Be Boy Buzz. Hooks, Bell. 2016. (ENG.). 32p. (J). (gr. -1 — 1). bds. 7.99 *(978-1-4847-8840-0(0),* Jump at the Sun) Hyperion Bks. for Children.

—Buggy Bug. 2014. (ENG.). 24p. (J). (gr. -1 — 1). 6.95 *(978-1-4197-1200-5(4),* Abrams Appleseed) Abrams, Inc.

—Clammy Clam. 2014. (ENG.). 24p. (J). (gr. -1 — 1). 6.95 *(978-1-4197-1201-2(2),* Abrams Appleseed) Abrams, Inc.

—Crabby Crab. 2014. (Thingy Things Ser.). (ENG.). 24p. (J). (gr. -1 — 1). 6.95 *(978-1-4197-1056-8(7),* Abrams Appleseed) Abrams, Inc.

—The Death of the Hat: A Brief History of Poetry in 50 Objects. Janeczko, Paul B. 80p. (J). (gr. 3-7). 2018. pap. 9.99 *(978-0-7636-9968-0(3))*; 2015. 17.99 *(978-0-7636-6963-8(6))* Candlewick Pr.

—Doggy Dog. 2014. (ENG.). 24p. (J). (gr. -1 — 1). 6.95 *(978-1-4197-1203-6(9),* Abrams Appleseed) Abrams, Inc.

—Fishing in the Air. Creech, Sharon. 2003. (ENG.). 32p. (J). (gr. -1-3). pap. 7.99 *(978-0-06-051606-2(2))* HarperCollins Pubs.

—Fishing in the Air. Creech, Sharon. 2003. pap. 9.95 incl. audio *(978-1-59112-223-4(6))*; (J). 25.95 incl. audio *(978-1-59112-225-8(2))*; (J). pap. 37.95 incl. audio *(978-1-59112-226-5(0))*; (J). pap. 39.95 incl. audio compact disk *(978-1-59112-521-1(9))* Live Oak Media.

—A Foot in the Mouth: Poems to Speak, Sing, & Shout. 2009. (ENG.). 64p. (J). (gr. 3-7). 17.99 *(978-0-7636-0663-3(4))* Candlewick Pr.

—A Foot in the Mouth: Poems to Speak, Sing, & Shout. Janeczko, Paul B. 2012. 64p. (J). (gr. 3-7). pap. 9.99 *(978-0-7636-6083-3(3))* Candlewick Pr.

—Fortune Cookies. Bitterman, Albert. 2011. (ENG.). 28p. (J). (gr. -1-k). 14.99 *(978-1-4169-6814-6(8),* Beach Lane Bks.) Beach Lane Bks.

—Good Sports: Rhymes about Running, Jumping, Throwing, & More. Prelutsky, Jack. 2011. 40p. (J). (gr. 1-4). pap. 7.99 *(978-0-375-86558-9(6),* Dragonfly Bks.) Random Hse. Children's Bks.

—Granny Torrelli Makes Soup. Creech, Sharon. 2004. (Joanna Cotler Bks.). 141p. (gr. 3-7). 17.00 *(978-0-7569-4604-3(2))* Perfection Learning Corp.

—Happy to Be Nappy. Hooks, Bell. 2017. (ENG.). 32p. (J). (gr. -1-1). bds. 7.99 *(978-1-4847-8841-7(9),* Jump at the Sun) Hyperion Bks. for Children.

—The Hello, Goodbye Window. Juster, Norton. 2005. (ENG.). 32p. (J). (gr. -1-3). 18.99 *(978-0-7868-0914-1(0),* di Capua, Michael Bks.) Hyperion Bks. for Children.

—I Pledge Allegiance. Martin, Bill, Jr. & Sampson, Michael. 2004. (ENG.). 40p. (J). (gr. 1-4). reprint ed. pap. 8.99 *(978-0-7636-2527-6(2))* Candlewick Pr.

—A Kick in the Head: An Everyday Guide to Poetic Forms. (ENG.). 64p. (J). (gr. 3-7). 2009. pap. 9.99 *(978-0-7636-4132-0(4))*; 2005. 26.19 *(978-0-7636-0662-6(6))* Candlewick Pr.

—Moosey Moose. 2014. (ENG.). 24p. (J). (gr. -1 — 1). 6.95 *(978-1-4197-1202-9(0),* Abrams Appleseed) Abrams, Inc.

—Old Dog Baby Baby. Fogliano, Julie. 2016. (ENG.). 32p. (J). 17.99 *(978-1-59643-853-8(3),* 9781596438538) Roaring Brook Pr.

—Otter & Odder: A Love Story. Howe, James. 2012. 40p. (J). (gr. 1-4). 14.00 *(978-0-7636-4174-0(X))* Candlewick Pr.

—Peter & the Wolf. Prokofiev, Sergei. 2008. (ENG.). 40p. (J). (gr. -1-2). 19.99 *(978-0-689-85652-5(0),* Atheneum/Richard Jackson Bks.) Simon & Schuster Children's Publishing.

—A Poke in the I: A Collection of Concrete Poems. Janeczko, Paul B., ed. 2006. (ENG.). 48p. (gr. 1-4). reprint ed. 7.99 *(978-0-7636-2376-0(8))* Candlewick Pr.

—A Primer about the Flag. Bell, Marvin. 2011. 32p. (J). (gr. -1-3). 15.99 *(978-0-7636-4991-3(0))* Candlewick Pr.

—Puddle. Jackson, Richard. 2019. (ENG.). 40p. (J). (gr. -1-3). 17.99 *(978-0-06-265195-2(1),* Greenwillow Bks.) HarperCollins Pubs.

—A Song about Myself. Keats, John. 2017. 40p. (J). (gr. 1-4). 17.99 *(978-0-7636-5090-2(0))* Candlewick Pr.

—Whaley Whale. 2014. (Thingy Things Ser.). (ENG.). 24p. (J). (gr. -1 — 1). 6.95 *(978-1-4197-1058-2(3),* Abrams Appleseed) Abrams, Inc.

—When Lions Roar. Harris, Robie H. 2013. (ENG.). 32p. (J). (gr. -1-k). 16.99 *(978-0-545-11283-3(4),* Orchard Bks.) Scholastic, Inc.

Raschka, Chris. A Ball for Daisy. Raschka, Chris. 32p. (J). (gr. -1-2). 2015. bds. 8.99 *(978-0-553-53723-9(7))*; 2011. 17.99 *(978-0-375-85861-1(X))* Random Hse. Children's Bks. (Schwartz & Wade Bks.).

—Daisy Gets Lost. Raschka, Chris. 2013. 32p. (J). (gr. -1-2). 17.99 *(978-0-449-81741-4(5),* Schwartz & Wade Bks.) Random Hse. Children's Bks.

—Everyone Can Learn to Ride a Bicycle. Raschka, Chris. 2013. 32p. (J). (gr. -1-3). 16.99 *(978-0-375-87007-1(5),* Schwartz & Wade Bks.) Random Hse. Children's Bks.

—Five for a Little One. Raschka, Chris. 2006. (ENG.). 48p. (J). (gr. -1-2). 19.99 *(978-0-689-84599-4(5),* Atheneum/Richard Jackson Bks.) Simon & Schuster Children's Publishing.

—John Coltrane's Giant Steps. Raschka, Chris. pap. 16.95 incl. audio *(978-0-87499-972-3(3))*; pap. incl. audio *(978-0-87499-974-7(X))*; pap. 18.95 incl. audio compact disk *(978-1-59112-416-0(6))*; pap. incl. audio compact disk *(978-1-59112-603-4(7))* Live Oak Media.

—The Magic Flute. Raschka, Chris. 2019. (ENG.). 48p. (J). (gr. -1-3). 17.99 *(978-1-4814-4902-1(8))* Simon & Schuster Children's Publishing.

—Mama Baby. Raschka, Chris. 2020. 32p. (J). (gr. -1-2). 14.99 *(978-0-7636-9060-1(0))* Candlewick Pr.

—Mysterious Thelonious. Raschka, Chris. pap. 18.95 incl. audio compact disk *(978-1-59112-421-4(2))* Live Oak Media.

—New Shoes. Raschka, Chris. 2018. (ENG.). 32p. (J). (gr. -1-3). 17.99 *(978-0-06-265752-7(6),* Greenwillow Bks.) HarperCollins Pubs.

—New York Is English, Chattanooga Is Creek. Raschka, Chris. 2018. (ENG.). 40p. (J). (gr. -1-2). 11.99 *(978-1-5344-3371-7(6),* Atheneum Bks. for Young Readers) Simon & Schuster Children's Publishing.

—Simple Gifts. Raschka, Chris. 2003. pap. 41.95 incl. audio *(978-0-87499-642-5(2))*; pap. 43.95 incl. audio compact disk *(978-1-59112-604-1(5))* Live Oak Media.

—Yo! Yes? Raschka, Chris. 2007. (Scholastic Bookshelf Ser.). (ENG.). 32p. (J). (gr. -1 — 1). pap. 7.99 *(978-0-439-92185-5(6))* Scholastic, Inc.

Raschka, Chris, jt. illus. see Williams, Vera B.

Raschke, Andrea. Barf's First Flight. Newcomer, Carolyn. 2009. 40p. (J). 14.95 *(978-0-9792583-8-1(3))* White Stag Pr.

Rasemas, Joe. My Favorite Time of Day (Mi Hora Preferida del Dia) Kondrchek, Jamie. Vega, Eida de la, tr. from ENG. 2009. (Day in the Life Ser.). (SPA & ENG.). 32p. (J). (gr. -1-1). lib. bdg. 25.70 *(978-1-58415-837-0(9))* Mitchell Lane Pubs.

—What It's Like to Be Ryan Howard: Como Es Ser Ryan Howard. Sherman, Patrice & Murica, Rebecca Thatcher. de la Vega, Eida, tr. from ENG. 2009. (What It's Like to Be Ser.). (SPA & ENG.). 32p. (J). (gr. -1-2). 25.70 *(978-1-58415-845-5(X))* Mitchell Lane Pubs.

Rasemas, Joe. On My Way to School (De Camino a la Escuela) Rasemas, Joe. Kondrchek, Jamie. Vega, Eida de la, tr. 2009. (Day in the Life Ser.). (SPA & ENG.). 32p. (J). (gr. -1-1). 25.70 *(978-1-58415-840-0(9))* Mitchell Lane Pubs.

—What Day Is It? (Que Dia Es Hoy?) Rasemas, Joe. Kondrchek, Jamie. Vega, Eida de la, tr. 2009. (Day in the Life Ser.). (SPA & ENG.). 32p. (J). (gr. -1-1). 25.70 *(978-1-58415-838-7(7))* Mitchell Lane Pubs.

—What Should I Wear Today? (Que Ropa Me Pondre Hoy?) Rasemas, Joe. Kondrchek, Jamie. Vega, Eida de la, tr. 2009. (Day in the Life Ser.). (ENG & SPA.). 32p. (J). (gr. -1-1). 25.70 *(978-1-58415-839-4(5))* Mitchell Lane Pubs.

Rash, Andy. Dweeb: Burgers, Beasts, & Brainwashed Bullies. Starmer, Aaron. 2011. (ENG.). 240p. (J). (gr. 4-6). 21.19 *(978-0-385-73705-0(X),* Delacorte Pr.) Random Hse. Children's Bks.

—May I Have a Word? Levis, Caron. 2017. (ENG.). 40p. (J). 16.99 *(978-0-374-34880-9(4),* 9780374348809, Farrar, Straus & Giroux (BYR)) Farrar, Straus & Giroux.

—Sea Monster & the Bossy Fish. Messner, Kate. 2013. (ENG.). 40p. (J). (gr. -1-k). 16.99 *(978-1-4521-1253-4(3))* Chronicle Bks. LLC.

—Sea Monster's First Day. Messner, Kate. 2011. (ENG.). 36p. (J). (gr. -1-3). 16.99 *(978-0-8118-7564-6(4))* Chronicle Bks. LLC.

—Superhero School. Reynolds, Aaron. 2009. 32p. (J). (gr. k-2). 17.99 *(978-1-59990-166-4(8),* 900048407, Bloomsbury USA Childrens) Bloomsbury Publishing USA.

Rash, Andy. The Happy Book. Rash, Andy. 2019. (ENG.). 40p. (J). (gr. -1-2). 17.99 *(978-0-451-47125-3(3),* Viking Books for Young Readers) Penguin Young Readers Group.

Rasheed, Iman. Once upon an Eid: Stories of Hope & Joy by 15 Muslim Voices. Ali, S. K. & Saeed, Aisha, eds. 2020. (ENG.). 304p. (J). (gr. 3-7). 17.99 *(978-1-4197-4083-1(0),* 1277801, Amulet Bks.) Abrams, Inc.

Rasheed, M. The Wicked Witch Pop Quiz. Peace, Bob. 2013. 132p. pap. 12.95 *(978-0-9824741-4-3(8))* Sojourner Publishing, Inc.

Rashid, Abdul. The Case of the Missing Pooch: Amanda's Amazing Adventures - Book One, 6 vols., Vol. 1. Cowan, C. C. Bauer, Cindy, ed. 2009. (ENG.). 100p. (J). pap. 14.95 *(978-0-9677385-1-2(2))* CCP Publishing & Entertainment.

Rashin. Hold Your Temper, Tiger. Roth, Carol. 2017. (ENG.). 32p. (J). (gr. -1-3). 17.95 *(978-0-7358-4274-8(4))* North-South Bks., Inc.

—The Seven Voyages of Sinbad the Sailor. Said. 2015. 64p. (J). 19.95 *(978-0-7358-4240-3(X))* North-South Bks., Inc.

—Two Parrots. 2014. 32p. (J). (gr. k-3). 17.95 *(978-0-7358-4171-0(3),* 9780735841710) North-South Bks., Inc.

Rasin, Ivana. When Hen Was on Her Way to Market: A Folktale-Inspired Story of Manners. Stanic Rasin, Irena. 2016. (ENG.). (J). (gr. k-4). pap. 7.99 *(978-0-9971333-1-8(7))* Perlina Pr.

—When Hen Was on Her Way to Market: A Folktale-Inspired Story of Manners & Nursery Rhyme. Stanic Rasin, Irena. 2018. (ENG.). 80p. (J). (gr. k-5). pap. 16.99 *(978-0-9971333-5-6(X))* Perlina Pr.

Raskauskas, Sally. Lyrical Earth Science: Geology. Elda, Doug & Elda, Dorry. 2003. 116p. (YA). (gr. 5-10). pap. 25.50 incl. audio *(978-0-9741635-2-9(X))* Lyrical Learning.

—Lyrical Earth Science: Geology. Elda, Doug & Elda, Dorry. 2003. 116p. (YA). (gr. 5-10). pap. 19.95 incl. audio *(978-0-9741635-7-4(0))* Lyrical Learning.

Raskavskas, Sally. Lyrical Earth Science: Geology. Eldon, Doug & Eldon, Dorry. 2003. 116p. (YA). (gr. 5-10). pap. 23.95 incl. audio compact disk *(978-0-9741635-8-1(9))* Lyrical Learning.

Raskin, Ellen. A Child's Christmas in Wales. Thomas, Dylan. 2003. (New Directions Paperbook Ser.: Vol. 972). (ENG.). 32p. reprint ed. pap. 8.00 *(978-0-8112-1560-2(1))* New Directions Publishing Corp.

Raskin, Ellen. Figgs & Phantoms. Raskin, Ellen. 2011. (Newbery Honor Ser.). 176p. (J). (gr. 6-8). 21.19 *(978-0-14-241169-8(8)*, Puffin) Penguin Publishing Group.

Rasmussen, Gerry. Crazy about Basketball! Lesynski, Loris. 2013. (Crazy about Sports Ser.). (ENG.). 32p. (J). (gr. 3-5). 22.95 *(978-1-55451-541-7(6)*, 9781554515417); pap. 12.95 *(978-1-55451-540-0(8)*, 9781554515400) Annick Pr., Ltd. CAN. Dist: Publishers Group West (PGW).

—Crazy about Hockey! Lesynski, Loris. 2015. (Crazy about Sports Ser.). (ENG.). 32p. (J). (gr. 3-5). pap. 9.95 *(978-1-55451-711-4(7)*, 9781554517114) Annick Pr., Ltd. CAN. Dist: Publishers Group West (PGW).

—Sniffy the Beagle. Eagle, Rita. 2007. (ENG.). 44p. per. 13.95 *(978-1-59800-537-0(5))* Outskirts Pr., Inc.

Rasmussen, Jennifer. What Do You See? Mellen, Wynette. 2012. 42p. (J). pap. 9.95 *(978-0-9839957-4-6(5))* Freundship Pr., LLC.

Rasmussen, Liz. Too Fat to Fly. 2007. 32p. (J). 16.95 *(978-0-9793517-0-9(7))* Silver Bells Publishing Hse.

Rasmussen, Wendy. The Tale of Benjamin Bunny. Potter, Beatrix. 2009. (Classic Tales by Beatrix Potter Ser.). (ENG.). 24p. (J). (gr. k-3). 28.50 *(978-1-60253-292-2(3)*, 200118) Child's World, Inc., The.

—The Tale of Johnny Town-Mouse. Potter, Beatrix & Aesop, Aesop. 2009. (Classic Tales by Beatrix Potter Ser.). (ENG.). 24p. (J). (gr. k-3). 28.50 *(978-1-60253-293-9(1)*, 200119) Child's World, Inc., The.

—The Tale of Mrs. Tittlemouse. Potter, Beatrix. 2009. (Classic Tales by Beatrix Potter Ser.). (ENG.). 24p. (J). (gr. k-3). 28.50 *(978-1-60253-294-6(X)*, 200120) Child's World, Inc., The.

—The Tale of Squirrel Nutkin. Potter, Beatrix. 2009. (Classic Tales by Beatrix Potter Ser.). (ENG.). 24p. (J). (gr. k-3). 28.50 *(978-1-60253-296-0(6)*, 200122) Child's World, Inc., The.

—The Tale of the Flopsy Bunnies. Potter, Beatrix. 2009. (Classic Tales by Beatrix Potter Ser.). (ENG.). 24p. (J). (gr. k-3). 28.50 *(978-1-60253-297-7(4)*, 200123) Child's World, Inc., The.

Rasmussen, Wendy. Marvelous Max, the Mansion Mouse. Rasmussen, Wendy, tr. Rowland, Patty. 2003. 32p. (J). 17.95 *(978-0-9649934-4-0(9))* Norfleet Pr., Inc.

Rassmus, Jens. Do Fish Sleep? Raschke, Jens. Cooper, Belinda, tr. 2019. 64p. (J). 16.95 *(978-1-59270-285-5(6))* Enchanted Lion Bks., LLC.

—I Need All of It. Postert, Petra. 2018. (ENG.). 32p. (J). 17.99 *(978-1-250-11271-2(0)*, 900170530) Feiwel & Friends.

Ratanavanh, Seng Soun. My Island. Demasse-Pottier, Stephanie. 2019. (ENG.). 25p. (J). (gr. -1-k). 16.95 *(978-1-61689-813-7(5))* Princeton Architectural Pr.

—Patience, Miyuki: (intergenerational Picture Book Ages 5-8 Teaches Life Lessons of Learning How to Wait, Japanese Art & Scenery) Galliez, Roxane Marie. 2019. (ENG.). 32p. (J). (gr. k-3). 17.95 *(978-1-61689-843-4(7))* Princeton Architectural Pr.

Ratanavanh, Seng Soun. Thank You, Miyuki. Galliez, Roxane Marie. 2020. (ENG.). 32p. (J). (gr. k-3). 17.95 ***(978-1-61689-901-1(8))*** Princeton Architectural Pr.

Ratanavanh, Seng Soun. Time for Bed, Miyuki. Galliez, Roxane Marie. 2018. (ENG.). 32p. (J). (gr. k-3). 17.95 *(978-1-61689-705-5(8))* Princeton Architectural Pr.

Ratchford, Casey. Hudson & the Missing Tiger: + the Treasure Hunt. Shepherd, Terry. 2020. (Waterford Detectives Ser.: Vol. 1). (ENG.). 54p. (J). pap. 5.50 ***(978-1-7929-3010-2(0))*** Independently Published.

Rath, Robert. Bug Feats of Montana. Oberbillig, Deborah Richie. 2009. 48p. (J). 7.95 *(978-1-56037-444-2(6))* Farcountry Pr.

—First Dog: Unleashed in the Montana Capitol. Solberg, Jessica L. 2007. (J). 11.95 *(978-1-56037-419-0(5))* Farcountry Pr.

—Fish Do WHAT in the Water? The Secret Lives of Marine Animals. Patterson, Caroline. 2012. 48p. (J). 14.95 *(978-1-56037-519-7(1))* Farcountry Pr.

—The Legend of Turtle Bridge. Stephen Coombs. 2019. (ENG.). 96p. (J). pap. 14.95 *(978-1-59152-215-7(3)*, Sweetgrass Bks.) Farcountry Pr.

—Saluting Grandpa: Celebrating Veterans & Honor Flight, 1 vol. Metivier, Gary. 2012. (ENG.). 32p. (J). (gr. k-3). 16.99 *(978-1-4556-1748-7(2)*, Pelican Publishing) Arcadia Publishing.

—Stanley: a Prairie Dog's Tale: Book One, Legend of the Star. Nehls, Robert. 2018. (Stanley: a Prairie Dog's Tale Ser.: Vol. 1). (ENG.). 184p. (J). pap. 14.95 *(978-1-59152-221-8(8)*, Sweetgrass Bks.) Farcountry Pr.

—Storm Chasers! on the Trail of Twisters. Davies, Jon & Reed, Jim, photos by. Davies, Jon. 2007. 48p. (J). (gr. 3-7). pap. 12.95 *(978-1-56037-407-7(1))* Farcountry Pr.

—Until Daddy Comes Home, 1 vol. Metivier, Gary. 2014. (ENG.). 32p. (J). (gr. k-3). 16.99 *(978-1-4556-1890-3(X)*, Pelican Publishing) Arcadia Publishing.

—Who Pooped in the Black Hills? Scats & Tracks for Kids. Robson, Gary D. 2006. (Who Pooped in the Park? Ser.). 48p. (J). (gr. 3-7). pap. 11.95 *(978-1-56037-387-2(3))* Farcountry Pr.

—Who Pooped in the Cascades? Scat & Tracks for Kids. Robson, Gary D. 2013. 48p. (J). pap. 11.95 *(978-1-56037-362-9(8))* Farcountry Pr.

—Who Pooped in the Park? Acadia National Park. Robson, Gary D. 2006. (Who Pooped in the Park? Ser.). 48p. (J). (gr. -1-3). pap. 11.95 *(978-1-56037-338-4(5))* Farcountry Pr.

—Who Pooped in the Park? Death Valley National Park: Scat & Tracks for Kids. Robson, Gary D. 2008. (ENG.). 48p. (J). (gr. 3-7). pap. 9.95 *(978-1-56037-403-9(9))* Farcountry Pr.

—Who Pooped in the Park? Great Smoky Mountains National Park. Kemp, Steve. 2005. 48p. (J). pap. 11.95 *(978-1-56037-321-6(0))* Farcountry Pr.

—Who Pooped in the Park? Red Rock Canyon National Conservation Area: Scats & Tracks for Kids. Robson, Gary D. 2005. (Who Pooped in the Park? Ser.). 48p. (J). (gr. -1-3). pap. 9.95 *(978-1-56037-371-1(7))* Farcountry Pr.

—Who Pooped in the Park? Shenandoah National Park: Scats & Tracks for Kids. Robson, Gary D. 2006. (Who Pooped in the Park? Ser.). 48p. (J). (gr. -1-3). pap. *(978-1-56037-339-1(3))* Farcountry Pr.

—Who Pooped in the Sonoran Desert? Scats & Tracks for Kids. Robson, Gary D. 2006. (Who Pooped in the Park? Ser.). 48p. (J). (gr. -1-3). pap. 11.95 *(978-1-56037-349-0(0))* Farcountry Pr.

—Who Pooped in the Zoo? Exploring the Weirdest, Wackiest, Grossest, & Most Surprising Facts about Zoo Poop. Patterson, Caroline. 2011. 40p. (J). 14.95 *(978-1-56037-504-3(3))* Farcountry Pr.

—Who Pooped in the Zoo? San Diego Zoo: Exploring the Weirdest, Wackiest, Grossest & Most Surprising Facts about Zoo Poo. Patterson, Caroline. 2007. (Farcountry Explorer Bks.). 41p. (J). (gr. 3-7). pap. 14.95 *(978-1-56037-421-3(7))* Farcountry Pr.

—Who Pooped on the Colorado Plateau? Scat & Tracks for Kids. Robson, Gary D. 2008. (Who Pooped in the Park? Ser.). 48p. (J). (gr. 1-7). pap. 11.95 *(978-1-56037-430-5(6))* Farcountry Pr.

Rath, Robert. Go Wild for Puzzles Glacier National Park. Rath, Robert. 2008. 32p. (J). (gr. k-3). pap. 5.95 *(978-1-56037-428-2(4))* Farcountry Pr.

Rath, Robert & Wilson, Phil. Digging up Dinosaurs. Horner, Jack. 2007. 49p. (J). (gr. 3-7). pap. 14.95 *(978-1-56037-396-4(2))* Farcountry Pr.

Rather, Sherri. Upside down Danny, 1 vol. Rather, Sherri. 2009. 27p. pap. 24.95 *(978-1-61582-924-8(5))* America Star Bks.

Rathke, Kathryn. Lewis Carroll's Alice in Wonderland. 2010. (Penguin Young Readers, Level 4 Ser.). (ENG.). 48p. (J). (gr. 3-4). 4.99 *(978-0-448-45269-2(3)*, Penguin Young Readers) Penguin Young Readers Group.

Rathmann, Peggy. Buenas Noches, Gorila. Rathmann, Peggy. Mayobre, María Francisca, tr. from ENG. 2004. (SPA.). 36p. (gr. k). 12.99 *(978-980-257-265-6(9))* Ekare, Ediciones VEN. Dist: Lectorum Pubns., Inc.

—Buenas Noches, Gorila. Rathmann, Peggy. 2004. (SPA.). 34p. (J). (gr. -1 — 1). bds. 7.99 *(978-0-399-24300-4(3)*, G.P. Putnam's Sons Books for Young Readers) Penguin Young Readers Group.

—The Day the Babies Crawled Away. Rathmann, Peggy. 2003. (ENG.). 40p. (J). (gr. -1-k). 17.99 *(978-0-399-23196-4(X)*, G.P. Putnam's Sons Books for Young Readers) Penguin Young Readers Group.

—Good Night, Gorilla Book & Plush Package. Rathmann, Peggy. 2019. (ENG.). 40p. (J). (-k). 17.99 *(978-1-9848-1374-9(9)*, G.P. Putnam's Sons Books for Young Readers) Penguin Young Readers Group.

—Good Night, Gorilla (oversized Board Book) Rathmann, Peggy. 2004. (ENG.). 34p. (J). (gr. -1 — 1). bds. 15.99 *(978-0-399-24260-1(0)*, G.P. Putnam's Sons Books for Young Readers) Penguin Young Readers Group.

—Ruby the Copycat. Rathmann, Peggy. 2006. (Scholastic Bookshelf Ser.). (ENG.). 32p. (J). (gr. -1-3). per. 6.99 *(978-0-439-47228-9(8)*, Teaching Resources) Scholastic, Inc.

Ratnayake, Kumari/Keiko. Monsieur Bagel's War. Ratnayake, Kumari/Keiko. 2007. 25p. (J). spiral bd. 15.00 net. *(978-0-9797015-1-1(1))* Augustana College Geology Dept. Pr.

Ratner, Phillip. The Passover Zoo Seder, 1 vol. Guttman, S. Daniel. 2011. (ENG.). 32p. (J). (gr. k-3). 16.99 *(978-1-58980-972-7(6)*, Pelican Publishing) Arcadia Publishing.

Rattee, Michael Anthony. The Watch. Rattee, Michael Anthony. Smith, Amy Lynn, ed. 2018. (ENG.). 34p. (J). pap. 9.99 *(978-1-9795-0920-6(4))* CreateSpace Independent Publishing Platform.

Ratterree, Alice. Dangerous Jane: the Life & Times of Jane Addams, Crusader for Peace. Slade, Suzanne. (ENG.). 40p. (J). (gr. 1-5). 2020. 8.99 ***(978-1-68263-206-2(7))***; 2017. 17.95 *(978-1-56145-913-1(5))* Peachtree Publishing Co. Inc.

Ratterree, Alice. Lilliput, 1 vol. Gayton, Sam. (ENG.). 256p. (J). (gr. 3-6). 2017. pap. 8.95 *(978-1-68263-006-8(4))*; 2015. 16.95 *(978-1-56145-806-6(6))* Peachtree Publishing Co. Inc.

—The Wolf Keepers. Broach, Elise. 2016. (ENG.). 352p. (J). 16.99 *(978-0-8050-9899-0(2)*, 900124013, Holt, Henry & Co. Bks. For Young Readers) Holt, Henry & Co.

—The Wolf Keepers. Broach, Elise. 2018. (ENG.). 368p. (J). pap. 7.99 *(978-1-250-16501-5(6)*, 900186931) Square Fish.

Ratto, Cinzia. Jack & the Beanstalk. Arengo, Sue. 2006. (ENG.). 24p. 5.50 *(978-0-19-422538-0(0))* Oxford Univ. Pr. GBR. Dist: Oxford Univ. Pr., Inc.

Ratyna, Linda. Max Goes to Kindy. Lamaro, Glenda. 2009. 36p. pap. 16.44 *(978-1-4251-8830-6(3))* Trafford Publishing.

Rau, Dinah M. Ted E. Bear the Labradoodle. Rau-Tobin, Joanna. 2013. 32p. 19.95 *(978-1-59299-849-4(6))* Inkwater Pr.

Rauch, Micah. Crazy Contraptions: Build Rube Goldberg Machines That Swoop, Spin, Stack, & Swivel: With Hands-On Engineering Activities. Perdew, Laura. 2019. (Build It Yourself Ser.). 128p. (J). (gr. 4-6). 22.95 *(978-1-61930-823-7(1)*, 4e47223f-3b0d-4d23-9913-4a72026a2a10); pap. 17.95 *(978-1-61930-826-8(6)*, 8caf3c2e-40ff-4b82-a5ec-3bfc4be86a97) Nomad Pr.

—Fairground Physics: Motion, Momentum, & Magnets with Hands-On Science Activities. Smibert, Angie. 2020. (Build It Yourself Ser.). (ENG.). 128p. (J). (gr. 4-7). 22.95 *(978-1-61930-888-6(6)*, 86bdeda7-3b12-452c-a1cd-7e2071178513); pap. 17.95 *(978-1-61930-891-6(6)*, ac9d6116-c5b4-4786-b34a-974a9f2eb4ae) Nomad Pr.

—Kitchen Chemistry: Cool Crystals, Rockin' Reactions, & Magical Mixtures with Hands-On Science Activities. Light Brown, Cynthia. 2020. (Build It Yourself Ser.). (ENG.). 128p. (J). (gr. 4-7). 22.95 *(978-1-61930-884-8(3)*, 2731e45d-d794-4815-8b6d-785080ee900c); pap. 17.95 *(978-1-61930-887-9(8)*, 810fd769-34bb-48f3-9df2-4d97a6acd6a2) Nomad Pr.

—Wobbles. Venegas, Leah. 2018. (ENG.). 42p. (J). (gr. k-2). 21.99 *(978-0-578-40046-4(4))* Leah Venegas.

Rauchwerger, Lisa. Holy Days, Holy Ways. Halper, Sharon D. 2004. (gr. k-3). stu. ed. 8.95 *(978-0-8074-0793-6(3)*, 102073) URJ Pr.

Rauchwerger, Lisa. Chocolate Chip Challah. Rauchwerger, Lisa. 2004. (gr. k-3). pap., act. bk. ed. 9.95 *(978-0-8074-0736-3(4)*, 104035) URJ Pr.

—Chocolate Chip Challah: And Other Twists on the Jewish Holiday Table. Rauchwerger, Lisa. 2004. 127p. (J). (gr. k-3). pap. 17.95 *(978-0-8074-0700-4(3)*, 510606) URJ Pr.

—P: Winter, Spring & Summer Holidays. Rauchwerger, Lisa. 2004. (gr. k-3). pap., act. bk. ed. 9.95 *(978-0-8074-0775-2(5)*, 104036) URJ Pr.

Raude, Karina. The Traitors' Gate. Avi. 2010. (ENG.). 368p. (J). (gr. 5-8). pap. 8.99 *(978-0-689-85336-4(X)*, Atheneum Bks. for Young Readers) Simon & Schuster Children's Publishing.

—The Traitors' Gate. Avi. 2010. (ENG.). 368p. (J). (gr. 6-8). 21.19 *(978-0-689-85335-7(1))* Simon & Schuster, Inc.

Raúl, III. Otto Es un Rinoceronte. 2003. (SPA.). 102p. (J). (gr. 3-5). pap. 12.95 *(978-958-24-0179-5(6))* Santillana USA Publishing Co., Inc.

—Todo Cambio con Jakob. Boie, Kirsten. 2003. (SPA.). 166p. (J). (gr. 3-5). pap. 8.95 *(978-84-204-4764-3(1))* Santillana USA Publishing Co., Inc.

Raúl, III & Gonzalez, Raul, III. Low Riders in Space. Camper, Cathy. 2014. (Lowriders Ser.). (ENG.). 112p. (J). (gr. 3-7). pap. 9.99 *(978-1-4521-2869-6(3))*;Bk. 1. 22.99 *(978-1-4521-2155-0(9))* Chronicle Bks. LLC.

Raul, Gonzalez. Lowriders to the Center of the Earth, Bk. 2. Camper, Cathy. 2016. (Lowriders Ser.). (ENG.). 128p. (J). (gr. 3-7). pap. 9.99 *(978-1-4521-3836-7(2))* Chronicle Bks. LLC.

Rauscher, Amariah. I Am a Super Girl! Greenawalt, Kelly. 2019. (Princess Truly Ser.: 1). (ENG.). 48p. (J). (gr. -1-1). pap. 4.99 *(978-1-338-33998-7(2))* Scholastic, Inc.

—I Am Truly. Greenawalt, Kelly. 2017. (Princess Truly Ser.). (ENG.). 40p. (J). (gr. -1-k). 16.99 *(978-1-338-16720-7(0)*, Orchard Bks.) Scholastic, Inc.

—The Off I Go! Greenawalt, Kelly. 2019. (Princess Truly Ser.: 2). (ENG.). 48p. (J). (gr. -1-1). 23.99 *(978-1-338-34006-8(9))* Scholastic, Inc.

—Off I Go! Greenawalt, Kelly. 2019. (Princess Truly Ser.: 2). (ENG.). 48p. (J). (gr. -1-1). pap. 4.99 *(978-1-338-34003-7(4))* Scholastic, Inc.

—Princess Truly in My Magical, Sparkling Curls. Greenawalt, Kelly. 2018. (Princess Truly Ser.). (ENG.). 40p. (J). (gr. -1-k). 16.99 *(978-1-338-16719-1(7)*, Orchard Bks.) Scholastic, Inc.

Rautkallio, Outi. A Birch Tree's Year. Pere, Tuula. Korman, Susan, ed. 2018. (ENG.). 34p. (J). (gr. k-4). *(978-952-357-018-4(8))*; pap. *(978-952-357-015-3(3))* Wickwick oy.

—Björkens År: Swedish Edition of a Birch Tree's Year. Pere, Tuula. Nikolowski-Bogomoloff, Angelika, tr. 2018. (SWE.). 34p. (J). (gr. k-4). *(978-952-357-020-7(X))*; pap. *(978-952-357-017-7(X))* Wickwick oy.

—Blåsångarens Berättelser: Swedish Edition of a Bluebird's Memories. Pere, Tuula. Torstensson, Elisabeth, tr. 2018. (SWE.). 36p. (J). (gr. k-4). pap. *(978-952-7107-77-5(6))* Wickwick oy.

—A Bluebird's Memories. Pere, Tuula. Korman, Susan, ed. 2018. (ENG.). 36p. (J). (gr. k-4). pap. *(978-952-7107-75-1(X))* Wickwick oy.

—The Gnome's Garden. Pere, Tuula. Korman, Susan, ed. 2018. (ENG.). 40p. (J). (gr. k-4). *(978-952-357-012-2(9))*; pap. *(978-952-357-009-2(9))* Wickwick oy.

—Koivun Vuosi: Finnish Edition of a Birch Tree's Year. Pere, Tuula. 2018. (FIN.). 34p. (J). (gr. k-4). *(978-952-357-019-1(6))*; pap. *(978-952-357-016-0(1))* Wickwick oy.

—Menninkäisen Puutarha: Finnish Edition of the Gnome's Garden. Pere, Tuula. 2018. (FIN.). 40p. (J). (gr. k-4). *(978-952-357-013-9(7))*; pap. *(978-952-357-010-8(2))* Wickwick oy.

—The Mouse of the Opera. Pere, Tuula. Korman, Susan, ed. 2018. (ENG.). 40p. (J). (gr. 1-4). *(978-952-7107-03-4(2))*; pap. *(978-952-5878-14-1(7))* Wickwick oy.

—Musen På Operan: Swedish Edition of the Mouse of the Opera. Pere, Tuula. Nikolowski-Bogomoloff, Angelika, tr. 2018. (SWE.). 40p. (J). (gr. k-4). *(978-952-7107-05-8(9))*; pap. *(978-952-5878-94-3(5))* Wickwick oy.

—Oopperan Hiiri: Finnish Edition of the Mouse of the Opera. Pere, Tuula. 2018. (FIN.). 40p. (J). (gr. k-4). *(978-952-7107-04-1(0))*; pap. *(978-952-5878-95-0(3))* Wickwick oy.

—Sininen Lintu Muistelee: Finnish Edition of a Bluebird's Memories. Pere, Tuula. 2018. (FIN.). 36p. (J). (gr. k-4). pap. *(978-952-7107-76-8(8))* Wickwick oy.

—Trollpojkens Trädgård: Swedish Edition of the Gnome's Garden. Pere, Tuula. Nikolowski-Bogomoloff, Angelika, tr. 2018. (SWE.). 40p. (J). (gr. k-4). *(978-952-357-014-6(5))*; pap. *(978-952-357-011-5(0))* Wickwick oy.

Ravaglia, Paola, et al. 365 Awesome Facts & Records about Everything. Davies, Gill. McRae, Anne, ed. 2008. (365 Awesome Facts & Records Ser.). (ENG.). 176p. (J). (gr. 1-18). 19.95 *(978-88-6098-001-4(1))* McRae Bks. Srl ITA. Dist: Independent Pubs. Group.

Ravanelli, Terry. Sportsercise: A School Story about Exercise-Induced Asthma. Gosselin, Kim. 2nd ed. 2004. (Children's Asthma Ser.). (J). per. 9.95 *(978-1-891383-25-0(6))* JayJo Bks., LLC.

Rave, Arte. Graphing the Mystery. Roger, Rachel & Lineberry, Joe. 2019. (Gift of Numbers Ser.: Vol. 3). (ENG.). 40p. (J). (gr. 2-3). 16.95 ***(978-1-943419-47-0(7))***; pap. 11.95 ***(978-1-943419-48-7(5))*** Prospective Pr.

Raven, Gloria. Jackie Jamis: Jumping in the Hay! Raven, Gloria. 2019. (Jackie Jamis Ser.). (ENG.). 50p. (J). (gr. k-3). 19.95 *(978-0-578-42837-6(7))* Mrs. Raven's World.

Raven, Scarlett, jt. illus. see Cunningham, S. C.

Ravenhill, John A., jt. illus. see Fitzpatrick, Meg.

Ravets, Elizabeth. Valentine, Shell-B & Friends: Rock-E's Crush. Ogbodo, Angel. 2018. (Valentine, Shell-B & Friends Ser.: Vol. 5). (ENG.). 48p. (J). pap. 10.99 *(978-1-7296-7702-5(9))* CreateSpace Independent Publishing Platform.

Rawal, Ishita. Sandy & Mitzi: Off to the Zoo. Crofoot, Nancy. 2013. 48p. pap. 24.95 *(978-1-62709-868-7(2))* America Star Bks.

Rawat, Tania. Anna the Cat. De Freitas, Freddy. 2019. (ENG.). 30p. (J). pap. 13.50 ***(978-1-0908-4451-4(4))*** Independently Published.

Rawat, Tania. Christmas in the Barn, 1 vol. Crofoot, Nancy. 2009. 37p. pap. 24.95 *(978-1-61582-585-1(1))* America Star Bks.

Rawat, Tania. Hank the Surfer Kangaroo. De Freitas, Freddy. 2018. (ENG.). 50p. (J). pap. 14.00 ***(978-1-9850-4915-4(5))*** CreateSpace Independent Publishing Platform.

—Py the Koala. De Freitas, Freddy. 2019. (ENG.). 30p. (J). pap. 13.00 ***(978-1-6500-2078-5(3))*** Independently Published.

Rawat, Tania. Sandy & Mitzi: Their First Adventure, 1 vol. Crofoot, Nancy. 2009. 31p. pap. 24.95 *(978-1-60836-707-8(X))* America Star Bks.

Rawcliffe, Lee. The Grumpy Troll, 1 vol. Manci, Arlene. 2009. 25p. pap. 19.95 *(978-1-4489-2456-1(1))* PublishAmerica, Inc.

Rawlings, Louise. Al Final del Dia. Rock, Lois. (Coleccion Luz de Noche). (SPA.). (J). (gr. k-3). *(978-84-236-5039-2(1))* Edebé ESP. Dist: Lectorum Pubns., Inc.

—La Estrella Que Brilló. Rock, Lois. (Coleccion Luz de Noche). (SPA.). 32p. (J). (gr. k-3). *(978-84-236-4915-0(6))* Edebé ESP. Dist: Lectorum Pubns., Inc.

—La Gran Noticia. Rock, Lois. (Coleccion Luz de Noche). (SPA.). (J). (gr. k-3). *(978-84-236-4917-4(2))* Edebé ESP. Dist: Lectorum Pubns., Inc.

—Todos los Dias Contigo. Rock, Lois. (Coleccion Luz de Noche). (SPA.). (J). (gr. k-3). *(978-84-236-4916-7(4))* Edebé ESP. Dist: Lectorum Pubns., Inc.

Rawlings, Stacey and Monterio. My Heart Is a House. Rawlings, Stacey. 2018. (ENG.). 26p. (J). pap. 12.95 *(978-1-64140-574-4(0))* Christian Faith Publishing.

Rawson, Maurice. James Monroe, Good Neighbor Boy: Childhood of Famous Americans Series. Widdemer, Mabel Cleland. 2011. 200p. 44.95 *(978-1-258-07964-2(X))* Literary Licensing, LLC.

Ray, Christie Jones. Eliz. Ray, Christie Jones. 2012. 28p. pap. 15.00 *(978-0-9853223-1-1(4))* Rose Water Cottage Pr.

—Eliza & a Cottage Door. Ray, Christie Jones. 2012. 40p. pap. 15.00 *(978-0-9853223-0-4(6))* Rose Water Cottage Pr.

—Eliza Celebrates a Royal Wedding. Ray, Christie Jones. 2012. 48p. pap. 15.00 *(978-0-9853223-6-6(5))* Rose Water Cottage Pr.

—Eliza Has a Cousin. Ray, Christie Jones. 2012. 32p. pap. 15.00 *(978-0-9853223-5-9(7))* Rose Water Cottage Pr.

—Eliza Will Not Be Afraid. Ray, Christie Jones. 2012. 24p. pap. 12.00 *(978-0-9853223-7-3(3))* Rose Water Cottage Pr.

—Fox Family of Franklin. Ray, Christie Jones. 2012. 16p. pap. 10.00 *(978-0-9853223-3-5(0))* Rose Water Cottage Pr.

—Goat's Milk & Gardening. Ray, Christie Jones. 2013. 42p. pap. 15.00 *(978-0-9853223-9-7(X))* Rose Water Cottage Pr.

—Pick-A-Pick-a-Pumpkin. Ray, Christie Jones. 2012. 36p. pap. 12.00 *(978-0-9853223-4-2(9))* Rose Water Cottage Pr.

Ray, Dale Marie & Ray, Joli. Moody Mae. Ray, Dale Marie. 2013. 22p. (J). pap. 7.95 *(978-1-935018-86-5(8))* International Localization Network.

Ray, Deborah Kogan. The Little Tree. Cummings, E. E. 2010. (Holiday Books: Christmas Ser.). (ENG.). 24p. (J). (gr. -1-2). 21.19 *(978-0-517-88178-1(0))* Random House Publishing Group.

Ray, Deborah Kogan. The Impossible Voyage of Kon-Tiki. Ray, Deborah Kogan. 2015. 40p. (J). (gr. 2-5). lib. bdg. 16.95 *(978-1-58089-620-7(0))* Charlesbridge Publishing, Inc.

Ray, Eric. Tommy's War: A Parent Goes to War, 1. Avery, Pat McGrath. 2003. 36p. (J). per. 5.95 *(978-0-9663276-8-7(3))* Red Engine Pr.

Ray, Jane. Arion y el Delfin. Seth, Vikram. Dieguez Dieguez, Remedios, tr. 2004. (SPA.). 40p. (J). (gr. 2-4). 14.95 *(978-84-95939-74-6(6))* Blume ESP. Dist: Independent Pubs. Group.

—Classic Fairy Tales: Candlewick Illustrated Classic. 2009. (Candlewick Illustrated Classics Ser.). (ENG.). 224p. (J). (gr. 5-4). pap. 12.99 *(978-0-7636-4212-9(6))* Candlewick Pr.

—Hummingbird. Davies, Nicola. 2019. (ENG.). 32p. (J). (gr. k-3). 16.99 *(978-1-5362-0538-1(9))* Candlewick Pr.

—Stories for a Fragile Planet: Traditional Tales about Caring for the Earth. Steven, Kenneth. ed. 2010. (ENG.). 48p. (J). (gr. 1-7). 13.99 *(978-0-7459-6157-6(6))* Lion Hudson PLC GBR. Dist: Independent Pubs. Group.

—The Unicorn Prince. Pirotta, Saviour. 2020. 32p. (J). (gr. -1-k). pap. 10.99 *(978-1-4083-3643-4(X)*, Orchard Bks.) Hachette Children's Group GBR. Dist: Hachette Bk. Group.

—William Shakespeare's the Tempest. Ellinas, Georgia. 2020. (ENG.). 32p. (J). (gr. 1-4). 17.99 *(978-1-5362-1144-3(3))* Candlewick Pr.

—Zeraffa Giraffa. Hofmeyr, Dianne. 2015. (ENG.). 40p. (J). pap. 9.99 *(978-1-84780-661-1(9)*, Frances Lincoln Children's Bks.) Quarto Publishing Group UK GBR. Dist: Littlehampton Bk Services, Ltd.

Ray, Jane. Adam & Eve & the Garden of Eden. Ray, Jane. 2005. 32p. (J). 17.00 *(978-0-8028-5278-6(5))* Eerdmans, William B. Publishing Co.

R

—Cinderella. Ray, Jane. 2012. (ENG.). 12p. (J). (gr. k-4). 19.99 (978-0-7636-6175-5(9)) Candlewick Pr.

Ray, Joli, jt. illus. see Ray, Dale Marie.

Ray, Michael. When Will I See Aunt Carole? Fairdoth, M. L. 2012. (J). 26p. 19.95 (978-1-61863-326-2(0)); 28p. pap. 9.99 (978-1-61863-324-8(4)) Bookstand Publishing.

Ray, Mike. Bad-Luck Basketball, 1 vol. Maddox, Jake. 2014. (Jake Maddox JV Ser.). (ENG.). 96p. (J). (gr. 4-6). 25.99 (978-1-4342-9156-1(1), Stone Arch Bks.) Capstone.

—Gridiron Showdown, 1 vol. Maddox, Jake. 2014. (Jake Maddox JV Ser.). (ENG.). 96p. (J). (gr. 4-6). 25.99 (978-1-4342-9155-4(3), Stone Arch Bks.) Capstone.

—Outfield Outcast, 1 vol. Maddox, Jake. 2014. (Jake Maddox JV Ser.). (ENG.). 96p. (J). (gr. 4-6). 25.99 (978-1-4342-9153-0(7), Stone Arch Bks.) Capstone.

—Picture a Slap Shot: A Hockey Drawing Book, 1 vol. Wacholtz, Anthony. 2013. (Drawing with Sports Illustrated Kids Ser.). (ENG.). 64p. (J). (gr. 5-9). 34.65 (978-1-4765-3105-2(6)) Capstone.

—Picture a Touchdown: A Football Drawing Book, 1 vol. Wacholtz, Anthony. 2013. (Drawing with Sports Illustrated Kids Ser.). (ENG.). 64p. (J). (gr. 5-9). 34.65 (978-1-4765-3104-5(8)) Capstone.

—Second-Chance Soccer, 1 vol. Maddox, Jake. 2014. (Jake Maddox JV Ser.). (ENG.). 96p. (J). (gr. 4-6). 25.99 (978-1-4342-9154-7(5), Stone Arch Bks.) Capstone.

Ray, Mike & Haya, Erwin. Drawing with Sports Illustrated Kids. Wacholtz, Anthony. 2013. (Drawing with Sports Illustrated Kids Ser.). (ENG.). 64p. (J). (gr. 5-9). lib. bdg., lib. bdg., lib. bdg. 138.60 (978-1-4765-3741-2(0)) Capstone.

Ray, Mike, jt. illus. see Haya, Erwin.

Ray, Noah. Otto the Otter Takes a Bath. Pichon, Lauren. 2019. (ENG.). 42p. (J). pap. 10.99 (978-1-0904-5015-9(X)) Independently Published.

Ray, Ralph. The Lion's Paw. White, Robb. 2008. 243p. (J). (gr. 4-7). 29.95 (978-0-9820932-0-7(9)) A. W. Ink, Inc.

Ray, Rex. 10,000 Dresses. Ewert, Marcus. 2008. (ENG.). 32p. (J). (gr. k-4). 16.95 (978-1-58322-850-0(0), Triangle Square) Seven Stories Pr.

Ray, Sarah. The Book of Me. Frost, Adam. 2017. 160p. (J). pap. (978-1-4088-7681-7(7), 297453, Bloomsbury Children's Bks.) Bloomsbury Publishing Plc.

Raye, Rebekah. The Secret Bay, 1 vol. Ridley, Kimberly. 2019. (Tilbury House Nature Book Ser.: 0). (ENG.). 40p. (J). (gr. 1-6). pap. 8.95 (978-0-88448-751-7(2), 884751) Tilbury Hse. Pubs.

—Secret Pool, 1 vol. Ridley, Kimberly. 2013. (Tilbury House Nature Book Ser.: 0). (ENG.). 32p. (J). (gr. 1-7). 16.95 (978-0-88448-339-7(8), 884339) Tilbury Hse. Pubs.

—The Secret Pool, 1 vol. Ridley, Kimberly. 2016. (Tilbury House Nature Book Ser.: 0). (ENG.). 36p. (J). (gr. 1-7). pap. 9.95 (978-0-88448-494-3(7), 884494) Tilbury Hse. Pubs.

—Swimming Home, 1 vol. Shetterly, Susan Hand. 2014. (Tilbury House Nature Book Ser.: 0). (ENG.). 32p. (J). (gr. 1-6). 16.95 (978-0-88448-354-0(1), 884354) Tilbury Hse. Pubs.

Raye, Rebekah. Bear-Ly There, 1 vol. Raye, Rebekah. 2009. (ENG.). 32p. (J). (gr. 3-6). 16.95 (978-0-88448-314-4(2), 884314) Tilbury Hse. Pubs.

—The Very Best Bed, 1 vol. Raye, Rebekah. 2015. (Tilbury House Nature Book Ser.: 0). (ENG.). 36p. (J). (gr. -1-3). pap. 9.95 (978-0-88448-410-3(6), 884410) Tilbury Hse. Pubs.

Rayevsky, Robert. Bernal & Florinda: A Spanish Tale. Kimmel, Eric A. 2004. 29p. (J). (gr. k-4). reprint ed. 16.00 (978-0-7567-7906-1(5)) DIANE Publishing Co.

—Hey, You! Poems to Skyscrapers, Mosquitoes, & Other Fun Things. Janeczko, Paul B. 2007. 40p. (J). (gr. 2-5). lib. bdg. 16.89 (978-0-06-052348-0(4)) HarperCollins Pubs.

—Two Fools & a Horse: An Orginal Tale, 1 vol. Derby, Sally. 2003. (ENG.). 32p. (J). (gr. k-3). 16.95 (978-0-7614-5119-8(6)) Marshall Cavendish Corp.

Rayla, Tim. The Wolf Who Cried Boy. Hartman, Bob. ed. 2004. (J). (gr. 1-3). spiral bd. (978-0-616-14574-6(8)) Canadian National Institute for the Blind/Institut National Canadien pour les Aveugles.

Raymond, Alejandro. I Bee the Bee, 1 vol. Milligan, Joe. 2016. (ENG.). 32p. (J). pap. 9.95 (978-1-4556-2201-6(X), Pelican Publishing) Arcadia Publishing.

Raymond, Janet Y. Pokey Pig's Picnic. Young, Polly G. 2007. (J). pap. 15.00 (978-0-8059-7298-6(6)) Dorrance Publishing Co., Inc.

Raymundo, Peter. The Monkey & the Bee. Bloom, C. P. 2015. (Monkey Goes Bananas Ser.). (ENG.). 40p. (J). (gr. -1-2). 14.95 (978-1-4197-0886-2(4), Abrams Bks. for Young Readers) Abrams, Inc.

—The Monkey Goes Bananas. Bloom, C. P. 2014. (ENG.). 40p. (J). (gr. -1-2). 14.95 (978-1-4197-0885-5(6), Abrams Bks. for Young Readers) Abrams, Inc.

Raymundo, Peter. I Am Not a Fish! Raymundo, Peter. 2019. 32p. (J). (-k). 17.99 (978-0-525-55459-2(9), Dial Bks) Penguin Young Readers Group.

Rayner, Catherine. The Further Adventures of Gobbolino & the Little Wooden Horse. Moray Williams, Ursula. 2018. (ENG.). 320p. (J). (gr. 2-4). 14.99 (978-1-5098-6037-1(1)) Pan Macmillan GBR. Dist: Independent Pubs. Group.

—Gobbolino the Witch's Cat. Moray Williams, Ursula. 2018. (ENG.). 256p. (J). (gr. k-3). 14.99 (978-1-5098-6036-4(3)) Pan Macmillan GBR. Dist: Independent Pubs. Group.

—Hello, Horse. French, Vivian. 2018. (ENG.). 40p. (J). (gr. k-3). 15.99 (978-1-5362-0167-3(7)) Candlewick Pr.

—Posy. Newbery, Linda. 2008. (ENG.). 32p. (J). (gr. -1-k). 16.99 (978-1-4169-7112-2(2), Atheneum Bks. for Young Readers) Simon & Schuster Children's Publishing.

Rayner, Catherine. Abigail. Rayner, Catherine. 2013. (ENG.). 32p. (J). (gr. -1-2). 14.99 (978-1-58925-147-2(4)) Tiger Tales.

Rayner, Catherine. Arlo the Lion Who Couldn't Sleep. Rayner, Catherine. 2020. (ENG.). 32p. (J). (gr. -1-1). 17.99 **(978-1-68263-222-2(9))** Peachtree Publishing Co. Inc.

Rayner, Catherine. Augustus & His Smile. Rayner, Catherine. 10th ed. 2016. (ENG.). 32p. (J). (gr. -1-2). 16.99 (978-1-68010-005-1(X)) Tiger Tales.

—Counting Stars. Rayner, Catherine. 2016. (ENG.). 28p. (J). (gr. -1-k). bds. 7.99 (978-1-58925-225-7(X)) Tiger Tales.

—Ernest, the Moose Who Doesn't Fit. Rayner, Catherine. 2010. (ENG.). 32p. (J). (gr. -1-1). 18.99 (978-0-374-32217-5(1), 9780374322175, Farrar, Straus & Giroux (BYR)) Farrar, Straus & Giroux.

—Harris Finds His Feet. Rayner, Catherine. 2020. (ENG.). 24p. (J). (-k). bds. 9.99 (978-1-68010-596-4(5)) Tiger Tales.

—One Happy Tiger. Rayner, Catherine. 2017. (ENG.). 24p. (J). (gr. -1-k). bds. 9.99 (978-1-58925-234-9(9)) Tiger Tales.

Rayner, Olivia. On the Farm: A Barnyard Book. Imperato, Teresa. 2005. 10p. (J). 7.95 (978-1-58117-270-6(2), Intervisual/Piggy Toes) Bendon, Inc.

—On the Go! A Transportation Book. Imperato, Teresa. 2005. 10p. (J). 7.95 (978-1-58117-271-3(0), Intervisual/Piggy Toes) Bendon, Inc.

—World Book Myths & Legends Series, 8 vols., Vol. 8. 2007. (World Book Myths & Legends Ser.). 64p. (gr. 4-8). 239.00 (978-0-7166-2613-8(6), 31020) World Bk., Inc.

Rayner, Shoo. Alien Invasion! (Mudpuddle Farm) Morpurgo, Michael. 2018. (Mudpuddle Farm Ser.). (ENG.). 144p. (J). 4.99 (978-0-00-826910-4(6), HarperCollins Children's Bks.) HarperCollins Pubs. Ltd. GBR. Dist: HarperCollins Pubs.

—The Big, Bad City. 2015. (Collins Big Cat Ser.). (ENG.). 24p. (J). (gr. 2-2). pap. 8.99 (978-0-00-759109-1(8)) HarperCollins Pubs. Ltd. GBR. Dist: Independent Pubs. Group.

—Cock-A-Doodle-Do! (Mudpuddle Farm) Morpurgo, Michael. 2018. (Mudpuddle Farm Ser.). (ENG.). 144p. (J). 4.99 (978-0-00-826911-1(4), HarperCollins Children's Bks.) HarperCollins Pubs. Ltd. GBR. Dist: HarperCollins Pubs.

—Pigs Might Fly! (Mudpuddle Farm) Morpurgo, Michael. 2018. (Mudpuddle Farm Ser.). (ENG.). 144p. (J). 4.99 (978-0-00-826909-8(2), HarperCollins Children's Bks.) HarperCollins Pubs. Ltd. GBR. Dist: HarperCollins Pubs.

—You Wait till I'm Older Than You! Rosen, Michael. 128p. (J). 7.95 (978-0-14-038014-9(0)) Penguin Bks., Ltd. GBR. Dist: Trafalgar Square Publishing.

Rayner, Shoo. Archimedes: The Man Who Invented the Death Ray. Rayner, Shoo. 2017. (ENG.). (J). (gr. 2-6). pap. (978-1-908944-35-1(8)) Rayner, Shoo.

—Collins Big Cat Phonics for Letters & Sounds - How to Draw Cat & Dog: Band 05/Green, Bd. 5. Rayner, Shoo. 2018. (Collins Big Cat Phonics Ser.). (ENG.). 24p. (J). (gr. k-1). pap. 8.99 (978-0-00-825171-0(1)) HarperCollins Pubs. Ltd. GBR. Dist: Independent Pubs. Group.

—Collins Big Cat Phonics for Letters & Sounds - Nibble, Nosh & Gnasher: Band 07/Turquoise. Rayner, Shoo. 2018. (Collins Big Cat Phonics Ser.). (ENG.). 24p. (J). (gr. 1-2). pap. 8.99 (978-0-00-825179-6(7)) HarperCollins Pubs. Ltd. GBR. Dist: Independent Pubs. Group.

—Euclid: The Man Who Invented Geometry. Rayner, Shoo. 2nd ed. 2017. (Mega Minds Ser.: Vol. 1). (ENG.). (J). (gr. 4-6). pap. (978-1-908944-36-8(6)) Rayner, Shoo.

—How to Draw Ancient Greek Stuff Real Easy: Easy Step by Step Drawing Guide. Rayner, Shoo. 2018. (Draw Stuff Real Easy Ser.: Vol. 1). (ENG.). (J). (gr. 3-6). 54p. (978-1-908944-39-9(0)); 52p. pap. (978-1-908944-38-2(2)) Rayner, Shoo.

—The Monster Joke Book: Band 12/Copper (Collins Big Cat) Rayner, Shoo. 2007. (Collins Big Cat Ser.). (ENG.). 32p. (J). (gr. 2-4). pap. 9.99 (978-0-00-723075-4(3)) HarperCollins Pubs. Ltd. GBR. Dist: Independent Pubs. Group.

—Pandora: The Most Curious Girl in the World. Rayner, Shoo. 2018. (ENG.). 32p. (J). (gr. k-4). (978-1-908944-41-2(2)) Rayner, Shoo.

Rayner, Shoo. Ricky Rocket - a Present from Earth: Space Boy, Ricky, Learns That Chocolate Is Not the Favourite Food in the Universe - Perfect for Newly Confident Readers. Rayner, Shoo. 2020. (Ricky Rocket Ser.: Vol. 2). (ENG.). 50p. (J). (gr. k-2). pap. 7.80 **(978-1-6611-7595-5(3))** Independently Published.

—Ricky Rocket - Sweet Disaster: Has Ricky Poisoned the New Neighbour's Kids! - Perfect for Newly Confident Readers. Rayner, Shoo. 2020. (Ricky Rocket Ser.: Vol. 3). (ENG.). 50p. (J). (gr. k-2). pap. 7.80 **(978-1-6611-1400-8(8))** Independently Published.

—Ricky Rocket - up & Away: Space Boy, Ricky, Learns to Ride His Rocket Without Stabilisers - Perfect for Newly Confident Readers. Rayner, Shoo. 2020. (Ricky Rocket Ser.: Vol. 1). (ENG.). 50p. (J). (gr. k-2). pap. 7.80 **(978-1-6610-1881-8(5))** Independently Published.

Rayner, Shoo. Viking Vik: Three Exciting Viking Stories. Rayner, Shoo. 2017. (ENG.). (J). (gr. 2-5). pap. (978-1-908944-33-7(1)) Rayner, Shoo.

Rayner, Shoo. Cat & Dog Play Hide & Seek: Band 02A/Red a (Collins Big Cat) Rayner, Shoo, concept. 2006. (Collins Big Cat Ser.). (ENG.). 16p. (J). (gr. -1-k). pap. 7.99 (978-0-00-718660-0(6)) HarperCollins Pubs. Ltd. GBR. Dist: Independent Pubs. Group.

Raynor, Jackie. Fairytale Mix-up. Smith, Jane. 2005. 12p. (J). (gr. -1-3). per. 10.95 (978-1-58117-419-9(5), Intervisual/Piggy Toes) Bendon, Inc.

Raynor, Maggie. Alan Apostrophe. Cooper, Barbara. 2004. (Meet the Puncs: A Remarkable Punctuation Family Ser.). 32p. (gr. 1-4). lib. bdg. 27.00 (978-0-8368-4223-4(5), Gareth Stevens Learning Library) Stevens, Gareth Publishing LLLP.

—Christopher Comma. Cooper, Barbara. 2004. (Meet the Puncs: A Remarkable Punctuation Family Ser.). 32p. (gr. 1-4). lib. bdg. 27.00 (978-0-8368-4224-1(3), Gareth Stevens Learning Library) Stevens, Gareth Publishing LLLP.

—Emma Exclamation Point. Cooper, Barbara. 2004. (Meet the Puncs: A Remarkable Punctuation Family Ser.). 32p. (gr. 1-4). lib. bdg. 27.00 (978-0-8368-4225-8(1), Gareth Stevens Learning Library) Stevens, Gareth Publishing LLLP.

—Hannah Hyphen-Hyphen. Cooper, Barbara. 2004. (Meet the Puncs: A Remarkable Punctuation Family Ser.). 32p. (gr. 1-4). lib. bdg. 27.00 (978-0-8368-4226-5(X), Gareth Stevens Learning Library) Stevens, Gareth Publishing LLLP.

Raysor, Joan. David & the Phoenix. Ormondroyd, Edward. 2012. (ENG.). 191p. (J). (gr. 3-6). pap. 2.99 (978-1-930900-58-5(9)) Purple Hse. Pr.

Rayyan, Omar. The Case of the Purloined Professor, 0 vols. Cox, Judy. 2009. (Tails of Frederick & Ishbu Ser.: 0). (ENG.). 256p. (J). (gr. 5-7). 16.99 (978-0-7614-5544-8(2), 9780761455448, Two Lions) Amazon Publishing.

—Castle Avamir. Duey, Kathleen. ed. 2005. 76p. (J). lib. bdg. 15.00 (978-1-59054-899-8(X)) Fitzgerald Bks.

—Castle Avamir. Duey, Kathleen. 2004. (Unicorn's Secret Ser.). 73p. (gr. 2-5). 15.00 (978-0-7569-3357-9(9)) Perfection Learning Corp.

—Castle Avamir. Duey, Kathleen. 2003. (Unicorn's Secret Ser.: 7). (ENG.). 80p. (J). (gr. 2-5). pap. 5.99 (978-0-689-85372-2(6), Simon & Schuster/Paula Wiseman Bks.) Simon & Schuster/Paula Wiseman Bks.

—Danger at Snow Hill, 3. Casanova, Mary. 2006. (Dog Watch Ser.: 3). (ENG.). 128p. (J). (gr. 3-7). pap. 4.99 (978-0-689-86812-2(X)) Simon & Schuster, Inc.

—Dog-Napped!, 2. Casanova, Mary. 2006. (Dog Watch Ser.: 2). (ENG.). 132p. (J). (gr. 3-6). 17.44 (978-0-689-86811-5(1)) Simon & Schuster, Inc.

—The Dragon of Never-Was. Downer, Ann. 2008. (ENG.). 320p. (J). (gr. 3-6). pap. 14.99 (978-1-4169-5453-8(8), Atheneum Bks. for Young Readers) Simon & Schuster Children's Publishing.

—Extreme Stunt Dogs. Casanova, Mary. 2007. (Dog Watch Ser.: 5). (ENG.). 144p. (J). (gr. 3-7). pap. 4.99 (978-1-4169-4782-0(5), Simon & Schuster/Paula Wiseman Bks.) Simon & Schuster/Paula Wiseman Bks.

—Hatching Magic. Downer, Ann. 2004. 242p. 16.00 (978-0-7569-3481-1(8)) Perfection Learning Corp.

—Joha Makes a Wish: A Middle Eastern Tale, 0 vols. Kimmel, Eric A. 2013. (ENG.). 40p. (J). (gr. k-3). pap. 7.99 (978-1-4778-1687-5(9), 9781477816875, Two Lions) Amazon Publishing.

—The Journey Home. Duey, Kathleen. 2003. (Unicorn's Secret Ser.: 8). (ENG.). 80p. (J). (gr. 2-5). pap. 5.99 (978-0-689-85374-6(2), Aladdin) Simon & Schuster Children's Publishing.

—The Mountains of the Moon. Duey, Kathleen. ed. 2005. 76p. (J). lib. bdg. 15.00 (978-1-59054-907-0(4)) Fitzgerald Bks.

—My Kitten's First Year. 2008. (ENG.). 24p. (J). (gr. -1-3). 12.99 (978-0-8249-5572-4(2), Ideal Pubns.) Worthy Publishing.

—The Mystery of the Burmese Bandicoot, 1 vol. Cox, Judy. 2007. (Tails of frederick & Ishbu Ser.). (ENG.). 224p. (J). (gr. 5-9). lib. bdg. 16.99 (978-0-7614-5376-5(8)) Marshall Cavendish Corp.

—Possum Summer. Blom, Jen K. 2011. (ENG.). 256p. (J). (gr. 3-7). 17.95 (978-0-8234-2331-6(X)) Holiday Hse., Inc.

—The Silver Bracelet. Duey, Kathleen. ed. 2005. 90p. (J). lib. bdg. 15.00 (978-1-59054-917-9(1)) Fitzgerald Bks.

—The Sunset Gates. Duey, Kathleen. ed. 2005. 76p. (J). lib. bdg. 15.00 (978-1-59054-918-6(X)) Fitzgerald Bks.

—To Catch a Burglar, 4. Casanova, Mary. 2007. (Dog Watch Ser.: 4). (ENG.). 144p. (J). (gr. 3-7). pap. 7.99 (978-0-689-86813-9(8)) Simon & Schuster, Inc.

—Trouble in Pembrook, 1. Casanova, Mary. 2006. (Dog Watch Ser.: 1). (ENG.). 128p. (J). (gr. 3-7). pap. 6.99 (978-0-689-86810-8(3)) Simon & Schuster, Inc.

—True Heart. Duey, Kathleen. ed. 2005. 76p. (J). lib. bdg. 15.00 (978-1-59054-920-9(1)) Fitzgerald Bks.

—True Heart. Duey, Kathleen. 2004. (Unicorn's Secret Ser.). 75p. (gr. 2-5). 15.00 (978-0-7569-3385-2(4)) Perfection Learning Corp.

—True Heart. Duey, Kathleen. 2003. (Unicorn's Secret Ser.: 6). (ENG.). 80p. (J). (gr. 2-5). pap. 5.99 (978-0-689-85370-8(X), Aladdin) Simon & Schuster Children's Publishing.

—The Turtle-Hatching Mystery, 5. Casanova, Mary. 2008. (Dog Watch Ser.: 6). (ENG.). 144p. (J). (gr. 3-7). pap. 8.99 (978-1-4169-4783-7(3)) Simon & Schuster, Inc.

—The Unicorn's Secret Collection: Moonsilver; the Silver Thread; the Silver Bracelet; the Mountains of the Moon; the Sunset Gates; True Heart; Castle Avamir; the Journey Home. Duey, Kathleen. ed. 2018. (Unicorn's Secret Ser.). (ENG.). 672p. (J). (gr. 2-5). pap. 46.99 (978-1-5344-3937-5(4), Aladdin) Simon & Schuster Children's Publishing.

—Waggit Again. Howe, Peter. 2010. (Waggit Ser.: 2). (ENG.). 320p. (J). (gr. 5). pap. 6.99 (978-0-06-124266-3(7)) HarperCollins Pubs.

—Waggit Forever. Howe, Peter. (Waggit Ser.: 3). (ENG.). (J). (gr. 5). 2011. 288p. pap. 7.99 (978-0-06-176516-2(3)); 2010. 272p. 16.99 (978-0-06-176517-9(1)) HarperCollins Pubs.

—Waggit's Tale. Howe, Peter. 2009. (Waggit Ser.: 1). (ENG.). 304p. (J). (gr. 5). pap. 6.99 (978-0-06-124263-2(2)) HarperCollins Pubs.

Rayyan, Sheila. Sacred Scars, No. 2. Duey, Kathleen. 2009. (Resurrection of Magic Ser.: 2). (ENG.). 560p. (YA). (gr. 7-18). 18.99 (978-0-689-84095-1(0), Atheneum Bks. for Young Readers) Simon & Schuster Children's Publishing.

—Skin Hunger, 1. Duey, Kathleen. 2007. (Resurrection of Magic Ser.: Bk. 1). (ENG.). 357p. (YA). (gr. 7-12). 24.94 (978-0-689-84093-7(4)) Simon & Schuster, Inc.

Raz, Rachel, photos by. The Colors of Israel, Vol. Raz, Rachel. 2015. (ENG., 24p. (J). (gr. -1-2). 7.99 (978-1-4677-5540-5(0), 9781467755405); lib. bdg. 17.99 (978-1-4677-5539-9(7), 9781467755399) Lerner Publishing Group. (Kar-Ben Publishing).

Razavi, Firouzeh. Jolly Talker. Razavi, Firouzeh. 2018. (ENG.). 38p. (J). pap. 9.95 (978-0-578-42265-7(4)) Razavi, Firouzeh Bks.

—The Squirrel Family Adventures. Razavi, Firouzeh. 2018. (ENG.). 62p. (J). pap. 12.75 (978-0-692-11249-6(9), FR Publishing) Razavi, Firouzeh Bks.

Razumova, Alena. One & Two. Copper, Jenny. 2019. (Touch, Feel, Explore! Ser.). (ENG.). 10p. (J). (— 1). 7.99 (978-1-78700-984-4(X)) Top That! Publishing PLC GBR. Dist: Independent Pubs. Group.

—Red & Blue. Copper, Jenny. 2019. (Touch, Feel, Explore! Ser.). (ENG.). 10p. (J). (— 1). 7.99 (978-1-78700-985-1(8)) Top That! Publishing PLC GBR. Dist: Independent Pubs. Group.

Razzi, Manuela. Brave. Ferrari, Alessandro. 2020. (Disney Princesses Ser.). (ENG.). 52p. (J). (gr. 2-6). lib. bdg. 28.50 **(978-1-5321-4559-9(4)**, 35206, Graphic Novels) Spotlight.

Rchards, Virginia Helen. I Pray the Stations of the Cross. Dateno, Maria Grace. 2006. (J). 4.50 (978-0-8198-3691-5(5)) Pauline Bks. & Media.

Rea, Arianna, et al. Inside Out. Ferrari, Alessandro. 2020. (Disney & Pixar Movies Ser.). (ENG.). 52p. (J). (gr. 2-6). lib. bdg. 28.50 **(978-1-5321-4552-0(7)**, 35199, Graphic Novels) Spotlight.

Rea, Ba. Monarch! Come Play with Me. Rea, Ba. 2006. 32p. (J). per. 10.95 (978-0-9657472-5-7(5)) Bas Relief, LLC.

Rea, Nathan. Anything Is Possible: The Ben Carson Story. Blum, Denise. 2015. (ENG.). 28p. (J). pap. 10.00 (978-0-9899479-1-6(2)) Mainstay Publishing.

Rea, Simone. Nasla's Dream. Roumiguière, Cécile. 2020. (ENG.). 32p. (J). (gr. -1-3). 17.95 **(978-1-61689-950-9(6))** Princeton Architectural Pr.

Read, Barbara. The Adventures of Boston: The Nosy Beagle. Culp, Elzie Lynn. 2018. (ENG.). 28p. (J). 22.95 (978-1-64300-174-6(4)); pap. 12.95 (978-1-64300-173-9(6)) Covenant Bks.

Read, Helen. ABCedar Key: An Island Alphabet. Needham, Miriam. 2018. (ENG.). 54p. (J). pap. 19.95 (978-1-62023-600-0(1), bf40f072-9b12-4462-bbda-9c8ccc8f3aa5) Atlantic Publishing Group, Inc.

Read, Kate. One Fox: A Counting Book Thriller. Read, Kate. 2019. (ENG.). 36p. (J). (gr. -1-1). 16.95 (978-1-68263-131-7(1)) Peachtree Publishing Co. Inc.

Read, Laura Catherine. Belly, Belly! Spray Ph D, Carrie G. Read. 2019. (ENG.). 24p. (J). pap. 9.99 **(978-1-6983-7836-7(X))** Independently Published.

Ready, D. M. The Opposites. Erickson, Sharon. 2008. 24p. pap. 24.95 (978-1-60672-551-1(3)) America Star Bks.

Reagan, Mike & Norstrand, Torstein. Seven Wonders Book 1: the Colossus Rises, Bk. 1. Lerangis, Peter. 2013. (Seven Wonders Ser.: 1). (ENG.). 368p. (J). (gr. 3-7). 17.99 (978-0-06-207040-1(1)) HarperCollins Pubs.

Reagan, Mike, jt. illus. see Norstrand, Torstein.

Reagan, Susan. Lights Out. Arnold, Marsha Diane. 2020. (ENG.). 32p. (J). (gr. 1-3). 18.99 **(978-1-56846-340-7(5)**, Creative Editions) Creative Co., The.

Reagan, Susan. My Sing-Along Bible: 50 Easy-Read Stories + 50 Fun Bible Songs. Elkins, Stephen. 2015. (ENG.). 96p. (J). 12.99 (978-1-4964-0543-2(9), 4612218) Tyndale Hse. Pubs.

—Randall Reindeer's Naughty & Nice Report. DePrisco, Dorothea. 2011. (ENG.). (J). (gr. -1-3). 24.95 (978-1-61524-365-5(8), Intervisual/Piggy Toes) Bendon, Inc.

—Simon Says Open the Book. Zebrowska, Emilia. 2019. (ENG.). 14p. (J). (gr. -1-1). 8.99 (978-1-56846-330-8(8), Creative Editions) Creative Co., The.

—You & Me. Dotlich, Rebecca Kai. 2018. 14p. (J). (gr. -1-1). bds. 9.99 (978-1-56846-321-6(9), Creative Editions) Creative Co., The.

Reagan, Susan Joy. Bitsy's Harvest Party. Carlson, Melody. 2005. 32p. (J). (gr. -1-4). 12.99 (978-0-8054-2684-7(1)) B&H Publishing Group.

—Forgive Others. Carlson, Melody. 2004. (Just Like Jesus Said Ser.). 32p. (J). (gr. -1-5). 12.99 (978-0-8054-2385-3(0)) B&H Publishing Group.

—Special Times Bible Prayers for Toddlers. Elkins, Stephen. 2004. (Special Times Ser.). 32p. (J). (gr. -1-18). 9.97 (978-0-8054-2660-1(4)) B&H Publishing Group.

—Special Times Bible Promises for Toddlers. Elkins, Stephen. 2005. (Special Times Ser.). 32p. (J). (gr. -1-18). 9.97 (978-0-8054-2678-6(7)) B&H Publishing Group.

—'Twas the Night: The Nativity Story. Carlson, Melody. 2005. 32p. (J). (gr. -1-4). 12.99 (978-0-8054-2683-0(3)) B&H Publishing Group.

—When the Creepy Things Come Out! Carlson, Melody. 2003. 32p. (J). (gr. -1-5). 12.99 (978-0-8054-2687-8(6)) B&H Publishing Group.

Ream, Robaire. Shadow on the Moon: A Child's Guide to the Discovery of the Universe. Matejovsky, Char. 2014. (J). (978-1-59815-151-0(7)) Polebridge Pr.

Reasoner, Charles. Bear Hugs. 2015. (J). (978-1-4795-5944-2(X), Picture Window Bks.) Capstone.

—A Day at the Zoo. Lee, Howard. 2009. (Inside Outside Board Bks.). 10p. (J). bds. 10.99 (978-1-934650-55-4(2)) Just For Kids Pr., LLC.

—Honey Bunny. 2015. (J). (978-1-4795-5945-9(8), Picture Window Bks.) Capstone.

—I'm Just a Little Pig. Thompson, Kate. 2014. (ENG.). 12p. (gr. -1). (978-1-78244-590-6(0)) Top That! Publishing PLC.

—Peep! Peep! 2015. (J). (978-1-4795-5943-5(1), Picture Window Bks.) Capstone.

—Puppy Love. 2015. (J). (978-1-4795-5946-6(6), Picture Window Bks.) Capstone.

—Who's There on Halloween? Beall, Pamela Conn & Nipp, Susan Hagen. 2003. 18p. (J). bds. 4.99 (978-0-8431-0495-0(3), Price Stern Sloan) Penguin Publishing Group.

—Who's There on Halloween? Beall, Pamela Conn & Nipp, Susan Hagen. 2003. 18p. (J). (gr. -1-k). bds. 5.99 (978-0-8431-0510-0(0), Price Stern Sloan) Penguin Young Readers Group.

Reasoner, Charles. I'm Just a Bird. Reasoner, Charles. 2007. (I'm Just Book Ser.). 12p. (J). (gr. -1). bds. (978-1-84666-289-8(3), Tide Mill Pr.) Top That! Publishing PLC.

—Inside Jolly Roger's Pirate Ship. Reasoner, Charles. 2007. (Story Book Ser.). 12p. (J). (gr. k). bds. (978-1-84666-149-5(8), Tide Mill Pr.) Top That! Publishing PLC.

—Inside Old Mcdonald's Barn. Reasoner, Charles. 2007. (Story Book Ser.). 12p. (J). (gr. k). bds.

(978-1-84666-287-4(7), Tide Mill Pr.) Top That! Publishing PLC.
—Inside Santa's Toy Shop. Reasoner, Charles. 2007. (Story Book Ser.). 12p. (J). (gr. k-3). bds. *(978-1-84666-151-8(X),* Tide Mill Pr.) Top That! Publishing PLC.
—The 3 Blind Mice Inside the Spooky Scary & Creepy Haunted House. Reasoner, Charles. 2007. (Story Book Ser.). 10p. (J). (gr. -1-3). bds. *(978-1-84666-381-9(4),* Tide Mill Pr.) Top That! Publishing PLC.
Reasoner, Charles & Reasoner, John. What's Following Us? Cooke, Brandy. 2011. (ENG.). 20p. (J). (gr. -1 — 1). bds. 6.99 *(978-1-4169-9673-6(7),* Little Simon) Little Simon.
Reasoner, John, jt. illus. see Reasoner, Charles.
Reasor, Mick. Trabajar y Jugar. Kleinhenz, Sydnie Meltzer. 2006. (Rookie Reader Español Ser.). (SPA.). 23p. (J). (gr. k-2). lib. bdg. 19.50 *(978-0-516-25306-0(9))* Scholastic Library Publishing.
—Work & Play. Meltzer Kleinhenz, Sydnie. 2011. (Rookie Ready to Learn Ser.). (ENG.). 32p. (J). pap. 5.95 *(978-0-531-26829-2(2),* Children's Pr.) Scholastic Library Publishing.
—Work & Play. Meltzer-Kleinhenz, Sydnie. 2011. (ENG.). 32p. (J). (gr. -1-1). lib. bdg. 25.00 *(978-0-531-27179-7(X))* Scholastic Library Publishing.
Reaveley, Trevor. Is Apatosaurus Okay? Nussbaum, Ben. 2005. (Smithsonian's Prehistoric Pals Ser.). (ENG.). (J). (gr. -1-2). 32p. 9.95 *(978-1-59249-510-8(9),* PS2458); 36p. pap. 2.95 *(978-1-59249-509-2(5),* S2458) Soundprints.
—Sabre-Tooth Tiger. Bailey, Gerry. 2011. (Smithsonian Prehistoric Zone Ser.). (ENG.). 32p. (J). (gr. k-3). *(978-0-7787-1801-7(8),* 1325447); pap. *(978-0-7787-1814-7(X),* 1325447) Crabtree Publishing Co.
Reavely, Trever. Saber-Tooth Trap. Bentley, Dawn. (Smithsonian's Prehistoric Pals Ser.). (ENG.). 36p. (J). (gr. -1-2). 8.95 *(978-1-59249-455-2(2),* SD2406); 2.95 *(978-1-59249-456-9(0),* S2456) Soundprints.
Reavely, Trevor. Is Apatosaurus Okay? Nussbaum, Ben. 2005. (ENG.). 36p. (J). (gr. -1-2). 8.95 *(978-1-59249-508-5(7),* SD2408); 14.95 *(978-1-59249-506-1(0),* H2408); pap. 6.95 *(978-1-59249-507-8(9),* S2408) Soundprints.
—Saber-Tooth Trap. Bentley, Dawn. 2005. (Smithsonian's Prehistoric Pals Ser.). (ENG.). 36p. (J). (gr. k-2). 14.95 *(978-1-59249-453-8(6),* H2406); pap. 6.95 *(978-1-59249-454-5(4),* S2406) Soundprints.
Reaves, Daniel. Invisible Julian. Hawes, Dorothy. 2011. 24p. pap. 24.95 *(978-1-4560-9583-3(8))* America Star Bks.
Rebecca, Rivard. Ben Has Autism. Ben Is Awesome. Zolty, Meredith. 2011. 32p. (J). lib. bdg. 15.95 *(978-0-944727-40-9(9),* Turtle Bks.) Jason & Nordic Pubs.
Rebecca, Spencer. Seaper Powers: The Rescue. Cameron, Kim. 2nd ed. 2017. (Seaper Powers Ser.: Vol. 3). (ENG.). (J). (gr. 1-4). 25.00 *(978-0-692-83666-8(7))* Side FX Partners, LLC.
Rebelka, Jakub. Spera: Ascension of the Starless Vol. 2. Tierney, Josh. 2017. (Spera Ser.: 2). (ENG.). 176p. (J). 24.99 *(978-1-68415-067-0(1),* Archaia Entertainment) Boom! Studios.
Rebora, Cecilia. Never Let a Ghost Borrow Your Library Book: Book Care Guidelines from the Library Secret Service. Casale, Karen. 2012. 32p. (J). 17.75 *(978-1-60213-061-6(2),* Upstart Bks.) Highsmith Inc.
—Ripple's Effect. Achor, Shawn & Blankson, Amy. O'Malley, Judy, ed. 2012. 32p. (J). (gr. -1-k). 18.95 *(978-0-9829938-7-3(0))* March 4th, Inc.
—Tower of Babel. Gadot, A. S. 2010. 32p. (J). (gr. k-4). lib. bdg. 17.95 *(978-0-8225-9917-3(1),* Kar-Ben Publishing) Lerner Publishing Group.
Recher, Andrew. Bats. Vogel, Julia. 2007. (Our Wild World Ser.). (ENG.). 48p. (J). (gr. 2-5). 10.95 *(978-1-55971-968-1(0));* pap. 7.95 *(978-1-55971-969-8(9))* Cooper Square Publishing Llc.
—Butterflies. Stewart, Melissa. 2007. (Our Wild World Ser.). (ENG.). 48p. (J). (gr. 2-5). 10.95 *(978-1-55971-966-7(4));* pap. 7.95 *(978-1-55971-967-4(2))* Cooper Square Publishing Llc.
Rechin, Kevin. Did You Know?, Vol. 2. Winter, Max. l.t. ed. 2005. (Little Books & Big Bks.: Vol. 8). 8p. (gr. k-2). 23.00 net. *(978-0-8215-7517-8(1))* Sadlier, William H. Inc.
—Guess Again! 1,001 Rib-Tickling Riddles from Highlights. 2012. (Highlights(TM) Laugh Attack! Joke Bks.). (ENG.). 256p. (J). (gr. 1-4). pap. 5.95 *(978-1-59078-919-3(9),* Highlights) Boyds Mills Pr.
—The Tumbleweed Came Back. Coyle, Carmela Lavigna. 2013. 32p. (J). 15.95 *(978-1-933855-83-7(5),* Rio Nuevo Pubs.) Rio Nuevo Pubs.
Rechlin. Dino Babies! 2018. (ENG.). 26p. (J). bds. 8.95 *(978-1-56037-734-4(8))* Farcountry Pr.
Recio, Ricardo. Manana es Domingo y Otras Rimas Infantiles. Puncel, Maria. 2003. (SPA.). 32p. 4.95 *(978-84-372-8021-9(4))* Altea, Ediciones, S.A. - Grupo Santillana ESP. Dist: Santillana USA Publishing Co., Inc.
Record, Adam. Elf in the House. Paquette, Ammi-Joan. 32p. (J). (gr. -1-2). 2019. 5.99 *(978-1-5362-0900-6(7));* 2017. 15.99 *(978-0-7636-8132-6(6))* Candlewick Pr.
—Even Superheroes Have to Sleep. Crow, Sara. (J). (— 1). 2018. 26p. bds. 6.99 *(978-0-399-55809-2(8));* 2017. 32p. 16.99 *(978-0-399-55806-1(3))* Random Hse. Children's Bks. (Doubleday Bks. for Young Readers).
—Even Superheroes Use the Potty. Crow, Sara. (J). (— 1). 2019. 26p. bds. 6.99 *(978-1-5247-6599-6(6));* 2018. 32p. 16.99 *(978-0-399-55934-1(5))* Random Hse. Children's Bks. (Doubleday Bks. for Young Readers).
—Ghost in the House. Paquette, Ammi-Joan. (ENG.). 32p. (J). (gr. -1-2). 2019. 5.99 *(978-0-7636-9892-8(X));* 2013. 15.99 *(978-0-7636-5529-7(5))* Candlewick Pr.
—Ghost in the House: a Lift-The-Flap Book. Paquette, Ammi-Joan. 2015. (ENG.). 20p. (J). (gr. -1-2). 9.99 *(978-0-7636-7622-3(5))* Candlewick Pr.
—Kit & Mateo Journey into the Clouds: Learning about Clouds, 1 vol. Meister, Cari. 2013. (Take It Outside Ser.). (ENG.). 24p. (J). (gr. -1-2). pap. 8.95 *(978-1-4795-1936-1(7),* Picture Window Bks.) Capstone.
—Little Dinos Don't Bite, 1 vol. Dahl, Michael. 2013. (Little Dinos Ser.). (ENG.). 20p. (J). (gr. -1-k). bds. 7.99 *(978-1-4048-7536-4(0),* Picture Window Bks.) Capstone.
—Little Dinos Don't Hit, 1 vol. Dahl, Michael. 2013. (Little Dinos Ser.). (ENG.). 20p. (J). (gr. -1-k). bds. 7.99 *(978-1-4048-7533-3(6),* Picture Window Bks.) Capstone.
—Little Dinos Don't Push, 1 vol. Dahl, Michael. 2013. (Little Dinos Ser.). (ENG.). 20p. (J). (gr. -1-k). bds. 7.99 *(978-1-4048-7534-0(4),* Picture Window Bks.) Capstone.
—Little Dinos Don't Yell, 1 vol. Dahl, Michael. 2013. (Little Dinos Ser.). (ENG.). 20p. (J). (gr. -1-k). bds. 7.99 *(978-1-4048-7912-6(9),* Picture Window Bks.) Capstone.
—Lost Treasure of Larry Longfoot: Learning to Use a Map. Meister, Cari. 2013. (Take It Outside Ser.). (ENG.). 24p. (J). (gr. -1-2). pap. 8.95 *(978-1-4795-1935-4(9),* Picture Window Bks.) Capstone.
—Marvin Redpost #1: Kidnapped at Birth? Sachar, Louis. 2015. (Marvin Redpost Ser.: 1). (ENG.). 96p. (J). (gr. 1-4). lib. bdg. 12.99 *(978-0-553-53540-2(4),* Random Hse. Bks. for Young Readers) Random Hse. Children's Bks.
—Marvin Redpost #3: Is He a Girl? Sachar, Louis. 2015. (Marvin Redpost Ser.: 3). (ENG.). 96p. (J). (gr. 1-4). lib. bdg. 12.99 *(978-0-553-53542-6(0),* Random Hse. Bks. for Young Readers) Random Hse. Children's Bks.
—Marvin Redpost #5: Class President. Sachar, Louis. 2015. (Marvin Redpost Ser.: 5). (ENG.). 96p. (J). (gr. 1-4). lib. bdg. 12.99 *(978-0-553-53543-3(9),* Random Hse. Bks. for Young Readers) Random Hse. Children's Bks.
—Marvin Redpost #6: a Flying Birthday Cake? Sachar, Louis. 2015. (Marvin Redpost Ser.: 6). (ENG.). 96p. (J). (gr. 1-4). lib. bdg. 12.99 *(978-0-553-53544-0(7),* Random Hse. Bks. for Young Readers) Random Hse. Children's Bks.
—Nick & Nack Build a Birdhouse. Budzi, Brandon. 2020. (Highlights Puzzle Readers Ser.). 32p. (J). (gr. -1-2). 16.99 *(978-1-68437-984-2(9));* pap. 4.99 *(978-1-68437-932-3(6))* Boyds Mills Pr. (Highlights).
—Nick & Nack Fly a Kite. Budzi, Brandon. 2020. (Highlights Puzzle Readers Ser.). 32p. (J). (gr. -1-2). 16.99 *(978-1-64472-111-7(2));* pap. 4.99 *(978-1-64472-112-4(0))* Boyds Mills Pr. (Highlights).
—Sadie's Seed Adventures: Learning about Seeds, 1 vol. Dybvik, Tina. 2013. (Take It Outside Ser.). (ENG.). 24p. (J). (gr. -1-2). pap. 8.95 *(978-1-4795-1937-8(5),* Picture Window Bks.) Capstone.
—Space Cowboy Caleb & the Night Sky Round-Up: Learning about the Night Sky, 1 vol. Dybvik, Tina. 2013. (Take It Outside Ser.). (ENG.). 24p. (J). (gr. -1-2). pap. 8.95 *(978-1-4795-1938-5(3),* Picture Window Bks.) Capstone.
—Super Fast, Out of Control. Sachar, Louis. 2015. (Marvin Redpost Ser.: 7). (ENG.). 96p. (J). (gr. 1-4). lib. bdg. 12.99 *(978-0-553-53545-7(5),* Random Hse. Bks. for Young Readers) Random Hse. Children's Bks.
—Take It Outside. Dybvik, Tina & Meister, Cari. 2013. (Take It Outside Ser.). (ENG.). 24p. (J). (gr. -1-2). pap., pap., pap. 35.80 *(978-1-4795-1998-9(7),* Picture Window Bks.) Capstone.
Record, Adam Michael. Little Dinos. Dahl, Michael. 2013. (Little Dinos Ser.). (ENG.). (J). (gr. -1-k). bds., bds., bds. 31.96 *(978-1-4795-2143-2(4),* Picture Window Bks.) Capstone.
Rectenbaugh, Marci. Jonathan Finds True Treasure. Adee, Donna & Adee, Ed. 2004. (Jonathan Ser.: Bk. 2). 344p. (J). per. 10.95 *(978-0-9654272-5-8(0))* Harvest Pubns.
Reczuch, Karen. The Auction, 1 vol. Andrews, Jan. 2nd ed. 2007. (ENG.). 32p. (J). (gr. k-2). pap. 6.95 *(978-0-88899-842-2(2))* Groundwood Bks. CAN. Dist: Publishers Group West (PGW).
—Ghost Cat. Abley, Mark. ed. 2004. (J). (gr. k-3). spiral bd. *(978-0-616-11091-1(X));* spiral bd. *(978-0-616-11092-8(8))* Canadian National Institute for the Blind/Institut National Canadien pour les Aveugles.
—Loon, 2 vols. Griek, Susan Vande. 2019. (ENG.). 48p. (J). (gr. k-2). 12.95 *(978-1-77306-236-5(0))* Groundwood Bks. CAN. Dist: Publishers Group West (PGW).
—Salmon Creek, 1 vol. LeBox, Annette. 2005. (ENG.). 48p. (J). pap. 12.95 *(978-0-88899-644-2(6))* Groundwood Bks. CAN. Dist: Publishers Group West (PGW).
—Turtle Pond, 1 vol. Gladstone, James. 2018. (ENG.). 32p. (J). (gr. k-3). 18.95 *(978-1-55498-910-2(8))* Groundwood Bks. CAN. Dist: Publishers Group West (PGW).
—Turtle Pond. Gladstone, James. 2018. (ENG.). 32p. E-Book *(978-1-55498-911-9(6))* Groundwood Bks.
—West Coast Wild: A Nature Alphabet, 1 vol. Hodge, Deborah. 2015. (ENG.). 48p. (J). (gr. -1-2). 18.95 *(978-1-55498-440-4(8))* Groundwood Bks. CAN. Dist: Publishers Group West (PGW).
—West Coast Wild Babies, 1 vol. Hodge, Deborah. 2020. (West Coast Wild Ser.: 2). 36p. (J). (gr. k-2). 19.95 *(978-1-77306-248-8(4))* Groundwood Bks. CAN. Dist: Publishers Group West (PGW).
Red Baklava, photos by. Blackbook Directory & Yearbook 2010-11: Black Business Year in Review, vol. 1. annuals Avista Products. Media Write, ed. aut. collector's ed. 2011. (ENG., 160p. 65.00 *(978-0-9798741-0-9(6))* Avista Products.
Red Nose Studio. Elvis Is King! Winter, Jonah. 2019. 40p. (J). (gr. -1-3). 17.99 *(978-0-399-55470-4(X),* Schwartz & Wade Bks.) Random Hse. Children's Bks.
REDCODE & Team, Air. Dinosaur Explorers Vol. 4: Trapped in the Triassic. Albbie. 2019. (Dinosaur Explorers Ser.: 4). (ENG.). 184p. (J). 16.99 *(978-1-5458-0205-2(X),* 900198503); pap. 12.99 *(978-1-5458-0204-5(1),* 900198504) Papercutz.
Redd, Zai & Josey, Clarke. The Mystery of the Missing Ring. 2019. (ENG.). 38p. (J). pap. 20.95 *(978-1-947656-07-9(4))* Butterfly Typeface, The.
Reddy, Sneha. The Ballad of Calvin the Cat. Harpan, Gaile. 2008. 24p. pap. 12.95 *(978-0-9817572-6-1(X))* Peppertree Pr., The.
—The Ballad of Furrio the Cat. Panks, Kristin & Harpan, Gaile. 2008. 24p. pap. 12.95 *(978-0-9822540-4-2(0))* Peppertree Pr., The.
—The Ballad of Omar the Cat. Harpan, Gaile. 2008. 28p. pap. 12.95 *(978-0-9820479-1-0(6))* Peppertree Pr., The.
—The Ballad of Snowball the Cat. Harpan, Gaile. 2009. 24p. pap. 12.95 *(978-1-936051-25-0(7))* Peppertree Pr., The.
—The Ballad of Victor the Cat. Harpan, Gaile. 2008. 20p. pap. 12.95 *(978-0-9814894-4-5(3))* Peppertree Pr., The.
Redel, Nicole. Odessa Bluegill - Out Shovels a Yellow Tractor. Gorman, Suzy, photos by. Session, Garry. Warren, Pamela, ed. 2003. 42p. (J). pap. 9.95 *(978-0-9658006-2-4(8))* Session Family.
Redenbaugh, Vicki. Skar's Picnic ... A Bear's Tale. Redenbaugh, Vicki. 2005. (J). 14.95 *(978-1-59091-034-4(6))* Eastern National.
Redenbaugh, Vicki Jo. Lots of Latkes: A Hanukkah Story, Vol. Lanton, Sandy. 2003. (ENG.). 32p. (J). (gr. -1-3). 14.95 *(978-1-58013-091-2(7),* Kar-Ben Publishing) Lerner Publishing Group.
Redfield, Nadine & Pickens, Macaeli. More Adventures with Clarissa & Gregory. Redfield, Nadine. 2019. (Children's Books for Grandparents Ser.). (ENG.). 38p. (J). (gr. k-2). 16.99 *(978-1-943492-45-9(X));* pap. 8.99 *(978-1-943492-46-6(8))* Elm Grove Publishing.
Redlich, Ben. Dragons vs Dinos. Bryant, Ann. 2014. (Race Ahead with Reading Ser.). (ENG.). 32p. (J). (gr. 2-2). *(978-0-7787-1328-9(8))* Crabtree Publishing Co.
—The Great Montefiasco. Thompson, Colin. 2004. 40p. (J). (gr. -1 — 1). 16.95 *(978-1-59572-008-5(1))* Star Bright Bks., Inc.
—Tortoise vs. Hare: The Rematch. Rutt, Preston. 2015. (ENG.). 24p. (J). (gr. -1-3). 7.99 *(978-1-85733-722-8(0))* Lerner Publishing Group.
Redmon, Angela M. The Adventures of Margaret Mouse: Hide 'n Seek. Wyatt, Cherokee. l.t. ed. 2005. 32p. (J). (gr. k-5). 6.95 *(978-0-9761326-4-6(8))* www.margaretmouse.com publishing co.
—The Adventures of Margaret Mouse: School Days. Wyatt, Cherokee. l.t. ed. 2004. 32p. (J). 6.95 *(978-0-9761326-0-8(5))* www.margaretmouse.com publishing co.
—The Adventures of Margaret Mouse: The Picnic. Wyatt, Cherokee. 2004. 32p. (J). 6.95 *(978-0-9761326-1-5(3))* www.margaretmouse.com publishing co.
Redmond, E. S. Bug Blonsky & His Very Long List of Don'ts. Redmond, E. S. 2018. 80p. (J). (gr. 1-4). 15.99 *(978-0-7636-8935-3(1))* Candlewick Pr.
—Felicity Floo Visits the Zoo. Redmond, E. S. 2010. (ENG.). 32p. (J). (-k). pap. 7.99 *(978-0-7636-4975-3(9))* Candlewick Pr.
—The Unruly Queen. Redmond, E. S. 2012. 32p. (J). (gr. -1-2). 15.99 *(978-0-7636-3445-2(X))* Candlewick Pr.
Redondo, Daniel. Lost Civilisations. Gutierrez, Pello. Publisher, Saure, ed. 2016. (Uncut Edition Ser.: Vol. 2). (ENG.). (YA). (gr. 7-9). *(978-84-16197-79-8(2))* Saure, Jean-Francois Editor.
Redondo, Fernando. Dulcita y el Burrito. Reyes, Carlos Jose. 2004. (Primer Acto: Teatro Infantil y Juvenil Ser.). (SPA.). 59p. (J). (gr. -1-7). pap. *(978-958-30-0313-4(1))* Panamericana Editorial.
Redondo, Jesus. Turtle Rescue! Chanda, J-P. 2004. (Teenage Mutant Ninja Turtles Ser.). 32p. (J). (gr. 4-7). 11.65 *(978-0-7569-5371-3(5))* Perfection Learning Corp.
Redondo, Jesus, jt. illus. see Vasquez, Ivan.
Redpath, Dale. Passages, 1 bk. Hulme, Lucy V. 2005. 40p. (J). 7.95 *(978-0-9769854-0-2(3),* 001) Combs-Hulme Publishing.
Reece, James A. Chocolate Puddles. Lovvorn, Ann R. 2010. 36p. pap. 15.49 *(978-1-4520-5158-1(5))* AuthorHouse.
Reece, Maynard. Animals under Your Feet. Green, Ivah E. 2011. 140p. 40.95 *(978-1-258-06244-6(5))* Literary Licensing, LLC.
Reed, Bill. Herbert Hilligan's SeaWorld Adventure. Epner, Paul. 2005. (J). 16.95 *(978-0-9743335-9-5(X))* Imaginative Publishing, Ltd.
—There's a Dachshund in My Bed! Epner, Paul. 2004. 56p. (J). 16.95 *(978-0-9743335-8-8(1))* Imaginative Publishing, Ltd.
Reed, C. W. Jack the Fisherman. Phelps, Elizabeth Stuart. 2005. reprint ed. pap. 15.95 *(978-1-4179-3778-3(5))* Kessinger Publishing, LLC.
Reed, Chris. Joke & Riddle Jackpot. Pellowski, Michael J. 2010. (Jokes & Riddles Ser.). (ENG.). 96p. (J). (gr. k-3). 17.44 *(978-1-4027-7849-0(X))* Sterling Publishing Co., Inc.
Reed, Emily. Millie, the Cross-Eyed Mole. Byrd, Frances. Byrd, Deborah, ed. 2019. (ENG.). 30p. (J). pap. 9.99 *(978-1-7967-5357-8(2))* Independently Published.
Reed, Gary & Miello, Tony. Irving's Icky Insects. 2020. (ENG.). 52p. (J). pap. 9.99 ***(978-1-63529-847-5(4))*** Caliber Comics.
Reed, Jay. Epic Athletes: Lionel Messi. Wetzel, Dan. 2019. (Epic Athletes Ser.: 6). (ENG.). 160p. (J). 16.99 *(978-1-250-29581-1(5),* 900195496, Holt, Henry & Co. Bks. For Young Readers) Holt, Henry & Co.
Reed, Jimmy, jt. illus. see Reed, Liz.
Reed, Joel B. Grandpa's New Kitty. Reed, Joel B. 2008. 28p. pap. 12.95 *(978-1-933482-65-1(6))* White Turtle Bks.
Reed, Kyle. Have You Ever Zeen a Ziz? Marshall, Linda Elovitz. 2020. (ENG.). 32p. (J). (gr. -1-3). 16.99 ***(978-0-8075-3173-0(1),*** 807531731) Whitman, Albert & Co.
Reed, Kyle. Ride the Whale: A Surfer Tail Tale. Apte, Sunita. 2006. 16p. (J). pap. *(978-0-439-74638-0(8))* Scholastic, Inc.
—Superheroes Don't Babysit. Hendricks, Amber. 2020. (ENG.). 32p. (J). (gr. k-3). 17.99 *(978-1-5064-5876-2(9),* Beaming Books) Augsburg Fortress, Pubs.
—Three Little Birds. Mullady, Lysa. 2019. 32p. (J). *(978-1-4338-2947-5(9),* Magination Pr.) American Psychological Assn.
Reed, Linda Davis. Adirondack ABCs. Snavlin, Joyce Burgess. 2009. 32p. (J). 9.95 *(978-1-59531-028-6(2))* North Country Bks., Inc.
Reed, Lisa. ABCs in the Bible. Moredock, Rebekah. 2020. 20p. (J). (gr. -1 — 1). bds. 9.99 *(978-1-5460-1428-7(4),* Worthy Kids/Ideals) Worthy Publishing.
—Animals in the Bible. Moredock, Rebekah. 2019. 20p. (J). (gr. -1-1). bds. 8.99 *(978-0-8249-1696-1(4),* Worthy Kids/Ideals) Worthy Publishing.
—Bob & Larry's Book of Colors. VeggieTales. 2019. (VeggieTales Ser.). 20p. (J). (gr. -1 — 1). bds. 7.99 *(978-1-5460-1436-2(5),* Worthy Kids/Ideals) Worthy Publishing.
—Bob & Larry's Book of Numbers. VeggieTales. 2019. (VeggieTales Ser.). 20p. (J). (gr. -1 — 1). bds. 7.99 *(978-1-5460-1437-9(3),* Worthy Kids/Ideals) Worthy Publishing.
—Count Your Blessings. Bostrom, Kathleen Long. 2017. (VeggieTales Ser.). 20p. (J). (gr. -1-k). bds. 7.99 *(978-0-8249-1664-0(6))* Worthy Publishing.
—Hooray! It's Easter Day! Bostrom, Kathleen Long. 2017. (VeggieTales Ser.). 20p. (J). (gr. -1-k). bds. 7.99 *(978-0-8249-1996-2(3))* Worthy Publishing.
—A Place Called Heaven for Kids. Jeffress, Robert. 2019. (ENG.). 32p. (J). 14.99 *(978-0-8010-9428-6(3))* Baker Bks.
—The Secret of the Hidden Scrolls: the King Is Born, Book 7, Bk. 7. Thomas, M. J. 2019. (Secret of the Hidden Scrolls Ser.: 7). (ENG.). 128p. (J). (gr. 1-4). pap. 6.99 *(978-1-5460-1463-8(2),* Worthy Kids/Ideals) Worthy Publishing.
—The Secret of the Hidden Scrolls: the Lion's Roar, Book 6. Thomas, M. J. 2019. (Secret of the Hidden Scrolls Ser.: 6). 128p. (J). (gr. 1-4). pap. 6.99 *(978-0-8249-5705-6(9),* Worthy Kids/Ideals) Worthy Publishing.
—VeggieTales Away in a Manger. Traditional. 2016. (VeggieTales Ser.). 16p. (J). bds. 12.99 *(978-0-8249-1989-4(0),* Worthy Kids/Ideals) Worthy Publishing.
—Very Veggie Bedtime Prayers. Kennedy, Pamela & Brady, Anne Kennedy. 2018. (VeggieTales Ser.). 26p. (J). (gr. -1-k). bds. 10.99 *(978-0-8249-1670-1(0))* Worthy Publishing.
—Very Veggie Devos for Little Ones. Kennedy, Pamela & Brady, Anne Kennedy. 2017. (VeggieTales Ser.). 32p. (J). (gr. -1-k). bds. 10.99 *(978-0-8249-1997-9(1))* Worthy Publishing.
—We Wish You a Merry Christmas! Kennedy, Pamela. 2017. (VeggieTales Ser.). 16p. (J). (gr. -1-k). bds. 12.99 *(978-0-8249-1663-3(8))* Worthy Publishing.
Reed, Liz & Reed, Jimmy. Sweet Competition. Reed, Liz & Reed, Jimmy. 2016. (ENG.). 40p. (J). (gr. -1-3). 17.99 *(978-0-06-240359-9(1),* HarperCollins) HarperCollins Pubs. Ltd. GBR. Dist: HarperCollins Pubs.
—Sweet Success. Reed, Liz & Reed, Jimmy. 2018. (ENG.). 40p. (J). (gr. -1-3). 17.99 *(978-0-06-240360-5(5))* HarperCollins Pubs.
Reed, Lynn Rowe. The Case of the Incapacitated Capitals. Pulver, Robin. 2012. (Language Arts Library). (ENG.). 32p. (J). (gr. -1-3). 16.95 *(978-0-8234-2402-3(2))* Holiday Hse., Inc.
—The Case of the Incapacitated Capitals. Pulver, Robin. 2013. (Language Arts Library). (ENG.). 32p. (J). (gr. -1-3). pap. 7.99 *(978-0-8234-2914-1(8))* Holiday Hse., Inc.
—Happy Endings: A Story about Suffixes. Pulver, Robin. 2012. (ENG.). 32p. (J). (gr. -1-3). pap. 8.99 *(978-0-8234-2434-4(0))* Holiday Hse., Inc.
—Happy Endings: A Story about Suffixes. Pulver, Robin. 2013. (ENG.). (J). (gr. 1-3). pap. 44.95 *(978-1-4301-1435-2(5))* Live Oak Media.
—Nouns & Verbs Have a Field Day. Pulver, Robin. 2007. (ENG.). 32p. (J). (gr. k-3). 8.99 *(978-0-8234-2097-1(3))* Holiday Hse., Inc.
—Nouns & Verbs Have a Field Day. Pulver, Robin. 2013. pap. 18.95 incl. audio compact disk *(978-1-4301-1115-3(1))* Live Oak Media.
—Punctuation Takes a Vacation. Pulver, Robin. 2004. (ENG.). 32p. (J). (gr. k-3). reprint ed. pap. 7.99 *(978-0-8234-1820-6(0))* Holiday Hse., Inc.
—Punctuation Takes a Vacation. Pulver, Robin. 2009. (J). (gr. 1-3). 29.95 incl. audio compact disk *(978-1-4301-0708-8(1))* Live Oak Media.
—Silent Letters Loud & Clear. Pulver, Robin. 2010. (ENG.). 32p. (J). (gr. 1-4). pap. 8.99 *(978-0-8234-2309-5(3))* Holiday Hse., Inc.
Reed, Lynn Rowe. Fireman Fred. Reed, Lynn Rowe. 2014. (I Like to Read Ser.). (ENG.). 24p. (J). (gr. -1-3). pap. 7.99 *(978-0-8234-3182-3(7))* Holiday Hse., Inc.
Reed, Mike. Andrew Lost #5: under Water. Greenburg, J. C. 2003. (Andrew Lost Ser.: 5). (ENG.). 96p. (J). (gr. 1-4). mass mkt. 4.99 *(978-0-375-82523-1(1),* Random Hse. Bks. for Young Readers) Random Hse. Children's Bks.
—Andrew Lost #6: in the Whale. Greenburg, J. C. 2003. (Andrew Lost Ser.: 6). (ENG.). 96p. (J). (gr. 1-4). 4.99 *(978-0-375-82524-8(X),* Random Hse. Bks. for Young Readers) Random Hse. Children's Bks.
—Bad to the Bone, 0 vols. Nolan, Lucy. 2011. (Down Girl & Sit Ser.: 3). (ENG.). 64p. (J). (gr. 1-4). pap. 9.99 *(978-0-7614-5834-0(4),* 9780761458340, Two Lions) Amazon Publishing.
—Catching the Wild Waiyuuzee. Williams-Garcia, Rita. 2007. (ENG.). 32p. (J). (gr. -1-1). 12.99 *(978-1-4169-6141-3(0),* Simon & Schuster/Paula Wiseman Bks.) Simon & Schuster/Paula Wiseman Bks.
—Cowboy Camp. Sauer, Tammi. (J). (gr. -1-k). 2015. 24p. bds. 6.95 *(978-1-4549-1389-4(4));* 2014. 32p. pap. 8.95 *(978-1-4549-1360-3(6))* Sterling Publishing Co., Inc.
—Even Firefighters Hug Their Moms. MacLean, Christine Kole. 2004. (ENG.). 32p. (J). (gr. k-3). pap. 6.99 *(978-0-14-240191-0(9),* Puffin Books) Penguin Young Readers Group.
—Home on the Range, 0 vols. Nolan, Lucy. 2010. (Down Girl & Sit Ser.: 4). (ENG.). 64p. (J). (gr. 1-4). 14.99 *(978-0-7614-5649-0(X),* 9780761456490, Two Lions) Amazon Publishing.
—Looking for Luna, 0 vols. Myers, Tim & Myers, Tim J. 2009. (ENG.). 32p. (J). (gr. -1-3). 17.99 *(978-0-7614-5564-6(7),* 9780761455646, Two Lions) Amazon Publishing.
—A Million Dots. Clements, Andrew. 2006. (ENG.). 48p. (J). (gr. -1-3). 19.99 *(978-0-689-85824-6(8),* Atheneum Bks.

R

for Young Readers) Simon & Schuster Children's Publishing.

—On the Road, 0 vols. Nolan, Lucy. unabr. ed. 2009. (Down Girl & Sit Ser.: 2). (ENG.). 68p. (J). (gr. 1-4). pap. 9.99 *(978-0-7614-5572-1(8)*, 9780761455721, Two Lions) Amazon Publishing.

—Peanut. Kilgras, Heidi. 2003. (Step into Reading Ser.). (ENG.). 32p. (J). (gr. -1-1). pap. 4.99 *(978-0-375-80618-6(0)*, Random Hse. Bks. for Young Readers) Random Hse. Children's Bks.

—Scholastic Children's Thesaurus. Bollard, John K. rev. ed. 2006. (ENG.). 240p. (J). (gr. 4-7). 17.99 *(978-0-439-79831-0(0)*, Scholastic Reference) Scholastic, Inc.

—Smarter Than Squirrels, 0 vols. Nolan, Lucy. unabr. ed. 2009. (Down Girl & Sit Ser.: 1). (ENG.). 68p. (J). (gr. 1-4). pap. 9.99 *(978-0-7614-5571-4(X)*, 9780761455714, Two Lions) Amazon Publishing.

Reed, Mike & Gerardi, Jan. On the Reef. Greenburg, J. C. Reed, Mike, tr. 2004. (Andrew Lost Ser.: 7). 96p. (J). (gr. 1-4). 4.99 *(978-0-375-82525-5(8)*, Random Hse. Bks. for Young Readers) Random Hse. Children's Bks.

Reed, Nathan. Brewing up (Witch-In-Training, Book 4), Vol. 4. Friel, Maeve. 2011. (Witch-In-Training Ser.: 4). (ENG.). 96p. (J). pap. 5.99 *(978-0-00-713344-4(8)*, HarperCollins Children's Bks.) HarperCollins Pubs. Ltd. GBR. Dist: HarperCollins Pubs.

—Broomstick Battles (Witch-In-Training, Book 5) Friel, Maeve. 2011. (Witch-In-Training Ser.: 5). (ENG.). 96p. (J). pap. 5.99 *(978-0-00-718524-5(3)*, HarperCollins Children's Bks.) HarperCollins Pubs. Ltd. GBR. Dist: HarperCollins Pubs.

—The Broomstick Collection: Books 1-4 (Witch-In-Training), Bks 1-4. Friel, Maeve. 2006. (Witch-In-Training Ser.). (ENG.). 368p. (J). (gr. 2-4). pap., pap., pap. 11.99 *(978-0-00-724072-2(4)*, HarperCollins Children's Bks.) HarperCollins Pubs. Ltd. GBR. Dist: HarperCollins Pubs.

—The Buskers of Bremen. 2004. 24p. (J). (POL & ENG.). *(978-1-85269-800-3(4))*; pap. *(978-1-85269-225-4(1))*; pap. *(978-1-85269-765-5(2))*; (ENG & CHI.). pap. *(978-1-85269-767-9(9))*; pap. *(978-1-85269-768-6(7))*; (GER & ENG.). pap. *(978-1-85269-770-9(9))*; pap. *(978-1-85269-771-6(7))*; (CZE & ENG.). pap. *(978-1-85269-773-0(3))*; pap. *(978-1-85269-774-7(1))*; (ENG.). pap. *(978-1-85269-775-4(X))*; pap. *(978-1-85269-776-1(8))*; (ITA & ENG.). pap. *(978-1-85269-777-8(6))*; (ENG & SPA.). pap. *(978-1-85269-778-5(4))*; pap. *(978-1-85269-779-2(2))*; (TUR & ENG.). pap. *(978-1-85269-780-8(6))* Mantra Lingua.

—The Buskers of Bremen. Barkow, Henriette. 2004. (ENG & PAN.). 24p. (J). pap. *(978-1-85269-772-3(5))* Mantra Lingua.

—Buskers of Bremen: Big Book English Only. 2004. (BEN & ENG.). (J). *(978-1-84444-301-7(9))* Mantra Lingua.

—Charming or What? (Witch-In-Training, Book 3), Vol. 3. Friel, Maeve. 2011. (Witch-In-Training Ser.: 3). (ENG.). 96p. (J). pap. 5.99 *(978-0-00-713343-7(X)*, HarperCollins Children's Bks.) HarperCollins Pubs. Ltd. GBR. Dist: HarperCollins Pubs.

—Flying Lessons (Witch-In-Training, Book 1), Vol. 1. Friel, Maeve. 2011. (Witch-In-Training Ser.: 1). (ENG.). 96p. (J). pap. 5.99 *(978-0-00-713341-3(3)*, HarperCollins Children's Bks.) HarperCollins Pubs. Ltd. GBR. Dist: HarperCollins Pubs.

—Grandma Dangerous & the Egg of Glory, Bk. 2. Mitchell, Kita. 2020. (Grandma Dangerous Ser.: 2). 272p. (J). (gr. 2-4). 10.99 *(978-1-4083-5550-3(7)*, Orchard Bks.) Hachette Children's Group GBR. Dist: Hachette Bk. Group.

—Grandma Dangerous & the Toe of Treachery. Mitchell, Kita. 2020. (Grandma Dangerous Ser.: 3). 272p. (J). (gr. 2-4). 10.99 *(978-1-4083-5552-7(3)*, Orchard Bks.) Hachette Children's Group GBR. Dist: Hachette Bk. Group.

Reed, Nathan. Incredible You. Brisenden, Rhys. 2019. (ENG.). 32p. (J). (gr. -1-3). 17.99 ***(978-1-84976-626-5(6))*** Tate Publishing, Ltd. GBR. Dist: Hachette Bk. Group.

Reed, Nathan. The Last Task (Witch-In-Training, Book 8) Friel, Maeve. 2011. (Witch-In-Training Ser.: 8). (ENG.). 96p. (J). (gr. 4-7). pap. 5.99 *(978-0-00-718527-6(8)*, HarperCollins Children's Bks.) HarperCollins Pubs. Ltd. GBR. Dist: HarperCollins Pubs.

—Moonlight Mischief (Witch-In-Training, Book 7) Friel, Maeve. 2011. (Witch-In-Training Ser.: 7). (ENG.). 96p. (J). per. 5.99 *(978-0-00-718526-9(X)*, HarperCollins Children's Bks.) HarperCollins Pubs. Ltd. GBR. Dist: HarperCollins Pubs.

—Sam Wu Is Not Afraid of Sharks. Tsang, Katie & Tsang, Kevin. 2019. (Sam Wu Is Not Afraid Ser.: 2). (ENG.). 240p. (J). (gr. 2-7). 12.95 *(978-1-4549-3256-7(2))* Sterling Publishing Co., Inc.

—Sam Wu Is Not Afraid of the Dark. Tsang, Katie & Tsang, Kevin. 2019. (Sam Wu Is Not Afraid Ser.: 3). (ENG.). 240p. (J). (gr. 2-7). 12.95 *(978-1-4549-3371-7(2))* Sterling Publishing Co., Inc.

—Samson, the Mighty Flea! McAllister, Angela. 2017. (ENG.). 40p. (J). (gr. -1-3). 17.99 *(978-1-5124-8123-5(8)*, 9781512481235) Lerner Publishing Group.

—Spelling Trouble (Witch-In-Training, Book 2) Vol. 2. Friel, Maeve. 2011. (Witch-In-Training Ser.: 2). (ENG.). 96p. (J). pap. 5.99 *(978-0-00-713342-0(1)*, HarperCollins Children's Bks.) HarperCollins Pubs. Ltd. GBR. Dist: HarperCollins Pubs.

—Witch Switch (Witch-In-Training, Book 6) Friel, Maeve. 2011. (Witch-In-Training Ser.: 6). (ENG.). 96p. (J). pap. 5.99 *(978-0-00-718525-2(1)*, HarperCollins Children's Bks.) HarperCollins Pubs. Ltd. GBR. Dist: HarperCollins Pubs.

Reed, Nathan, jt. illus. see Barkow, Henriette.

Reed, Neil. Nelson Mandela: The Life of an African Statesman. Shone, Rob. 2007. (Graphic Nonfiction Biographies Ser.). (ENG.). 48p. (J). (gr. 4-7). lib. bdg. 35.45 *(978-1-4042-0860-5(7))*; (gr. 5-8). pap. 14.05 *(978-1-4042-0923-7(9))* Rosen Publishing Group, Inc., The.

Reed, Philip. Granny's Cat. Parkin, Jessica. 2020. (ENG.). 32p. (J). pap. ***(978-1-913224-11-0(2))*** Jeffcock, Pippa.

Reed, Philip. Daddy's New Shed. Parkin, Jessica. 2019. (Tilly Tale Ser.: Vol. 2). (ENG.). 36p. (J). pap. *(978-1-913224-02-8(3))* Jeffcock, Pippa.

—My Silly Auntie: A Tilly Tale. Parkin, Jessica. 2019. (Tilly Tale Ser.: Vol. 1). (ENG.). 34p. (J). pap. *(978-1-9996427-6-1(7))* Jeffcock, Pippa.

Reed, Rebecca. The Train to Maine. Spencer, Jamie. 2008. (ENG.). 32p. (J). (gr. -1-3). 15.95 *(978-0-89272-767-4(5))* Down East Bks.

Reed, Rebecca Harrison, jt. illus. see Sollers, Jim.

Reed, Stephen. SpongeBob, Soccer Star! Lewman, David. 2010. (SpongeBob SquarePants Ser.). (ENG.). 24p. (J). (gr. -1-3). pap. 3.99 *(978-1-4169-9445-9(9)*, Simon Spotlight/Nickelodeon) Simon Spotlight/Nickelodeon.

Reed, Susan. Discovering the Sea. Mehrabi, Jacqueline. 2015. (Discovering Ser.). (ENG.). 218p. (J). (gr. 6-11). pap. 12.00 *(978-1-61851-093-8(2))* Baha'i Publishing.

—Discovering the Sun. Mehrabi, Jacqueline. 2015. (Discovering Ser.). (ENG.). 177p. (J). (gr. 6-11). pap. 12.00 *(978-1-61851-079-2(7))* Baha'i Publishing.

—Up up Up. Oldfield, Rachel. 2011. 24p. (J). (gr. -1-2). 9.99 *(978-1-84686-550-3(6))* Barefoot Bks., Inc.

Reed, Susan, jt. illus. see McDonald, Jill.

Reeder, Jayci. The Blue Lights. Driscoll, Stephanie. 2018. (ENG.). 38p. (J). 23.95 *(978-1-64300-134-0(5))*; pap. 13.95 *(978-1-64300-133-3(7))* Covenant Bks.

Rees, Mary. Little Brother & the Cough. Oram, Hiawyn. (ENG.). 32p. (J). (gr. -1-1). *(978-0-7112-0844-5(1))* ReiseArt Buchhandlung GmbH.

Reese, Amy. Illustrated Psalms of Praise: Psalmos de Albanza Ilustrados. 2005. (SPA & ENG.). 64p. (J). 16.95 *(978-1-56854-561-5(4))* Liturgy Training Pubns.

Reese, Bob. Do I Have To ... Picou, Lin. 2011. (Little Birdie Readers Ser.). (ENG.). 24p. (gr. 1-2). 29.93 *(978-1-61741-816-7(1)*, 9781617418167) Rourke Educational Media.

—Do I Have To... Picou, Lin. ed. 2011. (Little Birdie Readers Ser.). (ENG.). 24p. (gr. 1-2). pap. 8.95 *(978-1-61236-020-1(3)*, 9781612360201) Rourke Educational Media.

—Gator's Out, Said the Trout. Spaht-Gill, Janie. (J). (gr. k-2). 5.95 *(978-0-89868-305-9(X))* ARO Publishing Co.

—Habitat for Bats. Robbins, Maureen. ed. 2011. (Little Birdie Readers Ser.). (ENG.). 24p. (gr. 2-3). pap. 8.95 *(978-1-61236-037-9(8)*, 9781612360379) Rourke Educational Media.

—Monster Stew. Spaht-Gill, Janie. (J). 5.95 *(978-0-89868-307-3(6))* ARO Publishing Co.

—Ouch! Stitches. Karapetkova, Holly & Picou, Lin. ed. 2011. (Little Birdie Readers Ser.). (ENG.). 24p. (gr. 1-2). pap. 8.95 *(978-1-61236-023-2(8)*, 9781612360232) Rourke Educational Media.

—Puppy Trouble. Moreta, Gladys & Picou, Lin. ed. 2011. (Little Birdie Readers Ser.). (ENG.). 24p. (gr. 1-2). pap. 8.95 *(978-1-61236-018-8(1)*, 9781612360188) Rourke Educational Media.

—Ready, Set, Race! Robbins, Maureen & Steinkraus, Kyla. ed. 2011. (Little Birdie Readers Ser.). (ENG.). 24p. (gr. 2-3). pap. 8.95 *(978-1-61236-033-1(5)*, 9781612360331) Rourke Educational Media.

—Stop Arguing! Karapetkova, Holly & Robins, Maureen. ed. 2011. (Little Birdie Readers Ser.). (ENG.). 24p. (gr. 2-3). pap. 8.95 *(978-1-61236-032-4(7)*, 9781612360324) Rourke Educational Media.

—The Tree Fort. Steinkraus, Kyla. ed. 2011. (Little Birdie Readers Ser.). (ENG.). 24p. (gr. 2-3). pap. 8.95 *(978-1-61236-038-6(6)*, 9781612360386) Rourke Educational Media.

—The Trouble with Trading. Steinkraus, Kyla. ed. 2011. (Little Birdie Readers Ser.). (ENG.). 24p. (gr. 2-3). pap. 8.95 *(978-1-61236-034-8(3)*, 9781612360348) Rourke Educational Media.

Reese, Brandon. Amazing Animals: A Spin & Spot Book. Charlesworth, Liza. 2017. (ENG.). 16p. (J). (gr. -1 — 1). 8.99 *(978-0-545-78383-5(6)*, Cartwheel Bks.) Scholastic, Inc.

—Can You Canoe? & Other Adventure Songs. Okee Dokee Brothers Staff. 2016. 40p. (J). (gr. -1). 17.95 *(978-1-4549-1803-5(9))* Sterling Publishing Co., Inc.

—Print Writing: A Creepy-Crawly Alphabet. Flash Kids Editors, ed. 2012. (ENG.). 112p. (J). (gr. k-2). pap. 5.95 *(978-1-4114-6344-8(7)*, Spark Publishing Group) Sterling Publishing Co., Inc.

—Thousand Star Hotel. Okee Dokee Brothers Staff. 2017. 40p. (J). (gr. -1). 17.95 *(978-1-4549-1830-1(6))* Sterling Publishing Co., Inc.

Reese, Brandon. Draw Me Healthy! Reese, Brandon. 2012. 32p. (J). 7.99 *(978-0-8280-2680-2(7))* Review & Herald Publishing Assn.

Reese, Erica. My Almighty Daddy. 2007. 16p. (J). 10.00 *(978-0-9720773-3-0(2))* Christiangela Productions.

Reese, Jeff, photos by. A Is for Aloha. Feeney, Stephanie & Moravcik, Eva. 2nd ed. 2018. (ENG., 64p. (J). 16.99 *(978-0-8248-7654-8(7)*, 2604, Latitude 20) Univ. of Hawaii Pr.

Reese, Jonathan. In the Ocean. Taylor, Trace et al. 2012. (1-3Y Ecosystems Ser.). (ENG.). 16p. (J). (gr. k-1). pap. 8.00 *(978-1-59301-438-4(4))* American Reading Co.

Reese, Rick. Dream Town. Markel, Michelle. 2006. (J). 15.95 *(978-1-59714-022-5(8))* Heyday.

Reeve, Philip. The Snail Patrol. d'Lacey, Chris. 2005. 123p. (J). (gr. 2-5). per. 5.95 *(978-1-903015-30-8(8))* Barn Owl Bks, London GBR. Dist: Independent Pubs. Group.

Reeve, Philip. Esa Condenada Mala Suerte. Reeve, Philip. Poskitt, Kjartan. (SPA.). 176p. (YA). (gr. 5-8). pap. *(978-84-272-2091-1(X))* Molino, Editorial ESP. Dist: Lectorum Pubns., Inc.

—Esas Exasperantes Medidas de Longitud, Area y Volumen. Reeve, Philip. Poskitt, Kjartan. (SPA.). 178p. (YA). (gr. 5-8). *(978-84-272-2069-0(3))* Molino, Editorial ESP. Dist: Lectorum Pubns., Inc.

—Mas Mortiferas Mates. Reeve, Philip. Poskitt, Kjartan. (SPA.). 159p. (YA). (gr. 5-8). pap. *(978-84-272-2060-7(X))* Molino, Editorial ESP. Dist: Lectorum Pubns., Inc.

Reeve, Rosie. Mondays at Monster School. Symes, Ruth Louise. 2009. (ENG.). 32p. (J). (gr. -1-k). pap. 11.99 *(978-1-84255-536-1(7)*, Orion Children's Bks.) Hachette Children's Group GBR. Dist: Independent Pubs. Group.

—My Friend Fred. Oram, Hiawyn. 2012. (ENG.). 32p. (J). *(978-1-58925-105-2(9))* Tiger Tales.

—To Grandma, with Love. 2018. (Special Delivery Bks.). (ENG.). 8p. (J). (— 1). bds. 6.49 *(978-1-68412-270-7(8)*, Silver Dolphin Bks.) Printers Row Publishing Group.

Reeve, Tony. Esas Geniales Peliculas. Reeve, Tony, tr. Oliver, Martin. (Coleccion Esa Gran Cultura).Tr. of Groovy Movies. (SPA.). 160p. (YA). (gr. 5-8). 7.96 *(978-84-272-2133-8(9))* Molino, Editorial ESP. Dist: Lectorum Pubns., Inc.

Reeves, Eira. Would You Like to Know God?, 1 vol. Dowley, Tim & Jefferson, Graham. ed. 2016. (ENG.). 28p. (J). pap. 2.99 *(978-1-78128-275-5(7)*, Candle Bks.) Lion Hudson PLC GBR. Dist: Independent Pubs. Group.

—Would You Like to Know How to Pray?, 1 vol. Dowley, Tim. ed. 2014. (Would You Like to Know? Ser.). (ENG.). 28p. (J). (gr. -1-k). pap. 2.99 *(978-1-78128-158-1(0)*, Candle Bks.) Lion Hudson PLC GBR. Dist: Independent Pubs. Group.

—Would You Like to Know the Bible?, 1 vol. Dowley, Tim. ed. 2014. (Would You Like to Know? Ser.). (ENG.). 28p. (J). (gr. -1-k). pap. 2.99 *(978-1-78128-104-8(1)*, Candle Bks.) Lion Hudson PLC GBR. Dist: Independent Pubs. Group.

—Would You Like to Know the Story of Easter? Dowley, Tim. ed. 2017. (ENG.). 32p. (J). pap. 19.99 *(978-1-78128-360-8(5))* Lion Hudson PLC GBR. Dist: Independent Pubs. Group.

Reeves, Eira. Bible Storybook, 1 vol. Reeves, Eira. Dowley, Tim. ed. 2016. (Would You Like to Know? Ser.). (ENG.). 128p. (J). (gr. -1-k). pap. 9.99 *(978-1-78128-264-9(1)*, Candle Bks.) Lion Hudson PLC GBR. Dist: Independent Pubs. Group.

—The Complete Collection, 1 vol. Reeves, Eira. Dowley, Tim & Jefferson, Graham. ed. 2017. (Would You Like to Know? Ser.). (ENG.). 168p. (J). (gr. -1-k). pap. 12.99 *(978-1-78128-327-1(3)*, Candle Bks.) Lion Hudson PLC GBR. Dist: Independent Pubs. Group.

Reeves, Jeni. Anansi & the Box of Stories: A West African Folktale. 2007. (On My Own Folklore Ser.). 48p. (J). (gr. 2-5). lib. bdg. 25.26 *(978-0-8225-6741-7(5)*, Millbrook Pr.) Lerner Publishing Group.

—Anansi & the Box of Stories: [a West African Folktale]. Krensky, Stephen. 2008. (On My Own Folklore Ser.). (ENG.). 48p. (J). (gr. 2-4). pap. 7.99 *(978-0-8225-6545-5(8)*, First Avenue Editions) Lerner Publishing Group.

—Colors of Russia. Zemlicka, Shannon. (Colors of the World Ser.). 24p. (J). 2005. (gr. 3-6). lib. bdg. 19.93 *(978-1-57505-513-8(9))*; 2003. (gr. 1-4). pap. 5.95 *(978-1-57505-564-0(3))* Lerner Publishing Group.

—Enrique Esparza & the Battle of the Alamo. Brown, Susan Taylor. 2010. (History Speaks: Picture Books Plus Reader's Theater Ser.). (ENG.). 48p. (gr. 2-4). pap. 9.95 *(978-0-7613-3942-7(6))* Lerner Publishing Group.

—George Washington & the Story of the U. S. Constitution. Ransom, Candice. 2011. (History Speaks: Picture Books Plus Reader's Theater Ser.). 48p. pap. 56.72 *(978-0-7613-7632-3(1))*; (ENG.). (gr. 2-4). 27.93 *(978-0-7613-5877-0(3)*, Millbrook Pr.); (ENG.). (gr. 2-4). pap. 9.95 *(978-0-7613-7116-8(8))* Lerner Publishing Group.

—Mike Fink. Krensky, Stephen. 2007. (On My Own Folklore Ser.). (ENG.). 48p. (J). (gr. 2-4). per. 7.99 *(978-0-8225-6478-2(5)*, First Avenue Editions) Lerner Publishing Group.

—La Nina Que Poncho A Babe Ruth. Patrick, Jean L. S. 2007. (Yo Solo - Historia (on My Own - History) Ser.). 48p. (J). (gr. 4-7). per. 6.95 *(978-0-8225-7788-1(7))* Lerner Publishing Group.

—La Niña Que Ponchó a Babe Ruth. Patrick, Jean L. S. Translations.com Staff, tr. from ENG. 2007. (Yo Solo - Historia (on My Own - History) Ser.).Tr. of Girl Who Struck Out Babe Ruth. (SPA.). 48p. (gr. 2-4). lib. bdg. 25.26 *(978-0-8225-7765-0(2))* Lerner Publishing Group.

—Passover, Vol. Fishman, Cathy Goldberg. 2006. (On My Own Holidays Ser.). (ENG.). 48p. (gr. 2-4). per. 6.95 *(978-1-57505-695-1(X)*, First Avenue Editions) Lerner Publishing Group.

—Ramadan. Douglass, Susan L. 2004. (On My Own Holidays Ser.). 48p. (J). (gr. 2-4). lib. bdg. 25.26 *(978-0-87614-932-4(8))* Lerner Publishing Group.

—Willie Mclean & the Civil War Surrender. Ransom, Candice. 2004. (On My Own History Ser.). (ENG.). 48p. (J). (gr. 2-4). pap. 7.99 *(978-1-57505-698-2(4)*, First Avenue Editions) Lerner Publishing Group.

Reeves, Pauline. Attack of the Zombie Mermaids: A 4D Book. Steele, Michael Anthony. 2018. (Nearly Fearless Monkey Pirates Ser.). (ENG.). 48p. (J). (gr. k-2). lib. bdg. 23.99 *(978-1-5158-2677-4(5)*, 137832, Picture Window Bks.) Capstone.

—Battle of the Pirate Bands: A 4D Book. Steele, Michael Anthony. 2018. (Nearly Fearless Monkey Pirates Ser.). (ENG.). 48p. (J). (gr. k-2). pap. 7.95 *(978-1-5158-2687-3(2)*, 137838); lib. bdg. 23.99 *(978-1-5158-2679-8(1)*, 137834) Capstone. (Picture Window Bks.).

—Escape from Haunted Treasure Island: A 4D Book. Steele, Michael Anthony. 2018. (Nearly Fearless Monkey Pirates Ser.). (ENG.). 48p. (J). (gr. k-2). lib. bdg. 23.99 *(978-1-5158-2678-1(3)*, 137833, Picture Window Bks.) Capstone.

—Hunt for the Octo-Shark: A 4D Book. Steele, Michael Anthony. 2018. (Nearly Fearless Monkey Pirates Ser.). (ENG.). 48p. (J). (gr. k-2). lib. bdg. 23.99 *(978-1-5158-2680-4(5)*, 137835, Picture Window Bks.) Capstone.

—It Wasn't Me! Fehr, Daniel. 2019. (ENG.). 40p. (J). 15.95 *(978-84-17123-94-9(6))* NubeOcho Ediciones ESP. Dist: Consortium Bk. Sales & Distribution.

—Nearly Fearless Monkey Pirates. Steele, Michael Anthony. 2018. (Nearly Fearless Monkey Pirates Ser.). (ENG.). 48p. (J). (gr. k-2). 95.96 *(978-1-5158-2697-2(X)*, 27999, Picture Window Bks.) Capstone.

—¡Yo No Fui! Fehr, Daniel. 2019. (ENG.). 40p. (J). 15.95 *(978-84-17123-93-2(8))* NubeOcho Ediciones ESP. Dist: Consortium Bk. Sales & Distribution.

Reeves, Rick. United No More! Stories of the Civil War. Rappaport, Doreen & Verniero, Joan C. 2006. 144p. (J). (gr. 3-7). lib. bdg. 17.89 *(978-0-06-050600-1(8))* HarperCollins Pubs.

Reeves, Ruth. Tal, His Marvelous Adventures with Noom-Zor-Noom. Cooper, Paul Fenimore. 80th ed. 2009. 305p. (J). pap. 12.95 *(978-1-930900-41-7(4))* Purple Hse. Pr.

Regan, Dana. Away Went the Farmer's Hat: A Book about an Adventure. Moncure, Jane Belk. 2013. (Magic Castle Readers Ser.). (ENG.). 32p. (J). (gr. -1-2). 14.21 *(978-1-62323-572-7(3)*, 206309) Child's World, Inc., The.

—Brains vs. Brawn. Hoena, Blake. 2014. (Jess & Jaylen Ser.). (ENG.). 48p. (J). (gr. 1-4). 14.21 *(978-1-63143-436-5(5)*, 208260) Child's World, Inc., The.

—El Closet de Bessey, la Desordenada. McKissack, Patricia C. & McKissack, Fredrick L. 2003. (Rookie Reader Español Ser.).Tr. of Messy Bessey's Closet. (SPA.). 32p. (J). (gr. k-2). pap. 4.95 *(978-0-516-27796-7(0)*, Children's Pr.) Scholastic Library Publishing.

—Coming Clean. Hoena, Blake. 2014. (Jess & Jaylen Ser.). (ENG.). 48p. (J). (gr. 1-4). 14.21 *(978-1-63143-437-2(3)*, 208261) Child's World, Inc., The.

—Don't Let the Bedbugs Bite. Hawley, Greg. 2004. (J). *(978-0-9657612-7-7(4))* Paddle Wheel Publishing.

—A Dragon in a Wagon: A Book about Ways to Travel. Moncure, Jane Belk. 2013. (Magic Castle Readers Ser.). (ENG.). 32p. (J). (gr. -1-2). 14.21 *(978-1-62323-573-4(1)*, 206307) Child's World, Inc., The.

—Even the Sound Waves Obey Him: Bible Stories Brought to Life with Science. Kennedy, Nancy B. 2005. (CPH Teaching Resource Ser.). (ENG.). 64p. pap. 10.99 *(978-0-7586-0985-4(X))* Concordia Publishing Hse.

—Haiku on Your Shoes. Berry, Eileen M. 2005. 56p. (J). (gr. -1-3). per. 7.49 *(978-1-59166-374-4(1))* BJU Pr.

—Halloween Scream. Hoena, Blake. 2014. (Jess & Jaylen Ser.). (ENG.). 48p. (J). (gr. 1-4). 14.21 *(978-1-63143-438-9(1)*, 208262) Child's World, Inc., The.

—Hidden Pictures Alphabet. 2004. (ENG.). 32p. (J). pap. 2.99 *(978-1-58947-395-9(7)*, 02197) School Zone Publishing Co.

—I Can Learn Bible Stories. Ellis, Gwen. 2006. 10p. (J). spiral bd. 10.99 *(978-0-8254-5530-8(8))* Kregel Pubns.

—I Love Bathtime. Berry, Joy. 2010. (Teach Me About Ser.). (ENG.). 20p. (J). (gr. k — 1). pap. 5.99 *(978-1-60577-013-0(2))* Berry, Joy Enterprises.

—I Love Bedtime. Berry, Joy. 2010. (Teach Me About Ser.). (ENG.). 20p. (J). (gr. k — 1). pap. 5.99 *(978-1-60577-004-8(3))* Berry, Joy Enterprises.

—I Love Being Healthy. Berry, Joy. 2010. (Teach Me About Ser.). (ENG.). 20p. (J). (gr. k — 1). pap. 5.99 *(978-1-60577-005-5(1))* Berry, Joy Enterprises.

—I Love Brothers & Sisters. Berry, Joy. 2010. (Teach Me About Ser.). (ENG.). 20p. (J). (gr. k — 1). pap. 5.99 *(978-1-60577-002-4(7))* Berry, Joy Enterprises.

—I Love Daycare. Berry, Joy. 2010. (Teach Me About Ser.). (ENG.). 20p. (J). (gr. k — 1). bds. 5.99 *(978-1-60577-016-1(7))* Berry, Joy Enterprises.

—I Love Getting Dressed. Berry, Joy. 2010. (Teach Me About Ser.). (ENG.). 20p. (J). (gr. k — 1). bds. 5.99 *(978-1-60577-014-7(0))* Berry, Joy Enterprises.

—I Love Grandmas & Grandpas. Berry, Joy. 2010. (Teach Me About Ser.). (ENG.). 40p. (J). (gr. k — 1). pap. 5.99 *(978-1-60577-003-1(5))* Berry, Joy Enterprises.

—I Love Mealtime. Berry, Joy. 2010. (Teach Me About Ser.). (ENG.). 20p. (J). (gr. k — 1). pap. 5.99 *(978-1-60577-006-2(X))* Berry, Joy Enterprises.

—I Love Mommies & Daddies. Berry, Joy. 2010. (Teach Me About Ser.). (ENG.). 20p. (J). (gr. k — 1). pap. 5.99 *(978-1-60577-001-7(9))* Berry, Joy Enterprises.

—I Love My Friends. Berry, Joy. 2010. (Teach Me About Ser.). (ENG.). 20p. (J). (gr. k — 1). bds. 5.99 *(978-1-60577-017-8(5))* Berry, Joy Enterprises.

—I Love Preschool. Berry, Joy. 2010. (Teach Me About Ser.). (ENG.). 20p. (J). (gr. k — 1). bds. 5.99 *(978-1-60577-015-4(9))* Berry, Joy Enterprises.

Regan, Dana. Let's Go to the Fire Station. Harkrader, Lisa. 2020. (ENG.). 18p. (J). bds. ***(978-1-64269-254-9(9)***, 160eb70c-964e-4d3c-8362-266b1c741351, Sequoia Publishing & Media LLC) Phoenix International Publications, Inc.

Regan, Dana. Let's Talk Tails. English, June. 2004. 14p. (J). (gr. k-4). reprint ed. 4.00 *(978-0-7567-7832-3(8))* DIANE Publishing Co.

—Messy Bessey Vol. 2: Messy Bessey's Closet; Messy Bessey's Family Reunion; Messy Bessey's Garden. McKissack, Patricia C. & McKissack, Fredrick L. 2008. (Rookie Reader Ser.). (ENG.). 96p. (J). (gr. k-2). pap. 9.95 *(978-0-516-25301-5(8)*, Children's Pr.) Scholastic Library Publishing.

—Mr. Doodle Had a Poodle: A Book about Fun Activities. Moncure, Jane Belk. 2013. (Magic Castle Readers Ser.). (ENG.). 32p. (J). (gr. -1-2). 14.21 *(978-1-62323-574-1(X)*, 206310) Child's World, Inc., The.

—Museum Mystery. Hoena, Blake. 2014. (Jess & Jaylen Ser.). (ENG.). 48p. (J). (gr. 1-4). 14.21 *(978-1-63143-439-6(X)*, 208263) Child's World, Inc., The.

—My Little Easter Book. Steigemeyer, Julie. 2008. 20p. (J). (gr. -1-k). bds. 6.49 *(978-0-7586-1444-5(6))* Concordia Publishing Hse.

—Pinocho. Hillert, Margaret. 2018. (BeginningtoRead Ser.).Tr. of Pinocchio. (SPA.). 32p. (J). (gr. -1-2). pap. 11.94 *(978-1-68404-243-2(7))* Norwood Hse. Pr.

—Polka-Dot Puppy: A Just-for-Fun Book. Moncure, Jane Belk. 2013. (Magic Castle Readers Ser.). (ENG.). 32p. (J). (gr.

-1-2). 14.21 *(978-1-62323-575-8(8)*, 206311) Child's World, Inc., The.

—School Bus Bully. Hoena, Blake. 2014. (Jess & Jaylen Ser.). (ENG.). 48p. (J). (gr. 1-4). 14.21 *(978-1-63143-440-2(3)*, 208264) Child's World, Inc., The.

—Skateboard Scare. Hoena, Blake. 2014. (Jess & Jaylen Ser.). (ENG.). 48p. (J). (gr. 1-4). 14.21 *(978-1-63143-441-9(1)*, 208265) Child's World, Inc., The.

Regan, Dana, et al. Smart about the First Ladies: Smart about History. Warner, Sally. 2004. (Smart about History Ser.). (ENG.). 48p. (J). (gr. k-4). mass mkt. 6.99 *(978-0-448-43724-8(4)*, Grosset & Dunlap) Penguin Young Readers Group.

Regan, Dana. Train Your Brain with Activities of Odds & Chance, 1 vol. Hillman, Emilee. 2019. (Think Like a Programmer Ser.). (ENG.). 32p. (gr. 4-4). lib. bdg. 28.50 *(978-1-5026-4808-2(3))* Cavendish Square Publishing LLC.

—Train Your Brain with Activities Using Loops. Hillman, Emilee. 2019. (Think Like a Programmer Ser.). (ENG.). 32p. (gr. 4-4). 63.48 *(978-1-5026-4815-0(6))* Cavendish Square Publishing LLC.

—Train Your Brain with Collaboration Activities, 1 vol. Hillman, Emilee. 2019. (Think Like a Programmer Ser.). (ENG.). 32p. (gr. 4-4). lib. bdg. 28.50 *(978-1-5026-4812-9(1))* Cavendish Square Publishing LLC.

—Train Your Brain with Data Activities. Hillman, Emilee. 2019. (Think Like a Programmer Ser.). (ENG.). 32p. (gr. 4-4). 63.48 *(978-1-5026-4799-3(0))* Cavendish Square Publishing LLC.

—Train Your Brain with Parallel Computing & If/Then Activities, 1 vol. Hillman, Emilee. 2019. (Think Like a Programmer Ser.). (ENG.). 32p. (gr. 4-4). pap. 10.58 *(978-1-5026-4818-1(0))* Cavendish Square Publishing LLC.

—Train Your Brain with Problem-Solving Activities, 1 vol. Hillman, Emilie. 2019. (Think Like a Programmer Ser.). (ENG.). 32p. (gr. 4-4). pap. 10.58 *(978-1-5026-4802-0(4))* Cavendish Square Publishing LLC.

—Trouble with Cheating. Hoena, Blake. 2014. (Jess & Jaylen Ser.). (ENG.). 48p. (J). (gr. 1-4). 14.21 *(978-1-63143-442-6(X)*, 208266) Child's World, Inc., The.

—Video Game Zombie. Hoena, Blake. 2014. (Jess & Jaylen Ser.). (ENG.). 48p. (J). (gr. 1-4). 14.21 *(978-1-63143-443-3(8)*, 208267) Child's World, Inc., The.

Regan, Dana. Waiting for the Sun to Disappear. Silverman, Buffy. 2020. (ENG.). 26p. (J). pap. ***(978-1-925901-03-0(3))*** Library For All Limited.

Regan, Dana. What Gritty Kids Do When No One Is Looking. Grant, Jim & Grant, Caleb. 2016. (ENG.). pap. 10.95 *(978-1-63133-078-0(0))* Staff Development for Educators.

—When I Am/Cuando Estoy. Rosa-Mendoza, Gladys. (English Spanish Foundations Ser.). 20p. (gr. -1-k). 2007. pap. 19.95 *(978-1-931398-83-1(6))*; 2004. (SPA & ENG.). (J). bds. 6.95 *(978-1-931398-12-1(7))* Me+Mi Publishing.

—A Wish-For Dinosaur: A Just-for-Fun Book. Moncure, Jane Belk. 2013. (Magic Castle Readers Ser.). (ENG.). 32p. (J). (gr. -1-2). 14.21 *(978-1-62323-576-5(6)*, 206308) Child's World, Inc., The.

—5 Steps to Drawing Dogs & Cats. StJohn, Amanda. 2018. (5 Steps to Drawing Ser.). (ENG.). 32p. (J). (gr. k-3). 29.93 *(978-1-5038-2478-2(0)*, 212238) Child's World, Inc., The.

—5 Steps to Drawing Faces. Kesselring, Susan. 2018. (5 Steps to Drawing Ser.). (ENG.). 32p. (J). (gr. k-3). 29.93 *(978-1-5038-2479-9(9)*, 212239) Child's World, Inc., The.

Regan, Dana. Pinocho. Regan, Dana. Hillert, Margaret & Del Risco, Eida. 2018. (BeginningtoRead Ser.).Tr. of Pinocchio. (SPA.). 32p. (J). (gr. -1-2). lib. bdg. 22.60 *(978-1-59953-959-1(4))* Norwood Hse. Pr.

Regan, Dana, jt. illus. see Jack Pullan.

Regan, Dana, jt. illus. see Schwartz, Carol.

Regan, Laura. A Is for Anaconda: A Rainforest Alphabet. Fredericks, Anthony D. 2009. (Science Ser.). (ENG.). 40p. (J). (gr. 1-5). 17.95 *(978-1-58536-317-9(0))* Sleeping Bear Pr.

—Mama Mama/Papa Papa Flip Board Book. Marzollo, Jean. 2003. (Flip Boardbks.). (ENG.). 32p. (J). (gr. -1 — 1). bds. 7.99 *(978-0-06-051915-5(0)*, HarperFestival) HarperCollins Pubs.

—Pierre the Penguin. Marzollo, Jean. 2010. (ENG.). 32p. (J). (gr. -1-2). 15.95 *(978-1-58536-485-5(1))* Sleeping Bear Pr.

Regan, Lisa. Seek & Find Fairy: Find a Charm Book. Elliot, Rachel. 2014. (Seek & Find Bks.). (ENG.). 32p. (J). (gr. -1-1). 9.99 *(978-0-7641-6696-9(4)*, B.E.S. Publishing) Peterson's.

—Seek & Find Princess: Find a Charm Book. Elliot, Rachel. 2014. (Seek & Find Bks.). (ENG.). 32p. (J). (gr. -1-1). 9.99 *(978-0-7641-6697-6(2)*, B.E.S. Publishing) Peterson's.

Regan, Patricia. Little Christmas Tree: Open & Stand up the Tree! 2018. (ENG.). 16p. (J). (gr. -1-1). bds. 4.99 *(978-1-4380-5049-2(6)*, B.E.S. Publishing) Peterson's.

—Musical Christmas Tree. 2017. (ENG.). 16p. (J). (gr. -1-1). bds. 10.99 *(978-0-7641-6899-4(1)*, B.E.S. Publishing) Peterson's.

Regenold, Megan E. Winston's Halloween Scare. Regenold, Megan E. 2018. (ENG.). 36p. (J). pap. 9.99 *(978-1-7260-3123-3(3))* CreateSpace Independent Publishing Platform.

Reger, Rob. El Libro Secreto de las Cosas Extranas. Reger, Rob. 2006. (Emily the Strange (Spanish) Ser.). (SPA.). 64p. reprint ed. 19.95 *(978-1-59497-189-1(7))* Public Square Bks.

Reger, Rob & Brooks, Brian. Emily the Strange, Vol. 1. Reger, Rob. 2006. (Emily the Strange (Spanish) Ser.). (SPA.). 64p. 19.95 *(978-1-59497-188-4(9))* Public Square Bks.

Reger, Rob & Parker, Buzz. Emily the Strange: Dark Times. Reger, Rob & Gruner, Jessica. 2011. (Emily the Strange Ser.: 3). (ENG.). 248p. (YA). (gr. 8). pap. 9.99 *(978-0-06-145237-6(8))* HarperCollins Pubs.

—Emily the Strange: Piece of Mind. Reger, Rob & Gruner, Jessica. 2013. (Emily the Strange Ser.: 4). (ENG.). 288p. (YA). (gr. 8). pap. 9.99 *(978-0-06-145240-6(8))* HarperCollins Pubs.

—Emily the Strange: Stranger & Stranger. Reger, Rob & Gruner, Jessica. 2010. (Emily the Strange Ser.: 2). (ENG.). 272p. (YA). (gr. 8). pap. 9.99 *(978-0-06-145234-5(3))* HarperCollins Pubs.

Regier, Melanie B. The Animals' Guide to Weather Around the World & Other Natural Wonders. Cook, Mindy. 2015. (J). pap. *(978-0-692-03128-5(6))* Baron Ridge Productions.

Regis, Catienna. Chase Is Ready for Takeoff. John, Cousin. 2019. (Chase Bks.: Vol. 3). (ENG.). 44p. (J). pap. 15.00 ***(978-1-6753-2363-2(1))*** Independently Published.

Register, J. R. Tiny Paul the Tarantula Takes a Walk, 1 vol. Simpon, Tj. 2010. 70p. pap. 19.95 *(978-1-60703-117-8(5))* America Star Bks.

Regnier, Guylaine. Il Leone Pescatore. Ferre, Gil. 2017. (ITA.). (J). pap. *(978-2-930821-49-8(3))* Plannum.

Rehahn, Manuela. Robino ABC: Lernen Mit Den Sockenmonstern... 2017. (GER.). (J). (gr. k-2). pap. *(978-3-86467-059-6(4))* Rehahn., Ronny Spurenkreis-Verlag.

Rehahn, Manuela. Die Traurige Prinzessin. Rehahn, Manuela. 2019. (GER.). 28p. (J). *(978-3-86467-067-1(5))* Rehahn., Ronny Spurenkreis-Verlag.

Rehan, M. A Girl & Her Curls. Bermudez, Jenna & Bermudez, Jasia. 2020. (ENG.). 24p. (J). pap. 14.99 ***(978-1-0983-2318-9(1))*** BookBaby.

Rehan, Muhammad. Balloon Land. Armstrong, Marilyn & Barfi, Emmanuel. 2019. (ENG.). 54p. (J). pap. 15.99 *(978-1-0997-9575-6(3))* Independently Published.

Reiach, Margaret Amy. El Ciclo de Vida de la Mariposa. Kalman, Bobbie. 2005. (Serie Ciclos de Vida Ser.). (SPA.). 32p. (J). (gr. 1-4). pap. *(978-0-7787-8708-2(7))* Crabtree Publishing Co.

Reiach, Margaret Amy & Crabtree, Marc. Goldfish. Crabtree, Marc, photos by. MacAulay, Kelley & Kalman, Bobbie. 2004. (Pet Care Ser.). (ENG.). 32p. (J). pap. *(978-0-7787-1791-1(7))*; lib. bdg. *(978-0-7787-1759-1(3))* Crabtree Publishing Co.

Reibeling, Brandon. Awesome Air, 1 vol. Korb, Rena. 2007. (Science Rocks! Ser.). (ENG.). 32p. (J). (gr. k-4). 28.50 *(978-1-60270-036-9(2)*, 13188, Looking Glass Library) Magic Wagon.

—Crazy about Clouds, 1 vol. Korb, Rena. 2007. (Science Rocks! Ser.). (ENG.). 32p. (J). (gr. k-4). 28.50 *(978-1-60270-037-6(0)*, 13190, Looking Glass Library) Magic Wagon.

—Digging on Dirt, 1 vol. Korb, Rena. 2007. (Science Rocks! Ser.). (ENG.). 32p. (J). (gr. k-4). 28.50 *(978-1-60270-038-3(9)*, 13192, Looking Glass Library) Magic Wagon.

—Groovy Gravity, 1 vol. Korb, Rena. 2007. (Science Rocks! Ser.). (ENG.). 32p. (J). (gr. k-4). 28.50 *(978-1-60270-039-0(7)*, 13194, Looking Glass Library) Magic Wagon.

—Living Lights: Fireflies in Your Backyard. Loewen, Nancy. 2003. (Backyard Bugs Ser.). (ENG.). 24p. (J). (gr. -1-3). per. 8.95 *(978-1-4048-0447-0(1)*, Picture Window Bks.) Capstone.

—Radical Rocks, 1 vol. Korb, Rena. 2007. (Science Rocks! Ser.). (ENG.). 32p. (J). (gr. k-4). 28.50 *(978-1-60270-040-6(0)*, 13196, Looking Glass Library) Magic Wagon.

Reibeling, Brandon, jt. illus. see Haberstroh, Anne.

Reich, Carin. Shining Stars: A Colors Book. Robinson, Alise. 2005. (Space Craze Ser.). 16p. (J). (gr. -1-k). per., bds. 6.95 *(978-1-58117-392-5(X)*, Intervisual/Piggy Toes) Bendon, Inc.

Reich, Jonathan. Time Sandwich: A Start-In-the-Middle Book. Brennan, Matt. 2018. (Start in the Middle Book Ser.: Vol. 1). (ENG.). 38p. (J). (gr. k-6). 19.99 *(978-0-692-12587-8(6))* Brennan, Matt.

Reich, Kass. Carson Crosses Canada. Bailey, Linda. 2020. (ENG.). 36p. (J). (gr. -1-3). pap. 8.99 *(978-0-7352-6635-3(2)*, Tundra Bks.) Tundra Bks. CAN. Dist: Penguin Random Hse. LLC.

—Dr. Coo & the Pigeon Protest. Hampson, Sarah. 2018. (ENG.). 32p. (J). (gr. -1-2). 16.99 *(978-1-77138-361-5(5))* Kids Can Pr., Ltd. CAN. Dist: Hachette Bk. Group.

—Hamsters on the Go, 1 vol. 2016. (ENG.). 24p. (J). (gr. -1 — 1). bds. 9.95 *(978-1-4598-1016-7(3))* Orca Bk. Pubs. USA.

—Megabat. Humphrey, Anna. (Megabat Ser.: 1). (ENG.). 192p. (J). (gr. 2-5). 2020. pap. 8.99 *(978-0-7352-6695-7(6))*; 2018. 12.99 *(978-0-7352-6257-7(8))* Tundra Bks. CAN. (Tundra Bks.). Dist: Penguin Random Hse. LLC.

—Megabat & Fancy Cat. Humphrey, Anna. 2019. (Megabat Ser.: 2). (ENG.). 176p. (J). (gr. 2-5). 12.99 *(978-0-7352-6259-1(4)*, Tundra Bks.) Tundra Bks. CAN. Dist: Penguin Random Hse. LLC.

—Megabat Is a Fraidybat. Humphrey, Anna. 2020. (Megabat Ser.: 3). (ENG.). 192p. (J). (gr. 2-5). 12.99 *(978-0-7352-6602-5(6)*, Tundra Bks.) Tundra Bks. CAN. Dist: Penguin Random Hse. LLC.

—Sergeant Billy: The True Story of the Goat Who Went to War. Messier, Mireille. 2019. (ENG.). 40p. (J). (gr. -1-3). 17.99 *(978-0-7352-6442-7(2)*, Tundra Bks.) Tundra Bks. CAN. Dist: Penguin Random Hse. LLC.

—Up Hamster, down Hamster, 1 vol. 2015. (ENG.). 24p. (J). (gr. -1 — 1). bds. 9.95 *(978-1-4598-1013-6(9))* Orca Bk. Pubs. USA.

—What Grew in Larry's Garden. Alary, Laura. 2020. (ENG.). 32p. (J). (gr. -1-2). 17.99 *(978-1-5253-0108-7(X))* Kids Can Pr., Ltd. CAN. Dist: Hachette Bk. Group.

Reich, Robert E. Harry MacFly's the Old Mill Adventure. Reich, Robert E. 2013. (ENG.). 28p. (J). pap. 9.95 *(978-0-9895323-1-0(3))* Black Creek Publishing Group.

Reich, Tyler. Adventures of the Lions in the Most Magical Place on Earth. Reich, Austin. 2018. (ENG.). 64p. (J). (gr. -1-12). pap. 5.95 *(978-0-9986531-9-8(5))* Momosa Publishing LLC.

—The Adventures of the Rabbits in the Magic Kingdom. Reich, Austin. 2017. (Adventures of the Real Animals in the Most Magical Place on Earth Ser.). (ENG.). 64p. (J). (gr. -1-12). pap. 4.95 *(978-0-9970808-8-9(4))* Momosa Publishing LLC.

—Adventures of the Squirrels in Epcot. Reich, Austin. 2017. (Adventures of the Real Animals in the Most Magical Place on Earth Ser.). (ENG.). 64p. (J). (gr. -1-12). pap. 5.95 *(978-0-9986531-4-3(4))* Momosa Publishing LLC.

Reichman, Debbie. Kevin Can. Reichman, Beverley. 2019. (ENG.). 40p. (J). pap. 13.95 *(978-1-64096-655-0(2))* Newman Springs Publishing, Inc.

Reid, Barbara. The Night Before Christmas. Moore, Clement C. adapted ed. 2016. (ENG.). 36p. pap. 6.95 *(978-1-945546-47-1(6))* Frederic Thomas USA, Inc.

—Picture the Sky. 2019. (ENG.). 32p. (J). (gr. -1-k). 16.99 *(978-0-8075-9525-1(X)*, 080759525X) Whitman, Albert & Co.

—El Ternero Recien Nacido. Newlin-Chase, Edith. (SPA.). 32p. (J). (gr. -1-1). pap. 4.99 *(978-0-590-46106-1(0)*, SO30492) Scholastic, Inc.

Reid, Barbara. Picture a Tree. Reid, Barbara. 2013. (ENG.). 32p. (J). (gr. -1-3). 16.99 *(978-0-8075-6526-1(1)*, 807565261) Whitman, Albert & Co.

—The Subway Mouse. Reid, Barbara. 2017. 40p. (gr. 1-2). pap. 7.95 *(978-0-439-78917-2(6))*; 2005. (J). *(978-0-439-77430-7(6))* Scholastic, Inc.

Reid, Bill. The Raven Steals the Light. Reid, Bill. Bringhurst, Robert. 2nd ed. 2003. (ENG.). 128p. (C). (gr. -1-18). reprint ed. pap. 16.95 *(978-0-295-97524-5(5))* Univ. of Washington Pr.

Reid, Fiona. Mammals. Alden, Peter C. 2nd ed. 2013. (Peterson Field Guide Color-In Bks.). (ENG.). 10p. (J). 10.99 *(978-0-544-03254-5(3)*, 1530244) Houghton Mifflin Harcourt Publishing Co.

Reid, Gillian. Peanut Goes for the Gold. Van Ness, Jonathan. 2020. (ENG.). 32p. (J). (gr. -1-3). 18.99 *(978-0-06-294100-8(3)*, HarperCollins) HarperCollins Pubs. Ltd. GBR. Dist: HarperCollins Pubs.

Reid, Michael, et al. Laugh-Along Nursery Rhymes. (Rookie Read-Aloud Ser.). (ENG.). 32p. (J). (gr. -1-k). 2017. pap. 12.00 *(978-0-531-23046-6(5))*; 2016. 25.00 *(978-0-531-22879-1(7))* Scholastic Library Publishing. (Children's Pr.).

Reid, Mick. Boomerang Bob. Dale, Jenny. 2003. 105p. (J). *(978-0-439-45348-6(8))* Scholastic, Inc.

—Forever Sam. Dale, Jenny. 2003. 104p. (J). *(978-0-439-33801-1(8))* Scholastic, Inc.

—Homeward Bound. Dale, Jenny. 2003. 110p. (J). *(978-0-439-45354-7(2))* Scholastic, Inc.

—How Can I Get a Pet? Williams, Rozanne Lanczak. 2006. (Learn to Write Ser.). 8p. (J). (gr. k-2). pap. *(978-1-59198-290-6(1)*, 6184) Creative Teaching Pr., Inc.

—How Can I Get a Pet? Williams, Rozanne Lanczak. Maio, Barbara & Faulkner, Stacey, eds. 2006. (J). per. 6.99 *(978-1-59198-363-7(0))* Creative Teaching Pr., Inc.

—Husky Hero. Dale, Jenny. 2003. 108p. (J). *(978-0-439-54361-3(4))* Scholastic, Inc.

—If I Were a Cowboy, 1 vol. Braun, Eric. 2010. (Dream Big! Ser.). (ENG.). 24p. (J). (gr. k-3). lib. bdg. 27.32 *(978-1-4048-5531-1(9)*, Picture Window Bks.) Capstone.

—If I Were a Firefighter, 1 vol. Troupe, Thomas Kingsley. 2010. (Dream Big! Ser.). (ENG.). 24p. (J). (gr. k-3). lib. bdg. 27.32 *(978-1-4048-5535-9(1)*, Picture Window Bks.) Capstone.

—Jake's Progress. Dale, Jenny. 2003. 110p. (J). *(978-0-439-54365-1(7))* Scholastic, Inc.

—Jingle Belle. Dale, Jenny. 2003. 107p. (J). *(978-0-439-54366-8(5))* Scholastic, Inc.

—Little Star. Dale, Jenny. 2003. 109p. (J). *(978-0-439-54363-7(0))* Scholastic, Inc.

—Milly's Triumph. Dale, Jenny & Rowe, Michael. 2003. 102p. (J). *(978-0-439-45346-2(1))* Scholastic, Inc.

—Murphy's Mystery. Dale, Jenny. 2003. 110p. (J). *(978-0-439-54364-4(9))* Scholastic, Inc.

—The Puppy Express. Dale, Jenny. 2003. 108p. (J). *(978-0-439-45355-4(0))* Scholastic, Inc.

—Puppy Power. Dale, Jenny. 2003. 105p. (J). *(978-0-439-45351-6(8))* Scholastic, Inc.

—Signing Around Town: Sign Language for Kids, 1 vol. Clay, Kathryn & Vonne, Mira. 2013. (Time to Sign Ser.). (ENG.). 32p. (J). (gr. -1-2). 27.99 *(978-1-62065-053-0(3))* Capstone.

—Top Dog! Dale, Jenny. 2003. 107p. (J). *(978-0-439-54369-9(6))* Scholastic, Inc.

—Wait for Me! Gerver, Jane E. (My First Reader Ser.). (J). (gr. k-1). 2005. (ENG.). 32p. pap. 3.95 *(978-0-516-25116-5(3))*; 2004. 31p. 18.50 *(978-0-516-24676-5(3))* Scholastic Library Publishing. (Children's Pr.).

Reid, Mike. A Night of Nonsense. Arlington, Jane. 2006. 20p. (J). *(978-1-59939-103-8(1)*, Reader's Digest Young Families, Inc.) Studio Fun International.

Reid, Vince. The Clubhouse Mystery. McGann, Erika. 2017. (Cass & the Bubble Street Gang Ser.: 1). (ENG.). 160p. pap. 13.00 *(978-1-84717-920-3(7))* O'Brien Pr., Ltd., The IRL. Dist: Casemate Pubs. & Bk. Distributors, LLC.

—Diary Detectives. McGann, Erika. 2018. (Cass & the Bubble Street Gang Ser.: 3). (ENG.). 192p. 13.00 *(978-1-78849-022-1(3))* O'Brien Pr., Ltd., The IRL. Dist: Casemate Pubs. & Bk. Distributors, LLC.

—Making Millions. McGann, Erika. 2017. (Cass & the Bubble Street Gang Ser.: 2). (ENG.). 192p. pap. 13.00 *(978-1-84717-921-0(5))* O'Brien Pr., Ltd., The IRL. Dist: Casemate Pubs. & Bk. Distributors, LLC.

—Scavenger Hunt. McGann, Erika. 2019. (Cass & the Bubble Street Gang Ser.: 4). (ENG.). 224p. 13.00 *(978-1-78849-093-1(2))* O'Brien Pr., Ltd., The IRL. Dist: Casemate Pubs. & Bk. Distributors, LLC.

Reiff, Chris & Trevas, Chris. Darth Vader: A 3-D Reconstruction Log. Wallace, Daniel. 2011. (Star Wars Ser.). (ENG.). 24p. (J). bds. 19.99 *(978-0-545-31215-8(9))* Scholastic, Inc.

Reifsnyder, Scotty. Exploring the Bible: A Bible Reading Plan for Kids. Murray, David. 2017. (ENG.). 224p. 14.99 *(978-1-4335-5686-9(3))* Crossway.

Reilly, Joan & Katz, Avi. Bar Mitzvah, Bat Mitzvah: The Ceremony, the Party, & How the Day Came to Be. Metter, Bert & Metter, Bertram. 2007. (ENG.). 80p. (J). (gr. 5-7). pap. 8.95 *(978-0-618-76773-1(8)*, 100540) Houghton Mifflin Harcourt Publishing Co.

Reilly, Meghan M. What's Wrong with the New Girl? Jacques, Taryn Elise. 2004. 33p. pap. 24.95 *(978-1-4137-1999-4(6))* PublishAmerica, Inc.

Reilly, Michelle. In My Own Backyard. Larsen, Donna R. 2011. 30p. (J). *(978-0-615-52915-8(1))* DeuxRay Productions.

Reim, Melanie. The Cold War. Gottfried, Ted. 2003. (Rise & Fall of the Soviet Union Ser.). (ENG.). 160p. (gr. 7-12). lib. bdg. 29.20 *(978-0-7613-2560-4(3)*, Twenty-First Century Bks.) Lerner Publishing Group.

Reim, Melanie K. The Great Fatherland War: The Soviet Union in World War II. Gottfried, Ted. 2003. (Rise & Fall of the Soviet Union Ser.). 160p. (gr. 7-18). lib. bdg. 28.90 *(978-0-7613-2559-8(X)*, Twenty-First Century Bks.) Lerner Publishing Group.

Reimer, Jackie. No Thanks, but I'd Love to Dance! Choosing to Live Smoke Free. Reimer, Jackie. 2010. (ENG.). 32p. (J). (gr. 2-4). 14.95 *(978-1-60443-027-1(3))* American Cancer Society, Inc.

Reinford, Luanne & Horst, Melissa. Helping Grandfather. Witmer, Edith. 2016. (ENG.). 91p. (J). 4.75 *(978-0-7399-2537-9(7))* Rod & Staff Pubs., Inc.

Reingold, Alan. Liberty on 23rd Street. Glasthal, Jacqueline B. 2006. (Adventures in America Ser.). (gr. 4). 14.95 net. *(978-1-893110-45-8(1))* Silver Moon Pr.

Reinhardt, Jennifer Black. Footer Davis Probably Is Crazy. Vaught, Susan. 2015. (ENG.). 240p. (J). (gr. 5-9). 16.99 *(978-1-4814-2276-5(6)*, Simon & Schuster Bks. For Young Readers) Simon & Schuster Bks. For Young Readers.

—Gondra's Treasure. Park, Linda Sue. 2019. (ENG.). 40p. (J). (gr. -1-3). 17.99 *(978-0-544-54669-1(5)*, 1609531, Clarion Bks.) Houghton Mifflin Harcourt Trade & Reference Pubs.

—The Inventor's Secret: What Thomas Edison Told Henry Ford. Slade, Suzanne. 2015. 48p. (J). (gr. 1-4). lib. bdg. 16.95 *(978-1-58089-667-2(7))* Charlesbridge Publishing, Inc.

—Rabbi Benjamin's Buttons. McGinty, Alice B. 32p. (J). (gr. -1-3). 2017. pap. 7.99 *(978-1-58089-433-3(X))*; 2014. lib. bdg. 17.95 *(978-1-58089-432-6(1))* Charlesbridge Publishing, Inc.

—Sometimes You Fly. Applegate, Katherine. 2018. (ENG.). 40p. (J). (gr. -1-3). 17.99 *(978-0-547-63390-9(4)*, 1467767, Clarion Bks.) Houghton Mifflin Harcourt Trade & Reference Pubs.

—Sometimes You Fly (padded Board Book) Applegate, Katherine. 2020. (ENG.). 36p. (J). (— 1). bds. 8.99 *(978-0-358-21226-3(X)*, 1765192, HMH Books For Young Readers) Houghton Mifflin Harcourt Publishing Co.

—Yaks Yak: Animal Word Pairs. Park, Linda Sue. 2016. (ENG.). 40p. (J). (gr. -1-3). 16.99 *(978-0-544-39101-7(2)*, 1593193, Clarion Bks.) Houghton Mifflin Harcourt Trade & Reference Pubs.

Reinhart, Larry. Frank & the Balloon: Sapi y el Globo. Ross, Dev & Canetti, Yanitzia. 2010. (SPA & ENG.). 41p. (J). *(978-1-60115-041-7(5))* Treasure Bay, Inc.

—We Both Read Bilingual Edition-Frank & the Giant/Sapi y el Globo. Ross, Dev. ed. 2011. (ENG & SPA.). 44p. (J). pap. 4.99 *(978-1-60115-042-4(3))* Treasure Bay, Inc.

—We Both Read Bilingual Edition-Frank & the Tiger/Sapi y el Tigre. Ross, Dev. Canetti, Yanitzia, tr. from ENG. 2014. (We Both Read - Level K-1 (Quality) Ser.). (ENG & SPA.). 44p. (J). (gr. k-1). pap. 4.99 *(978-1-60115-058-5(X))* Treasure Bay, Inc.

—We Both Read-Fox's Best Trick Ever: Level 1. Ross, Dev. 2006. (We Both Read Ser.). 44p. (J). (gr. -1-3). 7.99 *(978-1-891327-69-8(0))* Treasure Bay, Inc.

—We Both Read-Frank & the Balloon: Level K-1. Ross, Dev. 2008. (We Both Read Ser.). 44p. (J). (gr. -1-2). per. 4.99 *(978-1-60115-012-7(1))* Treasure Bay, Inc.

—We Both Read-Frank & the Giant (Picture Book) Ross, Dev. 2007. (We Both Read Ser.). 44p. (J). (gr. -1-2). lib. bdg. 14.95 *(978-1-60115-006-6(7))* Treasure Bay, Inc.

—We Both Read-Frank & the Tiger. Ross, Dev. 2012. 44p. (J). pap. 4.99 *(978-1-60115-260-2(4))* Treasure Bay, Inc.

—We Both Read-Lulu's Lost Shoes. Blankenship, Paula. (We Both Read Ser.). (J). (gr. k-3). 2011. (ENG.). 48p. 17.44 *(978-1-891327-55-1(0))*; 2005. 44p. pap. 4.99 *(978-1-891327-56-8(9))* Treasure Bay, Inc.

—We Both Read-Lulu's Wild Party. Blankenship, Paula. 2009. (We Both Read Ser.). 44p. (J). 9.95 *(978-1-60115-231-2(0))*; pap. 4.99 *(978-1-60115-232-9(9))* Treasure Bay, Inc.

—We Read Phonics-Matt & Sid. McKay, Sindy. 2010. 32p. (J). 9.95 *(978-1-60115-315-9(5))*; pap. 4.99 *(978-1-60115-316-6(3))* Treasure Bay, Inc.

Reinhart, Matthew. My Little Pony: the Castles of Equestria: An Enchanted My Little Pony Pop-Up Book. 2015. 16p. (J). (gr. 1-17). 24.99 *(978-0-316-18832-6(8))* Little, Brown Bks. for Young Readers.

—No Biting, Louise. Palatini, Margie. 2007. 32p. (J). (gr. -1-3). 16.99 *(978-0-06-052627-6(0))*; (ENG.). lib. bdg. 17.89 *(978-0-06-052628-3(9))* HarperCollins Pubs. (Tegen, Katherine Bks).

Reinhart, Matthew. The Ark: A Pop-up Book. Reinhart, Matthew. 2006. 12p. (J). (gr. k-4). reprint ed. 17.00 *(978-1-4223-5673-9(6))* DIANE Publishing Co.

—Cinderella: A Pop-Up Fairy Tale. Reinhart, Matthew. 2005. (ENG.). 12p. (J). (gr. -1-3). 39.99 *(978-1-4169-0501-1(4)*, Little Simon) Little Simon.

—Disney*Pixar: A Pop-Up Celebration. Reinhart, Matthew. 2017. (ENG.). 12p. (YA). (gr. 7-17). 65.00 *(978-1-4847-9941-3(0)*, Disney Editions) Disney Pr.

—The Jungle Book: A Pop-Up Adventure. Reinhart, Matthew. 2006. (ENG.). 12p. (J). 39.99 *(978-1-4169-1824-0(8)*, Little Simon) Little Simon.

—A Pop-Up Book of Nursery Rhymes: A Classic Collectible Pop-Up. Reinhart, Matthew. 2009. (ENG.). 12p. (J). (gr. -1-3). 34.99 *(978-1-4169-1825-7(6)*, Little Simon) Little Simon.

R

Reinhart, Matthew & Sabuda, Robert. Encyclopedia Prehistorica Dinosaurs Pop-Up. Reinhart, Matthew & Sabuda, Robert. 2005. (Encyclopedia Prehistorica Ser.: 1). (ENG.). 12p. (J). (gr. k-4). 42.99 *(978-0-7636-2228-2(1))* Candlewick Pr.

—Encyclopedia Prehistorica Sharks & Other Sea Monsters. Reinhart, Matthew & Sabuda, Robert. 2006. (Encyclopedia Prehistorica Ser.: 2). 12p. (J). (gr. k-4). 42.99 *(978-0-7636-2229-9(X))* Candlewick Pr.

—Gods & Heroes. Reinhart, Matthew & Sabuda, Robert. 2010. (Encyclopedia Mythologica Ser.: 2). (ENG.). 12p. (J). (gr. k-4). 29.99 *(978-0-7636-3171-0(X))*; 250.00 *(978-0-7636-3486-5(7))* Candlewick Pr.

Reinoso, Carlos. Little Ducky Jr. & the Whirlwind Storm: A Tale of Loss, Hope,and Renewal. Reinoso, Carlos. I.t. ed. 2005. 50p. (J). 8.99 *(978-0-9777672-0-5(5))* Behavioral Health & Human Development Ctr.

Reis, Erica, et al. Rumors from the Other Side. Armand, Villavert et al. Schilling, Christine & Kim, Hyun-Joo, trs. 2017. (ENG.). 192p. (YA). (gr. 8-18). pap. 9.99 *(978-1-4278-0822-6(8),* c0f0d672-92f8-4989-9f56-25cae7413462) TOKYOPOP, Inc.

Reis, Ivan, et al. Dark Passage, Vol. 2. Pulido, Brian. 2004. (Lady Death Ser.: Vol. 2). 160p. (YA). pap. 9.95 *(978-1-59314-054-0(1))* CrossGeneration Comics, Inc.

Reis, Lauren. Pretend Friends: A Story about Schizophrenia & Other Illnesses That Can Cause Hallucinations. Hoyle, Alice. 2015. (ENG.). 36p. (J). 14.95 *(978-1-84905-624-3(2),* 693774) Kingsley, Jessica Pubs. GBR. Dist: Hachette UK Distribution.

Reis, Rod. New Mutants by Jonathan Hickman Vol. 1. 2020. (ENG.). 176p. (YA). (gr. 8-17). pap. 15.99 *(978-1-302-91992-4(X))* Marvel Worldwide, Inc.

—Winter Soldier: Second Chances. 2019. (ENG.). 112p. (YA). pap. 15.99 *(978-1-302-91587-2(8))* Marvel Worldwide, Inc.

Reis, Rod, jt. illus. see Quinones, Joe.

Reisberg, Mira. Baby Rattlesnake. Ata, Te. 2013. (ENG.). 32p. (J). (gr. -1). pap. 10.95 *(978-0-89239-216-2(9))* Lee & Low Bks., Inc.

—Baby Rattlesnake. Ata, Te. Alarcón, Francisco X., tr. 2013. (SPA & ENG.). 32p. (J). pap. 9.95 *(978-0-89239-188-2(X))* Lee & Low Bks., Inc.

—Baby Rattlesnake. Ata, Te et al. 2013. (ENG.). 32p. (J). (gr. -1-18). pap. 9.95 *(978-0-89239-049-6(2))* Lee & Low Bks., Inc.

—Uncle Nacho's Hat Flor Ada, Alma & Zubizarreta, Rosalma, trs. 2013.Tr. of El Sombrero Del Tio Nacho. (ENG & SPA.). 32p. (J). (gr. 1-18). pap. 8.95 *(978-0-89239-043-4(3),* CBP0433S) Lee & Low Bks., Inc.

—Uncle Nacho's Hat: El Sombrero Del to Nacho. Rohmer, Harriet. Flor Ada, Alma & Zubizarreta, Rosalma, trs. 2013. (ENG.). 32p. (J). (gr. k-18). pap. 10.95 *(978-0-89239-112-7(X))* Lee & Low Bks., Inc.

—Where Fireflies Dance: Ahi, Donde Bailan Las Luciernagas, 1 vol. Corpi, Lucha & National Geographic Learning Staff. 2013. (ENG & SPA.). 32p. (J). (gr. k-2). pap. 10.95 *(978-0-89239-177-6(4),* 903d1c63-639c-4e58-83a5-404613f4dcb8, Children's Book Press) Lee & Low Bks., Inc.

Reisch, Jesse. Bed in Summer. Stevenson, Robert Louis. 2011. (Poetry for Children Ser.). (ENG.). 24p. (J). (gr. k-3). 27.07 *(978-1-60973-151-9(4),* 201180) Child's World, Inc., The.

—The Drum Circle. Todd, Traci N. 2006. (J). *(978-1-58987-023-9(9))* Kindermusik International.

—I Am the Desert. Fredericks, Anthony D. 2012. (J). *(978-1-933855-73-8(8))* Rio Nuevo Pubs.

—The Shortest Day: Celebrating the Winter Solstice. Pfeffer, Wendy. 2014. (ENG.). 40p. (J). (gr. 1-4). 8.99 *(978-0-14-751284-0(0),* Puffin Books) Penguin Young Readers Group.

Reisch, Jessie. Ebony & Ivory: Discovering 10 Keys to Racial Harmony. Elkins, Stephen. 2003. 32p. (J). (gr. k-18). 14.99 incl. audio compact disk *(978-0-8054-2674-8(4))* B&H Publishing Group.

—Know God, No Fear. Elkins, Stephen. 2003. 32p. (J). (gr. k-5). 14.99 *(978-0-8054-2658-8(2))* B&H Publishing Group.

Reisenauer, Cynthia Mauro. Emerita. Reisenauer, Cynthia Mauro. 2007. 48p. (J). 18.95 *(978-0-9726487-5-2(5))* Puddle Jump Pr., Ltd.

Reiser, Lynn. My Way/a Mi Manera: Bilingual Spanish-English Children's Book. Reiser, Lynn. 2007. (SPA.). 32p. (J). (gr. -1-k). 16.99 *(978-0-06-084101-0(X),* Greenwillow Bks.) HarperCollins Pubs.

Reiss, John J. Numbers. Reiss, John J. 2016. (ENG.). 34p. (J). (gr. -1 — 1). bds. 8.99 *(978-1-4814-7647-8(5),* Little Simon) Little Simon.

—Shapes. Reiss, John J. 2016. (ENG.). 34p. (J). (gr. -1 — 1). bds. 8.99 *(978-1-4814-7645-4(9),* Little Simon) Little Simon.

Reiss, William, jt. illus. see Greenblatt, C. H.

Reitenour, Nick. The Life of Ellie. Block, Jan. Block, Erik, ed. 2019. (Stuffy Adventures Ser.: Vol. 1). (ENG.). 38p. (J). 23.95 ***(978-1-0878-6084-8(9))***; pap. 13.00 ***(978-0-578-60936-2(3))*** Block, Jan.

Reiter, Xee. The Shared Room. Yang, Kao Kalia. 2020. (ENG.). 32p. (J). (gr. k-5). 16.95 ***(978-1-5179-0794-5(2))*** Univ. of Minnesota Pr.

Reitmeyer, Shannon. The Proud Inchworm. Reitmeyer, Shannon. 2013. 24p. pap. 12.00 *(978-1-61286-161-6(X))* Avid Readers Publishing Group.

Reitze, Glenn Logan. Ernie the Easter Hippopotamus: A Comic Adventure for Anytime. Reitze, Glenn Logan. 2007. (ENG.). 48p. (J). lib. bdg. 19.95 *(978-0-88265-040-1(8),* Fine Art Editions) North American International.

Reitze, Glenn Logan. Ernie the Easter Hippotamus: A Comic Adventure for Anytime. Reitze, Glenn Logan, text. 2007. (J). pap. *(978-0-88265-041-8(6))* North American International.

Rejent, Renee. How High Can You Fly? DeVos, Janie. I.t. ed. 2005. 32p. 16.95 *(978-0-9663276-2-5(4))* Red Engine Pr.

Relf, Adam. Can Kittens Take a Catnap? Palfreman-Bunker, Claire. 2007. (J). pap. *(978-0-545-02595-9(8))* Scholastic, Inc.

—Sharks: Information for Young Readers - Level 1. Clarke, Catriona. 2007. (Usborne Beginners Ser.). 32p. (J). (gr. -1-3). 4.99 *(978-0-7945-1581-2(9),* Usborne) EDC Publishing.

Reller, Marcia Mattingly. Growing up in Wisdom: A Story of Jesus as a Baby & a Young Boy. Watson, Donn, ed. 2nd ed. 2011. 40p. (J). 14.95 *(978-0-9801975-4-9(6))* Blake-Virostko, Pamela.

Relyea, Alison. A Place in My Heart. Grossnickle, Mary. 2014. (ENG.). 36p. (J). 15.95 *(978-1-84905-771-4(0),* 694479) Kingsley, Jessica Pubs. GBR. Dist: Hachette UK Distribution.

Relyea, C. M. Caps & Capers: A Story of Boarding-School Life. Jackson, Gabrielle E. 2008. 136p. pap. *(978-1-4099-4255-9(4))* Dodo Pr.

—Caps & Capers: A Story of Boarding School Life (1901) Jackson, Gabrielle Emilie Snow. 284p. 2010. 35.16 *(978-1-164-31862-0(4))*; 2010. pap. 23.16 *(978-1-164-12697-3(0))*; 2008. 43.95 *(978-1-4366-0917-3(8))*; 2008. (ENG.). per. 28.95 *(978-0-548-82612-6(9))* Kessinger Publishing, LLC.

Relyea, Charles M. Catcher Craig. Mathewson, Christy. 2011. 360p. 51.95 *(978-1-258-06942-1(3))* Literary Licensing, LLC.

rem. Vampire Kisses: Blood Relatives, Volume II, Vol. II. Schreiber, Ellen. 2008. (Vampire Kisses: Blood Relatives Ser.: Vol. 2). (ENG.). 192p. (YA). (gr. 8-18). pap. 9.99 *(978-0-06-134082-6(0),* Tegen, Katherine Bks) HarperCollins Pubs.

rem, jt. illus. see Kwon, Elisa.

Rembert, Winfred. Don't Hold Me Back: My Life & Art. 2003. (ENG.). 48p. (J). 19.95 *(978-0-8126-2703-9(2))* Cricket Bks.

Remesz, Natasza. Oh, the Things I Can Be When I See Me. Coleman, Valerie. Johnson, Tenita C., ed. 2019. (ENG.). 34p. (J). (gr. 3-5). pap. 14.95 ***(978-0-9786066-8-8(X))*** Pen of the Writer, LLC.

Remey, Grace Anne. Lion's Pride: A Tail of Deployment. Remey, Grace Anne. 2012. (ENG.). 38p. pap. 12.95 *(978-0-9855445-0-8(3))* Remey, Lisa.

Remkiewicz, Frank. Arithme-Tickle: An Even Number of Odd Riddle-Rhymes. Lewis, J. Patrick. 2007. (ENG.). 32p. (J). (gr. k-3). 18.69 *(978-0-15-216418-8(9))* Harcourt Children's Bks.

—Arithme-Tickle: An Even Number of Odd Riddle-Rhymes. Lewis, J. Patrick. 2007. (ENG.). 32p. (J). (gr. 1-4). pap. 7.99 *(978-0-15-205848-7(6),* 1197563) Houghton Mifflin Harcourt Publishing Co.

—Down by the Station. Riggs Vetter, Jennifer. 2009. 32p. (J). (gr. -1-2). 16.99 *(978-1-58246-243-1(7),* Tricycle Pr.) Random Hse. Children's Bks.

—Froggy Builds a Snowman. London, Jonathan. 2020. (Froggy Ser.). 32p. (J). (-k). 16.99 *(978-1-9848-3636-6(6),* Viking Books for Young Readers) Penguin Young Readers Group.

—Froggy Eats Out. London, Jonathan. 2003. (Froggy Ser.). 32p. (J). (gr. -1-k). pap. 7.99 *(978-0-14-250061-3(5),* Puffin Books) Penguin Young Readers Group.

—Froggy Eats Out. London, Jonathan. 2003. (Froggy Ser.). 13.65 *(978-0-7569-1464-6(7))* Perfection Learning Corp.

—Froggy for President! London, Jonathan. 2020. (Froggy Ser.). 32p. (J). (-k). 16.99 *(978-0-451-47948-8(3),* Viking Books for Young Readers) Penguin Young Readers Group.

—Froggy Gets a Doggy. London, Jonathan. 2015. (Froggy Ser.). 32p. (J). (gr. -1-k). 7.99 *(978-0-14-242230-4(4),* Puffin Books) Penguin Young Readers Group.

—Froggy Goes to Camp. London, Jonathan. 2010. (Froggy Ser.). 32p. (J). (gr. -1-k). pap. 7.99 *(978-0-14-241604-4(5),* Puffin Books) Penguin Young Readers Group.

—Froggy Goes to Grandma's. London, Jonathan. 2019. (Froggy Ser.). 32p. (J). (-k). pap. 7.99 *(978-1-9848-3626-7(9),* Puffin Books) Penguin Young Readers Group.

—Froggy Goes to Hawaii. London, Jonathan. 2012. (Froggy Ser.). (ENG.). 32p. (J). (gr. -1-k). pap. 7.99 *(978-0-14-242119-2(7),* Puffin Books) Penguin Young Readers Group.

—Froggy Goes to School. London, Jonathan. 2006. (Froggy Ser.). 28p. (gr. -1-1). 16.00 *(978-0-7569-6986-8(7))* Perfection Learning Corp.

—Froggy Goes to the Doctor. London, Jonathan. 2004. (Froggy Ser.). 32p. (J). (gr. -1-k). pap. 7.99 *(978-0-14-240193-4(5),* Puffin Books) Penguin Young Readers Group.

—Froggy Goes to the Library. London, Jonathan. 2016. (Froggy Ser.). 32p. (J). (gr. -1-k). 16.99 *(978-0-670-01573-3(3),* Viking Books for Young Readers) Penguin Young Readers Group.

—Froggy Is the Best. London, Jonathan. 2015. (Froggy Ser.). (ENG.). 32p. (J). (gr. 1-2). pap. 4.99 *(978-0-448-48380-1(7),* Penguin Young Readers) Penguin Young Readers Group.

—Froggy Picks a Pumpkin. London, Jonathan. 2019. (Froggy Ser.). 32p. (J). (-k). 16.99 *(978-1-9848-3633-5(1),* Viking Books for Young Readers) Penguin Young Readers Group.

—Froggy Plays in the Band. London, Jonathan. 2004. (Froggy Ser.). 32p. (J). (gr. -1-k). 7.99 *(978-0-14-240051-7(3),* Puffin Books) Penguin Young Readers Group.

—Froggy Plays in the Band. London, Jonathan. 2004. (Froggy Ser.). (J). (gr. -1-3). 13.65 *(978-0-7569-2955-8(5))* Perfection Learning Corp.

—Froggy Plays T-Ball. London, Jonathan. 2009. (Froggy Ser.). 32p. (J). (gr. -1-k). pap. 7.99 *(978-0-14-241304-3(6),* Puffin Books) Penguin Young Readers Group.

—Froggy's Baby Sister. London, Jonathan. 2005. (Froggy Ser.). 32p. (J). (gr. -1-k). pap. 7.99 *(978-0-14-240342-6(3),* Puffin Books) Penguin Young Readers Group.

—Froggy's Best Babysitter. London, Jonathan. 2011. (Froggy Ser.). 32p. (J). (gr. -1-k). pap. 7.99 *(978-0-14-241899-4(4),* Puffin Books) Penguin Young Readers Group.

—Froggy's Birthday Wish. London, Jonathan. 2016. (Froggy Ser.). (ENG.). 32p. (J). (-k). pap. 7.99 *(978-0-14-751799-9(0),* Puffin Books) Penguin Young Readers Group.

—Froggy's Birthday Wish. London, Jonathan & Wells, Rosemary. 2015. (Froggy Ser.). 32p. (J). (gr. -1-k). bds. 16.99 *(978-0-670-01572-6(5),* Viking Books for Young Readers) Penguin Young Readers Group.

—Froggy's Day with Dad. London, Jonathan. 2006. (Froggy Ser.). 32p. (J). (gr. -1-k). pap. 7.99 *(978-0-14-240634-2(1),* Puffin Books) Penguin Young Readers Group.

—Froggy's Halloween. London, Jonathan. 2010. lib. bdg. 16.10 *(978-0-7569-8999-6(X))* Penguin Publishing Group.

—Froggy's Lemonade Stand. London, Jonathan. 2018. (Froggy Ser.). 32p. (J). (-k). 16.99 *(978-1-101-99967-7(5),* Viking Books for Young Readers) Penguin Young Readers Group.

—Froggy's Sleepover. London, Jonathan. 2007. (Froggy Ser.). (ENG.). 32p. (J). (gr. -1-k). pap. 7.99 *(978-0-14-240750-9(X),* Puffin Books) Penguin Young Readers Group.

—Froggy's Worst Playdate. London, Jonathan. 2015. (Froggy Ser.). 32p. (J). (gr. -1-k). 7.99 *(978-0-14-242229-8(0),* Puffin Books) Penguin Young Readers Group.

—Horrible Harry & the Dragon War. Kline, Suzy. 2003. (Horrible Harry Ser.: 14). (ENG.). 64p. (J). (gr. 2-4). 4.99 *(978-0-14-250166-5(2),* Puffin Books) Penguin Young Readers Group.

—Horrible Harry & the Goog. Kline, Suzy. 2006. (Horrible Harry Ser.). 56p. (gr. 2-5). 14.00 *(978-0-7569-6948-6(4))* Perfection Learning Corp.

—Horrible Harry & the Holidaze. Kline, Suzy. 2004. (Horrible Harry Ser.: 16). 80p. (J). (gr. 2-4). 4.99 *(978-0-14-240205-4(2),* Puffin Books) Penguin Young Readers Group.

—Horrible Harry & the Locked Closet. Kline, Suzy. 2005. (Horrible Harry Ser.: 17). (ENG.). 80p. (J). (gr. 2-4). 4.99 *(978-0-14-240451-5(9),* Puffin Books) Penguin Young Readers Group.

—Horrible Harry & the Locked Closet. Kline, Suzy. 2005. (Horrible Harry Ser.). 68p. (gr. 2-5). 14.00 *(978-0-7569-5825-1(3))* Perfection Learning Corp.

—Horrible Harry & the Mud Gremlins. Kline, Suzy. 2004. (Horrible Harry Ser.: 15). (ENG.). 64p. (J). (gr. 2-4). 4.99 *(978-0-14-240123-1(4),* Puffin Books) Penguin Young Readers Group.

—Horrible Harry & the Mud Gremlins. Kline, Suzy. 2004. (Horrible Harry Ser.). 50p. (gr. 2). 14.00 *(978-0-7569-2815-5(X))* Perfection Learning Corp.

—Horrible Harry Bugs the Three Bears. Kline, Suzy. 2009. (Horrible Harry Ser.: 22). 80p. (J). (gr. 2-4). 4.99 *(978-0-14-241295-4(3),* Puffin Books) Penguin Young Readers Group.

—Horrible Harry Cracks the Code. Kline, Suzy. 2008. (Horrible Harry Ser.: 21). 80p. (J). (gr. 2-4). 4.99 *(978-0-14-241247-3(3),* Puffin Books) Penguin Young Readers Group.

—Horrible Harry Goes to Sea: Puffine Chapters. Kline, Suzy. 2003. (Horrible Harry Ser.: 13). 64p. (J). (gr. 2-4). 4.99 *(978-0-14-250002-6(X),* Puffin Books) Penguin Young Readers Group.

—Horrible Harry Takes the Cake. Kline, Suzy. 2007. (Horrible Harry Ser.: 19). (ENG.). 64p. (J). (gr. 2-4). 4.99 *(978-0-14-240939-8(1),* Puffin Books) Penguin Young Readers Group.

—Horrible Harry Takes the Cake. Kline, Suzy. 2007. (Horrible Harry Ser.). 45p. (gr. 2-5). 14.00 *(978-0-7569-8158-7(1))* Perfection Learning Corp.

—Joe & Sparky Get New Wheels: Candlewick Sparks. Michalak, Jamie. 2013. (Candlewick Sparks Ser.). (ENG.). 48p. (J). (gr. k-4). pap. 4.99 *(978-0-7636-6641-5(6))* Candlewick Pr.

—Joe & Sparky Go to School. Michalak, Jamie. (Candlewick Sparks Ser.). 48p. (J). (gr. k-4). 2014. pap. 4.99 *(978-0-7636-7181-5(9))*; 2013. 15.99 *(978-0-7636-6278-3(X))* Candlewick Pr.

—Joe & Sparky, Party Animals! Michalak, Jamie. (Candlewick Sparks Ser.). 48p. (J). (gr. k-4). 2018. (ENG.). pap. 4.99 *(978-1-5362-0327-1(0))*; 2017. 15.99 *(978-0-7636-8206-4(3))* Candlewick Pr.

—Joe & Sparky, Superstars! Michalak, Jamie. (Candlewick Sparks Ser.). 48p. (J). (gr. k-4). 2013. (ENG.). pap. 4.99 *(978-0-7636-6642-2(4))*; 2011. 15.99 *(978-0-7636-4578-6(8))* Candlewick Pr.

—Less Than Zero. Murphy, Stuart J. 2003. (MathStart 3 Ser.: Vol. 49). (ENG.). 40p. (J). (gr. 2-18). pap. 5.99 *(978-0-06-000126-1(7))* HarperCollins Pubs.

—Piggy & Dad Play Big Book: Brand New Readers. Martin, David Lozell. 2009. (Brand New Readers Ser.). 48p. (J). (gr. -1-3). pap. 24.99 *(978-0-7636-4455-0(2))* Candlewick Pr.

—Seaweed Soup. Murphy, Stuart J. 2003. (Mathstart Ser.). 31p. (J). (gr. -1-3). pap. *(978-0-7398-6790-7(3))* Steck-Vaughn.

Remkiewicz, Frank. Suficientes Zanahorias: Just Enough Carrots (Spanish Edition) Murphy, Stuart J. 2020. (MathStart 1 Ser.). (ENG.). 40p. (J). (gr. -1-3). pap. 5.99 ***(978-0-06-298322-0(9)***, HarperCollins) HarperCollins Pubs. Ltd. GBR. Dist: HarperCollins Pubs.

Remkiewicz, Frank. The Twelve Days of Christmas in Florida. (Twelve Days of Christmas in America Ser.). (J). (-k). 2017. 22p. bds. 7.95 *(978-1-4549-2283-4(4))*; 2008. 40p. 12.95 *(978-1-4027-3817-3(X))* Sterling Publishing Co., Inc.

Remkiewicz, Frank & Frank, Remkiewicz. Horrible Harry & the Goog. Kline, Suzy. 2006. (Horrible Harry Ser.: 18). 64p. (J). (gr. 2-4). pap. 4.99 *(978-0-14-240728-8(3),* Puffin Books) Penguin Young Readers Group.

Remkiewicz, Frank & Wummer, Amy. Horrible Harry & the Dead Letters. Kline, Suzy. 2009. (Horrible Harry Ser.). 80p. (J). (gr. 2-4). 4.99 *(978-0-14-241457-6(3),* Puffin Books) Penguin Young Readers Group.

—Horrible Harry on the Ropes. Kline, Suzy. 2011. (Horrible Harry Ser.). 80p. (J). (gr. 2-4). 4.99 *(978-0-14-241695-2(9),* Puffin Books) Penguin Young Readers Group.

Rempel, Billi-Jo & Lascelles, Desireah. Cat. Beere, Lisa. 2018. (Cats Ser.: Vol. 2). (ENG.). 36p. (J). (gr. k-4). pap. 9.99 *(978-1-68160-622-4(4))* Crimson Cloak Publishing.

Rempel, Jennifer. Lavi the Lion Finds His Pride. 2005. (J). 15.95 *(978-0-9744715-2-5(6),* Towers Maguire Publishing) Local History Co., The.

Remphry, Martin. Cinderella's Big Foot. North, Laura. 2014. (Tadpoles: Fairytale Twists Ser.). (ENG.). 32p. (J). (gr. 1-2). *(978-0-7787-0440-9(8))*; pap. *(978-0-7787-0448-5(3))* Crabtree Publishing Co.

—A Gift for the King. Harvey, Damian. 2005. (Reading Corner Ser.). 24p. (J). (gr. k-3). lib. bdg. 22.80 *(978-1-59771-013-8(X))* Sea-To-Sea Pubns.

—Miss Pell Never Misspells: More Cool Ways to Remember Stuff. Martin, Steve. 2013. (ENG.). 128p. (J). (gr. 4-7). 12.99 *(978-0-545-49477-9(X),* Scholastic Reference) Scholastic, Inc.

—William Shakespeare. Fischel, Emma. 2010. (Famous People, Famous Lives Ser.). (KOR.). 46p. (J). *(978-89-491-8826-3(0))* Biryongso Publishing Co.

Remphry, Martin. Pirates Are Stealing Our Cows. Remphry, Martin. 2014. (Race Ahead with Reading Ser.). (ENG.). 32p. (J). (gr. 2-2). *(978-0-7787-1330-2(X))* Crabtree Publishing Co.

Ren, Amber. Because. Willems, Mo. 2019. (ENG.). 40p. (J). (gr. -1-k). 17.99 *(978-1-368-01901-9(3))* Hyperion Bks. for Children.

—The Colors of Summer. Smith, Danna. 2019. (Little Golden Book Ser.). 24p. (J). (-k). 4.99 *(978-1-5247-7343-4(3),* Golden Bks.) Random Hse. Children's Bks.

—The Colors of Winter. Smith, Danna. 2019. (Little Golden Book Ser.). (ENG.). 24p. (J). (-k). 4.99 *(978-1-5247-6892-8(8),* Golden Bks.) Random Hse. Children's Bks.

Rena, Keturah. Magenta Dahlia: Righteous Flower. Parach, Nitstsah. Judah, Princess, ed. 2019. (ENG.). 34p. (J). pap. 12.00 *(978-1-0731-2086-4(4))* Independently Published.

Renaud, Joanne. Runaway Train: Saved by Belle of the Mines & Mountains. Coleman, Wim & Perrin, Pat. 2015. (Setting the Stage for Fluency Ser.). (ENG.). 40p. (J). (gr. 3-5). lib. bdg. 27.99 *(978-1-939656-71-1(0))* Red Chair Pr.

Renaud, Paul. Tarot. 2020. (ENG.). 136p. (YA). (gr. 8-17). pap. 15.99 ***(978-1-302-91525-4(8))*** Marvel Worldwide, Inc.

Renda, Joseph, jt. illus. see Colson, A. W.

Rendeiro, Charlene. Been to Yesterdays: Poems of a Life. Hopkins, Lee Bennett. 2007. 64p. (gr. 3-7). 21.45 *(978-0-7569-7966-9(8))* Perfection Learning Corp.

Rendon, Amalia. The Egyptian Treasure. Beighton, Matt. 2018. (Monstacademy Ser.: Vol. 3). (ENG.). 108p. (J). (gr. 2-5). pap. 10.99 *(978-1-9997244-4-3(5),* Green Monkey Bks.) Purple Sword Pubns., LLC.

—The Egyptian Treasure: Dyslexia Friendly Edition. Beighton, Matt. 2018. (Monstacademy Ser.: Vol. 3). (ENG.). 156p. (J). (gr. 2-5). pap. 10.99 *(978-1-9997244-7-4(X),* Green Monkey Bks.) Purple Sword Pubns., LLC.

Rendon, Amalia. The Grand High Monster. Beighton, Matt. 2019. (Monstacademy Ser.: Vol. 3). (ENG.). 106p. (J). pap. ***(978-1-9161360-2-1(8))*** Green Monkey Pr.

Rendon, Amalia. The Halloween Parade. Beighton, Matt. 2017. (Monstacademy Ser.: Vol. 1). (ENG.). 128p. (J). (gr. 1-5). pap. 10.99 *(978-1-9997244-2-9(9),* Green Monkey Bks.) Purple Sword Pubns., LLC.

—The Halloween Parade: Dyslexia Friendly Edition. Beighton, Matt. 2017. (Monstacademy Ser.: Vol. 1). (ENG.). 166p. (J). (gr. 1-5). pap. 10.99 *(978-1-9997244-3-6(7),* Green Monkey Bks.) Purple Sword Pubns., LLC.

—The Magic Knight: You're the Monster! - Dyslexia Friendly Edition. Beighton, Matt. 2018. (Monstacademy Ser.: Vol. 2). (ENG.). 158p. (J). (gr. 1-5). pap. *(978-1-9997244-9-8(6))* Green Monkey Pr.

Rendon, Daniel, et al. The Opposite Numbers. Lobdell, Scott. 2006. 111p. (J). *(978-1-4156-9815-0(5))* Papercutz.

Rendon, Joel. La Invencion de Los Canibales. Navarrete, Federico. rev. ed. 2006. (Otra Escalera Ser.). (ENG.). 56p. (J). (gr. k-2). pap. 12.95 *(978-970-20-0774-6(7))* Castillo, Ediciones, S. A. de C. V. MEX. Dist: Macmillan.

Rene, Perez. No Bones about It. Heller, Andrew. I.t. ed. 2003. 12p. (J). 7.99 *(978-0-9722038-5-2(0))* Mr Do It All, Inc.

Renee, Ashley. Journey with Mr. Genorace. Clark, Johanna. Williams, Iris M., ed. 2016. (ENG.). 60p. (J). (gr. k-3). 20.00 *(978-1-942022-43-5(3))* Butterfly Typeface, The.

—Now This ... A Conting & Colors Book for Beginners. Williams, Iris M. 2016. (ENG.). (J). pap. 10.95 *(978-1-942022-44-2(1))* Butterfly Typeface, The.

Renee, Ashley, jt. illus. see Bembry, Shanylah.

Renee, Haley. Take a Trump. Pants, S'Mar T. 2019. (ENG.). 26p. (J). pap. 9.50 *(978-1-0734-0329-5(7))* Independently Published.

Renee, Heather. Good Morning, Mr. Chipmunk: Book 1: Gathering. Renee, Heather. Hazle, Vjange. 2018. (ENG.). 26p. (J). pap. 12.00 *(978-1-7906-1706-7(5))* Independently Published.

Renfro, Ed. Explorers Who Got Lost. Sansevere-Dreher, Diane. 2016. (ENG.). 176p. (J). pap. 14.99 *(978-0-7653-8151-4(6),* 900149518, Starscape) Doherty, Tom Assocs., LLC.

Renfroe, Emma. The Dog Who Loved Coffee. Lancaster, Camille. 2019. (ENG.). 24p. (J). (gr. k-4). pap. 8.99 ***(978-0-578-51597-7(0))*** Lancaster, Camille.

Renfroe, Leisa. A Whale Set Sail. Trechsel, Kelli. 2011. 28p. (J). pap. 14.95 *(978-1-936085-42-2(9))* Decent Hill.

Renger, Nikolai. Arnold the Brave. Herget, Gundi & Garlid, Ann. 2018. (J). *(978-1-4413-2650-8(2))* Peter Pauper Pr. Inc.

Renier, Aaron. The Adventures of Sir Balin the Ill-Fated. Morris, Gerald. 2013. (Knights' Tales Ser.: 4). (ENG.). 112p. (J). (gr. 1-4). pap. 6.99 *(978-0-544-10488-4(9),* 1540796) Houghton Mifflin Harcourt Publishing Co.

—The Adventures of Sir Gawain the True. Morris, Gerald. 2013. (Knights' Tales Ser.: 3). 128p. (J). (ENG.). (gr. 1-4). pap. 6.99 *(978-0-544-02264-5(5),* 1528486);3. (gr. 2-4).

21.19 *(978-0-547-41855-1(8))* Houghton Mifflin Harcourt Publishing Co.

—The Adventures of Sir Givret the Short. Morris, Gerald. 2009. (Knights' Tales Ser.: 2). (ENG.). 112p. (J). (gr. 1-4). pap. 8.95 *(978-0-547-24818-9(0),* 1100708) Houghton Mifflin Harcourt Publishing Co.

—The Lifters. Eggers, Dave. 2019. (ENG.). 352p. (J). (gr. 3-7). pap. 8.99 *(978-1-5247-6419-7(1),* Yearling) Random Hse. Children's Bks.

Renier, Aaron. Vampires of Blinsh. Pinkwater, Daniel M. 2020. (ENG.). 40p. (J). (gr. -1-3). 17.99 ***(978-1-4197-4681-9(2)**,* 1268001, Abrams Bks. for Young Readers) Abrams, Inc.

Renier, Aaron. The Unsinkable Walker Bean. Renier, Aaron. 2010. (Unsinkable Walker Bean Ser.: 1). (ENG.). 208p. (J). (gr. 4-9). pap. 16.99 *(978-1-59643-453-0(8),* 900055027, First Second Bks.) Roaring Brook Pr.

Renne, Philip K. Allosaurus vs. Brachiosaurus: Might Against Height. O'Hearn, Michael. 2010. (Dinosaur Wars Ser.). (ENG.). 32p. (J). (gr. 3-9). lib. bdg. 28.65 *(978-1-4296-3935-4(0),* Capstone Pr.) Capstone.

—Deinonychus vs. Styracosaurus: When Claws & Spikes Collide, 1 vol. O'Hearn, Michael. 2010. (Dinosaur Wars Ser.). (ENG.). 32p. (J). (gr. 3-9). lib. bdg. 28.65 *(978-1-4296-4757-1(4),* Capstone Pr.) Capstone.

—Triceratops vs. Stegosaurus: When Horns & Plates Collide. O'Hearn, Michael. 2010. (Dinosaur Wars Ser.). (ENG.). 32p. (J). (gr. 3-9). lib. bdg. 28.65 *(978-1-4296-3938-5(5),* Capstone Pr.) Capstone.

—Tyrannosaurus Rex vs. Velociraptor: Power Against Speed. O'Hearn, Michael. 2010. (Dinosaur Wars Ser.). (ENG.). 32p. (J). (gr. 3-9). lib. bdg. 28.65 *(978-1-4296-3937-8(7),* Capstone Pr.) Capstone.

Renne, Rachel, et al. Seth & Mattie's Big River Adventure. Owen, Sarah. 2020. (ENG.). 128p. (J). pap. 14.95 ***(978-1-59152-236-2(6)**,* Sweetgrass Bks.) Farcountry Pr.

Renner, Kate. Where Else Do Babies Come From? A Family Guide to Assisted Reproduction. Bentley, Hope A. C. 2018. (ENG.). 34p. (J). (gr. k-5). 19.99 *(978-1-7327645-1-4(4))* Golden Light Factory.

Rennocks, Sam. Zoom Ocean Adventure. Hayes, Susan. 2020. (Zoom Ser.). (ENG.). 36p. (J). (gr. -1 — 1). bds. 14.99 *(978-1-9999680-0-7(X))* What on Earth Books.

Reno, Stephanie. Lolly Learns about Joy. Wilson, Beth S. 2016. (Fruit of the Spirit Ser.: Vol. 2). (ENG.). (J). pap. 11.99 *(978-1-945620-07-2(2))* Hear My Heart Publishing.

Renon, Delphine. The Quiet Crocodile Goes to the Beach. Andriamirado, Natacha. 2019. (ENG.). (J). (gr. k-3). 17.95 *(978-1-61689-801-4(1))* Princeton Architectural Pr.

Renooy, "Cosmic" Ray. Rodney's SsssSolution - Big Book. Myracle, Lauren. 2003. (J). spiral bd. *(978-1-884272-88-2(6))* Premier Schl. Agendas.

Renouf, Michael. Malpas the Dragon. Cattanach, Ann. 2007. (ENG.). 28p. (J). (gr. 3-7). per. 15.95 *(978-1-84310-572-5(1),* 691969) Kingsley, Jessica Pubs. GBR. Dist: Hachette UK Distribution.

Rensink, Jessy. Gone to Toodoggone: Book 2 of the Wee Folk. MacLeod, Angus. 2018. (Wee Folk Ser.: Vol. 2). (ENG.). 32p. (J). (gr. k-6). pap. *(978-1-77143-370-9(1))* CCB Publishing.

Renta, Kathryn, jt. illus. see Bergting, Peter.

Renteria, Justin, jt. illus. see Gutierez, Francisco.

Renthrope, Damon. All Around Town. Wendel, Gretchen Schomel et al. 2007. 32p. (J). (gr. -1-3). 11.99 *(978-1-933754-10-9(9))* Waterside Publishing.

—All Around Town. Wendel, Gretchen Schomer & Schomer, Adam Anthony. 2009. (Becka & the Big Bubble Ser.). 32p. (J). (gr. -1-2). lib. bdg. 25.60 *(978-1-60754-104-2(1))* Windmill Bks.

—Becka Goes to Chicago. Wendel, Gretchen Schomer & Schomer, Adam Anthony. 2008. (ENG.). 36p. (J). (gr. -1-3). 11.99 *(978-1-933754-52-9(4))* Waterside Publishing.

—Becka Goes to India. Wendel, Gretchen Schomer & Schomer, Adam Anthony. 2009. (Becka & the Big Bubble Ser.). 32p. (J). (gr. -1-2). lib. bdg. 25.60 *(978-1-60754-110-3(6))* Windmill Bks.

—Becka Goes to India. Wendel, Gretchen Schomel et al. 2007. 32p. (J). 11.99 *(978-1-933754-13-0(3))* Waterside Publishing.

—Becka Goes to San Diego. Wendel, Gretchen Schomer & Schomer, Adam Anthony. 2008. 32p. (J). (gr. -1-3). 11.99 *(978-1-933754-51-2(6))* Waterside Publishing.

—Becka Goes to San Francisco. Wendel, Gretchen Schomel et al. 2007. 32p. (J). 11.99 *(978-1-933754-12-3(5))* Waterside Publishing.

—Becka Goes to the North Pole. Wendel, Gretchen Schomel et al. 2007. 28p. (J). 11.99 *(978-1-933754-11-6(7))* Waterside Publishing.

—Becka Goes to the North Pole. Wendel, Gretchen Schomer & Schomer, Adam Anthony. 2009. (Becka & the Big Bubble Ser.). 32p. (J). (gr. -1-2). lib. bdg. 25.60 *(978-1-60754-116-5(5))* Windmill Bks.

Rentta, Sharon. Charlie, the Home-Alone Kitten. Nolan, Tina. 2008. 96p. (J). (gr. 1-5). 3.99 *(978-1-56148-648-9(5),* Good Bks.) Skyhorse Publishing Co., Inc.

—Honey the Unwanted Puppy. Nolan, Tina. 2008. 96p. (J). (gr. 1-5). 3.99 *(978-1-56148-649-6(3),* Good Bks.) Skyhorse Publishing Co., Inc.

Reny, Todd, jt. illus. see Snider, Sharon.

Renzoni, Mark, photos by. The Baby Who Started a Revolution. Renzoni, Phil. Parise, Anna Maria, ed. 2016. (ENG., (J). pap. *(978-1-4602-9360-7(6))* FriesenPress.

Repetto, Laurie. A Dog Named Munson Finds the Missing Game Ball. Thomas, Charlene. 2012. 38p. (J). 14.95 *(978-1-62086-054-0(6))* Mascot Bks., Inc.

Reppel, Phyllis. Henriette Delille: Rebellious Saint, 1 vol. Martinez, Elsie & Stelly, Colette. 2010. (ENG.). 200p. (J). (gr. 3-7). 19.95 *(978-1-58980-839-3(8),* Pelican Publishing) Arcadia Publishing.

Rescek, Sanja. Animal Exercises. Ross, Mandy. 2006. (Poems for the Young Ser.). 32p. (J). (gr. 2-2). pap. *(978-1-84643-044-2(5))* Child's Play International Ltd.

—A Bedtime Prayer. Tiger Tales. 2013. (ENG.). 24p. (J). (gr. -1-k). bds. 8.99 *(978-1-58925-606-4(9))* Tiger Tales.

—Bedtime Songs: Deluxe Sound Book Wood Module. Wing, Scarlett. 2016. (Early Bird Song Ser.). (ENG.). 10p. (J). (gr. -1-2). bds. 18.99 *(978-1-68052-123-8(3),* 1001160) Cottage Door Pr.

—Bounce & Jiggle. 2007. (Baby Gym Ser.). 12p. (J). (gr. -1). spiral bd. *(978-1-84643-131-9(X))* Child's Play International Ltd.

—Calm & Soothe. 2007. (Baby Gym Ser.). 12p. (J). (gr. -1). spiral bd. *(978-1-84643-133-3(6))* Child's Play International Ltd.

—A Christmas Prayer. Tiger Tales. 2014. (ENG.). 22p. (J). (gr. -1-k). bds. 8.95 *(978-1-58925-596-8(8))* Tiger Tales.

—Dinosaur, Dinosaur, Say Good Night. Tiger Tales. 2019. (ENG.). 22p. (J). (gr. 2-k). bds. 9.99 *(978-1-68010-589-6(2))* Tiger Tales.

—Easter Bunny's Helpers. 2009. (ENG.). 12p. (J). 6.95 *(978-1-58117-870-8(0),* Intervisual/Piggy Toes) Bendon, Inc.

—A Gift for Baby's Dedication, 1 vol. Rock, Lois. ed. 2014. (ENG.). 48p. (J). (— 1). 9.99 *(978-0-7459-6491-1(5))* Lion Hudson PLC GBR. Dist: Kregel Pubns.

—I Do Not Want To. Schulz, Kathy. 2011. (Rookie Ready to Learn Ser.). 40p. (J). pap. 5.95 *(978-0-531-26707-3(5));* (gr. -1-k). lib. bdg. 23.00 *(978-0-531-26525-3(0))* Scholastic Library Publishing. (Children's Pr.).

—I'm a Little Vampire. Fry, Sonali. 2014. (ENG.). 16p. (J). (gr. -1 — 1). bds. 5.99 *(978-1-4814-0504-1(7),* Little Simon) Little Simon.

—The Itsy Bitsy Angel. Burton, Jeffrey. 2019. (Itsy Bitsy Ser.). (ENG.). 16p. (J). (gr. -1 — 1). bds. 5.99 *(978-1-5344-4340-2(1),* Little Simon) Little Simon.

—The Itsy Bitsy Bunny. Burton, Jeffrey. 2016. (Itsy Bitsy Ser.). (ENG.). 16p. (J). (gr. -1 — 1). bds. 5.99 *(978-1-4814-5621-0(0),* Little Simon) Little Simon.

—The Itsy Bitsy Dreidel. Burton, Jeffrey & Tornow, Chani. 2017. (Itsy Bitsy Ser.). (ENG.). 16p. (J). (gr. -1 — 1). bds. 5.99 *(978-1-5344-0022-1(2),* Little Simon) Little Simon.

—The Itsy Bitsy Leprechaun. Burton, Jeffrey. 2018. (Itsy Bitsy Ser.). (ENG.). 16p. (J). (gr. -1 — 1). bds. 5.99 *(978-1-5344-0024-5(9),* Little Simon) Little Simon.

—The Itsy Bitsy Pilgrim. Burton, Jeffrey. 2016. (Itsy Bitsy Ser.). (ENG.). 16p. (J). (gr. -1 — 1). bds. 5.99 *(978-1-4814-6852-7(9),* Little Simon) Little Simon.

—The Itsy Bitsy Pumpkin. Fry, Sonali. 2014. (Itsy Bitsy Ser.). (ENG.). 16p. (J). (gr. -1 — 1). bds. 5.99 *(978-1-4814-0505-8(5),* Little Simon) Little Simon.

—The Itsy Bitsy Reindeer. Burton, Jeffrey. 2016. (Itsy Bitsy Ser.). (ENG.). 16p. (J). (gr. -1 — 1). bds. 5.99 *(978-1-4814-6855-8(3),* Little Simon) Little Simon.

—The Itsy Bitsy School Bus. Burton, Jeffrey. 2018. (Itsy Bitsy Ser.). (ENG.). 16p. (J). (gr. -1 — 1). bds. 5.99 *(978-1-5344-1695-6(1),* Little Simon) Little Simon.

Rescek, Sanja, et al. Itsy Bitsy Spider & Other Clap-along Rhymes. 2004. (Clap-Alongs Ser.). (ENG.). 36p. (J). (gr. -1-k). 12.95 *(978-1-59249-522-1(2),* 1D025) Soundprints.

Rescek, Sanja. The Itsy Bitsy Sweetheart. Burton, Jeffrey. 2018. (Itsy Bitsy Ser.). (ENG.). 16p. (J). (gr. -1 — 1). bds. 5.99 *(978-1-5344-2689-4(2),* Little Simon) Little Simon.

Rescek, Sanja. Kittens: Seek & Find. Sequoia Children's Publishing. 2020. (ENG.). 10p. (J). bds. ***(978-1-64269-246-4(8)**,* 6adaff2a-e8a8-4b94-a412-8784f1e6b662, Sequoia Publishing & Media LLC) Phoenix International Publications, Inc.

Rescek, Sanja. Mr. Fox's Socks. Harvey, Damian. 2004. (ENG.). 16p. (J). lib. bdg. 23.65 *(978-1-59646-678-4(2))* Dingles & Co.

—My Guardian Angel, 1 vol. Piper, Sophie. ed. 2013. (ENG.). 48p. (J). (gr. -1-k). 7.99 *(978-0-7459-6397-6(8))* Lion Hudson PLC GBR. Dist: Independent Pubs. Group.

—One Elephant Went Out to Play. (Classic Books with Holes Big Book Ser.). (J). 2009. 16p. (gr. -1-1). spiral bd. *(978-1-84643-209-5(X));* 2009. (ENG.). 16p. (gr. -1-1). pap. incl. audio compact disk *(978-1-84643-258-3(8));* 2007. 14p. (gr. -1-1). spiral bd. *(978-1-84643-111-1(5));* 2007. 16p. (gr. 1-1). pap. *(978-1-84643-107-4(7))* Child's Play International Ltd.

Rescek, Sanja. Thank You God. Bradshaw, Sarah. 2018. (Tender Moments Ser.). (ENG.). 20p. (J). (gr. -1 — 1). bds. 8.99 ***(978-1-926444-47-5(7))*** Rainstorm Pr.

Rescek, Sanja. This Little Bunny. Fronis, Aly. 2016. (ENG.). 16p. (J). (gr. -1-k). bds. 5.99 *(978-1-4998-0105-7(X))* Little Bee Books Inc.

—Tim Feels Scared. Slater, Teddy. 2011. (J). *(978-0-545-35179-9(0))* Scholastic, Inc.

—Touch & Tickle. 2007. (Baby Gym Ser.). 12p. (J). (gr. -1). spiral bd. *(978-1-84643-130-2(1))* Child's Play International Ltd.

—Twinkle, Twinkle, Little Star. Tiger Tales. 2020. (ENG.). 22p. (J). (-k). bds. 9.99 *(978-1-68010-627-5(9));* pap. 5.99 ***(978-1-68010-466-0(7))*** Tiger Tales.

—Twinkle, Twinkle, Little Star: A Book of Bedtime Rhymes with a Soft Star Lovey. Tiger Tales. 2016. (ENG.). 10p. (J). (gr. -1 — 1). 14.99 *(978-1-58925-230-1(6))* Tiger Tales.

—Twinkle, Twinkle, Little Star: And Other Favorite Bedtime Rhymes. Tiger Tales. 2006. (ENG.). 22p. (J). (-k). bds. 7.95 *(978-1-58925-787-0(1))* Tiger Tales.

—Wiggle & Move. 2007. (Baby Gym Ser.). 12p. (J). (gr. -1). spiral bd. *(978-1-84643-132-6(8))* Child's Play International Ltd.

Rescek, Sanja, jt. illus. see Slater, Teddy.

Reschofsky, Jean. The Colors of Christmas: A Christmas Poem for Young & Old. Goff-Smith, Marie Jaume. 2013. (ENG.). 16p. (J). 12.95 *(978-1-939621-09-2(7))* ORO Editions.

Research & Education Association Editors & Leigh, Rob. Batman & the Monster Men. Wagner, Matt & Stewart, Dave. Schreck, Bob, ed. rev. ed. 2006. (ENG.). 144p. (YA). pap. 14.99 *(978-1-4012-1091-5(0))* DC Comics.

Research & Education Association Editors & Starkings, Richard. When in Rome. Loeb, Jeph & Sale, Tim. rev. ed. 2007. 160p. pap. 14.99 *(978-1-4012-0717-5(0))* DC Comics.

Reskala, Dannel. The Tallest House. Orenshein, Jesse. 2019. (ENG.). 28p. (J). pap. 9.99 ***(978-1-0743-8864-5(X))*** Independently Published.

Ressler-Horst, Lara. The World Is a Beautiful Place. Augsburger, A. Don. 2007. 48p. per. 14.95 *(978-1-934246-44-3(1))* Peppertree Pr., The.

Restelli, Grazia. We're Sailing to Galapagos: A Week in the Pacific. Krebs, Laurie. (ENG.). 32p. (J). (gr. k-1). 2007. pap. 8.99 *(978-1-84686-102-4(0));* 2005. 16.99 *(978-1-84148-902-5(6))* Barefoot Bks., Inc.

Restrepo, Andres. Out Loud: June's Venture. Friedman, Geddy & Hernandez, Michael, eds. 2019. (ENG.). 42p. (J). pap. 11.00 ***(978-0-9983011-9-8(1))*** MYTHIKAS.

Restrepo, Mayerlin. Wisteria Forest: The First Journey. Restrepo, Mayerlin. 2019. (Wisteria Forest the First Journey Ser.: Vol. 1). (ENG.). 34p. (J). pap. 11.13 *(978-1-7223-5458-9(5))* CreateSpace Independent Publishing Platform.

Rethi, Lili. Marie Curie. McKown, Robin. 2012. 128p. 40.95 *(978-1-258-23532-1(3));* pap. 25.95 *(978-1-258-24675-4(9))* Literary Licensing, LLC.

Rettenmund, Tamara, jt. illus. see Charlip, Remy.

Retwick, Roy. Opinions about Themes in Science Fiction: Two Stories about Valerie Logan, Interstellar Troubleshooter. Wood, Greg V. & Benchmark Education Co. 2014. (Text Connections Ser.). (J). (gr. 3). *(978-1-4509-9665-5(5))* Benchmark Education Co.

—Opinions about Themes in Science Fiction - Two Stories about Valerie Logan, Interstellar Troubleshooter: Set Of 6. Wood, Greg V. 2014. (Text Connections Ser.). (J). (gr. 3). 49.00 net. *(978-1-4900-0141-8(7))* Benchmark Education Co.

Retz, Zac. Too Much Glue. Lefebvre, Jason. 2013. (ENG.). 32p. (J). (gr. k-2). 16.95 *(978-1-936261-27-7(8))* Flashlight Pr.

Retzlaff, Shay. Annie the Texas Ranch Dog - Danger at Lost Maples. Shafer, Patty. 2012. (ENG.). 96p. (J). pap. 9.95 *(978-1-61899-009-9(8),* Tadpole Pr. 4 Kids) Mystic Harbor Pr., LLC.

—Annie the Texas Ranch Dog - Injured Hero. Shafer, Patty. 2012. 96p. (J). pap. 9.95 *(978-1-61899-008-2(X),* Tadpole Pr. 4 Kids) Mystic Harbor Pr., LLC.

—Annie the Texas Ranch Dog - New Life in Utopia. Shafer, Patty. 2012. 96p. (J). pap. 9.95 *(978-1-61899-007-5(1),* Tadpole Pr. 4 Kids) Mystic Harbor Pr., LLC.

Reuben, Borgen & Jenny, Lindley, photos by. God Loves You So Much... Learn As You Grow. 2010. (ENG.). 24p. (J). 12.95 *(978-0-9824652-3-3(8))* Learn As You Grow, L.L.C.

Reuder, Moran. Boto: The Environmental Hero. Abuthina, Hamed. Abuthina, Marion, ed. 2019. (ENG.). 42p. (J). pap. 15.00 ***(978-1-6988-0925-0(5))*** Independently Published.

Reul, Sarah Lynne. The Smith Family Secret: Book 1. Potoma, Alison. 2013. 122p. pap. 6.25 *(978-1-940602-00-4(9))* Potoma, Alison Elise.

Reul, Sarah Lynne. The Breaking News. Reul, Sarah Lynne. 2018. (ENG.). 48p. (J). 18.99 *(978-1-250-15356-2(5),* 900183878) Roaring Brook Pr.

—Farm the Farm: A Lift-The-Flap Book. Reul, Sarah Lynne. 2019. (ENG.). 18p. (J). (gr. -1 — 1). bds. 8.99 *(978-1-5344-0940-8(8),* Little Simon) Little Simon.

—Pet the Pets: A Lift-The-Flap Book. Reul, Sarah Lynne. 2018. (ENG.). 18p. (J). (gr. -1 — 1). bds. 8.99 *(978-1-5344-0939-2(4),* Little Simon) Little Simon.

Reusswig, William. What Does an Animal Eat? Lowery, Lawrence F. 2012. (I Wonder Why Ser.). (ENG.). 40p. (J). (gr. k-3). pap. 11.95 *(978-1-936959-46-4(1))* National Science Teachers Assn.

Revah, Patricia. Rimas y Numeros. Blanco, Alberto. 2015. (0). (ENG.). 32p. (J). pap. 14.99 ***(978-1-64101-178-5(5))*** Santillana USA Publishing Co., Inc.

Revell, Cindy. Bouki Cuts Wood: A Haitian Folktale. StJohn, Amanda. 2011. (Folktales from Around the World Ser.). (ENG.). 24p. (J). (gr. k-3). 28.50 *(978-1-60973-135-9(2),* 201140) Child's World, Inc., The.

—Clever Rachel, 1 vol. Waldman, Debby. 2009. (ENG.). 32p. (J). (gr. -1-k). 19.95 *(978-1-55469-081-7(1))* Orca Bk. Pubs. USA.

—Just Enough Series Bundle. Roberts, Jillian. 2020. (Just Enough Ser.). (ENG.). (J). (gr. 1-3). 69.95 *(978-1-4598-2532-1(2))* Orca Bk. Pubs. USA.

—Me & My Robot. West, Tracey. 2003. (Penguin Young Readers, Level 2 Ser.). 32p. (J). (gr. 1-2). mass mkt. 4.99 *(978-0-448-42895-6(4),* Penguin Young Readers) Penguin Young Readers Group.

—Room Enough for Daisy, 1 vol. Waldman, Debby & Feutl, Rita. 2011. (ENG.). 32p. (J). (gr. -1-k). 19.95 *(978-1-55469-255-2(5))* Orca Bk. Pubs. USA.

—A Sack Full of Feathers, 1 vol. Waldman, Debby. 2007. (ENG.). 32p. (J). (gr. -1-k). 9.95 *(978-1-55143-863-4(1))* Orca Bk. Pubs. USA.

—What Happens When a Loved One Dies? Our First Talk about Death, 1 vol. Roberts, Jillian. 2016. (Just Enough Ser.: 2). (ENG.). 32p. (J). (gr. -1-k). 19.95 *(978-1-4598-0945-1(9))* Orca Bk. Pubs. USA.

—Where Do Babies Come From? Our First Talk about Birth, 1 vol. Roberts, Jillian. 2015. (Just Enough Ser.: 1). (ENG.). 32p. (J). (gr. -1-k). 19.95 *(978-1-4598-0942-0(4))* Orca Bk. Pubs. USA.

Revell, Cindy. Why Do Families Change? Roberts, Jillian. 2020. (Just Enough Ser.: 4). (ENG.). 32p. (J). (gr. -1-k). 12.95 ***(978-1-4598-2644-1(2))*** Orca Bk. Pubs. USA.

Revell, Sharon. Be Brave, Sophia: Book 2 in the Lucy & Sophia Series. Criser, Starla K. 2019. (Lucy & Sophia Ser.: Vol. 2). (ENG.). 42p. (J). (gr. k-3). pap. 12.99 *(978-0-578-48303-0(3))* Starla Enterprises, Inc.

—Blossom Saves the Day: Book 3 in the Blossom & Matilda Series. Criser, Starla. 2018. (Blossom & Matilda Ser.: Vol. 3). (ENG.). 46p. (J). (gr. k-3). 16.95 *(978-0-692-12953-1(7))* Starla Enterprises, Inc.

—Blossom Sings with Her Friends: Book 2 in the Blossom & Matilda Series. Criser, Starla. 2017. (Blossom & Matilda Ser.: Vol. 2). (ENG.). 50p. (J). (gr. k-3). 16.95 *(978-0-692-97351-6(6))* Starla Enterprises, Inc.

—Cat Needs a Purpose: As Told by Brownee the Story Lizard. Brown, Sharon Lee. 2018. (Brownee the Story Lizard Ser.: Vol. 3). (ENG.). 38p. (J). (gr. k-4). 14.95 *(978-0-692-08944-6(6))* Starla Enterprises, Inc.

—A Family for Blossom: Book 1 in the Blossom & Matilda Series. Criser, Starla. 2017. (Blossom & Matilda Ser.: Vol. 1). (ENG.). 46p. (J). (gr. k-3). 16.95 *(978-0-692-97328-8(1))* Starla Enterprises, Inc.

—It'll Be Okay, Lucy. Criser, Starla. 2017. (ENG.). (J). (gr. k-3). 15.95 *(978-0-692-96659-4(5));* pap. 10.99 *(978-0-692-94596-4(2))* Starla Enterprises, Inc.

—Petie the Parrot's Amazing Adventure: As Told by Brownee the Story Lizard. Brown, Sharon Lee. 2018. (Brownee the Story Lizard Ser.: Vol. 1). (ENG.). 36p. (J). (gr. 2-4). 14.95 *(978-0-692-08941-5(1))* Starla Enterprises, Inc.

—Susie the Ladybug Makes New Friends: As Told by Brownee the Story Lizard. Brown, Sharon Lee. 2018. (Brownee the Story Lizard Ser.: Vol. 2). (ENG.). 50p. (J). (gr. k-4). 15.95 *(978-0-692-08943-9(8))* Starla Enterprises, Inc.

—TE the Toad Meets a Bully: As Told by Brownee the Story Lizard. Brown, Sharon Lee. 2019. (Brownee the Story Lizard Ser.: Vol. 4). (ENG.). 44p. (J). (gr. k-5). 17.95 *(978-0-578-52365-1(5))* Starla Enterprises, Inc.

—TE the Toad Meets a Bully: As Told by Brownee the Story Lizard. Brown, Sharon Lee. Criser, Starla, ed. 2019. (Brownee the Story Lizard Ser.: Vol. 4). (ENG.). 44p. (J). pap. 9.99 *(978-1-0714-4009-4(8))* Independently Published.

Revell, Sharon. Gracie Youngblood. Revell, Sharon. 2018. (ENG.). 32p. (J). (gr. k-4). 15.95 *(978-0-692-07934-8(3))* Starla Enterprises, Inc.

Revels, Robert, jt. illus. see Mori, Midori.

REVILLE, TONI-ANN. Freddie the Frog & Friends. Signoretti, Brenda. 2011. 32p. pap. 12.99 *(978-1-4634-4633-8(0))* AuthorHouse.

Revoir, Joyce. Austin Alligator: I'll See You Guys Later. Foust, Cindy G. 2003. (J). 12.95 *(978-0-9749220-0-3(5))* Alpha-kidZ.

—Benny Bear: Having A Baby Sister Isn't Fair. Foust, Cindy G. 2004. (J). 12.95 *(978-0-9749220-1-0(3))* Alpha-kidZ.

Revoy, Antoine. Anubis Speaks! A Guide to the Afterlife by the Egyptian God of the Dead. Shecter, Vicky Alvear. 2013. (Secrets of the Ancient Gods Ser.). (ENG.). 128p. (J). (gr. 4-7). 16.95 *(978-1-59078-995-7(4))* Boyds Mills Pr.

Revoy, Antoine, jt. illus. see Murphy, Kelly.

Revutsky, Helen Ross. Aimee's a Book: El Libro a de Aimee. Zocchi, Judith Mazzeo et al. 2005. (J). *(978-1-59646-421-6(6))* Dingles & Co.

—Bebe's "B" Book: El Libro "B" de Bibi. Zocchi, Judith Mazzeo et al. 2005. (SPA & ENG.). (J). *(978-1-59646-427-8(5))* Dingles & Co.

—Delia's D Book: El Libro D de Delia. Zocchi, Judith Mazzeo et al. 2005. (SPA.). (J). *(978-1-59646-439-1(9))* Dingles & Co.

—Uri's "U" Book. Zocchi, Judith Mazzeo. 2007. (J). *(978-1-59646-538-1(7))* Dingles & Co.

—Xavia's "X" Book: El Libro "X" de Xavia. Zocchi, Judith Mazzeo et al. 2005. (SPA.). *(978-1-59646-559-6(X))* Dingles & Co.

—Yola's "Y" Book. Zocchi, Judith Mazzeo. 2007. (J). *(978-1-59646-562-6(X))* Dingles & Co.

—Zach's "Z" Book: El Libro "Z" de Zach. Zocchi, Judith Mazzeo et al. 2005. (SPA & ENG.). (J). *(978-1-59646-571-8(9))* Dingles & Co.

Rew, Jen. Game Over. Hunter, Alex. 2012. 126p. pap. *(978-1-78176-771-9(8))* FeedARead.com.

Rewse, Katie. How to Grow an Apple Pie. Charles, Beth. 2020. (ENG.). 32p. (J). (gr. -1-3). 16.99 ***(978-0-8075-0401-7(7)**,* 0807504017) Whitman, Albert & Co.

Rex, Adam. Billy Twitters & His Blue Whale Problem. Barnett, Mac. 2009. 48p. (J). (gr. -1-2). 16.99 *(978-0-7868-4958-1(4))* Hyperion Pr.

—The Case of the Case of Mistaken Identity. Barnett, Mac. (Brixton Brothers Ser.: 1). (ENG.). (J). (gr. 3-7). 2010. 208p. pap. 7.99 *(978-1-4169-7816-9(X));* 2009. 192p. 15.99 *(978-1-4169-7815-2(1))* Simon & Schuster Bks. For Young Readers. (Simon & Schuster Bks. For Young Readers).

—Chloe & the Lion. Barnett, Mac. 2012. 48p. (J). (gr. -1-k). 16.99 *(978-1-4231-1334-8(9))* Hyperion Pr.

—Chu's Day. Gaiman, Neil. 2014. (ENG.). 40p. (J). (gr. -1-3). pap. 6.99 *(978-0-06-201783-3(7))* HarperCollins Pubs.

—Chu's Day. Gaiman, Neil. 2013. (ENG.). 32p. (J). (gr. -1-3). 17.99 *(978-0-06-201781-9(0),* HarperCollins) HarperCollins Pubs. Ltd. GBR. Dist: HarperCollins Pubs.

—Chu's Day at the Beach. Gaiman, Neil. 2015. (ENG.). 32p. (J). (gr. -1-3). 17.99 *(978-0-06-222399-9(2),* HarperCollins) HarperCollins Pubs. Ltd. GBR. Dist: HarperCollins Pubs.

—Chu's Day at the Beach Board Book. Gaiman, Neil. 2016. (ENG.). 36p. (J). (gr. -1 — 1). bds. 7.99 *(978-0-06-238124-8(5),* HarperFestival) HarperCollins Pubs.

—Chu's Day Board Book. Gaiman, Neil. 2014. (ENG.). 36p. (J). (gr. -1 — 1). bds. 7.99 *(978-0-06-234746-6(2),* HarperFestival) HarperCollins Pubs.

—Chu's First Day of School. Gaiman, Neil. 2014. (ENG.). 32p. (J). (gr. -1-3). 17.99 *(978-0-06-222397-5(6),* HarperCollins) HarperCollins Pubs. Ltd. GBR. Dist: HarperCollins Pubs.

—Chu's First Day of School Board Book. Gaiman, Neil. 2015. (ENG.). 36p. (J). (gr. -1 — 1). bds. 7.99 *(978-0-06-237149-2(5),* HarperFestival) HarperCollins Pubs.

—The Ghostwriter Secret. Barnett, Mac. (Brixton Brothers Ser.: 2). (ENG.). (J). (gr. 3-7). 2011. 256p. pap. 7.99 *(978-1-4169-7818-3(6));* 2010. 240p. 17.99 *(978-1-4169-7817-6(8))* Simon & Schuster Bks. For Young Readers. (Simon & Schuster Bks. For Young Readers).

—Guess Again! Barnett, Mac. 2009. (ENG.). 32p. (J). (gr. -1-3). 18.99 *(978-1-4169-5566-5(6),* Simon & Schuster

R

Bks. For Young Readers) Simon & Schuster Bks. For Young Readers.

—Here's the Thing about Me. Kelly, Katy. 2006. (Lucy Rose Ser.: 1). 160p. (J). (gr. 3-7). reprint ed. per. 7.99 *(978-0-440-42026-2(1)*, Yearling) Random Hse. Children's Bks.

—It Happened on a Train. Barnett, Mac. (Brixton Brothers Ser.: 3). (ENG.). (J). (gr. 3-7). 2012. 304p. pap. 7.99 *(978-1-4169-7820-6(8))*; 2011. 288p. 17.99 *(978-1-4169-7819-0(4))* Simon & Schuster Bks. For Young Readers. (Simon & Schuster Bks. For Young Readers).

—The Legend of Rock Paper Scissors. Daywalt, Drew. 2017. (ENG.). 48p. (J). (gr. -1-3). 18.99 *(978-0-06-243889-8(1)*, Balzer & Bray) HarperCollins Pubs.

—Lucy Rose: Busy Like You Can't Believe. Kelly, Katy. 2007. (Lucy Rose Ser.: 3). 192p. (J). (gr. 3-7). per. 6.99 *(978-0-440-42108-5(X)*, Yearling) Random Hse. Children's Bks.

Rex, Adam. Star Wars Are You Scared, Darth Vader? Rex, Adam. 2018. (ENG.). 48p. (J). (gr. k-3). 17.99 *(978-1-4847-0497-4(5)*, Disney Lucasfilm Press) Disney Publishing Worldwide.

—The True Meaning of Smekday, 1. Rex, Adam. 2009. (Smek Smeries Ser.: 1). (ENG.). 432p. (J). (gr. 3-7). pap. 7.99 *(978-0-7868-4901-7(0))* Hyperion Bks. for Children.

Rex, Adam & Myers, Matt. Brixton Brothers Mysterious Case of Cases: The Case of the Case of Mistaken Identity; the Ghostwriter Secret; It Happened on a Train; Danger Goes Berserk. Barnett, Mac. ed. 2013. (Brixton Brothers Ser.). (ENG.). 1024p. (J). (gr. 3-7). pap. 33.99 *(978-1-4424-9818-1(8)*, Simon & Schuster Bks. For Young Readers) Simon & Schuster Bks. For Young Readers.

Rex, Adam, jt. illus. see Teplin, Scott.

Rex, Annmarie. Black's Adventure in the Big, Scary, Hairy World. Rex, Annmarie. 2007. 46p. (J). (gr. -1-3). per. 15.99 *(978-1-59879-364-2(0)*, Lifevest) Lifevest Publishing, Inc.

Rex, Deloney. My Easter Story. Hoskins, Maria. 2017. (ENG.). (J). (gr. k-5). 21.99 *(978-0-9864036-5-1(2))* C&V 4 Seasons Publishing.

Rex, Michael. Jack the Builder. Murphy, Stuart J. 2006. (MathStart 1 Ser.). (ENG.). 40p. (J). (gr. -1-3). pap. 6.99 *(978-0-06-055775-1(3))* HarperCollins Pubs.

Rex, Michael. Jacobo, el Constructor: Jack the Builder (Spanish Edition) Murphy, Stuart J. 2020. (MathStart 1 Ser.). (ENG.). 40p. (J). (gr. -1-3). pap. 5.99 ***(978-0-06-298324-4(5)***, HarperCollins) HarperCollins Pubs. Ltd. GBR. Dist: HarperCollins Pubs.

Rex, Michael. My Dog Jack Is Fat, 0 vols. Bunting, Eve. 2011. (ENG.). 32p. (J). (gr. -1-3). 16.99 *(978-0-7614-5809-8(3)*, 9780761458098, Two Lions) Amazon Publishing.

—Sunshine Makes the Seasons. Branley, Franklyn M. 2005. (Let's-Read-And-Find-Out Science 2 Ser.). (ENG.). 40p. (J). (gr. k-4). pap. 5.99 *(978-0-06-059205-9(2)*, Collins) HarperCollins Pubs.

—Sunshine Makes the Seasons. Branley, Franklyn Mansfield. 2005. (Let's-Read-and-Find-Out-Science Ser.). (ENG.). 40p. (J). (gr. -1 — 1). 15.99 *(978-0-06-059203-5(6))* HarperCollins Pubs.

—Sunshine Makes the Seasons. Branley, Franklyn M. 2016. (Let's-Read-And-Find-Out Science 2 Ser.). (ENG.). 40p. (J). (gr. -1-3). pap. 6.99 *(978-0-06-238209-2(8))* HarperCollins Pubs.

—With Any Luck I'll Drive a Truck. Friend, David. 2019. (ENG.). 32p. (J). (-k). pap. 8.99 *(978-1-9848-1388-6(9)*, Puffin Books) Penguin Young Readers Group.

Rex, Michael. The Birthday Party of Dread. Rex, Michael. 2012. (Fangbone! Third Grade Barbarian Ser.: 3). 128p. (J). (gr. 2-4). pap. 7.99 *(978-0-399-25523-6(0)*, G.P. Putnam's Sons Books for Young Readers) Penguin Young Readers Group.

—Eat Pete. Rex, Michael. 2018. 32p. (J). (-k). 17.99 *(978-1-5247-3880-8(8)*, Nancy Paulsen Books) Penguin Young Readers Group.

—The Egg of Misery: Fangbone, Third Grade Barbarian. Rex, Michael. 2012. (Fangbone! Third Grade Barbarian Ser.: 2). 128p. (J). (gr. 2-4). 7.99 *(978-0-399-25522-9(2)*, G.P. Putnam's Sons Books for Young Readers) Penguin Young Readers Group.

—The End of the World, 2. Rex, Michael. 2013. (Icky Ricky Ser.). (ENG.). 128p. (J). (gr. 1-3). lib. bdg. 17.44 *(978-0-375-97102-0(5))* Random Hse. Bks. for Young Readers.

—Facts vs. Opinions vs. Robots. Rex, Michael. 2020. 32p. (J). (gr. k-3). 17.99 *(978-1-9848-1626-9(8)*, Nancy Paulsen Books) Penguin Young Readers Group.

—Fangbone! Third-Grade Barbarian. Rex, Michael. 2012. (Fangbone! Third Grade Barbarian Ser.: 1). (ENG.). 128p. (J). (gr. 2-4). 7.99 *(978-0-399-25521-2(4)*, G.P. Putnam's Sons Books for Young Readers) Penguin Young Readers Group.

—Goodnight Goon: A Petrifying Parody. Rex, Michael. (J). 2018. 30p. (— 1). bds. 14.99 *(978-0-525-51867-9(3))*; 2008. 32p. (gr. -1-k). 16.99 *(978-0-399-24534-3(0))* Penguin Young Readers Group. (G.P. Putnam's Sons Books for Young Readers).

—Goodnight Goon: a Petrifying Parody. Rex, Michael. 2012. (ENG.). 30p. (J). (gr. -1 — 1). bds. 6.99 *(978-0-399-26011-7(0)*, G.P. Putnam's Sons Books for Young Readers) Penguin Young Readers Group.

—Icky Ricky #2: the End of the World. Rex, Michael. 2013. (Icky Ricky Ser.: 2). 128p. (J). (gr. 1-4). 4.99 *(978-0-307-93169-6(2)*, Random Hse. Bks. for Young Readers) Random Hse. Children's Bks.

—Icky Ricky #3: the Dead Disco Raccoon. Rex, Michael. 2014. (Icky Ricky Ser.: 3). (ENG.). 128p. (J). (gr. 1-4). 4.99 *(978-0-307-93171-9(4)*, Random Hse. Bks. for Young Readers) Random Hse. Children's Bks.

—Scarecrow. Rex, Michael. 2003. (Scholastic Reader: Level 1 Ser.). (ENG.). 28p. (J). (gr. -1-1). 16.19 *(978-0-439-49311-6(0))* Scholastic, Inc.

—Toilet Paper Mummy. Rex, Michael. 2013. (Icky Ricky Ser.: 1). 128p. (J). (gr. 1-4). pap. 4.99 *(978-0-307-93167-2(6)*, Random Hse. Bks. for Young Readers) Random Hse. Children's Bks.

—Truck Duck. Rex, Michael. 2008. 26p. (J). (gr. -1 — 1). bds. 7.99 *(978-0-399-25092-7(1)*, G.P. Putnam's Sons Books for Young Readers) Penguin Young Readers Group.

—With Any Luck, I'll Drive a Truck. Rex, Michael. Friend, David. 2016. 32p. (J). (-k). 16.99 *(978-0-399-16956-4(3)*, Nancy Paulsen Books) Penguin Young Readers Group.

Rexroad, Susan. The Case of the Wounded Pigeon. Rexroad, Frederick. 2008. (ENG.). 194p. (J). (gr. 4-7). pap. 3.97 *(978-0-9817742-0-6(2)*, Rexroad Kids) Rexroad International.

Rey, H. A. & Hines, Anna Grossnickle. Curious George Learns to Count from 1 To. Rey, H. A. 2011. (Curious George Ser.). (ENG.). (J). (gr. -1-3). lib. bdg. 19.60 *(978-1-68065-138-6(2))* Perfection Learning Corp.

Rey, H. A. & Rey, Margret. Curious George's 1 to 10 & Back Again. 2003. (J). bds. 9.95 *(978-0-618-27711-7(0))* Houghton Mifflin Harcourt Trade & Reference Pubs.

—Curious George's ABCs. 2003. (J). bds. 9.95 *(978-0-618-27708-7(0))* Houghton Mifflin Harcourt Trade & Reference Pubs.

—Curious George's Are You Curious? 2003. (J). bds. 9.95 *(978-0-618-27710-0(2))* Houghton Mifflin Harcourt Trade & Reference Pubs.

—Curious George's Opposites. 2003. (J). bds. 9.95 *(978-0-618-27709-4(9))* Houghton Mifflin Harcourt Trade & Reference Pubs.

Rey, Luis. Dinosaurs in the Sea. Staunton, Joseph & Flinthart, Dirk. 2011. (Inside Crime Ser.). 48p. (YA). (gr. 5-9). 34.25 *(978-1-59920-393-5(6))* Black Rabbit Bks.

—Meat Eating Dinosaurs. Staunton, Joseph & Flinthart, Dirk. 2011. (Inside Crime Ser.). 48p. (YA). (gr. 5-9). 34.25 *(978-1-59920-395-9(2))* Black Rabbit Bks.

Rey, Luis & Trotter, Stuart. The Usborne Book of Dinosaurs. Mayes, Susan. rev. ed. 2005. 32p. (J). pap., pap. 6.95 *(978-0-7945-0849-4(9)*, Usborne) EDC Publishing.

Rey, Luis V. Dino Babies! Bakker, Robert T. 2010. (Pictureback Ser.). (ENG.). 24p. (J). (gr. k-3). lib. bdg. 16.19 *(978-0-375-96330-8(8))* Random House Publishing Group.

—Dinosaurs: The Most Complete, Up-to-Date Encyclopedia for Dinosaur Lovers of All Ages. Holtz, Thomas R. 2007. 432p. (J). (gr. 3-7). 39.99 *(978-0-375-82419-7(7)*, Random Hse. Bks. for Young Readers) Random Hse. Children's Bks.

—The Usborne Internet-Linked World Atlas of Dinosaurs. Davidson, Susanna et al. 2003. 144p. (J). *(978-0-439-81840-7(0))* Scholastic, Inc.

Rey, Margret & Vipah Interactive Staff. Curious George Makes Pancakes, 1 vol. Rey, H. A. 2008. (Curious George Ser.). (ENG.). 24p. (J). (gr. k-3). lib. bdg. 27.07 *(978-1-59961-417-5(0)*, 5058, Picture Bk.) Spotlight.

Rey, Margret, jt. illus. see Rey, H. A.

Reyes, Arlene. Carter Goes to a Funeral, 1 vol. Zorka, Shawna. 2009. 47p. pap. 24.95 *(978-1-60836-785-6(1))* America Star Bks.

Reyes, Citlali. Cuauhtémoc: A Bilingual Book of Shapes: Shapes - Formas, 1 vol. Rodriguez, Patty & Stein, Ariana. 2018.Tr. of Spanish. 22p. (J). (gr. -1-k). bds. 9.99 *(978-0-9861099-3-5(2))* Little Libros, LLC.

—Un Elefante: A Bilingual Counting Book: Numbers - Numeros, 1 vol. Rodriguez, Patty & Stein, Ariana. 2018.Tr. of Spanish. 22p. (J). (gr. -1-k). bds. 9.99 *(978-0-9861099-4-2(0))* Little Libros, LLC.

—Guadalupe, 1 vol. Rodriguez, Patty & Stein, Ariana. ed. 2018. (SPA.). 22p. (J). bds. 9.99 *(978-0-9861099-0-4(8))* Little Libros, LLC.

—The Life of / la Vida de Celia: A Bilingual Picture Book Biography, 1 vol. Rodriguez, Patty & Stein, Ariana. 2018. 22p. (J). (gr. -1-k). bds. 9.99 *(978-0-9861099-5-9(9))* Little Libros, LLC.

—The Life of / la Vida de Selena (Unauthorized) A Bilingual Picture Book Biography, 1 vol. Rodriguez, Patty & Stein, Ariana. 2018. (SPA.). 22p. (J). (gr. -1-k). bds. 9.99 *(978-0-9861099-9-7(1)*, Lil' Libros) Little Libros, LLC.

—La Llorona - Counting down / Contando Hacia Atras, 1 vol. Rodriguez, Patty & Stein, Ariana. 2018. 22p. (J). bds. 9.99 *(978-0-9861099-2-8(4))* Little Libros, LLC.

—Lucha Libre - Anatomy / Anatomia, 1 vol. Rodriguez, Patty & Stein, Ariana. 2018. 22p. (J). bds. 9.99 *(978-0-9861099-1-1(6))* Little Libros, LLC.

Reyes, Glendalys. The Three Little Explorers, 1 vol. Kittredge, James M. 2010. 16p. pap. 24.95 *(978-1-4489-8973-7(6))* PublishAmerica, Inc.

Reyes III, Romulo. This Is My Family. Gunawardana, Amani. 2019. (ENG.). 24p. (J). pap. *(978-1-925932-63-8(X))* Library For All Limited.

Reyes III, Romulo T. Bundy the Possum. Nicholls, Carol Khan. 2019. (ENG.). 42p. (J). pap. *(978-1-925986-10-5(1))* Library For All Limited.

Reyes, Maria Margarita. La Selva Maravillosa/the Wonderful Jungle. Aristizabal, Nora. 2005. (Bilingual Collection). (SPA.). 31p. (J). *(978-958-30-1966-1(6))* Panamericana Editorial.

Reyes, Paulina. Poemas de Juguete. Granados, Antonio. 2015. (Serie Azul Ser.).Tr. of Toy Poems. (SPA.). 144p. (J). pap. 10.95 *(978-1-64101-235-5(8))* Santillana USA Publishing Co., Inc.

Reyes, Pia. Breakfast at Grandma's. MacKenzie, Karin. 2018. (ENG.). 40p. (J). pap. *(978-1-5255-0979-7(9))* FriesenPress.

—Leaving Aleppo. Stube, Tahirih. 2019. (ENG.). 28p. (J). *(978-1-5255-2661-9(8))*; pap. *(978-1-5255-2662-6(6))* FriesenPress.

—My Mom Is an Octopus. Emrani, Nellie & Emrani, Melody. 2018. (ENG.). 48p. (J). *(978-1-5255-1057-1(6))*; pap. *(978-1-5255-1058-8(4))* FriesenPress.

Reyes, Pia. Sometimes It's Hard to Be Me: A Child's Struggle with Change. Hammond, Trish. 2020. (ENG.). 24p. (J). ***(978-1-5255-5291-5(0))***; pap. ***(978-1-5255-5292-2(9))*** FriesenPress.

Reyes, Romulo, III. Betty Likes Sea Animals (Tetun Edition) - Betty Gosta Balada Tasi Nian. Oluwond, Stanley. 2020. (TET.). 28p. (J). pap. ***(978-1-922331-51-9(1))*** Library For All Limited.

Reynarde, Niccola. Cowlick. Street-Ely, Linda. 2019. (ENG.). 32p. (J). pap. 9.99 *(978-1-947677-01-2(2))* Paper Airplane Publishing, LLC.

Reynolds, Adrian. Elephants Can't Jump! Willis, Jeanne. 2015. (ENG.). 32p. (J). (gr. -1-3). 16.95 *(978-1-4677-6316-5(0)*, 9781467763165); E-Book 27.99 *(978-1-4677-6320-2(9))* Lerner Publishing Group.

—Harry & the Bucketful of Dinosaurs. Whybrow, Ian. 2010. (Harry & the Dinosaurs Ser.). (ENG.). 32p. (J). (gr. -1-2). pap. 7.99 *(978-0-375-85119-3(4)*, Dragonfly Bks.) Random Hse. Children's Bks.

—Harry & the Dinosaurs Go to School. Whybrow, Ian. 2015. (ENG.). 32p. (J). (gr. -1-2). 7.99 *(978-0-553-53400-9(9)*, Dragonfly Bks.) Random Hse. Children's Bks.

—I'M Sure I Saw a Dinosaur. Willis, Jeanne. 2011. (Andersen Press Picture Books Ser.). (ENG.). 32p. 16.95 *(978-0-7613-8093-1(0))* Andersen Pr. GBR. Dist: Lerner Publishing Group.

—The Pets You Get. Taylor, Thomas. 2013. (ENG.). 32p. (J). (gr. -1-3). 16.95 *(978-1-4677-1143-2(8)*, 9781467711432) Lerner Publishing Group.

—The Tickle Test. White, Kathryn. 2017. (ENG.). 32p. (J). (gr. -1-3). 17.99 *(978-1-5124-8126-6(2)*, 9781512481266) Lerner Publishing Group.

—Upside down Babies. Willis, Jeanne. 2014. (ENG.). 32p. (J). (gr. -1-3). 16.95 *(978-1-4677-3424-0(1)*, 9781467734240) Lerner Publishing Group.

—What's Naughty? Oram, Hiawyn. (ENG.). 32p. (J). pap. 11.99 *(978-0-340-75447-4(8))* Hodder & Stoughton GBR. Dist: Trafalgar Square Publishing.

—Who's in the Loo? Willis, Jeanne. 10th ed. 2016. 12p. (J). (— 1). bds. 9.99 *(978-1-78344-420-5(7))* Andersen Pr. GBR. Dist: Independent Pubs. Group.

Reynolds, Barry. The Great Big Book of Irish Wildlife: Through the Seasons. Browne, Juanita. 2018. (ENG.). 80p. 29.00 *(978-1-84717-915-9(0))* O'Brien Pr., Ltd., The IRL. Dist: Casemate Pubs. & Bk. Distributors, LLC.

Reynolds, Calvin. Jayce: A Bee Adventure. Reynolds, Calvin. 2017. (ENG.). (J). pap. 11.99 *(978-0-9986630-1-2(8))*; (gr. 3-5). 19.99 *(978-0-9986630-2-9(6))* Concepts Redefined.

—Jayce the Bee: Journey to the Polka-Dot Village. Reynolds, Calvin. 2017. (ENG.). (J). (gr. k-5). 20.99 *(978-0-9986630-3-6(4))* Concepts Redefined.

Reynolds, Calvin. Jayce the Bee Activities & Coloring Book. Reynolds, Calvin. 2019. (ENG.). 40p. (J). pap. 6.99 ***(978-1-7330938-4-2(2))*** Concepts Redefined.

Reynolds, Candler. I'm Not Weird, I'm Wonderful. Stewart, Beth Roper. 2020. (ENG.). 28p. (J). 23.95 ***(978-1-64670-544-3(0))***; pap. 13.95 ***(978-1-64670-480-4(0))*** Covenant Bks.

Reynolds, Doris. Beth & Seth. Varble, Rachel McBrayer. 2012. 208p. 44.95 *(978-1-258-25079-9(9))*; pap. 29.95 *(978-1-258-25542-8(1))* Literary Licensing, LLC.

Reynolds, Emma. Rescuing Mrs. Birdley. Reynolds, Aaron. 2020. (ENG.). 40p. (J). (gr. -1-3). 17.99 ***(978-1-5344-2704-4(X)***, Simon & Schuster Bks. For Young Readers) Simon & Schuster Bks. For Young Readers.

Reynolds, Jan, photos by. Celebrate! Connections among Cultures, 1 vol. Reynolds, Jan. 2006. (ENG., 32p. (J). pap. 9.95 *(978-1-60060-452-8(8))* Lee & Low Bks., Inc.

—Cycle of Rice, Cycle of Life: A Story of Sustainable Farming. Reynolds, Jan. 2009. (ENG., 48p. (J). (gr. 2-7). 19.95 *(978-1-60060-254-2(1))* Lee & Low Bks., Inc.

—Only the Mountains Do Not Move: A Maasai Story of Culture & Conservation, 1 vol. Reynolds, Jan. 2011. (ENG., 40p. (J). (gr. 3-6). pap. 11.95 *(978-1-60060-844-5(2)*, c7c63daf-ac4c-4393-94b7-2e93b722c570); (gr. 1-6). pap. 18.95 *(978-1-60060-333-4(5))* Lee & Low Bks., Inc.

Reynolds, Pat. The Boy at the Park. Reilly, Carmel. 2009. 24p. pap. 10.67 *(978-1-4190-5517-1(8))* Rigby Education.

Reynolds, Paul A. & Reynolds, Peter H. Going Green! Reynolds, Paul A. 2015. (Sydney & Simon Ser.: 2). 48p. (J). (gr. 1-4). lib. bdg. 12.95 *(978-1-58089-677-1(4))* Charlesbridge Publishing, Inc.

Reynolds, Peter. Olivia Kidney. Potter, Ellen. 2003. (ENG.). 155p. (J). (gr. 4-6). 21.19 *(978-0-399-23850-5(6))* Penguin Young Readers Group.

—Olivia Kidney. Potter, Ellen. 2004. (ENG.). 176p. (J). (gr. 3-7). reprint ed. 6.99 *(978-0-14-240234-4(6)*, Puffin Books) Penguin Young Readers Group.

Reynolds, Peter H. Around the World in 8 1/2 Days. Mcdonald, Megan. 2010. (Judy Moody Ser.: 7). (ENG.). 176p. (J). (gr. 1-4). 15.99 *(978-0-7636-4864-0(7))*;Bk. 7. pap. 5.99 *(978-0-7636-4863-3(9))* Candlewick Pr.

—Bad Luck Charm. Mcdonald, Megan. 2013. (Judy Moody Ser.: 11). (ENG.). 176p. (J). (gr. 1-4). pap. 5.99 *(978-0-7636-4348-5(3))* Candlewick Pr.

—The Doctor Is In! Mcdonald, Megan. 2010. (Judy Moody Ser.: 5). (ENG.). 176p. (J). (gr. 1-4). 15.99 *(978-0-7636-4862-6(0))* Candlewick Pr.

—Guyku: A Year of Haiku for Boys. Raczka, Bob. 2018. (ENG.). 48p. (J). (gr. -1-3). pap. 6.99 *(978-1-328-86930-2(X)*, 1696693, HMH Books For Young Readers) Houghton Mifflin Harcourt Publishing Co.

—I Am ... a Box of Goodness. Verde, Susan. 2019. (I Am Bks.). (ENG.). 96p. (J). (gr. -1-3). 42.99 *(978-1-4197-4054-1(7)*, 1300807, Abrams Bks. for Young Readers) Abrams, Inc.

Reynolds, Peter H. I Am Human: A Book of Empathy. Verde, Susan. (I Am Bks.). (ENG.). (J). (gr. -1 — 1). 2020. 22p. bds. 8.99 ***(978-1-4197-4673-4(1)***, 1277610, Abrams Appleseed); 2018. 32p. 14.99 *(978-1-4197-3165-5(3)*, 1218601, Abrams Bks. for Young Readers) Abrams, Inc.

Reynolds, Peter H. I Am Love: A Book of Compassion. Verde, Susan. 2019. (ENG.). 32p. (J). (gr. -1-2). 14.99 *(978-1-4197-3726-8(0)*, 1277601) Abrams, Inc.

Reynolds, Peter H. I Am One: A Book of Action. Verde, Susan. 2020. (ENG.). 32p. (J). (gr. -1-3). 14.99 ***(978-1-4197-4238-5(8)***, 1263401, Abrams Bks. for Young Readers) Abrams, Inc.

Reynolds, Peter H. I Am Peace: A Book of Mindfulness. Verde, Susan. (I Am Bks.). (ENG.). (J). (gr. -1 — 1). 2019. 22p. bds. 8.99 *(978-1-4197-3152-5(1)*, 1192910, Abrams Appleseed); 2017. 32p. 14.95 *(978-1-4197-2701-6(X)*, 1192901, Abrams Bks. for Young Readers) Abrams, Inc.

—I Am Yoga. Verde, Susan. (I Am Bks.). (ENG.). (J). (gr. -1 — 1). 2017. 24p. bds. 8.95 *(978-1-4197-2697-2(8)*, 1191610, Abrams Appleseed); 2015. 32p. 14.95 *(978-1-4197-1664-5(6)*, 1085401, Abrams Bks. for Young Readers) Abrams, Inc.

—The Incredible Shrinking Kid. Mcdonald, Megan. 2013. (Stink Ser.: 1). (ENG.). 112p. (J). (gr. 1-4). 14.99 *(978-0-7636-6388-9(3))* Candlewick Pr.

—Judy Moody. McDonald, Megan. 2018. (Judy Moody Ser.: 1). (ENG.). 176p. (J). (gr. 1-4). pap. 5.99 *(978-1-5362-0071-3(9))* Candlewick Pr.

—Judy Moody & Stink: The Mad, Mad, Mad, Mad Treasure Hunt. Mcdonald, Megan. 2009. (Judy Moody & Stink Ser.: 2). 128p. (J). (gr. 1-4). 14.99 *(978-0-7636-3962-4(1))* Candlewick Pr.

—Judy Moody & Stink in the School's Out Collection. Mcdonald, Megan. 2015. (Judy Moody Ser.). (J). (gr. 1-4). 19.97 *(978-0-7636-8018-3(4))* Candlewick Pr.

—Judy Moody & Stink: the Big Bad Blackout. McDonald, Megan. 2015. (Judy Moody & Stink Ser.: 3). (ENG.). 144p. (J). (gr. 1-4). pap. 7.99 *(978-0-7636-7665-0(9))* Candlewick Pr.

—Judy Moody & Stink: the Holly Joliday. McDonald, Megan. 2008. (Judy Moody & Stink Ser.: 1). (ENG.). 96p. (J). (gr. k-3). pap. 7.99 *(978-0-7636-4113-9(8))* Candlewick Pr.

—Judy Moody & Stink: the Wishbone Wish. Mcdonald, Megan. (Judy Moody & Stink Ser.: 4). 128p. (J). (gr. 1-4). 2016. (ENG.). pap. 7.99 *(978-0-7636-9099-1(6))*; 2015. 14.99 *(978-0-7636-7206-5(8))* Candlewick Pr.

—Judy Moody & the Bad Luck Charm. Mcdonald, Megan. (Judy Moody Ser.: 11). 176p. (J). (gr. 1-4). 2018. (ENG.). pap. 5.99 *(978-1-5362-0080-5(8))*; 2012. 15.99 *(978-0-7636-3451-3(4))* Candlewick Pr.

—Judy Moody & the Bucket List. Mcdonald, Megan. (Judy Moody Ser.: 13). 176p. (J). (gr. 1-4). 2018. (ENG.). pap. 5.99 *(978-1-5362-0082-9(4))*; 2017. (ENG.). pap. 5.99 *(978-0-7636-9759-4(1))*; 2016. 15.99 *(978-0-7636-7995-8(X))* Candlewick Pr.

—Judy Moody & the NOT Bummer Summer. McDonald, Megan. 2018. (Judy Moody Ser.: 10). (ENG.). 208p. (J). (gr. 1-4). pap. 5.99 *(978-1-5362-0084-3(0))* Candlewick Pr.

—Judy Moody & the Not Bummer Summer. Mcdonald, Megan. movie tie-in ed. (J). 2011. (Judy Moody Movie Tie-Ins Ser.: Bk. 10). (ENG.). 128p. (gr. 3-6). 18.69 *(978-0-7636-5351-4(9))*; Bk. 10. 2012. (Judy Moody Ser.: 10). 208p. (gr. 1-4). 15.99 *(978-0-7636-5711-6(5))* Candlewick Pr.

—Judy Moody & the Right Royal Tea Party. McDonald, Megan. (Judy Moody Ser.: 14). 160p. (J). (gr. 1-4). 2019. (ENG.). pap. 5.99 *(978-1-5362-0332-5(7))*; 2018. 15.99 *(978-0-7636-9567-5(X))* Candlewick Pr.

—Judy Moody: Around the World in 8 1/2 Days. Mcdonald, Megan. 2018. (Judy Moody Ser.: 7). (ENG.). 176p. (J). (gr. 1-4). pap. 5.99 *(978-1-5362-0077-5(8))* Candlewick Pr.

Reynolds, Peter H. Judy Moody, Book Quiz Whiz. McDonald, Megan. (Judy Moody Ser.). (ENG.). 176p. (J). (gr. 1-4). 2020. pap. 5.99 ***(978-1-5362-1399-7(3))***; 2019. 15.99 *(978-1-5362-0484-1(6))* Candlewick Pr.

Reynolds, Peter H. Judy Moody Declares Independence. McDonald, Megan. 2018. (Judy Moody Ser.: 6). (ENG.). 160p. (J). (gr. 1-4). pap. 5.99 *(978-1-5362-0076-8(X))* Candlewick Pr.

—Judy Moody Declares Independence. Mcdonald, Megan. 2010. (Judy Moody Ser.: 6). (ENG.). 160p. (J). (gr. 1-4). 16.99 *(978-0-7636-4852-7(3))*; pap. 5.99 *(978-0-7636-4851-0(5))* Candlewick Pr.

—Judy Moody Declares Independence: #6. Mcdonald, Megan. 2019. (Judy Moody Ser.). (ENG.). 152p. (J). (gr. 1-5). lib. bdg. 27.07 *(978-1-5321-4310-6(9)*, 31840, Chapter Bks.) Spotlight.

—The Judy Moody Double-Rare Collection. Mcdonald, Megan. 2019. (Judy Moody Ser.). (ENG.). (J). (gr. 1-4). pap. 17.97 *(978-1-5362-0951-8(1))* Candlewick Pr.

—Judy Moody Gets Famous! McDonald, Megan. 2018. (Judy Moody Ser.: 2). (ENG.). 144p. (J). (gr. 1-4). pap. 5.99 *(978-1-5362-0073-7(5))* Candlewick Pr.

—Judy Moody Gets Famous! Mcdonald, Megan. 2010. (Judy Moody Ser.: 2). (ENG.). 144p. (J). (gr. 1-4). 16.99 *(978-0-7636-4854-1(X))*; pap. 5.99 *(978-0-7636-4853-4(1))* Candlewick Pr.

—Judy Moody Gets Famous!: #2. Mcdonald, Megan. 2019. (Judy Moody Ser.). (ENG.). 136p. (J). (gr. 1-5). lib. bdg. 27.07 *(978-1-5321-4306-9(0)*, 31836, Chapter Bks.) Spotlight.

—Judy Moody, Girl Detective. Mcdonald, Megan. (Judy Moody Ser.: 9). 192p. (J). (gr. 1-4). 2011. (ENG.). pap. 5.99 *(978-0-7636-4349-2(1))*; 2010. 15.99 *(978-0-7636-3450-6(6))* Candlewick Pr.

—Judy Moody, Girl Detective. McDonald, Megan. 2018. (Judy Moody Ser.: 9). (ENG.). 192p. (J). (gr. 1-4). pap. 5.99 *(978-1-5362-0079-9(4))* Candlewick Pr.

—Judy Moody Goes to College. Mcdonald, Megan. 2018. (Judy Moody Ser.: 8). (ENG.). 176p. (J). (gr. 1-4). pap. 5.99 *(978-1-5362-0078-2(6))* Candlewick Pr.

—Judy Moody Goes to College, Bk. 8. Mcdonald, Megan. 2010. (Judy Moody Ser.: 8). (ENG.). 144p. (J). (gr. 1-4). 15.99 *(978-0-7636-4856-5(6))* Candlewick Pr.

—Judy Moody, M. D. The Doctor Is In! McDonald, Megan. 2018. (Judy Moody Ser.: 5). (ENG.). 176p. (J). (gr. 1-4). pap. 5.99 *(978-1-5362-0074-4(3))* Candlewick Pr.

—Judy Moody, M. D.: the Doctor Is In!: #5. Mcdonald, Megan. 2019. (Judy Moody Ser.). (ENG.). 160p. (J). (gr. 1-5). lib. bdg. 27.07 *(978-1-5321-4309-0(5)*, 31839, Chapter Bks.) Spotlight.

—Judy Moody, Mood Martian. Mcdonald, Megan. (Judy Moody Ser.: 12). 208p. (J). (gr. 1-4). 2018. (ENG.). pap. 5.99 *(978-1-5362-0081-2(6))*; 2014. 15.99 *(978-0-7636-6698-9(X))* Candlewick Pr.

—The Judy Moody Most Mood-Tastic Collection Ever. McDonald, Megan. 2018. (Judy Moody Ser.). (ENG.). (J). (gr. 1-4). pap. 71.88 *(978-1-5362-0359-2(9))* Candlewick Pr.
—Judy Moody Predicts the Future. McDonald, Megan. 2018. (Judy Moody Ser.: 4). (ENG.). 160p. (J). (gr. 1-4). pap. 5.99 *(978-1-5362-0075-1(1))* Candlewick Pr.
—Judy Moody Predicts the Future. Mcdonald, Megan. 2010. (Judy Moody Ser.: 4). (ENG.). 160p. (J). (gr. 1-4). 15.99 *(978-0-7636-4858-9(2))*; pap. 5.99 *(978-0-7636-4857-2(4))* Candlewick Pr.
—Judy Moody Predicts the Future: #4. Mcdonald, Megan. 2019. (Judy Moody Ser.). (ENG.). 152p. (J). (gr. 1-5). lib. bdg. 27.07 *(978-1-5321-4308-3(7)*, 31838, Chapter Bks.) Spotlight.
—Judy Moody Saves the World! McDonald, Megan. 2004. (Judy Moody Ser.: Bk. 3). 144p. (J). (gr. 1-5). 13.65 *(978-0-7569-2588-8(6))* Perfection Learning Corp.
—Judy Moody Saves the World! McDonald, Megan. 2018. (Judy Moody Ser.: 3). (ENG.). 160p. (J). (gr. 1-4). pap. 5.99 *(978-1-5362-0072-0(7))* Candlewick Pr.
—Judy Moody Saves the World! Mcdonald, Megan. 2010. (Judy Moody Ser.: 3). (ENG.). 160p. (J). (gr. 1-4). 16.99 *(978-0-7636-4860-2(4))*;Bk. 3. pap. 5.99 *(978-0-7636-4859-6(0))* Candlewick Pr.
—Judy Moody Saves the World!: #3. Mcdonald, Megan. 2019. (Judy Moody Ser.). (ENG.). 152p. (J). (gr. 1-5). lib. bdg. 27.07 *(978-1-5321-4307-6(9)*, 31837, Chapter Bks.) Spotlight.
—Judy Moody (Set), 6 vols. Mcdonald, Megan. 2019. (Judy Moody Ser.). (ENG.). 136p. (J). (gr. 1-5). lib. bdg. 162.42 *(978-1-5321-4304-5(4)*, 31834, Chapter Bks.) Spotlight.
—The Judy Moody Star-Studded Collection. McDonald, Megan. 2018. (Judy Moody Ser.). (ENG.). (J). (gr. 1-4). pap. 17.97 *(978-1-5362-0360-8(2))* Candlewick Pr.
—Judy Moody: the Mad Rad Collection. Mcdonald, Megan. 2019. (Judy Moody Ser.). (ENG.). (J). (gr. 1-4). pap. 17.97 *(978-1-5362-0952-5(X))* Candlewick Pr.
—The Judy Moody Uber-Awesome Collection, 9 vols., Bks. 1-9. Mcdonald, Megan. 2011. (Judy Moody Ser.). 1488p. (J). (gr. 1-4). 48.00 *(978-0-7636-5411-5(6))* Candlewick Pr.
—Judy Moody Was in a Mood: #1. Mcdonald, Megan. 2019. (Judy Moody Ser.). (ENG.). 160p. (J). (gr. 1-5). lib. bdg. 27.07 *(978-1-5321-4305-2(2)*, 31835, Chapter Bks.) Spotlight.
—Judy Moody's Best Mood Ever Coloring & Activity Book. Mcdonald, Megan. 2011. (Judy Moody Ser.). 32p. (J). (gr. -1-2). pap. 3.99 *(978-0-7636-5707-9(7))* Candlewick Pr.
—Little Boy. McGhee, Alison. 2008. (ENG.). 40p. (J). (gr. -1-3). 17.99 *(978-1-4169-5872-7(X)*, Atheneum Bks. for Young Readers) Simon & Schuster Children's Publishing.
—Little Miss, Big Sis. Rosenthal, Amy Krouse. 2015. (ENG.). 40p. (J). (gr. -1-3). 17.99 *(978-0-06-230203-8(5))* HarperCollins Pubs.
—Little Miss, Big Sis Board Book. Rosenthal, Amy Krouse. 2020. (ENG.). 40p. (J). (gr. -1 — 1). bds. 7.99 *(978-0-06-299344-1(5)*, HarperFestival) HarperCollins Pubs.
—The Mad, Mad, Mad, Mad Treasure Hunt. Mcdonald, Megan. 2010. (Judy Moody & Stink Ser.: 2). 128p. (J). (gr. 1-4). pap. 7.99 *(978-0-7636-4351-5(3))* Candlewick Pr.
—Mad Rad. Mcdonald, Megan. 2012. (Judy Moody Ser.: Bks. 7-9). (ENG.). (J). (gr. 1-4). pap. 17.97 *(978-0-7636-5410-8(8))* Candlewick Pr.
—Mood Martian. Mcdonald, Megan. 2015. (Judy Moody Ser.). (ENG.). 208p. (J). (gr. 1-4). pap. 5.99 *(978-0-7636-8015-2(X))* Candlewick Pr.
—More Stink-Y Stuff from A to Z, Vol. 2. Mcdonald, Megan. 2012. (Stink Ser.: No. 2). (ENG.). 144p. (J). (gr. 1-5). 27.07 *(978-1-59961-196-9(1)*, 13837, Chapter Bks.) Spotlight.
—The Museum. Verde, Susan. 2013. (ENG.). 32p. (J). (gr. -1-2). 16.95 *(978-1-4197-0594-6(6)*, Abrams Bks. for Young Readers) Abrams, Inc.
—Off the Path Math with Tobbs, Vol. 1. O'Brien, Thomas C. 2003. 59p. (J). 14.50 *(978-1-891405-09-9(8))* FableVision Pr.
—Plant a Kiss. Rosenthal, Amy Krouse. 2011. (ENG.). 40p. (J). (gr. -1-3). 14.99 *(978-0-06-198675-8(5)*, HarperCollins) HarperCollins Pubs. Ltd. GBR. Dist: HarperCollins Pubs.
—Plant a Kiss Board Book. Rosenthal, Amy Krouse. 2015. (ENG.). 36p. (J). (gr. -1 — 1). bds. 7.99 *(978-0-06-241652-0(9)*, HarperFestival) HarperCollins Pubs.
—Solar System Superhero, Bk. 5. Mcdonald, Megan. 2013. (Stink Ser.: 5). (ENG.). 128p. (J). (gr. 1-4). 14.99 *(978-0-7636-6392-6(1))* Candlewick Pr.
—Solar System Superhero. Mcdonald, Megan. 2012. (Stink Ser.: No. 2). (ENG.). 144p. (J). (gr. 1-5). 27.07 *(978-1-59961-197-6(X)*, 13838, Chapter Bks.) Spotlight.
—Someday. Mcghee, Alison. 2008. (J). (gr. -1-2). 27.95 incl. audio *(978-0-8045-6975-0(4))*; 29.95 incl. audio compact disk *(978-0-8045-4200-5(7))* Spoken Arts, Inc.
—Someday. McGhee, Alison. 2015. (ENG.). 42p. (J). (gr. -1). bds. 9.99 *(978-1-4814-6012-5(9)*, Little Simon) Little Simon.
—Someday. McGhee, Alison. 2007. (ENG.). 40p. (J). (gr. -1-3). 17.99 *(978-1-4169-2811-9(1)*, Atheneum Bks. for Young Readers) Simon & Schuster Children's Publishing.
—Spf 40. FableVision. 2013. (Zebrafish Ser.). (ENG.). 128p. (J). (gr. 5-9). pap. 9.99 *(978-1-4169-9709-2(1)*, Atheneum Bks. for Young Readers) Simon & Schuster Children's Publishing.
—Star Bright: A Christmas Story. McGhee, Alison. 2014. (ENG.). 40p. (J). (gr. -1-3). 17.99 *(978-1-4169-5858-1(4)*, Atheneum Bks. for Young Readers) Simon & Schuster Children's Publishing.
—Stationery Studio Writing Collection Deluxe CD-ROM Single Computer License: The Irresistible Tool to Encourage Writing. Stearns, Peggy Healy. 2003. 112p. (J). 69.95 incl. cd-rom *(978-1-891405-07-5(1))* FableVision Pr.
—Stink: The Incredible Shrinking Kid. Mcdonald, Megan. 2010. (Stink Ser.: No. 1). (ENG.). 112p. (J). (gr. 1-5). 27.07 *(978-1-59961-686-5(6)*, 13833, Chapter Bks.) Spotlight.
—Stink: The Incredible Shrinking Kid. McDonald, Megan. 2013. (Stink Ser.: 1). (ENG.). 128p. (J). (gr. 1-4). pap. 4.99 *(978-0-7636-6426-8(X))* Candlewick Pr.
—Stink: Twice As Incredible. Mcdonald, Megan. 2016. (Stink Ser.). 277p. (J). (gr. 1-4). pap. 7.99 *(978-0-7636-8829-5(0))* Candlewick Pr.
—Stink & the Attack of the Slime Mold. Mcdonald, Megan. 2016. (Stink Ser.: 10). 144p. (J). (gr. 1-4). 12.99 *(978-0-7636-5554-9(6))* Candlewick Pr.
—Stink & the Attack of the Slime Mold. Mcdonald, Megan. 2019. (Stink Ser.). (ENG.). 136p. (J). (gr. 1-5). lib. bdg. 27.07 *(978-1-5321-4330-4(3)*, 31860, Chapter Bks.) Spotlight.
—Stink & the Attack of the Slime Mold. Mcdonald, Megan. ed. 2017. (Stink Ser.: 10). (ENG.). (J). (gr. 1-4). lib. bdg. 14.75 *(978-0-606-39836-7(8))* Turtleback.
—Stink & the Freaky Frog Freakout. Mcdonald, Megan. 2013. (Stink Ser.: 8). 160p. (J). (gr. 1-4). 12.99 *(978-0-7636-6140-3(6))* Candlewick Pr.
—Stink & the Freaky Frog Freakout. Mcdonald, Megan. 2019. (Stink Ser.). (ENG.). 160p. (J). (gr. 1-5). lib. bdg. 27.07 *(978-1-5321-4331-1(1)*, 31861, Chapter Bks.) Spotlight.
—Stink & the Great Guinea Pig Express. Mcdonald, Megan. 2010. (Stink Ser.: No. 4). (ENG.). 128p. (J). (gr. 1-5). 27.07 *(978-1-59961-683-4(1)*, 13830, Chapter Bks.) Spotlight.
—Stink & the Great Guinea Pig Express, Bk. 4. McDonald, Megan. 2013. (Stink Ser.: 4). (ENG.). 144p. (J). (gr. 1-4). pap. 4.99 *(978-0-7636-6421-3(9))* Candlewick Pr.
—Stink & the Great Guinea Pig Express, Bk. 4. Mcdonald, Megan. 2013. (Stink Ser.: 4). (ENG.). 128p. (J). (gr. 1-4). 12.99 *(978-0-7636-6391-9(3))* Candlewick Pr.
Reynolds, Peter H. Stink & the Hairy, Scary Spider. McDonald, Megan. 2020. (Stink Ser.). (ENG.). 160p. (J). (gr. 1-4). 14.99 ***(978-1-5362-0920-4(1))*** Candlewick Pr.
Reynolds, Peter H. Stink & the Incredible Super-Galactic Jawbreaker. Mcdonald, Megan. 2010. (Stink Ser.: No. 2). (ENG.). 128p. (J). (gr. 1-5). 27.07 *(978-1-59961-684-1(X)*, 13831, Chapter Bks.) Spotlight.
—Stink & the Incredible Super-Galactic Jawbreaker. McDonald, Megan. 2013. (Stink Ser.: 2). (ENG.). 144p. (J). (gr. 1-4). pap. 4.99 *(978-0-7636-6420-6(0))* Candlewick Pr.
—Stink & the Incredible Super-Galactic Jawbreaker, Bk. 2. Mcdonald, Megan. 2013. (Stink Ser.: 2). (ENG.). 128p. (J). (gr. 1-4). 14.99 *(978-0-7636-6389-6(1))* Candlewick Pr.
—Stink & the Midnight Zombie Walk. Mcdonald, Megan. 2013. (Stink Ser.: 7). (ENG.). 160p. (J). (gr. 1-4). 12.99 *(978-0-7636-6394-0(8))*; pap. 4.99 *(978-0-7636-6422-0(7))* Candlewick Pr.
—Stink & the Midnight Zombie Walk. Mcdonald, Megan. 2019. (Stink Ser.). (ENG.). 152p. (J). (gr. 1-5). lib. bdg. 27.07 *(978-1-5321-4332-8(X)*, 31862, Chapter Bks.) Spotlight.
—Stink & the Shark Sleepover. Mcdonald, Megan. (Stink Ser.: 9). 176p. (J). (gr. 1-4). 2014. 12.99 *(978-0-7636-6474-9(X))*; Bk. 9. 2015. (ENG.). pap. 4.99 *(978-0-7636-7678-0(0))* Candlewick Pr.
—Stink & the Shark Sleepover. Mcdonald, Megan. 2019. (Stink Ser.). (ENG.). 168p. (J). (gr. 1-5). lib. bdg. 27.07 *(978-1-5321-4333-5(8)*, 31863, Chapter Bks.) Spotlight.
—Stink & the Ultimate Thumb-Wrestling Smackdown. Mcdonald, Megan. 2013. (Stink Ser.: 6). (ENG.). 144p. (J). (gr. 1-4). pap. 4.99 *(978-0-7636-6423-7(5))*;Bk. 6. 12.99 *(978-0-7636-6393-3(X))* Candlewick Pr.
—Stink & the Ultimate Thumb-Wrestling Smackdown, 1 vol. Mcdonald, Megan. 2012. (Stink Ser.: No. 2). (ENG.). 144p. (J). (gr. 1-5). 27.07 *(978-1-59961-194-5(5)*, 13835, Chapter Bks.) Spotlight.
—Stink & the World's Worst Super-Stinky Sneakers. Mcdonald, Megan. 2010. (Stink Ser.: No. 3). (ENG.). 144p. (J). (gr. 1-5). 27.07 *(978-1-59961-685-8(8)*, 13832, Chapter Bks.) Spotlight.
—Stink & the World's Worst Super-Stinky Sneakers, Bk. 3. McDonald, Megan. 2013. (Stink Ser.: 3). (ENG.). 144p. (J). (gr. 1-4). pap. 4.99 *(978-0-7636-6424-4(3))* Candlewick Pr.
—Stink & the World's Worst Super-Stinky Sneakers, Bk. 3. Mcdonald, Megan. 2013. (Stink Ser.: 3). (ENG.). 144p. (J). (gr. 1-4). 14.99 *(978-0-7636-6390-2(5))* Candlewick Pr.
—Stink: Hamlet & Cheese. Mcdonald, Megan. (Stink Ser.). 144p. (J). (gr. 1-4). 2019. (ENG.). pap. 4.99 *(978-1-5362-0634-0(2))*; 2018. 14.99 *(978-0-7636-9163-9(1))* Candlewick Pr.
—Stink: Hamlet & Cheese. Mcdonald, Megan. 2019. (Stink Ser.). (ENG.). 136p. (J). (gr. 1-5). lib. bdg. 27.07 *(978-1-5321-4334-2(6)*, 31864, Chapter Bks.) Spotlight.
—Stink It Up! A Guide to the Gross, the Bad, & the Smelly. Mcdonald, Megan. 2013. (Stink Ser.). 128p. (J). (gr. 1-4). pap. 5.99 *(978-0-7636-5942-4(8))* Candlewick Pr.
—Stink-O-Pedia: Volume 1 Super Stink-Y Stuff from A to Zzzz. Mcdonald, Megan. 2012. (Stink Ser.: No. 2). (ENG.). 144p. (J). (gr. 1-5). 27.07 *(978-1-59961-195-2(3)*, 13836, Chapter Bks.) Spotlight.
—Stink Set 3 (Set), 5 vols. Mcdonald, Megan. 2019. (Stink Ser.). (ENG.). 136p. (J). (gr. 1-5). lib. bdg. 135.35 *(978-1-5321-4329-8(X)*, 31859, Chapter Bks.) Spotlight.
—Stink: Solar System Superhero. McDonald, Megan. 2013. (Stink Ser.: 5). (ENG.). 144p. (J). (gr. 1-4). pap. 4.99 *(978-0-7636-6425-1(1))* Candlewick Pr.
—Stink: the Absolutely Astronomical Collection: Books 4-6. McDonald, Megan. 2013. (Stink Ser.). (ENG.). 256p. (J). (gr. k-3). pap. 14.97 *(978-0-7636-6830-3(3))* Candlewick Pr.
—Stink: the Fabulously Freaky Collection. McDonald, Megan. 2016. (Stink Ser.). (J). (gr. 1-4). 14.97 *(978-0-7636-9076-2(7))* Candlewick Pr.
—Stink: the Super-Incredible Collection: Books 1-3, Bks. 1-3. McDonald, Megan. 2013. (Stink Ser.). 352p. (J). (gr. k-3). 14.97 *(978-0-7636-6831-0(1))* Candlewick Pr.
—Sydney & Simon: to the Moon! Reynolds, Paul. 2017. (Sydney & Simon Ser.: 3). 48p. (J). (gr. 1-4). pap. 4.99 *(978-1-58089-680-1(4))* Charlesbridge Publishing, Inc.
—Sydney & Simon: to the Moon! Reynolds, Paul. 2017. (Sydney & Simon Ser.: 3). 48p. (J). (gr. 1-4). lib. bdg. 12.99 *(978-1-58089-679-5(0))* Charlesbridge Publishing, Inc.
—Tess's Tree. Brallier, Jess M. 2010. (JPN.). 28p. (J). *(978-4-07-269392-6(8))* Shufunotomo Company, Limited.
—Twice as Moody. Mcdonald, Megan. 2011. (Judy Moody Ser.). (ENG.). 304p. (J). (gr. 1-4). pap. 8.99 *(978-0-7636-5740-6(9))* Candlewick Pr.
—Was in a Mood. Mcdonald, Megan. 2010. (Judy Moody Ser.: 1). (ENG.). 176p. (J). (gr. 1-4). pap. 5.99 *(978-0-7636-4849-7(3))* Candlewick Pr.
—Was in a Mood. Mcdonald, Megan. 2010. (Judy Moody Ser.: 1). (ENG.). 160p. (J). (gr. 1-4). 16.99 *(978-0-7636-4850-3(7))* Candlewick Pr.
—The Water Princess. Verde, Susan & Badiel, Georgie. 2016. (ENG.). 40p. (J). (gr. k-3). 17.99 *(978-0-399-17258-8(0)*, G.P. Putnam's Sons Books for Young Readers) Penguin Young Readers Group.
—What to Do If an Elephant Stands on Your Foot. Robinson, Michelle. 2012. 32p. (J). (gr. -1-k). 16.99 *(978-0-8037-3398-5(4)*, Dial Bks) Penguin Young Readers Group.
—The Wishbone Wish. Mcdonald, Megan. ed. 2016. (Judy Moody & Stink Ser.: 4). (ENG.). 116p. (J). (gr. 1-4). lib. bdg. 18.40 *(978-0-606-39093-4(6))* Turtleback.
—You & Me. Verde, Susan. 2015. (ENG.). 32p. (J). (gr. k-17). 14.95 *(978-1-4197-1197-8(0)*, Abrams Bks. for Young Readers) Abrams, Inc.
—Zebrafish. FableVision. 2012. (Zebrafish Ser.). (ENG.). 128p. (J). (gr. 5-9). pap. 11.99 *(978-1-4169-9707-8(5)*, Atheneum Bks. for Young Readers) Simon & Schuster Children's Publishing.
Reynolds, Peter H. Be You! Reynolds, Peter H. 2020. (ENG.). 32p. (J). (gr. -1-3). 17.99 *(978-1-338-57231-5(8)*, Orchard Bks.) Scholastic, Inc.
—The Best Kid in the World: A SugarLoaf Book. Reynolds, Peter H. 2012. (ENG.). 48p. (J). (gr. -1-2). pap. 22.99 *(978-1-4424-7178-8(6)*, Atheneum Bks. for Young Readers) Simon & Schuster Children's Publishing.
—¡Di algo! (Say Something!) Reynolds, Peter H. 2019.Tr. of Say Something!. (SPA.). 40p. (J). (gr. -1-k). pap. 7.99 *(978-1-338-56596-6(6)*, Scholastic en Espanol) Scholastic, Inc.
—The Dot. Reynolds, Peter H. 2005. 34p. (J). bds. 19.95 *(978-0-9769313-0-0(3))* BrailleInk.
—The Dot. Reynolds, Peter H. 2003. (Creatrilogy Ser.). (ENG.). 32p. (J). (gr. k-12). 15.00 *(978-0-7636-1961-9(2)*, 53509533) Candlewick Pr.
—The Dot: Make Your Mark Kit. Reynolds, Peter H. 2013. (Creatrilogy Ser.). (ENG.). (J). (gr. k-4). 24.99 *(978-0-7636-6978-2(4))* Candlewick Pr.
—Going Places. Reynolds, Peter H. Reynolds, Paul A. 2014. (ENG.). 40p. (J). (gr. -1-3). 17.99 *(978-1-4424-6608-1(1)*, Atheneum Bks. for Young Readers) Simon & Schuster Children's Publishing.
—Guyku: A Year of Haiku for Boys. Reynolds, Peter H. Raczka, Bob. 2010. (ENG.). 48p. (J). (gr. -1-3). 16.99 *(978-0-547-24003-9(1)*, 1098616) Houghton Mifflin Harcourt Publishing Co.
—I'm Here. Reynolds, Peter H. 2011. (ENG.). 32p. (J). (gr. -1-3). 17.99 *(978-1-4169-9649-1(4)*, Atheneum Bks. for Young Readers) Simon & Schuster Children's Publishing.
—Ish. Reynolds, Peter H. 2004. (Creatrilogy Ser.). (ENG.). 32p. (J). (gr. k-12). 15.00 *(978-0-7636-2344-9(X))* Candlewick Pr.
—Ish. Reynolds, Peter H. unabr. ed. 2005. (J). (gr. -1-4). 24.95 incl. audio *(978-0-439-80428-8(0)*, WHRA676) Scholastic, Inc.
—Ish. Reynolds, Peter H. 2005. (J). (gr. -1-4). 29.95 *(978-0-439-80429-5(9)*, WHCD676) Weston Woods Studios, Inc.
Reynolds, Peter H. Make Your Mark Gallery: a Coloring Book-Ish. Reynolds, Peter H. 2020. (ENG.). 96p. (J). (gr. -1-3). 9.99 ***(978-1-5362-0931-0(7))*** Candlewick Pr.
Reynolds, Peter H. My Very Big Little World. Reynolds, Peter H. 2006. (ENG.). 40p. (J). (gr. -1-3). 17.99 *(978-0-689-87621-9(1)*, Atheneum Bks. for Young Readers) Simon & Schuster Children's Publishing.
—The North Star. Reynolds, Peter H. 2009. (ENG.). 64p. (J). (gr. -1-2). 16.99 *(978-0-7636-3677-7(0))* Candlewick Pr.
—Playing from the Heart. Reynolds, Peter H. 2016. (ENG.). 32p. (J). (gr. k-12). 15.00 *(978-0-7636-7892-0(9))* Candlewick Pr.
—Rose's Garden. Reynolds, Peter H. 2009. (ENG.). 40p. (J). (gr. k-12). 15.99 *(978-0-7636-4641-7(5))* Candlewick Pr.
—Say Something! Reynolds, Peter H. 2019. (ENG.). 40p. (J). (gr. -1-3). 17.99 *(978-0-545-86503-6(4)*, Orchard Bks.) Scholastic, Inc.
—Sky Color. Reynolds, Peter H. 2012. (Creatrilogy Ser.). 32p. (J). (gr. k-12). 15.00 *(978-0-7636-2345-6(8))* Candlewick Pr.
—The Smallest Gift of Christmas. Reynolds, Peter H. 40p. (J). (gr. -1-2). 2015. 10.00 *(978-0-7636-7981-1(X))*; 2013. (ENG.). 14.00 *(978-0-7636-6103-8(1))* Candlewick Pr.
—So Few of Me. Reynolds, Peter H. 2006. (ENG.). 32p. (J). (gr. k-12). 15.00 *(978-0-7636-2623-5(6))* Candlewick Pr.
Reynolds, Peter H. & Candlewick Press Staff. Judy Moody Goes to Hollywood: Behind the Scenes with Judy Moody & Friends. Mcdonald, Megan. ed. 2011. (Judy Moody Ser.). (ENG.). 160p. (J). (gr. 1-4). 14.99 *(978-0-7636-5551-8(1))* Candlewick Pr.
—The Poop Picnic. Mcdonald, Megan & Michalak, Jamie. ed. 2011. (Judy Moody Ser.). 48p. (J). (gr. k-3). pap. 3.99 *(978-0-7636-5553-2(8))* Candlewick Pr.
Reynolds, Peter H. & FableVision. Charlie & Kiwi: An Evolutionary Adventure. New York Hall of Science, The. 2011. (ENG.). 48p. (J). (gr. -1-3). 16.99 *(978-1-4424-2112-7(6)*, Atheneum Bks. for Young Readers) Simon & Schuster Children's Publishing.
Reynolds, Peter H., jt. illus. see Reynolds, Paul A.
Reynolds, Rhonda. What Kind of War Was It, Anyhow? Reynolds, Rhonda, tr. Ekberg, Nancy. 2003. 45p. (J). pap. 8.95 *(978-1-58838-085-2(8)*, Junebug Bks.) NewSouth, Inc.
Reynolds, Sarah. Aunt Debra & My Favorite Things Poster. Pedrow, Debra A. Karper, Deborah, ed. 2003. 40p. (J). 15.95 *(978-1-928681-09-0(3))* Gladstone Publishing.
Rezaei, Heidi, jt. illus. see Ghaderi, Simin.
Rezai, Ehsan H. a. How Your Shoes Feel: A Story about Diversity. Hirsche, David. 2019. (ENG.). 32p. (J). pap. 9.99 ***(978-1-7204-0132-2(2))*** CreateSpace Independent Publishing Platform.
Reznicek, Curtis. Harold Discovers Santa's Secret: A Very Long Dog with a Very Big Heart. Witt, Janice. 2013. 40p. pap. 11.99 *(978-1-63022-442-4(1))* Speedy Publishing LLC.
RH Disney. Across the Sea (Disney Frozen) Homberg, Ruth. 2016. (Step into Reading Ser.). (ENG.). 24p. (J). (gr. -1-1). 4.99 *(978-0-7364-3398-3(8)*, RH/Disney) Random Hse. Children's Bks.
RH Disney, et al. The Adventures of Violet & Dash: Friend or Foe? (Disney/Pixar the Incredibles 2) RH Disney & Higginson, Sheila Sweeny. 2018. (Stepping Stone Book(TM) Ser.). (ENG.). 128p. (J). (gr. 1-4). 6.99 *(978-0-7364-3861-2(0))*; lib. bdg. 12.99 *(978-0-7364-8263-9(6))* Random Hse. Children's Bks. (RH/Disney).
RH Disney. The Best Birthday Ever (Disney Frozen) Green, Rico. 2016. (Little Golden Book Ser.). (ENG.). 24p. (J). (-k). 4.99 *(978-0-7364-3619-9(7)*, Golden/Disney) Random Hse. Children's Bks.
—Big Snowman, Little Snowman (Disney Frozen) Rabe, Tish. 2013. (Step into Reading Ser.). (ENG.). 32p. (J). (gr. -1-1). 4.99 *(978-0-7364-3119-4(5)*, RH/Disney) Random Hse. Children's Bks.
—Deputy Mater Saves the Day! (Disney/Pixar Cars) Berrios, Frank. 2013. (Little Golden Book Ser.). (ENG.). 24p. (J). (-k). 4.99 *(978-0-7364-2979-5(4)*, Golden/Disney) Random Hse. Children's Bks.
—Disney: Nine Classic Tales (Disney Mixed Property) 2014. (ENG.). 224p. (J). (-k). 12.99 *(978-0-7364-3260-3(4)*, Golden/Disney) Random Hse. Children's Bks.
—Disney Princess Beginnings: Moana's Big Leap (Disney Princess) Francis, Suzanne. 2019. (Stepping Stone Book(TM) Ser.). (ENG.). 128p. (J). (gr. 1-4). 6.99 *(978-0-7364-3794-3(0))*; 12.99 *(978-0-7364-8259-2(8))* Random Hse. Children's Bks. (RH/Disney).
—Disney Zombies Junior Novelization (Disney Zombies) Katschke, Judy. 2018. (ENG.). 144p. (J). (gr. 2-5). 6.99 *(978-0-7364-3963-3(3)*, RH/Disney) Random Hse. Children's Bks.
—Doc Mcstuffins Little Golden Book Library (Disney Junior: Doc Mcstuffins) As Big As a Whale; Snowman Surprise; Bubble-Rific!; Boomer Gets His Bounce Back; a Knight in Sticky Armor, 5 vols. 2015. (Little Golden Book Ser.). (ENG.). 120p. (J). (-k). 24.95 *(978-0-7364-3407-2(0)*, Golden/Disney) Random Hse. Children's Bks.
—Five Classic Tales (Disney Classics) 2014. (Step into Reading Ser.). (ENG.). 160p. (J). (gr. -1-1). 8.99 *(978-0-7364-3180-4(2)*, RH/Disney) Random Hse. Children's Bks.
—Five Enchanting Tales (Disney Princess) 2016. (Step into Reading Ser.). (ENG.). 160p. (J). (gr. -1-2). pap. 7.99 *(978-0-7364-3518-5(2)*, Random Hse. Bks. for Young Readers) Random Hse. Children's Bks.
—Ghost Hunt! (Disney Frozen) Lagonegro, Melissa. 2018. (Step into Reading Ser.). (ENG.). 24p. (J). (gr. -1-1). pap. 4.99 *(978-0-7364-3920-6(X)*, RH/Disney) Random Hse. Children's Bks.
—I Am Buzz Lightyear (Disney/Pixar Toy Story) Tillworth, Mary. 2011. (ENG.). 12p. (J). (— 1). bds. 4.99 *(978-0-7364-2821-7(6)*, Golden/Disney) Random Hse. Children's Bks.
—Lady & the Tramp (Disney Lady & the Tramp) Finnegan, Delphine. 2012. (Step into Reading Ser.). (ENG.). 32p. (J). (gr. -1-1). pap. 4.99 *(978-0-7364-3026-5(1)*, RH/Disney) Random Hse. Children's Bks.
—The Little Mermaid Step into Reading (Disney Princess) Homberg, Ruth. 2013. (Step into Reading Ser.). (ENG.). 32p. (J). (gr. -1-1). 4.99 *(978-0-7364-8128-1(1)*, RH/Disney) Random Hse. Children's Bks.
—Mickey Mouse & His Spaceship (Disney: Mickey Mouse) Werner, Jane. 2016. (Little Golden Book Ser.). (ENG.). 24p. (J). (-k). 4.99 *(978-0-7364-3633-5(2)*, Golden/Disney) Random Hse. Children's Bks.
—Mulan Deluxe Step into Reading (Disney Princess) Tillworth, Mary. 2020. (Step into Reading Ser.). (ENG.). 24p. (J). (gr. -1-1). 5.99 *(978-0-7364-4053-0(4))*; 12.99 *(978-0-7364-8290-5(3))* Random Hse. Children's Bks. (RH/Disney).
—The Never Girls Collection #1 (Disney: the Never Girls) Books 1-4, 4 vols. Thorpe, Kiki. 2013. (Never Girls Ser.). (ENG.). 128p. (J). (gr. 1-4). 23.96 *(978-0-7364-3141-5(1)*, RH/Disney) Random Hse. Children's Bks.
—Olaf Waits for Spring (Disney Frozen) Saxon, Victoria. 2018. (Little Golden Book Ser.). (ENG.). 24p. (J). (-k). 4.99 *(978-0-7364-3765-3(7)*, Golden/Disney) Random Hse. Children's Bks.
—Old Racers, New Racers (Disney/Pixar Cars 3) Tillworth, Mary. 2017. (Step into Reading Ser.). (ENG.). 24p. (J). (gr. -1-1). pap. 4.99 *(978-0-7364-3804-9(1)*, RH/Disney) Random Hse. Children's Bks.
—Onward: the Junior Novelization (Disney/Pixar Onward) Francis, Suzanne. 2020. (ENG.). 144p. (J). (gr. 2-5). 6.99 *(978-0-7364-3965-7(X)*, RH/Disney) Random Hse. Children's Bks.
—The Right Track (Disney Frozen: Northern Lights) Jordan, Apple. 2017. (Step into Reading Ser.). (ENG.). 24p. (J). (gr. -1-1). pap. 4.99 *(978-0-7364-3588-8(3)*, RH/Disney) Random Hse. Children's Bks.
—Shop with Minnie (Disney Junior: Mickey Mouse Clubhouse) Posner-Sanchez, Andrea. 2012. (Little Golden Book Ser.). (ENG.). 24p. (J). (gr. k-k). 4.99 *(978-0-7364-3031-9(8)*, Golden/Disney) Random Hse. Children's Bks.

R

—Sleeping Beauty Step into Reading (Disney Princess) Man-Kong, Mary. 2014. (Step into Reading Ser.). (ENG.). 32p. (J). (gr. -1-1). 5.99 *(978-0-7364-3226-9(4),* RH/Disney) Random Hse. Children's Bks.

—The Sword in the Stone (Disney) Memling, Carl. 2015. (Little Golden Book Ser.). (ENG.). 24p. (J). (-k). 4.99 *(978-0-7364-3374-7(0),* Golden/Disney) Random Hse. Children's Bks.

—Tales of Rapunzel #3: Friends & Enemies (Disney Tangled the Series) McCullough, Kathy. 2017. (Stepping Stone Book(TM) Ser.: 3). (ENG.). 128p. (J). (gr. 1-4). lib. bdg. 12.99 *(978-0-7364-3831-5(9),* RH/Disney) Random Hse. Children's Bks.

—This Little Piggy (Disney Junior: Minnie's Bow-Toons) Weinberg, Jennifer Liberts. 2014. (Little Golden Book Ser.). (ENG.). 24p. (J). (-k). 4.99 *(978-0-7364-3234-4(5),* Golden/Disney) Random Hse. Children's Bks.

—Tractor Trouble (Disney/Pixar Cars) Berrios, Frank. 2011. (Little Golden Book Ser.). (ENG.). 24p. (J). (gr. -1-2). 4.99 *(978-0-7364-2831-6(3),* Golden/Disney) Random Hse. Children's Bks.

—Where's Woody? (Disney/Pixar Toy Story) Depken, Kristen L. 2012. (Pictureback(R) Ser.). (ENG.). 16p. (J). (gr. -1-2). pap. 4.99 *(978-0-7364-2850-7(X),* RH/Disney) Random Hse. Children's Bks.

RH Disney. Aladdin Deluxe Step into Reading (Disney Aladdin) RH Disney. 2019. (Step into Reading Ser.). (ENG.). 24p. (J). (gr. -1-1). 5.99 *(978-0-7364-3947-3(1));* 12.99 *(978-0-7364-8266-0(0))* Random Hse. Children's Bks. (RH/Disney).

—Baby, You're Super! (Disney/Pixar the Incredibles 2) RH Disney. 2018. (ENG.). 22p. (J). (— 1). bds. 6.99 *(978-0-7364-3941-1(2),* RH/Disney) Random Hse. Children's Bks.

—Back on Track (Disney/Pixar Cars 3) RH Disney. 2017. (Step into Reading Ser.). (ENG.). 24p. (J). (gr. -1-1). pap. 4.99 *(978-0-7364-3680-9(4),* RH/Disney) Random Hse. Children's Bks.

—Belle's Story Collection (Disney Beauty & the Beast) RH Disney. 2017. (Step into Reading Ser.). (ENG.). 160p. (J). (gr. -1-1). pap. 7.99 *(978-0-7364-3916-9(1),* RH/Disney) Random Hse. Children's Bks.

—Beware the Kakamora! (Disney Moana) RH Disney. 2016. (Pictureback(R) Ser.). (ENG.). 24p. (J). (gr. -1-2). 4.99 *(978-0-7364-3601-4(4),* RH/Disney) Random Hse. Children's Bks.

—Big Hero 6 (Disney Big Hero 6) RH Disney. 2014. (Little Golden Book Ser.). (ENG.). 24p. (J). (-k). 4.99 *(978-0-7364-3168-2(3),* Golden Bks.) Random Hse. Children's Bks.

—Disney/Pixar Story Collection. RH Disney. 2008. (Step into Reading Ser.). (ENG.). 160p. (J). (gr. k-3). pap. 7.99 *(978-0-7364-2554-4(3),* RH/Disney) Random Hse. Children's Bks.

—Finding Nemo (Disney/Pixar Finding Nemo) RH Disney. 2003. (Little Golden Book Ser.). (ENG.). 24p. (J). (gr. -1-2). lib. bdg. 4.99 *(978-0-7364-2139-3(4),* Golden/Disney) Random Hse. Children's Bks.

—Frozen Big Golden Book (Disney Frozen) RH Disney. 2013. (Big Golden Book Ser.). (ENG.). 64p. (J). (gr. -1-2). 9.99 *(978-0-7364-3065-4(2),* Golden/Disney) Random Hse. Children's Bks.

—Frozen Story Collection (Disney Frozen) RH Disney. 2015. (Step into Reading Ser.). (ENG.). 160p. (J). (gr. -1-2). pap. 8.99 *(978-0-7364-3435-5(6),* RH/Disney) Random Hse. Children's Bks.

—Game Time! RH Disney. 2018. (Step into Reading Ser.). (ENG.). 32p. (J). (gr. -1-1). pap. 5.99 *(978-0-7364-3757-8(6));* lib. bdg. 12.99 *(978-0-7364-8258-5(X))* Random Hse. Children's Bks. (RH/Disney).

—A Home for a Princess: a Peek Inside 9 Disney Princess Castles (Disney Princess) RH Disney. 2019. (ENG.). 64p. (J). (gr. -1-3). 15.99 *(978-0-7364-4024-0(0),* RH/Disney) Random Hse. Children's Bks.

—Inside Out Big Golden Book (Disney/Pixar Inside Out) RH Disney. 2015. (Big Golden Book Ser.). (ENG.). 64p. (J). (gr. -1-2). 9.99 *(978-0-7364-3313-6(9),* RH/Disney) Random Hse. Children's Bks.

—The Jungle Book (Disney the Jungle Book) RH Disney. 2003. (Little Golden Book Ser.). (ENG.). 24p. (J). (gr. -1-k). 4.99 *(978-0-7364-2096-9(7),* Golden/Disney) Random Hse. Children's Bks.

—Moana Big Golden Book (Disney Moana) RH Disney. 2016. (Big Golden Book Ser.). (ENG.). 48p. (J). (gr. -1-2). 9.99 *(978-0-7364-3602-1(2),* Golden/Disney) Random Hse. Children's Bks.

—Monsters, Inc. Little Golden Book (Disney/Pixar Monsters, Inc.) RH Disney. 2012. (Little Golden Book Ser.). (ENG.). 24p. (J). (-k). 4.99 *(978-0-7364-2799-9(6),* Golden/Disney) Random Hse. Children's Bks.

RH Disney. Mulan's Happy Panda (Disney Princess: Palace Pets) RH Disney. 2020. (Step into Reading Ser.). (ENG.). 24p. (J). (gr. -1-1). 14.99 ***(978-0-7364-8299-8(7));*** 5.99 ***(978-0-7364-4112-4(3))*** Random Hse. Children's Bks. (RH/Disney).

RH Disney. Mulan's Perfect Present/Jasmine's New Friends (Disney Princess) RH Disney. 2019. (Pictureback(R) Ser.). (ENG.). 48p. (gr. -1-2). 5.99 *(978-0-7364-3753-0(3))* Perfection Learning Corp.

—Nine Disney Princess Tales (Disney Princess) RH Disney. 2016. (ENG.). 224p. (J). (-k). 12.99 *(978-0-7364-3617-5(0),* Golden/Disney) Random Hse. Children's Bks.

—Oh, Brother! (Disney/Pixar Onward) RH Disney. 2020. (Step into Reading Ser.). (ENG.). 24p. (J). (gr. -1-1). 5.99 *(978-0-7364-3949-7(8));* 12.99 *(978-0-7364-8267-7(9))* Random Hse. Children's Bks. (RH/Disney).

RH Disney. Olaf Loves to Read! (Disney Frozen 2) RH Disney. 2020. (Step into Reading Ser.). (ENG.). 24p. (J). (gr. -1-1). 5.99 ***(978-0-7364-4082-0(8));*** 14.99 ***(978-0-7364-8293-6(8))*** Random Hse. Children's Bks. (RH/Disney).

RH Disney. The Princess & the Frog Little Golden Book (Disney Princess & the Frog) RH Disney. 2009. (Little Golden Book Ser.). (ENG.). 24p. (J). (gr. -1-2). 4.99 *(978-0-7364-2628-2(0),* Golden/Disney) Random Hse. Children's Bks.

—Pua & Heihei (Disney Moana) RH Disney. 2017. (Step into Reading Ser.). (ENG.). 24p. (J). (gr. -1-1). pap. 4.99 *(978-0-7364-3684-7(7),* RH/Disney) Random Hse. Children's Bks.

—Quest for the Heart (Disney Moana) RH Disney. 2016. (Step into Reading Ser.). (ENG.). 32p. (J). (gr. -1-1). pap. 4.99 *(978-0-7364-3646-5(4),* RH/Disney) Random Hse. Children's Bks.

—Ralph Breaks the Internet. RH Disney. 2018. (ENG.). 144p. (J). (gr. 2-5). 6.99 *(978-0-7364-3763-9(0),* RH/Disney) Random Hse. Children's Bks.

RH Disney. Rapunzel's Perfect Pony (Disney Princess: Palace Pets) RH Disney. 2020. (Step into Reading Ser.). (ENG.). 24p. (J). (-k). 5.99 ***(978-0-7364-4113-1(1));*** 14.99 ***(978-0-7364-8297-4(0))*** Random Hse. Children's Bks. (RH/Disney).

RH Disney. Shapes, Colors, Counting & More! (Disney/Pixar Cars) RH Disney. 2013. (ENG.). 48p. (J). (gr. -1-2). bds. 10.99 *(978-0-7364-3105-7(5),* RH/Disney) Random Hse. Children's Bks.

—Snow White & the Seven Dwarfs (Disney Classic) RH Disney. 2003. (Little Golden Book Ser.). (ENG.). 24p. (J). (gr. -1-2). 4.99 *(978-0-7364-2186-7(6),* Golden/Disney) Random Hse. Children's Bks.

—Toy Story 4 Movie Storybook (Disney/Pixar Toy Story 4) RH Disney. 2019. (ENG.). 96p. (J). (gr. -1-2). 9.99 *(978-0-7364-4001-1(1),* RH/Disney) Random Hse. Children's Bks.

—WALL-E (Disney/Pixar WALL-e) RH Disney. 2008. (Little Golden Book Ser.). (ENG.). 24p. (J). (gr. -1-2). 4.99 *(978-0-7364-2422-6(9),* RH/Disney) Random Hse. Children's Bks.

—Wreck-It Ralph 2 Deluxe Hardcover Junior Novelization (Disney Wreck-It Ralph 2) RH Disney. 2018. (ENG.). 144p. (J). (gr. 2-5). 9.99 *(978-0-7364-3762-2(2),* RH/Disney) Random Hse. Children's Bks.

—Wreck-It Ralph Little Golden Book (Disney Wreck-It Ralph) RH Disney. 2012. (Little Golden Book Ser.). (ENG.). 24p. (J). (gr. k-k). 4.99 *(978-0-7364-2972-6(7),* Golden/Disney) Random Hse. Children's Bks.

—Zom-Azing Posters, Facts, & More! (Disney Zombies) RH Disney. 2018. (ENG.). 48p. (J). (gr. 1-4). pap. 7.99 *(978-0-7364-3964-0(1),* RH/Disney) Random Hse. Children's Bks.

RH Disney & Dale-Scott, Lindsay. Jasmine's Quest for the Stardust Sapphire (Disney Aladdin) RH Disney & McCullough, Kathy. 2019. (ENG.). 224p. (J). (gr. 3-7). 13.99 *(978-0-7364-3962-6(5),* RH/Disney) Random Hse. Children's Bks.

RH Disney & Syed, Anoosha. Daring Dreamers Club #1: Milla Takes Charge (Disney: Daring Dreamers Club) Soderberg, Erin. 2018. (Disney: Daring Dreamers Club Ser.: 1). (ENG.). 224p. (J). (gr. 3-7). 13.99 *(978-0-7364-3924-4(2));* lib. bdg. 16.99 *(978-0-7364-3881-0(5))* Random Hse. Children's Bks. (RH/Disney).

RH Disney Staff, et al. Anna & Elsa: A Warm Welcome (Disney Frozen), No. 3. David, Erica. 2015. (Stepping Stone Book(TM) Ser.: 3). (ENG.). 128p. (J). (gr. 1-4). 9.99 *(978-0-7364-3289-4(2));* lib. bdg. 12.99 *(978-0-7364-8247-9(4))* Random Hse. Children's Bks. (RH/Disney).

—Anna & Elsa: Anna Takes Charge (Disney Frozen), No. 9. David, Erica. 2017. (Stepping Stone Book(TM) Ser.: 9). (ENG.). 128p. (J). (gr. 1-4). 9.99 *(978-0-7364-3480-5(1),* RH/Disney) Random Hse. Children's Bks.

—Anna & Elsa: Princess in Charge. David, Erica. 2017. (Stepping Stone Book(TM) Ser.: 9). (ENG.). 128p. (J). (gr. 1-4). lib. bdg. 12.99 *(978-0-7364-8236-3(9),* RH/Disney) Random Hse. Children's Bks.

—Anna & Elsa: The Great Ice Engine (Disney Frozen), No. 4. David, Erica. 2015. (Stepping Stone Book(TM) Ser.: 4). (ENG.). 128p. (J). (gr. 1-4). 9.99 *(978-0-7364-3431-7(3),* RH/Disney) Random Hse. Children's Bks.

—Anna & Elsa #6: the Arendelle Cup (Disney Frozen) David, Erica. 2015. (Stepping Stone Book(TM) Ser.: 6). (ENG.). 128p. (J). (gr. 1-4). 9.99 *(978-0-7364-3437-9(2),* RH/Disney) Random Hse. Children's Bks.

RH Disney Staff. Anna & Elsa: Books 5-8 (Disney Frozen), 4 vols. David, Erica. 2016. (Stepping Stone Book(TM) Ser.). (ENG.). 512p. (J). (gr. 1-4). 39.96 *(978-0-7364-3631-1(6),* RH/Disney) Random Hse. Children's Bks.

—Anna & Elsa's Secret Playtime (Disney Frozen) Saxon, Victoria. 2016. (Big Golden Book Ser.). (ENG.). 32p. (J). (-k). 9.99 *(978-0-7364-3493-5(3),* Golden/Disney) Random Hse. Children's Bks.

—As Big As a Whale (Disney Junior: Doc Mcstuffins) Posner-Sanchez, Andrea. 2014. (Little Golden Book Ser.). (ENG.). 24p. (J). (-k). 4.99 *(978-0-7364-3087-6(3),* Golden/Disney) Random Hse. Children's Bks.

—Beauty & the Beast Big Golden Book (Disney Beauty & the Beast) Arps, Melissa & Lagonegro, Melissa. 2017. (Big Golden Book Ser.). (ENG.). 48p. (J). (gr. -1-2). 9.99 *(978-0-7364-3575-8(1),* Golden/Disney) Random Hse. Children's Bks.

—Beauty & the Beast Deluxe Step into Reading (Disney Beauty & the Beast) Lagonegro, Melissa. 2017. (Step into Reading Ser.). (ENG.). 24p. (J). (gr. -1-1). pap. 4.99 *(978-0-7364-3594-9(8),* RH/Disney) Random Hse. Children's Bks.

—Before Ever after (Disney Tangled: the Series) Deutsch, Stacia. 2017. (ENG.). 144p. (J). (gr. 3-7). 9.99 *(978-0-7364-3824-7(6),* RH/Disney) Random Hse. Children's Bks.

—Belle to the Rescue (Disney Beauty & the Beast) Richards, Kitty. 2017. (Big Golden Book Ser.). (ENG.). 32p. (J). (gr. -1-2). 10.99 *(978-0-7364-3915-2(3),* Golden/Disney) Random Hse. Children's Bks.

—Belle's Story. Arps, Melissa & Lagonegro, Melissa. 2017. (Pictureback(R) Ser.). (ENG.). 24p. (J). (gr. -1-1). pap. 4.99 *(978-0-7364-3592-5(1),* RH/Disney) Random Hse. Children's Bks.

—The Best Ball (Disney Palace Pets: Whisker Haven Tales) Homberg, Ruth. 2017. (Step into Reading Ser.). (ENG.). 24p. (J). (gr. -1-1). pap. 4.99 *(978-0-7364-3596-3(4),* RH/Disney) Random Hse. Children's Bks.

—Boomer Gets His Bounce Back (Disney Junior: Doc Mcstuffins) Posner-Sanchez, Andrea. 2013. (Little Golden Book Ser.). (ENG.). 24p. (J). (-k). 4.99 *(978-0-7364-3143-9(8),* Golden/Disney) Random Hse. Children's Bks.

—Bow-Bot Robot (Disney Junior: Minnie's Bow Toons) Posner-Sanchez, Andrea & Weinberg, Jennifer Liberts. 2014. (Little Golden Book Ser.). (ENG.). 24p. (J). (-k). 4.99 *(978-0-7364-3078-4(4),* Golden/Disney) Random Hse. Children's Bks.

—Bubble-Rific! Posner-Sanchez, Andrea. 2014. (Little Golden Book Ser.). (ENG.). 24p. (J). (-k). 4.99 *(978-0-7364-3236-8(1),* Golden/Disney) Random Hse. Children's Bks.

—Bunny Magic! (Disney Junior: Sofia the First) Posner-Sanchez, Andrea. 2015. (Little Golden Book Ser.). (ENG.). 24p. (J). (-k). 4.99 *(978-0-7364-3085-2(7),* Golden/Disney) Random Hse. Children's Bks.

—Cars 3 Tabbed Board Book (Disney/Pixar Cars 3) Manley, Victoria. 2017. (ENG.). 16p. (J). (— 1). bds. 7.99 *(978-0-7364-3748-6(7),* RH/Disney) Random Hse. Children's Bks.

RH Disney Staff, et al. Cinderella Is My Babysitter (Disney Princess) RH Disney Staff & Posner-Sanchez, Andrea. 2015. (Little Golden Book Ser.). (ENG.). 24p. (J). (-k). 3.99 *(978-0-7364-3324-2(4),* Golden/Disney) Random Hse. Children's Bks.

RH Disney Staff. The Cookie Boogie (Disney Palace Pets: Whisker Haven Tales) Lagonegro, Melissa. 2016. (Step into Reading Ser.). (ENG.). 24p. (J). (gr. -1-1). 4.99 *(978-0-7364-3623-6(5),* RH/Disney) Random Hse. Children's Bks.

—Disney Princess Beginnings: Tiana's Best Surprise (Disney Princess) Roehl, Tessa. 2018. (Stepping Stone Book(TM) Ser.). (ENG.). 128p. (J). (gr. 1-4). 6.99 *(978-0-7364-3759-2(2),* RH/Disney) Random Hse. Children's Bks.

—Driving School (Disney/Pixar Cars) Depken, Kristen L. 2013. (Step into Reading Ser.). (ENG.). 24p. (J). (gr. -1-1). 3.99 *(978-0-7364-2982-5(4),* RH/Disney) Random Hse. Children's Bks.

—A Fairy's Gift (Disney: the Never Girls) Thorpe, Kiki. 2015. (Never Girls Ser.). (ENG.). 224p. (J). (gr. 1-4). 14.99 *(978-0-7364-3278-8(7),* RH/Disney) Random Hse. Children's Bks.

—Forget This! West, Tracey. 2015. (Stepping Stone Book(TM) Ser.). (ENG.). 128p. (J). (gr. 1-4). 5.99 *(978-0-7364-3430-0(5),* RH/Disney) Random Hse. Children's Bks.

—The Friendship Code. Gownley, Jimmy. 2018. (ENG.). 96p. (J). (gr. 1-4). pap. 8.99 *(978-0-7364-3848-3(3),* RH/Disney) Random Hse. Children's Bks.

—Frozen Big Golden Book. Jordan, Apple. 2016. (Big Golden Book Ser.). (ENG.). 32p. (J). (gr. -1-2). 9.99 *(978-0-7364-3562-8(X),* Golden Bks.) Random Hse. Children's Bks.

—Ghost Moon (Disney Junior: Miles from Tomorrowland) Forte, Lauren. 2017. (Little Golden Book Ser.). (ENG.). 24p. (J). (-k). 4.99 *(978-0-7364-3717-2(7),* Golden/Disney) Random Hse. Children's Bks.

RH Disney Staff, et al. The Great Mountain Adventure. Redbank, Tennant. 2016. (ENG.). 64p. (J). (gr. 1-4). 5.99 *(978-0-7364-3636-6(7),* RH/Disney) Random Hse. Children's Bks.

RH Disney Staff. Happy Birthday, Mike! (Disney/Pixar Monsters, Inc.) Weinberg, Jennifer Liberts. 2014. (Step into Reading Ser.). (ENG.). 32p. (J). (gr. -1-1). 3.99 *(978-0-7364-3198-9(5),* RH/Disney) Random Hse. Children's Bks.

—How to Be a Princess (Disney Princess) Carbone, Courtney. 2015. (ENG.). 64p. (J). (gr. 1-4). 9.99 *(978-0-7364-3415-7(1),* RH/Disney) Random Hse. Children's Bks.

RH Disney Staff, et al. Jasmine Is My Babysitter (Disney Princess) Jordan, Apple. 2017. (Little Golden Book Ser.). (ENG.). 24p. (J). (-k). 4.99 *(978-0-7364-3715-8(0),* Golden/Disney) Random Hse. Children's Bks.

RH Disney Staff. Lights Out!; Tow Truck Trouble. Berrios, Frank. 2010. (Pictureback(R) Ser.). (ENG.). 32p. (J). (gr. -1-2). pap. 4.99 *(978-0-7364-2713-5(9),* RH/Disney) Random Hse. Children's Bks.

—Mad Hatter's Tea Party (Disney Alice in Wonderland) Werner, Jane. 2016. (Little Golden Book Ser.). (ENG.). 24p. (J). (-k). 4.99 *(978-0-7364-3627-4(8),* Golden/Disney) Random Hse. Children's Bks.

—Merida Is Our Babysitter (Disney Princess) Jordan, Apple. 2016. (Little Golden Book Ser.). (ENG.). 24p. (J). (-k). 4.99 *(978-0-7364-3614-4(6),* Golden/Disney) Random Hse. Children's Bks.

—Merry Christmas, Woody (Disney/Pixar Toy Story) Depken, Kristen L. 2013. (Pictureback(R) Ser.). (ENG.). 16p. (J). (gr. -1-2). 3.99 *(978-0-7364-3070-8(9),* RH/Disney) Random Hse. Children's Bks.

—A Midsummer Night's Dreamy (Disney Palace Pets: Whisker Haven Tales) Redbank, Tennant. 2017. (Stepping Stone Book(TM) Ser.). (ENG.). 64p. (J). (gr. 1-4). 5.99 *(978-0-7364-3598-7(0),* RH/Disney) Random Hse. Children's Bks.

—Miles from Tomorrowland (Disney Junior: Miles from Tomorrowland) Posner-Sanchez, Andrea. 2016. (Big Golden Book Ser.). (ENG.). 32p. (J). (-k). 9.99 *(978-0-7364-3494-2(1),* Golden/Disney) Random Hse. Children's Bks.

—Nemo's Big Adventure (Disney/Pixar Finding Nemo) Wrecks, Billy. 2012. (Pictureback(R) Ser.). (ENG.). 16p. (J). (gr. -1-2). pap. 4.99 *(978-0-7364-2968-9(9),* RH/Disney) Random Hse. Children's Bks.

—A New Reindeer Friend (Disney Frozen) Julius, Jessica. 2015. (Little Golden Book Ser.). (ENG.). 24p. (J). (-k). 4.99 *(978-0-7364-3351-8(1),* Golden/Disney) Random Hse. Children's Bks.

RH Disney Staff, et al. The Pet Pawlympics (Disney Palace Pets: Whisker Haven Tales) Redbank, Tennant. 2016. (ENG.). 64p. (J). (gr. 1-4). 5.99 *(978-0-7364-3513-0(1),* RH/Disney) Random Hse. Children's Bks.

—A Princess Can! (Disney Princess) Jordan, Apple. 2015. (Step into Reading Ser.). (ENG.). 24p. (J). (gr. -1-1). 4.99 *(978-0-7364-3341-9(4),* RH/Disney) Random Hse. Children's Bks.

—Pumpkin: Cinderella's Dancing Pup (Disney Princess: Palace Pets) Redbank, Tennant. 2015. (ENG.). 64p. (J). (gr. 1-4). 5.99 *(978-0-7364-3423-2(2),* RH/Disney) Random Hse. Children's Bks.

RH Disney Staff. Radiator Springs 500. Berrios, Frank. deluxe ed. 2015. (Pictureback(R) Ser.). (ENG.). 24p. (J). (gr. -1-2). 4.99 *(978-0-7364-3281-8(7),* RH/Disney) Random Hse. Children's Bks.

RH Disney Staff, et al. A Royal Easter (Disney Princess) Posner-Sanchez, Andrea. 2014. (Pictureback(R) Ser.). (ENG.). 16p. (J). (gr. -1-2). 4.99 *(978-0-7364-3084-5(9),* RH/Disney) Random Hse. Children's Bks.

RH Disney Staff. A Royal Pet Problem. Posner-Sanchez, Andrea. 2015. (Little Golden Book Ser.). (ENG.). 24p. (J). (-k). 4.99 *(978-0-7364-3308-2(2),* Golden/Disney) Random Hse. Children's Bks.

—A Royal Wedding Album (Disney Princess) Posner-Sanchez, Andrea. 2016. (Picture Book Ser.). (ENG.). 48p. (J). (gr. -1-2). 9.99 *(978-0-7364-3477-5(1),* RH/Disney) Random Hse. Children's Bks.

—Sadness Saves the Day! West, Tracey. 2016. (ENG.). 128p. (J). (gr. 1-4). 5.99 *(978-0-7364-3637-3(5),* RH/Disney) Random Hse. Children's Bks.

—Santa's Toy Shop (Disney) Dempster, Al. 2015. (Little Golden Book Ser.). (ENG.). 24p. (J). (-k). 4.99 *(978-0-7364-3401-0(1),* Golden/Disney) Random Hse. Children's Bks.

—Secret Spell. Bardhan-Quallen, Sudipta. 2017. (Stepping Stone Book(TM) Ser.). (ENG.). 128p. (J). (gr. 1-4). 9.99 *(978-0-7364-3616-8(2),* RH/Disney) Random Hse. Children's Bks.

RH Disney Staff, et al. Sharing & Caring. Lagonegro, Melissa et al. 2014. (Pictureback(R) Ser.). (ENG.). 16p. (J). (gr. -1-2). 4.99 *(978-0-7364-3334-1(1),* RH/Disney) Random Hse. Children's Bks.

RH Disney Staff. Sofia the Second (Disney Junior: Sofia the First) Posner-Sanchez, Andrea. 2014. (Little Golden Book Ser.). (ENG.). 24p. (J). (-k). 4.99 *(978-0-7364-3238-2(8),* Golden/Disney) Random Hse. Children's Bks.

RH Disney Staff, et al. Sweets & Treats (Disney Princess) Depken, Kristen L. 2016. (Pictureback(R) Ser.). (ENG.). 16p. (J). (-k). 4.99 *(978-0-7364-3353-2(8),* RH/Disney) Random Hse. Children's Bks.

RH Disney Staff. Toy Box Heroes! Webster, Christy. 2014. (Step into Reading Ser.). (ENG.). 32p. (J). (gr. -1-1). 4.99 *(978-0-7364-3270-2(1),* RH/Disney) Random Hse. Children's Bks.

RH Disney Staff, et al. Toy to Toy. RH Disney Staff & Redbank, Tennant. 2010. (Step into Reading Ser.). (ENG.). 32p. (J). (gr. k-3). pap. 3.99 *(978-0-7364-2665-7(5),* RH/Disney) Random Hse. Children's Bks.

—Travel Like a Princess (Disney Princess) Lagonegro, Melissa. 2014. (Step into Reading Ser.). (ENG.). 24p. (J). (gr. -1-1). 3.99 *(978-0-7364-3089-0(X),* RH/Disney) Random Hse. Children's Bks.

—Treasure: Ariel's Curious Kitten (Disney Princess: Palace Pets) Redbank, Tennant. 2015. (Stepping Stone Book(TM) Ser.). (ENG.). 64p. (J). (gr. 1-4). 5.99 *(978-0-7364-3346-4(5),* RH/Disney) Random Hse. Children's Bks.

RH Disney Staff. When You Wish upon a Well (Disney Junior: Sofia the First) Forte, Lauren. 2016. (Little Golden Book Ser.). (ENG.). 24p. (J). (-k). 4.99 *(978-0-7364-3508-6(5),* Golden/Disney) Random Hse. Children's Bks.

—Winter Fun for Everyone! (Disney Princess) Trimble, Irene. 2015. (Pictureback(R) Ser.). (ENG.). 16p. (J). (gr. -1-2). 5.99 *(978-0-7364-3416-4(X),* RH/Disney) Random Hse. Children's Bks.

—The Write Story. Gownley, Jimmy. 2018. (ENG.). 96p. (J). (gr. 1-4). pap. 8.99 *(978-0-7364-3849-0(1));* lib. bdg. 12.99 *(978-0-7364-9024-5(8))* Random Hse. Children's Bks. (RH/Disney).

RH Disney Staff. Amazing Ariel! (Disney Princess) RH Disney Staff. 2013. (Pictureback(R) Ser.). (ENG.). 16p. (J). (gr. -1-2). 4.99 *(978-0-7364-2994-8(8),* RH/Disney) Random Hse. Children's Bks.

—Anna's Birthday Surprise. RH Disney Staff. Julius, Jessica. 2015. (Pictureback(R) Ser.). (ENG.). 24p. (J). (gr. -1-2). 4.99 *(978-0-7364-3439-3(9),* RH/Disney) Random Hse. Children's Bks.

—Anna's Icy Adventure. RH Disney Staff. 2013. (Golden First Chapters Ser.). 80p. (J). (gr. 1-4). 4.99 *(978-0-7364-8132-8(X),* Golden/Disney) Random Hse. Children's Bks.

—Ariel's Royal Wedding/Aurora's Royal Wedding (Disney Princess) RH Disney Staff. 2014. (Pictureback(R) Ser.). (ENG.). 32p. (J). (gr. -1-2). 4.99 *(978-0-7364-3167-5(5),* RH/Disney) Random Hse. Children's Bks.

—Back on Track. RH Disney Staff. 2017. (Step into Reading Ser.). (ENG.). 24p. (J). (gr. -1-1). lib. bdg. 12.99 *(978-0-7364-8198-4(2),* RH/Disney) Random Hse. Children's Bks.

—Belle - Discovery. RH Disney Staff. 2017. (Stepping Stone Book(TM) Ser.). (ENG.). 128p. (J). (gr. 1-4). 6.99 *(978-0-7364-3579-6(4),* RH/Disney) Random Hse. Children's Bks.

—Belle's Friendship Invention/Tiana's Friendship Fix-Up (Disney Princess) RH Disney Staff. 2016. (Pictureback(R) Ser.). (ENG.). 48p. (J). (gr. -1-2). pap. 5.99 *(978-0-7364-3735-6(5),* RH/Disney) Random Hse. Children's Bks.

—Best Dad in the Sea. RH Disney Staff. Tyler, Amy J. 2003. (Step into Reading Ser.). (ENG.). 32p. (J). (gr. k-3). pap.

4.99 *(978-0-7364-2131-7(9)*, RH/Disney) Random Hse. Children's Bks.

—Brave Little Golden Book (Disney/Pixar Brave) RH Disney Staff. Redbank, Tennant. 2012. (Little Golden Book Ser.). (ENG.). 24p. (J). (gr. k-k). 4.99 *(978-0-7364-2901-6(8)*, Golden/Disney) Random Hse. Children's Bks.

—The Cake-Tillion (Disney Palace Pets: Whisker Haven Tales) RH Disney Staff. 2016. (Pictureback(R) Ser.). (ENG.). 16p. (J). (gr. -1-2). 5.99 *(978-0-7364-3387-7(2)*, RH/Disney) Random Hse. Children's Bks.

—Can You Find Dory? RH Disney Staff. 2016. (Lift-The-Flap Ser.). (ENG.). 12p. (J). (— 1). bds. 9.99 *(978-0-7364-3561-1(1)*, RH/Disney) Random Hse. Children's Bks.

—Cars 2 Little Golden Book (Disney/Pixar Cars 2) RH Disney Staff. 2011. (Little Golden Book Ser.). (ENG.). 24p. (J). (gr. -1-2). 4.99 *(978-0-7364-2781-4(3)*, Golden/Disney) Random Hse. Children's Bks.

—Cars 3 Big Golden Book (Disney/Pixar Cars 3) RH Disney Staff. 2017. (Big Golden Book Ser.). (ENG.). 48p. (J). (gr. -1-2). 9.99 *(978-0-7364-3674-8(X)*, Golden/Disney) Random Hse. Children's Bks.

—Cars 3 Deluxe Junior Novelization (Disney/Pixar Cars 3) RH Disney Staff. 2017. (ENG.). 144p. (J). (gr. 2-5). 9.99 *(978-0-7364-3725-7(8)*, RH/Disney) Random Hse. Children's Bks.

—Cars 3 Junior Novelization (Disney/Pixar Cars 3) RH Disney Staff. 2017. (ENG.). 144p. (J). (gr. 2-5). 6.99 *(978-0-7364-3726-4(6)*, RH/Disney) Random Hse. Children's Bks.

—Cars 3 Pictureback with Tattoos (Disney/Pixar Cars 3) RH Disney Staff. 2017. (Pictureback(R) Ser.). (ENG.). 16p. (J). (gr. -1-2). pap. 4.99 *(978-0-7364-3728-8(2)*, RH/Disney) Random Hse. Children's Bks.

—Cars Origins: Struck by Lightning. RH Disney Staff. Keane, Dave. 2017. (Stepping Stone Book(TM) Ser.). (ENG.). 128p. (J). (gr. 1-4). 5.99 *(978-0-7364-3820-9(3)*, RH/Disney) Random Hse. Children's Bks.

—Cinderella - Beginnings. RH Disney Staff. Roehl, Tessa. 2017. (Stepping Stone Book(TM) Ser.). (ENG.). 128p. (J). (gr. 1-4). 6.99 *(978-0-7364-3578-9(6)*, RH/Disney) Random Hse. Children's Bks.

—Cinderella's Best Creations/Snow White & the Three Giants (Disney Princess) RH Disney Staff. 2016. (Pictureback(R) Ser.). (ENG.). 48p. (J). (gr. -1-2). pap. 5.99 *(978-0-7364-3734-9(7)*, RH/Disney) Random Hse. Children's Bks.

—Coco Deluxe Hardcover Junior Novelization (Disney/Pixar Coco) RH Disney Staff. 2017. (ENG.). 144p. (J). (gr. 2-5). 9.99 *(978-0-7364-3807-0(6)*, RH/Disney) Random Hse. Children's Bks.

—Coco Deluxe Step into Reading with Cardstock (Disney/Pixar Coco) RH Disney Staff. 2017. (Step into Reading Ser.). (ENG.). 32p. (J). (gr. -1-1). lib. bdg. 12.99 *(978-0-7364-8252-3(0)*, RH/Disney) Random Hse. Children's Bks.

—Coco Deluxe Step into Reading with Stickers (Disney/Pixar Coco) RH Disney Staff. 2017. (Step into Reading Ser.). (ENG.). 32p. (J). (gr. -1-1). pap. 4.99 *(978-0-7364-3811-7(4))*; lib. bdg. 12.99 *(978-0-7364-8253-0(9))* Random Hse. Children's Bks. (RH/Disney).

—Coco Junior Novelization (Disney/Pixar Coco) RH Disney Staff. 2017. (ENG.). 144p. (J). (gr. 2-5). 6.99 *(978-0-7364-3806-3(8)*, RH/Disney) Random Hse. Children's Bks.

—The Critterzen Clue Contest (Disney Palace Pets: Whisker Haven Tales) RH Disney Staff. 2017. (Pictureback(R) Ser.). (ENG.). 24p. (J). (gr. -1-1). pap. 4.99 *(978-0-7364-3593-2(X)*, RH/Disney) Random Hse. Children's Bks.

—Disney Princess Beginnings: Ariel Makes Waves (Disney Princess) RH Disney Staff. 2017. (Stepping Stone Book(TM) Ser.). (ENG.). 128p. (J). (gr. 1-4). 6.99 *(978-0-7364-3733-2(9)*, RH/Disney) Random Hse. Children's Bks.

—Disney Princess Beginnings: Jasmine's New Rules (Disney Princess) RH Disney Staff. Francis, Suzanne. 2017. (Stepping Stone Book(TM) Ser.). (ENG.). 128p. (J). (gr. 1-4). 6.99 *(978-0-7364-3813-1(0))*; lib. bdg. 12.99 *(978-0-7364-8254-7(7))* Random Hse. Children's Bks. (RH/Disney).

—Disney Princess Heart Strong #2 (Disney Princess) RH Disney Staff. 2017. (Step into Reading Ser.). (ENG.). 48p. (J). (gr. -1-1). pap. 5.99 *(978-0-7364-3803-2(3)*, RH/Disney) Random Hse. Children's Bks.

—Dory's Sea of Wonders. RH Disney Staff. 2016. (Pictureback(R) Ser.). (ENG.). 24p. (J). (gr. -1-2). 4.99 *(978-0-7364-3507-9(7)*, RH/Disney) Random Hse. Children's Bks.

—Dory's Story. RH Disney Staff. 2016. (Step into Reading Ser.). (ENG.). 24p. (J). (gr. -1-1). 4.99 *(978-0-7364-3498-0(4)*, RH/Disney) Random Hse. Children's Bks.

—Driven to Win! RH Disney Staff. 2017. (Step into Reading Ser.). (ENG.). 32p. (J). (gr. -1-1). pap. 4.99 *(978-0-7364-3682-3(0))*; lib. bdg. 12.99 *(978-0-7364-8199-1(0))* Random Hse. Children's Bks. (RH/Disney).

—Elena of Avalor. RH Disney Staff. Olivas, Silvia. 2017. (Big Golden Book Ser.). (ENG.). 32p. (J). (gr. -1-2). 9.99 *(978-0-7364-3552-9(2)*, Golden/Disney) Random Hse. Children's Bks.

— Fairy's Fire. RH Disney Staff. 2016. (Never Girls Ser.). (ENG.). 224p. (J). (gr. 1-4). 14.99 *(978-0-7364-3556-7(5)*, RH/Disney) Random Hse. Children's Bks.

—A Family Mystery (Disney/Pixar Coco) RH Disney Staff. 2017. (Step into Reading Ser.). (ENG.). 32p. (J). (gr. -1-1). pap. 4.99 *(978-0-7364-3809-4(2)*, RH/Disney) Random Hse. Children's Bks.

—Finding Dory. RH Disney Staff. 2016. (ENG.). 144p. (J). (gr. 2-5). 6.99 *(978-0-7364-3486-7(0)*, RH/Disney) Random Hse. Children's Bks.

—Finding Dory Big Golden Book (Disney/Pixar Finding Dory) RH Disney Staff. 2016. (Big Golden Book Ser.). (ENG.). 48p. (J). (gr. -1-2). 9.99 *(978-0-7364-3506-2(9)*, Golden/Disney) Random Hse. Children's Bks.

—Finding Dory Deluxe Step into Reading (Disney/Pixar Finding Dory) RH Disney Staff. 2016. (Step into Reading Ser.). (ENG.). 24p. (J). (gr. -1-1). pap. 4.99 *(978-0-7364-3704-2(5))*; lib. bdg. 12.99 *(978-0-7364-8188-5(5))* Random Hse. Children's Bks. (RH/Disney).

—Finding Dory Little Golden Book (Disney/Pixar Finding Dory) RH Disney Staff. 2016. (Little Golden Book Ser.). (ENG.). 24p. (J). (-k). 4.99 *(978-0-7364-3511-6(5)*, Golden/Disney) Random Hse. Children's Bks.

—Finding Dory Padded Board Book (Disney/Pixar Finding Dory) RH Disney Staff. 2016. (ENG.). 30p. (J). (— 1). bds. 11.99 *(978-0-7364-3558-1(1)*, RH/Disney) Random Hse. Children's Bks.

—Finding Dory Pictureback with Stickers (Disney/Pixar Finding Dory) RH Disney Staff. 2016. (Pictureback(R) Ser.). (ENG.). 24p. (J). (gr. -1-2). pap. 4.99 *(978-0-7364-3708-0(8)*, RH/Disney) Random Hse. Children's Bks.

—Finding Dory: the Deluxe Junior Novelization (Disney/Pixar Finding Dory) RH Disney Staff. 2016. (ENG.). 144p. (J). (gr. 2-5). 9.99 *(978-0-7364-3573-4(5)*, RH/Disney) Random Hse. Children's Bks.

—Flounder Loves Ariel (Disney Princess) RH Disney Staff. 2016. (ENG.). 26p. (J). (gr. -1-1). bds. 9.99 *(978-0-7364-3707-3(X)*, RH/Disney) Random Hse. Children's Bks.

—Frozen - Big Snowman, Little Snowman. RH Disney Staff. Rabe, Tish. 2013. (Step into Reading Ser.). (ENG.). 32p. (J). (gr. -1-1). lib. bdg. 12.99 *(978-0-7364-8130-4(3)*, RH/Disney) Random Hse. Children's Bks.

—Frozen Fever. RH Disney Staff. Saxon, Victoria. deluxe ed. 2015. (Junior Novel Ser.). 96p. (J). (gr. 3-7). 9.99 *(978-0-7364-3440-9(2)*, RH/Disney) Random Hse. Children's Bks.

—Frozen Holiday Special Deluxe Junior Novelization (Disney Frozen) RH Disney Staff. 2017. (ENG.). 96p. (J). (gr. 3-7). 9.99 *(978-0-7364-3815-5(7)*, RH/Disney) Random Hse. Children's Bks.

—The Frozen Monster (Disney Frozen) RH Disney Staff. 2017. (Pictureback(R) Ser.). (ENG.). 24p. (J). (gr. -1-2). pap. 4.99 *(978-0-7364-3729-5(0)*, RH/Disney) Random Hse. Children's Bks.

—The Good Dinosaur Junior Novelization (Disney/Pixar the Good Dinosaur) RH Disney Staff. 2015. (ENG.). 128p. (J). (gr. 4-7). 5.99 *(978-0-7364-3140-8(3)*, RH/Disney) Random Hse. Children's Bks.

—Gus Loves Cinderella (Disney Princess) RH Disney Staff. 2016. (ENG.). 26p. (J). (gr. -1-1). bds. 9.99 *(978-0-7364-3706-6(1)*, RH/Disney) Random Hse. Children's Bks.

—Hank the Septopus. RH Disney Staff. deluxe ed. 2016. (Pictureback(R) Ser.). (ENG.). 24p. (J). (gr. -1-2). 4.99 *(978-0-7364-3510-9(7)*, RH/Disney) Random Hse. Children's Bks.

—Hello, Dory! RH Disney Staff. 2016. (ENG.). 16p. (J). (— 1). bds. 7.99 *(978-0-7364-3625-0(1)*, RH/Disney) Random Hse. Children's Bks.

—High-Flying Tea (Disney Palace Pets: Whisker Haven Tales) RH Disney Staff. 2016. (Pictureback(R) Ser.). (ENG.). 24p. (J). (gr. -1-2). pap. 4.99 *(978-0-7364-3551-2(4)*, Random Hse. Bks. for Young Readers) Random Hse. Children's Bks.

—I Love My Family! A Book of Memories. RH Disney Staff. 2017. (ENG.). 64p. (J). (gr. 4-7). 9.99 *(978-0-7364-3847-6(5)*, RH/Disney) Random Hse. Children's Bks.

—The Incredi-Files. RH Disney Staff. 2018. (ENG.). 96p. (J). (gr. 3-7). 9.99 *(978-0-7364-3860-5(2)*, RH/Disney) Random Hse. Children's Bks.

—Incredibles 2: the Deluxe Junior Novelization (Disney/Pixar the Incredibles 2) RH Disney Staff. 2018. (ENG.). 144p. (J). (gr. 3-7). 9.99 *(978-0-7364-3851-3(3)*, RH/Disney) Random Hse. Children's Bks.

—Incredibles 2: the Junior Novelization (Disney/Pixar the Incredibles 2) RH Disney Staff. 2018. (ENG.). 144p. (J). (gr. 3-7). 6.99 *(978-0-7364-3850-6(5)*, RH/Disney) Random Hse. Children's Bks.

—Journey to the Lights. RH Disney Staff. deluxe ed. 2016. (Stepping Stone Book(TM) Ser.). (ENG.). 224p. (J). (gr. 3-7). 14.99 *(978-0-7364-3659-5(6)*, RH/Disney) Random Hse. Children's Bks.

—M Is for Monster (Disney/Pixar Monsters, Inc.) RH Disney Staff. 2014. (Little Golden Book Ser.). (ENG.). 24p. (J). (-k). 4.99 *(978-0-7364-3170-5(5)*, Golden/Disney) Random Hse. Children's Bks.

—Meet the Emotions. RH Disney Staff. 2015. (ENG.). 12p. (J). (gr. -1-2). bds. 8.99 *(978-0-7364-3438-6(0)*, RH/Disney) Random Hse. Children's Bks.

—Miguel & the Amazing Alebrijes. RH Disney Staff. 2017. (Pictureback(R) Ser.). (ENG.). 24p. (J). (gr. -1-2). pap. 5.99 *(978-0-7364-3766-0(5)*, RH/Disney) Random Hse. Children's Bks.

—Moana Deluxe Step into Reading #1 (Disney Moana) RH Disney Staff. 2016. (Step into Reading Ser.). (ENG.). 24p. (J). (gr. -1-1). pap. 4.99 *(978-0-7364-3644-1(8)*, RH/Disney) Random Hse. Children's Bks.

—Moana Junior Novelization. RH Disney Staff. 2016. (ENG.). 144p. (J). (gr. 2-5). 6.99 *(978-0-7364-3600-7(6)*, RH/Disney) Random Hse. Children's Bks.

—Moana: the Deluxe Junior Novelization (Disney Moana) RH Disney Staff. 2016. (ENG.). 144p. (J). (gr. 2-5). 9.99 *(978-0-7364-3574-1(3)*, RH/Disney) Random Hse. Children's Bks.

—Monster Hide-and-Seek. RH Disney Staff. 2013. (ENG.). 12p. (J). (-k). bds. 6.99 *(978-0-7364-3032-6(6)*, Golden/Disney) Random Hse. Children's Bks.

—Monsters University Little Golden Book (Disney/Pixar Monsters University) RH Disney Staff. 2013. (Little Golden Book Ser.). (ENG.). 24p. (J). (-k). 3.99 *(978-0-7364-3034-0(2)*, Golden/Disney) Random Hse. Children's Bks.

—Mulan Is Loyal/Merida Is Brave (Disney Princess) RH Disney Staff. 2017. (Step into Reading Ser.). (ENG.). 48p. (J). (gr. -1-1). lib. bdg. 12.99 *(978-0-7364-9017-7(5)*, RH/Disney) Random Hse. Children's Bks.

—My Hero. RH Disney Staff. 2008. (Step into Reading Ser.). (ENG.). 32p. (J). (gr. k-3). pap. 3.99 *(978-0-375-84812-4(6)*, RH/Disney) Random Hse. Children's Bks.

—An Ocean Adventure. RH Disney Staff. 2016. (ENG.). 8p. (J). (-k). bds. 9.99 *(978-0-7364-3626-7(X)*, Random Hse. Bks. for Young Readers) Random Hse. Children's Bks.

—Olaf Loves ... Everything! (Disney Frozen) RH Disney Staff. Posner-Sanchez, Andrea. 2016. (Pictureback(R) Ser.). (ENG.). 16p. (J). (gr. -1-1). pap. 4.99 *(978-0-7364-3590-1(5)*, RH/Disney) Random Hse. Children's Bks.

—Olaf's 1-2-3. RH Disney Staff. 2013. (ENG.). 12p. (J). (— 1). bds. 6.99 *(978-0-7364-3064-7(4)*, Golden/Disney) Random Hse. Children's Bks.

—Opposites Attract. RH Disney Staff. 2017. (Stepping Stone Book(TM) Ser.: 3). (ENG.). 128p. (J). (gr. 1-4). 5.99 *(978-0-7364-3830-8(0)*, RH/Disney) Random Hse. Children's Bks.

—A Paw-Some Costume Party! (Disney Palace Pets Whisker Haven Tales) RH Disney Staff. 2017. (Little Golden Book Ser.). (ENG.). 24p. (J). (-k). 4.99 *(978-0-7364-3723-3(1)*, Golden/Disney) Random Hse. Children's Bks.

—Pete's Dragon (Disney: Pete's Dragon) RH Disney Staff. 2016. (Little Golden Book Ser.). (ENG.). 24p. (J). (-k). 4.99 *(978-0-7364-3522-2(0)*, Golden/Disney) Random Hse. Children's Bks.

—Princess Bedtime Stories (Disney Princess) RH Disney Staff. 2018. (Big Golden Book Ser.). (ENG.). 48p. (J). (gr. -1-2). 10.99 *(978-0-7364-3793-6(2)*, Golden Bks.) Random Hse. Children's Bks.

—Princess Spring-Themed Board Book (Disney Princess) RH Disney Staff. 2017. (ENG.). 22p. (J). (-k). bds. 6.99 *(978-0-7364-3736-3(3)*, RH/Disney) Random Hse. Children's Bks.

—Queen for a Day (Disney Tangled the Series) RH Disney Staff. 2017. (ENG.). 144p. (J). (gr. 3-7). 9.99 *(978-0-7364-3825-4(4)*, RH/Disney) Random Hse. Children's Bks.

—Quest for the Heart. RH Disney Staff. 2016. (Step into Reading Ser.). (ENG.). 32p. (J). (gr. -1-1). lib. bdg. 12.99 *(978-0-7364-8226-4(1)*, RH/Disney) Random Hse. Children's Bks.

—Rainbow of Emotions. RH Disney Staff. 2015. (Color Plus Rainbow Pencil Ser.). 128p. (J). (gr. -1-2). pap. 7.99 *(978-0-7364-3287-0(6)*, Golden/Disney) Random Hse. Children's Bks.

—Rapunzel's World (Disney Tangled: the Series) RH Disney Staff. 2017. (ENG.). 96p. (J). (gr. 1-4). pap. 9.99 *(978-0-7364-3817-9(3)*, RH/Disney) Random Hse. Children's Bks.

—The Royal Derby (Disney Palace Pets: Whisker Haven Tales) RH Disney Staff. 2016. (Pictureback(R) Ser.). (ENG.). 24p. (J). (gr. -1-2). 4.99 *(978-0-7364-3496-6(8)*, Random Hse. Bks. for Young Readers) Random Hse. Children's Bks.

—Scaring Lessons. RH Disney Staff. 2013. (Step into Reading Ser.). (ENG.). 32p. (J). (gr. -1-1). 3.99 *(978-0-7364-3035-7(0)*, RH/Disney) Random Hse. Children's Bks.

—Sleeping Beauty & the Good Fairies (Disney Classic) RH Disney Staff. 2018. (Little Golden Book Ser.). (ENG.). 24p. (J). (-k). 4.99 *(978-0-7364-3771-4(1)*, Golden/Disney) Random Hse. Children's Bks.

—Sleeping Beauty Big Golden Book (Disney Princess) RH Disney Staff. 2019. (Big Golden Book Ser.). (ENG.). 64p. (J). (gr. -1-2). 10.99 *(978-0-7364-3233-7(7)*, Golden/Disney) Random Hse. Children's Bks.

—Sparkle Magic! (Disney Frozen) RH Disney Staff. 2015. (Pictureback(R) Ser.). (ENG.). 16p. (J). (gr. -1-2). 5.99 *(978-0-7364-3366-2(X)*, RH/Disney) Random Hse. Children's Bks.

—Storm Chasing: Cars Origins. RH Disney Staff. Keane, Dave. 2017. (Stepping Stone Book(TM) Ser.). (ENG.). 128p. (J). (gr. 1-4). 5.99 *(978-0-7364-3821-6(1))*; lib. bdg. 12.99 *(978-0-7364-8257-8(1))* Random Hse. Children's Bks. (RH/Disney).

—Struck by Lightning. RH Disney Staff. Keane, Dave. 2017. (Stepping Stone Book(TM) Ser.). (ENG.). 128p. (J). (gr. 1-4). lib. bdg. 12.99 *(978-0-7364-8256-1(3)*, RH/Disney) Random Hse. Children's Bks.

—Taken by Storm/How to Be a Great Racer. RH Disney Staff. 2017. (Pictureback(R) Ser.). (ENG.). 48p. (J). (gr. -1-2). pap. 5.99 *(978-0-7364-3727-1(4)*, RH/Disney) Random Hse. Children's Bks.

—Tales of Rapunzel #4: the Search for the Sundrop (Disney Tangled the Series) RH Disney Staff. 2018. (Stepping Stone Book(TM) Ser.: 4). (ENG.). 128p. (J). (gr. 1-4). 5.99 *(978-0-7364-3764-6(9)*, RH/Disney) Random Hse. Children's Bks.

—Toy Story. RH Disney Staff. 2009. (Little Golden Book Ser.). (ENG.). 24p. (J). (gr. -1-2). 4.99 *(978-0-7364-2596-4(9)*, Golden/Disney) Random Hse. Children's Bks.

—The Unforgettable Joke Book. RH Disney Staff. 2016. (ENG.). 80p. (J). (gr. 1-4). 4.99 *(978-0-7364-3611-3(1)*, RH/Disney) Random Hse. Children's Bks.

—Walt Disney's Alice in Wonderland. RH Disney Staff. 2010. (Little Golden Book Ser.). (ENG.). 24p. (J). (gr. -1-2). 4.99 *(978-0-7364-2670-1(1)*, Golden/Disney) Random Hse. Children's Bks.

—Welcome to Whisker Haven (Disney Palace Pets: Whisker Haven Tales) RH Disney Staff. 2016. (Big Golden Book Ser.). (ENG.). 32p. (J). (gr. -1-2). 9.99 *(978-0-7364-3474-4(7)*, Golden/Disney) Random Hse. Children's Bks.

—Where Monsters Live. RH Disney Staff. 2016. (Pictureback(R) Ser.). (ENG.). 24p. (J). (gr. -1-2). 4.99 *(978-0-7364-3649-6(9)*, RH/Disney) Random Hse. Children's Bks.

RH Disney Staff & An, Jiyoung. I Can Be a Horse Rider (Barbie) Man-Kong, Mary. 2012. (Step into Reading Ser.). (ENG.). 32p. (J). (gr. -1-1). pap. 4.99 *(978-0-375-97030-6(4)*, Random Hse. Bks. for Young Readers) Random Hse. Children's Bks.

RH Disney Staff & Batson, Alan. I Am Ariel (Disney Princess) Posner-Sanchez, Andrea. 2018. (Little Golden Book Ser.). (ENG.). 24p. (J). (-k). 4.99 *(978-0-7364-3852-0(1)*, Golden/Disney) Random Hse. Children's Bks.

RH Disney Staff & Christy, Jana. Before the Bell. Thorpe, Kiki. 2015. (Never Girls Ser.: 9). (ENG.). 128p. (J). (gr. 1-4). lib. bdg. 12.99 *(978-0-7364-8167-0(2)*, RH/Disney) Random Hse. Children's Bks.

RH Disney Staff & Dale-Scott, Lindsay. Belle Takes Flight. McCullough, Kathy. 2018. (ENG.). 224p. (J). (gr. 3-7). 13.99 *(978-0-7364-3925-1(0))*; lib. bdg. 18.99 *(978-0-7364-8264-6(4))* Random Hse. Children's Bks. (RH/Disney).

RH Disney Staff & DiCicco, Sue. Sleepy Time with Aurora (Disney Princess) Posner-Sanchez, Andrea. 2015. (Board Book Ser.). (ENG.). 24p. (J). (— 1). bds. 6.99 *(978-0-7364-3311-2(2)*, RH/Disney) Random Hse. Children's Bks.

—Teacup to the Rescue! (Disney Princess: Palace Pets) Posner-Sanchez, Andrea. 2015. (Little Golden Book Ser.). (ENG.). 24p. (J). (-k). 4.99 *(978-0-7364-3364-8(3)*, Golden/Disney) Random Hse. Children's Bks.

—Treasure's Day at Sea (Disney Princess: Palace Pets) RH Disney Staff & Posner-Sanchez, Andrea. 2015. (Little Golden Book Ser.). (ENG.). 24p. (J). (-k). 4.99 *(978-0-7364-3335-8(X)*, Golden/Disney) Random Hse. Children's Bks.

RH Disney Staff & Disney Storybook Art Team. Fight to the Finish! RH Disney Staff & Scollon, Bill. 2014. (Step into Reading Ser.). (ENG.). 48p. (J). (gr. k-3). 4.99 *(978-0-7364-3189-7(6)*, RH/Disney) Random Hse. Children's Bks.

—The Journey Home, No. 2. Sher, Edie & Scollon, Bill. 2015. (Step into Reading Ser.). (ENG.). 24p. (J). (gr. -1-1). 4.99 *(978-0-7364-3093-7(8)*, RH/Disney) Random Hse. Children's Bks.

—The Journey Home, Vol. 2. RH Disney Staff et al. 2015. (Step into Reading Ser.). (ENG.). 24p. (J). (gr. -1-1). lib. bdg. 12.99 *(978-0-7364-8146-5(X)*, RH/Disney) Random Hse. Children's Bks.

—Ocean of Color. RH Disney Staff & Scollon, Bill. 2016. (Step into Reading Ser.). (ENG.). 24p. (J). (gr. -1-1). 4.99 *(978-0-7364-3519-2(0)*, RH/Disney) Random Hse. Children's Bks.

—Whisker Haven Birthday Pictureback (Disney Palace Pets: Whisker Haven Tales) RH Disney Staff & Orsi, Tea. 2017. (Pictureback(R) Ser.). (ENG.). 16p. (J). (gr. -1-2). pap. 4.99 *(978-0-7364-3696-0(0)*, RH/Disney) Random Hse. Children's Bks.

RH Disney Staff & Disney Storybook Artists Staff. The Incredible Elastigirl. RH Disney Staff & Bouchard, Natasha. 2018. (Step into Reading Ser.). (ENG.). 32p. (J). (gr. -1-1). lib. bdg. 12.99 *(978-0-7364-8262-2(8)*, RH/Disney) Random Hse. Children's Bks.

—Wings Around the Globe. RH Disney Staff & Scollon, Bill. 2013. (Pictureback(R) Ser.). (ENG.). 24p. (J). (gr. -1-2). pap. 3.99 *(978-0-7364-3016-6(4)*, RH/Disney) Random Hse. Children's Bks.

RH Disney Staff & Doescher, Erik. Ready to Play! (Disney Infinity) Saxon, Victoria. 2015. (Step into Reading Ser.). (ENG.). 32p. (J). (gr. k-3). 4.99 *(978-0-7364-3427-0(5)*, RH/Disney) Random Hse. Children's Bks.

RH Disney Staff & Egan, Caroline. The Pet Problem (Disney/Pixar Toy Story) RH Disney Staff & Depken, Kristen L. 2011. (Little Golden Book Ser.). (ENG.). 24p. (J). (gr. -1-2). 4.99 *(978-0-7364-2698-5(1)*, Golden/Disney) Random Hse. Children's Bks.

RH Disney Staff & Fruchter, Jason. Toby the Cowsitter (Disney Junior: Sheriff Callie's Wild West) Posner-Sanchez, Andrea. 2015. (Little Golden Book Ser.). (ENG.). 24p. (J). (-k). 4.99 *(978-0-7364-3299-3(X)*, Golden/Disney) Random Hse. Children's Bks.

RH Disney Staff & Hashimoto, Satoshi. Cars 3 ABC Book (Disney/Pixar Cars 3) RH Disney Staff & Wheeler, Lisa. 2017. (ENG.). 48p. (J). (-k). 8.99 *(978-0-7364-3818-6(1)*, RH/Disney) Random Hse. Children's Bks.

—Incredibles 2 Little Golden Book (Disney/Pixar Incredibles 2) RH Disney Staff. 2018. (Little Golden Book Ser.). (ENG.). 24p. (J). (-k). 4.99 *(978-0-7364-3855-1(6)*, Golden/Disney) Random Hse. Children's Bks.

RH Disney Staff & Hernandez, Sarah. Babysitting Mode (Disney/Pixar Incredibles 2) RH Disney Staff & Hernandez, Sarah. 2018. (Pictureback(R) Ser.). (ENG.). 24p. (J). (gr. -1-2). pap. 5.99 *(978-0-525-58159-8(6)*, RH/Disney) Random Hse. Children's Bks.

RH Disney Staff & Holtsclaw, Josh. A Roaring Adventure (Disney/Pixar Toy Story) Depken, Kristen L. 2012. (Little Golden Book Ser.). (ENG.). 24p. (J). (gr. k-k). 4.99 *(978-0-7364-2907-8(7)*, Golden/Disney) Random Hse. Children's Bks.

RH Disney Staff & Laguna, Fabio. Toy Box Trouble! RH Disney Staff & Weingartner, Amy. 2015. (Stepping Stone Book Ser.). (ENG.). 80p. (J). (gr. 1-4). 4.99 *(978-0-7364-3326-6(0)*, RH/Disney) Random Hse. Children's Bks.

RH Disney Staff & Loftis, Cory. The Stinky Cheese Caper. RH Disney Staff & Trine, Greg. 2016. (ENG.). 80p. (J). (gr. 1-4). 4.99 *(978-0-7364-3610-6(3)*, RH/Disney) Random Hse. Children's Bks.

RH Disney Staff & Molina, Adrian H. Toy Story 3. RH Disney Staff & Auerbach, Annie. 2010. (Little Golden Book Ser.). (ENG.). 24p. (J). (gr. -1-2). 4.99 *(978-0-7364-2668-8(X)*, Golden/Disney) Random Hse. Children's Bks.

RH Disney Staff & Random House Staff. I Can Be a Pastry Chef/I Can Be a Lifeguard (Barbie) Man-Kong, Mary et al. 2012. (Pictureback(R) Ser.). (ENG.). 32p. (J). (gr. -1-2). pap. 4.99 *(978-0-307-93114-6(5)*, Random Hse. Bks. for Young Readers) Random Hse. Children's Bks.

RH Disney Staff & Robinson, Bill. Anna & Elsa: All Hail the Queen (Disney Frozen), No. 1. David, Erica. 2015. (Stepping Stone Book(TM) Ser.: 1). (ENG.). 128p. (J). (gr. 1-4). lib. bdg. 12.99 *(978-0-7364-8216-5(4)*, RH/Disney) Random Hse. Children's Bks.

RH Disney Staff & Robinson, William E. Anna & Elsa: Memory & Magic (Disney Frozen), No. 2. David, Erica. 2015. (Stepping Stone Book(TM) Ser.: 2). (ENG.). 128p. (J). (gr. 1-4). 9.99 *(978-0-7364-3285-6(X)*, RH/Disney) Random Hse. Children's Bks.

RH Disney Staff & Rockwell, Lizzy. Don't Go up Haunted Hill... or Else! Swobud, I. K. 2008. (Holiday Books: Halloween Ser.). (ENG.). 24p. (J). (gr. k-3). 16.19 *(978-0-307-13309-0(5))* Random House Publishing Group.

RH Disney Staff & Sastrawinata-Lemay, Griselda. Moana Little Golden Book (Disney Moana) Posner-Sanchez, Andrea & Hitchcock, Laura. 2016. (Little Golden Book Ser.). (ENG.). 24p. (J). (-k). 4.99 *(978-0-7364-3603-8(0)*, Golden/Disney) Random Hse. Children's Bks.

RH Disney Staff & Studio IBOIX Staff. Two Princesses & a Baby (Disney Junior: Sofia the First) Posner-Sanchez, Andrea. 2015. (Little Golden Book Ser.). (ENG.). 24p. (J). (-k). 4.99 *(978-0-7364-3358-7(9)*, Golden/Disney) Random Hse. Children's Bks.

Rhead, Louis. Treasure Island. Stevenson, Robert Louis. 2015. (J). pap. *(978-1-4677-7821-3(4)*, First Avenue Editions) Lerner Publishing Group.

Rhead, Louis, jt. illus. see Wyeth, N. C.

Rheberg, Judy. The Hunting Safari. Matthews, T. J. 2003. (East African Adventures Ser.). 166p. (J). per. 11.95 *(978-0-938978-34-3(9))* Wycliffe Bible Translators.

Rheburg, Judy. The Canoeing Safari. Matthews, T. J. 2004. (J). *(978-0-938978-35-0(7))* Wycliffe Bible Translators.

—The Village Safari. Matthews, T. J. 2005. (J). *(978-0-938978-36-7(5))* Wycliffe Bible Translators.

Rheeder, Tina Heenop. Lucy's Way Home. Sylvester, Apara Mahal. 2020. (ENG.). 38p. (J). pap. 10.00 ***(978-1-6744-0253-6(8))*** Independently Published.

Rhine, Karen C. Princess Aisha & the Cave of Judgment. Taylor, Kay Lovelace. 2007. 32p. (J). 19.95 *(978-0-9799119-0-3(7))* KLT & Assocs.

—San Agustin (St Augustine) Lilly, Melinda. 2005. (Lecturas Historicas Norteamericanas (Reading American Histor Ser.). 24p. (J). (gr. 3-7). lib. bdg. 22.79 *(978-1-59515-637-2(2))* Rourke Educational Media.

Rhino, Black, jt. illus. see Hernandez, Rick.

Rhodes, Harry. Masks. Rhodes, Harry, photos by. Storey, Rita. 2014. (J). lib. bdg. 26.60 *(978-1-4677-4195-8(7)*, Lerner Pubns.) Lerner Publishing Group.

Rhodes, Julia. Daisy & Dawn. Rhodes, Julia. 2018. (ENG.). 36p. (J). pap. 9.25 *(978-1-7907-8393-9(3))* Independently Published.

Rhodes, Katie. Becky Bunny. Powell, Richard. 2004. (Fuzzy Friends Ser.). 10p. (J). 7.95 *(978-1-58925-723-8(5))* Tiger Tales.

—Leo Lion. Powell, Richard. 2004. (Fuzzy Friends Ser.). 10p. (J). 7.95 *(978-1-58925-719-1(7))* Tiger Tales.

—Lucy Lamb. Powell, Richard. 2004. (Fuzzy Friends Ser.). 8p. (J). 7.95 *(978-1-58925-724-5(3))* Tiger Tales.

—Mandy Monkey. Powell, Richard. 2004. (Fuzzy Friends Ser.). 10p. (J). 7.95 *(978-1-58925-720-7(0))* Tiger Tales.

—Peter Panda. Powell, Richard. 2004. (Fuzzy Friends Ser.). 10p. (J). 7.95 *(978-1-58925-721-4(9))* Tiger Tales.

—Timmy Tiger. Powell, Richard. 2004. (Fuzzy Friends Ser.). 10p. (J). 7.95 *(978-1-58925-722-1(7))* Tiger Tales.

Rhodes, Lisa. Animals of Africa. 2010. (Pruett Ser.). (ENG.). 32p. (J). pap. 3.95 *(978-0-87108-953-3(X)*, West Winds Pr.) West Margin Pr.

—Animals of the Mountain West Region. 2010. (Pruett Ser.). (ENG.). 32p. (J). pap. 3.95 *(978-0-87108-956-4(4)*, West Winds Pr.) West Margin Pr.

Rhys, Sara. Pony Poems for Little Pony Lovers. Meister, Cari. 2019. (ENG.). 40p. (J). (gr. -1-3). 17.99 *(978-1-4814-9814-2(2)*, Beach Lane Bks.) Beach Lane Bks.

Riano, Carlos. Koku-Yo, Mensajero del Sol. Espriella, Leopoldo Berdella De La. 2003. (Literatura Juvenil (Panamericana Editorial) Ser.). (SPA.). 90p. (YA). (gr. -1-7). per. *(978-958-30-0344-8(1))* Panamericana Editorial.

Ribbon, Lemon. Tiny Town Hide & Seek Counting. George, Joshua. 2018. (Tiny Town Hide & Seek Board Bks.). (ENG.). 12p. (J). (-k). bds. 6.99 *(978-1-78700-379-8(5))* Top That! Publishing PLC GBR. Dist: Independent Pubs. Group.

—Tiny Town Hide & Seek Words. George, Joshua. 2018. (Tiny Town Hide & Seek Board Bks.). (ENG.). 12p. (J). (-k). bds. 6.99 *(978-1-78700-380-4(9))* Top That! Publishing PLC GBR. Dist: Independent Pubs. Group.

—Tiny Town Let's Go Outside. George, Joshua. 2018. (Tiny Town Build-A-Scene Ser.). (ENG.). 12p. (J). (gr. -1-k). bds. 12.99 *(978-1-78700-381-1(7))* Top That! Publishing PLC GBR. Dist: Independent Pubs. Group.

—Tiny Town Let's Go to the Shops. George, Joshua. 2018. (Tiny Town Build-A-Scene Ser.). (ENG.). 12p. (J). (gr. -1-k). bds. 12.99 *(978-1-78700-387-3(6))* Top That! Publishing PLC GBR. Dist: Independent Pubs. Group.

—Tiny Town Picnic Fun. George, Joshua. 2018. (Soft Felt Play Bks.). (ENG.). 10p. (J). (gr. -1-k). bds. 9.99 *(978-1-78700-386-6(8))* Top That! Publishing PLC GBR. Dist: Independent Pubs. Group.

—Tiny Town What Did Busy Bee See? Graham, Oakley. 2018. (Tiny Town Touch & Trace Ser.). (ENG.). 10p. (J). (— 1). bds. 7.99 *(978-1-78700-377-4(9))* Top That! Publishing PLC GBR. Dist: Independent Pubs. Group.

—Tiny Town What Did Busy Bunny Hear? Graham, Oakley. 2018. (Tiny Town Touch & Trace Ser.). (ENG.). 10p. (J). (— 1). bds. 7.99 *(978-1-78700-378-1(7))* Top That! Publishing PLC GBR. Dist: Independent Pubs. Group.

Ribeira, Lili, jt. illus. see Graham, Andrew S.

Ribeiro, Gabriela. André e Os Animais! Monteiro, Nuno Antonio. 2019. (André Ser.: Vol. 1). (POR.). 110p. (J). pap. 8.00 *(978-1-0706-5052-4(8))* Independently Published.

Ribic, Esad. King Thor. 2020. 112p. (YA). (gr. 8-17). pap. 15.99 *(978-1-302-92102-6(9))* Marvel Worldwide, Inc.

—Marvel Legacy. 2018. (ENG.). (YA). (gr. 8-17). 224p. pap. 29.99 *(978-1-302-91102-7(3))*; 512p. 39.99 *(978-1-302-91101-0(5))* Marvel Worldwide, Inc.

—Marvel Monograph: the Art of Esad Ribic. 2019. (Marvel Monograph Ser.). (ENG.). 112p. (YA). (gr. 8-17). pap. 19.99 *(978-1-302-91760-9(9))* Marvel Worldwide, Inc.

—Thor: the God Butcher Marvel Select Edition. 2019. (ENG.). 136p. (YA). (gr. 8-17). 24.99 *(978-1-302-91892-7(3))* Marvel Worldwide, Inc.

Ribic, Esad, jt. illus. see Dauterman, Russell.

Ribic, Esad, jt. illus. see Larrazz, Pepe.

Ribina, Alena. Clyde the Rabbit Thief: An Exciting Instructive Story about the Transformation of a Rabbit Thief into a Friendly Farmer & Nurse. Sokolenko, Maxim. 2019. (ENG.). 28p. (J). pap. 9.99 ***(978-1-0869-6502-5(7))*** Independently Published.

Ricahrdson, Brittany. Metal Mike. Ricahrdson, Larry. 2010. 24p. (J). pap. 9.95 *(978-1-935706-26-7(8))* Wiggles Pr.

Ricardicus & Lopez, Ricard. Cuentos para niñas Sin Miedo / Stories for Fearless Girls. Sayalero, Myriam. 2020. (SPA.). 240p. (J). (gr. 7). 19.95 *(978-84-17605-04-9(5)*, Nube De Tinta) Penguin Random House Grupo Editorial ESP. Dist: Penguin Random Hse. LLC.

Ricceri, David, jt. illus. see Klossner, John.

Ricci, Andrés. Down for the Count. Riley, Zach. 2012. (Zach Riley Ser.). (ENG.). 80p. (J). (gr. 2-5). lib. bdg. 29.93 *(978-1-61783-533-9(1)*, 15857, Calico Chapter Bks.) ABDO Publishing Co.

—Quarterback Crisis. Riley, Zach. 2012. (Zach Riley Ser.). (ENG.). 80p. (J). (gr. 2-5). lib. bdg. 29.93 *(978-1-61783-534-6(X)*, 15859, Calico Chapter Bks.) ABDO Publishing Co.

—Sacred Stick. Riley, Zach. 2012. (Zach Riley Ser.). (ENG.). 80p. (J). (gr. 2-5). lib. bdg. 29.93 *(978-1-61783-535-3(8)*, 15861, Calico Chapter Bks.) ABDO Publishing Co.

—Surprise Kick. Riley, Zach. 2012. (Zach Riley Ser.). (ENG.). 80p. (J). (gr. 2-5). lib. bdg. 29.93 *(978-1-61783-536-0(6)*, 15863, Calico Chapter Bks.) ABDO Publishing Co.

Ricci, Andres Martinez. Electricity Is Everywhere, 1 vol. Higgins, Nadia. 2008. (Science Rocks! Ser.). (ENG.). 32p. (J). (gr. -1-4). 28.50 *(978-1-60270-276-9(4)*, 13202, Looking Glass Library) Magic Wagon.

—Marvelous Motion, 1 vol. Higgins, Nadia. 2008. (Science Rocks! Ser.). (ENG.). 32p. (J). (gr. -1-4). 28.50 *(978-1-60270-278-3(0)*, 13206, Looking Glass Library) Magic Wagon.

—Mighty Magnets, 1 vol. Higgins, Nadia. 2008. (Science Rocks! Ser.). (ENG.). 32p. (J). (gr. -1-4). 28.50 *(978-1-60270-279-0(9)*, 13208, Looking Glass Library) Magic Wagon.

—Stupendous Sound, 1 vol. Higgins, Nadia. 2008. (Science Rocks! Ser.). (ENG.). 32p. (J). (gr. -1-4). 28.50 *(978-1-60270-280-6(2)*, 13210, Looking Glass Library) Magic Wagon.

—Super Shadows. Higgins, Nadia & National Geographic Learning Staff. 2008. (Science Rocks! Ser.). (ENG.). 32p. (J). (gr. -1-4). 28.50 *(978-1-60270-281-3(0)*, 13212, Looking Glass Library) Magic Wagon.

Ricci, Andrés Martínez. Zap! Wile E. Coyote Experiments with Energy, 1 vol. Slade, Suzanne. 2014. (Wile E. Coyote, Physical Science Genius Ser.). (ENG.). 32p. (J). (gr. 3-6). 31.32 *(978-1-4765-4223-2(6))*; pap. 8.95 *(978-1-4765-5214-9(2))* Capstone. (Capstone Pr.).

Ricciardi, Charles. The Night the Bullies Were Bullied! Ricciardi, Charles. 2018. (ENG.). 46p. (J). pap. 10.99 *(978-0-9996986-1-7(3))* Ricciardi, Charles.

Riccio, Frank. Baseball for Breakfast: The Story of a Boy Who Hated to Wait. Myers, Bill. 2005. 29p. (J). (gr. 4-8). reprint ed. 15.00 *(978-0-7567-9248-0(7))* DIANE Publishing Co.

—The Little Soul & the Earth: I'm Somebody! Walsch, Neale Donald. 2005. (ENG.). 32p. (J). 20.00 *(978-1-57174-451-7(7))* Hampton Roads Publishing Co., Inc.

—Milton's Secret: An Adventure of Discovery Through Then, When, & the Power of Now. Tolle, Eckhart & Friedman, Robert S. 2008. (ENG.). 40p. (J). (gr. 3-7). 18.95 *(978-1-57174-577-4(7))* Hampton Roads Publishing Co., Inc.

Rice, Christie. The Spring Celebration, 1 vol. Umpherville, Tina. 2015. (ENG.). 32p. (Orig.). (J). (gr. 1-2). mass mkt. 10.95 *(978-0-921827-46-7(6)*, 1a2481c7-9a1b-4539-b7cd-5d00f3998955) Pemmican Pubns., Inc. CAN. Dist: Firefly Bks., Ltd.

Rice, Doug. The Magic Is Me. Rice, Donna. 2012. 34p. (J). mass mkt. 15.99 *(978-1-936497-16-4(6))* Searchlight Pr.

Rice, James. Country Music Night Before Christmas, 1 vol. Turner, Thomas N. 2003. (Night Before Christmas Ser.). (ENG.). 32p. (J). (gr. k-3). 16.99 *(978-1-58980-148-6(2)*, Pelican Publishing) Arcadia Publishing.

—Gaston Joins the Circus, 1 vol. 2015. (Gaston Ser.). (ENG.). 32p. (J). (gr. k-3). pap. 9.95 *(978-1-4556-2092-0(0)*, Pelican Publishing) Arcadia Publishing.

—Gaston® Joins the Circus, 1 vol. 2015. (Gaston Ser.). (ENG.). 32p. (J). (gr. k-3). 16.99 *(978-1-4556-2129-3(3)*, Pelican Publishing) Arcadia Publishing.

—An Irish Night Before Christmas, 1 vol. Blazek, Sarah Kirwan. 2009. (Night Before Christmas Ser.). (ENG.). 32p. (J). (gr. k-3). pap. 3.95 *(978-1-58980-704-4(9)*, Pelican Publishing) Arcadia Publishing.

—Nurse's Night Before Christmas, 1 vol. Davis, David. 2003. (Night Before Christmas Ser.). (ENG.). 32p. (J). (gr. k-3). 16.99 *(978-1-58980-152-3(0)*, Pelican Publishing) Arcadia Publishing.

—Ozark Night Before Christmas, 1 vol. McWilliams, Amanda & Moore, Clement C. 2004. (Night Before Christmas Ser.). (ENG.). 32p. (J). (gr. k-3). 16.99 *(978-1-58980-056-4(7)*, Pelican Publishing) Arcadia Publishing.

—The Principal's Night Before Christmas, 1 vol. Layne, Steven. 2004. (Night Before Christmas Ser.). (ENG.). 32p. (J). (gr. k-3). 16.99 *(978-1-58980-252-0(7)*, Pelican Publishing) Arcadia Publishing.

Rice, James. Gaston® Goes to Texas, 1 vol. Rice, James. 2007. (Gaston Ser.). (ENG.). 32p. (J). (gr. 1-3). 16.99 *(978-1-58980-531-6(3)*, Pelican Publishing) Arcadia Publishing.

—Gaston® Lays an Offshore Pipeline, 1 vol. Rice, James. 2007. (Gaston Ser.). (ENG.). 32p. (J). (gr. k-3). 16.99 *(978-1-58980-510-1(0)*, Pelican Publishing) Arcadia Publishing.

—Lyn & the Fuzzy, 1 vol. Rice, James. 2007. (ENG.). 40p. (J). (gr. k-3). 17.99 *(978-1-58980-508-8(9)*, Pelican Publishing) Arcadia Publishing.

—Santa's Revenge, 1 vol. Rice, James. 2005. (Night Before Christmas Ser.). (ENG.). 32p. (J). (gr. k-3). 16.99 *(978-1-58980-250-6(0)*, Pelican Publishing) Arcadia Publishing.

—Too Tall Thomas Rides the Grub Line, 1 vol. Rice, James. 2004. (ENG.). 32p. (J). (gr. k-3). 16.99 *(978-1-58980-177-6(6)*, Pelican Publishing) Arcadia Publishing.

Rice, James. Trail Boss: J. M. Daugherty. Rice, James, tr. 2003. (J). *(978-1-57168-769-2(6)*, Eakin Pr.) Eakin Pr.

Rice, John. What Happened to the Mammoths? And Other Explorations of Science in Action. Myers, Jack. 2004. (ENG.). 64p. (gr. 4-7). per. 11.95 *(978-1-59078-280-4(1))* Boyds Mills Pr.

Rice, Kaleb & Deasey, Kevin. The Day Kyle Met Nuf. Porrata, Mayra. 2013. 28p. pap. 12.95 *(978-0-9825480-2-8(8))* Sunny Day Publishing, LLC.

Rice, Rob. Effie's Chance to Dance. Dolcimascolo, Gelia. 2018. (ENG.). 48p. (J). (gr. k-3). pap. 10.00 *(978-0-9972158-1-6(X))* Autumn Gold Pr.

—I, Ixodes, the Mighty Tick: My True Story. Cox, Barbara G. 2017. (ENG.). (J). pap. 9.99 *(978-0-9973745-4-4(3))* Windhorse Bks.

Rice, Taj William. The Art of Taj: Colouring Book Volume 1. Rice, Taj William. 2019. (Art of Taj Ser.: Vol. 1). (ENG.). 26p. (J). pap. 12.99 *(978-1-0722-7720-0(4))* Independently Published.

Rich, Anna. Blacksmith's Song, 1 vol. Steenwyk, Elizabeth Van. 2018. (ENG.). 32p. (J). (gr. 1-5). 17.95 *(978-1-56145-580-5(6))* Peachtree Publishing Co. Inc.

—Coretta Scott King: Dare to Dream. Medearis, Angela Shelf. 2014. (Women of Our Time Ser.). (ENG.). 96p. (J). (gr. 3-7). 7.99 *(978-0-14-751363-2(4)*, Puffin Books) Penguin Young Readers Group.

—Joshua's Masai Mask, 1 vol. Hru, Dakari. 2013. (ENG.). 32p. (J). (gr. 1-4). pap. 10.95 *(978-1-880000-32-8(6)*, e6c9aa32-ad5e-43bf-9735-e094045f636f) Lee & Low Bks., Inc.

—Saturday at the New You, 1 vol. Barber, Barbara E. 2013. (ENG.). 32p. (J). (gr. 1-4). reprint ed. pap. 10.95 *(978-1-880000-43-4(1)*, c63af135-6506-4cba-a0c9-7a4258e7b8e3) Lee & Low Bks., Inc.

Rich, Bobbie. The Running Nose Book. Rich, Carol Bak. 2013. (ENG.). 41p. (J). pap. 9.95 *(978-1-4787-0062-3(9))* Outskirts Pr., Inc.

Rich, Christie. Captive of Dreams. Rich, Christie. Nottingham, Chase, ed. 2019. (Netherworld Ser.: Vol. 2). (ENG.). 346p. (J). pap. 14.99 ***(978-1-6887-7633-3(8))*** Independently Published.

—Keeper of Dreams. Rich, Christie. Nottingham, Chase, ed. 2019. (Netherworld Ser.: Vol. 3). (ENG.). 322p. (J). pap. 14.99 ***(978-1-6891-5483-3(7))*** Independently Published.

—Warrior of Dreams. Rich, Christie. Nottingham, Chase, ed. 2019. (Netherworld Ser.: Vol. 4). (ENG.). 380p. (J). pap. 14.99 ***(978-1-6891-6050-6(0))*** Independently Published.

—Weaver of Dreams. Rich, Christie. Circelli, Kristina, ed. 2019. (Netherworld Ser.: Vol. 1). (ENG.). 330p. (J). pap. 14.99 ***(978-1-6887-6050-9(4))*** Independently Published.

Rich, Graham. Brain Boosters: Adding & Subtracting Activities. Worms, Penny. 2019. (Brain Boosters Ser.: 6). (ENG.). 96p. (J). pap. 7.99 *(978-1-78950-604-4(2)*, d2d009e5-18bc-4ca3-8326-b93544f37cd4) Arcturus Publishing GBR. Dist: Baker & Taylor Publisher Services (BTPS).

—Brain Boosters: Times Tables Activities. Worms, Penny. 2019. (Brain Boosters Ser.: 7). (ENG.). 96p. (J). pap. 7.99 *(978-1-78950-609-9(3)*, 080d8a43-f319-4e8e-a88a-50a4ea4129b0) Arcturus Publishing GBR. Dist: Baker & Taylor Publisher Services (BTPS).

Rich, Sarita. Daddy, Me, & the Magic Hour. Melmed, Laura Krauss. 2018. 32p. (J). (gr. -1-k). 16.99 *(978-1-5107-0791-7(3)*, Sky Pony Pr.) Skyhorse Publishing Co., Inc.

—Hypnosis Harry. Bailey, Catherine. 2016. 40p. (J). (gr. -1-k). 16.99 *(978-1-63450-171-2(3)*, Sky Pony Pr.) Skyhorse Publishing Co., Inc.

Richa Kinra. Debra Meets Her Best Friend in Kindergarten. Debra Maymon. 2009. 36p. pap. 15.49 *(978-1-4389-6261-0(4))* AuthorHouse.

Richard, Ilene. The Author with the Fancy Purple Pen. Williams, Rozanne Lanczak. (Learn to Write Ser.). 16p. (J). 2007. (gr. -1-3). pap. 8.99 *(978-1-59198-346-0(0))*; 2006. (gr. k-2). pap. 2.99 *(978-1-59198-299-9(5)*, 6189) Creative Teaching Pr., Inc.

—Here Comes the Parade. Mishica, Clare. 2005. (Rookie Readers Ser.). (ENG.). 24p. (J). (gr. k-2). lib. bdg. 19.50 *(978-0-516-24857-8(X)*, Children's Pr.) Scholastic Library Publishing.

—Let My People Go!, Vol. Balsley, Tilda. 2008. (ENG.). 32p. (J). (gr. k-3). per. 7.99 *(978-0-8225-7241-1(9)*, Kar-Ben Publishing) Lerner Publishing Group.

—Luke & Leo Build a Limerick. Mataya, Marybeth. 2011. (Poetry Builders Ser.). 32p. (J). (gr. 2-4). lib. bdg. 25.27 *(978-1-59953-436-7(3))* Norwood Hse. Pr.

—The Queen Who Saved Her People, Vol. Balsley, Tilda. 2011. (ENG.). 32p. (J). (gr. 3-5). pap. 7.99 *(978-0-7613-5093-4(4)*, 9780761350934, Kar-Ben Publishing) Lerner Publishing Group.

—The Teacher with the Alligator Purse, Vol. 4259. Williams, Rozanne Lanczak. 2005. (Reading for Fluency Ser.). 16p. (J). pap. 3.49 *(978-1-59198-159-6(X))* Creative Teaching Pr., Inc.

Richard, Ilene, jt. illus. see Stott, Dorothy.

Richard, Keisha Luana. The Travels of Kui, the African Spurred Tortoise. Lynch, Stephen D. 2007. 36p. per. 24.95 *(978-1-4137-1802-7(7))* America Star Bks.

Richard, Laurent. Faster, Please! Vehicles on the Go. Leblanc, Catherine. 2020. (ENG.). 16p. (J). bds. 12.99 ***(978-0-7643-6032-9(9)***, 24683) Schiffer Publishing, Ltd.

Richard, P. M. Animals Animales: A Bilingual ABC Book for all Readers. Stanton, Laura. 2014. 32p. (J). 9.95 *(978-0-9860734-0-3(7))* Echo Valley Pr.

—Squirt the Otter: The True Story of an Orphaned Otter who Finds Friendship & Happiness. Mikowski, Tracy L. 2013. 32p. (J). 16.95 *(978-0-9860287-0-0(3))* Talking Crow Publishing.

Richards, C. E. King Arthur. 2010. (Classic Fiction Ser.). 72p. 4.75 *(978-1-4342-2603-7(4)*, Stone Arch Bks.) Capstone.

Richards, Charles. Bardolph Bedivere Wolf Returns. Richards, Pat. 2007. 42p. (J). *(978-0-9790796-4-1(0))* PJR Assocs., Ltd.

Richards, George M. Outdoor Visits (Yesterday's Classics) Patch, Edith M. & Howe, Harrison E. l.t. ed. 2018. (Nature & Science Readers Ser.: Vol. 2). (ENG.). 228p. (J). (gr. 1-3). pap. 11.95 *(978-1-63334-096-1(1))* Yesterday's Classics.

Richards, Ian, photos by. A Friend Like Iggy, 1 vol. Cole, Kathryn. 2019. (ENG., 32p. (J). (gr. 1-3). 18.95 *(978-1-77260-084-1(9))* Second Story Pr. CAN. Dist: Orca Bk. Pubs. USA.

Richards, Jon. Cosmo: A Cautionary Tale. Arkin, Alan. 2005. 40p. (J). 19.95 *(978-1-929115-12-9(1))* Azro Pr., Inc.

Richards, Kirsten. Big Brothers Are the Best, 1 vol. Manushkin, Fran. 2012. (Fiction Picture Bks.). (ENG.). 24p. (J). (gr. -1 — 1). 6.95 *(978-1-4048-7224-0(8))*; lib. bdg. 22.65 *(978-1-4048-7137-3(3))* Capstone. (Picture Window Bks.).

—Big Sisters Are the Best, 1 vol. Manushkin, Fran. 2012. (Fiction Picture Bks.). (ENG.). 24p. (J). (gr. -1 — 1). 6.95 *(978-1-4048-7225-7(6))*; lib. bdg. 22.65 *(978-1-4048-7138-0(1))* Capstone. (Picture Window Bks.).

—Count to 10 with a Mouse. Brown, Margaret Wise. (Margaret Wise Brown Classics Ser.). (ENG.). (J). (gr. -1-k). 2020. 28p. bds. 7.99 *(978-1-68412-966-9(4))*; 2019. 32p. 12.99 *(978-1-68412-741-2(6))* Printers Row Publishing Group. (Silver Dolphin Bks.).

—Easter Parade! Karr, Lily. 2013. (J). *(978-0-545-56401-4(8)*, Cartwheel Bks.) Scholastic, Inc.

—The Littlest Elf. Dougherty, Brandi. 2012. (Littlest Ser.). (ENG.). 24p. (J). (gr. -1-k). pap. 4.99 *(978-0-545-43654-0(0))* Scholastic, Inc.

—The Littlest Pilgrim. Dougherty, Brandi. 2008. (ENG.). 32p. (J). (gr. -1-k). pap. 3.99 *(978-0-545-05372-3(2)*, Cartwheel Bks.) Scholastic, Inc.

—Magical Mermaids. Trowell, Michelle. Top That Publishing Staff, ed. 2008. (Magnetic Story & Play Scene Ser.). 9p. (J). (gr. -1). *(978-1-84666-442-7(X)*, Tide Mill Pr.) Top That! Publishing PLC.

—My Little Beauty Shop: A Girly Girl Book. 2009. (ENG.). 12p. (J). bds. 6.95 *(978-1-58117-857-9(3)*, Intervisual/Piggy Toes) Bendon, Inc.

—My Pets, 1 vol. Dale, Jay. 2012. (Wonder Words Ser.). (ENG.). 32p. (gr. k-2). pap. 5.99 *(978-1-4296-8886-4(6)*, Capstone Pr.) Capstone.

—Woodland Fairies. Ranson, Erin. Top That Publishing Staff, ed. 2008. (Magnetic Story & Play Scene Ser.). 9p. (J). (gr. -1). bds. *(978-1-84666-440-3(3)*, Tide Mill Pr.) Top That! Publishing PLC.

Richards, Kirsten. Easter Parade! Richards, Kirsten. Karr, Lily. 2013. (ENG.). 24p. (J). (gr. -1-k). pap. 4.99 *(978-0-545-45824-5(2)*, Cartwheel Bks.) Scholastic, Inc.

Richards, Kris. Rusty's Gift. Springer, Audrey. 2012. 28p. 24.95 *(978-1-4626-6589-1(6))* America Star Bks.

Richards, Kristen. The Littlest Elf. Dougherty, Brandi. 2012. (J). pap. *(978-0-545-48978-2(4)*, WestBow Pr.) Scholastic, Inc.

Richards, Lucas. Lizzie's Lesson. Morrison-Andrews, Sharalyn. 2016. (ENG.). (J). 19.95 *(978-0-9975343-1-3(1))*; pap. 12.95 *(978-0-9975343-0-6(3))* Morrison-Andrews, Sharalyn.

Richards, Lucy. Animal Antics (with Header Card) 2004. (Cuddly Cuffs Ser.: No. 5). 10p. (J). tchr. ed. 5.95 *(978-1-58925-729-0(4))* Tiger Tales.

—Busy Bugs (W/Header Card) 2004. (Cuddly Cuffs Ser.: 6). 12p. (J). tchr. ed. 5.95 *(978-1-58925-730-6(8))* Tiger Tales.

—Jumping Jungle (W/Hang Tag) 2004. (Cuddly Cuffs Ser.: No. 7). 12p. (J). tchr. ed. 5.95 *(978-1-58925-727-6(8))* Tiger Tales.

—Jumping Jungle (W/Header Card) 2004. (Cuddly Cuffs Ser.: 7). 6p. (J). tchr. ed. 5.95 *(978-1-58925-731-3(6))* Tiger Tales.

—Night Monkey, Day Monkey. Donaldson, Julia. 2016. (ENG.). 26p. (J). (gr. -1-k). bds. 10.99 *(978-1-4052-8334-2(3))* Egmont Bks., Ltd. GBR. Dist: Independent Pubs. Group.

—Night Monkey, Day Monkey Magnet Book. Donaldson, Julia. 2019. (ENG.). 40p. (J). (gr. -1-k). 14.99 *(978-1-4052-8876-7(0))* Egmont Bks., Ltd. GBR. Dist: Independent Pubs. Group.

Richards, Lucy. Mairi's Mermaid. Richards, Lucy. Morpurgo, Michael. 2nd ed. 2016. (Reading Ladder Ser.). (ENG.). 48p. (J). (gr. k-2). pap. 7.99 *(978-1-4052-8201-7(0))* Egmont Bks., Ltd. GBR. Dist: Independent Pubs. Group.

—The Quick Brown Fox Cub. Richards, Lucy. Donaldson, Julia. 2nd ed. 2016. (Reading Ladder Ser.). (ENG.). 48p. (J). (gr. k-2). pap. 7.99 *(978-1-4052-8240-6(1))* Egmont Bks., Ltd. GBR. Dist: Independent Pubs. Group.

Richards, Lucy & Finn, Rebecca. Silly Sea (W/Hang Tag) 2004. (Cuddly Cuffs Ser.: No. 8). 10p. (J). tchr. ed. 5.95 *(978-1-58925-728-3(6))* Tiger Tales.

—Silly Sea (W/Header Card) 2004. (Cuddly Cuffs Ser.: 8). 10p. (J). tchr. ed. 5.95 *(978-1-58925-732-0(4))* Tiger Tales.

Richards, Steve & Farnsworth, Lauren. Hooray for Hexagons. Richards, Steve. 2018. (ENG.). 64p. (J). (gr. 3-7). pap. 9.99 *(978-1-78055-495-2(8))* O'Mara, Michael Bks., Ltd. GBR. Dist: Independent Pubs. Group.

Richards, Tanya. Let's Bake a Family. Paulin, Chrita. Burns, Rosalyn, ed. 2009. (ENG.). 32p. (J). pap. 12.95 *(978-0-9763400-1-0(1))* Coal Under Pr.ure, LLC.

Richards, Theodora. Gus & Me: The Story of My Granddad & My First Guitar. Richards, Keith. 2014. (ENG.). 32p. (J). (gr. -1-3). 18.00 *(978-0-316-32065-8(X))* Little, Brown Bks. for Young Readers.

Richards, Virginia Helen. The Beatitudes Coloring & Activity Book. Halpin, D. Thomas. 2006. (J). 1.95 *(978-0-8198-2359-5(7))* Pauline Bks. & Media.

—Feast Days & Holy Days: Dias Festivos de la Iglesia. Tebo, Mary Elizabeth. 2007. 32p. (J). lab manual ed. 1.95 *(978-0-8198-2682-4(0))* Pauline Bks. & Media.

—Holy Eucharist. Halpin, D. Thomas. 2005. 32p. (J). (gr. 4-7). 1.95 *(978-0-8198-3387-7(8)*, 332-425) Pauline Bks. & Media.

—No Room for Francie. MacDonald, Maryann. 2010. 64p. (J). (gr. 1-3). pap. 6.95 *(978-0-8198-5168-0(X))* Pauline Bks. & Media.

—Spotlight on Saints! A Year of Funny Readers Theater for Today's Catholic Kids. Jenkins, Diana R. 2009. 180p. (J). (gr. 4-7). pap. 18.95 *(978-0-8198-7119-0(2))* Pauline Bks. & Media.

—Starring Francie O'Leary. MacDonald, Maryann. 2010. 64p. (J). (gr. 1-3). pap. 6.95 *(978-0-8198-7132-9(X))* Pauline Bks. & Media.

—The Stations of the Cross for Children. Dateno, Maria Grace. Pompei, Maria Teresa, tr. 2006. (SPA.). 24p. (J). 1.25 *(978-0-8198-7095-7(1))* Pauline Bks. & Media.

Richards, Virginia Helen & Dick, Regina Frances. I Pray the Rosary! Scarfi, Margaret Rose. 2005. 47p. (J). (gr. -1-3). pap. 4.95 *(978-0-8198-3689-2(3)*, 332-141) Pauline Bks. & Media.

Richards, Virginia Helen & Halpin, D. Thomas. Blessed Miguel Pro. 2011. (J). pap. 2.95 *(978-0-8198-1192-9(0))* Pauline Bks. & Media.

—My Christmas Picture Book. 2005. 14p. (J). 4.95 *(978-0-8198-4829-1(8)*, 332-220) Pauline Bks. & Media.

—The Ten Commandments. Richards, Virginia Helen. 2007. (J). 1.95 *(978-0-8198-7420-7(5))* Pauline Bks. & Media.

Richards, Virginia Helen, jt. illus. see Halpin, D. Thomas.

Richardson, Cathie. The Christmas Tin. Eismann, Sheila F. & Putz, Ali F. 2013. 40p. pap. 9.95 *(978-0-9897133-8-2(5))* Desert Sage Pr.

Richardson, Doris, jt. illus. see Byj, Charlot.

Richardson, Frederick. East O' the Sun & West O' the Moon. Thorne-Thomsen, Gudrun. 2009. 148p. pap. 8.95 *(978-1-59915-337-7(8))* Yesterday's Classics.

—Mother Goose: A Classic Collection of Children's Nursery Rhymes. 2008. (ENG.). 24p. (J). 19.95 *(978-1-58117-687-2(2)*, Intervisual/Piggy Toes) Bendon, Inc.

—Mother Goose: More Than 100 Famous Rhymes! Grover, Eulalie Osgood. 2017. (Children's Classic Collections). (ENG.). 144p. (J). (gr. -1-3). 12.99 *(978-1-944686-09-3(6)*, Racehorse Publishing) Skyhorse Publishing Co., Inc.

—My Animal Story Book: A Treasury of Sunshine Stories for Children. Maltby, Ethel H. 2004. reprint ed. pap. 15.95 *(978-1-4191-7300-4(6))* Kessinger Publishing, LLC.

—Reading-Literature Second Reader. Treadwell, Harriette Taylor & Free, Margaret. 2008. 200p. pap. 9.95 *(978-1-59915-266-0(5))* Yesterday's Classics.

—Reading-Literature the Primer (Yesterday's Classics) Treadwell, Harriette Taylor & Free, Margaret. 2006. (J). per. 8.95 *(978-1-59915-129-8(4))* Yesterday's Classics.

—Reading-Literature Third Reader. Treadwell, Harriette Taylor & Free, Margaret. 2008. 264p. pap. 10.95 *(978-1-59915-267-7(3))* Yesterday's Classics.

Richardson, Frederick & Becker, Charlotte. The Flying Ship: Fairy Tales from the World Over. Faulkner, Georgene. 2011. 100p. 39.95 *(978-1-258-10171-8(8))* Literary Licensing, LLC.

—The Snow Maiden: Fairy Tales from the World Over. Faulkner, Georgene. 2011. 104p. 39.95 *(978-1-258-10524-2(1))* Literary Licensing, LLC.

—Squeaky & the Scare Box: Fairy Tales from the World Over. Faulkner, Georgene. 2011. 96p. 38.95 *(978-1-258-10158-9(0))* Literary Licensing, LLC.

Richardson-Jones, Tessa. Noah's Ark. Umansky, Kaye. 2012. *(978-0-88734-071-0(7))* Players Pr., Inc.

—Y Ddihangfa Anhygoel! Llyfr Drysfa Beiblaidd. Stowell, Gordon. Davies, Aled, ed. Wyn, Delyth, tr. 2005. (WEL.). 12p. *(978-1-85994-469-1(8))* Cyhoeddiadau'r Gair.

Richardson, Kae. Twinkle the Elf: A Copycat Who Finds Herself. Beere, Lisa. 2017. (ENG.). 34p. (J). (gr. k-5). pap. 9.49 *(978-1-68160-470-1(1))* Crimson Cloak Publishing.

Richardson, Kara. The Adventures of NanaCat & Her Children: Moving In. Moon, Catherine R. & Everette, Maureen C. 2003. 32p. (J). 6.95 *(978-0-930507-06-0(1))* GRAND Media, LLC.

—The Adventures of NanaCat & Her Children: Someone New. Moon, Catherine R. & Everette, Maureen C. 2004. 32p. (J). per. 6.95 *(978-0-930507-02-2(9))* GRAND Media, LLC.

Richardson, Kara. Little Bucket Beach Hat. Dundy, Melanie Richardson. 2019. (ENG.). 38p. (J). (gr. k-3). 24.95 ***(978-0-578-54083-2(5))*** M D C T Publishing.

Richardson, Kara. Simon & Barklee in Egypt. Scherer, Catherine W. 2006. (Another Country Calling Ser.). 65p. (J). per. 15.00 *(978-0-9714502-3-3(4)*, Explorer Media) Simon & Barklee, Inc./ExplorerMedia.

—Simon & Barklee in West Africa. Scherer, Catherine W. 2006. (Another Country Calling Ser.). 80p. (J). per. 15.00 *(978-0-9714502-4-0(2)*, Explorer Media) Simon & Barklee, Inc./ExplorerMedia.

Richardson, Kayla. Skip & Marty. Richardson, Levae. 2007. 20p. per. 24.95 *(978-1-4241-8469-9(X))* America Star Bks.

Richardson, Linda. Sea Treasure. Evans, Sally. 2004. (J). 16.95 *(978-1-59094-073-0(3)*, 1590940733, Jawbreakers for Kids) Jawbone Publishing Corp.

Richardson, Markayla & Cosley, Jamie. Punique's First Day of School. Hall, Richard. 2016. (ENG.). 32p. (J). (gr. k-5). pap. 10.00 *(978-0-692-07897-6(5))* Richard Hall II.

Richardson, Mike. Grandma's Crazy Chickens. Snyder, Susan E. 2012. 34p. (J). 14.95 *(978-0-9846428-8-5(9))* FireFly Publishings & Entertainment LLC.

Richardson, Owen. Bravelands #1: Broken Pride. Hunter, Erin. (Bravelands Ser.: 1). (ENG.). (J). (gr. 3-7). 2018. 352p. pap. 7.99 *(978-0-06-264204-2(9))*; 2017. 336p. 16.99 *(978-0-06-264202-8(2))*; 2017. 336p. lib. bdg. 17.89 *(978-0-06-264203-5(0))* HarperCollins Pubs.

—Iron Man: the Gauntlet. Colfer, Eoin. 2017. (ENG.). 288p. (J). (gr. 3-7). pap. 9.99 *(978-1-368-00851-8(8)*, Marvel Pr.) Disney Publishing Worldwide.

—Muppets Meet the Classics: the Phantom of the Opera. Jackson, Erik Forrest & Leroux, Gaston. 2017. (ENG.). 304p. 12.99 *(978-0-451-53437-8(9)*, Penguin Workshop) Penguin Young Readers Group.

—Unnaturals: the Battle Begins. Hughes, Devon. (Unnaturals Ser.: 1). (ENG.). (J). (gr. 3-7). 2017. 368p. pap. 6.99 *(978-0-06-225755-0(2)*, Tegen, Katherine Bks); 2015. 352p. 16.99 *(978-0-06-225754-3(4))* HarperCollins Pubs.

Richardson, Owen & Douglas, Allen. Warriors: Omen of the Stars #1: the Fourth Apprentice. Hunter, Erin. (Warriors: Omen of the Stars Ser.: 1). (ENG.). (J). (gr. 3-7). 2015. 384p. pap. 7.99 *(978-0-06-238257-3(8))*; 2009. 352p. 16.99 *(978-0-06-155509-1(6))* HarperCollins Pubs.

—Warriors: Omen of the Stars #2: Fading Echoes. Hunter, Erin. (Warriors: Omen of the Stars Ser.: 2). (ENG.). (J). (gr. 3-7). 2015. 384p. pap. 7.99 *(978-0-06-238259-7(4))*; 2010. 352p. 16.99 *(978-0-06-155512-1(6))* HarperCollins Pubs.

—Warriors: Omen of the Stars #3: Night Whispers. Hunter, Erin. (Warriors: Omen of the Stars Ser.: 3). (ENG.). (J). (gr. 3-7). 2015. 368p. pap. 7.99 *(978-0-06-238260-3(8))*; 2010. 352p. 16.99 *(978-0-06-155515-2(0))* HarperCollins Pubs.

—Warriors: Omen of the Stars #4: Sign of the Moon. Hunter, Erin. (Warriors: Omen of the Stars Ser.: 4). (ENG.). (J). (gr. 3-7). 2015. 368p. pap. 7.99 *(978-0-06-238261-0(6))*; 2011. 352p. 16.99 *(978-0-06-155518-3(5))* HarperCollins Pubs.

—Warriors: Omen of the Stars #5: the Forgotten Warrior. Hunter, Erin. (Warriors: Omen of the Stars Ser.: 5). (ENG.). (J). (gr. 3-7). 2015. 384p. pap. 7.99 *(978-0-06-238262-7(4))*; 2011. 368p. 16.99 *(978-0-06-155522-0(3))* HarperCollins Pubs.

—Warriors: Omen of the Stars #6: the Last Hope. Hunter, Erin. (Warriors: Omen of the Stars Ser.: 6). (ENG.). (J). (gr. 3-7). 2015. 400p. pap. 7.99 *(978-0-06-238263-4(2))*; 2012. 384p. 16.99 *(978-0-06-155527-5(4))* HarperCollins Pubs.

Richardson, Owen & Marvel Press Artist. Iron Man: the Gauntlet. Colfer, Eoin. 2016. (ENG.). 288p. (J). (gr. 3-7). 16.99 *(978-1-4847-4160-3(9)*, Marvel Pr.) Disney Publishing Worldwide.

Richardson, Owen, jt. illus. see Barry, James L.

Richardson, Penny. Haida Gwaii Treasures: Ali. Larocque, Donna-Lee. Salter, Amy Jo, ed. 2020. (Haida Gwaii Treasures Ser.: Vol. 1). (ENG.). 58p. (J). pap. ***(978-0-9949552-4-1(3))*** Mermaid Publishing.

—Haida Gwaii Treasures: Hunter. Larocque, Donna-Lee. Salter, Amy Jo, ed. 2020. (Haida Gwaii Treasures Ser.: Vol. 7). (ENG.). 58p. (J). pap. ***(978-0-9949552-8-9(6))*** Mermaid Publishing.

—Haida Gwaii Treasures: Issy. Larocque, Donna-Lee. Salter, Amy Jo, ed. 2020. (Haida Gwaii Treasures Ser.: Vol. 4). (ENG.). 58p. (J). pap. ***(978-0-9949552-7-2(8))*** Mermaid Publishing.

—Haida Gwaii Treasures: Luke. Larocque, Donna-Lee. Salter, Amy Jo, ed. 2020. (Haida Gwaii Treasures Ser.: Vol. 3). (ENG.). 58p. (J). pap. ***(978-0-9949552-6-5(X))*** Mermaid Publishing.

—Haida Gwaii Treasures: Stephie. Larocque, Donna-Lee. Salter, Amy Jo, ed. 2020. (Haida Gwaii Treasures Ser.: Vol. 2). (ENG.). 58p. (J). pap. ***(978-0-9949552-5-8(1))*** Mermaid Publishing.

Richardson, Peter. Solving Crimes with Trace Evidence. Jeffrey, Gary. 2008. (Graphic Forensic Science Ser.). (ENG.). 48p. (gr. 5-8). per. 14.05 *(978-1-4042-1432-3(1))*; (YA). lib. bdg. 35.45 *(978-1-4042-1431-6(3))* Rosen Publishing Group, Inc., The.

Richburg, Justin. Stop the Habit: A Guide for Youth Who Struggle with Trichotillomania. Farrington, Catinia. 2018. (ENG.). 42p. (YA). (gr. 8-12). 16.95 *(978-0-692-12809-1(3))* AR Thomas Publishing.

Riches, Aiden Vc. The Story of Kitty Girl: Created Together by a School Bus Driver & a Special Needs Student. Hanson, Sherry a. 2018. (ENG.). 28p. (J). pap. 9.95 *(978-1-9776-8294-9(4))* CreateSpace Independent Publishing Platform.

Riches Hall, Sara. Futuro: A Fable about Your Transformational Power. Bell, Michael J. 2017. (Futuro Cosmos Ser.: Vol. 1). (ENG.). 122p. (YA). pap. *(978-0-9957694-0-3(0))* Bell, Michael J.

Richie, Morgan W. The Sensitive Pirate. Richie, Morgan W. 2018. (ENG.). 48p. (J). (gr. k-2). pap. 8.99 *(978-0-692-06695-9(0))* Richie, Morgan W.

Richmond, Bob, jt. illus. see Gowens, Kyle.

Richmond, Jake. The CrossRoads of Eternity RPG: Core Rule Book. 2005. per. 24.99 *(978-0-9769951-0-4(7))* Arcadiam Games.

Richmond, Jamea. Grandma's Biscuits. Little, Robert. 2004. 32p. (J). (gr. -1-7). 15.95 *(978-0-9701863-5-5(5))* Rekle Publishing.

Richmond, Kip. Can You Hear Him Whisper? Kenny, Eileen. 2019. (ENG.). 34p. (J). (gr. k-4). 18.99 ***(978-0-578-54297-3(8))*** In Eileens Words.

Richmond, Lori. A Hop Is Up. Dempsey, Kristy. 2016. 40p. (J). 16.99 *(978-1-61963-390-2(6)*, 900135695, Bloomsbury USA Childrens) Bloomsbury Publishing USA.

—Oopsie-Do! Kubart, Tim. 2018. (ENG.). 32p. (J). (gr. -1-3). 17.99 *(978-0-06-257303-2(9))* HarperCollins Pubs.

—Pinky Got Out! Portis, Michael. 2019. 40p. (J). (gr. -1-2). 17.99 *(978-1-101-93298-8(8))*; (ENG.). lib. bdg. 20.99 *(978-1-101-93299-5(6))* Random Hse. Children's Bks. (Crown Books For Young Readers).

—Skelly's Halloween. Martin, David. 2018. (ENG.). 32p. (J). 16.99 *(978-1-250-12706-8(8)*, 900175312, Holt, Henry & Co. Bks. For Young Readers) Holt, Henry & Co.

Richmond, Lori. Pax & Blue. Richmond, Lori. 2017. (ENG.). 32p. (J). (gr. -1-3). 17.99 *(978-1-4814-5132-1(4)*, Simon & Schuster/Paula Wiseman Bks.) Simon & Schuster/Paula Wiseman Bks.

Richmond, Marianne. Big Boys Go Potty. Richmond, Marianne. 2012. (ENG.). 32p. (J). 9.99 *(978-1-4022-6659-1(6)*, Sourcebooks Jabberwocky) Sourcebooks, Inc.

—Big Girls Go Potty. Richmond, Marianne. 2012. 32p. (J). 9.99 *(978-1-4022-6662-1(6)*, Sourcebooks Jabberwocky) Sourcebooks, Inc.

—The Night Night Book. Richmond, Marianne. 2011. (Marianne Richmond Ser.: 0). 24p. (J). (gr. -1-3). bds. 7.95 *(978-1-934082-90-4(2)*, Sourcebooks Jabberwocky) Sourcebooks, Inc.

Richoll, Stephanie. Mrs. Mumford's Missing. DeLong, Lucianne. 2013. (Saloman Sawdust's Snappy Stories Ser.). (ENG.). 24p. (J). 4.99 *(978-0-9833237-5-4(5))* Krullstone Publishing, LLC.

Richter, Bernd. Listen to Alaskas Animals. Richter, Bernd. Richter, Susan. 12p. 2006. (J). act. bk. ed. 12.95 *(978-1-931353-25-0(5))*; 2003. bds. 12.95 *(978-1-931353-12-0(3))* Saddle Pal Creations, Inc.

Richter, Cheryl R., photos by. From Clay to Bricks. Taus-Bolstad, Stacy. 2003. (Start to Finish Ser.). (ENG., 24p. (J). (gr. k-3). lib. bdg. 19.93 *(978-0-8225-4663-4(9))* Lerner Publishing Group.

Richter, Hank. Little Critters. Sio, Betsy Menson. 2003. (Books for Young Learners). (ENG.). 16p. (J). 5.75 net. *(978-1-57274-532-2(0)*, 2458, Bks. for Young Learners) Owen, Richard C. Pubs., Inc.

Richter, Jeff, photos by. White Deer: Ghost of the Forest. 2007. 96p. pap. 19.95 *(978-0-9741883-1-7(X))* Nature's Pr.

Richter, Kevin. Dust Fairy Tales: Absolutely Aggie. Eastman, Michelle R. 2019. (ENG.). 48p. (J). pap. 9.99 ***(978-1-7080-5624-7(6))*** Independently Published.

—The Legend of Dust Bunnies, a Fairy's Tale. Eastman, Michelle R. 2019. (ENG.). 48p. (J). pap. 9.99 ***(978-1-7099-3214-4(7))*** Independently Published.

Rickard, Scarlett. Billy Mcgee & Tiny Mcflea. Henderson, Neil G. 2019. (ENG.). 24p. (J). pap. ***(978-0-9957943-3-7(2))*** Gluepot Bks.

Rickenbaker, Becky Hyatt. Would You Salute? One Child's Story of the Holocaust. Steele, D. Kelley. 2006. 48p. (J). (gr. 4-6). 22.95 *(978-0-9711534-2-4(6))* Hidden Path Pubn., Inc.

Rickerty, Simon. I Don't Want to Be a Pea! Bonwill, Ann. 2012. (ENG.). 32p. (J). (gr. -1-1). 14.99 *(978-1-4424-3614-5(X)*, Atheneum Bks. for Young Readers) Simon & Schuster Children's Publishing.

—Ten Little Elves. Brownlow, Mike. 2016. (J). *(978-1-4351-6404-8(0))* Barnes & Noble, Inc.

—Ten Little Monsters. Brownlow, Michael. 2016. 30p. (J). *(978-1-4351-6405-5(9))* Barnes & Noble, Inc.

—Ten Little Princesses. Brownlow, Michael. 2014. (J). *(978-1-4351-5735-4(4))* Barnes & Noble, Inc.

—Ug-a-Lug: Four Cavemen & a Prehistoric Pencil. Lewis, Jill. 2014. (ENG.). 32p. (J). 16.99 *(978-1-4711-1728-2(6))* Simon & Schuster, Ltd. GBR. Dist: Simon & Schuster, Inc.

—The Yoga Ogre. Bently, Peter. 2012. (ENG.). 32p. (J). 15.99 *(978-1-84738-902-2(3))* Simon & Schuster, Ltd. GBR. Dist: Simon & Schuster, Inc.

Rickerty, Simon. The Crayon: A Colorful Tale about Friendship. Rickerty, Simon. 2014. (ENG.). 32p. (J). (gr. -1-2). 15.99 *(978-1-4814-0475-4(X)*, Aladdin) Simon & Schuster Children's Publishing.

—The Peanut: A Nutty Tale about Sharing. Rickerty, Simon. 2013. (ENG.). 40p. (J). (gr. -1-2). 15.99 *(978-1-4424-8364-4(4)*, Simon & Schuster/Paula Wiseman Bks.) Simon & Schuster/Paula Wiseman Bks.

Ricketts, Mark Scott. Happy Birthday, Maine. Plourde, Lynn. 2020. (ENG.). 40p. (J). (gr. -1-1). 18.95 *(978-1-60893-711-0(9))* Down East Bks.

Ricketts, William. Teenage Winter Sports Stories. Owen, Frank, ed. 2011. 254p. 46.95 *(978-1-258-10167-1(X))* Literary Licensing, LLC.

Ricks, Melissa. Planting More Than Pansies: A Fable about Love. Bess, Stacey. 2003. (J). 14.95 *(978-1-57008-893-3(4)*, Shadow Mountain) Shadow Mountain Publishing.

Ricks, Sam. The Best of Iggy. Barrows, Annie. 2020. (Iggy Ser.: 1). 144p. (J). (gr. 3-7). 13.99 *(978-1-9848-1330-5(7)*, G.P. Putnam's Sons Books for Young Readers) Penguin Young Readers Group.

—A Case of the Clones. Hopper, Ada. 2016. (DATA Set Ser.: 5). (ENG.). 128p. (J). (gr. k-4). pap. 5.99 *(978-1-4814-7113-8(9)*, Little Simon) Little Simon.

—A Case of the Clones. Hopper, Ada. ed. 2018. 127p. (J). (gr. 1-4). 15.96 *(978-1-64310-201-6(X))* Penworthy Co., LLC, The.

—Don't Disturb the Dinosaurs. Hopper, Ada. 2016. (DATA Set Ser.: 2). (ENG.). 128p. (J). (gr. k-4). pap. 5.99 *(978-1-4814-5731-6(4)*, Little Simon) Little Simon.

—Don't Disturb the Dinosaurs. Hopper, Ada. ed. 2018. 125p. (J). (gr. 1-4). 15.96 *(978-1-64310-198-9(6))* Penworthy Co., LLC, The.

—Don't Throw It to Mo! Adler, David A. 2015. (Mo Jackson Ser.: 1). (ENG.). 32p. (J). (gr. 1-2). 14.99 *(978-0-670-01631-0(4)*, Penguin Young Readers) Penguin Young Readers Group.

Ricks, Sam. Eerie Elementary, Books 1-4: a Branches Box Set. Brallier, Max & Chabert, Jack. 2020. (Eerie Elementary Ser.). (ENG.). (J). (gr. 1-3). 19.96 ***(978-1-338-67797-3(7))*** Scholastic, Inc.

Ricks, Sam. ¡el Recreo Es una Jungla! Chabert, Jack. 2018. (Escuela de Espanto Ser.: 3). (SPA.). 96p. (J). (gr. 1-3). pap. 4.99 *(978-1-338-26906-2(2)*, Scholastic en Espanol) Scholastic, Inc.

—Get a Hit, Mo! Adler, David A. (Mo Jackson Ser.: 2). (ENG.). 32p. (J). (gr. 1-2). 2017. pap. 4.99 *(978-0-448-48010-7(7))*; 2016. 14.99 *(978-0-670-01632-7(2))* Penguin Young Readers Group. (Penguin Young Readers).

—Invasion of the Insects. Hopper, Ada. 2017. (DATA Set Ser.: 6). (ENG.). 128p. (J). (gr. -1-4). 16.99 *(978-1-4814-7117-6(1)*, Little Simon) Little Simon.

—The Locker Ate Lucy! Chabert, Jack. 2014. (Eerie Elementary Ser.: 2). (ENG.). 96p. (J). (gr. 1-3). 24.99 *(978-0-545-62396-4(0))*; pap. 4.99 *(978-0-545-62395-7(2))* Scholastic, Inc.

—The Locker Ate Lucy!: #2. Chabert, Jack. 2018. (Eerie Elementary Ser.). (ENG.). 96p. (J). (gr. 1-5). lib. bdg. 27.07 *(978-1-5321-4261-1(7)*, 31071, Chapter Bks.) Spotlight.

—March of the Mini Beasts. Hopper, Ada. 2016. (DATA Set Ser.: 1). (ENG.). 128p. (J). (gr. k-4). pap. 5.99 *(978-1-4814-5728-6(4)*, Little Simon) Little Simon.

—March of the Mini Beasts. Hopper, Ada. ed. 2018. 125p. (J). (gr. 1-4). 15.96 *(978-1-64310-195-8(1))* Penworthy Co., LLC, The.

—Pass the Ball, Mo! Adler, David A. (Mo Jackson Ser.: 3). (ENG.). 32p. (J). (gr. 1-2). 2019. pap. 4.99 *(978-0-425-28980-8(X))*; 2018. 14.99 *(978-0-425-28978-5(8))* Penguin Young Readers Group. (Penguin Young Readers).

—Recess Is a Jungle! Chabert, Jack. 2016. (Eerie Elementary Ser.: 3). (ENG.). 96p. (J). (gr. 1-3). 24.99 *(978-0-545-87353-6(3))* Scholastic, Inc.

—Recess Is a Jungle!: #3. Chabert, Jack. 2018. (Eerie Elementary Ser.). (ENG.). 96p. (J). (gr. 1-5). lib. bdg. 27.07 *(978-1-5321-4262-8(5)*, 31072, Chapter Bks.) Spotlight.

—Robots Rule the School. Hopper, Ada. 2016. (DATA Set Ser.: 4). (ENG.). 128p. (J). (gr. k-4). pap. 5.99 *(978-1-4814-6312-6(8)*, Little Simon) Little Simon.

—Robots Rule the School. Hopper, Ada. ed. 2018. 125p. (J). (gr. 1-4). 15.96 *(978-1-64310-199-6(4))* Penworthy Co., LLC, The.

—The Saddest Toilet in the World. Apple, Sam. 2016. (ENG.). 32p. (J). (gr. -1-2). 17.99 *(978-1-4814-5122-2(7)*, Aladdin) Simon & Schuster Children's Publishing.

—Sam Battles the Machine! Chabert, Jack. 2017. (Eerie Elementary Ser.: 6). (ENG.). 96p. (J). (gr. 1-3). pap. 4.99 *(978-0-545-87378-9(9))* Scholastic, Inc.

—Sam Battles the Machine!: #6. Chabert, Jack. 2018. (Eerie Elementary Ser.). (ENG.). 96p. (J). (gr. 1-5). lib. bdg. 27.07 *(978-1-5321-4265-9(X)*, 31075, Chapter Bks.) Spotlight.

—School Freezes Over! Chabert, Jack. 2016. (Eerie Elementary Ser.: 5). (ENG.). 96p. (J). (gr. 1-3). pap. 4.99 *(978-0-545-87373-4(8))* Scholastic, Inc.

—School Freezes Over!: #5. Chabert, Jack. 2018. (Eerie Elementary Ser.). (ENG.). 96p. (J). (gr. 1-5). lib. bdg. 27.07 *(978-1-5321-4264-2(1)*, 31074, Chapter Bks.) Spotlight.

—The School Is Alive! Chabert, Jack. 2014. (Eerie Elementary Ser.: 1). (ENG.). 96p. (J). (gr. 1-3). 24.99 *(978-0-545-62393-3(6))*; pap. 4.99 *(978-0-545-62392-6(8))* Scholastic, Inc.

—The School Is Alive!: #1. Chabert, Jack. 2018. (Eerie Elementary Ser.). (ENG.). 96p. (J). (gr. 1-5). lib. bdg. 27.07 *(978-1-5321-4260-4(9)*, 31070, Chapter Bks.) Spotlight.

—The Science Fair Is Freaky! Chabert, Jack. 2016. (Eerie Elementary Ser.: 4). (ENG.). 96p. (J). (gr. 1-3). pap. 4.99 *(978-0-545-87368-0(1))* Scholastic, Inc.

—The Science Fair Is Freaky!: #4. Chabert, Jack. 2018. (Eerie Elementary Ser.). (ENG.). 96p. (J). (gr. 1-5). lib. bdg. 27.07 *(978-1-5321-4263-5(3)*, 31073, Chapter Bks.) Spotlight.

—The Sky Is Falling. Hopper, Ada. 2016. (DATA Set Ser.: 3). (ENG.). 128p. (J). (gr. k-4). pap. 5.99 *(978-1-4814-6309-6(8)*, Little Simon) Little Simon.

—The Sky Is Falling. Hopper, Ada. ed. 2018. 125p. (J). (gr. 1-4). 15.96 *(978-1-64310-200-9(1))* Penworthy Co., LLC, The.

—Stinkbomb & Ketchup-Face & the Badness of Badgers. Dougherty, John. 2018. (Stinkbomb & Ketchup-Face Ser.: 1). (ENG.). 160p. (J). (gr. 3-7). 7.99 *(978-1-101-99663-8(3)*, Puffin Books) Penguin Young Readers Group.

—Stinkbomb & Ketchup-Face & the Pizza of Peril. Dougherty, John. 2019. (Stinkbomb & Ketchup-Face Ser.: 3). (ENG.). 176p. (J). (gr. 3-7). 16.99 *(978-0-525-51563-0(1)*, G.P. Putnam's Sons Books for Young Readers) Penguin Young Readers Group.

—Stinkbomb & Ketchup-Face & the Quest for the Magic Porcupine. Dougherty, John. 2019. (Stinkbomb & Ketchup-Face Ser.: 2). (ENG.). 176p. (J). (gr. 3-7). 7.99 *(978-1-101-99666-9(8)*, Puffin Books) Penguin Young Readers Group.

Rico, Gaby. Animals of My Land: Animales de Mi Tierra/Noyolkanyolkej. Lima, Rossy E. & Padilla, Gerald a. 2018. (ENG.). 38p. (J). (gr. k-3). 18.99 *(978-1-949299-07-6(4))* Jade Publishing.

Riddel, Leisha. Smooth Criminals Vol. 1. Smith, Kiwi & Lustgarten, Kurt. 2019. (ENG.). 112p. (YA). pap. 14.99 *(978-1-68415-385-5(9))* Boom! Studios.

—Smooth Criminals Vol. 2. Smith, Kiwi & Lustgarten, Kurt. 2019. (Smooth Criminals Ser.: 2). (ENG.). 112p. (YA). pap. 14.99 *(978-1-68415-463-0(4))* Boom! Studios.

Riddell, Chris. Castle Diary: The Journal of Tobias Burgess. Platt, Richard. 2003. (ENG.). 128p. (J). (gr. 4-7). 6.99 *(978-0-7636-2164-3(1))* Candlewick Pr.

—Giggly Wiggly: Playtime Rhymes. Rosen, Michael. 2019. (ENG.). 18p. (J). (— 1). bds. 8.99 *(978-1-5362-0673-9(3))* Candlewick Pr.

—A Great Big Cuddle: Poems for the Very Young. 2015. (ENG.). 80p. (J). (gr. -1-2). 19.99 *(978-0-7636-8116-6(4))* Candlewick Pr.

—Gulliver's Travels: Voyage to Lilliput. Swift, Jonathan. 2017. (ENG.). 48p. (J). (gr. 2-5). 8.99 *(978-0-7636-9349-7(9))* Candlewick Pr.

R

—Little Bit of Winter. Stewart, Paul. 2013. (Rabbit & Hedgehog Ser.). (ENG.). 32p. (J). (gr. -1-k). pap. 12.99 (978-0-86264-998-2(6)) Andersen Pr. GBR. Dist: Independent Pubs. Group.

—My Little Book of Big Freedoms. 2017. (ENG.). 40p. (J). (gr. -1-3). 9.99 (978-1-5247-8634-2(9), Penguin Workshop) Penguin Young Readers Group.

—Odd & the Frost Giants. Gaiman, Neil. 2016. (ENG.). 128p. (J). (gr. 3-7). 19.99 (978-0-06-256795-6(0), HarperCollins) HarperCollins Pubs. Ltd. GBR. Dist: HarperCollins Pubs.

—Pirate Diary: The Journal of Jake Carpenter. Platt, Richard. 2014. (ENG.). 128p. (J). (gr. 4-7). pap. 6.99 (978-0-7636-7361-1(7)) Candlewick Pr.

—Un Poquito de Invierno. Stewart, Paul & Stewart, Paul. 2003. (SPA.). 30p. (J). (gr. k-2). (978-84-348-6839-7(3), SM30933) SM Ediciones ESP. Dist: Lectorum Pubns., Inc.

—Rabbit & Hedgehog Treasury. Stewart, Paul. 2018. 112p. (J). (-2). 21.99 (978-1-78344-674-2(9)) Andersen Pr. GBR. Dist: Independent Pubs. Group.

—The Rabbits' Rebellion. Dorfman, Ariel. 2020. (ENG.). 64p. (J). (gr. 2). 13.95 (978-1-60980-937-9(8), Triangle Square) Seven Stories Pr.

—Un Regalo de Cumpleanos. Stewart, Paul. (SPA.). 30p. (J). (gr. k-2). (978-84-348-6840-3(7), SM30935) SM Ediciones ESP. Dist: Lectorum Pubns., Inc.

—The Sleeper & the Spindle. Gaiman, Neil. 2015. (ENG.). 64p. (YA). (gr. 8). 19.99 (978-0-06-239824-6(5), HarperCollins) HarperCollins Pubs.

—The Sleeper & the Spindle. Gaiman, Neil. 2019. (ENG.). 72p. (YA). (gr. 8). pap. 9.99 (978-0-06-239825-3(3), HarperCollins) HarperCollins Pubs. Ltd. GBR. Dist: HarperCollins Pubs.

—The Sleeper & the Spindle Deluxe Edition. Gaiman, Neil. 2017. (ENG.). 72p. (YA). (gr. 8). 35.00 (978-0-06-269792-9(7), HarperCollins) HarperCollins Pubs. Ltd. GBR. Dist: HarperCollins Pubs.

—Until I Met Dudley. McGough, Roger. 2012. (ENG.). 32p. (J). (gr. -1-2). pap. 8.99 (978-1-84780-350-4(4), Frances Lincoln Children's Bks.) Quarto Publishing Group UK GBR. Dist: Hachette Bk. Group.

—Zoid: Scavenger 1. Stewart, Paul. unabr. ed. 2016. (Scavenger Ser.: 1). (ENG.). 272p. (J). (gr. 4-7). pap. 9.99 (978-1-4472-9995-0(7)) Pan Macmillan GBR. Dist: Independent Pubs. Group.

Riddell, Chris. Dragon's Hoard. Riddell, Chris. Stewart, Paul. 2014. (Knight's Story Ser.: 3). (ENG.). 144p. (J). (gr. 2-6). pap. 13.99 (978-1-4814-2890-3(X), Atheneum Bks. for Young Readers) Simon & Schuster Children's Publishing.

—The Hunting of the Snark. Riddell, Chris. Carroll, Lewis. 2018. (ENG.). 96p. (J). (gr. 4-6). 18.99 (978-1-5098-1433-6(7)) Pan Macmillan GBR. Dist: Independent Pubs. Group.

—Joust of Honor. Riddell, Chris. Stewart, Paul. 2014. (Knight's Story Ser.: 2). (ENG.). 144p. (J). (gr. 2-6). pap. 13.99 (978-1-4814-2889-7(6), Atheneum Bks. for Young Readers) Simon & Schuster Children's Publishing.

—Lake of Skulls. Riddell, Chris. Stewart, Paul. 2014. (Knight's Story Ser.: 1). (ENG.). 144p. (J). (gr. 2-6). pap. 13.99 (978-1-4814-2888-0(8), Atheneum Bks. for Young Readers) Simon & Schuster Children's Publishing.

—Mr Underbed. Riddell, Chris. 2012. 32p. (J). (gr. -1-k). pap. 10.99 (978-1-84270-942-9(9)) Andersen Pr. GBR. Dist: Independent Pubs. Group.

—Poems to Live Your Life By. Riddell, Chris. 2019. (ENG.). 208p. (YA). (gr. 7-17). 14.99 (978-1-4197-4121-0(7), Amulet Bks.) Abrams, Inc.

Riddle, Scott. Arctic Mall Adventure. Stratton, Bart. 2010. 28p. pap. 15.95 (978-1-60844-558-5(5)) Dog Ear Publishing, LLC.

Riddle, Sue. Gotta Go! Gotta Go! A Picture Book. Swope, Sam. 2004. (ENG.). 32p. (J). (gr. -1-1). reprint ed. pap. 8.99 (978-0-374-42786-3(0), 900021953) Square Fish.

Riddle, Tohby. The Word Snoop. Dubosarsky, Ursula. 2009. (ENG.). 272p. (J). (gr. 5-18). 17.99 (978-0-8037-3406-7(9), Dial Bks) Penguin Young Readers Group.

Riddle, Tohby. Irving the Magician. Riddle, Tohby. 2005. 32p. (J). (978-0-670-89649-3(7)) Penguin Publishing Group.

Ridge, Rachel Anne. Flash the Donkey Makes New Friends. Ridge, Rachel Anne. 2016. (Flash the Donkey Ser.). (ENG.). 48p. (J). 12.99 (978-1-4964-1395-6(4), 20_11878, Tyndale Momentum) Tyndale Hse. Pubs.

Ridgell, Earl, jt. illus. see W., Earl.

Ridges, Kedrick. Lehi & His Dream. Bruderer, Brooke. 2005. (J). bds. 10.95 (978-1-58958-096-1(6)) Kofford, Greg Books, Inc.

Ridgway, Tony. All Animal Lives Matter. Ridgway, Tony. l.t. ed. 2018. (ENG.). 38p. (J). (gr. k-4). 14.95 (978-1-61477-361-0(0)) Bellissima Publishing, LLC.

Ridley, Alice. Lyra & the Adventure of the Flying Fish. Emina, Peter. 2013. 48p. (J). (gr. k-4). 17.99 (978-1-907912-01-6(0)) Phoenix Yard Bks. GBR. Dist: Independent Pubs. Group.

Ridley, Sharon. My Wildflower Friends. Phillips, Marilyn, photos by. 2006. (J). (978-0-9786168-0-9(4)) Rio Wildflower Pubns.

Riecks Goss, Carol. The Adventures of Giggles & Owen: A True Story. Holdman, Shirley Terrill. 2010. 26p. pap. 14.95 (978-1-60844-490-8(2)) Dog Ear Publishing, LLC.

Rieder, Floor. The Mystery of Life: How Nothing Became Everything. Schutten, Jan Paul. Watkinson, Laura, tr. from DUT. 2015. (ENG.). 240p. (YA). (gr. 5-9). 15.99 (978-1-58270-525-5(9), Simon & Schuster/Paula Wiseman Bks.) Simon & Schuster/Paula Wiseman Bks.

Rieger, Linda. A Good Heart. Rieger, Linda. 2007. 20p. (J). (978-0-9779427-4-9(0)) Pathways into Science.

Riegle, Janet. Piping Plover Summer. Riegle, Janet. 2008. 32p. (J). (gr. 1-2). 18.95 (978-0-9794202-9-0(6)); pap. 12.95 (978-0-9801045-4-7(8)) Raven Productions, Inc.

Rieley, Daniel. The Doctor with an Eye for Eyes: The Story of Dr. Patricia Bath. Mosca, Julia Finley. 2017. (Amazing Scientists Ser.: 2). 40p. (J). (gr. k-5). 17.99 (978-1-943147-31-1(0), c2080765-1770-4f0c-bdd0-61380f8fb5be) Innovation Pr., The.

—The Girl Who Thought in Pictures: The Story of Dr. Temple Grandin. Mosca, Julia Finley. (Amazing Scientists Ser.: 1). 40p. (J). 2019. pap. 9.95 (978-1-943147-61-8(2), 07249595-330d-4d6d-96fe-bd43fd9b36a2); 2017. 17.99 (978-1-943147-30-4(2), 8e78a8c3-7251-4de8-a85e-c2abf9be5965) Innovation Pr., The.

—The Girl with a Mind for Math: The Story of Raye Montague. Mosca, Julia Finley. 2018. (Amazing Scientists Ser.: 3). 40p. (J). (gr. 2-5). 17.99 (978-1-943147-42-7(6), 75d1da53-3d8e-48f8-995a-15a2dfda546a) Innovation Pr., The.

—Joe's New World: A Me & Mr. P Adventure. Farrer, Maria. 2019. (Me & Mister P. Ser.: 3). (ENG.). 288p. (J). (gr. 3-7). pap. 8.99 (978-1-5107-3911-6(4), Sky Pony Pr.) Skyhorse Publishing Co., Inc.

—Me & Mister P. Farrer, Maria. (Me & Mister P. Ser.). (ENG.). 224p. (J). (gr. 3-7). 2018. pap. 8.99 (978-1-5107-3942-0(4)); 2017. 16.99 (978-1-5107-2860-8(0)) Skyhorse Publishing Co., Inc. (Sky Pony Pr.).

—Penguins Don't Wear Sweaters! Tamura, Marikka. 2018. 32p. (J). (-k). 16.99 (978-1-101-99696-6(X), Nancy Paulsen Books) Penguin Young Readers Group.

—Ruby's Star: Me & Mister P. , Book Two. Farrer, Maria. 2018. (Me & Mister P. Ser.: 2). (ENG.). 224p. (J). (gr. 3-7). pap. 7.99 (978-1-5107-3910-9(6), Sky Pony Pr.) Skyhorse Publishing Co., Inc.

—This Is a Serious Book. Parachini, Jodie. 2016. (ENG.). 32p. (J). (gr. -1-3). 17.99 (978-0-06-247052-2(3), Greenwillow Bks.) HarperCollins Pubs.

Ries, Alex. Zoobots: Wild Robots Inspired by Real Animals, 0 vols. Becker, Helaine. 2014. (ENG.). 32p. (J). (gr. 3-7). 17.95 (978-1-55453-971-0(4)) Kids Can Pr., Ltd. CAN. Dist: Hachette Bk. Group.

Riette, Susanne. Rockafella Jones & the Hidden Treasure. Conroe, Lindy. 2011. 108p. (J). pap. 10.95 (978-1-935199-00-7(5)) Blue Mustang Pr.

Rietz, Kathleen. The ABCs of Yoga for Kids. Power, Teresa. 2009. (ENG.). 32p. (J). (gr. -1-3). 19.95 (978-0-9822587-0-5(4), 4e17cd6f-1cd3-4995-a291-23f8e9041df7) Stafford House.

—The ABCs of Yoga for Kids: A Book of Coloring. 2009. (ENG.). (J). (gr. -1-3). pap. 5.95 (978-0-9822587-2-9(0)) Stafford House.

—The ABCs of Yoga for Kids 56 Learning Cards. Power, Teresa Anne. 2011. (ENG.). 57p. (J). 19.95 (978-0-9822587-3-6(9)) Stafford House.

—ABECE de Yoga para Ninos. Power, Teresa Anne. 2011. (ENG.). 32p. (J). pap. 8.95 (978-0-9822587-4-3(7)) Stafford House.

—El árbol Que Trepó el Oso, 1 vol. Berkes, Marianne. 2012. (SPA.). 32p. (J). (gr. -1-3). 17.95 (978-1-60718-679-3(9)); pap. 11.95 (978-1-62855-426-7(6)) Arbordale Publishing.

—Champ's Story: Dogs Get Cancer Too!, 1 vol. North, Sherry. 2010. (ENG.). 32p. (J). (gr. -1-4). 16.95 (978-1-60718-077-7(4)); pap. 8.95 (978-1-60718-088-3(X)) Arbordale Publishing.

—Desert Baths, 1 vol. Pattison, Darcy. 2012. (SPA & ENG.). 32p. (J). (gr. -1-3). 17.95 (978-1-60718-525-3(3)); pap. 9.95 (978-1-60718-534-5(2)) Arbordale Publishing.

—La Historia de Campeona: la los Perros También les Da Cáncer! North, Sherry. 2010. (SPA & ENG.). 32p. (J). (gr. -1-4). 17.95 (978-1-60718-681-6(0)) Arbordale Publishing.

—Las Duchas en el Desierto, 1 vol. Pattison, Darcy. 2012. (SPA & ENG.). 32p. (J). (gr. -1-3). 17.95 (978-1-60718-676-2(4)) Arbordale Publishing.

—Little Black Ant on Park Street. Halfmann, Janet. 2009. (ENG.). 32p. 9.95 (978-1-60727-006-5(4)); 10.95 (978-1-60727-008-9(0)); 19.95 (978-1-60727-005-8(6)); (J). pap. 6.95 (978-1-60727-003-4(X)) Soundprints.

—Prairie Storms, 1 vol. Pattison, Darcy. 2011. (ENG.). 32p. (J). (gr. -1-4). 16.95 (978-1-60718-129-3(0)); pap. 8.95 (978-1-60718-139-2(8)) Arbordale Publishing.

—The Tree That Bear Climbed, 1 vol. Berkes, Marianne. 2012. (ENG & SPA.). 32p. (J). (gr. -1-3). 17.95 (978-1-60718-528-4(8)); pap. 9.95 (978-1-60718-537-6(7)) Arbordale Publishing.

Rifa, Fina. Barcelona, Tell Us about Gaudi. Cormand, Bernat. Kliczkowski, H., ed. 80p. (978-84-89439-29-0(X)) A. Asppan, S.L. Distribuidora Internacional de Libros y Revistas.

Rife, Ann Hollis. Daddy's Love. Leland, Debbie. ed. 2006. (J). 15.95 (978-0-9667086-4-6(4)) Wildflower Run.

Rift. The Wise Little Butterfly, 1 vol. Rift. 2009. 39p. pap. 19.95 (978-1-61546-493-7(X)) PublishAmerica, Inc.

Rigano, Giovanni. Illegal: A Graphic Novel Telling One Boy's Epic Journey of Hope & Survival. Colfer, Eoin & Donkin, Andrew. 2018. (ENG.). 144p. (J). (gr. 3-7). 19.99 (978-1-4926-6214-3(3)); pap. 14.99 (978-1-4926-6582-3(7)) Sourcebooks, Inc. (Sourcebooks Jabberwocky).

—Illegal: A Graphic Novel Telling One Boy's Epic Journey of Hope & Survival. Colfer, Eoin & Donkin, Andrew. ed. 2018. lib. bdg. 26.95 (978-0-606-41233-9(6)) Turtleback.

Rigano, Giovanni. The Incredibles. Ehrbar, Gregory. 2020. (Disney & Pixar Movies Ser.). (ENG.). 48p. (J). (gr. 2-6). lib. bdg. 28.50 (978-1-5321-4551-3(9), 35198, Graphic Novels) Spotlight.

Rigaudie, Mylène. Hello, I Am Lily from New York City. Husar, Jaco & Husar, Stephane. 2014. (AV2 Fiction Readalong Ser.: Vol. 129). (ENG.). 32p. (J). (gr. -1-3). lib. bdg. 34.28 (978-1-4896-2259-4(4), AV2 by Weigl) Weigl Pubs., Inc.

—Navani from Delhi. Benoit-Renard, Anne. 2014. (AV2 Fiction Readalong Ser.: Vol. 133). (ENG.). 32p. (J). (gr. -1-3). lib. bdg. 34.28 (978-1-4896-2271-6(3), AV2 by Weigl) Weigl Pubs., Inc.

Rigaudie, Mylene. Put Yourself in My Shoes. Isern, Susanna. 2020. (ENG.). 40p. (J). 15.95 (978-84-17673-37-6(7)) NubeOcho Ediciones ESP. Dist: Consortium Bk. Sales & Distribution.

Rigby, Amanda. Doris la Vache Qui Avait le Vertige. Mathew, Laura. Gavoille, Bastien, tr. 2018. (FRE.). 28p. (J). pap. (978-1-78623-395-0(9)) Grosvenor Hse. Publishing Ltd.

—Doris, the Dizzy Cow. Mathew, Laura. 2017. (ENG.). (J). pap. (978-1-78623-257-1(X)) Grosvenor Hse. Publishing Ltd.

Rigby, Deborah. The Mermaid & the Star. Baxter, Nicola. 2025. 14p. (J). bds. (978-1-84322-907-0(2), Armadillo) Anness Publishing.

—The Noisy Parrot. Scott, Janine. 2009. (Treasure Chest Readers Ser.). 24p. (J). (gr. -1-2). pap. 8.15 (978-1-60754-680-1(9)); lib. bdg. 25.60 (978-1-60754-679-5(5)) Windmill Bks.

—Stop That Stew! Mahy, Margaret. 2009. (Treasure Chest Readers Ser.). 24p. (J). (gr. -1-2). pap. 8.15 (978-1-60754-683-2(3)); lib. bdg. 25.60 (978-1-60754-682-5(5)) Windmill Bks.

Riggan, Brittany E. But God... Chose You! God's Story of Love in a 7-Day Devotional. Buck, Ginger K. 2020. (ENG.). 36p. (J). pap. 15.95 (978-1-9736-8522-7(1), WestBow Pr.) Author Solutions, Inc.

Riggs, Jenna. Finding Fairyland: A Picture Riddle Book. Engelman Berner, Beth. 2005. 12p. (J). 9.95 (978-1-58117-386-4(5), Intervisual/Piggy Toes) Bendon, Inc.

—What's in My Dresser?, 1 vol. Rizzi, Kathleen. 2013. (ENG.). 32p. (J). bds. 7.99 (978-1-59572-165-5(7)) Star Bright Bks., Inc.

Riggs, Ransom. Hollow City. Riggs, Ransom. 2014. 352p. (YA). (gr. 9). 18.99 (978-1-59474-612-3(5)) Quirk Bks.

—Hollow City. Riggs, Ransom. 2015. (Miss Peregrine's Peculiar Children Ser.: 2). lib. bdg. 22.10 (978-0-606-36394-5(7)) Turtleback.

Right, Mike. Kid Pickers: How to Turn Junk into Treasure. Wolfe, Mike & Sprengelmeyer, Lily. 2013. (ENG.). 128p. (J). (gr. 2-7). 19.99 (978-1-250-00848-0(4), 900083576); pap. 15.99 (978-1-250-01930-1(3), 900087856) Feiwel & Friends.

Riglietti, Serena. Fauna Mayor. d'Aquino, Alfonso. 2005. (SPA.). (J). (gr. k-2). pap. 10.95 (978-968-494-100-7(5)) Centro de Informacion y Desarrollo de la Comunicacion y la Literatura MEX. Dist: Iaconi, Mariuccia Bk. Imports.

—How Big Is a Million? Milbourne, Anna. Doherty, Gillian, ed. 2008. (Picture Books Ser.). 32p. (J). (gr. -1-3). 10.99 (978-0-7945-1924-7(5), Usborne) EDC Publishing.

—How Big Is a Million? Milbourne, Anna. 2008. (J). (978-0-545-11519-3(1)) Scholastic, Inc.

—How Deep Is the Sea? Milbourne, Anna. 2010. (Picture Bks). 24p. (J). 10.99 (978-0-7945-2311-4(0)) EDC Publishing.

—How High Is the Sky? Milbourne, Anna. 2009. (Picture Bks). 24p. (J). (gr. -1). 10.99 (978-0-7945-2273-5(4), Usborne) EDC Publishing.

—The Magician's Boy. Cooper, Susan. 2006. (ENG.). 112p. (J). (gr. 3-7). pap. 9.99 (978-1-4169-1555-3(9), McElderry, Margaret K. Bks.) McElderry, Margaret K. Bks.

—Under the Ground. Milbourne, Anna. 2006. 24p. (J). (gr. -1-3). 9.99 (978-0-7945-1264-4(X), Usborne) EDC Publishing.

Rigo, L. Little Bunny. 2012. (Mini Look at Me Bks.). (ENG.). 10p. (J). bds. 4.99 (978-0-7641-6509-2(7), B.E.S. Publishing) Peterson's.

—Little Duckling. (Mini Look at Me Bks.). 10p. (J). 2012. (ENG.). (gr. -1). bds. 5.99 (978-0-7641-6510-8(0)); 2011. bds. 8.99 (978-0-7641-6425-5(2)) Peterson's. (B.E.S. Publishing).

—Little Elephant. 2011. (Look at Me Bks.). 10p. (J). bds. 8.99 (978-0-7641-6426-2(0), B.E.S. Publishing) Peterson's.

—Little Lamb. 2012. (Mini Look at Me Bks.). (ENG.). 10p. (J). bds. 4.99 (978-0-7641-6511-5(9), B.E.S. Publishing) Peterson's.

—Little Monkey. 2011. (Mini Look at Me Bks.). 10p. (J). bds. 7.99 (978-0-7641-6428-6(7), B.E.S. Publishing) Peterson's.

—Little Panda Bear. 2014. (Mini Look at Me Bks.). (ENG.). 10p. (J). (gr. -1 — 1). bds. 5.99 (978-0-7641-6739-3(1), B.E.S. Publishing) Peterson's.

—Little Penguin. 2010. (Look at Me Bks.). (ENG.). 10p. (J). (gr. -1 — 1). bds. 8.99 (978-0-7641-6353-1(1), B.E.S. Publishing) Peterson's.

—Little Pig. 2010. (Mini Look at Me Bks.). (ENG.). 10p. (J). (gr. -1 — 1). bds. 8.99 (978-0-7641-6355-5(8), B.E.S. Publishing) Peterson's.

—Little Pony. 2014. (Mini Look at Me Bks.). 10p. (J). (gr. -1 — 1). bds. 4.99 (978-0-7641-6733-1(2), B.E.S. Publishing) Peterson's.

—Little Puppy. 2012. (Mini Look at Me Bks.). (ENG.). 10p. (J). (gr. -1). bds. 5.99 (978-0-7641-6512-2(7), B.E.S. Publishing) Peterson's.

Rigo, L. Little Penguin. Rigo, L. 2014. (Mini Look at Me Bks.). 10p. (J). (gr. -1 — 1). bds. 4.99 (978-0-7641-6731-7(6), B.E.S. Publishing) Peterson's.

Rigo, L. & Caviezel, Giovanni. Little Bunny. 2010. (Look at Me Bks.). (ENG.). 10p. (J). (gr. -1 — 1). bds. 8.99 (978-0-7641-6322-7(1), B.E.S. Publishing) Peterson's.

—Little Puppy. 2010. (Mini Look at Me Bks.). (ENG.). 10p. (J). (gr. -1 — 1). bds. 8.99 (978-0-7641-6324-1(8), B.E.S. Publishing) Peterson's.

Rigo, L., jt. illus. see Barron's Educational Series Staff.

Rigo, Laura. Furry Bunny. Auerbach, Annie. 2018. (Mini Friends Touch & Feel Ser.). 10p. (J). (gr. -1 — 1). bds. 5.99 (978-1-4380-5011-9(9), B.E.S. Publishing) Peterson's.

—Furry Chick. Auerbach, Annie. 2018. (Mini Friends Touch & Feel Bks.). 10p. (J). (gr. -1 — 1). bds. 5.99 (978-1-4380-5012-6(7), B.E.S. Publishing) Peterson's.

—Furry Lamb. Auerbach, Annie. 2018. (Mini Friends Touch & Feel Bks.). 10p. (J). (gr. -1 — 1). bds. 5.99 (978-1-4380-5013-3(5), B.E.S. Publishing) Peterson's.

—Furry Puppy. Auerbach, Annie. 2018. (Mini Friends Touch & Feel Bks.). 10p. (J). (gr. -1 — 1). bds. 5.99 (978-1-4380-5014-0(3), B.E.S. Publishing) Peterson's.

—Little Chimp. 2017. (Mini Look at Me Bks.). 10p. (J). (gr. -1 — 1). bds. 4.99 (978-0-7641-6878-9(9), B.E.S. Publishing) Peterson's.

—Little Elephant. 2017. (Mini Look at Me Bks.). 10p. (J). (gr. -1 — 1). bds. 5.99 (978-0-7641-6879-6(7), B.E.S. Publishing) Peterson's.

—Little Polar Bear. 2017. (Mini Look at Me Bks.). (ENG.). 10p. (J). (gr. -1 — 1). bds. 4.99 (978-0-7641-6880-2(0), B.E.S. Publishing) Peterson's.

—Little Tiger. 2017. (Mini Look at Me Bks.). 10p. (J). (gr. -1 — 1). bds. 4.99 (978-0-7641-6881-9(9), B.E.S. Publishing) Peterson's.

—A Spooky Halloween. Lorini, Andrea. 2016. (ENG.). 8p. (J). (gr. -1-1). bds. 6.99 (978-0-7641-6852-9(5), B.E.S. Publishing) Peterson's.

Rigo, Laura, jt. illus. see Pagnoni, Roberta.

Rigol, Francesc. Dan & Din Learn Colors. 2009. (Learning with Dan & Din Ser.). 12p. (J). (gr. -1-k). bds. 11.40 (978-1-60754-401-2(6)) Windmill Bks.

—Dan & Din Learn Numbers. 2009. (Learning with Dan & Din Ser.). 12p. (J). (gr. -1-k). bds. 11.40 (978-1-60754-402-9(4)) Windmill Bks.

—Dan & Din Learn Opposites. 2009. (Learning with Dan & Din Ser.). 12p. (J). (gr. -1-k). bds. 11.40 (978-1-60754-403-6(2)) Windmill Bks.

—Dan & Din Learn Shapes. 2009. (Learning with Dan & Din Ser.). 12p. (J). (gr. -1-k). bds. 11.40 (978-1-60754-400-5(8)) Windmill Bks.

—Pooh's Leaf Pile. Gaines, Isabel & Milne, A. A. 2012. (J). (978-1-4351-4190-2(3)) Disney Pr.

Rikaz, Sarah. Friends on My Street: A Celebration of Diversity. Probst, Erika Bracken. 2017. (ENG.). (J). (gr. -1-3). 18.99 (978-1-61984-797-2(3)) Gatekeeper Pr.

Riley, Andy. King Flashypants & the Creature from Crong. Riley, Andy. 2018. (King Flashypants Ser.: 2). (ENG.). 224p. (J). 13.99 (978-1-62779-811-2(0), 900160391, Holt, Henry & Co. Bks. For Young Readers) Holt, Henry & Co.

—King Flashypants & the Evil Emperor. Riley, Andy. 2017. (King Flashypants Ser.). (ENG.). 224p. (J). 13.99 (978-1-62779-809-9(9), 9781627798099, Holt, Henry & Co. Bks. For Young Readers) Holt, Henry & Co.

—King Flashypants & the Toys of Terror. Riley, Andy. 2018. (King Flashypants Ser.: 3). (ENG.). 192p. (J). 13.99 (978-1-62779-813-6(7), 900160395, Holt, Henry & Co. Bks. For Young Readers) Holt, Henry & Co.

Riley, Ashton. Bischero in Venice: Book 2. Milone, Janet Grace. Maltese-Perrie, Josette, ed. 2016. (Bischero Ser.: Vol. 2). (ENG.). (J). (gr. 3-6). pap. 9.99 (978-0-9820672-2-2(4)) Vista Italia.

Riley, David. Freedom Train. Coleman, Evelyn. 2012. (ENG.). 140p. (J). (gr. 3-6). 21.19 (978-0-689-84716-5(5)) Simon & Schuster, Inc.

—President Lincoln, Willie Kettles, & the Telegraph Machine. Figley, Marty Rhodes. 2010. (History Speaks: Picture Books Plus Reader's Theater Ser.). (ENG.). 48p. (gr. 2-4). pap. 9.95 (978-0-7613-6131-2(6)) Lerner Publishing Group.

Riley, Kellee. Before the Beginning Began. Cavalli, Frank. 2006. 56p. (J). (gr. -1-3). 19.95 (978-0-9766662-0-2(0)) Star Dome Publishing, LLC.

—Behold the Power of Gargamel! Gallo, Tina. 2011. (Smurfs Movie Ser.). (ENG.). 24p. (J). (gr. -1-3). pap. 6.99 (978-1-4424-2395-4(1), Simon Spotlight) Simon Spotlight.

—The Big Boat Race! (Team Umizoomi) Golden Books. 2012. (ENG.). 48p. (J). (gr. -1-2). pap. 3.99 (978-0-375-86215-1(3), Golden Bks.) Random Hse. Children's Bks.

—A Boo-Tiful Halloween! Man-Kong, Mary. 2013. (Pictureback Ser.). (ENG.). 16p. (J). (gr. -1-2). 4.99 (978-0-449-81860-2(8), Random Hse. Bks. for Young Readers) Random Hse. Children's Bks.

—An Egg-Cellent Easter! (Barbie) Frazer, Rebecca. 2012. (Pictureback(R) Ser.). (ENG.). 16p. (J). (gr. -1-2). pap. 3.99 (978-0-307-93025-5(4), Random Hse. Bks. for Young Readers) Random Hse. Children's Bks.

—Happy Birthday, Barbie! (Barbie) Man-Kong, Mary. 2014. (Pictureback(R) Ser.). (ENG.). 24p. (J). (gr. -1-2). 5.99 (978-0-385-37320-3(1), Random Hse. Bks. for Young Readers) Random Hse. Children's Bks.

—Happy Halloween, Kai-lan! A Lift-the-Flap Story. 2010. (Ni Hao, Kai-Lan Ser.). (ENG.). 16p. (J). pap. 6.99 (978-1-4424-0178-5(8), Simon Spotlight/Nickelodeon) Simon Spotlight/Nickelodeon.

—I Can Be a Farm Vet (Barbie) Jordan, Apple. 2016. (Step into Reading Ser.). (ENG.). 24p. (J). (gr. -1-1). 4.99 (978-1-101-93245-2(7), Random Hse. Bks. for Young Readers) Random Hse. Children's Bks.

—I Can Be... A Zoo Vet/I Can Be... A Cheerleader. Random House Staff. 2011. (Pictureback Ser.). (ENG.). 32p. (J). (gr. -1-2). pap. 4.99 (978-0-375-87265-5(5), Random Hse. Bks. for Young Readers) Random Hse. Children's Bks.

—My First Visit to the Doctor. Man-Kong, Mary. 2017. (Pictureback(R) Ser.). (ENG.). 16p. (J). (gr. -1-2). pap. 4.99 (978-0-399-55810-8(1), Random Hse. Bks. for Young Readers) Random Hse. Children's Bks.

—My Visit to the Doctor. Man-Kong, Mary. 2017. (J). (978-1-5182-2648-9(5)) Random Hse., Inc.

—Penny & Pepper. Betancourt, Jeanne. 2011. (Scholastic Reader Level 3 Ser.). (ENG.). 48p. (J). (gr. 1-4). pap. 3.99 (978-0-545-11508-7(6), Cartwheel Bks.) Scholastic, Inc.

—Tolee's Rhyme Time. 2009. (Ni Hao, Kai-Lan Ser.). (ENG.). 24p. (J). pap. 3.99 (978-1-4169-9024-6(0), Simon Spotlight/Nickelodeon) Simon Spotlight/Nickelodeon.

Riley, Kellee, jt. illus. see Golden Books Staff.

Riley, Kellee, jt. illus. see Random House Staff.

Riley, Kellee, jt. illus. see Spaziante, Patrick.

Riley, Kevin. Inky Winky Spider 1,2,3,4. Makeeff, Cyndi Sue. 2006. 32p. (J). pap. 7.99 (978-0-9778310-1-2(9)) New Vision Entertainment, LLC.

—Inky Winky Spider ABC's. Makeeff, Cyndi Sue. 2006. 32p. (J). pap. 7.99 (978-0-9778310-0-5(0)) New Vision Entertainment, LLC.

—Inky Winky Spider Colors by the Bay. Makeeff, Cyndi Sue. 2006. 32p. (J). pap. 7.99 *(978-0-9778310-2-9(7))* New Vision Entertainment, LLC.

Riley, Larry. Kiwi Phonics: Level 1: Basic Vowels & Consonants, 15 vols. Deighton-O'Flynn, Heather et al. 2004. 141p. 45.00 *(978-1-877276-69-9(3))* Otago University Pr. NZL. Dist: Independent Pubs. Group.

—Kiwi Phonics: Level 2: Consonant Clusters, 10 vols. Deighton-O'Flynn, Heather et al. 2004. 181p. 45.00 *(978-1-877276-70-5(7))* Otago University Pr. NZL. Dist: Independent Pubs. Group.

—Kiwi Phonics: Level 3: Complex Code, 20 vols. Deighton-O'Flynn, Heather et al. 2005. 280p. 85.00 *(978-1-877276-71-2(5))* Otago University Pr. NZL. Dist: Independent Pubs. Group.

Riley, Markie. I'll Be a Sunbeam. Chabot, Shersta. 2018. (ENG.). 32p. (J). (gr. k-3). 14.99 *(978-1-4621-2276-9(0))* Cedar Fort, Inc./CFI Distribution.

Riley, Melanie Ellis. Catie the Caterpillar: A Story to Help Break the Silence of Sexual Abuse. Schamburg, Tracy M. 2006. 31p. (J). (gr. -1). pap. 6.95 *(978-0-7648-1434-1(6))* Liguori Pubns.

Riley, Scott, jt. illus. see Darroch, Jane.

Riley, Terry. African Myths. Jeffrey, Gary & Newport, Kate. 2006. (Graphic Mythology Ser.). (ENG.). 48p. (J). (gr. 4-7). lib. bdg. 35.45 *(978-1-4042-0798-1(8))* Rosen Publishing Group, Inc., The.

—Allosaurus: The Strange Lizard. Shone, Rob. 2009. (Graphic Dinosaurs Ser.). (ENG.). 32p. (J). pap. 12.30 *(978-1-4358-8592-9(9))*; (gr. 2-5). 28.50 *(978-1-4358-8588-2(0))* Rosen Publishing Group, Inc., The. (PowerKids Pr.).

—Autopsies: Pathologists at Work. Jeffrey, Gary. 2008. (Graphic Forensic Science Ser.). (ENG.). (J). (gr. 5-8). lib. bdg. 22.55 *(978-1-68065-295-6(8))* Perfection Learning Corp.

—Autopsies: Pathologists at Work. Jeffrey, Gary. 2008. (Graphic Forensic Science Ser.). (ENG.). 48p. (gr. 5-8). per. 14.05 *(978-1-4042-1447-7(X))*; (YA). lib. bdg. 35.45 *(978-1-4042-1446-0(1))* Rosen Publishing Group, Inc., The.

—Bob Marley: The Life of a Musical Legend. Jeffrey, Gary. 2007. (Graphic Nonfiction Biographies Ser.). (ENG.). 48p. (YA). (gr. 4-7). lib. bdg. 35.45 *(978-1-4042-0854-4(2))* Rosen Publishing Group, Inc., The.

—Brachiosaurus: The Long-Limbed Dinosaur. Shone, Rob. 2009. (Graphic Dinosaurs Ser.). (ENG.). 32p. (J). pap. 12.30 *(978-1-4358-8600-1(3))*; (gr. 2-5). 28.50 *(978-1-4358-8589-9(9))* Rosen Publishing Group, Inc., The. (PowerKids Pr.).

—Crusades. Jeffrey, Gary. 2014. (Graphic Medieval History Ser.). (ENG.). 48p. (J). (gr. 5-5). *(978-0-7787-0397-6(5))* Crabtree Publishing Co.

—Defying Death at Sea. Jeffrey, Gary. 2010. (Graphic Survival Stories Ser.). 48p. (YA). 58.50 *(978-1-61532-897-0(1))*; (ENG.). pap. 14.05 *(978-1-61532-863-5(7))*; (gr. 5-8). 35.45 *(978-1-4358-3530-6(1))* Rosen Publishing Group, Inc., The. (Rosen Reference).

—Elasmosaurus: The Long-Necked Swimmer. Jeffrey, Gary. (Graphic Dinosaurs Ser.). (ENG.). 32p. 2009. (gr. 2-5). pap. 12.30 *(978-1-4042-7715-1(3)*, PowerKids Pr.); 2008. (J). 50.50 *(978-1-61532-138-4(1)*, PowerKids Pr.); 2008. (J). (gr. 2-5). lib. bdg. 28.50 *(978-1-4358-2505-5(5))* Rosen Publishing Group, Inc., The.

—The Explorations of Lewis & Clark. Jeffrey, Gary. 2012. (Graphic History of the American West Ser.). (ENG.). 24p. (J). (gr. 3-8). pap. 8.15 *(978-1-4339-6737-5(5)*, Gareth Stevens Learning Library); (gr. 4-7). lib. bdg. 24.95 *(978-1-4339-6735-1(9))* Stevens, Gareth Publishing LLLP.

—Ghosts & Poltergeists: Stories of the Supernatural. West, David. 2006. (Graphic Mysteries Ser.). (ENG.). 48p. (YA). (gr. 5-8). lib. bdg. 35.45 *(978-1-4042-0608-3(6))* Rosen Publishing Group, Inc., The.

—Giganotosaurus: The Giant Southern Lizard. Shone, Rob. (Graphic Dinosaurs Ser.). (ENG.). 32p. 2009. (gr. 2-5). pap. 12.30 *(978-1-4042-7712-0(9)*, PowerKids Pr.); 2008. (J). 50.50 *(978-1-61532-135-3(7)*, PowerKids Pr.); 2008. (J). (gr. 2-5). lib. bdg. 28.50 *(978-1-4358-2502-4(0))* Rosen Publishing Group, Inc., The.

—Hadrosaurus: The Duck-Billed Dinosaur. Shone, Rob. 2009. (Graphic Dinosaurs Ser.). (ENG.). 32p. (J). pap. 12.30 *(978-1-4358-8598-1(8))*; (gr. 2-5). 28.50 *(978-1-4358-8591-2(0))* Rosen Publishing Group, Inc., The. (PowerKids Pr.).

—Medical Breakthroughs. Jeffrey, Gary. 2008. (Graphic Discoveries Ser.). (ENG.). 48p. (YA). (gr. 5-9). lib. bdg. 35.45 *(978-1-4042-1086-8(5))* Rosen Publishing Group, Inc., The.

—Oprah Winfrey: The Life of a Media Superstar. Jeffrey, Gary. 2007. (Graphic Nonfiction Biographies Ser.). (ENG.). 48p. (YA). (gr. 4-7). lib. bdg. 35.45 *(978-1-4042-0862-9(3))* Rosen Publishing Group, Inc., The.

—The Pony Express. Jeffrey, Gary. 2012. (Graphic History of the American West Ser.). (ENG.). 24p. (J). (gr. 3-8). pap. 8.15 *(978-1-4339-6749-8(9)*, Gareth Stevens Learning Library); (gr. 4-7). lib. bdg. 24.95 *(978-1-4339-6747-4(2))* Stevens, Gareth Publishing LLLP.

—Rebellion & Revolt. Jeffrey, Gary. 2014. (Graphic Medieval History Ser.). (ENG.). 48p. (J). (gr. 5-5). *(978-0-7787-0399-0(1))* Crabtree Publishing Co.

—Secret Agents. Jeffrey, Gary. 2008. (Graphic Careers Ser.). (ENG.). 48p. (gr. 5-8). per. 14.05 *(978-1-4042-1465-1(8))*; (YA). lib. bdg. 35.45 *(978-1-4042-1464-4(X))* Rosen Publishing Group, Inc., The.

—Tornadoes & Superstorms. Jeffrey, Gary. 2007. (Graphic Natural Disasters Ser.). (ENG.). 48p. (gr. 5-8). pap. 14.05 *(978-1-4042-1985-4(4))*; (J). lib. bdg. 35.45 *(978-1-4042-1993-9(5))* Rosen Publishing Group, Inc., The.

—Volcanoes. Shone, Rob. 2007. (Graphic Natural Disasters Ser.). (ENG.). 48p. (J). (gr. 5-9). lib. bdg. 35.45 *(978-1-4042-1988-5(9))* Rosen Publishing Group, Inc., The.

Riley, Terry & Ball, Geoff. Pteranodon: Giant of the Sky. West, David. 2007. (Graphic Dinosaurs Ser.). (ENG.). 32p. (J). (gr. 2-5). lib. bdg. 28.50 *(978-1-4042-3895-4(6))* Rosen Publishing Group, Inc., The.

—Triceratops: The Three Horned Dinosaur. Shone, Rob. 2007. (Graphic Dinosaurs Ser.). (ENG.). 32p. (J). (gr. 2-5). lib. bdg. 28.50 *(978-1-4042-3896-1(4))* Rosen Publishing Group, Inc., The.

Riley, Terry, jt. illus. see Jeffrey, Gary.

Riley, Vicky. Bear Hugs. Walden, Libby. 2017. (ENG.). 18p. (J). (gr. -1-k). bds. 7.99 *(978-1-68010-519-3(1))* Tiger Tales.

Riley-Webb, Charlotte. Around Our Way on Neighbors' Day. Brown, Tameka Fryer. 2010. (ENG.). 32p. (J). (gr. -1-3). 17.95 *(978-0-8109-8971-9(9)*, Abrams Bks. for Young Readers) Abrams, Inc.

—Rent Party Jazz, 1 vol. Miller, William. 2005. (ENG.). 32p. (J). pap. 7.95 *(978-1-55041-972-6(2)*, b3affcff-1d96-4028-a6d8-c03e66074aa1) Fitzhenry & Whiteside, Ltd. CAN. Dist: Firefly Bks., Ltd.

—Rent Party Jazz. Miller, William. (ENG.). 32p. (J). (gr. 1-5). 2013. 16.95 *(978-1-58430-025-0(6))*; 2011. pap. 10.95 *(978-1-60060-344-0(0)*, 006a1279-91ee-4cb0-9cfc-1c224b4da487) Lee & Low Bks., Inc.

—Seed Magic, 1 vol. Buchanan, Jane. 2012. (ENG.). 32p. (J). 16.95 *(978-1-56145-622-2(5))* Peachtree Publishing Co. Inc.

—Strange Fruit: Billie Holiday & the Power of a Protest Song. Golio, Gary. 2017. (ENG.). 40p. (J). (gr. 3-6). 19.99 *(978-1-4677-5123-0(5)*, 9781467751230); E-Book 30.65 *(978-1-5124-2837-7(X))* Lerner Publishing Group. (Millbrook Pr.).

—Sweet Potato Pie. Lindsey, Kathleen D. 2003. (J). 16.95 *(978-1-58430-061-8(2))*; (ENG.). 32p. pap. 10.95 *(978-1-60060-277-1(0))* Lee & Low Bks., Inc.

Rim, Sujean. Project Paris. Barham, Lisa. 2007. (Fashion-Forward Adventures of Imogene Ser.). (ENG.). 224p. (YA). (gr. 7-12). pap. 10.99 *(978-1-4169-1444-0(7)*, Simon Pulse) Simon Pulse.

—The Secret Ingredient. Schaefer, Laura. (ENG.). 240p. (J). (gr. 4-8). 2012. pap. 6.99 *(978-1-4424-1960-5(1))*; 2011. 15.99 *(978-1-4424-1959-9(8))* Simon & Schuster/Paula Wiseman Bks. (Simon & Schuster/Paula Wiseman Bks.).

—The Teashop Girls. Schaefer, Laura. 2008. (ENG.). 256p. (J). (gr. 3-9). 15.99 *(978-1-4169-6793-4(1))* Simon & Schuster, Inc.

—The Teashop Girls. Schaefer, Laura. 2009. (ENG.). 272p. (J). (gr. 4-9). pap. 8.99 *(978-1-4169-6794-1(X)*, Simon & Schuster/Paula Wiseman Bks.) Simon & Schuster/Paula Wiseman Bks.

Rim, Sujean. Zoogie Boogie Fever! an Animal Dance Book: An Animal Dance Book. Rim, Sujean. 2018. (ENG.). 40p. (J). (gr. -1-k). 17.99 *(978-0-545-90005-8(0)*, Orchard Bks.) Scholastic, Inc.

Rimaszombati, Laura. Fantastical Finds. Lorens, Allyson. 2018. (ENG.). 34p. (J). pap. 12.99 *(978-1-7323065-8-5(3))* Horn, Jonathan.

Rimes, Nicole. Puppy Tales. Lattak, Cheryl. 2011. 28p. pap. 24.95 *(978-1-4560-2720-9(4))* America Star Bks.

Rimland, Mark. The Secret Night World of Cats. 2008. 32p. (YA). 15.00 *(978-0-9740360-6-9(4))* Autism Research Institute.

Rimmington, Natasha. Adding & Subtracting Activity Book. McLellan, Lorenzo. 2019. (Super Stars Activity Bks.). (ENG.). 96p. (J). pap. 9.99 *(978-1-78950-026-4(5)*, 5b0f305b-d568-483a-a4af-11817c117ab0) Arcturus Publishing GBR. Dist: Baker & Taylor Publisher Services (BTPS).

—Dios No Encuentra. Hilton, Jennifer & McCurry, Kristen. 2016. (SPA.). (J). *(978-1-5064-2091-2(5))* Augsburg Fortress, Pubs.

—God Made Feelings: A Book about Emotions, Vol. Bell, Lucy J. 2017. (ENG.). 10p. (J). 6.99 *(978-1-5064-1782-0(5)*, Sparkhouse Family) Augsburg Fortress, Pubs.

—Good Morning, World: A Book about Morning Routines, Vol. McCurry, Kristen & Hilton, Jennifer. 2017. (ENG.). (J). 6.99 *(978-1-5064-1785-1(X)*, Sparkhouse Family) Augsburg Fortress, Pubs.

Rimmington, Natasha. Magical Unicorn Wordsearch. Finnegan, Ivy. 2020. (ENG.). 96p. (J). pap. 9.99 ***(978-1-83940-587-7(2)***, 7a8b742a-dcfc-471a-8b60-95f0ec1c0d5c) Arcturus Publishing GBR. Dist: Baker & Taylor Publisher Services (BTPS).

Rimmington, Natasha. Max & Zap at the Museum, 35 vols. MacPherson, Molly. 2017. (ENG.). 32p. (J). 11.95 *(978-1-78250-423-8(0)*, Kelpies) Floris Bks. GBR. Dist: Consortium Bk. Sales & Distribution.

—Mi Primera Biblia. Reisch, J. A. 2016. (SPA.). (J). *(978-1-5064-2103-2(2))* Augsburg Fortress, Pubs.

—El Mundo Maravilloso de Dios. Hilton, Jennifer Sue & McCurry, Kristen. 2016. (SPA.). (J). *(978-1-5064-2094-3(X))* Augsburg Fortress, Pubs.

—My First Picture Puzzles: Over 50 Fantastic Puzzles. Butterfield, Moira. 2018. (My First Activity Bks.). (ENG.). 64p. (J). (gr. -1-2). pap. 5.99 *(978-1-4380-1144-8(X)*, B.E.S. Publishing) Peterson's.

—Super Stars! Phonics Activity Book. Worms, Penny. 2019. (ENG.). 96p. (J). pap. 9.99 *(978-1-78950-538-2(0)*, 11cad650-ac8f-4f99-8cb1-928ce6521ed4) Arcturus Publishing GBR. Dist: Baker & Taylor Publisher Services (BTPS).

—Super Stars! Spelling Activity Book. Worms, Penny. 2020. (ENG.). 96p. (J). pap. 9.99 *(978-1-78950-537-5(2)*, 49bc4ed8-6fdf-4f99-818d-7a8b224d9ff2) Arcturus Publishing GBR. Dist: Baker & Taylor Publisher Services (BTPS).

—Times Tables Activity Book. McLellan, Lorenzo. 2019. (Super Stars Activity Bks.). (ENG.). 96p. (J). pap. 9.99 *(978-1-78950-025-7(7)*, 77333797-ff4d-43b1-b32b-376c2abab9ce) Arcturus Publishing GBR. Dist: Baker & Taylor Publisher Services (BTPS).

Rinaldi, Angelo. The Gladiator's Victory. Hulme-Cross, Benjamin. 2015. (Warrior Heroes Ser.). (ENG.). 160p. (J). (gr. 6-6). *(978-0-7787-1764-5(X))* Crabtree Publishing Co.

—Horse. Doyle, Malachy. 2008. (ENG.). 32p. (J). (gr. k-4). 17.99 *(978-1-4169-2467-8(1)*, McElderry, Margaret K. Bks.) McElderry, Margaret K. Bks.

—The Knight's Enemies. Hulme-Cross, Benjamin. 2015. (Warrior Heroes Ser.). (ENG.). 160p. (J). (gr. 6-6). *(978-0-7787-1765-2(8))* Crabtree Publishing Co.

—Rainy Day. Haughton, Emma. (Carolrhoda Picture Books Ser.). 32p. (J). 2004. pap. 6.95 *(978-1-57505-668-5(2))*; 2003. (gr. -1-3). 6.95 *(978-1-57505-452-0(3)*, Carolrhoda Bks.) Lerner Publishing Group.

—The Samurai's Assassin. Hulme-Cross, Benjamin. 2015. (Warrior Heroes Ser.). (ENG.). 160p. (J). (gr. 6-6). *(978-0-7787-1766-9(6))* Crabtree Publishing Co.

—The Viking's Revenge. Hulme-Cross, Benjamin. 2015. (Warrior Heroes Ser.). (ENG.). 160p. (J). (gr. 6-6). *(978-0-7787-1767-6(4))* Crabtree Publishing Co.

Rinaldo, Luana. Bedtime Stories. 2015. (ENG.). 12p. (J). bds. 11.99 *(978-1-4472-7704-0(X))* Pan Macmillan GBR. Dist: Independent Pubs. Group.

—Butterphants & Eleflies. Froeb, Lori C. 2010. (Sliding Surprise Ser.). (ENG.). 10p. (J). bds. 7.99 *(978-0-7944-1932-5(1))* Reader's Digest Assn., Inc., The.

—God's Creation, 1 vol. Froeb, Lori C. 2008. 12p. (J). bds. 7.99 *(978-0-8254-5545-2(6))* Kregel Pubns.

—Matching Puzzle Cards - Colors. 2012. (ENG.). 36p. (J). (gr. k-12). 9.99 *(978-1-60905-220-1(X))* Blue Apple Bks.

—Noah's Ark, 1 vol. Froeb, Lori C. 2008. 12p. (J). bds. 7.99 *(978-0-8254-5546-9(4))* Kregel Pubns.

Rincon, Fernando. Los Papeles de Miguela. Nino, Jairo Anibal. 2003. (Literatura Juvenil (Panamericana Editorial) Ser.). (SPA.). 78p. (J). (gr. -1-7). pap. *(978-958-30-0336-3(0)*, PV30462) Centro de Informacion y Desarrollo de la Comunicacion y la Literatura MEX. Dist: Lectorum Pubns., Inc.

Riner, Christopher. Rose's Wish: An Unigo Adventure. Riner, Charlene. 2020. (Unigo Adventure Ser.: Vol. 2). (ENG.). 72p. (J). pap. 6.39 ***(978-1-6543-8380-0(5))*** Independently Published.

Ringgold, Faith. Bronzeville Boys & Girls. Brooks, Gwendolyn. 48p. (J). 2015. (ENG.). (gr. -1-3). pap. 7.99 *(978-0-06-443772-1(8)*, Amistad); 2007. (gr. 2-5). 18.89 *(978-0-06-029506-6(6))*; 2006. (ENG.). (gr. -1-3). 16.99 *(978-0-06-029505-9(8)*, Amistad) HarperCollins Pubs.

—O Holy Night: Christmas with the Boys Choir of Harlem. Boys Choir of Harlem Staff. 2004. 40p. (J). 19.89 *(978-0-06-051819-6(7))* HarperCollins Pubs.

—O Holy Night: Christmas with the Boys Choir of Harlem. 2006. 30p. (J). (gr. 4-8). 19.00 *(978-1-4223-5512-1(8))* DIANE Publishing Co.

—The Three Witches. Hurston, Zora Neale. 2006. 32p. (J). (gr. 1-5). 16.89 *(978-0-06-000650-1(1))* HarperCollins Pubs.

Ringgold, Faith. Cassie's Word Quilt. Ringgold, Faith. 2004. 32p. (J). (gr. -1-2). pap. 7.99 *(978-0-553-11233-7(3)*, Dragonfly Bks.) Random Hse. Children's Bks.

—Harlem Renaissance Party. Ringgold, Faith. 2015. (ENG.). 40p. (J). (gr. -1-3). 17.99 *(978-0-06-057911-1(0))* HarperCollins Pubs.

—Henry Ossawa Tanner: His Boyhood Dream Comes True. Ringgold, Faith. 2011. (ENG.). 32p. (J). (gr. 1-7). 17.50 *(978-1-59373-092-5(6))* Bunker Hill Publishing, Inc.

—If a Bus Could Talk: The Story of Rosa Parks. Ringgold, Faith. 2003. (ENG.). 32p. (J). (gr. k-4). pap. 8.99 *(978-0-689-85676-1(8)*, Aladdin) Simon & Schuster Children's Publishing.

Ringler, J. S. The Family Guide to Classic Movies. Ringler, J. S. 3rd ed. 2005. 354p. spiral bd. 11.95 *(978-0-9660286-0-7(0))* OSS Publishing Co.

Ringli, Andrea. I Wish I'd Been Born a Unicorn. Lyon, Rachel. 2019. (Early Bird Readers — Green (Early Bird Stories (tm)) Ser.). (ENG.). 32p. (J). (gr. k-3). 27.99 *(978-1-5415-4203-7(7)*, 9781541542037); pap. 7.99 *(978-1-5415-7408-3(7)*, 9781541574083) Lerner Publishing Group. (Lerner Pubns.).

Rink, Cynthia A. Where Does the Wind Blow? 2004. (Sharing Nature with Children Book Ser.). 32p. (J). pap. 7.95 *(978-1-58469-040-5(2))* Dawn Pubns.

Rink, Cynthia A. Where Does the Wind Blow? Rink, Cynthia A. 2004. (Sharing Nature with Children Book Ser.). 32p. (J). (gr. k-5). 16.95 *(978-1-58469-041-2(0))* Dawn Pubns.

Rinka, Kelci. The Adventures of Super Sophie: Cocoa Needs a Vet. Rich, Heidi Wilke. 2019. (ENG.). 20p. (J). pap. 9.99 *(978-1-64538-057-3(2))* Orange Hat Publishing.

Rinkel, Ken. Giant Machines. 2003. 12p. (J). (gr. k-3). 20.00 *(978-0-7567-6653-5(2))* DIANE Publishing Co.

Rino. Buzz Buzz, 1, Vol. 1. Rino. 2006. (Bambi Ser.: Vol. 1). 176p. (YA). per. 9.95 *(978-1-59697-012-0(X))* Infinity Studios LLC.

Rio, Adam del & Arroyo, David. Vines of the Earth. Rio, Adam del & Arroyo, David. 2006. (SPA & ENG.). 27p. *(978-0-9772852-7-3(8))*; pap. *(978-0-9772852-6-6(X))* Lectura Bks.

Rio, Adam del & Noel III. Teo & the Brick. Rio, Adam del & Noel III. 2006. (SPA & ENG.). 28p. *(978-0-9772852-4-2(3))*; *(978-0-9772852-5-9(1))* Lectura Bks.

Riojas, Edward. The World of the Wazzlewoods. Bramwell, Tyrel. 2018. (Fern & Dale Fairy Tale Ser.: Vol. 1). (ENG.). 104p. (J). pap. 7.99 *(978-1-7251-4025-7(X))* CreateSpace Independent Publishing Platform.

Rios, Daniela. The Adventures of Charlie & Betty. B, Maggie. 2020. (ENG.). 38p. (J). pap. ***(978-1-78830-449-8(7))*** Olympia Publishers.

Ríos, Esmeralda. Esquimales, Kwakiutl y Hurones. Llamas Camacho, Edith. 2015. (SPA.). 80p. (J). (gr. 4-7). pap. 11.95 *(978-607-8237-48-7(9))* Nostra Ediciones MEX. Dist: Independent Pubs. Group.

—Mayas: Los Indígenas de Mesoamérica III. Mariano Leyva, José. 2019. (Historias de Verdad Ser.). (SPA.). 80p. (J). (gr. 4-7). pap. 13.95 *(978-607-8469-54-3(1))* Nostra Ediciones MEX. Dist: Independent Pubs. Group.

Rios, Seth. I'm Looking for God. Cannon, Barney. 2010. (ENG.). 36p. (J). pap. 13.50 *(978-0-9829589-7-1(8))* Inkwell Books LLC.

Rioux, Jo. The Daughters of Ys. Anderson, M. T. 2020. (ENG.). 208p. 24.99 *(978-1-62672-878-3(X)*, 900176345, First Second Bks.) Roaring Brook Pr.

Rioux, Jo-Anne. Lake Monster Mix-Up, 2. Labatt, Mary. 2009. (Sam & Friends Mysteries Ser.). 96p. (J). (gr. 2-4). 21.19 *(978-1-55337-822-8(9))* Kids Can Pr., Ltd. CAN. Dist: Children's Plus, Inc.

—Mummy Mayhem. Labatt, Mary. 2010. (Sam & Friends Mystery Ser.). 96p. (J). (gr. 2-5). 16.95 *(978-1-55453-470-8(4))* Kids Can Pr., Ltd. CAN. Dist: Hachette Bk. Group.

—Sword Quest. Fan, Nancy Yi. 2008. (Swordbird Ser.). 288p. (J). (gr. 3-7). lib. bdg. 16.89 *(978-0-06-124336-3(1))* HarperCollins Pubs.

—Sword Quest. Fan, Nancy Y. 2008. (Swordbird Ser.). 176p. (J). (gr. 3-7). 15.99 *(978-0-06-124335-6(3))* HarperCollins Pubs.

—Witches' Brew. Labatt, Mary. 2011. (Sam & Friends Mystery Ser.). 96p. (J). (gr. 2-5). 16.95 *(978-1-55453-472-2(0))* Kids Can Pr., Ltd. CAN. Dist: Hachette Bk. Group.

Riphagen, Loes. Animals Home Alone. 2011. (ENG.). 32p. (J). (gr. -1-3). 15.95 *(978-1-934734-55-1(1))* Seven Footer Pr.

Ripley's Entertainment Inc., Staff. Ripley's Believe It or Not! Ripley's Entertainment Inc., Staff. 2017. (Ripley's Believe It or Not! Ser.). 144p. (J). (gr. 3-7). 16.99 *(978-1-338-20027-0(5))* Scholastic, Inc.

Ripper, Georgie. Abigail: The Breeze Fairy. Meadows, Daisy. 2006. (Weather Fairies Ser.: 2). (ENG.). 80p. (J). (gr. -1-3). 4.99 *(978-0-439-81386-0(7)*, Scholastic Paperbacks) Scholastic, Inc.

—Amber: The Orange Fairy. Meadows, Daisy. 2005. (Rainbow Magic Ser.: 2). (ENG.). 80p. (J). (gr. -1-3). pap. 4.99 *(978-0-439-74465-2(2))* Scholastic, Inc.

—Bella the Bunny Fairy. Meadows, Daisy. 2008. (Pet Fairies Ser.: 2). (ENG.). 80p. (J). (gr. -1-3). 4.99 *(978-0-545-04185-0(6)*, Scholastic Paperbacks) Scholastic, Inc.

—Bella the Bunny Fairy. Meadows, Daisy. ed. 2008. (Rainbow Magic — the Pet Fairies Ser.). 65p. (gr. 7). lib. bdg. 14.75 *(978-1-4178-2996-5(6))* Turtleback.

—Crystal: The Snow Fairy. Meadows, Daisy. 2006. (Weather Fairies Ser.: 1). (ENG.). 80p. (J). (gr. -1-3). mass mkt. 4.99 *(978-0-439-81387-7(5)*, Scholastic Paperbacks) Scholastic, Inc.

—Emily, the Emerald Fairy. Meadows, Daisy. 2005. 65p. (J). pap. *(978-0-545-01190-7(6))* Scholastic, Inc.

—Georgia the Guinea Pig Fairy. Meadows, Daisy. ed. 2008. (Rainbow Magic — the Pet Fairies Ser.). 65p. (gr. 3). lib. bdg. 14.75 *(978-1-4178-2997-2(4))* Turtleback.

—Heather the Violet Fairy. Meadows, Daisy. 2006. (Rainbow Magic Ser.: 7). (ENG.). 80p. (J). (gr. -1-3). 4.99 *(978-0-439-74686-1(8)*, Scholastic Paperbacks) Scholastic, Inc.

—Holly the Christmas Fairy. Meadows, Daisy. 2007. (Rainbow Magic Ser.). (ENG.). 176p. (Orig.). (J). (gr. -1-3). pap. 6.99 *(978-0-439-92880-9(X)*, Scholastic Paperbacks) Scholastic, Inc.

—Holly the Christmas Fairy. Meadows, Daisy. ed. 2007. (Rainbow Magic — Special Edition Ser.). 159p. (Orig.). (gr. -1-3). lib. bdg. 17.20 *(978-1-4178-1771-9(2))* Turtleback.

—Joy the Summer Vacation Fairy. Meadows, Daisy. 2007. (Rainbow Magic Ser.). (ENG.). 192p. (J). (gr. -1-3). 6.99 *(978-0-439-93442-8(7)*, Scholastic Paperbacks) Scholastic, Inc.

—Joy the Summer Vacation Fairy. Meadows, Daisy. ed. 2007. (Rainbow Magic — Special Edition Ser.). 177p. (gr. -1-3). lib. bdg. 17.20 *(978-1-4177-7081-6(3))* Turtleback.

—Katie the Kitten Fairy. Meadows, Daisy. 2008. (J). (Pet Fairies Ser.: 1). (ENG.). 80p. (gr. -1-3). pap. 4.99 *(978-0-545-02816-5(7)*, Scholastic Paperbacks); 65p. pap. *(978-0-545-13320-3(3))* Scholastic, Inc.

—Katie the Kitten Fairy. Meadows, Daisy. ed. 2008. (Rainbow Magic — the Pet Fairies Ser.). 65p. (gr. 1-4). lib. bdg. 14.75 *(978-1-4178-2999-6(0))* Turtleback.

—Molly the Goldfish Fairy. Meadows, Daisy. 2008. (Pet Fairies Ser.: 6). (ENG.). 80p. (J). (gr. -1-3). pap. 4.99 *(978-0-545-04189-8(9)*, Scholastic Paperbacks) Scholastic, Inc.

—Molly the Goldfish Fairy. Meadows, Daisy. ed. 2008. (Rainbow Magic — the Pet Fairies Ser.). 68p. (gr. -1-3). lib. bdg. 14.75 *(978-1-4178-3001-5(8))* Turtleback.

—Ruby the Red Fairy. Meadows, Daisy. 2005. (Rainbow Magic Ser.: 1). (ENG.). 80p. (Orig.). (J). (gr. -1-3). pap. 4.99 *(978-0-439-73861-3(X))* Scholastic, Inc.

—Saffron the Yellow Fairy. Meadows, Daisy. 2004. (Rainbow Magic Ser.). 69p. (Orig.). (J). *(978-0-439-69195-6(8))* Scholastic, Inc.

—Sky the Blue Fairy. Meadows, Daisy. 2005. (Rainbow Magic Ser.: 5). (ENG.). 80p. (Orig.). (J). (gr. -1-3). per. 4.99 *(978-0-439-74684-7(1)*, Scholastic Paperbacks) Scholastic, Inc.

—Stella the Star Fairy. Meadows, Daisy. ed. 2008. (Rainbow Magic Ser.). (ENG.). 192p. (J). (gr. -1-3). pap. 6.99 *(978-0-545-06776-8(6)*, Scholastic Paperbacks) Scholastic, Inc.

—Storm: The Lightning Fairy. Meadows, Daisy. 2007. (Weather Fairies Ser.: 6). (ENG.). 80p. (J). (gr. -1-3). pap. 4.99 *(978-0-439-81391-4(3)*, Scholastic Paperbacks) Scholastic, Inc.

Ripper, Peter. Hullo Sun. Hodgson, Joan. 2003. 32p. (gr. -1-3). 8.95 *(978-0-85487-072-1(5))* White Eagle Publishing Trust GBR. Dist: DeVorss & Co.

—Our Father. Hodgson, Joan. 2003. 24p. (gr. k-7). 5.95 *(978-0-85487-040-0(7))* White Eagle Publishing Trust GBR. Dist: DeVorss & Co.

Rippin, Sally. Mannie & the Long Brave Day. Murray, Martine. 2010. (ENG.). 32p. (J). (gr. -1-k). 17.99 *(978-1-74175-886-3(6))* Allen & Unwin AUS. Dist: Independent Pubs. Group.

R

—Meditation Is an Open Sky: Mindfulness for Kids. Stewart, Whitney. 2015. (ENG.). 32p. (J). (gr. -1-3). 12.99 *(978-0-8075-4908-7(8)*, 807549088) Whitman, Albert & Co.

Rippin, Sally. Where Is Baby? Rippin, Sally. 2009. (ENG.). 12p. (J). (gr. k — 1). bds. 7.99 *(978-1-74175-386-8(4))* Allen & Unwin AUS. Dist: Independent Pubs. Group.

Rippon, Jor-El. Princess, the Future Queen: A Mother's Guidance. Harris, Kandi. l.t. ed. 2006. 32p. (J). bds. 12.99 *(978-0-9770331-1-9(2))* Harris, K Publishing, Inc.

Ripps, Robert A., photos by. She's Out There! Essays by 35 Young Women Who Aspire to Lead the Nation - The Next Generation of Presidential Candidates. Sewell, Amy & Ogilvie, Heather. 2009. (ENG., 224p. 25.00 *(978-0-9816368-4-9(5))* LifeTime Media, Inc.

Risch, Christopher. In Mommy's Garden: A Book to Help Explain Cancer to Young Children. Ammary, Neyal J. 2004. 34p. (J). per. 10.95 *(978-0-9754221-0-6(3))* Canyon Beach Visual Communications.

Risi, Alice. EDGE: Tommy Donbavand's Funny Shorts: There's a Time Portal in My Pants! Donbavand, Tommy. ed. 2018. (EDGE: Tommy Donbavand's Funny Shorts Ser.). 64p. (J). (gr. 2-4). 12.99 *(978-1-4451-5388-9(2)*, Franklin Watts) Hachette Children's Group GBR. Dist: Hachette Bk. Group.

Rising Star Studios. Auto-B-Good - Citizen Miles: A Lesson in Citizenship. Walton, Phillip. 2010. 48p. (J). pap. 7.95 *(978-1-936086-52-8(2))*; lib. bdg. 14.95 *(978-1-936086-46-7(8))* Rising Star Studios, LLC.

Risley, Jacqueline & Tim. Alpha's ABC's Games: Spanish & English Ages 2-6. Risley, Jacqueline & Tim. 2007.Tr. of Alfa y sus Juegos de la A a la Z. (SPA & ENG.). 32p. (J). 6.99 *(978-0-9791680-0-0(7))* Alpha Learning World, Inc.

Risling, Lyn. A Is for Acorn: A California Indian ABC. Tripp, Analisa. 2015. (ENG.). 28p. (J). bds. 9.99 *(978-1-59714-316-5(2))* Heyday.

Risling-Sholl, Oona. Goober et Muffin. Lenihan, Kelly. Pledger, Dylan, tr. 2018. (FRE.). 50p. (J). 20.00 *(978-0-9991200-2-6(6))*; pap. 12.95 *(978-0-9991200-3-3(4))* Artisan Bookworks.

—Goober und Muffin. Lenihan, Kelly. Lenihan, Jutta, tr. 2018. (GER.). 50p. (J). 20.00 *(978-0-9979578-0-8(8))* Artisan Bookworks.

—Goober y Muffin. Lenihan, Kelly. Garcia, Norma, tr. 2018. (SPA.). 50p. (J). pap. 12.95 *(978-0-9979578-8-4(3))*; (gr. -1-3). 20.00 *(978-0-9979578-2-2(4))* Artisan Bookworks.

Risling-Sholl, Oona. Губер и Маффин; Lenihan, Kelly. Lazurin, Viacheslav, tr. 2020. (RUS.). 48p. (J). 20.00 ***(978-0-9991200-5-7(0))*** Artisan Bookworks.

Risling-Sholl, Oona & Bardoff, Naomi. La Piedra Que Salta. Lenihan, Kelly. 2018. (SPA.). 48p. (J). pap. 12.95 *(978-0-9979578-6-0(7))*; 20.00 *(978-0-9979578-3-9(2))* Artisan Bookworks.

—Le Ricochet. Lenihan, Kelly. 2018. (FRE.). 42p. (J). pap. 12.95 *(978-0-9991200-0-2(X))*; 17.95 *(978-0-9979578-9-1(1))* Artisan Bookworks.

Risling-Sholl, Oona & Bardoff, Naomi. Летит; камень; над; водой; Lenihan, Kelly. 2020. (RUS.). 42p. (J). 20.00 ***(978-0-9991200-7-1(7))*** Artisan Bookworks.

Risor, Katie. When Mommy Caught a Dragon. Carlson, Jon. 2018. (ENG.). 28p. (J). pap. 10.98 *(978-1-9814-9986-1(5))* CreateSpace Independent Publishing Platform.

Rissing, Karen. Snickerdoodle! a Tall Tale about a Powerful Pee-Wee! Grosgebauer, Clare Ham. 3rd ed. 2005. 40p. (J). (gr. -1-3). 12.99 *(978-0-9741888-2-9(4))* Small Wonders Enterprises.

—Snickerdoodle & the Roller-Skating Horse! Grosgebauer, Clare Ham. 3rd ed. 2005. 36p. (J). (gr. -1-3). 12.99 *(978-0-9741888-4-3(0))* Small Wonders Enterprises.

—Snickerdoodle's Star-Spangled Fourth of July! Grosgebauer, Clare Ham. 4th ed. 2005. 36p. (J). (gr. -1-3). 12.99 *(978-0-9741888-6-7(7))* Small Wonders Enterprises.

Rissland, Devon. The Spotted Zebra. McDonnell, Scott. Gulley, Robin, ed. 2017. (ENG.). (J). (gr. -1-3). pap. 14.99 *(978-0-9981252-3-7(7))* Gulley, Wayne.

Ristic, Milan. Menopause vs Puberty. Lumpkin, Tommalisa. Shaw, Robin, ed. 2019. (ENG.). 186p. (J). pap. 12.99 *(978-1-0818-8057-6(0))* Independently Published.

Ristord, Emmanuel. Touch & Explore: Animals at Night. Hedelin, Pascale. 2020. (Touch & Explore Ser.: 10). (ENG.). 16p. (J). (gr. -1-k). 14.99 *(978-2-408-01598-5(7))* Éditions Tourbillon FRA. Dist: Hachette Bk. Group.

Ristow, Trevor. Drawing a Blank: Or How I Tried to Solve a Mystery, End a Feud, & Land the Girl of My Dreams. Ehrenhaft, Daniel. 2009. (ENG.). 352p. (J). pap. 8.99 *(978-0-06-075254-5(8)*, HarperTeen) HarperCollins Pubs.

Riswold, Gilbert. The Highwayman. Noyes, Alfred. 2003. (ENG.). 31p. (gr. 6-6). cd-rom 147.47 net. *(978-0-13-036517-0(3)*, Prentice Hall) Savvas Learning Co.

Ritchey, Jessica. Curtis Gets Ready to Dream: A Bedtime Story to Guide Your Child to Sleep. Stiller, Catrina. 2017. (ENG.). 38p. (J). pap. 9.95 *(978-1-68350-102-2(0))* Morgan James Publishing.

Ritchie, Alex. Babies Are Boring. Ritchie, Jon. 2008. 40p. (J). *(978-0-9809970-0-2(3))* Purple Possum Publishing Inc.

Ritchie, Fern J. & Ritchie, Ralph W., photos by. Weaving with Rags & Leftovers: The Best of Recycling. Ritchie, Fern J. & Ritchie, Ralph W. 2005. 177p. (YA). cd-rom 14.95 *(978-0-939656-86-8(8)*, 0-939656-86-8) Ritchie Unlimited Pubns.

Ritchie, Ralph W., jt. photos by see Ritchie, Fern J.

Ritchie, Scot. How? The Most Awesome Question & Answer Book about Nature, Animals, People, Places — And You! Ripley, Catherine. 2019. (ENG.). 192p. (J). (gr. -1-4). pap. 17.95 *(978-1-77147-384-2(3))* Owlkids Bks. Inc. CAN. Dist: Publishers Group West (PGW).

—I'm Only Three¿ & Look at All the Things That I Can Do! Graves, Harmon. 2013. 30p. pap. 13.95 *(978-1-4349-3729-2(1))* Dorrance Publishing Co., Inc.

—See Saw Saskatchewan. Heidbreder, Robert. 2005. 32p. (J). (gr. -1-4). 7.95 *(978-1-55337-968-3(3))* Kids Can Pr., Ltd. CAN. Dist: Hachette Bk. Group.

—What Millie Did: The Remarkable Pioneer of Plastics Recycling, 1 vol. Moser, Elise. 2016. (ENG.). 48p. (J). (gr. 2-6). pap. 9.95 *(978-1-55498-893-8(4))* Groundwood Bks. CAN. Dist: Publishers Group West (PGW).

—Why? The Best Ever Question & Answer Book about Nature, Science & the World Around You. Ripley, Catherine. 2018. (ENG.). 192p. (J). (gr. -1-4). pap. 17.95 *(978-1-77147-321-7(5))* Owlkids Bks. Inc. CAN. Dist: Publishers Group West (PGW).

Ritchie, Scot. Follow That Bee! A First Book of Bees in the City. Ritchie, Scot. 2019. (Exploring Our Community Ser.). (ENG.). 32p. (J). (gr. -1-2). 16.99 *(978-1-5253-0034-9(2))* Kids Can Pr., Ltd. CAN. Dist: Hachette Bk. Group.

—Follow That Map! A First Book of Mapping Skills. Ritchie, Scot. 2009. (ENG.). 32p. (J). (gr. -1-2). 17.99 *(978-1-55453-274-2(4))* Kids Can Pr., Ltd. CAN. Dist: Hachette Bk. Group.

—Join the No-Plastic Challenge! A First Book of Reducing Waste. Ritchie, Scot. 2019. (Exploring Our Community Ser.). (ENG.). 32p. (J). (gr. -1-2). 16.99 *(978-1-5253-0240-4(X))* Kids Can Pr., Ltd. CAN. Dist: Hachette Bk. Group.

—Look at That Building! A First Book of Structures. Ritchie, Scot. 2011. (ENG.). 32p. (J). (gr. -1-2). 16.99 *(978-1-55453-696-2(0))* Kids Can Pr., Ltd. CAN. Dist: Hachette Bk. Group.

—Look Where We Live! A First Book of Community Building. Ritchie, Scot. 2015. (ENG.). 32p. (J). (gr. -1-2). 16.99 *(978-1-77138-102-4(7))* Kids Can Pr., Ltd. CAN. Dist: Hachette Bk. Group.

—See How We Move! A First Book of Health & Well-Being. Ritchie, Scot. 2018. (ENG.). 32p. (J). (gr. -1-2). 16.99 *(978-1-77138-967-9(2))* Kids Can Pr., Ltd. CAN. Dist: Hachette Bk. Group.

—See What We Eat! A First Book of Healthy Eating. Ritchie, Scot. 2017. (ENG.). 32p. (J). (gr. -1-2). 16.99 *(978-1-77138-618-0(5))* Kids Can Pr., Ltd. CAN. Dist: Hachette Bk. Group.

—Up, up & Away! Ritchie, Scot. 2005. (ENG.). 32p. pap. *(978-1-921049-01-9(4))* Little Hare Bks. AUS. Dist: HarperCollins Pubs. Australia.

Riti, Marsha. All about Ellie. Barkley, Callie. 2013. (Critter Club Ser.: 2). (ENG.). 128p. (J). (gr. k-2). 17.99 *(978-1-4424-5789-8(9))*; pap. 5.99 *(978-1-4424-5788-1(0))* Little Simon. (Little Simon).

—Amy & the Missing Puppy. Barkley, Callie. 2013. (Critter Club Ser.: 1). (ENG.). 128p. (J). (gr. k-2). 17.99 *(978-1-4424-5770-6(8))*; pap. 5.99 *(978-1-4424-5769-0(4))* Little Simon. (Little Simon).

—Amy Meets Her Stepsister. Barkley, Callie. 2013. (Critter Club Ser.: 5). (ENG.). 128p. (J). (gr. k-2). 17.99 *(978-1-4424-8216-6(8))*; pap. 5.99 *(978-1-4424-8215-9(X))* Little Simon. (Little Simon).

—The Critter Club: Amy & the Missing Puppy; All about Ellie; Liz Learns a Lesson. Barkley, Callie. 2014. (Critter Club Ser.). (ENG.). 368p. (J). (gr. k-4). pap. 8.99 *(978-1-4814-2770-8(9)*, Little Simon) Little Simon.

—Ellie & the Good-Luck Pig. Barkley, Callie. 2015. (Critter Club Ser.: 10). (ENG.). 128p. (J). (gr. k-4). pap. 5.99 *(978-1-4814-2402-8(5)*, Little Simon) Little Simon.

—Ellie's Lovely Idea. Barkley, Callie. 2013. (Critter Club Ser.: 6). (ENG.). 128p. (J). (gr. k-4). 17.99 *(978-1-4424-8219-7(2))*; pap. 5.99 *(978-1-4424-8218-0(4))* Little Simon. (Little Simon).

—Liz & the Sand Castle Contest. Barkley, Callie. 2015. (Critter Club Ser.: 11). (ENG.). 128p. (J). (gr. k-4). pap. 5.99 *(978-1-4814-2405-9(X)*, Little Simon) Little Simon.

—Liz at Marigold Lake. Barkley, Callie. 2014. (Critter Club Ser.: 7). (ENG.). 128p. (J). (gr. k-4). pap. 5.99 *(978-1-4424-9525-8(1)*, Little Simon) Little Simon.

—Liz Learns a Lesson. Barkley, Callie. 2013. (Critter Club Ser.: 3). (ENG.). 128p. (J). (gr. -1-2). 17.99 *(978-1-4424-6770-5(3))*; pap. 5.99 *(978-1-4424-6768-2(1))* Little Simon. (Little Simon).

—Marion Strikes a Pose. Barkley, Callie. 2014. (Critter Club Ser.: 8). (ENG.). 128p. (J). (gr. k-4). 16.99 *(978-1-4424-9529-6(4)*, Little Simon) Little Simon.

—Marion Takes a Break. Barkley, Callie. 2013. (Critter Club Ser.: 4). (ENG.). 128p. (J). (gr. k-2). 17.99 *(978-1-4424-6773-6(8))*; pap. 5.99 *(978-1-4424-6772-9(X))* Little Simon. (Little Simon).

—Marion Takes Charge. Barkley, Callie. 2015. (Critter Club Ser.: 12). (ENG.). 128p. (J). (gr. k-4). pap. 5.99 *(978-1-4814-2408-0(4)*, Little Simon) Little Simon.

—The Picky Little Witch, 1 vol. Brokamp, Elizabeth. 2011. (ENG.). 32p. (J). (gr. k-3). 16.99 *(978-1-58980-882-9(7)*, Pelican Publishing) Arcadia Publishing.

Ritter, Adam. Old Mo. Hsu, Stacey W. 2011. (Rookie Ready to Learn — Animals Ser.). 40p. (J). (gr. -1-k). lib. bdg. 25.00 *(978-0-531-26418-8(1))*; pap. 5.95 *(978-0-531-26699-1(0))* Scholastic Library Publishing. (Children's Pr.).

Rittmueller, Jeanne. Christopher's Bedtime Story. Haave, Meghan. 2012. 32p. (J). pap. 9.95 *(978-1-59530-459-9(2))* Hallmark Card, Inc.

Ritz, Gianna Rose. The Purple Forest. Iannelli, Joseph. 2020. (ENG.). 26p. (J). pap. 9.99 ***(978-1-6708-7451-1(6))*** Independently Published.

Ritz, Karen. Kate Shelley y el Tren de Medianoche. Wetterer, Margaret K. 2005. (Yo Solo - Historia (on My Own - History) Ser.).Tr. of Kate Shelley & the Midnight Express. (SPA.). 48p. (J). (gr. 2-5). per. 6.95 *(978-0-8225-3193-7(3))* Lerner Publishing Group.

—Kate Shelley y el Tren de Medianoche. Wetterer, Margaret K. Translations.com Staff, tr. 2005. (Yo Solo: Historia (on My Own History) Ser.).Tr. of Kate Shelley & the Midnight Express. (SPA.). 48p. (J). (gr. 2-4). lib. bdg. 25.32 *(978-0-8225-3096-1(1)*, Ediciones Lerner) Lerner Publishing Group.

—Martha Washington. Ransom, Candice. 2003. (On My Own Biographies Ser.). 48p. (J). 25.26 *(978-0-87614-918-8(2)*, Carolrhoda Bks.); (ENG.). (gr. 2-4). per. 7.99 *(978-0-87614-107-6(6)*, First Avenue Editions) Lerner Publishing Group.

—Max Talks to Me. Buchwald, Claire. 2007. (Sit! Stay! Read! Ser.). (ENG.). 24p. (J). (gr. k-2). 16.95 *(978-0-940719-03-3(7))* Gryphon Pr., The.

—Sadie Braves the Wilderness. Pearson, Yvonne. 2017. (ENG.). 32p. (J). (gr. -1-2). 16.95 *(978-1-68134-038-8(0))* Minnesota Historical Society Pr.

—Snowboarding on Monster Mountain. Bunting, Eve. 2003. (ENG.). 64p. (J). 15.95 *(978-0-8126-2704-6(0))* Cricket Bks.

Ritzmann, Mary B. L. I. B. B. Y. The Green Dog. Riachi, Ghassan Diab & Mitchell, Anna B. RJI Publishing, ed. 2011.Tr. of L. I. B. B. Y., el Perro Verde. 32p. (J). mass mkt. 9.95 *(978-1-885184-11-5(5))* RJI Publishing.

Rius, María. Los Tres Cerditos (The Three Little Pigs) Orihuela, Luz. Sarfatti, Esther, tr. 2006. (Bilingual Tales Ser.). (SPA & ENG.). 24p. (J). (gr. -1-3). pap. 3.99 *(978-0-439-77382-9(2)*, Scholastic en Espanol) Scholastic, Inc.

Rius, Roser. Ruth es un Torbellino. Rius, Roser. Rius Camps, Roser. Terzi, Marinella, tr. 2008. (SPA.). 24p. (J). *(978-84-675-2422-2(7))* SM Ediciones.

Rivard, Rebecca. Ben Has Autism. Ben Is Awesome. Zolty, Meredith. 2011. 32p. (J). pap. 9.95 *(978-0-944727-41-6(7)*, Turtle Bks.) Jason & Nordic Pubs.

Rivas, Miguel Díaz. FGTeeV Presents: into the Game! FGTeeV. 2020. (ENG.). 208p. (J). (gr. 3-7). 19.99 *(978-0-06-293367-6(1))* HarperCollins Pubs.

Rivas, Miguel Díaz. Red Riding Hood. Oxtra, Cristina. 2020. (Fairy Tales Ser.). (ENG.). 32p. (J). (gr. k-2). pap. 6.95 ***(978-1-5158-7275-7(0)***, 201236); lib. bdg. 21.32 ***(978-1-5158-7121-7(5)***, 199341) Capstone. (Picture Window Bks.).

Rivas, Victor. Bigfoot. Peabody, Erin. 2017. (Behind the Legend Ser.: 2). (ENG.). 128p. (J). (gr. 2-5). pap. 9.99 *(978-1-4998-0425-6(3))* Little Bee Books Inc.

—Campfire Stories. Miedoso, Andres. 2019. (Desmond Cole Ghost Patrol Ser.: 8). (ENG.). 128p. (J). (gr. k-4). 16.99 *(978-1-5344-3351-9(1))*; pap. 5.99 *(978-1-5344-3350-2(3))* Little Simon. (Little Simon).

—Caperucita Roja. Andersen, Hans & Stone Arch Books Staff. 2010. (Graphic Spin en Español Ser.). (SPA.). 40p. (J). (gr. 3-6). pap. 5.95 *(978-1-4342-2315-9(9)*, Stone Arch Bks.) Capstone.

—The Desmond Cole Ghost Patrol Collection: The Haunted House Next Door; Ghosts Don't Ride Bikes, Do They?; Surf's up, Creepy Stuff!; Night of the Zombie Zookeeper. Miedoso, Andres. ed. 2018. (Desmond Cole Ghost Patrol Ser.). (ENG.). 512p. (J). (gr. k-4). pap. 23.99 *(978-1-5344-3222-2(1)*, Little Simon) Little Simon.

Rivas, Victor. The Desmond Cole Ghost Patrol Collection #2: The Scary Library Shusher; Major Monster Mess; the Sleepwalking Snowman; Campfire Stories. Miedoso, Andres. ed. 2020. (Desmond Cole Ghost Patrol Ser.). (ENG.). 512p. (J). (gr. k-4). pap. 23.99 ***(978-1-5344-6534-3(0)***, Little Simon) Little Simon.

Rivas, Victor. Dragons. Peabody, Erin. 2018. (Behind the Legend Ser.). (ENG.). 128p. (J). (gr. 2-5). 17.99 *(978-1-4998-0572-7(1))*; pap. 9.99 *(978-1-4998-0571-0(3))* Little Bee Books Inc.

Rivas, Victor. Escape from the Roller Ghoster. Miedoso, Andres. 2020. (Desmond Cole Ghost Patrol Ser.: 11). (ENG.). 128p. (J). (gr. k-4). 17.99 ***(978-1-5344-6491-9(3))***; pap. 5.99 ***(978-1-5344-6490-2(5))*** Little Simon. (Little Simon).

Rivas, Victor. Ghosts Don't Ride Bikes, Do They? Miedoso, Andres. 2017. (Desmond Cole Ghost Patrol Ser.: 2). (ENG.). 128p. (J). (gr. k-4). 16.99 *(978-1-5344-1042-8(2))*; pap. 5.99 *(978-1-5344-1041-1(4))* Little Simon. (Little Simon).

—Ghouls Just Want to Have Fun. Miedoso, Andres. 2020. (Desmond Cole Ghost Patrol Ser.: 10). (ENG.). 128p. (J). (gr. k-4). 16.99 *(978-1-5344-6110-9(8))*; pap. 5.99 *(978-1-5344-6109-3(4))* Little Simon. (Little Simon).

—The Haunted House Next Door. Miedoso, Andres. 2017. (Desmond Cole Ghost Patrol Ser.: 1). (ENG.). 128p. (J). (gr. k-4). 16.99 *(978-1-5344-1039-8(2))*; pap. 5.99 *(978-1-5344-1038-1(4))* Little Simon. (Little Simon).

—In a Dark, Dark Room & Other Scary Stories: Reillustrated Edition. Schwartz, Alvin. 2017. (I Can Read Level 2 Ser.). (ENG.). 64p. (J). (gr. -1-3). 16.99 *(978-0-06-264338-4(X))*; pap. 4.99 *(978-0-06-264337-7(1))* HarperCollins Pubs.

—John Henry vs the Mighty Steam Drill, 1 vol. Meister, Cari. 2014. (American Folk Legends Ser.). (ENG.). 32p. (J). (gr. k-2). 27.99 *(978-1-4795-5430-0(8)*, Picture Window Bks.) Capstone.

—The Loch Ness Monster. Peabody, Erin. 2017. (Behind the Legend Ser.: 1). (ENG.). 128p. (J). (gr. 2-5). pap. 9.99 *(978-1-4998-0423-2(7))* Little Bee Books Inc.

—Major Monster Mess. Miedoso, Andres. 2018. (Desmond Cole Ghost Patrol Ser.: 6). (ENG.). 128p. (J). (gr. k-4). 16.99 *(978-1-5344-2695-5(7))*; pap. 5.99 *(978-1-5344-2694-8(9))* Little Simon. (Little Simon).

—Night of the Zombie Zookeeper. Miedoso, Andres. 2018. (Desmond Cole Ghost Patrol Ser.: 4). (ENG.). 128p. (J). (gr. k-4). 16.99 *(978-1-5344-1805-9(9))*; pap. 5.99 *(978-1-5344-1804-2(0))* Little Simon. (Little Simon).

—Now Museum, Now You Don't. Miedoso, Andres. 2019. (Desmond Cole Ghost Patrol Ser.: 9). (ENG.). 128p. (J). (gr. k-4). 16.99 *(978-1-5344-4952-7(3))*; pap. 5.99 *(978-1-5344-4951-0(5))* Little Simon. (Little Simon).

—Red Riding Hood: The Graphic Novel, 1 vol. Stone Arch Books Staff. 2008. (Graphic Spin Ser.). (ENG.). 40p. (J). (gr. 3-6). pap. 5.95 *(978-1-4342-0865-1(6)*, Stone Arch Bks.) Capstone.

—The Scary Library Shusher. Miedoso, Andres. 2018. (Desmond Cole Ghost Patrol Ser.: 5). (ENG.). 128p. (J). (gr. k-4). 16.99 *(978-1-5344-2692-4(2))*; pap. 5.99 *(978-1-5344-2691-7(4))* Little Simon. (Little Simon).

—The Sleepwalking Snowman. Miedoso, Andres. 2019. (Desmond Cole Ghost Patrol Ser.: 7). (ENG.). 128p. (J). (gr. k-4). 16.99 *(978-1-5344-3348-9(1))*; pap. 5.99 *(978-1-5344-3347-2(3))* Little Simon. (Little Simon).

—Surf's up, Creepy Stuff! Miedoso, Andres. 2018. (Desmond Cole Ghost Patrol Ser.: 3). (ENG.). 128p. (J). (gr. k-4). 16.99 *(978-1-5344-1802-8(4))*; pap. 5.99 *(978-1-5344-1801-1(6))* Little Simon. (Little Simon).

—Werewolves. Peabody, Erin. 2017. (Behind the Legend Ser.). (ENG.). 128p. (J). (gr. 2-5). pap. 9.99 *(978-1-4998-0458-4(X))* Little Bee Books Inc.

—100% Wolf. Lyons, Jayne. (ENG.). 256p. (J). (gr. 2-7). 2010. pap. 8.99 *(978-1-4424-0252-2(0))*; 2009. 16.99 *(978-1-4169-7474-1(1))* Simon & Schuster Children's Publishing. (Atheneum Bks. for Young Readers).

Rivera, Addy. Cleopatra. Platt, Christine. 2019. (Sheroes Ser.). (ENG.). 32p. (J). (gr. -1-3). lib. bdg. 28.50 *(978-1-5321-3641-2(2)*, 33728, Calico Chapter Bks) Magic Wagon.

—Harriet Tubman. Platt, Christine. 2019. (Sheroes Ser.). (ENG.). 32p. (J). (gr. -1-3). lib. bdg. 28.50 *(978-1-5321-3642-9(0)*, 33730, Calico Chapter Bks) Magic Wagon.

—Joan of Arc. Platt, Christine. 2019. (Sheroes Ser.). (ENG.). 32p. (J). (gr. -1-3). lib. bdg. 28.50 *(978-1-5321-3643-6(9)*, 33732, Calico Chapter Bks) Magic Wagon.

—Sacagawea. Platt, Christine. 2019. (Sheroes Ser.). (ENG.). 32p. (J). (gr. -1-3). lib. bdg. 28.50 *(978-1-5321-3644-3(7)*, 33734, Calico Chapter Bks) Magic Wagon.

—Sheroes (Set), 4 vols. Platt, Christine. 2019. (Sheroes Ser.). (ENG.). 32p. (J). (gr. -1-3). lib. bdg. 114.00 *(978-1-5321-3640-5(4)*, 33726, Calico Chapter Bks) Magic Wagon.

Rivera, Alba Marina. El Contador de Cuentos. Saki. Canales, Veronica & Guix, Juan Gabriel Lopez, trs. 2008. (SPA.). (J). (gr. 5-8). pap. 20.99 *(978-84-936504-3-8(9))* Ekaré Europa S.L. ESP. Dist: Lectorum Pubns., Inc.

Rivera, Alex. Bronxshapes. Rivera, Alex. 2020. (Bronx Baby Ser.). 14p. (J). (— 1). bds. 7.99 ***(978-0-593-11081-2(1)***, Kokila) Penguin Young Readers Group.

—Bronxtones. Rivera, Alex. 2020. (Bronx Baby Ser.). 14p. (J). (— 1). bds. 7.99 ***(978-0-593-11078-2(1)***, Kokila) Penguin Young Readers Group.

Rivera Carbajal, Adriana. El Tren Más Pesado Del Mundo. Moran Gama, Claudia Elena. 2019. (SPA.). 30p. (J). pap. 11.00 *(978-1-64086-313-2(3))* ibukku, LLC.

Rivera, Diego. My Papá Diego & Me (Mi Papa Diego y Yo) Memories of My Father & His Art (Recuerdos de Mi Padre y Su Arte) Marín, Guadalupe Rivera. 2013. (SPA & ENG.). 32p. (J). (gr. k-5). 18.95 *(978-0-89239-228-5(2))* Lee & Low Bks., Inc.

Rivera, Hanae. Kodoku. Justice, William E. 2012. (ENG.). 32p. (J). 16.95 *(978-1-59714-173-4(9))* Heyday.

Rivera, Juliana. Luna's Mission Trip. Riddering, Karenlie. 2019. (Luna Merina & the Shiny Club Ser.: Vol. 2). (ENG.). 132p. (J). pap. 9.99 ***(978-1-7094-9115-3(9))*** Independently Published.

Rivera, Matthew. I'm Happy-Sad Today: Making Sense of Mixed-Together Feelings. Britain, Lory. 2019. (ENG.). 40p. (J). (gr. -1-2). 15.99 *(978-1-63198-305-4(9)*, 83054) Free Spirit Publishing, Inc.

—Operation Photobomb. Cattie, Becky & Luebbe, Tara. 2019. (ENG.). 32p. (J). (gr. -1-3). 16.99 *(978-0-8075-6130-0(4)*, 807561304) Whitman, Albert & Co.

Rivera, Matthew. Roxy the Last Unisaurus Rex. Chen, Eva. 2020. (ENG.). 32p. (J). 18.99 ***(978-1-250-61992-1(0)***, 900223151) Feiwel & Friends.

Rivera, Matthew & Rivera, Matthew. Dinosaur Yoga. Gates, Mariam. 2019. (ENG.). 32p. (J). 17.95 *(978-1-68364-304-3(6)*, 900214682) Sounds True, Inc.

Rivera, Matthew, jt. illus. see Rivera, Matthew.

Rivera, Paolo Manuel. Spider-Man: One Moment in Time. 2011. (ENG.). 162p. (J). (gr. 4-17). pap. 19.99 *(978-0-7851-4620-9(2))* Marvel Worldwide, Inc.

Rivera, Rafael, et al. Baseball on Mars/Béisbol en Marte. Rivera, Rafael et al. 2009.Tr. of Béisbol en Marte. (SPA & ENG.). 32p. (J). (gr. -1-3). 16.95 *(978-1-55885-521-2(1))* Arte Publico Pr.

Rivera, Roberta. Missing Treasure Means Trouble. Krapp, JoAnn Vergona. 2012. 66p. (J). (gr. 3-5). pap. 12.95 *(978-0-9722576-3-3(2))* JoAnn Vergona Krapp & Gene Zaner.

Rivera Sonda, Addy. Felíz New Year, Ava Gabriela! Alessandri, Alexandra. 2020. (ENG.). 32p. (J). (gr. -1-3). 16.99 ***(978-0-8075-0450-5(5)***, 0807504505) Whitman, Albert & Co.

Rivero, Marcos Almada. Copo de Algodon. Esperon, Maria Garcia. 2010. (SPA.). 136p. (YA). (gr. 6-8). pap. *(978-607-7661-17-7(1))* Ediciones El Naranjo Sa De Cv.

—Señorita Mariposa. Gundersheimer (Mister G), Ben. 2019. (SPA & ENG.). 32p. (J). (-k). 17.99 *(978-1-5247-4070-2(5)*, Nancy Paulsen Books) Penguin Young Readers Group.

Rivers, Ruth. Bugs: Level 1. Bowman, Lucy. 2007. (Beginners Nature Ser.). 32p. (J). 4.99 *(978-0-7945-1705-2(6)*, Usborne) EDC Publishing.

—The Donkey That Went Too Fast. Orme, David. 2005. 32p. (J). lib. bdg. 9.00 *(978-1-4242-0890-6(4))* Fitzgerald Bks.

—It's Not Worth Making a Tzimmes Over! Rosenthal, Betsy R. 2006. 32p. (J). (gr. k-3). lib. bdg. 16.99 *(978-0-8075-3677-3(6))* Whitman, Albert & Co.

—Mary Had a Dinosaur. Browne, Eileen. 2009. (Get Ready (Windmill Books) Ser.). 32p. (J). (gr. k-2). lib. bdg. 25.60 *(978-1-60754-262-9(5))* Windmill Bks.

—Snowshoe the Hare. White, Kathryn. 2005. (Red Go Bananas Ser.). (ENG.). 48p. (J). (gr. 2-3). pap. *(978-0-7787-2699-9(1)*, 1253648); lib. bdg. *(978-0-7787-2677-7(0)*, 1253648) Crabtree Publishing Co.

—The Story Bible. 2018. (ENG.). 256p. (J). (gr. -1-2). 16.99 *(978-1-68099-198-7(1)*, Good Bks.) Skyhorse Publishing Co., Inc.

Rivers, Tess. Santa's Trip to the Bayou. Stewart, Rosanne. 2020. (ENG.). 32p. (J). pap. 13.95 ***(978-1-64468-186-2(2))*** Covenant Bks.

Rix, Fred. How to Build Your Own Country. Wyatt, Valerie. 2009. (CitizenKid Ser.). (ENG.). 40p. (J). (gr. 3-7). 17.99 *(978-1-55453-310-7(4))* Kids Can Pr., Ltd. CAN. Dist: Hachette Bk. Group.

Rizal, Clarissa, jt. illus. see Koch, Nobu.

Rizvi, Farah. Inca: Discover the Culture & Geography of a Lost Civilization with 25 Projects. Kovacs, Lawrence. 2013. (Build It Yourself Ser.). 128p. (J). (gr. 3-7). 21.95 *(978-1-61930-141-2(5),* 2181ad5e-6bfa-4d39-8731-42831eb73e24); pap. 15.95 *(978-1-61930-140-5(7),* 09e440d2-3267-42c8-883a-dd1faa923769) Nomad Pr.

—Seven Wonders of the World: Discover Amazing Monuments to Civilization with 20 Projects. Van Vleet, Carmella. 2011. (Build It Yourself Ser.). 128p. (J). (gr. 3-7). 21.95 *(978-1-934670-82-8(0),* b2850405-d527-4181-ad67-d4bb3ad0ca6a); pap. 15.95 *(978-1-936313-73-0(1),* 327bef82-5d10-4938-9f53-cd2b7d261a74) Nomad Pr.

Rizvi, Farah, jt. illus. see Carbaugh, Samuel.

Rizy, Brock. Emily Edison: Volume 1. 2006. 139p. (gr. 8-18). pap. 12.95 *(978-0-9777883-2-3(6))* Viper Comics.

Rizzi, Marco. Millie-Mop & Mamie-Moo. Lines, Josh. 2019. (ENG.). 26p. (J). pap. 9.99 *(978-1-0951-4370-4(0))* Independently Published.

Rizzo, Jerry. Fifty-Seven Stories of Saints. Heffernan, Eileen. 2003. (J). 552p. pap. 16.95 *(978-0-8198-2674-9(X),* 332-094); 549p. *(978-0-8198-2675-6(8))* Pauline Bks. & Media.

—57 Stories of Saints. Heffernan, Anne Eileen. 3rd ed. 2006. 531p. (J). pap. 16.95 *(978-0-8198-2681-7(2))* Pauline Bks. & Media.

Rizzo, Letizia. Big Bed for Little Bear: Shaped Board Book. Wing, Scarlett. 2017. (I Can Do It Ser.). (ENG.). 11p. (J). (gr. -1-k). bds. 6.99 *(978-1-68052-200-6(0),* 1001980) Cottage Door Pr.

Rizzo, Letizia. Bling Blaine: Throw Glitter, Not Shade. Sanders, Rob. 2020. 32p. (J). (gr. -1). 16.95 ***(978-1-4549-3456-1(5))*** Sterling Publishing Co., Inc.

—Tales of Sasha 11: the Best Birthday Party Ever. Pearl, Alexa. 2020. (Tales of Sasha Ser.: 11). (ENG.). 112p. (J). (gr. k-3). 16.99 ***(978-1-4998-0764-6(3))***; pap. 5.99 ***(978-1-4998-0763-9(5))*** Little Bee Books Inc.

Ro, August. One Black Cat. Rogge, Robie. 2020. (ENG.). 12p. (J). (gr. -1-k). bds. 7.99 ***(978-1-5344-6404-9(2),*** Little Simon) Little Simon.

Roach-Langille, Nancy. Fiddle Fantasy: A Selection of Fiddle Tunes by Maritime Composers. Roach-Langille, Nancy. Mitchell, Francis G. Mitchell, Francis G., ed. 2nd ed. 2004. (ENG.). 6p. pap. *(978-1-895814-28-6(6),* NWP103) New World Publishing.

Roan, Destry Love. Wahogicobi: Kinship Terms to Make Relationships with Each Other, 1 vol. Nakota Sioux Language Keepers. 2020. (ENG.). 24p. (J). bds. 7.95 ***(978-1-926696-86-7(7),*** 4d0b03c6-086d-4499-8dc2-ee886f3b5a23) Eschia Bks. CAN. Dist: Lone Pine Publishing USA.

Roba, Jean. Friends First. Roba, Jean. 2012. (Billy & Buddy Ser.: 3). (ENG.). 48p. (J). (gr. 3-12). pap. 11.95 *(978-1-84918-124-2(1))* CineBook GBR. Dist: National Bk. Network.

Robaard, Jedda. I'm Ready for Christmas. Robaard, Jedda. Melbourne, Australia. 2020. 14p. (J). (gr. -1-k). bds. 11.99 ***(978-1-76089-161-9(4),*** Picture Puffin) Penguin Random Hse. AUS. Dist: Independent Pubs. Group.

—I'm Ready for Preschool. Robaard, Jedda. Australia & Melbourne, Australia. 2020. 14p. (J). (gr. -1-k). bds. 11.99 ***(978-1-76089-160-2(6),*** Picture Puffin) Penguin Random Hse. AUS. Dist: Independent Pubs. Group.

Robaard, Jedda. Milo & Millie. Robaard, Jedda. 2014. (ENG.). 32p. (J). (-k). 14.99 *(978-0-7636-6783-2(8))* Candlewick Pr.

Robare, Jay. Pets in Heaven Activity Book: Children's Companion Book to: Do Pets & Other Animals Go to Heaven? 2003. 86p. (J). per. 12.95 *(978-0-9726363-1-5(5),* 6315) Brite Bks.

Robb, Donald. The Night Before Christmas: A Visit from St. Nicholas. Moore, Clement C. 2018. (ENG.). 24p. (J). pap. 14.99 *(978-1-7274-2290-0(2))* CreateSpace Independent Publishing Platform.

Robb, Jonathan. Doby's First Christmas. Wilkins, Nalini. 2012. 28p. pap. 12.50 *(978-1-62212-777-1(3),* Strategic Bk. Publishing) Strategic Book Publishing & Rights Agency (SBPRA).

Robberecht, Thierry. Perdí mi Sonrisa. Robberecht, Thierry. Goossens, Philippe. (SPA.). 28p. (J). (gr. k-3). 14.95 *(978-970-29-0667-4(9))* Santillana USA Publishing Co., Inc.

Robbins, Ashley. The Legend of Red Leaf. Watson, Don. l.t. ed. 2005. 125p. (J). pap. 9.95 *(978-0-9714358-6-5(3))* Longhorn Creek Pr.

Robbins, Carrie. Who Was Wolfgang Amadeus Mozart? McDonough, Yona Zeldis & Who HQ. 2003. (Who Was? Ser.). (ENG.). 112p. (J). (gr. 3-7). pap. 5.99 *(978-0-448-43104-8(1),* Penguin Workshop) Penguin Young Readers Group.

Robbins, Elizabeth. The Great & the Grand. Fox, Benjamin. 2015. (ENG.). 32p. (J). 16.95 *(978-1-942672-97-5(7),* 557297) Familius LLC.

Robbins, Frank, et al. Marvel Masterworks: Luke Cage, Power Man Vol. 3: Mercs for Money. 2019. (Marvel Masterworks: Luke Cage, Power Man Ser.: 3). (ENG.). 328p. (gr. 4-17). 75.00 *(978-1-302-91635-0(1))* Marvel Worldwide, Inc.

Robbins, Kathryn. That's What's Different about Me: Helping Children Understand Autism Spectrum Disorders. McKracken, Heather. 2006. (J). pap. 59.95 *(978-1-931282-96-3(X))* Autism Asperger Publishing Co.

—That's What's Different about Me! Helping Children Understand Autism Spectrum Disorders - Story & Coloring BK. Mccracken, Heather. 2006. (J). pap. 3.00 *(978-1-931282-97-0(8))* Autism Asperger Publishing Co.

Robbins, Ken. Fireflies at Midnight. Singer, Marilyn. 2003. (ENG.). 32p. (J). (gr. k-4). 19.99 *(978-0-689-82492-0(0),* Atheneum Bks. for Young Readers) Simon & Schuster Children's Publishing.

Robbins, Ken. Seeds. Robbins, Ken. 2005. (ENG.). 32p. (J). (gr. 1-4). 17.99 *(978-0-689-85041-7(7),* Atheneum Bks. for Young Readers) Simon & Schuster Children's Publishing.

—Thunder on the Plains: The Story of the American Buffalo. Robbins, Ken. 2009. (ENG.). 36p. (J). (gr. 2-5). pap. 10.99 *(978-1-4169-9536-4(6),* Atheneum Bks. for Young Readers) Simon & Schuster Children's Publishing.

—Trucks: Giants of the Highway. Robbins, Ken. 2013. (ENG.). 32p. (J). (gr. -1-3). pap. 16.99 *(978-1-4814-0164-7(5),* Atheneum Bks. for Young Readers) Simon & Schuster Children's Publishing.

Robbins, Trina, jt. illus. see Kremer, Warren.

Robbins, Wesley. Maravillas de Los EE. UU: Shine-A-light. Brown, Carron. 2019.Tr. of Wonders of the USA. (SPA.). (J). 12.99 *(978-1-61067-916-9(4))* Kane Miller.

—Secretos Del Planeta Tierra: Shine-A-light. Brown, Carron. 2019.Tr. of Secrets of Our Earth. (SPA.). (J). 12.99 *(978-1-61067-911-4(3))* Kane Miller.

Roberson, Ron. White Cloud: A Little Boy's Dream. Irwin, Esther. Puett, Gayle, ed. 2006. 16p. (J). spiral bd. 10.00 *(978-0-9778462-0-7(2))* Irwin, Esther L.

Robert, Bruno. A Cookie for Santa. Shaw, Stephanie. 2014. (ENG.). 32p. (J). (gr. 1-4). 15.99 *(978-1-58536-883-9(0),* 203675) Sleeping Bear Pr.

—The Cow Said Neigh! A Farm Story, 1 vol. Feek, Rory. 2018. (ENG.). 32p. (J). 16.99 *(978-1-4003-1171-2(3))* Nelson, Thomas Inc.

—The Cow Said Neigh! (board Book) A Farm Story, 1 vol. Feek, Rory. 2018. (ENG.). 26p. (J). bds. 9.99 *(978-1-4003-1189-7(6))* Nelson, Thomas Inc.

—Rabbit Cooks up a Cunning Plan. Fusek Peters, Andrew. (Traditional Tales with a Twist Ser.). 32p. (J). 2010. (gr. -1-2). *(978-1-84643-349-8(5))*; 2007. (gr. 2-2). pap. *(978-1-84643-097-8(6))* Child's Play International Ltd.

Robert, J. Martin. I Want You to Know, Son. Fink, Thad. 2007. 26p. (J). (gr. -1-3). per. 11.99 *(978-1-59879-260-7(1))* Lifevest Publishing, Inc.

Robert, LeyHonor. At the Market. Pink B Band. Hawes, Alison. 2016. (Cambridge Reading Adventures Ser.). (ENG.). 16p. pap. 7.37 *(978-1-107-54993-7(0))* Cambridge Univ. Pr.

Robert, Peters. Da Goodie Monsta. Robert, Peters. 2010. 30p. (J). pap. 9.95 *(978-0-9823906-4-1(5))* Wiggles Pr.

Robert, Yannick. The Frog Prince. Goodhart, Pippa. 2014. (Traditional Tales Ser.). (ENG.). 24p. (J). (gr. 1-2). pap. 6.95 *(978-1-62521-560-4(6),* Capstone Classroom) Capstone.

—Hello, I Am Charlie from London. Husar, Stephane. 2014. (AV2 Fiction Readalong Ser.: Vol. 127). (ENG.). 32p. (J). (gr. -1-3). lib. bdg. 34.28 *(978-1-4896-2256-3(X),* AV2 by Weigl) Weigl Pubs., Inc.

—The King of Spring. Page, Nick & Page, Claire. 2006. (Read with Me (Make Believe Ideas) Ser.). 31p. (J). (gr. k-2). *(978-1-84610-169-4(7))* Make Believe Ideas.

Roberti, Alessandra. Little Pony. Milbourne, Anna. 2009. (Picture Bks). 24p. (J). (gr. -1). 9.99 *(978-0-7945-2198-1(3),* Usborne) EDC Publishing.

—On the Farm. Milbourne, Anna. 2006. 24p. (J). (gr. -1-3). 9.99 *(978-0-7945-1282-8(8),* Usborne) EDC Publishing.

Roberts, Alice Jane. The Boy Who Dug. Woodcock, Jane. 2018. (ENG.). 20p. (J). pap. *(978-1-9993465-0-8(5))* IMPACT Investigative Media Productions.

—Shh ... Oes. Roberts, Trixie. 2018. (ENG.). 32p. (J). pap. *(978-0-9559177-7-6(8))* IMPACT Investigative Media Productions.

Roberts, Bruce, photos by. Ghosts of the Wild West. Roberts, Nancy. 2nd fac. ed. 2008. 110p. (J). (gr. 3-7). 24.95 *(978-1-57003-731-3(0))* Univ. of South Carolina Pr.

—Ghosts of the Wild West: Enlarged Edition Including Five Never-Before-Published Stories. Roberts, Nancy. 2nd enl. ed. 2008. (ENG., 120p. (gr. 3-7). pap. 15.99 *(978-1-57003-732-0(9))* Univ. of South Carolina Pr.

Roberts, Charlotte. Madeleine Goes to the Moon: 2nd Edition. Lynas, Peter. 2017. (Madeleine Goes Ser.: Vol. 1). (ENG.). 24p. (J). pap. *(978-0-9933403-4-5(2))* Lynas, P J.

Roberts, Cindy, jt. illus. see Davenport, Maxine.

Roberts, Curt & Traylor, Waverley. The Story of Scruffy of Smithfield, Virginia. Roberts, Curt. Traylor, Waverley, ed. l.t. ed. 2005. 14p. (J). (gr. k-6). pap. 3.95 *(978-0-9715068-4-8(1))* Traylor, Waverley Publishing.

Roberts, David. Ada Twist & the Perilous Pantaloons. Beaty, Andrea. 2019. (Questioneers Ser.). (ENG.). 112p. (J). (gr. 1-4). 11.63 *(978-1-4197-3901-9(8))* Abrams, Inc.

—Ada Twist & the Perilous Pants: The Questioneers Book #2. Beaty, Andrea. 2019. (Questioneers Ser.). (ENG.). 112p. (J). (gr. 1-4). 12.99 *(978-1-4197-3422-9(9),* Amulet Bks.) Abrams, Inc.

—Ada Twist, Scientist. Beaty, Andrea. 2016. (ENG.). 32p. (J). (gr. k-2). 18.99 *(978-1-4197-2137-3(2),* Abrams Bks. for Young Readers) Abrams, Inc.

—A Beginner's Guide to Bear Spotting. Robinson, Michelle. 2016. (ENG.). 32p. (J). 16.99 *(978-1-68119-026-6(5),* 900156322, Bloomsbury USA Childrens) Bloomsbury Publishing USA.

—The Bolds. Clary, Julian. 2017. (Bolds Ser.). (ENG.). 272p. (J). (gr. 3-6). pap. 6.99 *(978-1-5124-8174-7(2),* 9781512481747, Carolrhoda Bks.) Lerner Publishing Group.

—The Bolds' Christmas Cracker. Clary, Julian. 2020. 192p. (J). (gr. 1-6). pap. 13.99 *(978-1-78344-842-5(3))* Andersen Pr. GBR. Dist: Independent Pubs. Group.

—The Bolds Go Wild. Clary, Julian. 2019. 304p. (J). (gr. 1-6). 24.99 *(978-1-78344-804-3(0))* Andersen Pr. GBR. Dist: Independent Pubs. Group.

—The Bolds in Trouble. Clary, Julian. 2019. (Bolds Ser.). (ENG.). 304p. (J). (gr. 3-6). 16.99 *(978-1-5415-0045-7(8),* Carolrhoda Bks.) Lerner Publishing Group.

—The Bolds on Vacation. Clary, Julian. 2020. (Bolds Ser.). (ENG.). 320p. (J). (gr. 3-6). pap. 6.99 *(978-1-5415-8681-9(6),* Carolrhoda Bks.) Lerner Publishing Group.

—The Bolds to the Rescue. Clary, Julian. 2018. (Bolds Ser.). (ENG.). 288p. (J). (gr. 3-6). pap. 6.99 *(978-1-5415-3844-3(7),* Carolrhoda Bks.) Lerner Publishing Group.

—The Chinese Emperor's New Clothes. Compestine, Ying. 2017. (ENG.). 32p. (J). (gr. 1-4). 17.99 *(978-1-4197-2542-5(4),* Abrams Bks. for Young Readers) Abrams, Inc.

—The Cook & the King. Donaldson, Julia. 2019. (ENG.). 32p. (J). (gr. -1-2). 16.99 *(978-1-4197-3757-2(0),* Abrams Bks. for Young Readers) Abrams, Inc.

Roberts, David. Cuentos de Terror de la Boca Del T�nel. Priestley, Chris. 2018. (Torre Amarilla Ser.). (SPA.). 254p. (J). pap. ***(978-958-776-481-9(1))*** Norma Ediciones, S.A.

Roberts, David. Dear Tabby. Crimi, Carolyn. 2011. (ENG.). 32p. (J). (gr. -1-3). 16.99 *(978-0-06-114245-1(X))* HarperCollins Pubs.

—Dirty Bertie: Burp! Macdonald, Alan. 2008. 96p. (J). (gr. 1-5). 3.99 *(978-1-56148-644-1(2),* Good Bks.) Skyhorse Publishing Co., Inc.

—Dirty Bertie: Worms! Macdonald, Alan. 2008. 96p. (J). (gr. 4-7). 3.99 *(978-1-56148-645-8(0),* Good Bks.) Skyhorse Publishing Co., Inc.

—Don't Blink! Rosenthal, Amy Krouse. 2018. (ENG.). 40p. (J). (gr. -1-2). 20.99 *(978-0-375-97364-2(8),* Random Hse. Bks. for Young Readers) Random Hse. Children's Bks.

—Don't Blink! Rosenthal, Amy Krouse. 2020. (ENG.). 40p. (J). (gr. -1-2). pap. 7.99 *(978-0-593-17569-9(7),* Dragonfly Bks.) Random Hse. Children's Bks.

—The Dunderheads. Fleischman, Paul. 2012. (ENG.). 56p. (J). (gr. 1-4). pap. 6.99 *(978-0-7636-5239-5(3))* Candlewick Pr.

—The Dunderheads Behind Bars. Fleischman, Paul. 2012. (ENG.). 48p. (J). (gr. 1-4). 16.99 *(978-0-7636-4543-4(5))* Candlewick Pr.

—The Fall of Fergal. Ardagh, Philip. 2005. (Unlikely Exploits Trilogy Ser.: Bk. 1). (ENG.). 144p. (J). (gr. 4-7). reprint ed. per. 5.99 *(978-0-439-73014-3(7),* Scholastic Paperbacks) Scholastic, Inc.

—Fangs!, 1 vol. MacDonald, Alan. 2012. (Dirty Bertie Ser.). (ENG.). 112p. (J). (gr. 1-3). pap. 4.95 *(978-1-4342-4267-9(6))*; 25.32 *(978-1-4342-4601-1(9))* Capstone. (Stone Arch Bks.).

—Fleas!, 1 vol. MacDonald, Alan. 2013. (Dirty Bertie Ser.). (ENG.). 112p. (J). (gr. 1-3). pap. 4.95 *(978-1-4342-4822-0(4))*; lib. bdg. 25.32 *(978-1-4342-4618-9(3))* Capstone. (Stone Arch Bks.).

—The Flying Bath. Donaldson, Julia. 2016. (ENG.). 32p. (J). (gr. -1-k). pap. 9.99 *(978-1-4472-7711-8(2),* Macmillan Children's Bks.) Pan Macmillan GBR. Dist: Independent Pubs. Group.

—Germs!, 1 vol. MacDonald, Alan. 2012. (Dirty Bertie Ser.). (ENG.). 112p. (J). (gr. 1-3). pap. 4.95 *(978-1-4342-4266-2(8))*; 25.32 *(978-1-4342-4600-4(0))* Capstone. (Stone Arch Bks.).

—Happy Birthday, Madame Chapeau. Beaty, Andrea. 2014. (ENG.). 32p. (J). (gr. -1-3). 16.95 *(978-1-4197-1219-7(5),* Abrams Bks. for Young Readers) Abrams, Inc.

—Heir of Mystery. Ardagh, Philip. 2006. (Unlikely Exploits Trilogy Ser.: Bk. 2). (ENG.). 144p. (J). (gr. 4-7). per. 5.99 *(978-0-439-73017-4(1),* Scholastic Paperbacks) Scholastic, Inc.

—His Royal Highness, King Baby: A Terrible True Story. Lloyd-Jones, Sally. 2017. (ENG.). 48p. (J). (gr. -1-3). 16.99 *(978-0-7636-9793-8(1))* Candlewick Pr.

—Iggy Peck & the Mysterious Mansion. Beaty, Andrea. 2020. (Questioneers Ser.). (ENG.). 144p. (J). (gr. 1-4). 12.99 *(978-1-4197-3692-6(2),* 1204001, Amulet Bks.) Abrams, Inc.

—Iggy Peck, Architect. Beaty, Andrea. 2007. (ENG.). 32p. (J). (gr. k-17). 18.99 *(978-0-8109-1106-2(X),* Abrams Bks. for Young Readers) Abrams, Inc.

—Iggy Peck, Architect. Beaty, Andrea. 2010. (ENG.). 32p. (J). (gr. k-17). pap. 7.95 *(978-0-8109-8928-3(X))* UK Abrams Bks. for Young Readers.

—Iggy Peck's Big Project Book for Amazing Architects. Beaty, Andrea. 2017. (Questioneers Ser.). (ENG.). 96p. (J). (gr. k-2). pap. 14.99 *(978-1-4197-1892-2(4),* 1126707, Abrams Bks. for Young Readers) Abrams, Inc.

—Jack & the Flumflum Tree. Donaldson, Julia. 2016. (ENG.). 30p. (J). (gr. -1-k). bds. 9.99 *(978-1-4472-8549-6(2))* Pan Macmillan GBR. Dist: Independent Pubs. Group.

—Little Red: a Fizzingly Funny Fairy Tale. Roberts, Lynn. 2017. 40p. (J). (gr. k-2). pap. 9.99 *(978-1-84365-328-8(1),* Pavilion Children's Books) Pavilion Bks. GBR. Dist: Penguin Random Hse. LLC.

—Mrs. Crump's Cat. Smith, Linda. 2006. 32p. (J). (gr. -1-3). 17.89 *(978-0-06-443551-2(2))* HarperCollins Pubs.

—Operation Bunny. Gardner, Sally. 2014. (Wings & Co Ser.: 1). (ENG.). 208p. (J). (gr. 2-5). pap. 7.99 *(978-1-250-05053-3(7),* 900134108) Square Fish.

—The Prince & the Porker. Bently, Peter. 2017. (ENG.). 32p. (J). (gr. k-2). 16.95 *(978-1-4197-2312-4(X),* Abrams Bks. for Young Readers) Abrams, Inc.

—The Rise of the House of McNally, 3. Ardagh, Philip. 2006. (Unlikely Exploits Trilogy Ser.: Bk. 3). (ENG.). 160p. (J). (gr. 4-7). pap. 5.99 *(978-0-439-73018-1(X))* Scholastic, Inc.

Roberts, David. Rosa Pionera y Las Remachadoras Rechinantes / Rosie Revere & the Raucous Riveters. Beaty, Andrea. 2020. (Los Preguntones / the Questioneers Ser.: 1). (SPA.). 144p. (J). (gr. 2-4). pap. 11.95 ***(978-1-64473-185-7(1),*** Alfaguara) Penguin Random House Grupo Editorial ESP. Dist: Penguin Random Hse. LLC.

Roberts, David. Rosie Revere & the Raucous Riveters: The Questioneers Book #1. Beaty, Andrea. 2018. (ENG.). 144p. (J). (gr. 1-4). 12.99 *(978-1-4197-3360-4(5),* Amulet Bks.) Abrams, Inc.

—Rosie Revere, Engineer. Beaty, Andrea. 2013. (ENG.). 32p. (J). (gr. k-17). 18.99 *(978-1-4197-0845-9(7),* Abrams Bks. for Young Readers) Abrams, Inc.

—Rosie Revere's Big Project Book for Bold Engineers. Beaty, Andrea. 2017. (ENG.). 96p. (J). (gr. k-2). pap. 14.95 *(978-1-4197-1910-3(6),* Abrams Bks. for Young Readers) Abrams, Inc.

—Samantha Cardigan & the Genie's Revenge. Sutherland, David. 2005. (Red Bananas Ser.). (ENG.). 48p. (J). lib. bdg. *(978-0-7787-1070-7(X))* Crabtree Publishing Co.

—Samantha Cardigan & the Ghastly Twirling Sickness. Sutherland, David. 2005. (Red Bananas Ser.). (ENG.). 48p. (J). lib. bdg. *(978-0-7787-1069-1(6))* Crabtree Publishing Co.

—Siriol Llywelyn A'r Salwch Chwyrlio Erchyll. Sutherland, David et al. 2005. (WEL.). 48p. pap. *(978-1-85596-679-6(4))* Dref Wen.

—Sleeping Beauty: a Mid-Century Fairy Tale. Roberts, Lynn. 2017. 32p. (J). (gr. k-2). pap. 10.99 *(978-1-84365-339-4(7),* Pavilion Children's Books) Pavilion Bks. GBR. Dist: Penguin Random Hse. LLC.

—Sofia Valdez, Future Prez. Beaty, Andrea. 2019. (Questioneers Ser.). (ENG.). 40p. (J). (gr. k-2). 18.99 *(978-1-4197-3704-6(X),* 1217401, Abrams Bks. for Young Readers) Abrams, Inc.

—Those Magnificent Sheep in Their Flying Machines. Bently, Peter. 2014. (ENG.). 32p. (J). (gr. -1-3). 16.95 *(978-1-4677-4935-0(4),* 9781467749350) Lerner Publishing Group.

—The Vanishing of Billy Buckle. Gardner, Sally. 2015. (Wings & Co Ser.: 3). (ENG.). 240p. (J). (gr. 2-5). 13.99 *(978-0-8050-9915-7(8),* 9780805099157, Holt, Henry & Co. Bks. For Young Readers) Holt, Henry & Co.

—The Wind in the Willows. Grahame, Kenneth. 2013. (ENG.). 256p. (J). (gr. 5). 24.99 *(978-0-7636-6526-5(6))* Candlewick Pr.

—Worms!, 1 vol. MacDonald, Alan. 2013. (Dirty Bertie Ser.). (ENG.). 112p. (J). (gr. 1-3). pap. 4.95 *(978-1-4342-4823-7(2))*; lib. bdg. 25.32 *(978-1-4342-4619-6(1))* Capstone. (Stone Arch Bks.).

Roberts, David. Suffragette. Roberts, David. 2019. (ENG.). 128p. (J). (gr. 2-5). 25.00 *(978-1-5362-0841-2(8))* Candlewick Pr.

Roberts, David & Fletcher, Corina. Ghoul School. 2003. 10p. (J). (gr. k-4). reprint ed. 18.00 *(978-0-7567-7028-0(9))* DIANE Publishing Co.

Roberts, David, jt. illus. see Henry, Thomas.

Roberts, Gaylia. Felix's Fabulous Feathers, 1 vol. Bishop, Rhonda. 2009. 23p. pap. 24.95 *(978-1-60836-890-7(4))* America Star Bks.

Roberts, Gill. Josh in the Jungle. Lewis, Siân. 2005. (ENG.). 32p. pap. 12.95 *(978-1-84323-462-3(9))* Beekman Bks., Inc.

Roberts, J. P. Little Turtle Gets Lost. Gnap, Jean. 2017. (ENG.). (J). *(978-1-5255-0511-9(4))*; pap. *(978-1-4602-8755-2(X))* FriesenPress.

—Rock & Rhino Learn Responsibility. Lisbona, Margie Taylor. 2011. 48p. pap. *(978-1-77067-530-8(2))* FriesenPress.

Roberts, Jeremy. The Fate of Krypton. Sazaklis, John. 2013. (Man of Steel Ser.). (ENG.). 24p. (J). (gr. -1-3). pap. 3.99 *(978-0-06-223593-0(1),* HarperFestival) HarperCollins Pubs.

—Superman Saves Smallville. Sazaklis, John. 2013. (Man of Steel Ser.). (ENG.). 24p. (J). (gr. -1-3). pap. 3.99 *(978-0-06-223603-6(2),* HarperFestival) HarperCollins Pubs.

Roberts, Jeremy & Marion, V. Kenneth. Mind Games. 2016. (J). *(978-1-4844-9884-2(4))* HarperCollins Pubs. Ltd.

Roberts, Joel. Lenney the Lightning Bug. Williams Jr., Floyd. 2013. 20p. pap. 9.50 *(978-1-4276-1898-6(4))* Witty Publishing.

Roberts, Johanna. Mrs T & the Magic Pencil. Cummings, Elizabeth Mary. 2016. (Verityville Ser.: Vol. 3). (ENG.). 32p. (J). pap. *(978-1-911076-28-5(0))* Spiffing covers.

Roberts, Joshua, jt. illus. see Cole, Amy.

Roberts, Jp. B3 the Adult Eagle. Brooks, Karen a. 2019. (ENG.). 64p. (J). ***(978-1-5255-5303-5(8))***; pap. ***(978-1-5255-5304-2(6))*** FriesenPress.

Roberts, Jp. B3 the Juvenile Eagle. Brooks, Karen a. 2016. (ENG.). (J). *(978-1-4602-8844-3(0))*; pap. *(978-1-4602-8843-6(2))* FriesenPress.

—B3 the Subadult Eagle. Brooks, Karen a. 2017. (ENG.). (J). *(978-1-5255-1243-8(9))*; pap. *(978-1-5255-1244-5(7))* FriesenPress.

—I Love You More Than Most. Imbs, Nancy Schnoebelen. 2018. (ENG.). 28p. (J). *(978-1-5255-1154-7(8))*; pap. *(978-1-5255-1155-4(6))* FriesenPress.

Roberts, Jp. Mr. Aeroplane. Van Jaarsveld, Gernay. 2019. (ENG.). 28p. (J). ***(978-1-5255-4471-2(3))***; pap. ***(978-1-5255-4472-9(1))*** FriesenPress.

Roberts, Jp. On Top of the World. Stevenson, Lorie. 2018. (ENG.). 32p. (J). *(978-1-5255-0051-0(1))*; pap. *(978-1-5255-0052-7(X))* FriesenPress.

Roberts, Jp. Porter Flies up, up & Away. Moon, Debi. 2020. (ENG.). 24p. (J). ***(978-1-5255-4072-1(6))***; pap. ***(978-1-5255-4073-8(4))*** FriesenPress.

Roberts, Karen-Ann. Whistle Across the Banwy - Book Two: Brendan Badger's Journey Home. Byrne, Jeffrey Roy. 2019. (Whistle Across the Banwy Ser.: Vol. 2). (ENG.). 110p. (J). (gr. 2-5). pap. ***(978-1-78222-673-4(7))*** Paragon Publishing, Rothersthorpe.

Roberts, Ley Honor. The Big City Yellow Band. Rickards, Lynne. 2017. (Cambridge Reading Adventures Ser.). (ENG.). 16p. pap. 5.62 *(978-1-108-41079-3(0))* Cambridge Univ. Pr.

—Collins Big Cat Phonics for Letters & Sounds - Tip It: Band 01A/Pink A, Bd. 1A. Clarke, Zoë. 2018. (Collins Big Cat Phonics Ser.). (ENG.). 16p. (J). (gr. -1-k). pap. 6.99 *(978-0-00-825132-1(0))* HarperCollins Pubs. Ltd. GBR. Dist: Independent Pubs. Group.

—George Saves the World by Lunchtime. Readman, Jo. 2006. 32p. (J). (gr. k-2). pap. 15.99 *(978-1-903919-50-7(9))* Transworld Publishers Ltd. GBR. Dist: Independent Pubs. Group.

Roberts, Maggy. Billy Jones Dog Star. Roberts, Maggy, tr. Lewis, Siân. 2003. (ENG.). 56p. pap. 11.95 *(978-1-84323-169-1(7))* Beekman Bks., Inc.

Roberts, Marilyn. The Boy Who was President. Larichev, Andrei Borisovich. Moresco, Jamie, ed. 2004. 24p. (J). 9.95 *(978-0-9724386-0-5(2),* 2002096236) BlueSky Publishing.

Roberts, Mary Jo. The Pumpkin Fairy. Boyd, William T. 2003. 32p. (J). (gr. k-1). 14.95 *(978-0-9718161-0-7(7))* Wyatt Pr.

R

Roberts, Mary Sue, photos by. Down by the Shore. Crow, Marilee. 2011. 30p. 19.95 *(978-1-61633-087-3(2))* Guardian Angel Publishing, Inc.

Roberts, MarySue, photos by. Down by the Shore. Crow, Marilee. 2008. 28p. pap. 10.95 *(978-1-933090-39-9(1))* Guardian Angel Publishing, Inc.

—Gifts from God. Reeg, Cynthia. 2007. (J). 28p. 10.95 *(978-1-933090-33-7(2))*; 30p. E-Book 5.00 incl. cd-rom *(978-1-933090-34-4(0))* Guardian Angel Publishing, Inc.

—Wicky Wacky Things that Go! Airplanes 1. Burch, Lynda S. 2004. 28p. (J). E-Book 9.95 incl. cd-rom *(978-1-933090-07-8(3))* Guardian Angel Publishing, Inc.

—Wicky Wacky Things that Go! Hot Air Balloons. Burch, Lynda S. 2004. 28p. (J). E-Book 9.95 incl. cd-rom *(978-1-933090-08-5(1))* Guardian Angel Publishing, Inc.

Roberts, MarySue, jt. photos by see Burch, Lynda S.

Roberts, Megan, jt. illus. see Figert, Anya.

Roberts, Miranda. The Kid in My Closet. Meyer, Linda. 2008. (ENG.). 32p. (J). pap. 12.95 *(978-1-887542-94-4(9))* Bk. Pubs. Network.

Roberts, Nick. Apollo's Mystic Message! Tarakson, Stella. ed. 2019. (Hopeless Heroes Ser.: 5). (ENG.). 208p. (J). (gr. 2-6). *(978-1-78226-554-2(6)*, 9c4fb9cd-a314-4d6f-9e97-560f2356e008) Sweet Cherry Publishing.

—Arachne's Golden Gloves! Tarakson, Stella. ed. 2019. (Hopeless Heroes Ser.: 3). (ENG.). 208p. (J). (gr. 2-6). *(978-1-78226-552-8(X)*, db3d5867-4ca7-4b6b-8e8e-d5d3423963b0) Sweet Cherry Publishing.

—Circe's Beastly Feast! Tarakson, Stella. ed. 2020. (Hopeless Heroes Ser.: 7). (ENG.). 208p. (J). 6.99 *(978-1-78226-641-9(0)*, a36f490a-f298-4669-b13f-bd78d4aec37b) Sweet Cherry Publishing GBR. Dist: Baker & Taylor Publisher Services (BTPS).

—Hera's Terrible Trap! Tarakson, Stella. ed. 2019. (Hopeless Heroes Ser.). (ENG.). 208p. (J). (gr. 2-6). *(978-1-78226-551-1(1)*, ead449e9-1fa6-42da-815e-408c5a11dfca) Sweet Cherry Publishing.

—Here Comes Hercules! Tarakson, Stella. ed. 2019. (Hopeless Heroes Ser.: 1). (ENG.). 208p. (J). (gr. 2-6). *(978-1-78226-550-4(3)*, a484e513-a2c4-4468-81e8-ae90a9a493f4) Sweet Cherry Publishing.

—Jason's Wild Winds! Tarakson, Stella. ed. 2020. (Hopeless Heroes Ser.: 6). (ENG.). 208p. (J). pap. 6.99 *(978-1-78226-640-2(2)*, 17cac342-9925-43da-9072-95f84c27a0d7) Sweet Cherry Publishing GBR. Dist: Baker & Taylor Publisher Services (BTPS).

—Odysseus' Trojan Trick! Tarakson, Stella. ed. 2020. (Hopeless Heroes Ser.: 8). (ENG.). 208p. (J). 6.99 *(978-1-78226-642-6(9)*, 7857e639-38d8-4298-996a-699c7af5f430) Sweet Cherry Publishing GBR. Dist: Baker & Taylor Publisher Services (BTPS).

—Problems with Pythagoras! Tarakson, Stella. ed. 2019. (Hopeless Heroes Ser.: 4). (ENG.). 208p. (J). (gr. 2-6). *(978-1-78226-553-5(8)*, 160695ba-e299-45ea-a499-4a1eb8287d69) Sweet Cherry Publishing.

—Rocky Rocks & the Colourful Socks. Slowinski, Seniha. 2018. (ENG.). 26p. (J). pap. *(978-1-912262-27-4(4))* Clink Street Publishing.

—Tommy Twigtree & the Carrot Crunchers. Firman, Michael. 2018. (ENG.). 20p. (J). pap. *(978-1-912262-95-3(9))* Clink Street Publishing.

Roberts, Pam. The Hawk & the Turtles. Moses, Albert. 2011. 16p. pap. 24.95 *(978-1-4626-4261-8(6))* America Star Bks.

Roberts, Peter. The Awesome Book of Tornadoes & Other Storms. Petty, Kate. Paiva, Johannah Gilman, ed. 2014. (ENG.). 32p. (J). (gr. 3-7). 7.99 *(978-1-4867-0261-9(9))* Flowerpot Children's Pr. Inc. CAN. Dist: Cardinal Pubs. Group.

Roberts, Ramona. A Cat's Tale. Alexander, Troas. 2007. 36p. per. 14.95 *(978-1-59858-371-7(9))* Dog Ear Publishing, LLC.

Roberts, Rebecca. Sunshine, the Golden Unicorn. Pigg, Theresa. 2011. 20p. pap. 24.95 *(978-1-4626-0733-4(0))* America Star Bks.

Roberts, Scott. Andrew the Seeker. Nordling, Lee. 2017. (Game for Adventure Ser.). (ENG.). 32p. (J). (gr. k-3). 25.32 *(978-1-5124-1330-4(5)*, 9781512413304, Graphic Universe™) Lerner Publishing Group.

—Belinda the Unbeatable. Nordling, Lee. 2017. (Game for Adventure Ser.). (ENG.). 32p. (J). (gr. k-3). pap. 6.99 *(978-1-5124-5413-0(3)*, 9781512454130, Graphic Universe™) Lerner Publishing Group.

Roberts, Scott & Silva, Flavio B. Chavo the Invisible: A Graphic Novel for Children Without Words. Nordling, Lee. 2018. (Game for Adventure Ser.). 32p. (J). (gr. k-3). 25.32 *(978-1-5124-1332-8(1)*, 9781512413328, Graphic Universe™) Lerner Publishing Group.

Roberts, Smith. A House for a Mouse. Roberts, Smith. 2003. 56p. (J). per. 16.00 *(978-0-9727315-3-9(9))* Prospero's Pr.

Roberts, Steve. Animals. Hodge, Susie. 2010. (Let's Draw Ser.). (ENG.). 32p. (gr. 3-5). 25.60 *(978-1-61533-269-4(3))*; pap. 10.55 *(978-1-61533-270-0(7))* Windmill Bks.

—Bugs. Regan, Lisa. 2010. (Let's Draw Ser.). (ENG.). 32p. (J). (gr. 3-5). pap. 10.55 *(978-1-61533-268-7(5))*; lib. bdg. 25.60 *(978-1-61533-265-6(0))* Windmill Bks.

—Crocodiles. Parker, Steve. 2010. (I Love Animals Ser.). (ENG.). 24p. (gr. 1-5). 25.60 *(978-1-61533-247-2(2))*; pap. 8.15 *(978-1-61533-255-7(3))* Windmill Bks.

—Dinosaurs. Hodge, Susie. 2010. (Let's Draw Ser.). (ENG.). 32p. (gr. 3-5). 25.60 *(978-1-61533-264-9(2))* Windmill Bks.

—How to Draw Animals. Hodge, Susie. 2008. (How to Draw Ser.). 47p. (J). (gr. 4-7). *(978-1-84810-005-3(1))* Miles Kelly Publishing, Ltd.

—How to Draw Baby Animals. Regan, Lisa. 2008. (How to Draw Ser.). 47p. (J). (gr. 4-7). *(978-1-84810-066-4(3))* Miles Kelly Publishing, Ltd.

—How to Draw Bugs. Regan, Lisa. 2008. (How to Draw Ser.). 47p. (J). (gr. -1-3). *(978-1-84810-065-7(5))* Miles Kelly Publishing, Ltd.

—How to Draw Dinosaurs. Hodge, Susie. 2008. (How to Draw Ser.). 47p. (J). (gr. 4-7). *(978-1-84810-006-0(X))* Miles Kelly Publishing, Ltd.

—10 Things You Should Know about Crocodiles. Parker, Steve. Gallagher, Belinda & Borton, Paula, eds. 2004. (10 Things You Should Know Ser.). 24p. (J). 6.99 *(978-1-84236-121-4(X))* Miles Kelly Publishing, Ltd. GBR. Dist: Independent Pubs. Group.

Roberts, Tempie. Aspen Cat: Adventurer Extraordinaire. Brand, Mary. 2009. 44p. pap. 24.95 *(978-1-60749-165-1(6))* America Star Bks.

Roberts, Victoria. Halloweena. Glassman, Miriam. 2015. (ENG.). 40p. (J). (gr. -1-3). 13.99 *(978-1-4814-7996-7(2)*, Atheneum Bks. for Young Readers) Simon & Schuster Children's Publishing.

Robertson, Camille. A Guide to Sometimes Noise Is Big for Parents & Educators. Coelho, Angela & Seeley, Lori. 2017. (ENG.). 80p. (C). pap. 15.95 *(978-1-78592-374-6(9)*, 696626) Kingsley, Jessica Pubs. GBR. Dist: Hachette UK Distribution.

—Sometimes Noise Is Big: Life with Autism. Coelho, Angela. 2017. (ENG.). 40p. (C). 16.95 *(978-1-78592-373-9(0)*, 696629) Kingsley, Jessica Pubs. GBR. Dist: Hachette UK Distribution.

Robertson Campos, Halleluya. Vivie & Victor Vegan Adventures: In Costa Rica. Campos-P, Juan Diego & Robertson, Tracy Leeann. 2019. (Vegan Adventures Ser.: Vol. 4). (ENG.). 50p. (J). pap. 13.99 ***(978-1-0735-6179-7(8))*** Independently Published.

Robertson, Catherine. The Christmas Story As Told by Assellus the Christmas Donkey. Duggan, Janet. 2009. (ENG.). 44p. *(978-0-9563389-1-4(7))* Janet Duggan.

Robertson, Chris. If I Didn't Have You. Katz, Alan. 2018. (ENG.). 32p. (J). (gr. -1-3). 17.99 *(978-1-4169-7879-4(8)*, Simon & Schuster Bks. For Young Readers) Simon & Schuster Bks. For Young Readers.

Robertson, Chris. Knock Knock, Dino-Mite! Dinosaur Jokes for Kids. Rodriguez, Stephanie. 2020. (Illustrated Jokes Ser.). (ENG.). 28p. (J). (gr. 1-6). 12.99 ***(978-1-5324-2754-1(9))***; pap. 12.99 ***(978-1-5324-2753-4(0))*** Xist Publishing.

Robertson, Chris. Where Do Pants Go? Van Slyke, Rebecca. 2019. 22p. (J). (gr. -1). bds. 7.95 *(978-1-4549-3229-1(5))* Sterling Publishing Co., Inc.

Robertson, Chris. I'll Trade My Peanut Butter Sandwich. Robertson, Chris. 2017. (ENG.). 40p. (J). (gr. -1-k). pap. 9.99 *(978-1-5324-0174-9(4))* Xist Publishing.

—Little Miss Liberty. Robertson, Chris. 2017. (ENG.). 32p. (J). (gr. -1-2). pap. 9.99 *(978-1-5324-0173-2(6))* Xist Publishing.

—My Yellow Umbrella. Robertson, Chris. 2013. (ENG.). 36p. (J). (gr. -1-2). pap. 9.99 *(978-1-62395-543-4(2))* Xist Publishing.

Robertson, Darick, et al. New Warriors: Darkness & Light. 2018. (New Warriors: Darkness & Light (2018) Ser.: 1). (ENG.). 408p. (J). (gr. 4-17). pap. 34.99 *(978-1-302-91371-7(9))* Marvel Worldwide, Inc.

Robertson, Elysia Hill. Betsy Book: She Is A Smile. Robertson, Elysia Hill. 2005. 26p. (J). per. 6.95 *(978-0-9764444-7-3(X))* E. J. Publishing.

—Do Fish Cry ? Robertson, Elysia Hill. 2005. 116p. (J). per. 12.95 *(978-0-9764444-1-1(0)*, EJWV-002) E. J. Publishing.

—Dottie Goes to School. Robertson, Elysia Hill. 2005. 30p. (J). per. 6.95 *(978-0-9764444-8-0(8))* E. J. Publishing.

—Toley's Sleep over Learning Party. Robertson, Elysia Hill. 2005. 118p. (J). per. 12.95 *(978-0-9764444-4-2(5)*, EJWV-005) E. J. Publishing.

—Tool of Life My Pink School Books. Robertson, Elysia Hill. 2005. 112p. (J). per. 12.95 *(978-0-9764444-3-5(7)*, EJWV-004) E. J. Publishing.

Robertson, Elysia Hill & Bruce, Cindy. D. J. 's Sneakers. Robertson, Elysia Hill. 2005. 104p. (J). per. 12.95 *(978-0-9764444-2-8(9)*, EJWV-003) E. J. Publishing.

—We Make the World A Special Place. Robertson, Elysia Hill. 2005. 100p. (J). per. 12.95 *(978-0-9764444-0-4(2)*, EJWV-001) E. J. Publishing.

Robertson, Laura. Gordon the Goblin in Oh My! Is That a Pork Pie? Kurd, Tariq. 2012. 36p. pap. *(978-1-907762-10-9(8))* Malt Publishing.

Robertson, Maisie. Entrepreneur Academy. Martin, Steve. 2019. (ENG.). 64p. (J). pap. 12.99 *(978-1-61067-716-5(1))* Kane Miller.

Robertson, Maurice. The Playful Little Dog. Berg, Jean Horton. 2016. (G&d Vintage Ser.). 24p. (J). (-k). 7.99 *(978-0-448-48218-7(5)*, Grosset & Dunlap) Penguin Young Readers Group.

Robertson, Michael. Go to Bed, Blue. Bader, Bonnie. 2014. (Penguin Young Readers, Level 1 Ser.). 32p. (J). (gr. k-1). pap. 4.99 *(978-0-448-48219-4(3)*, Penguin Young Readers) Penguin Young Readers Group.

—Grandma Died & Mommy Really, Really Cried: Death - Dying. Frink-Hunter, Chene I. (J). (gr. -1-6). *(978-0-9654185-1-5(0))* Hunter Pubns.

—Monster Trouble. Fredrickson, Lane. 2015. 32p. (J). (gr. -1-2). 16.95 *(978-1-4549-1345-0(2))* Sterling Publishing Co., Inc.

—Play with Blue. Bader, Bonnie. 2013. (Penguin Young Readers, Level 1 Ser.). 32p. (J). (gr. k-1). mass mkt. 4.99 *(978-0-448-46254-7(0)*, Penguin Young Readers) Penguin Young Readers Group.

—The Three Little Pigs: a Finger Puppet Theater Book. 2017. (ENG.). 7p. (J). (— 1). 14.99 *(978-1-338-15162-6(2)*, Cartwheel Bks.) Scholastic, Inc.

Robertson, R. H. The Mystery Key at Camp Green Meadow. Gundel, Jean. 2011. (J). pap. 14.95 *(978-1-59571-730-6(7))* Word Association Pubs.

Robertson, Susan. Little Bunny. 2005. (Bedtime Babies Ser.). 8p. (J). (gr. -1). per., bds. 6.99 *(978-1-57755-503-2(1))* Flying Frog Publishing, Inc.

—Little Puppy. 2005. (Bedtime Babies Ser.). 8p. (J). (gr. -1). per., bds. 6.99 *(978-1-57755-501-8(5))* Flying Frog Publishing, Inc.

Robertson-Yeo, Jacqueline. Swifty the Guinea Pig & His New Super Powers. Robertson-Yeo, Jacqueline. 2018. (Swifty's Adventures Ser.). (ENG.). 134p. (J). pap. *(978-1-9164201-0-6(9))* Robertson-Yeo, Jacqueline.

Robertson-Yeo, Jacqueline. Swifty the Super Guinea Pig & the Disastrous Camping Adventure. Robertson-Yeo, Jacqueline. 2019. (Swifty's Adventures Ser.: Vol. 2). (ENG.). 140p. (J). (gr. 1-5). pap. ***(978-1-9164201-4-4(1))*** Robertson-Yeo, Jacqueline.

Robin, Clover. Across the Savannah. Walden, Libby. 2019. (ENG.). 12p. (J). ***(978-1-84857-723-7(0))*** Kane Miller.

Robin, Clover. Counting Birds: The Idea That Helped Save Our Feathered Friends. Stemple, Heidi E. Y. (ENG.). 32p. (J). (gr. -1-2). 2019. pap. 9.99 *(978-1-63322-819-1(3))*; 2018. 17.95 *(978-1-63322-604-3(2))* Quarto Publishing Group USA. (Seagrass).

—Origami & Poetry: Inspired by Nature. Nosy Crow. 2019. (ENG.). 132p. (J). (gr. 5). 15.00 *(978-1-5362-0580-0(X)*, Nosy Crow) Candlewick Pr.

Robin, Gulack. While You Were Gone Year Two. Garcia, Justine Marie. 2012. 26p. pap. 12.95 *(978-0-9836913-5-8(5))* Rose Bud Publishing Co. LLC.

Robin, Nelson T. Le Zoo en Papier: Une Aventure en Afrique du Sud: French Classroom Version. Woods, Leslie a. 3rd ed. 2020. (Colibri Ser.: Vol. 2). (FRE.). 38p. (J). pap. 6.95 ***(978-1-950323-05-0(6))*** Leaning Rock Pr.

—Zoológico de Papel: Una Aventura a Sudáfrica: Spanish Classroom Version. Leslie, Woods A. 4th ed. 2020. (Colibri Ser.: Vol. 2). (SPA.). 38p. (J). pap. 6.95 ***(978-1-950323-06-7(4))*** Leaning Rock Pr.

Robin, Sophie. The Secret Lives of Unicorns. Seraphini, Temisa. 2019. 64p. (J). (gr. 2-4). 18.95 *(978-1-911171-95-9(X))* Flying Eye Bks. GBR. Dist: Penguin Random Hse. LLC.

Robin, Thierry. Happy Halloween, Li'l Santa. Trondheim, Lewis & Robin, Thierry. 2003. (ENG.). 51p. 14.95 *(978-1-56163-361-6(5))* NBM Publishing Co.

Robins, Arthur. The Amazing Adventures of Chilly Billy. Mayle, Peter. 2013. 72p. pap. *(978-1-908191-69-4(4))* Escargot Bks. Online, Ltd.

—Dinosaur Olympics. Willis, Jeanne. 2012. (Downtown Dinosaurs Ser.). (ENG.). 176p. (J). (gr. k-3). pap. 9.99 *(978-1-84812-240-6(3))* Bonnier Publishing GBR. Dist: Independent Pubs. Group.

—Dinosaur Scramble. Willis, Jeanne. 2013. (Downtown Dinosaurs Ser.). (ENG.). 176p. (J). (gr. k-3). pap. 9.99 *(978-1-84812-315-1(9))* Bonnier Publishing GBR. Dist: Independent Pubs. Group.

—Macavity: The Mystery Cat. Eliot, T. S. 75th ed. 2016. (Old Possum Picture Bks.). (ENG.). 32p. (J). (-k). pap. 9.95 *(978-0-571-30813-2(9))* Faber & Faber, Inc.

—Macavity's Not There! A Lift-the-Flap Book. Eliot, T. S. 2017. (Old Possum Picture Bks.). (ENG.). 16p. (-k). 14.95 *(978-0-571-32863-5(6))* Faber & Faber, Inc.

—Macavity's Not There! A Lift-The-Flap Book. Eliot, T. S. 2018. (Old Possum Picture Bks.). (ENG.). 16p. (J). bds. 8.00 *(978-0-571-33528-2(4))* Faber & Faber, Inc.

—Mungojerrie & Rumpelteazer. Eliot, T. S. 2018. (Old Possum Picture Bks.). (ENG.). 32p. (J). pap. 9.95 *(978-0-571-32486-6(X)*, Faber & Faber Children's Bks.) Faber & Faber, Inc.

—My Granny Is a Pirate. McDermid, Val. 2012. 32p. (J). (gr. -1-k). pap. 9.99 *(978-1-4083-0927-8(0))* Hodder & Stoughton GBR. Dist: Hachette Bk. Group.

—Skimbleshanks: The Railway Cat. Eliot, T. S. 2016. (Old Possum Picture Bks.). (ENG.). 32p. (J). (-k). pap. 9.95 *(978-0-571-32483-5(5))* Faber & Faber, Inc.

Robins, James. What's That Bird? Getting to Know the Birds Around You, Coast to Coast. Vezo, Tom, photos by. Choiniere, Joseph & Golding, Claire Mowbray. 2005. (ENG.). 128p. (J). (gr. 3-8). pap. 14.95 *(978-1-58017-554-8(6)*, 67554) Storey Publishing, LLC.

Robins, Jim. Astronauts. West, David. 2008. (Graphic Careers Ser.). 48p. (gr. 5-8). per. 14.05 *(978-1-4042-1462-0(3))*; (YA). lib. bdg. 35.45 *(978-1-4042-1461-3(5))* Rosen Publishing Group, Inc., The.

Robins, Navi. The Robinson Brother's Adventure: Saving: Saving. Clark, Donita J. 2019. (ENG.). 24p. (J). (gr. k-6). pap. 10.00 ***(978-0-9984267-9-2(2))*** Extended Blessings.

Robins, Wesley. Amazing Evolution: The Journey of Life. Claybourne, Anna. 2019. (ENG.). 80p. (J). (gr. 4-7). 22.99 ***(978-1-78240-737-9(5)***, Ivy Kids) Ivy Group, The GBR. Dist: Hachette Bk. Group.

—Oceans in 30 Seconds: 30 Cool Topics for Junior Marine Explorers Explained in Half a Minute. Green, Jen. 2017. (Kids 30 Second Ser.). (ENG.). 96p. (J). (gr. 3-6). pap. 9.99 ***(978-1-78240-487-3(2)***, Ivy Kids) Ivy Group, The GBR. Dist: Hachette Bk. Group.

Robins, Wesley. Secrets of Animal Camouflage. Brown, Carron. 2016. (ENG.). 36p. (J). 12.99 *(978-1-61067-466-9(9))* Kane Miller.

—Secrets of Our Earth: Shine-A-light. Brown, Carron. 2017. (ENG.). 36p. (J). 12.99 *(978-1-61067-536-9(3))* Kane Miller.

Robinson, Alan James. Here Is the Arctic Winter. Dunphy, Madeleine. 2007. (Web of Life Ser.). 32p. (J). (gr. -1-3). (ENG.). 16.95 *(978-0-9777539-1-8(3))*; pap. 9.95 *(978-0-9777539-0-1(5))* Web of Life Children's Bks.

Robinson, Andrew, et al. Where Did Dinosaurs Go? Unwin, Mike. 2006. (Usborne Starting Point Science Ser.). 24p. (J). (gr. 1-4). pap. 4.99 *(978-0-7945-1410-5(3)*, Usborne) EDC Publishing.

Robinson, Aunya N. Irish the Fairy Baby - Hardcover. Robinson, Aunya N. 2018. (ENG.). 32p. (J). (gr. k-4). 15.99 *(978-1-7322949-8-1(4))* Rissarae Designs.

Robinson, Barbara J. Blue Turtle Moon Queen: The September Book. Blotnick, Elihu. 2009. (ENG.). 114p. (J). (gr. 6-12). pap. 7.25 *(978-0-915090-20-4(1)*, California Street) Firefall Editions.

—The Fog Line. Blotnick, Elihu. 2009. (Mr. Blot Ser.: No. 3). (ENG.). 56p. (YA). (gr. 6-18). pap. 9.00 *(978-0-915090-12-9(0)*, California Street) Firefall Editions.

Robinson, Bill. Game Night (Disney Junior Vampirina) Katschke, Judy. 2019. (Little Golden Book Ser.). (ENG.). 24p. (J). (-k). 4.99 *(978-0-7364-3931-2(5)*, Golden/Disney) Random Hse. Children's Bks.

Robinson, Bill, jt. illus. see RH Disney Staff.

Robinson, Charles. The Big Book of Fables. Jerrold, Walter. 2019. (Calla Editions Ser.). (ENG.). 384p. (J). (gr. -1-3). 40.00 *(978-1-60660-127-3(X))* Dover Pubns., Inc.

—The Big Book of Fairy Tales. Jerrold, Walter. 2018. (Calla Editions Ser.). (ENG.). 432p. (J). 40.00 *(978-1-60660-119-8(9))* Dover Pubns., Inc.

—The Big Book of Nursery Rhymes. Jerrold, Walter, ed. 2012. (Calla Editions Ser.). (ENG.). 352p. (gr. -1). 40.00 *(978-1-60660-030-6(3))* Dover Pubns., Inc.

—A Child's Garden of Verses. Stevenson, Robert Louis. 2020. (Children's Classic Collections). 96p. (J). (gr. -1-3). 14.99 *(978-1-63158-364-3(6)*, Racehorse Publishing) Skyhorse Publishing Co., Inc.

—Floramel & Esteban. Buchwald, Emilie. 2009. (ENG.). 80p. (J). (gr. 1-6). 16.95 *(978-1-57131-688-2(4))* Milkweed Editions.

—The Happy Prince & Other Stories. Wilde, Oscar. 2018. (Calla Editions Ser.). (ENG.). 160p. pap. 30.00 *(978-1-60660-117-4(2))* Dover Pubns., Inc.

—Lullaby Land: Songs of Childhood. Field, Eugene. 2006. 236p. per. 20.99 *(978-1-4255-1951-3(2))* Michigan Publishing.

—The Secret Garden. Burnett, Frances Hodgson. 2011. 304p. (J). *(978-1-4351-3344-0(7))* Barnes & Noble, Inc.

—The Secret Garden: (illustrated by Charles Robinson) Burnett, Frances Hodgson. 2019. (ENG.). 174p. (J). (gr. 7-12). pap. 6.99 *(978-1-4209-6127-0(6))* Digireads.com Publishing.

Robinson-Chavez, Kathryn A. & Madzel, D. E. Emma's House of Sound. Hayes, Mj. 2012. 80p. pap. 12.95 *(978-0-9819634-4-0(7))* St. Augustine Pr.

Robinson, Christian. Antoinette. DiPucchio, Kelly. 2017. (Gaston & Friends Ser.). (ENG.). 40p. (J). (gr. -1-3). 17.99 *(978-1-4814-5783-5(7))* Simon & Schuster Children's Publishing.

—Carmela Full of Wishes. de la Peña, Matt. 2018. 40p. (J). (gr. -1-3). 17.99 *(978-0-399-54904-5(8)*, G.P. Putnam's Sons Books for Young Readers) Penguin Young Readers Group.

—The Dead Bird. Brown, Margaret Wise. 2016. (ENG.). 32p. (J). (gr. -1-3). 17.99 *(978-0-06-028931-7(7))* HarperCollins Pubs.

—Gaston. DiPucchio, Kelly. (Gaston & Friends Ser.). (ENG.). (J). (gr. -1-3). 2014. 40p. 17.99 *(978-1-4424-5102-5(5))*; 2017. 80p. 35.99 *(978-1-5344-0002-3(8))* Simon & Schuster Children's Publishing. (Atheneum Bks. for Young Readers).

—Harlem's Little Blackbird: The Story of Florence Mills. Watson, Renée. 2012. 40p. (J). (gr. -1-2). 17.99 *(978-0-375-86973-0(5)*, Random Hse. Bks. for Young Readers) Random Hse. Children's Bks.

—Josephine: The Dazzling Life of Josephine Baker. Powell, Patricia Hruby. 2014. (ENG.). 104p. (J). (gr. 2-5). 17.99 *(978-1-4521-0314-3(3))* Chronicle Bks. LLC.

—Just in Case You Want to Fly. Fogliano, Julie. 2019. (ENG.). 40p. (J). (gr. -1-2). 18.99 *(978-0-8234-4344-4(2)*, Neal Porter Bks) Holiday Hse., Inc.

—Last Stop on Market Street. de la Peña, Matt. 2015. (ENG.). 32p. (J). (-k). 18.99 *(978-0-399-25774-2(8)*, G.P. Putnam's Sons Books for Young Readers) Penguin Young Readers Group.

—Last Stop on Market Street & Carmela Full of Wishes Box Set, 2 vols. de la Peña, Matt. 2019. (ENG.). 72p. (J). (gr. -1-3). 35.98 *(978-1-9848-1622-1(5)*, G.P. Putnam's Sons Books for Young Readers) Penguin Young Readers Group.

—Leo: A Ghost Story. Barnett, Mac. 2015. (ENG.). 52p. (J). (gr. -1-k). 16.99 *(978-1-4521-3156-6(2))* Chronicle Bks. LLC.

—Little Penguins. Rylant, Cynthia. (J). (gr. -1-2). 2019. 36p. bds. 8.99 *(978-1-9848-3058-6(9))*; 2016. 40p. 17.99 *(978-0-553-50770-6(2))* Random Hse. Children's Bks. (Schwartz & Wade Bks.).

—¡Lluvia!/ Rain! Ashman, Linda. Calvo, Carlos, tr. 2019. (SPA & ENG.). 30p. (J). (— 1). bds. 5.99 *(978-1-328-80871-4(8)*, 1688368, HMH Books For Young Readers) Houghton Mifflin Harcourt Publishing Co.

—Los Deseos de Carmela. de la Peña, Matt. 2018. 40p. (J). (gr. -1-3). 17.99 *(978-0-525-51870-9(3)*, G.P. Putnam's Sons Books for Young Readers) Penguin Young Readers Group.

—Rain! Ashman, Linda. (ENG.). (J). 2017. 30p. (— 1). bds. 7.99 *(978-0-544-88037-5(4)*, 1651189, HMH Books For Young Readers); 2013. 32p. (gr. -1-3). 18.99 *(978-0-547-73395-1(X)*, 1484490) Houghton Mifflin Harcourt Publishing Co.

—The Smallest Girl in the Smallest Grade. Roberts, Justin. 2014. (ENG.). 40p. (J). (gr. -1-k). 17.99 *(978-0-399-25743-8(8)*, G.P. Putnam's Sons Books for Young Readers) Penguin Young Readers Group.

—When's My Birthday? Fogliano, Julie. 2017. (ENG.). 40p. (J). 17.99 *(978-1-62672-293-4(5)*, 900150217) Roaring Brook Pr.

Robinson, Christian. Another. Robinson, Christian. 2019. (ENG.). 56p. (J). (gr. -1-3). 17.99 *(978-1-5344-2167-7(X)*, Atheneum Bks. for Young Readers) Simon & Schuster Children's Publishing.

Robinson, Christian. You Matter. Robinson, Christian. 2020. (ENG.). 40p. (J). (gr. -1-3). 17.99 ***(978-1-5344-2169-1(6)***, Atheneum Bks. for Young Readers) Simon & Schuster Children's Publishing.

Robinson, Cindy. Baby Baobab. Robinson, Cindy. 2010. (ENG.). 29p. (J). (gr. k-2). pap. 9.00 *(978-1-77009-671-4(X))* Jacana Media ZAF. Dist: Independent Pubs. Group.

Robinson, Don. Daddy, What Is Love? Shapiro, Jane. 2008. (ENG.). 28p. (J). (gr. -1-3). *(978-1-59700-244-8(5))* Island Heritage Publishing.

—G Is for Gecko: An Alphabet Adventure in Hawai'i. Gillespie, Jane. 2013. (ENG.). 26p. (J). (gr. -1-1). 12.95 *(978-1-933067-51-3(9))* Beachhouse Publishing, LLC.

—Kamehameha: The Boy Who Became a Warrior King. Crowe, Ellie. rev. ed. 2008. (ENG.). 62p. (J). (gr. k-k). pap. *(978-1-59700-591-3(6))* Island Heritage Publishing.

—Little Malia's Big Poi Idea. Calma, Jocelyn. 2009. 28p. (J). 12.99 *(978-1-59524-328-7(3))* Giddy Up, LLC.

—Mr. Miyataki's Marvelous Machine. Newsome, Tandy. 2004. 28p. (J). (gr. -1-3). 12.95 *(978-0-931548-68-0(3))* Island Heritage Publishing.

—Too Many Mangos. Paikai, Tammy. 2009. 28p. (J). (gr. -1). 11.95 *(978-1-59700-758-0(7))* Island Heritage Publishing.

Robinson, Erin. Only the Best: The Exceptional Life & Fashion of Ann Lowe. Messner, Kate & Powell, Margaret E. 2019. (J). *(978-1-4521-6160-0(7))* Chronicle Bks. LLC.

Robinson, Erin K. Brave. Black. First: 50 African American Women Who Led the Way. Hudson, Cheryl. 2020. 128p. (J). (gr. 3-7). 18.99 *(978-0-525-64581-8(0))*; (ENG.). lib. bdg. 21.99 *(978-0-525-64582-5(9))* Random Hse. Children's Bks. (Crown Books For Young Readers).

Robinson, Gordon. Alice's Adventures in Wonderland. Carroll, Lewis. 2009. 118p. (gr. 3-18). pap. 4.50 *(978-1-60450-761-4(6)*, Serenity Pubs.) Arc Manor.

Robinson, Heath. Hans Christian Andersen Fairy Tales. Andersen, Hans. 2018. (Arcturus Slipcased Classics Ser.). (ENG.). 384p. (J). 24.99 *(978-1-78888-323-8(3)*, f902a4f9-b450-4191-934a-53211c3a0661) Arcturus Publishing GBR. Dist: Baker & Taylor Publisher Services (BTPS).

Robinson, Hilda. Didn't We Have Fun! Robinson, Hilda. Kunkel, Jeff. 2012. 48p. (J). 19.95 *(978-1-933987-17-0(0)*, Crickhollow Bks.) Great Lakes Literary, LLC.

Robinson, James. The Wrong Adventure. Mountney, Ross. 2016. (ENG.). (J). pap. *(978-0-9932614-3-5(4))* Bird's Nest Bks.

Robinson, Jayme. The Unfortunate Tale of Kachuva the Tortoise: As Told by Chukwa Sulcata. Sapre, Reshme. 2012. (ENG.). 40p. 16.95 *(978-0-9829362-0-7(6))* Hathi Chiti Bks. for Kids.

Robinson, Jeleasa M. My Mum Says I'm a Wriggle Worm. Robinson, Jeleasa M. 2020. (ENG.). 24p. (J). (gr. k-4). pap. ***(978-0-6485775-1-5(1))*** Robinson, Jeleasa.

Robinson, Jo. Myrtle Makes a New Friend: Myrtle the Purple Turtle Series. Reyes-Grange, Lauren & Reyes, Cynthia. 2019. (Myrtle the Purple Turtle Ser.: Vol. 3). (ENG.). 34p. (J). pap. ***(978-0-6399914-2-9(4))*** Reyes, Cynthia.

Robinson, Jo. Myrtle the Purple Turtle. Reyes, Cynthia. 2017. (ENG.). 32p. (J). (gr. -1-3). *(978-0-620-77342-3(1))* Reyes, Cynthia.

—Myrtle's Game. Reyes-Grange, Lauren & Reyes, Cynthia. 2018. (Myrtle the Purple Turtle Ser.: Vol. 2). (ENG.). 32p. (J). pap. *(978-0-6399488-2-9(0))* Reyes, Cynthia.

—Vertu la Tortue Violette. Reyes, Cynthia. 2019. (Myrtle the Purple Turtle 1 Ser.). (FRE.). 30p. (J). pap. *(978-0-6399488-4-3(7))* Reyes, Cynthia.

Robinson, Kavion. Irie the Caterpilla: Patois (Patwa) Version. Wakefield, Latoya. 2019. (Irie Ser.: Vol. 1). (ENG.). 26p. (J). pap. 9.99 *(978-1-7940-3130-2(8))* Independently Published.

Robinson, Keith. The Magnus Chase Coloring Book (a Magnus Chase Book) Riordan, Rick. 2018. (Magnus Chase & the Gods of Asgard Ser.). (ENG.). 96p. (J). (gr. 3-7). pap. 15.99 *(978-1-368-00845-7(3))* Hyperion Bks. for Children.

—Speed Machines: A Pop-up Book with Moving Gears. Imperato, Teresa. 2005. 8p. (J). 14.95 *(978-1-58117-323-9(7)*, Intervisual/Piggy Toes) Bendon, Inc.

—Ugly. Hoge, Robert. 2016. (ENG.). 208p. (J). (gr. 3-7). 16.99 *(978-0-425-28775-0(0)*, Viking Books for Young Readers) Penguin Young Readers Group.

Robinson, Laura. Batley Needs Glasses, 10 vols., Vol. 12. Sargent, Dave & Sargent, Pat. 2004. (Learn to Read Ser.: 10).Tr. of Batley Necesita Anteojos. 18p. (J). pap. 10.95 *(978-1-56763-820-2(1))* Ozark Publishing.

—Batley Needs Glasses, 10 vols., Vol. 12. Sargent, Dave & Sargent, Pat. 2004. (Learn to Read Ser.: 10). 18p. (J). lib. bdg. 20.95 *(978-1-56763-819-6(8))* Ozark Publishing.

—Bo Bo's Big Imagination, 10 vols., Vol. 13. Sargent, Dave & Sargent, Pat. 2004. (Learn to Read Ser.: 10).Tr. of Gran Imaginacion de Bo Bo. 18p. (J). pap. 10.95 *(978-1-56763-822-6(8))* Ozark Publishing.

—Bo Bo's Big Imagination/la Gran Imaginacion de Bo Bo, 10 vols., Vol. 13. Sargent, Dave & Sargent, Pat. 2004. (Learn to Read Ser.: 10). (ENG & SPA.). 18p. (J). pap. 10.95 *(978-1-56763-986-5(0))* Ozark Publishing.

—Cat Who Barked, 10 vols., Vol. 18. Sargent, Dave & Sargent, Pat. 2004. (Learn to Read Ser.: 10). 18p. (J). pap. 10.95 *(978-1-56763-832-5(5))*; lib. bdg. 20.95 *(978-1-56763-831-8(7))* Ozark Publishing.

—Cat Who Barked/el gato que Ladró, 10. Sargent, Dave & Sargent, Pat. 2004. (Learn to Read Ser.: 10). (ENG & SPA.). 18p. (J). 18. pap. 9.95 *(978-1-56763-996-4(8))*; Vol. 18. lib. bdg. 20.95 *(978-1-56763-995-7(X))* Ozark Publishing.

—Do All Ducks Quack?, 10 vols., Vol. 14. Sargent, Dave & Sargent, Pat. 2004. (Learn to Read Ser.: 10). 18p. (J). lib. bdg. 20.95 *(978-1-56763-823-3(6))*; lib. bdg. 10.95 *(978-1-56763-824-0(4))* Ozark Publishing.

—Do All Ducks Quack?/¿Granznan todos los Patos?, 10 vols., Vol. 14. Sargent, Dave & Sargent, Pat. 2004. (Learn to Read Ser.: 10). (ENG & SPA.). 18p. (J). pap. 10.95 *(978-1-56763-988-9(7))*; lib. bdg. 20.95 *(978-1-56763-987-2(9))* Ozark Publishing.

—Do Frogs Have Tails?, 10 vols., Vol. 15. Sargent, Dave & Sargent, Pat. 2004. (Learn to Read Ser.: 10).Tr. of Tienen Colas las Ranas?. 18p. (J). pap. 10.95 *(978-1-56763-826-4(0))*; lib. bdg. 20.95 *(978-1-56763-825-7(2))* Ozark Publishing.

—Do Frogs Have Tails?/Tienen Colas las Ranas?, 10 vols. Sargent, Dave & Sargent, Pat. 2004. (Learn to Read Ser.: 10).Tr. of Tienen Colas las Ranas?. (ENG & SPA.). 18p. (J). lib. bdg. 20.95 *(978-1-56763-989-6(5))*; 15. pap. 9.95 *(978-1-56763-990-2(9))* Ozark Publishing.

—Fuzzy Bunny, 10 vols., Vol. 19. Sargent, Dave & Sargent, Pat. 2004. (Learn to Read Ser.: 10). 18p. (J). lib. bdg. 20.95 *(978-1-56763-833-2(3))*; lib. bdg. 10.95 *(978-1-56763-834-9(1))* Ozark Publishing.

—Fuzzy Bunny/el conejito Velloso, 10 vols., Vol. 19. Sargent, Dave & Sargent, Pat. 2004. (Learn to Read Ser.: 10). (ENG & SPA.). 18p. (J). pap. 10.95 *(978-1-56763-998-8(4))*; lib. bdg. 20.95 *(978-1-56763-997-1(6))* Ozark Publishing.

—I Can Read, Too/Puedo Leer, Tambien, 10 vols. Sargent, Dave & Sargent, Pat. 2003. (Puedo Leer Ser.). (SPA.). 24p. (J). Vol. 1. lib. bdg. 20.95 *(978-1-56763-943-8(7))*; Vol. 3. pap. 10.95 *(978-1-56763-948-3(8))*; Vol. 3. lib. bdg. 20.95 *(978-1-56763-947-6(X))*; Vol. 4. pap. 10.95 *(978-1-56763-950-6(X))*; Vol. 5. lib. bdg. 20.95 *(978-1-56763-951-3(8))*; Vol. 6. pap. 6.95 *(978-1-56763-954-4(2))*; Vol. 6. lib. bdg. 20.95 *(978-1-56763-953-7(4))*; Vol. 7. pap. 6.95 *(978-1-56763-956-8(9))*; Vol. 8. pap. 10.95 *(978-1-56763-958-2(5))*; Vol. 9. pap. 10.95 *(978-1-56763-960-5(7))*; Vol. 9. lib. bdg. 20.95 *(978-1-56763-959-9(3))*; Vol. 10. pap. 10.95 *(978-1-56763-962-9(3))*; Vol. 10. lib. bdg. 20.95 *(978-1-56763-961-2(5))* Ozark Publishing.

—Little Big Cat, 10 vols., Vol. 16. Sargent, Dave & Sargent, Pat. 2004. (Learn to Read Ser.: 10). 18p. (J). pap. 10.95 *(978-1-56763-828-8(7))*; lib. bdg. 20.95 *(978-1-56763-827-1(9))* Ozark Publishing.

—Little Big Cat/Gato pequeño y Grande, 10 vols., Vol. 16. Sargent, Dave & Sargent, Pat. 2004. (Learn to Read Ser.: 10). (ENG & SPA.). 18p. (J). pap. 10.95 *(978-1-56763-992-6(5))* Ozark Publishing.

—Little Big Cat/Gato Pequeño y Grande, 10 vols., Vol. 16. Sargent, Dave & Sargent, Pat. 2004. (Learn to Read Ser.: 10).Tr. of Gato Pequeno y Grande. (ENG & SPA.). 18p. (J). (gr. k-2). lib. bdg. 20.95 *(978-1-56763-991-9(7))* Ozark Publishing.

—Little Tadpole, 10. Sargent, Dave & Sargent, Pat. 2004. (Learn to Read Ser.: 10). 18p. (J). 20. lib. bdg. 9.95 *(978-1-56763-836-3(8))*; Vol. 20. lib. bdg. 20.95 *(978-1-56763-835-6(X))* Ozark Publishing.

—Little Tadpole/el Renacuajo Pequeño, 10 vols. Sargent, Dave & Sargent, Pat. 2004. (Learn to Read Ser.: 10). (ENG & SPA.). 18p. (J). pap. 10.95 *(978-1-56763-567-6(9))*; lib. bdg. 20.95 *(978-1-56763-999-5(2))* Ozark Publishing.

—Lizzy Lightning Bug, 10 vols., Vol. 17. Sargent, Dave & Sargent, Pat. 2004. (Learn to Read Ser.: 10). 18p. (J). lib. bdg. 20.95 *(978-1-56763-829-5(5))*; lib. bdg. 10.95 *(978-1-56763-830-1(9))* Ozark Publishing.

—Lizzy Lightning Bug/Lizzy la Luciérnaga, 10 vols. Sargent, Dave & Sargent, Pat. 2004. (Learn to Read Ser.: 10). (ENG & SPA.). 18p. (J). pap. 10.95 *(978-1-56763-994-0(1))* Ozark Publishing.

—Lizzy Lightning Bug/Lizzy la Luciérnaga, 10 vols., Vol. 17. Sargent, Dave & Sargent, Pat. 2004. (Learn to Read Ser.: 10).Tr. of Lizzy la Luciernaga. (ENG & SPA.). 18p. (J). (gr. k-2). lib. bdg. 20.95 *(978-1-56763-993-3(3))* Ozark Publishing.

—A Puppy for Bobby/un cachorro para Robertito, 10 vols. Sargent, Dave & Sargent, Pat. 2004. (Learn to Read Ser.: 10). (ENG & SPA.). 18p. (J). pap. 10.95 *(978-1-56763-982-7(8))* Ozark Publishing.

—Puppy for Bobby/un cachorro para Robertito, 10, 11. Sargent, Dave & Sargent, Pat. 2004. (Learn to Read Ser.: 10). (ENG & SPA.). 18p. (J). lib. bdg. 19.95 *(978-1-56763-981-0(X))* Ozark Publishing.

Robinson, Lee. Billy Burger, Model Citizen. Sazaklis, John. 2016. (Billy Burger, Model Citizen Ser.). (ENG.). 96p. (J). (gr. 2-4). lib. bdg., lib. bdg., lib. bdg. 90.60 *(978-1-4965-2733-2(X)*, Stone Arch Bks.) Capstone.

—The Dangers of Dog Walking. Sazaklis, John. 2016. (Billy Burger, Model Citizen Ser.). (ENG.). 96p. (J). (gr. 2-4). lib. bdg. 22.65 *(978-1-4965-2587-1(6)*, Stone Arch Bks.) Capstone.

—The Ferret Fiasco. Sazaklis, John. 2016. (Billy Burger, Model Citizen Ser.). (ENG.). 96p. (J). (gr. 2-4). lib. bdg. 22.65 *(978-1-4965-2589-5(2)*, Stone Arch Bks.) Capstone.

—Jumping for Junk Food. Sazaklis, John. 2016. (Billy Burger, Model Citizen Ser.). (ENG.). 96p. (J). (gr. 2-4). lib. bdg. 22.65 *(978-1-4965-2586-4(8)*, Stone Arch Bks.) Capstone.

Robinson, Lee, et al. Kung Fu Panda Collection - Ready, Set Po!, Vol. 1. Furman, Simon. 2016. (Kung Fu Panda Ser.: 1). 112p. (J). (gr. 1-4). pap. 12.99 *(978-1-78276-697-1(9))* Titan Bks. Ltd. GBR. Dist: Penguin Random Hse. LLC.

Robinson, Lee. Recess Is Ruined. Sazaklis, John. 2016. (Billy Burger, Model Citizen Ser.). (ENG.). 96p. (J). (gr. 2-4). lib. bdg. 22.65 *(978-1-4965-2588-8(4)*, Stone Arch Bks.) Capstone.

Robinson, Lee & Simmonds-Hurn, Zak. Kung Fu Panda, Vol. 1. Furman, Simon & Ferreyra, Lucas. 2016. (Kung Fu Panda Ser.: 1). 64p. (J). (gr. 3-7). pap. 6.99 *(978-1-78276-268-3(X))* Titan Bks. Ltd. GBR. Dist: Penguin Random Hse. LLC.

Robinson, Lenord. Brighton One Star's Journey to Shine. Speicher, Diane Carty. 2005. 84p. (J). 19.95 *(978-0-9749806-0-7(9))* Shine On Pubns.

Robinson, Linda. Lazar, the Good Deed Dog. Shanker, Myrna Gelman. 2010. (J). *(978-0-9829273-0-4(4))* IGI Pr.

—Little Me, Big Me. Gray, Stefanie. 2006. (ENG.). 24p. per. 19.99 *(978-1-4259-0919-2(1))* AuthorHouse.

Robinson, Marcus. My Life By: D. D. Duck. Branen, Kathy. 2012. 24p. pap. 12.95 *(978-0-9845904-1-4(2))* Joshua Tree Publishing.

Robinson, Michael. Little Lion Goes to School. Magnus, Kellie. I.t. ed. 2003. 16p. (J). 9.99 *(978-0-9744211-0-0(3))* Media Magic New York.

Robinson, Nikki Slade. Wanted: Witch's Cat - Apply Within. Davidson, Joy H. ed. 2020. (ENG.). 40p. (J). (gr. -1-1). 16.95 ***(978-1-912904-86-0(1)***, Scribblers) Book Hse. GBR. Dist: Sterling Publishing Co., Inc.

Robinson, Robin. L. Frank Baum's Wizard of Oz. 2013. (Penguin Young Readers, Level 4 Ser.). (ENG.). 48p. (J). (gr. 3-4). mass mkt. 4.99 *(978-0-448-45588-4(9)*, Penguin Young Readers) Penguin Young Readers Group.

—Maddie Hatter & the Timely Taffeta. Barnard, Jayne. 2017. (Maddie Hatter Adventures Ser.: Vol. 3). (ENG.). (YA). pap. *(978-1-928025-76-4(5))* Tyche Bks., Ltd.

Robinson, Roger & Igle, Jamal. Noble Vol. 2: Never Events. Thomas, Brandon. 2018. (ENG.). 144p. (YA). pap. 14.99 *(978-1-941302-74-3(2)*, 71336b96-3086-496d-9174-b72cb211959a, Lion Forge) Oni Pr., Inc.

Robinson, Roger, jt. illus. see Jeanty, Georges.

Robinson, Sade. Being Nice Is Magical. Fudge, Margie. 2018. (ENG.). 30p. (J). pap. 14.00 *(978-1-9865-1113-1(8))* Peterson, Kristi.

Robinson, Shantala. Forest Baby, 1 vol. Elmquist, Laurie. 2018. (ENG.). 24p. (J). (gr. -1 — 1). bds. 9.95 *(978-1-4598-1333-5(2))* Orca Bk. Pubs. USA.

Robinson, Stacey & Jennings, John. I Am Alfonso Jones, 1 vol. Medina, Tony. 2017. (ENG.). 176p. (YA). (gr. 6-12). pap. 18.95 *(978-1-62014-263-9(5)*, 8c63e30b-74bf-4708-865a-3d74f855e795, Tu Bks.) Lee & Low Bks., Inc.

Robinson, Susan. The Captain & Harry: A Trembling Tail of Thieves. Langley, Jan. 2006. 30p. (J). (gr. 4-7). pap. 10.95 *(978-1-892384-23-2(X))* Avery Color Studios, Inc.

—One Little Balsam Fir: A Northwoods Counting Book. DuTemple, Leslie A. 2006. 32p. (J). per. *(978-1-892384-37-9(X))* Avery Color Studios, Inc.

Robinson, Susan G. The Good Neighbors' Cheese Feast: A Cheesy Mouse Tale of Subtraction with Regrouping. Ramsay, Mark. 2010. (ENG.). 32p. (J). pap. 9.95 *(978-0-9842863-1-7(4))* Strategic Educational Tools.

—The Good Neighbors Store an Award: A Cheesy Mouse Tale of Addition with Regrouping. Ramsay, Mark. 2010. (ENG.). 32p. (J). pap. 9.95 *(978-0-9842863-0-0(6))* Strategic Educational Tools.

Robinson, T. H. A Child's Book of Saints. Canton, William. 2013. 268p. pap. 12.75 *(978-1-936639-22-9(X))* St. Augustine Academy Pr.

—The Heroes. Kingsley, Charles. 2009. 240p. pap. 10.95 *(978-1-59915-291-2(6))* Yesterday's Classics.

—Legends from River & Mountain (Illustrated Edition) Sylva, Carmen. Strettell, Alma, tr. 2016. (ENG.). (J). pap. *(978-1-4068-7943-8(6))* Echo Library.

Robinson, Tyler. Rhea the Great Detective & the Case of the Missing Mrs. Bearington. Briggs, Dominique S. 2019. (ENG.). 30p. (J). pap. 15.95 *(978-1-64471-194-1(X))* Covenant Bks.

Robinson, W. Heath. The Giant Crab & Other Tales from Old India - Illustrated by W. Heath Robinson. Rouse, W. H. D. 2016. (ENG.). (J). pap. *(978-1-4733-3467-0(5))* Read Bks.

—Hans Andersen's Fairy Tales - Illustrated by W. Heath Robinson. Andersen, Hans. 2016. (ENG.). (J). pap. *(978-1-4733-3464-9(0))* Read Bks.

—The Water-Babies - a Fairy Tale for a Land-Baby - Illustrated by W. Heath Robinson. Kingsley, Charles. 2016. (ENG.). (J). (gr. 1-6). pap. *(978-1-4733-3471-7(3))* Read Bks.

Robinson, W. Heath. Bill the Minder - Illustrated by W. Heath Robinson. Robinson, W. Heath. 2016. (ENG.). (J). (gr. 2-6). pap. *(978-1-4733-3465-6(9))* Read Bks.

Robinson, W. Heath & Rackham, Arthur. Fairy Tales & Stories from Hans Christian Andersen. Andersen, Hans Christian. 2018. (ENG.). 242p. (J). (gr. 4-7). *(978-1-910880-67-8(1))* Robin Bks. Ltd.

Robinson, William, et al. Anna & Elsa #5: the Polar Bear Piper (Disney Frozen) David, Erica. 2015. (Stepping Stone Book(TM) Ser.: 5). (ENG.). 128p. (J). (gr. 1-4). 9.99 *(978-0-7364-3436-2(4)*, RH/Disney) Random Hse. Children's Bks.

Robinson, William E. Anna & Elsa: All Hail the Queen/Memory & Magic (Disney Frozen), 2. David, Erica. 2019. (Stepping Stone Book(TM) Ser.). (ENG.). 256p. (J). (gr. 1-4). pap. 9.99 *(978-0-7364-4000-4(3)*, RH/Disney) Random Hse. Children's Bks.

Robinson, William E., jt. illus. see RH Disney Staff.

Robison Gamble Creative, photos by. Dan & Louie Vol. 1: The Greatest Stories Ever Told, Robison Gamble Creative, des. deluxe ed. 2005. (J). 89.95 incl. audio compact disk *(978-1-933497-00-6(9))* Robison Gamble Creative.

Robitzky, Marc. Les Cygnes Sauvages - de Wilde Zwanen (Français - Néerlandais). d'Après un Conte de Fées de Hans Christian Andersen: Livre Bilingue Pour Enfants À Partir de 4-6 Ans, Avec Livre Audio MP3 À Télécharger. Renz, Ulrich. Kleimaker, Christa, tr. 2018. (Sefa Albums Illustrés en Deux Langues Ser.). (FRE.). 30p. (J). pap. *(978-3-7399-5899-6(5))* Boedeker, Kirsten. Sefa Verlag.

—Les Cygnes Sauvages - Die Wilden Schwäne (Français - Allemand). d'Après un Conte de Fées de Hans Christian Andersen: Livre Bilingue Pour Enfants À Partir de 4-6 Ans, Avec Livre Audio MP3 À Télécharger. Renz, Ulrich. Andler, Martin, tr. 2018. (Sefa Albums Illustrés en Deux Langues Ser.). (FRE.). 30p. (J). pap. *(978-3-7399-5904-7(5))* Boedeker, Kirsten. Sefa Verlag.

—Les Cygnes Sauvages - I Cigni Selvatici (Français - Italien). d'Après un Conte de Fées de Hans Christian Andersen: Livre Bilingue Pour Enfants À Partir de 4-6 Ans, Avec Livre Audio MP3 À Télécharger. Renz, Ulrich. Galeati, Clara, tr. 2018. (Sefa Albums Illustrés en Deux Langues Ser.). (FRE.). 30p. (J). pap. *(978-3-7399-5903-0(7))* Boedeker, Kirsten. Sefa Verlag.

—Les Cygnes Sauvages - the Wild Swans (Français - Anglais). d'Après un Conte de Fées de Hans Christian Andersen: Livre Bilingue Pour Enfants À Partir de 4-6 Ans, Avec Livre Audio MP3 À Télécharger. Renz, Ulrich. Andler, Martin, tr. 2018. (Sefa Albums Illustrés en Deux Langues Ser.). (FRE.). 30p. (J). pap. *(978-3-7399-5902-3(9))* Boedeker, Kirsten. Sefa Verlag.

—De Vilda Svanarna - Khoo'hâye Wahshee (Svenska - Persiska, Farsi, Dari). Efter en Saga AV Hans Christian Andersen: Tvåspråkig Barnbok Med Ljudbok SOM Mp3-Nedladdning, Från 4-6 År. Renz, Ulrich. Thordsen, Narona, tr. 2018. (Sefa Bilderböcker På Två Språk Ser.). (SWE.). 30p. (J). pap. *(978-3-7399-5895-8(2))* Boedeker, Kirsten. Sefa Verlag.

Robitzky, Marc. Die Wilden Schw�ne - de Wilde Zwanen (Deutsch - Holl�ndisch). Nach Einem M�rchen Von Hans Christian Andersen: Zweisprachiges Kinderbuch Mit Mp3 H�rbuch Zum Herunterladen, Ab 4-6 Jahren. Andersen, Hans Christian. Kleimaker, Christa, tr. 2018. (GER.). 42p. (J). pap. ***(978-3-7399-7000-4(6))*** Boedeker, Kirsten. Sefa Verlag.

Robitzky, Marc. Die Wilden Schwäne - Albajae Albary (Deutsch - Arabisch). Nach Einem Märchen Von Hans Christian Andersen: Zweisprachiges Kinderbuch Mit MP3 Hörbuch Zum Herunterladen, AB 4-6 Jahren. Renz, Ulrich. Othman, Inana, tr. 2018. (Sefa Bilinguale Bilderbücher Ser.). (GER.). 30p. (J). pap. *(978-3-7399-5889-7(8))* Boedeker, Kirsten. Sefa Verlag.

—Die Wilden Schwäne - de Vilda Svanarna (Deutsch - Schwedisch). Nach Einem Märchen Von Hans Christian Andersen: Zweisprachiges Kinderbuch Mit MP3 Hörbuch Zum Herunterladen, AB 4-6 Jahren. Renz, Ulrich. Thordsen, Narona, tr. 2018. (Sefa Bilinguale Bilderbücher Ser.). (GER.). 30p. (J). pap. *(978-3-7399-5894-1(4))* Boedeker, Kirsten. Sefa Verlag.

—Die Wilden Schwäne - the Wild Swans (Deutsch - Englisch). Nach Einem Märchen Von Hans Christian Andersen: Zweisprachiges Kinderbuch Mit MP3 Hörbuch Zum Herunterladen, AB 4-6 Jahren. Renz, Ulrich. Savill, Pete, tr. 2018. (Sefa Bilinguale Bilderbücher Ser.). (GER.). 30p. (J). pap. *(978-3-7399-5890-3(1))* Boedeker, Kirsten. Sefa Verlag.

—Die Wilden Schwäne - Villijoutsenet (Deutsch - Finnisch). Nach Einem Märchen Von Hans Christian Andersen: Zweisprachiges Kinderbuch Mit MP3 Hörbuch Zum Herunterladen, AB 4-6 Jahren. Renz, Ulrich. Konttinen, Janika Tuulia, tr. 2018. (Sefa Bilinguale Bilderbücher Ser.). (GER.). 30p. (J). pap. *(978-3-7399-5896-5(0))* Boedeker, Kirsten. Sefa Verlag.

Robitzky, Marc. Los Cisnes Salvajes (espa�ol - Tigri�a) Libro Biling�e para ni�os Basado en un Cuento de Hadas de Hans Christian Andersen. Andersen, Hans Christian. Canedo, Marcos, tr. 2019. (SPA.). 42p. (J). pap. ***(978-3-7399-7258-9(0))*** Boedeker, Kirsten. Sefa Verlag.

Robitzky, Marc. The Wild Swans - Albajae Albary (English - Arabic). Based on a Fairy Tale by Hans Christian Andersen: Bilingual Children's Book with MP3 Audiobook for Download, Age 4-6 & Up. Renz, Ulrich. Othman, Inana, tr. 2018. (Sefa Picture Books in Two Languages Ser.). (ENG.). 30p. (J). pap. *(978-3-7399-5891-0(X))* Boedeker, Kirsten. Sefa Verlag.

—The Wild Swans - de Vilda Svanarna (English - Swedish). Based on a Fairy Tale by Hans Christian Andersen: Bilingual Children's Book with MP3 Audiobook for Download, Age 4-6 & Up. Renz, Ulrich. Thordsen, Narona, tr. 2018. (Sefa Picture Books in Two Languages Ser.). (ENG.). 30p. (J). pap. *(978-3-7399-5898-9(7))* Boedeker, Kirsten. Sefa Verlag.

—The Wild Swans - Khoo'hâye Wahshee (English - Persian, Farsi, Dari). Based on a Fairy Tale by Hans Christian Andersen: Bilingual Children's Book with MP3 Audiobook for Download, Age 4-6 & Up. Renz, Ulrich. Mortezai, Jahan, tr. 2018. (Sefa Picture Books in Two Languages Ser.). (ENG.). 30p. (J). pap. *(978-3-7399-5901-6(0))* Boedeker, Kirsten. Sefa Verlag.

—The Wild Swans - les Cygnes Sauvages (English - French). Based on a Fairy Tale by Hans Christian Andersen: Bilingual Children's Book with MP3 Audiobook for Download, Age 4-6 & Up. Renz, Ulrich. Andler, Martin, tr. 2018. (Sefa Picture Books in Two Languages Ser.). (ENG.). 30p. (J). pap. *(978-3-7399-5905-4(3))* Boedeker, Kirsten. Sefa Verlag.

—The Wild Swans - Los Cisnes Salvajes (English - Spanish). Based on a Fairy Tale by Hans Christian Andersen: Bilingual Children's Book with MP3 Audiobook for Download, Age 4-6 & Up. Renz, Ulrich. Canedo, Marcos, tr. 2018. (Sefa Picture Books in Two Languages Ser.). (ENG.). 30p. (J). pap. *(978-3-7399-5897-2(9))* Boedeker, Kirsten. Sefa Verlag.

Robjohns, Laura-Anne. Click, Click! Magic Pictures Change Color in Water! small world creations, Laura-Anne. 2018. (Magic Bath Bks.). (ENG.). 8p. (J). (gr. -1 — 1). 5.99 *(978-1-4380-7907-3(9)*, B.E.S. Publishing) Peterson's.

—Glub, Glub! Magic Pictures Change Color in Water! Small World Creations, Small World. 2018. (Magic Bath Bks.). (ENG.). 8p. (J). (gr. -1 — 1). 5.99 *(978-1-4380-7908-0(7)*, B.E.S. Publishing) Peterson's.

Robledo. The Dog Child. Black, Simon. 2006. (ENG.). 32p. (J). (gr. -1-3). 17.95 *(978-0-938317-42-5(3))* Cinco Puntos Pr.

Robledo, Emilia. The Birthday Party, 1 vol. Dale, Jay. 2012. (Engage Literacy Magenta Ser.). (ENG.). 32p. (gr. k-2). pap. 5.99 *(978-1-4296-8866-6(1)*, Capstone Pr.) Capstone.

—Cooking in Class, 1 vol. Dale, Jay. 2012. (Wonder Words Ser.). (ENG.). 32p. (gr. k-2). pap. 5.99 *(978-1-4296-8922-9(6)*, Capstone Pr.) Capstone.

Robledo, Honorio. ¡El Cucuy! A Bogeyman Cuento in English & Spanish. Hayes, Joe. 2003. (ENG.). 40p. (J). (gr. k-2). pap. 7.95 *(978-0-938317-78-4(4))* Cinco Puntos Pr.

Robledo Tapia, Honorio. La Supermina del Cilantro. Herrera, Juan Felipe & Herrera, Juan. 2003.Tr. of Super Cilantro Girl. (ENG & SPA.). 32p. (J). 16.95 *(978-0-89239-187-5(1))* Lee & Low Bks., Inc.

Robles, Nick & Hale, Kendall. Space Battles; Crypt Quest. Soria, Gabe. 2018. (Midnight Arcade Ser.: 1). 256p. (J). (gr. 5). 13.99 *(978-1-5247-8429-4(X)*, Penguin Workshop) Penguin Young Readers Group.

R

—Calvin Coconut: Dog Heaven. Salisbury, Graham. 2011. (Calvin Coconut Ser.: 3). (ENG.). 160p. (J). (gr. 3-7). 6.99 *(978-0-375-84602-1(6)*, Yearling) Random Hse. Children's Bks.

—Calvin Coconut: Man Trip. Salisbury, Graham. 2013. (Calvin Coconut Ser.). (ENG.). 144p. (J). (gr. 3-6). lib. bdg. 21.19 *(978-0-385-90798-9(2)*, Lamb, Wendy Bks.) Random Hse. Children's Bks.

—Calvin Coconut: Rocket Ride. Salisbury, Graham. 2013. (Calvin Coconut Ser.: 8). 160p. (J). (gr. 2-5). pap. 6.99 *(978-0-375-86508-4(X)*, Yearling) Random Hse. Children's Bks.

—Calvin Coconut: Zoo Breath. Salisbury, Graham. 2011. (Calvin Coconut Ser.: 4). (ENG.). 160p. (J). (gr. 3-7). 6.99 *(978-0-375-84603-8(4)*, Yearling) Random Hse. Children's Bks.

—The Complete 8-Book Ramona Collection: Beezus & Ramona, Ramona & Her Father, Ramona & Her Mother, Ramona Quimby, Age 8, Ramona Forever, Ramona the Brave, Ramona the Pest, Ramona's World. Cleary, Beverly. 2009. (Ramona Ser.). (ENG.). 1728p. (J). (gr. 3-7). pap. 63.92 *(978-0-06-196090-1(X)*, HarperCollins) HarperCollins Pubs. Ltd. GBR. Dist: HarperCollins Pubs.

—Dixie & the Best Day Ever. Gilman, Grace. 2014. (I Can Read Level 1 Ser.). (ENG.). 32p. (J). (gr. -1-3). pap. 4.99 *(978-0-06-208659-4(6))* HarperCollins Pubs.

—Dixie & the Class Treat. Gilman, Grace. 2012. (I Can Read Level 1 Ser.). (ENG.). 32p. (J). (gr. -1-3). pap. 4.99 *(978-0-06-208605-1(7))* HarperCollins Pubs.

—Dixie Wins the Race. Gilman, Grace. 2012. (I Can Read Level 1 Ser.). (ENG.). 32p. (J). (gr. -1-3). pap. 4.99 *(978-0-06-208614-3(6))* HarperCollins Pubs.

—Dog Heaven. Salisbury, Graham. 2011. (Calvin Coconut Ser.). (ENG.). 160p. (J). (gr. 3-6). lib. bdg. 21.19 *(978-0-385-90641-8(2)*, Lamb, Wendy Bks.) Random Hse. Children's Bks.

—The Enormous Turnip: Classic Tales Edition. Smith, Carrie. 2011. (Classic Tales Ser.). (J). *(978-1-936258-70-3(6))* Benchmark Education Co.

—Even More Short & Shivery: Thirty Spine-Tingling Tales. San Souci, Robert D. 2003. (ENG.). 176p. (J). (gr. 3-7). pap. 5.99 *(978-0-440-41877-1(1)*, Yearling) Random Hse. Children's Bks.

—Even More Short & Shivery: Thirty Spine-Tingling Tales. San Souci, Robert D. ed. 2003. 162p. (gr. 5-7). lib. bdg. 16.00 *(978-0-613-72191-2(8))* Turtleback.

—Five Bouncing Bunnies. Karr, Lily. 2013. (ENG.). 10p. (J). (gr. -1 — 1). bds. 6.99 *(978-0-545-45825-2(0)*, Cartwheel Bks.) Scholastic, Inc.

—The Gingerbread Man: Classic Tales Edition. Adams, Alison. 2011. (Classic Tales Ser.). (J). *(978-1-936258-67-3(6))* Benchmark Education Co.

—Goosed! Wallace, Bill. 2004. (ENG.). 128p. (J). (gr. 2-4). pap. 7.99 *(978-0-689-86681-4(X)*, Aladdin) Simon & Schuster Children's Publishing.

—Henry & Beezus. Cleary, Beverly. 2014. (Henry Huggins Ser.: 2). (ENG.). 224p. (J). (gr. 3-7). 16.99 *(978-0-688-21383-1(9))*; 50th anniv. ed. pap. 7.99 *(978-0-380-70914-4(7))* HarperCollins Pubs. Ltd. GBR. (HarperCollins). Dist: HarperCollins Pubs.

—Henry & Ribsy. Cleary, Beverly. 2014. (Henry Huggins Ser.: 3). (ENG.). 208p. (J). (gr. 3-7). 16.99 *(978-0-688-21382-4(0))*; 50th anniv. ed. pap. 7.99 *(978-0-380-70917-5(1))* HarperCollins Pubs. Ltd. GBR. (HarperCollins). Dist: HarperCollins Pubs.

—Henry & the Clubhouse. Cleary, Beverly. 2014. (Henry Huggins Ser.: 5). (ENG.). 224p. (J). (gr. 3-7). 16.99 *(978-0-688-21381-7(2))*; pap. 7.99 *(978-0-380-70915-1(5))* HarperCollins Pubs. Ltd. GBR. (HarperCollins). Dist: HarperCollins Pubs.

—Henry & the Paper Route. Cleary, Beverly. 2014. (Henry Huggins Ser.: 4). (ENG.). 224p. (J). (gr. 3-7). reprint ed. pap. 7.99 *(978-0-380-70921-2(X)*, HarperCollins) HarperCollins Pubs. Ltd. GBR. Dist: HarperCollins Pubs.

—Henry Huggins. Cleary, Beverly. (Henry Huggins Ser.: 1). (ENG.). 208p. (J). (gr. 3-7). 2014. 16.99 *(978-0-688-21385-5(5))*; 50th anniv. ed. 2016. pap. 7.99 *(978-0-380-70912-0(0))* HarperCollins Pubs. Ltd. GBR. (HarperCollins). Dist: HarperCollins Pubs.

—Hero of Hawaii. Salisbury, Graham. 2012. (Calvin Coconut Ser.: 5). (ENG.). 160p. (J). (gr. 2-5). pap. 6.99 *(978-0-375-86505-3(5)*, Yearling) Random Hse. Children's Bks.

—Kung Fooey. Salisbury, Graham. 2012. (Calvin Coconut Ser.: 6). 144p. (J). (gr. 2-5). 6.99 *(978-0-375-86506-0(3)*, Yearling) Random Hse. Children's Bks.

—Little Ree. Drummond, Ree. 2017. (J). *(978-0-06-266351-1(8))* Harper & Row Ltd.

—Little Ree. Drummond, Ree. 2017. (Little Ree Ser.). (ENG.). 40p. (J). (gr. -1-3). 17.99 *(978-0-06-245318-1(1))* HarperCollins Pubs.

—Little Ree #2 (signed Edition) Drummond, Ree. 2018. (Little Ree Ser.). 32p. (J). (gr. -1-3). 17.99 *(978-0-06-282077-8(X))* HarperCollins Pubs.

—Little Ree: Best Friends Forever! Drummond, Ree. 2018. (Little Ree Ser.). (ENG.). 40p. (J). (gr. -1-3). 17.99 *(978-0-06-245319-8(X))* HarperCollins Pubs.

—The Littles Have a Happy Valentine's Day. Peterson, John & Slater, Teddy. 2003. (Littles First Readers Ser.: No. 11). (ENG.). 32p. (J). (gr. k-2). pap. 3.99 *(978-0-439-42499-8(2)*, Scholastic Paperbacks) Scholastic, Inc.

—The Littlest Christmas Tree. Herman, R. A. 2007. (ENG.). 32p. (J). (gr. -1-3). pap. 3.99 *(978-0-439-54007-0(0))* Scholastic, Inc.

—The Mouse & the Motorcycle. Cleary, Beverly. (Ralph Mouse Ser.: 1). (ENG.). 208p. (J). (gr. 3-7). 2014. 16.99 *(978-0-688-21698-6(6))*; 2016. reprint ed. pap. 7.99 *(978-0-380-70924-3(4))* HarperCollins Pubs. Ltd. GBR. (HarperCollins). Dist: HarperCollins Pubs.

—The Mouse & the Motorcycle: a Harper Classic. Cleary, Beverly. 2017. (Harper Classic Ser.). (ENG.). 224p. (J). (gr. 3-7). 16.99 *(978-0-06-265798-5(4))* HarperCollins Pubs.

—One Tractor. Siy, Alexandra. 2018. (I Like to Read Ser.). (ENG.). 32p. (J). (gr. -1-3). 6.99 *(978-0-8234-4015-3(X))* Holiday Hse., Inc.

—Our Great Big Backyard. Bush, Laura & Hager, Jenna Bush. (ENG.). 40p. (J). (gr. -1-3). 2018. pap. 7.99 *(978-0-06-246841-3(3))*; 2016. 18.99 *(978-0-06-246835-2(9))*; 2016. lib. bdg. 19.89 *(978-0-06-246836-9(7))* HarperCollins Pubs.

—Ralph S. Mouse. Cleary, Beverly. 2014. (Ralph Mouse Ser.: 3). (ENG.). 192p. (J). (gr. 3-7). 16.99 *(978-0-688-01452-0(6))*; pap. 7.99 *(978-0-380-70957-1(0))* HarperCollins Pubs. Ltd. GBR. (HarperCollins). Dist: HarperCollins Pubs.

—The Ramona 4-Book Collection, Volume 1 Vol. 1: Beezus & Ramona, Ramona & Her Father, Ramona the Brave, Ramona the Pest, Vol. 1. Cleary, Beverly. 2020. (Ramona Ser.). (ENG.). 848p. (J). (gr. 3-7). pap. 22.99 *(978-0-06-124647-0(6)*, HarperCollins) HarperCollins Pubs. Ltd. GBR. Dist: HarperCollins Pubs.

—The Ramona 4-Book Collection, Volume 2 Vol. 2: Ramona & Her Mother; Ramona Quimby, Age 8; Ramona Forever; Ramona's World. Cleary, Beverly. 2020. (Ramona Ser.). (ENG.). 880p. (J). (gr. 3-7). pap. 22.99 *(978-0-06-124648-7(4)*, HarperCollins) HarperCollins Pubs. Ltd. GBR. Dist: HarperCollins Pubs.

—Ramona & Her Father. Cleary, Beverly. 2020. (Ramona Ser.: 4). (ENG.). 192p. (J). (gr. 3-7). 16.99 *(978-0-688-22114-0(9))*; pap. 7.99 *(978-0-380-70916-8(3))* HarperCollins Pubs. Ltd. GBR. (HarperCollins). Dist: HarperCollins Pubs.

—Ramona & Her Mother. Cleary, Beverly. 2020. (Ramona Ser.: 5). (ENG.). 224p. (J). (gr. 3-7). 16.99 *(978-0-688-22195-9(5))*; reprint ed. pap. 7.99 *(978-0-380-70952-6(X))* HarperCollins Pubs. Ltd. GBR. (HarperCollins). Dist: HarperCollins Pubs.

—Ramona Empieza el Curso: Ramona Quimby, Age 8 (Spanish Edition), 1 vol. Cleary, Beverly. 2006. (Ramona Ser.: 6).Tr. of Ramona Quimby, Age 8. (SPA.). 224p. (J). (gr. 3-7). pap. 6.99 *(978-0-688-15487-5(5)*, MR7554) HarperCollins Español.

—Ramona Forever. Cleary, Beverly. 2020. (Ramona Ser.: 7). (ENG.). 208p. (J). (gr. 3-7). 16.99 *(978-0-688-03785-7(2))*; reprint ed. pap. 7.99 *(978-0-380-70960-1(0))* HarperCollins Pubs. Ltd. GBR. (HarperCollins). Dist: HarperCollins Pubs.

—Ramona la Chinche: Ramona the Pest (Spanish Edition), 1 vol. Cleary, Beverly. 2006. (Ramona Ser.: 2).Tr. of Ramona the Pest. (SPA.). 192p. (J). (gr. 3-7). pap. 7.99 *(978-0-688-14888-1(3)*, MR2295) HarperCollins Español.

—Ramona Quimby, Age 8. Cleary, Beverly. 2016. (Ramona Ser.: 6). (ENG.). 208p. (J). (gr. 3-7). 12.99 *(978-0-06-246454-5(X))* HarperCollins Pubs.

—Ramona Quimby, Age 8. Cleary, Beverly. 2020. (Ramona Ser.: 6). (ENG.). 208p. (J). (gr. 3-7). 16.99 *(978-0-688-00477-4(6))*; pap. 7.99 *(978-0-380-70956-4(2))* HarperCollins Pubs. Ltd. GBR. (HarperCollins). Dist: HarperCollins Pubs.

—Ramona Quimby, Age 8 Read-Aloud Edition. Cleary, Beverly. 2016. (Ramona Ser.: 6). (ENG.). 208p. (J). (gr. 3-7). 17.99 *(978-0-06-245327-3(0))* HarperCollins Pubs.

—Ramona the Brave. Cleary, Beverly. 2020. (Ramona Ser.: 3). (ENG.). 208p. (J). (gr. 3-7). 16.99 *(978-0-688-22015-0(0))*; pap. 7.99 *(978-0-380-70959-5(7))* HarperCollins Pubs. Ltd. GBR. (HarperCollins). Dist: HarperCollins Pubs.

—Ramona the Pest. Cleary, Beverly. 2020. (Ramona Ser.: 2). (ENG.). 240p. (J). (gr. 3-7). 16.99 *(978-0-688-21721-1(4))*; pap. 7.99 *(978-0-380-70954-0(6))* HarperCollins Pubs. Ltd. GBR. (HarperCollins). Dist: HarperCollins Pubs.

—Ramona's World. Cleary, Beverly. 2020. (Ramona Ser.: 8). (ENG.). 240p. (J). (gr. 3-7). 16.99 *(978-0-688-16816-2(7))*; pap. 7.99 *(978-0-380-73272-2(6))* HarperCollins Pubs. Ltd. GBR. (HarperCollins). Dist: HarperCollins Pubs.

—Ribsy. Cleary, Beverly. 2014. (Henry Huggins Ser.: 6). (ENG.). 240p. (J). (gr. 3-7). 16.99 *(978-0-688-21662-7(5))*; pap. 7.99 *(978-0-380-70955-7(4))* HarperCollins Pubs. Ltd. GBR. (HarperCollins). Dist: HarperCollins Pubs.

—Runaway Ralph. Cleary, Beverly. 2014. (Ralph Mouse Ser.: 2). (ENG.). 224p. (J). (gr. 3-7). 16.99 *(978-0-688-21701-3(X))*; pap. 7.99 *(978-0-380-70953-3(8))* HarperCollins Pubs. Ltd. GBR. (HarperCollins). Dist: HarperCollins Pubs.

—Stone Soup: Classic Tales Edition. Smith, Carrie. 2011. (Classic Tales Ser.). (J). *(978-1-936258-72-7(2))* Benchmark Education Co.

—Trouble Magnet. Salisbury, Graham. (Calvin Coconut Ser.: 1). (ENG.). 160p. (J). 2010. (gr. 3-7). pap. 6.99 *(978-0-375-84600-7(X)*, Yearling); 2009. (gr. 4-6). lib. bdg. 21.19 *(978-0-385-90639-5(0)*, Lamb, Wendy Bks.) Random Hse. Children's Bks.

—The Ugly Duckling: Classic Tales Edition. Smith, Carrie. 2011. (Classic Tales Ser.). (J). *(978-1-936258-63-5(3))* Benchmark Education Co.

Rogers, Jacqueline. Goblin Moon. Rogers, Jacqueline. 2019. (ENG.). 32p. (J). (gr. -1-3). 17.99 *(978-0-06-279229-7(6))* HarperCollins Pubs.

Rogers, Jacqueline & Parlagreco, Aurora M. Just for Me: My Ramona Quimby Journal. Cleary, Beverly. 2013. (ENG.). 144p. (J). (gr. 3-7). 11.99 *(978-0-06-223049-2(2))* HarperCollins Pubs.

Rogers, Jacqueline, jt. illus. see Peterson, Joel.

Rogers, Jahshua. Dash on the Run! Rogers, Jahshua. 2016. (ENG.). (J). pap. 7.99 *(978-0-9863965-2-6(4))* OASYS Pr.

Rogers, Logan. The Big Sky Boys & Life on the Spinnin' Spur. Linder, Todd. 2019. (ENG.). 48p. (J). (gr. 4-6). 14.99 *(978-0-578-51100-9(2))* Monday Creek Publishing.

Rogers, Madalyn V. Your Own Little Silly Mcgilly. Liner, Robin. 2013. 38p. pap. 9.99 *(978-0-9910342-0-8(1))* East Stream Group, LLC.

Rogers, Marshall, et al. Marvel Masterworks: Doctor Strange Vol. 9. 2019. (Marvel Masterworks: Doctor Strange Ser.: 9). (ENG.). 336p. (YA). (gr. 4-17). 75.00 *(978-1-302-91704-3(8))* Marvel Worldwide, Inc.

Rogers, Melissa & Heran, Michelle. The Plot Thickens... Harry Potter Investigated by Fans for Fans. Waters, Galadriel, ed. 2015. (ENG.). 100p. (YA). pap. 18.95 *(978-0-9723936-3-8(3))* Wizarding World Pr.

Rogers, Nikki. A Beautiful Girl Like You. Rogers, Nikki. 2020. (ENG.). 30p. (J). (gr. k-5). *(978-0-6483562-5-7(6))* Created To Be.

Rogers, Nikki. A Hero Like You. Rogers, Nikki. 2020. (ENG.). 30p. (J). pap. ***(978-0-6487232-3-3(2))*** Created To Be.

Rogers, Paul. Forever Young. Dylan, Bob. 2008. (ENG.). 40p. (J). (gr. -1-4). 18.99 *(978-1-4169-5808-6(8)*, Atheneum Bks. for Young Readers) Simon & Schuster Children's Publishing.

—Jazz A-B-Z: An A to Z Collection of Jazz Portraits. Marsalis, Wynton. 2005. (ENG.). 76p. (J). (gr. 4-7). 24.99 *(978-0-7636-2135-3(8))* Candlewick Pr.

—Squeak, Rumble, Whomp! Whomp! Whomp! Marsalis, Wynton. 2012. (ENG.). 40p. (J). (gr. -1-3). 17.99 *(978-0-7636-3991-4(5))* Candlewick Pr.

Rogers, Peter. Evacuee's Return. Farrell, Tom. 2018. (ENG.). 238p. (gr. 3-6). 17.99 *(978-1-78719-711-4(5))*; pap. 13.99 *(978-1-78719-710-7(7))* New Generation Publishing GBR. Dist: Independent Pubs. Group.

Rogers, Ruth W., et al. Bible Stories in Pictures. Beck, William F. 2nd ed. 2003.Tr. of Bible Stories in Pictures. (ALB, SPA & SWE.). 376p. pap. 10.65 *(978-1-931891-08-0(7))* Multi-Language Pubns.

—Histori Biblike Me Llustrime: Nga Krijimi Ne Kishen e Hershme. Beck, William F. 2003.Tr. of Bible Stories in Pictures. (ALB, SPA & SWE.). 374p. (J). pap. 10.65 *(978-1-931891-07-3(9)*, 38-7378) Multi-Language Pubns.

Rogers, Sherry. Burro's Tortillas, 1 vol. Fields, Terri. 2007. (ENG.). 32p. (J). (gr. -1-3). 15.95 *(978-0-9768823-9-8(6))* Arbordale Publishing.

—¡Clasifícalo! Mariconda, Barbara. 2008.Tr. of Sort It Out!. (SPA.). 32p. (J). (gr. k-4). 17.95 *(978-1-60718-695-3(0))* Arbordale Publishing.

—La Dama de Los Pingüinos, 1 vol. Cole, Carol A. 2012. (SPA & ENG.). 32p. (J). (gr. -1-3). 17.95 *(978-1-60718-697-7(7))*; pap. 11.95 *(978-1-62855-420-5(7))* Arbordale Publishing.

—Le Détective Déductif: (the Deductive Detective in French) Rock, Brian. Troff, Sophie, tr. 2019. (FRE.). 32p. (J). (gr. k-3). pap. 11.95 *(978-1-64351-597-7(7))* Arbordale Publishing.

—El Detective Deductivo, 1 vol. Rock, Brian. 2013. (SPA.). 32p. (J). (gr. -1-2). pap. 11.95 *(978-1-62855-347-5(2))* Arbordale Publishing.

—First Fire. Allen, Nancy Kelly. 2014. (ENG.). (J). (gr. k-3). lib. bdg. 20.55 *(978-1-62765-712-9(6))* Perfection Learning Corp.

—Hey Diddle Diddle: A Food Chain Tale, 1 vol. Kapchinske, Pam. 2011. (ENG.). 32p. (J). (gr. -1-3). 16.95 *(978-1-60718-130-9(4))*; pap. 8.95 *(978-1-60718-140-8(1))* Arbordale Publishing.

—If You Were a Parrot, 1 vol. Rawson, Katherine. 2006. (ENG.). 32p. (J). (gr. -1-3). 15.95 *(978-0-9764943-9-3(6))* Arbordale Publishing.

—Kersplatypus, 1 vol. Mitchell, Susan K. 2008. (ENG.). 32p. (J). (gr. -1-2). 16.95 *(978-1-934359-07-5(6))*; pap. 8.95 *(978-1-934359-23-5(8))* Arbordale Publishing.

—Moose & Magpie, 1 vol. Restrepo, Bettina. 2009. (ENG.). 32p. (J). (gr. -1-3). pap. 9.95 *(978-1-60718-042-5(1))* Arbordale Publishing.

—Newton & Me. Mayer, Lynne. 2010. 32p. (J). (gr. -1-3). 16.95 *(978-1-60718-067-8(7))* Arbordale Publishing.

—Newton et Moi. Mayer, Lynne. Troff, Sophie, tr. 2019. (FRE.). 32p. (J). 11.95 *(978-1-64351-605-9(1))* Arbordale Publishing.

—Paws, Claws, Hands, & Feet, 1 vol. Hutmacher, Kimberly. 2009. (ENG.). 32p. (J). (gr. -1-2). 16.95 *(978-1-934359-88-4(2))*; pap. 8.95 *(978-1-934359-98-3(X)*, 9781934359983) Arbordale Publishing.

—The Penguin Lady, 1 vol. Cole, Carol A. 2012. (ENG.). 32p. (J). (gr. -1-3). 17.95 *(978-1-60718-527-7(X))*; pap. 9.95 *(978-1-60718-536-9(9))* Arbordale Publishing.

—Sort It Out!, 1 vol. Mariconda, Barbara. 2008. (ENG.). 32p. (J). (gr. k-4). 16.95 *(978-1-934359-11-2(4))*; pap. 8.95 *(978-1-934359-32-7(7))* Arbordale Publishing.

Rogers, Sherry. El Detective Deductivo, 1 vol. Rogers, Sherry. Rock, Brian. 2013. (SPA.). 32p. (J). (gr. -1-2). 17.95 *(978-1-60718-708-0(6))* Arbordale Publishing.

Rogers, Susie. The Color of Us. Hardee, Kathy. 2019. (ENG.). 40p. (J). pap. 14.59 *(978-1-68314-842-5(8))* Redemption Pr.

Rogers, Terry. Androcles & the Lion: A Roman Legend. 2003. (Dominie Collection of Myths & Legends). (SPA.). 20p. (J). lib. bdg. *(978-0-7685-2419-2(9))* Dominie Pr., Inc.

—Androcles & the Lion: A Roman Legend. 2004. (SPA & ENG.). 20p. (J). (gr. 3-3). pap. 6.47 net. *(978-0-7685-2122-1(X)*, Dominie Elementary) Savvas Learning Co.

Rogers, Walter S. Little Woodcrafters' Fun on the Farm. Roy, Lillian Elizabeth. 2011. 232p. 46.95 *(978-1-258-09314-3(6))* Literary Licensing, LLC.

Rogge, Rachel. Nature's Yucky! 2: The Desert Southwest. Landstrom, Lee Ann & Shragg, Karen. 2007. (Nature's Yucky Ser.). 48p. (J). (gr. k-7). pap. 12.00 *(978-0-87842-529-7(2))* Mountain Pr. Publishing Co., Inc.

—Nature's Yucky! 3: The Eastern United States. Landstrom, Lee Ann & Shragg, Karen I. 2013. 48p. (J). pap. 12.00 *(978-0-87842-601-0(9))* Mountain Pr. Publishing Co., Inc.

Roggenbuck, Kellen. Oomph: A World of Words. Lingelbach, Anne. 2018. (ENG.). 32p. (J). (gr. 3-6). pap. 14.99 *(978-1-948365-04-8(9))* Orange Hat Publishing.

Roguez, Jesus. The Littlest Smoke Detector. Brozman, Dave. 2006. (ENG.). 32p. per. 21.99 *(978-1-4259-6096-4(0))* AuthorHouse.

Roher, Michael. My New Granny. Steinkellner, Elisabeth. 2012. 32p. (J). (gr. -1-3). 16.95 *(978-1-62087-223-9(4)*, 620223, Sky Pony Pr.) Skyhorse Publishing Co., Inc.

Roher, Rebecca. Pete Milano's Guide to Being a Movie Star: A Charlie Joe Jackson Book. Greenwald, Tommy. 2018. (Charlie Joe Jackson Ser.). (ENG.). 272p. (J). pap. 7.99 *(978-1-250-14365-5(9)*, 9781250143655) Square Fish.

Rohmann, Eric. Bless This Mouse. Lois, Lowry. 2015. (ENG.). (J). (gr. 2-5). lib. bdg. 17.60 *(978-1-62765-702-0(9))* Perfection Learning Corp.

—Bulldozer Helps Out. Fleming, Candace. 2017. (Bulldozer Bks.). (ENG.). 40p. (J). (gr. -1-2). 17.99 *(978-1-4814-5894-8(9))* Simon & Schuster Children's Publishing.

—Bulldozer's Big Day. Fleming, Candace. 2015. (Bulldozer Bks.). (ENG.). 40p. (J). (gr. -1-2). 17.99 *(978-1-4814-0097-8(5)*, Atheneum Bks. for Young Readers) Simon & Schuster Children's Publishing.

—Giant Squid. Fleming, Candace. 2016. (ENG.). 40p. (J). (gr. 1-5). 18.99 *(978-1-59643-599-5(2)*, 900065585) Roaring Brook Pr.

—Honeybee: The Busy Life of Apis Mellifera. Fleming, Candace. 2020. (ENG.). 40p. (J). (gr. 1-4). 18.99 *(978-0-8234-4285-0(3)*, Neal Porter Bks) Holiday Hse., Inc.

—Oh, No! Fleming, Candace. 40p. (J). (gr. -1-2). 2018. (ENG.). 7.99 *(978-1-9848-5204-5(3)*, Dragonfly Bks.); 2012. 17.99 *(978-0-375-84271-9(3)*, Schwartz & Wade Bks.) Random Hse. Children's Bks.

—Strongheart: Wonder Dog of the Silver Screen. Fleming, Candace. 2018. (ENG.). 256p. (J). (gr. 3-7). lib. bdg. 20.99 *(978-1-101-93411-1(5)*, Schwartz & Wade Bks.) Random Hse. Children's Bks.

—Strongheart: Wonder Dog of the Silver Screen. Fleming, Candace. 2018. (ENG.). 256p. (J). (gr. 3-7). 17.99 *(978-1-101-93410-4(7)*, Schwartz & Wade Bks.) Random Hse. Children's Bks.

Rohmann, Eric. My Friend Rabbit: A Picture Book. Rohmann, Eric. 2011. (ENG.). 36p. (J). (gr. -1-3). bds. 7.99 *(978-1-59643-641-1(7)*, 900068766) Roaring Brook Pr.

—My Friend Rabbit: A Picture Book. Rohmann, Eric. 2007. (ENG.). 32p. (J). (gr. -1-1). pap. 7.99 *(978-0-312-36752-7(X)*, 900042356) Square Fish.

Rohner, Dorothia. Effie's Image. 2006. 32p. (J). (gr. -1-3). 17.95 *(978-0-9759829-5-2(8))* Prairieland Pr.

—Numbers in a Row: An Iowa Number Book. Patricia Pierce. 2006. (Count Your Way Across the U. S. A. Ser.). (ENG.). 40p. (J). (gr. -1-3). 17.95 *(978-1-58536-164-9(X))* Sleeping Bear Pr.

Röhr, Stéphanie. The Bad Easter Bunny. Atherton, Isabel. 2013. 32p. (J). (gr. -1-k). 12.95 *(978-1-62087-500-1(4)*, 620500, Sky Pony Pr.) Skyhorse Publishing Co., Inc.

—Count the Sheep to Sleep. Rae, Philippa. 2012. 28p. (J). (gr. -1-k). 12.95 *(978-1-61608-660-2(2)*, 608660, Sky Pony Pr.) Skyhorse Publishing Co., Inc.

Rohrbach, Sophie. Sherlock Holmes & a Scandal in Bohemia, No. 1. Doyle, A. Conan. 2010. (On the Case with Holmes & Watson Ser.: 1). 48p. (J). (gr. 4-6). lib. bdg. 27.99 *(978-0-7613-6185-5(5)*, 9780761361855, Graphic Universe™) Lerner Publishing Group.

—Sherlock Holmes & a Scandal in Bohemia: Case 1, No. 1. Doyle, A. Conan. 2010. (On the Case with Holmes & Watson Ser.: 1). (ENG.). 48p. (J). (gr. 4-6). pap. 9.99 *(978-0-7613-6197-8(9)*, 9780761361978, Graphic Universe™) Lerner Publishing Group.

—Sherlock Holmes & the Adventure of the Speckled Band: Case 5, No. 5. Doyle, A. Conan. 2010. (On the Case with Holmes & Watson Ser.: 5). (ENG.). 48p. (J). (gr. 4-6). pap. 9.99 *(978-0-7613-6198-5(7)*, 9780761361985, Graphic Universe™) Lerner Publishing Group.

Rohrbach, Sophie & Morrow, J. T. Sherlock Holmes & the Adventure of Black Peter. Doyle, A. Conan. 2012. (On the Case with Holmes & Watson Ser.). 48p. (J). (gr. 4-6). pap. 39.62 *(978-0-7613-9274-3(2)*, Graphic Universe™) Lerner Publishing Group.

—Sherlock Holmes & the Adventure of Black Peter, No. 11. Doyle, A. Conan. 2012. (On the Case with Holmes & Watson Ser.: 11). 48p. (J). (gr. 4-6). lib. bdg. 27.99 *(978-0-7613-7092-5(7)*, 9780761370925, Graphic Universe™) Lerner Publishing Group.

—Sherlock Holmes & the Adventure of the Cardboard Box. Doyle, A. Conan. 2012. (On the Case with Holmes & Watson Ser.). 48p. (J). (gr. 4-6). pap. 39.62 *(978-0-7613-9275-0(0)*, Graphic Universe™) Lerner Publishing Group.

—Sherlock Holmes & the Adventure of the Cardboard Box, No. 12. Doyle, A. Conan. 2012. (On the Case with Holmes & Watson Ser.: 12). 48p. (J). (gr. 4-6). lib. bdg. 27.99 *(978-0-7613-7090-1(0)*, 9780761370901, Graphic Universe™) Lerner Publishing Group.

—Sherlock Holmes & the Adventure of the Three Garridebs. Doyle, A. Conan. 2012. (On the Case with Holmes & Watson Ser.). 48p. (J). (gr. 4-6). pap. 39.62 *(978-0-7613-9276-7(9)*, Graphic Universe™) Lerner Publishing Group.

—Sherlock Holmes & the Boscombe Valley Mystery, No. 10. Doyle, A. Conan. 2011. (On the Case with Holmes & Watson Ser.: 10). 48p. (J). (gr. 4-6). 27.99 *(978-0-7613-7089-5(7)*, 9780761370895, Graphic Universe™) Lerner Publishing Group.

—Sherlock Holmes & the Gloria Scott. Doyle, A. Conan. 2012. (On the Case with Holmes & Watson Ser.). 48p. (J). (gr. 4-6). pap. 39.62 *(978-0-7613-9277-4(7)*, Graphic Universe™) Lerner Publishing Group.

Rohrbach, Sophie & Morrow, Jt. #07 Sherlock Holmes & the Redheaded League. Doyle, A. Conan. 2011. (On the Case with Holmes & Watson Set II Ser.). pap. 39.62 *(978-0-7613-7609-5(7)*, Graphic Universe™) Lerner Publishing Group.

—#08 Sherlock Holmes & the Adventure at the Copper Beeches. Doyle, A. Conan. 2011. (On the Case with Holmes & Watson Set II Ser.). (J). pap. 39.62 *(978-0-7613-7610-1(0)*, Graphic Universe™) Lerner Publishing Group.

—#09 Sherlock Holmes & the Adventure of the Six Napoleons. Doyle, A. Conan. 2011. (On the Case with Holmes & Watson Set II Ser.). pap. 39.62

(978-0-7613-7611-8(9), Graphic Universe™) Lerner Publishing Group.

—#10 Sherlock Holmes & the Boscombe Valley Mystery. Doyle, A. Conan. 2011. (On the Case with Holmes & Watson Set II Ser.). pap. 39.62 (978-0-7613-7612-5(7), Graphic Universe™) Lerner Publishing Group.

Rohrer, Neal. Rohrer's Fun Coloring & Games. Rohrer, Neal. 2003. 28p. 3.95 (978-0-9721138-0-9(0)) Rohrer Design.

Roi, Arnaud. Paper Toys: Speed Demons: 12 Paper Speed Demons to Build. 2017. (Paper Toys Ser.). (ENG.). 24p. (J). (gr. k-4). pap. 11.95 (978-1-58423-669-6(8), 27f83cf8-6210-48e9-a739-8147c86b5189, Gingko Pr.) Gingko Pr., Inc.

Roi Visual Staff. Robocar Poli: My Essential Guide to Traffic Safety. Chouette Publishing Staff, tr. 2018. 24p. (J). (gr. -1-1). bds. 7.99 (978-2-924786-59-8(2), CrackBoom! Bks.) Chouette Publishing CAN. Dist: Publishers Group West (PGW).

—Robocar Poli: Snow Mission: With 2-Way Sequins! ed. 2019. (ENG.). 24p. (J). (gr. k-2). 9.99 (978-2-89802-075-9(3), CrackBoom! Bks.) Chouette Publishing CAN. Dist: Publishers Group West (PGW).

ROI Visual Staff & Dupuis, Karina. Big Storm in Broomstown. Delporte, Corinne & Warriner, David. ed. 2019. (Robocar Poli Ser.). 24p. (J). (gr. -1-1). pap. 3.99 (978-2-924786-86-4(X), CrackBoom! Bks.) Chouette Publishing CAN. Dist: Publishers Group West (PGW).

—Helly's Wish. Delporte, Corinne & Warriner, David. ed. 2018. (Robocar Poli Ser.). 24p. (J). (gr. -1-1). pap. 3.99 (978-2-924786-88-8(6), CrackBoom! Bks.) Chouette Publishing CAN. Dist: Publishers Group West (PGW).

—Read with Robocar Poli: a Visit to the Farm (Level 1: Starting Reader) 2019. (Robocar Poli Ser.). (ENG.). 32p. (J). (gr. -1). 3.99 (978-2-924786-99-4(1), CrackBoom! Bks.) Chouette Publishing CAN. Dist: Publishers Group West (PGW).

—Read with Robocar Poli: Hooray for the Heroes! (Level 2: Qualified Reader) 2019. (Robocar Poli Ser.). (ENG.). 32p. (J). (gr. -1). 3.99 (978-2-89802-002-5(8), CrackBoom! Bks.) Chouette Publishing CAN. Dist: Publishers Group West (PGW).

—Robocar Poli: a Surprise Birthday Party: A Lift-The-Flap Book. 2019. 10p. (J). (gr. -1). bds. 7.99 (978-2-89802-032-2(X), CrackBoom! Bks.) Chouette Publishing CAN. Dist: Publishers Group West (PGW).

—Robocar Poli: My First Sticker Book. 2019. (Robocar Poli Ser.). 64p. (J). (gr. -1). bds. 10.99 (978-2-924786-92-5(4), CrackBoom! Bks.) Chouette Publishing CAN. Dist: Publishers Group West (PGW).

ROI Visual Staff & Legdani, Sanaa. Robocar Poli: Welcome to Broomstown! a Look & Find Book (Little Detectives) ed. 2019. 14p. (J). (gr. -1-1). bds. 9.99 (978-2-89802-011-7(7), CrackBoom! Bks.) Chouette Publishing CAN. Dist: Publishers Group West (PGW).

Roitman, Tanya. I'm Going to Boston to Visit the Ducks. 2006. (I'm Going to Read! Level 1 Ser.). (ENG.). 32p. (J). (gr. k-1). 16.19 (978-1-4027-3092-4(6)) Sterling Publishing Co., Inc.

—Long Vowels. Ziefert, Harriet. 2007. (I'm Going to Read® Ser.). 64p. (J). (gr. -1-1). pap. 5.95 (978-1-4027-5057-1(9)) Sterling Publishing Co., Inc.

—The More We Are Together. 2009. (Rookie Toddler Ser.). (ENG.). 12p. (J). (gr. -1 — 1). bds. 6.95 (978-0-531-24547-7(0), Children's Pr.) Scholastic Library Publishing.

—Sight Words. Ziefert, Harriet. 2007. (I'm Going to Read® Ser.). 64p. (J). (gr. -1-1). pap. 5.95 (978-1-4027-5058-8(7)) Sterling Publishing Co., Inc.

Rojankovsky, Feodor. The Three Bears. Golden Books. 2012. (Little Golden Book Ser.). 24p. (J). (gr. k-k). 4.99 (978-0-307-02140-3(8), Golden Bks.) Random Hse. Children's Bks.

Rojankovsky, Feodor & Gergely, Tibor. Little Golden Book Farm Favorites. McGinley, Phyllis et al. 2012. (Little Golden Book Favorites Ser.). 80p. (J). (gr. k-k). 7.99 (978-0-307-93020-0(3), Golden Bks.) Random Hse. Children's Bks.

Rojas, Jessica. Abecedarium Latinum. Sipes, Peter. 2011.Tr. of Latin Alphabet. 36p. (J). pap. 8.95 (978-1-937847-00-5(4)) Pluteo Pleno.

Rojas, Maria Fernanda. DOS Piratas y un Pincel. Mira, Katish. 2018. (SPA.). 32p. (J). (gr. k-3). (978-958-48-3873-5(3)) Restrepo, Ana.

Rojas, Mary. Before I Sleep I Say Thank You. Ekster, Carol Gordon. 2015. (J). 14.95 (978-0-8198-1225-4(0)) Pauline Bks. & Media.

—Siempre Tú: Un Libro Sobre Tu Cuerpo y Tu Alma. Lataif, Nicole. Pérez, Karen H., tr. from ENG. 2014.Tr. of Forever You: a Book about Your Body & Soul. (SPA.). (J). pap. 9.95 (978-0-8198-9009-2(X)) Pauline Bks. & Media.

Rojas, Mary & Grayson, Rick. Everyone's a Star. Allen, Margaret. Hults, Alaska, ed. 2003. (J). pap. 13.99 (978-1-59198-008-7(9), CTP2258) Creative Teaching Pr., Inc.

Rojas, Mary & Vangsgard, Amy. Jingle Jangles Vol. 2256: Fun, Interactive Reading Selections for Fluency Practice. Allen, Margaret. Walter, LaDawn, ed. 2004. 128p. (J). (gr. k-2). pap. 14.99 (978-1-59198-048-3(8), 2256) Creative Teaching Pr., Inc.

Rojas, Mary & Willardson, David. Leap into Literacy Spring. Geiser, Traci Ferguson & Boylan, Maureen McCourt. Cernek, Kim, ed. 2003. 160p. (J). (gr. k-2). pap. 17.99 (978-1-57471-959-8(9), 3375) Creative Teaching Pr., Inc.

Rojas, Mary Galan. Mrs. E's Extraordinary Number Activities. Etringer, Kathy. Mitchell, Judy & Sussman, Ellen, eds. 2006. 128p. (J). pap. 13.95 (978-1-57310-506-4(6)) Teaching & Learning Co.

Rojas, Saul Oscar. Habia una Vez una Casa. Montes, Graciela. 2005. (Pictocuentos Ser.). (SPA.). 24p. (J). 8.95 (978-1-59820-212-0(X), Alfaguara) Santillana USA Publishing Co., Inc.

Rojo, Sara. Baba Yaga: the Flying Witch. 2008. (Usborne First Reading: Level 4 Ser.). 48p. (J). 8.99 (978-0-7945-2078-6(2), Usborne) EDC Publishing.

—Why the Sea Is Salty. 2009. (First Reading Level 4 Ser.). 48p. (J). 6.99 (978-0-7945-2308-4(0), Usborne) EDC Publishing.

Rol, Agence, photos by. Carnet Blanc Voilier la France. 2016. (Bnf. Monum. Franc Ser.). (FRE., (J). pap. (978-2-01-126435-0(9)) Hachette Groupe Livre.

—Carnet Ligne Voilier la France: Librairie Dialogues Brest. 2016. (Bnf Monuments Ser.). (FRE., (J). pap. (978-2-01-359561-2(1)) Hachette Groupe Livre.

Roland, Timothy. Monkey Me & the New Neighbor. Roland, Timothy. 2014. (Monkey Me Ser.: 3). (ENG.). 96p. (J). (gr. 1-3). pap. 4.99 (978-0-545-55984-3(7)) Scholastic, Inc.

—Monkey Me & the School Ghost. Roland, Timothy. 2014. (Monkey Me Ser.: 4). (ENG.). 96p. (J). (gr. 1-3). pap. 4.99 (978-0-545-55989-8(8)); 15.99 (978-0-545-55990-4(1)) Scholastic, Inc.

—The Pet Show. Roland, Timothy. 2014. (Monkey Me Ser.: 2). (ENG.). 96p. (J). (gr. 1-3). pap. 4.99 (978-0-545-55980-5(4)) Scholastic, Inc.

Rold, Jenifer. A Night on Kingwood. Derowitsch, Jayson. 2019. (ENG.). 166p. (YA). 30.95 (978-1-4897-2100-6(2)); pap. 13.99 (978-1-4897-2101-3(0)) AuthorHouse. (Life Rich Publishing).

Roldan, Bree. Only Freaks Turn Things into Bones. Green, Steff. 2019. (ENG.). 40p. (J). (gr. 1-4). pap. 12.95 (978-1-925652-98-7(X), Pub. Obscura) Odyssey Bks. AUS. Dist: Ingram Content Group.

Roldan, Meg, jt. illus. see Mawhinney, Art.

Roldan, Patrict. The Hero: It's up to You. Burns, Judith. (Reader Friendly Bks.). (YA). (gr. 5-12). pap. 9.95 (978-0-9726099-9-9(7)) BurnsBooks.

Rolf, Heidi. Hey I'm Alex. Pellegrin, Leeann. 2012. 26p. pap. 12.95 (978-1-61244-049-1(5)) Halo Publishing International.

—My Pet Dinosaur. Elefritz, Erin. 2012. 24p. pap. 11.95 (978-1-61244-117-7(3)) Halo Publishing International.

Rolland, Leonard Le. Animal Jokes. Howell, Laura, ed. 2004. (Jokes Ser.). 96p. (J). pap. 6.95 (978-0-7945-0655-1(0), Usborne) EDC Publishing.

—The Usborne Encyclopedia of World Religions: Internet-Linked. Hickman, Clare & Meredith, Sue. Rogers, Kirsteen, ed. rev. ed. 2006. (Usborne Encyclopedia of World Religions Ser.). 128p. (J). (gr. 5-9). per. 14.95 (978-0-7945-1059-6(0), Usborne) EDC Publishing.

Rolland, Will. Brolga. Reilly, Pauline. (Picture Roo Bks.). 32p. (J). pap. (978-0-86417-719-3(4), Kangaroo Pr.) Simon & Schuster Australia.

Rolling, Beanic. Paper Boy Two: Over Whelming 0005. Veremiah, Omari. 2004. 74p. (YA). (gr. 7-12). pap. 12.99 (978-1-929188-10-9(2)) Morton Bks.

Rollinger, Marsha. Starlight Blue: A New Baby. Klingensmith, Ryan Lee & Klingensmith, Sherri Ann. 2012. 32p. pap. 24.95 (978-1-4626-8219-5(7)) America Star Bks.

Rollings, Brittany L. Molly Tailwagger. Rollings, Gwen C. 2016. (ENG.). (J). pap. 10.99 (978-1-4984-8588-3(X)) Salem Author Services.

—Molly Tailwagger & the Family Vacation. Rollings, Gwen C. 2016. (ENG.). (J). pap. 10.99 (978-1-4984-9194-5(4)) Salem Author Services.

—Molly Tailwagger & the Greatest Show on Earth. Rollings, Gwen C. 2016. (ENG.). (J). pap. 10.99 (978-1-4984-8926-3(5)) Salem Author Services.

—Molly Tailwagger Faces Her Fear. Rollings, Gwen C. 2019. (ENG.). 52p. (J). pap. 13.49 (978-1-5456-5666-2(5)) Salem Author Services.

—Molly Tailwagger You Could Be a Star. Rollings, Gwen C. 2017. (ENG.). (J). pap. 10.99 (978-1-5456-0028-3(7)) Salem Author Services.

Rollins, Anthony. Stage Fright. Perez, Trisha B. 2018. (Adventures of Josie & Bud Ser.: Vol. 1). (ENG.). 42p. (J). (gr. k-2). 19.95 (978-0-9995631-1-3(4)) Storm Praise Publishing, LLC.

Rollins, Berni. Paper Boy Four: L. O. E. P. S. Worst Nightmare. Jeremiah, Omari. 2007. 96p. (YA). (gr. 7-12). pap. 12.99 (978-1-929188-15-4(3)) Morton Bks.

Rollins, Bernic. Paper Boy. Jeremiatt, Omani. 2003. 40p. (J). (gr. 6-8). pap. 10.00 (978-1-929188-09-3(9)) Morton Bks.

Rollins, Bernie. Paperboy 3: The School of Doom. Jeremiah, Omari. 2006. 75p. pap. 12.99 (978-1-929188-13-0(7)) Morton Bks.

Rollins, Jay. My Name Is Shybo. Marotta, Teresa A. 2016. (ENG.). (J). (gr. 3-6). 18.95 (978-0-9980887-1-6(4)) Crary Pubns.

Rollins, Joe. Timmy the Turtle Learns to Swim. Crays, Lettie L. 2011. 44p. (J). pap. 11.95 (978-1-937089-06-1(1)) Truth Bk. Pubs.

Rollins, Joseph. Father & Son, Honey Hunt Has Begun! The Funniest Children Bear Book. Good Night Rhyming Story for Kids Ages 3 to 5 (ABC Books for Kids) Preschool, Kindergarten. Rollins, Shelly. 2019. (Father & Son Ser.: Vol. 1). (ENG.). 36p. (J). pap. 12.43 **(978-1-6746-7773-6(1))** Independently Published.

Rolseth, Ruthie. Tommie Turtle's Secret. Hicks, Robert Z. 2007. (ENG.). 40p. (J). 16.95 (978-0-9792031-0-7(4)) R.Z. Enterprises of Florida.

Rolston, Steve. The Great Motion Mission: A Surprising Story of Physics in Everyday Life. Lee, Cora. 2009. (ENG.). 120p. (J). (gr. 4-6). pap. 14.95 (978-1-55451-184-6(4), 9781554511846) Annick Pr., Ltd. CAN. Dist: Publishers Group West (PGW).

—In My House. Torres, J. 4th ed. 2007. (Degrassi the Next Generation Ser.). (ENG.). 120p. (J). pap. (978-1-55168-303-4(2)) Fenn, H. B. & Co., Ltd.

Romagna, Karen. Voyage. Collins, Billy. 2014. (ENG.). 32p. (J). (gr. 1-7). 16.95 (978-1-59373-154-0(X)) Bunker Hill Publishing, Inc.

Romagnoli, Robert. The Conifer Division. Stefoff, Rebecca. 2009. (Family Trees Ser.). 96p. (gr. 6-6). lib. bdg. 35.21 (978-0-7614-3077-3(6)) Cavendish Square Publishing LLC.

Romain, Trevor. Cliques, Phonies, & Other Baloney. Romain, Trevor. 2012. (Laugh & Learn Ser.). (ENG.). 136p. (J). (gr. 3-6). pap. 24.94 (978-1-57542-045-5(7)) Free Spirit Publishing, Inc.

Romain, Trevor & Mark, Steve. Bullying Is a Pain in the Brain. Romain, Trevor. rev. ed. 2016. (Laugh & Learn® Ser.). (ENG.). 112p. (J). pap. 9.99 (978-1-63198-065-7(3)) Free Spirit Publishing, Inc.

Roman, Dave, et al. Slappy's Tales of Horror. Hernández, Gabriel et al. 2015. 171p. (J). (978-0-545-87203-4(0), Graphix) Scholastic, Inc.

Roman, Dave. Astronaut Academy: Re-Entry. Roman, Dave. 2013. (Astronaut Academy Ser.: 2). (ENG.). 192p. (J). (gr. 5-9). pap. 10.99 (978-1-59643-621-3(2), 900066547, First Second Bks.) Roaring Brook Pr.

—Zero Gravity. Roman, Dave. 2011. (Astronaut Academy Ser.: 1). (ENG.). 192p. (J). (gr. 5-9). pap. 10.99 (978-1-59643-620-6(4), 900066546, First Second Bks.) Roaring Brook Pr.

Roman, Dave & Naifeh, Ted. Slappy's Tales of Horror (Goosebumps Graphix) Stine, R. L. 2015. (Goosebumps Graphix Ser.). (ENG.). 176p. (J). (gr. 3-7). pap. 12.99 (978-0-545-83595-4(X), Graphix) Scholastic, Inc.

Roman, Gabriel. MacKenzie Goes Adventuring. Baumann, J. L. 2017. (ENG.). (J). (gr. k-6). 24.95 (978-1-941880-16-6(9)); pap. 19.95 (978-1-941880-15-9(0)) Post Mortem Publications, Inc.

Roman, Gemma. Jesus Invites Me to Mass. Du Mesnil, Sabine. 2019. (ENG.). 20p. (J). (gr. k-3). 7.99 (978-1-62164-265-7(8)) Ignatius Pr.

Román, Gemma. Watch over Me Little Angel. Du Mesnil, Sabine. 2018. (ENG.). 24p. (J). (gr. -1-1). 7.99 (978-1-62164-247-3(X)) Ignatius Pr.

Roman-Stumpff, Bianca. The Little Witch & Wizard. Kontis, Alethea. 2019. (ENG.). 28p. (J). (gr. k-6). 19.99 (978-1-942541-40-0(6)) Kontis, Alethea.

Romanenko, Anna. The Royal Mail Snail. Bulbeck, Leonora, ed. 2019. (ENG.). 30p. (J). pap. 9.99 (978-1-0904-9685-0(0)) Independently Published.

Romanenko, Vasilisa, jt. illus. see Romanenko, Vitaliy.

Romanenko, Vitaliy & Romanenko, Vasilisa. A Car That Goes Far. Mermelstein, Yael. Rosenfeld, Dina, ed. 2009. 30p. (J). (gr. 1-3). 12.95 (978-1-929628-47-6(1)) Hachai Publishing.

Romanet, Caroline. The Girl & the Waterfall: A Tale from China. Samson, Lucretia. 2016. 24p. (J). pap. 9.95 (978-1-927244-61-6(7)) Flying Start Bks. NZL. Dist: Flying Start Bks.

—The Girl & the Waterfall (Big Book Edition) A Tale from China. Samson, Lucretia. 2016. 24p. (J). pap. (978-1-927244-71-5(4)) Flying Start Bks.

—Rumplestiltskin. Longstaff, Abie. 2015. (Collins Big Cat Ser.). (ENG.). 24p. (J). (gr. 2-2). pap. 8.99 (978-0-00-759117-6(9)) HarperCollins Pubs. Ltd. GBR. Dist: Independent Pubs. Group.

—The Science of Killer Dinosaurs. Parker, Steve. 2017. (ENG.). 32p. (J). (gr. 3). pap. 9.95 (978-0-531-26901-5(9), Watts, Franklin) Scholastic Library Publishing.

—The Science of Killer Dinosaurs: The Bloodcurdling Truth about T. Rex & Other Theropods. Parker, Steve. 2017. (Science of Dinosaurs Ser.). (ENG.). 32p. (J). (gr. 3). lib. bdg. 29.00 (978-0-531-25831-6(9), Watts, Franklin) Scholastic Library Publishing.

—The Science of Weather: The Changing Truth about Earth's Climate. Graham, Ian. 2018. (Science of the Earth Ser.). (ENG.). 32p. (J). (gr. 3-7). lib. bdg. 29.00 (978-0-531-22769-5(3), Watts, Franklin) Scholastic Library Publishing.

Romango, Jim. Rhymes for Teens: Poems Older Students Can Enjoy. Catalano, Tom. 2004. 80p. (YA). per. 9.95 (978-1-882646-48-7(7)) Wordsmith Bks.

Romanini, Davide. Mistero a Dog Town. Fadda, Liana. Hastur, R. D., ed. 2018. (ITA.). 146p. (J). pap. (978-88-6817-049-3(3)) Eclypsed Word.

—Morte Al Circo. Fadda, Liana. Hastur, R. D., ed. 2017. (ITA.). (J). pap. (978-88-6817-047-9(7)) Eclypsed Word.

Romano, Heidi Bosch. The Adventures of Amerina: The Sled. Romano, Heidi Bosch. Romano, Steve R. 2018. (Adventures of Amerina Ser.: Vol. 4). (ENG.). 36p. (J). pap. 10.99 (978-1-7217-5585-1(3)) CreateSpace Independent Publishing Platform.

Romano, Heidi Rosch & Romano, Steve R. The Adventures of Amerina: The Horse. Romano, Heidi Bosch. 2018. (Adventures of Amerina Ser.: Vol. 3). (ENG.). 34p. (J). pap. 10.99 (978-1-7291-4822-8(0)) Independently Published.

Romano, Steve R., jt. illus. see Romano, Heidi Rosch.

Romano, Tony, jt. illus. see Brett, Tyler.

Romberger, James, et al. Something Wicca This Way Comes, 7. Lansdale, John L. et al. 7th ed. 2009. (Tales from the Crypt Ser.: 7). (ENG.). 96p. (J). (gr. 5-12). 22.44 (978-1-59707-151-2(X), 900060948) Papercutz.

Rombough, John. Caribou Song, 1 vol. Highway, Tomson. 2016. (Songs of the North Wind Ser.). (ENG.). 32p. (J). (gr. 1-4). 14.95 (978-1-927083-49-9(4), d7500f3b-c37d-4891-9c55-c8207d82c677) Fifth Hse. Pubs. CAN. Dist: Firefly Bks., Ltd.

Romendik, Irena. The Musical Muffin Man. 2003. (Rub a Dub Books Ser.). 8p. (J). (gr. -1-k). vinyl bd. 7.00 (978-1-883043-45-2(X)) Straight Edge Pr., The.

Romendik, Irene. I've Been Working on the Railroad: Musical Book. 2003. (J). 6.49 (978-1-883043-48-3(4)) Straight Edge Pr., The.

Romens, Dan. Britta & the Boys. McIntyre, Lpc. 2020. (ENG.). 84p. (J). pap. 12.00 **(978-1-64538-146-4(3))** Orange Hat Publishing.

Romeo Pallar & Gim. Juicio de Piratas: Y el Caso Del Ladr. Romeo Pallar. 2018. (Juicio de Piratas Ser.: Vol. 1). (SPA.). 26p. (J). pap. 9.13 (978-1-7199-8596-3(0)) Independently Published.

Romer, Alejandra Barba. Bible Promises for Babies, 1 vol. Pedersen, Karoline Pahus. 2019. 16p. bds. 9.99 (978-0-8254-4611-5(2)) Kregel Pubns.

Romer, Valerie. Les Contes de Lucien le Lutin: Lucien et les Fourmis 1er Partie - Je Sais Lire. Gedall, Gary Edward. Buik, Graham, tr. 2018. (Peter the Pixie Ser.: Vol. 3). (FRE.). 36p. (J). pap. (978-2-940535-50-7(7)) From Words To Worlds, Gary Gedall.

—Peter the Pixie: Link&learn - I Can Count / I Know Colours. Gedall, Gary Edward. 2018. (Peter the Pixie Ser.: Vol. 15). (ENG.). 44p. (J). pap. (978-2-940535-63-7(9)) From Words To Worlds, Gary Gedall.

—Peter the Pixie: Lucien et les Fourmis 1er Partie - Je Lis Seul. Gedall, Gary Edward. 2018. (Peter the Pixie Ser.: Vol. 11). (FRE.). 34p. (J). pap. (978-2-940535-60-6(4)) From Words To Worlds, Gary Gedall.

—Peter the Pixie: Lucien et les Fourmis 1er Partie - Je Sais Lire - Fr - Eng. Gedall, Gary Edward. 2018. (Peter the Pixie Ser.: Vol. 13). (FRE.). 34p. (J). pap. (978-2-940535-56-9(6)) From Words To Worlds, Gary Gedall.

—Peter the Pixie: Peter & the Ants PT 1 - I Can Colour. Gedall, Gary Edward. 2018. (Peter the Pixie Ser.: Vol. 14). (ENG.). 38p. (J). pap. (978-2-940535-62-0(0)) From Words To Worlds, Gary Gedall.

—Peter the Pixie: Peter & the Ants PT 1 - I Can Read. Gedall, Gary Edward. 2018. (Peter the Pixie Ser.: Vol. 1). (ENG.). 36p. (J). pap. (978-2-940535-48-4(5)) From Words To Worlds, Gary Gedall.

—Peter the Pixie: Peter & the Ants PT 1 - I Can Read Eng - Al. Gedall, Gary Edward. 2018. (Peter the Pixie Ser.: Vol. 6). (ENG.). 34p. (J). pap. (978-2-940535-55-2(8)) From Words To Worlds, Gary Gedall.

—Peter the Pixie: Peter & the Ants PT 1 - I Read Alone. Gedall, Gary Edward. 2018. (Peter the Pixie Ser.: Vol. 10). (ENG.). 38p. (J). pap. (978-2-940535-59-0(0)) From Words To Worlds, Gary Gedall.

—Peter the Pixie: Peter & the Ants PT 1 - Je Sais Lire Fr - Al. Gedall, Gary Edward. 2018. (Peter the Pixie Ser.: Vol. 8). (FRE.). 34p. (J). pap. (978-2-940535-54-5(X)) From Words To Worlds, Gary Gedall.

—Peter the Pixie: Peter & the Ants PT 1 - Read to Me. Gedall, Gary Edward. 2018. (ENG.). 40p. (J). pap. (978-2-940535-49-1(3)) From Words To Worlds, Gary Gedall.

Romero, Alejandra. Croacatero. Cardoso, Marta Elena. 2019. (SPA.). 30p. (J). pap. 9.13 (978-1-0729-8736-9(8)) Independently Published.

—Los Amigos de Lucas. Cardoso, Marta Elena. 2019. (SPA.). 30p. (J). pap. 9.13 (978-1-0967-2837-5(0)) Independently Published.

Romero, Alejandra Barba. La Primera Biblia para Bebés: El Mensaje de le Biblia-Corto y Entrañable, 1 vol. Pedersen, Karoline Pahus. 2019. (SPA.). 16p. (J). bds. 7.99 (978-1-4041-0990-2(0)) Grupo Nelson.

Romero, Bernardita. Mummy, What's in Your Tummy? Romero, Bernardita. 2020. (ENG.). (J). bds. **(978-1-78285-976-5(4))** Barefoot Bks., Inc.

Romero, Danitza. The Long Walk. Guay, Tia. 2020. (ENG.). 44p. (J). pap. 29.99 **(978-1-0983-1933-5(8))** BookBaby.

Romero, Enric Badia. The Puppet Master. O'Donnell, Peter. 2006. (Modesty Blaise Ser.). (ENG.). 96p. per. 19.95 (978-1-84023-867-9(4), Titan Bks.) Titan Bks. Ltd. GBR. Dist: Penguin Random Hse. LLC.

Romero, Gina. Claude, the Clumsy Clydesdale. Altieri, Marion. 2011. (Alpha Mare Ser.: Vol. 1). 42p. (J). 16.47 (978-0-9840418-0-0(X)); pap. 14.47 (978-0-9840418-1-7(8)) Caballo Pr. of Ann Arbor. (Caballito Children's Bks.).

Romero, Leonardo. Hawkeye: Kate Bishop Vol. 3: Family Reunion. 2018. (ENG.). 112p. (YA). (gr. 8-17). pap. 15.99 (978-1-302-91097-6(3)) Marvel Worldwide, Inc.

Romero, Leonardo & Walsh, Michael. Hawkeye: Private Eye. 2019. (ENG.). 272p. (J). (gr. 4-7). pap. 12.99 (978-1-302-91795-1(1)) Marvel Worldwide, Inc.

Romero, Naomi. God Made the Animals, Vol. Turner, Marie B. 2017. (ENG.). (J). 6.99 (978-1-5064-2185-8(7), Sparkhouse Family) Augsburg Fortress, Pubs.

Romina Martí. Bears Make Dens. Raum, Elizabeth. 2017. (Animal Builders Ser.). (ENG.). 24p. (J). (gr. 1-4). 20.95 (978-1-68151-171-9(1), Amicus Illustrated) Amicus Publishing.

—Beavers Build Lodges. Raum, Elizabeth. 2017. (Animal Builders Ser.). (ENG.). 24p. (J). (gr. 1-4). 20.95 (978-1-68151-168-9(1), Amicus Illustrated) Amicus Publishing.

—Bees Build Beehives. Raum, Elizabeth. 2017. (Animal Builders Ser.). (ENG.). 24p. (J). (gr. 1-4). 20.95 (978-1-68151-169-6(X), Amicus Illustrated) Amicus Publishing.

—Birds Build Nests. Raum, Elizabeth. 2017. (Animal Builders Ser.). (ENG.). 24p. (J). (gr. 1-4). 20.95 (978-1-68151-170-2(3), Amicus Illustrated) Amicus Publishing.

—Las Abejas y Sus Colmenas (Bees Build Beehives) Raum, Elizabeth. 2017. (Animal Builders Ser.). (ENG & SPA.). 24p. (J). (gr. 1-4). 20.95 (978-1-68151-280-8(7), Amicus Illustrated) Amicus Publishing.

—Los Castores y Sus Madrigueras (Beavers Build Lodges) Raum, Elizabeth. 2017. (Animal Builders Ser.). (ENG & SPA.). 24p. (J). (gr. 1-4). 20.95 (978-1-68151-279-2(3), Amicus Illustrated) Amicus Publishing.

—Los Orangutanes y Sus Nidos (Orangutans Build Tree Nests) Raum, Elizabeth. 2017. (Animal Builders Ser.). (ENG & SPA.). 24p. (J). (gr. 1-4). 20.95 (978-1-68151-283-9(1), Amicus Illustrated) Amicus Publishing.

—Los Osos y Sus Guaridas (Bears Make Dens) Raum, Elizabeth. 2017. (Animal Builders Ser.). (ENG & SPA.). 24p. (J). (gr. 1-4). 20.95 (978-1-68151-282-2(3), Amicus Illustrated) Amicus Publishing.

—Los Pájaros y Sus Nidos (Birds Build Nests) Raum, Elizabeth. 2017. (Animal Builders Ser.). (ENG & SPA.). 24p. (J). (gr. 1-4). 20.95 (978-1-68151-281-5(5), Amicus Illustrated) Amicus Publishing.

—Orangutans Build Tree Nests. Raum, Elizabeth. 2017. (Animal Builders Ser.). (ENG.). 24p. (J). (gr. 1-4). 20.95 (978-1-68151-172-6(X), Amicus Illustrated) Amicus Publishing.

—Rabbits Dig Burrows. Raum, Elizabeth. 2017. (Animal Builders Ser.). (ENG.). 24p. (J). (gr. 1-4). 20.95 (978-1-68151-173-3(8), Amicus Illustrated) Amicus Publishing.

Romita, John, Jr. The Book of Ezekiel, Vol. 7. Straczynski, J. Michael. 2004. (Spider-Man Ser.). 144p. (YA). pap. 12.99 *(978-0-7851-1525-0(0))* Marvel Worldwide, Inc.
Romita, John, et al. Hulk: World War Hulk Omnibus. 2017. (ENG.). 1304p. (YA). (gr. 8-17). 125.00 *(978-1-302-90812-6(X))* Marvel Worldwide, Inc.
Romita, John. Marvel Visionaries: John Romita Sr. 2019. (ENG.). 336p. (YA). (gr. -1-17). pap. 34.99 *(978-1-302-91806-4(0))* Marvel Worldwide, Inc.
Romita, John, et al. Thor: Heroes Return Omnibus. 2017. (ENG.). 1232p. (YA). (gr. 8-17). 125.00 *(978-1-302-90813-3(8))* Marvel Worldwide, Inc.
Romita, John, Jr. Typhoid Mary, 4 vols. Nocenti, Ann. 2003. (Daredevil Legends Ser.: Vol. 4). 224p. (YA). pap. 19.99 *(978-0-7851-1041-5(0))* Marvel Worldwide, Inc.
Romita, John, et al. X-Force Epic Collection: X-Cutioner's Song. 2019. (ENG.). 496p. (YA). (gr. 4-17). pap. 34.99 *(978-1-302-92066-1(9))* Marvel Worldwide, Inc.
—X-Men Milestones: Mutant Massacre. 2019. (ENG.). 320p. (YA). (gr. 4-17). pap. 34.99 *(978-1-302-91853-8(2))* Marvel Worldwide, Inc.
Romita, John & Lieber, Larry. Spectacular Spider-Man: lo, This Monster. 2019. (ENG.). 128p. (YA). (gr. -1-17). pap. 19.99 *(978-1-302-92064-7(2))* Marvel Worldwide, Inc.
Romita, John & Romita, John, Jr. Daredevil: The Man Without Fear. 2010. 224p. (YA). (gr. 8-17). pap. 19.99 *(978-0-7851-3479-4(4))* Marvel Worldwide, Inc.
—Hulk: World War Hulk. Pak, Greg. 2019. 224p. (YA). (gr. 8-17). pap. 24.99 *(978-1-302-92077-7(4))* Marvel Worldwide, Inc.
—Marvel Visionaries: John Romita Jr. 2019. (ENG.). 360p. (YA). (gr. 8-17). pap. 34.99 *(978-1-302-91975-7(X))* Marvel Worldwide, Inc.
Romita, John, jt. illus. see Colan, Gene.
Romita, John, jt. illus. see Kremer, Warren.
Romita, John, Jr., jt. illus. see Romita, John.
Romo, Adriana. Felicia's Favorite Story. Newman, Lesléa. 2003. 24p. (J). pap. 9.95 *(978-0-9674468-5-1(6))* Two Lives Publishing.
Romo, Lennon. A Flower's Word: A Poetry Collection. Danielle, Amanda. 2019. (ENG.). 82p. (J). pap. 10.00 ***(978-1-0711-0661-7(9))*** Independently Published.
Romot, Rachel. A Million Amelias. McCalister, Joy. 2019. (ENG.). 34p. (J). pap. 12.75 *(978-1-0959-1928-6(8))* Independently Published.
Ron Frazier, photos by. Colleen Goes to the Farmer's Market. Janice Turner & Colleen Connelly. 2009. 20p. pap. 12.49 *(978-1-4389-6085-2(9))* AuthorHouse.
Ronald, Robrahn. Steven the Vegan. Bodenstein, Dan. 2012. 38p. (J). pap. 12.99 *(978-0-9843228-9-3(2))* Totem Tales Publishing.
Ronchi, Susanna. One Snowy Night. Harwood, Beth. 2005. 12p. (J). *(978-1-84011-627-4(7))* Templar Publishing.
Ronda Eden. The Brothers Foot: A Hair Raising Story. Steve Cormey. 2009. 56p. pap. 21.99 *(978-1-4389-4269-8(9))* AuthorHouse.
Ronda, Gilger. Lyssa Lamb. Bell, Debora. 2005. 32p. (J). 4.95 *(978-0-9768465-0-5(0))* Frontier Pr.
Rondo, Glenn. A Smile Made for Christmas. Perdue II, D. 2017. (ENG.). 30p. (J). pap. 12.99 *(978-0-9995675-0-0(0))* Here with an ear publishing.
Rong, Yap Kun. Dragon Theft Auto. Dahl, Michael. 2010. (Dragonblood Ser.). (ENG.). 40p. (J). (gr. 4-8). pap. 6.25 *(978-1-4342-2310-4(8))*, Stone Arch Bks.) Capstone.
Rong, Yap Kun & Kun Rong, Yap. It Screams at Night. Dahl, Michael. 2010. (Dragonblood Ser.). (ENG.). 40p. (J). (gr. 4-8). pap. 6.25 *(978-1-4342-2311-1(6))*, Stone Arch Bks.) Capstone.
Rong, Yu. Snowflake in My Pocket. Bright, Rachel. 2017. 32p. (J). 12.99 *(978-1-61067-551-2(7))* Kane Miller.
—Summer: Animals Share in a Poetic Tale of Kindness. Wenxuan, Cao. 2019. (ENG.). 48p. (J). 18.99 *(978-1-250-31006-4(7))*, 900198620) Imprint IND. Dist: Macmillan.
—Tracks of a Panda. Dowson, Nick. 2007. (ENG.). 32p. (J). (gr. k-3). 16.99 *(978-0-7636-3146-8(9))* Candlewick Pr.
—Tracks of a Panda: Read & Wonder. Dowson, Nick. 2010. (Read & Wonder Ser.). (ENG.). 32p. (J). (gr. -1-3). pap. 6.99 *(978-0-7636-4737-7(3))* Candlewick Pr.
Ronney, David. Tommy the Theatre Cat. Potter, Maureen. 3rd rev. ed. 2005. (ENG.). 80p. (J). pap. 10.95 *(978-0-86278-919-0(2))* O'Brien Pr., Ltd., The. IRL. Dist: Dufour Editions, Inc.
Ronney, Ronnie. Apes Find Shapes: A Book about Recognizing Shapes. Moncure, Jane Belk. 2013. (Magic Castle Readers Ser.). (ENG.). 32p. (J). (gr. -1-2). 14.21 *(978-1-62323-577-2(4))*, 206312) Child's World, Inc., The.
—The Smart Kid's Guide to Manners. Petersen, Christine. 2014. (Smart Kid's Guide to Everyday Life Ser.). (ENG.). 32p. (J). (gr. 2-5). 28.50 *(978-1-62687-344-5(5))*, 207184) Child's World, Inc., The.
Ronnquist, Debby. Child Out of Place: A Story for New England. Wall, Patricia Q. 2003. 116p. (J). (gr. 6-9). pap. 15.00 *(978-0-9742185-0-2(2))* Fall Rose Bks.
ronnybas. Secrets in Translation. Sorenson, Margo. 2018. (ENG.). 244p. (YA). (gr. 7). pap. 14.95 *(978-1-947548-20-6(4))*, Fitzroy Bks.) Regal Hse. Publishing, LLC.
Ronquillo, Nadia. Leap. Manning, Campbell. 2017. (ENG.). 32p. (J). (gr. k-2). *(978-1-4867-1267-0(3))* Flowerpot Children's Pr. Inc.
Ronstant, Paul. Adrift. Griffin, Paul. 2015. (ENG.). 240p. (YA). (gr. 7). 17.99 *(978-0-545-70939-2(3))*, Scholastic Pr.) Scholastic, Inc.
Rood, Brian. The Art of Brian Rood. 2003. 48p. (YA). (gr. 11-18). pap. *(978-0-86562-066-7(0))* Anabas Marketing, Ltd.
—Journey to Star Wars: the Last Jedi the Power of the Force. Siglain, Michael. 2017. (ENG.). 24p. (J). (gr. 1-3). pap. 5.99 *(978-1-4847-8075-6(2))*, Disney Lucasfilm Press) Disney Publishing Worldwide.
Rood, Brian. Star Wars. Hilton, Dave et al. 2015. 8p. (J). ***(978-1-5037-0033-8(X))*** Phoenix International Publications, Inc.
Rood, Brian. Star Wars: the Last Jedi Movie Storybook. Schaefer, Elizabeth. 2018. (ENG.). 128p. (J). (gr. 1-3). 16.99 *(978-1-4847-0556-8(4))*, Disney Lucasfilm Press) Disney Publishing Worldwide.
—Star Wars: the Last Jedi Rose & Finn's Secret Mission. Patrick, Ella. 2017. (ENG.). 24p. (J). (gr. 1-3). pap. 5.99 *(978-1-4847-0554-4(8))*, Disney Lucasfilm Press) Disney Publishing Worldwide.
—Star Wars the Original Trilogy Read-Along Storybook & CD Collection: Read-Along Storybook & CD. Thornton, Randy. 2018. (Read-Along Storybook & CD Ser.). (ENG.). 96p. (J). (gr. 1-3). pap. 9.99 *(978-1-368-00272-1(2))*, Disney Lucasfilm Press) Disney Publishing Worldwide.
—Star Wars the Skywalker Saga. Dawson, Delilah. 2019. (ENG.). 400p. (J). (gr. 5-9). 29.99 *(978-1-368-04153-9(1))*, Disney Lucasfilm Press) Disney Publishing Worldwide.
—World of Reading Journey to Star Wars: the Last Jedi: a Leader Named Leia (Level 2 Reader) (Level 2) Heddle, Jennifer. 2017. (World of Reading Ser.). (ENG.). 32p. (J). (gr. 1-3). pap. 4.99 *(978-1-368-00976-8(X))*, Disney Lucasfilm Press) Disney Publishing Worldwide.
—World of Reading Star Wars the Force Awakens: Finn & the First Order. Disney Book Group. 2015. (World of Reading Ser.). (ENG.). 32p. (J). (gr. 1-3). pap. 3.99 *(978-1-4847-0481-3(9))* Disney Pr.
—World of Reading Star Wars the Force Awakens: Rey Meets BB-8: Level 1. Schaefer, Elizabeth. 2015. (World of Reading Ser.). (ENG.). 32p. (J). (gr. -1-k). pap. 3.99 *(978-1-4847-0480-6(0))* Disney Pr.
Roode, Daniel. Dini Dinosaur. Beaumont, Karen. 2012. (ENG.). 32p. (J). (gr. -1-k). 14.99 *(978-0-06-207299-3(4))*, Greenwillow Bks.) HarperCollins Pubs.
—The Forever Tree. Surratt, Tereasa & Charlton-Perrin, Donna. 2018. (J). pap. *(978-0-553-52395-9(3))* Bantam Doubleday Dell Large Print Group, Inc.
—Moustache Up! A Playful Game of Opposites. Ainsworth, Kimberly. 2013. (ENG.). 18p. (J). (gr. -1-k). bds. 7.99 *(978-1-4424-7526-7(9))*, Little Simon) Little Simon.
—Peek-A-Boo Baby: Keepsake Greeting Card Board Book. Birdsong, Minnie. ed. 2017. (Little Bird Greetings Ser.). (ENG.). 8p. (J). (gr. -1-k). bds. 6.99 *(978-1-68052-207-5(8))*, 1000751) Cottage Door Pr.
—This Little Artist: An Art History Primer. Holub, Joan. 2019. (This Little Ser.). (ENG.). 26p. (J). (gr. -1-k). bds. 7.99 *(978-1-5344-4293-1(6))*, Little Simon) Little Simon.
—This Little Collection: This Little President, This Little Explorer, This Little Trailblazer, This Little Scientist. Holub, Joan. ed. 2018. (This Little Ser.). (ENG.). 104p. (J). (gr. -1-k). bds. 31.99 *(978-1-5344-2889-8(5))*, Little Simon) Little Simon.
—This Little Dreamer: An Inspirational Primer. Holub, Joan. 2020. (This Little Ser.). (ENG.). 26p. (J). (gr. -1-k). bds. 7.99 *(978-1-5344-4291-7(X))*, Little Simon) Little Simon.
—This Little Explorer: A Pioneer Primer. Holub, Joan. 2016. (This Little Ser.). (ENG.). 26p. (J). (gr. -1-k). bds. 7.99 *(978-1-4814-7175-6(9))*, Little Simon) Little Simon.
—This Little President: A Presidential Primer. Holub, Joan. 2016. (This Little Ser.). (ENG.). 26p. (J). (gr. -1-k). bds. 7.99 *(978-1-4814-5850-4(7))*, Little Simon) Little Simon.
—This Little Scientist: A Discovery Primer. Holub, Joan. 2018. (This Little Ser.). (ENG.). 26p. (J). (gr. -1-k). bds. 7.99 *(978-1-5344-0108-2(3))*, Little Simon) Little Simon.
—This Little Trailblazer: A Girl Power Primer. Holub, Joan. 2017. (This Little Ser.). (ENG.). 26p. (J). (gr. -1-k). bds. 7.99 *(978-1-5344-0106-8(7))*, Little Simon) Little Simon.
Roode, Daniel. Little Bea. Roode, Daniel. 2011. (ENG.). 32p. (J). (gr. -1-3). 12.99 *(978-0-06-199392-3(1))*, Greenwillow Bks.) HarperCollins Pubs.
—Little Bea & the Snowy Day. Roode, Daniel. 2011. (ENG.). 32p. (J). (gr. -1-k). 12.99 *(978-0-06-199395-4(6))*, Greenwillow Bks.) HarperCollins Pubs.
Roode, Laura. My Sweet Little Megabyte. Burton, Jeffrey. 2016. (ENG.). 16p. (J). (gr. -1 — 1). bds. 5.99 *(978-1-4814-6809-1(X))*, Little Simon) Little Simon.
Rooke, Veronica. My Silly Mum. Mulligan, Monique. 2016. (ENG.). 30p. *(978-0-9945265-5-7(5))* Serenity Press.
—Who Dresses God? ... for God's house Is this world we share & God Is in it Everywhere. Raffa-Mulligan, Teena. 2012. 32p. (J). pap. *(978-1-921883-28-6(6))* Pick-a-Woo Woo Pubs.
Rooks, Jo. Doug's Dung. 2020. (J). *(978-1-4338-3237-6(2))*, Magination Pr.) American Psychological Assn.
Rooks, Jo. Layla's Luck. 2020. (J). ***(978-1-4338-3238-3(0))***, Magination Pr.) American Psychological Assn.
Rooks, Jo. Lucy's Light. 2019. (J). *(978-1-4338-3088-4(4))*, Magination Pr.) American Psychological Assn.
—Sophie's Shell. 2019. 32p. (J). *(978-1-4338-3089-1(2))*, Magination Pr.) American Psychological Assn.
Rooney, C. J. Dream Come True. Pahls, Stevie Kay. Aerilyn Books, ed. 2018. 20p. (J). bds. 9.99 *(978-0-9997830-1-6(7))* Aerilyn Bks.
Rooney, David. Saint Patrick: Ireland's Patron Saint. Simms, George Otto. 3rd rev. ed. 2004. (Exploring Ser.). (ENG.). 104p. pap. 8.95 *(978-0-86278-749-3(1))* O'Brien Pr., Ltd., The. IRL. Dist: Dufour Editions, Inc.
Rooney, Ellen. Grandmother School. Singh, Rina. 2020. (ENG.). 32p. (J). (gr. 1-3). 19.95 ***(978-1-4598-1905-4(5))*** Orca Bk. Pubs. USA.
Rooney, Ellen. Her Fearless Run: Kathrine Switzer's Historic Boston Marathon. Chaffee, Kim. 2019. (ENG.). 40p. (J). 17.99 *(978-1-62414-654-1(6))*, 900196525) Page Street Publishing Co.
Rooney, Ronnie. Alimenta Tu Cuerpo. Tourville, Amanda Doering. 2011. (Cómo Mantenernos Saludables/How to Be Healthy Ser.).Tr. of Fuel the Body. (ENG.). 24p. (J). (gr. k-2). 27.32 *(978-1-4048-6890-8(9))*, Picture Window Bks.) Capstone.
—Batter Up! You Can Play Softball, 1 vol. Fauchald, Nick. 2005. (Game Day Ser.). (ENG.). 24p. (J). (gr. k-3). lib. bdg. 27.32 *(978-1-4048-1152-2(4))*, Picture Window Bks.) Capstone.
—Being a Good Guest. Ingalls, Ann. 2012. (Good Manners Ser.). (ENG.). 24p. (J). (gr. -1-2). 27.07 *(978-1-61473-224-2(8))*, 204919) Child's World, Inc., The.
—The Best Mud Pie. Quinn, Lin. 2011. (Rookie Ready to Learn Ser.). 40p. (J). (gr. -1-k). pap. 5.95 *(978-0-531-26650-2(8))*; lib. bdg. 23.00 *(978-0-531-26425-6(4))* Scholastic Library Publishing. (Children's Pr.).
—The Biggest Snowball of All: A Book about Sizes. Moncure, Jane Belk. 2013. (Magic Castle Readers Ser.). (ENG.). 32p. (J). (gr. -1-2). 14.21 *(978-1-62323-578-9(2))*, 206315) Child's World, Inc., The.
—Camiones Amigos/Truck Buddies, 1 vol. Crow, Melinda Melton. Heck, Claudia M., tr. 2012. (Camiones Amigos/Truck Buddies Ser.). (ENG.). 32p. (J). (gr. -1-1). pap. 5.05 *(978-1-4342-3913-6(6))*; lib. bdg. 22.65 *(978-1-4342-3774-3(5))* Capstone. (Stone Arch Bks.).
—Carrera en la Carretera. Crow, Melinda Melton. Heck, Claudia M., tr. 2012. (Camiones Amigos/Truck Buddies Ser.).Tr. of Road Race. (ENG.). 32p. (J). (gr. -1-1). pap. 5.05 *(978-1-4342-3915-0(2))*, Stone Arch Bks.) Capstone.
—The Christmas Baby. Kramer, Janice. 2008. (Arch Bks.). 16p. (J). (gr. k-4). pap. 1.99 *(978-0-7586-1454-4(3))* Concordia Publishing Hse.
—Evan & Erin Build an Essay. St. John, Amanda. 2012. (Writing Builders Ser.). 32p. (J). (gr. 2-4). lib. bdg. 25.27 *(978-1-59953-508-1(4))* Norwood Hse. Pr.
—Evan & Erin Build an Essay. StJohn, Amanda. 2012. (Writing Builders Ser.). 32p. (J). (gr. 2-4). pap. 11.94 *(978-1-60357-388-7(7))* Norwood Hse. Pr.
—Funky Chicken Enchiladas: And Other Mexican Dishes, 1 vol. Fauchald, Nick. 2009. (Kids Dish Ser.). (ENG.). 32p. (J). (gr. 1-3). lib. bdg. 27.99 *(978-1-4048-5189-4(5))*, Picture Window Bks.) Capstone.
—Get up & Go: Being Active, 1 vol. Tourville, Amanda Doering. 2008. (How to Be Healthy! Ser.). (ENG.). 24p. (J). (gr. k-2). 27.32 *(978-1-4048-4811-5(8))*, Picture Window Bks.) Capstone.
—Good Manners During Special Occasions. Ingalls, Ann. 2012. (Good Manners Ser.). (ENG.). 24p. (J). (gr. -1-2). 27.07 *(978-1-61473-229-7(9))*, 204921) Child's World, Inc., The.
—Good Manners on the Phone. Ingalls, Ann. 2012. (Good Manners Ser.). (ENG.). 24p. (J). (gr. -1-2). 27.07 *(978-1-61473-228-0(0))*, 204923) Child's World, Inc., The.
—Good Manners with Family. Ingalls, Ann. 2012. (Good Manners Ser.). (ENG.). 24p. (J). (gr. -1-2). 27.07 *(978-1-61473-227-3(2))*, 204924) Child's World, Inc., The.
—Good Table Manners. Ingalls, Ann. 2012. (Good Manners Ser.). (ENG.). 24p. (J). (gr. -1-2). 27.07 *(978-1-61473-230-3(2))*, 204925) Child's World, Inc., The.
—How Many Ways Can You Cut a Pie? A Book about Math. Moncure, Jane Belk. 2013. (Magic Castle Readers Ser.). (ENG.). 32p. (J). (gr. -1-2). 14.21 *(978-1-62323-579-6(0))*, 206313) Child's World, Inc., The.
—How the Camel Got Its Hump, 1 vol. Jones, Christianne C. 2011. (My First Classic Story Ser.). (ENG.). 32p. (J). (gr. k-3). pap. 7.10 *(978-1-4048-7358-2(9))*, Picture Window Bks.) Capstone.
—How the Camel Got Its Hump, 1 vol. Jones, Christianne C. & Kipling, Rudyard. 2010. (My First Classic Story Ser.). (ENG.). 32p. (J). (gr. k-3). lib. bdg. 22.65 *(978-1-4048-6075-9(4))*, Picture Window Bks.) Capstone.
—If I Were a Movie Star, 1 vol. Lyons, Shelly. 2010. (Dream Big! Ser.). (ENG.). 24p. (J). (gr. k-3). lib. bdg. 27.32 *(978-1-4048-6162-6(9))*, Picture Window Bks.) Capstone.
—Lávate. Tourville, Amanda Doering. 2011. (Cómo Mantenernos Saludables/How to Be Healthy Ser.).Tr. of Go Wash Up. (ENG.). 24p. (J). (gr. k-2). 27.32 *(978-1-4048-6892-2(5))*, Picture Window Bks.) Capstone.
—Líos en el Lodo. Crow, Melinda Melton. Heck, Claudia M., tr. 2012. (Camiones Amigos/Truck Buddies Ser.).Tr. of Mud Mess. (ENG.). 32p. (J). (gr. -1-1). pap. 5.05 *(978-1-4342-3916-7(0))*; lib. bdg. 22.65 *(978-1-4342-3777-4(X))* Capstone. (Stone Arch Bks.).
—Líos en la Nieve. Crow, Melinda Melton. Heck, Claudia M., tr. 2012. (Camiones Amigos/Truck Buddies Ser.).Tr. of Snow Trouble. (ENG.). 32p. (J). (gr. -1-1). pap. 5.05 *(978-1-4342-3914-3(4))*, Stone Arch Bks.) Capstone.
—The Magic Moon Machine: A Counting Adventure. Moncure, Jane Belk. 2013. (Magic Castle Readers Ser.). (ENG.). 32p. (J). (gr. -1-2). 14.21 *(978-1-62323-580-2(4))*, 206316) Child's World, Inc., The.
—Mud Mess, 1 vol. Crow, Melinda Melton. 2009. (Truck Buddies Ser.). (ENG.). 32p. (J). (gr. -1-1). pap. 6.25 *(978-1-4342-1753-0(1))*, Stone Arch Bks.) Capstone.
—November, 1 vol. Kesselring, Mari. 2009. (Months of the Year Ser.). (ENG.). 24p. (J). (gr. k-2). 27.07 *(978-1-60270-638-5(7))*, 11583, Looking Glass Library) Magic Wagon.
—October, 1 vol. Kesselring, Mari. 2009. (Months of the Year Ser.). (ENG.). 24p. (J). (gr. k-2). 27.07 *(978-1-60270-637-8(9))*, 11581, Looking Glass Library) Magic Wagon.
—On-the-Go Schwarmas: And Other Middle-Eastern Dishes. Fauchald, Nick. 2009. (Kids Dish Ser.). (ENG.). 32p. (J). (gr. 1-3). lib. bdg. 27.99 *(978-1-4048-5192-4(5))*, Picture Window Bks.) Capstone.
—One Tricky Monkey up on Top: A Counting Adventure. Moncure, Jane Belk. 2013. (Magic Castle Readers Ser.). (ENG.). 32p. (J). (gr. -1-2). 14.21 *(978-1-62323-581-9(2))*, 206314) Child's World, Inc., The.
—Road Race, 1 vol. Crow, Melinda Melton. 2009. (Truck Buddies Ser.). (ENG.). 32p. (J). (gr. -1-1). 22.65 *(978-1-4342-1623-6(3))*; pap. 6.25 *(978-1-4342-1754-7(X))* Capstone. (Stone Arch Bks.).
—Roly-Poly Ravioli: And Other Italian Dishes, 1 vol. Fauchald, Nick. 2009. (Kids Dish Ser.). (ENG.). 32p. (J). (gr. 1-3). lib. bdg. 27.99 *(978-1-4048-5186-3(0))*, Picture Window Bks.) Capstone.
—Ruth & Naomi. Sanders, Karen Nordberg. 2007. 16p. (J). (gr. k-4). 1.99 *(978-0-7586-1283-0(4))* Concordia Publishing Hse.
—September, 1 vol. Kesselring, Mari. 2009. (Months of the Year Ser.). (ENG.). 24p. (J). (gr. k-2). 27.07 *(978-1-60270-636-1(0))*, 11579, Looking Glass Library) Magic Wagon.
—The Smart Kid's Guide to Feeling Sad or Angry. Cosson, M. J. 2014. (Smart Kid's Guide to Everyday Life Ser.). (ENG.). 32p. (J). (gr. 2-5). 28.50 *(978-1-62687-341-4(0))*, 207181) Child's World, Inc., The.
—The Smart Kid's Guide to Knowing What to Say. Cosson, M. J. 2014. (Smart Kid's Guide to Everyday Life Ser.). (ENG.). 32p. (J). (gr. 2-5). 28.50 *(978-1-62687-343-8(7))*, 207183) Child's World, Inc., The.
—The Smart Kid's Guide to Losing a Pet. Petersen, Christine. 2014. (Smart Kid's Guide to Everyday Life Ser.). (ENG.). 32p. (J). (gr. 2-5). 28.50 *(978-1-62687-346-9(1))*, 207186) Child's World, Inc., The.
—The Smart Kid's Guide to Moving. Petersen, Christine. 2014. (Smart Kid's Guide to Everyday Life Ser.). (ENG.). 32p. (J). (gr. 2-5). 28.50 *(978-1-62687-345-2(3))*, 207185) Child's World, Inc., The.
—Snow Trouble, 1 vol. Crow, Melinda Melton. 2009. (Truck Buddies Ser.). (ENG.). 32p. (J). (gr. -1-1). pap. 6.25 *(978-1-4342-1755-4(8))*, Stone Arch Bks.) Capstone.
—Truck Buddies, 1 vol. Crow, Melinda Melton. 2009. (Truck Buddies Ser.). (ENG.). 32p. (J). (gr. -1-1). 22.65 *(978-1-4342-1625-0(X))*; pap. 6.25 *(978-1-4342-1756-1(6))* Capstone. (Stone Arch Bks.).
—Wrap-N-Bake Egg Rolls: And Other Chinese Dishes. Fauchald, Nick. 2009. (Kids Dish Ser.). (ENG.). 32p. (J). (gr. 1-3). lib. bdg. 27.99 *(978-1-4048-5183-2(6))*, Picture Window Bks.) Capstone.
Rooney, Ronnie. Thanksgiving Recipes, 1 vol. Rooney, Ronnie. 2010. (Thanksgiving Ser.). (ENG.). 24p. (J). (gr. k-3). lib. bdg. 27.99 *(978-1-4048-6283-8(8))*, Picture Window Bks.) Capstone.
—There Was a Crooked Man. Rooney, Ronnie. 2011. (Favorite Mother Goose Rhymes Ser.). (ENG.). 16p. (J). (gr. -1-2). lib. bdg. 14.21 *(978-1-60954-283-2(5))*, 200235) Child's World, Inc., The.
Rooney, Sandra. Ally M. & Ally G. Young, Lauren. 2006. 20p. (J). 9.95 *(978-1-4120-8518-2(7))* Trafford Publishing.
Roos, Maryn. Alphabetical Sleepy Sheep. Zuckerman, Rory. 2004. (J). bds. 12.95 *(978-0-9749305-3-4(9))* Castle Pacific Publishing.
—Alphabetical Sleepy Sheep. Zuckerman, Rory. 2007. (Sleepy Sheep Ser.). (J). (gr. -1-k). bds. 7.95 incl. audio compact disk *(978-0-9796393-1-9(X))* Little Lion Pr.
—Colorful Sleepy Sheep. Zuckerman, Rory. 2004. (J). bds. 12.95 *(978-0-9749305-1-0(2))* Castle Pacific Publishing.
—Colorful Sleepy Sheep. Zuckerman, Rory. 2007. (Sleepy Sheep Ser.). (J). (gr. -1). bds. 7.95 incl. audio compact disk *(978-0-9796393-2-6(8))* Little Lion Pr.
—Counting Sleepy Sheep. Zuckerman, Rory. 2004. (J). bds. 12.95 *(978-0-9749305-0-3(4))* Castle Pacific Publishing.
—Counting Sleepy Sheep. Zuckerman, Rory. 2007. (Sleepy Sheep Ser.). 16p. (J). (gr. -1). bds. 7.95 incl. audio compact disk *(978-0-9796393-3-3(6))* Little Lion Pr.
—Dancing Diva. Goldberg, Whoopi. 2012. (Sugar Plum Ballerinas Ser.: 6). 160p. (J). (gr. 1-5). pap. 4.99 *(978-0-7868-5265-9(8))*, Jump at the Sun) Hyperion Bks. for Children.
—How to Fish for Trouble. Wesley, Valerie Wilson. 2004. 89p. (J). lib. bdg. 15.00 *(978-1-4242-0643-8(X))* Fitzgerald Bks.
—Jump at the Sun Bible Classics David & Goliath. Schall, Jane. 2007. (ENG.). (J). (gr. -1-2). pap. 3.50 *(978-0-7868-5517-9(7))*, Jump at the Sun) Hyperion Bks. for Children.
—Jump at the Sun Bible Classics Jonah & the Whale. Schall, Jane. 2007. (ENG.). (J). (gr. -1-2). pap. 3.50 *(978-0-7868-5518-6(5))*, Jump at the Sun) Hyperion Bks. for Children.
—Perfectly Prima, No. 3. Goldberg, Whoopi & Underwood, Deborah. 2010. (Sugar Plum Ballerinas Ser.: 3). 160p. (J). (gr. 1-17). pap. 4.99 *(978-0-7868-5262-8(3))*, Jump at the Sun) Hyperion Bks. for Children.
—Plum Fantastic Bk. 1. Goldberg, Whoopi & Underwood, Deborah. 2008. (Sugar Plum Ballerinas Ser.: 1). 160p. (J). (gr. 1-5). pap. 4.99 *(978-0-7868-5260-4(7))*, Jump at the Sun) Hyperion Bks. for Children.
—Shapely Sleepy Sheep. Zuckerman, Rory. 2004. (J). bds. 12.95 *(978-0-9749305-2-7(0))* Castle Pacific Publishing.
—Shapely Sleepy Sheep. Zuckerman, Rory. 2007. (Sleepy Sheep Ser.). (J). (gr. -1). bds. 7.95 incl. audio compact disk *(978-0-9796393-4-0(4))* Little Lion Pr.
—Sugar Plum Ballerinas in Two Acts: Plum Fantastic & Toeshoe Trouble. Underwood, Deborah & Whoopi, Goldberg. 2020. (Sugar Plum Ballerinas Ser.). 304p. (J). (gr. 3-7). pap. 7.99 *(978-1-368-05459-1(5))* Hyperion Bks. for Children.
—Sugar Plums to the Rescue! Goldberg, Whoopi & Underwood, Deborah. 2011. (Sugar Plum Ballerinas Ser.: 5). 160p. (J). (gr. 1-5). pap. 4.99 *(978-0-7868-5264-2(X))*, Jump at the Sun) Hyperion Bks. for Children.
—Terrible Terrel. Goldberg, Whoopi & Underwood, Deborah. 2010. (Sugar Plum Ballerinas Ser.: 4). 160p. (J). (gr. 1-17). pap. 4.99 *(978-0-7868-5263-5(1))*, Jump at the Sun) Hyperion Bks. for Children.
—Toeshoe Trouble. Goldberg, Whoopi & Underwood, Deborah. 2009. (Sugar Plum Ballerinas Ser.: 2). 144p. (J). (gr. 1-5). pap. 4.99 *(978-0-7868-5261-1(5))*, Jump at the Sun) Hyperion Bks. for Children.
—Who Do I Look Like? Schulte, Mary. 2006. (Rookie Reader Skill Set Ser.). (ENG.). 32p. (J). (gr. k-2). pap. 4.95 *(978-0-516-24758-8(1))*, Children's Pr.) Scholastic Library Publishing.
Roosevelt, Michele Chopin. Gray Squirrel at Pacific Avenue. Harrington, Geri. 2011. (Smithsonian's Backyard Ser.). (ENG.). 32p. (J). (gr. -1-3). 19.95 *(978-1-60727-638-8(0))* Soundprints.
Roosevelt, Theodore. Simply Father: Life with Theodore Roosevelt As Seen through the Eyes of His Children. Selda, Toby. 2007. 28p. (J). 7.95 *(978-1-59091-030-6(3))* Eastern National.
Root, Barry. The Bell in the Bridge. Kooser, Ted. 2016. 32p. (J). (gr. 1-4). 16.99 *(978-0-7636-6481-7(2))* Candlewick Pr.
—The Birthday Tree. Fleischman, Paul. 2008. 40p. (J). (gr. -1-3). 16.99 *(978-0-7636-2604-4(X))* Candlewick Pr.

—By My Brother's Side. Barber, Tiki & Barber, Ronde. 2004. (ENG.). 32p. (J). (gr. 1-5). 18.99 *(978-0-689-86559-6(7)*, Simon & Schuster/Paula Wiseman Bks.) Simon & Schuster/Paula Wiseman Bks.
—Christmas Farm. Ray, Mary Lyn. (ENG.). 40p. (J). (gr. -1-3). 2008. 17.99 *(978-0-15-216290-0(9)*, 1200565); 2013. 7.99 *(978-0-544-10509-6(5)*, 1540809) Houghton Mifflin Harcourt Publishing Co.
—Dream Big: Michael Jordan & the Pursuit of Excellence. Jordan, Deloris. 2014. (ENG.). 32p. (J). (gr. -1-3). 8.99 *(978-1-4424-1270-5(4)*, Simon & Schuster/Paula Wiseman Bks.) Simon & Schuster/Paula Wiseman Bks.
—Dream Big: Michael Jordan & the Pursuit of Olympic Gold. Jordan, Deloris. 2012. (ENG.). 32p. (J). (gr. -1-3). 18.99 *(978-1-4424-1269-9(0)*, Simon & Schuster/Paula Wiseman Bks.) Simon & Schuster/Paula Wiseman Bks.
—Game Day. Barber, Tiki & Barber, Ronde. 2005. (ENG.). 32p. (J). (gr. k-5). 18.99 *(978-1-4169-0093-1(4)*, Simon & Schuster/Paula Wiseman Bks.) Simon & Schuster/Paula Wiseman Bks.
—Giant Peach Yodel, 1 vol. Peck, Jan. 2012. (ENG.). 32p. (J). (gr. k-3). 16.99 *(978-1-58980-980-2(7)*, Pelican Publishing) Arcadia Publishing.
—An Invisible Thread Christmas Story: A True Story Based on the #1 New York Times Bestseller. Schroff, Laura & Tresniowski, Alex. 2015. (ENG.). 32p. (J). (gr. -1-3). 17.99 *(978-1-4814-1930-7(7)*, Little Simon) Little Simon.
—Messenger, Messenger. Burleigh, Robert. 2011. (ENG.). 32p. (J). (gr. -1-3). pap. 16.99 *(978-1-4424-5335-7(4)*, Atheneum Bks. for Young Readers) Simon & Schuster Children's Publishing.
—Passing the Music Down. Sullivan, Sarah. 2011. 32p. (J). (gr. k-3). 17.99 *(978-0-7636-3753-8(X))* Candlewick Pr.
—Teammates. Barber, Tiki & Barber, Ronde. (ENG.). 32p. (J). (gr. 1-5). 2011. 8.99 *(978-1-4424-1262-0(3))*; 2006. 16.95 *(978-1-4169-2489-0(2))* Simon & Schuster/Paula Wiseman Bks. (Simon & Schuster/Paula Wiseman Bks.).
Root, Jeff. The Woollyhoodwinks: Vs. the Dark Patch. Dumesnil, Phil & Sanchez, Asa. 2008. (ENG.). 36p. (J). (gr. -1-3). 15.95 *(978-1-59702-012-1(5))* Immedium.
Root, Kimberly Bulcken. Born & Bred in the Great Depression. Winter, Jonah. 2011. 40p. (J). (gr. k-4). 17.99 *(978-0-375-86197-0(1)*, Schwartz & Wade Bks.) Random Hse. Children's Bks.
—Dadblamed Union Army Cow. Fletcher, Susan. 32p. (J). (gr. k-3). 2016. 7.99 *(978-0-7636-8770-0(7))*; 2007. (ENG.). 16.99 *(978-0-7636-2263-3(X))* Candlewick Pr.
—Don't Forget Winona. Peterson, Jeanne Whitehouse. 2004. 32p. (J). (gr. -1-3). lib. bdg. 15.89 *(978-0-06-027198-5(1))* HarperCollins Pubs.
Rooth, Mike. Beware the Vikings. Boyd, David. 2007. 48p. (J). lib. bdg. 23.08 *(978-1-4242-1624-6(9))* Fitzgerald Bks.
—Cave of Secrets. Low, Vicki. 2007. (Timeline Ser.). 48p. pap. 8.99 *(978-1-4190-4391-8(9))* Steck-Vaughn.
—A Time for Evron. Smillie, Bryan. 2004. 190p. 11.95 *(978-0-9689516-0-6(0))* Shabrya Publishing CAN. Dist: Hushion Hse. Publishing, Ltd.
—United Force. O'Donnell, Liam. 2007. 44p. (J). lib. bdg. 23.08 *(978-1-4242-1633-8(8))* Fitzgerald Bks.
Roots, Adrian, jt. illus. see Johnson, Staz.
Roper, Bob. Egg Surprise. Golden Books Staff. 2003. (ENG.). 32p. (J). (gr. -1-2). pap. 3.99 *(978-0-307-10043-6(X)*, Golden Bks.) Random Hse. Children's Bks.
—You Be the Jury: Courtroom Collection. Miller, Marvin. 2005. 361p. pap. *(978-0-439-77480-2(2))* Scholastic, Inc.
Roper, Clyde F. E., photos by. Giant Squid: Searching for a Sea Monster, 1 vol. Cerullo, Mary M. 2012. (Smithsonian Ser.). (ENG., 48p. (J). (gr. 2-6). pap. 8.95 *(978-1-4296-8023-3(7))*; lib. bdg. 29.99 *(978-1-4296-7541-3(1))* Capstone. (Capstone Pr.).
Roper, Robert. ¡A nadar, Boots! (Swim, Boots, Swim!) Beinstein, Phoebe. 2009. (Dora la Exploradora Ser.). (SPA.). 24p. (J). pap. 3.99 *(978-1-4169-7939-5(5)*, Libros Para Ninos) Libros Para Ninos.
—At the Carnival. Valdes, Leslie. 2005. (Dora the Explorer Ser.). (ENG.). 24p. (J). pap. 3.99 *(978-0-689-85841-3(8)*, Simon Spotlight/Nickelodeon) Simon Spotlight/Nickelodeon.
—Dolls of Danger. ed. 2005. 32p. (J). lib. bdg. 15.00 *(978-1-59054-989-6(9))* Fitzgerald Bks.
—Dora & the Baby Crab. Larsen, Kirsten. 2008. (Dora the Explorer Ser.: 17). (ENG.). 24p. (J). (gr. -1-1). pap. 3.99 *(978-1-4169-5451-4(1)*, Simon Spotlight/Nickelodeon) Simon Spotlight/Nickelodeon.
—Dora & the Stuck Truck. Beinstein, Phoebe. 2008. (Dora the Explorer Ser.: 25). (ENG & SPA.). 24p. (J). (gr. -1-2). pap. 3.99 *(978-1-4169-4799-8(X)*, Simon Spotlight/Nickelodeon) Simon Spotlight/Nickelodeon.
—Dora Goes to School. Valdes, Leslie. ed. 2005. (Dora the Explorer Ser.: 8). 22p. (J). lib. bdg. 15.00 *(978-1-59054-791-5(8))* Fitzgerald Bks.
—Dora Goes to School. 2004. (Dora the Explorer Ser.: Vol. 8). (ENG.). 24p. (J). pap. 3.99 *(978-0-689-86494-0(9)*, Simon Spotlight/Nickelodeon) Simon Spotlight/Nickelodeon.
—Dora in the Deep Sea. Ricci, Christine. 2003. (Dora the Explorer Ser.: Vol. 3). (ENG.). 24p. (J). pap. 3.99 *(978-0-689-85845-1(0)*, Simon Spotlight/Nickelodeon) Simon Spotlight/Nickelodeon.
—Dora y la Aventura de Cumpleaños. Domínguez, Adriana, tr. 2010. (Dora la Exploradora Ser.). (SPA.). 24p. (J). 6.99 *(978-1-4424-0286-7(5)*, Libros Para Ninos) Libros Para Ninos.
—Happy Birthday, Dora! 2010. (Dora the Explorer Ser.). (ENG.). 14p. (J). (gr. -1-k). bds. 6.99 *(978-1-4424-0333-8(0)*, Simon Spotlight/Nickelodeon) Simon Spotlight/Nickelodeon.
—The Little Flower Seed. Fisch, Sarah. 2007. (J). pap. *(978-0-439-90899-3(X))* Scholastic, Inc.
—Los Deseos de Dora. Beinstein, Phoebe. Ziegler, Argentina Palacios, tr. from ENG. 2008. (Dora la Exploradora Ser.).Tr. of Dora's Bedtime Wishes. (ENG.). 14p. (J). (gr. -1). bds. 4.99 *(978-1-4169-5036-3(2)*, Libros Para Ninos) Libros Para Ninos.
—La Mochila de Dora. Willson, Sarah. 2003. (Dora the Explorer Ser.).Tr. of Dora's Backpack. (SPA.). 24p. (J). pap. 3.99 *(978-0-689-86306-6(3)*, Libros Para Ninos) Libros Para Ninos.
—Show Me Your Smile! Ricci, Christine. ed. 2005. (Dora the Explorer Ser.: 11). 22p. (J). lib. bdg. 15.00 *(978-1-59054-800-4(0))* Fitzgerald Bks.
—Swim, Boots, Swim! Beinstein, Phoebe. 2009. (Dora the Explorer Ser.: 29). (ENG.). 24p. (J). (gr. -1-2). pap. 3.99 *(978-1-4169-7195-5(5)*, Simon Spotlight/Nickelodeon) Simon Spotlight/Nickelodeon.
Roper, Robert, jt. illus. see Angle, Scott.
Roper, Robert, jt. illus. see Hall, Susan.
Roraback, Robin. Fall Fun for Kit. Hoffmann, Sara E. 2013. (My Reading Neighborhood: Kindergarten Sight Word Stories Ser.). (ENG.). 16p. (J). (gr. -1-1). pap. 5.99 *(978-1-4677-1165-4(9)*, 9781467711654) Lerner Publishing Group.
—Fun Days. Hillert, Margaret. 2016. (BeginningtoRead Ser.). (ENG.). 32p. (J). (gr. -1-2). 22.60 *(978-1-59953-815-0(6))*; pap. 11.94 *(978-1-60357-977-3(X))* Norwood Hse. Pr.
—Nan Swims. Hoffmann, Sara E. 2013. (My Reading Neighborhood: Kindergarten Sight Word Stories Ser.). (ENG.). 16p. (J). (gr. -1-1). pap. 5.99 *(978-1-4677-1166-1(7)*, 9781467711661) Lerner Publishing Group.
—A Picnic with Kit. Hoffmann, Sara E. 2013. (My Reading Neighborhood: Kindergarten Sight Word Stories Ser.). (ENG.). 16p. (J). (gr. -1-1). pap. 5.99 *(978-1-4677-1168-5(3)*, 9781467711685) Lerner Publishing Group.
Roraback, Lori. Music of the City: In English & Afaan Oromo. Ready Set Go Books. Gemeda, Ahmed Dedo, tr. 2019. (ENG.). 34p. (J). pap. 11.99 ***(978-1-6774-7499-8(8))*** Independently Published.
—Music of the City: In English & Amharic. Ready Set Go Books. Eshetie, Amlaku B., tr. 2019. (Ready Set Go 10 Ser.: Vol. 1). (ENG.). 32p. (J). pap. 11.99 ***(978-1-6874-2333-7(4))*** Independently Published.
Roraback, Lori. Music of the City: In English & Tigrinya. Ready Set Go Books. Dessalegn, Aklilu, tr. 2019. (ENG.). 32p. (J). pap. 11.99 *(978-1-0731-4182-1(9))* Independently Published.
Rosa, Don, jt. illus. see Mebberson, Amy.
Rosa, Francesca. Ava, Seeker in the Snow. Stier, Catherine. 2020. (Dog's Day Ser.: 2). (ENG.). 96p. (J). (gr. 1-5). 12.99 ***(978-0-8075-1664-5(3)***, 807516643) Whitman, Albert & Co.
—I Am Ava, Seeker in the Snow. Stier, Catherine. 2020. (Dog's Day Ser.: 2). (ENG.). 96p. (J). (gr. 1-5). pap. 5.99 ***(978-0-8075-1670-6(8)***, 0807516708) Whitman, Albert & Co.
—I Am Bella, Star of the Show. Stier, Catherine. 2020. (Dog's Day Ser.). (ENG.). 96p. (J). (gr. 1-5). 12.99 ***(978-0-8075-1673-7(2)***, 0807516732) Whitman, Albert & Co.
—I Am Jax, Protector of the Ranch. Stier, Catherine. 2020. (Dog's Day Ser.). (ENG.). 96p. (J). (gr. 1-5). pap. 5.99 ***(978-0-8075-1671-3(6)***, 0807516716) Whitman, Albert & Co.
—I Am Sammy, Trusted Guide. Stier, Catherine. 2020. (Dog's Day Ser.). (ENG.). 96p. (J). (gr. 1-5). 12.99 ***(978-0-8075-1672-0(4)***, 0807516724) Whitman, Albert & Co.
—Jax, Protector of the Ranch. Stier, Catherine. 2020. (Dog's Day Ser.). (ENG.). 96p. (J). (gr. 1-5). 12.99 ***(978-0-8075-1663-8(5)***, 807516635) Whitman, Albert & Co.
Rosa, Leandra La. Being a Punch Line Is No Joke: A 4D Book. Green, D. L. 2018. (Funny Girl Ser.). (ENG.). 112p. (J). (gr. 3-5). pap. 7.95 *(978-1-4965-6473-3(1)*, 138382); lib. bdg. 25.99 *(978-1-4965-6469-6(3)*, 138378) Capstone. (Stone Arch Bks.).
—Good Deeds & Other Laughing Matters: A 4D Book. Green, D. L. 2018. (Funny Girl Ser.). (ENG.). 112p. (J). (gr. 3-5). pap. 7.95 *(978-1-4965-6474-0(X)*, 138383); lib. bdg. 25.99 *(978-1-4965-6470-2(7)*, 138379) Capstone. (Stone Arch Bks.).
—Making Friends & Horsing Around: A 4D Book. Green, D. L. 2018. (Funny Girl Ser.). (ENG.). 112p. (J). (gr. 3-5). pap. 7.95 *(978-1-4965-6471-9(5)*, 138380); lib. bdg. 25.99 *(978-1-4965-6467-2(7)*, 138376) Capstone. (Stone Arch Bks.).
—Something Smells Funny at the Talent Show: A 4D Book. Green, D. L. 2018. (Funny Girl Ser.). (ENG.). 112p. (J). (gr. 3-5). pap. 7.95 *(978-1-4965-6472-6(3)*, 138381); lib. bdg. 25.99 *(978-1-4965-6468-9(5)*, 138377) Capstone. (Stone Arch Bks.).
Rosa, Marrisa, photos by. Come the Morning. Harris, Mark Jonathan. 2nd ed. 2005. (Landscapes of Childhood Ser.). (ENG., 220p. (gr. 5-9). per. 25.99 *(978-0-8143-3241-2(2)*, 1366) Wayne State Univ. Pr.
Rosadiuk, Stacy. The Piano Mouse. Bayford, Lindsay. 2016. (ENG.) (J). *(978-1-4602-5694-7(8))*; pap. *(978-1-4602-5695-4(6))* FriesenPress.
Rosado, Michael. The Wishing Flower, 1 vol. Townsan, Judy. 2009. 13p. pap. 24.95 *(978-1-61546-179-0(5))* America Star Bks.
Rosado, Puig. Le Gentil Petit Diable: Et Autres Contes de la Rue Broca. Gripari, Pierre. 2007. (Folio Junior Ser.). 142p. (J). per. *(978-2-07-061255-0(4))* National Round Table on the Environment & the Economy (NRTEE)/Table ronde nationale sur l'environnement et l'economie (TRNEE).
—The Witch in the Broom Cupboard & Other Tales. Gripari, Pierre. Lewis, Sophie, tr. 2015. (ENG.). 144p. (J). (gr. 2-5). pap. 13.95 *(978-1-78269-066-5(2)*, Pushkin Press) Steerforth Pr.
Rosado, Rafael. Dragons Beware! Aguirre, Jorge. 2015. (Chronicles of Claudette Ser.). (ENG.). 160p. (J). (gr. 2-5). pap. 16.99 *(978-1-59643-878-1(9)*, 900118161, First Second Bks.) Roaring Brook Pr.
—Giants Beware! Aguirre, Jorge. 2012. (Chronicles of Claudette Ser.). (ENG.). 208p. (J). (gr. 2-5). pap. 16.99 *(978-1-59643-582-7(8)*, 900064169, First Second Bks.) Roaring Brook Pr.
—Monsters Beware! Aguirre, Jorge. 2018. (Chronicles of Claudette Ser.). (ENG.). 176p. (J). pap. 15.99 *(978-1-62672-180-7(7)*, 900143174, First Second Bks.) Roaring Brook Pr.
—Monsters Beware! Aguirre, Jorge Augusto & Novak, John. 2018. 171p. (J). *(978-0-7804-0062-7(3)*, First Second Bks.) Roaring Brook Pr.
Rosado, Veronica, jt. illus. see Greenfelder, Jill.
Rosado, Will. Incidentals Vol. 2: Balance of Power. Casey, Joe. 2018. (ENG.). 144p. (YA). pap. 14.99 *(978-1-941302-82-8(3)*, 9948537d-bf60-42a8-9aeb-ba34bb7f1b28, Lion Forge) Oni Pr., Inc.
Rosado, Will, et al. Silken Ghost. Dixon, Chuck. 2004. 160p. (YA). pap. 9.95 *(978-1-59314-036-6(3))* CrossGeneration Comics, Inc.
Rosado, Will, jt. illus. see Dallocchio, Federico.
Rosanas, Ramon. The Mighty Captain Marvel Vol. 1. 2017. (ENG.). 136p. (YA). (gr. 8-17). pap. 15.99 *(978-1-302-90605-4(4))* Marvel Worldwide, Inc.
—Star Wars: Age of Resistance - Heroes. 2019. 128p. (YA). (gr. 4-17). pap. 17.99 *(978-1-302-91712-8(9))* Marvel Worldwide, Inc.
Rosanbalm, Sunny. A Gift for Baby. 2009. (SPA & ENG.). *(978-0-9685754-7-5(1))* Natural Child Project Society, The.
Rosario, Andy Daniel. Llueve Llueve. Rosario, Andy Daniel. Alabi, Maria Aduke. 2020. (SPA.). 28p. (J). (gr. k-6). pap. 8.99 ***(978-1-0878-5930-9(1))*** Quisqueyana Pr.
Rosario, Joann. Bitty Witty Witty Witty Witty Monkey! Rosario, Joann. 2004. 10p. (J). pap. 10.00 *(978-0-9758746-9-1(1)*, 1246169) J.G.R. Enterprises.
—Double Diddley WHaaat! Rosario, Joann. 2004. (J). pap. *(978-0-9758746-8-4(3))* J.G.R. Enterprises.
—Happy- Go -Lucky Giraffe!! Rosario, Joann. 2004. 20p. (J). (gr. k-5). pap. 10.00 *(978-0-9758746-7-7(5)*, 1246169) J.G.R. Enterprises.
—Joey & His Famous Fish! Rosario, Joann. 2004. 20p. (J). (gr. -1-5). pap. 10.00 *(978-0-9758746-2-2(4)*, 1246169) J.G.R. Enterprises.
—The PenguinThat Boom- Booms to a Ferret That Zoom-Zoomed. Rosario, Joann. 2004. 28p. (J). (gr. -1-5). pap. 10.00 *(978-0-9758746-4-6(0)*, 1246169) J.G.R. Enterprises.
—Puddy Cat & the Chick Muck. Rosario, Joann. 2004. 15p. (J). (gr. -1-5). pap. 10.00 *(978-0-9758746-3-9(2)*, 1246169) J.G.R. Enterprises.
—Swiggly Swiggly Do! Rosario, Joann. 2004. 5p. (J). (gr. -1-5). pap. 10.00 *(978-0-9758746-6-0(7)*, 1246169) J.G.R. Enterprises.
—The Trick That Turned into Poop! Rosario, Joann. 2004. 20p. (J). (gr. -1-13). pap. 10.00 *(978-0-9758746-5-3(9)*, 1246169) J.G.R. Enterprises.
—Where Did Sabrina Go? Rosario, Joann. 2004. 13p. (J). (gr. -1-5). pap. 10.00 *(978-0-9758746-1-5(6))* J.G.R. Enterprises.
Rosario, Sherwin. Meet the Letters. 2005. 26p. (J). 9.99 *(978-0-9767008-0-7(8))* Preschool Prep Co.
—Meet the Numbers Lift the Flap Book. 2005. 12p. (J). bds. 9.99 *(978-0-9767008-1-4(6))* Preschool Prep Co.
—Meet the Numbers One to Ten. 2005. 10p. (J). bds. 7.99 *(978-0-9767008-3-8(2))* Preschool Prep Co.
—Meet the Vowels. 2005. 12p. (J). bds. 7.99 *(978-0-9767008-2-1(4))* Preschool Prep Co.
Rosas, Heather. ABC What Will I Be? Rosas, Heather. 2008. (ENG.). 16p. (J). 12.95 *(978-1-58117-681-0(3)*, Intervisual/Piggy Toes) Bendon, Inc.
Roscoe Robinson. Teddy's Bear, 1 vol. Robinson, Marquita E. 2009. 15p. pap. 24.95 *(978-1-60749-249-8(0))* America Star Bks.
Rose, Carolyn Maree. Pick-a-WooWoo - Angel Steps: Love You, Miss You, 16 vols., Vol. 10. Pretreger, Lidija. 2010. 32p. pap. *(978-0-9803669-9-0(2))* Pick-a-Woo Woo Pubs.
—Pick-a-WooWoo - My Angels Advice: A Story about Love, 16 vols., Vol. 3. Harper, Julie Ann. 2009. 32p. pap. *(978-0-9803669-2-1(5))* Pick-a-Woo Woo Pubs.
—Pick-a-WooWoo -Frolicking with the Fairies: Two Enchanting Fairytales, 16 vols., Vol. 1. Harper, Julie Ann. 2008. (ENG.). 32p. (J). pap. *(978-0-9803669-0-7(9))* Pick-a-Woo Woo Pubs.
Rose, Drew. Frosty the Snowman Returns. Ritchie, Joseph R. 2006. 14p. (J). (gr. -1-k). bds. 9.95 *(978-0-8249-6670-6(8)*, Ideal Pubns.) Worthy Publishing.
—God's Heroes. 2005. (Bible Activity Bks.). 94p. (J). (gr. -1-3). 2.99 *(978-0-7814-4313-5(X)*, 078144313X) Cook, David C.
—God's Son, Jesus. 2005. (Bible Activity Bks.). 94p. (J). (gr. -1-3). 2.99 *(978-0-7814-4314-2(8)*, 0781443148) Cook, David C.
—God's World. Keffer, Lois. ed. 2005. (Bible Activity Bks.). (ENG.). 96p. (J). (gr. -1-3). 2.99 *(978-0-7814-4312-8(1)*, 104553) Cook, David C.
—Knock, Knock, Who's There? Ritchie, Joseph R. 2005. (ENG.). 12p. (J). bds. 7.95 *(978-0-8249-6613-3(9)*, Ideal Pubns.) Worthy Publishing.
—Lost & Found. Poland, Pitch & Poland, Inglan. 2013. 30p. (J). *(978-0-9853430-0-2(1))* Little P Pr. Co.
—Noses & Toes. Pingry, Patricia A. 2005. (J). *(978-0-8249-6594-5(9)*, Ideal Pubns.) Worthy Publishing.
—Opposites. DeGrie, Eve. 2008. (ENG.). 12p. (J). bds. 6.95 *(978-0-8249-6559-4(0)*, Ideal Pubns.) Worthy Publishing.
—Sounds. Pingry, Patricia A. 2005. (J). *(978-0-8249-6596-9(5)*, Ideal Pubns.) Worthy Publishing.
—Tennis Court Conjunctions. Fisher, Doris & Gibbs, D. L. 2008. (Grammar All-Stars Ser.). 32p. (J). (gr. 2-5). lib. bdg. 27.00 *(978-0-8368-8905-5(3)*, Gareth Stevens Learning Library) Stevens, Gareth Publishing LLLP.
—Thomas Jefferson & the Ghostriders. Goldsmith, Howard. 2008. (Ready-to-Read Childhood of Famous Americans - Level 2 Ser.). (ENG.). (J). (gr. k-2). lib. bdg. 14.60 *(978-1-62765-949-9(8))* Perfection Learning Corp.
—Thomas Jefferson & the Ghostriders. Goldsmith, Howard. 2008. (Ready-To-Read Level 2 Ser.). (ENG.). 32p. (J). (gr. k-2). lib. bdg. 16.19 *(978-1-4169-2749-5(2)*, Aladdin) Simon & Schuster Children's Publishing.
—Thomas Jefferson & the Ghostriders. Goldsmith, Howard. 2008. (Ready-To-read COFA Ser.). (ENG.). 32p. (J). (gr. k-2). pap. 4.99 *(978-1-4169-2692-4(5)*, Simon Spotlight) Simon Spotlight.
Rose, Emme. Princess Aila & the Unicorns. Jameson, Bill. (ENG.). 32p. (J). 2019. 24.95 *(978-1-64438-371-1(3))*; 2018. pap. 14.95 *(978-1-64438-419-0(1))* Booklocker.com, Inc.
Rose, Giada. Penelope's Superpower. Cropsey, Melinda M. 2018. (ENG.). 32p. (J). 17.99 *(978-0-692-14348-3(3))* Breadcrumbs LLC.
Rose, Heidi. Squishy, Squishy: A Book about My Five Senses. Stihler, Cherie B. 2005. 23p. (J). pap. 5.95 *(978-0-8198-7078-0(1)*, 332-374) Pauline Bks. & Media.
—When Should I Pray? Pharr, Nancy Elizabeth. 2018. (ENG.). 40p. (J). (gr. -1-2). pap. 16.95 *(978-1-5127-9793-0(6)*, WestBow Pr.) Author Solutions, Inc.
—When Should I Pray? Pharr, Nancy Elizabeth. 2003. 40p. (J). pap. 8.95 *(978-0-8198-8304-9(2)*, 332-412) Pauline Bks. & Media.
Rose, Hilda. Freddy's Day at the Races, 1 vol. Chalker Browne, Susan. 2008. (ENG.). 32p. (J). (gr. 1-8). *(978-1-897174-36-4(5))* Breakwater Bks., Ltd.
—Freddy's Hockey Hero, 1 vol. Chalker Browne, Susan. 2010. (ENG.). 32p. (J). (gr. k-3). *(978-1-897174-62-3(4))* Breakwater Bks., Ltd.
—Hey Freddy, It's Canada's Birthday!, 1 vol. Chalker Browne, Susan. 2009. (ENG.). 32p. (J). (gr. k-5). *(978-1-897174-39-5(X))* Breakwater Bks., Ltd.
—Johnny & the Gypsy Moth, 1 vol. Sullivan-Fraser, Deannie. 2009. (ENG.). 32p. (J). (gr. k-5). *(978-1-897174-40-1(3))* Breakwater Bks., Ltd.
—Kisses Kisses Baby-O!, 1 vol. Fitch, Sheree. 2008. (ENG.). 12p. (J). (gr. -1 — 1). bds. 6.50 *(978-1-55109-646-9(3)*, 5415e9f4-e0fe-4011-a07b-77cf7a7e3547) Nimbus Publishing, Ltd. CAN. Dist: Baker & Taylor Publisher Services (BTPS).
Rose, Hilda, jt. illus. see HildaRose.
Rose, Jessica. Rafa & the Mist. Baird, Kade. 2017. (ENG.). 42p. (J). (gr. k-4). 24.00 *(978-0-692-99142-8(5))* Baird, Robert Kade.
Rose, Julianna. Go Out & Play! Favorite Outdoor Games from KaBOOM! KaBOOM!. 2012. 104p. (J). (gr. k-4). pap. 11.99 *(978-0-7636-5530-3(9))* Candlewick Pr.
Rose, Lucy. Animal Atlas, 1 vol. Lonely Planet Kids & Rooney, Anne. 2019. (ENG.). 32p. (J). (gr. 4-7). 18.99 *(978-1-78868-261-9(0))* Lonely Planet Global Ltd. IRL. Dist: Hachette Bk. Group.
Rose, Lucy. Wild City: Meet the Animals Who Share Our City Spaces. Hoare, Ben. 2020. (ENG.). 64p. (J). 19.99 ***(978-0-7534-7633-8(9)***, 900226424, Kingfisher) Roaring Brook Pr.
Rose, Melanie. A Is for Algonquin: An Ontario Alphabet. Gorman, Lovenia. rev. ed. 2005. (Discover Canada Province by Province Ser.). (ENG.). 40p. (J). (gr. k-5). 17.95 *(978-1-58536-263-9(8))* Sleeping Bear Pr.
— A Is for Amazing Moments: A Sports Alphabet. Herzog, Brad. 2008. (Sports Ser.). (ENG.). 40p. (J). (gr. -1-5). 17.95 *(978-1-58536-360-5(X))* Sleeping Bear Pr.
— A Is for Amazing Moments: A Sports Alphabet. Herzog, Brad. 2015. (Av2 Fiction Readalong 2016 Ser.). (ENG.). (J). (gr. 1-4). lib. bdg. 34.28 *(978-1-4896-3729-1(X)*, AV2 by Weigl) Weigl Pubs., Inc.
— A Is for Axel: An Ice Skating Alphabet. Browning, Kurt. rev. ed. 2005. (Sports Ser.). (ENG.). 40p. (J). (gr. -1-5). 17.95 *(978-1-58536-280-6(8))* Sleeping Bear Pr.
— A Is for Axel: An Ice Skating Alphabet. Browning, Kurt. 2015. (Av2 Fiction Readalong 2016 Ser.). (ENG.). (J). (gr. 1-4). lib. bdg. 34.28 *(978-1-4896-3732-1(X)*, AV2 by Weigl) Weigl Pubs., Inc.
—B Is for Big Ben: An England Alphabet. Edwards, Pamela Duncan. 2008. (Discover the World Ser.). (ENG.). 40p. (J). (gr. 1-3). 19.99 *(978-1-58536-305-6(7)*, 202110) Sleeping Bear Pr.
—E Is for Extreme: An Extreme Sports Alphabet. Herzog, Brad. rev. ed. 2007. (Sports Ser.). (ENG.). 40p. (J). (gr. -1-3). 17.95 *(978-1-58536-310-0(3))* Sleeping Bear Pr.
—E Is for Extreme: An Extreme Sports Alphabet. Herzog, Brad. 2015. (Av2 Fiction Readalong 2016 Ser.). (ENG.). (J). (gr. 1-4). lib. bdg. 34.28 *(978-1-4896-3735-2(4)*, AV2 by Weigl) Weigl Pubs., Inc.
—The Gift of the Inuksuk. Ulmer, Mike. rev. ed. 2004. (Tales of the World Ser.). (ENG.). 32p. (J). (gr. 1-4). 19.99 *(978-1-58536-214-1(X)*, 202045) Sleeping Bear Pr.
—H Is for Home Run: A Baseball Alphabet. Herzog, Brad. (Sports Alphabet Ser.). (ENG.). 40p. (J). (gr. 1-4). 2009. pap. 7.95 *(978-1-58536-475-6(4)*, 202311); 2004. 16.95 *(978-1-58536-219-6(0)*, 202049) Sleeping Bear Pr.
—H Is for Home Run: A Baseball Alphabet. Herzog, Brad. 2015. (Av2 Fiction Readalong 2016 Ser.). (ENG.). (J). (gr. 1-4). lib. bdg. 34.28 *(978-1-4896-3744-4(3)*, AV2 by Weigl) Weigl Pubs., Inc.
—Hat Tricks Count: A Hockey Number Book. Napier, Matt. rev. ed. 2005. (Sports Ser.). (ENG.). 40p. (J). (gr. k-5). 16.95 *(978-1-58536-163-2(1))* Sleeping Bear Pr.
—Hockey Numbers. Napier, Matt. (Numbers & Counting Ser.). (ENG.). 2009. 14p. 11.75 *(978-1-58536-495-4(9))*; 2007. 22p. (J). (gr. -1-1). 7.99 *(978-1-58536-346-9(4))* Sleeping Bear Pr.
—K Is for Kick: A Soccer Alphabet. Herzog, Brad. rev. ed. (Sports Ser.). (ENG.). 40p. (J). (gr. -1-3). 2006. pap. 7.95 *(978-1-58536-339-1(1))*; 2003. 16.95 *(978-1-58536-130-4(5))* Sleeping Bear Pr.
—K Is for Kick: A Soccer Alphabet. Herzog, Brad. 2015. (Av2 Fiction Readalong 2016 Ser.). (ENG.). (J). (gr. 1-4). lib. bdg. 34.28 *(978-1-4896-3756-7(7)*, AV2 by Weigl) Weigl Pubs., Inc.
—Loonies & Toonies: A Canadian Number Book. Ulmer, Mike. rev. ed. 2006. (ENG.). 40p. (J). (gr. k-6). 18.95 *(978-1-58536-239-4(5))* Sleeping Bear Pr.
—M Is for Maple: A Canadian Alphabet. Ulmer, Mike & Ulmer, Michael. rev. abr. ed. 2007. (Discover the World Ser.). (ENG.). 32p. (J). (gr. -1-1). 8.99 *(978-1-58536-345-2(6)*, 202380) Sleeping Bear Pr.
—M Is for Maple Leafs. Ulmer, Michael. 2014. 32p. (J). (gr. k-3). 19.95 *(978-1-77049-798-6(6)*, Tundra Bks.) Tundra Bks. CAN. Dist: Penguin Random Hse. LLC.

R

—P Is for Passport: A World Alphabet. Scillian, Devin. 2003. (Discover the World Ser.). (ENG.). 48p. (J). (gr. 1-3). 19.95 *(978-1-58536-157-1(7)*, 202017) Sleeping Bear Pr.

—W Is for Wind: A Weather Alphabet. Michaels, Pat. rev. ed. (Science Ser.). (ENG.). 40p. (J). 2006. (gr. -1-3). pap. 7.95 *(978-1-58536-330-8(8))*; 2005. 16.95 *(978-1-58536-237-0(9))* Sleeping Bear Pr.

—Z Is for Zamboni: A Hockey Alphabet. Napier, Matt. 2015. (Av2 Fiction Readalong 2016 Ser.). (ENG.). (J). (gr. -1-1). lib. bdg. 34.28 *(978-1-4896-3771-0(0)*, AV2 by Weigl) Weigl Pubs., Inc.

—Z Is for Zamboni: A Hockey Alphabet. Napier, Matt. rev. ed. 2006. (Sports Alphabet Ser.). (ENG.). 32p. (J). (gr. -1-1). 8.99 *(978-1-58536-303-2(0)*, 202288) Sleeping Bear Pr.

—1, 2, 3 Cheers for the Toronto Maple Leafs! An Official Toronto Maple Leafs Counting Book. Napier, Matt. 2016. 32p. (J). (gr. -1-2). 19.99 *(978-1-77049-801-3(X)*, Fenn-Tundra) Tundra Bks. CAN. Dist: Penguin Random Hse. LLC.

Rose, Melanie. Z Is for Zamboni: A Hockey Alphabet. Rose, Melanie. Napier, Matt. rev. ed. 2003. (Sports Alphabet Ser.). (ENG.). 40p. (J). (gr. -1-1). pap. 8.99 *(978-1-58536-238-7(7)*, 202277) Sleeping Bear Pr.

Rose, Melanie, jt. illus. see Megahan, John.

Rose, Micky, jt. illus. see Meurer, Caleb.

Rose, Mollie. Steven Universe: Harmony. Vidaurri, S. M. 2019. (Steven Universe Ser.). (ENG.). 144p. (J). pap. 14.99 *(978-1-68415-465-4(0))* Boom! Studios.

Rose, Naomi C. Where Snow Leopard Prowls: Wild Animals of Tibet. Rose, Naomi C. 2013. (ENG.). 32p. (J). 17.95 *(978-0-9836333-0-3(4))* Dancing Dakini Pr.

Rose, Nathalie. Nathalie's Socks. Jeanne, Diana. 2004. 51p. (J). mass mkt. 7.95 *(978-0-9727583-9-0(9))* Taylor-Dth Publishing.

Rose-Popp, Melanie. M Is for Maple: A Canadian Alphabet. Ulmer, Mike. rev. ed. 2004. (Discover the World Ser.). (ENG.). 48p. (J). (gr. -1-1). pap. 8.95 *(978-1-58536-235-6(2)*, 202276) Sleeping Bear Pr.

Rose, Shayla. Once upon a Time Far Away: There Was Helplessness. Pazzaglia, Gina. 2019. (Once upon a Time Far Away Ser.: Vol. 2). (ENG.). 40p. (J). pap. 15.99 ***(978-1-0797-7666-9(4))*** Independently Published.

—Once upon a Time Far Away: There Was Loneliness. Pazzaglia, Gina. 2019. (ENG.). 30p. (J). pap. 15.99 ***(978-1-7034-1029-7(7))*** Independently Published.

Rose, Silvia. Orinoco, AKA Bogeybum, Adventures of an African Pygmy Hedgehog. Harold, Jay. 2019. (ENG.). 38p. (J). pap. 6.00 ***(978-1-6763-5093-4(4))*** Independently Published.

Rosen, Anne. Good Night Colorado. Gamble, Adam & Mackey, Bill. 2012. (Good Night Our World Ser.). (ENG.). 20p. (J). (gr. k — 1). bds. 9.95 *(978-1-60219-055-9(0))* Good Night Bks.

—Good Night Connecticut. Vrba, Christina. 2009. (Good Night Our World Ser.). (ENG.). 20p. (J). (gr. k — 1). bds. 9.95 *(978-1-60219-035-1(6))* Good Night Bks.

—Good Night Florida Keys. Jasper, Mark. 2008. (Good Night Our World Ser.). (ENG.). 20p. (J). (gr. k — 1). bds. 9.95 *(978-1-60219-020-7(8))* Good Night Bks.

—Good Night Israel. Jasper, Mark. 2010. (Good Night Our World Ser.). (ENG.). 24p. (J). (gr. k — 1). bds. 9.95 *(978-1-60219-043-6(7))* Good Night Bks.

—Good Night Martha's Vineyard. Weeks, Megan. 2007. (Good Night Our World Ser.). (ENG.). 20p. (J). (gr. k — 1). bds. 9.95 *(978-1-60219-011-5(9))* Good Night Bks.

—Good Night Maryland. Gamble, Adam & Jasper, Mark. 2011. (Good Night Our World Ser.). (ENG.). 20p. (J). (gr. k — 1). bds. 9.95 *(978-1-60219-046-7(1))* Good Night Bks.

—Good Night Michigan. Gamble, Adam. 2011. (Good Night Our World Ser.). (ENG.). 20p. (J). (gr. k — 1). bds. 9.95 *(978-1-60219-054-2(2))* Good Night Bks.

—Good Night Nantucket. Gamble, Adam. 2007. (Good Night Our World Ser.). (ENG.). 20p. (J). (gr. k — 1). bds. 9.95 *(978-1-60219-013-9(5))* Good Night Bks.

—Good Night New Hampshire. Gamble, Adam. 2009. (Good Night Our World Ser.). (ENG.). 20p. (J). (gr. k — 1). bds. 9.95 *(978-1-60219-037-5(2))* Good Night Bks.

—Good Night North Carolina. Gamble, Adam. 2009. (Good Night Our World Ser.). (ENG.). 20p. (J). (gr. k — 1). bds. 9.95 *(978-1-60219-033-7(X))* Good Night Bks.

—Good Night Rhode Island. Gamble, Adam. 2008. (Good Night Our World Ser.). (ENG.). 20p. (J). (gr. k — 1). bds. 9.95 *(978-1-60219-024-5(0))* Good Night Bks.

—Good Night Vancouver. Adams, David J. 2010. (Good Night Our World Ser.). (ENG.). 20p. (J). (gr. k — 1). bds. 9.95 *(978-1-60219-039-9(9))* Good Night Bks.

Rosen, Anne & Jasper, Mark. Good Night Country Store. Gamble, Adam. 2010. (Good Night Our World Ser.). (ENG.). 20p. (J). (gr. k — 1). bds. 9.95 *(978-1-60219-044-3(5))* Good Night Bks.

Rosen, Anne & Veno, Joe. Good Night Georgia. Gamble, Adam. 2009. (Good Night Our World Ser.). (ENG.). 20p. (J). (gr. k — 1). bds. 9.95 *(978-1-60219-032-0(1))* Good Night Bks.

—Good Night Nevada. Gamble, Adam & Jasper, Mark. 2012. (Good Night Our World Ser.). (ENG.). 20p. (J). (gr. k — 1). bds. 9.95 *(978-1-60219-060-3(7))* Good Night Bks.

Rosen, Barry & Bell, Greg. Do You Know What a Stranger Is? Rosen, Barry. 2003. 34p. (J). pap. 7.25 *(978-0-9625593-4-1(2))* B.R. Publishing Co.

Rosen, Kim. 10 Plants That Shook the World. Richardson, Gillian. 2013. (World of Tens Ser.). (ENG.). 132p. (J). (gr. 5-7). pap. 14.95 *(978-1-55451-444-1(4)*, 9781554514441); 2nd ed. 24.95 *(978-1-55451-445-8(2)*, 9781554514458) Annick Pr., Ltd. CAN. Dist: Publishers Group West (PGW).

—10 Rivers That Shaped the World. Peters, Marilee. 2015. (World of Tens Ser.). (ENG.). 136p. (J). (gr. 4-7). pap. 14.95 *(978-1-55451-738-1(9)*, 9781554517381) Annick Pr., Ltd. CAN. Dist: Publishers Group West (PGW).

—10 Routes That Crossed the World. Richardson, Gillian. 2017. (ENG.). 164p. (J). (gr. 3-7). pap. 12.95 *(978-1-55451-875-3(X))* Annick Pr., Ltd. CAN. Dist: Publishers Group West (PGW).

—10 Ships That Rocked the World. Richardson, Gillian. 2015. (World of Tens Ser.). (ENG.). 176p. (J). (gr. 4-7). pap. 14.95 *(978-1-55451-781-7(8)*, 9781554517817) Annick Pr., Ltd. CAN. Dist: Publishers Group West (PGW).

Rosen, Michael & Oxenbury, Helen. Chung Ta Di Sian Gau. 2004. Orig. Title: We're Going on a Bear Hunt. (VIE & ENG.). 33p. (J). *(978-1-85269-722-8(9))* Mantra Lingua.

Rosenbaum, Andria Warmflash & Gill, Deirdre. Trains Don't Sleep. Rosenbaum, Andria Warmflash & Gill, Deirdre. 2017. (ENG.). 40p. (J). (gr. -1-3). 16.99 *(978-0-544-38074-5(6)*, 1591860, HMH Books For Young Readers) Houghton Mifflin Harcourt Publishing Co.

Rosenberg, Amye. My First Learn & Do Jewish Holiday Book. Gootel, Rifka. 64p. (J). (gr. k-2). pap. 4.95 *(978-0-87441-475-2(X))* Behrman Hse., Inc.

Rosenberg, Carol Killman. Ignatius: A Long Story about a Small Rock. Rosenberg, Carol Killman. 2015. (ENG.). (J). pap. 6.95 *(978-0-9908458-2-9(6))* Book Couple LLC, The.

Rosenberg, Natascha. Bake, Mice, Bake! Seltzer, Eric. 2012. (Penguin Young Readers, Level 1 Ser.). 32p. (J). (gr. k-1). mass mkt. 4.99 *(978-0-448-45763-5(6)*, Penguin Young Readers) Penguin Young Readers Group.

—Look!: Babies Head to Toe. Harris, Robie H. 2019. (ENG.). 20p. (J). (gr. -1 — 1). bds. 7.99 *(978-1-4197-3203-4(X)*, Abrams Appleseed) Abrams, Inc.

Rosenberg, Natascha. Mother Teresa. Sanchez Vegara, Maria Isabel. 2018. (Little People, Big Dreams Ser.: Vol. 18). (ENG.). 32p. (J). (gr. -1-2). ***(978-1-78603-230-0(9))*** Frances Lincoln Childrens Bks.

—Mother Teresa: My First Mother Teresa. Sanchez Vegara, Maria Isabel. 2019. (Little People, Big Dreams Ser.: Vol. 15). (ENG.). 24p. (J). (gr. -1). bds. ***(978-0-7112-4313-2(1))*** Frances Lincoln Childrens Bks.

Rosenberg, Natascha. Who? A Celebration of Babies. Harris, Robie. 2018. (ENG.). 20p. (J). (gr. -1 — 1). bds. 7.99 *(978-1-4197-2834-1(2)*, Abrams Appleseed) Abrams, Inc.

Rosenberg, Rachelle, jt. illus. see Araujo, Andre Lima.

Rosenberg, Rachelle, jt. illus. see Di Vito, Andrea.

Rosenberg, Rachelle, jt. illus. see Laiso, Emilio.

Rosenberg, Rachelle, jt. illus. see Lim, Ronald.

Rosenberg, Rachelle, jt. illus. see Lim, Ron.

Rosenberg, Rachelle, jt. illus. see Villanelli, Paolo.

Rosenberg, Rachelle, jt. illus. see Vito, Andrea Di.

Rosenberry, Vera. Baya, Baya, Lulla-By-a. McDonald, Megan. 2014. (ENG.). 32p. (J). (gr. -1-1). 16.99 *(978-1-4814-2533-9(1)*, Atheneum Bks. for Young Readers) Simon & Schuster Children's Publishing.

—Enviarme a Ti, Level 2. Guthrie, Woody. Flor Ada, Alma, tr. 2003. (Dejame Leer Ser.). (SPA.). 8p. (J). (gr. -1-1). 6.50 *(978-0-673-36301-5(5)*, Good Year Bks.) Celebration Pr.

—Monster Mischief. Jane, Pamela. 2014. (ENG.). 32p. (J). (gr. -1-2). 16.99 *(978-1-4814-2535-3(8)*, Atheneum Bks. for Young Readers) Simon & Schuster Children's Publishing.

Rosenberry, Vera. Princess of India: An Ancient Tale (30th Anniversary Edition) Shepard, Aaron. 2020. (ENG.). 44p. (J). 24.00 ***(978-1-62035-604-3(X))***; (gr. 2-6). pap. 12.00 ***(978-1-62035-603-6(1))*** Shepard Pubns. (Skyhook Pr.).

Rosenberry, Vera. When Vera Was Sick, 4 bks., Set. Rosenberry, Vera. unabr. ed. 2006. (Picture Book Readalong Ser.). (J). (gr. -1-3). pap. 37.95 incl. audio *(978-1-59519-652-1(8))*; pap. 39.95 incl. audio compact disk *(978-1-59519-653-8(6))* Live Oak Media.

Rosenblatt, Naomi. Furry Foot Notes. Rosenblatt, Judy, photos by. Wells, Leah. 2016. (ENG.). (J). pap. 7.50 *(978-1-942762-06-5(2))* Heliotrope Bks., LLC.

Rosendahl, Melissa M. Ebenezer Flea & the Right Thing to Do, 1 vol. Budic, Hannah Purdy. 2008. (ENG.). 30p. 24.95 *(978-1-60441-750-0(1))* America Star Bks.

Rosenfelder, Cheryl. Neddy the Nutty Acorn. Vos, Sharon. 2008. 40p. per. 24.95 *(978-1-60441-232-1(1))* America Star Bks.

Rosenstiehl, Agnès. Silly Lilly & the Four Seasons, 1 vol. Rosenstiehl, Agnès. 2013. (Toon Bks.). (ENG.). 36p. (J). (gr. -1-1). lib. bdg. 29.93 *(978-1-61479-155-3(4)*, 14847) Spotlight.

—Silly Lilly in What Will I Be Today?, 1 vol. Rosenstiehl, Agnès. 2013. (Toon Bks.). (ENG.). 36p. (J). (gr. -1-1). lib. bdg. 29.93 *(978-1-61479-156-0(2)*, 14848) Spotlight.

Rosenthal, Amy Krouse & Lichtenheld, Tom. The OK Book. Rosenthal, Amy Krouse & Lichtenheld, Tom. 2007. 40p. (J). (gr. -1-3). lib. bdg. 14.89 *(978-0-06-115256-6(0))* HarperCollins Pubs.

Rosenthal, Christina. When Rick Was Sick: About Stemmie, the Little Stem Cell. Darnall, Lyn. 2019. (1 Ser.: Vol. 1). (ENG.). 38p. (J). (gr. k-6). pap. 10.99 *(978-0-578-51928-9(3))* Chanticlair Publishing.

Rosenthal, Marc. All You Need Is Love. Lennon, John & McCartney, Paul. 2019. (ENG.). 40p. (J). (gr. -1-3). 17.99 *(978-1-5344-2981-9(6)*, Little Simon) Little Simon.

—Bobo the Sailor Man! Rosenthal, Eileen. 2013. (ENG.). 40p. (J). (gr. -1-1). 15.99 *(978-1-4424-4443-0(6))* Simon & Schuster Children's Publishing.

—Dig! Zimmerman, Andrea & Clemesha, David. 2014. (ENG.). 30p. (J). (— 1). bds. 7.99 *(978-0-544-17388-0(0)*, 1552172, HMH Books For Young Readers) Houghton Mifflin Harcourt Publishing Co.

—I Must Have Bobo! Rosenthal, Eileen. 2011. (ENG.). 40p. (J). (gr. -1-1). 14.99 *(978-1-4424-0377-2(2)*, Atheneum Bks. for Young Readers) Simon & Schuster Children's Publishing.

—I'll Save You Bobo! Rosenthal, Eileen. 2012. (ENG.). 40p. (J). (gr. -1-1). 14.99 *(978-1-4424-0378-9(0)*, Atheneum Bks. for Young Readers) Simon & Schuster Children's Publishing.

—Making a Friend. McGhee, Alison. 2011. (ENG.). 40p. (J). (gr. -1-3). 16.99 *(978-1-4169-8998-1(6)*, Atheneum Bks. for Young Readers) Simon & Schuster Children's Publishing.

—Mogie: The Heart of the House. Appelt, Kathi. 2014. (ENG.). 40p. (J). (gr. -1-3). 17.99 *(978-1-4424-8054-4(8)*, Atheneum Bks. for Young Readers) Simon & Schuster Children's Publishing.

—Small Walt. Verdick, Elizabeth. 2017. (ENG.). 40p. (J). (gr. -1-3). 17.99 *(978-1-4814-4845-1(5)*, Simon & Schuster Bks. For Young Readers) Simon & Schuster Bks. For Young Readers.

—Small Walt & Mo the Tow. Verdick, Elizabeth. 2018. (ENG.). 40p. (J). (gr. -1-3). 17.99 *(978-1-4814-6660-8(7)*, Simon & Schuster/Paula Wiseman Bks.) Simon & Schuster/Paula Wiseman Bks.

Rosenthal, Marc. The Small Walt Collection: Small Walt; Small Walt & Mo the Tow; Small Walt Spots Dot. Verdick, Elizabeth. ed. 2020. (ENG.). 120p. (J). (gr. -1-3). 53.99 ***(978-1-5344-7130-6(8))***, Simon & Schuster/Paula Wiseman Bks.) Simon & Schuster/Paula Wiseman Bks.

—Small Walt Spots Dot. Verdick, Elizabeth. 2020. (ENG.). 48p. (J). (gr. -1-3). 17.99 ***(978-1-5344-4284-9(7))***, Simon & Schuster/Paula Wiseman Bks.) Simon & Schuster/Paula Wiseman Bks.

Rosenthal, Marc. Archie & the Pirates. Rosenthal, Marc. 2075. 40p. (J). (gr. -1-3). pap. 6.99 *(978-0-06-144166-0(X))* HarperCollins Pubs.

—Phooey! Rosenthal, Marc. 2007. 40p. (J). (gr. -1-3). lib. bdg. 17.89 *(978-0-06-075249-1(1)*, Cotler, Joanna Books) HarperCollins Pubs.

Rosenthal, Robin. Big Ideas for Little Philosophers: Equality with Simone de Beauvoir. Armitage, Duane & McQuerry, Maureen. 2020. (Big Ideas for Little Philosophers Ser.: 1). (ENG.). 20p. (J). (— 1). bds. 8.99 ***(978-0-593-10884-0(1)***, G.P. Putnam's Sons Books for Young Readers) Penguin Young Readers Group.

—Big Ideas for Little Philosophers: Happiness with Aristotle. Armitage, Duane & McQuerry, Maureen. 2020. (Big Ideas for Little Philosophers Ser.: 2). (ENG.). 20p. (J). (— 1). bds. 8.99 ***(978-0-593-10881-9(7)***, G.P. Putnam's Sons Books for Young Readers) Penguin Young Readers Group.

—Big Ideas for Little Philosophers: Imagination with René Descartes. Armitage, Duane & McQuerry, Maureen. 2020. (Big Ideas for Little Philosophers Ser.: 3). (ENG.). 20p. (J). (— 1). bds. 8.99 ***(978-0-593-10878-9(7)***, G.P. Putnam's Sons Books for Young Readers) Penguin Young Readers Group.

—Big Ideas for Little Philosophers: Truth with Socrates. Armitage, Duane & McQuerry, Maureen. 2020. (Big Ideas for Little Philosophers Ser.: 4). (ENG.). 20p. (J). (— 1). bds. 8.99 ***(978-0-593-10875-8(2)***, G.P. Putnam's Sons Books for Young Readers) Penguin Young Readers Group.

Rosenthal, Robin. Two Dogs on a Trike. Snyder, Gabi. 2020. (ENG.). 32p. (J). (gr. -1-k). 16.99 *(978-1-4197-3891-3(7)*, 1291901, Abrams Appleseed) Abrams, Inc.

Rosenwasser, Robert. Biting Sun. Kitrilakis, Thalia. Rosenwasser, Rena, ed. 2011. 48p. (J). pap. 5.00 *(978-0-932716-17-0(2))* Kelsey Street Pr.

Rosenzweig, Sharon. The Comic Torah: Reimagining the Very Good Book. Rosenzweig, Sharon. Freeman, Aaron. 2010. (ENG.). 128p. (J). pap. 19.95 *(978-1-934730-54-6(8))* Yehuda, Ben Pr.

Roset, Conrad. Bob Dylan. Sanchez Vegara, Maria Isabel. ed. 2020. (Little People, BIG DREAMS Ser.: 37). (ENG.). 32p. (J). (gr. -1-2). 14.99 ***(978-0-7112-4674-4(2)***, 328350, Frances Lincoln Children's Bks.) Quarto Publishing Group UK GBR. Dist: Hachette UK Distribution.

Rosewarne, Graeme. My Book of Animals. Madgwick, Wendy. 2016. 48p. (J). (gr. -1-12). bds. 9.99 *(978-1-86147-768-2(6)*, Armadillo) Anness Publishing GBR. Dist: National Bk. Network.

Rosewarne, Graham. Alligator. Johnson, Jinny. 2007. (Zoo Animals in the Wild Ser.). 32p. (J). (gr. -1-3). lib. bdg. 28.50 *(978-1-58340-902-2(5))* Black Rabbit Bks.

—Brachiosaurus & Other Dinosaur Giants. Johnson, Jinny. 2009. (Dinosaurs Alive! Ser.). 32p. (J). (gr. 4-7). pap. 7.95 *(978-1-59920-182-5(8))* Black Rabbit Bks.

—Chimpanzee. Johnson, Jinny. 2007. (Zoo Animals in the Wild Ser.). 32p. (J). (gr. -1-3). lib. bdg. 28.50 *(978-1-58340-900-8(9))* Black Rabbit Bks.

—Dandelion. Johnson, Jinny. 2010. (J). 28.50 *(978-1-59920-351-5(0))* Black Rabbit Bks.

—Did Dinosaurs Lay Eggs? And Other Questions & Answers about Prehistoric Reptiles. Parker, Steve. 2016. 32p. 7.99 *(978-1-86147-481-0(4)*, Armadillo) Anness Publishing GBR. Dist: National Bk. Network.

Rosewarne, Graham, et al. Discover the Amazing World of Animals. 87p. (J). *(978-1-902272-27-6(7))* Tucker Slingsby, Ltd.

Rosewarne, Graham. Do Animals Go to School? And Other Questions & Answers about Animal Survival. Parker, Steve. 2016. 32p. 7.99 *(978-1-86147-479-7(2)*, Armadillo) Anness Publishing GBR. Dist: National Bk. Network.

—Do Animals Need Umbrellas? And Other Questions & Answers about Life in the Wild. Parker, Steve. 2016. 32p. 7.99 *(978-1-86147-478-0(4)*, Armadillo) Anness Publishing GBR. Dist: National Bk. Network.

—Elephant. Johnson, Jinny. 2005. (Zoo Animals in the Wild Ser.). 32p. (J). (gr. 2-5). lib. bdg. 27.10 *(978-1-58340-643-4(3))* Black Rabbit Bks.

—Fox. Johnson, Jinny. 2010. (J). 28.50 *(978-1-59920-354-6(5))* Black Rabbit Bks.

—Frog. Johnson, Jinny. 2010. (J). 28.50 *(978-1-59920-355-3(3))* Black Rabbit Bks.

—Iguanodon & Other Plant-Eating Dinosaurs. Johnson, Jinny. (Dinosaurs Alive! Ser.). 32p. (J). (gr. 4-7). 2009. pap. 7.95 *(978-1-59920-184-9(4))*; 2007. lib. bdg. 28.50 *(978-1-59920-067-5(8))* Black Rabbit Bks.

—Oak Tree. Johnson, Jinny. 2010. (J). 28.50 *(978-1-59920-356-0(1))* Black Rabbit Bks.

—Polar Bear. Johnson, Jinny. 2007. (Zoo Animals in the Wild Ser.). 32p. (J). (gr. -1-3). lib. bdg. 28.50 *(978-1-58340-901-5(7))* Black Rabbit Bks.

—Pteranodon & Other Flying Reptiles. Johnson, Jinny. (Dinosaurs Alive! Ser.). 32p. (J). (gr. 4-7). 2009. pap. 7.95 *(978-1-59920-185-6(2))*; 2007. lib. bdg. 28.50 *(978-1-59920-068-2(6))* Black Rabbit Bks.

—Triceratops & Other Horned & Armored Dinosaurs. Johnson, Jinny. 2009. (Dinosaurs Alive! Ser.). 32p. (J). (gr. 4-7). pap. 7.95 *(978-1-59920-181-8(X))* Black Rabbit Bks.

—Triceratops & Other Horned & Armored Dinosaurs. Johnson, Jinny. 2007. (Dinosaurs Alive! Ser.). 32p. (J). (gr. -1-3). lib. bdg. 28.50 *(978-1-59920-064-4(3))* Black Rabbit Bks.

—Tyrannosaurus & Other Mighty Hunters. Johnson, Jinny. (Dinosaurs Alive! Ser.). 32p. (J). 2009. (gr. 4-7). pap. 7.95 *(978-1-59920-180-1(1))*; 2007. (gr. -1-3). lib. bdg. 28.50 *(978-1-59920-063-7(5))* Black Rabbit Bks.

—Velociraptor & Other Speedy Killers. Johnson, Jinny. (Dinosaurs Alive! Ser.). 32p. (J). (gr. 4-7). 2009. pap. 7.95 *(978-1-59920-183-2(6))*; 2007. lib. bdg. 28.50 *(978-1-59920-066-8(X))* Black Rabbit Bks.

—Why Do Bugs Bite & Sting? And Other Questions & Answers about Creepy Crawlies. Parker, Steve. 2016. 32p. 7.99 *(978-1-86147-480-3(6)*, Armadillo) Anness Publishing GBR. Dist: National Bk. Network.

Rosinski. Giants. Hamme, Van. 2013. (Thorgal Ser.: 14). (ENG.). 48p. pap. 11.95 *(978-1-84918-156-3(X))* CineBook GBR. Dist: National Bk. Network.

—The Three Elders of Aran. Van Hamme, Jean. 2007. (Thorgal Ser.: 2). (ENG.). 96p. (J). (gr. 4-7). pap. 19.95 *(978-1-905460-31-1(7))* CineBook GBR. Dist: National Bk. Network.

Rosinski, Adolf. Child of the Stars. Van Hamme, Jean. 2007. (Thorgal Ser.: 1). (ENG.). 96p. per. 19.95 *(978-1-905460-23-6(6))* CineBook GBR. Dist: National Bk. Network.

Rosinski, Grzegorz. Beyond the Shadows. Van Hamme, Jean. 2008. (Thorgal Ser.: 3). (ENG.). 96p. pap. 19.95 *(978-1-905460-45-8(7))* CineBook GBR. Dist: National Bk. Network.

—Blackmore Vol. 2: Lament of the Lost Moors, Volume 2. Dufaux, Jean. 2014. (Lament of the Lost Moors Ser.: 2). (ENG.). 64p. pap. 15.95 *(978-1-84918-187-7(X))* CineBook GBR. Dist: National Bk. Network.

—The Brand of the Exiles. Van Hamme, Jean. 2013. (Thorgal Ser.: 12). (ENG.). 48p. (J). (gr. 7-12). pap. 11.95 *(978-1-84918-136-5(5))* CineBook GBR. Dist: National Bk. Network.

—The Cage, Vol. 15. Van Hamme, Jean. 2014. (Thorgal Ser.: 15). (ENG.). 48p. pap. 11.95 *(978-1-84918-186-0(1))* CineBook GBR. Dist: National Bk. Network.

—The Guardian of the Keys. Van Hamme, Jean. 2010. (Thorgal Ser.: 9). (ENG.). 48p. pap. 11.95 *(978-1-84918-050-4(4))* CineBook GBR. Dist: National Bk. Network.

—The Invisible Fortress. Van Hamme, Jean. 2012. (Thorgal Ser.: 11). (ENG.). 48p. (YA). (gr. 6-17). pap. 11.95 *(978-1-84918-103-7(9))* CineBook GBR. Dist: National Bk. Network.

—Mas alla de las Sombras, Vol. 5. Van Hamme, Jean. 2005. Orig. Title: Thorgal Vol. 5: Au-dela des Ombres. (SPA.). 48p. pap. 16.95 *(978-1-59497-010-8(6))* Public Square Bks.

—Ogotai's Crown. Van Hamme, Jean. 2013. (Thorgal Ser.: 13). (ENG.). 48p. pap. 11.95 *(978-1-84918-142-6(X))* CineBook GBR. Dist: National Bk. Network.

—Siobhan. Dufaux, Jean. 2014. (Lament of the Lost Moors Ser.: 1). (ENG.). 64p. pap. 15.95 *(978-1-84918-169-3(1))* CineBook GBR. Dist: National Bk. Network.

—Thorgal: La Isla de los Mares Helados, , Vol. 2. Van Hamme, Jean. 2004. Orig. Title: Thorgal vol. 2: L' ile des Mers Gelees. (SPA.). 48p. pap. 16.95 *(978-1-59497-007-8(6))* Public Square Bks.

—Thorgal: La Maga Traicionada. Van Hamme, Jean. 2004. Orig. Title: Thorgal vol. 1: la Magicienne Trahie. (SPA.). 48p. pap. 16.95 *(978-1-59497-006-1(8))* Public Square Bks.

—Thorgal Vol. 4: La Galera Negra. Van Hamme, Jean. 2004. Orig. Title: Thorgal: la Galere Negra. (SPA.). 48p. pap. 16.95 *(978-1-59497-009-2(2))* Public Square Bks.

—Thorgal - City of the Lost God, Vol. 6. van Hamme, Jean. 2009. (Thorgal Ser.: 6). (ENG.). 96p. pap. 19.95 *(978-1-84918-001-6(6))* CineBook GBR. Dist: National Bk. Network.

Roski, Gayle G. Endeavour's Long Journey/la Larga Travesía de Endeavour. Olivas, John D. 2016. (SPA.). 40p. (J). 19.95 *(978-0-9973947-2-6(2))* East West Discovery Pr.

Roski, Gayle Garner. Endeavour's Long Journey. Olivas, John D. 2013. (J). *(978-0-9856237-2-2(1))* East West Discovery Pr.

—Endeavour's Long Journey: Celebrating 19 Years of Space Exploration. Olivas, John D. 2013. (J). pap. *(978-0-9856237-3-9(X))* East West Discovery Pr.

—Mystery of the Giant Mask of Sanxingdui. Smith, Icy. 2015. (J). *(978-0-9913454-8-9(7))* East West Discovery Pr.

—Thomas the T. Rex: The Journey of a Young Dinosaur to Los Angeles. Smith, Michael. 2011. (J). *(978-0-9832278-4-7(5))*; 44p. (gr. 3-5). 19.95 *(978-0-9821675-3-3(9))* East West Discovery Pr.

Roski, Gayle Garner. Thomas the T. Rex: The Journey of a Young Dinosaur to Los Angeles. Roski, Gayle Garner. Smith, Michael. 2011. (SPA & ENG.). (J). *(978-0-9832278-2-3(9))* East West Discovery Pr.

Roskinski, Grzegorz. Los Tres Ancianos del pais de Aran, Vol. 3. Van Hamme, Jean. 2004. Orig. Title: Thorgal Vol. 3: les Trois Vieillards du Pays d'Aran. (SPA.). 48p. pap. 16.95 *(978-1-59497-008-5(4))* Public Square Bks.

Rosli, Shazana. Prophet Adam & Wicked Iblis. Taib, Saadah. 2019. (Prophets of Islam Activity Bks.). (ENG.). 16p. (J). pap. 3.95 *(978-0-86037-639-2(7))* Kube Publishing Ltd. GBR. Dist: Consortium Bk. Sales & Distribution.

—Prophet Ibrahim & the Little Bird Activity Book. Taib, Saadah. 2020. (Prophets of Islam Activity Bks.). (ENG.). 16p. (J). pap. 3.95 *(978-0-86037-740-5(7))* Kube Publishing Ltd. GBR. Dist: Consortium Bk. Sales & Distribution.

—Prophet Ismail & the ZamZam Well Activity Book. Taib, Saadah. 2020. (Prophets of Islam Activity Bks.). (ENG.). 16p. (J). pap. 3.95 *(978-0-86037-745-0(8))* Kube Publishing Ltd. GBR. Dist: Consortium Bk. Sales & Distribution.

—Prophet Muhammad & the Crying Camel Activity Book. Taib, Saadah. 2019. (Prophets of Islam Activity Bks.). (ENG.). 16p. (J). pap. 3.95 *(978-0-86037-634-7(6))* Kube Publishing Ltd. GBR. Dist: Consortium Bk. Sales & Distribution.

—Prophet Nuh & the Great Ark. Taib, Saadah. 2020. (Prophets of Islam Activity Bks.). (ENG.). 16p. (J). pap.

3.95 *(978-0-86037-644-6(3))* Kube Publishing Ltd. GBR. Dist: Consortium Bk. Sales & Distribution.

—Prophet Sulaiman & the Talking Ants. Taib, Saadah. 2020. (Prophets of Islam Activity Bks.). (ENG.). 16p. (J). pap. 3.95 *(978-0-86037-777-1(6))* Islamic Foundation, Ltd. GBR. Dist: Consortium Bk. Sales & Distribution.

Roslyn, Jacquelyn. The Peanut Pickle: A Story about Peanut Allergy. Ureel, Jessica & Jacobs, Jessica. 2012. 48p. (J). (gr. -1-3). 14.95 *(978-1-61608-672-5(6)*, 608672, Sky Pony Pr.) Skyhorse Publishing Co., Inc.

Ross. Don't Forget to Flush: A Bathroom Devotional for Kids, Vol. Alton, Kevin & Alton, Britta. 2017. (ENG.). 216p. (J). (gr. 4-6). pap. 14.99 *(978-1-5064-2701-0(4)*, Sparkhouse Family) Augsburg Fortress, Pubs.

Ross, Adam. Winston, the Polite St Bernard. Wainwright, Joann M. 2009. 28p. pap. 14.99 *(978-1-4389-2704-6(5))* AuthorHouse.

Ross, Alex. Marvels. Busiek, Kurt. Youngquist, Jeff, ed. 10th anniv. ed. 2004. (Marvel Heroes Ser.). 400p. (YA). 49.99 *(978-0-7851-1388-1(6))* Marvel Worldwide, Inc.

—Marvels 25th Anniversary Hardcover Edition. 2020. (ENG.). 504p. (YA). (gr. 4-17). 50.00 *(978-1-302-91987-0(3))* Marvel Worldwide, Inc.

—Marvels Monster-Sized Edition. 2019. (ENG.). 328p. (YA). (gr. 4-17). 75.00 *(978-1-302-91422-6(7))* Marvel Worldwide, Inc.

—Marvels Postcard Book. 2019. (ENG.). 84p. (YA). (gr. -1-17). pap. 19.99 *(978-1-302-91889-7(3))* Marvel Worldwide, Inc.

Ross, Alex & Braithwaite, Doug. Paradise X, 5 vols., Vol. 4. Kruger, Jim. 2003. (Universe X Ser.). 304p. (YA). pap. 29.99 *(978-0-7851-1120-7(4))* Marvel Worldwide, Inc.

Ross, Andrea. Turtles Go Slow. Ross, Andrea. 2003. 25p. (J). (gr. 1-3). pap. 7.95 *(978-1-887683-45-6(3))* Storybook Pr. & Productions.

Ross, Andrew J. Birthday on Mars! Schonfeld, Sara. 2019. 32p. (J). (gr. k-3). 8.99 *(978-1-5247-9122-3(9)*, Penguin Workshop) Penguin Young Readers Group.

Ross, Andrew J. Heart on Pluto. Jones, Karl. 2020. 32p. (J). (gr. k-3). 8.99 ***(978-0-593-09629-1(0)***, Penguin Workshop) Penguin Young Readers Group.

Ross, Bob & Kayser, Jason. Bob Ross & Peapod the Squirrel. Pearlman, Robb. 2019. (Bob Ross & Peapod Story Ser.). 32p. (J). (gr. -1-3). 17.99 *(978-0-7624-6779-2(7)*, Running Pr. Kids) Running Pr.

Ross, C. Century Club. Dorison, Xavier & Nury, Fabian. 2012. (Spooks Ser.: 2). (ENG.). 56p. (J). (gr. 10-12). pap. 13.95 *(978-1-84918-129-7(2))* CineBook GBR. Dist: National Bk. Network.

Ross, Christine. A Quick Picnic, 6 pack. Holden, Pam. 2009. (Red Rocket Readers Ser.). 16p. (gr. -1-1). pap. *(978-1-877363-22-1(7)*, Red Rocket Readers) Flying Start Bks.

—Weather: KinderConcepts Individual Title Six-Packs. Wallace, Jessica. (Kinderstarters Ser.). 8p. (gr. -1-1). 21.00 *(978-0-7635-8725-3(7))* Rigby Education.

Ross, Chrystal. God's Great Helper Featuring Ari the Dove. Ecclesiastes, Anthony. 2016. (ENG.). (J). pap. 18.95 *(978-0-9971037-2-4(8))* Abba's Hse. International Publishing.

Ross, Daniel Vaughn. The Fake Heir. Petrucha, Stefan et al. 2006. (J). *(978-1-59707-060-7(2))* Papercutz.

Ross, Dave, et al. Excalibur Epic Collection: Girl's School from Heck. 2019. (ENG.). 464p. (YA). (gr. 8-17). pap. 39.99 *(978-1-302-91652-7(1))* Marvel Worldwide, Inc.

Ross, Dave. Star Wars Legends Epic Collection: Legacy Vol. 3. 2020. 448p. (J). (gr. 4-17). pap. 39.99 ***(978-1-302-92375-4(7))*** Marvel Worldwide, Inc.

Ross, Dave. The Not-so-Scary Monster Handbook: Halloween. Ross, Dave. 2003. (J). 135.44 *(978-0-06-055492-7(4))* HarperCollins Pubs.

Ross, Dave, jt. illus. see Haynes, Rob.

Ross, Deborah. Ny Aiay Ako: Ako the Aye-Aye. Jolly, Alison. Rasamimanana, Hantanirina, tr. 2005. (MLA & ENG.). (J). 20.00 *(978-0-9766009-0-9(0))* Lemur Conservation Foundation.

Ross, Graham. And the Stink Spectacular. Sharpe, Luke. 2015. (Billy Sure Kid Entrepreneur Ser.: 2). (ENG.). 160p. (J). (gr. 3-7). 17.99 *(978-1-4814-3951-0(0)*, Simon Spotlight) Simon Spotlight.

—The Best Test. Sharpe, Luke. 2015. (Billy Sure Kid Entrepreneur Ser.: 4). (ENG.). 160p. (J). (gr. 3-7). 17.99 *(978-1-4814-4765-2(3)*, Simon Spotlight) Simon Spotlight.

—Billy Sure Kid Entrepreneur. Sharpe, Luke. 2015. (Billy Sure Kid Entrepreneur Ser.: 1). (ENG.). 160p. (J). (gr. 3-7). pap. 6.99 *(978-1-4814-3947-3(2)*, Simon Spotlight) Simon Spotlight.

—Billy Sure Kid Entrepreneur & the Attack of the Mysterious Lunch Meat. Sharpe, Luke. 2017. (Billy Sure Kid Entrepreneur Ser.: 12). (ENG.). 160p. (J). (gr. 3-7). pap. 6.99 *(978-1-4814-7909-7(1)*, Simon Spotlight) Simon Spotlight.

—Billy Sure, Kid Entrepreneur & the Best Test. Sharpe, Luke. 2015. 147p. (J). *(978-1-4242-6365-3(4)*, Simon Spotlight) Simon Spotlight.

—Billy Sure Kid Entrepreneur & the Best Test. Sharpe, Luke. 2015. (Billy Sure Kid Entrepreneur Ser.: 4). (ENG.). 160p. (J). (gr. 3-7). pap. 6.99 *(978-1-4814-4764-5(5)*, Simon Spotlight) Simon Spotlight.

—Billy Sure, Kid Entrepreneur & the Cat-Dog Translator. Sharpe, Luke. 2015. (Billy Sure Kid Entrepreneur Ser.: 3). (ENG.). 160p. (J). (gr. 3-7). 17.99 *(978-1-4814-4762-1(9)*, Simon Spotlight) Simon Spotlight.

—Billy Sure Kid Entrepreneur & the Cat-Dog Translator. Sharpe, Luke. 2015. (Billy Sure Kid Entrepreneur Ser.: 3). (ENG.). 160p. (J). (gr. 3-7). pap. 6.99 *(978-1-4814-4761-4(0)*, Simon Spotlight) Simon Spotlight.

—Billy Sure Kid Entrepreneur & the Everything Locator. Sharpe, Luke. 2016. (Billy Sure Kid Entrepreneur Ser.: 10). (ENG.). 160p. (J). (gr. 3-7). pap. 6.99 *(978-1-4814-6898-5(7)*, Simon Spotlight) Simon Spotlight.

—Billy Sure Kid Entrepreneur & the Haywire Hovercraft. Sharpe, Luke. 2016. (Billy Sure Kid Entrepreneur Ser.: 7). (ENG.). 160p. (J). (gr. 3-7). pap. 6.99 *(978-1-4814-6193-1(1)*, Simon Spotlight) Simon Spotlight.

—Billy Sure Kid Entrepreneur & the Invisible Inventor. Sharpe, Luke. 2016. (Billy Sure Kid Entrepreneur Ser.: 8). (ENG.). 160p. (J). (gr. 3-7). pap. 6.99 *(978-1-4814-6196-2(6)*, Simon Spotlight) Simon Spotlight.

—Billy Sure Kid Entrepreneur & the No-Trouble Bubble. Sharpe, Luke. 2016. (Billy Sure Kid Entrepreneur Ser.: 5). (ENG.). 160p. (J). (gr. 3-7). pap. 6.99 *(978-1-4814-5274-8(6)*, Simon Spotlight) Simon Spotlight.

—Billy Sure Kid Entrepreneur & the Stink Spectacular. Sharpe, Luke. 2015. (Billy Sure Kid Entrepreneur Ser.: 2). (ENG.). 160p. (J). (gr. 3-7). pap. 6.99 *(978-1-4814-3950-3(2)*, Simon Spotlight) Simon Spotlight.

—Billy Sure, Kid Entrepreneur Is a Spy! Sharpe, Luke. 2016. 141p. (J). *(978-1-4242-6367-7(0)*, Simon Spotlight) Simon Spotlight.

—Billy Sure Kid Entrepreneur Is NOT a SINGER! Sharpe, Luke. 2016. (Billy Sure Kid Entrepreneur Ser.: 9). (ENG.). 160p. (J). (gr. 3-7). pap. 6.99 *(978-1-4814-6895-4(2)*, Simon Spotlight) Simon Spotlight.

—Cheetah, 1 vol. Lewis, Wendy A. 2007. (Orca Echoes Ser.). (ENG.). 64p. (J). (gr. 1-3). per. 6.95 *(978-1-55143-465-0(2))* Orca Bk. Pubs. USA.

Ross, Graham. The DATA Set Collection #2: A Case of the Clones; Invasion of the Insects; Out of Remote Control; down the Brain Drain. Hopper, Ada. 2020. (DATA Set Ser.). (ENG.). 512p. (J). (gr. k-4). pap. 23.99 ***(978-1-5344-6535-0(9)***, Little Simon) Little Simon.

Ross, Graham. The No-Trouble Bubble. Sharpe, Luke. 2016. (Billy Sure Kid Entrepreneur Ser.: 5). (ENG.). 160p. (J). (gr. 3-7). 17.99 *(978-1-4814-5275-5(4)*, Simon Spotlight) Simon Spotlight.

—Out of Remote Control. Hopper, Ada. 2017. (DATA Set Ser.: 7). (ENG.). 128p. (J). (gr. k-4). 16.99 *(978-1-4814-9192-1(X))*; pap. 5.99 *(978-1-4814-9191-4(1))* Little Simon. (Little Simon).

—The Paper Wagon. Attema, Martha. 2005. 61p. (J). lib. bdg. 20.00 *(978-1-4242-1260-6(X))* Fitzgerald Bks.

—The Paper Wagon, 1 vol. Attema, Martha. 2005. (Orca Echoes Ser.). (ENG.). 64p. (J). (gr. 1-3). per. 6.95 *(978-1-55143-356-1(7))* Orca Bk. Pubs. USA.

—Timberwolf Prey, 1 vol. Brouwer, Sigmund. ed. 2010. (Orca Echoes Ser.). (ENG.). 64p. (J). (gr. 1-3). pap. 6.95 *(978-1-55469-109-8(5))* Orca Bk. Pubs. USA.

—Timberwolf Rivals, 1 vol. Brouwer, Sigmund. 2009. (Orca Echoes Ser.). (ENG.). 64p. (J). (gr. 1-3). pap. 6.95 *(978-1-55469-107-4(9))* Orca Bk. Pubs. USA.

—Timberwolf Tracks, 1 vol. Brouwer, Sigmund. 2009. (Orca Echoes Ser.). (ENG.). 64p. (J). (gr. 1-3). pap. 6.95 *(978-1-55143-734-7(1))* Orca Bk. Pubs. USA.

—What a Hippopota-Mess!, 1 vol. Skene, Pat. 2006. (Orca Echoes Ser.). (ENG.). 64p. (J). (gr. 1-3). per. 4.99 *(978-1-55143-402-5(4))* Orca Bk. Pubs. USA.

—The Wrong Shoes: A Book about Money & Self-Esteem, Vol. Rivadeneira, Caryn. 2018. (ENG.). 64p. (J). 14.99 *(978-1-5064-4681-3(7)*, Beaming Books) Augsburg Fortress, Pubs.

Ross, Graham T. Monster Lunch, 1 vol. Skene, Pat. 2008. (Orca Echoes Ser.). (ENG.). 64p. (J). (gr. 1-3). pap. 6.95 *(978-1-55143-941-9(7))* Orca Bk. Pubs. USA.

Ross, Heather. Crafty Chloe. DiPucchio, Kelly. 2012. (Crafty Chloe Ser.). (ENG.). 40p. (J). (gr. -1-3). 16.99 *(978-1-4424-2123-3(1)*, Atheneum Bks. for Young Readers) Simon & Schuster Children's Publishing.

—Dress-Up Mess-up. DiPucchio, Kelly. 2013. (Crafty Chloe Ser.). (ENG.). 40p. (J). (gr. -1-3). 16.99 *(978-1-4424-2124-0(X))* Simon & Schuster Children's Publishing.

—Fergus & Zeke. Messner, Kate. (Candlewick Sparks Ser.). 56p. (J). (gr. k-4). 2018. (ENG.). pap. 4.99 *(978-0-7636-9953-6(5))*; 2017. 14.99 *(978-0-7636-7846-3(5))* Candlewick Pr.

—Fergus & Zeke & the Field Day Challenge. Messner, Kate. 2020. (Fergus & Zeke Ser.). 56p. (J). (gr. k-3). 14.99 *(978-1-5362-0202-1(9))* Candlewick Pr.

—Fergus & Zeke at the Science Fair. Messner, Kate. (Candlewick Sparks Ser.). 48p. (J). 2019. (ENG.). (gr. k-4). pap. 4.99 *(978-1-5362-0899-3(X))*; 2018. (gr. 1-4). 14.99 *(978-0-7636-7847-0(3))* Candlewick Pr.

—Grimelda & the Spooktacular Pet Show. Murray, Diana. 2017. (ENG.). 40p. (J). (gr. -1-3). 16.99 *(978-0-06-226449-7(4)*, Tegen, Katherine Bks) HarperCollins Pubs.

—Grimelda: the Very Messy Witch. Murray, Diana. 2016. (ENG.). 32p. (J). (gr. -1-3). 16.99 *(978-0-06-226448-0(6)*, Tegen, Katherine Bks) HarperCollins Pubs.

—How to Behave at a Dog Show. Rosenberg, Madelyn. 2015. (ENG.). 32p. (J). (gr. -1-3). 17.99 *(978-0-06-227927-9(0))* HarperCollins Pubs.

—How to Behave at a Tea Party. Rosenberg, Madelyn. 2014. (ENG.). 32p. (J). (gr. -1-3). 17.99 *(978-0-06-227926-2(2)*, Tegen, Katherine Bks) HarperCollins Pubs.

—Mo Wren, Lost & Found. Springstubb, Tricia. 2011. (Fox Street Ser.: 2). (ENG.). 256p. (J). (gr. 3-7). 15.99 *(978-0-06-199039-7(6)*, Balzer & Bray) HarperCollins Pubs.

—No Dogs Allowed. Calmenson, Stephanie & Cole, Joanna. 2014. (Ready, Set, Dogs! Ser.: 1). (ENG.). 144p. (J). (gr. 1-4). pap. 5.99 *(978-1-250-04414-3(6)*, 9781250044143) Square Fish.

—Teacher's Pets. Calmenson, Stephanie & Cole, Joanna. 2015. (Ready, Set, Dogs! Ser.: 2). (ENG.). 144p. (J). (gr. 1-4). pap. 11.99 *(978-1-250-05705-1(1)*, 900139115) Square Fish.

—What Happened on Fox Street. Springstubb, Tricia. 2011. (Fox Street Ser.: 1). (ENG.). 240p. (J). (gr. 3-7). pap. 7.99 *(978-0-06-198636-9(4)*, Balzer & Bray) HarperCollins Pubs.

Ross, Julie. The Door in the Floor. Pimot, Karen Hutchins. 2009. 24p. pap. 12.95 *(978-0-9823002-6-8(3))* Peppertree Pr., The.

—Sam's Perfect Plan. Pimot, Karen Hutchins. 2008. 32p. pap. 12.95 *(978-0-9814894-8-3(6))* Peppertree Pr., The.

Ross Kennedy. Revenge of the Cannibal Chickens. Lihou, Gavin. 2013. 74p. pap. 10.50 *(978-1-62212-484-8(7)*, Strategic Bk. Publishing) Strategic Book Publishing & Rights Agency (SBPRA).

Ross, Leanne R. The Wandering Pirate Ship. Schmal, Mary I. 2018. (Children of the Light Ser.: Vol. 1). (ENG.). 220p. (J). 30.95 *(978-1-64140-191-3(5))* Christian Faith Publishing.

Ross, Luke. Star Wars: Darth Maul. 2017. 112p. (J). (gr. 4-17). pap. 16.99 *(978-0-7851-9589-4(0))* Marvel Worldwide, Inc.

—Star Wars: the Force Awakens Adaptation. 2017. (ENG.). 144p. (J). (gr. 4-17). pap. 19.99 *(978-1-302-90203-2(2))* Marvel Worldwide, Inc.

Ross, Luke & Martin, Frank. The Force Awakens: Volume 1. Wendig, Chuck. 2017. (Star Wars: the Force Awakens Ser.). (ENG.). 32p. (J). (gr. 6-12). lib. bdg. 27.07 *(978-1-5321-4022-8(3)*, 25454, Graphic Novels) Spotlight.

—The Force Awakens: Volume 2. Wendig, Chuck. 2017. (Star Wars: the Force Awakens Ser.). (ENG.). 24p. (J). (gr. 6-12). lib. bdg. 27.07 *(978-1-5321-4023-5(1)*, 25455, Graphic Novels) Spotlight.

—The Force Awakens: Volume 4. Wendig, Chuck. 2017. (Star Wars: the Force Awakens Ser.). (ENG.). 24p. (J). (gr. 6-12). lib. bdg. 27.07 *(978-1-5321-4025-9(8)*, 25457, Graphic Novels) Spotlight.

—The Force Awakens: Volume 5. Wendig, Chuck. 2017. (Star Wars: the Force Awakens Ser.). (ENG.). 24p. (J). (gr. 6-12). lib. bdg. 27.07 *(978-1-5321-4026-6(6)*, 25458, Graphic Novels) Spotlight.

—The Force Awakens: Volume 6. Wendig, Chuck. 2017. (Star Wars: the Force Awakens Ser.). (ENG.). 24p. (J). (gr. 6-12). lib. bdg. 27.07 *(978-1-5321-4027-3(4)*, 25459, Graphic Novels) Spotlight.

Ross, Luke & Smith, Cory. Star Wars: Age of Republic. 2020. (ENG.). 224p. (YA). (gr. 4-17). 34.99 *(978-1-302-91709-8(9))* Marvel Worldwide, Inc.

Ross, M. Flower Children: The Little Cousins of the Field & Garden. Gordon, Elizabeth. 2008. (ENG.). 96p. (J). (gr. -1-3). pap. 14.95 *(978-1-55709-086-7(6))* Applewood Bks.

Ross, M. T. Animal Children: The Friends of the Forest & the Plain. Kirkwood, Edith Brown. 2007. 100p. per. *(978-1-4065-2907-4(9))* Dodo Pr.

—Bird Children. Gordon, Elizabeth. 2011. (ENG.). (J). (gr. -1-3). 14.95 *(978-1-55709-083-6(1))* Applewood Bks.

—Bird Children: The Little Playmates of the Flower Children. Gordon, Elizabeth. 2008. (ENG.). 96p. (J). (gr. -1-3). pap. 14.95 *(978-1-55709-087-4(4))* Applewood Bks.

Ross, Melissa. Scriptures for Kids. Arbo, Barbara. 2013. 24p. 19.95 *(978-1-61633-402-4(9))*; pap. 10.95 *(978-1-61633-403-1(7))* Guardian Angel Publishing, Inc.

—Sparky & Jimmy: Sparky's Uganda Adventure. Brewer, Leanna. l.t. ed. 2018. (Sparky & Jimmy Ser.: Vol. 1). (ENG.). 24p. (J). (gr. k-4). pap. 10.95 *(978-1-61633-921-0(7))* Guardian Angel Publishing, Inc.

—Sparky's Amazon Adventure. Brewer, Leanna Jayne. l.t. ed. 2019. (ENG.). 24p. (J). (gr. k-3). pap. 10.95 *(978-1-61633-982-1(9))* Guardian Angel Publishing, Inc.

Ross, Melissa. Today I Am a Penguin. Ross, Melissa. 2012. 24p. pap. 10.95 *(978-1-61633-306-5(5))* Guardian Angel Publishing, Inc.

Ross, Sharon & Bergman, Shannon. Cookie Crisis! Willson, Sarah. ed. 2005. 32p. (J). lib. bdg. 15.00 *(978-1-59054-981-0(3))* Fitzgerald Bks.

Ross, Sonny. Duck Gets a Job. Ross, Sonny. 2018. (ENG.). 32p. (J). (gr. -1-2). 16.99 *(978-0-7636-9896-6(2)*, Templar) Candlewick Pr.

Ross, Suzy. Supporting Kids & Teens with Exam Stress in School: A Workbook. Steer, Joanne. 2019. (ENG.). 184p. wbk. ed. 32.95 ***(978-1-78592-467-5(2)***, 696764) Kingsley, Jessica Pubs. GBR. Dist: Hachette UK Distribution.

Ross, Sylvia. Lion Singer. Ross, Sylvia. 2005. 33p. (J). (gr. 3-7). 12.95 *(978-1-59714-009-6(0)*, Great Valley Bks.) Heyday.

Ross, Tony. The Adventures of Mademoiselle Charlotte, 3 vols. Demers, Dominique. 2019. 1p. (J). 29.97 *(978-1-84688-461-0(6)*, 442852) Alma Bks. GBR. Dist: Bloomsbury Publishing Plc.

—Alice's Adventures in Wonderland. Carroll, Lewis. 2008. (Puffin Classics Ser.). (ENG.). 176p. (J). (gr. 5-7). 6.99 *(978-0-14-132107-3(5)*, Puffin Books) Penguin Young Readers Group.

—Ámbar en Cuarto y Sin Su Amigo, Level 3.7. Danziger, Paula. 2003.Tr. of Amber Brown Goes Fourth. (SPA.). 136p. (J). (gr. 3-5). pap. 10.95 *(978-84-204-4412-3(X)*, SAN412X) Ediciones Alfaguara ESP. Dist: Santillana USA Publishing Co., Inc.

—Amber Brown Goes Fourth. Danziger, Paula. 2007. (Amber Brown Ser.: No. 3). 101p. (gr. 2-5). 15.00 *(978-0-7569-8197-6(2))* Perfection Learning Corp.

—Amber Brown Is Green with Envy. Danziger, Paula. 2004. (Amber Brown Ser.: No. 9). 151p. (J). (gr. 2-5). 12.65 *(978-0-7569-2978-7(4))* Perfection Learning Corp.

—Amber Brown Is Not a Crayon. Danziger, Paula. 2006. (Amber Brown Ser.: 1). (ENG.). 96p. (J). (gr. 2-5). 5.99 *(978-0-14-240619-8(8)*, Puffin Books) Penguin Young Readers Group.

—Amber Brown Is Tickled Pink. Danziger, Paula et al. 2013. (Amber Brown Ser.: 10). (ENG.). 176p. (J). (gr. 2-5). pap. 6.99 *(978-0-14-242757-6(8)*, Puffin Books) Penguin Young Readers Group.

—Amber Brown Wants Extra Credit. Danziger, Paula. 2008. (Amber Brown Ser.: 4). (ENG.). 144p. (J). (gr. 2-5). 6.99 *(978-0-14-241049-3(7)*, Puffin Books) Penguin Young Readers Group.

—Las Aventuras de Ulises. McCaughrean, Geraldine. Barroso, Paz, tr. 2005. (Mythology Series Collection Mitos Ser.).Tr. of Odysseus. (SPA.). 48p. (J). (gr. 2-3). 9.95 *(978-84-348-6426-9(6))* SM Ediciones ESP. Dist: Iaconi, Mariuccia Bk. Imports.

—Bad Dad. Walliams, David. 2019. (ENG.). 448p. (J). (gr. 3-7). 16.99 *(978-0-06-256110-7(3))* HarperCollins Pubs.

—Bad Dad. Walliams, David. 2017. (ENG.). 448p. (J). *(978-0-00-816466-9(5))* HarperCollins Pubs. Ltd.

—Bad Dad. Walliams, David. 2020. (ENG.). 464p. (J). (gr. 3-7). pap. 7.99 *(978-0-06-256109-1(X)*, HarperCollins) HarperCollins Pubs. Ltd. GBR. Dist: HarperCollins Pubs.

—Bah! Humbug! Rosen, Michael. 2018. (ENG.). 192p. (J). (gr. 3-7). 15.99 *(978-1-5362-0479-7(X))* Candlewick Pr.

—Barking for Bagels. Rosen, Michael. 2017. 96p. (J). (gr. 2-4). pap. 10.99 *(978-1-78344-505-9(X))* Andersen Pr. GBR. Dist: Independent Pubs. Group.

—The Bath Monster. Boyd, Colin. 2016. (ENG.). 32p. (J). (gr. -1-3). 17.99 *(978-1-5124-0426-5(8)*, 9781512404265) Lerner Publishing Group.

—Best Friends! Finney, Wendy. 2019. (Not-So-Little Princess Colour Readers Ser.: 2). 64p. (J). (gr. k-2). 9.99 *(978-1-78344-511-0(4))* Penguin Random Hse. AUS. Dist: Independent Pubs. Group.

—Bilal's Brilliant Bee. Rosen, Michael. 2016. 96p. (J). (gr. k-2). pap. 10.99 *(978-1-78344-395-6(2))* Andersen Pr. GBR. Dist: Independent Pubs. Group.

—Billionaire Baim: Billionaire Boy in Scots. Walliams, David. Fitt, Matthew, tr. 2015. 288p. (J). (gr. 1-7). pap. 10.99 *(978-1-84502-995-1(X)*, Itchy Coo) Black and White Publishing Ltd. GBR. Dist: Independent Pubs. Group.

—Binny Bewitched. McKay, Hilary. 2017. (ENG.). 240p. (J). (gr. 3-7). 17.99 *(978-1-4814-9102-0(4)*, McElderry, Margaret K. Bks.) McElderry, Margaret K. Bks.

Ross, Tony. The Binny Collection: Binny for Short; Binny in Secret; Binny Bewitched. McKay, Hilary. ed. 2020. (ENG.). 816p. (J). (gr. 3-7). pap. 24.99 ***(978-1-5344-6258-8(9)***, McElderry, Margaret K. Bks.) McElderry, Margaret K. Bks.

Ross, Tony. Boa's Bad Birthday. Willis, Jeanne. 2014. (ENG.). 32p. (J). (gr. -1-3). 16.95 *(978-1-4677-3450-9(0)*, 9781467734509) Lerner Publishing Group.

—Bob the Bursting Bear. Rosen, Michael. 2013. (ENG.). 32p. (J). (gr. -1-k). 17.99 *(978-1-84939-440-6(7))* Andersen Pr. GBR. Dist: Independent Pubs. Group.

—Bravo, Max! Grindley, Sally. 2007. (ENG.). 160p. (J). (gr. 1-4). pap. 8.99 *(978-1-4169-3645-9(9)*, Simon & Schuster/Paula Wiseman Bks.) Simon & Schuster/Paula Wiseman Bks.

—El Caballo de Madera. McCaughrean, Geraldine. Barroso, Paz, tr. 2005. (Mythology Series Collection Mitos Ser.).Tr. of Wooden Horse (Pandora's Box). (SPA.). 50p. (J). (gr. 2-3). 9.95 *(978-84-348-6432-0(0))* SM Ediciones ESP. Dist: Iaconi, Mariuccia Bk. Imports.

—Caterpillar Dreams. Willis, Jeanne. 2013. 32p. (J). (gr. -1-k). pap. 8.99 *(978-1-84939-025-5(8))* Andersen Pr. GBR. Dist: Independent Pubs. Group.

—Chicken Clicking. Willis, Jeanne. ed. 2015. (ENG.). 32p. (J). (gr. -1-k). pap. 14.99 *(978-1-78344-161-7(5))* Andersen Pr. GBR. Dist: Independent Pubs. Group.

—Class Six & the Very Big Rabbit: Band 10/White (Collins Big Cat) Waddell, Martin. 2005. (Collins Big Cat Ser.). (ENG.). 32p. (J). (gr. 1-3). pap. 9.99 *(978-0-00-718629-7(0))* HarperCollins Pubs. Ltd. GBR. Dist: Independent Pubs. Group.

—Cottonball Colin. Willis, Jeanne. 2008. 26p. (J). (gr. -1-4). 16.00 *(978-0-8028-5331-8(5)*, Eerdmans Bks For Young Readers) Eerdmans, William B. Publishing Co.

—Daft Bat. Willis, Jeanne. 2007. (ENG.). 32p. (J). (gr. k-2). 16.95 *(978-1-84270-476-9(1))* Transworld Publishers Ltd. GBR. Dist: Independent Pubs. Group.

—Dear Little Wolf. Whybrow, Ian. 2005. (Little Wolf Adventures Ser.). 64p. (J). (gr. 3-6). pap., lib. bdg. 14.95 *(978-0-87614-902-7(6))* Lerner Publishing Group.

—Dear Max. Grindley, Sally. 2006. (ENG.). 144p. (J). (gr. 2-4). 17.44 *(978-1-4169-0392-5(5))* Simon & Schuster, Inc.

—Dear Max. Grindley, Sally. 2007. (ENG.). 144p. (J). (gr. 1-4). pap. 7.99 *(978-1-4169-3443-1(X)*, Simon & Schuster/Paula Wiseman Bks.) Simon & Schuster/Paula Wiseman Bks.

—Dédalo e Ícaro: El Rey Midas. McCaughrean, Geraldine. Barroso, Paz, tr. 2nd ed. 2005. (Mythology Series Collection Mitos Ser.).Tr. of Daedalus & Icarus (King Midas). (SPA.). 48p. (J). (gr. 2-3). 9.95 *(978-84-348-6431-3(2))* SM Ediciones ESP. Dist: Iaconi, Mariuccia Bk. Imports.

—Demon Dentist. Walliams, David. 2016. (ENG.). (J). (gr. 3-7). 464p. pap. 7.99 *(978-0-06-241705-3(3))*; 448p. 16.99 *(978-0-06-241704-6(5))* HarperCollins Pubs.

—The Disappearing Daughter. Mitchelhill, Barbara. 2018. (No. 1 Boy Detective Ser.). 64p. (J). (gr. 2-4). pap. 9.99 *(978-1-78344-662-9(5))* Andersen Pr. GBR. Dist: Independent Pubs. Group.

—Los Doce Trabajos de Hércules: Eco y Narciso. McCaughrean, Geraldine. Barroso, Paz, tr. 2005. (Mythology Series Collection Mitos Ser.).Tr. of Twelve Labours of Heracles. (SPA.). 48p. (J). (gr. 2-3). 9.95 *(978-84-348-6429-0(0))* SM Ediciones ESP. Dist: Iaconi, Mariuccia Bk. Imports.

—Dog Snatchers. Mitchelhill, Barbara. 2018. (No. 1 Boy Detective Ser.). 64p. (J). (gr. 2-4). 9.99 *(978-1-78344-667-4(6))* Andersen Pr. GBR. Dist: Independent Pubs. Group.

—Dozy Mare. Willis, Jeanne. 2006. (ENG.). 32p. (J). (gr. k-2). pap. 9.99 *(978-1-84270-524-7(5))* Andersen Pr. GBR. Dist: Independent Pubs. Group.

—Dr Xargle's Book of Earth Relations. Willis, Jeanne. (ENG.). 32p. (J). pap. 9.99 *(978-1-84270-307-6(2))* Andersen Pr. GBR. Dist: Trafalgar Square Publishing.

—Dr Xargle's Book of Earth Tiggers. Willis, Jeanne. 2012. 28p. (J). (gr. -1-k). pap. 11.99 *(978-1-84939-297-6(8))* Andersen Pr. GBR. Dist: Independent Pubs. Group.

—Dr Xargle's Book of Earthlets. Willis, Jeanne. 2012. (ENG.). 28p. (J). (gr. -1-k). pap. 12.99 *(978-1-84939-292-1(7))* Andersen Pr. GBR. Dist: Independent Pubs. Group.

—Eric & the Green-Eyed God. Mitchelhill, Barbara. 2020. (Eric Ser.: 4). 64p. (J). (gr. 2-4). 11.99 *(978-1-78344-901-9(2))* Andersen Pr. GBR. Dist: Independent Pubs. Group.

—Eric & the Pimple Potion. Mitchelhill, Barbara. 2019. (Eric Ser.: 3). 64p. (J). (gr. k-2). pap. 11.99 *(978-1-78344-827-2(X))* Andersen Pr. GBR. Dist: Independent Pubs. Group.

R

—Eric & the Striped Horror. Mitchelhill, Barbara. 2019. 64p. (J). (gr. 2-4). pap. 11.99 *(978-1-78344-796-1(6))* Penguin Random Hse. AUS. Dist: Independent Pubs. Group.

Ross, Tony. Eric & the Voice of Doom. Mitchelhill, Barbara. 2020. (Eric Ser.: 5). 64p. (J). (gr. 2). 9.99 ***(978-1-78344-956-9(X))*** Andersen Pr. GBR. Dist: Independent Pubs. Group.

Ross, Tony. Eric & the Wishing Stone. Mitchelhill, Barbara. 2019. 64p. (J). (gr. 2-4). pap. 11.99 *(978-1-78344-797-8(4))* Penguin Random Hse. AUS. Dist: Independent Pubs. Group.

—Es Dia de Feria, Ambar Dorado. Danziger, Paula. 2007. (de Ámbar / a Is for Amber Easy-To-Read Ser.).Tr. of It's a Fair Day, Amber Brown. (SPA.). 48p. (gr. k-3). pap. 8.95 *(978-1-59820-596-1(X))* Santillana USA Publishing Co., Inc.

—Flabby Cat & Slobby Dog. Willis, Jeanne. 2009. (Andersen Press Picture Bks). (ENG.). 32p. (J). (gr. -1-3). 16.95 *(978-0-7613-5151-1(5)*, Carolrhoda Bks.) Lerner Publishing Group.

—Fly, Chick, Fly! Willis, Jeanne. 2012. (Andersen Press Picture Bks). (ENG.). 32p. (J). (gr. -1-3). 16.95 *(978-1-4677-0314-7(1))* Lerner Publishing Group.

—Football Forgery. Mitchelhill, Barbara. 2018. (No. 1 Boy Detective Ser.). 64p. (J). (gr. 2-4). pap. 9.99 *(978-1-78344-670-4(6))* Andersen Pr. GBR. Dist: Independent Pubs. Group.

—Get Ready for Second Grade, Amber Brown. Danziger, Paula. 2003. (Is for Amber Ser.: 4). (ENG.). 48p. (J). (gr. -1-3). mass mkt. 4.99 *(978-0-14-250081-1(X)*, Penguin Young Readers) Penguin Young Readers Group.

—Get Ready for Second Grade, Amber Brown. Danziger, Paula. 2004. (A Is for Amber Ser.). 48p. (gr. k-2). 14.00 *(978-0-7569-2177-4(5))* Perfection Learning Corp.

—Get Ready for Second Grade, Amber Brown. Danzinger, Paula. 2003. pap. 31.95 incl. audio compact disk *(978-1-59112-562-4(6))*; (J). 25.95 incl. audio *(978-1-59112-234-0(1))*; (J). pap. 29.95 incl. audio *(978-1-59112-235-7(X))* Live Oak Media.

—Goldilocks. Willis, Jeanne. 2019. (Online Safety Picture Bks.). 32p. (J). (gr. -1-k). 16.99 *(978-1-78344-717-6(6))* Penguin Random Hse. AUS. Dist: Independent Pubs. Group.

—Goldilocks (a Hashtag Cautionary Tale) Willis, Jeanne. 2020. (Online Safety Picture Bks.). 32p. (J). (gr. -1-k). pap. 12.99 *(978-1-78344-878-4(4))* Andersen Pr. GBR. Dist: Independent Pubs. Group.

—Grandpa's Great Escape. Walliams, David. (ENG.). (J). (gr. 3-7). 2018. 480p. pap. 7.99 *(978-0-06-256090-2(5))*; 2017. 464p. 16.99 *(978-0-06-256089-6(1))* HarperCollins Pubs.

—Gruesome Ghosts. Mitchelhill, Barbara. 2018. (No. 1 Boy Detective Ser.). 64p. (J). (gr. 2-4). pap. 9.99 *(978-1-78344-669-8(2))* Andersen Pr. GBR. Dist: Independent Pubs. Group.

—Hampstead the Hamster. Rosen, Michael. 2018. 80p. (J). (gr. k-2). 9.99 *(978-1-78344-732-9(X))* Andersen Pr. GBR. Dist: Independent Pubs. Group.

—Harry the Poisonous Centipede Goes to Sea. Banks, Lynne Reid. 2006. 203p. (J). (gr. 3-7). lib. bdg. 16.89 *(978-0-06-077549-0(1))* HarperCollins Pubs.

—Henry V, a Midsummer's Night Dream, the Merchant of Venice, Hamlet. 2017. (Shakespeare Stories Ser.). (ENG.). 256p. (J). (gr. 1-1). pap. 7.99 *(978-1-68412-163-2(9)*, Silver Dolphin Bks.) Printers Row Publishing Group.

—Hippospotamus. Willis, Jeanne. 2012. (Andersen Press Picture Bks). (ENG.). 32p. (J). (gr. -1-3). 16.95 *(978-1-4677-0316-1(8))* Lerner Publishing Group.

—Horrid Henry. Simon, Francesca. 2009. (J). Non-ISBN Publisher.

—Horrid Henry. Simon, Francesca. 2009. (Horrid Henry Ser.: 0). (ENG.). 112p. (J). (gr. 2-5). pap. 6.99 *(978-1-4022-1775-3(7)*, 9781402217753, Sourcebooks Jabberwocky) Sourcebooks, Inc.

—Horrid Henry, 1 vol. Simon, Francesca. 2012. (Horrid Henry Ser.). (ENG.). 112p. (J). (gr. 2-5). lib. bdg. 27.07 *(978-1-59961-185-3(6)*, 9618, Chapter Bks.) Spotlight.

—Horrid Henry & the Abominable Snowman. Simon, Francesca. 2010. (Horrid Henry Ser.: 0). (ENG.). 112p. (J). (gr. 2-5). pap. 6.99 *(978-1-4022-4256-4(5)*, 9781402242564, Sourcebooks Jabberwocky) Sourcebooks, Inc.

—Horrid Henry & the Abominable Snowman, 1 vol. Simon, Francesca. 2012. (Horrid Henry Ser.). (ENG.). 112p. (J). (gr. 2-5). lib. bdg. 27.07 *(978-1-59961-186-0(4)*, 9619, Chapter Bks.) Spotlight.

—Horrid Henry & the Mummy's Curse. Simon, Francesca. 2009. (Horrid Henry Ser.: 0). (ENG.). 112p. (J). (gr. 2-5). pap. 6.99 *(978-1-4022-1776-0(5)*, 9781402217760, Sourcebooks Jabberwocky) Sourcebooks, Inc.

—Horrid Henry & the Scary Sitter. Simon, Francesca. 2009. (Horrid Henry Ser.: 0). (ENG.). 112p. (J). (gr. 2-5). pap. 6.99 *(978-1-4022-1781-4(1)*, 9781402217814, Sourcebooks Jabberwocky) Sourcebooks, Inc.

—Horrid Henry & the Scary Sitter, 1 vol. Simon, Francesca. 2012. (Horrid Henry Ser.). (ENG.). 112p. (J). (gr. 2-5). lib. bdg. 27.07 *(978-1-59961-188-4(0)*, 9621, Chapter Bks.) Spotlight.

—Horrid Henry & the Soccer Fiend. Simon, Francesca. 2009. (Horrid Henry Ser.: 0). (ENG.). 112p. (J). (gr. 2-5). pap. 6.99 *(978-1-4022-1778-4(1)*, Sourcebooks Jabberwocky) Sourcebooks, Inc.

—Horrid Henry & the Soccer Fiend, 1 vol. Simon, Francesca. 2012. (Horrid Henry Ser.). (ENG.). 112p. (J). (gr. 2-5). lib. bdg. 27.07 *(978-1-59961-189-1(9)*, 9622, Chapter Bks.) Spotlight.

—Horrid Henry & the Zombie Vampire. Simon, Francesca. 2012. (Horrid Henry Ser.: 0). (ENG.). 112p. (J). (gr. 2-5). pap. 7.99 *(978-1-4022-6785-7(1)*, Sourcebooks Jabberwocky) Sourcebooks, Inc.

—Horrid Henry Annual 2020. Simon, Francesca. 2019. (Horrid Henry Ser.). 64p. (J). (gr. 2-4). 10.99 *(978-1-5101-0654-3(5)*, Orion Children's Bks.) Hachette Children's Group GBR. Dist: Hachette Bk. Group.

—Horrid Henry Robs the Bank. Simon, Francesca. 2013. (Horrid Henry Ser.: 0). (ENG.). 112p. (J). (gr. 2-5). pap. 8.99 *(978-1-4022-7995-9(7)*, 9781402279959, Sourcebooks Jabberwocky) Sourcebooks, Inc.

—Horrid Henry Rocks. Simon, Francesca. 2011. (Horrid Henry Ser.: 0). (ENG.). 112p. (J). (gr. 2-5). pap. 7.99 *(978-1-4022-5674-5(4)*, 9781402256745, Sourcebooks Jabberwocky) Sourcebooks, Inc.

—Horrid Henry Rocks, 1 vol. Simon, Francesca. 2012. (Horrid Henry Ser.). (ENG.). 112p. (J). (gr. 2-5). lib. bdg. 27.07 *(978-1-59961-190-7(2)*, 9623, Chapter Bks.) Spotlight.

—Horrid Henry's Christmas. Simon, Francesca. 2009. (Horrid Henry Ser.: 0). (ENG.). 112p. (J). (gr. 2-5). pap. 7.99 *(978-1-4022-1782-1(X)*, Sourcebooks Jabberwocky) Sourcebooks, Inc.

—Horrid Henry's Joke Book. Simon, Francesca. 2010. (Horrid Henry Ser.: 0). (ENG.). 112p. (J). (gr. 2-5). pap. 8.99 *(978-1-4022-4425-4(8)*, 9781402244254, Sourcebooks Jabberwocky) Sourcebooks, Inc.

—How to Be a Detective. Mitchelhill, Barbara. 2018. (No. 1 Boy Detective Ser.). 64p. (J). (gr. 2-4). pap. 9.99 *(978-1-78344-664-3(1))* Andersen Pr. GBR. Dist: Independent Pubs. Group.

—I, Amber Brown. Danziger, Paula. 2011. (Amber Brown Ser.: 8). (ENG.). 160p. (J). (gr. 2-5). 5.99 *(978-0-14-241965-6(6)*, Puffin Books) Penguin Young Readers Group.

—I Hate School. Willis, Jeanne. 2005. (ENG.). 32p. (J). (gr. -1-k). pap. 12.99 *(978-1-84270-463-9(X))* Andersen Pr. GBR. Dist: Independent Pubs. Group.

Ross, Tony. La Increíble Historia de... la Cosa Más Rara Del Mundo / Fing. Walliams, David. 2020. (Increíble Historia De... Ser.). (SPA.). 416p. (J). (gr. 4-7). pap. 14.95 ***(978-607-31-9023-7(9)***, Montena) Penguin Random House Grupo Editorial ESP. Dist: Penguin Random Hse. LLC.

Ross, Tony. It's a Fair Day, Amber Brown. Danziger, Paula. 2003. pap. 31.95 incl. audio compact disk *(978-1-59112-564-8(2))*; (J). 25.95 incl. audio *(978-1-59112-246-3(5))*; (J). pap. 29.95 incl. audio *(978-1-59112-247-0(3))*; (J). (gr. -1-2). audio compact disk 28.95 *(978-1-59112-565-5(0))* Live Oak Media.

—It's a Fair Day, Amber Brown. Danziger, Paula. 2003. (Is for Amber Ser.: 3). (ENG.). 48p. (J). (gr. -1-3). pap. 4.99 *(978-0-698-11982-6(7)*, Penguin Young Readers) Penguin Young Readers Group.

—It's Justin Time, Amber Brown. Danziger, Paula. (Amber Brown Ser.). 9.95 *(978-1-59112-294-4(5))* Live Oak Media.

—Jason y el Vellocino de Oro: Aracne, la Tejedora. McCaughrean, Geraldine. Barroso, Paz, tr. 2005. (Mythology Series Collection Mitos Ser.).Tr. of Jason & the Golden Fleece. (SPA.). 48p. (J). (gr. 2-3). 9.95 *(978-84-348-6425-2(8))* SM Ediciones ESP. Dist: Iaconi, Mariuccia Bk. Imports.

—Justo a Tiempo, Ambar Dorado. Danziger, Paula. 2007. (Amber Brown Ser.). (SPA.). 48p. (gr. k-3). per. 8.95 *(978-1-59820-595-4(1)*, Alfaguara) Santillana USA Publishing Co., Inc.

—Little Wolf, Forest Detective. Whybrow, Ian. 2005. (Middle Grade Fiction Ser.). 112p. (J). (gr. 3-6). 14.95 *(978-1-57505-413-1(2))*; pap. 6.95 *(978-1-57505-829-0(4))* Lerner Publishing Group.

—Little Wolf, Pack Leader. Whybrow, Ian. 2005. (Little Wolf Adventures Ser.). 126p. (gr. 3-6). 14.95 *(978-1-57505-400-1(0))* Lerner Publishing Group.

—Little Wolf, Terror of the Shivery Sea. Whybrow, Ian. 2004. (Little Wolf Adventures Ser.). (ENG.). 144p. (J). (gr. 3-6). 14.95 *(978-1-57505-629-6(1))* Lerner Publishing Group.

—Little Wolf's Diary of Daring Deeds. Whybrow, Ian. (Middle Grade Fiction Ser.). 132p. (gr. 3-6). 2005. 14.95 *(978-1-57505-411-7(6))*; 2003. (J). pap. 6.95 *(978-0-87614-536-4(5)*, Carolrhoda Bks.) Lerner Publishing Group.

—Little Wolf's Handy Book of Poems. Whybrow, Ian. 2005. (Little Wolf Adventures Ser.). 80p. (gr. 3-6). pap., lib. bdg. 14.95 *(978-0-87614-927-0(1))* Lerner Publishing Group.

—Little Wolf's Haunted Hall for Small Horrors. Whybrow, Ian. (Middle Grade Fiction Ser.). (J). 2005. 132p. (gr. 3-6). 14.95 *(978-1-57505-412-4(4))*; 2004. 125p. (gr. 4-7). per. 6.95 *(978-1-57505-794-1(8))* Lerner Publishing Group.

—Lobito Aprende a Ser Malo. Whybrow, Ian. Azaola, Miguel, tr. from ENG. 2007. (Ediciones Lerner Single Titles Ser.). (SPA.). 136p. (J). (gr. 3-6). per. 6.95 *(978-0-8225-8644-9(4)*, Ediciones Lerner) Lerner Publishing Group.

—Lucinda Belinda Melinda Mccool. Willis, Jeanne. 2016. (ENG.). 32p. (J). (-k). 23.99 *(978-1-78344-202-7(6))* Andersen Pr. GBR. Dist: Independent Pubs. Group.

—Malicia para Principiantes: Una Aventura de Lobito y Apestosito. Whybrow, Ian. Quintana, Joela, tr. 2005. (Libros Ilustrados (Picture Bks.)). (SPA.). 32p. (J). (gr. k-2). 16.95 *(978-0-8225-3211-8(5)*, Ediciones Lerner) Lerner Publishing Group.

—Mammoth Pie. Willis, Jeanne. 2013. (ENG.). 32p. (J). (gr. -1-k). pap. 8.99 *(978-1-84270-757-9(4))* Andersen Pr. GBR. Dist: Independent Pubs. Group.

—Mayfly Day. Ross, Melanie H. & Willis, Jeanne. 2012. (ENG.). 32p. (J). (gr. -1-k). pap. 10.99 *(978-1-84270-606-0(3))* Andersen Pr. GBR. Dist: Independent Pubs. Group.

—The Mega-Mean Time Machine. Simon, Francesca. 2009. (Horrid Henry Ser.: 0). (ENG.). 112p. (J). (gr. 2-5). pap. 6.99 *(978-1-4022-1780-7(3)*, 9781402217807, Sourcebooks Jabberwocky) Sourcebooks, Inc.

—The Mega-Mean Time Machine, 1 vol. Simon, Francesca. 2012. (Horrid Henry Ser.). (ENG.). 112p. (J). (gr. 2-5). lib. bdg. 27.07 *(978-1-59961-187-7(2)*, 9620, Chapter Bks.) Spotlight.

—The Mega Quiz. Mitchelhill, Barbara. 2018. (No. 1 Boy Detective Ser.). 64p. (J). (gr. 2-4). pap. 9.99 *(978-1-78344-671-1(4))* Andersen Pr. GBR. Dist: Independent Pubs. Group.

—The Midnight Gang. Walliams, David. 2018. (ENG.). 480p. (J). (gr. 3-7). 16.99 *(978-0-06-256106-0(5))* HarperCollins Pubs.

—The Midnight Gang. Walliams, David. 2019. (ENG.). 496p. (J). (gr. 3-7). pap. 7.99 *(978-0-06-256107-7(3))* HarperCollins Pubs.

—Mind the Door! Skidmore, Steve & Barlow, Steve. 2006. (Mad Myths Ser.). 121p. (J). (gr. 2-4). per. 6.95 *(978-1-903015-49-0(9))* Barn Owl Bks, London GBR. Dist: Independent Pubs. Group.

—Miss Dirt the Dustman's Daughter. Ahlberg, Allan. (ENG.). 24p. (J). pap. 6.95 *(978-0-14-037882-5(0))* Penguin Bks., Ltd. GBR. Dist: Trafalgar Square Publishing.

—Monster Movie. Simon, Francesca. 2012. (Horrid Henry Ser.: 0). (ENG.). 112p. (J). (gr. 2-5). pap. 7.99 *(978-1-4022-7737-5(7)*, Sourcebooks Jabberwocky) Sourcebooks, Inc.

—The New Football Coach. Demers, Dominique. Berg, Sander, tr. 2018. 96p. (J). pap. 9.99 *(978-1-84688-435-1(7)*, 382477) Alma Bks. GBR. Dist: Bloomsbury Publishing Plc.

—The Nights Before Christmas. 2018. (ENG.). 228p. (J). (gr. 4-8). pap. 23.95 *(978-1-78344-772-5(9))* Penguin Random Hse. AUS. Dist: Independent Pubs. Group.

—The Nights Before Christmas: 24 Classic Christmas Stories to Read Aloud. 2017. (ENG.). 240p. (J). (gr. 4-6). 26.99 *(978-1-84939-580-9(2))* Andersen Pr. GBR. Dist: Independent Pubs. Group.

—El Nino Que Perdio el Ombligo. Willis, Jeanne. (SPA.). (J). 8.95 *(978-958-04-5632-2(1))* Norma S.A. COL. Dist: Distribuidora Norma, Inc., Lectorum Pubns., Inc.

—Not Just a Book. Willis, Jeanne. 2018. (ENG.). 32p. (J). (gr. -1-3). 17.99 *(978-1-5415-3569-5(3))* Lerner Publishing Group.

—Orange You Glad It's Halloween, Amber Brown?, 4 bks., Set. Danziger, Paula. 2007. (Amber Brown Ser.). (J). (gr. 1-3). pap. 29.95 incl. audio *(978-1-4301-0080-5(X))* Live Oak Media.

—Orange You Glad It's Halloween, Amber Brown? Danziger, Paula. 2007. (Amber Brown Ser.). 48p. (J). (gr. k-3). 11.65 *(978-0-7569-8154-9(9))* Perfection Learning Corp.

—Perseo y la Gorgona Medisa. McCaughrean, Geraldine. Barroso, Paz, tr. 2005. (Mythology Series Collection Mitos Ser.).Tr. of Perseus & the Gorgon Medusa. (SPA.). 48p. (J). (gr. 2-3). 9.95 *(978-84-348-6430-6(4))* SM Ediciones ESP. Dist: Iaconi, Mariuccia Bk. Imports.

—The Pet Person. Willis, Jeanne. 2015. (ENG.). 32p. (J). (-k). pap. 9.99 *(978-1-78344-242-3(5))* Andersen Pr. GBR. Dist: Independent Pubs. Group.

—Pippi in the South Seas. Lindgren, Astrid. Turner, Marianne, tr. from SWE. ed. 2006. 128p. pap. *(978-0-19-275481-3(5))* Oxford Univ. Pr.

—The Popstar's Wedding. Mitchelhill, Barbara. 2018. 64p. (J). (gr. 2-4). pap. 9.99 *(978-1-78344-663-6(3))* Andersen Pr. GBR. Dist: Independent Pubs. Group.

—Por Que? Camp, Lindsay. (SPA.). 32p. *(978-84-233-3053-9(2)*, DS0265) Ediciones Destino ESP. Dist: Lectorum Pubns., Inc.

—Prince Charmless. Willis, Jeanne. 2014. 32p. (J). (gr. -1-k). pap. 14.99 *(978-1-84939-778-0(3))* Andersen Pr. GBR. Dist: Independent Pubs. Group.

—Querido Max. Grindley, Sally & Max, Querido. rev. ed. 2006. (Castillo de la Lectura Naranja Ser.). (ENG.). 120p. (J). pap. 7.95 *(978-970-20-0854-5(9))* Castillo, Ediciones, S. A. de C. V. MEX. Dist: Macmillan.

—Second Grade Rules, Amber Brown. Danziger, Paula. 2005. (Is for Amber Ser.: 5). (ENG.). 48p. (J). (gr. -1-3). mass mkt. 3.99 *(978-0-14-240421-8(7)*, Penguin Young Readers) Penguin Young Readers Group.

—Second Grade Rules, Amber Brown. Danziger, Paula. 2005. (Amber Brown Ser.). 48p. (gr. k-2). 14.00 *(978-0-7569-5521-2(1))* Perfection Learning Corp.

—Segundo Grado Es Increible, Ambar Dorado. Danziger, Paula. 2007. (de Ámbar / a Is for Amber Easy-To-Read Ser.).Tr. of Second Grade Rules, Amber Brown. (SPA.). 48p. (gr. k-3). pap. 8.95 *(978-1-59820-594-7(3))* Santillana USA Publishing Co., Inc.

—El Senor Browser y los Aflacerebros. Curtis, Philip. (SPA.). 112p. (YA). (gr. 5-8). *(978-84-239-2754-8(7)*, EC2750) Espasa Calpe, S.A. ESP. Dist: Lectorum Pubns., Inc.

—Serious Graffiti. Mitchelhill, Barbara. 2018. (No. 1 Boy Detective Ser.). 64p. (J). (gr. 2-4). pap. 9.99 *(978-1-78344-666-7(8))* Andersen Pr. GBR. Dist: Independent Pubs. Group.

Ross, Tony. Shakespeare Stories: The Tempest. Matthews, Andrew. 2003. 64p. (J). (gr. 4-6). pap. 6.99 ***(978-1-84121-346-0(2)***, Orchard Bks.) Hachette Children's Group GBR. Dist: Hachette Bk. Group.

Ross, Tony. The Shakespeare Stories: Much Ado about Nothing, the Taming of the Shrew, Macbeth, Romeo & Juliet. 2017. (Shakespeare Stories Ser.). (ENG.). 256p. (J). (gr. 1-1). pap. 7.99 *(978-1-68412-162-5(0)*, Silver Dolphin Bks.) Printers Row Publishing Group.

—Slug Needs a Hug! Willis, Jeanne. 2015. (ENG.). 32p. (J). (gr. -1-3). 17.99 *(978-1-4677-9309-4(4)*, 9781467793094); E-Book 27.99 *(978-1-4677-9317-9(5))* Lerner Publishing Group.

—Spooky Night! Finney, Wendy. 2020. (Not-So-Little Princess Colour Readers Ser.: 4). 64p. (J). (gr. k-2). pap. 9.99 *(978-1-78344-383-3(9))* Andersen Pr. GBR. Dist: Independent Pubs. Group.

—Spycatcher. Mitchelhill, Barbara. 2018. (No. 1 Boy Detective Ser.). 64p. (J). (gr. 2-4). 9.99 *(978-1-78344-665-0(X))* Andersen Pr. GBR. Dist: Independent Pubs. Group.

—Stinkbomb. Simon, Francesca. 2009. (Horrid Henry Ser.: 0). (ENG.). 112p. (J). (gr. 2-5). pap. 6.99 *(978-1-4022-1779-1(X)*, 9781402217791, Sourcebooks Jabberwocky) Sourcebooks, Inc.

—Stone Me! Barlow, Steve & Skidmore, Steve. 2005. (Mad Myths Ser.). 122p. (J). pap. 5.95 *(978-1-903015-43-8(X))* Barn Owl Bks, London GBR. Dist: Independent Pubs. Group.

—Swords, Sorcerers & Superheroes. Bradman, Tony. 2015. 127p. (J). *(978-1-4351-5960-0(8))* Barnes & Noble, Inc.

—The T-Rex Who Lost His Specs! Willis, Jeanne. 2018. (ENG.). 32p. (J). (gr. -1-3). 17.99 *(978-1-5415-1456-0(4))* Lerner Publishing Group.

—Tadpole's Promise. Willis, Jeanne. 15th ed. 2018. 32p. (J). (— 1). pap. 14.99 *(978-1-78344-586-8(6))* Andersen Pr. GBR. Dist: Independent Pubs. Group.

—Tom, Dad, & Colin. Burchett, Jan & Vogler, Sara. 2014. (Traditional Tales Ser.). (ENG.). 16p. (J). (gr. k-1). pap. 6.95 *(978-1-62521-604-5(1)*, Capstone Classroom) Capstone.

—Tricks the Tooth Fairy. Simon, Francesca. 2009. 90p. (J). Non-ISBN Publisher.

—Tricks the Tooth Fairy. Simon, Francesca. 2009. (Horrid Henry Ser.: 0). (ENG.). 112p. (J). (gr. 2-5). pap. 6.99 *(978-1-4022-2275-7(0)*, 9781402222757, Sourcebooks Jabberwocky) Sourcebooks, Inc.

—Tricks the Tooth Fairy, 1 vol. Simon, Francesca. 2012. (Horrid Henry Ser.). (ENG.). 112p. (J). (gr. 2-5). lib. bdg. 27.07 *(978-1-59961-191-4(0)*, 9624, Chapter Bks.) Spotlight.

—Troll Stinks. Willis, Jeanne. 2017. (ENG.). 32p. (J). (gr. -1-3). 17.99 *(978-1-5124-3948-9(7))* Lerner Publishing Group.

—Troll Stinks. Willis, Jeanne. 2017. (Andersen Press Picture Bks.). (ENG.). 32p. (gr. -1-3). 35.99 *(978-1-5124-3964-9(9))* Lerner Publishing Group.

—Under Cover. Mitchelhill, Barbara. 2018. (No. 1 Boy Detective Ser.). 64p. (J). (gr. 2-4). pap. 9.99 *(978-1-78344-668-1(4))* Andersen Pr. GBR. Dist: Independent Pubs. Group.

—Underpants. Simon, Francesca. 2009. 112p. (J). (gr. 2-5). (Horrid Henry Ser.: 0). (ENG.). pap. 6.99 *(978-1-4022-3825-3(8))*; pap. 4.99 *(978-1-4022-1777-7(3))* Sourcebooks, Inc. (Sourcebooks Jabberwocky).

—Wakes the Dead. Simon, Francesca. 2011. (Horrid Henry Ser.: 0). (ENG.). 112p. (J). (gr. 2-5). pap. 7.99 *(978-1-4022-5934-0(4)*, Sourcebooks Jabberwocky) Sourcebooks, Inc.

—Wakes the Dead, 1 vol. Simon, Francesca. 2012. (Horrid Henry Ser.). (ENG.). 112p. (J). (gr. 2-5). lib. bdg. 27.07 *(978-1-59961-192-1(9)*, 9625, Chapter Bks.) Spotlight.

—We're Going to a Party! Willis, Jeanne. 2015. 16p. (J). (-k). pap. 14.99 *(978-1-84939-456-7(3))* Andersen Pr. GBR. Dist: Independent Pubs. Group.

—What's My Name? Finney, Wendy. 2019. (Not-So-Little Princess Colour Readers Ser.: 1). 64p. (J). (gr. k-2). 9.99 *(978-1-78344-509-7(2))* Andersen Pr. GBR. Dist: Independent Pubs. Group.

—What's the Time, Little Wolf? A Little Wolf & Smellybreff Adventure. Whybrow, Ian. 2006. 32p. (J). (gr. -1-3). lib. bdg. 15.95 *(978-1-57505-939-6(8)*, Carolrhoda Bks.) Lerner Publishing Group.

—Where's Gilbert? Finney, Wendy. 2020. (Not-So-Little Princess Colour Readers Ser.: 3). 64p. (J). (gr. k-2). 9.99 *(978-1-78344-523-3(8))* Andersen Pr. GBR. Dist: Independent Pubs. Group.

—Who Am I? Phinn, Gervase. 2012. (ENG.). 32p. (J). (gr. -1-3). 16.95 *(978-0-7613-8996-5(2)*, 9780761389965) Lerner Publishing Group.

—The World's Worst Children. Walliams, David. 2016. (ENG.). 272p. (J). *(978-0-00-819703-2(2)*, HarperCollins Children's Bks.) HarperCollins Pubs. Ltd. GBR. Dist: HarperCollins Pubs.

—You Can't Eat Your Chicken Pox, Amber Brown. Danziger, Paula. 2006. (Amber Brown Ser.: No. 2). 100p. (gr. 2-5). 15.00 *(978-0-7569-6756-7(2))* Perfection Learning Corp.

—You Can't Eat Your Chicken Pox, Amber Brown. Danziger, Paula. 2006. (Amber Brown Ser.: 2). (ENG.). 128p. (J). (gr. 2-5). 6.99 *(978-0-14-240629-8(5)*, Puffin Books) Penguin Young Readers Group.

Ross, Tony. Alice - Through the Looking-Glass. Ross, Tony. Carroll, Lewis. 2016. 116p. (J). (-k). pap. 14.99 *(978-1-78344-412-0(6))* Andersen Pr. GBR. Dist: Independent Pubs. Group.

—An Anty-War Story. Ross, Tony. 2018. (ENG.). 32p. (J). (gr. 2-5). 17.99 *(978-1-5415-3564-0(2))* Lerner Publishing Group.

—Centipede's One Hundred Shoes. Ross, Tony. rev. ed. 2003. (ENG.). 32p. (J). (gr. -1-3). 19.99 *(978-0-8050-7298-3(5)*, 900019039, Holt, Henry & Co. Bks. For Young Readers) Holt, Henry & Co.

—Don't Do That! Ross, Tony. 2011. 32p. (J). (gr. k — 1). pap. 12.99 *(978-1-84270-936-8(4))* Andersen Pr. GBR. Dist: Independent Pubs. Group.

—I Didn't Do It! Ross, Tony. 2016. (Little Princess Ser.). (ENG.). 32p. (J). (gr. -1-3). 17.99 *(978-1-5124-0598-9(1)*, 9781512405989) Lerner Publishing Group.

—I Don't Want to Go to the Hospital! Ross, Tony. 2013. (ENG.). 32p. (J). (gr. -1-3). 16.95 *(978-1-4677-1155-5(1))* Lerner Publishing Group.

Ross, Tony. I Don't Want to Wash My Hands! Ross, Tony. 2020. (ENG.). 32p. (J). (-k). pap. 8.99 ***(978-0-593-32482-0(X)***, G.P. Putnam's Sons Books for Young Readers) Penguin Young Readers Group.

Ross, Tony. I Feel Sick! Ross, Tony. 2015. (ENG.). 32p. (J). (gr. -1-3). 16.99 *(978-1-4677-5797-3(7))* Andersen Pr. GBR. Dist: Lerner Publishing Group.

—I Feel Sick! Ross, Tony. ed. 2015. (Little Princess Ser.). (ENG.). 32p. (J). (gr. -1-3). E-Book 27.99 *(978-1-4677-5798-0(5))* Lerner Publishing Group.

—I Want a Bedtime Story! Ross, Tony. 2016. (Little Princess Ser.). (ENG.). 32p. (J). (gr. -1-3). 17.99 *(978-1-5124-1629-9(0)*, 9781512416299) Lerner Publishing Group.

—I Want a Cat! Ross, Tony. ed. 2008. 32p. (J). (gr. -1-k). pap. 12.99 *(978-1-84270-691-6(8))* Andersen Pr. GBR. Dist: Independent Pubs. Group.

—I Want a Friend! Ross, Tony. 2017. (Little Princess Ser.). (ENG.). 32p. (J). (gr. -1-3). 17.99 *(978-1-5124-0555-2(8)*, 9781512405552) Lerner Publishing Group.

—I Want a Sister! Ross, Tony. 2013. (ENG.). 32p. (J). (gr. -1-3). 16.95 *(978-1-4677-2047-2(X))* Andersen Pr. GBR. Dist: Lerner Publishing Group.

—I Want My Dad! Ross, Tony. 2018. (Little Princess Ser.). (ENG.). 32p. (J). (gr. -1-3). 17.99 *(978-1-5415-1453-9(X))* Lerner Publishing Group.
—I Want My Light On! Ross, Tony. 2010. (Little Princess Ser.). (ENG.). 32p. (J). (gr. -1-3). 16.95 *(978-0-7613-6443-6(9)*, 9780761364436) Lerner Publishing Group.
—I Want Snow! Ross, Tony. 2017. (Little Princess Ser.). (ENG.). 32p. (J). (gr. -1-3). 17.99 *(978-1-5124-8125-9(4)*, 9781512481259) Lerner Publishing Group.
—I Want to Do It Myself! Ross, Tony. 2011. (Andersen Press Picture Bks). (ENG.). 32p. (J). (gr. -1-3). 16.95 *(978-0-7613-7412-1(4))* Lerner Publishing Group.
—I Want to Go Home! Ross, Tony. 2014. (ENG.). 32p. (J). (gr. -1-3). 16.95 *(978-1-4677-5095-0(6))* Lerner Publishing Group.
—I Want to Win! Ross, Tony. 2012. (Little Princess Ser.). (ENG.). 32p. (J). (gr. -1-3). 16.95 *(978-0-7613-8993-4(8)*, 9780761389934) Lerner Publishing Group.
—My Favourite Fairy Tales. Ross, Tony. 2012. (ENG.). 96p. (J). (gr. -1-k). pap. 16.99 *(978-1-84939-211-2(0))* Andersen Pr. GBR. Dist: Independent Pubs. Group.
—Our Kid. Ross, Tony. 2017. (ENG.). 32p. (J). (gr. -1-3). 17.99 *(978-1-5124-8127-3(0)*, 9781512481273) Lerner Publishing Group.
—Paisajes. Ross, Tony. Delafosse, Claude & Jeunesse, Gallimard. (Coleccion Mundo Maravilloso). (SPA.). 168p. (J). (gr. 3-5). *(978-84-348-4450-6(8))* SM Ediciones.
—Rita's Rhino. Ross, Tony. ed. 2015. (ENG.). 32p. (J). (gr. -1-3). E-Book 27.99 *(978-1-4677-6319-6(5))* Lerner Publishing Group.
—Super Dooper Jezebel. Ross, Tony. 2010. (ENG.). 32p. (J). pap. 10.99 *(978-1-84939-016-3(9))* Andersen Pr. GBR. Dist: Independent Pubs. Group.

Ross, Tony, jt. illus. see Gledhill, Carly.

Ross, William. Willie the Wolf Goes to Wunderbar World. Ross, William. 2019. (ENG.). 34p. (J). pap. 9.99 ***(978-1-6880-4228-5(8))*** Independently Published.

Rossell, Judith. Me & You. Holmes, Janet A. 2009. (ENG.). 32p. (J). (gr. -1-3). 14.95 *(978-0-7358-2250-4(6))* North-South Bks., Inc.
—Mice Mischief: Math Facts in Action. Stills, Caroline. 2014. (ENG.). 24p. (J). (gr. -1-k). 16.95 *(978-0-8234-2947-9(4))* Holiday Hse., Inc.
—My Little Library - Me & You. Holmes, Janet A. 2014. (My Little Library). (ENG.). 24p. (J). (-k). 12.99 *(978-1-921541-58-2(X))* Little Hare Bks. AUS. Dist: Independent Pubs. Group.
—To Get to Me. Kerr, Eleanor. 2013. 32p. (J). (gr. -1-k). 18.99 *(978-1-74275-883-1(5))* Random Hse. Australia AUS. Dist: Independent Pubs. Group.
—Too Tight, Benito! Brian, Janeen. 2010. (ENG.). 32p. (J). (gr. -1-k). pap. 8.99 *(978-1-921272-94-3(5))* Little Hare Bks. AUS. Dist: Independent Pubs. Group.

Rossell, Judith. I Spy with Inspector Stilton. Rossell, Judith. 2003. (ENG.). 32p. (Orig.). pap., act. bk. ed. *(978-1-877003-29-5(8))* Little Hare Bks. AUS. Dist: HarperCollins Pubs. Australia.
—Inspector Stilton & the Missing Jewels. Rossell, Judith. 2005. (ENG.). 32p. pap. *(978-1-921049-09-5(X))* Little Hare Bks. AUS. Dist: HarperCollins Pubs. Australia.
—Oliver. Rossell, Judith. 2012. (ENG.). 32p. (J). (gr. -1-2). 16.99 *(978-0-06-202210-3(5))* HarperCollins Pubs.
—Withering-By-Sea. Rossell, Judith. 2017. (ENG.). 288p. (J). (gr. 3-7). pap. 8.99 *(978-1-4814-4368-5(2))* Simon & Schuster Children's Publishing.
—Wormwood Mire. Rossell, Judith. 2017. (ENG.). 288p. (J). (gr. 3-7). 16.99 *(978-1-4814-4370-8(4)*, Atheneum Bks. for Young Readers) Simon & Schuster Children's Publishing.

Rosser, Kelly. Turkey & Tinsel. Axtell, Paul & Davies, Eve Louise. 2019. (ENG.). 30p. (J). pap. 10.34 ***(978-1-7128-7303-8(2))*** Independently Published.

Rossetti, Carol. Love Your Body: Your Body Can Do Amazing Things... Sanders, Jessica. ed. 2020. (ENG.). 40p. (J). (gr. 3-7). 17.99 ***(978-0-7112-5242-4(4)***, Frances Lincoln Children's Bks.) Quarto Publishing Group UK GBR. Dist: Hachette Bk. Group.

Rossi, Andrea. Allison Marisa Burbank Gets into Trouble. Korobov, Kristine. Mahanov, Tanya, ed. 2008. 172p. 26.90 *(978-1-4251-8976-1(8))* Trafford Publishing.

Rossi, Christian. El Santero Vol. 3: Spooks. Dorison, Xavier & Nury, Fabien. 2014. (Spooks Ser.: 3). (ENG.). 56p. pap. 13.95 *(978-1-84918-170-9(5))* CineBook GBR. Dist: National Bk. Network.
—Spooks - The 46th State, Vol. 4. Dorison, Xavier & Nury, Fabien. 2014. (Spooks Ser.: 4). (ENG.). 64p. pap. 15.95 *(978-1-84918-185-3(3))* CineBook GBR. Dist: National Bk. Network.

Rossi, Francesca. The Greatest Fairy Tales. Perrault, Charles et al. 2018. (ENG.). 240p. (J). (gr. k). 19.95 *(978-88-544-1257-6(0))* White Star ITA. Dist: Sterling Publishing Co., Inc.
—Gulliver's Travels. Swift, Jonathan. 2017. (ENG.). 96p. (J). (gr. 1). 14.95 *(978-88-544-1184-5(1))* White Star ITA. Dist: Sterling Publishing Co., Inc.
—Journey to the Center of the Earth. Verne, Jules. 2018. (ENG.). 96p. (J). (gr. 1). 14.95 *(978-88-544-1292-7(9))* White Star ITA. Dist: Sterling Publishing Co., Inc.
—The Little Mermaid. 2015. (Fairy Tale Adventures Ser.). (ENG.). 64p. (J). (gr. 2-6). 7.95 *(978-1-4549-1509-6(9))* Sterling Publishing Co., Inc.
—Treasure Island. Stevenson, Robert Louis. 2018. (ENG.). 96p. (J). (gr. 1). 14.95 *(978-88-544-1291-0(0))* White Star ITA. Dist: Sterling Publishing Co., Inc.
—Twenty Thousand Leagues under the Sea. Verne, Jules. 2017. (ENG.). 96p. (J). (gr. 1). 14.95 *(978-88-544-1183-8(3))* White Star ITA. Dist: Sterling Publishing Co., Inc.

Rossi, Joe. Ariel Bradley, Spy for General Washington. Durrant, Lynda. 2013. (ENG.). 56p. (J). (gr. 1-5). 9.99 *(978-0-9832904-9-0(0))* VanitaBooks.
—Knees: The Mixed up World of a Boy with Dyslexia. Oelschlager, Vanita. 2012. (ENG.). 128p. (J). (gr. k-5). pap. 9.95 *(978-0-9826366-9-5(5))* VanitaBooks.

Rossi, Pamela. Grandmother's Song. Bauer, Marion Dane. 2007. (ENG.). 32p. (J). (gr. -1-3). 10.99 *(978-1-4169-6849-8(0)*, Simon & Schuster/Paula Wiseman Bks.) Simon & Schuster/Paula Wiseman Bks.

Rossi, Rich. The Twelve Days of Christmas in New Jersey. Woollatt, Margaret. 2018. (Twelve Days of Christmas in America Ser.). 22p. (J). (-k). bds. 7.95 *(978-1-4549-2916-1(2))* Sterling Publishing Co., Inc.

Rossi, Richard. The Twelve Days of Christmas in New Jersey. Woollatt, Margaret. 2008. (Twelve Days of Christmas in America Ser.). 40p. (J). (gr. k). 12.95 *(978-1-4027-3816-6(1))* Sterling Publishing Co., Inc.

Rossiter, Clair. A Dinosaur Alphabet: The ABCs of Prehistoric Beasts! Hasselius, Michelle M. 2016. (Alphabet Connection Ser.). (ENG.). 32p. (J). (gr. -1-2). lib. bdg. 27.99 *(978-1-4795-6884-0(8)*, Picture Window Bks.) Capstone.
—Easter Makes Me Feel Robin's Egg Blue. Michaels, Patty. 2020. (Crayola Ser.). (ENG.). 14p. (J). (gr. -1-k). bds. 6.99 *(978-1-5344-5388-3(1)*, Simon Spotlight) Simon Spotlight.
—Friends Make Me Feel Razzmatazz. Gallo, Tina. 2019. (Crayola Ser.). (ENG.). 24p. (J). (gr. -1-k). 12.99 *(978-1-5344-3265-9(5))*; pap. 4.99 *(978-1-5344-3264-2(7))* Simon Spotlight. (Simon Spotlight).
—Happiness Tastes Like Cotton Candy. Gallo, Tina. 2018. (Crayola Ser.). (ENG.). 24p. (J). (gr. -1-k). 12.99 *(978-1-5344-2524-8(1))*; pap. 4.99 *(978-1-5344-2523-1(3))* Simon Spotlight. (Simon Spotlight).
—I'm a True Blue Friend! Testa, Maggie. 2019. (Crayola Ser.). (ENG.). 24p. (J). (gr. -1-k). pap. 4.99 *(978-1-5344-5158-2(7)*, Simon Spotlight) Simon Spotlight.
—I'm Feeling Macaroni & Cheese: A Colorful Book about Feelings. Gallo, Tina. 2017. (Crayola Ser.). (J). (ENG.). 24p. (gr. -1-k). pap. 4.99 *(978-1-5344-0200-3(4))*; *(978-1-5379-7436-1(X))* Simon Spotlight. (Simon Spotlight).

Rossiter, Clair. I'm Feeling School Bus Yellow! A Colorful Book about School. Gallo, Tina. 2020. (Crayola Ser.). (ENG.). 14p. (J). (gr. -1-k). bds. 6.99 ***(978-1-5344-6433-9(6)***, Simon Spotlight) Simon Spotlight.

Rossiter, Clair. I'm Having a Sky Blue Day! A Colorful Book about Life. Testa, Maggie. 2018. (Crayola Ser.). (ENG.). 24p. (J). (gr. -1-k). 12.99 *(978-1-5344-1529-4(7))*; pap. 3.99 *(978-1-5344-1528-7(9))* Simon Spotlight. (Simon Spotlight).
—Nadiya's Bake Me a Celebration Story: Thirty Recipes & Activities Plus Original Stories for Children. Hussain, Nadiya. 2018. (ENG.). 160p. (J). (gr. 1-17). 13.99 *(978-1-4449-3958-3(0))* Hachette Children's Group GBR. Dist: Hachette Bk. Group.

Rossiter, Janina. 1, 2, 3, Who's Cleaning the Sea? A Counting Picture Book about Protecting Our Planet. Rossiter, Janina. 2019. (Early Childhood Concepts Ser.: Vol. 2). (ENG.). 48p. (J). pap. 11.99 *(978-1-7966-7019-6(7))* Independently Published.

Rosteck, Rachel. The Road Home. Speaker, Cathy. 2012. (ENG.). 45p. (J). pap. 15.95 *(978-1-4327-9146-9(X))* Outskirts Pr., Inc.

Roswell, Stacey. Garden Stories: Rosemarie's Garden, Rosemarie's Roof Garden & Rosemarie Returns to Her Garden. Alexander, Carmen. 2006. 60p. (J). pap. 14.99 *(978-1-886383-55-5(3))* Blue Forge Pr.
—Rosemarie Returns to Her Garden. Alexander, Carmen. 2009. (ENG.). 44p. (J). (gr. -1-4). pap. 10.99 *(978-1-886383-68-5(5))* Blue Forge Pr.
—Rosemarie's Garden. Alexander, Carmen. 2009. 44p. (J). (gr. -1-4). pap. 10.99 *(978-1-886383-66-1(9))* Blue Forge Pr.
—Rosemarie's Roof Garden. Alexander, Carmen. 2009. 44p. (J). (gr. -1-4). pap. 10.99 *(978-1-886383-67-8(7))* Blue Forge Pr.

Roszel, Karen. The Diamond Button. l.t. ed. 2005. 32p. (J). bds. 14.95 *(978-0-9709630-7-9(6))* Coal Hole Productions.

Roth, Jonathan. Beep & Bob 4 Books In 1! Too Much Space!; Party Crashers; Take Us to Your Sugar; Double Trouble. Roth, Jonathan. 2019. (Beep & Bob Ser.). (ENG.). 432p. (J). (gr. 1-4). 14.99 *(978-1-5344-5394-4(6)*, Aladdin) Simon & Schuster Children's Publishing.
—Beep & Bob's Astro Adventures: Too Much Space!; Party Crashers; Take Us to Your Sugar; Double Trouble. Roth, Jonathan. ed. 2019. (Beep & Bob Ser.). (ENG.). 512p. (J). (gr. 1-4). pap. 23.99 *(978-1-5344-3102-7(0)*, Aladdin) Simon & Schuster Children's Publishing.
—Double Trouble. Roth, Jonathan. 2018. (Beep & Bob Ser.: 4). (ENG.). 128p. (J). (gr. 1-4). 16.99 *(978-1-4814-8862-4(7))*; pap. 5.99 *(978-1-4814-8861-7(9))* Simon & Schuster Children's Publishing. (Aladdin).
—Party Crashers. Roth, Jonathan. 2018. (Beep & Bob Ser.: 2). (ENG.). 128p. (J). (gr. 1-4). 16.99 *(978-1-4814-8856-3(2))*; pap. 5.99 *(978-1-4814-8855-6(4))* Simon & Schuster Children's Publishing. (Aladdin).
—Take Us to Your Sugar. Roth, Jonathan. 2018. (Beep & Bob Ser.: 3). (ENG.). 128p. (J). (gr. 1-4). 16.99 *(978-1-4814-8859-4(7))*; pap. 5.99 *(978-1-4814-8858-7(9))* Simon & Schuster Children's Publishing. (Aladdin).
—Too Much Space! Roth, Jonathan. 2018. (Beep & Bob Ser.: 1). (ENG.). 128p. (J). (gr. 1-4). 17.99 *(978-1-4814-8853-2(8))*; pap. 5.99 *(978-1-4814-8852-5(X))* Simon & Schuster Children's Publishing. (Aladdin).

Roth, Judith L. & Rothshank, Brooke. Julia's Words. 2008. (J). (gr. -1-3). pap. 12.99 *(978-0-8361-9417-3(9))* Herald Pr.

Roth, Judy Langemo. Sun Rays: Tales for Children of Every Age. Livingston, Joshua. 2011. 136p. pap. 19.00 *(978-1-61097-261-1(9)*, Resource Pubns.(OR)) Wipf & Stock Pubs.

Roth, Justin. Baltazar & the Flying Pirates. Chin, Oliver. 2009. (ENG.). 36p. (J). (gr. -1-3). 15.95 *(978-1-59702-018-3(4))* Immedium.
—The Year of the Rabbit: Tales from the Chinese Zodiac. Chin, Oliver. 2010. (Tales from the Chinese Zodiac Ser.). (ENG.). 36p. (J). (gr. -1-3). 15.95 *(978-1-59702-023-7(0))* Immedium.
—The Year of the Tiger: Tales from the Chinese Zodiac. Chin, Oliver. 2010. (Tales from the Chinese Zodiac Ser.). (ENG.). 36p. (J). (gr. -1-3). 15.95 *(978-1-59702-020-6(6))* Immedium.

Roth, Leanne L. Tortoise on the Move. Roth, Leanne. 2017. (ENG.). (J). 20.00 *(978-0-9996326-0-4(4))* Torty2 Publishing.

Roth, R G. This Jazz Man. Ehrhardt, Karen. 2006. (ENG.). 32p. (J). (gr. -1-3). 17.99 *(978-0-15-205307-9(7)*, 1195991) Houghton Mifflin Harcourt Publishing Co.

Roth, R. G. This Jazz Man. Ehrhardt, Karen. 2010. (J). (gr. 1-5). 28.95 incl. audio compact disk *(978-1-4301-0740-8(5))* Live Oak Media.
—This Jazz Man. Ehrhardt, Karen. 2015. (ENG.). (J). (gr. -1-3). lib. bdg. 17.60 *(978-1-62765-689-4(8))* Perfection Learning Corp.
—This Jazz Man (4 Paperback/1 CD) Ehrhardt, Karen. 2010. (ENG.). (J). (gr. -1-3). pap. 40.95 *(978-1-4301-0741-5(3))* Live Oak Media.

Roth, Robert. Busing Brewster. Michelson, Richard. 2018. (ENG.). 32p. (J). pap. 10.95 *(978-1-56792-644-6(4))* Godine, David R. Pub.
—Journey of the Nightly Jaguar. Albert, Burton. 2007. (ENG.). 32p. (J). (gr. k-3). 10.99 *(978-1-4169-7092-7(4)*, Simon & Schuster/Paula Wiseman Bks.) Simon & Schuster/Paula Wiseman Bks.

Roth, Roger. The American Story: 100 True Tales from American History. Armstrong, Jennifer. 2006. (ENG.). 368p. (J). (gr. 3-7). 34.99 *(978-0-375-81256-9(3)*, Knopf Bks. for Young Readers) Random Hse. Children's Bks.
—The Giraffe That Walked to Paris. Milton, Nancy. 2013. (ENG.). 32p. (J). (gr. -1-3). 18.95 *(978-1-930900-67-7(8))* Purple Hse. Pr.

Roth, Roger, Sr. Roanoke, the Lost Colony: An Unsolved Mystery from History. Yolen, Jane & Stemple, Heidi E. Y. 2003. (Unsolved Mystery from History Ser.). (ENG.). 32p. (J). (gr. 1-5). 18.99 *(978-0-689-82321-3(5)*, Simon & Schuster Bks. For Young Readers) Simon & Schuster Bks. For Young Readers.
—The Salem Witch Trials: An Unsolved Mystery from History. Yolen, Jane & Stemple, Heidi E. Y. 2004. (Unsolved Mystery from History Ser.). (ENG.). 32p. (J). (gr. 1-5). 18.99 *(978-0-689-84620-5(7)*, Simon & Schuster Bks. For Young Readers) Simon & Schuster Bks. For Young Readers.

Roth, Roger. Star of the Week: A Story of Love, Adoption, & Brownies with Sprinkles. Friedman, Darlene. 2009. (ENG.). 32p. (J). (gr. k-3). 17.99 *(978-0-06-114136-2(4))* HarperCollins Pubs.

Roth, Ruby. That's Why We Don't Eat Animals: A Book about Vegans, Vegetarians, & All Living Things. Roth, Ruby. 2009. 48p. (J). (gr. 1-4). 16.95 *(978-1-55643-785-4(4))* North Atlantic Bks.
—V Is for Vegan: The ABCs of Being Kind. Roth, Ruby. 2013. 32p. (J). (gr. -1-2). 12.95 *(978-1-58394-649-7(7))* North Atlantic Bks.
—Vegan Is Love: Having Heart & Taking Action. Roth, Ruby. 2012. 44p. (J). (gr. 2-5). 16.95 *(978-1-58394-354-0(4))* North Atlantic Bks.

Roth, Ruchela. Who Am I? Schon, Ruchy. 2006. 26p. (J). (gr. -1-k). 14.99 *(978-1-59330-889-9(X))* Feldheim Pubs.

Roth Sisson, Stephanie. Princess Posey & the Crazy, Lazy Vacation. Greene, Stephanie. 2016. (Princess Posey, First Grader Ser.: 10). (ENG.). 96p. (J). (gr. k-3). 5.99 *(978-0-14-751293-2(X)*, Puffin Books) Penguin Young Readers Group.
—Princess Posey & the First Grade Ballet. Greene, Stephanie. 2014. (Princess Posey, First Grader Ser.: 9). 96p. (J). (gr. k-3). pap. 5.99 *(978-0-14-751292-5(1)*, Puffin Books) Penguin Young Readers Group.
—Princess Posey & the First-Grade Boys. Greene, Stephanie. 2014. (Princess Posey, First Grader Ser.: 8). 96p. (J). (gr. k-3). pap. 5.99 *(978-0-14-242735-4(7)*, Puffin Books) Penguin Young Readers Group.
—Princess Posey & the Flower Girl Fiasco. Greene, Stephanie. 2018. (Princess Posey, First Grader Ser.: 12). 96p. (J). (gr. k-3). 5.99 *(978-0-14-751720-3(6)*, Puffin Books); 14.99 *(978-0-399-17569-5(5)*, G.P. Putnam's Sons Books for Young Readers) Penguin Young Readers Group.
—Princess Posey & the New First Grader. Greene, Stephanie. 2013. (Princess Posey, First Grader Ser.: 6). (ENG.). 96p. (J). (gr. k-3). pap. 5.99 *(978-0-14-242763-7(2)*, Puffin Books) Penguin Young Readers Group.
—Princess Posey & the Perfect Present: Book 2, Bk. 2. Greene, Stephanie. 2011. (Princess Posey, First Grader Ser.: 2). 96p. (J). (gr. k-3). 5.99 *(978-0-14-241828-4(5)*, Puffin Books) Penguin Young Readers Group.

Roth Sisson, Stephanie. Spring after Spring: How Rachel Carson Inspired the Environmental Movement. Roth Sisson, Stephanie. 2018. (ENG.). 40p. (J). 17.99 *(978-1-62672-819-6(4)*, 900174864) Roaring Brook Pr.
—Star Stuff: Carl Sagan & the Mysteries of the Cosmos. Roth Sisson, Stephanie. 2014. (ENG.). 42p. (J). (gr. -1-3). 18.99 *(978-1-59643-960-3(2)*, 900125667) Roaring Brook Pr.

Roth, Stacy Schulstrom. It's Raining Outside & I'm Gonna Be Bored! Fenton, Karen B. 2006. (J). lib. bdg. 16.82 *(978-0-9778196-4-5(7))* Harbour Arts, LLC.

Roth, Stephanie. Bad Luck Brad: Probability. Herman, Gail. 2006. (Math Matters ® Ser.). (ENG.). 32p. (J). (gr. k-2). pap. 5.95 *(978-1-57565-112-5(2))* Astra Publishing Hse.

Roth, Susan L. Dream Something Big: The Story of the Watts Towers. Aston, Dianna Hutts. 2011. (ENG.). 40p. (J). (gr. k-3). 17.99 *(978-0-8037-3245-2(7)*, Dial Bks) Penguin Young Readers Group.
—Hands Around the Library: Protecting Egypt's Treasured Books. Leggett Abouraya, Karen. 2012. 40p. (J). (gr. -1-k). 17.99 *(978-0-8037-3747-1(5)*, Dial Bks) Penguin Young Readers Group.
—Listen to the Children: The Story of Dr. Greg & Stones into Schools. Mortenson, Greg & Husain, Farzana. 2011. (ENG.). 32p. (J). (gr. 1-3). 17.99 *(978-0-8037-3593-4(6)*, Dial) Penguin Publishing Group.
—Listen to the Wind: The Story of Dr. Greg & Three Cups of Tea. Mortenson, Greg. 2009. 32p. (J). (gr. 1-3). 17.99 *(978-0-8037-3058-8(6)*, Dial Bks) Penguin Young Readers Group.
—Pass the Fritters, Critters. Chapman, Cheryl. 2007. (ENG.). 40p. (J). (gr. -1-2). 11.99 *(978-1-4169-6160-4(7)*, Simon & Schuster/Paula Wiseman Bks.) Simon & Schuster/Paula Wiseman Bks.
—Playing with Osito - Jugando con Baby Bear: Bilingual English & Spanish. Burgess, Lisa Maria. 2018. (Kids' Books from Here & There Ser.). (ENG.). 40p. (J). (gr. k-3). pap. 9.99 *(978-1-939604-28-6(1))*; 19.95 *(978-1-939604-29-3(X))* Barranca Pr.
—See You Later, Amigo! an American Border Tale. Laufer, Peter. 2016. (Kids' Books from Here & There Ser.). (ENG.). (J). (gr. k-3). 19.95 *(978-1-939604-10-1(9))*; pap. 9.99 *(978-1-939604-11-8(7))* Barranca Pr.

Roth, Susan L. Do Re Mi: If You Can Read Music, Thank Guido D'Arezzo. Roth, Susan L. 2007. (ENG.). 40p. (J). (gr. -1-3). 18.99 *(978-0-618-46572-9(3)*, 595305) Houghton Mifflin Harcourt Publishing Co.
—The Mangrove Tree: Planting Trees to Feed Families. Roth, Susan L. Trumbore, Cindy. 2011. (ENG.). 40p. (J). (gr. 1-6). 19.95 *(978-1-60060-459-1(5))* Lee & Low Bks., Inc.
—Parrots over Puerto Rico, 1 vol. Roth, Susan L. Trumbore, Cindy. 2013. (ENG.). 48p. (J). 20.95 *(978-1-62014-004-8(7))* Lee & Low Bks., Inc.
—Prairie Dog Song. Roth, Susan L. Trumbore, Cindy. 2016. (ENG.). 40p. (J). (gr. 1-7). 18.95 *(978-1-62014-245-5(7))* Lee & Low Bks., Inc.

Rothan, Ann. Miranda's Magic Garden. Atnip, Linda. 2004. 32p. (gr. -1-7). 19.95 *(978-1-885394-21-7(7))* Bluestar Communications Corp.
—Who Can Help Me Sleep? Fox, Sabrina. 2004. 32p. (gr. -1-3). 16.95 *(978-1-885394-36-1(5))* Bluestar Communications Corp.

Rothenberg, Joan. Matzah Ball Soup. Rothenberg, Joan. 2005. 29p. (J). (gr. -1-2). reprint ed. 15.00 *(978-0-7567-8930-5(3))* DIANE Publishing Co.

Rothenberg, Joani. Shabbat Angels. Sigal, Maxine Handelman. 2003. (gr. k-3). 13.95 *(978-0-8074-0865-0(4)*, 164051) URJ Pr.

Rothenberg, Joani Keller. Adam & Eve's First Sunset: God's New Day. Sasso, Sandy Eisenberg. 2003. (ENG.). 32p. (gr. -1-3). 17.95 *(978-1-58023-177-0(2)*, 692cf3fe-f360-4e82-ab0c-aa132e13f90d, Jewish Lights Publishing) LongHill Partners, Inc.
—Adam & Eve's New Day. Sasso, Sandy Eisenberg. 2006. (ENG.). 24p. (gr. -1). bds. 7.99 *(978-1-59473-205-8(1)*, 316f8644-7638-4472-b248-c71e33b4d423, Skylight Paths Publishing) LongHill Partners, Inc.
—Butterflies under Our Hats. Sasso, Sandy Eisenberg. 2014. (ENG.). 32p. (J). (gr. k-5). pap. 15.99 *(978-1-61261-583-7(X)*, 5837) Paraclete Pr., Inc.
—The Shema in the Mezuzah: Listening to Each Other. Sasso, Sandy Eisenberg. 2012. (ENG.). 32p. (J). 18.99 *(978-1-58023-506-8(9)*, 2d784922-ed10-4d47-9068-9861ce43a990, Jewish Lights Publishing) LongHill Partners, Inc.
—The Story of And: The Little Word That Changed the World. Sasso, Sandy Eisenberg. 2019. (ENG.). 40p. (J). (gr. -1-2). 18.00 *(978-1-947888-05-0(6)*, 1947888056, Flyaway Bks.) Westminster John Knox Pr.

Rothenberger, Boyd & Bays, Gail. Kara's Kapers with Katy Pillar. Rothenberger, Charlene. 2006. 64p. per. 9.99 *(978-0-9776260-6-9(7))* Bearhead Publishing, LLC.

Rothero, Chris. Strawberry Fair. 2004. 96p. (gr. 1-6). 14.95 *(978-0-7136-2676-6(3)*, A&C Black) Bloomsbury Publishing Plc GBR. Dist: Consortium Bk. Sales & Distribution.

Rothero, Chris. Noah's Ark. Rothero, Chris. 2005. 20p. (J). 5.95 *(978-965-483-007-2(8)*, Devora Publishing) Simcha Media Group.

Rothfuss, Nina Marie. Quirky Miller & the Pirate. Rudkin, David. 2018. (Quirky Miller Ser.: Vol. 2). (ENG.). 38p. (J). (gr. k-1). pap. 11.99 *(978-1-942922-39-1(6))* Wee Creek Pr. LLC.
—When I Grow up I Want to Be Perfect. Olson, Abbey. 2018. (ENG.). 42p. (J). (gr. 1-2). pap. 11.99 *(978-1-942922-43-8(4))* Wee Creek Pr. LLC.

Rothfuss, Nina Marie. Low Belly Bunch. Rothfuss, Nina Marie. 2016. (ENG.). (J). (gr. k-2). pap. 9.99 *(978-1-942922-29-2(9))* Wee Creek Pr. LLC.

Röthlisberger, Simon. Ida & the Whale. Gugger, Rebecca. 2019. (ENG.). 32p. (J). (gr. -1-2). 17.95 *(978-0-7358-4341-7(4))* North-South Bks., Inc.

Rothman, Julia. What's Cooking? Stein, Joshua David. 2017. (ENG.). 40p. (J). (gr. -1-1). 16.95 *(978-0-7148-7508-8(2))* Phaidon Pr., Inc.

Rothman, Michael. At Home with the Gopher Tortoise: The Story of a Keystone Species. Dunphy, Madeleine. 2010. (ENG.). 32p. (J). (gr. k-4). 16.95 *(978-0-9777539-6-3(4))*; pap. 9.95 *(978-0-9777539-5-6(6))* Web of Life Children's Bks.
—Giant Lizards. Clarke, Ginjer L. 2005. (Penguin Young Readers, Level 3 Ser.). (ENG.). 48p. (J). (gr. 1-3). mass mkt. 4.99 *(978-0-448-43120-8(3)*, Penguin Young Readers) Penguin Young Readers Group.
—Here Is the Tropical Rain Forest. Dunphy, Madeleine. 2006. (Web of Life Ser.). (ENG.). 32p. (J). (gr. -1-3). 16.95 *(978-0-9773795-1-4(5))* Web of Life Children's Bks.
—Here Is the Tropical Rain Forest. Dunphy, Madeleine & National Geographic Learning Staff. 2006. (Web of Life Ser.). (ENG.). 32p. (J). (gr. -1-3). pap. 9.95 *(978-0-9773795-0-7(7))* Web of Life Children's Bks.

Rothshank, Brooke. Cups Held Out. 2006. 40p. (J). (gr. -1-3). per. 12.99 *(978-0-8361-9316-9(4))* Herald Pr.

R

—Plant a Seed of Peace. Seiling, Rebecca. 2007. 115p. (J). (gr. 3-7). per. 15.99 *(978-0-8361-9397-8(0))* Faith & Life Pr.

Rothshank, Brooke, jt. illus. see Roth, Judith L.

Rotman, Jeffrey L. Journey to Shark Island: A Shark Photographer's Close Encounters, 1 vol. Rotman, Jeffrey L., photos by. Cerullo, Mary M. 2014. (Shark Expedition Ser.). (ENG.). 40p. (J). (gr. 5-9). lib. bdg. 32.65 *(978-0-7565-4887-2(X)*, Compass Point Bks.) Capstone.

—Seeking Giant Sharks: A Shark Diver's Quest for Whale Sharks, Basking Sharks, & Manta Rays, 1 vol. Rotman, Jeffrey L., photos by. Cerullo, Mary M. 2014. (Shark Expedition Ser.). (ENG.). 40p. (J). (gr. 5-9). lib. bdg. 32.65 *(978-0-7565-4885-8(3)*, Compass Point Bks.) Capstone.

—Sharks of the Deep: A Shark Photographer's Search for Sharks at the Bottom of the Sea, 1 vol. Rotman, Jeffrey L., photos by. Cerullo, Mary M. 2014. (Shark Expedition Ser.). (ENG.). 40p. (J). (gr. 5-9). lib. bdg. 32.65 *(978-0-7565-4886-5(1)*, Compass Point Bks.) Capstone.

Rotman, Jeffrey L., photos by. City Fish Country Fish CL: How Fish Adapt to Tropical Seas & Cold Oceans, 1 vol. Cerullo, Mary M. 2nd ed. 2017. (How Nature Works: 0). (ENG., 40p. (J). (gr. 3-7). 17.95 *(978-0-88448-529-2(3)*, 884529) Tilbury Hse. Pubs.

—Searching for Great White Sharks: A Shark Diver's Quest for Mr. Big, 1 vol. Cerullo, Mary M. 2014. (Shark Expedition Ser.). (ENG., 40p. (J). (gr. 5-9). lib. bdg. 32.65 *(978-0-7565-4884-1(5)*, Compass Point Bks.) Capstone.

—Shark Expedition, 1 vol. Cerullo, Mary M. 2014. (Shark Expedition Ser.). (ENG., 40p. (J). (gr. 5-9). lib. bdg., lib. bdg., lib. bdg. 130.60 *(978-0-7565-4888-9(8)*, Compass Point Bks.) Capstone.

Rotner, Shelley. Nature Spy. Rotner, Shelley. Kreisler, Ken. 2014. (ENG.). 32p. (J). (gr. -1-1). pap. 13.99 *(978-1-4814-5042-3(5)*, Atheneum Bks. for Young Readers) Simon & Schuster Children's Publishing.

Rotner, Shelley, photos by. Garbage Helps Our Garden Grow: A Compost Story. Glaser, Linda. 2010. (ENG., 32p. (gr. k-3). lib. bdg. 25.26 *(978-0-7613-4911-2(1))* Lerner Publishing Group.

—Shapes. Woodhull, Anne. 2020. 32p. (J). (-k). 17.99 *(978-0-8234-4638-4(7))* Holiday Hse., Inc.

Rotner, Shelley, photos by. All Kinds of Friends. Rotner, Shelley. Kelly, Sheila M. 2017. (ENG., 32p. (J). (gr. k-2). pap. 7.99 *(978-1-5124-8632-2(9)*, 9781512486322); lib. bdg. 26.65 *(978-1-5124-3105-6(2)*, 9781512431056) Lerner Publishing Group. (Millbrook Pr.).

—De Muchas Maneras (Many Ways) Cómo Las Familias Practican Sus Creencias y Religiones. Rotner, Shelley. Kelly, Sheila M. 2006. (SPA., 32p. (J). (gr. k-3). lib. bdg. 15.95 *(978-0-8225-6506-2(4)*, Ediciones Lerner) Lerner Publishing Group.

—Families. Rotner, Shelley. Kelly, Sheila M. 2015. (ENG., 32p. (J). (gr. -1-k). 17.99 *(978-0-8234-3053-6(7))* Holiday Hse., Inc.

—I'm Adopted! Rotner, Shelley. Kelly, Sheila M. 2012. (ENG., 32p. (J). (-k). pap. 6.95 *(978-0-8234-2430-6(8))* Holiday Hse., Inc.

—Lots of Feelings. Rotner, Shelley. Kelly, Sheila M. 2003. (Shelley Rotner's Early Childhood Library). (ENG., 32p. (J). (gr. k-3). pap. 7.99 *(978-0-7613-2377-8(5)*, Millbrook Pr.) Lerner Publishing Group.

—Lots of Grandparents. Rotner, Shelley. Kelly, Sheila M. 2003. (Shelley Rotner's Early Childhood Library: Vol. 3). (ENG., 32p. (J). (gr. k-3). pap. 8.99 *(978-0-7613-1896-5(8)*, Millbrook Pr.) Lerner Publishing Group.

—Many Ways: How Families Practice Their Beliefs & Religions. Rotner, Shelley. Kelly, Sheila M. (Shelley Rotner's Early Childhood Library). (ENG., 32p. (gr. k-3). 2010. (J). pap. 11.99 *(978-0-7613-6531-0(1))*; 2005. lib. bdg. 22.60 *(978-0-7613-2873-5(4))* Lerner Publishing Group. (Millbrook Pr.).

—Senses at the Seashore. Rotner, Shelley. (Shelley Rotner's Early Childhood Library). (ENG., 32p. (gr. -1-2). 2010. (J). pap. 8.99 *(978-0-7613-6530-3(3)*, Millbrook Pr.); 2006. lib. bdg. 22.60 *(978-0-7613-2897-1(1))* Lerner Publishing Group.

—Shades of People. Rotner, Shelley. Kelly, Sheila M. 2009. (ENG., 32p. (J). (gr. -1-k). 17.99 *(978-0-8234-2191-6(0))* Holiday Hse., Inc.

—Whose Eye Am I? Rotner, Shelley. 2016. (ENG., 32p. (J). (gr. -1-3). 16.95 *(978-0-8234-3558-6(X))* Holiday Hse., Inc.

—Yummy! Rotner, Shelley. Kelly, Sheila M. 2013. (ENG., 32p. (J). (gr. -1-k). 16.95 *(978-0-8234-2426-9(X))* Holiday Hse., Inc.

Rottinger, Amy. Bailey's Heartstrings. Chicatelli, Joy. 2011. 28p. pap. 12.95 *(978-1-935268-96-3(1))* Halo Publishing International.

—Charlie's Gingerbread House. Staehli, Melissa. 2012. 24p. pap. 11.95 *(978-1-61244-063-7(0))* Halo Publishing International.

Rottinger, Amy. Freckle Face Fred. Cavitt, Deborah B. 2019. (ENG.). 28p. (J). (gr. k-3). 17.99 ***(978-1-950074-06-8(4))***; pap. 11.99 ***(978-1-950074-05-1(6))*** 4RV Pub.

Rottinger, Amy. Ian & the Great Silver Dragon: A Hero Is Reborn. Dilyard, Jim. 2018. (Ian & the Great Silver Dragon Ser.: Vol. 3). (ENG.). 368p. (J). pap. 15.95 *(978-1-7208-6367-0(9))* CreateSpace Independent Publishing Platform.

—Ian & the Great Silver Dragon a Friendship Begins. Dilyard, Jim. 2019. (Ian & the Great Silver Dragon Ser.: Vol. 2). (ENG.). 112p. (J). pap. 10.95 *(978-1-59098-646-2(6))* Wooster Bk. Co., The.

—My Mommy's Sweater. Torres, Veronica Hilda. 2013. 24p. pap. 12.95 *(978-1-61244-203-7(X))* Halo Publishing International.

—The Owl Who Couldn't Whoo. Kail, Leanna. 2013. 24p. pap. 11.95 *(978-1-61244-129-0(7))* Halo Publishing International.

—Skydive to Hive. Phelan, Anne. 2012. 24p. pap. 11.95 *(978-1-61244-098-9(3))* Halo Publishing International.

—Swanee Day. Consugar, Beth. 2013. 24p. pap. 12.95 *(978-1-61244-176-4(9))* Halo Publishing International.

—The Ticker That Needed a Fixer. Gibson, Donovan. 2011. 28p. pap. 12.95 *(978-1-935268-46-8(5))* Halo Publishing International.

—Tommy Gets Lost! Turner, Darlene. 2012. 24p. pap. 12.95 *(978-1-61244-064-4(9))* Halo Publishing International.

—When the Monsters Are Quiet. Lloyd, Alicia. 2013. 26p. pap. 11.95 *(978-1-61244-219-8(6))* Halo Publishing International.

Round, Graham. Dot-to-Dot Book: Combined Volume. Bryant-Mole, Karen & Tyler, Jenny. 2004. (Dot to Dot Ser.). 168p. (J). pap. 12.95 *(978-0-7945-0699-5(2)*, Usborne) EDC Publishing.

—Dot-to-Dot Machines. Bryant-Mole, Karen. Tyler, Jenny, ed. rev. ed. 2006. (Dot to Dot Ser.). 22p. (J). (gr. -1-2). pap. 3.99 *(978-0-7945-1495-2(2)*, Usborne) EDC Publishing.

—Dot-to-Dot on Seashore. Bryant-Mole, Karen. 2003. 24p. (J). pap. 3.99 *(978-0-7945-0494-6(9)*, Usborne) EDC Publishing.

Round, Graham, et al. How to Draw Cartoons & Caricatures. Tatchell, Judy. 2007. 40p. (J). (gr. 4). lib. bdg. 13.99 *(978-1-58086-895-2(9)*, Usborne) EDC Publishing.

Round, Graham. 42 Bible Stories for Little Ones: From Creation to Pentecost. Word Among Us Editorial Staff. 2008. 96p. pap. 13.95 *(978-1-59325-138-3(6))* Word Among Us Pr.

Rounds, Erin. Where's Winter. Rounds, Erin. Stevens, Tammie, ed. 2018. (ENG.). 36p. (J). (gr. 1-4). 15.99 *(978-0-9849155-8-3(3))*; pap. 9.99 *(978-0-9849155-6-9(7))* BillyFish Bks. LLC.

Rounds, Glen. A Wild Goose Tale. Gage, Wilson. 2012. 114p. 39.95 *(978-1-258-25188-8(4))*; pap. 24.95 *(978-1-258-25729-3(7))* Literary Licensing, LLC.

Rountree, Harry. Alice's Adventures in Wonderland. Carroll, Lewis. 2011. (Calla Editions Ser.). (ENG.). 248p. (gr. 3). 40.00 *(978-1-60660-014-6(1))* Dover Pubns., Inc.

Rouse, Andy, photos by. Busy Gorillas. Schindel, John. 2010. (Busy Book Ser.). 32p. (J). (— 1). bds. 6.99 *(978-1-58246-352-0(2)*, Tricycle Pr.) Random Hse. Children's Bks.

Rouse, Bonna. Les Arts Martiaux. Levigne, Heather. Briere, Marie-Josee, tr. from ENG. 2007. (Sans Limites Ser.). (FRE.). 32p. (J). pap. 9.95 *(978-2-89579-168-3(6))* Bayard Canada Livres CAN. Dist: Crabtree Publishing Co.

—El Ciclo de Vida de la Rana. Kalman, Bobbie & Smithyman, Kathryn. 2005. (Serie Ciclos de Vida Ser.). (SPA.). 32p. (J). (gr. 1-4). pap. *(978-0-7787-8709-9(5))* Crabtree Publishing Co.

—Les Grenouilles. Kalman, Bobbie & Smithyman, Kathryn. Briere, Marie-Josee, tr. from ENG. 2006. (Petit Monde Vivant Ser.). (FRE.). 32p. (J). (gr. -1-3). pap. 9.95 *(978-2-89579-080-8(9))* Bayard Canada Livres CAN. Dist: Crabtree Publishing Co.

—Porristas en Acción. Crabtree, Marc, photos by. Crossingham, John. 2005. (Deportes en Acción Ser.). (SPA & ENG.). 32p. (J). (gr. 3-4). lib. bdg. *(978-0-7787-8575-0(0))*; (gr. 6-9). pap. *(978-0-7787-8621-4(8))* Crabtree Publishing Co.

Rouse, Bonna, jt. illus. see Crabtree, Marc.

Rouse, Mark. Tembo's Roar: A Spiritual Journey of Discovery. Gow, Iain. 2019. (ENG.). 90p. (J). (gr. 3-7). ***(978-0-473-47684-7(3))*** Castle Publishing & Distribution.

Roush, April. My Baby Book. Wolf, Jackie. 2003. 10p. (J). (gr. -1-18). bds. 5.99 *(978-1-57151-712-8(X))* Playhouse Publishing.

—Picture Me One: Baby's First Year in Photos. D'Andrea, Deborah. 2004. (Picture Me Developmental Ser.). 10p. (J). (gr. -1-18). bds. 5.99 *(978-1-57151-736-4(7))* Playhouse Publishing.

—Picture Me Three Vol. 3: Child's Third Year in Photos. D'Andrea, Deborah. 2004. (Picture Me Developmental Ser.). 10p. (J). (gr. -1-18). bds. 5.99 *(978-1-57151-738-8(3))* Playhouse Publishing.

—Picture Me to the Rescue. Hapka, Cathy. 2003. (Role Play Ser.). 10p. (J). (gr. -1-18). bds. 6.99 *(978-1-57151-567-4(4))* Playhouse Publishing.

—Picture Me Two Vol. 2: Toddler's Second Year in Photos. D'Andrea, Deborah. 2004. (Picture Me Developmental Ser.). 10p. (J). (gr. -1-18). bds. 5.99 *(978-1-57151-737-1(5))* Playhouse Publishing.

Roush, April, jt. illus. see Hill, Heather C.

Rousseau, Craig. Big Red Machine. Caramagna, Joe. 2013. (Iron Man & the Armor Wars Ser.). (ENG.). 24p. (J). (gr. 2-6). lib. bdg. 27.07 *(978-1-61479-165-2(1)*, 10016, Marvel Age) Spotlight.

—Down & Out in Beverly Hills Hosted. Caramagna, Joe. 2013. (Iron Man & the Armor Wars Ser.). (ENG.). 24p. (J). (gr. 2-6). lib. bdg. 27.07 *(978-1-61479-164-5(3)*, 10015, Marvel Age) Spotlight.

—The Golden Avenger Strikes Back. Caramagna, Joe. 2013. (Iron Man & the Armor Wars Ser.). (ENG.). 24p. (J). (gr. 2-6). lib. bdg. 27.07 *(978-1-61479-167-6(8)*, 10018, Marvel Age) Spotlight.

—How I Learned to Love the Bomb. Caramagna, Joe. 2013. (Iron Man & the Armor Wars Ser.). (ENG.). 24p. (J). (gr. 2-6). lib. bdg. 27.07 *(978-1-61479-166-9(X)*, 10017, Marvel Age) Spotlight.

—The Invincible Iron Man. Thomas, Rich. 2012. (Marvel Origins Ser.). (ENG.). 48p. (J). (gr. k-5). lib. bdg. 27.07 *(978-1-61479-010-5(8)*, 11338, Marvel Age) Spotlight.

—Souljacker. McCool, Ben. 2012. (Captain America: the Korvac Saga Ser.). (ENG.). 24p. (J). (gr. 3-5). lib. bdg. 27.07 *(978-1-61479-020-4(5)*, 4111, Marvel Age) Spotlight.

—The Star Lord. McCool, Ben. 2012. (Captain America: the Korvac Saga Ser.). (ENG.). 24p. (J). (gr. 3-5). lib. bdg. 27.07 *(978-1-61479-022-8(1)*, 4113, Marvel Age) Spotlight.

—Strange Days. McCool, Ben. 2012. (Captain America: the Korvac Saga Ser.). (ENG.). 24p. (J). (gr. 3-5). lib. bdg. 27.07 *(978-1-61479-019-8(1)*, 4110, Marvel Age) Spotlight.

—The Traveler. McCool, Ben. 2012. (Captain America: the Korvac Saga Ser.). (ENG.). 24p. (J). (gr. 3-5). lib. bdg. 27.07 *(978-1-61479-021-1(3)*, 4112, Marvel Age) Spotlight.

Rousseau, Craig & Bancroft, Tom. Kim Possible Adventures. Stewart, Michael et al. 2019. (ENG.). 80p. (J). (gr. 4-7). pap. 9.99 *(978-1-68405-512-8(1))* Idea & Design Works, LLC.

Rousseau, Craig & Cliquet, Ronan. Marvel Vault of Heroes: Captain America. Tobin, Paul & Gray, Scott. 2020. 160p. (J). (gr. 4-7). pap. 15.99 ***(978-1-68405-678-1(0))*** Idea & Design Works, LLC.

Rousseff, Minnie & Maynard, Barbara. Bertram & His Fabulous Animals. Gilbert, Paul. 2016. 152p. (J). 24.95 *(978-0-7649-7539-4(0)*, POMEGRANATE KIDS) Pomegranate Communications, Inc.

Rousseff, Minnie H. Bertram & His Funny Animals. Gilbert, Paul T. 2016. (ENG.). 140p. (J). 24.95 *(978-0-7649-7372-7(X)*, POMEGRANATE KIDS) Pomegranate Communications, Inc.

Roussey, Christine. All My Treasures: A Book of Joy. Witek, Jo. 2016. (Growing Hearts Ser.). (ENG.). 32p. (J). (gr. -1 — 1). bds. 16.95 *(978-1-4197-2204-2(2)*, 1150201, Abrams Appleseed) Abrams, Inc.

—Brave As Can Be: A Book of Courage. Witek, Jo. 2015. (Growing Hearts Ser.). (ENG.). 32p. (J). (gr. -1 — 1). 16.95 *(978-1-4197-1923-3(8)*, 1130501, Abrams Appleseed) Abrams, Inc.

—Hello in There! A Big Sister's Book of Waiting. Witek, Jo. 2013. (ENG.). 28p. (J). (gr. -1 — 1). 16.95 *(978-1-4197-0371-3(4)*, 1037007, Abrams Appleseed) Abrams, Inc.

—In My Heart: A Book of Feelings. Witek, Jo. 2014. (ENG.). 32p. (J). (gr. -1 — 1). 16.95 *(978-1-4197-1310-1(8)*, 1089001, Abrams Appleseed) Abrams, Inc.

—In My Room: A Book of Creativity & Imagination. Witek, Jo. 2017. (Growing Hearts Ser.). (ENG.). 32p. (J). (gr. -1 — 1). 16.95 *(978-1-4197-2644-6(7)*, 1196601, Abrams Appleseed) Abrams, Inc.

—My Little Gifts: A Book of Sharing. Witek, Jo. 2018. (Growing Hearts Ser.). (ENG.). 30p. (J). (gr. -1 — 1). 16.99 *(978-1-4197-3320-8(6)*, 1257701, Abrams Appleseed) Abrams, Inc.

—My Tree & Me: A Book of Seasons. Witek, Jo. 2019. (Growing Hearts Ser.). (ENG.). 32p. (J). (gr. -1 — 1). 16.99 *(978-1-4197-3503-5(9)*, 1268201) Abrams, Inc.

—With My Daddy: A Book of Love & Family. Witek, Jo. 2018. (Growing Hearts Ser.). (ENG.). 34p. (J). (gr. -1 — 1). 16.99 *(978-1-4197-2822-8(9)*, 1194001, Abrams Appleseed) Abrams, Inc.

Roux, Stéphane. Escape from Darth Vader. Siglain, Michael. 2014. 30p. (J). *(978-1-4844-3969-2(4)*, Disney Lucasfilm Press) Disney Publishing Worldwide.

—Use the Force! Siglain, Michael. 2017. (World of Reading Level 2 Ser.). (ENG.). 32p. (J). (gr. k-3). 27.07 *(978-1-5321-4065-5(7)*, 25436) Spotlight.

Roux, Stéphane. Star Wars. Roux, Stéphane. Millici, Nate & Siglain, Michael. 2017. (J). ***(978-1-368-01493-9(3))*** Disney Publishing Worldwide.

Roux, Tony-George. Carnet Blanc Sport D'Hiver. 2016. (Bnf Sports Ser.). (FRE.). (J). pap. *(978-2-01-116971-6(2))* Hachette Groupe Livre.

—Carnet Ligne Sport D'Hiver. 2016. (Bnf Sports Ser.). (FRE.). (J). pap. *(978-2-01-116946-4(1))* Hachette Groupe Livre.

Rovira, Francesc. Caperucita Roja. Orihuela, Luz. Sarfatti, Esther, tr. 2006. (Bilingual Tales Ser.). (SPA & ENG.). 24p. (J). (gr. -1-3). pap. 3.99 *(978-0-439-77375-1(X)*, Scholastic en Espanol) Scholastic, Inc.

—Los Contrarios. Candel, Arianna. 2004. (Osito Estudiante / Little Bear's Firsts Ser.).Tr. of Opposites. (SPA.). 36p. (J). (gr. k-3). 21.19 *(978-0-7641-2993-3(7)*, B.E.S. Publishing) Peterson's.

—Donde Esta Mi Almohada? Maria Machado, Ana. 2015. (Serie Verde Ser.).Tr. of Where Is My Pillow?. (SPA.). 32p. (J). pap. 9.99 *(978-1-64101-170-9(X))* Santillana USA Publishing Co., Inc.

—Las Formas. Candel, Arianna. 2004. (Osito Estudiante / Little Bear's Firsts Ser.).Tr. of Shapes. (SPA.). 36p. (J). (gr. k-3). 21.19 *(978-0-7641-2995-7(3)*, B.E.S. Publishing) Peterson's.

—MMM Que Rico Esta! Maria Machado, Ana. 2015. (Serie Verde Ser.). (SPA.). 32p. (J). pap. 9.99 *(978-1-64101-171-6(8))* Santillana USA Publishing Co., Inc.

—Los Numeros. Candel, Arianna. 2004. (Osito Estudiante / Little Bear's Firsts Ser.).Tr. of Numbers. (SPA.). 36p. (J). (gr. k-3). 21.19 *(978-0-7641-2996-4(1)*, B.E.S. Publishing) Peterson's.

Row, Jan. Welcome to Doxieville. Martin, Darrin Todd. 2018. (ENG.). 42p. (J). pap. 9.99 *(978-0-9998569-1-8(X))* Roland Golf Services.

Row, Richard. The Kugel Valley Klezmer Band. Stuchner, Joan Betty. 2005. 30p. (J). (gr. 2-6). reprint ed. 16.00 *(978-0-7567-8605-2(3))* DIANE Publishing Co.

—The Kugel Valley Klezmer Band. Stuchner, Joan Betty. 2009. (PJ Library). (ENG.). 32p. (J). (gr. -1-3). pap. 7.95 *(978-1-56656-782-4(3)*, Crocodile Bks.) Interlink Publishing Group, Inc.

Rowberry, Ben. Toshi to the Moon: A Blockchain Adventure. Rowberry, Tim & Woodland, Jason W. 2018. (ENG.). 38p. (J). pap. 11.95 *(978-1-7288-2394-2(3))* Independently Published.

Rowe, Alan. Cracking Christmas. Locke, Ian. 21st ed. 2003. (ENG.). 64p. (J). pap. 3.99 *(978-0-330-37504-7(0)*, Pan) Pan Macmillan GBR. Dist: Trafalgar Square Publishing.

—What's up with Time? Heddle, Becca. 2017. (Collins Big Cat Ser.). (ENG.). 48p. (J). pap. 10.99 *(978-0-00-820884-4(0))* HarperCollins Pubs. Ltd. GBR. Dist: Independent Pubs. Group.

Rowe, Anne Burgess. The Newest Angel. 2015. 47p. (J). pap. *(978-1-63293-039-2(0))* Sunstone Pr.

Rowe, Colin. Grandpa's Noises. St John Thomas, Gareth. 2nd ed. 2020. (ENG.). 32p. (J). (gr. -1-3). pap. 14.99 *(978-1-925820-46-1(7)*, EK Bks.) Exisle Publishing Pty Ltd. AUS. Dist: Hachette Bk. Group.

Rowe, Eric. The Musicians of Bremen. 2004. (ENG.). 19p. (J). (gr. 1-3). pap. 6.47 net. *(978-0-7685-0332-6(9)*, Dominie Elementary) Savvas Learning Co.

Rowe, Eric F. Robin Hood. Rowe, Eric F. Sutton, Rosalind & Rosalind, Sutton. 4th ed. (Coleccion Clasicos en Accion). (SPA.). 80p. (YA). (gr. 5-8). 15.95 *(978-84-241-5782-1(6)*, EV1455) Everest Editora ESP. Dist: Lectorum Pubns., Inc.

Rowe, Harriet. I Don't Care! Said Claire. Hodgson, Karen J. 2010. 32p. (J). (gr. -1-2). pap. 9.99 *(978-1-907432-05-7(1))* Hogs Back Bks. GBR. Dist: Independent Pubs. Group.

Rowe, Helen. El Deseo de la Abuela. Lobo, Julia. Cottage Door Press, ed. 2020. (SPA.). 18p. (J). (gr. -1-2). bds. 9.99 *(978-1-68052-846-6(7)*, 1000090-SLA) Cottage Door Pr.

—Fun with Pets: A Pop-Up Book. 2016. (ENG.). 12p. (J). (gr. -1-k). bds. 8.99 *(978-1-4998-0300-6(1))* Little Bee Books Inc.

Rowe, Helen. Grandma Wishes. Lobo, Julia. 2015. (J). ***(978-1-68052-135-1(7))*** Cottage Door Pr.

Rowe, Helen. Grandma Wishes: Padded Board Book. Lobo, Julia. Cottage Door Press, ed. 2015. (Love You Always Ser.). (ENG.). 18p. (J). (gr. -1-1). bds. 9.99 *(978-1-68052-008-8(3)*, 1000090) Cottage Door Pr.

—Grandma Wishes Gift Set. Lobo, Julia. Cottage Door Press, ed. 2019. (Book & Cuddly Plush Toy Friend Ser.). (ENG.). 18p. (J). (gr. -1-k). bds. 16.99 *(978-1-68052-760-5(6)*, 1004710) Cottage Door Pr.

Rowe, Helen & Chin Mueller, Olivia. Love You Always: Grandma Wishes & All the Love in the World: Padded Board Book 2 Pack. Lobo, Julia & Bunting, Rose. Cottage Door Press, ed. 2016. (Love You Always Ser.). (ENG.). 18p. (J). (gr. -1-k). bds., bds., bds. 19.98 *(978-1-68052-249-5(3)*, 9000830) Cottage Door Pr.

Rowe, Jeannette. YoYo Goes Next Door. Rowe, Jeannette. 2003. 16p. (J). 5.95 *(978-1-58925-368-1(X))* Tiger Tales.

—YoYo Goes to the Park. Rowe, Jeannette. 2003. 12p. (J). pap. 5.95 *(978-1-58925-369-8(8))* Tiger Tales.

Rowe, John. I Wonder. Harris, Annaka. 2013. 32p. (J). 16.95 *(978-1-940051-04-8(5))* Four Elephants Pr.

—The Jungle Book. Kipling, Rudyard & Landolf, Diane Wright. 2008. (Stepping Stone Book(TM) Ser.). (ENG.). 112p. (J). (gr. 1-4). per. 4.99 *(978-0-375-84276-4(4)*, Random Hse. Bks. for Young Readers) Random Hse. Children's Bks.

Rowe, L. S. A Christmas Eve Tale. Draper, C. F. 2019. (ENG.). 42p. (J). pap. ***(978-1-78830-426-9(8))*** Olympia Publishers.

Rowe, Michael Langham. Wild Cats. Batten, Mary. 2004. (Step into Reading Ser.). 48p. (J). (gr. 2-4). pap. 4.99 *(978-0-375-82551-4(7)*, Random Hse. Bks. for Young Readers) Random Hse. Children's Bks.

Rowland, Andrew. Esther's Hanukkah Disaster. Sutton, Jane. 2013. (Hanukkah Ser.). 32p. (J). (gr. -1-3). lib. bdg. 17.95 *(978-0-7613-9043-5(X)*, Kar-Ben Publishing) Lerner Publishing Group.

—Hank Hammer, 1 vol. Klein, Adria F. 2011. (Tool School Ser.). (ENG.). 32p. (J). (gr. 1-2). pap. 6.25 *(978-1-4342-3385-1(5))*; lib. bdg. 22.65 *(978-1-4342-3043-0(0))* Capstone. (Stone Arch Bks.).

—Hank Hammer & the Puppy, 1 vol. Klein, Adria F. 2012. (Tool School Ser.). (ENG.). 32p. (J). (gr. 1-3). pap. 6.25 *(978-1-4342-4233-4(1))*; lib. bdg. 22.65 *(978-1-4342-4020-0(7))* Capstone. (Stone Arch Bks.).

—Journey into the Bible. Rock, Lois. ed. 2010. (ENG.). 48p. (J). (gr. 1-7). 11.99 *(978-0-7459-6088-3(X))* Lion Hudson PLC GBR. Dist: Independent Pubs. Group.

—Limericks. Cleary, Brian P. 2015. (Poetry Adventures Ser.). (ENG.). 32p. (J). (gr. 2-5). lib. bdg. 26.65 *(978-1-4677-2044-1(5)*, 9781467720441, Millbrook Pr.) Lerner Publishing Group.

—Little Lizards. Crow, Melinda Melton. 2013. (Little Lizards Ser.). (ENG.). 32p. (J). (gr. -1-1). lib. bdg., lib. bdg., lib. bdg. 135.90 *(978-1-4342-8840-0(4)*, Stone Arch Bks.) Capstone.

—Little Lizard's Big Party, 1 vol. Crow, Melinda Melton. 2010. (Little Lizards Ser.). (ENG.). 32p. (J). (gr. -1-1). lib. bdg. 22.65 *(978-1-4342-2007-3(9)*, Stone Arch Bks.) Capstone.

—Little Lizard's First Day, 1 vol. Crow, Melinda Melton. 2010. (Little Lizards Ser.). (ENG.). 32p. (J). (gr. -1-1). lib. bdg. 22.65 *(978-1-4342-2005-9(2)*, Stone Arch Bks.) Capstone.

—Little Lizard's New Baby, 1 vol. Crow, Melinda Melton. 2011. (Little Lizards Ser.). (ENG.). 32p. (J). (gr. -1-1). pap. 6.25 *(978-1-4342-3047-8(3)*, Stone Arch Bks.) Capstone.

—Little Lizard's New Bike, 1 vol. Crow, Melinda Melton. 2010. (Little Lizards Ser.). (ENG.). 32p. (J). (gr. -1-1). lib. bdg. 22.65 *(978-1-4342-2008-0(7)*, Stone Arch Bks.) Capstone.

—Little Lizard's New Friend, 1 vol. Crow, Melinda Melton. 2011. (Little Lizards Ser.). (ENG.). 32p. (J). (gr. -1-1). pap. 6.25 *(978-1-4342-3048-5(1)*, Stone Arch Bks.) Capstone.

—Little Lizard's New Pet, 1 vol. Crow, Melinda Melton. 2011. (Little Lizards Ser.). (ENG.). 32p. (J). (gr. -1-1). pap. 6.25 *(978-1-4342-3049-2(X))*; lib. bdg. 22.65 *(978-1-4342-2508-5(9))* Capstone. (Stone Arch Bks.).

—Little Lizard's New Shoes, 1 vol. Crow, Melinda Melton. 2011. (Little Lizards Ser.). (ENG.). 32p. (J). (gr. -1-1). pap. 6.25 *(978-1-4342-3050-8(3))*; lib. bdg. 22.65 *(978-1-4342-2509-2(7))* Capstone. (Stone Arch Bks.).

—Sammy Saw, 1 vol. Klein, Adria F. 2011. (Tool School Ser.). (ENG.). 32p. (J). (gr. 1-2). pap. 6.25 *(978-1-4342-3387-5(1))*; lib. bdg. 22.65 *(978-1-4342-3045-4(7))* Capstone. (Stone Arch Bks.).

—Sammy Saw & the Campout, 1 vol. Klein, Adria F. 2012. (Tool School Ser.). (ENG.). 32p. (J). (gr. 1-3). pap. 6.25 *(978-1-4342-4234-1(X))*; lib. bdg. 22.65 *(978-1-4342-4022-4(3))* Capstone. (Stone Arch Bks.).

—Sophie Screwdriver, 1 vol. Klein, Adria F. 2011. (Tool School Ser.). (ENG.). 32p. (J). (gr. 1-2). pap. 6.25 *(978-1-4342-3386-8(3))*; lib. bdg. 22.65 *(978-1-4342-3044-7(9))* Capstone. (Stone Arch Bks.).

—Sophie Screwdriver & the Classroom, 1 vol. Klein, Adria F. 2012. (Tool School Ser.). (ENG.). 32p. (J). (gr. 1-3). pap.

6.25 *(978-1-4342-4235-8(8))*; lib. bdg. 22.65 *(978-1-4342-4021-7(5))* Capstone. (Stone Arch Bks.).
—Space. 2015. 17p. (J). *(978-1-4351-5936-5(5))* Barnes & Noble, Inc.
—Tia Tape Measure, 1 vol. Klein, Adria F. 2011. (Tool School Ser.). (ENG.). 32p. (J). (gr. 1-2). pap. 6.25 *(978-1-4342-3388-2(X))*; lib. bdg. 22.65 *(978-1-4342-3046-1(5))* Capstone. (Stone Arch Bks.).
—Tia Tape Measure & the Move, 1 vol. Klein, Adria F. 2012. (Tool School Ser.). (ENG.). 32p. (J). (gr. 1-3). pap. 6.25 *(978-1-4342-4236-5(6))*; lib. bdg. 22.65 *(978-1-4342-4023-1(1))* Capstone. (Stone Arch Bks.).
—Tool School. Klein, Adria F. 2013. (Tool School Ser.). (ENG.). 32p. (J). (gr. -1-1). lib. bdg., lib. bdg., lib. bdg. 181.20 *(978-1-4342-8842-4(0)*, Stone Arch Bks.) Capstone.
—Viaje Por la Biblia. Rock, Lois. Pimentel, Alejandro, tr. 2011. (SPA.). 47p. (J). (gr. 4-7). 13.50 *(978-1-55883-030-1(8))* Libros Desafio.
Rowland, Andrew & Rowland, Andy. Snow White Sees the Light. Wallace, Karen. 2015. (Tadpoles: Fairytale Twists Ser.). (ENG.). 32p. (J). (gr. 1-2). *(978-0-7787-1931-1(6))* Crabtree Publishing Co.
Rowland, Andrew & Rowlands, Andy. Little Lizard's Big Party. Crow, Melinda Melton. 2010. (Little Lizards Ser.). (ENG.). 32p. (J). (gr. -1-1). pap. 6.25 *(978-1-4342-2791-1(X)*, Stone Arch Bks.) Capstone.
—Little Lizard's Family Fun. Crow, Melinda Melton. 2010. (Little Lizards Ser.). (ENG.). 32p. (J). (gr. -1-1). pap. 6.25 *(978-1-4342-2790-4(1)*, Stone Arch Bks.) Capstone.
—Little Lizard's First Day. Crow, Melinda Melton. 2010. (Little Lizards Ser.). (ENG.). 32p. (J). (gr. -1-1). pap. 6.25 *(978-1-4342-2789-8(8)*, Stone Arch Bks.) Capstone.
—Little Lizard's New Bike. Crow, Melinda Melton. 2010. (Little Lizards Ser.). (ENG.). 32p. (J). (gr. -1-1). pap. 6.25 *(978-1-4342-2792-8(8)*, Stone Arch Bks.) Capstone.
Rowland, Andy. The ABCs of Trucks, Boats Planes, & Trains. Sellers, Ronnie. 2020. (ENG.). 32p. (J). bds. 9.95 ***(978-1-5319-1222-2(2))*** Sellers Publishing, Inc.
Rowland, Andy. Bow-Tie Pasta: Acrostic Poems. Cleary, Brian P. 2015. (Poetry Adventures Ser.). (ENG.). 32p. (J). (gr. 2-5). 26.65 *(978-1-4677-2046-5(1)*, 9781467720465, Millbrook Pr.) Lerner Publishing Group.
—Esther's Hanukkah Disaster. Sutton, Jane. ed. 2013. (ENG.). 32p. (J). (gr. -1-3). E-Book 23.99 *(978-1-4677-1638-3(3)*, Kar-Ben Publishing) Lerner Publishing Group.
—Little Nelly's Big Book. Goodhart, Pippa. 2012. (ENG.). 32p. (J). (gr. -1-3). 16.99 *(978-1-59990-779-6(8)*, 9781599907796, Bloomsbury USA Childrens) Bloomsbury Publishing USA.
—Ode to a Commode: Concrete Poems. Cleary, Brian P. 2014. (Poetry Adventures Ser.). (ENG.). 32p. (J). (gr. 2-5). pap. 7.99 *(978-1-4677-4454-6(9)*, 9781467744546, Millbrook Pr.) Lerner Publishing Group.
—The Science of Sea Monsters: Prehistoric Reptiles of the Sea. Woolf, Alex. 2017. (Science of Dinosaurs Ser.). (ENG.). 32p. (J). (gr. 3). lib. bdg. 29.00 *(978-0-531-25832-3(7)*, Watts, Franklin) Scholastic Library Publishing.
—Something Sure Smells Around Here: Limericks. Cleary, Brian P. 2015. (Poetry Adventures Ser.). (ENG.). 32p. (J). (gr. 2-5). pap. 7.99 *(978-1-4677-6035-5(8)*, 9781467760355, Millbrook Pr.) Lerner Publishing Group.
Rowland, Andy, jt. illus. see Rowland, Andrew.
Rowland, Jada. Miss Tizzy. Gray, Libba Moore. 2014. 40p. pap. 8.00 *(978-1-61003-356-5(6))* Center for the Collaborative Classroom.
Rowland, Lauri. Grandma's Just Not Herself. Richards, Josie Aleardi. 2010. 36p. pap. 13.95 *(978-1-60911-236-3(9)*, Eloquent Bks.) Strategic Book Publishing & Rights Agency (SBPRA).
Rowland, Michael J. An Irish Tale: Tom Moore & the Seal Woman. Kasony_O'Malley, Michael R. 2007. (J). lib. bdg. 19.95 incl. audio compact disk *(978-0-9776170-3-6(3))* Green Igric Pr.
Rowlands, Andy. The Science of Natural Disasters: The Devastating Truth about Volcanoes, Earthquakes, & Tsunamis. Woolf, Alex. 2018. (Science of the Earth Ser.). (ENG.). 32p. (J). (gr. 3-7). lib. bdg. 29.00 *(978-0-531-22766-4(9)*, Watts, Franklin) Scholastic Library Publishing.
Rowlands, Andy, jt. illus. see Rowland, Andrew.
Rowles, Charles G., 3rd & Rowles, Steve. The Gods of Arr-Kelaan: Going Home (Book 2) Rowles, Charles G., 3rd. Pezzino, Martha, ed. 2005. 200p. (YA). per. 14.95 *(978-0-9748960-2-1(0))* Drunk Duck Comics.
Rowles, Chuck, et al. Drunk & Disorderly Vol. 2: The Drunk Duck Collection. Rowles, Chuck et al. 2004. (YA). per. 14.95 *(978-0-9748960-1-4(2))* Drunk Duck Comics.
Rowles, Steve, jt. illus. see Rowles, Charles G., 3rd.
Rowley, Jillian. The Tree & Annly el Árbol y Annly. Saavedra, Eusebio. 2011. 8p. (J). 7.00 *(978-0-9742432-9-0(9))* Flying Scroll Publishing, LLC.
Rowley, Tom. Brittle's Academy for the Magically Unstable: Charlie Makes a Discovery. Walters, Lily Mae. 2019. (Brittle's Academy Ser.: Vol. 1). (ENG.). 102p. (J). pap. 8.99 ***(978-1-68160-695-8(X))*** Crimson Cloak Publishing.
Rowntree, Winston. Your Presidential Fantasy Dream Team. O'Brien, Daniel. 2016. (ENG.). 272p. (J). (gr. 5). pap. 13.99 *(978-0-553-53747-5(4)*, Crown Books For Young Readers) Random Hse. Children's Bks.
Rowsey, Glenn. Steel Drums. Lakin, Patricia. 2018. (Made by Hand Ser.: 3). (ENG.). 32p. (J). (gr. 3-7). 17.99 *(978-1-4814-7898-4(2)*, Simon & Schuster/Paula Wiseman Bks.) Simon & Schuster/Paula Wiseman Bks.
Rowson, Kirstie. An Amazing Alphabet of Cake. Rowson, Kirstie. 2017. (ENG.). 32p. (J). pap. *(978-0-9928408-5-3(6))* And So We Begin Ltd.
Rowton, Caitlin. My Best Friend. Pruett, Nichole Lee. 2013. (ENG.). 46p. (J). pap. 14.95 *(978-1-936578-15-3(8))* Andy Sanders.
Roxas, Isabel. Hello, Universe. Kelly, Erin Entrada. (ENG.). (J). (gr. 3-7). 2020. 352p. pap. 8.99 *(978-0-06-241416-8(X))*; 2018. 320p. 8.99 ***(978-0-06-287750-5(X))***; 2017. 320p. 16.99 *(978-0-06-241415-1(1))* HarperCollins Pubs. (Greenwillow Bks.).
—Let Me Finish! Lê, Minh. 2016. (ENG.). 40p. (J). (gr. -1-3). 16.99 *(978-1-4847-2173-5(X))* Disney Pr.
—The Littlest Viking. Penfold, Alexandra. 2018. (ENG.). 40p. (J). (gr. -1-3). 17.99 *(978-0-399-55429-2(7))*; lib. bdg. 20.99 *(978-0-399-55430-8(0))* Random Hse. Children's Bks. (Knopf Bks. for Young Readers).
Roy, Avijit, jt. illus. see Basu, Sudipta.
Roy, Camille. Touch & Explore: Jungle. Mazas, Maria. 2019. (Touch & Explore Ser.: 9). (ENG.). 16p. (J). (gr. -1-k). 14.99 *(978-2-408-01284-7(8))* Editions Tourbillon FRA. Dist: Hachette Bk. Group.
Roy, Indrapramit. The Very Hungry Lion: A Folktale. Wolf, Gita. 2006. (ENG.). 24p. 20.95 *(978-81-86211-02-1(0))* Tara Publishing IND. Dist: Consortium Bk. Sales & Distribution.
Roy, Karen. A Royal Little Pest, 1 vol. Reynolds MacArthur, Anita. 2008. (ENG.). 32p. (J). (gr. k-2). 17.95 *(978-0-9810575-0-7(0))* Pollywog Bog Bks. CAN. Dist: Ingram Publisher Services.
Roy, Katherine. Buried Beneath Us: Discovering the Ancient Cities of the Americas. Aveni, Anthony. 2013. (ENG.). 96p. (J). (gr. 4-8). 18.99 *(978-1-59643-567-4(4)*, 900063100) Roaring Brook Pr.
—Otis & Will Discover the Deep: The Record-Setting Dive of the Bathysphere. Rosenstock, Barb. 2018. 48p. (J). (gr. -1-3). 18.99 *(978-0-316-39382-9(7))* Little, Brown Bks. for Young Readers.
—Red Rover: Curiosity on Mars. Ho, Richard. 2019. (ENG.). 44p. (J). 18.99 *(978-1-250-19833-4(X)*, 900194584) Roaring Brook Pr.
Roy, Rejean. Feuille de Lune et la Tribu des Mots. Pitre, Louÿs. 2014. (FRE.). 48p. (J). pap. *(978-2-349-72285-0(6))* Editions La Grande Maree.
Roy, Rejean. Glooscap, les Castors et le Mont Sugarloaf / Klu'skap Kopitk Aqq Sugarloaf Mountain / Glooscap, the Beavers & the Sugarloaf Mountain. Roy, Rejean. Sock, Serena M. 2010. (FRE.). 26p. (J). pap. *(978-2-89682-005-4(1))* Bouton d'or Acadie.
Roy, Suman. Origami Bible Stories for Kids Kit: Bring the Bible to Life with This Interactive Kit! Dewar, Andrew. 2018. 64p. 14.99 *(978-0-8048-4851-0(3))* Tuttle Publishing.
royal, bria. Missing Daddy. Kaba, Mariame. 2019. (ENG.). 36p. (J). 16.95 *(978-1-64259-036-4(3))* Haymarket Bks.
Royal British Columbia Museum Staff, photos by. Safari Beneath the Sea: The Wonder World of the North Pacific Coast, 1 vol. Swanson, Diane. (ENG., 64p. (J). pap. 12.95 *(978-1-55110-441-6(5))* Whitecap Bks., Ltd. CAN. Dist: Graphic Arts Ctr. Publishing Co.
Royal Jr, Andre. The Hippo-Critic: A Tale of Epic Proportions. Royal, Andre. 2020. (ENG.). 28p. (J). pap. ***(978-1-945432-36-1(5))*** Aurora Production AG.
Royder, Mike. Gullet the Mullet. Roper, Uncle Hardy. 2017. (ENG.). 38p. (J). (gr. -1-1). 12.99 *(978-1-59095-344-0(4)*, ExamWise) Total Recall Learning, Inc.
Roydon, Michael. B Is for Beaver: An Oregon Alphabet. Smith, Marie & Smith, Roland. 2003. (Discover America State by State Ser.). (ENG.). 40p. (J). 17.95 *(978-1-58536-071-0(6))* Sleeping Bear Pr.
Royer, Karen L. Time for Bed. Royer, Karen. 2019. (ENG.). 26p. (J). pap. 12.95 *(978-1-7205-5723-4(3))* CreateSpace Independent Publishing Platform.
Royo-Horodynska, Irena. Mnie Stworzye Bog - Ciebie Euolucya. Royo-Horodynska, Irena. 2004.Tr. of I am Created by God - Mov: By Evolution. (POL.). 160p. (YA). pap. *(978-83-88214-58-5(6))* Edytor, Wydawnictwo, Grzywacz, Halina i Franciszek.
Royo, Luis. The Ice Dragon. Martin, George R. R. 2014. (ENG.). 128p. (YA). (gr. 7-12). 14.99 *(978-0-7653-7877-4(9)*, 900140523, Tor Teen) Doherty, Tom Assocs., LLC.
Royse, Jane. Moozie's Cow Wisdom for Loving to the "Uddermost" Morton, Jane & Dreier, Ted. 2003. (J). pap. 4.95 *(978-0-9662268-3-6(6))* Children's Kindness Network.
Royse, Maria. Who Is Jesus? Kucharik, Elena & Goodings, Christina. ed. 2016. (ENG.). 64p. (J). (gr. 2-4). 16.99 *(978-0-7459-6596-3(2))* Lion Hudson PLC GBR. Dist: Independent Pubs. Group.
Roytman, Arkady. Extreme Sports. 2008. (Dover Coloring Bks.). (ENG.). 32p. (J). (gr. k-5). pap. 3.99 *(978-0-486-46688-0(4))* Dover Pubns., Inc.
Rozelaar, Angie. Artsy Cats Board Book. Mudpuppy. 2019. (ENG.). 28p. (J). (gr. -1-k). bds. 12.99 *(978-0-7353-6106-5(1)*, Mudpuppy) Galison.
—The Big Bad Mood. Jamieson, Tom & Demidova, Olga. 2017. 32p. (J). 16.99 *(978-1-4088-3919-5(9)*, 900187434, Bloomsbury Children's Bks.) Bloomsbury Publishing USA.
—Bookish Cats Board Book. Mudpuppy. 2020. (ENG.). 28p. (J). (gr. -1-k). bds. 12.99 *(978-0-7353-6378-6(1))* Mudpuppy Pr.
—Don't Call Me Sweet! Prasadam-Halls, Smriti. 2015. 32p. (J). (gr. -1-1). 18.99 *(978-1-4088-3881-5(8)*, 900140545, Bloomsbury Children's Bks.) Bloomsbury Publishing USA.
—I Love Cake! Starring Rabbit, Porcupine, & Moose. Sauer, Tammi. 2016. (ENG.). 40p. (J). (gr. -1-3). 17.99 *(978-0-06-227894-4(0)*, Tegen, Katherine Bks) HarperCollins Pubs.
Rozelaar, Angie. The Great Pumpkin Contest. Rozelaar, Angie. 2019. (ENG.). 40p. (J). (gr. -1-3). 17.99 *(978-0-06-274137-0(3)*, Tegen, Katherine Bks) HarperCollins Pubs.
Rozinski, Bob, jt. photos by see Shattil, Wendy.
Ru, Mic. Moose! the Reading Dog. Bruneau, Laura & Timmons, Beverly. 2018. (New Directions in the Human-Animal Bond Ser.). (ENG.). 74p. (J). pap. 12.99 *(978-1-55753-813-0(4)*, 3b02e5f2-8ccc-4b1a-9184-70d00ba512b4) Purdue Univ. Pr.
Ruano, Alfonso. The Composition, 1 vol. Skarmeta, Antonio. 2003. (ENG.). 36p. (J). (gr. 3-18). pap. 8.95 *(978-0-88899-550-6(4))* Groundwood Bks. CAN. Dist: Publishers Group West (PGW).
—My Friend, 1 vol. Amado, Elisa. 2019. (ENG.). 40p. (J). (gr. k-3). 18.95 *(978-1-55498-939-3(6))* Groundwood Bks. CAN. Dist: Publishers Group West (PGW).
—Somos Como las Nubes / We Are Like the Clouds, 1 vol. Argueta, Jorge. Amado, Elisa, tr. 2016. (SPA.). 36p. (J). (gr. 1-7). 18.95 *(978-1-55498-849-5(7))* Groundwood Bks. CAN. Dist: Publishers Group West (PGW).
Ruano, Kelsy C. Vuelos. Ruano, Tony. 2016. (SPA.). (J). pap. 15.99 *(978-0-9792972-4-3(9))* Ruano, José A.
Ruano, Kelsy C. & Valdes, Ernesto R. Fabulas para Gigantes. Ruano, Tony. 2016. (SPA.). (J). pap. 10.75 *(978-0-9792972-5-0(7))* Ruano, José A.
Ruban, Alina. Things That Go. Clever Publishing. 2019. (Look & Find, Clever Baby Ser.). (ENG.). 22p. (J). (gr. -1 — 1). bds. 7.99 *(978-1-948418-18-8(5))* Clever Media Group.
Rubbino, Salvatore. Harry Miller's Run. Almond, David. 2017. (ENG.). 64p. (J). (gr. 2-4). 16.99 *(978-0-7636-8975-9(0))* Candlewick Pr.
—Just Ducks! Davies, Nicola. 2012. (ENG.). 32p. (J). (gr. k-4). 15.99 *(978-0-7636-5936-3(3))* Candlewick Pr.
—Just Ducks. Davies, Nicola. 2014. (Read & Wonder Ser.). (ENG.). (J). (gr. k-3). lib. bdg. 17.60 *(978-1-62765-733-4(9))* Perfection Learning Corp.
—Our Very Own Dog. McCardie, Amanda. 2017. (ENG.). 32p. (J). (gr. -1-2). 15.99 *(978-0-7636-8948-3(3))* Candlewick Pr.
—Our Very Own Dog: Taking Care of Your First Pet. McCardie, Amanda. 2019. (Read & Wonder Ser.). (ENG.). 32p. (J). (gr. -1-2). 7.99 *(978-1-5362-0892-4(2))* Candlewick Pr.
Rubbino, Salvatore. A Walk in London. Rubbino, Salvatore. 2011. (ENG.). 40p. (J). (gr. k-3). 16.99 *(978-0-7636-5272-2(5))* Candlewick Pr.
—A Walk in New York. Rubbino, Salvatore. (ENG.). 40p. (J). (gr. -1-3). 2017. 8.99 *(978-0-7636-9510-1(6))*; 2009. 17.99 *(978-0-7636-3855-9(2))* Candlewick Pr.
—A Walk in Paris. Rubbino, Salvatore. 2014. (ENG.). 40p. (J). (gr. -1-3). 17.99 *(978-0-7636-6984-3(9))* Candlewick Pr.
Rubegni, Letizia. Shadow in the Woods & Other Scary Stories: an Acorn Book (Mister Shivers #2) Brallier, Max. 2020. (Mister Shivers Ser.: 2). (ENG.). 64p. (J). (gr. k-2). pap. 4.99 *(978-1-338-61541-8(6))*; lib. bdg. 23.99 *(978-1-338-61542-5(4))* Scholastic, Inc.
Rubel, Doris. Esa Eres Tu y Este Soy Yo. Caballero, D., tr. 2006. (Junior (Silver Dolphin) Ser.). (SPA.). 16p. (J). (gr. -1). 9.95 *(978-970-718-346-9(2))* Readerlink Distribution Services, LLC.
Rubel, Nicole. Best in Show for Rotten Ralph. Gantos, Jack. 2008. (Rotten Ralph Rotten Readers Ser.). (J). 25.95 incl. audio *(978-1-4301-0448-3(1))*; 28.95 incl. audio compact disk *(978-1-4301-0451-3(1))* Live Oak Media.
—Dino Riddles. Hall, Katy & Eisenberg, Lisa. 2003. (Easy-to-Read Ser.). 48p. (J). (gr. -1-3). 11.65 *(978-0-7569-2823-0(0))* Perfection Learning Corp.
—Practice Makes Perfect for Rotten Ralph: A Rotten Ralph Rotten Reader. Gantos, Jack. 2009. (Rotten Ralph Rotten Readers Ser.: 2). (ENG.). 48p. (J). (gr. 1-3). pap. 8.99 *(978-0-374-40002-6(4)*, 900038845) Square Fish.
—Rotten Ralph Feels Rotten. Gantos, Jack. 2007. (Rotten Ralph Ser.). (J). (gr. -1-3). 28.95 incl. audio compact disk *(978-1-4301-0098-0(2))* Live Oak Media.
—Rotten Ralph Helps Out. Gantos, Jack. unabr. ed. 2006. (Readalongs for Beginning Readers Ser.). (J). (gr. -1-3). 24.95 incl. audio *(978-1-59519-678-1(1))*; 28.95 incl. audio compact disk *(978-1-59519-679-8(X))* Live Oak Media.
—Rotten Ralph's Rotten Family: A Rotten Ralph Rotten Reader. Gantos, Jack. 2014. (Rotten Ralph Rotten Readers Ser.: 6). (ENG.). 48p. (J). (gr. 1-3). 16.99 *(978-0-374-36353-6(6)*, 900028351, Farrar, Straus & Giroux (BYR)) Farrar, Straus & Giroux.
Ruben, Paul L., photos by. Scream Machines: All about Roller Coasters. Karr, Susan Schott. 2004. 32p. (J). *(978-0-7652-3264-9(2))* Celebration Pr.
Rubenstein, Reva. The Thankyou Twins. Finkelstein, Ruth. 2006. 24p. (J). *(978-0-9628157-5-1(6))* Finkelstein, Ruth.
Rubin, David. The Fall of the House of West. Pope, Paul & Petty, J. T. 2015. (Battling Boy Ser.: 2). (ENG.). 160p. (J). (gr. 5). pap. 9.99 *(978-1-62672-010-7(X)*, 9781626720107, First Second Bks.) Roaring Brook Pr.
—The Fall of the House of West. Petty, J. T. & Pope, Paul. 2015. 157p. (J). *(978-1-5182-0095-3(8)*, First Second Bks.) Roaring Brook Pr.
—The Rise of Aurora West. Pope, Paul & Petty, J. T. 2014. (Battling Boy Ser.: 2). (ENG.). 160p. (J). (gr. 5-12). pap. 9.99 *(978-1-62672-009-1(6)*, 900129915, First Second Bks.) Roaring Brook Pr.
Rubine. Safari Survivor, No. 21. Smith, Owen & Smith, Anne. 2012. (Twisted Journeys ® Ser.: 21). (ENG.). 112p. (J). (gr. 4-7). lib. bdg. 27.99 *(978-0-7613-6727-7(6)*, 9780761367277, Graphic Universe™) Lerner Publishing Group.
Rubino, Alisa A. Bella: The Crooked Hat Witch. Serafin, Jordan. 2004. (J). *(978-0-932991-57-7(2))* Place In The Woods, The.
—Goldie, the Homeless Calico Cat. Stryker, Robin. 2005. (J). pap. *(978-0-932991-35-5(1))* Place In The Woods, The.
Rubino, Alisa A., jt. illus. see Brudos, Susan E.
Rubino, Maurizia. Big Bad Bunny. Joyce, Melanie. 2014. (ENG.). 26p. (J). bds. 8.95 *(978-1-78440-560-1(4))* Igloo Bks. GBR. Dist: Simon & Schuster, Inc.
—Rugrats Original Graphic Novel: the Last Token. Naujokaitis, Pranas. 2019. (Rugrats Ser.). (ENG.). 112p. (J). pap. 14.99 *(978-1-68415-462-3(6))* Boom! Studios.
Rubinroit, Sue. Where Shabbat Lives, Vol. Fabiyi, Jan Goldin. 2008. (ENG.). 12p. (J). (gr. -1 — 1). bds. 5.95 *(978-0-8225-8946-4(X)*, Kar-Ben Publishing) Lerner Publishing Group.
Rubio, Adrian, jt. illus. see Benatar, Raquel.
Rubio, Ayesha L. Buen Shabat, Shabbat Shalom. Aroeste, Sarah. 2020. (ENG.). 12p. (J). (gr. -1 — 1). bds. 6.99 *(978-1-5415-4246-4(0)*, Kar-Ben Publishing) Lerner Publishing Group.
—Sleeping Beauty. Askew, Amanda. 2018. (Once upon a Time ... Ser.). (ENG.). 24p. (J). (gr. -1-k). lib. bdg. 19.99 *(978-1-68297-299-1(2))* QEB Publishing Inc.
—The Universe Ate My Homework. Zeltser, David. 2018. (ENG.). 32p. (J). (gr. k-3). 17.99 *(978-1-5124-1798-2(X)*, Carolrhoda Bks.) Lerner Publishing Group.
Rubio, Gabriela. He Decidido Llamarme Max. Smadja, Bridgitte & Brigitte, Smadja. (SPA.). 96p. (J). *(978-84-392-8669-1(4))* Gaviota Ediciones ESP. Dist: Lectorum Pubns., Inc.
—Los Milagros de Max. Miracles, Max & Brigitte, Smadja. (SPA.). 84p. (J). *(978-84-392-8700-1(3))* Gaviota Ediciones ESP. Dist: Lectorum Pubns., Inc.
Ruble, Eugene. A Brainy Refrain: The Sum of Our Parts Book 4. Kirk, Bill. 2012. 24p. pap. 10.95 *(978-1-61633-231-0(X))* Guardian Angel Publishing, Inc.
—La Cabra Paisley. Monroy, Rocio. l.t. ed. 2017. (SPA.). 16p. (J). pap. 9.95 *(978-1-61633-907-4(1))* Guardian Angel Publishing, Inc.
—Circulation Celebration: The Sum of Our Parts Series. Kirk, Bill. 2010. 24p. pap. 10.95 *(978-1-61633-019-4(8))* Guardian Angel Publishing, Inc.
—Don't Give a Tiger Shark Indigestion. Ozmore, Kia Kelly. l.t. ed. 2018. (ENG.). 16p. (J). (gr. k-5). pap. 9.95 *(978-1-61633-957-9(8))* Guardian Angel Publishing, Inc.
—Earthquake! Berger, Susan J. 28p. 2013. 19.95 *(978-1-61633-430-7(4))*; 2009. pap. 11.95 *(978-1-933090-66-5(9))* Guardian Angel Publishing, Inc.
—Gatsby's Grand Adventure: Book 2 Renoir's the Apple Seller. Cairn, Barbara. 2013. 16p. pap. 9.95 *(978-1-61633-387-4(1))* Guardian Angel Publishing, Inc.
—Gatsby's Grand Adventures: Book 1 Winslow Homer's Snap the Whip. Cairns, Barbara. 2012. 16p. pap. 9.95 *(978-1-61633-350-8(2))* Guardian Angel Publishing, Inc.
—Gatsby's Grand Adventures Book 4: Vincent Van Gogh's First Steps. Cairns, Barbara. l.t. ed. 2017. (Gatsby's Grand Adventures Ser.: Vol. 4). (ENG.). (J). (gr. k-5). pap. 9.95 *(978-1-61633-874-9(1))* Guardian Angel Publishing, Inc.
—Great Gobs of Gustation- the Sum of Our Parts. Kirk, Bill. 2013. 24p. pap. 10.95 *(978-1-61633-358-4(8))* Guardian Angel Publishing, Inc.
—A Horse of Course. Lyle-Soffe, Shari. 2009. 20p. pap. 10.95 *(978-1-935137-82-5(4))* Guardian Angel Publishing, Inc.
—Liddil Gets Her Light. Cox, Tracey M. 2011. 16p. pap. 9.95 *(978-1-61633-151-1(8))* Guardian Angel Publishing, Inc.
—Little Shepherd. Malandrinos, Cheryl C. 2010. 16p. pap. 9.95 *(978-1-61633-085-9(6))* Guardian Angel Publishing, Inc.
—Muscles Make Us Move. Kirk, Bill. 2011. 32p. pap. 10.95 *(978-1-61633-134-4(8))* Guardian Angel Publishing, Inc.
—My Tooth Is Loose: The Sum of Our Parts. Kirk, Bill. 2012. 20p. pap. 10.95 *(978-1-61633-258-7(1))* Guardian Angel Publishing, Inc.
—Oh Yuck! I Sat on a Duck! Sasano, David. l.t. ed. 2016. (ENG.). (J). pap. 9.95 *(978-1-61633-825-1(3))* Guardian Angel Publishing, Inc.
—Secret Service Saint. Collins, Janet Ann. 2009. 16p. pap. 9.95 *(978-1-935137-98-6(0))* Guardian Angel Publishing, Inc.
—The Skin We're In: The Sum of Our Parts Series. Kirk, Bill. 2012. 24p. pap. 10.95 *(978-1-61633-296-9(4))* Guardian Angel Publishing, Inc.
—The Soggy Town of Hilltop. McNamee, Kevin. 2010. 20p. pap. 10.95 *(978-1-61633-041-5(4))* Guardian Angel Publishing, Inc.
—Tales from Indi: Character Counts! RESPECT. Vishpriya. 2009. 24p. pap. 10.95 *(978-1-933090-57-3(X))* Guardian Angel Publishing, Inc.
—Tissue Tantra: The Sum of Our Parts Series Book 9. Kirk, Bill. 2013. 28p. pap. 10.95 *(978-1-61633-448-2(7))* Guardian Angel Publishing, Inc.
Ruble, Eugene. Ancient Symbols, Artwork, Carvings & Alphabets: Book 3. Ruble, Eugene. l.t. ed. 2018. (Ancient Symbols, Artwork, Carvings & Alphabets Ser.: Vol. 3). (ENG.). 24p. (J). (gr. k-5). pap. 10.95 *(978-1-61633-929-6(2))* Guardian Angel Publishing, Inc.
—Counting 1 to 10 with Professor Hoot. Ruble, Eugene. 2008. 24p. pap. 10.95 *(978-1-935137-47-4(6))* Guardian Angel Publishing, Inc.
—Learning the Basics of Color. Ruble, Eugene. 2010. 16p. pap. 9.95 *(978-1-61633-063-7(5))* Guardian Angel Publishing, Inc.
Rucker, Georgia. Girl Activist. Kamps, Louisa et al. 2019. (Generation Girl Ser.). (ENG.). 160p. (J). (gr. 4). pap. 12.99 *(978-1-941367-64-3(X))* Downtown Bookworks.
—My Favorite Shoes: A Touch-And-feel Shoe-stravaganza. Merberg, Julie. 2013. (ENG.). 16p. (J). (gr. -1 — 1). bds. 12.99 *(978-1-935703-64-8(1))* Downtown Bookworks.
Rudd, Benton. The Heart of a Christmas Tree. Adair, Tammi. 2013. 32p. 16.99 *(978-0-9886409-1-7(0))* Mindstir Media.
—The Itty Bitty It. Ferguson, Scott. 2012. 26p. pap. 9.99 *(978-0-9858398-1-9(3))* Mindstir Media.
—The Poodle Tales: Book Eight. Faber, Toni Tuso. 2013. 24p. 16.99 *(978-0-9897168-0-2(5))*; pap. 10.99 *(978-0-9897168-1-9(3))* Mindstir Media.
—The Poodle Tales: Book Five. Faber, Toni Tuso. 2013. 24p. 16.99 *(978-0-9892711-0-3(2))*; pap. 10.99 *(978-0-9892711-1-0(0))* Mindstir Media.
—The Poodle Tales: Book Four. Faber, Toni Tuso. 2013. 24p. 16.99 *(978-0-9890288-9-9(5))*; pap. 10.99 *(978-0-9890288-8-2(7))* Mindstir Media.
—The Poodle Tales: Book Nine. Faber, Toni Tuso. 2013. 24p. 16.99 *(978-0-9897168-2-6(1))* Mindstir Media.
—The Poodle Tales: Book One. Faber, Toni Tuso. 2012. 26p. (-18). 16.99 *(978-0-9883162-9-4(3))* Mindstir Media.
—The Poodle Tales: Book Seven. Faber, Toni Tuso. 2013. 26p. 16.99 *(978-0-9894748-6-3(0))*; pap. 10.99 *(978-0-9894748-7-0(9))* Mindstir Media.

R

—The Poodle Tales: Book Six. Faber, Toni Tuso. 2013. 24p. 16.99 *(978-0-9892711-2-7(9))*; pap. 10.99 *(978-0-9892711-3-4(7))* Mindstir Media.

—The Poodle Tales: Book Ten. Faber, Toni Tuso. 2013. 24p. 16.99 *(978-0-9910324-1-9(1))* Mindstir Media.

—The Poodle Tales: Book Three. Faber, Toni Tuso. 2012. 24p. 16.99 *(978-0-9886409-9-3(6))*; pap. 10.99 *(978-0-9886409-8-6(8))* Mindstir Media.

—The Poodle Tales: Book Twelve. Faber, Toni Tuso. 2013. 24p. pap. 10.99 *(978-0-9913190-8-4(7))* Mindstir Media.

—The Poodle Tales: Book Two. Faber, Toni Tuso. 2012. 24p. 16.99 *(978-0-9885180-9-4(0))*; pap. 10.99 *(978-0-9885180-8-7(2))* Mindstir Media.

Rudd, Van Thanh. The Patchwork Bike. Clarke, Maxine Beneba. 2018. (ENG.). 40p. (J). (gr. 1-4). 15.99 *(978-1-5362-0031-7(X))* Candlewick Pr.

Rude, Steve. Captain America Legends: What Price Glory. Jones, Bruce. 2003. (Captain America Ser.). 96p. (YA). pap. 9.99 *(978-0-7851-1227-3(8))* Marvel Worldwide, Inc.

Rudebjer, Lars. I'm a Lot of Sometimes: A Growing-Up Story of Identity. Guinan, Jack. 2017. (Growing Up Ser.). (ENG.). 24p. (J). (gr. -1-1). lib. bdg. 19.99 *(978-1-63440-177-7(8))*; E-Book 30.65 *(978-1-63440-181-4(6))* Red Chair Pr. (Rocking Chair Kids).

—Middle Me: A Growing-Up Story of the Middle Child. Dinardo, Jeff. 2017. (Growing Up Ser.). (ENG.). 24p. (J). (gr. -1-1). lib. bdg. 19.99 *(978-1-63440-178-4(6)*, Rocking Chair Kids) Red Chair Pr.

—Middle Me: A Growing-Up Story of the Middle Child. Dinardo, Jeff. ed. 2017. (Growing Up Ser.). (ENG.). 24p. (J). (gr. -1-1). E-Book 30.65 *(978-1-63440-182-1(4)*, Rocking Chair Kids) Red Chair Pr.

Rudge, Leila. Duck for a Day. McKinlay, Meg. 2012. (ENG.). 96p. (J). (gr. 2-4). 12.99 *(978-0-7636-5784-0(0))* Candlewick Pr.

—Let Me Sleep, Sheep! McKinlay, Meg. 2019. (ENG.). 32p. (J). (gr. k-3). 15.99 *(978-1-5362-0547-3(8))* Candlewick Pr.

Rudge, Leila. Gary. Rudge, Leila. 2016. (ENG.). 32p. (J). (gr. -1-2). 16.99 *(978-0-7636-8954-4(8))* Candlewick Pr.

—A Perfect Place for Ted. Rudge, Leila. 2014. (ENG.). 32p. (J). (gr. -1-2). 16.99 *(978-0-7636-6781-8(1))* Candlewick Pr.

Rudi, Olga. Tony's Fantastic Sailing Trip! Schmidt, Carolin. 2019. (ENG.). 26p. (J). pap. 9.95 *(978-1-0821-5406-5(7))* Independently Published.

—Tonys Fantastische Segelreise. Schmidt, Carolin. 2019. (GER.). 26p. (J). pap. 10.40 *(978-1-0999-9941-3(3))* Independently Published.

Rudisill, J. J. Bloques. Koons, Linda. 2016. (Early Rising Readers Ser.). (SPA.). 16p. (J). (gr. 1-1). 6.67 *(978-1-4788-3739-8(X))* Newmark Learning LLC.

—Camino a la Escuela. Koons, Linda. 2016. (Early Rising Readers Ser.). (SPA.). 16p. (J). (gr. 1-1). 6.67 *(978-1-4788-3752-7(7))* Newmark Learning LLC.

—Mi Mitón. Koons, Linda. 2016. (Early Rising Readers Ser.). (SPA.). (J). (gr. -1). 6.67 *(978-1-4788-3660-5(1))* Newmark Learning LLC.

Rudkin, Tracy. Gift of Love, Vol. 2. Polk, James G. Rudkin, Shawn, ed. (YA). *(978-0-9727753-1-1(5))* New Wave Bks. & CD.

Rudner, Andrea. Sophie & Jack. Pelham, Fran & Balcer, Bernadette. 2006. (ENG.). 28p. pap. 10.96 *(978-1-4120-8047-7(9))* Trafford Publishing.

Rudnicki, Richard. Abigail's Wish, 1 vol. Wesley, Gloria Ann. 2016. (ENG.). 32p. (J). (gr. 1-3). 22.95 *(978-1-77108-439-0(1)*, a46dbbe1-5b86-4019-b802-c2986b29f307) Nimbus Publishing, Ltd. CAN. Dist: Baker & Taylor Publisher Services (BTPS).

—A Christmas Dollhouse, 1 vol. ed. 2011. (ENG.). 32p. (J). (gr. 1-3). 18.95 *(978-1-55109-868-5(7)*, 30583883-0270-450c-808d-7d6aa2ff6008) Nimbus Publishing, Ltd. CAN. Dist: Baker & Taylor Publisher Services (BTPS).

—Fania's Heart, 1 vol. Renaud, Anne. 2018. (ENG.). 32p. (J). (gr. 1-3). 18.95 *(978-1-77260-057-5(1))* Second Story Pr. CAN. Dist: Orca Bk. Pubs. USA.

—Gracie: The Public Gardens Duck. Meyrick, Judith. 2007. (ENG.). 32p. (J). (gr. -1-k). 14.95 *(978-1-55109-645-2(5)*, 9eb689e9-a7c5-450e-9f58-d500823a9d9f) Nimbus Publishing, Ltd. CAN. Dist: Baker & Taylor Publisher Services (BTPS).

—I Spy a Bunny, 1 vol. Dudar, Judy. ed. 2009. (ENG.). 32p. (J). (gr. -1-k). 17.95 *(978-1-55109-700-8(1)*, 0dad5ced-ae66-48d4-989f-409298d1ed89) Nimbus Publishing, Ltd. CAN. Dist: Baker & Taylor Publisher Services (BTPS).

—I Spy a Bunny (pb), 1 vol. Dudar, Judy. ed. 2012. (ENG.). 32p. (J). (gr. -1-k). pap. 12.95 *(978-1-55109-942-2(X)*, 887734f3-326e-43a6-bc25-f441dc754ace) Nimbus Publishing, Ltd. CAN. Dist: Baker & Taylor Publisher Services (BTPS).

—Making Contact! Marconi Goes Wireless. Kulling, Monica. 2013. (Great Idea Ser.: 5). (ENG.). 32p. (J). (gr. k-3). 17.95 *(978-1-77049-378-0(6)*, Tundra Bks.) Tundra Bks. CAN. Dist: Penguin Random Hse. LLC.

—Tecumseh, 1 vol. Laxer, James. 2012. (ENG.). 56p. (J). (gr. 3). 19.95 *(978-1-55498-123-6(9))* Groundwood Bks. CAN. Dist: Publishers Group West (PGW).

—Viola Desmond Won't Be Budged, 1 vol. Nyasha Warner, Jody. 2010. (ENG.). 32p. (J). (gr. k-4). 18.95 *(978-0-88899-779-1(5))* Groundwood Bks. CAN. Dist: Publishers Group West (PGW).

Rudnicki Rudnicki, Richard. Viola Desmond Won't Be Budged!, 1 vol. Warner, Jody Nyasha. 2018. (ENG.). 32p. (J). (gr. k-4). pap. 9.95 *(978-1-77306-035-4(X))* Groundwood Bks. CAN. Dist: Publishers Group West (PGW).

Rudolph, Ellen K., photos by. Willi Gets a History Lesson: In Virginia's Historic Triangle. Rudolph, Ellen K. 2007. (ENG., 80p. pap. 24.00 *(978-0-9791348-0-7(3))* EKR Pubns.

Rudolph, Stefanie. Stan & the Four Fantastic Powers: The First Ever Appreciative Inquiry Book for Kids. Levy, Shira et al. 2018. (ENG.). 40p. (J). (gr. 1-6). pap. 14.00 *(978-1-938552-65-6(2))* Taos Institute Pubns.

Rudy, Carol-Ann. Crossing to Freedom. Rudy, Carol-Ann. George, Paul S., ed. Date not set. (Hometown Heritage Ser.). 48p. (Orig.). (J). (gr. 2-4). pap. 4.95 *(978-1-889300-02-3(0))* Dormouse Productions, Inc.

Rudy, Maggie. I Wish I Had a Pet. Rudy, Maggie. 2014. (ENG.). 40p. (J). (gr. -1-3). 17.99 *(978-1-4424-5332-6(X)*, Beach Lane Bks.) Beach Lane Bks.

—Sootypaws: a Cinderella Story. Rudy, Maggie. 2020. (ENG.). 40p. (J). 17.99 *(978-1-250-18604-1(8)*, 900191474, Holt, Henry & Co. Bks. For Young Readers) Holt, Henry & Co.

Rudy, Marco. Odin. Denton, Shannon Eric. 2010. (Short Tales Norse Myths Ser.). (ENG.). 32p. (J). (gr. 1-4). 27.07 *(978-1-60270-568-5(2)*, 13465, Short Tales) Magic Wagon.

Ruebartsch, John, photos by. All about Wisconsin: Todo Acerca de Wisconsin. 2007.Tr. of Todo Acerca de Wisconsin. (ENG & SPA., 84p. (J). pap. 16.00 *(978-0-9770816-3-9(X))* SHARP Literacy, Inc.

—Friends & Neighbors: We Love to Learn. Cole, Kenneth. 2005. (J). pap. 9.95 *(978-0-9770816-1-5(3))* SHARP Literacy, Inc.

—Friends & Neighbors: We Love to Learn. Cole, Kenneth. ed. 2005. (J). 16.95 *(978-0-9770816-0-8(5))* SHARP Literacy, Inc.

Rueckel, Jeff. Wished for Me. Barragan, Kathleen. 2019. (ENG.). 28p. (J). pap. 9.99 *(978-1-7189-4472-5(1))* CreateSpace Independent Publishing Platform.

Rueda, Claudia. Celebrate Thanksgiving Day with Beto & Gaby. Flor Ada, Alma. Hayes, Joe & Franco, Sharon, trs. from SPA. 2006. (Cuentos para Celebrar / Stories to Celebrate Ser.). 30p. (J). (gr. k-6). per. 11.95 *(978-1-59820-133-8(6))* Santillana USA Publishing Co., Inc.

—Eency Weency Spider. Wang, Margaret. 2006. (ENG.). (J). 12p. bds. 5.95 *(978-1-58117-505-9(1))*; 22p. (gr. -1-3). bds. 10.95 *(978-1-58117-418-2(7))* Bendon, Inc. (Intervisual/Piggy Toes).

—Here Comes Teacher Cat. Underwood, Deborah. 2017. 80p. (J). (-k). 16.99 *(978-0-399-53905-3(0)*, Dial Bks) Penguin Young Readers Group.

—Here Comes the Easter Cat. Underwood, Deborah. 2014. 80p. (J). (gr. -1-k). 16.99 *(978-0-8037-3939-0(7)*, Dial Bks) Penguin Young Readers Group.

—Here Comes the Tooth Fairy Cat. Underwood, Deborah. 2015. 96p. (J). (gr. -1-k). 16.99 *(978-0-525-42774-2(0)*, Dial Bks) Penguin Young Readers Group.

—Here Comes Valentine Cat. Underwood, Deborah. 2015. 88p. (J). (-k). 16.99 *(978-0-525-42915-9(8)*, Dial Bks) Penguin Young Readers Group.

—I Know an Old Lady Who Swallowed a Fly. 2005. 14p. (J). 12.95 *(978-1-58117-267-6(2)*, Intervisual/Piggy Toes) Bendon, Inc.

Ruel, Adeline. Big Bear Can't Fall Asleep. Ruel, Adeline. 2017. (ENG.). 22p. (J). (— 1). bds. 9.99 *(978-988-8341-49-8(9)*, Minedition) Neugebauer, Michael (Publishing) Limited HKG. Dist: Penguin Random Hse. LLC.

Ruell, L J. Is That Funny? Patrick, B. & Schotz, Leo D. 2006. (ENG.). 32p. (J). (gr. -1-3). 15.95 *(978-0-9741319-6-2(2))* 4N Publishing LLC.

Ruelle, Karen. Bark Park, 1 vol. Ruelle, Karen Gray. (ENG.). 32p. (J). (gr. -1-1). 2014. pap. 7.95 *(978-1-56145-773-1(6))*; 2008. 15.95 *(978-1-56145-434-1(6))* Peachtree Publishing Co. Inc.

Ruelle, Karen Gray. Just in Time for New Year's! A Harry & Emily Adventure. Ruelle, Karen Gray. 2004. (Holiday House Readers Ser.). (ENG.). 32p. (J). pap. 4.95 *(978-0-8234-1842-8(1))* Holiday Hse., Inc.

Ruff, Jim, jt. illus. see Ruff, Zeata P.

Ruff, Zeata P. & Ruff, Jim. The Gumdrop Tree. Ruff, Zeata P. 2013. 34p. 16.95 *(978-1-937449-25-4(4))* YAV.

Ruffenach, France, photos by. Cupcakes! Klivans, Elinor. 2005. (ENG., 144p. (gr. 8-17). pap. 16.95 *(978-0-8118-4545-8(1))* Chronicle Bks. LLC.

—Everyday Celebrations: Savoring Food, Family, & Life at Home. Maggipinto, Donata. 2005. (ENG., 180p. (gr. 8-17). pap. 24.95 *(978-0-8118-4487-1(0))* Chronicle Bks. LLC.

Ruffieux, Jean-Marie & Chagnaud, Y. Pharaons et Dieux de l'Egypte Ancienne. Quesnel, Alain. 2010. (Mythes et Legendes Ser.: Vol. 2920940). (FRE.). (J). pap. *(978-2-01-292094-1(2))* Hachette Jeunesse.

Ruffin, Aurzella. Have You Ever Made Mud Pies on a Hot Summer Day? This Is a Bitty Book. Stevenson-Spurgon, Barbara J. 2006. 36p. (J). (gr. -1-4). per. 19.95 *(978-1-60002-234-0(0)*, 4073) Mountain Valley Publishing, LLC.

Ruffins, Reynold. Koi & the Kola Nuts. Gleeson, Brian. 2007. (Rabbit Ears-A Classic Tale Ser.). (ENG.). 36p. (J). (gr. 2-6). 28.50 *(978-1-59961-310-9(7)*, 12963, Picture Bk.) Spotlight.

—Marco's Run. Cartier, Wesley. ed. 2003. (Green Light Readers Level 2 Ser.). (ENG.). 24p. (J). (gr. -1-3). pap. 4.99 *(978-0-15-204828-0(6)*, 1194579) Houghton Mifflin Harcourt Publishing Co.

Ruffle, Mark. On the Track Blue Band. Llewellyn, Claire. 2016. (Cambridge Reading Adventures Ser.). (ENG.). 16p. pap. 7.37 *(978-1-316-50322-5(4))* Cambridge Univ. Pr.

Ruffle, Mark, jt. illus. see Bernstein, Galia.

Ruffolo, Rob, jt. illus. see Milne, Alex.

Rugg, Jim. Dr. Horrible. Whedon, Zack & Horse, Dark. 2010. (ENG.). 80p. pap. 9.99 *(978-1-59582-577-3(0))* Dark Horse Comics.

—Head, Vol. 1. Seagle, Steven T. rev. ed. 2006. (American Virgin Ser.). (ENG.). 112p. pap. 9.99 *(978-1-4012-1065-6(1)*, Vertigo) DC Comics.

Ruggeri, Alida. Pateandolo (Kickin It) Greve, Meg. 2017. (Beginning Chapter Bks.). (SPA.). 48p. (gr. k-3). pap. 8.95 *(978-1-68342-251-8(1)*, 9781683422518) Rourke Educational Media.

Ruhl, Greg. The Buried City of Pompeii: What It Was Like When Vesuvius Exploded. Christopher, Peter, photos by. Tanaka, Shelley. 2003. 48p. (J). (gr. 4-9). reprint ed. 17.00 *(978-0-7567-6722-8(9))* DIANE Publishing Co.

Rui, Paolo. Galileo's Journal, 1609-1610. Pettenati, Jeanne. 2006. 32p. (J). (gr. 1-4). pap. 7.95 *(978-1-57091-880-3(5))* Charlesbridge Publishing, Inc.

Ruis, Maria. Mi Gato. Sánchez, Isidro. (Coleccion Mis Animales Preferidos).Tr. of My Cat. (SPA.). 32p. (J). (gr. k-3). 6.36 *(978-84-342-1127-8(0)*, PR0482) Parramon Ediciones S.A. ESP. Dist: Lectorum Pubns., Inc.

—Mi Hamster. Sánchez, Isidro. (Coleccion Mis Animales Preferidos).Tr. of My Hamster. (SPA.). 32p. (J). (gr. k-3). 6.36 *(978-84-342-1129-2(7)*, PR0485) Parramon Ediciones S.A. ESP. Dist: Lectorum Pubns., Inc.

—Mi Pajaro. Sánchez, Isidro. (Coleccion Mis Animales Preferidos).Tr. of My Bird. (SPA.). 32p. (J). (gr. k-3). 6.36 *(978-84-342-1128-5(9)*, PR0483) Parramon Ediciones S.A. ESP. Dist: Lectorum Pubns., Inc.

—Mi Perro. Sánchez, Isidro. (Coleccion Mis Animales Preferidos).Tr. of My Dog. (SPA.). 32p. (J). (gr. k-3). *(978-84-342-1126-1(2)*, PR0481) Parramon Ediciones S.A. ESP. Dist: Lectorum Pubns., Inc.

Ruiz Abello, Margarita. PEDRITO Y EL REY GLOTÓN. 2004. (Troquelados Clásicos Ser.). (SPA & ENG.). 16p. (J). (gr. -1-k). pap. 3.95 *(978-84-7864-738-5(4))* Combel Editorial, S.A. ESP. Dist: Independent Pubs. Group.

—EL PEZ DE ORO. 2005. (Troquelados Clásicos Ser.). (SPA & ENG.). 16p. (J). (gr. -1-k). pap. 3.95 *(978-84-7864-897-9(6))* Combel Editorial, S.A. ESP. Dist: Independent Pubs. Group.

—UNA PRINCESA DE VERDAD. 2003. (Troquelados Clásicos Ser.). (SPA & ENG.). 16p. (J). (gr. -1-k). pap. 3.95 *(978-84-7864-677-7(9))* Combel Editorial, S.A. ESP. Dist: Independent Pubs. Group.

—EL RUISEÑOR. 2004. (Troquelados Clásicos Ser.). (SPA & ENG.). 16p. (J). (gr. -1-k). pap. 3.95 *(978-84-7864-737-8(6))* Combel Editorial, S.A. ESP. Dist: Independent Pubs. Group.

—EL SASTRECILLO VALIENTE. 2005. (Troquelados Clásicos Ser.). (SPA & ENG.). 16p. (J). (gr. -1-k). pap. 3.95 *(978-84-7864-896-2(8))* Combel Editorial, S.A. ESP. Dist: Independent Pubs. Group.

—LA VENDEDORA DE FÓSFOROS. 2003. (Troquelados Clásicos Ser.). (ENG & SPA.). 16p. (J). (gr. -1-k). pap. 3.95 *(978-84-7864-675-3(2))* Combel Editorial, S.A. ESP. Dist: Independent Pubs. Group.

—ZAPATOS BAILARINES. 2003. (Troquelados Clásicos Ser.). (SPA & ENG.). 16p. (J). (gr. -1-k). pap. 3.95 *(978-84-7864-678-4(7))* Combel Editorial, S.A. ESP. Dist: Independent Pubs. Group.

Ruiz, Alfonso. Drácula. Stoker, Bram. Schuler, Susan, tr. 2010. (Classic Fiction Ser.). (SPA.). 72p. (J). (gr. 5-9). pap. 7.15 *(978-1-4342-2277-0(2)*, Stone Arch Bks.) Capstone.

—Dracula. Stoker, Bram. Schuler, Susan, tr. 2010. (Classic Fiction Ser.). 72p. pap. 0.90 *(978-1-4342-2985-4(8)*, Stone Arch Bks.) Capstone.

—Full Court Pressure, 1 vol. Gunderson, Jessica & Gonzalez, Jorge. 2010. (Sports Illustrated Kids Graphic Novels Ser.). (ENG.). 56p. (J). (gr. 3-8). pap. 7.19 *(978-1-4342-2291-6(8)*, Stone Arch Bks.) Capstone.

—Full Court Pressure, 1 vol. Gunderson, Jessica. 2010. (Sports Illustrated Kids Graphic Novels Ser.). (ENG.). 56p. (J). (gr. 3-8). 26.65 *(978-1-4342-1911-4(9)*, Stone Arch Bks.) Capstone.

—Kickoff Blitz. Hoena, Blake A. & Gonzalez, Jorge. 2010. (Sports Illustrated Kids Graphic Novels Ser.). 56p. pap. 0.50 *(978-1-4342-3205-2(0))*; (ENG.). (J). (gr. 3-8). pap. 7.19 *(978-1-4342-2292-3(6))*; (ENG.). (J). (gr. 3-8). 26.65 *(978-1-4342-1909-1(7))* Capstone. (Stone Arch Bks.).

—Pinocchio, 1 vol. Gonzalez, Jorge & Collodi, Carlo. 2009. (Classic Fiction Ser.).Tr. of Avventure di Pinocchio. (ENG.). 72p. (J). (gr. 5-9). lib. bdg. 27.99 *(978-1-4342-1583-3(0)*, Stone Arch Bks.) Capstone.

Ruiz, Ana, jt. illus. see Gonzalez, Ralfka.

Ruiz, Ángeles. Hillel Builds a House. Lepon, Shoshana. 2020. (ENG.). 32p. (J). (gr. -1-3). 17.99 ***(978-1-5415-4402-4(1)**, Kar-Ben Publishing)* Lerner Publishing Group.

Ruiz, Aristides. From Army Ants to Zebrafish: Animals That Hop, Fly & Swish! (Dr. Seuss/Cat in the Hat) Golden Books. 2013. (ENG.). 64p. (J). (gr. -1-2). pap. 5.99 *(978-0-449-81432-1(7)*, Golden Bks.) Random Hse. Children's Bks.

—High? Low? Where Did It Go? All about Animal Camouflage. Rabe, Tish. 2016. (Cat in the Hat's Learning Library). (ENG.). 48p. (J). (gr. k-3). lib. bdg. 13.99 *(978-0-375-97169-3(6)*, Random Hse. Bks. for Young Readers) Random Hse. Children's Bks.

Ruiz, Aristides, et al. How to Help the Earth-By the Lorax. Rabe, Tish. 2012. (Step into Reading: Step 3 Ser.). (ENG.). 48p. (J). (gr. k-2). lib. bdg. 16.19 *(978-0-375-96977-5(2))* Random Hse. Bks. for Young Readers.

—How to Help the Earth-By the LORAX. Rabe, Tish. 2012. (Step into Reading Ser.). (ENG.). 48p. (J). (gr. k-3). pap. 4.99 *(978-0-375-86977-8(8)*, Random Hse. Bks. for Young Readers) Random Hse. Children's Bks.

Ruiz, Aristides. If I Ran the Rain Forest: All about Tropical Rain Forests. Worth, Bonnie. 2003. (Cat in the Hat's Learning Library). (ENG.). 48p. (J). (gr. -1-3). 9.99 *(978-0-375-81097-8(8)*, Random Hse. Bks. for Young Readers) Random Hse. Children's Bks.

—Inside Your Outside: All about the Human Body. Rabe, Tish. 2003. (Cat in the Hat's Learning Library). (ENG.). 48p. (J). (gr. -1-3). 9.99 *(978-0-375-81100-5(1)*, Random Hse. Bks. for Young Readers) Random Hse. Children's Bks.

—Oh Say Can You Say What's the Weather Today? All about Weather. Rabe, Tish. 2004. (Cat in the Hat's Learning Library). (ENG.). 48p. (J). (gr. -1-3). 9.99 *(978-0-375-82276-6(3)*, Random Hse. Bks. for Young Readers) Random Hse. Children's Bks.

—Oh, the Things Spring Brings! Golden Books Staff. 2013. (Color Plus Stencil Ser.). (ENG.). 64p. (J). (-k). pap. 5.99 *(978-0-307-98123-3(1)*, Golden Bks.) Random Hse. Children's Bks.

—Oh, the Things You Can Do That Are Good for You! All about Staying Healthy. Rabe, Tish. 2015. (Cat in the Hat's Learning Library). (ENG.). 64p. (J). (gr. k-3). lib. bdg. 13.99 *(978-0-375-91098-2(0)*, Random Hse. Bks. for Young Readers) Random Hse. Children's Bks.

—One Cent, Two Cents, Old Cent, New Cent: All about Money. Worth, Bonnie. 2008. (Cat in the Hat's Learning Library). (ENG.). 48p. (J). (gr. -1-3). 9.99 *(978-0-375-82881-2(8)*, Random Hse. Bks. for Young Readers) Random Hse. Children's Bks.

—A Whale of a Tale! All about Porpoises, Dolphins, & Whales. Worth, Bonnie. 2006. (Cat in the Hat's Learning Library). (ENG.). 48p. (J). (gr. -1-3). 9.99 *(978-0-375-82279-7(8)*, Random Hse. Bks. for Young Readers) Random Hse. Children's Bks.

—Wings & Paws & Fins & Claws. Rabe, Tish. 2010. (ENG.). 96p. (J). (gr. -1-2). pap. 3.99 *(978-0-375-85928-1(4)*, Golden Bks.) Random Hse. Children's Bks.

Ruiz, Aristides & Giles, Mike. Comic Book Heroes. Thomas, Jim. ed. 2005. 32p. (J). lib. bdg. 15.00 *(978-1-59054-990-2(2))* Fitzgerald Bks.

Ruiz, Aristides & Mathieu, Joe. Chasing Rainbows. Rabe, Tish. 2012. (Pictureback(R) Ser.). (ENG.). 16p. (J). (gr. -1-2). pap. 4.99 *(978-0-375-87124-5(1)*, Random Hse. Bks. for Young Readers) Random Hse. Children's Bks.

—Clam-I-Am! All about the Beach. Rabe, Tish. 2005. (Cat in the Hat's Learning Library). (ENG.). 48p. (J). (gr. -1-3). 9.99 *(978-0-375-82280-3(1)*, Random Hse. Bks. for Young Readers) Random Hse. Children's Bks.

—Happy Pi Day to You! Worth, Bonnie. 2020. (Cat in the Hat's Learning Library). (ENG.). 48p. (J). (gr. k-3). lib. bdg. 12.99 *(978-0-525-57994-6(X)*, Random Hse. Bks. for Young Readers) Random Hse. Children's Bks.

—Hark! a Shark! All about Sharks. Worth, Bonnie. 2013. (Cat in the Hat's Learning Library). (ENG.). 48p. (J). (gr. k-3). 9.99 *(978-0-375-87073-6(3)*, Random Hse. Bks. for Young Readers) Random Hse. Children's Bks.

—High? Low? Where Did It Go? All about Animal Camouflage. Rabe, Tish. 2016. (Cat in the Hat's Learning Library). (ENG.). 48p. (J). (gr. k-3). 9.99 *(978-0-449-81496-3(3)*, Random Hse. Bks. for Young Readers) Random Hse. Children's Bks.

—I Can Name 50 Trees Today! All about Trees. Worth, Bonnie. 2006. (Cat in the Hat's Learning Library). (ENG.). 48p. (J). (gr. -1-3). 9.99 *(978-0-375-82277-3(1)*, Random Hse. Bks. for Young Readers) Random Hse. Children's Bks.

—Ice Is Nice! All about the North & South Poles. Worth, Bonnie. 2010. (Cat in the Hat's Learning Library). (ENG.). 48p. (J). (gr. -1-3). 9.99 *(978-0-375-82885-0(0)*, Random Hse. Bks. for Young Readers) Random Hse. Children's Bks.

—If I Ran the Dog Show: All about Dogs. Rabe, Tish. 2012. (Cat in the Hat's Learning Library). (ENG.). 48p. (J). (gr. k-2). lib. bdg. 24.94 *(978-0-375-96682-8(X))* Random House Publishing Group.

—If I Ran the Dog Show: All about Dogs. Rabe, Tish. 2012. (Cat in the Hat's Learning Library). (ENG.). 48p. (J). (gr. k-3). 9.99 *(978-0-375-86682-1(5)*, Random Hse. Bks. for Young Readers) Random Hse. Children's Bks.

—If I Ran the Horse Show: All about Horses. Worth, Bonnie. 2012. (Cat in the Hat's Learning Library). (ENG.). 48p. (J). (gr. k-3). 9.99 *(978-0-375-86683-8(3)*, Random Hse. Bks. for Young Readers) Random Hse. Children's Bks.

—Miles & Miles of Reptiles: All about Reptiles. Rabe, Tish. 2009. (Cat in the Hat's Learning Library). (ENG.). 48p. (J). (gr. -1-3). 9.99 *(978-0-375-82884-3(2)*, Random Hse. Bks. for Young Readers) Random Hse. Children's Bks.

—My, Oh My — A Butterfly! All about Butterflies. Rabe, Tish. 2007. (Cat in the Hat's Learning Library). (ENG.). 48p. (J). (gr. -1-3). 9.99 *(978-0-375-82882-9(6)*, Random Hse. Bks. for Young Readers) Random Hse. Children's Bks.

—Night Lights (Dr. Seuss/Cat in the Hat) Rabe, Tish. 2014. (Pictureback(R) Ser.). (ENG.). 16p. (J). (gr. -1-2). pap. 4.99 *(978-0-385-37116-2(0)*, Random Hse. Bks. for Young Readers) Random Hse. Children's Bks.

—Oh, the Pets You Can Get! All about Our Animal Friends. Rabe, Tish. 2005. (Cat in the Hat's Learning Library). (ENG.). 48p. (J). (gr. -1-3). 9.99 *(978-0-375-82278-0(X)*, Random Hse. Bks. for Young Readers) Random Hse. Children's Bks.

—One Vote, Two Votes, I Vote, You Vote. Worth, Bonnie. 2016. (Cat in the Hat's Learning Library). (ENG.). 64p. (J). (gr. k-3). 9.99 *(978-0-399-55598-5(6))*; lib. bdg. 12.99 *(978-0-399-55599-2(4))* Random Hse. Children's Bks. (Random Hse. Bks. for Young Readers).

—Safari, So Good! All about African Wildlife. Worth, Bonnie. 2011. (Cat in the Hat's Learning Library). (ENG.). 48p. (J). (gr. -1-3). 9.99 *(978-0-375-86681-4(7)*, Random Hse. Bks. for Young Readers) Random Hse. Children's Bks.

—Trick-or-Treat!/Aye-Aye! Rabe, Tish. 2012. (Pictureback(R) Ser.). (ENG.). 32p. (J). (gr. -1-2). pap. 4.99 *(978-0-307-93056-9(4)*, Random Hse. Bks. for Young Readers) Random Hse. Children's Bks.

—What Cat Is That? All about Cats. Rabe, Tish. 2013. (Cat in the Hat's Learning Library). (ENG.). 48p. (J). (gr. k-3). 9.99 *(978-0-375-86640-1(X)*, Random Hse. Bks. for Young Readers) Random Hse. Children's Bks.

—Who Hatches the Egg? All about Eggs. Rabe, Tish. 2017. (Cat in the Hat's Learning Library). (ENG.). 48p. (J). (gr. k-3). lib. bdg. 13.99 *(978-0-375-97171-6(8)*, Random Hse. Bks. for Young Readers) Random Hse. Children's Bks.

—Why Oh Why Are Deserts Dry? All about Deserts. Rabe, Tish. 2011. (Cat in the Hat's Learning Library). (ENG.). 48p. (J). (gr. -1-3). 9.99 *(978-0-375-85868-0(7)*, Random Hse. Bks. for Young Readers) Random Hse. Children's Bks.

—The 100 Hats of the Cat in the Hat: A Celebration of the 100th Day of School. Rabe, Tish. 2019. (Cat in the Hat's Learning Library). 48p. (J). (gr. k-3). 9.99 *(978-0-525-57995-3(8)*, Random Hse. Bks. for Young Readers) Random Hse. Children's Bks.

Ruiz, Aristides & Mathieu, Joseph. Would You Rather Be a Pollywog? All about Pond Life. Worth, Bonnie. 2010. (Cat in the Hat's Learning Library). (ENG.). 48p. (J). (gr. -1-3). 9.99 *(978-0-375-82883-6(4)*, Random Hse. Bks. for Young Readers) Random Hse. Children's Bks.

Ruiz, Aristides, jt. illus. see Mathieu, Joe.

Ruiz, Cecilia. A Gift from Abuela. Ruiz, Cecilia. 2018. 38p. (J). (gr. -1-3). 16.99 *(978-0-7636-9267-4(0))* Candlewick Pr.

Ruiz, Christina. I Really CAN Do Anything! Thrower, Mykia. 2019. (ENG.). 38p. (J). pap. 12.99 ***(978-1-6749-4243-8(5))*** Independently Published.

Ruiz, Felix & Beaulieu, Jean-François. Disney Kingdoms: Big Thunder Mountain Railroad #3. Hopeless, Dennis. 2016. (Disney Kingdoms: Big Thunder Mountain Railroad Ser.). (ENG.). 24p. (J). (gr. k-5). lib. bdg. 27.07 *(978-1-61479-577-3(0)*, 24358, Graphic Novels) Spotlight.

Ruiz, Joe. Paul el Piloto Vuela a Barcelona: Aprendizaje de Idiomas Divertido para niños de 4 a 7 Años. Barton, Sarah & Wilkins, Ray. 2019. (Paul the Pilot Bilingual Storybooks - English & Spanish Ser.: Vol. 2). (SPA.). 76p. (J). pap. *(978-1-912761-07-4(6))* Nicier Publishing.

—Paul le Pilote S'Envole Pour Paris: Apprendre une Langue en S'Amusant Pour les 4-7 Ans. Barton, Sarah & Wilkins, Ray. 2019. (Paul the Pilot Bilingual Storybooks - English & French Ser.: Vol. 2). (FRE.). 72p. (J). pap. *(978-1-912761-01-2(7))* Nicier Publishing.

—Paul the Pilot Flies to Barcelona: Fun Language Learning for 4-7 Year Olds. Barton, Sarah & Wilkins, Ray. 2019. (Paul the Pilot Bilingual Storybooks - English & Spanish Ser.: Vol. 1). (ENG.). 76p. (J). pap. *(978-1-912761-06-7(8))* Nicier Publishing.

—Paul the Pilot Flies to Beijing: Fun Language Learning for 4-7 Year Olds. Barton, Sarah & Wilkins, Ray. 2019. (Paul the Pilot Bilingual Storybooks - English & Chinese Ser.: Vol. 1). (ENG.). 76p. (J). pap. *(978-1-912761-12-8(2))*; pap. *(978-1-912761-13-5(0))* Nicier Publishing.

—Paul the Pilot Flies to Beijing: Fun Language Learning for 4-7 Year Olds (with Pinyin) Barton, Sarah & Wilkins, Ray. 2019. (Paul the Pilot Bilingual Storybooks - English & Chinese Ser.: Vol. 4). (ENG.). 76p. (J). pap. *(978-1-912761-19-7(X))*; pap. *(978-1-912761-18-0(1))* Nicier Publishing.

Ruiz Johnson, Mariana. Le Colibri Chante et Danse: Chansons et Comptines Latino-Américaines. 2019. (FRE.). 64p. (J). (gr. -1-k). 16.95 *(978-2-924774-16-8(0))* La Montagne Secrete CAN. Dist: Independent Pubs. Group.

Ruiz Johnson, Mariana. Head, Shoulders, Knees & Toes. Silver, Skye. 2020. (ENG.). 32p. (J). pap. ***(978-1-64686-069-2(1))*** Barefoot Bks., Inc.

Ruiz, Jose Alfonso Ocampo & Woodman, Ned. The Last Rider: The Final Days of the Pony Express. Gunderson, J. 2007. (Historical Fiction Ser.). (ENG.). 56p. (J). (gr. 3-6). pap. 6.25 *(978-1-59889-407-3(2)*, Stone Arch Bks.) Capstone.

Ruiz, Joy Hwang. Every Little Letter. Underwood, Deborah. 2020. 40p. (J). (gr. -1-3). 17.99 ***(978-0-525-55402-8(5)***, Dial Bks) Penguin Young Readers Group.

Ruiz, Margarita. La Gallina de Los Huevos de Oro. 2020. (Troquelados Clásicos Ser.). (SPA.). 16p. (J). (gr. -1-k). pap. 3.95 ***(978-84-9825-401-3(9))*** Combel Editorial, S.A. ESP. Dist: Independent Pubs. Group.

Ruiz, Margarita. Pinocho. (SPA & ENG.). 24p. (J). (gr. -1-5). pap. 5.95 incl. audio compact disk *(978-88-8148-253-5(3))* EMC/Paradigm Publishing.

Ruiz, Margarita. Rapunzel. 2020. (Troquelados Clásicos Ser.). (SPA.). 16p. (J). (gr. -1-k). pap. 3.95 ***(978-84-9825-404-4(3))*** Combel Editorial, S.A. ESP. Dist: Independent Pubs. Group.

Ruiz Navarro, Jose. Rafael Alberti y los Niños. Ruiz Navarro, Jose. González, Lola et al. 2007. (SPA.). 50p. (J). (gr. 4-5). 23.99 *(978-84-241-2728-2(5))* Everest Editora ESP. Dist: Lectorum Pubns., Inc.

Ruiz, Pedro. Una Noche en el Tejado. Ruiz, Clarisa & Reyes, Yolanda. 2004. (Primer Acto: Teatro Infantil y Juvenil Ser.). (SPA.). 63p. (J). (gr. -1-7). pap. *(978-958-30-0320-2(4))* Panamericana Editorial.

Ruiz, Rosie. Have You Heard of the Little Boy Named Oliver? Costa, Gigi. 2018. (ENG.). 24p. (J). pap. 14.99 *(978-0-692-11572-5(2))* Gigi Costa.

Rukl, Antonin, jt. illus. see Tirion, Wil.

Rumble, Simon. Back on Track. Jackson, Kyle. 2018. (Mac's Sports Report). (ENG.). 128p. (J). pap. 7.99 *(978-1-63163-224-2(8)*, 1631632248); lib. bdg. 27.13 *(978-1-63163-223-5(X)*, 163163223X) North Star Editions. (Jolly Fish Pr.).

—Concussion Comeback. Jackson, Kyle. 2018. (Mac's Sports Report). (ENG.). 128p. (J). pap. 7.99 *(978-1-63163-228-0(0)*, 1631632280); lib. bdg. 27.13 *(978-1-63163-227-3(2)*, 1631632272) North Star Editions. (Jolly Fish Pr.).

—Mac's Sports Report (set Of 4) Jackson, Kyle. 2018. (Mac's Sports Report). (ENG.). 512p. (J). pap. 31.96 *(978-1-63163-220-4(5)*, 1631632205); lib. bdg. 108.52 *(978-1-63163-219-8(1)*, 1631632191) North Star Editions. (Jolly Fish Pr.).

—Racket Rumors. Jackson, Kyle. 2018. (Mac's Sports Report). (ENG.). 128p. (J). pap. 7.99 *(978-1-63163-232-7(9)*, 1631632329); lib. bdg. 27.13 *(978-1-63163-231-0(0)*, 1631632310) North Star Editions. (Jolly Fish Pr.).

—Sideline Pressure. Jackson, Kyle. 2018. (Mac's Sports Report). (ENG.). 128p. (J). pap. 7.99 *(978-1-63163-236-5(1)*, 1631632361, Jolly Fish Pr.) North Star Editions.

Rumford, James. Silent Music: A Story of Bagdad. Rumford, James. 2008. (ENG.). 32p. (J). (gr. -1-3). 18.99 *(978-1-59643-276-5(4)*, 900044099) Roaring Brook Pr.

Rumford, James. Beowulf: A Hero's Tale Retold. Rumford, James, retold by. 2006. (J). *(978-0-399-24391-2(7))* Penguin Publishing Group.

Rumikuu. Lily Clairet, Vol. 5. Ng, Kaye. 2020. (ENG.). 320p. (J). pap. ***(978-1-912792-06-1(0))*** Atsuko Pr.

Ruminski, Jeff. Taking Care of Pets. Mullican, Judy. l.t. ed. 2004. (HRL Big Book Ser.). 8p. (J). (gr. -1-1). pap. 10.95 *(978-1-57332-278-2(4))*; pap. 10.95 *(978-1-57332-279-9(2))* Carson-Dellosa Publishing, LLC. (HighReach Learning, Incorporated).

Rumiz, Susanna. Let's Draw Monsters with Crayola! Allen, Kathy. 2018. (Let's Draw with Crayola ® ! Ser.). (ENG.). 32p. (J). (gr. -1-3). 27.99 *(978-1-5124-3294-7(6)*, Lerner Pubns.) Lerner Publishing Group.

—Touch & Trace Farm. Litton, Jonathan. 2016. (ENG.). 26p. (J). (gr. -1-k). bds. 8.99 *(978-1-58925-220-2(9))* Tiger Tales.

—Zoom Space Adventure. Hayes, Susan. 2020. (Zoom Ser.). (ENG.). 36p. (J). (gr. -1 — 1). bds. 14.99 *(978-1-9999679-8-7(4))* What on Earth Books.

Runham, Isobel. Case Files of the Supernatural. Cockrill, Kathryn. 2018. (ENG.). 218p. (J). pap. *(978-1-988853-12-3(5))* Schreyer Ink Publishing.

Runnells, Patricia & Runnells, Treesha. Pig-a-Boo! A Farmyard Peekaboo Book. DePrisco, Dorothea. 2009. (ENG.). 14p. (J). (gr. -1-k). 9.99 *(978-1-4169-7226-6(9)*, Little Simon) Little Simon.

Runnells, Treesha. Pat Them Gently. O'Brien, Melanie. 2006. (ENG.). 10p. (J). (gr. -1-3). bds. 8.95 *(978-1-58117-462-5(4)*, Intervisual/Piggy Toes) Bendon, Inc.

Runnells, Treesha. Afraid of the Dark? Runnells, Treesha. 2005. (Stories to Share Ser.). 14p. (J). (gr. -1-2). 10.95 *(978-1-58117-107-5(2)*, Intervisual/Piggy Toes) Bendon, Inc.

—Forest Friends: A Fold-Out Fun Book. Runnells, Treesha. 2005. (Fold-Out Fun Ser.). 10p. (J). 4.95 *(978-1-58117-275-1(3)*, Intervisual/Piggy Toes) Bendon, Inc.

—Safari Friends: Fold-Out Fun. Runnells, Treesha. 2005. (Fold-Out Fun Ser.). 10p. (J). 4.95 *(978-1-58117-276-8(1)*, Intervisual/Piggy Toes) Bendon, Inc.

Runnells, Treesha, jt. illus. see Runnells, Patricia.

Runnentrom, Bengt-Arne. La Niña y la Anguila. Zak, Monica. Orea, Lucia, tr. 2009. (SPA.). 32p. (J). (gr. 1-3). pap. 13.95 *(978-99922-1-325-4(6))* Piedra Santa, Editorial GTM. Dist: Libros Sin Fronteras.

Runnerstrom, Bengt-Arne. Salven Mi Selva. Zak, Monica. (SPA.). 29p. (J). (gr. 3-18). pap. 12.95 *(978-968-6048-23-0(5))* volcano pr.

Runton, Andy. Owly & Wormy, Bright Lights & Starry Nights. Runton, Andy. 2012. (ENG.). 40p. (J). (gr. -1-3). 19.99 *(978-1-4169-5775-1(8)*, Atheneum Bks. for Young Readers) Simon & Schuster Children's Publishing.

—Owly & Wormy, Friends All Aflutter! Runton, Andy. 2011. (ENG.). 40p. (J). (gr. -1-2). 16.99 *(978-1-4169-5774-4(X)*, Atheneum Bks. for Young Readers) Simon & Schuster Children's Publishing.

Runyen, Elizabeth. Watch Me Draw Disney's Mickey Mouse Clubhouse. 2012. 24p. (J). *(978-1-936309-74-0(2))* Quarto Publishing Group USA.

Ruocco, Paul. Madison's Journey. Amarone, Morgan. 2011. 30p. (J). pap. 16.99 *(978-0-9841934-5-5(6))* Bryson Taylor Publishing.

Ruoff, Ian. Monte & Luna's Christmas. Saucier, Michelle Ann. 2019. (Monte & Luna Ser.: Vol. 4). (ENG.). 28p. (J). pap. 9.99 ***(978-1-6795-5536-7(7))*** Independently Published.

Ruoff, Ian. Monte Gets Lost in the Woods. Saucier, Michelle Ann. 2019. (Monte & Luna Ser.: Vol. 3). (ENG.). 32p. (J). pap. 9.99 *(978-1-0746-2348-7(7))* Independently Published.

Rupert, Chris, et al. Kitty Treats Cookbook. Bledsoe, Michele. 2010. (ENG.). 15p. (gr. 6). bds. 10.95 *(978-0-9753883-8-9(X))* Come & Get It Publishing.

Rupert, Mad & Sygh, Rian. Regular Show: Parks & Wreck. Ostertag, Molly Knox et al. 2017. (Regular Show Ser.). (ENG.). 112p. (J). (gr. 4-7). pap. 14.99 *(978-1-68415-042-7(6))* Boom! Studios.

Ruplin, Lois L. The Mystery of Sarah & the Gypsies: Illustrated by Lois L. Ruplin. Ruplin, Ferdinand A. 2004. (ENG.). 38p. pap. 15.99 *(978-1-4134-1560-5(1))* Xlibris Corp.

Rupp, Kristina. Cougars. Cline, Gina. 2013. (1G Predator Animals Ser.). (ENG.). 24p. (J). pap. 9.60 *(978-1-61406-244-8(7))* American Reading Co.

—The Gorilla Family. Fleischer, Jayson & Lynch, Michelle. 2009. (2G Animals Ser.). (ENG.). 40p. (J). pap. 8.00 *(978-1-61406-203-5(X))* American Reading Co.

—Lions. Cline, Gina. 2015. (1G Predator Animals Ser.). (ENG.). 24p. (J). pap. 9.60 *(978-1-61406-320-9(6))* American Reading Co.

Ruppelius, Conrad. Conrad's Hiking Adventure. Ruppelius, Conrad. Ruppelius, Jeffrey. 2006. (J). per. 12.95 *(978-0-9774143-3-8(7))* Little Dog Pubns.

Ruppert, Larry. Freddie & Flossie & the Leaf Monster. Hope, Laura Lee. 2005. (Bobbsey Twins Ser.). (ENG.). 32p. (J). (gr. -1-k). pap. 13.99 *(978-1-4169-0271-3(6)*, Simon Spotlight) Simon Spotlight.

Rus, Marta. Ride with My Dad. Sagata, Bruce. 2018. (ENG.). 22p. (J). (gr. k-3). pap. *(978-9980-900-26-5(1))* Library For All Limited.

Rusakova, Tatiana. Socktown: Published by Funky Dreamer Storytime. Wachs, Greg. 2018. (ENG.). 34p. (J). pap. 11.95 *(978-1-9858-9209-5(X))* CreateSpace Independent Publishing Platform.

Rusan Jeffers. McDuff & the Baby. Rosemary Wells. 2014. 28p. pap. 9.99 *(978-1-61003-384-8(1))* Center for the Collaborative Classroom.

Rusch, Amy. Busy, Busy Moose. Van Laan, Nancy. 2003. 48p. (J). (gr. k-2). tchr. ed. 21.19 *(978-0-395-96091-2(6))* Houghton Mifflin Harcourt Publishing Co.

Ruse, Jill, jt. illus. see Long, John.

Rush, Anne Kent. Go South to Freedom. Gaillard, Frye. 2016. (ENG.). 72p. (J). 17.95 *(978-1-58838-316-7(4)*, NewSouth Bks.) NewSouth, Inc.

Rush, Peter. Return to Sula, 72 vols. Derwent, Lavinia. 2003. (Kelpies Ser.). (ENG.). 128p. 10.00 *(978-0-86315-424-9(7))* Floris Bks. GBR. Dist: SteinerBooks, Inc.

Rushton, Adam. William Finds the Butterfly. Piper, Nikki. 2018. (ENG.). 20p. (J). (gr. k-3). pap. 11.99 *(978-1-78955-310-9(5))* New Generation Publishing GBR. Dist: Independent Pubs. Group.

—William Finds the Feather. Piper, Nikki. 2018. (ENG.). 20p. (J). (gr. k-3). pap. 11.99 *(978-1-78955-308-6(3))* New Generation Publishing GBR. Dist: Independent Pubs. Group.

—William Finds the Robin. Piper, Nikki. 2018. (ENG.). 24p. (J). (gr. k-3). pap. 11.99 *(978-1-78955-309-3(1))* New Generation Publishing GBR. Dist: Independent Pubs. Group.

Rushworth, Helen. Billy & Ant Fall Out: Pride. Minter, James. 2016. (Billy Growing Up Ser.: Vol. 2). (ENG.). (J). (gr. 2-3). *(978-1-910727-11-9(3))* Minter Publishing Ltd.

—Billy & Ant Lie: Lying. Minter, James. 2016. (Billy Growing Up Ser.: Vol. 4). (ENG.). 120p. (J). (gr. 3-6). pap. *(978-1-910727-15-7(6))* Minter Publishing Ltd.

—Billy Gets Bullied: Bullying. Minter, James. (Billy Growing Up Ser.: Vol. 1). (ENG.). (J). (gr. 2-3). 2018. 110p. *(978-1-910727-47-8(4))*; 2017. pap. *(978-1-910727-32-4(6))* Minter Publishing Ltd.

—Billy Has a Birthday: Bullying. Minter, James. 2016. (Billy Growing Up Ser.: Vol. 1). (ENG.). 133p. (J). (gr. 3-6). pap. *(978-1-910727-05-8(9))* Minter Publishing Ltd.

—Billy Helps Max: Stealing. Minter, James. 2016. (Billy Growing Up Ser.: Vol. 5). (ENG.). (J). (gr. 2-3). *(978-1-910727-20-1(2))* Minter Publishing Ltd.

—Billy Is Nasty to Ant: Jealousy. Minter, James. 2016. (Billy Growing Up Ser.: Vol. 3). (ENG.). (J). (gr. 2-3). *(978-1-910727-14-0(8))*; 143p. (gr. 3-6). pap. *(978-1-910727-12-6(1))* Minter Publishing Ltd.

—Billy Knows a Secret: Secrets. Minter, James. 2016. (Billy Growing Up Ser.: Vol. 8). (ENG.). (J). (gr. 2-3). *(978-1-910727-29-4(6))* Minter Publishing Ltd.

—Billy Saves the Day: Self-Belief. Minter, James. 2016. (Billy Growing Up Ser.: Vol. 6). (ENG.). (J). (gr. 2-3). *(978-1-910727-23-2(7))*; 148p. (gr. 3-6). pap. *(978-1-910727-21-8(0))* Minter Publishing Ltd.

—Billy Wants It All: Money. Minter, James. 2016. (Billy Growing Up Ser.: Vol. 7). (ENG.). (J). (gr. 3-6). *(978-1-910727-26-3(1))* Minter Publishing Ltd.

Rusky, Ann G. Mac s Mackinac Island Adventure. Vachon, Mary Beth. 2005. 216p. (J). pap. 17.95 *(978-0-9766104-1-0(8))* Arbutus Pr.

Russ Cardona. My Name Is Jeromy, 1. Jewell, Beverly. 2004. 28p. (J). 11.95 *(978-0-9701519-1-9(8))* All Gold Publishing Co.

Russ, Lamont. The Monster Bash: A Halloween Story. Sproles, Clay. 2019. (ENG.). 38p. (J). (gr. k-2). 14.49 ***(978-1-7340097-2-9(1))*** Cats Corner Publishing.

—Turkey's Thanksgiving Adventure. Sproles, Clay. 2019. (ENG.). 34p. (J). pap. 9.87 ***(978-1-7334195-4-3(3))*** Cats Corner Publishing.

—Turkey's Thanksgiving Adventure: A Barnyard Tale. Sproles, Clay. 2019. (ENG.). 34p. (J). (gr. k-2). 15.49 ***(978-1-7334195-6-7(X))***; pap. 9.49 ***(978-1-7334195-5-0(1))*** Cats Corner Publishing.

Russ, Sylvia, jt. illus. see Lowe, Sylbil.

Russell, A. A Little Maid in Toyland (Illustrated Edition) Sutton, Adah Louise. 2016. (ENG.). (J). pap. *(978-1-4068-7894-3(4))* Echo Library.

Russell, Bernadette. Be the Change, Make It Happen. Russell, Bernadette. 2017. (ENG.). 96p. (J). pap. 14.99 *(978-1-61067-404-1(9))* Kane Miller.

Russell, Brooklyn. Eddie & the Hot Cocoa Hot Rod. Williams-Sanchez, Valerie. 2015. 37p. (J). pap. *(978-1-4834-4173-3(3))* Lulu Pr., Inc.

Russell, Carol. No Eat Not Food: The Search for Intelligent Food on Planet Earth. Sanger, Rick. l.t. ed. 2006. 48p. (J). 15.95 *(978-0-9653149-2-3(8))* Mountain Path Pr.

Russell, Charity. Alicia y Cone Pintan un Mural. Ayuso, Pamela. 2nd ed. 2019. (SPA.). 30p. (J). *(978-1-989161-66-1(9))* Hasmark Services Publishing.

—I Can Do Hard Things: Mindful Affirmations for Kids. Garcia, Gabi. 2018. (ENG.). 36p. (J). pap. 12.95 *(978-0-9989580-8-8(5))* Skinned Knee Publishing.

Russell, Charity. In a Dream. Hoang, Ann. 2020. (ENG.). 24p. (J). pap. 10.99 ***(978-1-0983-3068-2(4))*** BookBaby.

Russell, Charity. Oh No! There's a Bully in Our School. Lunsford, Antoine. Harrison, Ron, ed. 2019. (Little Andy's World Ser.: Vol. 1). (ENG.). 42p. (J). pap. 17.00 *(978-1-0997-3994-1(2))* Independently Published.

Russell, Charity. Why Is My Piano Black & White? The Ultimate Fun Facts Guide. Holder, Nathan. Drazner, Joel, ed. 2020. (Why Music Ser.). (ENG.). 186p. (J). pap. ***(978-1-9997530-1-6(1))*** Holders Hill.

Russell, Charity. Yo Puedo Hacer Cosas Difíciles: Afirmaciones Conscientes para Niños. Garcia, Gabi. 2018. (SPA.). 36p. (J). pap. 11.95 *(978-1-949633-03-0(9))* Skinned Knee Publishing.

Russell, Danica. A Little Radical: The ABCs of Activism. Russell, Danica. Russell, Jason. 2017. (ENG.). 60p. (J). 20.00 *(978-0-692-82451-1(0))* Broomstick Engine LLC.

Russell, Elaine. Savannah Dreams. Stewart, Lolla. 2nd ed. 2020. (ENG.). 32p. (J). (gr. -1-k). pap. 13.99 ***(978-1-76050-592-9(7))*** Little Hare Bks. AUS. Dist: Independent Pubs. Group.

Russell, Elaine. The Shack That Dad Built. Russell, Elaine. 2005. (ENG.). 32p. (J). (gr. k-2). 13.95 *(978-1-877003-94-3(8))* Little Hare Bks. AUS. Dist: Independent Pubs. Group.

Russell, Fletch, photos by. I Like Rocks! Russell, Carol & Russell, Tally. 2011. 32p. pap. 12.95 *(978-1-4634-3271-3(2))* AuthorHouse.

Russell, Gayle. Kangaroo. Reilly, Pauline. (Picture Roo Bks.). 32p. (J). pap. *(978-0-86417-538-0(8)*, Kangaroo Pr.) Simon & Schuster Australia.

Russell, H. R. & Williams, Don. The Lion King (Disney the Lion King) Korman, Justine. 2003. (Little Golden Book Ser.). (ENG.). 24p. (J). (gr. -1-2). 4.99 *(978-0-7364-2095-2(9)*, Golden/Disney) Random Hse. Children's Bks.

Russell, Harriet. Animalsaurus: Incredible Creatures from Prehistoric & Modern Times. Turner, Tracey. 2017. (ENG.). 96p. (J). 14.99 *(978-1-68119-544-5(5)*, 900177245, Bloomsbury USA Childrens) Bloomsbury Publishing USA.

—Is It Still Cheating If I Don't Get Caught? Weinstein, Bruce D. 2009. (ENG.). 160p. (YA). (gr. 5-9). pap. 24.94 *(978-1-59643-306-9(X)*, 9781596433069) Roaring Brook Pr.

—This Book Thinks You're a Scientist: Experiment, Imagine, Create. London Science Museum Staff. 2016. (ENG.). 96p. (J). (gr. 2-5). pap. 14.95 *(978-0-500-65081-3(0)*, 565081) Thames & Hudson.

—This Book Thinks You're an Artist. 2018. (ENG.). 96p. (J). (gr. 2-6). pap. 14.95 *(978-0-500-65138-4(8)*, 565138) Thames & Hudson.

Russell, Howard. Bernard Jones Is Going Places: Book One. Bernard, Teko. 2018. (ENG.). 108p. (J). (gr. 2-5). pap. 9.99 *(978-0-9860593-3-9(1))* Elmdale Park Books.

Russell, Joyce. The Key of the Kingdom: A Book of Stories & Poems for Children, 1 vol. Gmeyner, Elizabeth. 2004. (ENG.). 100p. (J). pap. 15.00 *(978-0-88010-549-1(6)*, Bell Pond Bks.) SteinerBooks, Inc.

Russell, Kay. Murphy Moose & Garrett Goose. Macy-Mills, Phyllis. 2003. (J). spiral bd. *(978-1-932303-48-3(0)*, Llumina Pr.) Aeon Publishing Inc.

Russell, Kerri G. Get Ready... Get Set... Read!, 5 sets (35 bks.) Foster, Kelli C. & Erickson, Gina Clegg. (J). lib. bdg. 418.25Set. lib. bdg. 418.25 *(978-1-56674-920-6(4))* Forest Hse. Publishing Co., Inc.

Russell, Natalie. Donkey's Busy Day. Russell, Natalie. 2009. 32p. (J). (gr. k-k). pap. 11.95 *(978-0-7475-9547-2(X))* Bloomsbury Publishing Plc GBR. Dist: Independent Pubs. Group.

—Lost for Words, 1 vol. Russell, Natalie. (ENG.). 32p. (J). (gr. -1-3). 2020. pap. 7.99 *(978-1-68263-157-7(5))*; 2014. 16.95 *(978-1-56145-739-7(6))* Peachtree Publishing Co. Inc.

Russell, Nathaniel. My Listography: My Amazing Life in Lists. Nola, Lisa. 2008. (ENG.). 120p. (gr. 3-7). 12.95 *(978-0-8118-6399-5(9))* Chronicle Bks. LLC.

Russell, P. Craig. Coraline Graphic Novel. Gaiman, Neil. (ENG.). 192p. (J). (gr. 3-7). 2009. pap. 10.99 *(978-0-06-082545-4(6))*; 2008. 18.99 *(978-0-06-082543-0(X))* HarperCollins Pubs. Ltd. GBR. (HarperCollins). Dist: HarperCollins Pubs.

—Coraline Novela Grafica. Gaiman, Neil. Isern, Carol, tr. 2010. (SPA.). 186p. (YA). (gr. 5-8). pap. 20.95 *(978-84-9918-067-0(1))* Roca Editorial ESP. Dist: Spanish Pubs., LLC.

—The Fairy Tales of Oscar Wilde Collection Vol. 4: The Devoted Friend, The Nightengale, & the Rose. Wilde, Oscar. 2004. (Fairy Tales of Oscar Wilde Ser.: 4). (ENG.). 48p. 16.99 *(978-1-56163-391-3(7))* NBM Publishing Co.

—Fairy Tales of Oscar Wilde: the Complete Hardcover Set 1-5. Wilde, Oscar. 2014. (Fairy Tales of Oscar Wilde Ser.). (ENG.). 192p. (J). (gr. 4-7). 79.99 *(978-1-56163-890-1(0))* NBM Publishing Co.

—The Fairy Tales of Oscar Wilde: the Happy Prince Signed & Numbered. Wilde, Oscar. 2012. (Fairy Tales of Oscar Wilde Ser.). (ENG.). 32p. (J). (gr. 4-7). 49.99 *(978-1-56163-687-7(8))* NBM Publishing Co.

—The Giver: A Graphic Novel. Lowry, Lois. 2019. (Giver Quartet Ser.: 1). (ENG.). 192p. (YA). (gr. 7). 22.99 *(978-0-544-15788-0(5)*, 1550303, HMH Books For Young Readers) Houghton Mifflin Harcourt Publishing Co.

—The Giver (Graphic Novel) Lowry, Lois. 2020. (Giver Quartet Ser.: 1). (ENG.). 192p. (YA). (gr. 7). pap. 12.99 *(978-1-328-57548-7(9)*, 1727475, HMH Books For Young Readers) Houghton Mifflin Harcourt Publishing Co.

—The Graveyard Book Graphic Novel Single Volume. Gaiman, Neil. (ENG.). 368p. (J). (gr. 3-7). 2017. pap. 22.99 *(978-0-06-242189-0(1))*; 2016. 35.00 *(978-0-06-242188-3(3))* HarperCollins Pubs. Ltd. GBR. (HarperCollins). Dist: HarperCollins Pubs.

—The Graveyard Book Graphic Novel Single Volume Special Limited Edition. Gaiman, Neil. 2016. (ENG.). 384p. (J). (gr. 3-7). 175.00 *(978-0-06-239449-1(5)*, HarperCollins) HarperCollins Pubs. Ltd. GBR. Dist: HarperCollins Pubs.

—The Happy Prince. Wilde, Oscar. 5th ed. 2012. (Fairy Tales of Oscar Wilde Ser.: 5). (ENG.). 32p. (J). (gr. 4-7). 16.99 *(978-1-56163-626-6(6))* NBM Publishing Co.

—The Happy Prince Signed & Numbered. Wilde, Oscar. 2012. (Fairy Tales of Oscar Wilde Ser.). (ENG.). 32p. (J). (gr. 4-7). 50.00 *(978-1-56163-629-7(0))* NBM Publishing Co.

Russell, P. Craig. The Dark Horse Book of Hauntings. Russell, P. Craig. Mignola, Mike et al. 2003. (Dark Horse Book Of Ser.). (ENG.). 96p. 14.95 *(978-1-56971-958-9(6))* Dark Horse Comics.

—The Devoted Friend, the Nightengale, & the Rose. Russell, P. Craig. Wilde, Oscar. 2004. (Fairy Tales of Oscar Wilde Ser.: 4). (ENG.). 48p. pap. 8.99 *(978-1-56163-392-0(5))* NBM Publishing Co.

—Fairy Tales of Oscar Wilde: The Selfish Giant & the Star Child, Vol. 1. Russell, P. Craig. 2003. (Fairy Tales of Oscar Wilde Ser.: 1). (ENG.). 48p. pap. 9.99 *(978-1-56163-375-3(5))* NBM Publishing Co.

—The Graveyard Book Graphic Novel: Volume 1, Vol. 1. Russell, P. Craig. Gaiman, Neil. 2014. (ENG.). 192p. (J). (gr. 3-7). 19.99 *(978-0-06-219481-7(X)*, HarperCollins) HarperCollins Pubs.

—The Graveyard Book Graphic Novel: Volume 2, Vol. 2. Russell, P. Craig. Gaiman, Neil. 2014. (ENG.). 176p. (J). (gr. 3-7). 19.99 *(978-0-06-219483-1(6)*, HarperCollins) HarperCollins Pubs.

Russell, Rachel Renee. The Misadventures of Max Crumbly Collection: The Misadventures of Max Crumbly 1; the Misadventures of Max Crumbly 2; the Misadventures of Max Crumbly 3. Russell, Rachel Renée. ed. 2019. (Misadventures of Max Crumbly Ser.). (ENG.). 832p. (J). (gr. 4-7). 41.99 *(978-1-5344-5351-7(2)*, Aladdin) Simon & Schuster Children's Publishing.

R

Russell, Rachel Renée. Dork Diaries, Set. Russell, Rachel Renée. ed. 2013. (Dork Diaries: Nos. 4-6). (ENG.). 1056p. (J). (gr. 4-8). 41.99 *(978-1-4424-9859-4(5)*, Aladdin) Simon & Schuster Children's Publishing.

—Dork Diaries Set, Set. Russell, Rachel Renée. ed. 2011. (Dork Diaries: Nos. 1-3). (ENG.). 928p. (J). (gr. 4-8). 41.99 *(978-1-4424-2662-7(4)*, Aladdin) Simon & Schuster Children's Publishing.

—Dork Diaries 11: Tales from a Not-So-Friendly Frenemy. Russell, Rachel Renée. 2016. (Dork Diaries: 11). (ENG.). 288p. (J). (gr. 4-8). 13.99 *(978-1-4814-7920-2(2)*, Aladdin) Simon & Schuster Children's Publishing.

—Dork Diaries 12: Tales from a Not-So-Secret Crush Catastrophe. Russell, Rachel Renée. 2017. (Dork Diaries: 12). (ENG.). 272p. (J). (gr. 4-8). 13.99 *(978-1-5344-0560-8(7)*, Aladdin) Simon & Schuster Children's Publishing.

—Dork Diaries 13: Tales from a Not-So-Happy Birthday. Russell, Rachel Renée. 2018. (Dork Diaries: 13). (ENG.). 304p. (J). (gr. 4-8). 13.99 *(978-1-5344-2638-2(8)*, Aladdin) Simon & Schuster Children's Publishing.

—Dork Diaries 14: Tales from a Not-So-Best Friend Forever. Russell, Rachel Renée. 2019. (Dork Diaries: 14). (ENG.). 320p. (J). (gr. 4-8). 13.99 *(978-1-5344-2720-4(1)*, Aladdin) Simon & Schuster Children's Publishing.

—Dork Diaries 2: Tales from a Not-So-Popular Party Girl. Russell, Rachel Renée. 2010. (Dork Diaries: 2). (ENG.). 288p. (J). (gr. 4-8). 13.99 *(978-1-4169-8008-7(3)*, Aladdin) Simon & Schuster Children's Publishing.

—Dork Diaries 4: Tales from a Not-So-Graceful Ice Princess. Russell, Rachel Renée. 2012. (Dork Diaries: 4). (ENG.). 368p. (J). (gr. 4-8). 13.99 *(978-1-4424-1192-0(9)*, Aladdin) Simon & Schuster Children's Publishing.

—Dork Diaries 6: Tales from a Not-So-Happy Heartbreaker. Russell, Rachel Renée. 2013. (Dork Diaries: 6). (ENG.). 368p. (J). (gr. 4-8). 13.99 *(978-1-4424-4963-3(2)*, Aladdin) Simon & Schuster Children's Publishing.

—Dork Diaries 9: Tales from a Not-So-Dorky Drama Queen. Russell, Rachel Renée. 2015. (Dork Diaries: 9). (ENG.). 352p. (J). (gr. 4-8). 13.99 *(978-1-4424-8769-7(0)*, Aladdin Paperbacks) Simon & Schuster Children's Publishing.

—Dork Diaries Books 1-10 (Plus 3 1/2 & OMG!) Dork Diaries 1; Dork Diaries 2; Dork Diaries 3; Dork Diaries 3 1/2; Dork Diaries 4; Dork Diaries 5; Dork Diaries 6; Dork Diaries OMG!; Dork Diaries 7; Dork Diaries 8; Dork Diaries 9; Dork Diaries 10. Russell, Rachel Renée. ed. 2018. (Dork Diaries). (ENG.). 4000p. (J). (gr. 4-8). 166.99 *(978-1-5344-2459-3(8)*, Aladdin) Simon & Schuster Children's Publishing.

—Dork Diaries Books 10-12: Dork Diaries 10; Dork Diaries 11; Dork Diaries 12. Russell, Rachel Renée. ed. 2018. (Dork Diaries). (ENG.). 880p. (J). (gr. 4-8). 41.99 *(978-1-5344-2458-6(X)*, Aladdin) Simon & Schuster Children's Publishing.

—Dork Diaries Friendship Box. Russell, Rachel Renée. ed. 2018. (Dork Diaries). (ENG.). 352p. (J). (gr. 3). 24.99 *(978-1-5344-4062-3(3)*, Aladdin) Simon & Schuster Children's Publishing.

—How to Dork Your Diary. Russell, Rachel Renée. 2011. (Dork Diaries: No. 3.5). (ENG.). 288p. (J). (gr. 4-8). 13.99 *(978-1-4424-2233-9(5)*, Aladdin) Simon & Schuster Children's Publishing.

—Locker Hero. Russell, Rachel Renée. 2016. (Misadventures of Max Crumbly Ser.: 1). 320p. (J). (gr. 4-8). 13.99 *(978-1-4814-6001-9(3)*, Aladdin) Simon & Schuster Children's Publishing.

—The Misadventures of Max Crumbly 2: Middle School Mayhem. Russell, Rachel Renée. 2017. (Misadventures of Max Crumbly Ser.: 2). (ENG.). 240p. (J). (gr. 4-8). 13.99 *(978-1-4814-6003-3(X)*, Aladdin) Simon & Schuster Children's Publishing.

—The Misadventures of Max Crumbly 3: Masters of Mischief. Russell, Rachel Renée. 2019. (Misadventures of Max Crumbly Ser.: 3). (ENG.). 272p. (J). (gr. 4-7). 13.99 *(978-1-5344-5349-4(0)*, Aladdin) Simon & Schuster Children's Publishing.

—OMG!:All about Me Diary! Russell, Rachel Renée. 2013. (Dork Diaries). 272p. (J). (gr. 4-8). 13.99 *(978-1-4424-8771-0(2)*, Aladdin) Simon & Schuster Children's Publishing.

—Tales from a Not-So-Fabulous Life. Russell, Rachel Renée. 2009. (Dork Diaries: 1). (ENG.). 352p. (J). (gr. 4-8). 13.99 *(978-1-4169-8006-3(7)*, Aladdin) Simon & Schuster Children's Publishing.

—Tales from a Not-So-Glam TV Star. Russell, Rachel Renée. 2014. (Dork Diaries: 7). 336p. (J). (gr. 4-8). 13.99 *(978-1-4424-8767-3(4)*, Aladdin) Simon & Schuster Children's Publishing.

—Tales from a Not-So-Perfect Pet Sitter. Russell, Rachel Renée. 2015. (Dork Diaries: 10). (ENG.). 320p. (J). (gr. 4-8). 13.99 *(978-1-4814-5704-0(7)*, Aladdin) Simon & Schuster Children's Publishing.

—Tales from a Not-So-Perfect Pet Sitter. Russell, Rachel Renée. 2015. (Dork Diaries: 10). (ENG.). 320p. (J). (gr. 4-8). lib. bdg. 25.75 *(978-0-606-37923-6(1))* Turtleback.

—Tales from a Not-So-Smart Miss Know-It-All. Russell, Rachel Renée. 2012. (Dork Diaries: 5). (ENG.). 368p. (J). (gr. 4-8). 13.99 *(978-1-4424-4961-9(6)*, Aladdin) Simon & Schuster Children's Publishing.

—Tales from a Not-So-Talented Pop Star. Russell, Rachel Renée. 2011. (Dork Diaries: 3). (ENG.). 336p. (J). (gr. 4-8). 13.99 *(978-1-4424-1190-6(2)*, Aladdin) Simon & Schuster Children's Publishing.

Russell, Tom. Legend of the Hartwick Pines. Rancour, Thom. 2015. 32p. (J). 12.95 *(978-0-9860701-0-5(6))* Four Pines Farms.

Russik, Michael. Moon over the Mountain. Polette, Keith. 2010. (ENG.). 32p. (J). (gr. -1-3). pap. 7.95 *(978-1-934960-08-0(X)*, Raven Tree Pr.,Csi) Continental Sales, Inc.

Russita, Tanja. All in the Same Boat: A Cautionary Modern Fable about Greed Featuring a Rat, a Mouse & a Gerbil. Martin, Wilkie J. 2019. (ENG.). 52p. (J). (gr. 1-2). pap. *(978-1-912348-19-0(5))* Witcherley Bk. Co., The.

—All in the Same Boat: A Grim Modern Fable about Greed Featuring a Rat, a Mouse & a Gerbil. Martin, Wilkie J. 2019. (ENG.). 52p. (J). (gr. 2-3). *(978-1-912348-20-6(9))* Witcherley Bk. Co., The.

Russita, Tanja. The Bird That Couldn't Fly. Arrechea, Raquel. 2019. (ENG.). 58p. (J). (gr. k-2). 23.95 ***(978-0-578-42189-6(5))*** Azure Coast Pr.

Russita, Tanja. The Lazy Rabbit: A Grim Modern Fable about Laziness with a Rabbit, Vole & Fox. Martin, Wilkie J. 2019. (ENG.). 58p. (J). (gr. 2-3). *(978-1-912348-26-8(8))*; pap. *(978-1-912348-25-1(X))* Witcherley Bk. Co., The.

Russo, Blythe. My Daughters Are Smart! D Is for Daughters & S Is for Smart. Adhikary, Anita B. 2014. (ENG.). 24p. (J). (gr. -1-3). 14.95 *(978-1-62086-429-6(0))* Mascot Bks., Inc.

—One More Wheel! A Things-That-Go Counting Book. Venable, Colleen Af & Odd Dot. 2019. (ENG.). 22p. (J). bds. 12.99 *(978-1-250-30759-0(7)*, 900198063, Odd Dot) St. Martin's Pr.

Russo, Brian. Take Care. Hamill, Laura & Cramer, Jolene. 2020. (ENG.). 36p. (J). pap. 12.99 ***(978-1-0983-1492-7(1))*** BookBaby.

Russo, Brian. Yoga Bunny. Russo, Brian. 2016. (ENG.). 40p. (J). (gr. -1-3). 17.99 *(978-0-06-242952-0(3))* HarperCollins Pubs.

Russo, David Anson. Around the World: The Great Treasure Hunt. Russo, David Anson. 2011. (ENG.). 28p. (J). (gr. 4-6). pap. 14.99 *(978-1-4424-4343-3(X)*, Simon & Schuster Bks. For Young Readers) Simon & Schuster Bks. For Young Readers.

—The Great Treasure Hunt. Russo, David Anson. 2011. (ENG.). 28p. (J). (gr. k-3). pap. 14.99 *(978-1-4424-4342-6(1)*, Simon & Schuster Bks. For Young Readers) Simon & Schuster Bks. For Young Readers.

Russo, Erin. The Smidgeons & the Glugs II: The Rescue. Raven, J. E. 2018. (ENG.). 40p. (J). (gr. k-4). pap. 13.95 *(978-1-948365-65-9(0))* Orange Hat Publishing.

Russo, Erin. Angus Parker, Circus Tiger. Russo, Erin. 2018. (ENG.). 68p. (J). (gr. 3-6). pap. 12.99 *(978-1-948365-09-3(0))* Orange Hat Publishing.

Russo, Maria. We Are American. Aremu, Sharafa. 2018. (ENG.). 28p. (J). pap. 10.99 *(978-1-7278-9513-1(4))* CreateSpace Independent Publishing Platform.

Russo, Maria Octavia. Everybody Just Be Quiet. Wiley, Jennie. 2020. (ENG.). 54p. (J). 17.99 ***(978-1-948256-14-8(2))*** Willow Moon Publishing.

Russo, Marisabina. Always Remember Me: How One Family Survived World War II. Russo, Marisabina. 2005. (ENG.). 48p. (J). (gr. 1-5). 19.99 *(978-0-689-86920-4(7)*, Atheneum Bks. for Young Readers) Simon & Schuster Children's Publishing.

—The Bunnies Are Not in Their Beds. Russo, Marisabina. (J). 2019. 36p. (-k). bds. 8.99 *(978-0-525-58226-7(6)*, Schwartz & Wade Bks.); 2013. 40p. (gr. -1-2). 7.99 *(978-0-307-98126-4(6)*, Dragonfly Bks.) Random Hse. Children's Bks.

—Little Bird Takes a Bath. Russo, Marisabina. 2015. 40p. (J). (gr. -1-2). 16.99 *(978-0-385-37014-1(8)*, Schwartz & Wade Bks.) Random Hse. Children's Bks.

—The Trouble with Baby. Russo, Marisabina. 2003. 32p. (J). (gr. -1-18). 16.89 *(978-0-06-008925-2(3))* HarperCollins Pubs.

Russon, Anne E., jt. photos by see Smith, Dale.

Rust, Graham. A Little Princess: The Story of Sara Crewe. Burnett, Frances Hodgson. 2019. (ENG.). 192p. (J). (gr. 4-7). reprint ed. 18.95 *(978-0-87923-784-4(8))* Godine, David R. Pub.

—A Little Princess: The Story of Sara Crewe. Burnett, Frances Hodgson. (J). pap. 22.95 *(978-0-590-24079-6(X))* Scholastic, Inc.

Ruta, Angelo, et al. Christmas Around the World. Sims, Lesley. 2006. (Young Reading Series 1 Gift Bks.). 47p. (J). (gr. -1-3). 8.99 *(978-0-7945-1132-6(5)*, Usborne) EDC Publishing.

Ruta, Angelo. My First Holy Communion. Piper, Sophie. 2010. (ENG.). 64p. (J). (gr. 1-4). 14.99 *(978-1-55725-696-6(9)*, 6966) Paraclete Pr., Inc.

—The Plan: How God Got the World Ready for Jesus. Ferguson, Sinclair B. 2009. (Colour Bks.). (ENG.). 40p. (J). 9.99 *(978-1-84550-451-9(8)*, f1e68190-c1a7-43a3-9759-51910594be78) Christian Focus Pubns. GBR. Dist: Baker & Taylor Publisher Services (BTPS).

—The Story of Jesus. Skevington, Andrea. 2008. (ENG.). 128p. (J). (gr. 2-4). pap. 16.95 *(978-0-7459-6121-7(5))* Lion Hudson PLC GBR. Dist: Independent Pubs. Group.

Ruth, Annie. I Can Read. Ruth, Annie. l.t. ed. 2005. 32p. (J). (gr. -1-3). pap. 10.00 *(978-0-9656306-7-2(6))* Ruth, A. Creations.

Ruth, Greg. City of Orphans. Avi. (ENG.). 368p. (J). (gr. 5-9). 2012. pap. 8.99 *(978-1-4169-7108-5(4)*, Atheneum Bks. for Young Readers); 2011. 17.99 *(978-1-4169-7102-3(5)*, Atheneum/Richard Jackson Bks.) Simon & Schuster Children's Publishing.

—Fall of the Amazing Zalindas. Mack, Tracy & Citrin, Michael. 2009. (Sherlock Holmes & the Baker St. Irregulars Ser.: 1). (ENG.). 272p. (J). (gr. 3-7). 6.99 *(978-0-545-06939-7(4)*, Scholastic Paperbacks) Scholastic, Inc.

—Old Turtle: Questions of the Heart. Wood, Douglas. 2017. 56p. (J). (gr. -1-3). 19.99 *(978-0-439-32111-2(5)*, Scholastic Pr.) Scholastic, Inc.

—Our Enduring Spirit: President Barack Obama's First Words to America. Obama, Barack. 2009. 48p. (J). lib. bdg. 18.89 *(978-0-06-183456-1(4))* HarperCollins Pubs.

—A Pirate's Guide to First Grade. Preller, James. 2013. (ENG.). 48p. (J). (gr. -1-1). 8.99 *(978-1-250-02721-4(7)*, 9781250027214) Square Fish.

—Rolling Thunder. Messner, Kate. 2017. (ENG.). 32p. (J). (gr. -1-3). 17.99 *(978-0-545-47012-4(9)*, Scholastic Pr.) Scholastic, Inc.

—The Sea Wolves Bk. 2, Bk. 2. Golden, Christopher & Lebbon, Tim. 2012. (Secret Journeys of Jack London Ser.: 2). (ENG.). 400p. (YA). (gr. 8). 16.99 *(978-0-06-186320-2(3)*, HarperTeen) HarperCollins Pubs.

—The Wild. Golden, Christopher & Lebbon, Tim. 2011. (Secret Journeys of Jack London Ser.: 1). (ENG.). 368p. (YA). (gr. 5-18). 15.99 *(978-0-06-186317-2(3)*, HarperTeen) HarperCollins Pubs.

Ruth, Greg. Coming Home. Ruth, Greg. 2014. (ENG.). 32p. (J). (gr. -1-2). 16.99 *(978-1-250-05547-7(4)*, 900138235) Feiwel & Friends.

Ruthann, Keulen. Goodnight Cantata. Baker, Elizabeth D. 2020. (ENG.). 26p. (J). 14.99 ***(978-0-578-45052-0(6))*** Baker, Elizabeth.

Rutherford, Alexa. B Is for Bagpipes: A Scotland Alphabet. Kiehm, Eve Begley. 2010. (Discover the World Ser.). (ENG.). 40p. (J). (gr. 1-3). 19.99 *(978-1-58536-453-4(3)*, 202177) Sleeping Bear Pr.

—Nan's Rabbit. Bromilow, Mary. 2015. (ENG.). 27p. (J). pap. 10.95 *(978-1-908931-24-5(8))* Birlinn, Ltd. GBR. Dist: Casemate Pubs. & Bk. Distributors, LLC.

Rutherford, Courtney. The Church That Grew. Atchison, Lara Rebecca. 2019. (ENG.). 26p. (J). pap. 9.99 *(978-1-4993-0546-3(X))* CreateSpace Independent Publishing Platform.

Rutherford, Meg. Brave Lion, Scared Lion. Stimson, Joan. Rubio, Esther, tr. (J). (gr. k-1). pap. *(978-0-590-90985-3(1)*, SO3690) Scholastic, Inc.

Rutherford, Peter. A Claddagh Ring for Nuala, 1 vol. Crosbie, Duncan. gif. ed. 2003. (ENG.). 16p. (J). (gr. k-3). bds. 7.95 *(978-1-58980-175-2(X)*, Pelican Publishing) Arcadia Publishing.

—Giant Fun-to-Find Puzzles Busy Animals: Search for Pictures in Eight Exciting Scenes. 2015. 24p. pap. 6.99 *(978-1-86147-460-5(1)*, Armadillo) Anness Publishing GBR. Dist: National Bk. Network.

—Noah's Ark. 2015. 24p. bds. 6.99 *(978-1-86147-644-9(2)*, Armadillo) Anness Publishing GBR. Dist: National Bk. Network.

—The Twelve Labors of Hercules. Ford, James Evelyn & Salariya, David. 2013. 32p. (J). *(978-1-4351-5120-8(8))* Barnes & Noble, Inc.

Rutland, Elijah. Medal Club Kids: Winner's Circle. Manning, Justin & Waugh, Simone. 2019. (Winner's Circle Ser.: Vol. 1). (ENG.). 36p. (J). (gr. k-4). pap. 13.99 ***(978-0-578-61561-5(4))*** Medal Addict, Inc.

Rutland, Jarrett. The Best Parade Day: Spatz. Fair, Sherry. 2006. (Spatz Ser.). 40p. (J). (gr. -1-5). 18.95 *(978-1-57736-375-0(2))* Providence Hse Pubs.

—The Scratching Sound: Spatz. Fair, Sherry W. 2005. 28p. (J). (gr. -1-7). 16.98 *(978-1-57736-348-4(5))* Providence Hse Pubs.

Rutledge, Lauren. The Cheese Song: All Aboard the Orphan Train. Olson, Lisa Gammon. 2019. (Tales from American Herstory Ser.: Vol. 3). (ENG.). 38p. (J). (gr. k-5). pap. 9.99 *(978-1-63233-166-3(7))* Elfrig Publishing.

Rutledge, Lauren. Fig Newton Summer. Olson, Lisa Gammon. 2020. (ENG.). 110p. (J). (gr. 4-6). pap. 9.99 ***(978-1-63233-245-5(0))*** Elfrig Publishing.

Rutledge, Lauren. Sewing the Magic in at the Ringling Bros. & Barnum & Bailey Circus. Olson, Lisa Gammon. 2018. (ENG.). (J). (gr. k-5). pap. 9.99 *(978-1-63233-124-3(1))* Elfrig Publishing.

Ruttan, Molly. I Am a Thief! Rayner, Abigail. 2019. (ENG.). 40p. (J). (gr. -1-2). 17.95 *(978-0-7358-4289-2(2))* North-South Bks., Inc.

Ruttan, Molly. The Stray. Ruttan, Molly. 2020. 32p. (J). (gr. -1-2). 17.99 *(978-0-525-51446-6(5)*, Nancy Paulsen Books) Penguin Young Readers Group.

Rutten, Nicole. Not yet, Rose. Hill, Susanna Leonard. 2009. (ENG.). 34p. (J). (gr. -1-3). 16.50 *(978-0-8028-5326-4(9)*, Eerdmans Bks For Young Readers) Eerdmans, William B. Publishing Co.

—Sleepy Time Blessings. Conan, Sally Anne. 2009. (ENG.). 12p. (J). (gr. -1). bds. 8.00 *(978-0-8028-5350-9(1))* Eerdmans, William B. Publishing Co.

Rutylo, Iryna. The Jar of Dreams. Leigh, A. J. 2019. (ENG.). 38p. (J). pap. 9.99 ***(978-1-6534-7331-1(2))*** Independently Published.

RUZICKA, Carol. The Butterfly. Baker, Bill. 2012. 46p. pap. 15.00 *(978-0-9859132-0-5(7))* Asbury Heritage Publishing.

Ruzicka, Carol. Eva's Secret Name: Book 1 of the Adventures of Eva & Buckskin Charlie. Norton, John. 2018. (ENG.). 102p. (J). (gr. 2-6). pap. 8.99 *(978-1-947239-12-8(0))* Best Publishing Co.

Ruzicka, Delores F. The Star That Sparkled. Zachmeyer, Mary L. Date not set. 26p. (J). pap. 5.00 *(978-0-9646864-1-0(4))* Zachmeyer, Mary L.

Ruzzier, Sergio. And the Robot Went ... Robinson, Michelle. 2017. (ENG.). 32p. (J). (gr. -1-3). 16.99 *(978-0-544-58652-9(2)*, 1614145, Clarion Bks.) Houghton Mifflin Harcourt Trade & Reference Pubs.

—Broom, Zoom! Cohen, Caron Lee. 2010. (ENG.). 32p. (J). (gr. -1-3). 17.99 *(978-1-4169-9113-7(1)*, Simon & Schuster Bks. For Young Readers) Simon & Schuster Bks. For Young Readers.

—Fables You Shouldn't Pay Any Attention To. Heide, Florence Parry & Van Clief, Sylvia Worth. 2017. (ENG.). 112p. (J). (gr. 1-5). 16.99 *(978-1-4814-6382-9(9))* Simon & Schuster Children's Publishing.

—Have You Seen My New Blue Socks? Bunting, Eve. 2013. (ENG.). 32p. (J). (gr. -1-3). 16.99 *(978-0-547-75267-9(9)*, 1487502) Houghton Mifflin Harcourt Publishing Co.

—One Mean Ant. Yorinks, Arthur. 2020. (One Mean Ant Ser.). (ENG.). 48p. (J). (gr. -1-2). 16.99 *(978-0-7636-8394-8(9))* Candlewick Pr.

—Roar Like a Dandelion. Krauss, Ruth. 2019. (ENG.). 48p. (J). (gr. -1-3). 17.99 *(978-0-06-268007-5(2))* HarperCollins Pubs.

—A Round of Robins. Hesterman, Katie. 2018. 40p. (J). (gr. k-3). 16.99 *(978-0-399-54778-2(9)*, Nancy Paulsen Books) Penguin Young Readers Group.

—Tales for the Perfect Child. Heide, Florence Parry. (ENG.). 112p. (J). (gr. 1-5). 2018. pap. 6.99 *(978-1-4814-6380-5(2))*; 2017. 16.99 *(978-1-4814-6379-9(9))* Simon & Schuster Children's Publishing.

—Whose Shoe? Bunting, Eve. 2015. (ENG.). 32p. (J). (gr. -1-3). 16.99 *(978-0-544-30210-5(9)*, 1575895) Houghton Mifflin Harcourt Publishing Co.

Ruzzier, Sergio. Good Boy. Ruzzier, Sergio. 2019. (ENG.). 40p. (J). (gr. -1-3). 15.99 *(978-1-4814-9906-4(8))* Simon & Schuster Children's Publishing.

Ryan, Ann. The Little Wannabee. Ryan, Ann. 2006. (ENG.). 24p. (J). 16.95 *(978-1-933660-31-8(7)*, Tadpole Pr. 4 Kids) Mystic Harbor Pr., LLC.

Ryan, Elizabeth. Goosebumps, Giggles & Wagging Tails. Ryan, Elizabeth. 2018. (ENG.). 52p. (J). pap. 11.98 *(978-1-9850-3000-8(4))* CreateSpace Independent Publishing Platform.

Ryan, Eoin. My Ireland Counting Book. Webb, Mary & Ni Laoghaire, Ide. (ENG.). 32p. (J). 2012. pap. 12.95 *(978-1-84717-278-5(4))*; 2nd rev. ed. 2017. pap. 13.00 *(978-1-84717-931-9(2))* O'Brien Pr., Ltd., The IRL. Dist: Dufour Editions, Inc., Casemate Pubs. & Bk. Distributors, LLC.

Ryan, Hannah. Seal Mother: A Selkie Tale in Verse. English, Rose. 2018. (ENG.). 108p. (J). *(978-1-9999176-3-0(4))* Gillari Bks.

Ryan, Janice. When I Was Little. Puckett, Diane. 2019. (ENG.). 44p. (J). *(978-1-5255-4357-9(1))*; pap. *(978-1-5255-4358-6(X))* FriesenPress.

Ryan, Mary C. Twitcher Mcgee & the Wonderful Tree. Ryan, Mary C., text. 2008. 12p. (J). 4.95 *(978-0-9678115-3-6(8))* Dragonseed Pr.

Ryan, Michael & Azaceta, Paul. Crazy Like a Fox, Vol. 3. David, Peter. Youngquist, Jeff, ed. 2004. (Captain Marvel Ser.). 136p. pap. 14.99 *(978-0-7851-1340-9(1))* Marvel Worldwide, Inc.

Ryan, Nellie. Fabulous Fashion. Ryan, Nellie. 2014. (ENG.). 160p. (J). (gr. 3-7). pap. 12.99 *(978-1-907151-84-2(2))* O'Mara, Michael Bks., Ltd. GBR. Dist: Independent Pubs. Group.

Ryan, Nellie, jt. illus. see Davies, Hannah.

Ryan, Paul, et al. Iron Man Epic Collection: War Machine. 2020. (ENG.). 480p. (YA). (gr. 4-17). pap. 39.99 *(978-1-302-92351-8(X))* Marvel Worldwide, Inc.

Ryan, Rob. The Gift. Duffy, Carol Ann. 2009. 32p. (J). *(978-1-84686-354-7(6))* Barefoot Bks., Inc.

Ryan, Rob. The Gift. Ryan, Rob. Duffy, Carol Ann. 2010. 32p. (J). (gr. 3-18). 16.99 *(978-1-84686-355-4(4))* Barefoot Bks., Inc.

Ryan, Shari. Sir Thomas Take-It-Back. Marley, Pippa. 2019. (ENG.). 42p. (J). pap. 9.99 ***(978-1-7059-2949-0(4))*** Independently Published.

Ryan, Susannah. Coming to America. Maestro, Betsy. 2015. 40p. pap. 9.00 *(978-1-61003-543-9(7))* Center for the Collaborative Classroom.

Ryan, Victoria & Alley, R. W. When Your Pet Dies: A Healing Handbook for Kids. Ryan, Victoria. 2003. (Elf-Help Books for Kids). 32p. (J). per. 7.95 *(978-0-87029-376-4(1))* Abbey Pr.

Rycroft, Nina. Ballroom Bonanza: A Hidden Pictures ABC Book. Harris, Stephen. 2010. (ENG.). 48p. (J). (gr. -1-3). 16.95 *(978-0-8109-8842-2(9)*, Abrams Bks. for Young Readers) Abrams, Inc.

—Dinosaurs Love Cheese. French, Jackie. 32p. 2017. pap. 6.99 *(978-1-4607-5080-3(2))*; 2013. 17.99 *(978-0-7322-9264-5(6))* HarperCollins Pubs. Australia AUS. Dist: HarperCollins Pubs.

—No More Kisses. Wild, Margaret. 2012. (ENG.). 21p. (J). (gr. -1-k). pap. 9.99 *(978-1-921714-28-3(X))* Little Hare Bks. AUS. Dist: Independent Pubs. Group.

—No More Kisses! Wild, Margaret. 2011. (ENG.). 24p. (J). (gr. -1-k). 14.99 *(978-1-921541-52-0(0))* Little Hare Bks. AUS. Dist: Independent Pubs. Group.

Rydberg, Viktor. Our Fathers' Godsaga: Retold for the Young. Rydberg, Viktor. Reeves, William P. 2003. 223p. 25.95 *(978-0-595-66097-1(5))* iUniverse, Inc.

Ryden, Linda. Rosie's Brain. Ryden, Linda. 2016. (ENG.). (J). 14.99 *(978-0-9976954-2-7(0)*, Peace of Mind Pr.) Peace of Mind Inc.

Ryder, Abigail L. Seal Mother Retold. English, Rose. 2019. (ENG.). 54p. (YA). pap. ***(978-1-9999176-9-2(3))*** Gillari Bks.

Ryder, Michael Todd. Twins. 2012. 32p. (J). pap. 12.00 *(978-0-9847836-0-1(1))* Celtic Cat Publishing.

Ryding, Paul. Resist: 35 Profiles of Ordinary People Who Rose up Against Tyranny & Injustice. Chambers, Veronica. 2018. (ENG.). 224p. (J). (gr. 3-7). 16.99 *(978-0-06-279625-7(9))* HarperCollins Pubs.

Rylant, Cynthia. Creation. Rylant, Cynthia. 2016. (ENG.). 40p. (J). (gr. -1). 17.99 *(978-1-4814-7039-1(6)*, Beach Lane Bks.) Beach Lane Bks.

—Ecclesiastes: To Everything There Is a Season. Rylant, Cynthia. 2018. (ENG.). 40p. (J). (gr. -1-3). 17.99 *(978-1-4814-7654-6(8)*, Beach Lane Bks.) Beach Lane Bks.

—Everyday House. Rylant, Cynthia. 2018. (ENG.). 14p. (J). (gr. -1-k). bds. 6.99 *(978-1-5344-1812-7(1)*, Little Simon) Little Simon.

—Everyday Town. Rylant, Cynthia. 2018. (ENG.). 14p. (J). (gr. -1-k). bds. 6.99 *(978-1-5344-1814-1(8)*, Little Simon) Little Simon.

—Nativity. Rylant, Cynthia. 2017. (ENG.). 40p. (J). (gr. -1-3). 17.99 *(978-1-4814-7041-4(8)*, Beach Lane Bks.) Beach Lane Bks.

Ryley, David. Elijah/John the Baptist Flip-Over Book. Kovacs, Victoria. 2016. (Little Bible Heroes(tm) Ser.). (ENG.). 32p. (J). (gr. k-2). pap. 3.99 *(978-1-4336-4324-8(3)*, 005786142, B&H Kids) B&H Publishing Group.

—Heroes of Babylon/Ruth Flip-Over Book. Kovacs, Victoria. 2016. (Little Bible Heroes(tm) Ser.). (ENG.). 32p. (J). (gr. k-2). pap. 3.99 *(978-1-4336-4325-5(1)*, 005786143, B&H Kids) B&H Publishing Group.

—Joshua/Rahab Flip-Over Book. Kovacs, Victoria. 2015. (Little Bible Heroes(tm) Ser.). (ENG.). 32p. (J). (gr. k-2). pap. 3.99 *(978-1-4336-8716-7(X)*, 005742015, B&H Kids) B&H Publishing Group.

—The Little Giver/Zacchaeus Flip-Over Book. Kovacs, Victoria. 2016. (Little Bible Heroes(tm) Ser.). (ENG.). 32p.

(J). (gr. k-2). pap. 3.99 (978-1-4336-4326-2(X), 005786144, B&H Kids) B&H Publishing Group.
—Peter/Paul Flip-Over Book. Kovacs, Victoria. 2016. (Little Bible Heroes(tm) Ser.). (ENG.). 32p. (J). (gr. k-2). pap. 3.99 (978-1-4336-4327-9(8), 005786145, B&H Kids) B&H Publishing Group.
Ryley, David, jt. illus. see Krome, Mike.
Rymar, Yurko. Awesome Jokes That Every 5 Year Old Should Know! Waugh, Mat. 2018. (Awesome Jokes Ser.: Vol. 1). (ENG.). 68p. (J). (gr. k-1). pap. **(978-1-9999147-1-4(6))** Big Red Button Bks.
—Awesome Jokes That Every 6 Year Old Should Know! Waugh, Mat. 2018. (Awesome Jokes Ser.: Vol. 2). (ENG.). 70p. (J). (gr. 1-2). pap. **(978-1-9999147-2-1(4))** Big Red Button Bks.
Rymenants, Stef. Kinderguides Early Learning Guide to Herman Melville's Moby Dick. Colting, Fredrik & Medina, Melissa. 2018. (KinderGuides Early Learning Guide to Culture Classics Ser.). 50p. (J). 16.95 (978-0-9988205-4-5(7)) Moppet Bks.
Rymer, Alta M. Stars of Obron: Chambo Returns. Rymer, Alta M. (Tales of Planet Artembo Ser.: Bk. 3). 56p. (Orig.). (J). (gr. 5-7). pap. 20.00 (978-0-9600792-3-0(8)) Rymer Bks.
—Up from Uzam. Rymer, Alta M. (Tharma Lo Fairyland Ser.: Story 1). 28p. (Orig.). (J). (gr. 2-4). pap. 20.00 (978-0-9600792-8-5(9)) Rymer Bks.
Ryn, Aude van. The Life & Art of Claude Monet. Pappworth, Sara. 2016. (Lives of Great Artists Ser.). 00080p. (J). (gr. 8-8). 35.75 (978-1-4994-6584-6(X)) Rosen Publishing Group, Inc., The.
Ryn Katryn Digital Arts. Twice the Man. Barr, Stephanie. 2019. (Bete Ser.: Vol. 3). (ENG.). 284p. (J). pap. 14.00 (978-1-7975-9615-0(2)) Independently Published.
Rynhart, Kieran. The Genius of Bugs. Pollard, Simon. 2018. (ENG.). 24p. (J). (gr. 4-7). pap. 14.99 (978-0-9941362-0-6(X)) Te Papa Pr. NZL. Dist: Independent Pubs. Group.
—The New Zealand Art Activity Book. Lloyd, Helen. 2nd ed. 2018. (ENG.). 160p. (J). (gr. 4-7). pap. 29.99 (978-0-9941362-3-7(4)) Te Papa Pr. NZL. Dist: Independent Pubs. Group.
Ryniak, Christopher. The Word Eater. Amato, Mary. 2005. (ENG.). 151p. (J). (gr. 3-7). reprint ed. pap. 7.99 (978-0-8234-1940-1(1)) Holiday Hse., Inc.
Ryser, Nicolas. Clowns & Dragons!, No. 3. Richard, Laurent. Gauvin, Edward, tr. 2014. (Tao, the Little Samurai Ser.: 3). (ENG.). 56p. (J). (gr. 2-5). lib. bdg. 29.32 (978-1-4677-2096-0(8), 9781467720960, Graphic Universe™) Lerner Publishing Group.
—Ninjas & Knock Outs!, No. 2. Richard, Laurent. Gauvin, Edward, tr. 2014. (Tao, the Little Samurai Ser.: 2). (ENG.). 64p. (J). (gr. 2-5). lib. bdg. 29.32 (978-1-4677-3272-7(9), 9781467732727, Graphic Universe™) Lerner Publishing Group.
—Pranks & Attacks!, No. 1. Richard, Laurent. Gauvin, Edward, tr. 2014. (Tao, the Little Samurai Ser.: 1). (ENG.). 64p. (J). (gr. 2-5). lib. bdg. 29.32 (978-1-4677-2095-3(X), 9781467720953, Graphic Universe™) Lerner Publishing Group.
Ryski, Dawid. All My Animals. Napier, Lauren. 2016. (ENG.). 48p. (J). (gr. -1-2). 24.95 (978-3-89955-777-0(8)) Die Gestalten Verlag DEU. Dist: Ingram Publisher Services.
Ryskind, Sam. Los Santos Valientes de los Caballeros de Columbus. Drake, Tim. Alvarado, Tomas, tr. 2003.Tr. of Courageous Saints of the Knights of Columbus. (SPA.). (J). 5.00 (978-0-9747571-1-7(X)) Catholic World Mission.
Rzasa, Jennifer, et al. Drawing Fun Fashions. Bolte, Mari. 2013. (Drawing Fun Fashions Ser.). (ENG.). 32p. (J). (gr. 3-9). lib. bdg., lib. bdg., lib. bdg. 171.90 (978-1-62065-040-0(1)) Capstone.
Rzasa, Jennifer. Skater Chic Style: Fun Fashions You Can Sketch, 1 vol. Bolte, Mari. 2013. (Drawing Fun Fashions Ser.). (ENG.). 32p. (J). (gr. 3-9). lib. bdg. 28.65 (978-1-62065-038-7(X)) Capstone.

S

S, Agnes & Jenks, D. Birthday Balloon Panda Bear Notebook: Birthday Panda, Balloon Dance: Lined Notebook, Panda Bear Notebook for Girls, Teens & Tweens. Zoo Animal Parade. 2019. (Pandas on Parade Notebooks Ser.: Vol. 1). (ENG.). 122p. (J). pap. 6.99 **(978-1-0937-7244-9(1))** Independently Published.
S., Bijan, jt. illus. see Mukherjee, Aiswarya.
S. Fox, Culpeo. The Fox & the Crow. 2014. (ENG.). 28p. (J). (gr. -1). 17.95 (978-81-8190-303-7(X)) Karadi Tales Co. Pvt. Ltd. IND. Dist: Consortium Bk. Sales & Distribution.
S. I. Artists Staff. Fun & Games. 2003. 40p. (J). 3.95 (978-0-9729026-1-8(9)) Midwest Cylinder Management, Inc.
—Fun & Games. 2003. (J). per. (978-1-57657-854-4(2)) Paradise Pr., Inc.
S, Vera. Elfis the Singing Elf. N, Naila. 2019. (ENG.). 32p. (J). pap. **(978-99957-96-13-6(9))** Faraxa Publishing.
S Violette, Palumbo. Philo et le SuperDon Patience. Mishriky, Mireille. 2018. (Philo et les Superdons Ser.: Vol. 2). (FRE.). 26p. (J). (gr. 2-6). pap. (978-1-7753852-8-8(0)) Mishriky., Mireille.
S�ez, Sof�a. El Girasol. Freire De Matos, Isabel. 2019. (SPA.). 26p. (J). pap. 13.00 **(978-0-9994064-4-1(2))** Ediciones Cocolí.
Saa, Pitu. Frida Kahlo para Niñas y Niños. Fink, Nadia. ed. 2016.Tr. of Frida Kalho for Girls & Boys. (SPA.). (gr. 2-12). pap. 12.99 (978-0-9973280-0-4(2)) Bks. del Sur.
Saaf, Donald. Dan Zanes' House Party! A Family Roots Music Treasury. Zanes, Dan. 2018. (ENG.). 160p. (J). (gr. 3-17). spiral bd. 24.99 (978-0-7603-6201-3(7), Voyageur Pr.) Quarto Publishing Group USA.
Saavedra, Anthony. Justin's Very Own Drum. Cox, Steven. 2009. 24p. pap. 24.95 (978-1-60749-553-6(8)) America Star Bks.
Sabado, Joe. Mommy Teach Us to Pray. Fujii, Jason, photos by. l.t. ed. 2006. 31p. (J). 15.95 (978-1-59879-122-8(2)) Lifevest Publishing, Inc.
Sabaka, Donna. Seashells in My Pocket: AMC's Family Guide to Exploring the Coast from Maine to Florida. Hansen, Judith. 3rd ed. 2008. (ENG.). 160p. (gr. 3-7). per. 14.95 (978-1-929173-61-7(X)) Appalachian Mountain Club Bks.
Sabanski, Helen. The Very Best Friend There Ever Could Be. Fedderesen, Jill. 2004. 8p. pap. 5.73 (978-1-4116-0898-6(4)) Lulu Pr., Inc.
Sabater, Gaspar. Logic Lotty: The Fortune Teller's Spoon. Peterson, Paige. 2015. (ENG.). 82p. (J). pap. 6.99 (978-0-9907895-0-5(0)) Hollingale Bks. LLC.
Sabatini, Marie. Joseph's Hands. Sabatini, Kety. 2007. (ENG.). 36p. (J). per. 12.99 (978-0-9792258-8-8(4)) Bezalel Bks.
Sabatino, Chris. The Imitation of Christ for Children: A Guide to Following Jesus. Ficocelli, Elizabeth. 2006. 49p. (J). (gr. 3-7). per. 9.95 (978-0-8091-6733-3(6), 6733-6) Paulist Pr.
Sabbagh, Tatiana. Lebanon A to Z: A Middle Eastern Mosaic. Boutros, Jill et al. 2006. (ENG.). 40p. (J). (gr. -1-3). 25.00 (978-0-9744803-4-3(7)) PublishingWorks.
Sabbatini, Lorenzo. Lift-The-Flap Earth. 2020. (ENG.). 20p. (J). (gr. 2). 14.95 (978-88-544-1659-8(2)) White Star ITA. Dist: Sterling Publishing Co., Inc.
Sabel, Stacey. Do You Think Jesus Had a Dog? Koschak, Carianne. 2018. (ENG.). 30p. (J). pap. 13.95 (978-1-9736-2949-8(6), WestBow Pr.) Author Solutions, Inc.
Sabella, Elisa. Please Explain "Anxiety" to Me! Simple Biology & Solutions for Children & Parents. Zelinger, Laurie E. & Zelinger, Jordan. 2014. (J). pap. 15.95 (978-1-61599-216-4(2)) Loving Healing Pr., Inc.
—Please Explain Anxiety to Me! Simple Biology & Solutions for Children & Parents. Zelinger, Laurie & Zelinger, Jordan. 2010. 38p. 32.95 (978-1-61599-051-1(8)); 40p. pap. 21.95 (978-1-61599-029-0(1)) Loving Healing Pr., Inc.
Sabi, Wabi. El Misterio de Mi Mascota Verdesin. Mira, Katish. 2018. (SPA.). 34p. (J). (gr. k-3). **(978-958-48-3872-8(5))** Restrepo, Ana.
Sabin, Tracy. Fashion Rules! A Closer Look at Clothing in the Middle Ages. Skroback Hennessey, Gail. 2020. (ENG.). 40p. (J). (gr. 3-6). 18.99 **(978-1-63440-905-6(1))** Red Chair Pr.
Sabiston, Susan. The Bluff, 1. Gunther, Joseph. l.t. ed. 2006. 28p. (J). 14.95 (978-0-9789525-0-1(2)) Young Readers Publications.
Sabl�n Rodriguez, Mayra. Bigot�n: �lbum Infantil Ilustrado. Sabl�n Rodr�guez, Mayra & Sabl�n, Mayra. 2020. (SPA.). 24p. (J). pap. 10.08 **(978-1-6546-4530-4(3))** Independently Published.
Sable, Katherine. Hello Goldy! Aryal, Aimee. 2004. 24p. (J). 19.95 (978-0-9743442-4-9(9)) Mascot Bks., Inc.
Sabnani, Nina. The Boy Who Loved Colour. Shukla, Subir. 2004. (ENG & HIN.). (J). (978-81-8146-042-4(1)) Tulika Pubs.
—My Mother's Sari. Rao, Sandhya. 2009. 28p. (J). (gr. -1-3). 7.95 (978-0-7358-2233-7(6)) North-South Bks., Inc.
Sabol, Elizabeth. Day Is Done: A Lullaby, l.t. ed. 2004. 26p. (J). pap. incl. audio compact disk (978-0-9747382-0-8(4)) LeDor Publishing.
Saboten. Path of the Diamond. Cube Kid. 2017. 249p. (J). (978-1-5182-4674-6(5)) Andrews McMeel Publishing.
Sabrekova, Evgeniya. Warm & Busy Holidays. Clever Publishing. 2018. (Clever Activity Pad Ser.). (ENG.). 80p. (J). (gr. -1-1). pap. 4.99 (978-1-948418-25-6(8)) Clever Media Group.
Sabuda, Robert. Alice's Adventures in Wonderland. Carroll, Lewis. 2003. (ENG.). 12p. (J). (gr. -1-3). 34.99 (978-0-689-84743-1(2), Little Simon) Little Simon.
—America the Beautiful: America the Beautiful. 2004. (Classic Collectible Pop-Up Ser.). (ENG.). 16p. (J). (gr. -1-3). 39.99 (978-0-689-84744-8(0), Little Simon) Little Simon.
—Chanukah Lights. Rosen, Michael J. 2011. (ENG.). 16p. (J). (gr. k-4). 34.99 (978-0-7636-5533-4(3)) Candlewick Pr.
—I Hear America Singing. Whitman, Walt. 2004. 30p. (J). (gr. k-4). reprint ed. 15.00 (978-0-7567-8097-5(7)) DIANE Publishing Co.
—Peter Pan: Peter Pan. 2008. (ENG.). 16p. (J). 39.99 (978-0-689-85364-7(5), Little Simon) Little Simon.
—Winter's Tale: Winter's Tale. 2005. (ENG.). 12p. (J). (gr. -1-3). 39.99 (978-0-689-85363-0(7), Little Simon) Little Simon.
Sabuda, Robert. Beauty & the Beast: A Pop-Up Adaptation of the Classic Tale. Sabuda, Robert. 2010. (ENG.). 12p. (J). (gr. -1-2). 39.99 (978-1-4169-6079-9(1), Little Simon) Little Simon.
—Believe: A Pop-Up Book of Possibilities. Sabuda, Robert. 2019. 24p. (J). (gr. k-3). 27.99 (978-0-7636-6397-1(2)) Candlewick Pr.
—The Little Mermaid. Sabuda, Robert. 2013. (ENG.). 12p. (J). (gr. 1). 34.99 (978-1-4169-6080-5(5), Little Simon) Little Simon.
—Ten Horse Farm. Sabuda, Robert. 2018. 20p. (J). (gr. -1-2). 29.99 (978-0-7636-6398-8(0)) Candlewick Pr.
—Uh-Oh, Leonardo! The Adventures of Providence Traveler. Sabuda, Robert. 2007. (ENG.). 48p. (J). (gr. k-3). 12.99 (978-1-4169-6164-2(X), Aladdin) Simon & Schuster Children's Publishing.
—The White House: A Pop-Up of Our Nation's Home. Sabuda, Robert. 2015. (ENG.). 12p. (J). (gr. -1-3). 29.99 (978-0-545-54089-6(5), Orchard Bks.) Scholastic, Inc.
—Winter in White: A Mini Pop-Up Treat. Sabuda, Robert. 2007. (ENG.). 18p. (J). (gr. -1-3). 17.99 (978-0-689-85365-4(3), Little Simon) Little Simon.
—The 12 Days of Christmas. Sabuda, Robert. 10th anniv. ed. 2006. (ENG.). 14p. (J). (gr. -1-3). 39.99 (978-1-4169-2792-1(1), Little Simon) Little Simon.
Sabuda, Robert, jt. illus. see Reinhart, Matthew.
Saburi, Misa. Addition. Ghigna, Charles. 2017. (Winter Math Ser.). (ENG.). 24p. (J). (gr. -1-3). lib. bdg. 33.99 incl. audio compact disk (978-1-68410-007-1(0), 31591) Cantata Learning.
—Beamard's Book. Underwood, Deborah. 2019. (ENG.). 32p. (J). 17.99 (978-1-62779-757-3(2), 900159427, Holt, Henry & Co. Bks. For Young Readers) Holt, Henry & Co.
—Cats Are a Liquid. Donnelly, Rebecca. 2019. (ENG.). 32p. (J). 17.99 (978-1-250-20659-6(6), 900201486, Holt, Henry & Co. Bks. For Young Readers) Holt, Henry & Co.
—Count by 10 To 100. Ghigna, Charles. 2017. (Winter Math Ser.). (ENG.). 24p. (J). (gr. -1-3). lib. bdg. 33.99 incl. audio compact disk (978-1-68410-017-0(8), 31592) Cantata Learning.
—Even Numbers. Ghigna, Charles. 2017. (Winter Math Ser.). (ENG.). 24p. (J). (gr. -1-3). lib. bdg. 33.99 incl. audio compact disk (978-1-68410-023-1(2), 31593) Cantata Learning.
—Making 10. Ghigna, Charles. 2017. (Winter Math Ser.). (ENG.). 24p. (J). (gr. -1-3). lib. bdg. 33.99 incl. audio compact disk (978-1-68410-037-8(2), 31594) Cantata Learning.
—Natsumi's Song of Summer. Weston, Robert Paul. 2020. (ENG.). 40p. (J). (gr. -1-2). 17.99 (978-0-7352-6541-7(0), Tundra Bks.) Tundra Bks. CAN. Dist: Penguin Random Hse. LLC.
—Odd Numbers. Ghigna, Charles. 2017. (Winter Math Ser.). (ENG.). 24p. (J). (gr. -1-3). lib. bdg. 33.99 incl. audio compact disk (978-1-68410-043-9(7), 31595) Cantata Learning.
—Sakura's Cherry Blossoms. Weston, Robert Paul. 2018. (ENG.). 40p. (J). (gr. -1-2). 17.99 (978-1-101-91874-6(8), Tundra Bks.) Tundra Bks. CAN. Dist: Penguin Random Hse. LLC.
—Subtraction. Ghigna, Charles. 2017. (Winter Math Ser.). (ENG.). 24p. (J). (gr. -1-3). lib. bdg. 33.99 incl. audio compact disk (978-1-68410-053-8(4), 31596) Cantata Learning.
—Time Dogs: Balto & the Race Against Time. Moss, Helen. 2019. (Time Dogs Ser.: 1). (ENG.). 144p. (J). 15.99 (978-1-250-18633-1(1), 900191579, Holt, Henry & Co. Bks. For Young Readers) Holt, Henry & Co.
—Time Dogs: Balto & the Race Against Time. Moss, Helen. 2020. (Time Dogs Ser.: 1). (ENG.). 144p. (J). pap. 7.99 (978-1-250-25022-3(6), 900191580) Square Fish.
—Time Dogs: Barry & the Great Mountain Rescue. Moss, Helen. 2020. (Time Dogs Ser.: 3). (ENG.). 40p. (J). 15.99 (978-1-250-18637-9(4), 900191585, Holt, Henry & Co. Bks. For Young Readers) Holt, Henry & Co.
—Time Dogs: Seaman & the Great Northern Adventure. Moss, Helen. 2019. (Time Dogs Ser.: 2). (ENG.). 144p. (J). 15.99 (978-1-250-18635-5(8), 900191582, Holt, Henry & Co. Bks. For Young Readers) Holt, Henry & Co.
—Time Dogs: Seaman & the Great Northern Adventure. Moss, Helen. 2020. (Time Dogs Ser.: 2). (ENG.). 160p. (J). pap. 7.99 (978-1-250-25023-0(4), 900191583) Square Fish.
—Winter Math. Ghigna, Charles. 2017. (Winter Math Ser.). (ENG.). 24p. (J). (gr. -1-3). lib. bdg., lib. bdg., lib. bdg. 203.94 (978-1-68410-114-6(X), 27249) Cantata Learning.
Saccheri, Briana. The Secret to Easter Eggs. Saccheri, Josephine. 2008. 28p. pap. 24.95 (978-1-60474-210-7(0)) America Star Bks.
Sacco, Joe. One Flew over the Cuckoo's Nest: (Penguin Classics Deluxe Edition) Kesey, Ken. 2007. (Penguin Classics Deluxe Edition Ser.). (ENG.). 320p. (gr. 12-18). 18.00 (978-0-14-310502-2(7), Penguin Classics) Penguin Publishing Group.
Sacco, Mauro, jt. illus. see Vallarino, Elisa.
Sachs, Barry. Ghost Train to Freedom: An Adventure on the Underground Railroad. Reese Martin, Faith. 2012. (JMP Mystery Ser.: Bk. 3). (ENG.). 416p. (YA). pap. 14.99 (978-1-60800-014-2(1), American Literary Publishing) LifeReloaded Specialty Publishing LLC.
Sachs, Katrina. No More Pets. Sachs, Linda. 2018. (ENG.). 40p. (J). (978-1-5255-2889-7(0)); pap. (978-1-5255-2890-3(4)) FriesenPress.
Sachse, Dina. My Body: 12 Lift-N-Learn Flashcards about the Human Body, 12 vols. 2013. (Early Start Singles Ser.). (ENG.). 12p. (J). (978-1-77132-070-2(2)) SpiceBox Products Ltd.
—My Clothes: 12 Lift-N-Learn Flashcards about Clothes, 26 vols. 2013. (Early Start Singles Ser.). (ENG.). 12p. (J). (978-1-77132-101-3(6)) SpiceBox Products Ltd.
—My Food: 12 Lift-N-Learn Flashcards about Food!, 26 vols. 2013. (Early Start Singles Ser.). (ENG.). 12p. (J). (978-1-77132-102-0(4)) SpiceBox Products Ltd.
Sacré, Yohan. Timo the Adventurer. Garnier, Jonathan. 2020. (ENG.). 128p. (J). (gr. 3-7). 19.99 **(978-0-358-36012-4(9)**, 1783732); pap. 10.99 **(978-0-358-36011-7(0)**, 1783731) Houghton Mifflin Harcourt Publishing Co. (Etch).
Sacui, Alexandru. Leni the Pug: The Comet Christmas Caper. Fiore, Keith M. 2006. 95p. per. 29.50 (978-0-9785773-0-8(2)) Brownstone Monkey Productions, Inc.
Sada, Margarita. Una Canci�n Por Temo. Malpica, Tono. 2019. (Torre Azul Ser.). (SPA.). 136p. (J). pap. **(978-607-9107-91-8(0))** Norma Ediciones, S.A.
Sada, Margarita. The Dog. Mixter, Helen. 2017. 24p. (J). (gr. -1). 18.95 (978-1-77164-271-2(8)) Greystone Books Ltd. CAN. Dist: Publishers Group West (PGW).
—La Enfermedad del Beso. Ruiz, Maria Emilia Beyer. rev. ed. 2006. (Otra Escalera Ser.). (SPA & ENG.). 36p. (J). (gr. 5). pap. 9.95 (978-968-5920-82-7(6)) Castillo, Ediciones, S. A. de C. V. MEX. Dist: Macmillan.
—Forajidos: Historia y Poesia en Siete Corridos Mexicanos. Flores, Enrique. 2006. (SPA & ENG.). 48p. (J). (gr. 4). pap. 10.95 (978-968-5920-75-9(3)) Castillo, Ediciones, S. A. de C. V. MEX. Dist: Macmillan.
—Guacamole: Un Poema para Cocinar (A Cooking Poem), 1 vol. Argueta, Jorge. Amado, Elisa, tr. 2016. (Bilingual Cooking Poems Ser.). (SPA.). 32p. (J). (gr. -1-2). pap. 8.95 (978-1-55498-888-4(8)) Groundwood Bks. CAN. Dist: Publishers Group West (PGW).
Sada, Margarita. Los Cinco Guantes. Mansour Manzur, Vivian. 2019. (Torre Azul Ser.). (SPA.). 128p. (J). pap. **(978-607-722-129-6(5))** Norma Ediciones, S.A.
Sada, Margarita. Yo, Claudia. Arciniegas, Triunfo. rev. ed. 2006. (Castillo de la Lectura Preschool Ser.). (ENG.). 36p. (J). pap. 6.95 (978-970-20-0845-3(X)) Castillo, Ediciones, S. A. de C. V. MEX. Dist: Macmillan.
Sada, Margarita, jt. illus. see Mateo, Rosario.
Sadat, Madana. Trunk to Trunklet. Lujan, Jorge. 2016. (ENG.). 32p. (J). (gr. -1-2). 16.95 (978-1-59270-194-0(9)) Enchanted Lion Bks., LLC.
Sadeghi, Mina. Life Lessons for Mike. Seaton, William. 2018. (ENG.). 48p. (J). (gr. 2-6). 16.95 (978-1-63302-091-7(6), Total Publishing & Media) Yorkshire Publishing Group.
Sadeghian, Alireza. Everyone Prays: Celebrating Faith Around the World, Vol. York Lumbard, Alexis. 2014. 28p. (J). (gr. -1-3). 17.95 (978-1-937786-19-9(6), Wisdom Tales) World Wisdom, Inc.
—The Knight, the Princess, & the Magic Rock: A Classic Persian Tale, Vol. 2012. (ENG.). 32p. (J). (gr. -1-3). 15.95 (978-1-937786-01-4(3)) World Wisdom, Inc.
Sadler, Dale. More Than a Stove. Fussell, Bonnie. l.t. ed. 2004. 32p. (J). pap. 7.99 (978-0-615-12702-6(9)) Blackberry Pubs.
Sadler, Sonia Lynn. MaDear's Old Green House. Patrick, Denise Lewis. 2004. 32p. (J). (gr. k-3). 16.95 (978-0-940975-55-2(6), Sankofa Bks.) Just Us Bks., Inc.
—Seeds of Change, 1 vol. Johnson, Jen Cullerton. 2013. (ENG.). 40p. (J). (gr. 1-6). 19.95 (978-1-60060-367-9(X), cc3a946f-0d51-4b4c-a2f5-7d24cf2485f2) Lee & Low Bks., Inc.
—The Story of Environmentalist Wangari Maathai, 1 vol. Johnson, Jen Cullerton. 2020. (Story Of Ser.). (ENG.). 64p. (J). (gr. 3-7). pap. 9.95 (978-1-64379-012-1(9), 26644a3c-49cd-4718-a2ee-7d020ed38805) Lee & Low Bks., Inc.
Sadowski, Jeff. Cherry Pie Charlie & More Poems for Children. Tully, Sandra M. 2007. (J). 15.00 (978-1-933556-86-4(2)) Publishers' Graphics, L.L.C.
Sadr, Ayeshe, jt. illus. see Dasgupta, Ishaan.
Saefkow, Hans. King of Rome. Sudbury, Dave. 2008. (ENG.). 32p. (J). (gr. -1-3). 17.95 (978-1-894965-94-1(9)) Simply Read Bks. CAN. Dist: Ingram Publisher Services.
Saelig, S. M. Moonhorse. Osborne, Mary Pope. 2016. (ENG.). 40p. (J). (gr. -1-2). 16.99 (978-0-394-88960-3(6), Knopf Bks. for Young Readers) Random Hse. Children's Bks.
Saemann, Kara, jt. illus. see Trotta, Lee.
Saenger, Stefanie. Grow Healthy Little One. 2007. 24p. (J). pap. 16.95 (978-0-9796010-0-2(2)) Johnston, Ann.
Saez, Sofia. Una Carta de Delke. De Matos, Isabel Freire. 2004. (SPA.). 32p. (gr. k-3). pap. 8.95 (978-1-57581-573-2(7)) Santillana USA Publishing Co., Inc.
—Una Carta de Monica. De Matos, Isabel Freire. 2004. (SPA.). 32p. (gr. k-3). pap. 8.95 (978-1-57581-574-9(5)) Santillana USA Publishing Co., Inc.
Saez, Sofia. Toyita: Aventuras de una Hormiga. Freire De Matos, Isabel. 2019. (SPA.). 38p. (J). pap. 14.00 **(978-0-9994064-5-8(0))** Ediciones Cocolí.
Safar, Lina. The Forgotten Ornament. Shein, Erik Daniel & Reker, Martin. 2010. (J). pap. 11.95 (978-0-578-05938-9(X)) Ark Watch Holdings LLC.
—The Forgotten Ornament. Shein, Erik Daniel. Reker, Martin, ed. 2010. 32p. (J). pap. 16.95 (978-0-9765358-2-9(3)) Ark Watch Holdings LLC.
—How Did I Get Here? Maillis, Nicole. 2011. 4p. (J). 7.95 (978-1-60131-086-6(2)) Big Tent Bks.
—Pink Fire Trucks. Barberi, Gladys. 2013.Tr. of Los Camiones de Bomberos de Color Rosado. 30p. (J). 16.95 (978-1-60131-145-0(1)) Big Tent Bks.
Safarewicz, Evie. World of Ballet. Tatchell, Judy. Miles, Lisa, ed. 2006. (Kid Kits Ser.). 64p. (J). (gr. 5). lib. bdg. 17.95 (978-1-58086-514-2(3)) EDC Publishing.
Safarewicz, Evie & Smith, Guy. The World of Ballet: Internet-Linked. Tatchell, Judy. Miles, Lisa, ed. rev. ed. 2007. (World of Ballet Ser.). 64p. (J). (gr. 4-7). per. 9.99 (978-0-7945-1060-2(4), Usborne) EDC Publishing.
Safayiniya, Mahdiyah. Aya Man Buzurg Shudaham. Mastiri, Maryam. 2017. (PER.). 23p. (J). (978-964-337-842-4(X)) Ketab-e Neyestan.
—Ganj-i Sina. Mastiri, Maryam. 2017. (PER.). 23p. (J). (978-964-337-841-7(1)) Ketab-e Neyestan.
Safina, Carl. Beyond Words: What Elephants & Whales Think & Feel (a Young Reader's Adaptation) Safina, Carl. 2019. (Beyond Words Ser.). (ENG.). 176p. (J). 17.99 (978-1-250-14463-8(9), 900180670) Roaring Brook Pr.
—Beyond Words: What Wolves & Dogs Think & Feel (a Young Reader's Adaptation) Safina, Carl. 2020. (Beyond Words Ser.). (ENG.). 176p. (J). 19.99 (978-1-250-14465-2(5), 900180673) Roaring Brook Pr.
Saga-Whyte. Why the Naiads Dance: Book One of the Naiad Legends, 8 vols., Vol. 1. Saga-Whyte. 2007. 25p. (J). (978-90-8885-018-9(6)) Saga-Whyte Pr.
Sagar, Lindsey. Dinosaur Stomp! Copper, Jenny. 2019. (Push & Play Ser.). (ENG.). 16p. (J). (gr. -1-1). bds. 7.99 (978-1-78958-067-9(6)) Top That! Publishing PLC GBR. Dist: Independent Pubs. Group.
—Farm Scramble! Copper, Jenny. 2020. (Push & Play Ser.). (ENG.). 16p. (J). 7.99 (978-1-78958-068-6(4)) Top That! Publishing PLC GBR. Dist: Independent Pubs. Group.
—Fire Rescue! Copper, Jenny. 2020. (Push & Play Ser.). (ENG.). 16p. (J). bds. 7.99 (978-1-78958-346-5(2)) Top That! Publishing PLC GBR. Dist: Independent Pubs. Group.
Sagar, Lindsey. Peas on Earth. Marx, Jonny. 2020. (ENG.). 12p. (J). (gr. -1-k). bds. 8.99 **(978-1-64517-505-6(7)**, Silver Dolphin Bks.) Printers Row Publishing Group.
—The Story of Country. 2020. (Story Of Ser.). (ENG.). 24p. (J). (— 1). bds. 8.99 **(978-1-64517-177-5(9)**, Silver Dolphin Bks.) Printers Row Publishing Group.
—The Story of Pop. Editors of Caterpillar Books. 2020. (Story Of Ser.). (ENG.). 24p. (J). (— 1). bds. 8.99 **(978-1-64517-361-8(5)**, Silver Dolphin Bks.) Printers Row Publishing Group.

S

Sagar, Lindsey. The Story of Rap. Editors of Caterpillar Books. 2019. (Story Of Ser.). (ENG.). 24p. (J). (— 1). bds. 8.99 (978-1-68412-508-1(1), Silver Dolphin Bks.) Printers Row Publishing Group.

—The Story of Rock. Editors of Caterpillar Books. 2019. (Story Of Ser.). (ENG.). 24p. (J). (— 1). bds. 8.99 (978-1-68412-509-8(X), Silver Dolphin Bks.) Printers Row Publishing Group.

—Unicorn Dance! Copper, Jenny. 2019. (Push & Play Ser.). (ENG.). 16p. (J). (gr. -1-1). bds. 7.99 (978-1-78958-070-9(6)) Top That! Publishing PLC GBR. Dist: Independent Pubs. Group.

Sagasti, Miriam. The Leaves Are Falling One by One. Metzger, Steve. 2007. (J). (978-0-439-02444-0(7)) Scholastic, Inc.

—Thank You, Ruth & Naomi. Lundy, Charlotte. Waldrep, Evelyn L., ed. 2004. 32p. (J). (gr. k-4). 15.95 (978-0-9741817-0-7(6)) Bay Light Publishing.

—We Like Puddles. Kolodny, Cynthia. 2004. (ENG.). 12p. (gr. k-1). pap. 7.95 (978-1-57874-040-6(1), Kaeden Bks.) Kaeden Corp.

Sage, Molly. Things to Make & Do with Paper. Gulliver, Amanda & Turnbull, Stephanie. 2004. (Activity Books). 32p. (J). pap. 6.95 (978-0-7945-0674-2(7), Usborne) EDC Publishing.

Sage, Molly. Underwater. Sage, Molly. 2007. 6p. (J). (gr. k — 1). 6.99 (978-1-85602-498-3(9)) Pavilion Bks. GBR. Dist: Independent Pubs. Group.

Sage, Molly & Larkum, Adam. Little Children's Cookbook. Allman, Howard, photos by. Gilpin, Rebecca. 2005. (ENG.). 96p. (J). (gr. 4-7). 7.95 (978-0-7945-1113-5(9), Usborne) EDC Publishing.

Sage, Trina. Sarah's Most Perfect Day. Krohn, Kathryn T. 2007. 24p. (J). 13.99 (978-1-59879-325-3(X), Lifevest) Lifevest Publishing, Inc.

Saghy, Christopher. Growing Smarter. Wilson, Judith Vt. 2018. (ENG.). 30p. (J). (gr. 4-6). 18.95 (978-0-692-07753-5(7)) Judith VT Wilson.

Sagor, Jubayda. Buffy Goes Home. Phillips, Nicholas. 2010. (Buffy Ser.: Vol. 1). (ENG.). 46p. (J). pap. 10.00 (978-1-0967-4991-2(2)) Independently Published.

Sagor, Jubayda. Let's Hide: Nihi Ta Atok. Ulloa-Heath, Julie Manglona. 2019. (ENG.). 32p. (J). pap. 9.66 (978-1-6981-3547-2(5)) Independently Published.

Sagramola, Giulia. Girls Resist! A Guide to Activism, Leadership, & Starting a Revolution. Rich, KaeLyn. 2018. 208p. (YA). (gr. 9). pap. 14.99 (978-1-68369-059-7(1)) Quirk Bks.

Sah, Anup, photos by. The Tiger. Ledu-Frattini, Stéphanie. Uhlig, Elizabeth, tr. from FRE. 2004. (Animal Close-Ups Ser.). 28p. (J). pap. 6.95 (978-1-57091-373-0(0)) Charlesbridge Publishing, Inc.

Saha, Ayan. I Am Brown. Lewis, Latoya. 2020. (ENG.). 42p. (J). pap. 14.99 (978-1-7332980-5-6(3)) Ballard Publishing Group, LLC.

Saha, Sujata. Family Ticket. Fox, Julie G. Bulbeck, Leonora, ed. 2019. (ENG.). 30p. (J). pap. 9.99 (978-1-7943-5465-4(4)) Independently Published.

Sahai, Supriya. Once upon a Dinosaur Craft. Lim, Annalees. 2019. (Happily Ever Crafter Ser.). (ENG.). 32p. (J). (gr. 2-5). lib. bdg. 27.99 (978-1-5415-5881-6(2), 9781541558816, Lerner Pubns.) Lerner Publishing Group.

—Once upon a Fairy Tale Craft. Lim, Annalees. 2019. (Happily Ever Crafter Ser.). (ENG.). 32p. (J). (gr. 2-5). lib. bdg. 27.99 (978-1-5415-5877-9(4), 9781541558779, Lerner Pubns.) Lerner Publishing Group.

—Once upon a Medieval Craft. Lim, Annalees. 2019. (Happily Ever Crafter Ser.). (ENG.). 32p. (J). (gr. 2-5). lib. bdg. 27.99 (978-1-5415-5879-3(0), 9781541558793, Lerner Pubns.) Lerner Publishing Group.

—Once upon a Pirate Craft. Lim, Annalees. 2019. (Happily Ever Crafter Ser.). (ENG.). 32p. (J). (gr. 2-5). lib. bdg. 27.99 (978-1-5415-5878-6(2), 9781541558786, Lerner Pubns.) Lerner Publishing Group.

—Once upon a Robots & Aliens Craft. Lim, Annalees. 2019. (Happily Ever Crafter Ser.). (ENG.). 32p. (J). (gr. 2-5). 27.99 (978-1-5415-5880-9(4), 4f1bd0ea-a5be-4389-b703-9b4a32557a9d, Lerner Pubns.) Lerner Publishing Group.

—Once upon an Animal Craft. Lim, Annalees. 2019. (Happily Ever Crafter Ser.). (ENG.). 32p. (J). (gr. 2-5). 27.99 (978-1-5415-5882-3(0), 9781541558823, Lerner Pubns.) Lerner Publishing Group.

Saia, Jordan. Of Fire & Stars. Coulthurst, Audrey. (Of Fire & Stars Ser.: 1). (ENG.). (YA). (gr. 8). 2018. 416p. pap. 10.99 (978-0-06-243326-8(1), Balzer & Bray); 2016. 400p. 17.99 (978-0-06-243325-1(3)) HarperCollins Pubs.

Saichann, Alberto & Estudio, Pulsar. A Dream for a Princess (Disney Princess) Lagonegro, Melissa. 2016. (Step into Reading Ser.). (ENG.). 24p. (J). (gr. -1-1). pap. 4.99 (978-0-7364-3668-7(5), RH/Disney) Random Hse. Children's Bks.

Said, Shereen. The Incredible Tale of Mr. Wogglebug. Hanson, Cynthia. 2019. (Wogglebug Ser.: Vol. 1). (ENG.). 32p. (J). pap. 15.00 (978-1-9819-3056-2(6)) CreateSpace Independent Publishing Platform.

Saijyo, Shinji. Iron Wok Jan!, Vol. 12. Saijyo, Shinji. 2005. (Iron Wok Jan! Ser.). (ENG.). 200p. (YA). pap. 9.95 (978-1-58899-303-8(5)) DrMaster Pubns. Inc.

Saikia, Mayur. Anansi & His Children. 2010. (J). (978-1-60617-139-4(9)) Teaching Strategies, LLC.

Saillard, Remi. Funny Machines for George the Sheep: A Children's Book Inspired by Leonardo Da Vinci. 2014. (Children's Books Inspired by Famous Artworks Ser.). 32p. (J). (gr. -1-3). 14.95 (978-3-7913-7166-5(5)) Prestel Verlag GmbH & Co KG. DEU. Dist: Penguin Random Hse. LLC.

Saincilus, Larimer. Rita & the Parrot. Jeune, Marie Carole. 2010. (HAT.). 32p. (J). pap. 16.95 (978-1-60195-317-9(8)) International Step by Step Assn.

Sainio, Ulla. Bear & Fox Journal: Forest Animals Trekking in the Fall College Ruled Notebook. Publishing, Gentil Graphics. 2019. (Bear & Fox Notebooks Ser.: Vol. 1). (ENG.). 120p. (J). pap. 6.99 (978-1-0911-6642-4(0)) Independently Published.

Sainsilus, Ismer. A Mango for Grandpa. Hudicourt, Caroline. 2007. 32p. (J). (ARA & ENG.). pap. 14.95 (978-1-60195-085-7(3)); (POL.). pap. 14.95 (978-1-60195-093-2(4)) International Step by Step Assn.

Saint-James, Synthia. Dream a World: A Child's Journey to Self-Discovery Dreamer's Activity Kit. Hull, Bunny. 2004. 24p. (J). 16.95 incl. cd-rom (978-0-9721478-3-5(7)) BrassHeart Music.

Saint James, Synthia. Hallelujah! A Christmas Celebration. Nikola-lisa, W. & Nikola-lisa, W. 2009. (ENG.). 36p. (J). (gr. -1-3). 10.99 (978-1-4424-0224-9(5), Atheneum Bks. for Young Readers) Simon & Schuster Children's Publishing.

Saint-James, Synthia. Happy, Happy Kwanzaa: Kwanzaa for the World. Hull, Bunny. 2003. 24p. (J). (gr. k-5). pap. 16.95 incl. audio compact disk (978-0-9721478-1-1(0), KCC/HHKCD810, Kid's Creative Classics) BrassHeart Music.

Saint James, Synthia. No Mirrors in My Nana's House. Barnwell, Ysaye M. 2005. (ENG.). 32p. (J). (gr. -1-3). reprint ed. 10.99 (978-0-15-205243-0(7), 1195796) Houghton Mifflin Harcourt Publishing Co.

Saint Louis, Ahha Studios. Snazzy Razzy. Stotz, Allyn M. I.t. ed. 2017. (ENG.). (J). (gr. k-4). pap. 9.95 (978-1-61633-882-4(2)) Guardian Angel Publishing, Inc.

Saito, Chiho. Revolutionary Girl Utena, Vol. 3 (2nd Edition) Vol. 3: To Sprout. Saito, Chiho. 2nd ed. 2004. (Revolutionary Girl Utena Ser.: 3). (ENG.). 200p. pap. 9.95 (978-1-59116-207-0(6)) Viz Media.

Saito, Diogo, et al. Tangled: the Series - Let down Your Hair. Peterson, Scott. 2018. (Tangled Ser.). 72p. (J). (gr. 4-7). pap. 9.99 (978-1-68405-294-3(7)) Idea & Design Works, LLC.

Saito, Diogo & Aime, Luigi. Journey to Star Wars: the Rise of Skywalker First Order Villains (Level 2 Reader) Siglain, Michael. 2019. (World of Reading Ser.). (ENG.). 32p. (J). (gr. k-3). pap. 4.99 (978-1-368-05244-3(4), Disney Lucasfilm Press) Disney Publishing Worldwide.

—Journey to Star Wars: the Rise of Skywalker Resistance Heroes (Level 2 Reader) Siglain, Michael. 2019. (World of Reading Ser.). (ENG.). 32p. (J). (gr. k-3). pap. 4.99 (978-1-368-05245-0(2), Disney Lucasfilm Press) Disney Publishing Worldwide.

—Solo: a Star Wars Story Train Heist. Lucasfilm Press. 2018. (ENG.). 24p. (J). (gr. 1-3). pap. 5.99 (978-1-368-01627-8(8), Disney Lucasfilm Press) Disney Publishing Worldwide.

Saito, Diogo, jt. illus. see Sharvin, Ivan.

Saito, Ioe. The Adventure of Momotaro, the Peach Boy, 1 vol. McCarthy, Ralph F. 2013. (Kodansha's Children's Bilingual Classics Ser.: 2). (ENG.). 48p. (J). (gr. k-12). 11.95 (978-1-56836-528-2(4)) Kodansha International JPN. Dist: Penguin Random Hse. LLC.

Saito, Kazu, photos by. Shiki O Wataru Kaze. Pace, Teruko, tr. 2003. (JPN., (YA). pap. 20.00 (978-0-9743474-0-0(X)) Zuiho.

Saito, Masamitsu. Beach Feet. Konagaya, Kiyomi. 2012. (Being in the World Ser.). (ENG.). 32p. (J). (gr. k-k). 14.95 (978-1-59270-121-6(3)) Enchanted Lion Bks., LLC.

—Into the Snow. Kaneko, Yuki. 2016. (ENG.). 32p. (J). (gr. -1-2). 16.95 (978-1-59270-188-9(4)) Enchanted Lion Bks., LLC.

Saitou, Chiho. The World Exists for Me, Vol. 1. Be-Papas. 2005. 200p. per. 9.99 (978-1-59816-034-5(6), Tokyopop Adult) TOKYOPOP, Inc.

Saiz, Jesus, et al. Avengers: Standoff. 2017. (ENG.). 416p. (YA). (gr. 8-17). pap. 34.99 (978-1-302-90885-0(5)) Marvel Worldwide, Inc.

Saiz, Jesus. Doctor Strange by Mark Waid Vol. 1: Across the Universe. 2018. (Doctor Strange (2018) Ser.: 1). 112p. (YA). (gr. 8-17). pap. 15.99 (978-1-302-91233-8(X)) Marvel Worldwide, Inc.

—Doctor Strange by Mark Waid Vol. 4: The Choice. 2020. (ENG.). 112p. (YA). (gr. 8-17). pap. 15.99 (978-1-302-91458-5(8)) Marvel Worldwide, Inc.

Saiz, Jesus, jt. illus. see Pina, Javier.

Sajnani, Surya. Color Me: Who's in the Rain Forest? Sajnani, Surya. 2018. (Wee Gallery Bath Bks.). (ENG.). 8p. (J). (gr. -1 — 1). 12.95 (978-1-68297-343-1(3)) QEB Publishing Inc.

—Friendly Faces in the Forest (2020 Edition) Baby's First Soft Book. Sajnani, Surya. 2nd ed. 2020. (Wee Gallery Cloth Bks.). (ENG.). 6p. (J). (gr. -1 — 1). 16.95 (978-0-7112-5420-6(6), 336625, Words & Pictures) Quarto Publishing Group UK GBR. Dist: Hachette UK Distribution.

—Friendly Faces in the Garden (2020 Edition) Baby's First Soft Book. Sajnani, Surya. 2nd ed. 2020. (Wee Gallery Cloth Bks.). (ENG.). 4p. (J). (gr. -1 — 1). 16.95 (978-0-7112-5417-6(6), 336615, Words & Pictures) Quarto Publishing Group UK GBR. Dist: Hachette UK Distribution.

—Friendly Faces in the Wild (2020 Edition) Baby's First Soft Book. Sajnani, Surya. 2nd ed. 2020. (Wee Gallery Cloth Bks.). (ENG.). 6p. (J). (gr. -1 — 1). 16.95 (978-0-7112-5418-3(4), 336619, Words & Pictures) Quarto Publishing Group UK GBR. Dist: Hachette UK Distribution.

—Friendly Faces on the Farm (2020 Edition) Baby's First Soft Book. Sajnani, Surya. 2nd ed. 2020. (Wee Gallery Cloth Bks.). (ENG.). 6p. (J). (gr. -1 — 1). 16.95 (978-0-7112-5419-0(2), 336622, Words & Pictures) Quarto Publishing Group UK GBR. Dist: Hachette UK Distribution.

—Good Night You, Good Night Me: A Soft Bedtime Book with Mirrors. Sajnani, Surya. 2017. (Wee Gallery Ser.). (ENG.). 8p. (J). (gr. -1 — 1). pap. 14.95 (978-1-68297-207-6(0)) QEB Publishing Inc.

Sajnani, Surya. Moo, Cluck, Baa! the Farm Animals Are Hungry: A Press & Listen Sound Book. Sajnani, Surya. 2017. (Wee Gallery Ser.). (ENG.). 8p. (J). (gr. -1 — 1). bds. 12.95 (978-1-68297-209-0(7)) QEB Publishing Inc.

Sakai, Komako. The Fox Wish. Aman, Kimiko. 2017. (ENG.). 32p. (J). 16.99 (978-1-4521-5188-5(1)) Chronicle Bks. LLC.

—In the Meadow. Kato, Yukiko. 2011. (Being in the World Ser.). 32p. (J). (gr. k-k). 14.95 (978-1-59270-108-7(6)) Enchanted Lion Bks., LLC.

—Wait! Wait! Nakawaki, Hatsue. 2013. (ENG.). 24p. (J). 14.95 (978-1-59270-138-4(8)) Enchanted Lion Bks., LLC.

Sakai, Stan. The Adventures of Nilson Groundthumper & Hermy. Sakai, Stan. Wright, Brendan, ed. 2014. (ENG.). 112p. 14.99 (978-1-61655-341-8(3)) Dark Horse Comics.

—Usagi Yojimbo Saga Volume 3 Ltd. Ed. Sakai, Stan. 2015. (ENG.). 618p. 79.99 (978-1-61655-673-0(0)) Dark Horse Comics.

Sakamoto, Miki. I'm Like You, You're Like Me: A Book about Understanding & Appreciating Each Other. Gainer, Cindy. (J). (gr. -1-2). 2016. (SPA.). 36p. pap. 11.99 (978-1-63198-123-4(4)); 2013. (ENG.). 48p. pap. 11.99 (978-1-57542-436-1(3)); 2011. (ENG.). 48p. 14.99 (978-1-57542-383-8(9)) Free Spirit Publishing, Inc.

—Sofia's First Day of School. Bullard, Lisa. 2017. (Cloverleaf Books (tm) — off to School Ser.). (ENG.). 24p. (J). (gr. k-2). pap. 8.99 (978-1-5124-5579-3(2), 9781512455793); lib. bdg. 25.32 (978-1-5124-3936-6(3)) Lerner Publishing Group. (Millbrook Pr.).

—We're Going on a Leaf Hunt. Metzger, Steve. (J). 2008. (ENG.). 32p. (gr. -1-3). pap. 6.99 (978-0-439-87377-2(0), Cartwheel Bks.); 2005. pap. (978-0-439-77361-4(X)) Scholastic, Inc.

—What I Like about Me! Zobel-Nolan, Allia. 2005. (What I Like about Me Ser.). (ENG.). 16p. (J). (gr. k-4). tchr. ed., per. 20.99 (978-0-7944-1016-2(2), Reader's Digest Children's Bks.) Studio Fun International.

—What I Like about Me! A Book Celebrating Differences. Zobel Nolan, Allia. 2009. (What I Like about Me Ser.). (ENG.). 14p. (J). (gr. -1-k). 6.99 (978-0-7944-1945-5(3), Reader's Digest Children's Bks.) Studio Fun International.

Sakamoto-Sims, Serene. Tales Awaken. Medina, K. 2019. (ENG.). 322p. (J). pap. 15.95 (978-0-9991224-3-3(6)) Cricket Cottage Publishing, LLC.

Saker, Linda. Nana Star. Sills, Elizabeth & Patrice, Elena. 32p. (J). (gr. -1-3). 2007. 15.95 (978-0-9753843-5-0(X)); 2004. 17.99 (978-0-9753843-0-5(9)) ee publishing & productions, inc.

—Nana Star & the Moonman. Sills, Elizabeth & Patrice, Elena. 2008. 32p. (J). (gr. -1-3). 15.95 (978-0-9753843-6-7(8)) ee publishing & productions, inc.

Sakhavarz, Nazy. Orff Explorations: Classroom Projects in Music, Movement & Poetry. Brass, Alice. 2010. (ENG.). 80p. spiral bd. 20.00 (978-1-896941-34-9(6)) Brass, Robin Studio, Inc. CAN. Dist: Independent Pubs. Group.

Sakmar-Sullivan, Eva M. Kangaroo's Out of This World Restaurant, 1 vol. Sakmar-Sullivan, Eva M. 2013. (ENG.). 32p. (J). (gr. -1-3). 14.99 (978-0-7643-4519-7(2), 4889) Schiffer Publishing, Ltd.

Sakprayoonpong, Worachet Boon. Innovators in Action! Leonardo Da Vinci Gets a Do-Over, Vol. Friedlander, Mark P., Jr. 2014. (Innovators in Action Ser.: 1). (ENG.). 208p. (J). (gr. 5-9). pap. 12.95 (978-0-9678020-6-0(7)) Science, Naturally!.

Sakshi, Mangal. I Am Here: My Mindful Morning. Tucci, Lizelle Marpa. 2019. (ENG.). 38p. (J). (978-0-2288-1394-1(8)); pap. (978-0-2288-1393-4(X)) Tellwell Talent.

Sakti, Galih. Where I Live. Grant, Rick S. 2018. (J). pap. (978-1-934370-77-3(0)) Editorial Campana.

Sakupov, Bakhtiyar. The Bookshop: (Part 1) Sakupov, Bakhtiyar. 2019. (1 Ser.: Vol. 1). (ENG.). 40p. (J). pap. 9.13 (978-1-0776-7634-3(4)) Independently Published.

—The Bookshop: (Part 2) Sakupov, Bakhtiyar. 2019. (2 Ser.: Vol. 2). (ENG.). 26p. (J). pap. 9.13 (978-1-6888-9981-0(2)) Independently Published.

Sakurakoji, Kanoko. Black Bird, Vol. 3. Sakurakoji, Kanoko. 2010. (ENG.). 200p. pap. 9.99 (978-1-4215-2766-6(9)) Viz Media.

—Black Bird, Vol. 4. Sakurakoji, Kanoko. 2010. (ENG.). 200p. pap. 9.99 (978-1-4215-2767-3(7)) Viz Media.

Sala, Felicita. The Bog Beast (Big Foot & Little Foot #4) Potter, Ellen. 2020. (ENG.). 144p. (J). (gr. 1-4). 13.99 (978-1-4197-4322-1(8), 1682901, Amulet Bks.) Abrams, Inc.

Sala, Felicita. The Hideout. Mattiangeli, Susanna. 2019. (ENG.). 40p. (J). (gr. -1-3). 16.99 (978-1-4197-3416-8(4), Abrams Bks. for Young Readers) Abrams, Inc.

—I Don't Draw, I Color! Lehrhaupt, Adam. 2017. (ENG.). 32p. (J). (gr. -1-3). 17.99 (978-1-4814-6275-4(X), Simon & Schuster/Paula Wiseman Bks.) Simon & Schuster/Paula Wiseman Bks.

—Joan Procter, Dragon Doctor: The Woman Who Loved Reptiles. Valdez, Patricia. 2018. 40p. (J). (gr. -1-3). 17.99 (978-0-399-55725-5(3)); (ENG.). lib. bdg. 20.99 (978-0-399-55726-2(1)) Random Hse. Children's Bks. (Knopf Bks. for Young Readers).

—The Monster Detector (Big Foot & Little Foot #2) Potter, Ellen. 2018. (ENG.). 128p. (J). (gr. 1-4). 12.99 (978-1-4197-3122-8(X), Amulet Bks.) Abrams, Inc.

—The Monster Detector (Big Foot & Little Foot #2) Potter, Ellen. 2019. (ENG.). 144p. (J). (gr. 1-4). pap. 6.99 (978-1-4197-3386-4(9), Amulet Bks.) Abrams, Inc.

—Mr. Crum's Potato Predicament. Renaud, Anne. 2017. (ENG.). 40p. (J). (gr. -1-3). 17.99 (978-1-77138-619-7(3)) Kids Can Pr., Ltd. CAN. Dist: Hachette Bk. Group.

—Ode to an Onion: Pablo Neruda & His Muse. Giardino, Alexandria. 2018. (ENG.). 40p. (J). (gr. -1-3). 17.95 (978-1-944903-34-3(8), Cameron Kids) Cameron + Co.

—She Made a Monster: How Mary Shelley Created Frankenstein. Fulton, Lynn. 2018. (J). (gr. -1-3). 48p. 17.99 (978-0-525-57960-1(5)); (ENG.). 40p. lib. bdg. 20.99 (978-0-525-57961-8(3)) Random Hse. Children's Bks. (Knopf Bks. for Young Readers).

—The Squatchicorns (Big Foot & Little Foot #3) Potter, Ellen. 2019. (Big Foot & Little Foot Ser.). (ENG.). 144p. (J). (gr. 1-4). pap. 6.99 (978-1-4197-3701-5(5), 1200903); 12.99 (978-1-4197-3364-2(8)) Abrams, Inc. (Amulet Bks.).

Salaberria, Leire. Maya Angelou. Kaiser, Lisbeth. 2016. (Little People, BIG DREAMS Ser.: 4). (ENG.). 32p. (J). (gr. k-3). 15.99 (978-1-84780-889-9(1), Frances Lincoln Children's Bks.) Quarto Publishing Group UK GBR. Dist: Hachette Bk. Group.

—Peter Pan. Barrie, J. M. 2019. (ENG.). 256p. (J). 19.99 (978-1-78888-384-9(5), 9a933e72-0f7b-4f43-b43f-3b064b6fea6b) Arcturus Publishing GBR. Dist: Baker & Taylor Publisher Services (BTPS).

Salaberría, Leire. Todos Deberíamos Ser Feministas / We Should All Be Feminists. Ngozi Adichie, Chimamanda. 2020. (SPA.). 48p. (J). (gr. 2-5). pap. 18.95 (978-607-31-8869-2(2), Beascoa) Penguin Random House Grupo Editorial ESP. Dist: Penguin Random Hse. LLC.

Salaman, Rosy. MI29: Mouseweb International to the Rescue! Tozer, Sarah. 2014. (ENG.). 80p. (J). pap. 12.95 (978-1-84905-496-6(7), 694664) Kingsley, Jessica Pubs. GBR. Dist: Hachette UK Distribution.

—My Book of Feelings: A Book to Help Children with Attachment Difficulties, Learning or Developmental Disabilities Understand Their Emotions. Ross, Tracey. 2017. (ENG.). 40p. (J). 16.95 (978-1-78592-192-6(4), 696354) Kingsley, Jessica Pubs. GBR. Dist: Hachette UK Distribution.

Salamone, Jenna. Boardwalk Fries. Gagliardi, Alyssa. 2020. (ENG.). 18p. (J). 18.99 (978-1-952894-02-2(6)); pap. 13.99 (978-1-952894-84-8(0)) Pen It! Pubns., LLC.

Salan, Felipe Lopez. Jack & the Beanstalk. 2006. (ENG.). 32p. (J). (gr. -1). 15.95 (978-1-933327-11-2(1)) Purple Bear Bks., Inc.

Salanitro, Robert. Pizza Friday. Benhamu, Margaret. 2009. (Slide-Out Book Ser.). 9p. (J). 7.99 (978-1-60436-025-7(9)) Educational Publishing LLC.

—A Surprise in the Mail! Rosenberg, Amye. 2009. (Discovery Ser.). (ENG.). 12p. (J). 7.99 (978-1-60436-018-9(6)) Educational Publishing LLC.

Salariya, David & Scrace, Carolyn. The X-Ray Picture Book of Incredible Creatures. Legg, Gerald. 2004. 48p. (J). (gr. 4-8). pap. 9.00 (978-0-7567-7406-6(3)) DIANE Publishing Co.

Salas, Nadia. Alice's Musical Debut. Frazier, Duewa. 2019. (ENG.). 44p. (J). pap. 12.99 (978-1-5399-4555-0(3)) CreateSpace Independent Publishing Platform.

Salas, Nadia. Alice's Musical Debut. Frazier, Duewa. 2019. (ENG.). 44p. (J). (gr. 2-6). pap. 12.99 (978-0-578-50965-5(2)) Lit Noire Publishing.

Salati, Doug. In a Small Kingdom. dePaola, Tomie. 2016. (J). (978-0-8234-3551-7(2)) Holiday Hse., Inc.

—In a Small Kingdom. dePaola, Tomie. 2018. (ENG.). 48p. (J). (gr. -1-3). 17.99 (978-1-4814-9800-5(2), Simon & Schuster Bks. For Young Readers) Simon & Schuster Bks. For Young Readers.

Salazar, Amanda S. R. Fiona the Frog & Friends: Correcting Speech Delays in Children. Ondersma, Erin. 2019. (J). pap. (978-1-63293-244-0(X)) Sunstone Pr.

Salazar, Amanda S. R. Ricardo the Rabbit & Friends: One of a Series Devoted to Correcting Speech Delays in Children. Ondersma, Erin. 2020. (Correcting Speech Delays in Children Ser.: Vol. 2). (ENG.). 36p. (J). (gr. 3-7). pap. 16.95 (978-1-63293-301-0(2)) Sunstone Pr.

Salazar, Carrie. Mary & Joy Save Christmas. Harris-Wyrick, Wayne. 2016. (ENG.). (J). (gr. 4-6). 19.99 (978-1-940310-51-0(2)); pap. 14.99 (978-1-940310-50-3(4)) 4RV Pub.

—Odin, Dog Hero of the Fires. Smith, Emma Bland. 2020. (ENG.). 32p. (J). (gr. k-3). 16.99 (978-1-5132-6294-9(7), West Margin Pr.) West Margin Pr.

—Where Did Panther Go? A Panther Adventure. Zabel, Vivian. 2017. (Panther Adventure Ser.: Vol. 1). (ENG.). (J). (gr. k-2). pap. 15.99 (978-1-940310-69-5(5)) 4RV Pub.

Salazar, Edgar, et al. Six #1. Houser, Jody. 2019. (Stranger Things Ser.). (ENG.). 24p. (J). (gr. 6-12). lib. bdg. 27.07 (978-1-5321-4440-0(7), 33845, Graphic Novels) Spotlight.

—Six #2. Houser, Jody. 2019. (Stranger Things Ser.). (ENG.). 24p. (J). (gr. 6-12). lib. bdg. 27.07 (978-1-5321-4441-7(5), 33846, Graphic Novels) Spotlight.

—Six #3. Houser, Jody. 2019. (Stranger Things Ser.). (ENG.). 24p. (J). (gr. 6-12). lib. bdg. 27.07 (978-1-5321-4442-4(3), 33847, Graphic Novels) Spotlight.

—Six #4. Houser, Jody. 2019. (Stranger Things Ser.). (ENG.). 24p. (J). (gr. 6-12). lib. bdg. 27.07 (978-1-5321-4443-1(1), 33848, Graphic Novels) Spotlight.

—Stranger Things Set 2 (Set), 4 vols. Houser, Jody. 2019. (Stranger Things Ser.). (ENG.). 24p. (J). (gr. 6-12). lib. bdg. 108.28 (978-1-5321-4439-4(3), 33844, Graphic Novels) Spotlight.

Salazar, Edgar. Uncanny X-Men: Superior Vol. 4: IvX. 2017. (ENG.). 128p. (YA). (gr. 8-17). pap. 16.99 (978-1-302-90525-5(2)) Marvel Worldwide, Inc.

Salazar, Edgar & Sandoval, Gerardo. Venom & X-Men: Poison-X. 2018. (ENG.). 136p. (YA). (gr. 8-17). pap. 17.99 (978-1-302-91225-3(9)) Marvel Worldwide, Inc.

Salazar, Juliana. Pin Pin & Pon Pon. Castillo Lopez, Ana. Nunez, Miguel Angel, ed. 2019. (SPA.). 56p. (J). pap. 12.99 (978-1-0869-8815-4(9)) Independently Published.

Salazar, Riana. Pink Hat's Adventure with Kites. Roller, John, photos by. Roller, Pat Kellogg. 2009. 36p. pap. 10.95 (978-1-59858-957-3(1)) Dog Ear Publishing, LLC.

Salazar, Souther. Destined for Dizzyness. Salazar, Souther. 2005. 48p. pap. 5.95 (978-0-9766848-1-7(0)) Buenaventura Pr.

Salazar, Vivian. Santa Revisits His Secret Little Helper. Bass, William E. 2012. 26p. 24.95 (978-1-4626-5396-6(0)) America Star Bks.

Salazar, Vivian Rose. A Gift for Sant. Bass, William E. 2012. 36p. pap. 24.95 (978-1-4626-6731-4(7)) America Star Bks.

Salcedo Barrero, Juliana. Luisa Viaja en Tren. Castilla, Julia Mercedes. 2019. (Torre Azul Ser.). (SPA.). 122p. (J). (gr. 4-7). pap. (978-958-45-3922-9(1)) Norma Ediciones, S.A.

Salcedo, Erica. Georgia O'Keeffe. Sanchez Vegara, Maria Isabel. 2018. (Little People, Big Dreams Ser.: Vol. 13). (ENG.). 32p. (J). (gr. -1-2). (978-1-78603-122-8(1)) Frances Lincoln Childrens Bks.

Salcedo, Erica. How to Survive As a Firefly. Foote, Kristen. 2017. (How to Survive Ser.). 36p. (J). (gr. k-5). 16.99 *(978-1-943147-32-8(9),* afb519e0-4e59-4b26-acb9-24c71e1ea70e) Innovation Pr., The.
—How to Survive as a Shark. Foote, Kristen. 2017. (How to Survive Ser.). 44p. (J). (gr. 1-5). 16.99 *(978-1-943147-33-5(7),* 84651670-23de-4dab-a5d1-90165eb64f85) Innovation Pr., The.
—Kid Normal. James, Greg & Smith, Chris. (Kid Normal Ser.). (ENG.). 400p. (J). 2019. pap. 7.99 *(978-1-5476-0267-4(8),* 900209369); 2018. 13.99 *(978-1-68119-709-8(X),* 900182253) Bloomsbury Publishing USA. (Bloomsbury Children's Bks.).
—Kid Normal & the Rogue Heroes. James, Greg & Smith, Chris. 2019. (Kid Normal Ser.). (ENG.). 416p. (J). 13.99 *(978-1-5476-0098-4(5),* 900198464, Bloomsbury Children's Bks.) Bloomsbury Publishing USA.
—The Mosquito Brothers, 1 vol. Ondaatje, Griffin. 2015. (ENG.). 128p. (J). (gr. 1-4). 14.95 *(978-1-55498-437-4(8))* Groundwood Bks. CAN. Dist: Publishers Group West (PGW).
—Pigs in a Blanket. Wilhelm, Hans. 2019. (ENG.). 14p. (J). (gr. -1 — 1). bds. 9.99 *(978-1-4521-6451-9(7))* Chronicle Bks. LLC.
Salcedo, Erica. Who's That Cat? Clarkson, Steph. 2019. (ENG.). 28p. (J). bds. 8.99 ***(978-1-77402-120-0(X))*** Rainstorm Pr.
Saldana, Carmen. Bug Bear. Hegarty, Patricia. 2017. (ENG.). 32p. (J). (gr. -1-2). 16.99 *(978-1-68010-053-2(X))* Tiger Tales.
Saldaña, Carmen. Bunnybear. Loney, Andrea J. 2017. (ENG.). 32p. (J). (gr. -1-3). 16.99 *(978-0-8075-0938-8(8),* 807509388) Whitman, Albert & Co.
Saldana, Carmen. Finding Treasure: A Collection of Collections. Schaub, Michelle. 2019. 32p. (J). (gr. -1-3). lib. bdg. 16.99 *(978-1-58089-875-1(0))* Charlesbridge Publishing, Inc.
—I Give You the World. McCleary, Stacey. 2018. (ENG.). 32p. (J). (gr. -1-2). 16.99 *(978-1-68010-082-2(3))* Tiger Tales.
Saldaña, Carmen. Twinkle Twinkle Little Star, I Know Exactly What You Are. Kregenow, Julia. 2018. 40p. (J). (-3). 17.99 *(978-1-4926-7006-3(5),* Sourcebooks Jabberwocky) Sourcebooks, Inc.
—Will You Help Doug Find His Dog? Caston, Jane. 2017. (ENG.). 36p. (J). (gr. -1-1). 14.99 *(978-1-78285-320-6(0))* Barefoot Bks., Inc.
Sale, Graham. What Is Right? Boritzer, Etan. l.t. ed. 2005. (What Is? Ser.). 40p. (J). (gr. k-5). pap. 6.95 *(978-0-9762743-0-8(2)); (978-0-9762743-1-5(0))* Lane, Veronica Bks.
Sale, Tim. Blue. Loeb, Jeph. 2003. (Spider-Man Ser.). 160p. (YA). 21.99 *(978-0-7851-1062-0(3))* Marvel Worldwide, Inc.
—MARVEL KNIGHTS: Jeph Loeb & Tim Sale: Yellow, Blue, Gray & White Omnibus. 2018. (Jeph Loeb & Tim Sale: Yellow, Blue, Gray & White Omnibus Ser.: 1). (ENG.). 664p. (YA). (gr. 8-17). 100.00 *(978-1-302-91405-9(7))* Marvel Worldwide, Inc.
Salem, Eman. We're off to Pray. Munshey, Sana. 2016. (ENG.). 32p. (J). (gr. -1). 10.95 *(978-0-86037-529-6(3))* Kube Publishing Ltd. GBR. Dist: Consortium Bk. Sales & Distribution.
Salem, Iosi. The Great Friday Clean-up (French Flap) Fridman, Sashi. 2009. 32p. 12.95 *(978-1-934440-77-3(9),* Pitspopany Pr.) Simcha Media Group.
—The Great Friday Clean-up (Hard Cover) Fridman, Sashi. 2009. 32p. 17.95 *(978-1-934440-93-3(0),* Pitspopany Pr.) Simcha Media Group.
—The Mr. Mentch Coloring Book. 2008. (J). (gr. -1-3). 6.95 *(978-1-934440-37-7(X),* Pitspopany Pr.) Simcha Media Group.
Salem, Maru & Cabalu, Reimarie. Elias Zapple's Book of Slugs. Zapple, Elias. 2018. (ENG.). 70p. (J). (gr. 4-6). pap. *(978-1-912704-09-5(9))* Heads or Tales Pr.
—Elias Zapple's Book of Slugs: American-English Edition. Zapple, Elias. 2018. (ENG.). 70p. (J). (gr. 4-6). pap. *(978-1-912704-08-8(0))* Heads or Tales Pr.
Salemi, Lucia. A Book of Questions / un Libro de Preguntas. Meyer, Jane. 2017. (Xist Kids Bilingual Spanish English Ser.). (ENG & SPA.). 28p. (J). (gr. -1-3). pap. 9.99 *(978-1-5324-0082-7(9))* Xist Publishing.
Salenas, Bobbi. Cinderella Latina - Cinicienta Latina. Salenas, Bobbi. La Madrid, Enriquee, tr. 2003. (SPA.). (YA). (gr. 3-12). 19.95 *(978-0-934925-06-8(2))* Pinata Pubns.
Salerno, Joe. Fun Games & Activities for Children with Dyslexia. Winton, Alais. 2018. (ENG.). 136p. pap. 18.95 *(978-1-78592-292-3(0),* 696471) Kingsley, Jessica Pubs. GBR. Dist: Hachette UK Distribution.
Salerno, John. I've Got Mail! Messinger, Robert. 2003. 40p. (J). 12.95 *(978-1-893237-01-8(X))* Little Mai Pr.
Salerno, Steven. Bebé Goes Shopping. Elya, Susan Middleton. 2008. (ENG.). 36p. (J). (gr. -1-3). pap. 7.99 *(978-0-15-206142-5(8),* 1198442) Houghton Mifflin Harcourt Publishing Co.
—Brothers at Bat: The True Story of an Amazing All-Brother Baseball Team. Vernick, Audrey. 2012. (ENG.). 40p. (J). (gr. -1-3). 18.99 *(978-0-547-38557-0(9),* 1425838, Clarion Bks.) Houghton Mifflin Harcourt Trade & Reference Pubs.
—Counting Our Way to the 100th Day! Franco, Betsy. 2004. (ENG.). 48p. (J). (gr. -1-3). 19.99 *(978-0-689-84793-6(9),* McElderry, Margaret K. Bks.) McElderry, Margaret K. Bks.
—The Crayon Man: The True Story of the Invention of Crayola Crayons. Biebow, Natascha. 2019. (ENG.). 48p. (J). (gr. 1-4). 17.99 *(978-1-328-86684-4(X),* 1695835, HMH Books For Young Readers) Houghton Mifflin Harcourt Publishing Co.
—The Dirty Little Boy, 1 vol. Brown, Margaret Wise. 2005. (ENG.). 32p. (J). (gr. -1-1). pap. 5.95 *(978-0-7614-5180-8(3))* Marshall Cavendish Corp.
—The Fantastic Ferris Wheel: The Story of Inventor George Ferris. Kraft, Betsy Harvey. 2015. (ENG.). 42p. (J). (gr. k-4). 17.99 *(978-1-62779-072-7(1),* 900133755, Holt, Henry & Co. Bks. For Young Readers) Holt, Henry & Co.
—Goldenlocks & the Three Pirates. Prince, April Jones. 2017. (ENG.). 40p. (J). 17.99 *(978-0-374-30074-6(7),* 900134952, Farrar, Straus & Giroux (BYR)) Farrar, Straus & Giroux.
—Mrs. Wow Never Wanted a Cow. Freeman, Martha. 2006. (Beginner Books(R) Ser.). 48p. (J). (gr. -1-2). 9.99 *(978-0-375-83418-9(4),* Random Hse. Bks. for Young Readers) Random Hse. Children's Bks.
—Pass Go & Collect $200: The Real Story of How Monopoly Was Invented. Stone, Tanya Lee. 2018. (ENG.). 40p. (J). 18.99 *(978-1-62779-168-7(X),* 900138773, Holt, Henry & Co. Bks. For Young Readers) Holt, Henry & Co.
—Pride: the Story of Harvey Milk & the Rainbow Flag. Sanders, Rob. 2018. 40p. (J). (gr. k-3). 17.99 *(978-0-399-55531-2(5),* Random Hse. Bks. for Young Readers) Random Hse. Children's Bks.
—Puppy Princess. Fliess, Sue. 2016. (Little Golden Book Ser.). 24p. (J). (-k). 4.99 *(978-0-553-51209-0(9),* Golden Bks.) Random Hse. Children's Bks.
—Wild Horse Annie: Friend of the Mustangs. Fern, Tracey. 2019. (ENG.). 48p. (J). 17.99 *(978-0-374-30306-8(1),* 900153482, Farrar, Straus & Giroux (BYR)) Farrar, Straus & Giroux.
Salerno, Steven. Go-Go Baby!, 1 vol. Salerno, Steven, tr. Orgill, Roxane. 2004. (ENG.). 32p. (J). 14.95 *(978-0-7614-5157-0(9))* Marshall Cavendish Corp.
Salesse, Alain. Kung Fu Panda 3-D Puzzle Book. Chihak, Sheena. 2008. 10p. (J). 9.99 *(978-0-696-23485-9(8))* Meredith Bks.
Salg, Bert. Andy Blake's Comet Coaster. Edwards, Leo. 2011. 274p. 47.95 *(978-1-258-06587-4(8))* Literary Licensing, LLC.
—Bill Darrow's Victory. Heyliger, William. 2011. 202p. 44.95 *(978-1-258-07262-9(9))* Literary Licensing, LLC.
—Jerry Hicks, Explorer. Heyliger, William. 2011. 210p. 44.95 *(978-1-258-08964-1(5))* Literary Licensing, LLC.
—Jerry Hicks, Ghost Hunter. Heyliger, William. 2011. 210p. 44.95 *(978-1-258-08870-5(3))* Literary Licensing, LLC.
—The Lonesome Swamp Mystery: A Hal Keen Mystery Story. Lloyd, Hugh. 2011. 278p. 47.95 *(978-1-258-10174-9(2))* Literary Licensing, LLC.
—The Lost Mine of the Amazon. Lloyd, Hugh. 2011. 232p. 46.95 *(978-1-258-10175-6(0))* Literary Licensing, LLC.
—Poppy Ott Hits the Trail. Edwards, Leo. 2011. 218p. 44.95 *(978-1-258-10146-6(7))* Literary Licensing, LLC.
Salgado, Jimbo, jt. illus. see Milne, Alex.
Salguera, Eduardo. Fito: El Oso Que Quería Cantar. Blondell, Jessica. 2018. (SPA.). 28p. (J). pap. 9.95 *(978-1-7179-1088-2(2))* Independently Published.
Salim, Adunis. Uridu an Afuz! Ross, Tony. 2017. (ARA.). 32p. (J). 18.95 *(978-614-438-962-1(8))* Hachette Antoine.
—La Uridu an Utfiu Al-Dawi! Ross, Tony. 2017. (ARA.). 32p. (J). 18.95 *(978-614-438-960-7(1))* Hachette Antoine.
Salimkhan, Goldie. Pumpkin Head Loves Pumpkin Bread. Cain, Anika. 2019. (ENG.). 26p. (J). pap. 10.00 ***(978-1-6863-7579-8(4))*** Independently Published.
Salinas, Alex. James' Night of Terror. Martin, Bob. 2010. 120p. (gr. 4-6). 20.95 *(978-1-4502-6500-3(6));* pap. 10.95 *(978-1-4502-6498-3(0))* iUniverse, Inc.
Salinas, Erika. Friends. Whitman, David L. 2012. (ENG.). 32p. pap. 14.51 *(978-1-4669-6317-7(4))* Trafford Publishing.
Salino, Carolina. Why I Am Not a Princess. Salino, Carolina. 2018. (ENG.). 34p. (J). pap. *(978-1-7752931-1-8(4))* Pontes, Carolina Salino Freitas de.
Salle, Ludovic. Flames of Freedom. George, Sam. 2016. (History Files Ser.). (ENG.). 96p. (gr. 5-9). 29.93 *(978-1-68191-679-8(7),* 9781681916798) Rourke Educational Media.
Salmerón Lopez, Rafael, jt. illus. see Salmeron, Rafael.
Salmeron, Rafael. El Cernicalo Porque. Narváez, Concha López & Concha, López Narváez. (Pajaros de Cuento Coleccion). (SPA.). 84p. (YA). (gr. 5-8). *(978-84-241-7927-4(7))* Everest Editora ESP. Dist: Lectorum Pubns., Inc.
Salmeron, Rafael & Salmerón Lopez, Rafael. De la a a la Z con Mozart y la Música. Cruz-Contarini, Rafael & Rafael, Cruz-Contarini. 2005. (Montana Encantada Ser.). (SPA.). 36p. (gr. 1-3). pap. 8.99 *(978-84-241-1697-2(6))* Everest Editora ESP. Dist: Lectorum Pubns., Inc.
Salmieri, Daniel. Big Bad Bubble. Rubin, Adam. (ENG.). 40p. (J). (gr. -1-3). 2017. pap. 7.99 *(978-0-544-92782-7(6),* 1657202, HMH Books For Young Readers); 2014. 17.99 *(978-0-544-04549-1(1),* 1532278) Houghton Mifflin Harcourt Publishing Co.
—Big Bad Bubble. Rubin, Adam. ed. 2017. (ENG.). (J). (gr. -1-3). lib. bdg. 18.40 *(978-0-606-39829-9(5))* Turtleback.
—Dragones y Tacos 2: la Continuación. Rubin, Adam. 2018. 48p. (J). (-k). pap. 8.99 *(978-0-451-47920-4(3),* Puffin Books) Penguin Young Readers Group.
—Dragons Love Tacos. Rubin, Adam. 2012. (ENG.). 40p. (J). (gr. -1-2). 18.99 *(978-0-8037-3680-1(0),* Dial Bks) Penguin Young Readers Group.
—Dragons Love Tacos 2 Book & Toy Set. Rubin, Adam. 2019. 48p. (J). (gr. -1-2). 19.99 *(978-1-9848-1577-4(6),* Dial Bks) Penguin Young Readers Group.
—Dragons Love Tacos 2: the Sequel. Rubin, Adam. 2017. (ENG.). 48p. (J). (-k). 18.99 *(978-0-525-42888-6(7),* Dial Bks) Penguin Young Readers Group.
—Dragons Love Tacos: the Definitive Collection, 2 vols. Rubin, Adam. 2017. (ENG.). 88p. (J). (gr. -1-2). 36.00 *(978-0-7352-3017-0(X),* Dial Bks) Penguin Young Readers Group.
—Fiesta Secreta de Pizza. Rubin, Adam. 2015. 40p. (J). (gr. -1-k). 8.99 *(978-0-14-751560-5(2),* Puffin Books) Penguin Young Readers Group.
—High Five. Rubin, Adam. 2019. 64p. (J). (-k). 19.99 *(978-0-525-42889-3(5),* Dial Bks) Penguin Young Readers Group.
—Meet the Dullards. Pennypacker, Sara. 2015. (ENG.). 32p. (J). (gr. -1-3). 17.99 *(978-0-06-219856-3(4),* Balzer & Bray) HarperCollins Pubs.
—Robo-Sauce. Rubin, Adam. 2015. 48p. (J). (gr. -1-3). 18.99 *(978-0-525-42887-9(9),* Dial Bks) Penguin Young Readers Group.
—Secret Pizza Party. Rubin, Adam. 2013. 36p. (J). (gr. -1-2). 17.99 *(978-0-8037-3947-5(8),* Dial Bks) Penguin Young Readers Group.
—Those Darn Squirrels! Rubin, Adam. (ENG.). 32p. (J). (gr. -1-3). 2011. pap. 7.99 *(978-0-547-57681-7(1),* 1458442); 2008. 17.99 *(978-0-547-00703-8(5),* 1029826) Houghton Mifflin Harcourt Publishing Co.
—Those Darn Squirrels & the Cat Next Door. Rubin, Adam. 2011. (ENG.). 32p. (J). (gr. -1-3). 17.99 *(978-0-547-42922-9(3),* 1432155) Houghton Mifflin Harcourt Publishing Co.
—Those Darn Squirrels Fly South. Rubin, Adam. (ENG.). 32p. (J). (gr. -1-3). 2015. 7.99 *(978-0-544-55545-7(7),* 1610412, HMH Books For Young Readers); 2012. 17.99 *(978-0-547-67823-8(1),* 1475037) Houghton Mifflin Harcourt Publishing Co.
Salmon, Mica G. Mavis: A Genuine Heroine! Salmon, Mica G., ed. Crow Salmon, Caroline. 2018. (ENG.). 222p. (YA). (gr. 7-11). pap. *(978-0-6482277-0-0(7))* Turquoise Art.
Salmond, Jared. Mom Serves Monsters. Weimer, Brandon. 2018. (ENG.). 24p. (J). pap. 7.99 *(978-0-692-14609-5(1))* Weimer, Brandon Publishing.
Salmons, Tony, et al. Dakota North: Design for Dying. 2018. (ENG.). 280p. (YA). (gr. 8-17). pap. 29.99 *(978-1-302-91250-5(X))* Marvel Worldwide, Inc.
Salom, Ivette. Flow, Flow, Flow. Salom, Andrée. 2018. (ENG.). 40p. (J). 16.95 *(978-1-61429-330-9(9))* Wisdom Pubns.
—My New Best Friend. Marlowe, Sara. 2016. (ENG.). 32p. (J). 15.95 *(978-1-61429-353-8(8))* Wisdom Pubns.
—When the Anger Ogre Visits. Salom, Andree. 2015. (ENG.). 40p. (J). 18.95 *(978-1-61429-166-4(7))* Wisdom Pubns.
Salomo, Xavier. Grow, Baby, Grow! Watch Baby Grow Month by Month! Martí, Meritxell. 2019. (ENG.). 18p. (J). 24.99 *(978-1-64170-100-6(5),* 550100) Familius LLC.
Salopek, Kirk. I Can Be: A Child's Whimsical Introduction to Yoga. Sumner, Christine. 2008. 32p. (J). 8.95 *(978-0-615-15666-0(4))* Q & J Bird Pr., LLC.
Salter, Edward. The Boy & the Pebble. Salter, Sean. 2016. (ENG.). (J). pap. *(978-1-78623-050-8(X))* Grosvenor Hse. Publishing Ltd.
Salter, Safaya. Aesop's Fables. Handford, S. A. 2003. (Chrysalis Childrens Classics Ser.). 111p. (YA). pap. *(978-1-84365-035-5(5),* Pavilion Children's Books) Pavilion Bks.
—Just So Stories Set: For Little Children. Kipling, Rudyard. 2003. (Chrysalis Childrens Classics Ser.). 125p. (YA). pap. *(978-1-84365-036-2(3),* Pavilion Children's Books) Pavilion Bks.
Saltzberg, Barney. Chengdu Can Do. Saltzberg, Barney. 2017. (Chengdu Ser.: 1). (ENG.). 48p. (J). (gr. -1-3). 16.99 ***(978-1-4847-5847-2(1))*** Little, Brown Bks. for Young Readers.
—Chengdu Could Not Would Not Fall Asleep. Saltzberg, Barney. 2017. (Chengdu Ser.: 1). 32p. (J). (gr. -1 — 1). pap. 6.99 ***(978-1-4847-7565-3(1))*** Little, Brown Bks. for Young Readers.
Saltzberg, Barney. Cornelius P. Mud, Are You Ready for Baby? Saltzberg, Barney. 2009. (ENG.). 32p. (J). (gr. -1-k). 15.99 *(978-0-7636-3596-1(0))* Candlewick Pr.
—Crazy Hair Day. Saltzberg, Barney. 2008. (ENG.). 32p. (J). (gr. k-3). pap. 6.99 *(978-0-7636-2464-4(0))* Candlewick Pr.
—Crazy Hair Day. Saltzberg, Barney. 2011. (J). (gr. k-3). 29.95 *(978-0-545-13450-7(1))* Weston Woods Studios, Inc.
—Crazy Hair Day Big Book. Saltzberg, Barney. 2008. 32p. (J). (gr. k-3). pap. 24.99 *(978-0-7636-3969-3(9))* Candlewick Pr.
—Dog & Rabbit: A Story in Three Parts. Saltzberg, Barney. 2019. 48p. (J). (gr. -1-2). lib. bdg. 14.99 *(978-1-62354-107-1(7))* Charlesbridge Publishing, Inc.
—Enough Is Enough! Saltzberg, Barney. 2018. (ENG.). 32p. (J). (gr. -1-k). 16.99 *(978-1-939547-42-2(3))* Creston Bks.
—Star of the Week. Saltzberg, Barney. 2010. (ENG.). 32p. (J). (gr. k-3). pap. 7.99 *(978-0-7636-3076-8(4))* Candlewick Pr.
—Tea with Grandpa. Saltzberg, Barney. 2014. (ENG.). 40p. (J). (gr. -1-2). 15.99 *(978-1-59643-894-1(0),* 900119778) Roaring Brook Pr.
Salus, Diane. Understanding Katie: A Day in the Life Of. Do, Elisa Shipon-Blum. 2003. 28p. (J). (gr. -1-18). pap. *(978-0-9714800-3-2(6))* Selective Mutism Anxiety Research & Treatment Ctr.
Salvador, António. A Children's History of Portugal. Carvalho, Sérgio Luís de. Lima, Inês, tr. 2017. (Non-Series Titles from Tagus Press Ser.). (ENG.). 52p. (J). (gr. 3-6). 20.00 *(978-1-933227-79-5(6))* Tagus Pr.
Salvador, Martin. George Washington. Leighton, Marian. 2005. (Heroes of America Ser.). 239p. (gr. 3-8). lib. bdg. 27.07 *(978-1-59679-262-3(0),* Abdo & Daughters) ABDO Publishing Co.
Salvaje, Pablo. Animalkind. 2017. (ENG.). 72p. (J). (gr. -1-3). 19.95 *(978-3-7913-7302-7(1))* Prestel Verlag GmbH & Co KG. DEU. Dist: Penguin Random Hse. LLC.
Salvatus, Mark. Pan de Sal Saves the Day: An Award-Winning ChildrenAEs Story from the Philippines [New Bilingual English & Tagalog Edition]. Olizon-Chikiamco, Norma. ed. 2017. 28p. (J). (gr. -1-6). pap. 8.95 *(978-0-8048-4754-4(1))* Tuttle Publishing.
Salvo, Roberto Di, et al. The Mighty Thor: This Is Thor. West, Alexandra. 2019. (World of Reading Level 1 Ser.). (ENG.). 32p. (J). (gr. -1-3). lib. bdg. 27.07 *(978-1-5321-4404-2(0),* 33809) Spotlight.
Salway, Norma. My Maine School Bus Driver. Salway, Norma. 2019. (ENG.). 44p. (J). (gr. k-3). pap. 14.95 ***(978-1-944386-47-4(5))*** Just Write Bks.
Salyer, Adam Ernest. My Shadow. Salyer, Jennifer Marie. 2011. 32p. pap. *(978-1-77067-642-8(2))* FriesenPress.
Salzberg, Helen. What is an Angel? Falzon, Adrienne. 2012. (ENG.). 32p. 18.99 *(978-0-9855562-2-8(6))* Blue Note Pubns.
Sam, Ackerman. Language Quest Spanish B Blue. 2nd ed. 2008. (SPA & ENG.). (J). pap. *(978-0-9744691-1-9(4))* Language Quest Corp.
Sam, Hundley. There Goes a Mermaid - A NorFolktale. Suhay, Lisa. 2004. 32p. (J). pap. 7.95 *(978-0-9648308-2-0(5))* Virginian Pilot.
Sam, Joe. The Invisible Hunters (Los Cazadores Invisibles) (YA). (gr. 1-18). 25.95 incl. audio *(978-0-89239-036-6(0))* Lee & Low Bks., Inc.
Sam, Kagan. Mr. Duz Goes to the Doctor. Patrick, Wellman. 2007. 24p. (J). 5.95 *(978-0-9796226-6-3(2))* MrDuz.com.
—Mr. Duz Solves a Mystery. 2007. 24p. (J). 5.95 *(978-0-9796226-0-1(3))* MrDuz.com.
—Mr. Duz Trick or Treat. Patrick, Wellman. 2007. 24p. (J). 5.95 *(978-0-9796226-4-9(6))* MrDuz.com.
Sam Lam, Chris. Inspector Brunswick: the Case of the Missing Eyebrow. Keoghan, Angela. 2017. (ENG.). 32p. (J). (gr. k-17). 16.95 *(978-1-84976-444-5(1))* Tate Publishing, Ltd. GBR. Dist: Hachette Bk. Group.
Samanci, Ozge. Vincent & Me. Kohl, Dolores. 2018. (ENG.). 46p. (J). pap. 12.95 *(978-1-7903-7452-6(9))* Independently Published.
Samaniego, César. The Great Book of Explorers: With Augmented Realty. 2016. (ENG.). 112p. (J). 12.99 *(978-1-910596-92-0(2),* 3c8350e1-110e-4033-ab11-4c91022f6624) Design Media Publishing Ltd. HKG. Dist: Baker & Taylor Publisher Services (BTPS).
—Railway Jack: The True Story of an Amazing Baboon. Johnston, KT. 2020. (ENG.). 40p. (J). (gr. 3-5). 18.95 *(978-1-68446-088-5(3),* 141186, Capstone Editions) Capstone.
Samantha May Cerney. The Three Little Green Pigs, Llc: A Recycling Pig Tale. Oldenburg, Richard. 2013. 28p. 23.50 *(978-1-62516-753-8(9),* Strategic Bk. Publishing) Strategic Book Publishing & Rights Agency (SBPRA).
Samantha Nowak. Adam B Brave. Jessica Hoel. 2009. 20p. pap. 12.49 *(978-1-4389-3240-8(5))* AuthorHouse.
Samargedlis, Michelle. Nana's in the Attic. Peterson, Linda L. 2018. (ENG.). 36p. (J). pap. 14.00 *(978-1-7309-1780-6(1))* Independently Published.
Samartzi, Iris & Verne, Jules. From the Earth to the Moon: Or A Cannon for Peace. 2020. (Jules Verne's Adventure Stories Ser.). 36p. (J). (gr. k-2). 17.99 ***(978-1-9164091-5-6(6))*** Faros Bks. GBR. Dist: Independent Pubs. Group.
Sambourne, Linley. Friends & Foes from Fairy Land. Brabourne Baron, Edward Hugessen. Reitan, Zachary, ed. 2019. (ENG.). 376p. (J). pap. 13.40 *(978-1-0815-8329-3(0))* Independently Published.
Sambourne, Linley. The Water-Babies . Is a Children's Novel. / with ONE HUNDRED ILLUSTRATIONS/ Kingsley, Charles. 2019. (ENG.). 160p. (J). (gr. 2). pap. 9.40 ***(978-1-7044-8227-9(5))*** Independently Published.
Samnee, Chris. Black Widow by Waid & Samnee: the Complete Collection. 2020. (ENG.). 272p. (YA). (gr. 8-17). pap. 29.99 *(978-1-302-92129-3(0))* Marvel Worldwide, Inc.
Samnee, Chris, et al. Decades: Marvel in the 10s - Legends & Legacy. 2019. (ENG.). 248p. (YA). (gr. 8-17). pap. 24.99 *(978-1-302-91792-0(7))* Marvel Worldwide, Inc.
Samnee, Chris. Ryan Quinn & the Lion's Claw. McGee, Ron. 2017. (Ryan Quinn Ser.: 2). (ENG.). 352p. (J). (gr. 3-7). 16.99 *(978-0-06-242169-2(7))* HarperCollins Pubs.
—Ryan Quinn & the Rebel's Escape. McGee, Ron. 2016. (Ryan Quinn Ser.: 1). (ENG.). 368p. (J). (gr. 3-7). 16.99 *(978-0-06-242164-7(6))* HarperCollins Pubs.
Samol, Nanette & Prosofsky, Merle, photos by. The British Columbia Seasonal Cookbook: History, Folklore & Recipes with a Twist, 1 vol. Ogle, Jennifer et al. rev. ed. 2007. (Canadian Culinary Kitchen Ser.). (ENG., 160p. pap. 19.95 *(978-1-55105-584-8(8),* 1a1cacda-a0fe-46b9-aa46-8e3947d9e2a8) Lone Pine Publishing USA.
Sampar. Billy Stuart & the Sea of a Thousand Dangers, 1 vol. Bergeron, Alain M. Watson, Sophie B., tr. from FRE. 2019. (Billy Stuart Ser.: 3). (ENG.). 160p. (J). (gr. 1-3). pap. 9.95 *(978-1-4598-2343-3(5))* Orca Bk. Pubs. USA.
Sampar. Billy Stuart in the Eye of the Cyclops. Bergeron, Alain M. Watson, Sophie B., tr. from FRE. 2020. (Billy Stuart Ser.: 4). (ENG.). 160p. (J). (gr. 1-3). pap. 9.95 ***(978-1-4598-2346-4(X))*** Orca Bk. Pubs. USA.
Sampar. Billy Stuart in the Minotaur's Lair, 1 vol. Bergeron, Alain M. 2019. (Billy Stuart Ser.: 2). (ENG.). 160p. (J). (gr. 1-3). pap. 9.95 *(978-1-4598-1840-8(7))* Orca Bk. Pubs. USA.
—Do You Know Chameleons?, 1 vol. Bergeron, Alain M. & Quintin, Michel. 2013. (Do You Know? Ser.). (ENG.). 64p. (J). (gr. 2-4). 9.95 *(978-1-55455-299-3(0),* 24853fc8-6e07-4c03-9772-97e9492c1d84) éditeur, Annika Parance CAN. Dist: Firefly Bks., Ltd.
—Do You Know Crocodiles?, 1 vol. Bergeron, Alain M. & Quintin, Michel. 2013. (Do You Know? Ser.). (ENG.). 64p. (J). (gr. 2-4). 9.95 *(978-1-55455-304-4(0),* 4638515d-1a1f-4e76-b795-0c5920f81493) Trifolium Bks., Inc. CAN. Dist: Firefly Bks., Ltd.
—Do You Know Crows?, 1 vol. Bergeron, Alain M. & Quintin, Michel. 2013. (Do You Know? Ser.). (ENG.). 64p. (J). (gr. 2-4). pap. 9.95 *(978-1-55455-320-4(2),* 8aa0dc65-57b1-4a95-b8e4-4bc5cbb087cf) Trifolium Bks., Inc. CAN. Dist: Firefly Bks., Ltd.
—Do You Know Dinosaurs?, 1 vol. Bergeron, Alain M. & Quintin, Michel. 2014. (Do You Know? Ser.). (ENG.). 64p. (J). (gr. 2-4). pap. 9.95 *(978-1-55455-336-5(9),* 250058e1-b9cc-419d-81d7-d9f57c2d0a7a) Trifolium Bks., Inc. CAN. Dist: Firefly Bks., Ltd.
—Do You Know Hyenas?, 1 vol. Bergeron, Alain M. & Quintin, Michel. 2014. (Do You Know? Ser.). (ENG.). 64p. (J). (gr. 2-4). pap. 9.95 *(978-1-55455-338-9(5),* dc9fbde1-a654-412c-944d-ef8ac52e56b2) Fitzhenry & Whiteside, Ltd. CAN. Dist: Firefly Bks., Ltd.
—Do You Know Komodo Dragons?, 1 vol. Bergeron, Alain M. & Quintin, Michel. 2014. (Do You Know? Ser.). (ENG.). 64p. (J). (gr. 2-4). pap. 9.95 *(978-1-55455-339-6(3),* 982446e2-275e-4c5f-aace-918ed03b73f7) Trifolium Bks., Inc. CAN. Dist: Firefly Bks., Ltd.

S

—Do You Know Leeches?, 1 vol. Bergeron, Alain M. & Quintin, Michel. 2013. (Do You Know? Ser.). (ENG.). 64p. (J). (gr. 2-4). pap. 9.95 *(978-1-55455-318-1(0),* 39b99820-62ee-4051-a87f-4d06b5fa244d) Trifolium Bks., Inc. CAN. Dist: Firefly Bks., Ltd.

—Do You Know Porcupines?, 1 vol. Bergeron, Alain M. & Quintin, Michel. 2013. (Do You Know? Ser.). (ENG.). 64p. (J). (gr. 2-4). pap. 9.95 *(978-1-55455-321-1(0),* e5bf74ff-2e52-4213-845e-c991ad31f0f7) Trifolium Bks., Inc. CAN. Dist: Firefly Bks., Ltd.

—Do You Know Praying Mantises?, 1 vol. Bergeron, Alain M. & Quintin, Michel. 2014. (Do You Know? Ser.). (ENG.). 64p. (J). (gr. 2-4). pap. 9.95 *(978-1-55455-337-2(7),* 0b2cf7c3-8016-4fb5-8674-c46a23ac2fb3) Trifolium Bks., Inc. CAN. Dist: Firefly Bks., Ltd.

—Do You Know Rats?, 1 vol. Bergeron, Alain M. & Quintin, Michel. 2013. (Do You Know? Ser.). (ENG.). 64p. (J). (gr. 2-4). pap. 9.95 *(978-1-55455-319-8(9),* 1ade2265-bbce-4f07-9143-eb7cbdfd70d2) Trifolium Bks., Inc. CAN. Dist: Firefly Bks., Ltd.

—Do You Know Rhinoceros?, 1 vol. Quintin, Michel et al. Messier, Solange, tr. 2015. (Do You Know? Ser.). (ENG.). 64p. (J). (gr. 2-4). pap. 9.95 *(978-1-55455-354-9(7),* 6dd15e9e-bb1f-4fe4-af07-8a66d0438a59) Trifolium Bks., Inc. CAN. Dist: Firefly Bks., Ltd.

—Do You Know Spiders?, 1 vol. Bergeron, Alain M. & Quintin, Michel. 2013. (Do You Know? Ser.). (ENG.). 64p. (J). (gr. 2-4). 9.95 *(978-1-55455-302-0(4),* eee083c2-9508-468f-9166-37b5e072450e) Trifolium Bks., Inc. CAN. Dist: Firefly Bks., Ltd.

—Do You Know Tigers?, 1 vol. Quintin, Michel & Bergeron, Alain M. Messier, Solange, tr. 2015. (Do You Know? Ser.). (ENG.). 64p. (J). (gr. 2-4). pap. 9.95 *(978-1-55455-355-6(5),* 0f2029f9-3641-401e-ae9e-eff825f2f572) Trifolium Bks., Inc. CAN. Dist: Firefly Bks., Ltd.

—Do You Know Toads?, 1 vol. Bergeron, Alain M. & Quintin, Michel. 2013. (Do You Know? Ser.). (ENG.). 64p. (J). (gr. 2-4). 9.95 *(978-1-55455-303-7(2),* eb6668b1-271b-4661-8060-4e6ba08bc208) Trifolium Bks., Inc. CAN. Dist: Firefly Bks., Ltd.

Sampar, jt. illus. see Parent, Samuel.

Sample, Matthew & Sample, Matthew. Grandma's Moving In! Cone, Stephanie M. 2013. (Learning to Care Ser.). (ENG.). (J). 18.00 *(978-1-937460-68-6(1))* Vision Forum, Inc., The.

Sample, Matthew, jt. illus. see Sample, Matthew.

Sample, Matthew II. God's Great Plan. Cutrera, Melissa. 2013. 28p. (J). *(978-1-936908-81-3(6)); (978-1-936908-83-7(2)); (978-1-936908-82-0(4))* Shepherd Pr. Inc.

Sampson, Ajpril. Margarita y la Mariposa. Sampson, Ajpril. 2006. (SPA.). (J). 7.95 *(978-0-9774822-5-2(1))* Crosam Pr.

Sampson, April. Hallo, Mallo & Pallo: The Ostracized Ostrich Family. Stockton, Lucille. ed. 2005. 31p. (J). 19.95 *(978-1-59408-511-6(0))* Cork Hill Pr.

Sampson, Barbara. A Bethlehem Adventure. Maguire, Margie. 2019. (Rhyming Bible Stories for Children Ser.: Vol. 1). (ENG.). 24p. (J). pap. 9.20 *(978-1-7952-8085-3(9))* Independently Published.

Sampson, Jody. Abby. Russo, Anthony. 2003. 18p. (J). 7.95 *(978-1-59466-006-1(9),* Little Ones) Port Town Publishing.

—Tony the Pony. Kelly, Theresa. l.t. ed. 2003. 12p. (J). 5.95 *(978-1-59466-003-0(4))* Port Town Publishing.

—Tony the Pony: Bugs Are Not Bad. Kelly, Theresa. 2005. (J). per. 7.95 *(978-1-59466-030-6(1))* Port Town Publishing.

Sampson, Kathleen. Penelope's Piggies. Abbruzzi, Danielle. 2012. 42p. 24.95 *(978-1-4626-6264-7(1))* America Star Bks.

Sams, B. B. All about the ABC's. Gaydos, Nora. 2006. (ENG.). 112p. (J). (gr. -1-1). 16.99 *(978-1-58476-410-6(4),* IKIDS) Innovative Kids.

—Look Around! Now I'm Reading! For Beginning Readers. Gaydos, Nora. 2003. (NIR! Leveled Readers Ser.). 128p. (J). (gr. -1-2). 16.99 *(978-1-58476-167-9(9),* Now I'm Reading!) Random Hse. Children's Bks.

—My World: Now I'm Reading! For Beginning Readers. Gaydos, Nora. 2004. (NIR! Leveled Readers Ser.). 128p. (J). (gr. -1-2). 16.99 *(978-1-58476-263-8(2),* Now I'm Reading!) Random Hse. Children's Bks.

—Now I'm Reading! Big Fun. Gaydos, Nora. 2016. (NIR! Leveled Readers Ser.). 128p. (J). (gr. -1-3). 16.99 *(978-1-101-91960-6(4),* Now I'm Reading!) Random Hse. Children's Bks.

—Now I'm Reading! Pre-Reader - More Word Play. Gaydos, Nora. 2016. (NIR! Leveled Readers Ser.). 120p. (J). (gr. -1-2). 16.99 *(978-1-101-91962-0(0),* Now I'm Reading!) Random Hse. Children's Bks.

—Playful Pals, Level 1. Gaydos, Nora. 2003. (Now I'm Reading!). 128p. (J). (gr. -1-2). 14.99 *(978-1-58476-243-0(8))* Innovative Kids.

—Playful Pals: Now I'm Reading! For Beginning Readers. Gaydos, Nora. 2003. (NIR! Leveled Readers Ser.). 128p. (J). (gr. -1-3). 16.99 *(978-1-58476-203-4(9),* Now I'm Reading!) Random Hse. Children's Bks.

—Snack Attack: Now I'm Reading! For Beginning Readers. Gaydos, Nora. 2004. (NIR! Leveled Readers Ser.). 128p. (J). (gr. -1-3). 16.99 *(978-1-58476-264-5(0),* Now I'm Reading!) Random Hse. Children's Bks.

Sams, Carl R., II & Stoick, Jean, photos by. Happy Bird Day! Sams, Carl R., II & Stoick, Jean. 2012. (ENG., 14p. (J). bds. 7.95 *(978-0-9827625-2-3(6))* Sams, II, Carl R. Photography, Inc.

—Lost in the Woods: A Photographic Fantasy. 2004. (ENG., 48p. (J). 19.95 *(978-0-9671748-8-4(0))* Sams, II, Carl R. Photography, Inc.

Sams, Carl R., 2nd & Stoick, Jean, photos by. One Child, One Planet: Inspiration for the Young Conservationist. Llewellyn, Bridget McGovern. 2009. 48p. (J). 19.95 *(978-0-9841880-0-0(2))* Emerald Shamrock Pr. LLC.

Sams, Carl R., II & Stoick, Jean, photos by. Winter Friends. Sams, Carl R., II & Stoick, Jean. McDiarmid, Karen, ed. 2003. (ENG., 14p. (J). bds. 7.95 *(978-0-9671748-5-3(6))* Sams, II, Carl R. Photography, Inc.

Sams, Carl R., II, jt. photos by see Stoick, Jean.

Sams II, Carl R. & Stoick, Jean, photos by. When Snowflakes Fall. 2009. (ENG., 14p. bds. 7.95 *(978-0-9770108-9-9(9))* Sams, II, Carl R. Photography, Inc.

Samu, Juan. Marvel Action: Black Panther: Stormy Weather (Book One) Baker, Kyle. 2019. (Marvel Action: Black Panther Ser.: 1). 80p. (J). (gr. 4-7). pap. 9.99 *(978-1-68405-517-3(2))* Idea & Design Works, LLC.

Samuel, J. K. Swindlerella & Other Stories [grump-A-Log Book 2]. Samuel, J. K. 2018. (ENG.). 108p. (J). *(978-0-9550229-6-8(7))* Kingventor Publishing.

Samuel, Janet. Bible & Prayers for Teddy & Me, 1 vol. Goodings, Christina. ed. 2014. (ENG.). 64p. (J). (gr. -1-k). 12.99 *(978-0-7459-6452-2(4))* Lion Hudson PLC GBR. Dist: Kregel Pubns.

—The Grimpots. John, Gilly. 2019. (ENG.). 36p. (J). pap. 7.99 *(978-1-78461-696-0(6))* Y Lolfa GBR. Dist: Casemate Pubs. & Bk. Distributors, LLC.

—Guess Who's under the Sea. Mumme, Sarah. 2015. (Guess Who's... Bks.). (ENG.). 10p. (J). (gr. -1 — 1). 5.99 *(978-0-7641-6803-1(7),* B.E.S. Publishing) Peterson's.

—Imagine That! McKendry, Sam. 2007. (ENG.). 12p. (gr. -1-k). 9.95 *(978-1-58117-484-7(5),* Intervisual/Piggy Toes) Bendon, Inc.

Samuel, Janet. Kind Soup. Petersen, Jean. 2019. (ENG.). 34p. (J). (gr. 2-4). 16.99 ***(978-1-7332828-8-8(2));*** pap. 11.99 ***(978-1-7332828-4-0(X))*** Little Lamb Bks.

Samuel, Janet. One Sneaky Sheep: A Touch-and-Feel Fluffy Tale. 2007. (ENG.). 20p. (gr. -1). 14.95 *(978-1-58117-560-8(4),* Intervisual/Piggy Toes) Bendon, Inc.

—One Sneaky Sheep: The Sheep Who Didn't Want to Get Sheared. 2009. (ENG.). 20p. (J). 9.95 *(978-1-58117-841-8(7),* Intervisual/Piggy Toes) Bendon, Inc.

—The Ten Commandments for Little Ones. Nolan, Allia Zobel. 2009. (ENG.). 32p. (J). 14.99 *(978-0-7369-2545-7(7))* Harvest Hse. Pubs.

—Up on the Housetop. Hanby, Benjamin R. 2015. (ENG.). 20p. (Orig.). (J). (gr. -1-k). bds. 7.99 *(978-0-8249-1960-3(2),* Ideal Pubns.) Worthy Publishing.

Samuel, Karen. Why Transfer Day, Anyway? Sewer, Anecia. 2007. 16p. (J). 15.99 *(978-0-9752986-0-2(7))* Research Institute Pr., The.

Samuel, Karen L. The Lesson Box. Roach, Tregenza A. 2012. (J). *(978-1-934370-25-4(8))* Editorial Campana.

Samuels, Linda Nissen. Une Aventure D'Elly: Sauvons le Corail ! Samuels, Linda Nissen. 2018. (FRE.). 32p. (J). pap. *(978-0-9954790-4-3(6))* PatoPr.

—L' Aventure d'Elly Au Bord de la Mer. Samuels, Linda Nissen. 2016. (FRE.). (J). pap. *(978-0-9954790-2-9(X))* PatoPr.

—Cuando Elly Fue a la Reserva Ecologica. Samuels, Linda Nissen. 2013. 40p. pap. *(978-0-9511751-8-7(1))* Samuels, Linda Y.

—Elly e il Parco Degli Animali. Samuels, Linda Nissen. 2013. 40p. pap. *(978-0-9511751-7-0(3))* Samuels, Linda Y.

—When Elly Went to the Animal Park... Samuels, Linda Nissen. 2013. 40p. pap. *(978-0-9511751-5-6(7))* Samuels, Linda Y.

Samuelson, Norma. Noot the Root Goot. Ecke, Paul. 2019. (ENG.). 34p. (J). (gr. k-1). 16.99 *(978-1-7329192-0-4(8))* Samuelson, Norma.

Samworth, Kate. Liza Jane & the Dragon. Lippman, Laura. 2018. (ENG.). 32p. (J). 16.95 *(978-1-61775-661-0(X),* Black Sheep) Akashic Bks.

San Francisco School. Do I Bug You? A Who Am I? Book. Moog, Bob. 2006. (Spinner Books for Kids Ser.). (ENG.). 32p. (J). (gr. -1-12). 9.95 *(978-1-57528-898-7(2))* Univ. Games.

San Jorge, José. Variedades Poéticas. San Jorge, José. Hernández, René Mario, ed. l.t. ed. 2003. (SPA.). 154p. (YA). pap. *(978-1-931481-49-6(0))* LiArt-Literature & Art.

San Nicolas, Joshua M. Daisy, Ivy & Rose. Maurer, Eileen Reno. 2018. (ENG.). 26p. (J). (gr. 1-6). 20.00 *(978-0-692-16262-0(3))* Eileen Reno Maurer.

San Souci, Daniel. Little Pinto & the Wild Horses of Mustang Canyon. London, Jonathan. 2017. 40p. (J). (gr. k-3). 6.99 *(978-0-7636-9512-5(2))* Candlewick Pr.

—Yosemite's Songster: One Coyote's Story. Wadsworth, Ginger. 2013. (ENG.). 32p. (J). (gr. -1-2). 15.95 *(978-1-930238-34-3(7))* Yosemite Conservancy.

San Souci, Daniel, jt. illus. see San Souci, Robert D.

San Souci, Robert D. & San Souci, Daniel. Sister Tricksters: Rollicking Tales of Clever Females. 2006. (ENG.). 70p. (J). (gr. 3-7). 19.95 *(978-0-87483-791-9(X))* August Hse. Pubs., Inc.

San Vicente, Luis. The Festival of Bones / el Festival de Las Calaveras. 2014. (ENG.). 32p. (J). 7.95 *(978-1-941026-03-8(6))* Cinco Puntos Pr.

Sana, Maheen. Stuck. Gosselin, Matt. 2020. (ENG.). 56p. (J). (gr. k-3). pap. 12.99 ***(978-0-578-67389-9(4))*** Gosselin, Matthew S.

Sananmuang, Chatree. 20 Umbrellas. Pujari, M. Nathalie. 2007. (J). *(978-0-9715865-0-5(0))* Abuzz Bks.

Sanborn, Ashley. Boliche Polar: Un Cuento Sin Palabras. Beckstrand, Karl. 2020. (Stories Without Words Ser.: Vol. 5). (SPA.). 32p. (J). 26.55 ***(978-1-951599-06-5(3))*** Premio Publishing & Gozo Bks., LLC.

Sanborn, Ashley. Polar Bear Bowler: A Story Without Words. Beckstrand, Karl. 2017. (Stories Without Words Ser.: 1). (ENG.). (J). (gr. -1-1). 22.95 *(978-0-9853988-3-5(3))* Premio Publishing & Gozo Bks., LLC.

Sanborn, Casey. Close-Up: Forensic Photography, 5 vols. McIntosh, Kenneth. 2007. (Crime Scene Club Ser.: Bk. 5). 144p. (YA). (gr. 9-12). lib. bdg. 24.95 *(978-1-4222-0251-7(8))* Mason Crest.

—Dinosaur. Rader, Mark. 2008. (J). *(978-1-4127-9359-9(9))* Publications International, Ltd.

—Over the Edge: Forensic Accident Reconstruction, 2 vols. McIntosh, Kenneth. 2007. (Crime Scene Club Ser.: Bk. 2). 144p. (YA). (gr. 9-12). lib. bdg. 24.95 *(978-1-4222-0248-7(8))* Mason Crest.

Sanborn, F. C. & Railton, Fanny. More Mother Stories. Lindsay, Maud. 2008. 160p. pap. 9.95 *(978-1-59915-168-7(5))* Yesterday's Classics.

Sancartier, Emma. The World Is Your Oyster. James, Tamara. (ENG.). 50p. (J). (gr. -1-3). 2018. 16.95 *(978-1-927018-99-6(4));* 2010. 16.95 *(978-1-897476-22-2(1))* Simply Read Bks. CAN. Dist: Ingram Publisher Services.

Sanchez, Alejandro & Volley, Will. An Inspector Calls. 2012. (ENG.). 144p. pap. 16.95 *(978-1-907127-24-3(0));* (gr. 5). pap. 16.95 *(978-1-907127-23-6(2))* Classical Comics GBR. Dist: Publishers Group West (PGW).

Sanchez Almara, Dono & Almara, Dono Sanchez. A Christmas Carol. Dickens, Charles. 2015. (Graphic Revolve: Common Core Editions Ser.). (ENG.). 72p. (J). (gr. 5-9). lib. bdg. 27.99 *(978-1-4965-0370-1(8),* Stone Arch Bks.) Capstone.

Sánchez, Alvaro Iglesias, jt. illus. see Lokus, Rex.

Sanchez, Andres & Arte Y Diseno, Tane. Acoyani: El Nino y el Poeta. Peredo, Roberto. 2nd rev. ed. 2006. (Castillo de la Lectura Naranja Ser.). (SPA & ENG.). 166p. (J). (gr. 4-7). pap. 7.95 *(978-970-20-0146-1(3))* Castillo, Ediciones, S. A. de C. V. MEX. Dist: Macmillan.

Sanchez, Andres & Tagle. El Cinturón. Abodehman, Ahmed. Lovillo, Pilar Ortiz, tr. 2006. (la Orilla del Viento Ser.). (SPA.). 121p. (J). per. 8.50 *(978-968-16-6670-5(4))* Fondo de Cultura Economica USA.

—Sarah de Cordoba. Soci Et E de La Faune Et Des Parcs Du Qu Ebec. 2003. (la Orilla del Viento Ser.). (SPA.). 136p. (J). per. 8.50 *(978-968-16-7020-7(5))* Fondo de Cultura Economica USA.

Sanchez, Christina. Officer M. N. O. P. & Me: How Police Officers Serve the Community on & off Duty. Nop, Mony. Barley, Tammy, ed. 2018. (ENG.). 104p. (J). pap. 23.95 *(978-0-9997918-0-6(X))* Nop, Mony Publishing.

Sánchez, Diego Francisco. Incas. Riva Palacio, Mariana. 2014. (SPA.). 80p. (J). (gr. 4-7). pap. 11.95 *(978-607-8237-47-0(0))* Nostra Ediciones MEX. Dist: Independent Pubs. Group.

Sanchez, Edmundo. Caleb's Birthday Wish. Villanueva, David. 2006. 40p. (J). (gr. -1-3). per. 17.95 *(978-0-9771971-8-7(2))* W & B Pubs.

Sanchez, Elen. I'm a Princess Too. Kharoufeh, Nina. 2019. (ENG.). 66p. (J). pap. 18.95 ***(978-1-7283-2192-9(1))*** AuthorHouse.

Sanchez, Enrique O. Abuela's Weave. Castañeda, Omar S. 2013. (ENG.). 75p. (J). (gr. 1-4). pap. 10.95 *(978-1-880000-20-5(2))* Lee & Low Bks., Inc.

—Botas Negras. Gonzalez Jensen, Margarita. (SPA.). (J). (gr. 2-4). 3.96 net. *(978-0-590-26842-4(2))* Scholastic, Inc.

—Confeti: Poemas para Ninos, 1 vol. Mora, Pat. Mora, Pat & Fernandez, Queta, trs. 2006. (SPA.). 32p. (J). (gr. k-4). pap. 10.95 *(978-1-58430-270-4(4),* 21dbff8e-3713-401f-b539-a74c0fc79dc4) Lee & Low Bks., Inc.

—Estela en el Mercado de Pulgas, 1 vol. O'Neill, Alexis. de la Vega, Eida, tr. 2005. (SPA.). 32p. (J). (gr. 1-4). pap. 10.95 *(978-1-58430-246-9(1),* d5bfb7ee-a9ab-4457-9b6f-2aec5cd91e00) Lee & Low Bks., Inc.

—Estela en el Mercado de Pulgas. de la Vega, Eida, tr. from ENG. 2005. (SPA.). 32p. (J). (gr. -1-k). 16.95 *(978-1-58430-245-2(3))* Lee & Low Bks., Inc.

—La Flor de Oro: Un Mito Taino de Puerto Rico. Jaffe, Nina. Ventura, Gabriela Baeza, tr. from ENG. 2006. (SPA.). 32p. (J). (gr. -1-3). 16.95 *(978-1-55885-463-5(0),* Piñata Books) Arte Publico Pr.

—The Golden Flower: A Taino Myth from Puerto Rico. Jaffe, Nina. 2005. 32p. (J). (gr. -1-3). 16.95 *(978-1-55885-452-9(5),* Piñata Books) Arte Publico Pr.

—Una Muneca para el Dia de Reyes. Santiago, Esmeralda. Torres-Vidal, Nina, tr. from ENG. 2005.Tr. of Doll for Navidades. (SPA.). 32p. (J). (gr. -1-3). per. 5.99 *(978-0-439-75510-8(7))* Scholastic, Inc.

Sanchez, Evan. The Snail with Two Slippers. Shonka, Maria. 2011. 40p. pap. 24.95 *(978-1-60836-786-3(X))* America Star Bks.

Sanchez, Gary Donald. The Adventures of Pfreddy the Fetus. Nyce, B. E. 2017. (ENG.). (J). pap. 10.49 *(978-1-5456-1559-1(4))* Salem Author Services.

—In Search of the Great I Am. Jones, Monica. 2016. (ENG.). (J). pap. 10.99 *(978-1-4984-8156-4(6))* Salem Author Services.

—The Ugly Bug. Spates, Evelyn Eve Brown. 2017. (ENG.). (J). 24.49 *(978-1-5456-2091-5(1));* pap. 13.49 *(978-1-5456-1957-5(3))* Salem Author Services.

Sanchez-Gomez, Eva. Oleg the Giant. Fletcher, Graham. 2018. (ENG.). 36p. (J). pap. *(978-1-78830-136-7(6))* Olympia Publishers.

Sanchez Hernandez, Jorge. La Historia de Nuestra Seanora de Guadalupe, Emperatriz de America. Walsh, C. Lourdes. Johnson, Daniel J., ed. Zamorda, Maria Blanca, tr. 2008. (SPA.). 54p. pap. 23.75 *(978-1-4120-1198-3(1))* Trafford Publishing.

Sanchez, Israel. The Dinosaur Tooth Fairy. Brockenbrough, Martha. 2013. (ENG.). 32p. (J). (gr. -1-3). 17.99 *(978-0-545-24466-4(8),* Levine, Arthur A. Bks.) Scholastic, Inc.

Sanchez, James Rey. Irving Berlin: The Immigrant Boy Who Made America Sing. Churnin, Nancy. 2018. (ENG.). 32p. (J). (gr. 2-5). 17.99 *(978-1-939547-44-6(X))* Creston Bks.

Sanchez, Javier G. Un Rey sin Corona. Monkman, Olga. 2003. (SPA.). 39p. (J). (gr. k-3). pap. 7.95 *(978-950-511-368-2(4))* Santillana USA Publishing Co., Inc.

Sanchez, Jimena. Snow White & the Seven Robots. Simonson, Louise. 2015. (Far Out Fairy Tales Ser.). (ENG.). 40p. (J). (gr. 3-6). lib. bdg. 25.32 *(978-1-4342-9648-1(2),* Stone Arch Bks.) Capstone.

Sanchez, Jorge L. FonoCultura 1 - el Bebé. Diaz, Olga L. 2018. (SPA.). (gr. k-1). pap. *(978-1-949818-03-9(X),* LectoCultura) Diaz, Olga L.

Sanchez, Maria. Jose. Lazaro, Georgina. 2007. (J). 14.99 *(978-1-933032-08-5(1))* Lectorum Pubns., Inc.

Sanchez, Miguel R. Go Green! Join the Green Team & Learn How to Reduce, Reuse, & Recycle! Gogerly, Liz. 2019. (ENG.). 48p. (J). (gr. 3-6). 18.99 *(978-1-63198-430-3(6))* Free Spirit Publishing, Inc.

Sanchez S., Jimena. Blancanieves y Los Siete Robots: Una Novela Gráfica. Simonson, Louise. 2020. (Cuentos de Hadas Futuristas Ser.).Tr. of Snow White & the Seven Robots: a Graphic Novel. (SPA.). 40p. (J). (gr. 3-6). pap. 5.95 ***(978-1-4965-9960-5(8),*** 201606); lib. bdg. 25.32 ***(978-1-4965-9814-1(8),*** 200702) Capstone. (Stone Arch Bks.).

Sanchez, Sara. Ella WHO? Ashman, Linda. 2017. 32p. (J). (gr. -1). 14.95 *(978-1-4549-1904-9(3))* Sterling Publishing Co., Inc.

—Imagine That! Burlison, Tom. 2020. (ENG.). 32p. (J). (gr. -1-2). 17.99 *(978-1-68010-192-8(7))* Tiger Tales.

—Monkey in the Mirror. Zur Muehlen, Nersel. 2012. 56p. pap. 14.95 *(978-0-9829224-2-2(6))* BPM Research LLC.

—My Shadow. Stevenson, Robert Louis. 2016. (ENG.). 32p. (J). (gr. -1-k). 16.99 *(978-1-63450-178-1(0),* Sky Pony Pr.) Skyhorse Publishing Co., Inc.

—What Am I? A Let's Learn Spanish Book. de Anda, Diane. 2020. (ENG.). 16p. (J). (gr. -1-k). bds. 7.99 *(978-1-5344-2668-9(X),* Little Simon) Little Simon.

—Who Am I? A Let's Learn Spanish Book. de Anda, Diane. 2019. (ENG.). 16p. (J). (gr. -1-k). bds. 7.99 *(978-1-5344-2667-2(1),* Little Simon) Little Simon.

Sánchez, Sergio García. Lost in NYC: A Subway Adventure. Spiegelman, Nadja. 2016. (Toon Graphics Ser.). (ENG.). 52p. (J). (gr. 3-6). lib. bdg. 29.93 *(978-1-61479-499-8(5),* 21435, Graphic Novels) Spotlight.

Sanchez, Sergio Garcia. Lost in Nyc: a Subway Adventure. Spiegelman, Nadja. 2020. (ENG.). 52p. (J). pap. 9.99 *(978-1-943145-48-5(2))* TOON Books / RAW Junior, LLC.

Sánchez, Sonia. The Curious Cares of Bears. Florian, Douglas. (ENG.). (J). (gr. -1-k). 2018. 26p. bds. 7.99 *(978-1-4998-0743-1(0));* 2017. 32p. 16.99 *(978-1-4998-0462-1(8))* Little Bee Books Inc.

Sanchez, Sonia. Evelyn Del Rey Is Moving Away. Medina, Meg. 2020. (ENG.). 32p. (J). (gr. k-2). 17.99 ***(978-1-5362-0704-0(7))*** Candlewick Pr.

—Evelyn Del Rey Se Muda. Medina, Meg. 2020. (SPA.). 32p. (J). (gr. k-2). 17.99 ***(978-1-5362-1334-8(9))*** Candlewick Pr.

Sanchez, Sonia. El Fuertecito Rojo. Maier, Brenda. 2018. (SPA.). 40p. (J). (gr. -1-3). pap. 4.99 *(978-1-338-26901-7(1),* Scholastic en Espanol) Scholastic, Inc.

—Green Green: A Community Gardening Story. Lamba, Marie & Lamba, Baldev. 2017. (ENG.). 32p. (J). 17.99 *(978-0-374-32797-2(1),* 900147768, Farrar, Straus & Giroux (BYR)) Farrar, Straus & Giroux.

Sánchez, Sonia. Here I Am, 1 vol. Kim, Patti. 2015. (Na Ser.). (ENG.). 40p. (J). (gr. k-5). pap. 7.95 *(978-1-4795-1931-6(6),* Picture Window Bks.) Capstone.

—Here I Am. 2014. (J). *(978-1-4795-1932-3(4),* Picture Window Bks.) Capstone.

—Here I Am, 1 vol. Kim, Patti. 2013. (Na Ser.). (ENG.). 40p. (J). (gr. k-5). 29.32 *(978-1-4048-8299-7(5),* Picture Window Bks.) Capstone.

—The Little Red Fort. Maier, Brenda. 2018. (ENG.). 40p. (J). (gr. -1-3). 17.99 *(978-0-545-85919-6(0),* Scholastic Pr.) Scholastic, Inc.

Sanchez, Sonia. My Quiet Ship. Adelman, Hallee. 2018. (ENG.). 32p. (J). 16.99 *(978-0-8075-6713-5(2),* 807567132) Whitman, Albert & Co.

Sánchez, Sonia. Raisins & Almonds: A Yiddish Lullaby. Tarcov, Susan. 2019. (ENG.). 32p. (J). (gr. -1-2). 17.99 *(978-1-5415-2161-2(7),* Kar-Ben Publishing) Lerner Publishing Group.

—The Wonderful Habits of Rabbits. Florian, Douglas. (ENG.). (J). (gr. -1-3). 2018. 26p. bds. 7.99 *(978-1-4998-0622-9(1));* 2016. 32p. 16.99 *(978-1-4998-0104-0(1))* Little Bee Books Inc.

Sánchez, Sonia & Sánchez, Sonia. Sister Day! Mantchev, Lisa. 2017. (ENG.). 32p. (J). (gr. -1-3). 17.99 *(978-1-4814-3795-0(X),* Simon & Schuster Bks. For Young Readers) Simon & Schuster Bks. For Young Readers.

Sánchez, Sonia, jt. illus. see Sánchez, Sonia.

Sanchez, Sr. Algorithms: Solve a Problem! Hoena, Blake. 2018. (Code It! Ser.). (ENG.). (C). (gr. 1-3). lib. bdg. 33.99 *(978-1-68410-383-6(5),* 140357) Cantata Learning.

Sánchez, Sr. Ambulances / Ambulancias. Falligant, Erin. 2019. (Machines! / ¡Las Máquinas! Ser.). (MUL.). 24p. (J). (gr. -1-2). lib. bdg. 33.99 *(978-1-68410-336-2(3),* 140256) Cantata Learning.

—Bulldozers / Buldóceres. Falligant, Erin. 2019. (Machines! / ¡Las Máquinas! Ser.). (MUL.). 24p. (J). (gr. -1-2). lib. bdg. 33.99 *(978-1-68410-337-9(1),* 140257) Cantata Learning.

Sanchez, Sr. Code It! Higgins, Nadia et al. 2018. (Code It! Ser.). (ENG.). (C). (gr. 1-3). 135.96 *(978-1-68410-440-6(8),* 29691) Cantata Learning.

—Debugging: You Can Fix It! Stockland, Patricia M. 2018. (Code It! Ser.). (ENG.). 24p. (C). (gr. 1-3). lib. bdg. 33.99 *(978-1-68410-388-1(6),* 140361) Cantata Learning.

Sánchez, Sr. Dump Trucks / Camiones de Volteo. Falligant, Erin. 2019. (Machines! / ¡Las Máquinas! Ser.). (MUL.). 24p. (J). (gr. -1-2). lib. bdg. 33.99 *(978-1-68410-338-6(X),* 140258) Cantata Learning.

—Fire Trucks / Camiones de Bomberos. Higgins, Nadia. 2019. (Machines! / ¡Las Máquinas! Ser.). (MUL.). 24p. (J). (gr. -1-2). lib. bdg. 33.99 *(978-1-68410-339-3(8),* 140259) Cantata Learning.

Sanchez, Sr. Fire Trucks / Camiones de Bomberos. Higgins, Nadia. 2020. (Machines! / ¡Las Máquinas! Ser.). (MUL.). 20p. (J). (gr. -1-2). bds. 7.99 *(978-1-5158-6093-8(0),* 142373) Cantata Learning.

Sánchez, Sr. Garbage Trucks / Camiones de Basura. Higgins, Nadia. 2019. (Machines! / ¡Las Máquinas! Ser.). (MUL.). 24p. (J). (gr. -1-2). lib. bdg. 33.99 *(978-1-68410-340-9(1),* 140260) Cantata Learning.

Sanchez, Sr. Loops: Repeat, Repeat! Stockland, Patricia M. 2018. (Code It! Ser.). (ENG.). 24p. (C). (gr. 1-3). lib. bdg. 33.99 *(978-1-68410-390-4(8),* 140365) Cantata Learning.

—Machines! / ¡Las Máquinas! Falligant, Erin & Higgins, Nadia. 2019. (Machines! / ¡Las Máquinas! Ser.). (MUL.). (J). (gr -1-2). pap., pap., pap. 47.70 *(978-1-4966-1946-4(3),* 29280) Cantata Learning.

Sánchez, Sr. Sequences: Order Matters! Higgins, Nadia. 2018. (Code It! Ser.). (ENG.). 24p. (C). (gr. 1-3). lib. bdg. 33.99 incl. audio compact disk *(978-1-68410-119-1(0),* 31860) Cantata Learning.

Sanchez, Sr. Sequences: Order Matters! Higgins, Nadia. 2018. (Code It! Ser.). (ENG.). 24p. (C). (gr. 1-3). 33.99 *(978-1-68410-310-2(X),* 140702) Cantata Learning.

Sánchez, Sr. Trains / Trenes. Higgins, Nadia. 2019. (Machines! / ¡Las Máquinas! Ser.). (MUL.). 24p. (J). (gr. -1-2). lib. bdg. 33.99 *(978-1-68410-341-6(X),* 140261) Cantata Learning.

Sanchez, Yoss. Alpaca Pati's Fancy Fleece. Kyle, Tracey. 2019. 32p. (J). (gr. -1-3). 17.99 *(978-0-7624-9414-9(X),* Running Pr. Kids) Running Pr.

Sancton, Sylvaine, photos by. Some Birds ..., 1 vol. Sancton, Sylvaine. 2013. (ENG., 40p. (J). (gr. k-3). pap. 14.99 *(978-1-4556-1863-7(2),* Pelican Publishing) Arcadia Publishing.

Sanda-Ebosh, Mary. The Unfroggettable Fiona Fayetta Froggee: A Green Pond Memoir. Merriweather-Beech, Myrtle. 2009. 52p. pap. 24.99 *(978-1-4389-2585-1(9))* AuthorHouse.

Sandall, Diane. Small Graces. Sandall, Anne. 2004. (J). *(978-0-9741620-1-0(9))* Solsidan Hse.

Sandall, Ellie. Copycat Bear! Sandall, Ellie. 2013. (ENG.). 32p. (J). (gr. -1-k). 14.99 *(978-1-58925-120-5(2))* Tiger Tales.

—Daisy Plays Hide-and-Seek. Sandall, Ellie. (ENG.). 32p. (J). (gr. -1-k). 2012. pap. 8.99 *(978-1-4052-5457-1(2));* 2011. 17.99 *(978-1-4052-5419-9(X))* Egmont Bks., Ltd. GBR. Dist: Independent Pubs. Group.

—Everybunny Count! Sandall, Ellie. 2018. (ENG.). 32p. (J). (gr. -1-3). 17.99 *(978-1-5344-0014-6(1),* McElderry, Margaret K. Bks.) McElderry, Margaret K. Bks.

—Everybunny Dream! Sandall, Ellie. 2019. (ENG.). 32p. (J). (gr. -1-3). 17.99 *(978-1-5344-4004-3(6),* McElderry, Margaret K. Bks.) McElderry, Margaret K. Bks.

Sande, Ana. El Patito Feo. 2006. (Coleccion Libros para Sonar Ser.). (J). (gr. -1-3). *(978-84-96388-21-5(2))* Kalandraka Editora, S.L.

Sandemose, Iben. Gracie & Grandma. Sandemose, Iben. 2008. (Gracie & Grandma Ser.). 36p. (J). (gr. -1-1). 14.95 *(978-0-9790347-3-2(6))* Mackenzie Smiles, LLC.

—Gracie & Grandma & the Itsy, Bitsy Seed. Sandemose, Iben. Vetleseter, Tonje, tr. from NOR. 2008. (Gracie & Grandma Ser.). 40p. (J). (gr. -1-1). 14.95 *(978-0-9790347-5-6(2))* Mackenzie Smiles, LLC.

Sanders, Allan. Little Explorers: My Amazing Body. Martin, Ruth. 2015. (Little Explorers Ser.). (ENG.). 18p. (J). (gr. -1-3). 9.99 *(978-1-4998-0040-1(1))* Little Bee Books Inc.

—Little Explorers: Outer Space. Martin, Ruth. 2016. (Little Explorers Ser.). (ENG.). 18p. (J). (gr. -1-3). 9.99 *(978-1-4998-0250-4(1))* Little Bee Books Inc.

—Little Explorers: the Animal World. Martin, Ruth. 2016. (Little Explorers Ser.). (ENG.). 18p. (J). (gr. -1-3). 9.99 *(978-1-4998-0249-8(8))* Little Bee Books Inc.

Sanders, Allan. Search & Find A Number of Numbers. Wood, A. J. 2020. (ENG.). 48p. (J). (gr. -1-2). 17.99 ***(978-1-78603-536-3(7),*** 307578, Wide Eyed Editions) Quarto Publishing Group UK GBR. Dist: Hachette UK Distribution.

Sanders, Brian. Titanic. Jenkins, Martin. 2012. (ENG.). 32p. (J). (gr. 3-7). pap. 6.99 *(978-0-7636-6034-5(5))* Candlewick Pr.

Sanders, Khaili. Where the Road Begins: A Compilation of a Kid's Vivid Imagination. Dunn, Darin & Mills, Rosemary. 2019. (ENG.). 56p. (J). pap. 11.00 ***(978-1-6791-7355-4(3))*** Independently Published.

Sanders, Konnilaree Walker. The Legend of Little Bigfoot's Ice Cream Cone. Sanders, Konnilaree Walker. 2020. (ENG.). 32p. (J). 14.95 ***(978-1-7339106-9-7(7));*** pap. 9.95 ***(978-1-7339106-8-2(9))*** Stories By Mom.

—Pete & the Night Time Shadows. Sanders, Konnilaree Walker. 2020. (ENG.). 34p. (J). pap. 9.95 ***(978-1-7339106-7-5(0))*** Stories By Mom.

Sanders, Martin B., et al. Super Dentist Guy: Attack of the Yukkies. Xavier, Imbeus & Sanders, Martin B. 2003. 52p. 7.99 *(978-0-9708523-0-4(4))* DeMosi Publishing.

Sanders, Martin B. Super Dentist Guy: Attack of the Yukkies. Sanders, Martin B. Xavier, Imbeus. 2003. 64p. lib. bdg. 11.99 *(978-0-9708523-2-8(0))* DeMosi Publishing.

Sanders, Michelle. A Joyous Life. Sanders, Leslie. 2016. (ENG.). (J). pap. 12.95 *(978-1-63525-076-3(5))* Christian Faith Publishing.

Sanders, Rick. The Adventures of Callie the Curious Cat. Solomita, Cindy. 2017. (ENG.). (J). (gr. k-6). 19.99 *(978-0-9992479-4-5(8))* Theswordverve.

Sanders, Steven, et al. Uncanny X-Men by Kieron Gillen: the Complete Collection Vol. 1. 2019. (Uncanny X-Men by Kieron Gillen: the Complete Collection: 1). (ENG.). 504p. (YA). (gr. 8-17). pap. 39.99 *(978-1-302-91649-7(1))* Marvel Worldwide, Inc.

Sanderson, Constance. The Frog & the Fly. Webb, Heather. 2008. 29p. pap. 24.95 *(978-1-60441-380-9(8))* America Star Bks.

Sanderson, Jessica B. Global Heart Warming: Dream Believe Achieve Series. Symington, Martha M. 2009. 36p. pap. *(978-1-897435-34-2(7))* Agio Publishing Hse.

Sanderson, Ruth. Bell's Star: Horse Diaries #2. Hart, Alison. 2009. (Horse Diaries: 2). 144p. (J). (gr. 3-7). pap. 7.99 *(978-0-375-85204-6(2),* Random Hse. Bks. for Young Readers) Random Hse. Children's Bks.

—Calvino: Horse Diaries #14. Sanderson, Whitney. 2017. (Horse Diaries: 12). 160p. (J). (gr. 3-7). pap. 7.99 *(978-1-101-93779-2(3),* Random Hse. Bks. for Young Readers) Random Hse. Children's Bks.

—Darcy. Sanderson, Whitney. 2013. (Horse Diaries: 10). 160p. (J). (gr. 3-7). pap. 7.99 *(978-0-307-97635-2(1),* Random Hse. Bks. for Young Readers) Random Hse. Children's Bks.

—Horse Diaries #11: Jingle Bells (Horse Diaries Special Edition) Hapka, Catherine. 2014. (Horse Diaries: 11). 208p. (J). (gr. 3-7). pap. 7.99 *(978-0-385-38484-1(X),* Random Hse. Bks. for Young Readers) Random Hse. Children's Bks.

—Horse Diaries #12: Luna. Hapka, Catherine. 2015. (Horse Diaries: 12). (ENG.). 160p. (J). (gr. 3-7). lib. bdg. 12.99 *(978-0-553-53371-2(1),* Random Hse. Bks. for Young Readers) Random Hse. Children's Bks.

—Horse Diaries #13: Cinders (Horse Diaries Special Edition) Klimo, Kate. 2016. (Horse Diaries: 13). 160p. (J). (gr. 3-7). pap. 7.99 *(978-1-101-93690-0(8),* Random Hse. Bks. for Young Readers) Random Hse. Children's Bks.

—Horse Diaries #15: Lily. Sanderson, Whitney. 2018. (Horse Diaries: 15). (ENG.). 160p. (J). (gr. 3-7). lib. bdg. 12.99 *(978-1-5247-6655-9(0),* Random Hse. Bks. for Young Readers) Random Hse. Children's Bks.

—Horse Diaries #5: Golden Sun. Sanderson, Whitney. 2010. (Horse Diaries: 5). 160p. (J). (gr. 3-7). pap. 7.99 *(978-0-375-86194-9(7),* Random Hse. Bks. for Young Readers) Random Hse. Children's Bks.

—Koda. Hermes, Patricia. 2009. (Horse Diaries: 3). 160p. (J). (gr. 3-7). pap. 7.99 *(978-0-375-85199-5(2),* Random Hse. Bks. for Young Readers) Random Hse. Children's Bks.

—Lily: Horse Diaries #15. Sanderson, Whitney. 2018. (Horse Diaries: 15). 160p. (J). (gr. 3-7). pap. 7.99 *(978-1-5247-6654-2(2),* Random Hse. Bks. for Young Readers) Random Hse. Children's Bks.

—Maestoso Petra: Horse Diaries #4. Kendall, Jane F. 2010. (Horse Diaries: 4). 160p. (J). (gr. 3-7). pap. 7.99 *(978-0-375-85842-0(3),* Random Hse. Bks. for Young Readers) Random Hse. Children's Bks.

—Penny, Vol. 16. Sanderson, Whitney. 2019. (Horse Diaries: 16). 160p. (J). (gr. 3-7). pap. 7.99 *(978-0-525-64478-1(4),* Random Hse. Bks. for Young Readers) Random Hse. Children's Bks.

—Risky Chance. Hart, Alison. 2011. (Horse Diaries: 7). 176p. (J). (gr. 3-7). pap. 7.99 *(978-0-375-86833-7(X),* Random Hse. Bks. for Young Readers) Random Hse. Children's Bks.

—Summer Pony. Doty, Jean Slaughter. 2008. (Stepping Stone Book(TM) Ser.). (ENG.). 144p. (J). (gr. 1-4). pap. 4.99 *(978-0-375-84709-7(X),* Random Hse. Bks. for Young Readers) Random Hse. Children's Bks.

—Where Have the Unicorns Gone? Yolen, Jane. 2003. (ENG.). 32p. (J). (gr. -1-3). 9.99 *(978-0-689-86359-2(4),* Simon & Schuster/Paula Wiseman Bks.) Simon & Schuster Bks. For Young Readers.

—Winter Pony. Doty, Jean Slaughter. 2008. (Stepping Stones Chapter Book: Fiction Ser.). (ENG.). 128p. (J). (gr. 2-4). lib. bdg. 16.19 *(978-0-375-94710-0(8))* Random House Publishing Group.

—Winter Pony. Slaughter Doty, Jean. 2008. (Stepping Stone Book(TM) Ser.). (ENG.). 144p. (J). (gr. 1-4). 4.99 *(978-0-375-84710-3(3),* Random Hse. Bks. for Young Readers) Random Hse. Children's Bks.

—Yatimah: Horse Diaries #6. Hapka, Catherine. 2011. (Horse Diaries: 6). 176p. (J). (gr. 3-7). pap. 7.99 *(978-0-375-86719-4(8),* Random Hse. Bks. for Young Readers) Random Hse. Children's Bks.

Sanderson, Ruth. The Crystal Mountain. Sanderson, Ruth. (ENG.). 32p. (J). 2019. pap. 8.95 *(978-1-56656-007-8(1));* 2016. 17.95 *(978-1-56656-021-4(7))* Interlink Publishing Group, Inc. (Crocodile Bks.).

—The Enchanted Wood. Sanderson, Ruth. 2016. (ENG.). 32p. (J). 17.95 *(978-1-56656-057-3(8),* Crocodile Bks.) Interlink Publishing Group, Inc.

—More Saints: Lives & Illuminations. Sanderson, Ruth. 2007. 40p. (J). (gr. 1). 20.00 *(978-0-8028-5272-4(6),* Eerdmans Bks For Young Readers) Eerdmans, William B. Publishing Co.

—Papa Gatto: An Italian Fairy Tale. Sanderson, Ruth. 2015. (ENG.). 32p. (J). 17.95 *(978-1-56656-090-0(X))* Interlink Publishing Group, Inc.

—Rose Red & Snow White. Sanderson, Ruth. 2013. (ENG.). 32p. (J). 16.95 *(978-1-56656-910-1(9),* Crocodile Bks.) Interlink Publishing Group, Inc.

—Saints: Lives & Illuminations. Sanderson, Ruth. 2010. (ENG.). 160p. (J). (gr. 3-18). 16.00 *(978-0-8028-5365-3(X),* Eerdmans Bks For Young Readers); 2004. 40p. 20.00 *(978-0-8028-5220-5(3))* Eerdmans, William B. Publishing Co.

—The Snow Princess. Sanderson, Ruth. (ENG.). 32p. (J). 2017. pap. 8.95 *(978-1-56656-098-6(5));* 2014. 17.95 *(978-1-56656-985-9(0))* Interlink Publishing Group, Inc. (Crocodile Bks.).

Sanderson, Ruth, jt. illus. see Griffin-Scott, Janet.

Sanderson, Sean. Time for Bed Little Red. Scand, Sandra. 2009. 20p. pap. 10.00 *(978-1-934925-36-2(5),* Eloquent Bks.) Strategic Book Publishing & Rights Agency (SBPRA).

Sandford, Barbara. Grandma's Day. Anderson, P. G. 2013. 32p. 16.00 *(978-1-61170-133-3(3))* Robertson Publishing.

—Joe the Flea Finds a Home. Sribnick, Howard. 2018. (ENG.). 26p. (J). pap. 9.99 *(978-1-7268-4368-3(8))* Independently Published.

Sandford, Grace. Amazing Activities for Fans of Animal Crossing: An Unofficial Activity Book — Mazes, Crosswords, & Puzzles to Improve Your Skills. Weber, Jen Funk. 2020. 64p. (J). (gr. 3-5). pap. 9.99 ***(978-1-5107-6303-6(1),*** Sky Pony Pr.) Skyhorse Publishing Co., Inc.

Sandford, Grace. The Creeper Code: 5-Minute Mysteries for Minecrafters. Mann, Greyson. 2017. (5-Minute Stories for Minecrafters Ser.: 2). 112p. (J). pap. 7.99 *(978-1-5107-2369-6(2));* 120p. (gr. 2-6). 14.99 *(978-1-5107-2838-7(4))* Skyhorse Publishing Co., Inc. (Sky Pony Pr.).

—Extreme Stories from the Extreme Hills: 5-Minute Adventure Stories for Minecrafters. Mann, Greyson. 2017. (5-Minute Stories for Minecrafters Ser.: 1). 112p. (gr. 6-12). 14.99 *(978-1-5107-2839-4(2),* Sky Pony Pr.) Skyhorse Publishing Co., Inc.

—Extreme Stories from the Extreme Hills: 5-Minute Adventure Stories for Minecrafters. Mann, Greyson. 2017. (5-Minute Stories for Minecrafters Ser.: 1). 112p. (J). pap. 7.99 *(978-1-5107-2370-2(6),* Sky Pony Pr.) Skyhorse Publishing Co., Inc.

—Lost in the Jungle: Secrets of an Overworld Survivor, #1. Mann, Greyson. 2017. (Secrets of an Overworld Survivor Ser.). 112p. (J). (gr. 1-4). 13.99 *(978-1-5107-1325-3(5),* Sky Pony Pr.) Skyhorse Publishing Co., Inc.

—Tough Cookie. Louise, Kate. 2015. 32p. (J). (gr. -1-k). 16.99 *(978-1-63450-197-2(7),* Sky Pony Pr.) Skyhorse Publishing Co., Inc.

—When Lava Strikes: Secrets of an Overworld Survivor, #2. Mann, Greyson. 2017. (Secrets of an Overworld Survivor Ser.). (ENG.). 112p. (J). (gr. 1-4). 13.99 *(978-1-5107-1328-4(X),* Sky Pony Pr.) Skyhorse Publishing Co., Inc.

—The Witchas Warning: Secrets of an Overworld Survivor. Mann, Greyson. 2017. (Secrets of an Overworld Survivor Ser.). 112p. (J). (gr. 3-5). 13.99 *(978-1-5107-2706-9(X),* Sky Pony Pr.) Skyhorse Publishing Co., Inc.

—The Witch's Warning: Secrets of an Overworld Survivor, #5. Mann, Greyson. 2017. (Secrets of an Overworld Survivor Ser.). 112p. (J). (gr. 3-5). pap. 4.99 *(978-1-5107-2707-6(8),* Sky Pony Pr.) Skyhorse Publishing Co., Inc.

—Wolves vs. Zombies: Secrets of an Overworld Survivor, #3. Mann, Greyson. 2017. (Secrets of an Overworld Survivor Ser.). 112p. (J). (gr. 1-4). 13.99 *(978-1-5107-1331-4(X),* Sky Pony Pr.) Skyhorse Publishing Co., Inc.

Sandford, John. The Leprechaun in the Basement. Tucker, Kathy. 2010. (ENG.). 32p. (J). (gr. 1-3). 21.19 *(978-0-8075-4451-8(5))* Whitman, Albert & Co.

Sandford, John. Rules of the Game: Baseball Poems. Maddox, Marjorie. 2019. (ENG.). 34p. (J). (gr. 1-4). 24.00 ***(978-1-5326-9735-7(X))*** Resource Pubns., Inc.

Sandford, John. Little House Hotel. Sandford, John. 24p. (J). 2.99 *(978-1-59445-000-6(5))* Dogs in Hats Children's Publishing Co.

Sandham, Henry. Editha's Burglar. Burnett, Frances Hodgson. 2005. reprint ed. pap. 15.95 *(978-1-4179-0135-7(7))* Kessinger Publishing, LLC.

Sandheim, May. The Golden Heart, & Other Fairy Stories. Jacob, Violet. 2011. 168p. pap. *(978-1-84921-098-0(5))* Kennedy & Boyd.

Sandhu, Param. Tiger Tails. Trotman, Rita. 2020. (ENG.). 48p. (J). pap. ***(978-1-78324-149-1(7))*** Wordzworth Publishing.

Sandiford, Ted. Counting St. Lucian Style: A delightfully illustrated counting rhyme set in the Caribbean island of St. Lucia. Bousquet, Anthea. 2011. 16p. (J). pap. *(978-976-8238-01-6(1))* Maryli Pubs.

—Lucy's St. Lucian Alphabet: The ABCs of Caribbean Culture in Upbeat Rhyming Verse. Bousquet, Anthea. 2012. 20p. (J). pap. *(978-976-8238-02-3(X))* Maryli Pubs.

Sandiford, Ted M. Daddy's Mini-Me. Henry, Arnold. 2019. (ENG.). 34p. (J). pap. *(978-0-9940272-5-2(7))* Piton Bks.

Sandland, Amanda. Caribou. Aglukark, David & Aglukark, Dorothy. 2020. (Animals Illustrated Ser.). (ENG.). 28p. (J). 12.95 *(978-1-77227-234-5(5))* Inhabit Media Inc. CAN. Dist: Consortium Bk. Sales & Distribution.

Sandland, Amanda. Going Fishing (English), 1 vol. Vsetula, Maren. 2017. (Nunavummi Ser.). (ENG.). 8p. (gr. 1-1). pap. 7.95 ***(978-1-77266-536-9(3))*** Inhabit Education CAN. Dist: Consortium Bk. Sales & Distribution.

—I Want to Dance! (Inuktitut/English) Main, Heather. ed. 2020. (ENG.). 44p. (J). pap. 10.95 ***(978-0-2287-0490-4(1))*** Inhabit Education CAN. Dist: Consortium Bk. Sales & Distribution.

—Journey to the Winter Camp (English), 1 vol. Mallory, Carolyn & Mallory, Carolyn. 2017. (Nunavummi Ser.). (ENG.). 32p. (gr. 2-2). pap. 7.95 ***(978-1-77266-548-2(7))*** Inhabit Education CAN. Dist: Consortium Bk. Sales & Distribution.

—Owl & the Lemming, 1 vol. Akulukjuk, Roselynn. 2017. (Nunavummi Ser.). (ENG.). 28p. (J). (gr. 3-3). 24.95 ***(978-1-77266-590-1(8))*** Inhabit Education CAN. Dist: Consortium Bk. Sales & Distribution.

—Sometimes I Feel Angry, 1 vol. Inhabit Education. 2017. (Nunavummi Ser.). (ENG.). 24p. (J). (gr. 2-2). 8.95 ***(978-1-77266-510-9(X))*** Inhabit Education CAN. Dist: Consortium Bk. Sales & Distribution.

—Sometimes I Feel Jealous, 1 vol. Inhabit Education. 2017. (Nunavummi Ser.). (ENG.). 24p. (J). (gr. 2-2). 24.95 ***(978-1-77266-519-2(3))*** Inhabit Education CAN. Dist: Consortium Bk. Sales & Distribution.

—Sometimes I Feel Jealous (English), 1 vol. Inhabit Education. 2017. (Nunavummi Ser.). (ENG.). 24p. (J). (gr. 2-2). 8.95 ***(978-1-77266-516-1(9))*** Inhabit Education CAN. Dist: Consortium Bk. Sales & Distribution.

—Sometimes I Feel Lonely, 1 vol. Inhabit Education. 2017. (Nunavummi Ser.). (ENG.). 24p. (J). (gr. 2-2). 8.95 ***(978-1-77266-522-2(3))*** Inhabit Education CAN. Dist: Consortium Bk. Sales & Distribution.

—Sometimes I Feel Sad, 1 vol. Inhabit Education. 2017. (Nunavummi Ser.). (ENG.). 24p. (J). (gr. 2-2). 24.95 ***(978-1-77266-528-4(2))*** Inhabit Education CAN. Dist: Consortium Bk. Sales & Distribution.

—Ukaliq & Kalla Go Camping (English) Vsetula, Maren. ed. 2020. (Nunavummi Ser.). (ENG.). 32p. (J). (gr. 1-1). pap. 7.95 ***(978-1-77450-179-5(1))*** Inhabit Education CAN. Dist: Consortium Bk. Sales & Distribution.

—Ukaliq & Kalla Go Sliding, 1 vol. Hale, Jessie. 2017. (Nunavummi Ser.). (ENG.). 28p. (J). (gr. 2-2). 7.95 ***(978-1-77266-539-0(8))*** Inhabit Education CAN. Dist: Consortium Bk. Sales & Distribution.

—Ukaliq & Kalla Go Sliding: English Edition. Hale, Jessie. 2020. (Nunavummi Ser.). (ENG.). 28p. (J). (gr. 2-2). pap. 8.95 ***(978-1-77450-194-8(5))*** Inhabit Education CAN. Dist: Consortium Bk. Sales & Distribution.

—Ukaliq & Kalla Look for Bugs (English), 1 vol. 2018. (Nunavummi Ser.). (ENG.). 8p. (gr. 1-1). pap. 7.95 ***(978-0-2287-0153-8(8))*** Inhabit Education CAN. Dist: Consortium Bk. Sales & Distribution.

—Ukaliq & Kalla's Hunting Tools (English) 2018. (Nunavummi Ser.). (ENG.). 8p. (J). (gr. 1-1). pap. 7.95 ***(978-0-2287-0155-2(4))*** Inhabit Education CAN. Dist: Consortium Bk. Sales & Distribution.

—The Winter in Nunavut (English), 1 vol. Inhabit Education. 2017. (Nunavummi Ser.). (ENG.). 24p. (J). (gr. 2-2). pap. 8.95 ***(978-1-77266-525-3(8))*** Inhabit Education CAN. Dist: Consortium Bk. Sales & Distribution.

Sandland, Amanda & Sandland, Amanda. The Owl & the Lemming (English, Big Book), 1 vol. Bailey, Jenna. 2017. (Nunavummi Ser.). (ENG.). 28p. (J). (gr. 2-2). pap. 8.95 ***(978-1-77266-584-0(3))*** Inhabit Education CAN. Dist: Consortium Bk. Sales & Distribution.

—Sometimes I Feel Angry (English), 1 vol. Inhabit Education. 2017. (Nunavummi Ser.). (ENG.). 24p. (J). (gr. 2-2). pap. 8.95 ***(978-1-77266-513-0(4))*** Inhabit Education CAN. Dist: Consortium Bk. Sales & Distribution.

Sandland, Amanda, jt. illus. see Christopher, Danny.

Sandland, Amanda, jt. illus. see Sandland, Amanda.

Sandland, Reg. Good Friday. Ulmer, Louise. 2004. (Arch Bks.). (ENG.). 16p. (J). 1.99 *(978-0-7586-0638-9(9))* Concordia Publishing Hse.

Sandler, Martin W. America's Great Disasters. Sandler, Martin W. 2003. 96p. (J). (gr. 3-18). 17.99 *(978-0-06-029107-5(9))* HarperCollins Pubs.

Sandler, Vladik. Uncle Zucchini's Amazing Mustache. Shaked, S. 2016. (ENG.). 40p. (J). pap. *(978-965-92570-8-9(2))* Shaked, Shahaf.

Sandon, Gina. The Princes of Pleasant Valley: A Day in the Life of Zyler & Xavier, 1 vol. Proulx, Roxanna Darling. 2010. 46p. 24.95 *(978-1-4489-7641-6(3))* PublishAmerica, Inc.

Sandoval, Gerardo. BMX Breakthrough, 1 vol. Bowen, Carl & Fuentes, Benny. 2011. (Sports Illustrated Kids Graphic Novels Ser.). (ENG.). 56p. (J). (gr. 3-8). pap. 7.19 *(978-1-4342-3401-8(0));* lib. bdg. 26.65 *(978-1-4342-2240-4(3))* Capstone. (Stone Arch Bks.).

—End Zone Thunder, 1 vol. Ciencin, Scott & Fuentes, Benny. 2010. (Sports Illustrated Kids Graphic Novels Ser.). (ENG.). 56p. (J). (gr. 3-8). 26.65 *(978-1-4342-2010-3(9));* pap. 7.19 *(978-1-4342-2784-3(7))* Capstone. (Stone Arch Bks.).

—Full Court Flash, 1 vol. Ciencin, Scott & Fuentes, Benny. 2011. (Sports Illustrated Kids Graphic Novels Ser.). (ENG.). 56p. (J). (gr. 3-8). pap. 7.19 *(978-1-4342-3074-4(0));* lib. bdg. 26.65 *(978-1-4342-2225-1(X))* Capstone. (Stone Arch Bks.).

—Jason & the Golden Fleece, 1 vol. Yomtov, Nel et al. 2009. (Mythology Ser.). (ENG.). 72p. (J). (gr. 5-9). pap. 7.15 *(978-1-4342-1385-3(4));* lib. bdg. 27.99 *(978-1-4342-1172-9(X))* Capstone. (Stone Arch Bks.).

—Quarterback Scramble, 1 vol. Terrell, Brandon & Fuentes, Benny. 2011. (Sports Illustrated Kids Graphic Novels Ser.). (ENG.). 56p. (J). (gr. 3-8). pap. 7.19 *(978-1-4342-3070-6(8));* lib. bdg. 26.65 *(978-1-4342-2220-6(9))* Capstone. (Stone Arch Bks.).

—Reality Check, 1 vol. Yomtov, Nel & Fuentes, Benny. 2010. (Sports Illustrated Kids Graphic Novels Ser.). (ENG.). 56p. (J). (gr. 3-8). pap. 7.19 *(978-1-4342-2294-7(2));* 26.65 *(978-1-4342-1912-1(7))* Capstone. (Stone Arch Bks.).

—Sack Attack!, 1 vol. Fuentes, Benny & Hoena, Blake A. 2011. (Sports Illustrated Kids Graphic Novels Ser.). (ENG.). 56p. (J). (gr. 3-8). pap. 7.19 *(978-1-4342-3404-9(5));* lib. bdg. 26.65 *(978-1-4342-2243-5(8))* Capstone. (Stone Arch Bks.).

—Skateboard Breakdown, 1 vol. Fein, Eric & Fuentes, Benny. 2010. (Sports Illustrated Kids Graphic Novels Ser.). (ENG.). 56p. (J). (gr. 3-8). 26.65 *(978-1-4342-2011-0(7));* pap. 7.19 *(978-1-4342-2785-0(5))* Capstone. (Stone Arch Bks.).

—Skateboard Sonar, 1 vol. Stevens, Eric & Fuentes, Benny. 2010. (Sports Illustrated Kids Graphic Novels Ser.). (ENG.). 56p. (J). (gr. 3-8). pap. 7.19 *(978-1-4342-2295-4(0));* 26.65 *(978-1-4342-1910-7(0))* Capstone. (Stone Arch Bks.).

—Spotlight Striker, 1 vol. Hoena, Blake A. & Fuentes, Benny. 2010. (Sports Illustrated Kids Graphic Novels Ser.). (ENG.). 56p. (J). (gr. 3-8). 26.65 *(978-1-4342-2128-5(8));* pap. 7.19 *(978-1-4342-2787-4(1))* Capstone. (Stone Arch Bks.).

—Venom Vol. 1: Homecoming. Marvel Comics. 2017. (Venom (2017) Ser.: 1). (ENG.). 136p. (YA). (gr. 8-17). pap. 17.99 *(978-1-302-90602-3(X))* Marvel Worldwide, Inc.

—Wild Pitch, 1 vol. Fein, Eric & Fuentes, Benny. 2011. (Sports Illustrated Kids Graphic Novels Ser.). (ENG.). 56p. (J). (gr. 3-8). pap. 7.19 *(978-1-4342-3073-7(2));* lib. bdg. 26.65 *(978-1-4342-2221-3(7))* Capstone. (Stone Arch Bks.).

Sandoval, Gerardo & Level, Brian. Absolute Carnage: Scream. Bunn, Cullen & Chapman, Clay. 2020. (ENG.). 112p. (YA). (gr. 8-17). pap. 15.99 *(978-1-302-92015-9(4))* Marvel Worldwide, Inc.

Sandoval, Gerardo, jt. illus. see Salazar, Edgar.

Sandoval, Migs. Beauty & the Beast: Level 3: Learn Chinese Mandarin Through Fairy Tales. 2006. (Learn Chinese Through Fairy Tales Ser.). (ENG & CHI.). 29p. (J). (gr. -1-3). pap. 14.95 incl. audio compact disk *(978-1-891888-91-5(9))* Slangman Publishing.

—Beauty & the Beast: Level 3: Learn French Through Fairy Tales. Burke, David. 2006. (Learn French Through Fairy Tales Ser.). (ENG & FRE.). 29p. (J). (gr. -1-3). pap. 14.95 incl. audio compact disk *(978-1-891888-87-8(0))* Slangman Publishing.

—Beauty & the Beast: Level 3: Learn German Through Fairy Tales. Burke, David. 2006. (Learn German Through Fairy Tales Ser.). (ENG & GER.). 29p. (J). (gr. -1-3). pap. 14.95 incl. audio compact disk *(978-1-891888-88-5(9))* Slangman Publishing.

—Beauty & the Beast: Level 3: Learn Spanish Through Fairy Tales. Burke, David. 2006. (Learn Spanish Through Fairy Tales Ser.). (ENG & SPA.). 29p. (J). (gr. -1-3). pap. 14.95 incl. audio compact disk *(978-1-891888-86-1(2))* Slangman Publishing.

—La Bella y la Bestia: Nivel 3: Aprende Ingles con Cuentos de Hadas. Burke, David. Redoles, Marcela, tr. 2006. (Slangman para Ninos: Nivel 3 Ser.). (SPA & ENG.). 29p. (J). (gr. -1-3). pap. 14.95 incl. audio compact disk *(978-1-891888-97-7(8))* Slangman Publishing.

—La Cenicienta: Nivel 1: Aprende Ingles con Cuentos de Hadas. Burke, David. Bobrick, Julie, ed. Redoles,

S

Marcela, tr. 2006. (Slangman para Ninos: Nivel 1 Ser.). (SPA & ENG.). 29p. pap. 14.95 incl. cd-rom *(978-1-891888-95-3(1))* Slangman Publishing.
—Cinderella: Level 1: Learn French Through Fairy Tales. 2006. (Learn French Through Fairy Tales Ser.). (ENG & FRE.). 29p. (J). (gr. -1-3). pap. 14.95 incl. audio compact disk *(978-1-891888-75-5(7))* Slangman Publishing.
—Cinderella: Level 1: Learn German Through Fairy Tales. Burke, David. Bobrick, Julie, ed. Deese, Teut & Wirth, Petra, trs. 2006. (Learn German Through Fairy Tales Ser.). (ENG & GER.). 29p. pap. 14.95 incl. audio compact disk *(978-1-891888-76-2(5))* Slangman Publishing.
—Cinderella: Level 1: Learn Italian Through Fairy Tales. Burke, David. Bobrick, Julie, ed. Filippi, Alessio, tr. 2006. (Learn Italian Through Fairy Tales Ser.). (ENG & ITA.). 29p. pap. 14.95 incl. audio compact disk *(978-1-891888-77-9(3))* Slangman Publishing.
—Cinderella: Level 1: Learn Mandarin Chinese Through Fairy Tales. Bobrick, Julie, ed. Peters, Li Li & Tao, Ming, trs. 2006. (Learn Chinese Through Fairy Tales Ser.). (ENG & CHI.). 29p. pap. 14.95 incl. audio compact disk *(978-1-891888-79-3(X))* Slangman Publishing.
—Goldilocks & the 3 Bears: Level 2: Learn French Through Fairy Tales. 2006. (Learn French Through Fairy Tales Ser.). (ENG & FRE.). 29p. (J). (gr. -1-3). pap. 14.95 incl. audio compact disk *(978-1-891888-81-6(1))* Slangman Publishing.
—Goldilocks & the 3 Bears: Level 2: Learn Spanish Through Fairy Tales. Burke, David. 2006. (Learn Spanish Through Fairy Tales Ser.). (ENG & SPA.). 29p. (J). (gr. -1-3). pap. 14.95 incl. audio compact disk *(978-1-891888-80-9(3))* Slangman Publishing.

Sandoval, Rafa. The Simple Life. Van Lente, Fred. 2009. (Iron Man Ser.: No. 2). (ENG.). 24p. (J). (gr. 2-6). lib. bdg. 27.07 *(978-1-59961-592-9(4),* 10033, Marvel Age) Spotlight.
Sandoval, Rafa & Bonet, Roger. Pirated! Van Lente, Fred. 2009. (Iron Man Ser.: No. 2). (ENG.). 24p. (J). (gr. 2-6). lib. bdg. 27.07 *(978-1-59961-591-2(6),* 10032, Marvel Age) Spotlight.
Sandoval, Tony. Coco. Nitz, Jai. 2020. (Disney & Pixar Movies Ser.). (ENG.). 52p. (J). (gr. 2-6). lib. bdg. 28.50 ***(978-1-5321-4547-6(0),*** 35194, Graphic Novels) Spotlight.
Sandoval, Tony, jt. illus. see Corona, Jorge.
Sandoz, Matt. Doggie Bets. Howard, Assuanta. 2013. 32p. pap. 7.99 *(978-1-934947-76-0(8))* Asta Publications, LLC.
Sandro, Turburam. M Is for Mongolia. Ready, Tricia. 2013. (Alphabetical World Ser.). (ENG.). 48p. (J). (gr. k-4). 12.95 *(978-1-934159-27-9(1))* ThingsAsian Pr.
Sandstrom, Karen. Zombies! Evacuate the School. Holbrook, Sara E. 2010. (ENG.). 56p. (J). (gr. 4-7). 16.95 *(978-1-59078-820-2(6),* Wordsong) Boyds Mills Pr.
—Zombies! Evacuate the School! Holbrook, Sara E. 2014. (ENG.). 56p. (J). (gr. 4-7). pap. 7.99 *(978-1-62979-110-4(5),* Wordsong) Boyds Mills Pr.
Sandu, Anca. Gnu & Shrew. Schnitzlein, Danny. 2020. (ENG.). 32p. (J). (gr. -1-3). 16.99 ***(978-1-68263-146-1(X))*** Peachtree Publishing Co. Inc.
Sandu, Anca. Lana Lynn Howls at the Moon, 1 vol. Slyke, Rebecca van. 2019. (ENG.). 32p. (J). (gr. -1-3). 16.95 *(978-1-68263-050-1(1))* Peachtree Publishing Co. Inc.
Sandu, Anca. Churchill's Tale of Tails, 1 vol. Sandu, Anca. (ENG.). 32p. (J). (gr. -1-3). 2016. pap. 7.95 *(978-1-56145-782-3(5));* 2014. 16.95 *(978-1-56145-738-0(8))* Peachtree Publishing Co. Inc.
Sandvik, Lin-Marita, photos by. Bjornen Tor Blir Meisterbakar. Sandvik, Lin-Marita. 2017. (Bjornen Tor Ser.). (NNO., (J). *(978-82-93471-25-7(5))* Sandvikbok.
—Bjornen Tor Blir Mesterbaker. Sandvik, Lin-Marita. 2017. (Bjornen Tor Ser.). (NOB., (J). *(978-82-93471-21-9(2))* Sandvikbok.
—Bjornen Tor Feirar Jul. Sandvik, Lin-Marita. 2016. (Bjornen Tor Ser.). (NNO., (J). *(978-82-93471-29-5(8))* Sandvikbok.
—Bjornen Tor Feirer Jul. Sandvik, Lin-Marita. 2017. (Bjornen Tor Ser.). (NOB., (J). *(978-82-93471-32-5(8))* Sandvikbok.
—Bjornen Tor Finn Vikingskatten. Sandvik, Lin-Marita. 2017. (Bjornen Tor Ser.). (NNO., (J). *(978-82-93471-53-0(0))* Sandvikbok.
—Tor the Bear Becomes an Expert Baker. Sandvik, Lin-Marita. 2017. (Tor the Bear Ser.). (ENG., (J). *(978-82-93471-38-7(7))* Sandvikbok.
—Tor the Bear Celebrates Christmas. Sandvik, Lin-Marita. 2016. (ENG., (J). *(978-82-93471-35-6(2))* Sandvikbok.
—Tor the Bear Rescues a Friend. Sandvik, Lin-Marita. 2016. (Tor the Bear Ser.). (ENG., (J). *(978-82-93471-17-2(4))* Sandvikbok.
Sandy Flett. Edie's Experiments 1: How to Make Friends. Barkla, Charlotte. 2020. (Edie's Experiments Ser.: 1). (ENG.). 240p. (J). (gr. 4-7). 14.99 ***(978-1-76089-177-0(0),*** Puffin) Penguin Random Hse. AUS. Dist: Independent Pubs. Group.
—Edie's Experiments 2: How to Be the Best. Barkla, Charlotte. 2020. (Edie's Experiments Ser.: 2). 240p. (J). (gr. 3-5). 14.99 ***(978-1-76089-176-3(2),*** Puffin) Penguin Random Hse. AUS. Dist: Independent Pubs. Group.
Sandy, J. P. Mrs. Riley Bought Five Itchy Aardvarks & Other Painless Tricks for Memorizing Science Facts. Cleary, Brian P. 2008. (Adventures in Memory Ser.). (ENG.). 48p. (gr. 4-6). 26.60 *(978-0-8225-7819-2(0))* Lerner Publishing Group.
—Rhyme & Punishment: Adventures in Wordplay. Cleary, Brian P. 2006. (ENG.). 48p. (gr. 4-6). 26.60 *(978-1-57505-849-8(9),* Millbrook Pr.) Lerner Publishing Group.
—Washing Adam's Jeans & Other Painless Tricks for Memorizing Social Studies Facts. Cleary, Brian P. 2010. (Adventures in Memory Ser.). (ENG.). 48p. (gr. 4-6). lib. bdg. 26.60 *(978-0-8225-7821-5(2))* Lerner Publishing Group.
Sandy, John. The Laugh Stand: Adventures in Humor. Cleary, Brian P. 2008. (Exceptional Reading & Language Arts Titles for Intermediate Grades Ser.). (ENG.). 48p. (gr. 4-6). lib. bdg. 16.95 *(978-0-8225-7849-9(2))* Lerner Publishing Group.

Sane, Justin. Heart of a Corpse; an Undead Engagement Part One. Sane, Justin. 2012. 34p. pap. 5.95 *(978-1-59362-243-5(0),* Slave Labor Graphics) Slave Labor Bks.
Saneshige, Norio. Wu-lung & I-lung: Color Edition. 2004. 33p. (J). pap. 16.50 *(978-0-9759251-0-2(5),* FortuneChild) Forest Hill Publishing, LLC.
—Wu-lung & I-lung: Deluxe Edition. deluxe l.t. ed. 2004. 33p. (J). 24.50 *(978-0-9759251-1-9(3),* FortuneChild) Forest Hill Publishing, LLC.
Sanfelippo, Ana. Adoptar un Dinosaurio. Andres, Jose Carlos. 2019. (SPA.). 40p. (J). 16.95 *(978-84-17123-62-8(8))* NubeOcho Ediciones ESP. Dist: Consortium Bk. Sales & Distribution.
—Emmeline Pankhurst. Kaiser, Lisbeth. 2017. (Little People, BIG DREAMS Ser.: 8). (ENG.). 32p. (J). (gr. k-3). 14.99 *(978-1-78603-020-7(9),* Frances Lincoln Children's Bks.) Quarto Publishing Group UK GBR. Dist: Hachette Bk. Group.
Sanfelippo, Ana. Emmeline Pankhurst: My First Emmeline Pankhurst. Kaiser, Lisbeth. 2019. (Little People, Big Dreams Ser.: Vol. 8). (ENG.). 24p. (J). (gr. -1). bds. ***(978-1-78603-261-4(9))*** Frances Lincoln Childrens Bks.
Sanfilippo, Simona. Beauty & the Pea. Robinson, Hilary. 2013. (ENG.). 32p. (J). *(978-0-7787-1155-1(2));* pap. *(978-0-7787-1159-9(5))* Crabtree Publishing Co.
—Cinderella & the Beanstalk. Robinson, Hilary. 2013. (ENG.). 32p. (J). *(978-0-7787-1156-8(0));* pap. *(978-0-7787-1161-2(7))* Crabtree Publishing Co.
—The Elves & the Emperor. Robinson, Hilary. 2012. (ENG.). 32p. (J). *(978-0-7787-8025-0(2));* pap. *(978-0-7787-8036-6(8))* Crabtree Publishing Co.
—Goldilocks & the Wolf. Robinson, Hilary. 2012. (ENG.). 32p. (J). *(978-0-7787-8023-6(6));* pap. *(978-0-7787-8034-2(1))* Crabtree Publishing Co.
—The Good Samaritan. Box, Su. 2017. (My Bible Stories Ser.). (ENG.). 24p. (J). (gr. -1-k). lib. bdg. 19.99 *(978-1-68297-173-4(2))* QEB Publishing Inc.
—The Great Feast. Box, Su. 2018. (My Bible Stories Ser.). (ENG.). 24p. (J). (gr. -1-k). lib. bdg. 19.99 *(978-1-68297-178-9(3))* QEB Publishing Inc.
—The Grumpy Queen. Wilding, Valerie. 2011. (ENG.). 32p. (J). (gr. -1-k). pap. *(978-1-84089-637-4(X))* Zero to Ten, Ltd.
—Hansel, Gretel, & the Ugly Duckling. Robinson, Hilary. 2013. (ENG.). 32p. (J). *(978-0-7787-1157-5(9));* pap. *(978-0-7787-1166-7(8))* Crabtree Publishing Co.
—How to Track an Easter Bunny. Fliess, Sue. 2019. (Magical Creatures & Crafts Ser.: 2). (ENG.). 32p. (J). (gr. -1-k). 16.99 *(978-1-5107-4429-5(0),* Sky Pony Pr.) Skyhorse Publishing Co., Inc.
—The Lost Sheep. Box, Su. 2017. (My Bible Stories Ser.). (ENG.). 24p. (J). (gr. -1-k). lib. bdg. 19.99 *(978-1-68297-174-1(0))* QEB Publishing Inc.
—The Prodigal Son. Box, Su. 2018. (My Bible Stories Ser.). (ENG.). 24p. (J). (gr. -1-k). lib. bdg. 19.99 *(978-1-68297-177-2(5))* QEB Publishing Inc.
—Rapunzel. 2009. (Flip-Up Fairy Tales Ser.). 24p. (J). (gr. -1-2). *(978-1-84643-292-7(8));* pap. *(978-1-84643-249-1(9))* Child's Play International Ltd.
—Rapunzel & the Billy Goats. Robinson, Hilary. 2013. (ENG.). 32p. (J). pap. *(978-0-7787-1158-2(7))* Crabtree Publishing Co.
—Snow White & the Enormous Turnip. Robinson, Hilary. 2012. (ENG.). 32p. (J). pap. *(978-0-7787-8035-9(X))* Crabtree Publishing Co.
—The Sower. Box, Su. 2017. (My Bible Stories Ser.). (ENG.). 24p. (J). (gr. -1-k). lib. bdg. 19.99 *(978-1-68297-175-8(9))* QEB Publishing Inc.
—Three Pigs & a Gingerbread Man. Robinson, Hilary. 2012. (ENG.). 32p. (J). *(978-0-7787-8026-7(0));* pap. *(978-0-7787-8037-3(6))* Crabtree Publishing Co.
—The Two Houses. Box, Su. 2017. (My Bible Stories Ser.). (ENG.). 24p. (J). (gr. -1-k). lib. bdg. 19.99 *(978-1-68297-176-5(7))* QEB Publishing Inc.
Sanfilippo, Terry. The Land of Plaid. Sanfilippo, Terry. 2018. (ENG.). 34p. (J). 17.95 *(978-0-9997064-1-1(1))* Dancing Spirit Publishing, LLC.
Sanford, Grace. I Can Draw Cars & Trucks. Reynolds, Toby. 2018. (I Can Draw Ser.). 32p. (gr. 5-7). 28.50 *(978-1-5081-9728-7(8));* pap. 11.75 *(978-1-5383-9012-2(4))* Rosen Publishing Group, Inc., The. (Windmill Bks.).
—I Can Draw People. Reynolds, Toby. 2018. (I Can Draw Ser.). 32p. (gr. 5-7). 28.50 *(978-1-5081-9729-4(6));* pap. 11.75 *(978-1-5383-9015-3(9))* Rosen Publishing Group, Inc., The. (Windmill Bks.).
—I Can Draw Pets. Reynolds, Toby. 2018. (I Can Draw Ser.). 32p. (gr. 5-7). 28.50 *(978-1-5081-9730-0(X));* pap. 11.75 *(978-1-5383-9018-4(3))* Rosen Publishing Group, Inc., The. (Windmill Bks.).
—I Can Draw Wild Animals. Reynolds, Toby. 2018. (I Can Draw Ser.). 32p. (gr. 5-7). 28.50 *(978-1-5081-9731-7(8));* pap. 11.75 *(978-1-5383-9021-4(3))* Rosen Publishing Group, Inc., The. (Windmill Bks.).
Sanford, Lori Hood. Teach Them to Your Children: An Alphabet of Biblical Poems, Verses, & Stories. Wean, Sarah. 2006. 56p. (J). 17.00 *(978-0-9787559-5-9(2))* Vision Forum, Inc., The.
Sang-Sun, Park. Les Bijoux, Vol. I. Eun-Ha, Jo. 2004. 200p. pap. 14.99 *(978-1-59182-690-3(X),* Tokyopop Adult) TOKYOPOP, Inc.
—Les Bijoux, 6 vols., Vol. 2. Eun-Ha, Jo. Lee, Seung-Ah, tr. from KOR. rev. ed. 2004. 200p. pap. 14.99 *(978-1-59182-691-0(8),* Tokyopop Adult) TOKYOPOP, Inc.
—Les Bijoux, 6 vols., Vol. 3. Eun-Ha, Jo. rev. ed. 2004. 200p. pap. 14.99 *(978-1-59182-692-7(6),* Tokyopop Adult) TOKYOPOP, Inc.
Sangha Mitra, Ms Janice. Golden Bear: The Story of a Flowering Heart. Sangha Mitra, Ms Janice. 4th ed. 2013. (ENG.). 38p. pap. *(978-0-9805945-2-9(9))* Little Bear Values.

SanGiacomo, Scott. All about Castles. Duke, Nell K. et al. 2016. 32p. (J). *(978-0-87659-687-6(1))* Gryphon Hse., Inc.
—Tucker the Turtle Takes Time to Tuck & Think. Lentini, Rochelle et al. 2016. 16p. (J). pap. *(978-0-87659-705-7(3))* Gryphon Hse., Inc.
Sangngg. The Adventures of Derby & Charlie: Derby & Charlie Go to the Beach-The Power of Influence. Twede, Shane K. 2018. (Adventures of Derby & Charlie Ser.: Vol. 1). (ENG.). 32p. (J). (gr. k-3). 19.99 *(978-0-578-40186-7(X))* Kory Industries.
—The Adventures of Derby & Charlie: Derby & Charlie Go to the Beach-The Power of Influence. Twede, Shane K. 2018. (Adventures of Derby & Charlie Ser.: Vol. 1). (ENG.). 32p. (J). (gr. k-3). pap. 13.99 *(978-0-578-42596-2(3))* Kory Industries.
Sangregorio, Fernando, et al. Pictodiccionario: Diccionario en Im Genes. Santillana. 2003.Tr. of Child's First Spanish Dictionary. (SPA.). 144p. (gr. k-3). 29.95 *(978-1-58105-973-1(6),* Santillana) Santillana USA Publishing Co., Inc.
Sankaranarayanan, Ayswarya. The Story & the Song. Subramaniam, Manasi. 2013. (ENG.). 32p. (J). (gr. k). pap. 9.95 *(978-81-8190-273-3(4))* Karadi Tales Co. Pvt, Ltd. IND. Dist: Consortium Bk. Sales & Distribution.
Sankey, Tom. Camilla Gryski's Favorite String Games. Gryski, Camilla. 2005. 48p. *(978-0-439-77939-5(1))* Scholastic, Inc.
Sanna, Alessandro. Castle of Books. 2020. (ENG.). 48p. (J). (gr. -1-17). 17.95 *(978-1-84976-668-5(1))* Tate Publishing, Ltd. GBR. Dist: Hachette Bk. Group.
—Pinocchio: The Origin Story. 2016. 48p. (J). (gr. k-9). 19.95 *(978-1-59270-191-9(4))* Enchanted Lion Bks., LLC.
Sanna, Guillermo. Bullseye: the Colombian Connection. 2017. (ENG.). 120p. (YA). (gr. 8-17). pap. 15.99 *(978-1-302-90509-5(0))* Marvel Worldwide, Inc.
Sanna, Guillermo, jt. illus. see Blake, Nelson.
Sanne, Don. Lighthouse Mouse Meets Simon the Cat. Coons, Susan Anderson. 2012. 52p. pap. 10.03 *(978-1-4669-1223-6(5))* Trafford Publishing.
Sanregre Pelegrin, Ledys. El Se�or Big Eyes. Rebull Leon, Loreley. 2019. (SPA.). 44p. (J). pap. 22.50 ***(978-1-6985-7451-6(7))*** Independently Published.
Sans, Claparo. Arcadia's Ignoble Knight, Volume 3: The Sorceress' Knight's Tournament Part I. Varnell, Brandon. 2018. (Arcadia's Ignoble Knight Ser.: Vol. 3). (ENG.). 266p. (YA). (gr. 7-12). pap. 14.00 *(978-0-9978028-6-3(3))* Kitsune Inc.
—Arcadia's Ignoble Knight, Volume 4:: the Sorceress' Knight's Tournament Part II. Varnell, Brandon. 2018. (Arcadia's Ignoble Knight Ser.: Vol. 4). (ENG.). 312p. (YA). (gr. 7-12). pap. 14.00 *(978-0-9978028-8-7(X))* Kitsune Inc.
Sansevero, Tony. Just for Now: Kids & the People of the Court. Morris, Kimberly & Burke, Kathleen. 2007. 48p. (J). (gr. k-4). 16.95 *(978-0-9754953-9-1(9))* Child Advocates, Inc.
—Short Boat on a Long River. Cockrum, James L. 2013. 180p. (YA). pap. 14.95 *(978-0-9768586-1-4(4))* Pangloss Publishing.
—The World According to Rock. Wermund, Jerry. 2005. 48p. (J). pap. *(978-0-9726255-1-7(8))* Rockon Publishing.
Sansó, Bárbara. Camino de Plata: Poesía para Niños. Rincón, Gilda. 2018. (SPA.). 128p. (J). (— 1). pap. 18.00 *(978-607-8469-42-0(8))* Nostra Ediciones MEX. Dist: Independent Pubs. Group.
Sansom, Fiona. Egyptian Myths. Elgin, Kathy. 2009. (Myths from Many Lands Ser.). 48p. (YA). (gr. 2-6). pap. 12.85 *(978-1-60754-222-3(6));* (gr. 4-7). 32.25 *(978-1-60754-221-6(8))* Windmill Bks.
—Greek Myths. Claybourne, Anna. 2009. (Myths from Many Lands Ser.). 48p. (YA). (gr. 2-6). pap. 12.85 *(978-1-60754-225-4(0));* (gr. 4-7). 32.25 *(978-1-60754-224-7(2))* Windmill Bks.
—Roman Myths. Elgin, Kathy. 2009. (Myths from Many Lands Ser.). 48p. (YA). (gr. 2-6). pap. 12.85 *(978-1-60754-231-5(5));* (J). (gr. 4-7). 32.25 *(978-1-60754-230-8(7))* Windmill Bks.
Sansom, Fiona & Kennedy, Graham. African Myths. Morris, Neil. 2009. (Myths from Many Lands Ser.). 48p. (YA). (gr. 4-7). 32.25 *(978-1-60754-215-5(3))* Windmill Bks.
Sansom, Fiona, jt. illus. see Mims, Ashley.
Sanson, Rachel. The Cat Who Ruled the Town. Nakamura, May. 2019. (Tails from History Ser.). (ENG.). 32p. (J). (gr. k-2). 17.99 *(978-1-5344-3643-5(X));* pap. 4.99 *(978-1-5344-3642-8(1))* Simon Spotlight. (Simon Spotlight).
—A Parrot in the Painting: The Story of Frida Kahlo & Bonito. Feldman, Thea. 2018. (Tails from History Ser.). (ENG.). 32p. (J). (gr. k-2). 17.99 *(978-1-5344-2230-8(7));* pap. 4.99 *(978-1-5344-2229-2(3))* Simon Spotlight. (Simon Spotlight).
—A Pony with Her Writer: The Story of Marguerite Henry & Misty. Feldman, Thea. 2019. (Tails from History Ser.). (ENG.). 32p. (J). (gr. k-2). 17.99 *(978-1-5344-5154-4(4));* pap. 4.99 *(978-1-5344-5153-7(6))* Simon Spotlight. (Simon Spotlight).
—A Puppy for Helen Keller. Nakamura, May. 2018. (Tails from History Ser.). (ENG.). 32p. (J). (gr. k-2). 17.99 *(978-1-5344-2910-9(7));* pap. 4.99 *(978-1-5344-2909-3(3))* Simon Spotlight. (Simon Spotlight).
—A Raccoon at the White House. Dougherty, Rachel. 2018. (Tails from History Ser.). (ENG.). 32p. (J). (gr. k-2). 17.99 *(978-1-5344-0542-4(9));* pap. 4.99 *(978-1-5344-0541-7(0))* Simon Spotlight. (Simon Spotlight).
—A Sea Otter to the Rescue. Feldman, Thea. 2019. (Tails from History Ser.). (ENG.). 32p. (J). (gr. k-2). pap. 4.99 *(978-1-5344-4337-2(1),* Simon Spotlight) Simon Spotlight.
—Tails from History Collection: A Raccoon at the White House; a Parrot in the Painting; a Puppy for Helen Keller; the Cat Who Ruled the Town; a Sea Otter to the Rescue; a Pony with Her Writer. ed. 2019. (Tails from History Ser.). (ENG.). 192p. (J). (gr. k-2). pap. 17.99 *(978-1-5344-5324-1(5),* Simon Spotlight) Simon Spotlight.

Santa, Carlos Piedra. Los Animales Mensajeros. 2010. (SPA.). 16p. (J). (gr. -1-1). 10.95 *(978-99922-1-358-2(2))* Piedra Santa, Editorial GTM. Dist: Libros Sin Fronteras.
—Zico Perico. Zea, Amilcar. 2009. (SPA.). 16p. (J). (gr. -1-1). pap. 7.95 *(978-99922-1-345-2(0))* Piedra Santa, Editorial GTM. Dist: Libros Sin Fronteras.
Santacruz, Juan. Ego: The Loving Planet. Parker, Jeff. 2012. (Avengers Ser.). (ENG.). 24p. (J). (gr. 2-6). lib. bdg. 27.07 *(978-1-61479-014-3(0),* 33, Marvel Age) Spotlight.
—High Serpent Society. Parker, Jeff. 2012. (Avengers Ser.). (ENG.). 24p. (J). (gr. 2-6). lib. bdg. 27.07 *(978-1-61479-015-0(9),* 34, Marvel Age) Spotlight.
—The Hulks Take Manhattan. Benjamin, Paul. 2008. (Hulk Ser.: No. 2). (ENG.). 24p. (J). (gr. 2-6). 27.07 *(978-1-59961-546-2(0),* 9674, Marvel Age) Spotlight.
—Medieval Women. Parker, Jeff. 2012. (Avengers Ser.). (ENG.). 24p. (J). (gr. 2-6). lib. bdg. 27.07 *(978-1-61479-016-7(7),* 35, Marvel Age) Spotlight.
—A Not-So-Beautiful Mind. Parker, Jeff. 2012. (Avengers Ser.). (ENG.). 24p. (J). (gr. 2-6). lib. bdg. 27.07 *(978-1-61479-017-4(5),* 36, Marvel Age) Spotlight.
Santacruz, Juan & Fernandez, Raul. Doom, Where's My Car?! Parker, Jeff. 2007. (Fantastic Four Ser.: No. 2). (ENG.). 24p. (J). (gr. 2-6). lib. bdg. 27.07 *(978-1-59961-389-5(1),* 7227, Marvel Age) Spotlight.
Santana, Andrea. Los Gatos en la Luna/the Cats on the Moon. Castelli, Jeanette. 2005. (Bilingual Collection). (SPA.). 51p. (J). (gr. k-2). *(978-958-30-1767-4(1))* Panamericana Editorial.
Santana, Julia & Graham, Noelle. Cavernesia. 2019. (Keepers & Apprentices Ser.: Vol. 3). (ENG.). 204p. (J). pap. 10.00 *(978-1-0795-8775-3(6))* Independently Published.
Santanach, Tino. Jocelyn's Box of Socks, 1 vol. Jackson, Kristen L. 2019. (ENG.). 48p. (J). 16.99 *(978-0-7643-5693-3(3),* 9878) Schiffer Publishing, Ltd.
—The Mask of Power, 1. Beakman, Onk. 2013. (Skylanders Universe: Mask of Power Ser.). (ENG.). 160p. (J). (gr. 4-6). 18.69 *(978-0-448-46355-1(5))* Penguin Young Readers Group.
Santanach, Tino, et al. Nickelodeon. PI Kids. 2020. (My First Smart Pad Ser.). (ENG.). 192p. (J). ***(978-1-5037-5268-9(2),*** 5a00c6c8-084b-4ec7-aa64-27e7e56dbad3, p i kids) Phoenix International Publications, Inc.
Santat, Dan. The Adventures of Nanny Piggins. Spratt, R. A. 2012. (Nanny Piggins Ser.: 1). (ENG.). 272p. (J). (gr. 3-7). pap. 8.99 *(978-0-316-06818-5(7))* Little, Brown Bks. for Young Readers.
—The Adventures of Nanny Piggins. Spratt, R. A. 2012. (Nanny Piggins Ser.). (ENG.). (J). (gr. 3-7). lib. bdg. 17.60 *(978-1-61383-289-9(3))* Perfection Learning Corp.
—Because I'm Your Dad. Zappa, Ahmet. 2013. 32p. (J). (gr. -1-k). 15.99 *(978-1-4231-4774-9(X))* Disney Pr.
Santat, Dan. Because I'm Your Dad. Zappa, Ahmet. 2016. (ENG.). 32p. (J). (gr. -1-k). bds. 7.99 ***(978-1-4847-2661-7(8))*** Little, Brown Bks. for Young Readers.
Santat, Dan. Bobby the Brave (Sometimes) Yee, Lisa. 2012. (ENG.). 160p. (J). (gr. 2-5). pap. 5.99 *(978-0-545-05595-6(4),* Levine, Arthur A. Bks.) Scholastic, Inc.
—Bobby vs. Girls (Accidentally) Yee, Lisa. 2010. (ENG.). 176p. (J). (gr. 2-5). pap. 5.99 *(978-0-545-05593-2(8),* Levine, Arthur A. Bks.) Scholastic, Inc.
—Born to Drive. Perlman, Rhea. 2006. (Otto Undercover Ser.). 127p. (J). (gr. 4-7). 14.99 *(978-0-06-075496-9(6),* Tegen, Katherine Bks) HarperCollins Pubs.
—Canyon Catastrophe. Perlman, Rhea. 2006. (Otto Undercover Ser.). 128p. (J). (gr. 4-7). 14.99 *(978-0-06-075498-3(2))* HarperCollins Pubs.
—Carnivores. Reynolds, Aaron. 2013. (ENG.). 40p. (J). (gr. -1-3). 16.99 *(978-0-8118-6690-3(4))* Chronicle Bks. LLC.
—Chicken Dance. Sauer, Tammi. 2015. (ENG.). 40p. (J). (gr. -1-2). pap. 6.95 *(978-1-4549-1477-8(7))* Sterling Publishing Co., Inc.
—The Christmas Genie. Gutman, Dan. (ENG.). (J). (gr. 3-7). 2010. 176p. pap. 7.99 *(978-1-4169-9002-4(X));* 2009. 160p. 16.99 *(978-1-4169-9001-7(1))* Simon & Schuster Bks. For Young Readers. (Simon & Schuster Bks. For Young Readers).
—Crankenstein. Berger, Samantha. 2013. 40p. (J). (gr. -1-3). 17.99 *(978-0-316-12656-4(X))* Little Brown & Co.
—Crankenstein. Berger, Samantha. 2014. 24p. (J). (gr. -1 — 1). bds. 8.99 *(978-0-316-28232-1(4))* Little, Brown Bks. for Young Readers.
—A Crankenstein Valentine. Berger, Samantha. 2014. 48p. (J). (gr. -1-3). 17.99 *(978-0-316-37638-9(8))* Little, Brown Bks. for Young Readers.
—Dad & the Dinosaur. Choldenko, Gennifer. 2017. (ENG.). 40p. (J). (gr. k-3). 17.99 *(978-0-399-24353-0(4),* G.P. Putnam's Sons Books for Young Readers) Penguin Young Readers Group.
—Dog in Charge. Going, K. L. 2012. (ENG.). 40p. (J). (gr. -1-k). 16.99 *(978-0-8037-3479-1(4),* Dial Bks) Penguin Young Readers Group.
—Dude! Reynolds, Aaron. 2018. (ENG.). 40p. (J). 17.99 *(978-1-62672-603-1(5),* 900162895) Roaring Brook Pr.
—Dylan's Pets from A to Z. Marsoli, Lisa Ann. 2005. (J). bds. 14.99 *(978-0-9767325-1-8(3))* Toy Quest.
—The Fairy Swarm. Selfors, Suzanne. 2016. (Imaginary Veterinary Ser.: 6). (ENG.). 240p. (J). (gr. 2-7). pap. 7.99 *(978-0-316-28692-3(3))* Little, Brown Bks. for Young Readers.
—Fluffy Bunnies 2: The Schnoz of Doom. Beaty, Andrea. 2015. (Fluffy Bunnies Ser.). (ENG.). 192p. (J). (gr. 3-7). 12.95 *(978-1-4197-1051-3(6),* Amulet Bks.) Abrams, Inc.
—The Ghosts of Luckless Gulch. Isaacs, Anne. 2008. (ENG.). 48p. (J). (gr. k-3). 18.99 *(978-1-4169-0201-0(5),* Atheneum Bks. for Young Readers) Simon & Schuster Children's Publishing.
—The Great Santa Stakeout. Bird, Betsy. 2019. (ENG.). 40p. (J). (gr. -1-3). 17.99 *(978-1-338-16998-0(X),* Levine, Arthur A. Bks.) Scholastic, Inc.

—The Grimm Conclusion. Gidwitz, Adam. 2014. (ENG.). 384p. (J). (gr. 5). pap. 8.99 *(978-0-14-242736-1(5)*, Puffin Books) Penguin Young Readers Group.

—Guys Read: the Sports Pages. Scieszka, Jon et al. 2012. (Guys Read Ser.: 3). (ENG.). 272p. (J). (gr. 3-7). 16.99 *(978-0-06-196378-0(X))*; pap. 7.99 *(978-0-06-196377-3(1))* HarperCollins Pubs. (Waldon Pond Pr.).

—Hensel & Gretel, Ninja Chicks. Schwartz, Corey Rosen & Gomez, Rebecca J. 2016. (ENG.). 40p. (J). (gr. k-3). 17.99 *(978-0-399-17626-5(8)*, G.P. Putnam's Sons Books for Young Readers) Penguin Young Readers Group.

—In a Glass Grimmly. Gidwitz, Adam. 2013. (ENG.). 352p. (J). (gr. 5). pap. 8.99 *(978-0-14-242506-0(0)*, Puffin Books) Penguin Young Readers Group.

—Jurassic Jackrabbits from Jupiter. Pilkey, Dav. 2014. (Ricky Ricotta's Mighty Robot Ser.: 5). (ENG.). 128p. (J). (gr. -1-3). pap. 5.99 *(978-0-545-63013-9(4))* Scholastic, Inc.

—Lift. Lê, Minh. 2020. 56p. (J). (gr. -1-3). 17.99 *(978-1-368-03692-4(9))* Hyperion Bks. for Children.

—Lions & Liars. Beasley, Kate. 2018. (ENG.). 304p. (J). 16.99 *(978-0-374-30263-4(4)*, 900148156, Farrar, Straus & Giroux (BYR)) Farrar, Straus & Giroux.

—Lions & Liars. Beasley, Kate. 2019. (ENG.). 304p. (J). pap. 7.99 *(978-1-250-30851-1(8)*, 900198365) Square Fish.

—The Little Engine That Could: 90th Anniversary Edition. Piper, Watty. 2020. (Little Engine That Could Ser.). 48p. (J). (gr. -1-2). 18.99 *(978-0-593-09439-6(5)*, Grosset & Dunlap) Penguin Young Readers Group.

Santat, Dan. Little Fox & the Wild Imagination. Taccone, Jorma. 2020. (ENG.). 40p. (J). 18.99 ***(978-1-250-21250-4(2)***, 900203735) Roaring Brook Pr.

Santat, Dan. The Lonely Lake Monster. Selfors, Suzanne. 2014. (Imaginary Veterinary Ser.: 2). (ENG.). 240p. (J). (gr. 2-7). pap. 7.99 *(978-0-316-22561-8(4))* Little, Brown Bks. for Young Readers.

—Mighty Robot vs. the Mecha-Monkeys from Mars. Pilkey, Dav. 2014. (Ricky Ricotta's Mighty Robot Ser.: 4). (ENG.). 144p. (J). (gr. -1-3). pap. 5.99 *(978-0-545-63012-2(6))* Scholastic, Inc.

—Mighty Robot vs. the Mutant Mosquitoes from Mercury. Pilkey, Dav. 2014. (Ricky Ricotta's Mighty Robot Ser.: 2). (ENG.). 128p. (J). (gr. -1-3). pap. 5.99 *(978-0-545-63010-8(X))* Scholastic, Inc.

—Mighty Robot vs. the Naughty Nightcrawlers from Neptune. Pilkey, Dav. 2016. (Ricky Ricotta's Mighty Robot Ser.: 8). (ENG.). 128p. (J). (gr. -1-3). 15.99 *(978-0-439-37708-9(0))* Scholastic, Inc.

—Mighty Robot vs. the Stupid Stinkbugs from Saturn. 2015. (Ricky Ricotta's Mighty Robot Ser.: 6). (ENG.). 128p. (J). (gr. -1-3). 15.99 *(978-0-545-63121-1(1))* Scholastic, Inc.

—Ninja Red Riding Hood. Schwartz, Corey Rosen. 2014. (ENG.). 40p. (J). (gr. k-3). 17.99 *(978-0-399-16354-8(9)*, G.P. Putnam's Sons Books for Young Readers) Penguin Young Readers Group.

—Oh No! Or How My Science Project Destroyed the World. Barnett, Mac. 2010. 40p. (J). (gr. -1-2). 16.99 *(978-1-4231-2312-5(3))* Hyperion Pr.

—Oh No! Not Again! (or How I Built a Time Machine to Save History) (or at Least My History Grade) Barnett, Mac. 2012. (Oh No! Picture Book Ser.). 40p. (J). (gr. -1-k). 17.99 *(978-1-4231-4912-5(2))* Hyperion Pr.

—The Order of the Unicorn. Selfors, Suzanne. 2014. (ENG.). 208p. (J). E-Book *(978-0-316-32339-0(X))* Little Brown & Co.

—The Order of the Unicorn. Selfors, Suzanne. 2014. (Imaginary Veterinary Ser.: 4). 208p. (J). (gr. 2-7). 25.00 *(978-0-316-36406-5(1))* Little, Brown Bks. for Young Readers.

—The Perfect School Picture. Diesen, Deborah. 2019. (ENG.). 32p. (J). (gr. k-2). pap. 4.99 *(978-1-4197-3509-7(8)*, Abrams Bks. for Young Readers) Abrams, Inc.

—Picture Day Perfection. Diesen, Deborah. 2013. (ENG.). 32p. (J). (gr. -1-3). 17.95 *(978-1-4197-0844-2(9)*, Abrams Bks. for Young Readers) Abrams, Inc.

—The Princess & the Pit Stop. Angleberger, Tom. 2018. (ENG.). 48p. (J). (gr. k-2). 16.99 *(978-1-4197-2848-8(2)*, Abrams Bks. for Young Readers) Abrams, Inc.

—Ricky Ricotta's Mighty Robot. Pilkey, Dav. 2014. (Ricky Ricotta's Mighty Robot Ser.: 1). (ENG.). 112p. (J). (gr. -1-3). pap. 5.99 *(978-0-545-63009-2(6))*; lib. bdg. 15.99 *(978-0-545-63106-8(8))* Scholastic, Inc.

—Ricky Ricotta's Mighty Robot vs. the Naughty Nightcrawlers from Neptune. Pilkey, Dav. 2016. (Ricky Ricotta's Mighty Robot Ser.: 8). 128p. (J). (gr. -1-3). pap. 5.99 *(978-0-439-37709-6(9))* Scholastic, Inc.

—Ricky Ricotta's Mighty Robot vs. the Unpleasant Penguins from Pluto. Pilkey, Dav. 2016. (Ricky Ricotta's Mighty Robot Ser.: 9). (ENG.). 128p. (J). (gr. -1-3). 15.99 *(978-0-545-63016-0(9))* Scholastic, Inc.

—Ricky Ricotta's Mighty Robot vs. the Video Vultures from Venus. Pilkey, Dav. 2014. (Ricky Ricotta's Mighty Robot Ser.: 3). (ENG.). 128p. (J). (gr. -1-3). pap. 5.99 *(978-0-545-63011-5(8))* Scholastic, Inc.

—Rodzilla. Sanders, Rob. (ENG.). 48p. (J). (gr. -1-3). 2019. 7.99 *(978-1-5344-6692-0(4))*; 2017. 17.99 *(978-1-4814-5779-8(9))* McElderry, Margaret K. Bks. (McElderry, Margaret K. Bks.).

—The Sasquatch Escape. Selfors, Suzanne. 2014. (Imaginary Veterinary Ser.: 1). (ENG.). 240p. (J). (gr. 2-7). pap. 7.99 *(978-0-316-22569-4(X))* Little, Brown Bks. for Young Readers.

—Stupid Stinkbugs from Saturn. 2015. (Ricky Ricotta's Mighty Robot Ser.: 6). (ENG.). 128p. (J). (gr. -1-3). pap. 5.99 *(978-0-545-63014-6(2))* Scholastic, Inc.

—A Tale Dark & Grimm. Gidwitz, Adam. 2011. (ENG.). 288p. (J). (gr. 5-18). 8.99 *(978-0-14-241967-0(2)*, Puffin Books) Penguin Young Readers Group.

—The Three Ninja Pigs. Schwartz, Corey Rosen. 2012. (ENG.). 40p. (J). (gr. k-3). 17.99 *(978-0-399-25514-4(1)*, G.P. Putnam's Sons Books for Young Readers) Penguin Young Readers Group.

—Water Balloon Doom. Perlman, Rhea. 2006. (Otto Undercover Ser.: No. 3). 124p. (J). (gr. 2-6). 14.99 *(978-0-06-075500-3(8)*, Tegen, Katherine Bks) HarperCollins Pubs.

Santat, Dan. After the Fall (How Humpty Dumpty Got Back up Again) Santat, Dan. 2017. (ENG.). 40p. (J). 17.99 *(978-1-62672-682-6(5)*, 900170544) Roaring Brook Pr.

—Sidekicks. Santat, Dan. 2011. 224p. (J). (gr. 3-7). pap. 12.99 *(978-0-439-29819-3(9)*, Levine, Arthur A. Bks.) Scholastic, Inc.

Santat, Dan & Willems, Mo. The Cookie Fiasco (Elephant & Piggie Like Reading!) Santat, Dan & Willems, Mo. 2016. (Elephant & Piggie Like Reading! Ser.: 1). (ENG.). 64p. (J). (gr. 1-3). 9.99 *(978-1-4847-2636-5(7))* Hyperion Bks. for Children.

Santat, Dan, jt. illus. see Dantat, Dan.

Santiago McNeill, Lisa. Beyond the Shell: Finding You Beyond What Protects You. Brown, William. 2019. (Finding You Beyond What Protects You Ser.: Vol. 1). (ENG.). 26p. (J). pap. 14.95 *(978-1-0903-4171-6(7))* Independently Published.

—The Magical Christmas Tree. O'Banion, Sammy. 2018. (ENG.). 30p. (J). pap. 14.95 *(978-1-7907-2390-4(6))* Independently Published.

Santiago, Rose Mary. The Clever Boy & a Terrible, Dangerous Animal: English-Dari Edition. Shah, Idries. 2017. (Hoopoe Teaching-Stories Ser.). (ENG.). (J). (gr. k-6). pap. 9.99 *(978-1-946270-10-8(5)*, Hoopoe Bks.) I S H K.

—The Clever Boy & the Terrible, Dangerous Animal. Shah, Idries. 2005. 32p. (J). (gr. -1 — 1). pap. 6.99 *(978-1-883536-51-0(0)*, Hoopoe Bks.) I S H K.

—The Clever Boy & the Terrible Dangerous Animal: English-Pashto Edition. Shah, Idries. 2017. (Hoopoe Teaching-Stories Ser.). (ENG.). (J). (gr. 1-6). pap. 9.99 *(978-1-944493-55-4(7)*, Hoopoe Bks.) I S H K.

—The Clever Boy & the Terrible, Dangerous Animal/el Muchachito Listo y el Terrible y Peligroso Animal. Shah, Idries. Wirkala, Rita, tr. 2005. 32p. (J). (gr. -1-3). 18.00 *(978-1-883536-39-8(1))*; pap., per. 6.95 *(978-1-883536-40-4(5))* I S H K. (Hoopoe Bks.).

—The Farmer's Wife. Shah, Idries. 2005. 32p. (J). (gr. -1-3). pap., pap. 6.99 *(978-1-883536-49-7(9)*, Hoopoe Bks.) I S H K.

—The Farmer's Wife: English-Dari Edition. Shah, Idries. 2017. (ENG.). (J). (gr. k-6). pap. 9.99 *(978-1-946270-17-7(2)*, Hoopoe Bks.) I S H K.

—The Farmer's Wife: English-Pashto Edition. Shah, Idries. 2017. (Hoopoe Teaching-Stories Ser.). (ENG & PUS.). (J). (gr. k-6). pap. 9.99 *(978-1-944493-62-2(X)*, Hoopoe Bks.) I S H K.

—The Farmer's Wife: English-Urdu Bilingual Edition. Shah, Idries. 2016. (URD & ENG.). (J). (gr. k-6). pap. 9.99 *(978-1-942698-80-7(1)*, Hoopoe Bks.) I S H K.

—The Farmer's Wife HB/CD Combo English. Shah, Idries. 2005. (Sounds of Afghanistan Ser.). 32p. (J). (gr. -1-3). 28.95 incl. audio compact disk *(978-1-883536-67-1(7)*, FAWCB1, Hoopoe Bks.) I S H K.

—The Farmer's Wife (la Esposa Del Granjero) PB/CD Combo Bilingual. Shah, Idries. 2005. (ENG & SPA.). (J). (gr. -1-18). pap. 18.95 incl. audio compact disk *(978-1-883536-70-1(7)*, FAWCB4, Hoopoe Bks.) I S H K.

—The Farmer's Wife/la Esposa Del Granjero. Shah, Indries. 2003. (SPA & ENG.). (J). 6.95 *(978-1-883536-34-3(0)*, FAWI3, Hoopoe Bks.) I S H K.

—The Farmer's Wife/la Esposa Del Granjero. Shah, Idries. 2003. (SPA & ENG.). (J). 18.00 *(978-1-883536-33-6(2)*, FAWI2, Hoopoe Bks.) I S H K.

—The Farmer's Wife/la Esposa Del Granjero HB/CD Combo Bilingual. Shah, Idries. de Gonzales, Angelica Villagran, tr. 2005. (ENG & SPA.). 32p. (J). (gr. 4-7). 28.95 incl. audio compact disk *(978-1-883536-69-5(3)*, FAWCB3, Hoopoe Bks.) I S H K.

Santiago, Rose Mary. La Femme du Fermier: French-Arabic Edition. Shah, Idries. 2018. (Hoopoe Teaching-Stories Ser.). (FRE.). 40p. (J). (gr. k). pap. 9.99 ***(978-1-949358-45-2(3)***, Hoopoe Bks.) I S H K.

Santiago, Rose Mary. The Man with Bad Manners HB/CD Combo English. Shah, Idries. 2005. (Sounds of Afghanistan Ser.). (J). (gr. -1-3). 28.95 incl. audio compact disk *(978-1-883536-75-6(8)*, Hoopoe Bks.) I S H K.

Santiago, Rose Mary. Le Petit Gar�on Intelligent et la Terrible et Dangereuse B�te: French-Arabic Edition. Shah, Idries. 2018. (Hoopoe Teaching-Stories Ser.). (FRE.). 40p. (J). (gr. k-2). pap. 9.99 ***(978-1-949358-43-8(7)***, Hoopoe Bks.) I S H K.

Santiago, Rose Mary. The Man with Bad Manners. Santiago, Rose Mary, tr. Shah, Idries. 2003. 32p. (J). 18.00 *(978-1-883536-30-5(8)*, MABM1, Hoopoe Bks.) I S H K.

Santiago, Tony. A Greyhound's Tale: Running for Glory, Walking for Home. 2006. 40p. (J). 15.00 *(978-0-9762564-2-7(8))* Ideate Prairie.

—A Greyhound's Tale: Running for Glory, Walking for Home. Pierce, Craig. 2004. (J). per. 15.00 *(978-0-9762564-0-3(1)*, American Dog) Ideate Prairie.

—A Labrador's Tale: An Eye for Heroism. Pierce, Craig. 2006. 30p. (J). 15.00 *(978-0-9762564-3-4(6)*, American Dog) Ideate Prairie.

—A Labrador's Tale 2: The Incredible Thank You Gift, 1. Pierce, Craig. 2006. 34p. (J). 15.00 *(978-0-9762564-4-1(4)*, 2500, American Dog) Ideate Prairie.

—Sit. Stay. Work. Play: All Dogs Have Their Day. Pierce, Craig. 2008. 40p. (J). per. 5.95 *(978-0-9762564-5-8(2))* Ideate Prairie.

Santiago, Weberson. Old Man of the Sea. Elia, Stella. 2019. 40p. (J). (gr. k-2). 17.99 *(978-1-911373-54-4(4))* Lantana Publishing GBR. Dist: Lerner Publishing Group.

Santillan, Jorge. Alphabet of Music. Schwaeber, Barbie Heit. 2008. (ENG.). 40p. (J). (gr. k-2). 15.95 *(978-1-59249-770-6(5))* Soundprints.

—Drawing Baby Animals. Eason, Sarah. 2013. (Learn to Draw Ser.). 32p. (J). (gr. 2-5). pap. 63.00 *(978-1-4339-9526-2(3))* Stevens, Gareth Publishing LLLP.

—Drawing Dinosaurs. Eason, Sarah. 2013. (Learn to Draw Ser.). 32p. (J). (gr. 2-5). pap. 63.00 *(978-1-4339-9530-9(1))*; pap. 10.50 *(978-1-4339-9529-3(8))* Stevens, Gareth Publishing LLLP.

—Drawing Dragons. Eason, Sarah. 2013. (Learn to Draw Ser.). 32p. (J). (gr. 2-5). pap. 63.00 *(978-1-4339-9534-7(4))*; pap. 10.50 *(978-1-4339-9533-0(6))* Stevens, Gareth Publishing LLLP.

—Drawing Fairies, Mermaids, & Unicorns. Eason, Sarah. 2013. (Learn to Draw Ser.). 32p. (J). (gr. 2-5). pap. 63.00 *(978-1-4339-9538-5(7))*; pap. 10.50 *(978-1-4339-9537-8(9))* Stevens, Gareth Publishing LLLP.

—Drawing Knights & Castles. Eason, Sarah. 2013. (Learn to Draw Ser.). 32p. (J). (gr. 2-5). pap. 63.00 *(978-1-4339-9542-2(5))*; pap. 10.50 *(978-1-4339-9541-5(7))* Stevens, Gareth Publishing LLLP.

—Drawing Pirates & Pirate Ships. Eason, Sarah. 2013. (Learn to Draw Ser.). 32p. (J). (gr. 2-5). pap. 63.00 *(978-1-4339-9546-0(8))*; pap. 10.50 *(978-1-4339-9545-3(X))* Stevens, Gareth Publishing LLLP.

—Learn to Draw. Eason, Sarah. 2013. (Learn to Draw Ser.). 32p. (J). (gr. 2-5). 159.60 *(978-1-4339-9682-5(0))* Stevens, Gareth Publishing LLLP.

Santillan, Jorge & Clark, Debbie. Alphabet of Music. Schwaeber, Barbie Heit. 2011. (Alphabet Bks.). (ENG.). 40p. (J). (gr. -1-3). 9.95 *(978-1-60727-445-2(0))* Soundprints.

Santillan, Jorge H. Beach Volleyball Is No Joke, 1 vol. Yasuda, Anita. 2011. (Sports Illustrated Kids Victory School Superstars Ser.). (ENG.). 56p. (J). (gr. 1-3). pap. 5.95 *(978-1-4342-3393-6(6)*, Stone Arch Bks.) Capstone.

—Cheerleading Really Is a Sport, 1 vol. Gassman, Julie A. 2010. (Sports Illustrated Kids Victory School Superstars Ser.). (ENG.). 56p. (J). (gr. 1-3). 26.65 *(978-1-4342-2130-8(X))*; pap. 5.95 *(978-1-4342-2809-3(6))* Capstone. (Stone Arch Bks.).

—Don't Break the Balance Beam!, 1 vol. Gunderson, Jessica. 2010. (Sports Illustrated Kids Victory School Superstars Ser.). (ENG.). 56p. (J). (gr. 1-3). 26.65 *(978-1-4342-2057-8(5))*; pap. 5.95 *(978-1-4342-2807-9(X))* Capstone. (Stone Arch Bks.).

—Five Fouls & You're Out!, 1 vol. Priebe, Val. 2011. (Sports Illustrated Kids Victory School Superstars Ser.). (ENG.). 56p. (J). (gr. 1-3). pap. 5.95 *(978-1-4342-3075-1(9))*; lib. bdg. 26.65 *(978-1-4342-2228-2(4))* Capstone. (Stone Arch Bks.).

—I Am on Strike Against Softball, 1 vol. Gassman, Julie A. 2012. (Sports Illustrated Kids Victory School Superstars Ser.). (ENG.). 56p. (J). (gr. 1-3). pap. 5.95 *(978-1-4342-3870-2(9))*; lib. bdg. 26.65 *(978-1-4342-2247-3(0))* Capstone. (Stone Arch Bks.).

—I Broke into Gymnastics Camp, 1 vol. Gunderson, Jessica. 2012. (Sports Illustrated Kids Victory School Superstars Ser.). (ENG.). 56p. (J). (gr. 1-3). pap. 5.95 *(978-1-4342-3869-6(5))*; lib. bdg. 26.65 *(978-1-4342-2245-9(4))* Capstone. (Stone Arch Bks.).

—I Could Be a One-Man Relay, 1 vol. Nickel, Scott. 2012. (Sports Illustrated Kids Victory School Superstars Ser.). (ENG.). 56p. (J). (gr. 1-3). pap. 5.95 *(978-1-4342-3867-2(9))*; lib. bdg. 26.65 *(978-1-4342-2246-6(2))* Capstone. (Stone Arch Bks.).

—I Couldn't Land a Bunny Hop, 1 vol. Kreie, Chris. 2012. (Sports Illustrated Kids Victory School Superstars Ser.). (ENG.). 56p. (J). (gr. 1-3). pap. 5.95 *(978-1-4342-3865-8(2))*; lib. bdg. 26.65 *(978-1-4342-3762-0(1))* Capstone. (Stone Arch Bks.).

—I Don't Want to Live on the Tennis Court, 1 vol. Priebe, Val. 2012. (Sports Illustrated Kids Victory School Superstars Ser.). (ENG.). 56p. (J). (gr. 1-3). pap. 5.95 *(978-1-4342-3868-9(7))*; lib. bdg. 26.65 *(978-1-4342-3761-3(3))* Capstone. (Stone Arch Bks.).

—I Just Have to Ride the Halfpipe! Gunderson, Jessica. 2011. (Sports Illustrated Kids Victory School Superstars Ser.). (ENG.). 56p. (J). (gr. 1-3). pap. 5.95 *(978-1-4342-3397-4(9))*; lib. bdg. 26.65 *(978-1-4342-2236-7(5))* Capstone. (Stone Arch Bks.).

—I Only Surf Online, 1 vol. Priebe, Val. 2011. (Sports Illustrated Kids Victory School Superstars Ser.). (ENG.). 56p. (J). (gr. 1-3). pap. 5.95 *(978-1-4342-3394-3(4))*; lib. bdg. 26.65 *(978-1-4342-2233-6(0))* Capstone. (Stone Arch Bks.).

—It's a Wrestling Mat, Not a Dance Floor, 1 vol. Nickel, Scott. 2011. (Sports Illustrated Kids Victory School Superstars Ser.). (ENG.). 56p. (J). (gr. 1-3). lib. bdg. 26.65 *(978-1-4342-2227-5(6)*, Stone Arch Bks.) Capstone.

—It's Hard to Dribble with Your Feet, 1 vol. Priebe, Val. 2010. (Sports Illustrated Kids Victory School Superstars Ser.). (ENG.). 56p. (J). (gr. 1-3). 26.65 *(978-1-4342-2016-5(8))*; pap. 5.95 *(978-1-4342-2782-9(0))* Capstone. (Stone Arch Bks.).

—I've Got the No-Skateboard Blues, 1 vol. Yasuda, Anita. 2012. (Sports Illustrated Kids Victory School Superstars Ser.). (ENG.). 56p. (J). (gr. 1-3). pap. 5.95 *(978-1-4342-3866-5(0))*; lib. bdg. 26.65 *(978-1-4342-2244-2(6))* Capstone. (Stone Arch Bks.).

—Nobody Wants to Play with a Ball Hog, 1 vol. Gassman, Julie A. 2010. (Sports Illustrated Kids Victory School Superstars Ser.). (ENG.). 56p. (J). (gr. 1-3). 26.65 *(978-1-4342-2056-1(7))*; pap. 5.95 *(978-1-4342-2806-2(1))* Capstone. (Stone Arch Bks.).

—A Running Back Can't Always Rush, 1 vol. LeBoutillier, Nate. 2010. (Sports Illustrated Kids Victory School Superstars Ser.). (ENG.). 56p. (J). (gr. 1-3). 26.65 *(978-1-4342-2055-4(9))*; pap. 5.95 *(978-1-4342-2805-5(3))* Capstone. (Stone Arch Bks.).

—Skating Is Hard When You're Homesick, 1 vol. Gassman, Julie A. 2011. (Sports Illustrated Kids Victory School Superstars Ser.). (ENG.). 56p. (J). (gr. 1-3). pap. 5.95 *(978-1-4342-3398-1(7))*; lib. bdg. 26.65 *(978-1-4342-2237-4(3))* Capstone. (Stone Arch Bks.).

—Skiing Has Its Ups & Downs, 1 vol. Nickel, Scott. 2011. (Sports Illustrated Kids Victory School Superstars Ser.). (ENG.). 56p. (J). (gr. 1-3). pap. 5.95 *(978-1-4342-3395-0(2)*, Stone Arch Bks.) Capstone.

—There Are No Figure Eights in Hockey. Kreie, Chris. 2010. (Sports Illustrated Kids Victory School Superstars Ser.). (ENG.). 56p. (J). (gr. 1-3). pap. 5.95 *(978-1-4342-2808-6(8)*, Stone Arch Bks.) Capstone.

—There's a Hurricane in the Pool!, 1 vol. Gunderson, Jessica. 2011. (Sports Illustrated Kids Victory School Superstars Ser.). (ENG.). 56p. (J). (gr. 1-3). 26.65 *(978-1-4342-2230-5(6)*, Stone Arch Bks.) Capstone.

—There's No Crying in Baseball, 1 vol. Yasuda, Anita. 2011. (Sports Illustrated Kids Victory School Superstars Ser.). (ENG.). 56p. (J). (gr. 1-3). pap. 5.95 *(978-1-4342-3077-5(5))*; lib. bdg. 26.65 *(978-1-4342-2226-8(8))* Capstone. (Stone Arch Bks.).

—Who Wants to Play Just for Kicks?, 1 vol. Kreie, Chris. 2011. (Sports Illustrated Kids Victory School Superstars Ser.). (ENG.). 56p. (J). (gr. 1-3). pap. 5.95 *(978-1-4342-3079-9(1))*; lib. bdg. 26.65 *(978-1-4342-2229-9(2))* Capstone. (Stone Arch Bks.).

—You Can't Spike Your Serves, 1 vol. Gassman, Julie A. 2011. (Sports Illustrated Kids Victory School Superstars Ser.). (ENG.). 56p. (J). (gr. 1-3). pap. 5.95 *(978-1-4342-3080-5(5))*; lib. bdg. 26.65 *(978-1-4342-2231-2(4))* Capstone. (Stone Arch Bks.).

Santillan, Mariano. My Jewish Friend: A Young Catholic Learns about Judaism. Sirois, Celia. 2008. 47p. (J). (gr. 5-7). 15.95 *(978-0-8198-4857-4(3))* Pauline Bks. & Media.

—Trouble on the Blue Planet. Edison, Richard E. 2012. 47p. (J). 4.99 *(978-0-8280-2655-0(6))* Review & Herald Publishing Assn.

Santillanes, Alexander Vidal. So Many Feet. Mara, Nichole. 2017. (ENG.). 34p. (J). (gr. -1 — 1). bds. 12.95 *(978-1-4197-2318-6(9))* Abrams, Inc.

Santilli Wolfinger, Lorrie. Trouble in Treeville. Santilli, Shirley. 2013. 42p. 19.99 *(978-0-9910962-0-6(7))* Aperture Pr., LLC.

Santillo, LuAnn. At the Beach, 6 vols. Santillo, LuAnn. 2003. (Half-Pint Kids Readers Ser.). 42p. (J). (gr. -1-1). pap. 6.95 *(978-1-59256-084-4(9))* Half-Pint Kids, Inc.

—At the Circus, 6 vols. Santillo, LuAnn. 2003. (Half-Pint Kids Readers Ser.). 42p. (J). (gr. -1-1). pap. 6.95 *(978-1-59256-112-4(8))* Half-Pint Kids, Inc.

—The Bad Crab. Santillo, LuAnn. 2003. (Half-Pint Kids Readers Ser.). 7p. (J). (gr. -1-1). pap. 1.00 *(978-1-59256-094-3(6))* Half-Pint Kids, Inc.

—The Ball. Santillo, LuAnn. 2003. (Half-Pint Kids Readers Ser.). 7p. (J). (gr. -1-1). pap. 1.00 *(978-1-59256-081-3(4))* Half-Pint Kids, Inc.

—Barnyard Buddies, 6 vols. Santillo, LuAnn. 2003. (Half-Pint Kids Readers Ser.). 42p. (J). (gr. -1-1). pap. 6.95 *(978-1-59256-063-9(6))* Half-Pint Kids, Inc.

—Bee. Santillo, LuAnn. 2003. (Half-Pint Kids Readers Ser.). 7p. (J). (gr. -1-1). pap. *(978-1-59256-108-7(X))* Half-Pint Kids, Inc.

—The Best Show. Santillo, LuAnn. 2003. (Half-Pint Kids Readers Ser.). 7p. (J). (gr. -1-1). pap. 1.00 *(978-1-59256-117-9(9))* Half-Pint Kids, Inc.

—The Best Tricks. Santillo, LuAnn. 2003. (Half-Pint Kids Readers Ser.). 7p. (J). (gr. -1-1). pap. 1.00 *(978-1-59256-082-0(2))* Half-Pint Kids, Inc.

—The Big Hunt. Santillo, LuAnn. 2003. (Half-Pint Kids Readers Ser.). 7p. (J). (gr. -1-1). pap. 1.00 *(978-1-59256-076-9(8))* Half-Pint Kids, Inc.

—The Big Job. Santillo, LuAnn. 2003. (Half-Pint Kids Readers Ser.). 7p. (J). (gr. -1-1). pap. *(978-1-59256-044-8(X))* Half-Pint Kids, Inc.

—The Big Top. Santillo, LuAnn. 2003. (Half-Pint Kids Readers Ser.). 7p. (J). (gr. -1-1). pap. 1.00 *(978-1-59256-113-1(6))* Half-Pint Kids, Inc.

—Blends & Ends - Level B, 36 vols. Santillo, LuAnn. 2003. (Half-Pint Kids Readers Ser.). 7p. (J). (gr. -1-1). pap. 39.95 *(978-1-59256-127-8(6))* Half-Pint Kids, Inc.

—Bluejay. Santillo, LuAnn. 2003. (Half-Pint Kids Readers Ser.). 7p. (J). (gr. -1-1). pap. 1.00 *(978-1-59256-110-0(1))* Half-Pint Kids, Inc.

—Buzz. Santillo, LuAnn. 2003. (Half-Pint Kids Readers Ser.). 7p. (J). (gr. -1-1). pap. 1.00 *(978-1-59256-046-2(6))* Half-Pint Kids, Inc.

—The Cat. Santillo, LuAnn. 2003. (Half-Pint Kids Readers Ser.). 7p. (J). (gr. -1-1). pap. 1.00 *(978-1-59256-066-0(0))* Half-Pint Kids, Inc.

—The Chick. Santillo, LuAnn. 2003. (Half-Pint Kids Readers Ser.). 7p. (J). (gr. -1-1). pap. 1.00 *(978-1-59256-059-2(8))* Half-Pint Kids, Inc.

—Chip. Santillo, LuAnn. 2003. (Half-Pint Kids Readers Ser.). 7p. (J). (gr. -1-1). pap. *(978-1-59256-075-2(X))* Half-Pint Kids, Inc.

—Community Helpers, 6 vols. Santillo, LuAnn. 2003. (Half-Pint Kids Readers Ser.). 42p. (J). (gr. -1-1). pap. 6.95 *(978-1-59256-119-3(5))* Half-Pint Kids, Inc.

—The Cop. Santillo, LuAnn. 2003. (Half-Pint Kids Readers Ser.). 7p. (J). (gr. -1-1). pap. 1.00 *(978-1-59256-122-3(5))* Half-Pint Kids, Inc.

—The Dentist. Santillo, LuAnn. 2003. (Half-Pint Kids Readers Ser.). 7p. (J). (gr. -1-1). pap. 1.00 *(978-1-59256-120-9(9))* Half-Pint Kids, Inc.

—Digging for Clams. Santillo, LuAnn. 2003. (Half-Pint Kids Readers Ser.). 7p. (J). (gr. -1-1). pap. *(978-1-59256-092-9(X))* Half-Pint Kids, Inc.

—Dip & Sip. Santillo, LuAnn. 2003. (Half-Pint Kids Readers Ser.). 7p. (J). (gr. -1-1). pap. 1.00 *(978-1-59256-051-6(2))* Half-Pint Kids, Inc.

—The Doctor. Santillo, LuAnn. 2003. (Half-Pint Kids Readers Ser.). 7p. (J). (gr. -1-1). pap. 1.00 *(978-1-59256-121-6(7))* Half-Pint Kids, Inc.

—The Dog. Santillo, LuAnn. 2003. (Half-Pint Kids Readers Ser.). 7p. (J). (gr. -1-1). pap. 1.00 *(978-1-59256-065-3(2))* Half-Pint Kids, Inc.

—Down on the Farm, 6 vols. Santillo, LuAnn. 2003. (Half-Pint Kids Readers Ser.). 42p. (J). (gr. -1-1). pap. 6.95 *(978-1-59256-056-1(3))* Half-Pint Kids, Inc.

—The Duck. Santillo, LuAnn. 2003. (Half-Pint Kids Readers Ser.). 7p. (J). (gr. -1-1). pap. 1.00 *(978-1-59256-069-1(5))* Half-Pint Kids, Inc.

—The Eggs. Santillo, LuAnn. 2003. (Half-Pint Kids Readers Ser.). 7p. (J). (gr. -1-1). pap. *(978-1-59256-061-5(X))* Half-Pint Kids, Inc.

S

—Family Fun, 6 vols. Santillo, LuAnn. 2003. (Half-Pint Kids Readers Ser.). 42p. (J). (gr. -1-1). pap. 6.95 *(978-1-59256-098-1(9))* Half-Pint Kids, Inc.

—The Fire Fighter. Santillo, LuAnn. 2003. (Half-Pint Kids Readers Ser.). 7p. (J). (gr. -1-1). pap. 1.00 *(978-1-59256-124-7(1))* Half-Pint Kids, Inc.

—Fishing. Santillo, LuAnn. 2003. (Half-Pint Kids Readers Ser.). 7p. (J). (gr. -1-1). pap. 1.00 *(978-1-59256-093-6(8))* Half-Pint Kids, Inc.

—Flap. Santillo, LuAnn. 2003. (Half-Pint Kids Readers Ser.). 7p. (J). (gr. -1-1). pap. 1.00 *(978-1-59256-096-7(2))* Half-Pint Kids, Inc.

—Flipper. Santillo, LuAnn. 2003. (Half-Pint Kids Readers Ser.). 7p. (J). (gr. -1-1). pap. 1.00 *(978-1-59256-095-0(4))* Half-Pint Kids, Inc.

—Fred & Ed. Santillo, LuAnn. 2003. (Half-Pint Kids Readers Ser.). 7p. (J). (gr. -1-1). pap. 1.00 *(978-1-59256-074-5(1))* Half-Pint Kids, Inc.

—A Fun Trip. Santillo, LuAnn. 2003. (Half-Pint Kids Readers Ser.). 7p. (J). (gr. -1-1). pap. 1.00 *(978-1-59256-085-1(7))* Half-Pint Kids, Inc.

—Fun with Phonemes. Santillo, LuAnn. 2004. (Half-Pint Readers Ser.). 36p. (J). (gr. -1-1). pap. 11.95 *(978-1-59256-129-2(2))* Half-Pint Kids, Inc.

—Funny Clowns. Santillo, LuAnn. 2003. (Half-Pint Kids Readers Ser.). 7p. (J). (gr. -1-1). pap. 1.00 *(978-1-59256-116-2(0))* Half-Pint Kids, Inc.

—Go West. Santillo, LuAnn. 2003. (Half-Pint Kids Readers Ser.). 7p. (J). (gr. -1-1). pap. 1.00 *(978-1-59256-071-4(7))* Half-Pint Kids, Inc.

—Good Food. Santillo, LuAnn. 2003. (Half-Pint Kids Readers Ser.). 7p. (J). (gr. -1-1). pap. 1.00 *(978-1-59256-118-6(7))* Half-Pint Kids, Inc.

—Gum. Santillo, LuAnn. 2003. (Half-Pint Kids Readers Ser.). 7p. (J). (gr. -1-1). pap. 1.00 *(978-1-59256-087-5(3))* Half-Pint Kids, Inc.

—I Have Fun. Santillo, LuAnn. 2003. (Half-Pint Kids Readers Ser.). 7p. (J). (gr. -1-1). pap. 1.00 *(978-1-59256-055-4(5))* Half-Pint Kids, Inc.

—In the Meadow, 6 vols. Santillo, LuAnn. 2003. (Half-Pint Kids Readers Ser.). 42p. (J). (gr. -1-1). pap. 6.95 *(978-1-59256-105-6(5))* Half-Pint Kids, Inc.

—Jack. Santillo, LuAnn. 2003. (Half-Pint Kids Readers Ser.). 7p. (J). (gr. -1-1). pap. 1.00 *(978-1-59256-062-2(8))* Half-Pint Kids, Inc.

—Jake's Big Day. Santillo, LuAnn. 2003. (Half-Pint Kids Readers Ser.). 7p. (J). (gr. -1-1). pap. 1.00 *(978-1-59256-104-9(7))* Half-Pint Kids, Inc.

—Jane. Santillo, LuAnn. 2003. (Half-Pint Kids Readers Ser.). 7p. (J). (gr. -1-1). pap. 1.00 *(978-1-59256-099-8(7))* Half-Pint Kids, Inc.

—Jim & the Thug. Santillo, LuAnn. 2003. (Half-Pint Kids Readers Ser.). 7p. (J). (gr. -1-1). pap. 1.00 *(978-1-59256-078-3(4))* Half-Pint Kids, Inc.

—The King. Santillo, LuAnn. 2003. (Half-Pint Kids Readers Ser.). 7p. (J). (gr. -1-1). pap. 1.00 *(978-1-59256-050-9(4))* Half-Pint Kids, Inc.

—The Kiss. Santillo, LuAnn. 2003. (Half-Pint Kids Readers Ser.). 7p. (J). (gr. -1-1). pap. 1.00 *(978-1-59256-053-0(9))* Half-Pint Kids, Inc.

—Level A- Take Home Readers. Santillo, LuAnn. 2004. (Half-Pint Readers Ser.). 36p. (J). (gr. -1-1). pap. 79.95 *(978-1-59256-132-2(2))* Half-Pint Kids, Inc.

—Level B Take Home Readers. Santillo, LuAnn. 2004. (Half-Pint Readers Ser.). 36p. (J). (gr. -1-1). pap. 79.95 *(978-1-59256-133-9(0))* Half-Pint Kids, Inc.

—Level C - Take Home Readers. Santillo, LuAnn. 2004. (Half-Pint Readers Ser.). 36p. (J). (gr. -1-1). pap. 79.95 *(978-1-59256-134-6(9))* Half-Pint Kids, Inc.

—Lift-Off. Santillo, LuAnn. 2003. (Half-Pint Kids Readers Ser.). 7p. (J). (gr. -1-1). pap. 1.00 *(978-1-59256-043-1(1))* Half-Pint Kids, Inc.

—The Lion Tamer. Santillo, LuAnn. 2003. (Half-Pint Kids Readers Ser.). 7p. (J). (gr. -1-1). pap. 1.00 *(978-1-59256-115-5(2))* Half-Pint Kids, Inc.

—Liz. Santillo, LuAnn. 2003. (Half-Pint Kids Readers Ser.). 7p. (J). (gr. -1-1). pap. 1.00 *(978-1-59256-083-7(0))* Half-Pint Kids, Inc.

—Look at Me. Santillo, LuAnn. 2003. (Half-Pint Kids Readers Ser.). 7p. (J). (gr. -1-1). pap. 1.00 *(978-1-59256-052-3(0))* Half-Pint Kids, Inc.

—Lots More Fun with Phonemes. Santillo, LuAnn. 2004. (Half-Pint Readers Ser.). 36p. (J). (gr. -1-1). pap. 11.95 *(978-1-59256-131-5(4))* Half-Pint Kids, Inc.

—The Mailman. Santillo, LuAnn. 2003. (Half-Pint Kids Readers Ser.). 7p. (J). (gr. -1-1). pap. *(978-1-59256-125-4(X))* Half-Pint Kids, Inc.

—Medieval Magic, 6 vols. Santillo, LuAnn. 2003. (Half-Pint Kids Readers Ser.). 42p. (J). (gr. -1-1). pap. 6.95 *(978-1-59256-049-3(0))* Half-Pint Kids, Inc.

—Mike. Santillo, LuAnn. 2003. (Half-Pint Kids Readers Ser.). 7p. (J). (gr. -1-1). pap. 1.00 *(978-1-59256-100-1(4))* Half-Pint Kids, Inc.

—Mole. Santillo, LuAnn. 2003. (Half-Pint Kids Readers Ser.). 7p. (J). (gr. -1-1). pap. *(978-1-59256-111-7(X))* Half-Pint Kids, Inc.

—More Fun with Phonemes. Santillo, LuAnn. 2004. (Half-Pint Readers Ser.). 36p. (J). (gr. -1-1). pap. 11.95 *(978-1-59256-130-8(6))* Half-Pint Kids, Inc.

—Moving A-Long Level C, 36 vols. Santillo, LuAnn. 2003. (Half-Pint Kids Readers Ser.). 7p. (J). (gr. -1-1). pap. 39.95 *(978-1-59256-128-5(4))* Half-Pint Kids, Inc.

—Outerspace, 6 vols. Santillo, LuAnn. 2003. (Half-Pint Kids Readers Ser.). 42p. (J). (gr. -1-1). pap. 6.95 *(978-1-59256-042-4(3))* Half-Pint Kids, Inc.

—Packing. Santillo, LuAnn. 2003. (Half-Pint Kids Readers Ser.). 7p. (J). (gr. -1-1). pap. 1.00 *(978-1-59256-072-1(5))* Half-Pint Kids, Inc.

—The Picnic. Santillo, LuAnn. 2003. (Half-Pint Kids Readers Ser.). 7p. (J). (gr. -1-1). pap. 1.00 *(978-1-59256-090-5(3))* Half-Pint Kids, Inc.

—The Pig. Santillo, LuAnn. 2003. (Half-Pint Kids Readers Ser.). 7p. (J). (gr. -1-1). pap. 1.00 *(978-1-59256-064-6(4))* Half-Pint Kids, Inc.

—Pioneer Days, 6 vols. Santillo, LuAnn. 2003. (Half-Pint Kids Readers Ser.). 42p. (J). (gr. -1-1). pap. 6.95 *(978-1-59256-070-7(9))* Half-Pint Kids, Inc.

—Rags. Santillo, LuAnn. 2003. (Half-Pint Kids Readers Ser.). 7p. (J). (gr. -1-1). pap. 1.00 *(978-1-59256-073-8(3))* Half-Pint Kids, Inc.

—Rose. Santillo, LuAnn. 2003. (Half-Pint Kids Readers Ser.). 7p. (J). (gr. -1-1). pap. 1.00 *(978-1-59256-101-8(2))* Half-Pint Kids, Inc.

—Running Fox. Santillo, LuAnn. 2003. (Half-Pint Kids Readers Ser.). 7p. (J). (gr. -1-1). pap. 1.00 *(978-1-59256-079-0(2))* Half-Pint Kids, Inc.

—The Seeds. Santillo, LuAnn. 2003. (Half-Pint Kids Readers Ser.). 7p. (J). (gr. -1-1). pap. 1.00 *(978-1-59256-109-4(8))* Half-Pint Kids, Inc.

—Shag. Santillo, LuAnn. 2003. (Half-Pint Readers Ser.). 7p. (J). (gr. -1-1). pap. 1.00 *(978-1-59256-068-4(7))* Half-Pint Kids, Inc.

—A Sights & Sounds - Level, 36 vols. Santillo, LuAnn. 2003. (Half-Pint Kids Readers Ser.). 7p. (J). (gr. -1-1). pap. 39.95 *(978-1-59256-126-1(8))* Half-Pint Kids, Inc.

—Six Jobs. Santillo, LuAnn. 2003. (Half-Pint Kids Readers Ser.). 7p. (J). (gr. -1-1). pap. *(978-1-59256-058-5(X))* Half-Pint Kids, Inc.

—The Snack Shack. Santillo, LuAnn. 2003. (Half-Pint Kids Readers Ser.). 7p. (J). (gr. -1-1). pap. 1.00 *(978-1-59256-086-8(5))* Half-Pint Kids, Inc.

—Snail. Santillo, LuAnn. 2003. (Half-Pint Kids Readers Ser.). 7p. (J). (gr. -1-1). pap. 1.00 *(978-1-59256-106-3(3))* Half-Pint Kids, Inc.

—Steve & Pete. Santillo, LuAnn. 2003. (Half-Pint Kids Readers Ser.). 7p. (J). (gr. -1-1). pap. 1.00 *(978-1-59256-103-2(9))* Half-Pint Kids, Inc.

—Stop Hopping. Santillo, LuAnn. 2003. (Half-Pint Kids Readers Ser.). 7p. (J). (gr. -1-1). pap. 1.00 *(978-1-59256-054-7(7))* Half-Pint Kids, Inc.

—Stubs. Santillo, LuAnn. 2003. (Half-Pint Kids Readers Ser.). 7p. (J). (gr. -1-1). pap. 1.00 *(978-1-59256-097-4(0))* Half-Pint Kids, Inc.

—The Sun. Santillo, LuAnn. 2003. (Half-Pint Kids Readers Ser.). 7p. (J). (gr. -1-1). pap. 1.00 *(978-1-59256-047-9(4))* Half-Pint Kids, Inc.

—The Suntan. Santillo, LuAnn. 2003. (Half-Pint Kids Readers Ser.). 7p. (J). (gr. -1-1). pap. 1.00 *(978-1-59256-088-2(1))* Half-Pint Kids, Inc.

—Ted's Job. Santillo, LuAnn. 2003. (Half-Pint Kids Readers Ser.). 7p. (J). (gr. -1-1). pap. 1.00 *(978-1-59256-060-8(1))* Half-Pint Kids, Inc.

—The Tight Rope. Santillo, LuAnn. 2003. (Half-Pint Kids Readers Ser.). 7p. (J). (gr. -1-1). pap. 1.00 *(978-1-59256-114-8(4))* Half-Pint Kids, Inc.

—Toad. Santillo, LuAnn. 2003. (Half-Pint Kids Readers Ser.). 7p. (gr. -1-1). pap. 1.00 *(978-1-59256-107-0(1))* Half-Pint Kids, Inc.

—The Tracks. Santillo, LuAnn. 2003. (Half-Pint Kids Readers Ser.). 7p. (J). (gr. -1-1). pap. 1.00 *(978-1-59256-080-6(6))* Half-Pint Kids, Inc.

—The Trip. Santillo, LuAnn. 2003. (Half-Pint Kids Readers Ser.). 7p. (J). (gr. -1-1). pap. 1.00 *(978-1-59256-057-8(1))* Half-Pint Kids, Inc.

—Trot, Trot. Santillo, LuAnn. 2003. (Half-Pint Kids Readers Ser.). 7p. (J). (gr. -1-1). pap. 1.00 *(978-1-59256-067-7(9))* Half-Pint Kids, Inc.

—The Tune. Santillo, LuAnn. 2003. (Half-Pint Kids Readers Ser.). 7p. (J). (gr. -1-1). pap. 1.00 *(978-1-59256-102-5(0))* Half-Pint Kids, Inc.

—The UFO. Santillo, LuAnn. 2003. (Half-Pint Kids Readers Ser.). 7p. (J). (gr. -1-1). pap. 1.00 *(978-1-59256-045-5(8))* Half-Pint Kids, Inc.

—Under the Sea, 6 vols. Santillo, LuAnn. 2003. (Half-Pint Kids Readers Ser.). 42p. (J). (gr. -1-1). pap. 6.95 *(978-1-59256-091-2(1))* Half-Pint Kids, Inc.

—The Vet. Santillo, LuAnn. 2003. (Half-Pint Kids Readers Ser.). 7p. (J). (gr. -1-1). pap. 1.00 *(978-1-59256-123-0(3))* Half-Pint Kids, Inc.

—The Wet Dock. Santillo, LuAnn. 2003. (Half-Pint Kids Readers Ser.). 7p. (J). (gr. -1-1). pap. *(978-1-59256-089-9(X))* Half-Pint Kids, Inc.

—Wild West, 6 vols. Santillo, LuAnn. 2003. (Half-Pint Kids Readers Ser.). 42p. (J). (gr. -1-1). pap. 6.95 *(978-1-59256-077-6(6))* Half-Pint Kids, Inc.

—The Wish. Santillo, LuAnn. 2003. (Half-Pint Kids Readers Ser.). 7p. (J). (gr. -1-1). pap. 1.00 *(978-1-59256-048-6(2))* Half-Pint Kids, Inc.

Santini, Debrah L. Abby's Chairs. Santucci, Barbara. 2004. 32p. 16.00 *(978-0-8028-5205-2(X))* Eerdmans, William B. Publishing Co.

Santitoro, Theresa & Tumminello, Giovanna. It's Elementary, Funny Things Kids Say In School. Isler, Linda Germano. 2010. 32p. pap. 9.95 *(978-1-936343-00-3(2))* Peppertree Pr., The.

Santolouco, Mateus. Thor. Denton, Shannon Eric. 2010. (Short Tales Norse Myths Ser.). (ENG.). 32p. (J). (gr. 1-4). 27.07 *(978-1-60270-569-2(0),* 13467, Short Tales) Magic Wagon.

Santolouco, Mateus & Duncan, Dan. Teenage Mutant Ninja Turtles Enemies Old, Enemies New. Waltz, Tom & Eastman, Kevin B. 2016. (Teenage Mutant Ninja Turtles Ser.). 104p. pap. 17.99 *(978-1-63140-614-0(0),* 9781631406140) Idea & Design Works, LLC.

Santolouco, Mateus, jt. illus. see Duncan, Dan.

Santomauro, Fabio. The Whispering Town, Vol. Elvgren, Jennifer. 2014. (ENG.). 32p. (J). (gr. 2-5). 8.99 *(978-1-4677-1195-1(0),* 9781467711951, Kar-Ben Publishing) Lerner Publishing Group.

Santoni, Manuela. Jane Austen: Her Heart Did Whisper. Santoni, Manuela. Benassi, Matteo. 2018. (ENG.). 96p. (YA). (gr. 8-12). 30.65 *(978-1-5415-2366-1(0),* Graphic Universe™) Lerner Publishing Group.

Santora, Bud. Wise Bear William: A New Beginning. Wooten, Arthur. 2012. 44p. pap. 12.99 *(978-0-9850529-1-1(0))* Galaxias Productions.

Santora, Maureen Crethan. The Day the Towers Fell: The Story of September 11, 2001. Santora, Maureen Crethan. 2008. 32p. (J). 31.99 *(978-1-4257-7872-9(0))* Xlibris Corp.

Santore, Charles. Aesop's Fables: A Little Apple Classic. 2019. (Little Apple Bks.). (ENG.). 28p. (J). 4.99 *(978-1-60433-923-9(3),* Applesauce Pr.) Cider Mill Pr. Bk. Pubs., LLC.

—Aesop's Fables: The Classic Edition. 2018. (Classic Edition Ser.). (ENG.). 64p. (J). (gr. -1-6). 19.95 *(978-1-60433-810-2(5),* Applesauce Pr.) Cider Mill Pr. Bk. Pubs., LLC.

—Aesop's Fables Board Book: The Classic Edition. Aesop. 2020. (ENG.). 24p. (J). bds. 8.95 *(978-1-60433-949-9(7),* Applesauce Pr.) Cider Mill Pr. Bk. Pubs., LLC.

—The Alice in Wonderland Coloring Book: The Classic Edition. Carroll, Lewis. 2018. (Classic Edition Ser.: 11). (ENG.). 48p. (J). pap. 10.99 *(978-1-60433-712-9(5),* Applesauce Pr.) Cider Mill Pr. Bk. Pubs., LLC.

—Alice's Adventures in Wonderland (Hardcover) The Classic Edition. Carroll, Lewis. 2017. (Classic Edition Ser.: 10). (ENG.). 96p. (J). 19.95 *(978-1-60433-711-2(7),* Applesauce Pr.) Cider Mill Pr. Bk. Pubs., LLC.

—The Classic Tale of Benjamin Bunny Oversized Padded Board Book. Potter, Beatrix. 2020. (ENG.). 20p. (J). bds. 12.95 *(978-1-60433-939-0(X),* Applesauce Pr.) Cider Mill Pr. Bk. Pubs., LLC.

—The Classic Tale of Mr. Jeremy Fisher: The Classic Edition. Potter, Beatrix. 2015. (Classic Edition Ser.). (ENG.). 20p. (J). bds. 8.95 *(978-1-60433-548-4(3),* Applesauce Pr.) Cider Mill Pr. Bk. Pubs., LLC.

—The Classic Tale of Peter Rabbit: A Little Apple Classic. Potter, Beatrix. 2019. (Little Apple Bks.). (ENG.). 28p. (J). 4.99 *(978-1-60433-922-2(5),* Applesauce Pr.) Cider Mill Pr. Bk. Pubs., LLC.

—The Classic Tale of Peter Rabbit Board Book: The Classic Edition. Potter, Beatrix. 2014. (Classic Edition Ser.). (ENG.). 24p. (J). bds. 8.95 *(978-1-60433-511-8(4),* Applesauce Pr.) Cider Mill Pr. Bk. Pubs., LLC.

—The Classic Tale of Peter Rabbit Hardcover: And Other Cherished Stories (the Classic Edition) Potter, Beatrix. 2013. (Classic Edition Ser.). (ENG.). 74p. (J). 19.95 *(978-1-60433-376-3(6),* Applesauce Pr.) Cider Mill Pr. Bk. Pubs., LLC.

—The Classic Tale of Peter Rabbit Oversized Padded Board Book: The Classic Edition. Potter, Beatrix. 2018. (Classic Edition Ser.: 13). (ENG.). 24p. (J). bds. 12.95 *(978-1-60433-769-3(9),* Applesauce Pr.) Cider Mill Pr. Bk. Pubs., LLC.

—The Classic Tale of Peter Rabbit Touch-And-Feel Board Book: The Classic Edition. Potter, Beatrix. 2020. (Classic Edition Ser.). (ENG.). 16p. (J). bds. 12.95 *(978-1-60433-944-4(6),* Applesauce Pr.) Cider Mill Pr. Bk. Pubs., LLC.

—The Classic Tale of the Flopsy Bunnies: The Classic Edition. Potter, Beatrix. 2015. (Classic Edition Ser.). (ENG.). 20p. (J). bds. 8.95 *(978-1-60433-551-4(3),* Applesauce Pr.) Cider Mill Pr. Bk. Pubs., LLC.

—The Classic Tale of the Flopsy Bunnies Oversized Padded Board Book. Potter, Beatrix. 2020. (ENG.). 20p. (J). bds. 12.95 *(978-1-60433-940-6(3),* Applesauce Pr.) Cider Mill Pr. Bk. Pubs., LLC.

Santore, Charles. El Cuento Clásico de Pedrito, el Conejo Travieso: A Little Apple Classic (Spanish Edition of Classic Tale of Peter Rabbit) Potter, Beatrix. 2020. (Little Apple Bks.). (SPA.). 28p. (J). 4.99 ***(978-1-64643-034-5(4),*** Applesauce Pr.) Cider Mill Pr. Bk. Pubs., LLC.

—Cuento de Nochebuena, una Visita de San Nicolas: A Little Apple Classic. Moore, Clement C. 2020. (Little Apple Bks.). (SPA.). 28p. (J). 4.99 ***(978-1-64643-033-8(6),*** Applesauce Pr.) Cider Mill Pr. Bk. Pubs., LLC.

Santore, Charles. The Illustrated Treasury of Classic Children's Stories. 2019. (Classic Edition Ser.). (ENG.). 552p. (J). 39.95 *(978-1-60433-890-4(3),* Applesauce Pr.) Cider Mill Pr. Bk. Pubs., LLC.

Santore, Charles. Jabberwocky. Carroll, Lewis. 2020. 32p. (J). (gr. -1-3). 17.99 ***(978-0-7624-6543-9(3),*** Running Pr. Kids) Running Pr.

Santore, Charles. The Life & Adventures of Santa Claus. Baum, L. Frank. 2017. 56p. (J). (gr. -1-3). 16.99 *(978-0-7624-6313-8(9),* Running Pr. Kids) Running Pr.

—The Little Mermaid. Andersen, Hans. 2013. (Classic Edition Ser.). Orig. Title: Lille havfrue. (ENG.). 48p. (J). 19.95 *(978-1-60433-377-0(4),* Applesauce Pr.) Cider Mill Pr. Bk. Pubs., LLC.

—The Night Before Christmas: Or, a Visit from St. Nicholas. Moore, Clement C. 2011. 41p. (J). *(978-1-60464-033-5(2))* Appleseed Pr. Bk. Pub. LLC.

—The Night Before Christmas Board Book: The Classic Edition, the New York Times Bestseller. Moore, Clement. 2013. (Classic Edition Ser.). (ENG.). 24p. (J). bds. 8.95 *(978-1-60433-438-8(X),* Applesauce Pr.) Cider Mill Pr. Bk. Pubs., LLC.

—The Night Before Christmas Hardcover: The Classic Edition, the New York Times Bestseller. Moore, Clement. 2011. (Classic Edition Ser.). (ENG.). 48p. (J). (gr. -1). 19.95 *(978-1-60433-237-7(9),* Applesauce Pr.) Cider Mill Pr. Bk. Pubs., LLC.

—The Night Before Christmas Heirloom Edition: The Classic Edition Hardcover with Audio CD Narrated by Jeff Bridges. Moore, Clement. 2016. (Classic Edition Ser.). (ENG.). 48p. (J). 24.95 incl. audio compact disk *(978-1-60433-677-1(3),* Applesauce Pr.) Cider Mill Pr. Bk. Pubs., LLC.

—Night Before Christmas Keepsake Gift Set, Set. Moore, Clement. gif. ed. 2013. (ENG.). 48p. (J). 14.95 *(978-1-60433-437-1(1),* Applesauce Pr.) Cider Mill Pr. Bk. Pubs., LLC.

—The Night Before Christmas (Miniature Edition) The Classic Edition. Moore, Clement. 2011. (Little Seedling Edition Ser.: 1). (ENG.). 48p. (J). 6.95 *(978-1-60433-244-5(1),* Applesauce Pr.) Cider Mill Pr. Bk. Pubs., LLC.

—The Night Before Christmas Oversized Padded Board Book: The Classic Edition, the New York Times Bestseller. Moore, Clement. 2017. (Classic Edition Ser.: 13). (ENG.). 24p. (J). bds. 12.95 *(978-1-60433-749-5(4),* Applesauce Pr.) Cider Mill Pr. Bk. Pubs., LLC.

Santore, Charles. The Night Before Christmas Press & Play Storybook: The Classic Edition Hardcover Book Narrated by Jeff Bridges. Moore, Clement. 2020. (Classic Edition Ser.). (ENG.). 28p. (J). 19.95 ***(978-1-60433-989-5(6),*** Applesauce Pr.) Cider Mill Pr. Bk. Pubs., LLC.

Santore, Charles. The Night Before Christmas Sleigh Bell Gift Set. Moore, Clement. 2019. (Classic Edition Ser.). (ENG.). 26p. (J). bds. 16.95 *(978-1-60433-878-2(4),* Applesauce Pr.) Cider Mill Pr. Bk. Pubs., LLC.

—Paul Revere's Ride: The Classic Edition. Longfellow, Henry Wadsworth. Encarnacion, Elizabeth, ed. 2014. (Classic Edition Ser.). (ENG.). 36p. (J). 17.95 *(978-1-60433-493-7(2),* Applesauce Pr.) Cider Mill Pr. Bk. Pubs., LLC.

—Paul Revere's Ride: The Landlord's Tale. Longfellow, Henry. 2005. 28p. (J). (gr. 4-8). reprint ed. 17.00 *(978-0-7567-9202-2(9))* DIANE Publishing Co.

—Paul Revere's Ride: The Landlord's Tale. Longfellow, Henry. 2003. 40p. (J). lib. bdg. 17.89 *(978-0-06-623747-3(5))* HarperCollins Pubs.

—The Peter Rabbit Classic Tales Mini Gift Set: The Classic Collection. Potter, Beatrix. 2019. (Classic Edition Ser.). (ENG.). 160p. (J). pap. 10.95 *(978-1-60433-913-0(6),* Applesauce Pr.) Cider Mill Pr. Bk. Pubs., LLC.

—The Peter Rabbit Deluxe Plush Gift Set: The Classic Edition Board Book + Plush Stuffed Animal Toy Rabbit Gift Set. Potter, Beatrix. 2019. (Classic Edition Ser.). (ENG.). 64p. (J). bds. 29.95 *(978-1-60433-828-7(8),* Applesauce Pr.) Cider Mill Pr. Bk. Pubs., LLC.

—The Peter Rabbit Plush Gift Set: The Classic Edition Board Book + Plush Stuffed Animal Toy Rabbit Gift Set. Potter, Beatrix. 2017. (Classic Edition Ser.). (ENG.). 24p. (J). bds. 16.95 *(978-1-60433-685-6(4),* Applesauce Pr.) Cider Mill Pr. Bk. Pubs., LLC.

—Snow White: A Little Apple Classic. 2019. (Little Apple Bks.). (ENG.). 28p. (J). 4.99 *(978-1-60433-924-6(1),* Applesauce Pr.) Cider Mill Pr. Bk. Pubs., LLC.

—Snow White: The Classic Edition. Brothers Grimm, Brothers. 2019. (ENG.). 64p. (J). 19.95 *(978-1-60433-853-9(9),* Applesauce Pr.) Cider Mill Pr. Bk. Pubs., LLC.

—Timeless Tales Mini Gift Set: Big Stories for Little Hands. 2019. (Classic Edition Ser.). (ENG.). 160p. (J). pap. 10.95 *(978-1-60433-912-3(8),* Applesauce Pr.) Cider Mill Pr. Bk. Pubs., LLC.

—The Velveteen Rabbit: A Little Apple Classic. Williams Bianco, Margery. 2020. (Little Apple Bks.). (ENG.). 28p. (J). 4.99 *(978-1-60433-950-5(0),* Applesauce Pr.) Cider Mill Pr. Bk. Pubs., LLC.

—The Velveteen Rabbit Board Book: The Classic Edition. Williams, Margery. 2014. (Classic Edition Ser.). (ENG.). 24p. (J). bds. 8.95 *(978-1-60433-461-6(4),* Applesauce Pr.) Cider Mill Pr. Bk. Pubs., LLC.

—The Velveteen Rabbit Hardcover: The Classic Edition. Williams, Margery. 2013. (Classic Edition Ser.). (ENG.). 48p. (J). 17.95 *(978-1-60433-277-3(8),* Applesauce Pr.) Cider Mill Pr. Bk. Pubs., LLC.

—The Velveteen Rabbit Oversized Padded Board Book: The Classic Edition. Williams, Margery. 2018. (Classic Edition Ser.). (ENG.). 24p. (J). bds. 12.95 *(978-1-60433-811-9(3))* Cider Mill Pr. Bk. Pubs., LLC.

Santore, Charles. The Velveteen Rabbit Plush Gift Set: The Classic Edition Board Book + Plush Stuffed Animal Toy Rabbit Gift Set. Williams, Margery. 2020. (Classic Edition Ser.). (ENG.). 24p. (J). bds. 16.95 ***(978-1-60433-987-1(X),*** Applesauce Pr.) Cider Mill Pr. Bk. Pubs., LLC.

Santore, Charles. William the Curious: Knight of the Water Lilies. 2012. (J). *(978-1-60464-034-2(0))* Appleseed Pr. Bk. Pub. LLC.

—The Wizard of Oz Coloring Book: The Classic Edition. 2017. (Classic Edition Ser.). (ENG.). 52p. (J). pap. 10.99 *(978-1-60433-706-8(0),* Applesauce Pr.) Cider Mill Pr. Bk. Pubs., LLC.

Santore, Charles. The Silk Princess: The Classic Edition. Santore, Charles. 2020. (Classic Edition Ser.). (ENG.). 64p. (J). 19.95 *(978-1-60433-945-1(4),* Applesauce Pr.) Cider Mill Pr. Bk. Pubs., LLC.

—A Stowaway on Noah's Ark: The Classic Edition. Santore, Charles. 2015. (Classic Edition Ser.). (ENG.). 64p. (J). (gr. -1). 17.95 *(978-1-60433-543-9(2),* Applesauce Pr.) Cider Mill Pr. Bk. Pubs., LLC.

—A Stowaway on Noah's Ark Board Book: The Classic Edition. Santore, Charles. 2017. (Classic Edition Ser.: 12). (ENG.). 24p. (J). bds. 8.95 *(978-1-60433-742-6(7),* Applesauce Pr.) Cider Mill Pr. Bk. Pubs., LLC.

—A Stowaway on Noah's Ark Oversized Padded Board Book: The Classic Edition. Santore, Charles. 2018. (Classic Edition Ser.). (ENG.). 24p. (J). bds. 12.95 *(978-1-60433-801-0(6),* Applesauce Pr.) Cider Mill Pr. Bk. Pubs., LLC.

—William the Curious: Knight of the Water Lilies: The Classic Edition. Santore, Charles. 2014. (ENG.). 44p. (J). (gr. -1). 16.95 *(978-1-60433-474-6(6))* Cider Mill Pr. Bk. Pubs., LLC.

Santoro. Once upon a Gorjuss Time: Six Classic Tales to Dream By. Santoro Licensing. 2016. (Gorjuss Ser.). (ENG.). 112p. (J). (gr. 3-7). 19.99 *(978-0-7636-7742-8(6),* Candlewick Entertainment) Candlewick Pr.

Santoro. My Secret Place. Santoro. 2014. (Gorjuss Ser.). (ENG.). 128p. (J). (gr. 2-4). 12.99 *(978-0-7636-7453-3(2),* Candlewick Entertainment) Candlewick Pr.

Santoro, Christopher. Alabama. Hart, Joyce. 2007. (It's My State! (First Edition) ® Ser.). 80p. (gr. 4-4). lib. bdg. 32.36 *(978-0-7614-1925-9(X))* Cavendish Square Publishing LLC.

—Arizona. Bradley, Michael & Derzipilski, Kathleen. 2004. (It's My State! (First Edition) ® Ser.). 80p. (gr. 4-4). lib. bdg. 32.36 *(978-0-7614-1686-9(2))* Cavendish Square Publishing LLC.

—Arkansas. King, David C. 2007. (It's My State! (First Edition) ® Ser.). 80p. (gr. 4-4). lib. bdg. 32.36 *(978-0-7614-2215-0(3))* Cavendish Square Publishing LLC.

—Bang! Boom! Roar! a Busy Crew of Dinosaurs. Evans, Nate & Brown, Stephanie Gwyn. 2012. (ENG.). 40p. (J). (gr. -1-2). 15.99 *(978-0-06-087960-0(2))* HarperCollins Pubs.

—Bears Are Curious. Milton, Joyce. 2015. (Step into Reading Ser.). (ENG.). 32p. (J). (gr. -1-1). pap. 3.99 *(978-0-679-85301-5(4),* Random Hse. Bks. for Young Readers) Random Hse. Children's Bks.
—California. Burgan, Michael. 2003. (It's My State! (First Edition) ® Ser.). 80p. (gr. 4-4). 32.36 *(978-0-7614-1420-9(7))* Cavendish Square Publishing LLC.
—Colorado. Altman, Linda Jacobs. 2005. (It's My State! (First Edition) ® Ser.). 80p. (gr. 4-4). lib. bdg. 32.36 *(978-0-7614-1532-9(7))* Cavendish Square Publishing LLC.
—Delaware. King, David C. 2006. (It's My State! (First Edition) ® Ser.). 80p. (gr. 4-4). lib. bdg. 32.36 *(978-0-7614-1826-9(1))* Cavendish Square Publishing LLC.
—Dinosaur ABC. Evans, Nate & Brown, Stephanie Gwyn. 2011. (J). lib. bdg. 16.89 *(978-0-06-087962-4(9))* HarperCollins Pubs.
—Iowa. King, David C. 2007. (It's My State! (First Edition) ® Ser.). 80p. (gr. 4-4). lib. bdg. 32.36 *(978-0-7614-1928-0(4))* Cavendish Square Publishing LLC.
—Kansas. King, David C. 2004. (It's My State! (First Edition) ® Ser.). 80p. (gr. 4-4). lib. bdg. 32.36 *(978-0-7614-1688-3(9))* Cavendish Square Publishing LLC.
—Kentucky. Gaines, Ann Graham. 2003. (It's My State! (First Edition) ® Ser.). 80p. (gr. 4-4). 32.36 *(978-0-7614-1525-1(4))* Cavendish Square Publishing LLC.
—Louisiana. Bjorklund, Ruth. 2005. (It's My State! (First Edition) ® Ser.). 80p. (gr. 4-4). lib. bdg. 32.36 *(978-0-7614-1863-4(6))* Cavendish Square Publishing LLC.
—Maine. Hicks, Terry Allan. 2006. (It's My State! (First Edition) ® Ser.). 80p. (gr. 4-4). lib. bdg. 32.36 *(978-0-7614-1910-5(1))* Cavendish Square Publishing LLC.
—Michigan. Haney, Johannah. 2005. (It's My State! (First Edition) ® Ser.). 80p. (gr. 4-4). lib. bdg. 32.36 *(978-0-7614-1861-0(X))* Cavendish Square Publishing LLC.
—Mississippi. Gaines, Ann Graham. 2007. (It's My State! (First Edition) ® Ser.). 80p. (gr. 4-4). lib. bdg. 32.36 *(978-0-7614-2214-3(5))* Cavendish Square Publishing LLC.
—Missouri. Sanders, Doug. 2006. (It's My State! (First Edition) ® Ser.). 80p. (gr. 4-4). lib. bdg. 32.36 *(978-0-7614-1822-1(9))* Cavendish Square Publishing LLC.
—Montana. Bjorklund, Ruth. 2004. (It's My State! (First Edition) ® Ser.). 80p. (gr. 4-4). lib. bdg. 32.36 *(978-0-7614-1689-0(7))* Cavendish Square Publishing LLC.
—Nebraska. Sanders, Doug. 2006. (It's My State! (First Edition) ® Ser.). 80p. (gr. 4-4). lib. bdg. 32.36 *(978-0-7614-1911-2(X))* Cavendish Square Publishing LLC.
—Nevada. Hicks, Terry Allan. 2005. (It's My State! (First Edition) ® Ser.). 80p. (gr. 4-4). lib. bdg. 32.36 *(978-0-7614-1860-3(1))* Cavendish Square Publishing LLC.
—New Hampshire. Hicks, Terry Allan. 2006. (It's My State! (First Edition) ® Ser.). 80p. (gr. 4-4). lib. bdg. 32.36 *(978-0-7614-1825-2(3))* Cavendish Square Publishing LLC.
—Noah's Ark. Knudsen, Michelle. 2016. (Lift-The-Flap Ser.). 14p. (J). (gr. -1 — 1). bds. 6.99 *(978-0-553-53537-2(4),* Random Hse. Bks. for Young Readers) Random Hse. Children's Bks.
—North Dakota. Sanders, Doug. 2004. (It's My State! (First Edition) ® Ser.). 80p. (gr. 4-4). lib. bdg. 32.36 *(978-0-7614-1687-6(0))* Cavendish Square Publishing LLC.
—Ohio. Hart, Joyce. 2006. (It's My State! (First Edition) ® Ser.). 80p. (gr. 4-4). lib. bdg. 32.36 *(978-0-7614-1907-5(1))* Cavendish Square Publishing LLC.
—Oklahoma. Sanders, Doug. 2006. (It's My State! (First Edition) ® Ser.). 80p. (gr. 4-4). lib. bdg. 32.36 *(978-0-7614-1906-8(3))* Cavendish Square Publishing LLC.
—Old MacDonald Had a Dragon, 0 vols. Baker, Ken. 2012. (ENG.). 32p. (J). (gr. k-3). 16.99 *(978-0-7614-6175-3(2),* 9780761461753, Two Lions) Amazon Publishing.
—Open the Barn Door... Random House. 2016. 22p. (J). (— 1). bds. 6.99 *(978-0-399-54948-9(X),* Random Hse. Bks. for Young Readers) Random Hse. Children's Bks.
—Open the Church Door. 2020. (ENG.). 22p. (J). (— 1). bds. 6.99 *(978-0-593-12769-8(2),* Random Hse. Bks. for Young Readers) Random Hse. Children's Bks.
—Open the Preschool Door. 2019. 22p. (J). (— 1). bds. 6.99 *(978-1-5247-7174-4(0),* Random Hse. Bks. for Young Readers) Random Hse. Children's Bks.
—Oregon. Hart, Joyce. 2006. (It's My State! (First Edition) ® Ser.). 80p. (gr. 4-4). lib. bdg. 32.36 *(978-0-7614-1908-2(X))* Cavendish Square Publishing LLC.
—Pennsylvania. Hart, Joyce. 2004. (It's My State! (First Edition) ® Ser.). 80p. (gr. 4-4). lib. bdg. 32.36 *(978-0-7614-1691-3(9))* Cavendish Square Publishing LLC.
—Peter Cottontail. Stephens, Amanda. 2008. (ENG.). 60p. (J). (gr. -1-3). audio compact disk 18.95 *(978-0-545-05250-4(5))* Scholastic, Inc.
—Puerto Rico. Bjorklund, Ruth. 2007. (It's My State! (First Edition) ® Ser.). 80p. (gr. 4-4). lib. bdg. 32.36 *(978-0-7614-2218-1(8))* Cavendish Square Publishing LLC.
—Rhode Island. Petreycik, Rick. 2005. (It's My State! (First Edition) ® Ser.). 80p. (gr. 4-4). lib. bdg. 32.36 *(978-0-7614-1859-7(8))* Cavendish Square Publishing LLC.
—South Carolina. Hess, Debra. 2004. (It's My State! (First Edition) ® Ser.). 80p. (gr. 4-4). lib. bdg. 32.36 *(978-0-7614-1690-6(0))* Cavendish Square Publishing LLC.
—Tennessee. Petreycik, Rick. 2006. (It's My State! (First Edition) ® Ser.). 80p. (gr. 4-4). lib. bdg. 32.36 *(978-0-7614-1909-9(8))* Cavendish Square Publishing LLC.
—Vermont. Dornfeld, Margaret. 2005. (It's My State! (First Edition) ® Ser.). 80p. (gr. 4-4). lib. bdg. 32.36 *(978-0-7614-1864-1(4))* Cavendish Square Publishing LLC.
—Washington, D. C. Hicks, Terry Allan. 2007. (It's My State! (First Edition) ® Ser.). 80p. (gr. 4-4). lib. bdg. 32.36 *(978-0-7614-1929-7(2))* Cavendish Square Publishing LLC.
—West Virginia. Petreycik, Rick. 2007. (It's My State! (First Edition) ® Ser.). 80p. (gr. 4-4). lib. bdg. 32.36 *(978-0-7614-2216-7(1))* Cavendish Square Publishing LLC.
—Wyoming. Petreycik, Rick. 2007. (It's My State! (First Edition) ® Ser.). 80p. (gr. 4-4). lib. bdg. 32.36 *(978-0-7614-1930-3(6))* Cavendish Square Publishing LLC.
Santoro, Scott. Candy Cane Lane. Santoro, Scott. 2016. (ENG.). 48p. (J). (gr. -1-3). 17.99 *(978-1-4814-5661-6(X),* Simon & Schuster Bks. For Young Readers) Simon & Schuster Bks. For Young Readers.
—Which Way to Witch School? Santoro, Scott. (ENG.). 32p. (J). (gr. -1-2). 2012. pap. 5.99 *(978-0-06-078183-5(1));* 2010. 16.99 *(978-0-06-078181-1(5))* HarperCollins Pubs.
Santos, Adriana. Around the Passover Table. Newman, Tracy. 2019. (ENG.). 32p. (J). (gr. -1-3). 16.99 *(978-0-8075-0446-8(7),* 807504467) Whitman, Albert & Co.
Santos, Ana. Chronicles of a Barnyard Life: Smile Mr. Cow! Sun, Priya. 2017. (ENG.). (J). (gr. k-2). 16.99 *(978-0-692-83659-0(4))* Derry Lane Publishing.
Santos, Anthony Erazo. Nayan's Family Fruit Salad. Sandhu, Navjit. 2020. (Nayan's Bks.). (ENG.). 32p. (J). ***(978-1-5255-2975-7(7))***; pap. ***(978-1-5255-2976-4(5))*** FriesenPress.
Santos, Carriel Ann. A Straw Hat So Big. Bortnick, Lori. 2013. 52p. pap. 11.95 *(978-0-9851492-6-0(4))* Flying Turtle Publishing.
Santos, Emanuel. Superstar Cats: 25 Easy Tricks to Make Your Cat Shine in the Spotlight. Tottman, Julie. 2018. 112p. (J). *(978-1-5444-2388-3(8),* Running Pr.) Running Pr.
Santos, Genevieve. The Bad Luck Day. Anna, Holly. 2019. (Daisy Dreamer Ser.: 11). (ENG.). 128p. (J). (gr. k-4). 16.99 *(978-1-5344-4265-8(0));* pap. 5.99 *(978-1-5344-4264-1(2))* Little Simon. (Little Simon).
—A Daisy at the Beach. Anna, Holly. 2019. (Daisy Dreamer Ser.: 10). (ENG.). 128p. (J). (gr. k-4). 16.99 *(978-1-5344-4262-7(6));* pap. 5.99 *(978-1-5344-4261-0(8))* Little Simon. (Little Simon).
—Daisy Dreamer & the Totally True Imaginary Friend. Anna, Holly. 2017. (Daisy Dreamer Ser.: 1). (ENG.). 128p. (J). (gr. k-4). pap. 5.99 *(978-1-4814-8630-9(6),* Little Simon) Little Simon.
—Daisy Dreamer & the World of Make-Believe. Anna, Holly. 2017. (Daisy Dreamer Ser.: 2). (ENG.). 128p. (J). (gr. k-4). pap. 5.99 *(978-1-4814-8633-0(0),* Little Simon) Little Simon.
—The Daisy Dreamer Collection: Daisy Dreamer & the Totally True Imaginary Friend; Daisy Dreamer & the World of Make-Believe; Sparkle Fairies & the Imaginaries; the Not-So-Pretty Pixies. Anna, Holly. ed. 2018. (Daisy Dreamer Ser.). (ENG.). 512p. (J). (gr. k-4). pap. 23.99 *(978-1-5344-1504-1(1),* Little Simon) Little Simon.
—The Daisy Dreamer Collection #2: The Ice Castle; the Wishing-Well Spell; Posey, the Class Pest; Pop Goes the Bubble Trouble. Anna, Holly. ed. 2019. (Daisy Dreamer Ser.). (ENG.). 512p. (J). (gr. k-4). pap. 23.99 *(978-1-5344-4401-0(7),* Little Simon) Little Simon.
—The Great Bunny Escape. Anna, Holly. 2019. (Daisy Dreamer Ser.: 9). (ENG.). 128p. (J). (gr. k-4). 16.99 *(978-1-5344-2656-6(6));* pap. 5.99 *(978-1-5344-2655-9(8))* Little Simon. (Little Simon).
—The Ice Castle. Anna, Holly. 2017. (Daisy Dreamer Ser.: 5). (ENG.). 128p. (J). (gr. k-4). 16.99 *(978-1-4814-9893-7(2));* pap. 5.99 *(978-1-4814-9892-0(4))* Little Simon. (Little Simon).
—The Not-So-Pretty Pixies. Anna, Holly. 2017. (Daisy Dreamer Ser.: 4). (ENG.). 128p. (J). (gr. k-4). 16.99 *(978-1-4814-9888-3(6));* pap. 5.99 *(978-1-4814-9887-6(8))* Little Simon. (Little Simon).
—Pop Goes the Bubble Trouble. Anna, Holly. 2018. (Daisy Dreamer Ser.: 8). (ENG.). 128p. (J). (gr. k-4). 16.99 *(978-1-5344-2653-5(1));* pap. 5.99 *(978-1-5344-2652-8(3))* Little Simon. (Little Simon).
—Posey, the Class Pest. Anna, Holly. 2018. (Daisy Dreamer Ser.: 7). (ENG.). 128p. (J). (gr. k-4). 16.99 *(978-1-5344-1269-9(7));* pap. 5.99 *(978-1-5344-1268-2(9))* Little Simon. (Little Simon).
—Sparkle Fairies & the Imaginaries. Anna, Holly. 2017. (Daisy Dreamer Ser.: 3). (ENG.). 128p. (J). (gr. k-4). pap. 5.99 *(978-1-4814-9185-3(7),* Little Simon) Little Simon.
—The Wishing-Well Spell. Anna, Holly. 2018. (Daisy Dreamer Ser.: 6). (ENG.). 128p. (J). (gr. k-4). 16.99 *(978-1-5344-1266-8(2));* pap. 5.99 *(978-1-5344-1265-1(4))* Little Simon. (Little Simon).
Santos, Genevieve. I Yoga You. Santos, Genevieve. 2019. (ENG.). 26p. (J). (gr. -1). bds. 8.99 *(978-1-5344-5489-7(6),* Little Simon) Little Simon.
Santos, Wilton. Star Wars: Doctor Aphra Vol. 6. 2019. (Star Wars: Doctor Aphra Ser.: 6). (ENG.). 112p. (YA). (gr. 4-17). pap. 15.99 *(978-1-302-91488-2(X))* Marvel Worldwide, Inc.
Santoso, Charles. Bat & the End of Everything. Arnold, Elana K. (ENG.). 192p. (J). (gr. 1-5). 2020. pap. 6.99 *(978-0-06-279845-9(6));* 2019. 16.99 *(978-0-06-279844-2(8))* HarperCollins Pubs. (Waldon Pond Pr.).
—Bat & the Waiting Game. Arnold, Elana K. (ENG.). (J). (gr. 1-5). 2019. 208p. pap. 6.99 *(978-0-06-244586-5(3));* 2018. 192p. 16.99 *(978-0-06-244585-8(5))* HarperCollins Pubs. (Waldon Pond Pr.).
—A Boy Called Bat. Arnold, Elana K. (ENG.). 208p. (J). (gr. 1-5). 2018. pap. 6.99 *(978-0-06-244583-4(9));* 2017. 16.99 *(978-0-06-244582-7(0))* HarperCollins Pubs. (Waldon Pond Pr.).
—Dandy. Dyckman, Ame. 2019. 40p. (J). (gr. -1-3). 17.99 *(978-0-316-36295-5(6))* Little Brown & Co.
—Dragons Get Colds Too. Roan, Rebecca. 2019. 40p. (J). 17.99 *(978-1-68119-044-0(3),* 900156928, Bloomsbury Children's Bks.) Bloomsbury Publishing USA.
—I Don't Like Koala. Ferrell, Sean. 2015. (ENG.). 40p. (J). (gr. -1-3). 17.99 *(978-1-4814-0068-8(1),* Atheneum Bks. for Young Readers) Simon & Schuster Children's Publishing.
—Ida, Always. Levis, Caron. 2016. (ENG.). 40p. (J). (gr. -1-3). 18.99 *(978-1-4814-2640-4(0))* Simon & Schuster Children's Publishing.
—No Boring Stories! Falatko, Julie. 2018. 48p. (J). (gr. -1-3). 17.99 *(978-0-451-47682-1(4),* Viking Books for Young Readers) Penguin Young Readers Group.
—Peanut Butter & Aliens: A Zombie Culinary Tale. McGee, Joe. 2017. (ENG.). 32p. (J). (gr. -1-2). 16.95 *(978-1-4197-2530-2(0),* Abrams Bks. for Young Readers) Abrams, Inc.
—Peanut Butter & Brains: A Zombie Culinary Tale. McGee, Joe. 2015. (ENG.). 32p. (J). (gr. -1-3). 16.95 *(978-1-4197-1247-0(0),* Abrams Bks. for Young Readers) Abrams, Inc.
—Penguin & Tiny Shrimp Don't Do Bedtime! Berry, Cate. 2018. (ENG.). 32p. (J). (gr. -1-3). 17.99 *(978-0-06-249153-4(9),* Balzer & Bray) HarperCollins Pubs.
—The Snurtch. Ferrell, Sean. 2016. (ENG.). 40p. (J). (gr. -1-3). 17.99 *(978-1-4814-5656-2(3))* Simon & Schuster Children's Publishing.
—Spy Guy: The Not-So-Secret Agent. Young, Jessica. 2015. (ENG.). 40p. (J). (gr. -1-3). 16.99 *(978-0-544-20859-9(5),* 1560872, HMH Books For Young Readers) Houghton Mifflin Harcourt Publishing Co.
—This Way, Charlie. Levis, Caron. 2020. (ENG.). 40p. (J). (gr. -1-3). 17.99 *(978-1-4197-4206-4(X),* 1679101, Abrams Bks. for Young Readers) Abrams, Inc.
—This Way, Charlie: Inspired by a Real Animal Friendship. Levis, Caron. 2020. (J). *(978-1-5344-3063-1(6),* Atheneum Bks. for Young Readers) Simon & Schuster Children's Publishing.
Santoso, Charles. Watch Out for Wolf! Rissi, Anica Mrose. 2019. (ENG.). 32p. (J). (gr. -1-3). 17.99 ***(978-1-4847-8556-0(8))*** Little, Brown Bks. for Young Readers.
Santra, Ria, jt. illus. see Santra, Riya.
Santra, Riya. Rescuing Green Bean. Anderson, Brenda. 2019. (ENG.). 54p. (J). (gr. k-3). 23.99 ***(978-0-9965766-9-7(X))*** Slippers for Hannah (hardcover).
Santra, Riya & Santra, Ria. Rescuing Green Bean. Anderson, Brenda. 2019. (ENG.). 54p. (J). (gr. -1-4). pap. 14.99 *(978-0-9965766-7-3(3))* Little Lost Creations.
Santy, Elizabeth & Fisher, Jessie. I Believe in You: A Mother's Message to Her Son with Learning Differences. Debeer, Kristen. 2012. 32p. pap. 12.97 *(978-1-61897-802-8(0),* Strategic Bk. Publishing) Strategic Book Publishing & Rights Agency (SBPRA).
Sanz, Luis F. Why Juan Can't Sleep: A Mystery? Beckstrand, Karl. l.t. ed. 2019. (Mini-Mysteries for Minors Ser.: Vol. 4). (ENG.). 34p. (J). 26.55 ***(978-1-951599-04-1(7))*** Premio Publishing & Gozo Bks., LLC.
Sanzi, Desiderio. An Ant. Johnson, Jinny. 2015. (J). pap. *(978-1-68152-073-5(7))* Amicus Publishing.
—What's It Like to Be... Ant? Johnson, Jinny. 2011. (What's It Like to Be... ? Ser.). 24p. (J). (gr. -1-k). 25.65 *(978-1-60753-183-8(6))* Amicus Publishing.
—What's It Like to Be... Bee? Ganeri, Anita & Johnson, Jinny. 2011. (What's It Like to Be... ? Ser.). 24p. (J). (gr. -1-k). 25.65 *(978-1-60753-184-5(4))* Amicus Publishing.
—What's It Like to Be... Butterfly? Johnson, Jinny. 2011. (What's It Like to Be... ? Ser.). 24p. (J). (gr. -1-k). 25.65 *(978-1-60753-185-2(2))* Amicus Publishing.
—What's It Like to Be... Dragonfly? Ganeri, Anita & Johnson, Jinny. 2011. (What's It Like to Be... ? Ser.). 24p. (J). (gr. -1-k). 25.65 *(978-1-60753-186-9(0))* Amicus Publishing.
—What's It Like to Be... Grasshopper? Martineau, Susan & Jinny, Johnson. 2011. (What's It Like to Be... ? Ser.). 24p. (J). (gr. -1-k). 25.65 *(978-1-60753-193-7(3))* Amicus Publishing.
Sanzol, Jorge. Las Cosas Que Odio y Otras Exageraciones. Maria Shua, Ana. 2013. (Serie Naranja Ser.). (SPA.). 72p. (J). pap. 9.95 *(978-1-64101-128-0(9))* Santillana USA Publishing Co., Inc.
Saphin, Wendy. Rosie's Box: A Box Full of Surprises. Saphin, Wendy. 2012. 20p. pap. 10.95 *(978-1-62212-457-2(X),* Strategic Bk. Publishing) Strategic Book Publishing & Rights Agency (SBPRA).
Sapin, Mathieu. Akissi: Even More Tales of Mischief: Akissi Book 3. Abouet, Marguerite. 2020. 144p. (J). (gr. 3-7). pap. 14.95 ***(978-1-912497-41-6(7))*** Flying Eye Bks. GBR. Dist: Penguin Random Hse. LLC.
Sapin, Mathieu. Akissi: More Tales of Mischief: Akissi Book 2. Abouet, Marguerite. 2019. 176p. (J). (gr. 3-7). pap. 14.95 *(978-1-912497-17-1(4))* Flying Eye Bks. GBR. Dist: Penguin Random Hse. LLC.
—Akissi: Tales of Mischief: Akissi Book 1. Abouet, Marguerite. 2018. 184p. (J). (gr. 3-7). pap. 14.95 *(978-1-911171-47-8(X))* Flying Eye Bks. GBR. Dist: Penguin Random Hse. LLC.
Saponaro, Dominick. The Guns of Tortuga. Strickland, Brad & Fuller, Thomas E. 2003. (ENG.). 208p. (J). (gr. 3-7). pap. 10.99 *(978-0-689-85297-8(5),* Simon & Schuster/Paula Wiseman Bks.) Simon & Schuster/Paula Wiseman Bks.
Saport, Linda. Circles of Hope. Williams, Karen Lynn. 2005. (ENG.). 32p. (J). 16.00 *(978-0-8028-5276-2(9))* Eerdmans, William B. Publishing Co.
Saport, Linda. Before You Were Born. Saport, Linda. Carlstrom, Nancy White. 2004. 32p. (J). (gr. -1-k). 17.00 *(978-0-8028-5185-7(1))* Eerdmans, William B. Publishing Co.
Sapp, Allen. Nokum: Ma Voix et Mon Coeur, 1 vol. Bouchard, David. 2006. (FRE.). 32p. (J). (gr. 1-2). 24.95 *(978-0-88995-383-3(X),* 4fd75258-4639-4367-af1b-8adefb15e141) Red Deer Pr. CAN. Dist: Firefly Bks., Ltd.
—Nokum Is My Teacher, 1 vol. Bouchard, David & Bouchard, David. 2006. (ENG.). 32p. (J). (gr. 2-5). 24.95 *(978-0-88995-367-3(8),* 07eb83b6-4ced-4e78-a5bb-79378d37c75b) Red Deer Pr. CAN. Dist: Firefly Bks., Ltd.
—Nokum Is My Teacher, 1 vol. Bouchard, David et al. 2019. (ENG.). 32p. (J). (gr. k-4). pap. 16.95 *(978-0-88995-571-4(9),* ab7bcd18-4a24-46da-a65b-26ec5943a0a9) Red Deer Pr. CAN. Dist: Firefly Bks., Ltd.
Sapp, Karen. Barnaby the Bedbug Detective. Stier, Catherine. 2015. (Av2 Fiction Readalong 2016 Ser.). (ENG.). (J). (gr. k-3). lib. bdg. 34.28 *(978-1-4896-3849-6(0),* AV2 by Weigl) Weigl Pubs., Inc.
—Christmas Is... 2010. (ENG.). 24p. (J). (gr. -1-k). 8.99 *(978-0-00-730375-5(0))* HarperCollins Pubs. Ltd. GBR. Dist: Independent Pubs. Group.
—Counting on the Farm. Top That Publishing Staff, ed. 2007. (Magnetic Fun Ser.). 16p. (J). (gr. -1). *(978-1-84666-270-6(2),* Tide Mill Pr.) Top That! Publishing PLC.
—Ellie's Christmas. 2013. (J). *(978-1-4351-4835-2(5))* Barnes & Noble, Inc.
—The Star of the Show. McMillan, Sue. 2014. (J). *(978-0-545-81560-4(6))* Scholastic, Inc.
Sappington, Ray. Ben the Flying Cat, 1 vol. Randolph, Robert. 2009. 30p. pap. 24.95 *(978-1-60749-088-3(9))* America Star Bks.
Sapulich, Joseph. Day by Day Begin-to-Read Bible. Henley, Karyn. 2007. (ENG.). 448p. (J). (gr. -1-2). 16.99 *(978-1-4143-0934-7(1),* 6009341) Tyndale Hse. Pubs.
Sara Acton. Mr Walker Braves the Night. Black, Jess. 2020. (Mr Walker Ser.). (ENG.). 96p. (J). (gr. k-2). 12.99 ***(978-0-14-379310-6(1)***, Puffin) Penguin Random Hse. AUS. Dist: Independent Pubs. Group.
Saraceni, Claudia. Chinese Myths. Shone, Rob. 2006. (Graphic Mythology Ser.). (ENG.). 48p. (J). (gr. 4-7). lib. bdg. 35.45 *(978-1-4042-0799-8(6))* Rosen Publishing Group, Inc., The.
—Crime Scene Investigators. Shone, Rob. 2008. (Graphic Forensic Science Ser.). (ENG.). 48p. (YA). (gr. 5-8). lib. bdg. 35.45 *(978-1-4042-1443-9(7))* Rosen Publishing Group, Inc., The.
—Spectacular Shipwrecks. Jeffrey, Gary. 2008. (Graphic Nonfiction Ser.). (ENG.). 48p. (gr. 3-8). pap. 14.05 *(978-1-4042-9597-1(6));* (J). (gr. 5-9). lib. bdg. 35.45 *(978-1-4042-1091-2(1))* Rosen Publishing Group, Inc., The.
Sarago-Kendrick, Delphine. Djomi Dream Child. Fry, Christopher. 2004. (ENG.). 32p. (J). (gr. k-7). pap. 13.95 *(978-1-875641-82-6(3))* Magabala Bks. AUS. Dist: Independent Pubs. Group.
Sarago-Kendrick, Delphine. Nana's Land. Sarago-Kendrick, Delphine. 2004. 44p. (J). pap. *(978-1-875641-90-1(4))* Magabala Bks.
Sarah, Ackerley. Spaghetti Is Not a Finger Food (and Other Life Lessons) Carmichael, Jodi. 2013. (ENG.). 152p. (J). (gr. 1-5). pap. 6.95 *(978-1-939775-03-0(5),* Little Pickle Pr.) Sourcebooks, Inc.
Sarah, Waterfield. The Adventures of Mrs. B: Meeting the New Family. Benkendorf, Lynne. Shayla, Raquel, ed. 2018. (ENG.). 42p. (J). (gr. 1-2). 24.95 *(978-1-7321250-0-1(7))* Brown Spotted Dog Publishing.
—The Adventures of Mrs. B: Someone Who Understands Me. Benkendorf, Lynne. Shayla, Raquel, ed. 2019. (ENG.). 42p. (J). (gr. k-2). 24.95 *(978-1-7321250-1-8(5))* Brown Spotted Dog Publishing.
—Witch Wobblyknees: And the Wibbly Wobbly Wand. Bird, Rosita. 2016. (ENG.). (J). pap. 9.99 *(978-1-68160-185-4(0))* Crimson Cloak Publishing.
Sarah Wilkins. Abigail & the Birth of the Sun. Cunningham, Matthew. 2019. (ENG.). 32p. (J). (gr. -1-k). 17.99 ***(978-0-14-377270-5(8))*** Penguin Group New Zealand, Ltd. NZL. Dist: Independent Pubs. Group.
Saraniti, Carlos. La Polilla del Baul. Carvajal, Mario. 2003. (SPA.). 32p. (J). (gr. k-3). pap. 8.95 *(978-968-19-0483-8(4))* Santillana USA Publishing Co., Inc.
Sarcone-Roach, Julia. Excellent Ed. McAnulty, Stacy. 2016. 32p. (J). (gr. -1-3). 17.99 *(978-0-553-51023-2(1),* Knopf Bks. for Young Readers) Random Hse. Children's Bks.
—Incredible Inventions. Hopkins, Lee Bennett. 2009. 32p. (J). (gr. k-5). lib. bdg. 18.89 *(978-0-06-087246-5(2),* Greenwillow Bks.) HarperCollins Pubs.
—Incredible Inventions. Hopkins, Lee Bennett. 2009. (ENG.). 32p. (J). (gr. k-5). 17.99 *(978-0-06-087245-8(4),* Greenwillow Bks.) HarperCollins Pubs.
Sardà, Júlia. Duckworth, the Difficult Child. Sussman, Michael. 2019. (ENG.). 40p. (J). (gr. -1-3). 17.99 *(978-1-5344-0512-7(7))* Simon & Schuster Children's Publishing.
Sarda, Julia. The Liszts. Maclear, Kyo. 2016. (ENG.). 40p. (J). (gr. k-4). 16.99 *(978-1-77049-496-1(0),* Tundra Bks.) Tundra Bks. CAN. Dist: Penguin Random Hse. LLC.
Sardà, Júlia. Mary Poppins (Illustrated Gift Edition) Travers, P. L. 2018. (Mary Poppins Ser.). (ENG.). 248p. (J). (gr. 5-7). 24.99 *(978-1-328-49884-7(0),* 1717674, HMH Books For Young Readers) Houghton Mifflin Harcourt Publishing Co.
Sarda, Julia. Mary Who Wrote Frankenstein. Bailey, Linda. 2018. (ENG.). 56p. (J). (gr. k-3). 17.99 *(978-1-77049-559-3(2),* Tundra Bks.) Tundra Bks. CAN. Dist: Penguin Random Hse. LLC.

S

Sardà, Júlia. One Fun Day with Lewis Carroll: A Celebration of Wordplay & a Girl Named Alice. Krull, Kathleen. 2018. (ENG.). 32p. (J). (gr. 1-4). 17.99 *(978-0-544-34823-3(0)*, 1585762, HMH Books For Young Readers) Houghton Mifflin Harcourt Publishing Co.

—Sweep. Greig, Louise. 2019. (ENG.). 32p. (J). (gr. -1-3). 17.99 *(978-1-5344-3908-5(0)*, Simon & Schuster Bks. For Young Readers) Simon & Schuster Bks. For Young Readers.

—The Treasure of Barracuda. Campos, Llanos & Campos Martinez, Llanos. 2016. (ENG.). 156p. (J). (gr. 4-7). 15.95 *(978-1-939775-14-6(0)*, Little Pickle Pr.) Sourcebooks, Inc.

Sardinha, Rick. The Land of the Silver Apples. Farmer, Nancy. 2007. (ENG.). 512p. (J). (gr. 5-9). 21.99 *(978-1-4169-0735-0(1)*, Atheneum/Richard Jackson Bks.) Simon & Schuster Children's Publishing.

Sarecky, Melody. Apples, Bubbles, & Crystals: Your Science ABCs. Bennett, Andrea T. & Kessler, James H. 2004. (J). *(978-0-8412-3944-9(4))* American Chemical Society.

—Sunlight, Skyscrapers, & Soda-Pop: The Wherever-You-Look Science Book. Bennett, Andrea T. & Kessler, James H. 2003. (J). 12.95 *(978-0-8412-3870-1(7))* American Chemical Society.

Sarell, Nadja. Frankie Sparks & the Big Sled Challenge. Blakemore, Megan Frazer. 2019. (Frankie Sparks, Third-Grade Inventor Ser.: 3). (ENG.). 128p. (J). (gr. 2-5). 17.99 *(978-1-5344-3050-1(4))*; pap. 5.99 *(978-1-5344-3049-5(0))* Simon & Schuster Children's Publishing. (Aladdin).

—Frankie Sparks & the Class Pet. Blakemore, Megan Frazer. 2019. (Frankie Sparks, Third-Grade Inventor Ser.: 1). (ENG.). 144p. (J). (gr. 2-5). 17.99 *(978-1-5344-3044-0(X))*; pap. 5.99 *(978-1-5344-3043-3(1))* Simon & Schuster Children's Publishing. (Aladdin).

—Frankie Sparks & the Lucky Charm. Blakemore, Megan Frazer. 2020. (Frankie Sparks, Third-Grade Inventor Ser.: 4). (ENG.). 128p. (J). (gr. 2-5). 17.99 *(978-1-5344-3053-2(9))*; pap. 5.99 *(978-1-5344-3052-5(0))* Simon & Schuster Children's Publishing. (Aladdin).

—Frankie Sparks & the Talent Show Trick. Blakemore, Megan Frazer. 2019. (Frankie Sparks, Third-Grade Inventor Ser.: 2). (ENG.). 128p. (J). (gr. 2-5). 17.99 *(978-1-5344-3047-1(4))*; pap. 5.99 *(978-1-5344-3046-4(6))* Simon & Schuster Children's Publishing. (Aladdin).

—Frankie Sparks Invention Collection Books 1-4: Frankie Sparks & the Class Pet; Frankie Sparks & the Talent Show Trick; Frankie Sparks & the Big Sled Challenge; Frankie Sparks & the Lucky Charm. Blakemore, Megan Frazer. ed. 2020. (Frankie Sparks, Third-Grade Inventor Ser.). (ENG.). 528p. (J). (gr. 2-5). pap. 23.99 *(978-1-5344-5660-0(0)*, Aladdin) Simon & Schuster Children's Publishing.

—I Saw Santa in Cincinnati. Green, J. D. 2018. (I Saw Santa Ser.). (ENG.). 32p. (J). (-3). 12.99 *(978-1-4926-6838-1(9)*, Sourcebooks Jabberwocky) Sourcebooks, Inc.

—I Saw Santa in New Hampshire. Green, J. D. 2018. (I Saw Santa Ser.). (ENG.). 32p. (J). (-3). 12.99 *(978-1-4926-6868-8(0)*, Sourcebooks Jabberwocky) Sourcebooks, Inc.

—I Saw Santa in Philadelphia. Green, J. D. 2018. (I Saw Santa Ser.). (ENG.). 32p. (J). (-3). 12.99 *(978-1-4926-6881-7(8)*, Sourcebooks Jabberwocky) Sourcebooks, Inc.

—I Saw Santa in Rhode Island. Green, J. D. 2018. (I Saw Santa Ser.). (ENG.). 32p. (J). (-3). 12.99 *(978-1-4926-6883-1(4)*, Sourcebooks Jabberwocky) Sourcebooks, Inc.

—I Saw Santa in South Carolina. Green, J. D. 2018. (I Saw Santa Ser.). (ENG.). 32p. (J). (-3). 12.99 *(978-1-4926-6885-5(0)*, Sourcebooks Jabberwocky) Sourcebooks, Inc.

—I Saw Santa in Tennessee. Green, J. D. 2018. (I Saw Santa Ser.). (ENG.). 32p. (J). (-3). 12.99 *(978-1-4926-6888-6(5)*, Sourcebooks Jabberwocky) Sourcebooks, Inc.

—I Saw Santa in Texas. Green, J. D. 2018. (I Saw Santa Ser.). (ENG.). 32p. (J). (-3). 12.99 *(978-1-4926-6889-3(3)*, Sourcebooks Jabberwocky) Sourcebooks, Inc.

—Little Dove & the Story of Easter, 1 vol. 2019. (ENG.). 22p. (J). bds. 7.99 *(978-0-310-76668-1(0))* Zonderkidz.

Sarell, Nadja, et al. New England Books for Kids Gift Set. Green, J. D. et al. 2020. (ENG.). (J). 29.99 ***(978-1-7282-4192-0(8))*** Sourcebooks, Inc.

Sarell, Nadja. The One & Only Wolfgang: From Pet Rescue to One Big Happy Family, 1 vol. Greig, Steve & Hess, Mary Rand. 2019. (ENG.). 32p. (J). 17.99 *(978-0-310-76823-4(3))* Zonderkidz.

Sarell, Nadja, jt. illus. see Bassani, Srimalie.

Sarenac, Gorana. The Purloined Stamp. Phillips, Adam a. 2020. (Lenny & Janice Mystery Ser.: Vol. 2). (ENG.). 66p. (J). pap. 8.99 ***(978-1-6770-4249-4(4))*** Independently Published.

Sarganis, Brad. Mrs. Claus Saves Christmas. Wonder, Yvonne. 2018. (ENG.). 34p. (J). 19.95 *(978-1-949752-00-7(3))* Destination Wonder Pr.

Sargeant, Theresa. Shipwrecked on Gingerbeard's Island: Book 2 in the Chris & Andy Smythe Adventures. Sargeant, Theresa. 2018. (Chris & Andy Smythe Adventures Ser.: Vol. 2). (ENG.). 134p. (YA). pap. *(978-1-910882-91-7(7))* Abela Publishing.

Sargent, Claudia Karabaic. Nice Vine, Quite Fine, Vol. 2. Goldish, Meish. I.t. ed. 2005. (Little Books & Big Bks.: Vol. 7). 8p. (gr. k-2). 23.00 net. *(978-0-8215-7516-1(3))* Sadlier, William H. Inc.

Sargent, Shannon Marie. My Little One: A Mother's Lullaby. Wilt, Gerri Ann et al. 2008. (J). *(978-0-87839-299-5(8))* North Star Pr. of St. Cloud.

Sari. The Pink Maple House. Govan, Christine Noble. 2013. 292p. pap. 13.95 *(978-1-61427-443-8(6))* Martino Fine Bks.

—The Surprising Summer. Govan, Christine Noble. 2013. 178p. pap. 9.95 *(978-1-61427-449-0(5))* Martino Fine Bks.

Sarima. Conflicto: El Enigma de Los llenios II (Edicion V Aniversario) Urvi, Pedro. 2018. (Enigma de Los llenios Ser.: Vol. 2). (SPA.). 428p. (J). pap. 15.00 *(978-1-7177-8011-9(3))* Independently Published.

—Destino: El Enigma de Los llenios IV (Edición V Aniversario) Urvi, Pedro. 2018. (Enigma de Los llenios Ser.: Vol. 4). (SPA.). 444p. (J). pap. 19.00 *(978-1-7177-8041-6(5))* Independently Published.

Sarima. El Misterio de la Tundra: (el Sendero Del Guardabosques, Libro 3) Urvi, Pedro. 2019. (Sendero Del Guardabosques Ser.: Vol. 3). (SPA.). 374p. (J). pap. 15.99 ***(978-1-7116-1112-9(3))*** Independently Published.

—Traici�n en el Norte: (el Sendero Del Guardabosques, Libro 4) Urvi, Pedro. 2019. (Sendero Del Guardabosques Ser.: Vol. 4). (SPA.). 394p. (J). pap. 16.99 ***(978-1-7116-0833-4(5))*** Independently Published.

Sarin, Max. Giant Days Vol. 12. Allison, John. 2020. (Giant Days Ser.: 12). (ENG.). 112p. (YA). pap. 14.99 *(978-1-68415-484-5(7))* Boom! Studios.

—Giant Days Vol. 9. Allison, John. 2019. (Giant Days Ser.). (ENG.). 112p. (YA). (gr. 8-12). pap. 14.99 *(978-1-68415-310-7(7))* Boom! Studios.

Sarin, Max & Madrigal, Julia. Giant Days Vol. 10. Allison, John. 2019. (Giant Days Ser.: 10). (ENG.). 112p. (YA). pap. 14.99 *(978-1-68415-371-8(9))* Boom! Studios.

Sariola, Eulalia. El Libro de Las Mil y una Noches: Relatos de Hoy y Siempre. Castells, Margarita. 2006. (SPA & ENG.). 72p. (J). (gr. 4-7). pap. 15.00 *(978-84-666-1335-4(8))* Ediciones B ESP. Dist: Independent Pubs. Group.

Sarkar, Anjan. The Alien Next Door 1: the New Kid. Newton, A. I. 2018. (Alien Next Door Ser.: 1). (ENG.). 112p. (J). (gr. k-3). 16.99 *(978-1-4998-0559-8(4))*; pap. 5.99 *(978-1-4998-0558-1(6))* Little Bee Books Inc.

—The Alien Next Door 2: Aliens for Dinner?! Newton, A. I. 2018. (Alien Next Door Ser.: 2). (ENG.). 112p. (J). (gr. k-3). 16.99 *(978-1-4998-0562-8(4))*; pap. 5.99 *(978-1-4998-0561-1(6))* Little Bee Books Inc.

—The Alien Next Door 3: Alien Scout. Newton, A. I. 2018. (Alien Next Door Ser.: 3). (ENG.). 112p. (J). (gr. k-3). 16.99 *(978-1-4998-0581-9(0))*; pap. 5.99 *(978-1-4998-0580-2(2))* Little Bee Books Inc.

—The Alien Next Door: 4 Books In 1! Newton, A. I. 2019. (Alien Next Door Ser.: 1). (ENG.). 416p. (J). (gr. k-3). 14.99 *(978-1-4998-0992-3(1))* Little Bee Books Inc.

—The Alien Next Door 4: Trick or Cheat? Newton, A. I. 2018. (Alien Next Door Ser.: 4). (ENG.). 112p. (J). (gr. k-3). 16.99 *(978-1-4998-0584-0(5))*; pap. 5.99 *(978-1-4998-0583-3(7))* Little Bee Books Inc.

—The Alien Next Door 5: Baseball Blues. Newton, A. I. 2018. (Alien Next Door Ser.: 5). (ENG.). 112p. (J). (gr. k-3). 16.99 *(978-1-4998-0723-3(6))*; pap. 5.99 *(978-1-4998-0722-6(8))* Little Bee Books Inc.

—The Alien Next Door 6: the Mystery Valentine. Newton, A. I. 2018. (Alien Next Door Ser.: 6). (ENG.). 112p. (J). (gr. k-3). 16.99 *(978-1-4998-0726-4(0))*; pap. 5.99 *(978-1-4998-0725-7(2))* Little Bee Books Inc.

—The Alien Next Door 7: up, up, & Away! Newton, A. I. 2019. (Alien Next Door Ser.: 7). (ENG.). 112p. (J). (gr. k-3). 16.99 *(978-1-4998-0806-3(2))*; pap. 5.99 *(978-1-4998-0805-6(4))* Little Bee Books Inc.

—The Alien Next Door 8: a New Planet. Newton, A. I. 2020. (Alien Next Door Ser.: 8). (ENG.). 112p. (J). (gr. k-3). 16.99 *(978-1-4998-1003-5(2))*; pap. 5.99 *(978-1-4998-1002-8(4))* Little Bee Books Inc.

—Queen of the Hanukkah Dosas. Ehrenberg, Pamela. 2017. (ENG.). 40p. (J). 16.99 *(978-0-374-30444-7(0)*, 900159322, Farrar, Straus & Giroux (BYR)) Farrar, Straus & Giroux.

Sarkar, Anjan. Rum Pum Pum. Harrison, David L. & Yolen, Jane. 2020. (ENG.). 40p. (J). (gr. -1-2). 18.99 ***(978-0-8234-4100-6(8))*** Holiday Hse., Inc.

—Sadiq & the Bridge Builders. Nuurali, Siman. 2020. (Sadiq Ser.). (ENG.). 64p. (J). (gr. 1-3). pap. 6.95 ***(978-1-5158-7289-4(0)***, 201314); lib. bdg. 23.32 ***(978-1-5158-7103-3(7)***, 199200) Capstone. (Picture Window Bks.).

Sarkar, Anjan. Sadiq & the Desert Star. Nuurali, Siman. 2019. (Sadiq Ser.). (ENG.). 64p. (J). (gr. 1-3). 23.32 *(978-1-5158-3878-4(1)*, 139596, Picture Window Bks.) Capstone.

Sarkar, Anjan. Sadiq & the Explorers. Nuurali, Siman. 2020. (Sadiq Ser.). (ENG.). 64p. (J). (gr. 1-3). pap. 6.95 ***(978-1-5158-7290-0(4)***, 201315); lib. bdg. 23.32 ***(978-1-5158-7104-0(5)***, 199201) Capstone. (Picture Window Bks.).

Sarkar, Anjan. Sadiq & the Fun Run. Nuurali, Siman. 2019. (Sadiq Ser.). (ENG.). 64p. (J). (gr. 1-3). pap. 6.95 *(978-1-5158-4566-9(4)*, 141154, Picture Window Bks.) Capstone.

—Sadiq & the Green Thumbs. Nuurali, Siman. 2019. (Sadiq Ser.). (ENG.). 64p. (J). (gr. 1-3). pap. 6.95 *(978-1-5158-4567-6(2)*, 141155, Picture Window Bks.) Capstone.

Sarkar, Anjan. Sadiq & the Perfect Play. Nuurali, Siman. 2020. (Sadiq Ser.). (ENG.). 64p. (J). (gr. 1-3). pap. 6.95 ***(978-1-5158-7287-0(4)***, 201312); lib. bdg. 23.32 ***(978-1-5158-7101-9(0)***, 199197) Capstone. (Picture Window Bks.).

Sarkar, Anjan. Sadiq & the Pet Problem. Nuurali, Siman. 2019. (Sadiq Ser.). (ENG.). 64p. (J). (gr. 1-3). pap. 6.95 *(978-1-5158-4568-3(0)*, 141156, Picture Window Bks.) Capstone.

Sarkar, Anjan. Sadiq & the Ramadan Gift. Nuurali, Siman. 2020. (Sadiq Ser.). (ENG.). 64p. (J). (gr. 1-3). pap. 6.95 ***(978-1-5158-7288-7(2)***, 201313); lib. bdg. 23.32 ***(978-1-5158-7102-6(9)***, 199198) Capstone. (Picture Window Bks.).

Sarkar, Pratima. Peter the Little Irish Seal. Perkins, Dan. 2016. (ENG.). (J). *(978-1-5255-0030-5(9))*; pap. *(978-1-4602-9807-7(1))* FriesenPress.

Sarkar, Soumitro. Monkey's Drum. Moorthy, Anita. 2003. (ENG.). 24p. pap. 3.99 *(978-81-86211-15-1(2))* Penguin Publishing Group.

Sarna, Billy. Where Do Raindrops Go? Champagne, Elena. I.t. ed. 2006. 24p. (J). (gr. -1-3). per. 10.99 *(978-1-59879-233-1(4))* Lifevest Publishing, Inc.

Saroff, Phyllis. Belle: The Amazing, Astonishingly Magical Journey of an Artfully Painted Lady. Corlett, Mary Lee. 12th ed. 2011. (ENG.). 52p. (J). (gr. 3-9). pap. 25.00 *(978-1-59373-084-0(5))* Bunker Hill Publishing, Inc.

—Dear Tree. Weber, Rivka Doba. Rosenfeld, D. L., ed. 2010. 24p. (YA). 10.95 *(978-1-929628-48-3(X))* Hachai Publishing.

—Jesus, I Feel Close to You. Stuckey, Denise. 2005. 32p. (J). 10.95 *(978-0-8091-6718-0(2)*, 6718-2) Paulist Pr.

—Signal's Airport Adventure. Friday, Stormy. 2006. (J). 14.95 *(978-0-9717047-5-6(9))* Bay Media, Inc.

—Sonidos en la Sabana, 1 vol. Jennings, Terry Catasús. 2015. (SPA & ENG.). 32p. (J). (gr. k-3). pap. 9.95 *(978-1-62855-642-1(0))* Arbordale Publishing.

—Sounds of the Savanna, 1 vol. Jennings, Terry Catasús. 2015. (ENG.). 32p. (J). (gr. k-3). pap. 9.95 *(978-1-62855-637-7(4))* Arbordale Publishing.

—Time & the Tapestry. Plotz, John. 2014. (ENG.). 192p. (YA). (gr. 4-11). 18.50 *(978-1-59373-145-8(0))* Bunker Hill Publishing, Inc.

—Tuktuk: Tundra Tale, 1 vol. Currie, Robin. 2016. (ENG & SPA.). 32p. (J). (gr. k-3). 17.95 *(978-1-62855-879-1(2))* Arbordale Publishing.

—Tuktuk: Un Cuento Sobre la Tundra. Currie, Robin. 2016. (SPA.). 32p. (J). (gr. k-3). pap. 11.95 *(978-1-62855-881-4(4))* Arbordale Publishing.

—Vivian & the Legend of the Hoodoos. Jennings, Terry Catasús. 2017. (ENG & SPA.). 32p. (J). (gr. k-3). 17.95 *(978-1-62855-957-6(8))* Arbordale Publishing.

—Viviana y la Leyenda de Los Hoodoos. Jennings, Terry Catasús. 2017. (SPA.). 32p. (J). (gr. k-3). pap. 11.95 *(978-1-62855-959-0(4))* Arbordale Publishing.

Saroff, Phyllis V. A Journey into a Lake. Johnson, Rebecca L. 2004. (Biomes of North America Ser.). (J). pap. 6.95 *(978-0-8225-2043-6(5))*; 48p. (gr. 3-6). lib. bdg. 23.93 *(978-1-57505-594-7(5))* Lerner Publishing Group.

—A Journey into a River. Johnson, Rebecca L. 2004. (Biomes of North America Ser.). (J). pap. 8.95 *(978-0-8225-2044-3(3))*; 48p. (gr. 3-6). 23.93 *(978-1-57505-595-4(3))* Lerner Publishing Group.

—A Journey into a Wetland. Johnson, Rebecca L. 2004. (Biomes of North America Ser.). (J). pap. 8.95 *(978-0-8225-2047-4(8))*; 48p. (gr. 3-6). lib. bdg. 23.93 *(978-1-57505-593-0(7))* Lerner Publishing Group.

—A Journey into an Estuary. Johnson, Rebecca L. 2004. (Biomes of North America Ser.). (J). pap. 6.95 *(978-0-8225-2045-0(1))*; (ENG.). 48p. (gr. 3-6). lib. bdg. 23.93 *(978-1-57505-592-3(9))* Lerner Publishing Group.

—A Journey into the Ocean. Johnson, Rebecca L. 2004. (Biomes of North America Ser.). (ENG.). 48p. (gr. 3-6). lib. bdg. 23.93 *(978-1-57505-591-6(0))* Lerner Publishing Group.

—Mary Anning: Fossil Hunter. Walker, Sally M. 2007. (On My Own Biographies Ser.). 48p. (J). (gr. 2-5). per. 6.95 *(978-1-57505-457-5(4)*, First Avenue Editions) Lerner Publishing Group.

—Teeth. Collard, Sneed B., III. 2008. 32p. (J). (gr. k-3). per. 7.95 *(978-1-58089-121-9(7))*; (ENG.). 21.19 *(978-1-58089-120-2(9))* Charlesbridge Publishing, Inc.

—A Walk in the Deciduous Forest. Braasch, Gary, photos by. Johnson, Rebecca L. 2005. (Biomes of North America Ser.). 48p. (gr. 3-6). lib. bdg. 23.93 *(978-1-57505-155-0(9))* Lerner Publishing Group.

—A Walk in the Rain Forest. Braasch, Gary, photos by. Johnson, Rebecca L. 2005. (Biomes of North America Ser.). 48p. (gr. 3-6). 23.93 *(978-1-57505-154-3(0))* Lerner Publishing Group.

—A Walk in the Tundra. Braasch, Gary, photos by. Johnson, Rebecca L. 2005. (Biomes of North America Ser.). 48p. (gr. 3-6). lib. bdg. 23.93 *(978-1-57505-157-4(5))* Lerner Publishing Group.

Sarrazin, Jean-charles. El Mas Bonito de Todos los Regalos del Mundo. Teulade, Pascale. (SPA.). 40p. (J). (gr. k-1). 15.95 *(978-84-95150-27-1(1)*, COR30367) Corimbo, Editorial S.L. ESP. Dist: Lectorum Pubns., Inc., Distribooks, Inc.

Sarrazin, Marisol. Lizards Don't Wear Lip Gloss. Wiebe, Trina. 2004. (Abby & Tess Pet-Sitters Ser.). 91p. 15.95 *(978-0-7569-3425-5(7))* Perfection Learning Corp.

—Pizza for Sam. Labatt, Mary. 2003. (Kids Can Read Ser.). (ENG.). 32p. (J). (gr. k-1). 3.95 *(978-1-55337-331-5(6))* Kids Can Pr., Ltd. CAN. Dist: Hachette Bk. Group.

—Sam at the Seaside. Labatt, Mary. 2006. (Kids Can Read Ser.). (ENG.). 32p. (J). (gr. k-1). pap. 4.95 *(978-1-55337-877-8(6))* Kids Can Pr., Ltd. CAN. Dist: Hachette Bk. Group.

—Sam Finds a Monster. Labatt, Mary. 2003. 32p. (J). pap. *(978-0-439-58742-6(5))* Scholastic, Inc.

—Sam Finds a Monster. Labatt, Mary. 2003. (Kids Can Read Ser.). (ENG.). 32p. (J). (gr. k-1). 11.99 *(978-1-55337-352-0(9))* Kids Can Pr., Ltd. CAN. Dist: Hachette Bk. Group.

—Sam Gets Lost. Labatt, Mary. 2004. (Kids Can Read Ser.: Vol. 1). (ENG.). 32p. (J). (gr. k-1). 11.99 *(978-1-55337-563-0(7))* Kids Can Pr., Ltd. CAN. Dist: Hachette Bk. Group.

—Sam Goes to School. Labatt, Mary. 2004. (Kids Can Read Ser.: Vol. 1). (ENG.). 32p. (J). (gr. k-1). 4.95 *(978-1-55337-565-4(3))* Kids Can Pr., Ltd. CAN. Dist: Hachette Bk. Group.

—Sam's Snowy Day. Labatt, Mary. 2005. (Kids Can Read Level 1 Ser.). 32p. (J). (gr. -1-2). 16.19 *(978-1-55337-789-4(3))* Kids Can Pr., Ltd. CAN. Dist: Children's Plus, Inc.

Sarson, Jade. Heroes of Flight: Who Changed the World. Enz, Tammy L. 2019. (Graphic Greats Ser.). (ENG.). 128p. (J). (gr. 4-7). pap. 12.99 *(978-1-4380-1198-1(9)*, B.E.S. Publishing) Peterson's.

Sarter, Nicolas. L' Eveil: Les Chroniques D'Harmonie 1. Lecina, Patrice. 2020. (Chroniques D'Harmonie Ser.: Vol. 1). (FRE.). 370p. (J). pap. ***(978-2-9571277-0-2(9))*** Bekalle-Akwe (Henri Junior).

Sartor, Amanda. Fighting for Equal Rights: A Story about Susan B. Anthony. Sartor, Amanda, tr. Weidt, Maryann N. 2004. (Creative Minds Biography Ser.). 64p. (J). 22.60 *(978-1-57505-181-9(8)*, Carolrhoda Bks.) Lerner Publishing Group.

Sasaki, Chie. Someone Took Vanessa's Bike. Moran, Maggie A. 2003. 28p. (J). lib. bdg. 14.95 *(978-1-931642-03-3(6))* New Voices Publishing Co.

Sasaki, Chris. Home Is a Window. Ledyard, Stephanie. 2019. 40p. (J). (gr. -1-3). 18.99 *(978-0-8234-4156-3(3)*, Neal Porter Bks) Holiday Hse., Inc.

—Paper Son: the Inspiring Story of Tyrus Wong, Immigrant & Artist. Leung, Julie. 2019. (ENG.). 40p. (J). (gr. -1-3). 20.99 *(978-1-5247-7188-1(0)*, Schwartz & Wade Bks.) Random Hse. Children's Bks.

Sasaki, Ellen Joy. Gus, the Pilgrim Turkey. Bateman, Teresa. 2013. (AV2 Fiction Readalong Ser.). (ENG.). (J). (gr. k-3). 34.28 *(978-1-62127-879-5(4)*, AV2 by Weigl) Weigl Pubs., Inc.

Saseen, Sharon. Patience & the Flower Girl. 2004. *(978-0-9748425-0-9(8))* Saseen, Sharon.

Sasheva, Iva. Helen Thayer's Arctic Adventure: A Woman & a Dog Walk to the North Pole. Isaacs, Sally. 2016. (Encounter: Narrative Nonfiction Picture Bks.). (ENG.). 32p. (J). (gr. 4-5). lib. bdg. 29.32 *(978-1-4914-8044-1(0)*, Capstone Young Readers) Capstone.

—Helen Thayer's Arctic Adventure: A Woman & a Dog Walk to the North Pole. Isaacs, Sally Senzell. 2017. (Encounter: Narrative Nonfiction Picture Bks.). (ENG.). 32p. (J). (gr. 4-5). pap. 7.95 *(978-1-4914-8045-8(9)*, Capstone Young Readers) Capstone.

Sashigane, Richard. Solarspire. Oster, Aaron. 2019. (Rise to Omniscience Ser.: Vol. 4). (ENG.). 376p. (J). pap. 14.99 ***(978-1-7043-7800-8(1))*** Independently Published.

Sasiain, Leire, jt. illus. see Holliday, Jeremy Tinson.

Sasic, Natasha. Love Potion. Banks, Steven. ed. 2005. (Adventures of Jimmy Neutron Ser.: 7). 24p. (J). lib. bdg. 15.00 *(978-1-59054-784-7(5))* Fitzgerald Bks.

Sasky, Jazmin. What Grandma Built. Gilman, Michelle. 2016. (ENG.). 32p. (J). pap. 14.95 *(978-1-55017-753-4(2))* Harbour Publishing Co., Ltd. CAN. Dist: Publishers Group West (PGW).

Sasser, Mark. Mask of the Monkey. Foreman, Jay W. Lewis, Vicki, ed. 2018. (ENG.). 32p. (J). pap. 12.00 *(978-1-7239-8317-7(9))* Independently Published.

Sassin, Eva. Be a Tracker. Oxlade, Chris. 2015. (Go Wild Ser.). (ENG.). 32p. (J). (gr. 3-6). pap. 7.99 *(978-1-4677-7650-9(5)*, 9781467776509, Hungry Tomato ®) Lerner Publishing Group.

—Be an Adventurer. Oxlade, Chris. 2015. (Go Wild Ser.). (ENG.). 32p. (J). (gr. 3-6). pap. 7.99 *(978-1-4677-7647-9(5)*, 9781467776479, Hungry Tomato ®) Lerner Publishing Group.

—Be an Explorer. Oxlade, Chris. ed. 2015. (Go Wild Ser.). (ENG.). 32p. (J). (gr. 3-6). E-Book 42.65 *(978-1-4677-7223-5(2)*, Hungry Tomato ®) Lerner Publishing Group.

—Climbing Trees & Muddy Knees: The Kids Guide to Getting Unplugged & Getting Outside. Oxlade, Chris. 2020. (ENG.). 96p. (J). (gr. 2-6). 19.99 *(978-1-913077-18-1(7)*, e4142260-126f-4624-8b11-182ee33f21a8, Beetle Bks.) Hungry Tomato Ltd. GBR. Dist: Baker & Taylor Publisher Services (BTPS).

—Fun Experiments with Electricity: Mini Robots, Micro Lightning Strikes, & More. Ives, Rob. 2017. (Amazing Science Experiments Ser.). (ENG.). 32p. (J). (gr. 3-6). lib. bdg. 27.99 *(978-1-5124-3219-0(9)*, 9781512432190, Hungry Tomato ®) Lerner Publishing Group.

—Fun Experiments with Forces & Motion: Hovercrafts, Rockets, & More. Ives, Rob. 2017. (Amazing Science Experiments Ser.). (ENG.). 32p. (J). (gr. 3-6). lib. bdg. 27.99 *(978-1-5124-3217-6(2)*, 9781512432176, Hungry Tomato ®) Lerner Publishing Group.

—Fun Experiments with Light: Periscopes, Kaleidoscopes, & More. Ives, Rob. 2017. (Amazing Science Experiments Ser.). (ENG.). 32p. (J). (gr. 3-6). lib. bdg. 27.99 *(978-1-5124-3218-3(0)*, 9781512432183, Hungry Tomato ®) Lerner Publishing Group.

—Fun Experiments with Matter: Invisible Ink, Giant Bubbles, & More. Ives, Rob. 2017. (Amazing Science Experiments Ser.). (ENG.). 32p. (J). (gr. 3-6). lib. bdg. 27.99 *(978-1-5124-3216-9(4)*, 9781512432169, Hungry Tomato ®) Lerner Publishing Group.

—My Two Dogs. Crow, Melinda Melton. 2013. (My Two Dogs Ser.). (ENG.). 32p. (J). (gr. 1-3). lib. bdg., lib. bdg., lib. bdg. 181.20 *(978-1-4342-6069-7(0)*, Stone Arch Bks.) Capstone.

—Rocky & Daisy & the Birthday Party. Crow, Melinda Melton. 2013. (My Two Dogs Ser.). (ENG.). 32p. (gr. 1-3). pap. 29.70 *(978-1-4342-6296-7(0))*; (J). (gr. 2-3). pap. 5.95 *(978-1-4342-6205-9(7))*; (J). (gr. 2-3). lib. bdg. 22.65 *(978-1-4342-6011-6(9))* Capstone. (Stone Arch Bks.).

—Rocky & Daisy Go to the Vet. Crow, Melinda Melton. 2013. (My Two Dogs Ser.). (ENG.). 32p. (gr. 1-3). pap. 29.70 *(978-1-4342-6297-4(9))*; (J). (gr. 2-3). pap. 5.95 *(978-1-4342-6203-5(0))*; (J). (gr. 2-3). lib. bdg. 22.65 *(978-1-4342-6009-3(7))* Capstone. (Stone Arch Bks.).

—Rocky & Daisy Take a Vacation. Crow, Melinda Melton. 2013. (My Two Dogs Ser.). (ENG.). 32p. (gr. 1-3). pap. 29.70 *(978-1-4342-6298-1(7))*; (J). (gr. 2-3). lib. bdg. 22.65 *(978-1-4342-6008-6(9))* Capstone. (Stone Arch Bks.).

—Rocky & Daisy Wash the Van. Crow, Melinda Melton. 2013. (My Two Dogs Ser.). (ENG.). 32p. (gr. 1-3). pap. 29.70 *(978-1-4342-6299-8(5))*; (J). (gr. 2-3). pap. 5.95 *(978-1-4342-6204-2(9))*; (J). (gr. 2-3). lib. bdg. 22.65 *(978-1-4342-6010-9(0))* Capstone. (Stone Arch Bks.).

—25 Fun Things to Do for Your Neighbors. Mason, Paul. 2019. (100 Fun Things to Do to Unplug Ser.). (ENG.). 32p. (J). (gr. 3-6). lib. bdg. 27.99 *(978-1-5415-0136-2(5)*, Hungry Tomato ®) Lerner Publishing Group.

—25 Fun Things to Do on a Rainy Day. Mason, Paul. 2019. (100 Fun Things to Do to Unplug Ser.). (ENG.). 32p. (J). (gr. 3-6). lib. bdg. 27.99 *(978-1-5415-0134-8(9))*, Hungry Tomato ®) Lerner Publishing Group.
—25 Fun Things to Do Outside. Mason, Paul. 2019. (100 Fun Things to Do to Unplug Ser.). (ENG.). 32p. (J). (gr. 3-6). lib. bdg. 27.99 *(978-1-5415-0131-7(4))*, Hungry Tomato ®) Lerner Publishing Group.
—25 Fun Things to Do with Your Friends & Family. Mason, Paul. 2019. (100 Fun Things to Do to Unplug Ser.). (ENG.). 32p. (J). (gr. 3-6). lib. bdg. 27.99 *(978-1-5415-0135-5(7))*, Hungry Tomato ®) Lerner Publishing Group.
Sasso. Coloured Pictures. Bannerji, Himani. Date not set. 80p. pap. *(978-0-920813-86-7(0))* Sister Vision Pr.
—How the East Pond Got Its Flowers. Trotman, Althea. Date not set. 88p. (J). (gr. 3-7). pap. *(978-0-920813-85-0(2))* Sister Vision Pr.
Sassone, Richard. Galangous. Sassone, Richard. 2009. 62p. pap. 14.95 *(978-1-936051-14-4(1))* Peppertree Pr., The.
Sassouni, Maral. The Green Umbrella. Kramer, Jackie Azúa. 2017. (ENG.). 32p. (J). (gr. -1-3). 17.95 *(978-0-7358-4218-2(3))* North-South Bks., Inc.
Sastrawinata-Lemay, Griselda. Frozen 2: Bruni's Big Adventure. Francis, Suzanne. 2020. (ENG.). 40p. (J). (gr. -1-k). 12.99 ***(978-1-368-06478-1(7))*** Disney Pr.
Sastrawinata-Lemay, Griselda. Moana. Fejeran, Tony. 2016. (J). *(978-1-5182-2105-7(X)*, Golden Bks.) Random Hse. Children's Bks.
Sastrawinata-Lemay, Griselda. Blue Spot: Walt Disney Animation Studios Artist Showcase. Sastrawinata-Lemay, Griselda. 2019. (Artist Showcase Ser.). (ENG.). 48p. (J). (gr. -1-k). 16.99 *(978-1-368-02459-4(9))* Disney Publishing Worldwide.
Sastrawinata-Lemay, Griselda, jt. illus. see RH Disney Staff.
Satapathy, Adwita. Adventures of Lavender: A Journey of a Princess. . Acharya, Shyamashree. 2019. (ENG.). 42p. (J). pap. 9.99 *(978-1-7950-5940-4(0))* Independently Published.
Sati, Suruchi, jt. illus. see M M, Shanith.
Sato, Anna & Sato, Eriko. My First Japanese Kanji Book: Learning Kanji the Fun & Easy Way! Sato, Anna & Sato, Eriko. 2009. (ENG.). 64p. (J). (gr. 2-6). 19.95 *(978-4-8053-1037-3(5))* Tuttle Publishing.
Sato, Eriko, jt. illus. see Sato, Anna.
Sato, Kunio. The Restaurant of Many Colors. Miyazawa, Kenji. 2005. 31p. (J). 17.95 *(978-4-902216-24-0(8))* R.I.C. Publications Asia Co, Inc. JPN. Dist: Continental Enterprises Group, Inc. (CEG).
Sato, Miki. Golden Threads. Del Rizzo, Suzanne. 2020. (ENG.). 32p. (J). (gr. -1-4). 17.95 *(978-1-77147-360-6(6))* Owlkids Bks. Inc. CAN. Dist: Publishers Group West (PGW).
Sato, Yuki. Sherlock Bones 1, Vol. 1. Ando, Yuma. 2013. (Sherlock Bones Ser.: 1). (ENG.). 192p. (gr. 8-12). pap. 10.99 *(978-1-61262-444-0(8))* Kodansha America, Inc.
—Sherlock Bones 3, Vol. 3. Ando, Yuma. 2014. (Sherlock Bones Ser.: 3). (ENG.). 208p. (gr. 8-12). pap. 10.99 *(978-1-61262-446-4(4))* Kodansha America, Inc.
—Sherlock Bones 4, Vol. 4. Ando, Yuma. 2014. (Sherlock Bones Ser.: 4). (ENG.). 208p. (gr. 8-12). pap. 10.99 *(978-1-61262-447-1(2))* Kodansha America, Inc.
—Sherlock Bones 5. Ando, Yuma. 2014. (Sherlock Bones Ser.: 5). (ENG.). 192p. (gr. 8-12). pap. 10.99 *(978-1-61262-545-4(2))* Kodansha America, Inc.
Satoru, Akahori. Sorcerer Hunter, Vol. 13. Satoru, Akahori. 13th rev. ed. 2003. 192p. (gr. 11-18). pap. 12.99 *(978-1-59182-066-6(9))* TOKYOPOP, Inc.
Satoshi, Yamamoto. Pokémon Adventures (Gold & Silver), Vol. 11. Kusaka, Hidenori. 2011. (Pokemon Ser.: 11). (ENG.). 208p. (J). pap. 9.99 *(978-1-4215-3545-6(9))* Viz Media.
Satterfield, Jacob. Be Kind Shouted the Mime. Otter. 2016. (ENG.). (J). 21.99 *(978-1-943529-66-7(3))*; pap. 10.99 *(978-1-943529-65-0(5))* Yawn's Bks. & More, Inc.
Satterthwaite, Molly. Abracadabra. Spencer, Bevin Rolfs. 2016. (Backyard Players Ser.). (ENG.). 114p. (J). (gr. 1-3). pap. 7.99 *(978-1-5324-0079-7(9))* Xist Publishing.
Sattler, Jennifer. Bully. Sattler, Jennifer. 2018. (ENG.). 32p. (J). (gr. k-2). 16.99 *(978-1-58536-416-9(9)*, 204579) Sleeping Bear Pr.
—Dirty Birdies. Sattler, Jennifer. 2018. (ENG.). 22p. (J). (gr. -1-k). 7.99 *(978-1-58536-389-6(8)*, 204397) Sleeping Bear Pr.
—Jungle Gym. Sattler, Jennifer. Sattler, David. 2018. (ENG.). 22p. (J). (gr. -1-k). 7.99 *(978-1-58536-390-2(1)*, 204398) Sleeping Bear Pr.
—One Red Sock. Sattler, Jennifer. (ENG.). (J). (gr. -1-k). 2020. 30p. bds. 8.99 ***(978-1-5341-1104-2(2)***, 204929); 2019. 40p. 14.99 *(978-1-5341-1026-7(7)*, 204747) Sleeping Bear Pr.
Sauber, Robert. The Spirit Quest of Little Fox. Mayberry, Lynn M. 2017. (ENG.). 88p. (J). (gr. 3-6). 18.49 *(978-0-9993410-0-1(6))* Synchrony Hse. Publishing.
Sauer, Richard. A Hummingbird's Tale: Henry's Great Race. Wallace, K. K. 2017. (ENG.). 58p. (J). pap. *(978-1-945432-20-0(9))*; *(978-1-945432-19-4(5))* Aurora Production AG.
Saules, Tony de. Esa Repugnante Digestion. Saules, Tony de. Arnold, Nick. 2003. (Coleccion Esa Horrible Ciencia). (SPA.). 156p. (YA). pap. *(978-84-272-2057-7(X)*, ML4090) Molino, Editorial ESP. Dist: Lectorum Pubns., Inc.
—Esos Insoportables Sonidos. Saules, Tony de. Arnold, Nick. (SPA.). 160p. (YA). (gr. 5-8). *(978-84-272-2058-4(8))* Molino, Editorial ESP. Dist: Lectorum Pubns., Inc.
Saull, Eve. A Child's Garden: Introducing Your Child to the Joys of the Garden. Muse, Elizabeth St. Cloud. 2007. 45p. reprint ed. 15.00 *(978-1-4223-6638-7(3))* DIANE Publishing Co.
Sauls, Lynn B. Gabriel Goes to Washington: Through Big Brown Eyes; the Adventures of Gabriel the Poodle. Sauls, Lynn B. 2013. 26p. pap. 9.99 *(978-0-9893216-1-7(4))* Sauls, Lynn.
Saumell, Marina. I Have Two Moms. Lemaire, Colleen. 2019. (I Have Ser.: Vol. 4). (ENG.). 34p. (J). pap. 11.99 *(978-1-0779-0943-4(8))* Independently Published.
—Phantom Fishing with Gramps. Womick, Chip. 2018. (ENG.). 42p. (J). (gr. k-3). 22.95 *(978-0-9971661-2-5(6))*; pap. 12.99 *(978-0-9971661-3-2(4))* PeaceLight Pr.
—Ready, Set, Opa! Tsavaris-Lecourezos, Demetra. 2017. (Young World Travelers Ser.: Vol. 2). (ENG.). (J). (gr. 1-6). 22.00 *(978-1-941251-96-6(X))* Thewordverve.
Saumell, Marina, jt. illus. see Papeo, Maria Eugenia.
Saunders, Chris. God's Great Love for You, 1 vol. Warren, Rick. 2017. (ENG.). 32p. (J). 17.99 *(978-0-310-75247-9(7))* Zonderkidz.
Saunders, Chris. Wish. Saunders, Chris. 2019. (ENG.). 32p. (J). (gr. -1-1). 17.95 ***(978-1-78603-346-8(1)***, Words & Pictures) Quarto Publishing Group UK GBR. Dist: Hachette Bk. Group.
Saunders, Daniela Perea. Two Girls. Saunders, Tracy. 2019. (ENG.). 64p. (J). pap. 10.95 *(978-1-0721-6435-7(3))* Independently Published.
Saunders, Katie. Birthday Wishes: Large Little Bird Greetings. Birdsong, Minnie. Cottage Door Press, ed. 2018. (Little Bird Greetings Keepsake Book Ser.). (ENG.). 10p. (J). (gr. -1-2). bds. 6.99 *(978-1-68052-183-2(7)*, 1001810) Cottage Door Pr.
—Birthday Wishes: Little Bird Greetings. Birdsong, Minnie. Cottage Door Press, ed. 2019. (Little Bird Greetings Keepsake Book Ser.). (ENG.). 8p. (J). (gr. -1-2). bds. 6.99 *(978-1-68052-480-2(1)*, 1003610) Cottage Door Pr.
—Brandon's Birthday Surprise. Bullard, Lisa. 2012. (Holidays & Special Days Ser.). 24p. (J). (gr. k-2). pap. 39.62 *(978-0-7613-9246-0(7)*, Millbrook Pr.) Lerner Publishing Group.
—Carter's Christmas. Bullard, Lisa. 2012. (Cloverleaf Books (tm) — Fall & Winter Holidays Ser.). (ENG.). 24p. (J). (gr. k-2). lib. bdg. 25.32 *(978-0-7613-5074-3(8)*, 9780761350743, Millbrook Pr.) Lerner Publishing Group.
—Chelsea's Chinese New Year. Bullard, Lisa. 2012. (Cloverleaf Books (tm) — Holidays & Special Days Ser.). 24p. (J). (gr. k-2). (ENG.). pap. 8.99 *(978-0-7613-8579-0(7)*, 9780761385790); pap. 39.62 *(978-0-7613-9247-7(5))* Lerner Publishing Group. (Millbrook Pr.).
—Cloverleaf Books#8482; - Holidays & Special Days: 6Pack Set. Bullard, Lisa. 2012. (Holidays & Special Days Ser.). 24p. (J). (gr. k-2). pap. 237.69 *(978-0-7613-9252-1(1)*, Millbrook Pr.) Lerner Publishing Group.
—Cloverleaf Books#8482; - Holidays & Special Days: Single Copy Set. Bullard, Lisa. 2012. (Holidays & Special Days Ser.). 24p. (J). (gr. k-2). pap. 39.62 *(978-0-7613-9251-4(3)*, Millbrook Pr.) Lerner Publishing Group.
—Finger Friends Tickle Monsters. Bicknell, Joanna & Page, Nick. 2007. (Finger Puppet Books Ser.). 12p. (gr. -1). bds. *(978-1-84610-427-5(0))* Make Believe Ideas.
—Grace's Thanksgiving. Bullard, Lisa. 2012. (Cloverleaf Books (tm) — Fall & Winter Holidays Ser.). (ENG.). 24p. (J). (gr. k-2). lib. bdg. 25.32 *(978-0-7613-5076-7(4)*, 9780761350767, Millbrook Pr.) Lerner Publishing Group.
—I Am Brave. Porter, Jen. 2016. (ENG.). 16p. (J). (-3). bds. 7.99 *(978-1-4926-4165-0(0)*, 9781492641650, Sourcebooks Jabberwocky) Sourcebooks, Inc.
—I Am Kind. Porter, Jen. 2016. (ENG.). 16p. (J). (-3). bds. 7.99 *(978-1-4926-4169-8(3)*, 9781492641698, Sourcebooks Jabberwocky) Sourcebooks, Inc.
—I Am Tidy. Porter, Jen. 2016. (ENG.). 16p. (J). (-3). bds. 7.99 *(978-1-4926-4171-1(5)*, 9781492641711, Sourcebooks Jabberwocky) Sourcebooks, Inc.
—Let's Learn Opposites. 2013. 10p. (J). *(978-1-4351-4940-3(8))* Barnes & Noble, Inc.
—Little Reindeer. 2012. 10p. (J). *(978-1-4351-4314-2(0))* Barnes & Noble, Inc.
—My Family Celebrates Christmas. Bullard, Lisa. 2018. (Holiday Time (Early Bird Stories (tm)) Ser.). (ENG.). 24p. (J). (gr. k-2). 27.99 *(978-1-5415-2007-3(6)*, Lerner Pubns.) Lerner Publishing Group.
—My Family Celebrates Thanksgiving. Bullard, Lisa. 2018. (Holiday Time (Early Bird Stories (tm)) Ser.). (ENG.). 24p. (J). (gr. k-2). pap. 7.99 *(978-1-5415-2743-0(7))*; lib. bdg. 27.99 *(978-1-5415-2009-7(2)*, Lerner Pubns.) Lerner Publishing Group.
—Read with Me Three Billy Goats Gruff: Sticker Activity Book. Page, Nick & Page, Claire. 2006. (Read with Me (Make Believe Ideas) Ser.). 12p. (J). (gr. k-2). pap. *(978-1-84610-181-6(6))* Make Believe Ideas.
Saunders, M. D. Harry Meets Mathilda, 5 bks., Bk.1. Wisdom, Eileen Mary. 2007. 36p. (J). pap. 20.00 *(978-0-9771102-2-3(2))* Pelican Pr. Pensacola.
Saunders, Matt. The Bone Garden. Kassner, Heather. 2019. (ENG.). 272p. (J). 16.99 *(978-1-250-29689-4(7)*, 900195830, Holt, Henry & Co. Bks. For Young Readers) Holt, Henry & Co.
—The Bone Garden. Kassner, Heather. 2020. (ENG.). 288p. (J). pap. 7.99 *(978-1-250-25053-7(6)*, 900195831) Square Fish.
Saunders, Mike. You Can Draw Birds! Dicker, Katie. 2013. (Draw Your Pet! Ser.). 32p. (gr. 3-5). 27.60 *(978-1-4339-8723-6(2))*; pap. 10.50 *(978-1-4339-8724-3(4))* Stevens, Gareth Publishing LLLP. (Gareth Stevens Learning Library).
—You Can Draw Cats! Dicker, Katie. 2013. (Draw Your Pet! Ser.). 32p. (gr. 3-5). 27.60 *(978-1-4339-8727-4(9))*; pap. 10.50 *(978-1-4339-8728-1(7))* Stevens, Gareth Publishing LLLP. (Gareth Stevens Learning Library).
—You Can Draw Dogs! Dickler, Katie. 2013. (Draw Your Pet! Ser.). 32p. (J). (gr. 3-5). pap. 10.50 *(978-1-4339-8732-8(5))*; lib. bdg. 27.60 *(978-1-4339-8731-1(7))* Stevens, Gareth Publishing LLLP.
—You Can Draw Exotic Pets! Dicker, Katie. 2013. (Draw Your Pet! Ser.). 32p. (gr. 3-5). 27.60 *(978-1-4339-8735-9(X))*; pap. 10.50 *(978-1-4339-8736-6(8))* Stevens, Gareth Publishing LLLP. (Gareth Stevens Learning Library).
—You Can Draw Fish! Dicker, Katie. 2013. (Draw Your Pet! Ser.). 32p. (gr. 3-5). 27.60 *(978-1-4339-8739-7(2))*; pap. 10.50 *(978-1-4339-8740-3(6))* Stevens, Gareth Publishing LLLP. (Gareth Stevens Learning Library).
—You Can Draw Horses! Dicker, Katie. 2013. (Draw Your Pet! Ser.). 32p. (gr. 3-5). 27.60 *(978-1-4339-8743-4(0))*; pap. 10.50 *(978-1-4339-8744-1(9))* Stevens, Gareth Publishing LLLP. (Gareth Stevens Learning Library).
Saunders, Rachael. Boom! Bang! Royal Meringue! Doran, Sally. 2020. 32p. (J). (gr. -1-k). pap. 14.99 *(978-1-78344-879-1(2))* Andersen Pr. GBR. Dist: Independent Pubs. Group.
—Boom! Bang! Royal Meringue! Doran, Sally. 2019. 32p. (J). (gr. -1-k). 16.99 *(978-1-78344-415-1(0))* Penguin Random Hse. AUS. Dist: Independent Pubs. Group.
Saunders, Rachel. El Cuerpo Humano: Shine-A-light. Brown, Carron. 2019.Tr. of Human Body. (SPA.). (J). 12.99 *(978-1-61067-914-5(8))* Kane Miller.
—The Human Body. Brown, Carron. 2016. (ENG.). 36p. (J). 12.99 *(978-1-61067-465-2(0))* Kane Miller.
Saunders-Smith, Gail. Cool Soccer Facts. Czeskleba, Abby. 2011. (Cool Sports Facts Ser.). (ENG.). 24p. (gr. k-1). pap. 41.70 *(978-1-4296-7397-6(4)*, Capstone Pr.) Capstone.
Saunders, Zina. Dora Loves Boots. Inches, Alison & Weiner, Eric. 2004. (SPA & ENG.). (J). *(978-0-7383-3858-3(3)*, Simon Spotlight/Nickelodeon) Simon Spotlight/Nickelodeon.
—Dora Quiere Mucho a Boots. Inches, Alison. 2005. (Dora the Explorer Ser.). (SPA.). 24p. (J). (gr. -1-2). pap. 3.99 *(978-1-4169-0620-9(7)*, Libros Para Ninos) Libros Para Ninos.
—Dora's Costume Party! Ricci, Christine. 2005. (Dora the Explorer Ser.). (ENG.). 24p. (J). (gr. -1-2). pap. 3.99 *(978-1-4169-0010-8(1)*, Simon Spotlight/Nickelodeon) Simon Spotlight/Nickelodeon.
—¿Qué Voy a Ser? Beinstein, Phoebe. 2007. (Dora la Exploradora Ser.).Tr. of What Will I Be?. (ENG & SPA.). 14p. (J). (gr. -1). bds. 4.99 *(978-1-4169-3366-3(2)*, Libros Para Ninos) Libros Para Ninos.
—Say Please! A Book about Manners. 2006. (Backyardigans Ser.). (ENG.). 24p. (J). (gr. -1-2). pap. 3.99 *(978-1-4169-1386-3(6)*, Simon Spotlight/Nickelodeon) Simon Spotlight/Nickelodeon.
—SpongeBob Goes to the Doctor. Banks, Steven. 2005. (SpongeBob SquarePants Ser.: 9). (ENG.). 24p. (J). pap. 3.99 *(978-1-4169-0359-8(3)*, Simon Spotlight/Nickelodeon) Simon Spotlight/Nickelodeon.
—Spongebob Goes to the Doctor. Banks, Steven. 2005. 22p. (J). lib. bdg. 15.00 *(978-1-4242-0976-7(5))* Fitzgerald Bks.
—Trouble at the Krusty Krab! 2004. (SpongeBob SquarePants Ser.). (ENG.). 32p. (J). pap. 3.99 *(978-0-689-86838-2(3)*, Simon Spotlight/Nickelodeon) Simon Spotlight/Nickelodeon.
—U. S. Presidents: Feats & Foul-Ups. Fuqua, Nell & Jankowki, Dan. 2003. 48p. (J). pap. *(978-0-439-54081-0(X))* Lemondrop Pr.
—UFO! (SpongeBob SquarePants) Beechen, Adam. 2005. (SpongeBob SquarePants Ser.). (ENG.). 32p. (J). pap. 3.99 *(978-0-689-87202-0(X)*, Simon Spotlight/Nickelodeon) Simon Spotlight/Nickelodeon.
Saunders, Zoe. The Humble Seed. Appleby, Linda. 2019. (ENG.). 34p. (J). (gr. k-2). 14.99 ***(978-0-9600253-9-8(1))***; pap. 7.99 ***(978-0-9600253-4-3(0))*** Seeds of Imagination.
Saunders, Zoe. The Kindness Seed. Appleby, Linda. 2018. (Seeds of Imagination Ser.). (ENG.). 36p. (J). (gr. -1-3). 14.99 *(978-0-9600253-0-5(8))*; 7.99 *(978-0-9600253-1-2(6))* Seeds of Imagination.
—The Mindful Seed. Appleby, Linda. 2019. (Seeds of Imagination Ser.: Vol. 2). (ENG.). 34p. (J). (gr. k-3). 14.99 *(978-0-9600253-2-9(4))*; pap. 7.99 *(978-0-9600253-3-6(2))* Seeds of Imagination.
Saunders, Zoe. Monty & Friends African Adventure: The Mission to Save Kaluwa. Sanders, Mt. 2020. (ENG.). 38p. (J). (gr. k-5). pap. ***(978-1-913071-51-6(0))*** 2QT, Ltd. (Publishing).
—Monty & the Land of the Dinodogs. Sanders, Mt. 2020. (ENG.). 36p. (J). pap. ***(978-1-913071-60-8(X))*** 2QT, Ltd. (Publishing).
Saunders, Zoe. Monty & the Ocean Rescue: A Plastic Disaster. Sanders, Mt. 2019. (ENG.). 36p. (J). (gr. 1-3). *(978-1-913071-13-4(8))* 2QT, Ltd. (Publishing).
Saunderson, Chris. Climb up the Tree with Zacchaeus. Lane, Leena. Reynolds, Annette, ed. ed. 2007. (Action Rhymes Ser.). (ENG.). 16p. (J). (gr. -1-2). pap. 4.99 *(978-0-9789056-2-0(8))* New Day Publishing, Inc.
—Come into the Ark with Noah. Jeffs, Stephanie. Reynolds, Annette, ed. ed. 2007. (Action Rhymes Ser.). (ENG.). 16p. (J). (gr. -1-2). pap. 4.99 *(978-0-9789056-6-8(0))* New Day Publishing, Inc.
—Come to the Party with Jesus. Lane, Leena. Reynolds, Annette, ed. ed. 2007. (Action Rhymes Ser.). (ENG.). 16p. (J). (gr. -1-2). pap. 4.99 *(978-0-9789056-5-1(2))* New Day Publishing, Inc.
—Follow the Star with the Wise Men. Jeffs, Stephanie. Reynolds, Annette, ed. ed. 2007. (Action Rhymes Ser.). (ENG.). 16p. (J). (gr. -1-3). per. 4.99 *(978-0-9789056-3-7(6))* New Day Publishing, Inc.
—March Round the Walls with Joshua. Jeffs, Stephanie. Reynolds, Annette, ed. ed. 2007. (Action Rhymes Ser.). (ENG.). 16p. (J). (gr. -1-2). pap. 4.99 *(978-0-9789056-7-5(9))* New Day Publishing, Inc.
—Sail in the Boat with Jesus. Lane, Leena. Reynolds, Annette, ed. ed. 2007. (Action Rhymes Ser.). (ENG.). 16p. (J). (gr. -1-2). pap. 4.99 *(978-0-9789056-0-6(1))* New Day Publishing, Inc.
—Share Out the Food with Jesus. Jeffs, Stephanie. Reynolds, Annette, ed. ed. 2007. (Action Rhymes Ser.). (ENG.). 16p. (J). (gr. -1-2). pap. 4.99 *(978-0-9789056-1-3(X))* New Day Publishing, Inc.
—Stand up & Walk with Jesus. Lane, Leena. Reynolds, Annette, ed. ed. 2007. (Action Rhymes Ser.). (ENG.). 16p. (J). (gr. -1-2). pap. 4.99 *(978-0-9789056-4-4(4))* New Day Publishing, Inc.
Sautai, Raoul. Let's Look at the Rainforest. Fuhr, Ute & Allaire, Caroline. 2012. (ENG.). 38p. (J). (gr. 1-4). spiral bd. 11.99 *(978-1-85103-360-7(2))* Moonlight Publishing, Ltd. GBR. Dist: Independent Pubs. Group.
Sautai, Raoul. La Abeja. Sautai, Raoul. Fhur, Ute et al. Fhur, Ute & Barroso, Paz, trs. 3rd ed. (Coleccion Mundo Maravilloso). (SPA.). 40p. (J). (gr. 2-4). *(978-84-348-4036-2(7)*, SM5786) SM Ediciones ESP. Dist: Lectorum Pubns., Inc.
Sautai, Raoul, jt. illus. see Fuhr, Ute.
Sauvageot, Claude, photos by. Poland. Sein, Dominique. (Countries of the World Ser.: No. 27). 83p. (J). lib. bdg. 14.95 *(978-0-8288-3938-9(7))* French & European Pubns., Inc.
Sauve, Gordon. Car Smarts: Hot Tips for the Car Crazy. Edmonston, Phil & Sawa, Maureen. 2003. 80p. (J). (gr. 4-7). pap. 15.95 *(978-0-88776-646-6(3)*, Tundra Bks.) Tundra Bks. CAN. Dist: Penguin Random Hse. LLC.
Savadier, Elivia. I Love Saturdays y Domingos. Flor Ada, Alma. 2004. (ENG.). 32p. (J). (gr. -1-3). reprint ed. 7.99 *(978-0-689-87409-3(X)*, Atheneum Bks. for Young Readers) Simon & Schuster Children's Publishing.
Savage, Bridgette Z. Fly Like the Wind. Savage, Bridgette Z. Savage, Charles J., photos by. Savage, Charles J., ed. 2005. (ENG.). 112p. (YA). (gr. 5). per. 16.99 *(978-0-9771494-0-7(4))* Buckbeech Studios.
Savage, Jeff, photos by. Play-by-Play Football. 2005. (Play-by-Play Ser.). 80p. (gr. 4-8). lib. bdg. 23.93 *(978-0-8225-3935-3(7))* Lerner Publishing Group.
Savage, Marianne. Secrets in the Fairy Chimneys, 2nd Edition. Frank, Linda Maria. 2019. (Annie Tillery Mysteries Ser.: Vol. 6). (ENG.). 394p. (J). pap. 15.00 *(978-0-9989714-1-4(3))* Horn, Jonathan.
Savage, Stephen. The Fathers Are Coming Home. Brown, Margaret Wise. 2010. (ENG.). 32p. (J). (gr. -1-k). 19.99 *(978-0-689-83345-8(8)*, McElderry, Margaret K. Bks.) McElderry, Margaret K. Bks.
—Jack B. Ninja. McCanna, Tim. 2018. (ENG.). 32p. (J). (gr. -1-k). 16.99 *(978-0-545-91728-5(X)*, Orchard Bks.) Scholastic, Inc.
—Polar Bear Morning. Thompson, Lauren. 2013. (ENG.). 32p. (J). (gr. -1-k). 16.99 *(978-0-439-69885-6(5)*, Scholastic Pr.) Scholastic, Inc.
—Polar Bear Night. Thompson, Lauren. 2004. (ENG.). 32p. (J). (gr. -1-k). 17.99 *(978-0-439-49524-0(5)*, Scholastic Pr.) Scholastic, Inc.
Savage, Stephen. Little Tug. Savage, Stephen. 2015. (ENG.). 34p. (J). (gr. -1-1). bds. 7.99 *(978-1-62672-124-1(6)*, 900138367) Roaring Brook Pr.
—Sign Off. Savage, Stephen. 2019. (ENG.). 56p. (J). (gr. -1-3). 17.99 *(978-1-5344-1210-1(7)*, Beach Lane Bks.) Beach Lane Bks.
—Supertruck. Savage, Stephen. (ENG.). (J). 2018. 34p. bds. 7.99 *(978-1-250-14154-5(0)*, 900179942); 2015. 32p. (gr. -1-1). 12.99 *(978-1-59643-821-7(5)*, 9781596438217) Roaring Brook Pr.
—Where's Walrus? Savage, Stephen. 2011. (ENG.). 32p. (J). (gr. -1 — 1). 17.99 *(978-0-439-70049-8(3)*, Scholastic Pr.) Scholastic, Inc.
—Where's Walrus? & Penguin? Savage, Stephen. 2015. (ENG.). 32p. (J). (gr. -1-k). 16.99 *(978-0-545-40295-8(6)*, Scholastic Pr.) Scholastic, Inc.
Savage, Virginia, jt. illus. see Peterson, Roger Tory.
Savallo, Maria. Denny & the New Old Chair. Quigley, Nora Eberhardt. 2019. (ENG.). 34p. (J). pap. 9.95 *(978-1-7931-4232-0(7))* Independently Published.
Save, Ken. Dunamis Heroes: Issue #1: the Lost Kingdom. Bateman, Jordan. 2007. 120p. (J). per. *(978-0-9781953-0-4(2))* Dunamis Media.
Saville, Kathy Dee. Dance of the Eggshells: Baile de los Cascarones. Aragón, Carla et al. Aragon, Socorro, tr. 2010. (ENG.). 32p. (J). (gr. 1). 18.95 *(978-0-8263-4770-1(3))* Univ. of New Mexico Pr.
Savitsky, Steve, et al. Bug Hunt. Ricci, Christine & Golden Books Staff. 2008. (ENG.). 48p. (J). (gr. -1-2). pap. 3.99 *(978-0-375-84298-6(5)*, Golden Bks.) Random Hse. Children's Bks.
Savitsky, Steve. Dora Had a Little Lamb. Risco, Elle D. 2007. (Dora the Explorer Ser.). (J). (gr. -1-2). 11.65 *(978-0-7569-8294-2(4))* Perfection Learning Corp.
—Dora's Pirate Treasure Hunt. 2010. (Dora the Explorer Ser.). (ENG.). 12p. (J). (gr. -1-1). 6.99 *(978-1-4169-9927-0(2)*, Simon Spotlight/Nickelodeon) Simon Spotlight/Nickelodeon.
Savitsky, Steven. Dónde Está Boots? - Cuento para Levantar la Tapita. Thorpe, Kiki. 2005. (Dora the Explorer Ser.).Tr. of Where Is Boots? - A Lift-the-Flap Story. (SPA.). 16p. (J). pap. 5.99 *(978-1-4169-0621-6(5)*, Libros Para Ninos) Libros Para Ninos.
—Dora Had a Little Lamb. 2007. (Dora the Explorer Ser.: 23). (ENG.). 24p. (J). (gr. -1-2). pap. 3.99 *(978-1-4169-3368-7(9)*, Simon Spotlight/Nickelodeon) Simon Spotlight/Nickelodeon.
—Dora y el Día lluvioso. Echeverria, Jessica. 2009. (Dora la Exploradora Ser.). Orig. Title: Dora & the Rainy Day. (SPA.). 26p. (J). (gr. -1). bds. 5.99 *(978-1-4169-7186-3(6)*, Libros Para Ninos) Libros Para Ninos.
—Dora's Chilly Day. Thorpe, Kiki. ed. 2005. (Dora the Explorer Ser.: No. 10). 22p. (J). lib. bdg. 15.00 *(978-1-59054-794-6(2))* Fitzgerald Bks.
—Dora's Chilly Day. Thorpe, Kiki. 2004. (Dora the Explorer Ser.). (ENG.). 24p. (J). pap. 3.99 *(978-0-689-86795-8(6)*, Simon Spotlight/Nickelodeon) Simon Spotlight/Nickelodeon.
—Dora's Halloween Adventure. Willson, Sarah. 2003. (Dora the Explorer Ser.). (ENG.). 14p. (J). bds. 5.99 *(978-0-689-85844-4(2)*, Simon Spotlight/Nickelodeon) Simon Spotlight/Nickelodeon.
—Say Cheese! Ricci, Christine. ed. 2005. 22p. (J). lib. bdg. 15.00 *(978-1-59054-975-9(9))* Fitzgerald Bks.
—Say Cheese! Ricci, Christine. 2004. (Dora the Explorer Ser.). (ENG.). 24p. (J). pap. 3.99 *(978-0-689-86496-4(5)*, Simon Spotlight/Nickelodeon) Simon Spotlight/Nickelodeon.
Savitt, Sam. Buffalo Bill: Wild West Showman. Davidson, Mary Richmond. 2011. 80p. 37.95 *(978-1-258-01669-2(9))* Literary Licensing, LLC.

S

Saviuk, Alex, et al. Adventures of Spider-Man: Sinister Intentions. 2019. (ENG.). 168p. (J). (gr. 1-3). pap. 12.99 *(978-1-302-91779-1(X))* Marvel Worldwide, Inc.

Saviuk, Alex. Adventures of Spider-Man: Spectacular Foes. 2019. (ENG.). 280p. (J). (gr. 1-3). pap. 12.99 *(978-1-302-91984-9(9))* Marvel Worldwide, Inc.

Savoie, Karuna. The Lore of Ramridge: Book One of the Lore of Ramridge Series. Savoie, Karuna. 2018. (Lore of Ramridge Ser.: Vol. 1). (ENG.). 118p. (J). (gr. 7-12). pap. 6.99 *(978-1-7323192-5-7(1))* Hybrid Age Pr.

Savolainen, Laila. Hey, It's My Turn to Hide... Willard & Widget Go Wandering... Savolainen, Laila. 2017. (ENG.). (J). (gr. k-2). pap. *(978-0-9925164-6-8(3))* Laila.

Savoy, Angie. Hop's Case of Being Different. Michaelis, Noah Bella. 2018. (Adventure on. Explore More. Discover You Ser.: Vol. 1). (ENG.). 36p. (J). pap. 19.99 *(978-1-7325254-0-5(4))* Live Like Noah Foundation.

Savva, Ksenya. Zoo Animals: Create 10 Cute Pictures Using Simple Stickers. 2019. (First Sticker Art Ser.). (ENG.). 64p. (J). (gr. -1-2). pap. 8.99 *(978-1-4380-1248-3(9),* B.E.S. Publishing) Peterson's.

Sawa, Fumio. The Animal Garden. Thornton, Michael. 2020. (ENG.). 140p. (J). pap. 12.50 ***(978-1-5193-9967-0(7))*** CreateSpace Independent Publishing Platform.

Sawada, Hajime. Orphen, Vol. 3. Akita, Yoshinobu. 2005. (Orphen Ser.). 192p. (gr. 8-12). pap. 9.99 *(978-1-4139-0268-6(5))* ADV Manga.

Sawada, Sachiko. Can Yo Do What I Can Do? Castellanos, Graciela. 2019. (ENG.). 24p. (J). pap. 9.50 ***(978-1-6921-8769-9(4))*** Independently Published.

—�Puedes Hacer lo Que Yo Puedo Hacer? Castellanos, Graciela. 2019. (SPA.). 24p. (J). pap. 9.50 ***(978-1-6922-2992-4(3))*** Independently Published.

Sawvel, Gennai. Inviting a Giraffe to Tea: Teacher-Parent Guide. Huston-Holm, Patty & McFerin, Kathy. 2018. (ENG.). 80p. (J). (gr. 1-4). pap. 25.00 *(978-0-692-14271-4(1))* Patty Huston-Holm.

Sawvel, Gennai & Frink, Josh. Inviting a Giraffe to Tea: Color Me Different. Huston-Holm, Patty. 2017. (ENG.). 22p. (J). (gr. 1-4). pap. 9.99 *(978-0-692-04996-9(7))* Patty Huston-Holm.

Sawyer-Aitch, Anne. Nalah & the Pink Tiger. Sawyer-Aitch, Anne. 2013. (ENG.). 40p. pap. 13.95 *(978-1-938063-00-8(7),* Mighty Media Kids) Mighty Media Pr.

Sawyer, Darren, photos by. Guinea Pig. Rayner, Matthew. 2007. (I Am Your Pet Ser.). 32p. (gr. k-4). lib. bdg. 27.00 *(978-0-8368-8385-5(3),* Gareth Stevens Learning Library) Stevens, Gareth Publishing LLLP.

—Rat. Rayner, Matthew. 2007. (I Am Your Pet Ser.). 32p. (gr. k-4). lib. bdg. 27.00 *(978-0-8368-8386-2(1),* Gareth Stevens Learning Library) Stevens, Gareth Publishing LLLP.

Sawyer, Judith L. This Is How I Pray. Sawyer, Judith L. 2008. 24p. (J). pap. *(978-1-926585-11-6(9),* CCB Publishing) CCB Publishing.

Sawyer, Odessa. Believe, 1 vol. Bracken, Beth & Fraser, Kay. 2014. (Faerieground Ser.). (ENG.). 288p. (J). (gr. 4-8). 12.95 *(978-1-62370-113-0(9),* Capstone Young Readers) Capstone.

—Bloodfate, 1 vol. Bracken, Beth & Fraser, Kay. 2012. (Faerieground Ser.). (ENG.). 96p. (J). (gr. 5-9). lib. bdg. 23.99 *(978-1-4342-3305-9(7),* Stone Arch Bks.) Capstone.

—Fate of the Willow Queen. Bracken, Beth & Fraser, Kay. 2013. (Faerieground Ser.). (ENG.). 96p. (J). (gr. 5-9). 23.99 *(978-1-4342-4492-5(X),* Stone Arch Bks.) Capstone.

—Hope, 1 vol. Bracken, Beth & Fraser, Kay. 2013. (Faerieground Ser.). (ENG.). 288p. (J). (gr. 4-8). 12.95 *(978-1-62370-010-2(8),* Capstone Young Readers) Capstone.

—A Murder of Crows, 1 vol. Bracken, Beth & Fraser, Kay. 2013. (Faerieground Ser.). (ENG.). 96p. (J). (gr. 5-9). lib. bdg. 23.99 *(978-1-4342-4491-8(1),* Stone Arch Bks.) Capstone.

—The Seventh Kingdom, 1 vol. Bracken, Beth & Fraser, Kay. 2014. (Faerieground Ser.). (ENG.). 96p. (J). (gr. 5-9). 23.99 *(978-1-4342-9186-8(3),* Stone Arch Bks.) Capstone.

—The Shadows, 1 vol. Bracken, Beth & Fraser, Kay. 2012. (Faerieground Ser.). (ENG.). 96p. (J). (gr. 5-9). lib. bdg. 23.99 *(978-1-4342-3306-6(5),* Stone Arch Bks.) Capstone.

—Two Mothers. Bracken, Beth & Fraser, Kay. 2013. (Faerieground Ser.). (ENG.). 96p. (J). (gr. 5-9). 23.99 *(978-1-4342-4490-1(3),* Stone Arch Bks.) Capstone.

—Walk till You Disappear. Dembar Greene, Jacqueline. 2019. (ENG.). 208p. (J). (gr. 3-7). 15.99 *(978-1-5415-5722-2(0),* Kar-Ben Publishing) Lerner Publishing Group.

—The Willow Queen's Gate, 1 vol. Bracken, Beth & Fraser, Kay. 2012. (Faerieground Ser.). (ENG.). 96p. (J). (gr. 5-9). lib. bdg. 23.99 *(978-1-4342-3304-2(9),* Stone Arch Bks.) Capstone.

—Wish, 1 vol. Bracken, Beth & Fraser, Kay. 2013. (Faerieground Ser.). (ENG.). 304p. (J). (gr. 4-8). 12.95 *(978-1-62370-003-4(5),* Capstone Young Readers) Capstone.

—A Wish in the Woods, 1 vol. Bracken, Beth & Fraser, Kay. 2012. (Faerieground Ser.). (ENG.). 96p. (J). (gr. 5-9). lib. bdg. 23.99 *(978-1-4342-3303-5(0),* Stone Arch Bks.) Capstone.

Sawyer, Peter, jt. illus. see Burney, Laura.

Sax, Sarah. Escape This Book! Titanic. Doyle, Bill. 2019. (Escape This Book! Ser.). (ENG.). 192p. (J). (gr. 3-7). 10.99 *(978-0-525-64420-0(2),* Random Hse. Bks. for Young Readers) Random Hse. Children's Bks.

—Escape This Book! Tombs of Egypt. Doyle, Bill. 2020. (Escape This Book! Ser.). (ENG.). 192p. (J). (gr. 3-7). 10.99 *(978-0-525-64422-4(9),* Random Hse. Bks. for Young Readers) Random Hse. Children's Bks.

Saxelby, Anne. The Great Grace Escape. Saxelby, Pam. 2018. (ENG.). 38p. (J). (gr. k-4). 19.95 *(978-1-61244-695-0(7));* pap. 12.95 *(978-1-61244-653-0(1))* Halo Publishing International.

Saxton, Brenda. Reading Pals: Alphabet Recognition Gr. Pre K-K. 2007. (J). per. 6.99 *(978-1-59198-435-1(1))* Creative Teaching Pr., Inc.

Saxton, Patricia. A Book of Fairies. Saxton, Patricia. 2009. (ENG.). 32p. (J). (gr. 1-5). 14.95 *(978-1-934860-01-4(8))* Shenanigan Bks.

—The Book of Mermaids. Saxton, Patricia. 2006. (ENG.). 32p. (J). (gr. 1-5). 14.95 *(978-0-9726614-6-1(8))* Shenanigan Bks.

Say, Allen. Drawing from Memory. Say, Allen. 2011. (ENG.). 64p. (J). (gr. 3-7). 18.99 *(978-0-545-17686-6(7),* Scholastic Pr.) Scholastic, Inc.

—The Favorite Daughter. Say, Allen. 2013. (ENG.). 32p. (J). (gr. -1-3). 17.99 *(978-0-545-17662-0(X),* Levine, Arthur A. Bks.) Scholastic, Inc.

—Grandfather's Journey. Say, Allen. 2008. (ENG.). 32p. (J). (gr. -1-3). 7.99 *(978-0-547-07680-5(0),* 1042044) Houghton Mifflin Harcourt Publishing Co.

—Silent Days, Silent Dreams. Say, Allen. 2017. (ENG.). 64p. (J). (gr. 3-7). 21.99 *(978-0-545-92761-1(7),* Levine, Arthur A. Bks.) Scholastic, Inc.

—Tea with Milk. Say, Allen. 2009. (ENG.). 32p. (J). (gr. -1-3). pap. 7.99 *(978-0-547-23747-3(2),* 1083741, HMH Books For Young Readers) Houghton Mifflin Harcourt Publishing Co.

—Tree of Cranes. Say, Allen. 2009. (ENG.). 32p. (J). (gr. -1-3). pap. 7.99 *(978-0-547-24830-1(X),* 1100745) Houghton Mifflin Harcourt Publishing Co.

Sayegh, Rob. Santa's Big Day. Berry-Byrd, Holly. Cottage Door Press, ed. ed. 2020. (Finger Puppet Board Book Ser.). (ENG.). 12p. (J). (gr. -1 — 1). bds. 6.99 ***(978-1-64638-041-1(X),*** 1006170) Cottage Door Pr.

Sayekti, Sri & Fahim, Pranto. The Woman Who Invented Weaving. Davis Jr, Christopher. 2019. (Bmt Collection: Vol. 2). (ENG.). 30p. (J). (gr. k-6). pap. 14.99 *(978-0-578-43937-2(9))* Christopher Davis, Jr.

Sayer, Blair. William's Wet Week. Haley, Patty. 2010. (ENG.). 16p. (gr. k-2). pap. 7.95 *(978-1-61181-043-1(4),* Kaeden Bks.) Kaeden Corp.

Sayers, Myrna. Pound a Poem: The Winning Entries from the National Schools Poetry Competition. John Blake Publishing Staff. 2007. (ENG.). 256p. 19.95 *(978-1-84454-436-3(2))* Blake, John Publishing, Ltd. GBR. Dist: Independent Pubs. Group.

Sayers, Rachel. Nibbles. Heeney, Bronwyn. 2011. 26p. pap. 13.50 *(978-1-60860-278-0(8),* Eloquent Bks.) Strategic Book Publishing & Rights Agency (SBPRA).

Sayler, Machelle. Folkeminnevitskap II. 2004. 144p. *(978-0-9744422-1-1(6))* Erickson, Rakel L.

Sayles, Elizabeth. Americans. Wood, Douglas. 2018. (ENG.). 40p. (J). (gr. -1-3). 17.99 *(978-1-4169-2756-3(5),* Simon & Schuster Bks. For Young Readers) Simon & Schuster Bks. For Young Readers.

—I Already Know I Love You. Crystal, Billy. 40p. (J). 2007. (ENG.). (gr. -1-3). pap. 7.99 *(978-0-06-059393-3(8));* 2004. (ENG.). 16.99 *(978-0-06-059391-9(1));* 2004. lib. bdg. 17.89 *(978-0-06-059392-6(X))* HarperCollins Pubs.

—I Already Know I Love You Board Book. Crystal, Billy. 2008. (ENG.). 32p. (J). (gr. -1-3). bds. 7.99 *(978-0-06-145057-0(X),* HarperFestival) HarperCollins Pubs.

—Malala: A Hero for All. Corey, Shana. 2016. (Step into Reading Ser.). 48p. (J). (gr. 2-4). pap. 4.99 *(978-0-553-53761-1(X),* Random Hse. Bks. for Young Readers) Random Hse. Children's Bks.

—Moon Child. Krilanovich, Nadia. 2010. 32p. (J). (gr. -1-2). 15.99 *(978-1-58246-325-4(5),* Tricycle Pr.) Random Hse. Children's Bks.

—The Rainbow Tulip. Mora, Pat. 2003. 32p. (J). (gr. k-3). 7.99 *(978-0-14-250009-5(7),* Puffin Books) Penguin Young Readers Group.

—The Very Little Princess: Rose's Story. Bauer, Marion Dane. 2012. (Stepping Stones Chapter Book: Fantasy Ser.). (ENG.). 128p. (J). (gr. 2-4). lib. bdg. 17.44 *(978-0-375-95692-8(1))* Random House Publishing Group.

Sayles, Elizabeth, jt. illus. see Dooling, Michael.

Sayles, John. The Girl Who Reached for the Star. Lyons, Wendy Ackerman. 2007. (J). *(978-0-696-23982-3(5))* Meredith Bks.

Sayles, Susana. The Arborist. Holm, M. S. 2007. (ENG.). 104p. (J). 16.95 *(978-0-9796199-1-5(2));* pap. 11.95 *(978-0-9796199-3-9(9))* Great West Publishing. (Sentry Bks.).

Sayre, April Pulley. Being Frog. Sayre, April Pulley. 2020. (ENG.). 32p. (J). (gr. -1-3). 17.99 *(978-1-5344-2881-2(X),* Beach Lane Bks.) Beach Lane Bks.

—Cityscape: Where Science & Art Meet. Sayre, April Pulley. 2020. (ENG.). 40p. (J). (gr. -1-3). 17.99 *(978-0-06-289331-4(9),* Greenwillow Bks.) HarperCollins Pubs.

—Let's Go Nuts! Seeds We Eat. Sayre, April Pulley. 2013. (ENG.). 32p. (J). (gr. -1-3). 17.99 *(978-1-4424-6728-6(2),* Beach Lane Bks.) Beach Lane Bks.

—Thank You, Earth: A Love Letter to Our Planet. Sayre, April Pulley. 2018. (ENG.). 40p. (J). (gr. -1-3). 17.99 *(978-0-06-269734-9(X),* Greenwillow Bks.) HarperCollins Pubs.

Sayre, April Pulley, photos by. Bloom Boom! Sayre, April Pulley. 2019. (ENG., 40p. (J). (gr. -1-3). 18.99 *(978-1-4814-9472-4(4),* Beach Lane Bks.) Beach Lane Bks.

Sayre, April Pulley, photos by. Feel the Fog. Sayre, April Pulley. 2020. (Weather Walks Ser.). (ENG., 40p. (J). (gr. -1-3). 17.99 ***(978-1-5344-3760-9(6),*** Beach Lane Bks.) Beach Lane Bks.

Sayre, April Pulley, photos by. Go, Go, Grapes! A Fruit Chant. Sayre, April Pulley. 2012. (ENG., 32p. (J). (gr. -1-3). 17.99 *(978-1-4424-3390-8(6),* Beach Lane Bks.) Beach Lane Bks.

—Go, Go, Grapes! A Fruit Chant. Sayre, April Pulley. 2016. (Classic Board Bks.). (ENG., 34p. (J). (gr. -1 — 1). bds. 7.99 *(978-1-4814-5301-1(7),* Little Simon) Little Simon.

—Rah, Rah, Radishes! A Vegetable Chant. Sayre, April Pulley. 2011. (ENG., 32p. (J). (gr. -1-3). 17.99 *(978-1-4424-2141-7(X),* Beach Lane Bks.) Beach Lane Bks.

—Rah, Rah, Radishes! A Vegetable Chant. Sayre, April Pulley. 2014. (Classic Board Bks.). (ENG., 34p. (J). (gr. -1 — 1). bds. 7.99 *(978-1-4424-9927-0(3),* Little Simon) Little Simon.

Sayre, April Pulley, photos by. Rah, Rah, Radishes! Classroom Edition. Sayre, April Pulley. 2020. (ENG., 32p. (J). (gr. -1-3). 29.99 ***(978-1-5344-5987-8(1),*** Beach Lane Bks.) Beach Lane Bks.

Sayre, April Pulley, photos by. Raindrops Roll. Sayre, April Pulley. 2015. (Weather Walks Ser.). (ENG., 40p. (J). (gr. -1-3). 17.99 *(978-1-4814-2064-8(X),* Beach Lane Bks.) Beach Lane Bks.

—Warbler Wave. Sayre, April Pulley. 2018. (ENG., 32p. (J). (gr. -1-3). 17.99 *(978-1-4814-4829-1(3),* Beach Lane Bks.) Beach Lane Bks.

Sayre, Michael. Picture Girl. Brill, Marlene Targ. 2018. (Becoming American Kids Ser.: Vol. 1). (ENG.). 106p. (J). (gr. 3-6). pap. 7.99 *(978-1-7320276-0-2(9))* Golden Alley Pr.

Sayre, Michael S. No Seder Without You: Passover Past & Future. Parker, Joan Goldstein. 2018. (ENG.). 70p. (J). (gr. 3-6). pap. 9.95 *(978-0-9984429-6-9(8))* Golden Alley Pr.

Sayre, Tamara. Guide to Freshwater Animals Without Backbones. DeStrulle, Arlene & Johnson, Tora. Date not set. (Orig.). (J). (gr. 4-6). pap. 10.95 *(978-0-9616712-6-6(2))* Catskill Ctr. for Conservation & Development, Inc.

Sazaklis, John. The Lizard's Legacy. McVeigh, Mark W. 2009. (Spider-Man Ser.). 64p. (J). (gr. 2-5). pap. 4.99 *(978-0-06-162627-2(9),* HarperFestival) HarperCollins Pubs.

—The Secret Life of Black Cat. Teitelbaum, Michael. 2009. (Spider-Man Ser.). 64p. (J). (gr. 2-5). pap. 4.99 *(978-0-06-162626-5(0),* HarperFestival) HarperCollins Pubs.

Sazaklis, John, jt. illus. see Merkel, Joe F.

Sbandelli, Angela. The Fabulous Glitter Girl. Scheel, Morgan Lee. 2017. (ENG.). 54p. (J). pap. 9.95 *(978-1-63047-998-5(5))* Morgan James Publishing.

Sburelin, Glenda. Ogres & Giants: With Augmented Reality. 2017. (ENG.). 48p. (J). 8.99 *(978-1-910596-98-2(1),* ceff8988-04a3-4658-8412-c7ce5726ec9a) Design Media Publishing Ltd. HKG. Dist: Baker & Taylor Publisher Services (BTPS).

Scadden, Kathryn. Mr. Munson's Itvice on Bullying. Nolan, Nancy. 2015. (J). 16.95 *(978-1-59298-907-2(1))* Beaver's Pond Pr., Inc.

Scala, Susan. Captain Nathaniel Brown Palmer. Sanford, Candace. 2007. 96p. (YA). pap. 14.95 *(978-0-9773725-9-1(6))* Flat Hammock Pr.

Scales, Simon. Monsters, Mind Your Manners! Spurr, Elizabeth. 2012. (J). 34.28 *(978-1-61913-124-8(2))* Weigl Pubs., Inc.

Scalf, Chris. Spinosaurus in the Storm. Nussbaum, Ben. (Smithsonian's Prehistoric Pals Ser.). (ENG.). 36p. (J). (gr. -1-2). 9.95 *(978-1-59249-462-0(5),* PS2457) Soundprints.

—Spinosaurus in the Storm. Nussbaum, Ben & McIntosh, G. B. 2005. (Smithsonian's Prehistoric Pals Ser.). (ENG.). 36p. (J). (gr. -1-2). 2.95 *(978-1-59249-461-3(7),* S2457) Soundprints.

—Spinosaurus in the Storm. Nussbaum, Ben. 2005. (ENG.). 36p. (J). (gr. -1-2). 8.95 *(978-1-59249-460-6(9),* SD2407) Soundprints.

Scalf, Chris & McIntosh, Gabe. Spinosaurus. Bailey, Gerry. 2011. (Smithsonian Prehistoric Zone Ser.). (ENG.). 32p. (J). (gr. k-3). *(978-0-7787-1802-4(6));* pap. *(978-0-7787-1815-4(8))* Crabtree Publishing Co.

Scalf, Christopher. Spinosaurus in the Storm. Nussbaum, Ben. 2005. (Smithsonian's Prehistoric Pals Ser.). (ENG.). 36p. (J). (gr. -1 — 1). pap. 6.95 *(978-1-59249-459-0(5),* S2407) Soundprints.

Scalf, Christopher & McIntosh, Gabe. Spinosaurus in the Storm. Nussbaum, Ben. 2005. (Smithsonian's Prehistoric Pals Ser.). (ENG.). 36p. (J). (gr. 2-2). 14.95 *(978-1-59249-458-3(7),* H2407) Soundprints.

Scalia, Johnna. Wilmettie. Houser, Sue. 2020. (ENG.). 96p. (J). (gr. 4-6). pap. 17.95 ***(978-1-68283-065-9(9))*** Texas Tech Univ. Pr.

Scandella, Alessandra. Maria Callas. Capriolo, Paola. 2009. (SPA.). 116p. (YA). (gr. 7-18). 27.95 *(978-84-8483-351-2(8))* Ediciones del Laberinto ESP. Dist: Ediciones Universal.

Scanlon, Michael. Best Friends: A Chock-a-Block Book. Seiss, Ellie. 2010. (Yo Gabba Gabba! Ser.). (ENG.). 12p. (J). 5.99 *(978-1-4424-0970-5(3),* Simon Spotlight) Simon Spotlight.

—A Mystery in Gabba Land. McDoogle, Farrah. 2010. (Yo Gabba Gabba! Ser.). (ENG.). 24p. (J). (gr. -1-k). pap. 3.99 *(978-1-4424-0652-0(6),* Simon Spotlight) Simon Spotlight.

Scanlon, Michael, jt. illus. see Little Airplane Productions.

Scarborough, Casey. Cindy Lou Ella: A Country Fairy Tale. Ondrias, Rachel. 2007. (ENG.). 56p. (J). 18.95 *(978-1-933660-28-8(7),* Tadpole Pr. 4 Kids) Mystic Harbor Pr., LLC.

—Kolby, the Skating Bear: A Kalamazoo Christmas. Ondrias, Rachel. 2007. (ENG.). 32p. (J). 16.95 *(978-1-933660-29-5(5),* Tadpole Pr. 4 Kids) Mystic Harbor Pr., LLC.

—The Pumpkin Gift. Hollis, Ginger. 2006. (ENG.). 28p. (J). 16.95 *(978-1-933660-04-2(X),* Tadpole Pr. 4 Kids) Mystic Harbor Pr., LLC.

—There's a Pig in My Fridge. Ondrias, Rachel. 2006. (ENG.). 28p. (J). 16.95 *(978-1-933660-30-1(9),* Tadpole Pr. 4 Kids) Mystic Harbor Pr., LLC.

Scarborough, Rob. Brothers of the Fire Star. Arvidson, Douglas. 2012. 207p. (YA). pap. 15.95 *(978-1-890109-91-2(6),* Cross Time) Crossquarter Publishing Group.

Scardina, Chuck. Burt Bunny Gets Elected. Feller, Robert S. 2018. (Heidi the Lamb & Burt Bunny Ser.: Vol. 3). (ENG.). 34p. (J). pap. 10.00 *(978-1-7240-3900-2(8))* Independently Published.

Scardina, Tom. The Leaf That Was Afraid to Fall, 1 vol. Nunnery, Donna. 2010. 26p. 24.95 *(978-1-4489-5927-3(6))* PublishAmerica, Inc.

—Old Billy, the Bike. England, Don. 2011. 24p. pap. 24.95 *(978-1-4560-3049-0(3))* America Star Bks.

Scarlet, Tyler. Star Wars the Force Awakens: Tales from a Galaxy Far, Far Away. Walker, Landry Quinn. 2016. (ENG.). 352p. (J). (gr. 3-7). 12.99 *(978-1-4847-4141-2(2),* Disney Lucasfilm Press) Disney Publishing Worldwide.

Scarpa, Daniel. Bugs. Courtauld, Sarah. 2008. (Usborne First Reading: Level 3 Ser.). 47p. (J). 8.99 *(978-0-7945-1938-4(5),* Usborne) EDC Publishing.

Scarpa, Romano. Mickey Mouse: Dark Mines of the Phantom Metal. Castellan, Andrea et al. 2017. (Mickey Mouse Ser.: 5). 124p. (J). (gr. 4-7). pap. 12.99 *(978-1-63140-857-1(7))* Idea & Design Works, LLC.

Scarpulla, Caren. Super Kids: Ordinary Kids Who Have Done Extraordinary Things. Fitterman, Lisa. 2005. 96p. (J). (gr. 3-7). *(978-1-59258-136-8(6))* Hylas Publishing.

Scarrone, Gustavo. Insomnios. Villarreal, Francisco, photos by. Villalba Casas, Consuelo. l.t. ed. 2003. (SPA.). 100p. (YA). pap. *(978-1-931481-18-2(0))* LiArt-Literature & Art.

Scarry, Huck. All about Anne, 1 vol. 2018. (ENG.). 72p. (J). (gr. 4-7). 24.95 *(978-1-77260-060-5(1))* Second Story Pr. CAN. Dist: Orca Bk. Pubs. USA.

Scarry, Richard. The Animals' Merry Christmas. Jackson, Kathryn. 2005. 72p. (J). (gr. -1-2). 15.99 *(978-0-375-83341-0(2),* Golden Bks.) Random Hse. Children's Bks.

—The Bunny Book. Scarry, Patsy. 2016. (Little Golden Board Book Ser.). 26p. (J). (— 1). bds. 7.99 *(978-0-553-53587-7(0),* Random Hse. Bks. for Young Readers) Random Hse. Children's Bks.

—Counting to Ten Jigsaw Book: With Six 24-Piece Jigsaws Inside. 2004. 12p. (J). bds. *(978-1-74124-406-9(4))* Five Mile Australia.

—Duck & His Friends. Jackson, Kathryn & Jackson, Byron. 2019. (Little Golden Book Ser.). (ENG.). 24p. (J). (-k). 4.99 *(978-1-9848-4978-6(6),* Golden Bks.) Random Hse. Children's Bks.

—I Am a Bunny. Risom, Ole. 2004. (Golden Sturdy Book Ser.). (ENG.). 26p. (J). (gr. k — 1). bds. 7.99 *(978-0-375-82778-5(1),* Golden Bks.) Random Hse. Children's Bks.

—I Am a Bunny/Soy un Conejito. Risom, Ole. 2020. 26p. (J). (— 1). bds. 7.99 *(978-0-399-55290-8(1),* Golden Bks.) Random Hse. Children's Bks.

—Le Noël des Animaux. Jackson, Kathryn. Nikly, Michelle, tr. 2008. (A. M. Alb. Ill. A. Ser.). (FRE.). 70p. (J). (gr. -1-2). *(978-2-226-18340-8(X))* Albin-Michel, Editions.

—Richard Scarry's Best Little Golden Books Ever! Scarry, Patsy et al. 2014. 224p. (J). (-k). 12.99 *(978-0-385-37912-0(9),* Golden Bks.) Random Hse. Children's Bks.

—Richard Scarry's Colors. Daly, Kathleen N. 2017. (Little Golden Book Ser.). 20p. (J). (gr. -1-2). 5.99 *(978-0-399-55367-7(3),* Golden Bks.) Random Hse. Children's Bks.

—Richard Scarry's Good Night, Little Bear. Scarry, Patsy. 2014. (Big Golden Book Ser.). 32p. (J). (-k). 9.99 *(978-0-385-38729-3(6),* Golden Bks.) Random Hse. Children's Bks.

—Richard Scarry's Just for Fun. Scarry, Patricia. 2016. (Little Golden Book Ser.). 24p. (J). (gr. -1-k). 4.99 *(978-0-553-53662-1(1),* Golden Bks.) Random Hse. Children's Bks.

—Richard Scarry's the Animals' Merry Christmas. Jackson, Kathryn. 2016. (Little Golden Book Ser.). (J). (-k). 24p. 4.99 *(978-1-101-93842-3(0)); (978-1-5182-2103-3(3))* Random Hse. Children's Bks. (Golden Bks.).

—Richard Scarry's the Bunny Book. Scarry, Patsy. 2015. (Big Golden Book Ser.). 32p. (J). (-k). 9.99 *(978-0-385-39090-3(4),* Golden Bks.) Random Hse. Children's Bks.

—Richard Scarry's the Country Mouse & the City Mouse. Scarry, Patricia. 2018. (Little Golden Books Ser.). 24p. (J). (-k). 4.99 *(978-1-5247-7145-4(7),* Golden Bks.) Random Hse. Children's Bks.

—Richard Scarry's the Gingerbread Man. Nolte, Nancy. 2015. (Little Golden Book Ser.). 24p. (J). (-k). 4.99 *(978-0-385-37619-8(7),* Golden Bks.) Random Hse. Children's Bks.

—Richard Scarry's the Party Pig. Jackson, Kathryn & Jackson, Byron. 2019. (Little Golden Book Ser.). (ENG.). 24p. (J). (-k). 4.99 *(978-1-9848-4987-8(5),* Golden Bks.) Random Hse. Children's Bks.

Scarry, Richard. Boats. Scarry, Richard. 2015. 24p. (J). (— 1). bds. 4.99 *(978-0-385-39269-3(9),* Golden Bks.) Random Hse. Children's Bks.

—A Day at the Police Station. Scarry, Richard. Scarry, Huck. 2004. (Look-Look Ser.). 24p. (J). (gr. -1-2). pap. 4.99 *(978-0-375-82822-5(2),* Golden Bks.) Random Hse. Children's Bks.

—Mi Casa. Scarry, Richard. 2003. (Richard Scarry Ser.).Tr. of My Home. (SPA.). (J). (gr. -1-3). pap. *(978-970-690-845-2(5))* Planeta Mexicana Editorial S. A. de C. V.

—Planes. Scarry, Richard. 2015. 24p. (J). (— 1). bds. 4.99 *(978-0-385-39270-9(2),* Golden Bks.) Random Hse. Children's Bks.

—Richard Scarry's Best Bunny Book Ever! Scarry, Richard. 2014. 80p. (J). (-k). 7.99 *(978-0-385-38467-4(X),* Golden Bks.) Random Hse. Children's Bks.

—Richard Scarry's Best Counting Book Ever. Scarry, Richard. 2004. (SPA, ENG & MUL.). 40p. (J). (gr. -1-2). 14.95 *(978-0-87358-875-1(4));* pap. 8.95 *(978-0-87358-876-8(2))* Cooper Square Publishing Llc.

—Richard Scarry's Best Little Word Book Ever! Scarry, Richard. 2016. (Pictureback(R) Ser.). 24p. (J). (-k). pap. 4.99 *(978-0-385-39271-6(0),* Random Hse. Bks. for Young Readers) Random Hse. Children's Bks.

—Richard Scarry's Best Word Book Ever. Scarry, Richard. 2004. (SPA, ENG & MUL.). 64p. (J). (gr. -1-2). pap. 10.95 *(978-0-87358-874-4(6))* Cooper Square Publishing Llc.

—Richard Scarry's Bunnies. Scarry, Richard. 2014. 26p. (J). (-k). 8.99 *(978-0-385-38518-3(8)*, Golden Bks.) Random Hse. Children's Bks.

—Richard Scarry's Busy, Busy World. Scarry, Richard. 2015. (ENG.). 96p. (J). (gr. -1-2). 16.99 *(978-0-385-38480-3(7)*, Golden Bks.) Random Hse. Children's Bks.

Scarry, Richard. Richard Scarry's Busytown Seek & Find! Scarry, Richard. 2020. 18p. (J). (— 1). bds. 12.99 ***(978-0-593-17745-7(2)***, Golden Bks.) Random Hse. Children's Bks.

Scarry, Richard. Richard Scarry's Cars & Trucks. Scarry, Richard. 2017. (Little Golden Book Ser.). (ENG.). 24p. (J). (-k). 4.99 *(978-1-101-93927-7(3)*, Golden Bks.) Random Hse. Children's Bks.

—Richard Scarry's Christmas Mice. Scarry, Richard. 2014. (Little Golden Book Ser.). 24p. (J). (-k). 4.99 *(978-0-385-38421-6(1)*, Golden Bks.) Random Hse. Children's Bks.

—Richard Scarry's Just Right Word Book! Scarry, Richard. 2015. 24p. (J). (— 1). bds. 7.99 *(978-0-553-50902-1(0)*, Golden Bks.) Random Hse. Children's Bks.

—Richard Scarry's Lowly Worm Word Book. Scarry, Richard. 2014. (Chunky Book(R) Ser.). (ENG.). 28p. (J). (gr. -1 — 1). bds. 3.99 *(978-0-394-84728-3(8)*, Random Hse. Bks. for Young Readers) Random Hse. Children's Bks.

—Richard Scarry's Pig Will & Pig Won't. Scarry, Richard. 2014. (Pictureback(R) Ser.). (ENG.). 24p. (J). (gr. -1-2). 4.99 *(978-0-385-38337-0(1)*, Random Hse. Bks. for Young Readers) Random Hse. Children's Bks.

—Richard Scarry's Polite Elephant. Scarry, Richard. 2016. (Little Golden Book Ser.). 24p. (J). (-k). 4.99 *(978-1-101-93090-8(X)*, Golden Bks.) Random Hse. Children's Bks.

—Richard Scarry's Postman Pig & His Busy Neighbors. Scarry, Richard. 2015. (Pictureback(R) Ser.). 24p. (J). (gr. -1-2). pap. 4.99 *(978-0-385-38419-3(X)*, Random Hse. Bks. for Young Readers) Random Hse. Children's Bks.

—Richard Scarry's the Night Before the Night Before Christmas! Scarry, Richard. 2014. (ENG.). 48p. (J). (gr. -1-2). 16.99 *(978-0-385-38804-7(7)*, Golden Bks.) Random Hse. Children's Bks.

Scarry, Richard & Golden Books Staff. Little Golden Book Favorites. Golden Books Staff. 2008. 80p. (J). (gr. -1-2). 7.99 *(978-0-375-84580-2(1)*, Golden Bks.) Random Hse. Children's Bks.

Scauzillo, Tony. WonderChess - Chess Kit for Kids: Featuring unique, prize-fillable pieces & 3D illustrated lesson Book. Thyrion, Marie-Noelle, photos by. Alvarez, Michel J. 2004. 54p. (J). pap. 19.95 *(978-0-9771787-0-4(6))* Wonder Chess LLC.

—WonderChess - Chess Kit for Kids - Deluxe Edition in Tin: Featuring, unique prize fillable pieces & 3D illustrated lesson Book, 1. Thyrion, Marie-Noelle, photos by. Alvarez, Michel J. 2005. 54p. (J). 29.95 *(978-0-9771787-1-1(4))* Wonder Chess LLC.

Schaber, Kaylene. Three Short Stories & a Poem for Young Girls. Helm, Diane J. 2018. (Short Stories & Poems for Young Girls Ser.: Vol. 1). (ENG.). 42p. (J). pap. 9.95 *(978-1-9792-3081-0(1))* CreateSpace Independent Publishing Platform.

Schacher, Tracey. The Greatest Marriage Ever. Powell, Joyce. 2011. 26p. pap. 11.95 *(978-1-4575-0215-6(1))* Dog Ear Publishing, LLC.

Schachner, Judy. Dewey Bob. Schachner, Judy. 2015. 32p. (J). (gr. k-3). 17.99 *(978-0-8037-4120-1(0)*, Dial Bks) Penguin Young Readers Group.

—Skippyjon Jones. Schachner, Judy. (Skippyjon Jones Ser.). 32p. (J). 2003. (ENG.). (gr. -1-k). 17.99 *(978-0-525-47134-9(0)*, Dutton Books for Young Readers); 2005. (gr. k-k). reprint ed. pap. 7.99 *(978-0-14-240403-4(9)*, Puffin Books) Penguin Young Readers Group.

—Skippyjon Jones Book & Toy Set, Set. Schachner, Judy. 2007. (Skippyjon Jones Ser.). 32p. (J). (gr. -1-k). 17.99 *(978-0-525-47774-7(8)*, Dutton Books for Young Readers) Penguin Young Readers Group.

—Skippyjon Jones in Mummy Trouble. Schachner, Judy. 2006. (Skippyjon Jones Ser.). 32p. (J). (gr. -1-k). 17.99 *(978-0-525-47754-9(3)*, Dutton Books for Young Readers) Penguin Young Readers Group.

—Skippyjon Jones in the Doghouse. Schachner, Judy. 2007. (Skippyjon Jones Ser.). 32p. (J). (gr. -1-k). pap. 8.99 *(978-0-14-240749-3(6)*, Puffin Books) Penguin Young Readers Group.

—Skippyjon Jones in the Doghouse. Schachner, Judy. Wilhelm, James J., ed. 2005. (Skippyjon Jones Ser.). 32p. (J). (gr. -1-18). 17.99 *(978-0-525-47297-1(5)*, Dutton Books for Young Readers) Penguin Young Readers Group.

—Skippyjon Jones, Lost in Spice. Schachner, Judy. 2009. (Skippyjon Jones Ser.). 32p. (J). (gr. -1-k). 17.99 *(978-0-525-47965-9(1)*, Dutton Books for Young Readers) Penguin Young Readers Group.

—Stretchy Mchandsome. Schachner, Judy. 2019. 40p. (J). (-k). 17.99 *(978-0-8037-4121-8(9)*, Dial Bks) Penguin Young Readers Group.

—Up & Down. Schachner, Judy. 2007. (Skippyjon Jones Ser.). 14p. (J). (gr. -1 — 1). bds. 6.99 *(978-0-525-47807-2(8)*, Dutton Books for Young Readers) Penguin Young Readers Group.

Schaefer, Nikki. The Potty Train. Schaefer, Nikki. 2010. 24p. pap. 10.95 *(978-1-61633-043-9(0))* Guardian Angel Publishing, Inc.

Schaefer, Susi. Zoo Zen: A Yoga Story for Kids. Fischer, Kristen. 2017. (ENG.). 32p. (J). (gr. -1-2). 17.95 *(978-1-62203-891-6(6)*, 900220816) Sounds True, Inc.

Schaefer, Susi. Cat Ladies. Schaefer, Susi. 2020. (ENG.). 32p. (J). (gr. -1-3). 16.99 *(978-1-4197-4082-4(2)*, Abrams Bks. for Young Readers) Abrams, Inc.

Schaeffer, Bob. Peppy Learns to Play Baseball. Heller, Pete. Kinsey, Thomas D., ed. (Peppy Learns to Play Ser.). 32p. (J). (gr. k-5). pap. 3.95 *(978-0-932423-00-9(0))* Summa Bks.

Schaerer, Kathrin. Fox in the Library. Pauli, Lorenz. 2013. 32p. (J). (gr. -1-3). 17.95 *(978-0-7358-4150-5(0))* North-South Bks., Inc.

Schafbuch, Michael. R Is for Rocky Mountains. Kernahan, Maria. 2017. (ENG.). 56p. (J). (gr. -1-k). bds. 9.95 *(978-1-942402-46-6(5)*, 65071dde-a907-487a-872a-4c70274cd04f) Dry Climate Studios.

—W Is for Washington, DC. Kernahan, Maria. 2019. (Alphabet Cities Ser.). (ENG.). 56p. (J). (gr. k-2). 19.95 *(978-1-942402-30-5(9)*, 2f4222c5-9488-4935-97a8-b3bda1c659c7) Dry Climate Studios.

Schafer, Ann. A Home for the Winter. Lembke, Linda. 2018. (ENG.). 44p. (J). 19.99 *(978-0-578-41781-3(2))* Concordis Publishing.

Schafer, Holden J. Blue Tooth Sleuth. Steininger-Moore, Cheryl A. 2013. 26p. 16.50 *(978-1-61314-141-0(6))*; (J). pap. 9.99 *(978-1-61314-142-7(4)*, Innovo Pr.) Innovo Publishing, LLC.

Schafer, Rick, photos by. Cooking with the Seafood Steward: Taking the Mystery Out of Seafood Preparation. Puetz, Gary Rainer. 2008. (ENG., 198p. 24.95 *(978-0-9801942-5-8(3))* ACS, LLC Amica Creative Services.

—The Vintner's Kitchen: Celebrating the Wines of Oregon. King, William. 2008. (Chef's Bounty Ser.). (ENG., 187p. 29.95 *(978-0-9794771-3-3(1))* ACS, LLC Amica Creative Services.

Schafrath, Richard "ty". The Grasshopper. Wilkerson, Bessie T. 2020. (ENG.). 32p. (J). 21.99 ***(978-1-63050-522-6(6))***; pap. 19.99 ***(978-1-62952-999-8(0))*** Salem Author Services.

Schafrath, Ty. Feet. McCullough, Myrina D. 2013. 28p. pap. 15.00 *(978-0-9847740-1-2(7))* Systems Group, Inc., The.

—I Am Exceptional. Bender, Elaine. 2018. (ENG.). 34p. (J). 20.99 *(978-1-5456-4601-4(5))*; pap. 10.49 *(978-1-5456-4600-7(7))* Salem Author Services.

Schalkwijk, Bob, jt. photos by see Burgess, Don.

Schallmo, Carolyn. Ryan the Lion Finds His Roar. Lamb, Jim. 2011. 32p. 22.95 *(978-1-60844-880-7(0))*; pap. 12.95 *(978-1-60844-879-1(7))* Dog Ear Publishing, LLC.

Schamber, Kimberly. Rabbits on Mars. Wahl, Jan. 2005. 32p. (gr. k-2). 15.25 *(978-1-57505-511-4(2))* Lerner Publishing Group.

Schanck, Agnes. The Flower Pot Bunnies: Not A Good Place For A Nest. Rehm, Carolyn. 2004. 48p. (J). bds. 12.99 *(978-0-9755390-1-9(9))* Fifth Ave Pr.

Schandy, Rosita & Wooten, Neal. Spencer the Spring Chicken & Other Stories. Mitchell, Malinda. 2007. 88p. pap. 23.95 *(978-0-9800675-0-7(2))* Mirror Publishing.

Schanilec, Gaylord. My Mighty Journey: A Waterfall's Story. Coy, John. 2019. (ENG.). 40p. (J). 18.95 *(978-1-68134-008-1(9))* Minnesota Historical Society Pr.

Schank, Amanda. Origin of a Hero. West, Tracey. 2019. (She-Ra Ser.: 1). 128p. (J). (gr. 2-5). pap. 5.99 *(978-1-338-29841-3(0))* Scholastic, Inc.

Schank, Amanda & Häggman-Sund, Hedvig. Island of Magical Creatures, Bk. 2. Scholastic & West, Tracey. 2019. (She-Ra Ser.: 2). 128p. (J). (gr. 2-5). pap. 5.99 *(978-1-338-29843-7(7))* Scholastic, Inc.

Schanzer, Olivia. B'chol L'vavcha: With All Your Heart. rev. ed. 2004. (ENG & HEB.). xxiv, 261p. (gr. 7-9). pap. 14.00 *(978-0-8074-0777-6(1)*, 142611) URJ Pr.

Schanzer, Rosalyn. Ten Good Rules. Topek, Susan R. 2004. (General Jewish Interest Ser.). 24p. (J). (gr. -1-1). pap. 6.95 *(978-0-929371-30-6(5)*, Kar-Ben Publishing) Lerner Publishing Group.

—The True-or-False Book of Dogs. Lauber, Patricia. 2003. (ENG.). 32p. (J). 15.99 *(978-0-06-029767-1(0))* HarperCollins Pubs.

Schärer, Kathrin. The Fox in the Library. Pauli, Lorenz. 2015. 32p. (J). pap. 7.95 *(978-0-7358-4213-7(2))* North-South Bks., Inc.

Scharschmidt, Sherry. Tuck Me In! Hacohen, Dean. 2010. (ENG.). 40p. (J). (gr. -1 — 1). 14.00 *(978-0-7636-4728-5(4))* Candlewick Pr.

—Who's Hungry? Hacohen, Dean. 2015. (ENG.). 40p. (J). (— 1). 9.99 *(978-0-7636-6586-9(X))* Candlewick Pr.

Schartup, Adam. Hello, Beaker! Morehead State University. Aryal, Naren. 2013. (ENG.). (J). 14.95 *(978-1-62086-151-6(8))* Mascot Bks., Inc.

—Land of the Free, A to Z. Warner, Roxie & Warner, Christian. 2014. (J). *(978-1-62086-801-0(6))* Mascot Bks., Inc.

—The Secret Society of the Palos Verdes Lizards. Milani, Joan. 2013. (ENG.). (J). 14.95 *(978-1-62086-346-6(4))* Mascot Bks., Inc.

Schatell, Brian. On the First Night of Chanukah. Kaiser, Cecily. 2007. (ENG.). 24p. (J). (gr. -1-3). pap. 3.99 *(978-0-439-75802-4(5))* Scholastic, Inc.

Schaub, Stephen, photos by. Through a Glass Darkly: Photographs by Stephen M. Schaub. 2004. (ENG & FRE., 60p. 65.00 *(978-0-9669079-1-9(4))* Indian Hill Gallery of Fine Photography.

Schauer, Jane. Fantasy Park Book 1: The Doorman. Schauer, Jane. 2008. 36p. pap. *(978-0-9804633-2-3(7))* KREAV Publishing.

Schauer, Loretta. Good Little Bad Little Pig! Brown, Margaret Wise. 2019. (Margaret Wise Brown Classics Ser.). (ENG.). 32p. (J). (gr. -1-k). 12.99 *(978-1-68412-747-4(5)*, Silver Dolphin Bks.) Printers Row Publishing Group.

—A Monster Moved In! Knapman, Timothy. 2015. (ENG.). 32p. (J). (gr. -1-2). 16.99 *(978-1-58925-176-2(8))* Tiger Tales.

—Rumpelstiltskin. Tiger Tales. 2016. (My First Fairy Tales Ser.). (ENG.). 32p. (J). (gr. -1-2). pap. 7.99 *(978-1-58925-478-7(3))* Tiger Tales.

Schauer, Loretta. Sky Private Eye & the Case of the Missing Grandma: A Fairytale Mystery Starring Little Red Riding Hood, 1 vol. Clark, Jane. 2020. (Sky Private Eye Ser.). (ENG.). 32p. (J). (gr. 1-2). pap. 10.00 ***(978-1-4994-8670-4(7))***; lib. bdg. 27.25 ***(978-1-4994-8671-1(5))*** Rosen Publishing Group, Inc., The. (Windmill Bks.).

—Sky Private Eye & the Case of the Runaway Cookie: A Fairytale Mystery Starring the Gingerbread Boy, 1 vol. Clark, Jane. 2020. (Sky Private Eye Ser.). (ENG.). 32p. (J). (gr. 1-2). pap. 10.00 ***(978-1-4994-8673-5(1))***; lib. bdg. 27.25 ***(978-1-4994-8674-2(X))*** Rosen Publishing Group, Inc., The. (Windmill Bks.).

—Sky Private Eye & the Case of the Sparkly Slipper: A Fairytale Mystery Starring Cinderella, 1 vol. Clark, Jane. 2020. (Sky Private Eye Ser.). (ENG.). 32p. (J). (gr. 1-2). pap. 10.00 ***(978-1-4994-8667-4(7))***; lib. bdg. 27.25 ***(978-1-4994-8668-1(5))*** Rosen Publishing Group, Inc., The. (Windmill Bks.).

Schautz, Irmela. The Book of Time. Koller, Kathrin. 2020. (ENG.). 112p. (J). (gr. 2-5). 24.95 *(978-3-7913-7417-8(6))* Prestel Verlag GmbH & Co KG. DEU. Dist: Penguin Random Hse. LLC.

Schedeen, Minnie. Bleep Blop Bloop, 1. Arthur, Clint. 2006. 24p. (J). per. 8.99 net. *(978-1-4276-0218-3(2))* Aardvark Global Publishing.

Scheff, Marc. Gabe. Gill, Shelley. 2016. 64p. (J). (gr. 3-7). lib. bdg. 12.95 *(978-1-57091-354-9(4))* Charlesbridge Publishing, Inc.

Scheffler, Axel. The Bedtime Bear. Whybrow, Ian. 2016. (ENG.). 12p. (J). (gr. -1-2). bds. 9.99 *(978-1-5098-0695-9(4))* Pan Macmillan GBR. Dist: Independent Pubs. Group.

Scheffler, Axel. The Bedtime Bear Sticker Book. Whybrow, Ian. 2020. (Tom & Bear Ser.). (ENG.). 24p. (J). (gr. -1-k). pap. 9.99 ***(978-1-5290-1090-9(X))***, Macmillan Children's Bks.) Pan Macmillan GBR. Dist: Independent Pubs. Group.

Scheffler, Axel. Charlie Cook's Favorite Book. Donaldson, Julia. 2008. (ENG.). 32p. (J). (gr. -1-k). pap. 7.99 *(978-0-14-241138-4(8)*, Puffin Books) Penguin Young Readers Group.

—The Christmas Bear. Whybrow, Ian. 2016. (ENG.). 10p. (J). (gr. -1-2). bds. 8.99 *(978-1-5098-0696-6(2))* Pan Macmillan GBR. Dist: Independent Pubs. Group.

—The Christmas Bear Sticker Book. Whybrow, Ian. 2019. (Tom & Bear Ser.: 4). (ENG.). 24p. (J). (gr. -1-k). pap. 9.99 *(978-1-5098-8063-8(1))* Pan Macmillan GBR. Dist: Independent Pubs. Group.

—Christmas Poems. Morgan, Gaby. unabr. ed. 2014. (ENG.). 176p. (J). pap. 9.99 *(978-1-4472-5463-8(5))* Pan Macmillan GBR. Dist: Independent Pubs. Group.

—Cuddly Cow: A Farm Friends Sound Book. Nosy Crow Staff. 2017. (Farm Friends Sound Book Ser.). (ENG.). 12p. (J). (— 1). bds. 9.99 *(978-0-7636-9325-1(1)*, Nosy Crow) Candlewick Pr.

—The Fish Who Cried Wolf. Donaldson, Julia. (J). 2017. (ENG.). 40p. (gr. -1-k). 17.99 *(978-0-439-92825-0(7))*; 2008. pap. *(978-0-545-03454-8(X))* Scholastic, Inc. (Levine, Arthur A. Bks.).

—Flip Flap Dinosaurs. Nosy Crow. 2019. (Flip Flap Bks.). (ENG.). 28p. (J). (gr. -1-2). 11.99 *(978-1-5362-0826-9(4)*, Nosy Crow) Candlewick Pr.

—Flip Flap Farm. Crow, Nosy. 2014. (ENG.). 26p. (J). (gr. -1-2). 11.99 *(978-0-7636-7067-2(7)*, Nosy Crow) Candlewick Pr.

—Flip Flap Ocean. Nosy Crow. 2018. (Flip Flap Bks.). (ENG.). 28p. (J). (gr. -1-2). 11.99 *(978-0-7636-9942-0(X)*, Nosy Crow) Candlewick Pr.

—Flip Flap Safari. Nosy Crow Staff. 2015. (ENG.). 28p. (J). (gr. -1-2). 11.99 *(978-0-7636-7605-6(5)*, Nosy Crow) Candlewick Pr.

—Gobbly Goat: A Farm Friends Sound Book. Nosy Crow. 2018. (Farm Friends Sound Book Ser.). (ENG.). 12p. (J). (— 1). bds. 9.99 *(978-0-7636-9620-7(X)*, Nosy Crow) Candlewick Pr.

—A Gold Star for Zog. Donaldson, Julia. 2012. (ENG.). 32p. (J). (gr. -1-3). 18.99 *(978-0-545-41724-2(4)*, Levine, Arthur A. Bks.) Scholastic, Inc.

—El Grufalo. Donaldson, Julia. 2003. (SPA.). 32p. (J). (gr. k-2). 7.96 *(978-84-233-3145-1(8)*, DS4478) Ediciones Destino ESP. Dist: Lectorum Pubns., Inc.

—The Gruffalo. Donaldson, Julia. 2012. (ENG.). 32p. (J). (gr. -1-2). 20.99 *(978-0-230-75932-9(7))* Pan Macmillan GBR. Dist: Independent Pubs. Group.

—The Gruffalo. Donaldson, Julia. 2005. (ENG.). 26p. (J). (gr. -1-k). bds. 8.99 *(978-0-8037-3047-2(0)*, Dial Bks) Penguin Young Readers Group.

—The Gruffalo. Donaldson, Julia. 2005. (ENG.). 32p. (J). (gr. -1-2). 17.99 *(978-0-8037-3109-7(4)*, Dial Bks) Penguin Young Readers Group.

—The Gruffalo in Scots. Donaldson, Julia. Robertson, James, tr. 2012. 32p. (J). (-k). pap. 10.99 *(978-1-84502-503-8(2))* Black and White Publishing Ltd. GBR. Dist: Independent Pubs. Group.

—The Gruffalo's Child. Donaldson, Julia. 2007. (ENG.). 32p. (J). (gr. -1-2). pap. 7.99 *(978-0-14-240754-7(2)*, Puffin Books) Penguin Young Readers Group.

—Hamilton's Hats. Oborne, Martine. 2018. (ENG.). 32p. (J). (gr. -1-k). pap. 9.99 *(978-1-5098-5878-1(4))* Pan Macmillan GBR. Dist: Independent Pubs. Group.

—Higgly Hen: A Farm Friends Sound Book. Nosy Crow Staff. 2017. (Farm Friends Sound Book Ser.). (ENG.). 12p. (J). (— 1). bds. 9.99 *(978-0-7636-9324-4(3)*, Nosy Crow) Candlewick Pr.

—The Highway Rat. Donaldson, Julia. 2013. (ENG.). 32p. (J). (gr. -1-3). 16.99 *(978-0-545-47758-1(1)*, Levine, Arthur A. Bks.) Scholastic, Inc.

—Jeremy James: Never Say Moo to a Bull. Henry Wilson, David. 2017. (Jeremy James Ser.: 2). (ENG.). 128p. (J). (gr. k-5). pap. 8.99 *(978-1-5098-1878-5(2))* Pan Macmillan GBR. Dist: Independent Pubs. Group.

—On the Farm. 2020. (ENG.). 10p. (J). (gr. -1-k). bds. 9.99 *(978-1-5098-6694-6(9)*, Campbell Bks.) Pan Macmillan GBR. Dist: Independent Pubs. Group.

—Pip & Posy: the Bedtime Frog. Crow, Nosy. 2014. (Pip & Posy Ser.). (ENG.). 32p. (J). (-k). 12.99 *(978-0-7636-7068-9(5)*, Nosy Crow) Candlewick Pr.

—Pip & Posy: the Christmas Tree. Nosy Crow. 2018. (Pip & Posy Ser.). (ENG.). 32p. (J). (-k). 12.99 *(978-1-5362-0276-2(2)*, Nosy Crow) Candlewick Pr.

—Pip & Posy: the New Friend. Nosy Crow Staff. 2017. (Pip & Posy Ser.). (ENG.). 32p. (J). (-k). 12.99 *(978-0-7636-9339-8(1)*, Nosy Crow) Candlewick Pr.

—Porty Pig: A Farm Friends Sound Book. Nosy Crow. 2018. (Farm Friends Sound Book Ser.). (ENG.). 12p. (J). (— 1). bds. 9.99 *(978-0-7636-9621-4(8)*, Nosy Crow) Candlewick Pr.

—The Reiver Rat: The Highway Rat in Scots. Donaldson, Julia. Robertson, James, tr. 2015. 32p. (J). (-k). pap. 10.99 *(978-1-84502-996-8(8)*, Itchy Coo) Black and White Publishing Ltd. GBR. Dist: Independent Pubs. Group.

—Room on the Broom. Donaldson, Julia. (ENG.). (J). 2012. 24p. (— 1). bds. 7.99 *(978-0-8037-3841-6(2)*, Dial Bks); 2003. 32p. (gr. -1-2). pap. 7.99 *(978-0-14-250112-2(3)*, Puffin Books) Penguin Young Readers Group.

—Room on the Broom Big Activity Book. Donaldson, Julia. 2015. (ENG.). 48p. (J). (gr. -1-3). pap. 10.99 *(978-0-448-48944-5(9)*, Grosset & Dunlap) Penguin Young Readers Group.

—Room on the Broom in Scots. Donaldson, Julia & Robertson, James. 2014. 32p. (J). (-k). pap. 10.99 *(978-1-84502-753-7(1))* Black and White Publishing Ltd. GBR. Dist: Independent Pubs. Group.

—Room on the Broom Lap Board Book. Donaldson, Julia. 2017. (ENG.). 12p. (J). (-k). bds. 12.99 *(978-0-7352-3134-4(6)*, Dial Bks) Penguin Young Readers Group.

Scheffler, Axel. Room on the Broom Push-Pull-Slide. Donaldson, Julia. 2020. (ENG.). 8p. (J). (-k). bds. 8.99 ***(978-0-593-11040-9(4)***, Dial Bks) Penguin Young Readers Group.

Scheffler, Axel. The Scarecrows' Wedding. Donaldson, Julia. 2014. (ENG.). 32p. (J). (gr. -1-3). 17.99 *(978-0-545-72606-1(9)*, Levine, Arthur A. Bks.) Scholastic, Inc.

—The Snail & the Whale. Donaldson, Julia. 2006. (ENG.). 32p. (J). (gr. -1-2). reprint ed. pap. 8.99 *(978-0-14-240580-2(9)*, Puffin Books) Penguin Young Readers Group.

—The Spiffiest Giant in Town. Donaldson, Julia. 2005. (ENG.). 32p. (J). (gr. -1-2). reprint ed. pap. 7.99 *(978-0-14-240275-7(3)*, Puffin Books) Penguin Young Readers Group.

—A Squash & a Squeeze. Donaldson, Julia. 2016. (ENG.). 32p. (J). (gr. -1-k). 16.99 *(978-1-338-05220-6(9))* Scholastic, Inc.

—Stick Man. Donaldson, Julia. (ENG.). 32p. (J). (gr. -1-3). 2016. 12.99 *(978-0-545-94789-3(8))*; 2009. 16.99 *(978-0-545-15761-2(7))* Scholastic, Inc. (Levine, Arthur A. Bks.).

—Superworm. Donaldson, Julia. 2014. (ENG.). 32p. (J). (gr. -1-3). 16.99 *(978-0-545-59176-8(7)*, Levine, Arthur A. Bks.) Scholastic, Inc.

—Tabby McTat: The Musical Cat. Donaldson, Julia. 2012. (ENG.). 32p. (J). (gr. -1-3). 17.99 *(978-0-545-45168-0(X)*, Levine, Arthur A. Bks.) Scholastic, Inc.

—The Tickle Book. Whybrow, Ian. 2016. (ENG.). 12p. (J). (gr. -1-k). bds. 8.99 *(978-1-5098-0697-3(0))* Pan Macmillan GBR. Dist: Independent Pubs. Group.

—A Treasury of Songs: Book & CD. Donaldson, Julia. 2017. (ENG.). 96p. (J). (gr. -1-2). 14.99 *(978-1-5098-4613-9(1))* Pan Macmillan GBR. Dist: Independent Pubs. Group.

—The Ugly Five. Donaldson, Julia. 2018. (ENG.). 32p. (J). (gr. -1-3). 17.99 *(978-1-338-24953-8(3)*, Scholastic Pr.) Scholastic, Inc.

—Where's My Mom? Donaldson, Julia. 2008. (ENG.). 32p. (J). (gr. -1-2). 18.99 *(978-0-8037-3228-5(7)*, Dial Bks) Penguin Young Readers Group.

—Zog & the Flying Doctors. Donaldson, Julia. 2017. (ENG.). 32p. (J). (gr. -1-3). 17.99 *(978-1-338-13417-9(5)*, Levine, Arthur A. Bks.) Scholastic, Inc.

Scheffler, Axel. Mother Goose's Nursery Rhymes: And How She Came to Tell Them. Scheffler, Axel. Green, Alison. ed. 2006. (ENG.). 128p. *(978-0-333-96136-0(6)*, Macmillan Children's Bks.) Pan Macmillan.

—Pip & Posy: the Snowy Day. Scheffler, Axel. Nosy Crow Staff. 2013. (Pip & Posy Ser.). (ENG.). 32p. (J). (-k). 12.99 *(978-0-7636-6607-1(6)*, Nosy Crow) Candlewick Pr.

Scheibe, Adam. The Hungry Polar Bear. English, Wesley. 2018. (ENG.). 22p. (J). (gr. k-3). 17.95 *(978-0-9795389-1-9(2))* Tripping Light Pr.

Scheibe, Nancy. Loon & Moon: And Other Animal Stories. Strauss, Kevin. 2005. 48p. (J). (gr. 4-6). per. 12.95 *(978-0-9766264-3-5(8))* Raven Productions, Inc.

Scheideler, Lisa M. Chicken Pot Turtle Explores Nicaragua. Scheideler, Angela M. 2018. (ENG.). 34p. (J). pap. 11.99 *(978-1-7307-2604-0(6))* Independently Published.

Scheie, Jesse. Kisses to Heaven, 1 vol. Scheie, Jesse. 2009. 16p. pap. 24.95 *(978-1-61582-707-7(2))* America Star Bks.

Scheinberg, Shepsil. Out of the Woods. Lazewnik, Libby. 2011. 320p. (J). *(978-1-4226-1176-0(0))* Mesorah Pubns., Ltd.

Scheiner, A. & Wenckebach, L. W. R. The Nutcracker & the Mouse King. Hoffmann, E. T. A. 2013. Orig. Title: Nutcracker & the King of the Mice. 88p. pap. *(978-1-909115-77-4(0))* Planet, The.

Schellekens, Willem. UK & Piep: The Magic of a Tree & the Strength of Gnomes. Schellekens, Willem. 2017. (ENG.). (J). pap. 29.95 *(978-1-68394-571-0(9))* America Star Bks.

Schellpeper, Kathy, photos by. The Community of Lincoln. Manton, Charlotte. Stanley, Karen & Bornemeier, Pam, eds. 116p. (J). (gr. 3-6). pap. 10.50 *(978-0-9671920-0-0(5))* Lincoln Public Schls.

Schenker, Hilary. Same Sun Here. House, Silas & Vaswani, Neela. 2013. (ENG.). 304p. (J). (gr. 4-7). pap. 7.99 *(978-0-7636-6451-0(0))* Candlewick Pr.

Schenker, Sybille. The Frog Prince. Grimm, Jacob. 2018. (ENG.). 48p. (J). (gr. k-2). 29.99 *(978-988-8341-47-4(2)*, Minedition) Neugebauer, Michael (Publishing) Limited HKG. Dist: Penguin Random Hse. LLC.

Scherber, Diana. Millie & Pansy: Go to the Dog Park. Scherrer, Maura L. 2019. (Millie & Pansy Adventures Ser.: Vol. 1). (ENG.). 34p. (J). pap. 10.00 ***(978-1-0759-1651-9(8))*** Independently Published.

Scherberger, Patrick. Goom Got Game! Parker, Jeff & Lee, Stan. 2007. (Spider-Man Ser.: No. 2). (ENG.). 24p. (J). (gr. 2-6). lib. bdg. 27.07 *(978-1-59961-209-6(7)*, 13621, Marvel Age) Spotlight.

—Picture-Perfect Peril! Lee, Stan. 2007. (Spider-Man Ser.: No. 2). (ENG.). 24p. (J). (gr. 2-6). lib. bdg. 27.07 *(978-1-59961-212-6(7)*, 13624, Marvel Age) Spotlight.

—Power Struggle. McKeever, Sean & Lee, Stan. 2007. (Spider-Man Ser.: No. 2). (ENG.). 24p. (J). (gr. 2-6). lib. bdg. 27.07 *(978-1-59961-213-3(5)*, 13625, Marvel Age) Spotlight.

—Prison Break. David, Erica. 2007. (Spider-Man Ser.: No. 2). (ENG.). 24p. (J). (gr. 2-6). lib. bdg. 27.07 *(978-1-59961-214-0(3)*, 13626, Marvel Age) Spotlight.

—Rush Hour! McKeever, Sean. 2007. (Spider-Man Ser.: No. 2). (ENG.). 24p. (J). (gr. 2-6). lib. bdg. 27.07 *(978-1-59961-215-7(1)*, 13627, Marvel Age) Spotlight.

—Spider-Man & the Secret Wars GN. Tobin, Paul. 2010. (ENG.). 128p. pap. 14.99 *(978-0-7851-4443-4(9))* Marvel Worldwide, Inc.

Scherer, Donovan Harold. Fear & Sunshine. Scherer, Donovan Harold. 2009. 248p. (J). pap. 14.95 *(978-0-9841746-1-4(3))* Studio Moonfall.

Scherger, Joy. My Favourite Fairytales. Adam, Luisa. 2020. (ENG.). 56p. (J). (gr. 1-4). *(978-0-6484571-6-9(8)*, Brolly Bks.) Borghesi & Adam Pubs. Pty Ltd.

Schettle, Jane. Mad Maddie Maxwell, 1 vol. Maslyn, Stacie K. B. & Maslyn, Stacie K. 2007. (I Can Read! Ser.). (ENG.). 32p. (J). (gr. -1-1). pap. 4.99 *(978-0-310-71467-5(2))* Zonderkidz.

Scheuer, Lauren. Mini Mysteries 2: 20 More Tricky Tales to Untangle. Walton, Rick. 2006. 87p. (J). *(978-1-4156-6869-6(8)*, American Girl) American Girl Publishing, Inc.

—On the Job at a Farm. Cohn, Jessica. 2016. (Core Content Social Studies — on the Job Ser.). (ENG.). 32p. (J). (gr. 2-5). lib. bdg. 26.65 *(978-1-63440-112-8(3))* Red Chair Pr.

—On the Job at School. Cohn, Jessica. 2016. (Core Content Social Studies — on the Job Ser.). (ENG.). 32p. (J). (gr. 2-5). lib. bdg. 26.65 *(978-1-63440-108-1(5))* Red Chair Pr.

—On the Job in a Restaurant. Cohn, Jessica. 2016. (Core Content Social Studies — on the Job Ser.). (ENG.). 32p. (J). (gr. 2-5). lib. bdg. 26.65 *(978-1-63440-110-4(7))* Red Chair Pr.

—On the Job in Construction. Cohn, Jessica. 2016. (Core Content Social Studies — on the Job Ser.). (ENG.). 32p. (J). (gr. 2-5). lib. bdg. 26.65 *(978-1-63440-109-8(3))* Red Chair Pr.

—On the Job in the Game. Cohn, Jessica. 2016. (Core Content Social Studies — on the Job Ser.). (ENG.). 32p. (J). (gr. 2-5). lib. bdg. 26.65 *(978-1-63440-111-1(5))* Red Chair Pr.

—On the Job in the Theater. Cohn, Jessica. 2016. (Core Content Social Studies — on the Job Ser.). (ENG.). 32p. (J). (gr. 2-5). lib. bdg. 26.65 *(978-1-63440-113-5(1))* Red Chair Pr.

Schexnayder, Paul. In the Time of Joy & Wonder. 2017. (J). *(978-1-946160-08-9(3))* Univ. of Louisiana at Lafayette Pr.

—In the Time of Mission & Might. 2019. (J). *(978-1-946160-50-8(4))* Univ. of Louisiana at Lafayette Pr.

—In the Time of Shimmer & Light. 2018. (J). *(978-1-946160-29-4(6))* Univ. of Louisiana at Lafayette Pr.

—The Kajun Kween. 2003. (ENG.). 100p. (J). per. 22.00 *(978-0-9650977-1-0(4))* Border Pr.

—Mr. Tootles & the Polka-Dot Lollypops. Clement, Maryceleste. 2005. (Tootle Tales Ser.: Vol. 2). 32p. (J). 14.95 *(978-0-9721706-1-1(8))* Tootle Time Publishing Co.

Scheyder, Jacob P. One More Thing. Scheyder, S. Jane. 2013. (ENG.). 42p. (J). pap. 7.99 *(978-0-9830318-6-4(X))* Andres & Blanton.

Schiavello, Arlene, photos by. My Chosen Path: A Poetic Reflection of Teenage Emotions. Schiavello, Kira. 2005. 108p. (YA). 14.00 *(978-0-9761513-4-0(0))* ADR Inc.

Schick, Joel. The Jungle Book: A Story about Loyalty. 2006. (J). 6.99 *(978-1-59939-023-9(X))* Cornerstone Pr.

—The Magic School Bus in the Haunted Museum: A Book about Sound. Beech, Linda Ward. Duchesne, Lucie, tr. (Magic School Bus Ser.). (FRE.). 32p. (J). (gr. 1-4). pap. 5.99 *(978-0-590-24657-6(7))* Scholastic, Inc.

—Max Can Fix That. Albee, Sarah. 2006. (Step-By-Step Readers Ser.). (J). pap. *(978-1-59939-055-0(8)*, Reader's Digest Young Families, Inc.) Studio Fun International.

—Pumpkin Patch Party (Sesame Street) A Lift-The-Flap Board Book. St. Pierre, Stephanie. 2019. (ENG.). 22p. (J). (— 1). bds. 6.99 *(978-1-9848-4767-6(8)*, Random Hse. Bks. for Young Readers) Random Hse. Children's Bks.

Schickle, Ian. Behind the Door of Timothy Moore. Cameron, Kristy. 2013. 28p. pap. *(978-0-9859790-1-0(1))* LP Publishing.

Schiebold, Olivia, jt. illus. see Thomas, Leanne.

Schieldt, Jodi. Somebody's Gotta Get Rid of That Vacuum. Schieldt, Corine. 2008. 24p. per. 24.95 *(978-1-4241-9121-5(1))* America Star Bks.

Schifferli, Paul Phillip. Darryl's Daring Deed. Schifferli, Paul Phillip. 2006. (J). 9.95 *(978-0-9765304-7-3(3))* Windsor Media Enterprises, Inc.

Schiffers, Nicole. Old Vine & Little Branch. Bowen, Pamella. 2019. (ENG.). 34p. (J). pap. 9.99 *(978-1-7321212-8-7(1))* Green & Purple Publishing.

Schiffman, Jessica. The Doll Maker's Gift. Fridman, Sashi. 2011. 36p. 14.95 *(978-0-8266-0040-0(9))* Kehot Pubn. Society.

—Sybil Ludington: Freedom's Brave Rider. 2005. 32p. (J). pap. *(978-0-7367-2931-4(3))* Zaner-Bloser, Inc.

Schigiel, Gregg. Bat-Mite's Big Blunder, 1 vol. Kupperberg, Paul. 2013. (Batman Ser.). (ENG.). 56p. (J). (gr. 3-6). pap. 4.95 *(978-1-4342-2255-8(1)*, Stone Arch Bks.) Capstone.

—Batman Is Loyal. Harbo, Christopher. 2019. (DC Super Heroes Character Education Ser.). (ENG.). 24p. (J). (gr. k-2). lib. bdg. 27.32 *(978-1-5158-4019-0(0)*, 139806, Stone Arch Bks.) Capstone.

—The Deadly Dream Machine. Bright, J. E. (Superman Ser.). (ENG.). 56p. (J). (gr. 3-6). 2014. pap. 4.95 *(978-1-4342-2759-1(6))*; 2010. lib. bdg. 26.65 *(978-1-4342-1978-7(X))* Capstone. (Stone Arch Bks.).

Schigiel, Gregg. The Flash & the Storm of the Century. Steele, Michael Anthony. 2020. (DC Super Hero Adventures Ser.). (ENG.). 72p. (J). (gr. 3-5). pap. 6.95 ***(978-1-4965-9965-0(9)***, 201657); lib. bdg. 26.65 ***(978-1-4965-9791-5(5)***, 200585) Capstone. (Stone Arch Bks.).

Schigiel, Gregg. Mad Hatter's Movie Madness, 1 vol. Lemke, Donald B. 2014. (Batman Ser.). (ENG.). 56p. (J). (gr. 3-6). pap. 4.95 *(978-1-4342-1675-5(6)*, Stone Arch Bks.) Capstone.

—Mad Hatter's Movie Madness, 1 vol. Lemke, Donald B. & Loughridge, Lee. 2010. (Batman Ser.). (ENG.). 56p. (J). (gr. 3-6). lib. bdg. 26.65 *(978-1-4342-2131-5(8)*, Stone Arch Bks.) Capstone.

—My Frozen Valentine, 1 vol. Fein, Eric. 2013. (Batman Ser.). (ENG.). 56p. (J). (gr. 3-6). pap. 4.95 *(978-1-4342-1731-8(0)*, Stone Arch Bks.) Capstone.

—My Frozen Valentine, 1 vol. Fein, Eric & Loughridge, Lee. 2009. (Batman Ser.). (ENG.). 56p. (J). (gr. 3-6). 26.65 *(978-1-4342-1564-2(4)*, Stone Arch Bks.) Capstone.

—The Shrinking City, 1 vol. Dahl, Michael & Loughridge, Lee. 2009. (Superman Ser.). (ENG.). 56p. (J). (gr. 3-6). 26.65 *(978-1-4342-1569-7(5)*, Stone Arch Bks.) Capstone.

—Shrinking City. Dahl, Michael & Loughridge, Lee. 2013. (Superman Ser.). (ENG.). 56p. (J). (gr. 3-6). pap. 4.95 *(978-1-4342-1735-6(3)*, Stone Arch Bks.) Capstone.

—SpongeBob LovePants. Pass, Erica. 2006. (Ready-to-Read Ser.). (ENG.). 32p. (J). (gr. k-2). pap. 3.99 *(978-1-4169-1758-8(6)*, Simon Spotlight/Nickelodeon) Simon Spotlight/Nickelodeon.

—Supergirl Is Patient. Harbo, Christopher. 2019. (DC Super Heroes Character Education Ser.). (ENG.). 24p. (J). (gr. k-2). lib. bdg. 27.32 *(978-1-5158-4022-0(0)*, 139810, Stone Arch Bks.) Capstone.

—Superman & the Apokolips Attack. Cohen, Ivan. 2020. (DC Super Hero Adventures Ser.). (ENG.). 72p. (J). (gr. 3-5). pap. 6.95 *(978-1-4965-9201-9(8)*, 142229); lib. bdg. 26.65 *(978-1-4965-8723-7(5)*, 141592) Capstone. (Stone Arch Bks.).

—Superman & the Invasion of Earth: A Solar System Adventure. Korte, Steve. 2018. (Superman Solar System Adventures Ser.). (ENG.). 32p. (J). (gr. 4-8). lib. bdg. 27.99 *(978-1-5435-1565-7(7)*, 137923, Capstone Pr.) Capstone.

—Superman & the Mischief on Mars: A Solar System Adventure. Korte, Steve. 2018. (Superman Solar System Adventures Ser.). (ENG.). 32p. (J). (gr. 4-8). lib. bdg. 27.99 *(978-1-5435-1563-3(0)*, 137922, Capstone Pr.) Capstone.

—Superman & the Showdown at Saturn: A Solar System Adventure. Korte, Steve. 2018. (Superman Solar System Adventures Ser.). (ENG.). 32p. (J). (gr. 4-8). lib. bdg. 27.99 *(978-1-5435-1572-5(X)*, 137927, Capstone Pr.) Capstone.

—Superman & the Trials of Jupiter: A Solar System Adventure. Korte, Steve. 2018. (Superman Solar System Adventures Ser.). (ENG.). 32p. (J). (gr. 4-8). lib. bdg. 27.99 *(978-1-5435-1571-8(1)*, 137926, Capstone Pr.) Capstone.

—Superman Is Cooperative. Harbo, Christopher. 2019. (DC Super Heroes Character Education Ser.). (ENG.). 24p. (J). (gr. k-2). lib. bdg. 27.32 *(978-1-5158-4020-6(4)*, 139808, Stone Arch Bks.) Capstone.

—Wonder Woman & the Pandora Plot. Cohen, Ivan. 2020. (DC Super Hero Adventures Ser.). (ENG.). 72p. (J). (gr. 3-5). pap. 6.95 *(978-1-4965-9202-6(6)*, 142230); lib. bdg. 26.65 *(978-1-4965-8724-4(3)*, 141593) Capstone. (Stone Arch Bks.).

—Wonder Woman Perseveres. Harbo, Christopher. 2019. (DC Super Heroes Character Education Ser.). (ENG.). 24p. (J). (gr. k-2). lib. bdg. 27.32 *(978-1-5158-4021-3(2)*, 139809, Stone Arch Bks.) Capstone.

Schigiel, Gregg. Bat-Mite's Big Blunder, 1 vol. Schigiel, Gregg. Kupperberg, Paul & Loughridge, Lee. 2010. (Batman Ser.). (ENG.). 56p. (J). (gr. 3-6). lib. bdg. 26.65 *(978-1-4342-1877-3(5)*, Stone Arch Bks.) Capstone.

Schigiel, Gregg, jt. illus. see Castellani, Leonel.

Schilling, Deborah. Sago, A Very Special Service Dog: N/a. Davis, Beth. 2011.Tr. of N/a. 28p. (J). 15.00 *(978-0-9822974-9-0(1))*; lib. bdg. 24.00 *(978-0-9822974-8-3(3))* Rolemommy.

Schimler-Safford, Amy. Flood Warning. Kenah, Katharine. 2016. (Let's-Read-And-Find-Out Science 2 Ser.). (ENG.). 40p. (J). (gr. -1-3). pap. 6.99 *(978-0-06-238661-8(1))* HarperCollins Pubs.

—The Gray Adventure. Chong, Lisa. 2018. (ENG.). 32p. (J). pap. 25.00 *(978-0-9997557-0-9(6))* Chong, Lisa.

—Inky's Amazing Escape: How a Very Smart Octopus Found His Way Home. Montgomery, Sy. (ENG.). 32p. (J). (gr. -1-3). 2020. 7.99 ***(978-1-5344-8044-5(7))***; 2018. 17.99 *(978-1-5344-0191-4(1))* Simon & Schuster/Paula Wiseman Bks. (Simon & Schuster/Paula Wiseman Bks.).

Schimler-Safford, Amy. Splish Splash! A Touch & Hear Book. Schimler-Safford, Amy. 2011. (ENG.). 14p. (J). (gr. -1 — 1). bds. 6.99 *(978-1-4424-1354-2(9)*, Little Simon) Little Simon.

Schimmel, Beth. Abigail's New Home. Taylor, Dorothy L. (Valley View Farm Tales Ser.). 20p. (J). (gr. k-3). 7.50 *(978-0-9610640-0-6(5))* Taylor, Dorothy Loring.

Schimmel, Schim. Magic Planet: Pop-Up Fun. 2003. 12p. (J). (gr. k-5). 20.00 *(978-0-7567-6651-1(6))* DIANE Publishing Co.

—Our Precious World Stationery Set. Book Company Staff. 2003. (Stationery Ser.). (J). pap. 15.95 *(978-1-74047-215-9(2))* Book Co. Publishing Pty, Ltd., The AUS. Dist: Penton Overseas, Inc.

Schimmell, David. At the Bank with Dear Dragon, 10 vols. Conn, Marla. 2019. (Dear Dragon Developing Readers Ser.). (ENG.). 24p. (J). (gr. -1-k). pap. 10.60 *(978-1-68404-309-5(3))* Norwood Hse. Pr.

—At the Carnival with Dear Dragon, 10 vols. Conn, Marla. 2019. (Dear Dragon Developing Readers Ser.). (ENG.). 24p. (J). (gr. -1-k). pap. 10.60 *(978-1-68404-311-8(5))* Norwood Hse. Pr.

—At the Dentist with Dear Dragon, 10 vols. Conn, Marla. 2019. (Dear Dragon Developing Readers Ser.). (ENG.). 24p. (J). (gr. -1-k). pap. 10.60 *(978-1-68404-312-5(3))* Norwood Hse. Pr.

—At the Firehouse with Dear Dragon, 10 vols. Conn, Marla. 2019. (Dear Dragon Developing Readers Ser.). (ENG.). 24p. (J). (gr. -1-k). pap. 10.60 *(978-1-68404-313-2(1))* Norwood Hse. Pr.

—At the Hospital with Dear Dragon, 10 vols. Conn, Marla. 2019. (Dear Dragon Developing Readers Ser.). (ENG.). 24p. (J). (gr. -1-k). 21.27 *(978-1-68450-991-1(2))* Norwood Hse. Pr.

—At the Library with Dear Dragon, 10 vols. Conn, Marla. 2019. (Dear Dragon Developing Readers Ser.). (ENG.). 24p. (J). (gr. -1-k). pap. 10.60 *(978-1-68404-315-6(8))* Norwood Hse. Pr.

—At the Market with Dear Dragon, 10 vols. Conn, Marla. 2019. (Dear Dragon Developing Readers Ser.). (ENG.). 24p. (J). (gr. -1-k). pap. 10.60 *(978-1-68404-316-3(6))* Norwood Hse. Pr.

—At the Pond with Dear Dragon, 10 vols. Conn, Marla. 2019. (Dear Dragon Developing Readers Ser.). (ENG.). 24p. (J). (gr. -1-k). 21.27 *(978-1-68450-982-9(3))* Norwood Hse. Pr.

—At the Zoo with Dear Dragon, 10 vols. Conn, Marla. 2019. (Dear Dragon Developing Readers Ser.). (ENG.). 24p. (J). (gr. -1-k). pap. 10.60 *(978-1-68404-318-7(2))* Norwood Hse. Pr.

—Camping with Dear Dragon, 10 vols. Conn, Marla. 2019. (Dear Dragon Developing Readers Ser.). (ENG.). 24p. (J). (gr. -1-k). pap. 10.60 *(978-1-68404-306-4(9))* Norwood Hse. Pr.

—Dear Dragon Eats Out. Hillert, Margaret. rev. ed. 2014. (BeginningtoRead Ser.). (ENG.). 32p. (J). (gr. k-2). pap. 11.94 *(978-1-60357-637-6(1))*; lib. bdg. 22.60 *(978-1-59953-629-3(3))* Norwood Hse. Pr.

—Dear Dragon Goes Camping. Hillert, Margaret. 2010. (BeginningtoRead Ser.). 32p. (J). (gr. k-2). lib. bdg. 22.60 *(978-1-59953-345-2(6))* Norwood Hse. Pr.

—Dear Dragon Goes to the Bank. Hillert, Margaret. 2012. (BeginningtoRead Ser.). 32p. (J). (-2). lib. bdg. 22.60 *(978-1-59953-502-9(5))* Norwood Hse. Pr.

—Dear Dragon Goes to the Carnival. Hillert, Margaret. 2010. (BeginningtoRead Ser.). 32p. (J). (gr. k-2). lib. bdg. 22.60 *(978-1-59953-346-9(4))* Norwood Hse. Pr.

—Dear Dragon Goes to the Dentist. Hillert, Margaret. rev. ed. 2014. (BeginningtoRead Ser.). (ENG.). 32p. (J). (gr. k-2). lib. bdg. 22.60 *(978-1-59953-577-7(7))* Norwood Hse. Pr.

—Dear Dragon Goes to the Firehouse. Hillert, Margaret. 2010. (BeginningtoRead Ser.). 32p. (J). (gr. k-2). lib. bdg. 22.60 *(978-1-59953-375-9(8))* Norwood Hse. Pr.

—Dear Dragon Goes to the Hospital. Hillert, Margaret. rev. ed. 2014. (BeginningtoRead Ser.). (ENG.). 32p. (J). (gr. k-2). pap. 11.94 *(978-1-60357-422-8(0))*; lib. bdg. 22.60 *(978-1-59953-581-4(5))* Norwood Hse. Pr.

—Dear Dragon Goes to the Library. Hillert, Margaret. 2008. (BeginningtoRead Ser.). 32p. (J). (gr. k-2). lib. bdg. 22.60 *(978-1-59953-160-1(7))* Norwood Hse. Pr.

—Dear Dragon Goes to the Library (Querido Dragon Va a la Biblioteca) Hillert, Margaret. Del Risco, Eida, tr. from ENG. 2010. (BeginningtoRead Ser.). (SPA & ENG.). 32p. (J). (gr. k-2). lib. bdg. 22.60 *(978-1-59953-361-2(8))* Norwood Hse. Pr.

—Dear Dragon Goes to the Market. Hillert, Margaret. 2010. (BeginningtoRead Ser.). 32p. (J). (gr. k-2). lib. bdg. 22.60 *(978-1-59953-347-6(2))* Norwood Hse. Pr.

—Dear Dragon Goes to the Zoo. Hillert, Margaret. 2010. (BeginningtoRead Ser.). 32p. (J). (gr. k-2). lib. bdg. 22.60 *(978-1-59953-348-3(0))* Norwood Hse. Pr.

—Dear Dragon Grows a Garden. Hillert, Margaret. rev. ed. 2014. (BeginningtoRead Ser.). (ENG.). 32p. (J). (gr. k-2). pap. 11.94 *(978-1-60357-414-3(X))*; lib. bdg. 22.60 *(978-1-59953-578-4(5))* Norwood Hse. Pr.

—Dear Dragon Helps Out. Hillert, Margaret. 2012. (BeginningtoRead Ser.). 32p. (J). (-2). lib. bdg. 22.60 *(978-1-59953-505-0(X))* Norwood Hse. Pr.

—Dear Dragon Steps Out Volume 1. Hillert, Margaret. (Go Reader Read along Sets Ser.). (J). (-2). pap. 106.66 *(978-1-60357-418-1(2))* Norwood Hse. Pr.

—Dear Dragon's A Is for Apple. Hillert, Margaret. 2008. (BeginningtoRead Ser.). 32p. (J). (gr. k-2). lib. bdg. 22.60 *(978-1-59953-158-8(5))* Norwood Hse. Pr.

—Dear Dragon's Colors 1, 2, 3. Hillert, Margaret. 2010. (BeginningtoRead Ser.). 32p. (J). (-2). pap. 11.94 *(978-1-60357-100-5(0))* Norwood Hse. Pr.

—Dear Dragon's Colors 1 ,2, 3. Hillert, Margaret. 2010. (BeginningtoRead Ser.). 32p. (J). (gr. k-2). lib. bdg. 22.60 *(978-1-59953-376-6(6))* Norwood Hse. Pr.

—Dear Dragon's Day with Father. Hillert, Margaret. (BeginningtoRead Ser.). 32p. (J). (gr. k-2). 2017. (ENG.). pap. 11.94 *(978-1-68404-010-0(8))*; 2008. lib. bdg. 22.60 *(978-1-59953-162-5(3))* Norwood Hse. Pr.

—Dear Dragon's Day with Father (Querido Dragon Pasa el Dia con Papa) Hillert, Margaret. Del Risco, Eida, tr. from ENG. 2010. (BeginningtoRead Ser.). (SPA & ENG.). 32p. (J). (gr. k-2). lib. bdg. 22.60 *(978-1-59953-360-5(X))* Norwood Hse. Pr.

—Dear Dragon's Fun with Shapes. Hillert, Margaret. 2015. (BeginningtoRead Ser.). 32p. (J). (-2). lib. bdg. 22.60 *(978-1-59953-544-9(0))* Norwood Hse. Pr.

—Dear Dragon's Fun with Shapes. Hillert, Margaret. del Risco, Eida, tr. 2015. (BeginningtoRead Ser.). 32p. (J). (-2). pap. 11.94 *(978-1-60357-447-1(6))* Norwood Hse. Pr.

—Dear Dragon's Seasons Volume 2. Hillert, Margaret. (Go Reader Read along Sets Ser.). (J). (-2). pap. 106.66 *(978-1-60357-419-8(0))* Norwood Hse. Pr.

—¿Dónde Está Querido Dragón? Hillert, Margaret. Fernandez, Queta, tr. from ENG. 2014. (BeginningtoRead Ser.).Tr. of Where Is Dear Dragon?. (SPA & ENG.). 32p. (J). (-2). lib. bdg. 22.60 *(978-1-59953-615-6(3))* Norwood Hse. Pr.

—Es Hora de Ir a la Cama, Querido Dragón. Hillert, Margaret. Fernandez, Queta, tr. from ENG. 2014. (BeginningtoRead Ser.).Tr. of It's Bedtime, Dear Dragon. (ENG & SPA.). 32p. (J). (-2). lib. bdg. 22.60 *(978-1-59953-612-5(9))* Norwood Hse. Pr.

—Es Primavera, Querido Dragón/It's Spring, Dear Dragon. Hillert, Margaret. 2011. (BeginningtoRead Ser.). 32p. (J). (-2). pap. 11.94 *(978-1-60357-555-3(3))* Norwood Hse. Pr.

—Es Primavera, Querido Dragón/It's Spring, Dear Dragon. Hillert, Margaret. del Risco, Eida, tr. from ENG. 2011. (BeginningtoRead Ser.). 32p. (J). (gr. k-2). lib. bdg. 22.60 *(978-1-59953-471-8(1))* Norwood Hse. Pr.

—Es un Buen Juego, Querido Dragón/It's a Good Game, Dear Dragon. Hillert, Margaret. 2010. (BeginningtoRead Ser.). 32p. (J). (-2). pap. 11.94 *(978-1-60357-550-8(2))* Norwood Hse. Pr.

—Fun with Dear Dragon Volume 4. Hillert, Margaret. (Go Reader Read along Sets Ser.). (J). (-2). pap. 106.66 *(978-1-60357-421-1(2))* Norwood Hse. Pr.

—Happy Hanukkah, Dear Dragon. Hillert, Margaret. 2008. (BeginningtoRead Ser.). 32p. (J). (-2). (ENG.). pap. 11.94 *(978-1-68404-011-7(6))*; lib. bdg. 22.60 *(978-1-59953-159-5(3))* Norwood Hse. Pr.

—I Did It, Dear Dragon. Hillert, Margaret. 2009. (BeginningtoRead Ser.). 32p. (J). (gr. k-2). lib. bdg. 22.60 *(978-1-59953-295-0(6))* Norwood Hse. Pr.

—I See Colors, Dear Dragon, 10 vols. Conn, Marla. 2019. (Dear Dragon Developing Readers Ser.). (ENG.). 24p. (J). (gr. -1-k). pap. 10.60 *(978-1-68404-320-0(4))* Norwood Hse. Pr.

—I See Shapes, Dear Dragon, 10 vols. Conn, Marla. 2019. (Dear Dragon Developing Readers Ser.). (ENG.). 24p. (J). (gr. -1-k). pap. 10.60 *(978-1-68404-321-7(2))* Norwood Hse. Pr.

—In the Woods with Dear Dragon, 10 vols. Conn, Marla. 2019. (Dear Dragon Developing Readers Ser.). (ENG.). 24p. (J). (gr. -1-k). 21.27 *(978-1-68450-980-5(7))* Norwood Hse. Pr.

—A Is for Apple, Dear Dragon, 10 vols. Conn, Marla. 2019. (Dear Dragon Developing Readers Ser.). (ENG.). 24p. (J). (gr. -1-k). 21.27 *(978-1-68450-986-7(6))* Norwood Hse. Pr.

—It's a Good Game, Dear Dragon. Hillert, Margaret. 2009. (BeginningtoRead Ser.). 32p. (J). (gr. k-2). lib. bdg. 22.60 *(978-1-59953-293-6(X))* Norwood Hse. Pr.

—It's a Good Game, Dear Dragon (Es un Buen Juego, Querido Dragon) Hillert, Margaret. Del Risco, Eida, tr. from ENG. 2010. (BeginningtoRead Ser.). (SPA & ENG.). 32p. (J). (gr. k-2). lib. bdg. 22.60 *(978-1-59953-362-9(6))* Norwood Hse. Pr.

—It's Bedtime Dear Dragon. Hillert, Margaret. 2012. (BeginningtoRead Ser.). 32p. (J). (-2). lib. bdg. 22.60 *(978-1-59953-503-6(3))* Norwood Hse. Pr.

—It's Fall, Dear Dragon. Hillert, Margaret. 2009. (BeginningtoRead Ser.). 32p. (J). (gr. k-2). lib. bdg. 22.60 *(978-1-59953-311-7(1))* Norwood Hse. Pr.

—It's Ground Hog Day Dear Dragon. Hillert, Margaret. 2012. (BeginningtoRead Ser.). 32p. (J). (-2). lib. bdg. 22.60 *(978-1-59953-504-3(1))* Norwood Hse. Pr.

—It's Groundhog Day, Dear Dragon. Hillert, Margaret. 2012. (BeginningtoRead Ser.). 32p. (J). (-2). pap. 11.94 *(978-1-60357-384-9(4))* Norwood Hse. Pr.

—It's Spring, Dear Dragon. Hillert, Margaret. 2009. (BeginningtoRead Ser.). 32p. (J). (gr. k-2). lib. bdg. 22.60 *(978-1-59953-312-4(X))* Norwood Hse. Pr.

—It's St. Patrick's Day, Dear Dragon. Hillert, Margaret. 2008. (BeginningtoRead Ser.). 32p. (J). (gr. k-2). lib. bdg. 22.60 *(978-1-59953-161-8(5))* Norwood Hse. Pr.

—It's St. Patrick's Day, Dear Dragon. Hillert, Margaret. del Risco, Eida, tr. 2008. (BeginningtoRead Ser.). 32p. (J). (-2). pap. 11.94 *(978-1-60357-086-2(1))* Norwood Hse. Pr.

—It's Summer, Dear Dragon. Hillert, Margaret. 2009. (BeginningtoRead Ser.). 32p. (J). (gr. k-2). lib. bdg. 22.60 *(978-1-59953-313-1(8))* Norwood Hse. Pr.

—It's Time to Play, Dear Dragon Volume 3. Hillert, Margaret. (Go Reader Read along Sets Ser.). (J). (-2). pap. 106.66 *(978-1-60357-420-4(4))* Norwood Hse. Pr.

—It's Winter, Dear Dragon. Hillert, Margaret. 2009. (BeginningtoRead Ser.). 32p. (J). (gr. k-2). lib. bdg. 22.60 *(978-1-59953-314-8(6))* Norwood Hse. Pr.

—Juega, Juega, Juega, Querido Dragón/Play, Play, Play, Dear Dragon. Hillert, Margaret. del Risco, Eida, tr. 2010. (BeginningtoRead Ser.). 32p. (J). (-2). pap. 11.94 *(978-1-60357-551-5(0))* Norwood Hse. Pr.

—Look at the Sky, Dear Dragon, 10 vols. Conn, Marla. 2019. (Dear Dragon Developing Readers Ser.). (ENG.). 24p. (J). (gr. -1-k). pap. 10.60 *(978-1-68404-324-8(7))* Norwood Hse. Pr.

—Look in My Pocket, Dear Dragon, 10 vols. Conn, Marla. 2019. (Dear Dragon Developing Readers Ser.). (ENG.). 24p. (J). (gr. -1-k). pap. 10.60 *(978-1-68404-322-4(0))* Norwood Hse. Pr.

—Play, Play, Play Dear Dragon. Hillert, Margaret. 2009. (BeginningtoRead Ser.). 32p. (J). (gr. k-2). lib. bdg. 22.60 *(978-1-59953-294-3(8))* Norwood Hse. Pr.

—Play, Play, Play, Dear Dragon (Juega, Juega, Juega, Querido Dragon) Hillert, Margaret. Del Risco, Eida, tr. 2010. (BeginningtoRead Ser.). (SPA & ENG.). 32p. (J). (gr. k-2). lib. bdg. 22.60 *(978-1-59953-363-6(4))* Norwood Hse. Pr.

—¿Que Hay en el Bosque, Querido Dragon? Hillert, Margaret & Fernández, Queta. 2014. (BeginningtoRead Ser.).Tr. of What's in the Woods, Dear Dragon?. (ENG & SPA.). 32p. (J). (-2). lib. bdg. 22.60 *(978-1-59953-609-5(9))* Norwood Hse. Pr.

—¿Qué Hay en el Cielo, Querido Dragón? Hillert, Margaret. Fernandez, Queta, tr. from ENG. 2014. (BeginningtoRead Ser.).Tr. of What's in the Sky, Dear Dragon?. (ENG & SPA.). 32p. (J). (-2). lib. bdg. 22.60 *(978-1-59953-610-1(2))* Norwood Hse. Pr.

—¿Qué Hay en el Estanque, Querido Dragón? Hillert, Margaret. Fernandez, Queta, tr. from ENG. 2014. (BeginningtoRead Ser.).Tr. of What's in the Pond, Dear Dragon?. (ENG & SPA.). 32p. (J). (-2). lib. bdg. 22.60 *(978-1-59953-608-8(0))* Norwood Hse. Pr.

—¿Qué Tengo en el Bolsillo, Querido Dragón? Hillert, Margaret. Fernandez, Queta, tr. from ENG. 2014. (BeginningtoRead Ser.).Tr. of What's in My Pocket, Dear Dragon?. (ENG & SPA.). 32p. (J). (-2). lib. bdg. 22.60 *(978-1-59953-611-8(0))* Norwood Hse. Pr.

—Querido Dragón, Los Colores y 1, 2, 3 /Dear Dragon's Colors 1, 2, 3. Hillert, Margaret. del Risco, Eida, tr. 2011. (BeginningtoRead Ser.). 32p. (J). (-2). pap. 11.94 *(978-1-60357-554-6(5))* Norwood Hse. Pr.

—Querido Dragón, los Colores y 1, 2, 3 /Dear Dragon's Colors 1, 2, 3. Hillert, Margaret. del Risco, Eida, tr. from ENG. 2011. (BeginningtoRead Ser.). 32p. (J). (gr. k-2). lib. bdg. 22.60 *(978-1-59953-470-1(3))* Norwood Hse. Pr.

—Querido Dragón Quiere Ayudar. Hillert, Margaret. Fernandez, Queta, tr. from ENG. 2014. (BeginningtoRead Ser.).Tr. of Dear Dragon Helps Out. (ENG & SPA.). 32p. (J). (-2). lib. bdg. 22.60 *(978-1-59953-613-2(7))* Norwood Hse. Pr.

—Querido Dragón Va a la Biblioteca/Dear Dragon Goes to the Library. Hillert, Margaret. del Risco, Eida, tr. 2010. (BeginningtoRead Ser.). 32p. (J). (-2). pap. 11.94 *(978-1-60357-549-2(9))* Norwood Hse. Pr.

—Querido Dragón Va a la Estación de Bomberos / Dear Dragon Goes to the Firehouse. Hillert, Margaret. del Risco, Eida, tr. from ENG. 2011. (BeginningtoRead Ser.). 32p. (J). (gr. k-2). lib. bdg. 22.60 *(978-1-59953-468-8(1))* Norwood Hse. Pr.

—Querido Dragón Va a la Estación de Bomberos/Dear Dragon Goes to the Firehouse. Hillert, Margaret. del Risco, Eida, tr. 2011. (BeginningtoRead Ser.). 32p. (J). (-2). pap. 11.94 *(978-1-60357-552-2(9))* Norwood Hse. Pr.

—Querido Dragón Va Al Banco. Hillert, Margaret. Fernandez, Queta, tr. from ENG. 2014. (BeginningtoRead Ser.).Tr. of Dear Dragon Goes to the Bank. (ENG & SPA.). 32p. (J). (-2). lib. bdg. 22.60 *(978-1-59953-614-9(5))* Norwood Hse. Pr.

—Querido dragón va al mercado. Hillert, Margaret. del Risco, Eida, tr. from ENG. 2011. (BeginningtoRead Ser.).Tr. of Dear Dragon Goes to the Market. (SPA.). 32p. (J). (gr. k-2). lib. bdg. 22.60 *(978-1-59953-469-5(X))* Norwood Hse. Pr.

—Querido Dragón Va Al Mercado/Dear Dragon Goes to the Market. Hillert, Margaret. 2011. (BeginningtoRead Ser.). 32p. (J). (-2). pap. 11.94 *(978-1-60357-553-9(7))* Norwood Hse. Pr.

—Touchdown! Dear Dragon. Hillert, Margaret. 2009. (BeginningtoRead Ser.). 32p. (J). (gr. k-2). lib. bdg. 22.60 *(978-1-59953-296-7(4))* Norwood Hse. Pr.

—Up, up, up, Dear Dragon. Hillert, Margaret. 2012. (BeginningtoRead Ser.). 32p. (J). (-2). lib. bdg. 22.60 *(978-1-59953-545-6(9))* Norwood Hse. Pr.

—What's in My Pocket, Dear Dragon? Hillert, Margaret. 2014. (BeginningtoRead Ser.). (ENG.). 32p. (J). (-2). pap. 11.94 *(978-1-60357-415-0(8))*; lib. bdg. 22.60 *(978-1-59953-579-1(3))* Norwood Hse. Pr.

—What's in the Pond, Dear Dragon? Hillert, Margaret. 2014. (BeginningtoRead Ser.). (ENG.). 32p. (J). (-2). pap. 11.94 *(978-1-60357-601-7(0))*; lib. bdg. 22.60 *(978-1-59953-607-1(2))* Norwood Hse. Pr.

—What's in the Sky, Dear Dragon? Hillert, Margaret. 2014. (BeginningtoRead Ser.). (ENG.). 32p. (J). (-2). pap. 11.94 *(978-1-60357-416-7(6))*; lib. bdg. 22.60 *(978-1-59953-580-7(7))* Norwood Hse. Pr.

—What's in the Woods, Dear Dragon? Hillert, Margaret. 2014. (BeginningtoRead Ser.). (ENG.). 32p. (J). (-2). pap. 11.94 *(978-1-60357-599-7(5))*; lib. bdg. 22.60 *(978-1-59953-606-4(4))* Norwood Hse. Pr.

—Where Is Dear Dragon? Hillert, Margaret. 2012. (BeginningtoRead Ser.). 32p. (J). (-2). lib. bdg. 22.60 *(978-1-59953-546-3(7))* Norwood Hse. Pr.

Schimmelman, Alex. Buster & Snoopy. Zsikai-Spiker, Lisa Marie. 2012. 24p. 24.95 *(978-1-4626-7112-0(8))* America Star Bks.

Schindelman, Joseph, jt. illus. see Brunetti, Ivan.

Schindler, Roslyn. Zeon. Schindler, Roslyn. 2013. 28p. pap. 13.95 *(978-1-61493-192-8(5))* Peppertree Pr., The.

Schindler, S. D. Abraham Lincoln's Dueling Words, 1 vol. Bowman, Donna Janell. 2018. (ENG.). 36p. (J). (gr. 1-5). 17.95 *(978-1-56145-852-3(X))* Peachtree Publishing Co. Inc.

—Are We There Yet, Daddy? Walters, Virginia. 2005. 27p. (J). (gr. k-4). reprint ed. 16.00 *(978-0-7567-9708-9(X))* DIANE Publishing Co.

—Bat in the Dining Room, 1 vol. Dragonwagon, Crescent. 2005. (ENG.). 32p. (J). pap. 5.95 *(978-0-7614-5146-4(3))* Marshall Cavendish Corp.

—Ben Franklin's Big Splash: The Mostly True Story of His First Invention. Rosenstock, Barb. 2014. (ENG.). 32p. (J). (gr. 3-7). 17.95 *(978-1-62091-446-5(8)*, Calkins Creek) Boyds Mills Pr.

—A Big Cheese for the White House: The True Tale of a Tremendous Cheddar. Fleming, Candace. 2004. (ENG.). 32p. (J). (gr. -1-3). reprint ed. pap. 8.99 *(978-0-374-40627-1(8)*, 900021942) Square Fish.

—Boy, Were We Wrong about Dinosaurs! Kudlinski, Kathleen V. (ENG.). 32p. (J). (gr. 1-3). 2008. pap. 6.99 *(978-0-14-241193-3(0)*, Puffin Books); 2005. 16.99 *(978-0-525-46978-0(8)*, Dutton Books for Young Readers) Penguin Young Readers Group.

—Catwings Return. Le Guin, Ursula K. 2003. (Catwings Ser.: No. 2). (ENG.). 56p. (J). (gr. -1-3). 5.99 *(978-0-439-55190-8(0))* Scholastic, Inc.

—The Cod's Tale: A Biography of the Fish That Changed the World! Kurlansky, Mark. 2014. (ENG.). 48p. (J). (gr. 2-5). 8.99 *(978-0-14-751277-2(8)*, Puffin Books) Penguin Young Readers Group.

Schindler, S. D. Could It Be? Level 2. Oppenheim, Joanne. 2020. (ENG.). 34p. (J). pap. 9.95 ***(978-1-876965-69-3(X))*** ibooks, Inc.

Schindler, S. D. Don't Know Much about the Pilgrims. Davis, Kenneth C. 2006. (Don't Know Much About Ser.). (ENG.). 48p. (J). (gr. 1-4). pap. 7.99 *(978-0-06-446228-0(5))* HarperCollins Pubs.

—Honey in a Hive. Rockwell, Anne. 2005. (Let's-Read-And-Find-Out Science 2 Ser.). (ENG.). 40p. (J). (gr. k-4). pap. 5.99 *(978-0-06-445204-5(2))* HarperCollins Pubs.

—How Santa Lost His Job. Krensky, Stephen. 2004. (ENG.). 32p. (J). (gr. -1-3). 7.99 *(978-0-689-87147-4(3)*, Simon & Schuster Bks. For Young Readers) Simon & Schuster Bks. For Young Readers.

—Jane on Her Own. Le Guin, Ursula K. 2003. (Catwings Ser.: No. 4). (ENG.). 48p. (J). (gr. 2-5). 5.99 *(978-0-439-55192-2(7))* Scholastic, Inc.

—Monster Mess! Cuyler, Margery. 2008. (ENG.). 32p. (J). (gr. -1-1). 19.99 *(978-0-689-86405-6(1)*, McElderry, Margaret K. Bks.) McElderry, Margaret K. Bks.

Schindler, S. D., et al. Off to First Grade. Borden, Louise. 2008. (ENG.). 40p. (J). (gr. -1-3). 19.99 *(978-0-689-87395-9(6)*, McElderry, Margaret K. Bks.) McElderry, Margaret K. Bks.

Schindler, S. D. Skeleton Hiccups. Cuyler, Margery. 2005. (ENG.). 32p. (J). (gr. -1-3). reprint ed. 7.99 *(978-1-4169-0276-8(7)*, McElderry, Margaret K. Bks.) McElderry, Margaret K. Bks.

—The Snow Globe Family. O'Connor, Jane. 2008. (ENG.). 40p. (J). (gr. 1-3). pap. 7.99 *(978-0-14-241242-8(2)*, Puffin Books) Penguin Young Readers Group.

—Spinning Spiders. Berger, Melvin. 2015. 40p. pap. 6.00 *(978-1-61003-617-7(4))* Center for the Collaborative Classroom.

—Spinning Spiders. Berger, Melvin. 2003. 40p. (J). (gr. k-4). (Let's-Read-And-Find-Out Science Ser.). (ENG.). 15.99 *(978-0-06-028696-5(2))*; (Let's-Read-And-Find-Out Science 2 Ser.). (ENG.). pap. 5.99 *(978-0-06-445207-6(7))*; (Let's-Read-and-Find-Out-Science Ser.: Vol. 2). lib. bdg. 16.89 *(978-0-06-028697-2(0))* HarperCollins Pubs.

—Spinning Spiders. Berger, Melvin. 2003. (Let's-Read-and-Find-Out Science Ser.). 33p. (gr. k-4). 16.00 *(978-0-7569-1449-3(3))* Perfection Learning Corp.

—The Story of Salt. Kurlansky, Mark. (ENG.). 48p. (J). (gr. -1-3). 2014. 8.99 *(978-0-14-751166-9(6)*, Puffin Books); 2006. 18.99 *(978-0-399-23998-4(7)*, G.P. Putnam's Sons Books for Young Readers) Penguin Young Readers Group.

—Those Amazing Ants. Demuth, Patricia Brennan. 2012. (ENG.). 32p. (J). (gr. -1-3). pap. 16.99 *(978-1-4424-5932-8(8)*, Simon & Schuster Bks. For Young Readers) Simon & Schuster Bks. For Young Readers.

—Tricking the Tallyman. Davies, Jacqueline. 2014. 40p. (J). (gr. k-3). 7.99 *(978-0-385-75519-1(8)*, Dragonfly Bks.) Random Hse. Children's Bks.

—The Tyrannosaurus Game, 0 vols. Kroll, Steven. 2010. (ENG.). 32p. (J). (gr. -1-3). 17.99 *(978-0-7614-5603-2(1)*, 9780761456032, Two Lions) Amazon Publishing.

—We're Going on a Ghost Hunt, 0 vols. Pearson, Susan. 2012. (ENG.). 32p. (J). (gr. -1-3). 16.99 *(978-0-7614-6307-8(0)*, 9780761463078, Two Lions) Amazon Publishing.

—Whittington. Armstrong, Alan W. 2007. 191p. (gr. 3-7). 17.00 *(978-0-7569-7768-9(1))* Perfection Learning Corp.

—Wonderful Alexander & the Catwings. Le Guin, Ursula K. 2003. (Catwings Ser.: No. 3). (ENG.). 48p. (J). (gr. -1-3). 5.99 *(978-0-439-55191-5(9))* Scholastic, Inc.

Schinkel, Jeff. A Kid's Guide to Drawing Cartoon Animals: More Than 75 Fun Activities All about Cool Animals! Whiting, Vicki. 2019. (ENG.). 72p. (J). pap. 8.99 *(978-1-64124-032-1(6)*, 0321) Fox Chapel Publishing Co., Inc.

—Mind-Boggling Animal Puzzles: A Treasury of Fabulous Facts, Secret Codes, Games, Mazes, & More! 2019. (ENG.). 72p. (J). pap. 8.99 *(978-1-64124-044-4(X)*, 0444) Fox Chapel Publishing Co., Inc.

Schinkel, Jeff. Super Silly Jokes for Kids: Good, Clean Jokes, Riddles, & Puns. Whiting, Vicki. 2020. (ENG.). 80p. (J). pap. 5.99 ***(978-1-64124-067-3(9)***, 0673) Fox Chapel Publishing Co., Inc.

Schipper, Benjamin. Cap'n Rex & His Clever Crew. Herz, Henry L. 2017. 32p. (J). (gr. k). 16.95 *(978-1-4549-2088-5(2))* Sterling Publishing Co., Inc.

—Maybe I Can Love My Neighbor Too. Grant, Jennifer. 2019. (ENG.). 32p. (J). (gr. k-3). 16.99 *(978-1-5064-5201-2(9)*, Beaming Books) Augsburg Fortress, Pubs.

Schirack, Timm. The Night the Animals Spoke. Beres, Nancy. 2012. (J). 12.95 *(978-0-9752801-3-3(9))* Beres, Nancy.

Schirmer, Susan. A Little Dab of Paint. Frazin, Julian. 2012. 32p. (J). 22.95 *(978-0-9838846-5-1(X))* Berwick Court Publishing.

Schiti, Valerio. Donatello, 1 vol. Lynch, Brian & Waltz, Tom. 2015. (Teenage Mutant Ninja Turtles Ser.). (ENG.). 24p. (J). (gr. 3-7). 27.07 *(978-1-61479-338-0(7)*, 17338, Graphic Novels) Spotlight.

—Guardians of the Galaxy: New Guard Vol. 2: Wanted. 2017. (ENG.). 136p. (J). (gr. 4-17). pap. 19.99 *(978-0-7851-9951-9(9))* Marvel Worldwide, Inc.

—Guardians of the Galaxy: New Guard Vol. 4: Grounded. 2017. (ENG.). 136p. (J). (gr. 4-17). 24.99 *(978-1-302-90669-6(0))* Marvel Worldwide, Inc.

—Tony Stark: Iron Man Vol. 2: Stark Realities. 2019. 136p. (YA). pap. 17.99 *(978-1-302-91273-4(9))* Marvel Worldwide, Inc.

Schiti, Valerio & Villanelli, Paolo. Tony Stark: Iron Man Vol. 3: War of the Realms. 2019. (Tony Stark: Iron Man Ser.: 3). 136p. (YA). (gr. 8-17). pap. 15.99 *(978-1-302-91443-1(X))* Marvel Worldwide, Inc.

Schiti, Valerio, jt. illus. see Ramirez, Juanan.

Schlabach, Amy. Times of Trial: Poem Stories of Anabaptist Martyrs for Children. Schlabach, Amy. 2011. 46p. (J). (gr. 1-5). 14.99 *(978-1-933753-19-5(6))* Carlisle Pr.- Walnut Creek.

Schlafman, Dave. The Beast with 1000 Eyes #3. Dower, Laura. 2009. (Monster Squad Ser.: 3). 144p. (J). (gr. 3-7). pap. 5.99 *(978-0-448-44914-2(5)*, Grosset & Dunlap) Penguin Young Readers Group.

—The Slime That Would Not Die, 1. Dower, Laura. 2009. (Monster Squad Ser.: 1). (ENG.). 144p. (J). (gr. 4-6). 17.44 *(978-0-448-44912-8(9))* Penguin Young Readers Group.

—They Came from Planet Q. Dower, Laura. 2010. (Monster Squad Ser.: 4). 144p. (J). (gr. 2-4). pap. 5.99 *(978-0-448-44915-9(3)*, Grosset & Dunlap) Penguin Young Readers Group.

Schlechter, Annie, photos by. Celebrations: Easy Entertaining for Every Occasion. Rains, Valerie & Real Simple Magazine Staff. rev. ed. 2006. (ENG., 192p. (gr. 8-17). 27.95 *(978-1-933405-18-6(X)*, Real Simple Bks.) Time Inc. Bks.

Schleef, Vinciane. Ultimate Spotlight: Trains. Prénat, Sophie. 2020. (Ultimate Spotlight Ser.: 5). (ENG.). 14p. (J). (gr. k-3). 16.99 Éditions Tourbillon FRA. Dist: Hachette Bk. Group.

Schleihs, Kristin. Link & Rosie's Pets. Hubbard, Sharron/Y. 2007. (J). bds. *(978-0-9762434-3-4(1))* Link & Rosie Pr.

—Rosie's New Bike. Hubbard, Sharron/Y. 2006. (J). bds. 7.95 *(978-0-9762434-1-0(5))* Link & Rosie Pr.

Schleihs, Krostin. Link & Rosie Pick Berries. Hubbard, Sharron/Y. 2007. (J). bds. 7.95 *(978-0-9762434-2-7(3))* Link & Rosie Pr.

Schley, Cheri & Champagne, Heather. The Adventures of Hip Hop: Hip Hop & the Yellow Hat. Marshall, Denise. 2011. 36p. pap. 14.75 *(978-1-60976-342-8(4)*, Eloquent Bks.) Strategic Book Publishing & Rights Agency (SBPRA).

Schlingman, Dana. The Night Before Christmas in Ski Country. Brown, Suzanne. 2013. 32p. (J). 17.95 *(978-1-56579-658-4(6)*, Westcliffe Pubs.) Bower Hse.

Schlitt, RaRa. Two Little Birds. Hayton, Althea. 2012. 38p. pap. *(978-0-9557808-1-3(0))* Wren Pubns.

Schlitzkus, Dan. The International Space Station. Gifford, Clive. 2019. 32p. (J). (gr. 4-6). pap. 11.99 *(978-1-5263-0217-5(9)*, Wayland) Hachette Children's Group GBR. Dist: Hachette Bk. Group.

Schloesser, Natalie. The Donkey's Ear. 2005. 34p. (J). 10.00 *(978-0-9743850-1-3(8))* O'Brien, Gerard.

Schloss, E. Songs to Share. Goldstein, Rose B. (ENG & HEB.). 64p. (J). (gr. -1-5). 2.95 *(978-0-8381-0720-1(6)*, 10-720) United Synagogue of America Bk. Service.

Schlossberg, Elizabeth. On the Way to Kindergarten. Kroll, Virginia. 2008. (ENG.). 32p. (J). (gr. -1-k). pap. 6.99 *(978-0-14-241144-5(2)*, Puffin Books) Penguin Young Readers Group.

Schluenderfritz, T. Building the Way to Heaven: The Tower of Babel & Pentecost. McKeegan, Maura Roan. 2018. (Old & New Ser.: Vol. 3). (ENG.). 28p. (J). (gr. -1-2). 10.95 *(978-1-947792-77-7(6))*; 17.95 *(978-1-947792-78-4(4))* Emmaus Road Publishing.

Schluenderfritz, Ted. Darby O'Gill & the Crocks of Gold: And Other Irish Tales. Kavanagh, Herminie Templeton. 2003. ix, 155p. (J). pap. 14.95 *(978-1-928832-85-0(7))* Sophia Institute Pr.

Schluenderfritz, Theodore. Alvin Fernald, Foreign Trader. Hicks, Clifford B. 2007. (Secret Panel Mysteries Ser.). (ENG.). 181p. (J). (gr. 3-4). per. 11.95 *(978-1-883937-74-4(4))* Ignatius Pr.

Schlueter, Rachel. The Tree That Loved the Eagle. Pappas, Charles. 2013. 56p. (J). 19.95 *(978-1-58790-175-1(7))* Regent Pr.

Schlund, Mackenzie. Evelyn's Special Eggs. Mcinnes, Lisa. Duersch, Gretchen, ed. 2011. 32p. pap. *(978-1-77067-394-6(6))* FriesenPress.

Schlunke, Eva. Little Worm's Big Question, 1 vol. 2016. 36p. (J). (gr. -1-3). pap. 9.95 *(978-1-78026-261-1(2))* New Internationalist Pubns., Ltd. GBR. Dist: Consortium Bk. Sales & Distribution.

Schmeidler, Daniel. One Awesome School. J, Thais Sherell. 2015. (ENG.). 30p. (J). pap. 9.99 *(978-0-9814774-4-2(5))* N-Spired Productions.

Schmid, Debi. Plants in Disguise: Features of Creatures in Flowers & Foliage. Hedegaard, Lise. 2017. (J). 15.00 *(978-0-87842-673-7(6))* Mountain Pr. Publishing Co., Inc.

Schmid, Emma. Hey Diddle Diddle. (Classic Books with Holes 8x8 Ser.). 16p. (J). 2019. (ENG.). pap. *(978-1-78628-214-9(3))*; 2019. bds. *(978-1-78628-219-4(4))*; 2018. (ENG.). *(978-1-78628-235-4(6))*; 2018. (ENG.). *(978-1-78628-231-6(3))*; 2018. pap. *(978-1-78628-178-4(3))* Child's Play International Ltd.

Schmid, Paul. My Dog Is the Best. Thompson, Laurie Ann. 2015. (ENG.). 40p. (J). (gr. -1-1). 17.99 *(978-0-374-30051-7(8)*, 9780374300517, Farrar, Straus & Giroux (BYR)) Farrar, Straus & Giroux.

—The Wonder Book. Rosenthal, Amy Krouse. 2010. (ENG.). 80p. (J). (gr. -1-3). 17.99 *(978-0-06-142974-3(0)*, HarperCollins) HarperCollins Pubs. Ltd. GBR. Dist: HarperCollins Pubs.

—You See, I See: In the City. Colman, Michelle Sinclair. 2018. (You See, I See Ser.). 24p. (J). (— 1). bds. 7.99 *(978-1-5247-1500-7(X)*, Knopf Bks. for Young Readers) Random Hse. Children's Bks.

—You See, I See: on the Farm. Colman, Michelle Sinclair. 2018. (You See, I See Ser.). (ENG.). 24p. (J). (— 1). bds. 7.99 *(978-1-5247-1447-5(X)*, Knopf Bks. for Young Readers) Random Hse. Children's Bks.

Schmid, Paul. Hugs from Pearl. Schmid, Paul. 2011. (ENG.). 40p. (J). (gr. -1-2). 14.99 *(978-0-06-180434-2(7))* HarperCollins Pubs.

—Perfectly Percy. Schmid, Paul. 2013. (ENG.). 40p. (J). (gr. -1-3). 17.99 *(978-0-06-180436-6(3))* HarperCollins Pubs.

—A Pet for Petunia. Schmid, Paul. 2011. (ENG.). 40p. (J). (gr. -1-2). 12.99 *(978-0-06-196331-5(3))* HarperCollins Pubs.

—Petunia Goes Wild. Schmid, Paul. 2012. (ENG.). 40p. (J). (gr. -1-2). 12.99 *(978-0-06-196334-6(8))* HarperCollins Pubs.

Schmidt, Anita. On the Day You Were Baptized, Vol. DeYoung, Andrew. 2019. (ENG.). 32p. (J). (gr. -1 — 1). 17.99 *(978-1-5064-5552-5(2)*, Beaming Books) Augsburg Fortress, Pubs.

Schmidt, Anthony. Animals on the Truck. Craddock, Petra. 2015. (Early Rising Readers Ser.). (J). (gr. -1-k). 5.83 *(978-1-4788-1601-0(5))* Newmark Learning LLC.

Schmidt, Anthony & Schmidt, Erica. Samson Opens the Christmas Gifts. Liner-Ervin, Sharon. 2019. (ENG.). 34p. (J). pap. 14.95 ***(978-1-7020-5456-0(X))*** Independently Published.

Schmidt, Anthony & Schmidt, Erica Lyn. Animales en el Camión. Craddock, Petra. 2016. (Early Rising Readers Ser.). (SPA.). (J). (gr. -1). 6.67 *(978-1-4788-3677-3(6))* Newmark Learning LLC.

Schmidt, Ara. My Grandma Isn't Afraid of Alligators. Sisko, Diane Karkhoff. 2020. (ENG.). 26p. (J). pap. 9.56 ***(978-1-6542-7643-0(X))*** Independently Published.

Schmidt, Caleb & Schmidt, Carter. The Wonderful Adventures of Bradley the Bat. Paulding, Steve. 2013. 70p. pap. 18.95 *(978-0-615-74591-6(1))* Slow on the Draw Productions.

Schmidt, Carter, jt. illus. see Schmidt, Caleb.

Schmidt, Deborah. Squirrel Chronicles. Risch, Scott. 2018. (ENG.). 64p. (J). (gr. k-5). pap. 12.99 *(978-1-59095-385-3(1)*, ExamWise) Total Recall Learning, Inc.

Schmidt, Dennis. Our Federal Constitution, Our Michigan Constitution. Schmidt, Dennis, ed. Schmidt, Alex J. & Schmidt, Steven L. rev. ed. 2009. 72p. 8.00 *(978-1-892291-01-1(0))* AJS Pubns., Inc.

—Our Federal Constitution, Our Missouri Constitution. Schmidt, Dennis, ed. Schmidt, Alex & Schmidt, Steve. rev. ed. 2010. 72p. pap. 8.00 *(978-1-892291-00-4(2))* AJS Pubns., Inc.

—Our Federal Constitution, Our New Jersey Constitution. Schmidt, Dennis, ed. Schmidt, Alex & Schmidt, Steve. 2006. 72p. (YA). stu. ed. 8.00 *(978-1-892291-02-8(9))* AJS Pubns., Inc.

—Our Federal Constitution, Our Texas Constitution. Schmidt, Dennis, ed. Schmidt, Alex & Schmidt, Steve. rev. ed. 2008. 72p. pap. 8.00 *(978-1-892291-06-6(1))* AJS Pubns., Inc.

—Our Federal Constitution, Our Wisconsin Constitution. Schmidt, Dennis, ed. Schmidt, Alex & Schmidt, Steve. rev. ed. 2010. (ENG.). 72p. (YA). pap. 8.00 *(978-1-892291-04-2(5))* AJS Pubns., Inc.

Schmidt, Dennis & Schmidt, Esther, photos by. Baby Wild Animals, 1 vol. 2nd ed. 2015. (ENG., 48p. (J). (gr. -1-k). pap. 6.95 *(978-1-77203-090-7(2))* Heritage Hse. CAN. Dist: Orca Bk. Pubs. USA.

Schmidt, Erica. El Gigante. Koons, Linda. 2016. (Early Rising Readers Ser.). (SPA.). 16p. (J). (gr. 1-1). 6.67 *(978-1-4788-4212-5(1))* Newmark Learning LLC.

Schmidt, Erica, jt. illus. see Schmidt, Anthony.

Schmidt, Erica Lyn. Dinosaur Discovery: Everything You Need to Be a Paleontologist. McGowan, Chris. 2011. (ENG.). 48p. (J). (gr. 2-6). 18.99 *(978-1-4169-4764-6(7)*, Simon & Schuster Bks. For Young Readers) Simon & Schuster Bks. For Young Readers.

Schmidt, Erica Lyn, jt. illus. see Schmidt, Anthony.

Schmidt, Esther, jt. photos by see Schmidt, Dennis.

Schmidt, Frederico. Chubby: Die Wahre Geschichte Eines Teddybären, der Den Krebs Besiegte. Schmidt, Carola. Assis, Rogério, tr. 2019. (GER.). 42p. (J). pap. 10.90 *(978-1-0724-9180-4(X))* Independently Published.

Schmidt, J. Marc. The Sixsmiths: Volume 1. Franks, Jason. 2020. (Sixsmiths Ser.). (ENG.). 172p. (YA). pap. 16.99 ***(978-1-63529-857-4(1))*** Caliber Comics.

—The Sixsmiths: Volume One. Franks, Jason. 2020. (Sixsmiths Ser.: Vol. 1). (ENG.). 172p. (YA). pap. 16.99 ***(978-1-63529-853-6(9))*** Caliber Comics.

Schmidt, Jacqueline. Patchwork Helps a Friend. Greiner, Gail. 2013. (ENG.). 40p. (J). (gr. -1-2). 17.95 *(978-1-57687-642-8(X)*, powerHouse Bks.) powerHse. Bks.

Schmidt, Karenlee. The Jungle Baseball Game. Paxton, Tom. 2005. 30p. (J). (gr. -1-2). reprint ed. 16.00 *(978-0-7567-8932-9(X))* DIANE Publishing Co.

Schmidt, Katen. Max & Jax Plant a Garden. Nolen, Jerdine. Date not set. (J). 14.00 *(978-0-15-201672-2(4)*, Silver Whistle) Harcourt Children's Bks. CAN. Dist: Harcourt Trade Pubs.

Schmidt, M. Shadow & Friends Visit the Enchanted Forest. Jackson, S. & Raymond, A. 2020. (Shadow & Friends Ser.: Vol. 9). (ENG.). 36p. (J). (gr. k-4). 18.99 ***(978-0-578-64096-9(1))*** Schmidt, M. Productions.

Schmidt, Martin. Booger Cereal. Ledford, Paul. 2020. (ENG.). 32p. (J). pap. 10.99 ***(978-1-6594-4308-0(3))*** Independently Published.

Schmidt, Nathan. Zoey & the Zones: Coloring Book, 2. 2003. 0.99 *(978-0-9718120-7-9(1))* HealthSprings, LLC.

Schmidt, Ron. Back to Dog-Gone School. Schmidt, Amy. 2016. (Step into Reading Ser.). (ENG.). 32p. (J). (gr. -1-1). 4.99 *(978-1-101-93511-8(1)*, Random Hse. Bks. for Young Readers) Random Hse. Children's Bks.

Schmidt, Ron, photos by. Dog-Gone School. Schmidt, Amy. 2013. 40p. (J). (gr. -1-2). 16.99 *(978-0-375-86974-7(3)*, Random Hse. Bks. for Young Readers) Random Hse. Children's Bks.

Schmitt, Louis J. Goodnight Nola: An Endearing Bedtime Book for All Ages. Landry, Cornell P. 2009. (ENG.). 36p. (J). 16.95 *(978-0-9818126-4-9(3))* Ampersand, Inc.

Schmitt, Nannette Toups & Endres, Sharlene Duggan. Remember Last Island. Schmitt, Nannette Toups. Gorman, Carolyn Portier, ed. 2003. 206p. (YA). pap. 19.95 *(978-0-9740901-0-8(7)*, 11-May) Orage Publishing.

Schmitz, Cecile & Mouchet, Klutt. Father Damien Hawaii's Saint. 2009. 32p. (J). (gr. 4). pap. 14.95 *(978-1-57306-307-4(X))* Bess Pr., Inc.

Schmitz, Tamara. Back to School, Mallory. Friedman, Laurie. 2005. (Mallory Ser.: 2). (ENG.). 176p. (J). (gr. 2-5). per. 6.99 *(978-1-57505-865-8(0)*, Darby Creek) Lerner Publishing Group.

—Happy Birthday, Mallory! Friedman, Laurie. (J). (gr. 2-5). 2006. (Mallory Ser.: 4). (ENG.). 160p. per. 6.99 *(978-0-8225-6502-4(1)*, Darby Creek); 2005. 159p. per. 15.95 *(978-1-57505-823-8(5)*, Carolrhoda Bks.) Lerner Publishing Group.

—Mallory on the Move. Friedman, Laurie. 2005. (Mallory Ser.: 1). (ENG.). 160p. (J). (gr. 2-5). per. 6.99 *(978-1-57505-831-3(6)*, Darby Creek) Lerner Publishing Group.

—Mallory Se Muda. Friedman, Laurie. 2007. (Mallory en español (Mallory in Spanish) Ser.). (SPA.). 160p. (J). (gr. 4-7). per. 5.95 *(978-0-8225-7493-4(4)*, Ediciones Lerner) Lerner Publishing Group.

S

—Mallory vs. Max. Friedman, Laurie. 2006. (Mallory Ser.: 3). (ENG.). 160p. (J). (gr. 2-5). per. 6.99 *(978-1-57505-863-4(4)*, Darby Creek) Lerner Publishing Group.

—Playtime Devotions: Sharing Bible Moments with Your Baby or Toddler. Tangvald, Christine Harder. 2006. (Heritage Builders Ser.). 36p. (J). 15.99 *(978-0-7847-1361-7(8)*, 04024) Standard Publishing.

Schmolze, Ian. The Adventure of Paperman - Journey into Night. Larner, Eric. 2013. 194p. pap. 16.99 *(978-1-883651-68-8(9))* Winters Publishing.

Schnall, Emily. Dreaming of Boston: Counting down Around the Town. Everin, Gretchen. 2019. (Dreaming Of... Ser.). (ENG.). 16p. (J). bds. 9.95 *(978-1-64194-131-0(6)*, Commonwealth Editions) Applewood Bks.

Schneid, Frances E. Janey Junkfood's Fresh Adventure! Making Good Eating Great Fun! Storper, Barbara. 2008. 32p. (J). (gr. 3-7). 15.95 *(978-0-9642858-5-9(1))* FoodPlay Productions.

Schneider, Barbara Hoss. Remembering Pets: A Book for Children Who Have Lost a Special Friend. Dalpra-Berman, Gina. 2010. (ENG.). 30p. (gr. -1-3). 14.95 *(978-1-885003-68-3(4))* Reed, Robert D. Pubs.

Schneider, Cheryl. Bunnaby Bunny (L) Toddler Reader. Schneider, Cheryl. Olson, Carole. deluxe ed. 2006. 20p. (J). bds. 10.00 *(978-0-9712816-5-3(3))* Third Week Bks.

Schneider, Christine. Under Construction: A Moving Track Book. Perez, Jessica. 2005. (ENG.). 12p. (J). 12.95 *(978-1-58117-272-0(9)*, Intervisual/Piggy Toes) Bendon, Inc.

—Who Stole the Cookie from the Cookie Jar? Wang, Margaret. 2006. (ENG.). (J). 22p. bds. 10.95 *(978-1-58117-383-3(0))*; 12p. (gr. -1-3). 4.95 *(978-1-58117-429-8(2))* Bendon, Inc. (Intervisual/Piggy Toes).

—The World Is a Rainbow. Scelsa, Greg. Faulkner, Stacey, ed. 2006. (J). pap. 2.99 *(978-1-59198-319-4(3))* Creative Teaching Pr., Inc.

—Writing about Books. Williams, Rozanne Lanczak. 2006. (Learn to Write Ser.). 8p. (J). (gr. k-2). pap. 3.49 *(978-1-59198-289-0(8)*, 6183) Creative Teaching Pr., Inc.

—Writing about Books. Williams, Rozanne Lanczak. Maio, Barbara & Faulkner, Stacey, eds. 2006. (J). per. 6.99 *(978-1-59198-340-8(1))* Creative Teaching Pr., Inc.

Schneider, Christine M. Lily Learns about Wants & Needs. Bullard, Lisa. 2013. (Cloverleaf Books (tm) — Money Basics Ser.). (ENG.). 24p. (J). (gr. k-2). pap. 8.99 *(978-1-4677-1509-6(3)*, 9781467715096, Millbrook Pr.) Lerner Publishing Group.

—My Learn to Read Bible: Stories in Words & Pictures, 1 vol. Harrast, Tracy L. 2013. (ENG.). 240p. (J). 19.99 *(978-0-310-72740-8(5))* Zonderkidz.

—Shanti Saves Her Money. Bullard, Lisa. 2013. (Cloverleaf Books (tm) — Money Basics Ser.). (ENG.). 24p. (J). (gr. k-2). pap. 8.99 *(978-1-4677-1513-3(1)*, 9781467715133); lib. bdg. 25.32 *(978-1-4677-0765-7(1)*, 9781467707657) Lerner Publishing Group. (Millbrook Pr.).

—What Is It Made Of? Noticing Types of Materials. Rustad, Martha E. H. 2015. (Cloverleaf Books (tm) — Nature's Patterns Ser.). (ENG.). 24p. (J). (gr. k-2). 25.32 *(978-1-4677-8561-7(X)*, 9781467785617, Millbrook Pr.) Lerner Publishing Group.

Schneider, Claude. Vegetable Dreams/Huerto Sonado. Jeffers, Dawn. de La Vega, Eida, tr. 2006. (SPA & ENG.). 32p. (J). (gr. -1-3). 16.95 *(978-0-9741992-9-0(X)*, 626999, Raven Tree Pr.,Csi) Continental Sales, Inc.

Schneider, Josh. Tales for Very Picky Eaters. Schneider, Josh. 2014. (ENG.). (J). (gr. 1-4). lib. bdg. 16.60 *(978-1-62765-782-2(7))* Perfection Learning Corp.

Schneider, Katy. I Didn't Do It. Charest, Emily MacLachlan & MacLachlan, Patricia. 2010. (ENG.). 32p. (J). (gr. -1-3). 16.99 *(978-0-06-135833-3(9)*, Tegen, Katherine Bks) HarperCollins Pubs.

—Once I Ate a Pie. Charest, Emily MacLachlan & MacLachlan, Patricia. (ENG.). 40p. (J). (gr. -1-3). 2010. pap. 7.99 *(978-0-06-073533-3(3))*; 2006. 17.99 *(978-0-06-073531-9(7))* HarperCollins Pubs.

—Painting the Wind. MacLachlan, Patricia & Emily. 2006. (Joanna Cotler Bks.). (ENG.). 40p. (J). (gr. -1-3). reprint ed. pap. 7.99 *(978-0-06-443825-4(2))* HarperCollins Pubs.

Schneider, Leighanne. Tennessee Breeze. Achurch, Holly. 2018. (ENG.). (J). 15.00 *(978-0-9970690-1-3(5)*, Academy Park Pr.) Williamson County Public Library.

Schneider, Marine. I Am Life. 2017. (ENG.). 48p. (J). (gr. -1-3). 19.95 *(978-3-89955-793-0(X))* Die Gestalten Verlag DEU. Dist: Ingram Publisher Services.

—Life & I: A Story about Death. Helland Larsen, Elisabeth. 2016. (ENG.). 48p. (J). (gr. -1-3). 19.95 *(978-3-89955-771-8(9))* Die Gestalten Verlag DEU. Dist: Ingram Publisher Services.

Schneider, Rex. Tree House in a Storm. Burk, Rachelle. 2009. 42p. (J). pap. 11.95 *(978-0-88045-169-7(6))*; (ENG.). 16.95 *(978-0-916144-23-4(2))* Stemmer Hse. Pubs.

Schneider, Rex. Alice's Adventures in Wonderland: With a Discussion of Imagination. Schneider, Rex, tr. Carroll, Lewis. 2003. (J). *(978-1-59203-046-0(7))* Learning Challenge, Inc.

Schneider, Robin. Balloons for Grandpa, 1 vol. Smith-Eubanks, Jennifer. 2010. 20p. pap. 24.95 *(978-1-4489-5282-3(4))* PublishAmerica, Inc.

—Zoe the Zebra. Weaver, Amy Garrett. 2009. 33p. pap. 24.95 *(978-1-60749-552-9(X))* PublishAmerica, Inc.

Schneider, S. The Frontier Boys in Colorado, or Captured by Indians. Roosevelt, Wyn. 2014. (ENG.). (J). pap. 12.95 *(978-1-4794-1631-8(2))* Wildside Pr., LLC.

—The Frontier Boys in Hawaii, or the Mystery of the Hollow Mountain. Roosevelt, Wyn. 2014. (ENG.). (J). pap. 12.95 *(978-1-4794-1632-5(0))* Wildside Pr., LLC.

—The Frontier Boys in Mexico, or Mystery Mountain. Roosevelt, Wyn. 2014. (ENG.). (J). pap. 11.95 *(978-1-4794-1633-2(9))* Wildside Pr., LLC.

—The Frontier Boys on the Overland Trail. Roosevelt, Wyn. 2014. (ENG.). (J). pap. 12.95 *(978-1-4794-1635-6(5))* Wildside Pr., LLC.

schneider, Sandra. Secrets of the Symbols: Advanced Phonics Book including 54 skill Cards. schneider, Sandra. Hoppe, Gail, ed. 2008. 76p. (J). 18.00 *(978-0-9761987-5-8(4))* Magic Penny Reading.

Schneller, Lisa. The Five Keys to Wellness. Mather, Kelly. 2006. 46p. *(978-0-9787179-8-8(8))* Harmony Healing Hse.

Schnur-Fishman, Anna & Steele-Morgan, Alexandra. Tashlich at Turtle Rock. Schnur, Susan. 2010. (High Holidays Ser.). 32p. (J). (gr. k-4). lib. bdg. 17.95 *(978-0-7613-4509-1(4)*, Kar-Ben Publishing) Lerner Publishing Group.

Schoen-Smith, Sieglinde. Mother Earth & Her Children Coloring Book: Color the Wonderful World of Nature As You See It! 24 Magical, Mythical Coloring Scenes. von Olfers, Sibylle. Zipes, Jack, tr. 2015. (ENG.). 24p. (J). (gr. 2-4). pap. 6.95 *(978-1-933308-54-8(0))* Breckling Pr.

Schoenberg-Lam, Dahlia. My Synagogue Scrapbook. Person, Hara & Lewy, Faye Tillis. 2006. pap. 11.95 *(978-0-8074-0990-9(1)*, 164065) URJ Pr.

Schoenberg, Richard, photos by. Boot Camp - A Marine Legacy. Schoenberg, Richard. 2008. 100p. (YA). 129.95 *(978-0-9748208-3-5(0))* Schoenberg & Assocs.

Schoenbrun, Diana. The Gift Inside the Box. Grant, Adam & Grant, Allison Sweet. 2019. (ENG.). 40p. (J). (gr. k-3). 18.99 *(978-1-9848-1546-0(6)*, Dial Bks) Penguin Young Readers Group.

—Take Your Octopus to School Day. Vernick, Audrey. 2018. (ENG.). 40p. (J). (gr. -1-2). 17.99 *(978-0-399-55710-1(5))*; lib. bdg. 20.99 *(978-0-399-55711-8(3))* Random Hse. Children's Bks. (Knopf Bks. for Young Readers).

Schoenfeld, Wayne, photos by. American Photo Mission to India: Portrait of a Volunteer Surgical Team in Action. Weiner, Rex. 2006. 125p. 34.95 *(978-0-9727696-6-2(8)*, SWC Editions) Wayne, Steven Co.

Schoenherr, Ian. The After-Room. Meloy, Maile. 2015. (Apothecary Ser.: 3). (ENG.). 432p. (YA). (gr. 5). 17.99 *(978-0-399-17544-2(X)*, G.P. Putnam's Sons Books for Young Readers) Penguin Young Readers Group.

—The Apprentices. Meloy, Maile. (Apothecary Ser.: 2). (ENG.). (J). (gr. 5). 2014. 432p. pap. 9.99 *(978-0-14-242598-5(2)*, Puffin Books); 2013. 416p. 16.99 *(978-0-399-16245-9(3)*, G.P. Putnam's Sons Books for Young Readers) Penguin Young Readers Group.

—Bitterblue. Cashore, Kristin. 2013. (ENG.). 608p. (YA). (gr. 9). pap. 11.99 *(978-0-14-242601-2(6)*, Penguin Books) Penguin Young Readers Group.

—Castaways of the Flying Dutchman. Jacques, Brian. 2003. (Castaways of the Flying Dutchman Ser.). (ENG.). 336p. (J). (gr. 4-7). pap. 9.99 *(978-0-14-250118-4(2)*, Firebird) Penguin Young Readers Group.

—The Frame-Up. MacKnight, Wendy McLeod. (ENG.). (J). (gr. 3-7). 2019. 400p. pap. 7.99 *(978-0-06-266831-8(5))*; 2018. 384p. 16.99 *(978-0-06-266830-1(7))* HarperCollins Pubs. (Greenwillow Bks.).

—Sunrise, Sunset. Harnick, Sheldon. 2005. 32p. (J). (gr. -1-1). lib. bdg. 16.89 *(978-0-06-051527-0(9))* HarperCollins Pubs.

Schoenherr, Ian. Cat & Mouse. Schoenherr, Ian. 2008. 40p. (J). (gr. -1). lib. bdg. 17.89 *(978-0-06-136314-6(6)*, Greenwillow Bks.) HarperCollins Pubs.

—Pip & Squeak. Schoenherr, Ian. 2007. 32p. (J). (gr. -1-k). 18.89 *(978-0-06-087254-0(3))* HarperCollins Pubs.

—Read It, Don't Eat It! Schoenherr, Ian. 2009. (ENG.). 32p. (J). (gr. -1 — 1). 17.99 *(978-0-06-172455-8(6))*; lib. bdg. 18.89 *(978-0-06-178034-9(0))* HarperCollins Pubs. (Greenwillow Bks.).

Schoenherr, Ian, jt. illus. see Elliot, David.

Schoenherr, John. Gentle Ben. Morey, Walt. l.t. ed. 2004. (LRS Large Print Cornerstone Ser.). 264p. (J). lib. bdg. 33.95 *(978-1-58118-119-7(1))* LRS.

—Gentle Ben. Morey, Walt. 2006. 192p. (J). (gr. 3-7). 7.99 *(978-0-14-240551-2(5)*, Puffin Books) Penguin Young Readers Group.

—Julie of the Wolves. George, Jean Craighead. 2003. (Julie of the Wolves Ser.: 1). (ENG.). 208p. (J). (gr. 8-18). pap. 8.99 *(978-0-06-054095-1(8))* HarperCollins Pubs.

—Julie of the Wolves. George, Jean Craighead. 2019. (Julie of the Wolves Ser.: 1). (ENG.). 224p. (J). (gr. 8-18). pap. 7.99 *(978-0-06-440058-9(1)*, HarperCollins) HarperCollins Pubs. Ltd. GBR. Dist: HarperCollins Pubs.

—Julie y Los Lobos. Craighead George, Jean. 2014. (Serie Azul Ser.). (SPA.). 184p. (J). pap. 12.95 *(978-1-64101-134-1(3))* Santillana USA Publishing Co., Inc.

Schoening, Dan. Attack of the Cheetah, 1 vol. Mason, Jane B. 2013. (Wonder Woman Ser.). (ENG.). 56p. (J). (gr. 3-6). pap. 4.95 *(978-1-4342-2254-1(3)*, Stone Arch Bks.) Capstone.

—Batman. Dahl, Michael. 2019. (Batman Ser.). (ENG.). (J). (gr. 3-6). 106.60 *(978-1-4965-8668-1(9)*, 29757); pap., pap., pap. 27.80 *(978-1-4965-8669-8(7)*, 29761) Capstone. (Stone Arch Bks.).

—Battle of the Blue Lanterns, 1 vol. Acampora, Michael V. 2011. (Green Lantern Ser.). (ENG.). 56p. (J). (gr. 3-6). pap. 4.95 *(978-1-4342-3085-0(6))*; lib. bdg. 26.65 *(978-1-4342-2608-2(5))* Capstone. (Stone Arch Bks.).

—Beware Our Power! Sonnebom, Scott. 2011. (J). lib. bdg. (ENG.). 56p. (gr. 3-6). 26.65 *(978-1-4342-2607-5(7))*; (ENG.). 56p. (gr. 3-6). pap. 4.95 *(978-1-4342-3086-7(4))* Capstone. (Stone Arch Bks.).

—Catwoman's Classroom of Claws. Sonnebom, Scott. (Batman Ser.). (ENG.). 56p. (J). (gr. 3-6). 2013. pap. 4.95 *(978-1-4342-1732-5(9))*; 2009. lib. bdg. 26.65 *(978-1-4342-1565-9(2))* Capstone. (Stone Arch Bks.).

—Clock King's Time Bomb, 1 vol. Tulien, Sean et al. 2011. (Flash Ser.). (ENG.). 56p. (J). (gr. 3-6). lib. bdg. 26.65 *(978-1-4342-2626-6(3)*, Stone Arch Bks.) Capstone.

—Creature of Chaos. Stephens, Sarah Hines. (Wonder Woman Ser.). (ENG.). 56p. (J). (gr. 3-6). 2013. pap. 4.95 *(978-1-4342-2256-5(X))*; 2010. lib. bdg. 26.65 *(978-1-4342-1885-8(6))* Capstone. (Stone Arch Bks.).

—Deep Space Hijack. Sonnebom, Scott. (Superman Ser.). (ENG.). 56p. (J). (gr. 3-6). 2013. pap. 4.95 *(978-1-4342-2257-2(8))*; 2010. lib. bdg. 26.65 *(978-1-4342-1880-3(5))* Capstone. (Stone Arch Bks.).

Schoening, Dan, et al. Deepwater Disaster. Bright, J. E. 2011. (DC Super Heroes Ser.). (ENG.). 56p. (J). (gr. 3-6). 26.65 *(978-1-4342-3317-2(0)*, Stone Arch Bks.) Capstone.

Schoening, Dan. Dr. Psycho's Circus of Crime, 1 vol. Kupperberg, Paul. 2014. (Wonder Woman Ser.). (ENG.). 56p. (J). (gr. 3-6). pap. 4.95 *(978-1-4342-2761-4(8)*, Stone Arch Bks.) Capstone.

—Escape from the Orange Lanterns, 1 vol. Acampora, Michael Vincent. 2011. (Green Lantern Ser.). (ENG.). 56p. (J). (gr. 3-6). lib. bdg. 26.65 *(978-1-4342-2622-8(0)*, Stone Arch Bks.) Capstone.

—Fear the Shark, 1 vol. Sutton, Laurie S. 2011. (Green Lantern Ser.). (ENG.). 56p. (J). (gr. 3-6). pap. 4.95 *(978-1-4342-3406-3(1))*; lib. bdg. 26.65 *(978-1-4342-2620-4(4))* Capstone. (Stone Arch Bks.).

—Flower Power! (DC Super Friends) Carbone, Courtney. 2014. (Little Golden Book Ser.). (ENG.). 24p. (J). (-k). 4.99 *(978-0-385-37396-8(1)*, Golden Bks.) Random Hse. Children's Bks.

—The Fruit of All Evil. Crawford, Philip & Crawford, Philip Charles. 2014. (Wonder Woman Ser.). (ENG.). 56p. (J). (gr. 3-6). pap. 4.95 *(978-1-4342-2766-9(9)*, Stone Arch Bks.) Capstone.

—Ghostbusters: The Most Magical Place On Earth, Vol. 2. Burnham, Erik. 2012. (Ongoing (2012-2014) Ser.: 2). 104p. pap. 17.99 *(978-1-61377-279-9(3)*, 9781613772799) Idea & Design Works, LLC.

—Guardian of Earth, 1 vol. Dahl, Michael. 2011. (Green Lantern Ser.). (ENG.). 56p. (J). (gr. 3-6). pap. 4.95 *(978-1-4342-3081-2(3))*; lib. bdg. 26.65 *(978-1-4342-2611-2(5))* Capstone. (Stone Arch Bks.).

—Harley Quinn's Shocking Surprise, 1 vol. Hoena, Blake A. 2013. (Batman Ser.). (ENG.). 56p. (J). (gr. 3-6). pap. 4.95 *(978-1-4342-1729-5(9)*, Stone Arch Bks.) Capstone.

—High-Tech Terror, 1 vol. Steele, Michael A. 2011. (Green Lantern Ser.). (ENG.). 56p. (J). (gr. 3-6). pap. 4.95 *(978-1-4342-3084-3(8))*; lib. bdg. 26.65 *(978-1-4342-2609-9(3))* Capstone. (Stone Arch Bks.).

—The Last Super Hero, 1 vol. Dahl, Michael. 2011. (Green Lantern Ser.). (ENG.). 56p. (J). (gr. 3-6). pap. 4.95 *(978-1-4342-3082-9(1)*, Stone Arch Bks.) Capstone.

—The Light King Strikes!, 1 vol. Sutton, Laurie S. 2011. (Green Lantern Ser.). (ENG.). 56p. (J). (gr. 3-6). pap. 4.95 *(978-1-4342-3083-6(X))*; lib. bdg. 26.65 *(978-1-4342-2610-5(7))* Capstone. (Stone Arch Bks.).

—Livewire! Hoena, B. A. 2010. (J). pap. 34.99 *(978-1-4342-1766-0(3)*, Stone Arch Bks.) Capstone.

—Livewire!, 1 vol. Hoena, Blake A. & Hoena, B. A. 2013. (Superman Ser.). (ENG.). 56p. (J). (gr. 3-6). pap. 4.95 *(978-1-4342-1733-2(7)*, Stone Arch Bks.) Capstone.

—Livewire!, 1 vol. Hoena, Blake A. 2009. (Superman Ser.). (ENG.). 56p. (J). (gr. 3-6). lib. bdg. 26.65 *(978-1-4342-1566-6(0)*, Stone Arch Bks.) Capstone.

—The Man Behind the Mask. Dahl, Michael. 2019. (Batman Ser.). (ENG.). 56p. (J). (gr. 3-6). pap. 6.95 *(978-1-4965-8654-4(9)*, 141342); lib. bdg. 26.65 *(978-1-4965-8650-6(6)*, 141341) Capstone. (Stone Arch Bks.).

—Monster Magic. Simonson, Louise. (Wonder Woman Ser.). (ENG.). 56p. (J). (gr. 3-6). 2013. pap. 4.95 *(978-1-4342-2260-2(8))*; 2010. lib. bdg. 26.65 *(978-1-4342-1884-1(8))* Capstone. (Stone Arch Bks.).

—The Museum Monsters. Dahl, Michael. 2013. (Superman Ser.). (ENG.). 56p. (J). (gr. 3-6). pap. 4.95 *(978-1-4342-1372-3(2)*, Stone Arch Bks.) Capstone.

—Prisoner of the Ring, 1 vol. Sonnebom, Scott. 2011. (Green Lantern Ser.). (ENG.). 56p. (J). (gr. 3-6). pap. 4.95 *(978-1-4342-3410-0(X))*; lib. bdg. 26.65 *(978-1-4342-2624-2(7))* Capstone. (Stone Arch Bks.).

—Red Lanterns' Revenge, 1 vol. Acampora, Michael Vincent. 2011. (Green Lantern Ser.). (ENG.). 56p. (J). (gr. 3-6). lib. bdg. 26.65 *(978-1-4342-2623-5(9)*, Stone Arch Bks.) Capstone.

—Red Lanterns' Revenge, 1 vol. Acampora, Michael V. 2011. (Green Lantern Ser.). (ENG.). 56p. (J). (gr. 3-6). pap. 4.95 *(978-1-4342-3409-4(6)*, Stone Arch Bks.) Capstone.

—Rumble in the Rainforest, 1 vol. Stephens, Sarah Hines & Hines-Stephens, Sarah. 2014. (Wonder Woman Ser.). (ENG.). 56p. (J). (gr. 3-6). pap. 4.95 *(978-1-4342-2765-2(0)*, Stone Arch Bks.) Capstone.

—Savage Sands, 1 vol. Bright, J. E. 2011. (Green Lantern Ser.). (ENG.). 56p. (J). (gr. 3-6). pap. 4.95 *(978-1-4342-3405-6(3))*; lib. bdg. 26.65 *(978-1-4342-2619-8(0))* Capstone. (Stone Arch Bks.).

—Skyscraper Showdown. Wrecks, Billy. 2012. (Pictureback(R) Ser.). (ENG.). 16p. (J). (gr. -1-2). pap. 4.99 *(978-0-375-87299-0(X)*, Random Hse. Bks. for Young Readers) Random Hse. Children's Bks.

—Sword of the Dragon. Sutton, Laurie S. (Wonder Woman Ser.). (ENG.). 56p. (J). (gr. 3-6). 2014. pap. 4.95 *(978-1-4342-2760-7(X))*; 2010. 26.65 *(978-1-4342-1979-4(8))* Capstone. (Stone Arch Bks.).

—Trial of the Amazons. Dahl, Michael. 2010. (Wonder Woman Ser.). (ENG.). 56p. (J). (gr. 3-6). lib. bdg. 26.65 *(978-1-4342-1883-4(X)*, Stone Arch Bks.) Capstone.

—Under the Red Sun, 1 vol. Hoena, Blake A. (Superman Ser.). (ENG.). 56p. (J). (gr. 3-6). 2013. pap. 4.95 *(978-1-4342-1375-4(7))*; 2009. lib. bdg. 26.65 *(978-1-4342-1159-0(2))* Capstone. (Stone Arch Bks.).

—Web of Doom, 1 vol. Steele, Michael A. 2011. (Green Lantern Ser.). (ENG.). 56p. (J). (gr. 3-6). lib. bdg. 26.65 *(978-1-4342-2621-1(2)*, Stone Arch Bks.) Capstone.

Schoening, Dan & Delgado, Luis Antoni. Man from the Mirror. Burnham, Erik. 2016. (Ghostbusters Ser.). (ENG.). 24p. (J). (gr. 6-12). 27.07 *(978-1-61479-485-1(5)*, 21398, Graphic Novels) Spotlight.

Schoening, Dan & Delgado, Luis Antonio. Teenage Mutant Ninja Turtles/Ghostbusters (Set), 4 vols. Burnham, Erik & Waltz, Tom. 2016. (Teenage Mutant Ninja Turtles/Ghostbusters Ser.). (ENG.). 24p. (J). (gr. 6-12). lib. bdg. 108.28 *(978-1-61479-610-7(6)*, 24343, Graphic Novels) Spotlight.

—Teenage Mutant Ninja Turtles/Ghostbusters: Volume 1. Burnham, Erik & Waltz, Tom. 2016. (Teenage Mutant Ninja Turtles/Ghostbusters Ser.). (ENG.). 24p. (J). (gr. 6-12). lib. bdg. 27.07 *(978-1-61479-611-4(4)*, 24344, Graphic Novels) Spotlight.

—Teenage Mutant Ninja Turtles/Ghostbusters: Volume 2. Burnham, Erik & Waltz, Tom. 2016. (Teenage Mutant Ninja Turtles/Ghostbusters Ser.). (ENG.). 24p. (J). (gr. 6-12). lib. bdg. 27.07 *(978-1-61479-612-1(2)*, 24345, Graphic Novels) Spotlight.

—Teenage Mutant Ninja Turtles/Ghostbusters: Volume 3. Burnham, Erik & Waltz, Tom. 2016. (Teenage Mutant Ninja Turtles/Ghostbusters Ser.). (ENG.). 24p. (J). (gr. 6-12). lib. bdg. 27.07 *(978-1-61479-613-8(0)*, 24346, Graphic Novels) Spotlight.

—Teenage Mutant Ninja Turtles/Ghostbusters: Volume 4. Burnham, Erik & Waltz, Tom. 2016. (Teenage Mutant Ninja Turtles/Ghostbusters Ser.). (ENG.). 24p. (J). (gr. 6-12). lib. bdg. 27.07 *(978-1-61479-614-5(9)*, 24347, Graphic Novels) Spotlight.

Schofield, Angela. Why Is There Money? A Facinating Journey Through the Evolution of Money. Nourigat, Paul. 2011. (ENG.). 36p. (J). pap. 11.29 *(978-1-936872-00-8(5))* FarBeyond Publishing LLC.

Schofield, Christina Diane. Mrs. Rosey Posey & the Fine China Plate, 1 vol. Gunn, Robin Jones. 2008. (I Can Read! Ser.). (ENG.). 32p. (J). (gr. -1-3). pap. 4.99 *(978-0-310-71578-8(4))* Zonderkidz.

Schofield-Farmer, Twila. A Deaf Boy Meets Jesus. Entinger, Chad. 2011. 42p. (J). 10.00 *(978-1-59799-082-0(5))* Deaf Missions.

Schofield, Jayne. Peep & Find: Dragons. Schofield, Jayne, text. 2019. 10p. (J). (— 1). bds. 7.99 *(978-2-89802-024-7(9)*, CrackBoom! Bks.) Chouette Publishing CAN. Dist: Publishers Group West (PGW).

—Peep & Find: in the Jungle. Schofield, Jayne, text. 2019. 10p. (J). (— 1). bds. 7.99 *(978-2-89802-025-4(7)*, CrackBoom! Bks.) Chouette Publishing CAN. Dist: Publishers Group West (PGW).

—Peep & Find: under the Ocean. Schofield, Jayne, text. 2019. 10p. (J). (— 1). bds. 7.99 *(978-2-89802-026-1(5)*, CrackBoom! Bks.) Chouette Publishing CAN. Dist: Publishers Group West (PGW).

—Peep & Find: Unicorns. Schofield, Jayne, text. 2019. 10p. (J). (— 1). bds. 7.99 *(978-2-89802-023-0(0)*, CrackBoom! Bks.) Chouette Publishing CAN. Dist: Publishers Group West (PGW).

Schofield, Jayne & Dupuis, Karina. 10 Magical Mermaids. Weerasekera, Becky. 2019. 10p. (J). (gr. -1). bds. 9.99 *(978-2-89802-029-2(X)*, CrackBoom! Bks.) Chouette Publishing CAN. Dist: Publishers Group West (PGW).

—10 Pesky Pirates: a Lift-The-Flap Book. Weerasekera, Becky. 2019. 10p. (J). (gr. -1). bds. 9.99 *(978-2-89802-030-8(3)*, CrackBoom! Bks.) Chouette Publishing CAN. Dist: Publishers Group West (PGW).

Schofield, Vicki. Ben & Marty: A Forest Day. Schofield, Vicki. 2020. (Ben & Marty Ser.: Vol. 3). (ENG.). 36p. (J). pap. ***(978-1-9990033-4-0(9))*** Schofield, Vicki.

—Ben & Marty: A Rainy Day Parade. Schofield, Vicki. l.t. ed. 2020. (ENG.). 36p. (J). pap. ***(978-1-9990033-5-7(7))*** Schofield, Vicki.

—Ben & Marty: An Eggomatic Day. Schofield, Vicki. 2020. (ENG.). 36p. (J). pap. ***(978-1-9990033-7-1(3))*** Schofield, Vicki.

Scholastic. Batman's Guide to Being Cool. Dewin, Howie & Dewin, Howard. 2016. (LEGO Batman Movie Ser.). 128p. (J). (gr. 2-5). 9.99 *(978-1-338-11210-8(4))* Scholastic, Inc.

—The Lego Movie. Howard, Kate. movie tie-in ed. 2013. (LEGO: the LEGO Movie Ser.). (ENG.). 144p. (J). (gr. 1-3). pap. 5.99 *(978-0-545-62464-0(9))* Scholastic, Inc.

—Scratch & Sketch Secrets. Easton, Marilyn. 2019. (Beanie Boos Ser.). (ENG.). 64p. (J). (gr. -1-3). 12.99 *(978-1-338-29598-6(5))* Scholastic, Inc.

—Star Wars: Science Fair Book. Margles, Samantha. 2013. (Star Wars Ser.). (ENG.). 128p. (J). (gr. 5-9). pap. 9.99 *(978-0-545-52099-7(1))* Scholastic, Inc.

—Ultimate Sketch Challenge. Barbo, Maria S. 2nd ed. 2018. (Pokémon Ser.). 64p. (J). (gr. -1-3). 12.99 *(978-1-338-23756-6(X))* Scholastic, Inc.

—Unikitty - A Cuckoo Adventure. Brooke, Samantha. 2014. (LEGO: the LEGO Movie Ser.). (ENG.). 24p. (J). (gr. -1-3). pap. 3.99 *(978-0-545-79541-8(9))* Scholastic, Inc.

—Wacky Word Wedgies & Flushable Fill-Ins. Dewin, Howie & Dewin, Howard. 2017. (Captain Underpants Movie Ser.). (ENG.). 32p. (J). (gr. -1-3). pap. 4.99 *(978-1-338-19655-9(3))* Scholastic, Inc.

—Yo-Kai Watch. Rusu, Meredith. 2016. (Yo-Kai Watch Ser.). (ENG.). 32p. (J). (gr. -1-3). pap. 3.99 *(978-1-338-05444-6(9))* Scholastic, Inc.

—The Yoda Chronicles Trilogy. Landers, Ace. 2014. (LEGO Star Wars Ser.). (ENG.). 96p. (J). (gr. -1-3). 7.99 *(978-0-545-62901-0(2))* Scholastic, Inc.

Scholastic. Stats & Facts on over 150 Brand-New Pokémon! Scholastic. 2011. (Pokemon Ser.). (ENG.). 112p. (J). (gr. 2-5). pap., instr.'s hndbk. ed. 7.99 *(978-0-545-31652-1(9)*, Scholastic Paperbacks) Scholastic, Inc.

Scholastic, Inc. Staff. The Cabinet of Souls. Stine, R. L. & Ferguson, Jo Ann. 2016. (R. L. Stine's Monsterville Ser.: 1). 160p. (J). (gr. 3-7). pap. 6.99 *(978-1-338-03252-9(6))* Scholastic, Inc.

—Emmet's Awesome Day. Holmes, Anna. 2014. (LEGO: the LEGO Movie Ser.). (ENG.). 32p. (J). (gr. 1-3). pap. 3.99 *(978-0-545-79539-5(7))* Scholastic, Inc.

—Emmet's Guide to Being Awesome. Landers, Ace. 2014. (LEGO: the LEGO Movie Ser.). (ENG.). 128p. (J). (gr. 1-7). 9.99 *(978-0-545-79542-5(X))* Scholastic, Inc.

—Movie Novel. Stine, R. L. 2015. (ENG.). 144p. (J). (gr. 3-8). pap. 5.99 *(978-0-545-82124-7(X))* Scholastic, Inc.

Scholl, Larry. Trainer Tim's Camp Fitness. Green, Tim. 2019. (ENG.). 40p. (J). 12.99 ***(978-0-578-51360-7(9))*** Green, Tim.

Scholl, Larry. Trainer Tim's Camp Fitness. Green, Tim. 2018. (Trainer Tim Ser.: Vol. 1). (ENG.). 40p. (J). pap. 9.99 *(978-1-7267-3878-1(7))* Independently Published.

Scholl, Larry. Trainer Tim's down on the Farm. Green, Tim. 2019. (ENG.). 32p. (J). 12.99 ***(978-0-578-51390-4(0))*** Green, Tim.

Scholl, Larry. Trainer Tim's down on the Farm. Green, Tim. 2018. (Trainer Tim Ser.: Vol. 2). (ENG.). 32p. (J). pap. 9.99 *(978-1-7267-4116-3(8))* Independently Published.

Scholl, Larry. Trainer Tim's Gym. Green, Tim. 2019. (ENG.). 36p. (J). (gr. -1-3). 12.99 ***(978-0-578-51388-1(9))*** Green, Tim.

Scholl, Larry. Trainer Tim's Gym. Green, Tim. 2018. (Trainer Tim Ser.: Vol. 3). (ENG.). 36p. (J). pap. 9.99 *(978-1-7267-4192-7(3))* Independently Published.

Scholl, Larry. Trainer Tim's Troubled Friend. Green, Tim. 2019. (ENG.). 32p. (J). 12.99 ***(978-0-578-51389-8(7))*** Green, Tim.

Scholl, Larry. Trainer Tim's Troubled Friend. Green, Tim. 2018. (Trainer Tim Ser.: Vol. 4). (ENG.). 32p. (J). pap. 9.99 *(978-1-7267-4277-1(6))* Independently Published.

Scholten, Cheri. Ganz Gleich Mit Wem Wir Zusammen Sind. Vescio, Robert. Beer, Michele, tr. from ENG. 2013.Tr. of No Matter Who We're With. (GER.). 36p. pap. *(978-1-922120-48-9(0)*, IP Kidz) Interactive Pubns. Pty, Ltd.

—No Matter Who We're With. Vescio, Robert. 2012. 36p. pap. *(978-1-922120-21-2(9)*, IP Kidz) Interactive Pubns. Pty, Ltd.

Scholz, Barbara. Der Abc-Duden. 2nd ed. (Duden Ser.). (GER.). 96p. (J). *(978-3-411-70772-0(0))* Bibliographisches Institut & F. A. Brockhaus AG DEU. Dist: International Bk. Import Service, Inc.

Schomig, Michaelene A. P. Everybody Has a Guardian Angel: God Gives Every Child a Guardian Angel & Joins Them Together with One Heart. Fries, Marcella a. 2019. (ENG.). 36p. (J). pap. 9.13 *(978-1-7906-0830-0(9))* Independently Published.

Schon, Nick. Alien Swap. Cullimore, Stan. 2005. (ENG.). 24p. (J). lib. bdg. 23.65 *(978-1-59646-744-6(4))* Dingles & Co.

—The Amazing Adventures of Batbird: Band 11/Lime (Collins Big Cat) Clarke, Jane. 2005. (Collins Big Cat Ser.). (ENG.). 32p. (J). (gr. 2-3). pap. 9.99 *(978-0-00-718637-2(1))* HarperCollins Pubs. Ltd. GBR. Dist: Independent Pubs. Group.

—Sinbad & the Roc Purple Band. Whybrow, Ian. 2016. (Cambridge Reading Adventures Ser.). (ENG.). 24p. pap. 8.08 *(978-1-316-50340-9(2))* Cambridge Univ. Pr.

—Sinbad Goes to Sea Turquoise Band. Whybrow, Ian. 2016. (Cambridge Reading Adventures Ser.). (ENG.). 16p. pap. 7.37 *(978-1-316-50338-6(0))* Cambridge Univ. Pr.

Schönberg, John. Yussuf the Guide or the Mountain Bandits: Being the Strange Story of the Travels in Asia Minor of Burne the Lawyer, Preston the Professor, & Lawrenc. Fenn, George. 2007. 424p. 26.95 *(978-0-9776786-6-2(0))* Salem Ridge Press LLC.

—Yussuf the Guide or the Mountain Bandits: Being the Strange Story of the Travels in Asia Minor of Burne the Lawyer, Preston the Professor, & Lawrenc. Fenn, George Manville. 2008. 432p. pap. 16.95 *(978-1-934671-20-7(7))* Salem Ridge Press LLC.

Schonfeld, Shaya. Touched by a Story: For Children. Spero, Yechiel. 2004. (ArtScroll Youth Ser.). 48p. (J). *(978-1-57819-436-0(9))* Mesorah Pubns., Ltd.

Schongut, Emanuel. Christmas Eve Blizzard, 1 vol. Vlahakis, Andrea. 2005. (ENG.). 32p. (J). (gr. k-4). 15.95 *(978-0-9764943-3-1(7))* Arbordale Publishing.

—Turtles in My Sandbox, 1 vol. Curtis, Jennifer Keats. 2006. (ENG.). 32p. (J). (gr. 1-5). 16.95 *(978-0-9768823-7-4(X))* Arbordale Publishing.

Schons, Chris. Teen Angst? Naaah... A Quasi-Autobiography. Vizzini, Ned. 2004. 240p. (J). (gr. 8-18). pap. 12.95 *(978-1-57542-084-4(8))* Free Spirit Publishing, Inc.

Schons, Margaret. Pleasant Nightmares! Zach, Jacob. 2018. (ENG.). 40p. (J). pap. 25.00 *(978-0-692-93865-2(6))* Zach, Jacob.

Schoon-Tanis, Joel. At Psalms School/en la Escuela de Los Salmos: Learning the Multiple Elements of Christian Worship/Aprendiendo Los Múltiples Elementos de la Adoración Cristiana. Cornou, María Eugenia & Witvliet, John D. 2019. (ENG & SPA.). 40p. (J). (gr. k-2). 18.95 *(978-1-62277-372-5(1))* G I A Pubns., Inc.

Schoonmaker, Christina. Lucas & Leroy, 1 vol. Farrow, Nancy L. 2009. 32p. pap. 24.95 *(978-1-60836-232-5(9))* America Star Bks.

Schoonmaker, Elizabeth. Square Cat. Schoonmaker, Elizabeth. 2011. (ENG.). 32p. (J). (gr. -1-3). 18.99 *(978-1-4424-0619-3(4)*, Aladdin) Simon & Schuster Children's Publishing.

Schoonmaker, Gail. Do You Want a Friend? Piper, Noël. 2009. (ENG.). 32p. (J). (gr. -1-2). 12.99 *(978-1-4335-0621-5(1))* Crossway.

Schoonover, Brent. Ropes of Revolution: The Boston Tea Party, 1 vol. Gunderson, J. 2008. (Historical Fiction Ser.). (ENG.). 56p. (J). (gr. 3-6). pap. 6.25 *(978-1-4342-0492-9(8)*, Stone Arch Bks.) Capstone.

—Standoff: Remembering the Alamo, 1 vol. Trumbauer, Lisa. 2008. (Historical Fiction Ser.). (ENG.). 56p. (J). (gr. 3-6). pap. 6.25 *(978-1-4342-0849-1(4)*, Stone Arch Bks.) Capstone.

Schoonover, Brent, jt. illus. see Martin, Cynthia.

Schories, Pat. Biscuit. Capucilli, Alyssa Satin. 2017. (My First I Can Read Ser.). (ENG.). 32p. (J). (gr. -1-3). 9.99 *(978-0-06-257276-9(8))* HarperCollins Pubs.

—Biscuit. Capucilli, Alyssa Satin. 2006. (My First I Can Read Ser.). (ENG.). 32p. (J). (gr. -1 — 1). ed. reprint ed. pap. 4.99 *(978-0-06-444212-1(8))*; 10th anniv. ed. 16.99 *(978-0-06-026197-9(8))* HarperCollins Pubs. Ltd. GBR. (HarperCollins). Dist: HarperCollins Pubs.

—Biscuit. Capucilli, Alyssa Satin. ed. 2006. (Biscuit: My First I Can Read! Ser.). 26p. (J). (gr. -1-k). lib. bdg. 13.55 *(978-0-613-37688-4(9))* Turtleback.

—Biscuit 12-Book Phonics Fun! Includes 12 Mini-Books Featuring Short & Long Vowel Sounds. Capucilli, Alyssa Satin. 2008. (My First I Can Read Ser.). (ENG.). 100p. (J). (gr. -1 — 1). pap. 14.99 *(978-0-06-143204-0(0))* HarperCollins Pubs.

—Biscuit: 5-Minute Biscuit Stories: 12 Classic Stories! Capucilli, Alyssa Satin. 2017. (ENG.). 192p. (J). (gr. -1-3). 12.99 *(978-0-06-256725-3(X)*, HarperFestival) HarperCollins Pubs.

—Biscuit & the Baby. Capucilli, Alyssa Satin. 2005. (My First I Can Read Ser.). (ENG.). 32p. (J). (gr. -1 — 1). pap. 4.99 *(978-0-06-009461-4(3))*; 16.99 *(978-0-06-009459-1(1))* HarperCollins Pubs.

—Biscuit & the Big Parade! 2018. 29p. (J). *(978-1-5444-0450-9(6))* Harper & Row Ltd.

—Biscuit & the Big Parade! Capucilli, Alyssa Satin. 2018. (My First I Can Read Ser.). (ENG.). 32p. (J). (gr. -1-3). 16.99 *(978-0-06-243615-3(5))*; pap. 4.99 *(978-0-06-243614-6(7))* HarperCollins Pubs.

—Biscuit & the Little Pup. Capucilli, Alyssa Satin. 2007. (My First I Can Read Ser.). (ENG.). 32p. (J). (gr. -1 — 1). pap. 4.99 *(978-0-06-074172-3(4))* HarperCollins Pubs.

—Biscuit & the Little Pup. Capucilli, Alyssa Satin. 2007. (My First I Can Read Ser.). (ENG.). 32p. (J). (gr. -1 — 1). 16.99 *(978-0-06-074170-9(8))* HarperCollins Pubs.

—Biscuit & the Little Pup. Capucilli, Alyssa Satin. ed. 2007. (Biscuit: My First I Can Read! Ser.). 29p. (J). (gr. -1-3). lib. bdg. 13.55 *(978-1-4178-1002-4(5))* Turtleback.

—Biscuit & the Lost Teddy Bear. Capucilli, Alyssa Satin. 2011. (My First I Can Read Ser.). (ENG.). 32p. (J). (gr. -1 — 1). 16.99 *(978-0-06-117751-4(2))*; pap. 4.99 *(978-0-06-117753-8(9))* HarperCollins Pubs.

—A Biscuit Collection: 3 Woof-Tastic Tales: 3 Biscuit Stories in 1 Padded Board Book! Capucilli, Alyssa Satin. 2017. (Biscuit Ser.). (ENG.). 30p. (J). (gr. -1 — 1). bds. 11.99 *(978-0-06-274135-6(7)*, HarperFestival) HarperCollins Pubs.

—Biscuit Feeds the Pets. Capucilli, Alyssa Satin. 2016. (My First I Can Read Ser.). (ENG.). 32p. (J). (gr. -1-3). pap. 4.99 *(978-0-06-223696-8(2)*, HarperCollins) HarperCollins Pubs. Ltd. GBR. Dist: HarperCollins Pubs.

—Biscuit Flies a Kite. 2017. 29p. (J). *(978-0-605-96911-7(6))* Harper & Row Ltd.

—Biscuit Flies a Kite. Capucilli, Alyssa Satin. 2017. (My First I Can Read Ser.). (ENG.). 32p. (J). (gr. -1-3). pap. 4.99 *(978-0-06-223700-2(4))* HarperCollins Pubs.

—Biscuit Gives a Gift. Capucilli, Alyssa Satin. 2004. (ENG.). 16p. (J). (gr. -1-3). bds. 4.99 *(978-0-06-009467-6(2)*, HarperFestival) HarperCollins Pubs.

—Biscuit Goes Camping. Capucilli, Alyssa Satin. 2015. (My First I Can Read Ser.). (ENG.). 32p. (J). (gr. -1-3). pap. 4.99 *(978-0-06-223693-7(8))* HarperCollins Pubs.

—Biscuit Goes to School. Capucilli, Alyssa Satin. 2003. (My First I Can Read Ser.). (ENG.). 32p. (J). (gr. -1-3). pap. 4.99 *(978-0-06-443616-8(0))* HarperCollins Pubs.

—Biscuit Goes to School. Capucilli, Alyssa Satin. ed. 2003. (Biscuit: My First I Can Read! Ser.). 21p. (J). (gr. -1-3). lib. bdg. 13.55 *(978-0-613-66941-2(X))* Turtleback.

—Biscuit Goes to School Book & CD. Capucilli, Alyssa Satin. abr. ed. 2005. (My First I Can Read Ser.). (ENG.). 32p. (J). (gr. -1 — 1). audio compact disk 9.99 *(978-0-06-078686-1(8))* HarperCollins Pubs.

—Biscuit in the Garden. Capucilli, Alyssa Satin. 2013. (My First I Can Read Ser.). (ENG.). 32p. (J). (gr. -1-3). 16.99 *(978-0-06-193505-3(0))* HarperCollins Pubs.

—Biscuit in the Garden. Capucilli, Alyssa Satin. 2013. (My First I Can Read Ser.). (ENG.). 32p. (J). (gr. -1-3). pap. 4.99 *(978-0-06-193504-6(2)*, HarperCollins) HarperCollins Pubs. Ltd. GBR. Dist: HarperCollins Pubs.

—Biscuit Is Thankful. Capucilli, Alyssa Satin. 2003. (Biscuit Ser.). (ENG.). 16p. (J). (gr. -1-1). bds. 4.99 *(978-0-694-01519-1(9)*, HarperFestival) HarperCollins Pubs.

—Biscuit Loves School: a Lift-The-Flap Book. Capucilli, Alyssa Satin. 2020. (Biscuit Ser.). 12p. (J). (gr. -1-3). 6.99 *(978-0-06-296954-5(4)*, HarperFestival) HarperCollins Pubs.

—Biscuit Loves School Giant Lift-The-Flap. Capucilli, Alyssa Satin. 2003. (ENG.). 12p. (J). (gr. -1-3). 9.99 *(978-0-06-009454-6(0)*, HarperFestival) HarperCollins Pubs.

—Biscuit Loves the Library. Capucilli, Alyssa Satin. 2014. (My First I Can Read Ser.). (ENG.). 32p. (J). (gr. -1-3). 16.99 *(978-0-06-193507-7(7))*; pap. 4.99 *(978-0-06-193506-0(9))* HarperCollins Pubs.

—Biscuit Loves the Park. Capucilli, Alyssa Satin. 2018. (My First I Can Read Ser.). (ENG.). 32p. (J). (gr. -1-3). 16.99 *(978-0-06-243618-4(X))*; pap. 4.99 *(978-0-06-243617-7(1))* HarperCollins Pubs.

—Biscuit Meets the Class Pet. Capucilli, Alyssa Satin. 2009. (My First I Can Read Ser.). (ENG.). 32p. (J). (gr. -1-3). 16.99 *(978-0-06-117747-7(4))* HarperCollins Pubs.

—Biscuit Meets the Class Pet. Capucilli, Alyssa Satin. 2009. (My First I Can Read Ser.). (ENG.). 32p. (J). (gr. -1-3). pap. 4.99 *(978-0-06-117749-1(0)*, HarperCollins) HarperCollins Pubs. Ltd. GBR. Dist: HarperCollins Pubs.

—Biscuit Plays Ball. Capucilli, Alyssa Satin. 2012. (My First I Can Read Ser.). (ENG.). 32p. (J). (gr. -1-2). 16.99 *(978-0-06-193503-9(4))* HarperCollins Pubs.

—Biscuit Plays Ball. Capucilli, Alyssa Satin. 2012. (My First I Can Read Ser.). (ENG.). 32p. (J). (gr. -1-2). pap. 4.99 *(978-0-06-193502-2(6)*, HarperCollins) HarperCollins Pubs. Ltd. GBR. Dist: HarperCollins Pubs.

—Biscuit Storybook Favorites: Includes 10 Stories Plus Stickers! Capucilli, Alyssa Satin. 2019. (Biscuit Ser.). (ENG.). 192p. (J). (gr. -1-3). 13.99 *(978-0-06-289859-3(0))* HarperCollins Pubs.

—Biscuit Take-Along Storybook Set: 5 Biscuit Adventures. Capucilli, Alyssa Satin. 2017. (Biscuit Ser.). (ENG.). 120p. (J). (gr. -1-3). pap. 11.99 *(978-0-06-162516-9(7)*, HarperFestival) HarperCollins Pubs.

—Biscuit Takes a Walk. Capucilli, Alyssa Satin. 2009. (My First I Can Read Ser.). (ENG.). 32p. (J). (gr. -1 — 1). 16.99 *(978-0-06-117745-3(8))* HarperCollins Pubs.

—Biscuit Takes a Walk. Capucilli, Alyssa Satin. 2009. (My First I Can Read Ser.). (ENG.). 32p. (J). (gr. -1 — 1). pap. 4.99 *(978-0-06-117746-0(6)*, HarperCollins) HarperCollins Pubs. Ltd. GBR. Dist: HarperCollins Pubs.

—Biscuit Visits the Big City. Capucilli, Alyssa Satin. (My First I Can Read Ser.). (ENG.). 32p. (J). (gr. -1 — 1). 2007. pap. 4.99 *(978-0-06-074166-2(X))*; 2006. 16.99 *(978-0-06-074164-8(3))* HarperCollins Pubs.

—Biscuit Visits the Big City. Capucilli, Alyssa Satin. 2007. (Biscuit Ser.). 28p. (gr. -1-k). lib. bdg. 14.00 *(978-0-7569-8109-9(3))* Perfection Learning Corp.

—Biscuit Visits the Doctor. Capucilli, Alyssa Satin. 2008. (Biscuit Ser.). (ENG.). 24p. (J). (gr. -1-1). pap. 3.99 *(978-0-06-112843-1(0)*, HarperFestival) HarperCollins Pubs.

—Biscuit Visits the Farm. 2012. (J). *(978-1-4351-4383-8(3)*, HarperFestival) HarperCollins Pubs.

—Biscuit Visits the Pumpkin Patch. Capucilli, Alyssa Satin. 2004. (Biscuit Ser.). (ENG.). 16p. (J). (gr. -1-3). bds. 4.99 *(978-0-06-009466-9(4)*, HarperFestival) HarperCollins Pubs.

—Biscuit Wins a Prize. Capucilli, Alyssa Satin. 2003. (My First I Can Read Ser.). (ENG.). 32p. (J). (gr. -1-3). 16.99 *(978-0-06-009455-3(9))*; lib. bdg. 17.89 *(978-0-06-009457-7(5))* HarperCollins Pubs.

—Biscuit Wins a Prize. Capucilli, Alyssa Satin. 2005. (My First I Can Read Ser.). (ENG.). 32p. (J). (gr. -1-3). pap. 4.99 *(978-0-06-009458-4(3)*, HarperCollins) HarperCollins Pubs. Ltd. GBR. Dist: HarperCollins Pubs.

—Biscuit's 100th Day of School. Capucilli, Alyssa Satin. 2006. (Biscuit Ser.). (ENG.). 20p. (J). (gr. -1-1). pap. 6.99 *(978-0-06-079467-5(4)*, HarperFestival) HarperCollins Pubs.

—Biscuit's ABCs. Capucilli, Alyssa Satin. 2011. (Biscuit Ser.). (ENG.). 16p. (J). (gr. -1 — 1). 6.99 *(978-0-06-162518-3(3)*, HarperFestival) HarperCollins Pubs.

—Biscuit's Big Field Trip. Capucilli, Alyssa Satin. 2008. (Biscuit Ser.). 32p. (J). pap. 3.99 *(978-0-06-112844-8(9)*, HarperFestival) HarperCollins Pubs.

—Biscuit's Big Friend. Capucilli, Alyssa Satin. 2003. (My First I Can Read Ser.). (ENG.). 32p. (J). (gr. -1 — 1). pap. 4.99 *(978-0-06-444288-6(8))*; 16.99 *(978-0-06-029167-9(2))*; lib. bdg. 17.89 *(978-0-06-029168-6(0))* HarperCollins Pubs.

—Biscuit's Birthday. Capucilli, Alyssa Satin. 2005. (Biscuit Ser.). (ENG.). 24p. (J). (gr. -1-1). pap. 3.99 *(978-0-06-057845-9(9)*, HarperFestival) HarperCollins Pubs.

—Biscuit's Christmas Eve. Capucilli, Alyssa Satin. 2007. (Biscuit Ser.). (ENG.). 20p. (J). (gr. -1-1). pap. 6.99 *(978-0-06-112836-3(8)*, HarperFestival) HarperCollins Pubs.

—Biscuit's Christmas Storybook Collection. Capucilli, Alyssa Satin. 2013. 192p. (J). (gr. -1-3). pap. 11.99 *(978-0-06-228842-4(3)*, HarperFestival) HarperCollins Pubs.

—Biscuit's Christmas Storybook Collection (2nd Edition) Includes 9 Fun-Filled Stories! Capucilli, Alyssa Satin. 2018. (Biscuit Ser.). (ENG.). 192p. (J). (gr. -1-3). 11.99 *(978-0-06-269166-8(X))* HarperCollins Pubs.

Schories, Pat. Biscuit's Christmas Storybook Favorites: Includes 9 Stories Plus Stickers! Capucilli, Alyssa Satin. 2020. (Biscuit Ser.). 192p. (J). (gr. -1-3). 13.99 ***(978-0-06-304120-2(0)***, HarperCollins) HarperCollins Pubs. Ltd. GBR. Dist: HarperCollins Pubs.

Schories, Pat. Biscuit's Day at the Farm. Capucilli, Alyssa Satin. 2007. (My First I Can Read Ser.). (ENG.). 32p. (J). (gr. -1 — 1). pap. 4.99 *(978-0-06-074169-3(4))*; 16.99 *(978-0-06-074167-9(8))* HarperCollins Pubs.

—Biscuit's Earth Day Celebration. Capucilli, Alyssa Satin. 2010. (Biscuit Ser.). (ENG.). 24p. (J). (gr. -1-1). pap. 3.99 *(978-0-06-162514-5(0)*, HarperFestival) HarperCollins Pubs.

—Biscuit's First Beach Day. Capucilli, Alyssa Satin. 2010. (Biscuit Ser.). (ENG.). 24p. (J). (gr. -1-3). pap. 3.99 *(978-0-06-162515-2(9)*, HarperFestival) HarperCollins Pubs.

—Biscuit's First Sleepover. Capucilli, Alyssa Satin. 2008. (Biscuit Ser.). (ENG.). 24p. (J). (gr. -1-1). pap. 3.99 *(978-0-06-112842-4(2)*, HarperFestival) HarperCollins Pubs.

—Biscuit's First Trip. Capucilli, Alyssa Satin. 2010. (Biscuit Ser.). (ENG.). 24p. (J). (gr. -1-1). pap. 4.99 *(978-0-06-162524-4(8)*, HarperFestival) HarperCollins Pubs.

—Biscuit's Fourth of July. 2005. (J). *(978-1-4156-0311-6(1)*, HarperFestival) HarperCollins Pubs.

—Biscuit's Graduation Day. 2005. (J). *(978-1-4155-9660-9(3)*, HarperFestival) HarperCollins Pubs.

—Biscuit's My First I Can Read Book Collection. Capucilli, Alyssa Satin. 2003. (My First I Can Read Ser.). (ENG.). (J). (gr. -1 — 1). pap. 14.97 *(978-0-06-058933-2(7))* HarperCollins Pubs.

—Biscuit's Neighborhood: 5 Fun-Filled Stories in 1 Box! Capucilli, Alyssa Satin. 2018. (My First I Can Read Ser.). (ENG.). 160p. (J). (gr. -1-3). pap. 19.99 *(978-0-06-268826-2(X))* HarperCollins Pubs.

—Biscuit's Pet & Play Bedtime: A Touch & Feel Book. Capucilli, Alyssa Satin. 2017. (Biscuit Ser.). (ENG.). 12p. (J). (gr. -1 — 1). bds. 7.99 *(978-0-06-249039-1(7)*, HarperFestival) HarperCollins Pubs.

—Biscuit's Pet & Play Easter: A Touch & Feel Book. Capucilli, Alyssa Satin. 2008. (Biscuit Ser.). (ENG.). 12p. (J). (gr. -1 — 1). bds. 7.99 *(978-0-06-112839-4(2)*, HarperFestival) HarperCollins Pubs.

—Biscuit's Pet & Play Farm Animals: A Touch & Feel Book. Capucilli, Alyssa Satin. 2018. (Biscuit Ser.). (ENG.). 12p. (J). (gr. -1 — 1). bds. 8.99 *(978-0-06-249052-0(4)*, HarperFestival) HarperCollins Pubs.

—Biscuit's Pet & Play Halloween. Capucilli, Alyssa Satin. 2007. (Biscuit Ser.). (ENG.). 12p. (J). (gr. -1-1). bds. 7.99 *(978-0-06-112833-2(3)*, HarperFestival) HarperCollins Pubs.

—Biscuit's Show & Share Day. Capucilli, Alyssa Satin. 2007. (Biscuit Ser.). (ENG.). 24p. (J). (gr. -1-1). pap. 3.99 *(978-0-06-112832-5(5)*, HarperFestival) HarperCollins Pubs.

—Biscuit's Snow Day Race. Capucilli, Alyssa Satin. 2019. (My First I Can Read Ser.). (ENG.). 32p. (J). (gr. -1-3). 16.99 *(978-0-06-243621-4(X))* HarperCollins Pubs.

—Biscuit's Snow Day Race. Capucilli, Alyssa Satin. 2019. (My First I Can Read Ser.). (ENG.). 32p. (J). (gr. -1-3). pap. 4.99 *(978-0-06-243620-7(1)*, HarperCollins) HarperCollins Pubs. Ltd. GBR. Dist: HarperCollins Pubs.

—Biscuit's Valentine's Day. Capucilli, Alyssa Satin. 2019. (Biscuit Ser.). (ENG.). 20p. (J). (gr. -1-3). pap. 6.99 *(978-0-694-01222-0(X)*, HarperFestival) HarperCollins Pubs.

—Bizcocho Encuentra un Amigo: Biscuit Finds a Friend (Spanish Edition), 1 vol. Capucilli, Alyssa Satin. 2008. (My First I Can Read Ser.).Tr. of Biscuit Finds a Friend. (SPA.). 32p. (J). (gr. -1-3). pap. 4.99 *(978-0-06-143526-3(0)*, HarperCollins Español) HarperCollins Christian Publishing.

—Good Night, Biscuit: a Padded Board Book. Capucilli, Alyssa Satin. 2018. (Biscuit Ser.). (ENG.). 24p. (J). (gr. -1-3). bds. 9.99 *(978-0-06-266121-0(3)*, HarperFestival) HarperCollins Pubs.

—Happy Easter, Biscuit! A Lift-The-Flap Book. Capucilli, Alyssa Satin. 2020. (Biscuit Ser.). (ENG.). 20p. (J). (gr. -1-3). pap. 6.99 *(978-0-694-01223-7(8)*, HarperFestival) HarperCollins Pubs.

—Happy Halloween, Biscuit! Capucilli, Alyssa Satin. 2019. (Biscuit Ser.). (ENG.). 20p. (J). (gr. -1-3). pap. 6.99 *(978-0-694-01220-6(3)*, HarperFestival) HarperCollins Pubs.

—Happy Thanksgiving, Biscuit! Capucilli, Alyssa Satin. 2019. (Biscuit Ser.). (ENG.). 20p. (J). (gr. -1-3). pap. 6.99 *(978-0-694-01221-3(1)*, HarperFestival) HarperCollins Pubs.

—Meet Biscuit! Capucilli, Alyssa Satin. 2005. (Biscuit Ser.). (ENG.). 24p. (J). (gr. -1-1). pap. 3.99 *(978-0-06-057846-6(7)*, HarperFestival) HarperCollins Pubs.

—Mind Your Manners, Biscuit! Capucilli, Alyssa Satin. 2007. (Biscuit Ser.). (ENG.). 24p. (J). (gr. -1-1). pap. 3.99 *(978-0-06-112835-6(X)*, HarperFestival) HarperCollins Pubs.

—Where Is Love, Biscuit? A Touch & Feel Book. Capucilli, Alyssa Satin. 2009. (Biscuit Ser.). (ENG.). 12p. (J). (gr. -1 — 1). bds. 7.99 *(978-0-06-162521-3(3)*, HarperFestival) HarperCollins Pubs.

Schories, Pat & Berlin, Rose Mary. Biscuit's 123. Capucilli, Alyssa Satin. 2012. (Biscuit Ser.). (ENG.). 16p. (J). (gr. -1-1). 6.99 *(978-0-06-162523-7(X)*, HarperFestival) HarperCollins Pubs.

Schories, Pat & Young, Mary O'Keefe. Biscuit Loves Father's Day. Capucilli, Alyssa Satin. 2004. (ENG.). 20p. (J). (gr. -1-1). pap. 6.99 *(978-0-06-009463-8(X)*, HarperFestival) HarperCollins Pubs.

—Biscuit Loves Mother's Day. Capucilli, Alyssa Satin. 2004. (ENG.). 20p. (J). (gr. -1-1). pap. 6.99 *(978-0-06-009462-1(1)*, HarperFestival) HarperCollins Pubs.

—Biscuit's Hanukkah. Capucilli, Alyssa Satin. 2005. (Biscuit Ser.). (ENG.). 16p. (J). (gr. -1-3). bds. 4.99 *(978-0-06-009469-0(9)*, HarperFestival) HarperCollins Pubs.

—Biscuit's Pet & Play Christmas: A Touch & Feel Book. Capucilli, Alyssa Satin. 2006. (Biscuit Ser.). (ENG.). 12p. (J). (gr. -1 — 1). bds. 7.99 *(978-0-06-009470-6(2)*, HarperFestival) HarperCollins Pubs.

—Biscuit's Snowy Day. Capucilli, Alyssa Satin. 2005. (Biscuit Ser.). (ENG.). 16p. (J). (gr. -1-3). bds. 4.99 *(978-0-06-009468-3(0)*, HarperFestival) HarperCollins Pubs.

Schories, Pat, jt. illus. see Wenzel, David T.

Schorr, Bill. Red Roger to the Rescue. Riegelman, Rianna. 2012. (ENG.). 28p. (J). (gr. -1-3). 16.99 *(978-1-4494-2189-2(X))* Andrews McMeel Publishing.

Schorr, Jared. Better Together: A Book of Family. Lisberg, Anneke & Joosse, Barbara. 2017. (ENG.). 22p. (J). (gr. -1-k). bds. 14.95 *(978-1-4197-2538-8(6)*, Abrams Appleseed) Abrams, Inc.

Schorr, Jared Andrew. Peaceful Fights for Equal Rights. Sanders, Rob. 2018. (ENG.). 48p. (J). (gr. -1-3). 17.99 *(978-1-5344-2943-7(3)*, Simon & Schuster Bks. For Young Readers) Simon & Schuster Bks. For Young Readers.

Schossow, Peter. Where Is Grandma? Schossow, Peter. 2017. (ENG.). 64p. (J). (gr. k-5). 17.99 *(978-1-77657-154-3(1))* Gecko Pr. NZL. Dist: Lerner Publishing Group.

Schott, Elizabeth. Jake & Sam at the Empty Abbey. 2006. 96p. (J). per. 9.95 *(978-0-9724421-1-4(1))* Fountain Square Publishing.

Schpitalnik, Vladimir. Sasha & Babushka: A Story of Russia. Evans, Connie. (Make Friends Around the World Ser.). (ENG.). 32p. (J). (gr. k-3). 8.95 *(978-1-59249-446-0(3)*, SC8007) Soundprints.

Schrader, Gene. That Pesky Pickle. Cannon, Jamie. 2019. (ENG.). 36p. (J). (gr. k-3). 19.65 ***(978-0-578-57550-6(7))***; pap. 11.65 ***(978-1-0878-5992-7(1))*** Still Waters Transformation, LLC.

Schrader, Kimberly. Green Knee-High Farm. Schrader, Margaret. 2009. 28p. pap. 12.95 *(978-1-60844-000-9(1))* Dog Ear Publishing, LLC.

Schrader, Racheal. Doodlebugs: Trouble On Moss Farm. Schrader, Racheal. 2008. 156p. (YA). per. 7.99 *(978-0-9815274-0-6(X))* Schrader, Racheal.

Schrier, Albert. 50 States: A State-By-State Tour of the USA. McHugh, Erin. 2010. (ENG.). 240p. (J). (gr. -1-17). 24.95 *(978-1-57912-851-7(3)*, 81851, Black Dog & Leventhal Pubs. Inc.) Hachette Bks.

Schrier, Alfred. State Shapes: Arizona. McHugh, Erin. 2007. (ENG.). 48p. (J). (gr. -1-17). 9.95 *(978-1-57912-701-5(0)*, 81701, Black Dog & Leventhal Pubs. Inc.) Hachette Bks.

S

—State Shapes: Pennsylvania. McHugh, Erin. 2010. (ENG.). 52p. (J). (gr. -1-17). 9.95 *(978-1-57912-821-0(1)*, 81821, Black Dog & Leventhal Pubs. Inc.) Hachette Bks.

—State Shapes: Washington. McHugh, Erin. 2008. (ENG.). 48p. (J). (gr. -1-17). 9.95 *(978-1-57912-775-6(4)*, 81775, Black Dog & Leventhal Pubs. Inc.) Hachette Bks.

Schröder, Claudia. The Silver Eyes (Five Nights at Freddy's Graphic Novel) Cawthon, Scott & Breed-Wrisley, Kira. 2019. (Five Nights at Freddy's Ser.). (ENG.). 192p. (YA). (gr. 7-9). 24.99 *(978-1-338-62717-6(1))* Scholastic, Inc.

Schroder, Mark. Casey Jones. Krensky, Stephen. 2006. (On My Own Folklore Ser.). (ENG.). 48p. (J). (gr. 2-4). lib. bdg. 25.26 *(978-1-57505-890-0(1)*, Millbrook Pr.) Lerner Publishing Group.

—Casey Jones. Krensky, Stephen. 2007. (On My Own Folklore Ser.). (ENG.). 48p. (J). (gr. 2-4). per. 7.99 *(978-0-8225-6476-8(9)*, First Avenue Editions) Lerner Publishing Group.

—Cesar Chavez. Wadsworth, Ginger. 2005. (On My Own Biography Ser.). (ENG.). 48p. (J). (gr. 2-4). pap. 7.99 *(978-1-57505-826-9(X)*, First Avenue Editions) Lerner Publishing Group.

—César Chávez. Wadsworth, Ginger. Fitzpatrick, Julia, tr. 2005. (Yo Solo: Biografías (on My Own Biographies) Ser.). (SPA.). 48p. (J). (gr. 2-4). lib. bdg. 25.32 *(978-0-8225-3124-1(0)*, Ediciones Lerner) Lerner Publishing Group.

—Juneteenth. Nelson, Vaunda Micheaux & Nelson, Drew. 2006. (On My Own Holidays Ser.). 48p. (J). 25.26 *(978-1-57505-876-4(6))*; (ENG.). (gr. 2-4). per. 7.99 *(978-0-8225-5974-0(9)*, First Avenue Editions) Lerner Publishing Group.

Schroeder, Binette, jt. illus. see Hager, Christian.

Schroeder, Binnette, jt. illus. see Mogensen, Jan.

Schroeder, Erin. Oh no! it's the helpful hound... & the days of the Week. Schroeder, Erin, . 2006. (FRE, JPN, SPA & GER.). 27p. (J). per. 7.95 *(978-0-9779155-0-7(6))* Erinsillart.

Schroeder, Louise. The BLUES Go Birding Across America, 1 vol. Malnor, Carol L. & Fuller, Sandy F. 2010. (ENG.). 36p. (J). (gr. k-4). 16.95 *(978-1-58469-124-2(7)*, Dawn Pubns.) Sourcebooks, Inc.

—The BLUES Go Birding Across America, 1 vol. Malnor, Carol & Fuller, Sandy F. 2010. (ENG.). 36p. (J). (gr. k-4). pap. 8.99 *(978-1-58469-125-9(5)*, Dawn Pubns.) Sourcebooks, Inc.

—The BLUES Go Birding at Wild America's Shores, 1 vol. Malnor, Carol L. & Fuller, Sandy F. 2010. (ENG.). 36p. (J). 16.95 *(978-1-58469-131-0(X))* Dawn Pubns.

—The BLUES Go Birding at Wild America's Shores, 1 vol. Malnor, Carol L. & Fuller, Sandy F. 2010. (ENG.). 36p. (J). pap. 8.99 *(978-1-58469-132-7(8)*, Dawn Pubns.) Sourcebooks, Inc.

—The BLUES Go Extreme Birding, 1 vol. Malnor, Carol & Fuller, Sandy F. 2011. (ENG.). 36p. (J). (gr. k-4). pap. 8.95 *(978-1-58469-134-1(4))* Dawn Pubns.

—The BLUES Go Extreme Birding, 1 vol. Malnor, Carol & Fuller, Sandy F. 2011. (ENG.). 36p. (J). (gr. k-4). 16.95 *(978-1-58469-133-4(6)*, Dawn Pubns.) Sourcebooks, Inc.

Schroeder, Mark. Cesar Chavez. Wadsworth, Ginger. 2005. (Yo Solo - Biografías (on My Own - Biographies) Ser.). (SPA.). 48p. (J). (gr. 2-4). per. 6.95 *(978-0-8225-3125-8(9))* Lerner Publishing Group.

Schroeder, Mel. No More Flu for Suzie Sue: A Children's Coloring Book on Flu Awareness. Cirillo, Christine E. 2020. (Health Awareness Adventures Ser.: Vol. 3). (ENG.). 34p. (J). pap. 6.99 ***(978-1-6549-7643-9(1))*** Independently Published.

Schrom, Garren. Pepe & Lupita & the Great Yawn Jar. Lacy, Sandy Albee. 2013. 36p. pap. 10.95 *(978-1-60494-923-0(6))* Wheatmark, Inc.

Schrotter, Gustav. Robert Boyle, Founder of Modern Chemistry. Sootin, Harry. 2011. 142p. 40.95 *(978-1-258-00545-0(X))* Literary Licensing, LLC.

Schubbe, Matt. Gift of the Monkey Pajamas. Walsh, Sandy E. l.t. ed. 2015. (ENG.). 52p. (J). (gr. -1-4). pap. 12.95 *(978-1-68189-000-5(3)*, THEAQ Publishing) THEAQ LLC.

Schubert, Dieter. Opposites. Schubert, Dieter. 2013. (ENG.). 32p. (J). (gr. -1). 17.95 *(978-1-935954-26-2(1)*, 9781935954262) Lemniscaat USA.

Schubert, Jan. The Sun Seed, 1 vol. Schubert, Jan. 2007. (ENG.). 28p. (J). (gr. -1-k). lib. bdg. *(978-0-88010-585-9(2)*, Bell Pond Bks.) SteinerBooks, Inc.

Schubert, Karin. Extrano, Muy Extrano. Alonso, Manuel L. 2003. (SPA.). 124p. (J). (gr. 3-5). pap. 10.95 *(978-84-204-4906-7(7))* Santillana USA Publishing Co., Inc.

—Juan, Julia y Jerico. 2014. (ENG & SPA.). (J). (gr. 3-6). pap. *(978-607-01-1823-4(5))* Ediciones Alfaguara.

—Juan, Julia y Jerico. Nostlinger, Christine. 2005. (Serie Morada Ser.). (SPA.). 108p. (J). (gr. 2-5). pap. 9.95 *(978-1-64101-133-4(5))* Santillana USA Publishing Co., Inc.

Schuck, Tom. The Squirrels of Saltus Fidelis:: the Essential & Complete Book of Knowlege to All the Inhabitants of Saltus Fidelis. Schuck, Tom. 2019. (Squirrels of Saltus Fidelis Ser.: Vol. 1). (ENG.). 140p. (J). pap. 8.00 ***(978-1-6988-2859-6(4))*** Independently Published.

Schuepbach, Lynnette. Can You See Me Now? Dwyer, Cynthia. 2006. 24p. (J). 12.95 *(978-0-9677685-8-8(6))* Grannie Annie Family Story Celebration, The.

—Four-Eyed Philip. Dwyer, Cynthia. 2007. (J). 14.95 *(978-0-9793296-0-9(4))* Grannie Annie Family Story Celebration, The.

Schuepbach, Lynnette. Froggy Hollow. Schuepbach, Lynnette. l.t. ed. 2004. 32p. (J). pap. 7.00 net. *(978-0-9759613-0-8(6))* Creative Sources.

—Shhhh!!! Schuepbach, Lynnette. l.t. ed. 2004. (ENG.). 32p. (J). pap. 12.95 *(978-0-9759613-1-5(4))* Creative Sources.

Schuett, Stacey. Alex & the Wednesday Chess Club. Wong, Janet S. 2004. (ENG.). 40p. (J). (gr. -1-3). 19.99 *(978-0-689-85890-1(6)*, McElderry, Margaret K. Bks.) McElderry, Margaret K. Bks.

—America Is... Borden, Louise. 2005. (ENG.). 40p. (J). (gr. 1-4). 7.99 *(978-1-4169-0286-7(4)*, McElderry, Margaret K. Bks.) McElderry, Margaret K. Bks.

—Are Trees Alive? Miller, Debbie S. 2003. (ENG.). 32p. (J). (gr. -1-3). 17.99 *(978-0-8027-8801-6(7)*, 900034837, Bloomsbury USA Childrens) Bloomsbury Publishing USA.

—Halloween Howls: Holiday Poetry. Hopkins, Lee Bennett. 2005. (I Can Read Bks.). 32p. (J). (gr. k-3). 15.99 *(978-0-06-008060-0(4))*; lib. bdg. 16.89 *(978-0-06-008061-7(2))* HarperCollins Pubs.

—I Love to Write! Williams, Rozanne Lanczak. 2006. (Learn to Write Ser.). 8p. (J). (gr. k-2). pap. 3.49 *(978-1-59198-283-8(9)*, 6177) Creative Teaching Pr., Inc.

—I Love to Write! Williams, Rozanne Lanczak. Maio, Barbara & Faulkner, Stacey, eds. 2006. (J). per. 6.99 *(978-1-59198-334-7(7))* Creative Teaching Pr., Inc.

—Marching with Aunt Susan: Susan B. Anthony & the Fight for Women's Suffrage, 1 vol. Murphy, Claire Rudolf. (ENG.). 36p. (J). (gr. 1-5). 2017. pap. 7.95 *(978-1-56145-979-7(8))*; 2011. 16.95 *(978-1-56145-593-5(8)*, Peachtree Junior) Peachtree Publishing Co. Inc.

—Outside the Window. Smucker, Anna. 2005. 32p. (J). reprint ed. per. 7.95 *(978-1-891852-40-4(X))* Quarrier Pr.

—Pleasing the Ghost. Creech, Sharon. 2013. (Trophy Bk.). (ENG.). 112p. (J). (gr. 3-7). reprint ed. pap. 6.99 *(978-0-06-440686-4(5)*, HarperCollins) HarperCollins Pubs. Ltd. GBR. Dist: HarperCollins Pubs.

—Prairie Friends. Levinson, Nancy Smiler. 2003. (I Can Read Bks.). 64p. (J). (gr. k-3). 16.89 *(978-0-06-028002-4(6))*; 15.99 *(978-0-06-028001-7(8))* HarperCollins Pubs.

—Purple Mountain Majesties: The Story of Katharine Lee Bates & America the Beautiful. Younger, Barbara. 2005. 29p. (J). reprint ed. 16.00 *(978-0-7567-8984-8(2))* DIANE Publishing Co.

—A Tree Is a Plant. Bulla, Clyde Robert. 2016. (Let's-Read-And-Find-Out Science 1 Ser.). (ENG.). 40p. (J). (gr. -1-3). pap. 6.99 *(978-0-06-238210-8(1))* HarperCollins Pubs.

Schug, Sebastian. The Adventures of Daniel: Daniel Goes to the Farm. Ghazarian, Rene. 2019. (Adventures of Daniel Ser.: Vol. 29). (ENG.). 28p. (J). pap. 10.13 *(978-1-0993-6938-4(X))* Independently Published.

—The Adventures of Daniel: Daniel Visits the Farmer's Market. Ghazarian, Rene. 2019. (Adventures of Daniel Ser.: Vol. 30). (ENG.). 26p. (J). pap. 10.23 *(978-1-0994-5281-9(3))* Independently Published.

Schulbaum, Michael. Jyoti Meditation for Children. Singh, Rajinder. 2011. 24p. (J). (gr. -1-3). 10.00 *(978-0-918224-81-1(0))* Radiance Pubs.

Schuler, Carrie. Leo's Gift. Blackaby, Susan & Cicciarelli, Joellyn. 2017. (ENG.). 32p. (J). (gr. 1-7). 19.95 *(978-0-8294-4600-5(1))* Loyola Pr.

Schultz, Barbara, jt. illus. see Martin, Cynthia.

Schultz, Jolene. Albert Einstein: Scientist & Genius. Slade, Suzanne. 2007. (Biographies Ser.). (ENG.). 24p. (J). (gr. k-3). 25.99 *(978-1-4048-3730-0(2)*, Picture Window Bks.) Capstone.

Schultz, Michael. Mom, I Love Spaghetti. Fort, Gary W. 2011. 86p. pap. 24.00 *(978-1-60911-562-3(7)*, Eloquent Bks.) Strategic Book Publishing & Rights Agency (SBPRA).

Schultz, Paul, jt. illus. see Aiken, Lara.

Schultz, Rebecca. Not Just Any Donkey. Mayeaux, Stacy. 2008. (ENG.). 24p. pap. 12.49 *(978-1-4343-6598-9(0))* AuthorHouse.

Schulz, Barbara. The Curse of King Tut's Tomb, 1 vol. Burgan, Michael. 2005. (Graphic History Ser.). (ENG.). 32p. (J). (gr. 3-9). per. 8.10 *(978-0-7368-5244-9(1)*, Capstone Pr.) Capstone.

—Getting to the Bottom of Global Warming: An Isabel Soto Investigation. Collins, Terry. 2010. (Graphic Expeditions Ser.). (ENG.). 32p. (J). (gr. 3-9). lib. bdg. 31.32 *(978-1-4296-3972-9(5)*, Capstone Pr.) Capstone.

Schulz, Barbara & Kurth, Steve. Demeter & Persephone: Spring Held Hostage. Fontes, Justine & Fontes, Ron. 2007. (Graphic Myths & Legends Ser.). (ENG.). 48p. (J). (gr. 4-8). lib. bdg. 27.99 *(978-0-8225-5966-5(8)*, Graphic Universe™) Lerner Publishing Group.

Schulz, Barbara, jt. illus. see Kurth, Steve.

Schulz, Barbara, jt. illus. see Lohse, Otha Zackariah Edward.

Schulz, Barbara, jt. illus. see Martin, Cynthia.

Schulz, Barbara, jt. illus. see Purcell, Gordon.

Schulz, Barbara, jt. illus. see Seeley, Tim.

Schulz, Charles & Ellis, Kim. Where's Woodstock? (Peanuts) Lundell, Margo. 2015. (Little Golden Book Ser.). (ENG.). 24p. (J). (gr. -1-1). 4.99 *(978-1-101-93517-0(0)*, Golden Bks.) Random Hse. Children's Bks.

Schulz, Charles, jt. illus. see Ellis, Kim.

Schulz, Charles M. Peanuts: Christmas Time Is Here. Skwish, Emily. 2019. (Play-A-Song Ser.). (ENG.). 12p. (J). bds. *(978-1-5037-4678-7(X)*, 2ba50879-c630-466a-8c50-3a7307cdd265, p i kids) Phoenix International Publications, Inc.

Schulz, Janet. Will y Orv. Schulz, Walter A. Translations.com Staff, tr. from ENG. 2006. (Yo Solo - Historia (on My Own - History) Ser.). (SPA.). 48p. (J). (gr. 2-4). lib. bdg. 25.26 *(978-0-8225-6263-4(4))* Lerner Publishing Group.

Schulze, Marc-Alexander. A Child Is Born: The Nativity Story. 2010. 32p. (gr. -1 — 1). 16.95 *(978-0-7358-2321-1(9))* North-South Bks., Inc.

Schumaker, Ward. A Kids Guide to Giving. Zeiler, Freddi. 2006. (ENG.). 208p. (J). (gr. 7-17). 9.99 *(978-1-58476-489-2(9)*, IKIDS) Innovative Kids.

Schuna, Ramona. Aristotle: the Firefly's Message. Brown, Elizabeth. 2007. (ENG.). 40p. per. 19.95 *(978-1-59800-557-8(X))* Outskirts Pr., Inc.

Schunemann, Ryan. Gabriel's Magic Ornament. Bush, Randall B. 2003. 120p. (gr. 5-8). pap. 11.95 *(978-0-9716633-0-5(0))* Pristine Pubs., Inc.

Schuppert, David. What Do Roots Do? Kudlinski, Kathleen V. (ENG.). 32p. (J). (gr. k-3). 2007. pap. 7.95 *(978-1-55971-980-3(X))*; 2005. 15.95 *(978-1-55971-896-7(X))* Cooper Square Publishing Llc.

Schutzer, Dena. 3 Kids Dreamin' England, Linda. 2011. (ENG.). 32p. (J). (gr. 4-6). 6.99 *(978-1-4424-2944-4(5)*, McElderry, Margaret K. Bks.) McElderry, Margaret K. Bks.

Schuurmans, Hilde. Rosie & Roger. Dessers, Rik. 2015. (ENG.). 100p. (J). pap. 16.95 *(978-1-931290-09-8(1))* Tallfellow Pr.

Schuurmans, Hilde. Sidney Won't Swim. Schuurmans, Hilde. pap. 6.95 *(978-1-57091-515-4(6))* Charlesbridge Publishing, Inc.

Schwab, Alicia. The Mukluk Ball. Johnson, Katharine. 2018. (ENG.). 32p. (J). 16.95 *(978-1-68134-116-3(6))* Minnesota Historical Society Pr.

Schwab, Jordan. Pages, the Book-Maker Elf. Delrusso, Diana. 2008. 68p. pap. 23.49 *(978-1-4343-9844-4(7))* AuthorHouse.

Schwalm, Claudia, photos by. Folk Art of Mexico Book & Game. Schwalm, Claudia. Martinez Aydelott, Carmen, tr. 2005. (SPA., pap. 25.00 *(978-1-57371-050-3(4))* Cultural Connections.

Schwartz, Amy. A Little Kitty. Feder, Jane. 2009. 14p. (J). (— 1). bds. 4.99 *(978-0-7636-2650-1(3))* Candlewick Pr.

—The Night Flight. Ryder, Joanne. 2014. (ENG.). 32p. (J). (gr. k-2). 16.99 *(978-1-4814-2521-6(8)*, Simon & Schuster Bks. For Young Readers) Simon & Schuster Bks. For Young Readers.

—Things That Make Me Happy. 2017. (ENG.). 24p. (J). (gr. -1 — 1). bds. 7.95 *(978-1-4197-2367-4(7)*, Abrams Appleseed) Abrams, Inc.

—100 Things That Make Me Happy. 2014. (ENG.). 40p. (J). (gr. -1-1). 16.95 *(978-1-4197-0518-2(0)*, Abrams Appleseed) Abrams, Inc.

Schwartz, Amy. Begin at the Beginning: A Little Artist Learns about Life. Schwartz, Amy. 2005. 40p. (J). (gr. -1-2). lib. bdg. 16.89 *(978-0-06-000112-4(7))* HarperCollins Pubs.

—The Boys Team. Schwartz, Amy. 2014. (ENG.). 40p. (J). (gr. -1-1). 19.99 *(978-1-4814-2534-6(X)*, Atheneum Bks. for Young Readers) Simon & Schuster Children's Publishing.

—Busy Babies. Schwartz, Amy. 2019. (ENG.). 32p. (J). (gr. -1-3). 17.99 *(978-1-4814-4510-8(3)*, Beach Lane Bks.) Beach Lane Bks.

—A Glorious Day. Schwartz, Amy. 2010. (ENG.). 32p. (J). (gr. -1-k). 16.99 *(978-1-4424-2190-5(8)*, Atheneum Bks. for Young Readers) Simon & Schuster Children's Publishing.

—I Can't Wait! Schwartz, Amy. 2015. (ENG.). 40p. (J). (gr. k-3). 17.99 *(978-1-4424-8231-9(1)*, Beach Lane Bks.) Beach Lane Bks.

—Oscar: The Big Adventure of a Little Sock Monkey. Schwartz, Amy. Marcus, Leonard S. 2006. 32p. (J). (gr. -1-2). 16.99 *(978-0-06-072622-5(9)*, Tegen, Katherine Bks) HarperCollins Pubs.

—What James Likes Best. Schwartz, Amy. 2014. (ENG.). 32p. (J). (gr. -1-k). 16.99 *(978-1-4814-2536-0(6)*, Atheneum Bks. for Young Readers) Simon & Schuster Children's Publishing.

Schwartz, Carol. Best Friends: The True Story of Owen & Mzee. Edwards, Roberta. 2007. (Penguin Young Readers, Level 2 Ser.). 32p. (J). (gr. 1-2). mass mkt. 4.99 *(978-0-448-44567-0(0)*, Penguin Young Readers) Penguin Young Readers Group.

—Best Friends: The True Story of Owen & Mzee. Edwards, Roberta. 2007. (All Aboard Science Reader Ser.). 32p. (gr. -1-3). 14.00 *(978-0-7569-8167-9(0))* Perfection Learning Corp.

—Emperor Penguins. Edwards, Roberta. 2007. (Penguin Young Readers, Level 3 Ser.). 48p. (J). (gr. 1-3). mass mkt. 4.99 *(978-0-448-44664-6(2)*, Penguin Young Readers) Penguin Young Readers Group.

—How Does a Seed Sprout? And Other Questions about Plants. Stewart, Melissa. 2014. (Good Question! Ser.). (ENG.). 32p. (J). (gr. 1). pap. 6.95 *(978-1-4549-0671-1(5))* Sterling Publishing Co., Inc.

—My Busy Green Garden, 1 vol. Clough, David, photos by. Pierce, Terry & Hanson, Scott T. 2017. (Tilbury House Nature Book Ser.: 0). (ENG.). 36p. (J). (gr. -1-1). 16.95 *(978-0-88448-495-0(5)*, 884495) Tilbury Hse. Pubs.

—Shelley, the Hyperactive Turtle. Moss, Deborah. 2nd ed. 2006. (ENG.). 20p. (J). (gr. -1-2). *(978-1-890627-75-1(5))* Woodbine Hse.

—What If There Were No Bees? A Book about the Grassland Ecosystem, 1 vol. Slade, Suzanne. 2010. (Food Chain Reactions Ser.). (ENG.). 24p. (J). (gr. 2-4). pap. 9.95 *(978-1-4048-6394-1(X)*, Picture Window Bks.) Capstone.

—What If There Were No Gray Wolves? A Book about the Temperate Forest Ecosystem, 1 vol. Slade, Suzanne. 2010. (Food Chain Reactions Ser.). (ENG.). 24p. (J). (gr. 2-4). pap. 9.95 *(978-1-4048-6395-8(8)*, Picture Window Bks.) Capstone.

—What If There Were No Lemmings? A Book about the Tundra Ecosystem, 1 vol. Slade, Suzanne. 2010. (Food Chain Reactions Ser.). (ENG.). 24p. (J). (gr. 2-4). pap. 9.95 *(978-1-4048-6396-5(6))*; lib. bdg. 27.32 *(978-1-4048-6021-6(5))* Capstone. (Picture Window Bks.).

—What If There Were No Sea Otters? A Book about the Ocean Ecosystem, 1 vol. Slade, Suzanne. 2010. (Food Chain Reactions Ser.). (ENG.). 24p. (J). (gr. 2-4). pap. 9.95 *(978-1-4048-6397-2(4)*, Picture Window Bks.) Capstone.

—Wild Fibonacci: Nature's Secret Code Revealed. Hulme, Joy N. 2010. (ENG.). 32p. (J). (gr. -1-2). pap. 7.99 *(978-1-58246-324-7(7)*, Tricycle Pr.) Random Hse. Children's Bks.

—The World Never Sleeps, 1 vol. Rompella, Natalie. 2018. (Tilbury House Nature Book Ser.: 0). (ENG.). 36p. (J). (gr. -1-3). 17.95 *(978-0-88448-561-2(7)*, 884561) Tilbury Hse. Pubs.

Schwartz, Carol. Emperor Penguins. Schwartz, Carol. Edwards, Roberta. 2007. (All Aboard Science Reader Ser.). 48p. (gr. 1-3). 14.00 *(978-0-7569-8174-7(3))* Perfection Learning Corp.

—Old Mother Hubbard. Schwartz, Carol. 2010. (Favorite Mother Goose Rhymes Ser.). (ENG.). 16p. (J). (gr. -1-2). 14.21 *(978-1-60253-538-1(8)*, 200242) Child's World, Inc., The.

Schwartz, Carol & Regan, Dana. Pinocchio. Hillert, Margaret & Collodi, Carlo. 21st ed. 2016. (BeginningtoRead Ser.). (ENG.). 32p. (J). (-2). lib. bdg. 22.60 *(978-1-59953-786-3(9))* Norwood Hse. Pr.

—Pinocchio. Hillert, Margaret. 21st ed. 2016. (BeginningtoRead Ser.). (ENG.). 32p. (J). (gr. -1-2). pap. 11.94 *(978-1-60357-912-4(5))* Norwood Hse. Pr.

Schwartz, Kacey. June Sparrow & the Million-Dollar Penny. Chace, Rebecca. 2017. (ENG.). 352p. (J). (gr. 3-7). 16.99 *(978-0-06-246498-9(1))* HarperCollins Pubs.

Schwartz, Marty. Changing Statements to Questions Fun Deck: Fd55. Webber, Sharon. 2003. (J). 11.95 *(978-1-58650-248-5(4))* Super Duper Pubns.

Schwartz, Marty, jt. illus. see Ink, Bruce.

Schwartz, Robert, jt. illus. see Schwartz, Suzanne.

Schwartz, Suzanne & Schwartz, Robert. The Christmas Palm Tree: A Storybook to Color. Schwartz, Suzanne & Schwartz, Robert. l.t. ed. 2005. 22p. (J). spiral bd. 3.99 *(978-0-9764152-3-7(2))* Seascay Productions.

—Hibby's Coloring Book. 2005. 24p. (J). spiral bd. 3.95 *(978-0-9764152-1-3(6))* Seascay Productions.

—My Friend Hibby: A Tropical Adventure. Schwartz, Suzanne & Schwartz, Robert. 2005. 20p. (J). spiral bd. 6.00 *(978-0-9764152-0-6(8))* Seascay Productions.

Schwartz, Wendy. The Winged Pony. Beloat, Betty. 2005. 32p. (J). (gr. k-5). pap. 5.99 *(978-0-9701008-8-7(4))* Bicast, Inc.

Schwartzkopf, Jere. The Princess & the Talking Dog. Kizer, Amelia. 2017. (ENG.). 62p. (J). pap. 14.95 *(978-1-64028-817-1(1))* Christian Faith Publishing.

Schwarz, Renee. Birdfeeders. Schwarz, Renee. 2005. (Kids Can Do It Ser.). 40p. (J). (gr. 3-7). 6.95 *(978-1-55337-700-9(1))* Kids Can Pr., Ltd. CAN. Dist: Hachette Bk. Group.

—Birdhouses. Schwarz, Renee. 2005. (Kids Can Do It Ser.). 40p. (J). (gr. 3-7). 6.95 *(978-1-55337-550-0(5))*; (ENG.). 18.69 *(978-1-55337-549-4(1))* Kids Can Pr., Ltd. CAN. Dist: Hachette Bk. Group, Children's Plus, Inc.

—Wind Chimes & Whirligigs. Schwarz, Renee. 2007. (Kids Can Do It Ser.). 40p. (J). (gr. 3-18). (ENG.). 12.95 *(978-1-55337-868-6(7))*; pap. 6.95 *(978-1-55337-870-9(9))* Kids Can Pr., Ltd. CAN. Dist: Hachette Bk. Group.

Schwarz, Renée & Schwarz, Renée. Funky Junk: Cool Stuff to Make with Hardware. Schwarz, Renée & Schwarz, Renée. 2003. (Kids Can Do It Ser.). (ENG.). 40p. (J). (gr. 3-7). 5.95 *(978-1-55337-388-9(X))* Kids Can Pr., Ltd. CAN. Dist: Hachette Bk. Group.

Schwarz, Renée, jt. illus. see Schwarz, Renée.

Schwarz, Viviane. Cheese Belongs to You! Deacon, Alexis. 2013. (ENG.). 32p. (J). (gr. -1-1). 15.99 *(978-0-7636-6608-8(4))* Candlewick Pr.

—How to Put an Octopus to Bed: (Going to Bed Book, Read-Aloud Bedtime Book for Kids) Rinker, Sherri Duskey. 2020. (ENG.). 40p. (J). (gr. -1-k). 17.99 *(978-1-4521-4010-0(3))* Chronicle Bks. LLC.

—I Am Henry Finch. Deacon, Alexis. 2015. (ENG.). 40p. (J). (gr. k-3). 16.99 *(978-0-7636-7812-8(0))* Candlewick Pr.

—A Place to Call Home. Deacon, Alexis. 2011. (ENG.). 40p. (J). (gr. -1-2). 16.99 *(978-0-7636-5360-6(8))* Candlewick Pr.

—This Rock, That Rock: Poems Between You, Me & the Moon. Conlon, Dom. 2020. 80p. (J). (gr. 2-4). pap. 13.99 *(978-1-909991-92-7(9))* Troika Bks. GBR. Dist: Independent Pubs. Group.

Schwarz, Viviane. Animals with Tiny Cat. Schwarz, Viviane. 2018. (ENG.). 24p. (J). (-k). bds. 7.99 *(978-0-7636-9818-8(0))* Candlewick Pr.

—Counting with Tiny Cat. Schwarz, Viviane. (ENG.). (J). (-k). 2018. 24p. bds. 7.99 *(978-0-7636-9821-8(0))*; 2017. 32p. 14.99 *(978-0-7636-9462-3(2))* Candlewick Pr.

—How to Be on the Moon. Schwarz, Viviane. 2019. (ENG.). 32p. (J). (-k). 16.99 *(978-1-5362-0545-9(1))* Candlewick Pr.

—How to Find Gold. Schwarz, Viviane. 2016. 32p. (J). (-k). 16.99 *(978-0-7636-8104-3(0))* Candlewick Pr.

—Is There a Dog in This Book? Schwarz, Viviane. 2014. 32p. (J). (gr. -1-2). 16.99 *(978-0-7636-6991-1(1))* Candlewick Pr.

Schweitzer, Jeffrey. The Mundane Ghost. Schweitzer, Jeffrey. 2016. (ENG.). (J). (gr. 4-6). 30.00 *(978-0-692-77061-0(5))* Bindlestick Bks.

Schweitzer-Johnson, Betty. How Meg Changed Her Mind. Coffey, Ethel. 2014. (ENG.). 32p. (J). pap. 11.95 *(978-1-4525-8377-8(3)*, e7b1482b-f2d5-4e4b-92b8-2dccfac19860, Balboa Pr.) Author Solutions, Inc.

Schweitzer, Patty. The Fox, the Badger, & the Bunny: A Dales Tale. Wolcott, P. A. Wolcott, K. Hannah, ed. 2009. 20p. pap. 24.95 *(978-1-60749-525-3(2))* America Star Bks.

Schweninger, Ann. Amanda Pig & Her Big Brother Oliver. Van Leeuwen, Jean. (Oliver Pig Ser.). 56p. (J). (gr. k-2). pap. 3.99 *(978-0-8072-1341-4(1)*, Listening Library) Random Hse. Audio Publishing Group.

—Amanda Pig & the Awful, Scary Monster. Van Leeuwen, Jean. 2004. (Oliver & Amanda Ser.). (ENG.). 48p. (J). (gr. 1-3). mass mkt. 3.99 *(978-0-14-240203-0(6)*, Penguin Young Readers) Penguin Young Readers Group.

—Amanda Pig & the Really Hot Day. Van Leeuwen, Jean. 2007. (Oliver & Amanda Ser.). (ENG.). 48p. (J). (gr. 1-3). pap. 4.99 *(978-0-14-240775-2(5)*, Penguin Young Readers) Penguin Young Readers Group.

—Amanda Pig & the Really Hot Day. Van Leeuwen, Jean. 2007. (Oliver & Amanda Ser.). 47p. (J). (gr. -1-3). 11.65 *(978-0-7569-8152-5(2))* Perfection Learning Corp.

—Amanda Pig & the Wiggly Tooth. Van Leeuwen, Jean. 2009. (Oliver & Amanda Ser.). (ENG.). 48p. (J). (gr. 1-3). mass mkt. 4.99 *(978-0-14-241290-9(2)*, Penguin Young Readers) Penguin Young Readers Group.

—Amanda Pig, First Grader. Van Leeuwen, Jean. 2007. (Oliver & Amanda Ser.). 40p. (J). *(978-1-4287-4781-4(8)*, Dial) Penguin Publishing Group.

—Amanda Pig, First Grader. Van Leeuwen, Jean. 2009. (Oliver & Amanda Ser.). (ENG.). 48p. (J). (gr. 1-3). mass mkt. 4.99 *(978-0-14-241276-3(7),* Penguin Young Readers) Penguin Young Readers Group.

—Tales of Oliver Pig. Van Leeuwen, Jean. (Oliver Pig Ser.). 64p. (J). (gr. k-2). pap. 3.99 *(978-0-8072-1334-6(9),* Listening Library) Random Hse. Audio Publishing Group.

Schwortz, Anna M. A B C Rhymetime. Schwortz, Anna M. Schwortz, Anna M., ed. 2005. 48p. (J). (gr. k-3). pap. *(978-0-9769719-0-0(9))* AnnArt Pr.

Sciarrone, Claudio. Finding Nemo. Bazaldua, Charles. 2020. (Disney & Pixar Movies Ser.). (ENG.). 48p. (J). (gr. 2-6). lib. bdg. 28.50 ***(978-1-5321-4549-0(7),*** 35196, Graphic Novels) Spotlight.

—Wall*e. Ferrari, Alessandro. 2020. (Disney & Pixar Movies Ser.). (ENG.). 52p. (J). (gr. 2-6). lib. bdg. 28.50 ***(978-1-5321-4556-8(X),*** 35203, Graphic Novels) Spotlight.

Sciarrone, Claudio. Welcome to the City! (Dora & Friends) Golden Books. 2014. (ENG.). 48p. (J). (gr. -1-2). pap. 3.99 *(978-0-385-38412-4(2),* Golden Bks.) Random Hse. Children's Bks.

Sciarrone, Claudio, jt. illus. see Golden Books Staff.

Sciascia, Salvatore. Papá Guillermo y los Pájaros. Sartori, Gloria. Brignole, Giancarla, tr. rev. ed. 2007. (Fabulas De Familia Ser.). (SPA & ENG.). 32p. (J). pap. 6.95 *(978-970-20-0256-7(7))* Castillo, Ediciones, S. A. de C. V. MEX. Dist: Macmillan.

Sciulli, Erika. No Andy No! Brant, Dennis, Jr. 2008. 18p. pap. 24.95 *(978-1-60703-203-8(1))* America Star Bks.

Sciuto, Alex. Energy & Waves Through Infographics. Rowell, Rebecca. 2013. (Super Science Infographics Ser.). (ENG.). 32p. (J). (gr. 3-5). pap. 8.99 *(978-1-4677-1590-4(5))* Lerner Publishing Group.

—Natural Disasters Through Infographics. Higgins, Nadia. 2013. (Super Science Infographics Ser.). (ENG.). 32p. (J). (gr. 3-5). pap. 8.99 *(978-1-4677-1593-5(X));* lib. bdg. 26.65 *(978-1-4677-1287-3(6),* Lerner Pubns.) Lerner Publishing Group.

—US Government Through Infographics. Higgins, Nadia. 2014. (Super Social Studies Infographics Ser.). (ENG.). 32p. (J). (gr. 3-5). pap. 8.99 *(978-1-4677-4567-3(7));* lib. bdg. 26.65 *(978-1-4677-3463-9(2),* Lerner Pubns.) Lerner Publishing Group.

Scobie, Andrea. Erica from America & the Start of the Gang of Four. Waldman, Alan/A. 2013. 44p. pap. *(978-0-9840514-2-7(2))* Roxby Media Ltd.

Scobie, Lorna. Pairs! in the Garden. Prasadam-Halls, Smriti. 2017. (Pairs Ser.). (ENG.). 12p. (J). (gr. -1-k). bds. 12.99 *(978-1-84780-883-7(2),* Frances Lincoln Children's Bks.) Quarto Publishing Group UK GBR. Dist: Hachette UK Distribution.

—The Variety of Life. Davies, Nicola. 2018. (ENG.). 64p. (J). (gr. k). 16.95 *(978-1-4549-3188-1(4))* Sterling Publishing Co., Inc.

Scoggins, Jocelyn. Jocelyn's Theatre. Achilles, Carole. 2011. 20p. pap. 24.95 *(978-1-4560-8333-5(3))* America Star Bks.

Scolari, Silvano, jt. illus. see Legramandi, Francesco.

Scolero, Elizabeth. ABCs by Jesus & Me. Grapes, Elizabeth. 2015. 60p. 22.95 *(978-1-939930-57-6(X),* Belle Isle Bks.) Brandylane Pubs., Inc.

Scoles, Jessica. The Crow & the Earthquake: A Tale from the Oak Woodlands of California. Martin, Merci & Bishop, Wanda. 2017. (ENG.). 40p. (J). (gr. k-2). 17.99 *(978-0-9857932-3-4(6))* Cupola Pr.

Scoresby, Natassia a. Ark Tales. Hough, William E. 2019. (ENG.). 30p. (J). pap. 9.98 ***(978-1-6887-6389-0(9))*** Independently Published.

Scorey, John, jt. illus. see Shackell, John.

Scott, A. O. Treasure Trove of Pirate Stories: A Collection of Best Pirate Stories for Young People. Kessler, Ramon Wilke. 2011. 294p. 48.95 *(978-1-258-05706-0(9))* Literary Licensing, LLC.

Scott, Angela, photos by. Tigers of Ranthambore. Scott, Jonathan. 2017. (Cambridge Reading Adventures Ser.). (ENG., 24p. pap. 7.87 *(978-1-108-43613-7(7))* Cambridge Univ. Pr.

Scott, Angela, jt. illus. see Scott, Jonathan.

Scott, Ann. Isaac & the Red Jumper. Seyderhelm, Amanda. 2013. 26p. pap. *(978-0-9572146-1-3(8))* HARK Pubns.

Scott, Ashley. Ms. Abrams' Everything Garden. Colodny, Lisa & Colodny, Samantha. 2018. (ENG.). 58p. (J). (gr. k-6). pap. 9.99 *(978-1-970068-79-5(5))* Kingston Publishing Co.

Scott, Bob. Happiness Is a Warm Blanket, Charlie Brown! Pastis, Stephan & Schulz, Charles M. 2011. (Peanuts Ser.). (ENG.). 96p. (J). (gr. 3). 19.99 *(978-1-60886-682-3(3))* Boom! Studios.

—Peanuts Happiness Is a Warm Blanket, Charlie Brown. Pastis, Stephan & Schulz, Charles M. 2011. (Peanuts Ser.). (ENG.). 96p. (J). (gr. 3). pap. 9.99 *(978-1-60886-681-6(5))* Boom! Studios.

Scott, Brandon James. The Dog Who Wanted to Fly. Stinson, Kathy. 2019. (ENG.). 36p. (J). (gr. -1-1). 17.95 *(978-1-77321-280-7(X))* Annick Pr., Ltd. CAN. Dist: Publishers Group West (PGW).

—The Pancake Express. 2012. (Justin Time Ser.). (ENG.). 36p. (J). (gr. -1-3). 15.95 *(978-1-59702-035-0(4))* Immedium.

Scott, Chelsey. Ah-Choo - God Bless You. Jahn, Benny. 2009. 24p. pap. 11.95 *(978-1-60844-178-5(4))* Dog Ear Publishing, LLC.

Scott, Christopher L. I'm Mommy's Little Helper. Pendleton, Claudette M. 2012. 46p. 24.95 *(978-1-4626-9303-0(2));* 48p. pap. 24.95 *(978-1-4626-7427-5(5))* America Star Bks.

Scott, Concetta C. Move over, Mother Goose! Finger Plays, Action Verses & Funny Rhymes. Dowell, Ruth I. Charner, Kathy, ed. 2004. 126p. (Orig.). (gr. -1-1). pap. 12.95 *(978-0-87659-113-0(6),* 10006) Gryphon Hse., Inc.

Scott, Damion. Accel Vol. 2: Pop Quiz. Casey, Joe. 2018. (ENG.). 144p. (YA). pap. 14.99 *(978-1-941302-75-0(0),* 06c08c88-9f94-4ab0-9fd5-46c2a518cfdd, Lion Forge) Oni Pr., Inc.

—Accel Vol. 3: Turf Battles. Casey, Joe. 2018. (ENG.). 144p. (YA). pap. 14.99 *(978-1-941302-79-8(3),* 1c85a7ce-8037-43fb-ac9a-d94e7636559b, Lion Forge) Oni Pr., Inc.

—Here There Be the Monsters, Vol. 3. Jenkins, Paul. 2004. (Spider-Man Ser.). 144p. (YA). 9.99 *(978-0-7851-1333-1(9))* Marvel Worldwide, Inc.

Scott-Daniel, Toni. The Adventures of Super T: The Missing Blanket, Jackson, Gwendolyn. 2004. 32p. (J). lib. bdg. 15.95 *(978-0-9753434-0-1(8))* LeTay Publishing.

Scott, E. I Want My Kitty Cat Tv! Lee, G. 2012. 24p. pap. 24.95 *(978-1-4626-6610-2(8))* America Star Bks.

Scott Edgar. Derek Dool Supercool 2: Going Viral. Beck, Adrian. 2020. (Derek Dool Supercool Ser.: 2). 256p. (J). (gr. 2-4). 14.99 ***(978-1-76089-296-8(3),*** Puffin) Penguin Random Hse. AUS. Dist: Independent Pubs. Group.

Scott, Galvin. I Love You Because... Linn, Susie. 2020. (5-Minute Stories Portrait Padded Board B Ser.). (ENG.). 22p. (J). (— 1). bds. 9.99 ***(978-1-78958-635-0(6))*** Top That! Publishing PLC GBR. Dist: Independent Pubs. Group.

Scott, Gavin. Amemos Como Jesús, 1 vol. Fodor, Cecile Olesen. 2019. (SPA.). 10p. (J). 8.99 *(978-1-4041-0992-6(7))* Grupo Nelson.

—Biblia Dios Me Ama: Entrañables Historias Que Nos Hablan Del Amor de Dios, 1 vol. Fodor, Cecile Olesen. 2019. (SPA.). 40p. (J). bds. 12.99 *(978-1-4041-1010-6(0))* Grupo Nelson.

—Cuddle Bear. Freedman, Claire. (J). 2018. *(978-1-61067-730-1(7));* 2013. 28p. 12.99 *(978-1-61067-081-4(7))* Kane Miller.

Scott, Gavin. I Love You Because... Linn, Susie. 2020. (Padded Picture Storybook Ser.). (ENG.). 24p. (J). 12.99 ***(978-1-78958-629-9(1))*** Top That! Publishing PLC GBR. Dist: Independent Pubs. Group.

Scott, Gavin. My Bedtime Bible Prayers, 1 vol. Pedersen, Karoline Pahus. 2019. 96p. (J). (gr. 1). 10.99 *(978-0-8254-4633-7(3))* Kregel Pubns.

—My Christmas Story Tree, 1 vol. Simon, Mary Manz. 2018. (ENG.). 20p. (J). bds. 8.99 *(978-0-310-76125-9(5))* Zonderkidz.

—My God Loves Me Bible, 1 vol. Fodor, Cecilie. 2019. 40p. (J). (-k). bds. 12.99 *(978-0-8254-4632-0(5))* Kregel Pubns.

—My Precious Little Bear. Freedman, Claire. 2011. (ENG.). 20p. (J). (gr. k — 1). 8.99 *(978-0-545-27432-6(X),* Cartwheel Bks.) Scholastic, Inc.

—Oraciones Bíblicas para la Noche: Lindas Oraciones para la Hora de Dormir, 1 vol. Pedersen, Karoline Pahus. 2019. (SPA.). 96p. (J). 9.99 *(978-1-4041-0991-9(9))* Grupo Nelson.

—Sigamos a Jesús, 1 vol. Fodor, Cecile Olesen. 2019. (SPA.). 10p. (J). bds. 8.99 *(978-1-4041-0994-0(3))* Grupo Nelson.

—You're My Little Bunny. Freedman, Claire. 2010. (ENG.). 20p. (J). (gr. k — 1). bds. 8.99 *(978-0-545-20721-8(5),* Cartwheel Bks.) Scholastic, Inc.

Scott, Greg. X Isle, Vol.1. Cosby, Andrew & Nelson, Michael Alan. 2007. (ENG.). 128p. per. 14.99 *(978-1-934506-09-7(5))* Boom! Studios.

Scott, Greg, jt. illus. see Larroca, Salvador.

Scott, Jane Beecher. The Amazing Mosquito Bridge Secret. Scott, Jane Beecher, photos by. Scott, Jane Beecher. Scott, Jane Beecher, ed. 5th ed. 2004. 32p. (J). (gr. k-12). 12.95 *(978-0-9763077-0-9(7))* Beecher Scott.

Scott, Jane Wooster. Mitzi's World: Seek & Discover More Than 150 Details in 15 Works of Folk Art. Raffin, Deborah. 2009. (ENG.). 32p. (J). (gr. -1-3). 18.95 *(978-0-8109-8004-4(5),* Abrams Bks. for Young Readers) Abrams, Inc.

Scott, Jennifer. The Clumsiest Spider. Harney Jr., Robert. 2011. 44p. pap. 24.95 *(978-1-4626-2166-8(X))* America Star Bks.

Scott, Joanna. You Can Do It Tom Mouse! Barr, Dicky. 2018. (ENG.). 34p. (J). pap. *(978-1-9999569-0-5(7))* Tom Mouse Publishing.

Scott, John. The Adventures of Curious the Dragonfly - Search for Good Feelings. Fox, Stephanie. 2019. (Adventures of Curious the Dragonfly Ser.: Vol. 1). (ENG.). 48p. (J). pap. 10.99 *(978-1-0779-0768-3(0))* Independently Published.

Scott, Jonathan & Scott, Angela. Africa's Big Three: Band 07/Turquoise (Collins Big Cat) Scott, Jonathan & Scott, Angela. 2006. (Collins Big Cat Ser.). (ENG.). 24p. (J). (gr. 2-2). pap. 8.99 *(978-0-00-718693-8(2))* HarperCollins Pubs. Ltd. GBR. Dist: Independent Pubs. Group.

—Big Cat Babies: Band 05/Green (Collins Big Cat) Scott, Jonathan & Scott, Angela. 2005. (Collins Big Cat Ser.). (ENG.). 48p. (J). (gr. k-1). pap. 8.95 *(978-0-00-718594-8(4))* HarperCollins Pubs. Ltd. GBR. Dist: Independent Pubs. Group.

—Kings of the Wild: Band 13/Topaz (Collins Big Cat) Scott, Jonathan & Scott, Angela. 2007. (Collins Big Cat Ser.). (ENG.). 48p. (J). (gr. 2-4). pap. 10.99 *(978-0-00-723085-3(0))* HarperCollins Pubs. Ltd. GBR. Dist: Independent Pubs. Group.

—Living Dinosaurs: Band 08/Purple (Collins Big Cat) Scott, Jonathan & Scott, Angela. 2007. (Collins Big Cat Ser.). (ENG.). 24p. (J). (gr. k-1). pap. 8.99 *(978-0-00-718673-0(8))* HarperCollins Pubs. Ltd. GBR. Dist: Independent Pubs. Group.

—The Masai: Tribe of Warriors: Band 15/Emerald (Collins Big Cat) Scott, Jonathan & Scott, Angela. 2007. (Collins Big Cat Ser.). (ENG.). 48p. (J). (gr. 3-4). pap. 11.99 *(978-0-00-723097-6(4))* HarperCollins Pubs. Ltd. GBR. Dist: Independent Pubs. Group.

Scott, Judy. Can Daddy Stay Home & Play? Floyd, Gina. 2011. 28p. pap. 12.99 *(978-1-4567-1373-7(6))* AuthorHouse.

Scott, Julie. The Little Creek. Ward, Jennifer. 2005. 28p. (J). (gr. 3-7). pap. 7.95 *(978-1-58369-057-4(3))* Western National Parks Assn.

Scott, Katie. Animalium. Broom, Jenny. 2014. (Welcome to the Museum Ser.). (ENG.). 112p. (J). (gr. 3-7). 35.00 *(978-0-7636-7508-0(3),* Big Picture Press) Candlewick Pr.

—Animalium Activity Book. Big Picture Press, Big Picture. 2016. (ENG.). 72p. (J). (gr. 2-5). 14.99 *(978-0-7636-8919-3(X),* Big Picture Press) Candlewick Pr.

—Animalium Poster Book. Davidson, Susanna. 2017. (ENG.). 56p. (J). (gr. 2-4). pap. 22.00 *(978-0-7636-9318-3(9),* Big Picture Press) Candlewick Pr.

—Botanicum: Welcome to the Museum. Willis, Kathy. 2017. (Welcome to the Museum Ser.). (ENG.). 112p. (J). (gr. 3-7). 35.00 *(978-0-7636-8923-0(8),* Big Picture Press) Candlewick Pr.

Scott, Katie. Animalium Coloring Book. Scott, Katie. 2017. (ENG.). 96p. (J). (gr. 2-4). pap. 14.99 *(978-0-7636-9555-2(6),* Big Picture Press) Candlewick Pr.

Scott, Kimberley. The Black & White Club. Hemming, Alice. 2019. (Early Bird Readers — Orange (Early Bird Stories (tm)) Ser.). (ENG.). 32p. (J). (gr. k-3). pap. 7.99 *(978-1-5415-7411-3(7),* 9781541574113, Lerner Pubns.) Lerner Publishing Group.

—Cinderella: A Wheel-Y Silly Fairy Tale. Gallo, Tina. 2011. (Little Simon Sillies Ser.). (ENG.). 14p. (J). (gr. -1-1). lib. bdg. 5.99 *(978-1-4424-2106-6(1),* Little Simon) Little Simon.

—George & the New Craze. Hemming, Alice. 2019. (Early Bird Readers — Green (Early Bird Stories (tm)) Ser.). (ENG.). 32p. (J). (gr. k-3). pap. 7.99 *(978-1-5415-7406-9(0),* 9781541574069, Lerner Pubns.) Lerner Publishing Group.

—A Gold Star for George. Hemming, Alice. 2019. (Early Bird Readers — Orange (Early Bird Stories (tm)) Ser.). (ENG.). 32p. (J). (gr. k-3). pap. 7.99 *(978-1-5415-7413-7(3),* 9781541574137, Lerner Pubns.) Lerner Publishing Group.

—The Terrible Time Without Tilly. McKay, Hilary. 2014. (Red Bananas Ser.). (ENG.). 48p. (J). (gr. k-2). pap. 5.99 *(978-1-4052-6080-0(7))* Egmont Bks., Ltd. GBR. Dist: Independent Pubs. Group.

—Wipe-Clean First Math. 2014. (ENG.). (J). (gr. k-4). pap. 7.99 *(978-0-7945-3354-0(X),* Usborne) EDC Publishing.

—Wipe-Clean First Words. 2014. (ENG.). (J). (gr. k-2). pap. 7.99 *(978-0-7945-3331-1(0),* Usborne) EDC Publishing.

—Wipe-Clean Telling the Time. Greenwell, Jessica. 2013. (Usborne Wipe-Clean Ser.). (ENG.). 20p. (J). (gr. -1-3). pap. 7.99 *(978-0-7945-3403-5(1),* Usborne) EDC Publishing.

Scott, Kimberley, jt. illus. see Francis, John.

Scott, Kimberly & Dean, Venetia. Whiz Kid Science, 1 vol. Claybourne, Anna. 2014. (Whiz Kid Science Ser.). (ENG.). 32p. (J). (gr. 2-4). 183.90 *(978-1-4109-6751-0(4),* Raintree) Capstone.

Scott, Korey. The Energy Bus for Kids: A Story about Staying Positive & Overcoming Challenges. Gordon, Jon. 2012. (ENG.). 48p. (J). (gr. k-4). 17.00 *(978-1-118-28735-4(5),* Wiley) Wiley, John & Sons, Inc.

—Eric & the Enchanted Leaf: A Night with Echo. Frontiera, Deborah. 2007.Tr. of Eric y la hojita encantada: una noche con Eco. (SPA.). 32p. (J). *(978-0-9795474-2-3(3))* KAM Publishing.

—Eric & the Enchanted Leaf: The First Adventure, Frontiera, Deborah K. 2nd I.t. ed. 2004. 32p. (J). pap. 16.95 *(978-0-9753410-0-1(6))* Jade Enterprises.

—Eric & the Enchanted Leaf / Eric y la Hoja Encantada: A Visit with Canis Lupis / una Visita con Canis Lupis. Frontiera, Deborah K. Santillan-Cruz, Silvia R., tr. 2nd I.t. ed. 2005. (SPA & ENG.). 32p. (J). lib. bdg. 16.95 *(978-0-9663629-8-5(5))* By Grace Enterprises.

—How Do We Stay on Earth? A Gravity Mystery, 1 vol. Hansen, Amy S. 2011. (First Graphics: Science Mysteries Ser.). (ENG.). 24p. (J). (gr. k-3). pap. 6.29 *(978-1-4296-7174-3(2),* Capstone Pr.); (gr. 1-2). pap. 35.70 *(978-1-4296-7178-1(5))* Capstone.

—Simon & Company: Flea Market Mice. Wright, Mary H. & Frontiera, Deborah K. I.t. ed. 2016. (ENG.). 110p. (J). (gr. 2). pap. 11.99 *(978-1-940591-04-9(X))* By Grace Enterprises.

—Where Does the Sun Go at Night? An Earth Science Mystery, 1 vol. Hansen, Amy S. 2011. (First Graphics: Science Mysteries Ser.). (ENG.). 24p. (J). (gr. k-3). pap. 6.29 *(978-1-4296-7176-7(9));* (J). (gr. k-3). lib. bdg. 24.65 *(978-1-4296-6098-3(8));* (gr. 1-2). pap. 35.70 *(978-1-4296-7180-4(7))* Capstone.

Scott, Korey & McDee, Katie. First Graphics: Science Mysteries: A Science Mystery. Hansen, Amy S. & Olien, Rebecca. 2011. (First Graphics: Science Mysteries Ser.). (ENG.). 24p. (J). (gr. k-3). pap., pap., pap. 25.16 *(978-1-4296-7181-1(5));* (gr. 1-2). pap. 142.80 *(978-1-4296-7182-8(3))* Capstone.

Scott, Larry. Patsy Goes to a New Home: The Patsy Adventures Volume 1. Russell, Peggy. 2008. 16p. pap. 24.95 *(978-1-60703-799-6(8))* America Star Bks.

Scott, Lindsay. My Little Book of Bible Stories. 2016. (ENG.). 32p. (J). (gr. -1-k). mass mkt. 3.99 *(978-1-58925-487-9(2))* Tiger Tales.

Scott, Lucy. Busy Busy! Scott, Lucy. 2016. (ENG.). 32p. (J). (gr. -1-k). 15.99 *(978-1-939547-25-5(3))* Creston Bks.

Scott, Marc. We Both Read-the Oprah Winfrey Story. McKay, Sindy. 2009. (We Both Read Ser.). (ENG.). 44p. (J). (gr. k-3). 17.44 *(978-1-60115-241-1(8))* Treasure Bay, Inc.

Scott, Mario. I Am Smart, after All! Alves-Malcolm, Greta. 2018. (ENG.). 32p. (J). pap. *(978-976-96154-0-3(4))* Alves-Malcolm, Greta.

—¡todos Somos Inteligentes! Alves-Malcolm, Greta. Nelson Hudgson, Tanya Melisa, tr. 2018. (SPA.). 32p. (J). pap. *(978-976-96154-2-7(0))* Alves-Malcolm, Greta.

Scott, Matthew. Whizz Kidz: Brain Puzzles. Potter, William. 2018. (Whizz Kidz Puzzles Ser.). (ENG.). 96p. (J). pap. 9.99 *(978-1-78888-255-2(5),* 4ba03976-5c69-444c-a0fe-8135cb4c9f93) Arcturus Publishing GBR. Dist: Baker & Taylor Publisher Services (BTPS).

—Whizz Kidz: Number Puzzles. Potter, William. 2018. (Whizz Kidz Puzzles Ser.: 4). (ENG.). 96p. (J). pap. 9.99 *(978-1-78888-256-9(3),* 42373160-5ef3-44cb-b017-3144a072f4d5) Arcturus Publishing GBR. Dist: Baker & Taylor Publisher Services (BTPS).

Scott, Peter. Birds Lift-the-Flap. Khan, Sarah. 2004. (Luxury Lift-the-Flap Ser.). 16p. (J). (gr. 1-18). 11.95 *(978-0-7945-0714-5(X),* Usborne) EDC Publishing.

—Creepy Crawlies Lift-the-Flap. Khan, Sarah. 2005. (Luxury Lift-the-Flap Learners Ser.). 16p. (J). (gr. 1-18). 11.95 *(978-0-7945-0763-3(8),* Usborne) EDC Publishing.

—Los Dinosaurios Con Cuatro Puzzles Sencillos. Turnbull, Stephanie. 2004. (Titles in Spanish Ser.). (SPA.). 6p. (J). 8.95 *(978-0-7460-6109-1(9),* Usborne) EDC Publishing.

—Dinosaurs. Greenwell, Jessica. 2010. (Lift & Look Board Bks.). 12p. (J). bds. 9.99 *(978-0-7945-2585-9(7),* Usborne) EDC Publishing.

—Dragons Jigsaw Book. Tatchell, Judy & Rogers, Kirsteen. 2005. (Usborne Jigsaw Bks.). 12p. (J). (gr. -1-3). bds. 14.95 *(978-0-7945-1117-3(1),* Usborne) EDC Publishing.

—Dragons Lift-the-flap. Tatchell, Judy. 2005. 16p. (J). (gr. 1-18). 11.99 *(978-0-7945-0968-2(1),* Usborne) EDC Publishing.

—A Moment Like This: A Story of Love Between Parent & Child. Randall, Ronne. 2017. (ENG.). 26p. (J). 7.99 *(978-1-78670-311-8(4))* Igloo Bks. GBR. Dist: Simon & Schuster, Inc.

—See Inside the World of Dinosaurs. Frith, Alex. 2007. 16p. (J). bds. 13.99 *(978-0-7945-1436-5(7),* Usborne) EDC Publishing.

—Under the Sea Jigsaw Book. Rogers, Kirsteen. 2007. (Luxury Jigsaw Bks.). 14p. (J). bds. 14.99 *(978-0-7945-1330-6(1),* Usborne) EDC Publishing.

—Unicorns. Clarke, Phillip. 2006. (Luxury Lift-the-Flap Learners Ser.). 16p. (J). (gr. -1-3). 11.99 *(978-0-7945-1280-4(1),* Usborne) EDC Publishing.

Scott, Peter & JessT, Grant. Clarissa the Clown. Segal, Andrew. 2007. 32p. per. *(978-1-905823-20-8(7))* Panoma Pr. Ltd.

—Roberto the Robot. Segal, Andrew. 2007. 32p. per. *(978-1-905823-26-0(6))* Panoma Pr. Ltd.

Scott, Peter & Justine, Torode. Box of Bugs. 2005. 6p. (J). 11.95 *(978-0-7945-1023-7(X),* Usborne) EDC Publishing.

Scott, Peter David. Creepy Crawlies. Kahn, Sarah. 2006. (J). *(978-0-439-78702-4(5))* Scholastic, Inc.

—Dinosaur. 2006. 31p. (J). *(978-0-7607-7524-0(9))* backpackbook.

—Dinosaurs. Smith, Alastair & Tatchell, Judy. 2005. (J). *(978-0-439-68903-8(1))* Scholastic, Inc.

—Sharks. Clarke, Phillip & Furnival, Keith. 2005. (J). *(978-0-439-86358-2(9))* Scholastic, Inc.

—Under the Sea. Smith, Alastair & Tachell, Judy. 2007. (J). *(978-0-545-03305-3(5))* Scholastic, Inc.

Scott, Peter David & Furnival, Keith. Dragons. Tatchell, Judy. 2006. (J). *(978-0-439-82790-4(6))* Scholastic, Inc.

Scott, Rose Marie. Gentle Ones. Scott, Rose Marie. 2003. 60p. (J). lib. bdg. 22.95 *(978-1-59098-395-9(5))* Wooster Bk. Co., The.

Scott, Rosseau. The Snow That Just Wouldn't Stop. Ivan, Benson. 2008. 24p. (J). pap. 8.95 *(978-0-9774754-4-5(1))* Spiritbuilding Pubs.

Scott, Ruby & Farah, Jackie. Fifty Lemons: In English & Afaan Oromo. Ready Set Go Books. 2019. (ENG.). 30p. (J). pap. 9.99 ***(978-1-7030-6933-4(1))*** Independently Published.

Scott, Sarah C. Why Dogs Bark: & Other Tall Tales. Day, Ed D. 2006. 50p. (J). per. 12.95 *(978-1-933002-20-0(4))* PublishingWorks.

Scott, Sarah Chamberlin. Don't Slam the Door. Green, Holly G. 2005. (ENG.). 39p. (J). (gr. 2-7). 19.95 *(978-0-9744803-7-4(1))* PublishingWorks.

Scott, Stephen K. & Holbrook, Jef. The World According to Professor Petey. Scott, Stephen K. 2017. (ENG.). 46p. (J). pap. 12.95 *(978-0-9961370-4-1(1))* Kudzu King Productions.

Scott, Steve. Even a Hawkeye Can Cry. Parker, Jeff. 2014. (Avengers Ser.). (ENG.). 24p. (J). (gr. 2-6). lib. bdg. 27.07 *(978-1-61479-296-3(8),* 41, Marvel Age) Spotlight.

—Parrot in the Oven: Mi Vida. Martinez, Victor. rev. ed. 2004. (ENG.). 240p. (YA). (gr. 8-18). pap. 10.99 *(978-0-06-447186-2(1))* HarperCollins Español.

Scott, Summer. Cotton Tops on the Farm. Leffingwell, Paula. 2018. (ENG.). 27p. (J). 21.95 *(978-1-9772-0070-9(2))* Outskirts Pr., Inc.

Scott, Susan. An Amazing Adventure Back in Time. Cohen-Spence, Susan. 2013. 32p. pap. 14.99 *(978-0-9886360-4-0(2))* Kids At Heart Publishing, LLC.

—Gypsy. O'Connell, Isabel. 2012. 24p. pap. 12.99 *(978-0-9855202-8-1(0))* Kids At Heart Publishing, LLC.

Scott, Terri. The Little Island Bandit. Huber, Eric. 2019. (ENG.). 38p. (J). pap. 15.00 ***(978-1-0897-8675-7(1))*** Independently Published.

Scott, Vicki. Be a Good Sport, Charlie Brown! Schulz, Charles M. 2019. (Peanuts Ser.). (ENG.). 32p. (J). (gr. -1-2). pap. 4.99 *(978-1-5344-3028-0(8),* Simon Spotlight) Simon Spotlight.

—A Charlie Brown Christmas: Deluxe Edition. Schulz, Charles M. 2017. (Peanuts Ser.). (ENG.). 48p. (J). (gr. -1). 19.99 *(978-1-5344-0455-7(4),* Simon Spotlight) Simon Spotlight.

Scott, Vicki. A Charlie Brown Christmas: Pop-Up Edition. Schulz, Charles M. 2020. (Peanuts Ser.). (ENG.). 12p. (J). (gr. -1-3). 29.99 ***(978-1-5344-7087-3(5),*** Simon Spotlight) Simon Spotlight.

Scott, Vicki. It's the Easter Beagle, Charlie Brown. Schulz, Charles M. 2016. (Peanuts Ser.). (ENG.). 32p. (J). (gr. -1). 7.99 *(978-1-4814-6159-7(1),* Simon Spotlight) Simon Spotlight.

—It's the Great Pumpkin, Charlie Brown: Deluxe Edition. Schulz, Charles M. 2018. (Peanuts Ser.). (ENG.). 48p. (J). (gr. -1). 19.99 *(978-1-5344-1394-8(4),* Simon Spotlight) Simon Spotlight.

—My First 100 Peanuts Words. Schulz, Charles M. & Nakamura, May. 2018. (Peanuts Ser.). (ENG.). 26p. (J). (gr. -1-k). bds. 7.99 *(978-1-5344-2624-5(8),* Simon Spotlight) Simon Spotlight.

Scott, Vicki. Peanuts: Christmas Is Here! Holiday Gift Set. PI Kids. 2020. (Look & Find Ser.). (ENG.). 16p. (J). bds., bds. ***(978-1-5037-5661-8(0),*** d3031e1a-153b-48e5-a14d-0c05ba460eac, p i kids) Phoenix International Publications, Inc.

Scott, Vicki. Shoot for the Moon, Snoopy! Schulz, Charles M. 2019. (Peanuts Ser.). (ENG.). 24p. (J). (gr. -1-2). 12.99 (978-1-5344-5063-9(7)); pap. 6.99 (978-1-5344-5062-2(9)) Simon Spotlight. (Simon Spotlight).

—Snoopy Came to Play. Schulz, Charles M. 2018. (Peanuts Ser.). (ENG.). 32p. (J). (gr. -1-k). 17.99 (978-1-5344-1507-2(6)); pap. 4.99 (978-1-5344-1506-5(8)) Simon Spotlight. (Simon Spotlight).

—Snoopy's Christmas Surprise. Schulz, Charles M. 2018. (Peanuts Ser.). (ENG.). 16p. (J). (gr. -1-2). 5.99 (978-1-5344-2181-3(5), Simon Spotlight) Simon Spotlight.

—Who's Your Valentine, Charlie Brown? Schulz, Charles M. & Gallo, Tina. 2017. (Peanuts Ser.). (ENG.). 12p. (J). (gr. -1-k). bds. 5.99 (978-1-5344-0110-5(5), Simon Spotlight) Simon Spotlight.

—Woodstock's Sunny Day. Schulz, Charles M. 2019. (Peanuts Ser.). (ENG.). 14p. (J). (gr. -1-k). bds. 6.99 (978-1-5344-6016-4(0), Simon Spotlight) Simon Spotlight.

Scott, Vicki & Braddock, Paige. Charles M. Schulz' Snoopy. Schulz, Charles M. & Cooper, Jason. 2017. (Peanuts Ser.). (ENG.). 96p. (J). (gr. 3). 14.99 (978-1-68415-161-5(9)) Boom! Studios.

Scott, Vicki, jt. illus. see Braddock, Paige.

Scott, Vicki, jt. illus. see Charles M. Schulz Creative Associates.

Scott-Waters, Marilyn, jt. illus. see Everett, J. H.

Scotton, Rob, et al. I Love Snow: I Can Read 5-Book Box Set: Celebrate the Season by Snuggling up with 5 Snowy I Can Read Stories! George, Kallie et al. Drummond, Ree et al. 2019. (I Can Read Ser.). (ENG.). 160p. (J). (gr. -1-3). pap. 19.99 (978-0-06-289114-3(6)) HarperCollins Pubs.

Scotton, Rob. Love, Splat. Scotton, Rob. (Splat the Cat Ser.). (ENG.). 40p. (J). (gr. -1-2). 2011. 9.99 (978-0-06-207776-9(7)); 2008. 16.99 (978-0-06-083157-8(X)) HarperCollins Pubs.

—Merry Christmas, Splat. Scotton, Rob. (Splat the Cat Ser.). (ENG.). 40p. (J). (gr. -1-2). 2013. 9.99 (978-0-06-212450-0(1)); 2009. 16.99 (978-0-06-083160-8(X), HarperFestival) HarperCollins Pubs.

—Russell & the Lost Treasure. Scotton, Rob. 2006. (ENG.). 32p. (J). (gr. -1-2). 15.99 (978-0-06-059851-8(4)) HarperCollins Pubs.

—Russell the Sheep. Scotton, Rob. (ENG.). (J). (gr. -1-3). 2015. 32p. pap. 6.99 (978-0-06-239243-5(3), HarperFestival); 2011. 32p. pap. 6.99 (978-0-06-059850-1(6)); 2007. 16p. 9.99 (978-0-06-128434-2(3)); 2005. 32p. 17.99 (978-0-06-059848-8(4)) HarperCollins Pubs.

—Russell the Sheep Board Book. Scotton, Rob. 2009. (ENG.). 32p. (J). (gr. -1-3). bds. 7.99 (978-0-06-170996-8(4), HarperFestival) HarperCollins Pubs.

—Russell's Christmas Magic. Scotton, Rob. 2007. 32p. (J). (gr. -1-2). lib. bdg. 17.89 (978-0-06-059855-6(7)) HarperCollins Pubs.

—Scaredy-Cat, Splat! Scotton, Rob. (Splat the Cat Ser.). (ENG.). 40p. (J). (gr. -1-3). 2015. 9.99 (978-0-06-236897-3(4)); 2010. 16.99 (978-0-06-117760-6(1)); 2010. lib. bdg. 17.89 (978-0-06-117761-3(X)) HarperCollins Pubs. (HarperFestival).

—Secret Agent Splat! Scotton, Rob. 2012. (Splat the Cat Ser.). (ENG.). 40p. (J). (gr. -1-2). 16.99 (978-0-06-197871-5(X), HarperFestival) HarperCollins Pubs.

—Splat & the Cool School Trip. Scotton, Rob. 2013. (Splat the Cat Ser.). (ENG.). 40p. (J). (gr. -1-3). 17.99 (978-0-06-213386-1(1)) HarperCollins Pubs.

—Splat Says Thank You! Scotton, Rob. 2012. (Splat the Cat Ser.). (ENG.). 40p. (J). (gr. -1-3). 16.99 (978-0-06-197874-6(4), HarperFestival) HarperCollins Pubs.

—Splat the Cat. Scotton, Rob. 2008. (Splat the Cat Ser.). (ENG.). 40p. (J). (gr. -1-3). 17.99 (978-0-06-083154-7(5)); lib. bdg. 17.89 (978-0-06-083155-4(3)) HarperCollins Pubs.

—Splat the Cat: a Whale of a Tale. Scotton, Rob. 2013. (I Can Read Level 1 Ser.). (ENG.). 32p. (J). (gr. -1-3). 16.99 (978-0-06-209024-9(0)); pap. 4.99 (978-0-06-209022-5(4)) HarperCollins Pubs.

—Splat the Cat & the Big Secret. Scotton, Rob. 2016. (Splat the Cat Ser.). (ENG.). 24p. (J). (gr. -1-3). pap. 3.99 (978-0-06-229431-9(8), HarperFestival) HarperCollins Pubs.

Scotton, Rob. Splat the Cat & the Cat in the Moon. Scotton, Rob. 2020. (I Can Read Level 2 Ser.). (ENG.). 32p. (J). (gr. -1-3). pap. 4.99 **(978-0-06-269711-0(0)**, HarperCollins) HarperCollins Pubs. Ltd. GBR. Dist: HarperCollins Pubs.

Scotton, Rob. Splat the Cat & the Duck with No Quack. Scotton, Rob. 2011. (I Can Read Level 1 Ser.). (ENG.). 32p. (J). (gr. k-3). 16.99 (978-0-06-197858-6(2)); pap. 4.99 (978-0-06-197857-9(4)) HarperCollins Pubs.

—Splat the Cat & the Hotshot. Scotton, Rob. 2015. (I Can Read Level 1 Ser.). (ENG.). 32p. (J). (gr. -1-3). pap. 4.99 (978-0-06-229415-9(6)) HarperCollins Pubs.

—Splat the Cat & the Late Library Book. Scotton, Rob. 2016. (Splat the Cat Ser.). (ENG.). 24p. (J). (gr. -1-3). pap. 3.99 (978-0-06-229429-6(6), HarperFestival) HarperCollins Pubs.

—Splat the Cat & the Lemonade Stand. Scotton, Rob. 2019. (I Can Read Level 2 Ser.). (ENG.). 32p. (J). (gr. -1-3). 16.99 (978-0-06-269709-7(9)); pap. 4.99 (978-0-06-269708-0(0)) HarperCollins Pubs.

—Splat the Cat & the Pumpkin-Picking Plan: Includes More Than 30 Stickers! Scotton, Rob. 2014. (Splat the Cat Ser.). (ENG.). 24p. (J). (gr. -1-3). pap. 4.99 (978-0-06-211586-7(3)) HarperCollins Pubs.

—Splat the Cat & the Quick Chicks. Scotton, Rob. 2016. (I Can Read Level 1 Ser.). (ENG.). 32p. (J). (gr. -1-3). pap. 4.99 (978-0-06-229424-1(5)) HarperCollins Pubs.

—Splat the Cat & the Snowy Day Surprise. Scotton, Rob. 2014. (Splat the Cat Ser.). (ENG.). 16p. (J). (gr. -1-3). pap. 6.99 (978-0-06-197864-7(7), HarperFestival) HarperCollins Pubs.

—Splat the Cat: Back to School, Splat! Scotton, Rob. 2011. (Splat the Cat Ser.). (ENG.). 24p. (J). (gr. -1-3). pap. 3.99 (978-0-06-197851-7(5), HarperFestival) HarperCollins Pubs.

—Splat the Cat: Big Reading Collection. Scotton, Rob. 2012. (I Can Read Level 1 Ser.). (ENG.). 100p. (J). (gr. k-3). pap. 19.99 (978-0-06-209029-4(1)) HarperCollins Pubs.

—Splat the Cat: Blow, Snow, Blow. Scotton, Rob. 2013. (I Can Read Level 1 Ser.). (ENG.). 32p. (J). (gr. -1-3). 16.99 (978-0-06-209026-3(7)); pap. 4.99 (978-0-06-209027-0(5)) HarperCollins Pubs.

—Splat the Cat Board Book. Scotton, Rob. 2016. (Splat the Cat Ser.). (ENG.). 34p. (J). (gr. -1 — 1). bds. 7.99 (978-0-06-229436-4(9), HarperFestival) HarperCollins Pubs.

—Splat the Cat: Christmas Countdown. Scotton, Rob. 2015. (Splat the Cat Ser.). (ENG.). 12p. (J). (gr. -1 — 1). bds. 6.99 (978-0-06-197865-4(5), HarperFestival) HarperCollins Pubs.

—Splat the Cat: Doodle & Draw: A Coloring & Activity Book. Scotton, Rob. 2013. (Splat the Cat Ser.). (ENG.). 64p. (J). (gr. -1-3). 6.99 (978-0-06-211607-9(X), HarperFestival) HarperCollins Pubs.

—Splat the Cat Dreams Big. Scotton, Rob. 2013. (Splat the Cat Ser.). (ENG.). 24p. (J). (gr. -1-3). pap. 4.99 (978-0-06-209012-6(7), HarperFestival) HarperCollins Pubs.

—Splat the Cat: Fishy Tales. Scotton, Rob. 2012. (Splat the Cat Ser.). (ENG.). 24p. (J). (gr. -1-3). pap. 3.99 (978-0-06-197852-4(3), HarperFestival) HarperCollins Pubs.

—Splat the Cat for President. Scotton, Rob. 2016. (Splat the Cat Ser.). (ENG.). 24p. (J). (gr. -1-3). pap. 3.99 (978-0-06-229433-3(4), HarperFestival) HarperCollins Pubs.

—Splat the Cat: Funny Valentine. Scotton, Rob. 2012. (Splat the Cat Ser.). (ENG.). 16p. (J). (gr. -1-3). 6.99 (978-0-06-197862-3(0), HarperFestival) HarperCollins Pubs.

—Splat the Cat Gets a Job! Scotton, Rob. 2018. (I Can Read Level 2 Ser.). (ENG.). 32p. (J). (gr. -1-3). 16.99 (978-0-06-269706-6(4)); pap. 4.99 (978-0-06-269705-9(6)) HarperCollins Pubs.

—Splat the Cat Goes to the Doctor. Scotton, Rob. 2014. (Splat the Cat Ser.). (ENG.). 24p. (J). (gr. -1-3). pap. 4.99 (978-0-06-211588-1(X), HarperFestival) HarperCollins Pubs.

—Splat the Cat: Good Night, Sleep Tight. Scotton, Rob. 2011. (I Can Read Level 1 Ser.). (ENG.). 32p. (J). (gr. -1-3). 16.99 (978-0-06-197856-2(6)); pap. 4.99 (978-0-06-197855-5(8)) HarperCollins Pubs.

—Splat the Cat: I Scream for Ice Cream. Scotton, Rob. 2015. (I Can Read Level 1 Ser.). (ENG.). 32p. (J). (gr. -1-3). 16.99 (978-0-06-229419-7(9)); pap. 4.99 (978-0-06-229418-0(0)) HarperCollins Pubs.

—Splat the Cat Makes Dad Glad. Scotton, Rob. 2014. (I Can Read Level 1 Ser.). (ENG.). 32p. (J). (gr. -1-3). 16.99 (978-0-06-211599-7(5)); pap. 4.99 (978-0-06-211597-3(9)) HarperCollins Pubs.

—Splat the Cat: on with the Show. Scotton, Rob. 2013. (Splat the Cat Ser.). (ENG.). 24p. (J). (gr. -1-3). pap. 3.99 (978-0-06-209010-2(0), HarperFestival) HarperCollins Pubs.

—Splat the Cat: Oopsie-Daisy. Scotton, Rob. 2014. (Splat the Cat Ser.). (ENG.). 24p. (J). (gr. -1-3). pap. 4.99 (978-0-06-211585-0(5), HarperFestival) HarperCollins Pubs.

—Splat the Cat: Splat & Seymour, Best Friends Forevermore. Scotton, Rob. 2014. (I Can Read Level 1 Ser.). (ENG.). 32p. (J). (gr. -1-3). pap. 4.99 (978-0-06-211601-7(0)) HarperCollins Pubs.

—Splat the Cat: Splat & the New Baby. Scotton, Rob. 2018. (Splat the Cat Ser.). (ENG.). 40p. (J). (gr. -1-3). 17.99 (978-0-06-213389-2(6)) HarperCollins Pubs.

—Splat the Cat: Splat the Cat Sings Flat. Scotton, Rob. 2011. (I Can Read Level 1 Ser.). (ENG.). 32p. (J). (gr. -1-3). 16.99 (978-0-06-197854-8(X)); pap. 4.99 (978-0-06-197853-1(1)) HarperCollins Pubs.

—Splat the Cat: Sticker Fun. Scotton, Rob. 2013. (Splat the Cat Ser.). (ENG.). 100p. (J). (gr. -1-3). 12.99 (978-0-06-211594-2(4), HarperFestival) HarperCollins Pubs.

—Splat the Cat Takes the Cake. Scotton, Rob. 2012. (I Can Read Level 1 Ser.). (ENG.). 32p. (J). (gr. k-3). 16.99 (978-0-06-197860-9(4)); pap. 4.99 (978-0-06-197859-3(0)) HarperCollins Pubs.

—Splat the Cat: the Big Helper. Scotton, Rob. 2015. (Splat the Cat Ser.). (ENG.). 24p. (J). (gr. -1-3). pap. 4.99 (978-0-06-229427-2(X), HarperFestival) HarperCollins Pubs.

—Splat the Cat: the Name of the Game. Scotton, Rob. 2012. (I Can Read Level 1 Ser.). (ENG.). 32p. (J). (gr. -1-3). 16.99 (978-0-06-209015-7(1)) HarperCollins Pubs.

—Splat the Cat: the Perfect Present for Mom & Dad. Scotton, Rob. 2012. (Splat the Cat Ser.). (ENG.). 24p. (J). (gr. k-3). 4.99 (978-0-06-210009-2(2), HarperFestival) HarperCollins Pubs.

—Splat the Cat: the Rain Is a Pain. Scotton, Rob. 2012. (I Can Read Level 1 Ser.). (ENG.). 32p. (J). (gr. -1-3). 16.99 (978-0-06-209018-8(6)); pap. 4.99 (978-0-06-209017-1(8)) HarperCollins Pubs.

—Splat the Cat: Twice the Mice. Scotton, Rob. 2015. (I Can Read Level 1 Ser.). (ENG.). 32p. (J). (gr. -1-3). 16.99 (978-0-06-229422-7(9)); pap. 4.99 (978-0-06-229421-0(0)) HarperCollins Pubs.

—Splat the Cat: up in the Air at the Fair. Scotton, Rob. 2014. (I Can Read Level 1 Ser.). (ENG.). 32p. (J). (gr. -1-3). 16.99 (978-0-06-211596-6(0)); pap. 4.99 (978-0-06-211595-9(2)) HarperCollins Pubs.

—Splat the Cat: What Was That? Scotton, Rob. deluxe ed. 2013. (Splat the Cat Ser.). (ENG.). 12p. (J). (gr. k-3). pap. 6.99 (978-0-06-197863-0(9), HarperFestival) HarperCollins Pubs.

—Splat the Cat: Where's the Easter Bunny? Scotton, Rob. 2011. (Splat the Cat Ser.). (ENG.). 16p. (J). (gr. -1-1). pap. 6.99 (978-0-06-197861-6(2), HarperFestival) HarperCollins Pubs.

—Splat the Cat with a Bang & a Clang. Scotton, Rob. 2013. (I Can Read Level 1 Ser.). (ENG.). 32p. (J). (gr. -1-3). 16.99 (978-0-06-209021-8(6)) HarperCollins Pubs.

—Splish, Splash, Splat! Scotton, Rob. 2011. (Splat the Cat Ser.). (ENG.). 40p. (J). (gr. -1-3). 16.99 (978-0-06-197868-5(X)) HarperCollins Pubs.

—Splish, Splash, Splat! Board Book. Scotton, Rob. 2016. (Splat the Cat Ser.). (ENG.). 36p. (J). (gr. -1 — 1). bds. 7.99 (978-0-06-229438-8(5), HarperFestival) HarperCollins Pubs.

Scottorosano, Deborah. The Gift of Rainbows. Columbro, Judy. 2011. 24p. pap. 24.95 (978-1-4626-0355-8(6)) PublishAmerica, Inc.

—The Gift That Grows. Columbro, Judy. 2011. 28p. pap. 24.95 (978-1-4626-1800-2(6)) America Star Bks.

Scrace, Carolyn, jt. illus. see Lundie, Isobel.

Scrace, Carolyn, jt. illus. see Salariya, David.

Scrambly, Crab. The Floods #2: School Plot. Thompson, Colin. 2008. (Floods Ser.). (J). (ENG.). 224p. 15.99 (978-0-06-113861-4(4)); 256p. lib. bdg. 16.89 (978-0-06-113855-3(X)) HarperCollins Pubs.

—Good Neighbors. Thompson, Colin. 2008. (Floods Ser.: No. 1). 214p. (J). (gr. 3-7). 15.99 (978-0-06-113196-7(2)) HarperCollins Pubs.

Scribner, Carol A., photos by. To Life in the Small Corners, Scribner, Carol A. 2005. 232p. 48.00 (978-0-9752936-0-7(5)) Butterfly Productions, LLC.

Scribner, Margaret Rose. There's a Dragon in My Garden. Scribner, Benjamin. Scribner, Tina, ed. 2018. (ENG.). 34p. (J). pap. 9.50 (978-1-7266-6688-6(3)) Independently Published.

Scribner, Peter. Bennie & Thomas & the Rescue at Razor's Edge: Volume I. Scribner, Don. 2012. 44p. pap. 24.95 (978-1-4626-8957-6(4)) America Star Bks.

—Bennie & Thomas & the Rescue at Razor's Edge: Volume II. Scribner, Don. 2012. 48p. pap. 24.95 (978-1-4626-9472-3(1)) America Star Bks.

Scrivan, Maria. Nat Enough. Scrivan, Maria. 2020. (Nat Enough Ser.: 1). (ENG.). 240p. (J). (gr. 3-7). pap. 12.99 (978-1-338-53819-9(5)); lib. bdg. 24.99 (978-1-338-53821-2(7)) Scholastic, Inc. (Graphix).

Scriven, Luke. Tommy Tobotsky Tarantula III: The Sock Drawer Incident. Molinari, C. C. & Stanley, Elizabeth. 2019. (ENG.). 102p. (J). 26.95 **(978-1-64300-967-4(2))**; pap. 16.95 **(978-1-64300-966-7(4))** Covenant Bks.

Scroggs, Kirk. The Secret Spiral of Swamp Kid. Scroggs, Kirk. 2019. 160p. (J). (gr. 3-7). pap. 9.99 (978-1-4012-9068-9(X), DC Zoom) DC Comics.

Scruggs, Trina. Pinky & Peanut: The Adventure Begins. Cook, Deena & McIntosh, Cherie. 2007. 78p. (J). per. 4.99 (978-0-9797020-0-6(3)) P & P Publishing LLC.

Scruton, Ben. Romans. Gifford, Clive. 2016. (Reading Ladder Ser.). (ENG.). 32p. (J). (gr. 1-4). pap. 6.99 (978-1-4052-8043-3(3)) Egmont Bks., Ltd. GBR. Dist: Independent Pubs. Group.

Scruton, Clive. Dead Trouble. Gray, Keith. 90p. (J). pap. 7.50 (978-0-7497-4556-1(8)) Egmont Bks., Ltd. GBR. Dist: Trafalgar Square Publishing.

—Zack Can Fix It!, Vol. 4. Goldish, Meish. I.t. ed. 2005. (Sadlier Phonics Reading Program). 8p. (gr. -1-1). 23.00 net. (978-0-8215-7359-4(4)) Sadlier, William H. Inc.

Scudamore, Angelika. Collins Big Cat Phonics for Letters & Sounds - Tap It, Tip It!: Band 01A/Pink A. Ditchburn, Suzannah. 2020. (Collins Big Cat Phonics for Letters & Sounds Ser.). (ENG.). 16p. (J). (gr. -1-k). pap. 7.99 (978-0-00-835756-6(0)) HarperCollins Pubs. Ltd. GBR. Dist: Independent Pubs. Group.

Scudamore, Angelika, et al. Draw Your Own Animal Zendoodles. Huff, Abby. 2017. (Draw Your Own Zendoodles Ser.). (ENG.). 48p. (J). (gr. 4-8). lib. bdg. 31.99 (978-1-5157-4840-3(5), Capstone Pr.) Capstone.

Scudamore, Angelika. Happy Birthday to You! 2018. (Special Delivery Bks.). (ENG.). 8p. (J). (gr. -1 — 1). bds. 6.49 (978-1-68412-264-6(3), Silver Dolphin Bks.) Printers Row Publishing Group.

—I Love Matzah, Vol. Soban Biniashvili, Freidele Galya. 2020. (ENG.). 12p. (J). (gr. -1 — 1). bds. 6.99 (978-1-5415-5727-7(1), Kar-Ben Publishing) Lerner Publishing Group.

—Little Puppy's Busy Day. 2016. (J). (978-1-62885-142-7(2)) Kidsbooks, LLC.

—Math Mazes: Times Tables. Tafuni, Gabriele & Casey, Catherine. 2019. (Math Mazes Ser.). (ENG.). 96p. (J). pap. 9.99 (978-1-78950-023-3(0), 6ec05e46-f82d-45d7-9454-889d0dca3dbd) Arcturus Publishing GBR. Dist: Baker & Taylor Publisher Services (BTPS).

—My Easter Basket (die-Cut) The True Story of Easter. Simon, Mary Manz. 2016. (ENG.). 14p. (J). (gr. -1 — 1). bds. 12.99 (978-1-4336-8990-1(1), 005773752, B&H Kids) B&H Publishing Group.

—My March to the Manger: A Celebration of Jesus' Birth. Simon, Mary Manz. 2016. (ENG.). 14p. (J). (gr. -1 — 1). bds. 12.99 (978-1-4336-4525-9(4), 005788035, B&H Kids) B&H Publishing Group.

—Noah's Ark Animal ABCs, 1 vol. 2018. (ENG.). 28p. (J). bds. 9.99 (978-0-310-76700-8(8)) Zonderkidz.

—The Pumpkin Gospel (die-Cut) A Story of a New Start with God. Simon, Mary Manz. 2016. (ENG.). 14p. (J). (gr. -1 — 1). bds. 12.99 (978-1-4336-9163-8(9), 006102446, B&H Kids) B&H Publishing Group.

Scudamore, Angelika. Triceratops. Garnett, Jaye. Cottage Door Press, ed. 2020. (Smithsonian Kids Finger Puppet Board Book Ser.). (ENG.). 12p. (J). (gr. -1 — 1). bds. 6.99 **(978-1-68052-948-7(X)**, 1005910) Cottage Door Pr.

Scudamore, Angelika. Two by Two, 1 vol. Stauffer, Lisa Lowe. 2018. (ENG.). 18p. (J). bds. 8.99 (978-0-310-76273-7(1)) Zonderkidz.

Scudamore, Angelika. 1 2 3 4 Count Like a Dinosaur. Wage, Erin Rose. 2020. (Play-A-Sound Ser.). (ENG.). 20p. (J). bds. **(978-1-5037-4605-3(4)**, 0e4d07ef-fed2-4c6c-b64b-0f57f3740b88, p i kids) Phoenix International Publications, Inc.

Scull, Elaine. A Gift for the Children. Buck, Pearl S. 2020. (ENG.). 179p. (J). (gr. -1-3). pap. 17.99 **(978-1-5040-6014-1(8))** Open Road Integrated Media, Inc.

Scull, Marie-Louise. The Skit Book: 101 Skits from Kids. MacDonald, Margaret. 2006. (ENG.). 160p. (J). (gr. -1-12). per. 17.95 (978-0-87483-785-8(5)) August Hse. Pubs., Inc.

Scythe, Adam. Dark Oracle. Rayne, C. M. 2016. (ENG.). (J). pap. (978-615-80463-0-5(2)) GiziMap.

Seabaugh, Jan. Where Does the Water Come From? Shookuhi, Aminjon. Khodjibaev, Karim & Khodjibaeva, Moukhabbat, trs. 2009. 88p. (J). pap. 15.95 (978-0-9740551-2-1(3)) Smith, Viveca Publishing.

Seabaugh, Jan. Doctor Ouch. Seabaugh, Jan, tr. Chukovsky, Kornei. 2004. (Children's International Ser.: 1). Orig. Title: Aibolit. 43p. (J). pap. 6.99 (978-0-9740551-0-7(7)) Smith, Viveca Publishing.

Seabrooks, Lydia. The ed up Platypus. Young, Elizabeth. 2011. 20p. pap. 24.95 (978-1-4560-7028-1(2)) America Star Bks.

Seager, Maryann, et al. Sara Safety, School Safety: Kid's Activity Book. LaBerge, Margaret M. 2004. (J). pap. (978-0-9755561-1-5(8)) Reading Resc.

Seager, Patsy. Petey: Missing the Migration. Larter, Maureen. 2018. (Petey & His Family Ser.: Vol. 1). (ENG.). 70p. (J). pap. 14.50 (978-1-7274-0239-1(1)) CreateSpace Independent Publishing Platform.

Seager, Patsy. Petey: Missing the Migration. Larter, Maureen. 2018. (Petey & His Family Ser.: Vol. 1). (ENG.). 60p. (J). pap. **(978-0-9876393-8-7(2))** Sweetfields Publishing.

Seago, Ainsley. Bombo's Big Question. Will, Kipling. Arias, Elizabeth, tr. 2019. (SPA.). 36p. (J). pap. 9.13 (978-1-7296-4857-5(6)) CreateSpace Independent Publishing Platform.

—Bombo's Big Question. Will, Kipling. Amin, Shan, tr. 2019. (NOR.). 36p. (J). pap. 9.13 (978-1-7296-4866-7(5)) CreateSpace Independent Publishing Platform.

Seago, Danielle N. Faith over Fear. Hampton, Paige N. 2018. (ENG.). 24p. (J). pap. 9.99 (978-1-7287-1523-0(7)) Independently Published.

Seahorse, Risa. In the Swamp, Oh Yeah, in the Swamp. Ryan, Ruth. 2012. 54p. pap. (978-1-55483-922-3(X)) Insomniac Pr.

Seal, Julia. Abigail Santa's Secret Elf. Put Me In The Story & Sully, Katherine. 2018. (Santa's Secret Elf Ser.). (ENG.). 32p. (J). (-3). 5.99 **(978-1-4926-8111-3(3))** Sourcebooks, Inc.

—Addison Santa's Secret Elf. Put Me In The Story & Sully, Katherine. 2018. (Santa's Secret Elf Ser.). (ENG.). 32p. (J). (-3). 5.99 **(978-1-4926-8112-0(1))** Sourcebooks, Inc.

—Aiden Santa's Secret Elf. Put Me In The Story & Sully, Katherine. 2018. (Santa's Secret Elf Ser.). (ENG.). 32p. (J). (-3). 5.99 **(978-1-4926-8113-7(X))** Sourcebooks, Inc.

—Alexander Santa's Secret Elf. Put Me In The Story & Sully, Katherine. 2018. (Santa's Secret Elf Ser.). (ENG.). 32p. (J). (-3). 5.99 **(978-1-4926-8114-4(8))** Sourcebooks, Inc.

—Allison Santa's Secret Elf. Put Me In The Story & Sully, Katherine. 2018. (Santa's Secret Elf Ser.). (ENG.). 32p. (J). (-3). 5.99 **(978-1-4926-8115-1(6))** Sourcebooks, Inc.

—Amelia Santa's Secret Elf. Put Me In The Story & Sully, Katherine. 2018. (Santa's Secret Elf Ser.). (ENG.). 32p. (J). (-3). 5.99 **(978-1-4926-8116-8(4))** Sourcebooks, Inc.

—Andrew Santa's Secret Elf. Put Me In The Story & Sully, Katherine. 2018. (Santa's Secret Elf Ser.). (ENG.). 32p. (J). (-3). 5.99 **(978-1-4926-8117-5(2))** Sourcebooks, Inc.

—Anthony Santa's Secret Elf. Put Me In The Story & Sully, Katherine. 2018. (Santa's Secret Elf Ser.). (ENG.). 32p. (J). (-3). 5.99 **(978-1-4926-8118-2(0))** Sourcebooks, Inc.

—Aria Santa's Secret Elf. Put Me In The Story & Sully, Katherine. 2018. (Santa's Secret Elf Ser.). (ENG.). 32p. (J). (-3). 5.99 **(978-1-4926-8119-9(9))** Sourcebooks, Inc.

—Aubrey Santa's Secret Elf. Put Me In The Story & Sully, Katherine. 2018. (Santa's Secret Elf Ser.). (ENG.). 32p. (J). (-3). 5.99 **(978-1-4926-8120-5(2))** Sourcebooks, Inc.

—Ava Santa's Secret Elf. Put Me In The Story & Sully, Katherine. 2018. (Santa's Secret Elf Ser.). (ENG.). 32p. (J). (-3). 5.99 **(978-1-4926-8122-9(9))** Sourcebooks, Inc.

—Avery Santa's Secret Elf. Put Me In The Story & Sully, Katherine. 2018. (Santa's Secret Elf Ser.). (ENG.). 32p. (J). (-3). 5.99 **(978-1-4926-8123-6(7))** Sourcebooks, Inc.

Seal, Julia. Bad Dog & No, Nell, No! Dale, Elizabeth. 2019. (Early Bird Readers — Pink (Early Bird Stories (tm)) Ser.). (ENG.). 32p. (J). (gr. -1-2). pap. 7.99 (978-1-5415-4619-6(9)) Lerner Publishing Group.

Seal, Julia. Benjamin Santa's Secret Elf. Put Me In The Story & Sully, Katherine. 2018. (Santa's Secret Elf Ser.). (ENG.). 32p. (J). (-3). 5.99 **(978-1-4926-8124-3(5))** Sourcebooks, Inc.

—Brooklyn Santa's Secret Elf. Put Me In The Story & Sully, Katherine. 2018. (Santa's Secret Elf Ser.). (ENG.). 32p. (J). (-3). 5.99 **(978-1-4926-8125-0(3))** Sourcebooks, Inc.

—Camila Santa's Secret Elf. Put Me In The Story & Sully, Katherine. 2018. (Santa's Secret Elf Ser.). (ENG.). 32p. (J). (-3). 5.99 **(978-1-4926-8127-4(X))** Sourcebooks, Inc.

—Carter Santa's Secret Elf. Put Me In The Story & Sully, Katherine. 2018. (Santa's Secret Elf Ser.). (ENG.). 32p. (J). (-3). 5.99 **(978-1-4926-8128-1(8))** Sourcebooks, Inc.

—Charlotte Santa's Secret Elf. Put Me In The Story & Sully, Katherine. 2018. (Santa's Secret Elf Ser.). (ENG.). 32p. (J). (-3). 5.99 **(978-1-4926-8129-8(6))** Sourcebooks, Inc.

—Chloe Santa's Secret Elf. Put Me In The Story & Sully, Katherine. 2018. (Santa's Secret Elf Ser.). (ENG.). 32p. (J). (-3). 5.99 **(978-1-4926-8130-4(X))** Sourcebooks, Inc.

—Christopher Santa's Secret Elf. Put Me In The Story & Sully, Katherine. 2018. (Santa's Secret Elf Ser.). (ENG.). 32p. (J). (-3). 5.99 **(978-1-4926-8131-1(8))** Sourcebooks, Inc.

—Daniel Santa's Secret Elf. Put Me In The Story & Sully, Katherine. 2018. (Santa's Secret Elf Ser.). (ENG.). 32p. (J). (-3). 5.99 **(978-1-4926-8132-8(6))** Sourcebooks, Inc.

—David Santa's Secret Elf. Put Me In The Story & Sully, Katherine. 2018. (Santa's Secret Elf Ser.). (ENG.). 32p. (J). (-3). 5.99 ***(978-1-4926-8133-5(4))*** Sourcebooks, Inc.
—Dylan Santa's Secret Elf. Put Me In The Story & Sully, Katherine. 2018. (Santa's Secret Elf Ser.). (ENG.). 32p. (J). (-3). 5.99 ***(978-1-4926-8134-2(2))*** Sourcebooks, Inc.
—Elijah Santa's Secret Elf. Put Me In The Story & Sully, Katherine. 2018. (Santa's Secret Elf Ser.). (ENG.). 32p. (J). (-3). 5.99 ***(978-1-4926-8135-9(0))*** Sourcebooks, Inc.
—Elizabeth Santa's Secret Elf. Put Me In The Story & Sully, Katherine. 2018. (Santa's Secret Elf Ser.). (ENG.). 32p. (J). (-3). 5.99 ***(978-1-4926-8136-6(9))*** Sourcebooks, Inc.
—Ella Santa's Secret Elf. Put Me In The Story & Sully, Katherine. 2018. (Santa's Secret Elf Ser.). (ENG.). 32p. (J). (-3). 5.99 ***(978-1-4926-8137-3(7))*** Sourcebooks, Inc.
—Emily Santa's Secret Elf. Put Me In The Story & Sully, Katherine. 2018. (Santa's Secret Elf Ser.). (ENG.). 32p. (J). (-3). 5.99 ***(978-1-4926-8138-0(5))*** Sourcebooks, Inc.
—Emma Santa's Secret Elf. Put Me In The Story & Sully, Katherine. 2018. (Santa's Secret Elf Ser.). (ENG.). 32p. (J). (-3). 5.99 ***(978-1-4926-8139-7(3))*** Sourcebooks, Inc.
—Ethan Santa's Secret Elf. Put Me In The Story & Sully, Katherine. 2018. (Santa's Secret Elf Ser.). (ENG.). 32p. (J). (-3). 5.99 ***(978-1-4926-8140-3(7))*** Sourcebooks, Inc.
—Evelyn Santa's Secret Elf. Put Me In The Story & Sully, Katherine. 2018. (Santa's Secret Elf Ser.). (ENG.). 32p. (J). (-3). 5.99 ***(978-1-4926-8141-0(5))*** Sourcebooks, Inc.
Seal, Julia. Farmyard Words. 2016. (ENG.). 12p. (J). (gr. -1 — 1). bds. 6.99 *(978-1-4998-0260-3(9))* Little Bee Books Inc.
—Fly, Freddy, Fly. Joyce, Melanie. 2014. (J). *(978-1-4351-5806-1(7))* Barnes & Noble, Inc.
Seal, Julia. Gabriel Santa's Secret Elf. Put Me In The Story & Sully, Katherine. 2018. (Santa's Secret Elf Ser.). (ENG.). 32p. (J). (-3). 5.99 ***(978-1-4926-8142-7(3))*** Sourcebooks, Inc.
Seal, Julia. The Gift That I Can Give, 1 vol. Gifford, Kathie Lee. 2018. (ENG.). 32p. (J). 17.99 *(978-1-4002-0924-8(2))* Nelson, Thomas Inc.
—The Gift That I Can Give for Little Ones, 1 vol. Gifford, Kathie Lee. 2018. (ENG.). 26p. (J). bds. 9.99 *(978-1-4002-0925-5(0))* Nelson, Thomas Inc.
Seal, Julia. Grace Santa's Secret Elf. Put Me In The Story & Sully, Katherine. 2018. (Santa's Secret Elf Ser.). (ENG.). 32p. (J). (-3). 5.99 ***(978-1-4926-8143-4(1))*** Sourcebooks, Inc.
—Hannah Santa's Secret Elf. Put Me In The Story & Sully, Katherine. 2018. (Santa's Secret Elf Ser.). (ENG.). 32p. (J). (-3). 5.99 ***(978-1-4926-8144-1(X))*** Sourcebooks, Inc.
—Harper Santa's Secret Elf. Put Me In The Story & Sully, Katherine. 2018. (Santa's Secret Elf Ser.). (ENG.). 32p. (J). (-3). 5.99 ***(978-1-4926-8145-8(8))*** Sourcebooks, Inc.
—Henry Santa's Secret Elf. Put Me In The Story & Sully, Katherine. 2018. (Santa's Secret Elf Ser.). (ENG.). 32p. (J). (-3). 5.99 ***(978-1-4926-8146-5(6))*** Sourcebooks, Inc.
Seal, Julia. The Hungry Monster. Bucknell, Kate. 2018. (Little Monsters Ser.). (ENG.). 14p. (J). (gr. k-2). bds. 7.99 *(978-1-4867-1520-6(6),* c7d9fdeb-bb9e-47ad-8a2e-1b7392489284) Flowerpot Pr.
Seal, Julia. I Am Santa's Secret Elf. Put Me In The Story & Sully, Katherine. 2018. (Santa's Secret Elf Ser.). (ENG.). 32p. (J). (-3). 5.99 ***(978-1-4926-8182-3(2))***; 5.99 ***(978-1-4926-8181-6(4))*** Sourcebooks, Inc.
—Isaac Santa's Secret Elf. Put Me In The Story & Sully, Katherine. 2018. (Santa's Secret Elf Ser.). (ENG.). 32p. (J). (-3). 5.99 ***(978-1-4926-8147-2(4))*** Sourcebooks, Inc.
—Isabella Santa's Secret Elf. Put Me In The Story & Sully, Katherine. 2018. (Santa's Secret Elf Ser.). (ENG.). 32p. (J). (-3). 5.99 ***(978-1-4926-8148-9(2))*** Sourcebooks, Inc.
—Jackson Santa's Secret Elf. Put Me In The Story & Sully, Katherine. 2018. (Santa's Secret Elf Ser.). (ENG.). 32p. (J). (-3). 5.99 ***(978-1-4926-8149-6(0))*** Sourcebooks, Inc.
—Jacob Santa's Secret Elf. Put Me In The Story & Sully, Katherine. 2018. (Santa's Secret Elf Ser.). (ENG.). 32p. (J). (-3). 5.99 ***(978-1-4926-8150-2(4))*** Sourcebooks, Inc.
—James Santa's Secret Elf. Put Me In The Story & Sully, Katherine. 2018. (Santa's Secret Elf Ser.). (ENG.). 32p. (J). (-3). 5.99 ***(978-1-4926-8151-9(2))*** Sourcebooks, Inc.
—Jaxon Santa's Secret Elf. Put Me In The Story & Sully, Katherine. 2018. (Santa's Secret Elf Ser.). (ENG.). 32p. (J). (-3). 5.99 ***(978-1-4926-8556-2(9))*** Sourcebooks, Inc.
—Jayden Santa's Secret Elf. Put Me In The Story & Sully, Katherine. 2018. (Santa's Secret Elf Ser.). (ENG.). 32p. (J). (-3). 5.99 ***(978-1-4926-8152-6(0))*** Sourcebooks, Inc.
—John Santa's Secret Elf. Put Me In The Story & Sully, Katherine. 2018. (Santa's Secret Elf Ser.). (ENG.). 32p. (J). (-3). 5.99 ***(978-1-4926-8153-3(9))*** Sourcebooks, Inc.
—Joseph Santa's Secret Elf. Put Me In The Story & Sully, Katherine. 2018. (Santa's Secret Elf Ser.). (ENG.). 32p. (J). (-3). 5.99 ***(978-1-4926-8154-0(7))*** Sourcebooks, Inc.
—Joshua Santa's Secret Elf. Put Me In The Story & Sully, Katherine. 2018. (Santa's Secret Elf Ser.). (ENG.). 32p. (J). (-3). 5.99 ***(978-1-4926-8155-7(5))*** Sourcebooks, Inc.
Seal, Julia. Jungle 123. 2016. (ENG.). 12p. (J). (gr. -1 — 1). bds. 6.99 *(978-1-4998-0259-7(5))* Little Bee Books Inc.
Seal, Julia. Layla Santa's Secret Elf. Put Me In The Story & Sully, Katherine. 2018. (Santa's Secret Elf Ser.). (ENG.). 32p. (J). (-3). 5.99 ***(978-1-4926-8156-4(3))*** Sourcebooks, Inc.
Seal, Julia. The Lazy Monster. Bucknell, Kate. 2018. (Little Monsters Ser.). (ENG.). 14p. (J). (gr. k-2). bds. 7.99 *(978-1-4867-1521-3(4),* 945d1c58-1b80-45dc-bd27-e95c1e45cfdb) Flowerpot Pr.
Seal, Julia. Leah Santa's Secret Elf. Put Me In The Story & Sully, Katherine. 2018. (Santa's Secret Elf Ser.). (ENG.). 32p. (J). (-3). 5.99 ***(978-1-4926-8157-1(1))*** Sourcebooks, Inc.
—Liam Santa's Secret Elf. Put Me In The Story & Sully, Katherine. 2018. (Santa's Secret Elf Ser.). (ENG.). 32p. (J). (-3). 5.99 ***(978-1-4926-8158-8(X))*** Sourcebooks, Inc.
—Lillian Santa's Secret Elf. Put Me In The Story & Sully, Katherine. 2018. (Santa's Secret Elf Ser.). (ENG.). 32p. (J). (-3). 5.99 ***(978-1-4926-8159-5(8))*** Sourcebooks, Inc.
—Logan Santa's Secret Elf. Put Me In The Story & Sully, Katherine. 2018. (Santa's Secret Elf Ser.). (ENG.). 32p. (J). (-3). 5.99 ***(978-1-4926-8160-1(1))*** Sourcebooks, Inc.
—Lucas Santa's Secret Elf. Put Me In The Story & Sully, Katherine. 2018. (Santa's Secret Elf Ser.). (ENG.). 32p. (J). (-3). 5.99 ***(978-1-4926-8161-8(X))*** Sourcebooks, Inc.
—Madison Santa's Secret Elf. Put Me In The Story & Sully, Katherine. 2018. (Santa's Secret Elf Ser.). (ENG.). 32p. (J). (-3). 5.99 ***(978-1-4926-8162-5(8))*** Sourcebooks, Inc.
—Mason Santa's Secret Elf. Put Me In The Story & Sully, Katherine. 2018. (Santa's Secret Elf Ser.). (ENG.). 32p. (J). (-3). 5.99 ***(978-1-4926-8163-2(6))*** Sourcebooks, Inc.
—Matthew Santa's Secret Elf. Put Me In The Story & Sully, Katherine. 2018. (Santa's Secret Elf Ser.). (ENG.). 32p. (J). (-3). 5.99 ***(978-1-4926-8164-9(4))*** Sourcebooks, Inc.
—Mia Santa's Secret Elf. Put Me In The Story & Sully, Katherine. 2018. (Santa's Secret Elf Ser.). (ENG.). 32p. (J). (-3). 5.99 ***(978-1-4926-8165-6(2))*** Sourcebooks, Inc.
—Michael Santa's Secret Elf. Put Me In The Story & Sully, Katherine. 2018. (Santa's Secret Elf Ser.). (ENG.). 32p. (J). (-3). 5.99 ***(978-1-4926-8166-3(0))*** Sourcebooks, Inc.
—My Granddaughter Is Santa's Secret Elf. Put Me In The Story & Sully, Katherine. 2018. (Santa's Secret Elf Ser.). (ENG.). 32p. (J). (-3). 5.99 ***(978-1-4926-8171-7(7))*** Sourcebooks, Inc.
—My Grandson Is Santa's Secret Elf. Put Me In The Story & Sully, Katherine. 2018. (Santa's Secret Elf Ser.). (ENG.). 32p. (J). (-3). 5.99 ***(978-1-4926-8179-3(2))*** Sourcebooks, Inc.
—My Nephew Is Santa's Secret Elf. Put Me In The Story & Sully, Katherine. 2018. (Santa's Secret Elf Ser.). (ENG.). 32p. (J). (-3). 5.99 ***(978-1-4926-8126-7(1))*** Sourcebooks, Inc.
—My Niece Is Santa's Secret Elf. Put Me In The Story & Sully, Katherine. 2018. (Santa's Secret Elf Ser.). (ENG.). 32p. (J). (-3). 5.99 ***(978-1-4926-8121-2(0))*** Sourcebooks, Inc.
—Natalie Santa's Secret Elf. Put Me In The Story & Sully, Katherine. 2018. (Santa's Secret Elf Ser.). (ENG.). 32p. (J). (-3). 5.99 ***(978-1-4926-8167-0(9))*** Sourcebooks, Inc.
—Noah Santa's Secret Elf. Put Me In The Story & Sully, Katherine. 2018. (Santa's Secret Elf Ser.). (ENG.). 32p. (J). (-3). 5.99 ***(978-1-4926-8168-7(7))*** Sourcebooks, Inc.
—Oliver Santa's Secret Elf. Put Me In The Story & Sully, Katherine. 2018. (Santa's Secret Elf Ser.). (ENG.). 32p. (J). (-3). 5.99 ***(978-1-4926-8169-4(5))*** Sourcebooks, Inc.
—Olivia Santa's Secret Elf. Put Me In The Story & Sully, Katherine. 2018. (Santa's Secret Elf Ser.). (ENG.). 32p. (J). (-3). 5.99 ***(978-1-4926-8170-0(9))*** Sourcebooks, Inc.
—Samuel Santa's Secret Elf. Put Me In The Story & Sully, Katherine. 2018. (Santa's Secret Elf Ser.). (ENG.). 32p. (J). (-3). 5.99 ***(978-1-4926-8172-4(5))*** Sourcebooks, Inc.
—Savannah Santa's Secret Elf. Put Me In The Story & Sully, Katherine. 2018. (Santa's Secret Elf Ser.). (ENG.). 32p. (J). (-3). 5.99 ***(978-1-4926-8173-1(3))*** Sourcebooks, Inc.
—Scarlett Santa's Secret Elf. Put Me In The Story & Sully, Katherine. 2018. (Santa's Secret Elf Ser.). (ENG.). 32p. (J). (-3). 5.99 ***(978-1-4926-8174-8(1))*** Sourcebooks, Inc.
—Sebastian Santa's Secret Elf. Put Me In The Story & Sully, Katherine. 2018. (Santa's Secret Elf Ser.). (ENG.). 32p. (J). (-3). 5.99 ***(978-1-4926-8175-5(X))*** Sourcebooks, Inc.
Seal, Julia. The Silly Monster. Bucknell, Kate. 2018. (Little Monsters Ser.). (ENG.). 14p. (J). (gr. k-2). bds. 7.99 *(978-1-4867-1519-0(2),* 49312b4b-fc46-4968-a320-b24d781d9089) Flowerpot Pr.
—The Sketchbook. 2019. (J). *(978-1-4413-2937-0(4))* Peter Pauper Pr. Inc.
—The Sleepy Monster. Bucknell, Kate. 2018. (Little Monsters Ser.). (ENG.). 14p. (J). (gr. k-2). bds. 7.99 *(978-1-4867-1522-0(2),* 969fcb7e-8889-4222-9bd1-7558f721b2eb) Flowerpot Pr.
Seal, Julia. Sophia Santa's Secret Elf. Put Me In The Story & Sully, Katherine. 2018. (Santa's Secret Elf Ser.). (ENG.). 32p. (J). (-3). 5.99 ***(978-1-4926-8176-2(8))*** Sourcebooks, Inc.
Seal, Julia. Tag! & in Pip's Bag. Atkins, Jill. 2020. (Early Bird Readers — Pink (Early Bird Stories (tm)) Ser.). (ENG.). 32p. (J). (gr. -1-2). pap. 7.99 *(978-1-5415-8727-4(8),* Lerner Pubns.) Lerner Publishing Group.
Seal, Julia. Victoria Santa's Secret Elf. Put Me In The Story & Sully, Katherine. 2018. (Santa's Secret Elf Ser.). (ENG.). 32p. (J). (-3). 5.99 ***(978-1-4926-8177-9(6))*** Sourcebooks, Inc.
—William Santa's Secret Elf. Put Me In The Story & Sully, Katherine. 2018. (Santa's Secret Elf Ser.). (ENG.). 32p. (J). (-3). 5.99 ***(978-1-4926-8178-6(4))*** Sourcebooks, Inc.
—Zoey Santa's Secret Elf. Put Me In The Story & Sully, Katherine. 2018. (Santa's Secret Elf Ser.). (ENG.). 32p. (J). (-3). 5.99 ***(978-1-4926-8180-9(6))*** Sourcebooks, Inc.
Sealock, Rick. Widdermaker. Schnetzler, Pattie L. 2005. 32p. (gr. k-2). 15.95 *(978-0-87614-647-7(7))* Lerner Publishing Group.
Seaman, Paul. Feng Suey's Special Garden. Bell, Frank. 2004. 24p. pap. 7.00 *(978-1-84161-071-9(2))* Ravette Publishing, Ltd. GBR. Dist: Parkwest Pubns., Inc.
—How Slip Slap Slop Got His Name. Bell, Frank. 2004. 24p. pap. 7.00 *(978-1-84161-069-6(0))* Ravette Publishing, Ltd. GBR. Dist: Parkwest Pubns., Inc.
—Ma Jong & the Magic Carpet. Bell, Frank. 2004. 24p. pap. 7.00 *(978-1-84161-070-2(4))* Ravette Publishing, Ltd. GBR. Dist: Parkwest Pubns., Inc.
—Panda Patrol Go on Holiday. Bell, Frank & Bowler, Colin. 2004. 24p. pap. 7.00 *(978-1-84161-083-2(6))* Ravette Publishing, Ltd. GBR. Dist: Parkwest Pubns., Inc.
—Panda Patrol to the Rescue. Bell, Frank. 2004. 24p. pap. 7.00 *(978-1-84161-068-9(2))* Ravette Publishing, Ltd. GBR. Dist: Parkwest Pubns., Inc.
—Panda Power. Bell, Frank & Bowler, Colin. 2004. 24p. pap. 7.00 *(978-1-84161-084-9(4))* Ravette Publishing, Ltd. GBR. Dist: Parkwest Pubns., Inc.
Seamans, Amanda. Endangered Species & Friends in the U. S. A. Scott, Karen. unabr. ed. Date not set. (J). (gr. -1-6). 16.95 *(978-1-889667-00-3(5))* Second Ark Pubns.
Seapics.com Staff, photos by. Out of the Blue: A Journey Through the World's Oceans. Horsman, Paul. 2005. (ENG., 160p. (gr. 17). 32.95 *(978-0-262-08341-6(8),* 0262083418) MIT Pr.
Searle, Sarah Winifred. Sincerely, Harriet. Searle, Sarah Winifred. 2019. 176p. (J). (gr. 4-8). 29.32 *(978-1-5124-4019-5(1),* Graphic Universe™) Lerner Publishing Group.
Sears, Bart, et al. Blood on Snow, Vol. 2. Marz, Ron. 2003. (Path Ser.: Vol. 2). 160p. (YA). (gr. 7-18). pap. 15.95 *(978-1-931484-60-2(0))* CrossGeneration Comics, Inc.
—Death & Dishonor, Vol. 3. Marz, Ron. 2004. (Path Traveler Ser.: Vol. 3). 160p. (YA). pap. 9.95 *(978-1-59314-059-5(2))* CrossGeneration Comics, Inc.
—The Path, Vol. 3. Marz, Ron. 2003. (Path Ser.: Vol. 3). 160p. (YA). pap. 15.95 *(978-1-931484-88-6(0))* CrossGeneration Comics, Inc.
Sears, Bart. Sabretooth: Open Season. Way, Daniel. 2005. (Wolverine Ser.). 96p. pap. 9.99 *(978-0-7851-1507-6(2))* Marvel Worldwide, Inc.
Sears, Bart & Pennington, Mark. Crisis of Faith. Marz, Ron. 2003. (Path Traveler Ser.: Vol. 1). 192p. (YA). (gr. 7-18). pap. 9.95 *(978-1-59314-016-8(9))* CrossGeneration Comics, Inc.
Sears, Dovid. Rabbi Riddle Says... Look Who Dropped in for Yom Tov. Estrin, Leibel. 2005. (J). 10.95 *(978-1-931681-74-2(0))* Israel Bookshop Pubns.
Sears, Mary A. Vaulting: The Art of Gymnastics on Horseback. Sears, Mary A. Pakizer, Debi. Anderson, Julia & Barnette, Jackie, eds. 24p. (Orig.). (J). (gr. k-6). pap. 5.00 *(978-0-9639785-6-1(X))* Sears, M.A.
Seaton, Kit. Wonder Woman: Warbringer (the Graphic Novel) Bardugo, Leigh. 2020. 192p. (J). (gr. 7-7). 16.99 *(978-1-4012-8255-4(5))* DC Comics.
Seaton, Sierra. In a Forest Full of Trees. Ferguson, Tina L. 2019. (ENG.). 26p. (J). pap. 9.99 ***(978-1-0868-5968-3(5))*** Independently Published.
Seatter, Pamela. Dancer Girl M. C's Story: One Step at a Time. Douglass Thom, Kara. 2014. (Go! Go! Sports Girls Ser.). (ENG.). 32p. (J). (gr. k-2). pap. 4.99 *(978-1-940731-02-5(X))* Dream Big Toy Co.
—Mom & Me, Sweet As Can Bee. Skwish, Emily. 2019. (Play-A-Song Ser.). (ENG.). 14p. (J). *(978-1-5037-4535-3(X),* d364f8d8-3977-4253-a33e-bda7584aa5c9, p i kids) Phoenix International Publications, Inc.
—Soccer Girl Cassie's Story: Teamwork Is the Goal. Douglass Thom, Kara. 2014. (Go! Go! Sports Girls Ser.). (ENG.). 32p. (J). (gr. k-2). pap. 4.99 *(978-1-940731-00-1(3))* Dream Big Toy Co.
Seaver Keith, Emily. A Home for Webby. Seaver Keith, Emily. 2008. 23p. (J). (gr. -1-3). 16.95 *(978-0-9728646-1-9(X))* Bangzoom Pubs.
Seay, Christina. Silly Sally Sometime. Savannah. 2007. 188p. per. 24.95 *(978-0-60441-451-6(0))* America Star Bks.
Seay, Dave. Baxter's Big Teeth, Counce, Betty. 2011. (ENG.). 34p. (J). 16.95 *(978-0-9833155-0-6(7))* Keepworthy Creations LLC.
Sebastian. The Abc's of Character. Cabanillas, Laura Sabin. 2009. 60p. pap. 12.95 *(978-0-9818488-2-2(6))* Ajoyin Publishing, Inc.
Sebastian, Eleonore. Go Away, Mama! Fadden, Chelsea. 2018. (ENG.). 24p. (J). 16.95 *(978-1-59298-678-1(1))* Beaver's Pond Pr., Inc.
Sebastian Quigley, Sebastian. The Glow in the Dark Book of Space: The Book You Can Read in the Dark! Harris, Nicholas. 2013. (ENG.). 32p. (J). (gr. -1-2). 17.99 *(978-1-84780-417-4(9),* White Lion Publishing) Quarto Publishing Group UK GBR. Dist: Hachette Bk. Group.
Sebastián, Soledad. Cantaba la Rana. Scholastic, Inc. Staff. ed. 2011. (SPA & ENG.). 32p. (J). (gr. -1-3). pap. 6.99 *(978-0-545-27357-2(9),* Scholastic en Espanol) Scholastic, Inc.
Sebe, Masayuki. Let's Count To 100! Sebe, Masayuki. 2014. (ENG.). 24p. (J). (gr. -1-2). 7.95 *(978-1-55453-813-3(0))* Kids Can Pr., Ltd. CAN. Dist: Hachette Bk. Group.
—100 Animals on Parade! Sebe, Masayuki. 2013. (ENG.). 24p. (J). (gr. -1-2). 16.95 *(978-1-55453-871-3(8))* Kids Can Pr., Ltd. CAN. Dist: Hachette Bk. Group.
—100 Hungry Monkeys!, 0 vols. Sebe, Masayuki. 2014. (ENG.). 24p. (J). (gr. -1-2). 16.95 *(978-1-77138-045-4(4))* Kids Can Pr., Ltd. CAN. Dist: Hachette Bk. Group.
Sebern, Brian. Little Tree: A Story for Children with Serious Medical Illness. Mills, Joyce C. 2nd ed. 2003. 32p. (J). pap. 9.95 *(978-1-59147-042-7(0))*; 14.95 *(978-1-59147-041-0(2))* American Psychological Assn. (Magination Pr.).
Sebestyen, Adam. Characters of Letterworld. Sebestyen, Adam. 2019. (Letterworld Ser.: Vol. 1). (ENG.). 62p. (J). *(978-1-83853-034-1(7))* Independent Publishing Network.
Secchi, Riccardo. Ultraheroes Vol. 1: Save the World. Ghiglione, Marco. 2010. (Disney's Hero Squad Ser.). (ENG.). 112p. (J). pap. 9.99 *(978-1-60886-543-7(6))* Boom! Studios.
Secchi, Riccardo & Randoplh, Grace. Ultraheroes: Save the World. Ghiglione, Marco & Randolph, Grace. 2010. (Disney's Hero Squad Ser.: 1). (ENG.). 112p. (J). pap. 24.99 *(978-1-60886-552-9(5))* Boom! Studios.
Sechao, Annie & Legdani, Sanaa. 100 First Animals: a Carry along Book. 2018. 24p. (J). (gr. -1-1). bds. 7.99 *(978-2-924786-49-9(5),* CrackBoom! Bks.) Chouette Publishing CAN. Dist: Publishers Group West (PGW).
—100 First Vehicles & Things That Go. 2019. 24p. (J). (gr. -1-1). bds. 7.99 *(978-2-89802-052-0(4))*; bds. 7.99 *(978-2-89802-051-3(6))* Chouette Publishing CAN. (CrackBoom! Bks.). Dist: Publishers Group West (PGW).
—100 First Words: a Carry along Book. 2019. 24p. (J). (gr. -1-1). bds. 7.99 *(978-2-924786-98-7(3),* CrackBoom! Bks.) Chouette Publishing CAN. Dist: Publishers Group West (PGW).
—100 First Words for Your Litle Genius. 2019. 24p. (J). (gr. -1-1). bds. 7.99 *(978-2-89802-054-4(0),* CrackBoom! Bks.) Chouette Publishing CAN. Dist: Publishers Group West (PGW).
—100 First Words for Your Litle Genius: A Carry along Book. 2019. 24p. (J). (gr. -1-1). bds. 7.99 *(978-2-89802-053-7(2),* CrackBoom! Bks.) Chouette Publishing CAN. Dist: Publishers Group West (PGW).
Sécheret, Jessica. Art-Rageous. Young, Jessica. 2015. (Finley Flowers Ser.). (ENG.). 128p. (J). (gr. 1-3). 8.95 *(978-1-4795-5960-2(1),* Picture Window Bks.) Capstone.
—Fin-Tastic Fashion. Young, Jessica. 2017. (Finley Flowers Ser.). (ENG.). 128p. (J). (gr. 1-3). lib. bdg. 25.32 *(978-1-4795-9804-5(6),* 133579, Picture Window Bks.) Capstone.
—Finley Flowers Collection. Young, Jessica. 2016. (Finley Flowers Ser.). (ENG.). 256p. (J). (gr. 1-3). 9.99 *(978-1-4795-9850-2(X),* Picture Window Bks.) Capstone.
—Nature Calls. Young, Jessica. 2015. (Finley Flowers Ser.). (ENG.). 128p. (J). (gr. 1-3). 8.95 *(978-1-4795-5879-7(6),* Picture Window Bks.) Capstone.
—New & Improved. Young, Jessica. 2015. (Finley Flowers Ser.). (ENG.). 128p. (J). (gr. 1-3). 8.95 *(978-1-4795-5959-6(8),* Picture Window Bks.) Capstone.
—Original Recipe. Young, Jessica. 2015. (Finley Flowers Ser.). (ENG.). 128p. (J). (gr. 1-3). 8.95 *(978-1-4795-5878-0(8),* Picture Window Bks.) Capstone.
—Pet-Rified. Young, Jessica. 2017. (Finley Flowers Ser.). (ENG.). 128p. (J). (gr. 1-3). lib. bdg. 25.32 *(978-1-4795-9805-2(4),* 133580, Picture Window Bks.) Capstone.
—Room to Bloom. Young, Jessica. 2017. (Finley Flowers Ser.). (ENG.). 128p. (J). (gr. 1-3). lib. bdg. 25.32 *(978-1-4795-9806-9(2),* 133581, Picture Window Bks.) Capstone.
—Super Spooktacular. Young, Jessica. 2017. (Finley Flowers Ser.). (ENG.). 128p. (J). (gr. 1-3). lib. bdg. 25.32 *(978-1-4795-9807-6(0),* 133582, Picture Window Bks.) Capstone.
Seckel, Al. 50 Optical Illusions. Taplin, Sam. 2010. (Activity Cards Ser.). 50p. (J). 9.99 *(978-0-7945-2664-1(0),* Usborne) EDC Publishing.
Second Grade Class, Clay's 2001. The Awesome Alphabet Animal's Party. Stedelbauer, Joyce Carr. 2018. (ENG.). 42p. (J). (gr. k-4). pap. 12.99 *(978-1-945990-53-3(8))* High Tide Pubns.
Second Story Press Staff, jt. illus. see Ammirati, Christelle.
Second Story Press Staff, jt. illus. see Benoit, Renne.
Second Story Press Staff, jt. illus. see Jovanovic, Vanja Vuleta.
Second Story Press Staff, jt. illus. see Newland, Gillian.
Second Story Press Staff, jt. illus. see Steele-Card, Adrianna.
Seda, Alison. Dino Manners: Some Prehistoric Lessons Featuring Our Friends from the Cretaceous Period. Finch, Susan M. 2009. 32p. pap. 16.50 *(978-1-4490-5102-0(2))* AuthorHouse.
Sedalia, Rajan. In Search of Yourself Word Search Puzzles: Explorations into the Black Experience. Dunn, Kevin Ikim. 2005. (ENG.). 92p. per. 9.95 *(978-0-9767337-0-6(6))* Invision Pubns.
Seddon, Viola Anne. Swan Lake Ballet Theatre. Mahoney, Jean. 2009. (ENG.). 16p. (J). (gr. 1-4). 24.99 *(978-0-7636-4396-6(3))* Candlewick Pr.
Seeberger, Beverley. Razzle Dazzler. 2007. (J). per. 15.00 *(978-0-9713589-8-0(2))* Ubaviel's Gifts.
Seeger, Laura Vaccaro. Dog & Bear: Tricks & Treats. Seeger, Laura Vaccaro. 2014. (Dog & Bear Ser.). (ENG.). 32p. (J). (gr. -1-3). 14.99 *(978-1-59643-632-9(8),* 9781596436329) Roaring Brook Pr.
—Dog & Bear: Two Friends, Three Stories. Seeger, Laura Vaccaro. 2012. (My Readers Ser.). (ENG.). 32p. (J). (gr. k-2). pap. 4.99 *(978-0-312-54799-8(4),* 900074326) Square Fish.
—First the Egg. Seeger, Laura Vaccaro. 2007. (ENG.). 32p. (J). (gr. -1-1). 16.99 *(978-1-59643-272-7(1),* 900043980) Roaring Brook Pr.
—Green. Seeger, Laura Vaccaro. 2012. (ENG.). 36p. (J). (gr. -1-1). 18.99 *(978-1-59643-397-7(3),* 900051551) Roaring Brook Pr.
—Lemons Are Not Red. Seeger, Laura Vaccaro. 2006. (ENG.). 32p. (J). (gr. -1-k). pap. 8.99 *(978-1-59643-195-9(4),* 900039844) Square Fish.
—One Boy. Seeger, Laura Vaccaro. 2016. (ENG.). 48p. (J). 15.99 *(978-1-62672-252-1(8),* 900147590) Roaring Brook Pr.
—Two Friends, Three Stories. Seeger, Laura Vaccaro. 2007. (Dog & Bear Ser.). (ENG.). 32p. (J). (gr. -1-3). 15.99 *(978-1-59643-053-2(2),* 9781596430532) Roaring Brook Pr.
—Walter Was Worried. Seeger, Laura Vaccaro. 2006. (ENG.). 40p. (J). (gr. -1-3). pap. 8.99 *(978-1-59643-196-6(2),* 900039845) Square Fish.
—What If? Seeger, Laura Vaccaro. 2010. (ENG.). 32p. (J). (gr. -1-2). 18.99 *(978-1-59643-398-4(1),* 900051552) Roaring Brook Pr.
Seehafer, Ginger. Rudy's New Human. Elden, Roxanna. 2016. 32p. (J). (gr. -1-k). 16.99 *(978-1-63450-189-7(6),* Sky Pony Pr.) Skyhorse Publishing Co., Inc.
Seeley, Douglas A. Sun & Ponies, Wind & Sky. Lidard, Kelly, photos by. Seeley, Bonnie L. 2004. 32p. (J). lib. bdg. 11.95 *(978-0-9728380-1-6(5))* Seelcraft Publishing.
Seeley, Douglas A., jt. illus. see Lidard, Kelly.
Seeley, Laura L. Un Colchón de Plumas Para Ágata, 1 vol. Deedy, Carmen Agra. 2007. (SPA.). 32p. (J). (gr. k-3). 15.95 *(978-1-56145-426-6(5))*; pap. 7.95 *(978-1-56145-404-4(4))* Peachtree Publishing Co. Inc.
Seeley, Scott & Potts, Sam. The 82NYC Review. New York City Students Staff. 2008. (826NYC Review Ser.: 3). (ENG.). 256p. (J). (gr. 3-12). pap. 14.00 *(978-0-9790073-6-1(4))* 826 Valencia.
Seeley, Terre Lamb. The Little Black Dog Buccaneer. Spooner, J. B. 2011. (Little Black Dog Ser.). (ENG.). 32p. (J). (gr. -1-k). 16.95 *(978-1-61145-000-2(4),* 611000, Arcade Publishing) Skyhorse Publishing Co., Inc.
—The Little Black Dog Has Puppies. Spooner, J. B. 2011. (Little Black Dog Ser.). (ENG.). 32p. (J). (gr. -1-k). 16.95 *(978-1-61145-006-4(3),* 611006, Arcade Publishing) Skyhorse Publishing Co., Inc.
—The Story of the Little Black Dog. Spooner, J. B. 2011. (Little Black Dog Ser.). 32p. (J). (gr. -1-k). 16.95

S

(978-1-61145-001-9(2), 611001, Arcade Publishing) Skyhorse Publishing Co., Inc.

Seeley, Tim. Indoor Zoo. Ross, Michael Elsohn. 2003. (You Are the Scientist Ser.). 48p. (J). (gr. 3-6). lib. bdg. 23.93 (978-0-87614-621-7(3)) Lerner Publishing Group.

—Jason: Quest for the Golden Fleece [a Greek Myth]. Limke, Jeff. 2008. (Graphic Myths & Legends Ser.). (ENG.). 48p. (J). (gr. 4-8). per. 9.99 (978-0-8225-6571-0(4), 9780822565710, Graphic Universe™) Lerner Publishing Group.

—Kitchen Lab. Ross, Michael Elsohn. 2003. (You Are the Scientist Ser.). 48p. (J). (gr. 3-6). lib. bdg. 23.93 (978-0-87614-625-5(6)) Lerner Publishing Group.

—Toy Lab. Ross, Michael Elsohn. 2003. (You Are the Scientist Ser.). 48p. (J). (gr. 3-6). 23.93 (978-0-87614-456-5(3)) Lerner Publishing Group.

Seeley, Tim & Schulz, Barbara. Jason: Quest for the Golden Fleece. 2006. (Graphic Myths & Legends Ser.). 48p. (J). (gr. 4-7). lib. bdg. 26.60 (978-0-8225-5967-2(6)) Lerner Publishing Group.

Seelig, Renate. Mein Kleiner Brockhaus: Erste Woerter. 28p. (J). (gr. -1-18). (978-3-7653-2561-8(9)) Brockhaus, F. A., GmbH DEU. Dist: International Bk. Import Service, Inc.

—Mein Kleiner Brockhaus: Jahreszeiten. (GER.). 28p. (J). (gr. -1-18). (978-3-7653-2571-7(6)) Brockhaus, F. A., GmbH DEU. Dist: International Bk. Import Service, Inc.

Seely, Matthew. Dead Weight: Murder at Camp Bloom. Blas, Terry & Muldoon, Molly. 2018. (ENG.). 176p. pap. 19.99 (978-1-62010-481-1(4), Lion Forge) Oni Pr., Inc.

Sefati, Maryam. Counting Sheep (Disney Junior Puppy Dog Pals) Katschke, Judy. 2019. (Little Golden Book Ser.). (ENG.). 24p. (J). (-k). 4.99 (978-0-7364-3935-0(8), Golden/Disney) Random Hse. Children's Bks.

—Don't Rain on My Pug-Rade (Disney Junior Puppy Dog Pals) Forte, Lauren. 2018. (Little Golden Book Ser.). (ENG.). 24p. (J). (-k). 4.99 (978-0-7364-3900-8(5), Golden/Disney) Random Hse. Children's Bks.

—Walking the Bob (Disney Junior Puppy Dog Pals) Saxon, Victoria. 2019. (Little Golden Book Ser.). (ENG.). 24p. (J). (-k). 4.99 (978-0-7364-3972-5(2), Golden/Disney) Random Hse. Children's Bks.

Sefcik, Wendy. Gallery Eleven Twenty-Two. Brown, Tiffany M. 2013. 30p. 17.99 (978-0-9854423-0-9(1)); pap. 9.99 (978-0-9854423-1-6(X)) Brewster Moon.

—J Mac Is the Freestyle King! Thomas, Terri. 2010. 38p. pap. 20.00 (978-1-60844-453-3(8)) Dog Ear Publishing, LLC.

Segal, John. Sleepyhead. Wilson, Karma. 2012. (Classic Board Bks.). (ENG.). 32p. (J). (gr. -1 — 1). bds. 7.99 (978-1-4424-3433-2(3), Little Simon) Little Simon.

—Sleepyhead. Wilson, Karma. 2006. (ENG.). 32p. (J). (gr. -1-2). 16.99 (978-1-4169-1241-5(X), McElderry, Margaret K. Bks.) McElderry, Margaret K. Bks.

Segal, John. Alistair & Kip's Great Adventure! Segal, John. 2008. (ENG.). 32p. (J). (gr. -1-3). 17.99 (978-1-4169-0280-5(5), McElderry, Margaret K. Bks.) McElderry, Margaret K. Bks.

—Carrot Soup. Segal, John. 2006. (ENG.). 32p. (J). (gr. -1-3). 17.99 (978-0-689-87702-5(1), McElderry, Margaret K. Bks.) McElderry, Margaret K. Bks.

Segal, Nancy. Patchland USA. Segal, Mark. 2017. (ENG.). (J). (gr. k-3). 11.99 (978-1-943331-76-5(6)) Orange Hat Publishing.

Segarra, Angelo M. Coca Finds a Shell. Segarra, Angelo M. Segarra, Kirstie, ed. 2004. 24p. (J). 14.95 (978-0-9752664-0-3(3)) Segarra, Angelo.

Segawa, Michael. Mackenzie Blue #5: Double Trouble Vol. 5. Wells, Tina. 2014. (Mackenzie Blue Ser.: 5). (ENG.). 224p. (J). (gr. 3-7). pap. 6.99 (978-0-06-224412-3(4)) HarperCollins Pubs.

Segawa, Yasuo. Peek-A-Boo. Matsutani, Miyoko. 2006. 20p. (J). (gr. -1). 10.95 (978-1-74126-047-2(7)) R.I.C. Pubns. AUS. Dist: SCB Distributors.

Segner, Ellen. The Wild Dog of Edmonton. Grew, David. 2011. 208p. 44.95 (978-1-258-09902-2(0)) Literary Licensing, LLC.

Séguin-Magee, Luke. Boy Meets Squirrels. Nawrocki, Mike. 2019. (Dead Sea Squirrels Ser.: 2). (ENG.). 128p. (J). pap. 6.99 (978-1-4964-3502-6(8), 20_32041) Tyndale Hse. Pubs.

Seguin-Magee, Luke. Come Sit with Me. Gallo, Tina. 2019. (Crayola Ser.). (ENG.). 32p. (J). (gr. k-2). 17.99 (978-1-5344-5099-8(8), Simon Spotlight) Simon Spotlight.

—Come Sit with Me: Making Friends on the Buddy Bench. Gallo, Tina. 2019. (Crayola Ser.). (ENG.). 32p. (J). (gr. k-2). pap. 4.99 (978-1-5344-5080-6(7), Simon Spotlight) Simon Spotlight.

Séguin-Magee, Luke. Hanukkah. Morey, Allan. 2017. (Holidays in Rhythm & Rhyme Ser.). (ENG.). 24p. (J). (gr. -1-3). lib. bdg. 33.99 incl. audio compact disk (978-1-68410-033-0(X), 31520) Cantata Learning.

—Little Red Riding Hood: A Favorite Story in Rhythm & Rhyme. Peale, Jonathan. 2018. (Fairy Tale Tunes Ser.). (ENG.). 24p. (J). (gr. -1-3). lib. bdg. 33.99 (978-1-68410-395-9(9), 140349) Cantata Learning.

—Nutty Study Buddies. Nawrocki, Mike. 2019. (Dead Sea Squirrels Ser.: 3). (ENG.). 128p. (J). pap. 6.99 (978-1-4964-3506-4(0), 20_32045, Tyndale Kids) Tyndale Hse. Pubs.

—Squirreled Away. Nawrocki, Mike. 2019. (Dead Sea Squirrels Ser.: 1). (ENG.). 128p. (J). pap. 6.99 (978-1-4964-3498-2(6), 20_31671) Tyndale Hse. Pubs.

—Squirrelnapped! Nawrocki, Mike. 2019. (Dead Sea Squirrels Ser.: 4). (ENG.). 128p. (J). pap. 6.99 (978-1-4964-3510-1(9), 20_32049) Tyndale Hse. Pubs.

—Tree-Mendous Trouble. Nawrocki, Mike. 2020. (Dead Sea Squirrels Ser.: 5). (ENG.). 128p. (J). pap. 6.99 (978-1-4964-3514-9(1), 20_32053, Tyndale Kids) Tyndale Hse. Pubs.

—Whirly Squirrelies. Nawrocki, Mike. 2020. (Dead Sea Squirrels Ser.: 6). (ENG.). 128p. (J). pap. 6.99 (978-1-4964-3518-7(4), 20_32057, Tyndale Kids) Tyndale Hse. Pubs.

Segundo, Horazio. Snout & Blackie. Jones, Thomas Ernest. 2019. (ENG.). 52p. (J). pap. 14.99 (978-1-6885-8666-6(0)) Independently Published.

Segura, Jovan Carl. Let's Brush Our Teeth. Muncaster, Sandie. 2019. (ENG.). 28p. (J). pap. (978-1-925932-11-9(7)) Library For All Limited.

Sehler, Mark. The Porridge That Was Too Hot, 7 vols. Smith, Annette. 2005. (ENG.). (J). (gr. 1). pap. 54.80 (978-1-4189-1335-9(9)) Houghton Mifflin Harcourt Supplemental Pubs.

Seibel, Monique. Maddy & Mia: TriPaw Tales. Adler, Pamela. 2020. (ENG.). 56p. (J). (gr. 2-6). pap. 12.95 (978-1-947860-79-7(8), Belle Isle Bks.) Brandylane Pubs., Inc.

Seibold, J. Otto. Mind Your Manners, B. B. Wolf. Sierra, Judy. 2012. 40p. (J). (gr. -1-2). pap. 7.99 (978-0-307-93101-6(3), Dragonfly Bks.) Random Hse. Children's Bks.

—Seamore, the Very Forgetful Porpoise. Edgemon, Darcie. 2008. (J). 48p. (gr. -1-3). lib. bdg. 17.89 (978-0-06-085076-0(0)); (978-0-06-085075-3(2)) HarperCollins Pubs.

—Tell the Truth, B. B. Wolf. Sierra, Judy. 2010. 40p. (J). (gr. -1-2). 17.99 (978-0-375-85620-4(X), Knopf Bks. for Young Readers) Random Hse. Children's Bks.

Seibold, J. Otto. Olive, the Other Reindeer Pop-Up Advent Calendar. Seibold, J. Otto, creator. 2007. (Olive Ser.: OLIV). (ENG.). 4p. (J). (gr. -1-17). 9.95 (978-0-8118-5920-2(7)) Chronicle Bks. LLC.

Seiden, Art. Howdy Doody in Funland. Kean, Edward. 2011. 30p. 35.95 (978-1-258-02315-7(6)) Literary Licensing, LLC.

—Howdy Doody in the Wild West. Kean, Edward. 2011. 34p. 35.95 (978-1-258-02316-4(4)) Literary Licensing, LLC.

—Howdy Doody's Animal Friends. Daly, Kathleen. 2011. 26p. 35.95 (978-1-258-02771-1(2)) Literary Licensing, LLC.

—My ABC Book. Grosset and Dunlap Staff & dePaola, Tomie. 2015. (G&d Vintage Ser.). 24p. (J). (gr. -1-k). bds. 7.99 (978-0-448-48215-6(0), Grosset & Dunlap) Penguin Young Readers Group.

—The Noisy Clock Shop. Berg, Jean Horton & dePaola, Tomie. 2015. (G&d Vintage Ser.). 32p. (J). (gr. -1-k). bds. 7.99 (978-0-448-48216-3(9), Grosset & Dunlap) Penguin Young Readers Group.

—Tom Glazer's Treasury of Songs for Children. Glazer, Tom. 2nd ed. 2003. 256p. (J). (gr. 3-6). pap. 20.00 (978-1-58690-003-8(X)) Empire Publishing Service.

—The Train to Timbuctoo. Brown, Margaret Wise. 2018. (Little Golden Book Ser.). 24p. (J). (-k). 4.99 (978-0-553-53340-8(1), Golden Bks.) Random Hse. Children's Bks.

Seiders, Marian. Mommy, Am I A? Ali, Anila & Gottlieb, Karen. 2010. 28p. pap. 11.95 (978-1-935105-45-9(0)) Avid Readers Publishing Group.

Seidlitz, Serge. Geeger the Robot Goes to School: Geeger the Robot. Lerner, Jarrett. 2020. (Quix Ser.). (ENG.). 80p. (J). (gr. k-3). 17.99 (978-1-5344-5217-6(6)); pap. 5.99 (978-1-5344-5216-9(8)) Simon & Schuster Children's Publishing. (Aladdin).

Seiferling, Dena. Alice & Gert: An Ant & Grasshopper Story. Becker, Helaine. 2020. (ENG.). 24p. (J). (gr. k-4). 17.95 (978-1-77147-358-3(4)) Owlkids Bks. Inc. CAN. Dist: Publishers Group West (PGW).

Seiler, Jason & Farley, Jason. The Christmas Train. Bannister, Barbara. 2007. 61p. (J). (gr. 3-7). per. 7.95 (978-0-940895-54-6(4)) Cornerstone Pr. Chicago.

Seitzinger, Victoria. The Oz Odyssey. Baum, Roger S. 2006. 176p. (J). 19.95 (978-1-57072-299-8(4)) Overmountain Pr.

—Toto of Oz & the Surprise Party. Baum, Roger S. 2004. (ENG.). 32p. (J). 13.95 (978-1-57072-284-4(6), 1233723) Overmountain Pr.

Seivwright, Leonard. Rudy the Shy Car. Landy, Adrienne. 2009. 48p. pap. 13.75 (978-1-935125-43-3(5)) Robertson Publishing.

Seixas, Ana. My First Book of Comparisons: How the World Measures Up. Gifford, Clive. 2020. (ENG.). 48p. (J). (gr. k-2). 16.99 (978-1-78240-935-9(1), 327277, Ivy Kids) Ivy Group, The GBR. Dist: Hachette UK Distribution.

Seixas, Ana. Scratch & Learn Human Body: With 70 Things to Spot! Flint, Katy. 2019. (Scratch & Learn Ser.). (ENG.). 16p. (J). (gr. -1-1). 17.99 (978-1-78603-323-9(2), Wide Eyed Editions) Quarto Publishing Group UK GBR. Dist: Hachette Bk. Group.

Sekaz, Jennah. The Ecotarian Kids(tm) & the Big Four. Toney, Toni. 2019. (ENG.). 48p. (J). 21.99 (978-1-5456-6961-7(9)) Salem Author Services.

Seki, Sunny. The Tale of the Lucky Cat. Moon, Josephine. 2008. (KOR & ENG.). 32p. (J). (978-0-9799339-1-2(9)) East West Discovery Pr.

Seki, Sunny. The Last Kappa of Old Japan: A Magical Journey of Two Friends. Seki, Sunny. rev. ed. 2016. 32p. (J). (gr. k-8). 12.95 (978-4-8053-1399-2(4)) Tuttle Publishing.

—The Tale of the Lucky Cat. Seki, Sunny. 2008. (ENG & SPA.). 32p. (J). 18.95 (978-0-9669437-9-5(1)) East West Discovery Pr.

Seki, Sunny. The Tale of the Lucky Cat. Seki, Sunny, retold by. 32p. (J). 2008. (978-0-9669437-6-4(7)); 2007. (JPN & ENG.). 18.95 (978-0-9669437-5-7(9)) East West Discovery Pr.

Sekowsky, Mike. Justice League of America. Fox, Gardner & DC Comics Staff. Kahan, Bob, ed. rev. ed. 2006. (Justice League of America Archives Ser.: Vol. 3). (ENG.). 256p. (YA). 49.99 (978-1-56389-159-5(X)) DC Comics.

Sekula, John. The Little Car in Spring: Anti-Bullying. Villabona, Nancy Sue. Hooker, Terry, ed. 2019. (Villabona Voyager Book Ser.: Vol. 2). (ENG.). 42p. (J). pap. 14.95 (978-0-9996013-3-4(4)) Horn, Jonathan.

Sekulic, Britt. Vail's Tales. Payne, Ed & Johnson, Vail. 2019. (ENG.). 82p. (J). 18.00 (978-0-578-54481-6(4)) Proverbial Girl Publishing.

Selbert, Kathryn. The Fruit Salad Friend: A Guide to Finding True Friends. Dismondy, Maria. 2018. (ENG.). 32p. (J). (gr. 2-4). 10.95 (978-0-9976085-2-6(8), Cardinal Rule Pr.) Dismondy, Maria Inc.

—Hoppy Little Frog. Colombe, Rose. Cottage Door Press, ed. 2019. (Lamaze Activity Bks.). (ENG.). 10p. (J). (gr. -1-1). bds. 9.99 (978-1-68052-738-4(X), 1004590) Cottage Door Pr.

—I Like You More Than Ice Cream. Puffinton, Brick. Cottage Door Press, ed. 2020. (Finger Puppet Board Book Ser.). (ENG.). 12p. (J). (gr. -1 — 1). bds. 6.99 (978-1-68052-807-7(6), 1005200) Cottage Door Pr.

Selbert, Kathryn. Let's Play Football. Swift, Ginger. Cottage Door Press, ed. 2020. (Chunky Lift-A-Flap Board Book Ser.). (ENG.). 12p. (J). (gr. -1 — 1). bds. 7.99 (978-1-68052-981-4(1), 1006090) Cottage Door Pr.

Selbert, Kathryn. Let's Play Hockey: Chunky Lift a Flap Board Book. Swift, Ginger. Cottage Door Press, ed. 2019. (ENG.). 12p. (J). (gr. -1-k). bds. 7.99 (978-1-68052-376-8(7), 1003410) Cottage Door Pr.

—A Little Love: A Cuddle Close Book. Marx, Jonny. 2019. (ENG.). 18p. (J). (— 1). bds. 8.99 (978-1-64517-095-2(0), Silver Dolphin Bks.) Printers Row Publishing Group.

—More Bible Sliders, 1 vol. Williamson, Karen. ed. 2016. (Candle Tiny Tots Ser.). (ENG.). 10p. (J). (gr. -1). bds. 7.99 (978-1-78128-273-1(0), Candle Bks.) Lion Hudson PLC GBR. Dist: Independent Pubs. Group.

—Seeds & Stuck in the Tree. Jinks, Jenny. 2019. (Early Bird Readers — Red (Early Bird Stories (tm)) Ser.). (ENG.). 32p. (J). (gr. -1-2). 27.99 (978-1-5415-4165-8(0), Lerner Pubns.) Lerner Publishing Group.

—Wrapped in Love: Every Baby's First Blanket. Golden, Lucy. 2018. (ENG.). 16p. (J). (gr. -1-k). bds. 7.99 (978-1-4998-0818-6(6)) Little Bee Books Inc.

—Ye Cannae Shove Yer Granny off a Bus: A Favourite Scottish Rhyme with Moving Parts, 20 vols. 2018. (ENG.). 12p. (J). 9.95 (978-1-78250-478-8(8), Kelpies) Floris Bks. GBR. Dist: Consortium Bk. Sales & Distribution.

Selbert, Kathryn. War Dogs. Selbert, Kathryn. 2016. 48p. (J). (gr. 2-5). pap. 7.95 (978-1-58089-415-9(1)) Charlesbridge Publishing, Inc.

Selby, Ashley, jt. illus. see Selby, Joel.

Selby, Joel & Selby, Ashley. Peek-A-Bright Halloween: Tall Tiered Board Book. VonFeder, Rosa. Cottage Door Press, ed. 2018. (ENG.). 10p. (J). (gr. -1-k). bds. 9.99 (978-1-68052-342-3(2), 1003140) Cottage Door Pr.

Selby, Shannon. Lynnie Leonardson & the Weeping Willow. Coffey, Joe. 2011. 44p. pap. 24.95 (978-1-4560-6487-7(8)) America Star Bks.

Selivanova, Elena. Don't Blow Your Top! A Look Inside Volcanoes. Prokos, Anna. 2017. (Imagine That! Ser.). (ENG.). 32p. (J). (gr. 2-4). lib. bdg. 26.65 (978-1-63440-148-7(4)); E-Book 39.99 (978-1-63440-160-9(3)) Red Chair Pr.

—The Funny Ride. Hillert, Margaret. 2016. (BeginningtoRead Ser.). (ENG.). 32p. (J). (gr. -1-2). pap. 11.94 (978-1-60357-978-0(8)); (gr. k-2). 22.60 (978-1-59953-816-7(4)) Norwood Hse. Pr.

—Little Women: Band 18/Pearl (Collins Big Cat) Dale, Katie. 2016. (Collins Big Cat Ser.). (ENG.). 80p. (J). pap. 11.99 (978-0-00-814737-2(X)) HarperCollins Pubs. Ltd. GBR. Dist: Independent Pubs. Group.

—'Twas the Evening of Christmas, 1 vol. Nellist, Glenys. 2017. (ENG.). 32p. (J). 17.99 (978-0-310-74553-2(5)) Zonderkidz.

Sellaro, Brendan. Lily & Nana. Hamilton, Lily & Myers, Barbara. 2010. (J). (978-0-929915-38-8(0)) Headline Bks., Inc.

—Lily Goes to School. Hamilton, Lily & Myers, Barbara. 2012. (ENG.). 32p. (J). 17.95 (978-0-938467-59-5(X)) Headline Bks., Inc.

Sellers, Amy. Believe I-Can. Gallucci, Susie. 2006. (J). (978-0-9776074-1-9(0)) Pounce To Success International, Inc.

—Dream I-Can. Gallucci, Susie. 2006. (J). (978-0-9776074-2-6(9)) Pounce To Success International, Inc.

—Harry Spotter: The Incontinent Puppy. Hanson, Paige & Hanson, Jon. I.t. ed. 2005. 44p. (J). per. 20.00 (978-0-9721146-1-5(0)) Monroe Educational Media.

Selling, Mary. [BLACK & WHITE] - Drop Book Series - Based on the Writings of Luisa Piccarreta. 2019. (ENG.). 158p. (J). pap. 11.54 (978-1-6916-5373-7(X)) Independently Published.

Selmes, Caroline. The Curious Book of Lists: 263 Fun, Fascinating, & Fact-Filled Lists. Turner, Tracey. 2019. (Curious Lists Ser.). (ENG.). 160p. (J). 18.99 (978-0-7534-7514-0(6), 900207578, Kingfisher) Roaring Brook Pr.

Selover, Arthur, jt. illus. see Selover, Lisa.

Selover, Lisa & Selover, Arthur. Lynn Can Fly, 1 vol. Linkowski, Tami Leli. 2009. 15p. pap. 24.95 (978-1-60749-611-3(9)) America Star Bks.

Seltzer, Eric. Granny Doodle Day. Seltzer, Eric. 2006. (Doodle Dog Ser.). (ENG.). 32p. (J). (gr. -1-1). pap. 3.99 (978-0-689-85911-3(2), Simon & Schuster/Paula Wiseman Bks.) Simon & Schuster/Paula Wiseman Bks.

Seltzer, Jerry. Hannah the Magic Shelter Dog. Bogardus, Ray & Bogardus, Karin. 2005. 143p. (J). pap. 14.99 (978-1-932864-30-4(X)) Masthof Pr.

—Hover for a Day. Collins, Charles. 2006. (ENG.). 56p. (J). 19.95 (978-1-60131-004-0(8), Castlebridge Bks.) Big Tent Bks.

—A Pet for Me. Abbott, Rosalind. 2013. 24p. (J). 16.95 (978-1-60131-155-9(9), Castlebridge Bks.) Big Tent Bks.

—500 Presents for Penelope Potts. Yaldezian, Lisa M. 2006. (J). 16.95 (978-1-60131-005-7(6)) Big Tent Bks.

Seltzer, Jerry Joe. A Bump in the Road. Abbott, Roz. 2013. 26p. (J). 16.95 (978-1-60131-179-5(6)) Big Tent Bks.

Seltzer, Jerry Joe. There Are Fairies in My Tub. Seltzer, Jerry Joe. 2013. 20p. (J). 12.95 (978-1-60131-175-7(3), Castlebridge Bks.) Big Tent Bks.

Seluk, Nick. The Brain Is Kind of a Big Deal. Seluk, Nick. 2019. (ENG.). 40p. (J). (gr. 1-3). 17.99 (978-1-338-16700-9(6), Orchard Bks.) Scholastic, Inc.

—The Sun Is Kind of a Big Deal. Seluk, Nick. 2018. (ENG.). 40p. (J). (gr. -1-3). 17.99 (978-1-338-16697-2(2), Orchard Bks.) Scholastic, Inc.

Selway, Martina. Little Yoga: A Toddler's First Book of Yoga. Whitford, Rebecca. 2005. (ENG.). 32p. (J). (gr. -1 — 1). 12.99 (978-0-8050-7879-4(7), 900030787, Holt, Henry & Co. Bks. For Young Readers) Holt, Henry & Co.

—Sleepy Little Yoga. Whitford, Rebecca. 2007. (ENG.). 28p. (J). (gr. -1 — 1). 14.99 (978-0-8050-8193-0(3), 900040694, Holt, Henry & Co. Bks. For Young Readers) Holt, Henry & Co.

Selznick, Brian. The Dinosaurs of Waterhouse Hawkins: An Illuminating History of Mr. Warehouse Hawkins, Artist & Lecturer. Kerley, Barbara. 2011. (J). (gr. 2-5). 18.95 (978-0-545-19703-8(1)); 29.95 (978-0-545-19697-0(3)) Weston Woods Studios, Inc.

—The Doll People. Martin, Ann M. 2003. (Doll People Ser.: 1). (ENG.). 288p. (J). (gr. 3-7). pap. 7.99 (978-0-7868-1240-0(0)) Hyperion Pr.

—The Doll People. Martin, Ann M. & Godwin, Laura. pap. (978-0-439-05648-9(9)) Scholastic, Inc.

—The Doll People. Martin, Ann M. & Godwin, Laura. ed. 2003. (Doll People Ser.: 1). (J). (gr. 3-6). lib. bdg. 18.40 (978-0-613-49623-0(X)) Turtleback.

—The Doll People Set [3 Book Paperback Boxed Set + Paper Dolls]. Set. Martin, Ann M. & Godwin, Laura. 2014. (Doll People Ser.: 1). (ENG.). 944p. (J). (gr. 3-7). pap. 24.99 (978-1-4847-1299-3(4)) Hyperion Bks. for Children.

—The Dulcimer Boy. Seidler, Tor. 2003. 160p. (J). (gr. 3-7). lib. bdg. 16.89 (978-0-06-623610-0(X)) HarperCollins Pubs.

—The Dulcimer Boy. Seidler, Tor. 2004. 153p. (gr. 5-7). 17.00 (978-0-7569-3520-7(2)) Perfection Learning Corp.

—Frindle. Clements, Andrew. 105p. (J). (gr. 3-5). pap. 4.50 (978-0-8072-1522-7(8), Listening Library) Random Hse. Audio Publishing Group.

—Head of the Class: Frindle; the Landry News; the Janitor's Boy. Clements, Andrew. ed. 2007. (ENG.). 416p. (J). (gr. 3-7). pap. 23.99 (978-1-4169-4974-9(7), Atheneum Bks. for Young Readers) Simon & Schuster Children's Publishing.

—Lunch Money. Clements, Andrew. (ENG.). (J). (gr. 3-7). 2007. 240p. pap. 7.99 (978-0-689-86685-2(2)); 2005. 224p. 19.99 (978-0-689-86683-8(6)) Simon & Schuster Children's Publishing. (Atheneum Bks. for Young Readers).

—Marly's Ghost. Levithan, David. 2007. (ENG.). 208p. (YA). (gr. 7-18). 7.99 (978-0-14-240912-1(X), Speak) Penguin Young Readers Group.

—The Meanest Doll in the World. Martin, Ann M. & Godwin, Laura. 2005. (Doll People Ser.: 2). (ENG.). 304p. (J). (gr. 3-7). pap. 7.99 (978-0-7868-5297-0(6)) Hyperion Pr.

—El Periodico Landry. Clements, Andrew. 2004.Tr. of Landry News. (SPA.). (YA). pap. 9.99 (978-84-241-7886-4(6)) Everest Editora ESP. Dist: Lectorum Pubns., Inc.

—The Runaway Dolls. Martin, Ann M. & Godwin, Laura. 2010. (Doll People Ser.: 3). (ENG.). 352p. (J). (gr. 3-7). pap. 7.99 (978-0-7868-5585-8(1)) Hyperion Pr.

—The Runaway Dolls. Martin, Ann M. & Godwin, Laura. ed. 2010. (Doll People Ser.: 3). (J). lib. bdg. 18.40 (978-0-606-13987-8(7)) Turtleback.

—Walt Whitman: Words for America. Kerley, Barbara. 2004. (ENG.). 56p. (J). (gr. 2-5). 19.99 (978-0-439-35791-3(8), Scholastic Pr.) Scholastic, Inc.

—When Marian Sang: The True Recital of Marian Anderson. Ryan, Pam Muñoz. pap. 16.95 incl. audio (978-1-59112-943-1(5)); pap. incl. audio (978-1-59112-945-5(1)); pap. 18.95 incl. audio compact disk (978-1-59112-947-9(8)); pap. incl. audio compact disk (978-1-59112-949-3(4)); 2004. (J). 28.95 incl. audio compact disk (978-1-59112-948-6(6)) Live Oak Media.

Selznick, Brian. Baby Monkey, Private Eye. Selznick, Brian. Serlin, David. 2018. 192p. (J). (gr. -1-3). 16.99 (978-1-338-18061-9(4), Scholastic Pr.) Scholastic, Inc.

—The Boy of a Thousand Faces. Selznick, Brian. 2009. (ENG.). 48p. (gr. 3-18). 6.99 (978-0-06-441080-9(3)) Perfection Learning Corp.

—The Houdini Box. Selznick, Brian. 2008. (ENG.). 80p. (J). (gr. 2-5). 19.99 (978-1-4169-6878-8(4), Atheneum Bks. for Young Readers) Simon & Schuster Children's Publishing.

—The Invention of Hugo Cabret. Selznick, Brian. 2007. 544p. (J). (gr. 4-7). 24.99 (978-0-439-81378-5(6), Scholastic Pr.); (ENG.). 534p. (978-1-4071-0348-8(2)) Scholastic, Inc.

—The Marvels. Selznick, Brian. 2015. 640p. (J). (gr. 5-7). 32.99 (978-0-545-44868-0(9), Scholastic Pr.) Scholastic, Inc.

—Wonderstruck. Selznick, Brian. 2011. 640p. (J). (gr. 4-7). 29.99 (978-0-545-02789-2(6), Scholastic Pr.); (ENG.). 300.00 (978-0-545-38985-3(2)) Scholastic, Inc.

Selznick, Brian & GrandPré, Mary. Harry Potter & the Chamber of Secrets. Rowling, J. K. 2018. (Harry Potter Ser.: 2). (ENG.). 368p. (J). (gr. 3). pap. 12.99 (978-1-338-29915-1(8), Levine, Arthur A. Bks.) Scholastic, Inc.

—Harry Potter & the Deathly Hallows. Rowling, J. K. 2018. (Harry Potter Ser.: 7). (ENG.). 784p. (J). (gr. 3). pap. 16.99 (978-1-338-29920-5(4), Levine, Arthur A. Bks.) Scholastic, Inc.

—Harry Potter & the Goblet of Fire. Rowling, J. K. 2018. (Harry Potter Ser.: 4). (ENG.). 768p. (J). (gr. 3). pap. 14.99 (978-1-338-29917-5(4), Levine, Arthur A. Bks.) Scholastic, Inc.

—Harry Potter & the Half-Blood Prince. Rowling, J. K. 2018. (Harry Potter Ser.: 6). (ENG.). 688p. (J). (gr. 3). pap. 14.99 (978-1-338-29919-9(0), Levine, Arthur A. Bks.) Scholastic, Inc.

—Harry Potter & the Order of the Phoenix. Rowling, J. K. 2018. (Harry Potter Ser.: 5). (ENG.). 912p. (J). (gr. 3). pap. 14.99 (978-1-338-29918-2(2), Levine, Arthur A. Bks.) Scholastic, Inc.

—Harry Potter & the Prisoner of Azkaban. Rowling, J. K. 2018. (Harry Potter Ser.: 3). (ENG.). 464p. (J). (gr. 3). pap. 12.99 (978-1-338-29916-8(6), Levine, Arthur A. Bks.) Scholastic, Inc.

—Harry Potter & the Sorcerer's Stone. Rowling, J. K. 2018. (Harry Potter Ser.: 1). (ENG.). 336p. (J). (gr. 3). pap. 12.99

(978-1-338-29914-4(X), Levine, Arthur A. Bks.) Scholastic, Inc.

Sem. Carnet Blanc Statue de la Liberte. 2016. (Bnf Affiches Ser.). (FRE.). (J). pap. *(978-2-01-116960-0(7))* Hachette Groupe Livre.

—Carnet Ligne Statue de la Liberte. 2016. (Bnf Affiches Ser.). (FRE.). (J). pap. *(978-2-01-116937-2(2))* Hachette Groupe Livre.

Semeiks, Val, et al. Captain America: This Is Captain America. Dworkin, Brooke. 2017. (World of Reading Level 1 Ser.). (ENG.). 32p. (J). (gr. -1-3). lib. bdg. 27.07 *(978-1-5321-4051-8(7)*, 25422) Spotlight.

Semeiks, Val. The Courageous Captain America. Thomas, Rich. 2012. (Marvel Origins Ser.). (ENG.). 48p. (J). (gr. k-5). lib. bdg. 27.07 *(978-1-61479-008-2(6)*, 11336, Marvel Age) Spotlight.

—The Incredible Hulk. Thomas, Rich. 2012. (Marvel Origins Ser.). (ENG.). 48p. (J). (gr. k-5). lib. bdg. 27.07 *(978-1-61479-009-9(4)*, 11337, Marvel Age) Spotlight.

Semerad, Johnnie. Josh W. Time Out. Semerad, Johnnie. Semerad, Emma. 2003. 32p. (J). 15.00 *(978-0-9744251-0-8(9))* Quiet Man.

Semionov, Vlad. Snake Invasion. Wilhelm, Doug. 2016. (ENG.). 144p. (J). (gr. 4-8). pap. 6.99 *(978-1-937133-52-8(4))* Chooseco LLC.

Semionov, Vladimir. Chinese Dragons. Montgomery, R. A. 2009. (Choose Your Own Adventure Ser.: 30). (ENG.). 144p. (J). (gr. 4-8). pap. 6.99 *(978-1-933390-30-7(1))* Chooseco LLC.

—Forecast from Stonehenge. Montgomery, R. A. 2007. (Choose Your Own Adventure Ser.: 19). (ENG.). 127p. (J). (gr. 4-7). pap. 7.99 *(978-1-933390-19-2(0))* Chooseco LLC.

—Moon Quest. Montgomery, Anson. 2008. (Choose Your Own Adventure Ser.: 26). (ENG.). 144p. (J). (gr. 4-8). pap. 6.99 *(978-1-933390-26-0(3))* Chooseco LLC.

—Search for the Black Rhino. Gilligan, Alison. 2011. (ENG.). 144p. (J). (gr. 4-8). pap. 7.99 *(978-1-937133-01-6(X))* Chooseco LLC.

—Silver Wings. Montgomery, R. A. 2007. (Choose Your Own Adventure Ser.: 23). (ENG.). 107p. (J). (gr. 4-7). pap. 6.99 *(978-1-933390-23-9(9))* Chooseco LLC.

—Struggle down Under. Gilligan, Shannon. 2007. (Choose Your Own Adventure Ser.: 21). (ENG.). 144p. (J). (gr. 4-8). pap. 7.99 *(978-1-933390-21-5(2))* Chooseco LLC.

Semionov, Vladimir & Cannella, Marco. Project UFO. Montgomery, R. A. 2008. (ENG.). 144p. (J). (gr. 4-8). pap. 6.99 *(978-1-933390-27-7(1))* Chooseco LLC.

Sempe. Los Recreos Del Pequeno Nicolas. Goscinny, René. 2006. (Serie Naranja Ser.). (SPA.). 116p. (J). pap. 12.95 *(978-958-5403-22-2(6))* Santillana USA Publishing Co., Inc.

Sempé, Jean-Jacques. Nicholas on Vacation. Goscinny, René. Bell, Anthea, tr. 2013. (ENG.). 136p. (J). (gr. 1-4). pap. 9.95 *(978-0-7148-6224-8(X))* Phaidon Pr., Inc.

—Nicholas on Vacation. Goscinny, René. Bell, Anthea, tr. rev. ed. 2006. 132p. (gr. 8-17). 19.95 *(978-0-7148-4678-1(3))* Phaidon Pr., Inc.

Sempé, Jean-Jacques & Sempé, Jean-Jacques. Nicholas. Goscinny, René & Goscinny, René. 2011. (ENG.). 136p. (gr. 7-17). pap. 9.95 *(978-0-7148-6115-9(4))* Phaidon Pr., Inc.

—Nicholas Again. Goscinny, René & Goscinny, René. rev. ed. 2006. (ENG.). 120p. (gr. 8-17). 19.95 *(978-0-7148-4564-7(7))* Phaidon Pr., Inc.

Sempé, Jean-Jacques, jt. illus. see Sempé, Jean-Jacques.

Sempill. The Pulp7 Quartereader, Bk. 2. Storm, Michael. l.t. ed. 2005. Orig. Title: Pulp7. 265p. (YA). per. *(978-0-9744929-1-9(4))* Leeway Pubs.

Semple, Dave. The Fearless Four: Braced for Battle. Richards, Lynne. 2009. (ENG.). 24p. (J). (gr. 1-17). pap. 3.99 *(978-1-58476-814-2(2))* Innovative Kids.

—Phonics Comics: the Fearless Four - Level 2. Bergen, Lara Rice. 2007. (ENG.). 24p. (J). (gr. 1-17). per. 3.99 *(978-1-58476-564-6(X))* Innovative Kids.

Semple, David. Rory's Lost His Voice. Doyle, Malachy. 2005. (ENG.). 24p. (J). lib. bdg. 23.65 *(978-1-59646-714-9(2))* Dingles & Co.

—There Was a Crooked Man. Punter, Russell. 2010. (First Reading Level 2 Ser.). 32p. (J). 6.99 *(978-0-7945-2682-5(9)*, Usborne) EDC Publishing.

Semple, Lucy. Bird Singing, Bird Winging. Singer, Marilyn. 2020. (Ready-To-Reads Ser.). (ENG.). 32p. (J). (gr. -1-k). 17.99 ***(978-1-5344-4143-9(3))***; pap. 4.99 ***(978-1-5344-4142-2(5))*** Simon Spotlight. (Simon Spotlight).

—No Party Poopers! McLellan, Gretchen. 2020. (ENG.). 32p. (J). (gr. -1-3). 17.99 ***(978-1-4998-0988-6(3))*** Little Bee Books Inc.

Semple, Lucy. When I Grow up... Great Leaders: Kids Like You That Became Inspiring Leaders. DK. 2020. (When I Grow Up Ser.). (ENG.). 18p. (J). (-k). bds. 8.99 *(978-1-4654-9140-4(6)*, DK Children) Dorling Kindersley Publishing, Inc.

Semykina, Victoria. The Real Boat. Aromshtam, Marina. 2019. (ENG.). 64p. (J). (gr. k-3). 17.99 *(978-1-5362-0277-9(0)*, Templar) Candlewick Pr.

Sen, Giedre. Bob the Tooth Fairy. L. Treadwell, Jill, ed. 2018. (ENG.). 26p. (J). pap. 9.99 *(978-1-7292-1035-2(X))* Independently Published.

—Riwi the Kiwi (Opendyslexic) Goes to a Party. Nicholas-Holt, Lilla. 2016. (ENG.). (J). pap. *(978-0-473-36927-9(3))* Rare Design Ltd.

Sen Gupta, Subhadra & Gupta, Priyankar. A Children's History of India. 2015. 442p. (J). *(978-81-291-3697-8(X))* Rupa & Co.

Sendak, Maurice. Los Amigos de Osito. Minarik, Else Holmelund. Benavides, Rosa, tr. 2nd ed. (Infantil Alfaguara Ser.: 32).Tr. of Little Bear's Friends. (SPA.). 64p. (J). 7.95 *(978-84-204-3049-2(8))* Santillana USA Publishing Co., Inc.

—Bears. Krauss, Ruth. 2005. (ENG.). 24p. (J). 21.99 *(978-0-06-027994-3(X))* HarperCollins Pubs.

—Bears. Krauss, Ruth. 2005. (ENG.). 24p. *(978-0-00-720662-9(3)*, HarperCollins Children's Bks.) HarperCollins Pubs. Ltd.

—The Bee-Man of Orn. Stockton, Frank Richard. 2005. (Sendak Reissues Ser.). (ENG.). 56p. (J). (gr. -1-18). 15.95 *(978-0-06-029729-9(8))* HarperCollins Pubs.

—Un Beso para Osito. Minarik, Else Holmelund. Benavides, Rosa, tr. 2003. (Infantil Alfaguara Ser.: 31).Tr. of Kiss for Little Bear. (SPA.). 36p. (J). (gr. k-3). 11.95 *(978-84-204-3050-8(1)*, AF1633) Ediciones Alfaguara ESP. Dist: Lectorum Pubns., Inc., Santillana USA Publishing Co., Inc.

—The Big Green Book. Graves, Robert. 2018. (ENG.). 64p. (J). (gr. -1-3). 18.95 *(978-0-06-264483-1(1))* HarperCollins Pubs.

—Brundibar. Kushner, Tony. 2003. (ENG.). 56p. (J). (gr. 5-9). 24.99 *(978-0-7868-0904-2(3)*, di Capua, Michael Bks.) Hyperion Bks. for Children.

—The Griffin & the Minor Canon. Stockton, Frank Richard. 2005. (Sendak Reissues Ser.). (ENG.). 56p. (J). 15.95 *(978-0-06-029731-2(X))* HarperCollins Pubs.

—The Happy Rain. Sendak, Jack & Sendak, J. 2004. (Sendak Reissues Ser.). (ENG.). 48p. (J). reprint ed. 13.95 *(978-0-06-028785-6(3))* HarperCollins Pubs.

—In Grandpa's House. Sendak, Philip. 2003. (Sendak Reissues Ser.). (ENG.). 48p. (J). reprint ed. 16.95 *(978-0-06-028787-0(X))* HarperCollins Pubs.

—Little Bear. Minarik, Else Holmelund. 2003. (I Can Read Level 1 Ser.). (ENG.). 64p. (J). (gr. k-3). pap. 4.95 *(978-0-06-444004-2(4)*, HarperCollins) HarperCollins Pubs. Ltd. GBR. Dist: HarperCollins Pubs.

—Little Bear's Visit. Minarik, Else Holmelund. (J). pap. 12.95 incl. audio Weston Woods Studios, Inc.

—Lullabies & Night Songs. Engvick, William. 2004. (Sendak Reissues Ser.). 80p. (J). 40.00 *(978-0-06-029733-6(6))* HarperCollins Pubs.

—The Moon Jumpers. Udry, Janice May. 2013. (Sendak Reissues Ser.). (ENG.). 32p. (J). (gr. -1-3). 17.95 *(978-0-06-028460-2(9))* HarperCollins Pubs.

—No Fighting, No Biting! Minarik, Else Holmelund. 2004. 63p. (J). (gr. k-4). reprint ed. pap. 17.00 *(978-0-7567-7235-2(4))* DIANE Publishing Co.

—Nutcracker. Hoffmann, E. T. A. Manheim, Ralph, tr. 2012. 120p. (gr. 5). 24.99 *(978-0-385-34864-5(9)*, Crown) Potter/Ten Speed/Harmony/Rodale.

—Osito. Minarik, Else Holmelund. Aguilar, Joaquína, tr. 2003. (Infantil Alfaguara Ser.: 25).Tr. of Little Bear. (SPA.). 60p. (J). (gr. k-3). pap. 8.95 *(978-84-204-3044-7(7)*, AF1346) Santillana USA Publishing Co., Inc.

—El Oso Que No lo Era. Minarik, Else Holmelund & Tashlin, Frank. 2003. (Infantil Ser.).Tr. of Bear That Wasn't. (SPA.). 62p. (J). (gr. k-3). pap. 8.95 *(978-958-24-0002-6(1))* Santillana USA Publishing Co., Inc.

—Papa Oso Vuelve a Casa. Minarik, Else Holmelund. Benavides, Rosa, tr. 2nd ed. 2003. (Infantil Alfaguara Ser.: 29).Tr. of Father Bear Comes Home. (SPA.). 63p. (J). (gr. -1-3). pap. *(978-84-204-3048-5(X)*, AF1359) Ediciones Alfaguara ESP. Dist: Santillana USA Publishing Co., Inc.

—Pleasant Fieldmouse. Wahl, Jan. 2007. (Sendak Reissues Ser.). (ENG.). 72p. (J). 15.95 *(978-0-06-029725-1(5))* HarperCollins Pubs.

—Sarah's Room. Orgel, Doris. 2005. 47p. (J). (gr. k-4). reprint ed. 15.00 *(978-0-7567-9683-9(0))* DIANE Publishing Co.

—Sarah's Room. Orgel, Doris. 2003. (Sendak Reissues Ser.). (ENG.). 48p. (J). (gr. -1-3). 15.95 *(978-0-06-029727-5(1))* HarperCollins Pubs.

—La Visita de Osito. Minarik, Else Holmelund. Puncel, María, tr. 2006. (Osito / Little Bear Ser.).Tr. of Little Bear's Visit. (SPA.). 64p. (gr. k-3). pap. 8.95 *(978-968-19-0623-8(3)*, AF1060) Santillana USA Publishing Co., Inc.

—What Do You Say, Dear? Joslin, Sesyle. (J). (gr. k-2). 14.45 incl. audio *(978-0-8045-6525-7(2)*, SAC 6525) Spoken Arts, Inc.

Sendak, Maurice. Alligators All Around: An Alphabet. Sendak, Maurice. 2018. (ENG.). 32p. (J). (gr. -1-3). pap. 7.95 *(978-0-06-285436-0(4))* HarperCollins Pubs.

—Alligators All Around Board Book: An Alphabet. Sendak, Maurice. 2017. (ENG.). 32p. (J). (gr. -1-3). bds. 7.95 *(978-0-06-266807-3(2))* HarperCollins Pubs.

—Bumble-Ardy. Sendak, Maurice. 2011. (ENG.). 40p. (J). 17.95 *(978-0-06-205198-1(9))* HarperCollins Pubs.

—Chicken Soup with Rice: A Book of Months. Sendak, Maurice. 2018. (ENG.). 32p. (J). (gr. -1-3). pap. 7.95 *(978-0-06-285440-7(2))* HarperCollins Pubs.

—Chicken Soup with Rice Board Book: A Book of Months. Sendak, Maurice. 2017. (ENG.). 32p. (J). (gr. -1 — 1). bds. 7.95 *(978-0-06-266808-0(0))* HarperCollins Pubs.

—La Cocina de Noche. Sendak, Maurice. 2003. (Picture Books Collection). (SPA.). 40p. (J). (gr. k-3). 10.95 *(978-84-204-4570-0(3))* Ediciones Alfaguara ESP. Dist: Santillana USA Publishing Co., Inc.

—Kenny's Window. Sendak, Maurice. 2004. 54p. (J). (gr. k-4). reprint ed. 14.00 *(978-0-7567-7767-8(4))* DIANE Publishing Co.

—Kenny's Window. Sendak, Maurice. 2004. (Trophy Picture Bks.). (ENG.). 64p. (J). (gr. 3-6). pap. 11.95 *(978-0-06-443209-2(2))* HarperCollins Pubs.

—My Brother's Book. Sendak, Maurice. 2013. (ENG.). 32p. 18.95 *(978-0-06-223489-6(7))* HarperCollins Pubs.

—One Was Johnny: A Counting Book. Sendak, Maurice. 2018. (ENG.). 48p. (J). (gr. -1-3). pap. 7.95 *(978-0-06-285441-4(0))* HarperCollins Pubs.

—One Was Johnny Board Book: A Counting Book. Sendak, Maurice. 2017. (ENG.). 46p. (J). (gr. -1-3). bds. 7.95 *(978-0-06-266809-7(9))* HarperCollins Pubs.

—Pierre: A Cautionary Tale in Five Chapters & a Prologue. Sendak, Maurice. 2018. (ENG.). 48p. (J). (gr. -1-3). pap. 7.95 *(978-0-06-285442-1(9))* HarperCollins Pubs.

—Pierre Board Book: A Cautionary Tale in Five Chapters & a Prologue. Sendak, Maurice. 2017. (ENG.). 38p. (J). (gr. -1-3). bds. 7.95 *(978-0-06-266810-3(2))* HarperCollins Pubs.

—Presto & Zesto in Limboland. Sendak, Maurice. Yorinks, Arthur. 2018. (ENG.). 28p. (J). (gr. -1-3). 18.95 *(978-0-06-264465-7(3))* HarperCollins Pubs.

—Where the Wild Things Are. Sendak, Maurice. 25th anniv. ed. 2012. (ENG.). 48p. (J). (gr. -1-3). 19.95 *(978-0-06-025492-6(0))*; pap. 8.95 *(978-0-06-443178-1(9))* HarperCollins Pubs. Ltd. GBR. (HarperCollins). Dist: HarperCollins Pubs.

Sendak, Maurice. Un Beso para Osito. Sendak, Maurice, tr. Minarik, Else Holmelund.Tr. of Kiss for Little Bear. (SPA.). 34p. (J). (gr. k-3). pap. 8.95 *(978-84-204-4827-5(3))* Santillana USA Publishing Co., Inc.

Sender, Ana. ¿Por Qué Lloramos? Pintadera, Fran. 2019. (SPA.). 40p. (J). (gr. 2-4). pap. 17.95 *(978-84-17440-15-2(1))* Akiara Bks. ESP. Dist: Independent Pubs. Group.

—Why Do We Cry? Pintadera, Fran. 2020. (ENG.). 32p. (J). (gr. -1-2). 16.99 *(978-1-5253-0477-4(1))* Kids Can Pr., Ltd. CAN. Dist: Hachette Bk. Group.

Sénégas, Sthépane. ¿Qué ves? 2017. (SPA.). 40p. (J). (gr. k-2). *(978-84-16003-86-0(6))* Takatuka ESP. Dist: Lectorum Pubns., Inc.

Senior, Helen. See How They Grow - Pig. Ling, Bill, photos by. Ling, Mary & Dorling Kindersley Publishing Staff. 2007. (See How They Grow Ser.). (ENG.). 96p. (J). (gr. k-3). 16.19 *(978-0-7566-3018-8(5))* Dorling Kindersley Publishing, Inc.

Senisi, Ellen B., photos by. Friend Power. Marx, Trish. 2011. (J). (gr. k-5). 17.95 *(978-1-60060-233-7(9))* Lee & Low Bks., Inc.

Senisi, Ellen B., photos by. Berry Smudges & Leaf Prints: Finding & Making Colors from Nature. Senisi, Ellen B. 2005. 40p. (J). (gr. 4-8). reprint ed. 17.00 *(978-0-7567-9707-2(1))* DIANE Publishing Co.

Senkel, Nicholas. Celia & the Witches. Teare, Nellie. 2008. 24p. (J). 13.95 *(978-0-9820852-0-2(6))* Harmon Creek Pr.

Senn, Oscar. St. Augustine a to Z: A Young Reader's Guide to America's Oldest City. Calfee, Susan. 2016. (ENG.). (J). pap. 12.95 *(978-0-9895487-1-7(6))* Wordwhittler Bks.

Senner, Katja. Abre, Cierra y Aprende! Cuno, Sabine. Caballero, D., tr. 2007. 14p. (J). (gr. -1). *(978-970-718-489-3(2)*, Silver Dolphin en Español) Advanced Marketing, S. de R. L. de C. V.

Senning, Susan. A Sergeant in the House. Turnbull, Betty J. 2013. 44p. pap. 14.95 *(978-1-61153-060-5(1))* Light Messages Publishing.

—A Sergeant in the House. Turnbull, Betty. 2013. 44p. (J). 19.95 *(978-1-61153-059-9(8))* Light Messages Publishing.

Seo, Hong-Seock. Dragon Hunter, Vol. 13. Seo, Hong-Seock. 13th rev. ed. 2005. (Dragon Hunter Ser.). 176p. per. 9.99 *(978-1-59532-649-2(9))* TOKYOPOP, Inc.

Seo, Kaila Eunhye. Fred. 2015. (ENG.). 40p. (J). 15.99 *(978-1-4413-1731-5(7)*, 9781441317315) Peter Pauper Pr. Inc.

Seo, Tess. Fallen Angela. Kahng, Yuna. 2017. 32p. (J). (gr. 1-3). 18.00 *(978-1-56591-378-3(7))* Hollym International Corp.

Seoane, Jose Carlos. Los Sombreros Verdes. P Zabala. 2018. (SPA.). 98p. (J). pap. 25.00 *(978-1-7286-4919-1(6))* Independently Published.

Seock Seo, Hong. Dragon Hunter, Vol. 12. Im, Hye-Young, tr. rev. ed. 2005. 176p. pap. 9.99 *(978-1-59182-960-7(7))* TOKYOPOP, Inc.

Seon, JeongHyeon. Zippy the Runner. Kim, JiYu. rev. ed. 2014. (MySELF Bookshelf Ser.). (ENG.). 32p. (J). (gr. k-2). pap. 11.94 *(978-1-60357-656-7(8))*; lib. bdg. 25.27 *(978-1-59953-647-7(1))* Norwood Hse. Pr.

Seong-min, Kim. Dangun Wanggeom: Founder of the First Korean Kingdom. Chul-heon, Chung. Park, Christian J. & Park, Christian J., trs. 2011. (ENG.). 40p. 14.00 *(978-89-91913-50-9(4)*, 1330) Seoul Selection KOR. Dist: Univ. of Hawaii Pr.

Serafimovska, Biljana. The Men in Blue. Gatlin, Shawana D. 2019. (ENG.). 34p. (J). pap. 9.99 *(978-1-7957-3366-3(7))* Independently Published.

Serafini, Frank. Looking Closely Through the Forest, 0 vols. Serafini, Frank. 2014. (Looking Closely Ser.). (ENG.). 40p. (J). (gr. -1-2). pap. 7.99 *(978-1-77138-118-5(3))* Kids Can Pr., Ltd. CAN. Dist: Hachette Bk. Group.

Serbanescu, Luminita. Bee Paradise. Clackdoyle, Carolyn. 2019. (ENG.). 28p. (J). *(978-0-2288-0641-7(0))*; pap. *(978-0-2288-0640-0(2))* Tellwell Talent.

Sereda, Maja. A Kite's Flight. Gumede, William. 2011. (ENG.). 32p. (J). (gr. k-2). pap. 11.00 *(978-1-77009-804-6(6))* Jacana Media ZAF. Dist: Independent Pubs. Group.

Seredy, Kate. Winterbound. Bianco, Margery Williams. 2014. (ENG.). 256p. (J). (gr. 5-9). pap. 5.99 *(978-0-486-49290-2(7))* Dover Pubns., Inc.

Seredy, Kate. Philomena. Seredy, Kate. 2008. 93p. (J). pap. 11.95 *(978-1-932350-19-7(5))* Bethlehem Bks.

—A Tree for Peter. Seredy, Kate. 2004. 112p. (J). reprint ed. 19.95 *(978-1-930900-26-4(0))* Purple Hse. Pr.

Seren, Tara. Wings to Fly. Utsch, Jendala. 2018. (Scooter the Loquatian Ser.: Vol. 1). (ENG.). 26p. (J). pap. 10.95 *(978-1-7313-0182-6(0))* Independently Published.

Serena Geddes. Lulu Bell & the Arabian Nights. Murrell, Belinda. 2020. (Lulu Bell Ser.: 10). (ENG.). 96p. (J). (gr. 1-3). 9.99 ***(978-1-76089-180-0(0)**, Puffin)* Penguin Random Hse. AUS. Dist: Independent Pubs. Group.

—Lulu Bell & the Birthday Unicorn. Murrell, Belinda. 2020. (Lulu Bell Ser.: 1). (ENG.). 96p. (J). (gr. 1-3). 9.99 ***(978-1-76089-219-7(X)**, Puffin)* Penguin Random Hse. AUS. Dist: Independent Pubs. Group.

Serena Geddes. Lulu Bell & the Circus Pup. Murrell, Belinda. 2020. (Lulu Bell Ser.: 5). 96p. (J). (gr. 2-5). 9.99 *(978-1-76089-221-0(1)*, Puffin) Penguin Random Hse. AUS. Dist: Independent Pubs. Group.

—Lulu Bell & the Cubby Fort. Murrell, Belinda. 2020. (Lulu Bell Ser.: 3). 96p. (J). (gr. 2-5). 9.99 *(978-1-76089-222-7(X)*, Puffin) Penguin Random Hse. AUS. Dist: Independent Pubs. Group.

—Lulu Bell & the Fairy Penguin. Murrell, Belinda. 2020. (Lulu Bell Ser.: 2). 96p. (J). (gr. 2-5). 9.99 *(978-1-76089-223-4(8)*, Puffin) Penguin Random Hse. AUS. Dist: Independent Pubs. Group.

Serena Geddes. Lulu Bell & the Koala Joey. Murrell, Belinda. 2020. (Lulu Bell Ser.: 11). (ENG.). 96p. (J). (gr. 1-3). 9.99 ***(978-1-76089-224-1(6)**, Puffin)* Penguin Random Hse. AUS. Dist: Independent Pubs. Group.

Serena Geddes. Lulu Bell & the Moon Dragon. Murrell, Belinda. 2020. (Lulu Bell Ser.: 4). 96p. (J). (gr. 2-5). 9.99 *(978-1-76089-226-5(2)*, Puffin) Penguin Random Hse. AUS. Dist: Independent Pubs. Group.

Serena Geddes. Lulu Bell & the Pirate Fun. Murrell, Belinda. 2020. (Lulu Bell Ser.: 12). (ENG.). 96p. (J). (gr. 1-3). 9.99 ***(978-1-76089-227-2(0)**, Puffin)* Penguin Random Hse. AUS. Dist: Independent Pubs. Group.

Serfass, Jim. The Little Motorcycle. Link, C. Edward. 2004. (J). 9.95 *(978-0-9749615-0-7(7))* Roadracing World Publishing, Inc.

Sergeeva, Mary. Old MacDonald Had a Farm in Oregon. Everett, Forrest. 2018. (Old MacDonald Had a Farm Regional Board Bks.). (ENG.). 16p. (J). (gr. -1-3). bds. 12.99 *(978-1-64170-014-6(9)*, 550014) Familius LLC.

—Row, Row, Row Your Boat in Oregon. Everett, Forrest. 2018. (Row, Row, Row Your Boat Regional Board Bks.). (ENG.). 16p. (J). (gr. k-3). bds. 12.99 *(978-1-64170-015-3(7)*, 550015) Familius LLC.

Sergeeva, Masha. Finger Painting. Level 1: Stickers Inside! Strengthens Fine Motor Skills, Develops Patience, Sparks Conversation, Inspires Creativity. Uzorova, Olga & Nefedova, Elena. 2019. (Clever Hands Ser.). (ENG.). 32p. (J). (gr. -1 — 1). pap. 4.99 *(978-1-948418-14-0(2))* Clever Media Group.

—Finger Painting Level 2: Stickers Inside! Strengthens Fine Motor Skills, Develops Patience, Sparks Conversation, Inspires Creativity. Uzorova, Olga & Nefedova, Elena. 2019. (Clever Hands Ser.). (ENG.). 32p. (J). (gr. -1 — 1). pap. 4.99 *(978-1-948418-13-3(4))* Clever Media Group.

—Palm Painting Level 2: Stickers Inside! Strengthens Fine Motor Skills, Develops Patience, Sparks Conversation, Inspires Creativity. Uzorova, Olga & Nefedova, Elena. 2019. (Clever Hands Ser.). (ENG.). 32p. (J). (gr. -1 — 1). pap. 4.99 *(978-1-948418-11-9(8))* Clever Media Group.

Sergeyeva, Marina. Nikki & Nick Are Great Friends to Pick. Sergeyeva, Marina. 2012. 34p. 19.95 *(978-0-9834735-4-1(4))* Leo Publishing.

Serizawa, Naoki. Samurai Man, Vol.2. Serizawa, Naoki. 2005. 192p. (YA). pap. 9.99 *(978-1-58655-693-8(2)*, AWNOV-0562) Media Blasters, Inc.

Seroya, Tea. David & Jacko. Downie, David. Tatsi, Andreanna, tr. 2012. 52p. pap. *(978-1-922159-15-1(8))*; pap. *(978-1-922159-24-3(7))* Blue Peg Publishing.

—David & Jacko. Downie, David. Ivanova, Kalina, tr. 2012. 52p. pap. *(978-1-922159-01-4(8))* Blue Peg Publishing.

—David & Jacko. Downie, David. 2012. 52p. pap. *(978-1-922159-99-1(9))* Blue Peg Publishing.

—Horrible Stories My Dad Told Me. Downie, David. Tatsi, Andreanna, tr. 2012. 44p. pap. *(978-1-922159-95-3(6))* Blue Peg Publishing.

—Horrible Stories My Dad Told Me. Downie, David. M, Akiko, tr. 2012. 44p. pap. *(978-1-922159-94-6(8))* Blue Peg Publishing.

—Horrible Stories My Dad Told Me. Downie, David. Ivanova, Kalina, tr. 2012. 42p. pap. *(978-1-922159-96-0(4))* Blue Peg Publishing.

—Horrible Stories My Dad Told Me. Downie, David. Nanevych, Julia, tr. 2012. 44p. pap. *(978-1-922159-97-7(2))* Blue Peg Publishing.

—Horrible Stories My Dad Told Me. Downie, David. Nanevich, Julia, tr. 2012. 44p. pap. *(978-1-922159-90-8(5))* Blue Peg Publishing.

—Horrible Stories My Dad Told Me. Downie, David. 2012. 42p. pap. *(978-0-9873501-0-7(2))* Blue Peg Publishing.

—It's Not about You, Mr. Easter Bunny: A Love Letter about the True Meaning of Easter. Coffelt, Soraya. 2017. (Love Letters Book Ser.). (ENG.). 36p. (J). pap. 8.99 *(978-1-68350-063-6(6))* Morgan James Publishing.

Serpentelli, John. OUCH or AHHH - The Choice IS Easy!, 1 vol. Kelso, Susan. 2009. 47p. pap. 24.95 *(978-1-61546-148-6(5))* America Star Bks.

Serra, Adolfo. A Different Story. 2019. (ENG.). 32p. (J). *(978-0-8028-5527-5(X)*, Eerdmans Bks For Young Readers) Eerdmans, William B. Publishing Co.

Serra, Armando. La Familia de Nieve. Romero, Sensi. 2004. (Cuentos con miga Ser.). 47p. (J). (gr. 1-5). pap. 11.00 *(978-84-95895-22-6(6))* Editorial Brief ESP. Dist: Independent Pubs. Group.

Serra, Sebastià. Boy, Were We Wrong about the Weather! Kudlinski, Kathleen V. 2015. 32p. (J). (gr. -1-3). 16.99 *(978-0-8037-3793-8(9)*, Dial Bks) Penguin Young Readers Group.

Serra, Sebastia. The Dog Who Loved the Moon. Garcia, Cristina. 2011. (ENG.). 32p. (J). (gr. -1-3). 16.99 *(978-1-4424-3089-1(3)*, Atheneum Bks. for Young Readers) Simon & Schuster Children's Publishing.

—If You Were a Kid Aboard the Titanic. Gregory, Josh. 2017. (If You Were a Kid Ser.). (ENG.). 32p. (J). (gr. 2-4). lib. bdg. 26.00 *(978-0-531-22382-6(5)*, Children's Pr.) Scholastic Library Publishing.

Serra, Sebastiá. Inky's Great Escape: The Incredible & True Story of an Octopus Escape. Lyall, Casey. 2017. 32p. (J). (gr. k). 16.95 *(978-1-4549-2635-1(X))* Sterling Publishing Co., Inc.

Serra, Sebastia. A Mango in the Hand: A Story Told Through Proverbs. Sacre, Antonio. 2011. (ENG.). 32p. (J). (gr. -1-3). 17.99 *(978-0-8109-9734-9(7)*, Abrams Bks. for Young Readers) Abrams, Inc.

Serra, Sebastià. The Piñata That the Farm Maiden Hung. Vamos, Samantha R. 2019. 32p. (J). (gr. -1-3). lib. bdg. 17.99 *(978-1-58089-796-9(7))* Charlesbridge Publishing, Inc.

Serra, Sebastiá. A Pirate's Night Before Christmas. Yates, Philip. (J). 2020. 24p. (— 1). bds. 7.95 ***(978-1-4549-4264-1(9))***; 2014. (ENG.). 32p. (gr. -1-1). pap. 6.95 *(978-1-4549-1357-3(6))*; 2008. (ENG.). 32p. (gr. -1-1). 14.95 *(978-1-4027-4257-6(6))* Sterling Publishing Co., Inc.

Serra, Sebastià. A Pirate's Twelve Days of Christmas. Yates, Philip. 2015. 32p. (J). (gr. -1-1). pap. 6.95 *(978-1-4549-1682-6(6))* Sterling Publishing Co., Inc.

S

Serra, Sebastia. The Runaway Wok: A Chinese New Year Tale. Compestine, Ying Chang. 2011. (ENG.). 32p. (J). (gr. 1-3). 17.99 *(978-0-525-42068-2(1)*, Dutton Books for Young Readers) Penguin Young Readers Group.

Serrano, Javier. ¡¡¡Lambertooo!!! Serrano, Javier, tr. Sierra I. Fabra, Jordi & Sierra i Fabra, Jordi. 9th ed. 2004. (SPA.). 136p. (J). (gr. 6-12). pap. 14.99 *(978-84-207-2975-6(2))* Grupo Anaya, S.A. ESP. Dist: Lectorum Pubns., Inc.

Serrano, Javier U. Dias de Reyes Magos. Pascual, Emilio. 4th ed. 2003. (SPA.). 158p. *(978-84-207-9079-4(6)*, GS4140) Grupo Anaya, S.A. ESP. Dist: Lectorum Pubns., Inc.

Serrano, Pablo. La Malinche: The Princess Who Helped Cortés Conquer the Aztec Empire, 1 vol. Serrano, Francisco. Ourious, Susan, tr. 2012. (ENG.). 40p. (J). (gr. 3-7). 18.95 *(978-1-55498-111-3(5))* Groundwood Bks. CAN. Dist: Publishers Group West (PGW).

—Mi Mano. Ramos, Maria Cristina. 2007. (SPA.). 18p. (J). 11.95 *(978-968-494-213-4(3))* Centro de Informacion y Desarrollo de la Comunicacion y la Literatura MEX. Dist: Lectorum Pubns., Inc.

—The Poet King of Tezcoco: A Great Leader of Ancient Mexico, 1 vol. Serrano, Francisco. Balch, Trudy & Engelbert, Jo Anne, trs. 2007. (ENG.). 48p. (J). (gr. 3-6). 18.95 *(978-0-88899-787-6(6))* Groundwood Bks. CAN. Dist: Publishers Group West (PGW).

Servello, Joe. Double Trouble in Bugland. Kotzwinkle, William. 2016. (ENG.). 190p. (J). pap. 14.95 *(978-1-56792-564-7(2))* Godine, David R. Pub.

—Trouble in Bugland: A Collection of Inspector Mantis Mysteries. Kotzwinkle, William. 2015. (ENG.). 190p. (J). (gr. 4-7). reprint ed. pap. 14.95 *(978-1-56792-070-3(5))* Godine, David R. Pub.

Serwacki, Kevin & Pallace, Chris. Joey & Johnny, the Ninjas: Epic Fail. Serwacki, Kevin & Pallace, Chris. 2016. (Joey & Johnny, the Ninjas Ser.: 2). (ENG.). 384p. (J). (gr. 3-7). 12.99 *(978-0-06-229935-2(2))* HarperCollins Pubs.

—Joey & Johnny, the Ninjas: Get Mooned. Serwacki, Kevin & Pallace, Chris. 2015. (Joey & Johnny, the Ninjas Ser.: 1). (ENG.). 320p. (J). (gr. 3-7). 12.99 *(978-0-06-229933-8(6))* HarperCollins Pubs.

Sesame Workshop, jt. illus. see Brannon, Tom.

Sesma, Delia. Murci Solano Quiere Ser Vegano. Sesma, Delia. 2019. (SPA.). 26p. (J). pap. 19.90 ***(978-1-6887-1422-9(7))*** Independently Published.

Seth. All the Wrong Questions: Question 1: Also Published As Who Could That Be at This Hour? Snicket, Lemony. 2017. (All the Wrong Questions Ser.: 1). (ENG.). 288p. (J). (gr. 3-17). pap. 9.99 *(978-0-316-44546-7(0))* Little, Brown Bks. for Young Readers.

—File under: 13 Suspicious Incidents. Snicket, Lemony. (ENG.). (J). (gr. 3-17). 2016. 288p. pap. 8.99 *(978-0-316-39306-5(1))*; 2014. 272p. 13.99 *(978-0-316-28403-5(3))* Little, Brown Bks. for Young Readers.

—Shouldn't You Be in School? Snicket, Lemony. (All the Wrong Questions Ser.: 3). (ENG.). 352p. (J). (gr. 3-17). 2015. pap. 9.99 *(978-0-316-38060-7(1))*; 2014. 30.00 *(978-0-316-40968-1(5))* Little, Brown Bks. for Young Readers.

—When Did You See Her Last? Snicket, Lemony. (All the Wrong Questions Ser.: 2). (ENG.). 304p. (J). (gr. 3-17). 2014. pap. 8.99 *(978-0-316-33684-0(X))*; 2013. 28.00 *(978-0-316-23993-6(3))* Little, Brown Bks. for Young Readers.

—Who Could That Be at This Hour? Snicket, Lemony. l.t. ed. 2012. (All the Wrong Questions Ser.: 1). (ENG.). 304p. (J). (gr. 3-17). 25.00 *(978-0-316-22425-3(1))* Little, Brown Bks. for Young Readers.

—Who Could That Be at This Hour? Also Published As All the Wrong Questions: Question 1. Snicket, Lemony. (All the Wrong Questions Ser.: 1). (ENG.). (J). (gr. 3-17). 2014. 288p. pap. 9.99 *(978-0-316-33547-8(9))*; 2012. 272p. 15.99 *(978-0-316-12308-2(0))* Little, Brown Bks. for Young Readers.

Seton, Ernest Thompson. The Trail of the Sandhill Stag. Seton, Ernest Thompson. 2007. 94p. (YA). pap. 16.95 *(978-1-60355-055-0(0))* Juniper Grove.

—Two Little Savages: The Adventures of Two Boys Who Lived As American Indians. Seton, Ernest Thompson. 2010. (ENG.). 313p. (J). (gr. 4-7). pap. 18.00 *(978-1-60419-033-5(7))* Axios Pr.

Seton-Thompson, Grace Gallatin. Biography of a Grizzly. Seton, Ernest Thompson. 2008. 72p. pap. *(978-1-4099-1427-3(5))* Dodo Pr.

Setterlund, Donna J. Mouse in the House: For the Love of Peanut Butter. Callison, J. L. 2019. (Mouse in the House Ser.: Vol. 1). (ENG.). 42p. (J). (gr. k-2). 11.95 ***(978-0-9987771-5-3(3))***; 22.95 ***(978-0-9987771-4-6(5))*** Callison, J.L.

Settle, Zachary. Gaspar, the Flatulating Ghost, Flies a Kite. Burrell, Teresa. 2017. (ENG.). (J). pap. 11.99 *(978-1-938680-25-0(1))* Silent Thunder Publishing.

Seung-Man, Hwang. Zippy Ziggy, Vol. 2. Eun-Jeong, Kim. 2005. (Zippy Ziggy Ser.: Vol. 2). 192p. (YA). pap. 9.95 *(978-1-59697-162-2(2))* Infinity Studios LLC.

Seurat, Georges. Les Points de Seurat / Seurat's Dots: Learn Shapes in French & English. Oui Love Books. 2019. (First Impressions Ser.: Vol. 4). (ENG.). 32p. (J). pap. 12.95 *(978-1-947961-73-9(X)*, Oui Love Bks.) Odeon Livre.

Seuss. Oh, Baby, the Places You'll Go! Rabe, Tish. 2015. (ENG.). 32p. (J). (gr. k-12). 9.99 *(978-0-553-52057-6(1)*, Random Hse. Bks. for Young Readers) Random Hse. Children's Bks.

Seuss, Dr. Poisson Un - Poisson Deux - Poisson Rouge - Poisson Bleu. 2011. (FRE.). 64p. (J). (gr. -1-3). 12.95 *(978-1-61243-029-4(5))* Ulysses Pr.

Seuss, Dr. Gerald McBoing Boing. Seuss, Dr. 2004. (Little Golden Book Ser.). (ENG.). 24p. (J). (gr. -1-2). 4.99 *(978-0-375-82721-1(8)*, Golden Bks.) Random Hse. Children's Bks.

—How the Grinch Stole Christmas! Seuss, Dr. 50th ed. 2007. (ENG.). 64p. pap. *(978-0-00-725860-4(7)*, HarperCollins) HarperCollins Pubs. Ltd.

—How the Grinch Stole Christmas! Seuss, Dr. Jonaitis, Alice, ed. deluxe ed. 2014. (Classic Seuss Ser.). (ENG.). 64p. (J). (gr. k-4). 25.99 *(978-0-679-89153-6(6)*, Random Hse. Bks. for Young Readers) Random Hse. Children's Bks.

—The Lorax. Seuss, Dr. ed. 2010. (ENG.). 24p. bds. *(978-0-00-732618-1(1)*, HarperCollins Children's Bks.) HarperCollins Pubs. Ltd.

—Oh, the Places You'll Go! Seuss, Dr. 2003. (Dr Seuss - Yellow Back Book Ser.). (ENG.). 48p. pap. *(978-0-00-715852-2(1)*, HarperCollins Children's Bks.) HarperCollins Pubs. Ltd.

Seuss, Dr. Come Over to My House. Seuss, Dr., tr. Date not set. (J). lib. bdg. 11.99 *(978-0-679-98255-5(8))*; (gr. -1-3). 7.99 *(978-0-679-88255-8(3))* Random Hse. Children's Bks. (Random Hse. Bks. for Young Readers).

Seva. The Last Pair of Shoes. Fridman, Sashi. 2006. 32p. (J). 13.95 *(978-0-8266-0031-8(X))* Merkos L'Inyonei Chinuch.

—A Touch of the High Holidays: A Touch & Feel Book. Glazer, Devorah. 2006. 16p. (J). bds. 7.95 *(978-0-8266-0020-2(4))* Merkos L'Inyonei Chinuch.

Severance, Lyn. Pig. Older, Jules. 2004. 32p. (J). (gr. k-3). 16.95 *(978-0-88106-109-3(3))* Charlesbridge Publishing, Inc.

Severin, Marie, et al. Adventures of Spider-Man: Radioactive. 2019. (ENG.). 168p. (J). (gr. 1-3). pap. 12.99 *(978-1-302-92044-9(8))* Marvel Worldwide, Inc.

—Tigra: the Complete Collection. 2019. (ENG.). 424p. (YA). (gr. 8-17). pap. 39.99 *(978-1-302-92069-2(3))* Marvel Worldwide, Inc.

Severin, Marie. X-Men, Magneto's Master Plan. Gallagher, Michael. 24p. (YA). (gr. k-18). 12.95 *(978-0-9627001-6-3(9))* Futech Educational Products, Inc.

—X-Men, Scourge of the Savage Land. Gallagher, Michael. 24p. (YA). (gr. k-18). 12.95 *(978-0-9627001-7-0(7))* Futech Educational Products, Inc.

Severino, Philip. Getting Your First Allowance. Burke, Patrick J. 2008. 28p. pap. 24.95 *(978-1-60441-882-8(6))* America Star Bks.

Sevig, Kirsten. Goldilocks & the Three Pancakes: A Story of Shapes, Numbers, & Friendship. Cornell, Kari. 2016. 32p. (J). pap. *(978-0-87659-706-4(1))* Gryphon Hse., Inc.

Sevigny, Alexandra. Charlie Horse: Friends for Life. Leavitt, Gary. 2019. (Friends for Life Ser.: Vol. 1). (ENG.). 34p. (J). (gr. k-4). 23.95 *(978-1-64237-585-5(3))* Gatekeeper Pr.

Sévigny, Eric. As Good as New. 2012. (Ecology Club Ser.). (ENG.). 24p. (J). (gr. -1-1). pap. 5.95 *(978-2-89450-832-9(8))* Caillouet, Gerry.

—Caillou: Accidents Happen. 2014. (Clubhouse Ser.). (ENG.). 24p. (J). (gr. -1-1). pap. 3.99 *(978-2-89718-120-8(6))* Caillouet, Gerry.

—Caillou: Fresh from the Farm. 2013. (Ecology Club Ser.). (ENG.). 24p. (J). (gr. -1-1). 5.95 *(978-2-89718-026-3(9))* Caillouet, Gerry.

—Caillou: Happy Halloween. 2nd ed. 2012. (ENG.). 24p. (J). (gr. -1-1). pap. 4.99 *(978-2-89450-932-6(4))* Caillouet, Gerry.

Sévigny, Éric. Caillou: Jouons Au Cirque! Moeller, Rebecca Klevberg & Johnson, Marion. 2018. (Read with Caillou Ser.). (FRE.). 32p. (J). 4.95 *(978-2-89718-348-6(9))* Caillouet, Gerry.

Sévigny, Éric. Caillou: Le Jardin de Carottes. Paradis, Anne & Johnson, Marion. ed. 2017. (Lis Avec Caillou Ser.). (FRE.). 32p. (J). (gr. -1-1). 4.95 ***(978-2-89718-365-3(9))*** Caillouet, Gerry.

Sévigny, Éric. Caillou: Où Est Mon Chat? Moeller, Rebecca Klevberg & Johanson, Sarah Margaret. 2018. (Read with Caillou Ser.). (FRE.). 32p. (J). 4.95 *(978-2-89718-347-9(0))* Caillouet, Gerry.

—Caillou: Petites Chaussures, Nouvelles Chaussures. Moeller, Rebecca Klevberg & Johnson, Marion. 2018. (Read with Caillou Ser.). (FRE.). 32p. (J). 4.95 *(978-2-89718-346-2(2))* Caillouet, Gerry.

Sévigny, Eric. Caillou: Storybook Treasury. Chouette Publishing Staff. 2014. (ENG.). 256p. (J). (gr. -1-k). 15.99 *(978-2-89718-149-9(4))* Caillouet, Gerry.

Sevigny, Eric. Caillou: The Bike Lesson. Johanson, Sarah Margaret. ed. 2017. (Read with Caillou Ser.). (ENG.). 32p. (J). (gr. -1-1). 3.99 *(978-2-89718-366-0(7))* Caillouet, Gerry.

Sévigny, Eric. Caillou: The Birthday Party. 2014. (Clubhouse Ser.). (ENG.). 24p. (J). (gr. -1-1). pap. 4.99 *(978-2-89718-122-2(2))* Caillouet, Gerry.

Sevigny, Eric. Caillou: The Carrot Patch. Johnson, Marion. ed. 2017. (Read with Caillou Ser.). (ENG.). 32p. (J). (gr. -1-1). 3.99 *(978-2-89718-367-7(5))* Caillouet, Gerry.

Sévigny, Eric. Caillou: The Magic of Compost. 2011. (Ecology Club Ser.). (ENG.). 24p. (J). (gr. -1-1). pap. 5.95 *(978-2-89450-773-5(9))* Caillouet, Gerry.

—Caillou: Watches Rosie. rev. ed. 2008. (Playtime Ser.). (ENG.). 24p. (J). (gr. -1-1). pap. 4.95 *(978-2-89450-635-6(X))* Caillouet, Gerry.

—Caillou: When I Grow up ... Chouette Publishing Staff. 2011. (Pop-Up Ser.). (ENG.). 10p. (J). (gr. -1-1). 6.95 *(978-2-89450-760-5(7))* Caillouet, Gerry.

—Caillou - At the Beach. 2012. (Clubhouse Ser.). (ENG.). 24p. (J). (gr. -1-1). pap. 3.99 *(978-2-89450-942-5(1))* Caillouet, Gerry.

—Caillou - Backyard Olympics. 2016. (ENG.). 24p. (J). (gr. -1-k). pap. 3.99 *(978-2-89718-311-0(X))* Caillouet, Gerry.

—Caillou - Learns to Recycle. 2013. (Ecology Club Ser.). (ENG.). 24p. (J). (gr. -1-1). 5.95 *(978-2-89718-027-0(7))* Caillouet, Gerry.

—Caillou - The Firefighter. 2013. (Playtime Ser.). (ENG.). 24p. (J). (gr. -1-1). 4.99 *(978-2-89450-861-9(1))* Caillouet, Gerry.

Sevigny, Eric. Caillou - The Little Artist. Chouette Publishing Staff. 2011. (Activity Bks.). (ENG.). 96p. (J). (gr. -1-1). 7.95 *(978-2-89450-809-1(3))* Caillouet, Gerry.

Sévigny, Eric. Caillou - Training Wheels. 2010. (Clubhouse Ser.). (ENG.). 24p. (J). (gr. -1-1). pap. 3.99 *(978-2-89450-746-9(1))* Caillouet, Gerry.

Sevigny, Eric. Caillou & Friends (Little Detectives) 2018. (ENG.). 14p. (J). (gr. -1-1). bds. 9.99 *(978-2-89718-494-0(9)*, CrackBoom! Bks.) Chouette Publishing CAN. Dist: Publishers Group West (PGW).

Sévigny, Eric. Caillou & the Big Slide. 2012. (Clubhouse Ser.). (ENG.). 24p. (J). (gr. -1-1). pap. 3.99 *(978-2-89450-867-1(0))* Caillouet, Gerry.

—Caillou & the Rain. 2012. (Clubhouse Ser.). (ENG.). 24p. (J). (gr. -1-1). pap. 3.99 *(978-2-89450-870-1(0))* Caillouet, Gerry.

—Caillou Borrows a Book. 2014. (Clubhouse Ser.). (ENG.). 24p. (J). (gr. -1 — 1). pap. 3.99 *(978-2-89718-141-3(9))* Caillouet, Gerry.

—Caillou, Circus Fun. 2016. (Read with Caillou Ser.). (ENG.). 32p. (J). (gr. -1-1). 3.99 *(978-2-89718-343-1(8))* Caillouet, Gerry.

—Caillou, Easter Egg Surprise. Thompson, Kim. 2016. (Clubhouse Ser.). (ENG.). 24p. (J). (gr. -1-k). 9.99 *(978-2-89718-256-4(3))* Caillouet, Gerry.

—Caillou, Emma's Extra Snacks: Living with Diabetes. Paradis, Anne. 2015. (Playtime Ser.). (ENG.). 24p. (J). (gr. -1-1). pap. 4.99 *(978-2-89718-205-2(9))* Caillouet, Gerry.

Sevigny, Eric. Caillou en Spectacle - Lis Avec Caillou, Niveau 3 (French édition of Caillou: on Stage) ed. 2017. (Lis Avec Caillou Ser.). (FRE.). 32p. (J). (gr. k-2). 4.95 ***(978-2-89718-446-9(9))*** Caillouet, Gerry.

—Caillou: Everything Will Be Fine: A Story about Viruses. 2020. (Playtime Ser.). (ENG.). 24p. (J). (gr. -1-1). 3.99 ***(978-2-89718-603-6(8))*** Caillouet, Gerry.

Sevigny, Eric. Caillou: Family Fun Story Box: Includes 4 Board Books. ed. 2018. (ENG.). 48p. (J). (gr. -1). bds. 10.99 *(978-2-89718-476-6(0))* Caillouet, Gerry.

Sévigny, Eric. Caillou, Fun Tracing & Pen Control: Preschool Writing Activities. Paradis, Anne. 2016. (Write & Wipe Ser.). (ENG.). 24p. (J). (gr. -1-1). 9.99 *(978-2-89718-260-1(1))* Caillouet, Gerry.

—Caillou Gets the Hiccups! 2013. (Clubhouse Ser.). (ENG.). 24p. (J). (gr. -1-1). 3.99 *(978-2-89718-063-8(3))* Caillouet, Gerry.

—Caillou Goes Apple Picking. Patenaude, Danielle. 2014. (Clubhouse Ser.). (ENG.). 24p. (J). (gr. -1 — 1). pap. 3.99 *(978-2-89718-145-1(1))* Caillouet, Gerry.

—Caillou Goes Camping. Harvey, Roger. 2012. (Clubhouse Ser.). (ENG.). 24p. (J). (gr. -1-1). pap. 3.99 *(978-2-89450-856-5(5))* Caillouet, Gerry.

Sévigny, Éric. Caillou Goes to School. 2016. (Clubhouse Ser.). (ENG.). 24p. (J). (gr. -1-k). pap. 3.99 *(978-2-89718-313-4(6))* Caillouet, Gerry.

Sévigny, Eric. Caillou: Happy Holidays! Pleau-Murissi, Marilyn. ed. 2017. (ENG.). 56p. (J). (gr. -1). 14.95 *(978-2-89718-451-3(5))* Caillouet, Gerry.

Sévigny, Éric. Caillou, le Mystère de la Chaussette: Lis Avec Caillou, Niveau 2. Moeller, Rebecca Klevberg & Johanson, Sarah Margaret. ed. 2017. (Lis Avec Caillou Ser.). (FRE.). 32p. (J). (gr. k-2). 4.95 ***(978-2-89718-448-3(5))*** Caillouet, Gerry.

Sévigny, Eric. Caillou Makes a Meal: Includes a Simple Pizza Recipe. 2016. (Clubhouse Ser.). (ENG.). 24p. (J). (gr. -1 — 1). pap. 3.99 *(978-2-89718-258-8(X))* Caillouet, Gerry.

Sévigny, Éric. Caillou: My First Sticker Book: Includes 400 Fun Stickers. 2015. (Activity Bks.). (ENG.). 64p. (J). (gr. -1-1). 9.99 *(978-2-89718-179-6(6))* Caillouet, Gerry.

Sévigny, Eric. Caillou: Mystery Valentine. 2016. (Clubhouse Ser.). (ENG.). 24p. (J). (gr. -1-1). pap. 4.99 *(978-2-89718-181-9(8))* Caillouet, Gerry.

—Caillou, Old Shoes, New Shoes. 2016. (Read with Caillou Ser.). (ENG.). 32p. (J). (gr. -1-1). 3.99 *(978-2-89718-341-7(1))* Caillouet, Gerry.

Sévigny, Éric. Caillou, on Stage, Level 2. Pleau-Murissi, Marilyn. ed. 2017. (Read with Caillou Ser.). (ENG.). 32p. (J). (gr. 1-3). 3.99 *(978-2-89718-447-6(7))* Caillouet, Gerry.

Sévigny, Eric. Caillou: Parade of Colors. Johanson, Sarah Margaret. 2012. (Puzzle Bks.). (ENG.). 18p. (J). (gr. -1-1). bds. 12.95 *(978-2-89450-838-1(7))* Caillouet, Gerry.

—Caillou: Parade of Shapes. Johanson, Sarah Margaret. 2012. (Puzzle Bks.). (ENG.). 18p. (J). (gr. -1-1). bds. 12.95 *(978-2-89450-839-8(5))* Caillouet, Gerry.

—Caillou Plants a Tree. 2012. (Ecology Club Ser.). (ENG.). 24p. (J). (gr. -1-1). pap. 5.95 *(978-2-89450-834-3(4))* Caillouet, Gerry.

Sévigny, Éric. Caillou PreSchool Days: Includes 2 Stories. ed. 2018. (ENG.). 32p. (J). (gr. k-2). 7.99 *(978-2-89718-484-1(1))* Caillouet, Gerry.

Sévigny, Eric. Caillou Puts Away His Toys. 3rd ed. 2012. (Clubhouse Ser.). (ENG.). 24p. (J). (gr. -1-1). pap. 3.99 *(978-2-89450-938-8(3))* Caillouet, Gerry.

—Caillou, Search & Count: Fun Adventures! 2013. (Search & Count Ser.). (ENG.). 16p. (J). (gr. -1-1). bds. 9.99 *(978-2-89718-034-8(X))* Caillouet, Gerry.

—Caillou Sends a Letter. 2012. (Clubhouse Ser.). (ENG.). 24p. (J). (gr. -1-1). pap. 3.99 *(978-2-89450-866-4(2))* Caillouet, Gerry.

—Caillou: the Little Christmas Artist. Paradis, Anne. 2013. (Step by Step Ser.). (ENG.). 64p. (J). (gr. -1-1). 8.99 *(978-2-89718-065-2(X))* Caillouet, Gerry.

Sévigny, Éric. Caillou, the Sock Mystery. Johanson, Sarah Margaret. ed. 2017. (Read with Caillou Ser.). (ENG.). 32p. (J). (gr. k-2). 3.99 *(978-2-89718-449-0(3))* Caillouet, Gerry.

—Caillou Va À l'École. 2017. (Château de Cartes Ser.). (FRE.). 24p. (J). (gr. -1). 4.95 *(978-2-89718-314-1(4))* Caillouet, Gerry.

—Caillou Waits for Santa: Christmas Special Edition with Advent Calendar. Paradis, Anne. 2015. (ENG.). 24p. (J). (gr. -1-k). 9.99 *(978-2-89718-207-6(5))* Caillouet, Gerry.

Sevigny, Eric. Caillou Waits for Santa Gift Set: Book with 2 Stories & Gilbert Plush. 2018. (ENG.). 48p. (J). (gr. -1). 19.99 *(978-2-89718-509-1(0))* Caillouet, Gerry.

Sévigny, Éric. Caillou, Where Is My Cat? 2016. (Read with Caillou Ser.). (ENG.). 32p. (J). (gr. -1-1). 3.99 *(978-2-89718-342-4(X))* Caillouet, Gerry.

—Every Drop Counts! 2011. (Ecology Club Ser.). (ENG.). 24p. (J). (gr. -1-1). pap. 5.95 *(978-2-89450-772-8(0))* Caillouet, Gerry.

—Happy Holidays! Pleau-Murissi, Marilyn. 2008. (ENG.). 80p. (J). (gr. -1-1). 14.95 *(978-2-89450-644-8(9))* Caillouet, Gerry.

—In the Garden. 2005. (Playtime Ser.). (ENG.). 24p. (J). (gr. -1-1). pap. 4.95 *(978-2-89450-383-6(0))* Caillouet, Gerry.

—The Jungle Explorer. 2010. (Clubhouse Ser.). (ENG.). 24p. (J). (gr. -1-1). pap. 3.95 *(978-2-89450-724-7(0))* Caillouet, Gerry.

—My Imaginary Friend. 2003. (Clubhouse Ser.). (ENG.). 24p. (J). (gr. -1-1). pap. 3.95 *(978-2-89450-478-9(0))* Caillouet, Gerry.

—The Phone Call. 2003. (Clubhouse Ser.). (ENG.). 24p. (J). (gr. -1-1). pap. 3.99 *(978-2-89450-446-8(2))* Caillouet, Gerry.

—The School Bus. 2003. (Clubhouse Ser.). (ENG.). 24p. (J). (gr. -1-1). pap. 3.99 *(978-2-89450-421-5(7))* Caillouet, Gerry.

Sevigny, Eric & Dupuis, Karina. Caillou: My First Piano Book. 2017. (ENG.). 24p. (J). (gr. -1-1). 12.99 *(978-2-89718-453-7(1))* Caillouet, Gerry.

Sévigny, Eric & Sévigny, Eric. Caillou: Family Fun Story Box, 4 vols. 2014. (Boxset Ser.). (ENG.). 40p. (J). (gr. -1-k). bds. 12.99 *(978-2-89718-123-9(0))* Caillouet, Gerry.

—Caillou: My Little Bed. Chouette Publishing Staff & Paradis, Anne. 2012. (ENG.). 10p. (J). (gr. -1-k). 9.99 *(978-2-89450-951-7(0))* Caillouet, Gerry.

Sévigny, Eric, jt. illus. see Brignaud, Pierre.

Sévigny, Eric, jt. illus. see Sévigny, Eric.

Sevilla, Marta. Goldilocks, Go Home! Freeman, Martha. (J). (gr. 2-5). 2020. 176p. pap. 7.99 ***(978-0-8234-4538-7(0))***; 2019. 96p. 16.99 *(978-0-8234-3857-0(0))* Holiday Hse., Inc.

Sevilla, Marta. Witchy Things. Brusa, Mariasole. 2020. (ENG.). 40p. (J). 16.95 *(978-84-17673-60-4(1))* NubeOcho Ediciones ESP. Dist: Consortium Bk. Sales & Distribution.

Sevingy, Eric & Dupuis, Karina. Caillou: a Special Friend - Read with Caillou, Level 3. 2018. (Read with Caillou Ser.). (ENG.). 32p. (gr. -1). 3.99 *(978-2-89718-473-5(6))* Caillouet, Gerry.

—Caillou: Getting Dressed with Daddy - Read with Caillou, Level 1. Moeller, Rebecca Klevberg. 2018. (Read with Caillou Ser.). (ENG.). 32p. (gr. -1). 3.99 *(978-2-89718-471-1(X))* Caillouet, Gerry.

—Caillou: the Big Dance Contest - Read with Caillou, Level 1. Moeller, Rebecca Klevberg. 2018. (Read with Caillou Ser.). (ENG.). 32p. (gr. -1). 3.99 *(978-2-89718-469-8(8))* Caillouet, Gerry.

Sew, Susie. Betty Sue & Santa's Sleigh Christmas Story: Betty Sue & Santa's Sleigh Christmas & New Year Eve Story. Aholta, Julia. 2018. (Christmas Stories Ser.: Vol. 1). (ENG.). 26p. (J). pap. 9.99 *(978-1-7315-0765-5(8))* Independently Published.

Sewall, Marcia. Sable. Hesse, Karen. 2010. (ENG.). 96p. (J). (gr. 2-5). pap. 7.99 *(978-0-312-37610-9(3)*, 900048339) Square Fish.

—Stone Fox. Gardiner, John Reynolds. 25th anniv. ed. 2005. (ENG.). 96p. (J). (gr. 2-6). 16.99 *(978-0-690-03983-2(2)*, HarperCollins) HarperCollins Pubs. Ltd. GBR. Dist: HarperCollins Pubs.

Seward, Bernice. At the Haiku Zoo. Seward, Bernice. 2017. (ENG.). (J). (gr. k-3). pap. 9.99 *(978-0-9995378-0-0(6))* Seward, Bernice.

—Squawk Around the Clock. Seward, Bernice. 2019. (Bite-Size Books for Beginning Readers Ser.: Vol. 4). (ENG.). 32p. (J). (gr. k-1). pap. 7.99 *(978-0-9995378-4-8(9))* Seward, Bernice.

—Ten Swishy Fish. Seward, Bernice. 2018. (ENG.). 32p. (J). pap. 7.99 *(978-0-9995378-2-4(2))* Seward, Bernice.

Seward, Daniel. Hide & Seek, No Ticks Please. Fox, Nancy. 2014. (ENG.). 42p. (gr. k-6). pap. 9.95 *(978-1-61448-705-0(7))* Morgan James Publishing.

Seward, Daniel J. Quickly's Safari Adventure Coloring & Activity Book. Kronish, Miriam & Abelmann, Jeryl. 2016. (ENG.). (J). pap. 9.95 *(978-0-9971084-9-1(5))* Dancing Mommy Pr.

Seward, Prudence. Voyage to Tasmani. Parker, Richard. 2011. 128p. 40.95 *(978-1-258-08572-8(0))* Literary Licensing, LLC.

Sewell, Byron W. Snarkmaster: A Destiny in Eight Fits. a Tale Inspired by Lewis Carroll's the Hunting of the Snark. Sewell, Byron W. 2012. 138p. pap. *(978-1-78201-002-9(5))* Evertype.

Sewell, Helen. Old John. Cregan, Mairin. 2012. 198p. 44.95 *(978-1-258-23306-8(1))*; pap. 29.95 *(978-1-258-24727-0(5))* Literary Licensing, LLC.

—The Wonderful Day. Coatsworth, Elizabeth. 2006. (ENG.). 160p. (J). (gr. 10-12). pap. 11.95 *(978-1-883937-87-4(6))* Ignatius Pr.

Sexton, Brenda. Five Shiny Apples. Fleming, Maria. 2005. (ENG.). 16p. (J). (gr. -1-1). pap. 2.99 *(978-0-439-69014-0(5))* Scholastic, Inc.

—Monkey's Missing Bananas. Charlesworth, Liza & Scholastic, Inc. Staff. 2005. (ENG.). 16p. (J). (gr. -1-1). pap. 2.99 *(978-0-439-69032-4(3))* Scholastic, Inc.

—Rainbow of Colors. Scelsa, Greg. Faulkner, Stacey, ed. 2006. (J). pap. 2.99 *(978-1-59198-351-4(7))* Creative Teaching Pr., Inc.

—Reading Pals: Rhyming Words Using Blends & Digraphs Gr. K-1. Allen, Margaret. Taylor, Jennifer, ed. 2007. (J). per. 6.99 *(978-1-59198-437-5(8))* Creative Teaching Pr., Inc.

—Reading Pals: Short & Long Vowels Gr. K-1. Abrams, Majella. Taylor, Jennifer, ed. 2007. (J). per. 6.99 *(978-1-59198-436-8(X))* Creative Teaching Pr., Inc.

—Reading Pals: Sight Words Gr. K-1. Allen, Molly. Taylor, Jennifer, ed. 2007. (J). per. 6.99 *(978-1-59198-438-2(6))* Creative Teaching Pr., Inc.

Sexton, Brenda. Have a Crazy Christmas! Sexton, Brenda. Sloan, Price Stern. 2016. (Mad Libs Junior Ser.). 32p. (J). (gr. -1-k). bds., act. bk. ed. 7.99 *(978-0-8431-8939-1(8)*, Mad Libs) Penguin Young Readers Group.

—You Can Draw Fairies & Princesses, 1 vol. Sexton, Brenda. 2011. (You Can Draw Ser.). (ENG.). 24p. (J). (gr. k-3). lib. bdg. 27.32 *(978-1-4048-6808-3(9)*, Picture Window Bks.) Capstone.

—You Can Draw Pets, 1 vol. Sexton, Brenda. 2010. (You Can Draw Ser.). (ENG.). 24p. (J). (gr. k-3). lib. bdg. 27.32 *(978-1-4048-6277-7(3)*, Picture Window Bks.) Capstone.

—You Can Draw Planes, Trains, & Other Vehicles, 1 vol. Sexton, Brenda. Bruning, Matt. 2010. (You Can Draw Ser.). (ENG.). 24p. (J). (gr. k-3). lib. bdg. 27.32 *(978-1-4048-6278-4(1)*, Picture Window Bks.) Capstone.

Sexton, Brenda, jt. illus. see Cerato, Mattia.

Sexton, Brenton. The Little Golden Bible Storybook. Simeon, S. & Golden Books Staff. 2005. 168p. (J). (gr. -1 — 1). 6.99 *(978-0-375-83549-0(0)*, Golden Inspirational) Random Hse. Children's Bks.

Sexton, Jessa R., photos by. Mobert's Irish Experience. Sexton, Jessa R. 2012. 34p. pap. 10.00 *(978-0-9860150-3-8(2))* O'More Publishing.

Sexton, Laura. The Perfect Puppy. Koppers, Kristen. 2020. (ENG.). 32p. (J). 25.99 ***(978-1-970133-73-8(2))***; pap. 15.99 ***(978-1-970133-72-1(4))*** EduMatch.

Sexton, Richard, photos by. In the Victorian Style. Delehanty, Randolph. 2006. (ENG., 192p. (gr. 8-17). 40.00 *(978-0-8118-5360-6(8))* Chronicle Bks. LLC.

Seymour, Arlene. The Moon Book: A Lunar Pop-up Celebration. Seymour, Arlene. 2004. 14p. (YA). (gr. k-4). reprint ed. 22.00 *(978-0-7567-7645-9(7))* DIANE Publishing Co.

Sfar, Joann. The Little Prince Graphic Novel. De Saint-Exupéry, Antoine. ed. 2013. (Little Prince Ser.). (ENG.). 112p. (J). (gr. 5-7). 12.99 *(978-0-547-33800-2(7)*, 1418295) Houghton Mifflin Harcourt Publishing Co.

Sfar, Joann. Sardine in Outer Space, 4. Sfar, Joann. Guibert, Emmanuel. Gauvin, Edward, tr. 4th rev. ed. 2007. (Sardine in Outer Space Ser.: 4). (ENG.). 102p. (J). (gr. 3-6). 29.94 *(978-1-59643-129-4(6)*, 9781596431294, First Second Bks.) Roaring Brook Pr.

Sfar, Joann & Pezzali, Walter. Sardine in Outer Space. Guibert, Emmanuel & Sfar, Joann. Watson, Sasha, tr. 2006. (Sardine in Outer Space Ser.: 1). (ENG.). 128p. (J). deluxe ed. (gr. 1-5). pap. 17.99 *(978-1-59643-126-3(1)*, 900032000); 2. 2nd rev. ed. (gr. 3-6). 29.94 *(978-1-59643-127-0(X)*, 900032003) Roaring Brook Pr. (First Second Bks.).

Sfar, Joann, jt. illus. see Pezzali, Walter.

Sfetsios-Conover, Debra. Cyclone. Cronin, Doreen. (ENG.). (J). (gr. 4-8). 2018. 368p. pap. 8.99 *(978-1-4814-3526-0(4))*; 2017. 352p. 16.99 *(978-1-4814-3525-3(6)*, Atheneum/Caitlyn Dlouhy Books) Simon & Schuster Children's Publishing.

Sforza, Lucia. Lion, King, & Coin. Nam, Jeong-hee & Cowley, Joy. 2017. (J). 10.00 *(978-0-8028-5475-9(3)*, Eerdmans Bks For Young Readers) Eerdmans, William B. Publishing Co.

Sgarlata, Margherita. The Atlas of Women Explorers. Francaviglia, Riccardo. 2020. (ENG.). 96p. (J). (gr. 3). 16.95 ***(978-88-544-1667-3(3))*** White Star ITA. Dist: Sterling Publishing Co., Inc.

Sgouros, Yorgos. The First Christmas, 1 vol. 2020. (Stories of Christmas Ser.). (ENG.). 24p. (J). (gr. 1-2). lib. bdg. 24.60 ***(978-1-4994-8587-5(5))***; pap. 8.25 ***(978-1-4994-8585-1(9))*** Rosen Publishing Group, Inc., The. (Windmill Bks.).

Sgouros, Yorgos. My Toddler Bible. James, Bethan. 2008. (ENG.). 36p. (J). (gr. -1-k). 12.99 *(978-1-4143-2013-7(2)*, 4601003) Tyndale Hse. Pubs.

Sgroi, Tony. Annie Oakley in the Ghost Town Secret. Schroeder, Doris. 2011. 280p. 47.95 *(978-1-258-06482-2(0))* Literary Licensing, LLC.

Shabazz, Aminah. Arielle's Two Grand. Shabazz-Ugwumba, Sarah. Wag Publishing, ed. 2016. (ENG.). (J). pap. 10.50 *(978-0-9886117-5-7(9))* Gulley, Wayne.

—The Kwanzaa Family. Shabazz-Ugwumba, Sarah. Gulley, Robin, ed. 2017. (ENG.). (J). (gr. 4-6). pap. 10.50 *(978-0-9886117-2-6(4))* Gulley, Wayne.

—Modern Medicine. Shabazz-Ugwumba, Sarah. Wag Publishing, ed. 2016. (ENG.). (J). (gr. 2-4). pap. 10.50 *(978-0-9886117-6-4(7))* Gulley, Wayne.

—So Many Books. Shabazz-Ugwumba, Sarah. Wag Publishing, ed. 2016. (ENG.). (J). (gr. 1-3). pap. 10.50 *(978-0-9886117-7-1(5))* Gulley, Wayne.

Shachat, Andrew. Stop That Pickle! Armour, Peter. 2005. (ENG.). 32p. (J). (gr. -1-3). 7.99 *(978-0-618-54889-7(0)*, 480730) Houghton Mifflin Harcourt Publishing Co.

Shackelford, David. One Christmas Night. Henderson, Richard. 2008. 32p. (J). 15.95 *(978-0-615-17629-1(1))* St. Clair Publishing.

Shackell, John. French Dictionary for Beginners. Davies, Helen. Irving, Nicole, ed. 2006. (Beginner's Dictionaries Ser.). (FRE.). 128p. (J). (gr. 4). lib. bdg. 20.95 *(978-1-58086-475-6(9))* EDC Publishing.

—German Dictionary for Beginners. Davies, Helen. Irving, Nicole, ed. 2006. (Beginner's Dictionaries Ser.). (GER.). 128p. (J). (gr. 4). lib. bdg. 20.95 *(978-1-58086-487-9(2))* EDC Publishing.

—Italian Dictionary for Beginners. Davies, Helen. Irving, Nicole, ed. 2006. (Beginner's Dictionaries Ser.). (ITA.). 128p. (J). (gr. 4). lib. bdg. 20.95 *(978-1-58086-555-5(0))* EDC Publishing.

—Spanish Dictionary for Beginners. Davies, Helen. Irving, Nicole, ed. 2003. (Beginner's Dictionaries Ser.). (SPA.). 128p. lib. bdg. 20.99 *(978-1-58086-488-6(0))* EDC Publishing.

—Where Does Electricity Come From? Mayes, Susan. 2006. (Usborne Starting Point Science Ser.). 23p. (J). (gr. 4-7). lib. bdg. 12.99 *(978-1-58086-938-6(6)*, Usborne) EDC Publishing.

Shackell, John & Scorey, John. Where Does Electricity Come From? Mayes, Susan. 2006. (Usborne Starting Point Science Ser.). 23p. (J). (gr. 1-4). pap. 4.99 *(978-0-7945-1411-2(1)*, Usborne) EDC Publishing.

Shackleford, Smitty. The Jaguar Eye. Orr, Christoff. 2018. (ENG.). 240p. (J). pap. 12.00 *(978-1-7220-0126-1(7))* CreateSpace Independent Publishing Platform.

Shafer, Anders C. The Fantastic Journey of Pieter Bruegel. Shafer, Anders C. 2005. 38p. (J). 19.00 *(978-0-7567-9540-5(0))* DIANE Publishing Co.

Shaffer, Dale E. Marbles: A Forgotten Part of Salem History, 2 vols. Shaffer, Dale E. 2nd rev. ed. 2004. 38p. (Orig.). (YA). (gr. 3-18). mass mkt. 8.00 *(978-0-915060-34-4(5))* Shaffer, Dale E.

Shaffer, Eric. Make the Best of It! Ihaz lo Mejor Posible! Baker, Georgette. 2018. (ENG.). 30p. (J). pap. 9.95 *(978-1-892306-56-2(5))* Cantemos-bilingual bks. and music.

Shaffer, Grant. The Adventures of Honey & Leon. Cumming, Alan. 2017. (ENG.). 48p. (J). (gr. -1-2). lib. bdg. 20.99 *(978-0-399-55798-9(9)*, Random Hse. Bks. for Young Readers) Random Hse. Children's Bks.

—The Adventures of Honey & Leon. Cumming, Alan. 2017. (ENG.). 48p. (J). (gr. -1-2). 17.99 *(978-0-399-55797-2(0)*, Random Hse. Bks. for Young Readers) Random Hse. Children's Bks.

—Honey & Leon Take the High Road. Cumming, Alan. 2019. (ENG.). 48p. (J). (gr. -1-2). 17.99 *(978-0-399-55800-9(4)*, Random Hse. Bks. for Young Readers) Random Hse. Children's Bks.

—Three Magic Balloons. Margulies, Julianna & Margulies, Paul. 2016. (ENG.). 40p. (J). (gr. -1-2). 17.99 *(978-1-101-93523-1(5)*, Random Hse. Bks. for Young Readers) Random Hse. Children's Bks.

Shaffer, Paul. Grandpa's Tent. Kinney Gaventa, Sarah & Davila, Mary. 2018. (ENG.). 36p. (J). pap. 12.00 *(978-0-88028-440-0(4)*, 9780880284400) Forward Movement Pubns.

Shah, Nupur. In the Woods. Shah, Nupur. rev. ed. 2010. (1-3Y Ecosystems Ser.). (ENG.). 12p. (J). (gr. k-1). pap. 8.00 *(978-1-61541-458-1(4))* American Reading Co.

Shahan, Sherry. Feeding Time at the Zoo. Shahan, Sherry. 2014. (Step into Reading Ser.). (ENG.). 32p. (J). (gr. -1-1). lib. bdg. 12.99 *(978-0-375-97190-7(4)*, Random Hse. Bks. for Young Readers) Random Hse. Children's Bks.

Shahan, Sherry, photos by. Dashing Through the Snow: The Story of the Jr. Iditarod. 2nd ed. 2006. (J). pap. *(978-1-59336-714-5(7))* Mondo Publishing.

Shahid, Zeeshan. The Curious Adventures of the Super 3: Super! Murphy, Kimberly. 2019. (Curious Adventures of the Super 3 Ser.: Vol. 1). (ENG.). 26p. (J). pap. 9.99 ***(978-1-6919-5177-2(3))*** Independently Published.

Shahn, Ben. A Boy of Old Prague. Ish-Kishor, Sulamith. 2008. (Dover Children's Classics Ser.). (ENG.). 96p. (J). (gr. 4-6). pap. 3.99 *(978-0-486-46766-5(X))* Dover Pubns., Inc.

—Ounce, Dice, Trice. Reid, Alastair. 2009. 64p. (J). (gr. k-4). 15.95 *(978-1-59017-320-6(1)*, NYR Children's Collection) New York Review of Bks., Inc., The.

Shahzad-Naqvi, Sehreen. Joosh's Juice Bar: The Blue Banana Berry Adventure. Gottsegen, Josh. 2016. (ENG.). (J). 19.99 *(978-0-9909270-3-7(2))* OneLight Publishing.

—Joosh's Juice Bar: The Snackbook Adventure. Gottsegen, Josh. annot. ed. 2016. (ENG.). (J). 21.99 *(978-0-9909270-2-0(4))* OneLight Publishing.

—Joosh's Juice Bar: The Tropland Tee-Off. Gottsegen, Josh. 2016. (ENG.). (J). 19.99 *(978-0-9909270-9-9(1))* OneLight Publishing.

Shai, Moshe, photos by. It's Challah Time! 20th Anniversary Edition. Kropf, Latifa Berry. rev. ed. 2020. (ENG., 24p. (J). (gr. -1-1). pap. 7.99 ***(978-1-5415-7460-1(5)***, Kar-Ben Publishing) Lerner Publishing Group.

Shakespeare, Eleanor. Stormy Seas: Stories of Young Boat Refugees. Leatherdale, Mary Beth. 2017. (ENG.). 64p. (gr. 4). pap. 12.95 *(978-1-55451-895-1(4))* Annick Pr., Ltd. CAN. Dist: Publishers Group West (PGW).

Shakir, Susie. I Want to Potty. Neis, Izzy. 2005. 10p. (J). 9.95 *(978-1-58117-422-9(5)*, Intervisual/Piggy Toes) Bendon, Inc.

—One to Ten... & Back Again. Schwartz, Betty Ann. 2009. 24p. bds. 12.99 *(978-0-8249-1436-3(8)*, Ideal Pubns.) Worthy Publishing.

Shalaby, Asharaf. Resilient. Vanasse, Patricia. 2013. (ENG.). 328p. (YA). pap. 13.99 *(978-0-9860373-2-0(X))* Pants On Fire Pr.

Shalansky, Len. Aesop's Opposites: Interactive Aesop Fables. Enderle, Dotti. Mitchell, Judy, ed. 2004. 64p. (J). pap. 9.95 *(978-1-57310-424-1(8))* Teaching & Learning Co.

—100 Little Reading Comprehension Lessons, Grade 1-4: Fun-To-Read Stories with Skill-Building Exercises. Brinton, Margaret. 2004. (ENG.). 112p. pap. 12.95 *(978-1-57310-425-8(6))* Teaching & Learning Co.

Shalev, Michal. How to Be Famous. Shalev, Michal. ed. 2016. (ENG.). 32p. (J). (gr. -1-1). E-Book 9.99 *(978-1-77657-045-4(6)*, 9781776570454); E-Book 26.65 *(978-1-77657-047-8(2))*; E-Book 26.65 *(978-1-77657-057-7(X)*, 9781776570577) Gecko Pr. NZL. Dist: Lerner Publishing Group.

Shaloshvili, Natasha. Life, Loss, & Lemonade. Friedman, Laurie. ed. (Mostly Miserable Life of April Sinclair Ser.: 8). (ENG.). 168p. (J). (gr. 5-9). 2017. E-Book 27.99 *(978-1-5124-2699-1(7))*; Bk. 8. 2018. pap. 5.99 *(978-1-5415-0109-6(8)*, 9781541501096); No. 8. 2017. 17.95 *(978-1-4677-8591-4(1)*, 9781467785914) Lerner Publishing Group. (Darby Creek).

—Not What I Expected. Friedman, Laurie. ed. 2015. (Mostly Miserable Life of April Sinclair Ser.: 5). (ENG.). 176p. (J). (gr. 5-9). E-Book 27.99 *(978-1-4677-8829-8(5))*;No. 5. 17.95 *(978-1-4677-8588-4(1)*, 9781467785884) Lerner Publishing Group. (Darby Creek).

—Too Much Drama. Friedman, Laurie. ed. 2016. (Mostly Miserable Life of April Sinclair Ser.: 6). (ENG.). 184p. (J). (gr. 5-9). E-Book 27.99 *(978-1-4677-9570-8(4))*;No. 6. 17.95 *(978-1-4677-8589-1(X)*, 9781467785891) Lerner Publishing Group. (Darby Creek).

—A Twist of Fate. Friedman, Laurie. ed. 2016. (Mostly Miserable Life of April Sinclair Ser.: 7). (ENG.). 168p. (J). (gr. 5-9). E-Book 27.99 *(978-1-5124-0899-7(9))*;No. 7. 17.95 *(978-1-4677-8590-7(3)*, 9781467785907) Lerner Publishing Group. (Darby Creek).

Shalvey, Declan. Marvel Monograph: the Art of Declan Shalvey. 2020. (ENG.). 120p. (YA). (gr. 8-17). pap. 19.99 *(978-1-302-92254-2(8))* Marvel Worldwide, Inc.

Shalvey, Declan & Cardy, Jason. Sweeney Todd: The Demon Barber of Fleet Street. 2012. (ENG.). 176p. pap. 16.95 *(978-1-907127-10-6(0)*, Classical Comics, Ltd.); pap. 16.95 *(978-1-907127-09-0(7)*, Classical Comics, Ltd.); (gr. 9). lib. bdg. 24.95 *(978-1-907127-82-3(8))* Classical Comics GBR. Dist: Publishers Group West (PGW).

Shames, Stephen, photos by. Transforming Lives: Turning Uganda's Forgotten Children into Leaders. Shames, Stephen. 2009. 40p. (YA). pap. 12.95 *(978-1-59572-213-3(0))* Star Bright Bks., Inc.

Shamp, Danielle. When I Wished ... Tabor, Stephen A. 2009. 31p. pap. 24.95 *(978-1-60836-086-4(5))* America Star Bks.

Shamshirsaz, Shabab. A Tale of Two Sinbads 3 Explorers. Whybrow, Ian. 2017. (Cambridge Reading Adventures Ser.). (ENG.). 32p. pap. 7.87 *(978-1-108-43097-5(X))* Cambridge Univ. Pr.

Shanahan, Danny. The Bus Ride That Changed History: The Story of Rosa Parks. Edwards, Pamela Duncan. 2009. (ENG.). 32p. (J). (gr. -1-3). pap. 7.99 *(978-0-547-07674-4(6)*, 1042031) Houghton Mifflin Harcourt Publishing Co.

Shanahan, Sue. Sarah the Best Bridesmaid: Paper Doll Storybook. Rubins, Diane Teitel. 2004. (Dover Paper Dolls Ser.). (ENG.). 24p. (J). (gr. 2-5). pap. 5.95 *(978-0-486-43531-2(8))* Dover Pubns., Inc.

Shand, Stephan. What Rhymes with Cat? Wakefield, Latoya. 2019. (ENG.). 28p. (J). pap. 9.99 ***(978-1-6937-0443-7(9))*** Independently Published.

Shandler, Georgette, jt. illus. see Ramsdin-Firth, Bernice.

Shane, Nitzsche. Arizona Activity Book, 1 vol. Ellis, Paula. 2012. (Color & Learn Ser.). (ENG.). 64p. (J). (gr. k-5). pap. 6.95 *(978-1-59193-288-8(2)*, Adventure Pubns.) AdventureKEEN.

Shang, Lili. 19 Day Feast Pages for Kids: Introduction to the Bahá'í Months & Holy Days - Months 5 - 8. Shang, Lili. Shang, Wei. 2019. (Volume 1, Bundle Ser.: Vol. 2). (ENG.). 60p. (J). (gr. k-6). pap. 17.00 *(978-1-947485-51-8(2)*, Mine Rich In Gems) InnerPrize Group, LLC.

—19 Day Feast Pages for Kids: Introduction to the Bahá'í Months & Holy Days - Months 9 - 12. Shang, Lili. Shang, Wei. 2019. (Volume 1, Bundle Ser.: Vol. 3). (ENG.). 64p. (J). (gr. k-6). pap. 17.00 *(978-1-947485-52-5(0)*, Mine Rich In Gems) InnerPrize Group, LLC.

Shang, Lili. 19 Day Feast Pages for Kids: Introduction to the Bah&#65533;'&#65533; Months & Holy Days - Months 13 - 16: Qudrat, Qawl, Mas&#65533;'il, & Sharaf. Shang, Lili. Shang, Wei. 2019. (Volume 1, Bundle Ser.: Vol. 4). (ENG.). 64p. (J). (gr. k-6). pap. 17.00 ***(978-1-947485-53-2(9))*** InnerPrize Group, LLC.

—19 Day Feast Pages for Kids: Introduction to the Bah&#65533;'&#65533; Months & Holy Days - Months 17 - 19: Sult&#65533;n, Mulk, Ayy&#65533;m-I-H&#65533;, & 'Al&#65533;' Shang, Lili. Shang, Wei. 2019. (Volume Ser.: Vol. 5). (ENG.). 72p. (J). (gr. k-6). pap. 17.00 ***(978-1-947485-54-9(7))*** InnerPrize Group, LLC.

Shannacappo, Neal. If I Go Missing. Jonnie, Brianna. 2020. (ENG.). 64p. (YA). (gr. 7-12). lib. bdg. 24.95 *(978-1-4594-1451-8(9)*, 0551dd86-bf20-43b3-ba12-e715a442e1d6) James Lorimer & Co. Ltd., Pubs. CAN. Dist: Lerner Publishing Group.

Shannon, Ben. Cliques: Using What You Have Inside, 1 vol. Mototsune, Kat. (Lorimer Deal with It Ser.). (ENG.). 32p. (J). (gr. 4-9). 2016. lib. bdg. 24.95 *(978-1-55277-545-5(3)*, 70c4e0b0-cd98-4a60-b290-822f965ae4b5); 2011. pap. 12.95 *(978-1-55277-544-8(5)*, 9781552775448) James Lorimer & Co. Ltd., Pubs. CAN. Dist: Lerner Publishing Group, Orca Bk. Pubs. USA.

—Gaming: Before It Outplays You, 1 vol. Peters, Diane. 2016. (Lorimer Deal with It Ser.). (ENG.). 32p. (J). (gr. 4-9). 24.95 *(978-1-55277-490-8(2)*, a5535c19-fb08-4a03-8483-477be5c3dc4d) James Lorimer & Co. Ltd., Pubs. CAN. Dist: Lerner Publishing Group.

—Gaming: Deal with It Before It Outplays You, 1 vol. Peters, Diane. 2010. (Lorimer Deal with It Ser.). (ENG.). 32p. (J). (gr. 4-9). pap. 12.95 *(978-1-55277-434-2(1)*, 9781552774342) James Lorimer & Co. Ltd., Pubs. CAN. Dist: Orca Bk. Pubs. USA.

—Image: Deal with It from the Inside Out. Mototsune, Kat. (Lorimer Deal with It Ser.). (ENG.). 32p. (J). (gr. 4-9). 2017. lib. bdg. 22.65 *(978-1-4594-1188-3(9)*, 3b59c9e3-ad33-4676-9c02-9172c7e6aea9); 2007. pap. 12.95 *(978-1-55028-994-7(2)*, 994) James Lorimer & Co. Ltd., Pubs. CAN. Dist: Lerner Publishing Group, Formac Lorimer Bks. Ltd.

—Morgan & the Money, 1 vol. Staunton, Ted. ed. 2008. (Formac First Novels Ser.). (ENG.). 64p. (gr. 1-5). 4.95 *(978-0-88780-774-9(7)*, 774) Formac Publishing Co., Ltd. CAN. Dist: Formac Lorimer Bks. Ltd.

—Peer Pressure: Deal with It Without Losing Your Cool, 1 vol. Slavens, Elaine. 2016. (Lorimer Deal with It Ser.). (ENG.). 32p. (J). (gr. 4-9). 12.95 *(978-1-55028-815-5(6)*, f18e045a-5f04-48ba-9e75-e4b8dda954b9) James Lorimer & Co. Ltd., Pubs. CAN. Dist: Lerner Publishing Group.

—Walrus, 1 vol. Paniaq, Herve. 2017. (Animals Illustrated Ser.). (ENG.). 32p. (J). (gr. k-2). 12.95 *(978-1-77227-142-3(X))* Inhabit Media Inc. CAN. Dist: Consortium Bk. Sales & Distribution.

Shannon, Ben, jt. illus. see Slavin, Bill.

Shannon, David, et al. All Around Trucktown. Harper, Benjamin. 2008. (Jon Scieszka's Trucktown Ser.). (ENG.). 32p. (J). (gr. -1-1). 3.99 *(978-1-4169-4194-1(0)*, Simon Scribbles) Simon Scribbles.

—A Christmas Surprise. Mason, Tom & Danko, Dan. 2011. (Jon Scieszka's Trucktown Ser.). (ENG.). 12p. (J). (gr. -1-k). 7.99 *(978-1-4169-4193-4(2)*, Simon & Schuster Bks. For Young Readers) Simon & Schuster Bks. For Young Readers.

—Dizzy Izzy. Scieszka, Jon. (Jon Scieszka's Trucktown Ser.). (ENG.). 24p. (J). (gr. -1-1). 2014. 17.99 *(978-1-4814-1460-9(7))*; 2010. lib. bdg. 14.99 *(978-1-4169-4156-9(8))* Simon Spotlight. (Simon Spotlight).

—The Great Truck Rescue. Scieszka, Jon. 2010. (Jon Scieszka's Trucktown Ser.). (ENG.). 40p. (J). (gr. -1-3). pap. 4.99 *(978-1-4424-0932-3(0)*, Simon & Schuster Bks. For Young Readers) Simon & Schuster Bks. For Young Readers.

Shannon, David. Hiawatha & the Peacemaker. Robertson, Robbie. 2015. (ENG.). 48p. (J). (gr. -1-3). 19.95 *(978-1-4197-1220-3(9)*, Abrams Bks. for Young Readers) Abrams, Inc.

Shannon, David, et al. Honk That Horn! Mason, Tom et al. 2011. (Jon Scieszka's Trucktown Ser.). (ENG.). 24p. (J). (gr. -1-k). pap. 3.99 *(978-1-4169-4184-2(3)*, Simon & Schuster Bks. For Young Readers) Simon & Schuster Bks. For Young Readers.

Shannon, David. How I Became a Pirate. Long, Melinda. 2003. (ENG.). 44p. (J). (gr. -1-3). 17.99 *(978-0-15-201848-1(4)*, 1191067) Houghton Mifflin Harcourt Publishing Co.

—How I Became A Pirate. Long, Melinda. 2004. (J). *(978-0-439-66474-5(8)*, Scholastic) Scholastic, Inc.

Shannon, David, et al. Junkyard Dig! Building from a to Z. Auerbach, Annie. 2010. (Jon Scieszka's Trucktown Ser.). (ENG.). 26p. (J). (gr. -1-k). bds. 5.99 *(978-1-4169-4187-3(8)*, Little Simon) Little Simon.

—Kat's Maps. Scieszka, Jon. 2011. (Jon Scieszka's Trucktown Ser.). (ENG.). 24p. (J). (gr. -1-1). pap. 3.99 *(978-1-4169-4148-4(7)*, Simon Spotlight) Simon Spotlight.

—Kat's Mystery Gift. Scieszka, Jon. (Jon Scieszka's Trucktown Ser.). (ENG.). 24p. (J). (gr. -1-1). 2013. 16.99 *(978-1-4814-1459-3(3))*; 2009. lib. bdg. 14.99 *(978-1-4169-4154-5(1))* Simon Spotlight. (Simon Spotlight).

—Let's Dig It! Bergen, Lara. 2010. (Jon Scieszka's Trucktown Ser.). (ENG.). 12p. (J). (gr. -1-k). bds. 5.99 *(978-1-4169-4190-3(8)*, Little Simon) Little Simon.

—Max's Big Show. Testa, Maggie. 2010. (Jon Scieszka's Trucktown Ser.). (ENG.). 32p. (J). (gr. -1-1). 4.99 *(978-1-4169-4191-0(6)*, Simon Scribbles) Simon Scribbles.

—Meet Jack Truck! McKown, Hunter. 2008. (Jon Scieszka's Trucktown Ser.). (ENG.). 14p. (J). (gr. -1-1). bds. 5.99 *(978-1-4169-4173-6(8)*, Little Simon) Little Simon.

—Melvin's Valentine. Scieszka, Jon. (Jon Scieszka's Trucktown Ser.). (ENG.). 24p. (J). (gr. -1-1). 2014. 16.99 *(978-1-4814-1458-6(5))*; 2009. pap. 3.99 *(978-1-4169-4144-6(4))*; 2009. lib. bdg. 15.99 *(978-1-4169-4155-2(X))* Simon Spotlight. (Simon Spotlight).

—On the Move! Teitelbaum, Michael. 2009. (Jon Scieszka's Trucktown Ser.). (ENG.). 10p. (J). (gr. -1-k). bds. 6.99 *(978-1-4169-4178-1(9)*, Little Simon) Little Simon.

Shannon, David. Pirates Don't Change Diapers. Long, Melinda. 2007. (ENG.). 44p. (J). (gr. -1-3). 17.99 *(978-0-15-205353-6(0)*, 1196124) Houghton Mifflin Harcourt Publishing Co.

Shannon, David, et al. Playtime in Trucktown. Rao, Lisa. 2008. (Jon Scieszka's Trucktown Ser.). (ENG.). 24p. (J). (gr. -1-1). 5.99 *(978-1-4169-4197-2(5)*, Simon Scribbles) Simon Scribbles.

Shannon, David. The Rain Came Down. Johnson, Bruce Bailey. 2009. (ENG.). (J). (gr. -1-3). audio compact disk 10.99 *(978-0-545-13850-5(7))* Scholastic, Inc.

—Robot Zot! Scieszka, Jon. 2009. (ENG.). 40p. (J). (gr. -1-2). 17.99 *(978-1-4169-6394-3(4)*, Simon & Schuster Bks. For Young Readers) Simon & Schuster Bks. For Young Readers.

—Robot Zot! Scieszka, Jon. 2011. (J). (gr. -1-2). 29.95 *(978-0-545-32739-8(3))* Weston Woods Studios, Inc.

Shannon, David, et al. Sand Castle Bash: Counting from 1 To 10. McKown, Hunter. 2009. (Jon Scieszka's Trucktown Ser.). (ENG.). 26p. (J). (gr. -1-k). bds. 5.99 *(978-1-4169-4179-8(7)*, Little Simon) Little Simon.

—Scoop That Snow! Parker, Sydney. 2009. (Jon Scieszka's Trucktown Ser.). (ENG.). 12p. (J). (gr. -1-k). 7.99 *(978-1-4169-4182-8(7)*, Little Simon) Little Simon.

Shannon, David. The Shark God. Martin, Rafe. 2007. (Scholastic Bookshelf Ser.). (ENG.). 32p. (J). (gr. k-2). 18.69 *(978-0-590-39570-0(X))* Scholastic, Inc.

Shannon, David, et al. Smash That Trash! Sander, Sonia. 2009. (Jon Scieszka's Trucktown Ser.). (ENG.). 14p. (J). (gr. -1-k). 7.99 *(978-1-4169-4180-4(0)*, Little Simon) Little Simon.

—Smash!Crash! Scieszka, Jon. 2008. (Jon Scieszka's Trucktown Ser.). (ENG.). 42p. (J). (gr. -1-3). 19.99 *(978-1-4169-4133-0(9)*, Simon & Schuster Bks. For Young Readers) Simon & Schuster Bks. For Young Readers.

—The Spooky Tire. Scieszka, Jon. 2009. (Jon Scieszka's Trucktown Ser.). (ENG.). 24p. (J). (gr. -1-k). lib. bdg. 15.99 *(978-1-4169-4153-8(3))*; pap. 4.99 *(978-1-4169-4142-2(8))* Simon Spotlight. (Simon Spotlight).

—Steer the Wheel! Teitelbaum, Michael. 2011. (Jon Scieszka's Trucktown Ser.). (ENG.). 12p. (J). (gr. -1-1). bds. 7.99 *(978-1-4169-4185-9(1)*, Simon & Schuster Bks. For Young Readers) Simon & Schuster Bks. For Young Readers.

—Truckery Rhymes. Scieszka, Jon. 2009. (Jon Scieszka's Trucktown Ser.). (ENG.). 64p. (J). (gr. -1-3). 19.99 *(978-1-4169-4135-4(5)*, Simon & Schuster Bks. For Young Readers) Simon & Schuster Bks. For Young Readers.

—Trucks Line Up. Scieszka, Jon. 2011. (Jon Scieszka's Trucktown Ser.). (ENG.). 24p. (J). (gr. -1-1). 17.99 *(978-1-4169-4158-3(4)*, Simon Spotlight) Simon Spotlight.

—Trucksgiving. Scieszka, Jon. 2010. (Jon Scieszka's Trucktown Ser.). (ENG.). 24p. (J). (gr. -1-1). 16.99 *(978-1-4169-4157-6(6))*; pap. 4.99 *(978-1-4169-4146-0(0))* Simon Spotlight. (Simon Spotlight).

—Uh-Oh, Max. Scieszka, Jon. 2014. (Jon Scieszka's Trucktown Ser.). (ENG.). 24p. (J). (gr. -1-1). 16.99 *(978-1-4814-1461-6(5)*, Simon Spotlight) Simon Spotlight.

—Uh-Oh, Max. Scieszka, Jon. 2009. (Jon Scieszka's Trucktown Ser.). (ENG.). 24p. (J). (gr. -1-1). pap. 4.99 *(978-1-4169-4141-5(X)*, Simon Spotlight) Simon Spotlight.

—Welcome to Trucktown! Scieszka, Jon. 2010. (Jon Scieszka's Trucktown Ser.). (ENG.). 40p. (J). (gr. -1-3). pap. 4.99 *(978-1-4424-1271-2(2)*, Simon & Schuster Bks. For Young Readers) Simon & Schuster Bks. For Young Readers.

—Who's That Truck? Mason, Tom et al. 2008. (Jon Scieszka's Trucktown Ser.). (ENG.). 14p. (J). (gr. -1-1). bds. 7.99 *(978-1-4169-4175-0(4)*, Little Simon) Little Simon.

—Zoom! Boom! Bully. Scieszka, Jon. 2008. (Jon Scieszka's Trucktown Ser.). (ENG.). 24p. (J). (gr. -1-1). pap. 3.99 *(978-1-4169-4139-2(8)*, Simon Spotlight) Simon Spotlight.

Shannon, David. Alice the Fairy. Shannon, David. (ENG.). (J). 2009. (gr. -1-k). audio compact disk 10.99 *(978-0-545-11758-6(5))*; 2004. *(978-0-439-69379-0(9)*, Blue Sky Pr., The); 2004. 40p. (gr. -1-k). 17.99 *(978-0-439-49025-2(1)*, Blue Sky Pr., The) Scholastic, Inc.

—A Bad Case of Stripes. Shannon, David. (ENG.). 32p. (J). (gr. -1-3). 2006. audio compact disk 10.99 *(978-0-439-92494-8(4))*; 2004. reprint ed. pap. 6.99 *(978-0-439-59838-5(9)*, Scholastic Paperbacks) Scholastic, Inc.

—Bizzy Mizz Lizzie. Shannon, David. 2017. 40p. (J). (gr. -1-3). 17.99 *(978-0-545-61943-1(2))* Scholastic, Inc.

—Bugs in My Hair! Shannon, David. 2013. (ENG.). 32p. (J). (gr. -1-3). 17.99 *(978-0-545-14313-4(6)*, Blue Sky Pr., The) Scholastic, Inc.

—¡Crece Ya, David! Shannon, David. 2018. (David Bks.). (SPA.). 32p. (J). (gr. -1-k). pap. 6.99 *(978-1-338-29951-9(4)*, Scholastic en Espanol) Scholastic, Inc.

—David Smells! Shannon, David. 2005. (Diaper David Ser.). (ENG.). 12p. (J). (gr. -1-k). bds. 6.99 *(978-0-439-69138-3(9)*, Blue Sky Pr., The) Scholastic, Inc.

—David Va a la Escuela. Shannon, David. 2018. (David Bks.). (SPA.). 32p. (J). (gr. -1-k). pap. 6.99 *(978-1-338-26905-5(4)*, Scholastic en Espanol) Scholastic, Inc.

—Duck on a Tractor. Shannon, David. 2016. 40p. (J). (gr. -1-3). 16.99 *(978-0-545-61941-7(6)*, Blue Sky Pr., The) Scholastic, Inc.

—Good Boy, Fergus! Shannon, David. 2006. (ENG.). 40p. (J). (gr. -1-k). 17.99 *(978-0-439-49027-6(8)*, Blue Sky Pr., The) Scholastic, Inc.

—Grow up, David! Shannon, David. 2018. (David Bks.). 32p. (J). (gr. -1-k). 17.99 *(978-1-338-25097-8(3))* Scholastic, Inc.

—It's Christmas, David! Shannon, David. 2010. (David Books [Shannon] Ser.). (ENG.). 32p. (J). (gr. -1-3). 17.99 *(978-0-545-14311-0(X)*, Blue Sky Pr., The) Scholastic, Inc.

—Jangles: A Big Fish Story. Shannon, David. 2012. (ENG.). 32p. (J). (gr. -1-3). 17.99 *(978-0-545-14312-7(8)*, Blue Sky Pr., The) Scholastic, Inc.

—No, David! Shannon, David. 2018. (David Bks.). (ENG.). 32p. (J). (gr. -1 — 1). bds. 6.99 *(978-1-338-29958-8(1)*, Blue Sky Pr., The) Scholastic, Inc.

—¡No, David! Shannon, David. 2018. (David Bks.). (SPA.). 32p. (J). (gr. -1-k). pap. 6.99 *(978-1-338-26904-8(6)*, Scholastic en Espanol) Scholastic, Inc.

—Oh, David! A Diaper David Book. Shannon, David. 2005. (Diaper David Ser.). (ENG.). 12p. (J). (gr. -1-k). bds. 6.99 *(978-0-439-68881-9(7)*, Blue Sky Pr., The) Scholastic, Inc.

—Oops! A Diaper David Book. Shannon, David. 2005. (Diaper David Ser.). (ENG.). 12p. (J). (gr. -1-k). bds. 6.99 *(978-0-439-68882-6(5)*, Blue Sky Pr., The) Scholastic, Inc.

—Too Many Toys. Shannon, David. 2008. (ENG.). 32p. (J). (gr. -1-3). 16.99 *(978-0-439-49029-0(4))* Scholastic, Inc.

—Uh-Oh, David! A David Sticker Book. Shannon, David. 2013. 16p. (J). (gr. -1-k). 6.99 *(978-0-545-43768-4(7)*, Cartwheel Bks.) Scholastic, Inc.

Shannon, Doug. The Anxiety Survival Guide for Teens: CBT Skills to Overcome Fear, Worry, & Panic. Shannon, Jennifer. 2015. (Instant Help Solutions Ser.). (ENG.). 256p. (YA). (gr. 5-12). pap. 17.95 *(978-1-62625-243-1(2)*, 32431) New Harbinger Pubns.

Shannon, Drew. Extreme Battlefields: When War Meets the Forces of Nature. Lloyd Kyi, Tanya. 2016. (ENG.). 160p. (J). (gr. 4-8). pap. 14.95 *(978-1-55451-793-0(1))* Annick Pr., Ltd. CAN. Dist: Publishers Group West (PGW).

—The Montague Twins: the Witch's Hand. Page, Nathan. 2020. (Montague Twins Ser.: 1). 352p. (YA). (gr. 7). pap. 17.99 *(978-0-525-64677-8(9)*, Knopf Bks. for Young Readers) Random Hse. Children's Bks.

—Out of the Ice: How Climate Change Is Revealing the Past. Eamer, Claire. 2018. (ENG.). 32p. (J). (gr. 3-7). 17.99 *(978-1-77138-731-6(9))* Kids Can Pr., Ltd. CAN. Dist: Hachette Bk. Group.

Shannon, Drew. This Is Your Brain on Stereotypes: How Science Is Tackling Unconscious Bias. Lloyd Kyi, Tanya. 2020. (ENG.). 88p. (J). (gr. 6-9). 16.99 ***(978-1-5253-0016-5(4))*** Kids Can Pr., Ltd. CAN. Dist: Hachette Bk. Group.

Shannon, Kate. Coloring Book: Sidewalk Stories Meet Moby Mutt. Gray, Wendy K. 2019. (Sidewalk Stories Ser.: Vol. 3). (ENG.). 110p. (J). pap. 5.99 *(978-1-0971-6767-8(4))* Independently Published.

—Coloring Book: Sidewalk Stories Today Is the Day. Gray, Wendy K. 2019. (Sidewalk Stories Ser.: Vol. 4). (ENG.). 76p. (J). pap. 5.99 *(978-1-0971-1300-2(0))* Independently Published.

—Freddie, Bill & Irving. Bennett, Paul. 2009. 112p. (gr. 2-2). pap. 25.16 *(978-1-4251-7692-1(5))* Trafford Publishing.

—Sidewalk Stories: The Lemonade Landing Mat Big Coloring Book. Gray, Wendy K. 2019. (Sidewalk Stories Ser.: Vol. 1). (ENG.). 102p. (J). pap. 5.99 *(978-1-0993-3849-6(2))* Independently Published.

Shannon, Kenyon. The How & Why Wonder Book of Rocks & Minerals. Hyler, Nelson W. Blackwood, Paul E., ed. 2011. 52p. 36.95 *(978-1-258-10482-5(2))* Literary Licensing, LLC.

Shanower, Eric. The Living House of Oz. Einhorn, Edward. 2005. 239p. (J). 27.95 *(978-1-929527-08-3(X))* Hungry Tiger Pr.

Shanower, Eric. Adventures in Oz. Shanower, Eric. 2007. 256p. (J). (gr. 5-7). 75.00 *(978-1-60010-071-0(6))* Idea & Design Works, LLC.

—The Salt Sorcerer of Oz & Other Stories. Shanower, Eric. 2003. (Oz Ser.). 288p. (J). 24.95 *(978-1-929527-06-9(3))* Hungry Tiger Pr.

Shapiro, Alison Bonds. Just for Today. Phillips, Jan. 2005. (ENG.). 32p. (J). (gr. -1-5). 15.95 *(978-1-932073-07-2(8))* Kramer, H.J. Inc.

Shapiro, Alla. Tales from the Frog Forest. Lopatina, Irina. Lopatin, Dmitry, tr. 2012. (ENG.). 48p. (J). 18.00 *(978-1-61153-022-3(9))* Light Messages Publishing.

Shapiro, Deborah & Daniel, Alan. Letters from the Sea. Bjelke, Rolf, photos by. Shapiro, Deborah & Daniel, Lea. 2010. (ENG.). 96p. (J). (gr. 4-7). pap. 9.95 *(978-0-939837-03-8(X))* Paradise Cay Pubns.

Shapiro, Esmé. Eliza: the Story of Elizabeth Schuyler Hamilton: With an Afterword by Phillipa Soo, the Original Eliza from Hamilton: an American. McNamara, Margaret. 2018. (ENG.). 48p. (J). (gr. -1-3). 17.99 *(978-1-5247-6588-0(0)*, Schwartz & Wade Bks.) Random Hse. Children's Bks.

—Yak & Dove. Maclear, Kyo. 2017. (ENG.). 24p. (J). (gr. -1-3). 18.99 *(978-1-77049-494-7(4)*, Tundra Bks.) Tundra Bks. CAN. Dist: Penguin Random Hse. LLC.

Shapiro, Michelle. The Hanukkah Mice, 0 vols. Kroll, Steven. 2012. (ENG.). 42p. (J). (gr. -1-3). pap. 7.99 *(978-0-7614-5988-0(X)*, 9780761459880, Two Lions) Amazon Publishing.

—Happy Hanukkah Lights, Vol. Jules, Jacqueline. 2010. (ENG.). 12p. (J). (gr. -1 — 1). bds. 5.95 *(978-0-7613-5120-7(5)*, 9780761351207, Kar-Ben Publishing) Lerner Publishing Group.

—Rebecca's Journey Home. Sugarman, Brynn Olenberg. 2006. 32p. (J). (gr. -1-3). lib. bdg. 17.95 *(978-1-58013-157-5(3)*, Kar-Ben Publishing) Lerner Publishing Group.

Shapiro, Neil. The Amazing Menorah of Mazeltown. Dresner, Hal. 2009. (ENG.). 32p. (J). (gr. -1-3). 16.95 *(978-1-933176-28-4(8))* Red Rock Pr., Inc.

Shapiro, Pepper. The Journey of the Coconut. Meyer, Kim Shapiro. 2012. 34p. 24.95 *(978-1-4626-5576-2(9))*; 36p. pap. 24.95 *(978-1-4626-8641-4(9))* America Star Bks.

Shapiro, Rebecca. The Worry Worm. Brody, Lazer. 2007. 26p. (J). 26.95 *(978-0-9797530-1-5(5))* Kalcom Publishing.

Shapiro, Tikiri. The 12 Days of Yoga. Shapiro, Tikiri. 2018. (ENG.). 28p. (J). pap. 12.00 *(978-1-7308-0492-2(6))* Independently Published.

Shapur, Fredun. Singer & the Paint. Shapur, Mira. 2017. (ENG.). 32p. (J). (gr. -1-17). 16.95 *(978-1-84976-475-9(1))* Tate Publishing, Ltd. GBR. Dist: Hachette Bk. Group.

Share, Brian. There's a Dinosaur in My Room. Sharfe, Elaine. 2005. 20p. (J). pap. 7.95 *(978-1-894601-05-4(X))* Chestnut Publishing Group CAN. Dist: Hushion Hse. Publishing, Ltd.

Sharkey, Niamh. Dreams of Old Ireland. (J). *(978-1-84148-481-5(4))* Barefoot Bks., Inc.

—The Gigantic Turnip. Tolstoy, Aleksei. 2005. 40p. (J). (gr. -1-2). pap. 8.99 *(978-1-905236-58-9(1))* Barefoot Bks., Inc.

—Jack & the Beanstalk. Walker, Richard. 2019. (ENG.). 40p. (J). (gr. -1-2). pap. *(978-1-78285-416-6(9))* Barefoot Bks., Ltd.

—Tales from Old Ireland. Doyle, Malachy. (ENG.). 96p. 2017. pap. 16.99 *(978-1-78285-358-9(8))*; 2008. (J). 21.99 *(978-1-84686-241-0(8))* Barefoot Bks., Inc.

—Tales of Wisdom & Wonder. Lupton, Hugh. 64p. (J). 2008. 19.99 *(978-1-84686-243-4(4))*; 2006. 15.99 *(978-1-905236-84-8(0))* Barefoot Bks., Inc.

—Tales of Wisdom & Wonder. 2005. 64p. (J). *(978-1-84148-231-6(5))* Barefoot Bks., Inc.

Sharkey, Niamh. I'm a Happy Hugglewug: Laugh & Play the Hugglewug Way. Sharkey, Niamh. 2008. (ENG.). 34p. (J). (gr. k-k). bds. 6.99 *(978-0-7636-3981-5(8))* Candlewick Pr.

—Jack & the Beanstalk. Sharkey, Niamh. Walker, Richard. 2006. 40p. (J). (gr. -1-2). 10.99 *(978-1-905236-69-5(7))* Barefoot Bks., Inc.

—Santasaurus. Sharkey, Niamh. 2005. (ENG.). 32p. (J). (gr. -1-2). 15.99 *(978-0-7636-2671-6(6))* Candlewick Pr.

Sharma, Ishika. Little Bella's New Home. Gorrell, Sarah Walker. 2020. (ENG.). 48p. (J). pap. 7.99 ***(978-1-9759-6133-6(1))*** CreateSpace Independent Publishing Platform.

Sharma, Lalit Kumar. The Beautiful Game - Survival. Quinn, Jason. 2017. (Campfire Graphic Novels Ser.: 9). (ENG.). 160p. (J). (gr. 5). pap. 12.99 *(978-93-81182-11-6(6)*, Campfire) Steerforth Pr.

—Daredevil by Chip Zdarsky Vol. 2: No Devils, Only God. 2019. (Daredevil by Chip Zdarsky Ser.: 2). (ENG.). 136p. (YA). (gr. 8-17). pap. 15.99 *(978-1-302-91499-8(5))* Marvel Worldwide, Inc.

—In Defense of the Realm: Graphic Novel. Deshpande, Sanjay. 2011. (Campfire Graphic Novels Ser.: 2). (ENG.). 104p. (YA). (gr. 3-7). pap. 12.99 *(978-93-80028-64-4(4)*, Campfire) Steerforth Pr.

—Muhammad Ali: The King of the Ring. Helfand, Lewis. 2012. (Campfire Graphic Novels Ser.). (ENG.). 92p. (YA). (gr. 5-12). pap. 12.99 *(978-93-80741-23-9(5)*, Campfire) Steerforth Pr.

—World War One: 1914-1918. Cowsill, Alan. 2014. (Campfire Graphic Novels Ser.). (ENG.). 114p. (YA). (gr. 8-12). pap. 12.99 *(978-93-80741-85-7(5)*, Campfire) Steerforth Pr.

Sharma, Lalit Kumar, jt. illus. see Galindo, Diego.

Sharmat, Mitchell & Weston, Martha. Nate the Great on the Owl Express. Sharmat, Marjorie Weinman. 2004. (Nate the Great Ser.). (ENG.). 80p. (J). (gr. 1-4). 5.99 *(978-0-440-41927-3(1)*, Yearling) Random Hse. Children's Bks.

Sharon, Parker G. The Cave in Joseph's Yard. Ellis, Juanita B. 2018. (ENG.). 26p. (J). (gr. k-6). pap. 12.95 *(978-0-692-74049-1(X))* Parsons Porch Bks.

Sharp, Alice & Sharp, Paul. ¿Adivina Que? Historias de la Biblia, 1 vol. Harrast, Tracy. 2005. (SPA.). 192p. (J). (gr. 1-5). 13.99 *(978-0-8297-4448-4(7))* Vida Pubs.

Sharp, Anne, jt. illus. see Denchfield, Nick.

Sharp, Cheryl. The Mystery of Pineville Woods. Worley, Ashley. 2019. (ENG.). 148p. (YA). (gr. 7-12). pap. 12.95 ***(978-1-64458-897-0(8))*** Christian Faith Publishing.

Sharp, Chris. The ABCs of How I Love You. Berry, Ron. Smart Kidz, ed. (Parent Love Letters Ser.). (ENG.). 12p. (J). (gr. -1-2). 2020. bds. 9.99 ***(978-1-64123-398-9(2)***, 772222); 2019. bds. 14.99 *(978-1-64123-194-7(7)*, 770969) Smart Kidz Media, Inc.

Sharp, Chris. All Aboard! Charlie the Can-Do Choo Choo. Berry, Ron & Mead, David. 2009. (ENG.). 8p. 12.99 *(978-0-8249-1420-2(1)*, Ideal Pubns.) Worthy Publishing.

—Beware the Haunted House. Berry, Ron. 2008. (ENG.). 12p. (J). (gr. -1-k). bds. 12.99 *(978-0-8249-1815-6(0)*, Ideal Pubns.) Worthy Publishing.

—Beware the Haunted House. Berry, Ron. Smart Kidz, ed. 2019. (Halloween Safe Scare Ser.). (ENG.). 12p. (J). (gr. -1-2). bds. 9.99 *(978-1-64123-283-8(8)*, 771051) Smart Kidz Media, Inc.

—Can You Make Peter Rabbit Giggle? Berry, Ron. 2012. 10p. (J). bds. 10.99 *(978-0-8249-1418-9(X)*, Ideal Pubns.) Worthy Publishing.

—Can You Make the Monster Giggle? A Halloween Self-Scare Book! Mead, David & Berry, Ron. 2011. 16p. (J). 10.99 *(978-0-8249-1526-1(7)*, Ideal Pubns.) Worthy Publishing.

—Can You Roar Like a Lion? Berry, Ron. 2009. (ENG.). 14p. bds. 10.99 *(978-0-8249-1433-2(3)*, Ideal Pubns.) Worthy Publishing.

—Charlie the Can-Do Choo-Choo! Berry, Ron. 2006. (ENG.). 7p. (J). (gr. -1). bds. 12.95 *(978-0-8249-6678-2(3)*, Ideal Pubns.) Worthy Publishing.

—David & Goliath: A Story about Courage. Smart Kids Publishing Staff. 2006. (I Can Read the Bible Ser.). (ENG.). 12p. (J). (gr. -1-3). 14.95 *(978-0-8249-6659-1(7)*, Ideal Pubns.) Worthy Publishing.

—Faith-Filled Lullabies with Big Al & Annie. Kempf, Joe & Pescarino, Cathy. 2012. 32p. (J). *(978-1-61278-689-6(8))* Our Sunday Visitor, Publishing Div.

—The Forgetful Little Leprechaun. Mead, David. 2011. 18p. (J). (gr. -1-1). bds. 10.99 *(978-0-8249-1509-4(7)*, Ideal Pubns.) Worthy Publishing.

—God, Please Send Fire. Lashbrook, Marilyn. 2012. 32p. (J). pap. 8.00 *(978-1-935014-42-3(0))* Hutchings, John Pubs.

—How Do I Kiss You? Weimer, Heidi R. 2008. (ENG.). 18p. (J). (gr. -1-k). bds. 12.99 *(978-0-8249-1814-9(2)*, Ideal Pubns.) Worthy Publishing.

—It Was a Dark Dark Night. Berry, Ron. 2012. 14p. (J). bds. 12.99 *(978-0-8249-1602-2(6)*, Ideal Pubns.) Worthy Publishing.

—It's Potty Time for Boys. Berry, Ron. Smart Kidz, ed. 2019. (Time To... Book Ser.). (ENG.). 12p. (J). (gr. -1-2). bds. 9.99 *(978-1-64123-265-4(X)*, 771079) Smart Kidz Media, Inc.

—It's Potty Time for Girls. Smart Kidz, ed. 2019. (Time To... Book Ser.). (ENG.). 12p. (J). (gr. -1-2). bds. 9.99 *(978-1-64123-266-1(8)*, 771081) Smart Kidz Media, Inc.

—The Itsy Bitsy Spider. Berry, Ron. Smart Kidz, ed. 2019. (ENG.). 12p. (J). (gr. -1-2). bds. 14.99 *(978-1-64123-196-1(3)*, 770970) Smart Kidz Media, Inc.

—Jesus Loves Me! Berry, Ron. Smart Kidz, ed. 2019. (My Bible Sing along Book Ser.). (ENG.). 12p. (J). (gr. -1-2). bds. 9.99 *(978-1-64123-290-6(0)*, 771059); bds. 14.99 *(978-1-64123-197-8(1)*, 770972) Smart Kidz Media, Inc.

—Jesus Loves the Little Children. Berry, Ron. Smart Kidz, ed. 2019. (My Bible Sing along Book Ser.). (ENG.). 12p. (J). (gr. -1-2). bds. 9.99 *(978-1-64123-291-3(9)*, 771058); bds. 14.99 *(978-1-64123-206-7(4)*, 770980) Smart Kidz Media, Inc.

—Jingle Bells. Berry, Ron. Smart Kidz, ed. 2019. (Christmas Carol Book Ser.). (ENG.). 12p. (J). (gr. -1-2). bds. 14.99 *(978-1-64123-246-3(3))*; bds. 9.99 *(978-1-64123-288-3(9)*, 771057) Smart Kidz Media, Inc.

—Jonah & the Whale: A Story about Responsibility. Smart Kids Publishing Staff. 2006. (I Can Read the Bible Ser.). (ENG.). 12p. (J). (gr. -1-3). 14.95 *(978-0-8249-6661-4(9)*, Ideal Pubns.) Worthy Publishing.

—Joy to the World. Mead, David. 2010. 16p. (J). (gr. -1-1). 10.99 *(978-0-8249-1470-7(8)*, Ideal Pubns.) Worthy Publishing.

—Joy to the World. Mead, David. Smart Kidz, ed. 2019. (Christmas Carol Book Ser.). (ENG.). 12p. (J). (gr. -1-2). bds. 9.99 *(978-1-64123-297-5(8)*, 771027) Smart Kidz Media, Inc.

—Little Abe Lincoln Learns a Lesson in Honesty: Honesty. Mead, David. 2003. (American Virtues for Kids Ser.). (J). bds. 6.95 *(978-0-9746440-0-4(5)*, Ideal Pubns.) Worthy Publishing.

—Little Ben Franklin Learns a Lesson in Generosity: Generosity. Mead, David. 2003. (American Virtues for Kids Ser.). (J). bds. 6.95 *(978-0-9746440-2-8(1)*, Ideal Pubns.) Worthy Publishing.

—The Little Drummer Boy. Berry, Ron & Mead, David. 2009. (ENG.). 16p. 12.99 *(978-0-8249-1429-5(5)*, Ideal Pubns.) Worthy Publishing.

—Little George Washington Learns about Responsibility: Responsibility. Mead, David. 2004. (American Virtues for Kids Ser.). (J). bds. 6.95 *(978-0-9746440-1-1(3)*, Ideal Pubns.) Worthy Publishing.

—Little Teddy Roosevelt Learns a Lesson in Courage: Courage. Mead, David. 2003. (American Virtues for Kids Ser.). (J). bds. 6.95 *(978-0-9746440-3-5(X)*, Ideal Pubns.) Worthy Publishing.

—Look for the Rainbow! Berry, Ron. 2009. (ENG.). 18p. bds. 10.99 *(978-0-8249-1428-8(7)*, Ideal Pubns.) Worthy Publishing.

—Me 'n Mom: A Keepsake Scrapbook Journal. Barry, Ron & Fitzgerald, Paula. 2009. (ENG.). 33p. pap. 14.99 *(978-0-8249-1435-6(X)*, Ideal Pubns.) Worthy Publishing.

—My First Family Photo Album. Berry, Ron. 2008. (ENG.). 12p. (J). bds. 8.99 *(978-0-8249-6722-2(4)*, Ideal Pubns.) Worthy Publishing.

—My Guardian Angel. Berry, Ron. 2008. 12p. (J). (gr. -1-k). bds. 12.99 *(978-0-8249-1819-4(3)*, Ideal Pubns.) Worthy Publishing.

—O Little Town of Bethlehem. Berry, Ron. Smart Kidz, ed. 2019. (Christmas Carol Book Ser.). (ENG.). 12p. (J). (gr. -1-2). bds. 14.99 *(978-1-64123-242-5(0))*; bds. 9.99 *(978-1-64123-285-2(4)*, 771053) Smart Kidz Media, Inc.

—Rise & Shine! Berry, Ron. 2008. 14p. (J). bds. 12.99 *(978-0-8249-6735-2(6)*, Ideal Pubns.) Worthy Publishing.

—Silent Night. Mead, David. 2010. 16p. (J). (gr. -1-1). 10.99 *(978-0-8249-1427-1(9)*, Ideal Pubns.) Worthy Publishing.

—Silent Night. Berry, Ron. Smart Kidz, ed. 2019. (Christmas Carol Book Ser.). (ENG.). 12p. (J). (gr. -1-2). bds. 14.99 *(978-1-64123-244-9(7))*; bds. 9.99 *(978-1-64123-286-9(2)*, 771054) Smart Kidz Media, Inc.

—The Silly Safari Bus! Berry, Ron. 2008. (ENG.). 12p. (J). bds. 12.99 *(978-0-8249-6736-9(4)*, Ideal Pubns.) Worthy Publishing.

—Up on the Housetop. Berry, Ron. Smart Kidz, ed. 2019. (Christmas Carol Book Ser.). (ENG.). 12p. (J). (gr. -1-2). bds. 9.99 *(978-1-64123-287-6(0)*, 771055) Smart Kidz Media, Inc.

—We Wish You a Merry Christmas. Berry, Ron. 2011. 16p. (J). 10.99 *(978-0-8249-1464-6(3)*, Ideal Pubns.) Worthy Publishing.

—What's That Sound. Smart Kids Publishing Staff. 2005. 10p. (J). (gr. -1-k). 12.95 *(978-0-8249-6624-9(4)*, Ideal Pubns.) Worthy Publishing.

—Who's at the Door? Berry, Ron. Smart Kidz, ed. 2019. (ENG.). 12p. (J). (gr. -1-2). bds. 9.99 *(978-1-64123-284-5(6)*, 771052) Smart Kidz Media, Inc.

—You're My Little Love Bug. Weimer, Heidi. 2008. (ENG.). 16p. (J). bds. 12.99 *(978-0-8249-6589-1(2)*, Ideal Pubns.) Worthy Publishing.

Sharp, Chris. You're My Little Love Bug. Weimer, Heidi R. Smart Kidz, ed. 2019. (Parent Love Letters Ser.). (ENG.). 12p. (J). (gr. -1-2). bds. 9.99 ***(978-1-64123-376-7(1)***, 771142); bds. 14.99 *(978-1-64123-193-0(9)*, 770953) Smart Kidz Media, Inc.

Sharp, Chris. The 123s of How I Love You. Berry, Ron. 2012. 24p. (J). bds. 12.99 *(978-0-8249-1601-5(8)*, Ideal Pubns.) Worthy Publishing.

—The 123s of How I Love You. Berry, Ron. Smart Kidz, ed. (Parent Love Letters Ser.). (ENG.). 12p. (J). (gr. -1-2). 2020. bds. 9.99 *(978-1-64123-399-6(0)*, 772223); 2019. bds. 14.99 *(978-1-64123-195-4(5)*, 770954) Smart Kidz Media, Inc.

—131 Fun-Damental Facts for Catholic Kids: Liturgy, Litanies, Rituals, Rosaries, Symbols, Sacraments & Sacred Scripture. Synder, Bernadette. 2006. (Liguori's Fun Facts Ser.). 144p. (J). (gr. 3-7). per. 12.99 *(978-0-7648-1502-7(4))* Liguori Pubns.

Sharp, Chris & Currant, Gary. It's Bedtime. Berry, Ron & Sharp, Chris. 2003. (It's Time to Ser.). (ENG.). 14p. (J). (gr. -1-k). bds. 6.95 *(978-1-891100-61-1(0))* Smart Kidz Media, Inc.

—It's Potty Time for Boys. Berry, Ron. Smart Kidz, ed. 2019. (Time To... Book Ser.). (ENG.). 12p. (J). (gr. -1-2). bds. 14.99 *(978-1-64123-198-5(X)*, 770978) Smart Kidz Media, Inc.

—It's Potty Time for Girls. Smart Kidz, ed. 2019. (Time To... Book Ser.). (ENG.). 12p. (J). (gr. -1-2). bds. 14.99 *(978-1-64123-199-2(8)*, 770979) Smart Kidz Media, Inc.

Sharp, Craig. Mummy's Happy Tears. Bishop, Michele. 2013. 18p. pap. *(978-1-78148-186-8(5))* Grosvenor Hse. Publishing Ltd.

Sharp, Dan. Forever with Jesus. Mancini, Lee Ann. Lamson, Sharon, ed. 2018. (ENG.). 32p. (J). 12.99 *(978-0-9973325-3-7(0))* GLM Publishing.

Sharp, Gene. Please, Wind? Greene, Carol. 2011. (Rookie Ready to Learn - First Science Ser.). 40p. (J). (gr. -1-k). lib. bdg. 23.00 *(978-0-531-26502-4(1)*, Children's Pr.) Scholastic Library Publishing.

—Too Many Balloons. Matthias, Catherine. 2011. (Rookie Ready to Learn Ser.). 40p. (J). (gr. -1-k). pap. 5.95 *(978-0-531-26749-3(0))*; lib. bdg. 23.00 *(978-0-531-26449-2(1))* Scholastic Library Publishing. (Children's Pr.).

Sharp, Gene. Demasiados Globos. Sharp, Gene. Matthias, Catherine. 2011. (Rookie Ready to Learn Español Ser.).Tr. of Too Many Balloons. (SPA.). 40p. (J). pap. 5.95 *(978-0-531-26792-9(X))*; (gr. -1-1). lib. bdg. 23.00 *(978-0-531-26124-8(7))* Scholastic Library Publishing. (Children's Pr.).

Sharp, Kelley. Thisbe's Promise. Scott, Laurian. 2008. (ENG.). 32p. (J). 16.99 *(978-0-9816642-0-0(2))* ETS Publishing.

Sharp, Linda. The Grizzlies of Grouse Mountain: The True Adventures of Coola & Grinder. Hrdlitschka, Shelley & Schidlo, Rae. 2020. (ENG.). 48p. (J). (gr. 1-2). pap. ***(978-1-77203-355-7(3))*** Heritage Hse.

SHARP Literacy Students. The American Dream. SHARP Literacy Students, . 2008.Tr. of gran sueño Americano. (ENG & SPA.). 84p. pap. *(978-0-9770816-6-0(4))* SHARP Literacy, Inc.

Sharp, Melanie. Freddy's Teddy. De Marco, Clare. 2011. (Tadpoles Ser.). (ENG.). (J). (gr. -1-3). lib. bdg. 17.55 *(978-1-61383-937-9(5))* Perfection Learning Corp.

—In the Garden: Band 01A/Pink a (Collins Big Cat) Cronick, Mitch. 2005. (Collins Big Cat Ser.). (ENG.). 16p. (J). (gr. -1-k). pap. 6.99 *(978-0-00-718538-2(3))* HarperCollins Pubs. Ltd. GBR. Dist: Independent Pubs. Group.

—Ted's Party Bus. Robinson, Hilary. 2009. (Tadpoles Ser.). (ENG.). (J). (gr. k-k). lib. bdg. 17.55 *(978-1-61383-939-3(1))* Perfection Learning Corp.

Sharp, Pam. The Magical Journey of Bob Crane. Nicksich, Karen Marie. 2019. (ENG.). 54p. (J). (gr. 3-6). pap. 20.00 *(978-0-578-49282-7(2))* Nicksich, Karen M.

Sharp, Paul. Jovi Giraffe Learns to Look: A Lesson in Eye Contact. Bardina, Patricia & Burgess, Joanne. 2019. (Ducky Friends Ser.: Vol. 1). (ENG.). 36p. (J). (gr. k-2). 18.99 ***(978-1-64237-717-0(1))*** Gatekeeper Pr.

S

Sharp, Paul. My Little Doctor Bag Book. Hapka, Cathy. 2005. (J). *(978-1-57151-754-8(5))* Playhouse Publishing.
—Paul the Pitcher. 2011. (Rookie Ready to Learn: All about Me! Ser.). (ENG.). 40p. (J). (gr. -1-1). lib. bdg. 18.69 *(978-0-531-26426-3(2)*, Children's Pr.) Scholastic Library Publishing.
—Revony Rhinoceros Starts to Smile: A Lesson in Body Language. Bardina, Patricia & Burgess, Joanne. 2018. (Ducky Friends Ser.: Vol. 2). (ENG.). 36p. (J). (gr. k-3). 17.95 *(978-1-64237-193-2(9))* Gatekeeper Pr.
—Snow Joe. Greene, Carol. 2011. (Rookie Ready to Learn Ser.). 40p. (J). (ENG.). pap. 5.95 *(978-0-531-26804-9(7))*; (gr. -1-k). lib. bdg. 23.00 *(978-0-531-25644-2(8))* Scholastic Library Publishing. (Children's Pr.).
Sharp, Paul. Pablo el Lanzador. Sharp, Paul. 2011. (Rookie Ready to Learn Español Ser.). (SPA.). 40p. (J). pap. 5.95 *(978-0-531-26781-3(4))*; (gr. -1-1). lib. bdg. 23.00 *(978-0-531-26113-2(1))* Scholastic Library Publishing. (Children's Pr.).
—Paul the Pitcher. Sharp, Paul. 2011. (Rookie Ready to Learn Ser.). (ENG.). 40p. (J). pap. 5.95 *(978-0-531-26651-9(6)*, Children's Pr.) Scholastic Library Publishing.
Sharp, Paul, jt. illus. see Sharp, Alice.
Sharp, Rachel. How Flynn the Loh'li Conquered His Fears. Morris, A. R. 2019. (Flynn the Loh'li Ser.: Vol. 1). (ENG.). 26p. (J). (gr. k-6). 16.95 *(978-0-578-46224-0(9))* Morris, Amber.
Sharp, Rebecca. Monty & the Slobbernosserus. Sanders, Mt. 2017. (ENG.). 40p. (J). (gr. k-3). pap. *(978-1-912014-79-8(3))* 2QT, Ltd. (Publishing).
Sharp, Todd. Tom Tuff to the Rescue. Edgar, Robert. 2013. 26p. pap. *(978-0-9874832-0-1(X))* MoshPit Publishing.
—Who Caught the Yawn? & Where Did the Sneeze Go? Mosher, Jennifer. 2013. 38p. pap. *(978-0-9874832-3-2(4))* MoshPit Publishing.
Sharpe, Jemima. Mr Moon Wakes Up. Sharpe, Jemima. 2016. (Child's Play Library). 32p. (J). (ENG.). *(978-1-84643-694-9(X))*; pap. *(978-1-84643-693-2(1))* Child's Play International Ltd.
Sharpe, Jim, jt. illus. see Spector, Joel.
Sharpley, Kate. The Fantastic Christmas. Hughes, Julie. 2013. 34p. pap. *(978-0-9868344-9-3(1))* Yodoki Inc.
Sharpnack, Joe. The Magic Music Shop. Brenner, Vida. Sharp, Mary, ed. 2013. 102p. pap. 12.95 *(978-1-57216-094-1(2))* Penfield Bks.
Sharrat, Nick. Just Imagine. Goodhart, Pippa. 2014. 32p. (J). 12.99 *(978-1-61067-343-3(3))* Kane Miller.
Sharratt, Nick. Animal Music. Donaldson, Julia. (ENG.). (J). (-k). 2015. 20p. bds. 11.99 *(978-1-4472-7679-1(5))*; 2014. 24p. pap. 11.99 *(978-1-4472-1095-5(6))* Pan Macmillan GBR. Dist: Independent Pubs. Group.
—Best Friends. Wilson, Jacqueline. 2009. (ENG.). 256p. (J). (gr. 4-7). pap. 10.99 *(978-0-312-58144-2(0)*, 900061998) Square Fish.
—Candyfloss. Wilson, Jacqueline. 2008. (ENG.). 352p. (J). (gr. 4-7). pap. 10.99 *(978-0-312-38418-0(1)*, 900053319) Square Fish.
—Car, Car, Truck, Jeep. Charman, Katrina. 2018. (ENG.). 26p. (J). bds. 7.99 *(978-1-68119-895-8(9)*, 900191674, Bloomsbury Children's Bks.) Bloomsbury Publishing USA.
—Chocolate Mousse for Greedy Goose. Donaldson, Julia. (ENG.). (J). 2015. 18p. (-k). bds. 10.99 *(978-1-4472-8788-9(6))*; 2. 2006. 24p. (gr. -1-k). pap. 8.99 *(978-1-4050-2190-6(X))* Pan Macmillan GBR. Dist: Independent Pubs. Group.
—Cookie. Wilson, Jacqueline. 2010. (ENG.). 352p. (J). (gr. 4-7). pap. 17.99 *(978-0-312-64290-7(3)*, 900068061) Square Fish.
—Crazy Mayonnaisy Mum. Donaldson, Julia. 2015. (ENG.). 112p. (J). (gr. 2-4). pap. 8.99 *(978-1-4472-9322-4(3))* Pan Macmillan GBR. Dist: Independent Pubs. Group.
—Daisy & the Trouble with Sports Day. Gray, Kes. 2014. (Daisy Ser.). 320p. (J). (gr. 2-4). pap. 11.99 *(978-1-78295-285-5(3)*, Red Fox) Random House Children's Books GBR. Dist: Independent Pubs. Group.
—Daisy: Really, Really. Gray, Kes. 2016. (Daisy Picture Bks.: 2). 32p. (J). (gr. -1-k). pap. 11.99 *(978-1-78295-646-4(8)*, Red Fox) Random House Children's Books GBR. Dist: Independent Pubs. Group.
—Dinosaur Pox. Strong, Jeremy. (ENG.). 128p. (J). 7.95 *(978-0-14-038979-1(2))* Penguin Bks., Ltd. GBR. Dist: Trafalgar Square Publishing.
—Go, Go, Pirate Boat. Charman, Katrina. 2019. (ENG.). 24p. (J). bds. 7.99 *(978-1-5476-0319-0(4)*, 900211337, Bloomsbury Children's Bks.) Bloomsbury Publishing USA.
—Goat Goes to Playgroup. Donaldson, Julia. (ENG.). 24p. (J). 2015. (-k). bds. 10.99 *(978-1-4472-8791-9(6))*; 8. 2013. (gr. -1-k). pap. 9.99 *(978-1-4472-1094-8(8))* Pan Macmillan GBR. Dist: Independent Pubs. Group.
—Goldilocks, 2 vols. Tucker, Stephen. 2017. (Lift-The-Flap Fairy Tales Ser.). (ENG.). 24p. (J). (gr. -1-k). 11.99 *(978-1-5098-2818-0(4))* Pan Macmillan GBR. Dist: Independent Pubs. Group.
—Hippo Has a Hat. Donaldson, Julia. ed. 2007. (ENG.). 24p. (J). (gr. k-k). pap. 12.99 *(978-1-4050-2192-0(6))* Macmillan Pubs., Ltd. GBR. Dist: Independent Pubs. Group.
—The Indoor Pirates on Treasure Island. Strong, Jeremy. (ENG.). 96p. (J). 7.95 *(978-0-14-038637-0(8))* Penguin Bks., Ltd. GBR. Dist: Trafalgar Square Publishing.
—Jack & the Beanstalk, 2 vols. Tucker, Stephen. 2016. (Lift-The-Flap Fairy Tales Ser.). (ENG.). 24p. (J). (gr. -1-k). bds. 12.99 *(978-1-5098-1714-6(X))* Pan Macmillan GBR. Dist: Independent Pubs. Group.
—Little Baby's Busy Day: a Finger Wiggle Book. Symes, Sally. 2020. (ENG.). 22p. (J). (— 1). bds. 8.99 *(978-1-5362-1278-5(4))* Candlewick Pr.
—Little Baby's Playtime: a Finger Wiggle Book. Symes, Sally. 2020. (ENG.). 22p. (J). (— 1). bds. 8.99 *(978-1-5362-1279-2(2))* Candlewick Pr.
—Little Red Riding Hood, 2 vols. Tucker, Stephen. 2017. (Lift-The-Flap Fairy Tales Ser.). (ENG.). 24p. (J). (gr. -1-1). 10.99 *(978-1-5098-2815-9(X))* Pan Macmillan GBR. Dist: Independent Pubs. Group.
—Mixed up Fairy Tales. Robinson, Hilary. 2005. 32p. (J). (gr. -1-k). pap. 11.95 *(978-0-340-87558-2(5))* Hachette Children's Group GBR. Dist: Hachette Bk. Group.
—My First Animal Fun Sticker Book. Donaldson, Julia. 2016. (ENG.). 30p. (J). (gr. -1-2). pap. 8.99 *(978-1-5098-1622-4(4))* Pan Macmillan GBR. Dist: Independent Pubs. Group.
—One Mole Digging a Hole. Donaldson, Julia. 2015. (ENG.). 22p. (J). (-k). bds. 10.99 *(978-1-4472-8790-2(8))* Pan Macmillan GBR. Dist: Independent Pubs. Group.
—Shuffle & Squelch. Donaldson, Julia. 2015. (ENG.). 32p. (J). (-k). pap. 11.99 *(978-1-4472-7681-4(7))* Pan Macmillan GBR. Dist: Independent Pubs. Group.
—Socks. Lindsay, Elizabeth. 2018. (ENG.). 32p. (J). (— 1). pap. 12.99 *(978-0-552-57221-7(7))* Transworld Publishers Ltd. GBR. Dist: Independent Pubs. Group.
—The Story of Tracy Beaker. Wilson, Jacqueline. 2004. (ENG.). 133p. 16.00 *(978-0-7569-3205-3(X))* Perfection Learning Corp.
—The Three Billy Goats Gruff, 2 vols. Tucker, Stephen. 2017. (Lift-The-Flap Fairy Tales Ser.). (ENG.). 24p. (J). (gr. -1-k). 10.99 *(978-1-5098-2978-1(4))* Pan Macmillan GBR. Dist: Independent Pubs. Group.
—Tiger Ways. Gray, Kes. 2016. (Daisy Picture Bks.: 6). 32p. (J). (gr. -1-k). pap. 11.99 *(978-1-78295-649-5(2)*, Red Fox) Random House Children's Books GBR. Dist: Independent Pubs. Group.
—Toddle Waddle. Donaldson, Julia. 2015. (ENG.). 24p. (J). (-k). bds. 11.99 *(978-1-4472-8792-6(4))* Pan Macmillan GBR. Dist: Independent Pubs. Group.
Sharratt, Nick. The Whales on the Bus. Charman, Katrina. 2020. (ENG.). 26p. (J). bds. 7.99 ***(978-1-5476-0618-4(5)**,* 900234582, Bloomsbury Children's Bks.) Bloomsbury Publishing USA.
Sharratt, Nick. What the Jackdaw Saw: Book & CD Pack, 2 vols. Donaldson, Julia. 2015. (ENG.). 32p. (J). (gr. -1-k). 14.99 *(978-1-5098-0622-5(9)*, Macmillan Digital Audio) Pan Macmillan GBR. Dist: Independent Pubs. Group.
—Whose Toes Are Those? Symes, Sally. 2012. (ENG.). 22p. (J). (gr. k-12). bds. 7.99 *(978-0-7636-6274-5(7))* Candlewick Pr.
—Wriggle & Roar. Donaldson, Julia. 2015. (ENG.). 32p. (J). (gr. -1-1). pap. 9.99 *(978-1-4472-7665-4(5))* Pan Macmillan GBR. Dist: Independent Pubs. Group.
—Yawn. Symes, Sally. 2011. (ENG.). 24p. (J). (gr. -1-2). bds. 7.99 *(978-0-7636-5725-3(5))* Candlewick Pr.
Sharratt, Nick. Little Monster's Day Out with Dad. Sharratt, Nick. Goodhart, Pippa. 2017. (Little Monster Ser.). (ENG.). 14p. (J). (gr. -1-k). pap. 10.99 *(978-1-4052-7644-3(4))* Egmont Bks., Ltd. GBR. Dist: Independent Pubs. Group.
—The Three Little Pigs, 2 vols. Sharratt, Nick. Tucker, Stephen. 2016. (Lift-The-Flap Fairy Tales Ser.). (ENG.). 24p. (J). (gr. -1-k). bds. 11.99 *(978-1-5098-1713-9(1))* Pan Macmillan GBR. Dist: Independent Pubs. Group.
—What's in the Witch's Kitchen? Sharratt, Nick. 2011. (ENG.). 20p. (J). (gr. -1-2). 12.99 *(978-0-7636-5224-1(5))* Candlewick Pr.
Sharratt, Nick & Parsons, Garry. Daisy & the Trouble with Burglars. Gray, Kes. 2014. (Daisy Ser.: 8). (ENG.). 304p. (J). (gr. 2-4). pap. 11.99 *(978-1-84941-681-8(8)*, Red Fox) Random House Children's Books GBR. Dist: Independent Pubs. Group.
—Daisy & the Trouble with Coconuts. Gray, Kes. 2013. (Daisy Ser.). (ENG.). 272p. (J). (gr. 2-4). pap. 11.99 *(978-1-84941-678-8(8)*, Red Fox) Random House Children's Books GBR. Dist: Independent Pubs. Group.
—Daisy & the Trouble with Giants. Gray, Kes. 2010. (Daisy Ser.: 10). 256p. (J). (gr. 2-4). pap. 11.99 *(978-1-86230-495-6(5)*, Red Fox) Random House Children's Books GBR. Dist: Independent Pubs. Group.
—Daisy & the Trouble with Kittens. Gray, Kes. 2010. (Daisy Ser.). (ENG.). 256p. (J). (gr. 2-4). pap. 11.99 *(978-1-86230-834-3(9)*, Red Fox) Random House Children's Books GBR. Dist: Independent Pubs. Group.
—Daisy & the Trouble with Life. Gray, Kes. 2007. (Daisy Ser.: 12). 240p. (J). (gr. 2-4). pap. 11.95 *(978-1-86230-167-2(0)*, Red Fox) Random House Children's Books GBR. Dist: Independent Pubs. Group.
—Daisy & the Trouble with Maggots, No. 6. Gray, Kes. 2010. (Daisy Ser.: 6). 240p. (J). (gr. 2-4). pap. 11.99 *(978-1-86230-846-6(2)*, Red Fox) Random House Children's Books GBR. Dist: Independent Pubs. Group.
Sharrett, Nick. One Mole Digging a Hole, 2. Donaldson, Julia. ed. 2010. (ENG.). 32p. (J). (gr. k-k). pap. 8.99 *(978-0-230-70647-7(9))* Macmillan Pubs., Ltd. GBR. Dist: Independent Pubs. Group.
Sharum, Angel. Oliver & His Bff. MacKenzie, C. A. 2018. (ENG.). 64p. (J). pap. *(978-1-927529-52-2(2))* MacKenzie, Catherine A.
Sharvin, Ivan & Saito, Diogo. Tangled: the Series - Adventure Is Calling. Peterson, Scott & Ferrari, Alessandro. 2017. (Tangled Ser.). (ENG.). 72p. (J). (gr. 4-7). pap. 9.99 *(978-1-68405-198-4(3))* Idea & Design Works, LLC.
Shashkova, Vira. Positive Pants That Make You Dance: A Story about Two Friends Who Learn How to Share. Samarelli, Francesco & Dininno, Francesca. 2019. (ENG.). 32p. (J). pap. 11.00 ***(978-1-7123-7519-8(9))*** Independently Published.
Shaskan, Stephen. Art Panels, BAM! Speech Bubbles, POW! Writing Your Own Graphic Novel, 1 vol. Shaskan, Trisha Speed. 2010. (Writer's Toolbox Ser.). (ENG.). 32p. (J). (gr. 2-4). pap. 8.95 *(978-1-4048-6393-4(1)*, Picture Window Bks.) Capstone.
—The Case of the Missing Mola Lisa!, Bk. 1. Shaskan, Trisha Speed. 2017. (Q & Ray Ser.: 1). 48p. (J). (gr. 2-5). 26.65 *(978-1-5124-1147-8(7)*, 9781512411478, Graphic Universe™) Lerner Publishing Group.
—Meteorite or Meteor-Wrong? Case 2. Shaskan, Trisha Speed. 2018. (Q & Ray Ser.). (ENG.). 48p. (J). (gr. 2-5). pap. 7.99 *(978-1-5415-1047-0(X)*, 9781541510470, Graphic Universe™) Lerner Publishing Group.
—The Missing Mola Lisa: Case 1. Shaskan, Trisha Speed. 2017. (Q & Ray Ser.). (ENG.). 48p. (J). (gr. 2-5). pap. 7.99 *(978-1-5124-5414-7(1)*, 9781512454147, Graphic Universe™) Lerner Publishing Group.
—Punk Skunks. Shaskan, Trisha Speed. 2016. (ENG.). 40p. (J). (gr. -1-3). 17.99 *(978-0-06-236396-1(4))* HarperCollins Pubs.
Shaskan, Stephen. Max Speed. Shaskan, Stephen. 2016. (ENG.). 32p. (J). (gr. -1-3). 17.99 *(978-1-4814-4590-0(1)*, Simon & Schuster Bks. For Young Readers) Simon & Schuster Bks. For Young Readers.
—The Three Triceratops Tuff. Shaskan, Stephen. 2013. (ENG.). 32p. (J). (gr. -1-2). 16.99 *(978-1-4424-4397-6(9)*, Beach Lane Bks.) Beach Lane Bks.
—Toad on the Road: A Cautionary Tale. Shaskan, Stephen. 2017. (ENG.). 32p. (J). (gr. -1-3). 17.99 *(978-0-06-239347-0(2))* HarperCollins Pubs.
—Toad on the Road: Mama & Me. Shaskan, Stephen. 2018. (ENG.). 32p. (J). (gr. -1-3). 17.99 *(978-0-06-239349-4(9))* HarperCollins Pubs.
Shaskan, Stephen, jt. illus. see Shaskan, Trisha Speed.
Shaskan, Trisha Speed & Shaskan, Stephen. Foul Play at Elm Tree Park. Shaskan, Trisha Speed & Shaskan, Stephen. 2018. (Q & Ray Ser.). (ENG.). 48p. (J). (gr. 2-5). 26.65 *(978-1-5124-1149-2(3)*, Graphic Universe™) Lerner Publishing Group.
—Meteorite or Meteor-Wrong!, Bk. 2. Shaskan, Trisha Speed & Shaskan, Stephen. 2018. (Q & Ray Ser.). 48p. (J). (gr. 2-5). 26.65 *(978-1-5124-1148-5(5)*, 9781512411485, Graphic Universe™) Lerner Publishing Group.
Shattil, Wendy, et al, photos by. Sierra Babies. 2013. 26p. (J). 8.95 *(978-1-56037-557-9(4))* Farcountry Pr.
Shattil, Wendy & Rozinski, Bob, photos by. The Wildlife Detectives: How Forensic Scientists Fight Crimes Against Nature. Jackson, Donna M. 2005. (Scientists in the Field Ser.). 47p. (gr. 3-7). 20.00 *(978-0-7569-5191-7(7))* Perfection Learning Corp.
Shatto, Summer. This Is the Smile That Audrey Has. Banks, Glenn. Su, Chih-Huei Debby, tr. 2016. (CHI.). (J). pap. 9.49 *(978-1-943417-21-6(0))* B-Bright publishing.
Shauf, Rob. Erin's Gift. Williams, Patrick A. 2017. (ENG.). 46p. (J). *(978-1-988001-26-5(9))* Ahelia Publishing, Inc.
—Strong Together. Em, Charlie. 2018. (ENG.). 54p. (J). (gr. k-6). pap. *(978-1-988001-41-8(2))* Ahelia Publishing, Inc.
Shaughnessy, Mara. Downpour. Martin, Emily. 2013. (ENG.). 32p. (J). (gr. -1-k). 14.95 *(978-1-62087-545-2(4)*, 620545, Sky Pony Pr.) Skyhorse Publishing Co., Inc.
Shavers, Johnny L. The Bee in the Boot. Shavers, Latasha R. 2017. (ENG.). 26p. (J). pap. 9.99 *(978-1-5489-8596-7(1))* CreateSpace Independent Publishing Platform.
—I Love to Pretend. Shavers, Latasha R. 2018. (ENG.). 32p. (J). pap. 9.99 *(978-1-9793-8495-7(9))* CreateSpace Independent Publishing Platform.
Shavrin, Ivan. Disney PIXAR Toy Story 4 (Graphic Novel) Blackman, Haden. 2019. (ENG.). 72p. (J). (gr. 3-7). pap. 10.99 *(978-1-5067-1265-9(7)*, Dark Horse Books) Dark Horse Comics.
Shaw, Byam. The Adventures of Akbar: With an Essay from the Garden of Fidelity Being the Autobiography of Flora Annie Steel, by R. R. Clark. Steel, Flora Annie. 2020. (ENG.). 166p. (J). pap. ***(978-1-5287-1463-1(6))*** Read Bks.
Shaw, Charles. Big Cat Trouble. Smalley, Roger. 2005. (J). *(978-1-933248-13-4(0))* World Quest Learning.
—Gorilla Guardian. Smalley, Roger. 2005. (J). *(978-1-933248-14-1(9))* World Quest Learning.
Shaw, Daniel. Journey to Pansophigus. ed. 2005. (J). per. 9.95 *(978-0-9772168-0-2(2))* Water Lily Pr., Inc.
Shaw, David. The Brave Little Tailor: A Retelling of the Grimm's Fairy Tale, 1 vol. Blair, Eric. 2011. (My First Classic Story Ser.). (ENG.). 32p. (J). (gr. k-3). pap. 7.10 *(978-1-4048-7357-5(0)*, Picture Window Bks.) Capstone.
—Rumpelstiltskin. Blair, Eric. Abello, Patricia, tr. 2006. (Read-It! Readers en Español: Cuentos de Hadas Ser.). (SPA.). 32p. (J). (gr. k-3). 21.32 *(978-1-4048-1637-4(2)*, Picture Window Bks.) Capstone.
—Rumpelstiltskin: A Retelling of the Grimm's Fairy Tale, 1 vol. Blair, Eric. 2013. (My First Classic Story Ser.). (ENG.). 32p. (J). (gr. k-3). pap. 7.10 *(978-1-4795-1850-0(6)*, Picture Window Bks.) Capstone.
Shaw, Elizabeth. The Little Black Sheep. Shaw, Elizabeth. 2007. (Pandas Ser.: 06). (ENG.). 64p. (J). pap. 9.95 *(978-0-86278-463-8(8))* O'Brien Pr., Ltd., The IRL. Dist: Dufour Editions, Inc.
—The Little Black Sheep: Panda 6. Shaw, Elizabeth. 2nd rev. ed. 2017. (Pandas Ser.: 6). (ENG.). 64p. (J). 11.00 *(978-1-84717-918-0(5))* O'Brien Pr., Ltd., The IRL. Dist: Casemate Pubs. & Bk. Distributors, LLC.
Shaw, Geoff & Smith, Cory. Guardians of the Galaxy by Donny Cates Vol. 2: Faithless. 2020. (ENG.). 136p. (YA). (gr. 8-17). pap. 24.99 *(978-1-302-91589-6(4))* Marvel Worldwide, Inc.
Shaw, Gunner Alan. Building Bridges. Shaw, Daniel L. 2019. (ENG.). 30p. (J). pap. 9.25 ***(978-1-7127-1924-4(6))*** Independently Published.
Shaw, Hannah. The Great Dog Disaster. Davies, Katie. 2013. (Great Critter Capers Ser.). (ENG.). 208p. (J). (gr. 3-7). 12.99 *(978-1-4424-4517-8(3)*, Beach Lane Bks.) Beach Lane Bks.
—The Great Hamster Massacre. Davies, Katie. 2011. (Great Critter Capers Ser.). (ENG.). 208p. (J). (gr. 3-7). 12.99 *(978-1-4424-2062-5(6)*, Beach Lane Bks.) Beach Lane Bks.
—The Great Rabbit Rescue. Davies, Katie. 2011. (Great Critter Capers Ser.). (ENG.). 224p. (J). (gr. 3-7). 12.99 *(978-1-4424-2064-9(2)*, Beach Lane Bks.) Beach Lane Bks.
—I Don't Believe It, Archie! Norriss, Andrew. 2013. (ENG.). 128p. (J). (gr. 2-4). lib. bdg. 21.19 *(978-0-385-75251-0(2)*, David Fickling Bks.) Random Hse. Children's Bks.
—The World-Famous Cheese Shop Break-In. Taylor, Sean. 2015. (ENG.). 32p. (J). (gr. -1-2). 17.99 *(978-1-84780-430-3(6)*, 311699, Frances Lincoln Children's Bks.) Quarto Publishing Group UK GBR. Dist: Hachette UK Distribution.
Shaw, Hannah & Marttila, Andrew, photos by. Kitten Lady's Big Book of Little Kittens. Shaw, Hannah. 2019. (ENG., 56p. (J). (gr. -1-3). 18.99 *(978-1-5344-3894-1(7)*, Aladdin) Simon & Schuster Children's Publishing.
Shaw, Jaslyne. Dreamland. Dosanjh, R. K. & Lalli, Niyah. 2016. (Dreamland Ser.: Vol. 1). (ENG.). 18p. (J). (gr. 3-6). *(978-0-9939283-7-6(4))* Big Heart Publishing Inc.
Shaw, Jasper. A Place for Mulan. Chow, Marie. 2020. (ENG.). 40p. (J). (gr. 1-3). 16.99 *(978-1-368-02348-1(7))* Disney Pr.
Shaw, Peter. Hop, Little Hare! Wild, Margaret. 2008. (ENG.). 24p. (J). (gr. -1-2). pap. 10.95 *(978-1-921049-68-2(5))* Little Hare Bks. AUS. Dist: Independent Pubs. Group.
Shaw-Peterson, Kimberly. The Crayon Kids' Art Adventure. Ruprecht, Jennifer L. 2007. (ENG.). 32p. (J). per. 9.95 *(978-1-933916-10-1(9))* Nelson Publishing & Marketing.
—Darcy Daisy & the Firefly Festival: Learning about Bipolar Disorder & Community. Lewandowski, Lisa & Trost, Shannon. 2005. 32p. (J). (gr. -1-9). pap. 9.95 *(978-0-9785075-2-7(5)*, Ferne Pr.) Nelson Publishing & Marketing.
Shaw, Sarah. Davey the Detective: A Bird Brain Book. Chand, Emlyn. l.t. ed. 2012. (ENG.). 42p. (gr. k-1). 21.95 *(978-1-62253-107-3(8))*; pap. 10.95 *(978-1-62253-119-6(1))* Evolved Publishing.
—Honey the Hero: A Bird Brain Book. Chand, Emlyn. ed. 2012. (ENG.). 44p. (gr. k-1). (J). 21.95 *(978-1-62253-106-6(X))*; pap. 10.95 *(978-1-62253-118-9(3))* Evolved Publishing.
—Poppy the Proud: A Bird Brain Book. Chand, Emlyn. ed. 2012. (ENG.). 44p. (gr. k-3). 21.95 *(978-1-62253-108-0(6))*; pap. 10.95 *(978-1-62253-120-2(5))* Evolved Publishing.
Shaw-Smith, Emma. Bread Is for Eating. Gershator, David & Gershator, Phillis. 2003. (ENG & SPA.). 25p. (J). (gr. k-4). reprint ed. 16.00 *(978-0-7567-9033-2(6))* DIANE Publishing Co.
Shaw, Sonny. Papa Jon's Shed. Adams, Bill. 2016. (ENG.). 33p. (J). pap. *(978-0-9956247-0-2(4))* Hello Bks.
Shaw, Stan. Oscar Wilde, Vol. 16. Wilde, Oscar et al. Pomplun, Tom, ed. 2009. (ENG.). 144p. (YA). pap. 11.95 *(978-0-9787919-6-4(7)*, 80cd8909-efef-4be2-a412-1f402a4a9239) Eureka Productions.
Shaw, Yvonne. Priscilla & the Big Red Ball, 1 vol. Shaw, Laura. 2009. 19p. pap. 24.95 *(978-1-60749-523-9(6))* America Star Bks.
Shayan, Mohammad. Oink & Gobble & the Men in Black. Whaler, Norman. Firestone, Ellie, ed. 2019. (Oink & Gobble Series Book Ser.: Vol. 2). (ENG.). 30p. (J). (gr. k-2). 19.99 *(978-1-948131-38-4(2))* Whaler, Norman / Beneath Another Sky Bks.
Shayan, Mohammad. Oink & Gobble & the Missing Cupcakes. Whaler, Norman. Randell, Esther, ed. 2019. (Oink & Gobble Ser.: Vol. 3). (ENG.). 32p. (J). (gr. k-2). 19.99 ***(978-1-948131-47-6(1))*** Whaler, Norman / Beneath Another Sky Bks.
Shayan, Mohammad. Oink & Gobble & the 'no One Can Ever Know Secret' Whaler, Norman. Firestone, Ellie, ed. 2018. (Oink & Gobble Ser.: Vol. 1). (ENG.). 32p. (J). (gr. k-2). 19.99 *(978-1-948131-20-9(X))* Whaler, Norman / Beneath Another Sky Bks.
—Oink y Gobble y el 'secreto Que Nadie Debe Saber' Whaler, Norman. 2018. (Oink & Gobble Ser.: Vol. 1). (SPA.). 32p. (J). (gr. k-2). 19.99 *(978-1-948131-23-0(4))* Whaler, Norman / Beneath Another Sky Bks.
Shayan, Mohammad. Oink y Gobble y Los Cupcakes Desaparecidos. Whaler, Norman. Randell, Esther, ed. 2019. (Oink & Gobble Ser.: Vol. 3). (SPA.). 32p. (J). (gr. k-2). 19.99 ***(978-1-948131-50-6(1))*** Whaler, Norman / Beneath Another Sky Bks.
Shayibi, Sundus. Ahlam an Akun Katibah. Tahir, Samar. 2018. (ARA.). 24p. (J). *(978-614-03-2016-1(X))* Dar al saqi.
—Al-Ashkal Kharij Al-Lubah. Ata-Allah, Salma. 2018. (ARA.). 15p. (J). *(978-9953-37-292-1(6))* Academia.
Shchegoleva, Darya. My Favorite Morning. Jason, Juliana. 2018. (Georgia Honey Ser.: Vol. 1). (ENG.). 34p. (J). pap. 9.99 *(978-1-7903-4480-2(8))* Independently Published.
She, Liu. Chinese Fables & Folktales (I) Ma, Zheng & Li, Zheng. 2010. (ENG.). 48p. (J). (gr. -1-3). 16.95 *(978-1-60220-962-6(6))* Shanghai Translation Publishing Hse. CHN. Dist: Publishers Group West (PGW).
—Stories Behind Chinese Idioms (III) Ma, Zheng & Li, Zheng. 2010. (ENG.). 48p. (J). (gr. 3-6). 16.95 *(978-1-60220-967-1(7))* Shanghai Translation Publishing Hse. CHN. Dist: Publishers Group West (PGW).
Shea, Bob. Boo! Haiku. Caswell, Deanna. 2016. (ENG.). 24p. (J). (gr. -1-k). 12.95 *(978-1-4197-2118-2(6)*, Abrams Appleseed) Abrams, Inc.
—Gilbert Goldfish Wants a Pet. DiPucchio, Kelly. 2011. (ENG.). 32p. (J). (gr. -1-k). 16.99 *(978-0-8037-3394-7(1)*, Dial Bks) Penguin Young Readers Group.
—Guess Who, Haiku. Caswell, Deanna. 2016. (Guess Who Haiku Ser.). (ENG.). 24p. (J). (gr. -1-k). 14.95 *(978-1-4197-1889-2(4)*, Abrams Appleseed) Abrams, Inc.
—Love, Triangle. Colleen, Marcie. 2017. (ENG.). 32p. (J). (gr. -1-3). 17.99 *(978-0-06-241084-9(9))* HarperCollins Pubs.
—Me Want Pet! Sauer, Tammi. 2012. (ENG.). 40p. (J). (gr. -1-3). 19.99 *(978-1-4424-0810-4(3)*, Simon & Schuster/Paula Wiseman Bks.) Simon & Schuster/Paula Wiseman Bks.
—Quit Calling Me a Monster! John, Jory. 2016. (ENG.). 40p. (J). (gr. -1-2). 17.99 *(978-0-385-38990-7(6)*, Random Hse. Bks. for Young Readers) Random Hse. Children's Bks.
—Wedgieman & the Big Bunny Trouble. Harper, Charise Mericle. 2014. (Step into Reading Ser.). (ENG.). 48p. (J). (gr. k-3). 3.99 *(978-0-307-93073-6(4)*, Random Hse. Bks. for Young Readers) Random Hse. Children's Bks.
Shea, Bob. Ballet Cat What's Your Favorite Favorite? Shea, Bob. 2017. (Ballet Cat Ser.: 3). (ENG.). 56p. (J). (gr. 1-3). 9.99 ***(978-1-4847-7809-8(X))*** Little, Brown Bks. for Young Readers.
Shea, Bob. Cheetah Can't Lose. Shea, Bob. 2013. (ENG.). 40p. (J). (gr. -1-3). 17.99 *(978-0-06-173083-2(1))* HarperCollins Pubs.

—Dinosaur vs. Bedtime. Shea, Bob. (Dinosaur vs. Book Ser.: 1). (J). (gr. -1-k). 2011. 30p. bds. 6.99 *(978-1-4231-3788-7(4))*; 2008. 40p. 16.99 *(978-1-4231-1335-5(7))* Hyperion Pr.

—Dinosaur vs. School. Shea, Bob. 2016. (Dinosaur vs. Book Ser.: 5). 32p. (J). (gr. -1-k). bds. 7.99 *(978-1-4231-6094-6(0))* Hyperion Bks. for Children.

—Dinosaur vs. the Library. Shea, Bob. 2011. (Dinosaur vs. Book Ser.: 3). 40p. (J). (gr. -1-k). 16.99 *(978-1-4231-3338-4(2))* Hyperion Pr.

—Dinosaur vs. the Potty. Shea, Bob. 2012. (Dinosaur vs. Book Ser.: 2). 30p. (J). (gr. -1-k). bds. 6.99 *(978-1-4231-5179-1(8))* Hyperion Pr.

—I'm a Shark. Shea, Bob. 2011. (ENG.). 40p. (J). (gr. -1-1). 16.99 *(978-0-06-199846-1(X)*, Balzer & Bray) HarperCollins Pubs.

—Oh, Daddy! Shea, Bob. 2010. (ENG.). 40p. (J). (gr. -1-1). 16.99 *(978-0-06-173080-1(7))* HarperCollins Pubs.

—Race You to Bed. Shea, Bob. 2010. (ENG.). 40p. (J). (gr. -1-2). 16.99 *(978-0-06-170417-8(2)*, Tegen, Katherine Bks) HarperCollins Pubs.

Shea, Bob. Unicorn Is Maybe Not So Great after All. Shea, Bob. 2019. (ENG.). 40p. (J). (gr. -1-k). 17.99 ***(978-1-368-00944-7(1))*** Little, Brown Bks. for Young Readers.

Shea, Bob. Unicorn Thinks He's Pretty Great. Shea, Bob. 2013. (ENG.). 40p. (J). (gr. -1-k). 15.99 *(978-1-4231-5952-0(7))* Hyperion Pr.

Shea, Denise. Eye of the Storm: A Book about Hurricanes, 1 vol. Thomas, Rick & Picture Window Books Staff. 2005. (Amazing Science: Weather Ser.). (ENG.). 24p. (J). (gr. -1-3). per. 8.95 *(978-1-4048-1845-3(6)*, Picture Window Bks.) Capstone.

—Giran en el Espacio: Un Libro Sobre Los Planetas. Meachen Rau, Dana & Picture Window Books Staff. Robledo, Sol, tr. 2007. (Ciencia Asombrosa: Exploremos el Espacio Ser.). (SPA.). 24p. (J). (gr. k-4). 27.32 *(978-1-4048-3231-2(9)*, Picture Window Bks.) Capstone.

—El Ojo de la Tormenta: Un Libro Sobre Huracanes, 1 vol. Thomas, Rick & Picture Window Books Staff. Robledo, Sol, tr. 2007. (Ciencia Asombrosa: el Tiempo Ser.). (SPA.). 24p. (J). (gr. -1-3). 27.32 *(978-1-4048-3214-5(9)*, Picture Window Bks.) Capstone.

—Pull, Lift, & Lower: A Book about Pulleys, 1 vol. Dahl, Michael. 2006. (Amazing Science: Simple Machines Ser.). (ENG.). 24p. (J). (gr. k-4). lib. bdg. 27.32 *(978-1-4048-1305-2(5)*, 1253208, Picture Window Bks.) Capstone.

—¡Rambum! ¡Pum! Un Libro Sobre Tormentas. Thomas, Rick & Picture Window Books Staff. Robledo, Sol, tr. 2007. (Ciencia Asombrosa: el Tiempo Ser.). (SPA.). 24p. (J). (gr. -1-3). 27.32 *(978-1-4048-3227-5(0)*, Picture Window Bks.) Capstone.

—Spots of Light: A Book about Stars, 1 vol. Meachen Rau, Dana. 2005. (Amazing Science: Exploring the Sky Ser.). (ENG.). 24p. (J). (gr. k-4). lib. bdg. 25.99 *(978-1-4048-1139-3(7)*, Picture Window Bks.) Capstone.

Shea, Denise, jt. illus. see Alderman, Derrick.

Shea, Gary. Trading Places. Roller, Ellen. 2008. (J). pap. 11.95 *(978-0-9792645-0-4(2))* Edgewood Publishing, LLC.

Shea, Louis. We're Going on a Santa Hunt. Mitchell, Laine. 2017. (J). *(978-1-338-25514-0(2))* Scholastic, Inc.

Shea, Shawn. In Search of the Perfect Pumpkin. Evangelista, Gloria. 2008. (ENG.). 32p. (J). (gr. k). pap. 7.95 *(978-1-55591-697-8(X))* Fulcrum Publishing.

Shea, Therese. Soccer Stars. Shea, Therese. 2007. (Sports Stars Ser.). (ENG.). 48p. (J). (gr. 4-7). pap. 6.95 *(978-0-531-18705-0(5))* Scholastic Library Publishing.

Shearham, Victoria. Playing the Bully: (Black & White Illustrations) Fine, Esther Sokolov & Head, Jim. 2017. (ENG.). (J). pap. *(978-0-9880665-8-8(0))* Join In Pr.

—Playing the Bully: (black & White Illustrations) Fine, Esther Sokolov & Head, Jim. 2018. (ENG.). 102p. (J). pap. *(978-0-9880665-9-5(9))* Join In Pr.

—Playing the Bully: (Full Color Illustrations) Fine, Esther Sokolov & Head, Jim. 2017. (ENG.). (J). pap. *(978-0-9880665-6-4(4))* Join In Pr.

—Playing the Bully: (full Color Illustrations) Fine, Esther Sokolov & Head, Jim. 2018. (ENG.). 102p. (J). pap. *(978-1-7753121-0-9(0))* Join In Pr.

Shearing, Leonie. It's Fall! Ringler, Matt. 2006. 28p. (J). pap. *(978-0-439-87146-4(8))* Scholastic, Inc.

Shearring, Maisie Paradise. Go & Play with That Little Boy. Beauvais, Clémentine. 2018. (ENG.). 28p. (J). (gr. k-3). 14.95 *(978-0-500-65170-4(1)*, 565170) Thames & Hudson.

Sheban, Chris. Brooklyn Bridge: A Novel. Hesse, Karen. 2011. (ENG.). 256p. (J). (gr. 6-8). pap. 10.99 *(978-0-312-67428-1(7)*, 900072843) Square Fish.

—Christmas at Stony Creek. Greene, Stephanie. 2007. 96p. (gr. -1-3). lib. bdg. 15.89 *(978-0-06-121487-5(6))* HarperCollins Pubs.

—Firstborn. Seidler, Tor. 2015. (J). Non-ISBN Publisher.

—Firstborn. Seidler, Tor. 2015. (ENG.). 240p. (J). (gr. 4-9). 16.99 *(978-1-4814-1017-5(2)*, Atheneum Bks. for Young Readers) Simon & Schuster Children's Publishing.

—I Met a Dinosaur. Wahl, Jan. 2015. (ENG.). 32p. (J). (gr. 1-3). 17.99 *(978-1-56846-233-2(6)*, Creative Editions) Creative Co., The.

—Job Wanted. Bateman, Teresa. 32p. (J). (gr. k-3). 2019. pap. 8.99 *(978-0-8234-4444-1(9))*; 2015. (ENG.). 16.95 *(978-0-8234-3391-9(9))* Holiday Hse., Inc.

—The Lonely Book. Bernheimer, Kate. 2012. 40p. (J). (gr. -1-3). 17.99 *(978-0-375-86226-7(9)*, Schwartz & Wade Bks.) Random Hse. Children's Bks.

—A Night on the Range. Frisch, Aaron. (ENG.). 32p. (J). 2013. (gr. -1-17). pap. 7.99 *(978-0-89812-829-1(3)*, Creative Paperbacks); 2010. (gr. 1-3). 19.99 *(978-1-56846-205-9(0)*, Creative Editions) Creative Co., The.

Sheban, Chris. The Perfect Pillow. Pinder, Eric. 2018. 32p. (J). (gr. -1-3). 16.99 ***(978-1-4847-4646-2(5))*** Little, Brown Bks. for Young Readers.

Sheban, Chris. Red Fox at McCloskey's Farm. Heinz, Brian J. 2006. 32p. (J). (gr. -1-3). 17.95 *(978-1-56846-195-3(X)*, Creative Editions) Creative Co., The.

—The Story of a Seagull & the Cat Who Taught Her to Fly. Sepulveda, Luis. Peden, Margaret Sayers, tr. 2003. (Apple Signature Ser.).Tr. of Historia de Una Gaviota y Del Gato Que le Enseano a Volar. (ENG.). 126p. (J). (gr. 3-6). reprint ed. 18.69 *(978-0-439-40187-6(9))* Scholastic, Inc.

—Three Squeezes. Pratt, Jason. 2020. (ENG.). 32p. (J). 17.99 *(978-1-250-31345-4(7)*, 900199377) Roaring Brook Pr.

—The Tiger Rising. Dicamillo, Kate. 2006. 144p. (J). (gr. 5). pap. 5.99 *(978-0-7636-2916-8(2))* Candlewick Pr.

—What a Cold Needs. Bottner, Barbara. 2019. 32p. (J). (gr. -1-3). 17.99 *(978-0-8234-4172-3(5)*, Neal Porter Bks) Holiday Hse., Inc.

—What to Do with a Box. Yolen, Jane. (J). 2018. (ENG.). 14p. (gr. -1-1). bds. 8.99 *(978-1-56846-320-9(0))*; 2016. 32p. (gr. 1-3). 18.99 *(978-1-56846-289-9(1))* Creative Co., The. (Creative Editions).

Shebs, Stan & Hsu, Timothy, photos by. Axolotl! Fun Facts about the World's Coolest Salamander - an Info-Picturebook for Kids. Mason, Susan. 2016. (ENG.). 36p. (J). pap. *(978-0-9955707-0-2(1))* Bubble Publishing.

Sheckels, Astrid. Black Cloud, No. 8. Hermes, Patricia. 2012. (Horse Diaries: 8). 176p. (J). (gr. 3-7). pap. 7.99 *(978-0-375-86881-8(X)*, Random Hse. Bks. for Young Readers) Random Hse. Children's Bks.

—The Fish House Door. Baldwin, Robert F. ed. 2010. (ENG.). 36p. (J). 16.95 *(978-1-934031-30-8(5)*, 66ed2d28-c290-42c4-81d6-2399bb213738) Islandport Pr., Inc.

—Horse Diaries #9: Tennessee Rose. Kendall, Jane. 2012. (Horse Diaries: 9). (ENG.). 160p. (J). (gr. 3-7). pap. 7.99 *(978-0-375-87006-4(7)*, Random Hse. Bks. for Young Readers) Random Hse. Children's Bks.

—Nic & Nellie, 1 vol. 2013. (ENG.). 32p. (J). (gr. 1-4). 17.95 *(978-1-934031-52-0(6)*, 239d4b1c-1c35-4416-91c8-58b097eb61ac) Islandport Pr., Inc.

—The Scallop Christmas. Freeberg, Jane. ed. 2011. (ENG.). 36p. (J). 17.95 *(978-1-934031-25-4(9)*, 37b34ba8-9e23-4460-8138-c206f267ae57) Islandport Pr., Inc.

Shed, Greg. I Loved You Before You Were Born. Bowen, Anne. 2004. (ENG.). 32p. (J). (gr. -1-3). reprint ed. pap. 7.99 *(978-0-06-443631-1(4))* HarperCollins Pubs.

Shed, Greg. I Loved You Before You Were Born Board Book. Bowen, Anne. 2003. (ENG.). 36p. (J). (gr. -1 — 1). bds. 7.99 ***(978-0-06-051587-4(2)**, HarperFestival)* HarperCollins Pubs.

Shed, Greg. I Loved You Before You Were Born Board Book: A Love Letter from Grandma. Bowen, Anne. 2017. (ENG.). 30p. (J). (gr. -1 — 1). bds. 7.99 *(978-0-06-269094-4(9)*, HarperFestival) HarperCollins Pubs.

—The Secret of Saying Thanks. Wood, Douglas. 2005. (ENG.). 32p. (J). (gr. -1-3). 19.99 *(978-0-689-85410-1(2)*, Simon & Schuster Bks. For Young Readers) Simon & Schuster Bks. For Young Readers.

—Squanto's Journey: The Story of the First Thanksgiving. Bruchac, Joseph. 2007. (ENG.). 32p. (J). (gr. -1-3). pap. 7.99 *(978-0-15-206044-2(8)*, 1198153, HMH Books For Young Readers) Houghton Mifflin Harcourt Publishing Co.

—The Turning of the Year. Martin, Bill, Jr. 2007. (ENG.). 28p. (J). (gr. -1-3). pap. 7.99 *(978-0-15-204555-5(4)*, 1193717) Houghton Mifflin Harcourt Publishing Co.

Shed, Greg & Pham, Leuyen. Aunt Mary's Rose. Wood, Douglas. 2010. (ENG.). 32p. (J). (gr. -1-3). 16.99 *(978-0-7636-1090-6(9))* Candlewick Pr.

Sheehan, Lisa, et al. Bedtime Stories: 8 Timeless Tales by Margaret Wise Brown. Brown, Margaret Wise. 2019. (ENG.). 192p. (J). (gr. -1-k). 17.99 *(978-1-68412-735-1(1)*, Silver Dolphin Bks.) Printers Row Publishing Group.

Sheehan, Lisa. Nursery Rhyme Search & Find. Brown, Margaret Wise. 2019. (Margaret Wise Brown Classics Ser.). (ENG.). 32p. (J). (gr. -1-k). 12.99 *(978-1-68412-746-7(7)*, Silver Dolphin Bks.) Printers Row Publishing Group.

Sheehan, Monica. Be Happy! A Little Book for a Happy You. Sheehan, Monica. 2010. (ENG.). 38p. (J). (gr. -1-k). bds. 7.99 *(978-1-4424-0676-6(3)*, Little Simon) Little Simon.

—Be Happy! A Little Book for a Happy You & a Better World. Sheehan, Monica. 2014. (ENG.). 68p. (J). (gr. -1-3). 14.99 *(978-1-4424-9857-0(9)*, Little Simon) Little Simon.

—Love Is You & Me. Sheehan, Monica. (ENG.). (J). (gr. -1-3). 2013. 48p. 14.99 *(978-1-4424-3607-7(7))*; 2010. 38p. bds. 8.99 *(978-1-4424-0765-7(4))* Little Simon. (Little Simon).

Sheehy, Shawn. Welcome to the Neighborwood. Sheehy, Shawn. 2015. (ENG.). 18p. (J). (gr. -1-3). 29.99 *(978-0-7636-6594-4(0))* Candlewick Pr.

Sheeley, Mary. Swamp Tales. Savage, S. C. 2018. (ENG.). 252p. (J). pap. 9.75 *(978-1-7916-1781-3(6))* Independently Published.

Sheely, Tiffany. Captain William Clark's Great Montana Adventure. 2003. 32p. (J). mass mkt. 3.95 *(978-0-9711667-0-7(6))* Outlook Publishing, Inc.

Sheesley, Brian. Fizzopolis #2: Floozombies! Carman, Patrick. 2016. (Fizzopolis Ser.: 2). (ENG.). 176p. (J). (gr. 3-7). 12.99 *(978-0-06-239392-0(8)*, Tegen, Katherine Bks) HarperCollins Pubs.

—Fizzopolis #3: Snoodles! Carman, Patrick. 2017. (Fizzopolis Ser.: 3). (ENG.). 160p. (J). (gr. 3-7). 12.99 *(978-0-06-239394-4(4)*, Tegen, Katherine Bks) HarperCollins Pubs.

—Fizzopolis: the Trouble with Fuzzwonker Fizz. Carman, Patrick. 2016. (Fizzopolis Ser.: 1). (ENG.). 160p. (J). (gr. 3-7). 12.99 *(978-0-06-239390-6(1))* HarperCollins Pubs.

Sheets, Leslie. Brave Just Like Me. Ruff, Kimberly & Venturi-Pickett, Stacy. 2011. 32p. pap. 9.99 *(978-1-60888-106-2(7))* Nimble Bks. LLC.

Shefelman, Janice J. & Shefelman, Tom. Son of Spirit Horse. 2004. 74p. (J). *(978-1-57168-833-0(1)*, Eakin Pr.) Eakin Pr.

Shefelman, Janice Jordan & Shefelman, Tom. I, Vivaldi. Shefelman, Janice Jordan & Shefelman, Tom. Shefelman, Janice. 2008. (ENG.). 32p. (J). (gr. 2-6). 18.00 *(978-0-8028-5318-9(8))* Eerdmans, William B. Publishing Co.

Shefelman, Tom, jt. illus. see Shefelman, Janice Jordan.

Shefelman, Tom, jt. illus. see Shefelman, Janice J.

Sheffield, Heidi Woodward. Are Your Stars Like My Stars? Helakoski, Leslie. 2020. 32p. (J). (gr. -1-2). 16.95 *(978-1-4549-3013-6(6))* Sterling Publishing Co., Inc.

Sheffield, Heidi Woodward. Brick by Brick. Sheffield, Heidi Woodward. 2020. 32p. (J). (gr. -1-2). 17.99 *(978-0-525-51730-6(8)*, Nancy Paulsen Books) Penguin Young Readers Group.

Shefrin, Sima Elizabeth. Jewish Fairy Tale Feasts: A Literary Cookbook. Yolen, Jane & Stemple, Heidi E. Y. 2013. (ENG.). 160p. (J). 25.00 *(978-1-56656-909-5(5)*, Crocodile Bks.) Interlink Publishing Group, Inc.

—Once upon a Bathtime, 1 vol. Goss, Shelia M. & Hughes, Vi. 2011. (ENG.). 32p. (J). (gr. -1-k). 17.95 *(978-1-896580-54-8(8))* Tradewind Bks. CAN. Dist: Orca Bk. Pubs. USA.

Shehan, Terece. Mad about Miller. Thompson, Shannon Raines. Stone, Kathrine Thompson, ed. 2006. 24p. (YA). 12.95 *(978-1-59971-853-8(7))* Aardvark Global Publishing.

—Nuts about Neal. Thompson, Shannon Raines. Stone, Kathrine Thompson, ed. 2006. 24p. (YA). 12.95 *(978-1-59971-852-1(9))* Aardvark Global Publishing.

Shekailo, Pamela. Meet Angel & All Her Friends. Edwards-Wright, Tracy. 2012. 48p. pap. 24.95 *(978-1-4512-8280-1(X))* America Star Bks.

Sheldon, David. Guess Who? Namm, Diane. 2004. (My First Reader Ser.). (ENG.). 32p. (J). (gr. k-1). pap. 3.95 *(978-0-516-25503-3(7)*, Children's Pr.) Scholastic Library Publishing.

—The Little Golden Book of Jokes & Riddles. Brown, Peggy. 2013. (Little Golden Book Ser.). 24p. (J). (-k). 4.99 *(978-0-307-97916-2(4)*, Golden Bks.) Random Hse. Children's Bks.

—Matzo Frogs. Rosenthal, Sally. 2014. (ENG.). 32p. (J). 17.95 *(978-1-58838-302-0(4)*, NewSouth Bks.) NewSouth, Inc.

—Way down below Deep, 1 vol. Day, Nancy. 2014. (ENG.). 32p. (J). (gr. k-3). 16.99 *(978-1-4556-1945-0(0)*, Pelican Publishing) Arcadia Publishing.

Sheldon, Ian. Bugs of Ontario, 1 vol. Acorn, John Harrison. rev. ed. 2003. (ENG.). 160p. (gr. 4). pap. 16.95 *(978-1-55105-287-8(3)*, 95a8a06b-0982-42a0-85ec-616b9b8eb7e7) Lone Pine Publishing USA.

Sheldon, Ian. Seashore of Southern California, 1 vol. Sheldon, Ian. rev. ed. 2007. (ENG.). 216p. per. 14.95 *(978-1-55105-232-8(6)*, 8ee6851b-9c79-4a34-ab4b-6afbd604b4a8) Lone Pine Publishing USA.

Sheldon, Kristen. Required Reading for All Teenagers: (or at Least One Who Is Very Important to Me!) Pagels, Douglas. rev. ed. 2018. (ENG.). 96p. (YA). pap. 14.95 *(978-1-68088-252-0(X))* Blue Mountain Arts Inc.

Sheldon, Kristin. The Martha Is Mine: An Almost True Story. Hicks, Greg & Foster, Rick. 2007. (ENG.). 56p. (J). 16.95 *(978-0-9790709-0-7(2)*, 9780979070907) Foster, Hicks & Assocs.

Sheldon, Tamia. Toby the Flying Cat. Belshaw, Yvonne. 2013. (ENG.). 28p. (J). (gr. -1-2). pap. 9.99 *(978-1-62395-495-6(9))* Xist Publishing.

—The Zebra Said Shhh. Nelson, M. R. 2013. (ENG.). 32p. (J). (gr. -1-k). pap. 9.99 *(978-1-62395-440-6(1))* Xist Publishing.

Sheldon, Tamia. The Hungry Shark / el Tiburón Hambriento. Sheldon, Tamia. 2018. (Xist Kids Bilingual Spanish English Ser.). (ENG & SPA.). 26p. (J). (gr. -1-3). pap. 9.99 *(978-1-5324-0683-6(5))* Xist Publishing.

—Kids Cook: Global Recipes. Sheldon, Tamia. 2020. (ENG.). 32p. (J). (gr. 1-5). pap. 12.99 *(978-1-5324-1346-9(7))* Xist Publishing.

—The (Not) Sleepy Shark / el Tiburón Que (No) Tenía Sueño. Sheldon, Tamia. 2018. (Xist Kids Bilingual Spanish English Ser.). (ENG & SPA.). 40p. (J). (gr. -1-3). pap. 9.99 *(978-1-5324-0681-2(9))* Xist Publishing.

—El Tiburón Hambriento. Sheldon, Tamia. 2018. (Xist Kids Spanish Bks.). (SPA.). 24p. (J). (gr. -1-3). pap. 9.99 *(978-1-5324-0703-1(3))* Xist Publishing.

—El Tiburón Que (No) Tenía Sueño. Sheldon, Tamia. 2018. (Xist Kids Spanish Bks.). (SPA.). 40p. (J). (gr. -1-3). pap. 9.99 *(978-1-5324-0705-5(X))* Xist Publishing.

—What Is a Family? Sheldon, Tamia. 2013. 36p. pap. 9.99 *(978-1-62395-527-4(0))* Xist Publishing.

Sheldrake, Missy. Nothing's Too Hard for Me. Peine, Jan. 2013. 28p. (J). 7.00 *(978-0-9754575-4-2(3))* Ashway Pr.

Shelfer, Michael, jt. illus. see Jaro, Jose.

Shell-Aurora, Callie, photos by. TIME: President Obama: The Path to the White House. Ignatius, Adi et al, eds. 2009. 95p. (J). (gr. 5-13). 30.60 *(978-0-7613-5034-7(9))* Time Inc. Bks.

Shellabarger, Joan, jt. illus. see Shellabarger, Ruthie.

Shellabarger, Ruthie & Shellabarger, Joan. The Mysterious Neighbors. Parcells, Cynthia. 2019. (ENG.). 48p. (J). pap. 10.99 ***(978-1-7283-1980-3(3))*** AuthorHouse.

Shelley, Jeff. I Can Do It All. Pearson, Mary E. 2011. (Rookie Ready to Learn - I Can! Ser.). 32p. (J). (gr. -1-k). lib. bdg. 23.00 *(978-0-531-26429-4(7)*, Children's Pr.) Scholastic Library Publishing.

Shelley, John. Bella Baxter & the Lighthouse Mystery. Mason, Jane B. & Stephens, Sarah Hines. 2006. (Bella Baxter Ser.: 3). (ENG.). 80p. (J). (gr. 1-4). pap. 6.99 *(978-0-689-86282-3(2)*, Simon & Schuster/Paula Wiseman Bks.) Simon & Schuster/Paula Wiseman Bks.

—Crinkle, Crackle, Crack: It's Spring! Bauer, Marion Dane. 2015. (ENG.). 32p. (J). (gr. -1-3). 16.95 *(978-0-8234-2952-3(0))* Holiday Hse., Inc.

—Crinkle, Crackle, CRACK, It's Spring! Bauer, Marion Dane. 2019. 32p. (J). (gr. -1-3). pap. 7.99 *(978-0-8234-4177-8(6))* Holiday Hse., Inc.

—Family Reminders. Danneberg, Julie. 2013. 112p. (J). (gr. 3-7). pap. 6.95 *(978-1-58089-321-3(X))* Charlesbridge Publishing, Inc.

—Halloween Forest. Bauer, Marion Dane. 2018. 32p. (J). (gr. -1-3). pap. 7.99 *(978-0-8234-4038-2(9))* Holiday Hse., Inc.

—Magic for Sale. Clickard, Carrie. 2017. (ENG.). 32p. (J). (gr. -1-3). 16.95 *(978-0-8234-3559-3(8))* Holiday Hse., Inc.

—Mvp* Magellan Voyage Project. Evans, Douglas. (ENG.). 232p. (J). (gr. 4-7). 2008. pap. 10.95 *(978-1-59078-625-3(4))*; 2004. 16.95 *(978-1-932425-13-0(6))* Boyds Mills Pr. (Front Street).

—Stone Giant: Michelangelo's David & How He Came to Be. Sutcliffe, Jane. 2014. (J). 32p. pap. 16.95 *(978-1-60734-614-2(1))*; 32p. (gr. 1-4). lib. bdg. 16.95 *(978-1-58089-295-7(7))*; pap. *(978-1-58089-296-4(5))* Charlesbridge Publishing, Inc.

—Will's Words: How William Shakespeare Changed the Way You Talk. Sutcliffe, Jane. 2018. 40p. (J). (gr. 2-5). pap. 8.99 *(978-1-58089-639-9(1))* Charlesbridge Publishing, Inc.

Shellie, Shamari G. Be a Copycat of Jesus. Czerwinski, Lynn. 2018. (ENG.). 22p. (J). pap. 11.95 *(978-1-64349-246-9(2))* Christian Faith Publishing.

Shelly, Jeff. Alfred's Kid's Drum Course. Black, Dave & Houghton, Steve. 2004. (Kid's Drum Course Ser.: Bk 1). (ENG.). 48p. pap. 19.99 *(978-0-7390-3609-9(2)*, 23182) Alfred Publishing Co., Inc.

Shelly, Jeff, Sr. Dillan Mcmillan, Please Eat Your Peas. Schneider, David. 2016. (ENG.). 36p. (J). 16.95 *(978-0-9744446-4-2(2))* All About Kids Publishing.

Shelly, Jeff. Goodnight, Little Bug. Perez, Jessica. 2005. (J). bds. 14.99 *(978-0-9767325-2-5(1))* Toy Quest.

—How to Draw Dinosaurs: Step-By-step Instructions for 20 Prehistoric Creatures. 2018. (Learn to Draw Ser.). (ENG.). 32p. (J). (gr. 1-3). pap. 5.99 *(978-1-63322-758-3(8)*, Walter Foster Jr) Quarto Publishing Group USA.

—I Can Do It All. Pearson, Mary E. 2011. (Rookie Ready to Learn: I Can! Ser.). (ENG.). 40p. (J). (gr. -1-k). pap. 5.95 *(978-0-531-26654-0(0)*, Children's Pr.) Scholastic Library Publishing.

—Learn to Draw Cars & Trucks. 2012. (J). *(978-1-936309-49-8(1))* Quarto Publishing Group USA.

—Learn to Draw Dinosaurs. 2012. (J). *(978-1-936309-48-1(3))* Quarto Publishing Group USA.

—A Plump & Perky Turkey, 0 vols. Bateman, Teresa. 2013. (ENG.). 32p. (J). (gr. k-4). pap. 9.99 *(978-0-7614-5188-4(9)*, 9780761451884, Two Lions) Amazon Publishing.

Shelly, Jeff. Puedo Hacer de Todo. Shelly, Jeff. Pearson, Mary E. 2011. (Rookie Ready to Learn Español Ser.).Tr. of I Can Do It All. (SPA.). 40p. (J). pap. 5.95 *(978-0-531-26787-5(3))*; lib. bdg. 23.00 *(978-0-531-26119-4(0))* Scholastic Library Publishing. (Children's Pr.).

Shelly, Jeff, jt. illus. see Fisher, Diana.

Shelnutt, Charlene. Surprise, Little Mouse. Doxey, Carol E. 2019. (ENG.). 24p. (J). pap. 12.95 ***(978-1-942766-65-0(3))*** Vabella Publishing.

sheltrown, karen. The Adventures of AJ & Hunter: Lost in the Back Yard. Jones, Rachel. 2011. (ENG.). 24p. pap. 6.99 *(978-1-4681-0130-0(7))* CreateSpace Independent Publishing Platform.

Shems, Ed. Ancient Science: 40 Time-Traveling, World-Exploring, History-Making Activities for Kids. Wiese, Jim. 2003. (ENG.). 128p. (J). (gr. 3-7). pap. 16.00 *(978-0-471-21595-0(3)*, Wiley) Wiley, John & Sons, Inc.

—Baseball Buzz. Joven, C. C. 2017. (Sports Illustrated Kids Starting Line Readers Ser.). (ENG.). 32p. (J). (gr. -1-1). pap. 3.95 *(978-1-4965-4259-5(2))*; lib. bdg. 22.65 *(978-1-4965-4252-6(5))* Capstone. (Stone Arch Bks.).

—Gymnastics Jump. Joven, C. C. 2017. (Sports Illustrated Kids Starting Line Readers Ser.). (ENG.). 32p. (J). (gr. -1-1). lib. bdg. 22.65 *(978-1-4965-4250-2(9)*, Stone Arch Bks.) Capstone.

Shendrik, Svetlana. In the Park. Clever Publishing. 2019. (Look & Find, Clever Baby Ser.). (ENG.). 22p. (J). (gr. -1 — 1). bds. 7.99 *(978-1-948418-15-7(0))* Clever Media Group.

—123s: Memory Flash Cards. Clever Publishing. 2018. (Clever Big Box Of Ser.). (ENG.). 20p. (J). (gr. -1 — 1). 14.99 *(978-1-948418-41-6(X))* Clever Media Group.

Shene, Prescott. Mandy - The Alpha Dog: The Chronicles of the K-9 Boys & Girls on Locus Street. Shene, Paula. 2009. 36p. pap. 24.95 *(978-1-60836-710-8(X))* America Star Bks.

Sheng, Ann. Read, Wonder, Listen: Stories from the Bible for Young Readers. Alary, Laura. 2018. (ENG.). 244p. (YA). 24.95 *(978-1-77343-041-6(6))* Wood Lake Publishing, Inc. CAN. Dist: Westminster John Knox Pr.

Shenoi, Krishna Bala. Get Off That Camel! Benjamin, A. H. 2019. (ENG.). 40p. (J). 13.95 *(978-81-939033-1-5(5))* Karadi Tales Co. Pvt, Ltd. IND. Dist: Consortium Bk. Sales & Distribution.

—Jwala Kumar & the Gift of Fire: Adventures in Champakbagh. Shekhar, Hansda Sowvendra. 2018. (ENG.). 128p. (J). (gr. 4-6). pap. *(978-93-88070-43-0(7))* Speaking Tiger Publishing.

Shenton, Edward. Man of the Family. Moody, Ralph. 2019. 274p. (J). *(978-1-948959-07-0(0))* Purple Hse. Pr.

Shepard, Ernest H. Dream Days. Grahame, Kenneth. 2004. reprint ed. pap. 21.95 *(978-1-4179-0979-7(X))* Kessinger Publishing, LLC.

—An Gwyns I'n Helyk. Grahame, Kenneth & Williams, Nicholas. 2013. (COR.). 202p. pap. *(978-1-78201-029-6(7))* Evertype.

—The House at Pooh Corner. Milne, A. A. deluxe ed. 2009. (Winnie-The-Pooh Ser.). (ENG.). 192p. (J). (gr. 3-7). 19.99 *(978-0-525-47856-0(6)*, Dutton Books for Young Readers) Penguin Young Readers Group.

—The House at Pooh Corner, Set. Milne, A. A. (J). incl. audio *(978-1-57375-653-2(9)*, 71524) Audioscope.

—The House at Pooh Corner: Classic Gift Edition. Milne, A. A. 2018. (Winnie-The-Pooh Ser.). (ENG.). 192p. (J). (gr. 3-7). 16.00 *(978-0-525-55554-4(4)*, Dutton Books for Young Readers) Penguin Young Readers Group.

—In Which a House Is Built at Pooh Corner for Eeyore. Milne, A. A. unabr. ed. (Classic Pooh Treasury Ser.). (J). incl. audio *(978-1-57375-527-6(3)*, 71394) Audioscope.
—In Which Christopher Robin Gives Pooh a Party. Milne, A. A. unabr. ed. (Winnie-the-Pooh Ser.). (J). incl. audio *(978-1-57375-046-2(8)*, 70554) Audioscope.
—In Which Everyone Has a Birthday & Gets Two Presents. Milne, A. A. unabr. ed. (Winnie-the-Pooh Ser.). (J). incl. audio *(978-1-57375-015-8(8)*, 70134) Audioscope.
—In Which It Is Shown That Tiggers Don't Climb Trees. Milne, A. A. unabr. ed. (Classic Pooh Treasury Ser.). (J). incl. audio *(978-1-57375-529-0(X)*, 71414) Audioscope.
—In Which Piglet Meets a Heffalump. Milne, A. A. unabr. ed. (Winnie-the-Pooh Ser.). (J). incl. audio *(978-1-57375-014-1(X)*, 70124) Audioscope.
—In Which Pooh Goes Visiting & Gets into a Tight Place & in Which Pooh & Piglet Go Hunting & Nearly Catch a Woozle. Milne, A. A. unabr. ed. (Winnie-the-Pooh Ser.). (J). incl. audio *(978-1-57375-001-1(8)*, 70014) Audioscope.
—In Which Tigger Is Unbounced. Milne, A. A. unabr. ed. (Classic Pooh Treasury Ser.). (J). incl. audio *(978-1-57375-528-3(1)*, 71404) Audioscope.
—In Which We Are Introduced to Winnie the Pooh & Some Bees, & the Stories Begin. Milne, A. A. unabr. ed. (Winnie-the-Pooh Ser.). (J). incl. audio *(978-1-57375-000-4(X)*, 70004) Audioscope.
—Now We Are Six. Milne, A. A. deluxe ed. 2008. (Winnie-The-Pooh Ser.). (ENG.). 112p. (J). (gr. 3-7). 19.99 *(978-0-525-47929-1(5)*, Dutton Books for Young Readers) Penguin Young Readers Group.
Shepard, Ernest H. Now We Are Six: Classic Gift Edition. Milne, A. A. 2020. (Winnie-The-Pooh Ser.). (ENG.). 112p. (J). (gr. 3-7). 16.00 ***(978-0-593-11233-5(4)***, Dutton Books for Young Readers) Penguin Young Readers Group.
Shepard, Ernest H. Positively Pooh: Timeless Wisdom from Pooh. Milne, A. A. 2008. (Winnie-The-Pooh Ser.). (ENG.). 120p. (J). (gr. 3-7). 23.00 *(978-0-525-47931-4(7)*, Dutton Books for Young Readers) Penguin Young Readers Group.
—The Reluctant Dragon. Grahame, Kenneth. 75th ed. 2013. (ENG.). 64p. (J). (gr. 2-5). 16.95 *(978-0-8234-2820-5(6))* Holiday Hse., Inc.
—A Smackerel of Pooh: Ten Favorite Stories & Poems. Milne, A. A. 2006. 79p. (J). (gr. k-4). 16.00 *(978-1-4223-5283-0(8))* DIANE Publishing Co.
—Tigger Tales. Milne, A. A. 2006. 36p. (J). (gr. k-4). reprint ed. 15.00 *(978-1-4223-5453-7(9))* DIANE Publishing Co.
—When We Were Very Young. Milne, A. A. deluxe ed. 2009. (Winnie-The-Pooh Ser.). (ENG.). 112p. (J). (gr. 3-7). 19.99 *(978-0-525-47930-7(9)*, Dutton Books for Young Readers) Penguin Young Readers Group.
Shepard, Ernest H. When We Were Very Young: Classic Gift Edition. Milne, A. A. 2020. (Winnie-The-Pooh Ser.). (ENG.). 112p. (J). (gr. 3-7). 16.00 ***(978-0-593-11232-8(6)***, Dutton Books for Young Readers) Penguin Young Readers Group.
Shepard, Ernest H. The Wind in the Willows. Grahame, Kenneth. 2007. 259p. (J). (gr. 5-6). reprint ed. lib. bdg. 22.95 *(978-0-88411-877-0(0))* Amereon Ltd.
—Winnie Puh. Milne, A. A. Meddemmen, John, tr.Tr. of Winnie the Pooh. (ITA.). 164p. pap. 29.95 *(978-88-7782-278-9(3))* Salani ITA. Dist: Distribooks, Inc.
—Winnie the Pooh: Deluxe Edition. Milne, A. A. 80th anniv. deluxe ed. 2009. (Winnie-The-Pooh Ser.). (ENG.). 176p. (J). (gr. 3-7). 19.99 *(978-0-525-47768-6(3)*, Dutton Books for Young Readers) Penguin Young Readers Group.
—Winnie the Pooh & When We Were Young. Milne, A. A. 32p. (J). Boxed set. pap. incl. audio compact disk *(978-1-57375-583-2(4)*, 71512); Set. pap. incl. audio *(978-1-57375-652-5(0)*, 71514) Audioscope.
—Winnie-The-Pooh: Classic Gift Edition. Milne, A. A. 2017. (Winnie-The-Pooh Ser.). (ENG.). 176p. (J). (gr. 3-7). 16.00 *(978-0-525-55531-5(5)*, Dutton Books for Young Readers) Penguin Young Readers Group.
—The Winnie-the-Pooh Cookbook. Ellison, Virginia H. 2010. (Winnie-The-Pooh Ser.). 112p. (J). (gr. 3-7). 19.99 *(978-0-525-42359-1(1)*, Dutton Books for Young Readers) Penguin Young Readers Group.
—Winnie-The-Pooh (Puffin Modern Classics) Milne, A. A. 2005. (Winnie-The-Pooh Ser.). (ENG.). 176p. (J). (gr. 3-7). 7.99 *(978-0-14-240467-6(5)*, Puffin Books) Penguin Young Readers Group.
—Winnie the Pooh's 1,2,3. Milne, A. A. 2009. (Winnie-The-Pooh Ser.). 18p. (J). (gr. -1 — 1). bds. 6.99 *(978-0-525-42084-2(3)*, Dutton Books for Young Readers) Penguin Young Readers Group.
—Winnie-The-Pooh's ABC Book. Milne, A. A. 2004. (Winnie-The-Pooh Ser.). (ENG.). 26p. (J). (gr. -1-k). bds. 8.99 *(978-0-525-47280-3(0)*, Dutton Books for Young Readers) Penguin Young Readers Group.
—Winnie the Pooh's Colors. Milne, A. A. 2009. (Winnie-The-Pooh Ser.). (ENG.). 20p. (J). (gr. -1 — 1). bds. 7.99 *(978-0-525-42083-5(5)*, Dutton Books for Young Readers) Penguin Young Readers Group.
—Winnie the Pooh's Giant Lift The-Flap. Milne, A. A. 2009. (Winnie-The-Pooh Ser.). (ENG.). 12p. (J). (gr. -1-k). bds. 9.99 *(978-0-525-42088-0(6)*, Dutton Books for Young Readers) Penguin Young Readers Group.
—The World of Pooh: The Complete Winnie-the-Pooh & the House at Pooh Corner. Milne, A. A. 2010. (Winnie-The-Pooh Ser.). (ENG.). 384p. (J). (gr. 3-7). 26.99 *(978-0-525-44447-3(5)*, Dutton Books for Young Readers) Penguin Young Readers Group.
Shepard, Mary. Mary Poppins. Travers, P. L. 2006. (Mary Poppins Ser.: No. 1). (ENG.). 224p. (J). (gr. 5-7). 16.99 *(978-0-15-205810-4(9)*, 1197456) Houghton Mifflin Harcourt Publishing Co.
—Mary Poppins: 80th Anniversary Collection. Travers, P. L. 2014. (ENG.). 1024p. (J). (gr. 5-7). 24.99 *(978-0-544-34047-3(7)*, 1584771, HMH Books For Young Readers) Houghton Mifflin Harcourt Publishing Co.
—Mary Poppins & Mary Poppins Comes Back. Travers, P. L. 2007. (Mary Poppins Ser.: No 1 and 2). (ENG.). 368p. (J). (gr. 5-7). 19.99 *(978-0-15-205922-4(9)*, 1197779) Houghton Mifflin Harcourt Publishing Co.
—Mary Poppins Comes Back. Travers, P. L. 2006. (Mary Poppins Ser.: No. 2). (ENG.). 336p. (J). (gr. 5-7). 16.99 *(978-0-15-205816-6(8)*, 1197476) Houghton Mifflin Harcourt Publishing Co.
—Mary Poppins from A to Z. Travers, P. L. 2006. (Mary Poppins Ser.). (ENG.). 64p. (J). (gr. 5-7). 16.99 *(978-0-15-205834-0(6)*, 1197528) Houghton Mifflin Harcourt Publishing Co.
—Mary Poppins in the Kitchen: A Cookery Book with a Story. Travers, P. L. 2006. (Mary Poppins Ser.: No. 6). (ENG.). 88p. (J). (gr. 5-7). 16.99 *(978-0-15-206080-0(4)*, 1198263) Houghton Mifflin Harcourt Publishing Co.
—Mary Poppins in the Park. Travers, P. L. (Mary Poppins Ser.). (ENG.). (J). (gr. 5-7). 2015. 272p. pap. 7.99 *(978-0-544-51384-6(3)*, 1605889, HMH Books For Young Readers); 2006. 304p. 16.99 *(978-0-15-205828-9(1)*, 1197509) Houghton Mifflin Harcourt Publishing Co.
Shepard, Mary & Sims, Agnes. Mary Poppins Opens the Door. Travers, P. L. 2015. (Mary Poppins Ser.). (ENG.). 256p. (J). (gr. 5-7). pap. 7.99 *(978-0-544-43958-0(9)*, 1596852, HMH Books For Young Readers) Houghton Mifflin Harcourt Publishing Co.
Shepard, Mary, jt. illus. see Sims, Agnes.
Shephard, Dave. All Dolled Up! Fields, Jan. 2017. (Ghost Detectors Ser.: 21). (ENG.). 80p. (J). (gr. 2-5). lib. bdg. 29.93 *(978-1-5321-3153-0(4)*, 27050, Calico Chapter Bks.) ABDO Publishing Co.
—As It Lies! Fields, Jan. 2017. (Ghost Detectors Ser.: 22). (ENG.). 80p. (J). (gr. 2-5). lib. bdg. 29.93 *(978-1-5321-3154-7(2)*, 27051, Calico Chapter Bks.) ABDO Publishing Co.
—Heroes of Science: Who Changed the World. Biskup, Agnieska. 2019. (Graphic Greats Ser.). (ENG.). 128p. (J). (gr. 4-7). pap. 12.99 *(978-1-4380-1200-1(4)*, B.E.S. Publishing) Peterson's.
—Lions, Tiger & Bears, Oh My!, Bk. 24. Fields, Jan. 2017. (Ghost Detectors Ser.: 24). (ENG.). 80p. (J). (gr. 2-5). lib. bdg. 29.93 *(978-1-5321-3156-1(9)*, 27053, Calico Chapter Bks.) ABDO Publishing Co.
—One, Two, Three, Kick! Fields, Jan. 2017. (Ghost Detectors Ser.: 23). (ENG.). 80p. (J). (gr. 2-5). lib. bdg. 29.93 *(978-1-5321-3155-4(0)*, 27052, Calico Chapter Bks.) ABDO Publishing Co.
Shephard, David. Jackie Robinson. Hoena, B. A. 2020. (Athletes Who Made a Difference Ser.). 32p. (J). (gr. 3-6). 27.99 ***(978-1-5415-7816-6(3)***, Graphic Universe™) Lerner Publishing Group.
—Jackie Robinson: Athletes Who Made a Difference. Hoena, Blake. 2020. (Athletes Who Made a Difference Ser.). (ENG.). 32p. (J). (gr. 3-6). pap. 8.99 ***(978-1-7284-0294-9(8)***, Graphic Universe™) Lerner Publishing Group.
—Jesse Owens. Hoena, B. A. 2020. (Athletes Who Made a Difference Ser.). 32p. (J). (gr. 3-6). 27.99 ***(978-1-5415-7815-9(5)***, Graphic Universe™) Lerner Publishing Group.
—Jesse Owens: Athletes Who Made a Difference. Hoena, Blake. 2020. (Athletes Who Made a Difference Ser.). (ENG.). 32p. (J). (gr. 3-6). pap. 8.99 ***(978-1-7284-0295-6(6)***, Graphic Universe™) Lerner Publishing Group.
Shephard, David & Zamazing, Cherie. Let's Explore... Mountain, 1 vol. Webb, Christina & Lonely Planet Kids. 2017. (Let's Explore Ser.). (ENG.). 48p. (J). (gr. 1-3). pap. 9.99 *(978-1-78657-315-5(6)*, 5401) Lonely Planet Global Ltd. IRL. Dist: Hachette Bk. Group.
Shepherd, J. A. Old Hendrik's Tales - 13 South African Folk Tales. 2013. 198p. pap. *(978-1-909302-15-0(5))* Abela Publishing.
Shepherd, Keith D. Walking Home to Rosie Lee. LaFaye, A. 2011. (ENG.). 32p. (J). (gr. 1-6). 16.95 *(978-1-933693-97-2(5))* Cinco Puntos Pr.
Shepherd, Rosalie M. Women Who Fly, 1 vol. Homan, Lynn M. & Reilly, Thomas. 2004. (ENG.). 104p. (J). (gr. 3-7). 14.95 *(978-1-58980-160-8(1)*, Pelican Publishing) Arcadia Publishing.
Shepherd, Rosalie M. Girls Fly!, 1 vol. Shepherd, Rosalie M., tr. Homan, Lynn M. & Reilly, Thomas. 2003. (ENG.). 32p. (J). (gr. k-3). 16.99 *(978-1-58980-154-7(7)*, Pelican Publishing) Arcadia Publishing.
Shepherd, Rosalie M., jt. illus. see Lauve, Celia.
Sheppard, Kate. Keeper's Ball. Childs, Rob. 2005. (Corgi Pups Ser.). (ENG.). 64p. (J). pap. 7.50 *(978-0-552-55030-7(2))* Transworld Publishers Ltd. GBR. Dist: Independent Pubs. Group.
Sheppard, Vivien. Sven Och P�sen Med Silver. Wills, Michael E. Wills, Barbro K. E., tr. 2019. (SWE.). 36p. (J). pap. ***(978-1-78132-926-9(5))*** SilverWood Bks.
Shepperson, Claude A. The Diary of a Goose Girl. Wiggin, Kate Douglas. 2004. reprint ed. pap. 20.95 *(978-1-4179-1501-9(3))* Kessinger Publishing, LLC.
—The Diary of a Goose Girl: Illustrated. Smith Wiggin, Kate Douglas. 2018. (ENG.). 118p. (J). pap. 7.99 *(978-1-7903-3230-4(3))* Independently Published.
Shepperson, Claude Allin, jt. illus. see Lanos, Henri.
Shepperson, Rob. Blue Daisy. Frost, Helen. 2020. 96p. (J). (gr. 2-5). 15.99 *(978-0-8234-4414-4(7)*, Margaret Ferguson Books) Holiday Hse., Inc.
—Can I Just Take a Nap? Rauss, Ron. 2012. (ENG.). 32p. (J). (gr. -1-1). 15.99 *(978-1-4424-3497-4(X)*, Simon & Schuster/Paula Wiseman Bks.) Simon & Schuster/Paula Wiseman Bks.
—Don't Know Much about Abraham Lincoln, Vol. 4. Davis, Kenneth C. 2003. (Don't Know Much About Ser.). 144p. (J). (gr. 3-7). pap. 4.99 *(978-0-06-442127-0(9))* HarperCollins Pubs.
—Don't Know Much about Abraham Lincoln Abraham Lincoln, Vol. 4. Davis, Kenneth C. 2004. (Don't Know Much About Ser.). 144p. (J). (gr. 2-5). 15.89 *(978-0-06-028820-4(5))* HarperCollins Pubs.
—Don't Know Much about George Washington. Davis, Kenneth C. 2003. (Don't Know Much About Ser.). 128p. (J). (gr. 3). pap. 4.99 *(978-0-06-442124-9(4))* HarperCollins Pubs.
—Don't Know Much about Thomas Jefferson. Davis, Kenneth C. 2005. (Don't Know Much About Ser.). 128p. (J). (gr. 2-5). pap. 4.99 *(978-0-06-442128-7(7))* HarperCollins Pubs.
—Kelsey Green, Reading Queen. Mills, Claudia. 2014. (Franklin School Friends Ser.: 1). (ENG.). 144p. (J). (gr. 2-5). pap. 5.99 *(978-1-250-03405-2(1)*, 900120575) Square Fish.
—Lilly & the Pirates. Root, Phyllis. 2013. (ENG.). 180p. (J). (gr. 3-7). pap. 8.95 *(978-1-62091-027-6(6))* Boyds Mills Pr.
—The Memory Bank. Coman, Carolyn. 2010. (J). 263p. pap. *(978-0-545-21067-6(4))*; 288p. (gr. 3-7). 16.99 *(978-0-545-21066-9(6))* Scholastic, Inc. (Levine, Arthur A. Bks.).
—Sneaking Suspicions. Coman, Carolyn. 2007. (ENG.). 204p. (J). (gr. -1-2). 16.95 *(978-1-59078-491-4(X))* Boyds Mills Pr.
—Tummies on the Run. White, Andrea & Mimi, Vance. 2012. 32p. pap. 11.95 *(978-1-60898-134-2(7))* namelos llc.
Sheridan, Lucie. Find Me: Play for Little Hands. 2019. (Play for Little Hands Ser.). (ENG.). 14p. (J). (-k). bds. 10.99 *(978-1-910552-81-0(X))* O'Mara, Michael Bks., Ltd. GBR. Dist: Independent Pubs. Group.
—Follow Me: Play for Little Hands. 2019. (Play for Little Hands Ser.). (ENG.). 14p. (J). (— 1). bds. 9.99 *(978-1-910552-80-3(1))* O'Mara, Michael Bks., Ltd. GBR. Dist: Independent Pubs. Group.
Sherlock. The Misadventures of Prince Ivan. Duane, Diane. 2012. (ENG.). 108p. (YA). (gr. 8-11). pap. 9.99 *(978-1-936404-32-2(X))* About Comics.
Sherlock, Jean. Forests & Jungles. Radley, Gail. (Vanishing from Ser.). 32p. 2005. (gr. 6-12). lib. bdg. 22.60 *(978-1-57505-405-6(1))*; 2003. (J). (gr. 3-5). 6.95 *(978-1-57505-567-1(8))* Lerner Publishing Group.
—Grasslands & Deserts. Radley, Gail. (Vanishing from Ser.). 32p. 2005. (J). (gr. 6-12). lib. bdg. 22.60 *(978-1-57505-406-3(X))*; 2003. (YA). (gr. 3-5). 6.95 *(978-1-57505-568-8(6)*, Carolrhoda Bks.) Lerner Publishing Group.
—The Skies. Radley, Gail. (Vanishing from Ser.). 32p. 2005. (gr. 6-12). lib. bdg. 22.60 *(978-1-57505-407-0(8))*; 2003. (J). (gr. 3-5). pap. 6.95 *(978-1-57505-566-4(X))* Lerner Publishing Group.
—Waterways. Radley, Gail. 2003. (Vanishing from Ser.). 32p. (J). (gr. 3-5). 6.95 *(978-1-57505-569-5(4))* Lerner Publishing Group.
Sherlock, Jean & Matheny, Jean. Waterways. Radley, Gail. 2005. (Vanishing from Ser.). 32p. (gr. 6-12). lib. bdg. 22.60 *(978-1-57505-408-7(6))* Lerner Publishing Group.
Sherman, Joseph. How to Catch a Bear Who Loves to Read. Léveillé-Trudel, Juliana et al. 2018. (ENG.). 32p. (J). (gr. -1). 15.95 *(978-2-924786-47-5(9)*, CrackBoom! Bks.) Chouette Publishing CAN. Dist: Publishers Group West (PGW).
—El Viento. Koons, Linda. 2016. (Early Rising Readers Ser.). (SPA.). 16p. (J). (gr. 1-1). 6.67 *(978-1-4788-4220-0(2))* Newmark Learning LLC.
Sherman, Shandel. Something for Nothing. Early, Kelly. l.t. ed. 2007. 13p. (J). per. 8.95 *(978-1-59879-100-6(1))*; (gr. -1-3). 14.95 *(978-1-59879-131-0(1))* Lifevest Publishing, Inc.
Sheron, Jessica. Ghoul Power. Gold, Gina. 2016. (Passport to Reading: Level 2 Ser.). (ENG.). 32p. (J). (gr. 1-3). 16.19 *(978-1-4844-9253-6(6))* Little, Brown Bks. for Young Readers.
Sherrard, Laura. Silky: The Dog That Saved the Day. Innis-Weissenseder, Emma May. 2008. (ENG.). 65p. pap. 9.00 *(978-1-894372-43-5(3))* DreamCatcher Publishing CAN. Dist: Univ. of Toronto Pr.
Sherrell, Craig. Thando Rocker. Kowen, Dorothy. 2012. 24p. (J). (gr. k-2). pap. 7.95 *(978-1-4314-0087-4(4))* Jacana Media ZAF. Dist: Independent Pubs. Group.
Sherrill, Rusty. Kid Nitro & the Sinister Slorp. Sherrill, Rusty. Miers, Doug. Sherrill, Cathy, ed. 2007. 273p. (YA). per. 14.95 *(978-0-9787729-0-1(3))* RS Art Studio.
Sherron, Kate, et al. The Amazing World of Gumball: Scrimmage Scramble. Brennan, Megan. 2018. (Amazing World of Gumball Ser.: 4). (ENG.). 144p. (J). (gr. 4-7). pap. 14.99 *(978-1-68415-217-9(8))* Boom! Studios.
Sherron, Kate. The Amazing World of Gumball: Tunnel Kingdom. Brennan, Megan. 2018. (Amazing World of Gumball Ser.). (ENG.). 144p. (J). (gr. 4-7). pap. 14.99 *(978-1-68415-235-3(6))* Boom! Studios.
Sherron, Kate & Price, Andy. My Little Pony: Friendship Is Magic Volume 17. Anderson, Ted & Cook, Katie. 2019. (My Little Pony Ser.: 17). 144p. (J). (gr. 4-7). pap. 19.99 *(978-1-68405-526-5(1))* Idea & Design Works, LLC.
Sherron, Kate & Stresing, Fred C. Invader ZIM Vol. 4: Deluxe Edition. Trueheart, Eric & Logan, Sam. 2020. (Invader ZIM Ser.). (ENG.). 280p. (J). 49.99 ***(978-1-62010-750-8(3)***, Lion Forge) Oni Pr., Inc.
Sherron, Kate & Stresing, Fred C. Invader ZIM Vol. 8. Logan, Sam & Trueheart, Eric. 2019. (Invader ZIM Ser.: 8). (ENG.). 128p. (J). (gr. 4-7). pap. 19.99 *(978-1-62010-681-5(7)*, Lion Forge) Oni Pr., Inc.
Sherron, Kate, jt. illus. see Catalani, Ilaria.
Sherry, Kevin. Cat in the Box. 2019. 48p. (J). 17.99 *(978-1-4926-7123-7(1))* Sourcebooks, Inc.
—Swallow the Leader. Smith, Danna. 2016. (ENG.). 32p. (J). (gr. -1-3). 16.99 *(978-0-544-10518-8(4)*, 1540594, Clarion Bks.) Houghton Mifflin Harcourt Trade & Reference Pubs.
—Swallow the Leader (lap Board Book) Smith, Danna. 2018. (ENG.). 30p. (J). (— 1). bds. 12.99 *(978-1-328-48265-5(0)*, 1715795, HMH Books For Young Readers) Houghton Mifflin Harcourt Publishing Co.
Sherry, Kevin. Meet the Bigfeet. Sherry, Kevin. 2014. (Yeti Files Ser.: 1). (ENG.). 128p. (J). (gr. 2-5). 8.99 *(978-0-545-55617-0(1)*, Scholastic Pr.) Scholastic, Inc.
—Remy Sneakers & the Lost Treasure. Sherry, Kevin. 2018. (Remy Sneakers Ser.: 2). (ENG.). 128p. (J). (gr. 2-5). 9.99 *(978-1-338-03461-5(8)*, Scholastic Pr.) Scholastic, Inc.
—Remy Sneakers vs. the Robo-Rats. Sherry, Kevin. 2017. (Remy Sneakers Ser.: 1). (ENG.). 128p. (J). (gr. 2-5). 9.99 *(978-1-338-03460-8(X)*, Scholastic Pr.) Scholastic, Inc.
Sherry, Maureen & Stower, Adam. Walls Within Walls. Sherry, Maureen. 2012. (ENG.). (J). (gr. 3-7). lib. bdg. 17.60 *(978-1-68065-133-1(1))* Perfection Learning Corp.
Sherup. Tales of the Golden Corpse: Tibetan Folk Tales. Benson, Sandra. 2006. (ENG.). 224p. (gr. 9-18). per. 15.00 *(978-1-56656-632-2(0))* Interlink Publishing Group, Inc.
Sherwood, D. L. The Headless Snowman. Sherwood, D. L. 2020. (ENG.). 62p. (J). pap. 14.99 ***(978-1-5426-4553-9(0))*** CreateSpace Independent Publishing Platform.
Sherwood, Stewart. Legends in Their Time: Young Heroes & Victims of Canada. Sherwood, George. 2006. (ENG.). 272p. pap. 19.95 *(978-1-897045-10-7(7))* Natural Heritage/Natural History, Inc. CAN. Dist: Ingram Publisher Services.
Shetty, Lakshmi. Tales of Toy World. Shetty, Lalitha A. 2010. 48p. pap. 12.00 *(978-1-60911-157-1(5)*, Eloquent Bks.) Strategic Book Publishing & Rights Agency (SBPRA).
Sheuer, Lauren. The Pop Quiz Book: Tons of Trivia! Seip, Shannon Payette. 2008. (American Girl Library). (ENG.). 80p. (gr. 3-7). spiral bd. 7.95 *(978-1-58485-844-7(3)*, American Girl) American Girl Publishing, Inc.
Shewan-Friend, Hannah. Inky Babble. Shewan-Friend, Hannah. 2016. (ENG.). (J). pap. *(978-0-9954725-0-1(5))* Toil & Trouble Publishing.
Shi, Ellen. Construction People. Hopkins, Lee Bennett. 2020. (ENG.). 32p. (J). (gr. -1-3). 17.99 *(978-1-68437-361-1(1)*, Wordsong) Boyds Mills Pr.
—Do Doodlebugs Doodle?, 1 vol. Demas, Corinne & Roehrig, Artemis. 2018. (Do Animals Animate? Ser.: 2). (ENG.). 36p. (J). (gr. 1-3). 16.95 *(978-1-943978-35-9(2)*, 92c11fc4-f781-44ae-ab71-ebe3e719d60d, Persnickety Pr.) WunderMill, Inc.
—Do Jellyfish Like Peanut Butter? Amazing Sea Creature Facts, 1 vol. Demas, Corinne & Roehrig, Artemis. 2020. (Do Animals Animate? Ser.: 3). (ENG.). (J). 16.95 *(978-1-943978-44-1(1)*, 2abeac92-8afc-4644-aefa-a27c92624c5d, Persnickety Pr.) WunderMill, Inc.
—Little Frog & the Scary Autumn Thing. Yolen, Jane. 2019. (Little Frog & the Four Seasons Ser.: 1). (ENG.). 48p. (J). 8.95 *(978-1-943978-41-0(7)*, e43586bf-62fe-497b-8e35-5de5e7811af3, Persnickety Pr.) WunderMill, Inc.
—Little Frog & the Spring Polliwogs. Yolen, Jane. (Little Frog & the Four Seasons Ser.: 2). (ENG.). 32p. (J). 2019. 8.95 *(978-1-943978-37-3(9)*, d04e8426-e53c-4de4-871b-1ecdda4f699e, Persnickety Pr.); 2017. (gr. -1-k). 15.95 *(978-1-943978-22-9(0)*, af9d879a-cc02-4b02-8628-2b9916367771) WunderMill, Inc.
—School People. Hopkins, Lee Bennett. 2018. (ENG.). 32p. (J). (gr. k-3). 17.95 *(978-1-62979-703-8(0)*, Wordsong) Boyds Mills Pr.
Shi, Qian. The Weaver. Shi, Qian. 2018. (ENG.). 32p. (J). (gr. -1-3). 17.99 *(978-1-5415-1454-6(8))* Lerner Publishing Group.
Shibamoto, Thores. Kuklo Unbound. Suzukaze, Ryo. 2015. (Attack on Titan Ser.). (ENG.). 298p. (J). (gr. 7). pap. 14.95 *(978-1-939130-87-7(5)*, Vertical) Vertical, Inc.
Shickle, Ian. The Adventures of Herb the Wild Turkey - Herb Goes Camping. Cameron, Kristy. 2012. 38p. pap. *(978-0-9859790-0-3(3))* LP Publishing.
Shickle, Ian. The Adventures of Herb the Wild Turkey - Herb the Turkey Goes Skiing. Cameron, Kristy. 2019. (Herb the Turkey Ser.: Vol. 3). (ENG.). 32p. (J). (gr. k-5). pap. 12.00 ***(978-0-9859790-8-9(9))*** LP Publishing.
Shiei. Aoi House Omnibus 2, 2 vols. Arnold, Adam. 2008. (Aoi House Ser.: 2). (ENG.). 352p. pap. 13.99 *(978-1-934876-26-8(7)*, 9781934876268) Seven Seas Entertainment, LLC.
—The Warlock Diaries Omnibus. Roberts, Rachel. 2010. (Avalon: Web of Magic Ser.). (ENG.). 304p. (J). (gr. 3-6). pap. 11.99 *(978-1-934876-88-6(7)*, 9781934876886) Seven Seas Entertainment, LLC.
Shiela, Alejandro. Challah vs. Matza. Melissa, Berg. 2017. (ENG.). (J). (gr. k-6). pap. *(978-0-9921637-6-1(5))* Berg, Melissa.
Shields, Bonnie. Jasper: A Christmas Caper. Hodges, Meredith. 2004. 85p. (J). 24.95 *(978-1-928624-20-2(0))* Lucky 3 Ranch, Inc.
—Jasper: A Fabulous Fourth. Hodges, Meredith. 2006. 83p. (J). *(978-1-928624-24-0(3))* Lucky 3 Ranch, Inc.
—Jasper: The Story of a Mule. Hodges, Meredith. 2003. 245p. (J). (gr. k-7). 39.95 *(978-0-9702309-8-0(2))* Lucky 3 Ranch, Inc.
Shields, Chris, et al. Creepy Crawlies. Kilpatrick, Cathy. Jacquemier, Sue, ed. rev. ed. 2006. (First Nature Ser.). 24p. (J). pap. 4.99 *(978-0-7945-1494-5(4)*, Usborne) EDC Publishing.
Shields, Chris, jt. illus. see Gower, Jeremy.
Shields, Erik P., jt. illus. see Petersen, Darla.
Shields, Laurie. Burned & Beautiful. Tartakoff, Katy. 54p. (Orig.). (J). stu. ed. 14.95 *(978-0-9629365-1-7(0))* Children's Legacy.
—Let Me Show You My World. Tartakoff, Katy. 54p. (Orig.). (J). stu. ed. 14.95 *(978-0-9629365-2-4(9))* Children's Legacy.
Shields, Ruth. Il Goatino. Zyrro, Roggen. 2004. 32p. (J). 16.95 *(978-0-9762580-0-1(5))* Zyrro, Roggen.
Shields, Sue. Chameleons Are Cool. Jenkins, Martin. 2015. 32p. pap. 7.00 *(978-1-61003-406-7(6))* Center for the Collaborative Classroom.
—Clever Cleo. Ross, Stewart. (ENG.). 32p. pap. 9.99 *(978-0-7502-2853-4(9))* Hodder & Stoughton GBR. Dist: Trafalgar Square Publishing.
Shields, Susan. Don't Say No to Flo: The Story of Florence Nightingale. Ross, Stewart. (ENG.). 32p. (J). pap. *(978-0-7502-3273-9(0)*, Wayland) Hachette Children's Group.
—Sink the Armada! Sir Francis Drake & the Spanish Armada of 1588. Ross, Stewart. 62p. (J). pap. *(978-0-237-51959-9(3))* Evans Brothers, Ltd.

S

—Will's Dream. Ross, Stewart. (ENG.). 28p. pap. 9.99 (978-0-7502-2965-4(9)) Hodder & Stoughton GBR. Dist: Trafalgar Square Publishing.

Shiell, Mike. Jasper John Dooley: Lost & Found. Adderson, Caroline. 2015. (Jasper John Dooley Ser.). (ENG.). 128p. (J). (gr. 2-5). 15.95 (978-1-77138-014-0(4)) Kids Can Pr., Ltd. CAN. Dist: Hachette Bk. Group.

—Stinky Science: Why the Smelliest Smells Smell So Smelly. Kay, Edward. 2019. (ENG.). 44p. (J). (gr. 3-7). 17.99 (978-1-77138-382-0(8)) Kids Can Pr., Ltd. CAN. Dist: Hachette Bk. Group.

Shiffman, Lena. A Second Chance for Tina. Snyder, Marilyn. 2003. (Hello Reader! Ser.). (J). (978-0-439-44154-4(4)) Scholastic, Inc.

Shigeno, Shuichi. Initial D, 20 vols., Vol. 5. Shigeno, Shuichi. Hagihara, Rie, tr. from JPN. rev. ed. 2003. 232p. (gr. 8-18). pap. 14.99 (978-1-59182-038-3(3), Tokyopop Adult) TOKYOPOP, Inc.

—Initial D, 23 vols. Shigeno, Shuichi. Vol. 9. rev. ed. 2003. 200p. pap. 14.99 (978-1-59182-109-0(6)); Vol. 10. rev. ed. 2004. 192p. pap. 14.99 (978-1-59182-110-6(X)); Vol. 16. rev. ed. 2005. 240p. pap. 14.99 (978-1-59182-992-8(5)); Vol. 18. rev. ed. 2005. 192p. pap. 14.99 (978-1-59182-994-2(1)); Vol. 19. 19th rev. ed. 2005. 240p. pap. 14.99 (978-1-59182-995-9(X)); Vol. 20. 20th rev. ed. 2005. 192p. pap. 14.99 (978-1-59182-996-6(8)) TOKYOPOP, Inc. (Tokyopop Adult).

Shigeno, Shuichi. Initial D, Vol. 17. Shigeno, Shuichi, creator. rev. ed. 2005. 240p. (YA). pap. 14.99 (978-1-59182-993-5(3), Tokyopop Adult) TOKYOPOP, Inc.

Shih, Lin. Santa's Christmas Train. Caro, Joe. 2005. 32p. pap. (978-0-9628078-2-4(6)) Cowboy Collector Pubns.

—Santa's Christmas Train Coloring Book. Caro, Joe. 2005. 32p. pap. (978-0-9628078-5-5(0)) Cowboy Collector Pubns.

Shiina, You. Ascendance of a Bookworm: Part 1 Volume 1. Kazuki, Miya. Quof, tr. 2019. (Ascendance of a Bookworm (light Novel) Ser.: 1). 325p. pap. 14.99 (978-1-7183-5600-9(5)) J-Novel Club.

—Ascendance of a Bookworm: Part 1 Volume 2. Kazuki, Miya. Quof, tr. 2019. (Ascendance of a Bookworm (light Novel) Ser.: 2). 325p. pap. 14.99 (978-1-7183-5601-6(3)) J-Novel Club.

Shilliam, Jo-Anne. Will I Live Forever? Nystrom, Carolyn. 2006. 32p. (J). (gr. -1-3). 11.99 (978-0-8254-7306-7(3), Candle Bks.) Lion Hudson PLC GBR. Dist: Kregel Pubns.

Shillinglaw, Bruce, jt. illus. see Carrick, Paul.

Shiloh, Ramon. The Corn Whisperer. Houser, Sue. 2017. (ENG.). 48p. (J). (gr. 1-6). 20.00 (978-1-5154-3910-3(0)) Wilder Pubns., Corp.

—The Otter, the Spotted Frog & the Great Flood: A Creek Indian Story, Vol. Hausman, Gerald. 2013. 36p. (J). (gr. k-3). 17.95 (978-1-937786-12-0(9), Wisdom Tales) World Wisdom, Inc.

Shimabukuro, Denise. The Good Dinosaur. Ferrari, Alessandro. 2020. (Disney & Pixar Movies Ser.). (ENG.). 52p. (J). (gr. 2-6). lib. bdg. 28.50 (978-1-5321-4550-6(0), 35197, Graphic Novels) Spotlight.

Shimabukuro, Denise. How to Train Your Dragon. Newberger Speregen, Devra. 2017. (Little Golden Book Ser.). 24p. (J). (-k). 4.99 (978-1-5247-6774-7(3), Golden Bks.) Random Hse. Children's Bks.

Shimabukuro, Denise & Naggi, Elena. Frozen 2: Anna, Elsa, & the Secret River. Rosenbaum, Andria Warmflash. 2019. (ENG.). 40p. (J). (gr. -1-k). 16.99 (978-1-368-04362-5(3)) Disney Pr.

Shimabukuro, Denise, jt. illus. see Disney Storybook Art Team.

Shimabukuro, Denise, jt. illus. see Phillipson, Andrew.

Shimano, Chie. BioGraphic Novel: Che Guevara. 2008. (JPN.). 192p. (YA). pap. 14.95 (978-0-9817543-2-1(5)) Emotional Content, LLC.

Shimatsuka, Eri. Zen Scratch Art: Scandinavian Design. 2018. (ENG.). 6p. (YA). (gr. 6). 12.99 (978-4-05-621078-1(0)) Gakken Plus Co., Ltd. JPN. Dist: Simon & Schuster, Inc.

Shimin, Symeon. Zeely. Hamilton, Virginia. 2006. (ENG.). 128p. (J). (gr. 3-7). pap. 7.99 (978-1-4169-1413-6(7), Aladdin) Simon & Schuster Children's Publishing.

Shimizu, Aki. Qwan, Vol. 2. Kiefl, Mike, tr. from JPN. rev. ed. 2005. 192p. (YA). pap. 9.99 (978-1-59532-535-8(2)) TOKYOPOP, Inc.

Shimizu, Aki. Qwan, Vol. 1. Shimizu, Aki, creator. 2005. 192p. (YA). pap. 9.99 (978-1-59532-534-1(4)) TOKYOPOP, Inc.

Shimizu, Yuko. Barbed Wire Baseball. Moss, Marissa. 2013. (ENG.). 48p. (J). (gr. 1-5). 19.95 (978-1-4197-0521-2(0), Abrams Bks. for Young Readers) Abrams, Inc.

—The Fairy Tales of Oscar Wilde. Wilde, Oscar. 2020. (Illuminated Editions Ser.). 156p. (gr. 4-7). 100.00 (978-1-948886-01-7(4)) Beehive Bks.

—Guardian of the Darkness. Uehashi, Nahoko & Hirano, Cathy. 2009. (Moribito Ser.: No. 2). (J). pap. (978-0-545-10874-4(8), Levine, Arthur A. Bks.) Scholastic, Inc.

—Guardian of the Spirit. Uehashi, Nahoko. Hirano, Cathy, tr. 2008. (Moribito Ser.: 1). 288p. (J). (gr. 7-12). 22.44 (978-0-545-00543-2(4)) Scholastic, Inc.

—A Tear in the Ocean. Bouwman, H. M. 2020. 320p. (J). (gr. 5). 8.99 (978-0-399-54524-5(7), Puffin Books) Penguin Young Readers Group.

Shimmen, Cathy. Five Teddy Bears. Adeney, Anne. 2008. (Tadpoles Ser.). (ENG.). 24p. (J). (gr. -1-k). pap. (978-0-7787-3884-8(1)); lib. bdg. (978-0-7787-3853-4(1)) Crabtree Publishing Co.

—The Loaves & Fishes. Page, Nick & Page, Claire. 2006. (Read with Me (Make Believe Ideas) Ser.). 30p. (J). (gr. k-2). (978-1-84610-175-5(1)) Make Believe Ideas.

—Under the Sea. Milbourne, Anna. 2007. (Picture Bks). 32p. (J). 9.99 (978-0-7945-1801-1(X), Usborne) EDC Publishing.

—The Winter Prince. Page, Nick & Page, Claire. 2006. (Read with Me (Make Believe Ideas) Ser.). 31p. (J). (gr. k-2). (978-1-84610-172-4(7)) Make Believe Ideas.

Shimon, Diana. The Pilgrim Book of Bible Stories. Water, Mark. 2003. 320p. (J). 22.50 (978-0-8298-1487-3(6)) Pilgrim Pr., The/United Church Pr.

Shimone, MacKie. Garden of Virtues. Chelsea, Smith Lee. 2017. (ENG.). 52p. (J). (978-0-9876433-2-2(0)) Enable Me To Grow.

Shin, HaYoung. Thanksgiving Then & Now, 1 vol. Gunderson, Jessica. (Thanksgiving Ser.). (ENG.). 24p. (J). (gr. k-3). 2011. pap. 8.95 (978-1-4048-6723-9(6)); 2010. lib. bdg. 27.99 (978-1-4048-6286-9(2)) Capstone. (Picture Window Bks.).

Shin, Hwan. Threads of Time, Vol. 3. Noh, Mi Young. rev. ed. 2005. 192p. pap. 9.99 (978-1-59532-034-6(2)) TOKYOPOP, Inc.

Shin, Ji-Soo. So Lonely. Kim, Young-Ah. 2012. 32p. (J). (978-1-4338-1287-3(8)); pap. (978-1-4338-1288-0(6)) American Psychological Assn. (Magination Pr.).

Shin, Monte. Mirror Play. Shin, Monte. 2018. (ENG.). 26p. (J). (gr. -1-k). bds. 14.99 (978-988-8341-53-5(7), Minedition) Neugebauer, Michael (Publishing) Limited HKG. Dist: Penguin Random Hse. LLC.

Shin, Simone. Bumpety, Dunkety, Thumpety-Thump! Going, K. L. 2017. (ENG.). 48p. (J). (gr. -1-k). 17.99 (978-1-4424-3414-1(7), Beach Lane Bks.) Beach Lane Bks.

—Cuánto Mamá Te Quiere (Mama Loves You So) Pierce, Terry. 2018. (New Books for Newborns Ser.). (SPA.). 16p. (J). (gr. -1 — 1). bds. 7.99 (978-1-5344-2831-7(3), Libros Para Ninos) Libros Para Ninos.

—If I Could Drive, Mama. Best, Cari. 2016. (ENG.). 40p. (J). 17.99 (978-0-374-30205-4(7), 900143579, Farrar, Straus & Giroux (BYR)) Farrar, Straus & Giroux.

—Insults Aren't Funny: What to Do about Verbal Bullying. Doering, Amanda. 2015. (No More Bullies Ser.). (ENG.). 24p. (J). (gr. k-3). lib. bdg. 26.65 (978-1-4795-6942-7(9), Picture Window Bks.) Capstone.

Shin, Simone. The International Day of the Girl: Celebrating Girls Around the World. Humphreys, Jessica Dee & Ambrose, Rona. 2020. (CitizenKid Ser.). (ENG.). 32p. (J). (gr. 2-5). 18.99 (978-1-5253-0058-5(X)) Kids Can Pr., Ltd. CAN. Dist: Hachette Bk. Group.

Shin, Simone. Mama Loves You So. Pierce, Terry. 2017. (New Books for Newborns Ser.). (ENG.). 16p. (J). (gr. -1 — 1). bds. 7.99 (978-1-4814-8159-5(2), Little Simon) Little Simon.

—Niko Draws a Feeling. Raczka, Robert. 2017. (ENG.). 32p. (J). (gr. k-3). 17.99 (978-1-4677-9843-3(6), 9781467798433, Carolrhoda Bks.) Lerner Publishing Group.

—Niko Draws a Feeling. Raczka, Robert. ed. 2017. (ENG.). 32p. (J). (gr. k-3). E-Book 27.99 (978-1-5124-3275-6(X), 9781512432756); E-Book 27.99 (978-1-5124-2688-5(1)); E-Book 9.99 (978-1-5124-3276-3(8), 9781512432763) Lerner Publishing Group. (Carolrhoda Bks.).

—No More Bullies. Doering, Amanda F. & Higgins, Melissa. 2015. (No More Bullies Ser.). (ENG.). 24p. (J). (gr. k-3). 106.60 (978-1-4795-8007-1(4), 22959, Picture Window Bks.) Capstone.

—Pushing Isn't Funny: What to Do about Physical Bullying. Higgins, Melissa. 2015. (No More Bullies Ser.). (ENG.). 24p. (J). (gr. k-3). lib. bdg. 26.65 (978-1-4795-6941-0(0), Picture Window Bks.) Capstone.

—The Red Bicycle: The Extraordinary Story of One Ordinary Bicycle. Isabella, Jude. (CitizenKid Ser.). (ENG.). 32p. (J). (gr. 3-7). 2020. pap. 10.99 (978-1-77138-558-9(8)); 2015. 18.99 (978-1-77138-023-2(3)) Kids Can Pr., Ltd. CAN. Dist: Hachette Bk. Group.

—Rumble Grumble ... Hush. Banks, Kate. 2018. 40p. (J). (gr. -1-2). 17.99 (978-1-101-94049-5(2)); (ENG.). lib. bdg. 20.99 (978-1-101-94050-1(6)) Random Hse. Children's Bks. (Schwartz & Wade Bks.).

—Sometimes Jokes Aren't Funny: What to Do about Hidden Bullying. Doering, Amanda. 2015. (No More Bullies Ser.). (ENG.). 24p. (J). (gr. k-3). lib. bdg. 26.65 (978-1-4795-6943-4(7), Picture Window Bks.) Capstone.

—Teasing Isn't Funny: What to Do about Emotional Bullying. Higgins, Melissa. 2015. (No More Bullies Ser.). (ENG.). 24p. (J). (gr. k-3). lib. bdg. 26.65 (978-1-4795-6940-3(2), Picture Window Bks.) Capstone.

—Thank You, Garden. Scanlon, Liz Garton. 2020. (ENG.). 32p. (J). (gr. -1-2). 17.99 (978-1-4814-0350-4(8), Beach Lane Bks.) Beach Lane Bks.

Shin, Yujin. My Magical Mermaid. 2019. (ENG.). 8p. (J). (gr. -1 — 1). bds. 8.99 (978-1-4197-3730-5(9), Abrams Appleseed) Abrams, Inc.

Shine. Loon Summer. Santucci, Barbara. 2010. (ENG.). 32p. (YA). (gr. k-5). pap. 9.00 (978-0-8028-5389-9(7), Eerdmans Bks For Young Readers) Eerdmans, William B. Publishing Co.

Shine, Andrea. Family Reunion. Quattlebaum, Mary. 2004. 32p. (J). 16.00 (978-0-8028-5237-3(8)) Eerdmans, William B. Publishing Co.

—Loon Summer. Santucci, Barbara. 2004. 32p. (J). (gr. k-3). 16.00 (978-0-8028-5182-6(7)) Eerdmans, William B. Publishing Co.

—The Summer My Father Was Ten. Brisson, Pat. 2014. 32p. pap. 8.00 (978-1-61003-366-4(3)) Center for the Collaborative Classroom.

Shingle, Jude. Christopher Counts the Constellation, bks. 500, bk. 500. Moodey, Mary. 500th l.t. ed. 2012. (ENG.). 37p. 16.99 (978-0-9853579-0-0(8)) MarMooWorks,LLC.

Shinjo, Mayu. Sensual Phrase. Shinjo, Mayu. (Sensual Phrase Ser.). (ENG.). 5. 2004. 192p. pap. 9.95 (978-1-59116-560-6(1)); Vol. 3. 2004. 192p. pap. 9.95 (978-1-59116-449-4(4)); Vol. 4. 2004. 192p. (YA). pap. 9.95 (978-1-59116-411-1(7)); Vol. 6. 2005. 184p. pap. 9.99 (978-1-59116-671-9(3)); Vol. 7. 2005. 200p. (YA). pap. 9.99 (978-1-59116-734-1(5)); Vol. 9. 2005. 200p. pap. 9.99 (978-1-59116-867-6(8)); Vol. 11. 2005. 192p. pap. 9.99 (978-1-4215-0107-9(4)); Vol. 13. 2006. 208p. pap. 9.99 (978-1-4215-0395-0(6)) Viz Media.

Shinjo, Shelly. Bird. Elliott, Zetta & Terasaki, Stanley Todd. 2016. (ENG.). 32p. (J). (gr. 2-5). pap. 9.95 (978-1-62014-350-6(X)) Lee & Low Bks., Inc.

—Ghosts for Breakfast. Terasaki, Stanley Todd. 2013. (ENG.). 32p. (J). (gr. k-4). 16.95 (978-1-58430-046-5(9)) Lee & Low Bks., Inc.

Shinkewski, Sarah. Ava & Her Super Hero. McTaggart, Keven & McTaggart, Nathan. 2020. (ENG.). 32p. (J). (gr. k-5). pap. 15.25 (978-0-2288-2774-0(4)) CreateSpace Independent Publishing Platform.

Shiozaki, Yuji. Battle Vixens, Vol. 6. Shiozaki, Yuji. rev. ed. 2005. (Battle Vixens Ser.). 168p. pap. 9.99 (978-1-59182-948-5(8)) TOKYOPOP, Inc.

Shipe, Becky. Bend & Stretch: Learning about Your Bones & Muscles. Nettleton, Pamela Hill. 2004. (Amazing Body Ser.). (ENG.). 24p. (J). (gr. k-3). per. 8.95 (978-1-4048-0507-1(9), Picture Window Bks.) Capstone.

—Gurgles & Growls: Learning about Your Stomach. Nettleton, Pamela Hill. 2004. (Amazing Body Ser.). (ENG.). 24p. (J). (gr. k-3). per. 8.95 (978-1-4048-0504-0(4), Picture Window Bks.) Capstone.

—Look, Listen, Taste, Touch, & Smell: Learning about Your Five Senses. Nettleton, Pamela Hill. 2004. (Amazing Body Ser.). (ENG.). 24p. (J). (gr. k-3). per. 8.95 (978-1-4048-0508-8(7), Picture Window Bks.) Capstone.

—Think, Think, Think: Learning about Your Brain. Nettleton, Pamela Hill. 2004. (Amazing Body Ser.). (ENG.). 24p. (J). (gr. k-3). per. 8.95 (978-1-4048-0503-3(6), Picture Window Bks.) Capstone.

Shipley, Josh. This Is a Whoopsie! Cangelose, Andrew. 2018. (ENG.). 32p. (J). 15.99 (978-1-941302-87-3(4), 261b2858-1d42-49a2-a534-bbed80a47bc5, Lion Forge) Oni Pr., Inc.

Shipley, Marie. The Lion & the Lamb. Skoor, Susan. 2003. (ENG.). (J). pap. 12.95 (978-0-8309-1068-7(9)) Herald Publishing Hse.

Shipley, Matthew. B Is for Baller: The Ultimate Basketball Alphabet. Littlejohn, James. 2018. (ABC to MVP Ser.: 1). (ENG.). 32p. (J). (gr. -1-k). 17.95 (978-1-62937-588-5(8)) Triumph Bks.

Shipman, Gary. Pakkins' Land: Tavitah, 4. 2003. (Pakkins' Land: 4). 128p. pap. 16.95 (978-0-9700241-4-5(2)) Pakkins Presents.

Shipman, Josie. That's Not a Pickle! Part 7. Kruse, Donald W. 2018. (That's Not a Pickle! Ser.: Vol. 7). (ENG.). 48p. (J). (gr. k-5). pap. 14.95 (978-0-9994571-1-5(X)) Zaccheus Entertainment Co.

—Where's the Gold. Kruse, Donald W. 2012. 50p. pap. 12.95 (978-1-59663-857-0(5), Castle Keep Pr.) Rock, James A. & Co. Pubs.

Shipman, Talitha. Applesauce Day. Amstutz, Lisa. 2017. (ENG.). 32p. (J). (gr. -1-3). 16.99 (978-0-8075-0392-8(4), 807503924) Whitman, Albert & Co.

—First Snow. Viau, Nancy. 2018. (ENG.). 32p. (J). (gr. -1-k). 16.99 (978-0-8075-2440-4(9), 807524409) Whitman, Albert & Co.

—Judah Maccabee Goes to the Doctor. Koffsky, Ann D. 2017. (J). (978-1-68115-522-7(2)) Behrman Hse., Inc.

—On Your Way, Vol. Coy, John. 2019. (ENG.). 32p. (J). (gr. -1-k). 17.99 (978-1-5064-5258-6(2), Beaming Books) Augsburg Fortress, Pubs.

Shira, Arielle. Bubbles Bubbles Everywhere. Angues, Lisa. 2020. (ENG.). 32p. (J). (978-1-5255-6511-3(7)); pap. (978-1-5255-6512-0(5)) FriesenPress.

Shirasu, Nori. Solar System Song. Nono, Auntie. 2004. (J). bds. 1.25 (978-0-9754098-0-0(8)) Accordian Bks.

Shireen, Nadia. PlayShapes: Emperor Penguin. 2017. (PlayShapes Ser.). (ENG.). 12p. (J). (gr. -1 — 1). bds. 7.99 (978-2-7459-9074-7(8)) Éditions Tourbillon FRA. Dist: Hachette Bk. Group.

—PlayShapes: Seal. 2017. (PlayShapes Ser.). (ENG.). 12p. (J). (gr. -1 — 1). bds. 7.99 (978-2-7459-9075-4(6)) Éditions Tourbillon FRA. Dist: Hachette Bk. Group.

Shireen, Nadia. Yeti & the Bird. Shireen, Nadia. 2015. (ENG.). 32p. (J). (gr. -1-3). 18.99 (978-1-4814-0389-4(3), Atheneum Bks. for Young Readers) Simon & Schuster Children's Publishing.

Shirk, Linda. Happy Days with Daniel. Martin, Elaine S. Bowman. 2017. 108p. (J). (978-0-7399-2563-8(6)) Rod & Staff Pubs., Inc.

Shirk, Linda, jt. illus. see Higgins, Tabitha.

Shirk, Linda, jt. illus. see Whitehead, Victoria E.

Shirley, Hoskins. Letters from Scamper. Mary, Mize. 2012. 32p. pap. 10.00 (978-0-9832514-3-9(6)) Gypsy Heart Pr.

Shirley, John. Build Your Own Cars Sticker Book. Tudhope, Simon. 2013. (ENG.). 23p. (J). (gr. -1-3). 8.99 (978-0-7945-3379-3(5), Usborne) EDC Publishing.

Shirley-Smith, Sanette. A Donkey Is Not Stupid, a Donkey Can Think. Smith, Pieter Ernst. 2011. 24p. pap. 11.50 (978-1-61204-039-4(X), Eloquent Bks.) Strategic Book Publishing & Rights Agency (SBPRA).

Shirzad, Susanne. My Persian Haft Seen: An Iranian Nowruz Tradition. Shirzad, Susanne. 2018. (ENG.). 40p. (J). pap. 18.00 (978-1-58814-179-8(9)) Ibex Pubs., Inc.

—My Persian Haft Seen: The Iranian Nowruz Tradition. Shirzad, Susanne. 2018. 32p. (J). pap. 20.00 (978-1-58814-178-1(0)) Ibex Pubs., Inc.

Shivack, Nadia. Inside Out: Portrait of an Eating Disorder. Shivack, Nadia. 2007. (ENG.). 64p. (YA). (gr. 7-12). 19.99 (978-0-689-85216-9(9), Atheneum Bks. for Young Readers) Simon & Schuster Children's Publishing.

Shively, Julie. What Belongs? Baby Looney Tunes. Kurtz, John. 2004. 12p. bds. 6.95 (978-0-8249-6560-0(4), Ideal Pubns.) Worthy Publishing.

Shiver, Jennifer. Forever Home. Shiver, Ann. 2019. (ENG.). 32p. (J). pap. 14.99 (978-1-5456-6865-8(5), Mill City Press, Inc) Salem Author Services.

Shklovsky, Regina. Fun in the Mud: A Wetlands Tale. Bolger, Sally. 2018. (ENG.). 32p. (J). (gr. 3-3). 16.95 (978-1-944903-54-1(2), Roundtree Pr.) Cameron + Co.

Shleifer, Maya. Hand in Hand. Rosenbaum, Andria Warmflash. 2018. (J). (978-1-68115-538-8(9), Apples & Honey Pr.) Behrman Hse., Inc.

Shlichta, Joe. Eleven Nature Tales: A Multicultural Journey. DeSpain, Pleasant. 2005. (ENG.). 96p. (J). (gr. k-17). pap. 9.95 (978-0-87483-458-1(9)) August Hse. Pubs., Inc.

—Thirty-Three Multicultural Tales to Tell. DeSpain, Pleasant. 2005. (American Storytelling Ser.). (ENG.). 126p. (J). (gr. 2-5). pap. 16.95 (978-0-87483-266-2(7), AH2667) August Hse. Pubs., Inc.

Shoals, Melinda, jt. illus. see Worthington, Jennifer.

Shobaru, Moch Fajar. Go Bananers for Manners!! Olexa, Tony. 2019. (ENG.). 30p. (J). pap. 9.99 (978-1-0910-3930-8(5)) Independently Published.

Shockley, Aleah. Stop & Go Potty. Eytchison, Tami. 2018. (ENG.). 28p. (J). pap. 16.99 (978-1-5462-6547-4(3)) AuthorHouse.

Shoemaker, Kathryn. Floyd the Flamingo: And His Flock of Friends, 1 vol. Stone, Tiffany. 2004. (ENG.). 64p. (J). (gr. 1-3). per. 7.95 (978-1-896580-58-6(0)) Tradewind Bks. CAN. Dist: Orca Bk. Pubs. USA.

—My Animal Friends, 1 vol. Stephens, R. David. 2003. (ENG.). 32p. (J). (gr. -1-k). pap. 6.95 (978-1-896580-74-6(2)) Tradewind Bks. CAN. Dist: Orca Bk. Pubs. USA.

—Seeking Refuge, 1 vol. Watts, Irene. 2017. (ENG.). 128p. (J). (gr. 4-7). pap. 15.95 (978-1-926890-02-9(7)) Tradewind Bks. CAN. Dist: Orca Bk. Pubs. USA.

Shoemaker, Kathryn E. Good-Bye Marianne: A Story of Growing up in Nazi Germany. Watts, Irene N. 2008. 128p. (J). (gr. 4-7). pap. 12.95 (978-0-88776-830-9(X), Tundra Bks.) Tundra Bks. CAN. Dist: Penguin Random Hse. LLC.

—A Telling Time, 1 vol. Watts, Irene N. 2004. (ENG.). 32p. (J). (gr. 1-3). 17.95 (978-1-896580-39-5(4)); pap. 7.95 (978-1-896580-72-2(6)) Tradewind Bks. CAN. Dist: Orca Bk. Pubs. USA.

Shoemate, Ashley. Smoky Mountain Legacy: Smoky Mountain Heritage Series - Book 1. Shoemate, Linda. 2018. (Smoky Mountain Heritage Ser.: Vol. 1). (ENG.). 60p. (J). (gr. 3-6). pap. 6.95 (978-1-64373-137-7(8)) LPC.

Shogakukan & Mitsui-Kids. Duel Masters Vol. 3: The Champion of Tomorrow. 2004. (Teen Ser.). 96p. pap. 14.99 (978-1-59532-065-0(2), Tokyopop Kids) TOKYOPOP, Inc.

Sholto, Walker. Molly & the Giant. Jarman, Julia. 2005. (ENG.). 24p. (J). lib. bdg. 23.65 (978-1-59646-746-0(0)) Dingles & Co.

Shondeck, Betty. Liking Myself. Palmer, Pat. 2010. 102p. (J). pap. 12.99 (978-0-9622834-2-0(8)) Uplift Pr.

—The Mouse, the Monster & Me: Assertiveness for Young People. Palmer, Pat. rev. ed. 2010. 100p. (J). pap. 12.99 (978-0-9622834-3-7(6)) Uplift Pr.

Shone, Rob. Harriet Tubman: The Life of an African-American Abolitionist. Ganeri, Anita. 2005. (Graphic Biographies Ser.). (ENG.). 48p. (gr. 5-8). pap. 14.05 (978-1-4042-5172-4(3)) Rosen Publishing Group, Inc., The.

Shone, Rob & Field, James. Diplodocus: The Whip-Tailed Dinosaur. 2009. (Graphic Dinosaurs Ser.). (ENG.). 32p. (gr. 2-5). pap. 12.30 (978-1-4042-7714-4(5)) Rosen Publishing Group, Inc., The.

Shonkwiler, Martha. The Power of Self Ralph Waldo Emerson's Wonder Filled Life. Miller, Ruth L. 2013. 66p. pap. 12.00 (978-0-945385-85-1(4)) WiseWoman Pr.

Shoo, Rayner. Little Horrors: Shiver with Fear - Shake with Laughter! Rayner, Shoo. 2016. (ENG.). (J). (gr. 2-5). pap. (978-1-908944-34-4(X)) Rayner, Shoo.

—Monster Boy: Three Monster Stories. Rayner, Shoo. 2016. (ENG.). (J). (gr. 1-5). pap. (978-1-908944-37-5(4)) Rayner, Shoo.

—Scaredy Cats. Rayner, Shoo. 2016. (ENG.). (J). (gr. 3-6). pap. (978-1-908944-30-6(7)) Rayner, Shoo.

Shoop, Johanna. The Big Black Dog & the Big Blue Se. Lindeman, Craig. 2009. 40p. pap. 15.95 (978-1-60844-047-4(8)) Dog Ear Publishing, LLC.

Shoopik, Marina. Jessie's Big Move. Wilson, Nathaniel. 2010. (ENG.). 54p. (J). 16.95 (978-0-9744935-7-2(0)) Allwrite Publishing.

Shooter, Howard, photos by. DK Children's Cookbook. Dorling Kindersley Publishing Staff & Ibbs, Katharine. 2004. (ENG., 128p. (J). (gr. 3-7). 18.99 (978-0-7566-0597-1(0), 1235962, DK Children) Dorling Kindersley Publishing, Inc.

—Kids' Fun & Healthy Cookbook. Graimes, Nicola. 2007. (ENG., 128p. (J). (gr. 2-5). 18.99 (978-0-7566-2916-8(0), DK Children) Dorling Kindersley Publishing, Inc.

Shopsin, Tamara, jt. illus. see Fulford, Jason.

Shore, Judie. Naturaleza Divertida. Hickman, Pamela & Federation of Ontario Naturalists. (SPA.). 92p. (978-84-9754-095-7(6), 87821) Ediciones Oniro S.A.

—La Naturaleza y Tú. Hickman, Pamela & Federation of Ontario Naturalists. (SPA.). 63p. (978-84-9754-106-0(5), 87822) Ediciones Oniro S.A.

Shorrock, Claire. Snow Globe Wishes. Dealey, Erin. 2019. (ENG.). 32p. (J). (gr. k-2). 16.99 (978-1-5341-1031-1(3), 204763) Sleeping Bear Pr.

Short, Gregory T. Safety Sam, I Am: How to Avoid A Sticky Jelly Jam. Weathers, Regina Lorick. 2004. (J). per. 7.95 (978-0-9665909-6-8(1)) Kalawantis Publishing Services, Inc.

Short, Kasey. Betsy Beansprout Adventure Guide. Elmore, Amber. 2011. (J). pap. 15.99 (978-0-9822632-8-0(7)) ShadeTree Publishing, LLC.

Short, Robbie. Hiro Dragon Warrior: Battle at Mount Kamado. Weiss, Bobbi & Weiss, David. 2008. (ENG.). 24p. (J). (gr. 1-17). pap. 3.99 (978-1-58476-721-3(9)) Innovative Kids.

—Hiro: Dragon Warrior: Level 2. Weiss, Bobbi & Weiss, David. 2007. (ENG.). 24p. (J). (gr. 1-4). per. 3.99 (978-1-58476-616-2(6), IKIDS) Innovative Kids.

—I Want One Too! Ehrmantraut, Brenda. 2003. (J). lib. bdg. 16.95 (978-0-9729833-1-0(7)); per. 9.95 (978-0-9729833-0-3(9)) Bubble Gum Pr.

—I Want One Too! 2003. 32p. (J). lib. bdg. 12.95 (978-0-9729833-2-7(5)) Bubble Gum Pr.

Shortall, Leonard. Colors Are Nice. Holl, Adelaide. 2018. (Little Golden Book Ser.). 24p. (J). (-k). 4.99 (978-1-5247-7161-4(9), Golden Bks.) Random Hse. Children's Bks.

—Encyclopedia Brown, 13 vols., Set. Sobol, Donald J. 2015. (Encyclopedia Brown Ser.: Vol. 13). (ENG.). 96p. (J). (gr. 2-6). 351.91 (978-1-61479-307-6(7), 16933, Chapter Bks.) Spotlight.

—Encyclopedia Brown & the Case of the Dead Eagles, 1 vol. Sobol, Donald J. 2015. (Encyclopedia Brown Ser.). (ENG.). 96p. (J). (gr. 2-6). 27.07 *(978-1-61479-308-3(5),* 16934, Chapter Bks.) Spotlight.
—Encyclopedia Brown & the Case of the Secret Pitch, 1 vol. Sobol, Donald J. 2015. (Encyclopedia Brown Ser.). (ENG.). 96p. (J). (gr. 2-6). 27.07 *(978-1-61479-310-6(7),* 16936, Chapter Bks.) Spotlight.
—Encyclopedia Brown, Boy Detective, 1 vol. Sobol, Donald J. 2015. (Encyclopedia Brown Ser.). (ENG.). 96p. (J). (gr. 2-6). 27.07 *(978-1-61479-320-5(4),* 16946, Chapter Bks.) Spotlight.
—Encyclopedia Brown Finds the Clues, 1 vol. Sobol, Donald J. 2015. (Encyclopedia Brown Ser.). (ENG.). 96p. (J). (gr. 2-6). 27.07 *(978-1-61479-311-3(5),* 16937, Chapter Bks.) Spotlight.
—Encyclopedia Brown Gets His Man, 1 vol. Sobol, Donald J. 2015. (Encyclopedia Brown Ser.). (ENG.). 96p. (J). (gr. 2-6). 27.07 *(978-1-61479-312-0(3),* 16938, Chapter Bks.) Spotlight.
—Encyclopedia Brown Keeps the Peace, 1 vol. Sobol, Donald J. 2015. (Encyclopedia Brown Ser.). (ENG.). 96p. (J). (gr. 2-6). 27.07 *(978-1-61479-313-7(1),* 16939, Chapter Bks.) Spotlight.
—Encyclopedia Brown Lends a Hand, 1 vol. Sobol, Donald J. 2015. (Encyclopedia Brown Ser.). (ENG.). 96p. (J). (gr. 2-6). 27.07 *(978-1-61479-314-4(X),* 16940, Chapter Bks.) Spotlight.
—Encyclopedia Brown Saves the Day, 1 vol. Sobol, Donald J. 2015. (Encyclopedia Brown Ser.). (ENG.). 96p. (J). (gr. 2-6). 27.07 *(978-1-61479-315-1(8),* 16941, Chapter Bks.) Spotlight.
—Encyclopedia Brown Shows the Way, 1 vol. Sobol, Donald J. 2015. (Encyclopedia Brown Ser.). (ENG.). 96p. (J). (gr. 2-6). 27.07 *(978-1-61479-316-8(6),* 16942, Chapter Bks.) Spotlight.
—Encyclopedia Brown Solves Them All, 1 vol. Sobol, Donald J. 2015. (Encyclopedia Brown Ser.). (ENG.). 96p. (J). (gr. 2-6). 27.07 *(978-1-61479-317-5(4),* 16943, Chapter Bks.) Spotlight.
—Encyclopedia Brown Takes the Case, 1 vol. Sobol, Donald J. 2015. (Encyclopedia Brown Ser.). (ENG.). 96p. (J). (gr. 2-6). 27.07 *(978-1-61479-318-2(2),* 16944, Chapter Bks.) Spotlight.
—Encyclopedia Brown Tracks Them Down, 1 vol. Sobol, Donald J. 2015. (Encyclopedia Brown Ser.). (ENG.). 96p. (J). (gr. 2-6). 27.07 *(978-1-61479-319-9(0),* 16945, Chapter Bks.) Spotlight.
Shortall, Leonard, jt. illus. see Brandi, Lillian.
Shortall, Leonard W. Encyclopedia Brown, Boy Detective. Sobol, Donald J. 2009. (Encyclopedia Brown Ser.). 88p. lib. bdg. 15.00 *(978-1-60686-386-2(X))* Perfection Learning Corp.
—Encyclopedia Brown, Boy Detective. Sobol, Donald J. ed. 2007. (Encyclopedia Brown Ser.: 1). 88p. (J). (gr. 4-7). 14.75 *(978-1-4177-8622-0(1))* Turtleback.
—Encyclopedia Brown Finds the Clues. Sobol, Donald J. 2008. (Encyclopedia Brown Ser.). 96p. (gr. 4-7). 15.00 *(978-0-7569-8846-3(2))* Perfection Learning Corp.
—Encyclopedia Brown Gets His Man. Sobol, Donald J. 2009. (Encyclopedia Brown Ser.). 96p. lib. bdg. 15.00 *(978-1-60686-464-7(5))* Perfection Learning Corp.
—Encyclopedia Brown Shows the Way. Sobol, Donald J. 2008. (Encyclopedia Brown Ser.). 96p. (J). (gr. 2-5). 12.65 *(978-0-7569-8937-8(X))* Perfection Learning Corp.
—Encyclopedia Brown Takes the Case. Sobol, Donald J. 2008. (Encyclopedia Brown Ser.: 10). (ENG.). 96p. (J). (gr. 3-7). 5.99 *(978-0-14-241085-1(3),* Puffin Books) Penguin Young Readers Group.
—Encyclopedia Brown Takes the Case. Sobol, Donald J. 2008. (Encyclopedia Brown Ser.). 96p. (J). (gr. 3-7). 12.65 *(978-0-7569-9078-7(5))* Perfection Learning Corp.
—Secret Agents Four. Sobol, Donald J. 2003. (Adventure Library). (ENG.). 140p. (J). (gr. 4-6). pap. 10.95 *(978-1-883937-65-2(5))* Ignatius Pr.
Shortell, Stephen. Itchy Lee & Itchy Dee Mcgee. Rowe, Papa. Wilkins, Kevan & Mason, Shannon, eds. ed. 2006. (J). 15.99 *(978-0-9778858-0-0(1))* WowZee Works Inc.
Shortley, Michele. Malarkey & the Big Trap. Krensky, Stephen. 2011. 29p. (J). pap. *(978-0-7680-3487-5(6))* SAE Intl.
—Once upon a Time in the Woods. Krensky, Stephen. 2011. (J). pap. *(978-0-7680-3488-2(4))* SAE Intl.
—The Three Little Pigs' Sledding Adventure. Krensky, Stephen. 2011. 28p. (J). pap. *(978-0-7680-3486-8(8))* SAE Intl.
Shoup, Andrew J. Andy & Elmer's Apple Dumpling Adventure Coloring & Activity Book. Shoup, Andrew J. 2007. 36p. (J). 3.95 *(978-0-9720436-2-5(4))* TokoBooks, LLC.
Shoutarou, Harada. Na Na Na Na. Shoutarou, Harada. 2006. 208p. (YA). Vol. 3. (Café Au Cult Ser.: 3). per. 9.95 *(978-1-59697-103-5(7));* Vol. 4. (Na Na Na Na Ser.: Vol. 4). per. 9.95 *(978-1-59697-104-2(5))* Infinity Studios LLC.
Showalter, Kristin. When Dogs Dream. Olsen, S. R. 2013. 48p. pap. 13.95 *(978-0-9842560-2-0(4))* Sleepy Dog Publishing.
Showalter, Sarah Evelyn. Animals of the Bible from A to Z. 2007. (J). (gr. -1-3). 16.95 *(978-0-87946-331-1(7))* ACTA Pubns.
Shreder, Etienne & Aubin, Antoine. The Curse of the 30 Pieces of Silver, Vol. 14, Pt. 2. Van Hamme, Jean. 2012. (Blake & Mortimer Ser.: 14). (ENG.). 64p. (J). (gr. 5-12). pap. 15.95 *(978-1-84918-130-3(6))* CineBook GBR. Dist: National Bk. Network.
Shrestha, Anuj. Hello Big Jay! Aryal, Aimee. 2004. 24p. (J). 14.95 *(978-1-932888-41-6(1))* Mascot Bks., Inc.
—Hello Herbie Husker! Aryal, Aimee. 2004. 24p. (J). 14.95 *(978-1-932888-43-0(8))* Mascot Bks., Inc.
—Hello Otto! Aryal, Aimee. 2004. 22p. (J). 19.95 *(978-0-9743442-2-5(2))* Mascot Bks., Inc.
—Let's Go Hoosiers! Aryal, Aimee. 2004. 24p. (J). 19.95 *(978-1-932888-32-4(2))* Mascot Bks., Inc.
—Lets Go Illini! Aryal, Aimee. 2004. 24p. (J). lib. bdg. 19.95 *(978-1-932888-21-8(7))* Mascot Bks., Inc.
—Let's Go Irish! Aryal, Aimee. 2004. 24p. (J). 19.95 *(978-0-9743442-5-6(7))* Mascot Bks., Inc.
Shrestha, Sudesha. Myra Kemp - Vol 1: I Need a Vacation from My Family. McKiver, Debbie. 2018. (Myra Kemp Ser.: Vol. 1). (ENG.). 92p. (J). (gr. 1-6). 22.99 *(978-0-692-18080-8(X))* McKiver, Debbie dba Strong & Healthy Temple.
Shrestha, Sudesha & Gautam, Anamika. Scared at School: Robbie. Moore, Kate. 2019. (Love, Always Ser.: Vol. 2). (ENG.). 34p. (J). pap. *(978-1-9995539-1-3(8))* Moore, Kate.
Shreve, Steve. The Adventures of Charlie: Bigfoot or the Value of a Smelly Friend. Shreve, Steve. 2010. (Adventures of Charlie Ser.). 32p. pap. *(978-0-237-54284-9(6))* Evans Brothers, Ltd.
—The Bogey Man: Or a Good Argument for Not Picking Your Nose. Shreve, Steve. 2010. (Adventures of Charlie Ser.). 32p. pap. *(978-0-237-54287-0(0))* Evans Brothers, Ltd.
—Monkey Island: Or the Advantage of Opposable Thumbs. Shreve, Steve. 2010. (Adventures of Charlie Ser.). 32p. pap. *(978-0-237-54288-7(9))* Evans Brothers, Ltd.
—Pirates: Or the Truth about Life on the High Seas. Shreve, Steve. 2010. (Adventures of Charlie Ser.). 32p. pap. *(978-0-237-54286-3(2))* Evans Brothers, Ltd.
—Stan & the Toilet Monster. Shreve, Steve. 2019. (ENG.). 160p. (J). (gr. 2-6). pap. 9.99 *(978-1-4778-4744-2(8),* 9781477847442, Two Lions) Amazon Publishing.
Shroades, John. Dragon at the North Pole. Klimo, Kate. 2013. (Dragon Keepers Ser.: 6). 176p. (J). (gr. 3-7). 15.99 *(978-0-375-87066-8(0),* Random Hse. Bks. for Young Readers) Random Hse. Children's Bks.
—The Dragon in the Driveway, 2. Klimo, Kate. 2009. (Dragon Keepers Ser.). (ENG.). 176p. (J). (gr. 4-6). lib. bdg. 21.19 *(978-0-375-95589-1(5))* Random House Publishing Group.
—The Dragon in the Driveway. Klimo, Kate. 2010. (Dragon Keepers Ser.: 2). 176p. (J). (gr. 3-7). pap. 7.99 *(978-0-375-85590-0(4),* Yearling) Random Hse. Children's Bks.
—Dragon in the Library. Klimo, Kate. 2011. (Dragon Keepers Ser.: 3). 240p. (J). (gr. 3-7). 7.99 *(978-0-375-85592-4(0),* Yearling) Random Hse. Children's Bks.
—The Dragon in the Library, 3. Klimo, Kate. 2011. (Dragon Keepers Ser.: No. 3). (ENG.). 224p. (J). (gr. 4-6). lib. bdg. 21.19 *(978-0-375-95591-4(7),* Yearling) Random Hse. Children's Bks.
—The Dragon in the Sea, 5. Klimo, Kate. 2012. (Dragon Keepers Ser.). (ENG.). 224p. (J). (gr. 4-6). lib. bdg. 22.44 *(978-0-375-97065-8(7))* Random Hse. Bks. for Young Readers.
—The Dragon in the Sock Drawer. Klimo, Kate. 2009. (Dragon Keepers Ser.: 1). (ENG.). 192p. (J). (gr. 3-7). 6.99 *(978-0-375-85588-7(2),* Yearling) Random Hse. Children's Bks.
—Dragon Keepers #4: the Dragon in the Volcano. Klimo, Kate. 2012. (Dragon Keepers Ser.: 4). (ENG.). 256p. (J). (gr. 3-7). 7.99 *(978-0-375-86688-3(4),* Yearling) Random Hse. Children's Bks.
—Dragon Keepers #5: the Dragon in the Sea. Klimo, Kate. 2013. (Dragon Keepers Ser.: 5). 224p. (J). (gr. 3-7). 7.99 *(978-0-375-87116-0(0),* Yearling) Random Hse. Children's Bks.
—Dragon Keepers #6: the Dragon at the North Pole. Klimo, Kate. 2014. (Dragon Keepers Ser.: 6). 176p. (J). (gr. 3-7). 6.99 *(978-0-375-87117-7(9),* Yearling) Random Hse. Children's Bks.
—Magical Creatures. Torpie, Kate. 2007. (ENG.). 24p. (J). (gr. 2-7). 19.99 *(978-1-58476-619-3(0),* IKIDS) Innovative Kids.
Shroades, John / W. The Great Grand Canyon Time Train. Lowell, Susan. 2011. 32p. (J). 15.95 *(978-1-933855-63-9(0))* Rio Nuevo Pubs.
Shroom, Rahima. Nana Yaa & the Golden Stool. Odg, Fuse. 2018. (ENG.). 20p. (J). pap. *(978-1-78623-420-9(3))* Grosvenor Hse. Publishing Ltd.
Shropshire, Sandy. Bone Head: Story of the Longhorn. Webber, Desiree Morrison. 2003. 74p. (J). 16.95 *(978-1-57168-763-0(7));* pap. 9.95 *(978-1-57168-750-0(5))* Eakin Pr. (Eakin Pr.).
Shrum, Edgar. When I Was Little. Cortez, Linda. 2009. 44p. pap. 19.99 *(978-1-4389-5934-4(6))* AuthorHouse.
Shtereb, Ksenia. We Love You More. Collazo, Heather. 2019. (ENG.). 34p. (J). pap. 9.95 ***(978-1-7075-9923-3(8))*** Independently Published.
Shubin, Jon. The Fairytale Fracas: A Shubin Cousins Adventure. Shubin, Masha. 2012. 200p. pap. 7.95 *(978-0-9792145-8-5(0))* Anno Domini.
Shubin, Trinity. The Bad Hare Day: A Shubin Cousins Adventure. Shubin, Masha. 2018. (ENG.). 204p. (J). pap. 9.95 *(978-1-939689-01-6(5))* Anno Domini.
Shue, Linda Nicole, jt. illus. see Wilson, Elisa.
Shuler, Douglas. Peek & Boo Are Looking for You. Radman, David. 2019. (ENG.). 38p. (J). (gr. k-5). pap. 14.95 ***(978-1-68433-405-6(5))*** Black Rose Writing.
Shulevitz, Uri. Dusk. Shulevitz, Uri. 2013. (ENG.). 32p. (J). (gr. -1-3). 19.99 *(978-0-374-31903-8(0),* 900083618, Farrar, Straus & Giroux (BYR)) Farrar, Straus & Giroux.
—How I Learned Geography. Shulevitz, Uri. 2008. (ENG.). 32p. (J). (gr. -1-3). 19.99 *(978-0-374-33499-4(4),* 900030472, Farrar, Straus & Giroux (BYR)) Farrar, Straus & Giroux.
—One Monday Morning. Shulevitz, Uri. 2003. (ENG.). 48p. (J). (gr. -1-1). reprint ed. pap. 8.99 *(978-0-374-45648-1(8),* 900021257) Square Fish.
—Rain Rain Rivers. Shulevitz, Uri. National Geographic Learning Staff. 2006. (ENG.). 32p. (J). (gr. -1-3). reprint ed. pap. 8.99 *(978-0-374-46195-9(3),* 900012475) Square Fish.
—Snow, 1 vol. Shulevitz, Uri. 2012. (ENG.). 34p. (J). (gr. -1-2). bds. 7.99 *(978-0-374-37093-0(1),* 900078982, Farrar, Straus & Giroux (BYR)) Farrar, Straus & Giroux.
—Snow. Shulevitz, Uri. 2004. (ENG.). 32p. (J). (gr. -1-2). reprint ed. pap. 8.99 *(978-0-374-46862-0(1),* 900024515) Square Fish.
—Snow Storytime Set. Shulevitz, Uri. unabr. ed. 2013. (Macmillan Young Listeners Story Time Sets Ser.). (ENG.). (J). 12.99 *(978-1-4272-4370-6(0),* 900135924) Macmillan Audio.
Shulman, Dee. Songbooks - Alligator Raggedy-Mouth: Making Music with Poems & Rhymes. Hanke, Maureen & Leedham, Jacalyn. Sanderson, Ana, ed. (ENG.). 64p. (J). pap. *(978-0-7136-4281-0(5),* A&C Black) Bloomsbury Publishing Plc.
Shulman, Dee & Tinkler, Dennis. Abracadabra Brass - Abracadabra Tutors: Abracadabra Brass - Bass Clef: the Way to Learn Through Songs & Tunes. Fraser, Dot & Fraser, Noel. Sebba, Jane, ed. 2005. (Abracadabra Ser.). (ENG.). 64p. (J). pap. 13.95 *(978-0-7136-7184-1(X))* HarperCollins Pubs. Ltd. GBR. Dist: Independent Pubs. Group.
Shulman, Mark. Fillmore & Geary Take Off! Fickling, Phillip. 2003. 40p. (J). lib. bdg. *(978-1-58717-258-8(5),* SeaStar Bks.) Chronicle Bks. LLC.
Shulte, Sara. Sandy's Aunt. Shulte, Sharon. 2004. (J). per. 12.00 *(978-0-9747147-5-2(5))* MK Publishing.
Shultz, Kirsten, photos by. Mermaid Cookbook, 1 vol. Beery, Barbara. 2008. (ENG., 64p. (J). (gr. 1). spiral bd. 14.99 *(978-1-4236-0417-4(2))* Gibbs Smith, Publisher.
Shulz, Dirk Erik. President of the World: Axe Cop. Nicolle, Malachai. Edidin, Rachel, ed. 2013. (Axe Cop Ser.). (ENG.). 96p. (J). (gr. 5-12). pap. 12.99 *(978-1-61655-057-8(0))* Dark Horse Comics.
Shum, Benson. Go to Sheep. Sattler, Jennifer. 2019. (ENG.). 24p. (J). (gr. -1 — 1). bds. 7.99 *(978-1-5344-0395-6(7),* Little Simon) Little Simon.
—Hide 'n' Sheep. Sattler, Jennifer. 2019. (ENG.). 24p. (J). (gr. -1 — 1). bds. 7.99 *(978-1-5344-0397-0(3),* Little Simon) Little Simon.
—Sloth Went. Lehrhaupt, Adam. 2020. (ENG.). 32p. (J). 17.99 *(978-1-5476-0245-2(7),* 900207573, Bloomsbury Children's Bks.) Bloomsbury Publishing USA.
Shum, Benson. Holly's Day at the Pool: Walt Disney Animation Studios Artist Showcase. Shum, Benson. 2017. (Walt Disney Animation Studios Artist Showcase Ser.). (ENG.). 40p. (J). (gr. -1-k). 16.99 *(978-1-4847-0938-2(1))* Disney Pr.
Shumaker, Randi Bethel. Scoodles Gets Married. Plettner, Edith D. 2019. (Scoodles Gets Married Scoodles the Pup Ser.: Vol. 9). (ENG.). 36p. (J). pap. 10.00 *(978-1-9877-8865-5(6))* CreateSpace Independent Publishing Platform.
—Scoodles Proposes. Plettner, Edith D. 2019. (Scoodles Proposes Scoodles the Pup Ser.: Vol. 8). (ENG.). 38p. (J). pap. 10.00 *(978-1-9876-5585-8(0))* CreateSpace Independent Publishing Platform.
Shumate, A. Michael. Princess Foo & Bizaboo. Shumate, A. Michael. 2018. (ENG.). 34p. (J). (gr. k-3). pap. *(978-0-9950584-6-0(6))* Elfstone Press.
Shupe, Bobbi & Crum, Anna-Maria. Spiders: Read Well Level K Unit 1 Storybook. Sprick, Marilyn et al. 2003. (Read Well Level K Ser.). 20p. (J). *(978-1-57035-673-5(4))* Cambium Education, Inc.
—Spiders: Unit 1 Read Well Level K Teacher's Storybook. Sprick, Marilyn et al. 2003. (Read Well Level K Ser.). 20p. (J). *(978-1-57035-696-4(3))* Cambium Education, Inc.
Shupe, Kyla. Grammy Gets Treed. Saunders, Catherine. 2019. (Grammy Tales Ser.: Vol. 3). (ENG.). 48p. (J). pap. 10.99 ***(978-1-945669-97-2(7))*** Kids Bk. Pr.
Shurbet, Lilly. The Many Worlds of Rorlitzer Screw. Morgado, Juliana. 2019. (ENG.). 80p. (YA). pap. 8.99 *(978-1-4808-7500-5(7))* Archway Publishing.
Shurei, Kouyu. Return to Labyrinth, 4 vols., Vol. 2. Forbes, Jake T. & Jake, T. F. 2007. (Return to Labyrinth Ser.). 192p. pap. 9.99 *(978-1-59816-726-9(X))* TOKYOPOP, Inc.
Shurei, Kouyu. Alichino. Shurei, Kouyu. 2005. Vol. 1. 164p. pap. 14.99 *(978-1-59532-478-8(X));* Vol. 2. rev. ed. 160p. pap. 14.99 *(978-1-59532-479-5(8));* Vol. 3. 3rd rev. ed. 160p. per. 14.99 *(978-1-59532-480-1(1))* TOKYOPOP, Inc. (Tokyopop Kids).
Shurtliff, Ryan. The WoolaBulla & the Flaming Condor of Three-Finger Tower. Thurman, Jeffrey. 2019. (Woolabulla Adventures Ser.: Vol. 1). (ENG.). 92p. (J). pap. 7.99 ***(978-1-0830-2031-4(5))*** Independently Published.
Shurtliff, William. Today Someone I Love Passed Away. Ahern, Dianne. 2008. 82p. (J). *(978-0-9679437-4-9(4))* En Route Bks. & Media.
Shusterman, Brendan. Challenger Deep. Shusterman, Neal. (ENG.). 320p. (YA). (gr. 9). 2016. pap. 10.99 *(978-0-06-113414-2(7));* 2015. 17.99 *(978-0-06-113411-1(2))* HarperCollins Pubs. (HarperTeen).
Shusterman, Danielle. Chimps Use Sticks. Cline, Gina. 2012. (1B Animal Behaviors Ser.). (ENG.). 32p. (J). pap. 8.00 *(978-1-61406-689-7(2))* American Reading Co.
Shute, A. B. With Washington in the West or A Soldier Boy's Battles in the Wilderness. Stratemeyer, Edward. 2004. reprint ed. pap. 30.95 *(978-1-4179-2977-1(4))* Kessinger Publishing, LLC.
Shute, A. B. & Fitterling, Michael A. Fighting for the Right. Optic, Oliver. 2005. (Blue & Gray Ser.). (ENG.). 365p. (J). (gr. 4-7). reprint ed. pap. 19.99 *(978-1-890623-12-8(1))* Lost Classic Bks.
Shute, Linda. Captain John Smith's Big & Beautiful Bay, 1 vol. Jones, Rebecca C. 2011. (ENG.). 32p. (gr. 3-6). 14.99 *(978-0-7643-3869-4(2),* 9780764338694, Schiffer Publishing Ltd) Schiffer Publishing, Ltd.
Shutterstock. My First Book of What Is This? McFarland, Jake. 2020. (ENG.). 16p. (J). bds. ***(978-1-64269-257-0(3),*** 863ed8a6-d0e5-42ab-89dc-311d4c3190f6, Sequoia Publishing & Media LLC) Phoenix International Publications, Inc.
Shutterstock, photos by. Baby Einstein: Pop! Goes the Zebra. Wage, Erin Rose. 2019. (Play-A-Sound Ser.). (ENG., 20p. (J). bds. ***(978-1-5037-4657-2(7),*** 5935a215-7d11-487c-abc2-939c543a2fda, p i kids) Phoenix International Publications, Inc.
Shutterstock, photos by. Britannica Kids: Lift & Learn: Baby Animals. 2020. (ENG., 20p. (J). *(978-1-5037-5216-0(X),* d8d4ef28-8991-4b4e-b896-9d61383d1f61, p i kids) Phoenix International Publications, Inc.
Shutterstock.com. Apples & Oranges. Broderick, Kathy. 2019. (Brain Games for Babies Ser.). (ENG.). 20p. (J). *(978-1-5037-4651-0(8),* 6736fed5-40dc-4261-9f40-e1cc91d81a23, p i kids) Phoenix International Publications, Inc.
—Around the World. Broderick, Kathy. 2019. (What Do You See? Ser.). (ENG.). 20p. (J). *(978-1-5037-4628-2(3),* b7492c30-1b70-45ad-a6b0-f69b229e274c, p i kids) Phoenix International Publications, Inc.
—Fingers & Toes. Skwish, Emily. 2019. (Brain Games for Babies! Ser.). (ENG.). 20p. (J). *(978-1-5037-4652-7(6),* f20741ea-a96f-4ee1-9b01-71c092fcb5f0, p i kids) Phoenix International Publications, Inc.
Shutterstock.com, photos by. Baby Einstein: Busy World. Skwish, Emily. 2020. (ENG., 20p. (J). bds. *(978-1-5037-5237-5(2),* 12877cec-3203-4655-b1b2-c14e5eef0c9e, p i kids) Phoenix International Publications, Inc.
—Baby Einstein: Look & See with Me! Wagner, Veronica. 2020. (Look & Find Ser.). (ENG., 14p. (J). bds. *(978-1-5037-5257-3(7),* a60ebf97-9f2d-47fb-8c3e-3a5684d8b700, p i kids) Phoenix International Publications, Inc.
—Baby Einstein: Splish! Splash! Bath! Broderick, Kathy. 2019. (ENG., 6p. (J). *(978-1-5037-5133-0(3),* 5a08d0a3-00dd-4b06-833e-d99739a776e3, p i kids) Phoenix International Publications, Inc.
Shutterstock.com Staff, photos by. Baby Einstein: Rainbow Bath! Halpern, Rachel. 2019. (ENG., 6p. (J). *(978-1-5037-5134-7(1),* 444919ee-6322-47c9-98e0-cf15580635c8, p i kids) Phoenix International Publications, Inc.
Shuttlewood, Craig. Through the Town: A Follow-The-Trail Book. Howarth, Katie. 2015. (ENG.). 10p. (J). (gr. -1 — 1). bds. 6.99 *(978-1-4998-0076-0(2))* Little Bee Books Inc.
Shuttlewood, Craig. Awesome! Shuttlewood, Craig. 2018. (ENG.). 32p. (J). (gr. k-2). 15.95 *(978-1-68446-013-7(1),* 138906, Capstone Editions) Capstone.
Shuttleworth, Cathie. The Bunny Tales Collection: Twelve Lively Stories of Rascally Rabbits. Baxter, Nicola. 2014. 80p. (J). (gr. -1-3). pap. 9.99 *(978-1-84322-934-6(X),* Armadillo) Anness Publishing GBR. Dist: National Bk. Network.
—Celtic Tales & Legends. Baxter, Nicola. 2012. (ENG.). 80p. (J). (gr. 2-7). pap. 9.99 *(978-1-84322-950-6(1))* Anness Publishing GBR. Dist: National Bk. Network.
—The Children's Treasury of Classic Poetry. 176p. (J). pap. *(978-1-84322-143-2(8))* Bookmart Ltd.
—Classic Collection of Fairy Tales & Poems, 2 vols. 2014. (ENG.). 192p. (J). (gr. 2-12). 19.99 *(978-1-84322-972-8(2),* Armadillo) Anness Publishing GBR. Dist: National Bk. Network.
—Classic Poetry for Children. Baxter, Nicola. 2013. (ENG.). 80p. (J). (gr. k-4). pap. 9.99 *(978-1-84322-820-2(3))* Anness Publishing GBR. Dist: National Bk. Network.
—Little Tales for Toddlers: 35 Stories about Adorable Teddy Bears, Puppies & Bunnies. 2013. (ENG.). 256p. pap. 14.99 *(978-1-84322-925-4(0))* Anness Publishing GBR. Dist: National Bk. Network.
—My Book of Magical Pony Tales: 12 Beautifully Illustrated Stories. Baxter, Nicola. 2013. (ENG.). 80p. (J). (gr. -1-12). pap. 9.99 *(978-1-84322-965-0(X))* Anness Publishing GBR. Dist: National Bk. Network.
—The Puppy Tales Collection: Twelve Silly Stories from Houndsville. Baxter, Nicola. 2014. 80p. (J). (gr. k-5). pap. 9.99 *(978-1-84322-935-3(8),* Armadillo) Anness Publishing GBR. Dist: National Bk. Network.
—Rhymes for Playtime Fun. Baxter, Nicola. 2013. (ENG.). 80p. (J). (gr. -1-k). pap. 9.99 *(978-1-84322-921-6(8))* Anness Publishing GBR. Dist: National Bk. Network.
—Stories for Little Ones. Baxter, Nicola. 2018. (ENG.). 256p. (J). (gr. -1-12). 9.99 *(978-0-85723-894-8(9),* Armadillo) Anness Publishing GBR. Dist: National Bk. Network.
—Tales from the Farmyard: 12 Stories of Grunting Pigs, Quacking Ducks, Clucking Hens, Neighing Horses, Bleating Sheep & Other Animals. Baxter, Nicola. 2013. (ENG.). 80p. (J). (gr. 1-8). pap. 9.99 *(978-1-84322-899-8(8))* Anness Publishing GBR. Dist: National Bk. Network.
—Traditional Fairy Tales from Hans Christian Andersen & the Brothers Grimm. Baxter, Nicola. 2013. (ENG.). 192p. (J). (gr. 1-7). pap. 14.99 *(978-1-84322-971-1(4))* Anness Publishing GBR. Dist: National Bk. Network.
Shuttleworth, Cathy. The Classic Collection of Fairy Tales. Grimm, Jacob et al. 2011. (ENG.). 192p. (J). (gr. -1-12). 9.99 *(978-1-84322-787-8(8))* Anness Publishing GBR. Dist: National Bk. Network.
—Classic Poems for Children: Classic Verse from the Great Poets, Including Lewis Carroll, John Keats & Walt Whitman. 2011. (ENG.). 192p. (J). (gr. -1-12). 9.99 *(978-1-84322-788-5(6))* Anness Publishing GBR. Dist: National Bk. Network.
Shvart?s?man, L. Kotenok Po Imeni Gav. Oster, Grigorii. 2016. (RUS.). 61p. (J). *(978-5-17-092460-8(7))* AST Ltd., Izdatel'stvo.
Shyam. Kumari Loves a Monster: Kumariyin Ratcaca Katalan. Devadasan, Rashmi Ruth. 2010. (TAM & ENG.). 52p. pap. 17.95 *(978-93-80636-01-6(6))* Blaft Pubns.
Si, Zoe. The Sorry Plane. MacNamara, Deborah. 2019. (ENG.). 34p. (J). (gr. k-3). pap. ***(978-0-9950512-3-2(2))*** Aona Bks.
Si, Zoe. Wolfie & Fly. Fagan, Cary. 2018. (Wolfie & Fly Ser.). (ENG.). 96p. (J). (gr. 2-5). pap. 8.99 *(978-1-101-91939-2(6),* Tundra Bks.) Tundra Bks. CAN. Dist: Penguin Random Hse. LLC.
—Wolfie And Fly: Band On The Run. Fagan, Cary. 2018. (Wolfie & Fly Ser.). 96p. (J). (gr. 2-5). 14.99 *(978-1-101-91823-4(3),* Tundra Bks.) Tundra Bks. CAN. Dist: Penguin Random Hse. LLC.

Sias, Ryan. Meet Woof & Quack (reader) Swenson, Jamie. 2017. (Green Light Readers Level 1 Ser.). (ENG.). 32p. (J). (gr. -1-3). 12.99 *(978-0-544-95951-4(5)*, 1661276); pap. 3.99 *(978-0-544-95928-6(0)*, 1661274) Houghton Mifflin Harcourt Publishing Co. (HMH Books For Young Readers).

—Woof & Quack in Winter (reader) Swenson, Jamie. 2017. (Green Light Readers Level 1 Ser.). (ENG.). 32p. (J). (gr. -1-3). 12.99 *(978-0-544-95949-1(3)*, 1661275); pap. 3.99 *(978-0-544-95902-6(7)*, 1661277) Houghton Mifflin Harcourt Publishing Co. (HMH Books For Young Readers).

Siau, John. Retrieving with Evie. Harp, Susan. 2007. (ENG.). 24p. (J). lib. bdg. 12.95 *(978-1-932439-67-0(6))* M.T. Publishing Co., Inc.

Siau, Jon. Evie Goes Clean & Green. Harp, Susan. 2013. 24p. (J). lib. bdg. 14.95 *(978-1-938730-09-2(7))* M.T. Publishing Co., Inc.

Sibbick, John. My Favorite Dinosaurs. Ashby, Ruth. 2005. 32p. (J). (gr. 1-3). 16.95 *(978-0-689-03921-8(2))* ibooks, Inc.

Sibert, Stephanie Grace. A Royal Tea. Boyce, Catherine & Boyce, Peter. 2006. 32p. (J). per. 16.95 *(978-0-9778420-1-8(0))* Semper Studio.

—Tea with the Queen. Boyce, Catherine & Boyce, Peter. 2006. 32p. (J). per. 16.95 net. incl. audio compact disk *(978-0-9778420-0-1(2)*, 10,000) Semper Studio.

Sibley, Mason. Green Dinosaur Pancakes, 1 vol. Pigott, Kat. 2016. (ENG.). 32p. (J). (gr. k-3). 16.99 *(978-1-4556-2177-4(3)*, Pelican Publishing) Arcadia Publishing.

—I See You, Green Dinosaur, 1 vol. Pigott, Kat. 2019. (Green Dinosaur Ser.). (ENG.). 32p. (J). (gr. -1-3). 16.99 *(978-1-4556-2418-8(7)*, Pelican Publishing) Arcadia Publishing.

Sibley O'Brien, Anne. Moon Watchers: Shirin's Ramadan Miracle, 1 vol. Jalali, Reza. 2017. (ENG.). 32p. (J). (gr. 1-7). pap. 8.95 *(978-0-88448-587-2(0)*, 884587) Tilbury Hse. Pubs.

—Talking Walls: Discover Your World, 1 vol. Burns Knight, Margy. 2017. (ENG.). 64p. (J). (gr. 2-7). pap. 9.95 *(978-0-88448-576-6(5)*, 884576) Tilbury Hse. Pubs.

—Welcoming Babies, 1 vol. Burns Knight, Margy. 2nd ed. 2018. (ENG.). 40p. (J). (gr. -1-2). 13.95 *(978-0-88448-641-1(9)*, 884641) Tilbury Hse. Pubs.

—Who Belongs Here? An American Story, 1 vol. Burns Knight, Margy. 2nd ed. 2018. (ENG.). 48p. (J). (gr. 2-7). 17.95 *(978-0-88448-639-8(7)*, 884639) Tilbury Hse. Pubs.

Sichel, Harold. Captain Billie: Leads the way to the land of I don't want To. Gates, Josephine Scribner. 2007. 96p. (J). lib. bdg. 59.00 *(978-1-60304-019-8(6))* Dollworks.

Sickler, Jonas. Indestructibles: Frere Jacques. 2011. (Indestructibles Ser.). (ENG.). 12p. (J). (gr. k — 1). pap. 5.95 *(978-0-7611-5923-0(1)*, 15923) Workman Publishing Co., Inc.

—Indestructibles: Hey Diddle Diddle. 2010. (Indestructibles Ser.). (ENG.). 12p. (J). (gr. k — 1). pap. 5.95 *(978-0-7611-5862-2(6)*, 15862) Workman Publishing Co., Inc.

—Indestructibles: Hickory Dickory Dock. 2011. (Indestructibles Ser.). (ENG.). 12p. (J). (gr. k — 1). pap. 5.95 *(978-0-7611-5921-6(5)*, 15921) Workman Publishing Co., Inc.

—Indestructibles: Old MacDonald Had a Farm. 2011. (Indestructibles Ser.). (ENG.). 12p. (J). (gr. k — 1). pap. 5.95 *(978-0-7611-5922-3(3)*, 15922) Workman Publishing Co., Inc.

Sicolo, Daniel. Declan's Day. Lauder, Jessica. 2019. (ENG.). 32p. (J). *(978-1-5255-3608-3(7))*; pap. *(978-1-5255-3609-0(5))* FriesenPress.

Sicuro, Aimée. Bright Sky, Starry City, 1 vol. Krishnaswami, Uma. 2015. (ENG.). 32p. (J). (gr. k-4). 17.95 *(978-1-55498-405-3(X))* Groundwood Bks. CAN. Dist: Publishers Group West (PGW).

Sicuro, Aimee. Dancing Through Fields of Color: The Story of Helen Frankenthaler. Brown, Elizabeth. 2019. (ENG.). 40p. (J). (gr. -1-3). 18.99 *(978-1-4197-3410-6(5)*, Abrams Bks. for Young Readers) Abrams, Inc.

Sicuro, Aimée. I Feel Teal. Rille, Lauren. 2018. (ENG.). 40p. (J). (gr. -1-3). 17.99 *(978-1-4814-5846-7(9)*, Beach Lane Bks.) Beach Lane Bks.

—The Moon Inside, 1 vol. Feder, Sandra V. 2016. 32p. (J). (-k). 17.95 *(978-1-55498-823-5(3))* Groundwood Bks. CAN. Dist: Publishers Group West (PGW).

Siddiqa, Juma. My Arabic Words Book. 2007. (ENG.). 30p. (J). (gr. -1-6). 18.00 *(978-1-879402-33-1(5))* Tahrike Tarsile Quran, Inc.

Sidong, Li. Beowulf. 2010. (Graphic Classics Ser.). (ENG.). 48p. (J). (gr. 5-8). 19.95 *(978-0-7641-6301-2(9)*, B.E.S. Publishing) Peterson's.

Sidong, Li, jt. illus. see Gelev, Penko.

Sidwell, Kathy. Ethan Goes Green. Bell, Holly. 2009. 32p. pap. 12.99 *(978-1-4389-0115-2(1))* AuthorHouse.

Siebel, Fritz. Amelia Bedelia. Parish, Peggy. (I Can Read Level 2 Ser.). (ENG.). (J). 2017. 72p. (gr. -1-3). 9.99 *(978-0-06-257279-0(2))*; 50th ed. 2012. 64p. (gr. k-3). pap. 4.99 *(978-0-06-444155-1(5))* HarperCollins Pubs. (Greenwillow Bks.).

—Amelia Bedelia. Parish, Peggy. ed. 2012. (Amelia Bedelia: I Can Read! Ser.: 1). (J). (gr. 1-3). lib. bdg. 13.55 *(978-0-88103-916-0(0))* Turtleback.

—Amelia Bedelia Book & CD. Parish, Peggy. abr. ed. 2005. (I Can Read Level 2 Ser.). (ENG.). 64p. (J). (gr. k-3). audio compact disk 9.99 *(978-0-06-078700-4(7)*, HarperFestival) HarperCollins Pubs.

Siebel, Fritz, et al. Amelia Bedelia I Can Read Box Set #1: Amelia Bedelia Hit the Books, Set. Parish, Peggy. 2016. (I Can Read Level 2 Ser.). (ENG.). 320p. (J). (gr. -1-3). pap. 19.99 *(978-0-06-244356-4(9)*, Greenwillow Bks.) HarperCollins Pubs.

Siebel, Fritz. Cat & Dog. Minarik, Else Holmelund. 60th ed. 2017. (My First I Can Read Ser.). (ENG.). 40p. (J). (gr. -1-3). 9.99 *(978-0-06-265174-7(9))* HarperCollins Pubs.

—A Fly Went By. McClintock, Mike. 2007. (Beginner Ser.). (ENG.). 68p. pap. *(978-0-00-722482-1(6)*, HarperCollins Children's Bks.) HarperCollins Pubs. Ltd.

Siebel, Fritz, jt. illus. see Sweat, Lynn.

Siebold, Erin. Papa's Beach. Steeves, Lynn. 2020. (ENG.). 24p. (J). ***(978-1-5255-6150-4(2))***; pap. ***(978-1-5255-6151-1(0))*** FriesenPress.

Siebold, J. Otto. The Pig in the Spigot. Wilbur, Richard. 2004. (J). reprint ed. pap. 7.00 *(978-0-15-525066-6(3)*, Voyager Books/Libros Viajeros) Harcourt Children's Bks. CAN. Dist: Allen, Thomas & Son, Ltd.

Siebold, Kim. Starry Night, Hold Me Tight. Sagendorph, Jean. 2015. (ENG.). 18p. (J). (gr. -1 — 1). bds. 6.95 *(978-0-7624-5853-0(4)*, Running Pr. Kids) Running Pr.

Sieg, Katharina. Gnawed Stories. Andrés, Jose Carlos. 2019. (ENG.). 32p. (J). (gr. -1-k). 16.95 *(978-84-16566-95-2(X))* Ediciones La Fragatina ESP. Dist: Independent Pubs. Group.

Siegel, Mark. Boogie Knights. Wheeler, Lisa. 2008. (ENG.). 40p. (J). (gr. -1-3). 16.99 *(978-0-689-87639-4(4)*, Atheneum/Richard Jackson Bks.) Simon & Schuster Children's Publishing.

—How to Read a Story: (Illustrated Children's Book, Picture Book for Kids, Read Aloud Kindergarten Books) Messner, Kate. 2015. (ENG.). 32p. (J). (gr. k-3). 16.99 *(978-1-4521-1233-6(9))* Chronicle Bks. LLC.

—How to Write a Story: (Read-Aloud Book, Learn to Read & Write) Messner, Kate. 2020. (ENG.). 36p. (J). (gr. k-3). 17.99 *(978-1-4521-5666-8(2))* Chronicle Bks. LLC.

—Long Night Moon. Rylant, Cynthia. 2004. (ENG.). 32p. (J). (gr. -1-3). 18.99 *(978-0-689-85426-2(9)*, Simon & Schuster Bks. For Young Readers) Simon & Schuster Bks. For Young Readers.

—Oskar & the Eight Blessings. Simon, Tanya & Simon, Richard. 2015. (ENG.). 40p. (J). (gr. -1-3). 18.99 *(978-1-59643-949-8(1)*, 900123918) Roaring Brook Pr.

—Seadogs: An Epic Ocean Operetta. Wheeler, Lisa. 2006. (ENG.). 40p. (J). (gr. 2-5). reprint ed. 7.99 *(978-1-4169-4103-3(7)*, Atheneum Bks. for Young Readers) Simon & Schuster Children's Publishing.

—To Dance: Special Edition. Siegel, Siena Cherson. 2019. (ENG.). 88p. (J). (gr. 3-9). 19.99 *(978-1-4814-8663-7(2))*; pap. 11.99 *(978-1-4814-8664-4(0))* Simon & Schuster Children's Publishing. (Atheneum Bks. for Young Readers).

Siegel, Melanie. Isabella & Ivan Build an Interview. Ingalls, Ann. 2012. (Writing Builders Ser.). 32p. (J). (gr. 2-4). pap. 11.94 *(978-1-60357-389-4(5))*; lib. bdg. 25.27 *(978-1-59953-509-8(2))* Norwood Hse. Pr.

Siegel, Melanie. I Brought My Rat for Show-and-Tell. Siegel, Melanie, tr. Horton, Joan. 2004. (Penguin Young Readers, Level 3 Ser.). 48p. (J). (gr. 1-3). mass mkt. 4.99 *(978-0-448-43364-6(8)*, Penguin Young Readers) Penguin Young Readers Group.

Siegel, William. The Jumping-Off Place. McNeely, Marian Hurd. 2017. (ENG.). 320p. pap. 9.95 *(978-0-486-81568-8(4))* Dover Pubns., Inc.

—The Jumping-off Place. McNeely, Marian Hurd. 2008. 320p. (J). pap. 15.95 *(978-0-9798940-4-6(2)*, South Dakota State Historical Society Pr.) South Dakota Historical Society Pr.

Siegler, Karelyn. The First Thanksgiving. White, Amy. 2008. (Fácil de Leer / Easy to Read Ser.). (ENG.). 16p. (J). pap. 5.99 ***(978-1-59820-565-7(X)***, Santillana Texto) Santillana USA Publishing Co., Inc.

Siegrist, Wes. Realm of the Panther: A Story of South Florida's Forests. Costello, Emily. 2005. (Habitat Ser.). (ENG.). 32p. (J). (gr. 1-4). 15.95 *(978-1-56899-847-3(3))*; pap. 6.95 *(978-1-56899-848-0(1))* Soundprints.

Siema, Tony. Bundle of Secrets: Savita Returns Home. Kirmani, Mubina Hassanali. Castro, Isabel, tr. 2018. (SPA.). 34p. (J). pap. 9.90 *(978-1-7905-4803-3(9))* Independently Published.

Siemens, Wendy. Whatwhat! Damircheli, Majid. 2019. (ENG.). 42p. (J). 27.95 ***(978-1-64531-449-3(9))*** Newman Springs Publishing, Inc.

Siemensma, Hanneke. Little Wise Wolf. van der Hammen, Gijs. Watkinson, Laura, tr. 2020. (ENG.). 34p. (J). (gr. -1-2). 17.99 ***(978-1-5253-0549-8(2))*** Kids Can Pr., Ltd. CAN. Dist: Hachette Bk. Group.

Siems, Annika. Into the Deep: An Exploration of Our Oceans. Dreyer, Wolfgang. 2019. (ENG.). 96p. (J). (gr. 2). 25.00 *(978-3-7913-7390-4(0))* Prestel Verlag GmbH & Co KG. DEU. Dist: Penguin Random Hse. LLC.

Sienkiewicz, Bill & Green, Timothy. Trollhunters: Tales of Arcadia the Secret History of Trollkind. Dreamworks et al. 2018. (ENG.). 72p. (gr. 3-7). 10.99 *(978-1-5067-0289-6(9))* Dark Horse Comics.

Sierra, Holly. Cinabrio y la Isla de las Sombras, Bk. 7. Sweet, J. H. et al. Rabascall, Iolanda, tr. 2009. (SPA.). 124p. (J). (gr. 3-5). 11.95 *(978-84-92691-43-2(3))* Roca Editorial ESP. Dist: Spanish Pubs., LLC.

—Just Like Mom. Hiris, Monica. 2005. (ENG.). 8p. (gr. k-1). pap. 7.95 *(978-1-57874-088-8(6)*, Kaeden Bks.) Kaeden Corp.

—Snapdragon & the Odyssey of Élan. Sweet, J. H. 2009. (J). Non-ISBN Publisher.

Sierra, Juan. El Pirata de la Pata de Palo. Arciniegas, Triunfo. 2003. (Primer Acto: Teatro Infantil y Juvenil Ser.). (SPA.). 51p. (J). (gr. -1-7). pap. *(978-958-30-0321-9(2))* Panamericana Editorial.

—Thank You Universe. Roberts, Karen O. 2018. (ENG.). 24p. (J). pap. 9.95 *(978-1-5088-3523-3(3))* CreateSpace Independent Publishing Platform.

Sierra, Juan Ramon. El Intripido Simon: Aventuras del Libertador. Bastidas Padilla, Carlos. 2004. (Literatura Juvenil (Panamericana Editorial) Ser.). (SPA.). 252p. (YA). (gr. -1-7). pap. *(978-958-30-0354-7(9))* Panamericana Editorial.

—Razzgo, Indo y Zaz. Nino, Jairo Anibal. 2004. (Literatura Juvenil (Panamericana Editorial) Ser.). (SPA.). 128p. (YA). (gr. 4-7). pap. *(978-958-30-0292-2(5))* Panamericana Editorial.

Sievers, Lee. Beebear 2. Follett, Ross C. 2013. (ENG.). 52p. (J). (gr. -1-3). 15.95 *(978-0-9881748-0-1(4)*, Oddint Media) Greenwood Hill Pr.

Sievert, Claus. The Lion & the Puppy: And Other Stories for Children. Tolstoy, Leo & Riordan, James. Riordan, James, tr. 2012. 76p. (J). (gr. 4-7). 16.95 *(978-1-61608-484-4(7)*, 608484, Sky Pony Pr.) Skyhorse Publishing Co., Inc.

Sievert, Tim. The Big Book of Monsters: The Creepiest Creatures from Classic Literature. Johnson, Hal. 2019. (ENG.). 176p. (J). (gr. 4-8). 16.95 *(978-1-5235-0711-5(X)*, 100711) Workman Publishing Co., Inc.

Siewart, Pauline. Look What I Can Do! 2009. (Watch This! Ser.). 32p. (J). (gr. -1-k). 25.60 *(978-1-60754-452-4(0))*; pap. 10.55 *(978-1-60754-453-1(9))* Windmill Bks.

—Look What I Can Make! 2009. (Watch This! Ser.). 32p. (J). (gr. -1-k). 25.60 *(978-1-60754-446-3(6))*; pap. 10.55 *(978-1-60754-447-0(4))* Windmill Bks.

—Look What I Can Play! 2009. (Watch This! Ser.). 32p. (J). (gr. -1-k). 25.60 *(978-1-60754-458-6(X))*; pap. 10.55 *(978-1-60754-586-6(1))* Windmill Bks.

—See What I Can Do! 2009. (Watch This! Ser.). 32p. (J). (gr. -1-k). 25.60 *(978-1-60754-455-5(5))*; pap. 10.55 *(978-1-60754-456-2(3))* Windmill Bks.

—See What I Can Make! 2009. (Watch This! Ser.). 32p. (J). (gr. -1-k). 25.60 *(978-1-60754-449-4(0))*; pap. 10.55 *(978-1-60754-450-0(4))* Windmill Bks.

—See What I Can Play! 2009. (Watch This! Ser.). 32p. (J). (gr. -1-k). 25.60 *(978-1-60754-461-6(X))*; pap. 10.55 *(978-1-60754-462-3(8))* Windmill Bks.

—3-Minute Sleepytime Stories. Baxter, Nicola. 2013. (ENG.). 80p. (J). (gr. -1-3). pap. 9.99 *(978-1-84322-977-3(3)*, Armadillo) Anness Publishing GBR. Dist: National Bk. Network.

Siewert, Pauline. Christmas Cookie Day!, 1 vol. Knudson, Tara. 2018. (ENG.). 16p. (J). bds. 9.99 *(978-0-310-76289-8(8))* Zonderkidz.

—Easter Egg Day, 1 vol. Knudson, Tara. 2020. 16p. (J). bds. 9.99 *(978-0-310-76752-7(0))* Zonderkidz.

—Guided by His Light: A Child's Bedtime Prayer Book. Jones, Susan. 2017. (ENG.). 64p. (J). (gr. k). 9.99 *(978-1-68099-282-3(1)*, Good Bks.) Skyhorse Publishing Co., Inc.

—It's Valentine's Day! A Valentine Book & Activity Kit. 2005. 10p. (J). bds. 9.95 *(978-1-58117-377-2(6)*, Intervisual/Piggy Toes) Bendon, Inc.

—Jingle Bells. Pierpont, James Lord. 2015. (ENG.). 14p. (J). (— 1). 12.99 *(978-0-7636-8197-5(0))* Candlewick Pr.

—My Very First Christmas Story, 1 vol. David, Juliet. ed. 2015. (ENG.). 28p. (J). (gr. -1-k). 7.99 *(978-1-78128-231-1(5)*, Candle Bks.) Lion Hudson PLC GBR. Dist: Independent Pubs. Group.

Sif, Birgitta. Miss Hazeltine's Home for Shy & Fearful Cats. Potter, Alicia. 2015. (ENG.). 40p. (J). (gr. k-3). 16.99 *(978-0-385-75334-0(9))*; lib. bdg. 19.99 *(978-0-385-75335-7(7))* Random Hse. Children's Bks. (Knopf Bks. for Young Readers).

—My Big, Dumb, Invisible Dragon. Lucas, Angie. 2019. (ENG.). 32p. (J). 17.95 *(978-1-68364-184-1(1)*, 900220901) Sounds True, Inc.

—Snowboy & the Last Tree Standing. Oram, Hiawyn. 2018. (ENG.). 32p. (J). (gr. -1-2). 16.99 *(978-0-7636-9572-9(6))* Candlewick Pr.

—The Tall Man & the Small Mouse. Bergman, Mara. 2019. (ENG.). 32p. (J). (-k). 16.99 *(978-1-5362-0168-0(5))* Candlewick Pr.

Sif, Birgitta. Frances Dean Who Loved to Dance & Dance. Sif, Birgitta. 2014. 32p. (J). (gr. -1-3). 16.99 *(978-0-7636-7306-2(4))* Candlewick Pr.

—Oliver. Sif, Birgitta. 2012. (ENG.). 40p. (J). (gr. -1-3). 16.99 *(978-0-7636-6247-9(X))* Candlewick Pr.

Signorino, Slug. I Know an Old Lady Who Swallowed a Fly: A Traditional Rhyme. 2004. 16p. (J). (gr. k-4). reprint ed. pap. 10.00 *(978-0-7567-9066-0(2))* DIANE Publishing Co.

Sikorskaia, Margarita. Give Her a Pixie. Shaw, Nancy Jo. 2016. (ENG.). (J). *(978-1-59298-723-8(0))* Beaver's Pond Pr., Inc.

—If You Look up to the Sky. Dalton, Angela. 2017. (ENG.). (J). 17.95 *(978-1-59298-828-0(8))* Beaver's Pond Pr., Inc.

—Ozzie Finds a Home. Schrenk, Lorenz. 2016. (Roundhouse Cat Ser.: Vol. 1). (ENG.). (J). 14.95 *(978-1-59298-685-9(4))* Beaver's Pond Pr., Inc.

—Valentine Dilemma: A Josie Story. Shaw, Nancy Jo. 2017. (ENG.). (J). (gr. -1-3). 16.95 *(978-1-59298-657-6(9))* Beaver's Pond Pr., Inc.

Sikoryak, Bob, jt. illus. see Davis, Guy.

Siku & Thomas, Richard, Jr. The Lion Comic Book Hero Bible. Anderson, Jeff & Thomas, Richard. ed. 2015. (ENG.). 192p. 19.95 *(978-0-7459-5617-6(3)*, Lion Books) Lion Hudson PLC GBR. Dist: Independent Pubs. Group.

Sil, Avijit. The Epic Adventures of Chandrini Yogini: Chandrini Yogini Goes to India. Winzenried, Chandra. 2018. (Epic Adventures of Chandrini Yogini Ser.: Vol. 1). (ENG.). 40p. (J). (gr. 3-6). pap. 15.99 *(978-1-948365-02-4(2))* Orange Hat Publishing.

Silas, Thony & Valenza, Bryan. Mighty Morphin Power Rangers #6. Higgins, Kyle. 2019. (Mighty Morphin Power Rangers Ser.). (ENG.). 24p. (J). (gr. 6-12). lib. bdg. 27.07 *(978-1-5321-4428-8(8)*, 33833, Graphic Novels) Spotlight.

Silas, Thony, jt. illus. see Randolph, Khary.

Silberberg, Alan. The Awesome, Almost 100% True Adventures of Matt & Craz. Silberberg, Alan. 2014. (ENG.). 336p. (J). (gr. 4-8). pap. 7.99 *(978-1-4169-9433-6(5)*, Aladdin) Simon & Schuster Children's Publishing.

—Milo: Sticky Notes & Brain Freeze. Silberberg, Alan. (ENG.). 288p. (J). (gr. 4-8). 2011. pap. 7.99 *(978-1-4169-9431-2(9))*; 2010. 15.99 *(978-1-4169-9430-5(0))* Simon & Schuster Children's Publishing. (Aladdin).

Silbert, Ken. Black Bear Dreams. Lawrence, Anne Michelle. Mitten, Luana Kay. ed. 2019. (Aha! Readers Ser.). (ENG.). 52p. (J). (gr. k-4). 25.95 ***(978-0-9990924-5-3(6))***; pap. 16.95 ***(978-0-9990924-6-0(4))*** BeaLu Bks.

Silin-Palmer, Pamela. Unicorn Wings. Loehr, Mallory. 2006. (Step into Reading Ser.: Vol. 1). 32p. (J). (gr. -1-1). per. 4.99 *(978-0-375-83117-1(7)*, Random Hse. Bks. for Young Readers) Random Hse. Children's Bks.

Sill, Cathryn P. & Sill, John. About Mammals: A Guide for Children = Sobre Los Mamíferos: Una Guía para Niños. Torre, Cristina de la. 2014. (SPA & ENG.). (J). *(978-1-56145-815-8(5)*, Peachtree Junior) Peachtree Publishing Co. Inc.

Sill, John. About Amphibians: A Guide for Children, 1 vol. Sill, Cathryn. rev. ed. 2018. (About... Ser.: 5). (ENG.). 48p. (J). (gr. -1-2). 16.95 *(978-1-68263-031-0(5))*; pap. 7.95 *(978-1-68263-032-7(3))* Peachtree Publishing Co. Inc.

—About Amphibians / Sobre Los Anfibios: A Guide for Children / una Guía para Niños. Sill, Cathryn. ed. 2018. (About... Ser.: 22). (ENG.). 48p. (J). (gr. -1-2). pap. 8.95 *(978-1-68263-033-4(1))* Peachtree Publishing Co. Inc.

—About Arachnids: A Guide for Children, 1 vol. Sill, Cathryn. 2003. (About... Ser.: 7). (ENG.). 40p. (J). (gr. k-3). 16.95 *(978-1-56145-038-1(3))* Peachtree Publishing Co. Inc.

—About Arachnids: A Guide for Children, 1 vol. Sill, Cathryn. 2006. (About... Ser.: 7). (ENG.). 40p. (J). (gr. k-3). pap. 7.95 *(978-1-56145-364-1(1))* Peachtree Publishing Co. Inc.

—About Birds: A Guide for Children. Sill, Cathryn P. 2014. (ENG.). (J). *(978-1-56145-799-1(X))* Peachtree Publishing Co. Inc.

—About Birds: A Guide for Children, 1 vol. Sill, Cathryn. 2nd rev. ed. 2013. (About... Ser.: 1). (ENG.). 40p. (J). (gr. -1-2). 16.95 *(978-1-56145-688-8(8))*; 7.95 *(978-1-56145-699-4(3))* Peachtree Publishing Co. Inc.

—About Birds / Sobre Los Pájaros: A Guide for Children / una Guía para Niños, 1 vol. Sill, Cathryn. ed. 2014. (About... Ser.: 17). (ENG.). 40p. (J). (gr. -1-2). pap. 8.95 *(978-1-56145-783-0(3))* Peachtree Publishing Co. Inc.

—About Crustaceans: A Guide for Children, 1 vol. Sill, Cathryn. 2007. (About... Ser.: 8). (ENG.). 40p. (J). (gr. k-3). pap. 7.95 *(978-1-56145-405-1(2))* Peachtree Publishing Co. Inc.

—About Fish: A Guide for Children, 1 vol. Sill, Cathryn. rev. ed. 2017. (About... Ser.: 6). (ENG.). 48p. (J). (gr. -1-2). 16.95 *(978-1-56145-987-2(9))*; pap. 7.95 *(978-1-56145-988-9(7))* Peachtree Publishing Co. Inc.

—About Fish / Sobre Los Peces: A Guide for Children / una Guía para Niños, 1 vol. Sill, Cathryn. ed. 2017. (About... Ser.: 21). (ENG.). 48p. (J). (gr. -1-2). pap. 8.95 *(978-1-56145-989-6(5))* Peachtree Publishing Co. Inc.

—About Habitats-Deserts, 1 vol. Sill, Cathryn. 2007. (About Habitats Ser.). (ENG.). 48p. (J). (gr. k-3). 16.95 *(978-1-56145-390-0(0))* Peachtree Publishing Co. Inc.

—About Habitats: Deserts. Sill, Cathryn. 2012. (About Habitats Ser.: 1). (ENG.). 48p. (J). (gr. 4-7). 16.95 *(978-1-56145-641-3(1))* Peachtree Publishing Co. Inc.

—About Habitats: Forests, 1 vol. Sill, Cathryn. 2019. (About Habitats Ser.: 6). (ENG.). 48p. (J). (gr. -1-2). pap. 7.95 *(978-1-68263-126-3(5))* Peachtree Publishing Co. Inc.

—About Habitats: Grasslands, 1 vol. Sill, Cathryn. 2018. (About Habitats Ser.: 4). (ENG.). 48p. (J). (gr. -1-2). pap. 7.95 *(978-1-68263-034-1(X))* Peachtree Publishing Co. Inc.

—About Habitats: Grasslands, 1 vol. Sill, Cathryn. 2011. (About Habitats Ser.: 4). (ENG.). 48p. (J). (gr. -1-3). 16.95 *(978-1-56145-559-1(8))* Peachtree Publishing Co. Inc.

—About Habitats: Oceans, 1 vol. Sill, Cathryn. (About Habitats Ser.: 5). (ENG.). 48p. (J). 2016. (gr. -1-2). pap. 7.95 *(978-1-56145-960-5(7))*; 2012. 16.95 *(978-1-56145-618-5(7))* Peachtree Publishing Co. Inc.

—About Habitats: Polar Regions, 1 vol. Sill, Cathryn. 2015. (About Habitats Ser.: 7). (ENG.). 48p. (J). (gr. -1-2). 16.95 *(978-1-56145-832-5(5))* Peachtree Publishing Co. Inc.

—About Habitats: Rivers & Streams, 1 vol. Sill, Cathryn. 2019. (About Habitats Ser.: 9). (ENG.). 48p. (J). (gr. -1-2). 16.95 *(978-1-68263-091-4(9))* Peachtree Publishing Co. Inc.

—About Habitats: Seashores, 1 vol. Sill, Cathryn. 2017. (About Habitats Ser.: 8). (ENG.). 48p. (J). (gr. -1-2). 16.95 *(978-1-56145-968-1(2))* Peachtree Publishing Co. Inc.

—About Habitats: Wetlands, 1 vol. Sill, Cathryn. (About Habitats Ser.: 2). (ENG.). 48p. (J). 2013. (gr. -1-2). pap. 7.95 *(978-1-56145-689-5(6))*; 2008. (gr. k-3). 16.95 *(978-1-56145-432-7(X))* Peachtree Publishing Co. Inc.

—About Hummingbirds. Sill, Cathryn. 2015. (About Ser.). (ENG.). (J). (gr. -1-2). lib. bdg. 18.55 *(978-1-62765-964-2(1))* Perfection Learning Corp.

—About Hummingbirds: A Guide for Children, 1 vol. Sill, Cathryn. (About... Ser.: 14). (ENG.). 48p. (J). (gr. -1-2). 2015. pap. 7.95 *(978-1-56145-837-0(6))*; 2011. 16.95 *(978-1-56145-588-1(1))* Peachtree Publishing Co. Inc.

—About Insects / Sobre Los Insectos: A Guide for Children / una Guía para Niños, 1 vol. Sill, Cathryn. rev. ed. 2015. (About... Ser.: 18). (ENG.). 48p. (J). (gr. -1-2). pap. 8.95 *(978-1-56145-883-7(X))* Peachtree Publishing Co. Inc.

—About Mammals: A Guide for Children, 1 vol. Sill, Cathryn. rev. ed. 2014. (About... Ser.: 2). (ENG.). 48p. (J). (gr. -1-2). 16.95 *(978-1-56145-757-1(4))* Peachtree Publishing Co. Inc.

—About Marine Mammals: A Guide for Children, 1 vol. Sill, Cathryn. 2016. (About... Ser.: 19). (ENG.). 48p. (J). (gr. -1-2). 16.95 *(978-1-56145-906-3(2))* Peachtree Publishing Co. Inc.

—About Marsupials: A Guide for Children, 1 vol. Sill, Cathryn. (About... Ser.: 10). (ENG.). 48p. (J). 2009. pap. 7.95 *(978-1-56145-407-5(9))*; 2006. 15.95 *(978-1-56145-358-0(7))* Peachtree Publishing Co. Inc.

—About Mollusks: A Guide for Children, 1 vol. Sill, Cathryn. 2008. (About... Ser.: 9). (ENG.). 40p. (J). (gr. k-3). pap. 7.95 *(978-1-56145-406-8(0))* Peachtree Publishing Co. Inc.

—About Parrots: A Guide for Children, 1 vol. Sill, Cathryn. 2020. (About... Ser.: 16). (ENG.). 48p. (J). (gr. -1-2). pap. 7.99 *(978-1-68263-158-4(3))* Peachtree Publishing Co. Inc.

—About Penguins: A Guide for Children, 1 vol. Sill, Cathryn P. 2009. (ENG.). 48p. (J). (gr. -1-2). 15.95 *(978-1-56145-488-4(5))* Peachtree Publishing Co. Inc.

—About Penguins: A Guide for Children, 1 vol. Sill, Cathryn. 2nd rev. ed. (About... Ser.: 12). (ENG.). 48p. (J). (gr. -1-2). 2013. 7.95 *(978-1-56145-741-0(8))*; 2009. 16.95 *(978-1-56145-743-4(4))* Peachtree Publishing Co. Inc.

—About Raptors: A Guide for Children, 1 vol. Sill, Cathryn. 2010. (About... Ser.: 13). (ENG.). 48p. (J). (gr. -1-2). 16.95 *(978-1-56145-536-2(9))* Peachtree Publishing Co. Inc.

—About Reptiles: A Guide for Children, 1 vol. Sill, Cathryn P. & Sill, Cathryn. 2003. (About...Ser.). (ENG.). 40p. (J). (gr. k-3). pap. 7.95 *(978-1-56145-233-0(5))* Peachtree Publishing Co. Inc.

—About Reptiles / Sobre Los Reptiles: A Guide for Children / una Guía para Niños, 1 vol. Sill, Cathryn. ed. 2016. (About... Ser.: 20). (ENG.). 40p. (J). (gr. -1-2). pap. 8.95 *(978-1-56145-909-4(7))* Peachtree Publishing Co. Inc.

—About Rodents: A Guide for Children, 1 vol. Sill, Cathryn. (About... Ser.: 11). (ENG.). 48p. (J). 2016. (gr. -1-2). pap. 7.95 *(978-1-56145-914-8(3))*; 2008. (gr. k-3). 15.95 *(978-1-56145-454-9(0))* Peachtree Publishing Co. Inc.

Sill, John. About Seabirds: A Guide for Children. Sill, Cathryn. 2020. (About... Ser.: 28). (ENG.). 48p. (J). (gr. -1-2). 16.99 ***(978-1-68263-092-1(7))*** Peachtree Publishing Co. Inc.

Sill, John. About Woodpeckers: A Guide for Children. Sill, Cathryn. 2018. (About... Ser.: 23). (ENG.). 48p. (J). (gr. -1-2). 16.95 *(978-1-68263-004-4(8))* Peachtree Publishing Co. Inc.

—Birds. Alden, Peter C. & Peterson, Roger Tory. Peterson, Roger Tory, ed. 2nd ed. 2013. (Peterson Field Guide Color-In Bks.). (ENG.). 64p. (J). 10.99 *(978-0-544-02692-6(6)*, 1529289) Houghton Mifflin Harcourt Publishing Co.

—Curious about Birds. Sill, Cathryn. 2020. (Discovering Nature Ser.: 1). (ENG.). 22p. (J). (gr. -1-1). bds. 6.99 *(978-1-68263-190-4(7))* Peachtree Publishing Co. Inc.

—Sobre Los Insectos: Una Guía para Niños. Sill, Cathryn. 2020. (About... Ser.: 26). (SPA.). 48p. (J). (gr. -1-2). pap. 8.99 *(978-1-68263-155-3(9))* Peachtree Publishing Co. Inc.

—Sobre Los Mamíferos: Una Guía para Niños. Sill, Cathryn. 2019. (About... Ser.). (SPA.). 48p. (J). (gr. -1-2). pap. 8.95 *(978-1-68263-072-3(2))* Peachtree Publishing Co. Inc.

—Sobre Los Pájaros: Una Guía para Niños, 1 vol. Sill, Cathryn. 2019. (About... Ser.). (SPA.). 40p. (J). (gr. -1-2). pap. 8.95 *(978-1-68263-071-6(4))* Peachtree Publishing Co. Inc.

—Sobre Los Peces: Una Guía para Niños. Sill, Cathryn. 2020. (About... Ser.: 27). (SPA.). 48p. (J). (gr. -1-2). pap. 8.99 *(978-1-68263-154-6(0))* Peachtree Publishing Co. Inc.

Sill, John & Sill, John. About Crustaceans: A Guide for Children, 1 vol. Sill, Cathryn. 2004. (About... Ser.: 8). (ENG.). 40p. (J). (gr. k-3). 16.95 *(978-1-56145-301-6(3))* Peachtree Publishing Co. Inc.

—About Habitats: Mountains, 1 vol. Sill, Cathryn. 2009. (About Habitats Ser.: 3). (ENG.). 48p. (J). (gr. -1-2). 16.95 *(978-1-56145-469-3(9))* Peachtree Publishing Co. Inc.

Sill, John, jt. illus. see Sill, Cathryn P.

Sill, John, jt. illus. see Sill, John.

Sillani, Febe. Food Atlas: Discover All the Delicious Foods of the World. Malerba, Giulia. 2017. (ENG.). 72p. (J). (gr. 3-12). 19.95 *(978-1-77085-952-4(7)*, fbbeb15b-b2aa-42fe-ae7d-b9d653d60ffa) Firefly Bks., Ltd.

Siller, Germin. Los Frutos del Sol. Fuentes, Claudia Luna & Fuente, Claudia Luna. rev. ed. 2006. (Otra Escalera Ser.). (SPA & ENG.). 14p. (J). (gr. k). pap. 7.95 *(978-968-5920-54-4(0))* Castillo, Ediciones, S. A. de C. V. MEX. Dist: Macmillan.

Sills, Khalil. Honey & the New Vegetable. Taylor, Celeste & Finlay, Cynthia K. 2018. (ENG.). 34p. (J). pap. 12.00 *(978-1-7926-3533-5(8))* Independently Published.

Silswal, Kashvi. A Dog's Tail. Silswal, Kashvi. 2017. (Volume Ser.: Vol. 1). (ENG.). 184p. (J). (gr. 2-6). pap. 8.99 *(978-0-692-04749-1(2))* Kashvi'sArtwork.

Silva, Ana Camila. Olive the Sheep Can't Sleep. Almeida, Clementina. 2018. (ENG.). 32p. (J). (gr. -1-2). 12.99 *(978-1-58089-838-6(6))* Charlesbridge Publishing, Inc.

Silva, Augusto Alves da. Trisba & Sula: A Miskitu Folktale from Nicaragua (Una Leyenda de los Miskitos de Nicaragua) MacCracken, Joan. Macdonald, Isabel et al, trs. 2005. (ENG & SPA.). 16.95 *(978-0-9646018-2-6(6))* Tiffin Pr. of Maine.

Silva, David. Los Juguetes. Nunez, Jaclyn. 2016. (Early Rising Readers Ser.). (SPA.). (J). (gr. -1). 6.67 *(978-1-4788-3661-2(X))* Newmark Learning LLC.

Silva, David, jt. illus. see Gomez, Marcela.

Silva, Eliseo Art. Let's Cook Adobo!, 1 vol. Montoya, Carina Monica. 2010. 22p. pap. 24.95 *(978-1-4489-9022-1(X))* PublishAmerica, Inc.

Silva, Flávio B. Chavo the Invisible. Nordling, Lee. 2018. (Game for Adventure Ser.). (ENG.). 32p. (J). (gr. k-3). pap. 6.99 *(978-1-5415-1046-3(1)*, 9781541510463, Graphic Universe™) Lerner Publishing Group.

Silva, Flavio B., jt. illus. see Roberts, Scott.

Silva-Freimane, Jehanne. Anansi & Herald, the Fowl-Cock. Stoute, June. l.t. ed. 2010. (ENG.). 28p. (J). (gr. -1-3). pap. *(978-976-8233-08-0(7))* Word Ways Caribbean.

Silva, Keith, jt. illus. see Silva, Rachel M.

Silva, Kelsi Jo. Ela Cat in the Mountains. Knaub, Niki. 2018. (ENG.). 14p. (J). (— 1). bds. 7.99 *(978-0-9988846-1-5(8))* Good Luck Black Cat Bks.

Silva, Leandro Ricardo da & Dzioba, Wes. Disney Zootopia: Hard Day's Work (Younger Readers Graphic Novel) Gownley, Jimmy. 2019. (ENG.). 48p. (J). (gr. 3-7). 7.99 *(978-1-5067-1206-2(1))* Dark Horse Comics.

—Disney Zootopia: School Days (Younger Readers Graphic Novel) Gownley, Jimmy. 2019. (ENG.). 48p. (J). (gr. k-3). 7.99 *(978-1-5067-1205-5(3))* Dark Horse Comics.

Silva, Lucas. Ways to Say NUMBERS, чисел, Números, 数字 In Spanish, Portuguese, Japanese, Russian & English: Build Multilingual Minds. Kids, Multilingx & Stapleton, Inger. 2019. (Ways to Say Multilingual Development Bks.: Vol. 6). (ENG.). 26p. (J). pap. 9.99 *(978-1-0783-3619-2(9))* Independently Published.

Silva, Nill. Carlinhos, o Gnomo e o Curupira. Vasconcelos, Sandra. 2019. (POR.). 52p. (J). pap. 14.50 ***(978-1-6994-8543-9(7))*** Independently Published.

Silva, R. B., jt. illus. see Larraz, Pepe.

Silva, Rachel M. & Silva, Keith. My Extraordinary Brother. Cooper, Katie. 2018. (Life's Jungle Ser.: Vol. 1). (ENG.). 24p. (J). pap. 10.00 *(978-1-7288-6582-9(4))* Independently Published.

Silva, Reg & Woolley, Tom. Living in ... Italy. Perkins, Chloe. 2016. (Living In... Ser.). (ENG.). 32p. (J). (gr. k-2). pap. 4.99 *(978-1-4814-5200-7(2))* Simon & Schuster Children's Publishing.

Silva, Simon. La Mariposa. Jiménez, Francisco. 2004. 38p. (J). (gr. k-4). reprint ed. pap. 14.00 *(978-0-7567-8433-1(6))* DIANE Publishing Co.

Silva, Tom, jt. illus. see Hahn, Beverly.

Silver, Jago. Mr. Aesop's Story Shop. 2011. (ENG.). 48p. (J). (gr. 1-4). 14.99 *(978-0-7459-6915-2(1))* Lion Hudson PLC GBR. Dist: Independent Pubs. Group.

—Nachshon, Who Was Afraid to Swim: A Passover Story. Cohen, Deborah Bodin. (Passover Ser.). (ENG.). 32p. (J). (gr. -1-3). 2008. 17.95 *(978-0-8225-8764-4(5))*; Vol. 2009. pap. 8.95 *(978-0-8225-8765-1(3)*, 9780822587651) Lerner Publishing Group. (Kar-Ben Publishing).

—Oh No, Jonah! Balsley, Tilda. 2012. (Bible Ser.). (ENG.). 32p. (J). (gr. k-4). lib. bdg. 17.95 *(978-0-7613-5139-9(6)*, Kar-Ben Publishing) Lerner Publishing Group.

Silver, Jane. Sister Sun, Brother Storm. Matsakis, Cynthia. 2012. 32p. 24.95 *(978-1-4575-0768-7(4))* Dog Ear Publishing, LLC.

Silver, Maggie & Mayer, Uwe. How Flowers Grow. Helbrough, Emma. (Beginners Nature Ser.). 32p. (J). 2007. (gr. -1-3). 4.99 *(978-0-7945-1340-5(9)*, Usborne); 2006. (gr. 4-7). lib. bdg. 12.95 *(978-1-58086-508-1(9))* EDC Publishing.

Silver, Pattie. Kitty's Barn. 2005. 12p. (J). bds. 9.95 *(978-1-58117-385-7(7)*, Intervisual/Piggy Toes) Bendon, Inc.

Silver-Thompson, Pattie. Postcards from Kitty. Wang, Margaret. 2005. 12p. (J). (gr. -1-3). 9.95 *(978-1-58117-427-4(6)*, Intervisual/Piggy Toes) Bendon, Inc.

Silverberg-Kiss, Esti. Solomon & the Trees. Biers-Ariel, Matt. 2004. (J). (gr. k-3). 13.95 *(978-0-8074-0749-3(6)*, 101055) URJ Pr.

Silveria, Gordon. The Greedy Triangle. Burns, Marilyn. 2008. (Scholastic Bookshelf Ser.). (ENG.). 32p. (J). (gr. -1-3). pap. 6.99 *(978-0-545-04220-8(8)*, Scholastic Paperbacks) Scholastic, Inc.

Silverman, Dianne. Annie Oakley, 1 vol. Blair, Eric. 2013. (My First Classic Story Ser.). (ENG.). 32p. (J). (gr. k-3). pap. 7.10 *(978-1-4795-1846-3(8)*, Picture Window Bks.) Capstone.

—Belling the Cat: A Retelling of Aesop's Fable, 1 vol. Blair, Eric. 2013. (My First Classic Story Ser.). (ENG.). 24p. (J). (gr. k-3). pap. 7.10 *(978-1-4795-1854-8(9)*, Picture Window Bks.) Capstone.

—Belling the Cat: A Retelling of Aesop's Fable, 1 vol. Blair, Eric & Aesop Enterprise Inc. Staff. 2011. (My First Classic Story Ser.). (ENG.). 24p. (J). (gr. k-3). lib. bdg. 22.65 *(978-1-4048-6504-4(7)*, Picture Window Bks.) Capstone.

—The Boy Who Cried Wolf, 1 vol. Blair, Eric. 2011. (My First Classic Story Ser.). (ENG.). 24p. (J). (gr. k-3). pap. 7.10 *(978-1-4048-7364-3(3)*, Picture Window Bks.) Capstone.

—The Boy Who Cried Wolf: A Retelling of Aesop's Fable, 1 vol. Blair, Eric & Aesop Enterprise Inc. Staff. 2011. (My First Classic Story Ser.). (ENG.). 24p. (J). (gr. k-3). lib. bdg. 22.65 *(978-1-4048-6507-5(1)*, Picture Window Bks.) Capstone.

—The Country Mouse & the City Mouse: A Retelling of Aesop's Fable, 1 vol. Blair, Eric. 2013. (My First Classic Story Ser.). (ENG.). 24p. (J). (gr. k-3). pap. 7.10 *(978-1-4795-1858-6(1)*, Picture Window Bks.) Capstone.

—The Donkey in the Lion's Skin: A Retelling of Aesop's Fable, 1 vol. Blair, Eric. 2013. (My First Classic Story Ser.). (ENG.). 24p. (J). (gr. k-3). pap. 7.10 *(978-1-4795-1855-5(7)*, Picture Window Bks.) Capstone.

—The Donkey in the Lion's Skin: A Retelling of Aesop's Fable, 1 vol. Blair, Eric & Aesop Enterprise Inc. Staff. 2011. (My First Classic Story Ser.). (ENG.). 24p. (J). (gr. k-3). lib. bdg. 22.65 *(978-1-4048-6506-8(3)*, Picture Window Bks.) Capstone.

—El Pastorcito Mentiroso: Versión de la Fábula de Esopo. Blair, Eric. Abello, Patricia, tr. 2006. (Read-It! Readers en Español: Fábulas Ser.).Tr. of Boy Who Cried Wolf - A Retelling of Aesop's Fable. (SPA.). 24p. (J). (gr. k-3). 21.32 *(978-1-4048-1616-9(X)*, Picture Window Bks.) Capstone.

Silverstein, Ariel. Babies in the Snow: Chunky Lift a Flap Board Book. Swift, Ginger. Cottage Door Press, ed. 2017. (Lift a Flap Ser.). (ENG.). 12p. (J). (gr. -1-k). bds. 7.99 *(978-1-68052-228-0(0)*, 1002140) Cottage Door Pr.

—Noah: Peek-A-Flap. Garnett, Jaye. 2018. (ENG.). 12p. (J). (gr. -1-k). bds. 8.99 *(978-1-68052-370-6(8)*, 1003350) Cottage Door Pr.

Silverstein, Ariel. ¿Quién Está Aquí? ¡Yuju! Garnett, Jaye. Cottage Door Press, ed. 2020. (Peek-A-Flap Ser.). (SPA.). 12p. (J). (gr. -1-k). bds. 8.99 ***(978-1-64638-059-6(2)***, 1001180-SLA) Cottage Door Pr.

Silverstein, Ariel. Who Gift Set. Garnett, Jaye. Cottage Door Press, ed. 2019. (Book & Cuddly Plush Toy Friend Ser.). (ENG.). 12p. (J). (gr. -1-2). bds. 16.99 *(978-1-68052-759-9(2)*, 1004700) Cottage Door Pr.

Silverstein, Grant. Davey McGravy. Mason, David. 2015. (ENG.). 120p. (J). (gr. k). pap. 14.95 *(978-1-58988-099-3(4))* Dry, Paul Bks., Inc.

Silverstein, Shel. Different Dances 25th Anniversary Edition. Silverstein, Shel. 25th anniv. ed. 2004. (ENG.). 224p. 35.00 *(978-0-06-055430-9(4))* HarperCollins Pubs.

—Don't Bump the Glump! And Other Fantasies. Silverstein, Shel. 2014. (ENG.). 64p. (J). (gr. -1-3). 17.99 *(978-0-06-149338-6(4)*, HarperCollins) HarperCollins Pubs. Ltd. GBR. Dist: HarperCollins Pubs.

—Every Thing on It. Silverstein, Shel. 2011. (ENG.). 208p. (J). (gr. -1-3). 19.99 *(978-0-06-199816-4(8))*; lib. bdg. 20.89 *(978-0-06-199817-1(6))* HarperCollins Pubs.

—Falling Up. Silverstein, Shel. ed. 2006. (ENG.). 184p. (J). (gr. -1-3). 19.99 *(978-0-06-024802-4(5)*, HarperCollins) HarperCollins Pubs. Ltd. GBR. Dist: HarperCollins Pubs.

—Falling up Special Edition: With 12 New Poems. Silverstein, Shel. 2015. (ENG.). 200p. (J). (gr. -1-3). 19.99 *(978-0-06-232133-6(1))* HarperCollins Pubs.

—A Giraffe & a Half. Silverstein, Shel. 40th anniv. ed. 2014. (ENG.). 48p. (J). (gr. -1-3). 17.99 *(978-0-06-025655-5(9)*, HarperCollins) HarperCollins Pubs. Ltd. GBR. Dist: HarperCollins Pubs.

—The Giving Tree. Silverstein, Shel. gif. ed. 2007. 64p. 16.99 *(978-0-06-124001-0(X))* HarperCollins Pubs.

—The Giving Tree. Silverstein, Shel. (ENG.). 64p. (J). (gr. -1-3). 2003. lib. bdg. 18.89 *(978-0-06-025666-1(4))*; 50th anniv. ed. 2014. 17.99 *(978-0-06-025665-4(6)*, HC5567) HarperCollins Pubs. Ltd. GBR. (HarperCollins). Dist: HarperCollins Pubs.

—The Giving Tree with CD. Silverstein, Shel. anniv. ed. 2014. (ENG.). 64p. (J). (gr. -1-3). 19.99 *(978-0-06-058675-1(3)*, HarperCollins) HarperCollins Pubs. Ltd. GBR. Dist: HarperCollins Pubs.

—Lafcadio, the Lion Who Shot Back. Silverstein, Shel. 2013. (ENG.). 112p. (J). (gr. -1-3). 16.99 *(978-0-06-025675-3(3)*, HarperCollins) HarperCollins Pubs. Ltd. GBR. Dist: HarperCollins Pubs.

—A Light in the Attic. Silverstein, Shel. ed. 2005. (ENG.). 176p. (J). (gr. -1-3). 19.99 *(978-0-06-025673-9(7)*, HarperCollins) HarperCollins Pubs. Ltd. GBR. Dist: HarperCollins Pubs.

—A Light in the Attic Special Edition with 12 Extra Poems. Silverstein, Shel. ed. 2009. (ENG.). 192p. (J). (gr. -1-3). 19.99 *(978-0-06-190585-8(2)*, HarperCollins) HarperCollins Pubs. Ltd. GBR. Dist: HarperCollins Pubs.

—The Missing Piece. Silverstein, Shel. 30th anniv. ed. 2006. (Ursula Nordstrom Bk.). (ENG.). 112p. (J). (gr. -1-3). 17.99 *(978-0-06-025671-5(0)*, HarperCollins) HarperCollins Pubs. Ltd. GBR. Dist: HarperCollins Pubs.

—The Missing Piece Meets the Big O. Silverstein, Shel. ed. 2006. (ENG.). 104p. (J). (gr. -1-3). 16.99 *(978-0-06-025657-9(5)*, HarperCollins) HarperCollins Pubs. Ltd. GBR. Dist: HarperCollins Pubs.

—Runny Babbit: A Billy Sook. Silverstein, Shel. 2015. (ENG.). 96p. (J). (gr. -1-3). 18.99 *(978-0-06-025653-1(2)*, HarperCollins) HarperCollins Pubs.

—Runny Babbit Book & Abridged CD. Silverstein, Shel. abr. ed. 2006. (ENG.). 96p. (J). (gr. -1-3). 22.99 *(978-0-06-113047-2(8))* HarperCollins Pubs.

—Runny Babbit Returns: Another Billy Sook. Silverstein, Shel. 2017. (ENG.). 96p. (J). (gr. -1-3). 19.99 *(978-0-06-247939-6(3))*; lib. bdg. 20.89 *(978-0-06-247985-3(7))* HarperCollins Pubs.

—Shel Silverstein Pop-up Treasury. Silverstein, Shel. 2008. 16p. (J). 29.99 *(978-0-06-147269-5(7))* HarperCollins Pubs.

—Where the Sidewalk Ends: Poems & Drawings. Silverstein, Shel. 2014. (ENG.). 176p. (J). (gr. -1-3). 19.99 *(978-0-06-025667-8(2)*, HarperCollins) HarperCollins Pubs. Ltd. GBR. Dist: HarperCollins Pubs.

—Where the Sidewalk Ends Special Edition with 12 Extra Poems: Poems & Drawings. Silverstein, Shel. 30th anniv. ed. 2004. (ENG.). 192p. (J). (gr. -1-3). lib. bdg. 19.89 *(978-0-06-058653-9(2))* HarperCollins Pubs.

—Where the Sidewalk Ends Special Edition with 12 Extra Poems: Poems & Drawings. Silverstein, Shel. 30th anniv. ed. 2014. (ENG.). 192p. (J). (gr. -1-3). 18.99 *(978-0-06-057234-1(5)*, HarperCollins) HarperCollins Pubs. Ltd. GBR. Dist: HarperCollins Pubs.

—Who Wants a Cheap Rhinoceros? Silverstein, Shel. 50th anniv. ed. 2014. (ENG.). 64p. (J). (gr. -1-3). 19.99 *(978-1-4814-1593-4(X)*, Simon & Schuster Bks. For Young Readers) Simon & Schuster Bks. For Young Readers.

Silverstream, Bristol. Princess Space Rocket Cadet. Silverstream, Bristol. Sanchez, Tiffany, ed. 2019. (ENG.). 32p. (J). pap. 12.99 ***(978-1-6958-3745-4(2))*** Independently Published.

Silverthorne, Sandy. Surviving When You're Home Alone: How to Avoid Being Grounded for Life. Silverthorne, Sandy. 2006. 96p. (YA). (gr. 3-6). pap. 5.99 *(978-0-7847-1434-8(7)*, 42176) Standard Publishing.

—Surviving Zits: How to Cope with Your Changing Self. Silverthorne, Sandy. 2006. 96p. (YA). (gr. 3-6). pap. 5.99 *(978-0-7847-1435-5(5)*, 42177) Standard Publishing.

Silvestri, Boris. Duck Feet, 6 vols. Trussell-Cullen, Alan. 2006. (ENG.). (J). (gr. 2). pap., pap. 65.33 *(978-1-4189-1711-1(7))* Rigby Education.

Silvestri, Linda. Book of Mormon 1-2-3s. Eden, Kristena. 2016. (ENG.). (J). 14.99 *(978-1-4621-1651-5(5))* Cedar Fort, Inc./CFI Distribution.

—Prophet Joseph's 1-2-3s. Eden, Kristina. 2016. (ENG.). (gr. -1-1). 14.99 *(978-1-4621-1949-3(2))* Cedar Fort, Inc./CFI Distribution.

Silvestri, Marc, et al. Decades: Marvel in the 90s - the Mutant X-Plosion. 2019. (ENG.). 240p. (YA). (gr. -1-17). pap. 24.99 *(978-1-302-91772-2(2))* Marvel Worldwide, Inc.

—X-Men Milestones: Fall of the Mutants. 2019. (ENG.). 272p. (YA). (gr. 4-17). pap. 34.99 *(978-1-302-91851-4(6))* Marvel Worldwide, Inc.

—X-Men Milestones: Messiah Complex. 2020. (ENG.). 352p. (YA). (gr. 8-17). pap. 34.99 *(978-1-302-92280-1(7))* Marvel Worldwide, Inc.

Silvey, Allen, jt. illus. see Silvey, Joan.

Silvey, Joan & Silvey, Allen. Help Me Learn: Counting 1 - 10 in American Language, Silvey, Joan. Silvey, Allen, ed. l.t. ed. 2005. (Help Me Learn Ser.: Vol. 1). 24p. (J). per. 5.95 *(978-0-9762446-0-8(8))* Silvey Bk. Publishing.

Sim, David. Bear Boar. Robinson, Michelle. 2012. 12p. (J). (gr. -1-k). bds. *(978-1-4088-1704-9(7)*, 38575, Bloomsbury Children's Bks.) Bloomsbury Publishing Plc.

—Driving My Tractor. Dobbins, Jan & Songs, Steve. 2012. 32p. (J). (gr. -1-2). 9.99 *(978-1-84686-664-7(2))* Barefoot Bks., Inc.

—Driving My Tractor. Dobbins, Jan. 2009. 32p. (J). (gr. -1-3). 16.99 *(978-1-84686-358-5(9))* Barefoot Bks., Inc.

—Driving My Tractor Puzzle. Dobbins, Jan. 2011. (J). (gr. -1-1). 14.99 *(978-1-84686-573-2(5))* Barefoot Bks., Inc.

—Jungle School. Laird, Elizabeth & Davison, Roz. 2006. (Green Bananas Ser.). (ENG.). 48p. (J). (gr. -1-3). *(978-0-7787-1042-4(4))*; lib. bdg. *(978-0-7787-1026-4(2))* Crabtree Publishing Co.

—The Shape Song Singalong. SteveSongs Staff. 2011. 36p. (J). 16.99 *(978-1-84686-671-5(5))* Barefoot Bks., Inc.

—Shape Song Swingalong. SteveSongs Staff. 2011. 24p. (J). (gr. -1-2). 9.99 *(978-1-84686-679-1(0))* Barefoot Bks., Inc.

—Space Song Rocket Ride. Scribens, Sunny et al. 2014. 32p. (J). (gr. -1-2). 9.99 *(978-1-78285-098-4(8))* Barefoot Bks., Inc.

—Yak Yuk. Robinson, Michelle. 2012. 12p. (J). (gr. -1-k). bds. 10.99 *(978-1-4088-1703-2(9)*, 900086963, Bloomsbury Children's Bks.) Bloomsbury Publishing USA.

Sim, David. Matt's Hat: A Find the Hat Color Book, 2 bks. Sim, David. 2003. 10p. (J). 7.95 *(978-1-58117-197-6(8)*, Intervisual/Piggy Toes) Bendon, Inc.

—Matt's Mat: A Touch & Feel Counting Book, 2 vols. Sim, David. 2003. 10p. (J). 7.95 *(978-1-58117-198-3(6)*, Intervisual/Piggy Toes) Bendon, Inc.

Sim, Robert J. Bird Stories (Yesterday's Classics) Patch, Edith M. 2018. (ENG.). 206p. (J). (gr. 2-4). pap. 11.95 *(978-1-63334-095-4(3))* Yesterday's Classics.

—First Lessons in Nature Study (Yesterday's Classics) Patch, Edith M. 2018. (ENG.). 264p. (J). (gr. 4-6). pap. 12.95 *(978-1-63334-099-2(6))* Yesterday's Classics.

—Hexapod Stories (Yesterday's Classics) Patch, Edith M. 2018. (ENG.). 156p. (J). (gr. 2-4). pap. 11.95 *(978-1-63334-100-5(3))* Yesterday's Classics.

Sima, Jessie. Snow Pony & the Seven Miniature Ponies. Trimmer, Christian. 2018. (ENG.). 48p. (J). (gr. -1-3). 17.99 *(978-1-4814-6268-6(7)*, Simon & Schuster Bks. For Young Readers) Simon & Schuster Bks. For Young Readers.

Sima, Jessie. Harriet Gets Carried Away. Sima, Jessie. 2018. (ENG.). 48p. (J). (gr. -1-3). 17.99 *(978-1-4814-6911-1(8)*, Simon & Schuster Bks. For Young Readers) Simon & Schuster Bks. For Young Readers.

—Love, Z. Sima, Jessie. 2018. (ENG.). 48p. (J). (gr. -1-3). 17.99 *(978-1-4814-9677-3(8)*, Simon & Schuster Bks. For Young Readers) Simon & Schuster Bks. For Young Readers.

—Not Quite Narwhal. Sima, Jessie. 2017. (ENG.). 40p. (J). (gr. -1-3). 17.99 *(978-1-4814-6909-8(6)*, Simon & Schuster Bks. For Young Readers) Simon & Schuster Bks. For Young Readers.

—Spencer's New Pet. Sima, Jessie. 2019. (ENG.). 56p. (J). (gr. -1-3). 17.99 *(978-1-5344-1877-6(6)*, Simon & Schuster Bks. For Young Readers) Simon & Schuster Bks. For Young Readers.

Simard, Remy. Big Red School. Rusu, Meredith. 2019. (Clifford Ser.). (ENG.). 24p. (J). (gr. -1-k). pap. 4.99 *(978-1-338-53068-1(2))* Scholastic, Inc.

—Bus Ride Bully, 1 vol. Meister, Cari. (My First Graphic Novel Ser.). (ENG.). 32p. (J). (gr. k-2). 2011. pap. 6.25 *(978-1-4342-3101-7(1))*; 2010. 24.65 *(978-1-4342-2059-2(1))* Capstone. (Stone Arch Bks.).

—Busy Day Coloring Storybook. 2003. (Rainbow Fish & Friends Ser.). 24p. (J). mass mkt. 2.99 *(978-1-59014-132-8(6))* Night Sky Bks.

—The Cat That Disappeared, 1 vol. Mortensen, Lori. 2010. (My First Graphic Novel Ser.). (ENG.). 32p. (J). (gr. k-2). pap. 6.25 *(978-1-4342-2282-4(9)*, Stone Arch Bks.) Capstone.

—Clues in the Attic, 1 vol. Meister, Cari. 2010. (My First Graphic Novel Ser.). (ENG.). 32p. (J). (gr. k-2). pap. 6.25 *(978-1-4342-2283-1(7)*, Stone Arch Bks.) Capstone.

—Favorite Places Coloring Storybook. 2003. (Rainbow Fish & Friends Ser.). 24p. (J). mass mkt. 2.99 *(978-1-59014-133-5(4))* Night Sky Bks.

—First Day, No Way!, 1 vol. Mortensen, Lori. (My First Graphic Novel Ser.). (ENG.). 32p. (J). (gr. k-2). 2011. pap. 6.25 *(978-1-4342-3102-4(X))*; 2010. 24.65 *(978-1-4342-2015-8(X))* Capstone. (Stone Arch Bks.).

—It's My Birthday!/Es Mi Cumpleanos! Rosa-Mendoza, Gladys. 2006. (Englishspanish Foundations Ser.). (ENG & SPA.). 20p. (J). (gr. -1-k). bds. 6.95 *(978-1-931398-17-6(8))* Me+Mi Publishing.

—It's Pool Time! Rusu, Meredith. 2019. (Clifford Ser.). (ENG.). 24p. (J). (gr. -1-k). pap. 4.99 *(978-1-338-53067-4(4))* Scholastic, Inc.

—The Lost Lunch, 1 vol. Mortensen, Lori. (My First Graphic Novel Ser.). (ENG.). 32p. (J). (gr. k-2). 2011. pap. 6.25 *(978-1-4342-3103-1(8))*; 2010. 24.65 *(978-1-4342-2014-1(1))* Capstone. (Stone Arch Bks.).

—Mazes. School Zone Interactive Staff. rev. ed. 2006. (ENG.). 64p. (J). (gr. 1-2). wbk. ed. 7.99 *(978-1-58947-300-3(0))* School Zone Publishing Co.

—Meet the Sparkplugs, Level 3. Richards, Kitty. 2006. (ENG.). 24p. (J). (gr. 1-17). per. 3.99 *(978-1-58476-419-9(8)*, IKIDS) Innovative Kids.

—The Missing Monster Card, 1 vol. Mortensen, Lori. 2010. (My First Graphic Novel Ser.). (ENG.). 32p. (J). (gr. k-2). pap. 6.25 *(978-1-4342-2284-8(5))*; lib. bdg. 24.65 *(978-1-4342-1888-9(0))* Capstone. (Stone Arch Bks.).

—Morning Mystery, 1 vol. Jones, Christianne C. 2010. (My First Graphic Novel Ser.). (ENG.). 32p. (J). (gr. k-2). lib. bdg. 24.65 *(978-1-4342-1890-2(2)*, Stone Arch Bks.) Capstone.

—My Brain, 1 vol. Korb, Rena B. & Weinhaus, Anthony J. 2010. (My Body Ser.). (ENG.). 32p. (J). (gr. k-4). 28.50 *(978-1-60270-805-1(3)*, 11694, Looking Glass Library) Magic Wagon.

—My Mouth, 1 vol. Korb, Rena B. & Weinhaus, Anthony J. 2010. (My Body Ser.). (ENG.). 32p. (J). (gr. k-4). 28.50 *(978-1-60270-806-8(1)*, 11696, Looking Glass Library) Magic Wagon.

—My Muscles, 1 vol. Korb, Rena B. & Weinhaus, Anthony J. 2010. (My Body Ser.). (ENG.). 32p. (J). (gr. k-4). 28.50 *(978-1-60270-807-5(X)*, 11698, Looking Glass Library) Magic Wagon.

—My Nose, 1 vol. Korb, Rena B. & Weinhaus, Anthony J. 2010. (My Body Ser.). (ENG.). 32p. (J). (gr. k-4). 28.50 *(978-1-60270-808-2(8)*, 11700, Looking Glass Library) Magic Wagon.

—My Spine, 1 vol. Korb, Rena B. & Weinhaus, Anthony J. 2010. (My Body Ser.). (ENG.). 32p. (J). (gr. k-4). 28.50

(978-1-60270-809-9(6), 11702, Looking Glass Library) Magic Wagon.
—My Stomach, 1 vol. Korb, Rena B. & Weinhaus, Anthony J. 2010. (My Body Ser.). (ENG.). 32p. (J). (gr. k-4). 28.50 *(978-1-60270-810-5(X),* 11704, Looking Glass Library) Magic Wagon.
—Polly's Pen Pal. Murphy, Stuart J. 2005. (MathStart 3 Ser.). (ENG.). 40p. (J). (gr. 2-18). pap. 5.99 *(978-0-06-053170-6(3))* HarperCollins Pubs.
—Shark in the Library!, 1 vol. Meister, Cari. (My First Graphic Novel Ser.). (ENG.). 32p. (J). (gr. k-2). 2011. pap. 6.25 *(978-1-4342-3104-8(6));* 2010. 24.65 *(978-1-4342-2058-5(3))* Capstone. (Stone Arch Bks.).
—Top Secret. Hall, Kirsten. 2003. 64p. (J). *(978-0-439-50133-0(4))* Scholastic, Inc.
Simcic, Christina. We're Three: A Story About Families & The Only Child. Cameron-Gallo, Vivian. 2009. (ENG.). 28p. (gr. -1). pap. 10.96 *(978-1-4251-7215-2(6))* Trafford Publishing.
Siminovich, Lorena. In My Flower. Gillingham, Sara. 2009. (ENG.). 12p. (J). (gr. -1 — 1). bds. 8.99 *(978-0-8118-7339-0(0))* Chronicle Bks. LLC.
—In My Forest. Gillingham, Sara. 2010. (ENG.). 12p. (J). (gr. -1 — 1). bds. 8.99 *(978-0-8118-7566-0(0))* Chronicle Bks. LLC.
—In My Jungle. Gillingham, Sara. 2011. (ENG.). 12p. (J). (gr. -1 — 1). bds. 8.99 *(978-0-8118-7716-9(7))* Chronicle Bks. LLC.
—In My Ocean. Gillingham, Sara. 2011. (ENG.). 12p. (J). (gr. -1 — 1). bds. 8.99 *(978-0-8118-7717-6(5))* Chronicle Bks. LLC.
—My Favorite Things Flash Cards. 2010. (ENG.). 26p. (J). (gr. -1 — 1). 14.95 *(978-0-8118-6799-3(4))* Chronicle Bks. LLC.
—On My Leaf. Gillingham, Sara. 2012. (ENG.). 12p. (J). (gr. -1 — 1). bds. 8.99 *(978-1-4521-0813-1(7))* Chronicle Bks. LLC.
—You Are My Baby - Farm. 2013. (ENG.). 10p. (J). (gr. -1 — 1). bds. 8.99 *(978-1-4521-0643-4(6))* Chronicle Bks. LLC.
—You Are My Baby - Safari. 2013. (ENG.). 10p. (J). (gr. -1 — 1). bds. 8.99 *(978-1-4521-0642-7(8))* Chronicle Bks. LLC.
—You Are My Baby: Garden. 2014. (ENG.). 10p. (J). (gr. -1 — 1). bds. 8.99 *(978-1-4521-2649-4(6))* Chronicle Bks. LLC.
—You Are My Baby: Meadow: (Baby First Boards Books for Easter, Bunny Books, Whale Ocean Books) 2015. (ENG.). 10p. (J). (gr. -1 — 1). bds. 8.99 *(978-1-4521-4011-7(1))* Chronicle Bks. LLC.
—You Are My Baby: Ocean. 2014. (ENG.). 10p. (J). (gr. -1 — 1). bds. 8.99 *(978-1-4521-2650-0(X))* Chronicle Bks. LLC.
—You Are My Baby: Woodland. 2014. (ENG.). 10p. (J). (gr. -1 — 1). bds. 8.99 *(978-1-4521-3431-4(6))* Chronicle Bks. LLC.
Siminovich, Lorena. Alex & Lulu: Two of a Kind. Siminovich, Lorena. 2009. (ENG.). 32p. (J). (gr. -1-3). 14.99 *(978-0-7636-4423-9(4),* Templar) Candlewick Pr.
—I Like Toys. Siminovich, Lorena. 2011. (Petit Collage Ser.). (ENG.). 10p. (J). (— 1). bds. 6.99 *(978-0-7636-5074-2(9),* Templar) Candlewick Pr.
Simione, Allen. Mike the Microbe. Simione, Ruth. Date not set. 38p. (J). (gr. 4-8). pap. 14.70 *(978-1-877960-23-9(3))* Kemtec Educational Corp.
Simko, Joe. Big Billy & the Ice Cream Truck That Wouldn't Stop, 1 vol. Consiglio, Joe. 2012. (ENG.). 48p. (J). (gr. -1-3). 16.99 *(978-0-7643-4067-3(0),* 9780764340673) Schiffer Publishing, Ltd.
Simko, Joe. The Sweet Rot Book 3: The Purple Meltdown, 1 vol. Simko, Joe. 2012. (ENG.). 32p. (YA). (gr. 8-12). 19.99 *(978-0-7643-3977-6(X),* 9780764339776) Schiffer Publishing, Ltd.
Simko, Joe & Tidwell, Jeral. Spirit Warriors: Number Two. Baldwin, Stephen & Rosato, Bruno. 2007. (Spirit Warriors Ser.). 208p. (YA). per. 9.99 *(978-0-8054-4355-4(X))* B&H Publishing Group.
Simko, Joe & Zapata, Jeff. Welcome to Smellville (Garbage Pail Kids Book 1) Stine, R. L. & The Topps Company. 2020. (Garbage Pail Kids Ser.). (ENG.). 208p. (J). (gr. 3-7). 14.99 ***(978-1-4197-4361-0(9),*** 1685401, Amulet Bks.) Abrams, Inc.
Simko, Joe, jt. illus. see Zapata, Jeff.
Simler, Isabelle. The Blue Hour. 2017. (J). 19.00 *(978-0-8028-5488-9(5),* Eerdmans Bks For Young Readers) Eerdmans, William B. Publishing Co.
—My Wild Cat. 2019. (ENG.). 64p. (J). *(978-0-8028-5525-1(3),* Eerdmans Bks For Young Readers) Eerdmans, William B. Publishing Co.
—Sweet Dreamers. Ardizzone, Sarah. 2019. (ENG.). 80p. (J). *(978-0-8028-5517-6(2),* Eerdmans Bks For Young Readers) Eerdmans, William B. Publishing Co.
—A Web. 2018. (J). *(978-1-4413-2843-4(2))* Peter Pauper Pr. Inc.
Simmans, Sean. The War of the Worlds. Wells, H. G. 2005. 220p. (YA). per. *(978-0-9737282-1-7(3))* Coscom Entertainment.
Simmonds, Brian. In the Lamplight. Wolfer, Dianne. 2018. (Lighthouse Girl Ser.). 120p. (J). (gr. 6). 14.99 *(978-1-925591-22-4(0))* Fremantle Pr. AUS. Dist: Independent Pubs. Group.
Simmonds, Brian. Light Horse Boy. Wolfer, Dianne. 2020. 120p. (J). (gr. 4-7). 14.95 ***(978-1-925815-10-8(2))*** Fremantle Pr. AUS. Dist: Independent Pubs. Group.
Simmonds, Frank H. The Tale of Strawberry Snow, 1 vol. Caudle, P. L. 2012. (ENG.). 48p. (J). (gr. -1-3). 16.99 *(978-0-7643-4076-5(X),* 9780764340765) Schiffer Publishing, Ltd.
Simmonds-Hurn, Zak, jt. illus. see Robinson, Lee.
Simmonds, Posy. Baker Cat. Simmonds, Posy. 2015. 32p. (J). (gr. -1-k). pap. 11.99 *(978-1-78344-105-1(4))* Andersen Pr. GBR. Dist: Independent Pubs. Group.
Simmons, Ann. Jojo the Dappled Dachshund. Jones, Cheryl & Joseph, Rahzheena. 2013. 30p. pap. 15.95 *(978-1-4787-0560-4(4))* Outskirts Pr., Inc.
Simmons, Bethany. Spy Recruit, 1 vol. Osborne, Erin. 2010. (ENG.). 216p. (J). (gr. 3-6). pap. 8.95 *(978-1-58980-782-2(0),* Pelican Publishing) Arcadia Publishing.
Simmons, Elly. Calling the Doves, 1 vol. Herrera, Juan Felipe. 2014.Tr. of Canto De Las Palomos. (ENG & SPA.). 32p. (J). (gr. 2-5). pap. 10.95 *(978-0-89239-166-0(9),* c95d9020-965f-4883-837a-863185ec97f6) Lee & Low Bks., Inc.
Simmons, Jane. Ebb & Flo & the Baby Seal. Simmons, Jane. 2017. (ENG.). 32p. (J). (gr. -1-2). 13.99 *(978-1-5344-2234-6(X),* McElderry, Margaret K. Bks.) McElderry, Margaret K. Bks.
Simmons, Judy. The Story of God: All He Ever Wanted Was a Family. Elick, Celeste Kaufhold. 2019. (ENG.). 46p. (J). 23.95 ***(978-1-64559-233-4(2))*** Covenant Bks.
Simmons, Marc. Rollercoaster Grandma! The True Story of Dr. Ruth. Westheimer, Ruth K. & Lehu, Pierre A. 2018. (J). *(978-1-68115-532-6(X),* Apples & Honey Pr.) Behrman Hse., Inc.
Simmons, Mark. Claudette Colvin Refuses to Move: Courageous Kid of the Civil Rights Movement. Wilkins, Ebony Joy. 2020. (Courageous Kids Ser.). (ENG.). 32p. (J). (gr. 3-5). pap. 7.95 ***(978-1-4966-8803-3(1),*** 201688); lib. bdg. 31.32 ***(978-1-4966-8502-5(4),*** 200558) Capstone. (Capstone Pr.).
Simmons, Mark. Titanic Disaster! Nickolas Flux & the Sinking of the Great Ship. Yomtov, Nelson. 2015. (Nickolas Flux History Chronicles Ser.). (ENG.). 32p. (J). (gr. 3-9). lib. bdg. 31.32 *(978-1-4914-2070-6(7),* Capstone Pr.) Capstone.
—Trapped in Antarctica! Nickolas Flux & the Shackleton Expedition. Yomtov, Nelson. 2015. (Nickolas Flux History Chronicles Ser.). (ENG.). 32p. (J). (gr. 3-9). lib. bdg. 31.32 *(978-1-4914-2069-0(3))* Capstone.
Simmons, Mark, jt. illus. see Foster, Brad W.
Simmons, Matthew J. a. The Quest for Piggy Jon: Edited by Amy D. Miller Illustrated by Matthew J. A. Simmons. Hartshorn, Brian K. Miller, Amy D., ed. 2018. (ENG.). 64p. (J). pap. 14.00 *(978-1-7904-9870-3(8))* Independently Published.
Simmons, Nataly. Norton & Marvin & Dad & Me. Ciofalo, J. F. 2019. (ENG.). 24p. (J). 22.95 ***(978-1-4808-7955-3(X));*** pap. 12.45 ***(978-1-4808-7953-9(3))*** Archway Publishing.
Simmons, Nataly. The Tigers & the Exciting Inviting Meal. Cutelli, Nick. 2018. (Tiger Kittens Ser.: Vol. 1). (ENG.). 26p. (J). pap. 14.99 *(978-0-692-11508-4(0))* Cutelli, Nick.
Simmons, R. Itsy-Bitsy's Science Adventure. J Douglas. 2018. (Itsy-Bitsy Science Ser.). (ENG.). 24p. (J). *(978-1-5255-3191-0(3));* pap. *(978-1-5255-3192-7(1))* FriesenPress.
Simmons, Robert. The Wind & Little Cloud. Hancock, Susan G. 2006. (J). (ENG.). 40p. spiral bd. 17.95 *(978-0-9741743-3-4(5));* 48p. (gr. -1-3). per. 10.95 *(978-0-9741743-0-3(0))* Perlycross Pubs.
Simmons, Russell. Hannah's Homework. Mayer, Nicole & Mayer, Ryan. 2012. 36p. (J). 14.95 *(978-0-9849293-0-6(4))* Beaner Bks.
Simms, Genevieve. Ojiichan's Gift. Uegaki, Chieri. 2019. (ENG.). 32p. (J). (gr. -1-2). 16.99 *(978-1-77138-963-1(X))* Kids Can Pr., Ltd. CAN. Dist: Hachette Bk. Group.
Simms, Genevieve. Screech! Ghost Stories from Old Newfoundland, 1 vol. Cotter, Charis. 2020. (ENG.). 156p. (J). pap. 14.95 ***(978-1-77108-906-7(7),*** b996928b-874e-4226-9607-4500276c08fa) Nimbus Publishing, Ltd. CAN. Dist: Baker & Taylor Publisher Services (BTPS).
Simó, Roger. The Civil Rights Movement. Ohlin, Nancy. 2017. (Blast Back! Ser.). (ENG.). 112p. (J). (gr. 2-5). 16.99 *(978-1-4998-0455-3(5));* pap. 5.99 *(978-1-4998-0454-6(7))* Little Bee Books Inc.
—Pearl Harbor. Ohlin, Nancy. 2018. (Blast Back! Ser.). (ENG.). 112p. (J). (gr. 2-5). 16.99 *(978-1-4998-0621-2(3));* pap. 5.99 *(978-1-4998-0620-5(5))* Little Bee Books Inc.
—The Space Race. Ohlin, Nancy. 2017. (Blast Back! Ser.). (ENG.). 112p. (J). (gr. 2-5). pap. 5.99 *(978-1-4998-0452-2(0))* Little Bee Books Inc.
—The Statue of Liberty. Ohlin, Nancy. 2017. (Blast Back! Ser.). (ENG.). 112p. (J). (gr. 2-5). pap. 5.99 *(978-1-4998-0456-0(3));* 16.99 *(978-1-4998-0457-7(1))* Little Bee Books Inc.
—Women's Suffrage. Ohlin, Nancy. 2018. (Blast Back! Ser.). (ENG.). 112p. (J). (gr. 2-5). 16.99 *(978-1-4998-0619-9(1));* pap. 5.99 *(978-1-4998-0618-2(3))* Little Bee Books Inc.
—World War II. Ohlin, Nancy. 2016. (Blast Back! Ser.). (ENG.). 112p. (J). (gr. 2-5). pap. 5.99 *(978-1-4998-0275-7(7))* Little Bee Books Inc.
Simon, A. Christopher. Grandfather's Garden: Some Bedtime Stories for Little & Big Folk. Loye, David. 2019. (ENG.). 128p. (J). (gr. k-6). pap. 14.95 ***(978-0-578-43090-4(8),*** Osanto Univ. Pr.) Benjamin Franklin Pr.
Simon, Annette. Robot Zombie Frankenstein! Simon, Annette. 2012. (ENG.). 40p. (J). (gr. -1-3). 16.99 *(978-0-7636-5124-4(9))* Candlewick Pr.
Simon, Eric M. The Story of Mozart. Kaufmann, Helen L. Meadowcroft, Enid Lamonte, ed. 2011. 190p. 42.95 *(978-1-258-06631-4(9))* Literary Licensing, LLC.
Simon, Laurent. Line & Dot. Cauchy, Véronique. 2018. 32p. (J). *(978-1-4338-2873-7(1),* Magination Pr.) American Psychological Assn.
Simon, Loris. Sirol. Salum, Rose Mary. 2005. (J). *(978-0-9770287-0-2(4))* Literal Publishing Inc.
Simon, Madeline Gerstein. Voyage to Shelter Cove. Nunez, Ralph da Costa & Ellison, Jesse Andrews. 2005. (J). pap. 5.00 *(978-0-9724425-3-4(7))* Homes for the Homeless Institute, Inc.
Simon, Rainer. The Adventures of Pauli Broccoli. Kuehn, Birgit S. 2016. (ENG.). (J). 17.99 *(978-0-9982234-0-7(9))* Boutique Natural Health Solutions, LLC.
—The Adventures of Pauli Broccoli. Kuehn, Birgit. 2016. (ENG.). (J). pap. 8.99 *(978-0-9982234-2-1(5))* Boutique Natural Health Solutions, LLC.
—Die Abenteuer Von Pauli Broccoli. Kuehn, Birgit. Volz, Heiko, tr. 2017. (GER.). 42p. (J). 18.99 *(978-0-9982234-4-5(1))* Boutique Natural Health Solutions, LLC.
Simon, Romain. Forest Animals. 2011. 90p. 38.95 *(978-1-258-10284-5(6))* Literary Licensing, LLC.
Simon, Seymour. Cats. Simon, Seymour. 2004. 40p. (J). (gr. -1-3). lib. bdg. 17.89 *(978-0-06-028941-6(4))* HarperCollins Pubs.
Simon, Sue A., et al. Big Keep Books- Spanish Emergent Reader 1: Mira como Juego; ¡Curitas!; Los Animales del Zoológico; Construyendo una Casa; la Alberca; ¡Agua y Jabón!; Me Visto; Mi Gato, 8 bks., Set. Estice, Rose Mary & Fried, Mary. Elías, Annette, tr. 2005.Tr. of Emergent Reader 1. (SPA.). 8p. (J). 20.00 *(978-1-893986-42-8(X))* Keep Bks.
—Health & Safety 1: Gym Class; Shopping for Lunch; Good for You; My Happy Heart; Just Like Me; Staying Safe; Always Brush Your Teeth; A Visit to the Doctor, 8 bks. Cicola, Amanda et al. ed. 2005. (ENG.). 8p. (J). pap. 120.00 *(978-1-893986-26-8(8))* Keep Bks.
—Health & Safety 2: Safety First; Don't Be a Couch Potato; Birthday Shots; Just in Case; Time Out; Home Sick; the Eye Doctor; the Big Race, 8 bks., Set. Pinnell, Gay Su et al. ed. 2005. (ENG.). 8p. (J). pap. 120.00 *(978-1-893986-27-5(6))* Keep Bks.
Simon, Susan. No Rules for Michael, Vol. Rouss, Sylvia A. 2004. (ENG.). 24p. (J). (gr. -1-1). pap. 6.95 *(978-1-58013-044-8(5),* Kar-Ben Publishing) Lerner Publishing Group.
Simon, Ute. Albert Einstein. Norwich, Grace. 2012. (I Am Ser.). (ENG.). 112p. (J). (gr. 3-7). pap. 5.99 *(978-0-545-40575-1(0),* Scholastic Paperbacks) Scholastic, Inc.
—Dracula, 1 vol. Stoker, Bram. 2011. (Calico Illustrated Classics Ser.: No. 3). (ENG.). 112p. (J). (gr. 2-5). 29.93 *(978-1-61641-101-5(5),* 4009, Calico Chapter Bks.) ABDO Publishing Co.
—Good Night Great Lakes. Gamble, Adam & Jasper, Mark. 2020. (Good Night Our World Ser.). 20p. (J). (— 1). bds. 9.95 *(978-1-60219-848-7(9))* Good Night Bks.
—I Am #6: Harriet Tubman. Norwich, Grace. 2013. (I Am Ser.: 6). (ENG.). 128p. (J). (gr. 2-5). pap. 5.99 *(978-0-545-48436-7(7),* Scholastic Paperbacks) Scholastic, Inc.
—I Am Harriet Tubman. Norwich, Grace. 2013. 127p. (J). *(978-0-545-61344-6(2))* Scholastic, Inc.
—I Am Lebron James. Norwich, Grace. 2014. 127p. (J). *(978-0-545-79428-2(5))* Scholastic, Inc.
—The Merry Adventures of Robin Hood. Pyle, Howard. 2011. (Calico Illustrated Classics Ser.: No. 3). (ENG.). 112p. (J). (gr. 2-5). 29.93 *(978-1-61641-107-7(4),* 4021, Calico Chapter Bks.) ABDO Publishing Co.
—The Secret Garden, 1 vol. Burnett, Frances Hodgson. 2011. (Calico Illustrated Classics Ser.: No. 3). (ENG.). 112p. (J). (gr. 2-5). 29.93 *(978-1-61641-108-4(2),* 4023, Calico Chapter Bks.) ABDO Publishing Co.
—A Tale of Two Cities. Dickens, Charles. 2010. (Calico Illustrated Classics Ser.: No. 1). (ENG.). 112p. (J). (gr. 2-5). 29.93 *(978-1-60270-712-2(X),* 3977, Calico Chapter Bks.) ABDO Publishing Co.
Simone, Julia. Halo Cat. Simone, Julia. 2017. (ENG.). (J). (gr. 2-6). pap. 9.99 *(978-0-692-82697-3(1))* Simone, Julia.
Simonet, Evan. Jake & the Sailing Tree. 2009. (J). *(978-1-60108-019-6(0))* Red Cygnet Pr.
Simonis, Cheryl, jt. illus. see Lind, Kathleen.
Simonnet, Aurore. Why Can't I Jump Very High? A Book about Gravity. Prasad, Kamal S. 2004. 32p. (J). lib. bdg. 14.95 *(978-0-9740861-5-6(0))* Science Square Publishing.
Simons, Marijke. A Halifax Time-Travelling Tune, 1 vol. Coates, Jan. 2018. (ENG.). 32p. (J). (gr. 1-3). 22.95 *(978-1-77108-569-4(X),* 23ab592d-2fa7-4a11-9e5c-a0c615012742) Nimbus Publishing, Ltd. CAN. Dist: Baker & Taylor Publisher Services (BTPS).
Simons, Marijke. Who's a Scaredy Cat! A Story of the Halifax Explosion, 1 vol. Simons, Marijke, tr. Payzant, Joan M. 2005. (ENG.). 85p. (J). (gr. 4-7). pap. 11.95 *(978-1-55109-456-4(8),* 42d732c4-6d67-4cbd-ba78-4510bf26b6db) Nimbus Publishing, Ltd. CAN. Dist: Baker & Taylor Publisher Services (BTPS).
Simons, Sally. Plants Grow Almost Anywhere. Walker, Colin. 2012. (Concept Science: Plants Ser.). (ENG.). 16p. (J). (gr. k-3). pap. 8.50 *(978-0-8136-7331-8(3))* Modern Curriculum Pr.
Simonson, Bill. The Hungry Homeless Dog. Simonson, Bill. 2016. (ENG.). (J). 19.99 *(978-0-9977466-8-6(8))* Mindstir Media.
Simonson, C. A. Finding Your Superpowers! Right Choices - Super Power. Simonson, C. A. 2019. (ENG.). 72p. (J). pap. 6.95 ***(978-1-7059-3806-5(X))*** Independently Published.
Simonson, Louise, et al. Meltdown, 3 vols. Simonson, Walter. 2003. (Wolverine Legends Ser.: Vol. 2). 200p. (YA). pap. 19.99 *(978-0-7851-1048-4(8))* Marvel Worldwide, Inc.
Simonson, Walt, et al. Star Wars Legends: Forever Crimson. 2020. (ENG.). 152p. (YA). (gr. 4-17). pap. 19.99 *(978-1-302-92377-8(3))* Marvel Worldwide, Inc.
Simont, Marc. Un Arbol Es Hermoso: A Tree Is Nice (Spanish Edition) Udry, Janice May. 2006.Tr. of Tree Is Nice. (SPA.). 32p. (J). (gr. -1-3). pap. 7.99 *(978-0-06-088708-7(7),* HarperCollins Español) HarperCollins Christian Publishing.
—The Backward Day. Krauss, Ruth. 2007. 40p. (J). (gr. -1-2). 14.95 *(978-1-59017-237-7(X),* NYR Children's Collection) New York Review of Bks., Inc., The.
—In the Year of the Boar & Jackie Robinson. Lord, Bette Bao. 2019. (ENG.). 176p. (J). (gr. 3-7). pap. 6.99 *(978-0-06-440175-3(8),* HarperCollins) HarperCollins Pubs. Ltd. GBR. Dist: HarperCollins Pubs.
—Nate the Great. Sharmat, Marjorie Weinman. (Nate the Great Ser.: No. 1). 48p. (J). (gr. 1-4). pap. 4.50 *(978-0-8072-1351-3(9),* Listening Library) Random Hse. Audio Publishing Group.
—Nate the Great & the Halloween Hunt. Sharmat, Marjorie Weinman. (Nate the Great Ser.: No. 12). 48p. (J). (gr. 1-4). pap. 4.50 *(978-0-8072-1283-7(0),* Listening Library) Random Hse. Audio Publishing Group.
—Nate the Great & the Missing Key. Sharmat, Marjorie Weinman. (Nate the Great Ser.: No. 6). 48p. (J). (gr. 1-4). pap. 4.50 *(978-0-8072-1335-3(7),* Listening Library) Random Hse. Audio Publishing Group.
—Nate the Great Goes Undercover. Sharmat, Marjorie Weinman. (Nate the Great Ser.: No. 2). 48p. (J). (gr. 1-4). pap. 4.50 *(978-0-8072-1284-4(9));* 2004. pap. 17.00 incl. audio *(978-0-8072-0201-2(0),* FTR172SP) Random Hse. Audio Publishing Group. (Listening Library).
—The Wonderful O. Thurber, James. 2017. (Penguin Classics Deluxe Edition Ser.). (ENG.). 96p. pap. 17.00 *(978-0-14-313042-0(0),* Penguin Classics) Penguin Publishing Group.
Simont, Marc. El Perro Vagabundo: The Stray Dog (Spanish Edition), 1 vol. Simont, Marc. 2003.Tr. of Stray Dog. (SPA.). 32p. (J). (gr. -1-3). pap. 7.99 *(978-0-06-052274-2(7),* HarperCollins Español) HarperCollins Christian Publishing.
—The Stray Dog. Simont, Marc. 2003. (ENG.). 32p. (J). (gr. -1-3). pap. 7.99 *(978-0-06-443669-4(1))* HarperCollins Pubs.
—The Stray Dog. Simont, Marc. 2004. (gr. -1-3). 17.00 *(978-0-7569-1912-2(6))* Perfection Learning Corp.
Simonton, Tom. Hoops & Me. Furr, L. David. 2005. (ENG.). 16p. (J). 5.75 *(978-1-57274-751-7(X),* 2746, Bks. for Young Learners) Owen, Richard C. Pubs., Inc.
—Jeepers. Rondinone, Craig. 2005. (ENG.). 16p. (J). 5.75 *(978-1-57274-755-5(2),* 2750, Bks. for Young Learners) Owen, Richard C. Pubs., Inc.
—The Stone Hat. Hood, Douglas. 2005. (ENG.). 16p. (J). 5.75 *(978-1-57274-754-8(4),* 2784, Bks. for Young Learners) Owen, Richard C. Pubs., Inc.
Simpkins, Iravis. One Sunny Day. Buzzy. Martin, John, ed. 2003. 52p. (J). (gr. -1-2). pap. 7.99 *(978-0-9719054-1-2(X))* Buzzy's Bks.
Simpson, Adam. The Life & Art of Wassily Kandinsky. Howard, Annabel. 2016. (Lives of Great Artists Ser.). 00080p. (J). (gr. 8-8). 35.75 *(978-1-4994-6582-2(3),* Rosen Young Adult) Rosen Publishing Group, Inc., The.
Simpson, Dana. I'm Not a Girl: A Transgender Story. Verdi, Jessica & Lyons, Maddox. 2020. (ENG.). 40p. (J). 18.99 *(978-0-374-31068-4(8),* 900193892) Roaring Brook Pr.
—Phoebe & Her Unicorn in the Magic Storm. 2017. 157p. (J). *(978-1-5182-5085-9(8))* Andrews McMeel Publishing.
Simpson, Don, et al. Crazy. 2020. (ENG.). 248p. (YA). (gr. 8-17). pap. 19.99 *(978-1-302-92331-0(5))* Marvel Worldwide, Inc.
Simpson, Finn. Katie Mcginty Wants a Pet! Harrington, Jenna. 2015. (ENG.). 32p. (J). (gr. -1-2). 16.99 *(978-1-58925-192-2(X))* Tiger Tales.
Simpson, Howard. Afro-Bets Quotes for Kids: Words for Kids to Live By. Hudson, Katura J. 2004. (Afro-Bets Ser.). 64p. (J). (gr. k-4). pap. 5.95 *(978-0-940975-89-7(0),* Sankofa Bks.) Just Us Bks., Inc.
—Book of Opposites. Hudson, Cheryl Willis. (Afro-Bets Ser.). (J). pap. 4.95 *(978-0-940975-11-8(4))* Just Us Bks., Inc.
—Book of Seasons. Hudson, Cheryl Willis. (Afro-Bets Ser.). (J). pap. 4.95 *(978-0-940975-15-6(7))* Just Us Bks., Inc.
—Kim & Jones Investigations: Welcome to Elm City. Foster, William H. 2009. (ENG.). 48p. (YA). per. 14.95 *(978-0-9740212-4-9(5))* Cedar Grove Bks.
—Through Loona's Door: A Tammy & Owen Adventure with Carter G. Woodson. 2009. 80p. (J). per. 14.95 *(978-0-9740212-2-5(9))* Cedar Grove Bks.
Simpson, Howard, jt. illus. see Blair, Culverson.
Simpson, Kara. The Boy Who Built a Wall Around Himself. Redford, Ali. 2015. (ENG.). 32p. (J). 15.95 *(978-1-84905-683-0(8),* 693905) Kingsley, Jessica Pubs. GBR. Dist: Hachette UK Distribution.
—The Mermaid Who Couldn't. Redford, Ali. 2018. (ENG.). 32p. (C). 15.95 *(978-1-78592-395-1(1),* 696630) Kingsley, Jessica Pubs. GBR. Dist: Hachette UK Distribution.
Simpson, L. M., jt. illus. see Jackson, I. L.
Simpson, Mary. America Vol. 3: Art Activities about Lewis & Clark, Pioneers, & Plains Indians. Merrill, Yvonne Y. 2009. (Hands-on Ser.: 3). (ENG.). 82p. (gr. k-10). pap. 25.00 *(978-0-9778797-1-7(2))* KK.
—Ancient People: Art Activities about Mesopotamia, Egypt, & Islam. Merrill, Yvonne Y. 2003. (Hands-on Ser.). (ENG.). 88p. (J). (gr. 4-7). pap. 20.00 *(978-0-9643177-8-9(8))* KK.
—Ancient People Vol. 2: Art Activities about Minoans, Mycenaeans, Trojans, Ancient Greeks, Etruscans, & Romans. Merrill, Yvonne Y. 2nd ed. 2004. (Hands-on Ser.). (ENG.). 88p. (J). (gr. 3-7). pap. 20.00 *(978-0-9643177-6-6(X))* KK.
Simpson, Michelle. Back Home. Fatehali, Shaista Kaba. 2019. (ENG.). 36p. (J). (gr. k-3). 22.95 *(978-1-947860-44-5(5))* Brandylane Pubs., Inc.
—Backyard Biology: Discover the Life Cycles & Adaptations Outside Your Door with Hands-On Science Activities. Latham, Donna. 2020. (Build It Yourself Ser.). 128p. (J). (gr. 4-7). (ENG.). 22.95 *(978-1-61930-892-3(4),* 3af6eec6-60dc-4ba7-b143-5e8cb9cdff5a); pap. 17.95 *(978-1-61930-895-4(9),* 638ef513-c23f-44b2-a49c-1d7671ef87f3) Nomad Pr.
Simpson, Michelle. Cinderella. Fandel, Jennifer Lee. 2020. (Fairy Tales Ser.). (ENG.). 32p. (J). (gr. k-2). pap. 6.95 ***(978-1-5158-7272-6(6),*** 201231); lib. bdg. 21.32 ***(978-1-5158-7116-3(9),*** 199334) Capstone. (Picture Window Bks.).
Simpson, Michelle. Hanukkah Harvie vs. Santa Claus. Slater, David Michael. 2017. (ENG.). (J). (gr. k-2). pap. 14.99 *(978-0-9992758-2-5(8))* Library Tales Publishing, Inc.
Simpson, Michelle. The Power in Me. Axel, Meaghan. 2020. (ENG.). 32p. (J). (gr. -1-3). 21.95 ***(978-1-947860-82-7(8));*** pap. 13.95 ***(978-1-947860-83-4(6))*** Brandylane Pubs., Inc. (Belle Isle Bks.).
Simpson, Michelle. The Science of Weather & Climate: Rain, Sleet, & the Rising Tide. Danneberg, Julie. 2020. (Inquire & Investigate Ser.). (ENG.). 128p. (J). (gr. 7-9). 22.95 *(978-1-61930-847-3(9),* f6527f7f-9bab-4570-bfeb-034841f78298); pap. 17.95 *(978-1-61930-850-3(9),* dc5629b1-0618-4f02-98a6-90a6b7172a6f) Nomad Pr.

S

Simpson, Michelle. Stranger Danger. Slater, David Michael. 2020. (Mr. Mensch & His Magical Meshugenahmob Ser.: 1). (ENG.). 66p. (J). (gr. 2-4). pap. 7.99 ***(978-1-944589-40-0(6))*** Market Management Group.

Simpson, Rob. Majik the Flying Pug. Meenaghan, M. S. Margaret. 2018. (ENG.). 32p. (J). pap. *(978-1-9997094-3-3(8))* Trench Publishing.

Simpson, Steve. Billy Bully. Galan, Alvaro. 2009. (ENG.). 32p. (J). (gr. -1-3). pap. 3.99 *(978-0-545-11012-9(2))* Scholastic, Inc.

—Day of the Dead Activity Book. Jones, Karl. 2013. 16p. (J). (gr. 1-4). 9.99 *(978-0-8431-7300-0(9)*, Price Stern Sloan) Penguin Young Readers Group.

—The Farmer in the Dell. 2009. (J). *(978-0-545-06702-7(2))* Scholastic, Inc.

Simpson, Tynicka. Aniya & the Power of a Positive Kid! West, Melissa. 2017. (ENG.). (J). pap. *(978-1-4602-9785-8(7))* FriesenPress.

Simpson, William. Pirates, Bats, & Dragons. Davis, Mike. 2004. 174p. (J). 15.95 *(978-0-9747078-2-2(1))* Perceval Pr.

Sims, Agnes & Shepard, Mary. Mary Poppins Opens the Door. Travers, P. L. 2006. (Mary Poppins Ser.: No. 3). (ENG.). 288p. (J). (gr. 5-7). 16.99 *(978-0-15-205822-7(2)*, 1197494) Houghton Mifflin Harcourt Publishing Co.

Sims, Agnes, jt. illus. see Shepard, Mary.

Sims, Blanche. Abracadabra: Magia para Niños: 50 Divertido Trucos Mágicos. Charney, Steve. 2004. (SPA.). 144p. (gr. 3-4). *(978-84-9754-111-4(1)*, 87442) Ediciones Oniro S.A.

—Bugged! Mosquitoes. Knudsen, Michelle. 2008. (Science Solves It! ® Ser.). (ENG.). 32p. (J). (gr. 1-3). pap. 5.95 *(978-1-57565-259-7(5))* Astra Publishing Hse.

—Check It Out! Historical Evidence. Walker, Nan. 2006. (Social Studies Connects ® Ser.). (ENG.). 32p. (J). (gr. 1-3). pap. 5.95 *(978-1-57565-166-8(1))* Astra Publishing Hse.

—The Cupcake Thief: Justice System. Jackson, Ellen. 2007. (Social Studies Connects ® Ser.). (ENG.). 32p. (J). (gr. 1-3). pap. 5.95 *(978-1-57565-247-4(1))* Astra Publishing Hse.

—Lila the Fair: Conflict Resolution. Driscoll, Laura. 2006. (Social Studies Connects ® Ser.). (ENG.). 32p. (J). (gr. 1-3). pap. 5.95 *(978-1-57565-148-4(3))* Astra Publishing Hse.

—The Longest Yawn: Involuntary Reflexes. Dussling, Jennifer. 2006. (Science Solves It! ® Ser.). (ENG.). 32p. (J). (gr. 1-3). pap. 5.95 *(978-1-57565-160-6(2))* Astra Publishing Hse.

—Pete for President! Elections. Alberto, Daisy. 2006. (Social Studies Connects ® Ser.). (ENG.). 32p. (J). (gr. 1-3). pap. 5.95 *(978-1-57565-142-2(4))* Astra Publishing Hse.

—Sidewalk Chalk: Outdoor Fun & Games. McGillian, Jamie Kyle. 2006. 80p. (J). (gr. k-4). reprint ed. 18.00 *(978-1-4223-5580-0(2))* DIANE Publishing Co.

—Soccer Song. Giff, Patricia Reilly. 2008. (Green Light Readers Level 2 Ser.). (ENG.). 24p. (J). (gr. k-2). pap. 4.99 *(978-0-15-206565-2(2)*, 1199543) Houghton Mifflin Harcourt Publishing Co.

—Who Needs It? May, Eleanor. 2009. (Social Studies Connects ® Ser.). (ENG.). (gr. 1-3). pap. 33.92 *(978-0-7613-4804-7(2))* Lerner Publishing Group.

—Who Needs It? Wants & Needs. May, Eleanor. 2009. (Social Studies Connects ® Ser.). (ENG.). 32p. (J). (gr. 1-3). pap. 5.95 *(978-1-57565-281-8(1))* Astra Publishing Hse.

Sims, Bryan. My Little Golden Book about the First Moon Landing. Lovitt, Charles. 2019. (Little Golden Book Ser.). (ENG.). 24p. (J). (-k). 4.99 *(978-0-525-58007-2(7)*, Golden Bks.) Random Hse. Children's Bks.

Sims, David. Jungle School. Davison, Roz & Laird, Elizabeth. 2nd ed. 2016. (Reading Ladder Ser.). (ENG.). 48p. (J). (gr. k-2). pap. 7.99 *(978-1-4052-8226-0(6))* Egmont Bks., Ltd. GBR. Dist: Independent Pubs. Group.

Sims, Kathy C. Louisiana Potpourri from A to Z. Sims, Kathy C., text. 2004.Tr. of Potpourri Louisianais d' A à Z. (FRE.). 64p. (YA). lib. bdg. 24.95 *(978-0-9753435-0-0(5))* Louisiana Ladybug Pr.

Sims, Sean. The Adventures of Your Brain. Green, Dan. 2017. (ENG.). 14p. (J). (gr. k). 14.95 *(978-1-4549-2512-5(4))* Sterling Publishing Co., Inc.

—Dressing for the Weather Green Band. Harper, Kathryn. 2016. (Cambridge Reading Adventures Ser.). (ENG.). 16p. pap. 7.37 *(978-1-316-50324-9(0))* Cambridge Univ. Pr.

—Planet Earth. Green, Dan. 2017. (Reading Ladder Ser.). (ENG.). 32p. (J). (gr. 1-3). pap. 7.99 *(978-1-4052-8495-0(1))* Egmont Bks., Ltd. GBR. Dist: Independent Pubs. Group.

—The Water Cycle. Rose, Malcolm. 2017. (Reading Ladder Ser.). (ENG.). 32p. (J). (gr. 1-3). pap. 7.99 *(978-1-4052-8493-6(5))* Egmont Bks., Ltd. GBR. Dist: Independent Pubs. Group.

Simsek, Denise Michele, jt. illus. see Michelle, Aliyat.

Simson, Dana. Janey Monarch Seed. Dunlap, Julie. 2020. (ENG.). 32p. (J). (gr. k-2). 19.95 *(978-1-7336534-8-0(1))* Green Writers Pr.

Simson, Dana. Dreamland. Simson, Dana. Book Company Staff. 2003. (Pop-up Bks.). 14p. (J). 15.95 *(978-1-74047-211-1(X))* Book Co. Publishing Pty, Ltd., The AUS. Dist: Penton Overseas, Inc.

Sinclair, Alex, jt. illus. see Williams, Scott.

Sinclair, Bella. Ava's Secret Tea Party. Shepherd, Donna J. 2012. 24p. 19.95 *(978-1-61633-285-3(9))*; pap. 11.95 *(978-1-61633-286-0(7))* Guardian Angel Publishing, Inc.

—Lulu & the Witch Baby. O'Connor, Jane. 2014. (I Can Read Level 2 Ser.). (ENG.). 48p. (J). (gr. -1-3). pap. 4.99 *(978-0-06-230516-9(6)*, HarperCollins) HarperCollins Pubs. Ltd. GBR. Dist: HarperCollins Pubs.

—Lulu Goes to Witch School. O'Connor, Jane. 2013. (I Can Read Level 2 Ser.). (ENG.). 48p. (J). (gr. -1-3). 16.99 *(978-0-06-223351-6(3))*; pap. 4.99 *(978-0-06-223350-9(5))* HarperCollins Pubs. Ltd. GBR. (HarperCollins). Dist: HarperCollins Pubs.

Sinclair, Drew. Alana Loses a Tooth. Morgan, Rebecca. 2019. (ENG.). 42p. (J). pap. *(978-1-912551-58-3(6))* Conscious Dreams Publishing.

Sinclair, Drew. The Thief, the Witch, & the Shop of Curiosities. Isherwood, Mark. 2019. (ENG.). 204p. (J). (gr. 5-6). pap. 9.99 ***(978-1-63233-230-1(2))*** Elfrig Publishing.

Sinclair, James. Hellboy: Despierta al Demonio, Mignola, Mike. Abuli, Enrique Sánchez, tr. from ENG. 2004. Orig. Title: Hellboy: Wake the Devil. (SPA.). 144p. pap. 22.95 *(978-1-59497-027-6(0))* Public Square Bks.

Sinclair, Jeff. Mental Magic: Surefire Tricks to Amaze Your Friends. Gardner, Martin. 2010. (Dover Children's Activity Bks.). (ENG.). 96p. (J). (gr. 3-5). pap. 4.99 *(978-0-486-47495-3(X))* Dover Pubns., Inc.

Sinclair, Mandy. Septimus Pitt & the Grumbleoids, 22 vols. Whittingham, Brian. 2007. (ENG.). 48p. (J). 17.95 *(978-1-905222-81-0(5)*, 6ad3493d-bd75-480a-84c9-23c996ad6c41) Luath Pr. Ltd. GBR. Dist: Midpoint Trade Bks., Inc.

Sinclair, Peter. Grandpa's Crooked Smile: A Story of Stroke Survival. Reeves, Barbara. 2007. (J). *(978-1-4276-2013-2(X))* Aardvark Global Publishing.

Singer, Rhona Stein. There Can't Bee Two Queens in the Same Hive. Singer, Rhona Stein. l.t. ed. 2004. 32p. (J). pap. *(978-0-9687946-2-3(9))* Stone Woman Warrior Pr.

Singer, Ryan. Johonaa'éí: Bringer of Dawn. Tsinajinnie, Veronica. Thomas, Peter A., tr. from NAV. 2007. (ENG & NAV.). 32p. (J). (gr. -1-3). 17.95 *(978-1-893354-54-8(7))* Salina Bookshelf Inc.

Singh, Jen. Cheap Psychological Tricks for Parents: 62 Sure-Fire Secrets & Solutions for Successful Parenting, 1 vol. Buffington, Perry. 2003. (ENG.). 160p. pap. 9.95 *(978-1-56145-204-0(1))* Peachtree Publishing Co. Inc.

—It Can't Be Done, Nellie Bly! a Reporter's Race Around the World, 1 vol. Butcher, Nancy. 2003. (ENG.). 144p. (J). (gr. 2-5). 12.95 *(978-1-56145-289-7(0))* Peachtree Publishing Co. Inc.

Singh Kale, Kavita. Good Night Taj Mahal. Khemka, Nitya Mohan. 2019. (Good Night Our World Ser.). 20p. (J). (— 1). bds. 9.95 *(978-1-60219-673-5(7))* Good Night Bks.

Singh, Lalit Kumar. 400 BC: The Story of the Ten Thousand. Helfand, Lewis. 2011. (Campfire Graphic Novels Ser.). (ENG.). 72p. (YA). (gr. 5-12). pap. 9.99 *(978-93-80028-61-3(X)*, Campfire) Steerforth Pr.

Singh, Niharika. Snail's Dangerous Journey. Malloney, Gemma. 2016. (ENG.). 27p. (J). pap. *(978-0-9933603-2-9(7))* Bower Maze.

Singh, Nikhil. Salem Brownstone: All along the Watchtowers. Singh, Nikhil. Dunning, John Harris. 2010. (ENG.). 96p. (YA). (gr. 7-18). 18.99 *(978-0-7636-4735-3(7))* Candlewick Pr.

Singh, Parwinder. Collins Big Cat Phonics for Letters & Sounds - Tip It in!: Band 01A/Pink A. Wells, Alexandra. 2020. (Collins Big Cat Phonics for Letters & Sounds Ser.). (ENG.). 16p. (J). (gr. -1-k). pap. 6.99 *(978-0-00-835757-3(9))* HarperCollins Pubs. Ltd. GBR. Dist: Independent Pubs. Group.

—Let's Eat! Mealtime Around the World, Vol. Marie, Lynne. 2019. (ENG.). 32p. (J). (gr. -1-3). 17.99 *(978-1-5064-5194-7(2)*, Beaming Books) Augsburg Fortress, Pubs.

—Seymour, the Formerly Fearful. Feldman, Eve B. 2019. (ENG.). 184p. (J). (gr. 3-6). pap. 8.99 *(978-1-5415-3951-8(6)*, Kar-Ben Publishing) Lerner Publishing Group.

Singleton, Glen. No Way-Can't Believe It-Totally Freaky Facts. Bryant, Nick & Hewat, Katie. 2019. (ENG.). 208p. (J). (gr. 3-7). pap. 12.99 *(978-1-68412-593-7(6)*, Silver Dolphin Bks.) Printers Row Publishing Group.

—Topsy-Turvy Tongue Twisters & More. 2020. (ENG.). 208p. (J). (gr. 3-7). pap. 12.99 *(978-1-68412-594-4(4)*, Silver Dolphin Bks.) Printers Row Publishing Group.

—Yuck! Ick! Eww! the Grossest Jokes Ever. 2020. (ENG.). 208p. (J). (gr. 3-7). pap. 12.99 *(978-1-68412-592-0(8)*, Silver Dolphin Bks.) Printers Row Publishing Group.

Singleton, Waymond. The Moonlight Meeting. Hecht, Tracey & Dowling, Rumur. 2017. (Grow & Read Early Reader, Level 2 Ser.). 64p. (J). (gr. k-2). pap. 5.99 *(978-1-944020-14-9(4)*, Fabled Films Pr. LLC) Fabled Films LLC.

Sinha, Rhea. Latte's Vacation. Sinha, Rhea. 2011. 20p. pap. 7.50 *(978-1-61170-045-9(0))* Robertson Publishing.

Siniard, Ricky. Joel's Adventure at Sea. Fenton, Geleta. 2013. 50p. (J). mass mkt. 9.95 *(978-0-9824433-2-3(3))* Octopus Publishing Co.

Sink, Cynthia. The Nautical Road: A Straight Forward Approach to Learning the Navigation Rules. Pritchard, Herman S. Helwig, Teresa L., ed. 2nd rev. l.t. ed. 2004. 176p. (YA). 29.95 *(978-0-9716479-3-0(3))* Selby Dean Ventures, Inc.

Sinkovec, Igor. Blood Shark! Dahl, Michael. 2015. (Igor's Lab of Fear Ser.). (ENG.). 40p. (J). (gr. 4-8). lib. bdg. 23.99 *(978-1-4965-0456-2(9)*, Stone Arch Bks.) Capstone.

—How Long? Wacky Ways to Compare Length, 1 vol. Gunderson, Jessica. 2013. (Wacky Comparisons Ser.). (ENG.). 24p. (J). (gr. -1-2). 28.65 *(978-1-4048-8324-6(X))*; pap. 8.95 *(978-1-4795-1914-9(6))* Capstone. (Picture Window Bks.).

—How Tall? Wacky Ways to Compare Height, 1 vol. Weakland, Mark. 2013. (Wacky Comparisons Ser.). (ENG.). 24p. (J). (gr. -1-2). 28.65 *(978-1-4048-8323-9(1))*; pap. 8.95 *(978-1-4795-1913-2(8))* Capstone. (Picture Window Bks.).

—A Jar of Eyeballs. Dahl, Michael. 2015. (Igor's Lab of Fear Ser.). (ENG.). 40p. (J). (gr. 4-8). lib. bdg. 23.99 *(978-1-4965-0455-5(0)*, Stone Arch Bks.) Capstone.

—Ooze Is It? Dahl, Michael. 2015. (Igor's Lab of Fear Ser.). (ENG.). 40p. (J). (gr. 4-8). lib. bdg. 23.99 *(978-1-4965-0457-9(7)*, Stone Arch Bks.) Capstone.

—Werewolf Skin. Dahl, Michael. 2015. (Igor's Lab of Fear Ser.). (ENG.). 40p. (J). (gr. 4-8). lib. bdg. 23.99 *(978-1-4965-0458-6(5)*, Stone Arch Bks.) Capstone.

Sinnott, Adrian. Grasshopper Pie & Other Poems. Steinberg, D. J. 2004. (Penguin Young Readers, Level 3 Ser.). (ENG.). 48p. (J). (gr. 1-3). pap. 4.99 *(978-0-448-43347-9(8)*, Penguin Young Readers) Penguin Young Readers Group.

Sinnott, Jennie. Happy Tales of Happy Tails. Clough, Jean. 2017. (ENG.). (J). pap. *(978-1-78645-170-5(0))* Beaten Track Publishing.

Sinquett, Jaclyn. Farm Animals. Wing, Scarlett. Cottage Door Press, ed. 2020. (8-Button Early Bird Switch Sound Book Ser.). (ENG.). 18p. (J). (gr. -1 — 1). bds. 14.99 ***(978-1-68052-949-4(8)***, 1005920) Cottage Door Pr.

Siobhan, Bell. We All Go Traveling By. Sheena, Roberts & Roberts, Sheena. 2003. (ENG.). 24p. (J). pap. 6.99 *(978-1-84148-595-9(0))* Barefoot Bks., Inc.

Siqueira, Paulo. Wolverine: the Daughter of Wolverine. 2020. (ENG.). 120p. (gr. 10-17). pap. 15.99 *(978-1-302-91836-1(2))* Marvel Worldwide, Inc.

Sirac. Don't Put Gum in the Fish Bowl. Stuart, Wesley. l.t. ed. 2018. (ENG.). 16p. (J). (gr. k-3). pap. 9.95 *(978-1-61633-911-1(X))* Guardian Angel Publishing, Inc.

Siragusa, Renato. Brain Blitz. Lawrence, David. 2018. (Get in the Game Ser.). 32p. (J). (gr. 3-8). lib. bdg. 29.93 *(978-1-5321-3293-3(X)*, 28491, Graphic Planet - Fiction) Magic Wagon.

—Set & Spike. Yu, Bill. 2018. (Get in the Game Ser.). 32p. (J). (gr. 3-8). lib. bdg. 29.93 *(978-1-5321-3296-4(4)*, 28497, Graphic Planet - Fiction) Magic Wagon.

—Star Striker. Yu, Bill. 2018. (Get in the Game Ser.). 32p. (J). (gr. 3-8). lib. bdg. 29.93 *(978-1-5321-3297-1(2)*, 28499, Graphic Planet - Fiction) Magic Wagon.

Sirah, Rio. Be Your Own Boss. Abner, Lalanya. 2016. (Imagine Beyond Boundaries Bks.: Vol. 1). (ENG.). (J). pap. 16.50 *(978-0-692-63132-4(1))* LMA Publishing.

Siravo, Christina E. An Orphan's Promise: A Christmas Story. Davis, Dan. Davis, Jan, ed. 2006. 96p. (J). 14.95 *(978-0-9725977-5-3(1))* Second Star Creations.

Sirianni, Emily. Teddy Tippytoes. Edwards, Jean. 2019. (ENG.). 26p. (J). pap. 21.99 ***(978-1-7960-6548-0(X))*** Xlibris Corp.

Sirls, Jq. Hair. Styles, Angela C. 2018. (ENG.). (J). 16.99 *(978-0-9974495-1-8(9))* AngelaCstyles Holdngs LLC.

Sirois, Douglas A. Outrunning the Nazis: The Brave Escape of Resistance Fighter Sven Somme. Chandler, Matt. 2017. (Great Escapes of World War II Ser.). (ENG.). 32p. (J). (gr. 3-9). lib. bdg. 31.32 *(978-1-5157-3529-8(X)*, Capstone Pr.) Capstone.

Sirotich, Erica. JP & the Bossy Dinosaur: Feeling Unhappy. Crespo, Ana. 2016. (My Emotions & Me Ser.). (ENG.). 32p. (J). (gr. -1-3). 16.99 *(978-0-8075-3981-1(3)*, 807539813) Whitman, Albert & Co.

—JP & the Giant Octopus: Feeling Afraid. Crespo, Ana. 2015. (My Emotions & Me Ser.). (ENG.). 32p. (J). (gr. -1-3). 16.99 *(978-0-8075-3975-0(9)*, 807539759) Whitman, Albert & Co.

—JP & the Polka-Dotted Aliens: Feeling Angry. Crespo, Ana. 2015. (My Emotions & Me Ser.). (ENG.). 32p. (J). (gr. -1-3). 16.99 *(978-0-8075-3977-4(5)*, 807539775) Whitman, Albert & Co.

—JP & the Stinky Monster: Feeling Jealous. Crespo, Ana. 2016. (My Emotions & Me Ser.). (ENG.). 32p. (J). (gr. -1-3). 16.99 *(978-0-8075-3979-8(1)*, 807539791) Whitman, Albert & Co.

Sirrell, Terri. Power Reading: Chapter Books/Wizard of OZ. Cole, Bob. 2004. 94p. (J). (gr. 3-4). vinyl bd. 39.95 *(978-1-883186-64-7(1)*, PPCL1) National Reading Styles Institute, Inc.

—Power Reading: Chapter/Sci-Fi/Dr. Little. Cole, Bob. 2004. 25p. (J). (gr. 3-4). vinyl bd. 39.95 *(978-1-883186-63-0(3)*, PPSF1) National Reading Styles Institute, Inc.

—Power Reading: Comic Book/Dr. Little. Cole, Bob. 2005. 36p. (J). (gr. 2-4). vinyl bd. *(978-1-883186-77-7(3)*, PPSFC1) National Reading Styles Institute, Inc.

—Power Reading: Comic Book/Wizard of OZ. Cole, Bob. 2005. 60p. (J). (gr. 3-4). vinyl bd. 39.95 *(978-1-883186-80-7(3)*, PPCLC1) National Reading Styles Institute, Inc.

Sirrell, Terry. I Love Trees. Meister, Cari. 2011. (Rookie Ready to Learn Ser.). 40p. (J). pap. 5.95 *(978-0-531-26733-2(4))*; (ENG.). (gr. -1-1). lib. bdg. 23.00 *(978-0-531-26501-7(3))* Scholastic Library Publishing. (Children's Pr.).

Sirrell, Terry. Me Fascinan Los Árboles. Sirrell, Terry. Meister, Cari. 2005. (Rookie Reader Español Ser.). (ENG & SPA.). 32p. (J). (gr. k-2). 19.50 *(978-0-516-25253-7(4)*, Children's Pr.) Scholastic Library Publishing.

—Me Fascinan los Árboles. Sirrell, Terry. Meister, Cari. 2011. (Rookie Ready to Learn Español Ser.). (SPA.). 40p. (J). pap. 5.95 *(978-0-531-26786-8(5)*, Children's Pr.) Scholastic Library Publishing.

Sís, Peter. A Collection of Rudyard Kipling's Just So Stories. Kipling, Rudyard. 2004. (ENG.). 128p. (J). (gr. k-12). 22.99 *(978-0-7636-2629-7(5))* Candlewick Pr.

Sis, Peter. The Dream Stealer. Fleischman, Sid. (ENG.). (J). 2011. 128p. pap. 6.99 *(978-0-06-178729-4(9))*; 2009. 96p. (gr. 4-18). 16.99 *(978-0-06-175563-7(X))* HarperCollins Pubs. (Greenwillow Bks.).

Sís, Peter. The Dreamer. Ryan, Pam Muñoz. 2010. (ENG.). 384p. (J). (gr. 4-9). 21.99 *(978-0-439-26970-4(9)*, Scholastic Pr.) Scholastic, Inc.

Sis, Peter. The Ghost in the Noonday Sun. Fleischman, Sid. 2007. (ENG.). 256p. (J). (gr. 3-7). per. 5.99 *(978-0-06-134502-9(4)*, Greenwillow Bks.) HarperCollins Pubs.

Sís, Peter. The Little Wing Giver. Taravant, Jacques. Ignatowicz, Nina, tr. from FRE. 2004. 30p. (J). (gr. k-4). reprint ed. 15.00 *(978-0-7567-7970-2(7))* DIANE Publishing Co.

Sis, Peter. The Midnight Horse. Fleischman, Sid. 2004. (ENG.). 96p. (J). (gr. 3-7). pap. 5.99 *(978-0-06-072216-6(9)*, Greenwillow Bks.) HarperCollins Pubs.

—Scranimals. Prelutsky, Jack. 2006. (ENG.). 48p. (J). (gr. -1-3). reprint ed. pap. 7.99 *(978-0-06-075368-9(4)*, Greenwillow Bks.) HarperCollins Pubs.

Sís, Peter. El Soñador. Ryan, Pam Muñoz. 2010. (SPA.). 368p. (J). (gr. 4-7). pap. 8.99 *(978-0-545-17600-2(X)*, Scholastic en Espanol) Scholastic, Inc.

Sis, Peter. The Whipping Boy. Fleischman, Sid. 2003. (HarperClassics Ser.). (ENG.). 96p. (J). (gr. 3-8). pap. 6.99 *(978-0-06-052122-6(8)*, Greenwillow Bks.) HarperCollins Pubs.

—The 13th Floor: A Ghost Story. Fleischman, Sid. 2007. (ENG.). 240p. (J). (gr. 3-7). per. 7.99 *(978-0-06-134503-6(2)*, Greenwillow Bks.) HarperCollins Pubs.

Sis, Peter. Ballerina! Board Book. Sis, Peter. 2005. (ENG.). 30p. (J). (gr. -1-1). bds. 7.99 *(978-0-06-075966-7(6)*, Greenwillow Bks.) HarperCollins Pubs.

—Fire Truck Board Book. Sis, Peter. 2004. (ENG.). 28p. (J). (gr. -1-1). bds. 6.99 *(978-0-06-056259-5(5)*, Greenwillow Bks.) HarperCollins Pubs.

—Follow the Dream: The Story of Christopher Columbus. Sis, Peter. 2003. (ENG.). 40p. (J). (gr. -1-2). 15.95 *(978-0-679-80628-8(8)*, Knopf Bks. for Young Readers) Random Hse. Children's Bks.

Sís, Peter. Ice Cream Summer. Sís, Peter. 2015. (ENG.). 40p. (J). (gr. k-3). 17.99 *(978-0-545-73161-4(5)*, Scholastic Pr.) Scholastic, Inc.

—Play, Mozart, Play! Sís, Peter. 2006. 32p. (J). (gr. -1-3). 16.99 *(978-0-06-112181-4(9)*, Greenwillow Bks.) HarperCollins Pubs.

—Robinson. Sís, Peter. 2017. (ENG.). 48p. (J). (gr. -1-3). 17.99 *(978-0-545-73166-9(6)*, Scholastic Pr.) Scholastic, Inc.

—The Train of States. Sís, Peter. 2004. 64p. (J). (gr. 1-18). 17.99 *(978-0-06-057838-1(6))* HarperCollins Pubs.

Sis, Peter. The Train of States. Sis, Peter. 2007. (ENG.). 64p. (J). (gr. k-5). pap. 7.99 *(978-0-06-057840-4(8)*, Greenwillow Bks.) HarperCollins Pubs.

Sís, Peter. The Tree of Life: Charles Darwin. Sís, Peter. 2003. (ENG.). 44p. (J). (gr. k-3). 24.99 *(978-0-374-45628-3(3)*, 9780374456283, Farrar, Straus & Giroux (BYR)) Farrar, Straus & Giroux.

Sis, Peter. Trucks Trucks Trucks Board Book. Sis, Peter. 2004. (ENG.). 28p. (J). (gr. -1-1). bds. 8.99 *(978-0-06-056258-8(7)*, Greenwillow Bks.) HarperCollins Pubs.

Sís, Peter & Sís, Peter. The Dreamer. Ryan, Pam Muñoz. 2012. (ENG.). 384p. (J). (gr. 4-7). pap. 8.99 *(978-0-439-26998-8(9)*, Scholastic Paperbacks) Scholastic, Inc.

—Madlenka. Sís, Peter & Sís, Peter. 2010. (Madlenka Ser.). (ENG.). 48p. (J). (gr. k-2). pap. 9.99 *(978-0-312-65912-7(1)*, 900070485) Square Fish.

—The Pilot & the Little Prince: The Life of Antoine de Saint-Exupéry. Sís, Peter & Sís, Peter. 2014. (ENG.). 48p. (J). (gr. k-3). 18.99 *(978-0-374-38069-4(4)*, 900069447, Farrar, Straus & Giroux (BYR)) Farrar, Straus & Giroux.

—The Wall: Growing up Behind the Iron Curtain. Sís, Peter & Sís, Peter. 2007. (ENG.). 56p. (J). (gr. 3-7). 19.99 *(978-0-374-34701-7(8)*, 900029246, Farrar, Straus & Giroux (BYR)) Farrar, Straus & Giroux.

Sís, Peter, jt. illus. see Sís, Peter.

Sisco, Anthony G. The Miracle of Good Seed. Sisco, Anthony G. 2018. (ENG.). 40p. (J). pap. 12.00 *(978-1-7291-7557-6(0))* Independently Published.

Sislen, Dayne. The Girl Who Found Christmas: An Advent Calendar Storybook. Escher, Barbara. 2019. (ENG.). 146p. (J). (gr. -1-3). 17.99 *(978-1-7333034-1-5(3))* Red Mitten Bks., LLC.

—Shark Dentists & Other Stories. Immordino, Vincent. Krell, Stephanie, ed. 2017. (ENG.). (J). (gr. k-5). 15.99 *(978-0-9993322-0-7(1))* Intelligent Design Pr., Ltd.

Sisneros, Shawn. Shelby. Nyikos, Stacy. 2006. 32p. (J). (gr. -1-3). 15.95 *(978-0-9764199-1-4(2))* Stonehorse Publishing, LLC.

—Squirt. Nyikos, Stacy Ann. l.t. ed. 2005. 32p. (J). lib. bdg. 15.95 *(978-0-9764199-0-7(4))* Stonehorse Publishing, LLC.

Sisson, Elayna. Secret of the Magic Stones. Zimmerman, Nancy. 2018. (ENG.). 48p. (J). pap. 10.00 *(978-0-692-91758-9(6))* Hedgehog Hill Pr.

Sisson, Stephanie Roth. Persuading Miss Doover. Pulver, Robin. 32p. (J). 2020. (gr. -1-3). pap. 8.99 ***(978-0-8234-4672-8(7))***; 2018. (gr. 1-4). 17.99 *(978-0-8234-3426-8(5))* Holiday Hse., Inc.

Sisson, Stéphanie Roth. A Pocketful of Princess Posey: First Grade Parade-Perfect Present-Next-Door Dog. Greene, Stephanie. 2014. (Princess Posey, First Grader Ser.). 288p. (J). (gr. k-3). 8.99 *(978-0-14-751472-1(X)*, Puffin Books) Penguin Young Readers Group.

—Princess Posey & the First Grade Parade, Bk. 1. Greene, Stephanie. 2011. (Princess Posey, First Grader Ser.: 1). 96p. (J). (gr. k-3). 5.99 *(978-0-14-241827-7(7)*, Puffin Books) Penguin Young Readers Group.

Sisson, Stephanie Roth. Princess Posey & the First Grade Play. Greene, Stephanie. 2017. (Princess Posey, First Grader Ser.: 11). 96p. (J). (gr. k-3). 5.99 *(978-0-14-751719-7(2)*, Puffin Books) Penguin Young Readers Group.

Sisson, Stéphanie Roth. Princess Posey & the Monster Stew, 4 vols. Greene, Stephanie. 2012. (Princess Posey, First Grader Ser.: 4). 96p. (J). (gr. k-3). pap. 5.99 *(978-0-14-242105-5(7)*, Puffin Books) Penguin Young Readers Group.

—Princess Posey & the Next-Door Dog, 3 vols. Greene, Stephanie. 2011. (Princess Posey, First Grader Ser.: 3). 96p. (J). (gr. k-3). 5.99 *(978-0-14-241939-7(7)*, Puffin Books) Penguin Young Readers Group.

—Princess Posey & the Tiny Treasure. Greene, Stephanie. 2013. (Princess Posey, First Grader Ser.: 5). 96p. (J). (gr. k-3). pap. 5.99 *(978-0-14-242415-5(3)*, Puffin Books) Penguin Young Readers Group.

—The Sunhat. Ward, Jennifer. 2013. (ENG.). (J). 15.95 *(978-1-933855-78-3(9)*, Rio Nuevo Pubs.) Rio Nuevo Pubs.

Sister Mary of the Compassion. Saint John Masias: Marvelous Dominican Gatekeeper of Lima, Peru. Windeatt, Mary F. 2009. Orig. Title: Warrior in White. (ENG.). 156p. (J). (gr. 3-9). pap. 11.95 *(978-0-89555-428-4(3))* TAN Bks.

Sisters, Dominican & Cardinali, Diana. Catholic Arithmetic Grade 2. Andreski, Elaine, ed. 2019. (Catholic Arithmetic Ser.: Vol. 2). (ENG.). 272p. (J). pap. 21.95 (978-1-0949-0143-5(1)) Independently Published.
Sisterson, Sarah M. Sea Babies. Skwish, Emily. 2016. (ENG.). 12p. (J). bds. (978-1-5037-0516-6(1), 57005d09-bfd0-4f98-b593-c4ea4afdfbe8, p i kids) Phoenix International Publications, Inc.
Sistig, Heike. Prince Noah & the School Pirates. Schnee, Silke. 2016. (Prince Noah Book Ser.). (ENG.). 32p. (J). 16.00 (978-0-87486-765-7(7)) Plough Publishing Hse.
—The Prince Who Was Just Himself. Schnee, Silke. 2015. (Prince Noah Book Ser.). 32p. (J). (gr. -1-4). 16.00 (978-0-87486-682-7(0)) Plough Publishing Hse.
Sisung, Peter. Do You Know the Way to Find an A? A Rhyming ABC Book. Wildman, Dale. 2006. 24p. (J). per. 2.99 (978-1-59958-002-9(0)) Journey Stone Creations, LLC.
—Nicholas Knows: Big Brother Nicholas Knows It All! Wildman, Dale. 2006. 24p. (J). per. 2.99 (978-1-59958-005-0(5)) Journey Stone Creations, LLC.
Sita, Sofia. Twas the Night Before Christmas. Moore, Clement C. 2016. (ENG.). 32p. (J). (gr. -1-2). pap. 9.99 (978-1-5324-0083-4(7)) Xist Publishing.
—Yo Ho, Ha Ha! Pirate Jokes for Kids. Cressey, Debbie. 2019. (ENG.). 30p. (J). (gr. -1-3). pap. 9.99 (978-1-5324-1333-9(5)) Xist Publishing.
Sitaraman, Soumya. Chachaji's Cup. Krishnaswami, Uma. 2013. (ENG.). 32p. (J). (gr. 1-18). 16.95 (978-0-89239-178-3(2)) Lee & Low Bks., Inc.
Sites, Jennifer. Chloe, the Very Special Goat. Glover, Rosanne Harper. 2012. (ENG.). 48p. (J). 16.95 (978-0-938467-53-3(0)) Headline Bks., Inc.
Sith, Robert & Epps, Joesph. Follow the Ant. Girven, Brenda. 2019. (ENG.). 26p. (J). pap. 12.99 **(978-1-7107-6783-4(9))** Independently Published.
Siwek, Emily. A Monster on Main Street. Siwek, Emily. 2018. (ENG.). 32p. (J). (gr. -1-2). pap. 15.00 (978-1-947989-08-5(1), Fifth Avenue Pr.) Ann Arbor District Library.
Siwik, Patrick. Noun Neighborhood. Ward, Linda Lee. 2016. (ENG.). (J). (gr. k-3). pap. 9.95 (978-0-9974036-6-4(7)) Adventures in Print.
Siwinski, Deborah. The Adventures of Teddy & Freddy Summer Safari. Siwinski, Deborah. l.t. ed. 2006. 41p. (J). per. 8.95 (978-1-59879-097-9(8)) Lifevest Publishing, Inc.
Six, Stephanie. What Daddies Like. Carey Nevin, Judy. 2019. (ENG.). 26p. (J). (gr. -1-k). bds. 7.99 (978-1-4998-0800-1(3)) Little Bee Books Inc.
—What Daddies Like. Carey Nevin, Judy. 2017. (ENG.). 32p. (J). (gr. -1-3). 16.99 (978-1-4998-0197-2(1)) Little Bee Books Inc.
—What Mommies Like. Carey Nevin, Judy. (ENG.). (J). (gr. -1-k). 2019. 26p. bds. 7.99 (978-1-4998-0801-8(1)); 2018. 32p. 16.99 (978-1-4998-0528-4(4)) Little Bee Books Inc.
Siy, Alexandra & Kunkel, Dennis, photos by. Bug Shots: The Good, the Bad, & the Bugly. Siy, Alexandra. 2011. (ENG., 32p. (J). (gr. 1-4). 16.95 (978-0-8234-2286-9(0)) Holiday Hse., Inc.
Sizemore, Carmen. 10 Busy Bumble Bees, 1 vol. Pitman, Sandra. 2009. 20p. pap. 24.95 (978-1-60749-683-0(6)) America Star Bks.
Sizemore, Lisa. Be Careful Little Eyes: Helping Young Children Cope with Bad Pictures. Shivers, Frank. 2019. (ENG.). 34p. (J). (gr. 3-6). pap. 15.95 **(978-1-878127-41-9(1))** Shivers, Frank Evangelistic Assn.
Sizer, Irma. Designing Dandelions: An Engineering Everything Adventure. Hunt, Emily & Pantoya, Michelle. 2013. (Engineering Everything Ser.). (ENG.). 96p. (J). 14.95 (978-0-89672-849-3(8)) Texas Tech Univ. Pr.
Sjonger, Rebecca. Les Singes et Autres Primates. Kalman, Bobbie. 2012. (FRE.). 32p. (J). pap. 9.95 (978-2-89579-440-0(5)) Bayard Canada CAN. Dist: Crabtree Publishing Co.
Sjostrom, Nicole & Iseminger, Jonathan. Lucky. Carey-Costa, Denise. 2011. 34p. pap. 12.99 (978-1-61170-035-0(3)) Robertson Publishing.
Sjostrom, Nicole & Iseminger, Jonathon. A Tale of Three Tails. Carey-Costa, Denise. 2009. 81p. 10.99 (978-1-4251-8492-6(8)) Trafford Publishing.
Skaggs, Craig, et al. Altered Creatures: Essence of Gluic. 2018. (ENG.). 310p. (J). pap. 12.98 (978-1-7903-4372-0(0)) Independently Published.
—Altered Creatures: Plea of Avanda. 2018. (Thorik Dain's Journey Ser.: Vol. 6). (ENG.). 278p. (J). pap. 12.98 (978-1-7903-4811-4(0)) Independently Published.
—Altered Creatures: Rise of Rummon. 2018. (Thorik Dain's Journey Ser.: Vol. 4). (ENG.). 294p. (J). pap. 12.98 (978-1-7903-4577-9(4)) Independently Published.
—Altered Creatures: Sacrifice of Ericc. 2018. (Thorik Dain's Journey Ser.: Vol. 2). (ENG.). 272p. (J). pap. 12.98 (978-1-7903-4327-0(5)) Independently Published.
Skakandi, Viktoria. Aurora's Orchid. Weber, Vicky. 2019. (ENG.). (J). 34p. 17.99 **(978-1-7342129-2-1(6))**; 36p. (gr. 3-5). pap. 12.99 **(978-1-7342129-3-8(4))** Trunk Up Bks.
Skalak, Daniel. All Summer's Fun. Skalak, Daniel. 2006. 32p. (J). (gr. -1-3). 15.95 (978-1-60108-000-4(X)) Red Cygnet Pr.
Skardarasy, Doreen L. Gerry the Grape. Hereford, L. F. 2005. (J). pap. (978-0-9728969-9-3(6)) Acorn Publishing.
Skeate, Sarah, jt. illus. see Dunn, Fiona W.
Skeate, Sarah, jt. illus. see Katz, Pete.
Skeens, Matthew. The Bald Eagle, 1 vol. Pearl, Norman. 2007. (American Symbols Ser.). (ENG.). 24p. (J). (gr. 1-3). 9.95 (978-1-4048-2645-8(9), Picture Window Bks.) Capstone.
—The Bill of Rights, 1 vol. Pearl, Norman. 2007. (American Symbols Ser.). (ENG.). 24p. (J). (gr. 1-3). 9.95 (978-1-4048-2219-1(4), Picture Window Bks.) Capstone.
—The Bill of Rights, 1 vol. Pearl, Norman & Picture Window Books Staff. 2007. (American Symbols Ser.). (ENG.). 24p. (J). (gr. 1-3). 27.32 (978-1-4048-2213-9(5), Picture Window Bks.) Capstone.
—Celebrate America: A Guide to America's Greatest Symbols. Firestone, Mary et al. 2010. (American Symbols Ser.). (ENG.). 208p. (J). (gr. 1-3). pap. 15.95 (978-1-4048-6170-1(X), Picture Window Bks.) Capstone.
—Cows Sweat Through Their Noses: And Other Freaky Facts about Animal Habits, Characteristics, & Homes. Seuling, Barbara. 2010. (Freaky Facts Ser.). 40p. pap. 0.50 (978-1-4048-6200-5(5), Picture Window Bks.) Capstone.
—The Declaration of Independence, 1 vol. Mortensen, Lori. 2009. (American Symbols Ser.). (ENG.). 24p. (J). (gr. 1-3). lib. bdg. 27.32 (978-1-4048-5165-8(8), Picture Window Bks.) Capstone.
—Earth Is Like a Giant Magnet: And Other Freaky Facts about Planets, Oceans, & Volcanoes. Seuling, Barbara. (Freaky Facts Ser.). 40p. 2010. pap. 0.50 (978-1-4048-6202-9(1)); 2008. (gr. 3-5). pap. 3.00 (978-1-4048-5289-1(1)) Capstone. (Picture Window Bks.).
—The Great Seal of the United States. Pearl, Norman. 2006. (American Symbols Ser.). (ENG.). 24p. (J). (gr. 1-3). lib. bdg. 27.32 (978-1-4048-2214-6(3)); per. 9.95 (978-1-4048-2220-7(8)) Capstone. (Picture Window Bks.).
—The Liberty Bell, 1 vol. Firestone, Mary. 2007. (American Symbols Ser.). (ENG.). 24p. (J). (gr. 1-3). 9.95 (978-1-4048-3467-5(2), Picture Window Bks.) Capstone.
—The Liberty Bell, 1 vol. Firestone, Mary & Picture Window Books Staff. 2007. (American Symbols Ser.). (ENG.). 24p. (J). (gr. 1-3). 27.32 (978-1-4048-3101-8(0), Picture Window Bks.) Capstone.
—The Lincoln Memorial, 1 vol. Firestone, Mary. 2007. (American Symbols Ser.). (ENG.). 24p. (J). (gr. 1-3). lib. bdg. 27.32 (978-1-4048-3718-8(3), Picture Window Bks.) Capstone.
—Mount Rushmore, 1 vol. Troupe, Thomas Kingsley. 2009. (American Symbols Ser.). (ENG.). 24p. (J). (gr. 1-3). lib. bdg. 27.32 (978-1-4048-5168-9(2), Picture Window Bks.) Capstone.
—Our American Flag, 1 vol. Firestone, Mary. 2006. (American Symbols Ser.). (ENG.). 24p. (J). (gr. 1-3). 9.95 (978-1-4048-2218-4(6), 1258436, Picture Window Bks.) Capstone.
—Our National Anthem. Pearl, Norman. 2006. (American Symbols Ser.). (ENG.). 24p. (J). (gr. 1-3). lib. bdg. 27.32 (978-1-4048-2215-3(1), Picture Window Bks.) Capstone.
—Our National Anthem, 1 vol. Pearl, Norman. 2006. (American Symbols Ser.). (ENG.). 24p. (J). (gr. 1-3). 9.95 (978-1-4048-2221-4(6), Picture Window Bks.) Capstone.
—The Pledge of Allegiance, 1 vol. Pearl, Norman. 2007. (American Symbols Ser.). (ENG.). 24p. (J). (gr. 1-3). 9.95 (978-1-4048-2647-2(5), Picture Window Bks.) Capstone.
—The Statue of Liberty, 1 vol. Firestone, Mary. 2006. (American Symbols Ser.). (ENG.). 24p. (J). (gr. 1-3). 9.95 (978-1-4048-2222-1(4), Picture Window Bks.) Capstone.
—The U. S. Constitution, 1 vol. Pearl, Norman. 2006. (American Symbols Ser.). (ENG.). 24p. (J). (gr. 1-3). 9.95 (978-1-4048-2646-5(7), Picture Window Bks.) Capstone.
—The U. S. Supreme Court, 1 vol. Suen, Anastasia. 2008. (American Symbols Ser.). (ENG.). 24p. (J). (gr. 1-3). 27.32 (978-1-4048-4707-1(3), Picture Window Bks.) Capstone.
—The White House, 1 vol. Firestone, Mary. 2006. (American Symbols Ser.). (ENG.). 24p. (J). (gr. 1-3). 9.95 (978-1-4048-2223-8(2)); lib. bdg. 27.32 (978-1-4048-2217-7(8)) Capstone. (Picture Window Bks.).
Skeesuck, Justin & Waresak, Matt. The Push. Gray, Patrick. 2018. (ENG.). 32p. (J). 14.99 (978-1-4964-2880-6(3), 20_30836, Tyndale Kids) Tyndale Hse. Pubs.
Skehan, Krista. Alphabetica: Odes to the Alphabet. Spieker, Diana. 2009. (ENG.). 26p. 16.95 (978-0-9797491-0-0(7)) Personify Pr.
Skelley, Jen. Butterfly Color-In Locked Diary. Mudpuppy. 2017. (ENG.). 192p. (J). (gr. -1-7). 10.99 (978-0-7353-5213-1(5)) Mudpuppy Pr.
Skelton, J. R. Our Empire Story. Marshall, H. E. 2012. 402p. (978-1-78139-188-4(2)) Benediction Classics.
Skelton, J. R., et al. Scotland's Story (Yesterday's Classics) Marshall, H. E. 2005. 552p. (J). per. 17.95 (978-1-59915-056-7(5)) Yesterday's Classics.
Skerry, Brian, photos by. Adventures Beneath the Sea: Living in an Underwater Science Station. Mallory, Kenneth. 2010. (ENG., 48p. (J). (gr. 4-7). 18.95 (978-1-59078-607-9(6)) Boyds Mills Pr.
—Ocean Counting. Lawler, Janet. 2013. (ENG., 32p. (J). (gr. -1-k). lib. bdg. 25.90 (978-1-4263-1117-8(6), National Geographic Children's Bks.) National Geographic Society.
Skevington, Andrea. The Bible Story Retold in Twelve Chapters. Skevington, Andrea. ed. 2015. (ENG.). 224p. 17.99 (978-0-7459-7664-8(6), Lion Books) Lion Hudson PLC GBR. Dist: Independent Pubs. Group.
—Prayers & Verses Through the Bible. Skevington, Andrea. ed. 2016. (ENG.). 128p. 14.95 (978-0-7459-7663-1(8), Lion Books) Lion Hudson PLC GBR. Dist: Independent Pubs. Group.
Skewes, John. A Ticket to the Pennant: A Tale of Baseball in Seattle. Holtzen, Mark. 2016. 32p. (J). (gr. -1-3). 17.99 (978-1-63217-003-3(5), Little Bigfoot) Sasquatch Bks.
Skewes, John. Elliott the Otter: The Totally Untrue Story of Elliott Bay. Skewes, John. Ode, Eric. 2015. 32p. (J). (gr. -1-2). 16.99 (978-1-57061-952-6(2), Little Bigfoot) Sasquatch Bks.
—Larry Gets Lost in Alaska. Skewes, John. Mullin, Michael. 2013. (Larry Gets Lost Ser.). 32p. (J). (gr. -1-2). pap. 10.99 (978-1-57061-859-8(3), Little Bigfoot) Sasquatch Bks.
—Larry Gets Lost in Boston. Skewes, John. Mullin, Michael. 2013. (Larry Gets Lost Ser.). 32p. (J). (gr. -1-2). 17.99 (978-1-57061-793-5(7), Little Bigfoot) Sasquatch Bks.
—Larry Gets Lost in Chicago. Skewes, John. Mullin, Michael. 2010. (Larry Gets Lost Ser.). 32p. (J). (gr. -1-2). 17.99 (978-1-57061-619-8(1), Little Bigfoot) Sasquatch Bks.
—Larry Gets Lost in Los Angeles. Skewes, John. Mullin, Michael & ANZ014 Staff. 2009. (Larry Gets Lost Ser.). 32p. (J). (gr. -1-2). 17.99 (978-1-57061-568-9(3), Little Bigfoot) Sasquatch Bks.
—Larry Gets Lost in New York City. Skewes, John. Mullin, Michael. 2010. (Larry Gets Lost Ser.). 32p. (J). (gr. -1-2). 17.99 (978-1-57061-620-4(5), Little Bigfoot) Sasquatch Bks.
—Larry Gets Lost in Philadelphia. Skewes, John. Mullin, Michael. 2013. (Larry Gets Lost Ser.). 32p. (J). (gr. -1-2). 17.99 (978-1-57061-792-8(9), Little Bigfoot) Sasquatch Bks.
—Larry Gets Lost in Portland. Skewes, John. Mullin, Michael. 2012. (Larry Gets Lost Ser.). 32p. (J). (gr. -1-2). 17.99 (978-1-57061-679-2(5), Little Bigfoot) Sasquatch Bks.
—Larry Gets Lost in Prehistoric Times: From Dinosaurs to the Stone Age. Skewes, John. Fox, Andrew. 2013. (Larry Gets Lost Ser.). 32p. (J). (gr. -1-2). 16.99 (978-1-57061-862-8(3), Little Bigfoot) Sasquatch Bks.
—Larry Gets Lost in San Francisco. Skewes, John. Mullin, Michael & ANZ014 Staff. 2009. (Larry Gets Lost Ser.). 32p. (J). (gr. -1-2). 17.99 (978-1-57061-567-2(5), Little Bigfoot) Sasquatch Bks.
—Larry Gets Lost in Texas. Skewes, John. Mullin, Michael & ANZ014 Staff. 2010. (Larry Gets Lost Ser.). 32p. (J). (gr. -1-2). 17.99 (978-1-57061-680-8(9), Little Bigfoot) Sasquatch Bks.
—Larry Gets Lost in the Twin Cities. Skewes, John. Mullin, Michael. 2012. (Larry Gets Lost Ser.). 32p. (J). (gr. -1-2). 17.99 (978-1-57061-754-6(6), Little Bigfoot) Sasquatch Bks.
—Larry Gets Lost in Washington, DC. Skewes, John. Fox, Andrew. 2014. (Larry Gets Lost Ser.). 32p. (J). (gr. -1-2). 17.99 (978-1-57061-899-4(2), Little Bigfoot) Sasquatch Bks.
—Larry Gets Lost under the Sea. Skewes, John. Ode, Eric. 2015. (Larry Gets Lost Ser.). 32p. (J). (gr. -1-2). 16.99 (978-1-57061-925-0(5), Little Bigfoot) Sasquatch Bks.
—Larry Loves Chicago! A Larry Gets Lost Book. Skewes, John. 2014. (Larry Gets Lost Ser.). 20p. (J). (— 1). bds. 9.99 (978-1-57061-913-7(1), Little Bigfoot) Sasquatch Bks.
—Larry Loves New York City! Skewes, John. 2014. (Larry Gets Lost Ser.). 20p. (J). (— 1). bds. 9.99 (978-1-57061-936-6(0), Little Bigfoot) Sasquatch Bks.
—Larry Loves Portland! Skewes, John. 2014. (Larry Gets Lost Ser.). 20p. (J). (— 1). bds. 9.99 (978-1-57061-935-9(2), Little Bigfoot) Sasquatch Bks.
—Larry Loves San Francisco! Skewes, John. 2014. (Larry Gets Lost Ser.). 20p. (J). (— 1). bds. 9.99 (978-1-57061-912-0(3), Little Bigfoot) Sasquatch Bks.
Ski, Jenn. Soft Shapes: Dinosaurs (Baby's First Book + Puzzle) Ikids Staff. 2010. (ENG.). 8p. (J). (gr. -1 — 1). 10.99 (978-1-60169-043-2(6)) Innovative Kids.
—Soft Shapes: Trucks (Baby's First Book + Puzzle) Ikids Staff. 2010. (ENG.). 8p. (J). (gr. -1 — 1). 10.99 (978-1-60169-044-9(4)) Innovative Kids.
Skiadas, Melissa & Skiadas, Stephanie. The Forest of the Leprechauns. McMachan, Susan K. 2008. 36p. pap. 15.95 (978-1-4389-1325-4(7)) AuthorHouse.
Skiadas, Stephanie, jt. illus. see Skiadas, Melissa.
Skidmore, Donna. Color Me Panama * Coloreame Panama. Summer, Sunny W. 2016. (ENG.). 44p. (J). pap. **(978-9962-12-368-2(2))** Shute, Sunny W.
Skiles, Janet, jt. illus. see Armbrust, Janet.
Skinner, Gayle. Cinnamon the Adventurous Guinea Pig Goes to Devil's Island. Turner, Daniel. 2013. (ENG.). 48p. (J). pap. 10.95 (978-1-4787-1753-9(X)) Outskirts Pr., Inc.
Skinner, James W. T. The Raindrop Who Was Afraid to Drop. Dee. 2018. (ENG.). 30p. (J). pap. 13.95 (978-1-64028-780-8(9)) Christian Faith Publishing.
Skinner, Meg. I Am a Big Fish. Takuna, John Fred. 2019. (ENG.). 22p. (J). pap. (978-9980-89-918-7(2)) Library For All Limited.
—The Sea Is Everything to Me. Sevaru, Molly. 2018. (ENG.). 28p. (J). (gr. k-3). pap. (978-9980-900-27-2(X)) Library For All Limited.
Skinner, Russell Scott. Perry Panda: A Story about Parental Depression. Bashford, Helen. 2017. (ENG.). 32p. (J). 17.95 (978-1-78592-412-5(5), 696669) Kingsley, Jessica Pubs. GBR. Dist: Hachette UK Distribution.
Skipp, Hui. My Friend Robot! Scribens, Sunny. 2017. (ENG.). 32p. (J). (gr. -1-1). 16.99 (978-1-78285-322-0(7)); pap. 9.99 (978-1-78285-323-7(5)) Barefoot Bks., Inc.
—A Pandemonium of Parrots & Other Animals. Baker, Kate. 2018. (ENG.). 32p. (J). (gr. 2-4). 16.99 (978-1-5362-0279-3(7), Big Picture Press) Candlewick Pr.
Skirvan, Ted, 3rd. The Bad Day. Skirvan, Pamela. 2003. 12p. (J). (gr. k-6). pap. 4.95 (978-0-9742943-0-8(6)) Skirvan, Pamela.
Sklar, Andy. Undercover Kid: The Comic Book King. Kidd, Ronald. 2007. (All Aboard Mystery Reader Ser.). (ENG.). 48p. (J). pap. 3.99 (978-0-448-44438-3(0), Grosset & Dunlap) Penguin Publishing Group.
Skomorokhova, Olga. If There Never Was a You. Rowe, Amanda. 2019. (ENG.). 20p. (J). bds. 10.99 (978-1-64170-111-2(0), 550111) Familius LLC.
—Little Fingers Ballet. Mireles, Ashley Marie. 2019. (ENG.). 10p. (J). bds. 16.99 (978-1-64170-155-6(2), 550155) Familius LLC.
Skon, Sandy. Bianca the Dancing Crocodile. Lamb. 2008. 30p. pap. 24.95 (978-1-60563-447-0(6)) America Star Bks.
Skorpen, Neal. Oregon Is Fun! Rain or Sun! Klug, Kirsten. 2011. 20p. (J). pap. 7.95 (978-0-9798173-3-5(1)) Bamboo River Pr.
Skortcheva, Rossitza. Elijah's Tears: Stories for the Jewish Holidays, 1 vol. Pearl, Sydelle. 2004. (ENG.). 80p. (J). (gr. 3-7). 14.95 (978-1-58980-178-3(4), Pelican Publishing) Arcadia Publishing.
Skou, Nick. Fanakapan & the Fairies - a Children's Fairy Story. Jordan, Claire. 2013. 52p. pap. (978-1-78148-648-1(4)) Grosvenor Hse. Publishing Ltd.
Skovran, Victoria. Hair-Raising Hairstyles That Make a Statement: 4D an Augmented Reading & Fashion Experience. Rissman, Rebecca. 2018. (DIY Fearless Fashion Ser.). (ENG.). 48p. (J). (gr. 4-8). lib. bdg. 34.65 (978-1-5435-1101-7(5), 137707, Compass Point Bks.) Capstone.
Skrbic, Melissa. Touch of Christmas. Mumaugh, Lene. l.t. ed. 2003. 28p. per. 9.95 (978-1-932344-19-6(5)) Thornton Publishing, Inc.
Skrepnick, Michael. Raptor Pack. Bakker, Robert T. 2003. (Step into Reading Ser.). 48p. (J). (gr. 2-4). pap. 4.99 (978-0-375-82303-9(4), Random Hse. Bks. for Young Readers) Random Hse. Children's Bks.
Skrepnick, Michael W. Descubriendo Dinosaurios con un Cazador de Fsiles. Williams, Judith. 2008. (¡Me Gustan Las Ciencias! / I Like Science! Ser.).Tr. of Discovering Dinosaurs with a Fossil Hunter. (SPA & ENG.). 24p. (gr. k-2). lib. bdg. 23.60 (978-0-7660-2978-1(6), Enslow Elementary) Enslow Publishing, LLC.
Skrepnick, Michael William. Raptor Pack. Bakker, Robert T. 2003. (Step into Reading: Step 5 Ser.). (ENG.). 48p. (J). (gr. 2-4). lib. bdg. 16.19 (978-0-375-92303-6(9)) Random House Publishing Group.
Skromovas, Andrea. The Gifts You Cannot Buy: An Empowering Children's Book about Values & Gratitude. Skromovas, Andrea. 2020. (ENG.). 30p. (J). pap. 9.97 **(978-1-7322796-4-3(0))** Skromovas, Andrea.
—Os Presentes Que N�o Se Compram. Skromovas, Andrea. 2019. (POR.). 30p. (J). pap. 9.97 **(978-1-7322796-3-6(2))** Skromovas, Andrea.
Skye, Obert. Batneezer. Skye, Obert. 2016. (Creature from My Closet Ser.: 6). (ENG.). 208p. (J). 13.99 (978-1-62779-163-2(9), 9781627791632, Holt, Henry & Co. Bks. For Young Readers) Holt, Henry & Co.
—Batneezer: The Creature from My Closet. Skye, Obert. 2018. (Creature from My Closet Ser.: 6). (ENG.). 224p. (J). pap. 9.99 (978-1-250-17722-3(7), 900189673) Square Fish.
—Katfish. Skye, Obert. 2014. (Creature from My Closet Ser.: 4). (ENG.). 256p. (J). (gr. 4-7). 14.99 (978-0-8050-9690-3(6), 900096221, Holt, Henry & Co. Bks. For Young Readers) Holt, Henry & Co.
—Katfish. Skye, Obert. 2018. (Creature from My Closet Ser.: 4). (ENG.). 272p. (J). pap. 7.99 (978-1-250-14367-9(5), 900180541) Square Fish.
—Lord of the Hat. Skye, Obert. 2015. (Creature from My Closet Ser.: 5). (ENG.). 256p. (J). (gr. 4-7). 13.99 (978-1-62779-162-5(0), 900138586, Holt, Henry & Co. Bks. For Young Readers) Holt, Henry & Co.
—The Lord of the Hat. Skye, Obert. 2018. (Creature from My Closet Ser.: 5). (ENG.). 272p. (J). pap. 7.99 (978-1-250-15836-9(2), 900185488) Square Fish.
—Pinocula. Skye, Obert. 2013. (Creature from My Closet Ser.: 3). (ENG.). 256p. (J). (gr. 4-7). 12.99 (978-0-8050-9689-7(2), 900096220, Holt, Henry & Co. Bks. For Young Readers) Holt, Henry & Co.
—Wonkenstein. Skye, Obert. 2011. (Creature from My Closet Ser.: 1). (ENG.). 240p. (J). (gr. 4-7). 13.99 (978-0-8050-9268-4(4), 900068665, Holt, Henry & Co. Bks. For Young Readers) Holt, Henry & Co.
—Wonkenstein. Skye, Obert. 2015. (Creature from My Closet Ser.: 1). (ENG.). 256p. (J). (gr. 4-7). pap. 7.99 (978-1-250-01022-3(5), 900084759) Square Fish.
Slack, Alex. Penelope Pondhead. Surridge, David. 2017. (ENG.). 35p. (J). pap. (978-1-78623-052-2(6)) Grosvenor Hse. Publishing Ltd.
Slack, Jocelyn. P Is for Potato: An Idaho Alphabet. Steiner, Stan et al. 2005. (Discover America State by State Ser.). (ENG.). 40p. (J). 17.95 (978-1-58536-155-7(0)) Sleeping Bear Pr.
Slack, Michael. Edgar Allan Poe's Pie: Math Puzzlers in Classic Poems. Lewis, J. Patrick. 2012. (ENG.). 40p. (J). (gr. 1-4). 16.99 (978-0-547-51338-6(0), 1444189) Houghton Mifflin Harcourt Publishing Co.
—House: First Words Board Books - 5 Books Inside! 2018. (ENG.). 5p. (J). (gr. -1 — 1). bds. 18.99 (978-1-4521-6703-9(6)) Chronicle Bks. LLC.
—How Do You Burp in Space? And Other Tips Every Space Tourist Needs to Know. Goodman, Susan E. 2013. (ENG.). 80p. (J). (gr. 3-6). 16.99 (978-1-59990-068-1(8), 900042509); 17.89 (978-1-59990-934-9(0), 900085215) Bloomsbury Publishing USA. (Bloomsbury USA Childrens).
—Nugget & Fang: Friends Forever - Or Snack Time? Sauer, Tammi. 2013. (Nugget & Fang Ser.). (ENG.). 40p. (J). (gr. -1-3). 18.99 (978-0-547-85285-0(1), 1501493) Houghton Mifflin Harcourt Publishing Co.
—Nugget & Fang: Friends Forever — Or Snack Time? Sauer, Tammi. 2015. (Nugget & Fang Ser.). (ENG.). 40p. (J). (gr. -1-3). 7.99 (978-0-544-48171-8(2), 1602585, HMH Books For Young Readers) Houghton Mifflin Harcourt Publishing Co.
—Nugget & Fang: Race Around the Reef. Sauer, Tammi. 2019. (Nugget & Fang Ser.). (ENG.). 10p. (J). (— 1). 8.99 (978-0-358-04053-8(1), 1740901, HMH Books For Young Readers) Houghton Mifflin Harcourt Publishing Co.
—Nugget & Fang Go to School. Sauer, Tammi. 2019. (Nugget & Fang Ser.). (ENG.). 32p. (J). (gr. -1-3). 17.99 (978-1-328-54826-9(0), 1724057, Clarion Bks.) Houghton Mifflin Harcourt Trade & Reference Pubs.
—Nugget & Fang (lap Board Book) Friends Forever — Or Snack Time? Sauer, Tammi. 2018. (Nugget & Fang Ser.). (ENG.). 38p. (J). (— 1). bds. 12.99 (978-1-328-76839-1(2), 1681072, HMH Books For Young Readers) Houghton Mifflin Harcourt Publishing Co.
—Race Car Count. Dotlich, Rebecca Kai. 2015. (ENG.). 32p. (J). (gr. -1-k). 15.99 (978-1-62779-009-3(8), 900129911, Holt, Henry & Co. Bks. For Young Readers) Holt, Henry & Co.
—Sharks! Perl, Erica S. 2019. (Step into Reading Ser.). 48p. (J). (gr. k-3). pap. 4.99 (978-0-525-57879-6(X), Random Hse. Bks. for Young Readers) Random Hse. Children's Bks.
—Truth or Lie: Dinosaurs! Perl, Erica S. 2019. (Step into Reading Ser.). 48p. (J). (gr. k-3). pap. 4.99 (978-0-525-57882-6(X), Random Hse. Bks. for Young Readers) Random Hse. Children's Bks.
Slack, Michael. Bunny Built. Slack, Michael. 2018. (ENG.). 40p. (J). 17.99 (978-1-62779-270-7(8), 900144842, Holt, Henry & Co. Bks. For Young Readers) Holt, Henry & Co.

—Dragon Meets Boy. Slack, Michael. 2020. (ENG.). 40p. (J). 17.99 *(978-1-62779-271-4(6)*, 900144843, Holt, Henry & Co. Bks. For Young Readers) Holt, Henry & Co.

Slack, Michael. Kitties on Dinosaurs. Slack, Michael. 2020. (ENG.). 40p. (J). (-k). 17.99 ***(978-0-593-10838-3(8)***, Dial Bks) Penguin Young Readers Group.

Slack, Michael. Sharing Does Not Compute. Slack, Michael. 2018. (Standroid & Dandroid Ser.). (ENG.). 36p. (J). (gr. -1 — 1). bds. 7.99 *(978-1-5344-0569-1(0)*, Little Simon) Little Simon.

—Shorty & Clem. Slack, Michael. 2017. (ENG.). 40p. (J). (gr. -1-3). 17.99 *(978-0-06-242158-6(1))* HarperCollins Pubs.

—Shorty & Clem Blast Off! Slack, Michael. 2018. (ENG.). 40p. (J). (gr. -1-3). 17.99 *(978-0-06-242159-3(X))* HarperCollins Pubs.

—Standroid & Dandroid Make a Mess. Slack, Michael. 2018. (Standroid & Dandroid Ser.). (ENG.). 36p. (J). (gr. -1 — 1). bds. 7.99 *(978-1-5344-0567-7(4)*, Little Simon) Little Simon.

Slack, Michael H. Clot & Scab: Gross Stuff about Your Scrapes, Bumps, & Bruises. Lew, Kristi. 2009. (Gross Body Science Ser.). (ENG.). 48p. (gr. 3-5). lib. bdg. 29.27 *(978-0-8225-8965-5(6))* Lerner Publishing Group.

—Crust & Spray: Gross Stuff in Your Eyes, Ears, Nose, & Throat. Larsen, C. S. 2009. (Gross Body Science Ser.). (ENG.). 48p. (gr. 3-5). lib. bdg. 29.27 *(978-0-8225-8964-8(8))* Lerner Publishing Group.

—Hawk & Drool: Gross Stuff in Your Mouth. Donovan, Sandy. 2009. (Gross Body Science Ser.). (ENG.). 48p. (gr. 3-5). lib. bdg. 29.27 *(978-0-8225-8966-2(4))* Lerner Publishing Group.

—Itch & Ooze: Gross Stuff on Your Skin. Lew, Kristi & Lewandowski, Laura C. 2009. (Gross Body Science Ser.). (ENG.). 48p. (gr. 3-5). lib. bdg. 29.27 *(978-0-8225-8963-1(X))* Lerner Publishing Group.

—Pirasaurs! Funk, Josh. 2016. 40p. (J). (gr. -1-k). pap. 14.99 *(978-0-545-75049-3(0)*, Orchard Bks.) Scholastic, Inc.

—Rumble & Spew: Gross Stuff in Your Stomach & Intestines. Donovan, Sandy. 2009. (Gross Body Science Ser.). (ENG.). 48p. (gr. 3-5). lib. bdg. 29.27 *(978-0-8225-8899-3(4))* Lerner Publishing Group.

—Truth or Lie - Sharks! Perl, Erica S. 2019. (Step into Reading Ser.). 48p. (J). (gr. k-3). lib. bdg. 12.99 *(978-0-525-57880-2(3)*, Random Hse. Bks. for Young Readers) Random Hse. Children's Bks.

Slade, Christian. Aliens on Vacation. Smith, Clete Barrett. 2012. (Intergalactic Bed & Breakfast Ser.: 1). (ENG.). 272p. (J). (gr. 3-7). pap. 6.99 *(978-1-4231-5723-6(0))* Hyperion Pr.

—Aliens on Vacation. Smith, Clete Barrett. 2012. (Intergalactic Bed & Breakfast Ser.). (ENG.). (J). (gr. 3-7). lib. bdg. 17.60 *(978-1-68065-144-7(7))* Perfection Learning Corp.

—Angel of God, My Guardian Dear. Tebo, Mary Elizabeth. 2008. 14p. (J). (gr. -1). 8.95 *(978-0-8198-0784-7(2))* Pauline Bks. & Media.

—Music Star. Hannigan, Paula & Accord Publishing Staff. 2011. (ENG.). 16p. (J). (gr. -1-3). 14.99 *(978-1-4494-0173-3(2))* Andrews McMeel Publishing.

—Presidential Pets. Driscoll, Laura. 2009. (ENG.). 64p. (J). (gr. 1-3). 17.44 *(978-0-448-45250-0(2)*, Grosset & Dunlap) Penguin Publishing Group.

—Sunshine Picklelime. Ferguson, Pamela. 2011. (ENG.). 240p. (J). (gr. 4-6). 21.19 *(978-0-375-86175-8(0))* Random House Publishing Group.

—Where Do Diggers Celebrate Christmas? Sayres, Brianna Caplan. (Where Do... Ser.). (ENG.). (J). 2019. 26p. (— 1). bds. 8.99 *(978-0-525-57951-9(6))*; 2018. 32p. (gr. -1-2). 16.99 *(978-1-5247-7215-4(1))* Random Hse. Children's Bks. (Random Hse. Bks. for Young Readers).

—Where Do Diggers Sleep at Night? Sayres, Brianna Caplan. (Where Do... Ser.). (J). (-k). 2014. 26p. bds. 7.99 *(978-0-385-37415-6(1))*; 2012. (ENG.). 32p. 16.99 *(978-0-375-86848-1(8))* Random Hse. Children's Bks. (Random Hse. Bks. for Young Readers).

—Where Do Diggers, Trains, & Planes Sleep at Night? Board Book Boxed Set, 3 vols. Sayres, Brianna Caplan. 2019. (Where Do... Ser.). (ENG.). 26p. (J). (— 1). bds., bds., bds. 24.97 *(978-0-593-11968-6(1)*, Random Hse. Bks. for Young Readers) Random Hse. Children's Bks.

—Where Do Jet Planes Sleep at Night? Sayres, Brianna Caplan. 2017. 32p. (J). (gr. -1-2). 16.99 *(978-0-399-55448-3(3))*; (ENG.). lib. bdg. 19.99 *(978-0-399-55449-0(1))* Random Hse. Children's Bks. (Random Hse. Bks. for Young Readers).

Slade, Christian. Where Do Speedboats Sleep at Night? Sayres, Brianna Caplan. (ENG.). (J). (gr. -1-2). 2020. 26p. bds. 7.99 ***(978-1-5247-6578-1(3))***; 2019. 32p. 16.99 *(978-1-5247-6575-0(9))* Random Hse. Children's Bks. (Random Hse. Bks. for Young Readers).

Slade, Christian. Where Do Steam Trains Sleep at Night? Sayres, Brianna Caplan. (ENG.). (J). (gr. -1 — 1). 2017. 26p. bds. 7.99 *(978-0-553-52100-9(4))*; 2016. 32p. 19.99 *(978-0-375-97471-7(7))* Random Hse. Children's Bks. (Random Hse. Bks. for Young Readers).

Slade, Cody Graham and Sally. Invasion of the Bats in the Swamps. Slade, A. H. Slade and Sally. 2019. (ENG.). 38p. (J). pap. 10.00 *(978-1-7940-1085-7(8))* Independently Published.

Slade-Robinson, Nikki. The Seven Stars of Matariki. Rolleston-Cummins, Toni. 2009. (ENG.). 28p. pap. 12.00 *(978-1-86969-327-5(2)*, 4346) Huia Pubs. NZL. Dist: Univ. of Hawaii Pr.

Slaghekke, Harry. Meet Nancy Bird Walton. Atwood, Grace. 2015. 32p. (J). (gr. k). 19.99 *(978-0-85798-387-9(3))* Random Hse. Australia AUS. Dist: Independent Pubs. Group.

Slane, Andrea & Chen, Kuo Kang. Weather. Clarke, Catriona. 2006. (Beginners Science: Level 2 Ser.). 32p. (J). (gr. 1-3). 4.99 *(978-0-7945-1253-8(4)*, Usborne) EDC Publishing.

Slaney, Dave. Crocodile Legion. Turney, Sja. 2016. (ENG.). (J). pap. *(978-0-9935552-3-7(3))* Mulcahy Bks.

—Pirate Legion. Turney, Sja. 2017. (ENG.). (J). pap. *(978-0-9935552-4-4(1))* Mulcahy Bks.

Slater, Jason. The Solar System: Out of This World with Science Activities for Kids. Lopez, Delano. 2019. (Build It Yourself Ser.). 128p. (J). (gr. 4-6). 22.95 *(978-1-61930-794-0(4)*, 785d2018-ba08-4385-975f-2523ff3a4c04); pap. 17.95 *(978-1-61930-797-1(9)*, 3d0d44a3-92ff-48b4-b657-a20dfa37ef8a) Nomad Pr.

Slater, Jean M. The Adventures of Hopper. Slater, Jean M. 2003. 8p. (J). bds. 16.00 *(978-0-9743149-3-8(5))* Slater Software, Inc.

—Mixed up Morning. Slater, Jean M. 2003. 13p. (J). bds. 16.00 *(978-0-9743149-2-1(7))* Slater Software, Inc.

—Monkey Business: At the Market. Slater, Jean M. 2003. 10p. (J). bds. 16.00 *(978-0-9743149-5-3(5))* Slater Software, Inc.

—Wonderful Snow! Slater, Jean M. 2003. 9p. (J). bds. 16.00 *(978-0-9743149-1-4(9))* Slater Software, Inc.

Slater, Kate. After the River the Sun. Calhoun, Dia. 2013. (ENG.). 368p. (J). (gr. 4-7). 16.99 *(978-1-4424-3985-6(8))* Simon & Schuster Children's Publishing.

Slater, Kate. D Is for Dog. DK. 2020. (ENG.). 16p. (J). (— 1). bds. 7.99 ***(978-0-7440-2417-3(X)***, DK Children) Dorling Kindersley Publishing, Inc.

Slater, Kate. Eva of the Farm. Calhoun, Dia. (ENG.). (J). (gr. 4-7). 2013. 272p. pap. 6.99 *(978-1-4424-1701-4(3))*; 2012. 256p. 16.99 *(978-1-4424-1700-7(5))* Simon & Schuster Children's Publishing. (Atheneum Bks. for Young Readers).

—Goldilocks & the Three Bears. Bateson-Hill, Margaret. 2015. (J). *(978-1-84686-890-0(4))* Barefoot Bks., Inc.

—A Is for Ant. DK. 2020. (ENG.). 16p. (J). (— 1). bds. 7.99 *(978-1-4654-9743-7(9)*, DK Children) Dorling Kindersley Publishing, Inc.

—The King & His Wish. Hawes, Alison. 2014. (Traditional Tales Ser.). (ENG.). 16p. (J). (gr. -1-k). pap. 6.95 *(978-1-62521-574-1(6)*, Capstone Classroom) Capstone.

—The Little Red Hen. Finch, Mary & Messing, Debra. 32p. (J). 2018. (ENG.). (gr. k-3). pap. 8.99 *(978-1-78285-041-0(4))*; 2013. (gr. -1-2). 16.99 *(978-1-84686-575-6(1))*; 2013. (gr. -1-2). 9.99 *(978-1-84686-751-4(7))* Barefoot Bks., Inc.

Slater, Kate. La Gallinita Roja. Slater, Kate. Finch, Mary. 2013. (SPA.). 32p. (J). pap. 8.99 *(978-1-84686-753-8(3))* Barefoot Bks., Inc.

—Magpie's Treasure. Slater, Kate. 2012. (ENG.). 32p. (J). (gr. -1 — 1). pap. 10.99 *(978-1-84939-075-0(4))* Andersen Pr. GBR. Dist: Independent Pubs. Group.

Slater, Nicola. Acorn Farm. Bateson, Margaret. 2016. (J). *(978-1-4351-6320-1(6))* Barnes & Noble, Inc.

—Chihuawolf: A Tail of Mystery & Horror. Ganny, Charlee. 2011. (ENG.). 144p. (J). (gr. 4-6). pap. 8.99 *(978-1-4022-5940-1(9)*, Sourcebooks Jabberwocky) Sourcebooks, Inc.

—The Forever Tree. Surratt, Tereasa & Lukas, Donna. 2018. 40p. (J). (gr. -1-2). 17.99 *(978-0-553-52392-8(9))*; (ENG.). lib. bdg. 20.99 *(978-0-553-52393-5(7))* Random Hse. Children's Bks. (Crown Books For Young Readers).

—Happy Birthday to You: a Musical Instrument Song Book. Nosy Crow. 2018. (Musical Instrument Sound Book Ser.). (ENG.). 10p. (J). (gr. -1-3). bds. 17.99 *(978-0-7636-9943-7(8)*, Nosy Crow) Candlewick Pr.

—Leaping Lemmings! Briggs, John. 2016. 32p. (J). (gr. -1). 14.95 *(978-1-4549-1819-6(5))* Sterling Publishing Co., Inc.

—My Dog. Joy, Angela. 2005. 14p. (J). 12.95 *(978-1-58925-759-7(6))* Tiger Tales.

—A Skunk in My Bunk! Cerf, Christopher. 2019. (Beginner Books(R) Ser.). 48p. (J). (gr. k-3). 9.99 *(978-0-525-57872-7(2)*, Random Hse. Bks. for Young Readers) Random Hse. Children's Bks.

—¿Tú Serás Mi Rayito de Sol? Lobo, Julia. Cottage Door Press, ed. 2020. (SPA.). 18p. (J). (gr. -1-2). bds. 9.99 *(978-1-68052-847-3(5)*, 1000280-SLA) Cottage Door Pr.

—We're Bored. 2005. 12p. (J). 12.95 *(978-1-58117-384-0(9)*, Intervisual/Piggy Toes) Bendon, Inc.

—Will You Be My Sunshine: Padded Board Book. Lobo, Julia. 2015. (Love You Always Ser.). (ENG.). 18p. (J). (gr. -1-2). bds. 9.99 *(978-1-68052-027-9(X)*, 1000280) Cottage Door Pr.

—Will You Be My Sunshine Gift Set. Lobo, Julia. Cottage Door Press, ed. 2019. (Book & Cuddly Plush Toy Friend Ser.). (ENG.). 18p. (J). (gr. -1-k). bds. 16.99 *(978-1-68052-761-2(4)*, 1004720) Cottage Door Pr.

Slater, Teddy & Rescek, Sanja. I Can Say Please. 2012. (J). *(978-0-545-47249-4(0))* Scholastic, Inc.

Slater, Tim. The Wandering Wildebeest. Coleman, Martin. 2019. (ENG.). 32p. (J). (gr. -1-3). pap. 9.99 *(978-1-78711-386-2(8)*, Hubble & Hattie) Veloce Publishing Ltd. GBR. Dist: Hachette Bk. Group.

Slaughter, Tom. ABC X 3: English - Espanol - Francais. Jocelyn, Marthe. 2005. 32p. (J). (gr. k-k). 15.99 *(978-0-88776-707-4(9)*, Tundra Bks.) Tundra Bks. CAN. Dist: Penguin Random Hse. LLC.

—Eats. Jocelyn, Marthe. (J). (gr. k-k). 2010. 16p. 7.95 *(978-0-88776-988-7(8))*; 2007. 24p. 16.99 *(978-0-88776-820-0(2))* Tundra Bks. CAN. (Tundra Bks.). Dist: Penguin Random Hse. LLC.

—One Some Many. Jocelyn, Marthe. (J). (gr. k-k). 2006. 16p. 7.95 *(978-0-88776-789-0(3))*; 2004. 32p. 11.95 *(978-0-88776-675-6(7))* Tundra Bks. CAN. (Tundra Bks.). Dist: Penguin Random Hse. LLC.

—Over Under. Jocelyn, Marthe. (J). (gr. k-k). 2006. (ENG.). 16p. bds. 7.95 *(978-0-88776-790-6(7))*; 2005. 24p. 15.95 *(978-0-88776-708-1(7))* Tundra Bks. CAN. (Tundra Bks.). Dist: Penguin Random Hse. LLC.

—Same Same. Jocelyn, Marthe. (J). (gr. k-k). 2010. 16p. 7.95 *(978-0-88776-987-0(X))*; 2009. 24p. 15.95 *(978-0-88776-885-9(7))* Tundra Bks. CAN. (Tundra Bks.). Dist: Penguin Random Hse. LLC.

—Which Way? Jocelyn, Marthe. 2010. 24p. (J). (gr. k-k). 15.95 *(978-0-88776-970-2(5)*, Tundra Bks.) Tundra Bks. CAN. Dist: Penguin Random Hse. LLC.

Slaughter, Tom. Un, Deux, Trois. Slaughter, Tom. 2006. (FRE.). 24p. (J). (gr. k-k). pap. 7.95 *(978-0-88776-802-6(4))* Tundra Bks. CAN. Dist: Penguin Random Hse. LLC.

Slavens, Rick, photos by. Growing Pains: A Childhood on Bear Creek. Rieken, Ethel Plaep. Zander, Julie McDonald, ed. 2004. 140p. (YA). per. 23.00 *(978-0-9740348-2-9(7)*, Special Editions — Customized Biographies) Slavens Enterprises, LLC.

Slavin, Bill. Adventures in Ancient China. Bailey, Linda. 2003. (Good Times Travel Agency Ser.). (ENG.). 48p. (J). (gr. 3-7). 10.95 *(978-1-55337-454-1(1))* Kids Can Pr., Ltd. CAN. Dist: Hachette Bk. Group.

—All Aboard! Elijah McCoy's Steam Engine. Kulling, Monica. 2013. (Great Idea Ser.: 2). (ENG.). 32p. (J). (gr. k-3). pap. 7.95 *(978-1-77049-514-2(2)*, Tundra Bks.) Tundra Bks. CAN. Dist: Penguin Random Hse. LLC.

—The Big Book of Canada. Moore, Christopher. 2017. (ENG.). 256p. (J). (gr. 4-7). 34.99 *(978-1-101-91894-4(2)*, Tundra Bks.) Tundra Bks. CAN. Dist: Penguin Random Hse. LLC.

—The Bone Talker, 1 vol. Leedahl, Shelley A. 2005. (ENG.). 32p. (J). (gr. 1-3). pap. 8.95 *(978-1-55041-350-2(3)*, 39ade2e3-2ae8-4862-87ba-6da60833655e) Trifolium Bks., Inc. CAN. Dist: Firefly Bks., Ltd.

—Caedmon's Song. Ashby, Ruth. 2006. (ENG.). 32p. (J). (gr. k). 16.00 *(978-0-8028-5241-0(6)*, Eerdmans Bks For Young Readers) Eerdmans, William B. Publishing Co.

—Campfire Morgan, 1 vol. Staunton, Ted. (Formac First Novels Ser.: 36). (ENG.). 64p. (J). 2016. (gr. 1-5). 5.95 *(978-0-88780-721-3(6)*, 38f8bba5-9637-434f-a799-cd026c119cb5); 2007. (gr. 2-5). 14.95 *(978-0-88780-725-1(9)*, 725) Formac Publishing Co., Ltd. CAN. Dist: Lerner Publishing Group, Formac Lorimer Bks. Ltd.

—Daredevil Morgan. Staunton, Ted. 2018. (Be Brave, Morgan! Ser.). (ENG.). 96p. (J). (gr. k-3). 16.99 *(978-1-4595-0506-3(9)*, a32097ae-e72c-47fb-be73-ec03fcb5a52d) Formac Publishing Co., Ltd. CAN. Dist: Lerner Publishing Group.

—Discover Space. Nicolson, Cynthia. 2005. 32p. (J). lib. bdg. 15.38 *(978-1-4242-1193-7(X))* Fitzgerald Bks.

—Discover Space. Nicolson, Cynthia Pratt. 2005. (Kids Can Read! Ser.). 32p. (J). (gr. 1-3). 3.95 *(978-1-55337-824-2(5))* Kids Can Pr., Ltd. CAN. Dist: Hachette Bk. Group.

—Discover Space Rocks. Nicolson, Cynthia. 2006. 32p. (J). lib. bdg. 15.38 *(978-1-4242-1195-1(6))* Fitzgerald Bks.

—Discover the Planets. Nicolson, Cynthia. 2005. 32p. (J). lib. bdg. 15.38 *(978-1-4242-1194-4(8))* Fitzgerald Bks.

—Discover the Stars. Nicolson, Cynthia. 2006. 32p. (J). lib. bdg. 15.38 *(978-1-4242-1196-8(4))* Fitzgerald Bks.

Slavin, Bill, et al. Drumheller Dinosaur Dance. Heidbreder, Robert. 2006. (ENG.). 32p. (J). (gr. -1-2). pap. 7.95 *(978-1-55337-982-9(9))* Kids Can Pr., Ltd. CAN. Dist: Hachette Bk. Group.

Slavin, Bill. The Faceless Fiend: Being the Tale of a Criminal Mastermind, His Masked Minions & a Princess with a Butter Knife, Involving Explosives & a Certain Amount of Pushing & Shoving. Whitehouse, Howard. 2007. (Mad Misadventures of Emmaline & Rubberbones Ser.). (ENG.). 272p. (J). (gr. 4-7). 7.95 *(978-1-55453-180-6(2))* Kids Can Pr., Ltd. CAN. Dist: Hachette Bk. Group.

—Game on in Ancient Greece. Bailey, Linda. 2019. (ENG.). 56p. (J). (gr. 3-7). pap. 11.99 *(978-1-77138-988-4(5))* Kids Can Pr., Ltd. CAN. Dist: Hachette Bk. Group.

—Gonzalo Grabs the Good Life. Levy, Janice. 2009. (ENG.). 34p. (J). (gr. k-4). 17.50 *(978-0-8028-5328-8(5)*, Eerdmans Bks For Young Readers) Eerdmans, William B. Publishing Co.

—Great Play, Morgan. Staunton, Ted. 2008. (First Novel Ser.). (ENG.). 64p. (J). (gr. 2-6). *(978-0-88780-772-5(0))* Formac Publishing Co., Ltd. CAN. Dist: Casemate Pubs. & Bk. Distributors, LLC.

—Hot on the Trail in Ancient Egypt. Bailey, Linda. 2018. (Time Travel Guides). (ENG.). 56p. (J). (gr. 3-7). pap. 11.99 *(978-1-77138-985-3(0))* Kids Can Pr., Ltd. CAN. Dist: Hachette Bk. Group.

—How the Second Grade Got $8,205. 50 to Visit the Statue of Liberty. Zimelman, Nathan. 2017. (ENG.). 32p. (J). (gr. -1-3). pap. 7.99 *(978-0-8075-3435-9(8)*, 807534358) Whitman, Albert & Co.

—The Island of Mad Scientists: Being an Excursion to the Wilds of Scotland, Involving Many Marvels of Experimental Invention, Pirates, a Heroic Cat, a Mechanical Man & a Monkey. Whitehouse, Howard. 2008. (Mad Misadventures of Emmaline & Rubberbones Ser.). 264p. (J). (gr. 4-7). pap. 7.95 *(978-1-55453-237-7(X))* Kids Can Pr., Ltd. CAN. Dist: Hachette Bk. Group.

—It's a Snap! George Eastman's First Photograph. Kulling, Monica. (Great Idea Ser.: 1). 32p. (J). (gr. k-3). 2013. (ENG.). pap. 7.95 *(978-1-77049-513-5(4))*; 2009. 17.95 *(978-0-88776-881-1(4))* Tundra Bks. CAN. (Tundra Bks.). Dist: Penguin Random Hse. LLC.

—Little Chicken Duck. Beiser, Tim. 2013. (ENG.). 24p. (J). (gr. -1-2). 17.95 *(978-1-77049-392-6(1)*, Tundra Bks.) Tundra Bks. CAN. Dist: Penguin Random Hse. LLC.

—Morgan & the Dune Racer. Staunton, Ted. 2011. (Formac First Novels Ser.). (ENG.). 64p. (J). (gr. 2-3). 14.95 *(978-0-88780-966-8(9)*, 966) Formac Publishing Co., Ltd. CAN. Dist: Formac Lorimer Bks. Ltd.

—Morgan & the Money. Staunton, Ted. 2008. (First Novel Ser.). (ENG.). 64p. (J). (gr. 1-5). *(978-0-88780-776-3(3))* Formac Publishing Co., Ltd.

—Morgan Makes a Deal. Staunton, Ted. 2005. 60p. (J). lib. bdg. 12.00 *(978-1-4242-1205-7(7))* Fitzgerald Bks.

—Morgan Makes a Deal. Staunton, Ted. 2005. (Formac First Novels Ser.: 33). (ENG.). 64p. (J). (gr. 2-5). 14.95 *(978-0-88780-667-4(8)*, 667) Formac Publishing Co., Ltd. CAN. Dist: Formac Lorimer Bks. Ltd.

—Morgan Makes a Splash. Staunton, Ted. 2004. (Formac First Novels Ser.: 28). (ENG.). 64p. (J). (gr. 1-5). 14.95 *(978-0-88780-623-0(6)*, 623) Formac Publishing Co., Ltd. CAN. Dist: Formac Lorimer Bks. Ltd.

—Morgan on Ice. Staunton, Ted. (Be Brave, Morgan! Ser.). (ENG.). (J). 2018. 96p. (gr. k-3). 16.99 *(978-1-4595-0495-0(3)*, ff240a2d-c1b5-41f3-82ac-9428c9b47150); 2013. 56p. (gr. 2-3). 14.95 *(978-1-4595-0289-5(2)*, 0289) Formac Publishing Co., Ltd. CAN. Dist: Lerner Publishing Group, Formac Lorimer Bks. Ltd.

—Morgan the Brave. Staunton, Ted & Staunton, Will. 2018. (Be Brave, Morgan! Ser.). (ENG.). 96p. (J). (gr. k-3). 16.99 *(978-1-4595-0497-4(6)*, e9b7bb46-5a93-41b2-9fa5-97a737e0e09b) Formac Publishing Co., Ltd. CAN. Dist: Lerner Publishing Group.

—Morgan"s Got Game. Staunton, Ted. 2018. (Be Brave, Morgan! Ser.). (ENG.). 96p. (J). (gr. k-3). 16.99 *(978-1-4595-0508-7(5)*, 39f8bd8e-023f-49d5-8a7e-e7b800e068c0) Formac Publishing Co., Ltd. CAN. Dist: Lerner Publishing Group.

—Morgan's Pet Plot. Staunton, Ted. 2003. (Formac First Novels Ser.: 24). (ENG.). 64p. (J). (gr. 1-5). 14.95 *(978-0-88780-588-2(4)*, 588) Formac Publishing Co., Ltd. CAN. Dist: Formac Lorimer Bks. Ltd.

—Music by Morgan, 1 vol. Staunton, Ted. 2016. (Formac First Novels Ser.). (ENG.). 64p. (J). (gr. 1-5). pap. 5.95 *(978-0-88780-926-2(X)*, 9dfb569e-995d-4131-8e35-5d3e93c521a3) Formac Publishing Co., Ltd. CAN. Dist: Lerner Publishing Group.

—On the Run in Ancient China. Bailey, Linda. 2019. (Time Travel Guides: 3). (ENG.). 56p. (J). (gr. 3-7). pap. 11.99 *(978-1-5253-0112-4(8))* Kids Can Pr., Ltd. CAN. Dist: Hachette Bk. Group.

Slavin, Bill, et al. Our Flag: The Story of Canada's Maple Leaf. Owens, Ann-Maureen & Yealland, Jane. 2014. (ENG.). 32p. (J). (gr. 2-5). pap. 9.95 *(978-1-77138-112-3(4))* Kids Can Pr., Ltd. CAN. Dist: Hachette Bk. Group.

Slavin, Bill. Pandemic Survival: It's Why You're Alive. Drake, Jane & Love, Ann. 2013. (ENG.). 128p. (J). (gr. 4-7). 22.95 *(978-1-77049-268-4(2)*, Tundra Bks.) Tundra Bks. CAN. Dist: Penguin Random Hse. LLC.

—Pucker up, Morgan, 1 vol. Staunton, Ted. (Formac First Novels Ser.). (ENG.). 64p. (J). 2016. (gr. 1-5). 5.95 *(978-0-88780-744-2(5)*, afa4d09f-2e2c-4945-8ce2-6bbe53937c09); 2008. (gr. 2-5). 14.95 *(978-0-88780-746-6(1)*, 746) Formac Publishing Co., Ltd. CAN. Dist: Lerner Publishing Group, Formac Lorimer Bks. Ltd.

—Shapes in Math, Science & Nature: Squares, Triangles & Circles. Sheldrick Ross, Catherine. 2014. (ENG.). 192p. (J). (gr. 4-9). 24.95 *(978-1-77138-124-6(8))* Kids Can Pr., Ltd. CAN. Dist: Hachette Bk. Group.

—Le Soleil. Bourgeois, Paulette.Tr. of Destination Univers: Le Soleil. (FRE.). 40p. (J). pap. 8.99 *(978-0-590-16019-3(2))* Scholastic, Inc.

—Something to Tell the Grandcows. Spinelli, Eileen. 2004. 32p. (J). 16.00 *(978-0-8028-5236-6(X))*; (gr. -1-3). 8.00 *(978-0-8028-5304-2(8)*, Eerdmans Bks For Young Readers) Eerdmans, William B. Publishing Co.

—Stanley at School. Bailey, Linda. 2015. (ENG.). 32p. (J). (gr. -1-2). 17.95 *(978-1-77138-096-6(9))* Kids Can Pr., Ltd. CAN. Dist: Hachette Bk. Group.

—Stanley at Sea. Bailey, Linda. 2008. (ENG.). 32p. (J). (gr. -1-2). 16.95 *(978-1-55453-193-6(4))* Kids Can Pr., Ltd. CAN. Dist: Hachette Bk. Group.

—Stanley's Beauty Contest. Bailey, Linda. 2009. (ENG.). 32p. (J). (gr. -1-2). 17.95 *(978-1-55453-318-3(X))* Kids Can Pr., Ltd. CAN. Dist: Hachette Bk. Group.

—Stanley's Little Sister. Bailey, Linda. 2010. (ENG.). 32p. (J). (gr. -1-2). 17.95 *(978-1-55453-487-6(9))* Kids Can Pr., Ltd. CAN. Dist: Hachette Bk. Group.

—Stanley's Party. Bailey, Linda. 2004. (ENG.). 32p. (J). (gr. -1-2). pap. 8.99 *(978-1-55337-768-9(0))* Kids Can Pr., Ltd. CAN. Dist: Hachette Bk. Group.

—Stanley's Wild Ride. Bailey, Linda. 2008. (ENG.). 32p. (J). (gr. -1-2). pap. 7.95 *(978-1-55453-254-4(X))* Kids Can Pr., Ltd. CAN. Dist: Hachette Bk. Group.

—Stowing Away with the Vikings. Bailey, Linda. 2018. (Time Travel Guides: 2). (ENG.). 56p. (J). (gr. 3-7). pap. 11.99 *(978-1-77138-987-7(7))* Kids Can Pr., Ltd. CAN. Dist: Hachette Bk. Group.

—The Strictest School in the World: Being the Tale of a Clever Girl, a Rubber Boy & a Collection of Flying Machines, Mostly Broken. Whitehouse, Howard. 2006. (Mad Misadventures of Emmaline & Rubberbones Ser.). (ENG.). 256p. (J). (gr. 4-7). 16.95 *(978-1-55337-882-2(2))* Kids Can Pr., Ltd. CAN. Dist: Hachette Bk. Group.

—Super Move, Morgan! Staunton, Ted. 2006. (Formac First Novels Ser.: 35). (ENG.). 64p. (J). (gr. 2-5). 14.95 *(978-0-88780-704-6(6)*, 704); 4.95 *(978-0-88780-702-2(X)*, 702) Formac Publishing Co., Ltd. CAN. Dist: Formac Lorimer Bks. Ltd.

—Talking Tails: The Incredible Connection Between People & Their Pets. Love, Ann & Drake, Jane. (ENG.). 80p. (J). (gr. 4-7). 2012. pap. 9.95 *(978-1-77049-359-9(X))*; 2010. 22.95 *(978-0-88776-884-2(9))* Tundra Bks. CAN. (Tundra Bks.). Dist: Penguin Random Hse. LLC.

—Trash Revolution: Breaking the Waste Cycle. Fyvie, Erica. 2018. (ENG.). 64p. (J). (gr. 3-7). 18.99 *(978-1-77138-078-2(0))* Kids Can Pr., Ltd. CAN. Dist: Hachette Bk. Group.

—Zap! Nikola Tesla Takes Charge. Kulling, Monica. 2019. (Great Idea Ser.: 8). (ENG.). 32p. (J). (gr. k-3). pap. 6.99 *(978-0-7352-6481-6(3)*, Tundra Bks.) Tundra Bks. CAN. Dist: Penguin Random Hse. LLC.

Slavin, Bill. Big Top Otto. Slavin, Bill. 2013. (Elephants Never Forget Ser.). (ENG.). 88p. (J). (gr. 3-6). 16.95 *(978-1-55453-806-5(8))*; Vol. 2. pap. 7.95 *(978-1-55453-807-2(6))* Kids Can Pr., Ltd. CAN. Dist: Hachette Bk. Group.

—The Stone Lion, 1 vol. Slavin, Bill. 2003. (ENG.). 32p. (J). (gr. 1-3). pap. 6.95 *(978-0-88995-154-9(3)*, 354e7d80-4270-4d89-8848-219e051ec137) Red Deer Pr. CAN. Dist: Firefly Bks., Ltd.

—Transformed: How Everyday Things Are Made. Slavin, Bill. 2007. (ENG.). 160p. (J). (gr. 3-7). pap. 18.95 *(978-1-55453-244-5(2))* Kids Can Pr., Ltd. CAN. Dist: Hachette Bk. Group.

Slavin, Bill & Melo, Esperança. Our Flag: The Story of Canada's Maple Leaf. Owens, Ann-Maureen & Yealland, Jane. 2014. (ENG.). 32p. (J). (gr. 2-5). 17.95 *(978-1-77138-111-6(6))* Kids Can Pr., Ltd. CAN. Dist: Hachette Bk. Group.

Slavin, Bill & Melo, Esperanca. The Seven Seas. Jackson, Ellen B. 2010. (ENG.). 36p. (J). (gr. -1-3). 16.00 *(978-0-8028-5341-7(2),* Eerdmans Bks For Young Readers) Eerdmans, William B. Publishing Co.

Slavin, Bill & Shannon, Ben. Morgan Makes a Deal, 1 vol. Staunton, Ted. 2005. (Formac First Novels Ser.: 33). (ENG.). 64p. (J). (gr. 2-5). 4.95 *(978-0-88780-666-7(X),* 666) Formac Publishing Co., Ltd. CAN. Dist: Formac Lorimer Bks. Ltd.

—Morgan's Pet Plot, 1 vol. Staunton, Ted. 2003. (Formac First Novels Ser.: 24). (ENG.). 64p. (J). (gr. 1-5). 4.95 *(978-0-88780-587-5(6),* 587) Formac Publishing Co., Ltd. CAN. Dist: Formac Lorimer Bks. Ltd.

—Morgan's Secret, 1 vol. Staunton, Ted. 2016. (Formac First Novels Ser.: 15). (ENG.). 58p. (J). (gr. 1-5). 5.95 *(978-0-88780-494-6(2),* 3a230e1b-9f8e-4ee8-b93e-5df82cf1c7f4) Formac Publishing Co., Ltd. CAN. Dist: Lerner Publishing Group.

Slavin, Bill, jt. illus. see Nicolson, Cynthia Pratt.

Sleightholm, Heather. Snow on Martinmas. Sleightholm, Heather. 2017. (ENG.). 32p. (J). (gr. -1-3). pap. 9.99 *(978-1-5324-0170-1(1))* Xist Publishing.

Slettnes, Elisabeth. The Girl God. Hendren, Trista. 2019. (Hardcover Special Edition Ser.: Vol. 2). (ENG.). 50p. (J). (gr. k-6). *(978-978-8293-72-9(7))* Hendren, Trista.

—The Girl God. Hendren, Trista. 2012. (ENG.). (J). pap. 14.99 *(978-1-62209-484-4(0))* Primedia eLaunch LLC.

Slettnes, Elisabeth. Jenteguden. Hendren, Trista. Alfarnes, Oddvin, tr. 2019.Tr. of Girl God. (NOR.). 46p. (J). (gr. k-6). ***(978-82-93725-04-6(4))*** Hendren, Trista.

Sleva, Michael. 303 Kid-Approved Exercises & Active Games. Wechsler, Kimberly. 2013. (SmartFun Activity Bks.). (ENG.). 144p. (J). (gr. k-3). pap. 17.99 *(978-0-89793-619-4(1),* Hunter Hse.) Turner Publishing Co.

—303 Preschooler-Approved Exercises & Active Games. Wechsler, Kimberly. 2013. (SmartFun Activity Bks.). (ENG.). 168p. (J). (gr. k-k). pap. 14.95 *(978-0-89793-618-7(3));* spiral bd. 19.95 *(978-0-89793-623-1(X))* Turner Publishing Co. (Hunter Hse.).

—303 Tween-Approved Exercises & Active Games. Wechsler, Kimberly. 2013. (SmartFun Activity Bks.). (ENG.). 168p. (J). (gr. 3-6). pap. 14.95 *(978-0-89793-620-0(5));* spiral bd. 19.95 *(978-0-89793-625-5(6))* Turner Publishing Co. (Hunter Hse.).

Slim, Lillian, et al. Subsistence Adventures. Slim, Lillian et al. 2006. (Adventure Story Collection Ser.). 28p. (J). (gr. 2-6). pap. 10.00 *(978-1-58084-252-5(6))* Lower Kuskokwim Schl. District.

Slimp, Gwen H. The Winter Sleep: A Story of Hibernation. Rice, Joan W. 2004. 48p. (J). (gr. k-3). *(978-0-9755573-0-3(0))* Coastal Publishing, LLC.

Sliney, Will. Ben Reilly: Scarlet Spider Vol. 3: Slingers Return. 2018. (ENG.). 112p. (YA). (gr. 8-17). pap. 15.99 *(978-1-302-91115-7(5))* Marvel Worldwide, Inc.

—Ben Reilly: Scarlet Spider Vol. 5: Deal with the Devil. 2019. (Ben Reilly: Scarlet Spider Ser.: 5). (ENG.). 136p. (YA). (gr. 8-17). pap. 17.99 *(978-1-302-91504-9(5))* Marvel Worldwide, Inc.

—Spider-Man 2099 Vol. 6: Apocalypse Soon. 2017. (ENG.). 112p. (J). (gr. 4-17). pap. 15.99 *(978-1-302-90282-7(2))* Marvel Worldwide, Inc.

—Star Wars: Galaxy's Edge. 2019. 112p. (YA). (gr. 4-17). pap. 15.99 *(978-1-302-91786-9(2))* Marvel Worldwide, Inc.

Sliney, Will. Star Wars: the Rise of Kylo Ren. 2020. 112p. (J). (gr. 4-17). pap. 15.99 ***(978-1-302-92418-8(4))*** Marvel Worldwide, Inc.

Sloan, Jaclyn. The Awesome Opossum. Allen, Karen Mutchler. 2018. (This Is Me! Ser.: Vol. 1). (ENG.). 34p. (J). pap. 14.00 *(978-1-7238-1998-8(0))* Independently Published.

—The Couth Fairy. Allen, Karen Mutchler. 2018. (ENG.). 52p. (J). 21.99 *(978-1-948026-05-5(8))* Write Integrity Pr.

—The Couth Fairy Goes to School. Allen, Karen Mutchler. (ENG.). (J). 2017. pap. 13.99 *(978-1-948026-00-0(7));* 3rd ed. 2018. 32p. 21.99 *(978-1-948026-07-9(4))* Write Integrity Pr.

—The Couth Fairy Returns. Allen, Karen Mutchler. (ENG.). (J). 2016. pap. 13.99 *(978-0-9839485-7-5(7));* 2nd ed. 2018. 28p. 21.99 *(978-1-948026-06-2(6))* Write Integrity Pr.

Sloan, Michael. Glendale: Nashville's Magical Park. Lane, Andy. 2009. 88p. (J). 22.95 *(978-1-57736-408-5(2))* Providence Hse Pubs.

—My Anxious Mind: A Teen's Guide to Managing Anxiety & Panic. Tompkins, Michael A. & Martinez, Katherine A. 2009. 128p. (YA). (gr. 7-12). pap. 14.95 *(978-1-4338-0450-2(6),* Magination Pr.) American Psychological Assn.

Sloan, Monty, photos by. Wolves: For the Earliest Reader. Hillert, Margaret. Starfall Education, ed. 2006. (ENG., 32p. (J). *(978-1-59577-037-0(2));* pap. *(978-1-59577-038-7(0))* Starfall Education.

Sloan, Peter. Alice in Wonderland Made Simple for Kids. Carroll, Lewis. 2007. 126p. (J). per. 19.95 net. *(978-0-923891-91-6(9))* Ishi Pr. International.

Sloane, Roxy. Blueberry Pie: The Adventures of Blueberry Bear & Her Friends. Erin, K. c. 2009. 40p. pap. 16.99 *(978-1-4389-7592-4(9))* AuthorHouse.

Sloat, Teri. Dance on a Sealskin. Winslow, Barbara. 2015. (ENG.). 32p. (J). pap. 10.99 *(978-1-941821-80-0(4),* Alaska Northwest Bks.) West Margin Pr.

—How the Bear Lost This Tail. Alexie, Oscar. 2004. (J). pap. 14.00 *(978-1-58084-222-8(4))* Lower Kuskokwim Schl. District.

—My Bug Box. Blanchard, Patricia & Suhr, Joanne. 2003. (Books for Young Learners). 12p. (J). pap. 15.00 *(978-1-57274-701-2(3),* BB2473, Bks. for Young Learners) Owen, Richard C. Pubs., Inc.

Slobodkin, Louis. The Hundred Dresses. Estes, Eleanor. anniv. ed. 2004. (ENG.). 96p. (J). (gr. 1-4). 17.99 *(978-0-15-205170-9(8),* 1195595); pap. 8.99 *(978-0-15-205260-7(7),* 1195848) Houghton Mifflin Harcourt Publishing Co.

Slobodkina, Esphyr. Caps for Sale: A Tale of a Peddler, Some Monkeys & Their Monkey Business. Slobodkina, Esphyr. 2015. (Young Scott Bks.). (ENG.). 48p. (J). (gr. -1-3). 17.99 *(978-0-201-09147-2(X));* 75th ed. pap. 7.99 *(978-0-06-443143-9(6))* HarperCollins Pubs. Ltd. GBR. (HarperCollins). Dist: HarperCollins Pubs.

—Caps for Sale: A Tale of a Peddler, Some Monkeys & Their Monkey Businesss. Slobodkina, Esphyr. 2008. (Young Scott Bks.). (ENG.). 48p. (J). (gr. -1-3). lib. bdg. 17.89 *(978-0-06-025778-1(4),* HarperCollins) HarperCollins Pubs. Ltd. GBR. Dist: HarperCollins Pubs.

—Caps for Sale & the Mindful Monkeys. Slobodkina, Esphyr. Sayer, Ann Marie Mulhearn. 2017. (ENG.). 48p. (J). (gr. -1-3). 17.99 *(978-0-06-249988-2(2))* HarperCollins Pubs.

—Caps for Sale Board Book: A Tale of a Peddler, Some Monkeys & Their Monkey Business. Slobodkina, Esphyr. 75th ed. 2015. (Reading Rainbow Bks.). (ENG.). 32p. (J). (gr. -1-3). bds. 8.99 *(978-0-06-147453-8(3),* HarperFestival) HarperCollins Pubs.

—Circus Caps for Sale. Slobodkina, Esphyr. 2004. 40p. (J). (gr. -1-2). reprint ed. 17.00 *(978-0-7567-8345-7(3))* DIANE Publishing Co.

—Circus Caps for Sale. Slobodkina, Esphyr. 2004. (ENG.). 48p. (J). (gr. -1-3). reprint ed. pap. 7.99 *(978-0-06-443793-6(0))* HarperCollins Pubs.

—More Caps for Sale: Another Tale of Mischievous Monkeys. Slobodkina, Esphyr. Sayer, Ann Marie Mulhearn. (ENG.). 40p. (J). (gr. -1-3). 2017. pap. 8.99 *(978-0-06-249957-8(2));* 2015. 18.99 *(978-0-06-240545-6(4))* HarperCollins Pubs.

—More Caps for Sale: Another Tale of Mischievous Monkeys Board Book. Slobodkina, Esphyr. Sayer, Ann Marie Mulhearn. 2018. (ENG.). 32p. (J). (gr. -1-3). bds. 8.99 *(978-0-06-240560-9(8),* HarperFestival) HarperCollins Pubs.

Slocum, Bradley. A Tale of Too Many Cities - Egypt. Wax, Wendy & Weiss, Bobbi. Vargus, Nanci, ed. 2008. (ENG.). 24p. (J). (gr. 1-17). pap. 3.99 *(978-1-58476-722-0(7))* Innovative Kids.

Slonim, David. Bed Hog, 0 vols. Noullet, Georgette. 2011. (ENG.). 24p. (J). (gr. -1-3). 12.99 *(978-0-7614-5823-4(9),* 9780761458234, Two Lions) Amazon Publishing.

—The Deer Watch. Collins, Pat Lowery. 2013. 32p. (J). (gr. -1-2). 15.99 *(978-0-7636-4890-9(6))* Candlewick Pr.

—Digger, Dozer, Dumper. Vestergaard, Hope. (J). 2018. 32p. (gr. -1-3). 4.99 *(978-0-7636-9969-7(1));* 2016. (ENG.). 30p. (-k). bds. 7.99 *(978-0-7636-8893-6(2))* Candlewick Pr.

—How to Teach a Slug to Read, 0 vols. Pearson, Susan. 2011. (ENG.). 32p. (J). (gr. k-2). 16.99 *(978-0-7614-5805-0(0),* 9780761458050, Two Lions) Amazon Publishing.

—I Know an Old Lady Who Swallowed a Dreidel. Yacowitz, Caryn. 2014. (ENG.). 32p. (J). (gr. -1-3). 17.99 *(978-0-439-91530-4(9),* Levine, Arthur A. Bks.) Scholastic, Inc.

—Silly Tilly, 0 vols. Spinelli, Eileen. 2012. (ENG.). 32p. (J). (gr. -1-2). pap. 9.99 *(978-0-7614-5990-3(1),* 9780761459903, Two Lions) Amazon Publishing.

—Slugger, 0 vols. Pearson, Susan. 2013. (ENG.). 32p. (J). (gr. -1-2). 14.99 *(978-1-4778-1641-7(0),* 9781477816417, Two Lions) Amazon Publishing.

—A Sweet Passover. Newman, Lesléa & Newman, Lesléa. 2012. (ENG.). 40p. (J). (gr. -1-3). 17.95 *(978-0-8109-9737-0(1),* Abrams Bks. for Young Readers) Abrams, Inc.

—Who Swallowed Harold? And Other Poems about Pets, 0 vols. Pearson, Susan. 2013. (ENG.). 32p. (J). (gr. k-4). pap. 9.99 *(978-1-4778-1595-3(3),* 9781477815953, Two Lions) Amazon Publishing.

—Who Swallowed Harold? And Other Poems about Pets, 1 vol. Pearson, Susan. 2005. (ENG.). 32p. (J). (gr. k-4). 16.95 *(978-0-7614-5193-8(5))* Marshall Cavendish Corp.

—You Think It's Easy Being the Tooth Fairy? Bell-Rehwoldt, Sheri. 2007. (ENG.). 32p. (J). (gr. -1-3). 15.99 *(978-0-8118-5460-3(4))* Chronicle Bks. LLC.

Slonim, David. 10 Turkeys in the Road. Sturgis, Brenda Reeves. 2020. 32p. (J). (gr. -1-2). pap. 9.99 ***(978-1-5420-2537-9(0),*** 9781542025379, Two Lions) Amazon Publishing.

Slonim, David. He Came with the Couch. Slonim, David. 2005. (ENG.). 36p. (J). (gr. -1-3). 15.99 *(978-0-8118-4430-7(7))* Chronicle Bks. LLC.

—I Loathe You. Slonim, David. (ENG.). 24p. (J). (gr. -1-3). 2018. 7.99 *(978-1-5344-3311-3(2));* 2012. 15.99 *(978-1-4424-2244-5(0))* Simon & Schuster Children's Publishing. (Aladdin).

—Oh, Ducky! A Chocolate Calamity. Slonim, David. 2006. 28p. (J). (gr. k-4). 16.00 *(978-1-4223-5259-5(5))* DIANE Publishing Co.

Slonim, David, jt. illus. see Gurney, John Steven.

Slusser, Lauren & Birdy, Miss. Sugar Dragon Has a Problem. Birdy, Miss. 2019. (ENG.). 42p. (J). pap. 15.00 *(978-1-7933-8865-0(2))* Independently Published.

Slutz, Stephani. Ko 'Eku Tohi Lau Maau. Thompson, Richard & Thompson, Ofa. l.t. ed. 2005. (TON.). 16p. (J). (gr. -1-18). 5.00 *(978-0-9678979-4-3(7))* Friendly Isles Pr.

—Ko 'Eku Tohi 'oe Fanga Manu. Thompson, Richard & Thompson, Ofa. l.t. ed. 2004. (TON.). 16p. (J). (gr. -1-18). 5.00 *(978-0-9678979-2-9(0))* Friendly Isles Pr.

Sluyterman van Langeweyde, Ira. Mabel Opal Pear & the Rules for Spying. Hosch, Amanda. 2017. (Middle-Grade Novels Ser.). (ENG.). 272p. (J). (gr. 4-7). lib. bdg. 26.65 *(978-1-4965-4051-5(4),* 133353, Stone Arch Bks.) Capstone.

Smale, Denise L. & Blowars, Ryan. What If the Sun Didn't Rise. Smale, Denise L. 2011. 32p. pap. 24.95 *(978-1-4560-5032-0(X))* America Star Bks.

Small, David. Bloom. Cronin, Doreen. 2016. (ENG.). 40p. (J). (gr. -1-3). 17.99 *(978-1-4424-0620-9(8))* Simon & Schuster Children's Publishing.

—Catch That Cookie! Durand, Hallie. 2014. 32p. (J). (gr. -1-k). 17.99 *(978-0-525-42835-0(6),* Dial Bks) Penguin Young Readers Group.

—The Essential Worldwide Monster Guide. Ashman, Linda. 2010. (ENG.). 40p. (J). (gr. -1-3). 13.99 *(978-1-4424-1436-5(7),* Simon & Schuster Bks. For Young Readers) Simon & Schuster Bks. For Young Readers.

—The Gardener. Stewart, Sarah. 2003. (J). (gr. -1-2). 28.95 incl. audio compact disk *(978-1-59112-531-0(6))* Live Oak Media.

—The Gardener. Stewart, Sarah. 2007. (ENG.). 40p. (J). (gr. -1-2). per. 8.99 *(978-0-312-36749-7(X),* 900042354) Square Fish.

—Glamourpuss. Weeks, Sarah. 2015. (ENG.). 40p. (J). (gr. -1-1). 16.99 *(978-0-545-60954-8(2),* Scholastic Pr.) Scholastic, Inc.

—The Huckabuck Family: And How They Raised Popcorn in Nebraska & Quit & Came Back. Sandburg, Carl. 2006. 30p. (J). (gr. k-4). reprint ed. 16.00 *(978-1-4223-5854-2(2))* DIANE Publishing Co.

—The Journey. Stewart, Sarah. 2006. (ENG.). 40p. (J). (gr. k-4). reprint ed. pap. 9.99 *(978-0-374-40010-1(5),* 900039903) Square Fish.

—The Library. Stewart, Sarah. pap. 35.95 incl. audio compact disk *(978-1-59519-010-9(4));* 2004. (J). (gr. -1-2). 28.95 incl. audio compact disk *(978-1-59519-011-6(2))* Live Oak Media.

—The Mouse & His Child. Hoban, Russell. 2017. (ENG.). 272p. (J). (gr. 3-7). pap. 9.99 *(978-0-439-09827-4(0),* Scholastic Paperbacks) Scholastic, Inc.

—My Senator & Me: A Dog's-Eye View of Washington, D. C. Kennedy, Edward M. 2011. (J). (gr. 2-5). 29.95 *(978-0-545-04379-3(4))* Weston Woods Studios, Inc.

—Once upon a Banana. Armstrong, Jennifer. (ENG.). 48p. (J). (gr. -1-3). 2013. 6.99 *(978-0-689-85951-9(1));* 2006. 19.99 *(978-0-689-84251-1(1))* Simon & Schuster/Paula Wiseman Bks. (Simon & Schuster/Paula Wiseman Bks.).

—One Cool Friend. Buzzeo, Toni. 2012. (ENG.). 32p. (J). (gr. k-3). 17.99 *(978-0-8037-3413-5(1),* Dial Bks) Penguin Young Readers Group.

—One Cool Friend. Buzzeo, Toni. 2015. DVD 59.95 *(978-0-545-67553-6(7))* Scholastic, Inc.

—Princess Says Goodnight. Howland, Naomi. 2010. (ENG.). 32p. (J). (gr. -1-2). 16.99 *(978-0-06-145525-4(3));* lib. bdg. 17.89 *(978-0-06-145526-1(1))* HarperCollins Pubs.

—The Quiet Place, 1 vol. Stewart, Sarah. 2012. (ENG.). 44p. (J). (gr. k-4). 18.99 *(978-0-374-32565-7(0),* 900065971, Farrar, Straus & Giroux (BYR)) Farrar, Straus & Giroux.

—So You Want to Be an Inventor? St. George, Judith. 2005. 56p. (J). (gr. 2-5). pap. 7.99 *(978-0-14-240460-7(8),* Puffin Books) Penguin Young Readers Group.

—So You Want to Be President? St. George, Judith. 2004. (J). (gr. 1-6). 29.95 *(978-1-55592-132-3(9))* Weston Woods Studios, Inc.

—So You Want to Be President? The Revised & Updated Edition. St. George, Judith. rev. ed. 2004. (ENG.). 56p. (J). (gr. 2-5). 17.99 *(978-0-399-24317-2(8),* Philomel Bks.) Penguin Young Readers Group.

—That Book Woman. Henson, Heather. 2008. (ENG.). 40p. (J). (gr. -1-3). 17.99 *(978-1-4169-0812-8(9),* Atheneum Bks. for Young Readers) Simon & Schuster Children's Publishing.

—That Book Woman. Henson, Heather. 2011. (J). (gr. 2-4). 29.95 *(978-0-545-23715-4(7))* Weston Woods Studios, Inc.

—This Book of Mine: A Picture Book. Stewart, Sarah. 2019. (ENG.). 32p. (J). 17.99 *(978-0-374-30546-8(3),* 900163754, Farrar, Straus & Giroux (BYR)) Farrar, Straus & Giroux.

—The Underneath. Appelt, Kathi. 2010. (KOR.). 395p. (YA). pap. *(978-89-527-5767-8(X))* Sigongsa Co., Ltd.

—The Underneath. Appelt, Kathi. (ENG.). (J). (gr. 5-9). 2010. 336p. pap. 8.99 *(978-1-4169-5059-2(1));* 2008. 320p. 17.99 *(978-1-4169-5058-5(3))* Simon & Schuster Children's Publishing. (Atheneum Bks. for Young Readers).

—When Dinosaurs Came with Everything. Broach, Elise. (ENG.). 40p. (J). (gr. -1-3). 2019. 7.99 *(978-1-5344-5227-5(3));* 2007. 17.99 *(978-0-689-86922-8(3))* Simon & Schuster Children's Publishing. (Atheneum Bks. for Young Readers).

Small, David. Eulalie & the Hopping Head. Small, David. 2003. pap. 35.95 incl. audio compact disk *(978-1-59112-520-4(0));* (J). pap. 33.95 incl. audio *(978-1-59112-218-0(X))* Live Oak Media.

Small, Jan. Juni B. Dicello, Bob. 2013. 36p. 25.95 *(978-1-61493-157-7(7))* Peppertree Pr., The.

Small, Jessi Leigh. Ellie's Wish. David, Joan Mitchell. 2019. (ENG.). 42p. (J). (gr. 1-3). 14.95 ***(978-0-578-54664-3(7));*** pap. 6.95 ***(978-0-578-54665-0(5))*** Joan Mitchell David.

Small, Shannon. Dear You, Young Girl. Dixon, Nasheema S. 2018. (ENG.). 26p. (J). pap. 10.00 *(978-1-7321177-2-3(1))* Dear You.

Small, Steve. I'm Sticking with You. Prasadam-Halls, Smriti. 2020. (ENG.). 40p. (J). 18.99 *(978-1-250-61923-5(8),* 900223003, Holt, Henry & Co. Bks. For Young Readers) Holt, Henry & Co.

Small, Vanessa. Mystery at Pleasant Park. Small, Vanessa. 2017. (ENG.). (J). pap. 6.99 *(978-1-946257-01-7(X))* Small Publishing.

Small World Creations Ltd. Zippy Wheels: Diggers. 2016. (Zippy Wheels Ser.). (ENG.). 10p. (J). (gr. -1-k). bds. 8.99 *(978-0-7641-6825-3(8),* B.E.S. Publishing) Peterson's.

—Zippy Wheels: Dump Trucks. 2016. (Zippy Wheels Ser.). (ENG.). 10p. (J). (gr. -1-k). bds. 8.99 *(978-0-7641-6826-0(6),* B.E.S. Publishing) Peterson's.

—Zippy Wheels: Firetrucks. 2016. (Zippy Wheels Ser.). (ENG.). 10p. (J). (gr. -1-k). bds. 8.99 *(978-0-7641-6827-7(4),* B.E.S. Publishing) Peterson's.

—Zippy Wheels: Tractors. 2016. (Zippy Wheels Ser.). (ENG.). 10p. (J). (gr. -1-k). bds. 8.99 *(978-0-7641-6828-4(2),* B.E.S. Publishing) Peterson's.

Smallfield, Graeme. The Bedtime Treasury of Real Fairy Tales. Smallfield, Jane. 2005. 96p. 17.95 *(978-0-689-03923-2(9),* Milk & Cookies) ibooks, Inc.

Smallman, Steve. Bible Animals Story Collection, 1 vol. David, Juliet. ed. 2016. (ENG.). 136p. (J). (gr. -1-k). pap. 7.99 *(978-1-78128-286-1(2),* Candle Bks.) Lion Hudson PLC GBR. Dist: Independent Pubs. Group.

—Read & Share Bible: More Than 200 Best-Loved Bible Stories, 1 vol. Ellis, Gwen. 2007. (Read & Share (Tommy Nelson) Ser.). (ENG.). 440p. (J). (gr. k-3). 16.99 *(978-1-4003-0853-8(4))* Nelson, Thomas Inc.

—The Story of Easter, 1 vol. Ellis, Gwen. 2008. (Read & Share (Tommy Nelson) Ser.). (ENG.). 32p. (gr. -1-2). 7.99 *(978-1-4003-0855-2(0))* Nelson, Thomas Inc.

Smallman, Steve. Not-So-Brave Penguin: A Story about Overcoming Fears. Smallman, Steve. 2018. (Storytime Ser.). (ENG.). 24p. (J). (gr. -1-2). 16.95 ***(978-1-912413-90-4(6))*** QEB Publishing Inc.

Smalls, David. The Journey. Stewart, Sarah. pap. 16.95 incl. audio *(978-0-87499-922-8(7));* pap. incl. audio *(978-0-87499-924-2(3));* pap. 18.95 incl. audio compact disk *(978-1-59112-344-6(5));* pap. incl. audio compact disk *(978-1-59112-556-3(1))* Live Oak Media.

Smallwood, Sally. Sweet as a Strawberry. Smallwood, Sally. 2005. (Things I Eat Ser.: 1). (ENG.). 24p. (J). (gr. -1-k). *(978-1-84089-419-6(9))* Zero to Ten, Ltd.

Smantanica, Liviu. The Cuttlefish & the Elephant: Children's Stories. Poenaru, Vasile, ed. Isare, Simona, tr. 2019. (ENG.). 102p. (J). pap. 9.99 *(978-1-7931-3179-9(1))* Independently Published.

Smart, Andy. The Adventures of Wormie Wormington Book Three: Wormie & the Snowball. Brown, Adam. 2013. 48p. pap. *(978-0-9919196-3-5(7))* Beckon Creative.

—The Adventures of Wormie Wormington Book Two: Wormie & the Kite. Brown, Adam. 2013. 48p. pap. *(978-0-9919196-2-8(9))* Beckon Creative.

Smart, Andy. The Adventures of Wormie Wormington Book One: Wormie & the Fish. Smart, Andy. Brown, Adam. 2013. 50p. pap. *(978-0-9919196-0-4(2))* Beckon Creative.

—Bob'n Joe Book One: Lunch Time. Smart, Andy. 2013. 42p. (J). pap. *(978-0-9919196-1-1(0))* Beckon Creative.

Smart, Brooke. Families Belong. Saks, Dan. 2020. 24p. (J). (— 1). bds. 7.99 ***(978-0-593-22276-8(8))*** Penguin Young Readers Group.

Smart, George. Pupitukaar. Shield, Sophie. 2004. (J). pap. 10.00 *(978-1-58084-220-4(8))* Lower Kuskokwim Schl. District.

Smart, Jamie. Bunny vs. Monkey. Smart, Jamie. 2016. (Bunny vs. Monkey Ser.: 1). (ENG.). 64p. (J). (gr. 2-5). pap. 7.99 *(978-0-545-86184-7(5),* Graphix) Scholastic, Inc.

Smart Kids Publishing Staff. My Snuggle up Bedtime Book. Smart Kids Publishing Staff. 2007. 16p. 14.99 *(978-0-8249-6695-9(3),* Ideal Pubns.) Worthy Publishing.

Smart, Kyle, jt. illus. see Alfaro, Antonio.

Smarto, Luke. A Donde Te Vas? 2003. 16p. (J). per. 0.75 *(978-0-930201-05-0(1))* Frontline Pr.

Smath, Jerry. All Aboard! Reading Schedules. Skinner, Daphne. 2007. (Math Matters ® Ser.). (ENG.). 32p. (J). (gr. k-3). pap. 5.95 *(978-1-57565-239-9(0))* Astra Publishing Hse.

—¡Apaguen Las Luces! (Lights Out!) Subtraction. Penner, Lucille Recht. 2007. (Math Matters en Español Ser.). (SPA.). 32p. (J). (gr. k-2). pap. 5.95 *(978-1-57565-241-2(2))* Astra Publishing Hse.

—Bible Stories of Boys & Girls. Ditchfield, Christin. 2010. (Little Golden Book Ser.). 64p. (J). (gr. -1-2). 4.99 *(978-0-375-85461-3(4),* Golden Bks.) Random Hse. Children's Bks.

—Buried in the Backyard: Woolly Mammoths. Herman, Gail. 2006. (Science Solves It! ® Ser.). (ENG.). 32p. (J). (gr. k-2). pap. 5.95 *(978-1-57565-126-2(2))* Astra Publishing Hse.

—Butterfly Fever. Haskins, Lori. 2004. 31p. (J). lib. bdg. 20.00 *(978-1-4242-1087-9(9))* Fitzgerald Bks.

—David & Goliath. Ditchfield, Christin. 2019. (Little Golden Book Ser.). 24p. (J). (-k). 4.99 *(978-1-5247-7109-6(0),* Golden Bks.) Random Hse. Children's Bks.

—La Feria Musical de Matemáticas (Math Fair Blues) 2-D Shapes. Kassirer, Sue. 2006. (Math Matters en Español Ser.). (SPA.). 32p. (J). (gr. 1-3). pap. 5.95 *(978-1-57565-153-8(X))* Astra Publishing Hse.

—Keep Your Distance! Measurement: Distance. Herman, Gail. 2006. (Math Matters ® Ser.). (ENG.). 32p. (J). (gr. k-3). pap. 5.95 *(978-1-57565-107-1(6))* Astra Publishing Hse.

—Lights Out! Subtraction. Penner, Lucille Recht. 2006. (Math Matters ® Ser.). (ENG.). 32p. (J). (gr. k-2). pap. 5.95 *(978-1-57565-092-0(4))* Astra Publishing Hse.

—Locura Por Las Mariposas (Butterfly Fever) Haskins, Lori. 2009. (Science Solves It! ® en Espanol Ser.). (SPA.). (gr. 1-3). pap. 33.92 *(978-0-7613-4799-6(2))* Lerner Publishing Group.

—Mac & the Messmaker: Participation. Hudson, Iris. 2006. (Social Studies Connects ® Ser.). (ENG.). 32p. (J). (gr. k-2). pap. 5.95 *(978-1-57565-158-3(0))* Astra Publishing Hse.

—¡Mantén Tu Distancia! (Keep Your Distance!) Measurement: Distance. Herman, Gail. 2006. (Math Matters en Español Ser.). (SPA.). 32p. (J). (gr. 1-3). pap. 5.95 *(978-1-57565-168-2(8))* Astra Publishing Hse.

—Math Fair Blues: 2-D Shapes. Kassirer, Sue. 2006. (Math Matters ® Ser.). (ENG.). 32p. (J). (gr. k-3). pap. 5.95 *(978-1-57565-104-0(1))* Astra Publishing Hse.

—The Messiest Room on the Planet: Sequencing Events. Kulling, Monica & Walker, Nan. 2009. (Social Studies Connects ® Ser.). (ENG.). 32p. (J). (gr. k-2). pap. 5.95 *(978-1-57565-282-5(X))* Astra Publishing Hse.

—Miracles of Jesus. Broughton, Pamela. 2009. (Little Golden Book Ser.). 32p. (J). (gr. -1-2). 4.99 *(978-0-375-85623-5(4),* Golden Inspirational) Random Hse. Children's Bks.

—My Brother, the Knight: Past & Present. Driscoll, Laura. 2006. (Social Studies Connects ® Ser.). (ENG.). 32p. (J). (gr. 1-3). pap. 5.95 *(978-1-57565-140-8(8))* Astra Publishing Hse.

—No Rules for Rex! Rules & Laws. Alberto, Daisy. 2006. (Social Studies Connects ® Ser.). (ENG.). 32p. (J). (gr. k-2). pap. 5.95 *(978-1-57565-146-0(7))* Astra Publishing Hse.

—Palapalooza: Holidays. Skinner, Daphne. 2006. (Social Studies Connects ® Ser.). (ENG.). 32p. (J). (gr. k-2). pap. 5.95 *(978-1-57565-163-7(7))* Astra Publishing Hse.

—The Secret of the Circle-K Cave: Caves. Hays, Anna Jane. 2006. (Science Solves It! ® Ser.). (ENG.). 32p. (J). (gr. k-2). pap. 5.95 *(978-1-57565-189-7(0))* Astra Publishing Hse.

—Seven Little Hippos. Thaler, Mike. 2014. (ENG.). 36p. (J). (gr. -1-1). 16.99 *(978-1-4814-2541-4(2)*, Simon & Schuster Bks. For Young Readers) Simon & Schuster Bks. For Young Readers.

—The Story of Easter. Miller, Jean. 2018. (Little Golden Book Ser.). 24p. (J). (-k). 4.99 *(978-0-399-55514-5(5)*, Golden Bks.) Random Hse. Children's Bks.

—The Story of Jesus. Watson, Jane Werner. 2007. (Little Golden Book Ser.). (ENG.). 24p. (J). (gr. -1-k). 4.99 *(978-0-375-83941-2(0)*, Golden Bks.) Random Hse. Children's Bks.

—The Taming of Lola: A Shrew Story. Weiss, Ellen. 2010. (ENG.). 32p. (J). (gr. -1-3). 15.95 *(978-0-8109-4066-6(3)*, Abrams Bks. for Young Readers) Abrams, Inc.

—Tanya Tinker & the Gizmo Gang. Marks, Burton. 2003. 20p. (J). (gr. -1-3). reprint ed. 22.00 *(978-0-7567-6760-0(1))* DIANE Publishing Co.

—Wheels on the Bus. Grosset & Dunlap & dePaola, Tomie. 2016. (Pudgy Board Bks.). 18p. (J). (— 1). bds. 5.99 *(978-0-451-53270-1(8)*, Grosset & Dunlap) Penguin Young Readers Group.

—X Marks the Spot! Coordinate Graphing. Penner, Lucille Recht. 2006. (Math Matters ® Ser.). (ENG.). 32p. (J). (gr. k-3). pap. 5.95 *(978-1-57565-111-8(4))* Astra Publishing Hse.

Smedley, Chris. Pongwiffy. Umansky, Kaye. 2007. (ENG.). 192p. (J). (gr. 3-7). pap. 10.95 *(978-1-4169-6832-0(6)*, Simon & Schuster/Paula Wiseman Bks.) Simon & Schuster/Paula Wiseman Bks.

Smee, Nicola. My Big Rainy Day Activity Book. Dann, Penny. 2004. 96p. (J). act. bk. ed. 7.99 *(978-1-85854-554-7(4))* Brimax Books Ltd. GBR. Dist: Byeway Bks.

—Ten Little Babies. Impey, Rose. 2011. 32p. (J). (gr. -1-k). *(978-1-4088-1118-4(9)*, 38990, Bloomsbury Children's Bks.) Bloomsbury Publishing Plc.

—Two-Minute Bedtime Stories. Pasquali, Elena. 2010. (Two-Minute Stories Ser.). (ENG.). 48p. (J). (gr. -1-k). 12.99 *(978-0-7459-6079-1(0))* Lion Hudson PLC GBR. Dist: Independent Pubs. Group.

Smee, Nicola. Sleepyhead. Smee, Nicola. 2004. (ENG & BEN.). 10p. (J). bds. *(978-1-85269-095-3(X))*; bds. *(978-1-85269-097-7(6))* Mantra Lingua.

Smekhov, Zely. Seven Delightful Stories for Every Day. Elkins, Dov Peretz. 2005. 48p. (J). 16.95 *(978-1-930143-02-9(8)*, Devora Publishing) Simcha Media Group.

Smerdele, Laura. Yahyah & Mister Caterpillar. Osaze, Malik. 2020. (Yahyah & Friends Ser.: Vol. 1). (ENG.). 28p. (J). pap. 9.49 ***(978-1-6582-8239-0(6))*** Independently Published.

Smerek, Kim. What Is Zazu?, 1 bk. Smerek, Kim. 2003. 24p. (J). bds. 7.95 *(978-0-9745116-0-3(9))* Sunshine Bks. for Children.

Smid, Emmi. Minnie & Max are Ok! Calland, Chris & Hutchinson, Nicky. 2017. (ENG.). 40p. (J). 17.95 *(978-1-78592-233-6(5)*, 696284) Kingsley, Jessica Pubs. GBR. Dist: Hachette UK Distribution.

Smid, Emmi. Luna's Red Hat: An Illustrated Storybook to Help Children Cope with Loss & Suicide. Smid, Emmi. 2015. (ENG.). 34p. (J). pap. 19.95 *(978-1-84905-629-8(3)*, 693789) Kingsley, Jessica Pubs. GBR. Dist: Hachette UK Distribution.

Smietanka, Ela. PJ Time: 100 Devotions to Light up the Night, 1 vol. Thomas Nelson, Thomas. 2020. (ENG.). 208p. (J). 16.99 *(978-1-4002-1127-2(1))* Nelson, Thomas Inc.

—Unicorns & Rainbows: A Very Busy Board Book! Finch, Rusty. Cottage Door Press, ed. 2020. (Very Busy Board Book to Look, Match Search & Laugh! Ser.). (ENG.). 12p. (J). (gr. -1-1). bds. 14.99 *(978-1-68052-824-4(6)*, 1005370) Cottage Door Pr.

—Winter Cats. Lawler, Janet. 2019. (ENG.). 32p. (J). (gr. -1-3). 16.99 *(978-0-8075-9124-6(6)*, 807591246) Whitman, Albert & Co.

Smiley, Jess Smart. 10 Little Monsters Visit Oregon. Walton, Rick. 2014. (ENG.). 32p. (J). 16.95 *(978-1-939629-29-6(2)*, 552929) Familius LLC.

—10 Little Monsters Visit San Francisco. Walton, Rick. 2015. (ENG.). 32p. (J). 16.95 *(978-1-942672-99-9(3)*, 557299) Familius LLC.

—10 Little Monsters Visit Washington. Walton, Rick. 2015. (10 Little Monsters Ser.: 2). (ENG.). 32p. (J). 16.95 *(978-1-942672-98-2(5)*, 557298) Familius LLC.

Smiley, Mary Anne. Sam's Birthmark. Griffin, Martha & Griffin, Grant. 2013. (ENG.). 24p. (J). (gr. -1-3). 18.95 *(978-0-692-01920-7(0))* Griffin Group Publishing LLC.

Smileyworld Ltd. Staff. Where's Smiley? Smileyworld Ltd. Staff. 2010. (SmileyWorld Ser.). (ENG.). 34p. (J). (gr. k-3). 9.99 *(978-1-4424-0756-5(5)*, Little Simon) Little Simon.

Smillie, Natalie. ¡Abejas! Koons, Linda. 2016. (Early Rising Readers Ser.). (SPA.). (J). (gr. -1). 6.67 *(978-1-4788-3666-7(0))* Newmark Learning LLC.

—At My Home. Koons, Linda. 2015. (Early Rising Readers Ser.). (J). (gr. -1-k). 5.83 *(978-1-4788-2143-4(4))* Newmark Learning LLC.

—Bees! Koons, Linda. 2015. (Early Rising Readers Ser.). (J). (gr. -1-k). 5.83 *(978-1-4788-1597-6(3))* Newmark Learning LLC.

—The Best Little Bullfrog in the Forest Orange Band. Whybrow, Ian. 2016. (Cambridge Reading Adventures Ser.). (ENG.). 16p. pap. 8.08 *(978-1-107-56018-5(7))* Cambridge Univ. Pr.

—En Mi Casa. Koons, Linda. 2016. (Early Rising Readers Ser.). (SPA.). 16p. (J). (gr. 1-1). 6.67 *(978-1-4788-4183-8(4))* Newmark Learning LLC.

—Ensalada de Frutas. Craddock, Petra. 2016. (Early Rising Readers Ser.). (SPA.). (J). (gr. -1). 6.67 *(978-1-4788-3673-5(3))* Newmark Learning LLC.

—La Fiesta de la Gallina. Craddock, Petra. 2016. (Early Rising Readers Ser.). (SPA.). 16p. (J). (gr. 1-1). 29.00 *(978-1-4788-3889-0(2))* Newmark Learning LLC.

—Fruit Salad. Craddock, Petra. 2015. (Early Rising Readers Ser.). (J). (gr. -1-k). 5.83 *(978-1-4788-1583-9(3))* Newmark Learning LLC.

—How to Be a Princess. Fliess, Sue. 2018. (Little Golden Book Ser.). 24p. (J). (-k). 4.99 *(978-0-399-55642-5(7)*, Golden Bks.) Random Hse. Children's Bks.

—I Have a Playground. McGillian, Jamie Kyle. 2015. (Early Rising Readers Ser.). (J). (gr. -1-k). 5.83 *(978-1-4788-1690-4(2))* Newmark Learning LLC.

—Leela's Treasure. Shannon, Terry Miller. 2016. (Spring Forward Ser.). (J). (gr. 1). *(978-1-4900-9380-2(X))* Benchmark Education Co.

—Marigold Fairy Makes a Friend! Dennis, Elizabeth. 2018. (Flower Wings Ser.: 2). (ENG.). 24p. (J). (gr. -1-1). pap. 4.99 *(978-1-5344-1173-9(9)*, Simon Spotlight) Simon Spotlight.

—Marigold Fairy Makes a Friend. Dennis, Elizabeth. 2018. (J). *(978-1-5444-0276-5(7))* Simon & Schuster Children's Publishing.

—Marigold Fairy Makes a Friend. Dennis, Elizabeth. 2018. (Flower Wings Ser.: 2). (ENG.). 24p. (J). (gr. -1-1). 17.99 *(978-1-5344-1174-6(7)*, Simon Spotlight) Simon Spotlight.

—Violet Fairy Gets Her Wings. Dennis, Elizabeth. 2016. (J). *(978-1-5182-4501-5(3))* Simon & Schuster Children's Publishing.

—Yo Tengo un Parque. McGillian, Jamie Kyle. 2016. (Early Rising Readers Ser.). (SPA.). 16p. (J). (gr. 1-1). 6.67 *(978-1-4788-3722-0(5))* Newmark Learning LLC.

Smirnova, Irina. Princesses, Mermaids & Unicorns Activity Book: Tons of Fun Activities! Mazes, Drawing, Matching Games & More! Danilova, Lida & Clever Publishing. 2020. (Clever Activity Book Ser.). (ENG.). 48p. (J). (gr. -1-17). pap. 4.99 *(978-1-949998-86-3(X))* Clever Media Group.

Smishliaev, Anatoli. Grapette, the Runaway Who Rolled Away: A Timeless Tale of Love & Family: A Child Discovering the World. Konnikova, Svetlana. 2007. (Grapette's Adventures Ser.). (ENG.). 32p. (J). (gr. k-2). 15.95 *(978-0-9791758-0-0(1)*, Kids' Library) Aurora Pubs., Inc.

Smisson, John. The Go Yogi! Card Set: 50 Everyday Poses for Calm, Happy, Healthy Kids. Hughes, Emma. 2017. (ENG.). 50p. 15.95 *(978-1-84819-370-3(X)*, 700615, Singing Dragon) Kingsley, Jessica Pubs. GBR. Dist: Hachette UK Distribution.

—Striker, Slow Down! A Calming Book for Children Who Are Always on the Go. Hughes, Emma. 2016. (ENG.). 40p. (J). 16.95 *(978-1-84819-327-7(0)*, 696304, Singing Dragon) Kingsley, Jessica Pubs. GBR. Dist: Hachette UK Distribution.

Smit, Noelle. Snail's Birthday Wish. Rempt, Fiona. 2007. (ENG.). 32p. (J). (gr. -1-1). 14.95 *(978-1-905417-52-0(7))* Boxer Bks., Ltd. GBR. Dist: Sterling Publishing Co., Inc.

Smith, Abby. The Mysterious Money Tree: Little Tommy Learns a Lesson in Giving. Toombs, Tom. 2012. 28p. (J). pap. 12.95 *(978-1-61314-033-8(9)*, Innovo Pr.) Innovo Publishing, LLC.

Smith, Ahmara. Identity: A Story of Transitioning. Maison, Corey. 2020. (Zuiker Teen Topics Ser.). (ENG.). 88p. (YA). (gr. 6). 12.99 *(978-1-947378-24-7(4))* Zuiker Pr.

Smith, Alastair. On the Farm. Tatchell, Judy. 2004. (Lift-the-Flap Learners Ser.). (ENG.). 1p. (J). (gr. 1-18). pap. 8.95 *(978-0-7460-2775-2(3))* EDC Publishing.

Smith, Alex. Home. Smith, Alex. 2011. (ENG.). 32p. pap. 7.95 *(978-1-58925-433-6(3))* Tiger Tales.

Smith, Alex T. The Adventures of Egg Box Dragon. Adams, Richard. 2019. 32p. (J). (gr. -1-k). pap. 9.99 *(978-1-4449-3841-8(X))*; (ENG.). 16.99 ***(978-1-4449-3840-1(1)***, Hodder Children's Books) Hachette Children's Group GBR. Dist: Hachette Bk. Group.

—Eliot Jones Midnight Superhero. Cottringer, Anne. 2009. 24p. (J). (gr. -1-2). pap. 7.95 *(978-1-58925-416-9(3))* Tiger Tales.

—The Great Brain Robbery. Kemp, Anna. 2013. (ENG.). 288p. (J). pap. 6.99 *(978-0-85707-996-1(4)*, Simon & Schuster Children's) Simon & Schuster, Ltd. GBR. Dist: Simon & Schuster, Inc.

—My Mom Has X-Ray Vision. McAllister, Angela. 2011. (ENG.). 32p. (J). (gr. -1-2). 15.95 *(978-1-58925-097-0(4))*; pap. 7.95 *(978-1-58925-428-2(7))* Tiger Tales.

—The Tale of Angelino Brown. Almond, David. 2018. (ENG.). 272p. (J). (gr. 3-7). 16.99 *(978-0-7636-9563-7(7))* Candlewick Pr.

Smith, Alex T. Claude at the Beach, 1 vol. Smith, Alex T. (Claude Ser.). (ENG.). 96p. (J). (gr. 1-3). 2016. pap. 7.95 *(978-1-56145-919-3(4))*; 2014. 12.95 *(978-1-56145-703-8(5))* Peachtree Publishing Co. Inc.

—Claude at the Circus, 1 vol. Smith, Alex T. (Claude Ser.). (ENG.). 96p. (J). (gr. 2-4). 2017. pap. 7.95 *(978-1-56145-980-3(1))*; 2013. 12.95 *(978-1-56145-702-1(7))* Peachtree Publishing Co. Inc.

—Claude in the City, 1 vol. Smith, Alex T. (Claude Ser.). (ENG.). 96p. (J). (gr. 2-4). 2015. pap. 7.95 *(978-1-56145-843-1(0))*; 2013. 12.95 *(978-1-56145-697-0(7))* Peachtree Publishing Co. Inc.

—Claude in the Country, 1 vol. Smith, Alex T. 2016. (Claude Ser.). (ENG.). 96p. (J). (gr. 1-3). 12.95 *(978-1-56145-918-6(6))* Peachtree Publishing Co. Inc.

—Claude in the Spotlight, 1 vol. Smith, Alex T. 2015. (Claude Ser.). (ENG.). 96p. (J). (gr. 1-3). 12.95 *(978-1-56145-895-0(3))* Peachtree Publishing Co. Inc.

—Claude on the Big Screen, 1 vol. Smith, Alex T. 2017. (Claude Ser.). (ENG.). 96p. (J). (gr. 2-4). 12.95 *(978-1-68263-009-9(9))* Peachtree Publishing Co. Inc.

—Claude on the Slopes, 1 vol. Smith, Alex T. 2016. (Claude Ser.). (ENG.). 96p. (J). (gr. 1-3). pap. 7.95 *(978-1-56145-923-0(2))* Peachtree Publishing Co. Inc.

—Little Red & the Very Hungry Lion. Smith, Alex T. 2016. (ENG.). 32p. (J). (gr. -1-k). 17.99 *(978-0-545-91438-3(8)*, Scholastic Pr.) Scholastic, Inc.

Smith, Alex T. Mr. Penguin & the Catastrophic Cruise. Smith, Alex T. 2020. (Mr. Penguin Ser.). (ENG.). 288p. (J). (gr. 3-7). 16.99 ***(978-1-68263-213-0(X))*** Peachtree Publishing Co. Inc.

—Mr. Penguin & the Fortress of Secrets. Smith, Alex T. (Mr. Penguin Ser.). (ENG.). 288p. (J). (gr. 3-7). 2020. pap. 9.99 ***(978-1-68263-195-9(8))***; 2019. 16.95 *(978-1-68263-130-0(3))* Peachtree Publishing Co. Inc.

Smith, Alex T. Mr. Penguin & the Lost Treasure, 1 vol. Smith, Alex T. (Mr. Penguin Ser.). (ENG.). (J). (gr. 3-7). 2020. 206p. pap. 9.99 *(978-1-68263-170-6(2))*; 2019. 208p. 16.95 *(978-1-68263-120-1(6))* Peachtree Publishing Co. Inc.

Smith, Allie. Seeking a Bunny. DiTerlizzi, Angela. 2017. (ENG.). 30p. (J). (gr. -1 — 1). bds. 7.99 *(978-1-4814-7672-0(6)*, Little Simon) Little Simon.

—Seeking a Santa. Diterlizzi, Angela. 2016. (ENG.). 30p. (J). (gr. -1 — 1). bds. 7.99 *(978-1-4814-7674-4(2)*, Little Simon) Little Simon.

—There Are No Wrong Answers: A Book of Quizzes. Sector, Emma. 2016. (ENG.). 192p. (J). (gr. 3-7). pap. 7.99 *(978-1-4814-5932-7(5)*, Aladdin) Simon & Schuster Children's Publishing.

Smith, Andrew. Exile from Eden: Or, after the Hole. Smith, Andrew. 2019. (ENG.). 368p. (YA). (gr. 9). 18.99 *(978-1-5344-2223-0(4)*, Simon & Schuster Bks. For Young Readers) Simon & Schuster Bks. For Young Readers.

Smith, Andy, et al. The First, Vol. 5. Kesel, Barbara. 2003. (First Ser.: Vol. 5). 192p. (YA). pap. 15.95 *(978-1-59314-002-1(9))* CrossGeneration Comics, Inc.

—The First: Ragnarok, Vol. 6. Kesel, Barbara. 2004. (First Ser.). 160p. (YA). pap. 15.95 *(978-1-59314-035-9(5))* CrossGeneration Comics, Inc.

Smith, Andy. A Good Run: Maple Syrup's Sweet Journey. Smith, Judy. 2017. (ENG.). 32p. (J). pap. 10.95 *(978-1-4787-8152-3(1))* Outskirts Pr., Inc.

Smith, Andy. Into the Forest: The Journey of Sweetgrass. Smith, Judy. 2019. (ENG.). 37p. (J). pap. 16.95 ***(978-1-4787-9456-1(9))*** Outskirts Pr., Inc.

Smith, Andy. Superman: Day of Doom. Sazaklis, John & Vancata, Brad. 2013. (I Can Read Book: Level 2 Ser.). (ENG.). 32p. (YA). (gr. k-2). 16.19 *(978-1-4844-0620-5(6))* HarperCollins Pubs.

—Superman vs. the Silver Banshee. Lemke, Donald. 2013. (I Can Read Level 2 Ser.). (ENG.). 32p. (J). (gr. -1-3). pap. 3.99 *(978-0-06-188524-2(X))* HarperCollins Pubs.

Smith, Andy J. Attack of the Mutant Lunch Lady. Nickel, Scott. 2008. (Graphic Sparks Ser.). (ENG.). 40p. (J). (gr. 2-5). per. 5.95 *(978-1-4342-0501-8(0)*, Stone Arch Bks.) Capstone.

—Attack of the Mutant Lunch Lady: A Buzz Beaker Brainstorm. Vol. 1. Nickel, Scott. 2008. (Graphic Sparks Ser.). (ENG.). 40p. (J). (gr. 2-5). lib. bdg. 23.99 *(978-1-4342-0451-6(0)*, Stone Arch Bks.) Capstone.

—Backyard Bug Battle: A Buzz Beaker Brainstorm. Nickel, Scott. 2006. (Graphic Sparks Ser.). (ENG.). 40p. (J). (gr. 2-5). per. 5.95 *(978-1-59889-224-6(X)*, Stone Arch Bks.) Capstone.

—Billions of Bats. Nickel, Scott. 2007. (Graphic Sparks Ser.). (ENG.). 40p. (J). (gr. 2-5). per. 5.95 *(978-1-59889-408-0(0)*, Stone Arch Bks.) Capstone.

—Robot Rampage: A Buzz Beaker Brainstorm. Nickel, Scott. 2006. (Graphic Sparks Ser.). (ENG.). 40p. (J). (gr. 2-5). per. 5.95 *(978-1-59889-227-7(4)*, Stone Arch Bks.) Capstone.

—Wind Power Whiz Kid: A Buzz Beaker Brainstorm. Nickel, Scott. 2008. (Graphic Sparks Ser.). (ENG.). 40p. (J). (gr. 2-5). pap. 5.95 *(978-1-4342-0854-5(0)*, Stone Arch Bks.) Capstone.

Smith, Anne. Japan: Panorama Pops. Candlewick Press Staff. 2015. (Panorama Pops Ser.). (ENG.). 30p. (J). (gr. k-4). 8.99 *(978-0-7636-7504-2(0))* Candlewick Pr.

—Ox, House, Stick: The History of Our Alphabet. Robb, Don. 2007. 48p. (J). (gr. 3-7). pap. 7.95 *(978-1-57091-610-6(1))* Charlesbridge Publishing, Inc.

—The Whale Whisperers, 1 vol. Smith, John D. H. 2009. 17p. pap. 24.95 *(978-1-60749-211-5(3))* America Star Bks.

Smith, Ashley. Gooey Gummy Geese. Holzer, Angela. 2008. (ENG.). (J). lib. bdg. 8.99 *(978-0-9821563-1-5(6))* Good Sound Publishing.

Smith, Austin. Louie & the Lobster Lympics: Run Louie Run! Nabors, Wayne. 2018. (ENG.). 44p. (J). 24.95 *(978-1-64003-391-7(2))* Covenant Bks.

Smith, Barry. The Odyssey, Vol. 4. Redmond, Diane. unabr. ed. 2003. (Curtain Up Ser.: Vol. 4). 48p. (J). (gr. 1-4). pap. 15.00 *(978-0-7136-4628-3(4)*, A&C Black) Bloomsbury Publishing Plc GBR. Dist: Players Pr., Inc.

—The Odyssey. Redmond, Diane. 2012. 48p. *(978-0-88734-067-3(9))* Players Pr., Inc.

Smith, Bart, photos by. The Appalachian Trail: Calling Me Back to the Hills. 2007. (ENG., 128p. (YA). 39.95 *(978-0-9795659-0-8(1))* Shaffer, Earl Foundation, Inc.

Smith, Bernice. Where's Your Belly, Nelly. Essrow, Wende. 2016. (ENG.). (J). pap. 11.95 *(978-0-9977996-3-7(3))* Primedia eLaunch LLC.

Smith, Billi Rachelle. Engy, It's Time to Use the Potty. Smith, Billi Rachelle. 2019. (ENG.). 38p. (J). pap. 15.00 ***(978-1-7070-5384-1(7))*** Independently Published.

Smith, Brady. You're Missing It! Smith, Brady. Thiessen, Tiffani. 2019. 32p. (J). (-k). 17.99 *(978-0-525-51442-8(2)*, Nancy Paulsen Books) Penguin Young Readers Group.

Smith, Brenda. When Boo Boo Wakes Up!, 1 vol. Sister Flowers. 2009. 36p. pap. 24.95 *(978-1-61546-250-6(3))* America Star Bks.

Smith, Brian. Grow Up!, 4. Steinberg, D. J. 2010. (Adventures of Daniel Boom AKA Loudboy Ser.: 4). (ENG.). 96p. (J). (gr. 3-6). 21.19 *(978-0-448-44701-8(0))* Penguin Young Readers Group.

—Sound Off!, 1. Steinberg, D. J. 2008. (Adventures of Daniel Boom AKA Loudboy Ser.: 1). (ENG.). 96p. (J). (gr. 3-6). 18.69 *(978-0-448-44698-1(7))* Penguin Young Readers Group.

Smith, Briony May. Grab That Rabbit! Faber, Polly. 2018. 32p. (J). (gr. -1-k). (ENG.). 17.99 *(978-1-84365-378-3(8))*; pap. 9.99 *(978-1-84365-369-1(9))* Pavilion Bks. GBR. (Pavilion Children's Books). Dist: Penguin Random Hse. LLC.

—Stardust. Willis, Jeanne. 2019. (ENG.). 32p. (J). (-k). 16.99 *(978-1-5362-0265-6(7)*, Nosy Crow) Candlewick Pr.

—Tooth Fairy in Training. Robinson, Michelle. 2019. (ENG.). 40p. (J). (gr. -1-2). 16.99 *(978-1-5362-0939-6(2))* Candlewick Pr.

Smith, Brittney. My Baby's First Love. Perry, Lauren. 2020. (ENG.). 36p. (J). ***(978-1-5255-6358-4(0))***; pap. ***(978-1-5255-6359-1(9))*** FriesenPress.

Smith, Brock R. & Smith, Raissa B. Where Did Mommy Go? A Spiritual Tool to Help Children Grow from Grief to Peace. Smith, Brenda J. Smith, Brenda J. & Cloud, Olivia, eds. 2004. Orig. Title: Listed Above. 52p. (gr. 3-12). pap. 16.95 *(978-0-9744549-0-0(7))* Tall Through Bks.

Smith, Brody. A Cat Named Friend. Barbre, Mark. 2008. 18p. (J). pap. 9.95 *(978-0-615-20414-7(7))* Edgar Road Publishing.

Smith, Bron. Explorers of the New World Time Line. Fisher, Ann Richmond. Mitchell, Judy & Lindeen, Mary, eds. 2007. 112p. (J). pap. 12.95 *(978-1-57310-523-1(6))* Teaching & Learning Co.

—Language Fundamentals. Myers, R. E. Mitchell, Judith, ed. 2005. 96p. (J). Bk. 1. pap. 11.95 *(978-1-57310-450-0(7))*; Bk. 2. pap. 11.95 *(978-1-57310-451-7(5))* Teaching & Learning Co.

Smith, Buckley. Moonsailors. Smith, Buckley. 2007. (ENG.). 40p. (J). (gr. -1-7). 14.95 *(978-0-937822-95-1(7))* WoodenBoat Pubns.

Smith, Cat. Feliciana Feydra Leroux: A Cajun Tall Tale, 1 vol. Thomassie, Tynia. 2017. (Feliciana Ser.). (ENG.). 32p. (gr. -1-3). 9.95 *(978-1-4556-2381-5(4)*, Pelican Publishing) Arcadia Publishing.

Smith, Cat Bowman. Boom Town. Levitin, Sonia. 2004. 30p. (J). (gr. -1-3). 14.65 *(978-0-7569-3185-8(1))* Perfection Learning Corp.

—Feliciana Meets d'Loup Garou: A Cajun Tall Tale, 1 vol. Thomassie, Tynia. 2005. (ENG.). 32p. (J). (gr. k-3). 16.99 *(978-1-58980-287-2(X)*, Pelican Publishing) Arcadia Publishing.

—Joshua the Giant Frog, 1 vol. Thomas, Peggy. 2005. (ENG.). 32p. (J). (gr. k-3). 16.99 *(978-1-58980-267-4(5)*, Pelican Publishing) Arcadia Publishing.

Smith, Cat Bowman & Smith, Catharine Bowman. General Butterfingers. Gardiner, John Reynolds. 2007. (ENG.). 96p. (J). (gr. 5-7). 7.95 *(978-0-618-75922-4(0)*, 486370) Houghton Mifflin Harcourt Publishing Co.

Smith, Catharine Bowman, jt. illus. see Smith, Cat Bowman.

Smith, Charles R., Jr. Brown Sugar Babies. Smith, Charles R., Jr. 2020. 30p. (J). (gr. -1 — 1). bds. 7.99 *(978-1-368-05029-6(8)*, Jump at the Sun) Hyperion Bks. for Children.

Smith, Charles R., Jr. Pick-Up Game: A Full Day of Full Court. Smith, Charles R., Jr., ed. Aronson, Marc, ed. 2012. 176p. (YA). (gr. 9). pap. 7.99 *(978-0-7636-6068-0(X))*; 1. 18.69 *(978-0-7636-4562-5(1))* Candlewick Pr.

Smith, Charles R., Jr., photos by. If: A Father's Advice to His Son. Kipling, Rudyard. 2007. (ENG., 40p. (J). (gr. 1-5). 18.99 *(978-0-689-87799-5(4)*, Atheneum Bks. for Young Readers) Simon & Schuster Children's Publishing.

Smith, Charlie E. T. The Farmer & His Animals. MacNeil, Ben. 2013. 26p. pap. *(978-1-927625-02-6(5))* Quarter Castle Publishing.

Smith, Claire. Annie Elf Meets Mitty Mouse. Smith, Gloria. 2012. 24p. 29.95 *(978-1-62709-398-9(2))*; pap. 24.95 *(978-1-4626-8151-8(4))* America Star Bks.

Smith, Clara Batton. Colton & Chloe: A Trilingual Story-English Spanish French. Weaver, Nicole. 2018. (SPA.). 16p. (J). (gr. k-4). pap. 9.95 *(978-1-61633-951-7(9))* Guardian Angel Publishing, Inc.

Smith, Clara Batton. Elliott & Anastaci. Smith, Clara Batton. 2012. 16p. pap. 9.95 *(978-1-61633-233-4(6))* Guardian Angel Publishing, Inc.

Smith, Cory. Star Wars: Age of the Republic - Heroes. 2019. 112p. (YA). pap. 17.99 *(978-1-302-91710-4(2))* Marvel Worldwide, Inc.

Smith, Cory, jt. illus. see Ross, Luke.

Smith, Cory, jt. illus. see Shaw, Geoff.

Smith, Courtney. Fursey the Famous at the Farm. Ledford, Margaret. 2019. (ENG.). 34p. (J). pap. 10.00 *(978-1-0915-6852-5(9))* Independently Published.

Smith, Craig. Algunos Secretos Nunca Deben Guardarse. Sanders, Jayneen. abr. ed. 2013.Tr. of Some Secrets Should Never. (SPA.). 32p. (J). (gr. k-5). pap. *(978-0-9871860-2-7(7)*, Educate2Empower Publishing) UpLoad Publishing Pty, Ltd.

—Clown's Pants. Eggleton, Jill. 2003. (Rigby Sails Early Ser.). (ENG.). 16p. (gr. 1-2). pap. 6.95 *(978-0-7578-8723-9(6))* Houghton Mifflin Harcourt Publishing Co.

—Clown's Party. Eggleton, Jill. 2003. (Rigby Sails Early Ser.). (ENG.). 16p. (gr. 1-2). pap. 6.95 *(978-0-7578-8669-0(8))* Houghton Mifflin Harcourt Publishing Co.

—Emily Eyefinger & the Balloon Bandits. Ball, Duncan. 7th ed. 2003. 112p. *(978-0-207-19940-0(X))* HarperCollins Pubs. Australia.

—Emily Eyefinger & the City in the Sky. Ball, Duncan. 2006. 112p. *(978-0-207-20067-0(X))* HarperCollins Pubs. Australia.

—Emily Eyefinger & the Ghost Ship. Ball, Duncan. 2004. 112p. (Orig.). *(978-0-207-19869-4(1))* HarperCollins Pubs. Australia.

—Emily Eyefinger & the Puzzle in the Jungle. Ball, Duncan. 2005. 112p. (Orig.). (978-0-207-19903-5(5)) HarperCollins Pubs. Australia.

—First Friend. Mattingley, Christobel. 2020. (Puffin Nibbles Ser.). 80p. (J). (gr. k-2). pap. 9.99 (978-0-14-130894-4(X), Puffin) Penguin Random Hse. AUS. Dist: Independent Pubs. Group.

—Heather Fell in the Water. MacLeod, Doug. 2013. (ENG.). 32p. (J). (gr. -1-k). 19.99 (978-1-74237-648-6(7)) Allen & Unwin AUS. Dist: Independent Pubs. Group.

—Hush Baby Hush. Rippin, Sally. 2009. (ENG.). 12p. (J). (gr. k — 1). bds. 7.99 (978-1-74175-387-5(2)) Allen & Unwin AUS. Dist: Independent Pubs. Group.

—The Joker. Condon, Bill. 2004. iv, 36p. (J). pap. (978-0-7608-6742-6(9)) Sundance/Newbridge Educational Publishing.

—The Unforgettable What's His Name. Jennings, Paul. 2018. (ENG.). 224p. (J). (gr. 2-7). pap. 11.99 (978-1-76029-085-6(8)) Allen & Unwin AUS. Dist: Independent Pubs. Group.

Smith, Crystal & Lin, Albert. Questions for Kids: A Book to Discover a Child's Imagination & Knowledge. Smith, Michael. 2003. 209p. (J). (gr. k-4). 13.95 (978-0-9669437-3-3(2)) East West Discovery Pr.

Smith, Crystal, jt. illus. see Lin, Albert.

Smith, D. W. Tiger the Mule. Smith, John. 2019. (ENG.). 48p. (J). 20.00 (978-0-9990090-5-5(2)) Hilliard Pr.

Smith, Dale & Russon, Anne E., photos by. What the Orangutan Told Alice: A Rain Forest Adventure. Smith, Dale. 2003. 192p. (gr. 6-12). pap. 15.95 (978-0-9651452-8-2(X)) Deer Creek Publishing.

Smith, Dan. Portable Adventures: 8th Grade. Smith, Dan, ed. Nickoloff, Michael, ed. 2003. (YA). bds. 12.95 (978-0-9728526-2-3(X)) Third World Games, Inc.

—Portable Adventures: Lair of the Rat King. Smith, Dan, ed. Nickoloff, Michael, ed. 2003. (YA). bds. 12.95 (978-0-9728526-1-6(1)) Third World Games, Inc.

Smith, Dani. Fox & Faun. Smith, Dani. 2019. (Shale City Ser.: Vol. 1). (ENG.). 336p. (J). pap. 12.99 **(978-1-6978-9776-0(2))** Independently Published.

Smith, Dave. The Hair That Went Elsewhere. Musumeci, Andrew. 2019. (ENG.). (J). 40p. (978-1-9997558-2-9(0)); 38p. pap. (978-1-9997558-0-5(4)) MUZME.

—Paul, Man on a Mission: The Adventures of an Apostle, 1 vol. Hartman, Bob & Gempf, Conrad. ed. 2017. (ENG.). 160p. (J). (gr. 4-6). pap. 9.99 (978-0-7459-7739-3(1), Lion Children's) Lion Hudson PLC GBR. Dist: Independent Pubs. Group.

—Puzzle Heroes: People's Planet. Nilsen, Anna. 2019. (Puzzle Heroes Ser.). 32p. (J). (gr. 3-7). pap. 11.99 (978-1-4451-2135-2(2), Franklin Watts) Hachette Children's Group GBR. Dist: Hachette Bk. Group.

Smith, Dave. Puzzle Heroes: Wildlife Wonders. Nilsen, Anna. 2019. (Puzzle Heroes Ser.). 32p. (J). (gr. 3-7). pap. **(978-1-4451-2136-9(0)**, Franklin Watts) Hachette Children's Group.

Smith, Dave, jt. illus. see Cerisier, Emmanuel.

Smith, David. The Prehistoric Adventures of Dinosaur George: Jurassic Tigers. Blasing, George & Blasing, George. 2007. 16p. (J). 4.95 (978-0-9797304-0-5(6)) Raining Popcorn Media.

Smith, David Preston. Anne of Green Gables, 1 vol. Kessler, Deirdre & Montgomery, L. M. ed. 2008. (ENG.). 46p. (J). (gr. 1-3). pap. 12.95 (978-1-55109-662-9(5), d5ae0a47-d47b-48e7-b7af-dacf4b0d67dc) Nimbus Publishing, Ltd. CAN. Dist: Baker & Taylor Publisher Services (BTPS).

—Joe Howe to the Rescue, 1 vol. Bawtree, Michael. 2004. (ENG.). 152p. (J). (gr. 4-7). pap. 12.95 (978-1-55109-495-3(9), 359b6f07-7604-4ae0-874d-d3933b616162) Nimbus Publishing, Ltd. CAN. Dist: Baker & Taylor Publisher Services (BTPS).

—Tommy's New Block Skates, 1 vol. Vaughan, Garth. 2007. (ENG.). 36p. (J). (gr. 1-3). pap. 12.95 (978-1-55109-620-9(X), 645c3f1a-8ce3-4d9d-8ad2-e89ec6bc6cba) Nimbus Publishing, Ltd. CAN. Dist: Baker & Taylor Publisher Services (BTPS).

Smith, Debbie. Zig, Zag, Zoom. Smith Author, Debbie. 2019. (ENG.). 32p. (J). (gr. k-3). pap. 12.95 (978-1-0726-8074-1(2)) Independently Published.

Smith, Devin. The Real-Life Princess. Dunning, Rebecca. Rohman, Stefanie & Ritchie, Mary, eds. 2010. (ENG.). 40p. (J). pap. 13.99 (978-0-9826670-0-2(0)) Awen Hse. Publishing.

Smith, Diana, jt. illus. see Last, Ian.

Smith, Donald A. Heroes of the Revolution. Adler, David A. 2006. (ENG.). 32p. (J). (gr. 1-4). 7.99 (978-0-8234-2017-9(5)) Holiday Hse., Inc.

Smith, Duane. Mama's Window. Rubright, Lynn. 2005. 89p. (J). 16.95 (978-1-57480-160-6(0)) Lee & Low Bks., Inc.

—Seven Miles to Freedom: The Robert Smalls Story. Halfmann, Janet. 2008. 40p. (J). (gr. 1-6). 17.95 (978-1-60060-232-0(0)) Lee & Low Bks., Inc.

—The Story of Civil War Hero Robert Smalls, 1 vol. Halfmann, Janet. 2020. (Story Of Ser.). (ENG.). 80p. (J). pap. 9.95 (978-1-64379-016-9(1), 530e0916-6576-488f-8cfc-94fb032a32c2) Lee & Low Bks., Inc.

Smith, Duane A. Night Journey to Vicksburg. Masters, Susan Rowan. Killcoyne, Hope L., ed. 2003. (Adventures in America Ser.). 74p. (J). (gr. 4). 14.95 (978-1-893110-30-4(3)) Silver Moon Pr.

Smith, Duncan. People Are So Different! Clarke, Ann. 2008. 24p. 16.95 (978-0-9787235-0-7(3)) Precious Little Bks.

Smith, Duriel. The Myths of the Lechuza. Alexander, David E. Date not set. 78p. (Orig.). (J). pap. 12.95 (978-0-9623078-5-0(8)) Alexander Pubns.

Smith, Dwight. The Leaping Grasshopper. Archambault, Jeanne. 2006. 32p. (J). bds. 15.95 (978-0-9763031-2-1(4)) Jitterbug Bks.

Smith, E. Boyd. In the Days of Giants. Brown, Abbie Farwell. 2008. 204p. per. 9.95 (978-1-59915-044-4(1)) Yesterday's Classics.

—The Tortoise & the Geese & Other Fables of Bidpai. Dutton, Maude Barrows. 2008. 104p. pap. 7.95 (978-1-59915-249-3(5)) Yesterday's Classics.

Smith, Elise & Smith, Kimanne. The Missing Trumpet Blues. 2003. (ENG.). 56p. (J). (gr. 6-8). pap. 7.97 net. (978-0-7652-3276-2(6), Celebration Pr.) Savvas Learning Co.

Smith, Elwood. See How They Run: Campaign Dreams, Election Schemes, & the Race to the White House. Goodman, Susan E. (ENG.). 96p. (J). (gr. 3-6). 2008. 26.19 (978-1-59990-285-2(0), 9781599902852); 2nd rev. ed. 2012. pap. 9.99 (978-1-59990-897-7(2), 900083806, Bloomsbury USA Childrens) Bloomsbury Publishing USA.

—Señor Pancho Had a Rancho. Laínez, René Colato. 2014. (ENG.). 32p. (J). (gr. -1-k). 6.99 (978-0-8234-3173-1(8)) Holiday Hse., Inc.

Smith, Elwood. I'm Not a Pig in Underpants. Smith, Elwood. 2013. (ENG.). 40p. (J). (gr. 1-3). 18.99 (978-1-56846-229-5(8), Creative Editions) Creative Co., The.

Smith, Elwood H. Catfish Kate & the Sweet Swamp Band. Weeks, Sarah. 2009. (ENG.). 32p. (J). (gr. -1-3). 19.99 (978-1-4169-4026-5(X), Atheneum Bks. for Young Readers) Simon & Schuster Children's Publishing.

—Señor Pancho Had a Rancho. Laínez, René Colato. 2013. (ENG.). 32p. (J). (gr. -1-k). 16.95 (978-0-8234-2632-4(7)) Holiday Hse., Inc.

—Stalling. Katz, Alan. 2010. (ENG.). 40p. (J). (gr. -1-2). 16.99 (978-1-4169-5567-2(4), McElderry, Margaret K. Bks.) McElderry, Margaret K. Bks.

Smith, Eric. The Blue Moon Effect. Freidman, Mel. gif. ed. 2005. (Extreme Monsters Ser.). 96p. (J). (gr. 2-5). per. 3.99 (978-1-57791-178-4(4)) Brighter Minds Children's Publishing.

Smith, Eric. Engineer Academy: Marble Run. Colson, Rob. 2020. (Engineer Academy Ser.). (ENG.). 64p. (J). (gr. 3-7). pap. 21.99 **(978-1-68412-987-4(7)**, Silver Dolphin Bks.) Printers Row Publishing Group.

—Engineer Academy: Space. Colson, Rob. 2020. (Engineer Academy Ser.). (ENG.). 64p. (J). (gr. 3-7). pap. 21.99 **(978-1-68412-986-7(9)**, Silver Dolphin Bks.) Printers Row Publishing Group.

Smith, Eric. Mr. Rabbit the Farmer. Chandler, Pauline. 2005. (ENG.). 24p. (J). lib. bdg. 23.65 (978-1-59646-736-1(3)) Dingles & Co.

—Mummy's Little Monkey! Faulkner, Keith. 2006. 12p. (J). (978-0-86461-700-2(3), Koala Books) Scholastic Australia.

Smith, Eric, et al. This Little Piggy: And Other Favorite Rhymes. 2005. (Mother Goose Rhymes Ser.). (ENG.). 36p. (J). (gr. -1-k). 12.95 (978-1-59249-466-8(8), 1D013) Soundprints.

Smith, Eric. Water Views. Warren, Marion E., photos by. Carr, Stephen. 2003. 37.00 (978-1-884878-08-4(3)) Annapolis Publishing Co.

Smith, G. Michael. The Accidental Adventures of Bernie the Banana Slug. Smith, G. Michael. 2018. (ENG.). 86p. (J). pap. (978-1-927755-66-2(2)) Agio Publishing Hse.

Smith, Graham. Captain Ross & the Old Sea Ferry, 1 vol. Dale, Jay. 2012. (Engage Literacy Green Ser.). (ENG.). 32p. (gr. k-2). pap. 5.99 (978-1-4296-9016-4(X), Capstone Pr.) Capstone.

Smith, Graham. The Sideways Man: Imagine If You Kept Seeing Someone Around Your Neighbourhood but Only Ever Saw Him Sideways! Smith, Graham. 2016. (ENG.). 28p. (J). pap. (978-0-9942289-3-2(7)) My Literary Adventure.

Smith, Guy, jt. illus. see Chen, Kuo Kang.

Smith, Guy, jt. illus. see Safarewicz, Evie.

Smith, Haley Rachel. Ellie's Amazing Outfits. Potter, Patrick. 2018. (ENG.). 40p. (J). pap. 9.95 (978-1-908211-63-7(6)) Pro-Actif Communications GBR. Dist: Ingram Publisher Services.

Smith, Heidi. Jackie & Mona Lisa: How the First Lady of the United States Shared the First Lady of Art with a Nation. Gruener, Nina. 2019. (J). (978-1-338-16233-2(0), Orchard Bks.) Scholastic, Inc.

—Lovely Beasts: The Surprising Truth. Gardner, Kate. 2018. (ENG.). 48p. (J). (gr. -1-3). 17.99 (978-0-06-274161-5(6), Balzer & Bray) HarperCollins Pubs.

Smith, Helen. A Home for Virginia. St. John, Patricia. 2005. (ENG.). 24p. (J). (gr. 4-7). 9.99 (978-1-85792-961-4(6), 58264a35-84a8-4b5f-99b6-01a09dc28be7) Christian Focus Pubns. GBR. Dist: Baker & Taylor Publisher Services (BTPS).

—Princess Stories. Baxter, Nicola. 2013. (ENG.). 80p. (J). (gr. k-4). pap. 9.99 (978-1-84322-954-4(4)) Anness Publishing GBR. Dist: National Bk. Network.

Smith, Henry. Code Your Own Jungle Adventure. Wainewright, Max. 2017. (Little Coders Ser.). (ENG.). 32p. (J). (gr. 1-3). lib. bdg. 23.99 (978-1-68297-179-6(1)) QEB Publishing Inc.

—Code Your Own Knight Adventure. Wainewright, Max. 2017. (Little Coders Ser.). (ENG.). 32p. (J). (gr. 1-3). lib. bdg. 23.99 (978-1-68297-180-2(5)) QEB Publishing Inc.

Smith, Henry. My Dad Says Yes! Denson, Calvin. 2020. (ENG.). 24p. (J). 17.99 **(978-1-952320-27-9(5))**; pap. 9.99 **(978-1-952320-22-4(4))** Yorkshire Publishing Group.

Smith, Henry. Saving Adventure. Wainewright, Max. 2017. (Little Coders Ser.). (ENG.). 32p. (J). (gr. 1-3). lib. bdg. 23.99 (978-1-68297-181-9(3)) QEB Publishing Inc.

Smith, Huhana. Haere: Farewell, Jack, Farewell. Tipene, Tim. 2006. 32p. (J). (gr. -1-3). pap. 12.00 (978-1-86969-104-2(0)) Huia Pubs. NZL. Dist: Univ. of Hawaii Pr.

Smith, Iain. Angel Fish: A Pull & Lift Book. Smith, Iain. 2005. (Stories to Share Ser.). 12p. (J). 10.95 (978-1-58117-084-9(X), Intervisual/Piggy Toes) Bendon, Inc.

Smith, Ian. The Best Pet: An Animal Friends Reader. Charlesworth, Liza. 2015. 16p. (J). (978-0-545-85961-5(1)) Scholastic, Inc.

—Dog & Frog: An Animal Friends Reader. Charlesworth, Liza. 2015. 16p. (J). (978-0-545-85962-2(X)) Scholastic, Inc.

—Fish School: An Animal Friends Reader. Charlesworth, Liza. 2015. 16p. (J). pap. (978-0-545-85963-9(8)) Scholastic, Inc.

—Meet Our Class Pets. Charlesworth, Liza. 2017. 16p. (J). (978-1-338-18028-2(2)) Scholastic, Inc.

—Night on the Farm: An Animal Friends Reader. Charlesworth, Liza. 2015. 16p. (J). pap. (978-0-545-85964-6(6)) Scholastic, Inc.

—Norman the Naughty Knight. Prasadam-Halls, Smriti & Halls, Smriti. 2016. (Reading Ladder Ser.). (ENG.). 48p. (J). (gr. k-2). pap. 7.99 (978-1-4052-8214-7(2)) Egmont Bks., Ltd. GBR. Dist: Independent Pubs. Group.

—Pig Wants a Peach: An Animal Friends Reader. Charlesworth, Liza. 2015. 16p. (J). pap. (978-0-545-85965-3(4)) Scholastic, Inc.

—Six Silly Chicks: An Animal Friends Reader. Charlesworth, Liza. 2015. 16p. (J). pap. (978-0-545-85966-0(2)) Scholastic, Inc.

—Wake up, Rooster! An Animal Friends Reader. Charlesworth, Liza. 2015. 16p. (J). pap. (978-0-545-85971-4(9)) Scholastic, Inc.

Smith, Ian. Rooster's Alarm. Smith, Ian. Julian, Sean. 2009. (Tadpoles Ser.). (ENG.). 24p. (J). (gr. -1-2). pap. (978-0-7787-3905-0(8)); (gr. k-2). lib. bdg. (978-0-7787-3874-9(4)) Crabtree Publishing Co.

Smith, Ian & Clements, Ashley. Norman the Naughty Knight & the Flying Horse. Prasadam-Halls, Smriti & Halls, Smriti. 2017. (Reading Ladder Ser.). (ENG.). 48p. (J). (gr. k-2). pap. 7.99 (978-1-4052-8453-0(6)) Egmont Bks., Ltd. GBR. Dist: Independent Pubs. Group.

Smith, Jack K. Huey P. Long: Talker & Doer, 1 vol. Collins, David R. 2003. (ENG.). 32p. (J). (gr. k-3). 16.99 (978-1-56554-913-5(9), Pelican Publishing) Arcadia Publishing.

Smith, Jackson. A Nightmare in Oz: Founded on & Continuing the Famous Oz Stories by L. Frank Baum. Keyes, David M. 2020. (ENG.). 276p. (J). pap. 14.99 **(978-1-7028-4417-8(X))** Independently Published.

Smith, Jacquelyn & Kalafatis, John. Pitty the City Kitty; Tokyo. Smith, Jacquelyn. 2009. 32p. (J). 15.99 (978-1-935479-01-7(6)) A.M. Green Publishing.

Smith, Jacqui. The Rainbow Jars. Lincoln, James. 2013. 28p. (J). pap. 14.95 (978-1-60131-153-5(2), Castlebridge Bks.) Big Tent Bks.

Smith, Jamie. The Case of the Four-Leaf Clover. Barbo, Maria S. & Preller, James. 2008. 104p. (J). pap. (978-0-545-03837-9(5)) Scholastic, Inc.

—Home Safe Home. Slater, Teddy. 2010. 16p. (J). (978-0-545-24606-4(7)) Scholastic, Inc.

—Lee y Conoce la Biblia / the Lion Easy-Read Bible. Goodings, Christina. 2018. (SPA.). 320p. (J). (gr. k-2). 14.95 (978-1-945540-51-6(6)) Penguin Random House Grupo Editorial ESP. Dist: Penguin Random Hse. LLC.

—The Lion Easy-Read Bible, 1 vol. Goodings, Christina. ed. 2017. (ENG.). 320p. (J). (gr. k-2). 16.99 (978-0-7459-6553-6(9), Lion Children's) Lion Hudson PLC GBR. Dist: Kregel Pubns.

—The Littlest Dragon. Ryan, Margaret. ed. 2011. (ENG.). 80p. (J). (gr. 2-4). pap. 5.99 (978-0-00-714163-0(7), HarperCollins Children's Bks.) HarperCollins Pubs. Ltd. GBR. Dist: HarperCollins Pubs.

—The Littlest Dragon Gets the Giggles. Ryan, Margaret. ed. 2011. (ENG.). 80p. (J). pap. 5.99 (978-0-00-718029-5(2), HarperCollins Children's Bks.) HarperCollins Pubs. Ltd. GBR. Dist: HarperCollins Pubs.

—Littlest Dragon Goes for Goal. Ryan, Margaret. ed. 2011. (ENG.). 64p. (J). pap. 5.99 (978-0-00-719294-6(0), HarperCollins Children's Bks.) HarperCollins Pubs. Ltd. GBR. Dist: HarperCollins Pubs.

—Mystery at the Aquarium (a Nightlight Detective Book) Orloff, Karen Kaufman. 2014. (ENG.). 26p. (J). 12.99 (978-1-4413-1615-8(9), 9781441316158) Peter Pauper Pr. Inc.

—Nightlight Detective: Big Top Circus Mystery. Orloff, Karen Kaufman. 2013. 42p. spiral bd. 12.99 (978-1-4413-1227-3(7)) Peter Pauper Pr. Inc.

—Nightlight Detective: Mystery at the Museum. Orloff, Karen Kaufman. 2013. 42p. spiral bd. 12.99 (978-1-4413-1228-0(5)) Peter Pauper Pr. Inc.

—Safety in the Bus. Slater, Teddy. 2010. 16p. (J). (978-0-545-24602-6(4)) Scholastic, Inc.

—Street Safety. Slater, Teddy. 2010. 16p. (J). (978-0-545-24604-0(0)) Scholastic, Inc.

Smith, Jamie & Alley, R. W. The Case of the Groaning Ghost. Preller, James. 2008. (Jigsaw Jones Mysteries Ser.: Bk. 32). 89p. (gr. 1-5). 15.00 (978-0-7569-8302-4(9)) Perfection Learning Corp.

Smith, Jamie, jt. illus. see Waxman, Freesia.

Smith, Jan. Apple Countdown. Holub, Joan. 2012. (J). (978-1-61913-117-0(X)) Weigl Pubs., Inc.

—Apple Countdown. Holub, Joan. (ENG.). 32p. (J). 2018. (-3). pap. 7.99 (978-0-8075-0400-0(9), 807504009); 2009. (gr. -1-3). 16.99 (978-0-8075-0398-0(3), 807503983) Whitman, Albert & Co.

—Dot to Dot Coloring & Stickers Bk. 1, 1 vol., 1. David, Juliet. 2008. (Candle Activity Fun Ser.). 24p. (J). (gr. 4-7). pap. 6.99 (978-0-8254-7360-9(8), Candle Bks.) Lion Hudson PLC GBR. Dist: Kregel Pubns.

—Encyclopaedia Britannica: Animals All Around. 2016. (Look & Find Ser.). (ENG.). 24p. (J). (978-1-5037-1052-8(1), 9c3ec3d5-c327-4bdd-9cbc-98a0de6f9329, p i kids) Phoenix International Publications, Inc.

Smith, Jan. Jolly Phonics Orange Level Readers Complete Set: In Print Letters (American English Edition) Van-Pottelsberghe, Louise. 2019. (ENG.). (J). pap. 49.35 **(978-1-84414-589-8(1)**, Jolly Phonics) Jolly Learning, Ltd. GBR. Dist: American International Distribution Corp.

Smith, Jan. Miss Bubble's Troubles. Stanley, Malaika Rose. 2010. 40p. (J). (gr. 2-4). pap. 10.99 (978-1-84853-024-9(2)) Transworld Publishers Ltd. GBR. Dist: Independent Pubs. Group.

—Pumpkin Countdown. Holub, Joan. 2014. (AV2 Fiction Readalong Ser.: Vol. 147). (ENG.). (J). (gr. -1-2). lib. bdg. 34.28 (978-1-4896-2410-9(4), AV2 by Weigl) Weigl Pubs., Inc.

—Pumpkin Countdown. Holub, Joan. 2018. (ENG.). 32p. (J). (gr. -1-3). pap. 7.99 (978-0-8075-6662-6(4), 807566624) Whitman, Albert & Co.

Smith, Jane. Five Silly Pumpkins: A Pop-up Halloween Book. Seal, Kerry. 2009. 10p. (J). 5.95 (978-1-58117-908-8(1), Intervisual/Piggy Toes) Bendon, Inc.

—Kate & Caboodle. Pirc, Jerri J. 2015. pap. (978-0-473-32583-1(7)) Pirc, Jerri J.

Smith, Jane. Hello, New House. Smith, Jane. 2020. (ENG.). 32p. (J). (gr. -1-3). 16.99 **(978-0-8075-7226-9(8)**, 0807572268) Whitman, Albert & Co.

Smith, Jane. It's Easter, Chloe Zoe! Smith, Jane. 2016. (Chloe Zoe Ser.). (ENG.). 32p. (J). (gr. -1-3). 12.99 (978-0-8075-2460-2(3), 807524603) Whitman, Albert & Co.

—It's Halloween, Chloe Zoe! Smith, Jane. 2017. (Chloe Zoe Ser.). (ENG.). 32p. (J). (gr. -1-3). 12.99 (978-0-8075-1210-4(9), 807512109) Whitman, Albert & Co.

—It's Thanksgiving, Chloe Zoe! Smith, Jane. 2017. (Chloe Zoe Ser.). (ENG.). 32p. (J). (gr. -1-3). 12.99 (978-0-8075-1212-8(5), 807512125) Whitman, Albert & Co.

—It's the First Day of Kindergarten, Chloe Zoe! Smith, Jane. 2016. (Chloe Zoe Ser.). (ENG.). 32p. (J). (gr. -1-3). 12.99 (978-0-8075-2458-9(1), 807524581) Whitman, Albert & Co.

—It's the First Day of Preschool, Chloe Zoe! Smith, Jane. 2016. (Chloe Zoe Ser.). (ENG.). 32p. (J). (gr. -1-3). 12.99 (978-0-8075-2456-5(5), 807524565) Whitman, Albert & Co.

—It's Valentine's Day, Chloe Zoe! Smith, Jane. 2016. (Chloe Zoe Ser.). (ENG.). 32p. (J). (gr. -1-3). 12.99 (978-0-8075-2462-6(X), 080752462X) Whitman, Albert & Co.

Smith, Jay F. A Day to Remember: A Sam & Coco Story. Smith, Jay F. 2005. 32p. (J). (978-0-9764719-0-5(6)) MiceWorks.

Smith, Jeff. The Boy Who Wouldn't Sit Still!, Vol. 2. Lester, Sharon. 2nd ed. 2011. 40p. (J). 15.95 (978-0-9802302-2-2(5)) Privileged Communications, LLC.

—Quest for the Spark. Sniegoski, Tom. (ENG.). (J). 2012. (Bone Ser.). 240p. (gr. 4-7). pap. 10.99 (978-0-545-14104-8(4)); Bk. 1. 2011. (BONE: Quest for the Spark Ser.: 1). 224p. (gr. 3-7). 26.99 (978-0-545-14101-7(X)); Bk. 1. 2011. (BONE: Quest for the Spark Ser.: 1). 224p. (gr. 3-7). pap. 10.99 (978-0-545-14102-4(8)); Bk. 2. 2012. (Bone Ser.). 240p. (gr. 3-7). 26.99 (978-0-545-14103-1(6)); Bk. 3. 2013. (BONE: Quest for the Spark Ser.). 288p. (gr. 3-7). pap. 10.99 (978-0-545-14106-2(0)); No. 3. 2013. (BONE: Quest for the Spark Ser.). 288p. (gr. 3-7). 22.99 (978-0-545-14105-5(2)) Scholastic, Inc. (Graphix).

Smith, Jeff. Bone. Smith, Jeff. 2010. (Bone Ser.). (ENG.). 128p. (J). (gr. 4-7). pap., instr.'s hndbk. ed. 9.99 (978-0-545-21142-0(5), Graphix) Scholastic, Inc.

—Crown of Horns. Smith, Jeff. 2009. (Bone Ser.: 9). (ENG.). 224p. (J). (gr. 4-7). 26.99 (978-0-439-70631-5(9)); pap. 12.99 (978-0-439-70632-2(7)) Scholastic, Inc. (Graphix).

—The Dragonslayer. Smith, Jeff. 2006. (Bone Ser.: 4). (ENG.). 176p. (J). (gr. 3-7). 26.99 (978-0-439-70626-1(2)); pap. 12.99 (978-0-439-70637-7(8)) Scholastic, Inc. (Graphix).

—Eyes of the Storm. Smith, Jeff. 2006. (Bone Ser.: 3). (ENG.). 192p. (J). (gr. 3-7). 26.99 (978-0-439-70625-4(4)); pap. 12.99 (978-0-439-70638-4(6)) Scholastic, Inc. (Graphix).

—Ghost Circles. Smith, Jeff. 2008. (Bone Ser.: 7). (ENG.). 160p. (J). (gr. 4-7). pap. 12.99 (978-0-439-70634-6(3), Graphix) Scholastic, Inc.

—The Great Cow Race. Smith, Jeff. 2005. (Bone Ser.: 2). (ENG.). 144p. (J). (gr. 4-7). 26.99 (978-0-439-70624-7(6)); pap. 12.99 (978-0-439-70639-1(4)) Scholastic, Inc. (Graphix).

—Old Man's Cave. Smith, Jeff. 2009. (Bone Ser.: 6). (ENG.). 128p. (gr. 4-7). pap. 12.99 (978-0-439-70635-3(1)) Perfection Learning Corp.

—Out from Boneville. Smith, Jeff. 2005. (Bone Ser.: 1). (ENG.). 144p. (J). pap. 12.99 (978-0-439-70640-7(8)); pap. 26.99 (978-0-439-70623-0(8)) Scholastic, Inc. (Graphix).

—Rock Jaw: Master of the Eastern Border. Smith, Jeff. 2007. (Bone Ser.: 5). (ENG.). 128p. (J). (gr. -1-7). 26.99 (978-0-439-70627-8(0)); (gr. 4-7). pap. 12.99 (978-0-439-70636-0(X)) Scholastic, Inc. (Graphix).

—Tall Tales. Smith, Jeff. Sniegoski, Tom. 2010. (Bone Ser.). (ENG.). 128p. (J). (gr. 4-7). 26.99 (978-0-545-14095-9(1), Graphix) Scholastic, Inc.

—Tall Tales. Smith, Jeff. Sniegoski, Tom. 2010. (Bone Ser.). (ENG.). 128p. (J). (gr. 4-7). pap. 12.99 (978-0-545-14096-6(X), Graphix) Scholastic, Inc.

Smith, Jeff & Hamaker, Steve. Ghost Circles. Smith, Jeff. 2008. (Bone Ser.: 7). (ENG.). 160p. (J). (gr. 4-7). 26.99 (978-0-439-70629-2(7), Graphix) Scholastic, Inc.

—Old Man's Cave. Smith, Jeff. 2007. (Bone Ser.: 6). (ENG.). 128p. (J). (gr. 4-7). 26.99 (978-0-439-70628-5(9)) Scholastic, Inc.

Smith, Jeffrey. Peachboy. Metaxas, Eric. 2005. (Rabbit Ears-A Classic Tale Ser.). (ENG.). 36p. (J). (gr. 2-6). 28.50 (978-1-59679-227-2(2), 12935, Picture Bk.) Spotlight.

Smith, Jen. Big Ted's Guide to Tapping: Positive EFT Emotional Freedom Techniques for Children. Kent, Alex. 2013. 26p. pap. (978-1-908269-40-9(5)) DragonRising Publishing.

Smith, Jenni. The Inspired ABC's. Branch, Jennifer. 2008. 60p. (J). per. 16.99 (978-0-615-18948-2(2)) Laughing Baby Pubns.

Smith, Jennifer & Dutta, Dipali. Jack's Backyard. Smith, Scott P. 2016. (ENG.). (J). pap. 9.49 (978-0-9986381-0-2(2)) Glass Onion Publishing.

Smith, Jeremy. Zoo Force: Dear Eniko. Thomas, John Ira. 2003. 68p. per. 6.95 (978-0-9743147-1-6(4)) Candle Light Pr.

Smith, Jerry. The Adventures of Inka the Feline. Janowski, Alice. 2010. 36p. pap. 14.00 (978-1-60844-576-9(3)) Dog Ear Publishing, LLC.

Smith, Jessie Willcox. The Children of Dickens. Crothers, Samuel McChord. 2005. (ENG.). 150p. (gr. 4-7). pap. 14.95 *(978-0-89733-475-4(2)*, Academy Chicago Pubs., Ltd.) Chicago Review Pr., Inc.

—A Child's Book of Stories. Coussens, Penrhyn W. 2008. 608p. pap. 19.95 *(978-1-59915-248-6(7))* Yesterday's Classics.

—Twas the Night Before Christmas: A Visit from St. Nicholas. Moore, Clement C. 2015. vi, 29p. (J). pap. *(978-1-4677-7805-3(2)*, First Avenue Editions) Lerner Publishing Group.

Smith, Jessie Willcox. 'Twas the Night Before Christmas. Smith, Jessie Willcox. Moore, Clement C. 2005. (Holiday Classics Ser.). (ENG.). 32p. (J). (gr. -1-3). 6.99 *(978-0-618-61510-0(5)*, 451651); 14.00 *(978-0-618-61682-4(9)*, 551651) Houghton Mifflin Harcourt Publishing Co.

Smith, Jim. Christmas Fairy Tale Mix-Up. Robinson, Hilary. 2018. 30p. (J). (gr. -1-k). pap. 9.99 *(978-1-4449-3218-8(7))* Hachette Children's Group GBR. Dist: Hachette Bk. Group.

—Scoot! Blackburn, Katie. 2018. (ENG.). 32p. (J). pap. 9.95 *(978-0-571-33639-5(6)*, Faber & Faber Children's Bks.) Faber & Faber, Inc.

—Spooky Fairy Tale Mix-Up: Hundreds of Flip-Flap Stories. Robinson, Hilary. 2018. (ENG.). 26p. (J). (gr. -1-2). 11.99 *(978-1-4380-5066-9(6)*, B.E.S. Publishing) Peterson's.

Smith, Jim W. W., jt. illus. see Loxton, Daniel.

Smith, Jj. Math Workbooks Kindergarten: Math Workbook, Preschool to Kindergarten, Kindergarten Workbook - Ages 3 to 5, Early Reading & Writing, Count & Color Numbers 0-20, Basic Matching, Story Order & More. Skills, Academic. 2019. (Academic Skills Kindergarten Workbook Ser.: Vol. 1). (ENG.). 106p. (J). pap. 5.78 *(978-1-0823-4480-0(X))* Independently Published.

Smith, John H. Hello, My Name Is Tiff: A Little Dog's Life Story. Turner, Robert J. 2007. (ENG.). 24p. per. 15.99 *(978-1-4257-8661-8(8))* Xlibris Corp.

Smith, Jonathan. Comanche 1800-74. Meed, Douglas V. 2003. (Warrior Ser.: 75). 64p. pap. 18.95 *(978-1-84176-587-7(2)*, 900167871, Osprey) Bloomsbury Publishing USA.

Smith, Jordyn. Rich the Itch. McHaney, Eric & McHaney, Mandy. I.t. ed. 2005. 20p. (J). *(978-0-9769086-0-9(3))* RTI Publishing, LLC.

Smith, Jos. A. Bandit's Moon. Fleischman, Sid. 2008. (ENG.). 192p. (J). (gr. 3-7). pap. 6.99 *(978-0-06-145096-9(0)*, Greenwillow Bks.) HarperCollins Pubs.

—Gregor Mendel: The Friar Who Grew Peas. Bardoe, Cheryl. (ENG.). (J). (gr. k-4). 2015. 32p. pap. 9.95 *(978-1-4197-1840-3(1))*; 2006. 40p. 21.95 *(978-0-8109-5475-5(3))* Abrams, Inc. (Abrams Bks. for Young Readers).

—Jim Ugly. Fleischman, Sid. 2003. (ENG.). 144p. (J). (gr. 3-7). pap. 6.99 *(978-0-06-052121-9(X)*, Greenwillow Bks.) HarperCollins Pubs.

Smith Jr., Charles R. My People. Hughes, Langston. 2009. (ENG.). 40p. (J). (gr. -1-3). 19.99 *(978-1-4169-3540-7(1)*, Atheneum Bks. for Young Readers) Simon & Schuster Children's Publishing.

Smith, Kasey. Count to Ten & Look Again. Smith, Kiki. 2019. (ENG.). 42p. (J). pap. 15.00 ***(978-1-6950-1843-3(5))*** Independently Published.

—Do You Have a Penny? Smith, Kiki. 2019. (ENG.). 28p. (J). pap. 15.00 ***(978-1-7012-7774-8(3))*** Independently Published.

Smith, Kasey. Dots Spots & Chickenpox: Version II. Smith, Kiki. 2018. (ENG.). 30p. (J). pap. 15.00 *(978-1-7901-7031-9(1))* Independently Published.

Smith, Kate. The Colour Fairies Series Book 10: The Spring Ball. Jeffrey, Maggie. 2019. (Colour Fairies Ser.: Vol. 10). (ENG.). 42p. (J). pap. 9.13 *(978-1-7985-4606-2(X))* Independently Published.

—The Colour Fairies Series Book 15: The Colour Fairies Practise Their Magic. Jeffrey, Maggie. 2019. (Colour Fairies Ser.: Vol. 15). (ENG.). 38p. (J). pap. 9.13 *(978-1-0784-6938-8(5))* Independently Published.

—Twizzle & the Licked Clean Dish. Carter, Mike. 2016. (ENG.). (J). pap. *(978-1-78507-896-5(8))* Authors OnLine, Ltd.

Smith, Katya. Ben of the Island. Kett, Terrilyn. 2018. (ENG.). 32p. (J). (gr. 2-4). pap. *(978-1-987852-15-8(X))* Wood Islands Prints.

Smith, Keith. Dibe Lizhini Jiliigo Bee Shanah IDLI/Proud to Be a Blacksheep. John, Roberta. Thomas, Peter A., tr. from ENG. 2007. (NAV & ENG.). 32p. (J). (gr. 4-7). 17.95 *(978-1-893354-05-0(9))* Salina Bookshelf Inc.

—Little Prankster Girl: At'Eed Adilahi Yazhi. Blue, Martha. Ruffenach, Jessie, ed. Thomas, Peter, tr. from NAV. 2008. (NAV & ENG.). 32p. (J). (gr. -1-3). 17.95 *(978-1-893354-36-4(9))* Salina Bookshelf Inc.

Smith, Keri. Tear up This Book! The Sticker, Stencil, Stationery, Games, Crafts, Doodle, & Journal Book for Girls! Smith, Keri. Magruder, Trula, ed. 2005. (ENG.). 96p. (J). (gr. 3-7). spiral bd. 10.95 *(978-1-58485-977-2(6)*, American Girl) American Girl Publishing, Inc.

Smith, Kevin. Bumble! The Incredible Story of a Humble Bee & Her Famous Campaign. Bickerton, Andrew. 2018. (ENG.). 46p. (J). pap. *(978-1-78623-333-2(9))* Grosvenor Hse. Publishing Ltd.

Smith, Kim. Abuela's Birthday. Jules, Jacqueline. 2015. (Sofia Martinez Ser.). (ENG.). 32p. (J). (gr. k-2). lib. bdg. 21.32 *(978-1-4795-5775-2(7)*, Picture Window Bks.) Capstone.

—Abuela's Special Letters. Jules, Jacqueline. (Sofia Martinez Ser.). (ENG.). 32p. (J). (gr. k-2). 2018. pap. 5.95 *(978-1-5158-0730-8(4)*, 133612); 2017. lib. bdg. 21.32 *(978-1-5158-0728-5(2))* Capstone. (Picture Window Bks.).

—Back to the Future: The Classic Illustrated Storybook. 2018. (Pop Classics Ser.: 4). (ENG.). 40p. (J). (gr. -1-3). 18.99 *(978-1-68369-023-8(0))* Quirk Bks.

—The Beach Trip. Jules, Jacqueline. 2016. (Sofia Martinez Ser.). (ENG.). 32p. (J). (gr. k-2). lib. bdg. 21.32 *(978-1-4795-8719-3(2)*, Picture Window Bks.) Capstone.

—Bringing Back the Wolves: How a Predator Restored an Ecosystem. Isabella, Jude. 2020. (ENG.). 48p. (J). (gr. 3-7). 18.99 *(978-1-77138-625-8(8))* Kids Can Pr., Ltd. CAN. Dist: Hachette Bk. Group.

—Buffy the Vampire Slayer: A Picture Book. 2018. (Pop Classics Ser.: 5). (ENG.). 40p. (J). (gr. -1-3). 18.99 *(978-1-68369-069-6(9))* Quirk Bks.

—Builder Brothers: Better Together. Scott, Drew & Scott, Jonathan. 2019. (Builder Brothers Ser.). (ENG.). 32p. (J). (gr. -1-3). 17.99 *(978-0-06-284665-5(5))* HarperCollins Pubs.

—Builder Brothers: Big Plans. Scott, Drew & Scott, Jonathan. 2018. (Builder Brothers Ser.). (ENG.). 32p. (J). (gr. -1-3). 17.99 *(978-0-06-284662-4(0))* HarperCollins Pubs.

—Cantante Súper Estrella. Jules, Jacqueline. 2018. (Sofia Martinez en Español Ser.). (SPA.). 32p. (J). (gr. k-2). lib. bdg. 21.32 *(978-1-5158-2452-7(7)*, 137555, Picture Window Bks.) Capstone.

—El Cumpleaños de la Abuela. Jules, Jacqueline. 2018. (Sofia Martinez en Español Ser.). (SPA.). 32p. (J). (gr. k-2). lib. bdg. 21.32 *(978-1-5158-2443-5(8)*, 137546, Picture Window Bks.) Capstone.

—E. T. the Extra-Terrestrial: The Classic Illustrated Storybook. 2017. (Pop Classics Ser.: 3). (ENG.). 40p. (J). (gr. -1-3). 18.99 *(978-1-68369-010-8(9))* Quirk Bks.

—Every Day Is Exciting. Jules, Jacqueline. ed. 2018. (Sofia Martinez Ser.). (ENG.). 96p. (J). (gr. k-2). pap. 4.95 *(978-1-5158-2343-8(1)*, 137020, Picture Window Bks.) Capstone.

—The Ghost & Max Monroe, Case #1: The Magic Box. Falcone, L. M. 2014. (Ghost & Max Monroe Ser.). (ENG.). 88p. (J). (gr. 1-4). pap. 6.95 *(978-1-77138-017-1(9))* Kids Can Pr., Ltd. CAN. Dist: Hachette Bk. Group.

—The Ghost & Max Monroe, Case #3: The Dirty Trick. Falcone, L. M. 2015. (Ghost & Max Monroe Ser.). (ENG.). 96p. (J). (gr. 1-4). 6.95 *(978-1-77138-019-5(5))* Kids Can Pr., Ltd. CAN. Dist: Hachette Bk. Group.

—The Great Puppy Invasion. Heim, Alastair. 2017. (ENG.). 40p. (J). (gr. -1-3). 17.99 *(978-0-544-99917-6(7)*, 1666808) Houghton Mifflin Harcourt Publishing Co.

—The Great Puppy Invasion (padded Board Book) Heim, Alastair. 2019. (ENG.). 30p. (J). (— 1). bds. 8.99 *(978-1-328-60667-9(8)*, 1732423, HMH Books For Young Readers) Houghton Mifflin Harcourt Publishing Co.

—Hector's Hiccups. Jules, Jacqueline. 2018. (Sofia Martinez Ser.). (ENG.). 32p. (J). (gr. k-2). lib. bdg. 21.32 *(978-1-5158-2335-3(0)*, 137016, Picture Window Bks.) Capstone.

—Home Alone: The Classic Illustrated Storybook. 2015. (Pop Classics Ser.: 1). (ENG.). 40p. (J). (gr. -1-3). 18.95 *(978-1-59474-858-5(6))* Quirk Bks.

—The Ice Chips & the Haunted Hurricane: Ice Chips Series Book 2. MacGregor, Roy & MacGregor, Kerry. 2020. (Ice Chips Ser.). (ENG.). 176p. (J). (gr. 1-3). pap. 7.99 *(978-1-4434-5232-8(7)*, Harper Trophy) HarperCollins Pubs.

Smith, Kim. The Ice Chips & the Haunted Hurricane: Ice Chips Series Book 2. MacGregor, Roy & MacGregor, Kerry. 2018. (Ice Chips Ser.). (ENG.). 176p. (J). (gr. 1-3). 13.50 ***(978-1-4434-5231-1(9)***, HarperCollins) HarperCollins Pubs. Ltd. GBR. Dist: HarperCollins Pubs.

—The Ice Chips & the Invisible Puck: Ice Chips Series Book 3. MacGregor, Roy & MacGregor, Kerry. 2020. (Ice Chips Ser.). (ENG.). 176p. (J). (gr. 1-3). pap. 7.99 ***(978-1-4434-5235-9(1)***, Harper Trophy) HarperCollins Pubs.

Smith, Kim. The Ice Chips & the Magical Rink: Ice Chips Series. MacGregor, Roy & MacGregor, Kerry. 2019. (Ice Chips Ser.). (ENG.). 144p. (J). (gr. 1-3). pap. 6.99 *(978-1-4434-5963-1(1))* HarperCollins Pubs.

—The Ice Chips & the Stolen Cup: Ice Chips Series Book 4. MacGregor, Roy & MacGregor, Kerry. 2020. (Ice Chips Ser.). (ENG.). 208p. (J). (gr. 1-3). 13.50 *(978-1-4434-5999-0(2))* HarperCollins Pubs.

Smith, Kim. Jay Versus the Saxophone of Doom. Kootstra, Kara. 2020. 192p. (J). (gr. 3-7). pap. 8.99 ***(978-0-7352-6869-2(X)***, Puffin Canada) PRH Canada Young Readers CAN. Dist: Penguin Random Hse. LLC.

Smith, Kim. The Karate Kid: The Classic Illustrated Storybook. 2019. (Pop Classics Ser.: 6). (ENG.). 40p. (J). (gr. -1-3). 18.99 *(978-1-68369-092-4(3))* Quirk Bks.

—Kaugjagjuk, 1 vol. Lewis, Marion. 2011. (ENG.). 40p. (J). (gr. 1-3). 13.95 *(978-1-926569-39-0(3))* Inhabit Media Inc. CAN. Dist: Consortium Bk. Sales & Distribution.

—Las Cartas Especiales de la Abuela. Jules, Jacqueline. 2018. (Sofia Martinez en Español Ser.). (SPA.). 32p. (J). (gr. k-2). lib. bdg. 21.32 *(978-1-5158-2444-2(6)*, 137547, Picture Window Bks.) Capstone.

—Lights Out. Jules, Jacqueline. 2016. (Sofia Martinez Ser.). (ENG.). 32p. (J). (gr. k-2). lib. bdg. 21.32 *(978-1-4795-8718-6(4)*, Picture Window Bks.) Capstone.

—Lío de Caléndulas. Jules, Jacqueline. 2018. (Sofia Martinez en Español Ser.). (SPA.). 32p. (J). (gr. k-2). lib. bdg. 21.32 *(978-1-5158-2447-3(0)*, 137550, Picture Window Bks.) Capstone.

—Lista para la Foto. Jules, Jacqueline. 2018. (Sofia Martinez en Español Ser.). (SPA.). 32p. (J). (gr. k-2). lib. bdg. 21.32 *(978-1-5158-2449-7(7)*, 137552, Picture Window Bks.) Capstone.

—The Marigold Mess. Jules, Jacqueline. 2015. (Sofia Martinez Ser.). (ENG.). 32p. (J). (gr. k-2). lib. bdg. 21.32 *(978-1-4795-5776-9(5)*, Picture Window Bks.) Capstone.

—The Missing Mouse. Jules, Jacqueline. 2015. (Sofia Martinez Ser.). (ENG.). 32p. (J). (gr. k-2). lib. bdg. 21.32 *(978-1-4795-5774-5(9)*, Picture Window Bks.) Capstone.

—My Family Adventure. Jules, Jacqueline. 2015. (Sofia Martinez Ser.). (ENG.). 96p. (J). (gr. k-2). pap. 4.95 *(978-1-4795-5790-5(0)*, Picture Window Bks.) Capstone.

—My Fantástica Family. Jules, Jacqueline. 2017. (Sofia Martinez Ser.). (ENG.). 96p. (J). (gr. k-2). pap. 4.95 *(978-1-5158-0746-9(0)*, Picture Window Bks.) Capstone.

—My Vida Loca. Jules, Jacqueline. 2016. (Sofia Martinez Ser.). (ENG.). 96p. (J). (gr. k-2). pap. 4.95 *(978-1-4795-8720-9(6)*, Picture Window Bks.) Capstone.

—A Oscuras. Jules, Jacqueline. 2018. (Sofia Martinez en Español Ser.). (SPA.). 32p. (J). (gr. k-2). lib. bdg. 21.32 *(978-1-5158-2446-6(2)*, 137549, Picture Window Bks.) Capstone.

—Over the River & Through the Wood: A Holiday Adventure. Ashman, Linda. 2015. 32p. (J). (gr. -1). 14.95 *(978-1-4549-1024-4(0))* Sterling Publishing Co., Inc.

—Un Paseo de Compras Problemático. Jules, Jacqueline. 2018. (Sofia Martinez en Español Ser.). (SPA.). 32p. (J). (gr. k-2). lib. bdg. 21.32 *(978-1-5158-2451-0(9)*, 137554, Picture Window Bks.) Capstone.

—Picture Perfect. Jules, Jacqueline. 2015. (Sofia Martinez Ser.). (ENG.). 32p. (J). (gr. k-2). lib. bdg. 21.32 *(978-1-4795-5773-8(0)*, Picture Window Bks.) Capstone.

—El Ratón Perdido. Jules, Jacqueline. 2018. (Sofia Martinez en Español Ser.). (SPA.). 32p. (J). (gr. k-2). lib. bdg. 21.32 *(978-1-5158-2448-0(9)*, 137551, Picture Window Bks.) Capstone.

—The Raven & the Loon. Qitsualik-Tinsley, Rachel & Qitsualik-Tinsley, Sean. 2020. 32p. (J). 10.95 *(978-1-77227-270-3(1))* Inhabit Media Inc. CAN. Dist: Consortium Bk. Sales & Distribution.

—La Receta Secreta. Jules, Jacqueline. 2018. (Sofia Martinez en Español Ser.). (SPA.). 32p. (J). (gr. k-2). lib. bdg. 21.32 *(978-1-5158-2450-3(0)*, 137553, Picture Window Bks.) Capstone.

—The Secret Recipe. Jules, Jacqueline. 2016. (Sofia Martinez Ser.). (ENG.). 32p. (J). (gr. k-2). lib. bdg. 21.32 *(978-1-4795-8717-9(6)*, Picture Window Bks.) Capstone.

—Shopping Trip Trouble. Jules, Jacqueline. (Sofia Martinez Ser.). (ENG.). 32p. (J). (gr. k-2). 2018. pap. 5.95 *(978-1-5158-0731-5(2)*, 133613); 2017. lib. bdg. 21.32 *(978-1-5158-0729-2(0))* Capstone. (Picture Window Bks.).

—Singing Superstar. Jules, Jacqueline. 2016. (Sofia Martinez Ser.). (ENG.). 32p. (J). (gr. k-2). lib. bdg. 21.32 *(978-1-4795-8716-2(8)*, Picture Window Bks.) Capstone.

—Sofia's Party Shoes. Jules, Jacqueline. 2018. (Sofia Martinez Ser.). (ENG.). 32p. (J). (gr. k-2). lib. bdg. 21.32 *(978-1-5158-2336-0(9)*, 137017, Picture Window Bks.) Capstone.

—A Ticket Around the World. Diaz, Natalia & Owens, Melissa. 2019. (ENG.). 32p. (J). pap. 9.95 *(978-1-77147-352-1(5))* Owlkids Bks. Inc. CAN. Dist: Publishers Group West (PGW).

—The Twelve Days of Christmas in Canada. Warwick, Ellen. 2016. (Twelve Days of Christmas in America Ser.). 22p. (J). (-k). bds. 9.50 *(978-1-4549-2056-4(4))* Sterling Publishing Co., Inc.

—Viaja e a la Playa. Jules, Jacqueline. 2018. (Sofia Martinez en Español Ser.). (SPA.). 32p. (J). (gr. k-2). lib. bdg. 21.32 *(978-1-5158-2445-9(4)*, 137548, Picture Window Bks.) Capstone.

—The X-Files: Earth Children Are Weird: A Picture Book. 2017. (Pop Classics Ser.: 2). (ENG.). 40p. (J). (gr. -1-3). 18.99 *(978-1-59474-979-7(5))* Quirk Bks.

Smith, Kimanne. Demanding Justice: A Story about Mary Ann Shadd Cary. Ferris, Jeri Chase. 2003. (Creative Minds Biographies Ser.). (ENG.). 64p. (gr. 4-8). 22.60 *(978-1-57505-177-2(X))* Lerner Publishing Group.

Smith, Kimanne, jt. illus. see Smith, Elise.

Smith, Kimberly. The Twelve Days of Christmas in Canada. Warwick, Ellen. 2015. (Twelve Days of Christmas in America Ser.). 40p. (J). (gr. k). 12.95 *(978-1-4549-1431-0(9))* Sterling Publishing Co., Inc.

Smith, Kirsti. Dice Are for Rolling Eyes Are Not. Lash, Pam. 2019. (ENG.). 58p. (J). pap. 15.00 ***(978-1-7186-7859-0(2))*** CreateSpace Independent Publishing Platform.

Smith, Kuleigh. ¿Chili Texano? ¡Ay Dios! Vermillion, Patricia. Guadalupe, Jezabel, tr. 2013. (SPA & ENG.). 40p. 21.95 *(978-0-87565-584-0(X))* Texas Christian Univ. Pr.

—Texas Chili? Oh My! Vermillion, Patricia. 2013. (ENG.). 40p. 21.95 *(978-0-87565-568-0(8))* Texas Christian Univ. Pr.

Smith, Landa. Not Again, Mr. Cat! Johnson, Kimberly P. 2003. 36p. (J). (gr. k-3). 14.95 *(978-1-57197-362-7(1)*, Ivy House Publishing Group) Pentland Pr., Inc.

Smith, Lane. Baloney (Henry P.) Scieszka, Jon. 2005. (gr. -1-3). 17.00 *(978-0-7569-5494-9(0))* Perfection Learning Corp.

—Baloney (Henry P.) Scieszka, Jon. 2005. 40p. (J). (gr. k-k). pap. 7.99 *(978-0-14-240430-0(6)*, Puffin Books) Penguin Young Readers Group.

—Los Caballeros de la Mesa de la Cocina. Scieszka, Jon. (SPA.). (J). (gr. 5-8). 7.95 *(978-958-04-3400-9(X)*, NR4516) Norma S.A. COL. Dist: Distribuidora Norma, Inc., Lectorum Pubns., Inc.

Smith, Lane. Giraffe Problems. John, Jory. (Animal Problems Ser.). (ENG.). (J). 2020. 34p. (— 1). bds. 8.99 ***(978-0-593-12772-8(2))***; 2018. 42p. (gr. -1-2). 17.99 *(978-1-5247-7203-1(8))*; 2018. 42p. (gr. -1-2). lib. bdg. 20.99 *(978-1-5247-7204-8(6))* Random Hse. Children's Bks. (Random Hse. Bks. for Young Readers).

Smith, Lane. The Good, the Bad, & the Goofy. Scieszka, Jon. 2004. (Time Warp Trio Ser.: 3). 80p. (J). (gr. 2-4). pap. 5.99 *(978-0-14-240046-3(7)*, Puffin Books) Penguin Young Readers Group.

—The Good, the Bad, & the Goofy. Scieszka, Jon. 2005. (Time Warp Trio Ser.: No. 3). 70p. (gr. 4-7). 15.00 *(978-0-7569-5876-3(8))* Perfection Learning Corp.

—A House That Once Was. Fogliano, Julie. 2018. (ENG.). 48p. (J). 18.99 *(978-1-62672-314-6(1)*, 900151167) Roaring Brook Pr.

—It's All Greek to Me. Scieszka, Jon. 2006. (Time Warp Trio Ser.: No. 8). 71p. (gr. 4-7). 15.00 *(978-0-7569-6780-2(5))* Perfection Learning Corp.

—It's All Greek to Me #8, No. 8. Scieszka, Jon. 2004. (Time Warp Trio Ser.: 8). (ENG.). 80p. (J). (gr. 2-4). pap. 5.99 *(978-0-14-240116-3(1)*, Puffin Books) Penguin Young Readers Group.

—Kid Sheriff & the Terrible Toads. Shea, Bob. 2014. (ENG.). 32p. (J). (gr. -1-3). 17.99 *(978-1-59643-975-7(0)*, 900127683) Roaring Brook Pr.

—Lulu & the Brontosaurus. Viorst, Judith. (Lulu Ser.). (ENG.). 128p. (J). (gr. 1-5). 2012. pap. 8.99 *(978-1-4169-9962-1(0))*; 2010. 19.99 *(978-1-4169-9961-4(2))* Simon & Schuster Children's Publishing. (Atheneum Bks. for Young Readers).

—Lulu Walks the Dogs. Viorst, Judith. (Lulu Ser.). (ENG.). (J). (gr. 1-5). 2014. 176p. pap. 8.99 *(978-1-4424-3580-3(1))*; 2012. 160p. 19.99 *(978-1-4424-3579-7(8))* Simon & Schuster Children's Publishing. (Atheneum Bks. for Young Readers).

—Math Curse. Scieszka, Jon. 2011. (J). (gr. 1-4). 29.95 *(978-0-545-13458-3(7))* Weston Woods Studios, Inc.

—Penguin Problems. John, Jory. 2018. (ENG.). 32p. (J). (— 1). bds. 8.99 *(978-0-525-64575-7(6)*, Random Hse. Bks. for Young Readers) Random Hse. Children's Bks.

—El Pirata Barbanegra. Scieszka, Jon. (SPA.). (J). (gr. 5-8). 7.95 *(978-958-04-3401-6(8)*, NR8584) Norma S.A. COL. Dist: Distribuidora Norma, Inc., Lectorum Pubns., Inc.

—Princess Hyacinth. Heide, Florence Parry. 2009. 48p. (J). (gr. -1-3). 17.99 *(978-0-375-84501-7(1)*, Schwartz & Wade Bks.) Random Hse. Children's Bks.

—Princess Hyacinth (the Surprising Tale of a Girl Who Floated) Heide, Florence Parry. 2016. 48p. (J). (gr. -1-3). 7.99 *(978-0-553-53804-5(7)*, Dragonfly Bks.) Random Hse. Children's Bks.

—Science Verse. Scieszka, Jon. 2004. 40p. (J). (gr. 2-5). 18.99 *(978-0-670-91057-1(0)*, Viking Books for Young Readers) Penguin Young Readers Group.

—Squids Will Be Squids. Scieszka, Jon. 2003. 48p. (J). (gr. 3-7). pap. 8.99 *(978-0-14-250040-8(2)*, Puffin Books) Penguin Young Readers Group.

—Summer Reading Is Killing Me! Scieszka, Jon. 2004. (Time Warp Trio Ser.: No. 7). 73p. (J). (gr. 4-7). 12.65 *(978-0-7569-6781-9(3))* Perfection Learning Corp.

—Summer Reading Is Killing Me! #7. Scieszka, Jon. 2004. (Time Warp Trio Ser.: 7). 80p. (J). (gr. 2-4). pap. 5.99 *(978-0-14-240115-6(3)*, Puffin Books) Penguin Young Readers Group.

—Tomorrow Most Likely (Read Aloud Family Books, Mindfulness Books for Kids, Bedtime Books for Young Children, Bedtime Picture Books) Eggers, Dave. 2019. (ENG.). 40p. (J). (gr. -1-k). 17.99 *(978-1-4521-7278-1(1))* Chronicle Bks. LLC.

—The True Story of the 3 Little Pigs. Scieszka, Jon. 2011. (J). (gr. -1-3). 29.95 *(978-0-545-09457-3(7))*; 18.95 *(978-0-545-09459-7(3))* Weston Woods Studios, Inc.

—The True Story of the Three Little Pigs 25th Anniversary Edition. Scieszka, Jon. 25th anniv. ed. 2014. 32p. (J). (gr. k-3). 17.99 *(978-0-451-47195-6(4)*, Viking Books for Young Readers) Penguin Young Readers Group.

—Tu Mama Era Neanderthal. Scieszka, Jon. (SPA.). (J). (gr. 5-8). 7.95 *(978-958-04-5045-0(5)*, NR3076) Norma S.A. COL. Dist: Distribuidora Norma, Inc., Lectorum Pubns., Inc.

—Tut, Tut, No. 6. Scieszka, Jon. 2004. (Time Warp Trio Ser.: 6). 80p. (J). (gr. 2-4). pap. 5.99 *(978-0-14-240047-0(5)*, Puffin Books) Penguin Young Readers Group.

—Tut, Tut. Scieszka, Jon. 2004. (Time Warp Trio Ser.: No. 6). 74p. (gr. 4-7). 15.00 *(978-0-7569-4050-8(8))* Perfection Learning Corp.

—The Very Persistent Gappers of Frip. Saunders, George. 2015. (ENG.). 96p. 22.00 *(978-0-8129-8963-2(5)*, Random House) Random House Publishing Group.

—Your Mother Was a Neanderthal. Scieszka, Jon. 2006. (Time Warp Trio Ser.: No. 4). 78p. (gr. 4-7). 15.00 *(978-0-7569-6782-6(1))* Perfection Learning Corp.

—Your Mother Was a Neanderthal. Scieszka, Jon. ed. 2004. (Time Warp Trio Ser.: 4). 78p. (J). 16.00 *(978-1-4176-3603-7(3))* Turtleback.

—Your Mother Was a Neanderthal #4. Scieszka, Jon. 2004. (Time Warp Trio Ser.: 4). (ENG.). 80p. (J). (gr. 2-4). pap. 5.99 *(978-0-14-240048-7(3)*, Puffin Books) Penguin Young Readers Group.

—2095. Scieszka, Jon. 2004. (Time Warp Trio Ser.: 5). 80p. (J). (gr. 2-4). pap. 5.99 *(978-0-14-240044-9(0)*, Puffin Books) Penguin Young Readers Group.

—2095. Scieszka, Jon. 2005. (Time Warp Trio Ser.: No. 5). 72p. (gr. 4-7). 15.00 *(978-0-7569-5989-0(6))* Perfection Learning Corp.

Smith, Lane. Abe Lincoln's Dream. Smith, Lane. 2012. (ENG.). 32p. (J). (gr. k-4). 17.99 *(978-1-59643-608-4(5)*, 9781596436084) Roaring Brook Pr.

—Grandpa Green. Smith, Lane. 2011. (ENG.). 32p. (J). (gr. k-4). 16.99 *(978-1-59643-607-7(7)*, 900065871) Roaring Brook Pr.

—It's a Book. Smith, Lane. 2010. (ENG.). 32p. (J). (gr. 1-5). 16.99 *(978-1-59643-606-0(9)*, 900065870) Roaring Brook Pr.

—John, Paul, George & Ben. Smith, Lane. 2006. (ENG.). 40p. (J). (gr. -1 — 1). 17.99 *(978-0-7868-4893-5(6))* Hyperion Pr.

—Madam President. Smith, Lane. 2008. 40p. (J). (gr. -1-k). 16.99 *(978-1-4231-0846-7(9))* Hyperion Pr.

—A Perfect Day. Smith, Lane. 2017. (ENG.). 32p. (J). 17.99 *(978-1-62672-536-2(5)*, 900160579) Roaring Brook Pr.

—There Is a Tribe of Kids. Smith, Lane. 2016. (ENG.). 40p. (J). 18.99 *(978-1-62672-056-5(8)*, 900133365) Roaring Brook Pr.

Smith, Lane & Cornell, Kevin. The Lulu Collection (If You Don't Read Them, She Will NOT Be Pleased) Lulu & the Brontosaurus; Lulu Walks the Dogs; Lulu's Mysterious Mission; Lulu Is Getting a Sister. Viorst, Judith. ed. 2019. (Lulu Ser.). (ENG.). 688p. (J). (gr. 1-5). pap. 32.99 *(978-1-5344-5088-2(2)*, Atheneum/Caitlyn Dlouhy Books) Simon & Schuster Children's Publishing.

Smith, Lawrence Beall. Me & Caleb. Meyer, Franklyn E. 2006. (J). kivar 16.95 *(978-0-9789388-0-2(1))* Hester Publishing.

Smith, Lee. Animal Mama's House. Fox, Rachael. 2019. (Templetown Tales Ser.: Vol. 2). (ENG.). 36p. (J). pap. 9.95 *(978-1-7953-4831-7(3))* Independently Published.

—Friends Not Food. Fox, Rachael. 2019. (Plant Based Children Ser.: Vol. 2). (ENG.). 38p. (J). pap. 9.95 *(978-1-7958-5145-9(7))* Independently Published.

—Hey! Where Do You Get Your Protein? Fox, Rachael. 2019. (Plant Based Children Ser.: Vol. 1). (ENG.). 38p. (J). pap. 9.95 *(978-1-7955-7573-7(5))* Independently Published.

S

—The Kind Monk. Fox, Rachael. 2019. (Templetown Tales Ser.: Vol. 1). (ENG.). 42p. (J). pap. 9.95 *(978-1-7953-3891-2(1))* Independently Published.

Smith, Len. Día de Recoger Cachorritos (el Piquino Labrador N° 1) Puppy Pickup Day - Spanish Edition. Cox, April M. 2019. (Little Labradoodle Ser.). (SPA.). 36p. (J). (gr. k-4). 14.95 *(978-1-7339605-3-3(8))* Little Labradoodle Publishing, LLC.

—Puppy Pickup Day: Mom's Choice Award-Winner (GOLD), October 2018. Cox, April M. 2018. (Little Labradoodle Ser.: Vol. 1). (ENG.). 36p. (J). (gr. k-3). 14.95 *(978-1-7339605-1-9(1))* Little Labradoodle Publishing, LLC.

Smith, Lesley. Little Red Hen & the Wheat. Andrews, Jackie. 2012. (ENG.). 32p. pap. 6.50 *(978-1-84135-190-2(3))* Award Pubns. Ltd. GBR. Dist: Parkwest Pubns., Inc.

—My Big Book of Rhymes. 2012. (ENG.). 96p. (J). 13.50 *(978-1-84135-134-6(2))* Award Pubns. Ltd. GBR. Dist: Parkwest Pubns., Inc.

—Three Little Kittens. Andrews, Jackie. 2012. (ENG.). 32p. (J). pap. 6.50 *(978-1-84135-197-1(0))* Award Pubns. Ltd. GBR. Dist: Parkwest Pubns., Inc.

Smith, Lisa. Little Troll. Dolan, Penny. 2008. (Tadpoles Ser.). (ENG.). 24p. (J). (gr. -1-3). lib. bdg. *(978-0-7787-3856-5(6))* Crabtree Publishing Co.

—Plip & Plop. Dolan, Penny. 2004. (Read-It! Readers Ser.). (J). lib. bdg. 18.60 *(978-1-4048-0551-4(6))*, Picture Window Bks.) Capstone.

Smith, Lori. First Times, 1 vol. Ghigna, Charles. 2017. (ENG.). 32p. (J). (gr. -1-k). 19.95 *(978-1-4598-1198-0(4))* Orca Bk. Pubs. USA.

Smith, Lori Joy. Count Your Chickens. Bogart, Jo Ellen. (ENG.). 32p. (J). (— 1). 2020. bds. 7.99 *(978-0-7352-6713-8(8))*; 2017. 16.99 *(978-1-77049-792-4(7))* Tundra Bks. CAN. (Tundra Bks.). Dist: Penguin Random Hse. LLC.

—My Canada: An Illustrated Atlas. Dearlove, Katherine. 2019. (ENG.). 32p. (J). (gr. -1-3). pap. 9.95 *(978-1-77147-377-4(0))* Owlkids Bks. Inc. CAN. Dist: Publishers Group West (PGW).

—Run Salmon Run. Lolo, Bobs &. 2018. (ENG.). 34p. (J). (gr. k-3). pap. *(978-0-9938224-0-7(1))* Bobolo Productions Inc.

Smith, Lurs Schwarz. Sing a Song with Baby, 2 vol. Thienes-Schunemann, Mary. 2003. 50p. (J). 21.95 incl. audio compact disk *(978-0-9708397-5-6(8))* Naturally You Can Sing.

Smith, Maggie. Beach Day. Roosa, Karen. 2018. (ENG.). 30p. (J). (— 1). bds. 7.99 *(978-1-328-91069-1(5)*, 1701441, HMH Books For Young Readers) Houghton Mifflin Harcourt Publishing Co.

—Good Thing You're Not an Octopus! Markes, Julie. 2006. (ENG.). 40p. (J). (gr. -1-3). pap. 7.99 *(978-0-06-443586-4(5))* HarperCollins Pubs.

—Let's Talk about Being Away from Your Parents. Berry, Joy. 2010. (Let's Talk About Ser.). (ENG.). 32p. (J). (gr. -1-k). pap. 4.99 *(978-1-60577-202-8(X))* Berry, Joy Enterprises.

—Let's Talk about Being Patient. Berry, Joy. 2010. (Let's Talk About Ser.). (ENG.). 32p. (J). (gr. -1-k). pap. 4.99 *(978-1-60577-209-7(7))* Berry, Joy Enterprises.

—Let's Talk about Being Shy. Berry, Joy. 2010. (Let's Talk About Ser.). (ENG.). 32p. (J). (gr. -1-k). pap. 4.99 *(978-1-60577-220-2(8))* Berry, Joy Enterprises.

—Let's Talk about Feeling Afraid. Berry, Joy. 2010. (Let's Talk About Ser.). (ENG.). 32p. (J). (gr. -1-k). pap. 4.99 *(978-1-60577-205-9(4))* Berry, Joy Enterprises.

—Let's Talk about Feeling Angry. Berry, Joy. 2010. (Let's Talk About Ser.). (ENG.). 32p. (J). (gr. -1-k). pap. 4.99 *(978-1-60577-207-3(0))* Berry, Joy Enterprises.

—Let's Talk about Feeling Disappointed. Berry, Joy. 2010. (Let's Talk About Ser.). (ENG.). 32p. (J). (gr. -1-k). pap. 4.99 *(978-1-60577-204-2(6))* Berry, Joy Enterprises.

—Let's Talk about Feeling Jealous. Berry, Joy. 2010. (Let's Talk About Ser.). (ENG.). 32p. (J). (gr. -1-k). pap. 4.99 *(978-1-60577-223-3(2))* Berry, Joy Enterprises.

—Let's Talk about Feeling Sad. Berry, Joy. 2010. (Let's Talk About Ser.). (ENG.). 32p. (J). (gr. -1-k). pap. 4.99 *(978-1-60577-206-6(2))* Berry, Joy Enterprises.

—Let's Talk about Feeling Worried. Berry, Joy. 2010. (Let's Talk About Ser.). (ENG.). 32p. (J). (gr. -1-k). pap. 4.99 *(978-1-60577-221-9(6))* Berry, Joy Enterprises.

—Let's Talk about Getting Hurt. Berry, Joy. 2010. (Let's Talk About Ser.). (ENG.). 32p. (J). (gr. -1-k). pap. 4.99 *(978-1-60577-203-5(8))* Berry, Joy Enterprises.

—Let's Talk about Needing Attention. Berry, Joy. 2010. (Let's Talk About Ser.). (ENG.). 32p. (J). (gr. -1-k). pap. 4.99 *(978-1-60577-222-6(4))* Berry, Joy Enterprises.

—¡Libro! George, Kristine O'Connell. 2008. (ENG.). 30p. (J). (gr. k — 1). bds. 5.95 *(978-0-547-15406-0(2)*, 1052181) Houghton Mifflin Harcourt Publishing Co.

—What Does Bunny See? A Book of Colors & Flowers. Park, Linda Sue. 2018. (ENG.). 32p. (J). (gr. -1-3). pap. 7.99 *(978-1-328-88611-8(5)*, 1698480, HMH Books For Young Readers) Houghton Mifflin Harcourt Publishing Co.

Smith, Mandy M. Evan & Cassie Go on a Train Meet, 1 vol. Smith, B. M. 2009. 35p. pap. 24.95 *(978-1-60836-552-4(2))* America Star Bks.

Smith, Marcelle. Jasmine Finds a Doctor. Smith, Leone. 2011. 30p. pap. 12.50 *(978-1-61204-042-4(X)*, Strategic Bk. Publishing) Strategic Book Publishing & Rights Agency (SBPRA).

Smith, Mary Ann Free. Come Follow Me: A Child's Guide to Faith, Hope, & Charity. Newell, Karmel H. 2003. (J). 16.95 *(978-1-57008-809-4(8)*, Bookcraft, Inc.) Deseret Bk. Co.

Smith, Mary C. A Day in the Life of William Bray Goat. Smith, Mary C. Date not set. (J). 16.95 *(978-1-889668-11-6(7))* Smith & Daniel.

Smith, Mary Claire. The Nightspinners. Petty, Kate. 2004. (ENG.). 32p. (J). pap. 8.99 *(978-1-84255-105-9(1)*, Dolphin Paperbacks) Orion Publishing Group, Ltd. GBR. Dist: Trafalgar Square Publishing.

Smith, Mary Elizabeth. Coffee with Orange Sherbert: Friendship Can Be Found Where Eyes & Hearts Are Open. Shell, S. E. 2012. (ENG.). 42p. (J). pap. 14.99 *(978-0-9885461-2-7(4))* Osherbert Bks., LLC.

Smith, Matt. All God's Bugs. Derico, Laura Ring. 2015. (Faith That Sticks Bks.). (ENG.). 24p. (J). pap. 3.99 *(978-1-4964-0317-9(7)*, 4611992) Tyndale Hse. Pubs.

—Lenny Cyrus, School Virus. Schreiber, Joe. 2014. (ENG.). 288p. (J). (gr. 5-7). pap. 16.99 *(978-0-544-33628-5(3)*, 1584174, HMH Books For Young Readers) Houghton Mifflin Harcourt Publishing Co.

Smith, Matt. Barbarian Lord. Smith, Matt. 2014. (ENG.). 176p. (YA). (gr. 7-12). 17.99 *(978-0-547-85906-4(6)*, 1502475) Houghton Mifflin Harcourt Publishing Co.

Smith, Matthew, et al. Enemies & Allies, Vol. 4. Marz, Ron. 2004. (Path Ser.: Vol. 4). 160p. (YA). pap. 15.95 *(978-1-59314-052-6(5))* CrossGeneration Comics, Inc.

Smith, Mavis. Fluffy's Happy Halloween. McMullan, Kate. 2004. (Fluffy, the Classroom Guinea Pig Ser.). 40p. (J). lib. bdg. 15.00 *(978-1-59054-464-8(1))* Fitzgerald Bks.

Smith, Michelle. Travis Finds the Truth. Morrissey, Melissa. 2018. (ENG.). 54p. (J). (gr. 1-6). 24.00 *(978-0-9987057-7-4(2)*, Shining Hall) Twelve Winters Pr.

Smith, Mike. Amelia Earhart (the First Names Series) Prentice, Andrew. (First Names Ser.). (ENG.). (J). (gr. 3-7). 2020. 176p. pap. 6.99 *(978-1-4197-4089-3(X)*, 1279103); 2019. 160p. 9.99 *(978-1-4197-3741-1(4))* Abrams, Inc. (Abrams Bks. for Young Readers).

—Malala Yousafzai (the First Names Series) Williamson, Lisa. 2020. (First Names Ser.). (ENG.). 160p. (J). (gr. 3-7). 9.99 *(978-1-4197-4074-9(1)*, 1279301, Abrams Bks. for Young Readers) Abrams, Inc.

Smith, Miranda. Space: The Definitive Visual Catalog. Smith, Miranda. Callery, Sean. 2018. 208p. (J). (gr. 3-7). pap. 19.99 *(978-1-338-29196-4(3))* Scholastic, Inc.

Smith, Nancy C. The Chester Town Tea Party, 1 vol. Seabrooke, Brenda. 2009. (ENG.). 30p. (J). (gr. -1-3). 8.95 *(978-0-87033-422-1(0)*, 9780870334221, Cornell Maritime Pr./Tidewater Pubs.) Schiffer Publishing, Ltd.

Smith, Naniloa. The Children are Happy CD with Animals from the Southwest. Smith, Naniloa. 2004. (J). cd-rom 5.00 *(978-0-9744005-2-5(1))* In the Desert.

Smith, Nathan. Little Flathead & the Black Pearl. Wakefield, Nelida. 2009. 36p. pap. 12.99 *(978-1-59858-828-6(1))* Dog Ear Publishing, LLC.

Smith, Nikkolas. The Golden Girls of Rio. 2016. (ENG.). 32p. (J). (gr. -1-3). 16.99 *(978-1-5107-2247-7(5)*, Sky Pony Pr.) Skyhorse Publishing Co., Inc.

—World Cup Women: Megan, Alex, & the Team USA Soccer Champs. Walters, Meg. 2019. (ENG.). 32p. (J). (-3). 16.99 *(978-1-5107-5629-8(9)*, Sky Pony Pr.) Skyhorse Publishing Co., Inc.

Smith, Ora. A Christmas Story of Light. Smith, Ora. 2018. (ENG.). 34p. (J). (gr. k-2). 21.99 *(978-0-9980410-0-1(9))*; 12.99 *(978-0-9980410-1-8(7))* Lighten Pr.

Smith, Owen. Magnus at the Fire. Armstrong, Jennifer. 2005. (ENG.). 32p. (J). (gr. k-3). 18.99 *(978-0-689-83922-1(7)*, Simon & Schuster Bks. For Young Readers) Simon & Schuster Bks. For Young Readers.

Smith, P. Athene. Captive Birds in Health & Disease: A Practical Guide for Those Who Keep Gamebirds, Raptors, Parrots, Waterfowl & Other Species. Smith, P. Athene, tr. Cooper, John E. & Cooper, Margaret. 2003. (Act Ser.). (ENG.). 132p. 34.95 *(978-0-88839-538-2(8))* Hancock Hse. Pubs.

Smith, P. D. M. Phooey & the Dancing Pirates. Smith, P. D. M. 2018. (Adventures of Phooey Ser.: Vol. 3). (ENG.). 36p. (J). pap. 9.95 *(978-1-7287-8021-4(7))* Independently Published.

Smith, Phil. How Does a Plant Grow? Lowery, Lawrence F. (ENG.). (J). 2013. E-Book 11.95 *(978-1-936959-60-0(7))*; 2012. 40p. pap. 11.95 *(978-1-936959-47-1(X))* National Science Teachers Assn.

—How Tall Was Milton? Lowery, Lawrence F. 2012. (I Wonder Why Ser.). (ENG.). 40p. (J). (gr. k-3). pap. 11.95 *(978-1-936959-43-3(7))* National Science Teachers Assn.

—Rubber vs. Glass: I Wonder Why. Lowery, Lawrence F. 2014. (I Wonder Why Ser.). (ENG.). 36p. (J). (gr. k-3). pap. 11.95 *(978-1-938946-50-9(2))* National Science Teachers Assn.

Smith, R. M. An A to Z Walk in the Park (Animal Alphabet Book) Smith, R. M. 2008. (ENG.). 32p. (J). per. 7.95 *(978-0-615-19572-8(5))* Clarence-Henry Bks.

Smith, Rachael. Flying Solo. Stephas, Kristi. 2005. 40p. (J). 16.95 *(978-0-9764983-2-2(4))* Toy Truck Publishing.

Smith, Rachel. A Purple Hippopotamus Pillow & Pink Penguin Sheets. Maurer, Amy J. 2006. 52p. (J). 19.99 *(978-1-59879-239-3(3))*; per. 15.99 *(978-1-59879-167-9(2))* Lifevest Publishing, Inc.

Smith, Raissa B., jt. illus. see Smith, Brock R.

Smith, Richard. The Trouble with Adam's Heart. Bancroft, Myles. Brouillette, Peter, ed. 2004. (YA). per. 19.99 *(978-0-9760419-4-8(4))* ThatsMyLife Co.

Smith, Richard G. The Princess of Booray. Murphy, Emily. 2005. (J). *(978-0-9742891-2-0(4))* Marriwell Publishing.

Smith, Richard Shirley. The Prettiest Love Letters in the World: Letters Between Lucrezia Borgia & Pietro Bembo 1503 to 1519. Shankland, Hugh, tr. 2005. 111p. (YA). reprint ed. pap. 17.00 *(978-0-7567-9495-8(1))* DIANE Publishing Co.

Smith, Roberta. The Stories Huey Tells. Cameron, Ann. 2018. (Julian's World Ser.). (ENG.). 112p. (J). (gr. 1-4). lib. bdg. 12.99 *(978-0-525-57987-8(7)*, Random Hse. Bks. for Young Readers) Random Hse. Children's Bks.

Smith, Robin W. If You Got It a Truck Brought It: For We the People. Smith, Robin W. 2018. (If You Got It, a Truck Brought It Ser.: Vol. 2). (ENG.). 16p. (J). (gr. 2-4). pap. 11.00 *(978-1-64316-153-2(9))* Bright Tyke Creations LLC.

Smith, Robin Wayne. If You Got It, a Truck Brought It. Smith, Robin Wayne. 2012. 20p. pap. 6.00 *(978-0-615-63721-1(3))* Bright Tyke Creations LLC.

Smith, Ruth-Mary. Everybody Can Dance! Navolio, Kara. 2019. (ENG.). 32p. (J). (gr. k-3). 21.95 *(978-1-947860-36-0(4))*; 13.95 *(978-1-947860-39-1(9))* Brandylane Pubs., Inc.

Smith, Samayyah. I Say! Vaughn-Jackson, N. Vanessa. 2019. (ENG.). 42p. (J). (gr. k-6). 20.99 *(978-1-7337970-0-9(9))*; pap. 14.99 *(978-1-7337970-1-6(7))* Get the Word Out, Inc.

Smith, Sandra. Come Follow Me Bk. 1: Understanding One's Worth: Color Orange. Allgood, Jean. l.t. ed. 2004. 23p. (J). 14.95 *(978-0-9741627-3-7(6))* PricePoint+Publications.

Smith, Sarah. Where's My Mommy? 2009. (J). *(978-0-7607-8404-4(3))* Barnes & Noble, Inc.

Smith, Sarah. Home & Dry. Smith, Sarah. 2017. (Child's Play Library). (ENG.). 32p. (J). pap. *(978-1-84643-756-4(3))* Child's Play International Ltd.

Smith, Shane W. The Lesser Evil, Book 3 Comic Book. Smith, Shane W. 2012. 114p. pap. *(978-1-927384-04-6(4))* Zeta Comics.

Smith, Simon. Eggs, Legs, Wings: A Butterfly Life Cycle, 1 vol. Knudsen, Shannon. 2011. (First Graphics: Nature Cycles Ser.). (ENG.). 24p. (gr. 1-3). (J). pap. 6.29 *(978-1-4296-6228-4(X))*; pap. 35.70 *(978-1-4296-6397-7(9))* Capstone.

—Out-Of-This-World Aliens: Hidden Picture Puzzles, 1 vol. Kalz, Jill. 2013. (Seek It Out Ser.). (ENG.). 32p. (J). (gr. k-3). 27.32 *(978-1-4048-7942-3(0)*, Picture Window Bks.) Capstone.

Smith, Simon, et al. Poet in You, 1 vol. Fandel, Jennifer et al. 2014. (Poet in You Ser.). (ENG.). 32p. (J). (gr. 2-4). lib. bdg., lib. bdg., lib. bdg. 111.96 *(978-1-4795-3358-9(0)*, Picture Window Bks.) Capstone.

Smith, Simon. Seed, Sprout, Fruit: An Apple Tree Life Cycle, 1 vol. Knudsen, Shannon. 2011. (First Graphics: Nature Cycles Ser.). (ENG.). 24p. (gr. 1-3). (J). pap. 6.29 *(978-1-4296-6230-7(1))*; pap. 35.70 *(978-1-4296-6399-1(5))* Capstone.

Smith, Simon, et al. Tickles, Pickles, & Floofing Persnickles: Reading & Writing Nonsense Poems, 1 vol. Miller, Connie Colwell et al. 2014. (Poet in You Ser.). (ENG.). 32p. (J). (gr. 2-4). pap. 9.95 *(978-1-4795-2949-0(4))*; lib. bdg. 27.99 *(978-1-4795-2198-2(1))* Capstone. (Picture Window Bks.).

—Trust, Truth, & Ridiculous Goofs: Reading & Writing Friendship Poems, 1 vol. Fandel, Jennifer et al. 2014. (Poet in You Ser.). (ENG.). 32p. (J). (gr. 2-4). lib. bdg. 27.99 *(978-1-4795-2199-9(X)*, Picture Window Bks.) Capstone.

Smith, Simon & Epstein, Len. Seek It Out. Kalz, Jill. 2013. (Seek It Out Ser.). (ENG.). 32p. (J). (gr. k-3). 29.85 *(978-1-4048-8081-8(X)*, Picture Window Bks.) Capstone.

Smith, Simon, jt. illus. see Epstein, Len.

Smith, Sindy. Charlie the Chipmunk & the Lost Goldmine. Smith, Sindy. 2012. 38p. 29.95 *(978-1-4626-9865-3(4))* America Star Bks.

—Dadu the Dolphin. Smith, Sindy. 2012. 24p. 29.95 *(978-1-4626-9862-2(X))* America Star Bks.

—Indy the Unicorn Prince. Smith, Sindy. 2012. 46p. 29.95 *(978-1-4626-9864-6(6))* America Star Bks.

—Little Lucy Lou. Smith, Sindy. 2012. 38p. 29.95 *(978-1-4489-3350-1(1))* America Star Bks.

—Mr. Minko. Smith, Sindy. 2012. 38p. 29.95 *(978-1-4626-9863-9(8))* America Star Bks.

—Rosie the Rottweiler. Smith, Sindy. 2012. 26p. 29.95 *(978-1-4626-9860-8(3))* America Star Bks.

Smith, Stephan. The Day of the Sandwich. Salzman, Jeremiah. 2010. (Very Small Adventures of Daisie Pup! Ser.). 48p. (J). pap. 8.99 *(978-0-9842632-8-8(4))* Salzman Bks. LLC.

—Mike's Adventure Packs: England. Salzman, Jeremiah. 2010. (Mike's Adventure Packs Ser.). 144p. (J). pap. 16.95 *(978-0-9842632-5-7(X))* Salzman Bks. LLC.

Smith, Stephen, photos by. Choosing a Dance School: What Every Parent Should Consider. 2008. (ENG., 113p. (YA). spiral bd. 15.00 *(978-0-9801919-2-9(0))* Thacker Hse. Enterprises.

Smith, Steven. The Little Lost Egg. Smith, Paul. 2017. (ENG.). (gr. 1). pap. *(978-1-78222-500-3(5))* Paragon Publishing, Rothersthorpe.

Smith, Sue Millar. Raspberry & Turner. Reid, Joy. 2004. 32p. pap. 17.50 *(978-1-4120-2927-8(9))* Trafford Publishing.

Smith, Suzanna. Beautiful Mended Heart. Jethwa, Hemal. 2019. (ENG.). 38p. (J). pap. 12.99 ***(978-1-6971-8020-6(5))*** Independently Published.

Smith, Suzanna. Zavia the Stripeless Zebra. Benham, Tara. 2018. (ENG.). 40p. (J). pap. 12.00 *(978-1-7277-2391-5(0))* CreateSpace Independent Publishing Platform.

Smith, Sydney. Canada Year by Year. MacLeod, Elizabeth. 2016. (ENG.). 96p. (J). (gr. 3-7). 21.99 *(978-1-77138-397-4(6))* Kids Can Pr., Ltd. CAN. Dist: Hachette Bk. Group.

—The Dread Crew: Pirates of the Backwoods, 1 vol. Inglis, Kate. ed. 2010. (ENG.). 196p. (J). (gr. 4-7). pap. 12.95 *(978-1-55109-775-6(3)*, 8ae420af-4872-4d0b-9bf2-dc9b65a94548) Nimbus Publishing, Ltd. CAN. Dist: Baker & Taylor Publisher Services (BTPS).

—I Talk Like a River. Scott, Jordan. 2020. (ENG.). 40p. (J). (gr. -1-3). 18.99 *(978-0-8234-4559-2(3)*, Neal Porter Bks) Holiday Hse., Inc.

—Inkling. Oppel, Kenneth. (ENG.). 272p. (J). (gr. 3-7). 2020. 7.99 *(978-1-5247-7284-0(4)*, Yearling); 2018. 17.99 *(978-1-5247-7281-9(X)*, Knopf Bks. for Young Readers); 2018. lib. bdg. 20.99 *(978-1-5247-7282-6(8)*, Knopf Bks. for Young Readers) Random Hse. Children's Bks.

—Knock about with the Fitzgerald-Trouts. Spalding, Esta. 2017. 304p. (J). (gr. 3-7). 16.99 *(978-0-316-29860-5(3))* Little, Brown Bks. for Young Readers.

—Look Out for the Fitzgerald-Trouts. Spalding, Esta. 2017. 256p. (J). (gr. 3-7). pap. 6.99 *(978-0-316-29857-5(3))* Little, Brown Bks. for Young Readers.

—Mabel Murple, 1 vol. Fitch, Sheree. ed. 2011. (ENG.). 24p. (J). (gr. 1-3). pap. 13.95 *(978-1-55109-859-3(8)*, ad9ea123-b9f4-440e-b848-cf1c6fd659dc) Nimbus Publishing, Ltd. CAN. Dist: Baker & Taylor Publisher Services (BTPS).

—Music Is for Everyone, 1 vol. Barber, Jill. 2017. (ENG.). 32p. (J). (gr. 1-3). pap. 12.95 *(978-1-77108-535-9(5)*, 3e50ab72-6300-460b-929f-73af9255046d) Nimbus Publishing, Ltd. CAN. Dist: Baker & Taylor Publisher Services (BTPS).

—Pit Pony: The Picture Book. Barkhouse, Joyce & Barkhouse, Janet. 2012. (ENG.). 32p. (J). (gr. -1-2). 14.95 *(978-1-4595-0143-0(8)*, 0143) Formac Publishing Co., Ltd. CAN. Dist: Formac Lorimer Bks. Ltd.

—Sidewalk Flowers, 1 vol. Lawson, JonArno. 2015. (ENG.). 32p. (J). (gr. -1-2). 16.95 *(978-1-55498-431-2(9))* Groundwood Bks. CAN. Dist: Publishers Group West (PGW).

—There Were Monkeys in My Kitchen, 1 vol. Fitch, Sheree. 2nd ed. 2013. (ENG.). 32p. (J). (gr. k-2). pap. 12.95 *(978-1-55109-994-1(2)*, 6ca3dd63-afeb-401e-a8e3-fb16d5d873fc) Nimbus Publishing, Ltd. CAN. Dist: Baker & Taylor Publisher Services (BTPS).

—Town Is by the Sea, 1 vol. Schwartz, Joanne. 2017. (ENG.). 52p. (J). (gr. k-4). 19.95 *(978-1-55498-871-6(3))* Groundwood Bks. CAN. Dist: Publishers Group West (PGW).

—The White Cat & the Monk: A Retelling of the Poem Pangur Bán, 1 vol. Bogart, Jo Ellen. 2016. (ENG.). 32p. (J). (gr. -1-3). 18.95 *(978-1-55498-780-1(6))* Groundwood Bks. CAN. Dist: Publishers Group West (PGW).

Smith, Sydney . Smoot: A Rebellious Shadow. Cuevas, Michelle. 2017. 48p. (J). (gr. -1-3). 17.99 *(978-0-525-42969-2(7)*, Dial Bks) Penguin Young Readers Group.

Smith, Teri. Island Dream. Connelly, Susan. 2018. (ENG.). 16p. (J). pap. *(978-1-78623-240-3(5))* Grosvenor Hse. Publishing Ltd.

—Mangrove Fun in the Florida Sun. Connelly, Susan. 2016. (ENG.). 19p. (J). pap. *(978-1-78623-031-7(3))* Grosvenor Hse. Publishing Ltd.

Smith, Tim. Custer's Last Stand, 1 vol. Dunn, Joeming W. 2008. (Graphic History Ser.). (ENG.). 32p. (J). (gr. 3-8). 29.93 *(978-1-60270-181-6(4)*, 9054, Graphic Planet - Fiction) Magic Wagon.

—The Oregon Trail, 1 vol. Dunn, Joeming W. 2008. (Graphic History Ser.). (ENG.). 32p. (J). (gr. 3-8). 29.93 *(978-1-60270-183-0(0)*, 9058, Graphic Planet - Fiction) Magic Wagon.

Smith, Tim, jt. illus. see Young, Stephanie.

Smith, Tod. The Explosive World of Volcanoes with Max Axiom, Super Scientist, 1 vol. Harbo, Christopher L. (Graphic Science Ser.). (ENG.). 32p. (J). (gr. 3-9). 2008. pap. 8.10 *(978-1-4296-1770-3(5))*; 2007. 31.32 *(978-1-4296-0144-3(2))* Capstone. (Capstone Pr.).

—How to Draw Amazing Motorcycles, 1 vol. Sautter, Aaron. 2007. (Drawing Cool Stuff Ser.). (ENG.). 32p. (J). (gr. 3-9). 28.65 *(978-1-4296-0073-6(X)*, Capstone Pr.) Capstone.

Smith, Tod & Garcia, Eduardo. Norse Myths, 4 vols. Bowen, Carl et al. 2016. (Norse Myths: a Viking Graphic Novel Ser.). (ENG.). 56p. (J). (gr. 4-8). lib. bdg., lib. bdg., lib. bdg. 111.96 *(978-1-4965-3519-1(7)*, Stone Arch Bks.) Capstone.

Smith, Tod & Lokus, Rex. Loki & Thor. Bowen, Carl. 2016. (Norse Myths: a Viking Graphic Novel Ser.). (ENG.). 56p. (J). (gr. 4-8). pap. 5.95 *(978-1-4965-3494-1(8))*; lib. bdg. 27.99 *(978-1-4965-3490-3(5))* Capstone. (Stone Arch Bks.).

Smith, Tod G. Around the World in 80 Days. Verne, Jules & Lokus, Rex. 2015. (Graphic Revolve: Common Core Editions Ser.). (ENG.). 72p. (J). (gr. 5-9). pap. 6.95 *(978-1-4965-0381-7(3)*, Stone Arch Bks.) Capstone.

—Dead Man's Map, 1 vol. Peschke, Marci. 2008. (Vortex Bks.). (ENG.). 112p. (J). (gr. 5-9). pap. 7.19 *(978-1-59889-921-4(X)*, 1271328, Stone Arch Bks.) Capstone.

—Exploring Ecosystems with Max Axiom, Super Scientist, 1 vol. Biskup, Agnieszka. 2007. (Graphic Science Ser.). (ENG.). 32p. (J). (gr. 3-9). per. 8.10 *(978-0-7368-7894-4(7))* Capstone.

—Exploring Ecosystems with Max Axiom Super Scientist: 4D an Augmented Reading Science Experience. Biskup, Agnieszka. 2018. (Graphic Science 4D Ser.). (ENG.). 32p. (J). (gr. 3-9). lib. bdg. 34.65 *(978-1-5435-2946-3(1)*, 138535, Capstone Pr.) Capstone.

—Exploring Ecosystems with Max Axiom Super Scientist: An Augmented Reading Science Experience. Biskup, Agnieszka. 2018. (Graphic Science 4D Ser.). (ENG.). 32p. (J). (gr. 3-9). pap. 7.95 *(978-1-5435-2957-9(7)*, 138557, Capstone Pr.) Capstone.

—The Explosive World of Volcanoes with Max Axiom Super Scientist: 4D an Augmented Reading Science Experience. Harbo, Christopher L. 2018. (Graphic Science 4D Ser.). (ENG.). 32p. (J). (gr. 3-9). lib. bdg. 34.65 *(978-1-5435-2947-0(X)*, 138536, Capstone Pr.) Capstone.

—The Explosive World of Volcanoes with Max Axiom Super Scientist: An Augmented Reading Science Experience. Harbo, Christopher L. 2018. (Graphic Science 4D Ser.). (ENG.). 32p. (J). (gr. 3-9). pap. 7.95 *(978-1-5435-2958-6(5)*, 138558, Capstone Pr.) Capstone.

—Johann Gutenberg & the Printing Press, 1 vol. Olson, Kay Melchisedech. 2006. (Inventions & Discovery Ser.). (ENG.). 32p. (J). (gr. 3-9). pap. 8.10 *(978-0-7368-9644-3(9)*, Capstone Pr.) Capstone.

—Lecciones Sobre la Seguridad en el Trabajo Científico. Lemke, Donald B. & Adamson, Thomas K. 2013. (Ciencia Gráfica Ser.). (SPA.). 32p. (J). (gr. 3-9). lib. bdg. 31.32 *(978-1-62065-183-4(1))* Capstone.

—Lessons in Science Safety with Max Axiom, Super Scientist, 1 vol. Lemke, Donald B. & Adamson, Thomas K. 2007. (Graphic Science Ser.). (ENG.). 32p. (J). (gr. 3-9). 31.32 *(978-0-7368-6834-1(8))*; per. 8.10 *(978-0-7368-7887-6(4))* Capstone.

—Lessons in Science Safety with Max Axiom Super Scientist: 4D an Augmented Reading Science Experience. Lemke, Donald B. & Adamson, Thomas K. 2018. (Graphic Science 4D Ser.). (ENG.). 32p. (J). (gr. 3-9). lib. bdg. 34.65 *(978-1-5435-2948-7(8)*, 138537, Capstone Pr.) Capstone.

—Lessons in Science Safety with Max Axiom Super Scientist: An Augmented Reading Science Experience. Lemke, Donald B. & Adamson, Thomas K. 2018. (Graphic

Science 4D Ser.). (ENG.). 32p. (J). (gr. 3-9). pap. 7.95 *(978-1-5435-2959-3(3)*, 138559, Capstone Pr.) Capstone.

—La Leyenda Del Jinete Sin Cabeza, 1 vol. Irving, Washington & Gutierrez, Dave. Tobon, Sara, tr. 2009. (Classic Fiction Ser.). (SPA.). 72p. (J). (gr. 5-9). lib. bdg. 27.99 *(978-1-4342-1688-5(8)*, Stone Arch Bks.) Capstone.

—El Mundo Explosivo de los Volcanes con Max Axiom, Supercientífico. Harbo, Christopher L. Strictly Spanish, LLC., tr. 2012. (Ciencia Gráfica Ser.). (SPA.). 32p. (J). (gr. 3-9). lib. bdg. 31.32 *(978-1-4296-9237-3(5))* Capstone.

—The Surprising World of Bacteria with Max Axiom, Super Scientist: 4D an Augmented Reading Science Experience. Biskup, Agnieszka Jòzefina. 2019. (Graphic Science 4D Ser.). (ENG.). 32p. (J). (gr. 3-9). pap. 7.95 *(978-1-5435-7546-0(3)*, 141078); lib. bdg. 34.65 *(978-1-5435-7249-0(9)*, 140590) Capstone.

—Theseus & the Minotaur, 1 vol. Yomtov, Nel et al. (Mythology Ser.). (ENG.). 72p. (J). (gr. 5-9). 2010. pap. 7.15 *(978-1-4342-1387-7(0))*; 2009. lib. bdg. 27.99 *(978-1-4342-1171-2(1))* Capstone. (Stone Arch Bks.).

Smith, Tod G. & Milgram, Al. The Earth-Shaking Facts about Earthquakes with Max Axiom, Super Scientist, 1 vol. Krohn, Katherine. 2008. (Graphic Science Ser.). (ENG.). 32p. (J). (gr. 3-9). per. 8.10 *(978-1-4296-1759-8(4))* Capstone.

—Investigating the Scientific Method with Max Axiom, Super Scientist, 1 vol. Lemke, Donald B. 2008. (Graphic Science Ser.). (ENG.). 32p. (J). (gr. 3-9). per. 8.10 *(978-1-4296-1760-4(8)*, Capstone Pr.) Capstone.

Smith, Tod G. & Milgrom, Al. The Earth-Shaking Facts about Earthquakes with Max Axiom, Super Scientist. Krohn, Katherine E. 2008. (Graphic Science Ser.). (ENG.). 32p. (J). (gr. 3-9). 31.32 *(978-1-4296-1328-6(9))* Capstone.

—Steve Jobs, Steve Wozniak, & the Personal Computer, 1 vol. Lemke, Donald B. 2006. (Inventions & Discovery Ser.). (ENG.). 32p. (J). (gr. 3-9). 31.32 *(978-0-7368-6488-6(1)*, Capstone Pr.) Capstone.

Smith, Tod G., jt. illus. see Milgrom, Al.

Smith, Tod G., jt. illus. see Smith, Todd Aaron.

Smith, Todd Aaron. The Average Monkey. Smith, Todd Aaron. 2003. (Higby the Monkey Ser.). 32p. (J). pap. 4.97 *(978-1-58660-857-6(6))* Barbour Publishing, Inc.

—Higby Throws a Fit. Smith, Todd Aaron. 2003. (Higby the Monkey Ser.). 32p. (J). pap. 4.97 *(978-1-58660-858-3(4))* Barbour Publishing, Inc.

Smith, Todd Aaron & Smith, Tod G. Exploring Ecosystems with Max Axiom, Super Scientist, 1 vol. Biskup, Agnieszka. 2007. (Graphic Science Ser.). (ENG.). 32p. (J). (gr. 3-9). 31.32 *(978-0-7368-6842-6(9))* Capstone.

Smith, Tracy. Mommy Has 1 Foot: Learning about Numbers - Learning about People. Derke, Connie Butterfield. 2003. (Kayla's Learning Books). 24p. (J). (gr. 1-6). pap. 5.95 *(978-0-9747063-0-6(2))* Derke, Connie.

Smith, Vernon. Jokes for Crescent City Kids, 1 vol. Strecker, Michael. 2018. (ENG.). 64p. (gr. k-2). pap. 8.95 *(978-1-4556-2427-0(6)*, Pelican Publishing) Arcadia Publishing.

—The King Cake Baby, 1 vol. Dawson, Keila. 2015. (ENG.). 32p. (J). (gr. k-3). 8.99 *(978-1-4556-2013-5(0)*, Pelican Publishing) Arcadia Publishing.

—When the Morning Comes, 1 vol. Pardo, Juan. 2019. (ENG.). 32p. (gr. -1-3). 16.99 *(978-1-4556-2439-3(X)*, Pelican Publishing) Arcadia Publishing.

Smith, W. D. A Puppy for Athena. Wilkie, G. Lamar. 2016. (ENG.). 48p. (J). pap. 10.75 *(978-0-9971141-0-2(X))* G. Lamar Wilkie.

Smith, Wd. Christopher's Tornado. Wilkie, G. Lamar. 2016. (ENG.). 42p. (J). pap. 9.75 *(978-0-9971141-1-9(8))* G. Lamar Wilkie.

Smith, Wendy. Exploring the Earth with John Wesley Powell. Ross, Michael Elsohn. 2005. (Naturalist's Apprentice Biographies Ser.). 48p. (gr. 3-6). lib. bdg. 19.93 *(978-1-57505-254-0(7))* Lerner Publishing Group.

—Fish Watching with Eugenie Clark. Ross, Michael Elsohn. 2005. (Naturalist's Apprentice Biographies Ser.). 48p. (gr. 3-6). lib. bdg. 19.93 *(978-1-57505-384-4(5))* Lerner Publishing Group.

—Nature Art with Chiura Obata. Ross, Michael Elsohn. 2005. (Naturalist's Apprentice Biographies Ser.). 48p. (gr. 3-6). lib. bdg. 19.93 *(978-1-57505-378-3(0))* Lerner Publishing Group.

—Pond Watching with Ann Morgan. Ross, Michael Elsohn. 2005. (Naturalist's Apprentice Biographies Ser.). 48p. (gr. 3-6). lib. bdg. 19.93 *(978-1-57505-385-1(3))* Lerner Publishing Group.

—Red Fox at Hickory Lane. Hollenbeck, Kathleen M. 2005. (Smithsonian's Backyard Ser.). (ENG.). 32p. (J). (gr. -1-2). 8.95 *(978-1-59249-117-9(0)*, SC5025); 19.95 *(978-1-59249-116-2(2)*, BC5025); 9.95 *(978-1-59249-120-9(0)*, PB5075); 4.95 *(978-1-59249-114-8(6)*, B5075) Soundprints.

—We Both Read Bilingual Edition-About Bats/Acerca de Los Murcielagos. McKay, Sindy. Canetti, Yanitzia, tr. 2014. (We Both Read - Level K-1 (Quality) Ser.). (ENG & SPA.). 44p. (J). (gr. k-1). pap. 4.99 *(978-1-60115-060-8(1))* Treasure Bay, Inc.

Smith, Wendy. Red Fox at Hickory Lane. Smith, Wendy, tr. Hollenbeck, Kathleen M. 2005. (Smithsonian's Backyard Ser.). (ENG.). 32p. (J). (gr. -1-2). 15.95 *(978-1-59249-113-1(8)*, B5025); pap. 6.95 *(978-1-59249-115-5(4)*, S5025) Soundprints.

Smith, Wendy, jt. illus. see Hunt, Judith.

Smith, William. Alby's Letters to Henry: Written from Isle of Mull. Tennant Iain Staff. 2007. (ENG.). 176p. (J). pap. 15.99 *(978-1-903071-14-4(3))* Bene Factum Publishing, Ltd. GBR. Dist: Independent Pubs. Group.

Smith, William E. Hank & Kale Visit the Aquarium. Snowden, Gary. 2012. 24p. pap. 8.99 *(978-1-938768-05-7(1))* Gypsy Pubns.

Smith, Zak. Worst Breakfast. Mieville, China. 2016. (ENG.). 32p. (J). (gr. -1-2). 16.95 *(978-1-61775-486-9(2)*, Black Sheep) Akashic Bks.

Smithers, J. Megan. Emma: An Interactive Storybook. 2nd ed. 2005. 60p. (J). (gr. k-4). pap. 9.00 *(978-0-9713342-6-7(9))* B V Wespat.

Smitherton, Jeb. Dinos are Big Babies & Dylan's Pets. Marsoli, Lisa Ann. 2005. (J). bds. 19.99 *(978-0-9767325-7-0(2))* Toy Quest.

—Dinosaurs are Big Babies. Marsoli, Lisa Ann. 2005. (J). bds. 14.99 *(978-0-9767325-0-1(5))* Toy Quest.

—Let's Go to the Zoo. Marsoli, Lisa Ann. 2005. (J). bds. 14.99 *(978-0-9767325-4-9(8))* Toy Quest.

—Let's Go to the Zoo & Leaping Lilly. Marsoli, Lisa Ann. 2005. (J). bds. 19.99 *(978-0-9767325-6-3(4))* Toy Quest.

Smithsonian Kids, photos by. Butterflies & Moths: First Discovery Books. Wing, Scarlett. Cottage Door Press, ed. 2019. (Smithsonian Kids First Discovery Bks.). (ENG., 12p. (J). (gr. -1-1). bds. 7.99 *(978-1-68052-495-6(X)*, 1003700) Cottage Door Pr.

—Planets: And the Solar System. Murphy, Patricia J. Cottage Door Press, ed. 2019. (Smithsonian Kids First Discovery Bks.). (ENG., 12p. (J). (gr. -1-1). bds. 7.99 *(978-1-68052-706-3(1)*, 1004390) Cottage Door Pr.

—Trains Then & Now: First Discovery Books. Wing, Scarlett. Cottage Door Press, ed. 2019. (Smithsonian Kids First Discovery Bks.). (ENG., 12p. (J). (gr. -1-1). bds. 7.99 *(978-1-68052-496-3(8)*, 1003710) Cottage Door Pr.

—100 Curious Things to Count: Case Bound Big Book. Wing, Scarlett. Cottage Door Press, ed. 2018. (Smithsonian Kids Ser.). (ENG., 22p. (J). (gr. -1-2). bds. 9.99 *(978-1-68052-353-9(8)*, 1003250) Cottage Door Pr.

—100 Curious Words to Know: Case Bound Big Book. Wing, Scarlett & Cottage Door Press. 2018. (Smithsonian Kids Ser.). (ENG., 22p. (J). (gr. -1-2). bds. 9.99 *(978-1-68052-352-2(X)*, 1003240) Cottage Door Pr.

Smits, Josh. The Grumble Rumble Mumbler. Drewery, Melanie. 36p. pap. 13.00 *(978-1-86969-284-1(5))* Univ. of Hawaii Pr.

Smoak, I. W. & Washington, C. E. Brave Enough: The Story of Rob Sanford, Vermont Pioneer Boy. Washington, Ida H. 2003. vii, 128p. (J). (gr. 4-6). pap. 12.95 *(978-0-9666832-7-1(7))* Cherry Tree Bks.

Smolin, Michael. Sesame Street: the Monster at the End of This Sound Book. Stone, Jon. 2020. (Play-A-Sound Ser.). (ENG.). 28p. (J). ***(978-1-5037-5664-9(5)***, d03b9b4d-8ea4-4572-9f6e-57b5b116df77, p i kids) Phoenix International Publications, Inc.

Smoljan, Marina. Little Earth: Little Earth Says: Children, Come Outside & Play. Brooks, D. K. 2019. (ENG.). 28p. (J). ***(978-0-2288-1981-3(4))***; pap. ***(978-0-2288-1980-6(6))*** Tellwell Talent.

Smollin, Michael. Another Monster at the End of This Book (Sesame Street) Stone, Jon. 2016. (ENG.). 26p. (J). (-k). bds. 7.99 *(978-1-101-93137-0(X)*, Golden Bks.) Random Hse. Children's Bks.

—Big Bird's Red Book (Sesame Street) Cerf, Roseanne. 2019. (Little Golden Book Ser.). (ENG.). 24p. (J). (-k). 4.99 *(978-0-525-64726-3(0)*, Golden Bks.) Random Hse. Children's Bks.

—The Monster at the End of This Book. Stone, Jon. 2015. (ENG.). 26p. (J). (— 1). bds. 7.99 *(978-0-553-50873-4(3)*, Golden Bks.) Random Hse. Children's Bks.

—The Monster at the End of This Book (Sesame Street) Stone, Jon. 2004. (Big Little Golden Book Ser.). (ENG.). 32p. (J). (gr. -1-2). 8.99 *(978-0-375-82913-0(X)*, Golden Bks.) Random Hse. Children's Bks.

Smollin, Michael. Monsters at the End of This Book (Sesame Street) Stone, Jon. 2020. (Big Golden Book Ser.). (ENG.). 64p. (J). (-k). 10.99 ***(978-0-593-17781-5(9)***, Golden Bks.) Random Hse. Children's Bks.

Smollin, Michael & Swanson, Maggie. Sesame Street Little Golden Book Library 5-Book Boxed Set: My Name Is Elmo; Elmo Loves You; Elmo's Tricky Tongue Twisters; the Monster on the Bus; the Monster at the End of This Book, 5 vols. Stone, Jon & Albee, Sarah. 2017. (Little Golden Book Ser.). (ENG.). 120p. (J). (-k). 24.95 *(978-1-5247-2077-3(1)*, Golden Bks.) Random Hse. Children's Bks.

Smouse, Phil A. Jesus Wants All of Me: Based on the Classic Devotional My Utmost for His Highest. Chambers, Oswald. ltd. ed. 2003. 384p. (J). pap. 4.99 *(978-1-58660-841-5(X))* Barbour Publishing, Inc.

Smyth, Bambi. Favourite Nursery Rhymes. 15p. (J). bds. *(978-1-86503-636-6(6))* Five Mile Australia.

Smyth, Fiona. ¿Cómo Se Hace un Bebé? Spanish Language Edition. Silverberg, Cory. 2017. 36p. (J). (gr. -1-2). 11.95 *(978-1-60980-769-6(3)*, Siete Cuentos Editorial) Seven Stories Pr.

—Sex Is a Funny Word: A Book about Bodies, Feelings, & YOU. Silverberg, Cory. 2015. (ENG.). 160p. (J). (gr. 2-5). 23.95 *(978-1-60980-606-4(9)*, Triangle Square) Seven Stories Pr.

—What Makes a Baby. Silverberg, Cory. 2013. (ENG.). 36p. (J). (gr. -1-2). 18.95 *(978-1-60980-485-5(6)*, Triangle Square) Seven Stories Pr.

Smyth, Iain. The Eye of the Pharaoh: A Pop-up Whodunit. Smyth, Iain. 2005. 12p. (J). (gr. 4-8). reprint ed. pap. 17.00 *(978-0-7567-8840-7(4))* DIANE Publishing Co.

Smyth, Iain, jt. illus. see Goulding, June.

Smythe, Richard. Dozy Bear & the Secret of Food. Blackburn, Katie. 2018. (Dozy Bear Ser.). (ENG.). 32p. (J). pap. 9.95 *(978-0-571-33443-8(1)*, Faber & Faber Children's Bks.) Faber & Faber, Inc.

—Dozy Bear & the Secret of Sleep. Blackburn, Katie. 2017. (ENG.). 32p. (J). (gr. -1-3). 17.99 *(978-0-06-256426-9(9))* HarperCollins Pubs.

—Fox Explores the Night: a First Science Storybook. Jenkins, Martin. 2018. (Science Storybooks Ser.). (ENG.). 32p. (J). (-k). 16.99 *(978-0-7636-9883-6(0))* Candlewick Pr.

—Half a Giraffe? Parachini, Jodie. 2018. (ENG.). 32p. (J). 16.99 *(978-0-8075-3144-0(8)*, 807531448) Whitman, Albert & Co.

—The Messy Book. Powell-Tuck, Maudie. 2016. (ENG.). 32p. (J). (gr. -1-2). 16.99 *(978-1-68010-037-2(8))* Tiger Tales.

—The Mighty Steam Engine. Ng, Yvonne. 2019. (ENG.). 32p. (J). (gr. 1-3). 17.99 *(978-1-68152-237-1(3))* Amicus.

—Watersong. McCanna, Tim. 2017. (ENG.). 32p. (J). (gr. -1-3). 17.99 *(978-1-4814-6881-7(2)*, Simon & Schuster/Paula Wiseman Bks.) Simon & Schuster/Paula Wiseman Bks.

Smythe, Theresa. Chester's Colorful Easter Eggs. Smythe, Theresa. 2013. (ENG.). 24p. (J). (gr. -1-k). 12.99 *(978-0-8050-9326-1(5)*, 9780805093261, Holt, Henry & Co. Bks. For Young Readers) Holt, Henry & Co.

Snader, Gregory. Sadie. Krone, Thelma Smith. 2008. 6p. (J). pap. 7.95 *(978-1-934696-02-6(1)*, Shooting Star Edition) American Literary Pr.

Snaith, Andy, photos by. Lift & Learn 123. Donoghue, Stella. 2006. 24p. (gr. -1). per., bds. *(978-1-84610-030-7(5))* Make Believe Ideas.

—Lift & Learn ABC. Phillips, Sarah. 2006. 24p. (gr. -1). per., bds. *(978-1-84610-029-1(1))* Make Believe Ideas.

—Lift & Learn Colors. Gordon, Bob. 2006. 24p. (gr. -1 — 1). per., bds. *(978-1-84610-028-4(3))* Make Believe Ideas.

—Lift & Learn Opposites. Holmen, Lene. 2006. 24p. (gr. -1 — 1). per., bds. *(978-1-84610-031-4(3))* Make Believe Ideas.

—Look at Me! I'm a Ballerina! Bicknell, Joanna & Page, Nick. 2005. 23p. (J). (gr. -1-3). *(978-1-905051-72-4(7))* Make Believe Ideas.

Snape, Emily. Hey! Look at You... in the Jungle. 2018. (Hey! Look at You Bks.). (ENG.). 10p. (J). (gr. -1 — 1). bds. 7.99 *(978-1-4380-5063-8(1)*, B.E.S. Publishing) Peterson's.

—Hey! Look at You... on the Move. 2018. (Hey! Look at You Bks.). (ENG.). 10p. (J). (gr. -1 — 1). bds. 7.99 *(978-1-4380-5064-5(X)*, B.E.S. Publishing) Peterson's.

Snape, Jenny. Charlie's Harmonica. Robertson, J. Jean. 2012. (Little Birdie Bks.). (ENG.). 24p. (gr. 1-2). pap. 8.95 *(978-1-61810-312-3(1)*, 9781618103123) Rourke Educational Media.

Sneed, Brad. Big Bad Wolves at School. Krensky, Stephen. 2007. (ENG.). 32p. (J). (gr. -1-3). 18.99 *(978-0-689-83799-9(2)*, Simon & Schuster Bks. For Young Readers) Simon & Schuster Bks. For Young Readers.

—The Boy Who Was Raised by Librarians. Morris, Carla. 2019. (ENG.). 32p. (J). (gr. -1-3). pap. 7.95 *(978-1-68263-123-2(0))* Peachtree Publishing Co. Inc.

—The Boy Who Was Raised by Librarians, 1 vol. Morris, Carla. 2007. (ENG.). 32p. (J). (gr. k-3). 16.95 *(978-1-56145-391-7(9))* Peachtree Publishing Co. Inc.

—Johnny Kaw: A Tall Tale. Scillian, Devin. 2013. (ENG.). 32p. (J). (gr. 1-4). 15.95 *(978-1-58536-791-7(5)*, 202353) Sleeping Bear Pr.

—Mr. President Goes to School, 1 vol. Walton, Rick. (ENG.). 32p. (J). (gr. -1-3). 2015. pap. 7.95 *(978-1-56145-892-9(9))*; 2010. 15.95 *(978-1-56145-538-6(5))* Peachtree Publishing Co. Inc.

—Thumbelina. Andersen, Hans Christian. 2004. Orig. Title: Tummelisa. (ENG.). 40p. (J). (gr. -1-3). 17.99 *(978-0-8037-2812-7(3)*, Dial Bks) Penguin Young Readers Group.

—Washday. Bunting, Eve. 2014. (ENG.). 32p. (J). (gr. -1-3). 16.95 *(978-0-8234-2868-7(0))* Holiday Hse., Inc.

—When the Wind Blows. Clark, Stacy. 2015. (ENG.). 32p. (J). (gr. -1-3). 16.95 *(978-0-8234-3069-7(3))* Holiday Hse., Inc.

Sneed, Brad. The Boy Who Was Raised by Librarians. Sneed, Brad. 2008. (J). (gr. k-3). 27.95 incl. audio *(978-0-8045-6965-1(7))* Spoken Arts, Inc.

Sneed, Patty. Hailey's Dream. Kuhns, Jennifer. 2013. 32p. pap. 13.95 *(978-0-9846811-8-1(3))* Shalako Pr.

Sneider, Jonathan. Teddy the Dog: Be Your Own Dog. Boyle, Keri Claiborne. 2016. (Teddy the Dog Ser.: 1). (ENG.). 32p. (J). (gr. -1-3). 17.99 *(978-0-06-238283-2(7))* HarperCollins Pubs.

—Teddy the Dog: (Almost) Best in Show. Boyle, Keri Claiborne. 2017. (Teddy the Dog Ser.). (ENG.). 32p. (J). (gr. -1-3). 17.99 *(978-0-06-238284-9(5))* HarperCollins Pubs.

Snell, Alexis. The Head of the Saint. Acioli, Socorro. Hahn, Daniel, tr. from POR. 2016. (ENG.). 192p. (YA). (gr. 7). 16.99 *(978-0-553-53792-5(X)*, Delacorte Pr.) Random Hse. Children's Bks.

Snellenberger, Bonita, jt. illus. see Snellenberger, Earl.

Snellenberger, Earl & Snellenberger, Bonita. Dinosaur Activity Book: The Wonder's of God's World. Snellenberger, Earl & Snellenberger, Bonita. 2008. (ENG.). 128p. (J). (gr. 4-6). per. 9.99 *(978-0-89051-515-0(8)*, Master Books) New Leaf Publishing Group.

—Noah's Ark Pre-School Activity Book. Snellenberger, Earl & Snellenberger, Bonita. 2014. (ENG.). 98p. (J). (gr. -1-3). pap. 8.99 *(978-0-89051-832-8(7)*, Master Books) New Leaf Publishing Group.

Snerling, Tina. An Aussie Year: Twelve Months in the Life of Australian Kids. McCartney, Tania. 2nd rev. ed. 2019. (Kids' Year Ser.). (ENG.). 32p. (J). (gr. -1-6). 14.99 *(978-1-925820-27-0(0)*, 334880, EK Bks.) Exisle Publishing Pty Ltd. AUS. Dist: Hachette Bk. Group.

Snerling, Tina. A Canadian Year: Twelve Months in the Life of Canada's Kids. McCartney, Tania. 3rd ed. 2020. (Kids' Year Ser.). (ENG.). 32p. (J). (gr. -1-6). pap. 7.99 ***(978-1-925820-66-9(1)***, 337664) Exisle Publishing Pty Ltd. AUS. Dist: Hachette UK Distribution.

Snerling, Tina. An English Year: Twelve Months in the Life of England's Kids. McCartney, Tania. 2015. (Kids' Year Ser.). (ENG.). 32p. (J). (gr. -1-3). 17.99 *(978-1-921966-86-6(6)*, EK Bks.) Exisle Publishing Pty Ltd. AUS. Dist: Hachette Bk. Group.

—A New York Year: Twelve Months in the Life of New York's Kids. McCartney, Tania. 2016. (Kids' Year Ser.). (ENG.). 32p. (J). (gr. -1-3). 17.99 *(978-1-925335-07-1(0)*, EK Bks.) Exisle Publishing Pty Ltd. AUS. Dist: Hachette Bk. Group.

—Peas in a Pod. McCartney, Tania. (ENG.). 32p. (J). (gr. -1-2). 2016. pap. 9.99 *(978-1-925335-28-6(3)*, EK Bks.); 2015. 17.95 *(978-1-921966-71-2(8))* Exisle Publishing Pty Ltd. AUS. Dist: Hachette Bk. Group.

—A Scottish Year: Twelve Months in the Life of Scotland's Kids. McCartney, Tania. 2015. (Kids' Year Ser.). (ENG.). 32p. (J). (gr. -1-3). 17.99 *(978-1-921966-87-3(4)*, EK Bks.) Exisle Publishing Pty Ltd. AUS. Dist: Hachette Bk. Group.

—Tottie & Dot. McCartney, Tania. 2015. (ENG.). 32p. (J). (gr. -1-2). 17.99 *(978-1-921966-49-1(1)*, 220719) Exisle Publishing Pty Ltd. AUS. Dist: Hachette UK Distribution.

Sneyers, Joachim. Marvelous but True. Mission to the Bottom of the Sea. Leyssens, Jan. 2020. (Marvelous but True Ser.: 1). 32p. (J). (gr. 1). 16.95 *(978-1-60537-531-1(4))* Clavis Publishing.

Snider, Grant. Quiet Power: The Secret Strengths of Introverted Kids. Cain, Susan et al. 2017. (ENG.). 288p. (J). (gr. 5). 9.99 *(978-0-14-750992-5(0)*, Puffin Books) Penguin Young Readers Group.

—Quiet Power: The Secret Strengths of Introverts. Cain, Susan et al. 2016. (ENG.). 288p. (J). (gr. 5). 17.99 *(978-0-8037-4060-0(3)*, Dial Bks) Penguin Young Readers Group.

Snider, Jackie. Eight Legs Are Great! Charlesworth, Liza & Scholastic Canada Ltd. Staff. 2005. (ENG.). 16p. (J). (gr. -1-1). pap. 2.99 *(978-0-439-69019-5(6))* Scholastic, Inc.

—My Family. Cifuentes, Carolina. 2010. (My World Ser.). (ENG.). 24p. (J). (gr. -1-1). lib. bdg. 25.60 *(978-1-60754-946-8(8))* Windmill Bks.

—My Family. Cifuentes, Carolina, ed. 2010. (My World Ser.). (ENG.). 24p. (J). (gr. -1-1). pap. 8.15 *(978-1-61533-025-6(9))* Windmill Bks.

—My Family & I. Rosa-Mendoza, Gladys. Cifuentes, Carolina, ed. 2004. (English-Spanish Foundations Ser.: Vol. 4).Tr. of Mi Familia y Yo. (ENG & SPA.). 20p. (J). (gr. -1-4). bds. 6.95 *(978-0-9679748-4-2(4))* Me+Mi Publishing.

—My Family & I/Mi Familia y Yo. Rosa-Mendoza, Gladys. 2007. (English Spanish Foundations Ser.). 20p. (gr. -1-k). pap. 19.95 *(978-1-931398-80-0(1))* Me+Mi Publishing.

—The Perfect Pet. Baker, Courtney. 2003. (Hello Reader! Ser.). (J). pap. *(978-0-439-47111-4(7))* Scholastic, Inc.

Snider, K. C. The Adventures of Andy & Spirit: Book 1. Kelso, Mary Jean. 2010. 64p. pap. 9.95 *(978-1-61633-069-9(4))* Guardian Angel Publishing, Inc.

—Andy & Spirit Go to the Fair. Kelso, Mary Jean. 2008. 24p. pap. 10.95 *(978-1-935137-03-0(4))* Guardian Angel Publishing, Inc.

—Andy & Spirit in the Big Rescue. Kelso, Mary Jean. 2009. 24p. pap. 10.95 *(978-1-935137-67-2(0))* Guardian Angel Publishing, Inc.

—Andy & Spirit Meet the Rodeo Queen. Kelso, Mary Jean. 2010. 24p. pap. 10.95 *(978-1-61633-031-6(7))* Guardian Angel Publishing, Inc.

—Baby Jesus Is Missing. Phillips, Dixie. 2009. 16p. pap. 9.95 *(978-1-61633-000-2(7))* Guardian Angel Publishing, Inc.

—A Bad Mad Sad Day for Mama Bear. Calvani, Mayra. 2013. 24p. 19.95 *(978-1-61633-434-5(7))* Guardian Angel Publishing, Inc.

—Benjamin Jay Was a Bully. Glover, Emma M. 2012. 16p. pap. 9.95 *(978-1-61633-327-0(8))* Guardian Angel Publishing, Inc.

—Cartwheel Annie. Crow, Marilee. 2009. 24p. pap. 10.95 *(978-1-935137-71-9(9))* Guardian Angel Publishing, Inc.

—The Christmas Angel. Kelso, Mary Jean. 2007. 32p. (J). 11.95 *(978-1-933090-58-0(8))* Guardian Angel Publishing, Inc.

—Cowboy James. Kelso, Mary Jean. 2011. 24p. pap. 10.95 *(978-1-61633-174-0(7))*; 19.95 *(978-1-61633-178-8(X))* Guardian Angel Publishing, Inc.

—Does Heaven Get Mail? Crow, Marilee. 2008. 24p. pap. 10.95 *(978-1-935137-12-2(3))* Guardian Angel Publishing, Inc.

—God Loves You Whoever You Are. Reece, Colleen L. & DeMarco, Julie Reece. 2011. 20p. pap. 10.95 *(978-1-61633-183-2(6))* Guardian Angel Publishing, Inc.

—The Milk Horse. Luce, Catherine. 2011. 20p. pap. 10.95 *(978-1-61633-168-9(2))* Guardian Angel Publishing, Inc.

—Monster Maddie. Stephenson, Susan. 2010. 20p. pap. 10.95 *(978-1-61633-027-9(9))* Guardian Angel Publishing, Inc.

—One Family's Christmas. Kelso, Mary Jean. 24p. 2012. 19.95 *(978-1-61633-308-9(1))*; 2008. pap. 10.95 *(978-1-935137-05-4(0))* Guardian Angel Publishing, Inc.

—A Pocketful of Manners. Crow, Marilee. 2011. 16p. pap. 9.95 *(978-1-61633-176-4(3))* Guardian Angel Publishing, Inc.

—Preston, the Not-So-Perfect-Pig. Robinson, Janie. 2009. 20p. pap. 10.95 *(978-1-935137-84-9(0))* Guardian Angel Publishing, Inc.

—Ruthie & the Hippo's Fat Behind. Finke, Margot. 2010. 16p. pap. 10.95 *(978-1-61633-059-0(7))* Guardian Angel Publishing, Inc.

—Rv Mouse. Kelso, Mary Jean. 2010. 24p. pap. 10.95 *(978-1-61633-025-5(2))* Guardian Angel Publishing, Inc.

—A Short Tale about a Long Tail. Crow, Marilee. 2010. 16p. pap. 10.95 *(978-1-61633-067-5(8))* Guardian Angel Publishing, Inc.

—So Silly. Crow, Marilee. 2013. 28p. pap. 10.95 *(978-1-61633-443-7(6))* Guardian Angel Publishing, Inc.

—The Town of Masquerade. Samuels, Jack. 2012. 20p. pap. 9.95 *(978-1-61633-329-4(4))* Guardian Angel Publishing, Inc.

—What Is That Thing? McNamee, Kevin. 2011. 16p. pap. 9.95 *(978-1-61633-141-2(0))* Guardian Angel Publishing, Inc.

Snider, Kc. Andy & Spirit in Search & Rescue. Kelso, Mary Jean. 2013. 28p. 19.95 *(978-1-61633-410-9(X))*; pap. 10.95 *(978-1-61633-408-6(8))* Guardian Angel Publishing, Inc.

—Andy & Spirit Ride a Train. Kelso, Mary Jean. 2018. (Andy & Spirit Ser.: Vol. 7). (ENG.). 22p. (J). (gr. k-5). pap. 10.95 *(978-1-61633-949-4(7))* Guardian Angel Publishing, Inc.

—The Best Kind of String. Dubbeld, Janene a. l.t. ed. 2016. (ENG.). (J). pap. 9.95 *(978-1-61633-775-9(3))* Guardian Angel Publishing, Inc.

Snider, Kc. Big Bad Reunion. Gibson, Jacob & Phillips, Dixie. l.t. ed. 2019. (ENG.). 16p. (J). (gr. k-4). pap. 9.95 ***(978-1-61633-991-3(8))*** Guardian Angel Publishing, Inc.

Snider, Kc. Bubba & Bridgette's Adventure. Kelso, Mary Jean. l.t. ed. 2019. (ENG.). 26p. (J). (gr. 1-6). pap. 9.95 *(978-1-61633-967-8(5))* Guardian Angel Publishing, Inc.

Snider, Kc. Dragon Amy's Flames. Nott, Michelle. l.t. ed. 2019. (ENG.). 20p. (J). (gr. k-1). pap. 10.95 ***(978-1-951545-00-0(1))*** Guardian Angel Publishing, Inc.

Snider, Kc. The First Reindeer. Barker, Susan. l.t. ed. 2018. (ENG.). 20p. (J). (gr. k-1). pap. 10.95 *(978-1-61633-944-9(6))* Guardian Angel Publishing, Inc.

—Kitsy's Mischief & Horses. Glover, Emma M. l.t. ed. 2017. (ENG.). (J). pap. 9.95 *(978-1-61633-840-4(7))* Guardian Angel Publishing, Inc.

—Mamá, Existe Santa Claus? Berger, Susan J. l.t. ed. 2018. (SPA.). 24p. (J). (gr. 3-5). pap. 10.95 *(978-1-61633-942-5(X))* Guardian Angel Publishing, Inc.

—Mom Is There a Santa Claus? Berger, Susan J. l.t. ed. 2016. (ENG.). (J). (gr. 4-6). pap. 10.95 *(978-1-61633-798-8(2))* Guardian Angel Publishing, Inc.

—Powder Monkey. McDine, Donna M. 2013. 24p. 19.95 *(978-1-61633-384-3(7))*; pap. 10.95 *(978-1-61633-385-0(5))* Guardian Angel Publishing, Inc.

—Seagrass Surprise. Hunter, Christopher. 2017. (ENG.). 30p. (J). (gr. 2-5). pap. 10.95 *(978-1-61633-898-5(9))* Guardian Angel Publishing, Inc.

—Ulysses the Befuddled Basset. Glover, Emma M. l.t. ed. 2018. (ENG.). 16p. (J). (gr. k-2). pap. 9.95 *(978-1-61633-918-0(7))* Guardian Angel Publishing, Inc.

Snider, Kc. Silence. Snider, Kc. 2013. 28p. 19.95 *(978-1-61633-437-6(1))* Guardian Angel Publishing, Inc.

Snider, Sharon. Responza the Bull Learns the Ropes of Friendship. Dunlap, Sonya. 2009. 32p. pap. 17.95 *(978-0-9815245-8-0(3))* Accelerator Bks.

Snider, Sharon & Reny, Todd. Yummy Yummy Nummy Nummy, Should I Put This in My Tummy? MacGregor, Kim. Ioannou, Gregory Phillip, ed. 2004. 24p. *(978-0-9731301-0-2(5))* Beautiful Beginnings Youth, Inc.

Snook, Randy, photos by. Many Ideas Open the Way: A Collection of Hmong Proverbs. 2003. 32p. (J). 16.95 *(978-1-885008-23-7(6)*, Shen's Bks.) Lee & Low Bks., Inc.

Snortum, Marty, photos by. Pink Princess Cookbook, 1 vol. Beery, Barbara. 2006. (ENG., 64p. (J). (gr. -1-3). spiral bd. 14.99 *(978-1-4236-0173-9(4))* Gibbs Smith, Publisher.

Snow, Alan. On a Tall, Tall Cliff. Murray, Andrew. 2005. (ENG.). 32p. (J). (gr. k-2). 19.99 *(978-0-00-712155-7(5))* HarperCollins Pubs. Ltd. GBR. Dist: Independent Pubs. Group.

—A Spell Behind Bars. Bowvayne. 2006. (Misadventures of Danny Cloke Ser.). (J). 207p. per. 4.99 *(978-0-7945-1293-4(3))*; 208p. (gr. 6). lib. bdg. 12.99 *(978-1-58086-926-3(2))* EDC Publishing. (Usborne).

—A Turn in the Grave. Bowvayne. 2006. (Misadventures of Danny Cloke Ser.). 143p. (J). per. 4.99 *(978-0-7945-1292-7(5)*, Usborne) EDC Publishing.

Snow, Alan. Here Be Monsters! Snow, Alan. (Ratbridge Chronicles Ser.: 1). (ENG.). 544p. (J). (gr. 3-9). 2007. per. 9.99 *(978-0-689-87048-4(5))*; 2006. 17.95 *(978-0-689-87047-7(7))* Simon & Schuster Children's Publishing. (Atheneum Bks. for Young Readers).

—How Dinosaurs Really Work! Snow, Alan. 2013. (ENG.). 32p. (J). (gr. -1-3). 17.99 *(978-1-4424-8294-4(X)*, Atheneum Bks. for Young Readers) Simon & Schuster Children's Publishing.

—How Kids Really Work. Snow, Alan. 2013. (ENG.). 40p. (J). (gr. -1-5). 16.99 *(978-0-689-85818-5(3)*, Atheneum Bks. for Young Readers) Simon & Schuster Children's Publishing.

—How Santa Really Works. Snow, Alan. 2007. (ENG.). 48p. (J). (gr. -1-3). 7.99 *(978-1-4169-5000-4(1)*, Atheneum Bks. for Young Readers) Simon & Schuster Children's Publishing.

—Worse Things Happen at Sea! A Tale of Pirates, Poison, & Monsters. Snow, Alan. 2013. (Ratbridge Chronicles Ser.: 2). (ENG.). 352p. (J). (gr. 3-9). 17.99 *(978-0-689-87049-1(3)*, Atheneum Bks. for Young Readers) Simon & Schuster Children's Publishing.

Snow, Jeff. Beasts in the Closet. Snow, Jeff. 2006. 32p. (J). 17.95 *(978-1-932362-11-4(8))* Snowbound Pr., Inc.

Snow, Jess X. The Ocean Calls: A Haenyeo Mermaid Story. Cho, Tina. 2020. 48p. (J). (gr. k-3). 17.99 ***(978-1-9848-1486-9(9)***, Kokila) Penguin Young Readers Group.

Snow, Philip. Animals of the Bible. Snow, Philip. 2005. (Bible Discover & Colour Ser.). 32p. (J). (gr. -1-7). 4.00 *(978-1-903087-88-6(0))* DayOne Pubns. GBR. Dist: Send The Light Distribution LLC.

—Birds of the Bible. Snow, Philip. 2005. (Bible Discover & Colour Ser.). 32p. (J). (gr. -1-7). 4.00 *(978-1-903087-89-3(9))* DayOne Pubns. GBR. Dist: Send The Light Distribution LLC.

—Places of the Bible. Snow, Philip. 2005. (Bible Discover & Colour Ser.). 32p. (J). (gr. -1-7). 4.00 *(978-1-903087-90-9(2))* DayOne Pubns. GBR. Dist: Send The Light Distribution LLC.

—Plants of the Bible. Snow, Philip. 2005. (Bible Discover & Colour Ser.). 32p. (J). (gr. -1-7). 4.00 *(978-1-903087-91-6(0))* DayOne Pubns. GBR. Dist: Send The Light Distribution LLC.

Snow, Ravay L. Hildegarde & the Great Green Shirt Factory. Snow, Ravay L. 2005. (Hildegarde Ser.). 32p. (J). 16.95 *(978-1-932362-10-7(X))* Snowbound Pr., Inc.

Snow, Sarah. These Bees Count! Formento, Alison. 2013. (AV2 Fiction Readalong Ser.). (ENG.). (J). (gr. -1-2). 34.28 *(978-1-62127-901-3(4)*, AV2 by Weigl) Weigl Pubs., Inc.

—These Bees Count! Formento, Alison. 2012. (These Things Count! Ser.). (ENG.). 32p. (J). (gr. -1-3). 16.99 *(978-0-8075-7868-1(1)*, 807578681) Whitman, Albert & Co.

—These Rocks Count! Formento, Alison. 2014. (AV2 Fiction Readalong Ser.: Vol. 152). (ENG.). (J). (gr. -1-2). lib. bdg. 34.28 *(978-1-4896-2422-2(8)*, AV2 by Weigl) Weigl Pubs., Inc.

—These Seas Count! Formento, Alison. 2013. (AV2 Fiction Readalong Ser.: Vol. 71). (ENG.). (J). (gr. -1-2). 34.28 *(978-1-62127-903-7(0)*, AV2 by Weigl) Weigl Pubs., Inc.

—This Tree Counts! Formento, Alison. 2013. (AV2 Fiction Readalong Ser.: Vol. 72). (ENG.). (J). (gr. k-3). 34.28 *(978-1-62127-902-0(2)*, AV2 by Weigl) Weigl Pubs., Inc.

—This Tree Counts! Formento, Alison. 2019. (These Things Count! Ser.). (ENG.). 32p. (J). (gr. -1-3). pap. 7.99 *(978-0-8075-7897-1(5)*, 807578975) Whitman, Albert & Co.

Snow, Scott. In the Eye of the Storm. Kimmel, Elizabeth Cody. 2003. (Adventures of Young Buffalo Bill Ser.). 144p. (J). (gr. 3-7). lib. bdg. 16.89 *(978-0-06-029116-7(8))* HarperCollins Pubs.

—In the Eye of the Storm. Kimmel, E. Cody. 2003. (Adventures of Young Buffalo Bill Ser.). (ENG.). 144p. (J). (gr. 3-7). 15.99 *(978-0-06-029115-0(X))* HarperCollins Pubs.

—West on the Wagon Train. Kimmel, E. Cody. 2003. (Adventures of Young Buffalo Bill Ser.). (ENG.). 160p. (J). 15.99 *(978-0-06-029113-6(3))* HarperCollins Pubs.

Snow, Stephanie. Dreaming of Orlando: Counting down Around the Town. Everin, Gretchen. 2019. (Dreaming Of... Ser.). (ENG.). 16p. (J). bds. 9.95 *(978-1-64194-133-4(2)*, Commonwealth Editions) Applewood Bks.

Snowden-Fine, Lily. Why Do Dogs Sniff Butts? Curious Questions about Your Favorite Pets. 2020. (ENG.). 48p. (J). (gr. k-7). 16.95 *(978-0-500-65223-7(6)*, 565223) Thames & Hudson.

Snowden, Linda. Uncle Moishy Visits Torah Island. Safran, Faigy. (J). pap. 5.99 *(978-0-89906-806-0(5)*, UM1P) Mesorah Pubns., Ltd.

Snowdon, Ellie. Jasmine Green Rescues: a Collie Called Sky. Peters, Helen. 2020. (Jasmine Green Ser.). (ENG.). 160p. (J). (gr. 2-4). 14.99 ***(978-1-5362-1026-2(9))***; pap. 6.99 ***(978-1-5362-1571-7(6))*** Candlewick Pr.

Snowdon, Ellie. Jasmine Green Rescues: a Duckling Called Button. Peters, Helen. 2020. (Jasmine Green Ser.). (ENG.). 160p. (J). (gr. 2-4). 14.99 *(978-1-5362-1025-5(0))*; pap. 6.99 *(978-1-5362-1458-1(2))* Candlewick Pr.

Snowdon, Ellie. Jasmine Green Rescues: a Kitten Called Holly. Peters, Helen. 2020. (Jasmine Green Ser.). (ENG.). 160p. (J). (gr. 2-4). 14.99 ***(978-1-5362-1027-9(7))***; pap. 6.99 ***(978-1-5362-1572-4(4))*** Candlewick Pr.

Snowdon, Ellie. Jasmine Green Rescues: a Piglet Called Truffle. Peters, Helen. 2020. (Jasmine Green Ser.). (ENG.). 160p. (J). (gr. 2-4). 14.99 *(978-1-5362-1024-8(2))*; pap. 6.99 *(978-1-5362-1459-8(0))* Candlewick Pr.

Snowman, Tracy L. Snowy Secrets Vol. 1: Santa's Special Reindeer. Snowman, Tracy L. Snowman, Scott M. 2018. (Snowy Secrets Ser.: Vol. 1). (ENG.). 38p. (J). pap. 10.95 *(978-1-7211-7977-0(1))* CreateSpace Independent Publishing Platform.

Snyder, Betsy. Don't Throw That Away! A Lift-The-Flap Book about Recycling & Reusing. Bergen, Lara. 2009. (Little Green Bks.). (ENG.). 14p. (J). (gr. -1-1). bds. 7.99 *(978-1-4169-7517-5(9)*, Little Simon) Little Simon.

—I Can Dream. 2018. (ENG.). 14p. (J). (gr. -1 — 1). bds. 8.99 *(978-1-4521-6214-0(X))* Chronicle Bks. LLC.

—I Can Explore. 2018. (ENG.). 14p. (J). (gr. -1 — 1). bds. 8.99 *(978-1-4521-6213-3(1))* Chronicle Bks. LLC.

Snyder, Betsy E. I Can Dance. 2015. (ENG.). 14p. (J). (gr. -1 — 1). bds. 8.99 *(978-1-4521-2929-7(0))* Chronicle Bks. LLC.

—Lily's Potty. 2010. 16p. (J). bds. *(978-1-60906-001-5(6))* Begin Smart LLC.

—Peanut Butter & Jellyfishes: A Very Silly Alphabet Book. Cleary, Brian P. 2007. (ENG.). 32p. (J). (gr. -1-2). 15.95 *(978-0-8225-6188-0(3)*, Millbrook Pr.) Lerner Publishing Group.

—Tons of Trucks. Fliess, Sue. 2012. (ENG.). 18p. (J). (gr. k — 1). 13.99 *(978-0-547-44927-2(5)*, 1435126) Houghton Mifflin Harcourt Publishing Co.

Snyder, Betsy E. Haiku Baby. Snyder, Betsy E. 2008. 14p. (J). (gr. k — 1). bds. 6.99 *(978-0-375-84395-2(7)*, Random Hse. Bks. for Young Readers) Random Hse. Children's Bks.

Snyder, Diana, jt. illus. see Sun Star, Elan.

Snyder, Don, photos by. Swatches. La Prade, Erik. 2008. (ENG., 26p. pap. 10.00 *(978-0-9817678-1-9(8))* Poets Wear Prada.

Snyder, Harold E. A Frontier Girl of New York. Curtis, Alice Turner. 2011. 282p. 48.95 *(978-1-258-01096-6(8))* Literary Licensing, LLC.

Snyder, Iii, jt. illus. see Snyder, Max.

Snyder, Joe. Pokey & the Rooster. Helsel, Sandra. 2009. 28p. pap. 9.95 *(978-0-9818488-1-5(8))* Ajoyin Publishing, Inc.

Snyder, Joel. Fawn at Woodland Way. Zoehfeld, Kathleen Weidner. 2011. (Smithsonian's Backyard Ser.). (ENG.). 32p. (J). (gr. -1-3). 19.95 *(978-1-60727-637-1(2))* Soundprints.

—Good News for Naaman. Konzen, Lisa M. 2004. (ENG.). 16p. (J). 1.99 *(978-0-570-07573-8(4))* Concordia Publishing Hse.

—Joshua James Likes Trucks. Petrie, Catherine. 2011. (Rookie Ready to Learn: Out & about in My Community Ser.). (ENG.). 32p. (J). (gr. -1-k). lib. bdg. 18.69 *(978-0-531-27177-3(3))*; pap. 5.95 *(978-0-531-26827-8(6))* Scholastic Library Publishing. (Children's Pr.).

—Opossum at Sycamore Road. Walker, Sally M. 2011. (Smithsonian's Backyard Ser.). (ENG.). 32p. (J). (gr. -1-3). 8.95 *(978-1-60727-640-1(2))* Soundprints.

—Screech Owl at Midnight Hollow. Lamm, C. Drew. 2011. (Smithsonian's Backyard Ser.). (ENG.). 32p. (J). (gr. -1-3). 19.95 *(978-1-60727-643-2(7))* Soundprints.

—Timothy Joins Paul. Rottmann, Erik. 2005. (ENG.). 16p. (J). 1.99 *(978-0-7586-0506-1(4))* Concordia Publishing Hse.

Snyder, Kari. Lullaby Luna. Donovan, Patricia. 2018. (ENG.). 18p. (J). pap. 9.99 *(978-0-578-41284-9(5))* All Systems Grow.

Snyder, Max & Snyder, Iii. The King with No Kingdom. Snyder, Max. 2013. 42p. 18.99 *(978-0-9911512-9-5(1))* Mindstir Media.

Snyder, Peter Etril. Winterberries & Apple Blossoms: Reflections & Flavors of a Mennonite Year. Forler, Nan. 2011. 40p. (J). (gr. k-4). 22.95 *(978-1-77049-254-7(2)*, Tundra Bks.) Tundra Bks. CAN. Dist: Penguin Random Hse. LLC.

Snyder, Ronda. The Kingdom of Wish & Why. Milliner, Donna L. 2013. 30p. pap. 11.95 *(978-1-938743-06-1(7))* Reimann Bks.

Snyder, Sally. Hold the Fort. Snyder, Sally. 2003. 45p. (J). 20.00 *(978-1-882203-99-4(2))* Orange Frazer Pr.

—If It's to Be, It's up to Me! The ABC's of Character Building. Snyder, Sally. 2008. (ENG.). 59p. (J). (gr. -1-3). 22.50 *(978-1-933197-57-9(9))* Orange Frazer Pr.

Snyder, Scott, photos by. N Is for New Hampshire. Rule, Rebecca. 2016. (ENG., 32p. (J). 17.95 *(978-1-934031-68-1(2)*, 6c8c54b1-142e-40d5-9be7-2f88a203620b) Islandport Pr., Inc.

Snyman, Hedley. Maya & the Magical Flower. Riege, Diana. Zehmke, Justin, tr. 2018. (ENG.). 66p. (J). pap. 15.00 *(978-1-7178-4559-7(2))* Independently Published.

—Naughty Rhymes for Nice Children. Zehmke, Justin. 2018. (ENG.). 54p. (J). pap. 12.00 *(978-1-7178-4521-4(5))* Independently Published.

So, Meilo. El Agua Rueda, el Agua Sube. Mora, Pat & Domínguez, Adriana. 2014.Tr. of Water Rolls, Water Rises. (ENG & SPA.). 32p. (J). 18.95 *(978-0-89239-325-1(4))* Lee & Low Bks., Inc.

—Bronze & Sunflower. Wenxuan, Cao. 2019. (ENG.). 400p. (J). (gr. 4-7). pap. 9.99 *(978-1-5362-0637-1(7))* Candlewick Pr.

—Bronze & Sunflower. Wenxuan, Cao. Wang, Helen, tr. from CHI. 2017. (ENG.). 400p. (J). (gr. 4-7). 17.99 *(978-0-7636-8816-5(9))* Candlewick Pr.

—Brush of the Gods. Look, Lenore. 2013. 40p. (J). (gr. -1-3). 17.99 *(978-0-375-87001-9(6)*, Schwartz & Wade Bks.) Random Hse. Children's Bks.

—Butterflies Belong Here: A Story of One Idea, Thirty Kids, & a World of Butterflies. Hopkinson, Deborah. 2020. (ENG.). 68p. (J). (gr. k-3). 18.99 *(978-1-4521-7680-2(9))* Chronicle Bks. LLC.

—By Day, by Night. Gibson, Amy. 2014. (ENG.). 32p. (J). (gr. -1-3). 16.95 *(978-1-59078-991-9(1))* Boyds Mills Pr.

—Follow the Moon Home: A Tale of One Idea, Twenty Kids, & a Hundred Sea Turtles. Cousteau, Philippe & Hopkinson, Deborah. 2016. (ENG.). 48p. (J). (gr. k-3). 16.99 *(978-1-4521-1241-1(X))* Chronicle Bks. LLC.

—Hurry & the Monarch. O Flatharta, Antoine. 2009. (ENG.). 40p. (J). (gr. k-3). pap. 7.99 *(978-0-385-73719-7(X)*, Dragonfly Bks.) Random Hse. Children's Bks.

—The Magic Paintbrush. Miles, Liz. 2014. (Traditional Tales Ser.). (ENG.). 24p. (J). (gr. k-1). pap. 6.95 *(978-1-62521-584-0(3)*, Capstone Classroom) Capstone.

—Noodle Magic. Thong, Roseanne Greenfield. 2014. (ENG.). 32p. (J). (gr. -1-3). 17.99 *(978-0-545-52167-3(X))* Scholastic, Inc.

—Otters Love to Play. London, Jonathan. (Read & Wonder Ser.). 32p. (J). (gr. k-4). 2018. 7.99 *(978-1-5362-0324-0(6))*; 2016. 16.99 *(978-0-7636-6913-3(X))* Candlewick Pr.

—Read a Rhyme, Write a Rhyme. 2009. (ENG.). 32p. (J). (gr. 1-4). pap. 7.99 *(978-0-385-73727-2(0)*, Dragonfly Bks.) Random Hse. Children's Bks.

So, Meilo. Water Rolls, Water Rises / el Agua Rueda, el Agua Sube, 1 vol. Mora, Pat. 2020. (ENG & SPA.). 32p. (J). (gr. 1-6). pap. 10.95 ***(978-1-64379-239-2(3)***, 81b9cee1-9789-4cb9-ae99-a5bea3b66d90, Children's Book Press) Lee & Low Bks., Inc.

So, Meilo. Water Sings Blue: (Blue Book of Ocean & Water, Books for Kids about Sea Castles) Coombs, Kate. 2012. (ENG.). 36p. (J). (gr. -1-3). 16.99 *(978-0-8118-7284-3(X))* Chronicle Bks. LLC.

—Wonderful You: An Adoption Story. McLaughlin, Lauren. 2017. (ENG.). 40p. (J). (gr. -1-2). 17.99 *(978-0-553-51001-0(0)*, Random Hse. Bks. for Young Readers) Random Hse. Children's Bks.

So, Meilo. Water Rolls, Water Rises, 1 vol. So, Meilo. Mora, Pat & Dominguez, Adriana. 2014. (SPA & ENG.). 32p. (J). 18.95 *(978-1-60060-899-5(X))* Lee & Low Bks., Inc.

So, Patty. So Simple Sightwords at-Home Volume 3. So, Patty. 2008. 117p. (J). spiral bd. *(978-0-9772158-4-3(9))* So Simple Learning.

So-Young, Lee. Model, Vol. 5. So-Young, Lee. rev. ed. 2005. 192p. pap. 9.99 *(978-1-59532-007-0(5))* TOKYOPOP, Inc.

Sobieski, Aniela. The Day We Lost Pet. Young, Chuck. 2018. (ENG.). 48p. (J). 16.95 *(978-0-9987999-3-3(9))* Penny Candy Bks., LLC.

Sobol, Richard. Construction Zone. Hudson, Cheryl Willis. 2017. 32p. (J). (gr. -1-3). 6.99 *(978-0-7636-9344-2(8))* Candlewick Pr.

Sobol, Richard. The Story of Silk: From Worm Spit to Woven Scarves. Sobol, Richard. 2012. (Traveling Photographer Ser.). 40p. (J). (gr. 1-4). 17.99 *(978-0-7636-4165-8(0))* Candlewick Pr.

Sobol, Richard, photos by. An Elephant in the Backyard. 2004. (J). *(978-0-525-46970-4(2)*, Dutton Juvenile) Penguin Publishing Group.

Sobol, Richard, photos by. Breakfast in the Rainforest: A Visit with Mountain Gorillas. Sobol, Richard. 2010. (Traveling Photographer Ser.). 48p. (J). (gr. 1-4). pap. 7.99 *(978-0-7636-5134-3(6))* Candlewick Pr.

Sochard, Fred. A Dragon on the Roof: A Children's Book Inspired by Antoni Gaudí. Alix, Cecile. 2019. (Children's Books Inspired by Famous Artworks Ser.). (ENG.). 32p. (J). (gr. -1-3). 14.95 *(978-3-7913-7391-1(9))* Prestel Verlag GmbH & Co KG. DEU. Dist: Penguin Random Hse. LLC.

Sochor, Lesia. A Moose's Morning. Love, Pamela. ed. 2007. (ENG.). 32p. (J). (gr. -1-3). 15.95 *(978-0-89272-733-9(0))* Down East Bks.

Soda, Masahito. Firefighter! Soda, Masahito. 2005. (Firefighter Ser.: Vol. 12). (ENG.). 200p. pap. 9.95 *(978-1-59116-980-2(1))* Viz Media.

—Firefighter! Daigo of Fire Company M. Soda, Masahito. (Firefighter Ser.: Vol. 11). (ENG.). 200p. 2005. pap. 9.95 *(978-1-59116-795-2(7))*; 2004. pap. 9.95 *(978-1-59116-464-7(8))* Viz Media.

—Firefighter! Vol. 10: Daigo of Fire Company M. Soda, Masahito. 2005. (Firefighter Ser.: Vol. 10). (ENG.). 208p. pap. 9.95 *(978-1-59116-635-1(7))* Viz Media.

—Firefighter, Vol. 3. Soda, Masahito. collector's ed. 2003. (ENG.). 192p. pap. 9.95 *(978-1-56931-881-2(6))* Viz Media.

—Firefighter, Vol. 4. Soda, Masahito. 2003. (ENG.). 200p. pap. 9.95 *(978-1-56931-991-8(X))* Viz Media.

—Firefighter, Vol. 5. Soda, Masahito. 2003. (ENG.). 192p. pap. 9.95 *(978-1-59116-093-9(6))* Viz Media.

—Firefighter, Vol. 7. Soda, Masahito. 2004. (ENG.). 200p. pap. 9.95 *(978-1-59116-315-2(3))* Viz Media.

—Privileged to Kill. Soda, Masahito. 2004. (Firefighter Ser.: Vol. 9). (ENG.). 200p. pap. 9.95 *(978-1-59116-634-4(9))* Viz Media.

Sodano, Meg. Lila's Harbor. Talbert, Cj. 2017. (ENG.). (J). pap. 11.95 *(978-0-692-83362-9(5))* CJT Publishing.

—Salamander Sky. Farber, Katy. 2018. (ENG.). 32p. (J). (gr. -1-8). 17.95 *(978-0-9990766-4-4(7))* Green Writers Pr.

Soderberg, Kimberly. Ruth the Sleuth & the Messy Room. Ekster, Carol Gordon. l.t. ed. 2018. (Building Character Ser.: Vol. 8). (ENG.). 34p. (J). 17.95 *(978-1-946124-33-3(8))* Mazo Pubs.

Soderlund, Birgit. Pacific Halibut Flat or Fiction?, 1. Sadorus, Lauri. 2005. 24p. (J). per. *(978-0-9776931-0-8(4))* International Pacific Halibut Commission.

Sodré, Julie. Baby Farm Animals. Grimm, Sandra. 2012. 20p. (J). (gr. -1-1). 12.95 *(978-1-61608-654-1(8)*, 608654, Sky Pony Pr.) Skyhorse Publishing Co., Inc.

Soekarno, Sonya Abby. Gritty & Graceful: 15 Inspiring Women of the Bible, Vol. Rivadeneira, Caryn. 2019. (ENG.). 32p. (J). (gr. k-3). 16.99 *(978-1-5064-5206-7(X)*, Beaming Books) Augsburg Fortress, Pubs.

Soelver, Anita. An Amazing & Almost Always Accurate Alliterative Alphabet. Stemp, Patrick S. 2017. (ENG.). 60p. (J). pap. *(978-1-988023-12-0(2))* Stirling Bay.

—The Great Escape (Goblin & Pig 1) Stemp, Patrick S. 2016. (Goblin & Pig Ser.: Vol. 1). (ENG.). 34p. (J). pap. *(978-1-988023-02-1(5))* Stirling Bay.

—The Lonely Snowflake. Stemp, Patrick S. 2015. (ENG.). (J). pap. *(978-0-9938503-7-0(5))* Stirling Bay.

—The New Cat. Stemp, Patrick S. 2015. (ENG.). (J). pap. *(978-1-988023-01-4(7))* Stirling Bay.

Soentpiet, Chris. My Brother Martin: A Sister Remembers Growing up with the Rev. Dr. Martin Luther King Jr. Farris, Christine King. 2003. (ENG.). 32p. (J). (gr. 1-6). 19.99 *(978-0-689-84387-7(9)*, Simon & Schuster Bks. For Young Readers) Simon & Schuster Bks. For Young Readers.

—My Brother Martin: A Sister Remembers Growing up with the Rev. Dr. Martin Luther King Jr. Farris, Christine King. 2006. (ENG.). 40p. (J). (gr. 1-6). 8.99 *(978-0-689-84388-4(7)*, Aladdin) Simon & Schuster Children's Publishing.

—Saturdays & Teacakes, 1 vol. Laminack, Lester L. 2004. (ENG.). 32p. (J). (gr. k-3). 16.95 *(978-1-56145-303-0(X))* Peachtree Publishing Co. Inc.

Soentpiet, Chris & Hale, Christy. Amazing Places. 2018. (ENG.). 40p. (J). pap. 11.95 *(978-1-62014-805-1(6))* Lee & Low Bks., Inc.

Soentpiet, Chris K. Amazing Faces, 1 vol. Hopkins, Lee Bennett. ed. 2015. (ENG.). 40p. (J). (gr. 2-5). pap. 11.95 *(978-1-62014-223-3(6))* Lee & Low Bks., Inc.

—Amazing Faces. Hopkins, Lee Bennett. 2011. (ENG.). 40p. (J). (gr. 1-18). 18.95 *(978-1-60060-334-1(3))* Lee & Low Bks., Inc.

—Coolies. Yin. 2003. 40p. (J). (gr. 2-5). 7.99 *(978-0-14-250055-2(0)*, Puffin Books) Penguin Young Readers Group.

—Coolies. Yin. 2003. (gr. k). 18.00 *(978-0-7569-1545-2(7))* Perfection Learning Corp.

—Happy Birthday to You! The Mystery Behind the Most Famous Song in the World. Raven, Margot Theis. 2008. (ENG.). 40p. (J). (gr. 1-4). 19.99 *(978-1-58536-169-4(0)*, 202025) Sleeping Bear Pr.

—My Brother Martin: A Sister Remembers Growing up with the Rev. Dr. Martin Luther King Jr. King Farris, Christine. 2005. 35p. (J). (gr. 4-7). 15.65 *(978-0-7569-6552-5(7))* Perfection Learning Corp.

—Saturdays & Teacakes, 1 vol. Laminack, Lester L. 2009. (ENG.). 32p. (J). 19.95 *(978-1-56145-513-3(X))* Peachtree Publishing Co. Inc.

—So Far from the Sea. Bunting, Eve. 2009. (ENG.). 32p. (J). (gr. 5-7). pap. 7.99 *(978-0-547-23752-7(9)*, 1083866) Houghton Mifflin Harcourt Publishing Co.

Soentpiet, Chris K. & Hale, Christy. Amazing Places. 2015. (ENG.). 40p. (J). 18.95 *(978-1-60060-653-3(9))* Lee & Low Bks., Inc.

Soffritti, Donald. Disney: Minnie's Starry, Starry Night. Parent, Nancy. 2020. (Disney Classic 8 X 8 Ser.). (ENG.). 24p. (J). (gr. -1-k). pap. 4.99 ***(978-0-7944-4527-0(6)***, Studio Fun International) Printers Row Publishing Group.

Soffritti, Donald. Double Duck. Enna, Bruno. 2010. (ENG.). 112p. (J). pap. 9.99 *(978-1-60886-545-1(2))* Boom! Studios.

Sofilas, Mark. Hello, I Am Fiona from Scotland. Graham, Mark. 2014. (AV2 Fiction Readalong Ser.: Vol. 128). (ENG.). 32p. (J). (gr. -1-3). lib. bdg. 34.28 *(978-1-4896-2253-2(5)*, AV2 by Weigl) Weigl Pubs., Inc.

—Hello, I Am Max from Sydney. Husar, Stephane. 2014. (AV2 Fiction Readalong Ser.: Vol. 130). (ENG.). 32p. (J). (gr. -1-3). lib. bdg. 34.28 *(978-1-4896-2250-1(0)*, AV2 by Weigl) Weigl Pubs., Inc.

Sofroniou, Miranda. Billie Jean King. Sanchez Vegara, Maria Isabel. 2020. (Little People, Big Dreams Ser.: Vol. 39). (ENG.). 32p. (J). (gr. -1-2). ***(978-0-7112-4693-5(9))*** Frances Lincoln Childrens Bks.

Sogabe, Aki. The Origami Master. Lachenmeyer, Nathaniel. 2013. (AV2 Fiction Readalong Ser.: Vol. 88). (ENG.). (J). (gr. -1-3). 34.28 *(978-1-62127-897-9(2)*, AV2 by Weigl) Weigl Pubs., Inc.

Sohn, Jeana. Laffy the Lamb. Bee, Granny. Werthiemer, Beverly, ed. 2006. 32p. (J). 16.95 *(978-1-932367-00-3(4))* BookBound Publishing.

Soileau, Hodges. The Black Widow Spider Mystery. 2004. (Boxcar Children Special Ser.). 130p. (gr. 2-7). 15.50 *(978-0-7569-3266-4(1))* Perfection Learning Corp.

—The Comic Book Mystery. 2003. (Boxcar Children Ser.). 106p. (gr. 4-7). 15.00 *(978-0-7569-1611-4(9))* Perfection Learning Corp.

—The Great Shark Mystery. 2003. (Boxcar Children Mystery & Activities Specials Ser.: 20). (ENG.). 160p. (J). (gr. 1-5). pap. 6.99 *(978-0-8075-5532-3(0),* 807555320) Whitman, Albert & Co.

—The Great Shark Mystery. 2003. (Boxcar Children Special Ser.). 130p. (gr. 4-7). 15.50 *(978-0-7569-1616-9(X))* Perfection Learning Corp.

—The Mystery at Skeleton Point. 2003. (Boxcar Children Ser.). 120p. (gr. 4-7). 15.00 *(978-0-7569-1609-1(7))* Perfection Learning Corp.

—The Mystery in the Fortune Cookie. 2003. (Boxcar Children Mysteries Ser.: 96). (ENG.). 144p. (J). (gr. 2-5). pap. 6.99 *(978-0-8075-5540-8(1),* 807555401) Whitman, Albert & Co.

—The Mystery of the Haunted Boxcar. 2004. (Boxcar Children Mysteries Ser.: 100). (ENG.). 128p. (J). (gr. 1-5). mass mkt. 6.99 *(978-0-8075-5554-5(1),* 807555541) Whitman, Albert & Co.

—The Mystery of the Runaway Ghost. Warner, Gertrude Chandler. 2004. (Boxcar Children Ser.). 135p. (J). 12.65 *(978-0-7569-3264-0(5))* Perfection Learning Corp.

—The Mystery of the Runaway Ghost. 2004. (Boxcar Children Mysteries Ser.: 98). (ENG.). 144p. (J). (gr. 1-5). pap. 5.99 *(978-0-8075-5551-4(7),* 807555517) Whitman, Albert & Co.

—The Radio Mystery. 2003. (Boxcar Children Mysteries Ser.: 97). (ENG.). 128p. (J). (gr. 1-5). mass mkt. 6.99 *(978-0-8075-5547-7(9),* 807555479) Whitman, Albert & Co.

Sojdr, Martin. Beehive. Bartikova, Petra. 2020. (ENG.). 14p. (J). bds. 9.99 ***(978-1-64124-086-4(5),*** 0864) Fox Chapel Publishing Co., Inc.

Sokol, Bill. Alvin Fernald, Mayor for a Day. Hicks, Clifford B. 2015. 138p. (J). pap. 9.99 *(978-1-930900-86-8(4))* Purple Hse. Pr.

—Alvin's Secret Code. Hicks, Clifford B. 2015. (J). pap. 9.99 *(978-1-930900-85-1(6))* Purple Hse. Pr.

Sokolava, Valerie. Cinderella. McFadden, Deanna. 2013. (Silver Penny Stories Ser.). 48p. (J). (gr. -1-1). 4.95 *(978-1-4027-8333-3(7))* Sterling Publishing Co., Inc.

—Thumbelina. Olmstead, Kathleen et al. 2013. (Silver Penny Stories Ser.). 48p. (J). (gr. -1-1). 4.95 *(978-1-4027-8352-4(3))* Sterling Publishing Co., Inc.

Sokoloff, David. The Queen of Persia. Moscowitz, Moshe & Resnick, Yael. 2004. 107p. *(978-1-930925-09-0(3),* Shazak Productions) Torah Excel.

Sokolova, Valerie. Bella Basset Ballerina. Garn, Laura Aimee. 2006. 32p. (J). (gr. -1-3). 15.95 *(978-0-9759378-0-8(4))* Pretty Please Pr., Inc.

—Jesus Feeds the Five Thousand, 1 vol. Bowman, Crystal. 2011. (I Can Read! / Bible Stories Ser.). (ENG.). 32p. (J). (gr. -1-2). pap. 4.99 *(978-0-310-72157-4(1))* Zonderkidz.

—Jesus Raises Lazarus, 1 vol. Bowman, Crystal. 2011. (I Can Read! / Bible Stories Ser.). (ENG.). 32p. (J). (gr. -1-2). pap. 4.99 *(978-0-310-72158-1(X))* Zonderkidz.

—Joshua Crosses the Jordan, 1 vol. Bowman, Crystal. 2011. (I Can Read! / Bible Stories Ser.). (ENG.). 32p. (J). (gr. -1-2). pap. 4.99 *(978-0-310-72156-7(3))* Zonderkidz.

—The Magic of Merlin. Spinner, Stephanie. 2004. (Stepping Stones: A Chapter Book: Fantasy Ser.). 42p. (J). 11.65 *(978-0-7569-0905-5(8))* Perfection Learning Corp.

—The Prodigal Son, 1 vol. Bowman, Crystal. 2011. (I Can Read! / Bible Stories Ser.). (ENG.). 32p. (J). (gr. -1-2). pap. 4.99 *(978-0-310-72155-0(5))* Zonderkidz.

—Thankful Together. Davis, Holly. 2006. 36p. (J). 5.99 *(978-0-7847-1436-2(3),* 04077) Standard Publishing.

Sol, Anne, photos by. Of Course They Do! Boys & Girls Can Do Anything. Roger, Marie-Sabine. 2014. (ENG., 40p. (J). (-k). lib. bdg. 9.95 *(978-1-58089-669-6(3))* Charlesbridge Publishing, Inc.

Solak, Daria. Dolly Parton. Sanchez Vegara, Maria Isabel. 2019. (Little People, Big Dreams Ser.: Vol. 28). (ENG.). 32p. (J). (gr. -1-2). ***(978-1-78603-760-2(2))*** Frances Lincoln Childrens Bks.

Solana, Javier. Poesias para Todos los Dias: Versos Fritos. Solana, Javier, tr. Fuertes, Gloria. 2003. (SPA.). 126p. *(978-84-305-7805-4(6),* SU4857) Susaeta Ediciones, S.A. ESP. Dist: Lectorum Pubns., Inc.

Solano, Jordi. Beyond the Sixth Extinction: A Post-Apocalyptic Pop-Up. Sheehy, Shawn. 2018. (ENG.). 40p. (J). (gr. 9). 65.00 *(978-0-7636-8788-5(X))* Candlewick Pr.

—Hu-Wan & the Sleeping Dragon. Young, Judy. 2017. (ENG.). 32p. (J). (gr. 1-4). 16.99 *(978-1-58536-977-5(2),* 204324) Sleeping Bear Pr.

—Miep & the Most Famous Diary: The Woman Who Rescued Anne Frank's Diary. Pincus, Meeg. 2019. (ENG.). 40p. (J). (gr. 1-4). 17.99 *(978-1-5341-1025-0(9),* 204761) Sleeping Bear Pr.

—Rónán & the Mermaid: a Tale of Old Ireland. McShane, Marianne. 2020. (ENG.). 32p. (J). (gr. k-3). 16.99 *(978-1-5362-0022-5(0))* Candlewick Pr.

—Swimming with Sharks: The Daring Discoveries of Eugenie Clark. Lang, Heather. 2016. (ENG.). 32p. (J). (gr. -1-3). 16.99 *(978-0-8075-2187-8(6),* 807521876) Whitman, Albert & Co.

Solares, Rosario. The Horse Andaluz: A Different Way of Reading. Villasana, Jenny. 2018. (ENG.). 28p. (J). pap. 14.99 *(978-1-7929-2929-8(3))* Independently Published.

Solari, Kylee. Forces on Earth: Bridges Edition, Set Of 10. Pelleschi, Andrea. 2013. (Prime Plus Ser.). (J). (gr. 6-8). 99.00 net. *(978-1-4509-9952-6(2))* Benchmark Education Co.

—Forces on Earth: Prime Bridges Edition. Pelleschi, Andrea. 2013. (Prime Ser.). (YA). (gr. 6-8). pap. *(978-1-4509-9703-4(1))* Benchmark Education Co.

—Forces on Earth: Set Of 10. Pelleschi, Andrea. 2013. (Prime Plus Ser.). (J). (gr. 6-8). 99.00 net. *(978-1-4509-9928-1(X))* Benchmark Education Co.

—The Nature of Motion: Bridges Edition, Set Of 10. Pelleschi, Andrea. 2013. (Prime Plus Ser.). (J). (gr. 6-8). 99.00 net. *(978-1-4509-9951-9(4))* Benchmark Education Co.

—The Nature of Motion: Prime Bridges Edition. Pelleschi, Andrea. 2013. (Prime Ser.). (YA). (gr. 6-8). pap. *(978-1-4509-9702-7(3))* Benchmark Education Co.

—The Nature of Motion: Set Of 10. Pelleschi, Andrea. 2013. (Prime Plus Ser.). (J). (gr. 6-8). 99.00 net. *(978-1-4509-9927-4(1))* Benchmark Education Co.

—Simple & Complex Machines: Bridges Edition, Set Of 10. Pelleschi, Andrea. 2013. (Prime Plus Ser.). (J). (gr. 6-8). 99.00 net. *(978-1-4509-9953-3(0))* Benchmark Education Co.

—Simple & Complex Machines: Prime Bridges Edition. Pelleschi, Andrea. 2013. (Prime Ser.). (YA). (gr. 6-8). pap. *(978-1-4509-9704-1(X))* Benchmark Education Co.

—Simple & Complex Machines: Set Of 10. Pelleschi, Andrea. 2013. (Prime Plus Ser.). (J). (gr. 6-8). 99.00 net. *(978-1-4509-9929-8(8))* Benchmark Education Co.

Solbert, Ronni. The Elephant Who Liked to Smash Small Cars. Merrill, Jean. 2015. (ENG.). 40p. (J). (gr. -1-2). 16.95 *(978-1-59017-872-0(6),* NYR Children's Collection) New York Review of Bks., Inc., The.

—The Pushcart War. Merrill, Jean. 50th ed. 2015. 232p. (J). (gr. 3-7). pap. 11.99 *(978-1-59017-936-9(6),* NYRB Kids) New York Review of Bks., Inc., The.

—The Pushcart War. Merrill, Jean. 50th anniv. ed. 2014. 222p. (J). (gr. 3-7). 15.95 *(978-1-59017-819-5(X),* NYR Children's Collection) New York Review of Bks., Inc., The.

Sole, Francisco. El Senor del Cero. Molina, Maria Isabel. 2003. (SPA.). 153p. (J). (gr. 5-8). pap. 10.95 *(978-968-19-0388-6(9))* Santillana USA Publishing Co., Inc.

Solé, Francisco. La Isla del Tesoro. Solé, Francisco, tr. Ruiz, Celia & Stevenson, Robert Louis. 3rd ed. 2003. (Timeless Classics Ser.). (SPA.). 92p. (J). (gr. 5-8). pap. 12.95 *(978-84-204-5729-1(9))* Santillana USA Publishing Co., Inc.

Sole, Julien. The Little Book of Knowledge: Sharks. Seret, Bernard. 2018. (Little Book Ser.). (ENG.). 88p. 14.99 *(978-1-68405-066-6(9))* Idea & Design Works, LLC.

Solecki, Kristen. The 826 Quarterly, Volume 27. Students of the 826 Valencia writing programs, Students of the 826 Valencia writing. 2018. (826 Quarterly Ser.). (ENG.). 216p. (J). pap. 18.00 *(978-1-948644-20-4(7))* 826 Valencia.

Soleiman, Serg & Parks, Phil. The Mothman's Shadow, 1 vol. Strange, Jason. 2011. (Jason Strange Ser.). (ENG.). 72p. (J). (gr. 3-6). lib. bdg. 25.32 *(978-1-4342-2965-6(3),* Stone Arch Bks.) Capstone.

—Zombie Winter, 1 vol. Strange, Jason. 2011. (Jason Strange Ser.). (ENG.). 72p. (J). (gr. 3-6). lib. bdg. 25.32 *(978-1-4342-2964-9(5),* Stone Arch Bks.) Capstone.

Solenne and Thomas. The Big Book of Christians Around the World. de Mullenheim, Sophie. 2020. (ENG.). 85p. (J). (gr. k-2). 16.99 ***(978-1-62164-358-6(1))*** Ignatius Pr.

Solenova, Kate. The Architect Fairy. Gordon, Lisa. 2016. (Fairy Village Ser.: Vol. 3). (ENG.). (J). 19.95 *(978-0-9973594-1-1(2))* Magical Beginnings.

Soler, Sara, jt. illus. see Chan, Ron.

Soley, Liesel. Can You Be an Artist? Soley, Liesel. 2011. 28p. (J). (gr. -1-3). 16.95 *(978-1-935359-69-2(X))* Bk. Pubs. Network.

Solheim, Kermit. Callie Cow. Hogan, Jayne. Reiter, Cheryl, ed. (J). (gr. -1). mass mkt. 12.99 *(978-1-887327-55-8(X))* TOMY International, Inc.

Soli, Tina. When Two Are Angry at Each Other. Bringsvaerd, Tor Age. Vetleseter, Tonje, tr. from NOR. 2008. 32p. (J). (gr. -1-1). 14.95 *(978-0-9790347-8-7(7))* Mackenzie Smiles, LLC.

—When Two Get Up. Bringsvaerd, Tor Age. 2009. (When Two Ser.). 36p. (J). (gr. -1-1). 14.95 *(978-0-9815761-4-5(1))* Mackenzie Smiles, LLC.

—When Two Say Goodnight. Bringsvaerd, Tor Age. 2009. (When Two Ser.). 36p. (J). (gr. -1-1). 14.95 *(978-0-9815761-3-8(3))* Mackenzie Smiles, LLC.

—When Two Take a Bath. Bringsvaerd, Tor Age. 2009. (When Two Ser.). 36p. (J). (gr. -1-3). 14.95 *(978-0-9815761-1-4(7))* Mackenzie Smiles, LLC.

Solimine, John. Does Frankenstein Get Hungry? Solimine, John. 2018. 32p. (J). (gr. k-3). 17.99 *(978-0-399-54641-9(3),* G.P. Putnam's Sons Books for Young Readers) Penguin Young Readers Group.

Solino, Ali. Alligator, Bayou, Crawfish. Solino, Ali. Huber, Candice, ed. 2018. (ENG.). 33p. (J). (gr. -1-2). 19.99 *(978-1-7322794-3-8(8))* Tubby & Coo's Mid-City Bk. Shop.

Solis, Fermin. Counting Elephants. Young, Dawn. 2020. 32p. (J). (gr. -1-1). 17.99 *(978-0-7624-6694-8(4),* Running Pr. Kids) Running Pr.

—Eek! Yikes! Boo! ed. 2019. (Booktacular Ser.). 30p. (J). (— 1). 9.95 *(978-1-912904-48-8(9),* Scribblers) Book Hse. GBR. Dist: Sterling Publishing Co., Inc.

—I Am the Sky. Schmauss, Judy Kentor. 2015. (Early Rising Readers Ser.). (J). (gr. -1-k). 5.83 *(978-1-4788-2154-0(X))* Newmark Learning LLC.

Solís, Fermín. Search & Find: Dinosaurs. Walden, Libby. 2018. (Search & Find Ser.). (ENG.). 12p. (J). (gr. -1-k). 9.99 *(978-1-68412-263-9(5),* Silver Dolphin Bks.) Printers Row Publishing Group.

Solis, Fermin. Who's That Hiding in the Chimney? Townsend, John. ed. 2018. 14p. (J). (gr. -1). bds. 6.95 *(978-1-912537-32-7(X),* Scribblers) Book Hse. GBR. Dist: Sterling Publishing Co., Inc.

—Who's That Hiding in the Dark? Townsend, John. ed. 2018. 14p. (J). (gr. -1). bds. 6.95 *(978-1-912537-33-4(8),* Scribblers) Book Hse. GBR. Dist: Sterling Publishing Co., Inc.

—Yo Se Dibujar. Schmauss, Judy Kentor. 2016. (Early Rising Readers Ser.). (SPA.). 16p. (J). (gr. 1-1). 6.67 *(978-1-4788-4166-1(4))* Newmark Learning LLC.

—Yo Soy el Cielo. Schmauss, Judy Kentor. 2016. (Early Rising Readers Ser.). (SPA.). 16p. (J). (gr. 1-1). 6.67 *(978-1-4788-4175-3(3))* Newmark Learning LLC.

Sollano, Gennel Marie. Ellie & Emma Share the Moon. Sunderland, Lisa. 2019. (ENG.). 26p. (J). pap. 13.95 ***(978-1-9736-7624-9(9),*** WestBow Pr.) Author Solutions, Inc.

—God Made You. McGowan, Stefanie. 2019. (ENG.). 30p. (J). pap. 13.95 ***(978-1-9736-7657-7(5),*** WestBow Pr.) Author Solutions, Inc.

Sollers, Jim. Beau Beaver Goes to Town. Bloxam, Frances. ed. 2009. (ENG.). 32p. (J). (gr. -1-3). 16.95 *(978-0-89272-792-6(6))* Down East Bks.

Sollers, Jim & Reed, Rebecca Harrison. Only Cows Allowed!, 1 vol. Plourde, Lynn. 2011. (ENG.). 32p. (gr. -1-3). 16.95 *(978-0-89272-790-2(X))* Down East Bks.

Solly, Gloria, jt. illus. see Cruzan, Patricia.

Solly, Gloria D. Max Does It Again. Cruzan, Patricia. 2009. 118p. (J). (gr. 2-2). pap. 14.00 *(978-1-4120-6581-8(X))* Trafford Publishing.

Solner Heimer, Patricia. Li'l Earth. Solner Heimer, Patricia. 2010. 32p. (J). (gr. k-4). 15.99 *(978-0-9844453-0-1(7))* Maple Road Publishing, Inc.

Solomon, Debra. How Come? Every Kid's Science Questions Explained. Wollard, Kathy. ed. 2014. (ENG.). 416p. (J). pap. 16.95 *(978-0-7611-7978-8(X),* 17978) Workman Publishing Co., Inc.

Solomon, Debra. El Libro de Los Porqués 2: Las Preguntas Más Difíciles y Las Respuestas Más Fáciles Sobre Las Personas, Los Animales y Las Cosas. Solomon, Debra. Wollard, Kathy. 2004. (SPA.). 208p. 28.99 *(978-84-9754-047-6(6),* 87432) Ediciones Oniro S.A. ESP. Dist: Lectorum Pubns., Inc.

Solomon, Harry. The Day Silver Snowed. Solomon, Harry. 2009. 112p. 80.00 *(978-0-9630376-1-9(7))* Figure 8 Pr.

Solomon, Heather. Ugly Pie. Wheeler, Lisa. 2014. (ENG.). 32p. (J). (gr. -1-3). pap. 7.99 *(978-0-544-23961-6(X),* 1565437, HMH Books For Young Readers) Houghton Mifflin Harcourt Publishing Co.

Solomon, Heather M. Clever Beatrice. Willey, Margaret. 2004. (ENG.). 40p. (J). (gr. -1-3). reprint ed. 8.99 *(978-0-689-87068-2(X),* Atheneum Bks. for Young Readers) Simon & Schuster Children's Publishing.

—Clever Beatrice & the Best Little Pony. Willey, Margaret. 2004. (ENG.). 40p. (J). (gr. -1-3). 18.99 *(978-0-689-85339-5(4),* Atheneum Bks. for Young Readers) Simon & Schuster Children's Publishing.

—A Clever Beatrice Christmas. Willey, Margaret. 2006. (ENG.). 40p. (J). (gr. -1-2). 19.99 *(978-0-689-87017-0(5),* Atheneum Bks. for Young Readers) Simon & Schuster Children's Publishing.

—If I Were a Lion. Weeks, Sarah. (ENG.). 40p. (J). (gr. -1-2). 2007. 8.99 *(978-1-4169-3837-8(0));* 2004. 19.99 *(978-0-689-84836-0(6))* Simon & Schuster Children's Publishing. (Atheneum Bks. for Young Readers).

—The Secret-Keeper. Coombs, Kate. 2006. (ENG.). 32p. (J). (gr. -1-3). 17.99 *(978-0-689-83963-4(4),* Atheneum Bks. for Young Readers) Simon & Schuster Children's Publishing.

—Willa & the Wind, 1 vol. Del Negro, Janice M. 2005. (ENG.). 32p. (J). (gr. k-3). 16.95 *(978-0-7614-5232-4(X))* Marshall Cavendish Corp.

—The 3 Bears & Goldilocks. Willey, Margaret. 2008. (ENG.). 32p. (J). (gr. -1-3). 19.99 *(978-1-4169-2494-4(9),* Atheneum Bks. for Young Readers) Simon & Schuster Children's Publishing.

Solomon, Kerita & W, Chris. The Pancake Kids: Introduction Story. Shivers, Ellen C. 2017. (ENG.). 52p. (J). *(978-1-5255-1020-5(7));* pap. *(978-1-5255-1021-2(5))* FriesenPress.

Solotareff, Gregoire. Wolfy. Solotareff, Gregoire. 2018. (ENG.). 36p. (J). (gr. k-3). 16.99 *(978-1-77657-156-7(8))* Gecko Pr. NZL. Dist: Lerner Publishing Group.

Soltau, Gabriele K. I Love the World: And I Will Make It a Better Place. Soltau, Gabriele K. 2018. (ENG.). 38p. (J). pap. 9.90 *(978-1-7267-7218-1(7))* Independently Published.

Soltero, Emilio. A Very Special Athlete. Flynn, Dale Bachm. 2004. 32p. (J). lib. bdg. 14.95 *(978-0-9741332-1-8(3),* 1237268) Pearl Pr.

Soltero, Emilio. Draw the Line. Soltero, Emilio, text. 2003. 128p. (YA). per. 15.95 *(978-0-9741332-0-1(5))* Pearl Pr.

Solutions (P) Ltd, Matrix Media. One Amazing Day with Papa. Jensen, Fredrich William. 2019. (ENG.). 26p. (J). pap. *(978-1-989161-74-6(X))* Hasmark Services Publishing.

Solutions Ltd, Matrix Media. My Best Buddy Is Forever with Me. Dunn, Lynn. 2018. (ENG.). 26p. (J). pap. *(978-1-988071-81-7(X))* Hasmark Services Publishing.

Solway, Jeff. Maritime Monsters, 1 vol. Vernon, Steve. (ENG.). (J). ed. 2009. 32p. (gr. 4-7). 12.95 *(978-1-55109-727-5(3),* 733962a2-bdba-4cde-8b5d-143f1024a139); 2nd ed. 2019. 48p. pap. 11.95 *(978-1-77108-814-5(1),* 7e6870d7-7d79-4458-9cc1-91dd2623a821) Nimbus Publishing, Ltd. CAN. Dist: Baker & Taylor Publisher Services (BTPS).

Somà, Marco. The Call of the Swamp. Cali, Davide. 2017. (ENG.). 26p. (J). 16.00 *(978-0-8028-5486-5(9),* Eerdmans Bks For Young Readers) Eerdmans, William B. Publishing Co.

Soma, Marco. The Dormouse & His Seven Beds. Isern, Susanna. 2018. (ENG.). 40p. (J). 16.95 *(978-84-946926-6-6(6))* NubeOcho Ediciones ESP. Dist: Consortium Bk. Sales & Distribution.

Somà, Marco. Just Right Time. Isern Iñigo, Susanna. 2019. (ENG.). 32p. (J). (— 1). 16.95 *(978-84-16566-52-5(6))* Ediciones La Fragatina ESP. Dist: Independent Pubs. Group.

Soma, Marco. Las Siete Camas de Lirón. Isern, Susanna. 2018. (SPA.). 40p. (J). 16.95 *(978-84-946926-5-9(8))* NubeOcho Ediciones ESP. Dist: Consortium Bk. Sales & Distribution.

Somaiah, B. Ranjan, jt. illus. see Somaiah, Ranjan.

Somaiah, Ranjan. Indian Children's Favorite Stories. Somaiah, Ranjan. Somaiah, Rosemarie. 2006. (ENG.). 80p. (J). (gr. k-8). 18.95 *(978-0-8048-3687-6(6))* Tuttle Publishing.

Somaiah, Ranjan & Somaiah, B. Ranjan. Indian Children's Favorite Stories: Fables, Myths & Fairy Tales. Somaiah, Rosemarie. 2020. 64p. (J). (gr. k-5). 14.99 *(978-0-8048-5016-2(X))* Tuttle Publishing.

Soman, David. The Amazing Adventures of Bumblebee Boy. Davis, Jacky. 2011. (Ladybug Girl Ser.). (ENG.). 40p. (J). (gr. -1-k). 17.99 *(978-0-8037-3418-0(2),* Dial Bks) Penguin Young Readers Group.

—Bumblebee Boy Loves... Davis, Jacky. 2017. (ENG.). 12p. (J). (-k). bds. 5.99 *(978-0-7352-2869-6(8),* Dial Bks) Penguin Young Readers Group.

—Do You Like These Boots? Davis, Jacky. 2014. (Ladybug Girl Ser.). (ENG.). 32p. (J). (gr. k-1). pap. 4.99 *(978-0-448-46503-6(5),* Penguin Young Readers) Penguin Young Readers Group.

—I Love You, Bingo. Davis, Jacky. 2015. (Ladybug Girl Ser.). (ENG.). 32p. (J). (gr. 1-2). pap. 4.99 *(978-0-448-48756-4(X),* Penguin Young Readers) Penguin Young Readers Group.

—Ladybug Girl. Davis, Jacky. 2008. (Ladybug Girl Ser.). (ENG.). 40p. (J). (gr. -1-k). 17.99 *(978-0-8037-3195-0(7),* Dial Bks) Penguin Young Readers Group.

—Ladybug Girl & Bingo. Davis, Jacky. 2012. (Ladybug Girl Ser.). (ENG.). 40p. (J). (gr. -1-k). 17.99 *(978-0-8037-3582-8(0),* Dial Bks) Penguin Young Readers Group.

—Ladybug Girl & Bumblebee Boy. Davis, Jacky. 2009. (Ladybug Girl Ser.). (ENG.). 40p. (J). (gr. -1-k). 17.99 *(978-0-8037-3339-8(9),* Dial Bks) Penguin Young Readers Group.

—Ladybug Girl & Her Mama. Davis, Jacky. 2013. (Ladybug Girl Ser.). (ENG.). 12p. (J). (gr. -1 — 1). bds. 7.99 *(978-0-8037-3891-1(9),* Dial Bks) Penguin Young Readers Group.

—Ladybug Girl & Her Papa. Davis, Jacky. 2017. (Ladybug Girl Ser.). (ENG.). 12p. (J). (— 1). bds. 6.99 *(978-0-8037-4035-8(2),* Dial Bks) Penguin Young Readers Group.

—Ladybug Girl & the Best Ever Playdate. Davis, Jacky. 2015. (Ladybug Girl Ser.). (ENG.). 40p. (J). (gr. -1-k). 17.99 *(978-0-8037-4030-3(1),* Dial Bks) Penguin Young Readers Group.

—Ladybug Girl & the Big Snow. Davis, Jacky. 2013. (Ladybug Girl Ser.). (ENG.). 40p. (J). (gr. -1-k). 17.99 *(978-0-8037-3583-5(9),* Dial Bks) Penguin Young Readers Group.

—Ladybug Girl & the Bug Squad. Davis, Jacky. 2011. (Ladybug Girl Ser.). (ENG.). 40p. (J). (gr. -1-k). 17.99 *(978-0-8037-3419-7(0),* Dial Bks) Penguin Young Readers Group.

—Ladybug Girl & the Dress-Up Dilemma. Davis, Jacky. 2014. (Ladybug Girl Ser.). (ENG.). 40p. (J). (gr. -1-k). 17.99 *(978-0-8037-3584-2(7),* Dial Bks) Penguin Young Readers Group.

—Ladybug Girl & the Rescue Dogs. Davis, Jacky. 2018. (Ladybug Girl Ser.). (ENG.). 40p. (J). (-k). 17.99 *(978-0-399-18640-0(9),* Dial Bks) Penguin Young Readers Group.

—Ladybug Girl at the Beach. Davis, Jacky. 2010. (Ladybug Girl Ser.). (ENG.). 40p. (J). (gr. -1-k). 17.99 *(978-0-8037-3416-6(6),* Dial Bks) Penguin Young Readers Group.

—Ladybug Girl Feels Happy. Davis, Jacky. 2012. (Ladybug Girl Ser.). (ENG.). 12p. (J). (gr. -1 — 1). bds. 5.99 *(978-0-8037-3890-4(0),* Dial Bks) Penguin Young Readers Group.

—Ladybug Girl Plays. Davis, Jacky. 2013. (Ladybug Girl Ser.). (ENG.). 12p. (J). (gr. -1 — 1). bds. 5.99 *(978-0-8037-3892-8(7),* Dial Bks) Penguin Young Readers Group.

—Ladybug Girl Ready for Snow. Davis, Jacky. 2014. (Ladybug Girl Ser.). (ENG.). 14p. (J). (gr. -1 — 1). bds. 7.99 *(978-0-8037-4137-9(5),* Dial Bks) Penguin Young Readers Group.

—Ladybug Girl Says Good Night. Davis, Jacky. 2014. (Ladybug Girl Ser.). (ENG.). 12p. (J). (gr. -1 — 1). bds. 6.99 *(978-0-8037-3893-5(5),* Dial Bks) Penguin Young Readers Group.

—Ladybug Girl: the Super Fun Edition. Davis, Jacky. 2015. (Ladybug Girl Ser.). (ENG.). 40p. (J). (-k). 18.99 *(978-1-101-99433-7(9),* Dial Bks) Penguin Young Readers Group.

—Ladybug Girl's Day Out with Grandpa. Davis, Jacky. 2017. (Ladybug Girl Ser.). (ENG.). 40p. (J). (-k). 17.99 *(978-0-8037-4032-7(8),* Dial Bks) Penguin Young Readers Group.

—My Big Sister's First Day of School. Heller, Maryellen. 2009. (J). *(978-0-8037-3246-9(5),* Dial) Penguin Publishing Group.

—Who Can Play? Davis, Jacky. 2013. (Ladybug Girl Ser.). (ENG.). 32p. (J). (gr. k-1). pap. 4.99 *(978-0-448-46501-2(9),* Penguin Young Readers) Penguin Young Readers Group.

Soman, David. Agent Lion. Soman, David. Davis, Jacky. 2020. (ENG.). 40p. (J). (gr. -1-3). 17.99 *(978-0-06-286917-3(5))* HarperCollins Pubs.

—Ladybug Girl Dresses Up! Soman, David. Davis, Jacky. 2010. (Ladybug Girl Ser.). (ENG.). 12p. (J). (gr. -1 — 1). bds. 5.99 *(978-0-448-45373-6(8),* Grosset & Dunlap) Penguin Young Readers Group.

—Ladybug Girl Loves... Soman, David. Davis, Jacky. 2010. (Ladybug Girl Ser.). (ENG.). 12p. (J). (gr. -1 — 1). bds. 6.99 *(978-0-448-45374-3(6),* Grosset & Dunlap) Penguin Young Readers Group.

—Ladybug Girl Makes Friends. Soman, David. Davis, Jacky. 2012. (Ladybug Girl Ser.). (ENG.). 12p. (J). (gr. -1 — 1). bds. 5.99 *(978-0-448-45764-2(4),* Grosset & Dunlap) Penguin Young Readers Group.

—Ladybug Girl Visits the Farm. Soman, David. Davis, Jacky. 2011. (Ladybug Girl Ser.). (ENG.). 16p. (J). (gr. -1-k). pap. 6.99 *(978-0-448-45598-3(6),* Grosset & Dunlap) Penguin Young Readers Group.

—Little Box of Ladybug Girl, 4 vols. Soman, David. Davis, Jacky. 2013. (Ladybug Girl Ser.). 14p. (J). (gr. -1-k). bds. 23.96 *(978-0-8037-4102-7(2),* Dial Bks) Penguin Young Readers Group.

—Play All Day with Ladybug Girl. Soman, David. Davis, Jacky. 2013. (Ladybug Girl Ser.). (ENG.). 16p. (J). (gr. -1-k). 6.99

S

(978-0-448-46686-6(4), Grosset & Dunlap) Penguin Young Readers Group.
—Super Catarina y los Super Insectos. Soman, David. Davis, Jacky. 2012. (Ladybug Girl Ser.).Tr. of Ladybug Girl & the Bug Squad. 40p. (J). (gr. -1-k). mass mkt. 6.99 *(978-0-14-242582-4(6)*, Puffin Books) Penguin Young Readers Group.
—Three Bears in a Boat. Soman, David. 2014. 34p. (J). (gr. -1-k). 17.99 *(978-0-8037-3993-2(1)*, Dial Bks) Penguin Publishing Group.
Somerville, Charles C. E Is for Egypt. Somerville, Charles C. 2015. (Is for Alphabet Ser.). 32p. (J). (gr. -1-3). pap. 9.99 *(978-1-907432-15-6(9))* Hogs Back Bks. GBR. Dist: Independent Pubs. Group.
—F Is for Football. Somerville, Charles C. Elliott, Ned. 2014. 32p. (J). (gr. -1-3). pap. 9.99 *(978-1-907432-16-3(7))* Hogs Back Bks. GBR. Dist: Independent Pubs. Group.
Somerville, Hannah. I Just Couldn't Wait to Meet You. Ritchie, Kate. 2015. 32p. (J). (-k). 22.99 *(978-0-85798-970-3(7))* Random Hse. Australia AUS. Dist: Independent Pubs. Group.
Somerville, Sheila. The Adventures of Walter the Weremouse; the Adventures of Mishka the Mousewere. Dashney, John. 2005. 202p. (J). pap. *(978-0-9633236-7-5(9))* Storm Peak Pr.
—The Pig That Bethlehem Never Knew. Copeland, Colene. 2003. 56p. (J). 14.95 *(978-0-939810-26-0(3)*, Q) Jordan Valley Heritage Hse.
Somerville/ Lampstand Press, David. South America: The Continent & Its Countries. Rohwer/Lampstand Press, Lauren. 2008. (ENG.). 56p. (J). pap. 8.95 *(978-1-935301-01-1(2))* Lampstand Pr., Ltd.
Somina, Yulia. Bekalu: From Ethiopia with Love. Wigglesworth, Laura. 2017. (ENG.). 26p. (J). (gr. k-2). 13.99 *(978-0-692-98820-6(3))* Retzler, Laura.
Somina, Yuliya. Porridge the Tartan Cat & the Brawsome Bagpipes, 27 vols. Dapre, Alan. 2017. (Porridge the Tartan Cat Ser.). (ENG.). 152p. (J). pap. 6.95 *(978-1-78250-355-2(2)*, Kelpies) Floris Bks. GBR. Dist: Consortium Bk. Sales & Distribution.
—Porridge the Tartan Cat & the Kittycat Kidnap, 13 vols. Dapre, Alan. 2017. (Porridge the Tartan Cat Ser.). (ENG.). 152p. (J). pap. 6.95 *(978-1-78250-357-6(9)*, Kelpies) Floris Bks. GBR. Dist: Consortium Bk. Sales & Distribution.
—Porridge the Tartan Cat & the Loch Ness Mess, 30 vols. Dapre, Alan. 2017. (Porridge the Tartan Cat Ser.). (ENG.). 152p. (J). pap. 6.95 *(978-1-78250-358-3(7)*, Kelpies) Floris Bks. GBR. Dist: Consortium Bk. Sales & Distribution.
—Porridge the Tartan Cat & the Pet Show Show-Off, 28 vols. Dapre, Alan. 2018. (Porridge the Tartan Cat Ser.: 6). (ENG.). 152p. (J). pap. 6.95 *(978-1-78250-360-6(9)*, Kelpies) Floris Bks. GBR. Dist: Consortium Bk. Sales & Distribution.
—Porridge the Tartan Cat & the Unfair Funfair, 28 vols. Dapre, Alan. 2017. (Porridge the Tartan Cat Ser.). (ENG.). 144p. (J). pap. 6.95 *(978-1-78250-359-0(5)*, Kelpies) Floris Bks. GBR. Dist: Consortium Bk. Sales & Distribution.
Sommariva, Jon. Batman / Teenage Mutant Ninja Turtles Adventures. Manning, Matthew K. 2018. (Batman / Teenage Mutant Ninja Turtles Adventures Ser.). (ENG.). 32p. (J). (gr. 2-6). 131.58 *(978-1-4965-7388-9(9)*, 28659, Stone Arch Bks.) Capstone.
—Batman/Teenage Mutant Ninja Turtles Adventures. Manning, Matthew K. 2017. 144p. (J). (gr. 4-7). pap. 19.99 *(978-1-63140-909-7(3))* Idea & Design Works, LLC.
—The Clown & the Clan. Manning, Matthew K. 2018. (Batman / Teenage Mutant Ninja Turtles Adventures Ser.). (ENG.). 32p. (J). (gr. 2-6). lib. bdg. 28.95 *(978-1-4965-7382-7(X)*, 138940, Stone Arch Bks.) Capstone.
—The Face of Two Worlds. Manning, Matthew K. 2018. (Batman / Teenage Mutant Ninja Turtles Adventures Ser.). (ENG.). 32p. (J). (gr. 2-6). lib. bdg. 28.95 *(978-1-4965-7381-0(1)*, 138939, Stone Arch Bks.) Capstone.
—Greener on the Other Side. Manning, Matthew K. 2018. (Batman / Teenage Mutant Ninja Turtles Adventures Ser.). (ENG.). 32p. (J). (gr. 2-6). lib. bdg. 28.95 *(978-1-4965-7383-4(8)*, 138941, Stone Arch Bks.) Capstone.
—Marvel Action: Avengers: the New Danger (Book One) Manning, Matthew K. 2019. (Marvel Action: Avengers Ser.: 1). 80p. (J). (gr. 4-7). pap. 9.99 *(978-1-68405-515-9(6))* Idea & Design Works, LLC.
—Marvel Action: Avengers: the Ruby Egress (Book Two) Manning, Matthew K. 2019. (Marvel Action: Avengers Ser.: 2). 80p. (J). (gr. 4-7). pap. 9.99 *(978-1-68405-522-7(9))* Idea & Design Works, LLC.
—The Terror of the Kraang. Manning, Matthew K. 2018. (Batman / Teenage Mutant Ninja Turtles Adventures Ser.). (ENG.). 32p. (J). (gr. 2-6). lib. bdg. 28.95 *(978-1-4965-7387-2(0)*, 138944, Stone Arch Bks.) Capstone.
—Through the Looking Glass. Manning, Matthew K. 2018. (Batman / Teenage Mutant Ninja Turtles Adventures Ser.). (ENG.). 32p. (J). (gr. 2-6). lib. bdg. 28.95 *(978-1-4965-7386-5(2)*, 138943, Stone Arch Bks.) Capstone.
—To Laugh So Not to Cry. Manning, Matthew K. 2018. (Batman / Teenage Mutant Ninja Turtles Adventures Ser.). (ENG.). 32p. (J). (gr. 2-6). lib. bdg. 28.95 *(978-1-4965-7385-8(4)*, 138942, Stone Arch Bks.) Capstone.
Sommariva, Jon & Pinto, Valentina. Star Wars Adventures Vol. 7: Pomp & Circumstance. Jackson Miller, John et al. 2019. (Star Wars Adventures Ser.: 7). (ENG.). 96p. (J). (gr. 4-7). pap. 9.99 *(978-1-68405-569-2(5))* Idea & Design Works, LLC.
Sommariva, Jon, jt. illus. see Charm, Derek.
Sommerfeldt Cone, Christine. Lasuris. Sommerfeldt, Lorna. 2020. (ENG.). 318p. (J). pap. 12.95 ***(978-1-6547-6670-2(4))*** Independently Published.
Sommerset, Rowan. Baa Baa Smart Sheep. Sommerset, Mark. 2016. (ENG.). 32p. (J). (gr. k-3). 14.00 *(978-0-7636-8066-4(4))* Candlewick Pr.
—I Love Lemonade. Sommerset, Mark. 2016. (ENG.). 32p. (J). (gr. k-3). 14.00 *(978-0-7636-8067-1(2))* Candlewick Pr.
Sommerville, Hannah. My Friend Ernest. Allen, Emma. 2019. 32p. pap. 6.99 *(978-1-4607-5054-4(3))* HarperCollins Pubs.
Somova, Masha. Snowflake Dreams: A Mountain Tale. Halverson, Kristen. 2018. (ENG.). 34p. (J). pap. 16.99 *(978-1-7295-6254-3(X))* CreateSpace Independent Publishing Platform.
—Star Moon: The Lullaby Horse. Halverson, Kristen. 2019. (ENG.). 34p. (J). 21.99 *(978-1-64570-944-2(2))* The Tale of Noel: The Holiday Horse Angel, The.
—Star Moon, the Lullaby Horse. Halverson, Kristen. 2019. (ENG.). 34p. (J). pap. 12.99 *(978-1-7264-4254-1(3))* CreateSpace Independent Publishing Platform.
Somova, Masha. The Tale of Prince Misha: The Lost Snow Maiden. Halverson, Kristen. 2019. (ENG.). 42p. (J). (gr. 3-6). 24.99 ***(978-0-578-54889-0(5))*** The Tale of Noel: The Holiday Horse Angel, The.
Son, Hee-Joon. Phantasy Degree, Vol. 4. Son, Hee-Joon. rev. ed. 2005. (PhD: Phantasy Degree Ser.). 192p. pap. 9.99 *(978-1-59532-322-4(8))* TOKYOPOP, Inc.
Sona & Jacob. Counting. Singhal, Sheetal. 2007.Tr. of Ginti. (ENG, HIN, GUJ & PAN.). 24p. (J). pap. 8.00 *(978-0-9773645-8-9(5))* MeeraMasi, Inc.
—Diwali: A Festival of Lights & Fun. Kumar, Monica & Kumar, Manisha. 2006.Tr. of Diwali: Khushiyon Ka Tyohaar. (ENG & HIN.). 32p. (J). 11.00 *(978-0-9773645-7-2(7))* MeeraMasi, Inc.
—Jay & Juhi: Taj Mahal Kee Saahsik Khoj. Kumar, Monica. Aggarwal, Madhu, tr. 2008.Tr. of Jay & Juhi: the Taj Mahal Adventure. (HIN & ENG.). 32p. (J). pap. 14.99 *(978-0-9797191-4-1(3))* MeeraMasi, Inc.
—Opposites. Singhal, Sheetal. 2007.Tr. of Vipareet Shabdh. (ENG, HIN, GUJ & PAN.). 32p. (J). pap. 8.00 *(978-0-9773645-9-6(3))* MeeraMasi, Inc.
—Varnamala Geet. 2006. (HIN & ENG.). 3p. (J). 12.00 *(978-0-9773645-6-5(9))* MeeraMasi, Inc.
Sona and Jacob. Hide-n-seek Monday. Darling, Helen. Glickstein, Jennifer, ed. 2007. (J). 10.00 *(978-0-9797674-0-1(7))* My Darling-Tots Pubns.
Sonda, Addy Rivera. Heart of Gold (Cutiecorns #1) Penney, Shannon. 2020. (Cutiecorns Ser.: 1). (ENG.). 112p. (J). (gr. 2-5). pap. 5.99 *(978-1-338-54036-9(X)*, Scholastic Paperbacks) Scholastic, Inc.
—Purrfect Pranksters (Cutiecorns #2) Penney, Shannon. 2020. (Cutiecorns Ser.: 2). (ENG.). 112p. (J). (gr. 2-5). pap. 5.99 *(978-1-338-54038-3(6)*, Scholastic Paperbacks) Scholastic, Inc.
Song, C. & Song, E. El Daddy Jefe de Cocina. Song, Robyn. 2019. (ENG.). 40p. (J). pap. 9.99 *(978-1-7957-1235-4(X))* Independently Published.
Song, Christina. Winter, Winter, Cold & Snow. Palermo, Sharon Gibson. 2016. (ENG.). 24p. (J). (gr. -1-k). 16.99 *(978-1-58536-953-9(5)*, 204110) Sleeping Bear Pr.
Song, Claudine. Respect Me, Respect You: Treating People with Respect Makes Our World a Nicer Place to Live In. Song, Claudine. 2020. (ENG.). 26p. (J). pap. 10.00 ***(978-1-7207-0573-4(9))*** CreateSpace Independent Publishing Platform.
Song, Danielle, jt. illus. see Payne, Rachel.
Song, E., jt. illus. see Song, C.
Song, Jeong-Hwa. Creating a Concert: Sound. Lee, Mi-Ae. 2020. (Science Storybooks Ser.). (ENG.). 32p. (J). (gr. k-4). pap. 8.99 *(978-1-925235-52-4(1))*; lib. bdg. 27.99 *(978-1-925235-56-2(4))* ChoiceMaker Pty. Ltd., The AUS. (Big and SMALL). Dist: Lerner Publishing Group.
Song, Kori. Found in Melbourne. O'Callaghan, Joanne. 2018. (ENG.). 36p. (J). (gr. -1-1). 19.99 *(978-1-76052-341-1(0))* Allen & Unwin AUS. Dist: Independent Pubs. Group.
Song, Mika. Cancer Hates Kisses. Sliwerski, Jessica Reid. 2017. 40p. (J). (-k). 17.99 *(978-0-7352-2781-1(0)*, Dial Bks) Penguin Young Readers Group.
—A Friend for Henry. Bailey, Jenn. 2019. (ENG.). 36p. (J). (gr. k-3). 16.99 *(978-1-4521-6791-6(5))* Chronicle Bks. LLC.
—Ho'onani: Hula Warrior. Gale, Heather. 2019. (ENG.). 40p. (J). (gr. -1-3). 17.99 *(978-0-7352-6449-6(X)*, Tundra Bks.) Tundra Bks. CAN. Dist: Penguin Random Hse. LLC.
Song, Mika. Love, Sophia on the Moon. Rissi, Anica Mrose. 2020. 32p. (J). (gr. -1-3). 17.99 ***(978-1-368-02285-9(5))*** Little, Brown Bks. for Young Readers.
Song, Mika. A New School Year: Poem Stories in Six Voices. Derby, Sally. 2017. 48p. (J). (gr. k-4). lib. bdg. 16.99 *(978-1-58089-730-3(4))* Charlesbridge Publishing, Inc.
Song, Mika. Picnic with Oliver. Song, Mika. 2018. (ENG.). 32p. (J). (gr. -1-3). 17.99 *(978-0-06-242950-6(7))* HarperCollins Pubs.
—Tea with Oliver. Song, Mika. 2017. (ENG.). 40p. (J). (gr. -1-3). 17.99 *(978-0-06-242948-3(5))* HarperCollins Pubs.
Song, Sok. Everyday Origami: A Foldable Fashion Guide. Song, Sok. 2016. (Fashion Origami Ser.). (ENG.). 48p. (J). (gr. 4-8). lib. bdg. 32.65 *(978-1-5157-1630-3(9)*, Capstone Pr.) Capstone.
—Fashion Origami. Song, Sok. 2016. (Fashion Origami Ser.). (ENG.). 48p. (J). (gr. 4-8). lib. bdg., lib. bdg., lib. bdg. 97.95 *(978-1-5157-1653-2(8)*, Capstone Pr.) Capstone.
—Origami Accessories: A Foldable Fashion Guide. Song, Sok. 2016. (Fashion Origami Ser.). (ENG.). 48p. (J). (gr. 4-8). lib. bdg. 32.65 *(978-1-5157-1623-5(6)*, Capstone Pr.) Capstone.
—Origami Chic: A Guide to Foldable Fashion. Song, Sok. 2016. (ENG.). 240p. (J). (gr. 3-3). pap. 14.95 *(978-1-62370-771-2(4)*, Capstone Young Readers) Capstone.
—Origami Outfits: A Foldable Fashion Guide. Song, Sok. 2016. (Fashion Origami Ser.). (ENG.). 48p. (J). (gr. 4-8). lib. bdg. 32.65 *(978-1-5157-1631-0(7)*, Capstone Pr.) Capstone.
Songer, Steve. Joseph Smith: The Boy ... the Prophet. Parry, Jay A. 2019. (ENG.). 48p. (J). (gr. k-6). pap. 14.95 ***(978-1-62730-119-0(4))*** Stonewell Pr.
Songs, Steve. Knick Knack Paddy Whack. Engel, Christiane. 2009. 24p. (J). pap. 6.99 *(978-1-84686-305-9(8))* Barefoot Bks., Inc.
Soni, M. S. Ruhi, jt. illus. see Majumder, Ankur.
Soni, Parwinder Singh. Little Red Riding Hood. 2010. (J). *(978-1-60617-132-5(1))* Teaching Strategies, LLC.
Sonishi, Kenji. Leave It to PET!, Vol. 2. Sonishi, Kenji. 2009. (Leave It to PET! Ser.: 2). (ENG.). 196p. (J). pap. 7.99 *(978-1-4215-2650-8(6))* Viz Media.
—Leave It to PET!, Vol. 3. Sonishi, Kenji. 2009. (Leave It to PET! Ser.: 3). (ENG.). 192p. (J). pap. 7.99 *(978-1-4215-2651-5(4))* Viz Media.
—Leave It to PET!, Vol. 4. Sonishi, Kenji. 2010. (ENG.). 192p. (J). pap. 7.99 *(978-1-4215-2652-2(2))* Viz Media.
Sonke, Sandie. The Little I Who Lost His Dot. Gard, Kimberlee. 2018. (Language Is Fun! Ser.: 1). (ENG.). 32p. (J). (gr. k-2). 16.99 *(978-1-64170-016-0(5)*, 550016) Familius LLC.
—The Triplet Ballerinas. Witwer, Beverly. 2019. (ENG.). 28p. (J). (gr. k-2). pap. 10.99 *(978-1-7328429-0-8(6))* Triple Ballerina Pr.
Sonkin, Jessica. Standing for Socks. Weissman, Elissa Brent. 2009. (ENG.). 224p. (J). (gr. 3-7). 15.99 *(978-1-4169-4801-8(5)*, Atheneum Bks. for Young Readers) Simon & Schuster Children's Publishing.
Sonnenmair, Jan. Cowboy Up: Ride the Navajo Rodeo. Flood, Nancy Bo. 2013. (ENG.). 48p. (J). (gr. 3-7). 17.95 *(978-1-59078-893-6(1)*, Wordsong) Boyds Mills Pr.
Sonsky, Kim. Stamp It! Brush-Free Art Prints & Paint Projects. Sonsky, Kim. Garry-McCord, Kathleen. 2006. 48p. (J). *(978-0-439-81340-2(9))* Scholastic, Inc.
Soo, Kean. The Baker's Run. 2015. (March Grand Prix Ser.). (ENG.). 48p. (J). (gr. 3-6). lib. bdg. 33.32 *(978-1-4342-9640-5(7)*, Capstone Young Readers) Capstone.
—The Fake-Chicken Kung Fu Fighting Blues. Lam, Aaron. 2018. (Lorimer Illustrated Humor Ser.). (ENG.). 152p. (J). (gr. 4-7). pap. 8.99 *(978-1-4594-1272-9(9)*, b49e414f-ae25-4a00-9d3f-e4865422332f); lib. bdg. 27.99 *(978-1-4594-1274-3(5)*, 555d8557-4ae4-4253-938f-55791db879ea) James Lorimer & Co. Ltd., Pubs. CAN. Dist: Lerner Publishing Group.
—The Great Desert Rally. 2015. (March Grand Prix Ser.). (ENG.). 48p. (J). (gr. 3-6). lib. bdg. 33.32 *(978-1-4342-9641-2(5)*, Capstone Young Readers) Capstone.
—March Grand Prix: The Fast & the Furriest. 2015. (March Grand Prix Ser.). (ENG.). 144p. (J). (gr. 3-6). pap. 14.95 *(978-1-62370-171-0(6)*, Capstone Young Readers) Capstone.
Soo, Kean. The Race at Harewood. Soo, Kean. 2015. (March Grand Prix Ser.). (ENG.). 48p. (J). (gr. 3-6). lib. bdg. 33.32 *(978-1-4342-9639-9(3)*, Capstone Young Readers) Capstone.
Sookocheff, Carey. Buddy & Earl, 1 vol. Fergus, Maureen. (Buddy & Earl Ser.: 1). (ENG.). 32p. (J). 2018. (-2). pap. 7.95 *(978-1-77306-119-1(4))*; 2015. (gr. -1-2). 16.95 *(978-1-55498-712-2(1))* Groundwood Bks. CAN. Dist: Publishers Group West (PGW).
—Buddy & Earl & the Great Big Baby, 1 vol. Fergus, Maureen. 2016. (Buddy & Earl Ser.). (ENG.). 32p. (J). (gr. -1-2). 16.95 *(978-1-55498-716-0(4))* Groundwood Bks. CAN. Dist: Publishers Group West (PGW).
—Buddy & Earl Go Exploring, 1 vol. Fergus, Maureen. (Buddy & Earl Ser.: 2). (ENG.). 32p. (J). (gr. k-2). 2018. 7.95 *(978-1-77306-120-7(8))*; 2016. 16.95 *(978-1-55498-714-6(8))* Groundwood Bks. CAN. Dist: Publishers Group West (PGW).
—Buddy & Earl Go to School, 1 vol. Ferguson, Maureen. 2017. (Buddy & Earl Ser.: 4). (ENG.). 32p. (J). (gr. k-2). 16.95 *(978-1-55498-927-0(2))* Groundwood Bks. CAN. Dist: Publishers Group West (PGW).
Sookocheff, Carey. I Do Not Like Stories. Larsen, Andrew. 2020. (ENG.). 32p. (J). (gr. -1-3). 17.95 ***(978-1-77147-378-1(9))*** Owlkids Bks. Inc. CAN. Dist: Publishers Group West (PGW).
Soon, Ileana. Night Train: A Journey from Dusk to Dawn. Cronin Romano, Annie. 2019. (ENG.). 32p. (J). 17.99 *(978-1-62414-657-2(0)*, 900196533) Page Street Publishing Co.
Soper, Patrick. Jolie Blonde & the Three Héberts: A Cajun Twist to an Old Tale, 1 vol. Hébert-Collins, Sheila. 2019. (Cajun Tall Tales Ser.). (ENG.). 32p. (J). (gr. -1-3). 9.99 *(978-1-4556-2480-5(2)*, Pelican Publishing) Arcadia Publishing.
Soper, Vernon. The Magic Walking Stick & Stories from the Arabian Nights. Buchan, John. 2007. 336p. per. 19.95 *(978-0-9791702-8-7(1))* Capricorn Hse. Publishing.
Soprano, Sophie. Laughing All the Way. 2008. (J). *(978-1-59811-642-7(8))* Covenant Communications.
Sorasan, Sorin. L. Ormsby, Mike. 2018. (FRE.). 70p. (J). pap. 14.99 *(978-1-7312-8536-2(1))* Independently Published.
Sorba, Richard. Getting to Know Your Emotional Needs. Dombrower, Jan. Date not set. (J). *(978-1-55864-021-4(5))* Kidsrights.
Sordo, Paco. Corre, Corre, Caballito. Canetti, Yanitzia. 2017. (Rising Readers Ser.). (SPA.). 32p. (J). (gr. k). 5.83 *(978-1-4788-2721-4(1))* Newmark Learning LLC.
—Delivery Bear. Gehl, Laura. 2018. (ENG.). 32p. (J). 16.99 *(978-0-8075-1532-7(9)*, 807515329) Whitman, Albert & Co.
—Fire Truck to the Rescue! Copeland, Alan. 2018. (Take the Wheel! Ser.). (ENG.). 14p. (J). (gr. -1-k). bds. 8.99 *(978-1-4998-0597-0(7))* Little Bee Books Inc.
—Fred Flintstone's Adventures with Pulleys: Work Smarter, Not Harder. Weakland, Mark. 2016. (Flintstones Explain Simple Machines Ser.). (ENG.). 24p. (J). (gr. k-2). lib. bdg. 27.99 *(978-1-4914-8475-3(6))* Capstone.
—Goodnight Lagoon. Ann Scott, Lisa. 2019. (ENG.). 40p. (J). (gr. -1-3). 17.99 *(978-1-4998-0845-2(3))* Little Bee Books Inc.
—Rocket Ship Adventure! Strickland, Stanley. 2018. (Take the Wheel! Ser.). (ENG.). 14p. (J). (gr. -1-k). bds. 8.99 *(978-1-4998-0596-3(9))* Little Bee Books Inc.
—The Science of Rocks & Minerals: The Hard Truth about the Stuff Beneath Our Feet. Woolf, Alex. 2018. (Science of the Earth Ser.). (ENG.). 32p. (J). (gr. 3-7). lib. bdg. 29.00 *(978-0-531-22768-8(5)*, Watts, Franklin) Scholastic Library Publishing.
—Tales of Sasha 1: the Big Secret. Pearl, Alexa. 2017. (Tales of Sasha Ser.: 1). (ENG.). 112p. (J). (gr. k-3). pap. 5.99 *(978-1-4998-0389-1(3))* Little Bee Books Inc.
—Tales of Sasha 10: a Mystery Message. Pearl, Alexa. 2018. (Tales of Sasha Ser.: 10). (ENG.). 112p. (J). (gr. k-3). 16.99 *(978-1-4998-0609-0(4))*; pap. 5.99 *(978-1-4998-0608-3(6))* Little Bee Books Inc.
—Tales of Sasha 2: Journey Beyond the Trees. Pearl, Alexa. 2017. (Tales of Sasha Ser.: 2). (ENG.). 112p. (J). (gr. k-3). pap. 5.99 *(978-1-4998-0391-4(5))* Little Bee Books Inc.
—Tales of Sasha 3: a New Friend. Pearl, Alexa. 2017. (Tales of Sasha Ser.: 3). (ENG.). 112p. (J). (gr. k-3). pap. 5.99 *(978-1-4998-0397-6(4))* Little Bee Books Inc.
—Tales of Sasha: 4 Books In 1! Pearl, Alexa. 2019. (Tales of Sasha Ser.: 1). (ENG.). 416p. (J). (gr. k-3). 14.99 *(978-1-4998-0997-8(2))* Little Bee Books Inc.
—Tales of Sasha 4: Princess Lessons. Pearl, Alexa. 2017. (Tales of Sasha Ser.: 4). (ENG.). 112p. (J). (gr. k-3). pap. 5.99 *(978-1-4998-0399-0(0))* Little Bee Books Inc.
—Tales of Sasha 5: the Plant Pixies. Pearl, Alexa. 2017. (Tales of Sasha Ser.: 5). (ENG.). 112p. (J). (gr. k-3). 16.99 *(978-1-4998-0464-5(4))*; pap. 5.99 *(978-1-4998-0463-8(6))* Little Bee Books Inc.
—Tales of Sasha 6: Wings for Wyatt. Pearl, Alexa. 2017. (Tales of Sasha Ser.: 6). (ENG.). 112p. (J). (gr. k-3). 16.99 *(978-1-4998-0466-9(0))*; pap. 5.99 *(978-1-4998-0465-2(2))* Little Bee Books Inc.
—Tales of Sasha 7: the Royal Island. Pearl, Alexa. 2018. (Tales of Sasha Ser.: 7). (ENG.). 112p. (J). (gr. k-3). 16.99 *(978-1-4998-0603-8(5))*; pap. 5.99 *(978-1-4998-0602-1(7))* Little Bee Books Inc.
—Tales of Sasha 8: Showtime! Pearl, Alexa. 2018. (Tales of Sasha Ser.: 8). (ENG.). 112p. (J). (gr. k-3). 16.99 *(978-1-4998-0605-2(1))*; pap. 5.99 *(978-1-4998-0604-5(3))* Little Bee Books Inc.
—Tales of Sasha 9: the Disappearing History. Pearl, Alexa. 2018. (Tales of Sasha Ser.: 9). (ENG.). 112p. (J). (gr. k-3). 16.99 *(978-1-4998-0607-6(8))*; pap. 5.99 *(978-1-4998-0606-9(X))* Little Bee Books Inc.
—Zoom! Wile E. Coyote Experiments with Speed & Velocity. Weakland, Mark. 2017. (Wile E. Coyote, Physical Science Genius Ser.). (ENG.). 32p. (J). (gr. 3-5). lib. bdg. 31.32 *(978-1-5157-3734-6(9)*, Capstone Pr.) Capstone.
Sordo, Sharon. Ana & Andrew (Spanish Version) (Set), 4 vols. Platt, Christine. 2019. (Ana & Andrew (Spanish Version) Ser.). (SPA.). 32p. (J). (gr. -1-3). lib. bdg. 114.00 *(978-1-5321-3755-6(9)*, 33776, Calico Chapter Bks) Magic Wagon.
—Bailando en el Carnaval (Dancing at Carnival) Platt, Christine. 2019. (Ana & Andrew (Spanish Version) Ser.). (SPA.). 32p. (J). (gr. -1-3). lib. bdg. 28.50 *(978-1-5321-3756-3(7)*, 33778, Calico Chapter Bks) Magic Wagon.
—Dancing at Carnival. Platt, Christine. 2018. (Ana & Andrew Ser.). (ENG.). 32p. (J). (gr. -1-3). lib. bdg. 28.50 *(978-1-5321-3351-0(0)*, 31125, Calico Chapter Bks) Magic Wagon.
—A Day at the Museum. Platt, Christine. 2018. (Ana & Andrew Ser.). (ENG.). 32p. (J). (gr. -1-3). lib. bdg. 28.50 *(978-1-5321-3352-7(9)*, 31127, Calico Chapter Bks) Magic Wagon.
—Un día de Nieve (a Snowy Day) Platt, Christine. 2019. (Ana & Andrew (Spanish Version) Ser.). (SPA.). 32p. (J). (gr. -1-3). lib. bdg. 28.50 *(978-1-5321-3758-7(3)*, 33782, Calico Chapter Bks) Magic Wagon.
—Un día en el Museo (a Day at the Museum) Platt, Christine. 2019. (Ana & Andrew (Spanish Version) Ser.). (SPA.). 32p. (J). (gr. -1-3). lib. bdg. 28.50 *(978-1-5321-3757-0(5)*, 33780, Calico Chapter Bks) Magic Wagon.
—My Food, Your Food, Our Food. Berne, Emma Carlson. 2018. (How Are We Alike & Different? Ser.). (ENG.). 24p. (J). (gr. -1-2). pap. 7.95 *(978-1-68410-290-7(1)*, 139061); lib. bdg. 33.99 *(978-1-68410-238-9(3)*, 138442) Cantata Learning.
—A Snowy Day. Platt, Christine. 2018. (Ana & Andrew Ser.). (ENG.). 32p. (J). (gr. -1-3). lib. bdg. 28.50 *(978-1-5321-3353-4(7)*, 31129, Calico Chapter Bks) Magic Wagon.
—Summer in Savannah. Platt, Christine. 2018. (Ana & Andrew Ser.). (ENG.). 32p. (J). (gr. -1-3). lib. bdg. 28.50 *(978-1-5321-3354-1(5)*, 31131, Calico Chapter Bks) Magic Wagon.
—Summer in Savannah. Patrick, C. P. & Platt, Christine. 2019. (Ana & Andrew Ser.). (ENG.). 32p. (J). pap. 6.95 *(978-1-64494-258-1(5)*, 1644942585, Calico Kid) ABDO Publishing Co.
—El Verano en Savannah (Summer in Savannah) Platt, Christine. 2019. (Ana & Andrew (Spanish Version) Ser.). (SPA.). 32p. (J). (gr. -1-3). lib. bdg. 28.50 *(978-1-5321-3759-4(1)*, 33784, Calico Chapter Bks) Magic Wagon.
Sorel, Edward. Jack & the Beanstalk, 1 vol. Metaxas, Eric. 2005. (Rabbit Ears-A Classic Tale Ser.). (ENG.). 36p. (J). (gr. 2-6). 28.50 *(978-1-59679-345-3(7)*, 12946, Picture Bk.) Spotlight.
Sorensen, Heather. Bugs, Bugs, Bugs! Davies, Kathern. 2010. 24p. pap. 12.99 *(978-1-4520-1624-5(0))* AuthorHouse.
Sorensen, Henri. Daddy Played Music for the Cows. Weidt, Maryann N. 2nd ed. 2004. 32p. (J). pap. 7.95 *(978-0-89317-060-8(7)*, WW-0607, Windward Publishing) Finney Co., Inc.
—My Love Will Be with You. Melmed, Laura Krauss. 2009. (ENG.). 24p. (J). (gr. -1-2). 17.99 *(978-0-06-155260-1(7))* HarperCollins Pubs.
—Ol' Bloo's Boogie-Woogie Band & Blues Ensemble, 1 vol. Huling, Jan. 2010. (ENG.). 32p. (J). (gr. 1-5). 16.95 *(978-1-56145-436-5(2))* Peachtree Publishing Co. Inc.
—Poetry for Young People: Robert Frost. Schmidt, Gary D., ed. 2014. (Poetry for Young People Ser.: 1). 48p. (J). (gr.

3). 14.95 *(978-1-4549-0288-1(4))* Sterling Publishing Co., Inc.

—The Printer, 1 vol. Uhlberg, Myron. (ENG.). 32p. (J). 2009. (gr. -1-3). pap. 8.99 *(978-1-56145-483-9(4))*; 2003. (gr. k-3). 16.95 *(978-1-56145-221-7(1))* Peachtree Publishing Co. Inc.

—Robert Frost. Schmidt, Gary D., ed. 2008. (Poetry for Young People Ser.: 1). 48p. (J). (gr. 3). pap. 6.95 *(978-1-4027-5475-3(2))* Sterling Publishing Co., Inc.

—Wishes for You. Tobias, Tobi. 40p. (J). (gr. -1-2). 2005. pap. 6.99 *(978-0-06-443730-1(2))*; 2003. 16.99 *(978-0-688-10838-0(5))* HarperCollins Pubs.

—The Yellow Star: The Legend of King Christian X of Denmark. Deedy, Carmen Agra. 2020. (ENG.). 32p. (J). (gr. 3-6). pap. 8.99 *(978-1-68263-189-8(3))* Peachtree Publishing Co. Inc.

Sorensen, Peter, jt. illus. see Liss, Ira.

Sorge, Rebecca. The Everything Princess Book: 101 Crafts, Recipes, Stories, Hairstyles, & More! Beery, Barbara et al. 2016. (ENG.). 160p. (J). 19.95 *(978-1-942934-65-3(3)*, 553465) Familius LLC.

—Full of Empty. Myers, Tim J. & Myers, Priscilla. 2016. (ENG.). 32p. (J). 16.95 *(978-1-942934-35-6(1)*, 553435) Familius LLC.

—King Arthur & His Knights. Weiss, Jim. 2nd ed. 2017. (Companion Reader Ser.: 0). (ENG.). (J). (gr. 2-12). audio compact disk 14.95 *(978-1-945841-14-9(1)*, 458414) Well-Trained Mind Pr.

—Spider's Gift: A Christmas Story. Marshall, Geraldine Ann. 2016. 40p. (J). pap. 14.95 *(978-0-8198-9058-0(8))* Pauline Bks. & Media.

—The Sword & the Cape: A Tale of Saint Martin of Tours. Love, Pamela. 2018. 29p. (J). pap. *(978-0-8198-7544-0(9))* Pauline Bks. & Media.

—The Wonderful Wizard of Oz Book & Puzzle Box Set. Baum, Frank. 2017. (Classic Book & Puzzle Set Ser.). (ENG.). 248p. (J). 19.99 *(978-1-944822-51-4(8)*, 552251) Familius LLC.

Sorghienti, Mauro. Alien: Mysterious Monsters (book Two) Slater, David Michael. 2018. (Mysterious Monsters Ser.: 2). (ENG.). 106p. (J). (gr. 2-4). pap. 8.99 *(978-1-944589-26-4(0))* Market Management Group.

—Bigfoot: Mysterious Monsters. Slater, David Michael. 2017. (Mysterious Monsters Ser.: 1). (ENG.). 78p. (J). (gr. 1-4). pap. 7.99 *(978-1-944589-23-3(6))* Market Management Group.

—The Collector: Mysterious Monsters (book Six) Slater, David Michael. 2019. (Mysterious Monsters Ser.: 6). (ENG.). 120p. (J). (gr. 2-4). pap. 8.99 *(978-1-944589-38-7(4))* Market Management Group.

—Ghost: Mysterious Monsters (Book Four) Slater, David Michael. 2019. (Mysterious Monsters Ser.: 4). (ENG.). 100p. (J). pap. 8.99 *(978-1-944589-32-5(5))* Market Management Group.

Sorghienti, Mauro. Mysterious Monsters: The Complete Series. Slater, David Michael. 2019. (Mysterious Monsters Ser.: 1). (ENG.). 470p. (J). (gr. 2-4). pap. 34.95 ***(978-1-944589-34-9(1))*** Market Management Group.

Sorghienti, Mauro. Vampire: Mysterious Monsters (book Three) Slater, David Michael. 2019. (Mysterious Monsters Ser.: 3). (ENG.). 100p. (J). (gr. 1-3). pap. 8.99 *(978-1-944589-29-5(5))* Market Management Group.

—Werewolf: Mysterious Monsters (book Five) Slater, David Michael. 2019. (Mysterious Monsters Ser.: 5). (ENG.). 120p. (J). (gr. 1-4). pap. 8.99 *(978-1-944589-35-6(X))* Market Management Group.

Sorra, Kristin. Groundhog Weather School: Fun Facts about Weather & Groundhogs. Holub, Joan. 2013. (ENG.). 32p. (J). (gr. k-3). 7.99 *(978-0-14-750945-1(9)*, Puffin Books) Penguin Young Readers Group.

—King o' the Cats. Shepard, Aaron. 2010. (ENG.). 32p. (J). (gr. -1-3). 11.99 *(978-1-4424-1256-9(9)*, Atheneum Bks. for Young Readers) Simon & Schuster Children's Publishing.

—My Friend Has ADHD, 1 vol. Tourville, Amanda Doering. 2010. (Friends with Disabilities Ser.). (ENG.). 24p. (J). (gr. k-3). lib. bdg. 26.65 *(978-1-4048-5749-0(4)*, Picture Window Bks.) Capstone.

—My Friend Has ADHD, 1 vol. Doering Tourville, Amanda. 2010. (Friends with Disabilities Ser.). (ENG.). 24p. (J). (gr. k-3). pap. 7.49 *(978-1-4048-6108-4(4)*, Picture Window Bks.) Capstone.

—My Friend Has ADHD [Readers World]. Doering Tourville, Amanda. 2010. (Friends with Disabilities Ser.). 24p. pap. 6.00 *(978-1-4048-6701-7(5)*, Picture Window Bks.) Capstone.

—My Friend Has Autism, 1 vol. Tourville, Amanda Doering. 2010. (Friends with Disabilities Ser.). (ENG.). 24p. (J). (gr. k-3). lib. bdg. 26.65 *(978-1-4048-5750-6(8)*, Picture Window Bks.) Capstone.

—My Friend Has Autism, 1 vol. Doering Tourville, Amanda. 2010. (Friends with Disabilities Ser.). (ENG.). 24p. (J). (gr. k-3). pap. 7.49 *(978-1-4048-6109-1(2)*, Picture Window Bks.) Capstone.

—My Friend Has Autism [Readers World]. Doering Tourville, Amanda. 2010. (Friends with Disabilities Ser.). 24p. pap. 6.00 *(978-1-4048-6702-4(3)*, Picture Window Bks.) Capstone.

—My Friend Has down Syndrome, 1 vol. Doering Tourville, Amanda. 2010. (Friends with Disabilities Ser.). (ENG.). 24p. (J). (gr. k-3). pap. 7.49 *(978-1-4048-6110-7(6)*, Picture Window Bks.) Capstone.

—My Friend Has down Syndrome, 1 vol. Tourville, Amanda Doering. 2010. (Friends with Disabilities Ser.). (ENG.). 24p. (J). (gr. k-3). lib. bdg. 26.65 *(978-1-4048-5751-3(6)*, Picture Window Bks.) Capstone.

—My Friend Has down Syndrome [Readers World]. Doering Tourville, Amanda. 2010. (Friends with Disabilities Ser.). 24p. pap. 6.00 *(978-1-4048-6703-1(1)*, Picture Window Bks.) Capstone.

—My Friend Has Dyslexia, 1 vol. Tourville, Amanda Doering. 2010. (Friends with Disabilities Ser.). (ENG.). 24p. (J). (gr. k-3). lib. bdg. 26.65 *(978-1-4048-5752-0(4)*, Picture Window Bks.) Capstone.

—My Friend Has Dyslexia [Readers World]. Doering Tourville, Amanda. 2010. (Friends with Disabilities Ser.). 24p. pap. 6.00 *(978-1-4048-6704-8(X)*, Picture Window Bks.) Capstone.

—Scarlett the Cat to the Rescue: Fire Hero, 1 vol. Loewen, Nancy. 2014. (Animal Heroes Ser.). (ENG.). 32p. (J). (gr. k-2). 29.32 *(978-1-4795-5464-5(2)*, Picture Window Bks.) Capstone.

Sorra, Kristin. Mi Amiga Tiene Síndrome de Down. Sorra, Kristin. Tourville, Amanda Doering. Translations.com Staff, tr. 2012. (Amigos con Discapacidades/Friends with Disabilities Ser.). (ENG.). 24p. (J). (gr. k-3). lib. bdg. 26.65 *(978-1-4048-7313-1(9)*, Picture Window Bks.) Capstone.

—Mi Amigo Tiene ADHD. Sorra, Kristin. Tourville, Amanda Doering. Translations.com Staff, tr. 2012. (Amigos con Discapacidades/Friends with Disabilities Ser.).Tr. of My Friend Has ADHD. (ENG.). 24p. (J). (gr. k-3). lib. bdg. 26.65 *(978-1-4048-7311-7(2)*, Picture Window Bks.) Capstone.

Sorrentino, Alessandra, jt. illus. see Random House.

Sorrentino, Andrea, jt. illus. see Leon, Nico.

Sorrentino, Andrea, jt. illus. see Marquez, David.

Sorrentino, Flavia. The Big Book of Twisted Fairy Tales: Stories about Kindness, Responsibility, Honesty, & Teamwork. Nicholson, Sue. 2019. (Fairytale Friends Ser.). (ENG.). 96p. (J). (gr. k-2). 14.99 ***(978-1-78603-988-0(5))*** QEB Publishing Inc.

Sorrentino, Flavia. Book 1: the Howler. Gohmann, Johanna. 2017. (Ursula's Funland Ser.). (ENG.). 48p. (J). (gr. 3-7). lib. bdg. 29.93 *(978-1-5321-3011-3(2)*, 25568, Spellbound) Magic Wagon.

—Book 2: the Face in the Photo. Gohmann, Johanna. 2017. (Ursula's Funland Ser.). (ENG.). 48p. (J). (gr. 3-7). lib. bdg. 29.93 *(978-1-5321-3012-0(0)*, 25570, Spellbound) Magic Wagon.

—Book 3: the Fortune Teller. Gohmann, Johanna. 2017. (Ursula's Funland Ser.). (ENG.). 48p. (J). (gr. 3-7). lib. bdg. 29.93 *(978-1-5321-3013-7(9)*, 25572, Spellbound) Magic Wagon.

—Book 4: the Hall of Mirrors. Gohmann, Johanna. 2017. (Ursula's Funland Ser.). (ENG.). 48p. (J). (gr. 3-7). lib. bdg. 29.93 *(978-1-5321-3014-4(7)*, 25574, Spellbound) Magic Wagon.

—The Boy Who Cried Wolf. Hoena, Blake. 2018. (Classic Fables in Rhythm & Rhyme Ser.). (ENG.). 24p. (C). (gr. k-2). lib. bdg. 33.99 *(978-1-68410-385-0(1)*, 140359) Cantata Learning.

—Cinderella's Ballet Shoes. Nicholson, Sue. 2019. (Fairytale Friends Ser.). (ENG.). 24p. (J). (gr. -1-k). lib. bdg. 27.99 *(978-1-78603-565-3(0))* QEB Publishing Inc.

—Diwali. Morey, Allan. 2018. (Holidays in Rhythm & Rhyme Ser.). (ENG.). 24p. (J). (gr. -1-3). lib. bdg. 33.99 *(978-1-68410-381-2(9)*, 140354) Cantata Learning.

—Jack Breaks the Beanstalk. Nicholson, Sue. 2019. (Fairytale Friends Ser.). (ENG.). 24p. (J). (gr. -1-k). lib. bdg. 27.99 *(978-1-78603-568-4(5))* QEB Publishing Inc.

—Snow White, Star Striker. Nicholson, Sue. 2019. (Fairytale Friends Ser.). (ENG.). 24p. (J). (gr. -1-k). lib. bdg. 27.99 *(978-1-78603-571-4(5))* QEB Publishing Inc.

—Ursula's Funland (Set), 4 vols. Gohmann, Johanna. 2017. (Ursula's Funland Ser.). 48p. (J). (gr. 3-7). lib. bdg. 114.00 *(978-1-5321-3010-6(4)*, 25566, Spellbound) Magic Wagon.

—Wake up, Sleepy Beauty! Nicholson, Sue. 2019. (Fairytale Friends Ser.). (ENG.). 24p. (J). (gr. -1-k). lib. bdg. 27.99 *(978-1-78603-574-5(X))* QEB Publishing Inc.

Sorrentino, Natalie. Will It. Kotloski, Courtney. 2019. (ENG.). 32p. (J). 15.99 *(978-1-948365-96-3(0))* Orange Hat Publishing.

Sorrow, Casey. The Cats of Copenhagen. Joyce, James. 2012. (ENG.). 32p. 19.99 *(978-1-4767-0894-2(0)*, Scribner) Scribner.

Sorte, Marta. Weird & Amazing Things Pets Do! Fiedler, Heidi. 2018. (Wacky Things Ser.). (ENG.). 32p. (J). (gr. 3-5). lib. bdg. 27.99 *(978-1-60058-788-7(7)*, 9781600587887); lib. bdg. 27.99 *(978-1-60058-789-4(5)*, 9781600587894) Quarto Publishing Group USA. (Walter Foster Jr).

Sosa, Daniela. All God's Creatures: Chunky Lift a Flap Board Book. Swift, Ginger. Cottage Door Press, ed. 2019. (ENG.). 12p. (J). (gr. -1-2). bds. 7.99 *(978-1-68052-523-6(9)*, 1003790) Cottage Door Pr.

Sosa, Daniela. Away in a Manger. Berry-Byrd, Holly. Cottage Door Press, ed. ed. 2020. (3-Button Early Bird Sound Bks.). (ENG.). 12p. (J). (gr. -1 — 1). bds. 9.99 ***(978-1-68052-988-3(9)****, 1006150)* Cottage Door Pr.

Sosa, Daniela. Bless This Food. Swift, Ginger. Cottage Door Press, ed. 2019. (ENG.). 12p. (J). (gr. -1-k). bds. 7.99 *(978-1-68052-524-3(7)*, 1003800) Cottage Door Pr.

—Good Morning, God: Chunky Lift a Flap Board Book. Swift, Ginger. Cottage Door Press, ed. 2018. (Little Sunbeams Ser.). (ENG.). 12p. (J). (gr. -1-k). bds. 7.99 *(978-1-68052-377-5(5)*, 1003420) Cottage Door Pr.

—Good Night, God: Chunky Lift a Flap Board Book. Swift, Ginger. Cottage Door Press, ed. 2018. (Little Sunbeams Ser.). (ENG.). 12p. (J). (gr. -1-k). bds. 7.99 *(978-1-68052-375-1(9)*, 1003400) Cottage Door Pr.

Sosa, Daniela. Me & Mcgee. Uhlberg, Myron. 2020. (ENG.). 32p. (J). (gr. -1-3). 16.99 ***(978-0-8075-5028-1(0)****,* 807550280) Whitman, Albert & Co.

Sosa, Hernan. Armando & the Blue Tarp School, 1 vol. Fine, Edith H. & Josephson, Judith P. 2007. (ENG.). 32p. (J). (gr. -1-3). lib. bdg. 17.95 *(978-1-58430-278-0(X))* Lee & Low Bks., Inc.

—Armando y la Escuela de Lona Azul. Fine, Edith H. & Josephson, Judith P. 2015.Tr. of Armando & the Blue Tarp School. (SPA.). 32p. (J). (gr. k-4). pap. 11.95 *(978-1-60060-449-2(8))* Lee & Low Bks., Inc.

—Mimi's Parranda/la Parranda de Mimi. Gil, Lydia M. 2007. (SPA & ENG.). 32p. (J). (gr. -1-2). 16.95 *(978-1-55885-477-2(0)*, Piñata Books) Arte Publico Pr.

Sosa, Marcelo. The Aeneid: A Graphic Novel. Agrimbau, Diego. 2018. (Classic Fiction Ser.). (ENG.). 80p. (J). (gr. 5-9). lib. bdg. 27.32 *(978-1-4965-6113-8(9)*, 137710, Stone Arch Bks.) Capstone.

Sosebee, Cheryl. Bobby's Dove. Hamilton, Matthew. 2005. (J). bds. 9.99 *(978-1-4183-0061-6(6))* Christ Inspired, Inc.

Sosnowski, Tiffany. Ace's Wish for a Forever Home. Written By Kimberly M Sosnowski; Illustr. 2011. 28p. pap. 24.95 *(978-1-4626-3031-8(6))* America Star Bks.

Sossella, David. American Revolution: A Handbook for Time Travelers. Stokes, Jonathan W. 2019. (Thrifty Guides: 2). 150p. (J). (gr. 3-7). pap. 8.99 *(978-1-101-99813-7(X)*, Puffin Books) Penguin Young Readers Group.

Sossella, David. Lukezilla Beats the Game. Scaletta, Kurtis. 2020. (ENG.). 240p. (J). (gr. 4-8). 16.99 ***(978-1-68446-204-9(5)****,* 200652, Capstone Editions) Capstone.

Sossella, David. The Thrifty Guide to Ancient Rome. Stokes, Jonathan W. 2018. (Thrifty Guides: 1). 144p. (J). (gr. 3-7). 13.99 *(978-0-451-47960-0(2)*, Viking Books for Young Readers) Penguin Young Readers Group.

—Thrifty Guide to Ancient Rome: The a Handbook for Time Travelers. Stokes, Jonathan W. 2019. (Thrifty Guides: 1). 144p. (J). (gr. 3-7). pap. 8.99 *(978-1-101-99810-6(5)*, Puffin Books) Penguin Young Readers Group.

—The Thrifty Guide to the American Revolution. Stokes, Jonathan W. 2018. (Thrifty Guides: 2). 160p. (J). (gr. 3-7). 13.99 *(978-0-451-47961-7(0)*, Viking Books for Young Readers) Penguin Young Readers Group.

Sotirovski, Aleksandar. Ali-A Adventures: Game on! the Graphic Novel. Ali-A & Scott, Cavan. 2017. (ENG.). 192p. (J). (gr. 3-7). 19.99 *(978-1-5247-7095-2(7))*; lib. bdg. 22.99 *(978-1-5247-7096-9(5))* Random Hse. Children's Bks. (Random Hse. Bks. for Young Readers).

Sotirovski, Aleksandar. Drummer Boys Lead the Charge: Courageous Kids of the Civil War. Berglund, Bruce. 2020. (Courageous Kids Ser.). (ENG.). 32p. (J). (gr. 3-5). pap. 7.95 ***(978-1-4966-8805-7(8)****,* 201690); lib. bdg. 31.32 ***(978-1-4966-8504-9(0)****,* 200560) Capstone. (Capstone Pr.).

Sotirovski, Aleksandar. Earthquakes!, 1 vol. Gray-Wilburn, Renée. 2012. (First Graphics: Wild Earth Ser.). (ENG.). 24p. (J). (gr. k-3). pap. 6.29 *(978-1-4296-7950-3(6))*; (J). (gr. k-3). lib. bdg. 24.65 *(978-1-4296-7605-2(1))*; (gr. 1-2). pap. 35.70 *(978-1-4296-8370-8(8))* Capstone.

—First Graphics: Wild Earth. Aboff, Marcie & Gray-Wilburn, Renée. 2012. (First Graphics: Wild Earth Ser.). (ENG.). 24p. (J). (gr. k-3). pap., pap., pap. 25.16 *(978-1-4296-8374-6(0))*; (J). (gr. k-3). lib. bdg., lib. bdg., lib. bdg. 73.95 *(978-1-4296-8146-9(2))*; (gr. 1-2). pap. 142.80 *(978-1-4296-8375-3(9))* Capstone.

—Hurricanes!, 1 vol. Aboff, Marcie. 2012. (First Graphics: Wild Earth Ser.). (ENG.). 24p. (J). (gr. k-3). pap. 6.29 *(978-1-4296-7951-0(4))*; (J). (gr. k-3). lib. bdg. 24.65 *(978-1-4296-7607-6(8))*; (gr. 1-2). pap. 35.70 *(978-1-4296-8371-5(6))* Capstone.

—Tornadoes!, 1 vol. Aboff, Marcie. 2012. (First Graphics: Wild Earth Ser.). (ENG.). 24p. (J). (gr. k-3). pap. 6.29 *(978-1-4296-7952-7(2))*; (J). (gr. k-3). lib. bdg. 24.65 *(978-1-4296-7608-3(6))*; (gr. 1-2). pap. 35.70 *(978-1-4296-8372-2(4))* Capstone.

—Volcanoes!, 1 vol. Gray-Wilburn, Renée & Beehive Illustrations Staff. 2012. (First Graphics: Wild Earth Ser.). (ENG.). 24p. (J). (gr. k-3). pap. 6.29 *(978-1-4296-7953-4(0))* Capstone.

—Volcanoes! Gray-Wilburn, Renée. 2012. (First Graphics: Wild Earth Ser.). 24p. (gr. 1-2). pap. 35.70 *(978-1-4296-8373-9(2))* Capstone.

Sotnik, Katherine. Choirs of Angels Coloring Book. Maritain, Jacques. 2012. (ENG.). 195p. (gr. -1-3). 17.95 *(978-1-58617-588-7(2))* Ignatius Pr.

Soto, Lucia. Uncle Bobby's Wedding (2020) Brannen, Sarah S. 2020. (ENG.). 32p. (J). (gr. -1-1). 17.99 ***(978-1-4998-1008-0(3))*** Little Bee Books Inc.

Soto, Michelle. What Good Is a Mushroom? A Fictional Look at the Interactions of Living Things. Anderson, Kimberly Griffith. 2020. (ENG.). 28p. (J). pap. 9.99 ***(978-1-7186-8710-3(9))*** CreateSpace Independent Publishing Platform.

Sotomayor, Chris, jt. illus. see Pham, Khoi.

Sotomayor, Chris, jt. illus. see Qualano, Pascale.

Sotomayor, Chris, jt. illus. see Qualano, Pasquale.

Sotomayor, Dario Brizuela Chris. Inferno! McCann, Jim. 2019. (Marvel Super Hero Adventures Graphic Novels Ser.). (ENG.). 24p. (J). (gr. 1-5). lib. bdg. 27.07 *(978-1-5321-4449-3(0)*, 33853, Marvel Age) Spotlight.

—Ms. Marvel & the Teleporting Dog. McCann, Jim. 2019. (Marvel Super Hero Adventures Graphic Novels Ser.). (ENG.). 24p. (J). (gr. 1-5). lib. bdg. 27.07 *(978-1-5321-4450-9(4)*, 33855, Marvel Age) Spotlight.

—Webs & Arrows & Ants, Oh My! McCann, Jim. 2019. (Marvel Super Hero Adventures Graphic Novels Ser.). (ENG.). 24p. (J). (gr. 1-5). lib. bdg. 27.07 *(978-1-5321-4457-8(1)*, 33862, Marvel Age) Spotlight.

Sotuyo, Ayme. Lumberjanes Vol. 10: Parents' Day. Leyh, Kat. 2018. (Lumberjanes Ser.: 10). (ENG.). 112p. (J). (gr. 5). pap. 14.99 *(978-1-68415-278-0(X))* Boom! Studios.

—Lumberjanes Vol. 11. Leyh, Kat. 2019. (Lumberjanes Ser.). (ENG.). 112p. (J). (gr. 4-7). pap. 14.99 *(978-1-68415-325-1(5))* Boom! Studios.

Sotuyo, Ayme, jt. illus. see Nowak, Carolyn.

Soud. Abraham Lincoln: 16th U. S. President, 1 vol. Hall, Margaret. 2008. (Beginner Biographies Ser.). (ENG.). 32p. (J). (gr. k-4). 28.50 *(978-1-60270-250-9(0)*, 3451, Looking Glass Library) Magic Wagon.

—Being You. Pate, Alexs. 2018. (ENG.). 32p. (J). (gr. -1-4). 17.95 *(978-1-68446-021-2(2)*, 139169, Capstone Editions) Capstone.

—George Washington: 1st U. S. President, 1 vol. Cosson, Jody. 2008. (Beginner Biographies Ser.). (ENG.). 32p. (J). (gr. k-4). 28.50 *(978-1-60270-253-0(5)*, 3457, Looking Glass Library) Magic Wagon.

—Jane Goodall: Friend of the Apes, 1 vol. Lindeen, Mary. 2008. (Beginner Biographies Ser.). (ENG.). 32p. (J). (gr. k-4). 28.50 *(978-1-60270-249-3(7)*, 3449, Looking Glass Library) Magic Wagon.

—Kate, the Ghost Dog: Coping with the Death of a Pet. Wilson, Wayne L. 2009. 48p. (J). (gr. 3-8). 14.95 *(978-1-4338-0554-7(5))*; pap. 9.95 *(978-1-4338-0555-4(3))* American Psychological Assn. (Magination Pr.).

—Marie Curie: Scientist, 1 vol. Lindeen, Mary. 2008. (Beginner Biographies Ser.). (ENG.). 32p. (J). (gr. k-4). 28.50 *(978-1-60270-248-6(9)*, 3447, Looking Glass Library) Magic Wagon.

—Martin Luther King, Jr. Civil Rights Leader, 1 vol. Hall, M. C. 2008. (Beginner Biographies Ser.). (ENG.). 32p. (J). (gr. k-4). 28.50 *(978-1-60270-251-6(9)*, 3453, Looking Glass Library) Magic Wagon.

—Sacagawea: Indian Guide, 1 vol. Cosson, Jody. 2008. (Beginner Biographies Ser.). (ENG.). 32p. (J). (gr. k-4). 28.50 *(978-1-60270-252-3(7)*, 3455, Looking Glass Library) Magic Wagon.

Souhami, Jessica. The Leopard's Drum: An Asante Tale from West Africa. 2006. (ENG.). 36p. (J). (gr. -1-2). 8.99 *(978-1-84507-506-4(4)*, Frances Lincoln Children's Bks.) Quarto Publishing Group UK GBR. Dist: Hachette Bk. Group.

Souleiman, Serg. The Golden Book of Death. Dahl, Michael. 2008. (Library of Doom Ser.). (ENG.). 40p. (J). (gr. 4-8). lib. bdg. 23.99 *(978-1-4342-0487-5(1))*; per. 6.25 *(978-1-4342-0547-6(9))* Capstone. (Stone Arch Bks.).

—El Libro Dorado de la Muerte. Dahl, Michael. 2020. (Biblioteca Maldita Ser.).Tr. of Golden Book of Death. (SPA.). 40p. (J). (gr. 4-8). pap. 6.95 *(978-1-4965-9308-5(1)*, 142320); lib. bdg. 23.99 *(978-1-4965-9169-2(0)*, 142082) Capstone. (Stone Arch Bks.).

Soulier, Daniel. Pateando Lunas. Berocay, Roy. 2003. (SPA.). 166p. (J). (gr. 3). pap. 12.95 *(978-9974-590-63-2(9))* Santillana S. A. URY. Dist: Santillana USA Publishing Co., Inc.

—Pateando Lunas. Berocay, Roy. 2015. (Serie Naranja Ser.). (SPA.). 128p. (J). pap. 10.99 *(978-1-64101-140-2(8))* Santillana USA Publishing Co., Inc.

Soumagnac, Virginie. Zero Kisses for Me. Monari, Manuela. 2010. (ENG.). 24p. (J). (gr. -1-1). 12.95 *(978-1-77049-208-0(9)*, Tundra Bks.) Tundra Bks. CAN. Dist: Penguin Random Hse. LLC.

Sourwine, David. The Dragon Prince. Blum, Vicki. 2005. (ENG.). 160p. pap. *(978-0-439-95668-0(4))* Scholastic Canada, Ltd.

Sousa, Agusti. Great Streets of the World: From London to San Francisco. Berchtig, Frauke. 2019. (ENG.). 40p. (J). (gr. k-4). 14.95 *(978-3-7913-7403-1(6))* Prestel Verlag GmbH & Co KG. DEU. Dist: Penguin Random Hse. LLC.

Sousa, Jay, photos by. How to Build a California Mission: Santa Barbara, 20 vols. Campodonica, Carol A. Wardup, Shirley et al, eds. Date not set. (How to Build a California Mission Ser.). (J). (gr. 4-5). pap. *(978-0-9648488-3-2(X))* Buzzard Pr. International.

Southard, Jan. Ookie! Stoll, Emily. 2012. 28p. pap. 12.00 *(978-1-4575-0859-2(1))* Dog Ear Publishing, LLC.

Southerland, Christina. A True Princess. Bishop, Carrie. 2018. (ENG.). 30p. (J). pap. 12.50 *(978-1-9841-2608-5(3))* CreateSpace Independent Publishing Platform.

Southerland, Taylor. The Savvy Cyber Kids at Home: The Defeat of the Cyber Bully. Halpert, Ben. 2011. (J). 22.99 *(978-0-9827968-4-9(6))* Savvy Cyber Kids, Inc.

Southorn, Michael. The Mystery of the Golden Tower. Newman, Elaine. 2016. (ENG.). 91p. (J). (gr. k-2). pap. *(978-0-9956190-2-9(6))* Pixel Tweaks Pub.

Souva, Jacob. The Boy with Big, Big Feelings, Vol. Lee, Britney Winn. 2019. (ENG.). 32p. (J). (gr. -1-3). 17.99 *(978-1-5064-5450-4(X)*, Beaming Books) Augsburg Fortress, Pubs.

—Hide-And-Seek Ladybugs. Bright, Paul. 2020. (ENG.). (J). 26p. (-k). bds. 9.99 *(978-1-68010-606-0(6))*; 32p. (gr. -1-2). 17.99 *(978-1-68010-206-2(0))* Tiger Tales.

—Pedro's Pan: A Gold Rush Story. Lasley, Matthew. 2019. (ENG.). 32p. (J). (gr. k-2). 17.99 *(978-1-5132-6187-4(8)*, Alaska Northwest Bks.) West Margin Pr.

—Where Does a Cowgirl Go Potty? Prochovnic, Dawn Babb. 2019. (ENG.). 32p. (J). (gr. k-3). 16.99 *(978-1-5132-6238-3(6)*, West Margin Pr.) West Margin Pr.

—Where Does a Pirate Go Potty? Prochovnic, Dawn Babb. 2019. (ENG.). 32p. (J). (gr. k-3). 16.99 *(978-1-5132-6240-6(8)*, West Margin Pr.) West Margin Pr.

Souza, Jared. Dreaming of New Orleans: Counting down Around the Town. Everin, Gretchen. 2019. (Dreaming Of... Ser.). (ENG.). 16p. (J). bds. 9.95 *(978-1-64194-132-7(4)*, Commonwealth Editions) Applewood Bks.

Souza, Paul. Roy Rogers & the Desert Treasure. Sankey, Alice. 2011. 26p. 35.95 *(978-1-258-03927-1(3))* Literary Licensing, LLC.

Sovak, Jean-Marc Superville. Deadly. Chibbaro, Julie. (ENG.). 304p. (YA). (gr. 7). 2012. pap. 10.99 *(978-0-689-85739-3(X))*; 2011. 17.99 *(978-0-689-85738-6(1))* Simon & Schuster Children's Publishing. (Atheneum Bks. for Young Readers).

Sowards, Ben. Christmas Oranges. 2004. 32p. 17.95 *(978-1-59156-098-2(5))* Covenant Communications, Inc.

—The Eyes of the Want. Skye, Obert. 2008. (Leven Thumps Ser.: 3). (ENG.). 464p. (J). (gr. 3-7). pap. 10.99 *(978-1-4169-4719-6(1)*, Aladdin) Simon & Schuster Children's Publishing.

—He Took My Lickin' for Me: A Classic Folk Tale. 2003. 32p. (J). (gr. 3-7). 16.95 *(978-1-57008-953-4(1)*, Shadow Mountain) Shadow Mountain Publishing.

—Leven Thumps the Complete Series: The Gateway; the Whispered Secret; the Eyes of the Want; the Wrath of Ezra; the Ruins of Alder. Skye, Obert. ed. 2018. (Leven Thumps Ser.). (ENG.). 2208p. (J). (gr. 3-7). pap. 49.99 *(978-1-5344-1876-9(8)*, Aladdin) Simon & Schuster Children's Publishing.

—Penny's Christmas Jar Party. Wright, Jason F. 2009. 32p. (J). 17.95 *(978-1-60641-167-4(5)*, Shadow Mountain) Shadow Mountain Publishing.

—The Ruins of Alder. Skye, Obert. 2010. (Leven Thumps Ser.: 5). (ENG.). 416p. (J). (gr. 4-9). pap. 10.99 *(978-1-4169-9093-2(3)*, Aladdin) Simon & Schuster Children's Publishing.

—The Whispered Secret. Skye, Obert. 2007. (Leven Thumps Ser.: 2). (ENG.). 464p. (J). (gr. 3-7). pap. 10.99 (978-1-4169-4718-9(3), Aladdin) Simon & Schuster Children's Publishing.

—The Wrath of Ezra. Skye, Obert. 2009. (Leven Thumps Ser.: 4). (ENG.). 464p. (J). (gr. 4-9). pap. 10.99 (978-1-4169-9092-5(5), Aladdin) Simon & Schuster Children's Publishing.

—You Are Priceless: The Parable of the Bicycle. Robinson, Stephen Edward. 2004. 32p. (J). (gr. -1-3). 18.95 (978-1-59038-361-2(3), Shadow Mountain) Shadow Mountain Publishing.

Sowards, Ben. Asleep on the Hay: A Dust Bowl Christmas. Sowards, Ben. 2015. (ENG.). 32p. (J). (gr. 3). 17.99 (978-1-62972-067-8(4), Ensign Peak) Shadow Mountain Publishing.

Sowerby, Githa & Sowerby, Millicent. Cinderella. 2012. (J). (978-1-59583-458-4(3)) Laughing Elephant.

Sowerby, Malcolm. Sid & the Wicked Weta King: The Awesome Adventures of a Spider Named Sid. Wyeth, Tony. 2019. (ENG.). 36p. (J). pap. **(978-0-473-49724-8(7))** HookMedia Co. Ltd.

Sowerby, Millicent, jt. illus. see Sowerby, Githa.

Soye, Alison. Maggie's Monsters. Clayton, Coo. 2018. (Maggie Ser.). 36p. (J). (gr. -1-k). pap. 12.99 (978-1-78530-177-3(2)) Black and White Publishing Ltd. GBR. Dist: Independent Pubs. Group.

Sozapato. Monstruos (Libro + CD) Williams, Ricardo. 2015. (Serie Verde / Álbum Ilustrado Ser.). (SPA.). 24p. (J). (gr. -1-2). pap. 14.95 (978-9942-19-336-0(7)) Santillana Ecuador ECU. Dist: Santillana USA Publishing Co., Inc.

Spaceheater, Dreamstime Com. My Book of Sleepy Time Tales. Cubbinz, Zenaida. 2nd ed. 2018. (ENG.). 80p. (J). (gr. k-1). pap. (978-1-912315-34-5(3)) Stergiou Ltd.

Spachner, Karen D. Volcano Adventures of Keikilani. Jackson, Kimberly. 2009. 32p. pap. 8.95 (978-0-9643512-1-9(8)) Mouse! Publishing.

Spackman, Jeff. Boo! Halloween Poems & Limericks, 1 vol. Hubbell, Patricia. 2005. (ENG.). 32p. (YA). pap. 5.95 (978-0-7614-5151-8(X)) Marshall Cavendish Corp.

Spada, Maria. The Lost Legends. Marie, Cait. Craven, Melissa, ed. 2020. (Nihryst Ser.: Vol. 1). (ENG.). 358p. (J). pap. 14.99 **(978-1-6737-9552-3(8))** Independently Published.

Spadaccini, Cheryl. Where Will We Fly. Seymour, Marysue. 2013. 20p. pap. 9.95 (978-1-61633-417-8(7)) Guardian Angel Publishing, Inc.

Spafford, Suzy. My Little Book of Prayers. gif. ed. 2005. 32p. 9.99 (978-0-7369-1495-6(1)) Harvest Hse. Pubs.

—Periwinkle's Journey. Petersen-Fleming, Judy & Spafford, Judy. 2016. (ENG.). (J). 16.99 (978-1-943198-03-0(9)) Southwestern Publishing Hse., Inc.

Spafford, Suzy. Helping-Out Day? Hooray! Spafford, Suzy. 2003. (Tales from Duckport Ser.). (ENG.). 40p. (J). (gr. k-3). pap. 3.99 (978-0-439-38358-5(7)) Scholastic, Inc.

Spagarino, Cristina, jt. illus. see Boeri, Irene.

Spagnol, Hannah & Spagnol, Tayleigh. Life with Daddy... & His Boyfriend. Spagnol, Noreen. 2019. (Life With... Ser.). (ENG.). 36p. (J). (978-1-5255-4504-7(3)); pap. (978-1-5255-4505-4(1)) FriesenPress.

Spagnol, Tayleigh, jt. illus. see Spagnol, Hannah.

Spahn, Jerrold. Pearl Harbor: A Day of Infamy. White, Steve D. 2007. (Graphic Battles of World War II Ser.). (ENG.). 48p. (YA). (gr. 4-7). lib. bdg. 35.45 (978-1-4042-0785-1(6)) Rosen Publishing Group, Inc., The.

Spalinski, Amanda. El circo llega al Pueblo: Version de Lectura Temprana. Scalzo, Linda V. Torres, Marcela H., tr. I.t. ed. 2005. (SPA.). 24p. per. 9.99 (978-0-9753724-2-5(4)) Carazona Creations LLC.

—The Circus Is coming to Town: Early Reader Version. Scalzo, Linda V. I.t. ed. 2005. 24p. (J). per. 9.99 (978-0-9753724-1-8(6)) Carazona Creations LLC.

Spangler, Brie. We Both Read-The Mystery of Pirate's Point: Level 3. 2008. (We Both Read Ser.). 40p. (J). (gr. 1-5). per. 4.99 (978-1-60115-010-3(5)) Treasure Bay, Inc.

Spanjer, Kendra. All Me, All the Time: The Authorized Art-O-Biography Of... Oceanak, Karla. 2012. (Aldo Zelnick Comic Novel Ser.). (ENG.). 80p. (J). (gr. 3-7). pap. 7.95 (978-1-934649-20-6(1)) Bailiwick Pr.

—Artsy-Fartsy. Oceanak, Karla. 2016. (Aldo Zelnick Comic Novel Ser.: 1). (ENG.). 160p. (J). (gr. 1-8). pap. 8.95 (978-1-934649-65-7(1)) Bailiwick Pr.

—Bogus: An Aldo Zelnick Comic Novel. Oceanak, Karla. 2016. (Aldo Zelnick Comic Novel Ser.: 2). (ENG.). 160p. (J). (gr. 3-7). pap. 8.95 (978-1-934649-66-4(X)) Bailiwick Pr.

—Cahoots. Oceanak, Karla. 2011. (Aldo Zelnick Comic Novel Ser.: 3). (ENG.). 151p. (J). (gr. 3-7). 12.95 (978-1-934649-08-4(2)) Bailiwick Pr.

—Cahoots: An Aldo Zelnick Comic Novel. Oceanak, Karla. 2016. (Aldo Zelnick Comic Novel Ser.: 3). (ENG.). 160p. (J). (gr. 1-8). pap. 8.95 (978-1-934649-67-1(8)) Bailiwick Pr.

—Dumbstruck. Oceanak, Karla. 2011. (Aldo Zelnick Comic Novel Ser.: 4). (ENG.). 160p. (J). (gr. 3-7). 12.95 (978-1-934649-16-9(3)) Bailiwick Pr.

—Dumbstruck: An Aldo Zelnick Comic Novel. Oceanak, Karla. 2016. (Aldo Zelnick Comic Novel Ser.: 4). (ENG.). 160p. (J). (gr. 1-8). pap. 8.95 (978-1-934649-68-8(6)) Bailiwick Pr.

—Egghead. Oceanak, Karla. 2012. (Aldo Zelnick Comic Novel Ser.: 5). (ENG.). 160p. (J). (gr. 1-8). 12.95 (978-1-934649-17-6(1)) Bailiwick Pr.

—Egghead: An Aldo Zelnick Comic Novel. Oceanak, Karla. 2016. (Aldo Zelnick Comic Novel Ser.: 5). (ENG.). 160p. (J). (gr. 1-8). pap. 8.95 (978-1-934649-69-5(4)) Bailiwick Pr.

—Finicky. Oceanak, Karla. 2012. (Aldo Zelnick Comic Novel Ser.: 6). (ENG.). 160p. (J). (gr. 3-7). 12.95 (978-1-934649-24-4(4)) Bailiwick Pr.

—Finicky: An Aldo Zelnick Comic Novel. Oceanak, Karla. 2016. (Aldo Zelnick Comic Novel Ser.: 6). (ENG.). 160p. (J). (gr. 1-8). pap. 8.95 (978-1-934649-70-1(8)) Bailiwick Pr.

—Glitch. Oceanak, Karla. 2012. (Aldo Zelnick Comic Novel Ser.: 7). (ENG.). 160p. (J). (gr. 3-7). 12.95 (978-1-934649-25-1(2)) Bailiwick Pr.

—Glitch: An Aldo Zelnick Comic Novel. Oceanak, Karla. 2016. (Aldo Zelnick Comic Novel Ser.: 7). (ENG.). 160p. (J). (gr. 1-8). pap. 8.95 (978-1-934649-71-8(6)) Bailiwick Pr.

—Goodnight Unicorn: A Magical Parody. Oceanak, Karla. 2016. 32p. (gr. -1-3). 16.95 (978-1-934649-63-3(5)) Bailiwick Pr.

—Hotdogger. Oceanak, Karla. 2013. (Aldo Zelnick Comic Novel Ser.: 8). (ENG.). 160p. (J). (gr. 3-7). 12.95 (978-1-934649-37-4(6)) Bailiwick Pr.

—Hotdogger: An Aldo Zelnick Comic Novel. Oceanak, Karla. 2016. (Aldo Zelnick Comic Novel Ser.: 8). (ENG.). 160p. (J). (gr. 1-8). pap. 8.95 (978-1-934649-72-5(4)) Bailiwick Pr.

—Ignoramus. Oceanak, Karla. 2013. (Aldo Zelnick Comic Novel Ser.: 9). (ENG.). 160p. (J). (gr. 3-7). 12.95 (978-1-934649-41-1(4), 1365432) Bailiwick Pr.

—Ignoramus: An Aldo Zelnick Comic Novel. Oceanak, Karla. 2016. (Aldo Zelnick Comic Novel Ser.: 9). (ENG.). 160p. (J). (gr. 1-8). pap. 8.95 (978-1-934649-73-2(2)) Bailiwick Pr.

—Jackpot: An Aldo Zelnick Comic Novel. Oceanak, Karla. 2016. (Aldo Zelnick Comic Novel Ser.: 10). (ENG.). 160p. (J). (gr. 1-8). pap. 8.95 (978-1-934649-74-9(0)) Bailiwick Pr.

—Kerfuffle. Oceanak, Karla. 2015. (Aldo Zelnick Comic Novel Ser.: 11). (ENG.). 160p. (gr. 1-8). 12.95 (978-1-934649-53-4(8)) Bailiwick Pr.

—Kerfuffle: An Aldo Zelnick Comic Novel. Oceanak, Karla. 2016. (Aldo Zelnick Comic Novel Ser.: 11). (ENG.). 160p. (J). (gr. 1-8). pap. 8.95 (978-1-934649-75-6(9)) Bailiwick Pr.

—Logjam. Oceanak, Karla. 2016. (Aldo Zelnick Comic Novel Ser.: 12). (ENG.). 160p. (gr. 1-8). 12.95 (978-1-934649-64-0(3)) Bailiwick Pr.

—Logjam: Book 12. Oceanak, Karla. 2018. (Aldo Zelnick Comic Novel Ser.: 12). (ENG.). 160p. (gr. 1-8). pap. 8.95 (978-1-934649-78-7(3)) Bailiwick Pr.

—Mooch. Oceanak, Karla. 2018. (Aldo Zelnick Comic Novel Ser.: 13). (ENG.). 160p. (J). 12.95 (978-1-934649-76-3(7)) Bailiwick Pr.

Spanyol, Jessica. All about Clive Board Book Set Of 8. Spanyol, Jessica. 2020. (Social & Emotional Learning Sets Ser.). (ENG.). 56p. (J). bds., bds., bds. **(978-1-78628-532-4(0))** Child's Play International Ltd.

—All about Rosa Board Book Set Of 4. Spanyol, Jessica. 2020. (Social & Emotional Learning Sets Ser.). (ENG.). 48p. (J). bds., bds., bds. **(978-1-78628-534-8(7))** Child's Play International Ltd.

Spanyol, Jessica. Clive & His Art. Spanyol, Jessica. 2016. (All about Clive Ser.: 4). 14p. (J). spiral bd. (978-1-84643-883-7(7)) Child's Play International Ltd.

—Clive & His Babies. Spanyol, Jessica. 2016. (All about Clive Ser.). 14p. (J). spiral bd. (978-1-84643-882-0(9)) Child's Play International Ltd.

—Clive & His Bags. Spanyol, Jessica. 2016. (All about Clive Ser.). 14p. (J). spiral bd. (978-1-84643-884-4(5)) Child's Play International Ltd.

—Clive & His Hats. Spanyol, Jessica. 2016. (All about Clive Ser.). 14p. (J). spiral bd. (978-1-84643-885-1(3)) Child's Play International Ltd.

—Clive Is a Librarian. Spanyol, Jessica. 2017. (Clive's Jobs Ser.: 4). 14p. (J). spiral bd. (978-1-84643-989-6(2)) Child's Play International Ltd.

—Clive Is a Nurse. Spanyol, Jessica. 2017. (Clive's Jobs Ser.: 4). 14p. (J). spiral bd. (978-1-84643-991-9(4)) Child's Play International Ltd.

—Clive Is a Teacher. Spanyol, Jessica. 2017. (Clive's Jobs Ser.: 4). 14p. (J). spiral bd. (978-1-84643-990-2(6)) Child's Play International Ltd.

—Clive Is a Waiter. Spanyol, Jessica. 2017. (Clive's Jobs Ser.: 4). 14p. (J). spiral bd. (978-1-84643-992-6(2)) Child's Play International Ltd.

—Keith & His Super-Stunt Rally Racer. Spanyol, Jessica. 2008. (MiniBug Bks.). (ENG.). 24p. (J). (gr. k-k). 5.99 (978-0-7636-3742-2(4)) Candlewick Pr.

—Rosa Loves Cars. Spanyol, Jessica. 2018. (All about Rosa Ser.: 4). 14p. (J). bds. (978-1-78628-125-8(2)) Child's Play International Ltd.

—Rosa Loves Dinosaurs. Spanyol, Jessica. 2018. (All about Rosa Ser.: 4). 14p. (J). bds. (978-1-78628-124-1(4)) Child's Play International Ltd.

—Rosa Plays Ball. Spanyol, Jessica. 2018. (All about Rosa Ser.: 4). 14p. (J). bds. (978-1-78628-126-5(0)) Child's Play International Ltd.

—Rosa Rides Her Scooter. Spanyol, Jessica. 2018. (All about Rosa Ser.: 4). 14p. (J). bds. (978-1-78628-123-4(6)) Child's Play International Ltd.

—Rosa's Big Boat Experiment. Spanyol, Jessica. 2020. (Rosa's Workshop Ser.: 4). (ENG.). 20p. (J). (978-1-78628-363-4(8)) Child's Play International Ltd.

—Rosa's Big Bridge Experiment. Spanyol, Jessica. 2020. (Rosa's Workshop Ser.: 4). (ENG.). 20p. (J). (978-1-78628-362-7(X)) Child's Play International Ltd.

—Rosa's Big Pizza Experiment. Spanyol, Jessica. 2020. (Rosa's Workshop Ser.: 4). (ENG.). 20p. (J). (978-1-78628-361-0(1)) Child's Play International Ltd.

—Rosa's Big Sunflower Experiment. Spanyol, Jessica. 2020. (Rosa's Workshop Ser.: 4). (ENG.). 20p. (J). (978-1-78628-364-1(6)) Child's Play International Ltd.

Sparks, Beverly, photos by. Busy Doggies. Schindel, John. 2003. (Busy Book Ser.). 20p. (J). (— 1). bds. 6.99 (978-1-58246-090-1(6), Knopf Bks. for Young Readers) Random Hse. Children's Bks.

Sparks, David. Flat-Top Sam & the Junkyard Elephant. Sparks, David. 2008. 36p. pap. 12.95 (978-1-59858-587-2(8)) Dog Ear Publishing, LLC.

Sparks, Jenni. Unfolding Journeys Amazon Adventure, 1 vol. Ross, Stewart & Lonely Planet Kids. 2016. (Unfolding Journeys Ser.). (ENG.). 16p. (J). (gr. 4-7). 17.99 (978-1-78657-106-9(4), 5246) Lonely Planet Global Ltd. IRL. Dist: Hachette Bk. Group.

Sparks, Jolene. Mr. Squirrel. Sparks, Joanne. 2009. 29p. pap. 24.95 (978-1-61546-375-6(5)) America Star Bks.

Sparks, Michal. Reagandoodle & Little Buddy Find a Forever Family. Swiridoff, Sandi & Dunham, Wendy. 2019. (ENG.). 32p. (J). (gr. -1-2). 14.99 (978-0-7369-7468-4(7), 6974684) Harvest Hse. Pubs.

—The Sweetest Story Ever Told: A New Christmas Tradition for Families. TerKeurst, Lysa. 2003. 32p. 9.99 (978-0-8024-7094-2(7)) Moody Pubs.

—The Sweetest Story Ever Told Activity Kit. TerKeurst, Lysa. 2003. 14.99 (978-0-8024-7093-5(9)) Moody Pubs.

Sparling, Bren M. Through the Fairy Door. Reintjes, Susan B. 2012. 128p. (J). pap. 16.95 (978-1-59715-085-9(1)) Chapel Hill Press, Inc.

Sparrow, K. Time Grafters - Running Out of Time: Book One of Origins. Somerset, Pg. 2019. (Time Grafters Ser.: Vol. 1). (ENG.). 140p. (J). pap. 9.95 (978-1-7964-3223-7(7)) Independently Published.

Sparrow, K. Time Grafters Book 3: Order: Foundation: Book One. Somerset, Pg. 2019. (Time Grafters Ser.: Vol. 3). (ENG.). 138p. (J). pap. 9.95 **(978-1-7979-3882-0(7))** Independently Published.

Spartels, Stephanie. The Big Adventure. Rippin, Sally. 2015. 41p. (J). (978-1-61067-453-9(7)) Kane Miller.

—The Big Adventure: Hey Jack! Rippin, Sally. 2016. (ENG.). 48p. (J). pap. 4.99 (978-1-61067-393-8(X)) Kane Miller.

—The Circus Lesson. Rippin, Sally. 2013. 41p. (J). (978-1-61067-236-8(4)) Kane Miller.

—The Crazy Cousins. Rippin, Sally. (J). 2013. (ENG.). 48p. pap. 4.99 (978-1-61067-121-7(X)); 2012. 42p. (978-1-61067-135-4(X)) Kane Miller.

—The Scary Solo. Rippin, Sally. (J). 2013. (ENG.). 48p. pap. 4.99 (978-1-61067-122-4(8)); 2012. 43p. (978-1-61067-136-1(8)) Kane Miller.

—The Top Team. Rippin, Sally. 2014. 42p. (J). (978-1-61067-293-1(3)) Kane Miller.

—The Toy Sale. Rippin, Sally. 2015. 41p. (J). (978-1-61067-454-6(5)) Kane Miller.

—The Toy Sale: Hey Jack! Rippin, Sally. 2016. (ENG.). 48p. (J). pap. 4.99 (978-1-61067-394-5(8)) Kane Miller.

—The Winning Goal. Rippin, Sally. (J). 2013. (ENG.). 48p. pap. 4.99 (978-1-61067-123-1(6)); 2012. 43p. (978-1-61067-137-8(6)) Kane Miller.

Spatrisano, Kimberly, jt. illus. see Lawson, Robert.

Spay, Anthony & Campbell, Alex. Louis Armstrong. O'Hern, Kerri & Holland, Gini. 2007. (Biografías Gráficas (Graphic Biographies) Ser.). (SPA.). 32p. (gr. 5-8). pap. 10.50 (978-0-8368-7885-1(X)) Stevens, Gareth Publishing LLLP.

Spay, Anthony, jt. illus. see Campbell, Alex.

Spay, Anthony, jt. illus. see Floor, Guus.

Spaziante, Patrick. Allura's Story. Spinner, Cala. 2018. (Voltron Legendary Defender Ser.). (ENG.). 32p. (J). (gr. k-2). 17.99 (978-1-5344-3035-8(0)); pap. 4.99 (978-1-5344-3034-1(2)) Simon Spotlight. (Simon Spotlight).

—Ant-Man. Wrecks, Billy. 2016. (Little Golden Book Ser.). (ENG.). 24p. (J). (-k). 4.99 (978-0-399-55097-3(6), Golden Bks.) Random Hse. Children's Bks.

—Batman Strikes Back. Cregg, R. J. ed. 2016. (Batman Unlimited Ser.). (ENG.). 24p. (J). (gr. -1-2). 13.55 (978-0-606-39249-5(1)) Turtleback.

—Batman Unlimited: Heroes of Gotham City. Bright, J. E. ed. 2016. (Simon & Schuster Ready-To-Read Level 2 Ser.). (ENG.). 32p. (J). (gr. k-2). lib. bdg. 13.55 (978-0-606-39245-7(9)) Turtleback.

—Beware of Bebop & Rocksteady! (Teenage Mutant Ninja Turtles) Random House. 2016. (ENG.). 24p. (J). (gr. -1-2). pap. 6.99 (978-0-399-55468-1(8), Random Hse. Bks. for Young Readers) Random Hse. Children's Bks.

—Bigfoot's Spring Break (Teenage Mutant Ninja Turtles) Random House. 2016. (Pictureback(R) Ser.). (ENG.). 16p. (J). (gr. -1-2). 4.99 (978-1-101-93174-5(4), Random Hse. Bks. for Young Readers) Random Hse. Children's Bks.

—Bizarro's Last Laugh. Lemke, Donald B. 2017. 31p. (J). (978-1-5182-3834-5(3)) Harper & Row Ltd.

—Black Panther. Berrios, Frank. 2018. (J). (978-1-5444-0200-0(7), Golden Bks.) Random Hse. Children's Bks.

—Black Panther Little Golden Book (Marvel: Black Panther) Berrios, Frank. 2018. (Little Golden Book Ser.). (ENG.). 24p. (J). (-k). 4.99 (978-1-5247-6388-6(8), Golden Bks.) Random Hse. Children's Bks.

—Blackout! Peterson, Scott. ed. 2005. (Teenage Mutant Ninja Turtles Ser.: Garden & No. 6). 24p. (J). lib. bdg. 15.00 (978-1-59054-831-8(0)) Fitzgerald Bks.

—Bug Battle! Mangual, C. Ines. 2017. 20p. (J). (978-1-5182-2750-9(3)) Random Hse., Inc.

Spaziante, Patrick. Cape. Hannigan, Kate. 2020. (League of Secret Heroes Ser.: 1). (ENG.). 352p. (J). (gr. 3-7). pap. 8.99 **(978-1-5344-3912-2(9)**, Aladdin) Simon & Schuster Children's Publishing.

Spaziante, Patrick. Cape. Hannigan, Kate. 2019. (League of Secret Heroes Ser.: 1). (ENG.). 336p. (J). (gr. 3-7). 17.99 (978-1-5344-3911-5(0), Simon & Schuster/Paula Wiseman Bks.) Simon & Schuster/Paula Wiseman Bks.

—Double-Team! (Teenage Mutant Ninja Turtles) Webster, Christy. 2014. (Step into Reading Ser.). (ENG.). 48p. (J). (gr. 2-4). 4.99 (978-0-385-37434-7(8), Random Hse. Bks. for Young Readers) Random Hse. Children's Bks.

—Eye of the Dragon (Marvel: Iron Man) Wrecks, Billy. 2016. (Little Golden Book Ser.). (ENG.). 24p. (J). (-k). 4.99 (978-0-307-97654-3(8), Golden Bks.) Random Hse. Children's Bks.

—Flip the Lid! (Teenage Mutant Ninja Turtles: Half-Shell Heroes) Random House. 2016. (Lift-The-Flap Ser.). (ENG.). 12p. (J). (— 1). bds. 6.99 (978-0-553-53909-7(4), Random Hse. Bks. for Young Readers) Random Hse. Children's Bks.

—Green Team! (Teenage Mutant Ninja Turtles) Webster, Christy. 2012. (Step into Reading Ser.). (ENG.). 48p. (J). (gr. k-3). pap. 4.99 (978-0-307-98070-0(7), Random Hse. Bks. for Young Readers) Random Hse. Children's Bks.

—Grumpy Cat - This Book Stinks! Webster, Christy & Random House Staff. 2019. 24p. (J). (gr. -1-2). 9.99 (978-1-9848-5129-1(2), Random Hse. Bks. for Young Readers) Random Hse. Children's Bks.

—A Grumpy Easter (Grumpy Cat) Berrios, Frank. 2020. (Pictureback(R) Ser.). 24p. (J). (gr. -1-2). 5.99 (978-0-593-12264-8(X), Random Hse. Bks. for Young Readers) Random Hse. Children's Bks.

—Happy, Sad, Mad, & Glad! (Thomas & Friends) Random House. 2020. (ENG.). 12p. (J). (— 1). bds. 9.99 (978-0-593-12431-4(6), Random Hse. Bks. for Young Readers) Random Hse. Children's Bks.

—Harley Quinn: Wild Card. Marsham, Liz. 2016. 127p. (J). (978-1-5182-1359-5(6)) Scholastic, Inc.

—Homecoming. 2019. (How to Train Your Dragon: Hidden World Ser.). (ENG.). 24p. (J). (gr. -1-3). pap. 4.99 (978-1-5344-5235-0(4), Simon Spotlight) Simon Spotlight.

—Hunk's Story. Spinner, Cala. 2018. (Voltron Legendary Defender Ser.). (ENG.). 32p. (J). (gr. k-2). 17.99 (978-1-5344-3209-3(4)); pap. 4.99 (978-1-5344-3208-6(6)) Simon Spotlight. (Simon Spotlight).

—The Incredible Hulk (Marvel: Incredible Hulk) Wrecks, Billy. 2016. (Little Golden Book Ser.). (ENG.). 24p. (J). (gr. k-k). 4.99 (978-0-307-93194-8(3), Golden Bks.) Random Hse. Children's Bks.

—The Invincible Iron Man (Marvel: Iron Man) Wrecks, Billy. 2016. (Little Golden Book Ser.). (ENG.). 24p. (J). (gr. k-k). 4.99 (978-0-307-93064-4(5), Golden Bks.) Random Hse. Children's Bks.

—Journey to New Berk. ed. 2019. (How to Train Your Dragon: Hidden World Ser.). (ENG.). 24p. (J). (gr. -1-2). pap. 4.99 (978-1-5344-3840-8(8), Simon Spotlight) Simon Spotlight.

—Justice League Classic: Battle of the Power Ring. Lemke, Donald. 2016. (I Can Read Level 2 Ser.). 32p. (J). (gr. -1-3). pap. 3.99 (978-0-06-234494-6(3)) HarperCollins Pubs.

—Justice League Classic: Storm Surge. Lemke, Donald. 2017. 24p. (J). (gr. -1-3). pap. 3.99 (978-0-06-236079-3(5), HarperFestival) HarperCollins Pubs.

—Keith's Story. Burton, Jesse. 2018. (Voltron Legendary Defender Ser.). (ENG.). 32p. (J). (gr. k-2). 17.99 (978-1-5344-2041-0(X)); pap. 4.99 (978-1-5344-2040-3(1)) Simon Spotlight. (Simon Spotlight).

—Lance's Story. Spinner, Cala. 2018. (Voltron Legendary Defender Ser.). (ENG.). 32p. (J). (gr. k-2). 17.99 (978-1-5344-2540-8(3)); pap. 4.99 (978-1-5344-2539-2(X)) Simon Spotlight. (Simon Spotlight).

—Lights Out! (Marvel: Mighty Avengers) Carbone, Courtney. 2016. (Little Golden Book Ser.). (ENG.). 24p. (J). (-k). 4.99 (978-0-307-97658-1(0), Golden Bks.) Random Hse. Children's Bks.

—The Lost Scrolls: Fire. Mason, Tom & Danko, Dan. 2006. (Avatar Ser.). (ENG.). 64p. (J). pap. 4.99 (978-1-4169-1880-6(9), Simon Spotlight/Nickelodeon) Simon Spotlight/Nickelodeon.

—The Lost Scrolls: Water. Teitelbaum, Michael. 2006. (Avatar, the Last Airbender: Lost Scrolls Ser.). (ENG.). 64p. (J). (gr. 2-4). 17.44 (978-1-4169-1878-3(7)) Simon & Schuster, Inc.

Spaziante, Patrick. Mask. Hannigan, Kate. 2020. (League of Secret Heroes Ser.: 2). (ENG.). 272p. (J). (gr. 3-7). 17.99 **(978-1-5344-3914-6(5)**, Aladdin) Simon & Schuster Children's Publishing.

Spaziante, Patrick. Mean Team. Random House Editors. ed. 2016. (Step into Reading Level 2 Ser.). (ENG.). 24p. (J). (gr. -1-1). 14.75 (978-0-606-39354-6(4)) Turtleback.

—Meet Casey Jones. ed. 2005. (Teenage Mutant Ninja Turtles Ser.: No. 1). 24p. (J). lib. bdg. 15.00 (978-1-59054-836-3(1)) Fitzgerald Bks.

—Meet Leatherhead. Wax, Wendy. 2005. 22p. (J). lib. bdg. 15.00 (978-1-4242-0972-9(2)) Fitzgerald Bks.

—The Mighty Avengers (Marvel: the Avengers) Wrecks, Billy. 2016. (Little Golden Book Ser.). (ENG.). 24p. (J). (gr. k-k). 4.99 (978-0-307-93109-2(9), Golden Bks.) Random Hse. Children's Bks.

—Mikey's Monster (Teenage Mutant Ninja Turtles) Smith, James J. & James, Hollis. 2013. (Step into Reading Ser.). (ENG.). 48p. (J). (gr. k-3). 4.99 (978-0-449-81826-8(8), Random Hse. Bks. for Young Readers) Random Hse. Children's Bks.

—My Best Friend Is a Yeti! 2019. (Abominable Ser.). (ENG.). 32p. (gr. k-2). (J). pap. 4.99 (978-1-5344-5065-3(3)); (YA). 17.99 (978-1-5344-5066-0(1)) Simon Spotlight. (Simon Spotlight).

—Night of the T-Machines (Teenage Mutant Ninja Turtles) Gilbert, Matthew. 2016. (Pictureback(R) Ser.). (ENG.). 16p. (J). (gr. -1-2). 4.99 (978-1-101-93866-9(8), Random Hse. Bks. for Young Readers) Random Hse. Children's Bks.

—Ninjas on Ice! (Teenage Mutant Ninja Turtles) Random House. 2015. (ENG.). 16p. (J). (gr. -1-2). 5.99 (978-0-553-52272-3(8), Random Hse. Bks. for Young Readers) Random Hse. Children's Bks.

—Olivia & the Kite Party. Harvey, Alex. ed. 2012. (Olivia Ready-To-Read Level 1 Ser.). lib. bdg. 13.55 (978-0-606-26360-3(8)) Turtleback.

—Olivia Makes Memories. Considine-Johnson, Joan. 2015. (J). (978-1-4806-9185-8(2), Simon Spotlight) Simon Spotlight.

—Paladins of Voltron Collector's Set (with More Than 30 Stickers!) Allura's Story; Keith's Story; Lance's Story; Shiro's Story; Pidge's Story; Hunk's Story. ed. 2019. (Voltron Legendary Defender Ser.). (ENG.). 192p. (J). (gr. k-2). pap. 17.99 (978-1-5344-4047-0(X), Simon Spotlight) Simon Spotlight.

—Pidge's Story. Shaw, Natalie. 2018. (Voltron Legendary Defender Ser.). (ENG.). 32p. (J). (gr. k-2). 17.99 (978-1-5344-1512-6(2)); pap. 4.99 (978-1-5344-1511-9(4)) Simon Spotlight. (Simon Spotlight).

—Pizza Patrol! (Rise of the Teenage Mutant Ninja Turtles) Webster, Christy. 2020. (Step into Reading Ser.). (ENG.). 32p. (J). (gr. -1-1). 5.99 (978-0-593-12373-7(5)); 12.99 (978-0-593-12373-7(5)) Random Hse. Children's Bks. (Random Hse. Bks. for Young Readers).
—Red Alert! (Teenage Mutant Ninja Turtles) Random House. 2015. (Pictureback(R) Ser.). (ENG.). 16p. (J). (gr. -1-2). 4.99 (978-0-553-50901-4(2), Random Hse. Bks. for Young Readers) Random Hse. Children's Bks.
—The Rise of Voltron. 2017. (Voltron Legendary Defender Ser.: 1). (ENG.). 64p. (J). (gr. k-4). 17.99 (978-1-5344-0920-0(3)); pap. 6.99 (978-1-5344-0919-4(X)) Simon Spotlight. (Simon Spotlight).
—Rough-And-Tumble Turtles! (Teenage Mutant Ninja Turtles: Half-Shell Heroes) Random House. 2016. (Touch-And-Feel Ser.). (ENG.). 10p. (J). (— 1). bds. 12.99 (978-1-101-94029-7(8), Random Hse. Bks. for Young Readers) Random Hse. Children's Bks.
—The Santa Snatcher. Gerver, Jane E. 2004. 32p. (J). lib. bdg. 15.00 (978-1-4242-0959-0(5)) Fitzgerald Bks.
—Shiro's Story. Spinner, Cala. 2018. (Voltron Legendary Defender Ser.). (ENG.). 32p. (J). (gr. k-2). 17.99 (978-1-5344-1831-8(8)); pap. 4.99 (978-1-5344-1830-1(X)) Simon Spotlight. (Simon Spotlight).
—Show Your Colors! (Teenage Mutant Ninja Turtles) Random House. 2015. (Board Book Ser.). (ENG.). 24p. (J). (— 1). bds. 4.99 (978-0-553-49776-2(6), Random Hse. Bks. for Young Readers) Random Hse. Children's Bks.
Spaziante, Patrick. Sleeper Shift. Marsham, Liz. 2020. (Fast & Furious: Spy Racers Ser.). (ENG.). 80p. (J). (gr. 2-5). 6.99 (978-0-593-09496-9(4), Penguin Young Readers Licenses) Penguin Young Readers Group.
Spaziante, Patrick. So, You Want to Be a Boss? 2020. (Boss Baby TV Ser.). (ENG.). 64p. (J). (gr. k-4). 17.99 (978-1-5344-5776-8(3)); pap. 6.99 (978-1-5344-5775-1(5)) Simon Spotlight. (Simon Spotlight).
—Sokka, the Sword Master. 2008. (Avatar Ser.: 1). (ENG.). 32p. (J). (gr. 1-3). pap. 3.99 (978-1-4169-5491-0(0), Simon Spotlight/Nickelodeon) Simon Spotlight/Nickelodeon.
—Sonic & the Tales of Terror. Phegley, Kiel. 2018. (Sonic the Hedgehog Ser.). (ENG.). 64p. (J). (gr. 2-5). 6.99 (978-1-5247-8731-8(0), Penguin Young Readers Licenses) Penguin Young Readers Group.
—Space Shark! (Teenage Mutant Ninja Turtles) James, Hollis. 2016. (Step into Reading Ser.). (ENG.). 24p. (J). (gr. -1-1). 4.99 (978-1-101-93708-2(4), Random Hse. Bks. for Young Readers) Random Hse. Children's Bks.
—Star Wars: Revenge of the Sith (Star Wars) Smith, Geof. 2015. (Little Golden Book Ser.). (ENG.). 24p. (J). (-k). 4.99 (978-0-7364-3540-6(9), Golden Bks.) Random Hse. Children's Bks.
Spaziante, Patrick. The Stolen Vault. Walker, Landry Q. 2020. (Fast & Furious: Spy Racers Ser.). (ENG.). 80p. (J). (gr. 2-5). 6.99 (978-0-593-09497-6(2), Penguin Young Readers Licenses) Penguin Young Readers Group.
Spaziante, Patrick. Super Slam Turtles! Thomas, Jim. 2005. 22p. (J). lib. bdg. 15.00 (978-1-4242-0971-2(4)) Fitzgerald Bks.
—Supergirl: Daughter of Krypton (Backstories) Wallace, Daniel. 2016. (Backstories Ser.: 5). (ENG.). 128p. (J). (gr. 3-7). pap. 5.99 (978-1-338-02981-9(9)) Scholastic, Inc.
—Superman Classic: Pranking News. Lemke, Donald. 2016. (I Can Read Level 2 Ser.). 32p. (J). (gr. -1-3). pap. 3.99 (978-0-06-236085-4(X)) HarperCollins Pubs.
—T-Machines Turbo Guide (Teenage Mutant Ninja Turtles) Random House. 2015. (Pictureback(R) Ser.). (ENG.). 16p. (J). (gr. -1-2). 4.99 (978-0-553-53867-0(5), Random Hse. Bks. for Young Readers) Random Hse. Children's Bks.
—Tale of Zuko. Teitelbaum, Michael. 2008. (Avatar Ser.). (ENG.). 96p. (J). (gr. 2-6). pap. 5.99 (978-1-4169-4984-8(4), Simon Spotlight/Nickelodeon) Simon Spotlight/Nickelodeon.
—Thunder Strike. Sazaklis, John. 2017. (J). (978-1-5379-5735-7(X), Golden Bks.) Random Hse. Children's Bks.
—Thunder Strike! (Marvel: Thor) Sazaklis, John. 2017. (Little Golden Book Ser.). (ENG.). 24p. (J). (-k). 4.99 (978-1-5247-1730-8(4), Golden Bks.) Random Hse. Children's Bks.
—The Voltron Legendary Defender Chapter Book Collection: The Rise of Voltron; Battle for the Black Lion; Space Mall; the Blade of Marmora. ed. 2018. (Voltron Legendary Defender Ser.). (ENG.). 256p. (J). (gr. k-4). pap. 27.99 (978-1-5344-2996-3(4), Simon Spotlight) Simon Spotlight.
Spaziante, Patrick. Welcome to Camp! (Jurassic World: Camp Cretaceous) Behling, Steve. 2020. (Step into Reading Ser.). (ENG.). 32p. (J). (gr. k-3). pap. 5.99 (978-0-593-30335-1(0)); lib. bdg. 14.99 (978-0-593-30336-8(9)) Random Hse. Children's Bks. (Random Hse. Bks. for Young Readers).
Spaziante, Patrick. World of Dragons. Nakamura, May. ed. 2019. (How to Train Your Dragon: Hidden World Ser.). (ENG.). 96p. (J). (gr. -1-5). 14.99 (978-1-5344-3738-8(X), Simon Spotlight) Simon Spotlight.
Spaziante, Patrick & Giles, Mike. Dino Disaster! Mattern, Joanne. ed. 2005. (Adventures of Jimmy Neutron Ser.: 9). 24p. (J). lib. bdg. 15.00 (978-1-59054-782-3(9)) Fitzgerald Bks.
Spaziante, Patrick & Riley, Kellee. Crushed, Bk. 5. Black, Allyson. 2011. (Scarlett & Crimson Ser.). (ENG.). 112p. (J). pap. 6.99 (978-1-4169-9648-4(6), Simon Spotlight) Simon Spotlight.
Spaziante, Patrick & Style Guide Staff. The Blade of Marmora. 2017. (Voltron Legendary Defender Ser.: 4). (ENG.). 64p. (J). (gr. k-2). 17.99 (978-1-5344-1019-0(8)); pap. 6.99 (978-1-5344-1018-3(X)) Simon Spotlight. (Simon Spotlight).
Spaziante, Patrick, jt. illus. see Doescher, Erik.
Spaziante, Patrick, jt. illus. see Random House Editors.
Spaziante, Patrick, jt. illus. see Random House Staff.
Spaziante, Patrick, jt. illus. see Random House.
Spaziante, Patrick 'Spaz'. Mega Man 8: Redemption. Flynn, Ian. 2015. (Mega Man Ser.: 8). (ENG.). 104p. (J). (gr. 4-7). pap. 11.99 (978-1-61988-944-6(7)) Archie Comic Pubns., Inc.
Spear, Kevin. What's a Bathtub Doing in My Church? Fifteen Questions Kids Ask about Baptism, Salvation & Snorkels. Spear, Kevin. 2006. (ENG.). 32p. (J). per. 5.99 (978-1-59317-155-1(2)) Warner Pr., Inc.
Spear, Rebecca. The Christmas Star. Roach, Christina. 2016. (ENG.). (J). (gr. k-5). 17.95 (978-0-9982115-0-3(8)) CR Publishing.
Spearing, Craig J. Our Texas. Hopkins, Jackie Mims. 2010. 44p. (J). (gr. 1-4). pap. 8.95 (978-1-57091-726-4(4)) Charlesbridge Publishing, Inc.
Spearman, Davidx & Spearman, Terry. What Will I Grow up to Be?, 1 vol. Spearman, David. 2009. 34p. pap. 24.95 (978-1-60749-728-8(X)) America Star Bks.
Spearman, Terry, jt. illus. see Spearman, Davidx.
Spears, Ashley, jt. illus. see Clayton, Sean.
Spears, Ashley E. Cloudy. Stover, Anne Long. 2005. 20p. (J). (978-0-9762389-0-4(X)) Trent's Prints.
—The Piggle. Shams, K. I.t. ed. 2004. 20p. (J). 9.99 (978-0-9728872-9-8(6)) Trent's Prints.
—Young Eagle, Pretty Flower. Forester, MaMa Eagle. 2004. 16p. (J). 7.95 (978-0-9762389-4-2(2)) Trent's Prints.
Spears, Rick. Cryptid Creatures: A Field Guide. Halls, Kelly Milner. 2019. 224p. (J). (gr. 2). pap. 16.99 (978-1-63217-210-5(0), Little Bigfoot) Sasquatch Bks.
—Dinosaur Mummies: Beyond Bare-Bone Fossils. Halls, Kelly Milner. 2003. (Junior Library Guild Selection Ser.). 48p. (J). (gr. 4-18). 17.95 (978-1-58196-000-6(X), Darby Creek) Lerner Publishing Group.
Spears, Rick. C. Alien Investigation: Searching for the Truth about UFOs & Aliens. Halls, Kelly Milner. ed. 2015. (ENG.). 64p. (J). (gr. 5-12). E-Book 53.32 (978-1-4677-5987-8(2), 9781467759878, Lerner Digital) Lerner Publishing Group.
Spears, Rick C. Tales of the Cryptids: Mysterious Creatures That May or May Not Exist. Spears, Rick C. Halls, Kelly Milner & Young, Roxyanne. 2006. (ENG.). 72p. (J). (gr. 5-12). 19.99 (978-1-58196-049-5(2), Millbrook Pr.) Lerner Publishing Group.
Spears, Sheri. Pee Wee Pickle Goes to Kinder-Garden. Schmitt, H. D. 2008. 20p. pap. 24.95 (978-1-60672-731-7(1)) America Star Bks.
Speas, Joann. Meet Mister Muttley. Leduc-Lenmark, MaryAlice. 2004. 25p. (J). 16.95 (978-0-9760733-0-7(7)) Heartstrings Publishing.
Specht, Jessica. Call Me Charly. Michaels, Joanna. 2012. 92p. pap. 10.95 (978-1-61493-102-7(X)) Peppertree Pr., The.
Specialty Publishing Company. Fearless Faith: And the New School. Newmark, Rachel J. 2006. (J). pap. 7.95 (978-0-9755199-4-3(8)) Specialty Publishing Co.
Spector, Joel. And Still They Bloom: A Family's Journey of Loss & Healing. Rovere, Amy. 2012. (ENG.). 48p. (J). (gr. 4-7). 14.95 (978-1-60443-036-3(2)) American Cancer Society, Inc.
Spector, Joel & Sharpe, Jim. Poetry for Young People: Rudyard Kipling. Gillooly, Eileen, ed. 2010. (Poetry for Young People Ser.: 8). 48p. (J). (gr. 3). pap. 6.95 (978-1-4027-7293-1(9)) Sterling Publishing Co., Inc.
Spee, Gitte. Detective Gordon: A Case in Any Case. Nilsson, Ulf. 2017. (Detective Gordon Ser.). (ENG.). 108p. (gr. k-5). 9.99 (978-1-77657-110-9(X)) Gecko Pr. NZL. Dist: Lerner Publishing Group.
—Detective Gordon: a Case for Buffy. Nilsson, Ulf. 2018. (Detective Gordon Ser.). (ENG.). 108p. (J). (gr. k-5). 16.99 (978-1-77657-178-9(9)) Gecko Pr. NZL. Dist: Lerner Publishing Group.
—Detective Gordon: a Case in Any Case. Nilsson, Ulf. 2017. (Detective Gordon Ser.). (ENG.). 108p. (J). (gr. k-5). 16.99 (978-1-77657-108-6(8)) Gecko Pr. NZL. Dist: Lerner Publishing Group.
—Detective Gordon: the First Case. Nilsson, Ulf. 2015. (Detective Gordon Ser.). (ENG.). 96p. (J). (gr. k-5). 16.99 (978-1-927271-49-0(5), 9781927271490) Gecko Pr. NZL. Dist: Lerner Publishing Group.
Speer, Cheryl. Scuby the Farting Hot Dog Goes to the Animal Hospital. Cray Cray, Shoo Shoo. Hanson, Jan, ed. 2019. (ENG.). 56p. (J). (gr. k-5). pap. 15.99 (978-0-578-45598-3(6)) Scuby's DogHse.
Speer, Julie & Davis, Christopher Owen. Farmer Dillo Paints His Barn. Adams, Jesse. 2007. (J). (gr. -1-1). 21p. (978-1-59166-481-9(0)); pap. 12.95 (978-1-59166-808-4(5)) BJU Pr.
Speer, Julie & Polhamus, Bruce. Farmer Dillo Shapes Things Up. Adams, Jesse. 2009. 24p. (gr. -1-1). pap. 7.99 (978-1-59166-865-7(4)) BJU Pr.
Speer, Julie & Rogers, David. Farmer Dillo Counts His Chickens. Adams, Jesse. 2008. 22p. (gr. -1-1). pap. 7.99 (978-1-59166-868-8(9)) BJU Pr.
Speidel, Sandra. What's Heaven? Shriver, Maria. 2007. (ENG.). 32p. (J). (gr. -1-3). 16.99 (978-0-312-38241-4(3), 900051561, Golden Bks. Adult Publishing Group) St. Martin's Pr.
Speigel, Amber. Best Friends Forever. Fritz, Laura & Good, Michael. 2019. (ENG.). 32p. (J). pap. 10.99 (978-1-947773-56-1(9)) Yawn's Bks. & More, Inc.
Speigel, Beth. Samantha Jane's Missing Smile: A Story about Coping with the Loss of a Parent. Pincus, Donna & Kaplow, Julie. 2007. 32p. (J). (gr. -1-3). 14.95 (978-1-59147-808-9(1)); per. 9.95 (978-1-59147-809-6(X)) American Psychological Assn. (Magination Pr.).
Speir, Nancy. Check It Out! Reading, Finding, Helping, 0 vols. Hubbell, Patricia. 2011. (ENG.). 32p. (J). (gr. -1-3). 16.99 (978-0-7614-5803-6(4), 9780761458036, Two Lions) Amazon Publishing.
—Eliza's Kindergarten Pet, 0 vols. McGinty, Alice B. 2010. (ENG.). 32p. (J). (gr. k-3). 15.99 (978-0-7614-5702-2(X), 9780761457022, Two Lions) Amazon Publishing.
—Eliza's Kindergarten Surprise, 0 vols. McGinty, Alice B. 2013. (ENG.). 34p. (J). (gr. k-3). pap. 9.99 (978-1-4778-1683-7(6), 9781477816837, Two Lions) Amazon Publishing.
—My First Airplane Ride, 0 vols. Hubbell, Patricia. 2013. (ENG.). 42p. (J). (gr. -1-2). pap. 9.99 (978-1-4778-1675-2(5), 9781477816752, Two Lions) Amazon Publishing.
Speir, Nancy. Teacher! Sharing, Helping, Caring. Hubbell, Patricia. 2020. (ENG.). 34p. (J). (gr. -1-3). pap. 9.99 (978-1-4778-1091-0(9), 9781477810910, Two Lions) Amazon Publishing.
Speirs, John. Amazing Magnetism. Carmi, Rebecca. 2003. (Magic School Bus Science Chapter Bks.). 76p. (gr. 2-4). 15.00 (978-0-7569-1576-6(7)) Perfection Learning Corp.
—Animal Tracks: Wild Poems to Read Aloud. Ghigna, Charles. 2004. (ENG.). 36p. (J). (gr. -1-1). 14.95 (978-0-8109-4841-9(9)) Abrams, Inc.
—Food Chain Frenzy. Capeci, Anne. 2004. (Magic School Bus Science Chapter Bks.). 91p. (gr. 2-5). 15.00 (978-0-7569-2206-1(2)) Perfection Learning Corp.
—It's about Time! Murphy, Stuart J. 2005. (MathStart Ser.). 40p. (J). 16.99 (978-0-06-055768-3(0)); (ENG.). (gr. -1). pap. 5.99 (978-0-06-055769-0(9)) HarperCollins Pubs.
—It's about Time! Murphy, Stuart J. 2005. (Mathstart Ser.). 33p. (gr. -1-3). 16.00 (978-0-7569-5224-2(7)) Perfection Learning Corp.
—Twister Trouble. Schreiber, Ann. 2010. (Magic School Bus Science Chapter Bks.). (KOR.). 82p. (J). (978-89-491-5320-9(3)) Biryongso Publishing Co.
—Voyage to the Volcano. Stamper, Judith. 2010. (Magic School Bus Science Chapter Bks.). (KOR.). 101p. (J). (978-89-491-5322-3(X)) Biryongso Publishing Co.
—Voyage to the Volcano. Stamper, Judith. 2003. (Magic School Bus Science Chapter Bks.). 87p. (gr. 3-6). 15.00 (978-0-7569-1581-0(3)) Perfection Learning Corp.
Speirs, Wendy. The Tree Beyond. Tomanio, Ronald. 2019. (Children Story Ser.: Vol. 1). (ENG.). 56p. (J). pap. 12.99 (978-1-0720-9658-0(7)) Independently Published.
Speiser, Mike. Carried & Cuddled / Consentido y Cargado. Platypus, Editors at. 2018. (ENG.). 32p. (J). (gr. -1-k). 14.95 (978-1-930775-96-1(2)) Platypus Media, L.L.C.
—Cuddled & Carried. Michels, Dia L. 2018. (ENG.). 32p. (J). (gr. -1-k). 14.95 (978-1-930775-99-2(7)); pap. 9.95 (978-1-930775-98-5(9)) Platypus Media, L.L.C.
—Cuddled & Carried / Consentido y Cargado. Michels, Dia. 2018. (ENG.). 32p. (J). (gr. -1-k). pap. 9.95 (978-1-930775-95-4(4)) Platypus Media, L.L.C.
Spellman, Susan. Bright Easter Day. Stiegemeyer, Julie. 2005. 32p. (J). 10.49 (978-0-7586-0818-5(7)) Concordia Publishing Hse.
—How Timbo & Trevor Got Together. Towle, Barbara E. 2007. (ENG.). 38p. (J). (gr. -1-3). 19.95 (978-1-933002-21-7(2)) PublishingWorks.
—Hurricane Mia: A Caribbean Adventure. Seim, Donna Marie. 2010. 168p. (J). (gr. 3-7). pap. 12.95 (978-0-9826911-0-6(6), Peapod Pr.) PublishingWorks.
—Pinky & Bubs' Stinky Night Out. Spellman, Frankie. 2005. (ENG.). 32p. (J). (gr. -1-3). per. 12.95 (978-1-933002-16-3(6)) PublishingWorks.
Spence, Kiya. Little Tree. Moodie, Natashia. Eaglespeaker, Jason, ed. 2019. (ENG.). 34p. (J). pap. 10.99 (978-1-9779-7798-4(7)) CreateSpace Independent Publishing Platform.
Spenceley, Annabel. Beauty & the Beast. 2017. 24p. pap. 7.99 (978-1-86147-817-7(8)); 2013. (ENG.). 48p. (J). (gr. -1-4). pap. 7.99 (978-1-84322-789-2(4)) Anness Publishing GBR. (Armadillo). Dist: National Bk. Network.
—Cinderella. 2016. 24p. pap. 7.99 (978-1-86147-813-9(5), Armadillo) Anness Publishing GBR. Dist: National Bk. Network.
—First Prayers for Baby, 1 vol. Piper, Sophie. ed. 2016. (ENG.). 48p. (J). (— 1). 12.99 (978-0-7459-7665-5(4)) Lion Hudson PLC GBR. Dist: Kregel Pubs.
—Jesus in Pictures for Little Eyes. Taylor, Kenneth N. ed. 2003. (ENG.). 128p. (J). (gr. k-3). 9.99 (978-0-8024-3059-5(7)) Moody Pubs.
—The New Bible in Pictures for Little Eyes. Taylor, Kenneth N. gif. ed. 2004. (ENG.). 384p. (J). 24.99 (978-0-8024-3078-6(3)) Moody Pubs.
—Puzzle Journey through Time. Heddle, Rebecca. 2003. 32p. (J). pap. 6.95 (978-0-7945-0440-3(X), Usborne) EDC Publishing.
—A Storyteller Book: Cinderella. Perrault, Charles. 2014. (ENG.). 48p. (J). (gr. k-5). pap. 7.99 (978-1-84322-883-7(1)) Anness Publishing GBR. Dist: National Bk. Network.
Spenceley, Annabel & Chen, Kuo Kang. What Makes You Ill? Unwin, Mike & Woodward, Kate. Meredith, Susan, ed. rev. ed. 2006. (Starting Point Science Ser.). 24p. (J). (gr. -1-3). pap. 4.99 (978-0-7945-1624-6(6), Usborne) EDC Publishing.
—Why Do People Eat? Needham, Kate. rev. ed. 2007. (Starting Point Science Ser.). 24p. (J). (gr. 1-4). pap. 4.99 (978-0-7945-1623-9(8), Usborne) EDC Publishing.
Spencer, Alison. Cinders. Stewart, Maddie. 2007. (Panda Cubs Ser.: 05). (ENG.). 48p. (J). pap. 9.95 (978-1-84717-027-9(7)) O'Brien Pr., Ltd., The IRL. Dist: Dufour Editions, Inc.
Spencer, Bob. The One & Only Sam: A Story Explaining Idioms for Children with Asperger Syndrome & Other Communication Difficulties. Stalker, Aileen. 2009. (ENG.). 64p. (gr. 1-3). 19.95 (978-1-84905-040-1(6), 693161) Kingsley, Jessica Pubs. GBR. Dist: Hachette UK Distribution.
Spencer, Brent. Eeko & the Nosy Neighbour. Charbonneau, Diane. 2019. (Adventures of Eeko, the Friendly Alien Ser.). (ENG.). 48p. (J). (978-1-5255-5544-2(8)); pap. (978-1-5255-5545-9(6)) FriesenPress.
Spencer, Brent. Eeko Returns to Earth: The Adventures of Eeko, the Friendly Alien. Charbonneau, Diane. 2018. (Adventures of Eeko the Friendly Alien Ser.). (ENG.). 54p. (J). pap. (978-1-5255-1175-2(0)) FriesenPress.
Spencer, Carolyn Royer. Lord Computesalot, Ruler of Aurora Bullyalis, & His Secret Quest to End Bullying. Davis, Regina. 2013. (ENG.). 40p. 38.95 (978-1-5246-2785-0(2)) AuthorHouse.
Spencer, Chip. Porka-Bella-Snu & the Mystery of the Letters. Hays, Phillip. 2013. 54p. pap. 6.95 (978-1-938679-05-6(9)) Written World Communications.
Spencer, David. The Epic Adventures of Huggie & Stick. Daywalt, Drew. 2018. 40p. (J). (gr. -1-3). 17.99 (978-0-399-17276-2(9), Philomel Bks.) Penguin Young Readers Group.
Spencer, Hugh. Billy Bunny & Daddy Fox: By David Cory *LATEST EDITION* Cory, David. 2019. (ENG.). 124p. (J). pap. 6.99 (978-1-0722-8690-5(4)) Independently Published.
Spencer, Kay Kincannon. Sleigh Ride with Santa. Spencer, John Nicholas. 2012. (ENG.). 26p. (J). pap. 14.95 (978-1-61296-140-8(1)) Black Rose Writing.
Spencer, Monica. The Bell That Wouldn't Ring. Kline, Karen E. 2008. 16p. pap. 24.95 (978-1-60672-497-2(5)) PublishAmerica, Inc.
Spencer, Nicola. Carlin. Ariel, BiVi. 2018. (ENG.). 30p. (J). pap. 6.99 (978-1-9996490-1-2(X)) Blossom Spring Publishing.
—Meo the Meerkat. Crookes, Kevin. 2016. (ENG.). (J). pap. (978-0-9956006-1-4(9)) Blossom Spring Publishing.
—A Naughty Little Angel. Ariel, BiVi. 2016. (ENG.). (J). pap. (978-0-9956006-2-1(7)) Blossom Spring Publishing.
—Paddy the Wee Leprechaun. Doyle Heagy, Viki. 2018. (ENG.). 28p. (J). pap. (978-1-9996490-0-5(1)) Blossom Spring Publishing.
Spencer, Tim. Oops! the Fish Died. Rome, Jamie & Curry, Paul. 2019. (ENG.). 28p. (J). (gr. k-6). 15.99 (978-0-578-46373-5(3)) Rome, Jamie.
Spencer, Trevor. Teddy Mars Book #1: Almost a World Record Breaker. Burnham, Molly B. (Teddy Mars Ser.: 1). (ENG.). (J). (gr. 3-7). 2016. 240p. pap. 6.99 (978-0-06-227811-1(8), Tegen, Katherine Bks); 2015. 224p. 16.99 (978-0-06-227810-4(X)) HarperCollins Pubs.
—Teddy Mars Book #2: Almost a Winner. Burnham, Molly B. (Teddy Mars Ser.: 2). (ENG.). 288p. (J). (gr. 3-7). 2017. pap. 6.99 (978-0-06-227814-2(2)); 2016. 16.99 (978-0-06-227813-5(4)) HarperCollins Pubs. (Tegen, Katherine Bks).
—Teddy Mars Book #3: Almost an Outlaw. Burnham, Molly B. (Teddy Mars Ser.: 3). (ENG.). 288p. (J). (gr. 3-7). 2018. pap. 6.99 (978-0-06-227818-0(5)); 2017. 16.99 (978-0-06-227816-6(9)) HarperCollins Pubs. (Tegen, Katherine Bks).
Spender, Nick. Ancient Treasures. Shone, Rob. 2008. (Graphic Nonfiction Ser.). (ENG.). 48p. (gr. 3-8). pap. 14.05 (978-1-4042-9593-3(3)); (YA). (gr. 5-9). lib. bdg. 35.45 (978-1-4042-1089-9(X)) Rosen Publishing Group, Inc., The.
—The Battle of the Alamo. Jeffrey, Gary. 2012. (Graphic History of the American West Ser.). (ENG.). 24p. (J). (gr. 3-8). pap. 8.15 (978-1-4339-6729-0(4), Gareth Stevens Learning Library); (gr. 4-7). lib. bdg. 24.95 (978-1-4339-6727-6(8)) Stevens, Gareth Publishing LLLP.
—The Battle of the Little Bighorn. Jeffrey, Gary. 2012. (Graphic History of the American West Ser.). (ENG.). 24p. (J). (gr. 3-8). pap. 8.15 (978-1-4339-6733-7(2), Gareth Stevens Learning Library); (gr. 4-7). lib. bdg. 24.95 (978-1-4339-6731-3(6)) Stevens, Gareth Publishing LLLP.
—Bigfoot & Other Strange Beasts. Shone, Rob. 2006. (Graphic Mysteries Ser.). (ENG.). 48p. (YA). (gr. k-3). lib. bdg. 35.45 (978-1-4042-0793-6(7)) Rosen Publishing Group, Inc., The.
—Castles. Jeffrey, Gary. 2014. (Graphic Medieval History Ser.). (ENG.). 48p. (J). (gr. 5-5). (978-0-7787-0396-9(7)) Crabtree Publishing Co.
—Corpses & Skeletons: The Science of Forensic Anthropology. Shone, Rob. 2008. (Graphic Forensic Science Ser.). (ENG.). (J). (gr. 5-8). lib. bdg. 22.55 (978-1-68065-314-4(8)) Perfection Learning Corp.
—Corpses & Skeletons: The Science of Forensic Anthropology. Shone, Rob. 2008. (Graphic Forensic Science Ser.). (ENG.). 48p. (gr. 5-8). per. 14.05 (978-1-4042-1441-5(0)); (YA). lib. bdg. 35.45 (978-1-4042-1440-8(2)) Rosen Publishing Group, Inc., The.
—The Dark Ages & the Vikings. Jeffrey, Gary. 2014. (Graphic Medieval History Ser.). (ENG.). 48p. (J). (gr. 5-5). (978-0-7787-0401-0(7)) Crabtree Publishing Co.
—Defying Death in the Mountains. Shone, Rob. 2010. (Graphic Survival Stories Ser.). 48p. (YA). 58.50 (978-1-61532-901-4(3), Rosen Reference) Rosen Publishing Group, Inc., The.
—Earthquakes. Shone, Rob. 2007. (Graphic Natural Disasters Ser.). (ENG.). 48p. (YA). (gr. 5-9). lib. bdg. 35.45 (978-1-4042-1989-2(7)) Rosen Publishing Group, Inc., The.
—Knights. Jeffrey, Gary. 2014. (Graphic Medieval History Ser.). (ENG.). 48p. (J). (gr. 5-5). (978-0-7787-0398-3(3)); pap. (978-0-7787-0404-1(1)) Crabtree Publishing Co.
—Muhammad Ali: The Life of a Boxing Hero. Shone, Rob. 2007. (Graphic Nonfiction Biographies Ser.). (ENG.). 48p. (J). (gr. 4-7). lib. bdg. 35.45 (978-1-4042-0856-8(9)); (gr. 5-8). pap. 14.05 (978-1-4042-0919-0(0)) Rosen Publishing Group, Inc., The.
—Rosa Parks: The Life of a Civil Rights Heroine. Shone, Rob. 2007. (Graphic Nonfiction Biographies Ser.). (ENG.). 48p. (J). (gr. 4-7). lib. bdg. 35.45 (978-1-4042-0864-3(X)) Rosen Publishing Group, Inc., The.
—Solving Crimes Through Criminal Profiling. Shone, Rob. 2008. (Graphic Forensic Science Ser.). (ENG.). 48p. (gr. 5-8). per. 14.05 (978-1-4042-1438-5(0)); (YA). lib. bdg. 35.45 (978-1-4042-1437-8(2)) Rosen Publishing Group, Inc., The.
Spender, Nik. Bigfoot & Other Strange Beasts. Shone, Rob. 2006. (Graphic Mysteries Ser.). (ENG.). 48p. (gr. 5-8). pap. 14.05 (978-1-4042-0804-9(6)) Rosen Publishing Group, Inc., The.
—Defying Death at the North & South Poles. Jeffrey, Gary & Shone, Rob. 2010. (Graphic Survival Stories Ser.). 48p. (YA). (gr. 5-8). 35.45 (978-1-4358-3527-6(1), Rosen Reference) Rosen Publishing Group, Inc., The.
—Defying Death in the Mountains. Shone, Rob. 2010. (Graphic Survival Stories Ser.). 48p. (YA). (ENG.). pap. 14.05 (978-1-61532-866-6(1)); (gr. 5-8). 35.45

S

(978-1-4358-3532-0(8)) Rosen Publishing Group, Inc., The. (Rosen Reference).
—Rosa Parks: The Life of a Civil Rights Heroine. Shone, Rob. 2007. (Graphic Biographies Ser.). (ENG.). 48p. (gr. 5-8). pap. 14.05 *(978-1-4042-0927-5(1))* Rosen Publishing Group, Inc., The.
—The Soviet War in Afghanistan. Jeffrey, Gary. 2013. (ENG.). 48p. (J). *(978-0-7787-1235-0(4))*; pap. *(978-0-7787-1239-8(7))* Crabtree Publishing Co.
Spender, Nik & Moulder, Bob. The Loch Ness Monster & Other Lake Mysteries. Jeffrey, Gary. 2006. (Graphic Mysteries Ser.). (ENG.). 48p. (YA). (gr. 5-8). lib. bdg. 35.45 *(978-1-4042-0796-7(1))* Rosen Publishing Group, Inc., The.
Spender, Nik, jt. illus. see Jeffrey, Gary.
Spender, Nik, jt. illus. see West, David.
Spengler, Ken. Oh My, Pumpkin Pie! Ghigna, Charles. 2005. (Step into Reading Ser.). 32p. (J). (gr. -1-1). pap. 4.99 *(978-0-375-82945-1(8)*, Random Hse. Bks. for Young Readers) Random Hse. Children's Bks.
Spengler, Kenneth. Mountain Night Mountain Day. Fredericks, Anthony D. 2014. (ENG.). 32p. (J). 15.95 *(978-1-933855-98-1(3)*, Rio Nuevo Pubs.) Rio Nuevo Pubs.
—Whose Tail on the Trail at Grand Canyon. Stephenson, Midji. 2012. (J). *(978-1-934656-55-6(0))* Grand Canyon Conservancy.
Spengler, Kenneth. Hotel Jungle. Spengler, Kenneth, tr. Napoli, Donna Jo & Johnston, Shelagh. 2004. 33p. (J). 15.95 *(978-1-59336-002-3(9))*; pap. *(978-1-59336-003-0(7))* Mondo Publishing.
Spengler, Kenneth J. Buster. Sudduth, Brent H. 2003. 32p. (J). 15.95 *(978-1-59034-478-1(2))* Mondo Publishing.
—Desert Night Desert Day. Fredericks, Anthony D. 2011. 32p. (J). 15.95 *(978-1-933855-70-7(3))* Rio Nuevo Pubs.
—Way up in the Arctic. Ward, Jennifer. 2007. (ENG.). 32p. (J). (gr. -1-3). 15.95 *(978-0-87358-928-4(9))* Cooper Square Publishing Llc.
Spengler, Margaret. Animal Strike at the Zoo. It's True! Wilson, Karma. 2006. (ENG.). 32p. (J). (gr. -1-1). 16.99 *(978-0-06-057502-1(6))* HarperCollins Pubs.
—Little Red Hen Gets Help. Spengler, Kenneth. 2007. (Green Light Reader Level 2 Ser.). 24p. (J). (gr. k-2). 16.19 *(978-0-15-206195-1(9))* Houghton Mifflin Harcourt Publishing Co.
—One, Two, Buckle My Shoe. 2004. (J). bds. 6.99 *(978-1-890647-12-4(8))* TOMY International, Inc.
—See Through Safari. Hawksley, Gerald. 2005. (J). bds. *(978-1-890647-15-5(2))* TOMY International, Inc.
—Storm Is Coming! Tekavec, Heather. 2004. 32p. (J). (gr. -1-3). reprint ed. pap. 6.99 *(978-0-14-240070-8(X)*, Puffin Books) Penguin Young Readers Group.
Spengler, Margaret L. Noah & the Mighty Ark, 1 vol. Greene, Rhonda Gowler. 2014. (ENG.). 32p. (J). 9.99 *(978-0-310-73217-4(4))* Zonderkidz.
Sper, Emily. Follow the Yarn: A Book of Colors. Sper, Emily. 2016. (ENG.). 24p. (J). (gr. -1 — 1). bds. 7.99 *(978-0-9754902-8-0(1)*, 9780975490280) Jump Pr.
—The Kids' Fun Book of Jewish Time. Sper, Emily. 2006. (HEB & ENG.). 24p. (J). (gr. -1-1). 16.99 *(978-1-58023-311-8(2)*, 1260461, Jewish Lights Publishing) LongHill Partners, Inc.
Sperling, Alia, jt. illus. see Sperling, Karima.
Sperling, Karima. Animal Salams. Sperling, Karima. 2020. (ENG.). 28p. (J). pap. 10.00 ***(978-0-9913003-8-9(6))*** Little Bird Bks.
Sperling, Karima & Sperling, Alia. Links of Light: The Golden Chain: A Child's Version of the Naqshbandi Sufi Way. Kabbani, Shaykh Muhamma & Kabbani, Muhammad Hisham. 2009. xi, 217p. (J). *(978-1-930409-68-2(0))* Islamic Supreme Council of America.
Sperling, S. David, jt. illus. see Mantell, Ahuva.
Sperling, Thomas. Chicken Licken. 2005. (J). *(978-0-7664-1050-3(1))* Abrams, Inc.
—Let's Celebrate Columbus Day. deRubertis, Barbara. 2014. (Holidays & Heroes Ser.). (ENG.). 32p. (J). (gr. 1-4). pap. 7.95 *(978-1-57565-634-2(5)*, 9781575656342) Astra Publishing Hse.
—Let's Celebrate Presidents' Day. deRubertis, Barbara. 2014. (Holidays & Heroes Ser.). (ENG.). 32p. (J). (gr. 1-4). pap. 7.95 *(978-1-57565-649-6(3)*, 9781575656496) Astra Publishing Hse.
—Let's Celebrate Thanksgiving Day. deRubertis, Barbara. (Holidays & Heroes Ser.). (ENG.). 32p. (J). (gr. 1-4). 2014. lib. bdg. 25.32 *(978-1-57565-723-3(6)*, 9781575657233); 2013. pap. 7.95 *(978-1-57565-636-6(1)*, 9781575656366) Astra Publishing Hse.
—The Little Red Hen. 2005. (J). *(978-0-7664-1052-7(8))* Abrams, Inc.
—Little Red Riding Hood. 2005. (J). *(978-0-7664-1055-8(2))* Abrams, Inc.
—Stone Cheese. 2005. (J). *(978-0-7664-1053-4(6))* Abrams, Inc.
—The Three Billy Goats Gruff. Asbjømsen, Peter Christen. 2005. (J). *(978-0-7664-1054-1(4))* Abrams, Inc.
—The Three Little Pigs. 2005. (J). *(978-0-7664-1051-0(X))* Abrams, Inc.
Sperling, Tom. The Refugee Camp 4 Voyagers. Eldridge, Jim. 2017. (Cambridge Reading Adventures Ser.). (ENG.). 32p. pap. 7.87 *(978-1-108-40108-1(2))* Cambridge Univ. Pr.
Sperling, Tom, jt. illus. see Paget, Walter Stanley.
Sperry, Armstrong. Wagons Westward: The Old Trail to Santa Fe. Sperry, Armstrong. 2005. 200p. (YA). (gr. 6-11). reprint ed. pap. 15.00 *(978-0-7567-9693-8(8))* DIANE Publishing Co.
Speth, Brandilyn. Some Secrets Hurt: A Story of Healing. Garner, Linda. 2009. 64p. (J). (gr. 1). 15.95 *(978-1-60641-135-3(7))* Deseret Bk. Co.
Spetter, Jung-Hee. Bye, Bye! Kaufmann, Nancy. 2004. (ENG.). 32p. (J). (gr. -1-1). 14.95 *(978-1-886910-95-9(2)*, Lemniscaat) Boyds Mills Pr.
Spicer, Bridgett. Earl Joins the Circus. Scheber, George. I.t. ed. 2005. (Adventures of Earl the Squirrel Ser.). 32p. (J). (gr. -1-3). 12.95 *(978-1-878847-01-0(5))* Make Me A Story Pr.
—Earl the Squirrel. Scheber, George. l.t. ed. 2005. (Adventures of Earl the Squirrel Ser.). 32p. (J). (gr. -1-2). 12.95 *(978-1-878847-00-3(7))* Make Me A Story Pr.
Spicer, Morgan. Are You My Daddy? - Paperback. Medina, Sylvia M. Hill, Krista, ed. 2019. (ENG.). 44p. (J). (gr. k-3). pap. 17.00 *(978-1-939871-67-1(0))* Green Kids Club, Inc.
Spicer, Morgan. Benjamin Birdie & the Tree Dwellers. Dotsikas, Michael. 2019. (ENG.). 50p. (J). (gr. 1-2). pap. 14.99 ***(978-1-61254-377-2(4))*** Brown Books Publishing Group.
—Benjamin Birdie's First Flight. Dotsikas, Michael. 2019. (ENG.). 54p. (J). (gr. -1-3). pap. 14.99 ***(978-1-61254-376-5(6))*** Brown Books Publishing Group.
Spicer, Morgan. The Fire Elephant - Translated in Setswana Paperback. Medina, Sylvia M. & Hill, Krista. 2018. (Baby Animal Environmental Heroes Ser.: Vol. 2). (ENG.). 44p. (J). (gr. k-2). pap. 15.50 *(978-1-939871-74-9(3))* Green Kids Club, Inc.
Spicer, Morgan. Grizzly 399 - Hardback: Environmental Heroes Series. Medina, Sylvia M. 2020. (ENG.). 43p. (J). 29.99 ***(978-1-939871-53-4(0))*** Green Kids Club, Inc.
Spicer, Morgan. The Last Rhino. Stevenson, Deborah. Hill, Krista, ed. 2018. (ENG.). 88p. (J). (gr. 2-5). pap. 11.95 *(978-1-7325410-4-7(3))* Frog Prince Bks.
Spicer, Morgan. Little Moyo - Hardback: Baby Animal Environmental Heroes. Medina, Sylvia M. 2019. (ENG.). 43p. (J). (gr. k-3). 25.00 ***(978-1-939871-92-3(1))*** Green Kids Club, Inc.
—Little Moyo - Paperback: Baby Animal Environmental Heroes. Medina, Sylvia M. 2019. (ENG.). 43p. (J). (gr. k-3). pap. 16.00 ***(978-1-939871-91-6(3))*** Green Kids Club, Inc.
Spicer, Morgan. Oy, Elephants! Stevenson, Deborah. Hill, Krista, ed. 2nd ed. 2019. (ENG.). 38p. (J). (gr. k-4). 18.95 *(978-1-7325410-1-6(9))*; pap. 12.95 *(978-1-7325410-2-3(7))* Frog Prince Bks.
—Princess - Hardback: Baby Animal Environmental Heroes. Medina, Sylvia M. & Shapiro, Gary. 2019. (ENG.). 44p. (J). (gr. k-3). 25.75 *(978-1-939871-64-0(6))* Green Kids Club, Inc.
—Princess - Paperback: Baby Animal Environmental Heroes. Medina, Sylvia M. & Shapiro, Gary. 2019. (ENG.). 44p. (J). (gr. k-3). pap. 15.75 *(978-1-939871-65-7(4))* Green Kids Club, Inc.
Spicer, Morgan. Sashi Adopts a Brother. Greiner, Linda. 2019. (ENG.). 42p. (J). (gr. k-3). pap. 12.95 ***(978-1-61254-393-2(6))*** Brown Books Publishing Group.
—Sashi & the Puppy Mill Girl. Greiner, Linda. 2019. (ENG.). 42p. (J). (gr. k-3). pap. 12.95 ***(978-1-61254-394-9(4))*** Brown Books Publishing Group.
—Sashi, the Scared Little Sheltie. Greiner, Linda. 2019. (ENG.). 34p. (J). (gr. k-3). pap. 12.95 ***(978-1-61254-392-5(8))*** Brown Books Publishing Group.
Spicer, Morgen. Grizzly 399 - Paperback: Environmental Heroes Series. Medina, Sylvia M. 2020. (ENG.). 43p. (J). pap. 19.99 ***(978-1-939871-62-6(X))*** Green Kids Club, Inc.
Spiegel, Beth. First Grade Stinks!, 1 vol. Rodman, Mary Ann. (ENG.). 32p. (J). (gr. k-3). 2008. pap. 8.95 *(978-1-56145-462-4(1))*; 2006. 15.95 *(978-1-56145-377-1(3))* Peachtree Publishing Co. Inc.
—Rosa's Room, 1 vol. Bottner, Barbara. (ENG.). 32p. (J). 2014. (gr. -1-3). pap. 7.95 *(978-1-56145-776-2(0))*; 2004. (gr. k-3). 15.95 *(978-1-56145-302-3(1))* Peachtree Publishing Co. Inc.
—Will It Be a Baby Brother? Bunting, Eve. 2010. (ENG.). 32p. (J). (gr. -1-k). 16.95 *(978-1-59078-439-6(1))* Boyds Mills Pr.
Spiegelman, Art. Jack & the Box, 1 vol. Spiegelman, Art. 2013. (Toon Bks.). (ENG.). 36p. (J). (gr. -1-1). lib. bdg. 29.93 *(978-1-61479-151-5(1)*, 14843) Spotlight.
Spiegelman, Art & Mouly, Françoise. It Was a Dark & Silly Night... Spiegelman, Art & Mouly, Françoise. 2003. (Little Lit Ser.: Vol. 3). 48p. (J). (gr. 1-18). 19.99 *(978-0-06-028628-6(8))* HarperCollins Pubs.
Spiegle, Dan. Pocahontas. Foster, Bob. 2020. (Disney Princesses Ser.). (ENG.). 48p. (J). (gr. 2-6). lib. bdg. 28.50 ***(978-1-5321-4565-0(9)***, 35212, Graphic Novels) Spotlight.
Spieler, Leah. ThumBie Character Kit. Spieler, Leah. 2004. (J). pap. 29.95 *(978-0-9761408-2-5(9))* Creative Marketing Concepts, Inc.
Spier, Jo. The Story of Louis Pasteur. Malkus, Alida Sims. Meadowcroft, Enid Lamonte, ed. 2011. 190p. 42.95 *(978-1-258-05476-2(0))* Literary Licensing, LLC.
Spier, Peter. The Fox Went Out on a Chilly Night: An Old Song. unabr. ed. 2006. (J). (gr. -1-3). pap. 16.95 incl. audio *(978-1-59112-440-5(9))*;Set. pap. 37.95 incl. audio *(978-1-59112-442-9(5))*;Set. pap. 39.95 incl. audio compact disk *(978-1-59112-443-6(3))* Live Oak Media.
Spies, Robert. Weirdo. Spies, Ben. 2015. (ENG.). 54p. (J). pap. *(978-0-473-33563-2(8))* Spies Publishing.
Spiker, Sue Ann. The Day the Snapdragons Snapped Back. Chambers, Melinda. 2007. 32p. (J). 16.95 *(978-0-929915-72-2(0))* Headline Bks., Inc.
—We Are Whoooo We Are. Chambers, Melinda. 2006. 32p. (J). 16.95 *(978-0-929915-46-3(1))* Headline Bks., Inc.
Spiker, Sue Ann Maxwell. Tails, Trails & Pies: An Appalachian Cattle Drive. Hedrick, Helen Groves. 2008. 32p. 15.95 *(978-0-929915-87-6(9))* Headline Bks., Inc.
Spikes, Leon, Jr. Taffey Pop Kids Presents the Adventures of Lemmon Head & Mudd Duck: What to Do if Someone Tries to Grab YOU!!! Spikes, James L. 2007. 32p. (J). 14.95 *(978-0-9771438-0-1(5))* Taffey Pop Kids Publishing.
Spikings, Ashley. Philbert Larue Had a Hole in His Shoe. Pelicano, Matt. 2018. (ENG.). 32p. (J). (gr. k-6). 18.95 *(978-0-692-16938-4(5))* April Fool Publishing.
Spillane, Lisa. Six Healing Sounds with Lisa & Ted: Qigong for Children. Spillane, Lisa. 2011. (ENG.). 78p. (J). 14.95 *(978-1-84819-051-1(4)*, 694631, Singing Dragon) Kingsley, Jessica Pubs. GBR. Dist: Hachette UK Distribution.
Spiller, Michael. The Sandman. Milligan, Domino. 2008. 16p. pap. 24.95 *(978-1-60703-728-6(9))* America Star Bks.
Spina Dixon, Debra, jt. illus. see Dixon, Debra Spina.
Spinelli, Patti. Alphabet Book with Mackenzie & Emma. Spinelli, Patti. 2003. 32p. (Orig.). (J). (gr. k-4). pap. 11.95 *(978-1-892066-00-8(9))* Nicolin Fields Publishing, Inc.
—Mackenzie & Emma Visit York Beach. Spinelli, Patti. 2003. (J). *(978-0-9742328-0-5(7))* Spinelli, Patti.
Spinks, Lindsey. Ancient Wonders - Then & Now, 1 vol. Hill, Stuart & Lonely Planet Kids. 2018. (Then & Now Ser.). (ENG.). 24p. (J). (gr. 4-7). 18.99 *(978-1-78701-340-7(5)*, 5746) Lonely Planet Global Ltd. IRL. Dist: Hachette Bk. Group.
Spinks, Scott. Mommy, Am I Strong? Lazurek, Michelle S. 2015. 25p. (J). pap. *(978-0-8198-4948-9(0))* Pauline Bks. & Media.
—Up, up, & Away. Hillert, Margaret. 2016. (BeginningtoRead Ser.). (ENG.). 32p. (J). (gr. -1-2). pap. 11.94 *(978-1-60357-947-6(8))*; (gr. 1-2). 22.60 *(978-1-59953-806-8(7))* Norwood Hse. Pr.
Spinks, Stefphany (Snider). When the Moon Was Born, 1 vol. Eubanks-Adkison, Eufa. 2010. 16p. 24.95 *(978-1-4512-1367-6(0))* PublishAmerica, Inc.
Spino, Bonnie. Wild about Friends. Loria, Lorraine. (ENG.). 28p. (J). 2019. pap. 11.99 *(978-0-9881889-3-8(7))*; 2018. (Wild About Ser.: Vol. 2). 18.00 *(978-0-9881889-4-5(5))* Piccolo Tales.
—Wild about Manners. Lorraine, Loria. 2013. 36p. pap. 11.95 *(978-0-9881889-0-7(2))* Piccolo Tales.
Spiotto, Joey. Attack! Boss! Cheat Code! A Gamer's Alphabet. Barton, Chris. 2014. (ENG.). 32p. (J). (gr. 1-4). 14.95 *(978-1-57687-701-2(9)*, powerHouse Bks.) powerHse. Bks.
Spires, Ashley. Book or Bell? Barton, Chris. 2017. 40p. (J). 16.99 *(978-1-68119-729-6(4)*, 900182504, Bloomsbury USA Childrens) Bloomsbury Publishing USA.
—C'mere, Boy! Jennings, Sharon. 2010. 32p. (J). (gr. -1-2). 16.95 *(978-1-55453-440-1(2))* Kids Can Pr., Ltd. CAN. Dist: Hachette Bk. Group.
—Ella's Umbrellas. Lloyd, Jennifer. (J). (gr. -1-3). 2017. 36p. 8.99 *(978-1-77229-010-3(6))*; 2010. (ENG.). 32p. 16.95 *(978-1-897476-23-9(X))* Simply Read Bks. CAN. Dist: Ingram Publisher Services.
—Go to Sleep, Little Creep. Quinn, David. 2018. 32p. (J). (-k). 17.99 *(978-1-101-93944-4(3))*; (ENG.). lib. bdg. 20.99 *(978-1-101-93945-1(1))* Random Hse. Children's Bks. (Crown Books For Young Readers).
—Mae & June & the Wonder Wheel. Harper, Charise Mericle. (ENG.). 128p. (J). (gr. 1-4). 2018. pap. 6.99 *(978-1-328-90012-8(6)*, 1700041); 2017. 15.99 *(978-0-544-63063-5(7)*, 1619505) Houghton Mifflin Harcourt Publishing Co. (HMH Books For Young Readers).
—My Mom Loves Me More Than Sushi. Gomes, Filomena. 2006. 24p. (J). pap. *(978-1-897187-13-5(0))* Second Story Pr.
—My Mom Loves Me More Than Sushi, 1 vol. Gomes, Filomena. 2006. (ENG.). 32p. (J). (gr. 1-3). 15.95 *(978-1-897187-09-8(2))* Second Story Pr. CAN. Dist: Orca Bk. Pubs. USA.
—The Red Shoes. Glass, Eleri. (J). (gr. -1-3). 2017. 40p. 8.99 *(978-1-927018-85-9(4))*; 2008. (ENG.). 36p. 16.95 *(978-1-894965-78-1(7))* Simply Read Bks. CAN. Dist: Ingram Publisher Services.
—Turtle & Tortoise Are Not Friends. Reiss, Mike. 2019. (ENG.). 32p. (J). (gr. -1-3). 17.99 *(978-0-06-074031-3(0))* HarperCollins Pubs.
Spires, Ashley. Binky: License to Scratch. Spires, Ashley. 2013. (Binky Adventure Ser.). (ENG.). 64p. (J). (gr. 2-5). pap. 7.95 *(978-1-55453-964-2(1))* Kids Can Pr., Ltd. CAN. Dist: Hachette Bk. Group.
—Binky Takes Charge. Spires, Ashley. 2012. (Binky Adventure Ser.: 4). (ENG.). 64p. (J). (gr. 2-5). 7.99 *(978-1-55453-768-6(1))*; 16.95 *(978-1-55453-703-7(7))* Kids Can Pr., Ltd. CAN. Dist: Hachette Bk. Group.
—Binky the Space Cat. Spires, Ashley. 2009. (Binky Adventure Ser.). (ENG.). 64p. (J). (gr. 2-5). 7.95 *(978-1-55453-419-7(4))*; 16.95 *(978-1-55453-309-1(0))* Kids Can Pr., Ltd. CAN. Dist: Hachette Bk. Group.
—Binky to the Rescue. Spires, Ashley. 2010. (Binky Adventure Ser.). (ENG.). 64p. (J). (gr. 2-5). 7.95 *(978-1-55453-597-2(2))* Kids Can Pr., Ltd. CAN. Dist: Hachette Bk. Group.
—Larf. Spires, Ashley. 2012. (ENG.). 32p. (J). (gr. -1-2). 16.95 *(978-1-55453-701-3(0))* Kids Can Pr., Ltd. CAN. Dist: Hachette Bk. Group.
—The Most Magnificent Thing, 0 vols. Spires, Ashley. 2014. (ENG.). 32p. (J). (gr. -1-2). 16.95 *(978-1-55453-704-4(5))* Kids Can Pr., Ltd. CAN. Dist: Hachette Bk. Group.
—Small Saul. Spires, Ashley. 2011. (ENG.). 32p. (J). (gr. -1-2). 16.95 *(978-1-55453-503-3(4))* Kids Can Pr., Ltd. CAN. Dist: Hachette Bk. Group.
Spiridellis, Evan, jt. illus. see Spiridellis, Gregg.
Spiridellis, Gregg & Spiridellis, Evan. Grumpy Santa. Moore, Clement C. 2003. (ENG.). (J). *(978-0-439-53039-2(3)*, Orchard Bks.) Scholastic, Inc.
Spirin, Gennady. Frog Song. Guiberson, Brenda Z. 2013. (ENG.). 40p. (J). (gr. -1-3). 18.99 *(978-0-8050-9254-7(4)*, 900068332, Holt, Henry & Co. Bks. For Young Readers) Holt, Henry & Co.
—The Greatest Dinosaur Ever. Z. Guiberson, Brenda. 2013. (ENG.). 32p. (J). (gr. -1-3). 18.99 *(978-0-8050-9625-5(6)*, 900086243, Holt, Henry & Co. Bks. For Young Readers) Holt, Henry & Co.
—La Hija del Rey de los Mares. Shepard, Aaron. (SPA.). 32p. (J). (gr. 3-5). *(978-84-264-3725-9(7)*, LM5051) Editorial Lumen ESP. Dist: Lectorum Pubns., Inc.
—Jesus: His Life in Verses from the King James Holy Bible, 0 vols. Cuyler, Margery. 2010. (ENG.). 36p. (J). (gr. 3-7). 21.00 *(978-0-7614-5630-8(9)*, 9780761456308, Two Lions) Amazon Publishing.
—The Little Black Hen. Pogorelsky, Antony. 2003. (ENG.). 32p. (J). (gr. k-4). 16.95 *(978-1-894965-03-3(5))* Simply Read Bks. CAN. Dist: Ingram Publisher Services.
—The Most Amazing Creature in the Sea. Guiberson, Brenda Z. 2015. (ENG.). 32p. (J). (gr. -1-3). 17.99 *(978-0-8050-9961-4(1)*, 900127879, Holt, Henry & Co. Bks. For Young Readers) Holt, Henry & Co.
—The Night Before Christmas, 0 vols. Moore, Clement Clarke. ltd. ed. 2006. (ENG.). 32p. (J). (gr. -1-3). 16.99 *(978-0-7614-5298-0(2)*, 9780761452980, Two Lions) Amazon Publishing.
—Perceval: King Arthur's Knight of the Holy Grail, 1 vol. Perkins, John. 2007. (ENG.). 40p. (J). (gr. 3-7). 16.99 *(978-0-7614-5339-0(3))* Marshall Cavendish Corp.
—The Sea King's Daughter: A Russian Legend. Shepard, Aaron. 15th ed. 2017. (ENG.). (J). (gr. 2-7). pap. 10.00 *(978-1-62035-504-6(3)*, Skyhook Pr.) Shepard Pubns.
—Simeon's Gift. Andrews, Julie & Hamilton, Emma Walton. 2006. 30p. (J). (gr. 4-8). reprint ed. 17.00 *(978-1-4223-5855-9(0))* DIANE Publishing Co.
—Simeon's Gift. Andrews, Julie & Hamilton, Emma Walton. 2003. (Julie Andrews Collection). 40p. (J). 17.89 *(978-0-06-008915-3(6)*, Julie Andrews Collection) HarperCollins Pubs.
—Simeon's Gift. Andrews, Julie et al. 2003. (Julie Andrews Collection). (ENG.). 40p. (J). (gr. k-4). 19.99 *(978-0-06-008914-6(8))* HarperCollins Pubs.
—The Velveteen Rabbit, 0 vols. Williams, Margery. 2011. (ENG.). 48p. (gr. 3-7). 17.99 *(978-0-7614-5848-7(4)*, 9780761458487, Two Lions) Amazon Publishing.
Spirin, Gennady. Goldilocks & the Three Bears, 0 vols. Spirin, Gennady. 2009. (ENG.). 32p. (J). (gr. -1-2). 17.99 *(978-0-7614-5596-7(5)*, 9780761455967, Two Lions) Amazon Publishing.
—The Twelve Days of Christmas, 0 vols. Spirin, Gennady. 2009. (ENG.). 32p. (J). (gr. 1-3). 16.99 *(978-0-7614-5551-6(5)*, 9780761455516, Two Lions) Amazon Publishing.
—The Twelve Days of Christmas. Spirin, Gennady. ltd. ed. 2009. 32p. (J). (gr. -1-3). 16.99 *(978-0-7614-5607-0(4))* Marshall Cavendish Corp.
Spirin, Ilya. Ice Bears. Guiberson, Brenda Z. 2014. (ENG.). (J). (gr. k-3). lib. bdg. 18.60 *(978-1-62765-376-3(7))* Perfection Learning Corp.
—Little Lost Tiger, 0 vols. London, Jonathan. 2012. (ENG.). 32p. (J). (gr. k-3). 17.99 *(978-0-7614-6130-2(2)*, 9780761461302, Two Lions) Amazon Publishing.
Spivey Gilchrist, Jan. The Thumbtack Dancer. Tyron, Leslie. 2017. (ENG.). 32p. (J). (gr. k-2). 17.95 *(978-0-9977720-0-5(X)*, Alazar Pr.) Royal Swan Enterprises, Inc.
Spizzirri, Peter M. Prehistoric Birds. Spizzirri, Linda, ed. 32p. (J). (gr. 1-8). pap. 4.98 incl. audio *(978-0-86545-023-3(4))* Spizzirri Pr., Inc.
—Space Craft. Spizzirri, Linda, ed. 32p. (J). (gr. 1-8). pap. 4.98 incl. audio *(978-0-86545-036-3(6))* Spizzirri Pr., Inc.
Splho, Michal. Repair for Teens: A Program for Recovery from Incest & Childhood Sexual Abuse. McKinnon, Margie. 2012. 138p. (J). 28.95 *(978-1-61599-127-3(1))*; pap. 16.95 *(978-1-61599-126-6(3))* Loving Healing Pr., Inc.
Splink, jt. illus. see Loki.
Spoerl, Amber. Dee Dee's First Shot, 1 vol. Dusablon, David. 2009. 17p. pap. 24.95 *(978-1-60749-113-2(3))* America Star Bks.
—The Dentist, 1 vol. Dusablon, David. 2009. 11p. pap. 24.95 *(978-1-60836-186-1(1))* America Star Bks.
Spohn, David. The Creation Story: In Words & Sign Language. Audia, John P. 2007. (ENG.). 16p. (gr. 3-7). 9.95 *(978-0-8146-3174-4(6))* Liturgical Pr.
Spohn, Kate. Turtle & Snake's Day at the Beach. Spohn, Kate. 2004. (Penguin Young Readers, Level 2 Ser.). 32p. (J). (gr. 1-2). mass mkt. 4.99 *(978-0-14-240157-6(9)*, Penguin Young Readers) Penguin Young Readers Group.
—Turtle & Snake's Day at the Beach. Spohn, Kate. 2004. (Puffin Easy-to-Read Ser.). 32p. (gr. k-3). 14.00 *(978-0-7569-2826-1(5))* Perfection Learning Corp.
—Turtle & Snake's Spooky Halloween. Spohn, Kate. 2003. (Easy-to-Read Ser.). 32p. (J). (gr. -1-3). 11.65 *(978-0-7569-1949-8(5))* Perfection Learning Corp.
Sponaugle, Kim. Amari's Great Adventures: The Magical Playground. Harris, Deborah D. 2018. (ENG.). (J). (gr. -1-2). 19.99 *(978-1-5456-3621-3(4))* Salem Author Services.
—Angel Eyes. Phillips, Dixie. 2008. 24p. pap. 10.95 *(978-1-933090-74-0(X))* Guardian Angel Publishing, Inc.
—Dusty the Dustball & Family: Their Adventure Begins. Pickhardt Jr, Edward. 2018. (ENG.). 80p. (J). (gr. 7-9). pap. 15.95 *(978-1-61244-594-6(2))* Halo Publishing International.
—Forever Evergreen. Roberts, Kay. 2018. (ENG.). 30p. (J). (gr. k-6). 24.95 *(978-1-61244-596-0(9))* Halo Publishing International.
—Grandma Kathy Has Cancer. Buckley, Colleen. 2007. 24p. per. 11.50 *(978-1-59858-422-6(7))* Dog Ear Publishing, LLC.
—Jeremy & Red Jeep Car Show. Lenser, Debra. 2019. (ENG.). 34p. (J). (gr. k-2). 21.95 *(978-1-938796-58-6(6))* Fruitbearer Publishing, LLC.
—Just a Quilt? Keys, Dalen. 2nd ed. 2012. (ENG.). 32p. (J). 16.00 *(978-1-886068-56-8(9))* Fruitbearer Publishing, LLC.
—One Noble Journey. Phillips, Dixie. 2009. 16p. pap. 9.95 *(978-1-935137-86-3(7))* Guardian Angel Publishing, Inc.
—Seymour the Semi- Space Truckin' Spoonmore, Scott. 2012. 24p. 19.95 *(978-1-61633-282-2(4))*; pap. 11.95 *(978-1-61633-283-9(2))* Guardian Angel Publishing, Inc.
—Sweet Sweet Carabee. Gresham, Evelyn. 2013. 24p. pap. 11.95 *(978-1-61244-233-4(1))* Halo Publishing International.
—Willoughby: And the Lumpy Bumpy Cake. Halter, Pam. 2018. (Willoughby & Friends Ser.: Vol. 2). (ENG.). 34p. (J). (gr. k-2). pap. 14.95 *(978-1-938796-48-7(9))* Fruitbearer Publishing, LLC.
Sponaugle, Kim. Willoughby: Goes a Wee Bit Batty. Halter, Pam. 2019. (Willoughby & Friends Ser.: Vol. 3). (ENG.). 38p. (J). (gr. k-2). pap. 14.95 ***(978-1-938796-59-3(4))*** Fruitbearer Publishing, LLC.

Spong, Clive. King Arthur & the Magic Sword: An English Legend. 2004. (ENG.). 24p. (J). (gr. 3-3). pap. 6.47 net. *(978-0-7685-2123-8(8)*, Dominie Elementary) Savvas Learning Co.
—Let's Look on the Move. Rutherford, Peter. 2015. 24p. (J). (gr. -1-2). bds. 6.99 *(978-1-86147-414-8(8)*, Armadillo) Anness Publishing GBR. Dist: National Bk. Network.
—Rapunzel. McCafferty, Catherine. ed. 2008. (Keepsake Stories Ser.). (ENG.). 32p. (gr. -1-3). pap. 3.99 *(978-0-7696-5418-8(5)*, 0769654185, Brighter Child) Carson-Dellosa Publishing, LLC.
Sponheimer, Katheryne. The Sun Tea Fish. Callahan, Ann Marie. 2008. 16p. pap. 24.95 *(978-1-60672-160-5(7))* America Star Bks.
Spont, Ursula. What Is Therapy & Why Do I Have to Go? Domowski Lcsw, Patience. 2018. (ENG.). 28p. (J). pap. 10.00 *(978-1-7181-9700-8(4))* Independently Published.
Spookytooth, T. S. Bone by Bone: Comparing Animal Skeletons. Levine, Sara C. 2013. (Animal by Animal Ser.). (ENG.). 32p. (J). (gr. k-4). lib. bdg. 26.65 *(978-0-7613-8464-9(2)*, 9780761384649, Millbrook Pr.) Lerner Publishing Group.
Spookytooth, T. S. Eye by Eye: Comparing How Animals See. Levine, Sara. 2020. (Animal by Animal Ser.). (ENG.). 32p. (J). (gr. k-4). 26.65 ***(978-1-5415-3838-2(2)***, Millbrook Pr.) Lerner Publishing Group.
Spookytooth, T. S. Fossil by Fossil: Comparing Dinosaur Bones. Levine, Sara C. 2018. (Animal by Animal Ser.). (ENG.). 32p. (J). (gr. k-4). 26.65 *(978-1-4677-9489-3(9)*, Millbrook Pr.) Lerner Publishing Group.
—Tooth by Tooth: Comparing Fangs, Tusks, & Chompers. Levine, Sara. 2016. (Animal by Animal Ser.). (ENG.). 32p. (J). (gr. k-4). 26.65 *(978-1-4677-5215-2(0)*, 9781467752152); E-Book 39.99 *(978-1-4677-9727-6(8))*; E-Book 39.99 *(978-1-5124-0732-7(1)*, 9781512407327) Lerner Publishing Group. (Millbrook Pr.).
Spooner, Joe. Max's Moving Adventure: A Coloring Book for Kids on the Move. Till, Danelle. 2006. 52p. (J). 8.95 *(978-0-912301-64-8(3))* First Bks.
Spooner, Joe. The Elephant Walk. Spooner, Joe. McCann, Michelle, ed. 2005. (ENG.). 36p. (J). (gr. -1-3). 15.00 *(978-0-9745686-3-8(5))* ACS, LLC Amica Creative Services.
Spooner, Luke. Emlyn & the Gremlin: Emlyn & the Gremlin Series. Kneff, Steff F. I.t. ed. 2014. (ENG.). 52p. (gr. k-3). 26.95 *(978-1-62253-399-2(2))*; pap. 10.95 *(978-1-62253-398-5(4))* Evolved Publishing.
Spoor, Mike. Alice's Birthday Pig. Kennemore, Tim. 2008. 54p. (J). (gr. 2-5). 12.00 *(978-0-8028-5335-6(8))* Eerdmans, William B. Publishing Co.
—Alice's World Record. Kennemore, Tim. 2008. 85p. (J). (gr. 4-7). 12.00 *(978-0-8028-5336-3(6))* Eerdmans, William B. Publishing Co.
—Benjamin the Bear: A Tale of Selfishness. Law, Felicia. 2010. (Animal Fair Values Ser.). (ENG.). 32p. (J). (gr. -1-3). pap. 10.55 *(978-1-60754-915-4(8))*; lib. bdg. 25.60 *(978-1-60754-905-5(0))* Windmill Bks.
—Blackbeard's Sword: The Pirate King of the Carolinas. O'Donnell, Liam. 2007. (Historical Fiction Ser.). (ENG.). 56p. (J). (gr. 3-6). pap. 6.25 *(978-1-59889-404-2(8)*, Stone Arch Bks.) Capstone.
—Desperate Measures: Units of Measurement in Action. 2010. (Mandrill Mountain Math Mysteries Ser.). (ENG.). 32p. (J). (gr. 2-6). pap. 10.55 *(978-1-60754-925-3(5))* Windmill Bks.
—Desperate Measures: Units of Measurement in Action. 2010. (Mandrill Mountain Math Mysteries Ser.). (ENG.). 32p. (J). (gr. 2-6). lib. bdg. 25.60 *(978-1-60754-920-8(4))* Windmill Bks.
—The Emperor's Guards: Concepts of Time. 2010. (Mandrill Mountain Math Mysteries Ser.). (ENG.). 32p. (J). (gr. 2-6). pap. 10.55 *(978-1-60754-927-7(1))*; lib. bdg. 25.60 *(978-1-60754-922-2(0))* Windmill Bks.
—The Emperor's Last Command: Problem-solving in Action. 2010. (Mandrill Mountain Math Mysteries Ser.). (ENG.). 32p. (J). (gr. 2-6). pap. 10.55 *(978-1-60754-928-4(X))* Windmill Bks.
—The Emperor's Last Command: Problem-Solving in Action. 2010. (Mandrill Mountain Math Mysteries Ser.). (ENG.). 32p. (J). (gr. 2-6). lib. bdg. 25.60 *(978-1-60754-923-9(9))* Windmill Bks.
—Farmer Ham. Sillifant, Alec. import ed. 2004. 24p. *(978-1-904511-93-9(7))* Meadowside Children's Bks.
—The Hidden Valley: Reasoning in Action. 2010. (Mandrill Mountain Math Mysteries Ser.). (ENG.). 32p. (J). (gr. 2-6). pap. 10.55 *(978-1-60754-924-6(7))*; lib. bdg. 25.60 *(978-1-60754-919-2(0))* Windmill Bks.
—Lightning Flash: Probability in Action. 2010. (Mandrill Mountain Math Mysteries Ser.). (ENG.). 32p. (J). (gr. 2-6). pap. 10.55 *(978-1-60754-926-0(3))*; lib. bdg. 25.60 *(978-1-60754-921-5(2))* Windmill Bks.
—Monster under the Stairs. Dhami, Narinder. 2005. (ENG.). 24p. (J). lib. bdg. 23.65 *(978-1-59646-718-7(5))* Dingles & Co.
—The Mystery of the Vampire Boy: Dare You Peek Through the Pop-Up Windows? Taylor, Dereen. 2014. 12p. (J). (gr. k-5). 16.99 *(978-1-86147-410-0(5)*, Armadillo) Anness Publishing GBR. Dist: National Bk. Network.
—Olivia the Orangutan: A Tale of Helpfulness. Law, Felicia. 2010. (Animal Fair Values Ser.). (ENG.). 32p. (J). (gr. -1-3). pap. 10.55 *(978-1-60754-917-8(4))*; lib. bdg. 25.60 *(978-1-60754-906-2(9))* Windmill Bks.
—Pressing Down: The Lever. Bailey, Gerry. 2014. (Robotx Get Help from Simple Machines Ser.). (ENG.). 32p. (J). (gr. 2-3). *(978-0-7787-0416-4(5))*; pap. *(978-0-7787-0422-5(X))* Crabtree Publishing Co.
—Pulling Up: The Pulley. Bailey, Gerry. 2014. (Robotx Get Help from Simple Machines Ser.). (ENG.). 32p. (J). (gr. 2-3). *(978-0-7787-0417-1(3))*; pap. *(978-0-7787-0423-2(8))* Crabtree Publishing Co.
—Rolling Along: Wheels & Axles. Bailey, Gerry. 2014. (Robotx Get Help from Simple Machines Ser.). (ENG.). 32p. (J). (gr. 2-3). *(978-0-7787-0418-8(1))*; pap. *(978-0-7787-0424-9(6))* Crabtree Publishing Co.
—Sloping up & Down: The Ramp. Bailey, Gerry & Law, Felicia. 2014. (Robotx Get Help from Simple Machines Ser.). (ENG.). 32p. (J). (gr. 2-3). *(978-0-7787-0419-5(X))*; pap. *(978-0-7787-0425-6(4))* Crabtree Publishing Co.
—Splitting Apart: The Wedge. Bailey, Gerry. 2014. (Robotx Get Help from Simple Machines Ser.). (ENG.). 32p. (J). (gr. 2-3). *(978-0-7787-0420-1(3))*; pap. *(978-0-7787-0426-3(2))* Crabtree Publishing Co.
—Winding Around: The Screw. Bailey, Gerry. 2014. (Robotx Get Help from Simple Machines Ser.). (ENG.). 32p. (J). (gr. 2-3). *(978-0-7787-0421-8(1))*; pap. *(978-0-7787-0427-0(0))* Crabtree Publishing Co.
Spoor, Mike & Mostyn, David. Crocodile Teeth: Geometric Shapes in Action. Law, Felicia & Way, Steve. 2010. (Mandrill Mountain Math Mysteries Ser.). 32p. (J). (gr. 2-6). 25.60 *(978-1-60754-816-4(X))*; pap. 10.55 *(978-1-60754-821-8(6))* Windmill Bks.
—Mirage in the Mist: Measurement in Action. Law, Felicia & Way, Steve. 2010. (Mandrill Mountain Math Mysteries Ser.). 32p. (J). (gr. 2-6). pap. 10.55 *(978-1-60754-823-2(2))* Windmill Bks.
—Mirage in the Mist: Measurements in Action. Law, Felicia & Way, Steve. 2010. (Mandrill Mountain Math Mysteries Ser.). 32p. (J). (gr. 2-6). 25.60 *(978-1-60754-818-8(6))* Windmill Bks.
—The Mystery of Nine: Number Place & Value in Action. Law, Felicia & Way, Steve. 2010. (Mandrill Mountain Math Mysteries Ser.). 32p. (J). (gr. 2-6). 25.60 *(978-1-60754-819-5(4))*; pap. 10.55 *(978-1-60754-824-9(0))* Windmill Bks.
—A Storm at Sea: Sorting, Mapping, & Grids in Action. Law, Felicia & Way, Steve. 2010. (Mandrill Mountain Math Mysteries Ser.). 32p. (J). (gr. 2-6). 25.60 *(978-1-60754-815-7(1))*; pap. 10.55 *(978-1-60754-820-1(8))* Windmill Bks.
Spory, Sheila K. Grandma's Adventures with God's Creatures. Heiser, Connie. I.t. ed. 2017. (Grandma's Adventures Ser.: Vol. 2). (ENG.). (J). (gr. k-5). pap. 9.95 *(978-1-61633-888-6(1))* Guardian Angel Publishing, Inc.
—Stories from Grandma's Heart. Heiser, Connie. I.t. ed. 2017. (ENG.). 60p. (J). pap. 9.95 *(978-1-61633-905-0(5))* Guardian Angel Publishing, Inc.
Spotts, Ana. The Voices of Nature: Stories for Young Readers. Walker, Cindy. 2010. (ENG.). 144p. (J). pap. 9.95 *(978-1-7944-5065-3(3))* Independently Published.
Spradlin, Leslie. H Is for Heaven: The Bible Alphabet Book. Gilbert, Drexel. 2011. 36p. (J). pap. *(978-0-9818464-3-9(2))* Gilbert, Drexel Enterprises, Inc.
—Merry Christmas Sandy. Thomas, J.D. 2018. (ENG.). 40p. (J). pap. 24.99 *(978-1-5456-5059-2(4))* Salem Author Services.
Sprague, Dean. The Adventure of Pushy Octopus & His Friends. Trimble, Marcia. 2005. 18p. (J). (gr. k-2). 4.95 *(978-1-891577-61-1(1)*, SAN2994844) Images Pr.
Sprague, Jonathan, photos by. Paper Craft Kit Kit: Materials & Instructions for Beautiful Handmade Paper Creations. Murray-Clark, Sidd. 2006. (ENG., 80p. (gr. 8-17). 24.95 *(978-0-8118-4828-2(0))* Chronicle Bks. LLC.
Sprague, Lois. The Sandal Artist, 1 vol. Pelley, Kathleen T. 2012. (ENG.). 32p. (J). (gr. k-3). 16.99 *(978-1-58980-910-9(6)*, Pelican Publishing) Arcadia Publishing.
Sprague, Lois Rosio. The Goodnight Thing. Hurst, Rich. 2006. 25p. (J). (gr. 4-7). 10.99 *(978-0-9763770-1-6(2))* Red Door Pr.
Sprague, Terrell Eastman. The Nutcracker. Groover, David L. & Tchaikovsky, Peter Ilich. 2018. (J). *(978-1-942945-63-5(9))* Night Heron Media.
Spreen, Kathe. Ann Paints & Plays. Kalar, Bonnie. Date not set. 12p. (J). (gr. -1-2). pap. *(978-1-891619-40-3(3))* Corona Pr.
—At Dawn. Kalar, Bonnie. Date not set. 8p. (J). (gr. -1-2). pap. *(978-1-891619-24-3(1))* Corona Pr.
—At the Lake. Kalar, Bonnie. Date not set. 12p. (J). (gr. -1-2). pap. *(978-1-891619-34-2(9))* Corona Pr.
—At the Pond. Kalar, Bonnie. Date not set. 8p. (J). (gr. -1-2). pap. *(978-1-891619-07-6(1))* Corona Pr.
—At the Zoo. Kalar, Bonnie. Date not set. 8p. (J). (gr. -1-2). pap. *(978-1-891619-18-2(7))* Corona Pr.
—Beth & Thad. Kalar, Bonnie. Date not set. 12p. (J). (gr. -1-2). pap. *(978-1-891619-17-5(9))* Corona Pr.
—The Bird & the Shirt. Kalar, Bonnie. Date not set. 12p. (J). (gr. -1-2). pap. *(978-1-891619-30-4(6))* Corona Pr.
—Burt. Kalar, Bonnie. Date not set. 8p. (J). (gr. -1-2). pap. *(978-1-891619-31-1(4))* Corona Pr.
—Chuck & the Chick. Kalar, Bonnie. Date not set. 8p. (J). (gr. -1-2). pap. *(978-1-891619-16-8(0))* Corona Pr.
—Clair at Home. Kalar, Bonnie. Date not set. 12p. (J). (gr. -1-2). pap. *(978-1-891619-44-1(6))* Corona Pr.
—The Clown. Kalar, Bonnie. Date not set. 12p. (J). (gr. -1-2). pap. *(978-1-891619-22-9(5))* Corona Pr.
—The Cook & the Crook. Kalar, Bonnie. Date not set. 12p. (J). (gr. -1-2). pap. *(978-1-891619-29-8(2))* Corona Pr.
—The Crows. Kalar, Bonnie. Date not set. 8p. (J). (gr. -1-2). pap. *(978-1-891619-28-1(4))* Corona Pr.
—A Dream. Kalar, Bonnie. Date not set. 12p. (J). (gr. -1-2). pap. *(978-1-891619-23-6(3))* Corona Pr.
—Fran & the Doll. Kalar, Bonnie. Date not set. 8p. (J). (gr. -1-2). pap. *(978-1-891619-09-0(8))* Corona Pr.
—Fred. Kalar, Bonnie. Date not set. 8p. (J). (gr. -1-2). pap. *(978-1-891619-10-6(1))* Corona Pr.
—Gail Sails. Kalar, Bonnie. Date not set. 12p. (J). (gr. -1-2). pap. *(978-1-891619-20-5(9))* Corona Pr.
—Gay & Jay Play. Kalar, Bonnie. Date not set. 8p. (J). (gr. -1-2). pap. *(978-1-891619-19-9(5))* Corona Pr.
—A Good Day. Kalar, Bonnie. Date not set. 12p. (J). (gr. -1-2). pap. *(978-1-891619-41-0(1))* Corona Pr.
—Jack. Kalar, Bonnie. Date not set. 12p. (J). (gr. -1-2). pap. *(978-1-891619-13-7(6))* Corona Pr.
—Joan's Coat. Kalar, Bonnie. Date not set. 12p. (J). (gr. -1-2). pap. *(978-1-891619-21-2(7))* Corona Pr.
—Josh & the Fish. Kalar, Bonnie. Date not set. 8p. (J). (gr. -1-2). pap. *(978-1-891619-14-4(4))* Corona Pr.
—Kirk & the Deer. Kalar, Bonnie. Date not set. 12p. (J). (gr. -1-2). pap. *(978-1-891619-43-4(8))* Corona Pr.
—Lew & His New Cap. Kalar, Bonnie. Date not set. 8p. (J). (gr. -1-2). pap. *(978-1-891619-27-4(6))* Corona Pr.
—Mark at the Farm. Kalar, Bonnie. Date not set. 12p. (J). (gr. -1-2). pap. *(978-1-891619-25-0(X))* Corona Pr.
—Mike. Kalar, Bonnie. Date not set. 8p. (J). (gr. -1-2). pap. *(978-1-891619-35-9(7))* Corona Pr.
—Miss Lane's Class. Kalar, Bonnie. Date not set. 12p. (J). (gr. -1-2). pap. *(978-1-891619-38-0(1))* Corona Pr.
—Neal Camps Out. Kalar, Bonnie. Date not set. 12p. (J). (gr. -1-2). pap. *(978-1-891619-39-7(X))* Corona Pr.
—Rose & the Mole. Kalar, Bonnie. Date not set. 12p. (J). (gr. -1-2). pap. *(978-1-891619-36-6(5))* Corona Pr.
—The Scouts. Kalar, Bonnie. Date not set. 8p. (J). (gr. -1-2). pap. *(978-1-891619-26-7(8))* Corona Pr.
—The Sheep & the Bee. Kalar, Bonnie. Date not set. 8p. (J). (gr. -1-2). pap. *(978-1-891619-15-1(2))* Corona Pr.
—Stan & His Sled. Kalar, Bonnie. Date not set. 8p. (J). (gr. -1-2). pap. *(978-1-891619-08-3(X))* Corona Pr.
—The Trip. Kalar, Bonnie. Date not set. 8p. (J). (gr. -1-2). pap. *(978-1-891619-11-3(X))* Corona Pr.
—A Trip to the Beach. Kalar, Bonnie. Date not set. 12p. (J). (gr. -1-2). pap. *(978-1-891619-42-7(X))* Corona Pr.
Spremulli, Pam. Woof! Markey, Neil. 2011. (ENG.). 34p. (J). (gr. k-k). 14.00 *(978-1-935557-77-7(7))* Purple Bear Bks., Inc.
Springer, Cherish. Appropriate Behavior Counts: A Guide for Young Athletes. Uhrich, Jeremy. 2018. (ENG.). 60p. (J). pap. 15.00 *(978-0-692-18457-8(0))* Children's Bk. Publishing.
Springer, Mary Jane. The Story of Baby 'I' Baby L. Springer, Mary Jane. 2019. (ENG.). 34p. (J). pap. 18.99 ***(978-0-578-22443-5(7))*** Springer, Mary Jane.
Springer, Sally. I'll Take My Chances, 1 vol. Burrows, Mark. 2015. (ENG.). 32p. (J). (gr. -1-3). 16.99 *(978-1-4556-2106-4(4)*, Pelican Publishing) Arcadia Publishing.
—Monster Parade. Stamper, Judith Bauer & Keyes, Joan Ross. 2004. (Oxford Picture Dictionary for Kids Ser.). (ENG.). 16p. 7.00 *(978-0-19-430929-5(0))* Oxford Univ. Pr., Inc.
—Patty & the Pink Princesses. Slater, Teddy. 2007. (J). pap. *(978-0-439-89707-5(6))* Scholastic, Inc.
—Rainbow Candles: A Hanukkah Counting Book, Vol. Shostak, Myra. 2003. (ENG.). 12p. (J). (gr. -1-18). 4.95 *(978-1-58013-031-8(3)*, Kar-Ben Publishing) Lerner Publishing Group.
—The Shapes of My Jewish Year, Vol. Gold-Vukson, Marji. 2003. (Very First Board Bks.). (ENG.). 12p. (J). (gr. -1 — 1). bds. 4.95 *(978-1-58013-049-3(6)*, Kar-Ben Publishing) Lerner Publishing Group.
Springett, Isobel, photos by. Kate & Pippin: An Unlikely Love Story. Springett, Martin. 2012. (My Readers Ser.). (ENG.). 32p. (J). (gr. -1-3). 16.99 *(978-0-8050-9487-9(3)*, 900080048, Holt, Henry & Co. Bks. For Young Readers) Holt, Henry & Co.
Springett, Martin. Come Like Shadows. Katz, Welwyn W. 2005. 318p. (gr. 7-12). 7.95 *(978-1-55050-170-4(4))* Coteau Bks. CAN. Dist: Fitzhenry & Whiteside, Ltd.
—The Follower, 1 vol. Thompson, Springett & Thompson, Richard. 2003. (ENG.). 32p. (J). (gr. 1-3). pap. 7.95 *(978-1-55041-880-4(7)*, 031379c5-8520-4061-9498-7e486914a220) Fitzhenry & Whiteside, Ltd. CAN. Dist: Firefly Bks., Ltd.
Sprouls, Bridget. Gnome at the Laundromat. Sprouls, Bridget. 2018. (ENG.). 32p. (J). (gr. k-2). pap. 12.95 *(978-0-692-09142-5(4))* Sprouls, Bridget.
—Shore Buddies: A Guide to Making Friends at the Beach. Sprouls, Bridget. 2018. (ENG.). 36p. (J). (gr. k-1). pap. 12.95 *(978-0-692-11034-8(8))* Sprouls, Bridget.
Sprouse, Chris, et al. Amazing Spider-Man: Full Circle. 2020. (ENG.). 128p. (YA). (gr. 4-17). 29.99 *(978-1-302-92138-5(X))* Marvel Worldwide, Inc.
Sprouse, Chris. Infinity Countdown Companion. 2018. (Infinity Countdown Companion (2018) Ser.: 1). (ENG.). 112p. (YA). (gr. 8-17). pap. 17.99 *(978-1-302-91309-0(3))* Marvel Worldwide, Inc.
Sprouse, Chris, et al. Marvel Universe: Time & Again. 2019. (Marvel Universe: Time & Again Ser.: 1). (ENG.). 232p. (YA). (gr. 8-17). pap. 24.99 *(978-1-302-91597-1(5))* Marvel Worldwide, Inc.
—A Nation under Our Feet: Part 5. Coates, Ta-Nehisi. 2019. (Black Panther Ser.). (ENG.). 24p. (J). (gr. 6-12). lib. bdg. 27.07 *(978-1-5321-4355-7(9)*, 31875, Marvel Age) Spotlight.
—A Nation under Our Feet: Part 6. Coates, Ta-Nehisi. 2019. (Black Panther Ser.). (ENG.). 24p. (J). (gr. 6-12). lib. bdg. 27.07 *(978-1-5321-4356-4(7)*, 31876, Marvel Age) Spotlight.
Sprouse, Chris. Star Wars: Age of the Rebellion - Heroes. 2019. 112p. (YA). (gr. 4-17). pap. 17.99 *(978-1-302-91708-1(0))* Marvel Worldwide, Inc.
—Star Wars: Age of the Rebellion - Villains. 2019. (ENG.). 128p. (YA). (gr. 4-17). pap. 17.99 *(978-1-302-91728-9(5))* Marvel Worldwide, Inc.
Sprouse, Chris & Kirk, Leonard. Black Panther Book 5: Avengers of the New World Part 2. 2018. 136p. (J). (gr. 4-17). pap. 19.99 *(978-1-302-90988-8(6))* Marvel Worldwide, Inc.
Sprouse, Chris, jt. illus. see Stelfreeze, Brian.
Sprout. But It's the Truth! Sprout. Eeebs, Aunt Eeebs. 2017. (ENG.). (J). pap. 9.95 *(978-1-946027-60-3(X))* RiverCrest Publishing.
Sprunger, Reed. Eleanor Roosevelt: First Lady & Civil Rights Activist, 1 vol. Stille, Darlene R. 2013. (Beginner Biographies Ser.). (ENG.). 32p. (J). (gr. k-4). 28.50 *(978-1-61641-941-7(5)*, 3471, Looking Glass Library) Magic Wagon.
Spudvilas, Anne. The Silver Donkey. Hartnett, Sonya. 2004. viii, 193p. (J). *(978-0-670-04240-1(4)*, Viking Adult) Penguin Publishing Group.
Spuras, Priscilla Vilela. El Lazo Convertido en Abrazo. George, Maria Vilela. Mendes, David, ed. 2020. (SPA.). 38p. (J). pap. 9.99 ***(978-1-7064-6617-8(X))*** Independently Published.
—Il Nastro Che Divenne un Abbraccio. George, Maria Vilela. Mendes, David, ed. 2020. (ITA.). 38p. (J). pap. 9.99 ***(978-1-7041-2880-1(3))*** Independently Published.
Spurgeon, Aaron. Dinosaurs Live On! And Other Fun Facts. DiSiena, Laura Lyn & Eliot, Hannah. 2015. (Did You Know? Ser.). (ENG.). 32p. (J). (gr. -1-3). pap. 6.99 *(978-1-4814-2424-0(6)*, Little Simon) Little Simon.
—Monsters Are Real! And Other Fun Facts. Eliot, Hannah. 2016. (Did You Know? Ser.). (ENG.). 32p. (J). (gr. -1-3). pap. 6.99 *(978-1-4814-6781-0(6)*, Little Simon) Little Simon.
—Turkeys Strike Out. Eliot, Hannah. 2016. (Did You Know? Ser.). (ENG.). 32p. (J). (gr. -1-3). 17.99 *(978-1-4814-5169-7(3))*; pap. 6.99 *(978-1-4814-5168-0(5))* Little Simon. (Little Simon).
Spurgeon, Aaron, jt. illus. see Oswald, Pete.
Spurll, Barbara. Ashley's Elephant: The Pond Hockey Challenge. Zaretsky, Evan. 2005. (ENG.). 32p. (gr. k-2). pap. 9.06 *(978-1-57874-095-6(9)*, Kaeden Bks.) Kaeden Corp.
—The Easter Bunny Is Missing! Metzger, Steve. 2007. (J). pap. *(978-0-439-92959-2(8))* Scholastic, Inc.
—Emma at the Fair, 1 vol. Ruurs, Margriet. 2007. (ENG.). 32p. (J). (gr. -1-2). per. 9.95 *(978-1-55005-127-8(X)*, 47fc39e6-4af4-4e71-8244-e05ba2709198) Fitzhenry & Whiteside, Ltd. CAN. Dist: Firefly Bks., Ltd.
—Emma's Cold Day, 1 vol. Ruurs, Margriet. 2003. (ENG.). 24p. (J). (gr. -1-2). pap. 10.95 *(978-1-55005-076-9(1)*, e91ee9ea-f72a-457a-876e-71ae429e3016) Trifolium Bks., Inc. CAN. Dist: Firefly Bks., Ltd.
—Rhinos for Lunch & Elephants for Supper!, 1 vol. Mollel, Tololwa M. 2012. (ENG.). 32p. (J). pap. 9.95 *(978-1-55455-197-2(8)*, 216d483d-c0d2-4570-b571-6156517b12da) Fitzhenry & Whiteside, Ltd. CAN. Dist: Firefly Bks., Ltd.
—Theodora Bear, 1 vol. Jones, Carolyn. 2007. (Orca Echoes Ser.). (ENG.). 64p. (J). (gr. 1-3). per. 4.99 *(978-1-55143-496-4(2))* Orca Bk. Pubs. USA.
Spurrell, Hailey. The Turdsons: Tp's Revenge. Spurrell, Chris. 2017. (ENG.). 152p. (J). pap. *(978-0-9959338-0-4(4))* Spurrell, Christopher.
Spusta, Marq. All the Way to the Ocean. Harper, Joel. 2006. (J). 14.95 *(978-0-9714254-1-5(8))* Freedom Three Publishing.
Squier, Robert. Aphrodite: Goddess of Love & Beauty. Temple, Teri. 2012. (Greek Mythology Ser.). (ENG.). 32p. (J). (gr. 2-5). 29.93 *(978-1-61473-253-2(1)*, 204926) Child's World, Inc., The.
—Aphrodite: Goddess of Love & Beauty. Temple, Teri. 2019. (Greek Gods & Goddesses Ser.). (ENG.). 32p. (J). (gr. 3-6). lib. bdg. 29.93 *(978-1-5038-3251-0(1)*, 213019) Child's World, Inc., The.
—Apollo: God of the Sun, Healing, Music, & Poetry. Temple, Teri. 2019. (Greek Gods & Goddesses Ser.). (ENG.). 32p. (J). (gr. 3-6). lib. bdg. 29.93 *(978-1-5038-3252-7(X)*, 213020) Child's World, Inc., The.
—Ares: God of War. Temple, Teri. 2012. (Greek Mythology Ser.). (ENG.). 32p. (J). (gr. 2-5). 29.93 *(978-1-61473-255-6(8)*, 204928) Child's World, Inc., The.
—Ares: God of War. Temple, Teri. 2019. (Greek Gods & Goddesses Ser.). (ENG.). 32p. (J). (gr. 3-6). lib. bdg. 29.93 *(978-1-5038-3253-4(8)*, 213021) Child's World, Inc., The.
—Artemis: Goddess of Hunting & Protector of Animals. Temple, Teri. 2019. (Greek Gods & Goddesses Ser.). (ENG.). 32p. (J). (gr. 3-6). lib. bdg. 29.93 *(978-1-5038-3254-1(6)*, 213022) Child's World, Inc., The.
—Athena: Goddess of Wisdom, War, & Crafts. Temple, Teri. 2012. (Greek Mythology Ser.). (ENG.). 32p. (J). (gr. 2-5). 29.93 *(978-1-61473-257-0(4)*, 204930) Child's World, Inc., The.
—Athena: Goddess of Wisdom, War, & Crafts. Temple, Teri. 2019. (Greek Gods & Goddesses Ser.). (ENG.). 32p. (J). (gr. 3-6). lib. bdg. 29.93 *(978-1-5038-3255-8(4)*, 213023) Child's World, Inc., The.
—Eros: God of Love. Temple, Teri. 2012. (Greek Mythology Ser.). (ENG.). 32p. (J). (gr. 2-5). 29.93 *(978-1-61473-258-7(2)*, 204931) Child's World, Inc., The.
—Eros: God of Love. Temple, Teri. 2019. (Greek Gods & Goddesses Ser.). (ENG.). 32p. (J). (gr. 3-6). lib. bdg. 29.93 *(978-1-5038-3256-5(2)*, 213024) Child's World, Inc., The.
—Follow the Drinking Gourd: An Underground Railroad Story, 1 vol. 2012. (Night Sky Stories Ser.). (ENG.). 24p. (J). (gr. 2-4). pap. 8.95 *(978-1-4048-7714-6(2)*, Picture Window Bks.) Capstone.
—Follow the Drinking Gourd: An Underground Railroad Story, 1 vol. Capstone Press Staff. 2012. (Night Sky Stories Ser.). (ENG.). 24p. (J). (gr. 2-4). lib. bdg. 27.32 *(978-1-4048-7375-9(9)*, Picture Window Bks.) Capstone.
—Hades: God of the Underworld. Temple, Teri. 2019. (Greek Gods & Goddesses Ser.). (ENG.). 32p. (J). (gr. 3-6). lib. bdg. 29.93 *(978-1-5038-3258-9(9)*, 213025) Child's World, Inc., The.
—Hephaestus: God of Fire, Metalwork, & Building. Temple, Teri. 2019. (Greek Gods & Goddesses Ser.). (ENG.). 32p. (J). (gr. 3-6). lib. bdg. 29.93 *(978-1-5038-3257-2(0)*, 213026) Child's World, Inc., The.
—Hera: Queen of the Gods, Goddess of Marriage. Temple, Teri. 2019. (Greek Gods & Goddesses Ser.). (ENG.). 32p. (J). (gr. 3-6). lib. bdg. 29.93 *(978-1-5038-3259-6(7)*, 213027) Child's World, Inc., The.
—Hermes: God of Travels & Trade. Temple, Teri. 2019. (Greek Gods & Goddesses Ser.). (ENG.). 32p. (J). (gr. 3-6). lib. bdg. 29.93 *(978-1-5038-3260-2(0)*, 213028) Child's World, Inc., The.
—The Lost Sheep. Berendes, Mary. 2011. (Parables Ser.). (ENG.). 24p. (J). (gr. k-3). lib. bdg. 14.21 *(978-1-60954-392-1(0)*, 201187) Child's World, Inc., The.
—Poseidon: God of the Sea & Earthquakes. Temple, Teri. 2019. (Greek Gods & Goddesses Ser.). (ENG.). 32p. (J). (gr. 3-6). lib. bdg. 29.93 *(978-1-5038-3261-9(9)*, 213029) Child's World, Inc., The.

S

—The Prodigal Son. Berendes, Mary. 2011. (Parables Ser.). (ENG.). 24p. (J). (gr. k-3). lib. bdg. 14.21 *(978-1-60954-393-8(9),* 201188) Child's World, Inc., The.
—The Sower & the Seeds. Berendes, Mary. 2011. (Parables Ser.). (ENG.). 24p. (J). (gr. k-3). lib. bdg. 14.21 *(978-1-60954-394-5(7),* 201189) Child's World, Inc., The.
—The Story of Cassiopeia: A Roman Constellation Myth, 1 vol. 2012. (Night Sky Stories Ser.). (ENG.). 24p. (J). (gr. 2-4). pap. 8.95 *(978-1-4048-7716-0(9),* Picture Window Bks.) Capstone.
—The Story of Cassiopeia: A Roman Constellation Myth, 1 vol. Capstone Press Staff. 2012. (Night Sky Stories Ser.). (ENG.). 24p. (J). (gr. 2-4). lib. bdg. 27.32 *(978-1-4048-7376-6(7),* Picture Window Bks.) Capstone.
—The Ten Bridesmaids. Berendes, Mary. 2011. (Parables Ser.). (ENG.). 24p. (J). (gr. k-3). lib. bdg. 14.21 *(978-1-60954-395-2(5),* 201190) Child's World, Inc., The.
—The Truth about Elves, 1 vol. Troupe, Thomas Kingsley. 2010. (Fairy-Tale Superstars Ser.). (ENG.). 32p. (J). (gr. 1-3). lib. bdg. 27.99 *(978-1-4048-6047-6(9),* Picture Window Bks.) Capstone.
—The Truth about Witches, 1 vol. Braun, Eric. 2010. (Fairy-Tale Superstars Ser.). (ENG.). 32p. (J). (gr. 1-3). lib. bdg. 27.99 *(978-1-4048-6160-2(2),* Picture Window Bks.) Capstone.
—The Unmerciful Servant. Berendes, Mary. 2011. (Parables Ser.). (ENG.). 24p. (J). (gr. k-3). lib. bdg. 14.21 *(978-1-60954-396-9(3),* 201191) Child's World, Inc., The.
Squier, Robert. What Is a Presidential Election? With Activities, Stickers, & a Poster! Yacka, Douglas & Who HQ. 2020. (What Was? Ser.). (ENG.). 112p. (J). (gr. 3-7). 7.99 ***(978-0-593-09561-4(8),*** Penguin Workshop) Penguin Young Readers Group.
Squier, Robert. What Is the Story of the Wizard of Oz? Anderson, Kirsten & Who HQ. 2019. (What Is the Story Of? Ser.). 112p. (J). (gr. 3-7). 6.99 *(978-1-5247-8830-8(9));* 15.99 *(978-1-5247-8831-5(7))* Penguin Young Readers Group. (Penguin Workshop).
—Who Is Temple Grandin? Demuth, Patricia Brennan & Who HQ. 2020. (Who Was? Ser.). 112p. (J). (gr. 3-7). 5.99 *(978-0-451-53251-0(1));* 15.99 *(978-0-451-53253-4(8))* Penguin Young Readers Group. (Penguin Workshop).
—The Who Was? History of the World. Manzanero, Paula K. & Who HQ. 2019. (Who Was? Ser.). (ENG.). 176p. (J). (gr. 3-7). 9.99 *(978-1-5247-8800-1(7),* Penguin Workshop) Penguin Young Readers Group.
—Who Was Davy Crockett? Herman, Gail & Who HQ. 2013. (Who Was? Ser.). (ENG.). 112p. (J). (gr. 3-7). 5.99 *(978-0-448-46704-7(6),* Penguin Workshop) Penguin Young Readers Group.
—Who Was Frederick Douglass? Prince, April Jones & Who HQ. 2014. (Who Was? Ser.). (ENG.). 112p. (J). (gr. 3-7). 5.99 *(978-0-448-47911-8(7),* Penguin Workshop) Penguin Young Readers Group.
—Who Was Louis Braille? Frith, Margaret & Who HQ. 2014. (Who Was? Ser.). (ENG.). 112p. (J). (gr. 3-7). 5.99 *(978-0-448-47903-3(6),* Penguin Workshop) Penguin Young Readers Group.
—Who Was Louis Braille? Frith, Margaret. 2014. (Who Was... ? Ser.). (ENG.). (J). (gr. 3-7). lib. bdg. 16.60 *(978-1-62765-915-4(3))* Perfection Learning Corp.
—Zeus: King of the Gods, God of Sky & Storms. Temple, Teri. 2019. (Greek Gods & Goddesses Ser.). (ENG.). 32p. (J). (gr. 3-6). lib. bdg. 29.93 *(978-1-5038-3262-6(7),* 213030) Child's World, Inc., The.
Squier, Robert, jt. illus. see Johnson, Pamela.
Squillace, Elisa. Down in the Jungle. (Classic Books with Holes 8x8 with CD Ser.). (J). 2013. (ENG.). 16p. (gr. -1). pap. incl. audio compact disk *(978-1-84643-623-9(0));* 2006. 16p. (gr. -1-3). spiral bd. *(978-1-84643-009-1(7));* 2005. 14p. (gr. -1-1). spiral bd. *(978-1-904550-61-7(4));* 2005. 16p. pap. *(978-1-904550-32-7(0))* Child's Play International Ltd.
—Three Wishes. 2009. (First Reading Level 1 Ser.). 32p. (J). (gr. 2). 6.99 *(978-0-7945-2278-0(5),* Usborne) EDC Publishing.
Squire, M H & Mars, E. Heroes of Greek Mythology. Kingsley, Charles. 2006. (Dover Children's Classics Ser.). (ENG.). 240p. (YA). (gr. 3-12). per. 9.95 *(978-0-486-44854-1(1))* Dover Pubns., Inc.
Squire, Mariah. What Could It Be? Peterson, Melanie. 2019. (ENG.). 26p. (J). pap. 11.99 ***(978-1-6953-8424-8(5))*** Independently Published.
Squire, Maud Hunt. Hindu Stories. Williston, Teresa Peirce. 2011. 110p. 39.95 *(978-1-258-02581-6(7))* Literary Licensing, LLC.
—Hindu Tales. Williston, Teresa Peirce. 2011. 86p. 37.95 *(978-1-258-02582-3(5))* Literary Licensing, LLC.
Sreckovic, Sandra. Where Did Thaddeus Go? A Small, Lost Dog's Adventure Through the Big Wonderful World of Los Angeles. Barrielle, Barbara. 2018. (Thaddeus Ser.: Vol. 101). (ENG.). 28p. (J). pap. 12.95 *(978-1-7291-8466-0(9))* Independently Published.
Sreenivasan, Archana. Desert Girl, Monsoon Boy. Dairman, Tara. 2020. (ENG.). 32p. (J). (gr. -1-3). 17.99 *(978-0-525-51806-8(1),* G.P. Putnam's Sons Books for Young Readers) Penguin Young Readers Group.
—Diwali. Eliot, Hannah. 2018. (Celebrate the World Ser.). (ENG.). 24p. (J). (gr. -1 — 1). bds. 8.99 *(978-1-5344-1990-2(X),* Little Simon) Little Simon.
—Old Mummy Card Game. Samoun, Abigail. 2019. (ENG.). 51p. (J). (gr. -1-5). 12.99 *(978-1-4521-7486-0(5))* Chronicle Bks. LLC.
—Rapunzel. Perkins, Chloe. 2017. (Once upon a World Ser.). (ENG.). 24p. (J). (gr. -1 — 1). bds. 8.99 *(978-1-4814-9072-6(9),* Little Simon) Little Simon.
Srejber, Leah. Baby Tom Is on the Driveway. Mitchell, Jennifer Scott. 2016. (Sidewalk Children Ser.). (ENG.). (gr. -1-4). pap. *(978-0-9875050-8-8(4),* Baby Tom Series) Wild Orange Publishing.
Srejber, Leah Rose. Baby Tom Can't Run Left Hand Drive Edition. Mitchell, Jennifer Scott. 2016. (Sidewalk Children Ser.). (ENG.). (gr. -1-4). pap. *(978-0-9875050-6-4(8),* Baby Tom Series) Wild Orange Publishing.
—Baby Tom Can't Run Right Hand Drive Edition. Mitchell, Jennifer. 2016. (Sidewalk Children Ser.). (ENG.). (gr. -1-4). pap. *(978-0-9875050-7-1(6),* Baby Tom Series) Wild Orange Publishing.
Srinivasan, Divya. Cinnamon. Gaiman, Neil. 2017. (ENG.). 40p. (J). (gr. -1-3). 17.99 *(978-0-06-239961-8(6),* HarperCollins) HarperCollins Pubs. Ltd. GBR. Dist: HarperCollins Pubs.
Srinivasan, Divya. Little Owl's 1-2-3. Srinivasan, Divya. 2015. (ENG.). 18p. (J). (— 1). bds. 5.99 *(978-0-451-47454-4(6),* Viking Books for Young Readers) Penguin Young Readers Group.
—Little Owl's Colors. Srinivasan, Divya. 2015. (ENG.). 18p. (J). (— 1). bds. 5.99 *(978-0-451-47456-8(2),* Viking Books for Young Readers) Penguin Young Readers Group.
—Little Owl's Day. Srinivasan, Divya. 2014. (ENG.). 32p. (J). (gr. -1-k). 16.99 *(978-0-670-01650-1(0),* Viking Books for Young Readers) Penguin Young Readers Group.
Srivi. Hanuman's Adventures in the Nether World: A 600 Year Old Classic Retold. Mahadevan, Madhavi S. 2005. (J). *(978-81-89020-30-9(7))* Katha.
Srkalova', Anna. Grandma's Tales Coloring Book: Let Your Light Shine. Asbill, Nancy. 2019. (ENG.). 84p. (J). pap. 5.38 ***(978-1-6910-9164-5(2))*** Independently Published.
Ssebulime, John. Dragon Baked Bread, 32 vols. Cohen, Warren Lee. 2005. (ENG.). 32p. (J). *(978-1-902636-70-2(8))* Clairview Bks.
St. Angelo, Ron, photos by. Princess Bible, 1 vol. Hitzges, Norm. 2007. (Compact Kids Ser.). (ENG., 1152p. pap. 24.99 *(978-1-4003-0987-0(5))* Nelson, Thomas Inc.
St Anthony, Gus. Tutti Frutti. Marcucci, Vince. 2005. 32p. (J). (gr. -1-3). pap. 8.99 *(978-0-9769198-0-3(X))* Chick Light Publishing.
St. Aubin, Bruno. Corre, Nicolas, Corre! Tibo, Gilles. Rioja, Alberto Jimenez, tr. from FRE. 2009. (SPA & ENG.). 32p. (J). (gr. 2-4). pap. 6.99 *(978-1-933032-57-3(X))* Lectorum Pubns., Inc.
St-Aubin, Bruno. Fred & the Mysterious Letter. Croteau, Marie-Danielle. 2005. 61p. (J). lib. bdg. 12.00 *(978-1-4242-1199-9(9))* Fitzgerald Bks.
—Fred & the Mysterious Letter, 1 vol. Croteau, Marie-Danielle. Cummins, Sarah, tr. 2005. (Formac First Novels Ser.). (ENG.). 64p. (J). (gr. 2-5). 4.95 *(978-0-88780-688-9(0),* 688) Formac Publishing Co., Ltd. CAN. Dist: Formac Lorimer Bks. Ltd.
—Fred & the Pig Race, 1 vol. Croteau, Marie-Danielle. Cummins, Sarah, tr. (Formac First Novels Ser.). (ENG.). 64p. 2016. (J). (gr. 1-5). 5.95 *(978-0-88780-731-2(3),* 00bb04c7-d313-45db-9e17-da46ba2f5cb9); 2007. (gr. 2-5). 14.95 *(978-0-88780-733-6(X),* 733) Formac Publishing Co., Ltd. CAN. Dist: Lerner Publishing Group, Formac Lorimer Bks. Ltd.
St. Aubin, Bruno. La Petite Reine au Nez Rouge. Croteau, Marie-Danielle. 2004. (Premier Roman Ser.). (FRE.). 64p. (J). (gr. 1-4). pap. *(978-2-89021-706-5(X))* Diffusion du livre Mirabel (DLM).
St-Aubin, Bruno. The Several Lives of Orphan Jack, 1 vol. Ellis, Sarah. 2005. (ENG.). 88p. (J). pap. 8.95 *(978-0-88899-618-3(7))* Groundwood Bks. CAN. Dist: Publishers Group West (PGW).
St. Aubin, Claude. Captured off Guard: The Attack on Pearl Harbor, 1 vol. Lemke, Donald B. 2008. (Historical Fiction Ser.). (ENG.). 56p. (J). (gr. 3-6). pap. 6.25 *(978-1-4342-0493-6(6),* Stone Arch Bks.) Capstone.
—A Totally True Princess Story. Patton, Chris. Wellman, Mike, ed. 2009. 72p. 12.99 *(978-0-615-27602-1(4))* Atomic Basement.
St Aubin, Mallari. The Adventures of Peanut: The Fox & the Crows. Pope, Debra K. 2013. (ENG.). 26p. (J). pap. 12.95 *(978-0-9885108-0-7(4))* Networking Univ.
St Clair, Stan. The Choo-Choo Clock & the Donkey. St Clair, Stan. St Clair, Scott. 2017. (ENG.). 38p. (J). pap. 14.95 *(978-1-935786-92-4(X))* St. Clair Pubns.
St Clair, Stanley J. A Man for the Ages. Bacheller, Irving. 2012. (ENG.). 376p. (J). pap. 15.95 *(978-1-935786-43-6(1))* St. Clair Pubns.
St Denis, Stefanie. Your Inner Compass That Could. Pierce, Kristin. 2018. (ENG.). 38p. (J). (gr. k-3). ***(978-1-77370-601-6(2))*** Inner Compass Bks.
St Denis, Stephanie. Your Inner Compass That Could. Pierce, Kristin. 2018. (ENG.). 38p. (J). (gr. k-3). pap. ***(978-1-77370-600-9(4))*** Inner Compass Bks.
St. George, Carolyn. Vine & Branches. Hakowski, Maryann. 2003. (Resources for Youth Retreats Ser.: Vol. 1). 160p. (YA). (gr. 7-12). spiral bd. 24.95 *(978-0-88489-255-7(7))* Saint Mary's Press of Minnesota.
—Vine & Branches, Vol. 2. Hakowski, Maryann. Stamschror, Robert P., ed. 2003. (Resources for Youth Retreats Ser.: Vol. 2). 168p. (YA). (gr. 7-12). spiral bd. 24.95 *(978-0-88489-278-6(6))* Saint Mary's Press of Minnesota.
St. John Taylor, Jeannie, jt. illus. see Taylor, Jeannie St. John.
St Louis, Juleigh. Fly Balloon, Fly! St Louis, Juleigh. 2018. (ENG.). 24p. (J). pap. 9.99 *(978-1-7905-1497-7(5))* Independently Published.
St Louis, Julie. Good Morning, Goodnight. St Louis, Julie. 2018. (ENG.). 34p. (J). pap. 9.99 *(978-1-7918-7253-3(0))* Independently Published.
St. Pierre, Joe & Max, Iman. Graphic STEM Adventures with Max Axiom, Super Scientist. Biskup, Agnieszka Józefina et al. ed. 2020. (STEM Adventures Ser.). (ENG.). 112p. (J). (gr. 3-9). pap. 9.95 *(978-1-4966-6662-8(3),* 142372) Capstone.
Staadecker, Peter. Just One More Page: A Book about a Tame Dragon Gone Wild. Staadecker, Peter. 2017. (ENG.). 68p. (J). pap. *(978-0-9959251-4-4(3))* Staadecker, Robert Peter.
Staake, Bob. Bugs Galore. Stein, Peter. 2013. 32p. (J). (— 1). bds. 7.99 *(978-0-7636-6220-2(8))* Candlewick Pr.
—Cars Galore. Stein, Peter. (J). (gr. -1-3). 2012. 30p. bds. 7.99 *(978-0-7636-6148-9(1));* 2011. 32p. 15.99 *(978-0-7636-4743-8(8))* Candlewick Pr.
Staake, Bob, et al. Favorites: I'm a Truck/The Happy Man & His Dump Truck/I'm a Monster Truck. Shealy, Dennis & Miryam. 2011. 80p. (J). (gr. -1-2). 7.99 *(978-0-375-86549-7(7),* Golden Bks.) Random Hse. Children's Bks.
—Hot Summer Fun, Cool Summer Stars. Thomas, Stephen, ed. Date not set. 28p. (Orig.). (J). (gr. 3-7). pap. *(978-1-886749-26-9(4))* Sports Illustrated For Kids.
Staake, Bob. I Love Cats! Stainton, Sue. 2017. (ENG.). 32p. (J). (gr. -1-3). 17.99 *(978-0-06-243882-9(4),* Tegen, Katherine Bks) HarperCollins Pubs.
—I Love Dogs! Stainton, Sue. 2014. (ENG.). 32p. (J). (gr. -1-3). 14.99 *(978-0-06-117057-7(7))* HarperCollins Pubs.
—I'm a Monster Truck. Shealy, Dennis. 2016. 26p. (J). (gr. -1-k). bds. 7.99 *(978-0-553-53586-0(2),* Random Hse. Bks. for Young Readers) Random Hse. Children's Bks.
—I'm a Monster Truck. Shealy, Dennis R. 2011. (Little Golden Book Ser.). 32p. (J). (gr. -1-2). 4.99 *(978-0-375-86132-1(7),* Golden Bks.) Random Hse. Children's Bks.
Staake, Bob. I'm a Snowplow. Shealy, Dennis R. 2020. (Little Golden Book Ser.). 24p. (J). (-k). 4.99 ***(978-0-593-12559-5(2),*** Golden Bks.) Random Hse. Children's Bks.
Staake, Bob. I'm a Truck. Shealy, Dennis R. 2006. (Little Golden Book Ser.). (ENG.). 24p. (J). (gr. -1-2). 4.99 *(978-0-375-83263-5(7),* Golden Bks.) Random Hse. Children's Bks.
—Margaret Wise Brown's the Steam Roller. Brown, Margaret Wise. 2017. (Little Golden Book Ser.). 24p. (J). (-k). 4.99 *(978-0-399-55653-1(2),* Golden Bks.) Random Hse. Children's Bks.
—Margaret Wise Brown's the Steam Roller. Brown, Margaret Wise. (J). *(978-1-5379-5883-5(6))* Follett School Solutions.
—Robots, Robots Everywhere! Fliess, Sue. 2013. (Little Golden Book Ser.). 24p. (J). (-k). 4.99 *(978-0-449-81079-8(8),* Golden Bks.) Random Hse. Children's Bks.
—Sputter, Sputter, Sput! Bell, Babs. 2008. 32p. (J). (gr. -1-k). lib. bdg. 17.89 *(978-0-06-056223-6(4))* HarperCollins Pubs.
—Toys Galore. Stein, Peter. 2013. 32p. (J). (gr. -1-3). 16.99 *(978-0-7636-6254-7(2))* Candlewick Pr.
—Trucks Galore. Stein, Peter. 2017. 32p. (J). (gr. -1-3). 15.99 *(978-0-7636-8978-0(5))* Candlewick Pr.
—We Planted a Tree. Muldrow, Diane. 2016. 40p. (J). (gr. -1-2). 7.99 *(978-0-553-53903-5(5),* Dragonfly Bks.) Random Hse. Children's Bks.
Staake, Bob. Bluebird. Staake, Bob. 2013. 40p. (J). (gr. -1-3). 17.99 *(978-0-375-87037-8(7),* Schwartz & Wade Bks.) Random Hse. Children's Bks.
—The Book of Gold. Staake, Bob. 2017. 40p. (J). (gr. -1-3). 17.99 *(978-0-553-51077-5(0),* Schwartz & Wade Bks.) Random Hse. Children's Bks.
—The Donut Chef. Staake, Bob. 2013. 40p. (J). (gr. -1-2). 7.99 *(978-0-385-36992-3(1),* Dragonfly Bks.) Random Hse. Children's Bks.
—The Red Lemon. Staake, Bob. 2012. 32p. (J). (gr. -1-3). pap. 7.99 *(978-0-307-97846-2(X),* Dragonfly Bks.) Random Hse. Children's Bks.
—This Is Not a Pumpkin. Staake, Bob. 2007. (ENG.). 32p. (J). (gr. -1 — 1). bds. 7.99 *(978-1-4169-3353-3(0),* Little Simon) Little Simon.
Stabile, Nicolette. Why Am I Brown? A Child's View of Multi-cultural Adoption, 1 vol. Meissner, Jacqueline. 2009. 22p. pap. 24.95 *(978-1-60836-234-9(5))* America Star Bks.
Stacey, Alan. Round Up: A Texas Number Book. Crane, Carol. 2003. (America by the Numbers Ser.). (ENG.). 40p. (J). (gr. k-6). 16.95 *(978-1-58536-133-5(X))* Sleeping Bear Pr.
Stacey, Mark. Wizards: From Merlin to Faust. McIntee, David & McIntee, Lesley. 2014. (Myths & Legends Ser.: 9). 80p. pap. *(978-1-4728-0339-9(6),* 303249, Osprey Publishing) Bloomsbury Publishing Plc.
Stacey, Tim. Camden & the Eyecants. Calandro, Joseph. 2020. (ENG.). 28p. (J). pap. 11.99 ***(978-1-6777-8012-9(6))*** Independently Published.
Stacey, W. The Martyr's Victory: A Story of Danish England. Leslie, Emma. 2007. 300p. 24.95 *(978-1-934671-08-5(8));* per. 14.95 *(978-1-934671-09-2(6))* Salem Ridge Press LLC.
Stacey, W. S., jt. illus. see Hymper, W.
Stachnick, Lisa. Zauberpfote Bei Den Piraten. Sapotnik, Juli. 2018. (Zauberpfotes Abenteuer Ser.: Vol. 2). (GER.). 80p. (J). pap. 6.99 *(978-1-7181-6251-8(0))* Independently Published.
Stacy, Alan. Alaskan Night Before Christmas, 1 vol. Brown, Tricia. 2008. (Night Before Christmas Ser.). (ENG.). 32p. (J). (gr. 1-3). 16.99 *(978-1-58980-554-5(2),* Pelican Publishing) Arcadia Publishing.
—Discover Texas, 2 bks. Crane, Carol. 2003. (ENG.). 40p. (J). 27.95 *(978-1-58536-227-1(1))* Sleeping Bear Pr.
—G Is for Galaxy: An Out of This World Alphabet. Collison, Cathy & Campbell, Janis. (World/Country Alphabet Ser.). (ENG.). 40p. (J). (gr. k-5). 2005. 16.95 *(978-1-58536-255-4(7));* 2006. pap. 7.95 *(978-1-58536-335-3(9))* Sleeping Bear Pr.
—Pennsylvania Dutch Alphabet, 1 vol. Williamson, Chet. 2007. (ABC Ser.). (ENG.). 32p. (J). (gr. k-3). 16.99 *(978-1-58980-496-8(1),* Pelican Publishing) Arcadia Publishing.
—Texas Zeke & the Longhorn, 1 vol. Davis, David. 2018. (ENG.). 36p. (gr. -1-3). 10.95 *(978-1-4556-2421-8(7),* Pelican Publishing) Arcadia Publishing.
Stacy, Alan & Braught, Mark. T Is for Touchdown: A Football Alphabet. Herzog, Brad. 2004. (Sports Ser.). (ENG.). 40p. (J). (gr. -1-5). 16.95 *(978-1-58536-233-2(6))* Sleeping Bear Pr.
Stacy, Alan F. Ross the Reader & the Great Balloon Race. Dailey, Reid. 2011. 46p. pap. 13.95 *(978-1-4575-0154-8(6))* Dog Ear Publishing, LLC.
Stacy, Dorothy. Erie Canal Cousins. Stacy, Dorothy. 2007. 110p. (J). per. 9.95 *(978-0-9792947-0-9(3))* Blackberry Hill Pr.
—Three Weeks in Utica. Stacy, Dorothy. 2008. 120p. (J). pap. 9.95 *(978-0-9792947-1-6(1))* Blackberry Hill Pr.
Stadelmann, Amy Marie. The Super-Smelly Moldy Blob. Stadelmann, Amy Marie. 2016. (Olive & Beatrix Ser.: 2). (ENG.). 80p. (J). (gr. k-2). 15.99 *(978-0-545-81485-0(5))* Scholastic, Inc.
Stader, Kristina & Stroede, Paul. Frog on my Head. Stadler, Kristina. 2011. 24p. (J). lib. bdg. 11.95 *(978-1-59598-138-7(1),* Goblin Fern Pr.) HenschelHAUS Publishing, Inc.
Stadler, John. Catilda. Stadler, John. 2010. (ENG.). 32p. (J). (gr. -1-k). 16.99 *(978-1-4424-2939-0(9),* Atheneum Bks. for Young Readers) Simon & Schuster Children's Publishing.
—Los Gatos de la Señora Calamari: The Cats of Mrs. Calamari. Stadler, John. 2019. (ENG & SPA.). 32p. (J). pap. 6.99 *(978-1-59572-832-6(5))* Star Bright Bks., Inc.
Stadther, Michael. Secrets of the Alchemist Dar. Stadther, Michael. 2006. (Treasure's Trove Ser.). (ENG.). 144p. (J). 21.99 *(978-1-4169-2653-5(4));* 39.99 *(978-1-4169-2661-0(5))* Treasure Trove, Inc.
—101 New Puzzles Clues, Maps, Tantalizing Tales: And Stories of Real Treasure. Stadther, Michael. 2006. (Treasure's Trove Ser.). (ENG.). 112p. (J). pap. 12.99 *(978-1-4169-2655-9(0))* Treasure Trove, Inc.
Stadtlander, Becca. Genevieve's War. Giff, Patricia Reilly. 2017. (ENG.). 240p. (J). (gr. 3-7). 16.95 *(978-0-8234-3800-6(7))* Holiday Hse., Inc.
—The Greatest Table. Rosen, Michael J. 2019. (ENG.). 32p. (J). (gr. 1-3). 19.99 *(978-1-56846-303-2(0),* Creative Editions) Creative Co., The.
—Look! What Do You See? An Art Puzzle Book of American & Chinese Songs. Xu, Bing. 2017. 48p. (J). (gr. 2-5). 18.99 *(978-0-451-47377-6(9),* Viking Books for Young Readers) Penguin Young Readers Group.
—Made by Hand: a Crafts Sampler. Schaefer, Carole Lexa. 2018. 48p. (J). (gr. 3-7). 17.99 *(978-0-7636-7433-5(8))* Candlewick Pr.
—On the Wing. Elliott, David. 32p. (J). (gr. -1-2). 2017. 6.99 *(978-0-7636-9302-2(2));* 2014. 16.99 *(978-0-7636-5324-8(1))* Candlewick Pr.
—On Wings of Words: The Extraordinary Life of Emily Dickinson (Emily Dickinson for Kids, Biography of Female Poet for Kids) Berne, Jennifer. 2020. (ENG.). 52p. (J). (gr. k-3). 18.99 *(978-1-4521-4297-5(1))* Chronicle Bks. LLC.
—Sleep Tight Farm: A Farm Prepares for Winter. Doyle, Eugenie. 2016. (ENG.). 36p. (J). (gr. -1-k). 16.99 *(978-1-4521-2901-3(0))* Chronicle Bks. LLC.
—Style Guide - Fashion from Head to Toe: 35 Prints to Colour. Slee, Natasha. 2015. (ENG.). 72p. (J). pap. 19.99 *(978-1-84780-734-2(8),* Wide Eyed Editions) Quarto Publishing Group UK GBR. Dist: Littlehampton Bk Services, Ltd.
—Style Guide: Fashion from Head to Toe. Slee, Natasha. 2016. (ENG.). 72p. (J). (gr. 1-4). pap. 19.99 *(978-1-84780-830-1(1),* Wide Eyed Editions) Quarto Publishing Group UK GBR. Dist: Hachette Bk. Group.
—Things That Grow. Walden, Libby. 2017. (ENG.). 76p. (J). (gr. 2-12). 12.99 *(978-1-944530-05-1(3),* 360 Degrees) Tiger Tales.
Staehle, Will. Warren the 13th & the All-Seeing Eye. del Rio, Tania. 2015. (Warren The 13th Ser.: 1). 256p. (J). (gr. 5). 16.95 *(978-1-59474-803-5(9))* Quirk Bks.
—Warren the 13th & the Thirteen-Year Curse: A Novel. del Rio, Tania. 2020. (Warren The 13th Ser.: 3). (ENG.). 224p. (J). (gr. 5). 16.99 *(978-1-68369-090-0(7))* Quirk Bks.
Stafford, Jordan. The Legend of the Sweet Potato Pie. Mitchell, Shirley Lipscomb. Tombers, Monica, ed. 2012. 40p. (-18). pap. 12.95 *(978-0-9851996-0-9(1))* HMSI, Inc.
—Poetino Piccolino Saves the Day. Gambini, Josephine. 2011. (ENG.). (J). pap. 19.95 *(978-0-9829496-3-4(4))* Giusti-Gambini, J.M. Publishing, LLC.
Stafford, Justin. Tiny World: Quilting! Stafford, Justin. Odd Dot. 2020. (Tiny World Ser.: 7). (ENG.). 32p. (J). pap. 14.99 *(978-1-250-20818-7(1),* 900203029, Odd Dot) St. Martin's Pr.
Stafford, Rosalee. Wood's New Collar. Salyers, Rita. 2006. (J). per. 11.95 *(978-0-9760129-3-1(6))* The Publishing Place LLC.
Stafford, Tiffany. Treasure in Catclaw Canyon. Stafford, Anita. 2019. (Legend of Sassafras House Ser.: Vol. 2). (ENG.). 98p. (J). pap. 8.00 *(978-1-0817-3945-4(2))* Independently Published.
Staggenborg, Kim. Stories of the Saints V1, 4 vols. Woodfield, Elaine. 2009. (J). pap. 13.95 *(978-0-9788376-8-6(1))* Catholic Heritage Curricula.
—Stories of the Saints V2, 4 vols. Woodfield, Elaine. 2009. (J). pap. 0.00 *(978-0-9788376-9-3(X))* Catholic Heritage Curricula.
Stahl, Bethany. Breathe & Squeeze. Andrus, Kendra. 2019. (ENG.). 30p. (J). pap. 11.95 *(978-0-9995444-4-0(6))* Wild Willow Pr.
Stahl, Todd. Me & IMAGI. Binder, Bettina. 2019. (ENG.). 36p. (J). pap. 24.99 ***(978-1-5456-7257-0(1))*** Salem Author Services.
Stahlberg, Carina. Lucia Morning in Sweden. Rydaker, Ewa. Lewis, Anne Gillespie, ed. 2014. (ENG.). 35p. (J). (gr. -1-3). pap. 8.99 *(978-1-935666-65-3(7))* Nodin Pr.
—A Perfect Tree for Christmas. Lewis, Anne G. 2013. (ENG.). (J). pap. 7.99 *(978-1-935666-55-4(X))* Nodin Pr.
Staige, Pat & Stanton, Janet. Farmer Carpenter's Barn & the Cow's Saturday Night Dance. Banicki, Patsy & Staige, Pat. Date not set. (Orig.). (J). (gr. k-4). pap. *(978-0-9641375-1-6(8))* Staige Productions.
Staino, Franco. The Adventures of Pinocchio, Vol. 2012. (ENG.). 312p. *(978-88-492-2206-7(8))* Gangemi.
Stalio, Ivan. The Human Body. Starry Dog Books. 2007. (Back to Basics Ser.). 31p. (J). lib. bdg. *(978-88-6098-050-2(X))* McRae Bks. Srl.

Stalio, Ivan & Fabbrucci, Fabiano. What Is It? Hillert, Margaret. 2016. (BeginningtoRead Ser.). (ENG.). 32p. (J). (gr. k-2). 22.60 (978-1-59953-807-5(5)) Norwood Hse. Pr.

Stallings, Bree. Alisa's First Adventure. Ball, Liz. 2018. (ENG.). 24p. (J). (gr. k-3). pap. 10.95 (978-0-692-18141-6(5)) Tree Farm Pr.

Stallop, Christy. There's a Yak in my Bed. Pluta, K. 2007. (ENG.). 32p. (J). (gr. -1 — 1). 16.95 (978-0-9769417-4-3(0)) Blooming Tree Pr.

Stalsjo, Eva. Goldie at the Farm, 25 vols. Sandwall-Bergstrom, Martha. (ENG.). 24p. 17.95 (978-0-86315-485-0(9)) Floris Bks. GBR. Dist: SteinerBooks, Inc.

Stålsjö, Eva. Goldie at the Orphanage, 25 vols. Sandwall-Bergström, Martha. 2004. (ENG.). 24p. (J). 16.95 (978-0-86315-443-0(3)) Floris Bks. GBR. Dist: SteinerBooks, Inc.

Sta.Maria, Ian & Blanden, Neale. Edgar Allan Poe's Tales of Mystery, Vol. 21. Caputo, Antonella et al. 2011. (ENG.). 144p. (YA). pap. 17.95 (978-0-9825630-2-1(7), a0ed2097-8015-4509-8a5d-141116b314f2) Eureka Productions.

Stamatiadi, Daniela. The Edelweiss Pirates. Elvgren, Jennifer. 2018. (ENG.). 32p. (J). (gr. 3-6). 17.99 (978-1-5124-8360-4(5), Kar-Ben Publishing) Lerner Publishing Group.

Stamato, Fátima. Family Stew for Dads: Building a Family with an Egg Donor & Surrogate. Stamm, Linda J. 2018. (J). pap. (978-1-938313-26-4(7)) Graphite Pr.

Stamaty, Mark Alan. Yellow Yellow. Asch, Frank. 2019. (ENG.). 48p. 15.95 (978-1-77046-358-5(5), 900208054) Drawn & Quarterly Pubns. CAN. Dist: Macmillan.

Stammen, Jo Ellen McAllister. Hero Cat, 0 vols. Spinelli, Eileen. 2011. (ENG.). 32p. (J). (gr. -1-3). pap. 9.99 (978-0-7614-5837-1(9), 9780761458371, Two Lions) Amazon Publishing.

Stammen, JoEllen McAllister. Wild Fox: A True Story. Mason, Cherie. 2013. (ENG.). 56p. 14.99 (978-1-60893-212-2(5)) Down East Bks.

Stammschroer, Danielle. Zoe's Princess Pants. Pontefract, Michelle. 2019. (ENG.). 36p. (J). pap. **(978-1-7753119-9-7(6))** Pandamonium Publishing Hse.

Stamper, Claire. Let's Draw Kooky Characters with Crayola ® ! Allen, Kathy. 2019. (Let's Draw with Crayola ® ! Ser.). (ENG.). 32p. (J). (gr. -1-3). pap. 6.99 (978-1-5415-4609-7(1), Lerner Pubns.) Lerner Publishing Group.

—Let's Draw Kooky Characters with Crayola®! Allen, Kathy. 2019. (Let's Draw with Crayola ® ! Ser.). (ENG.). 32p. (J). (gr. -1-3). 27.99 (978-1-5415-1104-0(2), Lerner Pubns.) Lerner Publishing Group.

Stan, Jaskiel. Dumplings are Delicious Learning & Activity Guide. Deb, Capone. 2007. 20p. (J). 9.95 (978-0-9728666-9-9(8)) As Simple As That Publishing.

—Families are Forever Learning & Activity Guide. 2007. 20p. (J). 9.95 (978-0-9728666-2-0(0)) As Simple As That Publishing.

Stanbury, Emily. Fin & the Red Deer. Cooper, V. I. X. J. 2020. (ENG.). 28p. (J). **(978-1-78132-995-5(8))** SilverWood Bks.

Stanbury, Emily. Philomena, the Cat Who Thinks She's a Dog. Wall, Jessie. 2020. (ENG.). 80p. (J). (gr. -1-1). pap. 9.99 (978-0-9931109-7-9(5)) Wacky Bee Bks. GBR. Dist: Independent Pubs. Group.

Stanciulescu, Diana. The Following: Behind the Eyes of Beniwan. Terbush, Tom. 2016. (ENG.). (J). pap. 14.95 (978-0-9838068-3-7(7)) Missing Lid Bk.Hse.

Stancliffe, Bethany. Lost on the Titanic (Out of Time Book 1) Rinker, Jessica. 2020. (Out of Time Ser.). (ENG.). 136p. (J). 12.99 **(978-1-5248-6043-1(3))**; pap. 6.99 **(978-1-5248-5825-4(0))** Andrews McMeel Publishing.

Standing, Ian. William Shakes a Beer. Mason, P. Harry. 2017. (ENG.). 54p. (YA). (gr. 8-12). pap. (978-1-911589-37-2(7), Choir Pr., The) Action Publishing Technology Ltd.

Standley, Leigh. Sweet Dreams: Bedtime Visualizations for Kids. Gates, Mariam. 2019. (ENG.). 32p. (J). 17.95 (978-1-68364-170-4(1), 900220892) Sounds True, Inc.

Stanek, Joyce Huntington. Sarah 'n' Dippity. Stanek, Gerald. 2004. (ENG.). 28p. (J). 14.95 (978-0-9747417-0-3(1)) Shiver Hill Bks.

Stanek, Mary Beth. The Fire Keepers: Mystery at Manitou Beach. Stanek, Mary Beth. Stanek, Linda, photos by. 2003. (J). pap. 20.00 (978-0-9747556-0-1(5)) Stanek, Mary Beth.

Stanek, Robert, pseud. The Kingdoms & the Elves of the Reaches. Stanek, Robert. alt. gif. ed. 2004. 176p. (YA). pap. 10.99 (978-1-57545-501-3(3), Reagent Pr. Echo) RP Media.

—The Kingdoms & the Elves of the Reaches II. Stanek, Robert. alt. gif. ed. 2004. (ENG.). 180p. (YA). pap. 10.99 (978-1-57545-502-0(1), Reagent Pr. Echo) RP Media.

—The Kingdoms & the Elves of the Reaches III. Stanek, Robert. alt. gif. ed. 2004. (ENG.). 172p. (YA). pap. 10.99 (978-1-57545-503-7(X), Reagent Pr. Echo) RP Media.

—The Kingdoms & the Elves of the Reaches IV. Stanek, Robert. alt. gif. ed. 2005. 172p. (YA). pap. 10.99 (978-1-57545-504-4(8), Reagent Pr. Echo) RP Media.

Stanghini, Simone. El Hada Del Solsticio. Amiti, Loreley. 2017. (SPA.). (J). pap. (978-0-9956761-9-0(4)) Littwitz Pr.

—Halloween Holler: Picture Book for Children 3+ Amiti, Loreley. 2017. (ENG.). (J). pap. (978-0-9956761-0-7(0)) Littwitz Pr.

—Hollenlarm an Halloween. Amiti, Loreley. 2017. (GER.). (J). pap. (978-0-9956761-3-8(5)) Littwitz Pr.

—The Solstice Fairy: Picture Book for Children 5+ Amiti, Loreley. 2016. (ENG.). (J). pap. (978-0-9956761-2-1(7)) Littwitz Pr.

Stangl, Katrin. Strong As a Bear. 2016. 40p. (J). (gr. -1-3). 16.95 (978-1-59270-198-8(1)) Enchanted Lion Bks., LLC.

Stangl, Sonja. Gwen the Rescue Hen. Crawford, Leslie. 2018. (ENG.). 40p. (J). 17.99 (978-0-9988623-2-3(0)) Stone Pier Pr.

—Sprig the Rescue Pig. Crawford, Leslie. 2018. (ENG.). 40p. (J). 17.99 (978-0-9988623-0-9(4)) Stone Pier Pr.

Staniland, C. Gytha's Message: A Tale of Saxon England. Leslie, Emma. 2007. 256p. 22.95 (978-1-934671-11-5(8)) Salem Ridge Press LLC.

Stankiewicz, Steven. Economics Through Infographics. Kenney, Karen Latchana. 2014. (Super Social Studies Infographics Ser.). (ENG.). 32p. (J). (gr. 3-5). pap. 8.99 (978-1-4677-4564-2(2)); lib. bdg. 26.65 (978-1-4677-3460-8(8), Lerner Pubns.) Lerner Publishing Group.

Stanley, Anne. Listen in Addition. 2007. (ENG.). 16p. (J). 16.99 (978-0-9796150-0-9(3)) Jandie Jams Music LLC.

Stanley, Christopher Heath & Parsons, Arielle. The Castle Rock Critter. Stanley, Phillip Orin, 2nd. l.t. ed. 2004. 16p. (J). 8.00 (978-0-9761355-0-0(7)) Floodgate Publishing.

Stanley, Diane. Bard of Avon: the Story of William Shakespeare. Stanley, Diane. Vennema, Peter. 2015. (ENG.). 48p. (J). (gr. 1-5). pap. 7.99 (978-0-06-241925-5(0)) HarperCollins Pubs.

—Goldie & the Three Bears. Stanley, Diane. 2007. (ENG.). 40p. (J). (gr. k-3). pap. 7.99 (978-0-06-113611-5(5)) HarperCollins Pubs.

—Michelangelo. Stanley, Diane. 2003. (ENG.). 48p. (J). (gr. 2-18). pap. 7.99 (978-0-06-052113-4(9)) HarperCollins Pubs.

—Raising Sweetness, 4 bks. Stanley, Diane. 2003. (J). pap. 37.95 incl. audio (978-1-59112-267-8(8)) Live Oak Media.

—The Trouble with Wishes. Stanley, Diane. 2007. 32p. (J). (gr. k-3). lib. bdg. 17.89 (978-0-06-055452-1(5)) HarperCollins Pubs.

Stanley, Evan. Sonic the Hedgehog: Tangle & Whisper. Flynn, Ian. 2020. 144p. (J). (gr. 4-7). pap. 19.99 (978-1-68405-583-8(0)) Idea & Design Works, LLC.

Stanley, Evan & Herms, Matt. Fallout Part 4. Flynn, Ian. 2019. (Sonic the Hedgehog Ser.). (ENG.). 24p. (J). (gr. 2-8). lib. bdg. 27.07 (978-1-5321-4436-3(9), 33841, Graphic Novels) Spotlight.

Stanley, Evan, jt. illus. see Yardley, Tracy.

Stanley, Gemma. Emily Gray & the Resurrection Men. Kent, R. W. 2018. (ENG.). 296p. (J). (gr. 4-6). pap. (978-1-9164451-0-9(1)) Kent, R. W.

Stanley, Heather. Mademoiselle Grands Doigts: A Cajun New Year's Eve Tale, 1 vol. Downing, Johnette. 2018. (ENG.). 32p. (gr. -1-3). 16.99 (978-1-4556-2393-8(8), Pelican Publishing) Arcadia Publishing.

—Petit Pierre & the Floating Marsh, 1 vol. Downing, Johnette. 2016. (ENG.). 32p. (J). (gr. k-3). 16.99 (978-1-4556-2279-5(6), Pelican Publishing) Arcadia Publishing.

Stanley, Joshua Rodriguez. I've Always Wanted to Eat a Rainbow. Bradfute, Jan. 2020. (ENG.). 58p. (J). pap. 14.95 **(978-1-0999-5015-5(5))** Independently Published.

Stanley, Mandy. Arty Words. 2016. (Arty Mouse Wipe Clean with Pen Ser.). (ENG.). 24p. (J). (gr. -1-2). pap. 7.99 (978-1-78445-858-4(9)) Top That! Publishing PLC GBR. Dist: Independent Pubs. Group.

—Baby Blessings Baby's Bible. 2005. 6p. (YA). (gr. -1 — 1). 15.99 (978-0-7847-1739-4(7), 04382) Standard Publishing.

—Birdy & Bou. Bedford, David. 2018. (J). (978-1-4351-6727-8(9)) Barnes & Noble, Inc.

—Busy Bear's Counting. 2014. (J). bds. 0.00 (978-0-9906156-8-2(5)) Bookworks, LLC.

—Cassie & Charm. McKain, Kelly. 2019. (Pony Camp Diaries). (ENG.). 128p. (J). (gr. 1-4). 4.99 (978-1-68010-442-4(X)); lib. bdg. 19.99 (978-1-68010-164-5(1)) Tiger Tales.

—Christmas Blessings Baby's Holiday Photo Album. Davidson, Alice Joyce. 2005. (Baby Blessings Ser.). 10p. (YA). (gr. -1-k). 15.99 (978-0-7847-1771-4(0), 04723) Standard Publishing.

—Daddy Loves Me. Moore, Karen. gif. ed. 2005. 10p. (J). (gr. -1-1). per., bds. 6.99 (978-1-57791-183-8(0)) Brighter Minds Children's Publishing.

—Emily & Emerald. McKain, Kelly. 2019. (Pony Camp Diaries). (ENG.). 128p. (J). (gr. 1-4). 4.99 (978-1-68010-443-1(8)); lib. bdg. 19.99 (978-1-68010-165-2(X)) Tiger Tales.

—Good Puppy. Hawksley, Gerald. 2005. (J). (978-1-890647-14-8(4)) TOMY International, Inc.

—Jack & Jill & Other Nursery Favourites. 2010. (Time for a Rhyme Ser.). (ENG.). 24p. (J). (gr. k — 1). 6.99 (978-0-00-731564-2(3)) HarperCollins Pubs. Ltd. GBR. Dist: Independent Pubs. Group.

—Jessica & Jewel. McKain, Kelly. 2020. (Pony Camp Diaries). (ENG.). 128p. (J). (gr. 1-4). 21.99 (978-1-68010-178-2(1)); pap. 5.99 (978-1-68010-452-3(7)) Tiger Tales.

—Lauren & Lucky. McKain, Kelly. 2020. (Pony Camp Diaries). (ENG.). 128p. (J). (gr. 1-4). 21.99 (978-1-68010-179-9(X)); pap. 5.99 (978-1-68010-453-0(5)) Tiger Tales.

—Lift & Look Daniel. 2005. 8p. (J). (gr. -1-k). 7.99 (978-0-7847-1751-6(6), 04377) Standard Publishing.

—Mommy Loves Me. Moore, Karen. gif. ed. 2005. 10p. (J). (gr. -1-1). per., bds. 6.99 (978-1-57791-182-1(2)) Brighter Minds Children's Publishing.

—My First Mandarin Word Book. 2020. (ENG.). 48p. (J). pap. 7.99 (978-0-7534-7545-4(6), 900211420, Kingfisher) Roaring Brook Pr.

—Roo the Roaring Dinosaur. Bedford, David. 2015. (J). (978-1-4351-6481-9(4)) Barnes & Noble, Inc.

—Tracing: Early Learning Through Art. George, Joshua. 2017. (Arty Mouse Creativity Bks.). (ENG.). 48p. (J). (gr. -1-k). pap. 6.99 (978-1-78445-624-5(1)) Top That! Publishing PLC GBR. Dist: Independent Pubs. Group.

Stanley, Mandy. Who Do You Love? Stanley, Mandy. 2007. (ENG.). 24p. (J). (gr. -1 — 1). bds. 8.99 (978-1-4169-3929-0(6), Little Simon) Little Simon.

Stanley, Sanna. Amistad: The Story of a Slave Ship. McKissack, Patricia. 2005. (Penguin Young Readers, Level 4 Ser.). (ENG.). 48p. (J). (gr. 3-4). mass mkt. 4.99 (978-0-448-43900-6(X), Penguin Young Readers) Penguin Young Readers Group.

Stanley, Stephen. Kanga Santa. Stanley, David. 2015. 24p. (J). pap. (978-1-326-21343-5(1)) Stanley, Stephen.

Stanley, Susan. The GOSPEL According to TUFFY TURTLE: The LIFE of JESUS As Told by TUFFY TURTLE the Seventy-Seventh Generation of Spiriturtlelus Family. McNamara, Joni Lundin. 2019. (ENG.). 142p. (J). pap. 15.99 **(978-1-5456-6457-5(9))** Salem Author Services.

Stanley, Susan. Marv the Moose Is on the Loose. Scaling, Sam T. 2012. 32p. (J). (978-0-9798806-4-3(5)) STS Publishing.

Stansfield, Laurie. Halloween, Here I Come! Steinberg, D. J. 2020. (Here I Come! Ser.). 32p. (J). (gr. -1-1). pap. 5.99 **(978-0-593-09420-4(4)**, Grosset & Dunlap) Penguin Young Readers Group.

Stanton, Brandon, photos by. Little Humans. Stanton, Brandon. 2014. (ENG., 40p. (J). (gr. -1-1). 17.99 (978-0-374-37456-3(2), 900123448, Farrar, Straus & Giroux (BYR)) Farrar, Straus & Giroux.

Stanton, Brian, photos by. Van Fleet Animal Trio: Moo; Cat; Dog. Van Fleet, Matthew. ed. 2013. (ENG., 58p. (J). (gr. -1-2). 51.99 (978-1-4424-8450-4(0), Simon & Schuster/Paula Wiseman Bks.) Simon & Schuster/Paula Wiseman Bks.

Stanton, Elizabeth Rose. Bub. Stanton, Elizabeth Rose. 2018. (ENG.). 40p. (J). (gr. -1-3). 17.99 (978-1-4814-8757-3(4), Simon & Schuster/Paula Wiseman Bks.) Simon & Schuster/Paula Wiseman Bks.

—Cowie. Stanton, Elizabeth Rose. 2020. (ENG.). 40p. (J). (gr. -1-3). 18.99 (978-1-5344-2174-5(2), Simon & Schuster/Paula Wiseman Bks.) Simon & Schuster/Paula Wiseman Bks.

—Henny. Stanton, Elizabeth Rose. 2014. (ENG.). 40p. (J). (gr. -1-3). 18.99 (978-1-4424-8436-8(5), Simon & Schuster/Paula Wiseman Bks.) Simon & Schuster/Paula Wiseman Bks.

—Peddles. Stanton, Elizabeth Rose. 2016. (ENG.). 40p. (J). (gr. -1-3). 17.99 (978-1-4814-1691-7(X), Simon & Schuster Bks. For Young Readers) Simon & Schuster Bks. For Young Readers.

Stanton, Janet, jt. illus. see Staige, Pat.

Stanton, Joe. Heroes of History. Ganeri, Anita. 2015. (Heroes of History Ser.). (ENG.). 176p. (J). (gr. 2-5). 11.99 (978-1-4998-0079-1(7)) Little Bee Books Inc.

Stanton, Karen. Monday, Wednesday, & Every Other Weekend. Stanton, Karen. 2014. (ENG.). 40p. (J). (gr. -1-1). 16.99 (978-1-250-03489-2(2), 900120992) Feiwel & Friends.

Stanton, Matt. The Moose Is Loose! Carthew, Mark. 2015. 32p. 17.99 (978-0-7333-3101-5(7)) ABC Bks. AUS. Dist: HarperCollins Pubs.

Stanton, Matt. Funny Kid #3: Prank Wars. Stanton, Matt. 2019. (Funny Kid Ser.: 3). (ENG.). 256p. (J). (gr. 3-7). 12.99 (978-0-06-257297-4(0)) HarperCollins Pubs.

—Funny Kid for President. Stanton, Matt. 2018. (Funny Kid Ser.: 1). (ENG.). 240p. (J). (gr. 3-7). 12.99 (978-0-06-257291-2(1)) HarperCollins Pubs.

—Funny Kid Stand Up. Stanton, Matt. 2018. (Funny Kid Ser.: 2). (ENG.). 272p. (J). (gr. 3-7). 12.99 (978-0-06-257294-3(6)) HarperCollins Pubs.

Stanton, Philip. Got Geography! Hopkins, Lee Bennett. 2006. (ENG.). 32p. (J). (gr. k-5). 16.99 (978-0-06-055601-3(3), Greenwillow Bks.) HarperCollins Pubs.

Stapelkamp, Brent, photos by. Cecil's Pride: The True Story of a Lion King. Hatkoff, Craig et al. 2016. 40p. (J). (gr. -1-3). 17.99 (978-1-338-03445-5(6)) Scholastic, Inc.

Staples, Students of Rf. The Stormy Night. Polefka-Proulx, Monika. 2017. (ENG.). (J). pap. 11.39 (978-1-366-83628-1(6)) Blurb, Inc.

Stapley, Craig. I Believe in Jesus Too. Nielson, Mark S. 2011. (J). 17.99 (978-1-60908-741-8(0)) Deseret Bk. Co.

Star, Brenda. Grandpa's Magical Accordion. Errico, Jessica / C. 2007. 28p. (J). pap. 17.95 incl. cd-rom (978-0-9800577-0-6(1)) Three Part Harmony LLC.

Starace, Tom. Easter Fun. Knudsen, Michelle. 2006. (ENG.). 12p. (J). bds. 4.99 (978-0-689-87894-7(X), Little Simon) Little Simon.

Starbuck-McMillan, Elizabeth. The Little Ferry Travels with Virginia Bk. 6: The Little Ferry Goes to Yorktown. Briggs, Martha Wren. 2007. (The Little Ferry Travels with Virginia Ser.: Vol. 6). 30p. (YA). (gr. 5-8). pap. 6.95 (978-0-9633240-8-5(X)) Dory Pr.

Starfall Education. Dragon Goes to the Farm: For the Earliest Reader. Hillert, Margaret. 2006. (ENG.). 32p. (J). (978-1-59577-032-5(1)); pap. (978-1-59577-034-9(8)) Starfall Education.

—Happy Mother's Day, Dear Dragon, 5 bks. Hillert, Margaret. 2005. (ENG.). 32p. (J). 6.95 (978-1-59577-022-6(4)); pap. (978-1-59577-023-3(2)) Starfall Education.

—I Can Do It: For the Earliest Reader. Hillert, Margaret. 2006. (ENG.). 32p. (J). (978-1-59577-039-4(9)); pap. (978-1-59577-040-0(2)) Starfall Education.

—It's Earth Day, Dear Dragon: For the Earliest Reader. Hillert, Margaret. 2006. (ENG.). 32p. (J). (978-1-59577-041-7(0)); pap. (978-1-59577-042-4(9)) Starfall Education.

—The No-Tail Cat or, I Like What I Am: For the Earliest Reader, 5 bks. Hillert, Margaret. 2005. (ENG.). 32p. (J). 6.95 (978-1-59577-024-0(0)); pap. (978-1-59577-025-7(9)) Starfall Education.

—Not Too Little to Help, 5 bks. Hillert, Margaret. 2005. (ENG.). 32p. (J). 6.95 (978-1-59577-026-4(7)); pap. (978-1-59577-027-1(5)) Starfall Education.

—Three Little Plays, 5 bks. Hillert, Margaret. 2005. (ENG.). 32p. (J). 6.95 (978-1-59577-018-9(6)); pap. (978-1-59577-019-6(4)) Starfall Education.

Starfall Education. The Big Hit. Starfall Education. 2004. (ENG.). 8p. (J). pap. (978-1-59577-003-5(8)) Starfall Education.

—Car Race. Starfall Education. 2004. (ENG.). 8p. (J). pap. (978-1-59577-012-7(7)) Starfall Education.

—Dune Buggy. Starfall Education. 2004. (ENG.). 8p. (J). pap. (978-1-59577-010-3(0)) Starfall Education.

—Gus the Duck. Starfall Education. 2004. (ENG.). 8p. (J). pap. (978-1-59577-005-9(4)) Starfall Education.

—Jake's Tale. Starfall Education. 2004. (ENG.). 8p. (J). pap. (978-1-59577-006-6(2)) Starfall Education.

—Level I Reading & Writing Journal: Starfall Manuscript. Starfall Education. 2004. (ENG.). 96p. (J). (gr. k-2). (978-1-59577-017-2(8), WK301m) Starfall Education.

—Level I Reading & Writing Journal - Block Print: WK201b. Starfall Education. 2011. (ENG.). 96p. (J). (978-1-59577-045-5(3)) Starfall Education.

—Mox's Shop. Starfall Education. 2004. (ENG.). 8p. (J). pap. (978-1-59577-004-2(6)) Starfall Education.

—My Family. Starfall Education. 2004. (ENG.). 8p. (J). pap. (978-1-59577-015-8(1)) Starfall Education.

—My Horse Glory. Starfall Education. 2004. (ENG.). 8p. (J). pap. (978-1-59577-013-4(5)) Starfall Education.

—Peg the Hen. Starfall Education. 2004. (ENG.). 8p. (J). pap. (978-1-59577-002-8(X)) Starfall Education.

—Pete's Sheep. Starfall Education. 2004. (ENG.). 8p. (J). pap. (978-1-59577-007-3(0)) Starfall Education.

—Robot & Mr. Mole. Starfall Education. 2004. (ENG.). 8p. (J). pap. (978-1-59577-009-7(7)) Starfall Education.

—Sky Ride. Starfall Education. 2004. (ENG.). 8p. (J). pap. (978-1-59577-008-0(9)) Starfall Education.

—Soap Boat. Starfall Education. 2004. (ENG.). 8p. (J). pap. (978-1-59577-011-0(9)) Starfall Education.

—Surfer Girl. Starfall Education. 2004. (ENG.). 8p. (J). pap. (978-1-59577-014-1(3)) Starfall Education.

—Zac the Rat. Starfall Education. 2004. (ENG.). 8p. (J). pap. (978-1-59577-001-1(1)) Starfall Education.

Starfall Education, photos by. Pumpkin, Pumpkin: For the Earliest Reader. Hillert, Margaret. 2006. (ENG., 32p. (J). (978-1-59577-035-6(6)); pap. (978-1-59577-036-3(4)) Starfall Education.

Stargeon, Bobbi. Haunted Doghouse II: Halloween Night, 3 vols., bk. 2. Johnson, Sandi et al. Durant, Sybrina, ed. l.t. ed. 2014. (ENG.). 36p. (J). (gr. k-5). pap. 12.99 (978-1-929063-27-7(X), 351) Moons & Stars Publishing For Children.

Starikova, Natalia. Kikitu Saves Christmas. Conner, Tommy. 2018. (Kikitu Ser.). (ENG.). 92p. (J). (978-1-5255-2664-0(2)); pap. (978-1-5255-2665-7(0)) FriesenPress.

Starikova, Natalia. Who's Mostly Scared? Holman, Aj. 2020. (ENG.). 36p. (J). **(978-1-4602-7599-3(3))**; pap. **(978-1-4602-7556-6(X))** FriesenPress.

Starin, Liz. Captain Monty Takes the Plunge. Mook-Sang, Jennifer. 2017. (ENG.). 32p. (J). (gr. -1-2). 16.99 (978-1-77138-626-5(6)) Kids Can Pr., Ltd. CAN. Dist: Hachette Bk. Group.

—Roar! Sauer, Tammi. 2015. (ENG.). 32p. (J). (gr. -1-3). 17.99 (978-1-4814-0224-8(2), Simon & Schuster Bks. For Young Readers) Simon & Schuster Bks. For Young Readers.

Stark, Andy. Ample Animals. Peters, Gemma. 2019. (ENG.). 62p. (J). pap. 25.94 (978-1-5462-9272-2(1)) AuthorHouse.

Stark, Kathleen. Carrie's Doll. Murphy, Elizabeth R. 2018. (ENG.). 26p. (J). 24.99 (978-1-4897-1454-1(5)); pap. 16.99 (978-1-4897-1453-4(7)) AuthorHouse. (Life Rich Publishing).

Stark, Kayla. The Fox & the Crow. Berne, Emma Carlson. 2019. (Classic Fables in Rhythm & Rhyme Ser.). (ENG.). 24p. (J). (gr. -1-2). lib. bdg. 33.99 (978-1-68410-332-4(0), 140252) Cantata Learning.

—Mr. Pack Rat Really Wants That. Ewert, Marcus. 2018. 40p. (J). (gr. -1-3). 14.95 (978-1-946764-25-6(6), Plum Blossom Bks.) Parallax Pr.

—Trying Again. Arrow, Emily. 2019. (My Feelings, My Choices Ser.). (ENG.). 24p. (J). (gr. -1-2). 33.99 (978-1-68410-407-9(6), 141217) Cantata Learning.

Stark, Mindy C. A Is for Alligator. Bringhurst, Nancy J. 2004. 32p. (J). 17.95 (978-1-883991-96-8(X)) White Cloud Pr.

Stark, Regina. Meghan's World: The Story of One Girl's Triumph Over Sensory Processing Disorder. Renna, Diane M. 2007. 32p. (J). 17.95 (978-0-9788339-0-9(2)) Indigo Impressions.

Stark, Ryan. We Like to Invent! Dunham, Bandhu Scott. 2010. (J). pap. (978-1-935387-13-8(8)) Hohm Pr.

Starkey, Fiona. The Amazing Adventure of Tiptoe & the Yellow Balloon. White, June. 2011. 32p. pap. (978-0-7552-1345-0(9)) Authors OnLine, Ltd.

Starkings, Richard, jt. illus. see Norman, Justin.

Starkings, Richard, jt. illus. see Research & Education Association Editors.

Starkoff, Vanina. From My Window. Júnior, Otavio. 2020. (ENG.). (J). pap. **(978-1-78285-978-9(0))** Barefoot Bks., Inc.

—From My Window. Júnior, Otávio & Dias, Beatriz C. 2020. (J). **(978-1-78285-977-2(2))** Barefoot Bks., Inc.

Starkoff, Vanina. Unfolding Journeys - Wonders of Egypt, 1 vol. Ross, Stewart & Lonely Planet Kids. 2017. (Unfolding Journeys Ser.). (ENG.). 16p. (J). (gr. 4-7). 17.99 (978-1-78657-538-8(8), 5376) Lonely Planet Global Ltd. IRL. Dist: Hachette Bk. Group.

Starlin, Jim. Thanos Vol. 3: Marvel Universe - The End, 3 vols. Starlin, Jim. 2003. (Marvel Heroes Ser.). 160p. (YA). (gr. 7-18). pap. 16.99 (978-0-7851-1116-0(6)) Marvel Worldwide, Inc.

—Thanos Vol. 4: Epiphany. Starlin, Jim. Youngquist, Jeff, ed. 2004. (Marvel Heroes Ser.). 144p. pap. 14.99 (978-0-7851-1355-3(X)) Marvel Worldwide, Inc.

Starling, Robert. Super Sloth. Starling, Robert. 2019. (ENG.). 32p. (J). (gr. -1-3). 17.99 (978-1-5415-5511-2(2)) Lerner Publishing Group.

Starmer, Anika & Wertz, Michael. Bliss Live It! Bliss Give It! Thomas, Wendy Russell & Ruchman, Laura. 2010. 60p. (YA). (978-0-88441-754-5(9)) Girl Scouts of the USA.

Starner, Lynn. The Day Cagney Lost Her Wag. Salzler, Laurie. 2018. (ENG.). 36p. (J). (gr. 2-4). pap. 12.95 (978-1-945805-72-1(2)) Bedazzled Ink Publishing Co.

Staron, Berangere. At Home. Clever Publishing. 2019. (My First Words Ser.). (ENG.). 192p. (J). (gr. -1 — 1). pap. 7.99 (978-1-948418-63-8(0)) Clever Media Group.

Starr, Branka. Quimble Wood. Bodecker, N. M. 2004. (ENG.). 32p. (J). reprint ed. (978-1-931561-97-6(4)) MacAdam/Cage Publishing, Inc.

Starr, Branka, jt. illus. see Blegvad, Erik.

Starr, Jim. Big Sam: A Rosh Hashanah Tall Tale. Kimmel, Eric A. 2017. (J). (978-1-68115-525-8(7)) Behrman Hse., Inc.

Starr, Lisa. Paddy the Penguin's Adventure. McGuinness, Jeff. I.t. ed. 2006. 33p. (J). 27.95 (978-1-59879-231-7(8)); (gr. -1-3). per. 15.95 (978-1-59879-229-4(6)) Lifevest Publishing, Inc.

Starr Taylor, Bridget. Happy Hippo Holiday: Set Of 6. Parkes, Brenda. 2014. (Shared Reading Foundations Ser.). (J). (gr. 1). 36.00 net. (978-1-4900-0029-9(1)) Benchmark Education Co.

—Happy Hippo Holiday Book Set. Parkes, Brenda. 2014. (Shared Reading Foundations Ser.). (J). (gr. 1). 72.00 net. (978-1-4509-9999-1(9)) Benchmark Education Co.

—Old MacDonald's Funny Farm, Vol. 4261. Williams, Rozanne Lanczak. 2005. (Reading for Fluency Ser.). 16p. (J). pap. 3.49 (978-1-59198-161-9(1), 4261) Creative Teaching Pr., Inc.

Stasiuk, Max. Anastasia Rose Sleeps in Her Own Room, 1 vol. Kopczynski, Megan. 2010. 26p. pap. 24.95 (978-1-4489-4923-6(8)) PublishAmerica, Inc.

Stasolla, Mario. The Bright Blue Button & the Button-Hole. Peck, Judith. 2004. 28p. (J). 18.95 (978-0-9746119-5-2(6)) Imagination Arts Pubns.

Stasuyk, Max. Daddy's Picture. Levine, Karen R. 2013. 24p. pap. 14.95 (978-1-57258-794-6(6), Aspect Bk.) TEACH Services, Inc.

—Five Little Children at the Zoo. Rolle, Elvy P. 2016. (ENG.). 26p. (J). pap. 13.95 (978-1-4796-0534-7(4), Aspect) Grand Central Publishing.

Stasyuk, Max. The Blue Wizard. Edwards, Garth. 2011. (Adventures of Titch & Mitch Ser.). (J). pap. (978-0-9567449-9-9(0)) Inside Pocket Publishing, Ltd.

—The King of the Castle. Edwards, Garth. 2011. (Adventures of Titch & Mitch Ser.). (J). pap. (978-0-9567449-7-5(4)) Inside Pocket Publishing, Ltd.

—The Magic Boots. Edwards, Garth. 2011. (Adventures of Titch & Mitch Ser.). (J). pap. (978-0-9567449-8-2(2)) Inside Pocket Publishing, Ltd.

—The Trolls of Sugar Loaf Wood. Edwards, Garth. 2011. (Adventures of Titch & Mitch Ser.). (J). pap. (978-0-9567449-6-8(6)) Inside Pocket Publishing, Ltd.

—#01 Shipwrecked! Edwards, Garth. 2011. (Adventures of Titch & Mitch, the Ser.). (J). pap. (978-0-7613-8421-2(9)) Inside Pocket Publishing, Ltd.

—The #02 Trolls of Sugar Loaf Wood. Edwards, Garth. 2011. (Adventures of Titch & Mitch, the Ser.). (J). pap. (978-0-7613-8422-9(7)) Inside Pocket Publishing, Ltd.

—The #03 King of the Castle. Edwards, Garth. 2011. (Adventures of Titch & Mitch, the Ser.). (J). pap. (978-0-7613-8423-6(5)) Inside Pocket Publishing, Ltd.

—The #04 Magic Boots. Edwards, Garth. 2011. (Adventures of Titch & Mitch, the Ser.). (J). pap. (978-0-7613-8424-3(3)) Inside Pocket Publishing, Ltd.

—The #05 Blue Wizard. Edwards, Garth. 2011. (Adventures of Titch & Mitch, the Ser.). (J). pap. (978-0-7613-8425-0(1)) Inside Pocket Publishing, Ltd.

States, Anna. The Unordinary Elephant. Yamada, Rikako. 2005.Tr. of Chiisana mimi no Kozou. (JPN.). 26p. (J). per. 14.99 (978-0-9761606-0-1(9)) WonderToast.

Statia, Andy. Down the Dark Well. Statia, Andy. 2019. (Worlds Within Ser.: Vol. 4). (ENG.). 62p. (J). (gr. 3-6). **(978-1-988419-05-3(0))** Never Dot.

Statia, Andy. Run, Monster, Run. Statia, Andy. 2018. (Worlds Within Ser.: Vol. 3). (ENG.). 54p. (J). (gr. 3-6). (978-1-988419-04-6(2)) Never Dot.

Staton, Joe & Mcrae, Scott. Scooby-Doo in Trick or Treat! Fisch, Sholly. 2010. (Scooby-Doo Graphic Novels Ser.: No. 1). (ENG.). 24p. (J). (gr. 2-6). 27.07 (978-1-59961-699-5(8), 567, Graphic Novels) Spotlight.

Staton, Joe, jt. illus. see Brizuela, Dario.

Statuti, Laura. Butterbean Finds a Home. Statuti, Laura. 2019. (ENG.). 32p. (J). (gr. k-3). 9.99 **(978-0-578-51935-7(6))** STATUTI, LAURA.

Staub, Frank J., photos by. America's Forests & Woodlands. 2006. 48p. (J). pap. (978-1-59034-806-2(0)) Mondo Publishing.

Staub, Leslie. Mama's Nightingale: A Story of Immigration & Separation. Danticat, Edwidge. 2015. 32p. (J). (gr. k-3). 17.99 (978-0-525-42809-1(7), Dial Bks) Penguin Young Readers Group.

—Whoever You Are. Fox, Mem. 2017.Tr. of Sé de¿it Mak Ó. (ENG.). 28p. (J). (— 1). bds. 7.99 (978-1-328-89581-3(5), 1699665, HMH Books For Young Readers) Houghton Mifflin Harcourt Publishing Co.

—Whoever You Are (Quienquiera Que Seas) Fox, Mem. Flor Ada, Alma & Campoy, F. Isabel, trs. 2007. (ENG.). 28p. (J). (gr. k — 1). bds. 6.95 (978-0-15-205891-3(5), 1197688) Houghton Mifflin Harcourt Publishing Co.

Stauffer, Lori. Let's Talk about Safety Skills for Kids: A Personal Safety Activity Book for Children. Stauffer, Lori. Deblinger, Esther. 2004. 32p. (J). (gr. k-6). 5.00 (978-0-9676489-3-4(9)) Hope for Families, Inc.

Stauffer, Lori. Let's Talk about Coping & Safety Skills: A Workbook about Taking Care of Me! Stauffer, Lori, photos by. Deblinger, Esther. 2005. (J). (gr. k-6). pap. 10.00 (978-0-9676489-4-1(7)) Hope for Families, Inc.

—Let's Talk about Taking Care of Me: An Educational Book about Body Safety for Young Children. Stauffer, Lori, photos by. Deblinger, Esther. 2004. 64p. (J). (gr. -1-1). pap. 12.00 (978-0-9676489-2-7(0)) Hope for Families, Inc.

Stauffer, Lori & Moyer, Brett. Let's Talk about Taking Care of Me: An Educational Book about Body Safety. Stauffer, Lori & Deblinger, Esther. 2nd rev. ed. 2003. 96p. (J). (gr. k-6). pap. 18.00 (978-0-9676489-1-0(2)) Hope for Families, Inc.

Staunton, Mathew. I Met a Man from Artikelly: Verse for the Young & Young at Heart. Rosenstock, Gabriel. 2013. 96p. pap. (978-1-78201-032-6(7)) Evertype.

Stayte, James. Forces & Motion: Investigating a Car Crash, 1 vol. Graham, Ian. 2013. (Anatomy of an Investigation Ser.). (ENG.). 56p. (YA). (gr. 6-11). pap. 9.95 (978-1-4329-7608-8(7), Heinemann) Capstone.

—Human Body: Investigating an Unexplained Death. Solway, Andrew. 2013. (Anatomy of an Investigation Ser.). (ENG.). 56p. (YA). (gr. 6-11). 35.32 (978-1-4329-7604-0(4)); pap. 9.95 (978-1-4329-7610-1(9)) Capstone. (Heinemann).

Ste Marie, Julia. ... & Then Some. O'Neil, Jeremiah. 2019. (ENG.). 28p. (J). pap. 10.00 **(978-1-0864-3119-3(7))** Independently Published.

Steacy, Ken. Bessie Coleman: Daring Stunt Pilot, 1 vol. Robbins, Trina. 2007. (Graphic Biographies Ser.). (ENG.). 32p. (J). (gr. 3-9). per. 8.10 (978-0-7368-7903-3(X)) Capstone.

Stead, April-Nicole. If I Called You a Hippopotamus! Stevens, Gary J. 2010. 24p. pap. 11.50 (978-1-60911-280-6(6), Eloquent Bks.) Strategic Book Publishing & Rights Agency (SBPRA).

Stead, Erin. Music for Mister Moon. Stead, Philip C. 2019. 40p. (J). (gr. -1-3). 18.99 (978-0-8234-4160-0(1), Neal Porter Bks) Holiday Hse., Inc.

—The Purloining of Prince Oleomargarine. Twain, Mark & Stead, Philip C. 2017. (ENG.). 160p. (J). (gr. 3-7). 24.99 (978-0-553-52322-5(8)); lib. bdg. 27.99 (978-0-553-52323-2(6)) Random Hse. Children's Bks. (Doubleday Bks. for Young Readers).

Stead, Erin E. And Then It's Spring. Fogliano, Julie. 2012. (ENG.). 32p. (J). (gr. -1-2). 18.99 (978-1-59643-624-4(7), 900066722) Roaring Brook Pr.

—Bear Has a Story to Tell. Stead, Philip C. (ENG.). (J). 2019. 34p. bds. 7.99 (978-1-250-22194-0(3), 900207876); 2012. 32p. (gr. -1-1). 18.99 (978-1-59643-745-6(6), 900077930) Roaring Brook Pr.

—If You Want to See a Whale. Fogliano, Julie. 2013. (ENG.). 32p. (J). (gr. -1-2). 18.99 (978-1-59643-731-9(6), 900076361) Roaring Brook Pr.

—Lenny & Lucy. Stead, Philip C. 2015. (ENG.). 40p. (J). (gr. -1-2). 17.99 (978-1-59643-932-0(7), 900122425) Roaring Brook Pr.

Stead, Erin E. A Sick Day for Amos McGee. Stead, Philip C. 2010. (JPN.). 32p. (J). (gr. -1-1). **(978-4-89572-814-0(5))** Hisakata-Child.

Stead, Erin E. A Sick Day for Amos Mcgee. Stead, Philip C. (ENG.). (J). 2018. 34p. bds. 8.99 (978-1-250-17110-8(5), 900188204); 2010. 32p. (gr. -1-1). 18.99 (978-1-59643-402-8(3), 900051603) Roaring Brook Pr.

—A Sick Day for Amos McGee. Stead, Philip C. ed. 2019. (ENG.). 40p. (J). 29.99 (978-1-62672-105-0(X), 900136450) Roaring Brook Pr.

—A Sick Day for Amos Mcgee: Book & CD Storytime Set. Stead, Philip C. 2017. (Macmillan Young Listeners Story Time Sets Ser.). (ENG.). 32p. (J). 12.99 (978-1-4272-8722-9(8), 900178665) Macmillan Audio.

—Tony. Galing, Ed. 2017. (ENG.). 32p. (J). 16.99 (978-1-62672-308-5(7), 900150587) Roaring Brook Pr.

—The Uncorker of Ocean Bottles. Cuevas, Michelle. 2016. 34p. (J). (gr. -1-3). 17.99 (978-0-8037-3868-3(4), Dial Bks) Penguin Young Readers Group.

Stead, Judy. Isabel's Car Wash. Bair, Sheila. 2012. (J). 34.28 (978-1-61913-118-7(6)) Weigl Pubs., Inc.

—Isabel's Car Wash. Bair, Sheila. 2011. (ENG.). 32p. (J). (gr. -1-3). 7.99 (978-0-8075-3653-7(9), 807536539) Whitman, Albert & Co.

—Mister Sun. 2006. (J). (978-1-58987-097-0(2)) Kindermusik International.

—Summer Wonders. Raczka, Bob. 2012. (J). 34.28 (978-1-61913-125-5(0)) Weigl Pubs., Inc.

—The Twelve Days of Christmas in North Carolina. 2017. (Twelve Days of Christmas in America Ser.). 22p. (J). (-k). bds. 7.95 (978-1-4549-2285-8(0)) Sterling Publishing Co., Inc.

—What a Way to Start a New Year! A Rosh Hashanah Story. Jules, Jacqueline. 2013. (ENG.). 24p. (J). (gr. -1-2). lib. bdg. 8.99 (978-0-7613-8116-7(3), 9780761381167, Kar-Ben Publishing) Lerner Publishing Group.

Stead, Judy. The Twelve Days of Christmas in North Carolina. Stead, Judy. 2009. (Twelve Days of Christmas in America Ser.). 40p. (J). (gr. k). 12.95 (978-1-4027-4467-9(6)) Sterling Publishing Co., Inc.

Stead, Natalie. Henry. Brookes, John. Hardcastle, E. Rachael, ed. 2020. (ENG.). 24p. (J). (gr. k-4). pap. 6.49 **(978-1-9999688-5-4(9),** Curious Cat Bks.) Legacy Bound.

Stead, Philip C. In My Garden. Zolotow, Charlotte. 2020. 40p. (J). (-k). 18.99 (978-0-8234-4320-8(5), Neal Porter Bks) Holiday Hse., Inc.

Stead, Philip C. Hello, My Name Is Ruby: A Picture Book. Stead, Philip C. 2013. (ENG.). 36p. (J). (gr. -1-1). 16.99 (978-1-59643-809-5(6), 900086606) Roaring Brook Pr.

—A Home for Bird. Stead, Philip C. 2012. (ENG.). 32p. (J). (gr. -1-3). 18.99 (978-1-59643-711-1(1), 900074736) Roaring Brook Pr.

—Sebastian & the Balloon: A Picture Book. Stead, Philip C. 2014. (ENG.). 40p. (J). (gr. -1-2). 17.99 (978-1-59643-930-6(0), 900122420) Roaring Brook Pr.

Steadman, Barbara. Russian Picture Word Book: Learn over 500 Commonly Used Russian Words Through Pictures. Rogers, Svetlana. 2003. (Dover Children's Language Activity Bks.). (ENG.). 32p. (J). (gr. 1-5). pap. 3.99 (978-0-486-42671-6(8)) Dover Pubns., Inc.

Steadman, Ralph. Alice in Wonderland. Carroll, Lewis. 2010. 128p. pap. 19.95 (978-1-55407-203-3(4), ea76a9e4-0069-4d3b-ad99-48b591b057d2) Firefly Bks., Ltd.

—The Big Red Squirrel & the Little Rhinoceros. Damjan, Mischa. 2010. 32p. (J). (gr. -1-k). 15.99 (978-1-84365-130-7(0), Pavilion Children's Books) Pavilion Bks. GBR. Dist: Penguin Random Hse. LLC.

—The False Flamingoes. Damjan, Mischa. 32p. (J). (gr. -1-3). 13.95 (978-0-87592-016-0(0)) Scroll Pr., Inc.

Steadman, Ralph. The Jelly Book. Steadman, Ralph. 32p. (J). (gr. -1-3). 14.95 (978-0-87592-026-9(8)) Scroll Pr., Inc.

Steadman-Robert, Ava & Steadman-Robert, Esme. Pin & the Magic Butterflies. Steadman, Amanda. 2019. (ENG.). 28p. (J). (gr. k-4). pap. **(978-0-9576365-2-1(0))** Steadman, Amanda.

Steadman-Robert, Esme, jt. illus. see Steadman-Robert, Ava.

Stearns, Forest. The Wonderful Adventures of Ozzie Sea Otter (Spanish) Dohlke, Nora. 2009. (ENG.). 98p. 19.95 (978-0-9822046-2-7(0)) Bay Publishing.

—The Wonderful Adventures of Ozzie the Sea Otter. Dohlke, Nora. 2009. 98p. (J). 19.95 (978-0-9822046-0-3(4)) Bay Publishing.

—The Wonderful Adventures of Ozzie the Sea Otter (Book & CD) Dohlke, Nora. 2009. (ENG.). 98p. 26.95 (978-0-9822046-1-0(2)) Bay Publishing.

Stebakova, Elena. I Am a Rainbow Child Coloring-Story Book. Yacoubou, Jeanne. 2005. 16p. (J). (978-0-9788737-4-5(2)) Alaafia Kids Co.

—Wanna Play? Coloring-Story Book. Yacoubou, Jeanne. 2005. 16p. (J). (978-0-9788737-5-2(0)) Alaafia Kids Co.

—What's My Heritage? Coloring-Story Book. Yacoubou, Jeanne. 2006. 24p. (J). (978-0-9788737-2-1(6)) Alaafia Kids Co.

Steccati, Eve. The Secret of Stoneship Woods. Barba, Rick. 2006. (Spy Gear Adventures Ser.: 1). (ENG.). 160p. (J). (gr. 3-7). pap. 8.99 (978-1-4169-0887-6(0), Simon & Schuster/Paula Wiseman Bks.) Simon & Schuster/Paula Wiseman Bks.

Steck, Jim. Flipping Out! How to Draw Flip Animation. Bellen-Berthézène, Cyndie. 2005. 48p. (J). (978-0-439-81335-8(2)) Scholastic, Inc.

Steckel, Michele, photos by. My Teeth. Steckel, Richard. 2008. 20p. (J). (gr. k — 1). bds. 6.99 (978-1-58246-212-7(7), Tricycle Pr.) Random Hse. Children's Bks.

Steckler, Elaine. Bella the Dragon. Nick, Barbara. 2013. 36p. pap. 11.75 (978-1-938078-05-7(5)) Catto Creations, LLC.

Steckler, Kerren Barbas. Ready, Set, Draw... under the Sea! Conlon, Mara. 2009. (Activity Bks). 40p. (J). spiral bd. 15.99 (978-1-59359-837-2(8)) Peter Pauper Pr. Inc.

—Water Magic. Paulding, Barbara. 2009. (Young Artist Ser.). 24p. (J). (gr. -1). 15.99 (978-1-59359-842-6(4)) Peter Pauper Pr. Inc.

Steckler, Megan. Boots. Roman, Lisa. 2009. 24p. pap. 24.95 (978-1-60749-329-7(2)) America Star Bks.

—Finding the Perfect Fit. Ayres, S. C. 2011. 28p. pap. 24.95 (978-1-4560-0912-0(5)) America Star Bks.

—Krissy & the Indians, 1 vol. Fitzsimmons, Christy. 2009. 28p. pap. 24.95 (978-1-61546-206-3(6)) America Star Bks.

Steckley, Ed. Rube Goldberg's Simple Normal Humdrum School Day. George, Jennifer. 2017. (ENG.). 40p. (J). (gr. k-2). 17.95 (978-1-4197-2558-6(0), Abrams Bks. for Young Readers) Abrams, Inc.

Steege, Joanna. Hooray! I'm Catholic. Cole, Hana. 2010. 32p. (J). 14.95 (978-0-8091-6746-3(8), Ambassador Bks.) Paulist Pr.

Steel, John. Roy Rogers' Surprise for Donnie. Sankey, Alice. 2011. 32p. pap. 35.95 (978-1-258-03591-4(X)) Literary Licensing, LLC.

Steele, Andrea M. Princess Zoe & the Mer-Bird. Brower, Sandra Shane. 2013. 46p. pap. 10.95 (978-1-936688-77-7(8), Compass Flower Pr.) AKA:yoLa.

—Zoe & the Cocoa-Brown Tutu. Brower. 2nd ed. 2013. 56p. pap. 10.95 (978-1-936688-79-1(4)) AKA:yoLa.

Steele, Andrew & Clement, Devyn. The Paperweight. Young, Francis Kerr. 2008. 39p. pap. 24.95 (978-1-60610-034-9(3)) America Star Bks.

Steele-Card, Adrianna & Second Story Press Staff. Sandy's Incredible Shrinking Footprint, 1 vol. Handy, Femida & Carpenter, Carole H. 2010. (ENG.). 24p. (J). (gr. 1-3). 15.95 (978-1-897187-69-2(6)) Second Story Pr. CAN. Dist: Orca Bk. Pubs. USA.

Steele, Gregory D. The Adventures of Maximillian P. Dogg - Rescue Dog: Max Finds a New Home. Tveite, William P. 2012. (ENG.). 30p. (J). pap. 12.95 (978-1-61863-289-0(2)) Bookstand Publishing.

Steele, K-Fai. I've Been Kissed. Joyce, John Owen. 2016. (ENG.). 39p. (J). 18.95 (978-1-4787-6738-1(3)) Outskirts Pr., Inc.

—Noodlephant. Kramer, Jacob. 2019. 80p. (J). 18.95 (978-1-59270-266-4(X)) Enchanted Lion Bks., LLC.

—Old MacDonald Had a Baby. Snape, Emily. 2019. (ENG.). 40p. (J). 17.99 (978-1-250-30281-6(1), 900196974) Feiwel & Friends.

Steele, K-Fai. A Normal Pig. Steele, K-Fai. 2019. (ENG.). 40p. (J). (gr. -1-3). 17.99 (978-0-06-274857-7(2), Balzer & Bray) HarperCollins Pubs.

Steele, Kris. Journey to Cahokia. Steele, Kris. 32p. (Orig.). (J). (gr. 4-6). pap. 4.95 (978-1-881563-02-0(2)) Cahokia Mounds Museum Society.

Steele-Morgan, Alex. Tashlich at Turtle Rock, Vol. Schnur, Susan & Schnur-Fishman, Anna. 2010. (ENG.). 32p. (J). (gr. k-3). pap. 7.95 (978-0-7613-4510-7(8), 9780761345107, Kar-Ben Publishing) Lerner Publishing Group.

—Touch & Feel Bible Animal Friends. Nolan, Allia Zobel. 2004. (Touch & Feel Ser.). 12p. (J). bds. 10.99 (978-0-8254-5512-4(X)) Kregel Pubns.

Steele-Morgan, Alexandra, jt. illus. see Schnur-Fishman, Anna.

Steele, Paul. The Bonsai Coloring Book. Baran, Robert J. 2005. 5.95 net. (978-0-9659913-5-3(0)) Pyramid Dancer Pubns.

Steele, Robert G. Dad & Me in the Morning. Lakin, Patricia. 2019. (ENG.). 32p. (J). (gr. -1-k). pap. 7.99 (978-0-8075-1420-7(9), 807514209) Whitman, Albert & Co.

Steele, Robert Gantt. Lily's Victory Garden. Wilbur, Helen L. 2010. (Tales of Young Americans Ser.). (ENG.). 32p. (J). (gr. 1-4). 16.95 (978-1-58536-450-3(9), 202175) Sleeping Bear Pr.

Steelhammer, Ilona. Storybook Readers, 5 bks. Cosgrove, Stephen. (J). lib. bdg. 73.75 (978-1-56674-921-3(2)) Forest Hse. Publishing Co., Inc.

Steen, Rob. Flanimals Pop-Up. Gervais, Ricky. 2010. (ENG.). 14p. (J). (gr. k-4). 19.99 (978-0-7636-4781-0(0)) Candlewick Pr.

Steenholdt, Jeff. Come, Ye Children: A Bible Storybook for Young Children. Hoeksema, Gertrude. 3rd ed. 2010. (ENG.). 599p. (J). reprint ed. 47.95 (978-0-916206-27-7(0)) Reformed Free Publishing Assn.

Steenz. Archival Quality. Weir, Ivy Noelle. 2018. (ENG.). 280p. pap. 19.99 (978-1-62010-470-5(9), 9781620104705, Lion Forge) Oni Pr., Inc.

Steers, Billy. Tractor Mac Learns to Fly. 2007. (J). 7.95 (978-0-9788496-2-7(0)) Tractor Mac Inc.

Steers, Billy. Tractor Mac: Autumn Is Here. Steers, Billy. 2019. (Tractor Mac Ser.: 1). (ENG.). 40p. (J). 17.99 (978-0-374-30920-6(5), 900189990, Farrar, Straus & Giroux (BYR)) Farrar, Straus & Giroux.

—Tractor Mac Colors on the Farm. Steers, Billy. 2018. (Tractor Mac Ser.). (ENG.). 16p. (J). bds. 5.99 (978-0-374-30633-5(8), 900175318, Farrar, Straus & Giroux (BYR)) Farrar, Straus & Giroux.

—Tractor Mac Farmers Market: Farmer's Market. Steers, Billy. 2009. (ENG.). (J). 7.95 (978-0-9826870-1-7(X)) Tractor Mac Inc.

Stefano, Micaela. Keith & Kevin & the Santa Claus Mystery. Pierce, Keith. 2018. (Keith & Kevin Ser.: Vol. 5). (ENG.). 36p. (J). pap. 10.95 **(978-1-7180-8676-0(8))** Independently Published.

Steffen, Jennifer. The Wonder of a Summer Day. Becker, Laura. 2008. (ENG.). 40p. (J). (gr. -1-3). lib. bdg. (978-1-934363-25-6(1)) Zoe Life Publishing.

Steffen, Jeremy. What Hurricane? My Solar-Powered History on a Supply Ship to the Jamestown Colony. Terry, Alana. 2013. 136p. pap. 12.99 (978-1-937848-05-7(1)) Do Life Right, Inc.

—What, No Sushi? Terry, Alana. 2013. 116p. pap. 7.99 (978-1-937848-04-0(3)) Do Life Right, Inc.

Steffen, Randy. Roy Rogers & the Sure 'Nough Cowpoke. Beecher, Elizabeth. 2011. 32p. pap. 35.95 (978-1-258-03587-7(1)) Literary Licensing, LLC.

Steffibauer, Thomas. I See You. Jackson, P. D. 2019. (ENG.). 32p. (J). (978-0-578-21528-0(4)) ISeeYou Media I.G.

—Queen Nzinga. Panev, Aleksandar. 2007. 48p. (J). lib. bdg. 23.08 (978-1-4242-1641-3(9)) Fitzgerald Bks.

Stegall, Joel E. I'm Happy Being Me. Johns, Isabel G. 2012. 32p. pap. 14.95 (978-1-61493-093-8(7)) Peppertree Pr., The.

Steger, Volker, photos by. Buzz: The Intimate Bond Between Humans & Insects. 2004. (ENG.). 144p. (gr. 8-17). pap. 24.95 (978-0-8118-3789-7(0)) Chronicle Bks. LLC.

Stegman, Ryan. Absolute Carnage. 2020. (ENG.). 136p. (YA). (gr. 8-17). pap. 29.99 (978-1-302-91908-5(3)) Marvel Worldwide, Inc.

Stegman, Ryan, et al. Sif: Journey into Mystery - the Complete Collection. 2017. (ENG.). 248p. (YA). (gr. 8-17). pap. 29.99 (978-1-302-90683-2(6)) Marvel Worldwide, Inc.

Stegman, Ryan. Venom by Donny Cates Vol. 1: Rex. 2018. (Venom (2018) Ser.: 1). 136p. (YA). (gr. 8-17). pap. 17.99 (978-1-302-91306-9(9)) Marvel Worldwide, Inc.

Stegman, Ryan, et al. Venom Unleashed Vol. 1. 2019. 136p. (YA). (gr. 8-17). pap. 17.99 (978-1-302-91723-4(4)) Marvel Worldwide, Inc.

Stegman, Ryan, jt. illus. see Coello, Iban.

Stegos, Daniel. Canada Goose at Cat Tail Lane. Halfmann, Janet. 2006. (ENG.). 32p. (J). (gr. -1-2). 9.95 (978-1-59249-499-6(4), PB5079) Soundprints.

—Penguins Family: Story of a Humboldt Penguin Hardcover. Hollenbeck, Kathleen. 2005. (ENG.). 32p. (J). (gr. -1-2). 19.95 (978-1-59249-349-4(1), BC4027) Soundprints.

—Penguin's Family: The Story of a Humboldt Penguin. Hollenbeck, Kathleen. 2005. (ENG.). 32p. (J). (gr. -1-2). 9.95 (978-1-59249-351-7(3), PB4027); 15.95 (978-1-59249-346-3(7), B4027) Soundprints.

—Penguins Family: The Story of a Humboldt Penguin. Hollenbeck, Kathleen. 2005. (ENG.). 32p. (J). (gr. -1-2). 4.95 (978-1-59249-348-7(3), B4077); pap. 6.95 (978-1-59249-347-0(5), S4027) Soundprints.

—Red Bat at Sleep Hollow Lane. Halfmann, Janet. 2005. (ENG.). 32p. (J). (gr. -1-2). 19.95 (978-1-59249-343-2(2), BC5027); 15.95 (978-1-59249-340-1(8), B5027); 4.95 (978-1-59249-342-5(4), B5077) Soundprints.

—Red Bat at Sleepy Hollow Lane. Halfmann, Janet. 2005. (Smithsonian's Backyard Ser.). (ENG.). 32p. (J). (gr. -1-2). pap. 6.95 (978-1-59249-341-8(6), S5027) Soundprints.

—Swordfish Returns. Korman, Susan. (ENG.). 32p. (J). 2005. (gr. -1-2). 9.95 (978-1-59249-132-2(4), PB4075); 2005. (gr. -1-2). 4.95 (978-1-59249-126-1(X), B4075); 2004. (gr. 2-2). pap. 6.95 (978-1-59249-127-8(8), S4025); 2003. (gr. -1-2). 8.95 (978-1-59249-129-2(4), SC4025); 2003. (gr. -1-2). 19.95 (978-1-59249-128-5(6), BC4025) Soundprints.

Stegos, Daniel J. Canada Goose at Cattail Lane. Halfmann, Janet. (Smithsonian's Backyard Ser.). (ENG.). 32p. (J). 2011. (gr. -1-3). 19.95 (978-1-60727-632-6(1)); 2011. (gr. -1-3). pap. 8.95 (978-1-60727-633-3(X)); 2006. (gr. -1-2). 8.95 (978-1-59249-498-9(6), SC5029); 2006. (gr. -1-2). pap. 6.95 (978-1-59249-495-8(1), S5029); 2006. (gr. k-2). 19.95 (978-1-59249-497-2(8), BC5029); 2005. (gr. k-2). 15.95 (978-1-59249-494-1(3), B5029) Soundprints.

—Penguin's Family: The Story of a Humboldt Penguin. Hollenbeck, Kathleen M. 2008. (ENG.). 32p. (J). (gr. -1-3). 19.95 (978-1-59249-765-2(9)) Soundprints.

—Swordfish Returns. Korman, Susan. (Smithsonian Oceanic Collection Ser.). (ENG.). 32p. (J). 2011. (gr. -1-3). 8.95 (978-1-60727-666-1(6)); 2011. (gr. -1-3). 19.95 (978-1-60727-665-4(8)); 2003. (gr. 2-2). 15.95 (978-1-59249-125-4(1), B4025) Soundprints.

Stehr, Frederic. Bim Bam Boom. Stehr, Frederic. 2018. (ENG.). 26p. (J). (gr. -1-k). bds. 12.99 (978-1-77657-136-9(3)) Gecko Pr. NZL. Dist: Lerner Publishing Group.

Stehrenberger, Michiko. Bikini Bonini: Queen of the Cul-De-Sac. Duignan, Patricia Rose. 2018. (ENG.). 126p. (J). pap. 24.00 (978-1-7190-5243-6(3)) CreateSpace Independent Publishing Platform.

Steig, William. Alpha Beta Chowder. Steig, Jeanne. 2016. (ENG.). 48p. (J). (gr. -1-3). 17.99 (978-1-4814-4060-8(8), Atheneum/Caitlyn Dlouhy Books) Simon & Schuster Children's Publishing.

—Consider the Lemming. Steig, Jeanne. 2016. (ENG.). 48p. (J). (gr. -1-3). 19.99 (978-1-4814-3963-3(4), Atheneum/Caitlyn Dlouhy Books) Simon & Schuster Children's Publishing.

—Divine Comedies: The Old Testament Made Easy & a Gift from Zeus. Steig, Jeanne. 2016. (ENG.). 200p. (YA). (gr. 7). 19.99 (978-1-4814-3957-2(X)) Simon & Schuster Children's Publishing.

—The Flying Latke. Yorinks, Arthur. 2017. (ENG.). 32p. (J). (gr. -1-3). 13.99 (978-1-5344-0948-4(3), Simon & Schuster Bks. For Young Readers) Simon & Schuster Bks. For Young Readers.

—A Handful of Beans. Steig, Jeanne. 2016. (ENG.). 128p. (YA). (gr. 7). 17.99 (978-1-4814-3961-9(8), Atheneum/Caitlyn Dlouhy Books) Simon & Schuster Children's Publishing.

Steig, William. Abel's Island. Steig, William. 2007. (ENG.). 128p. (J). (gr. 3-7). per. 6.99 (978-0-312-37143-2(8), 900044681) Square Fish.

—The Amazing Bone. Steig, William. 2011. (ENG.). 32p. (J). (gr. k-3). pap. 8.99 (978-0-312-56421-6(X), 900074774) Square Fish.

—Amos & Boris. Steig, William. 2009. (ENG.). 32p. (J). (gr. k-3). pap. 8.99 (978-0-312-53566-7(X), 900054745) Square Fish.

—Brave Irene: A Picture Book. Steig, William. 2011. (ENG.). 32p. (J). (gr. -1-3). pap. 8.99 (978-0-312-56422-3(8), 900074775) Square Fish.

—C d C ? Steig, William. 2008. (ENG.). 64p. (J). (gr. 1-4). pap. 9.99 (978-0-312-38012-0(7), 900050537) Square Fish.

—Cdb! Steig, William. 2003. (ENG.). 48p. (J). (gr. k-3). pap. 8.99 (978-0-689-85706-5(3), Aladdin) Simon & Schuster Children's Publishing.

—Doctor de Soto. Steig, William. 2010. (ENG.). 32p. (J). (gr. -1-3). pap. 8.99 (978-0-312-61189-7(7), 900065535) Square Fish.

—Doctor de Soto Book & CD Storytime Set, 1 vol. Steig, William. unabr. ed. 2012. (Macmillan Young Listeners Story Time Sets Ser.). (ENG.). (J). (gr. k-3). 12.99 (978-1-4272-3219-9(9), 900122268) Macmillan Audio.

—Farmer Palmer's Wagon Ride. Steig, William. 2014. (ENG.). 32p. (J). (gr. -1-3). 6.99 (978-1-250-05791-4(4), 900139546) Square Fish.

—Grown-Ups Get to Do All the Driving. Steig, William. gif. ed. 2003. (ENG.). 48p. (J). (gr. k-3). 10.95 (978-1-57505-617-3(8)) Lerner Publishing Group.

—Pete's a Pizza Board Book. Steig, William. 2003. (ENG.). 34p. (J). (gr. -1 — 1). bds. 7.99 (978-0-06-052754-9(4), HarperFestival) HarperCollins Pubs.

—The Real Thief. Steig, William. 2007. (ENG.). 64p. (J). (gr. 2-5). per. 8.99 (978-0-312-37145-6(4), 900044683) Square Fish.

—Shrek! Steig, William. 20th anniv. ed. 2010. (ENG.). 40p. (J). (gr. -1-3). 18.99 (978-0-374-36879-1(1), 900065703, Farrar, Straus & Giroux (BYR)) Farrar, Straus & Giroux.

—Shrek! Steig, William. 2003. (J). (gr. -1-2). pap. 35.95 incl. audio compact disk (978-1-59112-551-8(0)) Live Oak Media.

—Shrek! Steig, William. 2008. (ENG.). 32p. (J). (gr. -1-3). pap. 8.99 (978-0-312-38449-4(1), 900053435) Square Fish.

—Shrek! (Book & CD Set), Set. Steig, William. unabr. ed. 2009. (Macmillan Young Listeners Story Time Sets Ser.). (ENG.). (J). (gr. -1-3). 9.99 (978-1-4272-0827-9(1), 900063826) Macmillan Audio.

—Spinky Sulks. Steig, William. 2011. (ENG.). 32p. (J). (gr. -1-1). pap. 8.99 (978-0-312-67246-1(2), 900072229) Square Fish.

—Sylvester & the Magic Pebble. Steig, William. 2012. (ENG.). 32p. (J). (gr. -1-2). pap. 9.99 (978-1-4424-3560-5(7), Little Simon) Little Simon.

—Sylvester & the Magic Pebble. Steig, William. 2005. (ENG.). 42p. (J). (gr. -1-3). 19.99 (978-1-4169-0206-5(6), Simon & Schuster Bks. For Young Readers) Simon & Schuster Bks. For Young Readers.

—Sylvester & the Magic Pebble. Steig, William. 2006. (Stories to Go! Ser.). 32p. (J). (gr. -1-3). 4.99 (978-1-4169-1857-8(4), Simon & Schuster/Paula Wiseman Bks.) Simon & Schuster/Paula Wiseman Bks.

—When Everybody Wore a Hat. Steig, William. 40p. (J). 2003. (gr. k-5). lib. bdg. 18.89 (978-0-06-009701-1(9), Cotler, Joanna Books); 2005. (ENG.). (gr. -1-3). reprint ed. pap. 8.99 (978-0-06-009702-8(7)) HarperCollins Pubs.

Stein, David Ezra. Because Amelia Smiled. Stein, David Ezra. 2012. (ENG.). 40p. (J). (gr. -1-2). 17.99 (978-0-7636-4169-6(3)) Candlewick Pr.

—Cowboy Ned & Andy. Stein, David Ezra. (ENG.). 32p. (J). (gr. -1-1). 2011. 6.99 (978-1-4424-3619-0(0)); 2006. 16.99 (978-1-4169-0041-2(1)) Simon & Schuster/Paula Wiseman Bks. (Simon & Schuster/Paula Wiseman Bks.).

—Dinosaur Kisses. Stein, David Ezra. (J). (-k). 2014. 34p. bds. 6.99 (978-0-7636-7389-5(7)); 2013. 32p. 15.99 (978-0-7636-6104-5(X)) Candlewick Pr.

—Honey. Stein, David Ezra. (ENG.). (J). (— 1). 2020. 34p. bds. 7.99 (978-0-593-10820-8(5)); 2018. 32p. 16.99 (978-1-5247-3786-3(0)) Penguin Young Readers Group. (Nancy Paulsen Books).

—Hush, Little Bunny. Stein, David Ezra. 2019. (ENG.). 40p. (J). (gr. -1-3). 17.99 (978-0-06-284522-1(5), Balzer & Bray) HarperCollins Pubs.

—Ice Boy. Stein, David Ezra. (J). (gr. -1-2). 2019. 32p. 6.99 (978-1-5362-0893-1(0)); 2017. (ENG.). 40p. 15.99 (978-0-7636-8203-3(9)) Candlewick Pr.

—I'm My Own Dog. Stein, David Ezra. 2014. 32p. (J). (gr. -1-3). 16.99 (978-0-7636-6139-7(2)) Candlewick Pr.

—Interrupting Chicken. Stein, David Ezra. (J). 2019. 34p. (-k). bds. 8.99 (978-1-5362-0672-2(5)); 2016. (ENG.). 40p. (gr. -1-3). 7.99 (978-0-7636-8903-2(3)); 2010. (ENG.). 40p. (gr. -1-3). 16.99 (978-0-7636-4168-9(5)) Candlewick Pr.

—Interrupting Chicken & the Elephant of Surprise. Stein, David Ezra. 2018. (ENG.). 40p. (J). (gr. -1-3). 16.99 (978-0-7636-8842-4(8)) Candlewick Pr.

—Leaves. Stein, David Ezra. (ENG.). (J). (gr. -1 — 1). 2010. 30p. bds. 7.99 (978-0-399-25497-0(8)); 2007. 32p. 16.99 (978-0-399-24636-4(3)) Penguin Young Readers Group. (G.P. Putnam's Sons Books for Young Readers).

—The Nice Book. Stein, David Ezra. 2013. (ENG.). 32p. (J). (gr. -1 — 1). bds. 7.99 (978-0-399-16534-4(7), Nancy Paulsen Books) Penguin Young Readers Group.

—Pouch! Stein, David Ezra. 2012. (ENG.). 32p. (J). (gr. -1 — 1). bds. 7.99 (978-0-399-25738-4(1), Nancy Paulsen Books) Penguin Young Readers Group.

Stein, Harve. Young Cowboys at the Broken Arrow. Bell, Marion R. & Geyer, Donna M. 2011. 256p. 47.95 (978-1-258-10205-0(6)) Literary Licensing, LLC.

Stein, Laurie. Fred's Wish for Fish. Landman, Yael & Hill, Barbara. 2009. 8p. (J). (978-0-545-16144-2(4)) Scholastic, Inc.

—Spectacularly Beautiful: A Refugee's Story. Lucas, Lisa. 2018. (ENG.). 32p. (J). (gr. -1-2). 16.99 (978-1-57687-891-0(0), powerHouse Bks.) powerHse. Bks.

Steinbach, Coreen. My Dad Is an Ironman. Hoese, Ray. 2004. (ENG.). 32p. (J). 15.00 (978-1-891369-51-3(2)) Breakaway Bks.

Steinbach, Hans. A Midnight Opera: Act 2, Vol. 2. Steinbach, Hans. 2006. 176p. per. 14.99 (978-1-59816-471-8(6), Tokyopop Adult) TOKYOPOP, Inc.

Steinbauer, Larry. Tommy the Timid Turtle. Swartz, Neva. 2004. (ENG.). 24p. (J). 19.95 (978-1-878044-75-4(3)) Mayhaven Publishing, Inc.

Steiner, Elke. Bella's Brazilian Football. Steiner, Elke. Guillain, Adam. 2007. (Bella Balistica Ser.). (ENG.). 32p. (J). (gr. k-2). pap. 8.95 (978-1-84059-488-1(8)) Milet Publishing.

Steiner, Maria. God Gave Us Fathers & Mothers. Newswanger, Rebecca. 2009. (Little Jewel Book Ser.). 24p. (J). (gr. 2). pap. 2.70 (978-0-7399-2408-2(7)) Rod & Staff Pubs., Inc.

Steiner, Sage. Emma Goes to School. Pack, Kristin. 2017. (ENG.). (J). 19.99 (978-0-9993624-0-2(2)) Pack, Kristin.

Steinfeld, Allison. Kid Activists: True Tales of Childhood from Champions of Change. Stevenson, Robin. 2019. (Kid Legends Ser.: 6). 208p. (J). (gr. 4-7). 13.99 (978-1-68369-141-9(5)) Quirk Bks.

Steinhardt, Marge. Letters to Antonio Andrew Anderson from His Mother. Mills Inc. 2011. 36p. pap. 35.95 (978-1-258-10331-6(1)) Literary Licensing, LLC.

Steinke, Aron Nels. The Zoo Box. Cohn, Ariel. 2014. (ENG.). 48p. (J). (gr. k-2). 17.99 (978-1-62672-052-7(5), 900133006, First Second Bks.) Roaring Brook Pr.

Steinkellner, Emma. The Okay Witch. Steinkellner, Emma. 2019. (Okay Witch Ser.: 1). (ENG.). 272p. (J). (gr. 3-7). 20.99 (978-1-5344-3146-1(2)); pap. 12.99 (978-1-5344-3145-4(4)) Simon & Schuster Children's Publishing. (Aladdin).

Steinlage, Kelly. Frollica & Frenzi: New York City Friends. Ramsey, Charmaine J. 2009. 36p. pap. 15.49 (978-1-4490-0487-3(3)) AuthorHouse.

Steinle, Shelley a. Birds of Paradise. Wight, Pamela S. 2018. (ENG.). 32p. (J). (gr. k-3). 17.99 (978-0-9984606-1-1(3)) Borgo Publishing.

Steinle, Shelley a. Molly FInds Her Purr. Wight, Pamela S. 2019. (ENG.). 32p. (J). 17.99 **(978-1-7339165-6-1(3))** Borgo Publishing.

Steinmark, Fran. The Little House in the Village. Steinmark, Fran. 2019. (ENG.). 30p. (J). (gr. k-4). 19.95 (978-0-9977582-2-1(8)) Steinmark, Frances.

Steinmark, Sharyl. Marvin Mallard & the Magic Medallion. Riva, Jim. 2004. 64p. (YA). pap. 14.95 (978-1-891262-03-6(3)) Soaring Sparrow Pr.

Steinwart, Coe. The Elf on the Shelf: Spanish Boy Dark Elf. Aebersold, Carol V. & Bell, Chanda. 2012. 32p. (J). lib. bdg. 15.00 net. (978-0-9769907-5-8(X)) CCA & B, LLC.

—The Elf on the Shelf: Spanish Girl Dark Elf. Aebersold, Carol V. & Chanda, Bell. 2012. (J). lib. bdg. 29.95 (978-0-9843651-6-6(8)) CCA & B, LLC.

—The Elf on the Shelf - a Christmas Tradition: Boy Light. Bell, Chanda & Aebersold, Carol. 2009. 32p. (J). lib. bdg. 29.95 (978-0-9769907-0-3(9)) CCA & B, LLC.

—The Elf on the Shelf - a Christmas Tradition: Girl Dark. Aebersold, Carol V. & Bell, Chanda. 2012. (J). lib. bdg. 29.95 (978-0-9843651-5-9(X)) CCA & B, LLC.

Stelfreeze, Brian & Martin, Laura. A Nation under Our Feet: Part 1. Coates, Ta-Nehisi. 2019. (Black Panther Ser.). (ENG.). 28p. (J). (gr. 6-12). lib. bdg. 27.07 (978-1-5321-4351-9(6), 31871, Marvel Age) Spotlight.

—A Nation under Our Feet: Part 2. Coates, Ta-Nehisi. 2019. (Black Panther Ser.). (ENG.). 28p. (J). (gr. 6-12). lib. bdg. 27.07 (978-1-5321-4352-6(4), 31872, Marvel Age) Spotlight.

—A Nation under Our Feet: Part 3. Coates, Ta-Nehisi. 2019. (Black Panther Ser.). (ENG.). 24p. (J). (gr. 6-12). lib. bdg. 27.07 (978-1-5321-4353-3(2), 31873, Marvel Age) Spotlight.

—A Nation under Our Feet: Part 4. Coates, Ta-Nehisi. 2019. (Black Panther Ser.). (ENG.). 24p. (J). (gr. 6-12). lib. bdg. 27.07 (978-1-5321-4354-0(0), 31874, Marvel Age) Spotlight.

Stelfreeze, Brian & Sprouse, Chris. Black Panther Vol. 1. 2017. (ENG.). 344p. (J). (gr. 4-17). 34.99 (978-1-302-90415-9(9)) Marvel Worldwide, Inc.

Stella D, Luna. Walter Is a Pig. Maxwell, David. 2020. (Goodnight Walter the Pig Bks.: Vol. 1). (ENG.). 28p. (J). pap. 14.95 **(978-1-6984-5567-9(4))** Independently Published.

Stelluto, Jessica. Pancakes for Breakfast, Pancakes for Lunch. Lloyd, Veronica M. 2017. (ENG.). (J). (gr. k-4). (978-0-9951879-4-8(0)) V Lloyd.

Steltzer, Ulli, photos by. Building an Igloo. Steltzer, Ulli. (ENG., 100p. (J). (gr. -1-2). (978-0-88899-118-8(5)) Groundwood Bks.

Stemen, Jeffrey. Critter Giggles. 2006. (J). (978-1-58987-035-2(2)) Kindermusik International.

Stemple, Jason, photos by. The Alligator's Smile: And Other Poems. Yolen, Jane. 2016. (ENG., 32p. (J). (gr. 3-6). 19.99 (978-1-4677-5575-7(3), 9781467755757); E-Book 30.65 (978-1-5124-1110-2(8)) Lerner Publishing Group. (Millbrook Pr.).

—Birds of a Feather. Yolen, Jane. 2011. (ENG., 32p. (J). (gr. 4-7). 17.95 (978-1-59078-830-1(3), Wordsong) Boyds Mills Pr.

—Bug off! Creepy, Crawly Poems: Creepy, Crawly Poems. Yolen, Jane. 2012. (ENG., 32p. (J). (gr. k-4). 17.95 (978-1-59078-862-2(1), Wordsong) Boyds Mills Pr.

—Color Me a Rhyme: Nature Poems for Young People. Yolen, Jane. 2003. (ENG., 32p. (J). (gr. -1-1). pap. 7.95 (978-1-59078-172-2(4), Wordsong) Boyds Mills Pr.

—Count Me a Rhyme: Animal Poems by the Numbers. Yolen, Jane. 2014. (ENG., 32p. (J). (gr. 1-4). pap. 7.95 (978-1-62091-733-6(5), Wordsong) Boyds Mills Pr.

—An Egret's Day. Yolen, Jane. 2010. (ENG., 32p. (J). (gr. 4-7). 17.95 (978-1-59078-650-5(5), Wordsong) Boyds Mills Pr.

—A Mirror to Nature: Poems about Reflection. Yolen, Jane. 32p. (J). (gr. 2). 2019. pap. 8.95 (978-1-68437-278-2(X)); 2009. (ENG., 17.95 (978-1-59078-624-6(6)) Boyds Mills Pr. (Wordsong).

—On the Slant. Yolen, Jane. 2009. (ENG., 56p. (J). pap. 8.00 (978-1-57274-978-8(4), Author at Work) Owen, Richard C. Pubs., Inc.

—Shape Me a Rhyme: Nature's Forms in Poetry. Yolen, Jane. 2015. (ENG., 32p. (J). (gr. 1-4). 7.99 (978-1-62091-791-6(2), Wordsong) Boyds Mills Pr.

—Snow, Snow: Winter Poems for Children. Yolen, Jane. 2005. (ENG., 32p. (J). (gr. 4-7). pap. 12.95 (978-1-59078-346-7(8)) Boyds Mills Pr.

—Water Music: Poems for Children. Yolen, Jane. 2003. (ENG., 40p. (J). (gr. 4-7). pap. 9.99 (978-1-59078-251-4(8), Wordsong) Boyds Mills Pr.

Stengel, Michelle, photos by. Terror in the Darkness (Confessions of a Stalked Fan) Darnell, Yolanda. 2005. 260p. (YA). (gr. 9-18). pap. 14.99 (978-1-884429-28-6(9), B-104) Papilion Pr.

Stensaas, Martin & Strasburg, Sunny. Gingerbread Jimmi: Magical Storybook. Holbrook, John Robert. Scott, Catherine, ed. 2004. (J). 19.95 (978-0-9762440-0-4(4)) Holbrook Studios.

Stensen, Cindy. I Never Get Scared. Knutson, Eric. 2010. (J). (978-1-930596-99-3(5)) Amherst Pr.

Stenton, Murray. Justin Fights Sleep. Vien, Ashley. 2018. (J). pap. (978-1-61599-376-5(2)); (978-1-61599-383-3(5)) Loving Healing Pr., Inc.

—Logan & the Magic Tree. Hanif, Cristina. 2019. (J). (978-1-61599-422-9(X)) Loving Healing Pr., Inc.

Stenton, Murray. Miss Popular Steals the Show: Girls in Wheelchairs Rule! Kats, Jewel. (J). 2019. (ENG.). 42p. (gr. 2-4). 26.95 **(978-1-61599-477-9(7)**, Marvelous Spirit Pr.); 2014. 37p. pap. 14.95 (978-1-61599-236-2(7)) Loving Healing Pr., Inc.

Stenton, Murray. My Brother Is Special: A Sibling with Cerebral Palsy. 2016. (J). pap. (978-1-61599-309-3(6)) Loving Healing Pr., Inc.

Stenton, Murray. My Brother Is Special: A Cerebral Palsy Story. Stenton, Murray. 2017. (ENG.). (J). (gr. k-2). 27.95 (978-1-61599-326-0(6)) Loving Healing Pr., Inc.

Stephen, Alice Barbar. Mother Carey's Chickens: Illustrated. Wiggin, Kate Douglas. 2019. (ENG.). 384p. (J). (gr. 4-6). pap. 9.99 **(978-1-68422-399-2(7))** Martino Fine Bks.

Stephen, Lib. The Bird House, 4 Bks., Pack. Wernham, Sara. 2008. (Jolly Phonics Readers, Complete Set Level 4 Ser.). (ENG.). 16p. (J). pap. 14.00 (978-1-84414-054-1(7)) Jolly Learning, Ltd. GBR. Dist: American International Distribution Corp.

—Dictionary. Wernham, Sara & Lloyd, Sue. 2003. (Jolly Grammar Ser.: DICTIONARY). (ENG.). 300p. (J). pap. 13.95 (978-1-84414-001-5(6), JL016, Jolly Learning) Jolly Learning, Ltd. GBR. Dist: American International Distribution Corp.

—Finger Phonics,, 1-7 Bks., Set. Wernham, Sara & Lloyd, Sue. 2013. (ENG.). (J). pap. 124.95 (978-1-84414-386-3(4), Jolly Phonics) Jolly Learning, Ltd. GBR. Dist: American International Distribution Corp.

—Grammar, Bk. 1-7. Wernham, Sara & Lloyd, Sue. 2015. (ENG.). (J). pap., wbk. ed. 22.50 (978-1-84414-470-9(4), Jolly Learning) Jolly Learning, Ltd. GBR. Dist: American International Distribution Corp.

—Grammar 1. Wernham, Sara & Lloyd, Sue. 2015. (Grammar 1 Workbooks 1-6 (in Print Letters) Ser.). (ENG.). (J). pap., wbk. ed. 3.75 (978-1-84414-464-8(X), Jolly Learning) Jolly Learning, Ltd. GBR. Dist: American International Distribution Corp.

—Grammar 1, Ages 5+ Wernham, Sara & Lloyd, Sue. 2015. (Grammar 1 Workbooks 1-6 (in Print Letters) Ser.). (ENG.). (J). pap., wbk. ed. 3.75 (978-1-84414-466-2(6)); pap., wbk. ed. 3.75 (978-1-84414-468-6(2)); pap., wbk. ed. 3.75 (978-1-84414-469-3(0)); pap., wbk. ed. 3.75 (978-1-84414-465-5(8)); pap., wbk. ed. 3.75 (978-1-84414-467-9(4)) Jolly Learning, Ltd. GBR. (Jolly Learning). Dist: American International Distribution Corp.

—Grammar 6 Student Book: In Print Letters (American English Edition) Wernham, Sara & Lloyd, Sue. 2018. (ENG.). (J). (gr. 6-6). pap., stu. ed. 8.20 (978-1-84414-517-1(4), Jolly Phonics) Jolly Learning, Ltd. GBR. Dist: American International Distribution Corp.

—Grammar 6 Teacher's Book: In Print Letters (American English Edition) Wernham, Sara & Lloyd, Sue. 2018. (ENG.). (J). (gr. 6). pap., tchr. ed. 9.40 (978-1-84414-518-8(2), Jolly Phonics) Jolly Learning, Ltd. GBR. Dist: American International Distribution Corp.

—Grammar Big Book 1: In Print Letters (American English Edition) Wernham, Sara & Lloyd, Sue. 2019. (ENG.). 24p. (J). pap. 27.75 (978-1-84414-401-3(1), Jolly Phonics) Jolly Learning, Ltd. GBR. Dist: American International Distribution Corp.

—Grammar Big Book 2: In Print Letters (American English Edition) Wernham, Sara & Lloyd, Sue. 2019. (ENG.). (J). pap. 27.75 (978-1-84414-402-0(X), Jolly Phonics) Jolly Learning, Ltd. GBR. Dist: American International Distribution Corp.

—Jolly Phonics Activity Book 4: Ai, J, Oa, Ie, Ee, Or, 7 vols. Wernham, Sara & Lloyd, Sue. 2010. (Jolly Phonics Activity Books, Set 1-7 Ser.). (ENG.). 7p. (J). pap. (978-1-84414-156-2(X)) Jolly Learning, Ltd.

—Letter Sound Strips, 30 vols. Lloyd, Sue. 2012. (Jolly Phonics Ser.). (ENG.). (J). (gr. k-2). 14.50 (978-1-84414-030-5(X), Jolly Phonics) Jolly Learning, Ltd. GBR. Dist: American International Distribution Corp.

—My First Letter Sounds. Wernham, Sara & Lloyd, Sue. 2015. (ENG.). (J). bds. 9.50 (978-1-84414-475-4(5), Jolly Learning) Jolly Learning, Ltd. GBR. Dist: American International Distribution Corp.

—Phonic, 6 Bks., Pack. Wernham, Sara. 2003. (Jolly Phonics Readers, Complete Set Level 2 Ser.). (ENG.). 12p. (J). pap. 12.50 (978-1-903619-86-5(6), JL866, Jolly Learning) Jolly Learning, Ltd. GBR. Dist: American International Distribution Corp.

—Songs. Fyke, Laurie & Sinclair, Kerrie. 2005. (ENG.). (J). pap. 17.50 incl. audio compact disk (978-1-84414-079-4(2), Jolly Learning) Jolly Learning, Ltd. GBR. Dist: American International Distribution Corp.

—Stories: Join Our Adventures & Learn Your Sounds. Lloyd, Sue & Wernham, Sara. 2008. (ENG.). 80p. (J). 29.50 (978-1-84414-081-7(4), Jolly Learning) Jolly Learning, Ltd. GBR. Dist: American International Distribution Corp.

—The Tree That Blinked, 6 Bks., Vol. 3. Wernham, Sara. 2004. (Jolly Phonics Readers, Complete Set Level 3 Ser.). (ENG.). (J). pap. 14.00 (978-1-84414-008-4(3), Jolly Learning) Jolly Learning, Ltd. GBR. Dist: American International Distribution Corp.

—Word Book. Lloyd, Sue & Wernham, Sara. 2003. (ENG.). 48p. (J). (gr. k-2). pap. 4.50 (978-1-84414-028-2(8), Jolly Phonics) Jolly Learning, Ltd. GBR. Dist: American International Distribution Corp.

Stephen, Lib & Maddison, Kevin. The Bird House & Other Stories. Wernham, Sara. 2014. (ENG.). (J). pap. 14.50 (978-1-84414-427-3(5), Jolly Learning) Jolly Learning, Ltd. GBR. Dist: American International Distribution Corp.

—The Enormous Turnip, 6 Bks., Pack. Wernham, Sara. 2008. (Jolly Phonics Readers, Complete Set Level 4 Ser.). (ENG.). (J). pap. 14.00 (978-1-84414-061-9(X), Jolly Learning) Jolly Learning, Ltd. GBR. Dist: American International Distribution Corp.

—The Enormous Turnip & Other Stories. Wernham, Sara. 2014. (ENG.). (J). pap. 14.50 (978-1-84414-428-0(3), Jolly Learning) Jolly Learning, Ltd. GBR. Dist: American International Distribution Corp.

—Monster Party & Other Stories. Wernham, Sara. 2014. (ENG.). (J). pap. 13.00 (978-1-84414-422-8(4), Jolly Learning) Jolly Learning, Ltd. GBR. Dist: American International Distribution Corp.

—Phonic & Other Stories. Wernham, Sara. 2014. (ENG.). (J). pap. 13.00 (978-1-84414-421-1(6), Jolly Learning) Jolly Learning, Ltd. GBR. Dist: American International Distribution Corp.

—Phonic; Rainforests; Monster Party, 18 vols., Pack, Set. Wernham, Sara. 2003. (ENG.). (J). pap. 37.50 (978-1-84414-091-6(1), Jolly Learning) Jolly Learning, Ltd. GBR. Dist: American International Distribution Corp.

—Rainforests & More Nonfiction. Wernham, Sara. 2014. (ENG.). (J). pap. 13.00 (978-1-84414-423-5(2), Jolly Learning) Jolly Learning, Ltd. GBR. Dist: American International Distribution Corp.

—Snakes & More Nonfiction. Wernham, Sara. 2014. (ENG.). (J). pap. 14.50 (978-1-84414-426-6(7), Jolly Learning) Jolly Learning, Ltd. GBR. Dist: American International Distribution Corp.

—Soccer, 6 Bks., Set. Wernham, Sara. 2008. (Jolly Phonics Readers, Complete Set Level 4 Ser.). (ENG.). (J). pap. 14.00 (978-1-84414-068-8(7), Jolly Learning) Jolly Learning, Ltd. GBR. Dist: American International Distribution Corp.

—Soccer & More Nonfiction. Wernham, Sara. 2014. (ENG.). (J). pap. 14.50 (978-1-84414-429-7(1), Jolly Learning) Jolly Learning, Ltd. GBR. Dist: American International Distribution Corp.

—The Rocket & Other Stories. Wernham, Sara. 2014. (ENG.). (J). pap. 11.50 (978-1-84414-419-8(4), Jolly Learning) Jolly Learning, Ltd. GBR. Dist: American International Distribution Corp.

—The Three Billy Goats Gruff & Other Stories. Wernham, Sara. 2014. (ENG.). (J). pap. 14.50 (978-1-84414-425-9(9), Jolly Learning) Jolly Learning, Ltd. GBR. Dist: American International Distribution Corp.

—The Tree That Blinked & Other Stories. Wernham, Sara. 2014. (ENG.). (J). pap. 14.50 (978-1-84414-424-2(0), Jolly Learning) Jolly Learning, Ltd. GBR. Dist: American International Distribution Corp.

Stephen, Lib, jt. illus. see Maddison, Kevin.

Stephen, Marchesi, jt. illus. see Pukac, Michael.

Stephens, Bonnie. Yummy Yoga: Playful Poses & Tasty Treats. Bauer, Joy. 2019. (ENG.). 24p. (J). (gr. -1-17). 14.99 (978-1-4197-3824-1(0), Abrams Bks. for Young Readers) Abrams, Inc.

Stephens, Cyndi. ABCs Are Delicious. Stephens, Heather. 2019. (ENG.). 20p. (J). (978-1-5255-4162-9(5)); pap. (978-1-5255-4163-6(3)) FriesenPress.

Stephens, Erika Benitez. Charlie the Cat Gets Envious: Charlie Turns Green. Stephens, Erika Benitez. 2019. (ENG.). 38p. (J). pap. 9.25 (978-1-7976-4289-5(8)) Independently Published.

Stephens, Helen. Oliver Elephant. Peacock, Lou. 2018. (ENG.). 32p. (J). (-k). 16.99 (978-1-5362-0266-3(5), Nosy Crow) Candlewick Pr.

Stephens, Helen. The Big Adventure of the Smalls. Stephens, Helen. 2012. (ENG.). 32p. (J). (gr. -1-3). 15.99 (978-1-4424-5058-5(4), Aladdin) Simon & Schuster Children's Publishing.

—How to Hide a Lion. Stephens, Helen. 2013. (How to Hide a Lion Ser.: 1). (ENG.). 32p. (J). (gr. -1-3). 16.99 (978-0-8050-9834-1(8), 900121823, Holt, Henry & Co. Bks. For Young Readers) Holt, Henry & Co.

—How to Hide a Lion at Christmas. Stephens, Helen. 2019. (How to Hide a Lion Ser.: 2). (ENG.). 40p. (J). 17.99 (978-1-250-23079-9(9), 900209514, Holt, Henry & Co. Bks. For Young Readers) Holt, Henry & Co.

—Witchety Sticks & the Magic Buttons. Stephens, Helen. 2010. (ENG.). 32p. (J). (gr. -1-k). pap. 8.99 (978-1-4169-1107-4(3), Simon & Schuster Children's) Simon & Schuster, Ltd. GBR. Dist: Simon & Schuster, Inc.

Stephens, Jay. Eat It Up! Lip-Smacking Recipes for Kids. de Mariaffi, Elisabeth. 2004. 88p. 15.95 (978-2-89507-549-3(2)) Bayard Canada Livres CAN. Dist: Univ. of Toronto Pr.

S

Stephens, Joan Wilson. Wethechildren, Future Leaders - Patriotic 123. Catalani, Dorothy Kon & Catalani, Jim. 2010. 16p. pap. 10.95 *(978-1-936343-19-5(3))* Peppertree Pr., The.

Stephens, Matt. The Foolish Fox. Hawes, Alison. 2014. (Traditional Tales Ser.). (ENG.). 16p. (J). (gr. k-1). pap. 6.95 *(978-1-62521-558-1(4),* Capstone Classroom) Capstone.

Stephens, Matte. Tigers & Tea with Toppy. Kerley, Barbara & Kalt, Rhoda Knight. 2018. (ENG.). 48p. (J). (gr. -1-3). 18.99 *(978-1-338-13427-8(2),* Scholastic Pr.) Scholastic, Inc.

Stephens, Pat. Animal Groups: How Animals Live Together. Kaner, Etta. 2004. (Animal Behavior Ser.). (ENG.). 40p. (J). (gr. 2-6). 12.99 *(978-1-55337-338-4(3))* Kids Can Pr., Ltd. CAN. Dist: Hachette Bk. Group.

—Animals & Their Mates: How Animals Attract, Fight for & Protect Each Other. Hickman, Pamela. 2004. (Animal Behavior Ser.). (ENG.). 40p. (J). (gr. 2-6). 5.95 *(978-1-55337-546-3(7))* Kids Can Pr., Ltd. CAN. Dist: Hachette Bk. Group.

—Animals Hibernating: How Animals Survive Extreme Conditions. Hickman, Pamela. 2005. (Animal Behavior Ser.). (ENG.). 40p. (J). (gr. 2-6). 12.99 *(978-1-55337-663-7(3))* Kids Can Pr., Ltd. CAN. Dist: Hachette Bk. Group.

—Desert Animals. Hodge, Deborah. 2008. (Who Lives Here? Ser.). 24p. (J). (gr. -1-2). 14.95 *(978-1-55453-047-2(4))* Kids Can Pr., Ltd. CAN. Dist: Hachette Bk. Group.

—How Animals Eat. Hickman, Pamela. 2007. (Kids Can Read Ser.). 32p. (J). (gr. 1-3). 14.95 *(978-1-55453-031-1(8))* Kids Can Pr., Ltd. CAN. Dist: Hachette Bk. Group.

—How Animals Use Their Senses. Hickman, Pamela. 2006. (Kids Can Read Ser.). 32p. (J). (gr. 1-3). 14.95 *(978-1-55337-902-7(0))* Kids Can Pr., Ltd. CAN. Dist: Hachette Bk. Group.

—Rain Forest Animals. Hodge, Deborah. 2008. (Who Lives Here? Ser.). 24p. (J). (gr. -1-2). 14.95 *(978-1-55453-041-0(5))* Kids Can Pr., Ltd. CAN. Dist: Hachette Bk. Group.

—Savanna Animals. Hodge, Deborah. 2009. (Who Lives Here? Ser.). 24p. (J). (gr. -1-2). 18.69 *(978-1-55453-072-4(5))* Kids Can Pr., Ltd. CAN. Dist: Children's Plus, Inc.

—Wetland Animals. Hodge, Deborah. 2008. (Who Lives Here? Ser.). 24p. (J). (gr. -1-2). 14.95 *(978-1-55453-045-8(8))* Kids Can Pr., Ltd. CAN. Dist: Hachette Bk. Group.

—Who Lives Here? Desert Animals. Hodge, Deborah. 2008. (Who Lives Here? Ser.). (ENG.). 24p. (J). (gr. -1-2). pap. 12.99 *(978-1-55453-048-9(2))* Kids Can Pr., Ltd. CAN. Dist: Hachette Bk. Group.

—Who Lives Here? Forest Animals. Hodge, Deborah. 2009. (Who Lives Here? Ser.). (ENG.). 24p. (J). (gr. -1-2). 5.95 *(978-1-55453-071-7(7))* Kids Can Pr., Ltd. CAN. Dist: Hachette Bk. Group.

—Who Lives Here? Polar Animals. Hodge, Deborah. 2008. (Who Lives Here? Ser.). (ENG.). 24p. (J). (gr. -1-2). pap. 5.99 *(978-1-55453-044-1(X))* Kids Can Pr., Ltd. CAN. Dist: Hachette Bk. Group.

—Who Lives Here? Rain Forest Animals. Hodge, Deborah. 2008. (Who Lives Here? Ser.). (ENG.). 24p. (J). (gr. -1-2). pap. 12.99 *(978-1-55453-042-7(3))* Kids Can Pr., Ltd. CAN. Dist: Hachette Bk. Group.

—Who Lives Here? Savanna Animals. Hodge, Deborah. 2009. (Who Lives Here? Ser.). (ENG.). 24p. (J). (gr. -1-2). 5.95 *(978-1-55453-073-1(3))* Kids Can Pr., Ltd. CAN. Dist: Hachette Bk. Group.

Stephens, Sherry & Finnell, Cyndy. Don't You See It? Jungle Edition, 1 vol. Argo, Sandi & Argo, Kaitlyn. 2009. 39p. pap. 19.95 *(978-1-61546-322-0(4))* PublishAmerica, Inc.

Stephens, Surplus. Bryson's Big Adventure: My First Year. Carter, Kendra. 2019. (ENG.). 26p. (J). pap. 20.95 ***(978-1-4808-8393-2(X))*** Archway Publishing.

Stephenson, Alex. The Land of the Great Turtles. Wagnon, Brad. 2018. (ENG.). (J). (gr. k-4). pap. 14.00 *(978-1-939054-90-6(7))* Rowe Publishing.

Stephenson, Kristina. The Angel & the Dove: A Story for Easter, 1 vol. Piper, Sophie. 2010. 32p. (J). 12.99 *(978-0-8254-7897-0(9),* Lion Children's); (ENG.). (gr. -1-k). 12.99 *(978-0-7459-6123-1(1))* Lion Hudson PLC GBR. Dist: Kregel Pubns., Independent Pubs. Group.

—The Angel & the Lamb: A Story for Christmas, 1 vol. Piper, Sophie. 2009. 32p. (J). 12.99 *(978-0-8254-7887-1(1),* Lion Children's) Lion Hudson PLC GBR. Dist: Kregel Pubns.

Stephenson, Kristina. Baby's Little Bible, 1 vol. Toulmin, Sarah. 2020. 160p. (J). 9.99 ***(978-0-8254-4662-7(7))***; 9.99 ***(978-0-8254-4661-0(9))*** Kregel Pubns.

Stephenson, Kristina. Baby's Little Bible & Prayers, 2 vols. Toulmin, Sarah. ed. 2008. (ENG.). 1p. (J). (gr. k — 1). pap. 16.99 *(978-0-7459-6039-5(1))* Lion Hudson PLC GBR. Dist: Independent Pubs. Group.

—From the Day You Were Born, 1 vol. Piper, Sophie. ed. 2014. (ENG.). 24p. (J). (— 1). bds. 6.99 *(978-0-7459-6237-5(8))* Lion Hudson PLC GBR. Dist: Kregel Pubns.

—Thank You for Me! Bauer, Marion Dane. 2010. (ENG.). 32p. (J). (gr. -1-3). 17.99 *(978-0-689-85788-1(8),* Simon & Schuster Bks. For Young Readers) Simon & Schuster Bks. For Young Readers.

—The Time-for-Bed Angel. Stromberg, Ronica. ed. 2010. (ENG.). 32p. (J). (gr. -1-k). pap. 9.99 *(978-0-7459-6066-1(9))* Lion Hudson PLC GBR. Dist: Independent Pubs. Group.

Steptoe, Javaka. All of the Above. Pearsall, Shelley. 2007. 234p. (gr. 3-7). 18.00 *(978-0-7569-8144-0(1))* Perfection Learning Corp.

—Hot Day on Abbott Avenue. English, Karen. 2019. (ENG.). 32p. (J). (gr. -1-3). pap. 7.99 *(978-1-328-50006-9(3),* 1718045, Clarion Bks.) Houghton Mifflin Harcourt Trade & Reference Pubs.

—In Daddy's Arms I Am Tall: African Americans Celebrating Fathers. Schoeder, Alan. 2013. (ENG.). 32p. (J). pap. 10.95 *(978-1-58430-016-8(7))* Lee & Low Bks., Inc.

—Jimi: Sounds Like a Rainbow - A Story of the Young Jimi Hendrix. Golio, Gary. 2010. (ENG.). 32p. (J). (gr. 1-4). 17.99 *(978-0-618-85279-6(4),* 100567) Houghton Mifflin Harcourt Publishing Co.

—A Pocketful of Poems. Grimes, Nikki. 2018. (ENG.). 32p. (J). (gr. -1-3). pap. 7.99 *(978-1-328-49796-3(8),* 1717849, HMH Books For Young Readers) Houghton Mifflin Harcourt Publishing Co.

Steptoe, Javaka, jt. illus. see Christie, R. Gregory.

Steptoe, John. She Come Bringing Me That Little Baby Girl. Greenfield, Eloise. 2014. 32p. pap. 7.00 *(978-1-61003-336-7(1))* Center for the Collaborative Classroom.

Steptoe, John. Baby Says. Steptoe, John. 2018. (ENG.). 32p. (J). (gr. -1-4). 17.99 *(978-0-688-07423-4(5),* HarperCollins) HarperCollins Pubs. Ltd. GBR. Dist: HarperCollins Pubs.

—Baby Says Board Book. Steptoe, John. 2018. (ENG.). 26p. (J). (gr. -1-4). bds. 7.99 *(978-0-06-284753-9(8),* HarperFestival) HarperCollins Pubs.

—Mufaro's Beautiful Daughters. Steptoe, John. 2018. (Amistad Ser.). (ENG.). 32p. (J). (gr. -1-3). 17.99 *(978-0-688-04045-1(4),* Amistad) HarperCollins Pubs.

—Stevie. Steptoe, John. 2018. (Trophy Picture Bks.). (ENG.). 24p. (J). (gr. -1-3). pap. 7.99 *(978-0-06-443122-4(3),* HarperCollins) HarperCollins Pubs. Ltd. GBR. Dist: HarperCollins Pubs.

Steranka-Petit, Heather. Becky Says WOOF! A Story about a Dog Named Becky & Her Friends Around the World. Steranka-Petit, Heather. 2019. (ENG.). 34p. (J). pap. 12.95 *(978-1-0762-0574-2(7))* Independently Published.

Steranko. Compliments of the Domino Lady. Anderson, Lars. Harvey, Rich, ed. 2004. 96p. per. 14.95 *(978-0-9712246-6-7(8))* Bold Venture Pr.

—Magnus, Robot Fighter, Vol. 1. Simonson, Louise & Hendricks, Damion. 2005. (ENG.). 48p. pap. 6.95 *(978-1-59687-833-4(9))* IBks., Inc.

Stergios, Tina. Tell Me-Tell Me More.... Amazing Animals a to Z. Wong, Linda L. 2020. (ENG.). 34p. (J). (gr. k-2). 22.95 ***(978-1-941247-71-6(7))***; pap. 19.95 ***(978-1-941247-67-9(9))*** 3G Publishing, Inc.

Stergulz, Richard. Barack Obama: 44th U.S. President, 1 vol. Stille, Darlene R. 2013. (Beginner Biographies Ser.). (ENG.). 32p. (J). (gr. k-4). 28.50 *(978-1-61641-939-4(3),* 3467, Looking Glass Library) Magic Wagon.

—Jackie Robinson: Amazing Athlete & Activist, 1 vol. Stille, Darlene R. 2013. (Beginner Biographies Ser.). (ENG.). 32p. (J). (gr. k-4). 28.50 *(978-1-61641-940-0(7),* 3469, Looking Glass Library) Magic Wagon.

Sterle, Lisa. Steven Universe Original Graphic Novel: Camp Pining Play. Mannino, Nicole. 2019. (Steven Universe Ser.). (ENG.). 144p. (J). (gr. 4-7). pap. 14.99 *(978-1-68415-340-4(9))* Boom! Studios.

Sterling, Holly. Everybody Feels Jealous (Lerner Edition) Harvey, Moira. 2020. (Everybody Feels ... Ser.). (ENG.). 24p. (J). (gr. k-2). 27.99 ***(978-0-7112-5019-2(7))*** QEB Publishing Inc.

—Everybody Feels Lonely (Lerner Edition) Harvey, Moira. 2020. (Everybody Feels ... Ser.). (ENG.). 24p. (J). (gr. k-2). 27.99 ***(978-0-7112-5040-6(5))*** QEB Publishing Inc.

—Everybody Feels Shy (Lerner Edition) Harvey, Moira. 2020. (Everybody Feels ... Ser.). (ENG.). 24p. (J). (gr. k-2). 27.99 ***(978-0-7112-5044-4(8))*** QEB Publishing Inc.

—Everybody Feels Worried (Lerner Edition) Harvey, Moira. 2020. (Everybody Feels ... Ser.). (ENG.). 24p. (J). (gr. k-2). 27.99 ***(978-0-7112-5048-2(0))*** QEB Publishing Inc.

Sterling, Holly. 15 Things Not to Do with a Grandma. McAllister, Margaret. 2016. (15 Things Not to Do Ser.). (ENG.). 32p. (J). (gr. -1-2). 17.99 *(978-1-84780-854-7(9),* Frances Lincoln Children's Bks.) Quarto Publishing Group UK GBR. Dist: Hachette Bk. Group.

—15 Things Not to Do with a Puppy. McAllister, Margaret. 2018. (15 Things Not to Do Ser.). (ENG.). 32p. (J). (gr. -1-k). 17.99 *(978-1-78603-047-4(0),* Frances Lincoln Children's Bks.) Quarto Publishing Group UK GBR. Dist: Hachette Bk. Group.

Sterling, Holly. Karate Kids. Sterling, Holly. 2020. (ENG.). 32p. (J). (gr. -1-2). 16.99 *(978-1-5362-1457-4(4))* Candlewick Pr.

Sterling, Louse. The Lost Beach. Ezinwoke, Patience. 2017. (ENG.). (J). pap. 5.99 *(978-978-100-656-2(0))* Lantern Publishing & Media.

Sterling, Susan Fisher. Everett, the Incredibly Helpful Helper. 2008. (ENG.). 40p. (J). (gr. -1-k). 14.95 *(978-0-7892-1001-2(0),* 791001, Abbeville Kids) Abbeville Pr., Inc.

Sterling, Zachary. Adventure Time Original Graphic Novel: Marceline the Pirate Queen: Marceline the Pirate Queen. Williams, Leah. 2019. (Adventure Time Ser.). (ENG.). 144p. (J). (gr. 4-7). pap. 14.99 *(978-1-68415-305-3(0))* Boom! Studios.

—Adventure Time Original Graphic Novel Vol. 11: Princess & Princess. Sorese, Jeremy. 2018. (Adventure Time Ser.: 11). (ENG.). 144p. (J). (gr. 4-7). pap. 14.99 *(978-1-68415-025-0(6))* Boom! Studios.

—Adventure Time Original Graphic Novel Vol. 12: Thunder Road: Thunder Road. Sorese, Jeremy. 2018. (ENG.). 144p. (J). (gr. 4-7). pap. 14.99 *(978-1-68415-179-0(1))* Boom! Studios.

Sterling, Zack. Adventure Time Original Graphic Novel Vol. 2: Pixel Princesses: Pixel Princesses, Vol. 2. Corsetto, Danielle. 2013. (Adventure Time Ser.: 2). (ENG.). 160p. (J). (gr. 4-7). pap. 11.99 *(978-1-60886-329-7(8))* Boom! Studios.

Stern, Chani. Making Hashem Proud: Stories of Kiddush Hashem in Everyday Life. Pfeiffer, Chaviva Krohn. 2014. 48p. (J). *(978-1-4226-1464-8(6))* Mesorah Pubns., Ltd.

Stern, Elsa Charretier: Sarah. Leia. Charretier, Elsa & Colinet, Pierrick. 2018. (Star Wars: Forces of Destiny Ser.). (ENG.). 24p. (J). (gr. 4-9). lib. bdg. 27.07 *(978-1-5321-4294-9(3),* 31120, Graphic Novels) Spotlight.

Stern, Marie Simchow. Favorite Psalms for Children. 2011. 40p. pap. 35.95 *(978-1-258-07228-5(9))* Literary Licensing, LLC.

Sternberg, Kate. Oh, Brother! Growing up with a Special Needs Sibling. Sternberg, Kate, tr. Hale, Natalie. 2004. 48p. (J). 14.95 *(978-1-59147-060-1(9))*; pap. 9.95 *(978-1-59147-061-8(7))* American Psychological Assn. (Magination Pr.).

Sterne, René & De Spiegeleer, Chantal. The Curse of the 30 Pieces of Silver, Pt. 1. Van Hamme, Jean. 2012. (Blake & Mortimer Ser.: 13). (ENG.). 62p. (J). (gr. 5-12). pap. 15.95 *(978-1-84918-125-9(X))* CineBook GBR. Dist: National Bk. Network.

Sternhagen, Mimi. The Beatitudes for Children. Gortler, Rosemarie & Piscitelli, Donna. 2009. 64p. (J). (gr. -1-3). pap. 6.95 *(978-1-59276-545-4(9))* Our Sunday Visitor, Publishing Div.

—Just Like Mary. Gortler, Rosemarie & Piscitelli, Donna. 2003. 48p. (J). 5.95 *(978-1-931709-79-8(3))* Our Sunday Visitor, Publishing Div.

—Living the 10 Commandments for Children. Piscitelli, Donna & Gortler, Rosemarie. 2006. 48p. (J). pap. 6.95 *(978-1-59276-231-6(X))* Our Sunday Visitor, Publishing Div.

—The Mass Book for Children. Gortler, Rosemarie & Piscitelli, Donna. 2004. 48p. per. 5.95 *(978-1-59276-075-6(9))* Our Sunday Visitor, Publishing Div.

Sterns, Megan. Amazing Africa Projects. Mooney, Carla. 2010. (Build It Yourself Ser.). 128p. (J). (gr. 3-7). pap. 15.95 *(978-1-934670-41-5(3),* 4fd3eb69-fb4a-4d42-8456-a3bc7eccf519) Nomad Pr.

Sterrett, Virginia. Tanglewood Tales. Hawthorne, Nathaniel. 2012. (Calla Editions Ser.). (ENG.). 304p. (gr. 4). 40.00 *(978-1-60660-026-9(5))* Dover Pubns., Inc.

Sterrett, Virginia Frances. Arabian Nights. 2010. (ENG.). 182p. (J). pap. *(978-606-92253-4-9(1))* Mediamorphosis.

—Old French Fairy Tales (Vol. 1) Comtesse De Segur, Sophie Rostopchine & Saegur, Sophie. 2010. (ENG.). 128p. (J). (gr. 3-7). pap. *(978-606-92253-0-1(9))* Mediamorphosis.

—Old French Fairy Tales (Vol. 2) Comtesse De Segur, Sophie Rostopchine & Saegur, Sophie. 2010. (ENG.). 130p. (J). (gr. 3-7). pap. *(978-606-92253-1-8(7))* Mediamorphosis.

—Tanglewood Tales. Hawthorne, Nathaniel. 2010. (ENG.). 198p. (J). (gr. 4-7). pap. *(978-606-92253-3-2(3))* Mediamorphosis.

Stetz, Ken. Christmas Tails. Leeds, Robert X. rev. ed. 2005. 55p. (J). 16.95 *(978-0-9674025-7-4(3))* EPIC Publishing Co.

—Words of Promise: A Story about James Weldon Johnson. Shull, Jodie A. 2005. (Creative Minds Biographies Ser.). (ENG.). 64p. (gr. 4-8). lib. bdg. 22.60 *(978-1-57505-755-2(7),* Carolrhoda Bks.) Lerner Publishing Group.

Steuerwald, Joy. A Little Piglet. Wren, Rosalee. Cottage Door Press, ed. 2018. (ENG.). 10p. (J). (gr. -1-k). bds. 4.99 *(978-1-68052-383-6(X),* 1003481) Cottage Door Pr.

—Moo Gift Set. Garnett, Jaye. Cottage Door Press, ed. 2019. (Book & Cuddly Plush Toy Friend Ser.). (ENG.). 12p. (J). (gr. -1-1). bds. 16.99 *(978-1-68052-758-2(4),* 1004690) Cottage Door Pr.

—Muu: Tapitas Curiosas en la Granja. Garnett, Jaye. Cottage Door Press, ed. 2019. (Peek-A-Flap Children's Interactive Lift-a-Flap Board Book Ser.). (SPA.). 12p. (J). (gr. -1-1). bds. 8.99 *(978-1-68052-843-5(2),* 1001170-SLA) Cottage Door Pr.

—On the Farm. Jordan, Karen. 2015. (Highlights(TM) Find It Board Bks.). (ENG.). 14p. (J). (— 1). bds. 7.99 *(978-1-62979-413-6(9),* Highlights) Boyds Mills Pr.

—One Christmas Story. Harper, Stephan J. 2003. 32p. (J). lib. bdg. 16.95 *(978-0-9741800-0-7(9))* Inspire Press, Inc.

Steuerwald, Joy. Tractor Tales. Redwing, Jack. Cottage Door Press, ed. 2020. (John Deere Rolling Tractor Toy Book Ser.). (ENG.). 24p. (J). (gr. -1-k). bds. 16.99 ***(978-1-68052-951-7(X),*** 1005940) Cottage Door Pr.

Steuerwald, Joy. The Peculiar Pig. Steuerwald, Joy. 2019. 32p. (J). (-k). 17.99 *(978-0-399-54887-1(4),* Nancy Paulsen Books) Penguin Young Readers Group.

Steuerwald, Joy, jt. illus. see Couvillian, Shelley.

Steuerwald, Joy, jt. illus. see Nowowiejska, Kasia.

Stevanovic, Ivica. Hercules & the Pooper-Scooper Peril. Hoena, Blake. 2019. (Michael Dahl Presents: Gross Gods Ser.). (ENG.). 64p. (J). (gr. 3-5). pap. 6.95 *(978-1-4965-8458-8(9),* 140983); lib. bdg. 21.99 *(978-1-4965-8357-4(4),* 140646) Capstone. (Stone Arch Bks.).

—Jack & the Wild Life, No. 2. Doan, Lisa. 2014. (Berenson Schemes Ser.: 2). (ENG.). 144p. (J). (gr. 4-6). 17.95 *(978-1-4677-1077-0(6),* 9781467710770, Darby Creek) Lerner Publishing Group.

—Jack at the Helm. Doan, Lisa. ed. 2015. (Berenson Schemes Ser.). (ENG.). 152p. (J). (gr. 4-6). E-Book 6.99 *(978-1-4677-7787-2(0),* 9781467777872, Darby Creek) Lerner Publishing Group.

—Jason & the Totally Funky Fleece. Hoena, Blake. 2019. (Michael Dahl Presents: Gross Gods Ser.). (ENG.). 64p. (J). (gr. 3-5). pap. 6.95 *(978-1-4965-8461-8(9),* 140986); lib. bdg. 21.99 *(978-1-4965-8360-4(4),* 140649) Capstone. (Stone Arch Bks.).

—Medusa & Her Oh-So-Stinky Snakes. Hoena, Blake. 2019. (Michael Dahl Presents: Gross Gods Ser.). (ENG.). 64p. (J). (gr. 3-5). pap. 6.95 *(978-1-4965-8460-1(0),* 140985); lib. bdg. 21.99 *(978-1-4965-8359-8(0),* 140648) Capstone. (Stone Arch Bks.).

—Michael Dahl Presents: Gross Gods. Hoena, Blake. 2019. (Michael Dahl Presents: Gross Gods Ser.). (ENG.). (J). (gr. 3-5). 87.96 *(978-1-4965-8361-1(2),* 29349); pap., pap., pap. 27.80 *(978-1-4965-8514-1(3),* 29595) Capstone. (Stone Arch Bks.).

—Monsters Can Mosey: Understanding Shades of Meaning, 1 vol. Olson, Gillia M. 2013. (Language on the Loose Ser.). (ENG.). 24p. (J). (gr. 2-4). 28.65 *(978-1-4048-8320-8(7))*; pap. 7.95 *(978-1-4795-1919-4(7))* Capstone. (Picture Window Bks.).

—Scarlett & Sam: Escape from Egypt. Kimmel, Eric A. 2015. (Scarlett & Sam Ser.). (ENG.). 168p. (J). (gr. 1-3). lib. bdg. 15.95 *(978-1-4677-3850-7(6),* 9781467738507); E-Book 23.99 *(978-1-4677-6207-6(5))* Lerner Publishing Group. (Kar-Ben Publishing).

—Search for the Shamir, Vol. Kimmel, Eric A. 2018. (Scarlett & Sam Ser.). (ENG.). 152p. (J). (gr. 1-3). pap. 6.99 *(978-1-5124-2938-1(4),* 9781512429381, Kar-Ben Publishing) Lerner Publishing Group.

—Theseus & the Maze-O-Muck. Hoena, Blake. 2019. (Michael Dahl Presents: Gross Gods Ser.). (ENG.). 64p. (J). (gr. 3-5). pap. 6.95 *(978-1-4965-8459-5(7),* 140984); lib. bdg. 21.99 *(978-1-4965-8358-1(2),* 140647) Capstone. (Stone Arch Bks.).

—Whale of a Tale. Kimmel, Eric A. 2019. (Scarlett & Sam Ser.). (ENG.). 152p. (J). (gr. 1-3). 15.99 *(978-1-5415-2216-9(8))*; pap. 6.99 *(978-1-5415-2217-6(6))* Lerner Publishing Group. (Kar-Ben Publishing).

Stevanovic, Tanja. My Pets, Your Pets, Our Pets. Berne, Emma Carlson. 2018. (How Are We Alike & Different? Ser.). (ENG.). 24p. (J). (gr. -1-2). pap. 7.95 *(978-1-68410-292-1(8),* 139063); lib. bdg. 33.99 *(978-1-68410-240-2(5),* 138444) Cantata Learning.

Steve, Lavigne. Shine Like a Lighthouse. Janis, Tim. 2nd ed. 2007. (J). 12.95 *(978-0-9773335-1-6(5))* Janis, Tim Ensemble, Inc.

Stevens. From Bobcat to Wolf: The Story of Den Seven, Pack Four. Gardner, L. S. 2011. 192p. 42.95 *(978-1-258-04225-7(8))* Literary Licensing, LLC.

Stevens, Art, jt. illus. see Paul, Leonard.

Stevens, Arthur A. The Sharing Circle: Stories about First Nations Culture, 1 vol. Meuse, Theresa. 2003. (ENG.). 52p. (J). (gr. 1-3). pap. 12.95 *(978-1-55109-450-2(9),* a5bfeeaa-46d9-4980-addf-2dc49fa73fb3) Nimbus Publishing, Ltd. CAN. Dist: Baker & Taylor Publisher Services (BTPS).

Stevens, Chris & Udon. G. I. Joe Master & Apprentice vol II. Jerwa, Brandon. 2006. (YA). per. 14.95 *(978-1-932796-45-2(2))* Devil's Due Publishing, Inc.

Stevens, Daniel. Can't & Able: An Inspirational Story. Fabian, Cynthia. 2012. 28p. pap. 12.50 *(978-1-61204-327-2(5),* Strategic Bk. Publishing) Strategic Book Publishing & Rights Agency (SBPRA).

—Orchestra in Our Brain: The Story of a Child with Epilepsy. Fabian, Cynthia. 2011. 20p. pap. 10.95 *(978-1-60976-783-9(7),* Eloquent Bks.) Strategic Book Publishing & Rights Agency (SBPRA).

Stevens, Dave. Weirdly Wonderful a to Z: Exotic, Aquatic Creatures from the West Coast of British Columbia, Canada. Stevens, Dave. 2016. (ENG.). 32p. (J). *(978-0-9950594-0-5(3))* Treewind Publishing.

Stevens, David S. Stepping Stones for Boys & Girls. Stevens, Margaret M. 2003. 32p. (gr. 5-18). 5.95 *(978-0-87516-248-5(7))* DeVorss & Co.

—Stepping Stones for Little Feet. Stevens, Margaret M. 2003. 31p. (gr. 4-6). 4.50 *(978-0-87516-202-7(9),* Devorss Pubns.) DeVorss & Co.

Stevens, David T. Eccnetric Earthlings A-Z: Fun Land Creatures from British Columbia, Canada. Stevens, Diane M. R. 2018. (ENG.). 32p. (J). *(978-0-9950594-2-9(X))* Treewind Publishing.

Stevens, Debra. Whos' Riley? Van Kersen, Elizabeth. l.t. ed. 2006. 23p. (J). 15.99 *(978-1-59879-173-0(7))* Lifevest Publishing, Inc.

Stevens, Helen. Moose Eggs: Or, Why Moose Has Flat Antlers. Beckhorn, Susan Williams. ed. 2007. (ENG.). 32p. (J). (gr. -1-3). 15.95 *(978-0-89272-689-9(X))* Down East Bks.

—Spirit of the Snowpeople. Keyes, Diane. ed. 2008. (ENG.). 32p. (J). (gr. -1-3). 15.95 *(978-0-89272-710-0(1))* Down East Bks.

Stevens, Janet. Anansi & the Magic Stick. Kimmel, Eric A. 2003. (J). 25.95 incl. audio *(978-1-59112-482-5(4))*; pap. 37.95 incl. audio *(978-1-59112-483-2(2))*; pap. 39.95 incl. audio compact disk *(978-1-59112-519-8(7))* Live Oak Media.

—Anansi Series. Kimmel, Eric A. 2003. pap. 68.95 incl. audio compact disk *(978-1-59112-840-3(4))*;Set. (J). pap. 61.95 incl. audio *(978-0-87499-469-8(1))* Live Oak Media.

—Anansi's Party Time. Kimmel, Eric A. (Anansi the Trickster Ser.: 5). (ENG.). 32p. (J). (gr. -1-3). 2009. pap. 7.99 *(978-0-8234-2241-8(0))*; 2008. 17.95 *(978-0-8234-1922-7(3))* Holiday Hse., Inc.

—Epossumondas Plays Possum. Salley, Coleen. 2009. (ENG.). 40p. (J). (gr. -1-3). 17.99 *(978-0-15-206420-4(6),* 1199212) Houghton Mifflin Harcourt Publishing Co.

—Tumbleweed Stew. Crummel, Susan Stevens. 2003. (Green Light Readers Level 2 Ser.). (ENG.). 32p. (J). (gr. -1-3). pap. 4.99 *(978-0-15-204830-3(8),* 1194585) Houghton Mifflin Harcourt Publishing Co.

—The Weighty Word Book. Levitt, Paul M. et al. 3rd ed. 2009. (ENG.). 96p. (J). 21.95 *(978-0-8263-4555-4(7))* Univ. of New Mexico Pr.

—Wild about Us! Beaumont, Karen. 2015. (ENG.). 40p. (J). (gr. -1-3). 17.99 *(978-0-15-206294-1(7),* 1198860, HMH Books For Young Readers) Houghton Mifflin Harcourt Publishing Co.

Stevens, Janet. Find a Cow Now! Stevens, Janet. Crummel, Susan Stevens. 2012. (ENG.). 32p. (J). (gr. -1-3). 16.95 *(978-0-8234-2218-0(6))* Holiday Hse., Inc.

—The Little Red Pen. Stevens, Janet. Crummel, Susan Stevens. 2011. (ENG.). 56p. (J). (gr. 1-4). 17.99 *(978-0-15-206432-7(X),* 1199238) Houghton Mifflin Harcourt Publishing Co.

—My Big Dog. Stevens, Janet. Stevens Crummel, Susan. 2009. (Golden Classic Ser.). (ENG.). 32p. (J). (gr. -1-2). pap. 7.99 *(978-0-375-85103-2(8),* Dragonfly Bks.) Random Hse. Children's Bks.

—Tumbleweed Stew/Sopa de Matojos. Stevens, Janet. Crummel, Susan Stevens. Flor Ada, Alma & Campoy, F. Isabel, trs. 2009. (Green Light Readers Level 2 Ser.). (ENG.). 36p. (J). (gr. -1-3). pap. 4.99 *(978-0-547-25261-2(7),* 1271215) Houghton Mifflin Harcourt Publishing Co.

S

Stevens, Judy. Stories of the Saints. Denham, Joyce. 2003. 48p. (J). pap. 11.99 *(978-0-7459-4637-5(2),* Lion Books) Lion Hudson PLC GBR. Dist: Trafalgar Square Publishing.

—Stories of the Saints. Denham, Joyce. 2007. (ENG.). 48p. (J). (gr. 4-7). pap. 9.95 *(978-1-55725-534-1(2))* Paraclete Pr., Inc.

Stevens, Mary. Good Old Archibald. Parkinson, Ethelyn. 2014. 145p. (J). pap. 14.95 *(978-1-932350-42-5(X))* Bethlehem Bks.

—Palace Wagon Family: A True Story of the Donner Party. Sutton, Margaret. 2011. 224p. 44.95 *(978-1-258-00668-6(5))* Literary Licensing, LLC.

—The Secret of the Mansion. Campbell, Julie. 2003. (Trixie Belden Ser.: 1). 272p. (J). (gr. 3-7). 8.99 *(978-0-375-82412-8(X),* Random Hse. Bks. for Young Readers) Random Hse. Children's Bks.

Stevens-Marzo, Bridget. The Big Book of Shapes. Cocagne, Marie-Pascale. 2009. (ENG.). 60p. (J). (gr. -1-3). 15.95 *(978-1-85437-851-4(1))* Tate Publishing, Ltd. GBR. Dist: Hachette Bk. Group.

Stevens, Matt. Encountering Chupacabra & Other Cryptids: Eyewitness Accounts, 1 vol. Peterson, Megan Cooley & Rustad, Martha E. H. 2014. (Eyewitness to the Unexplained Ser.). (ENG.). 32p. (J). (gr. 3-9). 31.32 *(978-1-4914-0242-9(3),* Capstone Pr.) Capstone.

—Special God. Melilli, Julie. 2018. 64p. (J). 16.99 *(978-1-4335-6251-8(0))* Crossway.

Stevens, Melissa. Sophie's Tails. Beynon, M. C. Bacher, Trish, ed. 2019. (ENG.). 58p. (J). pap. 5.99 *(978-1-5450-5814-5(8))* CreateSpace Independent Publishing Platform.

Stevens, Melissa. Sophie's Tails. Beynon, M. C. Bacher, Trish, ed. 2019. (ENG.). 62p. (J). (gr. k-4). pap. 4.99 ***(978-0-578-49900-0(2))*** M.C. Beynon.

—Sophie's Tails: Nothing but Trouble. Beynon, M. C. Bacher, Trish, ed. 2020. (Sophie's Tails Ser.: Vol. 2). (ENG.). 98p. (J). (gr. k-4). pap. 5.99 ***(978-1-7349499-0-2(2))*** M.C. Beynon.

Stevens, Tim. Brother Aelred's Feet: Band 15/Emerald (Collins Big Cat) Cross, Gillian. 2007. (Collins Big Cat Ser.). (ENG.). 40p. (J). (gr. 3-4). pap. 11.99 *(978-0-00-723093-8(1))* HarperCollins Pubs. Ltd. GBR. Dist: Independent Pubs. Group.

—Down with the Dirty Danes! Cross, Gillian. 2011. (ENG.). 64p. (J). pap. 5.99 *(978-0-00-715842-3(4),* HarperCollins Children's Bks.) HarperCollins Pubs. Ltd. GBR. Dist: HarperCollins Pubs.

Stevens, Tim & Wyatt, David. Troll Blood. Langrish, Katherine. 2008. 352p. (YA). (gr. 5-8). lib. bdg. 17.89 *(978-0-06-111675-9(0),* Eos) HarperCollins Pubs.

Stevens, Tracey. Chalice of the Goddess. Stevens, Tracey. Snowden, Susan, ed. 2004. 313p. (YA). per. 17.95 *(978-0-9719628-4-2(7))* Amazing Dreams Publishing.

Stevenson, Dave. A Dangerous Path. Hunter, Erin. 2005. (Warriors: the Prophecies Begin Ser.: 5). (ENG.). 336p. (J). (gr. 3-7). pap. 6.99 *(978-0-06-052565-1(7))* HarperCollins Pubs.

—The Darkest Hour. Hunter, Erin. 2005. (Warriors: the Prophecies Begin Ser.: 6). (ENG.). 368p. (J). (gr. 3-7). pap. 6.99 *(978-0-06-052585-9(1))* HarperCollins Pubs.

—Dawn. Hunter, Erin. 2006. (Warriors: the New Prophecy Ser.: 3). (ENG.). 400p. (J). (gr. 3-7). pap. 6.99 *(978-0-06-074457-1(X))* HarperCollins Pubs.

—The Dragon's Gate. Wolverton, Barry. (Chronicles of the Black Tulip Ser.: 2). (ENG.). (J). (gr. 3-7). 2017. 352p. pap. 6.99 *(978-0-06-222194-0(9));* 2016. 336p. 16.99 *(978-0-06-222193-3(0))* HarperCollins Pubs. (Walden Pond Pr.).

—Forest of Secrets. Hunter, Erin. 2004. (Warriors: the Prophecies Begin Ser.: 3). (ENG.). 336p. (J). (gr. 3-7). pap. 6.99 *(978-0-06-052561-3(4))* HarperCollins Pubs.

—Into the Wild. Hunter, Erin. 2004. (Warriors: the Prophecies Begin Ser.: 1). (ENG.). 288p. (J). (gr. 3-7). pap. 6.99 *(978-0-06-052550-7(9))* HarperCollins Pubs.

—Midnight. Hunter, Erin. 2006. (Warriors: the New Prophecy Ser.: 1). (ENG.). 352p. (J). (gr. 3-7). pap. 6.99 *(978-0-06-074451-9(0))* HarperCollins Pubs.

—Moonrise. Hunter, Erin. 2006. (Warriors: the New Prophecy Ser.: 2). (ENG.). 336p. (J). (gr. 3-7). pap. 6.99 *(978-0-06-074454-0(5))* HarperCollins Pubs.

—Rising Storm. Hunter, Erin. 2005. (Warriors: the Prophecies Begin Ser.: 4). (ENG.). 368p. (J). (gr. 3-7). pap. 6.99 *(978-0-06-052563-7(0))* HarperCollins Pubs.

—Twilight. Hunter, Erin. 2007. (Warriors: the New Prophecy Ser.: 5). (ENG.). 368p. (J). (gr. 3-7). pap. 6.99 *(978-0-06-082767-0(X))* HarperCollins Pubs.

—The Vanishing Island. Wolverton, Barry. (Chronicles of the Black Tulip Ser.: 1). (ENG.). (J). (gr. 3-7). 2016. 368p. pap. 6.99 *(978-0-06-222191-9(4));* 2015. 352p. 16.99 *(978-0-06-222190-2(6))* HarperCollins Pubs. (Walden Pond Pr.).

—The Vanishing Island. Wolverton, Barry. ed. 2016. (Chronicles of the Black Tulip Ser.: Vol. 1). (ENG.). 368p. (J). (gr. 3-7). 17.20 *(978-0-606-39260-0(2))* Turtleback.

—Warriors #1: into the Wild. Hunter, Erin. (Warriors: the Prophecies Begin Ser.: 1). (ENG.). (J). (gr. 3-7). 2015. 320p. pap. 7.99 *(978-0-06-236696-2(3));* 2003. 288p. 16.99 *(978-0-06-000002-8(3))* HarperCollins Pubs.

—Warriors #2: Fire & Ice. Hunter, Erin. (Warriors: the Prophecies Begin Ser.: 2). (ENG.). (J). (gr. 3-7). 2015. 368p. pap. 7.99 *(978-0-06-236697-9(1));* 2003. 336p. 16.99 *(978-0-06-000003-5(1))* HarperCollins Pubs.

—Warriors #3: Forest of Secrets. Hunter, Erin. (Warriors: the Prophecies Begin Ser.: 3). (ENG.). (J). (gr. 3-7). 2015. 368p. pap. 7.99 *(978-0-06-236698-6(X));* 2003. 336p. 16.99 *(978-0-06-000004-2(X));* 2003. 336p. lib. bdg. 17.89 *(978-0-06-052560-6(6))* HarperCollins Pubs.

—Warriors #4: Rising Storm. Hunter, Erin. (Warriors: the Prophecies Begin Ser.: 4). (ENG.). (J). (gr. 3-7). 2015. 368p. pap. 7.99 *(978-0-06-236699-3(8));* 2004. 336p. 16.99 *(978-0-06-000005-9(8))* HarperCollins Pubs.

—Warriors #5: a Dangerous Path. Hunter, Erin. 2015. (Warriors: the Prophecies Begin Ser.: 5). (ENG.). 368p. (J). (gr. 3-7). pap. 7.99 *(978-0-06-236700-6(5))* HarperCollins Pubs.

—Warriors #5: a Dangerous Path. Hunter, Erin. 2004. (Warriors: the Prophecies Begin Ser.: 5). (ENG.). 336p. (J). (gr. 3-7). 16.99 *(978-0-06-000006-6(6),* HarperCollins) HarperCollins Pubs. Ltd. GBR. Dist: HarperCollins Pubs.

—Warriors #6: the Darkest Hour. Hunter, Erin. (Warriors: the Prophecies Begin Ser.: 6). (ENG.). (J). (gr. 3-7). 2015. 368p. pap. 7.99 *(978-0-06-236701-3(3));* 2004. 336p. 17.99 *(978-0-06-000007-3(4))* HarperCollins Pubs.

—Warriors: the New Prophecy #1: Midnight. Hunter, Erin. (Warriors: the New Prophecy Ser.: 1). (ENG.). (J). (gr. 3-7). 2015. 352p. pap. 7.99 *(978-0-06-236702-0(1));* 2005. 320p. 17.99 *(978-0-06-074449-6(9))* HarperCollins Pubs.

—Warriors: the New Prophecy #2: Moonrise. Hunter, Erin. 2015. (Warriors: the New Prophecy Ser.: 2). (ENG.). 336p. (J). (gr. 3-7). pap. 7.99 *(978-0-06-236703-7(X))* HarperCollins Pubs.

—Warriors: the New Prophecy #2: Moonrise. Hunter, Erin. 2005. (Warriors: the New Prophecy Ser.: 2). (ENG.). 304p. (J). (gr. 3-7). 16.99 *(978-0-06-074452-6(9),* HarperCollins) HarperCollins Pubs. Ltd. GBR. Dist: HarperCollins Pubs.

—Warriors: the New Prophecy #3: Dawn. Hunter, Erin. (Warriors: the New Prophecy Ser.: 3). (ENG.). (J). (gr. 3-7). 2015. 400p. pap. 7.99 *(978-0-06-236704-4(8));* 2005. 352p. 16.99 *(978-0-06-074455-7(3))* HarperCollins Pubs.

—Warriors: the New Prophecy #4: Starlight. Hunter, Erin. (Warriors: the New Prophecy Ser.: 4). (ENG.). (J). (gr. 3-7). 2015. 368p. pap. 7.99 *(978-0-06-236705-1(6));* 2006. 336p. 16.99 *(978-0-06-082758-8(0))* HarperCollins Pubs.

—Warriors: the New Prophecy #5: Twilight. Hunter, Erin. (Warriors: the New Prophecy Ser.: 5). (ENG.). (J). (gr. 3-7). 2015. 368p. pap. 7.99 *(978-0-06-236706-8(4));* 2006. 336p. 16.99 *(978-0-06-082764-9(5))* HarperCollins Pubs.

—Warriors: the New Prophecy #6: Sunset. Hunter, Erin. (Warriors: the New Prophecy Ser.: 6). (ENG.). (J). (gr. 3-7). 2015. 352p. pap. 7.99 *(978-0-06-236707-5(2));* 2006. 320p. 16.99 *(978-0-06-082769-4(6))* HarperCollins Pubs.

—York: the Shadow Cipher. Ruby, Laura. (York Ser.: 1). (ENG.). 496p. (J). (gr. 3-7). 2018. pap. 7.99 *(978-0-06-230694-4(4));* 2017. E-Book *(978-0-06-230695-1(2));* 2017. 17.99 *(978-0-06-230693-7(6))* HarperCollins Pubs. (Walden Pond Pr.).

Stevenson, Emma. Hide-and-Seek Science: Animal Camouflage. Stevenson, Emma. 2014. (ENG.). 32p. (J). (gr. 1-4). 7.99 *(978-0-8234-3187-8(8))* Holiday Hse., Inc.

Stevenson, Harvey. Wilhe'mina Miles: After the Stork Night. Carter, Dorothy. 2005. 30p. (J). (gr. k-4). reprint ed. 16.00 *(978-0-7567-9421-7(8))* DIANE Publishing Co.

Stevenson, Harvey. Looking at Liberty. Stevenson, Harvey. 2003. 40p. (J). (gr. -1-2). 17.89 *(978-0-06-000101-8(1))* HarperCollins Pubs.

Stevenson, Irene. Archie the Inchworm That Wasn't. Boyce, Carla. 2019. (ENG.). 24p. (J). ***(978-1-5255-5850-4(1));*** pap. ***(978-1-5255-5851-1(X))*** FriesenPress.

Stevenson, James. Cool Zone with the Pain & the Great One. Blume, Judy. 2009. (Pain & the Great One Ser.: 2). (ENG.). 128p. (J). (gr. 3-7). 5.99 *(978-0-440-42093-4(8),* Yearling) Random Hse. Children's Bks.

—Friend or Fiend? with the Pain & the Great One. Blume, Judy. 2010. (Pain & the Great One Ser.: 4). (ENG.). 128p. (J). (gr. 3-7). 5.99 *(978-0-440-42095-8(4),* Yearling) Random Hse. Children's Bks.

—Going, Going, Gone! with the Pain & the Great One. Blume, Judy. 2010. (Pain & the Great One Ser.: 3). (ENG.). 128p. (J). (gr. 3-7). 5.99 *(978-0-440-42094-1(6),* Yearling) Random Hse. Children's Bks.

—Going, Going, Gone! with the Pain & Thegreat One. Blume, Judy. 2010. (Pain & the Great One (Quality) Ser.). (ENG.). (J). (gr. 3-7). lib. bdg. 16.60 *(978-1-60686-608-5(7))* Perfection Learning Corp.

—It's Raining Pigs & Noodles. Prelutsky, Jack. 2012. (ENG.). 160p. (J). (gr. k-5). reprint ed. pap. 9.99 *(978-0-06-076390-9(6),* Greenwillow Bks.) HarperCollins Pubs.

—My Dog May Be a Genius. Prelutsky, Jack. 2008. (ENG.). 160p. (J). (gr. k-5). 18.99 *(978-0-06-623862-3(5),* Greenwillow Bks.) HarperCollins Pubs.

—The New Kid on the Block. Prelutsky, Jack. 2013. (ENG.). 160p. (J). (gr. k-5). pap. 9.99 *(978-0-06-223950-1(3),* Greenwillow Bks.) HarperCollins Pubs.

—Something Big Has Been Here. Prelutsky, Jack. 2010. (ENG.). 160p. (J). (gr. k-5). pap. 10.99 *(978-0-06-185775-1(0),* Greenwillow Bks.) HarperCollins Pubs.

—Soupy Saturdays with the Pain & the Great One. Blume, Judy. 2007. (Pain & the Great One Ser.). (ENG.). 108p. (J). (gr. 2-4). lib. bdg. 18.69 *(978-0-385-90324-0(3),* Delacorte Pr.) Random Hse. Children's Bks.

—Soupy Saturdays with the Pain & the Great One. Blume, Judy. 2009. (Pain & the Great One Ser.: 1). (ENG.). 128p. (J). (gr. 3-7). 5.99 *(978-0-440-42092-7(X),* Yearling) Random Hse. Children's Bks.

Stevenson, James. Flying Feet: A Mud Flat Story. Stevenson, James. 2004. 48p. (J). 15.99 *(978-0-06-051975-9(4))* HarperCollins Pubs.

Stevenson, Noelle. The Fire Never Goes Out: A Memoir in Pictures. Stevenson, Noelle. 2020. (ENG.). 208p. (J). (gr. 9). 19.99 *(978-0-06-227827-2(4),* HarperTeen) HarperCollins Pubs.

—Nimona. Stevenson, Noelle. 2015. (ENG.). 272p. (J). (gr. 8). 18.99 *(978-0-06-227823-4(1));* pap. 14.99 *(978-0-06-227822-7(3))* HarperCollins Pubs. (HarperTeen).

Stevenson, Peter. Baby's First Nativity. ed. 2016. (ENG.). 20p. (J). (gr. -1-k). bds. 9.99 *(978-0-7944-3850-0(4))* Studio Fun International.

—Baby's First Nativity: A CarryAlong Treasury. ed. 2016. (Carry along Treasury Ser.: 1). (ENG.). 20p. (J). (gr. -1-k). bds. 14.99 *(978-0-7944-3836-4(9))* Studio Fun International.

—Catholic Baby's Bedtime Bible Stories. Zobel-Nolan, Allia. 2006. (First Bible Collection). (gr. -1-k). bds. 15.95 *(978-0-88271-067-9(2))* Regina Pr., Malhame & Co.

Stevenson, Robert, photos by. Already Legends: Stevenson Studios Sports Photo Journal. 2005. 160p. per. 29.95 *(978-0-9753434-5-6(9))* LeTay Publishing.

Stevenson, Seline. The Street Cats of Marrakech. Tóth-Jones, Dee S. 2013. 34p. pap. *(978-1-908794-08-6(9))* Chiaroscuro Bks.

Stevenson, Suçie. Annie & Snowball & the Cozy Nest. Rylant, Cynthia. 2009. (Ready-To-Read Level 2 Ser.: 5). (ENG.). 40p. (J). (gr. k-2). 16.19 *(978-1-4169-3943-6(1))* Simon & Schuster, Inc.

—Annie & Snowball & the Dress-Up Birthday. Rylant, Cynthia. 2008. (Annie & Snowball Ser.: 1). (ENG.). 40p. (J). (gr. k-2). pap. 4.99 *(978-1-4169-1459-4(5),* Simon Spotlight) Simon Spotlight.

—Annie & Snowball & the Magical House. Rylant, Cynthia. 2011. (Annie & Snowball Ser.: 7). (ENG.). 40p. (J). (gr. k-2). pap. 4.99 *(978-1-4169-3949-8(0),* Simon Spotlight) Simon Spotlight.

—Annie & Snowball & the Prettiest House. Rylant, Cynthia. 2007. (Annie & Snowball Ser.: 2). (ENG.). 40p. (J). (gr. k-2). 16.99 *(978-1-4169-0939-2(7),* Simon Spotlight) Simon Spotlight.

—Annie & Snowball & the Shining Star. Rylant, Cynthia. 2009. (Annie & Snowball Ser.: 6). (ENG.). 40p. (J). (gr. k-2). 17.99 *(978-1-4169-3946-7(6),* Simon Spotlight) Simon Spotlight.

—Annie & Snowball & the Surprise Day. Rylant, Cynthia. 2012. (Annie & Snowball Ser.: 11). (ENG.). 40p. (J). (gr. k-2). 16.99 *(978-1-4169-3944-3(X),* Simon Spotlight) Simon Spotlight.

—Annie & Snowball & the Teacup Club. Rylant, Cynthia. 2008. (Annie & Snowball Ser.: 3). (ENG.). 40p. (J). (gr. k-2). 16.99 *(978-1-4169-0940-8(0),* Simon Spotlight) Simon Spotlight.

—Annie & Snowball & the Thankful Friends. Rylant, Cynthia. (Annie & Snowball Ser.: 10). (ENG.). 40p. (J). (gr. k-2). 2012. pap. 4.99 *(978-1-4169-7202-0(1));* 2011. 15.99 *(978-1-4169-7200-6(5))* Simon Spotlight. (Simon Spotlight).

—Annie & Snowball & the Wedding Day. Rylant, Cynthia. 2014. (Annie & Snowball Ser.: 13). (ENG.). 40p. (J). (gr. k-2). 16.99 *(978-1-4169-7485-7(7),* Simon Spotlight) Simon Spotlight.

—Annie & Snowball & the Wintry Freeze. Rylant, Cynthia. 2011. (Annie & Snowball Ser.: 8). (ENG.). 40p. (J). (gr. k-2). pap. 3.99 *(978-1-4169-7206-8(4),* Simon Spotlight) Simon Spotlight.

—Annie & Snowball Collector's Set 2: Annie & Snowball & the Magical House; Annie & Snowball & the Wintry Freeze; Annie & Snowball & the Book Bugs Club; Annie & Snowball & the Thankful Friends; Annie & Snowball & the Surprise Day; Annie & Snowball & the Grandmother Night. Rylant, Cynthia. ed. 2019. (Annie & Snowball Ser.). (ENG.). 240p. (J). (gr. k-2). pap. 17.99 *(978-1-5344-3810-1(6),* Simon Spotlight) Simon Spotlight.

—Family Stories You Can Relate To: A Reading Rainbow Reader. Rylant, Cynthia. 2004. 64p. (J). (gr. 1-4). reprint ed. 15.00 *(978-0-7567-7150-8(1))* DIANE Publishing Co.

—Henry & Mudge & a Very Merry Christmas. Rylant, Cynthia. 2005. (Henry & Mudge Ser.). 40p. (gr. -1-3). 14.00 *(978-0-7569-5816-9(4))* Perfection Learning Corp.

—Henry & Mudge & the Big Sleepover. Rylant, Cynthia. 2007. (Henry & Mudge Ser.). 40p. (gr. k-2). lib. bdg. 14.00 *(978-0-7569-8117-4(4))* Perfection Learning Corp.

—Henry & Mudge & the Big Sleepover. Rylant, Cynthia. ed. 2007. (Henry & Mudge Ready-To-Read Ser.: 28). 40p. (gr. -1-3). lib. bdg. 13.55 *(978-1-4177-8140-9(8))* Turtleback.

—Henry & Mudge & the Great Grandpas. Rylant, Cynthia. 2006. (Henry & Mudge Ser.). 40p. (gr. k-2). 14.00 *(978-0-7569-6793-2(7))* Perfection Learning Corp.

—Henry & Mudge & the Great Grandpas. Rylant, Cynthia. 2006. (Henry & Mudge Ser.: 26). (ENG.). 40p. (J). (gr. k-2). pap. 4.99 *(978-0-689-83447-9(0),* Simon Spotlight) Simon Spotlight.

Stevenson, Suçie, et al. Henry & Mudge & the Great Grandpas. Rylant, Cynthia. 2005. (Henry & Mudge Ser.: 26). (ENG.). 40p. (J). (gr. k-2). 17.99 *(978-0-689-81170-8(5),* Simon Spotlight) Simon Spotlight.

Stevenson, Suçie. Henry & Mudge Get the Cold Shivers. Rylant, Cynthia. (Henry & Mudge Ser.). 9.95 *(978-1-59112-290-6(2))* Live Oak Media.

—Henry & Mudge Ready-To-Read Value Pack #2: Henry & Mudge & the Long Weekend; Henry & Mudge & the Bedtime Thumps; Henry & Mudge & the Big Sleepover; Henry & Mudge & the Funny Lunch; Henry & Mudge & the Great Grandpas; Henry & Mudge & the Tall Tree House. Rylant, Cynthia. 2013. (Henry & Mudge Ser.). (ENG.). 240p. (J). (gr. k-2). pap. 17.96 *(978-1-4424-9441-1(7),* Simon Spotlight) Simon Spotlight.

—Henry & Mudge the Complete Collection: Henry & Mudge; Henry & Mudge in Puddle Trouble; Henry & Mudge & the Bedtime Thumps; Henry & Mudge in the Green Time; Henry & Mudge & the Happy Cat; Henry & Mudge Get the Cold Shivers; Henry & Mudge under the Yellow Moon, Etc. Rylant, Cynthia. ed. 2018. (Henry & Mudge Ser.). (ENG.). 1120p. (J). (gr. k-2). pap. 111.99 *(978-1-5344-2713-6(9),* Simon Spotlight) Simon Spotlight.

—Puppy Mudge Finds a Friend. Rylant, Cynthia. 2004. (Puppy Mudge Ser.). (ENG.). 32p. (J). (gr. -1-k). 17.99 *(978-0-689-83982-5(0),* Simon Spotlight) Simon Spotlight.

—Puppy Mudge Wants to Play. Rylant, Cynthia. 2005. (Puppy Mudge Ser.). (ENG.). 32p. (J). (gr. -1-k). 16.99 *(978-0-689-83984-9(7),* Simon Spotlight) Simon Spotlight.

Stevenson, Suçie & Stevenson, Suçie. Annie & Snowball & the Book Bugs Club. Rylant, Cynthia. (Annie & Snowball Ser.: 9). (ENG.). 40p. (J). (gr. k-2). 2012. pap. 4.99 *(978-1-4169-7201-3(3));* 2011. 16.99 *(978-1-4169-7199-3(8))* Simon Spotlight. (Simon Spotlight).

—Annie & Snowball & the Cozy Nest. Rylant, Cynthia. 2010. (Annie & Snowball Ser.: 5). (ENG.). 40p. (J). (gr. k-2). pap. 4.99 *(978-1-4169-3947-4(4),* Simon Spotlight) Simon Spotlight.

—Annie & Snowball & the Dress-Up Birthday. Rylant, Cynthia. 2007. (Annie & Snowball Ser.: 1). (ENG.). 40p. (J). (gr. k-2). 16.99 *(978-1-4169-0938-5(9),* Simon Spotlight) Simon Spotlight.

—Annie & Snowball & the Grandmother Night. Rylant, Cynthia. (Annie & Snowball Ser.: 12). (ENG.). 40p. (J). (gr. k-2). 2013. pap. 4.99 *(978-1-4169-7204-4(8));* 2012. 16.99 *(978-1-4169-7203-7(X))* Simon Spotlight. (Simon Spotlight).

—Annie & Snowball & the Magical House. Rylant, Cynthia. 2010. (Annie & Snowball Ser.: 7). (ENG.). 40p. (J). (gr. k-2). 17.99 *(978-1-4169-3945-0(8),* Simon Spotlight) Simon Spotlight.

—Annie & Snowball & the Pink Surprise. Rylant, Cynthia. (Annie & Snowball Ser.: 4). (ENG.). 40p. (J). (gr. k-2). 2010. pap. 4.99 *(978-1-4169-1462-4(5));* 2008. 16.99 *(978-1-4169-0941-5(9))* Simon Spotlight. (Simon Spotlight).

—Annie & Snowball & the Prettiest House. Rylant, Cynthia. 2008. (Annie & Snowball Ser.: 2). (ENG.). 40p. (J). (gr. k-2). pap. 4.99 *(978-1-4169-1460-0(9),* Simon Spotlight) Simon Spotlight.

—Annie & Snowball & the Shining Star. Rylant, Cynthia. 2010. (Annie & Snowball Ser.: 6). (ENG.). 40p. (J). (gr. k-2). pap. 4.99 *(978-1-4169-3950-4(4),* Simon Spotlight) Simon Spotlight.

—Annie & Snowball & the Surprise Day. Rylant, Cynthia. 2013. (Annie & Snowball Ser.: 11). (ENG.). 40p. (J). (gr. k-2). pap. 4.99 *(978-1-4169-3948-1(2),* Simon Spotlight) Simon Spotlight.

—Annie & Snowball & the Teacup Club. Rylant, Cynthia. 2009. (Annie & Snowball Ser.: 3). (ENG.). 40p. (J). (gr. k-2). pap. 4.99 *(978-1-4169-1461-7(7),* Simon Spotlight) Simon Spotlight.

—Annie & Snowball & the Wedding Day. Rylant, Cynthia. 2015. (Annie & Snowball Ser.: 13). (ENG.). 40p. (J). (gr. k-2). pap. 4.99 *(978-1-4169-7486-4(5),* Simon Spotlight) Simon Spotlight.

—Annie & Snowball & the Wintry Freeze. Rylant, Cynthia. 2010. (Annie & Snowball Ser.: 8). (ENG.). 40p. (J). (gr. k-2). 16.99 *(978-1-4169-7205-1(6),* Simon Spotlight) Simon Spotlight.

—Henry & Mudge & a Very Merry Christmas. Rylant, Cynthia. 2004. (Henry & Mudge Ser.: 25). (ENG.). 40p. (J). (gr. k-2). 17.99 *(978-0-689-81168-5(3),* Simon Spotlight) Simon Spotlight.

—Henry & Mudge & the Big Sleepover. Rylant, Cynthia. (Henry & Mudge Ser.: 28). (ENG.). 40p. (J). (gr. k-2). 2006. 17.99 *(978-0-689-81171-5(3));* Bk. 28. 2007. pap. 4.99 *(978-0-689-83451-6(9))* Simon Spotlight. (Simon Spotlight).

—Henry & Mudge Ready-To-Read Value Pack: Henry & Mudge; Henry & Mudge & Annie's Good Move; Henry & Mudge in the Green Time; Henry & Mudge & the Forever Sea; Henry & Mudge in Puddle Trouble; Henry & Mudge & the Happy Cat. Rylant, Cynthia. 2012. (Henry & Mudge Ser.). (ENG.). 280p. (J). (gr. k-2). pap. 17.96 *(978-1-4424-4952-7(7),* Simon Spotlight) Simon Spotlight.

—Puppy Mudge Finds a Friend. Rylant, Cynthia. 2005. (Puppy Mudge Ser.). (ENG.). 32p. (J). (gr. -1-k). pap. 4.99 *(978-1-4169-0369-7(0),* Simon Spotlight) Simon Spotlight.

—Puppy Mudge Wants to Play. Rylant, Cynthia. 2006. (Puppy Mudge Ser.). (ENG.). 32p. (J). (gr. -1-k). pap. 4.99 *(978-1-4169-1556-0(7),* Simon Spotlight) Simon Spotlight.

Stevenson, Suçie, jt. illus. see Stevenson, Suçie.

Stewart, Ashley. Full Moon Lore. Wahl, Ellen. 2017. (ENG.). 32p. (J). (gr. k-3). 16.99 *(978-1-58536-965-2(9),* 204301) Sleeping Bear Pr.

Stewart, Cameron. One Thing Missing. Stewart, Beth Roper. 2019. (ENG.). 30p. (J). 24.95 *(978-1-64300-832-5(3));* pap. 15.95 *(978-1-64300-831-8(5))* Covenant Bks.

Stewart, Chantal. Dependable Dan. Zail, Suzy. 2004. iv, 36p. (J). pap. *(978-0-7608-6747-1(X))* Sundance/Newbridge Educational Publishing.

—Diary Disaster. Smith Dinbergs, Holly. 2005. (Girlz Rock! Ser.). (J). pap. *(978-1-59336-700-8(7))* Mondo Publishing.

—Hair Scare. Dinbergs, Holly Smith. 2005. (Girlz Rock! Ser.). (J). pap. *(978-1-59336-702-2(3))* Mondo Publishing.

—To the Light. Flynn, Pat. 2005. 120p. (Orig.). (YA). pap. *(978-0-7022-3492-7(3))* Univ. of Queensland Pr.

—Tortoise Soup! 2009. 24p. pap. 10.67 *(978-1-4190-5523-2(2))* Rigby Education.

Stewart, Dave, jt. illus. see Mignola, Mike.

Stewart, David. World of Gods & Goddesses. Morley, Jacqueline. 2013. (Mythology Ser.). (ENG.). 64p. (gr. 3-6). lib. bdg. 41.35 *(978-1-908973-92-4(7))* Book Hse. GBR. Dist: Black Rabbit Bks.

Stewart, Don. Blessed Pier Giorgio Frassati: Journey to the Summit. Vazquez, Ana Maria & Dean, Jennings. 2004. (Encounter Ser.: 18). 144p. (J). pap. 5.95 *(978-0-8198-1165-3(3),* 332-028) Pauline Bks. & Media.

Stewart, Edgar. They Dance in the Sky: Native American Star Myths. Williamson, Ray A. & Monroe, Jean Guard. 2007. (ENG.). 144p. (J). (gr. 5-7). pap. 8.95 *(978-0-618-80912-7(0),* 491700) Houghton Mifflin Harcourt Publishing Co.

Stewart, Emily D. Pink Baby Alligator. Barrett, Judith A. 2016. (ENG.). (J). pap. 9.99 *(978-0-9967207-5-5(8))* Marcinson Pr.

Stewart, Fion. On the Way Home. Chen, Julia. 2009. (J). *(978-0-9787550-6-5(5))* Heryin Publishing Corp.

Stewart, James. Guitar Method for Young Beginners, Book 1. Turner, Gary. 2006. (Young Beginner Giant Coloring Bks.). 36p. pap. incl. audio compact disk *(978-1-86469-096-5(8))* LearnToPlayMusic.com Pty Ltd.

—Keyboard Method for Young Beginners, Book 1. Turner, Gary. 2006. (Young Beginner Giant Coloring Bks.). 48p. pap. incl. audio compact disk *(978-1-86469-097-2(6))* LearnToPlayMusic.com Pty Ltd.

—Piano Method for Young Beginners, Book 1. Turner, Gary. 2006. (Young Beginner Giant Coloring Bks.). 44p. pap. incl. audio compact disk *(978-1-86469-098-9(4))* LearnToPlayMusic.com Pty Ltd.

—Recorder Method for Young Beginners, Book 1. Turner, Gary. 2006. (Young Beginner Giant Coloring Bks.). 36p. pap. *(978-1-86469-099-6(2))* LearnToPlayMusic.com Pty Ltd.

Stewart, Joel. The Cow Tripped over the Moon: a Nursery Rhyme Emergency. Willis, Jeanne. 2015. (ENG.). 32p. (J). (gr. -1-2). 15.99 *(978-0-7636-7402-1(8))* Candlewick Pr.

—The Magic Paintbrush. Donaldson, Julia. 2017. (ENG.). 32p. (J). (gr. -1-1). pap. 9.99 *(978-1-5098-3046-6(4))* Pan Macmillan GBR. Dist: Independent Pubs. Group.

—Moon Zoo. Duffy, Carol Ann. 2011. (ENG.). 32p. (J). (gr. -1-k). pap. 8.99 *(978-0-230-74805-7(8))* Pan Macmillan GBR. Dist: Independent Pubs. Group.

—Shark & Lobster's Amazing Undersea Adventure. Schwarz, Viviane. 2006. 34p. (J). *(978-1-4156-8140-4(6))* Candlewick Pr.

—Tales of Hans Christian Andersen. Andersen, Hans. 2010. (Candlewick Illustrated Classics Ser.). (ENG.). 208p. (J). (gr. 3-7). pap. 12.99 *(978-0-7636-4892-3(2))* Candlewick Pr.

Stewart, K. L. Happy the Hippo: Eats Healthy Food. Hoyes, Amy & Reimann, A. J. 2013. 24p. pap. 9.99 *(978-1-938743-08-5(3))* Reimann Bks.

Stewart, Lisa. Jam for Nana. Kelly, Deborah. 2014. 32p. (J). (gr. k-2). 9.99 *(978-0-85798-001-4(7))* Random Hse. Australia AUS. Dist: Independent Pubs. Group.

Stewart, Michael G. Noises from under the Rug: The Barry Louis Polisar Songbook. Polisar, Barry Louis. rev. ed. 2006. (ENG.). 32p. (gr. 4-7). per. 7.95 *(978-0-938663-24-9(0))* Rainbow Morning Music Alternatives.

Stewart, Muriel. My Mommy's Getting Married. Chambers, Pamela G. 2009. 32p. (gr. -1-3). 17.95 *(978-0-9799487-0-1(3))* Infinity Publishing Co.

Stewart, Pat, jt. illus. see Kerr, George.

Stewart, Pat Ronson, jt. illus. see Cady, Harrison.

Stewart, Pat Ronson, jt. illus. see Kerr, George.

Stewart, Phoebe E. L. A Flying Visit: Book One of the Salute Islands Treasury. Stewart, Lindzi J. 2019. (Salute Islands Treasury Ser.: Vol. 1). (ENG.). 258p. (J). pap. ***(978-1-913166-19-9(8))*** Heddon Publishing.

Stewart, Roger. Build a Birdhouse. Miller, Mirella S. 2016. (Earth-Friendly Projects Ser.). (ENG.). 24p. (J). (gr. 2-5). 28.50 *(978-1-5038-0783-9(5)*, 210619) Child's World, Inc., The.

—Build a Compact Garden. Bell, Samantha S. 2016. (Earth-Friendly Projects Ser.). (ENG.). 24p. (J). (gr. 2-5). 28.50 *(978-1-5038-0784-6(3)*, 210620) Child's World, Inc., The.

—Build a Compost Tumbler. Abell, Tracy. 2016. (Earth-Friendly Projects Ser.). (ENG.). 24p. (J). (gr. 2-5). 28.50 *(978-1-5038-0785-3(1)*, 210621) Child's World, Inc., The.

—Build a Flytrap. Bell, Samantha S. 2016. (Earth-Friendly Projects Ser.). (ENG.). 24p. (J). (gr. 2-5). 28.50 *(978-1-5038-0786-0(X)*, 210622) Child's World, Inc., The.

—Build a Neighborhood Library. Gulati, Annette. 2016. (Earth-Friendly Projects Ser.). (ENG.). 24p. (J). (gr. 2-5). 28.50 *(978-1-5038-0790-7(8)*, 210623) Child's World, Inc., The.

—Build a Rain Barrel. McGraw, Sally. 2016. (Earth-Friendly Projects Ser.). (ENG.). 24p. (J). (gr. 2-5). 28.50 *(978-1-5038-0787-7(8)*, 210624) Child's World, Inc., The.

—Build a Solar Cooker. Bell, Samantha S. 2016. (Earth-Friendly Projects Ser.). (ENG.). 24p. (J). (gr. 2-5). 28.50 *(978-1-5038-0788-4(6)*, 210625) Child's World, Inc., The.

—Build a Weather Station. Hand, Carol. 2016. (Earth-Friendly Projects Ser.). (ENG.). 24p. (J). (gr. 2-5). 28.50 *(978-1-5038-0789-1(4)*, 210626) Child's World, Inc., The.

—Captured by Pirates! An Isabel Soto History Adventure. Biskup, Agnieszka. 2012. (Graphic Expeditions Ser.). (ENG.). 32p. (gr. 3-4). pap. 47.70 *(978-1-4296-8471-2(2))*; (J). lib. bdg. 31.32 *(978-1-4296-7545-1(4))* Capstone. (Capstone Pr.).

—Egypt's Mysterious Pyramids: An Isabel Soto Archaeology Adventure. Biskup, Agnieszka. 2012. (Graphic Expeditions Ser.). (ENG.). 32p. (gr. 3-4). pap. 47.70 *(978-1-4296-8472-9(0)*, Capstone Pr.) Capstone.

—Graphic Expeditions. Biskup, Agnieszka. (Graphic Expeditions Ser.). (ENG.). 32p. (gr. 3-9). 2016. (J). lib. bdg., lib. bdg., lib. bdg. 250.56 *(978-1-5157-4023-0(4))*; 2012. pap. 667.80 *(978-1-4296-8474-3(7))* Capstone. (Capstone Pr.).

Stewart, Scott. Robo Monster. Black, Jake & Meredith Books Staff. 2008. 22p. (J). pap. 3.99 *(978-0-696-23957-1(4))* Meredith Bks.

Stewart, Todd. Flow, Spin, Grow: Looking for Patterns in Nature. Barss, Patchen. 2018. (ENG.). 32p. (J). (gr. k-5). 18.95 *(978-1-77147-287-6(1))* Owlkids Bks. Inc. CAN. Dist: Publishers Group West (PGW).

Stewart, Yale. Alien Superman!, 1 vol. Stewart, Yale. 2014. (Amazing Adventures of Superman! Ser.). (ENG.). 32p. (J). (gr. k-2). lib. bdg. 25.32 *(978-1-4795-5733-2(1)*, Stone Arch Bks.) Capstone.

—Battle of the Super Heroes!, 1 vol. Stewart, Yale. 2014. (Amazing Adventures of Superman! Ser.). (ENG.). 32p. (J). (gr. k-2). 25.32 *(978-1-4795-5731-8(5)*, Stone Arch Bks.) Capstone.

—Creatures from Planet X!, 1 vol. Stewart, Yale. 2014. (Amazing Adventures of Superman! Ser.). (ENG.). 32p. (J). (gr. k-2). lib. bdg. 25.32 *(978-1-4795-5734-9(X)*, Stone Arch Bks.) Capstone.

—Escape from Future World!, 1 vol. Stewart, Yale. 2014. (Amazing Adventures of Superman! Ser.). (ENG.). 32p. (J). (gr. k-2). lib. bdg. 25.32 *(978-1-4795-5732-5(3)*, Stone Arch Bks.) Capstone.

Steyert, Bill. Queen Esther's New Coloring Book. Brodsky, Irene. 2011. 39p. pap. 17.95 *(978-1-4327-6771-6(2))* Outskirts Pr., Inc.

Stich, Carlolyn R. The Barefoot Boys of Fayette. Henry, Regene. 2005. 180p. (J). (gr. 4-7). pap. 9.95 *(978-0-9749412-3-3(9))* EDCO Publishing, Inc.

—Water Words Rhymed & Defined. McKinney, Barbara Shaw. 2007. 30p. (J). (gr. 4-7). 19.95 *(978-0-9712692-8-6(9))* EDCO Publishing, Inc.

Stich, Carolyn R. Atsa & Ga: A Story from the High Desert. Stroschin, Jane H. 2005. 32p. (J). (gr. k-6). *(978-1-883960-29-2(0))* Henry Quill Pr.

Stickland, Shadra. A Place Where Hurricanes Happen. Watson, Renée. 2014. 40p. (J). (gr. k-4). 7.99 *(978-0-385-37668-6(5)*, Dragonfly Bks.) Random Hse. Children's Bks.

—White Water. Bandy, Michael S. & Stein, Eric. 2015. 40p. (J). (gr. k-3). 7.99 *(978-0-7636-7945-3(3))* Candlewick Pr.

Stickler, Eidi Helen. Angelfly. Ness, Nikki. Eikli, M. Amelia, tr. 2017. (ENG.). 136p. (J). pap. *(978-82-690749-3-2(4))* FlyFly.

Stickley, Kelly. Little Train! Mysak, Mary. 2004. 16p. (J). 7.50 *(978-0-9762274-0-3(1))* Helping Hands Children's Bks.

Stickley, Lisa. Bernard Makes a Splash. 2020. (ENG.). 32p. (J). (gr. -1-17). 16.99 *(978-1-84976-660-9(6))* Tate Publishing, Ltd. GBR. Dist: Hachette Bk. Group.

Stieber, Joel. Secret of the Tree: Marcus Speer's Ecosentinel. MacDonald, Tom. 2009. 300p. 28.95 *(978-0-595-51985-9(7))*; pap. 18.95 *(978-0-595-52402-0(8))* iUniverse, Inc.

Stiefvater, Maggie. Pip Bartlett's Guide to Magical Creatures. Stiefvater, Maggie. Pearce, Jackson. 2016. (Pip Bartlett Ser.: 1). (ENG.). 192p. (J). (gr. 3-7). 9.99 *(978-1-338-08815-1(7))* Scholastic, Inc.

Stier, Justin. Santa's Tiniest Elves Meet the Keeper of the Northern Lights. Love, T. & Children's Foundation, Sojihuggles. 2019. (ENG.). 32p. (J). pap. 14.99 *(978-0-9600237-4-5(7))* Mindstir Media.

Stier, Justin, jt. illus. see Kickingbird, Samantha.

Stietencron, Bettina. Hut in the Forest, 20 vols. Grimm, Jacob & Grimm, Wilhelm K. Lawson, Polly, tr. 2007. (Grimm's Fairy Tales Ser.). (ENG.). 28p. (J). *(978-0-86315-615-1(0))* Floris Bks.

Stiffler, Michael. You Are a Twisting Tornado. Malavolti, Angela. 2011. 28p. (J). 16.99 *(978-0-9834092-0-5(X))* Jungle Wagon Pr.

Stigler, Marilyn. Into the Hidden Lands: A Castle Rose Adventure. Franz, Kevin. 2004. 112p. (J). per. 7.99 *(978-0-9747774-0-5(4))* Starbell Bks.

—The Princess Sisters & the Underwater City. Franz, Kevin. 2004. 112p. (J). per. 7.99 *(978-0-9747774-1-2(2))* Starbell Bks.

Stiglich, Tom. Goin' to the Zoo / Vamos Al Zoologico. Adams, William J. 2007. (ENG & SPA.). 58p. (J). pap. 10.95 *(978-0-9772757-2-4(8))* Mandy & Andy Bks., Inc.

—Goin' to the Zoo Coloring Book: Vamos Al Zoologico. Adams, William J. 2007. (ENG & SPA.). (J). pap. 3.95 *(978-0-9772757-3-1(6))* Mandy & Andy Bks., Inc.

—Hate that Thunder. Adams, William J. 2005. 24p. (J). pap. 8.95 *(978-0-9772757-0-0(1))* Mandy & Andy Bks., Inc.

—Hate That Thunder/Odio Ese Trueno, 1 vol. Adams, William J. 2007. (Mandy & Andy Bks.). (ENG & SPA.). 49p. (J). (gr. k-2). per. 10.95 *(978-0-9772757-1-7(X))* Mandy & Andy Bks., Inc.

—Visiting the Farm / Visitando la Granja. Adams, William J. 2008. (ENG & SPA.). (J). pap. 10.95 *(978-0-9772757-4-8(4))* Mandy & Andy Bks., Inc.

—Visiting the Farm / Visitando la Granja Coloring Book. Adams, William J. 2008. (ENG & SPA.). 26p. (J). pap. 3.95 *(978-0-9772757-5-5(2))* Mandy & Andy Bks., Inc.

Stilchen, Julia. Little Astronomer: The Moon. Stilchen, Julia. 2019. (Kid Lit Science Ser.: Vol. 3). (ENG.). 26p. (J). pap. 11.99 *(978-1-0791-6302-5(6))* Independently Published.

Stileman, Kali. Big Book of My World. 2012. (ENG.). 48p. (J). *(978-1-58925-114-4(8))* Tiger Tales.

—Never Feed a Queen a Jellybean. Make Believe Ideas Ltd. 2019. (ENG.). 12p. (J). bds. *(978-1-78947-049-9(8))* Make Believe Ideas.

Stileman, Kali. Never Feed a Troll a Casserole. Make Believe Ideas Ltd & Greening, Rosie. 2020. (Felt Teeth Ser.). (ENG.). 12p. (J). bds. ***(978-1-78947-375-9(6))*** Make Believe Ideas.

—There Was an Old Lady Who Swallowed a Fly. Make Believe Ideas Ltd & Greening, Rosie. 2020. (Felt Teeth Ser.). (ENG.). 12p. (J). bds. ***(978-1-78947-376-6(4))*** Make Believe Ideas.

Stiles, Tim. William Penn: Founder of Pennsylvania. Jacobson, Ryan. 2006. (Graphic Biographies Ser.). (ENG.). 32p. (J). (gr. 3-9). 31.32 *(978-0-7368-6501-2(2)*, Capstone Pr.) Capstone.

Still, Wayne A. A Salute to African American Architects: Learning Activities. Chandler, Alton. Chapman, Loring F., ed. 24p. (Orig.). (J). (gr. 3-8). pap. 1.75 *(978-1-877804-16-8(9))* Chandler/White Publishing Co.

—A Salute to African American in Medicine: Learning. Chandler, Alton. Chapman, L., ed. 24p. (Orig.). (J). (gr. 3-8). pap. 1.75 *(978-1-877804-17-5(7))* Chandler/White Publishing Co.

—A Salute to Black Inventors Vol. 2: Coloring Learning Activities. Howell, Ann C. & Chandler, Alton. Chapman, L., ed. 96p. (J). (gr. 3-8). pap. 6.95 *(978-1-877804-19-9(3))* Chandler/White Publishing Co.

Still, Wayne A. & Hayden, Seitu. A Salute to Black Inventor, Dr. Georde Washington Carver: The Peanut Wizard. Chandler, Alton. Chapman, L., ed. 24p. (Orig.). (J). (gr. 3-8). pap. 1.75 *(978-1-877804-15-1(0))* Chandler/White Publishing Co.

Stillerman, Robbie. Make Your Own Laptop: Color & Build Your Own Computer! Pearlstein, Don. 2011. (Dover Children's Activity Bks.). (ENG.). 24p. (J). (gr. k-3). pap. 9.99 *(978-0-486-48532-4(3))* Dover Pubns., Inc.

Stillview, photos by. Mini Temporary Tattoos. Top That! Team Staff. 2005. 51p. (J). (gr. 4-8). reprint ed. pap. 8.00 *(978-0-7567-9417-0(X))* DIANE Publishing Co.

Stillwell, Heath. The Haunted Dog House. Johnson, Sandi. Brundige, Britt & Durant, Sybrina, eds. 2014. (Spooky Ser.). 32p. (J). (gr. -1-6). pap. 12.99 *(978-1-929063-50-5(4)*, 149) Moons & Stars Publishing For Children.

Stillwell, Heath. The Haunted Dog House. Brundige, Britt & Durant, Sybrina, eds. 2019. (Haunted Dog House Ser.: Vol. 1). (ENG.). 34p. (J). pap. 12.99 ***(978-1-6755-9168-0(7))*** Independently Published.

Stillwell, Jennifer. The I Love You Mom Coupon Book: 28 Ways to Show Mom You Appreciate Her Every Day, 4. Loveland-Coen, Victoria. 2007. (Give a Little Love Ser.: 4). 62p. (J). pap. 5.95 *(978-0-9644765-8-5(4))* Self-Mastery Pr.

Stilton, Thea. A Mouseford Musical. Stilton, Thea. 2018. (Thea Stilton Mouseford Academy Ser.: 6). (ENG.). 128p. (J). (gr. 2-5). pap. 7.99 *(978-0-545-78905-9(2))* Scholastic, Inc.

—The Secret Invention. Stilton, Thea. 2018. (Thea Stilton Mouseford Academy Ser.: 5). (ENG.). 128p. (J). (gr. 2-5). pap. 7.99 *(978-0-545-78904-2(4)*, Scholastic Paperbacks) Scholastic, Inc.

—Thea Stilton & the Riddle of the Ruins: A Geronimo Stilton Adventure. Stilton, Thea. Schaffer, Andrea, tr. 2018. (Thea Stilton Ser.: 28). 176p. (J). (gr. 2-5). pap. 8.99 *(978-1-338-26857-7(0)*, Scholastic Paperbacks) Scholastic, Inc.

Stimpson, Colin. Germs! Howard, Martin. 2012. (ENG.). 32p. (J). (gr. k-k). 16.99 *(978-1-84365-119-2(X)*, Pavilion Children's Books) Pavilion Bks. GBR. Dist: Penguin Random Hse. LLC.

—How to Cook Children: A Grisly Recipe Book for Gruesome Witches. Howard, Martin. 2011. (ENG.). 80p. (J). (gr. 4-7). pap. 10.99 *(978-1-84365-179-6(3)*, Pavilion) Pavilion Bks. GBR. Dist: Independent Pubs. Group.

Stimson, James. The Bully Goat Grim: A Maynard Moose Tale. 2012. 32p. (J). (gr. 2-6). 18.95 *(978-0-87483-952-4(1))* August Hse. Pubs., Inc.

—The Little Moose Who Couldn't Go to Sleep, Vol. Claflin, Willy. 2014. (ENG.). 36p. 18.95 *(978-1-939160-67-6(7))* August Hse. Pubs., Inc.

—Rapunzel & the Seven Dwarfs: A Maynard Moose Tale. Claflin, Willy. 2011. (ENG.). 33p. (J). (gr. -1-3). 18.95 *(978-0-87483-914-2(9))* August Hse. Pubs., Inc.

—The Uglified Ducky. Claflin, Willy. 2011. 32p. (J). (gr. -1-3). pap. 9.95 *(978-0-87483-953-1(X))* August Hse. Pubs., Inc.

Stipe, Bonnie. Bossy Rosie: A Second Grader Book. Hess, Steve. 2018. (Second Grader Bks.: Vol. 1). (ENG.). 26p. (J). pap. 5.99 *(978-1-7315-4980-8(6))* Independently Published.

Stites, Theresa. I'll Be There Everyday but in a Different Kind of Way. Goodluck, Marquita. 2018. (ENG.). 24p. (J). (gr. k-6). 15.99 *(978-0-692-19942-8(X))* goodluck, marquita Publishing.

—El Misterio Del Dinero Perdido. Wood, Debbie. Duval, Milagros, tr. 2018. (Olliezoodle's Hope Ser.: Vol. 1). (SPA.). 32p. (J). (gr. k-6). pap. 14.27 *(978-0-578-43189-5(0))* Debra L. Wood.

—Wolf. Porter, Harry. 2012. 28p. pap. 14.99 *(978-0-9838018-5-6(1))* 4RV Pub.

Stites, Theresa & Blake, Joshua. William Warrior Bear. Wood, Debbie. 2020. (Olliezoodle's Hope Ser.: Vol. 5). (ENG.). 34p. (J). (gr. k-6). pap. 14.27 ***(978-0-578-64475-2(4))*** Debra L. Wood.

Stitt, Sue. Big Book of Things to Do: Combined Volume. Gibson, Ray. 2004. (What Shall I Do Today? Ser.). 192p. (J). pap. 18.95 *(978-0-7945-0442-7(6)*, Usborne) EDC Publishing.

—Who Built the Pyramids? Chisholm, Jane & Reid, Straun. 2004. (Starting Point History Ser.). 32p. (J). (gr. 1). lib. bdg. 12.95 *(978-1-58086-629-3(8)*, Usborne) EDC Publishing.

Stiver, Megan. The Great Bellybutton Cover-Up. 2011. 32p. *(978-0-9810634-7-8(0))* Susan Ross (self publishing).

—Say Please to the Honeybees. 2010. 33p. *(978-0-9810634-3-0(8))* Susan Ross (self publishing).

Stjean, Todd. Cranky Bear Wakes Up: An Animal Kingdom Story Sketchbook. Stjean, Shawn. 2018. (Cranky Bear Ser.: Vol. 1). (ENG.). 42p. (J). (gr. k-4). 16.99 *(978-1-5380-6993-6(8))* Glas Daggre Publishing.

sto. The Chess Set in the Mirror. Bontempelli, Massimo. Gilson, Estelle, tr. 2007. (Nautilus Ser.). (ENG.). 114p. (J). (gr. 7-9). per. 9.95 *(978-1-58988-031-3(5))* Dry, Paul Bks., Inc.

Stock, Catherine. After the Kill. Lunde, Darrin. 2011. 32p. (J). (gr. 1-4). pap. 7.99 *(978-1-57091-744-8(2))* Charlesbridge Publishing, Inc.

—Ballerina Gets Ready. Kent, Allegra. (ENG.). 40p. (J). (gr. -1-3). 2017. 6.99 *(978-0-8234-3765-8(5))*; 2016. 16.95 *(978-0-8234-3563-0(6))* Holiday Hse., Inc.

—Emily & Carlo. Figley, Marty Rhodes. 2012. 32p. (J). (gr. k-3). 15.95 *(978-1-58089-274-2(4))* Charlesbridge Publishing, Inc.

—Galimoto. Williams, Karen Lynn. 2015. 32p. pap. 7.00 *(978-1-61003-604-7(2))* Center for the Collaborative Classroom.

—Justin & the Best Biscuits in the World. Walter, Mildred Pitts. 2010. (ENG.). 144p. (J). (gr. 3-7). pap. 6.99 *(978-0-06-195891-5(3))* HarperCollins Pubs.

—Karl, Get Out of the Garden! Carolus Linnaeus & the Naming of Everything. Sanchez, Anita. 2017. (ENG.). 48p. (J). (gr. 2-5). lib. bdg. 17.99 *(978-1-58089-606-1(5))* Charlesbridge Publishing, Inc.

—My Name Is Sangoel. Mohammed, Khadra & Williams, Karen Lynn. 2009. (ENG.). 36p. (J). (gr. 1-5). 17.00 *(978-0-8028-5307-3(2)*, Eerdmans Bks For Young Readers) Eerdmans, William B. Publishing Co.

—Ready & Waiting for You. Moreillon, Judi. 2013. (ENG.). 26p. (J). 17.00 *(978-0-8028-5355-4(2)*, Eerdmans Bks For Young Readers) Eerdmans, William B. Publishing Co.

—Vinnie & Abraham. FitzGerald, Dawn. 2007. (ENG.). 48p. (J). (gr. k-3). lib. bdg. 16.95 *(978-1-57091-658-8(6))* Charlesbridge Publishing, Inc.

Stockdale, Susan. Bring on the Birds, 1 vol. Stockdale, Susan. (ENG.). (J). (gr. -1 — 1). 2013. 22p. bds. 6.99 *(978-1-56145-692-5(6))*; 2011. 32p. 16.95 *(978-1-56145-560-7(1))* Peachtree Publishing Co. Inc.

—Carry Me! Animal Babies on the Move, 1 vol. Stockdale, Susan. (ENG.). 32p. (J). (gr. k-1). 2008. pap. 7.95 *(978-1-56145-449-5(4))*; 2005. 15.95 *(978-1-56145-328-3(5))* Peachtree Publishing Co. Inc.

—Fabulous Fishes, 1 vol. Stockdale, Susan. (ENG.). 32p. (J). 2019. (gr. -1-1). pap. 7.95 *(978-1-68263-099-0(4))*; 2008. (gr. k-1). 16.95 *(978-1-56145-429-7(X))* Peachtree Publishing Co. Inc.

—Fantastic Flowers, 1 vol. Stockdale, Susan. 2017. (ENG.). 32p. (J). (gr. -1-1). 16.95 *(978-1-56145-952-0(6))* Peachtree Publishing Co. Inc.

—Spectacular Spots, 1 vol. Stockdale, Susan. 2015. (ENG.). 32p. (J). (gr. 1-1). 15.95 *(978-1-56145-817-2(1))* Peachtree Publishing Co. Inc.

—Spectacular Spots / Magníficas Manchas, 1 vol. Stockdale, Susan. rev. ed. 2017. (ENG.). 32p. (J). (gr. -1-1). pap. 8.99 *(978-1-56145-978-0(X))* Peachtree Publishing Co. Inc.

—Stripes of All Types, 1 vol. Stockdale, Susan. 2013. (ENG.). 32p. (J). (gr. -1-1). 16.95 *(978-1-56145-695-6(0))* Peachtree Publishing Co. Inc.

—Stripes of All Types / Rayas de Todas Las Tallas, 1 vol. Stockdale, Susan. ed. 2014. (ENG.). 32p. (J). (gr. -1-1). pap. 8.99 *(978-1-56145-793-9(0))* Peachtree Publishing Co. Inc.

Stockelbach, Ed. The Little Girl Who Did... What?!!! Dupuy, Diane. 2004. 32p. 12.95 *(978-0-9730736-0-7(8))* Beyond Light CAN. Dist: Hushion Hse. Publishing, Ltd.

Stockham, Jess. Baby Sitter. 2009. (First Time Ser.). 24p. (J). (gr. -1-k). *(978-1-84643-279-8(0))* Child's Play International Ltd.

—Beauty & the Beast. 2007. (Flip-Up Fairy Tales Ser.). 24p. (J). (gr. -1-2). *(978-1-84643-155-5(7))*; (gr. 2-2). *(978-1-84643-114-2(X))* Child's Play International Ltd.

—Big Day Out. 2009. (First Time Ser.). 24p. (J). (gr. -1-k). *(978-1-84643-282-8(0))* Child's Play International Ltd.

—The Boy Who Cried Wolf. 2011. (Flip-Up Fairy Tales Ser.). 24p. (J). *(978-1-84643-407-5(6))*; (gr. 2-2). *(978-1-84643-368-9(1))* Child's Play International Ltd.

—Cinderella. (Flip-Up Fairy Tales Ser.). 24p. (J). 2007. (gr. -1-2). *(978-1-84643-091-6(7))*; 2006. (gr. 2-2). *(978-1-904550-74-7(6))* Child's Play International Ltd.

—The Cockerel, the Mouse & the Little Red Hen. (Flip-Up Fairy Tales Ser.). 24p. (J). 2007. (gr. -1-2). *(978-1-84643-092-3(5))*; 2006. (ENG.). (gr. 2-2). *(978-1-904550-75-4(4))* Child's Play International Ltd.

—Dentist. 2011. (First Time Ser.). 24p. (J). (gr. 2-2). pap. *(978-1-84643-335-1(5))* Child's Play International Ltd.

—Doctor. 2011. (First Time Ser.). 24p. (J). (gr. 2-2). pap. *(978-1-84643-334-4(7))* Child's Play International Ltd.

—Down by the Station. (Classic Books with Holes 8x8 with CD Ser.). (ENG.). 16p. (J). 2007. (gr. -1-1). pap. incl. audio compact disk *(978-1-904550-68-6(1))*; 2003. *(978-0-85953-132-0(5))* Child's Play International Ltd.

—Eating Well!/¡Comer Bien! Mlawer, Teresa, tr. ed. 2013. (Child's Play - Bilingual Titles Ser.). (SPA.). 12p. (J). bds. *(978-1-84643-562-1(5))* Child's Play International Ltd.

—Feeling Great!/¡Sentirse Bien! Mlawer, Teresa, tr. ed. 2013. (Child's Play - Bilingual Titles Ser.). (SPA.). 12p. (J). (gr. -1). bds. *(978-1-84643-561-4(7))* Child's Play International Ltd.

—The Frog Prince. 2007. (Flip-Up Fairy Tales Ser.). 24p. (J). *(978-1-84643-143-2(3))*; (gr. 2-2). pap. *(978-1-84643-077-0(1))* Child's Play International Ltd.

—Hospital. 2011. (First Time Ser.). 24p. (J). (gr. 2-2). pap. *(978-1-84643-336-8(3))* Child's Play International Ltd.

—Little Red Riding Hood. (Flip-Up Fairy Tales Ser.). 24p. (J). 2007. (gr. -1-2). *(978-1-84643-088-6(7))*; 2005. pap. *(978-1-904550-22-8(3))* Child's Play International Ltd.

—Looking Good!/¡Lucir Bien! Mlawer, Teresa, tr. ed. 2013. (Child's Play - Bilingual Titles Ser.). (SPA.). 12p. (J). (gr. -1). bds. *(978-1-84643-560-7(9))* Child's Play International Ltd.

—Moving Day! 2011. (Helping Hands Ser.). 24p. (J). *(978-1-84643-414-3(9))* Child's Play International Ltd.

—Nursery. 2009. (First Time Ser.). 24p. (J). (gr. -1-k). *(978-1-84643-281-1(2))* Child's Play International Ltd.

—Oh Baby! Baker, Sue. 2006. (Blanket Babies Ser.). (ENG.). 12p. (J). (gr. -1-k). bds. *(978-1-904550-87-7(8))* Child's Play International Ltd.

—On the Go!/¡a Moverse! Mlawer, Teresa, tr. ed. 2013. (Child's Play - Bilingual Titles Ser.). (SPA.). 12p. (J). (gr. -1). bds. *(978-1-84643-563-8(3))* Child's Play International Ltd.

—Party! 2011. (Helping Hands Ser.). 24p. (J). *(978-1-84643-413-6(0))* Child's Play International Ltd.

—Peep-O! Baker, Sue. 2006. (Blanket Babies Ser.). (ENG.). 12p. (J). (gr. -1-k). bds. *(978-1-904550-88-4(6))* Child's Play International Ltd.

—The Princess & the Pea. (Flip-Up Fairy Tales Ser.). 24p. (J). (gr. -1-2). 2010. *(978-1-84643-332-0(0))*; 2009. pap. *(978-1-84643-326-9(6))* Child's Play International Ltd.

—Recycling! 2011. (Helping Hands Ser.). 24p. (J). *(978-1-84643-415-0(7))* Child's Play International Ltd.

—Shopping! 2011. (Helping Hands Ser.). 24p. (J). *(978-1-84643-412-9(2))* Child's Play International Ltd.

—Sleep Tight! Baker, Sue & Stockham, Jessica. 2006. (Blanket Babies Ser.). (ENG.). 12p. (J). (gr. -1-k). bds. *(978-1-904550-90-7(8))* Child's Play International Ltd.

—Sleepover. 2009. (First Time Ser.). 24p. (J). (gr. -1-k). *(978-1-84643-280-4(4))* Child's Play International Ltd.

—The Steadfast Tin Soldier. 2012. (Flip-Up Fairy Tales Ser.). 24p. (J). *(978-1-84643-477-8(7))* Child's Play International Ltd.

—Stone Soup. (Flip-Up Fairy Tales Ser.). 24p. (J). 2007. (gr. -1-2). *(978-1-84643-094-7(1))*; 2006. (gr. 2-2). pap. *(978-1-84643-021-3(6))* Child's Play International Ltd.

—Vet. 2011. (First Time Ser.). 24p. (J). (gr. 2-2). pap. *(978-1-84643-337-5(1))* Child's Play International Ltd.

—Wash Day! Baker, Sue. 2006. (Blanket Babies Ser.). (ENG.). 12p. (J). (gr. -1-k). bds. *(978-1-904550-89-1(4))* Child's Play International Ltd.

Stockham, Jess. The Big Red Rock, 1 vol. Stockham, Jess. 2018. (Child's Play Library). 32p. (J). *(978-1-78628-003-9(5))*; pap. *(978-1-78628-002-2(7))* Child's Play International Ltd.

Stockham, Jess, jt. illus. see Birkett, Georgie.

Stockley, Gerry. Mac, Information Detective, in the Curious Kids... - Digging for Answers: A Storybook Approach to Introducing Research Skills, 2 vols. Arnone, Marilyn P. & Coatney, Sharon. 2006. 104p. 35.00 *(978-1-59158-397-4(7)*, LU3977, Libraries Unlimited) ABC-CLIO, LLC.

Stockman, Jack. Benjamin's Box: The Story of the Resurrection Eggs, 1 vol. Carlson, Melody. rev. ed. 2008. (ENG.). 40p. (J). (gr. -1-3). 8.99 *(978-0-310-71505-4(9))* Zonderkidz.

Stockman, Nathan. Iceman Vol. 3: Amazing Friends. 2019. (ENG.). 112p. (YA). (gr. 8-17). pap. 17.99 *(978-1-302-91483-7(9))* Marvel Worldwide, Inc.

—Spidey #11: Missing Out. Thompson, Robbie. 2017. (Spidey Ser.). (ENG.). 24p. (J). (gr. 2-8). lib. bdg. 27.07 *(978-1-5321-4159-1(9)*, 27032, Marvel Age) Spotlight.

—Spidey #12: Spidey No More! Thompson, Robbie. 2017. (Spidey Ser.). (ENG.). 24p. (J). (gr. 2-8). lib. bdg. 27.07 *(978-1-5321-4160-7(2)*, 27033, Marvel Age) Spotlight.

—Spidey #9: To Catch a Spider! Thompson, Robbie. 2017. (Spidey Ser.). (ENG.). 24p. (J). (gr. 2-8). lib. bdg. 27.07 *(978-1-5321-4157-7(2)*, 27030, Marvel Age) Spotlight.

Stockton, Frank. World Without Fish. Kurlansky, Mark. 2014. (ENG.). 208p. (J). (gr. 5). pap. 14.95 *(978-0-7611-8500-0(3)*, 18500) Workman Publishing Co., Inc.

Stockton, Greta & Philbrick, Katie. Goddesses of Legend & Myth: A Coloring Book Celebrating the Heroines of Ancient Europe. Toutz-Hager, Tanya. Date not set. 40p. (YA). (gr. 4-12). pap. 8.95 *(978-0-9672107-0-4(4))* MoonStar Pr.

Stockton, Liz. The Knight in Battered Armor. Tibbetts, Brianna. 2019. (ENG.). 58p. (J). 27.99 *(978-1-68314-767-1(7))*; pap. 17.99 *(978-1-68314-766-4(9))* Redemption Pr.

Stockwell, Pel. Fandango: The Key to the Wind. Stockwell, Jeff. 2007. 58p. (YA). per. 22.50 *(978-0-9785594-0-3(1))* Stockwell Publishing.

Stoddard, Jeff. The Garden Wall: A Story of Love Based on I Corinthians 13. Bishop, Jennie. 2006. (ENG.). 32p. (J). (gr. 2-7). 12.99 *(978-1-59317-168-1(4))* Warner Pr., Inc.

Stoddard, Jeffery. Pete & Pillar: A Story of Friendship Based on John 15:13: the Big Rain. Stoddard, Jeffery. 2007. (Pete & Pillar Ser.). (ENG.). 32p. (J). (gr. -1-2). 12.99 *(978-1-59317-203-9(6))* Warner Pr., Inc.

—Skid & the Too Tiny Tunnel: A Story of Courage Based on Deuteronomy 31:6. Stoddard, Jeffery. Fogle, Robin & Rhodes, Karen, eds. 2009. (ENG.). 32p. (J). (gr. -1-2). 12.99 *(978-1-59317-355-5(5))* Warner Pr., Inc.

Stodden, Lindsay. Our Cat Hogan - Could He Be Part Dog? Powell, Anthony. 2012. 24p. (J). 19.95 *(978-1-61863-358-3(9))* Bookstand Publishing.

Stoeckigt, Anja. How Many Ways Can You Say Hello? Moahloli, Refiloe. 2017. (ENG.). 32p. 12.95 *(978-1-4859-0030-6(1))* Penguin Random House South Africa ZAF. Dist: Casemate Pubs. & Bk. Distributors, LLC.

Stoeke, Janet Morgan. Letting Go. Stoeke, Janet Morgan. Bader, Bonnie. 2015. (Loopy Coop Hens Ser.). (ENG.). 32p. (J). (gr. 1-2). pap. 3.99 *(978-0-448-48458-7(7)*, Penguin Young Readers) Penguin Young Readers Group.

—The Loopy Coop Hens. Stoeke, Janet Morgan. 2013. (Loopy Coop Hens Ser.). (ENG.). 32p. (J). (gr. 1-2). mass mkt. 3.99 *(978-0-448-46272-1(9)*, Penguin Young Readers) Penguin Young Readers Group.

Stoffel, Dominique, jt. photos by see Amann, Remy.

Stoh, Judy. Roger Meets Sam. Stoh, Emily. 2009. 24p. pap. 9.95 *(978-1-935105-41-1(8))* Avid Readers Publishing Group.

Stoick, Jean & Sams, Carl R., II, photos by. First Snow in the Woods. 2007. (ENG., 49p. (J). (gr. -1-3). 19.95 *(978-0-9770108-6-8(4))* Sams, II, Carl R. Photography, Inc.

Stoick, Jean & Sams, Carl R., photos by. Stranger in the Woods: Snowflake Edition. 2010. (ENG., 48p. 21.95 *(978-0-9827625-0-9(X))* Sams, II, Carl R. Photography, Inc.

Stoick, Jean, jt. photos by see Sams, Carl R., II.

Stoick, Jean, jt. photos by see Sams, Carl R., 2nd.

Stoick, Jean, jt. photos by see Sams, Carl R., II.

Stoick, Jean, jt. photos by see Sams II, Carl R.

Stojanova, Elena. Oranges for Everyone. Zake, Daiga. 2007. 32p. (J). (ARA.). pap. 12.95 *(978-1-60195-306-3(2))*; (POL & ENG.). pap. 12.95 *(978-1-60195-104-5(3))* International Step by Step Assn.

Stojanović, Bojana. Buddy & Emil Count To 10. Michaelis, Nils. 2018. (ENG.). 26p. (J). (gr. k-4). ***(978-87-970623-0-2(8))*** Michaelis, Nils.

Stojic, Manja. Polar Bear's Story. Blackford, Harriet. 2019. (ENG.). 32p. (J). (gr. -1-1). 16.95 *(978-1-912757-10-7(9))* Boxer Bks., Ltd. GBR. Dist: Sterling Publishing Co., Inc.

Stojic, Manya. Baby Goes Too. Roddie, Shen. 2003. 32p. (YA). *(978-1-85602-460-0(1)*, Pavilion Children's Books) Pavilion Bks.

—Weather Report: Band 02A/Red a (Collins Big Cat) Hawes, Alison. 2007. (Collins Big Cat Ser.). (ENG.). 16p. (J). (gr. -1-k). pap. 6.99 *(978-0-00-718655-6(X))* HarperCollins Pubs. Ltd. GBR. Dist: Independent Pubs. Group.

Stojic, Manya. Rain. Stojic, Manya. 2009. (ENG.). 32p. (J). (gr. -1-2). pap. 7.99 *(978-0-385-73729-6(7)*, Dragonfly Bks.) Random Hse. Children's Bks.

Stojic, Manya & Hamilton, Allen. Happy Cat, Me! A Slide-the-Spot Book of Animals. Wilson-Max, Ken. 2005. 10p. (J). (gr. k-4). reprint ed. 10.00 *(978-0-7567-9364-7(5))* DIANE Publishing Co.

Stokely, Jeff. Piper. Asher, Jay & Freeburg, Jessica. 2017. 140p. (YA). (gr. 7). pap. 17.99 *(978-0-448-49366-4(7)*, Razorbill) Penguin Young Readers Group.

Stokes, Brett. Haja Plays Basketball. Fitzpatrick, Dawn & Kovic, James, eds. 2019. (Haja Ser.: Vol. 2). (ENG.). 30p. (J). pap. 12.00 *(978-1-7297-2691-4(7))* CreateSpace Independent Publishing Platform.

Stokes, John. The Importance of Being Earnest. Wilde, Oscar. 2014. (ENG.). 136p. (gr. 5). pap. 16.95 *(978-1-907127-31-1(3))* Classical Comics GBR. Dist: Publishers Group West (PGW).

—The Importance of Being Earnest the Graphic Novel Quick Text: (American English) Wilde, Oscar. 2012. 144p. (J). pap. *(978-1-907127-32-8(1)*, Classical Comics, Ltd.) Classical Comics.

Stokes, Malcolm. The Legend of the Blue Bonnets: A Native American Legend. 2004. (ENG.). 20p. (J). (gr. 3-3). pap. 6.47 net. *(978-0-7685-2129-0(7)*, Dominie Elementary) Savvas Learning Co.

Stokoe, James, et al. Moon Knight Vol. 2: Reincarnations. 2017. (ENG.). 112p. (YA). (gr. 8-17). pap. 15.99 *(978-0-7851-9954-0(3))* Marvel Worldwide, Inc.

Stoliarchuk, Roman. Teddy Bear from Peru. Pidopryghora, Olja. 2018. (ENG.). 30p. (J). pap. 9.99 ***(978-1-6616-1548-2(1))*** Independently Published.

Stollinger, Heide. Donkeys. Dahiméne, Adelheid. 2014. (ENG.). 48p. (J). (gr. k-3). 17.95 *(978-0-7358-4160-4(8))* North-South Bks., Inc.

Stoltenberg, Nathan. Lily Hates Goodbyes. Marler, Jerilyn. 2012. 32p. pap. 6.95 *(978-1-936214-78-5(4))* Wyatt-MacKenzie Publishing.

Stomann, Allan. Selby Santa. Ball, Duncan. ed. 2007. 192p. *(978-0-7322-8679-8(4))* HarperCollins Pubs. Australia.

—Selby Scrambled. Ball, Duncan. 2004. 208p. *(978-0-207-19911-0(6))* HarperCollins Pubs. Australia.

—Selby Screams. Ball, Duncan. 2004. 192p. *(978-0-207-20023-6(8))* HarperCollins Pubs. Australia.

—Selby Shattered. Ball, Duncan. 2006. 192p. *(978-0-207-20066-3(1))* HarperCollins Pubs. Australia.

—Selby Snaps. Ball, Duncan. 2004. 208p. (Orig.). *(978-0-207-20020-5(3))* HarperCollins Pubs. Australia.

—Selby Snowbound. Ball, Duncan. 2004. 192p. (Orig.). *(978-0-207-20019-9(X))* HarperCollins Pubs. Australia.

—Selby Sorcerer. Ball, Duncan. 2003. 208p. *(978-0-207-19861-8(6))* HarperCollins Pubs. Australia.

—Selby Spacedog. Ball, Duncan. 2003. 176p. *(978-0-207-20006-9(8))* HarperCollins Pubs. Australia.

—Selby Speaks. Ball, Duncan. 2004. 176p. *(978-0-207-20024-3(6))* HarperCollins Pubs. Australia.

—Selby Splits. Ball, Duncan. 2004. 224p. *(978-0-207-20025-0(4))* HarperCollins Pubs. Australia.

—Selby Supersnoop. Ball, Duncan. 2003. 176p. *(978-0-207-20005-2(X))* HarperCollins Pubs. Australia.

—Selby Surfs. Ball, Duncan. 2003. 208p. *(978-0-207-20003-8(3))* HarperCollins Pubs. Australia.

—Selby's Secret. Ball, Duncan. 2003. 160p. *(978-0-207-20004-5(1))* HarperCollins Pubs. Australia.

—Selby's Selection. Ball, Duncan. 2006. 192p. *(978-0-207-20040-3(8))* HarperCollins Pubs. Australia.

—Selby's Shemozzle. Ball, Duncan. 2005. 192p. (J). *(978-0-207-20030-4(0))* HarperCollins Pubs. Australia.

—Selby's Side-Splitting Joke Book. Ball, Duncan. 2006. 160p. *(978-0-207-20041-0(6))* HarperCollins Pubs. Australia.

—Selby's Stardom. Ball, Duncan. 2004. 192p. *(978-0-207-20021-2(1))* HarperCollins Pubs. Australia.

Stone, A. R. Lion in the Living Room. McKinna, Caelaach. 2008. 24p. (J). pap. 14.99 *(978-0-9797513-4-9(9))* 4RV Pub.

Stone, Adrian. Macbeth: Band 18/Pearl (Collins Big Cat) Mayhew, Jon. 2014. (Collins Big Cat Ser.). (ENG.). 176p. (J). (gr. 5). pap. 12.99 *(978-0-00-753013-7(7))* HarperCollins Pubs. Ltd. GBR. Dist: Independent Pubs. Group.

Stone, Ana F. Dare to Be... A Series of Inspiring & Uplifting Poems for Children. Life Lessons for Young People, from Tots to Teens. Kaufman, Kendra L. 2019. (ENG.). 50p. (J). (gr. 2-7). pap. 16.95 ***(978-1-64559-210-5(3))*** Covenant Bks.

Stone-Barker, Holly. The Biggest Pumpkin, 1 vol. Horning, Sandra. 2014. (ENG.). 32p. 16.99 *(978-1-4556-1925-2(6)*, Pelican Publishing) Arcadia Publishing.

—Blue Frog: The Legend of Chocolate, 1 vol. de Las Casas, Dianne. 2011. (ENG.). 32p. (J). (gr. k-3). 16.99 *(978-1-4556-1459-2(9)*, Pelican Publishing) Arcadia Publishing.

—The House That Santa Built, 1 vol. de Las Casas, Dianne. 2013. (ENG.). 32p. (J). (gr. -1-k). 16.99 *(978-1-4556-1750-0(4)*, Pelican Publishing) Arcadia Publishing.

—The House That Witchy Built, 1 vol. de Las Casas, Dianne. 2011. (ENG.). 32p. (J). (gr. k-k). 16.99 *(978-1-58980-965-9(3)*, Pelican Publishing) Arcadia Publishing.

—The Little Read Hen, 1 vol. de Las Casas, Dianne. 2013. (ENG.). 32p. (J). (gr. -1-k). 16.99 *(978-1-4556-1702-9(4)*, Pelican Publishing) Arcadia Publishing.

—Mama's Bayou, 1 vol. de Las Casas, Dianne. 2010. (ENG.). 32p. (J). (gr. k-k). 16.99 *(978-1-58980-787-7(1)*, Pelican Publishing) Arcadia Publishing.

Stone, Bryan. Bridges! With 25 Science Projects for Kids. Swanson, Jennifer. 2018. (Explore Your World Ser.). 96p. (J). (gr. 3-4). pap. 14.95 *(978-1-61930-591-5(7)*, 6f5314fe-dee9-4f29-a636-dc20e46f9f7d); 19.95 *(978-1-61930-587-8(9)*, 36fbfb3f-0f50-43cb-9f65-c1a2ffd221a0) Nomad Pr.

—Explore Colonial America! 25 Great Projects, Activities, Experiments. Fisher, Verna. 2009. (Explore Your World Ser.). 96p. (J). (gr. k-4). pap. 12.95 *(978-1-934670-37-8(5)*, 9cc9faa0-6c49-4859-b2f1-b0182dd4c52b) Nomad Pr.

—Explore Comets & Asteroids! With 25 Great Projects. Yasuda, Anita. 2017. (Explore Your World Ser.). 96p. (J). (gr. 1-5). 19.95 *(978-1-61930-511-3(9)*, c9b7ea46-fc6f-4d61-8f2e-4a2c8c6a7320) Nomad Pr.

—Explore Electricity! With 25 Great Projects. Van Vleet, Carmella. 2013. (Explore Your World Ser.). 96p. (J). (gr. k-4). pap. 13.95 *(978-1-61930-180-1(6)*, 10cb319d-08e7-4ed4-95c0-aea2e9274d02) Nomad Pr.

—Explore Flight! With 25 Great Projects. Yasuda, Anita. 2013. (Explore Your World Ser.). 96p. (J). (gr. k-4). pap. 13.95 *(978-1-61930-176-4(8)*, c3bd016b-501d-456c-91c2-faebfcf0a66d) Nomad Pr.

—Explore Force & Motion! With 25 Great Projects. Swanson, Jennifer. 2016. (Explore Your World Ser.). 96p. (J). (gr. 1-5). 19.95 *(978-1-61930-351-5(5)*, fcbe3145-cf40-4e15-b389-7575caf3b0da) Nomad Pr.

—Explore Fossils! With 25 Great Projects. Brown, Cynthia Light & Brown, Grace. 2016. (Explore Your World Ser.). 96p. (J). (gr. 1-5). 19.95 *(978-1-61930-331-7(0)*, b1b0b3fd-0790-4ded-ac9b-adf6d84c6387) Nomad Pr.

—Explore Gravity! With 25 Great Projects. Blobaum, Cindy. 2013. (Explore Your World Ser.). 96p. (J). (gr. k-4). pap. 13.95 *(978-1-61930-207-5(1)*, c424d7d0-5b62-4dcb-88ef-cbc734c790e6) Nomad Pr.

—Explore Honey Bees! With 25 Great Projects. Blobaum, Cindy. 2015. (Explore Your World Ser.). 96p. (J). (gr. 1-5). 19.95 *(978-1-61930-286-0(1)*, b68dc93c-0064-48df-8624-ddd7edb0cb7f) Nomad Pr.

—Explore Life Cycles! 25 Great Projects, Activities, Experiments. Reilly, Kathleen M. 2011. (Explore Your World Ser.). 96p. (J). (gr. k-4). pap. 12.95 *(978-1-934670-80-4(4)*, 0c582c68-d1a4-465f-b7bc-47d405c23c03) Nomad Pr.

—Explore Light & Optics! With 25 Great Projects. Yasuda, Anita. 2016. (Explore Your World Ser.). 96p. (J). (gr. 1-5). 19.95 *(978-1-61930-376-8(0)*, f9e714d9-3d6c-4e7e-b7ab-98743f7025c5); pap. 14.95 *(978-1-61930-380-5(9)*, 181023aa-e9e5-49e8-a3a7-263fd4265e00) Nomad Pr.

—Explore Night Science! With 25 Great Projects. Blobaum, Cindy. 2012. (Explore Your World Ser.). 96p. (J). (gr. k-4). pap. 12.95 *(978-1-61930-156-6(3)*, 80b6b3a0-169c-4283-908a-ba96d250b8b9) Nomad Pr.

—Explore Norse Myths! With 25 Great Projects. Yasuda, Anita. 2015. (Explore Your World Ser.). 96p. (J). (gr. 1-5). 19.95 *(978-1-61930-316-4(7)*, 6390f641-1a8a-4dc7-84a8-26fd052805b8) Nomad Pr.

—Explore Poetry! With 25 Great Projects. Diehn, Andi. 2015. (Explore Your World Ser.). 96p. (J). (gr. 1-5). 19.95 *(978-1-61930-279-2(9)*, 0eeba188-e22e-49a4-8831-62de536fc66b) Nomad Pr.

—Explore Rivers & Ponds! With 25 Great Projects. Mooney, Carla. 2012. (Explore Your World Ser.). 96p. (J). (gr. k-4). pap. 12.95 *(978-1-936749-80-5(7)*, 19cc1d5c-d2eb-45a8-b365-b1e73b379f11) Nomad Pr.

—Explore Rocks & Minerals! 20 Great Projects, Activities, Experiments. Brown, Cynthia Light & Brown, Nick. 2010. (Explore Your World Ser.). 96p. (J). (gr. k-4). pap. 12.95 *(978-1-934670-61-3(8)*, 378282a2-7646-4cad-bcb2-c0b9f020919f) Nomad Pr.

—Explore Soil! With 25 Great Projects. Reilly, Kathleen M. 2015. (Explore Your World Ser.). 96p. (J). (gr. 1-5). pap. 14.95 *(978-1-61930-295-2(0)*, 8d1cc1b2-cfcf-4436-aa2a-945ed2c42243) Nomad Pr.

—Explore Solids & Liquids! With 25 Great Projects. Reilly, Kathleen M. 2014. (Explore Your World Ser.). 96p. (J). (gr. 1-5). 19.95 *(978-1-61930-171-9(7)*, b795221b-5c50-4f79-8e10-54324a165874) Nomad Pr.

—Explore the Ice Age! With 25 Great Projects. Blobaum, Cindy. 2017. (Explore Your World Ser.). 96p. (J). (gr. 3-4). 19.95 *(978-1-61930-577-9(1)*, 141977c8-d46d-4cb8-b2c6-483c5d3c3cfc) Nomad Pr.

—Explore Water! 25 Great Projects, Activities, Experiments. Yasuda, Anita. 2011. (Explore Your World Ser.). 96p. (J). (gr. k-4). pap. 12.95 *(978-1-936313-42-6(1)*, c04c5337-4b1a-4adf-b5dd-b3592fb1b07c) Nomad Pr.

—Music: Investigate the Evolution of American Sound. Latham, Donna. 2013. (Inquire & Investigate Ser.). 128p. (J). (gr. 6-10). 21.95 *(978-1-61930-199-3(7)*, 9fb11901-2e12-4905-9cd9-2c250d34d671); pap. 16.95 *(978-1-61930-203-7(9)*, 13c9906f-e90e-4726-b4df-05e0af834b47) Nomad Pr.

—Simple Machines! With 25 Science Projects for Kids. Yasuda, Anita. 2019. (Explore Your World Ser.). 96p. (J). (gr. 3-4). 19.95 *(978-1-61930-814-5(2)*, 328ab615-22f5-4d58-a960-ec71173722a0); pap. 14.95 *(978-1-61930-817-6(7)*, 3f99a360-925b-4594-8795-590b559b3d04) Nomad Pr.

Stone, Bryan, jt. illus. see Kim, Alex.

Stone, David. The Mystery of Arroyo Seco. Ryan, Jessica. 2011. 186p. 42.95 *(978-1-258-08470-7(8))* Literary Licensing, LLC.

—The Secret of the Old Coach Inn. Evatt, Harriet. 2011. 190p. 42.95 *(978-1-258-08239-0(X))* Literary Licensing, LLC.

Stone, Helen. Little Witch: 60th Anniversay Edition. Bennett, Anna Elizabeth. 60th anniv. ed. 2013. (ENG.). 128p. (J). (gr. k-3). pap. 12.95 *(978-1-61608-964-1(4)*, 608964, Sky Pony Pr.) Skyhorse Publishing Co., Inc.

Stone, Joanie. Hanukkah: The Festival of Lights. Bader, Bonnie. 2020. (Big Golden Book Ser.). 32p. (J). (gr. -1-2). 10.99 ***(978-1-9848-5249-6(3)***, Golden Bks.) Random Hse. Children's Bks.

Stone, Joanie. The Kid & the Chameleon. Mabry Bestor, Sheri. 2019. (Time to Read Ser.). (ENG.). 48p. (J). (gr. k-2). 12.99 *(978-0-8075-4179-1(6)*, 807541796) Whitman, Albert & Co.

Stone, Joanie. The Kid & the Chameleon Go to School (the Kid & the Chameleon: Time to Read, Level 3) Mabry, Sheri. (Time to Read Ser.). (ENG.). 48p. (J). (gr. k-2). 2020. pap. 3.99 ***(978-0-8075-4164-7(8)***, 807541648); 2019. 12.99 *(978-0-8075-4177-7(X)*, 080754177X) Whitman, Albert & Co.

Stone, Joanie. The Kid & the Chameleon Sleepover. Mabry Bestor, Sheri. 2019. (Time to Read Ser.). (ENG.). 48p. (J). (gr. k-2). 12.99 *(978-0-8075-4180-7(X)*, 080754180X) Whitman, Albert & Co.

—The Kid & the Chameleon Sleepover (the Kid & the Chameleon: Time to Read, Level 3) Mabry, Sheri. 2019. (Time to Read Ser.). (ENG.). 48p. (J). (gr. k-2). pap. 3.99 *(978-0-8075-4166-1(4)*, 807541664) Whitman, Albert & Co.

—The Kid & the Chameleon (the Kid & the Chameleon: Time to Read, Level 3) Mabry, Sheri. 2019. (Time to Read Ser.). (ENG.). 48p. (J). (gr. k-2). pap. 3.99 *(978-0-8075-4167-8(2)*, 0807541672) Whitman, Albert & Co.

—Me & the Sky: Captain Beverley Bass, Pioneering Pilot. Bass, Beverley & Williams, Cynthia. 2019. 40p. (J). (gr. -1-3). 17.99 *(978-0-525-64549-8(7))*; (ENG.). lib. bdg. 20.99 *(978-0-525-64550-4(0))* Random Hse. Children's Bks. (Knopf Bks. for Young Readers).

—Purple. Doering, Amanda. 2018. (Sing Your Colors! Ser.). (ENG.). 24p. (J). (gr. -1-2). 33.99 *(978-1-68410-313-3(4)*, 140701); lib. bdg. 33.99 incl. audio compact disk *(978-1-68410-132-0(8)*, 31854) Cantata Learning.

Stone, Joanie. Teeny-Tiny Mermaid. Puffinton, Brick. Cottage Door Press, ed. 2020. (Finger Puppet Board Book Ser.). (ENG.). 12p. (J). (gr. -1 — 1). bds. 6.99 ***(978-1-68052-938-8(2)***, 1005810) Cottage Door Pr.

Stone, Joanie. Unbeatable Betty: Betty Robinson, the First Female Olympic Track & Field Gold Medalist. Kimmel, Allison Crotzer. 2020. 40p. (J). (gr. -1-3). 17.99 *(978-0-06-289607-0(5)*, HarperCollins) HarperCollins Pubs. Ltd. GBR. Dist: HarperCollins Pubs.

Stone, John. The Amazing Adventures of Andy Owl: A Children's Guide to Understanding Music. Russell, D. Z. 2003. 34p. (J). per. 7.95 *(978-0-9725398-0-7(8))* World Famous Children's Bks.

Stone, Jonny. The Kitty Who Found His Meeooww. Salter, Michelle Lewis. 2011. 40p. pap. 24.95 *(978-1-4560-5953-8(X))* America Star Bks.

Stone, Joyce M., jt. illus. see Stone, Kelly P.

Stone, Kate. ABC Train. 2013. (ENG.). 20p. (J). bds. 10.99 *(978-1-4494-3157-0(7))* Andrews McMeel Publishing.

—Colors. Andrews McMeel Publishing, LLC Staff. 2015. (ENG.). 12p. (J). bds. 10.99 *(978-1-4494-5587-3(5))* Andrews McMeel Publishing.

—Heads & Tails. 2013. (ENG.). 20p. (J). bds. 10.99 *(978-1-4494-3246-1(8))* Andrews McMeel Publishing.

Stone, Kazuko. Ten Oni Drummers / Diez Tamborileros Oni. Gollub, Matthew. 2019. (SPA & ENG.). 32p. (J). (gr. -1-k). 17.95 *(978-1-889910-53-6(8))* Tortuga Pr.

Stone, Kazuko G. Cool Melons - Turn to Frogs! The Life & Poems of Issa. Gollub, Matthew W. 2013. (ENG.). (J). (gr. 3-6). lib. bdg. 21.55 *(978-0-7569-4774-3(X))* Perfection Learning Corp.

—Cool Melons-Turn to Frogs! The Life & Poems of Issa, 1 vol. Gollub, Matthew. 2013. (ENG.). 30p. (J). (gr. 1-6). pap. 11.95 *(978-1-58430-241-4(0)*, 3fb00599-3d33-48fa-8ac8-8db7b40cdc84) Lee & Low Bks., Inc.

—Ten Oni Drummers. Gollub, Matthew. 2018. (ENG.). 32p. (J). (gr. -1-k). 17.95 *(978-1-889910-51-2(1))* Tortuga Pr.

Stone, Kazuko G. Cool Melons — Turn to Frogs! The Life & Poems of Issa. Stone, Kazuko G. Gollub, Matthew & Kobayashi, Issa. 2nd ed. 2017. (ENG.). 40p. (J). (gr. 2-4). 17.95 *(978-1-889910-50-5(3))* Tortuga Pr.

Stone, Kelly P. & Stone, Joyce M. What Do Pets Do When They Go up to Heaven?, 1 vol. Stone, Kelly P. 2009. 13p. pap. 24.95 *(978-1-61546-212-4(0))* America Star Bks.

Stone, Kyle M. Please Bury Me in the Library. Lewis, J. Patrick. 2005. (ENG.). 32p. (J). (gr. -1-3). 17.99 *(978-0-15-216387-7(5)*, 1200853) Houghton Mifflin Harcourt Publishing Co.

Stone, Lyn. The Fairy Midnight Surprise Party. Taylor, Dereen. 2012. 12p. (J). (gr. 1-6). 16.99 *(978-1-84322-763-2(0))* Anness Publishing GBR. Dist: National Bk. Network.

—Rosie Rides to the Rescue: Peek Inside the Pop-Up Windows! Taylor, Dereen. 2015. (ENG.). 12p. 16.99 *(978-1-86147-488-9(1)*, Armadillo) Anness Publishing GBR. Dist: National Bk. Network.

Stone, Lynn M., photos by. Box Turtles. Stone, Lynn M. 2007. (Nature Watch Ser.). (ENG., 48p. (gr. 4-8). lib. bdg. 27.93 *(978-1-57505-869-6(3)*, Lerner Pubns.) Lerner Publishing Group.

—Grizzlies. Stone, Lynn M. rev. ed. 2007. (Nature Watch Ser.). (ENG., 48p. (gr. 4-8). lib. bdg. 27.93 *(978-0-8225-6601-4(X)*, Lerner Pubns.) Lerner Publishing Group.

Stone, Mitzie. #bookpusher. White, Porchanee a. 2018. (ENG.). 48p. (J). pap. 12.99 *(978-1-59755-465-7(0)*, Advantage BibleStudy) Advantage Bks.

Stone, Norman. Horace & the Christmas Mystery. Magnusson, Sally. 2015. 48p. (J). (gr. k). 14.99 *(978-1-84502-791-9(4))* Black and White Publishing Ltd. GBR. Dist: Independent Pubs. Group.

Stone, Phoebe. In God's Name. Sasso, Sandy Eisenberg. 2004. (ENG.). (J). (gr. -1-2). 38p. pap. 11.99 *(978-1-68442-409-2(7))*; 32p. 24.99 *(978-1-879045-26-2(5)*, b3f69034-af51-480e-8ee7-09d0d505f579, Jewish Lights Publishing) LongHill Partners, Inc.

Stone, Sandra, et al, photos by. The Alaska We Love. Stone, Sandra & Stone, James. 2007. 70p. *(978-0-9800019-0-7(0))* Blue Skies Above Texas Co.

Stone, Steve. Bugs Don't Hug: Six-Legged Parents & Their Kids. Montgomery, Heather L. 2018. 32p. (J). (gr. -1-2). lib. bdg. 14.99 *(978-1-58089-816-4(5))* Charlesbridge Publishing, Inc.

—Grumpy King Colin. Allcock, Phil. 2019. (Early Bird Readers — Purple (Early Bird Stories (tm)) Ser.). (ENG.). 32p. (J). (gr. k-3). 27.99 *(978-1-5415-4223-5(1)*, 9781541542235); pap. 7.99 *(978-1-5415-7423-6(0)*, 9781541574236) Lerner Publishing Group. (Lerner Pubns.).

—Rumpelstiltskin Returns. Pearson, Maggie. 2014. (Race Ahead with Reading Ser.). (ENG.). 32p. (J). (gr. 2-2). *(978-0-7787-1332-6(6))* Crabtree Publishing Co.

Stone, Tess. Buzz! Hirsh, Ananth. 2013. (ENG.). 144p. pap. 19.99 *(978-1-62010-088-2(6)*, 9781620100882, Lion Forge) Oni Pr., Inc.

Stoner, Alexis. Especially Me! Gerbracht, Edie. 2012. 34p. pap. 11.77 *(978-0-9843855-5-3(X))* aBASK Publishing.

Stones, Greg. The Backup Bunny. Rayner, Abigail. 2018. (ENG.). 32p. (J). (gr. -1-3). 17.95 *(978-0-7358-4282-3(5))* North-South Bks., Inc.

Stoney, Annaliese. Ada Lovelace & Computing. Canavan, Roger. ed. 2020. (Eureka Moment! Ser.). 128p. (J). (gr. 4). pap. 8.95 *(978-1-912904-04-4(7))* Book Hse. GBR. Dist: Sterling Publishing Co., Inc.

—Charles Darwin & Evolution. Graham, Ian. ed. 2020. (Eureka Moment! Ser.). 128p. (J). (gr. 4). pap. 8.95 *(978-1-912537-43-3(5))* Book Hse. GBR. Dist: Sterling Publishing Co., Inc.

—Isaac Newton & Gravity. Woolf, Alex. ed. 2020. (Eureka Moment! Ser.). 128p. (J). (gr. 4). pap. 8.95 *(978-1-912904-05-1(5))* Book Hse. GBR. Dist: Sterling Publishing Co., Inc.

—Marie Curie & Radioactivity. Graham, Ian. ed. 2020. (Eureka Moment! Ser.). 128p. (J). (gr. 4). pap. 8.95 *(978-1-912537-42-6(7))* Book Hse. GBR. Dist: Sterling Publishing Co., Inc.

—Samira's Garden (Ballet School, Book 2) Macdonald, Fiona. 2017. (Ballet School Ser.). (ENG.). 240p. (J). (gr. 3-7). pap. 7.95 *(978-1-912006-61-8(8),* Scribo) Book Hse. GBR. Dist: Sterling Publishing Co., Inc.

Stooke, Andrew. Bafana Bafana: A Story of Soccer, Magic & Mandela. Blacklaws, Troy. 2010. (ENG.). 64p. pap. 24.00 *(978-1-77009-718-6(X))* Jacana Media ZAF. Dist: Independent Pubs. Group.

Stoop, Naoko. All Creatures Great & Small. 2012. 22p. (J). (gr. k — 1). bds. 6.95 *(978-1-4027-8581-8(X))* Sterling Publishing Co., Inc.

—Jonah & the Big Fish. Thoms, Susan Collins. 2016. 22p. (J). (— 1). bds. 6.95 *(978-1-4549-1493-8(9),* 1402423) Sterling Publishing Co., Inc.

—Love Is Patient, Love Is Kind. 2017. 22p. (J). (— 1). bds. 6.95 *(978-1-4549-1767-0(9))* Sterling Publishing Co., Inc.

—Noah's Ark. Collins Thoms, Susan. 2013. 22p. (J). (— 1). bds. 6.95 *(978-1-4027-8549-8(6))* Sterling Publishing Co., Inc.

—Pup & Bear. Banks, Kate. 2017. (J). (gr. -1-2). 32p. 17.99 *(978-0-399-55409-4(2));* (ENG.). 40p. lib. bdg. 20.99 *(978-0-399-55410-0(6))* Random Hse. Children's Bks. (Schwartz & Wade Bks.).

—Sun & Moon Have a Tea Party. Heo, Yumi. 2020. 40p. (J). (gr. -1-2). 17.99 *(978-0-385-39033-0(5),* Schwartz & Wade Bks.) Random Hse. Children's Bks.

Stoqnova, Kremena P. Beyond Reach. Davis, Siobhan. Hartigan, Kelly, ed. 2015. (ENG.). 416p. (J). pap. *(978-0-9929304-4-8(8))* Davis, Siobhan.

Storch, Ellen N. At the Circus. Muench-Williams, Heather. I.t. ed. 2005. (HRL Board Book Ser.). 10p. (J). (gr. -1-1). bds. 10.95 *(978-1-57332-285-0(7),* HighReach Learning, Incorporated) Carson-Dellosa Publishing, LLC.

—Building a Sand Castle. Mullican, Judy & Williams, Heather L. I.t. ed. 2004. (HRL Big Book Ser.). (J). (gr. -1). pap. 10.95 *(978-1-57332-297-3(0));* pap. 10.95 *(978-1-57332-298-0(9))* Carson-Dellosa Publishing, LLC. (HighReach Learning, Incorporated).

—Caillou & the Storyteller. Mullican, Judy. I.t. ed. 2006. (HRL Board Book Ser.). (J). (gr. k-18). pap. 10.95 *(978-1-57332-330-7(6),* HighReach Learning, Incorporated) Carson-Dellosa Publishing, LLC.

—Caillou Finds a Caterpillar. Jarrell, Pamela R. I.t. ed. 2005. (HRL Board Book Ser.). (J). (gr. -1-1). pap. 10.95 *(978-1-57332-292-8(X),* HighReach Learning, Incorporated) Carson-Dellosa Publishing, LLC.

—Caillou's Community. Vonthron, Satanta C. I.t. ed. 2006. (HRL Board Book Ser.). (J). (gr. k-18). pap. 10.95 *(978-1-57332-332-1(2),* HighReach Learning, Incorporated) Carson-Dellosa Publishing, LLC.

—Caillou's Hiking Adventure. Muench-Williams, Heather & Jarrell, Pamela R. I.t. ed. 2005. (HRL Board Book Ser.). (J). (gr. k-18). pap. 10.95 *(978-1-57332-329-1(2),* HighReach Learning, Incorporated) Carson-Dellosa Publishing, LLC.

—Caillov Learns about Space. Williams, Heather L. & Muench-Williams, Heather. I.t. ed. 2005. (HRL Board Book Ser.). (J). (gr. -1-k). bds. 10.95 *(978-1-57332-308-6(X),* HighReach Learning, Incorporated) Carson-Dellosa Publishing, LLC.

—Caillov Visits the Circus. Hensley, Sarah M. I.t. ed. 2005. (HRL Board Book Ser.). (J). (gr. -1-k). pap. 10.95 *(978-1-57332-309-3(8),* HighReach Learning, Incorporated) Carson-Dellosa Publishing, LLC.

—Down at the Shore. Vonthron, Satanta C. I.t. ed. 2005. (HRL Board Book Ser.). (J). (gr. -1-k). pap. 10.95 *(978-1-57332-306-2(3),* HighReach Learning, Incorporated) Carson-Dellosa Publishing, LLC.

—In the Kitchen. Vonthron, Satanta C. I.t. ed. 2004. (HRL Big Book Ser.). (J). (gr. -1-k). pap. 10.95 *(978-1-57332-316-1(0));* pap. 10.95 *(978-1-57332-317-8(9))* Carson-Dellosa Publishing, LLC. (HighReach Learning, Incorporated).

—Mary & Marsha Make Cookies. Mullican, Judy. I.t. ed. 2005. 18p. (J). (gr. -1-k). pap. 10.95 *(978-1-57332-346-8(2),* HighReach Learning, Incorporated) Carson-Dellosa Publishing, LLC.

—What's at the Beach? Heady, Heather. I.t. ed. 2005. 10p. (J). (gr. -1-k). pap. 10.95 *(978-1-57332-355-0(1),* HighReach Learning, Incorporated) Carson-Dellosa Publishing, LLC.

Storch, Ellen N. Here We Go! Storch, Ellen N. I.t. ed. 2005. (HRL Board Book Ser.). (J). (gr. -1-k). pap. 10.95 *(978-1-57332-322-2(5),* HighReach Learning, Incorporated) Carson-Dellosa Publishing, LLC.

Storch, Ellen N. & Gillen, Lisa P. Someone New in the Neighborhood. Mullican, Judy. I.t. ed. 2005. 20p. (J). (gr. -1-k). pap. 10.95 *(978-1-57332-356-7(X),* HighReach Learning, Incorporated) Carson-Dellosa Publishing, LLC.

Storer, Florence. Christmas Tales & Christmas Verse. Field, Eugene. 2007. 100p. per. *(978-1-4065-2387-4(9))* Dodo Pr.

Storey, Geri. Peter Puck & the Stolen Stanley Cup. McFarlane, Brian. 2015. (Adv. Hockey's Greatest Mascot Ser.). 64p. (J). (gr. 1-4). 10.99 *(978-1-77049-581-4(9),* Fenn-Tundra) Tundra Bks. CAN. Dist: Penguin Random Hse. LLC.

Storey, Jim. Animal Art, 6 vols. Holden, Pam. 2009. (Red Rocket Readers Ser.). 16p. (gr. 1-1). pap. *(978-1-877419-73-7(7),* Red Rocket Readers) Flying Start Bks.

—Huff & Puff!, 6 pack. Holden, Pam. 2009. (Red Rocket Readers Ser.). 16p. (gr. 2-2). pap. *(978-1-877363-58-0(8),* Red Rocket Readers) Flying Start Bks.

—The Long, Long Ride, 6 pack. Holden, Pam. 2009. (Red Rocket Readers Ser.). 22p. (gr. 2-2). pap. *(978-1-877363-76-4(6))* Flying Start Bks.

—Make a Scarecrow. Holden, Pam. 2015. 16p. (-1). pap. *(978-1-77654-133-1(2),* Red Rocket Readers) Flying Start Bks.

—Sailor Sam in Trouble. Eggleton, Jill. 2004. (Rigby Sails Early Ser.). (ENG.). 16p. (gr. 1-2). pap. 6.95 *(978-0-7578-9295-0(7))* Houghton Mifflin Harcourt Publishing Co.

—Sally Snip Snap's Party, 6 pack. Holden, Pam. 2009. (Red Rocket Readers Ser.). 19p. (gr. 2-1). pap. *(978-1-877363-57-3(X),* Red Rocket Readers) Flying Start Bks.

—Sneaky Spider, 6 pack. Holden, Pam. 2009. (Red Rocket Readers Ser.). 17p. (gr. 2-2). pap. *(978-1-877363-83-2(9))* Flying Start Bks.

—Three Little Pigs, 6 pack. Holden, Pam. 2009. (Red Rocket Readers Ser.). 16p. (gr. -1-1). pap. *(978-1-877363-11-5(1),* Red Rocket Readers) Flying Start Bks.

Storey, Jim & Hawley, Kelvin. Dinosaur Hunters, 6 pack. Holden, Pam. 2009. (Red Rocket Readers Ser.). 16p. (gr. 2-2). pap. *(978-1-877363-59-7(6),* Red Rocket Readers) Flying Start Bks.

Storey, Lela Belle. The Mystery of the Vanishing Chickens. Lozzi, Annette. 2013. 32p. pap. *(978-1-922120-68-7(5))* Interactive Pubns. Pty, Ltd.

Storey, Linda & Nielson, Doug. Angie the Aviator. Carlson, Glenn E. Robinson, Helen, ed. I.t. ed. 2004. 55p. (J). (gr. 2-9). 21.95 *(978-0-9611954-4-1(4))* Watosh Publishing.

Stories, Brimoral. The Hotel Hero. Stories, Brimoral. 2019. (ENG.). 30p. (J). (gr. k-4). 15.99 *(978-1-7332425-2-3(X))* BriMoral Stories.

Storino, Sara, et al. Alice in Wonderland. Corteggiani, François. 2020. (Disney Classics Ser.). (ENG.). 48p. (J). (gr. 2-6). lib. bdg. 28.50 ***(978-1-5321-4534-6(9)***, 35180, Graphic Novels) Spotlight.

Storms, Patricia. Edward & the Eureka Lucky Wish Company. Todd, Barbara. 2009. 32p. (J). (gr. -1-2). 16.95 *(978-1-55453-264-3(7))* Kids Can Pr., Ltd. CAN. Dist: Hachette Bk. Group.

—The Ghosts Go Scaring. Bozik, Chrissy. 2016. (ENG.). 24p. (J). (gr. -1-k). 14.99 *(978-1-5107-1228-7(3),* Sky Pony Pr.) Skyhorse Publishing Co., Inc.

—Kid Confidential: An Insider's Guide to Grown-Ups. Montgomery, Monte. 2012. (ENG.). 160p. (J). (gr. 3-6). 24.94 *(978-0-8027-8643-2(X),* 9780802786432) Walker & Co.

—Saints of Note: The Comic Collection. Jenkins, Diana R. 2009. 93p. (J). (gr. 2-5). pap. 9.95 *(978-0-8198-7120-6(6))* Pauline Bks. & Media.

Storr, Nicola. Grandma's Basket. Sims, Janice. 2010. 28p. pap. *(978-1-904408-68-0(0))* Bank House Bks.

Story Rhyme Staff. Self-Esteem: Stories, Poetry & Activity Pages. Story Rhyme Staff. Date not set. 28p. (YA). (gr. 4-9). ring bd. 19.95 *(978-1-56820-107-8(9))* Story Time Stories That Rhyme.

Storybook Art Team, Disney. Disney Baby: ABCs. Broderick, Kathy. 2019. (Look & Find Ser.). (ENG.). 18p. (J). *(978-1-5037-4569-8(4),* 6024dd07-8809-459d-a3c7-42e4e4aadf6f, p i kids) Phoenix International Publications, Inc.

—Disney Baby: Best Friends. Harmening, Derek. 2018. (What Do You See? Ser.). (ENG.). 20p. (J). *(978-1-5037-4360-1(8),* 413fe94b-4424-48ee-a82c-19789571a48a, p i kids) Phoenix International Publications, Inc.

—Disney Baby: Busy Day. Broderick, Kathy. 2019. (ENG.). 20p. (J). *(978-1-5037-4659-6(3),* 3e1ba637-b2a9-4608-a856-53e738f12054, p i kids) Phoenix International Publications, Inc.

—Disney Baby: Let's Play! Skwish, Emily. 2019. (What Do You See? Ser.). (ENG.). 20p. (J). *(978-1-5037-4566-7(X),* 7ec45078-f322-4aab-ac1e-8c42d470c7ce, p i kids) Phoenix International Publications, Inc.

—Disney Baby: Polka Dot Day! Brooke, Susan Rich. 2019. (Play-A-Sound Ser.). (ENG.). 20p. (J). bds. *(978-1-5037-4658-9(5),* f18409de-43b1-4b36-bda8-601033cf8c20, p i kids) Phoenix International Publications, Inc.

—Disney Frozen. 2015. (Me Reader Ser.). (ENG.). 192p. (J). *(978-1-5037-0038-3(0),* d7371f2e-d70c-47e5-8f2e-9d4e78cf1017, p i kids) Phoenix International Publications, Inc.

—Disney Frozen: A Starry Night. Keast, Jennifer H. 2015. (Play-A-Sound Ser.). (ENG.). 10p. (J). pap. *(978-1-5037-0062-8(3),* f627739b-cdff-4314-8aa6-03b648826b8d, p i kids) Phoenix International Publications, Inc.

—Disney Minnie Mouse: Daisy's Bright Idea. Keast, Jennifer H. 2017. (Play-A-Sound Ser.). (ENG.). 10p. (J). *(978-1-4508-7440-3(1),* 0d9ada57-6225-4677-bcf0-4c0bb7015d97, p i kids) Phoenix International Publications, Inc.

—Disney: the Lion King: Friends Forever. 2019. (Play-A-Sound Ser.). (ENG.). 12p. (J). *(978-1-5037-4356-4(X),* b2283e46-6ec4-41de-ae8d-f827b42633b7, p i kids) Phoenix International Publications, Inc.

—Disney: the Lion King: Songs with Simba. 2019. (ENG.). 12p. (J). *(978-1-5037-4590-2(2),* b56ea6b4-0efa-464b-939e-56f3add5ff67, p i kids) Phoenix International Publications, Inc.

Storybook Art Team, Disney, jt. illus. see Inc., Loter.

Stossel, Sage. Season of Angels. Wile, Mary Lee. 2013. *(978-0-88028-367-0(X))* Forward Movement Pubns.

Stott, Apryl. Brigid & the Butter: A Legend about Saint Brigid of Ireland. 2017. 25p. (J). pap. *(978-0-8198-1233-9(1))* Pauline Bks. & Media.

—Daddy, Am I Beautiful? Lazurek, Michelle S. 2015. 24p. (J). pap. *(978-0-8198-1905-5(0))* Pauline Bks. & Media.

Stott, Apryl. Historias de la Biblia para Los Pequeñitos. Monchamp, Genny. 2014.Tr. of Bible Stories for Little Ones. (SPA.). (J). 16.95 *(978-0-8198-3443-0(2))* Pauline Bks. & Media.

Stott, Dorothy. Bunny Loves Others. Simon, Mary Manz. 2006. (First Virtues for Toddlers Ser.). 20p. (J). 5.99 *(978-0-7847-1409-6(6),* 04037) Standard Publishing.

—First Feelings (padded Cover) Twelve Stories for Toddlers. Simon, Mary Manz. rev. ed. 2017. (ENG.). 256p. (J). (gr. -1-k). 12.99 *(978-1-4336-4384-2(7),* 005786469, B&H Kids) B&H Publishing Group.

—Hannah Is a Big Sister. Capucilli, Alyssa Satin. 2014. (Hannah & Henry Ser.). 32p. (J). (gr. -1-k). 5.99 *(978-0-7641-6750-8(2),* B.E.S. Publishing) Peterson's.

—Henry Is a Big Brother. Capucilli, Alyssa Satin. 2014. (Hannah & Henry Ser.). (ENG.). 32p. (J). (gr. -1-k). 5.99 *(978-0-7641-6749-2(9),* B.E.S. Publishing) Peterson's.

—Piglet Tells the Truth. Simon, Mary Manz. 2006. (First Virtues for Toddlers Ser.). 20p. (J). 5.99 *(978-0-7847-1407-2(X),* 04035) Standard Publishing.

—Ten in the Bed. 2010. (Padded Board Book W/CD Ser.). 8p. (J). (gr. k-2). bds. 10.99 incl. audio compact disk *(978-1-59922-578-4(6))* Twin Sisters IP, LLC.

Stott, Dorothy & Richard, Ilene. Ten Hungry Turkeys, 1 vol. Balsley, Tilda. 2018. (ENG.). 32p. (J). (gr. -1-3). 16.99 *(978-1-4556-2235-1(4),* Pelican Publishing) Arcadia Publishing.

Stotts, Jasmyn & Jayda. When I Learned to Read. Toles-Stotts, LaShunda. I.t. ed. 2005. 36p. (J). per. 11.99 *(978-1-59879-071-9(4))* Lifevest Publishing, Inc.

Stouch, Ryan. Bailey & Friends. Kiick, Lisa. 2008. 40p. pap. 14.95 *(978-1-59858-743-2(9))* Dog Ear Publishing, LLC.

Stouffer, Rebecca. At the Cabin: In the Woods by the Lake up North. Wilke, Cheryl Weibye. 2017. (J). pap. *(978-0-9835189-7-6(1))* Raven Productions, Inc.

Stout, William. Abu & the 7 Marvels. Matheson, Richard. 2003. 128p. (YA). pap. 21.95 *(978-1-887368-49-0(3))* Gauntlet, Inc.

—The Emerald Wand of Oz. Smith, Sherwood. 2007. 262p. (J). 17.00 *(978-1-4223-6710-0(X))* DIANE Publishing Co.

—The Emerald Wand of Oz. Smith, Sherwood. 2005. (ENG.). 272p. (J). (gr. -1-17). 16.99 *(978-0-06-029607-0(0))* HarperCollins Pubs.

Stover, Beth. Busy Little Beaver. Bentley, Dawn. 2003. (ENG.). 32p. (J). (gr. -1-1). pap. 3.95 *(978-1-59249-011-0(5),* S2029); 12.95 *(978-1-59249-012-7(3),* PS2079) Soundprints.

—The Prickly Porcupine. Bentley, Dawn. 2003. (Soundprints' Read-and-Discover Ser.). (ENG.). 32p. (J). (gr. -1-3). 12.95 *(978-1-59249-014-1(X),* PS2065); pap. 3.95 *(978-1-59249-013-4(1),* S2015) Soundprints.

—Wake up, Black Bear! Bentley, Dawn. 2003. (ENG.). 32p. (J). (gr. -1-17). pap. 4.35 *(978-1-59249-007-3(7),* S2020); 12.95 *(978-1-59249-008-0(5),* PS2070) Soundprints.

—Welcome Back, Puffin! Bentley, Dawn. 2003. (Soundprints' Read-and-Discover Ser.). (ENG.). 32p. (J). (gr. -1-k). 12.95 *(978-1-59249-010-3(7),* PS2064); pap. 3.95 *(978-1-59249-009-7(3),* S2014) Soundprints.

Stover, Breanna. Little Susie Patch. Jones, Judith M. 2020. (ENG.). 44p. (J). 29.99 ***(978-1-7283-6246-5(6))***; pap. 20.99 ***(978-1-7283-6244-1(X))*** AuthorHouse.

Stover, Kellan. Brown. Doering, Amanda. 2018. (Sing Your Colors! Ser.). (ENG.). 24p. (J). (gr. -1-2). lib. bdg. 33.99 *(978-1-68410-317-1(7),* 140863); lib. bdg. 33.99 incl. audio compact disk *(978-1-68410-139-9(5),* 31855) Cantata Learning.

Stowell, Elena. Winging It! A Monarch Love Story. Davis, Bev. 2019. (ENG.). 38p. (J). (gr. k-6). 19.99 ***(978-1-948225-78-6(6))*** Thewordverve.

Stowell, Elena. Frango & Chicken. Stowell, Elena. 2018. (ENG.). 46p. (J). (gr. k-6). 19.99 *(978-0-9992479-5-2(6))* Thewordverve.

—Frango & Chicken: (in Portugese) Stowell, Elena. 2018. (POR.). 46p. (J). (gr. k-6). 19.99 *(978-1-948225-20-5(4))* Thewordverve.

Stower, Adam. Children's English History in Verse. Baker, Kenneth, ed. 2007. 289p. pap. 20.00 *(978-1-4223-9012-2(8))* DIANE Publishing Co.

—Fangs for Everything. Greenwald, Tommy. 2019. (Crimebiters Ser.: 4). (ENG.). 224p. (J). (gr. 3-7). 12.99 *(978-1-338-19328-2(7),* Scholastic Pr.) Scholastic, Inc.

—Fear Itself. Clements, Andrew. 2011. (Benjamin Pratt & the Keepers of the School Ser.: 2). (ENG.). (J). (gr. 2-5). 240p. pap. 8.99 *(978-1-4169-3908-5(3));* 224p. 16.99 *(978-1-4169-3887-3(7))* Simon & Schuster Children's Publishing. (Atheneum Bks. for Young Readers).

—In Harm's Way. Clements, Andrew. (Benjamin Pratt & the Keepers of the School Ser.: 4). (ENG.). (J). (gr. 2-5). 2014. 240p. pap. 8.99 *(978-1-4169-3910-8(5));* 2013. 224p. 14.99 *(978-1-4169-3889-7(3))* Simon & Schuster Children's Publishing. (Atheneum Bks. for Young Readers).

—Legends of the Shadow World: The Secret Country; the Shadow World; Dragon's Fire. Johnson, Jane. 2010. (ENG.). 1120p. (J). (gr. 3-7). pap. 14.99 *(978-1-4169-9082-6(8),* Simon & Schuster Bks. For Young Readers) Simon & Schuster Bks. For Young Readers.

—Mrs. Noodlekugel. Pinkwater, Daniel M. 2012. (Mrs. Noodlekugel Ser.: 1). 80p. (J). (gr. k-4). 14.99 *(978-0-7636-5053-7(6))* Candlewick Pr.

—Mrs. Noodlekugel. Pinkwater, Daniel M. 2013. (Mrs. Noodlekugel Ser.: 1). 80p. (J). (gr. k-4). pap. 6.99 *(978-0-7636-6452-7(9))* Candlewick Pr.

—Mrs. Noodlekugel & Drooly the Bear. Pinkwater, Daniel M. 2015. (Mrs. Noodlekugel Ser.: 3). 96p. (J). (gr. k-4). 14.99 *(978-0-7636-6645-3(9))* Candlewick Pr.

—Mrs. Noodlekugel & Four Blind Mice. Pinkwater, Daniel M. (Mrs. Noodlekugel Ser.: 2). 96p. (J). (gr. k-4). 2015. pap. 5.99 *(978-0-7636-7658-2(6));* 2013. 14.99 *(978-0-7636-5054-4(4))* Candlewick Pr.

—Mrs. Noodlekugel & Four Blind Mice. Pinkwater, Daniel M. 2015. (Mrs. Noodlekugel Ser.). (ENG.). (J). (gr. k-4). lib. bdg. 16.60 *(978-1-62765-746-4(0))* Perfection Learning Corp.

—My Dog Is Better Than Your Dog. Greenwald, Tom. 2015. 198p. (J). pap. *(978-0-545-91669-1(0),* Scholastic Pr.) Scholastic, Inc.

—My Dog Is Better Than Your Dog. Greenwald, Tommy. 2015. (Crimebiters Ser.: 1). (ENG.). 208p. (J). (gr. 3-7). 12.99 *(978-0-545-77332-4(6),* Scholastic Pr.) Scholastic, Inc.

—Piggy Hero. Jones, Pip. 2018. (Piggy Handsome Ser.). (ENG.). 192p. (J). pap. 9.95 *(978-0-571-32756-0(7),* Faber & Faber Children's Bks.) Faber & Faber, Inc.

—The Secret Country. Johnson, Jane. 2007. (Eidolon Chronicles Ser.: 1). (ENG.). 336p. (J). (gr. 3-7). per. 15.99 *(978-1-4169-3815-6(X),* Simon & Schuster Bks. For Young Readers) Simon & Schuster Bks. For Young Readers.

—This Side of Magic, 1. Jones, Marcia & Dadey, Debbie. 2009. (Keyholders Ser.: 1). (ENG.). 144p. (J). (gr. 4-7). 17.44 *(978-0-7653-5982-7(0),* 900050018) Doherty, Tom Assocs., LLC.

—Walls Within Walls. Sherry, Maureen. (ENG.). 368p. (J). (gr. 3-7). 2012. pap. 7.99 *(978-0-06-176703-6(4));* 2010. 16.99 *(978-0-06-176700-5(X))* HarperCollins Pubs. (Tegen, Katherine Bks).

—We Hold These Truths. Clements, Andrew. 2013. (Benjamin Pratt & the Keepers of the School Ser.: 5). (ENG.). 272p. (J). (gr. 2-5). 14.99 *(978-1-4169-3890-3(7),* Atheneum Bks. for Young Readers) Simon & Schuster Children's Publishing.

—We the Children, 1. Clements, Andrew. 2010. (Benjamin Pratt & the Keepers of the School Ser.: 1). (ENG.). 160p. (J). (gr. 2-5). 16.99 *(978-1-4169-3886-6(9))* Simon & Schuster, Inc.

—The Whites of Their Eyes. Clements, Andrew. 2013. (Benjamin Pratt & the Keepers of the School Ser.: 3). (ENG.). 240p. (J). (gr. 2-5). pap. 6.99 *(978-1-4169-3909-2(1),* Atheneum Bks. for Young Readers) Simon & Schuster Children's Publishing.

Stower, Adam. Naughty Kitty! Stower, Adam. 2014. (ENG.). 40p. (J). (gr. -1-k). 16.99 *(978-0-545-57604-8(0),* Orchard Bks.) Scholastic, Inc.

—Troll & the Oliver. Stower, Adam. 2015. (ENG.). 40p. (J). (gr. -1-2). 16.99 *(978-0-7636-7956-9(9),* Templar) Candlewick Pr.

Stower, Adam, jt. illus. see Henry, Thomas.

Stower, Adam, jt. illus. see Sherry, Maureen.

Stowers, B. J., photos by. Hal Stowers & the Art of Life Blending: How to Keep Your Creative Juices Flowing, 2 vols., 1 bk, Stowers, B. J. Stowers, Hal. 2004. (Life Blending Ser.: Vols. 1-2). 276p. 90.00 *(978-0-9749832-0-2(9))* Walking Tree, Inc.

Stoyanova, Mariya. It's Okay to Be Different. Holiday, Josalyn Ironette. 2017. (ENG.). (J). 19.99 *(978-0-9985781-1-8(8))* Mindstir Media.

—Saying Goodbye to Stein: A Rhyming Storybook to Help Little Ones Overcome the Loss of a Pet. Sarkisyan, Mary. 2018. (ENG.). 24p. (J). pap. 7.00 *(978-0-692-15938-5(X))* Sarkisyan, Mary.

Støyva, Mei. Baby's First Christmas. Birdsong, Minnie. Cottage Door Press, ed. 2019. (Little Bird Greetings Keepsake Book Ser.). (ENG.). 8p. (J). (gr. -1). bds. 6.99 *(978-1-68052-491-8(7),* 1003660) Cottage Door Pr.

—Baby's First Halloween. VonFeder, Rosa. Cottage Door Press, ed. 2019. (Little Bird Greetings Keepsake Book Ser.). (ENG.). 16p. (J). (gr. -1-k). bds. 6.99 *(978-1-68052-312-6(0),* 1002870) Cottage Door Pr.

—Happy Halloween, Little Baby! VonFeder, Rosa. Cottage Door Press, ed. 2019. (Little Bird Greetings: Keepsake Board Book with Personalization Flap Ser.). (ENG.). 10p. (J). (gr. -1-2). bds. 6.99 *(978-1-68052-313-3(9),* 1002880) Cottage Door Pr.

—Hello! Please! Thank You! Wooden Slider Book with Sound. Byrd, Ruby. Cottage Door Press, ed. 2018. (Early Bird Sound Books Slide & Sound Ser.). (ENG.). 16p. (J). (gr. -1-1). bds. 19.99 *(978-1-68052-300-3(7),* 1002781) Cottage Door Pr.

—How Many Do I Love You? a Valentine Counting Book: Square Padded Board Picture Book. Love-Byrd, Cheri. Cottage Door Press, ed. 2017. (Square Padded Picture Book Ser.). (ENG.). 13p. (J). (gr. -1-k). bds. 7.99 *(978-1-68052-274-7(4),* 1002590) Cottage Door Pr.

—Merry Christmas, Little Baby! Birdsong, Minnie. Cottage Door Press, ed. 2019. (Little Bird Greetings: Keepsake Board Book with Personalization Flap Ser.). (ENG.). 10p. (J). (gr. -1-2). bds. 6.99 *(978-1-68052-492-5(5),* 1003670) Cottage Door Pr.

St.Pierre, Joe. Great White Shark Adventure. Fraioli, James O. & Cousteau, Fabien. 2019. (Fabien Cousteau Expeditions Ser.). (ENG.). 112p. (J). (gr. 3-7). 12.99 *(978-1-5344-2087-8(8),* McElderry, Margaret K. Bks.) McElderry, Margaret K. Bks.

—Journey under the Arctic. Cousteau, Fabien & Fraioli, James O. 2020. (Fabien Cousteau Expeditions Ser.). (ENG.). 112p. (J). (gr. 3-7). 12.99 *(978-1-5344-2090-8(8));* 19.99 *(978-1-5344-2091-5(6))* McElderry, Margaret K. Bks. (McElderry, Margaret K. Bks.).

Straathof, Alette. 100 Dinosaur & Prehistoric Words to Know. Wing, Scarlett. Cottage Door Press, ed. 2019. (Smithsonian Kids Ser.). (ENG.). 22p. (J). (gr. -1-2). bds. 9.99 *(978-1-68052-702-5(9),* 1004350) Cottage Door Pr.

Strain, Shiloh. Aloha Beach Chicken. Clower, Dawn. 2017. (Beach Chicken Ser.: Vol. 2). (ENG.). (J). (gr. k-2). pap. 12.99 *(978-0-692-96780-5(X))* hart Hse. publishing's.

Straker, Bethany. Belly Laugh Jokes for Kids: 350 Hilarious Jokes. Sky Pony Editors. 2015. 144p. (J). (gr. k). 9.99 *(978-1-63450-156-9(X),* Sky Pony Pr.) Skyhorse Publishing Co., Inc.

—Belly Laugh Knock-Knock Jokes for Kids: 350 Hilarious Knock-Knock Jokes. Sky Pony Editors. 2015. 144p. (J). (gr. k). 9.99 *(978-1-63220-437-0(1),* Sky Pony Pr.) Skyhorse Publishing Co., Inc.

—Belly Laugh Riddles & Puns for Kids: 350 Hilarious Riddles & Puns. Sky Pony Editors. 2016. 144p. (J). (gr. k). 9.99 *(978-1-5107-1198-3(8)*, Sky Pony Pr.) Skyhorse Publishing Co., Inc.

—Boo's Beard. Mannering, Rose. 2015. 32p. (J). (gr. -1-k). 16.99 *(978-1-63450-207-8(8)*, Sky Pony Pr.) Skyhorse Publishing Co., Inc.

—A Curious Robot on Mars! Duffett-Smith, James. 2013. (ENG.). 32p. (J). (gr. -1-k). 14.95 *(978-1-62087-994-8(8)*, 620994, Sky Pony Pr.) Skyhorse Publishing Co., Inc.

—Fantastic Fugitives: Criminals, Cutthroats, & Slaves Who Changed History (While on the Run!) DuMont, Brianna. 2016. (Changed History Ser.). 192p. (J). (gr. 3-7). 16.99 *(978-1-63220-412-7(6)*, Sky Pony Pr.) Skyhorse Publishing Co., Inc.

—The Funny Bunny Fly. 2014. 32p. (J). (gr. -1-k). 14.95 *(978-1-62914-610-2(2)*, Sky Pony Pr.) Skyhorse Publishing Co., Inc.

—Pierre the French Bulldog Recycles. Louise, Kate. 2015. (ENG.). 32p. (J). (gr. -1-k). 14.99 *(978-1-63220-411-0(8)*, Sky Pony Pr.) Skyhorse Publishing Co., Inc.

—Ruby Moo's Deep-Sea Adventure! Atherton, Isabel. 2014. (ENG.). 32p. (J). (gr. -1-k). 14.95 *(978-1-62914-625-6(0)*, Sky Pony Pr.) Skyhorse Publishing Co., Inc.

—Smelly Ghost. Atherton, Isabel. 2013. (ENG.). 32p. (J). (gr. -1-k). 14.95 *(978-1-62087-989-4(1)*, 620989, Sky Pony Pr.) Skyhorse Publishing Co., Inc.

—The Spotty Dotty Daffodil. Mannering, Rose. 2014. 32p. (J). (gr. -1-k). 16.95 *(978-1-62636-346-5(3)*, Sky Pony Pr.) Skyhorse Publishing Co., Inc.

—Stella & Steve Travel Through Space! Duffett-Smith, James. 2014. 32p. (J). (gr. -1-k). 14.95 *(978-1-62873-815-5(4)*, Sky Pony Pr.) Skyhorse Publishing Co., Inc.

Straker, Bethany. Springy Chicken. Straker, Bethany. Atherton, Isabel. 2014. 32p. (J). (gr. -1-k). 14.95 *(978-1-62636-161-4(4)*, Sky Pony Pr.) Skyhorse Publishing Co., Inc.

Strambini, Karla. The Extraordinary Mr. Qwerty. Strambini, Karla. 2014. (ENG.). 32p. (J). (gr. k-3). 16.99 *(978-0-7636-7324-6(2))* Candlewick Pr.

Strand, Vivian. I Am Utterly Unique: Celebrating the Strengths of Children with Asperger Syndrome & High-Functioning Autism. Larson, Elaine M. et al. 2006. 56p. (J). (gr. -1-3). 18.95 *(978-1-931282-89-5(7))* Autism Asperger Publishing Co.

—The Kaleidoscope Kid: Focusing on the Strengths of Children with Asperger Syndrome & High-Functioning Autism. Larson, Elaine Marie. 2007. 35p. 17.95 *(978-1-931282-41-3(2))* Autism Asperger Publishing Co.

Strange, Katie. Ana & the Pet Show. Hoffmann, Sara E. 2013. (My Reading Neighborhood: First-Grade Sight Word Stories Ser.). (ENG.). 16p. (J). (gr. -1-1). pap. 5.99 *(978-1-4677-1170-8(5)*, 9781467711708) Lerner Publishing Group.

—Nia Bakes Cookies. Hoffmann, Sara E. 2013. (My Reading Neighborhood: First-Grade Sight Word Stories Ser.). (ENG.). 16p. (J). (gr. -1-1). pap. 5.99 *(978-1-4677-1172-2(1)*, 9781467711722) Lerner Publishing Group.

Strapec, Amy. The Garbage Grandma. Silverman, Toby. 2005. 23p. (J). 9.50 *(978-0-9793475-0-4(5))* Silverman, Toby.

Strasburg, Sunny, jt. illus. see Stensaas, Martin.

Strassburg, Brian. More-If You Had to Choose, What Would You Do?, Vol. Humphrey, Sandra McLeod & Barker, Dan. 2003. (ENG.). 132p. (gr. 4-7). pap. 14.99 *(978-1-59102-077-6(8))* Prometheus Bks., Pubs.

Strasser, Susanne. So Far Up. Strasser, Susanne. 2018. (ENG.). 22p. (J). (— 1). bds. 7.99 *(978-1-58089-848-5(3))* Charlesbridge Publishing, Inc.

—So Light, So Heavy. Strasser, Susanne. 2018. (ENG.). 22p. (J). (— 1). bds. 7.99 *(978-1-58089-849-2(1))* Charlesbridge Publishing, Inc.

Stratford, Stevan. Allah Gave Me a Nose to Smell. Qamaruddin, Rizwana. 2015. (ENG.). 32p. (J). 8.95 *(978-0-86037-333-9(9))* Kube Publishing Ltd. GBR. Dist: Consortium Bk. Sales & Distribution.

—Allah Gave Me a Tongue to Taste. Jones, Ayesha. 2016. (ENG.). 32p. (J). 8.95 *(978-0-86037-338-4(X))* Kube Publishing Ltd. GBR. Dist: Consortium Bk. Sales & Distribution.

Stratford, Steven. Allah Gave Me Two Eyes to See.... D'Oyen, Fatima M. 2007. (ENG.). 24p. pap. *(978-0-86037-283-7(9))* Kube Publishing Ltd. GBR. Dist: Consortium Bk. Sales & Distribution.

Stratman, Kay. The Christmas Crown. Martin, Maria G. 2010. 20p. pap. 10.95 *(978-1-60911-442-8(6)*, Eloquent Bks.) Strategic Book Publishing & Rights Agency (SBPRA).

Stratton, Helen. The Princess & Curdie. MacDonald, George. 2003. 162p. pap. 12.99 *(978-1-57646-634-6(5))* Quiet Vision Publishing.

Strauss, Michael L. Timothy Cooper's- Boone's Magical Adventure: Boone's Magical Adventure. Strauss, Michael L. 2019. (Timothy Cooper Ser.: Vol. 2). (ENG.). 46p. (J). (gr. k-6). 21.99 *(978-0-578-51104-7(5))* Strauss, Michael L.

Straw, Wendy. Action Rhymes Musical Songbook. 2019. (Wendy Straw's Songbooks Ser.). (ENG.). 16p. (J). (— 1). 14.99 *(978-1-925386-92-9(9)*, Brolly Bks.) Borghesi & Adam Pubs. Pty Ltd AUS. Dist: Independent Pubs. Group.

—Counting Rhymes Musical Songbook. 2019. (Wendy Straw's Songbooks Ser.). (ENG.). 16p. (J). (— 1). 14.99 *(978-1-925386-94-3(5)*, Brolly Bks.) Borghesi & Adam Pubs. Pty Ltd AUS. Dist: Independent Pubs. Group.

Straw, Wendy. Itsy Bitsy Spider. Adam, Luisa. 2020. (Wendy Straw's Nursery Rhyme Collection). (ENG.). 12p. (J). (— 1). pap. 4.99 ***(978-1-921756-79-5(9)***, Brolly Bks.) Borghesi & Adam Pubs. Pty Ltd AUS. Dist: Independent Pubs. Group.

—Twinkle Twinkle Little Star Book N' Puzzle Pack. 2020. (KiddieJigs Ser.). (ENG.). 12p. (J). (— 1). bds. 15.99 ***(978-0-6486918-4-6(5)***, Brolly Bks.) Borghesi & Adam Pubs. Pty Ltd AUS. Dist: Independent Pubs. Group.

Straw, Wendy. Wheels on the Bus. 2016. (ENG.). 24p. (J). (gr. -1-k). bds. *(978-1-925386-74-5(0)*, Brolly Bks.) Borghesi & Adam Pubs. Pty Ltd.

Straw, Wendy. The Wheels on the Bus Book N' Puzzle Pack. 2020. (KiddieJigs Ser.). (ENG.). 12p. (J). (— 1). bds. 15.99 ***(978-0-6486918-3-9(7)***, Brolly Bks.) Borghesi & Adam Pubs. Pty Ltd AUS. Dist: Independent Pubs. Group.

Straw, Wendy. 7 Dark Tales. Grace, Christine. 2019. (ENG.). 96p. (YA). (gr. 7). *(978-1-925386-84-4(8))*; pap. *(978-1-925386-72-1(4))* Borghesi & Adam Pubs. Pty Ltd. (Brolly Bks.).

—7 Mór Dark Tales. Grace, Christine. 2020. (ENG.). 96p. (YA). (gr. 7). *(978-0-6484571-5-2(X)*, Brolly Bks.) Borghesi & Adam Pubs. Pty Ltd.

—7 Mór Dark Tales. Grace, Christine. 2020. (ENG.). 96p. (YA). (gr. 7). pap. 15.99 *(978-0-6484571-8-3(4)*, Brolly Bks.) Borghesi & Adam Pubs. Pty Ltd AUS. Dist: Independent Pubs. Group.

Strecker, Darren. Leelah at the Lake. Fettig, Pamela. 2010. 28p. pap. 9.99 *(978-1-60844-697-1(2))* Dog Ear Publishing, LLC.

Streed, Sam. Alfred's Book of Monsters. Streed, Sam. 2019. 32p. (J). (gr. -1-2). lib. bdg. 15.99 *(978-1-58089-833-1(5))* Charlesbridge Publishing, Inc.

Street, James. Santa's Elves & the Tickets. Garner, Ellen. 2012. 56p. pap. 12.99 *(978-0-615-55920-9(4))* EG Bks.

Street Level Studio. Math & Stories, Grades K-3. Bartch, Marian. 2007. 173p. per. 17.95 *(978-1-59647-222-8(7))* Good Year Bks.

Streeter, Talena. Loving Baby Louie: Hope in the Midst of Grief. Currie, Colleen & Currie, David. 2015. (ENG.). 54p. (J). 24.95 *(978-1-941447-44-4(9))* Emmaus Road Publishing.

Stref. The Tattoo Fox, 1 vol. Hutton, Alasdair. ed. 2014. (ENG.). 96p. (J). (gr. 2-8). pap. 9.95 *(978-1-908373-93-9(8)*, 05bb3c63-d284-4013-a546-b01345c542c5) Luath Pr. Ltd. GBR. Dist: Independent Pubs. Group.

Stremanos, A. M. Rosemary's Taken over My Potatoes. 2008. 20p. (J). 5.00 *(978-0-9801372-0-0(9))* Benedetti, Jef.

Stresing, Fred C., jt. illus. see Sherron, Kate.

Stresing, Fred C., jt. illus. see Wucinich, Warren.

Stevens-Marzo, Bridget. Daddy Does the Cha Cha Cha! Bedford, David. 2010. (ENG.). 32p. (J). (gr. -1-k). pap. 8.99 *(978-1-921541-16-2(4))* Little Hare Bks. AUS. Dist: Independent Pubs. Group.

—How Do You Make a Baby Smile? Sturges, Philemon. 2007. 24p. (J). (gr. -1-k). lib. bdg. 17.89 *(978-0-06-076073-1(7))* HarperCollins Pubs.

—Kiss Kiss! Wild, Margaret. 2004. 26p. pap. *(978-1-877003-51-6(4))* Little Hare Bks. AUS. Dist: HarperCollins Pubs. Australia.

—Kiss, Kiss! Wild, Margaret. 2008. 26p. bds. *(978-1-921272-33-2(3))* Little Hare Bks. AUS. Dist: HarperCollins Pubs. Australia.

—Kiss Kiss! Wild, Margaret. ed. 2006. (J). *(978-1-921049-24-8(3))* Little Hare Bks. AUS. Dist: HarperCollins Pubs. Australia.

Strickland, Shadra. The Diary of B. B. Bright, Possible Princess. Randall, Alice & Randall Williams, Caroline. 2012. (ENG.). 192p. (J). (gr. 2-6). 25.99 *(978-1-61858-015-3(9))* Turner Publishing Co.

—Eliza's Freedom Road: An Underground Railroad Diary. Nolen, Jerdine. 2011. (ENG.). 160p. (J). (gr. 3-7). 17.99 *(978-1-4169-5814-7(2)*, Simon & Schuster/Paula Wiseman Bks.) Simon & Schuster/Paula Wiseman Bks.

—Loving vs. Virginia: A Documentary Novel of the Landmark Civil Rights Case. Powell, Patricia Hruby. 2017. (ENG.). 260p. (YA). (gr. 7-12). 21.99 *(978-1-4521-2590-9(2))* Chronicle Bks. LLC.

—A Place Where Hurricanes Happen. Watson, Renée. 2010. 40p. (J). (gr. k-4). 17.99 *(978-0-375-85609-9(9)*, Random Hse. Bks. for Young Readers) Random Hse. Children's Bks.

—Please, Louise. Morrison, Toni & Morrison, Slade. 2014. (ENG.). 32p. (J). (gr. -1-3). 17.99 *(978-1-4169-8338-5(4)*, Simon & Schuster Bks. For Young Readers) Simon & Schuster Bks. For Young Readers.

—Sunday Shopping, 1 vol. Derby, Sally. 2015. (ENG.). 32p. (J). 17.95 *(978-1-60060-438-6(2)*, 9781600000000) Lee & Low Bks., Inc.

—White Water. Bandy, Michael S. & Stein, Eric. 2011. 40p. (J). (gr. k-3). 16.99 *(978-0-7636-3678-4(9))* Candlewick Pr.

Stringer, Karen. The Light of Stars. Glowatsky, Phyllis. 2003. 32p. (J). 19.95 *(978-1-931650-18-2(7))* Coastal Publishing Carolina, Inc.

Stringer, Lauren. Deer Dancer. Ray, Mary Lyn. 2014. (ENG.). 40p. (J). (gr. -1-3). 17.99 *(978-1-4424-3421-9(X)*, Beach Lane Bks.) Beach Lane Bks.

—Fold Me a Poem. George, Kristine O'Connell. 2005. (ENG.). 56p. (J). (gr. 1-4). 17.99 *(978-0-15-202501-4(4)*, 1192988) Houghton Mifflin Harcourt Publishing Co.

—Our Family Tree: An Evolution Story. Peters, Lisa Westberg. 2003. (ENG.). 48p. (J). (gr. -1-3). 17.99 *(978-0-15-201772-9(0)*, 1190844) Houghton Mifflin Harcourt Publishing Co.

—The Princess & Her Panther. Orr, Wendy. 2010. (ENG.). 40p. (J). (gr. -1-3). 16.99 *(978-1-4169-9780-1(6)*, Beach Lane Bks.) Beach Lane Bks.

—Red Rubber Boot Day. Ray, Mary Lyn. 2005. (ENG.). 32p. (J). (gr. -1-3). pap. 7.99 *(978-0-15-205398-7(0)*, 1196251) Houghton Mifflin Harcourt Publishing Co.

—Scarecrow. Rylant, Cynthia. 2014. 32p. pap. 7.00 *(978-1-61003-181-3(4))* Center for the Collaborative Classroom.

—The Shape of the World: A Portrait of Frank Lloyd Wright. Going, K. L. 2017. (ENG.). 40p. (J). (gr. k-5). 18.99 *(978-1-4424-7821-3(7))* Beach Lane Bks.

—Snow. Rylant, Cynthia. (ENG.). 40p. (J). (gr. -1-3). 2017. pap. 7.99 *(978-1-328-74055-7(2)*, 1677027, HMH Books For Young Readers); 2008. 17.99 *(978-0-15-205303-1(4)*, 1195978) Houghton Mifflin Harcourt Publishing Co.

—Tell Me about Your Day Today. Fox, Mem. 2012. (ENG.). 40p. (J). (gr. -1-3). 17.99 *(978-1-4169-9006-2(2)*, Beach Lane Bks.) Beach Lane Bks.

Stringer, Lauren. Yellow Time. Stringer, Lauren. 2016. (ENG.). 40p. (J). (gr. -1-3). 17.99 *(978-1-4814-3156-9(0)*, Beach Lane Bks.) Beach Lane Bks.

Stringer, Margaret. Googus, the Toothless Alligator. Shaffert, Charles. I.t. ed. 2003. 30p. (J). per. 7.95 *(978-1-932338-27-0(6))* Lifevest Publishing, Inc.

—Googus to the Rescue. Shaffert, Charles F. I.t. ed. 2005. 31p. (J). per. 10.00 *(978-1-59879-043-6(9))* Lifevest Publishing, Inc.

Stringfield, Joni. Circle of Three: Enough Friendship to Go Around? Brokamp, Elizabeth. 2008. 48p. (J). (gr. 3-7). 14.95 *(978-1-4338-0321-5(6))*; pap. 9.95 *(978-1-4338-0322-2(4))* American Psychological Assn. (Magination Pr.).

Stringle, Sam, jt. illus. see Duncan, Karen.

Strock, Carren. Grandpa & Me & the Park in the City. Strock, Carren. (ENG.). (J). 2016. pap. 10.00 *(978-1-5154-0050-9(6))*; 2nd ed. 2019. 34p. 20.00 ***(978-1-5154-2403-1(0))***; 2nd ed. 2019. 34p. pap. 10.00 ***(978-1-5154-2402-4(2))*** Wilder Pubns., Corp.

Stroede, Paul. The Dog Days of Christmas. Rogala, Judy. 2012. 32p. (J). 12.95 *(978-1-59598-219-3(1)*, Goblin Fern Pr.) HenschelHAUS Publishing, Inc.

Stroede, Paul, jt. illus. see Stader, Kristina.

Stroer, Barbara. No Shrinking, Violet: A Teaching Resource about Exclusion. Pinner, Vivian. 2019. (ENG.). (J). 38p. 24.95 ***(978-1-7340908-1-9(2))***; 48p. pap. 14.95 ***(978-1-7340908-0-2(4))*** McNeil Publishing.

Strologo, Doriano. No Jack Don't Play with the Wall Socket. George, Anya. 2017. (ENG.). 34p. (J). pap. *(978-0-9957094-1-6(6))* Silver Bk. Publishing.

Strom, Allison. All's Fairy in Love & War: Avalon Web of Magic Book 8. Roberts, Rachel. 2018. (ENG.). 178p. (J). (gr. 2-6). pap. 9.99 *(978-1-941015-38-4(7))* Red Sky Presents.

—Song of the Unicorns: Avalon Web of Magic Book 7. Roberts, Rachel. 2018. (ENG.). 182p. (J). (gr. 4-7). pap. 9.99 *(978-1-941015-37-7(9))* Red Sky Presents.

—Trial by Fire: Avalon Web of Magic Book 6. Roberts, Rachel. 2018. (ENG.). 216p. (J). (gr. 4-7). pap. 9.99 *(978-1-941015-36-0(0))* Red Sky Presents.

Strom, Jillian. Where Is Bucket?! Strom, Nolan. 2019. (ENG.). 46p. (J). pap. 9.99 *(978-1-0822-9573-7(6))* Independently Published.

Strom, Maria Diaz. Joe Arco Iris y Yo, 1 vol. Strom, Maria Diaz. 2008.Tr. of Rainbow Joe & Me. (SPA.). 32p. (J). (gr. -1-3). pap. 10.95 *(978-1-60060-278-8(9)*, 9801b9ed-8446-41f1-87f8-e072a05e2a85) Lee & Low Bks., Inc.

Strömgård, Katarina. The Secret Cat. 2019. (ENG.). 32p. (J). *(978-0-8028-5511-4(3)*, Eerdmans Bks For Young Readers) Eerdmans, William B. Publishing Co.

Stromoski, Rick. Bats in My Attic. Meltzer Kleinhenz, Sydnie. 2005. (Rookie Readers Ser.). (ENG.). 32p. (J). (gr. k-2). lib. bdg. 19.50 *(978-0-516-24865-3(0)*, Children's Pr.) Scholastic Library Publishing.

—Chairs, Chairs, Chairs! Cappetta, Cynthia. 2004. (Rookie Readers Ser.). 31p. (gr. k-3). 14.95 *(978-0-7569-3639-6(X))* Perfection Learning Corp.

—Willie's Word World. Curry, Don L. 2011. (Rookie Ready to Learn: I Can! Ser.). (ENG.). 40p. (J). (gr. -1-1). lib. bdg. 18.69 *(978-0-531-26374-7(6))*; pap. 5.95 *(978-0-531-26679-3(6)*, Children's Pr.) Scholastic Library Publishing.

Strong, Belinda. Everybody Potties: Shaped Board Book down SPEC. Vogel, Cheri. Cottage Door Press, ed. ed. 2017. (I Can Do It Ser.). (ENG.). 11p. (J). (gr. -1-k). bds. 6.99 *(978-1-68052-238-9(8)*, 1002240) Cottage Door Pr.

Strong, Belinda, et al. Peas Please, Night Octopus, Everybody Potties, Safety Bugs 4 Pack: Shaped Board Book 4 Pack. Hane, Tori et al. Cottage Door Press, ed. 2015. (I Can Do It Ser.). (ENG.). 20p. (J). (gr. -1-k). bds. 35.96 *(978-1-68052-140-5(3)*, 9000320) Cottage Door Pr.

Strong, Belinda. The Peas Say Please: I Can Do It 2. 0. Hane, Tori. Cottage Door Press, ed. 2018. (ENG.). 12p. (J). (gr. -1-k). bds. 6.99 *(978-1-68052-396-6(1)*, 1003580) Cottage Door Pr.

Strong, Gerry. Ghost at the Lake: Pug Detective Charlotte. Strong, Gerry. 2019. (ENG.). 110p. (J). (gr. k-3). pap. 5.99 ***(978-1-0816-9903-1(5))*** Independently Published.

Strong, Melodee. You Are Beautiful. Snow, Todd. 2007. (You Are Important Ser.). (ENG.). 24p. (J). (gr. -1-k). bds. 7.99 *(978-1-934277-10-2(X))* Maren Green Publishing, Inc.

—You Are Brave. Snow, Todd. 2007. (ENG.). 24p. (J). bds. 7.99 *(978-1-934277-08-9(8))* Maren Green Publishing, Inc.

—You Are Brave (PB) Snow, Todd. 2008. (ENG.). 24p. (J). pap. 8.99 *(978-1-934277-19-5(3))* Maren Green Publishing, Inc.

—You Are Creative. Snow, Todd. 2007. (ENG.). 24p. (J). bds. 7.99 *(978-1-934277-07-2(X))* Maren Green Publishing, Inc.

—You Are Friendly. Snow, Todd. 2007. (You Are Important Ser.). (ENG.). 24p. (J). (gr. -1-k). bds. 7.99 *(978-1-934277-09-6(6))* Maren Green Publishing, Inc.

—You Are Friendly (PB) Snow, Todd. 2008. (ENG.). 24p. (J). pap. 8.99 *(978-1-934277-18-8(5))* Maren Green Publishing, Inc.

—You Are Healthy (PB) Snow, Todd. 2008. (ENG.). 24p. (J). pap. 8.99 *(978-1-934277-22-5(3))* Maren Green Publishing, Inc.

—You Are Helpful. Snow, Todd. 2008. (You Are Important Ser.). (ENG.). 24p. (J). (gr. -1-3). pap. 8.99 *(978-1-934277-23-2(1))* Maren Green Publishing, Inc.

—You Are Important. Snow, Todd. 2007. (You Are Important Ser.). (ENG.). 24p. (J). (gr. -1-k). bds. 7.99 *(978-1-934277-06-5(1))* Maren Green Publishing, Inc.

Stroniarz, Christina V. Let's Sing & Celebrate! 105 Original Songs for Seasons & Festivals. 2003. 224p. pap. 24.95 *(978-0-9720913-9-8(4))* Songbird Pr.

Stroud, Brenda. The Thursday Surprise: A Story about Kids & Autism. Ennis, Ryan R. 2011. 86p. pap. 9.95 *(978-0-9843426-7-9(2))* G Publishing LLC.

Stroud, Brenda D. A Proper Place for Boogers. Finley, Ucal P. 2011. 54p. pap. 12.95 *(978-0-9834307-0-4(5))* G Publishing LLC.

Stroud, David Wayne. Wiggles the White Blood Cell. Stroud, David Wayne. 2005. (J). 14.95 *(978-0-9762835-1-5(4))* Shooting Star Publishing.

Stroud, Joanne. 365 Silly Jokes for Kids. West, Tracey. West, Simon, ed. 2013. 100p. pap. *(978-1-910094-05-1(6))* Magic Oxygen.

S

Strouse, Stephanie. Annie's Jar of Patience: Feeling Impatient & Learning Patience. Day, Sophia & Johnson, Megan. 2019. (Help Me Understand Ser.: 10). 72p. (J). (ENG.). 14.99 *(978-1-64370-756-3(6)*, 4b38963b-53eb-408f-9f39-4d19ec1f62ad); pap. 9.99 *(978-1-64370-757-0(4)*, 0bb74f17-aae1-44ed-92a3-ed9c0c398aec) MVP Kids Media.

—Blake Rewires the Failure Circuit: Feeling Failure & Learning Success. Day, Sophia & Johnson, Megan. 2020. (Help Me Understand Ser.: 3). (ENG.). 72p. (J). pap. 9.99 *(978-1-64204-798-1(8)*, 90d1a924-4da6-486f-8511-b550e1b739b9) MVP Kids Media.

—Check up with the Doctor: Celebrate! Doctors. Day, Sophia & Johnson, Megan. 2019. (Celebrate! Ser.: 22). (ENG.). 32p. (J). pap. 4.99 *(978-1-64255-234-8(8)*, 75d99afc-8e9c-4786-b44d-23b9113d8c46) MVP Kids Media.

—Ezekiel Builds on His Mistakes: Feeling Regret & Learning Wisdom. Day, Sophia & Johnson, Megan. 2019. (Help Me Understand Ser.: 7). 72p. (J). (ENG.). 14.99 *(978-1-64370-750-1(7)*, d3ac855a-23e8-459a-bcf7-1d2e37e8a668); pap. 9.99 *(978-1-64370-751-8(5)*, cbee36a0-acc1-4dba-93e4-9385485c1539) MVP Kids Media.

—Gabby Bears with Embarrassment: Feeling Embarrassment & Learning Humor. Day, Sophia & Johnson, Megan. 2019. (Help Me Understand Ser.: 8). 72p. (J). 14.99 *(978-1-64370-752-5(3)*, bd16ea35-a3ba-48b8-aa01-26b1afb66310); pap. 9.99 *(978-1-64370-753-2(1)*, cd060871-4c56-498d-8500-b346a7578929) MVP Kids Media.

—Leo's Pent up Feelings: Hiding Feelings & Learning Authenticity. Day, Sophia & Johnson, Megan. 2019. (Help Me Understand Ser.: 9). (ENG.). 72p. (J). 14.99 *(978-1-64370-754-9(X)*, bd7c7d25-725f-4e6a-813d-c09ebe50500f); pap. 9.99 *(978-1-64370-755-6(8)*, 47066c0f-8648-4110-8c52-f3e072039679) MVP Kids Media.

—Lucas Tames the Anger Dragon: Feeling Anger & Learning Delight. Day, Sophia & Johnson, Megan. 2019. (Help Me Understand Ser.: 1). (ENG.). 72p. (J). pap. 9.99 *(978-1-64370-758-7(2)*, 255e06f0-cecf-4c41-9213-b83d2d0a0514) MVP Kids Media.

—Miriam Lassoes the Worry Whirlwind: Feeling Worry & Learning Comfort. Day, Sophia & Johnson, Megan. 2019. (Help Me Understand Ser.: 2). (ENG.). 72p. (J). pap. 9.99 *(978-1-64204-797-4(X)*, 3c09b7d2-3c50-41ea-8d1d-b0281cb70f6e) MVP Kids Media.

—My Family Loves Me: Celebrate! Families. Day, Sophia & Johnson, Megan. 2019. (Celebrate! Ser.: 23). (ENG.). 32p. (J). pap. 4.99 *(978-1-64255-235-5(6)*, a6e9862c-108d-4b0c-9256-df317c4ae3a3) MVP Kids Media.

—Smile for the Dentist: Celebrate! Dentists. Day, Sophia & Johnson, Megan. 2019. (Celebrate! Ser.: 21). (ENG.). 32p. (J). pap. 4.99 *(978-1-64204-793-6(7)*, 32301202-1291-484d-b08a-9fa74b16d35d) MVP Kids Media.

—Yong Breaks Out of the Boredom Box: Feeling Bored & Learning Curiosity. Day, Sophia & Johnson, Megan. 2019. (Help Me Understand Ser.: 5). (ENG.). 68p. (J). 14.99 *(978-1-64255-231-7(3)*, 7c36fc83-872c-4185-9a04-09ec862a0c54) MVP Kids Media.

Strouse, Stephanie & Zowada, Timothy. Counting Critters: Celebrate! Number Sense. Day, Sophia et al. 2019. (Celebrate! Ser.: 15). 32p. (J). pap. 4.99 *(978-1-64370-760-0(4)*, 59f29ee7-4e5a-4719-ba39-a40fc06bdf2b) MVP Kids Media.

—We're More Alike Than Different: Celebrate! Diversity. Day, Sophia et al. 2019. (Celebrate! Ser.: 16). (ENG.). 36p. (J). pap. 4.99 *(978-1-64370-761-7(2)*, 13c10228-4e4b-4e19-b0a5-1373611a5e01) MVP Kids Media.

Strudwick, Gina. Mummy Sometimes Goes Funny! Strudwick, Gina. 2019. (ENG.). 28p. (J). (gr. 5-6). pap. *(978-1-912358-03-8(4))* Stellium Ltd.

Strugnell, Ann. Julian, Dream Doctor. Cameron, Ann. 2018. (Julian's World Ser.). (ENG.). 80p. (J). (gr. 1-4). lib. bdg. 12.99 *(978-0-525-57984-7(2)*, Random Hse. Bks. for Young Readers) Random Hse. Children's Bks.

—More Stories Julian Tells. Cameron, Ann. 2018. (Julian's World Ser.). (ENG.). 96p. (J). (gr. 1-4). lib. bdg. 12.99 *(978-0-525-57982-3(6)*, Random Hse. Bks. for Young Readers) Random Hse. Children's Bks.

—The Stories Julian Tells. Cameron, Ann. 2018. (Julian's World Ser.). (ENG.). 96p. (J). (gr. 1-4). lib. bdg. 12.99 *(978-0-525-57981-6(8)*, Random Hse. Bks. for Young Readers) Random Hse. Children's Bks.

Strunk, Peter. Two Inch Hero: The Adventures of Lorenzo Lizard. Strunk, Peter, creator. 2006. (J). 17.95 *(978-0-9785961-0-1(2))* Smile Time Publishing.

Struntz, D. J., photos by. Cold Waves, Cold Blood: Sku 2370000777256. Doherty, Patrick. 2015. (ENG., 256p. (YA). (gr. 9-12). pap. 11.95 *(978-0-9963756-3-4(5))* All About Kids Publishing.

Strychalski, Irene, et al. Mealtime Mayhem. McGuire, Seanan et al. 2019. (Marvel Super Hero Adventures Graphic Novels Ser.). (ENG.). 24p. (J). (gr. 1-5). lib. bdg. 27.07 *(978-1-5321-4448-6(2)*, 33854, Marvel Age) Spotlight.

Strychalski, Irene. Silk Vol. 3: The Clone Conspiracy. 2017. (ENG.). 136p. (J). (gr. 4-17). pap. 17.99 *(978-1-302-90593-4(7))* Marvel Worldwide, Inc.

Strydom, Sanette. KAA of the Great Kalahari. Du Toit, Lydia. 2019. (ENG.). 40p. (J). pap. ***(978-0-9922302-3-4(3))*** Mirror Word Publishing.

Stryk, Suzanne, jt. illus. see Hooper, Hadley.

Stryker, Dale, jt. illus. see Stryker, Stephanie.

Stryker, Stephanie & Stryker, Dale. Speech Illustrated Numero Uno: Pictured Nouns & Verbs. Stryker, Stephanie & Stryker, Dale. 2008.Tr. of Numero uno -Sustantivos Imaginados y Verbos. (SPA.). 48p. 24.95 net. *(978-0-9821038-7-6(5))* Stryker Illustrations.

Stuart, B. S. One day in Betty,s Life. Gates, Josephine Scribner. 2007. 58p. (J). lib. bdg. 59.00 *(978-1-60304-018-1(8))* Dollworks.

Stuart, Catterson. Ruby & Alfie Don't Push That Button. Hil, Gibb. 2020. (Ruby & Alfie Ser.: Vol. 2). (ENG.). 38p. (J). (gr. 1-3). pap. ***(978-0-9571911-4-3(6))*** Haruki Publishing.

Stuart, Emma. Perry & Perky's Fun-Filled Adventures. Grace, Lani. 2020. (ENG.). 66p. (J). ***(978-0-6485137-7-3(7))***; pap. ***(978-0-6485137-6-6(9))*** Grace, Lani.

Stuart, Jon. Collins Big Cat Phonics for Letters & Sounds - Pick It up!: Band 01B/Pink B. Baker, Catherine. 2020. (Collins Big Cat Phonics for Letters & Sounds Ser.). (ENG.). 16p. (J). (gr. -1-k). pap. 7.99 *(978-0-00-835762-7(5))* HarperCollins Pubs. Ltd. GBR. Dist: Independent Pubs. Group.

—Help! Yellow Band. Pritchard, Gabby. 2017. (Cambridge Reading Adventures Ser.). (ENG.). 16p. pap. 5.62 *(978-1-108-40815-8(X))* Cambridge Univ. Pr.

—Journey to Callisto 3 Explorers. DeRidder, Mauritz. 2017. (Cambridge Reading Adventures Ser.). (ENG.). 40p. pap. 10.11 *(978-1-108-40581-2(9))* Cambridge Univ. Pr.

—Lost! Blue Band. Pritchard, Gabby. 2016. (Cambridge Reading Adventures Ser.). (ENG.). 16p. pap. 7.37 *(978-1-316-60078-8(5))* Cambridge Univ. Pr.

—What's for Breakfast: Band 02B/Red B (Collins Big Cat) Shipton, Paul. 2006. (Collins Big Cat Ser.). (ENG.). 16p. (J). (gr. -1-k). pap. 6.99 *(978-0-00-718668-6(1))* HarperCollins Pubs. Ltd. GBR. Dist: Independent Pubs. Group.

Stuart, Mitchell. The Curious Adventures of India Sophia. Stewart, Angela. 2004. (Juvenile Novel Ser.). 176p. (J). (gr. 4-6). pap. 9.95 *(978-1-895836-78-3(6))* River Bks. CAN. Dist: Fitzhenry & Whiteside, Ltd.

Stuart, Walter. Little Walrus Warning. Young, Carol. (Smithsonian Oceanic Collection). (J). 2009. 24.95 incl. audio compact disk *(978-1-59249-667-9(9))*; 2005. (ENG.). 32p. (gr. -1-2). 8.95 *(978-1-59249-070-7(0)*, SC4009); 2005. (ENG.). 32p. (gr. -1-3). 6.95 *(978-1-56899-937-1(2)*, S4009) Soundprints.

Stubbing, Lori. Little Hero's Frown. Rjk. 2012. 36p. pap. 24.95 *(978-1-4626-7786-3(X))* America Star Bks.

Stubbings, Ellen. Baby Beats: Let's Learn 2/4 Time! Odd Dot. 2020. (Baby Beats Ser.: 3). (ENG.). 10p. (J). bds. 8.99 *(978-1-250-24147-4(2)*, 900211835, Odd Dot) St. Martin's Pr.

—Baby Beats: Let's Learn 3/4 Time! Odd Dot. 2020. (Baby Beats Ser.: 2). (ENG.). 10p. (J). bds. 8.99 *(978-1-250-24146-7(4)*, 900211834, Odd Dot) St. Martin's Pr.

—Baby Beats: Let's Learn 4/4 Time! Odd Dot. 2020. (Baby Beats Ser.: 1). (ENG.). 480p. (J). bds. 8.99 *(978-1-250-24145-0(6)*, 900211833, Odd Dot) St. Martin's Pr.

Stubbings, Ellen. The Itty Bitty Princess Kitty Collection: The Newest Princess; the Royal Ball; the Puppy Prince; Star Showers. Mews, Melody. ed. 2020. (Itty Bitty Princess Kitty Ser.). (ENG.). 512p. (J). (gr. k-4). pap. 23.99 ***(978-1-5344-6908-2(7)***, Little Simon) Little Simon.

—The Puppy Prince. Mews, Melody. 2020. (Itty Bitty Princess Kitty Ser.: 3). (ENG.). 128p. (J). (gr. k-4). 17.99 ***(978-1-5344-6358-5(5))***; pap. 5.99 ***(978-1-5344-6357-8(7))*** Little Simon. (Little Simon).

—Star Showers. Mews, Melody. 2020. (Itty Bitty Princess Kitty Ser.: 4). (ENG.). 128p. (J). (gr. k-4). 17.99 ***(978-1-5344-6361-5(5))***; pap. 5.99 ***(978-1-5344-6360-8(7))*** Little Simon. (Little Simon).

Stubbings, Ellen. TinkerActive Workbooks: Kindergarten Math. Le Du, Nathalie & Odd Dot. 2019. (TinkerActive Workbooks Ser.: 1). (ENG.). 128p. (J). pap. 12.99 *(978-1-250-30721-7(X)*, 900197981, Odd Dot) St. Martin's Pr.

Stubbs, Lisa. Grumpy Feet. Stubbs, Lisa. 2017. (Lily & Bear Ser.). (ENG.). 32p. (J). (gr. -1-3). 17.99 *(978-1-4814-7167-1(8)*, Simon & Schuster/Paula Wiseman Bks.) Simon & Schuster/Paula Wiseman Bks.

—Lily & Bear. Stubbs, Lisa. 2015. (Lily & Bear Ser.). (ENG.). 32p. (J). (gr. -1-3). 17.99 *(978-1-4814-4416-3(6)*, Simon & Schuster Bks. For Young Readers) Simon & Schuster Bks. For Young Readers.

Stubbs, Robert Earl. Fearfully & Wonderfully Made: A Christian Health & Puberty Guide for Preteen Boys & Girls. Stubbs, Lori. 2nd ed. 2005. 40p. (J). (gr. -1 — 1). pap. 10.00 *(978-1-58597-174-9(X))* Leathers Publishing.

Stubbs, Tommy. Best Birthday Ever! (Thomas & Friends) Webster, Christy. 2020. (ENG.). 24p. (J). (gr. -1-2). 9.99 *(978-1-5247-1651-6(0)*, Random Hse. Bks. for Young Readers) Random Hse. Children's Bks.

—Big World, Big Adventure. Golden Books. 2018. (Little Golden Book Ser.). (ENG.). 24p. (J). (-k). 4.99 *(978-1-5247-7316-8(6)*, Golden Bks.) Random Hse. Children's Bks.

—Blue Mountain Mystery (Thomas & Friends) Awdry, Wilbert V. 2012. (Big Golden Book Ser.). (ENG.). 48p. (J). (gr. -1-2). 9.99 *(978-0-307-93149-8(8)*, Golden Bks.) Random Hse. Children's Bks.

—Blue Train, Green Train. Awdry, Wilbert V. & Awdry, W. 2007. (Bright & Early Board Books(TM) Ser.). (ENG.). 24p. (J). (— 1). bds. 4.99 *(978-0-375-83984-9(4)*, Random Hse. Bks. for Young Readers) Random Hse. Children's Bks.

—Busy, Busy Thomas. Awdry, W. 2013. (ENG.). 12p. (J). (— 1). bds. 5.99 *(978-0-449-81642-4(7)*, Random Hse. Bks. for Young Readers) Random Hse. Children's Bks.

—A Crack in the Track. 2004. (Bright & Early Board Books(TM) Ser.). (ENG.). 24p. (J). (— 1). bds. 4.99 *(978-0-375-82755-6(2)*, Random Hse. Bks. for Young Readers) Random Hse. Children's Bks.

—The Fearsome Footprints/Thomas the Brave (Thomas & Friends) Random House. 2014. (Pictureback(R) Ser.). (ENG.). 24p. (J). (gr. -1-2). 4.99 *(978-0-385-37392-0(9)*, Random Hse. Bks. for Young Readers) Random Hse. Children's Bks.

—Go, Train, Go! Thomas & Friends. Awdry, Wilbert V. 2006. (Bright & Early Board Books(TM) Ser.). (ENG.). 24p. (J). (— 1). bds. 4.99 *(978-0-375-83461-5(3)*, Random Hse. Bks. for Young Readers) Random Hse. Children's Bks.

—Journey Beyond Sodor. Golden Books. 2017. (Little Golden Book Ser.). (ENG.). 24p. (J). (-k). 4.99 *(978-1-5247-1653-0(7)*, Golden Bks.) Random Hse. Children's Bks.

—Lost at Sea! Hit Entertainment. 2010. (Pictureback(R) Ser.). (ENG.). 24p. (J). (gr. -1-2). pap. 3.99 *(978-0-375-84754-7(5)*, Random Hse. Bks. for Young Readers) Random Hse. Children's Bks.

—May the Best Engine Win! Courtney, Richard, photos by. Golden Books Staff. 2008. (Little Golden Book Ser.). (ENG.). 24p. (J). (gr. -1-2). 4.99 *(978-0-375-84381-5(7)*, Golden Bks.) Random Hse. Children's Bks.

—The Missing Christmas Tree. Awdry, Wilbert Were. 2013. (ENG.). 12p. (J). (— 1). bds. 6.99 *(978-0-449-81713-1(X)*, Golden Bks.) Random Hse. Children's Bks.

—Ride the Rails with Thomas (Thomas & Friends) Awdry, W. 2015. (Pictureback(R) Ser.). (ENG.). 24p. (J). (gr. -1-2). 5.99 *(978-0-385-38538-1(2)*, Random Hse. Bks. for Young Readers) Random Hse. Children's Bks.

—Steam Team! Awdry, W. 2011. (ENG.). 12p. (J). (gr. -1-2). pap. 6.99 *(978-0-375-87162-7(4)*, Golden Bks.) Random Hse. Children's Bks.

—Tale of the Brave (Thomas & Friends) Awdry, W. 2014. (Big Golden Book Ser.). (ENG.). 48p. (J). (gr. -1-2). 9.99 *(978-0-385-37915-1(3)*, Golden Bks.) Random Hse. Children's Bks.

—Thomas & Friends: Blue Train, Green Train (Thomas & Friends) Awdry, W. 2006. (Bright & Early Books(R) Ser.). (ENG.). 36p. (J). (gr. k-k). 9.99 *(978-0-375-83463-9(X)*, Random Hse. Bks. for Young Readers) Random Hse. Children's Bks.

—Thomas & Friends: Go, Train, Go! (Thomas & Friends) Terrill, Elizabeth & Awdry, W. 2005. (Beginner Books(R) Ser.). (ENG.). 48p. (J). (gr. -1-1). 9.99 *(978-0-375-83177-5(0)*, Random Hse. Bks. for Young Readers) Random Hse. Children's Bks.

—Thomas & Friends Little Golden Book Library (Thomas & Friends), 5 vols. Awdry, W. 2013. (Little Golden Book Ser.). (ENG.). 120p. (J). (-k). 24.95 *(978-0-449-81482-6(3)*, Golden Bks.) Random Hse. Children's Bks.

—Thomas & Friends: My Red Railway Book Box (Thomas & Friends) Go, Train, GO!; Stop, Train, Stop!; a Crack in the Track!; & Blue Train, Green Train. Awdry, W. 2008. (Bright & Early Board Books(TM) Ser.). (ENG.). 96p. (J). (— 1). bds. 14.99 *(978-0-375-84322-8(1)*, Random Hse. Bks. for Young Readers) Random Hse. Children's Bks.

—Thomas & Friends Summer 2017 Movie Big Golden Book (Thomas & Friends) Golden Books. 2017. (Big Golden Book Ser.). (ENG.). 32p. (J). (gr. -1-2). 9.99 *(978-1-5247-1662-2(6)*, Golden Bks.) Random Hse. Children's Bks.

—Thomas & Friends the Great Railway Show/off to the Races. Random House Disney Staff. 2016. (Pictureback(R) Ser.). (ENG.). 24p. (J). (gr. -1-2). 4.99 *(978-1-101-93202-5(3)*, Random Hse. Bks. for Young Readers) Random Hse. Children's Bks.

—Thomas & the Great Discovery (Thomas & Friends) Awdry, W. 2009. (Little Golden Book Ser.). (ENG.). 24p. (J). (gr. -1-2). 4.99 *(978-0-375-85153-7(4)*, Golden Bks.) Random Hse. Children's Bks.

—Thomas & the Lost Pirate / the Sunken Treasure, 2 bks. in 1. Random House. 2015. (Pictureback(R) Ser.). (ENG.). 24p. (J). (gr. -1-2). 4.99 *(978-0-553-52078-1(4)*, Random Hse. Bks. for Young Readers) Random Hse. Children's Bks.

—Thomas' Favorite Places & Faces. Awdry, Wilbert V. 2014. (Reusable Sticker Book Ser.). (ENG.). 24p. (J). (gr. -1-2). pap. 6.99 *(978-0-449-81712-4(1)*, Golden Bks.) Random Hse. Children's Bks.

—Thomas in Africa/Friends Around the World. Random House. 2018. (Pictureback(R) Ser.). (ENG.). 24p. (J). (gr. -1-2). pap. 4.99 *(978-1-5247-7317-5(4)*, Random Hse. Bks. for Young Readers) Random Hse. Children's Bks.

—Thomas Saves Easter! (Thomas & Friends) Awdry, W. 2013. (ENG.). 12p. (J). (-k). bds. 6.99 *(978-0-307-98158-5(4)*, Golden Bks.) Random Hse. Children's Bks.

—Thomas's Christmas Delivery. Awdry, W. 2004. (Sparkle Storybook Ser.). (ENG.). 32p. (J). (gr. -1-2). 8.99 *(978-0-375-82877-5(X)*, Random Hse. Bks. for Young Readers) Random Hse. Children's Bks.

—Trains, Cranes & Troublesome Trucks. Awdry, Wilbert V. 2008. (Beginner Books(R) Ser.). (ENG.). 36p. (J). (gr. -1-1). 8.99 *(978-0-375-84977-0(7)*, Random Hse. Bks. for Young Readers) Random Hse. Children's Bks.

Stubbs, Tommy, jt. illus. see Courtney, Richard.

Stuby, Tim. Extreme Monsters Joke Book. Bataille Lange, Nikki. gif. ed. 2005. 95p. (J). (gr. 2-5). per. 3.99 *(978-1-57791-181-4(4))* Brighter Minds Children's Publishing.

Stucki, Ron. Edgar & the Tattle-Tale Heart, 1 vol. Adams, Jennifer. 2014. 32p. (J). 16.99 *(978-1-4236-3766-0(6))* Gibbs Smith, Publisher.

—Edgar & the Tattle-Tale Heart Board Book, 1 vol. Adams, Jennifer. 2015. 34p. (J). bds. 9.99 *(978-1-4236-4176-6(0))* Gibbs Smith, Publisher.

—Edgar & the Tree House of Usher: Inspired by Edgar Allan Poe's the Fall of the House of Usher, 1 vol. Adams, Jennifer. 2016. 22p. (J). bds. 9.99 *(978-1-4236-4493-4(X))* Gibbs Smith, Publisher.

—Edgar & the Treehouse of Usher: A BabyLit First Steps Book, 1 vol. Adams, Jennifer. 2015. (ENG.). 32p. (J). 16.99 *(978-1-4236-4043-1(8))* Gibbs Smith, Publisher.

—Edgar Gets Ready for Bed, 1 vol. Adams, Jennifer. ed. 2014. 32p. (J). 16.99 *(978-1-4236-3528-4(0))* Gibbs Smith, Publisher.

—Edgar Gets Ready for Bed Board Book, 1 vol. Adams, Jennifer. 2015. (ENG.). 22p. (J). bds. 9.99 *(978-1-4236-4175-9(2))* Gibbs Smith, Publisher.

Students and Instructors at Clark Colleg & Students from Findley School. I See You: The Beauty of Ethiopia, in Amharic & English. Ready Set Go Books. 2020. (ENG.). 38p. (J). pap. 9.99 ***(978-1-6591-1794-3(1))*** Independently Published.

Students from Christa McAuliffe Elementa, jt. illus. see Iwicki, Lizzie.

Students from Clark College Continuing E & Mitsein, Rebekah. Trees Are Life: In English & Amharic. Ready Set Go Books. 2019. (ENG.). 36p. (J). pap. 9.99 ***(978-1-6880-1382-7(2))*** Independently Published.

Students from Findley School, jt. illus. see Students and Instructors at Clark Colleg.

Students from Riverview Elementary Schoo, jt. illus. see Bradley, Katie.

Studio, Alifstyle. The Social Skills Workbook. Jatau, Z. Andrew. 2017. (ENG.). 126p. (J). pap. 19.95 *(978-0-9964154-5-3(9))* Mylemarks LLC.

Studio, Balarupa. Grrrrrrr, Do I Have To? Biddy, Natasha. 2019. (ENG.). 28p. (J). pap. *(978-1-9990856-0-5(4))* Gauvin, Jacques.

Studio, Character Building & Team, Disney Storybook Art. Doc Mcstuffins: Brave Dragon. Scollon, Bill & Redeker, Kent. 2018. (World of Reading Level Pre-1 Ser.). (ENG.). 32p. (J). (gr. -1-2). lib. bdg. 27.07 *(978-1-5321-4175-1(0)*, 28524) Spotlight.

—Doc Mcstuffins: Brontosaurus Breath. Higginson, Sheila Sweeny & Nee, Chris. 2018. (World of Reading Level Pre-1 Ser.). (ENG.). 32p. (J). (gr. -1-2). lib. bdg. 27.07 *(978-1-5321-4176-8(9)*, 28525) Spotlight.

—Doc Mcstuffins: Starry, Starry Night. Scollon, Bill & Rabb, Michael. 2018. (World of Reading Level 1 Ser.). (ENG.). 32p. (J). (gr. -1-3). lib. bdg. 27.07 *(978-1-5321-4187-4(4)*, 31064) Spotlight.

—Doc Mcstuffins: Take Your Pet to the Vet. Miller, Sara & Riley, Ford. 2018. (World of Reading Level 1 Ser.). (ENG.). 32p. (J). (gr. -1-3). lib. bdg. 27.07 *(978-1-5321-4188-1(2)*, 28531) Spotlight.

—Doc Mcstuffins: Peaches Pie, Take a Bath! Scollon, Bill & Valentine, Ed. 2018. (World of Reading Level Pre-1 Ser.). (ENG.). 32p. (J). (gr. -1-2). lib. bdg. 27.07 *(978-1-5321-4178-2(5)*, 31060) Spotlight.

—Jake & the Never Land Pirates: Surfin' Turf. LaRose, Melinda & Dubuc, Nicole. 2018. (World of Reading Level 1 Ser.). (ENG.). 32p. (J). (gr. -1-3). lib. bdg. 27.07 *(978-1-5321-4189-8(0)*, 31065) Spotlight.

—Sofia the First: Just One of the Princes. Baer, Jill & Gerber, Craig. 2018. (World of Reading Level 1 Ser.). (ENG.). 32p. (J). (gr. -1-3). lib. bdg. 27.07 *(978-1-5321-4194-2(7)*, 28535) Spotlight.

—Sofia the First: Sofia Takes the Lead. Marsoli, Lisa Ann & Cooney, Doug. 2018. (World of Reading Level 1 Ser.). (ENG.). 32p. (J). (gr. -1-3). lib. bdg. 27.07 *(978-1-5321-4197-3(1)*, 31068) Spotlight.

—Sofia the First: The Missing Necklace. Marsoli, Lisa Ann & Ruderman, Rachel. 2018. (World of Reading Level 1 Ser.). (ENG.). 32p. (J). (gr. -1-3). lib. bdg. 27.07 *(978-1-5321-4195-9(5)*, 28536) Spotlight.

—Sofia the First: Riches to Rags. Amerikaner, Susan et al. 2018. (World of Reading Level 1 Ser.). (ENG.). 32p. (J). (gr. -1-3). lib. bdg. 27.07 *(978-1-5321-4196-6(3)*, 31067) Spotlight.

Studio, Dekree. Wednesday. Ludwig, Mike. 2019. (ENG.). 26p. (J). pap. 9.99 *(978-1-7242-7092-4(3))* CreateSpace Independent Publishing Platform.

—Wednesday. Ludwig, Mike. 2019. (ENG.). 26p. (J). (gr. k-6). 20.99 *(978-1-64570-578-9(1))* Ludwig, Michael.

Studio, Franfrou. Frank the Cat: A Sing-Along Book. Kelman, Angela. 2016. (ENG.). 16p. (J). pap. *(978-0-9864733-0-2(8))* Polyester Music Productions.

Studio, Fx and Color. Roller Skating Ralph. Blom, Tracy. 2019. (ENG.). 32p. (J). 16.99 ***(978-1-7336349-5-3(9))*** Blom Pubns.

Studio, Fx and Color. The Wave. Sheridan, Scott & Blom, Tracy. 2019. (ENG.). 30p. (J). pap. 11.99 *(978-1-7336349-6-0(7))* Hom, Jonathan.

Studio, Gau Family. Toodle's Big Race: Interactive for Children That Don't Like to Sit Still! Jusino, Cindy M. 2013. 44p. 20.00 *(978-0-9888003-2-8(2))* Sensational Pubns.

Studio IBOIX & Disney Storybook Artists Staff. Rapunzel & the Golden Rule/Jasmine & the Two Tigers (Disney Princess) Bazaldua, Barbara & Bergen, Lara. 2011. (Pictureback(R) Ser.). (ENG.). 32p. (J). (gr. -1-2). pap. 4.99 *(978-0-7364-2829-3(1)*, RH/Disney) Random Hse. Children's Bks.

Studio IBOIX, jt. illus. see Cagol, Andrea.

Studio IBOIX Staff. Aurora: The Perfect Party. Loggia, Wendy. 2012. (Disney Princess Ser.). (ENG.). 96p. (J). (gr. 2-6). lib. bdg. 27.07 *(978-1-59961-181-5(3)*, 5182, Chapter Bks.) Spotlight.

—Belle: The Mysterious Message. Richards, Kitty. 2011. (Disney Princess Ser.). (ENG.). 96p. (J). (gr. 2-6). 27.07 *(978-1-59961-878-4(8)*, 5178, Chapter Bks.) Spotlight.

—Cinderella: The Great Mouse Mistake. O'Ryan, Ellie. 2011. (Disney Princess Ser.). (ENG.). 96p. (J). (gr. 2-6). 27.07 *(978-1-59961-879-1(6)*, 5179, Chapter Bks.) Spotlight.

—Jasmine: The Missing Coin. Nathan, Sarah. 2012. (Disney Princess Ser.). (ENG.). 96p. (J). (gr. 2-6). lib. bdg. 27.07 *(978-1-59961-182-2(1)*, 5183, Chapter Bks.) Spotlight.

—Rapunzel: A Day to Remember, 1 vol. Perelman, Helen. 2012. (Disney Princess Ser.). (ENG.). 96p. (J). (gr. 2-6). lib. bdg. 27.07 *(978-1-59961-183-9(X)*, 5184, Chapter Bks.) Spotlight.

—Tiana: The Grand Opening. Perelman, Helen. 2011. (Disney Princess Ser.). (ENG.). 96p. (J). (gr. 2-6). 27.07 *(978-1-59961-880-7(X)*, 5180, Chapter Bks.) Spotlight.

Studio Iboix Staff, jt. illus. see Disney Storybook Artists Staff.

Studio IBOIX Staff, jt. illus. see RH Disney Staff.

Studio, Imaginism & Team, The Disney Storybook Art. Going Batty. Beyl, Chelsea & Nee, Chris. 2019. (Vampirina Ser.). (ENG.). 24p. (J). (gr. -1-2). 27.07 *(978-1-5321-4300-7(1)*, 31830, Picture Bk.) Spotlight.

—Meet Vampirina. Miller, Sara. 2019. (Vampirina Ser.). (ENG.). 24p. (J). (gr. -1-2). 27.07 *(978-1-5321-4301-4(X)*, 31831, Picture Bk.) Spotlight.

—Vampirina (Set), 4 vols. 2019. (Vampirina Ser.). (ENG.). 24p. (J). (gr. -1-2). 108.28 *(978-1-5321-4299-4(4)*, 31829, Picture Bk.) Spotlight.

—Vee Is for Valentine. Beyl, Chelsea. 2019. (Vampirina Ser.). (ENG.). 24p. (J). (gr. -1-2). 27.07 *(978-1-5321-4302-1(8)*, 31832, Picture Bk.) Spotlight.

—Vee's Monster Bash. Beyl, Chelsea & Braun, Travis. 2019. (Vampirina Ser.). (ENG.). 24p. (J). (gr. -1-2). 27.07 *(978-1-5321-4303-8(6)*, 31833, Picture Bk.) Spotlight.

Studio, Imaginism and Team. Vampirina: Scare B & B. Beyl, Chelsea & King, Jeff. 2019. (World of Reading Level 1 Ser.). (ENG.). 32p. (J). (gr. -1-3). lib. bdg. 27.07 *(978-1-5321-4407-3(5)*, 33812) Spotlight.

—Vampirina: the Surprise Party. Beyl, Chelsea & King, Jeff. 2019. (World of Reading Level Pre-1 Ser.). (ENG.). 32p. (J). (gr. -1-2). lib. bdg. 27.07 *(978-1-5321-4395-3(8)*, 33800) Spotlight.

—Vampirina: Vampirina in the Fall. Miller, Sara. 2019. (World of Reading Level 1 Ser.). (ENG.). 32p. (J). (gr. -1-3). lib. bdg. 27.07 *(978-1-5321-4408-0(3)*, 33813) Spotlight.

Studio, Pilot. Star Wars: the Fight in the Forest. Millici, Nate. 2019. (World of Reading Level 2 Ser.). (ENG.). 32p. (J). (gr. k-3). lib. bdg. 27.07 *(978-1-5321-4412-7(1)*, 33817) Spotlight.

—Star Wars: Trapped in the Death Star! Siglain, Michael. 2019. (World of Reading Level 2 Ser.). (ENG.). 32p. (J). (gr. k-3). lib. bdg. 27.07 *(978-1-5321-4413-4(X)*, 33818) Spotlight.

—Star Wars: Trouble on Tatooine. Millici, Nate. 2019. (World of Reading Level 2 Ser.). (ENG.). 32p. (J). (gr. k-3). lib. bdg. 27.07 *(978-1-5321-4414-1(8)*, 33819) Spotlight.

Studio Stalio. Abejas: Por Dentro y Por Fuera. Houghton, Gillian. Velazquez De Leon, Mauricio, tr. 2004. (Explora la Naturaleza (Getting into Nature) Ser.). (SPA.). 32p. (YA). (gr. 3-6). lib. bdg. 27.25 *(978-1-4042-2862-7(4))* Rosen Publishing Group, Inc., The.

—Aranas: Por Dentro y Por Fuera. Houghton, Gillian. Gonzalez, Tomas, tr. 2004. (Explora la Naturaleza (Getting into Nature) Ser.). (SPA.). 27p. (YA). (gr. 3-6). lib. bdg. 27.25 *(978-1-4042-2867-2(5))* Rosen Publishing Group, Inc., The.

—Buhos: Por Dentro y Por Fuera. Houghton, Gillian. Gonzalez, Tomas, tr. 2004. (Explora la Naturaleza (Getting into Nature) Ser.). (SPA.). 27p. (YA). (gr. 3-6). lib. bdg. 27.25 *(978-1-4042-2866-5(7))* Rosen Publishing Group, Inc., The.

—Tortugas: Por Dentro y Por Fuera. Houghton, Gillian. Gonzalez, Tomas, tr. 2004. (Explora la Naturaleza (Getting into Nature) Ser.). (SPA.). 32p. (J). (gr. k-5). lib. bdg. 27.25 *(978-1-4042-2869-6(1))* Rosen Publishing Group, Inc., The.

StudioMDHR Entertainment Inc. Cuphead in Carnival Chaos: A Cuphead Novel. Bates, Ron. 2020. 272p. (J). (gr. 3-7). 14.99 *(978-0-316-45654-8(3))* Little, Brown Bks. for Young Readers.

Studios, A&J. Dora's Starry Christmas. Ricci, Christine. 2005. 24p. (J). lib. bdg. 9.00 *(978-1-4242-0980-4(3))* Fitzgerald Bks.

Studios, Anisoft. Noodle Makes New Friends. Bayes, Erica. Bearden, Brittany, ed. 2019. (ENG.). 26p. (J). pap. 19.99 *(978-1-7239-9554-5(1))* Independently Published.

Studios, Aveira. Julia Bops to the Beat'. Bradshaw, Felisha. Osio, Raymundo, ed. 2018. (Julia Learns Knows & Grows Ser.: Vol. 1). (ENG.). 42p. (J). pap. 12.99 *(978-0-692-19898-8(9))* Brand New Happy moon Pub.

Studios, Caravan. Avengers: Ms. Marvel's Fists of Fury. Glass, Calliope. 2018. (Mighty Marvel Chapter Bks.). (ENG.). 128p. (J). (gr. 2-7). lib. bdg. 27.07 *(978-1-5321-4213-0(7)*, 28550, Chapter Bks.) Spotlight.

—Black Panther: The Battle for Wakanda. Snider, Brandon T. 2018. (Mighty Marvel Chapter Bks.). (ENG.). 128p. (J). (gr. 2-7). lib. bdg. 27.07 *(978-1-5321-4214-7(5)*, 28551, Chapter Bks.) Spotlight.

Studios, Marvel. Marvel's Avengers: Endgame - the Art of the Movie. 2019. 240p. (YA). (gr. -1-17). 50.00 *(978-1-302-91798-2(6))* Marvel Worldwide, Inc.

Studios, Marvel Animation. Adapting to Change #1. Caramagna, Joe & Son, Eugene. 2019. (Avengers: Ultron Revolution Ser.). (ENG.). 24p. (J). (gr. 2-6). lib. bdg. 27.07 *(978-1-5321-4346-5(X)*, 31866, Marvel Age) Spotlight.

—Avengers: Ultron Revolution (Set), 4 vols. 2019. (Avengers: Ultron Revolution Ser.). (ENG.). 24p. (J). (gr. 2-6). lib. bdg. 108.28 *(978-1-5321-4345-8(1)*, 31865, Marvel Age) Spotlight.

—Dehulked #4. Caramagna, Joe & Giacoppo, Paul. 2019. (Avengers: Ultron Revolution Ser.). (ENG.). 24p. (J). (gr. 2-6). lib. bdg. 27.07 *(978-1-5321-4349-6(4)*, 31869, Marvel Age) Spotlight.

—Guardians of the Galaxy Set 3 (Set), 6 vols. 2019. (Guardians of the Galaxy Ser.). (ENG.). 24p. (J). (gr. 2-6). lib. bdg. 162.42 *(978-1-5321-4357-1(5)*, 31877, Marvel Age) Spotlight.

—Saving Captain Rogers #3. Caramagna, Joe & Scott, Mairghread. 2019. (Avengers: Ultron Revolution Ser.).

(ENG.). 24p. (J). (gr. 2-6). lib. bdg. 27.07 *(978-1-5321-4348-9(6)*, 31868, Marvel Age) Spotlight.
—The Ultimates #2. Caramagna, Joe & Wolff, Danielle. 2019. (Avengers: Ultron Revolution Ser.). (ENG.). 24p. (J). (gr. 2-6). lib. bdg. 27.07 *(978-1-5321-4347-2(8)*, 31867, Marvel Age) Spotlight.
—Volume 10: Bad Moon Rising. Caramagna, Joe & Wayne, Matt. 2019. (Guardians of the Galaxy Ser.). (ENG.). 24p. (J). (gr. 2-6). lib. bdg. 27.07 *(978-1-5321-4361-8(3)*, 31881, Marvel Age) Spotlight.
—Volume 11: Space Cowboys. Caramagna, Joe & Scott, Mairghread. 2019. (Guardians of the Galaxy Ser.). (ENG.). 24p. (J). (gr. 2-6). lib. bdg. 27.07 *(978-1-5321-4362-5(1)*, 31882, Marvel Age) Spotlight.
—Volume 12: Crystal Blue Persuasion. Caramagna, Joe & McDermott, David. 2019. (Guardians of the Galaxy Ser.). (ENG.). 24p. (J). (gr. 2-6). lib. bdg. 27.07 *(978-1-5321-4363-2(X)*, 31883, Marvel Age) Spotlight.
—Volume 7: the Backstabbers. Caramagna, Joe & Robinson, Andrew R. 2019. (Guardians of the Galaxy Ser.). (ENG.). 24p. (J). (gr. 2-6). lib. bdg. 27.07 *(978-1-5321-4358-8(3)*, 31878, Marvel Age) Spotlight.
—Volume 8: Hitchin' a Ride. Caramagna, Joe & McDermott, David. 2019. (Guardians of the Galaxy Ser.). (ENG.). 24p. (J). (gr. 2-6). lib. bdg. 27.07 *(978-1-5321-4359-5(1)*, 31879, Marvel Age) Spotlight.
—Volume 9: We Are Family. Caramagna, Joe & Melching, Steven. 2019. (Guardians of the Galaxy Ser.). (ENG.). 24p. (J). (gr. 2-6). lib. bdg. 27.07 *(978-1-5321-4360-1(5)*, 31880, Marvel Age) Spotlight.
Studios, Milktee, jt. illus. see Creations, Adriatica.
Studios, Yellowhale. Manosaurs Vol. 1: Walk Like a Manosaur. Petrucha, Stefan. 2017. (Manosaurs Ser.: 1). (ENG.). 64p. (J). 12.99 *(978-1-62991-814-3(8)*, 9781629918143); pap. 7.99 *(978-1-62991-813-6(X)*, 9781629918136) Papercutz.
Stukey, James. Playground Personalities. Vermillion, Gail. 2017. (ENG.). (J). pap. 12.95 *(978-1-63525-621-5(6))* Christian Faith Publishing.
Stukey, Jim. Lovely Things: The Blessings of the Seasons. Stubby, Jolene. l.t. ed. 2018. (ENG.). 22p. (J). (gr. k-3). pap. 10.95 *(978-1-61633-916-6(0))* Guardian Angel Publishing, Inc.
—A Shoe Full of Pets. Stubby, Jolene. l.t. ed. 2019. (ENG.). 24p. (J). (gr. k-4). 19.95 *(978-1-61633-986-9(1))*; pap. 10.95 *(978-1-61633-984-5(5))* Guardian Angel Publishing, Inc.
Stumpf, Hannah Viktoria. Tricksy & the Mama Cardinal. Garrido, Theresa Jenner. 2019. (ENG.). 64p. (J). pap. 13.99 *(978-1-0928-3282-3(3))* Independently Published.
Sturcke, Otto. A Heart That Finds His Way: More on the Line. List, Gloria A. 2005. 18p. (J). pap. 7.95 *(978-0-9709861-0-8(6))* Fingerprint Bks.
Sturgen, Bobbi. Black Ridge Mountain. Johnson, Sandi. Durant, Sybrina, ed. 2014. (ENG.). 34p. (J). (gr. k-5). pap. 12.99 *(978-1-929063-66-6(0)*, 165) Moons & Stars Publishing For Children.
—Chip Dude from Outer Space. Johnson, Sandi. Johnson, Britt, ed. l.t. ed. 2014. (ENG.). 28p. (J). (gr. k-5). pap. 12.99 *(978-1-929063-81-9(4)*, 254) Moons & Stars Publishing For Children.
—Dittle's Christmas Wish. Johnson, Sandi. Durant, Sybrina, ed. 2014. 40p. (J). (gr. k-5). pap. 12.99 *(978-1-929063-65-9(2)*, 164) Moons & Stars Publishing For Children.
—My Teacher Is an Alien. Johnson, Sandi. Durant, Sybrina, ed. 2014. (ENG.). 30p. (J). (gr. k-5). pap. 12.99 *(978-1-929063-75-8(X)*, 285) Moons & Stars Publishing For Children.
—White Wolf at Dawn. Johnson, Sandi. Johnson, Britt, ed. 2014. (ENG.). 30p. (J). (gr. k-5). pap. 12.99 *(978-1-929063-72-7(5)*, 171) Moons & Stars Publishing For Children.
Sturgeon, Bobbi. Blackridge Mountain. Johnson, Sandi. Durant, Sybrina, ed. 2019. (ENG.). 34p. (J). pap. 12.99 ***(978-1-6704-0895-2(7))*** Independently Published.
—Cats on Extreme Vacation. Brundige, Britt & Durant, Sybrina, eds. 2019. (ENG.). 36p. (J). pap. 12.99 ***(978-1-6794-6188-0(5))*** Independently Published.
—Chip Dude from Outer Space. Brundige, Britt & Durant, Sybrina, eds. 2019. (ENG.). 28p. (J). pap. 12.99 ***(978-1-6749-2127-3(6))*** Independently Published.
—Harold the Hopping Hamster. Brundige, Britt & Durant, Sybrina, eds. 2019. (ENG.). 26p. (J). pap. 12.99 ***(978-1-6790-6776-1(1))*** Independently Published.
Sturgeon, Bobbi. Harold the Hopping Hamster. Johnson, Sandi. Johnson, Britt, ed. l.t. ed. 2003. (ENG.). 34p. (J). (gr. k-5). pap. 12.99 *(978-1-929063-91-8(1)*, 322) Moons & Stars Publishing For Children.
Sturgeon, Bobbi. The Haunted Doghouse - Book 2. Brundige, Britt & Durant, Sybrina, eds. 2019. (Haunted Doghouse Ser.: Vol. 2). (ENG.). 38p. (J). pap. 12.99 ***(978-1-6756-0063-4(5))*** Independently Published.
—Lost Island. Brundige, Britt & Durant, Sybrina, eds. 2019. (ENG.). 32p. (J). pap. 12.99 ***(978-1-6741-7426-6(8))*** Independently Published.
Sturgeon, Bobbi. Lost Island. Johnson, Sandi. Johnson, Britt & Durant, Sybrina, eds. l.t. ed. 2014. 28p. (J). (gr. k-5). pap. 12.99 *(978-1-929063-69-7(5)*, 168) Moons & Stars Publishing For Children.
Sturgeon, Bobbi. White Wolf at Dawn. Brundige, Britt & Durant, Sybrina, eds. 2019. (ENG.). 32p. (J). pap. 12.99 ***(978-1-6755-7309-9(3))*** Independently Published.
Sturgeon, Bobbi & Brundige, Britt. Dittle's Christmas Wish. Durant, Sybrina, ed. 2019. (ENG.). 42p. (J). pap. 12.99 ***(978-1-6708-8173-1(3))*** Independently Published.
—My Teacher Is an Alien! Durant, Sybrina, ed. 2019. (ENG.). 32p. (J). pap. 12.99 ***(978-1-6745-4450-2(2))*** Independently Published.
Sturgeon, Bobbi, jt. illus. see Brundige, Britt.
Sturgeon, Brad. The Wonder of Keys for Kids. Cruz-Martinez, George. 2006. 43p. (J). *(978-1-55452-013-8(4))* Essence Publishing.
Sturm, Adrienne. Sticksville. Scheer, Jacqueline. 2016. (ENG.). (J). *(978-1-4602-9446-8(7))*; pap. *(978-1-4602-9447-5(5))* FriesenPress.
Sturm, James. Characters in Action! Sturm, James. Arnold, Andrew & Frederick-Frost, Alexis. 2013. (Adventures in Cartooning Ser.). (ENG.). 64p. (J). (gr. 1-5). pap. 12.99 *(978-1-59643-732-6(4)*, 900076820, First Second Bks.) Roaring Brook Pr.
Stutz, Chris. Lady, 1 vol. Depucci, Diana M. 2009. 25p. pap. 24.95 *(978-1-61546-677-1(0))* America Star Bks.
—My Mom Inside My Pocket, 1 vol. Barr, Barbara Jean. 2010. 16p. 24.95 *(978-1-4489-5704-0(4))* America Star Bks.
—Never Never Be a Bully. Pam, Miss. 2011. 24p. pap. 24.95 *(978-1-4626-4325-7(6))* America Star Bks.
—The Story of Chris Moose, 1 vol. McArthur, Cathy E. 2009. 24p. pap. 24.95 *(978-1-4489-0928-5(7))* America Star Bks.
Stutzman, Laura. B Is for Blue Crab: A Maryland Alphabet. Menendez, Shirley. 2004. (Discover America State by State Ser.). (ENG.). 40p. (J). (gr. 1-3). 17.95 *(978-1-58536-160-1(7)*, 202020) Sleeping Bear Pr.
—The Happy Prince. Wilde, Oscar & Grodin, Elissa. rev. ed. 2006. (ENG.). 48p. (J). (gr. k-6). 17.95 *(978-1-58536-264-6(6))* Sleeping Bear Pr.
Style Guide. Meet the Heroes ... & the Villains, Too! Testa, Maggie. 2016. (PJ Masks Ser.). (ENG.). 14p. (J). (gr. -1-k). bds. 7.99 *(978-1-4814-8650-7(0)*, Simon Spotlight) Simon Spotlight.
—Owlette & the Giving Owl. Pendergrass, Daphne. 2017. (PJ Masks Ser.). (ENG.). 32p. (J). (gr. -1-1). 16.99 *(978-1-5344-0376-5(0))*; pap. 4.99 *(978-1-5344-0375-8(2))* Simon Spotlight. (Simon Spotlight).
—The Paladin's Handbook: Official Guidebook of Voltron Legendary Defender. Cregg, R. J. 2017. (Voltron Legendary Defender Ser.). (ENG.). 96p. (J). (gr. 1). pap. 7.99 *(978-1-5344-0903-3(3)*, Simon Spotlight) Simon Spotlight.
—PJ Masks Make Friends! 2016. (PJ Masks Ser.). (ENG.). 24p. (J). (gr. -1-2). pap. 3.99 *(978-1-4814-8907-2(0)*, Simon Spotlight) Simon Spotlight.
—PJ Masks Save Headquarters! 2017. (PJ Masks Ser.). (ENG.). 12p. (J). (gr. -1-k). bds. 12.99 *(978-1-4814-9552-3(6)*, Simon Spotlight) Simon Spotlight.
—PJ Masks Save the Library! 2016. (PJ Masks Ser.). (ENG.). 32p. (J). (gr. -1-1). pap. 3.99 *(978-1-4814-8892-1(9)*, Simon Spotlight) Simon Spotlight.
—A Ride Through the Neighborhood. Testa, Maggie. 2014. (Daniel Tiger's Neighborhood Ser.). (ENG.). 12p. (J). (gr. -1-1). bds. 7.99 *(978-1-4424-9839-6(0)*, Simon Spotlight) Simon Spotlight.
—Super Team. 2016. (PJ Masks Ser.). (ENG.). 16p. (J). (gr. -1-3). pap. 5.99 *(978-1-4814-8978-2(X)*, Simon Spotlight) Simon Spotlight.
—Time to Be a Hero. 2016. (PJ Masks Ser.). (ENG.). 32p. (J). (gr. -1-1). 16.99 *(978-1-4814-8648-4(9))*; pap. 3.99 *(978-1-4814-8647-7(0))* Simon Spotlight. (Simon Spotlight).
Style Guide Staff. Battle for the Black Lion. 2017. (Voltron Legendary Defender Ser.: 2). (ENG.). 64p. (J). (gr. k-4). 17.99 *(978-1-5344-0923-1(8))*; pap. 6.99 *(978-1-5344-0922-4(X))* Simon Spotlight. (Simon Spotlight).
—Goodnight, Daniel Tiger. Santomero, Angela C. 2014. (Daniel Tiger's Neighborhood Ser.). (ENG.). 26p. (J). (gr. -1-2). 12.99 *(978-1-4814-0048-0(7)*, Simon Spotlight) Simon Spotlight.
—Hello, Teletubbies! Testa, Maggie. 2017. (Teletubbies Ser.). (ENG.). 12p. (J). (gr. -1 — 1). bds. 8.99 *(978-1-5344-0428-1(7)*, Simon Spotlight) Simon Spotlight.
—Lovely, Love My Family. 2011. (Yo Gabba Gabba! Ser.). (ENG.). 14p. (J). (gr. -1-1). bds. 5.99 *(978-1-4424-2134-9(7)*, Simon Spotlight) Simon Spotlight.
—Meet Po! Gallo, Tina. 2017. (Teletubbies Ser.). (ENG.). 14p. (J). (gr. -1-k). bds. 5.99 *(978-1-5344-0148-8(2)*, Simon Spotlight) Simon Spotlight.
—Meet the Neighbors! Shaw, Natalie. 2014. (Daniel Tiger's Neighborhood Ser.). (ENG.). 16p. (J). (gr. -1-k). bds. 7.99 *(978-1-4424-9837-2(4)*, Simon Spotlight) Simon Spotlight.
—Meet the Penguins! Pendergrass, Daphne. 2014. (Penguins of Madagascar Ser.). (ENG.). 24p. (J). (gr. -1-3). pap. 3.99 *(978-1-4814-3734-9(8)*, Simon Spotlight) Simon Spotlight.
—Meet the Teletubbies! Shaw, Natalie. 2017. (Teletubbies Ser.). (ENG.). 14p. (J). (gr. -1-k). bds. 7.99 *(978-1-4814-8530-2(X)*, Simon Spotlight) Simon Spotlight.
—Miffy's Yummy Cake. 2017. (Miffy's Adventures Big & Small Ser.). (ENG.). 24p. (J). (gr. -1-2). pap. 3.99 *(978-1-4814-6977-7(0)*, Simon Spotlight) Simon Spotlight.
—Oh, Barnacles! SpongeBob's Handbook for Bad Days. Lewman, David. 2005. (SpongeBob SquarePants Ser.). (ENG.). 48p. (J). pap. 3.99 *(978-1-4169-0641-4(X)*, Simon Spotlight/Nickelodeon) Simon Spotlight/Nickelodeon.
—Patricks Backpack Book. 2003. (SpongeBob SquarePants Ser.). (ENG.). 16p. (J). bds. 6.99 *(978-0-689-85649-5(0)*, Simon Spotlight/Nickelodeon) Simon Spotlight/Nickelodeon.
—Proud to Be a Ghostbuster. 2016. (Ghostbusters 2016 Movie Ser.). (ENG.). 40p. (J). (gr. 1-3). pap. 3.99 *(978-1-4814-7503-7(7)*, Simon Spotlight) Simon Spotlight.
—SpongeBob SpookyPants. Silverhardt, Lauryn. 2004. (SpongeBob SquarePants Ser.). (ENG.). 16p. (J). bds. 5.99 *(978-0-689-87320-1(4)*, Simon Spotlight/Nickelodeon) Simon Spotlight/Nickelodeon.
—SpongeBob's Backpack Book. 2003. (SpongeBob SquarePants Ser.). (ENG.). 16p. (J). bds. 6.99 *(978-0-689-85648-8(2)*, Simon Spotlight/Nickelodeon) Simon Spotlight/Nickelodeon.
Style Guide Staff, jt. illus. see Spaziante, Patrick.
Stylou, Georgia. Cloud City: A Child's Journey Through Bereavement. Spergel, Heather. 2013. (ENG.). 40p. (J). 15.95 *(978-1-938501-45-6(4))* Turn the Page Publishing.
—Hallonröd: Swedish Edition of Raspberry Red. Pere, Tuula. Nikolowski-Bogomoloff, Angelika, tr. 2018. (History Ser.: Vol. 2). (SWE.). 40p. (J). (gr. k-4). pap. *(978-952-5878-98-1(8))* Wickwick oy.
Styloy, Georgia. Raspberry Red. Pere, Tuula. Korman, Susan, ed. 2018. (History Ser.: Vol. 2). (ENG.). 40p. (J). (gr. k-4). pap. *(978-952-5878-97-4(X))* Wickwick oy.
—The Shoemaker's Splendid Lamp. Pere, Tuula. Korman, Susan, ed. 2018. (History Ser.: Vol. 1). (ENG.). 32p. (J). (gr. k-4). pap. *(978-952-5878-79-0(1))* Wickwick oy.
—Skomakarens Sagolika Lampa: Swedish Edition of the Shoemaker's Splendid Lamp. Pere, Tuula. Timonen Wahlstrom, Mai-Le, tr. 2018. (History Ser.: Vol. 1). (SWE.). 32p. (J). (gr. k-4). pap. *(978-952-5878-80-6(5))* Wickwick oy.
—Suutarin Hieno Lamppu: Finnish Edition of the Shoemaker's Splendid Lamp. Pere, Tuula. 2018. (History Ser.: Vol. 1). (FIN.). 32p. (J). (gr. k-4). pap. *(978-952-5878-81-3(3))* Wickwick oy.
—Vadelmanpunainen: Finnish Edition of Raspberry Red. Pere, Tuula. 2018. (History Ser.: Vol. 2). (FIN.). 40p. (J). (gr. k-4). pap. *(978-952-5878-99-8(6))* Wickwick oy.
Su, Keren, photos by. Giant Pandas. Stone, Lynn M. 2003. (Nature Watch Ser.). (ENG., 48p. (gr. 4-8). 27.93 *(978-1-57505-343-1(8)*, Carolrhoda Bks.) Lerner Publishing Group.
Su, Kim. A Day in the Garden. Su, Kim. 2019. (ENG.). 28p. (J). (gr. -1-3). pap. 9.99 *(978-1-5324-1212-7(6))* Xist Publishing.
Su, Lucy. Children of Lir Jigsaw Book. 2005. 12p. (J). 24.95 *(978-0-7171-3942-2(5))* M.H. Gill & Co. U. C. IRL. Dist: Dufour Editions, Inc.
Su, Lucy. Make a Picnic. Su, Lucy. 2003. (Kitten & Baby Kitten Ser.). 32p. (YA). *(978-1-85602-445-7(8)*, Pavilion Children's Books) Pavilion Bks.
—Make Cards. Su, Lucy. 2003. (Kitten & Baby Kitten Ser.). 32p. (YA). *(978-1-85602-446-4(6)*, Pavilion Children's Books) Pavilion Bks.
—Play Dressing Up. Su, Lucy. 2003. (Kitten & Baby Kitten Ser.). 24p. (J). bds. *(978-1-85602-463-1(6)*, Pavilion Children's Books) Pavilion Bks.
—Play Hide & Seek. Su, Lucy. 2003. (Kitten & Baby Kitten Ser.). 42p. (J). pap. *(978-1-85602-538-6(1)*, Pavilion Children's Books) Pavilion Bks.
—Say Good Morning. Su, Lucy. 2003. (Kitten & Baby Kitten Ser.). 42p. (J). bds. *(978-1-85602-466-2(0)*, Pavilion Children's Books) Pavilion Bks.
—Say Good Night. Su, Lucy. 2003. (Kitten & Baby Kitten Ser.). 42p. (J). bds. *(978-1-85602-537-9(3)*, Pavilion Children's Books) Pavilion Bks.
Su, Qin. At Home in This World: A China Adoption Story. MacLeod, Jean. 2nd ed. 2004. 32p. 15.95 *(978-0-9726244-1-1(4))* EMK Pr.
Sua, Laura. The Pumpkin Monster Blue Band. Gates, Susan. 2016. (Cambridge Reading Adventures Ser.). (ENG.). 16p. pap. 7.37 *(978-1-316-60576-9(0))* Cambridge Univ. Pr.
Suad, Laura. The Great Chapatti Chase. Dolan, Penny. 2015. (Collins Big Cat Ser.). (ENG.). 32p. (J). (gr. 2-2). pap. 9.99 *(978-0-00-759121-3(7))* HarperCollins Pubs. Ltd. GBR. Dist: Independent Pubs. Group.
Suarez, Florencia. Cuentos para Pensar. Suarez, Florencia. 2018. (SPA.). 58p. (J). pap. 28.00 *(978-1-7179-1355-5(5))* Independently Published.
Suarez Inclan, Maria. The Big Book of Everything You Need to Get the Job Done. Cassany, Mia. 2019. (ENG.). 32p. (J). (-k). 14.95 *(978-3-7913-7404-8(4))* Prestel Verlag GmbH & Co KG. DEU. Dist: Penguin Random Hse. LLC.
Suarez, Maribel. Dreams. Santillana USA. (Rowing Frog's Rhymes Ser.). 16p. (J). (gr. k-3). 7.95 *(978-1-59437-842-3(8))* Santillana USA Publishing Co., Inc.
—Este Soy Yo. Robleda, Margarita. 2006. (Rana, Rema, Rimas Ser.).Tr. of This Is Me. (SPA.). 12p. (J). (gr. -1-k). 7.95 *(978-1-59820-207-6(3)*, Alfaguara) Santillana USA Publishing Co., Inc.
—Here, Kitty, Kitty! (Ven, Gatita, Ven!) Mora, Pat. 2008. (My Family: Mi Familia Ser.). (SPA & ENG.). 24p. (J). (gr. 4-7). lib. bdg. 15.89 *(978-0-06-085045-6(0)*, Rayo) HarperCollins Pubs.
—Here, Kitty, Kitty!/Ven, Gatita, Ven! Bilingual Spanish-English Children's Book. Mora, Pat. 2008. (My Family: Mi Familia Ser.). (ENG.). 24p. (J). (gr. -1-3). 14.99 *(978-0-06-085044-9(2)*, HarperCollins Español) HarperCollins Christian Publishing.
—Jugando con Las Vocales. Robleda, Margarita. 2006. (Rana, Rema, Rimas Ser.).Tr. of Playing with Vowels. (SPA.). 12p. (J). (gr. -1-k). 7.95 *(978-1-59820-210-6(3)*, Alfaguara) Santillana USA Publishing Co., Inc.
—Let's Eat!/a Comer! Bilingual Spanish-English Children's Book. Mora, Pat. 2008. (My Family: Mi Familia Ser.). (ENG.). 24p. (J). (gr. -1-3). 12.99 *(978-0-06-085038-8(8)*, HarperCollins Español) HarperCollins Christian Publishing.
Suarez, Maribel. Mamá Goose: Bilingual Lullabies Nanas. Ada, Alma Flor & Campoy, F. Isabel. 2019. 18p. (J). (gr. -1 — 1). bds. 7.99 ***(978-1-368-04541-4(3))*** Little, Brown Bks. for Young Readers.
Suarez, Maribel. Muneca de Trapo. Robleda, Margarita. 2006. (Rana, Rema, Rimas Ser.). (SPA.). 12p. (J). (gr. -1-k). 7.95 *(978-1-59820-209-0(X)*, Alfaguara) Santillana USA Publishing Co., Inc.
—Patito, Donde Estas? Robleda, Margarita. 2006. (Rana, Rema, Rimas Ser.).Tr. of Where Are You Little Ducky?. (SPA.). 12p. (J). (gr. -1-k). 7.95 *(978-1-59820-208-3(1)*, Alfaguara) Santillana USA Publishing Co., Inc.
—Ramon & His Mouse. (Rowing Frog's Rhymes Ser.). 16p. (J). (gr. k-3). 7.95 *(978-1-59437-839-3(8))* Santillana USA Publishing Co., Inc.
—Ramon y Su Raton. Robleda, Margarita. (Rana, Rema, Rimas Ser.). (SPA.). 16p. (J). (gr. k-3). 7.95 *(978-1-59437-818-8(5))* Santillana USA Publishing Co., Inc.
Suárez, Maribel. Ramón y Su Ratón. Robleda, Margarita. 2007. (Rana, Rema, Rimas / Rowing Rhyming Frog Ser.). (SPA.). 16p. (J). (gr. k-3). pap. 6.99 *(978-1-63113-942-0(8))* Santillana USA Publishing Co., Inc.
Suarez, Maribel. Rebeca. Robleda, Margarita. (Rana, Rema, Rimas Ser.).Tr. of Rebecca. (SPA.). 16p. (J). (gr. k-3). 7.95 *(978-1-59437-819-5(3))* Santillana USA Publishing Co., Inc.
—Rebecca. (Rowing Frog's Rhymes Ser.). 16p. (J). (gr. k-3). 7.95 *(978-1-59437-840-9(1))* Santillana USA Publishing Co., Inc.
—Sana Ranita, Sana. Robleda, Margarita. (Rana, Rema, Rimas Ser.).Tr. of Kiss Away My Boo-Boo. (SPA.). 16p. (J). (gr. k-3). 7.95 *(978-1-59437-820-1(7))* Santillana USA Publishing Co., Inc.
—Suenos. Robleda, Margarita. (Rana, Rema, Rimas Ser.). (SPA.). 16p. (J). (gr. k-3). 7.95 *(978-1-59437-821-8(5))* Santillana USA Publishing Co., Inc.
—Sweet Dreams/Dulces Suenos: Bilingual Spanish-English Children's Book. Mora, Pat. 2008. (My Family: Mi Familia Ser.). (ENG.). 24p. (J). (gr. -1-3). 12.99 *(978-0-06-085041-8(8)*, HarperCollins Español) HarperCollins Christian Publishing.
—Wiggling Pockets/Los Bolsillos Saltarines: Bilingual Spanish-English Children's Book. Mora, Pat. 2009. (My Family: Mi Familia Ser.). (ENG.). 24p. (J). (gr. -1-3). 12.99 *(978-0-06-085047-0(7)*, HarperCollins Español) HarperCollins Christian Publishing.
Suarez, Maribel, tr. Namm, Diane. 2004. (My First Reader Ser.). (ENG.). 31p. (J). 18.50 *(978-0-516-24417-4(5)*, Children's Pr.) Scholastic Library Publishing.

Suarez, Maribel. Pick a Pet. Suarez, Maribel, tr. Namm, Diane. 2004. (My First Reader Ser.). (ENG.). 31p. (J). 18.50 *(978-0-516-24417-4(5)*, Children's Pr.) Scholastic Library Publishing.
Suarez, Rosa Virginia Urdaneta, photos by. Un Caballo en la Ciudad. Pantin, Yolanda. 2003. (Playco's Best Collection). (SPA., 36p. (J). (gr. 2-7). *(978-980-6437-40-1(3))* Playco Editores, C.A.
Suarez, Sergio Lopez. Huakala! a los Miedos. Suarez, Sergio Lopez. 2003. (SPA.). 32p. (J). (gr. k-3). 9.95 *(978-968-19-0556-9(3))* Aguilar, Altea, Taurus, Alfaguara, S.A. de C.V MEX. Dist: Santillana USA Publishing Co., Inc.
Suarez, Vince. Goodnight, Goodly Tree. Takizadeh, Rosario. 2019. (Goodly Tree Ser.: Vol. 3). (ENG.). 28p. (J). pap. 9.49 *(978-1-0738-1956-0(6))* Independently Published.
Suber, Melissa. Tough Chicks (lap Board Book) Meng, Cece. 2018. (ENG.). 28p. (J). (— 1). bds. 12.99 *(978-1-328-95985-0(6)*, 1706952, HMH Books For Young Readers) Houghton Mifflin Harcourt Publishing Co.
—Tough Chicks Love Their Mama (tabbed Touch-And-feel) Meng, Cece. 2019. (ENG.). 12p. (J). (— 1). 8.99 *(978-0-358-12653-9(3)*, 1752368, HMH Books For Young Readers) Houghton Mifflin Harcourt Publishing Co.
—Tough Chicks to the Rescue! (tabbed Touch-And-feel) Meng, Cece. 2019. (ENG.). 12p. (J). (— 1). 8.99 *(978-1-328-45057-9(0)*, 1711428, HMH Books For Young Readers) Houghton Mifflin Harcourt Publishing Co.
Subi. Las Aventuras de Don Quijote. Palacio, Carla, tr. 2005. (SPA.). 32p. *(978-84-264-1492-2(3))* Editorial Lumen.
—Stegosaurus: the Friendliest Dinosaur. Obiols, Anna. 2012. (Dinosaur Bks.). (ENG.). 36p. (J). (gr. -1-1). pap. 7.99 *(978-1-4380-0107-4(X)*, B.E.S. Publishing) Peterson's.
—Triceratops: the Strongest Dinosaur. Obiols, Anna. 2012. (Dinosaur Bks.). (ENG.). 36p. (J). (gr. -1-1). pap. 7.99 *(978-1-4380-0108-1(8)*, B.E.S. Publishing) Peterson's.
Subirana, Joan. El León y el Ratón. Bailer, Darice et al. 2007. (SPA & ENG.). 28p. (J). *(978-0-545-02449-5(8))* Scholastic, Inc.
Subisak, Tracy. Cy Makes a Friend. Stephens, Ann Marie. 2017. (ENG.). 32p. (J). (gr. -1-3). 16.95 *(978-1-62979-578-2(X))* Boyds Mills Pr.
—Grizzly Boy. Davis-Pyles, Barbara. 2018. 32p. (J). (gr. -1-2). 17.99 *(978-1-63217-168-9(6)*, Little Bigfoot) Sasquatch Bks.
—Wood, Wire, Wings: Emma Lilian Todd Invents an Airplane. Larson, Kirsten W. 2020. (ENG.). 48p. (J). (gr. 2-5). 18.99 *(978-1-62979-938-4(6)*, Calkins Creek) Boyds Mills Pr.
Sudipta, Dasgupta. Sea Dreams. Blom, Tracy. 2018. (ENG.). 22p. (J). pap. 10.00 *(978-0-9906871-3-9(9))* Blom Pubns.
Sudo, Kumiko. Coco-Chan's Kimono. Sudo, Kumiko. 2010. (ENG.). 32p. (J). (gr. k-2). 16.95 *(978-1-933308-26-5(5))* Breckling Pr.
Sudyka, Diana. Every Single Second. Springstubb, Tricia. (ENG.). 368p. (J). (gr. 3-7). 2017. pap. 6.99 *(978-0-06-236629-0(7)*, Balzer & Bray); 2016. 16.99 *(978-0-06-236628-3(9))* HarperCollins Pubs.
—The Extraordinary Education of Nicholas Benedict. Stewart, Trenton Lee. (Mysterious Benedict Society Ser.). (ENG.). (J). (gr. 3-7). 2013. 496p. pap. 9.99 *(978-0-316-17620-0(6))*; 2012. 480p. 33.00 *(978-0-316-17619-4(2))* Little, Brown Bks. for Young Readers.
—How to Find a Bird. Ward, Jennifer. 2020. (ENG.). 48p. (J). (gr. -1-3). 17.99 *(978-1-4814-6705-6(0)*, Beach Lane Bks.) Beach Lane Bks.
—The Mysterious Benedict Society & the Perilous Journey. Stewart, Trenton Lee. 2009. (Mysterious Benedict Society Ser.: 2). (ENG.). 464p. (J). (gr. 3-7). pap. 9.99 *(978-0-316-03673-3(0))* Little Brown & Co.
—The Mysterious Benedict Society & the Perilous Journey. Stewart, Trenton Lee. 2008. (Mysterious Benedict Society Ser.: 2). (ENG.). 448p. (J). (gr. 3-7). 18.99 *(978-0-316-05780-6(0))* Little, Brown Bks. for Young Readers.
—The Mysterious Benedict Society & the Prisoner's Dilemma. Stewart, Trenton Lee. (Mysterious Benedict Society Ser.: 3). (ENG.). 400p. (J). (gr. 3-7). 2010. pap. 9.99 *(978-0-316-04550-6(0))*; 2009. 31.00 *(978-0-316-04552-0(7))* Little, Brown Bks. for Young Readers.
—The Mysterious Benedict Society: Mr. Benedict's Book of Perplexing Puzzles, Elusive Enigmas, & Curious Conundrums. Stewart, Trenton Lee. (Mysterious Benedict Society Ser.). 176p. (J). (gr. 3-7). 2016. (ENG.). pap. 9.99 *(978-0-316-39475-8(0))*; 2011. 17.99

S

(978-0-316-18193-8(5)) Little, Brown Bks. for Young Readers.

—The Secret Keepers. Stewart, Trenton Lee. (ENG.). 512p. (J). (gr. 3-7). 2017. pap. 9.99 *(978-0-316-38954-9(4))*; 2016. 18.99 *(978-0-316-38955-6(2))* Little, Brown Bks. for Young Readers.

—Sometimes Rain. Fleming, Meg. 2018. (ENG.). 40p. (J). (gr. -1-3). 17.99 *(978-1-4814-5918-1(X)*, Beach Lane Bks.) Beach Lane Bks.

—What Miss Mitchell Saw. Barrett, Hayley. 2019. (ENG.). 40p. (J). (gr. -1-3). 17.99 *(978-1-4814-8759-7(0)*, Beach Lane Bks.) Beach Lane Bks.

—When Sue Found Sue: Sue Hendrickson Discovers Her T. Rex. Buzzeo, Toni. 2019. (ENG.). 32p. (J). (gr. -1-3). 17.99 *(978-1-4197-3163-1(7)*, Abrams Bks. for Young Readers) Abrams, Inc.

Sudzuka, Goran, et al. Daredevil: Back in Black Vol. 4: Identity. 2017. (ENG.). 136p. (YA). (gr. 8-17). pap. 17.99 *(978-1-302-90562-0(7))* Marvel Worldwide, Inc.

Suenobu, Keiko. Life, Vol. 1. Suenobu, Keiko. 2006. (Life (Tokyopop) Ser.). 200p. (YA). pap. 14.99 *(978-1-59532-931-8(5)*, Tokyopop Adult) TOKYOPOP, Inc.

Sugarman, S. Allan. The Heroes of Masada. Rosenfield, Geraldine. 38p. (J). (gr. 6-10). pap. 1.50 *(978-0-8381-0733-1(8)*, 10-732) United Synagogue of America Bk. Service.

Suggs, Aisha. The Boy Who Did Not Want to Read, 1 vol. Williams, Tova. 2010. 36p. pap. 24.95 *(978-1-4489-5705-7(2))* PublishAmerica, Inc.

Suggs, Margaret. Blue, Where Are You? Magee, Wes. 2007. (Flyers Ser.: 16). (ENG.). 64p. (J). pap. 11.00 *(978-1-84717-009-5(9))* O'Brien Pr., Ltd., The. IRL. Dist: Casemate Pubs. & Bk. Distributors, LLC.

Suggs, Margaret Anne. Cuppa Tea. La Branche, Eric. 2017. (ENG.). 32p. (J). (gr. -1 — 1). 17.95 *(978-1-60537-281-5(1))* Clavis ROM. Dist: Publishers Group West (PGW).

—The Growing up Book for Boys: What Boys on the Autism Spectrum Need to Know! Hartman, Davida. 2015. (Growing Up Ser.). (ENG.). 72p. (J). 16.95 *(978-1-84905-575-8(0)*, 693097) Kingsley, Jessica Pubs. GBR. Dist: Hachette UK Distribution.

—The Growing up Guide for Girls: What Girls on the Autism Spectrum Need to Know! Hartman, Davida. 2015. (Growing Up Ser.). (ENG.). 72p. (J). 16.95 *(978-1-84905-574-1(2)*, 693027) Kingsley, Jessica Pubs. GBR. Dist: Hachette UK Distribution.

—The Naughty Naughty Chair. Jessop, Connie. 2019. (ENG.). 30p. (J). pap. *(978-1-78324-112-5(8))* Wordzworth Publishing.

—Pigín of Howth. Watkins, Kathleen. 2017. (ENG.). 64p. (J). 28.00 *(978-0-7171-6972-6(3))* Gill Bks. IRL. Dist: Casemate Pubs. & Bk. Distributors, LLC.

Sugisaki, Yukiru. Brain Powered, 3 vols., Vol. 3. Tomino, Yoshiyuki. rev. ed. 2003. 192p. pap. 9.99 *(978-1-59182-391-9(9))* TOKYOPOP, Inc.

—Brain Powered, 4 vols., Vol. 4. Tomino, Yoshiyuki. Matsunaga, Aya, tr. from JPN. rev. ed. 2004. 192p. pap. 9.99 *(978-1-59182-392-6(7))* TOKYOPOP, Inc.

Sugisaki, Yukiru. D. N. Angel, Vol. 6. Sugisaki, Yukiru. Nibley, Alethea & Nibley, Athena, trs. from JPN. rev. ed. 2005. 176p. (YA). pap. 9.99 *(978-1-59182-955-3(0))* TOKYOPOP, Inc.

—D. N. Angel. Sugisaki, Yukiru. 2005. Vol. 7. 7th rev. ed. 176p. pap. 9.99 *(978-1-59182-956-0(9))*; Vol. 8. rev. ed. 192p. (YA). pap. 9.99 *(978-1-59182-957-7(7))* TOKYOPOP, Inc.

—Rizelmine, Vol. 1. Sugisaki, Yukiru. 2005. 144p. per. 9.99 *(978-1-59532-901-1(3)*, Tokyopop Adult) TOKYOPOP, Inc.

Sugita, Yataka. Good Morning-Sun's Up. Beach, Stewart. 32p. (J). (gr. -1-3). 13.95 *(978-0-87592-021-4(7))* Scroll Pr., Inc.

Sugita, Yutaka. Goodnight, One, Two, Three. Sugita, Yutaka. 32p. (J). (gr. -1-2). 14.95 *(978-0-87592-022-1(5))* Scroll Pr., Inc.

Suhr, James W. Like a Cat: Creep, Sleep, Pounce, & Peek. . . Donlon, Diane Youngblood. 2003. 32p. (J). 16.95 *(978-0-9720427-2-7(5))* OLLY Publishing Co.

—Tippee Tippee Tiptoe. Donlon, Diane Youngblood. 2003. (J). 16.95 *(978-0-9720427-0-3(9))* OLLY Publishing Co.

Suits, Rosella. Leggys in Number-land. Ostrom, Gladys. 2011. 40p. (J). pap. 12.95 *(978-0-9841721-6-0(5))* Open Door Publishers, Inc.

Sukanada, I. Gusti Made. Gecko's Complaint: A Balinese Folktale. Bowler, Ann Martin. ed. 2009. (ENG.). 32p. (J). (gr. k-3). 14.95 *(978-0-7946-0484-4(6))* Tuttle Publishing.

Sukarno, Achmad. The Why-Entist & the Wild Weather. Lowry, Jane. 2019. (Ask-A-Lot Kids Ser.: Vol. 1). (ENG.). 44p. (J). (gr. 1-5). 17.95 ***(978-1-7338375-0-7(7))*** Quoi Happens LLC.

Sukmanindya, Windha. Ella's Big Catch. Reich, Tina. 2019. (ENG.). 44p. (J). pap. 9.99 ***(978-1-7343186-2-3(7))*** Reich, Tina.

SukWon, Sa. Bubbly & Grumpy. SungJa, Cho. rev. ed. 2014. (MySELF Bookshelf Ser.). (ENG.). 32p. (J). (gr. k-2). pap. 11.94 *(978-1-60357-660-4(6))*; lib. bdg. 25.27 *(978-1-59953-651-4(X))* Norwood Hse. Pr.

Suleman, Shilo Shiv. The Bookworm. R. N., Lavanya. 2013. (ENG.). 32p. (J). (gr. k). pap. 9.95 *(978-81-8190-180-4(0))* Karadi Tales Co. Pvt, Ltd. IND. Dist: Consortium Bk. Sales & Distribution.

—Tak-Tak! Ranade, Soumitra. 2013. (ENG.). 32p. (J). (gr. k). pap. 9.95 *(978-81-8190-183-5(5))* Karadi Tales Co. Pvt, Ltd. IND. Dist: Consortium Bk. Sales & Distribution.

Sulik, Alberta, jt. illus. see Gartler, Monica.

Sulit, William. Wild Blues. Kephart, Beth. (ENG.). (J). (gr. 5-9). 2019. 352p. pap. 9.99 *(978-1-4814-9154-9(7))*; 2018. 336p. 17.99 *(978-1-4814-9153-2(9)*, Atheneum/Caitlyn Dlouhy Books) Simon & Schuster Children's Publishing.

Sullens, Anais. The Hyena & the Rabbit. Diabate, Keba & Sumnicht, Patricia. 2015. (J). pap. 10.00 *(978-1-59598-370-1(8))* HenschelHAUS Publishing, Inc.

Sullivan, Carolyn Rose. The Music Box: Songs, Rhymes, & Games for Young Children, 1 box. 2006. 200p. (J). 49.95 *(978-0-9772717-1-9(4))* ELZ Publishing.

Sullivan, Dana. Bob Books: First Stories. Kertell, Lynn Maslen. 2015. (Bob Bks.). (ENG.). 12p. (J). (gr. -1-1). 16.99 *(978-0-545-73409-7(6))* Scholastic, Inc.

—Digger & Daisy Go Camping. Young, Judy. 2019. (I AM a READER: Digger & Daisy Ser.). (ENG.). 32p. (J). (gr. k-2). 9.99 *(978-1-5341-1022-9(4)*, 204655); pap. 4.99 *(978-1-5341-1023-6(2)*, 204663) Sleeping Bear Pr.

—Digger & Daisy Go on a Picnic. Young, Judy. 2014. (I Am a Reader: Digger & Daisy Ser.). (ENG.). 32p. (J). (gr. k-1). 9.99 *(978-1-58536-843-3(1)*, 203006) Sleeping Bear Pr.

—Digger & Daisy Go to the Doctor. Young, Judy. 2014. (I AM a READER!: Digger & Daisy Ser.). (ENG.). 32p. (J). (gr. k-2). 9.99 *(978-1-58536-845-7(8)*, 203674); pap. 4.99 *(978-1-58536-846-4(6)*, 203728) Sleeping Bear Pr.

—Digger & Daisy Plant a Garden. Young, Judy. 2016. (I AM a READER: Digger & Daisy Ser.). (ENG.). 32p. (J). (gr. k-2). 9.99 *(978-1-58536-931-7(4)*, 204030) Sleeping Bear Pr.

—Digger et Daisy Vont Au Docteur (Digger & Daisy Go to the Doctor) Young, Judy. 2016. (I AM a READER: Digger & Daisy Ser.). (ENG.). 32p. (J). (gr. k-2). 12.95 *(978-1-62753-949-4(2)*, 204172) Sleeping Bear Pr.

—Digger y Daisy Van a la Ciudad (Digger & Daisy Go to the City) Young, Judy. 2016. (I AM a READER: Digger & Daisy Ser.). (ENG.). 32p. (J). (gr. k-2). 9.99 *(978-1-62753-954-8(9)*, 204177) Sleeping Bear Pr.

—Digger y Daisy Van Al Médico (Digger & Daisy Go to the Doctor) Young, Judy. 2016. (I AM a READER: Digger & Daisy Ser.). (ENG.). 32p. (J). (gr. k-2). 9.99 *(978-1-62753-953-1(0)*, 204176) Sleeping Bear Pr.

—Digger y Daisy Van Al Zoológico (Digger & Daisy Go to the Zoo) Young, Judy. 2016. (I AM a READER: Digger & Daisy Ser.). (ENG.). 32p. (J). (gr. k-2). 9.99 *(978-1-62753-951-7(4)*, 204174) Sleeping Bear Pr.

—Digger y Daisy Van de Picnic (Digger & Daisy Go on a Picnic) Young, Judy. 2016. (I AM a READER: Digger & Daisy Ser.). (ENG.). 32p. (J). (gr. k-2). 9.99 *(978-1-62753-952-4(2)*, 204175) Sleeping Bear Pr.

—Rhyming Words. Kertell, Lynn Maslen. 2013. (Bob Bks.). (ENG.). (J). (gr. -1-1). 17.99 *(978-0-545-51322-7(7))* Scholastic, Inc.

—Star in a Play. Young, Judy. 2015. (I AM a READER: Digger & Daisy Ser.). (ENG.). 32p. (J). (gr. k-2). 9.99 *(978-1-58536-929-4(2)*, 203950) Sleeping Bear Pr.

Sullivan, Dana. The Deadening: Book 1. Sullivan, Dana. 2020. (Dead Max Comix Ser.). (ENG.). 64p. (J). (gr. 4-8). 18.99 *(978-1-63440-852-3(7))*; pap. 8.99 *(978-1-63440-853-0(5))* Red Chair Pr.

—Kay Kay's Alphabet Safari. Sullivan, Dana. 2014. (ENG.). 40p. (J). (gr. 1-4). 15.99 *(978-1-58536-905-8(5)*, 203666) Sleeping Bear Pr.

—My Red Velvet Cape. Sullivan, Dana. 2018. (ENG.). 32p. (J). (gr. k-3). 16.99 *(978-1-58536-393-3(6)*, 204399) Sleeping Bear Pr.

—Ozzie & the Art Contest. Sullivan, Dana. 2013. (ENG.). 15.99 *(978-1-58536-820-4(2))* Sleeping Bear Pr.

Sullivan, Dana. The Rocking Dead: Book 2. Sullivan, Dana. 2020. (Dead Max Comix Ser.). (ENG.). 64p. (J). (gr. 4-8). 18.99 ***(978-1-63440-858-5(6))***; pap. 8.99 ***(978-1-63440-859-2(4))*** Red Chair Pr.

Sullivan, Derek. Don't Eat Me, Chupacabra! / ¡No Me Comas, Chupacabra! A Delicious Story with Digestible Spanish Vocabulary. Sullivan, Kyle. 2018. (Hazy Dell Press Monster Ser.). 30p. (J). bds. 13.95 *(978-0-9965787-7-6(3))* Hazy Dell Pr.

—Get Dressed, Sasquatch! Sullivan, Kyle. 2018. (Hazy Dell Press Monster Ser.). 30p. (J). bds. 13.95 *(978-0-9965787-3-8(0))* Hazy Dell Pr.

—Goodnight Krampus. Sullivan, Kyle. 2018. (Hazy Dell Press Monster Ser.). (ENG.). 30p. (J). (gr. -1-12). bds. 13.95 *(978-0-9965787-2-1(2))* Hazy Dell Pr.

—Hazy Dell Press 5-Book Gift Set: Monster ABC, Goodnight Krampus, Get Dressed, Sasquatch!, Hush Now Banshee! & Don't Eat Me, Chupacabra!/¡No Me Comas, Chupacabra! Sullivan, Kyle. 2018. (Hazy Dell Press Monster Ser.). (ENG.). 150p. (J). 59.95 *(978-0-9965787-8-3(1))* Hazy Dell Pr.

—Hush Now, Banshee! A Not-So-Quiet Counting Book. Sullivan, Kyle. 2018. (Hazy Dell Press Monster Ser.). 30p. (J). bds. 13.95 *(978-0-9965787-5-2(7))* Hazy Dell Pr.

—Monster ABC. Sullivan, Kyle. 2018. (Hazy Dell Press Monster Ser.). 30p. (J). bds. 13.95 *(978-0-9965787-0-7(6))* Hazy Dell Pr.

—Party Croc! A Folktale from Zimbabwe. MacDonald, Margaret Read. 2015. (ENG.). 32p. (J). (gr. -1-3). 16.99 *(978-0-8075-6320-5(X)*, 080756320X) Whitman, Albert & Co.

Sullivan, Don. El Tronco de Arbol, Level 1. Forbes, Chris. Flor Ada, Alma, tr. 2003. (Dejame Leer Ser.). (SPA.). 8p. (J). (gr. -1-k). 6.50 *(978-0-673-36300-8(7)*, Good Year Bks.) Celebration Pr.

Sullivan, James Kevin. What Went Right Today? Journal: WWRT Journal. 2007. 72p. (J). spiral bd. 12.95 *(978-0-9766990-1-9(X))* Buz-Land Presentations, Inc.

Sullivan, Kate. On Linden Square. Sullivan, Kate. 2013. (ENG.). 40p. 15.99 *(978-1-58536-832-7(6))* Sleeping Bear Pr.

Sullivan, Mary. Bella's Boat Surprise, 1 vol. Jones, Christianne C. (My First Graphic Novel Ser.). (ENG.). 32p. (J). (gr. k-2). 2010. pap. 6.25 *(978-1-4342-2287-9(X))*; 2009. 24.65 *(978-1-4342-1617-5(9))* Capstone. (Stone Arch Bks.).

—Bree's Bike Jump, 1 vol. Mortensen, Lori. 2009. (My First Graphic Novel Ser.). (ENG.). 32p. (J). (gr. k-2). 24.65 *(978-1-4342-1620-5(9)*, Stone Arch Bks.) Capstone.

—The End Zone, 1 vol. Mortensen, Lori. 2009. (My First Graphic Novel Ser.). (ENG.). 32p. (J). (gr. k-2). pap. 6.25 *(978-1-4342-1408-9(7)*, Stone Arch Bks.) Capstone.

—Hidden Pictures. School Zone Interactive Staff. rev. ed. 2006. (ENG.). 64p. (J). (gr. 1-2). 7.99 *(978-1-58947-301-0(9))* School Zone Publishing Co.

—Joy's Journey Home. Connolly, Timothy. 2012. (ENG.). 92p. (J). 17.95 *(978-0-9859986-2-2(8))*; pap. 8.95 *(978-0-9859986-1-5(X))* Nectar Pubns.

—The Lunchroom Fight. Sateren, Shelley Swanson. 2013. (Max & Zoe Ser.). (ENG.). 32p. (J). (gr. k-2). lib. bdg. 21.32 *(978-1-4048-7199-1(3)*, Picture Window Bks.) Capstone.

—Max & Zoe. Sateren, Shelley Swanson. 2013. (Max & Zoe Ser.). (ENG.). 32p. (J). (gr. k-2). lib. bdg., lib. bdg., lib. bdg. 255.84 *(978-1-4795-1695-7(3)*, Picture Window Bks.) Capstone.

—Max & Zoe. Swanson Sateren, Shelley. 2014. (Max & Zoe Ser.). (ENG.). (J). (gr. k-2). pap., pap., pap. 41.52 *(978-1-4795-1820-3(4)*, Picture Window Bks.) Capstone.

—Max & Zoe at Recess, 1 vol. Sateren, Shelley Swanson. 2012. (Max & Zoe Ser.). (ENG.). 32p. (J). (gr. k-2). lib. bdg. 21.32 *(978-1-4048-7200-4(0)*, Picture Window Bks.) Capstone.

—Max & Zoe at School, 1 vol. Sateren, Shelley Swanson. (Max & Zoe Ser.). (ENG.). 32p. (J). (gr. k-2). 2013. pap. 5.19 *(978-1-4048-8059-7(3))*; 2011. lib. bdg. 21.32 *(978-1-4048-6211-1(0))* Capstone. (Picture Window Bks.).

—Max & Zoe at Soccer Practice, 1 vol. Sateren, Shelley Swanson. 2012. (Max & Zoe Ser.). (ENG.). 32p. (J). (gr. k-2). lib. bdg. 21.32 *(978-1-4048-6213-5(7)*, Picture Window Bks.) Capstone.

—Max & Zoe at the Dentist, 1 vol. Sateren, Shelley Swanson. (Max & Zoe Ser.). (ENG.). 32p. (J). (gr. k-2). 2013. pap. 5.19 *(978-1-4048-8057-3(7))*; 2011. lib. bdg. 21.32 *(978-1-4048-6206-7(4))* Capstone. (Picture Window Bks.).

—Max & Zoe at the Doctor, 1 vol. Sateren, Shelley Swanson. (Max & Zoe Ser.). (ENG.). 32p. (J). (gr. k-2). 2013. pap. 5.19 *(978-1-4048-8060-3(7))*; 2011. lib. bdg. 21.32 *(978-1-4048-6212-8(9))* Capstone. (Picture Window Bks.).

—Max & Zoe at the Library, 1 vol. Sateren, Shelley Swanson. (Max & Zoe Ser.). (ENG.). 32p. (J). (gr. k-2). 2013. pap. 5.19 *(978-1-4048-8058-0(5))*; 2011. lib. bdg. 21.32 *(978-1-4048-6210-4(2))* Capstone. (Picture Window Bks.).

—Max & Zoe Celebrate Mother's Day, 1 vol. Sateren, Shelley Swanson. 2012. (Max & Zoe Ser.). (ENG.). 32p. (J). (gr. k-2). lib. bdg. 21.32 *(978-1-4048-6214-2(5)*, Picture Window Bks.) Capstone.

—Max & Zoe: the Lunchroom Fight, 1 vol. Sateren, Shelley Swanson. 2013. (Max & Zoe Ser.). (ENG.). 32p. (J). (gr. k-2). pap. 5.19 *(978-1-4795-2328-3(3)*, Picture Window Bks.) Capstone.

—Max & Zoe: the Science Fair, 1 vol. Sateren, Shelley Swanson. 2013. (Max & Zoe Ser.). (ENG.). 32p. (J). (gr. k-2). pap. 5.19 *(978-1-4795-2330-6(5)*, Picture Window Bks.) Capstone.

—Max & Zoe: the Very Best Art Project, 1 vol. Sateren, Shelley Swanson. 2013. (Max & Zoe Ser.). (ENG.). 32p. (J). (gr. k-2). pap. 5.19 *(978-1-4795-2329-0(1)*, Picture Window Bks.) Capstone.

—Max & Zoe: Too Many Tricks, 1 vol. Sateren, Shelley Swanson. 2013. (Max & Zoe Ser.). (ENG.). 32p. (J). (gr. k-2). pap. 5.19 *(978-1-4795-2327-6(5)*, Picture Window Bks.) Capstone.

—My Name Is Wakawakaloch! Stiefel, Chana. 2019. (ENG.). 32p. (J). (gr. -1-3). 17.99 *(978-1-328-73209-5(6)*, 1675985, HMH Books For Young Readers) Houghton Mifflin Harcourt Publishing Co.

—Now I'm Reading! Pre-Reader: Word Play. Gaydos, Nora. 2008. (NIR! Leveled Readers Ser.). 128p. (J). (gr. -1-2). 16.99 *(978-1-58476-725-1(1)*, Now I'm Reading!) Random Hse. Children's Bks.

—Phonics Comics: Clara the Klutz - Level 2. Wax, Wendy. 2007. (ENG.). 24p. (J). (gr. 1-17). per. 3.99 *(978-1-58476-565-3(8))* Innovative Kids.

—The School Concert. Sateren, Shelley Swanson. 2012. (Max & Zoe Ser.). (ENG.). 32p. (J). (gr. k-2). lib. bdg. 21.32 *(978-1-4048-7198-4(5)*, Picture Window Bks.) Capstone.

—The Science Fair. Sateren, Shelley Swanson. 2013. (Max & Zoe Ser.). (ENG.). 32p. (J). (gr. k-2). lib. bdg. 21.32 *(978-1-4048-7202-8(7)*, Picture Window Bks.) Capstone.

—Secret Scooter, 1 vol. Jones, Christianne C. 2009. (My First Graphic Novel Ser.). (ENG.). 32p. (J). (gr. k-2). 24.65 *(978-1-4342-1619-9(5)*, Stone Arch Bks.) Capstone.

—Too Many Tricks. Sateren, Shelley Swanson. 2013. (Max & Zoe Ser.). (ENG.). 32p. (J). (gr. k-2). lib. bdg. 21.32 *(978-1-4048-7197-7(7)*, Picture Window Bks.) Capstone.

—The Very Best Art Project. Sateren, Shelley Swanson. 2013. (Max & Zoe Ser.). (ENG.). 32p. (J). (gr. k-2). lib. bdg. 21.32 *(978-1-4048-7201-1(9)*, Picture Window Bks.) Capstone.

Sullivan, Mary & Gray, Steve. Clever Critters: Now I'm Reading! For Beginning Readers. Gaydos, Nora. 2008. (NIR! Leveled Readers Ser.). 128p. (J). (gr. -1-3). 16.99 *(978-1-58476-666-7(2)*, Now I'm Reading!) Random Hse. Children's Bks.

Sullivan, Mary C. Bugs! a Counting Book. Sullivan, Mary C. 2013. 32p. 18.95 *(978-0-9859986-6-0(0))* Nectar Pubns.

Sullivan, Rosana. Mommy Sayang: Pixar Animation Studios Artist Showcase. Sullivan, Rosana. 2019. (Artist Showcase Ser.). (ENG.). 48p. (J). (gr. -1-k). 16.99 *(978-1-368-01590-5(5))* Disney Pr.

Sullivan, Simon. Clara Barton: Spirit of the American Red Cross. Lakin, Patricia. 2004. (Ready-To-read SOFA Ser.). (ENG.). 48p. (J). (gr. 1-3). pap. 4.99 *(978-0-689-86513-8(9)*, Simon Spotlight) Simon Spotlight.

—Clara Barton Spirit of the American Red Cross. Lakin, Patricia. ed. 2005. (Ready-to-Read Ser.). 48p. (J). lib. bdg. 15.00 *(978-1-59054-958-2(9))* Fitzgerald Bks.

—The Dog That Dug for Dinosaurs. Redmond, Shirley Raye & Redmond, Shirley Raye. 2004. (Ready-To-Reads Ser.). (ENG.). 32p. (J). (gr. 1-3). pap. 4.99 *(978-0-689-85708-9(X)*, Simon Spotlight) Simon Spotlight.

Sullivan, Sonja. I Am A Kumeyaay. Sullivan, Sonja. Stanley, Barbara, ed. 2007. 29p. (J). *(978-0-9790951-1-5(5))* Sycuan Pr.

Sullivan, Tom. Blue vs. Yellow. Sullivan, Tom. 2017. (ENG.). 48p. (J). (gr. -1-3). 17.99 *(978-0-06-245295-5(9))* HarperCollins Pubs.

—I Used to Be a Fish. Sullivan, Tom. 2016. (ENG.). 48p. (J). (gr. -1-3). 17.99 *(978-0-06-245198-9(7))* HarperCollins Pubs.

—Out There. Sullivan, Tom. 2019. (ENG.). 32p. (J). (gr. -1-3). 17.99 *(978-0-06-285449-0(6)*, Balzer & Bray) HarperCollins Pubs.

Sullivan, Troy. Scribble & Grin: 53 Rhymes for Inspiring Times. Giuffre, Mary & Clark, Paul L. 2013. 142p. *(978-0-9919101-0-6(9))* inspirtainment ink.

Suman, Surendra. Classic Collection: 22 Short Stories. Menon, Geeta. 2005. 143p. (J). *(978-81-7011-970-8(7))* Children's Bk. Trust.

Sumberac, Manuel. A Midsummer Night's Dream: Band 18/Pearl (Collins Big Cat) Dougherty, John. 2014. (Collins Big Cat Ser.). (ENG.). 80p. (J). (gr. 5-6). pap. 11.99 *(978-0-00-753012-0(9))* HarperCollins Pubs. Ltd. GBR. Dist: Independent Pubs. Group.

—The Snow Queen. Andersen, Hans. 2014. (J). *(978-1-4351-5587-9(4))* Barnes & Noble, Inc.

Sumberac, Manuel, jt. illus. see Basic, Zdenko.

Sume, Lori Anne. Sorry, Sorry, Sorry: Learning to Choose the Right. 2004. (J). bds. 9.95 *(978-1-59156-298-6(8))* Covenant Communications, Inc.

Summerhayes, Roger, photos by. Whatever Happened to Baby Harry: The True Story of the First Child Born to an Officer's Family at Camp Apache, Arizona Territory. Ruffner, Melissa. 2003. 19p. (YA). pap. 12.95 *(978-0-9673171-1-3(8))* Primrose Pr.

Summers, Dana. Run, Dogs, Run! Higdon, Hal. 2003. 56p. (J). *(978-0-9636346-3-4(1))* Roadrunner Pr.

Summers, Mark. Pirates at the Plate. Frisch, Aaron. 2012. (ENG.). 32p. (J). (gr. 1-3). 17.99 *(978-1-56846-210-3(7)*, Creative Editions) Creative Co., The.

Summy, Margaret A. Imagine Me... Love My Body. l.t. ed. 2005. 60p. per. *(978-1-880292-96-9(3))* LangMarc Publishing.

Sumner, William. Saving the Baghdad Zoo: A True Story of Hope & Heroes. Sumner, William. Halls, Kelly Milner. 2010. (ENG.). 64p. (J). (gr. 3-18). 17.99 *(978-0-06-177202-3(X)*, Greenwillow Bks.) HarperCollins Pubs.

Sumpter, Rachell. InStyle Getting Gorgeous: The Step-by-Step Guide to Your Best Hair, Makeup & Skin. Tung, Jennifer. rev. ed. 2004. (ENG.). 192p. (gr. 8-17). 27.95 *(978-1-932273-55-7(7)*, Liberty St.) Time Inc. Bks.

—The Wizard of Oz: And Other Wonderful Books of Oz - The Emerald City of Oz & Glinda of Oz. Baum, L. Frank. deluxe ed. 2012. (Penguin Classics Deluxe Edition Ser.). 432p. (gr. 5). pap. 17.00 *(978-0-14-310663-0(5)*, Penguin Classics) Penguin Publishing Group.

Sun, Ann Ruozhu. Boxer & the Fish. Hughes, Mónica. 2014. (Traditional Tales Ser.). (ENG.). 16p. (J). (gr. k-1). pap. 6.95 *(978-1-62521-540-6(1)*, Capstone Classroom) Capstone.

Sun, Antuanette. Pat-A-Cake, Pat-a-Cake... We Made a Mistake! Dellas, Melanie & Woodworth, John. 2012. 24p. pap. 9.95 *(978-0-9830163-2-8(1))* Dellas, Melanie.

Sun, Jun. The Musical. Chen, Bill. 2013. (J). *(978-0-9845523-1-3(6))* Heryin Publishing Corp.

Sun Rise Illustration and Computer Animation Staff. Zagros & Nature Force: Coloring Book. Esmaili, Roza. Date not set. 74p. (J). (gr. k-8). pap. 2.49 *(978-0-9656185-1-9(X))* Esmaili, Inc.

Sun Star, Elan & Snyder, Diana. Megan... A Child of God I Am. Chauvin, Belinda N. 2008. 40p. (J). 14.75 *(978-0-9801675-2-8(3))* Robertson Publishing.

Sundaravej, Sittisan. Behind the Wheel. Montgomery, R. A. 2010. (ENG.). 144p. (J). (gr. 4-8). pap. 6.99 *(978-1-933390-35-2(2))* Chooseco LLC.

—House of Danger. Montgomery, R. A. 2006. (Choose Your Own Adventure Ser.: No. 6). (ENG.). 144p. (J). (gr. 4-8). per. 6.99 *(978-1-933390-06-2(9)*, CHCL06) Chooseco LLC.

—Journey under the Sea. Montgomery, R. A. 2006. (Choose Your Own Adventure Ser.). (ENG.). 144p. (J). (gr. 4-8). per. 7.99 *(978-1-933390-02-4(6)*, CHCL02) Chooseco LLC.

—Race Forever. Montgomery, R. A. 2006. (Choose Your Own Adventure Ser.: No. 7). (ENG.). 144p. (J). (gr. 4-8). per. 6.99 *(978-1-933390-07-9(7)*, CHCL07) Chooseco LLC.

—Return to Atlantis. Montgomery, R. A. 2006. (Choose Your Own Adventure Ser.: 18). (ENG.). 144p. (J). (gr. 4-8). per. 7.99 *(978-1-933390-18-5(2)*, CHCL18) Chooseco LLC.

—Terror on the Titanic. Wallace, Jim. 2007. (Choose Your Own Adventure Ser.: 24). (ENG.). 144p. (J). (gr. 4-8). pap. 7.99 *(978-1-933390-24-6(7))* Chooseco LLC.

Sundberg, Angela M., et al. The Pottamus Family & the Unhappy Pottamus. Sundberg, Angela M. et al. 2007. (J). pap. 16.00 *(978-0-8059-7478-2(4))* Dorrance Publishing Co., Inc.

Sundblom, Haddon H. The Night Before Christmas: A Family Treasury of Songs, Poems, & Stories. 2007. 32p. (J). (gr. -1-3). 7.98 *(978-1-4127-8961-5(3))* Publications International, Ltd.

Sunderland, John. The Rocking Horse Diary. Combes, Alan. 2018. (ENG.). 174p. (J). pap. *(978-1-912053-78-0(0))* Fantastic Bks. Publishing.

Sundram, Steve. Three Whales: Who Won the Heart of the World. Kita, Suzanne. 2010. (ENG.). 40p. (J). (gr. 3). *(978-1-59700-761-0(7))* Island Heritage Publishing.

Sundy, Jonathan. El Conejito de Pascua: El Cuento de un Dia Extraordinario. Benoist, Cathy & Gilmore, Cathy. 2014. (SPA.). 40p. (J). (gr. 4-7). 16.99 *(978-0-7648-2456-2(2)*, Libros Liguori) Liguori Pubns.

—Easter Bunny's AMAZING Day. Gilmore, Cathy & Benoist, Carol. 2011. (ENG.). 40p. (J). 15.99 *(978-0-9847656-1-4(1))* I.H.S. Pubs.

Sung, Amber. A Day at the Park: My 1st Seek & Find Book. Bullock, Laura. 2020. (ENG.). 24p. (J). pap. 9.99 ***(978-1-7040-8263-9(3))*** Independently Published.

Sung, Haeun. Green, Black or White. Ludwig, Mike. Worthington, Katharine, ed. 2020. (Green, Black or White Ser.: Vol. 1). (ENG.). 30p. (J). (gr. k-6). 22.99 ***(978-1-64633-647-0(X))*** Ludwig, Michael.
—Green, Black or White. Ludwig, Mike. 2020. (Green, Black or White Ser.: Vol. 1). (ENG.). 30p. (J). pap. 9.99 ***(978-1-7242-7147-1(4))*** CreateSpace Independent Publishing Platform.
Sung Ku, Min. The Body Book for Boys. Paley, Rebecca et al. 2010. (ENG.). 128p. (J). (gr. 5-10). pap. 9.99 *(978-0-545-23751-2(3)*, Scholastic Paperbacks) Scholastic, Inc.
Suni, Hanna. Giacomo e il Cilindro Magico. Tucci, Michele M. 2018. (ITA.). 20p. (J). (gr. k-3). 19.99 *(978-0-9778932-8-7(6))* Art&Media Communications LLC.
Sunluvr, Amy. The Ballet Slippers. Bates, Melony. 2016. (ENG.). (J). pap. 7.99 *(978-1-945595-01-1(9))* Blue Cove Publishing.
Sunni Brannan, jt. illus. see Phil Brannan.
Sunset Producciones & Producciones, Sunset. El Huevo Azul. Cordero, Silvia Jaeger & Cordero, Silvia Jaeger. rev. ed. 2005. (Castillo de la Lectura Verde Ser.). (SPA & ENG.). 136p. (J). (gr. -1-7). pap. 7.95 *(978-970-20-0127-0(7))* Castillo, Ediciones, S. A. de C. V. MEX. Dist: Macmillan.
Sunshine, Mary Lou. Happy Days: Book 1. Orth, Jack. 2013. 50p. (J). pap. 9.95 *(978-1-61863-545-7(X))* Bookstand Publishing.
—Happy Days: Book 2. Orth, Jack. 2013. 50p. (J). pap. 9.95 *(978-1-61863-546-4(8))* Bookstand Publishing.
—Happy Days: Book 3. Orth, Jack. 2013. 50p. (J). pap. 9.95 *(978-1-61863-547-1(6))* Bookstand Publishing.
Suorsa, Michael. Puppy Stew. Gregory, Caroline. 2009. (ENG.). 28p. (J). pap. 8.99 *(978-0-9772025-9-1(3))* Sortis Publishing.
Sur, Duendes Del. Catnapped Caper, 1 vol. Barbo, Maria S. 2013. (Scooby-Doo! Picture Clue Bks.). (ENG.). 24p. (J). (gr. k-2). lib. bdg. 27.07 *(978-1-61479-035-8(3)*, 13229) Spotlight.
—Clues at the Carnival, 1 vol. Ip, Ivy S. 2013. (Scooby-Doo! Picture Clue Bks.). (ENG.). 24p. (J). (gr. k-2). lib. bdg. 27.07 *(978-1-61479-036-5(1)*, 13230) Spotlight.
—Dinosaur Dig, 1 vol. Soderberg, Erin. 2013. (Scooby-Doo! Picture Clue Bks.). (ENG.). 24p. (J). (gr. k-2). lib. bdg. 27.07 *(978-1-61479-037-2(X)*, 13231) Spotlight.
—Pizza Place Ghost, 1 vol. Class 1-208. 2013. (Scooby-Doo! Picture Clue Bks.). (ENG.). 24p. (J). (gr. k-2). lib. bdg. 27.07 *(978-1-61479-038-9(8)*, 13232) Spotlight.
—Scooby-Doo & Museum Madness, 1 vol. McCann, Jesse Leon. 2011. (Scooby-Doo! Ser.: No. 2). (ENG.). 24p. (J). (gr. k-4). lib. bdg. 27.07 *(978-1-59961-867-8(2)*, 13245, Picture Bk.) Spotlight.
—Scooby-Doo! & the Carnival Creeper, 1 vol. Gelsey, James. 2013. (Scooby-Doo Mysteries Ser.). (ENG.). 64p. (J). (gr. 3-6). lib. bdg. 27.07 *(978-1-61479-042-6(6)*, 13222, Chapter Bks.) Spotlight.
Sur, Duendes del. Scooby-Doo & the Dinosaur Ghost, 1 vol. Soderberg, Erin. 2016. (Scooby-Doo Early Reading Adventures Ser.). (ENG.). 24p. (J). (gr. -1-2). lib. bdg. 27.07 *(978-1-61479-464-6(2)*, 21377) Spotlight.
Sur, Duendes Del. Scooby-Doo & the Fishy Phantom, 1 vol. McCann, Jesse Leon. 2011. (Scooby-Doo! Ser.: No. 2). (ENG.). 24p. (J). (gr. k-4). lib. bdg. 27.07 *(978-1-59961-866-1(4)*, 13244, Picture Bk.) Spotlight.
—Scooby-Doo! & the Frankenstein Monster, 1 vol. Gelsey, James. 2013. (Scooby-Doo Mysteries Ser.). (ENG.). 64p. (J). (gr. 3-6). lib. bdg. 27.07 *(978-1-61479-043-3(4)*, 13223, Chapter Bks.) Spotlight.
—Scooby-Doo! & the Groovy Ghost, 1 vol. Gelsey, James. 2013. (Scooby-Doo Mysteries Ser.). (ENG.). 64p. (J). (gr. 3-6). lib. bdg. 27.07 *(978-1-61479-044-0(2)*, 13224, Chapter Bks.) Spotlight.
—Scooby-Doo! & the Gruesome Goblin, 1 vol. Gelsey, James. 2013. (Scooby-Doo Mysteries Ser.). (ENG.). 64p. (J). (gr. 3-6). lib. bdg. 27.07 *(978-1-61479-045-7(0)*, 13225, Chapter Bks.) Spotlight.
—Scooby-Doo! & the Howling Wolfman, 1 vol. Gelsey, James. 2013. (Scooby-Doo Mysteries Ser.). (ENG.). 64p. (J). (gr. 3-6). lib. bdg. 27.07 *(978-1-61479-046-4(9)*, 13226, Chapter Bks.) Spotlight.
—Scooby-Doo & the Karate Caper, 1 vol. Gelsey, James. 2011. (Scooby-Doo Mysteries Ser.). (ENG.). 64p. (J). (gr. 3-6). 27.07 *(978-1-59961-891-3(5)*, 13215, Chapter Bks.) Spotlight.
Sur, Duendes del. Scooby-Doo & the Kitty Cat Caper, 1 vol. Barbo, Maria S. 2016. (Scooby-Doo Early Reading Adventures Ser.). (ENG.). 24p. (J). (gr. -1-2). lib. bdg. 27.07 *(978-1-61479-465-3(0)*, 21378) Spotlight.
—Scooby-Doo & the Missing Scooby-Snacks, 1 vol. Wasserman, Robin. 2016. (Scooby-Doo Early Reading Adventures Ser.). (ENG.). 24p. (J). (gr. -1-2). lib. bdg. 27.07 *(978-1-61479-467-7(7)*, 21380) Spotlight.
—Scooby-Doo & the Monster in the Woods, 1 vol. Nagler, Michelle H. 2016. (Scooby-Doo Early Reading Adventures Ser.). (ENG.). 24p. (J). (gr. -1-2). lib. bdg. 27.07 *(978-1-61479-468-4(5)*, 21381) Spotlight.
Sur, Duendes Del. Scooby-Doo & the Mummy's Curse, 1 vol. McCann, Jesse Leon. 2010. (Scooby-Doo! Ser.: No. 1). (ENG.). 24p. (J). (gr. k-4). lib. bdg. 27.07 *(978-1-59961-677-3(7)*, 13237, Picture Bk.) Spotlight.
Sur, Duendes del. Scooby-Doo & the Mystery at the Park, 1 vol. Soderberg, Erin. 2016. (Scooby-Doo Early Reading Adventures Ser.). (ENG.). 24p. (J). (gr. -1-2). lib. bdg. 27.07 *(978-1-61479-469-1(3)*, 21382) Spotlight.
—Scooby-Doo & the Rock 'n' Roll Zombie, 1 vol. McCann, Jesse Leon. 2010. (Scooby-Doo! Ser.: No. 1). (ENG.). 24p. (J). (gr. k-4). lib. bdg. 27.07 *(978-1-59961-678-0(5)*, 13238, Picture Bk.) Spotlight.
Sur, Duendes Del. Scooby-Doo & the Rotten Robot, 1 vol. Balaban, Mariah. 2011. (Scooby-Doo! Ser.: No. 2). (ENG.). 24p. (J). (gr. k-4). lib. bdg. 27.07 *(978-1-59961-868-5(0)*, 13246, Picture Bk.) Spotlight.
—Scooby-Doo & the Scary Snowman, 1 vol. Balaban, Mariah. 2011. (Scooby-Doo! Ser.: No. 2). (ENG.). 24p. (J). (gr. k-4). lib. bdg. 27.07 *(978-1-59961-869-2(9)*, 13247, Picture Bk.) Spotlight.
Sur, Duendes del. Scooby-Doo & the Snow Monster Scare, 1 vol. Wasserman, Robin. 2016. (Scooby-Doo Early Reading Adventures Ser.). (ENG.). 24p. (J). (gr. -1-2). lib. bdg. 27.07 *(978-1-61479-473-8(1)*, 21386) Spotlight.
Sur, Duendes Del. Scooby-Doo! & the Spooky Strikeout, 1 vol. Gelsey, James. 2013. (Scooby-Doo Mysteries Ser.). (ENG.). 64p. (J). (gr. 3-6). lib. bdg. 27.07 *(978-1-61479-047-1(7)*, 13227, Chapter Bks.) Spotlight.
—Scooby-Doo & the Sunken Ship, 1 vol. Gelsey, James. 2011. (Scooby-Doo Mysteries Ser.). (ENG.). 64p. (J). (gr. 3-6). 27.07 *(978-1-59961-893-7(1)*, 13217, Chapter Bks.) Spotlight.
—Scooby-Doo & the Vampire's Revenge, 1 vol. Gelsey, James. 2011. (Scooby-Doo Mysteries Ser.). (ENG.). 64p. (J). (gr. 3-6). 27.07 *(978-1-59961-894-4(X)*, 13218, Chapter Bks.) Spotlight.
—Scooby-Doo & the Werewolf, 1 vol. McCann, Jesse Leon. 2010. (Scooby-Doo! Ser.: No. 1). (ENG.). 24p. (J). (gr. k-4). lib. bdg. 27.07 *(978-1-59961-681-0(5)*, 13241, Picture Bk.) Spotlight.
—Scooby-Doo & the Zombie's Treasure, 1 vol. Gelsey, James. 2011. (Scooby-Doo Mysteries Ser.). (ENG.). 64p. (J). (gr. 3-6). 27.07 *(978-1-59961-896-8(6)*, 13220, Chapter Bks.) Spotlight.
Sur, Duendes del. Scooby-Doo Early Reading Adventures, 14 vols. ABDO Publishing Company Staff. 2016. (Scooby-Doo Early Reading Adventures Ser.). (ENG.). 24p. (J). (gr. -1-2). lib. bdg. 378.98 *(978-1-61479-463-9(4)*, 21376) Spotlight.
—Scooby-Doo in Lights Out at the Ball Game, 1 vol. Guidone, Ellen. 2016. (Scooby-Doo Early Reading Adventures Ser.). (ENG.). 24p. (J). (gr. -1-2). lib. bdg. 27.07 *(978-1-61479-475-2(8)*, 21388) Spotlight.
—Scooby-Doo in Lost at Sea, 1 vol. Nagler, Michelle H. 2016. (Scooby-Doo Early Reading Adventures Ser.). (ENG.). 24p. (J). (gr. -1-2). lib. bdg. 27.07 *(978-1-61479-476-9(6)*, 21389) Spotlight.
Sur, Duendes Del. Scooby-Doo Mysteries, 6 vols., Set. Abdo Publishing & Gelsey, James. 2013. (Scooby-Doo Mysteries Ser.: 6). (ENG.). 64p. (J). (gr. 3-6). lib. bdg. 162.42 *(978-1-61479-041-9(8)*, 13221, Chapter Bks.) Spotlight.
—Scooby-Doo! Picture Clue Books, 6 vols. 2013. (Scooby-Doo! Picture Clue Bks.: 6). (ENG.). 24p. (J). (gr. -1-2). lib. bdg. 162.42 *(978-1-61479-034-1(5)*, 13228) Spotlight.
—Search for Scooby Snacks, 1 vol. Wasserman, Robin. 2013. (Scooby-Doo! Picture Clue Bks.). (ENG.). 24p. (J). (gr. k-2). lib. bdg. 27.07 *(978-1-61479-039-6(6)*, 13233) Spotlight.
—Treasure Hunt, 1 vol. Barbo, Maria S. 2013. (Scooby-Doo! Picture Clue Bks.). (ENG.). 24p. (J). (gr. k-2). lib. bdg. 27.07 *(978-1-61479-040-2(X)*, 13234) Spotlight.
Suratos, Don. Dynomike: Proud to Be Me: (Children's Book on Anti-Bullying, Self-Esteem, Self Confidence) Mendolla, Robyn & Rabbit, Frankie B. 2019. (Dynomike Teaches Ser.: Vol. 9). (ENG.). 56p. (J). (gr. k-2). pap. 14.99 *(978-1-0918-0465-4(6))* Independently Published.
Surber, Shawn-Michelle. Hope, 1. Surber, Shawn-Michelle. collector's ed. 2007. 35p. (J). 19.99 *(978-0-9763534-0-9(7)*, Momin'Light Media) Momin' Light Media.
Surducan, Maria. Gabriel's Horn. Kimmel, Eric A. 2016. (ENG.). 32p. (J). (gr. -1-3). 9.99 *(978-1-4677-8936-3(4)*, 9781467789363, Kar-Ben Publishing) Lerner Publishing Group.
Surein, Manuel. My First 1000 Animals. Besson, Agnès. 2016. (ENG.). 64p. (J). (gr. -1 — 1). 19.95 *(978-1-77085-796-4(6)*, 03420b5a-c0ef-4401-a109-610b1b771e41) Firefly Bks., Ltd.
Surendranath, Nayantara. The Clever Tailor. Venkat, Srividhya. 2019. (ENG.). 40p. (J). 13.95 *(978-81-933889-0-7(9))* Karadi Tales Co. Pvt, Ltd. IND. Dist: Consortium Bk. Sales & Distribution.
Suriano, Andy & Davis, Dan W. Menace of the Time Thief, 1 vol. Wayne, Matt. 2012. (Batman: the Brave & the Bold Ser.). (ENG.). 32p. (J). (gr. 2-5). lib. bdg. 22.60 *(978-1-4342-4548-9(9)*, Stone Arch Bks.) Capstone.
—Panic of the Composite Creatures. Wayne, Matt. 2012. (Batman: the Brave & the Bold Ser.). (ENG.). 32p. (J). (gr. 2-5). lib. bdg. 22.60 *(978-1-4342-4545-8(4)*, Stone Arch Bks.) Capstone.
—President Batman, 1 vol. Wayne, Matt. 2012. (Batman: the Brave & the Bold Ser.). (ENG.). 32p. (J). (gr. 2-5). lib. bdg. 22.60 *(978-1-4342-4547-2(0)*, Stone Arch Bks.) Capstone.
Suriano, Andy, jt. illus. see Davis, Dan.
Surnaite, Margarita. Meditate with Me: A Step-By-Step Mindfulness Journey. Gates, Mariam. 2017. 40p. (J). (gr. -1-3). 17.99 *(978-0-399-18661-5(1)*, Dial Bks) Penguin Young Readers Group.
Surojegin, Pirkko-Liisa. The Kalevala: Tales of Magic & Adventure. Makinen, Kirsti, ed. Brooks, Kaarina, tr. 2009. (ENG.). 214p. (YA). (gr. 4-18). 24.95 *(978-1-897476-00-0(0))* Simply Read Bks. CAN. Dist: Ingram Publisher Services.
—Otto & the Secret Light of Christmas, 18 vols. Surojegin, Nora. Timbers, Jill, tr. 2016. Orig. Title: Untu Ja Sydäntalven Salaisuus. (ENG.). 108p. (J). 24.95 *(978-1-78250-323-1(4))* Floris Bks. GBR. Dist: Consortium Bk. Sales & Distribution.
Surovec, Yasmine. I See Kitty. Surovec, Yasmine. 2015. (ENG.). 34p. (J). (gr. -1-1). bds. 7.99 *(978-1-62672-093-0(2)*, 9781626720930) Roaring Brook Pr.
Surplice, Holly. Hush-A-Bye Bunny. Nosy Crow. 2017. (ENG.). 16p. (J). (-k). bds. 8.99 *(978-0-7636-9459-3(2)*, Nosy Crow) Candlewick Pr.
Surplice, Holly. About a Bear. Surplice, Holly. 2012. (ENG.). 32p. (J). *(978-1-58925-112-0(1))* Tiger Tales.
—I Love You, Little One. Surplice, Holly. 2019. (ENG.). 24p. (J). (-k). bds. 8.99 *(978-1-5362-0578-7(8)*, Nosy Crow) Candlewick Pr.
—Peek-A-Boo Bunny. Surplice, Holly. 2014. (ENG.). 32p. (J). (gr. -1-3). 9.99 *(978-0-06-224265-5(2))* HarperCollins Pubs.
—Snow Still. Surplice, Holly. 2019. (ENG.). 22p. (J). (— 1). bds. 8.99 *(978-1-5362-0834-4(5)*, Nosy Crow) Candlewick Pr.
Surrey, Ellen. Giving Thanks: More Than 100 Ways to Say Thank You. 2016. (ENG.). 32p. (J). (gr. 1-4). 19.99 *(978-1-84780-879-0(4)*, Frances Lincoln Children's Bks.) Quarto Publishing Group UK GBR. Dist: Hachette Bk. Group.
Surrey, Michael. Cool It Frida! Hamer, Ron. 2008. 40p. pap. 11.95 *(978-1-59858-654-1(8))* Dog Ear Publishing, LLC.
—Move It Milton! Hamer, Ron. 2009. 36p. pap. 11.95 *(978-1-59858-738-8(2))* Dog Ear Publishing, LLC.
—Suck It up Tate! Hamer, Ron. 2008. 36p. pap. 11.95 *(978-1-59858-512-4(6))* Dog Ear Publishing, LLC.
Susan, Krupp. Harvey Bear Gets Rescued. Gonzalez de Freire, Aurora Margarita. 2019. (ENG.). 62p. (J). 19.95 ***(978-1-950685-20-2(9))*** Inspire Bks.
Susan, Lisbin. Mommy, What's an MRI? Soloway, Cindy. Steve, Sumner, ed. 2006. (J). mass mkt. *(978-0-9765060-2-7(5))* TouchSmart Publishing, LLC.
Susan, Paradis. Edna. Susan, Paradis. 2013. 32p. pap. 11.95 *(978-1-60898-153-3(3))* namelos llc.
Susan, Turnbull. The Raccoon & the Bee Tree. Eastman, Charles A. & Eastman, Elaine Goodale. 2013. (J). 40p. 9.95 *(978-0-9798940-8-4(5))*; 32p. *(978-0-9860355-4-8(8))* South Dakota Historical Society Pr.
Susini, Brigitte. Les Fables de la Fontaine. La Fontaine, Jean de. 2011. (Petits Gautier Ser.: Vol. 3934809). (FRE.). (J). pap. *(978-2-01-393480-0(7))* Gautier-Languereau.
Suska, Monika. The Great Grizzly Race. Lumsden, Zoa. 2019. (Early Bird Readers — Purple (Early Bird Stories (tm)) Ser.). (ENG.). 32p. (J). (gr. k-3). 27.99 *(978-1-5415-4231-0(2)*, 9781541542310); pap. 7.99 *(978-1-5415-7419-9(2)*, 9781541574199) Lerner Publishing Group. (Lerner Pubns.).
Sutanto, Tommy. Friends in the Garden. Gopinath, Karin Ursula. 2008. 34p. (J). per. 19.95 *(978-0-9800637-0-7(1))* Lotus Art Works Inc.
Sutcliffe, Tim. The Elves Help Puss in Boots. Harrison, Paul. 2016. (Fairy Tale Mix-Ups Ser.). (ENG.). 24p. (J). (gr. k-2). lib. bdg. 23.99 *(978-1-4109-8303-9(X)*, Raintree) Capstone.
Suteski, Monika. Secret Lives of the Civil War: What Your Teachers Never Told You about the War Between the States. O'Brien, Cormac. 2007. (Secret Lives Ser.: 3). (ENG.). 320p. (gr. 9-18). pap. 16.95 *(978-1-59474-138-8(7))* Quirk Bks.
Sutherland, Celeste. Kerri Berry Lynn. Ballantyne, Sonya. Sage, ed. 2018. (ENG.). 32p. (J). *(978-1-5255-3875-9(6))*; pap. *(978-1-5255-3876-6(4))* FriesenPress.
Sutherland, Dianne. Rashiecoat: A Story in Scots for Young Readers. 16p. pap. 6.95 *(978-1-899827-19-0(6))* Scottish Children's Pr. GBR. Dist: Gatewood Pr.
Sutherland, Karen. Katie's a Tae Z: An Alphabet for Wee Folk. Robertson, James. 2014. 20p. (J). (-k). bds. 12.99 *(978-1-84502-754-4(X))* Black and White Publishing Ltd. GBR. Dist: Independent Pubs. Group.
Sutherland, Leah. For Girls Only! Devotions. Larsen, Carolyn. 2009. (ENG.). 256p. (J). pap. 9.99 *(978-1-4143-2209-4(7)*, 4601199, Tyndale Kids) Tyndale Hse. Pubs.
Sutherland, Marc. The Waiting Place. Sutherland, Marc. 2004. 24p. (J). (gr. k-4). reprint ed. 15.00 *(978-0-7567-8382-2(8))* DIANE Publishing Co.
Sutherland, Nicholas. Snuffley. Shumate, Robert O. 2008. 28p. pap. 24.95 *(978-1-60610-707-2(0))* America Star Bks.
Sutphin, Joe. Dr. Critchlore's School for Minions: Book One. Grau, Sheila. 2016. (ENG.). 304p. (J). (gr. 3-7). pap. 7.95 *(978-1-4197-2029-1(5)*, Amulet Bks.) Abrams, Inc.
—Monster's Trucks. Van Slyke, Rebecca. 2020. (ENG.). 40p. (J). 17.99 *(978-1-68119-301-4(9)*, 900165544, Bloomsbury Children's Bks.) Bloomsbury Publishing USA.
—Polar Distress: Dr. Critchlore's School for Minions #3. Grau, Sheila. 2017. (ENG.). 288p. (J). (gr. 3-7). 14.95 *(978-1-4197-2294-3(8)*, Amulet Bks.) Abrams, Inc.
—The Society of Extraordinary Raccoon Society. Goodgame, Randall. 2019. (Slugs & Bugs Ser.). (ENG.). 32p. (J). (gr. -1-3). 9.99 *(978-1-5359-4094-8(8)*, 005811433, B&H Kids) B&H Publishing Group.
—The Society of Extraordinary Raccoon Society on Boasting. Goodgame, Randall. 2019. (Slugs & Bugs Ser.). (ENG.). 32p. (J). (gr. -1-3). 9.99 *(978-1-5359-4095-5(6)*, 005811434, B&H Kids) B&H Publishing Group.
—Twice Cursed (Dr. Critchlore's School for Minions #4) Grau, Sheila. 2018. (ENG.). 304p. (J). (gr. 3-7). 14.99 *(978-1-4197-2863-1(6)*, Amulet Bks.) Abrams, Inc.
—Word of Mouse. Patterson, James & Grabenstein, Chris. 2018. (ENG.). 320p. (J). (gr. 3-7). pap. 7.99 *(978-0-316-41401-2(8)*, Jimmy Patterson) Little Brown & Co.
—Word of Mouse. Patterson, James. 2016. (ENG.). 304p. (J). (gr. 3-7). 13.99 *(978-0-316-34956-7(9)*, Jimmy Patterson) Little Brown & Co.
Suttie, Alan, jt. illus. see Jackson, Ian.
Sutton, Emily. The Christmas Eve Tree. Huddy, Delia. (ENG.). 40p. (J). (gr. k-3). 2018. 9.99 *(978-1-5362-0002-7(6))*; 2016. 16.99 *(978-0-7636-7917-0(8))* Candlewick Pr.
—Ernestine's Milky Way. Madden-Lunsford, Kerry. 2019. (ENG.). 40p. (J). (gr. -1-2). lib. bdg. 20.99 *(978-1-5247-1485-7(2)*, Schwartz & Wade Bks.) Random Hse. Children's Bks.
—Ernestine's Milky Way. Madden-Lunsford, Kerry. 2019. (ENG.). 40p. (J). (gr. -1-2). 17.99 *(978-1-5247-1484-0(4)*, Schwartz & Wade Bks.) Random Hse. Children's Bks.
—A First Book of the Sea. Davies, Nicola. 2018. (ENG.). 104p. (J). (gr. -1-2). 22.00 *(978-0-7636-9882-9(2))* Candlewick Pr.
Sutton, Emily. Grow: Secrets of Our DNA. Davies, Nicola. 2020. (ENG.). 40p. (J). (gr. k-4). 17.99 ***(978-1-5362-1272-3(5))*** Candlewick Pr.
Sutton, Emily. Many: the Diversity of Life on Earth. Davies, Nicola. 2017. (ENG.). 40p. (J). (gr. k-3). 15.99 *(978-0-7636-9483-8(5))* Candlewick Pr.
—One Christmas Wish. Rundell, Katherine. 2018. (ENG.). 64p. (J). (gr. k-4). 18.99 *(978-1-4814-9161-7(X)*, Simon & Schuster Bks. For Young Readers) Simon & Schuster Bks. For Young Readers.
—Tiny Creatures: The World of Microbes. Davies, Nicola. (ENG.). 40p. (J). (gr. k-3). 2016. pap. 7.99 *(978-0-7636-8904-9(1))*; 2014. 15.99 *(978-0-7636-7315-4(3))* Candlewick Pr.
Sutton, George Miksch. The Burgess Seashore Book for Children. Burgess, Thornton W. 2005. (Dover Children's Classics Ser.). (ENG.). 288p. (J). (gr. k-3). per. 12.95 *(978-0-486-44253-2(5)*, 442535) Dover Pubns., Inc.
Sutton, Hannah. Dodo. Jones, Jack. 2nd ed. 2020. (ENG.). 72p. (J). (gr. 3-6). pap. ***(978-1-989092-34-7(9))*** Celticfrog Publishing.
Sutton, Mikayla. The Return of Sancho, the Not-So-Silly Billy Goat. Moreno, Elizabeth Dettling. 2019. (ENG.). 34p. (J). (gr. k-6). pap. 12.95 *(978-1-970079-49-4(5))* Dettling Moreno, Elizabeth.
—Sancho, the Silly Billy Goat. Moreno, Elizabeth Dettling. 2018. (ENG.). 20p. (J). (gr. 2-5). pap. 12.45 *(978-0-692-18190-4(3))* Dettling Moreno, Elizabeth.
Sutton, Tom, et al. Hellstrom: Evil Origins. 2020. (ENG.). 192p. (YA). (gr. 8-17). pap. 24.99 ***(978-1-302-92516-1(4))*** Marvel Worldwide, Inc.
Sutula, Hollie. Uncle Bills Farm: True Stories of His Crazy Farm Animals. Susedik, Tina & Heers, Alli. 2014. 29p. (J). pap. 10.00 *(978-0-9667527-6-2(7))* Maple Lane Writing & Desktop Publishing.
Suvorova, Anastasia. Shadow. Christopher, Lucy. 2019. 40p. (J). (gr. k-2). 17.99 *(978-1-911373-83-4(8))* Lantana Publishing GBR. Dist: Lerner Publishing Group.
Suvorova, Viktoriia. Your Planet Is Inside. Makise, Ul. 2019. (ENG.). 34p. (J). pap. 9.13 ***(978-1-6864-1684-2(9))*** Independently Published.
Suwanda, Teguh & Getty. The Half-Full Glass of Water. Spud Getty. 2018. (ENG.). 34p. (J). pap. 6.99 *(978-1-7200-1944-2(4))* Independently Published.
Suwanda, Teguh & Getty, Spud. The Half-Full Glass of Water. Getty, Spud. 2018. (ENG.). 34p. (J). pap. 10.99 *(978-1-7268-8502-7(X))* Independently Published.
Suwannakit, Tul. How the Tooth Mouse Met the Tooth Fairy. Vries, Lizzette de & Vries, Cecile de. 2010. (J). 19.95 *(978-0-86715-507-5(8))* Quintessence Publishing Co., Inc.
Suwannakit, Tull. Sad, the Dog. Fussell, Sandy. 2015. (ENG.). 32p. (J). (gr. -1-2). 15.99 *(978-0-7636-7826-5(0))* Candlewick Pr.
Suzan, Gerardo. Arbol Del Tropico. Pellicer, Carlos. 2015. (Serie Roja Ser.). (SPA.). 120p. (J). pap. 9.95 *(978-1-64101-225-6(0))* Santillana USA Publishing Co., Inc.
—Jardin del Mar. Bracho, Coral. 2005. (SPA.). (J). (gr. k-2). pap. 10.95 *(978-968-494-055-0(6)*, CI6078) Centro de Informacion y Desarrollo de la Comunicacion y la Literatura MEX. Dist: Iaconi, Mariuccia Bk. Imports, Lectorum Pubns., Inc.
—My New Town. Hall, Kirsten. 2005. (My First Reader Ser.). (ENG.). 32p. (J). (gr. k-1). lib. bdg. 18.50 *(978-0-516-24877-6(4)*, Children's Pr.) Scholastic Library Publishing.
Suzanne, Rachel. Bears Don't Eat Egg Sandwiches. Fulton, Julie. 2019. (ENG.). 32p. (J). (gr. -1-3). 17.99 *(978-1-84886-358-3(6))* Maverick Arts Publishing GBR. Dist: Lerner Publishing Group.
Suzn, Gerardo. Al Vientoantolog-As de Haiks. 2014. (ENG & SPA.). (J). pap. *(978-607-01-2203-3(8))* Ediciones Alfaguara.
Suzuki, Tomoko. Pancakes to Parathas: Breakfast Around the World. McGinty, Alice B. 2019. (ENG.). 40p. (J). (gr. -1-3). 17.99 *(978-1-4998-0712-7(0))* Little Bee Books Inc.
Süßbauer, Anna. Rock-A-Bye Tree Sloth. Fronis, Aly. 2019. (ENG.). 16p. (J). (gr. -1-k). bds. 5.99 *(978-1-4998-0968-8(9))* Little Bee Books Inc.
Svendsen, Julius, jt. illus. see Walt Disney Studio.
Svensson, Richard. The Sweeet Old Lady Coloring & Activity Book. Killam, Catherine D. 2013. 62p. pap. 6.99 *(978-0-9910700-4-6(6))* Enchanted Forest Publishing.
—The Sweeet Old Lady down the Street. Killam, Catherine D. 2013. 42p. pap. 9.99 *(978-0-9910700-2-2(X))* Enchanted Forest Publishing.
Svetlin. Don Quijote. Cervantes, Miguel de. 2005. 159p. (J). (gr. 6-8). per. 14.99 *(978-84-316-7637-7(X))* Vicens-Vives, Editorial, S.A. ESP. Dist: Lectorum Pubns., Inc.
Svieta. Ivy Lost & Found. Sparrow, September. 2016. (Ivy Stories Ser.: Vol. 1). (ENG.). (J). 14.95 *(978-0-9978198-0-9(4))*; pap. 8.95 *(978-0-9978198-1-6(2))* Colby Studio.
Svobodova, Zuzana. Zetta the Poinsettia. Hammond, Alma. 2018. (ENG.). 34p. (J). (gr. -1-2). 17.95 *(978-0-9985362-7-9(X))*; pap. 11.95 *(978-0-9985362-6-2(1))* Sweetbeet Bks.
Swaab, Neil. Abigail Adams, Pirate of the Caribbean. Sheinkin, Steve. (Time Twisters Ser.). (ENG.). (J). 2019. 176p. pap. 6.99 *(978-1-250-20788-3(6)*, 900201776); 2018. 160p. 13.99 *(978-1-250-14893-3(6)*, 900182117) Roaring Brook Pr.
—Abraham Lincoln, Pro Wrestler. Sheinkin, Steve. (Time Twisters Ser.). (ENG.). (J). 2019. 176p. pap. 6.99 *(978-1-250-20787-6(8)*, 900201775); 2018. 160p. 13.99 *(978-1-250-14891-9(X)*, 900182114) Roaring Brook Pr.
—Amelia Earhart & the Flying Chariot. Sheinkin, Steve. 2019. (Time Twisters Ser.). (ENG.). 176p. (J). 13.99 *(978-1-250-14899-5(5)*, 900182127); pap. 6.99 *(978-1-250-15257-2(7)*, 900182128) Roaring Brook Pr.
—The Immortal Fire. Ursu, Anne. 2010. (Cronus Chronicles Ser.: 3). (ENG.). 528p. (J). (gr. 3-7). pap. 7.99 *(978-1-4169-0592-9(8)*, Atheneum Bks. for Young Readers) Simon & Schuster Children's Publishing.

S

—Middle School: Big Fat Liar. Patterson, James & Papademetriou, Lisa. 2014. (Middle School Ser.: 3). (ENG.). 304p. (J). (gr. 3-7). 13.99 (978-0-316-32203-4(2), Jimmy Patterson) Little Brown & Co.
—Middle School: Born to Rock. Patterson, James & Tebbetts, Chris. 2019. (Middle School Ser.: 11). (ENG.). 320p. (J). (gr. 3-7). 13.99 (978-0-316-34952-9(6), Jimmy Patterson) Little Brown & Co.
—Middle School: My Brother Is a Big, Fat Liar. Patterson, James & Papademetriou, Lisa. 2013. (Middle School Ser.: Bk. 3). (ENG.). 304p. (J). (gr. 3-7). 28.00 (978-0-316-20754-6(3), Jimmy Patterson) Little Brown & Co.
—Neil Armstrong & Nat Love, Space Cowboys. Sheinkin, Steve. 2019. (Time Twisters Ser.). (ENG.). 176p. (J). 13.99 (978-1-250-14897-1(9), 900182122); pap. 6.99 (978-1-250-15258-9(5), 900182123) Roaring Brook Pr.
Swaab, Neil, jt. illus. see Papademetriou, Lisa.
Swaim. The King & the Queen & the Jelly Bean. Crichton, Julie. l.t. ed. 2005. (SPA.). 24p. (J). bds. 7.95 (978-0-9761990-0-7(9)) Bean Bk. Publishing.
Swaim, Michael. The Adventures of Rodger Dodger Dog. Britland, Jan. 2009. 40p. pap. 15.95 (978-1-936051-23-6(0)) Peppertree Pr., The.
—The Adventures of Rodger Dodger Dog: A Christmas Story. Britland, Jan. 2009. 52p. pap. 18.95 (978-1-936051-48-9(6)) Peppertree Pr., The.
—Max & Voltaire Treasure in the Snow. Bail, Mina Mauerstein. 2017. (Max & Voltaire Series(tm) Book Four Ser.: Vol. 4). (ENG.). (J). (gr. k-6). pap. 14.95 (978-1-59095-547-5(1), ExamWise) Total Recall Learning, Inc.
Swaim, Michael. Max y Voltaire: La Excursión y el Secuestro. Bail, Mina Mauerstein. 2020. (Segundo Libro de la Serie Max y Voltaire Ser.: Vol. 2). (SPA.). 98p. (YA). pap. 15.00 **(978-1-59095-157-6(3)**, ExamWise) Total Recall Learning, Inc.
Swaim, Mike. I Wonder What a Fish Would Wish For? Clish, Marian L. 2009. 29p. pap. 24.95 (978-1-60836-289-9(2)) America Star Bks.
—Noodles - a Lunchtime Adventure. MacDonald, Alysha. 2012. 28p. pap. (978-0-9735526-8-3(9)) Cold Rock Publishing.
Swaim, Ramon. El rey y la reina y el frijolito de Goma. Crichton, Julie. l.t. ed. 2005. 24p. (J). bds. 7.95 (978-0-9761990-1-4(7)) Bean Bk. Publishing.
Swain, Alison Campbell. Bobby the Bush Pilot. Baker, Kane. 2003. (J). pap. (978-1-932046-02-1(X)) Pastime Pr.
Swain, Wilson. A Nutty Nutcracker Christmas. Covert, Ralph & Mills, G. Riley. 2009. (ENG.). 40p. (J). (gr. -1-2). 18.99 (978-0-8118-6111-3(2)) Chronicle Bks. LLC.
—The Misfits, Level 3. MacDonald, Kimber. 2006. (ENG.). 24p. (J). (gr. 1-17). per. 3.99 (978-1-58476-421-2(X), IKIDS) Innovative Kids.
Swampy, Lloyd. Nanabosho & the Cranberries, 1 vol. McLellan, Joe et al. 2015. (ENG.). 32p. (J). mass mkt. 10.95 (978-0-921827-63-4(6), d8f24a0c-8d5b-481c-b388-a143aad0c681) Pemmican Pubns., Inc. CAN. Dist: Firefly Bks., Ltd.
—Nanabosho Grants a Wish, 1 vol. McLellan, Joseph et al. 2015. (ENG.). 32p. (J). mass mkt. 10.95 (978-0-921827-66-5(0), 8d9d9f89-76ad-4839-8bab-25feb37c4f85) Pemmican Pubns., Inc. CAN. Dist: Firefly Bks., Ltd.
Swampy, Lloyd, jt. illus. see Burling, Jeff.
Swan, Angela. Chocolate Wishes #1. Bentley, Sue. 2013. (Magic Bunny Ser.: 1). (ENG.). 128p. (J). (gr. 1-3). pap. 5.99 (978-0-448-46727-6(5), Grosset & Dunlap) Penguin Young Readers Group.
—A Christmas Surprise. Bentley, Sue. 2008. (Magic Kitten Ser.). (ENG.). 128p. (J). (gr. 1-3). pap. 5.99 (978-0-448-45001-8(1), Grosset & Dunlap) Penguin Young Readers Group.
—Circus Surprise #7. Bentley, Sue. 2014. (Magic Ponies Ser.: 7). (ENG.). 128p. (J). (gr. 1-3). 5.99 (978-0-448-46734-4(8), Grosset & Dunlap) Penguin Young Readers Group.
—A Circus Wish #6, 6 vols. Bentley, Sue. 2009. (Magic Kitten Ser.: 6). (ENG.). 128p. (J). (gr. 1-3). pap. 5.99 (978-0-448-45062-9(3), Grosset & Dunlap) Penguin Young Readers Group.
—Classroom Capers #4. Bentley, Sue. 2014. (Magic Bunny Ser.: 4). (ENG.). 128p. (J). (gr. 1-3). 5.99 (978-0-448-46792-4(5), Grosset & Dunlap) Penguin Young Readers Group.
—Classroom Chaos #2, 2 vols. Bentley, Sue. 2008. (Magic Kitten Ser.: 2). (ENG.). 128p. (J). (gr. 1-3). pap. 5.99 (978-0-448-44999-9(4), Grosset & Dunlap) Penguin Young Readers Group.
—Classroom Princess #9. Bentley, Sue. 2013. (Magic Puppy Ser.: 9). (ENG.). 128p. (J). (gr. 1-3). 5.99 (978-0-448-46732-0(1), Grosset & Dunlap) Penguin Young Readers Group.
—Cloud Capers #3, 3 vols., 3. Bentley, Sue. 2009. (Magic Puppy Ser.: 3). (ENG.). 128p. (J). (gr. 1-3). 5.99 (978-0-448-45046-9(1), Grosset & Dunlap) Penguin Young Readers Group.
—Dancing Days #5. Bentley, Sue. 2014. (Magic Bunny Ser.: 5). (ENG.). 128p. (J). (gr. 1-3). 5.99 (978-0-448-46793-1(3), Grosset & Dunlap) Penguin Young Readers Group.
—Double Trouble #4, 4 vols. Bentley, Sue. 2009. (Magic Kitten Ser.: 4). (ENG.). 128p. (J). (gr. 1-3). pap. 5.99 (978-0-448-45060-5(7), Grosset & Dunlap) Penguin Young Readers Group.
—Firelight Friends #10. Bentley, Sue. 2014. (Magic Kitten Ser.: 10). (ENG.). 128p. (J). (gr. 1-3). 5.99 (978-0-448-46788-7(7), Grosset & Dunlap) Penguin Young Readers Group.
—A Forest Charm #6, 6 vols. Bentley, Sue. 2010. (Magic Puppy Ser.: 6). (ENG.). 128p. (J). (gr. 1-3). pap. 5.99 (978-0-448-45065-0(8), Grosset & Dunlap) Penguin Young Readers Group.
—Friendship Forever #10. Bentley, Sue. 2013. (Magic Puppy Ser.: 10). (ENG.). 128p. (J). (gr. 1-3). 5.99 (978-0-448-46733-7(X), Grosset & Dunlap) Penguin Young Readers Group.
—A Glittering Gallop #8, No. 8. Bentley, Sue. 2013. (Magic Kitten Ser.: 8). (ENG.). 128p. (J). (gr. 1-3). 5.99 (978-0-448-46730-6(5), Grosset & Dunlap) Penguin Young Readers Group.
—Magic Christmas. Bentley, Sue. 2019. (ENG.). 384p. (J). (gr. 1-3). 9.99 (978-0-593-09644-4(4), Grosset & Dunlap) Penguin Young Readers Group.
Swan, Angela. Magic Kitten: Books 1-2. Bentley, Sue. 2020. (Magic Kitten Ser.). (ENG.). 256p. (J). (gr. 1-3). 6.99 **(978-0-593-22500-4(7)**, Grosset & Dunlap) Penguin Young Readers Group.
Swan, Angela. Magic Puppy: Books 1-2. Bentley, Sue. 2019. (Magic Puppy Ser.). (ENG.). 256p. (J). (gr. 1-3). 6.99 (978-0-593-22214-0(8), Grosset & Dunlap) Penguin Young Readers Group.
—Magic Puppy: Books 1-3. Bentley, Sue. 2014. (Magic Puppy Ser.). (ENG.). 368p. (J). (gr. 1-3). 9.99 (978-0-448-48460-0(9), Grosset & Dunlap) Penguin Young Readers Group.
—Moonlight Mischief #5, 5 vols. Bentley, Sue. 2009. (Magic Kitten Ser.: 5). (ENG.). 128p. (J). (gr. 1-3). pap. 5.99 (978-0-448-45061-2(5), Grosset & Dunlap) Penguin Young Readers Group.
—Muddy Paws #2, No. 2. Bentley, Sue. 2009. (Magic Puppy Ser.: 2). (ENG.). 128p. (J). (gr. 1-3). pap. 5.99 (978-0-448-45045-2(3), Grosset & Dunlap) Penguin Young Readers Group.
—A New Beginning #1, No. 1. Bentley, Sue. 2009. (Magic Puppy Ser.: 1). (ENG.). 128p. (J). (gr. 1-3). pap. 5.99 (978-0-448-45044-5(5), Grosset & Dunlap) Penguin Young Readers Group.
—A New Friend #1, 1. Bentley, Sue. 2013. (Magic Ponies Ser.: 1). (ENG.). 128p. (J). (gr. 1-3). 5.99 (978-0-448-46205-9(2), Grosset & Dunlap) Penguin Young Readers Group.
—Party Dreams #5, 5 vols., 5. Bentley, Sue. 2010. (Magic Puppy Ser.: 5). (ENG.). 128p. (J). (gr. 1-3). 5.99 (978-0-448-45064-3(X), Grosset & Dunlap) Penguin Young Readers Group.
—The Perfect Secret #14. Bentley, Sue. 2014. (Magic Puppy Ser.: 14). (ENG.). 128p. (J). (gr. 1-3). 5.99 (978-0-448-46799-3(2), Grosset & Dunlap) Penguin Young Readers Group.
—Picture Perfect #13. Bentley, Sue. 2014. (Magic Kitten Ser.: 13). (ENG.). 128p. (J). (gr. 1-3). 5.99 (978-0-448-46796-2(8), Grosset & Dunlap) Penguin Young Readers Group.
—Pony Camp #8. Bentley, Sue. 2014. (Magic Ponies Ser.: 8). (ENG.). 128p. (J). (gr. 1-3). 5.99 (978-0-448-46787-0(9), Grosset & Dunlap) Penguin Young Readers Group.
—A Puzzle of Paws #12. Bentley, Sue. 2014. (Magic Kitten Ser.: 12). (ENG.). 128p. (J). (gr. 1-3). 5.99 (978-0-448-46795-5(X), Grosset & Dunlap) Penguin Young Readers Group.
—Riding Rescue #6. Bentley, Sue. 2013. (Magic Ponies Ser.: 6). (ENG.). 128p. (J). (gr. 1-3). 5.99 (978-0-448-46735-1(6), Grosset & Dunlap) Penguin Young Readers Group.
—School of Mischief #8, 8 vols., 8. Bentley, Sue. 2010. (Magic Puppy Ser.: 8). (ENG.). 128p. (J). (gr. 1-3). 5.99 (978-0-448-45067-4(4), Grosset & Dunlap) Penguin Young Readers Group.
—Seaside Mystery #9. Bentley, Sue. 2013. (Magic Kitten Ser.: 9). (ENG.). 128p. (J). (gr. 1-3). 5.99 (978-0-448-46731-3(3), Grosset & Dunlap) Penguin Young Readers Group.
—A Shimmering Splash #11. Bentley, Sue. 2014. (Magic Kitten Ser.: 11). (ENG.). 128p. (J). (gr. 1-3). 5.99 (978-0-448-46789-4(5), Grosset & Dunlap) Penguin Young Readers Group.
—Show-Jumping Dreams #4. Bentley, Sue. 2013. (Magic Ponies Ser.: 4). (ENG.). 128p. (J). (gr. 1-3). pap. 5.99 (978-0-448-46208-0(7), Grosset & Dunlap) Penguin Young Readers Group.
—Snowy Wishes. Bentley, Sue. 2013. (Magic Puppy Ser.). (ENG.). 128p. (J). (gr. 1-3). 5.99 (978-0-448-46737-5(2), Grosset & Dunlap) Penguin Young Readers Group.
—Sparkling Skates #13. Bentley, Sue. 2014. (Magic Puppy Ser.: 13). (ENG.). 128p. (J). (gr. 1-3). 5.99 (978-0-448-46798-6(4), Grosset & Dunlap) Penguin Young Readers Group.
—Sparkling Steps #7, 7 vols., 7. Bentley, Sue. 2009. (Magic Kitten Ser.: 7). (ENG.). 128p. (J). (gr. 1-3). 5.99 (978-0-448-45063-6(1), Grosset & Dunlap) Penguin Young Readers Group.
—A Special Wish #2, No. 2. Bentley, Sue. 2013. (Magic Ponies Ser.: 2). (ENG.). 128p. (J). (gr. 1-3). pap. 5.99 (978-0-448-46206-6(0), Grosset & Dunlap) Penguin Young Readers Group.
—Spellbound at School #11. Bentley, Sue. 2014. (Magic Puppy Ser.: 11). (ENG.). 128p. (J). (gr. 1-3). 5.99 (978-0-448-46790-0(9), Grosset & Dunlap) Penguin Young Readers Group.
—A Splash of Forever #14. Bentley, Sue. 2014. (Magic Kitten Ser.: 14). (ENG.). 128p. (J). (gr. 1-3). 5.99 (978-0-448-46797-9(6), Grosset & Dunlap) Penguin Young Readers Group.
—A Splash of Magic #3. Bentley, Sue. 2013. (Magic Bunny Ser.: 3). (ENG.). 128p. (J). (gr. 1-3). pap. 5.99 (978-0-448-46729-0(1), Grosset & Dunlap) Penguin Young Readers Group.
—Star Dreams #3, 3 vols. Bentley, Sue. 2008. (Magic Kitten Ser.: 3). (ENG.). 128p. (J). (gr. 1-3). pap. 5.99 (978-0-448-45000-1(3), Grosset & Dunlap) Penguin Young Readers Group.
—Star of the Show #4, 4 vols. Bentley, Sue. 2009. (Magic Puppy Ser.: 4). (ENG.). 128p. (J). (gr. 1-3). pap. 5.99 (978-0-448-45047-6(X), Grosset & Dunlap) Penguin Young Readers Group.
—A Summer Spell #1. Bentley, Sue. 2008. (Magic Kitten Ser.: 1). (ENG.). 128p. (J). (gr. 1-3). pap. 5.99 (978-0-448-44998-2(6), Grosset & Dunlap) Penguin Young Readers Group.
—Sunshine Shimmers #12. Bentley, Sue. 2014. (Magic Puppy Ser.: 12). (ENG.). 128p. (J). (gr. 1-3). 5.99 (978-0-448-46791-7(7), Grosset & Dunlap) Penguin Young Readers Group.
—A Twinkle of Hooves #3. Bentley, Sue. 2013. (Magic Ponies Ser.: 3). (ENG.). 128p. (J). (gr. 1-3). pap. 5.99 (978-0-448-46207-3(9), Grosset & Dunlap) Penguin Young Readers Group.
—Twirling Tails #7, 7 vols. Bentley, Sue. 2010. (Magic Puppy Ser.: 7). (ENG.). 128p. (J). (gr. 1-3). pap. 5.99 (978-0-448-45066-7(6), Grosset & Dunlap) Penguin Young Readers Group.
—Vacation Dreams #2. Bentley, Sue. 2013. (Magic Bunny Ser.: 2). (ENG.). 128p. (J). (gr. 1-3). pap. 5.99 (978-0-448-46728-3(3), Grosset & Dunlap) Penguin Young Readers Group.
—Winter Wonderland #5. Bentley, Sue. 2013. (Magic Ponies Ser.: 5). (ENG.). 128p. (J). (gr. 1-3). 5.99 (978-0-448-46786-3(0), Grosset & Dunlap) Penguin Young Readers Group.
Swan, Felicity. The Dragon Princess. Hirschi, Hans M. 2018. (ENG.). 40p. (J). pap. (978-1-78645-274-0(X)) Beaten Track Publishing.
Swan, Finn. The Vampire Who Lost Her Fangs. Hirschi, Hans M. 2020. (ENG.). 26p. (J). pap. **(978-1-78645-435-5(1))** Beaten Track Publishing.
Swan, Gloria. Mama Grizzly Bear. Finke, Margot. 2012. 16p. (-18). pap. 9.95 (978-1-61633-304-1(9)) Guardian Angel Publishing, Inc.
Swan, Owen. My Friend Tertius. Fenton, Corinne. 2017. (ENG.). 32p. (J). (gr. k-3). 19.99 (978-1-76011-382-7(4)) Allen & Unwin AUS. Dist: Independent Pubs. Group.
—Newspaper Hats. Cummings, Phil. 2016. (ENG.). 32p. (J). (gr. -1-2). lib. bdg. 16.95 (978-1-58089-783-9(5)) Charlesbridge Publishing, Inc.
Swan, Phoebe. King Leonard's Teddy. Swan, Phoebe. 2019. (Child's Play Library). (ENG.). 36p. (J). (978-1-78628-184-5(8)); pap. (978-1-78628-183-8(X)) Child's Play International Ltd.
Swan, S. How Reindeer Learn How to Fly. Swan, S. 2019. (ENG.). 32p. (J). 16.99 **(978-1-7342991-1-3(8))**; pap. 9.99 **(978-1-7342991-0-6(X))** S. Swan.
Swan, Susan. Guess Who's in the Desert. Profiri, Charline. 2013. (J). (978-1-933855-79-0(7)) Rio Nuevo Pubs.
—It's Fall! Glaser, Linda. 2003. (Celebrate the Seasons Ser.). (ENG.). 32p. (J). (gr. k-3). pap. 7.95 (978-0-7613-1342-7(7), First Avenue Editions) Lerner Publishing Group.
—It's Spring! Glaser, Linda. 2003. (Celebrate the Seasons Ser.). (ENG.). 32p. (J). (gr. k-3). pap. 7.95 (978-0-7613-1345-8(1), First Avenue Editions) Lerner Publishing Group.
—A Monarch Butterfly's Journey, 1 vol. Slade, Suzanne. 2011. (Follow It! Ser.). (ENG.). 24p. (J). (gr. 1-3). pap. 7.49 (978-1-4048-7029-1(6)); lib. bdg. 27.32 (978-1-4048-6655-3(8)) Capstone. (Picture Window Bks.).
—Stretch to the Sun: From a Tiny Sprout to the Tallest Tree on Earth. Pearson, Carrie A. 2018. (ENG.). 32p. (J). (gr. k-3). 16.99 (978-1-58089-771-6(1)) Charlesbridge Publishing, Inc.
—Sugar White Snow & Evergreens. Chernesky, Felicia Sanzari. 2015. (Av2 Fiction Readalong 2016 Ser.). (ENG.). (J). (gr. -1-2). lib. bdg. 34.28 (978-1-4896-3876-2(8), AV2 by Weigl) Weigl Pubs., Inc.
—Volcano Rising. Rusch, Elizabeth. 2013. 32p. (J). (gr. 1-4). pap. 7.95 (978-1-58089-409-8(7)) Charlesbridge Publishing, Inc.
Swaney, Julianna. Book Uncle & Me, 1 vol. Krishnaswami, Uma. 2018. (ENG.). 152p. (gr. 2-5). pap. 8.95 (978-1-55498-809-9(8)) Groundwood Bks. CAN. Dist: Publishers Group West (PGW).
—Dr. Jo: How Sara Josephine Baker Saved the Lives of America's Children. Kulling, Monica. 2018. (ENG.). 32p. (J). (gr. k-3). 17.99 (978-1-101-91789-3(X), Tundra Bks.) Tundra Bks. CAN. Dist: Penguin Random Hse. LLC.
—I Will Always Be Your Bunny: Love from the Velveteen Rabbit. Gilbert, Frances. 2019. (ENG.). 32p. (J). (gr. -1-2). 8.99 (978-1-9848-9341-3(6), Doubleday Bks. for Young Readers) Random Hse. Children's Bks.
—Mermaid School. Wetzel, JoAnne Stewart. 2018. 32p. (J). (gr. -1-2). 17.99 (978-0-399-55716-3(4), Knopf Bks. for Young Readers) Random Hse. Children's Bks.
—We Are the Gardeners, 1 vol. Gaines, Joanna. 2019. (ENG.). 40p. (J). 19.99 (978-1-4003-1422-5(4)) Nelson, Thomas Inc.
Swann, Mary. A Fearsome Day. Swann, Mary. 2007. 56p. (J). (gr. 1-3). 19.95 (978-0-932616-87-6(9)) BrickHouse Bks., Inc.
Swanson, Christine Mason. Agnes Had a Secret. Swanson, Christine Mason. 2019. (ENG.). 34p. (J). pap. 9.99 (978-1-7933-7763-0(4)) Independently Published.
Swanson, Jacqueline Rose. I Can Do Yoga. Life, This Beautiful & Bliss, Stasia. 2019. (I Can Ser.: Vol. 1). (ENG.). 38p. (J). pap. 13.13 (978-1-5141-8038-9(3)) CreateSpace Independent Publishing Platform.
Swanson, Karl. John Muir & Stickeen: An Alaskan Adventure. Koehler-Pentacoff, Elizabeth. 2003. (Single Titles Ser.). (ENG.). 32p. (J). (gr. 4-8). lib. bdg. 15.95 (978-0-7613-2769-1(X), Millbrook Pr.) Lerner Publishing Group.
Swanson, Karl W. John Muir & Stickeen: An Alaskan Adventure. Koehler-Pentacoff, Elizabeth. 2003. (Single Titles Ser.). 32p. (J). 14.95 (978-0-7613-1997-9(2)) Lerner Publishing Group.
Swanson, Maggie. The Bunny Hop (Sesame Street) Albee, Sarah. (J). (— 1). 2018. 26p. bds. 7.99 (978-0-525-57819-2(6), Golden Bks.); 2015. 24p. 4.99 (978-0-553-50798-0(2), Golden Bks.); 2004. (ENG.). 24p. bds. 4.99 (978-0-375-82693-1(9), Random Hse. Bks. for Young Readers) Random Hse. Children's Bks.
—Elmo Can... Taste! Touch! Smell! See! Hear! (Sesame Street) Muntean, Michaela. 2013. (Big Bird's Favorites Board Bks.). (ENG.). 24p. (J). (— 1). bds. 4.99 (978-0-307-98078-6(2), Random Hse. Bks. for Young Readers) Random Hse. Children's Bks.
—Elmo's 12 Days of Christmas. Albee, Sarah. 2015. (Little Golden Book Ser.). (ENG.). 24p. (J). (-k). 4.99 (978-0-553-52430-7(5), Golden Bks.) Random Hse. Children's Bks.
Swanson, Maggie. Elmo's 12 Days of Christmas (Sesame Street) Albee, Sarah. (ENG.). (J). (— 1). 2020. 26p. bds. 7.99 **(978-0-593-17673-3(1))**; 2003. 24p. bds. 4.99 (978-0-375-82506-4(1)) Random Hse. Children's Bks. (Random Hse. Bks. for Young Readers).
Swanson, Maggie. Elmo's Mother Goose Rhymes (Sesame Street) Allen, Constance. 2017. (Little Golden Book Ser.). 24p. (J). (-k). 4.99 (978-1-101-93994-9(X), Golden Bks.) Random Hse. Children's Bks.
—Elmo's Tricky Tongue Twisters. Albee, Sarah. 2016. 24p. (J). (978-1-4806-9705-8(2), Golden Bks.) Random Hse. Children's Bks.
—Elmo's Tricky Tongue Twisters (Sesame Street) Albee, Sarah. (Little Golden Book Ser.). 24p. (J). 2016. (gr. -1-k). 4.99 (978-1-101-93138-7(8), Golden Bks.); 2011. (ENG.). (gr. k — 1). bds. 4.99 (978-0-375-87249-5(3), Random Hse. Bks. for Young Readers) Random Hse. Children's Bks.
—Goldilocks & the Three Bears: A Tale about Respecting Others. 2006. (J). 6.99 (978-1-59939-006-2(X)) Cornerstone Pr.
—My Name Is Elmo (Sesame Street) Allen, Constance. (J). (— 1). 2016. (ENG.). 26p. bds. 7.99 (978-1-101-93746-4(7)); 2013. 24p. 4.99 (978-0-449-81066-8(6)) Random Hse. Children's Bks. (Golden Bks.).
—Shake a Leg! (Sesame Street) Allen, Constance. 2010. (Big Bird's Favorites Board Bks.). (ENG.). 24p. (J). (gr. k — 1). bds. 4.99 (978-0-375-85424-8(X), Random Hse. Bks. for Young Readers) Random Hse. Children's Bks.
—St. Francis & the Animals. Davidson, Alice Joyce. 2006. 24p. (J). 7.95 (978-0-88271-003-7(6)) Regina Pr., Malhame & Co.
—St. Therese: the Little Flower. Davidson, Alice Joyce. 2006. 24p. (J). 7.95 (978-0-88271-214-7(4)) Regina Pr., Malhame & Co.
—The Tale of Two Bad Mice. 2006. (J). 6.99 (978-1-59939-030-7(2)) Cornerstone Pr.
—Time for Bed, Elmo! (Sesame Street) Albee, Sarah. 2014. (Little Golden Book Ser.). (ENG.). 24p. (J). (-k). 4.99 (978-0-385-37138-4(1), Golden Bks.) Random Hse. Children's Bks.
Swanson, Maggie. My First Christmas. Swanson, Maggie. 2006. 10p. (gr. -1). bds. 7.95 (978-0-88271-707-4(3)) Regina Pr., Malhame & Co.
Swanson, Maggie. The Kitten's Christmas Lullaby. Swanson, Maggie, retold by. 2007. (J). (gr. -1-3). 8.95 (978-0-88271-064-8(8)) Regina Pr., Malhame & Co.
Swanson, Maggie. Grow, Tree, Grow! Swanson, Maggie, tr. Dreyer, Ellen. 2003. (Hello Reader! Ser.). (J). (978-0-439-43964-0(7)) Scholastic, Inc.
Swanson, Maggie & Leigh, Tom. Elmo's Little Library (Sesame Street) Elmo's Mother Goose; Elmo's Tricky Tongue Twisters; Elmo Says; Elmo's ABC Book. Albee, Sarah et al. 2013. (ENG.). 24p. (J). (— 1). bds. 14.99 (978-0-449-81740-7(7), Random Hse. Bks. for Young Readers) Random Hse. Children's Bks.
Swanson, Maggie, jt. illus. see Smollin, Michael.
Swanson, Peter Joseph. Tedoul. Bond, Alan. 2009. 28p. pap. 8.95 (978-1-60076-137-9(2)) StoneGarden.net Publishing.
Swanson, Tom. Twas the Night Before Christmas. ed. 2011. (Recordable Bks). 12p. (J). ring bd. 24.99 (978-1-60130-261-8(4), Usborne) EDC Publishing.
Sward, Adam. The Best Saturday Ever! Cook, Gary. 2013. (Robbie's Big Adventures Ser.). (ENG.). 40p. (J). (gr. k-3). 15.95 (978-1-938063-25-1(2), Mighty Media Kids) Mighty Media Pr.
Swarmer, Kristina. Festival Poems. 2017. (Poems Just for Me Ser.). 32p. (gr. 7-8). 27.25 (978-1-4994-8386-4(4), Windmill Bks.) Rosen Publishing Group, Inc., The.
Swarner, Kristina. The Bedtime Sh'ma: A Good Night Book. 2007. (ENG & HEB.). 40p. (J). 17.95 (978-0-939144-55-6(7)); pap. 10.95 (978-0-939144-54-9(9)) EKS Publishing Co.
—The BEDTIME SH'MA, Book & CD Set. 2007. (ENG & HEB.). 40p. (J). 24.95 incl. audio compact disk (978-0-939144-58-7(1)) EKS Publishing Co.
Swarner, Kristina. A Crowded Farmhouse Folktale. Rostoker-Gruber, Karen. 2020. (ENG.). 32p. (J). (gr. -1-3). 16.99 **(978-0-8075-5692-4(0)**, 0807556920) Whitman, Albert & Co.
Swarner, Kristina. The Gift of Christmas: The Boy Who Blessed the World. Joslin, Mary. ed. 2020. (ENG.). 32p. (J). (gr. -1-k). pap. 8.99 (978-0-7459-7751-5(0), Lion Children's) Lion Hudson PLC GBR. Dist: Independent Pubs. Group.
—Good People Everywhere. Gillen, Lynea. 2012. (ENG.). 32p. (J). (gr. -1-2). 15.95 (978-0-9799289-8-7(2)) Three Pebble Pr., LLC.
—Light the Menorah! A Hanukkah Handbook, Vol. Jules, Jacqueline. 2018. (ENG.). 40p. (J). (gr. -1-5). pap. 8.99 (978-1-5124-8369-7(9), Kar-Ben Publishing) Lerner Publishing Group.
—Modeh Ani: A Good Morning Book. 2010. (HEB & ENG.). 32p. (J). 17.95 (978-0-939144-64-8(6)); pap. 10.95 (978-0-939144-63-1(8)) EKS Publishing Co.
—The Nutcracker: A Magic Theater Book. McCaughrean, Geraldine & Hoffmann, E. T. A. 2012. (ENG.). 24p. (J). (gr. 1-17). 19.99 (978-1-4521-0669-4(X)) Handprint Bks.
Swarte, Joost. Thrice Told Tales: Three Mice Full of Writing Advice. Lewis, Catherine. 2013. (ENG.). 144p. (YA). (gr. 7). 17.99 (978-1-4169-5784-3(7)) Simon & Schuster Children's Publishing.
Swartz, Daniel. Duckville. Drury, David. 2013. 32p. (J). (978-0-89827-721-0(3)) Wesleyan Publishing Hse.
Swartz, Karen, jt. illus. see Flores, Catty.

Swearingen, Greg. The Giants & the Joneses. Donaldson, Julia. 2008. (ENG.). 218p. (J). (gr. 4-6). 21.19 *(978-0-312-37961-2(7)*, 9780312379612) Square Fish.

—Is That an Unlucky Leprechaun in Your Lunch? Strasser, Todd. 2009. 184p. (J). *(978-0-545-11034-1(3))* Scholastic, Inc.

—Mr. Worry: A Story about OCD. Niner, Holly L. 2003. (ENG.). 32p. (J). (gr. 2-3). 16.99 *(978-0-8075-5182-0(1)*, 807551821) Whitman, Albert & Co.

—The Outlandish Adventures of Liberty Aimes. Easton, Kelly. 2011. 224p. (J). (ENG.). (gr. 4-6). lib. bdg. 21.19 *(978-0-375-93771-2(4)*, Lamb, Wendy Bks.); (gr. 3-7). pap. 6.99 *(978-0-375-83772-2(8)*, Yearling) Random Hse. Children's Bks.

Swearingen, Hala Wittwer. Spring Surprises. Hays, Anna Jane. 2010. (Step into Reading: Step 2 Ser.). (ENG.). 24p. (J). (gr. -1-1). lib. bdg. 16.19 *(978-0-375-95840-3(1))* Random House Publishing Group.

Sweat, Lynn. Amelia Bedelia & the Baby. Parish, Peggy. 2004. (I Can Read Level 2 Ser.). (ENG.). 64p. (J). (gr. k-3). pap. 4.99 *(978-0-06-051105-0(2)*, Greenwillow Bks.) HarperCollins Pubs.

—Amelia Bedelia & the Cat. Parish, Herman. (I Can Read Level 2 Ser.). (ENG.). 48p. (J). (gr. k-3). 2009. pap. 4.99 *(978-0-06-084351-9(9))*; 2008. 16.99 *(978-0-06-084349-6(7))* HarperCollins Pubs. (Greenwillow Bks.).

—Amelia Bedelia Bakes Off. Parish, Herman. 2010. (I Can Read Level 2 Ser.). (ENG.). 64p. (J). (gr. k-3). pap. 4.99 *(978-0-06-084360-1(8))*; 17.99 *(978-0-06-084358-8(6))*; lib. bdg. 18.89 *(978-0-06-084359-5(4))* HarperCollins Pubs. (Greenwillow Bks.).

—Amelia Bedelia, Bookworm. Parish, Herman. (I Can Read Level 2 Ser.). (ENG.). 64p. (J). (gr. k-3). 2005. pap. 4.99 *(978-0-06-051892-9(8))*; 2003. 17.99 *(978-0-06-051890-5(1))* HarperCollins Pubs. (Greenwillow Bks.).

—Amelia Bedelia, Bookworm. Parish, Herman. 2005. (I Can Read Bks.). 63p. (gr. -1-3). 14.00 *(978-0-7569-5766-7(4))* Perfection Learning Corp.

—Amelia Bedelia, Cub Reporter. Parish, Herman. 2012. (I Can Read Level 2 Ser.). (ENG.). 64p. (J). (gr. -1-3). pap. 4.99 *(978-0-06-209509-1(9)*, Greenwillow Bks.) HarperCollins Pubs.

—Amelia Bedelia Goes Back to School. Parish, Herman. 2004. (Amelia Bedelia Ser.). (ENG.). 20p. (J). (gr. -1-3). pap. 6.99 *(978-0-06-051873-8(1)*, Greenwillow Bks.) HarperCollins Pubs.

—Amelia Bedelia Goes Camping. Parish, Peggy. 2003. (I Can Read Level 2 Ser.). (ENG.). 64p. (J). (gr. k-3). pap. 4.99 *(978-0-06-051106-7(0)*, Greenwillow Bks.) HarperCollins Pubs.

—Amelia Bedelia Helps Out. Parish, Peggy. 2005. (I Can Read Level 2 Ser.). (ENG.). 64p. (J). (gr. k-3). pap. 4.99 *(978-0-06-051111-1(7)*, Greenwillow Bks.) HarperCollins Pubs.

—Amelia Bedelia, Rocket Scientist? Parish, Herman. (I Can Read Level 2 Ser.). 64p. (J). 2007. (ENG.). (gr. k-3). pap. 4.99 *(978-0-06-051889-9(8)*, Greenwillow Bks.); 2005. (gr. 1-18). 15.99 *(978-0-06-051887-5(1))*; 2005. (ENG.). (gr. k-4). lib. bdg. 17.89 *(978-0-06-051888-2(X)*, Greenwillow Bks.) HarperCollins Pubs.

—Amelia Bedelia, Rocket Scientist? Parish, Herman. 2007. (I Can Read Ser.). 64p. 14.00 *(978-0-7569-8058-0(5))* Perfection Learning Corp.

—Amelia Bedelia, Rocket Scientist? Parish, Herman. ed. 2007. (Amelia Bedelia: I Can Read! Ser.: 19). (J). lib. bdg. 13.55 *(978-1-4177-8068-6(1))* Turtleback.

—Amelia Bedelia Storybook Treasury #2 (Classic) Calling Doctor Amelia Bedelia; Amelia Bedelia & the Cat; Amelia Bedelia Bakes Off. Parish, Herman. 2016. (Amelia Bedelia Ser.). (ENG.). 192p. (J). (gr. 1-5). 11.99 *(978-0-06-246908-3(8)*, Greenwillow Bks.) HarperCollins Pubs.

—Amelia Bedelia Talks Turkey. Parish, Herman. (I Can Read Level 2 Ser.). (ENG.). 64p. (J). (gr. k-3). 2009. pap. 4.99 *(978-0-06-084354-0(3))*; 2008. 16.99 *(978-0-06-084352-6(7))* HarperCollins Pubs. (Greenwillow Bks.).

—Amelia Bedelia under Construction. Parish, Herman. (I Can Read Level 2 Ser.). (ENG.). 64p. (J). (gr. k-3). 2007. pap. 4.99 *(978-0-06-084346-5(2))*; 2006. 15.99 *(978-0-06-084344-1(6))* HarperCollins Pubs. (Greenwillow Bks.).

—Amelia Bedelia under Construction. Parish, Herman. 2007. (I Can Read Bks.). 64p. (gr. k-3). 14.00 *(978-0-7569-8054-2(2))* Perfection Learning Corp.

—Amelia Bedelia's Backpack Bundle. Parish, Herman. 2012. 192p. (J). *(978-1-4351-4392-0(2)*, Greenwillow Bks.) HarperCollins Pubs.

—Amelia Bedelia's Family Album. Parish, Peggy. 2003. (I Can Read Level 2 Ser.). (ENG.). 48p. (J). (gr. k-3). pap. 4.99 *(978-0-06-051116-6(8)*, Greenwillow Bks.) HarperCollins Pubs.

—Amelia Bedelia's Masterpiece. Parish, Herman. (I Can Read Level 2 Ser.). (ENG.). 64p. (J). (gr. k-3). 2008. pap. 4.99 *(978-0-06-084357-1(8))*; 2007. 16.99 *(978-0-06-084355-7(1))* HarperCollins Pubs. (Greenwillow Bks.).

—Be My Valentine, Amelia Bedelia. Parish, Herman. 2004. (Amelia Bedelia Ser.). (ENG.). 20p. (J). (gr. -1-3). pap. 6.99 *(978-0-06-051886-8(3)*, Greenwillow Bks.) HarperCollins Pubs.

—Calling Doctor Amelia Bedelia. Parish, Herman. 2004. (I Can Read Level 2 Ser.). (ENG.). 64p. (J). (gr. k-3). pap. 4.99 *(978-0-06-008780-7(3)*, Greenwillow Bks.) HarperCollins Pubs.

—Calling Doctor Amelia Bedelia. Parish, Herman. 2004. (Amelia Bedelia Ser.). 64p. (gr. -1-2). 14.00 *(978-0-7569-3209-1(2))* Perfection Learning Corp.

—Go West, Amelia Bedelia! Parish, Herman. (I Can Read Level 2 Ser.). (ENG.). 64p. (J). (gr. k-4). 2012. pap. 4.99 *(978-0-06-084363-2(2))*; 2011. 17.99 *(978-0-06-084361-8(6))*; 2011. lib. bdg. 18.89 *(978-0-06-084362-5(4))* HarperCollins Pubs. (Greenwillow Bks.).

—Good Work, Amelia Bedelia. Parish, Peggy. 2003. (I Can Read Level 2 Ser.). (ENG.). 64p. (J). (gr. k-3). pap. 4.99 *(978-0-06-051115-9(X)*, Greenwillow Bks.) HarperCollins Pubs.

—Happy Haunting, Amelia Bedelia. Parish, Herman. (I Can Read Level 2 Ser.). (ENG.). 64p. (J). (gr. k-3). 2006. pap. 4.99 *(978-0-06-051895-0(2))*; 2004. 16.99 *(978-0-06-051893-6(6))*; 2004. lib. bdg. 16.89 *(978-0-06-051894-3(4))* HarperCollins Pubs. (Greenwillow Bks.).

—Teach Us, Amelia Bedelia. Parish, Peggy. 2004. (I Can Read Level 2 Ser.). (ENG.). 64p. (J). (gr. k-3). pap. 4.99 *(978-0-06-051114-2(1)*, Greenwillow Bks.) HarperCollins Pubs.

—Teach Us, Amelia Bedelia. Parish, Peggy. 2005. (Amelia Bedelia Ser.). 58p. (gr. -1-3). 14.00 *(978-0-7569-4804-7(5))* Perfection Learning Corp.

Sweat, Lynn & Siebel, Fritz. An Amelia Bedelia Celebration: Four Stories Tall. Parish, Peggy & Parish, Herman. 2009. (Amelia Bedelia Ser.). (ENG.). 224p. (J). (gr. -1-3). 19.99 *(978-0-06-171030-8(X)*, Greenwillow Bks.) HarperCollins Pubs.

Sweeny, Elizabeth Mifflin. Second Hand Cat. Sweeny, Vell. 2013. (ENG.). 48p. (gr. -1-6). 14.95 *(978-0-9816360-2-3(0)*, 4eca5dfc-ae38-48db-8d19-a525c97f2c25) Pink Pig Pr.

Sweet Briar School. Bea's Almost Bad Day. Wolf, Penny et al. 2011. 32p. (J). 8.00 *(978-0-9802015-1-2(9))* Sweetbriar Crafts & Pubns.

Sweet, Darrell & Allen, Douglas. The How & Why Wonder Book of Reptiles & Amphibians. Mathewson, Robert F. 2011. 48p. pap. 35.95 *(978-1-258-09940-4(3))* Literary Licensing, LLC.

Sweet, Glenn. Fuzzy. Sweet, Glenn. 2003. (ENG.). (J). lib. bdg. *(978-0-9766674-0-7(1))* Cactus Publishing, LLC.

Sweet, Melissa. Alphamaniacs: Builders of 26 Wonders of the Word. Fleischman, Paul. 2020. (ENG.). 160p. (J). (gr. 7). 19.99 *(978-0-7636-9066-3(X))* Candlewick Pr.

—Baabwaa & Wooliam: A Tale of Literacy, Dental Hygiene, & Friendship. Elliott, David. 2017. 40p. (J). (gr. -1-3). 16.99 *(978-0-7636-6074-1(4))* Candlewick Pr.

—Bat Jamboree. Appelt, Kathi. 2004. 17.00 *(978-0-7569-4074-4(5))* Perfection Learning Corp.

—The Boy Who Drew Birds: A Story of John James Audubon. Davies, Jacqueline. 2004. (ENG.). 32p. (J). (gr. -1-3). tchr. ed. 17.99 *(978-0-618-24343-3(7)*, 584353, HMH Books For Young Readers) Houghton Mifflin Harcourt Publishing Co.

—Brave Girl: Clara & the Shirtwaist Makers' Strike Of 1909. Markel, Michelle. 2013. (ENG.). 32p. (J). (gr. -1-3). 17.99 *(978-0-06-180442-7(8)*, Balzer & Bray) HarperCollins Pubs.

—Christmas Tree. Martin, David Lozell. 2009. 26p. (J). (— 1). bds. 5.99 *(978-0-7636-3030-0(6))* Candlewick Pr.

—Christmas Tree. Martin, David. 2015. 26p. (J). (gr. -1-2). 5.99 *(978-0-7636-7968-2(2))* Candlewick Pr.

—Firefly July: A Year of Very Short Poems. Janeczko, Paul B. 2018. 48p. (J). (gr. -1-3). pap. 7.99 *(978-0-7636-9971-0(3))* Candlewick Pr.

—Girls Think of Everything: Stories of Ingenious Inventions by Women. Thimmesh, Catherine. 2018. (ENG.). 112p. (J). (gr. 5-7). 17.99 *(978-1-328-77253-4(5)*, 1681294, HMH Books For Young Readers) Houghton Mifflin Harcourt Publishing Co.

—Hanukkah Lights. Martin, David Lozell. 2009. (ENG.). 26p. (J). (gr. -1 — 1). bds. 5.99 *(978-0-7636-3029-4(2))* Candlewick Pr.

—Hanukkah Lights. Martin, David. 2015. 26p. (J). (gr. -1-2). 5.99 *(978-0-7636-7972-9(0))* Candlewick Pr.

—How to Read a Book. Alexander, Kwame. 2019. (ENG.). 32p. (J). (gr. -1-3). 17.99 *(978-0-06-230781-1(9)*, HarperCollins) HarperCollins Pubs. Ltd. GBR. Dist: HarperCollins Pubs.

—I Love You, Too! Bunting, Eve. 2015. 24p. (J). (— 1). bds. 7.99 *(978-0-545-81390-7(5)*, Cartwheel Bks.) Scholastic, Inc.

—It's Spring! Berger, Samantha & Chanko, Pamela. (StoryPlay Ser.). (ENG.). (J). (gr. -1-k). 2017. 40p. 5.99 *(978-1-338-23218-9(5))*; 2003. 30p. bds. 6.99 *(978-0-439-44238-1(9)*, Cartwheel Bks.) Scholastic, Inc.

—Listen to Our World. Martin, Bill, Jr. & Sampson, Michael. 2016. (ENG.). 40p. (J). (gr. -1-3). 17.99 *(978-1-4424-5472-9(5)*, Simon & Schuster Bks. For Young Readers) Simon & Schuster Bks. For Young Readers.

—Little Red Writing. Holub, Joan. (ENG.). 36p. (J). (gr. k-3). 2016. pap. 7.99 *(978-1-4521-5209-7(8))*; 2013. 16.99 *(978-0-8118-7869-2(4))* Chronicle Bks. LLC.

—Moonlight: The Halloween Cat. Rylant, Cynthia. (ENG.). 32p. (J). (gr. -1-3). 2009. pap. 7.99 *(978-0-06-443814-8(7))*; 2003. 17.99 *(978-0-06-029711-4(5))* HarperCollins Pubs.

—Mrs. Harkness & the Panda. Potter, Alicia. 2012. (ENG.). 40p. (J). (gr. k-3). 17.99 *(978-0-375-84448-5(1)*, Knopf Bks. for Young Readers) Random Hse. Children's Bks.

—The Right Word: Roget & His Thesaurus. Bryant, Jen. 2014. (ENG.). 42p. (J). 17.50 *(978-0-8028-5385-1(4)*, Eerdmans Bks For Young Readers) Eerdmans, William B. Publishing Co.

—A River of Words: The Story of William Carlos Williams. Bryant, Jennifer. 2008. 34p. (J). (gr. 4-7). 17.50 *(978-0-8028-5302-8(1)*, Eerdmans Bks For Young Readers) Eerdmans, William B. Publishing Co.

—The Sky's the Limit: Stories of Discovery by Women & Girls. Thimmesh, Catherine. 2005. 73p. (J). (gr. 4-8). reprint ed. 16.00 *(978-0-7567-9631-0(8))* DIANE Publishing Co.

—Sleepy Little Alphabet: A Bedtime Story from Alphabet Town. Sierra, Judy. 2009. (ENG.). 40p. (J). (gr. -1 — 1). 17.99 *(978-0-375-84002-9(8)*, Knopf Bks. for Young Readers) Random Hse. Children's Bks.

—The Sleepy Little Alphabet: A Bedtime Story from Alphabet Town. Sierra, Judy. 2014. 34p. (J). (— 1). bds. 7.99 *(978-0-385-75400-2(0)*, Knopf Bks. for Young Readers) Random Hse. Children's Bks.

—Spike: The Mixed-Up Monster. Hood, Susan. 2012. (ENG.). 40p. (J). (gr. -1-3). 16.99 *(978-1-4424-0601-8(1)*, Simon & Schuster/Paula Wiseman Bks.) Simon & Schuster/Paula Wiseman Bks.

—A Splash of Red: The Life & Art of Horace Pippin. Bryant, Jennifer. 2013. 40p. (J). (gr. k-3). 17.99 *(978-0-375-86712-5(0)*, Knopf Bks. for Young Readers) Random Hse. Children's Bks.

—Won't You Be My Kissaroo? Ryder, Joanne. (ENG.). (J). (gr. -1 — 1). 2015. 40p. pap. 6.99 *(978-0-15-205820-3(6)*, 1197487, HMH Books For Young Readers); 2008. 15p. bds. 6.95 *(978-0-15-206060-2(X)*, 1198201) Houghton Mifflin Harcourt Publishing Co.

—Won't You Be My Kissaroo? (padded Board Book) Ryder, Joanne. 2018. (ENG.). 30p. (J). (— 1). bds. 8.99 *(978-1-328-48262-4(6)*, 1715789, HMH Books For Young Readers) Houghton Mifflin Harcourt Publishing Co.

—You Nest Here with Me. Yolen, Jane & Stemple, Heidi E. Y. (J). 2019. 28p. (— 1). bds. 7.99 *(978-1-68437-371-0(9))*; 2015. (ENG.). 40p. (gr. -1-3). 17.95 *(978-1-59078-923-0(7))* Boyds Mills Pr.

Sweet, Melissa, jt. illus. see Nap, Dug.

Sweet, Stephen. Cars. Parker, Steve. 2005. (Twenty4Sevens Ser.). 48p. (J). pap. *(978-0-439-78528-0(6))* Scholastic, Inc.

Sweet, Stephen. Out-Of-This-World Space. Mobberley, Martin. 2019. (Lightspeed Science Ser.). (ENG.). 48p. (J). (gr. 2-6). pap. ***(978-1-78700-983-7(1))*** Top That! Publishing PLC.

Sweeten, Sami. Snow Dog. Blackman, Malorie. 2014. 80p. (J). (gr. k-2). pap. 9.99 *(978-0-552-56891-3(0))* Transworld Publishers Ltd. GBR. Dist: Independent Pubs. Group.

Sweetland, Robert. My Pal Victor. Bertrand, Diane Gonzales. 2010.Tr. of Mi Amigo, Victor. (ENG.). 32p. (J). (gr. 4-7). 16.95 *(978-1-934960-84-4(5)*, Raven Tree Pr.,Csi) Continental Sales, Inc.

Sweetman, Gary W., photos by. Pockets: Book: Nonfiction_Juvenile, The Molly Brave Preschool Series Vol. 1. Deveny, Mary Alice. 2011. 40p. (J). pap. 14.95 *(978-1-61245-000-1(8))* Molly Brave.

Swiatkowska, Gabi. Arrowhawk. Schaefer, Lola M. 2014. (ENG.). (J). (gr. -1-3). lib. bdg. 18.60 *(978-1-62765-386-2(4))* Perfection Learning Corp.

—Arrowhawk: A True Survival Story. Schaefer, Lola M. 2014. (ENG.). 32p. (J). (gr. -1-3). 8.99 *(978-1-250-03988-0(6)*, 900123691) Square Fish.

—The Golden Rule. Cooper, Ilene. (J). (gr. k-4). 2008. 27.95 incl. audio *(978-0-8045-6968-2(1))*; 2007. 29.95 incl. audio compact disk *(978-0-8045-4191-6(4))* Spoken Arts, Inc.

—Golden Rule. Cooper, Ilene. 2019. (ENG.). 40p. (J). (gr. -1-3). 18.99 *(978-1-4197-4069-5(5)*, Abrams Bks. for Young Readers) Abrams, Inc.

—How the Queen Found the Perfect Cup of Tea. Hosford, Kate. 2017. (ENG.). 40p. (J). (gr. k-3). 18.99 *(978-1-4677-3904-7(9)*, 9781467739047); E-Book 29.32 *(978-1-4677-9563-0(1))*; E-Book 29.32 *(978-1-5124-3272-5(5)*, 9781512432725); E-Book 9.99 *(978-1-5124-3273-2(3)*, 9781512432732) Lerner Publishing Group. (Carolrhoda Bks.).

—Infinity & Me. Hosford, Kate. 2012. (ENG.). 32p. (J). (gr. k-4). lib. bdg. 17.99 *(978-0-7613-6726-0(8)*, 9780761367260, Carolrhoda Bks.) Lerner Publishing Group.

—Mary Cassatt: Extraordinary Impressionist Painter. Herkert, Barbara. 2015. (ENG.). 32p. (J). (gr. -1-3). 17.99 *(978-1-62779-016-1(0)*, 900130253, Holt, Henry & Co. Bks. For Young Readers) Holt, Henry & Co.

—Me Llama Yoon. Recorvits, Helen. 2003.Tr. of My Name is Yoon. (SPA.). 32p. (gr. k-2). 18.99 *(978-84-261-3335-9(5))* Juventud, Editorial ESP. Dist: Lectorum Pubns., Inc.

—My Name Is Yoon. Recorvits, Helen. 2003. (ENG.). 32p. (J). (gr. -1-3). 17.99 *(978-0-374-35114-4(7)*, 9780374351144, Farrar, Straus & Giroux (BYR)) Farrar, Straus & Giroux.

—My Name Is Yoon. Recorvits, Helen. 2014. (ENG.). 32p. (J). (gr. -1-3). 7.99 *(978-1-250-05711-2(6)*, 900139124) Square Fish.

Swiatkowska, Gabi. Queen on Wednesday. Swiatkowska, Gabi. 2014. (ENG.). 36p. (J). (gr. -1-3). 17.99 *(978-0-374-37446-4(5)*, 900079440, Farrar, Straus & Giroux (BYR)) Farrar, Straus & Giroux.

Swiatoviak, Jeri. Buddy & the Poi Puppy. Gissing, Kathleen. 2012. 24p. pap. 24.95 *(978-1-4626-8089-4(5))* America Star Bks.

Swiderska, Barbara. The Fisherman's Bride. Swiderska, Barbara. 32p. (J). (gr. -1-3). 12.95 *(978-0-87592-018-4(7))* Scroll Pr., Inc.

Swift, Anne. The Christmas Tree Wish. Inglis, Karen. 2019. (ENG.). 34p. (J). (gr. k). pap. ***(978-0-9954543-6-1(1))*** Well Said Pr.

Swift, Drew. Isis: Imitation of Life. James, Shawn. 2018. (ENG.). 146p. (J). pap. 14.00 *(978-1-5302-6650-0(5))* CreateSpace Independent Publishing Platform.

Swift, Gary. The Bug Book. Fleming, Maria. 2004. (Grammar Tales Ser.). (ENG.). 16p. (J). (gr. 3-7). pap. 3.25 *(978-0-439-45818-4(8))* Scholastic, Inc.

—The Fantastic Fruit Group, 1 vol. Aboff, Marcie. 2011. (First Graphics: Myplate & Healthy Eating Ser.). (ENG.). 24p. (J). (gr. k-3). lib. bdg. 24.65 *(978-1-4296-6090-7(2))*; (gr. 1-2). pap. 35.70 *(978-1-4296-7166-8(1))* Capstone.

—Flying Butter. Trattles, Patricia. 2005. (Rookie Reader: Compound Words Ser.). (ENG.). 24p. (J). (gr. k-2). 17.44 *(978-0-516-25150-9(3)*, Children's Pr.) Scholastic Library Publishing.

—Healthy Snacks, Healthy You!, 1 vol. Lee, Sally. 2011. (First Graphics: Myplate & Healthy Eating Ser.). (ENG.). 24p. (J). (gr. k-3). pap. 6.29 *(978-1-4296-7162-0(9))*; (gr. 1-2). pap. 35.70 *(978-1-4296-7168-2(8))* Capstone.

—Healthy Snacks, Healthy You! [Scholastic]. Lee, Sally. 2013. (First Graphics: Myplate & Healthy Eating Ser.). (ENG.). (gr. 1-2). pap. 0.50 *(978-1-4765-3129-8(3))* Capstone.

—The Powerful Protein Group, 1 vol. Lee, Sally. 2011. (First Graphics: Myplate & Healthy Eating Ser.). (ENG.). 24p. (J). (gr. k-3). lib. bdg. 24.65 *(978-1-4296-6091-4(0))*; (gr. 1-2). pap. 35.70 *(978-1-4296-7170-5(X))* Capstone.

Swift, Gary, jt. illus. see Poling, Kyle.

Swigelson, Kayce M. The Grand Adventures of Petit Louis. Swigelson, Kayce M. 2013. 54p. 24.95 *(978-0-9889643-1-0(7))* MathisJones Communications, LLC.

Swinford, Charles. Breakfast with Bigfoot. Cotter, Amelia. 2013. 30p. pap. 11.95 *(978-1-61876-017-3(3))* Black Oak Media, Inc.

Swing, Michael. My Florida Facts, Vol. Johnson, Russell W. & Johnson, Annie P. 2009. (ENG.). 64p. (J). (gr. -1-12). 14.95 *(978-1-56164-430-8(7))* Pineapple Pr., Inc.

Swingler, Simon. Locked In. Fraillon, Z. 2011. (Monstrum House Ser.: 1). (ENG.). 176p. (J). (gr. 4-7). pap. 8.99 *(978-1-921564-25-3(3))* Hardie Grant Egmont Pty, Ltd. AUS. Dist: Independent Pubs. Group.

—When Robots Go Bad. Badger, M. C. 2014. (Super Baddies Ser.: 2). (ENG.). 48p. (J). (gr. k-2). pap. 9.99 *(978-1-921848-43-8(X))* Hardie Grant Egmont Pty, Ltd. AUS. Dist: Independent Pubs. Group.

Swisher, Elizabeth, et al. Celebrate with Jesus: A Child's Book of the Sacraments. Larkin, Jean, ed. 2007. 32p. pap. 3.95 *(978-1-933178-67-7(1))* Pflaum Publishing Group.

Swisher, Elizabeth. Days of Faith: Student Planner & Assignment Book/Primary Grades 2005-2006. Ward, Hadley & Castano, Marie. Cannizzo, Karen, ed. 2005. (J). spiral bd. 4.99 *(978-1-933178-05-9(1)*, 9806) Pflaum Publishing Group.

—Jesus Walks on the Water. Sanders, Nancy I. 2005. (ENG.). 16p. (J). 1.99 *(978-0-7586-0864-2(0))* Concordia Publishing Hse.

—The Lord Calls Samuel. Susan, Hammond. 2005. (Arch Bks.). 16p. (J). 1.99 *(978-0-7586-0639-6(7))* Concordia Publishing Hse.

Swisher, Michael-Che. Secret along the St. Mary's. Swisher, Michael-Che, tr. Troeger, Virginia B. 2003. (Mysteries in Time Ser.). 92p. (gr. 4). 14.95 *(978-1-893110-35-9(4))* Silver Moon Pr.

Switzer, Bobbi. The Adventures of Pj & Split Pea. Moore, S. D. 2008. 36p. per. 12.95 *(978-1-4327-1288-4(8))* Outskirts Pr., Inc.

—Aidan's Shoes. Sampson, Brent. 2006. (ENG.). 28p. per. 12.95 *(978-1-59800-684-1(3))* Outskirts Pr., Inc.

—Onyx. Barreto, Sonia. 2008. 36p. pap. 13.95 *(978-1-4327-1787-2(1))* Outskirts Pr., Inc.

—Queen Vernita's Visitors. Menge, Dawn. 2008. 36p. pap. 19.95 *(978-1-59800-714-5(9))* Outskirts Pr., Inc.

—When Little Pinkie Gets Her Wings. Elliott, Linda. 2007. 28p. per. 11.95 *(978-1-59800-871-5(4))* Outskirts Pr., Inc.

Switzer, Bobby. Angus & the Triplets. Rhoton, Lesa. 2006. 28p. (J). (gr. -1-3). per. 13.95 *(978-1-58939-852-8(1))* Virtualbookworm.com Publishing, Inc.

Switzer Hutson, Betty. History of the Christian Methodist Episcopal Church for Children. 2010. 48p. (YA). pap. 15.00 *(978-0-615-37424-6(7))* leharperwilliamsdesign group.

Swofford, Morgan. Salvados Por la Suma. Rogers, Rachel & Lineberry, Joe. 2018. (Gift of Numbers Ser.: Vol. 1). (SPA.). 34p. (J). (gr. 2-3). pap. 11.95 *(978-1-943419-73-9(6))* Prospective Pr.

—Saved by Addition. Rogers, Rachel & Lineberry, Joe. 2016. (ENG.). (J). (gr. 2-3). pap. 11.95 *(978-1-943419-35-7(3))*; (Gift of Numbers Ser.: Vol. 1). 16.95 *(978-1-943419-34-0(5))* Prospective Pr.

—Surprised by Subtraction. Rogers, Rachel & Lineberry, Joe. 2017. (Gift of Numbers Ser.: Vol. 2). (ENG.). 38p. (J). (gr. 2-3). pap. 11.95 *(978-1-943419-46-3(9))* Prospective Pr.

Swope, Brenda. The Adventures of Katie Koala: Oops! My Momma Is Lost!, 1 vol. Robinson Ed. D., Shannon R. 2009. 23p. pap. 24.95 *(978-1-60749-733-2(6))* America Star Bks.

—Beethoven. Cardona, Nancy. 2011. 28p. pap. 24.95 *(978-1-4560-0961-8(3))* America Star Bks.

—Bob the Lizard, 1 vol. Ramirez, Iz. 2009. 26p. pap. 24.95 *(978-1-60749-232-0(6))* America Star Bks.

—Bobby & Bun Bun's Afternoon Adventure. Murray, Rosalie. 2012. 32p. pap. 24.95 *(978-1-4560-5090-0(7))* America Star Bks.

—Chicken Church. Mattingly, Robin. 2011. 28p. pap. 24.95 *(978-1-4560-0962-5(1))* America Star Bks.

—Dollop the Cloud & Dee the Bee. Ferry, Ann. 2012. 28p. pap. 24.95 *(978-1-4626-7433-6(X))* America Star Bks.

—Don't Forget about Me. Joseph, Beverly L. 2011. 28p. pap. 24.95 *(978-1-4560-0972-4(9))* America Star Bks.

—Farm Friends. Fass, Amanda L. 2011. 28p. pap. 24.95 *(978-1-4560-0894-9(3))* America Star Bks.

—Gusty the Cloud & Streakie the Snail. Ferry, Ann. 2011. 28p. pap. 24.95 *(978-1-4560-0928-1(1))* America Star Bks.

—Huff the Magicless Dragon, 1 vol. Lawson, Barbara. 2009. 35p. pap. 24.95 *(978-1-61546-419-7(0))* PublishAmerica, Inc.

—I Guess I'll Be, 1 vol. Kelty, Colleen Alyce. 2010. 24p. 24.95 *(978-1-4489-4937-3(8))* PublishAmerica, Inc.

—Little Bird & the Wind. Hart-Plaugher, Teresa. 2011. 28p. pap. 24.95 *(978-1-4512-9102-5(7))* America Star Bks.

—Little John, God, & the Circus. Dubrule, Jackie. 2011. 32p. pap. 24.95 *(978-1-4560-0978-6(8))* America Star Bks.

—Lunie Balloonies. Blace, Maria. 2011. 24p. pap. 24.95 *(978-1-4560-0947-2(8))* America Star Bks.

—Malcolm's Cubby House. Stewart, Mark R. 2011. 28p. pap. 24.95 *(978-1-4560-0958-8(3))* America Star Bks.

—Mi Mi's Mini Tea Party. Kirkland, Kim M. 2011. 28p. pap. 24.95 *(978-1-4512-8099-9(8))* America Star Bks.

—Miranda, God & the Park. Dubrule, Jackie. 2011. 32p. pap. 24.95 *(978-1-4560-0966-3(4))* America Star Bks.

—Mr Mouse Morgan. Seaman, Lucy. 2011. 28p. pap. 24.95 *(978-1-4560-0916-8(8))* America Star Bks.

—My Dad's off to War. Calabrese, Diane Marie. 2011. 28p. pap. 24.95 *(978-1-4560-0942-7(7))* America Star Bks.

—Nine & a Half Dozen, 1 vol. V. 2010. 24p. 24.95 *(978-1-4489-2596-4(7))* PublishAmerica, Inc.

—The Puppy Tree, 1 vol. Emanuel, Lora. 2009. 30p. pap. 24.95 *(978-1-60749-614-4(3))* America Star Bks.

—The Rivers. Trimoglie, Mario. 2012. 26p. 24.95 *(978-1-4560-3907-3(5))* America Star Bks.

—Tree Talkers: A Christmas Story, 1 vol. Doman, Dave. 2009. 32p. pap. 24.95 *(978-1-61546-180-6(9))* America Star Bks.

—Why Santa Claus Comes at Christmas. McDade Jr, Bert M. 2011. 32p. pap. 24.95 *(978-1-4560-0921-2(4))* America Star Bks.

—Zoey Finds a New Home. Wade, Joan. 2011. 28p. pap. 24.95 *(978-1-4560-0899-4(4))* PublishAmerica, Inc.

Sy, Cleoward. Kitty Ballou's Sanctuary Zoo. Shirley, Cindy. Shirley, Cailey, ed. 2019. (ENG.). 66p. (J). (gr. 2-6). 18.95 *(978-1-7324256-4-4(7))* Let's Pretend Childrens Bks.

—Kitty Ballou's Sanctuary Zoo: Color Illustration Edition. Shirley, Cindy L. Shirley, Cailey, ed. 2019. (ENG.). 66p. (J). pap. 14.95 *(978-1-7324256-3-7(9))* Let's Pretend Childrens Bks.

—The Lonely Balloon. Mallorey, Gemma. 2016. (ENG.). 27p. (J). pap. *(978-0-9933603-3-6(5))* Bower Maze.

—What Does Christmas Mean to You? Hurst, Tasheira Nichole & Trafton, V. A. 2018. (ENG.). 40p. (J). pap. 10.00 *(978-1-7311-0756-5(0))* Independently Published.

Sy, Jan Michael Vincent. Anthology of Chaconia Creations: 2Nd Edition. Wattley, Jason J. 2020. (ENG.). 24p. (J). pap. 15.99 ***(978-1-7960-8156-5(6))*** Xlibris Corp.

Sy, Jan Michael Vincent. Willy the Worm Gets Lost. Miller, H. James. 2011. (ENG.). 24p. pap. 15.99 *(978-1-4568-9801-4(9))* Xlibris Corp.

Sycamore-Batty, Sharon. The Cat Who Wanted to Be a Reindeer. Gwynn, Michele E. 2018. (Cat Who Ser.: Vol. 1). (ENG.). 38p. (J). pap. 9.99 *(978-1-7902-4406-5(4))* Independently Published.

Sycamore, Hilary, jt. illus. see O'Connor, George.

Syder, Andrew. The Chronicles of Mike Bike Hall. Howard, Mike. 2016. (ENG.). (J). (gr. 1-5). pap. *(978-1-78222-488-4(2))* Paragon Publishing, Rothersthorpe.

—The Chronicles of Mike Bike Hall: Book Two. Howard, Mike. 2017. (ENG.). (J). (gr. 1-2). pap. *(978-1-78222-552-2(8))* Paragon Publishing, Rothersthorpe.

Syed, Anoosha. Bilal Cooks Daal. Saeed, Aisha. 2019. (ENG.). 40p. (J). (gr. -1-3). 17.99 *(978-1-5344-1810-3(5),* Salaam Reads) Simon & Schuster Bks. For Young Readers.

—Book 1: Otis the Very Large Dog. Harrington, Claudia. 2016. (Hank the Pet Sitter Ser.). (ENG.). 32p. (J). (gr. -1-3). lib. bdg. 28.50 *(978-1-62402-187-9(5),* 24553, Calico Chapter Bks) Magic Wagon.

—Book 2: Pickles the Very Hungry Pig. Harrington, Claudia. 2016. (Hank the Pet Sitter Ser.). (ENG.). 32p. (J). (gr. -1-3). lib. bdg. 28.50 *(978-1-62402-188-6(3),* 24555, Calico Chapter Bks) Magic Wagon.

—Book 3: Yum-Yum the Very Spoiled Fish. Harrington, Claudia. 2016. (Hank the Pet Sitter Ser.). (ENG.). 32p. (J). (gr. -1-3). lib. bdg. 28.50 *(978-1-62402-189-3(1),* 24557, Calico Chapter Bks) Magic Wagon.

—Book 4: Elmer the Very Sneaky Sheep. Harrington, Claudia. 2016. (Hank the Pet Sitter Ser.). (ENG.). 32p. (J). (gr. -1-3). lib. bdg. 28.50 *(978-1-62402-190-9(5),* 24559, Calico Chapter Bks) Magic Wagon.

—Book 5: Ralph the Very Quick Chick. Harrington, Claudia. 2018. (Hank the Pet Sitter Ser.). (ENG.). 32p. (J). (gr. -1-3). lib. bdg. 28.50 *(978-1-5321-3173-8(9),* 28441, Calico Chapter Bks) Magic Wagon.

—Book 6: Pete the Very Chatty Parrot. Harrington, Claudia. 2018. (Hank the Pet Sitter Ser.). (ENG.). 32p. (J). (gr. -1-3). lib. bdg. 28.50 *(978-1-5321-3174-5(7),* 28443, Calico Chapter Bks) Magic Wagon.

—Book 7: Fawn the Very Small Deer. Harrington, Claudia. 2018. (Hank the Pet Sitter Ser.). (ENG.). 32p. (J). (gr. -1-3). lib. bdg. 28.50 *(978-1-5321-3175-2(5),* 28445, Calico Chapter Bks) Magic Wagon.

—Book 8: Otis the Very Scared Dog. Harrington, Claudia. 2018. (Hank the Pet Sitter Ser.). (ENG.). 32p. (J). (gr. -1-3). lib. bdg. 28.50 *(978-1-5321-3176-9(3),* 28447, Calico Chapter Bks) Magic Wagon.

—Bug Girl. Harper, Benjamin et al. 2017. (Bug Girl Ser.: 1). (ENG.). 304p. (J). 14.99 *(978-1-250-10661-2(3),* 900164625) Imprint IND. Dist: Macmillan.

—Bug Girl: Fury on the Dance Floor. Harper, Benjamin & Stephens, Sarah Hines. 2018. (Bug Girl Ser.: 2). (ENG.). 304p. (J). 14.99 *(978-1-250-10663-6(X),* 900164628) Imprint IND. Dist: Macmillan.

—Hank el Cuida-Mascotas Set 2 (Hank the Pet Sitter Set 2) (Set), 4 vols. Harrington, Claudia. 2019. (Hank el Cuida-Mascotas (Hank the Pet Sitter) Ser.). (SPA.). 32p. (J). (gr. -1-3). lib. bdg. 114.00 *(978-1-5321-3760-0(5),* 33786, Calico Chapter Bks) Magic Wagon.

—Hank the Pet Sitter Set 2 (Set), 4 vols. Harrington, Claudia. 2018. (Hank the Pet Sitter Ser.). 32p. (J). (gr. -1-3). lib. bdg. 108.28 *(978-1-5321-3172-1(0),* 28439, Calico Chapter Bks) Magic Wagon.

—How I Did It. Ragsdale, Linda. 2017. (Peace Dragon Tales Ser.). (ENG.). 32p. (J). (gr. -1-3). 16.99 *(978-1-4867-1211-3(8),* 7b35ff60-0fae-47e0-9cca-41c6ff71c8df) Flowerpot Pr.

—I Am Perfectly Designed. Brown, Karamo & Brown, Jason "Rachel". 2019. (ENG.). 40p. (J). 18.99 *(978-1-250-23221-2(X),* 900209767, Holt, Henry & Co. Bks. For Young Readers) Holt, Henry & Co.

—Kid Scientists: True Tales of Childhood from Science Superstars. Stabler, David. 2018. (Kid Legends Ser.: 5). 208p. (J). (gr. 4-7). 13.99 *(978-1-68369-074-0(5))* Quirk Bks.

—Monster & Boy. Barnaby, Hannah. 2020. (Monster & Boy Ser.: 1). (ENG.). 144p. (J). 13.99 *(978-1-250-21783-7(0),* 900207062, Holt, Henry & Co. Bks. For Young Readers) Holt, Henry & Co.

—Piper Cooks up a Plan. Soderberg, Erin. 2019. (Disney: Daring Dreamers Club Ser.: 2). (ENG.). 224p. (J). (gr. 3-7). 13.99 *(978-0-7364-3944-2(7),* RH/Disney) Random Hse. Children's Bks.

—#1 Otis el Grandísimo Perro (Book 1: Otis the Very Large Dog) Harrington, Claudia. 2018. (Hank el Cuida-Mascotas (Hank the Pet Sitter) Ser.). (SPA.). 32p. (J). (gr. -1-3). lib. bdg. 28.50 *(978-1-5321-3326-8(X),* 28515, Calico Chapter Bks) Magic Wagon.

—#2 Pickles el Cerdito Muy Hambriento (Book 2: Pickles the Very Hungry Pig) Harrington, Claudia. 2018. (Hank el Cuida-Mascotas (Hank the Pet Sitter) Ser.). (SPA.). 32p. (J). (gr. -1-3). lib. bdg. 28.50 *(978-1-5321-3327-5(8),* 28517, Calico Chapter Bks) Magic Wagon.

—#3 Ñam-Ñam el Pececito Muy Consentido (Book 3: Yum-Yum the Very Spoiled Fish) Harrington, Claudia. 2018. (Hank el Cuida-Mascotas (Hank the Pet Sitter) Ser.). (SPA.). 32p. (J). (gr. -1-3). lib. bdg. 28.50 *(978-1-5321-3328-2(6),* 28519, Calico Chapter Bks) Magic Wagon.

—#4 Elmer la Oveja Sigilosa (Book 4: Elmer the Very Sneaky Sheep) Harrington, Claudia. 2018. (Hank el Cuida-Mascotas (Hank the Pet Sitter) Ser.). (SPA.). 32p. (J). (gr. -1-3). lib. bdg. 28.50 *(978-1-5321-3329-9(4),* 28521, Calico Chapter Bks) Magic Wagon.

—#5 Raúl el Pollito Muy Rápido (Book 5: Ralph the Very Quick Chick) Harrington, Claudia. 2019. (Hank el Cuida-Mascotas (Hank the Pet Sitter) Ser.). (SPA.). 32p. (J). (gr. -1-3). lib. bdg. 28.50 *(978-1-5321-3761-7(3),* 33788, Calico Chapter Bks) Magic Wagon.

—#6 Pedro el Loro Muy Hablador (Book 6: Pete the Very Chatty Parrot) Harrington, Claudia. 2019. (Hank el Cuida-Mascotas (Hank the Pet Sitter) Ser.). (SPA.). 32p. (J). (gr. -1-3). lib. bdg. 28.50 *(978-1-5321-3762-4(1),* 33790, Calico Chapter Bks) Magic Wagon.

—#7 Fawn el Ciervo Muy Pequeño (Book 7: Fawn the Very Small Deer) Harrington, Claudia. 2019. (Hank el Cuida-Mascotas (Hank the Pet Sitter) Ser.). (SPA.). 32p. (J). (gr. -1-3). lib. bdg. 28.50 *(978-1-5321-3763-1(X),* 33792, Calico Chapter Bks) Magic Wagon.

—#8 Otis el Perro Muy Asustado (Book 8: Otis the Very Scared Dog) Harrington, Claudia. 2019. (Hank el Cuida-Mascotas (Hank the Pet Sitter) Ser.). (SPA.). 32p. (J). (gr. -1-3). lib. bdg. 28.50 *(978-1-5321-3764-8(8),* 33794, Calico Chapter Bks) Magic Wagon.

Syed, Anoosha, jt. illus. see RH Disney.

Sygh, Rian, et al. The Backstagers Vol. 3. Tynion Iv, James & Johns, Sam. 2019. (Backstagers Ser.). (ENG.). 96p. (J). (gr. 8-12). pap. 14.99 *(978-1-68415-332-9(8))* Boom! Studios.

Sygh, Rian & BOOM! Studios. The Backstagers & the Final Blackout (Backstagers #3) Mientus, Andy. 2019. (Backstagers Ser.). (ENG.). 208p. (J). (gr. 5-9). 14.99 *(978-1-4197-3865-4(8),* Amulet Bks.) Abrams, Inc.

—The Backstagers & the Ghost Light (Backstagers #1) Mientus, Andy. 2018. (ENG.). 208p. (J). (gr. 5-9). 14.99 *(978-1-4197-3120-4(3),* Amulet Bks.) Abrams, Inc.

Sygh, Rian & BOOM! Studios. The Backstagers & the Ghost Light (Backstagers #1) Mientus, Andy. 2020. (ENG.). 224p. (J). (gr. 5-9). pap. 8.99 ***(978-1-4197-3694-0(9),*** Amulet Bks.) Abrams, Inc.

Sygh, Rian & BOOM! Studios. The Backstagers & the Theater of the Ancients (Backstagers #2) Mientus, Andy. 2020. (ENG.). 208p. (J). (gr. 5-9). pap. 8.99 *(978-1-4197-4270-5(1),* Amulet Bks.) Abrams, Inc.

—The Backstagers & the Theater of the Ancients (Backstagers #2) Mientus, Andy. 2019. (ENG.). 192p. (J). (gr. 5-9). 14.99 *(978-1-4197-3365-9(6),* Amulet Bks.) Abrams, Inc.

Sygh, Rian, jt. illus. see Rupert, Mad.

Sykes, Christine. The Adventures of Charlie & Mae: A Puppy Comes Home. Devlin, Julia. 2019. (ENG.). 30p. (J). 29.95 *(978-1-9772-0975-7(0))* Outskirts Pr., Inc.

Sykes M D, Robin a. MacGregor. MacGregor, Nancy. 2018. (ENG.). 28p. (J). *(978-1-5255-2925-2(0));* pap. *(978-1-5255-2926-9(9))* FriesenPress.

Sykes M D, Robin a. Macgregor & the Sea Turtles. MacGregor, Nancy. 2019. (ENG.). 28p. (J). ***(978-1-5255-6409-3(9));*** pap. ***(978-1-5255-6410-9(2))*** FriesenPress.

Sykes, Shannon. A Cub Explores. Love, Pamela. ed. 2004. (ENG.). 32p. (J). (gr. -1-17). 15.95 *(978-0-89272-593-9(1))* Down East Bks.

Syler, Rachel. The Heart of a Princess. Ivey, Casi. 2018. (ENG.). 30p. (J). 20.00 *(978-0-9990716-6-3(1))* Grassleaf Publishing.

Sylvada, Peter. Firefly Mountain, 1 vol. Thomas, Patricia. 2007. (ENG.). 32p. (J). (gr. 1-5). 16.95 *(978-1-56145-360-3(9))* Peachtree Publishing Co. Inc.

—Gleam & Glow. Bunting, Eve. 2005. (ENG.). 32p. (J). (gr. -1-3). reprint ed. pap. 7.99 *(978-0-15-205380-2(8),* 1196199) Houghton Mifflin Harcourt Publishing Co.

—Yatandou. Whelan, Gloria. rev. ed. 2007. (Tales of the World Ser.). (ENG.). 32p. (J). (gr. 1-4). 17.95 *(978-1-58536-211-0(5),* 202042) Sleeping Bear Pr.

Sylvaine, Jenny. The Mouse & the Wizard: A Hindu Folktale. Malaspina, Ann. 2013. (Folktales from Around the World Ser.). (ENG.). 24p. (J). (gr. k-3). 28.50 *(978-1-62323-633-5(9),* 206384) Child's World, Inc., The.

Sylvester, Kevin. And the Crowd Goes Wild! A Global Gathering of Sports Poems. Hoyte, Carol-Ann. Roemer, Heidi Bee, ed. 2012. 80p. pap. *(978-1-77097-953-6(0))* FriesenPress.

—Don't Touch That Toad & Other Strange Things Adults Tell You. Rondina, Catherine. 96p. (J). (gr. 2-5). 2014. (ENG.). pap. 8.95 *(978-1-55453-455-5(0));* 2010. 14.95 *(978-1-55453-454-8(2))* Kids Can Pr., Ltd. CAN. Dist: Hachette Bk. Group.

—Great. Holomis, Lauri & Gretzky, Glen. 32p. (J). (gr. -1-3). 2018. pap. 8.99 *(978-0-7352-6513-4(5));* 2016. 16.99 *(978-0-670-06990-3(6))* PRH Canada Young Readers CAN. (Puffin Canada). Dist: Penguin Random Hse. LLC.

—Neil Flambé & the Aztec Abduction. 2010. (Neil Flambé Capers Ser.: No. 2). 304p. (J). (gr. 4-7). *(978-1-55470-329-6(8))* Me to We.

Sylvester, Kevin. Neil Flambé & the Aztec Abduction. Sylvester, Kevin. 2014. (Neil Flambe Capers Ser.: 2). (ENG.). 336p. (J). (gr. 3-7). pap. 8.99 *(978-1-4424-4608-3(0),* Simon & Schuster Bks. For Young Readers) Simon & Schuster Bks. For Young Readers.

—Neil Flambé & the Bard's Banquet. Sylvester, Kevin. 2015. (Neil Flambe Capers Ser.: 5). (ENG.). 320p. (J). (gr. 3-7). 12.99 *(978-1-4814-1038-0(5),* Simon & Schuster Bks. For Young Readers) Simon & Schuster Bks. For Young Readers.

—Neil Flambé & the Crusader's Curse. Sylvester, Kevin. 2014. (Neil Flambe Capers Ser.: 3). (ENG.). 320p. (J). (gr. 3-7). pap. 7.99 *(978-1-4424-4287-0(5),* Simon & Schuster Bks. For Young Readers) Simon & Schuster Bks. For Young Readers.

—Neil Flambé & the Duel in the Desert. Sylvester, Kevin. (Neil Flambe Capers Ser.: 6). (ENG.). 304p. (J). (gr. 3-7). 2017. pap. 8.99 *(978-1-4814-1042-7(3));* 2016. 13.99 *(978-1-4814-1041-0(5))* Simon & Schuster Bks. For Young Readers. (Simon & Schuster Bks. For Young Readers).

—Neil Flambé & the Marco Polo Murders. Sylvester, Kevin. (Neil Flambe Capers Ser.: 1). (ENG.). (J). (gr. 3-7). 2014. 320p. pap. 8.99 *(978-1-4424-4605-2(6));* 2012. 304p. 14.99 *(978-1-4424-4604-5(8))* Simon & Schuster Bks. For Young Readers. (Simon & Schuster Bks. For Young Readers).

—Neil Flambé & the Tokyo Treasure. Sylvester, Kevin. (Neil Flambe Capers Ser.: 4). (ENG.). (J). (gr. 3-7). 2014. 368p. pap. 7.99 *(978-1-4424-4289-4(1));* 2012. 352p. 13.99 *(978-1-4424-4288-7(3))* Simon & Schuster Bks. For Young Readers. (Simon & Schuster Bks. For Young Readers).

—The Neil Flambé Capers Collection: Neil Flambé & the Marco Polo Murders; Neil Flambé & the Aztec Abduction; Neil Flambé & the Crusader's Curse; Neil Flambé & the Tokyo Treasure. Sylvester, Kevin. ed. 2014. (Neil Flambe Capers Ser.). (ENG.). 1344p. (J). (gr. 3-7). pap. 31.99 *(978-1-4814-3238-2(9),* Simon & Schuster Bks. For Young Readers) Simon & Schuster Bks. For Young Readers.

Sylvestre, Daniel. Aimez-Vous la Musique? Desrosiers, Sylvie. 2004. (Roman Jeunesse Ser.). (FRE.). 96p. (J). (gr. 4-7). pap. *(978-2-89021-709-6(4))* Diffusion du livre Mirabel (DLM).

—Deux Squelettes au Téléphone. Duggan, Paul. 2004. (Picture Bks.). (FRE.). 32p. (J). (gr. 4). *(978-2-89021-677-8(2))* Diffusion du livre Mirabel (DLM).

—Ophelia, 1 vol. Gingras, Charlotte. Morelli, Christelle & Ouriou, Susan, trs. 2018. (ENG.). 264p. (YA). (gr. 8). 16.95 *(978-1-77306-099-6(6))* Groundwood Bks. CAN. Dist: Publishers Group West (PGW).

—Qui Veut Entrer dans la Legende? Desrosiers, Sylvie. 2003. (Roman Jeunesse Ser.). (FRE.). 96p. (YA). (gr. 4-7). pap. *(978-2-89021-269-5(6))* Diffusion du livre Mirabel (DLM).

Symington, Lindsay. An Alphabet of Saints. Benson, Robert Hugh. 2013. (ENG.). 32p. (J). (gr. -1-k). reprint ed. 16.95 *(978-1-930873-12-4(3),* Neumann Pr.) TAN Bks.

—The Children's Hour of Heaven on Earth. McNabb, Vincent. 2007. 48p. per. 21.95 *(978-0-9782985-2-4(7))* Catholic Authors Pr.

Symington, Sabrina. The Junk Drawer. Karten, Ryan. 2017. (ENG.). 34p. (J). (gr. 2-6). 13.99 *(978-0-9987424-1-0(4))* Karten, Ryan.

Symmons, Sheeres. From Bondage to Freedom: A Tale of the Times of Mohammed. Leslie, Emma. 2007. 308p. 24.95 *(978-1-934671-10-8(X))* Salem Ridge Press LLC.

Synarski, Susan & Johnson, Karen. Cool Tricks for Kids. Gordon, Lynn & Chronicle Books Staff. 2008. (ENG.). 54p. (gr. 8-17). 6.95 *(978-0-8118-6374-2(3))* Chronicle Bks. LLC.

Synarski, Susan, jt. illus. see Johnson, Karen.

Synepolsky, I. & Belomlinsky, M. Volleyball with the Family: Fife Steps to Success. Slupskiy, Leon. 2003. 105/35p. (YA). pap. *(978-0-9728301-3-3(8))* Publishing Hse. Gelany.

Synge, E. M. The Awakening of Europe (Yesterday's Classics) Synge, M. B. I.t. ed. 2006. 268p. (J). per. 11.95 *(978-1-59915-015-4(8))* Yesterday's Classics.

—The Discovery of New Worlds (Yesterday's Classics) Synge, M. B. I.t. ed. 2006. 252p. (J). per. *(978-1-59915-014-7(X))* Yesterday's Classics.

—The Growth of the British Empire (Yesterday's Classics) Synge, M. B. 2006. 284p. (YA). per. 11.95 *(978-1-59915-017-8(4))* Yesterday's Classics.

—On the Shores of the Great Sea (Yesterday's Classics) Synge, M. B. I.t. ed. 2006. 240p. (J). per. 11.95 *(978-1-59915-013-0(1))* Yesterday's Classics.

Synge, E. M. The Struggle for Sea Power: A History of the British, French & Spanish Empires & Their Naval Wars Across Europe. Synge, M. B. 2020. (ENG.). 120p. (J). pap. ***(978-1-78987-248-4(0))*** Pantianos Classics.

Synge, E. M. The Struggle for Sea Power (Yesterday's Classics) Synge, M. B. I.t. ed. 2006. 276p. (J). per. 11.95 *(978-1-59915-016-1(6))* Yesterday's Classics.

System, Eminence. The Forgetful Chicken. Patterson, Keyonna. 2019. (ENG.). 20p. (J). 17.99 ***(978-0-578-55517-1(4))*** Patterson, Keyonna.

System, Eminence. The Happyfeet Kids Load the Train. Dione, Donald. Dione, Donna, ed. 2017. (Happyfeet Kids Ser.: Vol. 2). (ENG.). 34p. (J). 19.99 *(978-0-9992492-2-2(3))* HappyFeet Bks.

—The Happyfeet Kids Make New Friends. Dione, Donald. Dione, Donna, ed. 2018. (Happyfeet Kids Ser.: Vol. 1). (ENG.). 34p. (J). 19.99 *(978-0-9992492-5-3(8))* HappyFeet Bks.

Szabo, Levente. Elementals: Battle Born. Kaufman, Amie. 2020. (Elementals Ser.: 3). (ENG.). 272p. (J). (gr. 3-7). 16.99 *(978-0-06-245804-9(3),* HarperCollins) HarperCollins Pubs. Ltd. GBR. Dist: HarperCollins Pubs.

—Elementals: Ice Wolves. Kaufman, Amie. (Elementals Ser.: 1). (ENG.). (J). (gr. 3-7). 2019. 368p. pap. 6.99 *(978-0-06-245799-8(3));* 2018. 352p. 16.99 *(978-0-06-245798-1(5))* HarperCollins Pubs.

—Ice Wolves. Kaufman, Amie. 2018. 432p. *(978-1-4607-5527-3(8))* Harper & Row Ltd.

Szafranski, Keith. Barrington Bear Visits the Emperor - the Emperor Penguin That Is. Szafranski, Keith. 2008. (ENG.). 48p. (J). 19.95 *(978-0-9801662-0-0(9))* Small Bear Publishing.

Szalay, Dave. The True Story of Zippy Chippy: The Little Horse That Couldn't. Bennett, Artie. 2020. (ENG.). 40p. (J). (gr. -1-3). 17.95 *(978-0-7358-4396-7(1))* North-South Bks., Inc.

Szanyi, Joshua. The Purple Polka-Dotted Peanut Butter Eater. Roemisch, Matt. 2019. (ENG.). 32p. (J). (gr. k-5). 17.99 ***(978-0-578-53394-0(4))*** Roemisch, Matt Graphic Design.

Szecsi, Susan. On the Walk Trail: Japan. Carlson, Jon C. 2017. (On the Walk Trail Ser.). (ENG.). 34p. (J). (gr. k-2). 17.95 *(978-1-63132-045-3(9))* Advanced Publishing LLC.

—Synchro Sisters Forever: Mermaid Dreams. Migliore, John, photos by. Reveno, Katie. 2017. (ENG.). (J). (gr. k-5). pap. 14.99 *(978-0-692-94881-1(3))* Reveno, Katherine.

—Yes, I Can Listen! Metzger, Steve. 2019. (ENG.). 32p. (J). (gr. k-2). 16.99 *(978-1-64160-174-0(4))* Parenting Pr., Inc.

Szegedi, Katalin. Ambrose & the Cathedral Dream. Sorenson, Margo. 2006. (ENG.). 32p. (J). (gr. -1-3). pap. 4.24 *(978-0-8146-3004-4(9))* Liturgical Pr.

—Ambrose & the Princess. Sorenson, Margo. 2005. (ENG.). 32p. (J). (gr. -1-3). 16.95 *(978-0-8146-3043-3(X))* Liturgical Pr.

—El Peso de Una Misa: Un Relato de Fe. Nobisso, Josephine. 2003. Orig. Title: The Weight of a Mass a Tale of Faith. (SPA.). 32p. (J). (gr. k-2). pap. 9.95 *(978-0-940112-17-9(5))* Gingerbread Hse.

—El Peso de Una Misa: Un Relato de Fe. Nobisso, Josephine. 2003. Orig. Title: The Weight of a Mass a Tale of Faith. (SPA.). 32p. (J). (gr. k-2). 17.95 *(978-0-940112-15-5(9))* Gingerbread Hse.

—Take It to the Queen: A Tale of Hope. Nobisso, Josephine. 2008. (ENG.). 32p. (J). (gr. k-2). 17.95 *(978-0-940112-19-3(1));* pap. 9.95 *(978-0-940112-21-6(3))* Gingerbread Hse.

Szekeres, Cyndy & McElmurry, Jill. When Otis Courted Mama. Appelt, Kathi. 2015. (ENG.). 40p. (J). (gr. -1-3). 17.99 *(978-0-15-216688-5(2),* 1201655, HMH Books For Young Readers) Houghton Mifflin Harcourt Publishing Co.

Szereszewski, Haley Rose. Two Dark Moons. Silver, Avi. Tristen, Sienna, ed. 2019. (Sãoni Cycle Ser.: Vol. 1). (ENG.). 250p. (YA). (gr. 8-12). pap. *(978-1-7752427-2-7(2))* Molewhale Pr.

Szewczyk, Manda. Messy Penny. Weber, Roopa. 2013. 38p. pap. 11.99 *(978-0-9896966-2-3(6))* Karma Kollection LLC.

Szijgyarto, Cynthia, jt. illus. see Broughton, Ilona.

Szilagyi, Mary. Big & Little. Krauss, Ruth. 2003. (J). pap. 12.95 *(978-0-590-40698-7(1))* Scholastic, Inc.

—Night in the Country. Rylant, Cynthia. 2014. 32p. pap. 7.00 *(978-1-61003-359-6(0))* Center for the Collaborative Classroom.

Szlapa, Rafal. The Unbreakable Zamperini: A World War II Survivor's Brave Story. Yomtov, Nel. 2019. (Amazing World War II Stories Ser.). (ENG.). 32p. (J). (gr. 3-9). pap. 7.95 *(978-1-5435-7548-4(X),* 141080); lib. bdg. 34.65 *(978-1-5435-7313-8(4),* 140618) Capstone.

Szmidt, Aleksandra. Grandma Hugs. Hall, Hannah C. 2019. (ENG.). 20p. (J). (gr. -1-1). bds. 6.99 *(978-0-8249-5697-4(4),* Worthy Kids/Ideals) Worthy Publishing.

—Grandpa Love. Hall, Hannah C. 2019. 20p. (J). (gr. -1-1). bds. 6.99 *(978-0-8249-5698-1(2),* Worthy Kids/Ideals) Worthy Publishing.

Szuc, Jeff. Have You Ever Seen a Stork Build a Log Cabin? Kaner, Etta. 2010. (Have You Ever Seen Ser.). 32p. (J). (gr. -1-2). 14.95 *(978-1-55453-336-7(8))* Kids Can Pr., Ltd. CAN. Dist: Hachette Bk. Group.

—Have You Ever Seen an Octopus with a Broom? Kaner, Etta. 2009. (Have You Ever Seen Ser.). 32p. (J). (gr. -1-2). 14.95 *(978-1-55453-247-6(7))* Kids Can Pr., Ltd. CAN. Dist: Hachette Bk. Group.

Szucs, Barbara Szepesi. If You're Happy & You Know It, 1 vol. 2017. (Sing-Along Book Ser.). (ENG.). 20p. (J). bds. 8.99 *(978-0-310-75922-5(6))* Zonderkidz.

Szulyovszky, Sarolta. The Boy & the Goats. Hillert, Margaret. 2016. (BeginningtoRead Ser.). (ENG.). 32p. (J). (-2). lib. bdg. 22.60 *(978-1-59953-777-1(X))* Norwood Hse. Pr.

—El niño y los Chivos. Hillert, Margaret. 2018. (BeginningtoRead Ser.). (SPA.). 32p. (J). (gr. -1-2). pap. 11.94 *(978-1-68404-236-4(4))* Norwood Hse. Pr.

Szulyovszky, Sarolta. El Nino y Los Chivos. Szulyovszky, Sarolta. Hillert, Margaret & Del Risco, Eida. 2018. (BeginningtoRead Ser.). (SPA.). 32p. (J). (gr. -1-2). lib. bdg. 22.60 *(978-1-59953-952-2(7))* Norwood Hse. Pr.

Szulyovszky, Sarolta, jt. illus. see Jack Pullan.

T

T, M. O. My Secret Super-Powers 2: A Hilarious Adventure for Kids of All Ages 2. Wolly, Paul T. Adventure Books, ed. 2017. (ENG.). 72p. (J). pap. *(978-3-946819-11-0(7))* Obst, Hartmut. be-to-ce_publishing.

T, N. Magic in Us. the Power of Imagination: The Power of Imagination, bks. 1, vol. 2. Tinti, Natalie. ed. 2013. (Sewing a Friendship Ser.). (ENG.). 116p. (J). pap. 12.95 *(978-0-9842625-3-3(9))* Tintinatie Publishing Hse.

T. W. Zimmerman. The Day the Horse Was Free. Dodgson, Y. K. 2004. 16p. (J). 11.95 *(978-0-9748091-0-6(1))* Alaska Avenue Pr.

T?s?ygankova, I. Veselye Stikhi. Usache?v, Andrei?. 2017. (RUS.). 63p. (J). *(978-5-17-101509-1(0))* AST Ltd., Izdatel'stvo.

Taback, Simms. Road Builders. Hennessy, B. G. 2018. (ENG.). 32p. (J). (— 1). bds. 6.99 *(978-0-425-29121-4(9),* Viking Books for Young Readers) Penguin Young Readers Group.

—Two Little Witches: A Halloween Counting Story. Ziefert, Harriet. 2007. (ENG.). 32p. (J). (gr. k-k). pap. 3.99 *(978-0-7636-3309-7(7))* Candlewick Pr.

Taback, Simms. Joseph Had a Little Overcoat. Taback, Simms. pap. incl. audio compact disk *(978-1-59112-608-9(8))* Live Oak Media.

Tabacon, Marvin. Growing up Lucky: A Young Magician's Travels in the American Civil War. Copeland, Billy M. 2018. (ENG.). 236p. (YA). (gr. 7-12). 28.99 *(978-1-943492-40-4(9))*; pap. 15.99 *(978-1-943492-41-1(7))* Elm Grove Publishing.

Tabaranza, Jeanelle. Las Aventuras de Mar. Richards, Anthony. 2018. (SPA.). 26p. (J). pap. 10.99 *(978-1-7290-0886-7(0))* Independently Published.

—A Magical Journey of Jamie's Big Adventure. Richards, Anthony. 2018. (Ten Minute Tales Ser.: Vol. 4). (ENG.). 28p. (J). pap. 10.99 *(978-1-7908-3221-7(7))* Independently Published.

Tabares, Bridgitt. Monkeys on an Island. Tabares, Veronica. 2012. 32p. (J). pap. 14.50 *(978-1-60916-005-0(3))* Sun Break Publishing.

Tabary. The Grand Vizier Iznogoud, Vol. 9. Goscinny, René. 2012. (Iznogoud Ser.: 9). (ENG.). 52p. (J). (gr. 3-12). pap. 13.95 *(978-1-84918-131-0(4))* CineBook GBR. Dist: National Bk. Network.

—Iznogoud - The Infamous, Vol. 7. Goscinny, René. 2011. (Iznogoud Ser.: 7). (ENG.). 48p. (gr. 3-17). pap. 11.95 *(978-1-84918-074-0(1))* CineBook GBR. Dist: National Bk. Network.

—Iznogoud & the Magic Carpet. Goscinny, René. 2010. (Iznogoud Ser.: 6). (ENG.). 46p. (J). (gr. 3-17). pap. 11.95 *(978-1-84918-044-3(X))* CineBook GBR. Dist: National Bk. Network.

—Rockets to Stardom - Iznogoud, Vol. 8. Goscinny, René. 2011. (Iznogoud Ser.: 8). (ENG.). 48p. pap. 11.95 *(978-1-84918-092-4(X))* CineBook GBR. Dist: National Bk. Network.

Tabary, Armelle. The Wicked Wiles of Iznogoud, Vol. 1. Goscinny, René. 2008. (Iznogoud Ser.: 1). (ENG.). 48p. (J). (gr. -1-12). pap. 13.95 *(978-1-905460-46-5(5))* CineBook GBR. Dist: National Bk. Network.

Tabary, Jean. Iznogoud Vol. 10: Iznogoud the Relentless. Goscinny, René. 2013. (Iznogoud Ser.: 10). (ENG.). 48p. (J). (gr. 3-12). pap. 11.95 *(978-1-84918-181-5(0))* CineBook GBR. Dist: National Bk. Network.

Tabatabaei, Maryam. Stone Soup with Matzoh Balls: A Passover Tale in Chelm. Glaser, Linda. 2014. (AV2 Fiction Readalong Ser.: Vol. 111). (ENG.). (J). (gr. -1-2). lib. bdg. 34.28 *(978-1-4896-2416-1(3)*, AV2 by Weigl) Weigl Pubs., Inc.

—Stone Soup with Matzoh Balls: A Passover Tale in Chelm. Glaser, Linda. 2014. (ENG.). 32p. (J). (gr. -1-2). 16.99 *(978-0-8075-7620-5(4))* Whitman, Albert & Co.

Tabbutt, Steven. Alphabet of Art. Gates Galvin, Laura. 2011. (ENG.). 40p. (J). 9.95 *(978-1-60727-196-3(6))* Soundprints.

Taber, Melissa. Virginia (Jennie) Claypool Meredith: An Amazing Woman, Ahead of Her Time. Hamilton, Bailey & Hormel, Margaret. 2014. 25p. (J). *(978-0-9899472-5-1(4))* Kids At Heart Publishing, LLC.

Tabilio, Marco. Marco Polo: Dangers & Visions. Tabilio, Marco. 2017. (ENG.). 208p. (YA). (gr. 9-12). pap. 11.99 *(978-1-5124-3069-1(2)*, 9781512430691, Graphic Universe™) Lerner Publishing Group.

—Marco Polo: The Silk Road. Tabilio, Marco. Schwandt, Kerstin. 2017. 208p. (YA). (gr. 9-12). 29.32 *(978-1-5124-1182-9(5)*, 9781512411829, Graphic Universe™) Lerner Publishing Group.

Tablason, Jamie. Hawaiian Christmas Day. Greenway, Beth. 2018. (ENG.). 28p. (J). (gr. -1-2). 12.95 *(978-1-949000-01-6(X))* Beachhouse Publishing, LLC.

—Ice Queen: Exploring Icebergs & Glaciers. Prokos, Anna. 2017. (Imagine That! Ser.). (ENG.). 32p. (J). (gr. 2-4). lib. bdg. 26.65 *(978-1-63440-149-4(2))*; E-Book 39.99 *(978-1-63440-161-6(1))* Red Chair Pr.

—Sippi Sue & the Cool Cat Blues, 1 vol. Greenway, Beth. 2017. (ENG.). 32p. (J). (gr. -1-8). 16.99 *(978-1-4556-2267-2(2)*, Pelican Publishing) Arcadia Publishing.

Tabler, Marie. One Pea. Tabler, Marie. Meyer, Julia. 2013. 36p. 14.95 *(978-1-62314-139-4(7))* ePub Bud.

Tableson, Jamie. Big Brave Bold Sergio. Wagenbach, Debbie. 2018. 32p. (J). *(978-1-4338-2794-5(8))* American Psychological Assn.

Tabor, Corey R. Fox & the Bike Ride. Tabor, Corey R. 2017. (ENG.). 32p. (J). (gr. -1-3). 17.99 *(978-0-06-239875-8(X)*, Balzer & Bray) HarperCollins Pubs.

—Fox & the Jumping Contest. Tabor, Corey R. 2016. (ENG.). 32p. (J). (gr. -1-3). 17.99 *(978-0-06-239874-1(1))* HarperCollins Pubs.

—Fox Is Late. Tabor, Corey R. 2018. (My First I Can Read Ser.). (ENG.). 32p. (J). (gr. -1-3). 16.99 *(978-0-06-239872-7(5))*; pap. 4.99 *(978-0-06-239871-0(7))* HarperCollins Pubs. (Balzer & Bray).

—Fox the Tiger. Tabor, Corey R. 2018. (My First I Can Read Ser.). (ENG.). 32p. (J). (gr. -1-3). 16.99 *(978-0-06-239869-7(5))*; pap. 4.99 *(978-0-06-239867-3(9))* HarperCollins Pubs. (Balzer & Bray).

—Snail Crossing. Tabor, Corey R. 2020. (ENG.). 40p. (J). (gr. -1-3). 17.99 *(978-0-06-287800-7(X)*, Balzer & Bray) HarperCollins Pubs.

Tabor, Nancy Maria Grande. Celebraciones: Dias Feriados de los Estados Unidos y Mexico. Tabor, Nancy Maria Grande. ed. 2004. (Charlesbridge Bilingual Bks.).Tr. of Celebrations - Holidays of the United States of America & Mexico. 32p. (J). (gr. -1-2). pap. 7.95 *(978-1-57091-550-5(4))* Charlesbridge Publishing, Inc.

—Somos un Arco Iris (We Are a Rainbow) Tabor, Nancy Maria Grande. 2006. (ENG & SPA.). 28p. (gr. -1-3). 17.95 *(978-0-7569-7027-7(X))* Perfection Learning Corp.

Tabor, Nathan. Peekaboo Barn. Sims, Nat. 2014. (Peekaboo Ser.). (ENG.). 20p. (J). (— 1). bds. 7.99 *(978-0-7636-7557-8(1)*, Candlewick Entertainment) Candlewick Pr.

—Peekaboo Barn / ¿Quién Está en el Granero? Sims, Nat. 2017. (SPA.). 20p. (J). (— 1). bds. 7.99 *(978-0-7636-9315-2(4)*, Candlewick Entertainment) Candlewick Pr.

Tacey, Romaine. Avery Sleeps More Readily: A Whispered Good Night Fairy Book. Frances, Renee. Curk, Mary, ed. 2018. (Good Night Fairy Book Ser.: Vol. 3). (ENG.). 24p. (J). (gr. k-6). pap. *(978-0-9950247-3-1(1))*; (gr. 1-6). *(978-0-9950247-4-8(X))* Stuff, Somnus.

—Tiger the Dog. del Re, Joey. 2017. (ENG.). 40p. (J). (gr. k-3). 24.99 *(978-0-692-99876-2(4))* Re, Joseph Del.

Tachibana, Yutaka. Gatcha Gacha, 8 vols., Vol. 1. Tachibana, Yutaka. Tachibana, Yutaka. 2006. (Gatcha Gacha Ser.). 208p. pap. 9.99 *(978-1-59816-153-3(9))* TOKYOPOP, Inc.

Tackett, Mike. Kai: The Honu Didn't Know He Was Brave. Mora, Ebie. 2005. 24p. (J). 12.95 *(978-1-56647-755-0(7))* Mutual Publishing LLC.

Tadema-Wielandt, Rebecca. Arizona Lucy. Truchan - Schulte, Carol. 2007. (ENG.). 34p. per. 14.99 *(978-1-4257-7368-7(0))* Xlibris Corp.

Tadgell, Nicole. Astronaut Annie. Slade, Suzanne. (ENG.). 36p. (J). (gr. k-3). 2020. pap. 9.95 ***(978-0-88448-574-2(9)***, 884574); 2018. 17.95 *(978-0-88448-523-0(4)*, 884523) Tilbury Hse. Pubs.

Tadgell, Nicole. A Day with Daddy. Scholastic, Inc. Staff & Grimes, Nikki. 2004. (Just for You Ser.). (ENG.). 32p. pap. 3.99 *(978-0-439-56850-0(1)*, Teaching Resources) Scholastic, Inc.

—First Peas to the Table. Grigsby, Susan. 2013. (AV2 Fiction Readalong Ser.). (ENG.). (J). (gr. 1-4). 34.28 *(978-1-62127-876-4(X)*, AV2 by Weigl) Weigl Pubs., Inc.

—First Peas to the Table: How Thomas Jefferson Inspired a School Garden. Grigsby, Susan. 2012. (ENG.). 32p. (J). (gr. 1-3). 16.99 *(978-0-8075-2452-7(2)*, 807524522) Whitman, Albert & Co.

—A Fist for Joe Louis & Me. Noble, Trinka Hakes. 2019. (Tales of Young Americans Ser.). (ENG.). 40p. (J). (gr. 1-4). 17.99 *(978-1-5341-1016-8(X)*, 204748) Sleeping Bear Pr.

—Follow Me down to Nicodemus Town: Based on the True Story of the African American Pioneer Settlement. LaFaye, A. 2019. (ENG.). 32p. (J). 16.99 *(978-0-8075-2535-7(9)*, 807525359) Whitman, Albert & Co.

—Frederick Douglass: Voice for Justice, Voice for Freedom. Murphy, Frank. 2019. (Step into Reading Ser.). (ENG.). 48p. (J). (gr. k-3). pap. 4.99 *(978-1-5247-7235-2(6))*; lib. bdg. 12.99 *(978-1-5247-7236-9(4))* Random Hse. Children's Bks. (Random Hse. Bks. for Young Readers).

—Friends for Freedom: The Story of Susan B. Anthony & Frederick Douglass. Slade, Suzanne. 2014. 40p. (J). (gr. 1-4). 16.95 *(978-1-58089-568-2(9))* Charlesbridge Publishing, Inc.

—I'll Do the Right Thing. Elster, Jean Alicia. 2010. (ENG.). 32p. (J). pap. 11.99 *(978-0-8170-1658-6(9))* Judson Pr.

—In the Garden with Dr. Carver. Grigsby, Susan. 2012. (J). *(978-1-61913-157-6(9))* Weigl Pubs., Inc.

—In the Garden with Dr. Carver. Grigsby, Susan. 2010. (ENG.). 32p. (J). (gr. -1-3). 16.99 *(978-0-8075-3630-8(X)*, 080753630X) Whitman, Albert & Co.

—Lucky Beans. Birtha, Becky. 2012. (J). 34.28 *(978-1-61913-129-3(3))* Weigl Pubs., Inc.

—My Cancer Days. Filigenzi, Courtney. 2015. (ENG.). 24p. (J). (gr. 2-4). 12.95 *(978-1-60443-091-2(5))* American Cancer Society, Inc.

—Nelson Mandela: From Prisoner to President. Capozzi, Suzy. 2016. (Step into Reading Ser.). (ENG.). 48p. (J). (gr. 2-4). 12.99 *(978-0-375-97467-0(9)*, Random Hse. Bks. for Young Readers) Random Hse. Children's Bks.

—No Mush Today, 1 vol. Derby, Sally. 2008. (ENG.). 32p. (J). (gr. -1-3). 17.95 *(978-1-60060-238-2(X))* Lee & Low Bks., Inc.

Tadgell, Nicole. Tiara's Hat Parade. Lyons, Kelly Starling. 2020. (ENG.). 32p. (J). (gr. -1-3). 16.99 ***(978-0-8075-7945-9(9)***, 807579459) Whitman, Albert & Co.

Tadgell, Nicole. With Books & Bricks: How Booker T. Washington Built a School. Slade, Suzanne. 2014. (ENG.). 32p. (J). (gr. 2-3). 16.99 *(978-0-8075-0897-8(7)*, 807508977) Whitman, Albert & Co.

Tadgell, Nicole, jt. illus. see Carmb, Sara Lynn.

Tadiello, Ed. Rebecca of Sunnybrook Farm. Wiggin, Kate Douglas. Warren, Eliza Gatewood, ed. 2006. 240p. (YA). (gr. 4-8). reprint ed. 10.00 *(978-0-7567-9830-7(2))* DIANE Publishing Co.

Tae-Hyung, Kim. Planet Blood. Tae-Hyung, Kim. (J). Vol. 1. 2005. 200p. pap. 9.99 *(978-1-59532-537-2(9))*; Vol. 4. 4th rev. ed. 2006. 184p. per. 9.99 *(978-1-59532-540-2(9))* TOKYOPOP, Inc.

Taesoo Kim, John. Oliver: The Second-Largest Living Thing on Earth. Crute, Josh. 2018. (ENG.). 32p. (J). 17.99 *(978-1-62414-577-3(9)*, 900192298) Page Street Publishing Co.

Tafalla, Ortiz. Benjamin Franklin. Kelly, Jack. 2005. (Heroes of America Ser.). 239p. (gr. 3-8). 27.07 *(978-1-59679-257-9(4)*, Abdo & Daughters) ABDO Publishing Co.

Tafuni, Gabriele. Very Silly Jokes. Fullman, Joe & Lindley, Sally. 2019. (Pocket Fun Ser.: 3). (ENG.). 96p. (J). pap. 6.99 *(978-1-78888-748-9(4)*, 877ccde5-f5cc-4a8c-9efc-a654d7262f83) Arcturus Publishing GBR. Dist: Baker & Taylor Publisher Services (BTPS).

Tafuri, Nancy. The Big Storm: A Very Soggy Counting Book. Tafuri, Nancy. 2013. (Classic Board Bks.). (ENG.). 34p. (J). (gr. -1 — 1). bds. 7.99 *(978-1-4424-8179-4(X)*, Little Simon) Little Simon.

—The Big Storm: A Very Soggy Counting Book. Tafuri, Nancy. 2009. (ENG.). 32p. (J). (gr. -1-2). 18.99 *(978-1-4169-6795-8(8)*, Simon & Schuster Bks. For Young Readers) Simon & Schuster Bks. For Young Readers.

—Blue Goose. Tafuri, Nancy. 2010. (Classic Board Bks.). (ENG.). 34p. (J). (gr. -1 — 1). bds. 7.99 *(978-1-4169-2835-5(9)*, Little Simon) Little Simon.

—Blue Goose. Tafuri, Nancy. 2008. (ENG.). 32p. (J). (gr. -1-3). 19.99 *(978-1-4169-2834-8(0)*, Simon & Schuster Bks. For Young Readers) Simon & Schuster Bks. For Young Readers.

—The Busy Little Squirrel. Tafuri, Nancy. 2010. (Classic Board Bks.). (ENG.). 34p. (J). (gr. -1 — 1). bds. 7.99 *(978-1-4424-0721-3(2)*, Little Simon) Little Simon.

—The Busy Little Squirrel. Tafuri, Nancy. 2007. (ENG.). 32p. (J). (gr. -1-3). 17.99 *(978-0-689-87341-6(7)*, Simon & Schuster Bks. For Young Readers) Simon & Schuster Bks. For Young Readers.

—Five Little Chicks. Tafuri, Nancy. 2011. (Classic Board Bks.). (ENG.). 34p. (J). (gr. -1 — 1). bds. 7.99 *(978-1-4424-0722-0(0)*, Little Simon) Little Simon.

—Five Little Chicks. Tafuri, Nancy. 2006. (ENG.). 32p. (J). (gr. -1-3). 18.99 *(978-0-689-87342-3(5)*, Simon & Schuster Bks. For Young Readers) Simon & Schuster Bks. For Young Readers.

—Have You Seen My Duckling? Tafuri, Nancy. 2007. (gr. -1-k). 17.00 *(978-0-7569-7869-3(6))* Perfection Learning Corp.

—Whose Chick Are You? Tafuri, Nancy. 2007. (ENG.). 40p. (J). (gr. -1-k). 16.99 *(978-0-06-082514-0(6)*, Greenwillow Bks.) HarperCollins Pubs.

—Whose Chick Are You? Board Book. Tafuri, Nancy. 2019. (ENG.). 38p. (J). (gr. -1 — 1). bds. 7.99 *(978-0-06-285739-2(8)*, Greenwillow Bks.) HarperCollins Pubs.

Tageau, Jerry. Who Were the Beatles? Edgers, Geoff. 2006. (Who Was... ? Ser.). 106p. (J). *(978-0-448-43907-5(7)*, Grosset & Dunlap) Penguin Publishing Group.

Tagel, Peggy. Animal Safari. 2003. (Squishy Shapes Ser.). 10p. (J). 12.95 *(978-1-57145-741-7(0)*, Silver Dolphin Bks.) Readerlink Distribution Services, LLC.

—Birthday Counting. McGrath, Barbara Barbieri. 2017. (First Celebrations Ser.: 7). 12p. (J). (— 1). bds. 6.99 *(978-1-58089-537-8(9))* Charlesbridge Publishing, Inc.

—Christmas Colors & Counting. McGrath, Barbara Barbieri. 2016. (First Celebrations Ser.: 3). 12p. (J). (— 1). bds. 6.95 *(978-1-58089-531-6(X))* Charlesbridge Publishing, Inc.

—Color My World Blue. 2005. (J). *(978-1-58987-101-4(4))* Kindermusik International.

—Dinosaurs. 2003. (Squishy Shapes Ser.). 10p. (J). 12.95 *(978-1-57145-740-0(2)*, Silver Dolphin Bks.) Readerlink Distribution Services, LLC.

—Easter Counting. McGrath, Barbara Barbieri. 2017. (First Celebrations Ser.: 5). 12p. (J). (— 1). bds. 6.99 *(978-1-58089-535-4(2))* Charlesbridge Publishing, Inc.

—Halloween Colors. McGrath, Barbara Barbieri. 2016. (First Celebrations Ser.: 1). 12p. (J). (— 1). bds. 6.95 *(978-1-58089-533-0(6))* Charlesbridge Publishing, Inc.

—The M & M's® Brand All-American Parade Book. McGrath, Barbara Barbieri. 2004. 12p. (J). (gr. -1-k). bds. 6.95 *(978-1-57091-430-0(3))* Charlesbridge Publishing, Inc.

—The M & M's® Brand Birthday Book. McGrath, Barbara Barbieri. 2004. 12p. (J). (gr. -1-3). bds. 6.95 *(978-1-57091-480-5(X))* Charlesbridge Publishing, Inc.

—The M & M's® Brand Easter Egg Hunt. McGrath, Barbara Barbieri. 2004. 12p. (J). (gr. -1-3). bds. 6.95 *(978-1-57091-423-2(0))* Charlesbridge Publishing, Inc.

—The M & M's® Brand Valentine Book. McGrath, Barbara Barbieri. 2004. 12p. (J). (gr. -1-k). bds. 6.95 *(978-1-57091-422-5(2))* Charlesbridge Publishing, Inc.

—On the Go. 2003. (Squishy Shapes Ser.). 10p. (J). 12.95 *(978-1-57145-739-4(9)*, Silver Dolphin Bks.) Readerlink Distribution Services, LLC.

—Parade Colors. McGrath, Barbara Barbieri. 2017. (First Celebrations Ser.: 6). 12p. (J). (— 1). bds. 6.99 *(978-1-58089-536-1(0))* Charlesbridge Publishing, Inc.

—Valentine's Shapes. McGrath, Barbara Barbieri. 2016. (First Celebrations Ser.: 4). 12p. (J). (— 1). bds. 6.95 *(978-1-58089-532-3(8))* Charlesbridge Publishing, Inc.

Taggart, Katy, et al. Workin' on the Railroad: And Other Favorite Rhymes. 2004. (Mother Goose Ser.). (ENG.). 32p. (J). 15.95 *(978-1-59249-385-2(8)*, 1D004) Soundprints.

Tagle, jt. illus. see Sanchez, Andres.

Taglietti, Emanuele. John Calvin. Carr, Simonetta. 2008. (ENG.). 63p. (J). 18.00 *(978-1-60178-055-3(9))* Reformation Heritage Bks.

Taguchi, Masayuki. Battle Royale, 5 vols., Vol. 1. Takami, Koushun. 2003. 192p. pap. 9.99 *(978-1-59182-314-8(5))* TOKYOPOP, Inc.

Taher, Ronak. Sonam & the Silence. Ayres, Eddie. 2018. (ENG.). 32p. (J). (gr. 2-4). 19.99 *(978-1-76029-366-6(0))* Allen & Unwin AUS. Dist: Independent Pubs. Group.

Taherian, Elaheh. Khalil & Mr. Hagerty & the Backyard Treasures. Springstubb, Tricia. 2020. 32p. (J). (gr. k-3). 16.99 *(978-1-5362-0306-6(8))* Candlewick Pr.

Tahleh, Eleykaa. The Legend of Kalikimaka: Alohalani, Kalikimaka Auntie. Westerman, Rob. 2003. 32p. (J). 12.95 *(978-0-9761992-0-5(3))* Gold Boy Music & Pubn.

Taiki. Infinite Dendrogram: Volume 1. Kaidou, Sakon. Nomura, Nick & Hodgson, Andrew, trs. 2019. (Infinite Dendrogram (light Novel) Ser.: 1). 250p. pap. 14.99 *(978-1-7183-5500-2(9))* J-Novel Club.

—Infinite Dendrogram: Volume 2. Kaidou, Sakon. Hodgson, Andrew, tr. 2019. (Infinite Dendrogram (light Novel) Ser.: 2). 250p. pap. 14.99 *(978-1-7183-5501-9(7))* J-Novel Club.

—Infinite Dendrogram: Volume 3. Kaidou, Sakon. Hodgson, Andrew, tr. 2019. (Infinite Dendrogram (light Novel) Ser.: 3). (ENG.). 250p. pap. 14.99 *(978-1-7183-5502-6(5))* J-Novel Club.

Taimy Studios. Isobel's New World. Turnbull, Betty Turnbull. 2011. 48p. (J). 11.95 *(978-1-61153-016-2(4))* Light Messages Publishing.

Tait, Carys. A Drop of Rain Green Band. Landman, Tanya. 2016. (Cambridge Reading Adventures Ser.). (ENG.). 16p. pap. 7.37 *(978-1-107-55060-5(2))* Cambridge Univ. Pr.

Tait, Mat. The Adventures of Tupaia. Meredith, Courtney Sina. 2019. (ENG.). 64p. (J). (gr. 3-7). 22.99 ***(978-1-988547-14-5(8))*** Allen & Unwin AUS. Dist: Independent Pubs. Group.

Tait, Tristan. There Was a Rabbit. Ruberto, Carolyn. 2019. (ENG.). 32p. (J). pap. 16.95 ***(978-1-5043-1937-9(0)***, Balboa Pr.) Author Solutions, Inc.

Taixi, Su. Stories Behind Chinese Idioms (I) Ma, Zheng & Li, Zheng. 2010. 48p. (J). (gr. 3-6). 16.95 *(978-1-60220-965-7(0))* Shanghai Translation Publishing Hse. CHN. Dist: Publishers Group West (PGW).

Takabatake, Jun. Dear Professor Whale. Iwasa, Megumi. 2018. (ENG.). 104p. (J). (gr. k-3). 16.99 *(978-1-77657-206-9(8))* Gecko Pr. NZL. Dist: Lerner Publishing Group.

—Yours Sincerely, Giraffe. Iwasa, Megumi. 2017. (ENG.). 104p. (gr. k-3). (J). 16.99 *(978-1-927271-88-9(6))*; 9.99 *(978-1-77657-114-7(2))* Gecko Pr. NZL. Dist: Lerner Publishing Group.

Takacova, Magdalena. Anthill. Bartikova, Petra. 2020. (ENG.). 14p. (J). bds. 9.99 ***(978-1-64124-085-7(7)***, 0857) Fox Chapel Publishing Co., Inc.

—Tree. Bartikova, Petra. 2020. (ENG.). 12p. (J). bds. 9.99 ***(978-1-64124-087-1(3)***, 0871) Fox Chapel Publishing Co., Inc.

Takacs-Moore, Mary. Energy: 25 Projects Investigate Why We Need Power & How We Get It. Takacs-Moore, Mary. Reilly, Kathleen M. 2009. (Build It Yourself Ser.). 128p. (J). (gr. 3-7). pap. 15.95 *(978-1-934670-34-7(0)*, 01a0b3b3-54b4-460c-8b75-ae33e2898b4d) Nomad Pr.

Takada, Rie. Gaba Kawa, Vol. 1. Takada, Rie. 2008. (Gaba Kawa Ser.: 1). (ENG.). 192p. (J). (gr. 8-18). pap. 8.99 *(978-1-4215-2259-3(4))* Viz Media.

Takahashi, Hideko. Eight Is Great, Vol. Balsley, Tilda. 2013. (ENG.). 12p. (J). (gr. -1 — 1). bds. 5.95 *(978-0-7613-6623-2(7)*, 9780761366232, Kar-Ben Publishing) Lerner Publishing Group.

—Hello, New Baby. 2005. 12p. (J). (gr. -1-18). 9.95 *(978-1-58117-345-1(8)*, Intervisual/Piggy Toes) Bendon, Inc.

Takahashi, Rumiko. Inu Yasha Ani-Manga, Vol. 11. Takahashi, Rumiko. 2005. (Inuyasha Ser.: 11). (ENG.). 216p. pap. 11.99 *(978-1-4215-0022-5(1))* Viz Media.

—Inuyasha Ani-Manga, Vol. 14. Takahashi, Rumiko. 2006. (Inuyasha Ser.: 14). (ENG.). 208p. pap. 11.99 *(978-1-4215-0384-4(0))* Viz Media.

—Inuyasha Ani-Manga, Vol. 10. Takahashi, Rumiko. 2005. (ENG.). 216p. pap. 11.99 *(978-1-59116-859-1(7))* Viz Media.

—Inuyasha Ani-Manga, Vol. 7. Takahashi, Rumiko. 2005. (ENG.). 216p. pap. 11.95 *(978-1-59116-612-2(8))* Viz Media.

—Inuyasha the Movie Ani-Manga: Affections Touching Across Time. Takahashi, Rumiko. 2005. (Inuyasha Ser.). (ENG.). 432p. (YA). pap. 24.99 *(978-1-59116-828-7(7))* Viz Media.

—Inuyasha, Vol. 44, Set. Takahashi, Rumiko. 2003. (Inuyasha Ser.). (ENG.). 200p. (YA). pap. 39.98 *(978-1-59116-235-3(1)*, Viz Comics) Viz Media.

—Maison Ikkoku. Takahashi, Rumiko. 2005. (Maison Ikkoku Ser.: 11). (ENG.). Vol. 11. 2nd ed. 232p. pap. 9.95 *(978-1-59116-804-1(X))*; Vol. 12. 323p. pap. 9.95 *(978-1-59116-869-0(4))*; Vol. 13. 2nd ed. 232p. pap. 9.95 *(978-1-4215-0141-3(4))*; Vol. 14. 2nd ed. 240p. pap. 9.95 *(978-1-4215-0142-0(2))* Viz Media.

—Maison Ikkoku, Vol. 7: Intensive Care, Vol. 7. Takahashi, Rumiko. 2nd ed. 2004. (Maison Ikkoku Ser.: 7). (ENG.). 288p. pap. 9.95 *(978-1-59116-485-2(0))* Viz Media.

—Mermaid Saga. Takahashi, Rumiko. 2004. (Mermaid Saga Ser.). (ENG.). (YA). 3. 176p. pap. 9.99 *(978-1-59116-483-8(4))*; Vol. 4. 2nd ed. 192p. pap. 9.99 *(978-1-59116-482-1(6))* Viz Media.

—RIN-NE, Vol. 2. Takahashi, Rumiko. 2010. (ENG.). 192p. (YA). pap. 9.99 *(978-1-4215-3486-2(X))* Viz Media.

Takahashi, Shin. Saikano, Vol. 4. Takahashi, Shin. 2005. (Saikano Ser.). (ENG.). 248p. (YA). pap. 9.95 *(978-1-59116-476-0(1))* Viz Media.

—Saikano: The Last Love Song on This Little Planet. Takahashi, Shin. 2005. (Saikano Ser.: 5). (ENG.). 248p. pap. 9.95 *(978-1-59116-477-7(X))* Viz Media.

—Saikano, Vol. 2. Takahashi, Shin. 2004. (ENG.). 200p. pap. 9.95 *(978-1-59116-474-6(5))* Viz Media.

—Saikano, Vol. 3. Takahashi, Shin. 2004. (Saikano Ser.: 3). (ENG.). 200p. pap. 9.95 *(978-1-59116-475-3(3))* Viz Media.

Takamisaki, Ryo. Megaman NT Warrior W/Trading Card (no foil Wrap) Takamisaki, Ryo. 2004. (Megaman Nt Warrior Ser.). (ENG.). 192p. (YA). pap. 7.95 *(978-1-59116-827-0(9))* Viz Media.

—MEGAMAN, Vol. 5, 13 vols. Takamisaki, Ryo. 2005. (ENG.). 200p. (J). pap. 7.95 *(978-1-59116-561-3(X))* Viz Media.

Takamiya, Satoru. Heaven's Will. Takamiya, Satoru. 2009. (ENG.). 200p. (gr. 8-18). pap. 8.99 *(978-1-4215-2258-6(6))* Viz Media.

Takara, Marcio. City of Incredibles, Vol. 2. Waid, Mark. 2010. (Incredibles Ser.). (ENG.). 112p. (J). 24.99 *(978-1-60886-529-1(0))* Boom! Studios.

—Family Matters. Waid, Mark. 2009. (Incredibles Ser.). (ENG.). 128p. (J). 24.99 *(978-1-60886-525-3(8))*; pap. 9.99 *(978-1-934506-83-7(4))* Boom! Studios.

—Incorruptible. Waid, Mark. 2012. (ENG.). 128p. Vol. 6. (Incorruptible Ser.: 6). (gr. 10). pap. 16.99 *(978-1-60886-084-5(1))*; Vol. 7. (gr. 9). pap. 16.99 *(978-1-60886-085-2(X))* Boom! Studios.

—The Incredibles: City of Incredibles, Vol. 2. Waid, Mark. 2010. (Incredibles Ser.). (ENG.). 112p. (J). pap. 9.99 *(978-1-60886-503-1(7))* Boom! Studios.

—Revenge from Below. Waid, Mark & Walker, Landry. 2011. (Kaboom! Graphic Novels Ser.). (ENG.). 112p. (J). (gr. 4-7). 26.19 *(978-1-60886-518-5(5))* Boom! Studios.

—Secrets & Lies. Walker, Landry. 2010. (Incredibles Ser.). 112p. (J). (gr. 3-8). pap. 9.99 *(978-1-60886-583-3(5))* Boom! Studios.

Takashi, Fuuji. Anya Goes to India. Fungchung, Nikko M. 2017. (Anya's World Adventures Ser.: Vol. 2). (ENG.). (J). (gr. k-4). pap. 9.99 *(978-0-9981497-5-2(6))* FungChung, Nikko M.

—Anya Goes to Jamaica. Fungchung, Nikko M. 2016. (Anya's World Adventures Ser.: Vol. 1). (ENG.). (J). (gr. k-4). pap.

T

9.99 *(978-0-9981497-3-8(X))*; 17.99 *(978-0-9981497-0-7(5))* FungChung, Nikko M.

—Anya Va en Inde. Fungchung, Nikko M. 2017. (Aventures d'Anya Autour du Monde Ser.: Vol. 2). (FRE.). 30p. (J). (gr. k-4). pap. 9.99 *(978-0-9981497-8-3(0))* FungChung, Nikko M.

—Anya Va en Jamaique. Fungchung, Nikko M. 2017. (Aventures d'Anya Autour du Monde Ser.: Vol. 1). (FRE.). 32p. (J). (gr. k-4). pap. 9.99 *(978-0-9981497-2-1(1))* FungChung, Nikko M.

—Juju 'round the World: Japan. Boston, Jennifer. 2018. (ENG.). 28p. (J). (gr. 2-5). *(978-1-78222-579-9(X))* Paragon Publishing, Rothersthorpe.

—Little Lady Rose. Grigsby, Tamar. 2019. (ENG.). 28p. (J). pap. 16.99 *(978-1-7283-0859-3(3))* AuthorHouse.

Takaya, Natsuki. Fruits Basket, Vol. 7. Takaya, Natsuki. Nibley, Alethea & Nibley, Athena, trs. from JPN. rev. ed. 2005. 208p. (YA). pap. 9.99 *(978-1-59532-402-3(X))* TOKYOPOP, Inc.

—Fruits Basket. Takaya, Natsuki. (Fruits Basket Ser.). 208p. Vol. 10. 10th rev. ed. 2005. pap. 9.99 *(978-1-59532-405-4(4))*; Vol. 13. 13th rev. ed. 2006. pap. 9.99 *(978-1-59532-408-5(9))* TOKYOPOP, Inc.

Takaya, Natsuki. Fruits Basket, Vol. 11. Takaya, Natsuki, creator. rev. ed. 2005. (Fruits Basket Ser.). 208p. pap. 9.99 *(978-1-59532-406-1(2))* TOKYOPOP, Inc.

Takeshita, Gene. True Blue Friend. Block, Cheryl. 2006. 32p. (J). 21.95 *(978-0-9761625-2-0(0))* Block Publishing.

Takeuchi, Chihiro. Colors. Takeuchi, Chihiro. 2019. (Paper Peek Ser.). (ENG.). 38p. (J). (— 1). bds. 14.99 *(978-1-5362-1148-1(6))* Candlewick Pr.

Takeuchi, Chihiro. Paper Peek: Animals. Takeuchi, Chihiro. 2020. (Paper Peek Ser.). (ENG.). 34p. (J). (— 1). bds. 14.99 ***(978-1-5362-1149-8(4))*** Candlewick Pr.

Takeuchi, Kana. Death Trance. Takeuchi, Kana. 2005. 152p. (YA). Bk. 2, Vol. 2. pap. 9.99 *(978-1-58655-652-5(5)*, TSNOV-0514); Vol. 3. pap. 9.99 *(978-1-58655-691-4(6)*, TSNOV-0515) Media Blasters, Inc.

Takhar, Jodi & Jones, Paul. Four Seasons of Fun. Takhar, Jodi. 14p. (J). (gr. -1-3). 19.95 *(978-1-886000-02-5(6))* Takhar's, Jodi Spilt Milk Collection.

—What Can I Do Today? Takhar, Jodi. 14p. (J). (gr. -1-3). 19.95 *(978-1-886000-03-2(4))* Takhar's, Jodi Spilt Milk Collection.

Taki, Emiko, photos by. A Taste of Home. Jamison, Heather & Meckenstock, Shay. Marconette, Gennifer, ed. 2008. (ENG.). 128p. (YA). 24.95 *(978-0-9794167-2-9(8))* Simple Ink, LLC.

Takvorian, Nadine. Apples, Apples Everywhere! Learning about Apple Harvests, 1 vol. Koontz, Robin. 2010. (Autumn Ser.). (ENG.). 24p. (J). (gr. -1-3). pap. 8.95 *(978-1-4048-6388-0(5)*, Picture Window Bks.) Capstone.

—Busy Animals: Learning about Animals in Autumn, 1 vol. Bullard, Lisa. 2010. (Autumn Ser.). (ENG.). 24p. (J). (gr. -1-3). lib. bdg. 27.32 *(978-1-4048-6014-8(2)*, Picture Window Bks.) Capstone.

—Hades & the Underworld: An Interactive Mythological Adventure. Hoena, Blake. 2017. (You Choose: Ancient Greek Myths Ser.). (ENG.). 112p. (J). (gr. 3-7). lib. bdg. 32.65 *(978-1-5157-4823-6(5)*, Capstone Pr.) Capstone.

—Jason & the Argonauts, 1 vol. 2011. (Greek Myths Ser.). (ENG.). 32p. (J). (gr. 3-5). lib. bdg. 29.32 *(978-1-4048-6669-0(8)*, 1329957, Picture Window Bks.) Capstone.

—Leaves Fall Down: Learning about Autumn Leaves, 1 vol. Bullard, Lisa. 2010. (Autumn Ser.). (ENG.). 24p. (J). (gr. -1-3). pap. 8.95 *(978-1-4048-6390-3(7)*, Picture Window Bks.) Capstone.

—Odysseus & the Cyclops, 1 vol. 2011. (Greek Myths Ser.). (ENG.). 32p. (J). (gr. 3-5). lib. bdg. 29.32 *(978-1-4048-6666-9(3)*, 1329959, Picture Window Bks.) Capstone.

—Pick a Perfect Pumpkin: Learning about Pumpkin Harvests, 1 vol. Koontz, Robin Michal. 2010. (Autumn Ser.). (ENG.). 24p. (J). (gr. -1-3). lib. bdg. 27.32 *(978-1-4048-6011-7(8)*, Picture Window Bks.) Capstone.

—Thanksgiving Crafts, 1 vol. Muehlenhardt, Amy Bailey. 2010. (Thanksgiving Ser.). (ENG.). 24p. (J). (gr. k-3). lib. bdg. 27.99 *(978-1-4048-6282-1(X)*, Picture Window Bks.) Capstone.

—The Trojan War: An Interactive Mythological Adventure. Hoena, Blake. 2017. (You Choose: Ancient Greek Myths Ser.). (ENG.). 112p. (J). (gr. 3-7). lib. bdg. 32.65 *(978-1-5157-4822-9(7)*, Capstone Pr.) Capstone.

Talayssat, Lucille. Das Tagebuch Von J. Lemouton. Giuliano, Danielle. 2019. (Tome Ser.: Vol. 1). (GER.). 28p. (J). pap. 10.00 *(978-1-0912-8578-1(0))* Independently Published.

Talbert, Nick. Love Is the Way. Hardrick, Joseline. 2020. (ENG.). 32p. (J). pap. 12.99 ***(978-1-6921-1851-8(X))*** Independently Published.

Talbot, Jim. Whoa! Amusement Park Gone Wild! Lerangis, Peter. 2003. (Abracadabra Ser.: No. 7). (ENG.). 112p. (J). pap. 3.99 *(978-0-439-38938-9(0)*, Scholastic Paperbacks) Scholastic, Inc.

—Wow! Blast from the Past! Lerangis, Peter. 2003. (Abracadabra Ser.: No. 8). (ENG.). 112p. (J). pap. 3.99 *(978-0-439-38939-6(9)*, Scholastic Paperbacks) Scholastic, Inc.

Talbot, Josh. Jesus Was Just Like Me. Doxey, Heidi. 2017. (ENG.). (J). (gr. -1-k). bds. 12.99 *(978-1-4621-2120-5(9))* Cedar Fort, Inc./CFI Distribution.

—No Biggy! A Story about Overcoming Everyday Obstacles. Rubin, Elycia. 32p. (J). 2019. (— 1). pap. 7.99 *(978-1-9848-9249-2(5)*, Dragonfly Bks.); 2018. (gr. -1-3). 17.99 *(978-1-63565-048-8(8)*, 9781635650488, Rodale Kids) Random Hse. Children's Bks.

Talbot, Michael. Jamaican Mi Seh Mi ABCs. Kemp-Davis, Valrie. 2017. (ENG.). 62p. (J). (gr. k-6). 22.00 ***(978-0-578-53389-6(8))*** Carradice Collection.

Talbott, Hudson. The Lost Colony of Roanoke. Fritz, Jean. 2004. (ENG.). 64p. (J). (gr. 2-5). 18.99 *(978-0-399-24027-0(6)*, G.P. Putnam's Sons Books for Young Readers) Penguin Young Readers Group.

—Show Way. Woodson, Jacqueline. 2005. (ENG.). 48p. (J). (gr. -1-3). 17.99 *(978-0-399-23749-2(6)*, G.P. Putnam's Sons Books for Young Readers) Penguin Young Readers Group.

Talbott, Hudson. From Wolf to Woof: The Story of Dogs. Talbott, Hudson. 2016. 40p. (J). (gr. k-3). 16.99 *(978-0-399-25404-8(8)*, Nancy Paulsen Books) Penguin Young Readers Group.

—It's All about Me-Ow. Talbott, Hudson. 2012. 32p. (J). (gr. -1-2). 17.99 *(978-0-399-25403-1(X)*, Nancy Paulsen Books) Penguin Young Readers Group.

—Picturing America: Thomas Cole & the Birth of American Art. Talbott, Hudson. 2018. 32p. (J). (gr. 1-3). 17.99 *(978-0-399-54867-3(X)*, Nancy Paulsen Books) Penguin Young Readers Group.

—River of Dreams: The Story of the Hudson River. Talbott, Hudson. 2009. 40p. (J). (gr. 1-3). 17.99 *(978-0-399-24521-3(9)*, G.P. Putnam's Sons Books for Young Readers) Penguin Young Readers Group.

—United Tweets of America: 50 State Birds Their Stories, Their Glories. Talbott, Hudson. 2015. 64p. (J). (gr. 1-3). 8.99 *(978-0-14-751557-5(2)*, Puffin Books) Penguin Young Readers Group.

Talbott, Sherri. My Mom Has Wheels. Rose, Sandra. 2009. 28p. pap. 24.95 *(978-1-60836-889-1(0))* America Star Bks.

Taliaferro, Al. The Complete Sunday Comics, 1939-1942. Karp, Bob. 2016. (DONALD DUCK Sunday Comics Ser.: 1). 168p. 49.99 *(978-1-63140-530-3(6)*, 9781631405303) Idea & Design Works, LLC.

Taliana, Philip, jt. illus. see Galea, Ryan.

Talib, Binny. Hello, My Name Is Octicorn. Diller, Kevin & Lowe, Justin. 2016. (ENG.). 48p. (J). (gr. -1-3). 17.99 *(978-0-06-238793-6(6))* HarperCollins Pubs.

—The Perfect Flower Girl. Chandab, Taghred. 2012. (ENG.). 32p. (J). (gr. -1-k). 19.99 *(978-1-74237-573-1(1))* Allen & Unwin AUS. Dist: Independent Pubs. Group.

—The Very Stuffed Turkey. Kenah, Katharine. 2015. (ENG.). 32p. (J). (gr. -1-k). pap. 6.99 *(978-0-545-76109-3(3)*, Cartwheel Bks.) Scholastic, Inc.

Tallack, Bethany. The Magical Jump. Fuhrer, Kyle. 2019. (ENG.). 24p. (J). pap. 10.00 *(978-1-0816-9909-3(4))* Independently Published.

Tallardy, Laura. The Girls Body Book: Everything You Need to Know for Growing up YOU. Dunham, Kelli. 2013. (ENG.). 116p. (J). pap. 11.95 *(978-1-60433-353-4(7)*, Applesauce Pr.) Cider Mill Pr. Bk. Pubs., LLC.

—The Girls Body Book: Fifth Edition. Dunham, Kelli. 2019. (ENG.). 148p. (J). pap. 12.95 *(978-1-60433-833-1(4)*, Applesauce Pr.) Cider Mill Pr. Bk. Pubs., LLC.

—The Girls Body Book: Third Edition: Everything You Need to Know for Growing up YOU. Dunham, Kelli. 3rd rev. ed. 2015. (ENG.). 132p. (J). pap. 12.95 *(978-1-60433-575-0(0)*, Applesauce Pr.) Cider Mill Pr. Bk. Pubs., LLC.

—Party Girl: How to Throw a Fab Fest. Speregen, Debra Newberger. 2008. 48p. pap. *(978-0-545-04093-8(0))* Scholastic, Inc.

—Sophie the Awesome. Bergen, Lara. 2010. 99p. (J). *(978-0-545-24231-8(2))* Scholastic, Inc.

—Sophie the Hero. Bergen, Lara. 2010. (Sophie Ser.: 2). (ENG.). 112p. (J). (gr. 2-5). pap. 4.99 *(978-0-545-14605-0(4)*, Scholastic Paperbacks) Scholastic, Inc.

Tallarico, Tony. Ultimate Sticker Puzzles: License Plates Across the States: Travel Puzzles & Games. Tallarico, Tony. 2005. (ENG.). 24p. (J). (gr. -1-2). mass mkt. 6.99 *(978-0-8431-7737-4(3)*, Price Stern Sloan) Penguin Young Readers Group.

Tallec, Olivier. The Bathing Costume. Moundlic, Charlotte. 2013. (ENG.). 40p. (J). (gr. k-3). 15.95 *(978-1-59270-141-4(8))* Enchanted Lion Bks., LLC.

—Big Wolf & Little Wolf. Brun-Cosme, Nadine. 2009. 32p. (J). (gr. -1-2). 16.95 *(978-1-59270-084-4(5))* Enchanted Lion Bks., LLC.

—Big Wolf & Little Wolf: The Little Leaf That Wouldn't Fall. Brun-Cosme, Nadine. 2009. 32p. (J). (gr. -1-2). 16.95 *(978-1-59270-088-2(8))* Enchanted Lion Bks., LLC.

—Big Wolf & Little Wolf, Such a Beautiful Orange! Brun-Cosme, Nadine. 2011. 32p. (J). (gr. -1-3). 16.95 *(978-1-59270-106-3(0))* Enchanted Lion Bks., LLC.

—Blob: The Ugliest Creature in the World. Sorman, Joy. Klinger, Sarah, tr. 2017. 48p. (J). (gr. k-4). 16.95 *(978-1-59270-207-7(4))* Enchanted Lion Bks., LLC.

—Five Minutes: (That's a Lot of Time) (No, It's Not) (Yes, It Is) Scanlon, Liz Garton & Vernick, Audrey. 2019. (ENG.). 32p. (J). (gr. -1-2). 16.99 *(978-0-525-51631-6(X)*, G.P. Putnam's Sons Books for Young Readers) Penguin Young Readers Group.

—Gus Is a Fish. Babin, Claire. 2008. (ENG.). 32p. (J). (gr. -1-2). 14.95 *(978-1-59270-101-8(9))* Enchanted Lion Bks., LLC.

—Gus Is a Tree. Babin, Claire. 2009. 32p. (J). (gr. -1-2). 14.95 *(978-1-59270-078-3(0))* Enchanted Lion Bks., LLC.

—Un libro de Mono y Pastel: ¿Qué hay en la caja? Daywalt, Drew. 2019. (Monkey & Cake Ser.: 1). (SPA.). 56p. (J). (gr. -1-3). pap. 4.99 *(978-1-338-35910-7(X)*, Scholastic en Espanol) Scholastic, Inc.

—The Scar. Moundlic, Charlotte. 2011. (ENG.). 32p. (J). (gr. k-4). 15.99 *(978-0-7636-5341-5(1))* Candlewick Pr.

—Sealed with a Kiss. Ferry, Beth. 2019. (ENG.). 32p. (J). (gr. -1-3). 17.99 *(978-0-06-247577-0(0))* HarperCollins Pubs.

—This Book Will Not Be Fun. Dunlap, Cirocco. 2017. 32p. (J). (gr. -1-2). 17.99 *(978-0-399-55061-4(5))*; (ENG.). lib. bdg. 20.99 *(978-0-399-55062-1(3))* Random Hse. Children's Bks. (Random Hse. Bks. for Young Readers).

—This Is My Fort! Daywalt, Drew. 2019. (Monkey & Cake Ser.: 2). (ENG.). 56p. (J). (gr. -1-3). 9.99 *(978-1-338-14390-4(5)*, Orchard Bks.) Scholastic, Inc.

—Thumbelina of Toulaba. Picouly, Daniel. 2007. (ENG.). 36p. (J). (gr. -1-3). 16.95 *(978-1-59270-069-1(1))* Enchanted Lion Bks., LLC.

—What If... ? Lenain, Thierry. Bedrick, Claudia Zoe, tr. from FRE. 2019. (ENG.). 32p. (J). 17.95 *(978-1-59270-281-7(3))* Enchanted Lion Bks., LLC.

—What Is Inside This Box? Daywalt, Drew. 2019. (Monkey & Cake Ser.: 1). (ENG.). 56p. (J). (gr. -1-3). 9.99 *(978-1-338-14386-7(7)*, Orchard Bks.) Scholastic, Inc.

—What's Going on Here? A Tell-Your-Own-Tale Book. 2019. (ENG.). 28p. (J). (gr. -1-k). 15.99 *(978-1-4521-7317-7(6))* Chronicle Bks. LLC.

—Who Done It? 2015. (ENG.). 32p. (J). (gr. -1-k). 15.99 *(978-1-4521-4198-5(3))* Chronicle Bks. LLC.

—Who Was That? 2018. (ENG.). 32p. (J). (gr. -1-k). 15.99 *(978-1-4521-6990-3(X))* Chronicle Bks. LLC.

—Who What Where? 2016. (ENG.). 32p. (J). (gr. -1-k). 15.99 *(978-1-4521-5693-4(X))* Chronicle Bks. LLC.

Tallec, Olivier. It's MY Tree. Tallec, Olivier. 2020. (ENG.). 30p. (J). (gr. -1-2). 17.99 ***(978-1-5253-0547-4(6))*** Kids Can Pr., Ltd. CAN. Dist: Hachette Bk. Group.

Tallent, Alyssa. A Bright Easter. Christensen, Catherine. 2019. (ENG.). 32p. (J). 15.99 *(978-1-4621-2298-1(1))* Cedar Fort, Inc./CFI Distribution.

—Danny Calloway & the Puzzle House. Bolger, Z. C. Robinson, Garrett, ed. 2013. 346p. 24.99 *(978-1-939898-01-2(3))* Story Road Publishing, Inc.

Talley, Pam. Two Foals, a Dash of Sprinkles & a Cherry on Top! Bevis, Brittany. 2011. 32p. (J). 18.47 *(978-0-9824766-7-3(1))*; pap. 18.47 *(978-0-9824766-8-0(X))* Caballo Pr. of Ann Arbor. (Caballito Children's Bks.).

Talsma, Nynke. YA Know What? Gordon Ekster, Carol. 2017. 32p. (J). (gr. -1 — 1). 17.95 *(978-1-60537-278-5(1))* Clavis Publishing.

Talsma, Nynke Mare. Plastic Soup. Koppens, Judith & Engel, Andy. 2020. 32p. (J). (gr. -1). 16.95 *(978-1-60537-530-4(6))* Clavis Publishing.

Talvitie, Virpi. Bicycling to the Moon. Parvela, Timo. 2016. (ENG.). 128p. (gr. k-5). 9.99 *(978-1-77657-078-2(2))*; 16.99 *(978-1-77657-080-5(4))*; 16.99 *(978-1-77657-091-1(X))* Gecko Pr. NZL. Dist: Lerner Publishing Group.

Talwar, Roshni. Money & Kids: WOW, I AM RICH ! (I): Roshni Gets Her First Money Lesson. Talwar, Manish C. & Walia Talwar, Rachna. 2019. (Wow, I Am Rich! Ser.: Vol. 1). (ENG.). 38p. (J). pap. 10.00 *(978-1-7287-7612-5(0))* Independently Published.

Tamaki, Jillian. Gertie's Leap to Greatness. Beasley, Kate. 2016. (ENG.). 256p. (J). 16.99 *(978-0-374-30261-0(8)*, 9780374302610, Farrar, Straus & Giroux (BYR)) Farrar, Straus & Giroux.

—Gertie's Leap to Greatness. Beasley, Kate. 2018. (ENG.). 272p. (J). pap. 7.99 *(978-1-250-14374-7(8)*, 900180551) Square Fish.

—My Best Friend. Fogliano, Julie. 2020. (ENG.). 32p. (J). (gr. -1-3). 17.99 *(978-1-5344-2722-8(8)*, Atheneum Bks. for Young Readers) Simon & Schuster Children's Publishing.

—They Say Blue. 2020. (ENG.). 38p. (J). (gr. k-2). bds. 9.99 *(978-1-4197-4096-1(2)*, Abrams Appleseed) Abrams, Inc.

—This One Summer. Tamaki, Mariko. 2014. (ENG.). 320p. (YA). (gr. 7). 21.99 *(978-1-62672-094-7(0)*, 900135617); pap. 18.99 *(978-1-59643-774-6(X)*, 900081621) Roaring Brook Pr. (First Second Bks.).

Tamaki, Lauren. You Are Mighty: A Guide to Changing the World. Paul, Caroline. 2018. 128p. (J). 17.99 *(978-1-68119-822-4(3)*, 900188032, Bloomsbury Children's Bks.) Bloomsbury Publishing USA.

Tamaki, Nozomu. The Most Original Vampire Story in Centuries! Tamaki, Nozomu. 2008. (Dance in the Vampire Bund Ser.: 3). (ENG.). 208p. pap. 10.99 *(978-1-934876-15-2(1)*, 9781934876152); 192p. pap. 10.99 *(978-1-933164-81-6(6)*, 9781933164816) Seven Seas Entertainment, LLC.

Tamang, Mayan. The Adventures of Captain Remarkable: Companion chapter book to Captain Remarkable. O'Neal-Thorpe, Rochelle. 2nd ed. 2010. 124p. (J). pap. 10.95 *(978-0-9823906-0-3(2))* Wiggles Pr.

—Captain Remarkable; Girls can be Superheroes Too! 2009. 28p. (J). pap. 10.95 *(978-0-9823906-1-0(0))* Wiggles Pr.

Tamara, Visco. Dinero the Frog Learns to Save Energy. Colon De Mejias, Leticia. 2013. 32p. pap. 7.00 *(978-0-9822168-9-7(0))* Independent Pub.

Tamarin, Nicole. Little Yellow Pear Tomatoes. Yumel, Demain. 2005. 32p. (J). 15.95 *(978-0-9740190-2-4(X))* Illumination Arts Publishing Co., Inc.

Tamarit, Núria. Season of the Witch: A Spellbinding History of Witches & Other Magical Folk. Ralphs, Matt. 2020. (ENG.). 80p. (J). (gr. 4-7). 18.95 *(978-1-912497-71-3(9))* Flying Eye Bks. GBR. Dist: Penguin Random Hse. LLC.

Tamarkin, Annette. Mon Petit Busy Day. Tamarkin, Annette. 2018. (ENG.). 12p. (J). (gr. -1-k). bds. 14.99 *(978-1-5344-1296-5(4)*, Little Simon) Little Simon.

Tamas, Emanuel. Sagas Taggiga Vän: Swedish Edition of Stella & Her Spiky Friend. Pere, Tuula. Nikolowski-Bogomoloff, Angelika, tr. 2018. (Saga Ser.: Vol. 3). (SWE.). 42p. (J). (gr. k-4). *(978-952-357-008-5(0))*; pap. *(978-952-357-005-4(6))* Wickwick oy.

—Sanni Ja Apteekin Salmiakki: Finnish Edition of Stella & Her Spiky Friend. Pere, Tuula. 2018. (Sanni Ser.: Vol. 3). (FIN.). 42p. (J). (gr. k-4). *(978-952-357-007-8(2))*; pap. *(978-952-357-004-7(8))* Wickwick oy.

—Stella & Her Spiky Friend. Pere, Tuula. Korman, Susan, ed. 2018. (Stella Ser.: Vol. 3). (ENG.). 42p. (J). (gr. k-4). *(978-952-357-006-1(4))*; pap. *(978-952-357-003-0(X))* Wickwick oy.

Tamayo, Natalia. Paso A Paso. Vasco, Irene. 2003. (Literatura Juvenil (Panamericana Editorial) Ser.). (SPA.). 77p. (YA). (gr. -1-7). pap. *(978-958-30-0374-5(3))* Panamericana Editorial.

Tambellini, Stefano. Frightlopedia: An Encyclopedia of Everything Scary, Creepy, & Spine-Chilling, from Arachnids to Zombies. 2016. ix, 213p. (J). *(978-1-5181-5609-0(6))* Workman Publishing Co., Inc.

—Girls Miscellany: Fascinating Information Every Girl Should Know. Stride, Lottie. 2013. 128p. (J). *(978-1-4351-5048-5(1))* Barnes & Noble, Inc.

—The Signalman: Two Ghost Stories: Band 14/Ruby (Collins Big Cat) Dolan, Penny. 2015. (Collins Big Cat Ser.). (ENG.). 48p. (J). (gr. 3-4). pap. 10.99 *(978-0-00-812780-0(8))* HarperCollins Pubs. Ltd. GBR. Dist: Independent Pubs. Group.

Tamir, Rony. Masada: Judea's Last Stand. 2014. (ENG.). (J). (gr. -1-3). pap. *(978-965-7607-21-3(3))* Gefen Publishing Hse., Ltd.

Tamponi, Joe. The Banana Notebook: Lined, Soft Cover, Letter Size (8. 5x11) Ruled Notebook & Journal for Students, Kids & Teens. for School & College, Writing & Notes. Tamponi, Joe. 2019. (ENG.). 102p. (J). pap. 5.99 ***(978-1-6927-5340-5(1))*** Independently Published.

—The Black Widow Notebook: Lined, Soft Cover, Letter Size (8. 5x11) Ruled Notebook & Journal for Students, Kids & Teens. for School & College, Writing & Notes. Tamponi, Joe. 2019. (ENG.). 102p. (J). pap. 5.99 ***(978-1-6914-1842-8(0))*** Independently Published.

—The Creepy Notebook: Lined, Soft Cover, Letter Size (8. 5x11) Ruled Notebook & Journal for Students, Kids & Teens. for School & College, Writing & Notes. Tamponi, Joe. 2019. (ENG.). 102p. (J). pap. 5.99 ***(978-1-6921-9827-5(0))*** Independently Published.

—The Dynamite Bomb Notebook: Lined, Soft Cover, Letter Size (8. 5x11) Ruled Notebook & Journal for Students, Kids & Teens. for School & College, Writing & Notes. Tamponi, Joe. 2019. (ENG.). 102p. (J). pap. 5.99 ***(978-1-6921-8462-9(8))*** Independently Published.

—The Psychedelic Notebook: Lined, Soft Cover, Letter Size (8. 5x11) Ruled Notebook & Journal for Students, Kids & Teens. for School & College, Writing & Notes. Tamponi, Joe. 2019. (ENG.). 102p. (J). pap. 5.99 ***(978-1-6921-9552-6(2))*** Independently Published.

—The Smoking Sunset Notebook: Lined, Soft Cover, Letter Size (8. 5x11) Ruled Notebook & Journal for Students, Kids & Teens. for School & College, Writing & Notes. Tamponi, Joe. 2019. (ENG.). 102p. (J). pap. 5.99 ***(978-1-6921-9293-8(0))*** Independently Published.

—The Surfer Wolf Notebook: Lined, Soft Cover, Letter Size (8. 5x11) Ruled Notebook & Journal for Students, Kids & Teens. for School & College, Writing & Notes. Tamponi, Joe. 2019. (ENG.). 102p. (J). pap. 5.99 ***(978-1-6914-1508-3(1))*** Independently Published.

—The Tropical Turbo Toucan Notebook: Lined, Soft Cover, Letter Size (8. 5x11) Ruled Notebook & Journal for Students, Kids & Teens. for School & College, Writing & Notes. Tamponi, Joe. 2019. (ENG.). 102p. (J). pap. 5.99 ***(978-1-6922-0413-6(0))*** Independently Published.

—The Vacation Notebook: Lined, Soft Cover, Letter Size (8. 5x11) Ruled Notebook & Journal for Students, Kids & Teens. for School & College, Writing & Notes. Tamponi, Joe. 2019. (ENG.). 102p. (J). pap. 5.99 ***(978-1-6922-3004-3(2))*** Independently Published.

Tamula, Elis. La Faiseuse de Neige. Lhuissier, Marie. 2018. (Contes Mathematiques Ser.: Vol. 2). (FRE.). 40p. (J). pap. *(978-2-9560767-2-8(8))* Marie, Lhuissier.

—Kuu. Lhuissier, Marie. 2017. (EST.). 50p. (J). pap. *(978-2-9560767-1-1(X))* Marie, Lhuissier.

—Lune. Lhuissier, Marie. 2017. (FRE.). 50p. (J). pap. *(978-2-9560767-0-4(1))* Marie, Lhuissier.

Tamura, Mitsuhisa. Bakegyamon. Tamura, Mitsuhisa. 2009. (Bakégyamon Ser.: 5). (ENG.). 216p. (J). pap. 7.99 *(978-1-4215-2171-8(7))* Viz Media.

—BakéGyamon. Tamura, Mitsuhisa. 2009. (Bakégyamon Ser.: 3). (ENG.). 216p. (J). Vol. 3. pap. 7.99 *(978-1-4215-1795-7(7))*; Vol. 4. pap. 7.99 *(978-1-4215-1882-4(1))* Viz Media.

Tamura, Yumi. Book of Justice. Tamura, Yumi. 2003. (Chicago Ser.: Vol. 2). (ENG.). 200p. pap. 15.95 *(978-1-56931-829-4(8))* Viz Media.

—Wild Com. Tamura, Yumi. 2004. (Wild Com Ser.). (ENG.). 192p. (YA). pap. 9.95 *(978-1-59116-559-0(8))* Viz Media.

Tan, Abigail. Marsha's Special Gift. Breen, Deborah. 2019. (ENG.). 26p. (J). pap. 9.50 ***(978-1-6712-2588-6(0))*** Independently Published.

Tan, Anthony. Bratz: Super-Bratz. Christine, Peymani. 2008. 96p. pap. 6.99 *(978-1-4278-0789-2(2))* TOKYOPOP, Inc.

Tan, Billy. League of Legends: Lux. 2019. 144p. (YA). (gr. 8-17). pap. 15.99 *(978-1-302-91943-6(1))* Marvel Worldwide, Inc.

Tan, Billy, et al. Thor by Kieron Gillen: the Complete Collection. 2019. (ENG.). 312p. (YA). (gr. 8-17). pap. 34.99 *(978-1-302-91561-2(4))* Marvel Worldwide, Inc.

Tan, Philip, et al. X-Men: Trial of the Juggernaut. 2019. (ENG.). 392p. (YA). (gr. 8-17). pap. 34.99 *(978-1-302-92037-1(5))* Marvel Worldwide, Inc.

Tan, Shaun. Memorial. Crew, Gary. 32p. *(978-0-85091-983-7(5)*, Lothian Children's Bks.) Hachette Australia.

—The Viewer. Crew, Gary. 2003. (ENG.). 32p. (J). (gr. 1-6). 16.95 *(978-1-894965-02-6(7))* Simply Read Bks. CAN. Dist: Ingram Publisher Services.

Tan, Shaun. The Arrival. Tan, Shaun. 2007. (ENG.). 128p. (J). (gr. 7-12). 21.99 *(978-0-439-89529-3(4)*, Levine, Arthur A. Bks.) Scholastic, Inc.

—Cicada. Tan, Shaun. 2019. (ENG.). 32p. (J). (gr. 7-7). 19.99 *(978-1-338-29839-0(9)*, Levine, Arthur A. Bks.) Scholastic, Inc.

—Lost & Found. Tan, Shaun. 2011. (ENG.). 128p. (J). (gr. 7-3). 21.99 *(978-0-545-22924-1(3)*, Levine, Arthur A. Bks.) Scholastic, Inc.

—Rules of Summer. Tan, Shaun. 2014. (ENG.). 48p. (J). (gr. -1-3). 18.99 *(978-0-545-63912-5(3)*, Levine, Arthur A. Bks.) Scholastic, Inc.

—The Singing Bones. Tan, Shaun. 2016. (ENG.). 192p. (J). (gr. 7). 24.99 *(978-0-545-94612-4(3)*, Levine, Arthur A. Bks.) Scholastic, Inc.

—Tales from Outer Suburbia. Tan, Shaun. 2009. (ENG.). 96p. (J). (gr. 7-18). 21.99 *(978-0-545-05587-1(3)*, Levine, Arthur A. Bks.) Scholastic, Inc.

Tan, Ying Hui. Escuchando a Mi Cuerpo: Una Guía para Ayudar a Los niños Entender la Conexión Entre Las Sensaciones Físicas y Sus Sentimientos. Garcia, Gabi. 2018. (SPA.). 34p. (J). (gr. -1-3). pap. 11.95 *(978-1-949633-01-6(2))* Skinned Knee Publishing.

—Escuchando con Mi Corazón: Una Cuento de Bondad y Autocompasión. Garcia, Gabi. 2018. (SPA.). 36p. (J).

pap. 11.95 *(978-0-9989580-6-4(9))* Skinned Knee Publishing.

Tan, Ying Hui. Listening to My Body: A Guide to Helping Kids Understand the Connection Between Their Sensations (what the Heck Are Those?) & Feelings So That They Can Get Better at Figuring Out What They Need. Garcia, Gabi. 2019. (ENG.). 34p. (J). (gr. k-4). 21.99 ***(978-0-9989580-1-9(8))*** Skinned Knee Publishing.

Tan, Ying Hui. Listening to My Body: A Guide to Helping Kids Understand the Connection Between Their Sensations (What the Heck Are Those?) & Feelings So That They Can Get Better at Figuring Out What They Need. Garcia, Gabi. 2017. (ENG.). 34p. (J). (gr. -1-3). pap. 12.99 *(978-0-9989580-0-2(X))* Skinned Knee Publishing.

—Listening with My Heart: A Story of Kindness & Self-Compassion. Garcia, Gabi. (ENG.). 36p. (J). 2018. (gr. 1-5). 21.99 *(978-0-9989580-4-0(2))*; 2017. pap. 12.95 *(978-0-9989580-3-3(4))* Skinned Knee Publishing.

Tanaka, Shinsuke. Wings. 2006. (ENG.). 80p. (J). (gr. -1). 14.95 *(978-1-933327-19-8(7))* Purple Bear Bks., Inc.

Tanaka, Suzuki. Menkui!, Vol. 1. Tanaka, Suzuki. 2006. (Menkui! Ser.). 192p. pap. 9.99 *(978-1-59816-358-2(2))* TOKYOPOP, Inc.

Tanaka, Usa. Give Me That! Tanaka, Usa. 2007. (ENG.). 32p. (J). 15.95 *(978-0-9741319-0-0(3))* 4N Publishing LLC.

Tanaka, Yoko. The Magician's Elephant. DiCamillo, Kate. (J). (gr. 3-7). 2015. 224p. pap. 7.99 *(978-0-7636-8088-6(5))*; 2009. 208p. 17.99 *(978-0-7636-4410-9(2))* Candlewick Pr.

—One Moon, Two Cats. Godwin, Laura. 2011. (ENG.). 32p. (J). (gr. -1-1). 16.99 *(978-1-4424-1202-6(X)*, Atheneum Bks. for Young Readers) Simon & Schuster Children's Publishing.

—Sparrow Girl. Pennypacker, Sara. 2009. 40p. (J). (gr. 1-5). 16.99 *(978-1-4231-1187-0(7))* Hyperion Pr.

—Theodosia & the Eyes of Horus. LaFevers, R. L. 2011. (Theodosia Ser.). (ENG.). 384p. (J). (gr. 3-7). pap. 7.99 *(978-0-547-55011-4(1)*, 1450219) Houghton Mifflin Harcourt Publishing Co.

—Theodosia & the Last Pharaoh, 4. LaFevers, R. L. 2012. (Theodosia Ser.: 4). 400p. (J). (gr. 4-6). 21.19 *(978-0-547-39018-5(1))* Houghton Mifflin Harcourt Publishing Co.

—Theodosia & the Serpents of Chaos. LaFevers, R. L. (Theodosia Ser.). (J). 2008. (ENG.). 352p. (gr. 3-7). pap. 7.99 *(978-0-618-99976-7(0)*, 1027887); 1. 2007. 343p. (gr. 4-6). 22.44 *(978-0-618-75638-4(8))* Houghton Mifflin Harcourt Publishing Co.

—Theodosia & the Staff of Osiris. LaFevers, R. L. 2009. (Theodosia Ser.). (ENG.). 400p. (J). (gr. 3-7). pap. 7.99 *(978-0-547-24819-6(9)*, 1100709) Houghton Mifflin Harcourt Publishing Co.

—The Witch's Guide to Cooking with Children, 1. McGowan, Keith. 2011. (Witch's Guide to Cooking with Children Ser.). (ENG.). 192p. (J). (gr. 4-6). pap. 21.19 *(978-0-312-67486-1(4)*, 900072904) Square Fish.

Tanaka, Yoko. Dandelion's Dream. Tanaka, Yoko. 2020. (ENG.). 40p. (J). (gr. -1-2). 16.99 *(978-1-5362-0453-7(6))* Candlewick Pr.

Tanana, Mary. Christmas to Color: Coloring Book for Adults & Kids to Share. Tanana, Mary. 2015. (ENG.). 96p. (J). (gr. -1). pap. 15.99 *(978-0-06-244379-3(8))* HarperCollins Pubs.

Tanant, T'Uy. Squamish People of the Sunset Coast. Wyss, Barbara. 2006. (ENG.). 36p. (J). pap. 21.73 ***(978-1-4120-7643-2(9))*** Trafford Publishing.

Tanchak, Diane. The True Story of Federico Fish & Ana Alligator. Beckenstein, Cara. 2003. 32p. 11.95 *(978-0-9726699-0-0(6))* Laughing Gull Pr.

Tanchez, Plinio. El Viaje de Lucita. Garcia, Elizabeth. 2010. (SPA.). (J). (gr. -1-1). pap. *(978-99922-1-343-8(4))* Piedra Santa, Editorial.

Tanco, Miguel. Great Dog. Call, Davide. 2018. (ENG.). 46p. (J). (gr. -1-2). 17.99 *(978-1-101-91917-0(5)*, Tundra Bks.) Tundra Bks. CAN. Dist: Penguin Random Hse. LLC.

—My Best Buddy. Kim, YeShil. 2014. (MySELF Bookshelf Ser.). (ENG.). 32p. (J). (gr. k-2). pap. 11.94 *(978-1-60357-693-2(2))*; lib. bdg. 25.27 *(978-1-59953-658-3(7))* Norwood Hse. Pr.

Tandy, Russell H. The Clue in the Jewel Box, No. 20. Keene, Carolyn. 2005. (Nancy Drew Mystery Stories Ser.). (ENG.). 228p. (J). (gr. 5-9). 17.95 *(978-1-55709-277-9(X))* Applewood Bks.

Tang, Betty. Jacky Ha-Ha: a Graphic Novel, 232 vols. Patterson, James & Grabenstein, Chris. 2020. (Jacky Ha-Ha Ser.: 1). (ENG.). 240p. (J). (gr. 3-9). pap. 12.99 *(978-0-316-49195-2(0)*, Jimmy Patterson) Little Brown & Co.

Tang, Charles. The Amusement Park Mystery. Warner, Gertrude Chandler. 2020. (Boxcar Children Ser.). (ENG.). 128p. (J). (gr. 2-6). lib. bdg. 27.07 ***(978-1-5321-4471-4(7)***, 35161, Chapter Bks.) Spotlight.

—The Castle Mystery. Warner, Gertrude Chandler. 2020. (Boxcar Children Ser.). (ENG.). 128p. (J). (gr. 2-6). lib. bdg. 27.07 ***(978-1-5321-4474-5(1)***, 35164, Chapter Bks.) Spotlight.

—The Haunted Cabin Mystery. Warner, Gertrude Chandler. 2020. (Boxcar Children Ser.). (ENG.). 128p. (J). (gr. 2-6). lib. bdg. 27.07 ***(978-1-5321-4475-2(X)***, 35165, Chapter Bks.) Spotlight.

—The Pizza Mystery. Warner, Gertrude Chandler. 2020. (Boxcar Children Ser.). (ENG.). 128p. (J). (gr. 2-6). lib. bdg. 27.07 ***(978-1-5321-4478-3(4)***, 35168, Chapter Bks.) Spotlight.

Tang, Ge. The Dragon Emperor. Wang, Ping. 2007. (J). lib. bdg. 6.95 *(978-0-8225-6744-8(X)*, Millbrook Pr.) Lerner Publishing Group.

T'Ang, Li Chu. A Chinese Wonder Book: [Illustrated Edition]. Pitman, Norman Hinsdale. 2019. (ENG.). 194p. (J). (gr. k-3). ***(978-605-7748-53-9(0))*** Uhrayoglu, Murat E Kitap Projesi.

Tang, Sandara. Following Magic. Duey, Kathleen. 2010. (Faeries' Promise Ser.: 2). (ENG.). 128p. (J). (gr. 2-5). pap. 6.99 *(978-1-4169-8459-7(3)*, Aladdin) Simon & Schuster Children's Publishing.

—Following Magic. Duey, Kathleen. 2010. (Faeries' Promise Ser.: 2). (ENG.). 128p. (J). (gr. 2-5). 15.99 *(978-1-4169-8458-0(5)*, Simon & Schuster/Paula Wiseman Bks.) Simon & Schuster/Paula Wiseman Bks.

—The Full Moon. Duey, Kathleen. (Faeries' Promise Ser.: 4). (ENG.). 128p. (J). (gr. 2-5). 2011. pap. 4.99 *(978-1-4169-8463-4(1))*; 4. 2012. lib. bdg. 17.44 *(978-1-4169-8462-7(3))* Simon & Schuster Children's Publishing. (Aladdin).

—Silence & Stone. Duey, Kathleen. 2010. (Faeries' Promise Ser.: 1). (ENG.). 128p. (J). (gr. 2-5). pap. 6.99 *(978-1-4169-8457-3(7)*, Aladdin) Simon & Schuster Children's Publishing.

—Silence & Stone. Duey, Kathleen. 2010. (Faeries' Promise Ser.: 1). (ENG.). 128p. (J). (gr. 2-5). 15.99 *(978-1-4169-8456-6(9)*, Simon & Schuster/Paula Wiseman Bks.) Simon & Schuster/Paula Wiseman Bks.

—Wishes & Wings. Duey, Kathleen. 2011. (Faeries' Promise Ser.: 3). (ENG.). 128p. (J). (gr. 2-5). pap. 4.99 *(978-1-4169-8461-0(5)*, Aladdin) Simon & Schuster Children's Publishing.

—Wishes & Wings. Duey, Kathleen. 2011. (Faeries' Promise Ser.: 3). (ENG.). 128p. (J). (gr. 2-5). 15.99 *(978-1-4169-8460-3(7)*, Simon & Schuster/Paula Wiseman Bks.) Simon & Schuster/Paula Wiseman Bks.

Tang, Sanmu. Celebrating the Chinese New Year. Tang, Sanmu. Ying, Wu, tr. 2010. (Chinese Festivals Ser.). 32p. (J). (gr. -1-3). pap. 4.95 *(978-1-60220-958-9(8))* Shanghai Translation Publishing Hse. CHN. Dist: Publishers Group West (PGW).

—Celebrating the Dragon Boat Festival. Tang, Sanmu. Tenison, Mina, tr. 2010. (Chinese Festivals Ser.). (ENG.). 32p. (J). (gr. -1-3). pap. 4.95 *(978-1-60220-968-8(5))* Shanghai Translation Publishing Hse. CHN. Dist: Publishers Group West (PGW).

—Celebrating the Mid-Autumn Festival. Tang, Sanmu. Tenison, Mina, tr. 2010. (Chinese Festivals Ser.). (ENG.). 32p. (J). (gr. -1-3). pap. 4.95 *(978-1-60220-969-5(3))* Shanghai Translation Publishing Hse. CHN. Dist: Publishers Group West (PGW).

Tang, Wenjia. I Am a Tractor. Redwing, Jack. Cottage Door Press, ed. 2020. (John Deere Finger Puppet Board Book Ser.). (ENG.). 12p. (J). (gr. -1 — 1). bds. 6.99 ***(978-1-68052-806-0(8)***, 1005190) Cottage Door Pr.

Tang, Wenjia. Under Your Feet... Soil, Sand & Everything Underground. Royal Horticultural Society. 2020. (ENG.). 64p. (J). (gr. k-3). 14.99 *(978-1-4654-9095-7(7)*, DK Children) Dorling Kindersley Publishing, Inc.

Tang, You-shan. Striking It Rich: Treasures from Gold Mountain. Yamada, Debbie Leung. l.t. ed. 2004. 128p. (J). (gr. 4-8). pap. 13.95 *(978-1-879965-21-8(6))* Polychrome Publishing Corp.

Tang, Youshan. Abadeha: The Philippine Cinderella. De La Paz, Myrna J. 2014. (ENG.). 32p. (J). (gr. 3-7). 16.95 *(978-1-885008-17-6(1)*, Shen's Bks.) Lee & Low Bks., Inc.

—Abadeha: The Philippine Cinderella. de la Paz, Myrna J. 2014. (ENG.). 32p. (J). pap. 8.95 *(978-1-885008-44-2(9)*, Shen's Bks.) Lee & Low Bks., Inc.

—Anklet for a Princess: A Cinderella Story from India. Mehta, Lila. 2014. (ENG.). 32p. (J). pap. 10.95 *(978-1-885008-46-6(5)*, Shen's Bks.) Lee & Low Bks., Inc.

—The Magical Monkey King: Mischief in Heaven. 2004. 113p. (J). (gr. 2-5). 14.95 *(978-1-885008-24-4(4))*; (ENG.). per. 12.95 *(978-1-885008-25-1(2)*, 1e04e654-76e1-44f7-8613-0675562d5dfe) Lee & Low Bks., Inc. (Shen's Bks.).

Tangen, Nick. Trains & Tow Boats. Trombello, William. 2013. 34p. pap. *(978-0-9842998-1-2(5))* Roxby Media Ltd.

Tango-Schurmann, Ann. Olivia Macallister, Who Are You? A Ghost Mystery Set in Maine. Mariotti, Celine Rose. 2004. 85p. (YA). (gr. 3-6). pap. 12.95 *(978-0-9721389-6-3(X))* Rock Village Publishing.

Tani, Toshihiko. The Deer King. Yamanushi, Toshiko. 2014. (J). 8.95 *(978-1-935523-70-3(8))* World Tribune Pr.

Taniguchi, Tomoko. Aquarium, Vol. 1. Taniguchi, Tomoko. 2nd rev. ed. 2003. 200p. pap. 9.99 *(978-1-58664-900-5(0)*, CMX 62801MM, CPM Manga) Central Park Media Corp.

—Call Me Princess. Taniguchi, Tomoko. 2nd rev. ed. 2003. 192p. pap. 9.99 *(978-1-58664-898-5(5)*, CMX 61601MM, CPM Manga) Central Park Media Corp.

—Just a Girl, 2 bks., Bk. 1. Taniguchi, Tomoko. Pannone, Frank, ed. Hiroe, Ikoi, tr. from JPN. 2004. 184p. (YA). pap. 9.99 *(978-1-58664-911-1(6)*, CMX 64801G, CPM Manga) Central Park Media Corp.

—Just a Girl 2, 2 vols., Vol. 2. Taniguchi, Tomoko. Pannone, Frank, ed. Hiroe, Ikoi, tr. from JPN. 2004. 168p. pap. 9.99 *(978-1-58664-912-8(4)*, CMX 64802G, CPM Manga) Central Park Media Corp.

—Let's Stay Together Forever. Taniguchi, Tomoko. Pannone, Frank, ed. Rose, Julia, tr. from JPN. 2003. 192p. pap. 15.95 *(978-1-58664-881-7(0)*, CMX 62701G, CPM Manga) Central Park Media Corp.

—Miss Me? Taniguchi, Tomoko. Pannone, Frank, ed. Hiroe, Ikoi, tr. from JPN. 2004. 184p. pap. 9.99 *(978-1-58664-905-0(1)*, CMX 64701G, CPM Manga) Central Park Media Corp.

—Popcorn Romance. Taniguchi, Tomoko. 2003. Orig. Title: Love & Peace in a Cornfield. 192p. pap. 9.99 *(978-1-58664-901-2(9)*, CMX 64901G, CPM Manga) Central Park Media Corp.

—Princess Prince. Taniguchi, Tomoko. 2003. 336p. (YA). pap. 15.95 *(978-1-58664-860-2(8)*, CMX 62601G, CPM Manhwa) Central Park Media Corp.

Tanis, Joel E. Swing! Klein, Pamela. 2006. (ENG.). (J). 15.95 *(978-1-932514-05-6(8))* College of DuPage Pr.

Tanis, Katy. Animal Olympics: Creatures Great & Small Competing in Incredible, Impressive, & Extraordinary Events! Discover Nature's Sporting Stars. CARRON BROWN. 2020. (ENG.). 32p. (J). (gr. k-2). 16.99 ***(978-1-78240-987-8(4)***, Ivy Kids) Ivy Group, The GBR. Dist: Hachette Bk. Group.

Tanis, Katy. I Am the Jungle: A Yoga Adventure. Hurt, Melissa. 2020. (ENG.). 32p. (J). 17.99 *(978-1-68364-382-1(8)*, 900220040) Sounds True, Inc.

Taniwan, Andrias. Sweet Annie See, Sweet Annie Do. Kennard, Jennifer Lynne. 2019. (ENG.). 38p. (J). pap. 10.95 *(978-0-578-43066-9(5))* Jennifer Lynne Kennard.

Tank, Daniel, jt. illus. see Pennington, Jack.

Tank, Daniel, jt. illus. see Vitale, Raoul.

Tank, Daniel, jt. illus. see White, John, Jr.

Tankard, Jeremy. It's a Tiger! LaRochelle, David. 2012. (ENG.). 36p. (J). (gr. -1-k). 16.99 *(978-0-8118-6925-6(3))* Chronicle Bks. LLC.

—Privacy: Deal with It Like Nobody's Business, 1 vol. Peters, Diane. 2016. (Lorimer Deal with It Ser.). (ENG.). 32p. (J). (gr. 4-9). pap. 12.95 *(978-1-55028-907-7(1)*, fe4cd6df-f6ff-4b7e-98e7-a9473a027066) James Lorimer & Co. Ltd., Pubs. CAN. Dist: Lerner Publishing Group.

—Procrastination: Deal with It All in Good Time, 1 vol. Peters, Diane. 2016. (Lorimer Deal with It Ser.). (ENG.). 32p. (J). (gr. 4-9). pap. 12.95 *(978-1-55028-947-3(0)*, a0fe15cd-483b-45ff-988f-aeaa84a45459) James Lorimer & Co. Ltd., Pubs. CAN. Dist: Lerner Publishing Group.

Tankard, Jeremy. Boo Hoo Bird. Tankard, Jeremy. 2009. (ENG.). 32p. (J). (gr. -1-k). 16.99 *(978-0-545-06570-2(4)*, Scholastic Pr.) Scholastic, Inc.

—Grumpy Bird. Tankard, Jeremy. 2007. (ENG.). 32p. (J). (gr. -1-k). 16.99 *(978-0-439-85147-3(5)*, Scholastic Pr.) Scholastic, Inc.

—Hungry Bird. Tankard, Jeremy. 2016. 32p. (J). (gr. -1-k). 16.99 *(978-0-545-86417-6(8)*, Scholastic Pr.) Scholastic, Inc.

—Me Hungry! Tankard, Jeremy. 2008. (ENG.). 40p. (J). (gr. -1-2). 15.99 *(978-0-7636-3360-8(7))* Candlewick Pr.

—Sleepy Bird. Tankard, Jeremy. 2018. (ENG.). 32p. (J). (gr. -1-k). 16.99 *(978-1-338-15785-7(X)*, Scholastic Pr.) Scholastic, Inc.

—Yorick & Bones. Tankard, Jeremy. Tankard, Hermione. 2020. (ENG.). 144p. (J). (gr. 3-7). 16.99 *(978-0-06-285430-8(5))*; pap. 9.99 *(978-0-06-285431-5(3))* HarperCollins Pubs.

Tanksley, Ann. The Six Fools. Hurston, Zora Neale. 2006. (ENG.). 40p. (J). (gr. 1-5). 15.99 *(978-0-06-000646-4(3))* HarperCollins Pubs.

—The Six Fools. Hurston, Zora Neale & Thomas, Joyce Carol. 2005. 40p. (J). (gr. 1-5). lib. bdg. 18.89 *(978-0-06-000647-1(1))* HarperCollins Pubs.

Tannehill, Mary Jo. The Little Acorn. Kauble, Christa. Natural Resources Conservation Service (U.S.), ed. 2008. (ENG.). 24p. (gr. -1-4). pap. 5.00 *(978-0-16-081701-4(3)*, Forest Service) United States Government Printing Office.

Tannenbaum, Rose. Theo: The Blue Rider Pigeon, 1 vol. Sireau, Christine. 2005. (ENG.). 20p. (J). (gr. -1-3). pap. 15.00 *(978-0-88010-561-3(5))* SteinerBooks, Inc.

Tanner, Jane. Soldier's Gift. Palmer, Anthony. 2017. 44p. (J). (gr. 3-7). 16.99 *(978-0-14-350716-1(8))* Penguin Random Hse. AUS. Dist: Independent Pubs. Group.

—Storm Whale. Brennan, Sarah. 2019. (ENG.). 32p. (J). (gr. -1-3). 16.99 *(978-1-76029-364-2(4))* Allen & Unwin AUS. Dist: Independent Pubs. Group.

Tanner, Jennifer. Robin Hood, 1 vol. Stone Arch Books Staff. Tobon, Sara, tr. 2009. (Classic Fiction Ser.). (SPA.). 72p. (J). (gr. 5-9). lib. bdg. 27.99 *(978-1-4342-1689-2(6)*, Stone Arch Bks.) Capstone.

—Robin Hood. 2010. (Classic Fiction Ser.). 72p. lib. bdg. 4.95 *(978-1-4342-2604-4(2)*, Stone Arch Bks.) Capstone.

—Robin Hood, 1 vol. Stone Arch Books Staff. Tobon, Sara, tr. 2010. (Classic Fiction Ser.). (SPA.). 72p. (J). (gr. 5-9). pap. 7.15 *(978-1-4342-2275-6(6)*, Stone Arch Bks.) Capstone.

Tanner, Shandra. Bubby Books: From Ragamuffin to Lovestuffin! Guytwins, Dj & Guytwins, Denise. 2019. (ENG.). 40p. (J). pap. 16.99 ***(978-1-7283-3256-7(7))*** AuthorHouse.

Tanner, Stephanie. Sam's Mission Call. Brown, Gary. 24p. (J). 12.95 *(978-0-910523-13-4(4))* Grandin Bk. Co.

Tanner, Suzy-Jane. Nursery Rhymes. 2012. 24p. (J). 9.95 *(978-1-84135-743-0(X))* Award Pubns. Ltd. GBR. Dist: Parkwest Pubns., Inc.

Tanner Voyles. Mickey's Mini Farm. Myers, Jean Emily. 2009. 32p. pap. 21.99 *(978-1-4389-5544-5(8))* AuthorHouse.

Tans, Adrian. The Emperor's Army, 1 vol. Pilegard, Virginia. 2010. (ENG.). 32p. (J). (gr. k-3). 16.99 *(978-1-58980-690-0(5)*, Pelican Publishing) Arcadia Publishing.

—Kick the Cowboy, 1 vol. Gribnau, Joe. 2009. (ENG.). 32p. (J). (gr. k-3). 16.99 *(978-1-58980-605-4(0)*, Pelican Publishing) Arcadia Publishing.

—Pirate Treasure Hunt!, 1 vol. Peck, Jan. 2008. (ENG.). 32p. (J). (gr. k-3). 16.99 *(978-1-58980-549-1(6)*, Pelican Publishing) Arcadia Publishing.

—Pirates Don't Say Please!, 1 vol. Knowlton, Laurie Lazzaro. 2012. (ENG.). 32p. (J). (gr. k-3). 16.99 *(978-1-58980-982-6(3)*, Pelican Publishing) Arcadia Publishing.

—Witches' Night Before Halloween, 1 vol. Bannatyne, Lesley Pratt. 2007. (ENG.). 32p. (J). (gr. k-3). 16.99 *(978-1-58980-485-2(6)*, Pelican Publishing) Arcadia Publishing.

Tansley, Eric. Ajax: Golden Dog of the Australian Bush. Patchett, Mary Elwyn. 2011. 172p. 42.95 *(978-1-258-01103-1(4))* Literary Licensing, LLC.

Tanwar, Rajesh. Goldilocks & the Three Bears. 2010. (J). *(978-1-60617-147-9(X))* Teaching Strategies, LLC.

Tanzosh, Edward. Cinder Yeti. McKenzie, Precious. 2019. (ENG.). 34p. (J). (gr. k-2). 22.95 ***(978-1-7333092-9-5(2))***; pap. 11.95 ***(978-1-7341065-0-3(6))*** BeaLu Bks.

Tapia, Alfredo. Pounce de Leon, 1 vol. Wynne-Jones, Tim. 2014. (ENG.). 32p. (J). (gr. -1-2). pap. 9.95 *(978-0-88995-510-3(7)*, cb934c96-990c-4b71-ab00-657f78d17b5a) Red Deer Pr. CAN. Dist: Firefly Bks., Ltd.

Tapia, Guillermo D. Starlight. Cox, Hayley. 2019. (ENG.). 34p. (J). pap. 9.99 *(978-1-7982-3915-5(9))* Independently Published.

Taplinger, Lee, jt. photos by see Florian, Douglas.

Tapper, Lucy. Hedgehugs & the Hattiepillar. Wilson, Steve. 2016. (Hedgehugs Ser.: 2). (ENG.). 32p. (J). 16.99 *(978-1-62779-414-5(X)*, 900149940, Holt, Henry & Co. Bks. For Young Readers) Holt, Henry & Co.

—Hedgehugs: Autumn Hide-And-Squeak. Wilson, Steve. 2017. (Hedgehugs Ser.: 3). (ENG.). 32p. (J). 16.99 *(978-1-250-11248-4(6)*, 9781250112484, Holt, Henry & Co. Bks. For Young Readers) Holt, Henry & Co.

—Horace & Hattiepillar. Wilson, Steve. 2015. (Hedgehugs Ser.: 1). (ENG.). 32p. (J). (gr. -1-3). 17.99 *(978-1-62779-404-6(2)*, 900149648, Holt, Henry & Co. Bks. For Young Readers) Holt, Henry & Co.

Tappin, Christine. Whose Lovely Child Can You Be? Viswanath, Shobha. 2013. (ENG.). 32p. (J). (gr. -1). pap. 9.95 *(978-81-8190-304-4(8))* Karadi Tales Co. Pvt. Ltd. IND. Dist: Consortium Bk. Sales & Distribution.

Taraba, Catherine. Joyful Noises: 20 Original Catholic Prayers Sung to Classic Children's Tunes. Sharpe, Jennifer. 2018. (ENG.). 56p. (J). pap. 12.99 *(978-1-7246-2547-2(0))* CreateSpace Independent Publishing Platform.

Taranggana. See Me Don't Judge Me. Denchukwu, Nkem. Shann, Melissa, ed. 2019. (ENG.). 36p. (J). pap. 9.99 *(978-1-7331416-3-5(4))* Elevlv Publishing Group.

Tarazona, Oscar. Volando con Alas Propias. l.t. ed. 2004. (SPA.). 116p. (YA). pap. 12.00 *(978-1-931481-88-5(1))* LiArt-Literature & Art.

Tarbett, Debbie. Ten Cheepy, Chirpy Chicks. 2017. (J). *(978-1-84857-576-9(9))* Little Tiger Pr. Group.

—Ten Splishy, Splashy Fish. 2017. (J). *(978-1-84857-577-6(7))* Little Tiger Pr. Group.

—Ten Splishy, Splashy Fish. Tiger Tales. 2017. (ENG.). 26p. (J). (gr. -1-k). mass mkt. 4.99 *(978-1-68010-412-7(8))* Tiger Tales.

—Ten Wriggly, Wiggly Caterpillars. 2017. (J). *(978-1-84857-562-2(9))* Little Tiger Pr. Group.

—5 Cheeky Monkeys. Brooks, Susie. 2016. (J). *(978-1-84857-539-4(4))* Little Tiger Pr. Group.

—5 Chirpy Birds. Brooks, Susie. 2016. (J). *(978-1-84857-540-0(8))* Little Tiger Pr.

—5 Little Ducks. 2016. (J). *(978-1-84857-541-7(6))* Little Tiger Pr.

—5 Stomping Elephants. 2016. (J). *(978-1-84857-542-4(4))* Little Tiger Pr.

Tardif, Benoit. Metropolis. Tardif, Benoit. 2016. (ENG.). 72p. (J). (gr. -1-3). 17.95 *(978-1-77138-721-7(1))* Kids Can Pr., Ltd. CAN. Dist: Hachette Bk. Group.

Tarkela, Johanna. Orangutan & Baby. Garnett, Jaye. Cottage Door Press, ed. 2020. (Smithsonian Kids Big Head Board Book Ser.). (ENG.). 12p. (J). (gr. -1-1). bds. 12.99 ***(978-1-68052-805-3(X)***, 1005180) Cottage Door Pr.

Tarnowski, Mark. The Sun Stone. Treanor, H. T. 2012. 16p. pap. 10.00 *(978-1-60976-125-7(1)*, Strategic Bk. Publishing) Strategic Book Publishing & Rights Agency (SBPRA).

Tarr, Lisa M. Colorado Fun: Activities for on the Road & at Home. Perry, Phyllis J. 2007. 80p. (J). (gr. 1-7). pap. 12.95 *(978-1-55566-402-2(4)*, Johnson Bks.) Bower Hse.

Tarrant, Daniel. Park Here (Time to Read, Level 1) Lakin, Patricia. 2020. (Time to Read Ser.). (ENG.). 32p. (J). (gr. k-2). pap. 3.99 ***(978-0-8075-6369-4(2)***, 0807563692); 12.99 ***(978-0-8075-6366-3(8)***, 807563668) Whitman, Albert & Co.

Tarrant, Percy. Tom & Some Other Girls. Vaizey, George de Horne. 2007. 208p. per. *(978-1-4065-4698-9(4))* Dodo Pr.

Tarrier, Keith. Have You Seen My Undies? Tarrier, Keith. 2019. (ENG.). 44p. (J). pap. 9.99 *(978-1-7968-5706-1(8))* Independently Published.

Tarver, Monroe S. Little Light Shine Bright. Tarver, Monroe S. l.t. ed. 2004. 32p. (J). 6.99 *(978-0-9743568-4-6(0))* Tarver, Monroe.

Tashiro, Chisato. Five Nice Mice & the Great Car Race. Tashiro, Chisato. 2014. (Five Nice Mice Ser.). (ENG.). 40p. (J). (gr. k-2). 17.99 *(978-988-8240-73-9(0)*, Minedition) Neugebauer, Michael (Publishing) Limited HKG. Dist: Penguin Random Hse. LLC.

Tashjian, Jake. Einstein the Class Hamster. Tashjian, Janet. 2013. (Einstein the Class Hamster Ser.: 1). (ENG.). 160p. (J). (gr. 2-5). 12.99 *(978-0-8050-9610-1(8)*, 900085726, Holt, Henry & Co. Bks. For Young Readers) Holt, Henry & Co.

—Einstein the Class Hamster & the Very Real Game Show. Tashjian, Janet. 2014. (Einstein the Class Hamster Ser.: 2). (ENG.). 176p. (J). (gr. 2-5). 12.99 *(978-1-62779-026-0(8)*, 9781627790260, Holt, Henry & Co. Bks. For Young Readers) Holt, Henry & Co.

—Einstein the Class Hamster Saves the Library. Tashjian, Janet. 2015. (Einstein the Class Hamster Ser.: 3). (ENG.). 192p. (J). (gr. 2-5). 13.99 *(978-1-62779-061-1(6)*, 9781627790611, Holt, Henry & Co. Bks. For Young Readers) Holt, Henry & Co.

—My Life As a Book. Tashjian, Janet. 2010. (My Life Ser.: 1). (ENG.). 224p. (J). (gr. 4-7). 19.99 *(978-0-8050-8903-5(9)*, 900054649, Holt, Henry & Co. Bks. For Young Readers) Holt, Henry & Co.

—My Life As a Cartoonist. Tashjian, Janet. 2013. (My Life Ser.: 3). (ENG.). 272p. (J). (gr. 4-7). 13.99 *(978-0-8050-9609-5(4)*, 900085725, Holt, Henry & Co. Bks. For Young Readers) Holt, Henry & Co.

—My Life As a Coder. Tashjian, Janet. 2020. (My Life Ser.: 9). (ENG.). 40p. (J). 13.99 *(978-1-250-26179-3(1)*, 900221423, Holt, Henry & Co. Bks. For Young Readers) Holt, Henry & Co.

—My Life As a Gamer. Tashjian, Janet. 2015. (My Life Ser.: 5). (ENG.). 272p. (J). (gr. 4-7). 13.99 *(978-0-8050-9851-8(8)*, 900122325, Holt, Henry & Co. Bks. For Young Readers) Holt, Henry & Co.

—My Life As a Gamer. Tashjian, Janet. 2018. (My Life Ser.: 5). (ENG.). 288p. (J). pap. 7.99 *(978-1-250-14368-6(3)*, 900180543) Square Fish.

—My Life As a Joke. Tashjian, Janet. 2014. (My Life Ser.: 4). (ENG.). 272p. (J). (gr. 4-7). 13.99 *(978-0-8050-9850-1(X)*, 900122324, Holt, Henry & Co. Bks. For Young Readers) Holt, Henry & Co.

—My Life As a Meme. Tashjian, Janet. 2019. (My Life Ser.: 8). (ENG.). 272p. (J). 13.99 *(978-1-250-19657-6(4)*, 900194128, Holt, Henry & Co. Bks. For Young Readers) Holt, Henry & Co.

—My Life As a Ninja. Tashjian, Janet. 2017. (My Life Ser.: 6). (ENG.). 240p. (J). 13.99 *(978-1-62779-889-1(7)*, 900161971, Holt, Henry & Co. Bks. For Young Readers) Holt, Henry & Co.

—My Life As a Ninja. Tashjian, Janet. 2019. (My Life Ser.: 6). (ENG.). 256p. (J). pap. 7.99 *(978-1-250-29415-9(0)*, 900161972) Square Fish.

—My Life as a Stuntboy. Tashjian, Janet. 2011. (My Life Ser.: 2). (ENG.). 272p. (J). (gr. 4-7). 15.99 *(978-0-8050-8904-2(7)*, 900054652, Holt, Henry & Co. Bks. For Young Readers) Holt, Henry & Co.

—My Life As a Stuntboy. Tashjian, Janet. 2015. (My Life Ser.: 2). (ENG.). 288p. (J). (gr. 4-7). pap. 7.99 *(978-1-250-01038-4(1)*, 900084784) Square Fish.

—My Life As a Youtuber. Tashjian, Janet. 2018. (My Life Ser.: 7). (ENG.). 272p. (J). 13.99 *(978-1-62779-892-1(7)*, 900161978, Holt, Henry & Co. Bks. For Young Readers) Holt, Henry & Co.

—My Life As a Youtuber. Tashjian, Janet. 2020. (My Life Ser.: 7). (ENG.). 240p. (J). pap. 7.99 *(978-1-250-23367-7(4)*, 900161979) Square Fish.

Taso, Alex. The Wind in the Willows. Grahame, Kenneth. 2006. (ENG.). 240p. (J). (gr. 5-18). 5.95 *(978-0-451-53014-1(4)*, Signet) Penguin Publishing Group.

Tatarnikau, Pavel. Arthur of Albion. Matthews, John & Matthe, John. 2008. 96p. (J). (gr. 3-6). 24.99 *(978-1-84686-049-2(0))* Barefoot Bks., Inc.

Tatarnikov, Pavel. The Snow Queen. Andersen, Hans. 2006.Tr. of ??????? ????????. (ENG.). 48p. (J). (gr. 1). 15.95 *(978-1-933327-22-8(7))*; lib. bdg. 16.50 *(978-1-933327-23-5(5))* Purple Bear Bks., Inc.

Tatcheva, Eva. Witch Zelda's Birthday Cake: A Wild & Wicked Pop-up, Pull-the-Tab Book. Tatcheva, Eva. 2004. 12p. (J). (gr. k-3). reprint ed. 18.00 *(978-0-7567-7225-3(7))* DIANE Publishing Co.

Tate, Danielle. Spartacus Gets Adopted. Suber, Sonia. 2019. (ENG.). 40p. (J). pap. 12.99 ***(978-1-0932-8714-1(4))*** Independently Published.

Tate, Don. The Amazing Age of John Roy Lynch. Barton, Chris. 2015. (ENG.). 50p. (J). 17.00 *(978-0-8028-5379-0(X)*, Eerdmans Bks For Young Readers) Eerdmans, William B. Publishing Co.

—Black All Around! Hubbell, Patricia. 2003. (ENG.). 32p. (J). 16.95 *(978-1-58430-048-9(5))* Lee & Low Bks., Inc.

—The Cart That Carried Martin. Bunting, Eve. 2013. 32p. (J). (gr. 1-4). lib. bdg. 16.95 *(978-1-58089-387-9(2))* Charlesbridge Publishing, Inc.

—Carter Reads the Newspaper. Hopkinson, Deborah. 2019. (ENG.). 36p. (J). (gr. 1-5). 17.95 *(978-1-56145-934-6(8))* Peachtree Publishing Co. Inc.

—Duke Ellington's Nutcracker Suite. Celenza, Anna Harwell. 2018. (Once upon a Masterpiece Ser.: 5). 32p. (J). (gr. 1-4). 16.99 *(978-1-57091-701-1(9))* Charlesbridge Publishing, Inc.

—¡fushhh! El Chorro de Inventos Súper Húmedos de Lonnie Johnson. Barton, Chris. 2019. 32p. (J). (gr. 2-5). 7.99 *(978-1-58089-523-1(9))*; 17.99 *(978-1-58089-233-9(7))* Charlesbridge Publishing, Inc.

—Greg & the Cheat Sheets, 1 vol. Wiggins, Thalia. 2012. (Making Choices: the Mcnair Cousins Ser.). (ENG.). 64p. (J). (gr. 2-5). 29.93 *(978-1-61641-630-0(0)*, 11301, Calico Chapter Bks.) ABDO Publishing Co.

—Greg & the Mural, 1 vol. Wiggins, Thalia. 2012. (Making Choices: the Mcnair Cousins Ser.). (ENG.). 64p. (J). (gr. 2-5). 29.93 *(978-1-61641-631-7(9)*, 11303, Calico Chapter Bks.) ABDO Publishing Co.

—Greg's Game Dilemma, 1 vol. Wiggins, Thalia. 2012. (Making Choices: the Mcnair Cousins Ser.). (ENG.). 64p. (J). (gr. 2-5). 29.93 *(978-1-61641-632-4(7)*, 11305, Calico Chapter Bks.) ABDO Publishing Co.

—The Hidden Feast: A Folktale from the American South. Hamilton, Martha & Weiss, Mitch. 2006. (ENG.). 32p. (J). (gr. k-3). 16.95 *(978-0-87483-758-2(8))* August Hse. Pubs., Inc.

—Hope's Gift. Lyons, Kelly Starling. 2012. (ENG.). 32p. (J). (gr. 1-3). 16.99 *(978-0-399-16001-1(9)*, G.P. Putnam's Sons Books for Young Readers) Penguin Young Readers Group.

—I Am My Grandpa's Enkelin. Wangerin, Walter, Jr. 2008. 30p. (J). (gr. 3-7). 18.95 *(978-1-55725-468-9(0))* Paraclete Pr., Inc.

—It Jes' Happened: When Bill Traylor Started to Draw, 1 vol. Christie, R. Gregory. 2012. (ENG.). 1p. (J). 17.95 *(978-1-60060-260-3(6))* Lee & Low Bks., Inc.

—James Cheats!, 1 vol. Wiggins, Thalia. 2012. (Making Choices: the Mcnair Cousins Ser.). (ENG.). 64p. (J). (gr. 2-5). 29.93 *(978-1-61641-633-1(5)*, 11307, Calico Chapter Bks.) ABDO Publishing Co.

—James Makes a Choice, 1 vol. Wiggins, Thalia. 2012. (Making Choices: the Mcnair Cousins Ser.). (ENG.). 64p. (J). (gr. 2-5). 29.93 *(978-1-61641-634-8(3)*, 11309, Calico Chapter Bks.) ABDO Publishing Co.

—James the Rock's Boys, 1 vol. Wiggins, Thalia. 2012. (Making Choices: the Mcnair Cousins Ser.). (ENG.). 64p. (J). (gr. 2-5). 29.93 *(978-1-61641-635-5(1)*, 11311, Calico Chapter Bks.) ABDO Publishing Co.

—No Small Potatoes: Junius G. Groves & His Kingdom in Kansas. Bolden, Tonya. 2018. 40p. (J). (gr. -1-3). 17.99 *(978-0-385-75276-3(8)*, Knopf Bks. for Young Readers) Random Hse. Children's Bks.

—No Small Potatoes: Junius G. Groves & His Kingdom in Kansas. Bolden, Tonya. 2018. (ENG.). 40p. (J). (gr. -1-3). lib. bdg. 20.99 *(978-0-385-75277-0(6)*, Knopf Bks. for Young Readers) Random Hse. Children's Bks.

—Par-Tay: Dance of the Veggies (and Their Friends) Greenfield, Eloise. 2018. (ENG.). 32p. (J). (gr. k-2). 17.95 *(978-0-9977720-2-9(6)*, Alazar Pr.) Royal Swan Enterprises, Inc.

—Ron's Big Mission. Blue, Rose & Naden, Corinne. 2009. (ENG.). 32p. (J). (gr. 1-3). 17.99 *(978-0-525-47849-2(3)*, Dutton Books for Young Readers) Penguin Young Readers Group.

—Say Hey! A Song of Willie Mays. Mandel, Peter. 2004. 30p. (J). (gr. k-2). reprint ed. 16.00 *(978-0-7567-8162-0(0))* DIANE Publishing Co.

—She Loved Baseball: The Effa Manley Story. Vernick, Audrey. 2010. (ENG.). 32p. (J). (gr. k-5). 16.99 *(978-0-06-134920-1(8)*, Collins) HarperCollins Pubs.

—Stalebread Charlie & the Razzy Dazzy Spasm Band. Mahin, Michael. 2018. (ENG.). 40p. (J). (gr. -1-3). 17.99 *(978-0-547-94201-8(X)*, 1517145) Houghton Mifflin Harcourt Publishing Co.

—Whoosh! Lonnie Johnson's Super-Soaking Stream of Inventions. Barton, Chris & Tate, Don, II. 2019. 32p. (J). (gr. 2-5). pap. 7.99 *(978-1-58089-298-8(1))* Charlesbridge Publishing, Inc.

—Whoosh! Lonnie Johnson's Super-Soaking Stream of Inventions. Barton, Chris. 2016. 32p. (J). (gr. 2-5). lib. bdg. 16.95 *(978-1-58089-297-1(3))* Charlesbridge Publishing, Inc.

Tate, Don. Poet: The Remarkable Story of George Moses Horton. Tate, Don. (ENG.). 36p. (J). (gr. 1-5). 2018. pap. 8.99 *(978-1-68263-062-4(5))*; 2015. 16.95 *(978-1-56145-825-7(2))* Peachtree Publishing Co. Inc.

Tate, Don. William Still & His Freedom Stories: The Father of the Underground Railroad. Tate, Don. 2020. (ENG.). 40p. (J). (gr. 1-5). 18.99 ***(978-1-56145-935-3(6))*** Peachtree Publishing Co. Inc.

Tate, Lizzy. I Love My Church. Tate, Andy. 2008. 16p. pap. 24.95 *(978-1-60441-419-6(7))* America Star Bks.

Tate, M., photos by. My Little Life: A Cancer Survivor's Story As Told by Nature. Tate, M. 2004. (YA). pap. 10.00 *(978-0-9761969-0-7(5))* Heads First (1st).

Tate, Richard. Jack Bates & the Wizard's Spell. Grantham, Leslie. 2016. (ENG.). 362p. (J). pap. *(978-1-9993063-2-8(5))* Mambi Bks. Ltd.

Tatic, Mihailo. Trixy & the Troublesome Egg: Trixy & Friends. Zapple, Elias. 2018. ('you Decide the Story' Interactive Picture Book Ser.: Vol. 1). (ENG.). 132p. (YA). pap. *(978-1-912704-33-0(1))* Heads or Tales Pr.

Tatlow-Lord, Robin. Go Away, Worry Monster! Graham, Brooke. 2020. (ENG.). 32p. (J). (gr. -1-5). 18.99 ***(978-1-925820-39-3(4)***, 335043, EK Bks.) Exisle Publishing Pty Ltd. AUS. Dist: Hachette Bk. Group.

Tatsuyama, Sayuri. Happy Happy Clover, Vol. 2. Tatsuyama, Sayuri. 2009. (ENG.). 192p. (J). pap. 9.99 *(978-1-4215-2657-7(3))* Viz Media.

—Happy Happy Clover, Vol. 3. Tatsuyama, Sayuri. 2009. (ENG.). 192p. (J). pap. 7.99 *(978-1-4215-2658-4(1))* Viz Media.

—Happy Happy Clover, Vol. 4. Tatsuyama, Sayuri. 2010. (ENG.). 192p. (J). pap. 7.99 *(978-1-4215-2735-2(9))* Viz Media.

Taub, Udi. A Chanukah Story. Davis, Linda. 2003. 24p. 12.99 *(978-1-58330-652-9(8))* Feldheim Pubs.

—When the Oomp & the Floomp Met the Groomp of Lake Bloomp. Shaked, S. 2016. (ENG.). 28p. (J). (gr. k-2). pap. *(978-965-92570-9-6(0))* Shaked, Shahaf.

Taulo, Tuija. King Solomon Figures It Out. Steinberg, Sari. 2005. 32p. (J). (gr. k-3). 9.95 *(978-965-465-004-5(5)*, Devora Publishing) Simcha Media Group.

Tauss, Marc. Desiderata: Words to Live By. Ehrmann, Max. 2003. (Desiderata Ser.). (ENG.). 48p. (J). 15.95 *(978-0-439-37293-0(3)*, Scholastic Pr.) Scholastic, Inc.

Tavares, Matt. A Ben of All Trades: the Most Inventive Boyhood of Benjamin Franklin. Rosen, Michael J. 2020. 32p. (J). (gr. k-4). 16.99 *(978-1-5362-0121-5(9))* Candlewick Pr.

—The Gingerbread Pirates. Kladstrup, Kristin. 2009. 32p. (J). (gr. -1-3). 16.99 *(978-0-7636-3223-6(6))* Candlewick Pr.

—The Gingerbread Pirates Gift Edition. Kladstrup, Kristin. gif. ed. 2012. 32p. (J). (gr. -1-3). 9.99 *(978-0-7636-6233-2(X))* Candlewick Pr.

—Helen's Big World: The Life of Helen Keller. Rappaport, Doreen. 2012. (Big Words Book Ser.: 4). (ENG.). 48p. (J). (gr. 1-3). 17.99 *(978-0-7868-0890-8(X))* Hyperion Pr.

—Jack & the Beanstalk. Nesbit, E. 2006. (ENG.). 48p. (J). (gr. -1-2). 18.99 *(978-0-7636-2124-7(2))* Candlewick Pr.

—Jack's Path of Courage: The Life of John F. Kennedy. Rappaport, Doreen. 2016. (Big Words Book Ser.: 3). 48p. (J). (gr. -1-3). pap. 8.99 *(978-1-4847-4961-6(8))* Hyperion Bks. for Children.

—Jack's Path of Courage: The Life of John F. Kennedy. Rappaport, Doreen. 2010. (Big Words Book Ser.: 3). 48p. (J). (gr. 1-3). 17.99 *(978-1-4231-2272-2(0))* Hyperion Pr.

—Lady Liberty: A Biography. Rappaport, Doreen. (Candlewick Biographies Ser.). (J). (gr. 3-7). 2014. (ENG.). 48p. 14.99 *(978-0-7636-7114-3(2))*; 2011. 40p. pap. 8.99 *(978-0-7636-5301-9(2))* Candlewick Pr.

—Lady Liberty: A Biography. Rappaport, Doreen. 2011. (ENG.). (J). (gr. 4-7). lib. bdg. 19.60 *(978-1-61383-052-9(1))* Perfection Learning Corp.

—Lighter Than Air: Sophie Blanchard, the First Woman Pilot. Smith, Matthew Clark. 2017. 32p. (J). (gr. 1-4). 16.99 *(978-0-7636-7732-9(9))* Candlewick Pr.

—Lighter Than Air: Sophie Blanchard, the First Woman Pilot: Candlewick Biographies. Smith, Matthew Clark. 2019. (Candlewick Biographies Ser.). (ENG.). 40p. (J). (gr. 1-4). pap. 4.99 *(978-1-5362-0555-8(9))* Candlewick Pr.

—'Twas the Night Before Christmas: Or Account of a Visit from St. Nicholas. Anonymous. 2006. (ENG.). 32p. (J). (gr. k-12). 9.99 *(978-0-7636-3118-5(3))* Candlewick Pr.

Tavares, Matt. Becoming Babe Ruth. Tavares, Matt. (Candlewick Biographies Ser.). (J). (gr. k-3). 2016. (ENG.). 48p. 14.99 *(978-0-7636-8767-0(7))*; 2013. 40p. 16.99 *(978-0-7636-5646-1(1))* Candlewick Pr.

—Crossing Niagara: The Death-Defying Tightrope Adventures of the Great Blondin. Tavares, Matt. (Candlewick Biographies Ser.). (J). (gr. 1-4). 2018. (ENG.). 40p. 14.99 *(978-1-5362-0341-7(6))*; 2018. (ENG.). 40p. pap. 4.99 *(978-1-5362-0342-4(4))*; 2016. 36p. 17.99 *(978-0-7636-6823-5(0))* Candlewick Pr.

—Dasher: How a Brave Little Doe Changed Christmas Forever. Tavares, Matt. 2019. (ENG.). (J). E-Book 17.99 *(978-1-5362-1490-1(6)*, 85751); 40p. (gr. -1-3). 17.99 *(978-1-5362-0137-6(5))* Candlewick Pr.

—Growing up Pedro: How the Martinez Brothers Made It from the Dominican Republic All the Way to the Major Leagues. Tavares, Matt. 2015. 40p. (J). (gr. 3-7). 16.99 *(978-0-7636-6824-2(9))* Candlewick Pr.

—Growing up Pedro: Candlewick Biographies: How the Martinez Brothers Made It from the Dominican Republic All the Way to the Major Leagues. Tavares, Matt. 2017. (Candlewick Biographies Ser.). 48p. (J). (gr. 3-7). 14.99 *(978-0-7636-9310-7(3))* Candlewick Pr.

—Henry Aaron's Dream. Tavares, Matt. (Candlewick Biographies Ser.). (J). 2015. (ENG.). 48p. (gr. k-3). 14.99 *(978-0-7636-7653-7(5))*; 2012. 40p. (gr. 3-7). pap. 6.99 *(978-0-7636-5820-5(0))*; 2010. (ENG.). 40p. (gr. 3-7). 16.99 *(978-0-7636-3224-3(4))* Candlewick Pr.

—Mudball. Tavares, Matt. 2011. 32p. (J). (gr. 1-4). pap. 7.99 *(978-0-7636-4136-8(7))* Candlewick Pr.

—Oliver's Game. Tavares, Matt. (Tavares Baseball Bks.). 32p. (J). (gr. 1-4). 2009. pap. 6.99 *(978-0-7636-4137-5(5))*; 2004. (ENG.). 15.99 *(978-0-7636-1852-0(7))* Candlewick Pr.

—Red & Lulu. Tavares, Matt. 2017. (ENG.). 40p. (J). (gr. -1-2). 17.99 *(978-0-7636-7733-6(7))* Candlewick Pr.

—There Goes Ted Williams: The Greatest Hitter Who Ever Lived. Tavares, Matt. 2015. (Candlewick Biographies Ser.). (ENG.). 48p. (J). (gr. 1-4). 14.99 *(978-0-7636-7655-1(1))* Candlewick Pr.

—Zachary's Ball. Tavares, Matt. anniv. ed. 2012. (Tavares Baseball Bks.). (ENG.). 32p. (J). (gr. 1-4). pap. 6.99 *(978-0-7636-5977-6(0))*; (gr. k-2). 21.19 *(978-0-7636-5033-9(1))* Candlewick Pr.

Tavares, Victor. Beauty & the Beast. 2007. (Picture Book Classics Ser.). (J). 24p. (gr. -1-3). 9.99 *(978-0-7945-1855-4(9))*; 63p. 8.99 *(978-0-7945-1456-3(1))* EDC Publishing. (Usborne).

—Lin Yi's Lantern: A Moon Festival Tale. Williams, Brenda. 2008. 32p. (J). *(978-1-84686-148-2(9))* Barefoot Bks., Inc.

—The Magical Book. Sims, Lesley. 2007. (Young Reading Series 2 Gift Bks). 64p. (J). (gr. 4-7). 8.99 *(978-0-7945-1703-8(X)*, Usborne) EDC Publishing.

Tavares, Victor. Star Seeker: A Journey to Outer Space. Tavares, Victor. Heine, Theresa. 2006. (ENG.). 32p. (J). (gr. -1-3). 16.99 *(978-1-905236-36-7(0))* Barefoot Bks., Inc.

Tavares, Victore. Three Musketeers. Levene, Rebecca, ed. 2009. (Young Reading 3 Ser.). 64p. (J). (gr. 2). 6.99 *(978-0-7945-1946-9(6)*, Usborne) EDC Publishing.

Tavcar, Samantha, jt. illus. see Eagle, Joy.

Tavernier, Sarah, jt. illus. see Verhille, Alexandre.

Taxali, Gary. Apple. DePrisco, Dorothea. 2005. (Plush Learning Books Ser.). 10p. (J). bds. 6.95 *(978-1-58117-191-4(9)*, Intervisual/Piggy Toes) Bendon, Inc.

—Lemon. DePrisco, Dorothea. 2005. (Plush Learning Books Ser.). 10p. (J). bds. 6.95 *(978-1-58117-194-5(3)*, Intervisual/Piggy Toes) Bendon, Inc.

—Orange. DePrisco, Dorothea. 2005. (Plush Learning Books Ser.). 10p. (J). bds. 6.95 *(978-1-58117-192-1(7)*, Intervisual/Piggy Toes) Bendon, Inc.

—Pear. DePrisco, Dorothea. 2005. (Plush Learning Books Ser.). 10p. (J). bds. 6.95 *(978-1-58117-193-8(5)*, Intervisual/Piggy Toes) Bendon, Inc.

—A Perfect Idiot. Iodice, Frank. 2017. (ENG.). 164p. (J). pap. *(978-88-943762-2-7(2))* Associazione culturale Articoli Liberi.

Tay-Audouard, L. K. Monkey King: A Classic Chinese Tale for Children. Seow, David. 2017. 32p. (J). (gr. -1-3). 9.95 *(978-0-8048-4840-4(8))* Tuttle Publishing.

Tay-Audouard, L. K. Singapore Children's Favorite Stories. Tay-Audouard, L. K. Taylor, Diane. 2003. (ENG.). 96p. (J). (gr. k-8). 18.95 *(978-0-7946-0097-6(2)*, PeriplusEdition) Tuttle Publishing.

Tay-Audouard, Lak-Khee. Chinese Fables: The Dragon Slayer & Other Timeless Tales of Wisdom. Tay-Audouard, Lak-Khee. Nunes, Shiho S. 2013. 64p. (J). (gr. 3-6). 16.95 *(978-0-8048-4152-8(7))* Tuttle Publishing.

Tayal, Amit. Carma Comes Home. Troupe, Thomas Kingsley. 2017. (Star Belchers Ser.). (ENG.). 128p. (J). (gr. 3-6). pap. 7.95 *(978-1-4965-4877-1(9)*, 135642); lib. bdg. 25.99 *(978-1-4965-4873-3(6)*, 135638) Capstone. (Stone Arch Bks.).

—Conquering Everest: the Lives of Edmund Hillary & Tenzing Norgay: A Graphic Novel. Helfand, Lewis. 2011. (Campfire Graphic Novels Ser.). (ENG.). 96p. (YA). (gr. 5-12). pap. 12.99 *(978-93-80741-24-6(3)*, Campfire) Steerforth Pr.

—Jack & the Beanstalk: An Interactive Fairy Tale Adventure. Hoena, B. A. 2015. (You Choose: Fractured Fairy Tales Ser.). (ENG.). 112p. (J). (gr. 3-7). pap. 6.95 *(978-1-4914-5930-0(1)*, Capstone Pr.) Capstone.

—Jewel of the Galaxy. Troupe, Thomas Kingsley. 2017. (Star Belchers Ser.). (ENG.). 128p. (J). (gr. 3-6). lib. bdg. 25.99 *(978-1-4965-4874-0(4)*, 135639, Stone Arch Bks.) Capstone.

—No Kidding, Mermaids Are a Joke! The Story of the Little Mermaid As Told by the Prince. Loewen, Nancy. 2013. (Other Side of the Story Ser.). (ENG.). 24p. (J). (gr. -1-3). 9.95 *(978-1-4795-1947-7(2)*, Picture Window Bks.) Capstone.

—No Kidding, Mermaids Are a Joke! The Story of the Little Mermaid As Told by the Prince. Loewen, Nancy. 2013. (Other Side of the Story Ser.). (ENG.). 24p. (J). (gr. -1-3). 27.99 *(978-1-4048-8303-1(7)*, Picture Window Bks.) Capstone.

—Robot Ruckus. Troupe, Thomas Kingsley. 2017. (Star Belchers Ser.). 128p. (J). (gr. 3-6). lib. bdg. 25.99 *(978-1-4965-4872-6(8)*, 135637, Stone Arch Bks.) Capstone.

—A Spaceship Named Judy. Troupe, Thomas Kingsley. 2017. (Star Belchers Ser.). (ENG.). 128p. (J). (gr. 3-6). pap. 7.95 *(978-1-4965-4875-7(2)*, 135640); lib. bdg. 25.99 *(978-1-4965-4871-9(X)*, 135636) Capstone. (Stone Arch Bks.).

—The Swiss Family Robinson. Wyss, Johann David. 2011. (Campfire Graphic Novels Ser.). (ENG.). 88p. (YA). (gr. 3-7). pap. 11.99 *(978-93-80028-47-7(4)*, Campfire) Steerforth Pr.

—The Three Musketeers. Dumas, Alexandre. 2011. (Campfire Graphic Novels Ser.). (ENG.). 104p. (YA). (gr. 3-7). pap. 12.99 *(978-93-80028-57-6(1)*, Campfire) Steerforth Pr.

—Truly, We Both Loved Beauty Dearly! The Story of Sleeping Beauty as Told by the Good & Bad Fairies. Shaskan, Trisha Speed. 2013. (Other Side of the Story Ser.). (ENG.). 24p. (J). (gr. -1-3). 27.99 *(978-1-4048-7940-9(4)*, Picture Window Bks.) Capstone.

—Truly, We Both Loved Beauty Dearly! The Story of Sleeping Beauty As Told by the Good & Bad Fairies. Shaskan, Trisha Speed. 2013. (Other Side of the Story Ser.). (ENG.). 24p. (J). (gr. -1-3). 9.95 *(978-1-4795-1945-3(6)*, Picture Window Bks.) Capstone.

Tayal, Amit & Alsonso, Denis. No Kidding, Mermaids Are a Joke! The Story of the Little Mermaid, As Told by the Prince. Loewen, Nancy. 2013. (Other Side of the Story Ser.). (ENG.). 24p. (J). (gr. -1-3). pap. 6.95 *(978-1-4795-1951-4(0)*, Picture Window Bks.) Capstone.

—Truly, We Both Loved Beauty Dearly! The Story of Sleeping Beauty, As Told by the Good & Bad Fairies. Shaskan, Trisha Speed & Loewen, Nancy. 2013. (Other Side of the Story Ser.). (ENG.). 24p. (J). (gr. -1-3). pap. 6.95 *(978-1-4795-1949-1(9)*, Picture Window Bks.) Capstone.

Tayal, Amit & Nagar, Sachin. Escape from Hotel Infinity (Numbers) Poskitt, Kjartan. 2017. (Mission Math Ser.). (ENG.). 48p. (J). (gr. 2-4). lib. bdg. 31.99 *(978-1-68297-188-8(0))* QEB Publishing Inc.

Tayal, Amit, jt. illus. see Alonso, Denis.

Tayama, Thomas. Mother Goose on the Loose in Guam A Chamorro Adaptation of Traditional Nursery Rhymes. Jackson, Marilyn Malloy, ed. 2006. (J). 6.50 net. *(978-0-9790111-5-3(9))* M-m-mauleg Publishing.

Taylor, Adam. The Exasperated Clock. Hickman, Debbie. 2013. 40p. pap. *(978-1-4602-1811-2(6))* FriesenPress.

—Little Red Fire. Heidari, Mahdi. 2012. 40p. (J). pap. 12.99 *(978-0-9838321-8-8(8))* Higher Ground Pr.

—Saving Santa's Seals. Murphy, T. M. 2009. (LeapKids Ser.). (ENG.). 170p. (J). (gr. 1-5). pap. 10.95 *(978-0-9815148-8-8(X))* Leapfrog Pr.

Taylor, Adam. George in the UK: The Unknown Kingdom. Taylor, Adam. West, Jeannette, ed. 2011. 28p. (J). 8.99 *(978-0-9766062-9-1(1))* Higher Ground Pr.

Taylor, Amber. Mommy Does a Lot So I Want to Too, 1 vol. Reyes, S. L. 2010. 30p. 24.95 *(978-1-4489-5420-9(7))* PublishAmerica, Inc.

Taylor, Amber L. I'm Two, So What Should I Do?, 1 vol. Reyes, Shawntie L. 2010. 34p. 24.95 *(978-1-4489-7869-4(6))* PublishAmerica, Inc.

Taylor, Ann Creal. Lydia Ann & Scraggles: The Adventures of a Girl & Her Dog. Taylor, Ann Creal. Creal, Nancy. 2013. 28p. (J). 12.00 *(978-0-9800059-4-3(9))* Taylor, Ann.

Taylor, Ashley. It's Your Universe: You Have the Power to Make It Happen. Eckstein, Ashley & Kravetz, Stacy. 2018. (ENG.). 208p. (YA). (gr. 7-12). 17.99 *(978-1-368-02132-6(8)*, Disney Editions) Disney Pr.

Taylor, Brian. Escape from Hat. Kline, Adam. 2020. (ENG.). 176p. (J). (gr. 3-7). 17.99 *(978-0-06-283997-8(7)*, HarperCollins) HarperCollins Pubs. Ltd. GBR. Dist: HarperCollins Pubs.

Taylor, Bridget Starr. The Truth about Trolls, 1 vol. Troupe, Thomas Kingsley. 2010. (Fairy-Tale Superstars Ser.). (ENG.). 32p. (J). (gr. 1-3). lib. bdg. 27.99 *(978-1-4048-5984-5(5)*, Picture Window Bks.) Capstone.

—Why the Stomach Growls. Edwards, Pamela Duncan. 2006. (ENG.). 32p. (J). (gr. k-6). 15.95 *(978-1-58536-298-1(0))* Sleeping Bear Pr.

Taylor, Byron. Ghost Stories from the American South. McNeil, W. K., ed. 2005. (ENG.). 176p. (J). (gr. 4-17). pap. 15.95 *(978-0-935304-84-8(3))* August Hse. Pubs., Inc.

Taylor, Carol. The Pony Princess. Watts, Ana Dearborn & Dearborn, Dorothy. 2008. (ENG.). 32p. pap. 6.00 *(978-1-896543-32-1(4))* DreamCatcher Publishing CAN. Dist: Univ. of Toronto Pr.

Taylor, Carolyn. The Princess & the Garden. Johnson, Esther A. 2012. 34p. pap. 19.99 *(978-1-62419-614-0(4))* Salem Author Services.

Taylor, Catherine. Downtown Ducks. Taylor, Douglas. 2005. 62p. (J). per. 22.99 *(978-1-4134-3803-1(2))* Xlibris Corp.

Taylor, Chet. Brother Dragon. Branson, Terri. 2004. (J). 18.99 *(978-0-9755888-5-7(0))* Dragonfly Publishing, Inc.

—Little Lost Leprechaun. Gorgas, Paula Blais. l.t. ed. 2005. 20p. (J). 17.99 *(978-0-9755888-4-0(2))* Dragonfly Publishing, Inc.

—Perky Turkey Finds a Friend. Goodspeed, Judy. l.t. ed. 2006. 24p. (J). pap. 14.99 *(978-0-9765786-6-6(2))* Dragonfly Publishing, Inc.

—Perky Turkey's Perfect Plan. Goodspeed, Judy. 2005. 22p. (J). 18.99 *(978-0-9765786-0-4(3))* Dragonfly Publishing, Inc.

—Pete, the Peacock, Goes to Town. Branson, Terri. l.t. ed. 2005. 22p. (J). lib. bdg. 24.95 *(978-0-9765786-1-1(1))* Dragonfly Publishing, Inc.

—Tyler on the Moon. Branson, Terri. l.t. ed. 24p. (J). 2005. lib. bdg. 24.95 *(978-0-9765786-2-8(X))*; 2004. 18.99 *(978-0-9755888-2-6(6))* Dragonfly Publishing, Inc.

Taylor, Chet. Last, but Not Least. Taylor, Chet. l.t. ed. 2004. 20p. (J). 17.99 *(978-0-9755888-6-4(9))*; lib. bdg. 22.99 *(978-0-9755888-1-9(8))* Dragonfly Publishing, Inc.

Taylor, Chris. How to Speak Cow. Irwin, Jonathan. 2019. (ENG.). 24p. (J). (gr. 4-2). 14.99 *(978-1-7282-0520-5(4)*, Sourcebooks Jabberwocky) Sourcebooks, Inc.

Taylor, Clive. Brave Mouse, 3 vols., Pack. Eggleton, Jill. (Sails Literacy Ser.). 24p. (gr. 1-18). 57.00 *(978-0-7578-3205-5(9))* Rigby Education.

—Rabbit & Rooster's Ride: 3-in-1 Package. Eggleton, Jill. (Sails Literacy Ser.). 24p. (gr. k-18). 57.00 *(978-0-7578-8617-1(5))* Rigby Education.

—Rabbit & Rooster's Ride: 6 Small Books. Eggleton, Jill. (Sails Literacy Ser.). 24p. (gr. k-18). 25.00 *(978-0-7578-7727-8(3))* Rigby Education.

—Rabbit & Rooster's Ride: Big Book Only. Eggleton, Jill. (Sails Literacy Ser.). 24p. (gr. k-18). 27.00 (978-0-7578-6200-7(4)) Rigby Education.

Taylor, Dan. But the Bear Came Back. Sauer, Tammi. 2018. 32p. (J). (gr. -1). 16.95 (978-1-4549-2098-4(X)) Sterling Publishing Co., Inc.

—First Stories: Nutcracker. 2018. (First Stories Ser.). (ENG.). 10p. (J). (— 1). bds. 8.99 (978-1-68412-380-3(1), Silver Dolphin Bks.) Printers Row Publishing Group.

—Goodnight Sleepyheads. Fischer, Maggie. 2019. (ENG.). 12p. (J). (— 1). bds. 8.99 (978-1-68412-612-5(6), Silver Dolphin Bks.) Printers Row Publishing Group.

Taylor, Dan. Iguanodon: The Noisy Night, 1 vol. Veitch, Catherine. 2020. (Dinosaur Adventures Ser.). (ENG.). 24p. (gr. 1-2). pap. 8.25 **(978-1-4994-8493-9(3)**, Windmill Bks.) Rosen Publishing Group, Inc., The.

Taylor, Dan. A Little Chicken. Sauer, Tammi. 2019. 32p. (J). (gr. -1). 16.95 (978-1-4549-2900-0(6)) Sterling Publishing Co., Inc.

—My First Day. Sparrow, Leilani. 2015. (ENG.). 32p. (J). (gr. -1-k). 16.99 (978-1-4998-0111-8(4)) Little Bee Books Inc.

—My New Friends. Sparrow, Leilani. 2018. (ENG.). 32p. (J). (gr. -1-k). 16.95 (978-1-910716-75-5(8)) Boxer Bks., Ltd. GBR. Dist: Sterling Publishing Co., Inc.

—My New Shoes. Sparrow, Leilani. (Mini Bee Board Bks.). (ENG.). (J). (gr. -1-1). 2018. 24p. bds. 7.99 (978-1-4998-0729-5(5)); 2016. 32p. 16.99 (978-1-4998-0363-1(X)) Little Bee Books Inc.

—Old MacDonald Had a Band: Board Book with Handle. Wing, Scarlett. Cottage Door Press, ed. 2015. (Sing & Smile Stories Ser.). (ENG.). 10p. (J). (gr. -1-k). bds. 8.99 (978-1-68052-003-3(2), 1000040) Cottage Door Pr.

Taylor, David A. Bandit Raccoon. McCorkle, Barbara. l.t. ed. 2006. 39p. (J). 19.95 (978-1-59879-170-9(2)); per. 13.99 (978-1-59879-123-5(0)) Lifevest Publishing, Inc.

—Brutis' New Friend. McCorkle, Barbara. 2007. 30p. (J). 13.99 (978-1-59879-439-7(6)) Lifevest Publishing, Inc.

Taylor, David C. The Adventures of Theo & Gus Gus. Hughes, Megan Hoert. 2018. (ENG.). 32p. (J). pap. 10.00 (978-1-59715-190-0(4)) Chapel Hill Press, Inc.

Taylor, David W. Christian Kids Explore Biology. Redmond, Stephanie L. 2007. (Christian Kids Explore Ser.). 291p. per. 34.95 (978-1-892427-05-2(2)) Bright Ideas! Educational Resources.

Taylor, David W., Jr. & Northcutt, Leslie L. Earth & Space. Redmond, Stephanie L. 2006. (Christian Kids Explore Ser.). 363p. (J). (gr. 3-7). per. (978-1-892427-19-9(2)) Bright Ideas! Educational Resources.

Taylor, Debbie. Merry Kissmus, Lincoln! Fletcher, E. B. 2019. (ENG.). 36p. (J). pap. 16.99 **(978-1-7283-3005-1(X))** AuthorHouse.

Taylor, E. Dee. Lots of Cats. Taylor, E. Dee. 2018. (ENG.). 40p. (J). (gr. -1-3). 16.99 (978-0-06-267569-9(9)) HarperCollins Pubs.

Taylor, Edwardian. It's Not Hansel & Gretel. Funk, Josh. 2019. (It's Not a Fairy Tale Ser.: 2). 40p. (J). (gr. k-3). 17.99 (978-1-5039-0294-7(3), 9781503902947, Two Lions) Amazon Publishing.

—Race! Fliess, Sue. 2017. (ENG.). 32p. (J). (gr. -1-3). 16.99 (978-1-4998-0237-5(4)) Little Bee Books Inc.

—Ready for Action. Lynch, Brian. 2019. (Toy Academy Ser.: 2). (ENG.). 192p. (J). (gr. 2-5). 14.99 (978-1-338-14916-6(4), Scholastic Pr.) Scholastic, Inc.

—Toy Academy: Some Assembly Required (Toy Academy #1) Lynch, Brian. 2017. (Toy Academy Ser.: 1). (ENG.). 192p. (J). (gr. 2-5). 12.99 (978-1-338-14845-9(1), Scholastic Pr.) Scholastic, Inc.

Taylor, Eleanor. Cha-Cha Chimps. Durango, Julia. 2010. (ENG.). 32p. (J). (gr. -1-3). 7.99 (978-1-4169-9574-6(9), Simon & Schuster Bks. For Young Readers) Simon & Schuster Bks. For Young Readers.

—The Christmas Tale of Peter Rabbit. Thompson, Emma. 2013. (Peter Rabbit Ser.). (ENG.). 72p. (J). (gr. -1-2). 20.00 (978-0-7232-7694-4(3), Warne) Penguin Young Readers Group.

—A Christmas Wish: A Peter Rabbit Tale. Potter, Beatrix. 2017. (Peter Rabbit Ser.). (ENG.). 16p. (J). (-k). bds. 7.99 (978-0-241-29334-8(0), Warne) Penguin Young Readers Group.

—The Further Tale of Peter Rabbit. Thompson, Emma. 2012. (Peter Rabbit Ser.). (ENG.). 72p. (J). (gr. -1-2). 20.00 (978-0-7232-6910-6(6), Warne) Penguin Young Readers Group.

—Go-Go Gorillas. Durango, Julia. 2010. (ENG.). 32p. (J). (gr. -1-3). 19.99 (978-1-4169-3779-1(X), Simon & Schuster Bks. For Young Readers) Simon & Schuster Bks. For Young Readers.

—Half a Creature from the Sea: A Life in Stories. Almond, David. 2015. (ENG.). 240p. (YA). (gr. 7). 16.99 (978-0-7636-7877-7(5)) Candlewick Pr.

—A Little Guide to Gardening. Elworthy, Jo. 2018. (Little Guide Ser.). (ENG.). 80p. (J). (gr. k-2). pap. 15.99 (978-0-9574907-2-7(0)) Transworld Publishers Ltd. GBR. Dist: Independent Pubs. Group.

—The Spectacular Tale of Peter Rabbit. Thompson, Emma. 2014. (Peter Rabbit Ser.). (ENG.). 72p. (J). (gr. -1-2). 20.00 (978-0-7232-7116-1(X), Warne) Penguin Young Readers Group.

Taylor, Eleonor. Sgeulachd Eile Mu Pheader Rabaid. Thompson, Emma et al. 2012.Tr. of Further Tale of Peter Rabbit. (GLA.). 80p. (J). (978-1-907676-12-3(0)) Grace Note Pubns.

Taylor, Erin. The Adventures of the Little Prince. Evans, Rosemary R. 2011. (ENG.). 44p. (J). 16.95 (978-1-61658-706-2(7)) Independent Pub.

—Collins Big Cat Phonics for Letters & Sounds - Bad Luck, Dad: Band 01B/Pink B, Bd. 1B. Coe, Catherine. 2018. (Collins Big Cat Phonics Ser.). (ENG.). 16p. (J). pap. 6.99 (978-0-00-825140-6(1)) HarperCollins Pubs. Ltd. GBR. Dist: Independent Pubs. Group.

—Go Go Sadie. Lee, Bonnie. 2011. 46p. 24.00 (978-1-4349-8679-5(9), RoseDog Bks.) Dorrance Publishing Co., Inc.

—Grandma Hugs: Large Little Bird Greetings. Birdsong, Minnie. Cottage Door Press, ed. 2018. (Little Bird Greetings Keepsake Book Ser.). (ENG.). 10p. (J). (gr. -1-2). bds. 6.99 (978-1-68052-380-5(5), 1003450) Cottage Door Pr.

—Grandma Hugs: Little Bird Greetings. Birdsong, Minnie. Cottage Door Press, ed. 2019. (Little Bird Greetings Keepsake Book Ser.). (ENG.). 8p. (J). (gr. -1-2). bds. 6.99 (978-1-68052-478-9(X), 1003590) Cottage Door Pr.

—The Little Princesses Magial Party. Evans, Rosemary R. 2012. 40p. (J). 16.95 (978-1-60743-759-8(7)) Wink Publishing.

Taylor, Erin. A Magical Day in Grandpa's Garden. Meadowsweet, Felicity. 2019. (Magical Garden Ser.: Vol. 1). (ENG.). 36p. (J). (gr. k-5). pap. 9.99 **(978-1-7338765-0-6(2))** Magic Mountain Pr.

Taylor, Erin. Pat Roll Pull: A Challah Braiding Story. Heald, Robin. Rosenfeld, Dina, ed. 2012. 32p. (J). 10.95 (978-1-929628-64-3(1)) Hachai Publishing.

Taylor, Geoff. Chronicles of Ancient Darkness #1: Wolf Brother. Paver, Michelle. 2006. (Chronicles of Ancient Darkness Ser.: 1). (ENG.). 320p. (J). (gr. 5-9). reprint ed. per. 6.99 (978-0-06-072827-4(2), Tegen, Katherine Bks) HarperCollins Pubs.

—Chronicles of Ancient Darkness #2: Spirit Walker, 2. Paver, Michelle. 2007. (Chronicles of Ancient Darkness Ser.: 2). (ENG.). 384p. (J). (gr. 5-8). pap. 6.99 (978-0-06-072830-4(2)) HarperCollins Pubs.

—Chronicles of Ancient Darkness #3: Soul Eater. Paver, Michelle. 2008. (Chronicles of Ancient Darkness Ser.: 3). (ENG.). 352p. (J). (gr. 5). pap. 7.99 (978-0-06-072833-5(7), Tegen, Katherine Bks) HarperCollins Pubs.

—Chronicles of Ancient Darkness #4: Outcast, 4. Paver, Michelle. 2009. (Chronicles of Ancient Darkness Ser.: 4). (ENG.). 352p. (J). (gr. 5-8). pap. 6.99 (978-0-06-072836-6(1)) HarperCollins Pubs.

—Chronicles of Ancient Darkness #5: Oath Breaker. Paver, Michelle. (Chronicles of Ancient Darkness Ser.: 5). (ENG.). (J). (gr. 5-18). 2009. 304p. 16.99 (978-0-06-072837-3(X), Tegen, Katherine Bks); 5. 2010. 320p. pap. 6.99 (978-0-06-072839-7(6)) HarperCollins Pubs.

—Chronicles of Ancient Darkness #6: Ghost Hunter, 6. Paver, Michelle. 2011. (Chronicles of Ancient Darkness Ser.: 6). (ENG.). 304p. (J). (gr. 5-8). pap. 7.99 (978-0-06-072842-7(6)) HarperCollins Pubs.

Taylor, Gerad. The Real Story of the Exodus. Maier, Paul L. 2009. 32p. (J). (gr. -1-3). 16.99 (978-0-7586-1268-7(0)) Concordia Publishing Hse.

Taylor, Gypsy. Pearlie & Great Aunt Garnet. Harmer, Wendy. 2014. (Pearlie Ser.: 7). 48p. (Orig.). (J). (gr. 2-4). pap. 8.99 (978-1-74166-131-6(5)) Random Hse. Australia AUS. Dist: Independent Pubs. Group.

—Pearlie & Sapphire. Harmer, Wendy. 2014. (Pearlie Ser.: 8). 48p. (J). (gr. 2-4). pap. 8.99 (978-1-74166-137-8(4)) Random Hse. Australia AUS. Dist: Independent Pubs. Group.

—Pearlie & the Fairy Queen. Harmer, Wendy. 2014. (Pearlie Ser.: 10). 48p. (J). (gr. 2-4). pap. 8.99 (978-1-74166-149-1(8)) Random Hse. Australia AUS. Dist: Independent Pubs. Group.

—Pearlie Goes to Rio. Harmer, Wendy. 2015. (Pearlie Ser.: 16). 48p. (J). (gr. 2-4). pap. 8.99 (978-0-85798-216-2(8)) Random Hse. Australia AUS. Dist: Independent Pubs. Group.

—Pearlie in Central Park. Harmer, Wendy. 2014. (Pearlie Ser.: 11). 48p. (J). (gr. 2-4). pap. 8.00 (978-1-74166-377-8(6)) Random Hse. Australia AUS. Dist: Independent Pubs. Group.

—Pearlie in Paris. Harmer, Wendy. 2015. (Pearlie Ser.: 14). 48p. (J). (gr. 2-4). pap. 7.99 (978-1-74166-380-8(6)) Random Hse. Australia AUS. Dist: Independent Pubs. Group.

Taylor Harris Photography, photos by. I Believe I'll Testify: A True Story about the Power of Prayer. Harris, Patricia Taylor. 2008. (ENG., 53p. (YA). pap. 18.95 (978-0-615-24897-4(7)) Blue Scribbles Publishing.

Taylor, Jacqui. Chizi's Tale. Jones, Jack. 2nd ed. 2016. (ENG.). 28p. (J). (gr. k-2). pap. 3.99 (978-1-943154-00-5(7)) Peek-A-Boo Publishing.

Taylor, Jane. Actau. Mackenzie, Carine & Gair, Cyhoeddiadau'r. 2005. (WEL.). 16p. pap. (978-1-85994-271-0(7)) Cyhoeddiadau'r Gair.

—Hosea - Malachi. Mackenzie, Carine & Gair, Cyhoeddiadau'r. 2005. (WEL.). 16p. pap. (978-1-85994-272-7(5)) Cyhoeddiadau'r Gair.

—6 1 Timotheus - Datguddiad. Mackenzie, Carine & Gair, Cyhoeddiadau'r. 2005. (WEL.). 16p. pap. (978-1-85994-269-7(5)) Cyhoeddiadau'r Gair.

Taylor, JaRabia. The Big Rig Kids. Brown, Renee. 2016. 119p. (J). (978-0-692-79625-2(8)) Big Rig LLC.

Taylor, Jeannie St. John & St. John Taylor, Jeannie. Who Did It? Mehl, Ron & Taylor, Jeannie St. John. St. John Taylor, Jeannie. 2004. 32p. (J). (gr. k-4). 12.99 (978-0-8254-3168-5(9)) Kregel Pubns.

Taylor, Jen. Brave Little Camper: Sound Book Wood Button Module. Crowe, Carmen. 2016. (Early Bird Sound Bks.). (ENG.). 10p. (J). (gr. -1-k). bds. 12.99 (978-1-68052-074-3(1), 1000770) Cottage Door Pr.

—Brave Little Camper Saves Christmas: Square Padded Board Picture Book. Berry Byrd, Holly. Cottage Door Press, ed. 2017. (ENG.). 13p. (J). (gr. -1-k). bds. 7.99 (978-1-68052-232-7(9), 1002180) Cottage Door Pr.

—Brave Little Camper Saves Halloween: Square Padded Board Book. VonFeder, Rosa. Cottage Door Press, ed. 2018. (ENG.). 14p. (J). (gr. -1-k). bds. 7.99 (978-1-68052-172-6(1), 1001700) Cottage Door Pr.

Taylor, Jen. Dirt: Peek-A-Flap. Redwing, Jack. Cottage Door Press, ed. 2020. (John Deere Peek-A-Flap Board Book Ser.). (ENG.). 12p. (J). (gr. -1-1). bds. 8.99 **(978-1-68052-810-7(6)**, 1005230) Cottage Door Pr.

Taylor, Jen. Earth Day Extravaganza: Book 4. Bovis, Ali. 2019. (Sylvie Ser.). (ENG.). 112p. (J). (gr. 2-5). lib. bdg. 29.93 (978-1-5321-3654-2(4), 33754, Calico Chapter Bks.) ABDO Publishing Co.

—Flash, the Little Fire Engine. Calvert, Pam. 2019. (ENG.). 40p. (J). (gr. -1-1). 17.99 (978-1-5420-4178-2(3), 9781542041782, Two Lions) Amazon Publishing.

—Ninja Camp. Fliess, Sue. 2019. 384p. (J). (gr. -1-3). 17.99 (978-0-7624-6331-2(7), Running Pr. Kids) Running Pr.

—Organizer Extraordinaire: Book 3. Bovis, Ali. 2019. (Sylvie Ser.). (ENG.). 112p. (J). (gr. 2-5). lib. bdg. 29.93 (978-1-5321-3653-5(6), 33752, Calico Chapter Bks.) ABDO Publishing Co.

—Save the Beach: Book 2. Bovis, Ali. 2019. (Sylvie Ser.). (ENG.). 112p. (J). (gr. 2-5). lib. bdg. 29.93 (978-1-5321-3652-8(8), 33750, Calico Chapter Bks.) ABDO Publishing Co.

—Sea View Star: Book 1. Bovis, Ali. 2019. (Sylvie Ser.). (ENG.). 112p. (J). (gr. 2-5). lib. bdg. 29.93 (978-1-5321-3651-1(X), 33748, Calico Chapter Bks.) ABDO Publishing Co.

—Sylvie (Set), 4 vols. Bovis, Ali. 2019. (Sylvie Ser.). (ENG.). 112p. (J). (gr. 2-5). lib. bdg. 119.72 (978-1-5321-3650-4(1), 33746, Calico Chapter Bks.) ABDO Publishing Co.

Taylor, Jennifer. The Life of Riley the Cat. Akerson, Julie Chicos. 2005. 28p. (J). 15.50 (978-1-4120-5858-2(9)) Trafford Publishing.

—A Little Nana Story. Hall, Wanda. 2007. (ENG.). 26p. pap. 12.99 (978-1-4257-4109-9(6)) Xlibris Corp.

—The Rising Star Ball. Rickman, Jeanie Parker. 2006. 32p. per. 17.95 (978-1-59858-201-7(1)) Dog Ear Publishing, LLC.

—Way down Yonder in the Paw Paw Patch. Clark, Abbie. 2006. 32p. (J). (gr. -1-3). per. 16.95 (978-1-59858-129-4(5)) Dog Ear Publishing, LLC.

Taylor, Jennifer Louise. The Cookie Crumb Trail. Johnson, Doris M. 2008. (ENG.). 28p. pap. 15.99 (978-1-4196-9127-0(9)) CreateSpace Independent Publishing Platform.

Taylor, Jenny. Anna the Goanna: And Other Poems. McDougall, Jill. 2009. 48p. (J). (gr. k-6). pap. 17.95 (978-0-85575-616-1(0)) Aboriginal Studies Pr. AUS. Dist: Independent Pubs. Group.

Taylor, Jill. Little Wolf's Christmas. Hopkins, Suzette. 2004. (Little Wolf & Friends Ser.). 19p. (J). 12.95 (978-1-932133-72-1(0)) Writers' Collective, The.

Taylor, Jo. Family Fix-It Plan. Higgins, M. G. 2016. (Sibling Split Ser.). (ENG.). 112p. (J). (gr. 3-6). lib. bdg. 25.32 (978-1-4965-2590-1(6), Stone Arch Bks.) Capstone.

—The Impossible Wish. Higgins, M. G. 2016. (Sibling Split Ser.). (ENG.). 112p. (J). (gr. 3-6). lib. bdg. 25.32 (978-1-4965-2593-2(0), Stone Arch Bks.) Capstone.

—Party of Nine. Higgins, M. G. 2016. (Sibling Split Ser.). (ENG.). 112p. (J). (gr. 3-6). lib. bdg. 25.32 (978-1-4965-2592-5(2), Stone Arch Bks.) Capstone.

—Sibling Split, 4 vols. Higgins, M. G. 2016. (Sibling Split Ser.). (ENG.). 112p. (J). (gr. 3-6). lib. bdg., lib. bdg., lib. bdg. 101.28 (978-1-4965-2721-9(6), Stone Arch Bks.) Capstone.

—Trouble in the City. Higgins, M. G. 2016. (Sibling Split Ser.). (ENG.). 112p. (J). (gr. 3-6). lib. bdg. 25.32 (978-1-4965-2591-8(4), Stone Arch Bks.) Capstone.

Taylor, John. Lucky Dip, Vol. Boddy, Catharine. 2016. (ENG.). 36p. (J). (gr. 2-6). pap. 6.99 (978-1-908853-79-0(4)) Valley Pr.

Taylor, Jon. Tower of Babel. 2007. 24p. (J). (gr. 4-7). 14.99 (978-0-89051-487-0(9), Master Books) New Leaf Publishing Group.

Taylor, Jonathan. My Creation Bible: Teaching Kids to Trust the Bible from the Very First Verse. Ham, Ken. 2006. (ENG.). 12p. (J). (gr. -1-1). bds., bds. 11.99 (978-0-89051-462-7(3), Master Books) New Leaf Publishing Group.

Taylor, Josephine. Lawrence the Laughing Cookie Jar. Marks, William C. 2003. 16.95 (978-0-9715541-0-8(2)) MPC Pr. International.

Taylor, Josh. Joshua & the Spider. Blocker, Adam P. 2013. (ENG.). 72p. 17.99 (978-1-939418-08-1(9)) Writer of the Round Table Pr.

Taylor, Kathleen. Eddie & Bingo: A Friendship Tale. Taylor, Kathleen. 2011. 42p. (J). pap. 21.95 (978-1-59299-558-5(6)) Inkwater Pr.

Taylor, Kathy. Max is Mad... Mad about Everything!! Cartwright, Genita. 2005. (ENG.). 26p. per. 13.99 (978-1-4134-6750-5(4)) Xlibris Corp.

Taylor-Kielty, Simon. The Special Christmas Tree. Walters, Catherine. 2012. (J). (978-1-4351-4315-9(9)) Barnes & Noble, Inc.

Taylor, Kristen Michelle. Tatiana. Mbonu, Ngozi Elizabeth. 2013. (ENG.). (J). 14.95 (978-1-62086-307-7(3)) Mascot Bks., Inc.

Taylor, Lawrie. Goldilocks & the Three Bears. Andrews, Jackie. 2012. (ENG.). 32p. (J). pap. 6.50 (978-1-84135-191-9(1)) Award Pubns. Ltd. GBR. Dist: Parkwest Pubns., Inc.

—Great Big Enormous Turnip. Andrews, Jackie. 2012. (ENG.). 32p. (J). pap. 6.50 (978-1-84135-192-6(X)) Award Pubns. Ltd. GBR. Dist: Parkwest Pubns., Inc.

—Henny Penny. Andrews, Jackie. 2012. (ENG.). 32p. (J). pap. 6.50 (978-1-84135-194-0(6)) Award Pubns. Ltd. GBR. Dist: Parkwest Pubns., Inc.

Taylor, Linda. Wisdom Weaver/Bina'nitin Bidziilgo Atł'óhí. Johnson, Jann A. Manavi, Lorraine Begay, tr. from ENG. 2006. (ENG.). 32p. (J). (gr. -1-3). 17.95 (978-1-893354-82-1(2)) Salina Bookshelf Inc.

Taylor, Lori. What to Do When Your Hoof Turns Blue!!! Taylor, Lori. l.t. ed. 2006. 28p. (J). pap. 20.99 (978-1-59879-220-1(2)) Lifevest Publishing, Inc.

Taylor, Marjorie. Challenger. Bricker, Sandra D. Miller, Zachary N., ed. rev. ed. 2003. (Take Ten Ser.). 47p. (J). (gr. 4-18). pap. 4.95 (978-1-58659-021-5(9)) Artesian Pr.

—The Kuwaiti Oil Fires. Skip Press Staff. Miller, Zachary N., ed. rev. ed. 2003. (Take Ten Ser.). 46p. (J). (gr. 4-18). pap. 4.95 (978-1-58659-024-6(3)) Artesian Pr.

—The Mount St. Helens Volcano. Bankier, William. Miller, Zachary N., ed. rev. ed. 2003. (Take Ten Ser.). 45p. (J). (gr. 4-12). pap. 4.95 (978-1-58659-023-9(5)) Artesian Pr.

—The Nuclear Disaster at Chernobyl. Cruise, Robin. rev. ed. 2003. (Take Ten Ser.). 46p. (J). (gr. 4-18). pap. 4.95 (978-1-58659-022-2(7)) Artesian Pr.

Taylor, Mark. The Tale of Sidney Elderberry - an Ordinary Boy with Extraordinary Bowels. Younge, Cathy. 2013. 32p. pap. (978-1-78148-838-6(X)) Grosvenor Hse. Publishing Ltd.

Taylor, Matt. Randolph the Christmas Moose: A Yuletide Fable of Empowerment. Gibson, Gerry. 2020. (ENG.). 46p. (J). 27.95 **(978-1-61599-500-4(5))**; pap. 15.95 **(978-1-61599-499-1(8))** Loving Healing Pr., Inc.

Taylor, Matt, jt. illus. see Bruff, Alex.

Taylor, Mike. Mesoamerican Myths. West, David. 2006. (Graphic Mythology Ser.). (ENG.). 48p. (J). (gr. 4-7). lib. bdg. 35.45 (978-1-4042-0802-5(X)) Rosen Publishing Group, Inc., The.

Taylor, Nadia. Into the Forest. Baker, Laura. 2018. (ENG.). 10p. (J). (gr. -1-k). bds. 9.99 (978-1-4197-3354-3(0), Abrams Appleseed) Abrams, Inc.

Taylor, Nancy Simms. Little Manger, Oh, Little Manger! Taylor, Nancy Simms. Taylor, Randy Mark. 2020. (ENG.). 32p. (J). pap. 10.95 **(978-1-6548-2723-6(1))** Independently Published.

Taylor, Natascha. Angry Potato Man: ... & the Jellybellies! Taylor, Natascha Rosina. 2016. (ENG.). (J). pap. (978-0-9566666-7-3(1)) nischnasch.

—The Beetle, Barabus. Taylor, Natascha Rosina. 2016. (ENG.). (J). pap. (978-0-9566666-8-0(X)) nischnasch.

Taylor, Nate. The Adventures of the Princess & Mr. Whiffle: The Thing Beneath the Bed. Rothfuss, Patrick. 2010. 68p. 25.00 (978-1-59606-313-6(0)) Subterranean Pr.

Taylor, Ned. A Letter to Santa. Davies, Gill. 2015. (J). (978-1-4351-6225-9(0)) Barnes & Noble, Inc.

—The Night Before Christmas. 2016. (ENG.). 26p. (J). (-k). bds. 8.95 (978-1-78557-515-0(5)) Igloo Bks. GBR. Dist: Simon & Schuster, Inc.

—Santa's Snow Globe: Join the Snowy Fun & Discover Adventure Friends & Love. 2017. (ENG.). 24p. (J). 9.95 (978-1-78670-963-9(5)) Igloo Bks. GBR. Dist: Simon & Schuster, Inc.

Taylor, Nicole. Hug-A-Bug Travels to Greece. Church, Anna. 2012. 44p. pap. 12.00 (978-0-9831449-5-3(8)) Mighty Lion Ventures.

Taylor, Nicole, jt. illus. see Church, Anna.

Taylor, Nina. The Day We Asked the Fish to Climb the Tree. Kee, Kate. 2019. (ENG.). 36p. (J). (gr. 1-2). pap. (978-1-9996213-7-7(9)) Cavalcade Bks.

Taylor, Nina. Tilly Millpepper & the Enchanted Book. Narracott, J. E. 2020. (ENG.). 210p. (J). (gr. 3-6). pap. **(978-1-9996213-8-4(7))** Cavalcade Bks.

Taylor, Nina. Tilly Millpepper & the Wishing Stone. Narracott, J. E. 2019. (ENG.). 184p. (J). (gr. 3-6). pap. (978-1-9996213-6-0(0)) Cavalcade Bks.

Taylor, Nina. Tilly Millpepper & the Wishing Stone. Narracott, J. E. 2020. (ENG.). 180p. (J). (gr. 3-6). **(978-1-9996213-9-1(5))** Cavalcade Bks.

Taylor, Non, et al. Yummy Little Cookbook. Gilpin, Rebecca & Atkinson, Catherine. rev. ed. 2007. (Children's Cooking Ser.). (ENG.). 96p. (J). (gr. -1-3). 7.99 (978-0-7945-1655-0(6), Usborne) EDC Publishing.

Taylor, Peter Lane & Nicola, Christos, photos by. The Secret of Priest's Grotto: A Holocaust Survival Story, Vol. Taylor, Peter Lane & Nicola, Christos. 2007. (ENG., 64p. (YA). (gr. 5-12). per. 8.95 (978-1-58013-261-9(8), Kar-Ben Publishing) Lerner Publishing Group.

Taylor, R. For Merrie England: A Tale of the Weavers of Norfolk. Leslie, Emma. 2010. 168p. 20.95 (978-1-934671-38-2(X)); pap. 10.95 (978-1-934671-39-9(8)) Salem Ridge Press LLC.

Taylor, Rachaele. A Family of One. Brenneman, Kenneth M. 2019. (ENG.). 44p. (J). pap. 12.00 **(978-1-6884-0089-4(3))** Independently Published.

Taylor, Roger. The Special Birthday. MacKenzie, Carine. 2010. (Bible Art Ser.). (ENG.). 16p. (J). pap., act. bk. ed. 2.50 (978-1-85792-307-0(3), 6618a232-d277-46c3-9ff9-4f07facdcb67) Christian Focus Pubns. GBR. Dist: Baker & Taylor Publisher Services (BTPS).

Taylor, Sally & van Deelen, Fred. Changeling. Gregory, Philippa. 2012. (Order of Darkness Ser.: 1). (ENG.). 272p. (YA). (gr. 9). 18.99 (978-1-4424-5344-9(3), Simon Pulse) Simon Pulse.

Taylor, Sally, jt. illus. see van Deelen, Fred.

Taylor, Sol. Te Amare Siempre. Margot, Recast. 2015. (SPA.). 292p. (J). pap. (978-84-606-9254-6(X)) Castro, Emma Requejo.

Taylor, Stephen. Cakewalk. Helmso, Candy Grant. 2003. (Books for Young Learners). (ENG.). 16p. (J). pap. 5.75 net. (978-1-57274-250-5(X), 2727, Bks. for Young Learners) Owen, Richard C. Pubs., Inc.

—Gift Days, 1 vol. Winters, Kari-Lynn. 2012. (ENG.). 32p. (J). (gr. k-3). 18.95 (978-1-55455-192-7(7), edaa418b-b268-43f3-b4b6-f2437f545a7a) Trifolium Bks., Inc. CAN. Dist: Firefly Bks., Ltd.

—Like You, Like Me, 1 vol. Morgan, Cliff. 2010. 20p. 24.95 (978-1-4489-5140-6(2)) PublishAmerica, Inc.

Taylor, Sue. Yarns of Ballpoint II. Olofson, Darrell. 2005. (ENG.). 44p. (J). spiral bd. (978-1-60225-002-4(2)) Motherhood Printing & Etc.

Taylor, Theodore. Buzzing with Questions: The Inquisitive Mind of Charles Henry Turner. Harrington, Janice N. 2019. 48p. (J). (gr. 2-5). 18.99 (978-1-62979-558-4(5), Calkins Creek) Boyds Mills Pr.

—Little Shaq. O'Neal, Shaquille. 2015. 73p. (J). (978-1-68119-119-5(9)) Bloomsbury Pr.

Taylor, Theodore, III. Little Shaq. O'Neal, Shaquille. (ENG.). 80p. (J). 2016. pap. 6.99 (978-1-61963-722-1(7), 900146361); 2015. 9.99 (978-1-61963-721-4(9), 900146374) Bloomsbury Publishing USA. (Bloomsbury USA Childrens).

—Little Shaq: Star of the Week. O'Neal, Shaquille. 2016. (ENG.). 80p. (J). 9.99 (978-1-61963-879-2(7), 900150926, Bloomsbury USA Childrens) Bloomsbury Publishing USA.

—Little Shaq Takes a Chance. O'Neal, Shaquille. 2016. (ENG.). 80p. (J). 9.99 (978-1-61963-844-0(4),

T

900150245, Bloomsbury USA Childrens) Bloomsbury Publishing USA.
—Trailblazer: The Story of Ballerina Raven Wilkinson. Schubert, Leda. 2018. (ENG.). 40p. (J). (gr. k-4). 17.99 *(978-1-4998-0592-5(6))* Little Bee Books Inc.
—When the Beat Was Born: DJ Kool Herc & the Creation of Hip Hop. Hill, Laban Carrick. 2013. (ENG.). 32p. (J). (gr. 1-5). 18.99 *(978-1-59643-540-7(2)*, 900061866) Roaring Brook Pr.
—Woke: A Young Poet's Call to Justice. Browne, Mahogany L. et al. 2020. (ENG.). 56p. (J). 18.99 *(978-1-250-31120-7(9)*, 900198839) Roaring Brook Pr.
—Woke Baby. Browne, Mahogany L. 2018. (ENG.). 22p. (J). bds. 7.99 *(978-1-250-30898-6(4)*, 900198423) Roaring Brook Pr.
Taylor, Thomas. Franklin's Bear. d'Lacey, Chris. 2005. (Red Go Bananas Ser.). (ENG.). 48p. (J). (gr. 2-3). *(978-0-7787-2696-8(7))*; lib. bdg. *(978-0-7787-2674-6(6))* Crabtree Publishing Co.
—It's Hard to Hurry When You're a Snail, 1 vol. Stewart, Dorothy. 2009. 32p. (J). 14.95 *(978-0-8254-7838-3(3)*, Lion Children's) Lion Hudson PLC GBR. Dist: Kregel Pubns.
—The Red Ribbon: A Book about Friendship. Reader's Digest Editors, ed. 2004. (ENG.). 14p. (J). 12.99 *(978-0-7944-0401-7(4)*, Reader's Digest Children's Bks.) Studio Fun International.
—Scarlett Hart: Monster Hunter. Sedgwick, Marcus. 2018. (ENG.). 208p. (J). 23.99 *(978-1-250-15984-7(9)*, 900185794); pap. 14.99 *(978-1-62672-026-8(6)*, 900131764) Roaring Brook Pr. (First Second Bks.).
Taylor, Trace. Viento. Sánchez, Lucia M. 2010. (1B Nuestro Mundo Natural Ser.). (SPA.). 40p. (J). pap. 9.60 *(978-1-61406-207-3(2))* American Reading Co.
Taylor, Trace. Baseball. Taylor, Trace. 2009. (2G Sports Ser.). (ENG.). 16p. (J). (gr. k-2). pap. 8.00 *(978-1-59301-877-1(0))* American Reading Co.
—Basketball. Taylor, Trace. 2011. (2G Sports Ser.). (ENG.). 12p. (J). (gr. k-2). pap. 8.00 *(978-1-59301-876-4(2))* American Reading Co.
—Bikes. Taylor, Trace. 2015. (1-3Y Getting Around Ser.). (ENG.). 24p. (J). (gr. k-2). pap. 8.00 *(978-1-59301-465-0(1))* American Reading Co.
—Cobras. Taylor, Trace. Lynch, Michelle. 2015. (2G Predator Animals Ser.). (ENG.). 24p. (J). (gr. k-2). pap. 8.00 *(978-1-61541-504-5(1))* American Reading Co.
—Dogtown Diner. Taylor, Trace. 2010. (1G ARC Press Comics Ser.). (ENG.). 24p. (J). (gr. k-2). pap. 8.00 *(978-1-61541-073-6(2))* American Reading Co.
—Jumping Spiders. Taylor, Trace. 2012. (1-3Y Bugs Ser.). (ENG.). 20p. (J). pap. 8.00 *(978-1-61406-687-3(6))* American Reading Co.
—Lions of Africa. Taylor, Trace. 2015. (1-3Y Wild Animals Ser.). (ENG.). 24p. (J). (gr. k-2). pap. 8.00 *(978-1-59301-654-8(9))* American Reading Co.
—Nile Crocodiles. Taylor, Trace. 2016. (1-3Y Reptiles Ser.). (ENG.). 24p. (J). (gr. k-2). pap. 8.00 *(978-1-59301-655-5(7))* American Reading Co.
—Owls. Taylor, Trace. Cline, Gina. 2017. (2G Predator Animals Ser.). (ENG.). 32p. (J). pap. 8.00 *(978-1-61406-133-5(5))* American Reading Co.
—Sea Turtles. Taylor, Trace. 2010. (1-3Y Marine Life Ser.). (ENG.). 16p. (J). pap. 8.00 *(978-1-61541-483-3(5))* American Reading Co.
—Soccer. Taylor, Trace. 2009. (2G Sports Ser.). (ENG.). 16p. (J). (gr. k-2). pap. 9.60 *(978-1-59301-878-8(9))* American Reading Co.
—The Tree Truck. Taylor, Trace. 2015. (1-3Y Jobs & Careers Ser.). (ENG.). 24p. (J). (gr. k-2). pap. 8.00 *(978-1-59301-463-6(5))* American Reading Co.
—Wheels. Taylor, Trace. 2009. (1-3Y Getting Around Ser.). (ENG.). 16p. (J). pap. 8.00 *(978-1-61406-201-1(3))* American Reading Co.
—Who Took That Dog? Taylor, Trace. 2012. (1B Graphic Novels Ser.). (ENG.). 32p. (J). (gr. k-2). pap. 8.00 *(978-1-59301-757-6(X))* American Reading Co.
—You Think You Know Giraffes. Taylor, Trace. 2013. (1-3Y Mammals Ser.). (ENG.). 20p. (J). (gr. k-2). pap. 9.60 *(978-1-59301-437-7(6))* American Reading Co.
—You Think You Know Hippos. Taylor, Trace. 2008. (1-3Y Wild Animals Ser.). (ENG.). 24p. (J). (gr. k-2). pap. 5.99 *(978-1-59301-267-0(5))* American Reading Co.
Taylor, Trace, jt. illus. see Bianchi, John.
Taylor, Val Paul. Who Is Maria Tallchief? Gourley, Catherine. 2003. (Who Was... ? Ser.). 103p. 15.00 *(978-0-7569-1592-6(9))* Perfection Learning Corp.
Taylor, Victoria. Billy the Kid & Crooked Jim: Book 6. Gleason, Mike. 2018. (Hideout Kids Ser.). (ENG.). 130p. (J). (gr. k-4). *(978-1-912207-16-9(8))*; pap. *(978-1-912207-15-2(X))* Farm Street Publishing.
—The Parrot Gang & Wild West Ghosts: Book 5. Gleason, Mike. 2018. (Hideout Kids Ser.: Vol. 5). (ENG.). 130p. (J). (gr. k-4). *(978-1-912207-13-8(3))*; pap. *(978-1-912207-12-1(5))* Farm Street Publishing.
Taylor, Yvonne. Hartlie: The Streak. Taylor, Yvonne. (Hartlie: Vol. 1). 32p. (J). 10.99 *(978-0-9709187-0-3(4))* Peaceable Productions.
Taylour-Simone. The Fish Boy. Kalivas, Marleen. 2018. (ENG.). 82p. (J). pap. 18.95 *(978-1-64258-678-7(1))* Christian Faith Publishing.
Tayts, Alexandra. Celeste & the Adorable Kitten. Typaldos, Melanie. 2013. 244p. 14.99 *(978-0-9899847-0-6(2))* Capybara Madness.
Tazzyman, David. Circus of Thieves & the Comeback Caper. Sutcliffe, William. 2017. (ENG.). 272p. (J). pap. 7.99 *(978-1-4711-4535-3(2)*, Simon & Schuster Children's) Simon & Schuster, Ltd. GBR. Dist: Simon & Schuster, Inc.
—Circus of Thieves & the Raffle of Doom. Sutcliffe, William. 2016. (ENG.). 224p. (J). pap. 7.99 *(978-1-4711-2023-7(6)*, Simon & Schuster Children's) Simon & Schuster, Ltd. GBR. Dist: Simon & Schuster, Inc.
—Circus of Thieves on the Rampage. Sutcliffe, William. 2017. (ENG.). 288p. (J). pap. 7.99 *(978-1-4711-2025-1(2)*, Simon & Schuster Children's) Simon & Schuster, Ltd. GBR. Dist: Simon & Schuster, Inc.
—Mr Gum & the Biscuit Billionaire. Stanton, Andy. 2019. (Mr Gum Ser.: 2). (ENG.). 192p. (J). (gr. 2-6). pap. 10.99 *(978-1-4052-9370-9(5))* Egmont Bks., Ltd. GBR. Dist: Independent Pubs. Group.
—Mr Gum & the Goblins. Stanton, Andy. 2019. (Mr Gum Ser.: 3). (ENG.). 208p. (J). (gr. 2-6). pap. 10.99 *(978-1-4052-9371-6(3))* Egmont Bks., Ltd. GBR. Dist: Independent Pubs. Group.
—Natboff! One Million Years of Stupidity. Stanton, Andy. 2019. (ENG.). 288p. (J). (gr. 2-7). pap. 10.99 *(978-1-4052-9098-2(6))* Egmont Bks., Ltd. GBR. Dist: Independent Pubs. Group.
—You're a Bad Man, Mr. Gum! Stanton, Andy. 2019. (Mr Gum Ser.: 1). (ENG.). 192p. (J). (gr. 2-6). pap. 10.99 *(978-1-4052-9369-3(1))* Egmont Bks., Ltd. GBR. Dist: Independent Pubs. Group.
TBD, T. B. D. Great Expectations: A BabyLit Storybook, 1 vol. 2018. 28p. (J). 12.99 *(978-1-4236-4984-7(2))* Gibbs Smith, Publisher.
Tcherevkoff, Michel, jt. illus. see Barrager, Brigette.
Tchoukriel, Emmanuelle. Animal Atlas. Aladjidi, Virginia. Ramsey, Cecelia, tr. 2016. (ENG.). 112p. (J). (gr. 5-8). 24.99 *(978-1-4926-4163-6(4)*, 9781492641636, Sourcebooks Jabberwocky) Sourcebooks, Inc.
te Loo, Sanne. Cherry Blossom & Paper Planes, 23 vols. Aerts, Jef. 2020. (ENG.). 48p. (J). 17.95 *(978-1-78250-561-7(X))* Floris Bks. GBR. Dist: Consortium Bk. Sales & Distribution.
—On the Spot: Countless Funny Stories. Rosenthal, Amy Krouse & Redmond, Lea. 2017. (ENG.). 32p. (J). (gr. -1-2). 16.99 *(978-1-101-93230-8(9)*, Random Hse. Bks. for Young Readers) Random Hse. Children's Bks.
Te Selle, Davis. Whitefoot: A Story from the Center of the World. Berry, Wendell. 2010. (ENG.). 64p. pap. 12.95 *(978-1-58243-640-1(1)*, Counterpoint) Counterpoint Pr.
—Whitefoot: A Story from the Center of the World. Berry, Wendell & Rorer, Abigail. 2008. (Port William Ser.). (ENG.). 64p. (gr. 2-7). 22.00 *(978-1-58243-432-2(8)*, Counterpoint) Counterpoint Pr.
Te Whata, Munro. We Are the Rock! Niue Heroes. Tamua, Evotia, photos by. Riley, David. 2012. (ENG.). 106p. pap. 28.00 *(978-1-877484-21-6(0)*, 11775) Little Island Press NZL. Dist: Univ. of Hawaii Pr.
Teagle, Caitlyn. Just Batty. Spalding, Brenda M. 2011. 26p. pap. 12.00 *(978-1-61204-156-8(6)*, Strategic Bk. Publishing) Strategic Book Publishing & Rights Agency (SBPRA).
Teague, Mark. ¿Cómo Aprenden los Colores los Dinosaurios? Yolen, Jane. 2006. (How Do Dinosaurs... Ser.).Tr. of How Do Dinosaurs Learn Their Colors?. (SPA.). 12p. (J). (gr. -1-k). bds. 6.99 *(978-0-439-87192-1(1)*, Scholastic en Espanol) Scholastic, Inc.
—¿Cómo Comen los Dinosaurios? Yolen, Jane. 2006. (How Do Dinosaurs... Ser.). (SPA.). 40p. (J). (gr. -1-k). pap. 6.99 *(978-0-439-76404-9(1)*, Scholastic en Espanol) Scholastic, Inc.
—Como Dicen Estoy Enojado los Dinosaurios? Yolen, Jane. 2014. (SPA.). 40p. (J). (gr. -1-k). pap. 6.99 *(978-0-545-62780-1(X)*, Scholastic en Espanol) Scholastic, Inc.
—¿Cómo Eligen Sus Mascotas Los Dinosaurios? Yolen, Jane. 2017. (SPA.). 40p. (J). (gr. -1-k). 6.99 *(978-1-338-16020-8(6)*, Scholastic en Espanol) Scholastic, Inc.
—How Do Dinosaurs Choose Their Pets? Yolen, Jane. 2016. (How Do Dinosaurs... ? Ser.). (ENG.). 40p. (J). (gr. -1-k). 16.99 *(978-1-338-03278-9(X)*, Blue Sky Pr., The) Scholastic, Inc.
—How Do Dinosaurs Clean Their Rooms? Yolen, Jane. 2004. (How Do Dinosaurs... ? Ser.). (ENG.). 12p. (J). (gr. -1-k). bds. 6.99 *(978-0-439-64950-6(1)*, Blue Sky Pr., The) Scholastic, Inc.
—How Do Dinosaurs Count to Ten? Yolen, Jane. 2004. (How Do Dinosaurs... ? Ser.). (ENG.). 12p. (J). (gr. -1-k). bds. 7.99 *(978-0-439-64949-0(8)*, Blue Sky Pr., The) Scholastic, Inc.
—How Do Dinosaurs Eat Cookies? Yolen, Jane. 2012. (How Do Dinosaurs... Ser.). (ENG.). 14p. (J). (gr. -1-k). 7.99 *(978-0-545-38253-3(X)*, Cartwheel Bks.) Scholastic, Inc.
—How Do Dinosaurs Eat Their Food? Yolen, Jane. 2005. (How Do Dinosaurs... ? Ser.). (ENG.). 40p. (J). (gr. -1-k). 17.99 *(978-0-439-24102-1(2)*, Blue Sky Pr., The) Scholastic, Inc.
—How Do Dinosaurs Get Well Soon? Yolen, Jane. 2003. (How Do Dinosaurs... ? Ser.). (ENG.). 40p. (J). (gr. -1-3). 16.99 *(978-0-439-24100-7(6)*, Blue Sky Pr., The) Scholastic, Inc.
—How Do Dinosaurs Go to School? Yolen, Jane. 2007. (How Do Dinosaurs... ? Ser.). (ENG.). 40p. (J). (gr. -1-k). 17.99 *(978-0-439-02081-7(6))* Scholastic, Inc.
—How Do Dinosaurs Go to School? Yolen, Jane. 2011. (J). (gr. -1-3). 29.95 *(978-0-545-19700-7(7))*; 18.95 *(978-0-545-19707-6(4))* Weston Woods Studios, Inc.
—How Do Dinosaurs Go to Sleep? Yolen, Jane. 2016. (How Do Dinosaurs... ? Ser.). (ENG.). 12p. (J). (— 1). bds. 6.99 *(978-0-545-94120-4(2)*, Blue Sky Pr., The) Scholastic, Inc.
—How Do Dinosaurs Laugh Out Loud? Yolen, Jane. 2010. (How Do Dinosaurs... Ser.). (ENG.). 16p. (J). (gr. -1-k). pap. 7.99 *(978-0-545-23652-2(5)*, Cartwheel Bks.) Scholastic, Inc.
—How Do Dinosaurs Learn Their Colors? Yolen, Jane. 2006. (How Do Dinosaurs... ? Ser.). (ENG.). 12p. (J). (gr. -1-k). bds. 7.99 *(978-0-439-85653-9(1)*, Blue Sky Pr., The) Scholastic, Inc.
—How Do Dinosaurs Learn to Read? Yolen, Jane. 2018. (How Do Dinosaurs... ? Ser.). (ENG.). 40p. (J). (gr. -1-k). 16.99 *(978-1-338-23301-8(7)*, Blue Sky Pr., The) Scholastic, Inc.
—How Do Dinosaurs Love Their Cats? Yolen, Jane. 2010. (How Do Dinosaurs... ? Ser.). (ENG.). 14p. (J). (gr. -1-k). bds. 7.99 *(978-0-545-15354-6(9))* Scholastic, Inc.
—How Do Dinosaurs Love Their Dogs? Yolen, Jane. 2010. (How Do Dinosaurs... ? Ser.). (ENG.). 14p. (J). (gr. -1-k). bds. 7.99 *(978-0-545-15352-2(2))* Scholastic, Inc.
—How Do Dinosaurs Play with Their Friends? Yolen, Jane. 2006. (How Do Dinosaurs... ? Ser.). (ENG.). 6p. (J). (gr. -1-k). bds. 7.99 *(978-0-439-85654-6(X)*, Blue Sky Pr., The) Scholastic, Inc.
—How Do Dinosaurs Say Good Night? Yolen, Jane. (How Do Dinosaurs... ? Ser.). (ENG.). (J). (gr. -1 — 1). 2020. 34p. bds. 7.99 *(978-0-545-15351-5(4)*, Blue Sky Pr., The); 2008. audio compact disk 10.99 *(978-0-545-09319-4(8))* Scholastic, Inc.
—How Do Dinosaurs Say Good Night? Yolen, Jane. 2004. (J). (gr. -1-3). 29.95 *(978-1-55592-138-5(8))* Weston Woods Studios, Inc.
—How Do Dinosaurs Say Happy Birthday? Yolen, Jane. 2011. (How Do Dinosaurs... ? Ser.). (ENG.). 12p. (J). (gr. -1-k). bds. 7.99 *(978-0-545-15353-9(0)*, Blue Sky Pr., The) Scholastic, Inc.
—How Do Dinosaurs Say Happy Chanukah? Yolen, Jane. 2012. (How Do Dinosaurs... ? Ser.). (ENG.). 40p. (J). (gr. -1 — 1). 16.99 *(978-0-545-41677-1(9)*, Blue Sky Pr., The) Scholastic, Inc.
—How Do Dinosaurs Say I Love You? Yolen, Jane. (J). 2011. pap. *(978-0-545-33076-3(9))*; 2009. (ENG.). 40p. (gr. -1 — 1). 16.99 *(978-0-545-14314-1(4)*, Blue Sky Pr., The) Scholastic, Inc.
—How Do Dinosaurs Say I'm Mad? Yolen, Jane. 2013. (How Do Dinosaurs... ? Ser.). (ENG.). 40p. (J). (gr. -1-k). 16.99 *(978-0-545-14315-8(2)*, Blue Sky Pr., The) Scholastic, Inc.
—How Do Dinosaurs Say Merry Christmas? Yolen, Jane. 2012. (How Do Dinosaurs... ? Ser.). (ENG.). 40p. (J). (gr. -1-k). 16.99 *(978-0-545-41678-8(7)*, Blue Sky Pr., The) Scholastic, Inc.
—How Do Dinosaurs Stay Friends? Yolen, Jane. 2016. (How Do Dinosaurs... ? Ser.). (ENG.). 40p. (J). (gr. -1-k). 16.99 *(978-0-545-82934-2(8)*, Exhibit A) Scholastic, Inc.
—How Do Dinosaurs Stay Safe? Yolen, Jane. 2015. (How Do Dinosaurs... ? Ser.). (ENG.). 40p. (J). (gr. -1-k). 16.99 *(978-0-439-24104-5(9)*, Blue Sky Pr., The) Scholastic, Inc.
—How Do Dinosaurs Write Their ABC's with Chalk? Yolen, Jane. 2016. (How Do Dinosaurs... ? Ser.). (ENG.). 16p. (J). (gr. -1-k). 10.99 *(978-0-545-89052-6(7)*, Blue Sky Pr., The) Scholastic, Inc.
—Poppleton. Rylant, Cynthia. 2015. 56p. pap. 4.00 *(978-1-61003-551-4(8))* Center for the Collaborative Classroom.
—Poppleton in Spring. Rylant, Cynthia. 2009. (Scholastic Reader Level 3 Ser.). (ENG.). 48p. (J). (gr. -1-3). pap. 3.99 *(978-0-545-07867-2(9)*, Cartwheel Bks.) Scholastic, Inc.
—Poppleton in Winter. Rylant, Cynthia. 2008. 48p. (gr. -1-3). 14.00 *(978-0-7569-8910-1(8))* Perfection Learning Corp.
—Poppleton in Winter, Level 3. Rylant, Cynthia. 2008. (Scholastic Reader Level 3 Ser.). (ENG.). 48p. (J). (gr. -1-3). pap. 3.99 *(978-0-545-06823-9(1)*, Cartwheel Bks.) Scholastic, Inc.
—Poppleton Se Divierte. Rylant, Cynthia. 2006. (Poppleton Ser.). (SPA.). 48p. pap. 11.73 *(978-0-15-356487-1(3))* Harcourt Children's Bks.
—The Tree House That Jack Built. Verburg, Bonnie. 2014. (ENG.). 40p. (J). (gr. -1-k). 17.99 *(978-0-439-85338-5(9)*, Orchard Bks.) Scholastic, Inc.
Teague, Mark. Dear Mrs. LaRue: Letters from Obedience School. Teague, Mark. 2003. (LaRue Bks.). (ENG.). 32p. (J). (gr. -1-3). 17.99 *(978-0-439-20663-1(4)*, Scholastic Pr.) Scholastic, Inc.
—Detective LaRue: Letters from the Investigation. Teague, Mark. 2004. (LaRue Bks.). (ENG.). 32p. (J). (gr. -1-3). 17.99 *(978-0-439-45868-9(4)*, Scholastic Pr.) Scholastic, Inc.
—Felipe & Claudette. Teague, Mark. 2019. (ENG.). 40p. (J). (gr. -1-k). 17.99 *(978-0-545-91432-1(9)*, Orchard Bks.) Scholastic, Inc.
—Firehouse! Teague, Mark. 2017. (StoryPlay Ser.). (ENG.). 40p. (J). (gr. -1-k). 5.99 *(978-1-338-18159-3(9)*, Cartwheel Bks.) Scholastic, Inc.
—Fly! Teague, Mark. 2019. (ENG.). 40p. (J). (-3). 17.99 *(978-1-5344-5128-5(5)*, Beach Lane Bks.) Beach Lane Bks.
—Jack & the Beanstalk & the French Fries. Teague, Mark. 2017. (ENG.). 40p. (J). (gr. -1-k). 18.99 *(978-0-545-91431-4(0))* Scholastic, Inc.
—Pigsty. Teague, Mark. 2007. (ENG.). (J). (gr. -1-3). audio compact disk 9.99 *(978-0-545-00361-2(X))* Scholastic, Inc.
—The Pirate Jamboree. Teague, Mark. 2016. 32p. (J). (gr. -1-k). 17.99 *(978-0-545-63221-8(8))* Scholastic, Inc.
—The Sky Is Falling! Teague, Mark. 2015. (ENG.). 32p. (J). (gr. -1-k). 16.99 *(978-0-545-63217-1(X))* Scholastic, Inc.
—The Three Little Pigs & the Somewhat Bad Wolf. Teague, Mark. 2013. (ENG.). 48p. (J). (gr. -1-k). 17.99 *(978-0-439-91501-4(5)*, Orchard Bks.) Scholastic, Inc.
—The Three Little Pigs & the Somewhat Bad Wolf (a StoryPlay Book) Teague, Mark. 2017. (StoryPlay Ser.). (ENG.). 48p. (J). (gr. -1-k). 5.99 *(978-1-338-15774-1(4)*, Cartwheel Bks.) Scholastic, Inc.
Teakle, Hannah. Joshua Wonders: What Does the Tooth Fairy Do with My Teeth? Teakle, Ruth. 2020. (ENG.). 32p. (J). ***(978-1-5255-6811-4(6))***; pap. ***(978-1-5255-6812-1(4))*** FriesenPress.
Teakle, Hannah. M. Chat Rencontre Chaton! Teakle, Hannah. 2019. (FRE.). 28p. (J). pap. 10.99 ***(978-1-7128-9792-8(6))*** Independently Published.
Team, Air. Dinosaur Explorers Vol. 5: Lost in the Jurassic. REDCODE & Albbie. 2019. (Dinosaur Explorers Ser.: 5). (ENG.). 184p. (J). 16.99 *(978-1-5458-0315-8(3)*, 900207089); pap. 12.99 *(978-1-5458-0316-5(1)*, 900207090) Papercutz.
—Dinosaur Explorers Vol. 6: Escaping the Jurassic. REDCODE & Albbie. 2020. (Dinosaur Explorers Ser.: 6). (ENG.). 184p. (J). 16.99 *(978-1-5458-0415-5(X)*, 900211164); pap. 12.99 *(978-1-5458-0416-2(8)*, 900211165) Papercutz.
Team, Air. Dinosaur Explorers Vol. 7: Cretaceous Craziness. REDCODE & Albbie. 2020. (Dinosaur Explorers Ser.: 7). (ENG.). 184p. (J). 16.99 ***(978-1-5458-0547-3(4)***, 900225111); pap. 12.99 ***(978-1-5458-0548-0(2)***, 900225112) Papercutz.
Team, Air, jt. illus. see REDCODE.
Team, Black Ink. X-Venture Xplorers #1: The Kingdom of Animals — Lion vs Tiger. Meng, Author & Slaium, Author. 2020. (X-Venture Explorers Ser.: 1). (ENG.). 160p. (J). 16.99 ***(978-1-5458-0549-7(0)***, 900225118); pap. 12.99 ***(978-1-5458-0550-3(4)***, 900225119) Papercutz.
Team, Disney Storybook Art. Adventures in Puppy-Sitting. Auerbach, Annie & Carleton, Jessica. 2018. (Puppy Dog Pals Ser.). (ENG.). 32p. (J). (gr. -1-3). 27.07 *(978-1-5321-4250-5(1)*, 28538, Picture Bk.) Spotlight.
—Design-A-Dog. Olson, Michael & Carleton, Jessica. 2018. (Puppy Dog Pals Ser.). (ENG.). 24p. (J). (gr. -1-3). 27.07 *(978-1-5321-4251-2(X)*, 28539, Picture Bk.) Spotlight.
—Elena of Avalor: the Secret Spell Book. Rogers, Tom. 2019. (World of Reading Level 2 Ser.). (ENG.). 32p. (J). (gr. k-3). lib. bdg. 27.07 *(978-1-5321-4410-3(5)*, 33815) Spotlight.
—Happy Birthday, Puppy Pals! Olson, Michael & Carleton, Jessica. 2018. (Puppy Dog Pals Ser.). (ENG.). 24p. (J). (gr. -1-3). 27.07 *(978-1-5321-4252-9(8)*, 28540, Picture Bk.) Spotlight.
—Hawaii Pug-O. Olson, Michael & Williams, Harland. 2018. (Puppy Dog Pals Ser.). (ENG.). 24p. (J). (gr. -1-3). 27.07 *(978-1-5321-4253-6(6)*, 28541, Picture Bk.) Spotlight.
—The Lion Guard: Pride Lands Patrol. Group, Disney Book. 2019. (World of Reading Level 1 Ser.). (ENG.). 32p. (J). (gr. -1-3). lib. bdg. 27.07 *(978-1-5321-4400-4(8)*, 33805) Spotlight.
—Miles from Tomorrowland: How I Saved My Summer Vacation. Higginson, Sheila Sweeny & Ansolabehere, Joe. 2018. (World of Reading Level 1 Ser.). (ENG.). 32p. (J). (gr. -1-3). lib. bdg. 27.07 *(978-1-5321-4192-8(0)*, 28534) Spotlight.
—Miles from Tomorrowland: Who Stole the Stellosphere? Scollon, Bill & Johnson, Greg. 2018. (World of Reading Level 1 Ser.). (ENG.). 32p. (J). (gr. -1-3). lib. bdg. 27.07 *(978-1-5321-4193-5(9)*, 31066) Spotlight.
—Puppy Dog Pals: Ice, Ice, Puggy. Miller, Sara & Rose, Darrin. 2019. (World of Reading Level 1 Ser.). (ENG.). 32p. (J). (gr. -1-3). lib. bdg. 27.07 *(978-1-5321-4405-9(9)*, 33810) Spotlight.
Team, Disney Storybook Art, jt. illus. see Studio, Character Building.
Team, The Disney Storybook Art, jt. illus. see Studio, Imaginism.
Teare, Steve. Manners Fun Book: A Fun Workbook with Activities for Pre-K Through Elementary School Years. Ericson, Staci. 2016. (ENG.). (J). pap. 7.50 *(978-0-9964175-3-2(2))* Golly Gee-pers.
Teba, Alicia. Score for Imagination. Eig, Jonathan. 2020. (Lola Jones Book Ser.). (ENG.). (J). (gr. 1-5). 96p. 12.99 ***(978-0-8075-6565-0(2)***, 0807565652); pap. 5.99 ***(978-0-8075-6569-8(5)***, 0807565695) Whitman, Albert & Co.
—Some Pigtails. Eig, Jonathan. 2020. (Lola Jones Book Ser.). (ENG.). (J). (gr. 1-5). 96p. 12.99 ***(978-0-8075-6564-3(4)***, 0807565644); pap. 5.99 ***(978-0-8075-6568-1(7)***, 0807565687) Whitman, Albert & Co.
Tebalan, Helman. El Vaso de Miel. Menchú, Rigoberta & Liano, Dante. 2003. (SPA.). 96p. (J). (gr. 5-8). pap. 13.95 *(978-970-29-0985-9(6))* Santillana USA Publishing Co., Inc.
Tebbit, Jake. Grandpa & the Raccoon. Odom, Rebecca. 2009. 36p. pap. 24.95 *(978-1-60749-912-1(6))* America Star Bks.
—My Sister Sophie. MacKey, Cindy. 2013. 30p. pap. 12.99 *(978-0-9892699-9-5(X))* Cyrano Bks.
Tech-It-Fwd, *. The Super Duper CSS Coloring-In-Book. 2016. (ENG.). (J). pap. *(978-0-9933981-2-4(X))* Tech-it-FWD.
Techau, Ashlyn. Rosie: The Patchwork Bunny. Midden, Maribeth Grubb. 2011. 24p. (gr. 1-2). pap. 12.99 *(978-1-4269-5671-3(1))* Trafford Publishing.
Teckentrup, Britta. Big & Small. Books, Barefoot. 2013. 14p. (J). (gr. -1-k). bds. 6.99 *(978-1-84686-951-8(X))* Barefoot Bks., Inc.
—Bugs Everywhere. Murray, Lily. 2020. (ENG.). 32p. (J). (gr. 1-4). 16.99 *(978-1-5362-1042-2(0)*, Big Picture Press) Candlewick Pr.
—Fast & Slow. Books, Barefoot. 2013. 14p. (J). (gr. -1-k). bds. 6.99 *(978-1-84686-952-5(8))* Barefoot Bks., Inc.
—Fast & Slow Spanish. 2013. 14p. (J). (gr. -1-k). bds. 6.99 *(978-1-78285-035-9(X))* Barefoot Bks., Inc.
—Firefly Home. Clarke, Jane. 2019. (ENG.). 24p. (J). (-k). 14.99 *(978-1-5362-0587-9(7)*, Nosy Crow) Candlewick Pr.
—Get Out of My Bath! Nosy Crow Staff. 2015. (ENG.). 24p. (J). (gr. -1-2). 15.99 *(978-0-7636-8006-0(0)*, Nosy Crow) Candlewick Pr.
—Grande y Pequeno. 2013. 14p. (J). (gr. -1-k). bds. 6.99 *(978-1-78285-034-2(1))* Barefoot Bks., Inc.
Teckentrup, Britta. The House by the Lake: the True Story of a House, Its History, & the Four Families Who Made It Home. Harding, Thomas. 2020. (ENG.). 48p. (J). (gr. 2-5). 17.99 ***(978-1-5362-1274-7(1))*** Candlewick Pr.
Teckentrup, Britta. Leap Frog. Clarke, Jane. 2020. (ENG.). 24p. (J). (gr. -1-1). 14.99 *(978-1-5362-1205-1(9)*, Nosy Crow) Candlewick Pr.
—My Book of Opposites. 2014. (J). *(978-1-4351-5678-4(1))* Barnes & Noble, Inc.
—An Oval Submarine & Other Shapes. 2020. (ENG.). 18p. (J). (— 1). bds. 7.95 *(978-1-912757-22-0(2))* Boxer Bks., Ltd. GBR. Dist: Sterling Publishing Co., Inc.
—Playbook Pirates. Fletcher, Corina. 2013. (ENG.). 12p. (J). (gr. -1-2). 24.00 *(978-0-7636-6606-4(8)*, Nosy Crow) Candlewick Pr.
—A Red Train & Other Colors. 2020. (ENG.). 18p. (J). (— 1). bds. 7.95 *(978-1-912757-24-4(9))* Boxer Bks., Ltd. GBR. Dist: Sterling Publishing Co., Inc.
Teckentrup, Britta. Don't Wake up the Tiger. Teckentrup, Britta. 2016. (ENG.). 30p. (J). (-k). 15.99 *(978-0-7636-8996-4(3)*, Nosy Crow) Candlewick Pr.

—Fish Everywhere. Teckentrup, Britta. 2019. (ENG.). 32p. (J). (gr. 1-4). 16.99 *(978-1-5362-0625-8(3)*, Big Picture Press) Candlewick Pr.

—Get Out of My Bath! Teckentrup, Britta. 2018. (ENG.). 22p. (J). (— 1). bds. 7.99 *(978-1-5362-0274-8(6)*, Nosy Crow) Candlewick Pr.

Teckentrup, Britta. Kindness Grows. Teckentrup, Britta. 2020. (ENG.). 32p. (J). (gr. -1-2). 17.99 ***(978-1-68010-229-1(X))*** Tiger Tales.

Teckentrup, Britta. The Odd One Out. Teckentrup, Britta. 2014. (ENG.). 32p. (J). (-k). 14.99 *(978-0-7636-7127-3(4)*, Big Picture Press) Candlewick Pr.

—One Is Not a Pair. Teckentrup, Britta. 2017. (ENG.). 32p. (J). (-k). 14.99 *(978-0-7636-9319-0(7)*, Big Picture Press) Candlewick Pr.

—Up & Down. Teckentrup, Britta. 2014. (ENG.). 28p. (J). (-k). 17.99 *(978-0-7636-7129-7(0)*, Templar) Candlewick Pr.

—We Are Together. Teckentrup, Britta. 2020. (ENG.). 32p. (J). (gr. -1-2). 17.99 *(978-1-68010-177-5(3))* Tiger Tales.

—Where's the Baby? Teckentrup, Britta. 2018. (ENG.). 32p. (J). (-k). 14.99 *(978-0-7636-9901-7(2)*, Big Picture Press) Candlewick Pr.

—Where's the Pair? Teckentrup, Britta. 2015. (ENG.). 32p. (J). (-k). 14.99 *(978-0-7636-7772-5(8)*, Big Picture Press) Candlewick Pr.

Ted, Hood, Jr., photos by. The Cardinal Nest: Where the Life Cycle Begins. Dealia, Yancey. 2013. 30p. (J). pap. 9.95 *(978-0-578-05005-8(6))* Four Seasons Publishing.

Tedder, Elizabeth. Alphabet & Numbers in a New Way. 2011. 32p. pap. 35.95 *(978-1-258-06357-3(3))* Literary Licensing, LLC.

—The Three Bears. 2011. 20p. 35.95 *(978-1-258-10100-8(9))* Literary Licensing, LLC.

Tee, Jacqueline. The Adventures of Jenny & Philip: We All Need Friends. France, Dawn Maria. 2018. (ENG.). 26p. (J). pap. *(978-1-78623-372-1(X))* Grosvenor Hse. Publishing Ltd.

—The Aliens Who Loved Lemon Curd. Piddington, Lorraine. 2016. (ENG.). 21p. (J). pap. *(978-1-78623-810-8(1))* Grosvenor Hse. Publishing Ltd.

—Anton the Viking & the King of Crumbly Castle. Halvorsen, Lyn. 2019. (ENG.). 22p. (J). pap. *(978-1-78623-513-8(7))* Grosvenor Hse. Publishing Ltd.

—Come & Count with Us. Smith, Paul. 2017. (ENG.). 24p. (J). pap. *(978-1-78623-990-7(6))* Grosvenor Hse. Publishing Ltd.

Tee, Jacqueline. The Eagle Project. Imlay, Mandy. 2020. (ENG.). 106p. (J). pap. ***(978-1-83975-051-9(0))*** Grosvenor Hse. Publishing Ltd.

Tee, Jacqueline. Remember Remember the Fifth of November. Webb, Deborah. 2018. (ENG.). 42p. (J). pap. *(978-1-78623-271-7(5))* Grosvenor Hse. Publishing Ltd.

—Socks in a Window Box. Blackwell, Michelle. 2017. (ENG.). 28p. (J). pap. *(978-1-78623-985-3(X))* Grosvenor Hse. Publishing Ltd.

—Thumper's Great Escape. Newman, P. R. 2019. (ENG.). 110p. (J). *(978-1-78623-468-1(8))*; pap. *(978-1-78623-490-2(4))* Grosvenor Hse. Publishing Ltd.

Tee, Jacqueline. The Waterboy & the Tomb. Heath, Liz. 2020. (ENG.). 28p. (J). pap. ***(978-1-83975-028-1(6))*** Grosvenor Hse. Publishing Ltd.

Teeple, Jackie. Amy Washes Her Hands. Muench-Williams, Heather. l.t. ed. 2004. (HRL Board Book Ser.). (J). (gr. -1-k). pap. 10.95 *(978-1-57332-314-7(4))*; pap. 10.95 *(978-1-57332-315-4(2))* Carson-Dellosa Publishing, LLC. (HighReach Learning, Incorporated).

—I Can Be. Hensley, Sarab M. l.t. ed. 2006. 12p. (J). (gr. -1-k). pap. 10.95 *(978-1-57332-339-0(X)*, HighReach Learning, Incorporated) Carson-Dellosa Publishing, LLC.

—I Want a Pet. Muench-Williams, Heather. l.t. ed. 2006. 12p. (J). (gr. -1-k). pap. 10.95 *(978-1-57332-353-6(5)*, HighReach Learning, Incorporated) Carson-Dellosa Publishing, LLC.

—Loving Our Country. Howard-Parham, Pam. l.t. ed. 2004. (HRL Little Book Ser.). (J). (gr. -1-1). pap. 10.95 *(978-1-57332-302-4(0))*; pap. 10.95 *(978-1-57332-301-7(2))* Carson-Dellosa Publishing, LLC. (HighReach Learning, Incorporated).

—Marsy's Perfect Eyesight. Vonthron, Satanta C. l.t. ed. 2005. (J). (gr. -1-k). pap. 10.95 *(978-1-57332-344-4(6))*; pap. 10.95 *(978-1-57332-345-1(4))* Carson-Dellosa Publishing, LLC. (HighReach Learning, Incorporated).

—A Nice Cool Drink. Jarrell, Pamela R. l.t. ed. 2005. (J). (gr. -1-k). pap. 10.95 *(978-1-57332-340-6(3))*; pap. 10.95 *(978-1-57332-341-3(1))* Carson-Dellosa Publishing, LLC. (HighReach Learning, Incorporated).

—Spending Time Outdoors. Howard-Parham, Pam. l.t. ed. 2005. (HRL Big Book Ser.). (J). (gr. k-18). pap. 10.95 *(978-1-57332-333-8(0))*; pap. 10.95 *(978-1-57332-334-5(9))* Carson-Dellosa Publishing, LLC. (HighReach Learning, Incorporated).

Teets, Ashley. Dori's Gift. Wilson, Angie. 2013. (ENG.). 32p. (J). (gr. -1-3). 16.95 *(978-0-938467-85-4(9))* Headline Bks., Inc.

—Robot Rhymes. Teel, Karen. 2013. (ENG.). 31p. (J). (gr. -1-3). 16.95 *(978-0-938467-79-3(4))* Headline Bks., Inc.

—Season of Play. Benedetti, Debra. 2011. 32p. (J). *(978-0-929915-99-9(2))* Headline Bks., Inc.

Teets, Ashley, jt. illus. see McNeal, Drema.

Teffeteller, Juniper. Rescuing Jack & Jill: A Real Jack & Jill Story. Heil, Jill. 2019. (ENG.). 40p. (J). (gr. -1-3). 14.95 *(978-1-947937-81-9(2))* Aviva Publishing.

Tegan-Olsen, Sandra. Joey's adventures by the Sea: Jellyfish Everywhere! 2008. 20p. (J). per. 9.95 *(978-0-9801527-0-8(4))* Freefox Publishing.

Teich, Karsten. Jonah & the Whale. Grosche, Erwin. 2016. (ENG.). 28p. (J). (gr. k-3). 12.99 *(978-1-5064-0882-8(6)*, Sparkhouse Family) Augsburg Fortress, Pubs.

Teich, Melle. Sly the Fly: The Doctor's Office. Harter, Gage. 2003. 16p. (J). 7.95 *(978-1-59466-009-2(3)*, Little Ones) Port Town Publishing.

Teichreb, Mike. Space Pug. McGilvery, Alex. 2020. (ENG.). 82p. (J). (gr. 3-6). pap. ***(978-1-989092-22-4(5))*** Celticfrog Publishing.

Teis, Kyra. Read to Me, 1 vol. Moreillon, Judi. (J). 2004. (ENG.). 32p. (gr. -1). bds. 6.95 *(978-1-59572-014-6(6))*; 2003. 24p. 6.95 *(978-1-932065-49-7(0)*, 1-718-784-9112) Star Bright Bks., Inc.

Teis, Kyra. Sometimes When I'm Sad. Serani, Deborah. 2020. (ENG.). 40p. (J). (gr. -1-2). 14.99 ***(978-1-63198-382-5(2)***, 83825) Free Spirit Publishing, Inc.

Teis, Kyra. Speaking of Me... Stepping Stones to a Better Life, 1 vol. Mathers, Beth. 2006. (ENG.). 32p. (YA). (gr. 5-9). pap. 15.95 *(978-1-59572-039-9(1))* Star Bright Bks., Inc.

—Vamos a Leer. Moreillon, Judi. Mercado, Mary M., tr. from ENG.Tr. of Read to Me. (SPA.). 12p. (J). 2005. bds. 6.95 *(978-1-59572-015-3(4))*; 2004. 6.95 *(978-1-932065-50-3(4))* Star Bright Bks., Inc.

—Words are like Faces, 1 vol. Baer, Edith. 2007. (ENG.). 32p. (J). 15.95 *(978-1-59572-108-2(8))* Star Bright Bks., Inc.

Teixeira, Doug. Mystery at the O'Reilly Farm. Teixeira, G. Ann. 2010. 30p. pap. 10.00 *(978-1-60911-336-0(5)*, Eloquent Bks.) Strategic Book Publishing & Rights Agency (SBPRA).

Tejado, Irene. The Adventures of a Water Drop. Ibarrola, Begonia. 2013. (ENG.). 32p. (J). *(978-84-95923-96-7(3))* Primera Persona.

Tejido, Jomike. Apollo's First Moon Landing: A Fly on the Wall History. Troupe, Thomas Kingsley. 2018. (Fly on the Wall History Ser.). (ENG.). 32p. (J). (gr. 1-3). lib. bdg. 27.99 *(978-1-5158-1598-3(6)*, 136251, Picture Window Bks.) Capstone.

—Birth of the Star-Spangled Banner: A Fly on the Wall History. Troupe, Thomas Kingsley. 2018. (Fly on the Wall History Ser.). (ENG.). 32p. (J). (gr. 1-3). lib. bdg. 27.99 *(978-1-5158-1601-0(X)*, 136254, Picture Window Bks.) Capstone.

—Buddy Blues: An Emily Story. Abrams, Kelsey. 2019. (Second Chance Ranch Ser.). (ENG.). 120p. (J). pap. 7.99 *(978-1-63163-252-5(3)*, 1631632523); lib. bdg. 27.13 *(978-1-63163-251-8(5)*, 1631632515) North Star Editions. (Jolly Fish Pr.).

—Bunny Surprise. Edgar, Amy. 2017. (Scholastic Reader, Level 2 Ser.). (ENG.). 32p. (J). (gr. k-2). pap. 5.99 *(978-1-338-04590-1(3))* Scholastic, Inc.

—Fly on the Wall History. Troupe, Thomas Kingsley. 2017. (Fly on the Wall History Ser.). (ENG.). 32p. (J). (gr. 1-3). 111.96 *(978-1-4795-9801-4(1)*, 25372, Picture Window Bks.) Capstone.

—Fly on the Wall History. Troupe, Thomas Kingsley. 2018. (Fly on the Wall History Ser.). (ENG.). 32p. (J). (gr. 1-3). 223.92 *(978-1-5158-1619-5(2)*, 27059, Picture Window Bks.) Capstone.

—Forever Amigo: An Abby Story. Abrams, Kelsey. 2019. (Second Chance Ranch Ser.). (ENG.). 120p. (J). pap. 7.99 *(978-1-63163-256-3(6)*, 1631632566); lib. bdg. 27.13 *(978-1-63163-255-6(8)*, 1631632558) North Star Editions. (Jolly Fish Pr.).

—Harriet Tubman's Escape: a Fly on the Wall History. Troupe, Thomas Kingsley. 2017. (Fly on the Wall History Ser.). (ENG.). 32p. (J). (gr. 1-3). lib. bdg. 27.99 *(978-1-4795-9788-8(0)*, Picture Window Bks.) Capstone.

—Heart Horse: A Natalie Story. Abrams, Kelsey. 2019. (Second Chance Ranch Ser.). (ENG.). 120p. (J). pap. 7.99 *(978-1-63163-260-0(4)*, 1631632604); lib. bdg. 27.13 *(978-1-63163-259-4(0)*, 1631632590) North Star Editions. (Jolly Fish Pr.).

—Heart Song: Book 1. Sanderson, Whitney. 2020. (Unicorns of the Secret Stable Ser.). (ENG.). 72p. (J). lib. bdg. 25.32 *(978-1-63163-391-1(0)*, 1631633910, Jolly Fish Pr.) North Star Editions.

—Heartsong's Missing Foal: Book 1. Sanderson, Whitney. 2020. (Unicorns of the Secret Stable Ser.). (ENG.). 72p. (J). pap. 4.99 *(978-1-63163-392-8(9)*, 1631633929, Jolly Fish Pr.) North Star Editions.

—Here, Kitty, Kitty. Edgar, Amy. 2017. (Scholastic Reader, Level 2 Ser.). (ENG.). 32p. (J). (gr. k-2). pap. 5.99 *(978-1-338-04591-8(1))* Scholastic, Inc.

—I Funny: School of Laughs. Patterson, James & Grabenstein, Chris. 2017. 299p. (J). *(978-0-316-50853-7(5))* Little Brown & Co.

—I Want to Be a Brachiosaurus. Troupe, Thomas Kingsley. 2016. (I Want to Be... Ser.). (ENG.). 24p. (J). (gr. k-3). lib. bdg. 27.32 *(978-1-4795-8770-4(2)*, Picture Window Bks.) Capstone.

—I Want to Be a Triceratops. Troupe, Thomas Kingsley. 2016. (I Want to Be... Ser.). (ENG.). 24p. (J). (gr. k-3). lib. bdg. 27.32 *(978-1-4795-8768-1(0)*, Picture Window Bks.) Capstone.

—I Want to Be a Tyrannosaurus Rex. Troupe, Thomas Kingsley. 2016. (I Want to Be... Ser.). (ENG.). 24p. (J). (gr. k-3). lib. bdg. 27.32 *(978-1-4795-8767-4(2)*, Picture Window Bks.) Capstone.

—I Want to Be a Velociraptor. Troupe, Thomas Kingsley. 2016. (I Want to Be... Ser.). (ENG.). 24p. (J). (gr. k-3). lib. bdg. 27.32 *(978-1-4795-8769-8(9)*, Picture Window Bks.) Capstone.

—It's Not Destiny. Abrams, Kelsey. 2018. (Second Chance Ranch Ser.). (ENG.). 120p. (J). pap. 7.99 *(978-1-63163-145-0(4)*, 1631631454, Jolly Fish Pr.) North Star Editions.

—It's Not Destiny: An Abby Story. Abrams, Kelsey. 2018. (Second Chance Ranch Ser.). (ENG.). 120p. (J). lib. bdg. 27.13 *(978-1-63163-144-3(6)*, 1631631446, Jolly Fish Pr.) North Star Editions.

—Jumbo Stickers for Little Hands: Things That Go: Includes 75 Stickers. 2017. (Jumbo Stickers for Little Hands Ser.). (ENG.). 24p. (J). (gr. -1-k). pap. 7.95 *(978-1-63322-157-4(1)*, Moondance) Quarto Publishing Group USA.

—Jumbo Stickers for Little Hands: under the Sea: Includes 75 Stickers. 2017. (Jumbo Stickers for Little Hands Ser.). (ENG.). 24p. (J). (gr. -1-k). pap. 7.95 *(978-1-63322-156-7(3)*, Moondance) Quarto Publishing Group USA.

—Keep It Simple, Rapunzel! The Fairy-Tale Physics of Simple Machines. Troupe, Thomas Kingsley. 2018. (STEM-Twisted Fairy Tales Ser.). (ENG.). 32p. (J). (gr. k-3). pap. 7.95 *(978-1-5158-2899-0(9)*, 138421); lib. bdg. 27.99 *(978-1-5158-2895-2(6)*, 138417) Capstone. (Picture Window Bks.).

—Llama Drama: A Grace Story. Abrams, Kelsey. 2019. (Second Chance Ranch Ser.). (ENG.). 120p. (J). pap. 7.99 *(978-1-63163-264-8(7)*, 1631632647); lib. bdg. 27.13 *(978-1-63163-263-1(9)*, 1631632639) North Star Editions. (Jolly Fish Pr.).

—Middle School: Dog's Best Friend. Patterson, James & Tebbetts, Chris. 2016. (Middle School Ser.: 8). (ENG.). 256p. (J). (gr. 3-7). 13.99 *(978-0-316-34954-3(2)*, Jimmy Patterson) Little Brown & Co.

—Middle School: Master of Disaster. Patterson, James. 2020. (Middle School Ser.: 12). (ENG.). 352p. (J). (gr. 3-7). 13.99 *(978-0-316-42049-5(2)*, Jimmy Patterson) Little Brown & Co.

—Move on up That Beanstalk, Jack! The Fairy-Tale Physics of Forces & Motion. Troupe, Thomas Kingsley. 2018. (STEM-Twisted Fairy Tales Ser.). (ENG.). 32p. (J). (gr. k-3). pap. 7.95 *(978-1-5158-2898-3(0)*, 138420); lib. bdg. 27.99 *(978-1-5158-2894-5(8)*, 138416) Capstone. (Picture Window Bks.).

—Paul Revere's Ride: a Fly on the Wall History. Troupe, Thomas Kingsley. 2017. (Fly on the Wall History Ser.). (ENG.). 32p. (J). (gr. 1-3). lib. bdg. 27.99 *(978-1-4795-9785-7(6)*, Picture Window Bks.) Capstone.

—The Pilgrims' Voyage to America: a Fly on the Wall History. Troupe, Thomas Kingsley. 2017. (Fly on the Wall History Ser.). (ENG.). 32p. (J). (gr. 1-3). lib. bdg. 27.99 *(978-1-4795-9786-4(4)*, Picture Window Bks.) Capstone.

—The Red Key: Book 4. Sanderson, Whitney. 2020. (Unicorns of the Secret Stable Ser.). (ENG.). 72p. (J). pap. 4.99 *(978-1-63163-396-6(1)*, 1631633961); lib. bdg. 25.32 *(978-1-63163-395-9(3)*, 1631633953) North Star Editions. (Jolly Fish Pr.).

—Second Chance Ranch Set 2 (Set Of 4) Abrams, Kelsey. 2019. (Second Chance Ranch Ser.). (ENG.). 480p. (J). pap. 31.96 *(978-1-63163-248-8(5)*, 1631632485); lib. bdg. 108.52 *(978-1-63163-247-1(7)*, 1631632477) North Star Editions. (Jolly Fish Pr.).

—Second Chance Ranch (Set Of 4) Abrams, Kelsey. 2018. (Second Chance Ranch (Paperback Set Of 4) Ser.). (ENG.). 480p. (J). pap. 31.96 *(978-1-63163-175-7(6)*, 1631631756); lib. bdg. 108.52 *(978-1-63163-174-0(8))* North Star Editions. (Jolly Fish Pr.).

—Stolen Magic: Book 3. Sanderson, Whitney. 2020. (Unicorns of the Secret Stable Ser.). (ENG.). 72p. (J). pap. 4.99 *(978-1-63163-400-0(3)*, 1631634003); lib. bdg. 25.32 *(978-1-63163-399-7(6)*, 1631633996) North Star Editions. (Jolly Fish Pr.).

—Taking Chances. Abrams, Kelsey. 2018. (Second Chance Ranch Ser.). (ENG.). 120p. (J). pap. 7.99 *(978-1-63163-149-8(7)*, 1631631497, Jolly Fish Pr.) North Star Editions.

—Taking Chances: A Grace Story. Abrams, Kelsey. 2018. (Second Chance Ranch Ser.). (ENG.). 120p. (J). lib. bdg. 27.13 *(978-1-63163-148-1(9)*, 1631631489, Jolly Fish Pr.) North Star Editions.

—Titanic's Tragic Journey: A Fly on the Wall History. Troupe, Thomas Kingsley. 2018. (Fly on the Wall History Ser.). (ENG.). 32p. (J). (gr. 1-3). lib. bdg. 27.99 *(978-1-5158-1599-0(4)*, 136252, Picture Window Bks.) Capstone.

—The Tuskegee Airmen's Mission to Berlin: A Fly on the Wall History. Troupe, Thomas Kingsley. 2018. (Fly on the Wall History Ser.). (ENG.). 32p. (J). (gr. 1-3). lib. bdg. 27.99 *(978-1-5158-1600-3(1)*, 136253, Picture Window Bks.) Capstone.

—Two to Tango. Abrams, Kelsey. 2018. (Second Chance Ranch Ser.). (ENG.). 120p. (J). pap. 7.99 *(978-1-63163-153-5(5)*, 1631631535, Jolly Fish Pr.) North Star Editions.

—Two to Tango: A Natalie Story. Abrams, Kelsey. 2018. (Second Chance Ranch Ser.). (ENG.). 120p. (J). lib. bdg. 27.13 *(978-1-63163-152-8(7)*, 1631631527, Jolly Fish Pr.) North Star Editions.

—Unicorn Uncovered: Book 2. Sanderson, Whitney. 2020. (Unicorns of the Secret Stable Ser.). (ENG.). 72p. (J). pap. 4.99 *(978-1-63163-404-8(6)*, 1631634046); lib. bdg. 25.32 *(978-1-63163-403-1(8)*, 1631634038) North Star Editions. (Jolly Fish Pr.).

—Unicorns. Peabody, Erin. 2018. (Behind the Legend Ser.). (ENG.). 128p. (J). (gr. 2-5). pap. 9.99 *(978-1-4998-0574-1(8))* Little Bee Books Inc.

—Unicorns of the Secret Stable (Set Of 4) Sanderson, Whitney. 2020. (Unicorns of the Secret Stable Ser.). (ENG.). 288p. (J). pap. 19.96 *(978-1-63163-388-1(0)*, 1631633880); lib. bdg. 101.28 *(978-1-63163-387-4(2)*, 1631633872) North Star Editions. (Jolly Fish Pr.).

—What's That Sound, Cinderella? The Fairy-Tale Physics of Sound. Troupe, Thomas Kingsley. 2018. (STEM-Twisted Fairy Tales Ser.). (ENG.). 32p. (J). (gr. k-3). pap. 7.95 *(978-1-5158-2901-0(4)*, 138423); lib. bdg. 27.99 *(978-1-5158-2897-6(2)*, 138419) Capstone. (Picture Window Bks.).

—What's the Matter with the Three Little Pigs? The Fairy-Tale Physics of Matter. Troupe, Thomas Kingsley. 2018. (STEM-Twisted Fairy Tales Ser.). (ENG.). 32p. (J). (gr. k-3). pap. 7.95 *(978-1-5158-2900-3(6)*, 138422); lib. bdg. 27.99 *(978-1-5158-2896-9(4)*, 138418) Capstone. (Picture Window Bks.).

—Wild Midnight. Abrams, Kelsey. 2018. (Second Chance Ranch Ser.). (ENG.). 120p. (J). pap. 7.99 *(978-1-63163-157-3(8)*, 1631631578, Jolly Fish Pr.) North Star Editions.

—Wild Midnight: An Emily Story. Abrams, Kelsey. 2018. (Second Chance Ranch Ser.). (ENG.). 120p. (J). lib. bdg. 27.13 *(978-1-63163-156-6(X)*, 163163156X, Jolly Fish Pr.) North Star Editions.

—The Wright Brothers' First Flight: a Fly on the Wall History. Troupe, Thomas Kingsley. 2017. (Fly on the Wall History Ser.). (ENG.). 32p. (J). (gr. 1-3). pap. 7.95 *(978-1-4795-9791-8(0))*; lib. bdg. 27.99 *(978-1-4795-9787-1(2))* Capstone. (Picture Window Bks.).

—Zombies. Peabody, Erin. 2017. (Behind the Legend Ser.). (ENG.). 128p. (J). (gr. 2-5). 17.99 *(978-1-4998-0461-4(X))*; pap. 9.99 *(978-1-4998-0460-7(1))* Little Bee Books Inc.

Tejpar, Iman. A Manual for Marco: Living, Learning, & Laughing with an Autistic Sibling. Abdullah, Shaila. 2015. (J). *(978-1-61599-248-5(0))* Loving Healing Pr., Inc.

Tekiela, Stan, photos by. Baby Bear Discovers the World, 1 vol. Bauer, Marion Dane. 2006. (Wildlife Picture Bks.). (ENG., 64p. (J). (gr. -1-3). 14.95 *(978-1-59193-165-2(7)*, Adventure Pubns.) AdventureKEEN.

—Jump, Little Wood Ducks. Bauer, Marion Dane. 2017. (Wildlife Picture Bks.). (ENG., 32p. (J). (gr. -1-3). 14.95 *(978-1-59193-585-8(7)*, Adventure Pubns.) AdventureKEEN.

Tela, Donna L. Squnky's Big Awakening. Tela, Carl M. 2009. 140p. pap. 14.99 *(978-1-4251-8145-1(7))* Trafford Publishing.

Telapary, Michael. Andy & the Bully! The Real Super-Man. Rushin, Paul R. 2016. (ENG.). (J). pap. 14.95 *(978-1-68273-876-4(0))* BookPatch LLC, The.

Telford, Jane. Can I Tell You about Asperger Syndrome? A Guide for Friends & Family. Welton, Jude. 2003. (Can I Tell You About... ? Ser.). (ENG.). 48p. pap. 13.95 *(978-1-84310-206-9(4)*, 695770) Kingsley, Jessica Pubs. GBR. Dist: Hachette UK Distribution.

—Tomas Loves... A Rhyming Book about Fun, Friendship - & Autism. Welton, Jude. 2015. (ENG.). 32p. 15.95 *(978-1-84905-544-4(0)*, 693420) Kingsley, Jessica Pubs. GBR. Dist: Hachette UK Distribution.

Telgemeier, Raina. Claudia & Mean Janine. Martin, Ann M. & Martin Ann, M. 2016. (Baby-Sitters Club Graphix Ser.: 4). (ENG.). 176p. (J). (gr. 3-7). lib. bdg. 22.10 *(978-0-606-38056-0(6))* Turtleback.

—Claudia & Mean Janine. Martin Ann, M. ed. 2016. (Baby-Sitters Club Graphic Novel Ser.: 4). (ENG.). 176p. (J). (gr. 3-7). 24.99 *(978-0-545-88623-9(6)*, Graphix) Scholastic, Inc.

—Claudia & Mean Janine. Martin, Ann M. rev. ed. 2016. (Baby-Sitters Club Graphic Novel Ser.: 4). 176p. (J). (gr. 3-7). pap. 10.99 *(978-0-545-88622-2(8)*, Graphix) Scholastic, Inc.

—Kristy's Great Idea. Martin, Ann M. rev. ed. 2015. (Baby-Sitters Club Graphic Novel Ser.: 1). (ENG.). 192p. (J). (gr. 3-7). 24.99 *(978-0-545-81386-0(7)*, Graphix) Scholastic, Inc.

—Mary Anne Saves the Day. Martin, Ann M. rev. ed. 2015. (Baby-Sitters Club Graphix Ser.: 3). 160p. (J). (gr. 3-7). (ENG.). 24.99 *(978-0-545-88617-8(1))*; pap. 10.99 *(978-0-545-88621-5(X))* Scholastic, Inc. (Graphix).

—The Truth about Stacey. Martin, Ann M. rev. ed. 2015. (Baby-Sitters Club Graphix Ser.: 2). 144p. (J). (gr. 3-7). (ENG.). 24.99 *(978-0-545-81388-4(3))*; pap. 10.99 *(978-0-545-81389-1(1))* Scholastic, Inc. (Graphix).

Telgemeier, Raina. Drama. Telgemeier, Raina. 240p. (J). 2018. (SPA.). (gr. 4-7). pap. 10.99 *(978-1-338-26916-1(X)*, Scholastic en Espanol); 2012. (ENG.). (gr. 5-9). 24.99 *(978-0-545-32698-8(2)*, Graphix); 2012. (gr. 5-9). pap. 10.99 *(978-0-545-32699-5(0)*, Graphix) Scholastic, Inc.

—Ghosts. Telgemeier, Raina. 2016. (ENG.). 256p. (J). (gr. 3-7). 24.99 *(978-0-545-54061-2(5)*, Graphix) Scholastic, Inc.

—Sisters. Telgemeier, Raina. 2014. 208p. (J). (gr. 3-7). (ENG.). 24.99 *(978-0-545-54059-9(3))*; pap. 10.99 *(978-0-545-54060-5(7))* Scholastic, Inc. (Graphix).

—Smile. Telgemeier, Raina. 2010. 224p. (J). (gr. 3-7). pap. 10.99 *(978-0-545-13206-0(1)*, Graphix) Scholastic, Inc.

Telielska, M. Magdalena. Old Fairy Tales Anew. Doolittle, Eva M. 2008. 88p. (J). *(978-0-9791065-0-7(8))* Vesta Bks., LLC.

Tellekamp, Lynda. Waiting for Ding. McKnight, Alex. 2013. 20p. pap. 24.95 *(978-1-62709-362-0(1))* America Star Bks.

Tello, Jorge. Here Come the Blobbies. Tello, Jorge. 2004. 32p. (J). pap. 15.89 incl. audio compact disk *(978-1-932179-32-3(1))* Pers Publishing.

—Pookie & Tushka Find a Little Piano. Tello, Jorge. 2004. 32p. (J). 15.89 incl. cd-rom *(978-1-932179-23-1(2))* Pers Publishing.

Temairik, Jaime. Bigfoot Does Not Like Birthday Parties. Ode, Eric. 2015. 40p. (J). (gr. -1-3). 16.99 *(978-1-63217-004-0(3)*, Little Bigfoot) Sasquatch Bks.

—How to Negotiate Everything. Spellman, David & Lutz, Lisa. 2013. (ENG.). 32p. (J). (gr. -1-3). 16.99 *(978-1-4424-5119-3(X)*, Simon & Schuster Bks. For Young Readers) Simon & Schuster Bks. For Young Readers.

Tempest, Annabel. Alice in Wonderland: A BabyLit Storybook, 1 vol. 2018. 28p. (J). 12.99 *(978-1-4236-4983-0(4))* Gibbs Smith, Publisher.

—Anne of Green Gables: A BabyLit Storybook, 1 vol. 2018. 28p. (J). 12.99 *(978-1-4236-5071-3(9))* Gibbs Smith, Publisher.

—The Big Book of Bible Questions. Parker, Amy & Powell, Doug. 2020. (ENG.). 144p. (J). 14.99 *(978-1-4964-3524-8(9)*, 20_31884) Tyndale Hse. Pubs.

—The Jungle Book, 1 vol. 2018. 28p. (J). 12.99 *(978-1-4236-4922-9(2))* Gibbs Smith, Publisher.

—Llamaste & Friends: Being Kind Through Yoga. Pat-A-Cake. import ed. 2020. (ENG.). 20p. (J). (— 1). bds. 8.99 *(978-0-593-17923-9(4)*, Rodale Kids) Random Hse. Children's Bks.

—Moby-Dick, 1 vol. Wakeham, Kate. 2017. 28p. 12.99 *(978-1-4236-4784-3(X))* Gibbs Smith, Publisher.

—Pride & Prejudice, 1 vol. Wakeham, Kate. 2017. 28p. (J). 12.99 *(978-1-4236-4783-6(1))* Gibbs Smith, Publisher.

—Wow! The Good News in Four Words, 1 vol. Mackall, Dandi Daley. 2017. (ENG.). 32p. (J). 14.99 *(978-1-4964-1814-2(X)*, 20_27690, Tyndale Kids) Tyndale Hse. Pubs.

Tempesta, Franco. Discovery: Roar with the Dinosaurs! Acampora, Courtney. 2020. (39-Button Sound Bks.). (ENG.). 34p. (J). (gr. -1-k). bds. 24.99 ***(978-1-68412-819-8(6)***, Silver Dolphin Bks.) Printers Row Publishing Group.

Tempesta, Franco. Smithsonian Reader Level 2: Dinosaur Discoveries. Acampora, Courtney. 2018. (Smithsonian Leveled Readers Ser.). (ENG.). 32p. (J). (gr. 1-3). pap. 4.99 *(978-1-68412-467-1(0)*, Silver Dolphin Bks.) Printers Row Publishing Group.

Tempesta, Franco. Ultimate Dinopedia. Lessem, Don. 2nd ed. 2017. (ENG.). 296p. (J). (gr. 2-5). 24.99 ***(978-1-4263-3134-3(7))*** National Geographic Society.

Temple, Chuck. Brady Brady & the B Team, 12 vols. Shaw, Mary. l.t. ed. 2006. 32p. (J). per. *(978-1-897169-09-4(4))* Brady Brady, Inc.

—Brady Brady & the Ballpark Bark. Shaw, Mary. 2007. (J). *(978-1-897169-10-0(8))* Brady Brady, Inc.

—Brady Brady & the Big Mistake, 11vols. Shaw, Mary. l.t. ed. 2004. 32p. (J). per. *(978-0-9735557-4-5(2))* Brady Brady, Inc.

—Brady Brady & the Cleanup Hitters. Shaw, Mary. 2008. 32p. (J). pap. *(978-1-897169-11-7(6))* Brady Brady, Inc.

—Brady Brady & the Great Exchange, 11 vols. Shaw, Mary. l.t. ed. 2003. 32p. (J). per. *(978-0-9735557-5-2(0))* Brady Brady, Inc.

—Brady Brady & the Great Rink, 11 vols. Shaw, Mary. l.t. ed. 2004. 32p. (J). per. *(978-0-9735557-0-7(X))* Brady Brady, Inc.

—Brady Brady & the Most Important Game, 11 vols. Shaw, Mary. l.t. ed. 2004. 32p. (J). per. *(978-0-9735557-6-9(9))* Brady Brady, Inc.

—Brady Brady & the MVP, 11 vols. Shaw, Mary. l.t. ed. 2004. 32p. (J). per. *(978-0-9735557-7-6(7))* Brady Brady, Inc.

—Brady Brady & the Puck on the Pond, 11 vols. Shaw, Mary. l.t. ed. 2005. 32p. (J). per. *(978-1-897169-07-0(8))* Brady Brady, Inc.

—Brady Brady & the Runaway Goalie, 11 vols. Shaw, Mary. l.t. ed. 2004. 32p. (J). per. *(978-0-9735557-1-4(8))* Brady Brady, Inc.

—Brady Brady & the Singing Tree, 11 vols. Shaw, Mary. l.t. ed. 2004. 32p. (J). per. *(978-0-9735557-3-8(4))* Brady Brady, Inc.

—Brady Brady & the Super Skater, 11 vols. Shaw, Mary. l.t. ed. 2005. 32p. (J). per. *(978-1-897169-06-3(X))* Brady Brady, Inc.

—Brady Brady & the Twirlin' Torpedo, 11 vols. Shaw, Mary. l.t. ed. 2004. 32p. (J). per. *(978-0-9735557-2-1(6))* Brady Brady, Inc.

Temple, Ed, jt. illus. see Grosshauser, Peter.

Templer, Hannah. Captain Marvel: Higher, Further, Faster. Palmer, Liza. 2019. (ENG.). 256p. (YA). (gr. 7-17). 17.99 *(978-1-368-04780-7(7)*, Marvel Pr.) Disney Publishing Worldwide.

Templer, Stephen. The Grumbles. Page, L. E. 2019. (ENG.). 24p. pap. 13.99 ***(978-1-5434-9583-6(4))*** Xlibris Corp.

Templeton, Robyn. Tell Me Why. Templeton, Robyn. Jackson, Sarah. 2004. 32p. (Orig.). (J). pap. *(978-1-875641-96-3(3))* Magabala Bks.

Templeton, Ty. Bill the Boy Wonder: The Secret Co-Creator of Batman. Nobleman, Marc Tyler. 2012. (J). pap. 17.95 *(978-1-58089-290-2(6))*; 48p. (gr. 3-7). 17.99 *(978-1-58089-289-6(2))* Charlesbridge Publishing, Inc.

Templeton, Ty, et al. Captain Marvel: First Day of School! Fisch, Sholly & Templeton, Ty. 2019. (Marvel Super Hero Adventures Graphic Novels Ser.). (ENG.). 24p. (J). (gr. 1-5). lib. bdg. 27.07 *(978-1-5321-4445-5(8)*, 33850, Marvel Age) Spotlight.

—Captain Marvel: Frost Giants among Us! Caramagna, Joe et al. 2019. (Marvel Super Hero Adventures Graphic Novels Ser.). (ENG.). 24p. (J). (gr. 1-5). lib. bdg. 27.07 *(978-1-5321-4446-2(6)*, 33851, Marvel Age) Spotlight.

Templeton, Ty. Need to Know, 1 vol. Templeton, Ty. Slott, Dan. 2012. (Batman Adventures Ser.). (ENG.). 32p. (J). (gr. 3-6). lib. bdg. 22.60 *(978-1-4342-4560-1(8)*, Stone Arch Bks.) Capstone.

Temporin, Elena. The Gingerbread Man. 2007. (Picture Book Classics Ser.). 24p. (J). 9.99 *(978-0-7945-1786-1(2)*, Usborne) EDC Publishing.

—Saint Francis of Assisi. Denham, Joyce. 2008. (ENG.). 32p. (J). (gr. k-6). pap. 10.00 *(978-1-55725-571-6(7))* Paraclete Pr., Inc.

—The Snowy Day. Milbourne, Anna. 2005. 24p. (J). (gr. -1-3). 9.99 *(978-0-7945-1147-0(3)*, Usborne) EDC Publishing.

—The Snowy Day. Milbourne, Anna. 2007. (J). *(978-0-439-88988-9(X))* Scholastic, Inc.

—The Usborne Book of Christmas Lullabies. 2006. (Christmas Lullabies Ser.). 8p. (J). bds. 14.99 incl. audio compact disk *(978-0-7945-1469-3(3)*, Usborne) EDC Publishing.

—Usborne Stories from Shakespeare. Fearn, Laura. 2006. 191p. pap. *(978-0-439-88984-1(7))* Scholastic, Inc.

—The Windy Day. Milbourne, Anna. 2007. (Picture Bks). 24p. (J). (gr. -1-3). 9.99 *(978-0-7945-1616-1(5)*, Usborne) EDC Publishing.

Ten Berge, Marieke. Rhino & Narwhal. Oranje, Corien. ed. 2020. (ENG.). 32p. (J). (gr. -1-1). 16.99 *(978-0-7459-7846-8(0)*, Lion Children's) Lion Hudson PLC GBR. Dist: Independent Pubs. Group.

Tenenbaum, Linda. Confident Carly. Schnick, Bernice. 2018. (ENG.). 32p. (J). pap. *(978-0-9920106-0-7(8))* LoGreco, Bruno.

Teng, Lee. Collins Big Cat Phonics for Letters & Sounds - Food on the Farm: Band 02B/Red B. Casey, Catherine. 2020. (Collins Big Cat Phonics for Letters & Sounds Ser.). (ENG.). 16p. (J). (gr. -1-k). pap. 6.99 *(978-0-00-835769-6(2))* HarperCollins Pubs. Ltd. GBR. Dist: Independent Pubs. Group.

Tenggren, Gustaf. The Poky Little Puppy. Lowrey, Janette Sebring. 2011. (Little Golden Book Ser.). 24p. (J). (— 1). bds. 6.99 *(978-0-375-86129-1(7)*, Golden Bks.) Random Hse. Children's Bks.

—The Poky Little Puppy. Lowrey, Janette Sebring. 2007. (Little Golden Book Ser.). 26p. (J). (gr. k — 1). bds. 4.99 *(978-0-375-83925-2(9)*, Golden Bks.) Random Hse. Children's Bks.

—The Poky Little Puppy. Lowrey, Janette Sebring. deluxe ed. Date not set. 23p. (J). (gr. -1-2). reprint ed. *(978-1-929566-56-3(5))*; *(978-1-929566-50-1(6))* Cronies.

—The Poky Little Puppy Book & Vinyl Record. Lowrey, Janette Sebring. 2018. 24p. (J). (-k). 12.99 *(978-0-525-57979-3(6)*, Golden Bks.) Random Hse. Children's Bks.

—Poky Little Puppy Tales. Sebring Lowrey, Janette. 2015. (ENG.). 80p. (J). (-k). 7.99 *(978-0-553-51208-3(0)*, Golden Bks.) Random Hse. Children's Bks.

—The Saggy Baggy Elephant. Jackson, Kathryn & Jackson, B. deluxe ed. Date not set. (J). (gr. -1-2). reprint ed. *(978-1-929566-60-0(3))* Cronies.

—The Saggy Baggy Elephant: Classic Edition. Jackson, Kathryn & Jackson, B. Date not set. 23p. (J). (gr. -1-1). *(978-1-929566-54-9(9))* Cronies.

—The Shy Little Kitten. Schurr, Cathleen. deluxe ed. Date not set. (J). (gr. -1-2). reprint ed. *(978-1-929566-57-0(3))* Cronies.

—The Shy Little Kitten: Classic Edition. Schurr, Cathleen. Date not set. (J). (gr. -1-1). reprint ed. *(978-1-929566-51-8(4))* Cronies.

—The Shy Little Kitten Book & Vinyl Record. Schurr, Cathleen. 2018. 24p. (J). (-k). 12.99 *(978-0-525-57980-9(X)*, Golden Bks.) Random Hse. Children's Bks.

—Tawney Scrawny Lion. Jackson, Kathryn. deluxe ed. Date not set. (J). (gr. -1-2). reprint ed. *(978-1-929566-61-7(1))* Cronies.

—Tawny Scrawny Lion: Classic Edition. Jackson, Kathryn. Date not set. 23p. (J). (gr. -1-1). reprint ed. *(978-1-929566-55-6(7))* Cronies.

—Where Is the Poky Little Puppy? Lowrey, Janette Sebring. 2015. (Little Golden Book Ser.). 24p. (J). (-k). 4.99 *(978-0-375-84750-9(2)*, Golden Bks.) Random Hse. Children's Bks.

Tennant, Harry. Darwin's Rival: Alfred Russel Wallace & the Search for Evolution. Dorion, Christiane. 2020. (ENG.). 64p. (J). (gr. 5). 24.99 *(978-1-5362-0932-7(5))* Candlewick Pr.

TenNapel, Doug. Cardboard. TenNapel, Doug. 2012. (ENG.). 288p. (J). (gr. 4-7). pap. 12.99 *(978-0-545-41873-7(9)*, Graphix) Scholastic, Inc.

—Ghostopolis. TenNapel, Doug. 2010. (ENG.). 272p. (J). (gr. 5-7). pap. 12.99 *(978-0-545-21028-7(3)*, Graphix) Scholastic, Inc.

Tenney, Rose Marie. The Community Helper Mice; Los Ratoncitos Ayudantes de la Comunidad. Puerto, Ledezna. 2018. (MUL.). 44p. (J). pap. 13.95 *(978-1-64003-728-1(4))* Covenant Bks.

Tenney, Shawna J. C. Brunhilda's Backwards Day. 2016. (ENG.). 32p. (J). (gr. -1-k). 16.99 *(978-1-63450-691-5(X)*, Sky Pony Pr.) Skyhorse Publishing Co., Inc.

—The Mismatched Nativity. Boyack, Merrilee. 2016. (J). 18.99 *(978-1-62972-239-9(1))* Deseret Bk. Co.

—Peter Pan, 1 vol. Barrie, J. M. 2010. (Calico Illustrated Classics Ser.: No. 1). (ENG.). 112p. (J). (gr. 2-5). 29.93 *(978-1-60270-710-8(3)*, 3973, Calico Chapter Bks.) ABDO Publishing Co.

—The Truth about Ogres, 1 vol. Braun, Eric. 2010. (Fairy-Tale Superstars Ser.). (ENG.). 32p. (J). (gr. 1-3). lib. bdg. 27.99 *(978-1-4048-6159-6(9)*, Picture Window Bks.) Capstone.

—When I Take the Sacrament, I Remember Jesus. Gudmundson, C. J. 2012. (J). *(978-1-62108-020-6(X))* Covenant Communications, Inc.

Tenniel, John. Alice Au Pays des Merveilles. Carroll, Lewis. Bue, Henri, tr. 2018. (FRE.). 176p. (J). pap. *(978-2-35455-003-5(0))* Livio Informatique.

—Alice in Wonderland: Alice's Adventures in Wonderland & Through the Looking Glass. Carroll, Lewis. 2018. (ENG.). 304p. (J). (gr. 3-8). 14.99 *(978-1-63158-275-2(5)*, Racehorse Publishing) Skyhorse Publishing Co., Inc.

—Alice in Wonderland Giant Poster & Coloring Book. Carroll, Lewis. 2012. (ENG.). 48p. (gr. -1-17). pap. 12.95 *(978-1-4197-0089-7(8)*, Abrams Image) Abrams, Inc.

—Alice Through the Looking Glass. Carroll, Lewis. 2016. (ENG.). 133p. (J). (gr. 3). pap. *(978-1-911249-01-6(0))* Jam, Huge.

—Alice's Abenteuer im Wunderland. Carroll, Lewis. Zimmermann, Antonie, tr. 2012. (Dover Dual Language German Ser.).Tr. of Alice's Adventures in Wonderland. (GER.). 192p. (J). reprint ed. pap. 8.95 *(978-0-486-20668-4(8))* Dover Pubns., Inc.

—Alice's Adventures in Drawing Prompts. Carroll, Lewis. 2019. (Draw Classic Lit! Ser.: Vol. 1). (ENG.). 66p. (J). pap. 9.99 *(978-1-0959-1924-8(5))* Independently Published.

—Alice's Adventures in Wonderland. Carroll, Lewis. 2018. (ENG.). 256p. (J). 19.99 *(978-1-78888-387-0(X)*, b775fafc-527b-4d87-baa2-eda2dfaf9006) Arcturus Publishing GBR. Dist: Baker & Taylor Publisher Services (BTPS).

—Alice's Adventures in Wonderland. Carroll, Lewis. 2017. (ENG.). 122p. (J). 14.75 *(978-1-947844-18-6(0))* Athanatos Publishing Group.

—Alice's Adventures in Wonderland. Carroll, Lewis. Date not set. 248p. (YA). 14.95 *(978-1-884807-19-0(4))* Blushing Rose Publishing.

—Alice's Adventures in Wonderland. Carroll, Lewis. 2013. (Cambridge Library Collection - Fiction & Poetry Ser.). (ENG.). 210p. 59.99 *(978-1-108-06037-0(4))*; pap. 30.99 *(978-1-108-05958-9(9))* Cambridge Univ. Pr.

—Alice's Adventures in Wonderland. Carroll, Lewis. 2007. 204p. (J). 24.95 *(978-1-58218-791-4(6))*; (ENG.). (YA). per. 14.95 *(978-1-58218-790-7(8))* Digital Scanning, Inc.

—Alice's Adventures in Wonderland. Carroll, Lewis. 2009. 68p. pap. 14.14 *(978-1-151-46988-5(2))* General Bks. LLC.

—Alice's Adventures in Wonderland. Carroll, Lewis. 2008. (Vintage Classics Ser.). 336p. (gr. 4-7). pap. 11.95 *(978-0-09-951207-3(6))* Penguin Random Hse. GBR. Dist: Independent Pubs. Group.

—Alice's Adventures in Wonderland & Other Stories. Carroll, Lewis. 2013. (Leather-Bound Classics Ser.). (ENG.). 544p. lthr. 24.99 *(978-1-60710-933-4(6)*, Canterbury Classics) Printers Row Publishing Group.

—Alice's Adventures in Wonderland & Through the Looking-Glass. Carroll, Lewis & Frith, Barbara. 2013. (ENG.). 288p. *(978-1-907360-36-7(0)*, Collector's Library, The) Pan Macmillan.

—Alice's Adventures in Wonderland & Through the Looking-Glass. Carroll, Lewis. Haughton, Hugh, ed. rev. ed. 2003. 448p. (gr. 12-18). pap. 11.00 *(978-0-14-143976-1(9)*, Penguin Classics) Penguin Publishing Group.

—Alice's Adventures in Wonderland (illustrated) Carroll, Lewis. 2019. (ENG.). 182p. (J). pap. 9.99 *(978-1-0782-9725-7(8))* Independently Published.

—Les Aventures d'Alice Au Pays des Merveilles (illustré) Carroll, Lewis. Bue, Henri, tr. 2019. (FRE.). 202p. (J). pap. 11.00 *(978-1-0803-4812-1(3))* Independently Published.

—Eachdraidh Ealasaid Ann an Tìr Nan Iongantas. Carroll, Lewis. Watson, Moray, tr. from ENG. 2012. 156p. pap. *(978-1-78201-015-9(7))* Evertype.

—The Nursery Alice. Carroll, Lewis. 2010. 86p. pap. *(978-1-904808-42-8(5))* Evertype.

—The Nursery Alice. Carroll, Lewis. 2013. 74p. (J). pap. 18.58 *(978-1-939652-68-3(5))* Lire Bks.

—The Nursery Alice. Carroll, Lewis. 2009. 56p. *(978-973-88826-8-3(0))* Mediamorphosis.

—The Nursery Alice (illustrated) Illustrated by John Tenniel. Carroll, Lewis. 2019. (ENG.). 68p. (J). pap. 16.90 *(978-1-0801-1207-4(3))* Independently Published.

—'O Tafaoga a 'Alise I Le Nu'u O Mea Ofoofogia. Carroll, Lewis. Simanu-Klutz, Luafata, tr. from ENG. 2013. 152p. pap. *(978-1-78201-023-4(8))* Evertype.

—Sense & Nonsense Stories from Lewis Carroll: Alice, Sylvie & Bruno, & More. Carroll, Lewis. 2009. 672p. pap. 24.95 *(978-1-930585-75-1(6))* Coachwhip Pubns.

—Through the Looking Glass. Carroll, Lewis. 2012. *(978-1-897093-65-8(9))* Qualitas Publishing.

Tenniel, John. Through the Looking-Glass & What Alice Found There. Carroll, Lewis. 2020. (ENG.). 242p. (J). (gr. 2-13). ***(978-1-5287-1640-6(X))***; pap. ***(978-1-5287-1639-0(6))*** Read Bks.

Tenniel, John. Through the Looking-Glass, & What Alice Found There, Original Version: Alice Through the Looking Glass. Carroll, Lewis. 2010. (ENG.). 210p. pap. 25.95 *(978-4-87187-304-8(8))* Ishi Pr. International.

—Trans la Speguło Kaj Kion Alico Trovis Tie. Carroll, Lewis. Broadribb, Donald, tr. from ENG. 2012. 180p. pap. *(978-1-78201-001-2(7))* Evertype.

Tenniel, John & Bickford-Smith, Coralie. Alice's Adventures in Wonderland & Through the Looking Glass. Carroll, Lewis & Bickford-Smith, Coralie. 2010. (Penguin Clothbound Classics Ser.). 448p. (gr. 12). 24.00 *(978-0-14-119246-8(1)*, Penguin Classics) Penguin Publishing Group.

Tenniel, John & Holiday, Henry. Alice in Wonderland (Illustrated) Alice's Adventures in Wonderland, Through the Looking-Glass, & the Hunting of the Snark. Carroll, Lewis. 2020. (Top Five Classics Ser.). (ENG.). 324p. (J). (gr. 2-6). pap. 16.00 ***(978-1-938938-44-3(5))*** Top Five Bks.

Tenniel, John & Thomson, E. Gertrude. The Nursery Alice. Carroll, Lewis. 2010. 64p. pap. *(978-1-907960-00-0(7))* English Rose Publishing.

Tenniel, Sir John. The Nursery Alice. Carroll, Lewis. 2015. (Macmillan Alice Ser.). (ENG.). 72p. (J). (-k). 19.99 *(978-1-4472-8711-7(8))* Pan Macmillan GBR. Dist: Independent Pubs. Group.

Tenniel, Sir John & Thomson, E. Gertrude. The Nursery Alice. Carroll, Lewis. 2014. 64p. *(978-1-907960-09-3(0))* English Rose Publishing.

Tenorio, Audrey. Skyway: Clairvoyance- a Science Fiction Space Saga. Cavalida, J. D. 2018. (Skyway Ser.: Vol. 1). (ENG.). 74p. (J). pap. 11.99 *(978-1-7294-0150-7(3))* Independently Published.

Tentler-Krylov, Victoria. Cyclops of Central Park. Rosenberg, Madelyn. 2020. 32p. (J). (gr. -1-2). 17.99 *(978-0-525-51470-1(8)*, G.P. Putnam's Sons Books for Young Readers) Penguin Young Readers Group.

—Just Read! Degman, Lori. 2019. 32p. (J). (gr. -1). 16.95 *(978-1-4549-2572-9(8))* Sterling Publishing Co., Inc.

Tenud, Trish. Baby's First Bible & Book of Prayers Gift Set, 1 vol. Carlson, Melody. 2020. 192p. (J). 16.99 ***(978-0-310-76889-0(6))*** Zonderkidz.

Teo, Ali. Barnaby Bennett, 1 vol. Rainforth, Hannah. 2008. (ENG.). 32p. (J). (gr. -1-3). pap. 5.95 *(978-1-59572-156-3(8))* Star Bright Bks., Inc.

—Barnaby Bennett. Rainforth, Hannah. 2007. 32p. (J). (gr. -1-3). pap. 10.00 *(978-1-86969-232-2(2))* Univ. of Hawaii Pr.

—In My Garden. Buxton, Jane. 2010. (ENG.). 8p. (gr. k-1). pap. 7.95 *(978-1-61181-033-2(7)*, Kaeden Bks.) Kaeden Corp.

—The Seagull & the Fish. Trussell-Cullen, Alan. 2010. (ENG.). 16p. (gr. k-2). pap. 7.95 *(978-1-61181-039-4(6)*, Kaeden Bks.) Kaeden Corp.

Teo, Ali & O'Reilly, John. Kiss! Kiss! Yuck! Yuck!, 1 vol. Mewburn, Kyle. (ENG.). 32p. (J). (gr. -1-3). 2017. pap. 7.95 *(978-1-56145-759-5(0))*; 2008. 16.95 *(978-1-56145-457-0(5))* Peachtree Publishing Co. Inc.

Teo, Ali, jt. illus. see Jensen, Astrid.

Teplin, Scott & Rex, Adam. The Clock Without a Face. Barnett, Mac et al. 2010. 30p. (J). (gr. 2-18). bds. 19.95 *(978-1-934781-71-5(1)*, 58d07e96-8b05-496a-aa15-e78c32d0d649) McSweeney's Publishing.

Teplow, Rotem. The Eternal Soldier: The True Story of How a Dog Became a Civil War Hero. Crotzer Kimmel, Allison. 2019. (ENG.). 40p. (J). (gr. k-4). 17.99 *(978-1-4998-0863-6(1))* Little Bee Books Inc.

Terada, Junzo. Animal Friends on Parade Puzzle. 2017. (ENG.). 12p. (J). (gr. -1-k). 14.99 *(978-1-4521-5190-8(3))* Chronicle Bks. LLC.

Terblanche, Adrien. I've Heard of a Herd: But How about a Homophone? Nally, Martin P. 2018. (ENG.). 32p. (J). pap. *(978-0-6484131-0-3(1))* Incharge Investments.

Terceira, Anna. Bermuda's Flying Flowers Activity Book. Mykkal, Ras, photos by. 2016. (ENG.). (J). (gr. k-6). pap. *(978-0-947480-44-8(7))* Bermuda National Trust.

Tercio, Ricardo. Aesop's Fables. McGovern, Ann. 2013. (ENG.). 80p. (J). (gr. 2-5). pap. 4.99 *(978-0-545-46722-3(5))* Scholastic, Inc.

—Jack & the Beanstalk: The Graphic Novel. 2008. (Graphic Spin Ser.). (ENG.). 40p. (J). (gr. 3-6). 25.32 *(978-1-4342-0766-1(8)*, Stone Arch Bks.) Capstone.

—Jack & the Beanstalk: The Graphic Novel, 1 vol. Stone Arch Books Staff. 2008. (Graphic Spin Ser.). (ENG.). 40p. (J). (gr. 3-6). pap. 5.95 *(978-1-4342-0862-0(1)*, Stone Arch Bks.) Capstone.

—Jack y los Frijoles Magicos. Andersen, Hans & Stone Arch Books Staff. 2010. (Graphic Spin en Español Ser.). (SPA.). 40p. (J). (gr. 3-6). pap. 5.95 *(978-1-4342-2272-5(1)*, Stone Arch Bks.) Capstone.

—Jack y los Frijoles Magicos. Andersen, Hans & Capstone Press Staff. 2010. (Graphic Spin en Español Ser.). (SPA.). 40p. (J). (gr. 3-6). lib. bdg. 25.32 *(978-1-4342-1902-2(X)*, Stone Arch Bks.) Capstone.

Terkulova, Marina. The Secret of Moon Lake. Nova, Sofia. 2019. (ENG.). 286p. (J). pap. 14.99 ***(978-0-578-59944-1(9))*** GOLDEN LIBERTY.

Termure, Catalin Bogdan. Noaptea Magica: Povesti Pentru Copii. Termure, Gabriela Georgeta. 2017. (RUM.). 82p. (J). pap. *(978-606-94356-2-5(1))* Letras.

Terrana-Hollis, Kristen. My Big Book of Feelings: 200+ Awesome Activities to Grow Every Kid's Emotional Well-Being. Ginns, Russell. 2020. 256p. (J). (gr. -1-2). pap. 12.99 ***(978-0-525-57140-7(X)***, Rodale Kids) Random Hse. Children's Bks.

Terrazzini, Daniela Jaglenka. The Call of the Wild. London, Jack. 2011. (Puffin Classics Ser.). (ENG.). 160p. (J). (gr. 5-7). 16.99 *(978-0-14-133654-1(4)*, Puffin Books) Penguin Young Readers Group.

Terrazzini, Daniela Jaglenka, jt. illus. see Blake, Quentin.

Terrazzini, Daniela Jaglenka, jt. illus. see Hall, Arthur.

Terron Tamez, Irma Ilia. Ana & Her Dog Nana. Ortiz Bello, Frank Joseph, ed. Marcano, Edgar J., tr. 2019. (ENG.). 38p. (J). pap. 15.00 ***(978-1-881741-93-0(1))*** Ediciones Eleos.

Terry, Brian. The Lemonade Crash. Hafer, Tom. 2010. 24p. 16.95 *(978-1-4520-1439-5(6))* AuthorHouse.

Terry, Laura. Anna Strong & the Revolutionary War Culper Spy Ring, Library Edition: A Spy on History Book. Alberti, Enigma. 2019. (Spy on History Ser.). (ENG.). 96p. (gr. 3-9). 15.95 *(978-1-5235-0794-8(2)*, 100794) Workman Publishing Co., Inc.

Terry, Laura. Graveyard Shakes. Terry, Laura. 2017. (ENG.). 208p. (J). (gr. 3-7). 24.99 *(978-0-545-88955-1(3))*; pap. 12.99 *(978-0-545-88954-4(5))* Scholastic, Inc. (Graphix).

Terry, Michael. Gossipy Parrot. Roddie, Shen. 2003. (J). pap. 9.99 *(978-0-7475-6489-8(2))* Bloomsbury Publishing Plc GBR. Dist: Independent Pubs. Group.

—Lonely Giraffe. Blight, Peter. Matthewson, Emma, ed. 2005. 32p. (J). 19.99 *(978-0-7475-6894-0(4))* Bloomsbury Publishing Plc GBR. Dist: Independent Pubs. Group.

—The Lonely Giraffe. Blight, Peter. 2006. (Bloomsbury Paperbacks Ser.). 32p. (J). (gr. -1-3). pap. 12.99 *(978-0-7475-7144-5(9))* Bloomsbury Publishing Plc GBR. Dist: Trafalgar Square Publishing.

—See the Sea! A Book about Colors. Reader's Digest Editors & Zobel-Nolan, Allia. 2004. (Googly Eyes Ser.). (ENG.). 10p. (J). (-1). bds. 7.99 *(978-0-7944-0291-4(7)*, Reader's Digest Children's Bks.) Studio Fun International.

—The Selfish Crocodile Anniversary Edition. Charles, Faustin. 20th anniv. ed. 2018. (Selfish Crocodile Ser.). 32p. (J). 9.99 *(978-1-4088-8525-3(5)*, 900208407, Bloomsbury Children's Bks.) Bloomsbury Publishing USA.

—The Selfish Crocodile Book of Colours. Charles, Faustin. 2013. (Selfish Crocodile Ser.). (ENG.). 14p. (J). bds. 10.99 *(978-1-4088-1449-9(8)*, 900121647, Bloomsbury Children's Bks.) Bloomsbury Publishing USA.

—The Selfish Crocodile Book of Sounds. Charles, Faustin. 2012. (Selfish Crocodile Ser.). 14p. (J). (gr. -1-3). bds. 10.99 *(978-1-4088-1450-5(1)*, 900097234, Bloomsbury Children's Bks.) Bloomsbury Publishing USA.

—The Selfish Crocodile Counting Book. Charles, Faustin. l.t. ed. 2008. 12p. (J). (gr. k-k). bds. 8.95 *(978-0-7475-9238-9(1))* Bloomsbury Publishing Plc GBR. Dist: Independent Pubs. Group.

Terry, Michael. Captain Wag & the Big Blue Whale. Terry, Michael. 2008. (Captain Wag Ser.). 32p. (J). (gr. k-k). pap. 13.95 *(978-0-7475-9254-9(3))* Bloomsbury Publishing Plc GBR. Dist: Independent Pubs. Group.

—The Selfish Crocodile Book of Nursery Rhymes. Terry, Michael. Charles, Faustin. 2008. (J). (gr. -1-k). audio compact disk 25.95 *(978-0-7475-9523-6(2))* Bloomsbury Publishing Plc GBR. Dist: Independent Pubs. Group.

Terry, Michael. The Gossipy Parrot. Terry, Michael, tr. Roddie, Shen. 2004. 32p. (J). (gr. k-2). 20.00 *(978-0-7475-6079-1(X))* Bloomsbury Publishing Plc GBR. Dist: Independent Pubs. Group.

Terry, Roger. How 'Pilly-Pine', the Alpaca, Lost His Quills. Miceli, Mary Anne. 2012. 44p. pap. 20.00 *(978-0-578-10145-3(9))* Miceli, Mary Anne.

Terry, Will. Armadilly Chili. Ketteman, Helen. 2012. (J). *(978-1-61913-143-9(9))* Weigl Pubs., Inc.

—Armadilly Chili. Ketteman, Helen. 2004. (ENG.). 32p. (J). (gr. -1-3). pap. 7.99 *(978-0-8075-0458-1(0)*, 807504580) Whitman, Albert & Co.

—Big Heart! A Valentine's Day Tale. Holub, Joan. 2007. (Ant Hill Ser.). (ENG.). 24p. (J). (gr. -1-k). lib. bdg. 13.89 *(978-1-4169-2562-0(7)*, Simon & Schuster/Paula Wiseman Bks.) Simon & Schuster/Paula Wiseman Bks.

—Big Heart! A Valentine's Day Tale. Holub, Joan. 2007. (Ant Hill Ser.). (ENG.). 24p. (J). (gr. -1-k). pap. 4.99 *(978-1-4169-0957-6(5)*, Simon Spotlight) Simon Spotlight.

—Bonaparte Falls Apart. Cuyler, Margery. 2020. 40p. (J). (gr. -1-2). 7.99 *(978-1-101-93772-3(6)*, Dragonfly Bks.) Random Hse. Children's Bks.

—The Frog with the Big Mouth. 2012. (J). 34.28 *(978-1-61913-146-0(3))* Weigl Pubs., Inc.

—Good Luck! A St. Patrick's Day Story. Holub, Joan. 2007. (Ant Hill Ser.). (ENG.). 24p. (J). (gr. -1-k). lib. bdg. 11.89 *(978-1-4169-2560-6(0),* Aladdin Library) Simon & Schuster Children's Publishing.

—Good Luck! A St. Patrick's Day Story. Holub, Joan. 2007. (Ant Hill Ser.). (ENG.). 24p. (J). (gr. -1-k). pap. 4.99 *(978-1-4169-0955-2(9),* Simon Spotlight) Simon Spotlight.

—Little Rooster's Diamond Button. 2012. (J). *(978-1-61913-156-9(0))* Weigl Pubs., Inc.

—Monster Parade. Corey, Shana. 2009. (Step into Reading: Step 2 Ser.). (ENG.). 24p. (J). (gr. -1-1). lib. bdg. 16.19 *(978-0-375-95638-6(7))* Random House Publishing Group.

—Monster Parade. Corey, Shana. 2009. (Step into Reading Ser.). 24p. (J). (gr. -1-1). 4.99 *(978-0-375-85638-9(2),* Random Hse. Bks. for Young Readers) Random Hse. Children's Bks.

—More Snacks! A Thanksgiving Play. Holub, Joan. 2006. (Ant Hill Ser.: 1). (ENG.). 24p. (J). (gr. -1-k). pap. 4.99 *(978-1-4169-0954-5(0));* lib. bdg. 11.89 *(978-1-4169-2559-0(7))* Simon Spotlight. (Simon Spotlight).

—Picnic! A Day in the Park. Holub, Joan. 2008. (Ant Hill Ser.). (ENG.). 24p. (J). (gr. -1-k). pap. 4.99 *(978-1-4169-5133-9/4),* Simon Spotlight) Simon Spotlight.

—Santa Pups. Pallotta, Jerry. 2016. (ENG.). 32p. (J). (gr. -1-k). 6.99 *(978-0-545-48479-4(0))* Scholastic, Inc.

—Santa Pups. Pallotta, Jerry. ed. 2016. (ENG.). 32p. (J). (gr. -1-k). 17.20 *(978-0-606-39130-6(4))* Turtleback.

—Scaredy-Pants! A Halloween Story. Holub, Joan. 2007. (Ant Hill Ser.). (ENG.). 24p. (J). (gr. -1-k). pap. 3.99 *(978-1-4169-0956-9(7),* Simon Spotlight/Nickelodeon) Simon Spotlight/Nickelodeon.

—Senorita Gordita. Ketteman, Helen. 2012. (ENG.). 32p. (J). (gr. -1-3). 16.99 *(978-0-8075-7302-0(7),* 807573027) Whitman, Albert & Co.

Terry, Will. Skeleton for Dinner. Cuyler, Margery. 2020. (ENG.). 32p. (J). (gr. -1-3). pap. 7.99 ***(978-0-8075-7402-7(3),*** 0807574023) Whitman, Albert & Co.

Terry, Will. Snow Day! A Winter Tale. Holub, Joan. 2008. (Ant Hill Ser.). (ENG.). 24p. (J). (gr. -1-k). pap. 4.99 *(978-1-4169-5135-3(0),* Simon Spotlight) Simon Spotlight.

—Spring Is Here! A Story about Seeds. Holub, Joan. 2008. (Ant Hill Ser.). (ENG.). 24p. (J). (gr. -1-k). lib. bdg. 13.89 *(978-1-4169-5132-2(6),* Simon & Schuster/Paula Wiseman Bks.) Simon & Schuster/Paula Wiseman Bks.

—Spring Is Here! A Story about Seeds. Holub, Joan. 2008. (Ant Hill Ser.). (ENG.). 24p. (J). (gr. -1-k). pap. 3.99 *(978-1-4169-5131-5(8),* Simon Spotlight) Simon Spotlight.

—There Once Was a Cowpoke Who Swallowed an Ant. Ketteman, Helen. 2014. (ENG.). 32p. (J). (gr. -1-3). 16.99 *(978-0-8075-7850-6(9),* 807578509) Whitman, Albert & Co.

—The Three Bully Goats. Kimmelman, Leslie. 2012. (J). *(978-1-61913-136-1(6))* Weigl Pubs., Inc.

—The Three Bully Goats. Kimmelman, Leslie. 2011. (ENG.). 32p. (J). (gr. -1-3). 16.99 *(978-0-8075-7900-8(9),* 807579009) Whitman, Albert & Co.

—The Three Little Gators. Ketteman, Helen. 2012. (J). 34.28 *(978-1-61913-140-8(4))* Weigl Pubs., Inc.

—The Three Little Gators. Ketteman, Helen. 2009. (ENG.). 32p. (J). (gr. -1-3). 16.99 *(978-0-8075-7824-7(X),* 080757824X) Whitman, Albert & Co.

—The Treasure of Ghostwood Gully: A Southwest Mystery. Vaughan, Marcia. 2004. (ENG.). 32p. (J). (gr. 1-3). 15.95 *(978-0-87358-858-4(4))* Cooper Square Publishing Llc.

Terzi, Merve. Fun at the Playground! Ladi, Liz & CAM. Lassa, Julia. 2017. (Ladi, Liz & CAM Ser.: Vol. 3). (ENG.). 32p. (J). *(978-0-9956683-2-4(9));* pap. *(978-0-9956683-3-1(7))* Bower Maze.

—The Hungry City Fox. Mallorey, Gemma. 2016. (ENG.). (J). pap. *(978-0-9933603-4-3(3))* Bower Maze.

—Let's Bake! Ladi, Liz & CAM. Lassa, Julia. 2017. (Ladi, Liz & CAM Ser.: Vol. 2). (ENG.). (J). *(978-0-9956683-1-7(0))* Bower Maze.

—MC Veggie Fresh Rocks the Mic. Morris, Shanon. 2018. (MC Veggie Fresh Ser.: Vol. 1). (ENG.). 50p. (J). (gr. k-4). 19.99 *(978-1-7325821-1-8(4));* pap. 14.99 *(978-1-7325821-0-1(6))* Morris, Shanon.

—On Your Marks, Get Set, Go! Ladi, Liz & CAM. Lassa, Julia. 2017. (Ladi, Liz & CAM Ser.: Vol. 1). (ENG.). (J). *(978-0-9956683-0-0(2))* Bower Maze.

Teskey, Donald. The Táin: Ireland's Epic Adventure. MacUistin, Liam. 2012. (ENG.). 112p. (J). pap. 10.95 *(978-1-84717-288-4(1))* O'Brien Pr., Ltd., The IRL. Dist: Casemate Pubs. & Bk. Distributors, LLC.

—Under the Hawthorn Tree. Conlon-McKenna, Marita. 2003. (ENG.). 160p. pap. 5.95 *(978-0-86278-206-1(6))* O'Brien Pr., Ltd., The IRL. Dist: Independent Pubs. Group.

Tessama, C. Eeny, Meeny, Miney, Moe, Four Alaskan Ravens. Johannes, Avril & Branham, Jan. 2003. 32p. (J). 7.95 *(978-0-9749360-0-0(6))* Icicle Falls Publishing Co.

Tessier, Beth Marie, photos by. Debbie's Eyes. Barry, Debra R. 2011. 32p. pap. 24.95 *(978-1-4560-5272-0(1))* America Star Bks.

Tessler, Daria. Young Henry & the Dragon. Kaufman, Jeanne. 2011. (J). *(978-1-934860-11-3(5))* Shenanigan Bks.

Testa, Fulvio. Aesop's Forgotten Fables. Waters, Fiona. 2014. (ENG.). 96p. (J). (gr. 2-4). 24.99 *(978-1-84939-706-3(6))* Andersen Pr. GBR. Dist: Independent Pubs. Group.

—Pinocchio. Collodi, Carlo. Brock, Geoffrey, tr. from ITA. ed. 2012.Tr. of Avventure di Pinocchio. (ENG.). 184p. (J). (gr. k-4). 24.95 *(978-1-59017-588-0(3),* NYR Children's Collection) New York Review of Bks., Inc., The.

Testa, Fulvio. Aesop's Fables. Testa, Fulvio. Waters, Fiona & Aesop, Aesop. Waters, Fiona, ed. 2015. 128p. (J). (gr. 2-4). pap. 18.99 *(978-1-84939-247-1(1))* Andersen Pr. GBR. Dist: Independent Pubs. Group.

—Aesop's Fables. Testa, Fulvio. Waters, Fiona & Aesop Enterprise Inc. Staff. Waters, Fiona, ed. 2011. (ENG.). 128p. (J). (gr. 2-4). 24.99 *(978-1-84939-049-1(5))* Andersen Pr. GBR. Dist: Independent Pubs. Group.

Testar, Sue, jt. illus. see Francis, John.

Tetrault, Jamison, jt. illus. see Tetrault, Parker.

Tetrault, Parker. Summit Searches for Squeaky. Tetrault, Suzanne. 2019. (ENG.). 26p. (J). pap. 9.79 *(978-1-7940-5932-0(6))* Independently Published.

Tetrault, Parker & Tetrault, Jamison. Summit Saves Her Pet: Based on a True Story about a Dog... Written by Her Pets. Tetrault, Suzanne. 2019. (Summit's Stories Ser.: Vol. 2). (ENG.). 30p. (J). pap. 9.97 *(978-1-7954-2231-4(9))* Independently Published.

Tetri, Emily. Tiger vs. Nightmare. Tetri, Emily. 2018. (ENG.). 64p. (J). 17.99 *(978-1-62672-535-5(7),* 900160471, First Second Bks.) Roaring Brook Pr.

Teves, Miles. The Dragon Hunter's Handbook. 2008. (J). *(978-1-4351-0204-0(5))* Metro Bks.

Tewinkel, Naomi. Marci's Gift. Winchester, Tonia. 2019. (ENG.). 40p. (J). pap. ***(978-1-9991841-0-0(6))*** Gauvin, Jacques.

Texier, Jean. Alfie Green & the Bee-Bottle Gang. O'Brien, Joe. 2nd rev. ed. 2007. (Alfie Green Ser.). (ENG.). 80p. (J). pap. 13.00 *(978-1-84717-054-5(4))* O'Brien Pr., Ltd., The IRL. Dist: Dufour Editions, Inc.

—Alfie Green & the Conker King. O'Brien, Joe. 2012. (Alfie Green Ser.). (ENG.). 80p. (J). pap. 13.00 *(978-1-84717-283-9(0))* O'Brien Pr., Ltd., The IRL. Dist: Dufour Editions, Inc.

Tey, Priscilla. In-Between Things. Tey, Priscilla. 2018. 40p. (J). (gr. -1-3). 16.99 *(978-0-7636-8983-4(1))* Candlewick Pr.

Teymorian, Anahita. There's Room for Everyone. Teymorian, Anahita. Ghanimifard, Delaram, tr. 2019. (ENG.). 32p. (J). 16.99 *(978-1-910328-53-8(7))* Tiny Owl Publishing Ltd. GBR. Dist: Consortium Bk. Sales & Distribution.

Tezuka, Osamu. Astro Boy. Tezuka, Osamu. 2003. (ENG.). Vol. 11. 216p. pap. 9.95 *(978-1-56971-812-4(1));* Vol. 20. 224p. pap. 9.95 *(978-1-56971-901-5(2))* Dark Horse Comics.

—Karma. Tezuka, Osamu. 2004. (Phoenix Ser.: Vol. 4). (ENG.). 368p. pap. 15.95 *(978-1-59116-300-8(5))* Viz Media.

—Nextworld, Vol. 1. Tezuka, Osamu. 2003. (ENG.). 168p. pap. 13.95 *(978-1-56971-866-7(0))* Dark Horse Comics.

—Phoenix, Vol. 1. Tezuka, Osamu. 2003. (ENG.). 344p. pap. 15.95 *(978-1-56931-868-3(9))* Viz Media.

—Resurrection. Tezuka, Osamu. 2004. (Phoenix Ser.). (ENG.). 200p. pap. 15.95 *(978-1-59116-593-4(8))* Viz Media.

—Yamato/Space, Vol. 3. Tezuka, Osamu. 2003. (Phoenix Ser.). (ENG.). 336p. pap. 15.95 *(978-1-59116-100-4(2))* Viz Media.

Th, H. Nh Ninh. A Most Unlikely Hero, Vol. 1. Varnell, Brandon. 2017. (Most Unlikely Hero Ser.: Vol. 1). (ENG.). (YA). (gr. 7-12). pap. 13.00 *(978-0-9978028-4-9(7))* Kitsune Inc.

Thacker, Becky. The Chorus Kids' Memorial Day Parade. Thacker, Becky. 2006. (J). 10.95 *(978-0-9786276-1-4(X))* Mentzer Printing Ink.

Thacker, Kat. The First Olympic Games: A Gruesome Greek Myth with a Happy Ending. Richards, Jean. 2004. 32p. pap. 10.95 *(978-0-7613-2443-0(7),* Millbrook Pr.) Lerner Publishing Group.

Thacker, Marci. Big Daddy & Rico Visit Indian Springs. Jacobs, Mary T. 2018. (ENG.). 40p. (J). (gr. k-2). (Big Daddy Ser.: Vol. 3). 22.99 *(978-1-948026-17-8(1));* pap. 14.99 *(978-1-948026-14-7(7))* Write Integrity Pr.

Thai, Thu. Camille's Mermaid Tale. Tripp, Valerie. 2017. 100p. (J). *(978-1-5182-4321-9(5),* American Girl) American Girl Publishing, Inc.

—The Clippity-Cloppity Carnival. Tripp, Valerie. 2018. 91p. (J). *(978-1-5444-0756-2(4),* American Girl) American Girl Publishing, Inc.

—Emerson & Princess Peep. Tripp, Valerie. 2018. 97p. (J). *(978-1-5444-0754-8(8),* American Girl) American Girl Publishing, Inc.

—The Mystery of Mr. E. Tripp, Valerie. 2017. (American Girl: WellieWishers Ser.). (ENG.). 96p. (J). (gr. 2-4). 18.69 *(978-1-5364-1784-5(X))* American Girl Publishing, Inc.

—The Rainstorm Brainstorm. Tripp, Valerie. 2017. 83p. (J). *(978-1-5182-4311-0(8),* American Girl) American Girl Publishing, Inc.

—Willa's Wilderness Campout. Tripp, Valerie. 2018. 87p. (J). *(978-1-5444-0755-5(6),* American Girl) American Girl Publishing, Inc.

Thaipinnarong, Tidawan. Invent-A-Pet. Fang, Vicky. 2020. 32p. (J). (gr. -1-2). 16.95 ***(978-1-4549-3381-6(X))*** Sterling Publishing Co., Inc.

Thaler, Shmuel, photos by. Bread Comes to Life: A Garden of Wheat & a Loaf to Eat. Levenson, George. 2008. 32p. (J). (gr. -1-2). pap. 7.99 *(978-1-58246-273-8(9),* Tricycle Pr.) Random Hse. Children's Bks.

—Piece = Part = Portion. Gifford, Scott. 2008. 32p. (J). (gr. 1-4). pap. 7.99 *(978-1-58246-261-5(5),* Tricycle Pr.) Random Hse. Children's Bks.

Thames, Bob. Hermy the Hermit Crab Goes Shrimping. 2007. 44p. (J). 16.99 *(978-0-933101-05-0(8))* Legacy Pubns.

Thames, Leona & Williams, Kareem Paul. I Love My Scaredy Cat. Thames, Leona. 2019. (I Love My Scaredy Cat Ser.: Vol. 1). (ENG.). 34p. (J). pap. 9.13 ***(978-1-7311-0004-7(3))*** Independently Published.

Thammavongsa, Christine, jt. illus. see Disney Storybook Artists Staff.

Thanh Le, Xuan. The Easter Story. Elliot, Rachel. Cottage Door Press & Parragon Books, eds. ed. 2019. (ENG.). 32p. (J). (gr. -1-3). 9.99 *(978-1-68052-515-1(8),* 2000870, Parragon Books) Cottage Door Pr.

Thannhauser, Stephanie. Baa Quack Moo. Make Believe Ideas Ltd. 2020. (ENG.). 12p. (J). bds. ***(978-1-78947-351-3(9))*** Make Believe Ideas.

—Rhinocorn. Make Believe Ideas Ltd & Best, Elanor. 2020. (Two-Way Sequin Picture Bks.). (ENG.). 32p. (J). (gr. -1-7). ***(978-1-78947-388-9(8))*** Make Believe Ideas.

—Rhinocorn. Best, Elanor. 2020. (Two-Way Sequin Picture Bks.). (ENG.). 32p. (J). (gr. -1-7). pap. ***(978-1-78947-387-2(X));*** pap. ***(978-1-78947-389-6(6))*** Make Believe Ideas.

—A School of Fish. Creese, Sarah. 2020. (ENG.). 12p. (J). bds. ***(978-1-78843-989-3(9))*** Make Believe Ideas.

Thapa, Diptee. Monkey - Dagens Superhelt:: Da Tigeren Mistede Sine Striber. Bramsted, Dino Theodoor. Bramsted, Natalina Atlanta, ed. 2016. (Monkey - Dagens Superhelt Ser.: Vol. 1). (DAN.). (J). (gr. k-2). *(978-87-93084-29-2(3))* Piffz.

—Monkey - Dagens Superhelt: Elefanten der Ikke Kunne Hore. Bramsted, Dino Theodoor. Bramsted, Natalina Atlanta, ed. 2017. (Monkey - Dagens Superhelt Ser.: Vol. 2). (DAN.). 50p. (J). (gr. k-2). *(978-87-93084-31-5(5))* Piffz.

—Monkey - Dagens Superhelt: En Knude der Skal Losnes. Bramsted, Dino Theodoor. Bramsted, Natalina Atlanta, ed. 2017. (Monkey - Dagens Superhelt Ser.: Vol. 3). (DAN.). 50p. (J). (gr. k-2). *(978-87-93084-33-9(1))* Piffz.

—Monkey - Hero of the Jungle: A Knot to Be Loosened. Bramsted, Dino Theodoor. Bramsted, Natalina Atlanta, ed. 2017. (Monkey - Hero of the Jungle Ser.: Vol. 3). (ENG.). (J). (gr. k-2). *(978-87-93084-32-2(3))* Piffz.

—Monkey - Hero of the Jungle: The Elephant Who Could Not Hear. Bramsted, Dino Theodoor. Bramsted, Natalina Atlanta, ed. 2017. (Monkey - Hero of the Jungle Ser.: Vol. 2). (ENG.). (J). (gr. k-2). *(978-87-93084-30-8(7))* Piffz.

—Monkey - Hero of the Jungle: When the Tiger Lost Its Stripes. Bramsted, Dino Theodoor. Bramsted, Natalina Atlanta, ed. 2016. (Monkey: Hero of the Jungle Ser.: Vol. 1). (ENG.). (J). (gr. k-2). *(978-87-93084-28-5(5))* Piffz.

Thapar, Bindia. The Magic Raindrop. Dharmarajan, Geeta. 2005. (J). *(978-81-89020-28-6(5))* Katha.

Thapp, Manjit. Can I Tell You about down Syndrome? A Guide for Friends, Family & Professionals. Elliott, Elizabeth. 2015. (Can I Tell You About...? Ser.). (ENG.). 48p. pap. 14.95 *(978-1-84905-501-7(7),* 693004) Kingsley, Jessica Pubs. GBR. Dist: Hachette UK Distribution.

—Women's Art Work: More Than 30 Female Artists Who Changed the World. Bennett, Sophia. 2020. (ENG.). 112p. (J). (gr. 5-9). 19.99 *(978-1-4197-4118-0(7),* 1303801, Abrams Bks. for Young Readers) Abrams, Inc.

Tharani, Nadir. When Trees Walked Miti Ilipokuwa Yatembea: Bilingual English & Swahili. Tharani, Nishant. Kitunga, Demere, tr. 2016. (Kids' Books from Here & There Ser.). (ENG.). (J). (gr. k-3). 19.95 *(978-1-939604-12-5(5));* pap. 9.99 *(978-1-939604-13-2(3))* Barranca Pr.

Tharlet, Eve. Blue Pebble. Balpe, Anne-Gaëlle. 2019. (ENG.). 32p. (J). (gr. k-2). 17.99 *(978-988-8341-75-7(8),* Minedition) Neugebauer, Michael (Publishing) Limited HKG. Dist: Penguin Random Hse. LLC.

—Davy Loves the Baby. Weninger, Brigitte. 2015. 32p. (J). 15.95 *(978-0-7358-4210-6(8))* North-South Bks., Inc.

—Davy's Summer Vacation. Weninger, Brigitte. 2018. (Davy Ser.: 6). (ENG.). 32p. (J). (gr. -1-3). 16.95 *(978-0-7358-4278-6(7))* North-South Bks., Inc.

—Happy Birthday, Davy! Weninger, Brigitte. 2nd rev. ed. 2015. 32p. (J). 15.95 *(978-0-7358-4224-3(8))* North-South Bks., Inc.

—Happy Easter, Davy! Weninger, Brigitte. 2014. 32p. (J). (gr. k-3). 15.95 *(978-0-7358-4161-1(6))* North-South Bks., Inc.

—How Will We Get to the Beach? Luciani, Brigitte. 2003. (ENG.). 32p. (J). (gr. -1). pap. 7.95 *(978-0-7358-1783-8(9))* North-South Bks., Inc.

—A Hubbub: Book 2, No. 2. Luciani, Brigitte. 2010. (Mr. Badger & Mrs. Fox Ser.: 2). (ENG.). 32p. (J). (gr. k-3). pap. 7.99 *(978-0-7613-5632-5(0),* 9780761356325, Graphic Universe™) Lerner Publishing Group.

—Just in Case You Ever Wonder, 1 vol. Lucado, Max. 2019. (ENG.). (J). 30p. bds. 8.99 *(978-0-7180-7539-2(0));* 32p. 17.99 *(978-0-7180-7538-5(2))* Nelson, Thomas Inc.

—The Little Red Thread. Balpe, Anne-Gaëlle. 2019. (ENG.). 32p. (J). (gr. -1-2). 17.99 *(978-988-8341-90-0(1),* Minedition) Neugebauer, Michael (Publishing) Limited HKG. Dist: Penguin Random Hse. LLC.

—The Meeting: Book 1, No. 1. Luciani, Brigitte. 2010. (Mr. Badger & Mrs. Fox Ser.: 1). (ENG.). 32p. (J). (gr. k-3). pap. 7.99 *(978-0-7613-5631-8(2),* 9780761356318, Graphic Universe™) Lerner Publishing Group.

—Merry Christmas Davy. Weninger, Brigitte. 2014. 32p. (J). 15.95 *(978-0-7358-4186-4(1))* North-South Bks., Inc.

—Peace & Quiet: Book 4, No. 4. Luciani, Brigitte. 2012. (Mr. Badger & Mrs. Fox Ser.: 4). (ENG.). 32p. (J). (gr. k-3). pap. 7.99 *(978-0-8225-9163-4(4),* 9780822591634, Graphic Universe™) Lerner Publishing Group.

—Sweet Dreams, Bruno. Knister. 2017. (ENG.). 32p. (J). (gr. -1-k). 17.99 *(978-988-8341-21-4(9),* Minedition) Neugebauer, Michael (Publishing) Limited HKG. Dist: Penguin Random Hse. LLC.

—Too Big, Too Small. Leblanc, Catherine. 2017. (ENG.). 32p. (J). (gr. -1-k). 17.99 *(978-988-8341-42-9(1),* Minedition) Neugebauer, Michael (Publishing) Limited HKG. Dist: Penguin Random Hse. LLC.

—What a Team! Luciani, Brigitte. Gauvin, Edward, tr. from FRE. 2011. (Mr. Badger & Mrs. Fox Ser.: 3). (ENG.). 32p. (J). (gr. k-3). 25.26 *(978-0-7613-5627-1(4))* Lerner Publishing Group.

—What a Team! Book 3, No. 3. Luciani, Brigitte. 2011. (Mr. Badger & Mrs. Fox Ser.: 3). (ENG.). 32p. (J). (gr. k-3). pap. 7.99 *(978-0-7613-5633-2(9),* 9780761356332, Graphic Universe™) Lerner Publishing Group.

—The Wild Cat. Luciani, Brigitte & Sacks, Nathan. 2018. (Mr. Badger & Mrs. Fox Ser.). (ENG.). 32p. (J). (gr. k-3). 26.65 *(978-1-5415-0086-0(5),* Graphic Universe™) Lerner Publishing Group.

—24 Stories for Advent. Weninger, Brigitte. 2015. 120p. (J). (gr. -1-2). 19.95 *(978-0-7358-4229-8(9))* North-South Bks., Inc.

Tharp, Jason. Bunny Will Not Be Quiet! Tharp, Jason. 2020. (Ready-To-Reads Ser.). (ENG.). 32p. (J). (gr. -1-1). 17.99 ***(978-1-5344-6638-8(X));*** pap. 4.99 ***(978-1-5344-6637-1(1))*** Simon Spotlight. (Simon Spotlight).

Tharp, Jason. Bunny Will Not Smile! Ready-To-Read Level 1. Tharp, Jason. 2019. (Ready-To-Reads Ser.). (ENG.). 32p. (J). (gr. -1-1). 17.99 *(978-1-5344-2509-5(8));* pap. 4.99 *(978-1-5344-2508-8(X))* Simon Spotlight. (Simon Spotlight).

—The Haunted Halls. Tharp, Jason. Rose, J. B. 2018. (Peachy & Keen Ser.: 3). (ENG.). 96p. (J). (gr. 2-5). pap. 4.99 *(978-1-338-27130-0(X))* Scholastic, Inc.

—It's Okay to Be a Unicorn! Tharp, Jason. 2020. (ENG.). 40p. (J). 17.99 *(978-1-250-31132-0(2),* 900198865) Imprint IND. Dist: Macmillan.

—Kiwi Cannot Reach! Tharp, Jason. 2019. (Ready-To-Reads Ser.). (ENG.). 32p. (J). (gr. -1-1). 17.99 *(978-1-5344-2512-5(8));* pap. 4.99 *(978-1-5344-2511-8(X))* Simon Spotlight. (Simon Spotlight).

—A School Tail, Bk. 1. Tharp, Jason. Rose, J. B. 2018. (Peachy & Keen Ser.: 1). (ENG.). 80p. (J). (gr. 2-5). pap. 4.99 *(978-1-338-11043-2(8))* Scholastic, Inc.

Tharp, Lauren R. Scary Man. Barlow, C. E. 2009. 44p. pap. 18.99 *(978-1-4269-1060-9(6))* Trafford Publishing.

Tharp, Tricia. I Love You! Lee, Calee M. 2013. (ENG.). 32p. (J). (gr. -1-k). pap. 9.99 *(978-1-62395-471-0(1))* Xist Publishing.

Thatcher, Emily. Dogs & Data Science. Denning, Camille. 2019. (ENG.). 24p. (J). pap. 10.00 *(978-1-0753-7223-0(2))* Independently Published.

Thayer, Elizabeth. The Trouble with Jeremy Chance. Harrar, George. 2007. (Historical Fiction for Young Readers Ser.). (ENG.). 168p. (J). (gr. 2-8). per. 6.95 *(978-1-57131-669-1(8))* Milkweed Editions.

Thayer, Pam. Carteles de Seguridad. Lindeen, Mary. 2016. (Early Rising Readers Ser.). (SPA.). 16p. (J). (gr. 1-1). 6.67 *(978-1-4788-4188-3(5))* Newmark Learning LLC.

Thayer, Pamela D. I Am Safe! Corriols, Carmen. 2015. (Early Rising Readers Ser.). (J). (gr. -1-k). 5.83 *(978-1-4788-2144-1(2))* Newmark Learning LLC.

—Para, Mira, Pasa. Corriols, Carmen. 2016. (Early Rising Readers Ser.). (SPA.). 16p. (J). (gr. 1-1). 6.67 *(978-1-4788-4179-1(6))* Newmark Learning LLC.

—Safety Posters. Lindeen, Mary. 2015. (Early Rising Readers Ser.). (J). (gr. -1-k). 5.83 *(978-1-4788-2146-5(9))* Newmark Learning LLC.

—Stop, Look, Go. Corriols, Carmen. 2015. (Early Rising Readers Ser.). (J). (gr. -1-k). 5.83 *(978-1-4788-2145-8(0))* Newmark Learning LLC.

Thayer, Pamela D. I Can Draw. Thayer, Pamela D. 2015. (Early Rising Readers Ser.). (J). (gr. -1-k). 5.83 *(978-1-4788-2150-2(7))* Newmark Learning LLC.

Thayne, Tamira Ci. Puddles on the Floor. Estep, Lorena. 2008. 24p. 15.95 *(978-0-615-21952-3(7))* Who Chains You Bks.

The Aguilar Sisters, The Aguilar. Count Me In: A Parade of Mexican Folk Art Numbers in English & Spanish. Weill, Cynthia. 2012. (First Concepts in Mexican Folk Art Ser.). (ENG.). 32p. (J). (gr. k-k). 14.95 *(978-1-935955-39-9(X))* Cinco Puntos Pr.

The Artifact Group. Lost in Time. Banks, Steven. 2006. 22p. (J). lib. bdg. 15.00 *(978-1-4242-0977-4(3))* Fitzgerald Bks.

The Artist, Eleven. Spirit Comes to Earth: Fearless Love. The Artist, Eleven. 2007. 128p. lib. bdg. 9.95 *(978-0-9743540-3-3(1))* Peace Love Karma Publishing.

—Spirit Comes to Earth: Renewing Your Heart's Mission. The Artist, Eleven. 2005. 128p. (YA). lib. bdg. 19.95 *(978-0-9743540-2-6(3))* Peace Love Karma Publishing.

The Author, By. El Oso, el Mejor Amigo Del Hombre. Fernanda Heredia, Maria. 2015. (Serie Verde / Album Ilustrado Ser.). (SPA.). 24p. (J). pap. 12.95 *(978-9942-19-326-1(X))* Santillana USA Publishing Co., Inc.

The Boy Fitz Hammond, The Boy. My Hamster Is an Astronaut. Lowe, Dave. 2019. (Stinky & Jinks Ser.: 2). (ENG.). 144p. (J). (gr. 1-4). pap. 9.99 *(978-1-84812-656-5(5))* Bonnier Publishing GBR. Dist: Independent Pubs. Group.

—My Hamster's Got Talent. Lowe, Dave. 2019. (Stinky & Jinks Ser.: 4). (ENG.). 112p. (J). (gr. 1-4). pap. 9.99 *(978-1-84812-658-9(1))* Bonnier Publishing GBR. Dist: Independent Pubs. Group.

The Ciletti Publishing Group. Story Time Cafe Maisy's Blue Bath Set. The Ciletti Publishing Group. 2010. (J). 24.95 *(978-0-917665-71-4(6))* Ciletti Publishing Group, Inc., The.

The Disney Storybook Art Team. Big Fish, Little Fish (Disney/Pixar Finding Dory) Webster, Christy. 2016. (Step into Reading Ser.). (ENG.). 24p. (J). (gr. -1-1). E-Book *(978-0-7364-3705-9(3),* RH/Disney) Random Hse. Children's Bks.

—Coco Little Golden Book (Disney/Pixar Coco) RH Disney. 2017. (Little Golden Book Ser.). (ENG.). 24p. (J). (-k). 4.99 *(978-0-7364-3800-1(9),* Golden/Disney) Random Hse. Children's Bks.

—Crash, Boom, Roar! (Disney/Pixar the Good Dinosaur) Amerikaner, Susan. 2015. (Step into Reading Ser.). (ENG.). 24p. (J). (gr. -1-1). 4.99 *(978-0-7364-3367-9(8),* Random Hse. Bks. for Young Readers) Random Hse. Children's Bks.

—Meet the Muppet Babies! Depken, Kristen L. 2018. (ENG.). 14p. (J). (— 1). bds. 8.99 *(978-0-7364-3967-1(6),* RH/Disney) Random Hse. Children's Bks.

—Olaf's Perfect Day (Disney Frozen) Julius, Jessica. 2015. (Little Golden Book Ser.). (ENG.). 24p. (J). (-k). 4.99 *(978-0-7364-3356-3(2),* Golden/Disney) Random Hse. Children's Bks.

—Show-and-Tell. RH Disney. 2018. (Little Golden Book Ser.). (ENG.). 24p. (J). (-k). 4.99 *(978-0-7364-3966-4(8),* Golden/Disney) Random Hse. Children's Bks.

The Disney Storybook Art Team, jt. illus. see Thomas, Jeffrey.

The Fan Brothers. The Darkest Dark. Hadfield, Chris. 2016. (ENG.). 48p. (J). (gr. -1-3). 17.99 *(978-0-316-39472-7(6))* Little, Brown Bks. for Young Readers.

The Indigo Bunting & Jang, Erin. Little Learner Board Book Set. Mudpuppy. 2020. (ENG.). 32p. (J). (gr. -1-k). bds. 14.99 *(978-0-7353-6380-9(3))* Mudpuppy Pr.

The Jim Henson Company. Dot: for Pet's Sake. Candlewick Press. 2020. (ENG.). 80p. (J). (gr. k-3). 14.99 ***(978-1-5362-1656-1(9),*** Candlewick Entertainment) Candlewick Pr.

T

The Jim Henson Company. Dot Goes Fishing. Candlewick Press. 2020. (Dot Ser.). 80p. (J). (gr. k-3). 14.99 *(978-1-5362-1333-1(0)*, Candlewick Entertainment) Candlewick Pr.

—Dot Unplugged. Candlewick Press. 2020. (Dot Ser.). (ENG.). 32p. (J). (gr. -1-1). 16.99 *(978-1-5362-0983-9(X)*, Candlewick Entertainment) Candlewick Pr.

—Leaf It to Dot. Cascardi, Andrea. 2019. (Dot Ser.). (ENG.). 48p. (J). (gr. k-3). 12.99 *(978-1-5362-0261-8(4))*; pap. 4.99 *(978-1-5362-0262-5(2))* Candlewick Pr. (Candlewick Entertainment).

—Rocket Out of the Park. Cascardi, Andrea. 2019. (Dot Ser.). (ENG.). 48p. (J). (gr. k-3). 12.99 *(978-1-5362-0009-6(3))*; 4.99 *(978-1-5362-0312-7(2))* Candlewick Pr. (Candlewick Entertainment).

the Mad, Johanna. Fence Vol. 2. Pacat, C. S. 2019. (Fence Ser.). (ENG.). 112p. (YA). pap. 14.99 *(978-1-68415-297-1(6))* Boom! Studios.

—Fence Vol. 3. Pacat, C. S. 2019. (Fence Ser.). (ENG.). 112p. (YA). pap. 14.99 *(978-1-68415-334-3(4))* Boom! Studios.

The Metropolitan Museum of Art. Degas, Painter of Ballerinas. Rubin, Susan Goldman. 2019. (ENG.). 64p. (J). (gr. 3-7). 19.99 *(978-1-4197-2843-3(1)*, Abrams Bks. for Young Readers) Abrams, Inc.

The Mousekins Staff. Letters from Space. Knaus, Patricia. 2004. 112p. (J). (gr. 3-4). pap. 8.50 *(978-0-9758742-0-2(9)*, 10704) KnausWorks.

The Pope Twins. We Are Proud of You. Kim, YeShil. rev. ed. 2014. (MySELF Bookshelf Ser.). (ENG.). 32p. (J). (gr. k-2). pap. 11.94 *(978-1-60357-651-2(7))*; lib. bdg. 25.27 *(978-1-59953-642-2(0))* Norwood Hse. Pr.

The Puppet Company Ltd. Goldilocks & the Three Bears Finger Puppets & Book Set. 2013. (ENG.). (J). *(978-1-908633-10-1(7))* Puppet Company Ltd., The.

The, Tienny. An Instrument for Eddie. Lee, Karen. 2012. 30p. pap. 12.97 *(978-1-61204-302-9(X)*, Strategic Bk. Publishing) Strategic Book Publishing & Rights Agency (SBPRA).

The Toy Box. Pull the Lever: Who Are You? Wolfe, Jane. 2014. (ENG.). 8p. (J). (gr. -1-2). bds. 6.99 *(978-1-86147-391-2(5)*, Armadillo) Anness Publishing GBR. Dist: National Bk. Network.

The Trustees of the British Museum. ABC: Early Learning at the Museum. Nosy Crow. 2018. (Early Learning at the Museum Ser.). (ENG.). 22p. (J). (— 1). bds. 7.99 *(978-1-5362-0268-7(1)*, Nosy Crow) Candlewick Pr.

—Animals: Early Learning at the Museum. Nosy Crow. 2019. (Early Learning at the Museum Ser.). (ENG.). 22p. (J). (— 1). bds. 7.99 *(978-1-5362-0583-1(4)*, Nosy Crow) Candlewick Pr.

—Colors: Early Learning at the Museum. Nosy Crow. 2018. (Early Learning at the Museum Ser.). (ENG.). 22p. (J). (— 1). bds. 7.99 *(978-1-5362-0269-4(X)*, Nosy Crow) Candlewick Pr.

—First Words: Early Learning at the Museum. Nosy Crow. 2019. (Early Learning at the Museum Ser.). (ENG.). 22p. (J). (— 1). bds. 7.99 *(978-1-5362-0584-8(2)*, Nosy Crow) Candlewick Pr.

The Trustees of the British Museum. Nature: Early Learning at the Museum. Nosy Crow. 2020. (Early Learning at the Museum Ser.). (ENG.). 22p. (J). (— 1). bds. 7.99 ***(978-1-5362-1212-9(1)***, Nosy Crow) Candlewick Pr.

The Trustees of the British Museum. Opposites: Early Learning at the Museum. Nosy Crow. 2018. (Early Learning at the Museum Ser.). (ENG.). 20p. (J). (— 1). bds. 7.99 *(978-1-5362-0270-0(3)*, Nosy Crow) Candlewick Pr.

—Origami & Haiku: Inspired by Japanese Artwork. Nosy Crow. 2018. (ENG.). 132p. (J). (gr. 5). 15.00 *(978-1-5362-0273-1(8)*, Nosy Crow) Candlewick Pr.

—This or That? What Will You Choose at the British Museum? Goodhart, Pippa. 2020. (Early Learning at the Museum Ser.). (ENG.). 32p. (J). (gr. -1-2). 16.99 *(978-1-5362-1223-5(7)*, Nosy Crow) Candlewick Pr.

—123: Early Learning at the Museum. Nosy Crow. 2018. (Early Learning at the Museum Ser.). (ENG.). 22p. (J). (— 1). bds. 7.99 *(978-1-5362-0267-0(3)*, Nosy Crow) Candlewick Pr.

Theagene, Jeannisse. Bunnies & Butterflies in the Backyard & the Pirates Who Know Where They Live: Stories That Help Children Learn & Remember Their Address & Telephone Number. Jackman, Vernon. I.t. ed. 2010. (ENG.). 32p. (J). pap. 6.99 *(978-0-9829371-1-2(3))* New Kid Safety.

Theisen, Patricia. A Magical Mystery Tour of hte Senses: What Does it Mean to be a Human? All about Your Body & You, 1 CD. Theisen, Patricia. I.t. ed. 2007. 160p. (YA). *(978-0-9793076-1-4(9))* Theisen, Patricia.

Theiss, Nicole. Newton's Little Tail. Merecoulias, Mia. 2019. (ENG.). 36p. (J). pap. 10.45 ***(978-1-9798-2971-7(3))*** CreateSpace Independent Publishing Platform.

Thelan, Mary. Little Red Hen Makes Soup. Williams, Rozanne Lanczak. Hamaguchi, Carla, ed. 2003. (Sight Word Readers Ser.). 16p. (J). (gr. k-2). pap. 3.49 *(978-1-57471-969-7(6)*, 3591) Creative Teaching Pr., Inc.

Thelen, John. Lil' Bro' Pete Lost His Sheep. Thelen, John. 2019. (ENG.). 30p. (J). pap. 14.00 *(978-1-5087-4720-8(2))* CreateSpace Independent Publishing Platform.

Thelen, Mary. The Jazzy Alphabet. Shahan, Sherry. 2006. 30p. (J). (gr. k-4). reprint ed. 16.00 *(978-1-4223-5730-9(9))* DIANE Publishing Co.

—Postcards from Barney Bear. Williams, Rozanne Lanczak. Maio, Barbara & Faulkner, Stacey, eds. 2006. (Learn to Write Ser.). 8p. (J). pap. 3.49 *(978-1-59198-287-6(1)*, 6181) Creative Teaching Pr., Inc.

Theobald, Denise. Baby, the Poodle Cow Dog. Webb, Willyn. 2007. 32p. (J). 13.95 *(978-1-932738-40-7(1))* Western Reflections Publishing Co.

—Toliver in Time: For a Fourth of July Celebration. Hein, Connie L. 2003. 40p. (J). lib. bdg. 19.95 *(978-0-9740855-8-6(8))*; per. 12.95 *(978-0-9740855-9-3(6))* Still Water Publishing.

—Toliver in Time; for a Journey West: History in a Nutshell. Hein, Connie L. I.t. ed. 2005. 28p. (J). lib. bdg. 17.95 *(978-0-9740855-6-2(1))*; per. 9.95 *(978-0-9740855-7-9(X))* Still Water Publishing.

Theobald, Joseph. Marvin Wanted More! Theobald, Joseph. 32p. (J). (gr. -1-k). 2005. pap. 12.99 *(978-0-7475-6481-2(7))*; 2004. 16.99 *(978-0-7475-5631-2(8))* Bloomsbury Publishing Plc GBR. Dist: Independent Pubs. Group.

—When Arthur Wouldn't Sleep: Band 06/Orange (Collins Big Cat) Theobald, Joseph. 2006. (Collins Big Cat Ser.). (ENG.). 24p. (J). (gr. 2-2). pap. 8.99 *(978-0-00-718688-4(6))* HarperCollins Pubs. Ltd. GBR. Dist: Independent Pubs. Group.

Theophilopoulos, Andrew. Junior & Bo's Trip to the Olympics. Panayotis. 2007. 104p. per. 10.95 *(978-1-934246-26-9(3))* Peppertree Pr., The.

Therian, Francis Patrick & Bruha, Victor. Tommy Too. Therian, Francis Patrick. 96p. (J). (gr. 4-6). pap. 5.99 *(978-0-9702944-0-1(9))* Pennywise Pubns., Inc.

Thermes, Jennifer. Bear & Bird. Skofield, James. 2014. (ENG.). 40p. (J). (gr. 1-3). 15.99 *(978-1-58536-835-8(0)*, 203012) Sleeping Bear Pr.

—Beginning Again: Immigrating to America. Kule, Elaine A. 2006. 40p. *(978-1-59137-473-2(1))* Options Publishing.

—Freya & Zoose. Butler, Emily. 2019. 208p. (J). (gr. 3-7). 16.99 *(978-1-5247-1771-1(1)*, Crown Books For Young Readers) Random Hse. Children's Bks.

—Helen Keller's Best Friend Belle. Barry, Holly M. 2014. (AV2 Fiction Readalong Ser.: Vol. 140). (ENG.). (J). (gr. -1-2). lib. bdg. 34.28 *(978-1-4896-2338-6(8)*, AV2 by Weigl) Weigl Pubs., Inc.

—The Iciest, Diciest, Scariest Sled Ride Ever!, 1 vol. Rule, Rebecca. 2012. (ENG.). 36p. (J). 17.95 *(978-1-934031-88-9(7)*, 4d30e478-2fdd-45fa-b952-91842108bc2d) Islandport Pr., Inc.

—Little Author in the Big Woods: A Biography of Laura Ingalls Wilder. McDonough, Yona Zeldis. 2014. (ENG.). 176p. (J). (gr. 3-7). 16.99 *(978-0-8050-9542-5(X)*, 9780805095425, Holt, Henry & Co. Bks. For Young Readers) Holt, Henry & Co.

—Maggie & Oliver or a Bone of One's Own. Hobbs, Valerie. 2013. (ENG.). 208p. (J). (gr. 8-12). pap. 21.19 *(978-1-250-01672-0(X)*, 9781250016720) Square Fish.

—There Are No Moose on This Island, 1 vol. Calmenson, Stephanie. 2013. (ENG.). 32p. (J). 17.95 *(978-1-934031-34-6(8)*, 1a9ce3a1-750c-455a-8b29-bebe9f3d3dd6) Islandport Pr., Inc.

Therrian, John. Why the Hyena Has Short Hind Legs. Kimani, Kamande. 2011. 40p. pap. 24.95 *(978-1-4560-5468-7(6))* America Star Bks.

Therrien, Melanie. Elsbeth & the Freedom Fighters: Book II in the Cape Cod Witch Series. Palmer, J. Bean. 3rd ed. 2018. (Cape Cod Witch Ser.: Vol. 2). (ENG.). 196p. (J). (gr. 3-6). pap. 9.95 *(978-0-578-41542-0(9))* Holly Hill Pr.

Thi, Hanh Ninh. A Most Unlikely Hero, Vol. 3. Varnell, Brandon. Goodall, Dominique, ed. 2018. (Most Unlikely Hero Ser.: Vol. 3). (ENG.). 222p. (YA). (gr. 7-12). pap. 13.00 *(978-0-9989942-4-6(3))* Kitsune Inc.

Thi Hop, Nguyen. Each Breath a Smile. Sister Susan, Sister. 2005. 32p. (J). (gr. -1-2). pap. 10.95 *(978-1-888375-22-0(1)*, Plum Blossom Bks.) Parallax Pr.

Thibodeau, Piper. North Pole Ninjas: MISSION: Christmas! Gregson, Tyler Knott & Linden, Sarah. 2018. (ENG.). 40p. (J). (gr. -1-2). 10.99 *(978-1-5247-9079-0(6)*, Penguin Workshop) Penguin Young Readers Group.

Thibodeaux, Rebecca. Tenan & Colleen: I Don't Want to Go to Bed. Moffett, Elzater. 2010. 36p. 15.49 *(978-1-4490-6633-8(X))* AuthorHouse.

Thiébaux-Heikalo, Tamara. Mayann's Train Ride, 1 vol. Francis, Mayann. 2015. (ENG.). 32p. (J). (gr. 1-3). 22.95 *(978-1-77108-348-5(4)*, de80fa04-925c-4029-b375-aafe87930b1c) Nimbus Publishing, Ltd. CAN. Dist: Baker & Taylor Publisher Services (BTPS).

Thies, Michelle. Cleo & Cornelius: A Tale of Two Cities & Two Kitties. Nicholson, Elizabeth et al. 2018. (ENG.). 32p. (J). (gr. -1-k). 16.99 *(978-1-947440-03-6(9))* Getty Pubns.

Thiessen, Marci. Timeout's Great Baseball Adventure: How Fresno State's Favorite Bulldog Helped the Diamond Dogs Win the College World Series. Takata, George. 2011. (ENG.). 28p. (J). (gr. -1-2). 19.95 *(978-1-61035-002-0(2))* Linden Publishing Co., Inc.

Thisdale, François. Bird Child. Forler, Nan. 2009. (ENG.). 32p. (J). (gr. k-3). 19.95 *(978-0-88776-894-1(6)*, Tundra Bks.) Tundra Bks. CAN. Dist: Penguin Random Hse. LLC.

—The Birdman: A Journey with the Underground Railroad's Most Daring Abolitionist, 1 vol. Harrison, Troon. 2019. (ENG.). 36p. (J). (gr. 1-5). 24.95 *(978-0-88995-506-6(9)*, 4e560030-f5f4-4446-bb89-a8156d970d30) Red Deer Pr. CAN. Dist: Firefly Bks., Ltd.

—French Toast. Winters, Kari-Lynn. 2016. (ENG.). 32p. (J). (gr. k-2). 17.95 *(978-1-77278-006-2(5))* Pajama Pr. CAN. Dist: Ingram Publisher Services.

Thisdale, François. Nini. Thisdale, François. 2011. (ENG.). 40p. (J). (gr. -1-2). 15.95 *(978-1-77049-270-7(4)*, Tundra Bks.) Tundra Bks. CAN. Dist: Penguin Random Hse. LLC.

Thisdale, François & Thisdale, François. Bon Voyage, Mister Rodriguez. Duchesne, Christiane. 2019. (ENG.). 32p. (J). (gr. k-3). 18.95 *(978-1-77278-089-5(8))* Pajama Pr. CAN. Dist: Ingram Publisher Services.

Thisdale, François, jt. illus. see Thisdale, François.

Thivierge, Claude. Platypus Creek. Giancamilli, Vanessa. 2005. (Soundprints' Amazing Animal Adventures! Ser.). (ENG.). 36p. (J). (gr. -1-2). 19.95 *(978-1-59249-355-5(6)*, BC7109); (gr. -1-2). 2.95 *(978-1-59249-354-8(8)*, S7159); (gr. -1-2). 9.95 *(978-1-59249-357-9(2)*, PS7159); (gr. -1-2). 15.95 *(978-1-59249-352-4(1)*, B7109); (gr. -1-2). pap. 6.95 *(978-1-59249-353-1(X)*, S7109); (gr. 2-6). 8.95 *(978-1-59249-356-2(4)*, SC7109) Soundprints.

Thoburn, Michelle. Tres Mures Caeci. Noe, David C. 2005. (LAT.). 48p. (J). (gr. k-12). 11.99 *(978-0-9714458-1-9(8))* Patrick Henry College Pr.

Tholen, Shane. Groovy Granny. Haynes, Cate. 2003. 32p. (J). pap. 13.50 *(978-1-86368-332-6(1))* Fremantle Pr. AUS. Dist: Independent Pubs. Group.

Thomann, Nani. La Scuola Speciale. Nunez, Miguel Angel. Cupertino, Lidia, tr. 2019. (ITA.). 58p. (J). pap. 13.75 ***(978-1-0861-6592-0(6))*** Independently Published.

Thomas, Adam Bryce. Fallout Part 2. Flynn, Ian. 2019. (Sonic the Hedgehog Ser.). (ENG.). 24p. (J). (gr. 2-8). lib. bdg. 27.07 *(978-1-5321-4434-9(2)*, 33839, Graphic Novels) Spotlight.

Thomas, Adam Bryce, et al. Sonic the Hedgehog, Vol. 2: the Fate of Dr. Eggman. Flynn, Ian. 2019. (Sonic the Hedgehog Ser.: 2). 96p. (J). (gr. 4-7). pap. 15.99 *(978-1-68405-406-0(0))* Idea & Design Works, LLC.

—Sonic the Hedgehog, Vol. 4: Infection, Vol. 4. Flynn, Ian. 2019. (Sonic the Hedgehog Ser.: 4). 96p. (J). (gr. 4-7). pap. 15.99 *(978-1-68405-544-9(X))* Idea & Design Works, LLC.

Thomas, Adele K. Magic Pearl. Davis, Delphine. 2020. (Mermaid Holidays Ser.: 2). (ENG.). 128p. (J). (gr. 1-4). 9.99 ***(978-0-14-379649-7(6)***, Puffin) Penguin Random Hse. AUS. Dist: Independent Pubs. Group.

Thomas, Adele K. Pearl the Flying Unicorn. Odgers, Sally. 2020. (Pearl the Magical Unicorn Ser.: 2). (ENG.). 128p. (J). 13.99 *(978-1-250-23552-7(9)*, 900210323) Feiwel & Friends.

—Pearl the Magical Unicorn. Odgers, Sally. 2020. (Pearl the Magical Unicorn Ser.: 1). (ENG.). 128p. (J). 13.99 *(978-1-250-23550-3(2)*, 900210320) Feiwel & Friends.

Thomas, Adele K. Talent Show. Davis, Delphine. 2020. (Mermaid Holidays Ser.: 1). (ENG.). 128p. (J). (gr. 1-3). 9.99 ***(978-0-14-379651-0(8)***, Puffin) Penguin Random Hse. AUS. Dist: Independent Pubs. Group.

Thomas Anderson, Joy. How Sunny the Skunk Found His Smell. Israel, Antalaya. 2018. (ENG.). 26p. (J). pap. 9.95 *(978-0-9987161-9-0(7))* Tre H Publishing a division of Tre H Productions, LLC.

Thomas, Andrew. Ambitious Abbey. Duplaga, Abbey. 2018. (Ambitious Abbey Ser.: Vol. 1). (ENG.). 34p. (J). (gr. k-4). 15.95 *(978-0-692-10005-9(9))* Ambitious Abbey, LLC.

—Successville. Harris, Noah. 2019. (ENG.). 34p. (J). (gr. k-2). 21.99 *(978-0-578-46408-4(X))*; pap. 12.99 *(978-0-578-42504-7(1))* Harris, Noah.

Thomas, Angela Trotta. The Monster from the Sea: Level 2. Hooks, William H. 2020. (ENG.). 34p. (J). pap. 9.95 ***(978-1-876965-81-5(9))*** ibooks, Inc.

Thomas, B. K. Logs. Thomas, B. K. 2013. 36p. 24.95 *(978-1-4512-2170-1(3))* America Star Bks.

Thomas, Bill. Asking about Sex & Growing Up: A Question-And-Answer Book for Kids. Cole, Joanna. rev. ed. 2009. (ENG.). 96p. (J). (gr. 3-18). pap. 6.99 *(978-0-06-142986-6(4))* HarperCollins Pubs.

—Girls' Life Guide to Being the Most Amazing You. Scholastic, Inc. Staff. Bokram, Karen, ed. 2010. (ENG.). 128p. (J). (gr. 5-9). pap. 8.99 *(978-0-545-21494-0(7)*, Scholastic Paperbacks) Scholastic, Inc.

—Head-to-Toe Guide to You. Bokram, Karen, ed. 2010. (ENG.). 128p. (J). (gr. 5-9). pap. 8.99 *(978-0-545-20236-7(1)*, Scholastic Paperbacks) Scholastic, Inc.

Thomas, Cassia. I Love My Baby Because... Simons, Paullina. 2015. (ENG.). 24p. (J). 17.99 *(978-0-00-810211-1(2)*, HarperCollins Children's Bks.) HarperCollins Pubs. Ltd. GBR. Dist: HarperCollins Pubs.

Thomas, Chad. Peel + Discover: Dinosaurs. Workman Publishing. 2019. (Peel + Discover Ser.). (ENG.). 26p. (J). (gr. -1-5). 8.95 *(978-1-5235-0358-2(0)*, 100358) Workman Publishing Co., Inc.

—Peel + Discover: Horses. Workman Publishing. 2019. (Peel + Discover Ser.). (ENG.). 26p. (J). (gr. k-5). 8.95 *(978-1-5235-0360-5(2)*, 100360) Workman Publishing Co., Inc.

—Peel + Discover: Washington, DC. Workman Publishing. 2019. (Peel + Discover Ser.). (ENG.). 26p. (J). (gr. k-5). 8.95 *(978-1-5235-0359-9(9)*, 100359) Workman Publishing Co., Inc.

—Rise of the Teenage Mutant Ninja Turtles. Manning, Matthew K. 2019. (Rise of TMNT Ser.). (ENG.). 72p. (J). (gr. 4-7). pap. 9.99 *(978-1-68405-454-1(0))* Idea & Design Works, LLC.

—Rise of the Teenage Mutant Ninja Turtles: Sound Off! Manning, Matthew K. 2020. (Rise of TMNT Ser.). (ENG.). 72p. (J). (gr. 4-7). pap. 9.99 *(978-1-68405-616-3(0))* Idea & Design Works, LLC.

—Rise of the Teenage Mutant Ninja Turtles: the Big Reveal. Manning, Matthew K. 2019. (Rise of TMNT Ser.). (ENG.). 72p. (J). (gr. 4-7). pap. 9.99 *(978-1-68405-530-2(X))* Idea & Design Works, LLC.

—Star Wars Adventures Vol. 5: Mechanical Mayhem. Barber, John et al. 2019. (Star Wars Adventures Ser.: 5). (ENG.). 80p. (J). (gr. 2-5). pap. 9.99 *(978-1-68405-422-0(2))* Idea & Design Works, LLC.

—Teenage Mutant Ninja Turtles Amazing Adventures: Robotanimals! Goellner, Caleb. 2018. (TMNT Amazing Adventures Ser.). (ENG.). 72p. (J). (gr. 4-7). 12.99 *(978-1-68405-101-4(0))* Idea & Design Works, LLC.

Thomas, Chad, et al. Teenage Mutant Ninja Turtles Amazing Adventures: Tea-Time for a Turtle. Flynn, Ian & Goellner, Caleb. 2017. (TMNT Amazing Adventures Ser.). (ENG.). 84p. (J). (gr. 4-7). 12.99 *(978-1-63140-886-1(0))* Idea & Design Works, LLC.

Thomas, Chad. TinkerActive Workbooks: 1st Grade Math. Krasner, Justin & Odd Dot. 2019. (TinkerActive Workbooks Ser.: 2). (ENG.). 128p. (J). pap. 12.99 *(978-1-250-30722-4(8)*, 900197982, Odd Dot) St. Martin's Pr.

—Tricky Coyote Tales. Schweizer, Chris. 2011. (Tricky Journeys Ser.: 1). (ENG.). (J). (gr. 2-4). pap. 39.62 *(978-0-7613-8625-4(4))* Lerner Publishing Group.

—Tricky Monkey Tales. Schweizer, Chris. 2011. (Tricky Journeys Ser.: 6). (ENG.). (J). (gr. 2-4). pap. 39.62 *(978-0-7613-8630-8(0))* Lerner Publishing Group.

Thomas, Chad & Yan, Edison. Summer Brain Quest: Between Grades 4 And 5. Heos, Bridget et al. 2017. (Summer Brain Quest Ser.). (ENG.). 160p. (J). (gr. 4-5). pap. 12.95 *(978-0-7611-8920-6(3)*, 18920) Workman Publishing Co., Inc.

Thomas, Chad Allen. Tricky Coyote Tales: Book 1, No. 1. Schweizer, Chris. 2011. (Tricky Journeys (tm) Ser.: 1). (ENG.). 64p. (J). (gr. 2-4). pap. 7.99 *(978-0-7613-7859-4(6)*, 9780761378594, Graphic Universe™) Lerner Publishing Group.

Thomas, Cory. Epic Athletes: Alex Morgan. Wetzel, Dan. 2019. (Epic Athletes Ser.: 2). (ENG.). 160p. (J). 16.99 *(978-1-250-29577-4(7)*, 900195183, Holt, Henry & Co. Bks. For Young Readers) Holt, Henry & Co.

—Epic Athletes: Alex Morgan. Wetzel, Dan. 2020. (Epic Athletes Ser.: 2). (ENG.). 176p. (J). pap. 7.99 *(978-1-250-25071-1(4)*, 900195184) Square Fish.

—Public School Superhero. Patterson, James & Tebbetts, Chris. 2016. (ENG.). 304p. (J). (gr. 3-7). pap. 8.99 *(978-0-316-26598-0(5)*, Jimmy Patterson) Little Brown & Co.

Thomas, Cristine. Can I Catch Cancer? Explaing cancer to Children. Thomas, Cristine. 2007. 44p. (J). 10.95 *(978-0-9778796-9-4(0))* Brittany's Bks.

Thomas, Cristine Leeann. I Can Too! Cancer Kids Can Too African American Series. Thomas, Cristine Leeann. 2006. (J). *(978-0-9778796-4-9(X))* Brittany's Bks.

Thomas, Deborah. Today Is Monday in Louisiana, 1 vol. Downing, Johnette. 2016. (ENG.). 8p. (J). bds. 9.95 *(978-1-4556-2306-8(7)*, Pelican Publishing) Arcadia Publishing.

Thomas, Deborah. Grandma's Gumbo, 1 vol. Thomas, Deborah. 2017. (ENG.). 10p. bds. 9.95 *(978-1-4556-2343-3(1)*, Pelican Publishing) Arcadia Publishing.

—I Spy in the Texas Sky, 1 vol. Thomas, Deborah. 2018. (I Spy Ser.). (ENG.). 32p. (J). (gr. -1-3). 8.99 *(978-1-4556-2420-1(9)*, Pelican Publishing) Arcadia Publishing.

Thomas, Deborah Kadiar. Cemetery Jamboree, 1 vol. Thomas, Deborah Kadiar. 2016. (ENG.). 32p. (J). (gr. k-5). pap. 9.95 *(978-1-4556-2239-9(7)*, Pelican Publishing) Arcadia Publishing.

Thomas, Dylan. Morus Yr Ystlum. Thomas-Christensen, Sheelagh. 2005. (Cyfres Llyfrau Llawen Ser.: Vol. 1). (WEL.). 36p. pap. *(978-0-86243-396-3(7))* Y Lolfa.

Thomas, Eric. The Children's Illustrated Bible. Hastings, Selina. 3rd ed. 2004. (ENG.). 320p. (J). (gr. 5-12). 24.99 *(978-0-7566-0261-1(0)*, DK Children) Dorling Kindersley Publishing, Inc.

—Children's Illustrated Jewish Bible. DK. 2007. (ENG.). 192p. (J). (gr. k-3). 19.99 *(978-0-7566-2665-5(X)*, DK Children) Dorling Kindersley Publishing, Inc.

—Delivering Your Mail: A Book about Mail Carriers. Owen, Ann & National Geographic Learning Staff. 2003. (Community Workers Ser.). (ENG.). 24p. (J). (gr. -1-3). per. 8.95 *(978-1-4048-0485-2(4)*, Picture Window Bks.) Capstone.

—Helping You Heal: A Book about Nurses, 1 vol. Wohlrabe, Sarah C. 2003. (Community Workers Ser.). (ENG.). 24p. (J). (gr. -1-3). per. 8.95 *(978-1-4048-0480-7(3)*, Picture Window Bks.) Capstone.

—Helping You Learn: A Book about Teachers, 1 vol. Wohlrabe, Sarah C. 2003. (Community Workers Ser.). (ENG.). 24p. (J). (gr. -1-3). per. 8.95 *(978-1-4048-0478-4(1)*, Picture Window Bks.) Capstone.

—Keeping You Healthy: A Book about Doctors, 1 vol. Owen, Ann & Picture Window Books Staff. 2003. (Community Workers Ser.). (ENG.). 24p. (J). (gr. -1-3). per. 8.95 *(978-1-4048-0479-1(X)*, Picture Window Bks.) Capstone.

—Keeping You Safe: A Book about Police Officers, 1 vol. Owen, Ann. 2003. (Community Workers Ser.). (ENG.). 24p. (J). (gr. -1-3). per. 8.95 *(978-1-4048-0483-8(8)*, Picture Window Bks.) Capstone.

—Protecting Your Home: A Book about Firefighters, 1 vol. Owen, Ann. 2003. (Community Workers Ser.). (ENG.). 24p. (J). (gr. -1-3). per. 8.95 *(978-1-4048-0482-1(X)*, Picture Window Bks.) Capstone.

—Taking You Places: A Book about Bus Drivers, 1 vol. Owen, Ann. 2003. (Community Workers Ser.). (ENG.). 24p. (J). (gr. -1-3). per. 8.95 *(978-1-4048-0484-5(6)*, Picture Window Bks.) Capstone.

Thomas, Erika & Treg, Mccoy. Petey Yikes! A very, very true story about a homeless little blue bird in New York City. 2006. (J). *(978-0-9789642-0-7(9))* Petey, Rock & Roo Children's Pubns.

Thomas, Franselica, jt. illus. see Isabel, Michelle.

Thomas, Glenn. Dial 911! Ghigna, Charles. (Fire Safety Ser.). (ENG.). 24p. (J). (gr. -1-3). 2018. lib. bdg. 33.99 *(978-1-68410-394-2(0)*, 140351); 2017. lib. bdg. 33.99 incl. audio compact disk *(978-1-68410-019-4(4)*, 31509) Cantata Learning.

—Get Out. Stay Out! Ghigna, Charles. 2017. (Fire Safety Ser.). (ENG.). 24p. (J). (gr. -1-3). lib. bdg. 33.99 incl. audio compact disk *(978-1-68410-029-3(1)*, 31512) Cantata Learning.

—I'm Not Little! Inches, Alison. 2017. (ENG.). 32p. (J). (gr. -1-3). 16.99 *(978-1-4998-0377-8(X))* Little Bee Books Inc.

—My Little Pony Best Gift Ever: a Perfectly Pinkie Present. Ventura, Bonnie. 2019. (Little Golden Book Ser.). (ENG.). 24p. (J). (-k). 4.99 *(978-1-9848-9709-1(8)*, Golden Bks.) Random Hse. Children's Bks.

—Orange. Doering, Amanda. 2018. (Sing Your Colors! Ser.). (ENG.). 24p. (J). (gr. -1-2). lib. bdg. 33.99 *(978-1-68410-318-8(5)*, 140864); lib. bdg. 33.99 incl. audio compact disk *(978-1-68410-127-6(1)*, 31852) Cantata Learning.

—Plan & Prepare! Ghigna, Charles. 2017. (Fire Safety Ser.). (ENG.). 24p. (J). (gr. -1-3). lib. bdg. 33.99 incl. audio compact disk *(978-1-68410-045-3(3)*, 31510) Cantata Learning.

—Stop, Drop, & Roll! Ghigna, Charles. (Fire Safety Ser.). (ENG.). 24p. (J). (gr. -1-3). 2018. lib. bdg. 33.99 *(978-1-68410-379-9(7)*, 140352); 2017. pap. 7.95 *(978-1-68410-094-1(1)*, 136415) Cantata Learning.

—Stretchy Shapes! Straight, Curved, & Twisty. Hoena, Blake. 2018. (Creative Movement Ser.). (ENG.). 24p. (J). (gr. -1-2). lib. bdg. 33.99 *(978-1-68410-245-7(6),* 138435) Cantata Learning.

—The Supernormal Sleuthing Service #1: the Lost Legacy. Bond, Gwenda & Rowe, Christopher. (Supernormal Sleuthing Service Ser.: 1). (ENG.). (J). (gr. 3-7). 2018. 432p. pap. 6.99 *(978-0-06-245995-4(3));* 2017. 416p. 16.99 *(978-0-06-245994-7(5))* HarperCollins Pubs. (Greenwillow Bks.).

Thomas, Iulian. Buddy the Bear: First Day of School. Allen, Victoria. 2019. (ENG.). 58p. (J). (gr. k-1). 17.00 ***(978-0-9600605-0-4(2))*** Marshlands Group LLC.

Thomas, James. The Adventures of Mr. Feeny & Cinnamon. Kesecker, Jennifer. 2012. 20p. pap. 24.95 *(978-1-4626-8858-6(6))* America Star Bks.

—God Loves Me! Traywick-Jones, Andrea. 2003. 24p. (J). *(978-1-55306-459-6(3),* Guardian Bks.) Essence Publishing.

Thomas, Jan. Let's Count Goats! Fox, Mem. 2010. (ENG.). 40p. (J). (gr. -1-3). 17.99 *(978-1-4424-0598-1(8),* Beach Lane Bks.) Beach Lane Bks.

Thomas, Jan. Can You Make a Scary Face? Thomas, Jan. 2009. (ENG.). 40p. (J). (gr. -1-3). 16.99 *(978-1-4169-8581-5(6),* Beach Lane Bks.) Beach Lane Bks.

—The Easter Bunny's Assistant. Thomas, Jan. 2012. (ENG.). 40p. (J). (gr. -1-3). 12.99 *(978-0-06-169286-4(7))* HarperCollins Pubs.

—Here Comes the Big, Mean Dust Bunny! Thomas, Jan. 2009. (ENG.). 40p. (J). (gr. -1-3). 15.99 *(978-1-4169-9150-2(6),* Beach Lane Bks.) Beach Lane Bks.

—Is Everyone Ready for Fun? Thomas, Jan. 2011. (ENG.). 40p. (J). (gr. -1-3). 15.99 *(978-1-4424-2364-0(1),* Beach Lane Bks.) Beach Lane Bks.

Thomas, Jan. Is Everyone Ready for Fun? Classroom Edition. Thomas, Jan. 2020. (ENG.). 40p. (J). (gr. -1-3). 29.99 ***(978-1-5344-5986-1(3),*** Beach Lane Bks.) Beach Lane Bks.

Thomas, Jan. Is That Wise, Pig? Thomas, Jan. 2016. (ENG.). 40p. (J). (gr. -1-3). 16.99 *(978-1-4169-8582-2(4),* Beach Lane Bks.) Beach Lane Bks.

—Let's Sing a Lullaby with the Brave Cowboy. Thomas, Jan. 2012. (ENG.). 40p. (J). (gr. -1-3). 12.99 *(978-1-4424-4276-4(X),* Beach Lane Bks.) Beach Lane Bks.

—Pumpkin Trouble. Thomas, Jan. 2011. (ENG.). 40p. (J). (gr. -1-3). 9.99 *(978-0-06-169284-0(0))* HarperCollins Pubs.

—Rhyming Dust Bunnies. Thomas, Jan. 2009. (ENG.). 40p. (J). (gr. -1-3). 16.99 *(978-1-4169-7976-0(X),* Beach Lane Bks.) Beach Lane Bks.

Thomas, Jeffrey. Ariel & the Big Baby/Rapunzel Finds a Friend (Disney Princess) Sky Koster, Amy & Patrick, Ella. 2017. (Pictureback(R) Ser.). (ENG.). 48p. (J). (gr. -1-2). pap. 5.99 *(978-0-7364-3747-9(9),* RH/Disney) Random Hse. Children's Bks.

Thomas, Jeffrey & The Disney Storybook Art Team. Ariel Is Fearless/Jasmine Is Helpful (Disney Princess) Marsham, Liz & Francis, Suzanne. 2017. (Step into Reading Ser.). (ENG.). 48p. (J). (gr. -1-1). pap. 5.99 *(978-0-7364-3802-5(5),* RH/Disney) Random Hse. Children's Bks.

Thomas, John, Jr., jt. illus. see Thomas, Wes.

Thomas, John Wes. Choose to Reuse. Bullard, Lisa. 2011. (Cloverleaf Books (tm) — Planet Protectors Ser.). (ENG.). 24p. (J). (gr. k-2). pap. 8.99 *(978-0-7613-8511-0(8),* 9780761385110, Millbrook Pr.) Lerner Publishing Group.

—Go Easy on Energy. Bullard, Lisa. 2011. (Cloverleaf Books (tm) — Planet Protectors Ser.). (ENG.). 24p. (J). (gr. k-2). pap. 8.99 *(978-0-7613-8513-4(4),* 9780761385134, Millbrook Pr.) Lerner Publishing Group.

—Go Green by Fighting Pollution. Bullard, Lisa. 2018. (Go Green (Early Bird Stories (tm)) Ser.). (ENG.). 24p. (J). (gr. k-2). pap. 7.99 *(978-1-5415-2713-3(5));* lib. bdg. 27.99 *(978-1-5415-2016-5(5),* Lerner Pubns.) Lerner Publishing Group.

—Go Green by Recycling. Bullard, Lisa. 2018. (Go Green (Early Bird Stories (tm)) Ser.). (ENG.). 24p. (J). (gr. k-2). pap. 7.99 *(978-1-5415-2714-0(3));* lib. bdg. 27.99 *(978-1-5415-2013-4(0),* Lerner Pubns.) Lerner Publishing Group.

—Go Green by Reusing. Bullard, Lisa. 2018. (Go Green (Early Bird Stories (tm)) Ser.). (ENG.). 24p. (J). (gr. k-2). pap. 7.99 *(978-1-5415-2715-7(1));* lib. bdg. 27.99 *(978-1-5415-2012-7(2),* Lerner Pubns.) Lerner Publishing Group.

—Go Green by Saving Energy. Bullard, Lisa. 2018. (Go Green (Early Bird Stories (tm)) Ser.). (ENG.). 24p. (J). (gr. k-2). pap. 7.99 *(978-1-5415-2716-4(X));* lib. bdg. 27.99 *(978-1-5415-2015-8(7),* Lerner Pubns.) Lerner Publishing Group.

—Power up to Fight Pollution. Bullard, Lisa. 2011. (Cloverleaf Books (tm) — Planet Protectors Ser.). (ENG.). 24p. (J). (gr. k-2). pap. 8.99 *(978-0-7613-8515-8(0),* 9780761385158, Millbrook Pr.) Lerner Publishing Group.

—Rally for Recycling. Bullard, Lisa. 2011. (Cloverleaf Books (tm) — Planet Protectors Ser.). (ENG.). 24p. (J). (gr. k-2). pap. 8.99 *(978-0-7613-8516-5(9),* 9780761385165, Millbrook Pr.) Lerner Publishing Group.

Thomas, Julian. I Keep Forgetting Stuff. Thompson, Isaiah W. 2018. (ENG.). 40p. (J). pap. 10.00 *(978-1-7307-8642-6(1))* Independently Published.

Thomas, Keith A. Cross-Lengua Coloring Book for Kids. Thomas, Keith A. l.t. ed. 2004. (ENG & SPA.). 22p. (J). (gr. 3-18). pap. *(978-0-9617451-2-7(6))* KALEXT Productions, LLC.

—The Idioms. Thomas, Keith A. (ENG & SPA.). 44p. (J). (gr. 3-18). pap. *(978-0-9617451-4-1(2))* KALEXT Productions, LLC.

Thomas, Leanne & Schiebold, Olivia. Puppylicious. 2010. 96p. (J). *(978-0-545-26020-6(5))* Scholastic, Inc.

Thomas, LeSean. Out of the Shadows. David, Peter. 2007. (ENG.). 96p. pap. 12.95 *(978-1-84576-146-2(4),* Titan Bks.) Titan Bks. Ltd. GBR. Dist: Penguin Random Hse. LLC.

Thomas, Lillie Michelle. When the Carnival Comes to Town. Q., Bev. 2009. 28p. pap. 24.95 *(978-1-60749-682-3(8))* America Star Bks.

Thomas, Louis. Crash! #1. Krulik, Nancy. 2017. (Kid from Planet Z Ser.: 1). 96p. (J). (gr. 1-3). 5.99 *(978-0-448-49012-0(9),* Grosset & Dunlap) Penguin Young Readers Group.

—Don't Sneeze! Krulik, Nancy. 2017. (Kid from Planet Z Ser.: 2). 96p. (J). (gr. 1-3). 5.99 *(978-0-451-53343-2(7),* Grosset & Dunlap) Penguin Young Readers Group.

—Why Do I Have to Eat My Greens? Big Issues for Little People about Health & Well-Being. McCurry, Chris & Waddington, Emma. 2016. (Life & Soul Library). (ENG.). 32p. (J). (gr. -1-3). 12.99 *(978-1-84780-865-3(4),* Frances Lincoln Children's Bks.) Quarto Publishing Group UK GBR. Dist: Hachette Bk. Group.

—88 Instruments. Barton, Chris. 2016. 32p. (J). (gr. -1-2). 17.99 *(978-0-553-53814-4(4),* Knopf Bks. for Young Readers) Random Hse. Children's Bks.

Thomas, Louis, jt. illus. see Campbell, Scott.

Thomas, Marc, jt. illus. see Elder, Jennifer.

Thomas, Meredith. Girl Pirates. Kettle, Shey. 2005. (Girlz Rock! Ser.). (J). pap. *(978-1-59336-701-5(5))* Mondo Publishing.

—Surf Girls. Kettle, Shey. 2005. (Girlz Rock! Ser.). (J). pap. *(978-1-59336-708-4(2))* Mondo Publishing.

Thomas, Michael. The Church Fathers for Young People, , Grube, George. 2007. (ENG.). 35p. (J). pap. 7.95 *(978-1-933654-07-2(4))* Light & Life Publishing Co.

Thomas, Michael Lee. A Father for Me. James-Carde, Genice. 2011. 20p. pap. 24.95 *(978-1-4560-3951-6(2))* America Star Bks.

Thomas, Middy. Gooney Bird & All Her Charms. Lois, Lowry. (Gooney Bird Greene Ser.). (ENG.). 160p. (J). (gr. 1-4). 2015. pap. 6.99 *(978-0-544-45596-2(7),* 1599321, HMH Books For Young Readers); 2014. 16.99 *(978-0-544-11354-1(3),* 1542003) Houghton Mifflin Harcourt Publishing Co.

—Gooney Bird & the Room Mother. Lowry, Lois. 2006. (Gooney Bird Ser.: No. 2). (ENG.). 80p. (J). (gr. 3-7). 5.99 *(978-0-440-42133-7(0),* Yearling) Random Hse. Children's Bks.

—Gooney Bird Greene. Lois, Lowry. 2015. (Gooney Bird Greene Ser.). (ENG.). (J). (gr. 1-4). lib. bdg. 16.60 *(978-1-62765-992-5(7))* Perfection Learning Corp.

—Gooney Bird Is So Absurd. Lois, Lowry. 2013. (Gooney Bird Greene Ser.). (ENG.). 112p. (J). (gr. 1-4). pap. 6.99 *(978-0-547-87559-0(2),* 1505831) Houghton Mifflin Harcourt Publishing Co.

—Gooney Bird on the Map. Lois, Lowry. 2013. (Gooney Bird Greene Ser.). (ENG.). 128p. (J). (gr. 1-4). pap. 7.99 *(978-0-547-85088-7(3),* 1501066) Houghton Mifflin Harcourt Publishing Co.

Thomas, Pamela L. Do I Have to Go to Church Today? Rome, Jacqueline Thomas. 2010. 36p. pap. 14.95 *(978-0-9841899-6-0(3))* PearlStone Publishing, Inc.

Thomas, Richard, Jr., jt. illus. see Siku.

Thomas, Richard A. Lucky & Me. Lamuth, Nancy. 2012. 20p. pap. 24.95 *(978-1-4626-0665-8(2))* America Star Bks.

Thomas, Rita J. Seeds: Erin's Dream Journey. Blommer, Brian James. 2019. (ENG.). 196p. (J). pap. 11.11 ***(978-1-6868-3209-3(5))*** Independently Published.

Thomas, Robyn. The Cricket Winter. Holman, Felice. 2006. 91p. (J). (gr. 3-7). 15.00 *(978-0-8028-5289-2(0),* Eerdmans Bks For Young Readers) Eerdmans, William B. Publishing Co.

Thomas, Sam. Fletcher Babysits a Crocodile. Kooistra, Adrian. 2018. (ENG.). 32p. (J). pap. *(978-0-6484531-0-9(3))* Lilly Pilly Publishing.

Thomas, Sonya. Today I Got Saved, 1 book. Magee, Kanika A. M. 2003. 20p. (J). 10.00 net. *(978-0-9748834-0-3(9))* Ebenezer A.M.E. Church.

—Where Is God at Midnight?? Magee, Kanika. 2003. (J). 10.00 net. *(978-0-9748834-1-0(7))* Ebenezer A.M.E. Church.

Thomas, Tamara. ABC Poem Book. Thomas, Tamara. 2004. (YA). (gr. 1-6). pap. *(978-1-930200-28-9(5))* Martell Publishing Co.

Thomas, Tasha. Bj's Beaver Bridge. Cox, Amy R. 2019. (ENG.). 20p. (J). pap. 7.99 *(978-1-945464-95-9(X))* Cox & Castelluccio.

Thomas, Tim. Do You Know Where Sea Turtles Go? Lowery, Paul. 2005. (J). lib. bdg. 15.99 *(978-0-9771059-9-1(7))* Thomas Expressions, LLC.

—Fruitman. 2007. 32p. (J). *(978-0-9790487-0-8(2))* J & K Publishing.

—What Happened to Willie? Dixon, Virginia. 2007. 32p. (J). 16.00 *(978-0-9795386-0-5(2))* Grand Productions.

Thomas, Titus V. Everybody Eats Lunch. Azima, Cricket. 2008. (ENG.). 16p. (J). (gr. -1-3). 16.00 *(978-0-9793384-4-1(1))* G Arts LLC.

Thomas, Toi. Camie Loves Books. Thomas, Toi. 2018. (Camie Loves Bks.: Vol. 1). (ENG.). 30p. (J). pap. 9.99 *(978-1-7286-9251-7(2))* Independently Published.

Thomas, Tria M., photos by. The Artful Journey: The Artwork of Andy Thomas. Thomas, Dina M. & Thomas, Andy, eds. l.t. ed. 2003. 122p. 50.00 *(978-0-9742285-0-1(8))* Maze Creek Studio.

Thomas, Wes. Choose to Reuse. Bullard, Lisa. 2011. (Planet Protectors Ser.). pap. 39.62 *(978-0-7613-8651-3(3),* Millbrook Pr.) Lerner Publishing Group.

—Go Easy on Energy. Bullard, Lisa. 2011. (Planet Protectors Ser.). pap. 39.62 *(978-0-7613-8653-7(X),* Millbrook Pr.) Lerner Publishing Group.

—Phil & His Fabulous Feathers, 1 vol. Blazek, Frank. 2005. (ENG.). 32p. (J). (gr. k-3). 16.99 *(978-1-58980-280-3(2),* Pelican Publishing) Arcadia Publishing.

—Power up to Fight Pollution. Bullard, Lisa. 2011. (Planet Protectors Ser.). pap. 39.62 *(978-0-7613-8655-1(6),* Millbrook Pr.) Lerner Publishing Group.

—Rally for Recycling. Bullard, Lisa. 2011. (Planet Protectors Ser.). pap. 39.62 *(978-0-7613-8656-8(4),* Millbrook Pr.) Lerner Publishing Group.

Thomas, Wes. Down the Crawfish Hole, 1 vol. Thomas, Wes. 2004. (Cajun Tall Tales Ser.). (ENG.). 32p. (J). (gr. k-3). 16.99 *(978-1-58980-163-9(6),* Pelican Publishing) Arcadia Publishing.

Thomas, Wes & Thomas, John, Jr. Choose to Reuse. Bullard, Lisa. 2011. (Cloverleaf Books (tm) — Planet Protectors Ser.). (ENG.). 24p. (J). (gr. k-2). lib. bdg. 25.32 *(978-0-7613-6104-6(9),* 9780761361046, Millbrook Pr.) Lerner Publishing Group.

Thomason, Annabel. Mabel Moves Abroad. Rees, Bethan. 2019. (Mabel Moves Abroad Ser.: Vol. 1). (ENG.). 38p. (J). pap. 10.00 ***(978-1-0729-0423-6(3))*** Independently Published.

Thomassen, Hellen. The Featherless Chicken. Nunez, Marisa. 2003. 32p. (J). 14.95 *(978-84-95730-36-7(7))* Kalandraka Catalunya, Edicions, S.L. ESP. Dist: Independent Pubs. Group.

Thomburgh, Rebecca. Alphabet. Connelly, Neil O. 10p. (J). (gr. -1). bds. 3.95 *(978-1-58989-004-6(3))* Thurman Hse., LLC.

—Colors. Connelly, Neil O. 10p. (J). (gr. -1). bds. 3.95 *(978-1-58989-003-9(5))* Thurman Hse., LLC.

—Numbers. Connelly, Neil O. (Cuddly Beasties Ser.). 10p. (J). (gr. -1). bds. 3.95 *(978-1-58989-001-5(9))* Thurman Hse., LLC.

—Shapes. Connelly, Neil O. 10p. (J). (gr. -1). bds. 3.95 *(978-1-58989-002-2(7))* Thurman Hse., LLC.

Thompkins, Michelle. Meet Bobby the Buzzlebee: The Buzzlebee Series. Gonzalez, Kristin Selby. 2020. (ENG.). 26p. (J). pap. 9.99 ***(978-1-7034-3806-2(X))*** Independently Published.

Thompson, Alexandra. A Family for Louie. Thompson, Alexandra. 2020. 40p. (J). (gr. -1-2). 17.99 *(978-1-9848-1321-3(8),* G.P. Putnam's Sons Books for Young Readers) Penguin Young Readers Group.

Thompson, Allissa. Freckles & the Less Fortunate. Caswell, Vickianne. 4 Paws Games and Publishing, ed. 2016. (Freckles the Bunny Ser.: Vol. 2). (ENG.). (J). (gr. k-4). pap. *(978-1-988345-37-6(5))* Caswell, Vickianne.

—Freckles Is Scared of School. Caswell, Vickianne. 4 Paws Games and Publishing, ed. 2016. (Freckles the Bunny Ser.: Vol. 1). (ENG.). (J). (gr. k-4). pap. *(978-1-988345-38-3(3))* Caswell, Vickianne.

Thompson, Angie. We Like to Read: A Picture Book for Pre-Readers & Parents. April, Elyse. 2008. (ENG.). 32p. (J). (gr. 3-7). pap. 9.95 *(978-1-890772-80-2(1))* Kalindi Pr.

Thompson, Brett. Alpaca Snow Removal. Joseph, Kathy a. 2018. (Life with Petie the Alpaca Ser.: Vol. 4). (ENG.). 44p. (J). pap. 9.95 *(978-1-7263-0393-4(4))* CreateSpace Independent Publishing Platform.

Thompson, Brian. The Dyerville Tales. Kozlowsky, M. P. 2014. (ENG.). 336p. (J). (gr. 3-7). 16.99 *(978-0-06-199871-3(0),* Waldon Pond Pr.) HarperCollins Pubs.

Thompson Brothers Studio Staff. Estrellita. Willson, Sarah & Thompson Bros. 2003. (Dora la Exploradora Ser.).Tr. of Little Star. (SPA.). 24p. (J). pap. 3.99 *(978-0-689-86307-3(1),* Libros Para Ninos) Libros Para Ninos.

Thompson, Bryon & Kulihin, Vic. US Culture Through Infographics. Higgins, Nadia. 2014. (Super Social Studies Infographics Ser.). (ENG.). 32p. (J). (gr. 3-5). lib. bdg. 26.65 *(978-1-4677-3464-6(0),* Lerner Pubns.) Lerner Publishing Group.

Thompson, Carol. Daddy, Papa, & Me. Newman, Lesléa. 2009. 20p. (J). (gr. -1 — 1). bds. 7.99 *(978-1-58246-262-2(3),* Tricycle Pr.) Random Hse. Children's Bks.

—Hold My Hand: Five Stories of Love & Family. Zolotow, Charlotte. 2003. (ENG.). 64p. (gr. -1-k). 19.99 *(978-0-7868-0518-1(8))* Hyperion Pr.

—Molly & Her Dad. Ormerod, Jan. 2008. 32p. *(978-1-921272-55-4(4))* Little Hare Bks. AUS. Dist: HarperCollins Pubs. Australia.

—Mommy, Mama, & Me. Newman, Lesléa. 2009. 20p. (J). (gr. -1-2). bds. 7.99 *(978-1-58246-263-9(1),* Tricycle Pr.) Random Hse. Children's Bks.

—My Turtle & Me. Bernstein, Owen. 2012. (ENG.). 10p. (J). (— 1). bds. 9.99 *(978-0-545-43387-7(8))* Scholastic, Inc.

—Thunder-Boomer! Crum, Shutta. 2009. (ENG.). 40p. (J). (gr. -1-3). 17.99 *(978-0-618-61865-1(1),* 100451) Houghton Mifflin Harcourt Publishing Co.

—Two Times the Fun. Cleary, Beverly. ed. 2005. (ENG.). 96p. (J). (gr. -1-2). 16.99 *(978-0-06-057921-0(8))* HarperCollins Pubs.

—Winners Never Quit! Hamm, Mia. 2006. (ENG.). 32p. (J). (gr. -1-2). pap. 7.99 *(978-0-06-074052-8(3))* HarperCollins Pubs.

Thompson, Carol. Amazing Me! Board Book Set Of 4. Thompson, Carol. 2020. (Social & Emotional Learning Sets Ser.). (ENG.). 48p. (J). bds., bds., bds. ***(978-1-78628-531-7(2))*** Child's Play International Ltd.

Thompson, Carol. ¡Bailo!/Dance! ¡Soy Sorprendente!/Amazing Me! Thompson, Carol. Mlawer, Teresa, tr. ed. 2019. (Spanish/English Bilingual Editions Ser.). (ENG & SPA.). 12p. (J). (gr. k-k). bds. *(978-1-78628-299-6(2))* Child's Play International Ltd.

—¡Canto!/Sing! ¡Soy Sorprendente!/Amazing Me! Thompson, Carol. Mlawer, Teresa, tr. ed. 2019. (Spanish/English Bilingual Editions Ser.). (ENG & SPA.). 12p. (J). (gr. k-k). bds. *(978-1-78628-300-9(X))* Child's Play International Ltd.

—Climb! Thompson, Carol. 2013. (Little Movers Ser.). 12p. (J). spiral bd. *(978-1-84643-617-8(6))* Child's Play International Ltd.

—Crawl! Thompson, Carol. 2013. (Little Movers Ser.). 12p. (J). spiral bd. *(978-1-84643-614-7(1))* Child's Play International Ltd.

—Dance. Thompson, Carol. 2018. (Amazing Me! Ser.: 4). 12p. (J). (gr. k-k). spiral bd. *(978-1-84643-959-9(0))* Child's Play International Ltd.

—Dressing Up. Thompson, Carol. 2018. (Amazing Me! Ser.: 4). 12p. (J). (gr. k-k). spiral bd. *(978-1-84643-960-5(4))* Child's Play International Ltd.

—Jump! Thompson, Carol. 2013. (Little Movers Ser.). 12p. (J). spiral bd. *(978-1-84643-615-4(X))* Child's Play International Ltd.

—Lluvia. Thompson, Carol. Mlawer, Teresa, tr. from ENG. 2017. (¡Haga el Tiempo Que Haga! - Whatever the Weather (Spanish) Ser.: 4). Orig. Title: Rain. (SPA.). 12p. (J). (gr. k-k). bds. *(978-1-84643-979-7(5))* Child's Play International Ltd.

—¡Me Disfrazo!/Dressing Up! ¡Soy Sorprendente!/Amazing Me! Thompson, Carol. Mlawer, Teresa, tr. ed. 2019. (Spanish/English Bilingual Editions Ser.). (ENG & SPA.). 12p. (J). (gr. k-k). bds. *(978-1-78628-301-6(8))* Child's Play International Ltd.

—Music. Thompson, Carol. 2018. (Amazing Me! Ser.: 4). 12p. (J). (gr. k-k). spiral bd. *(978-1-84643-961-2(2))* Child's Play International Ltd.

—Nieve. Thompson, Carol. Mlawer, Teresa, tr. from ENG. 2017. (¡Haga el Tiempo Que Haga! - Whatever the Weather (Spanish) Ser.). Orig. Title: Snow. (SPA.). 12p. (J). (gr. k-k). bds. *(978-1-84643-978-0(7))* Child's Play International Ltd.

—Rain. Thompson, Carol. 2014. (Whatever the Weather Ser.: 4). 12p. (J). (gr. k-k). spiral bd. *(978-1-84643-683-3(4))* Child's Play International Ltd.

—Run! Thompson, Carol. 2013. (Little Movers Ser.). 12p. (J). spiral bd. *(978-1-84643-616-1(8))* Child's Play International Ltd.

—Sing. Thompson, Carol. 2018. (Amazing Me! Ser.: 4). 12p. (J). (gr. k-k). spiral bd. *(978-1-84643-962-9(0))* Child's Play International Ltd.

—Snow. Thompson, Carol. 2014. (Whatever the Weather Ser.). 12p. (J). (gr. k-k). spiral bd. *(978-1-84643-681-9(8))* Child's Play International Ltd.

—Sol. Thompson, Carol. Mlawer, Teresa, tr. from ENG. 2017. (¡Haga el Tiempo Que Haga! - Whatever the Weather (Spanish) Ser.: 4). Orig. Title: Sun. (SPA.). 12p. (J). (gr. k-k). bds. *(978-1-84643-980-3(9))* Child's Play International Ltd.

—Sun. Thompson, Carol. 2014. (Whatever the Weather Ser.). 12p. (J). (gr. k-k). spiral bd. *(978-1-84643-680-2(X))* Child's Play International Ltd.

—¡Toco Música!/Music! ¡Soy Sorprendente!/Amazing Me! Thompson, Carol. Mlawer, Teresa, tr. ed. 2019. (Spanish/English Bilingual Editions Ser.). (ENG & SPA.). 12p. (J). (gr. k-k). bds. *(978-1-78628-302-3(6))* Child's Play International Ltd.

—Viento. Thompson, Carol. Mlawer, Teresa, tr. from ENG. 2017. (¡Haga el Tiempo Que Haga! - Whatever the Weather (Spanish) Ser.). Orig. Title: Wind. (SPA.). 12p. (J). (gr. k-k). bds. *(978-1-84643-977-3(9))* Child's Play International Ltd.

—Wind. Thompson, Carol. 2014. (Whatever the Weather Ser.). 12p. (J). (gr. k-k). spiral bd. *(978-1-84643-682-6(6))* Child's Play International Ltd.

Thompson, Chad. Brave Fire Truck, 1 vol. Crow, Melinda Melton. 2011. (Wonder Wheels Ser.). (ENG.). 32p. (J). (gr. -1-1). pap. 6.25 *(978-1-4342-3384-4(7));* lib. bdg. 22.65 *(978-1-4342-3029-4(5))* Capstone. (Stone Arch Bks.).

—Bully Bill. Birky, Joy. 2007. 40p. (J). (gr. 3-7). per. 12.99 *(978-0-8361-9382-4(2))* Herald Pr.

—Busy, Busy Train, 1 vol. Crow, Melinda Melton. 2011. (Wonder Wheels Ser.). (ENG.). 32p. (J). (gr. -1-1). pap. 6.25 *(978-1-4342-3383-7(9));* lib. bdg. 22.65 *(978-1-4342-3028-7(7))* Capstone. (Stone Arch Bks.).

Thompson, Chad. Daphne the Blind Dog Gets Adopted. Gibbons, Dawn M. 2019. (Daphne the Blind Dog Ser.). (ENG.). 32p. (J). ***(978-1-5255-4916-8(2));*** pap. ***(978-1-5255-4917-5(0))*** FriesenPress.

Thompson, Chad. Field Trip for School Bus, 1 vol. Crow, Melinda Melton. 2012. (Wonder Wheels Ser.). (ENG.). 32p. (J). (gr. -1-1). pap. 6.25 *(978-1-4342-4237-2(4),* Stone Arch Bks.) Capstone.

Thompson, Chad. From Ditches to Riches. Brohart, Karen. 2020. (Adventures of Sully Ser.). (ENG.). 24p. (J). ***(978-1-5255-5108-6(6));*** pap. ***(978-1-5255-5109-3(4))*** FriesenPress.

Thompson, Chad. Gluten-Free Me Beckman Goes to School. Bykowski, Christy. 2013. 24p. pap. 11.95 *(978-1-61244-228-0(5))* Halo Publishing International.

—Helpful Tractor, 1 vol. Crow, Melinda Melton. 2011. (Wonder Wheels Ser.). (ENG.). 32p. (J). (gr. -1-1). pap. 6.25 *(978-1-4342-3382-0(0));* lib. bdg. 22.65 *(978-1-4342-3027-0(9))* Capstone. (Stone Arch Bks.).

—Let's Paint the Garage!, 1 vol. Crow, Melinda Melton. 2012. (Wonder Wheels Ser.). (ENG.). 32p. (J). (gr. -1-1). pap. 6.25 *(978-1-4342-4238-9(2));* lib. bdg. 22.65 *(978-1-4342-4016-3(9))* Capstone. (Stone Arch Bks.).

—Let's Volunteer. Houghton, Jill Zierels. 2013. 28p. pap. 10.95 *(978-1-61244-211-2(0))* Halo Publishing International.

—The Long Train Ride, 1 vol. Crow, Melinda Melton. 2012. (Wonder Wheels Ser.). (ENG.). 32p. (J). (gr. -1-1). pap. 6.25 *(978-1-4342-4239-6(0));* lib. bdg. 22.65 *(978-1-4342-4018-7(5))* Capstone. (Stone Arch Bks.).

—Lucky School Bus, 1 vol. Crow, Melinda Melton. 2011. (Wonder Wheels Ser.). (ENG.). 32p. (J). (gr. -1-1). pap. 6.25 *(978-1-4342-3381-3(2));* lib. bdg. 22.65 *(978-1-4342-3026-3(0))* Capstone. (Stone Arch Bks.).

—Milo Finds His Best Friend. Umina, Lisa. 2013. 30p. 15.95 *(978-1-61244-182-5(3))* Halo Publishing International.

—Truck Parade, 1 vol. Crow, Melinda Melton. 2012. (Wonder Wheels Ser.). (ENG.). 32p. (J). (gr. -1-1). pap. 6.25 *(978-1-4342-4240-2(4));* lib. bdg. 22.65 *(978-1-4342-4017-0(7))* Capstone. (Stone Arch Bks.).

—Will Old Rusty Ever Get to Go to the Classic Car Show? Gnap, Jean. 2017. (ENG.). (J). *(978-1-5255-0510-2(6));* pap. *(978-1-4602-8753-8(3))* FriesenPress.

Thompson, Chad J. Rhymes with Claire. Thompson, Chad J. 2019. (ENG.). 40p. (J). (gr. -1-3). 17.99 *(978-1-4814-7097-1(3),* Aladdin) Simon & Schuster Children's Publishing.

T

—Rhymes with Doug. Thompson, Chad J. 2016. (ENG.). 40p. (J). (gr. -1-3). 16.99 *(978-1-4814-7095-7(7)*, Aladdin) Simon & Schuster Children's Publishing.

Thompson, Chelsea. Nytemares & Dreamscapes: Beyond Here #2. Matthews, D. F. 2019. (Beyond Here Ser.: Vol. 2). (ENG.). 242p. (J). pap. 17.99 *(978-1-7178-0932-2(4))* Independently Published.

Thompson, Colin. The Amazing Illustrated Floodsopedia. Thompson, Colin. 2013. (Floods Ser.). 96p. (J). (gr. 4-7). pap. 17.99 *(978-1-74275-104-7(0))* Random Hse. Australia AUS. Dist: Independent Pubs. Group.

—Barry. Thompson, Colin. 2013. 32p. (J). (gr. k-4). pap. 9.99 *(978-1-86471-884-3(6))* Random Hse. Australia AUS. Dist: Independent Pubs. Group.

—Castles. Thompson, Colin. 2007. 32p. (J). (gr. k-2). pap. 17.99 *(978-0-09-943942-4(5)*, Red Fox) Random House Children's Books GBR. Dist: Independent Pubs. Group.

—The Floods Family Files. Thompson, Colin. 2012. (Floods Ser.: 1). (ENG.). 32p. (J). (gr. 4-7). pap. 12.99 *(978-1-86471-942-0(7))* Random Hse. Australia AUS. Dist: Independent Pubs. Group.

—Home & Away. Thompson, Colin. 2006. (Floods Ser.: 3). 240p. (J). (gr. 3-7). 9.99 *(978-1-74166-032-6(7))* Random Hse. Australia AUS. Dist: Independent Pubs. Group.

—The Last Alchemist. Thompson, Colin. 2003. 30p. (J). (gr. k-3). reprint ed. 17.00 *(978-0-7567-6164-6(6))* DIANE Publishing Co.

—Playschool. Thompson, Colin. 2006. (Floods Ser.: 2). 224p. (Orig.). (J). (gr. 3-7). 13.99 *(978-1-74166-026-5(2))* Random Hse. Australia AUS. Dist: Independent Pubs. Group.

—Top Gear, Vol. 7. Thompson, Colin. 2008. (Floods Ser.: 7). 224p. (J). (gr. 3-7). pap. 9.99 *(978-1-74166-254-2(0))* Random Hse. Australia AUS. Dist: Independent Pubs. Group.

Thompson, Craig. Space Dumplins. Thompson, Craig. 2015. (ENG.). 320p. (J). (gr. 3-7). 24.99 *(978-0-545-56541-7(3))*; pap. 16.99 *(978-0-545-56543-1(X))* Scholastic, Inc. (Graphix).

Thompson, Dana. Nick Newton: The Highest Bidder. Ishida, S. E. M. 2018. 128p. (J). *(978-1-62856-511-9(X))* BJU Pr.

Thompson, Del, et al. Tony Salerno's Good News Express. Salerno, Tony et al. 64p. (Orig.). (J). (gr. k-6). pap. *(978-1-881597-00-1(8))* Magination.

Thompson, Elizabeth. Thrill in The 'Ville. Trollinger, Patsi B. 2012. 128p. (J). pap. 6.99 *(978-0-9836106-1-8(4))* Benjamin Pr.

Thompson, Floyd. The Key: The Adventure Begins. Hambrick, Brandy Yvonne. Benston, Rebecca, ed. 2018. (ENG.). 216p. (J). pap. 10.99 *(978-0-578-21029-2(0))* Hambrick, Brandy .

Thompson, George. Vlad the Drac. Jungman, Ann. 2006. (Vlad the Drac Ser.). 124p. (J). (gr. 2-4). per. 6.95 *(978-1-903015-22-3(7))* Barn Owl Bks, London GBR. Dist: Independent Pubs. Group.

—Vlad the Drac Superstar. Jungman, Ann. 2006. (Vlad the Drac Ser.). 122p. (J). (gr. 2-4). pap. 6.95 *(978-1-903015-45-2(6))* Barn Owl Bks, London GBR. Dist: Independent Pubs. Group.

Thompson, Haley a. Scout Goes to School. Almendinger, Barbara-Jo. 2018. (ENG.). 28p. (J). 14.99 *(978-1-63337-223-8(5))*; pap. 11.99 *(978-1-63337-222-1(7))* Roland Golf Services.

Thompson, Ian, jt. illus. see Various.

Thompson, Janet M., jt. illus. see Thompson, Michelle Gormican.

Thompson, Jeffrey. A Day at the Fire Station. Mortensen, Lori. 2010. (First Graphics: My Community Ser.). (ENG.). 24p. (gr. 1-2). pap. 35.70 *(978-1-4296-5613-9(1))* Capstone.

—Going to the Dentist. Mortensen, Lori. 2010. (First Graphics: My Community Ser.). (ENG.). 24p. (gr. 1-2). pap. 35.70 *(978-1-4296-5611-5(5))*; (J). 24.65 *(978-1-4296-4507-2(5))* Capstone.

—Thomas Edison: Inventor, Scientist, & Genius, 1 vol. Mortensen, Lori & Picture Window Books Staff. 2007. (Biographies Ser.). (ENG.). 24p. (J). (gr. k-3). 27.32 *(978-1-4048-3105-6(3)*, Picture Window Bks.) Capstone.

—Transportation in the City, 1 vol. Tourville, Amanda Doering. 2010. (First Graphics: My Community Ser.). (ENG.). 24p. (J). (gr. 1-3). lib. bdg. 24.65 *(978-1-4296-5370-1(1))* Capstone.

—Transportation in the City. Doering Tourville, Amanda. 2011. (First Graphics: My Community Ser.). (ENG.). 24p. (gr. 1-2). pap. 35.70 *(978-1-4296-6403-5(7))* Capstone.

—A Visit to the Library. Wohlrabe, Sarah C. (First Graphics: My Community Ser.). (ENG.). 24p. (gr. 1-2). 2011. pap. 35.70 *(978-1-4296-6404-2(5))*; 2010. (J). lib. bdg. 24.65 *(978-1-4296-5371-8(X))* Capstone.

—A Visit to the Police Station. Doering Tourville, Amanda. 2011. (First Graphics: My Community Ser.). (ENG.). 24p. (gr. 1-2). pap. 35.70 *(978-1-4296-6402-8(9))* Capstone.

—Working on the Farm, 1 vol. Mortensen, Lori. 2010. (First Graphics: My Community Ser.). (ENG.). 24p. (gr. 1-3). (J). pap. 6.29 *(978-1-4296-5616-0(6))*; pap. 35.70 *(978-1-4296-5617-7(4))* Capstone.

Thompson, Jenean. All in a Day's Play. Thompson, Jenean. l.t. ed. 2005. 40p. (J). 14.95 *(978-1-59879-066-5(8))* Lifevest Publishing, Inc.

Thompson, Jessica. Alvin the Proud Prankster. Burt, Vickie. 2011. 24p. pap. 13.99 *(978-1-937129-10-1(1))* Faithful Life Pubs.

Thompson, Jill. The Neil Gaiman Coloring Book: Coloring Book for Adults & Kids to Share. Gaiman, Neil. 2017. (ENG.). 96p. (J). (gr. 3-7). pap. 15.99 *(978-0-06-265297-3(4)*, HarperCollins) HarperCollins Pubs. Ltd. GBR. Dist: HarperCollins Pubs.

Thompson, Jill, et al. Terror Trips. Stine, R. L. 2007. (Goosebumps Graphic Novels Ser.: 2). (ENG.). 144p. (J). (gr. 3-5). pap. 9.99 *(978-0-439-85780-2(5)*, Graphix) Scholastic, Inc.

Thompson, Jill. Magic Trixie. Thompson, Jill. 2008. 96p. (J). (gr. 3-7). pap. 8.99 *(978-0-06-117045-4(3))* HarperCollins Pubs.

—Magic Trixie & the Dragon. Thompson, Jill. 2009. 96p. (J). (gr. 3-7). pap. 7.99 *(978-0-06-117050-8(X))* HarperCollins Pubs.

Thompson, Jimmy. Los Angeles 1 To 10. Greene, Sara Beth. 2019. (City 1 To 10 Ser.). 22p. (J). (— 1). bds. 9.99 *(978-1-63217-239-6(9)*, Little Bigfoot) Sasquatch Bks.

—Portland 1 To 10. Greene, Sara Beth. 2019. (City 1 To 10 Ser.). 22p. (J). (— 1). bds. 9.99 *(978-1-63217-254-9(2)*, Little Bigfoot) Sasquatch Bks.

Thompson, John. Always, Jackie. Lewis, J. Patrick. 2020. (ENG.). 32p. (J). (gr. 1-3). pap. 18.99 *(978-1-56846-307-0(3)*, Creative Editions) Creative Co., The.

—Hattie on Her Way. Clark, Clara Gillow. 2005. (Trials of Hattie Belle Basket Ser.). (ENG.). 208p. (J). (gr. 5-18). 15.99 *(978-0-7636-2286-2(9))* Candlewick Pr.

—Prairie Train. Chall, Marsha Wilson. 2003. 40p. (J). (gr. -1-3). 16.89 *(978-0-688-13434-1(3))* HarperCollins Pubs.

Thompson, Josephine. Big Book of Science Things to Make & Do. Gilpin, Rebecca & Pratt, Leonie. 2008. (Big Book of Science Things to Make & Do Ser.). 95p. (J). (gr. 1). pap. 14.99 *(978-0-7945-1923-0(7)*, Usborne) EDC Publishing.

Thompson, Josephine & Day, Caroline. Big Drawing Book. Watt, Fiona. ed. 2013. (Doodle Bks). 95p. (J). pap. 11.99 *(978-0-7945-3365-6(5)*, Usborne) EDC Publishing.

Thompson, Josephine Et Al. Knights & Castles Things to Make & Do. Pratt, Leonie. 2006. 32p. (J). pap. 6.99 *(978-0-7945-1355-9(7)*, Usborne) EDC Publishing.

Thompson, Justin K., jt. illus. see Oswald, Pete.

Thompson, K. Dyble. Cartwheel to the Moon: My Sicilian Childhood. di Pasquale, Emanuel. 2003. (ENG.). 64p. (J). (gr. 3-7). 16.95 *(978-0-8126-2679-7(6))* Cricket Bks.

Thompson, Karin. The Night the Moon Went Out. Lord, Pia. 2011. 28p. pap. 24.95 *(978-1-4626-0010-6(7))* America Star Bks.

Thompson, Keith. Behemoth. Westerfeld, Scott. (Leviathan Trilogy Ser.). (ENG.). (YA). (gr. 7). 2011. 512p. pap. 14.99 *(978-1-4169-7176-4(9))*; 2010. 496p. 18.99 *(978-1-4169-7175-7(0))* Simon Pulse. (Simon Pulse).

—Behemoth. Westerfeld, Scott. l.t. ed. 2010. (Leviathan Trilogy: Bk. 2). (ENG.). 540p. 23.99 *(978-1-4104-3066-3(9))* Thorndike Pr.

—Darkwing. Oppel, Kenneth. 2007. (Silverwing Ser.: 1). (ENG.). 432p. (J). (gr. 5-9). 17.99 *(978-0-06-085054-8(X))* HarperCollins Pubs.

—Goliath. Westerfeld, Scott. (Leviathan Trilogy Ser.). (ENG.). (YA). (gr. 7). 2012. 576p. pap. 14.99 *(978-1-4169-7178-8(5))*; 2011. 560p. 19.99 *(978-1-4169-7177-1(7))* Simon Pulse. (Simon Pulse).

—Leviathan. Westerfeld, Scott. (Leviathan Trilogy Ser.). (ENG.). (YA). (gr. 7-18). 2010. 464p. pap. 14.99 *(978-1-4169-7174-0(2))*; 2009. 448p. 24.99 *(978-1-4169-7173-3(4))* Simon Pulse. (Simon Pulse).

—Leviathan: Leviathan; Behemoth; Goliath. Westerfeld, Scott. ed. 2012. (Leviathan Trilogy Ser.). (ENG.). 1552p. (YA). (gr. 7). pap. 44.99 *(978-1-4424-8377-4(6)*, Simon Pulse) Simon Pulse.

—The Manual of Aeronautics: An Illustrated Guide to the Leviathan Series. Westerfeld, Scott. 2012. (ENG.). 64p. (YA). (gr. 7). 19.99 *(978-1-4169-7179-5(3)*, Simon Pulse) Simon Pulse.

Thompson, Kim. Farm Animals. Regan, Lisa. 2010. (I Love Animals Ser.). (ENG.). 24p. (J). (gr. 1-5). pap. 8.15 *(978-1-61533-233-5(2))*; lib. bdg. 25.60 *(978-1-61533-227-4(8))* Windmill Bks.

Thompson, Kristi June. Molly, the Good Furry Friend. Thompson, Holly Sue. 2011. 36p. pap. 14.75 *(978-1-60911-431-2(0)*, Eloquent Bks.) Strategic Book Publishing & Rights Agency (SBPRA).

Thompson, Leslie. Millie the Octopus Learn to Surf. Makhlouf, Jack. 2011. (ENG.). 26p. (J). pap. 9.99 *(978-0-9843297-5-5(7))* Octobooks.

—Millie the Octopus Learns Yoga. Makhlouf, Jack. 2011. (ENG.). 26p. (J). pap. 9.99 *(978-0-9843297-4-8(9))* Octobooks.

Thompson, Leslie Thompson. Millie the Octopus Learns to Hula Dance. Makhlouf, Jack. 2011. (ENG.). 26p. (J). pap. 9.99 *(978-0-9843297-3-1(0))* Octobooks.

Thompson, Lydia. Welby the Worm Who Lost His Wiggle. Hunter, Lee Hargus. 2004. 32p. (J). (gr. -1-1). *(978-1-930093-04-1(7))* Brookfield Reader, Inc., The.

Thompson, Margot. Biomimicry: Inventions Inspired by Nature. Lee, Dora. 2011. (ENG.). 40p. (J). (gr. 3-7). 18.95 *(978-1-55453-467-8(4))* Kids Can Pr., Ltd. CAN. Dist: Hachette Bk. Group.

—Planet Ark: Preserving Earth's Biodiversity. Mason, Adrienne. 2013. (CitizenKid Ser.). (ENG.). 32p. (J). (gr. 3-7). 18.95 *(978-1-55453-753-2(3))* Kids Can Pr., Ltd. CAN. Dist: Hachette Bk. Group.

—Tree of Life: The Incredible Biodiversity of Life on Earth. Strauss, Rochelle. 2013. (CitizenKid Ser.). (ENG.). 40p. (J). (gr. 3-7). pap. 12.99 *(978-1-55453-961-1(7))* Kids Can Pr., Ltd. CAN. Dist: Hachette Bk. Group.

Thompson, Maria. Exploring the Native Plant World: A Life Science Curriculum, 5th-6th Grade: Adaptations in the Native Plant World. Russell, Margaret. 2004. 63p. (J). (gr. 5-6). per. 14.95 *(978-1-57168-851-4(X)*, Eakin Pr.) Eakin Pr.

Thompson, Michael. Los Otros Osos, 1 vol. Thompson, Michael. 2013. (SPA.). 32p. (J). pap. 6.99 *(978-1-59572-664-3(0))* Star Bright Bks., Inc.

—Los Otros Osos / the Other Bears. Thompson, Michael. 2013. (ENG & SPA.). (J). 16.99 *(978-1-59572-644-5(6))* Star Bright Bks., Inc.

—The Other Bears, 1 vol. Thompson, Michael. 2013.Tr. of Os Outros Ursos. (ENG.). 32p. (J). 16.99 *(978-1-59572-638-4(1))*; pap. 6.99 *(978-1-59572-639-1(X))* Star Bright Bks., Inc.

Thompson, Michelle Gormican & Thompson, Janet M. Wyatt Walker Turbo Talker. Hierl, Christine Gormican. 2004. 28p. *(978-0-9760680-0-6(1))* Cedar Shamrock Publishing.

Thompson, Mike. Chicken Boy & the Wrath of Dr. Dimwad. Thompson, Mike. 2008. 102p. (J). per. 9.95 *(978-0-9799216-0-5(0))* Thompson Original Productions LLC.

Thompson, Mills. Half-A-Dozen Housekeepers (Illustrated Edition) Wiggin, Kate Douglas. 2017. (ENG.). (J). pap. *(978-1-4068-8562-0(2))* Echo Library.

Thompson, Richard. BrainJuice: Science, Fresh Squeezed! Shields, Carol Diggory. 2003. (ENG.). 64p. (J). (gr. -1-7). 14.95 *(978-1-59354-005-0(1)*, Handprint Bks.) Chronicle Bks. LLC.

Thompson, Robin. Plum. Hayes, Sean & Icenogle, Scott. 2018. (ENG.). 48p. (J). (gr. -1-3). 17.99 *(978-1-5344-0404-5(X)*, Simon & Schuster Bks. For Young Readers) Simon & Schuster Bks. For Young Readers.

Thompson, Sally Jane. Conspiracy of Ravens. Moore, Leah & Reppion, John. 2018. (ENG.). 136p. (J). (gr. 5). 14.99 *(978-1-5067-0883-6(8))* Dark Horse Comics.

Thompson, Scott M. Color. Lilly, Melinda. 2003. 24p. (J). 22.79 *(978-1-58952-646-4(5))* Rourke Educational Media.

—Dirty & Clean. Lilly, Melinda. 2003. 24p. (J). 22.79 *(978-1-58952-636-5(8))* Rourke Educational Media.

—Gravity. Lilly, Melinda. 2003. (Read & Do Science Ser.). 24p. (J). 22.79 *(978-1-58952-642-6(2))* Rourke Educational Media.

—Make It Grow. Lilly, Melinda. 2003. (Rourke Discovery Library). 24p. (J). 22.79 *(978-1-58952-637-2(6))* Rourke Educational Media.

—Solid, Liquid, & Gas. Lilly, Melinda. 2003. 24p. (J). 20.64 *(978-1-58952-648-8(1))* Rourke Educational Media.

—Sound up & Down. Lilly, Melinda. 2003. 24p. (J). 20.64 *(978-1-58952-644-0(9))* Rourke Educational Media.

Thompson, Scott M., photos by. Energy. Lilly, Melinda. 2005. (Rourke Discovery Library). 24p. (J). (gr. 1-4). lib. bdg. 22.79 *(978-1-59515-401-9(9)*, 1244272) Rourke Educational Media.

—Rocks. Lilly, Melinda. 2005. (Rourke Discovery Library). 24p. (J). (gr. 1-4). lib. bdg. 14.95 *(978-1-59515-404-0(3)*, 1244275) Rourke Educational Media.

—Sun & Moon. Lilly, Melinda. 2005. (Rourke Discovery Library). 24p. (J). (gr. 1-4). lib. bdg. 14.95 *(978-1-59515-405-7(1)*, 1244276) Rourke Educational Media.

Thompson, Sharon. Horse Mad. Wolfer, Dianne. 2005. 62p. (Orig.). (J). 10.95 *(978-1-920731-47-2(4))* Fremantle Pr. AUS. Dist: Independent Pubs. Group.

—The Judas Donkey. Broome, Errol. 2003. 144p. pap. 13.50 *(978-1-920731-18-2(0))* Fremantle Pr. AUS. Dist: Independent Pubs. Group.

—Rainbow Jackets. Forrestal, Elaine. 2003. 64p. (YA). pap. 11.95 *(978-1-920731-67-0(9))* Fremantle Pr. AUS. Dist: Independent Pubs. Group.

Thompson, Sunnie R. What's So Great about Silent E? The Thoughts of Sunnie Rae. Thompson, Deanna T. 2010. 28p. pap. 13.99 *(978-1-4490-9274-0(8))* AuthorHouse.

Thompson, Susan. The Invitation. Allen, Mary. l.t. ed. 2017. (ENG.). 25p. (J). 12.95 *(978-0-9887841-3-0(0))* Farrand Avenue Faith Publishing.

Thompson, Taylor. Bonus Love. Dooley, Jessica. 2020. (ENG.). 36p. (J). pap. 20.99 ***(978-1-7283-6631-9(3))*** AuthorHouse.

Thompson, Travis a. Always Just Be You! Thompson, Travis a. 2019. (ENG.). 36p. (J). (gr. k-5). 20.95 *(978-0-578-50746-0(3))* SivART Gallery, The.

Thompson, Veronica, photos by. Earth-Friendly Animal Crafts. Thompson, Veronica. 2018. (Green STEAM Ser.). (ENG., 32p. (J). (gr. 3-5). pap. 9.99 *(978-1-5415-2778-2(X))*; lib. bdg. 29.32 *(978-1-5415-2421-7(7)*, Lerner Pubns.) Lerner Publishing Group.

—Earth-Friendly Earth Day Crafts. Thompson, Veronica. 2018. (Green STEAM Ser.). (ENG., 32p. (J). (gr. 3-5). 29.32 *(978-1-5415-2420-0(9)*, Lerner Pubns.) Lerner Publishing Group.

—Earth-Friendly Engineering Crafts. Thompson, Veronica. 2018. (Green STEAM Ser.). (ENG., 32p. (J). (gr. 3-5). pap. 9.99 *(978-1-5415-2780-5(1))*; lib. bdg. 29.32 *(978-1-5415-2418-7(7)*, Lerner Pubns.) Lerner Publishing Group.

—Earth-Friendly Math Crafts. Thompson, Veronica. 2018. (Green STEAM Ser.). (ENG., 32p. (J). (gr. 3-5). 29.32 *(978-1-5415-2419-4(5)*, Lerner Pubns.) Lerner Publishing Group.

—Earth-Friendly Tech Crafts. Thompson, Veronica. 2018. (Green STEAM Ser.). (ENG., 32p. (J). (gr. 3-5). pap. 9.99 *(978-1-5415-2783-6(6))*; lib. bdg. 29.32 *(978-1-5415-2417-0(9)*, Lerner Pubns.) Lerner Publishing Group.

Thompson, Veronica M., photos by. Earth-Friendly Science Crafts. Thompson, Veronica M. 2018. (Green STEAM Ser.). (ENG., 32p. (J). (gr. 3-5). 29.32 *(978-1-5415-2416-3(0)*, Lerner Pubns.) Lerner Publishing Group.

Thompsongriffin, Bea. Esty's Mistake. Medeiros, Lisa. 2019. (ENG.). 32p. (J). pap. 12.50 ***(978-1-6956-8974-9(7))*** Independently Published.

Thomson, Andrew. Knock! Knock! Where Is There? Elling, Brian & Who HQ. 2019. (Where Is? Ser.). 128p. (J). (gr. 3-7). 6.99 *(978-1-5247-9208-4(X)*, Penguin Workshop) Penguin Young Readers Group.

—Knock! Knock! Who Was There? Elling, Brian & Who HQ. 2018. (Who Was? Ser.). 128p. (J). (gr. 3-7). 6.99 *(978-0-515-15932-5(8)*, Penguin Workshop) Penguin Young Readers Group.

—What Are the Paralympic Games? Herman, Gail & Who HQ. 2020. (What Was? Ser.). 112p. (J). (gr. 3-7). 5.99 *(978-1-5247-9262-6(4))*; lib. bdg. 15.99 *(978-1-5247-9263-3(2))* Penguin Young Readers Group. (Penguin Workshop).

—What Is the Story of Scooby-Doo? Payne, M. D. & Who HQ. 2019. (What Is the Story Of? Ser.). 112p. (J). (gr. 3-7). 6.99 *(978-1-5247-8824-7(4))*; lib. bdg. 15.99 *(978-1-5247-8825-4(2))* Penguin Young Readers Group. (Penguin Workshop).

—Who Are the Rolling Stones? Rau, Dana Meachen. 2017. 107p. (J). *(978-1-5182-4233-5(2)*, Grosset & Dunlap) Penguin Young Readers Group.

—Who Are Venus & Serena Williams? Buckley, James, Jr. et al. 2017. (Who Was? Ser.). 112p. (J). (gr. 3-7). 5.99 *(978-0-515-15803-8(8)*, Penguin Workshop) Penguin Young Readers Group.

—Who Is Bono? Pollack, Pam et al. 2018. (Who Was? Ser.). 112p. (J). (gr. 3-7). 5.99 *(978-0-448-48868-4(X))*; lib. bdg. 15.99 *(978-1-5247-8851-3(1))* Penguin Young Readers Group. (Penguin Workshop).

—Who Is Derek Jeter? Herman, Gail & Who HQ. 2015. (Who Was? Ser.). 112p. (J). (gr. 3-7). 5.99 *(978-0-448-48697-0(0)*, Penguin Workshop) Penguin Young Readers Group.

—Who Is Malala Yousafzai? Brown, Dinah. 2015. (Who Was-? Chapters Ser.). (ENG.). 112p. (J). (gr. 4-6). 18.69 *(978-1-4844-6131-0(2))* Penguin Publishing Group.

—Who Is Malala Yousafzai? Brown, Dinah & Who HQ. 2015. (Who Was? Ser.). 112p. (J). (gr. 3-7). 5.99 *(978-0-448-48937-7(6)*, Penguin Workshop) Penguin Young Readers Group.

—Who Is Pele? Buckley, James & Who HQ. 2018. (Who Was? Ser.). 112p. (J). (gr. 3-7). 5.99 *(978-0-399-54261-9(2))*; lib. bdg. 15.99 *(978-0-399-54262-6(0))* Penguin Young Readers Group. (Penguin Workshop).

—Who Was Alexander the Great? Waterfield, Kathryn et al. 2016. (Who Was? Ser.). 112p. (J). (gr. 3-7). 15.99 *(978-0-399-54235-0(3)*, Penguin Workshop) Penguin Young Readers Group.

—Who Was Genghis Khan? Medina, Nico & Who HQ. 2014. (Who Was? Ser.). 112p. (J). (gr. 3-7). pap. 5.99 *(978-0-448-48260-6(6)*, Penguin Workshop) Penguin Young Readers Group.

—Who Was Joan of Arc? Pollack, Pam & Belviso, Meg. 2016. (Who Was-? Chapters Ser.). (ENG.). 112p. (J). (gr. 4-6). 18.69 *(978-1-4844-7648-2(4))* Penguin Publishing Group.

—Who Was Joan of Arc? Belviso, Meg et al. 2016. (Who Was? Ser.). 112p. (J). (gr. 3-7). pap. 5.99 *(978-0-448-48304-7(1)*, Penguin Workshop) Penguin Young Readers Group.

—Who Was Woodrow Wilson? Frith, Margaret & Who HQ. 2015. (Who Was? Ser.). 112p. (J). (gr. 3-7). 5.99 *(978-0-448-48428-0(5)*, Penguin Workshop) Penguin Young Readers Group.

Thomson, Andy. I Told You So! The Journey Continues. Gunning, Mark. 2019. (I Told You So! Ser.: Vol. 2). (ENG.). 124p. (J). pap. *(978-0-9950670-8-0(2))* Itchygooney Bks.

Thomson, Andy. I Told You So! The Journey Continues. Gunning, Mark. Sims, Stephanie, ed. 2nd ed. 2019. (I Told You So! Ser.: Vol. 2). (ENG.). 124p. (J). (gr. 2-6). ***(978-1-9992007-2-5(1))*** Itchygooney Bks.

Thomson, Andy. I Told You So! Book 2: The Journey Continues. Gunning, Mark. 2018. (ENG.). 98p. (J). pap. *(978-0-9950670-2-8(3))* Itchygooney Bks.

Thomson, Bill. Baseball Hour. Nevius, Carol. 2020. (ENG.). 34p. (J). (gr. -1-3). pap. 9.99 ***(978-1-4778-1042-2(0)***, 9781477810422, Two Lions) Amazon Publishing.

Thomson, Bill. Building with Dad, 0 vols. Nevius, Carol. 2012. (ENG.). 32p. (J). (gr. -1-2). pap. 9.99 *(978-0-7614-5984-2(7)*, 9780761459842, Two Lions) Amazon Publishing.

—Karate Hour, 0 vols. Nevius, Carol. 2011. (ENG.). 34p. (J). (gr. -1-2). pap. 7.99 *(978-0-7614-5840-1(9)*, 9780761458401, Two Lions) Amazon Publishing.

Thomson, Bill. Fossil, 0 vols. Thomson, Bill. 2013. (ENG.). 40p. (J). (gr. k-3). 17.99 *(978-1-4778-4700-8(6)*, 9781477847008, Two Lions) Amazon Publishing.

Thomson, E. Gertrude, jt. illus. see Tenniel, John.

Thomson, E. Gertrude, jt. illus. see Tenniel, Sir John.

Thomson, Regan. The Boy in Number Four. Kootstra, Kara. 2014. (ENG.). 32p. (J). (gr. k-3). 14.99 *(978-0-670-06713-8(X)*, Puffin Canada) PRH Canada Young Readers CAN. Dist: Penguin Random Hse. LLC.

Thoraval, Carly & Buchanan, Jessie. The Mystical Noise, 1 vol. Belanger, Madeleine. 2010. 40p. 24.95 *(978-1-4512-9062-2(4))* PublishAmerica, Inc.

Thorgeirsson, Sigmundur. Inuit Games: English Edition. Johnston, Thomas Anguti. ed. 2020. (Nunavummi Ser.). (ENG.). 24p. (J). 18.95 ***(978-1-77450-175-7(9))*** Inhabit Education CAN. Dist: Consortium Bk. Sales & Distribution.

Thorgeirsson, Sigmundur, jt. illus. see Lawrence, Margaret.

Thorn, Shawn. Don't Tease Mr. Beeze. Thorn, Shawn. Coia, Vincenzo, ed. 2017. (ENG.). (J). *(978-1-5255-1587-3(X))*; pap. *(978-1-5255-1588-0(8))* FriesenPress.

Thornborrow, Nick. Brain Quest Workbook: Grade 6. Walker, Persephone. 2015. (Brain Quest Workbooks Ser.). (ENG.). 320p. (J). (gr. 6-6). pap. 12.95 *(978-0-7611-8243-6(8)*, 18243) Workman Publishing Co., Inc.

—Stories of the Saints: Bold & Inspiring Tales of Adventure, Grace, & Courage. Wallace, Carey. 2020. (ENG.). 232p. (J). (gr. 2-8). 24.95 *(978-0-7611-9327-2(8)*, 19327) Workman Publishing Co., Inc.

Thornburgh, Rebecca. The Blast off Kid: Number Sense: Place Value. Driscoll, Laura. 2006. (Math Matters ® Ser.). (ENG.). 32p. (J). (gr. k-2). pap. 5.95 *(978-1-57565-130-9(0))* Astra Publishing Hse.

—Count on Pablo: Counting & Skip Counting. deRubertis, Barbara. 2006. (Math Matters ® Ser.). (ENG.). 32p. (J). (gr. k-2). pap. 5.95 *(978-1-57565-090-6(8))* Astra Publishing Hse.

—Cuenta con Pablo (Count on Pablo) Counting & Skip Counting. deRubertis, Barbara. 2006. (Math Matters en Español Ser.). (SPA.). 32p. (J). (gr. k-2). pap. 5.95 *(978-1-57565-151-4(3))* Astra Publishing Hse.

—Frosty the Snowman Sticker Book. Rollins, Jack & Nelson, Steve. 2012. 24p. (J). 5.99 *(978-0-8249-5646-2(X)*, Ideal Pubns.) Worthy Publishing.

—My First Book. Moncure, Jane Belk. 2018. (Jane Belk Moncure's Sound Box Bks.). (ENG.). 32p. (J). (gr. -1-2).

27.07 *(978-1-5038-2302-0(4)*, 212157); 14.21 *(978-1-5038-3124-7(8)*, 212971) Child's World, Inc., The.
—My Sound Parade. Moncure, Jane Belk. 2018. (Jane Belk Moncure's Sound Box Bks.). (ENG.). 32p. (J). (gr. -1-2). 27.07 *(978-1-5038-2303-7(2)*, 212158); 14.21 *(978-1-5038-3125-4(6)*, 212996) Child's World, Inc., The.
—Picture Book & Library Lessons. Hopkins, Jackie Mims. 2004. 32p. (gr. -1-2). 16.95 *(978-1-932146-27-1(X)*, K67-39703, Upstart Bks.) Highsmith Inc.
—El Problema de 100 Libras (the 100-Pound Problem) Weight. Dussling, Jennifer. 2006. (Math Matters en Español Ser.). (SPA.). 32p. (J). (gr. k-2). pap. 5.95 *(978-1-57565-154-5(8))* Astra Publishing Hse.
—The Story of Adam & Eve. Pingry, Patricia A. 2003. (ENG.). 24p. (J). bds. 6.95 *(978-0-8249-4229-8(9)*, Ideal Pubns.) Worthy Publishing.
—Take a Walk, Johnny. Hillert, Margaret. 2016. (BeginningtoRead Ser.). (ENG.). 32p. (J). (gr. -1-2). pap. 11.94 *(978-1-60357-946-9(X))*; (gr. 1-2). 22.60 *(978-1-59953-805-1(9))* Norwood Hse. Pr.
—Which Way, Wendy? Map Symbols. Redbank, Tennant. 2006. (Social Studies Connects ® Ser.). (ENG.). 32p. (J). (gr. 1-3). pap. 5.95 *(978-1-57565-147-7(5))* Astra Publishing Hse.
—The 100-Pound Problem: Weight. Dussling, Jennifer. 2006. (Math Matters ® Ser.). (ENG.). 32p. (J). (gr. k-2). pap. 5.95 *(978-1-57565-095-1(9))* Astra Publishing Hse.
Thornburgh, Rebecca McKillip. El Chico del Despegue. Driscoll, Laura. Ramirez, Alma, tr. from ENG. 2009. (Math Matters en Espanol Ser.). (SPA.). 32p. (J). (gr. k-2). pap. 5.95 *(978-1-57565-267-2(6))* Astra Publishing Hse.
—The Little Land. Stevenson, Robert Louis. 2011. (Poetry for Children Ser.). (ENG.). 24p. (J). (gr. k-3). 27.07 *(978-1-60973-153-3(0)*, 201184) Child's World, Inc., The.
—Search for the Hidden Garden: A Discovery with Saint Thérèse. Smith, Sherry Weaver. 2016. 128p. (J). pap. 9.95 *(978-0-8198-9050-4(2))* Pauline Bks. & Media.
—The Shelf Elf. Hopkins, Jackie Mims. 2004. (J). (gr. k-3). 17.95 *(978-1-932146-16-5(4)*, 1237659) Highsmith Inc.
—The Shelf Elf Helps Out. Hopkins, Jackie Mims. 2006. (J). *(978-1-932146-45-5(8)*, Upstart Bks.) Highsmith Inc.
Thorne, Jenny. Alice Through the Needle's Eye: The Further Adventures of Lewis Carroll's Alice. Adair, Gilbert. 4th ed. 2012. 150p. pap. *(978-1-78201-000-5(9))* Evertype.
—A Child's Treasury of Classic Stories: Charles Dickens, William Shakespeare, Oscar Wilde. Baxter, Nicola. 2012. 240p. (J). (gr. 2-7). 18.99 *(978-1-84322-948-3(X))* Anness Publishing GBR. Dist: National Bk. Network.
—Classic Stories: Charles Dickens, William Shakespeare & Oscar Wilde - A Treasury for Children. Baxter, Nicola, ed. 2015. 240p. 16.99 *(978-0-85723-756-9(X)*, Armadillo) Anness Publishing GBR. Dist: National Bk. Network.
—The Jungle Book. Kipling, Rudyard. 2014. 48p. (J). (gr. k-5). pap. 7.99 *(978-1-84322-882-0(3)*, Armadillo) Anness Publishing GBR. Dist: National Bk. Network.
—The Jungle Book. 2016. 24p. pap. 7.99 *(978-1-86147-814-6(3)*, Armadillo) Anness Publishing GBR. Dist: National Bk. Network.
—Llygoden y Nadolig. Jeffs, Stephanie. Wyn, Delyth, tr. from ENG. 2005. (WEL.). 28p. *(978-1-85994-497-4(3))* Cyhoeddiadau'r Gair.
—A Midsummer Night's Dream & Other Classic Tales of the Plays: Six Illustrated Stories from Shakespeare. Baxter, Nicola, ed. 2015. 80p. pap. 9.99 *(978-1-86147-466-7(0)*, Armadillo) Anness Publishing GBR. Dist: National Bk. Network.
—Oliver Twist & Other Classic Tales. Dickens, Charles. 2015. 80p. (J). (gr. -1-12). pap. 9.99 *(978-1-86147-408-7(3)*, Armadillo) Anness Publishing GBR. Dist: National Bk. Network.
—The Selfish Giant & Other Classic Tales. Wilde, Oscar. 2014. 96p. (J). (gr. k-5). pap. 9.99 *(978-1-86147-403-2(2)*, Armadillo) Anness Publishing GBR. Dist: National Bk. Network.
Thorne, Sean. When Do You Grow? Captain, Tamira. 2003. (J). pap. 6.95 *(978-0-9742288-0-8(X))* Stories From Four Publishing Co.
Thorne-Thomsen, Kathleen. A Shaker's Dozen: Counting Book. Thorne-Thomsen, Kathleen. Rocheleau, Paul, photos by. 2003. 27p. (J). (gr. k-13). reprint ed. 16.00 *(978-0-7567-9041-7(7))* DIANE Publishing Co.
Thornhill, Jan. The Wildlife ABC: A Nature Alphabet Book. Thornhill, Jan. 2012. (ENG.). 32p. (J). (gr. -1-2). pap. 7.95 *(978-1-926973-08-1(9)*, Owlkids) Owlkids Bks. Inc. CAN. Dist: Publishers Group West (PGW).
Thornley, Blair. Why We Are in Need of Tails. Tillmanns, Maria Davenza. 2020. (ENG.). 36p. (J). (gr. 1-6). ***(978-1-77180-390-8(8))***; pap. ***(978-1-77180-372-4(X))*** Iguana Bks.
Thornton, Barbara. Classroom Times: Charactoons & Rhymes. Stolz, Donald R. 2011. 266p. 76.95 *(978-1-60976-951-2(1)*, Strategic Bk. Publishing) Strategic Book Publishing & Rights Agency (SBPRA).
Thornton, Christine. Heading to the Wedding: You're Invited to Join Patrick & Evie on the Great Adventure of Becoming (Almost) Perfect Guests. Shacter, Sara F. 2006. (ENG.). 32p. (J). (gr. -1-3). 18.95 *(978-1-933176-05-5(9))* Red Rock Pr., Inc.
Thornton, Peter J. Everybody Brings Noodles. Dooley, Norah. 40p. (J). 2005. (ENG.). (gr. k-3). pap. 7.99 *(978-1-57505-916-7(9)*, First Avenue Editions); 2003. (gr. -1-3). 15.95 *(978-0-87614-455-8(5)*, Carolrhoda Bks.) Lerner Publishing Group.
—Everybody Cooks Rice. Dooley, Norah. 2015. 32p. pap. 7.00 *(978-1-61003-603-0(4))* Center for the Collaborative Classroom.
—Everybody Serves Soup. Dooley, Norah. 2004. (Picture Bks.). 40p. (J). (gr. -1-3). 15.95 *(978-1-57505-422-3(1))*; (ENG.). (gr. k-3). per. 7.99 *(978-1-57505-791-0(3)*, First Avenue Editions) Lerner Publishing Group.
Thornton, Susan Ann. The Adventures of Baby Cat in Cherry Grove: Finding Faith. Thornton, Susan Ann. Steffen, Tim. 2007. 50p. (J). per. 12.00 *(978-0-9779518-1-9(2))* Cardinal Pr.
—The Golden Dragonfly: The Adventures of Baby Cat in Cherry Grove. Thornton, Susan Ann. Steffen, Tim. 2009. 76p. pap. 8.95 *(978-1-4401-4804-0(X))* iUniverse, Inc.
Thorp, Cameron. Beat the Clock Sports. Miller, Ray et al. 2007. 48p. (J). *(978-0-439-02189-0(8))* Scholastic, Inc.
—Mwangi: A Young African Boy's Journey of Faith. Ritsi, Renee. 2006. 32p. (J). 17.95 *(978-1-888212-67-9(5))* Ancient Faith Publishing.
Thorpe, Darell & Thorpe, James. Unchained Dragon: & the Legend of the Wandering Prophetess, Christkindl, That Unchained & Changed Him. Thorpe, Darell. 2018. (ENG.). 102p. (J). pap. 29.99 *(978-1-7913-0797-4(3))* Independently Published.
Thorpe, Darell & Thorpe, James Eldon. Unchained Dragon: & the Legend of the Wandering Prophetess, Christkindl, That Unchained & Changed Him. Thorpe, Darell. 2018. (1 Ser.: Vol. 1). (ENG.). 100p. (J). pap. 39.99 *(978-1-7916-8660-4(5))* Independently Published.
Thorpe, Del. Space on Earth. Kanani, Sheila. 2019. 128p. (J). pap. 11.00 *(978-1-84688-455-9(1)*, 900210530) Alma Bks. GBR. Dist: Macmillan.
Thorpe, James, jt. illus. see Thorpe, Darell.
Thorpe, James Eldon, jt. illus. see Thorpe, Darell.
Thorpe, McKenzie. The Adventures of Finn & Jj: Spell Slingers. Helein, Collin Matthew. 2019. (Adventures of Finn & Jj Ser.: Vol. 2). (ENG.). 36p. (J). (gr. -1-2). pap. 9.95 *(978-1-9877-2841-5(6))* CreateSpace Independent Publishing Platform.
Thorpe, Nicholas. Don't Call Me Turtle. Powers, Elaine A. 2017. (ENG.). (J). 19.95 *(978-0-9991669-3-2(X))* Powers, Elaine A.
Thrall, Gordon & Heflin, Jenifer. Puertas Abiertas Student Workbook Level 1: Open Doors to Spanish. 2003. Orig. Title: Puertas Abiertas. 212p. (J). pap., wbk. ed. 15.00 *(978-0-9723341-1-2(4))* Heflin & Thrall Language Pubns., Inc.
Thrash, Maggie. Honor Girl: A Graphic Memoir. Thrash, Maggie. 272p. (YA). (gr. 9). 2017. pap. 14.99 *(978-0-7636-8755-7(3))*; 2015. 19.99 *(978-0-7636-7382-6(X))* Candlewick Pr.
—Lost Soul, Be at Peace. Thrash, Maggie. 192p. (YA). (gr. 9). 2020. pap. 12.99 *(978-1-5362-1315-7(2))*; 2018. 18.99 *(978-0-7636-9419-7(3))* Candlewick Pr.
Thrasher, Brian. Wandering Sam. Bowlin, Serina. 2011. 20p. pap. 9.97 *(978-1-61204-280-0(5)*, Eloquent Bks.) Strategic Book Publishing & Rights Agency (SBPRA).
Three-Thirty, Inc. A Bug's Life. Bazaldua, Barbara. 2020. (Disney & Pixar Movies Ser.). (ENG.). 48p. (J). (gr. 2-6). lib. bdg. 28.50 ***(978-1-5321-4545-2(4)***, 35192, Graphic Novels) Spotlight.
Throckmorton, Sylvestra, et al. Star Baby. Throckmorton, Sylvestra. 2006. (ENG & RAJ.). 16p. (J). 14.95 *(978-0-9761723-1-4(3))* Greene, A.S. & Co.
Thuillier, Eleonore. The Wolf Who Discovered the Museum. Lallemand, Orianne. 2019. (Wolf Who ... Ser.). 32p. (J). 14.95 *(978-2-7338-6740-2(7))* Auzou, Philippe Editions FRA. Dist: Consortium Bk. Sales & Distribution.
—The Wolf Who Learned Self-Control. Lallemand, Orianne. 2018. (Wolf Who ... Ser.). 32p. (J). 14.95 *(978-2-7338-6147-9(6))* Auzou, Philippe Editions FRA. Dist: Consortium Bk. Sales & Distribution.
—The Wolf Who Visited the Land of Fairy Tales. Lallemand, Orianne. 2018. (Wolf Who ... Ser.). 32p. (J). 14.95 *(978-2-7338-5962-9(5))* Auzou, Philippe Editions FRA. Dist: Consortium Bk. Sales & Distribution.
Thuillier, Eléonore. The Wolf Who Was Looking for Love. Lallemand, Orianne. 2017. (Wolf Who ... Ser.). (ENG.). 32p. (J). (gr. -1). 14.95 *(978-2-7338-5244-6(2))* Auzou, Philippe Editions FRA. Dist: Consortium Bk. Sales & Distribution.
Thumann, Robin K. Peaceful Thoughts: An Interactive Journey in Positive Thinking for Children & Their Parents. Thumann, Robin K. 2003. 44p. (J). (gr. -1-4). 19.95 *(978-0-9725118-0-3(6))* Peaceful Thoughts Pr.
Thummler, Brenna. Anne of Green Gables: A Graphic Novel. Marsden, Mariah. 2017. (ENG.). (J). (gr. 2-6). 39.99 *(978-1-4494-9454-4(4))* Andrews McMeel Publishing.
—Anne of Green Gables: A Graphic Novel. Marsden, Mariah. Phipps, Kendra & Kuster, Erika, eds. 2017. (ENG.). 232p. (J). pap. 10.99 *(978-1-4494-7960-2(X))* Andrews McMeel Publishing.
Thunder, Jonathan. Bowwow Powwow. Child, Brenda J. Jourdain, Gordon, tr. 2018. (ENG.). 32p. (J). 16.95 *(978-1-68134-077-7(1))* Minnesota Historical Society Pr.
Thurlby, Paul. Paul Thurlby's Alphabet. Thurlby, Paul. 2011. (ENG.). 64p. (J). (gr. -1-2). 16.99 *(978-0-7636-5565-5(1)*, Templar) Candlewick Pr.
—Paul Thurlby's Wildlife. Thurlby, Paul. 2013. (ENG.). 32p. (J). (gr. k-4). 17.99 *(978-0-7636-6563-0(0)*, Templar) Candlewick Pr.
Thurman, Mark. Alien Invaders: Species That Threaten Our World. Drake, Jane & Love, Ann. (ENG.). 56p. (J). (gr. 4-7). 2013. pap. 8.95 *(978-1-77049-512-8(6))*; 2008. 19.95 *(978-0-88776-798-2(2))* Tundra Bks. CAN. (Tundra Bks.). Dist: Penguin Random Hse. LLC.
—Carrie Loses Her Nerve, 1 vol. Choyce, Lesley. 2003. (Formac First Novels Ser.: 26). (ENG.). 64p. (J). (gr. 1-5). 4.95 *(978-0-88780-591-2(4)*, 591); 14.95 *(978-0-88780-592-9(2)*, 592) Formac Publishing Co., Ltd. CAN. Dist: Formac Lorimer Bks. Ltd.
—Carrie's Camping Adventure, 1 vol. Choyce, Lesley. 2016. (Formac First Novels Ser.: 17). (ENG.). 64p. (J). (gr. 1-5). 5.95 *(978-0-88780-534-9(5)*, 5b9b8a1b-d27d-46f5-9b0d-9193642b4ebb) Formac Publishing Co., Ltd. CAN. Dist: Lerner Publishing Group.
—Franny & the Music Girl, 1 vol. Hearn, Emily. 2005. (ENG.). 24p. (J). (gr. 1-3). pap. 4.95 *(978-0-929005-03-4(1))* Second Story Pr. CAN. Dist: Orca Bk. Pubs. USA.
—Snow Amazing: Cool Facts & Warm Tales. Drake, Jane & Love, Ann. 2004. 80p. (J). (gr. 4-7). 19.95 *(978-0-88776-670-1(6)*, Tundra Bks.) Tundra Bks. CAN. Dist: Penguin Random Hse. LLC.
Thurn, David Ryan, jt. illus. see Thurn, Gwen.
Thurn, Gwen & Thurn, David Ryan. Hong Kong Kitty. Crotty, Martha. 2005. (J). per. 14.00 *(978-0-9766017-0-8(2))* Ironcreek Pr.
Thuysbaert, Pat. Lady the LadyBug Dyslexic Edition: Dyslexic Font. Thuysbaert, Emily. 2020. (ENG.). 30p. (J). (gr. k-6). 19.99 ***(978-1-64372-546-8(7))***; pap. 15.99 ***(978-1-64372-547-5(5))*** MacLaren-Cochrane Publishing, Inc.
—Mia - My Incredible Adventures on the Titanic Dyslexic Edition: Dyslexic Font. Thuysbaert, Emily. 2020. (ENG.). 34p. (J). (gr. k-6). 19.99 ***(978-1-64372-548-2(3))*** MacLaren-Cochrane Publishing, Inc.
—Mia - My Incredible Adventures on the Titanic Dyslexic Edition: Dyslexic Font. Thuysbaert, Emily. 2020. (ENG.). 34p. (J). (gr. k-6). pap. 15.99 ***(978-1-64372-549-9(1))*** MacLaren-Cochrane Publishing, Inc.
Thymer, Olman. Tumblegum. Hamster, Uncle. 2019. (Callers Ser.: Vol. 2). (ENG.). 174p. (J). pap. 8.99 ***(978-1-6893-6938-1(8))*** Independently Published.
Thyssen, Emma. I Am Never Bored: the Best Ever Craft & Activity Book for Kids: 100 Great Ideas for Kids to Do When There Is Nothing to Do. Devos, Sarah. 2018. (ENG.). 144p. (J). (gr. k-5). pap. 15.99 *(978-1-63159-468-7(0)*, Quarry Bks.) Quarto Publishing Group USA.
Tian, Celia. Use Your Body for God. Penny, Kristy. 2018. (ENG.). 28p. (J). 15.99 *(978-1-9994101-1-7(4))*; pap. 8.99 *(978-1-9994101-0-0(6))* Kris.
Tian, Elli. Silly nursery Rhymes. Tian, Elli. 2007. 12p. (J). 9.49 *(978-0-9798611-5-4(2))* Byte Me! Inc.
Tian, Iris. 5-Minute Amazing Animal Stories. Howden, Sarah. 2019. (ENG.). 176p. (J). (gr. -1-2). 16.99 *(978-1-4434-5941-9(0)*, Collins) HarperCollins Pubs.
Tibbles, Jean-Paul. The Cry of the Loon: A Samantha Mystery. Steiner, Barbara. 2006. (ENG.). 192p. (gr. 4-18). 10.95 *(978-1-59369-479-1(2))* American Girl Publishing, Inc.
—Josefina Story Collection. Tripp, Valerie. 2008. 420p. pap. 29.95 *(978-1-59369-453-1(9))* American Girl Publishing, Inc.
—The Tangled Web: A Julie Mystery. Reiss, Kathryn. 2009. (ENG.). 168p. (J). (gr. 4-18). 10.95 *(978-1-59369-475-3(X))*; pap. 21.19 *(978-1-59369-476-0(8))* American Girl Publishing, Inc.
Tibo, Gilles. Pikolo's Night Voyage. Filion, Pierre. 2004. 28p. (J). (gr. k-4). reprint ed. 16.00 *(978-0-7567-7818-7(2))* DIANE Publishing Co.
Tiburcio, Tom. Houdini Weenie: Le Chien du Mystere. Jansen, Mike. 2019. (ENG.). 38p. (J). (gr. k-3). 17.99 *(978-0-578-41166-8(0))* Jansen, Michael.
Tickle, Jack. The Crunching Munching Caterpillar. Cain, Sheridan. (J). 2013. (ENG.). 20p. (gr. -1). 9.99 *(978-1-58925-616-3(6))*; 2005. 18p. bds. 6.95 *(978-1-58925-757-3(X))* Tiger Tales.
—Crunching Munching Caterpillar. Cain, Sheridan. 2003. 32p. (J). tchr. ed. 15.95 *(978-1-58925-025-3(7))* Tiger Tales.
—The Crunching Munching Caterpillar Pop-up. Cain, Sheridan. 2006. 16p. (J). 15.95 *(978-1-58925-771-9(5))* Tiger Tales.
—Itsy Bitsy Spider. Chapman, Keith. (Tiger Tales Ser.). (J). 2008. 24p. (gr. -1-2). pap. 6.95 *(978-1-58925-407-7(4))*; 2006. 32p. 15.95 *(978-1-58925-050-5(9))* Tiger Tales.
—The Teeny Weeny Tadpole. Cain, Sheridan. 2005. 32p. (J). 15.95 *(978-1-58925-047-5(8))* Tiger Tales.
—The Very Greedy Bee. Smallman, Steve. 2010. (ENG.). 32p. (J). (gr. -1-2). pap. 7.95 *(978-1-58925-422-0(8))* Tiger Tales.
—The Very Lazy Ladybug. Finn, Isobel. 2005. 16p. (J). bds. 6.95 *(978-1-58925-758-0(8))* Tiger Tales.
—The Very Sleepy Sloth. Murray, Andrew. 2020. (Favorite Stories Ser.). (ENG.). 32p. (J). (gr. -1-2). 23.99 *(978-1-68010-196-6(X))* Tiger Tales.
—Yummy Yummy! Food for My Tummy. Lloyd, Sam R. 2004. 32p. (J). tchr. ed. 15.95 *(978-1-58925-035-2(4))* Tiger Tales.
Tickle, Jack. Fish on a Dish! Tickle, Jack. 2015. (ENG.). 24p. (J). (gr. -1-2). 16.99 *(978-1-58925-191-5(1))* Tiger Tales.
—Look Out, Ladybug! Tickle, Jack. 2013. (ENG.). 32p. (J). (gr. -1-2). 12.95 *(978-1-58925-128-1(8))* Tiger Tales.
Tickle, Jack. The Very Sleepy Sloth. Tickle, Jack, tr. Murray, Andrew. 2003. 32p. (J). tchr. ed. 15.95 *(978-1-58925-033-8(8))* Tiger Tales.
Tickle, Jessica Courtney. Cinderella. Jones, Ursula. 2020. 32p. (J). (gr. -1-k). pap. 10.99 ***(978-1-4083-4570-2(6)***, Orchard Bks.) Hachette Children's Group GBR. Dist: Hachette Bk. Group.
—The Story Orchestra: Carnival of the Animals: Press the Note to Hear Saint-Saëns' Music. Flint, Katy. 2020. (Story Orchestra Ser.). (ENG.). 24p. (J). (gr. -1-2). 24.99 ***(978-0-7112-4952-3(0)***, 329689, Frances Lincoln Children's Bks.) Quarto Publishing Group UK GBR. Dist: Hachette Bk. Group.
Tickle, Jessica Courtney. The Story Orchestra: Swan Lake: Press the Note to Hear Tchaikovsky's Music. Flint, Katy. ed. 2019. (Story Orchestra Ser.). (ENG.). 24p. (J). (gr. k-3). 24.99 *(978-0-7112-4150-3(3)*, 322634, Frances Lincoln Children's Bks.) Quarto Publishing Group UK GBR. Dist: Hachette UK Distribution.
—The Story Orchestra: the Sleeping Beauty: Press the Note to Hear Tchaikovsky's Music. 2018. (Story Orchestra Ser.). (ENG.). 24p. (J). (gr. -1-2). 24.99 *(978-1-78603-093-1(4)*, 301239, Frances Lincoln Children's Bks.) Quarto Publishing Group UK GBR. Dist: Hachette Bk. Group.
Tidwell, Jeral, jt. illus. see Simko, Joe.
Tidwell, Susan. Three Virtuous Brothers: A Story of the Three Acts of Goodness. Tidwell, Susan. 2012. 47p. (J). pap. 9.95 *(978-1-932293-63-0(9))* Buddha's Light Publications USA Corp.
Tiegreen, Alan. Cookies & Crutches. Delton, Judy & Pee Wee Scouts Staff. 2007. (PeeWee Scouts Ser.: No. 1). 69p. (J). (gr. k-3). 17.44 *(978-0-440-40010-3(4))* Random House Publishing Group.
—Rosy Noses, Freezing Toes. Delton, Judy. 2008. (PeeWee Scouts Ser.: No. 13). (ENG.). 86p. (J). (gr. k-3). 17.44 *(978-0-440-40384-5(7))* Random House Publishing Group.
—Yours till Banana Splits: 201 Autograph Rhymes. Cole, Joanna & Calmenson, Stephanie. 2004. 64p. (J). (gr. 6-8). reprint ed. pap. 7.00 *(978-0-7567-7349-6(0))* DIANE Publishing Co.
Tiegren, Alan. Tons of Fun: Over 300 Action Rhymes, Old & New Riddles, Tongue Twisters, & Play Rhymes. Cole, Joanna & Calmenson, Stephanie, eds. 2004. 229p. (J). (gr. k-4). reprint ed. pap. 15.00 *(978-0-7567-8222-1(8))* DIANE Publishing Co.
Tien, Wai. The Land of Os: John Ramsay. Robertson, David A. 2014. (Tales from Big Spirit Ser.: 6). (ENG.). 30p. (J). (gr. 4-6). pap. *(978-1-55379-491-2(5)*, 71d193fb-9d6f-4711-9ca7-63e7716b3ed2, HighWater Pr.) Portage & Main Pr.
—The Peacemaker: Thanadelthur. Robertson, David A. 2014. (Tales from Big Spirit Ser.: 6). (ENG.). 30p. (J). (gr. 4-6). pap. *(978-1-55379-479-0(6)*, 51f7764c-c947-4547-8ce4-63887e0f4e03, HighWater Pr.) Portage & Main Pr.
Tierney, Jim. The Boundless. Oppel, Kenneth. 2014. (ENG.). 336p. (J). (gr. 3-7). 17.99 *(978-1-4424-7288-4(X)*, Simon & Schuster Bks. For Young Readers) Simon & Schuster Bks. For Young Readers.
Tierney, Jim. The Night Country: A Hazel Wood Novel. Albert, Melissa. 2020. ***(978-1-250-25813-7(8))*** St. Martin's Pr.
Tierney, Tiffany N. Scoodles Digs for Buried Treasure. Plettner, Edith D. 2019. (Scoodles Digs for Buried Treasure Scoodles the Pup Ser.: Vol. 2). (ENG.). 40p. (J). pap. 10.00 *(978-1-9877-8844-0(3))* CreateSpace Independent Publishing Platform.
—Scoodles Falls in Love. Plettner, Edith D. 2019. (Scoodles Falls in Love Scoodles the Pup Ser.: Vol. 7). (ENG.). 34p. (J). pap. 10.00 *(978-1-9876-5572-8(9))* CreateSpace Independent Publishing Platform.
Tierney, Tom. Life's a Drag! Paper Dolls. 2012. (Dover Celebrity Paper Dolls Ser.). (ENG.). 32p. (gr. 7-8). pap. 9.99 *(978-0-486-48313-9(4))* Dover Pubns., Inc.
Tietjens, Harold, photos by. Cybertronian Transformers Index. Tietjens, Harold. 2003. (ENG., 128p. (YA). pap. 29.95 *(978-0-9663588-3-4(X)*, 10a07fd0-715f-4de3-a12c-ebb183c329bf) Antarctic Pr., Inc.
—Cybertronian TRG Unofficial Transformers Guide to Beast Wars. Tietjens, Harold. Diin, Douglas. 2003. (ENG., 96p. (YA). pap. 24.95 *(978-0-9663588-8-9(0)*, a0b029c6-b02d-4785-a902-43de1312a111) Antarctic Pr., Inc.
Tiffany, Sean. Backup Goalie, 1 vol. Maddox, Jake. 2008. (Jake Maddox Sports Stories Ser.). (ENG.). 72p. (J). (gr. 3-6). pap. 5.95 *(978-1-4342-0517-9(7))*; lib. bdg. 25.32 *(978-1-4342-0467-7(7))* Capstone. (Stone Arch Bks.).
—Batter Up!, 1 vol. Maddox, Jake. 2008. (Jake Maddox Sports Stories Ser.). (ENG.). 72p. (J). (gr. 3-6). lib. bdg. 25.32 *(978-1-4342-0465-3(0))*; per. 5.95 *(978-1-4342-0515-5(0))* Capstone. (Stone Arch Bks.).
—Behind the Plate, 1 vol. Maddox, Jake. 2012. (Jake Maddox Sports Stories Ser.). (ENG.). 72p. (J). (gr. 3-6). pap. 5.95 *(978-1-4342-4205-1(6))*; lib. bdg. 25.32 *(978-1-4342-4010-1(X))* Capstone. (Stone Arch Bks.).
—Blizzard! A Survive! Story, 1 vol. Maddox, Jake. 2009. (Jake Maddox Sports Stories Ser.). (ENG.). 72p. (J). (gr. 3-6). 25.32 *(978-1-4342-1206-1(8)*, Stone Arch Bks.) Capstone.
—Blueline Breakaway. Maddox, Jake. 2018. (Jake Maddox Sports Stories Ser.). (ENG.). 72p. (J). (gr. 3-6). pap. 5.95 *(978-1-4965-6319-4(0)*, 138058); lib. bdg. 25.32 *(978-1-4965-6317-0(4)*, 138049) Capstone. (Stone Arch Bks.).
—BMX Bully, 1 vol. Suen, Anastasia & Maddox, Jake. 2006. (Jake Maddox Sports Stories Ser.). (ENG.). 72p. (J). (gr. 3-6). pap. 5.95 *(978-1-59889-236-9(3))*; lib. bdg. 25.32 *(978-1-59889-059-4(X))* Capstone. (Stone Arch Bks.).
—BMX Challenge, 1 vol. Maddox, Jake. 2011. (Jake Maddox Sports Stories Ser.). (ENG.). 72p. (J). (gr. 3-6). pap. 5.95 *(978-1-4342-3423-0(1)*, Stone Arch Bks.) Capstone.
—Board Rebel. Maddox, Jake. 2007. (Jake Maddox Sports Stories Ser.). (ENG.). 72p. (J). (gr. 3-6). pap. 5.95 *(978-1-59889-414-1(5))*; lib. bdg. 25.32 *(978-1-59889-319-9(X))* Capstone. (Stone Arch Bks.).
—Cowboy Up, 1 vol. Maddox, Jake. 2011. (Jake Maddox Sports Stories Ser.). (ENG.). 72p. (J). (gr. 3-6). pap. 5.95 *(978-1-4342-3425-4(8))*; lib. bdg. 25.32 *(978-1-4342-2989-2(0))* Capstone. (Stone Arch Bks.).
—Definición por Penales. Maddox, Jake. Heck, Claudia M., tr. 2012. (Jake Maddox en Español Ser.). (SPA.). 72p. (J). (gr. 3-6). 25.32 *(978-1-4342-3814-6(8)*, Stone Arch Bks.) Capstone.
—Diamond Double Play. Maddox, Jake. 2019. (Jake Maddox Sports Stories Ser.). (ENG.). 72p. (J). (gr. 3-6). pap. 5.95 *(978-1-4965-8452-6(X)*, 140977, Stone Arch Bks.) Capstone.
—Diamond Double Play. Pryor, Shawn & Maddox, Jake. 2019. (Jake Maddox Sports Stories Ser.). (ENG.). 72p. (J). (gr. 3-6). 25.32 *(978-1-4965-8329-1(9)*, 140498, Stone Arch Bks.) Capstone.
—Disc Golf Drive, 1 vol. Maddox, Jake. 2009. (Jake Maddox Sports Stories Ser.). (ENG.). 72p. (J). (gr. 3-6). 25.32 *(978-1-4342-1599-4(7)*, Stone Arch Bks.) Capstone.
—Diving off the Edge, 1 vol. Maddox, Jake. 2009. (Jake Maddox Sports Stories Ser.). (ENG.). 72p. (J). (gr. 3-6). lib. bdg. 25.32 *(978-1-4342-1205-4(X)*, Stone Arch Bks.) Capstone.
—Doubles Trouble. Maddox, Jake. 2017. (Jake Maddox Sports Stories Ser.). (ENG.). 72p. (J). (gr. 3-6). lib. bdg. 25.32 *(978-1-4965-4957-0(0)*, 135852, Stone Arch Bks.) Capstone.
—En la línea de Ataque. Maddox, Jake. Heck, Claudia M., tr. 2012. (Jake Maddox en Español Ser.). (SPA.). 72p. (J). (gr. 3-6). 25.32 *(978-1-4342-3813-9(X)*, Stone Arch Bks.) Capstone.
—Face-Off, 1 vol. Maddox, Jake. 2006. (Jake Maddox Sports Stories Ser.). (ENG.). 72p. (J). (gr. 3-6). lib. bdg. 25.32 *(978-1-59889-063-1(8)*, Stone Arch Bks.) Capstone.

T

—Face-Off, 1 vol. Maddox, Jake. 2006. (Jake Maddox Sports Stories Ser.). (ENG.). 72p. (J). (gr. 3-6). pap. 5.95 (978-1-59889-237-6(1), Stone Arch Bks.) Capstone.

—Free Climb. Maddox, Jake. 2008. (Jake Maddox Sports Stories Ser.). (ENG.). 72p. (J). (gr. 3-6). 25.32 (978-1-4342-0784-5(6)); pap. 5.95 (978-1-4342-0880-4(X)) Capstone. (Stone Arch Bks.).

—Free Throw, 1 vol. Maddox, Jake. 2006. (Jake Maddox Sports Stories Ser.). (ENG.). 72p. (J). (gr. 3-6). pap. 5.95 (978-1-59889-238-3(X)); lib. bdg. 25.32 (978-1-59889-060-0(3)) Capstone. (Stone Arch Bks.).

—Geocache Surprise, 1 vol. Maddox, Jake. 2011. (Jake Maddox Sports Stories Ser.). (ENG.). 72p. (J). (gr. 3-6). lib. bdg. 25.32 (978-1-4342-2600-6(X), Stone Arch Bks.) Capstone.

—Go-Kart Rush. Maddox, Jake. 2007. (Jake Maddox Sports Stories Ser.). (ENG.). 72p. (J). (gr. 3-6). pap. 5.95 (978-1-59889-415-8(3), Stone Arch Bks.) Capstone.

—Gridiron Bully, 1 vol. Maddox, Jake. 2009. (Jake Maddox Sports Stories Ser.). (ENG.). 72p. (J). (gr. 3-6). 25.32 (978-1-4342-1201-6(7), Stone Arch Bks.) Capstone.

—Hockey Meltdown, 1 vol. Maddox, Jake. 2011. (Jake Maddox Sports Stories Ser.). (ENG.). 72p. (J). (gr. 3-6). pap. 5.95 (978-1-4342-3426-1(6)); lib. bdg. 25.32 (978-1-4342-2990-8(4)) Capstone. (Stone Arch Bks.).

—Home-Field Football, 1 vol. Maddox, Jake. 2012. (Jake Maddox Sports Stories Ser.). (ENG.). 72p. (J). (gr. 3-6). pap. 5.95 (978-1-4342-4206-8(4)); 25.32 (978-1-4342-4008-8(8)) Capstone. (Stone Arch Bks.).

—Hoop Hotshot, 1 vol. Maddox, Jake. 2009. (Jake Maddox Sports Stories Ser.). (ENG.). 72p. (J). (gr. 3-6). lib. bdg. 25.32 (978-1-4342-1202-3(5), Stone Arch Bks.) Capstone.

—The Hunter's Code. Maddox, Jake. 2008. (Jake Maddox Sports Stories Ser.). (ENG.). 72p. (J). (gr. 3-6). 25.32 (978-1-4342-0782-1(X)); pap. 5.95 (978-1-4342-0878-1(8)) Capstone. (Stone Arch Bks.).

Tiffany, Sean. Jake Maddox Sports Stories. Maddox, Jake. (Jake Maddox Sports Stories Ser.). (ENG.). (J). (gr. 3-6). 2020. 1899.00 **(978-1-4965-9770-0(2)**, 199574); 2020. pap., pap., pap. 345.10 **(978-1-4965-9937-7(3)**, 201374); 2019. pap., pap., pap. 333.20 (978-1-4965-8508-0(9), 29589) Capstone. (Stone Arch Bks.).

Tiffany, Sean. Karate Countdown, 1 vol. Maddox, Jake. 2009. (Jake Maddox Sports Stories Ser.). (ENG.). 72p. (J). (gr. 3-6). lib. bdg. 25.32 (978-1-4342-1200-9(9), Stone Arch Bks.) Capstone.

—Kart Crash, 1 vol. Maddox, Jake. 2008. (Jake Maddox Sports Stories Ser.). (ENG.). 72p. (J). (gr. 3-6). 25.32 (978-1-4342-0777-7(3)); pap. 5.95 (978-1-4342-0873-6(7)) Capstone. (Stone Arch Bks.).

—Lacrosse Attack. Maddox, Jake. 2008. (Jake Maddox Sports Stories Ser.). (ENG.). 72p. (J). (gr. 3-6). 25.32 (978-1-4342-0776-0(5)); pap. 5.95 (978-1-4342-0872-9(9)) Capstone. (Stone Arch Bks.).

—El Lanzador Bajo Presión. Maddox, Jake. Heck, Claudia M., tr. 2012. (Jake Maddox en Español Ser.). (SPA.). 72p. (J). (gr. 3-6). 25.32 (978-1-4342-3815-3(6), Stone Arch Bks.) Capstone.

—Legend of the Lure, 1 vol. Maddox, Jake. 2008. (Jake Maddox Sports Stories Ser.). (ENG.). 72p. (J). (gr. 3-6). 25.32 (978-1-4342-0783-8(8)); pap. 5.95 (978-1-4342-0879-8(6)) Capstone. (Stone Arch Bks.).

—Linebacker Block, 1 vol. Maddox, Jake. 2010. (Team Jake Maddox Sports Stories Ser.). (ENG.). 72p. (J). (gr. 3-6). lib. bdg. 25.32 (978-1-4342-1635-9(7)); pap. 5.95 (978-1-4342-2779-9(0)) Capstone. (Stone Arch Bks.).

—Motocross Double-Cross. Maddox, Jake. 2007. (Jake Maddox Sports Stories Ser.). (ENG.). 72p. (J). (gr. 3-6). pap. 5.95 (978-1-59889-897-2(3)); lib. bdg. 25.32 (978-1-59889-845-3(0)) Capstone. (Stone Arch Bks.).

—Mountain Bike Hero, 1 vol. Maddox, Jake. 2011. (Jake Maddox Sports Stories Ser.). (ENG.). 72p. (J). (gr. 3-6). lib. bdg. 25.32 (978-1-4342-2536-8(4), Stone Arch Bks.) Capstone.

—Mr. Strike Out, 1 vol. Maddox, Jake. 2006. (Jake Maddox Sports Stories Ser.). (ENG.). 72p. (J). (gr. 3-6). 25.32 (978-1-59889-061-7(1), Stone Arch Bks.) Capstone.

—Off the Bench, 1 vol. Maddox, Jake. 2010. (Team Jake Maddox Sports Stories Ser.). (ENG.). 72p. (J). (gr. 3-6). pap. 5.95 (978-1-4342-2278-7(0)); lib. bdg. 25.32 (978-1-4342-1922-0(4)) Capstone. (Stone Arch Bks.).

—On Guard, 1 vol. Maddox, Jake. 2010. (Team Jake Maddox Sports Stories Ser.). (ENG.). 72p. (J). (gr. 3-6). pap. 5.95 (978-1-4342-2279-4(9)); lib. bdg. 25.32 (978-1-4342-1920-6(8)) Capstone. (Stone Arch Bks.).

—On the Line, 1 vol. Maddox, Jake. 2006. (Jake Maddox Sports Stories Ser.). (ENG.). 72p. (J). (gr. 3-6). 25.32 (978-1-59889-062-4(X)); pap. 5.95 (978-1-59889-240-6(1)) Capstone. (Stone Arch Bks.).

—On the Speedway, 1 vol. Maddox, Jake. 2011. (Jake Maddox Sports Stories Ser.). (ENG.). 208p. (J). (gr. 3-6). pap. 7.95 (978-1-4342-3030-0(9), Stone Arch Bks.) Capstone.

—Paintball Blast. Maddox, Jake. 2007. (Jake Maddox Sports Stories Ser.). (ENG.). 72p. (J). (gr. 3-6). pap. 5.95 (978-1-59889-417-2(X)); lib. bdg. 25.32 (978-1-59889-322-9(X)) Capstone. (Stone Arch Bks.).

—Paintball Invasion, 1 vol. Maddox, Jake. 2008. (Jake Maddox Sports Stories Ser.). (ENG.). 72p. (J). (gr. 3-6). lib. bdg. 25.32 (978-1-4342-0466-0(9)); per. 5.95 (978-1-4342-0516-2(9)) Capstone. (Stone Arch Bks.).

—Pick & Roll. Maddox, Jake. 2018. (Jake Maddox Sports Stories Ser.). (ENG.). 72p. (J). (gr. 3-6). pap. 5.95 (978-1-4965-6320-0(4), 138059); lib. bdg. 25.32 (978-1-4965-6318-7(2), 138050) Capstone. (Stone Arch Bks.).

—Pit Crew Crunch, 1 vol. Maddox, Jake. 2009. (Jake Maddox Sports Stories Ser.). (ENG.). 72p. (J). (gr. 3-6). 25.32 (978-1-4342-1600-7(4), Stone Arch Bks.) Capstone.

—Pitcher Pressure, 1 vol. Maddox, Jake. 2009. (Jake Maddox Sports Stories Ser.). (ENG.). 72p. (J). (gr. 3-6). 25.32 (978-1-4342-1596-3(2), Stone Arch Bks.) Capstone.

—Playing Forward. Maddox, Jake. 2010. (Team Jake Maddox Sports Stories Ser.). (ENG.). 72p. (J). (gr. 3-6). pap. 5.95 (978-1-4342-2280-0(2), Stone Arch Bks.) Capstone.

—Playing Forward. Stevens, Eric & Maddox, Jake. 2010. (Jake Maddox Sports Story Ser.). 72p. pap. 0.60 (978-1-4342-3206-9(9), Stone Arch Bks.) Capstone.

—Point Guard Prank, 1 vol. Maddox, Jake. 2012. (Jake Maddox Sports Stories Ser.). (ENG.). 72p. (J). (gr. 3-6). pap. 5.95 (978-1-4342-4207-5(2)); 25.32 (978-1-4342-4009-5(6)) Capstone. (Stone Arch Bks.).

—Punter's Pride. Maddox, Jake. 2017. (Jake Maddox Sports Stories Ser.). (ENG.). 72p. (J). (gr. 3-6). lib. bdg. 25.32 (978-1-4965-4956-3(2), 135851, Stone Arch Bks.) Capstone.

—Quarterback Comeback, 1 vol. Maddox, Jake. 2010. (Team Jake Maddox Sports Stories Ser.). (ENG.). 72p. (J). (gr. 3-6). lib. bdg. 25.32 (978-1-4342-1634-2(9)); pap. 5.95 (978-1-4342-2778-2(2)) Capstone. (Stone Arch Bks.).

—Quarterback Sneak, 1 vol. Maddox, Jake. 2008. (Jake Maddox Sports Stories Ser.). (ENG.). 72p. (J). (gr. 3-6). lib. bdg. 25.32 (978-1-4342-0464-6(2)); per. 5.95 (978-1-4342-0514-8(2)) Capstone. (Stone Arch Bks.).

—Race Car Rival, 1 vol. Maddox, Jake. 2009. (Jake Maddox Sports Stories Ser.). (ENG.). 72p. (J). (gr. 3-6). 25.32 (978-1-4342-1601-4(2), Stone Arch Bks.) Capstone.

—El Rebelde de la Patineta, 1 vol. Maddox, Jake. Heck, Claudia, tr. 2012. (Jake Maddox en Español Ser.). (SPA.). 72p. (J). (gr. 3-6). 25.32 (978-1-4342-3816-0(4), Stone Arch Bks.) Capstone.

—Running Back Dreams, 1 vol. Maddox, Jake. 2010. (Team Jake Maddox Sports Stories Ser.). (ENG.). 72p. (J). (gr. 3-6). lib. bdg. 25.32 (978-1-4342-1637-3(3)); pap. 5.95 (978-1-4342-2781-2(2)) Capstone. (Stone Arch Bks.).

—Shark Attack! Maddox, Jake. 2009. (Jake Maddox Sports Stories Ser.). (ENG.). 72p. (J). (gr. 3-6). 25.32 (978-1-4342-1210-8(6), Stone Arch Bks.) Capstone.

—Shipwreck! Maddox, Jake. 2009. (Jake Maddox Sports Stories Ser.). (ENG.). 72p. (J). (gr. 3-6). 25.32 (978-1-4342-1207-8(6), Stone Arch Bks.) Capstone.

—Skate Park Challenge, 1 vol. Maddox, Jake. 2006. (Jake Maddox Sports Stories Ser.). (ENG.). 72p. (J). (gr. 3-6). 25.32 (978-1-59889-064-8(6), Stone Arch Bks.) Capstone.

—Skateboard Save, 1 vol. Maddox, Jake. 2008. (Jake Maddox Sports Stories Ser.). (ENG.). 72p. (J). (gr. 3-6). pap. 5.95 (978-1-4342-0871-2(0), Stone Arch Bks.) Capstone.

—Skateboard Struggle, 1 vol. Maddox, Jake. 2011. (Jake Maddox Sports Stories Ser.). (ENG.). 72p. (J). (gr. 3-6). pap. 5.95 (978-1-4342-3424-7(X)); lib. bdg. 25.32 (978-1-4342-2987-8(4)) Capstone. (Stone Arch Bks.).

—Skatepark Challenge. Maddox, Jake. 2010. (Jake Maddox Sports Story Ser.). 72p. pap. 0.60 (978-1-4342-3207-6(7), Stone Arch Bks.) Capstone.

—Slam Dunk Shoes, 1 vol. Maddox, Jake. 2007. (Jake Maddox Sports Stories Ser.). (ENG.). 72p. (J). (gr. 3-6). 25.32 (978-1-59889-842-2(6)); per. 5.95 (978-1-59889-894-1(9)) Capstone. (Stone Arch Bks.).

—Snowboard Duel, 1 vol. Maddox, Jake. 2007. (Jake Maddox Sports Stories Ser.). (ENG.). 72p. (J). (gr. 3-6). pap. 5.95 (978-1-59889-895-8(7), Stone Arch Bks.) Capstone.

—Soccer Shootout, 1 vol. Maddox, Jake. 2007. (Jake Maddox Sports Stories Ser.). (ENG.). 72p. (J). (gr. 3-6). 25.32 (978-1-59889-844-6(2)); per. 5.95 (978-1-59889-896-5(5)) Capstone. (Stone Arch Bks.).

—Speed Camp, 1 vol. Maddox, Jake. 2009. (Jake Maddox Sports Stories Ser.). (ENG.). 72p. (J). (gr. 3-6). 25.32 (978-1-4342-1602-1(0), Stone Arch Bks.) Capstone.

—Speed Receiver, 1 vol. Maddox, Jake. 2010. (Team Jake Maddox Sports Stories Ser.). (ENG.). 72p. (J). (gr. 3-6). lib. bdg. 25.32 (978-1-4342-1636-6(5)); pap. 5.95 (978-1-4342-2780-5(4)) Capstone. (Stone Arch Bks.).

—Speedway Switch. Maddox, Jake. 2007. (Jake Maddox Sports Stories Ser.). (ENG.). 72p. (J). (gr. 3-6). pap. 5.95 (978-1-59889-416-5(1)); lib. bdg. 25.32 (978-1-59889-321-2(1)) Capstone. (Stone Arch Bks.).

—Striker Assist, 1 vol. Maddox, Jake. 2012. (Jake Maddox Sports Stories Ser.). (ENG.). 72p. (J). (gr. 3-6). pap. 5.95 (978-1-4342-4208-2(0)); 25.32 (978-1-4342-4011-8(8)) Capstone. (Stone Arch Bks.).

—Takedown. Maddox, Jake. 2008. (Jake Maddox Sports Stories Ser.). (ENG.). 72p. (J). (gr. 3-6). 25.32 (978-1-4342-0774-6(9)); pap. 5.95 (978-1-4342-0870-5(2)) Capstone. (Stone Arch Bks.).

—Tiro Libre, 1 vol. Maddox, Jake. Heck, Claudia M., tr. 2012. (Jake Maddox en Español Ser.). (SPA.). 72p. (J). (gr. 3-6). 25.32 (978-1-4342-3812-2(1), Stone Arch Bks.) Capstone.

—El Tramposo de BMX, 1 vol. Maddox, Jake. Heck, Claudia M., tr. 2012. (Jake Maddox en Español Ser.). (SPA.). 72p. (J). (gr. 3-6). 25.32 (978-1-4342-3817-7(2), Stone Arch Bks.) Capstone.

—Undercover BMX. Maddox, Jake. 2019. (Jake Maddox Sports Stories Ser.). (ENG.). 72p. (J). (gr. 3-6). pap. 5.95 (978-1-4965-8453-3(8), 140978); lib. bdg. 25.32 (978-1-4965-8330-7(2), 140499) Capstone. (Stone Arch Bks.).

—Volcano! A Survive! Story. Maddox, Jake. 2009. (Jake Maddox Sports Stories Ser.). (ENG.). 72p. (J). (gr. 3-6). 25.32 (978-1-4342-1208-5(4), Stone Arch Bks.) Capstone.

—Whitewater Courage, 1 vol. Maddox, Jake. 2011. (Jake Maddox Sports Stories Ser.). (ENG.). 72p. (J). (gr. 3-6). lib. bdg. 25.32 (978-1-4342-2530-6(5), Stone Arch Bks.) Capstone.

—Wild Hike. Maddox, Jake. 2008. (Jake Maddox Sports Stories Ser.). (ENG.). 72p. (J). (gr. 3-6). 25.32 (978-1-4342-0785-2(4)); pap. 5.95 (978-1-4342-0881-1(8)) Capstone. (Stone Arch Bks.).

—Wildcats Slam Dunk, 1 vol. Maddox, Jake. 2010. (Team Jake Maddox Sports Stories Ser.). (ENG.). 208p. (J). (gr. 3-6). pap. 7.95 (978-1-4342-2886-4(X), Stone Arch Bks.) Capstone.

—Win or Lose. Maddox, Jake. 2010. (Team Jake Maddox Sports Stories Ser.). (ENG.). 72p. (J). (gr. 3-6). pap. 5.95 (978-1-4342-2281-7(0), Stone Arch Bks.) Capstone.

—Windsurfing Winner, 1 vol. Maddox, Jake. 2011. (Jake Maddox Sports Stories Ser.). (ENG.). 72p. (J). (gr. 3-6). lib. bdg. 25.32 (978-1-4342-2535-1(6), Stone Arch Bks.) Capstone.

Tiffany, Sean. Mr. Strike Out, 1 vol. Tiffany, Sean. Maddox, Jake. 2006. (Jake Maddox Sports Stories Ser.). (ENG.). 72p. (J). (gr. 3-6). per. 5.95 (978-1-59889-239-0(8), Stone Arch Bks.) Capstone.

Tiger Tales. Funny Faces Sticker Fun! Tiger Tales. 2014. (ENG.). 14p. (J). (gr. -1-k). 3.99 (978-1-58925-304-9(3)); 3.99 (978-1-58925-305-6(1)) Tiger Tales.

Tigga, Amrit. Bentley. Clouser, Lisa M. 2016. (ENG.). (J). (gr. k-3). pap. 6.99 (978-0-9977202-0-4(4)) Clouser, Lisa M.

Tigue, Terry & Turner, Diane. The Gift: A Woodsong Story. Mundy, Dawn. 2003. (J). lib. bdg. (978-1-932139-16-7(8)) DEMDACO.

Tiitinen, Nikolai. Drops of Life. Tiitinen, Esko-Pekka. Claret Pyrhonen, Emma, tr. 2012. (ENG.). 24p. (J). (gr. k-2). 14.95 (978-84-15241-31-7(3)) Cuento de Luz SL ESP. Dist: Publishers Group West (PGW).

Tiki Papier, Tiki. How to Be a Fashion Designer. Ware, Lesley. 2018. (Careers for Kids Ser.). (ENG.). 96p. (J). (gr. 2-4). pap. 16.99 (978-1-4654-6761-4(0), DK Children) Dorling Kindersley Publishing, Inc.

Tikulin, Tomislav. Asylum: Refugees of Mars. Collins, A. L. 2018. (Redworld Ser.). (ENG.). 128p. (J). (gr. 3-8). lib. bdg. 25.99 (978-1-4965-5886-2(3), 137024, Stone Arch Bks.) Capstone.

—Homestead: A New Life on Mars. Collins, A. L. 2017. (Redworld Ser.). (ENG.). 128p. (J). (gr. 3-8). lib. bdg. 25.99 (978-1-4965-4819-1(1), 135341, Stone Arch Bks.) Capstone.

—Legacy: Relics of Mars. Collins, A. L. 2017. (Redworld Ser.). (ENG.). 128p. (J). (gr. 3-8). lib. bdg. 25.99 (978-1-4965-4822-1(1), 135344, Stone Arch Bks.) Capstone.

—Outcry: Defenders of Mars. Collins, A. L. 2018. (Redworld Ser.). (ENG.). 128p. (J). (gr. 3-8). lib. bdg. 25.99 (978-1-4965-5887-9(1), 137025, Stone Arch Bks.) Capstone.

—Raiders: Water Thieves of Mars. Collins, A. L. 2017. (Redworld Ser.). (ENG.). 128p. (J). (gr. 3-8). lib. bdg. 25.99 (978-1-4965-4820-7(5), 135342, Stone Arch Bks.) Capstone.

—Redworld, 6 vols. Collins, A. L. (Redworld Ser.). (ENG.). 128p. (J). (gr. 3-8). 2018. 155.94 (978-1-4965-5892-3(8), 27538); 2017. 103.96 (978-1-4965-4839-9(6), 26585) Capstone. (Stone Arch Bks.).

—Redworld: Year One. Collins, A. L. ed. 2018. (Redworld Ser.). (ENG.). 320p. (J). (gr. 3-8). pap. 8.95 (978-1-62370-986-0(5), 137317, Capstone Young Readers) Capstone.

—Tharsis City: The Wonder of Mars. Collins, A. L. 2017. (Redworld Ser.). (ENG.). 128p. (J). (gr. 3-8). lib. bdg. 25.99 (978-1-4965-4821-4(3), 135343, Stone Arch Bks.) Capstone.

Tilak, Brian, jt. illus. see Moore, Sasha.

Tilde, photos by. How Does a Seed Grow? A Book with Foldout Pages. Kim, Sue. 2010. (ENG., 14p. (J). (gr. -1-1). bds. 9.99 (978-1-4169-9435-0(1), Little Simon) Little Simon.

Tildes, Phyllis L. The Garden Wall. Tildes, Phyllis L. 2005. (J). per. 7.95 (978-0-9723729-1-6(1)) Imagination Stage, Inc.

Tildes, Phyllis Limbacher. Apples. Farmer, Jacqueline. 2007. 32p. (J). (gr. k-3). 7.99 (978-1-57091-695-3(0)) Charlesbridge Publishing, Inc.

—Baby Animals Take a Bath. Arnold, Marsha Diane. 2017. 10p. (J). (— 1). bds. 6.99 (978-1-58089-538-5(7)) Charlesbridge Publishing, Inc.

—Baby Animals Take a Nap. Arnold, Marsha Diane. 2017. 10p. (J). (— 1). bds. 6.99 (978-1-58089-539-2(5)) Charlesbridge Publishing, Inc.

—Plant Secrets. Goodman, Emily. 2009. 40p. (J). (gr. -1-3). pap. 7.95 (978-1-58089-205-6(1)) Charlesbridge Publishing, Inc.

—Pumpkins. Farmer, Jacqueline. 2004. 32p. (J). (gr. k-3). pap. 7.95 (978-1-57091-558-1(X)) Charlesbridge Publishing, Inc.

Tildes, Phyllis Limbacher. Baby Animals Day & Night. Tildes, Phyllis Limbacher. 2016. 12p. (J). (— 1). bds. 6.95 (978-1-58089-609-2(X)) Charlesbridge Publishing, Inc.

—Baby Animals Spots & Stripes. Tildes, Phyllis Limbacher. 2015. 12p. (J). (— 1). bds. 6.95 (978-1-58089-608-5(1)) Charlesbridge Publishing, Inc.

—Baby's First Book of Birds & Colors. Tildes, Phyllis Limbacher. 2017. 18p. (J). (— 1). bds. 8.99 (978-1-58089-742-6(8)) Charlesbridge Publishing, Inc.

—Bunny's Big Surprise. Tildes, Phyllis Limbacher. 2020. 32p. (J). (-k). lib. bdg. 16.99 (978-1-58089-684-9(7)) Charlesbridge Publishing, Inc.

—Eye Guess: A Foldout Guessing Game. Tildes, Phyllis Limbacher. 2005. 36p. (J). (gr. -1-2). 11.95 (978-1-57091-650-2(0)) Charlesbridge Publishing, Inc.

—The Magic Babushka. Tildes, Phyllis Limbacher. 2009. 32p. (J). (gr. k-3). pap. 7.95 (978-1-58089-225-4(6)) Charlesbridge Publishing, Inc.

—Will You Be Mine? A Nursery Rhyme Romance. Tildes, Phyllis Limbacher. 2011. 32p. (J). (gr. -1-2). pap. 7.95 (978-1-58089-245-2(0)) Charlesbridge Publishing, Inc.

Till, Tom, photos by. Photographing the World: A Guide to Photographing 201 of the Most Beautiful Places on Earth. Till, Tom. Martres, Laurent, ed. 2012. 336p. pap. (978-0-9916189-22-8(8)) Graphic International, Inc.

Tiller, Amy. My Sister Is Like a Baby Bird. Tiller, Amy. 2009. (ENG.). 26p. (J). 12.95 (978-1-935130-02-4(1)) Grateful Steps.

Tiller, Bill. Kimmy the Kangaroo Goes to the Doctor. Kobren, Myles Scott. 2019. (Adventures of Kimmy the Kangaroo Ser.). (ENG.). 44p. (J). (978-1-5255-4615-0(5)); pap. **(978-1-5255-4616-7(3))** FriesenPress.

Tiller, Paul. Sammy's Day at the Fair: The Digestive System,featuring Gut Feelings & Reactions. Tiller, Jerome. 2nd ed. 2018. (ENG.). 48p. (J). (gr. 4-6). pap. 17.95 (978-0-9777693-9-1(9)) ArtWrite Productions.

Tiller, Richard. Sid Smart: Moving. Tiller, Richard. 2020. (ENG.). 36p. (J). pap. **(978-1-8380028-3-1(9))** Crossbridge Bks.

Tillery, Paul, IV, et al. Thundercluck! Tillery, Paul, IV & Tillery, Paul. 2018. (Thundercluck! Ser.). (ENG.). 240p. (J). 14.99 (978-1-250-15528-3(2), 900184615) Roaring Brook Pr.

Tillery, Paul, IV & Wittwer, Meg. Thundercluck! Chicken of Thor: Recipe for Revenge. Tillery, Paul, IV. 2020. (Thundercluck! Ser.). (ENG.). 224p. (J). pap. 7.99 **(978-1-250-61978-5(5)**, 900184619) Square Fish.

Tillery, Paul, IV, jt. illus. see Wittwer, Meg.

Tilley, Debbie. Babies Don't Eat Pizza: A Big Kids' Book about Baby Brothers & Baby Sisters. Danzig, Dianne. 2009. 32p. (J). (gr. -1-k). 17.99 (978-0-525-47441-8(2), Dutton Books for Young Readers) Penguin Young Readers Group.

—Boy, Were We Wrong about the Human Body! Kudlinski, Kathleen V. 2015. 32p. (J). (gr. -1-3). 16.99 (978-0-8037-3792-1(0), Dial Bks) Penguin Young Readers Group.

—E Is for Elisa. Hurwitz, Johanna. 2003. (Riverside Kids Ser.). (ENG.). 96p. (J). (gr. 1-4). pap. 4.25 (978-0-06-054374-7(4)) HarperCollins Pubs.

—My Teacher Is an Idiom. Gilson, Jamie. 2015. (ENG.). 144p. (J). (gr. 1-4). 16.99 (978-0-544-05680-0(9), 1533561) Houghton Mifflin Harcourt Publishing Co.

—Oye, Hormiguita (Hey, Little Ant Spanish Edition) Hoose, Phillip & Hoose, Hannah. 2004.Tr. of Hey Little Ant!. 32p. (J). (gr. -1-2). pap. 7.99 (978-1-58246-089-5(2), Tricycle Pr.) Random Hse. Children's Bks.

—Spaghetti & Meatballs for All! A Mathematical Story. Burns, Marilyn. 2008. (Scholastic Bookshelf Ser.). (ENG.). 40p. (J). (gr. -1-3). pap. 6.99 (978-0-545-04445-5(6), Scholastic Paperbacks) Scholastic, Inc.

—Swimming Upstream: Middle School Poems. George, Kristine O'Connell. 2018. (ENG.). 80p. (J). (gr. 5-7). pap. 7.99 (978-1-328-90018-0(5), 1700053, HMH Books For Young Readers) Houghton Mifflin Harcourt Publishing Co.

—Winky Blue Goes Wild! Jane, Pamela. 2003. 64p. (J). 13.95 (978-1-59034-588-7(6)); pap. (978-1-59034-589-4(4)) Mondo Publishing.

Tilley, Scott. The Bing Bong Book. Uyeda, Laura. 2015. (Little Golden Book Ser.). (ENG.). 24p. (J). (-k). 4.99 (978-0-7364-3321-1(X), Golden/Disney) Random Hse. Children's Bks.

—Boo on the Loose (Disney/Pixar Monsters, Inc.) Herman, Gail. 2012. (Step into Reading Ser.). (ENG.). 32p. (J). (gr. -1-1). pap. 3.99 (978-0-7364-2860-6(7), RH/Disney) Random Hse. Children's Bks.

Tilley, Scott & Orpinas, Jean-Paul. Ratatouille. Saxon, Victoria & RH Disney Staff. 2007. (Little Golden Book Ser.). (ENG.). 24p. (J). (gr. -1-2). 3.99 (978-0-7364-2423-3(7), RH/Disney) Random Hse. Children's Bks.

Tilley, Scott, jt. illus. see Orpinas, Jean-Paul.

Tilley, Shiho, jt. illus. see Ford, Melissa.

Tillie, Chiquanda. Imani's Bad Day. Tillie, C. Dawn. 2020. (ENG.). 36p. (J). pap. 14.99 **(978-1-7341903-1-1(0))** Tickle Me Purple, LLC.

Tillie, Chiquanda. Mommy, Mommy! Alston, Ronalyn T. 2019. (ENG.). 24p. (J). pap. 9.99 (978-0-9990536-8-3(X)) Tickle Me Purple, LLC.

Tillie, Chiquanda. Believe: A Coloring Book of Positive Affirmations: Coloring Book. Tillie, Chiquanda. 2018. (ENG.). 60p. (J). pap. 7.00 (978-0-9990536-7-6(1)) Tickle Me Purple, LLC.

Tillis, Carrie. Rudy the Rabbit. Tillis, Doris. 2005. 32p. per. 17.95 (978-1-58961-410-9(0)) PageFree Publishing, Inc.

Tillman, Gloria J. Teeth for Thanksgiving. Tillman, Gloria J. 2021. (ENG.). 36p. (J). lib. bdg. 12.99 (978-0-9841260-7-1(4)) Tamaja Pr.

Tillman, Nancy. Let There Be Light, 1 vol. Tutu, Desmond. 2014. (ENG.). 30p. (J). bds. 7.99 (978-0-310-73396-6(0)) Zonderkidz.

Tillman, Nancy. The Crown on Your Head. Tillman, Nancy. (ENG.). (J). (gr. -1-3). 2014. 34p. bds. 7.99 (978-1-250-04045-9(0), 900123921); 2011. 32p. 17.99 (978-0-312-64521-2(X), 900068684) Feiwel & Friends.

—The Heaven of Animals. Tillman, Nancy. 2014. (ENG.). 32p. (J). (gr. -1-3). 18.99 (978-0-312-55369-2(2), 900077347) Feiwel & Friends.

—I Knew You Could Do It! Tillman, Nancy. 2019. (ENG.). 32p. (J). 17.99 (978-1-250-11377-1(6), 900171050) Feiwel & Friends.

—I'd Know You Anywhere, My Love. Tillman, Nancy. (ENG.). (J). 2015. 16p. bds. 7.99 (978-1-250-07292-4(1), 900150647); 2013. 32p. (gr. -1-3). 17.99 (978-0-312-55368-5(4), 9780312553685) Feiwel & Friends.

—It's Time to Sleep, My Love. Tillman, Nancy. Metaxas, Eric. (ENG.). (J). 2011. 34p. (— 1). bds. 7.99 (978-0-312-67336-9(1), 900072514); 2008. 32p. (gr. -1 — 1). 16.95 (978-0-312-38371-8(1), 900053023) Feiwel & Friends.

—On the Night You Were Born. Tillman, Nancy. 2006. (ENG.). 32p. (J). (gr. -1 — 1). 17.99 (978-0-312-34606-5(9), 900041898) Feiwel & Friends.

—The Spirit of Christmas. Tillman, Nancy. 2009. (ENG.). 32p. (J). (gr. -1-3). 17.99 (978-0-312-54965-7(2), 900055822) Feiwel & Friends.

—Tumford the Terrible. Tillman, Nancy. 2015. (Tumford Ser.). (ENG.). 32p. (J). (gr. -1-1). bds. 8.99 (978-1-250-03364-2(0), 900120149) Feiwel & Friends.

—Wherever You Are: My Love Will Find You. Tillman, Nancy. (ENG.). 32p. (J). (gr. -1-3). 2012. bds. 7.99 (978-1-250-01797-0(1), 900087504); 2010. 17.99 (978-0-312-54966-4(0), 900055823) Feiwel & Friends.

—You're All Kinds of Wonderful. Tillman, Nancy. 2017. (ENG.). 32p. (J). 17.99 (978-1-250-11376-4(8), 900171049) Feiwel & Friends.

Tillotson, Katherine. All Ears, All Eyes. Jackson, Richard. 2017. (ENG.). 40p. (J). (gr. -1-3). 17.99 *(978-1-4814-1571-2(9))* Simon & Schuster Children's Publishing.
—All the Water in the World. Lyon, George Ella. 2011. (ENG.). 40p. (J). (gr. -1-3). 18.99 *(978-1-4169-7130-6(0),* Atheneum/Richard Jackson Bks.) Simon & Schuster Children's Publishing.
—It's Picture Day Today! Mcdonald, Megan. 2009. (ENG.). 36p. (J). (gr. -1-3). 16.99 *(978-1-4169-2434-0(5),* Atheneum/Richard Jackson Bks.) Simon & Schuster Children's Publishing.
—Nice Try, Tooth Fairy. Olson, Mary W. 2003. Orig. Title: Dear Tooth Fairy. (ENG.). 32p. (J). (gr. -1-2). 13.99 *(978-0-689-86141-3(9),* Aladdin) Simon & Schuster Children's Publishing.
—Shoe Dog. Mcdonald, Megan. 2014. (ENG.). 40p. (J). (gr. -1-2). 17.99 *(978-1-4169-7932-6(8),* Atheneum/Richard Jackson Bks.) Simon & Schuster Children's Publishing.
—The Three Billy Goats Gruff — The FULL Story. Jackson, Richard. 2020. (ENG.). 48p. (J). (gr. -1-3). 17.99 *(978-1-4814-1573-6(5))* Simon & Schuster Children's Publishing.
—When the Library Lights Go Out. Mcdonald, Megan. (ENG.). 40p. (J). (gr. -1-1). 2009. 9.99 *(978-1-4169-8028-5(8),* Atheneum Bks. for Young Readers); 2005. 19.99 *(978-0-689-86170-3(2),* Atheneum/Richard Jackson Bks.) Simon & Schuster Children's Publishing.
Tillson, Linda L. The Moon & the Mouse. Ryan, Christopher. 2011. 32p. pap. 24.95 *(978-1-4626-1586-5(4))* America Star Bks.
Tilly. Where's Will? Find Shakespeare Hidden in His Plays. Claybourne, Anna. 2015. (J). *(978-1-61067-407-2(3))* Kane Miller.
Tilma, Taralee. It's OK to Cry. Reid, Kimm. 2020. (ENG.). 50p. (J). pap. ***(978-1-988001-49-4(8))*** Ahelia Publishing, Inc.
Tilma, Taralee. Rocky & Penelope: The Perfect Exchange. Em, Charlie. 2018. (ENG.). 66p. (YA). (gr. 7-12). pap. *(978-1-988001-19-7(6))* Ahelia Publishing, Inc.
Tim, Hamilton. Treasure Island: The Graphic Novel. Stevenson, Robert Louis. 2005. (ENG.). 176p. (J). (gr. 3-7). 10.99 *(978-0-14-240470-6(5),* Puffin Books) Penguin Young Readers Group.
Timbers, Suzanne. Sepia & the Big Ocean. Timbers, Suzanne. 2019. (ENG.). 32p. (J). (gr. -1-2). 17.99 *(978-988-8341-84-9(7),* Minedition) Neugebauer, Michael (Publishing) Limited HKG. Dist: Penguin Random Hse. LLC.
Timmers, Carol. Max Magee. Morgan, Railin. 2020. (ENG.). 36p. (J). ***(978-1-5255-7053-7(6))***; pap. ***(978-1-5255-7054-4(4))*** FriesenPress.
Timmers, Leo. All Through My Town. Reidy, Jean. (ENG.). (J). (gr. -1-k). 2015. 26p. bds. 7.99 *(978-1-61963-562-3(3),* 900140699); 2013. 32p. 17.99 *(978-1-59990-785-7(2),* 900080105) Bloomsbury Publishing USA. (Bloomsbury USA Childrens).
—Busy Builders, Busy Week! Reidy, Jean. 2016. 32p. (J). 16.99 *(978-1-61963-556-2(9),* 900140134, Bloomsbury USA Childrens) Bloomsbury Publishing USA.
Timmers, Leo. Franky. Timmers, Leo. 2016. (ENG.). 40p. (J). (gr. -1-2). 16.99 *(978-1-927271-93-3(2),* 9781927271933); E-Book 26.65 *(978-1-77657-054-6(5),* 9781776570546); E-Book 26.65 *(978-1-77657-053-9(7))* Gecko Pr. NZL. Dist: Lerner Publishing Group.
—Gus's Garage. Timmers, Leo. 2017. (ENG.). 32p. (gr. -1-k). (J). 16.99 *(978-1-77657-092-8(8))*; 9.99 *(978-1-77657-094-2(4))* Gecko Pr. NZL. Dist: Lerner Publishing Group.
—Monkey on the Run. Timmers, Leo. 2019. (ENG.). 32p. (J). (gr. -1-k). 17.99 *(978-1-77657-250-2(5))* Gecko Pr. NZL. Dist: Lerner Publishing Group.
—Who Is Driving? Timmers, Leo. 2014. (ENG.). 30p. (J). (gr. -1-1). bds. 7.99 *(978-1-61963-169-4(5),* 900125789, Bloomsbury USA Childrens) Bloomsbury Publishing USA.
Timmins, Jeffrey Stewart. Cenicienta. Andersen, Hans & Capstone Press Staff. Feely, Maria Luisa, tr. 2010. (Graphic Spin en Español Ser.). (SPA.). 40p. (J). (gr. 3-6). lib. bdg. 25.32 *(978-1-4342-1900-8(3),* Stone Arch Bks.) Capstone.
—Cenicienta: La Novela Grafica. Andersen, Hans & Stone Arch Books Staff. 2010. (Graphic Spin en Español Ser.). (SPA.). 40p. (J). (gr. 3-6). pap. 5.95 *(978-1-4342-2270-1(5),* Stone Arch Bks.) Capstone.
—Cinderella: The Graphic Novel, 1 vol. 2008. (Graphic Spin Ser.). (ENG.). 40p. (J). (gr. 3-6). 25.32 *(978-1-4342-0764-7(1),* Stone Arch Bks.) Capstone.
—Cinderella: The Graphic Novel, 1 vol. Stone Arch Books Staff. 2008. (Graphic Spin Ser.). (ENG.). 40p. (J). (gr. 3-6). pap. 5.95 *(978-1-4342-0860-6(5),* Stone Arch Bks.) Capstone.
—The Emperor's New Clothes: The Graphic Novel, 1 vol. Andersen, Hans. 2009. (Graphic Spin Ser.). (ENG.). 40p. (J). (gr. 3-6). pap. 5.95 *(978-1-4342-1744-8(2),* Stone Arch Bks.) Capstone.
—Last Laughs: Animal Epitaphs. Lewis, J. Patrick & Yolen, Jane. 2012. 32p. (J). (gr. 2-5). 16.95 *(978-1-58089-260-5(4))* Charlesbridge Publishing, Inc.
—Last Laughs: Prehistoric Epitaphs. Yolen, Jane & Lewis, J. Patrick. 2017. 32p. (J). (gr. 2-5). 16.99 *(978-1-58089-706-8(1))* Charlesbridge Publishing, Inc.
—Rapunzel. Capstone Press Staff. 2009. (Graphic Spin Ser.). (ENG.). 40p. (J). (gr. 3-6). pap. 5.95 *(978-1-4342-1392-1(7),* Stone Arch Bks.) Capstone.
—A Whole Nother Story. Soup, Cuthbert. 2010. (Whole Nother Story Ser.). (ENG.). 288p. (YA). (gr. 3-6). pap. 8.99 *(978-1-59990-518-1(3),* 9781599905181, Bloomsbury USA Childrens) Bloomsbury Publishing USA.
Timmins, William. Wild Bill Hickok & Deputy Marshal Joey. Stone, Ethel B. 2011. 32p. pap. 35.95 *(978-1-258-05913-2(4))* Literary Licensing, LLC.
Timmons, Anne. Florence Nightingale: Lady with the Lamp, 1 vol. Robbins, Trina & Capstone Press Staff. 2007. (Graphic Biographies Ser.). (ENG.). 32p. (J). (gr. 3-9). 31.32 *(978-0-7368-6850-1(X),* Capstone Pr.) Capstone.
—Florence Nightingale: Lady with the Lamp, 1 vol. Robbins, Trina. 2007. (Graphic Biographies Ser.). (ENG.). 32p. (J). (gr. 3-9). per. 8.10 *(978-0-7368-7902-6(1),* 1264942, Capstone Pr.) Capstone.
Timmons, Anne, et al. Lily Renée, Escape Artist: From Holocaust Survivor to Comic Book Pioneer, Vol. Robbins, Trina. 2011. (ENG.). 96p. (J). (gr. 5-8). pap. 9.99 *(978-0-7613-8114-3(7),* 9780761381143, Graphic Universe™) Lerner Publishing Group.
Timmons, Anne. Pigling: A Cinderella Story [a Korean Tale]. Jolley, Dan. 2009. (Graphic Myths & Legends Ser.). (ENG.). 48p. (J). (gr. 4-8). pap. 9.99 *(978-1-58013-825-3(X),* Graphic Universe™) Lerner Publishing Group.
Timmons, Anne & Oh, Mo. Lily Renée, Escape Artist: From Holocaust Survivor to Comic Book Pioneer. Robbins, Trina. 2011. (Single Titles Ser.). (ENG.). 96p. (J). (gr. 5-8). lib. bdg. 29.27 *(978-0-7613-6010-0(7),* Graphic Universe™) Lerner Publishing Group.
Timmons, Anne, jt. illus. see Martin, Cynthia.
Timmons, Bonnie. Eats MORE, Shoots & Leaves: Why, ALL Punctuation Marks Matter! Truss, Lynne. 2019. (ENG.). 64p. (J). (gr. 1-4). pap. 9.99 *(978-1-9848-1574-3(1),* G.P. Putnam's Sons Books for Young Readers) Penguin Young Readers Group.
—Eats, Shoots & Leaves: Why, Commas Really Do Make a Difference! Truss, Lynne. 2006. (ENG.). 32p. (J). (gr. 1-4). 16.99 *(978-0-399-24491-9(3),* G.P. Putnam's Sons Books for Young Readers) Penguin Young Readers Group.
—The Girl's Like Spaghetti: Why, You Can't Manage Without Apostrophes! Truss, Lynne. 2007. (ENG.). 32p. (J). (gr. 1-4). 16.99 *(978-0-399-24706-4(8),* G.P. Putnam's Sons Books for Young Readers) Penguin Young Readers Group.
—Twenty-Odd Ducks: Why, Every Punctuation Mark Counts! Truss, Lynne. 2008. (ENG.). 32p. (J). (gr. 1-3). 16.99 *(978-0-399-25058-3(1),* G.P. Putnam's Sons Books for Young Readers) Penguin Young Readers Group.
—Your Amazing Skin from Outside In. Settel, Joanne. 2018. (Your Amazing Body Bks.). (ENG.). 96p. (J). (gr. 3-7). 18.99 *(978-1-4814-2205-5(7))* Simon & Schuster Children's Publishing.
Timmons, Gayle. Do You Love Me Best? Schad, Kristine. 2007. 40p. (J). lib. bdg. 23.95 *(978-1-58374-156-6(9))* Chicago Spectrum Pr.
Timmons, Johnny & Grabe, Robert. The Odyssey of Flight 33. Serling, Rod & Kneece, Mark. 2009. (Twilight Zone Graphic Novels Ser.). (ENG.). 72p. (J). (gr. 7-12). 26.19 *(978-0-8027-9718-6(0),* 9780802797186) Walker & Co.
Timmons, Jonathan, jt. illus. see Isaacs, Rebekah.
Timmons, Joshua. The Adventures of Lil' Kenny: Vol. 1 - Kenny Finds Basketball. Babaian, Edward & Anderson, Kenny. 2019. (ENG.). 24p. (J). (gr. k-6). pap. 16.99 ***(978-1-7331068-0-1(4))*** BABAIAN, Edward.
Timothy, Chanté. A Black Woman Did That. Adero, Malaika. 2020. (ENG.). 160p. (J). (gr. 5-6). pap. 11.99 *(978-1-941367-51-3(8))* Downtown Bookworks.
Timreck, Caitlyn. Khanda's Adventures: Beyond the Milky Way. Harkins, Debra Ann. 2018. (ENG.). 26p. (J). pap. 9.49 *(978-1-7326371-0-8(5))* Purple Owl Publishing.
Tina, Dunnier. The Gentle Elephant. Kneisley, Amy. 2013. 24p. pap. 8.99 *(978-1-938768-21-7(3))* Gypsy Pubns.
Tinarelli, Beatrice. Let's Learn: Time to Explore. Holowaty, Lauren. 2020. (Let's Learn Ser.). (ENG.). 18p. (J). (gr. -1-k). 14.99 ***(978-1-64517-204-8(X),*** Silver Dolphin Bks.) Printers Row Publishing Group.
Tinarelli, Beatrice. T. rex: From Head to Tail. Murphy, Patricia J. Cottage Door Press, ed. 2019. (Smithsonian Kids First Discovery Bks.). (ENG.). 12p. (J). (gr. -1-1). bds. 7.99 *(978-1-68052-705-6(3),* 1004380) Cottage Door Pr.
Tinari, Leah. Limitless: 24 Remarkable American Women of Vision, Grit, & Guts. Tinari, Leah. 2018. (ENG.). 56p. (J). (gr. 5-3). 19.99 *(978-1-5344-1855-4(5),* Aladdin) Simon & Schuster Children's Publishing.
—The Presidents: Portraits of History. Tinari, Leah. 2019. (ENG.). 96p. (J). (gr. 5). 19.99 *(978-1-5344-1857-8(1),* Aladdin) Simon & Schuster Children's Publishing.
Tindall, Kelly. Alexander Hamilton: the Fighting Founding Father! Shulman, Mark. 2019. (Show Me History! Ser.). (ENG.). 96p. (J). (gr. 3-7). 12.99 *(978-1-68412-543-2(X),* Portable Pr.) Printers Row Publishing Group.
—Amelia Earhart: Pioneer of the Sky! Buckley, James, Jr. 2019. (Show Me History! Ser.). (ENG.). 96p. (J). (gr. 3-7). 12.99 *(978-1-68412-545-6(6),* Portable Pr.) Printers Row Publishing Group.
—Babe Ruth: Baseball's All-Time Best! Buckley, James, Jr. 2020. (Show Me History! Ser.). (ENG.). 96p. (J). (gr. 3-7). 12.99 *(978-1-64517-071-6(3),* Portable Pr.) Printers Row Publishing Group.
—Benjamin Franklin: Inventor of the Nation! Shulman, Mark. 2020. (Show Me History! Ser.). (ENG.). 96p. (J). (gr. 3-7). 12.99 *(978-1-64517-072-3(1),* Portable Pr.) Printers Row Publishing Group.
—Susan B. Anthony: Champion for Voting Rights! Shulman, Mark. 2020. (Show Me History! Ser.). (ENG.). 96p. (J). (gr. 3-7). 12.99 *(978-1-64517-074-7(8),* Portable Pr.) Printers Row Publishing Group.
Ting, Jasmine. What Does Super Jonny Do When Mom Gets Sick? (CANCER Version). Colwill, Simone. 2020. (Super Jonny Ser.: Vol. 1). (ENG.). 38p. (J). (gr. k-6). pap. ***(978-0-9941297-4-1(2))*** Sick Mom.
—What Does Super Jonny Do When Mom Gets Sick? (CROHN's Disease Version). Colwill, Simone. 2020. (Super Jonny Ser.: Vol. 1). (ENG.). 36p. (J). (gr. k-6). pap. ***(978-0-9941297-7-2(7))*** Sick Mom.
—What Does Super Jonny Do When Mom Gets Sick? (DIABETES Version). Colwill, Simone. 2020. (Super Jonny Ser.: Vol. 1). (ENG.). 36p. (J). (gr. k-6). pap. ***(978-0-9941297-6-5(9))*** Sick Mom.
—What Does Super Jonny Do When Mom Gets Sick? (HEART Disease Version). Colwill, Simone. 2020. (Super Jonny Ser.: Vol. 1). (ENG.). 36p. (J). (gr. k-6). pap. ***(978-0-9941297-5-8(0))*** Sick Mom.
Tingley, Janice Ramos. Nolan's Dream. Tingley, Janice Ramos. 2018. (ENG.). 32p. (J). (gr. -1-3). *(978-1-5255-0645-1(5))*; pap. *(978-1-5255-0646-8(3))* FriesenPress.
Tinkelman, Murray. Pigeon Flight. Stolz, Mary. 2012. 62p. 36.95 *(978-1-258-25234-2(1))*; pap. 21.95 *(978-1-258-25387-5(9))* Literary Licensing, LLC.
Tinker, Jason. My Wish, Our Little Oat. Martin, Tamra. 2007. 36p. (J). 21.99 *(978-1-59879-522-6(8),* Lifevest) Lifevest Publishing, Inc.
Tinkler, Dennis, jt. illus. see Shulman, Dee.
Tinling, Molly. Shanie June Jumped over the Moon. Wand, Dana. 2013. 32p. pap. *(978-1-4602-0466-5(2))* FriesenPress.
Tino. La Panza del Tepozteco. Agustin, Jose. 2003. (SPA.). 118p. (J). (gr. 8-12). pap. 12.95 *(978-968-19-0187-5(8))* Santillana USA Publishing Co., Inc.
Tinsley, Larry. Fun in the Rain. Li, Marci. 2018. (ENG.). 26p. (J). pap. 19.99 *(978-0-578-43404-9(0))* INDICOMM.
Tinsman, Kaya. Platinums. Borzilleri, Sophia. 2018. (ENG.). 224p. (YA). 29.95 *(978-1-64300-003-9(9))*; pap. 16.95 *(978-1-64300-002-2(0))* Covenant Bks.
Tinti, Natalie. Magic in Us. the Healing Circle, bks. 2, vol. 2. Tinti, Natalie. ed. 2013. (Sewing a Friendship Ser.). (ENG.). 96p. (J). 25.95 *(978-0-9830884-4-8(6))* Tintinatie Publishing Hse.
—Magic in Us. the Healing Circle: The Healing Circle, bks. 2, vol. 2. Tinti, Natalie. ed. 2013. (Sewing a Friendship Ser.: 3). (ENG.). 96p. (J). pap. 12.95 *(978-0-9830884-0-0(3))* Tintinatie Publishing Hse.
—Magic in Us. the Power of Imagination, bks. 1, vol. 2. Tinti, Natalie. ed. 2013. (Sewing a Friendship Ser.: 2). (ENG.). 116p. (J). 25.95 *(978-0-9830884-1-7(1))* Tintinatie Publishing Hse.
—Sewing a Friendship. Tinti, Natalie. ed. 2009. (Sewing a Friendship Ser.: 1). (ENG.). 88p. (J). pap. 12.95 *(978-0-9842625-1-9(2))* Tintinatie Publishing Hse.
—Sewing a Friendship 1: I Wish I Have Friends. Tinti, Natalie. 2009. (Sewing a Friendship Ser.: Vol. 1). (ENG.). 104p. (J). pap. 21.17 *(978-0-9966540-9-8(7))* Hom, Jonathan.
Tintjer, Birgit. Stary's Secret. Wilson, Jessica. 2007. 28p. pap. 24.95 *(978-1-4241-9089-8(4))* America Star Bks.
Tinto, Davide. Marvel Action: Spider-Man: Venom (Book Four) Dawson, Delilah S. 2020. (Marvel Action: Spider-Man Ser.: 4). (ENG.). 72p. (J). (gr. 4-7). pap. 9.99 *(978-1-68405-632-3(2))* Idea & Design Works, LLC.
Tipeo. Caillou: Los Contrarios. Savary, Fabien & Vadeboncoeur, Isabelle. 2004. (Caillou Ser.).Tr. of What's the Difference?. (SPA & ENG.). 12p. (J). (gr. -1-17). bds. 4.95 *(978-1-58728-348-2(4))* Cooper Square Publishing Llc.
Tipping, Naomi. Bully. Safran, Sheri. 2012. (ENG.). 12p. (J). (gr. -1). 12.99 *(978-1-60887-163-6(0))* Insight Editions.
Tipsey, Carlianne. Ray & Mia's Adventure: レイとミアの冒険 Weaver, Catherine. 2019. (ENG.). 30p. (J). pap. 9.95 ***(978-1-0830-3711-4(0))*** Independently Published.
Tipton, Erica. A Monkey Named Haha. Tipton, Erica. 2019. (ENG.). 36p. (J). pap. 9.99 *(978-0-359-22383-1(4))* Wright Bks.
Tirabosco, Tom. Weekend with Purpose. Wazem, Pierre. 2003. 108p. (YA). pap. 9.95 *(978-1-930652-98-9(4))* Humanoids, Inc.
Tirey, Rodney. Coppershoo Saves the Sarge's Saddle! Tirey, Rodney. 2007. 32p. (J). 16.95 *(978-0-9789591-0-4(8))* MirthMarks Publishing.
Tirion, Wil & Rukl, Antonin. Atlas of the Night Sky. Storm, Dunlop. 2005. (Smithsonian Institution Ser.). 224p. 29.95 *(978-0-06-081891-3(3))* HarperCollins Pubs.
Tiritilli, Robert. Adventures in Sportsand - the Baseball Bully (with accompanying CD) The Baseball Bully. Hellman, Charles. 2008. (Adventures in SportsLand: the Bully Ser.). 32p. pap. 19.95 *(978-0-935938-27-2(3))* Stogo, Malcolm Assocs.
—Adventures in SportsLand - the Basketball Bully (with accompanying CD) Hellman, Charles. 2008. (Adventures in SportsLand: the Bully Ser.). 32p. (J). (gr. -1-3). 19.95 *(978-0-935938-28-9(1))* Stogo, Malcolm Assocs.
—Adventures in SportsLand - the Football Bully (with accompanying CD) Hellman, Charles. 2008. (Adventures in SportsLand: the Bully Ser.). 32p. (J). (gr. -1-3). 19.95 *(978-0-935938-30-2(3))* Williams, Michael.
—Adventures in SportsLand - the Soccer Bully (with accompanying CD) Hellman, Charles. 2008. (Adventures in SportsLand: the Bully Ser.). 32p. (gr. -1-3). pap. 19.95 *(978-0-935938-26-5(5))* Stogo, Malcolm Assocs.
—Adventures in SportsLand - the Tennis Bully (with accompanying CD) Hellman, Charles. 2008. (Adventures in SportsLand: the Bully Ser.). 32p. (J). (gr. -1-3). 19.95 *(978-0-935938-32-6(X))* Stogo, Malcolm Assocs.
Tiritilli, Robert A. The Baseball Bully. Hellman, Charles S. 2013. 34p. pap. 9.25 *(978-0-935938-19-7(2))* LuckySports.
—The Baseball Challenge: Defenders of Sportsland. Hellman, Charles S. 2013. 54p. pap. 11.25 *(978-0-935938-52-4(4))* LuckySports.
—Discovering Sportsland. Hellman, Charles S. 2013. 44p. pap. 9.49 *(978-0-935938-51-7(6))* LuckySports.
—The Football Bully. Hellman, Charles S. 2013. 34p. pap. 9.25 *(978-0-935938-22-7(2))* LuckySports.
—The Hockey Bully. Hellman, Charles S. 2013. 34p. pap. 9.25 *(978-0-935938-23-4(0))* LuckySports.
—Luckysports Abc's Coloring Book. Hellman, Charles S. 2013. 50p. pap. 5.40 *(978-0-935938-46-3(X))* LuckySports.
—The Volleyball Bully. Hellman, Charles S. 2013. 34p. pap. 9.25 *(978-0-935938-53-1(2))* LuckySports.
Tisdall, Sarah. You're Thinking about Doughnuts. Rosen, Michael. 2006. 90p. (J). (gr. 2-4). per. 6.95 *(978-1-903015-03-2(0))* Barn Owl Bks, London GBR. Dist: Independent Pubs. Group.
Tisdel, L. L. The Incredibly Awesome Adventures of Puggie Liddel, the Graphic Novel. Bryson, Karen Mueller. 2013. 108p. pap. *(978-1-927384-09-1(5))* Zeta Comics.
Titonis, George. The Gift of the Giggles. 2005. 24p. (J). 16.95 *(978-0-9765398-0-3(2))* Bellaboozle Books, Inc.
Titra, Stephen. We'll Ring in God's Name. Thiry, Joan. 2009. (ENG.). 44p. (YA). tchr. ed. 5.00 *(978-0-935046-06-9(2))* Chateau Thierry Pr.
Tiwari, Saral. Abraham Lincoln: The Civil War President, 2004. 48p. (J). 15.95 *(978-0-9742502-0-5(1))* Gossamer Bks., LLC.
—Thirteen Americas: American Revolution & Constitution. Pettinato, Laura. 2004. (J). 18.95 *(978-0-9742502-7-4(9))* Gossamer Bks., LLC.
—Thirteen Americas: The Declaration of Independence. Pettinato, Laura. 2nd ed. 2004. (J). lib. bdg. *(978-0-9742502-6-7(0))* Gossamer Bks., LLC.
Tiwi College Students, jt. illus. see McMaster, Anne.
Tjia, Sherwin. Black Stars in a White Night Sky. Lawson, JonArno. 2006. (ENG.). 80p. *(978-1-897141-07-6(6))* Pedlar Pr.
—The Man in the Moon-Fixer's Mask. Lawson, JonArno. 2004. (ENG.). 88p. (J). (gr. 3-7). *(978-0-9732140-9-3(0))* Pedlar Pr.
Tkachenko, Olha. The Ladybug Story. Mitchell, Liliana. 2018. (ENG.). 56p. (J). 19.99 *(978-0-9996085-9-3(2))*; pap. 13.99 *(978-0-9996085-3-1(3))* Mindstir Media.
To Be Announced. Meechee's Top-Secret Society. 2018. (Smallfoot Ser.). (ENG.). 24p. (J). (gr. -1-2). pap. 4.99 *(978-1-5344-3170-6(5),* Simon Spotlight) Simon Spotlight.
To, Marcus. Age of X-Man: NextGen. 2019. (ENG.). 112p. (YA). (gr. 8-17). pap. 15.99 *(978-1-302-91576-6(2))* Marvel Worldwide, Inc.
—All-New Guardians of the Galaxy Vol. 3: Infinity Quest. 2018. (ENG.). 136p. (YA). (gr. 8-17). pap. 15.99 *(978-1-302-90546-0(5))* Marvel Worldwide, Inc.
—Excalibur by Tini Howard Vol. 1. 2020. (ENG.). 176p. (YA). (gr. 8-17). pap. 17.99 *(978-1-302-91991-7(1))* Marvel Worldwide, Inc.
To, Vivienne. A Babysitter's Guide to Monster Hunting #1. Ballarini, Joe. (Babysitter's Guide to Monsters Ser.: 1). (ENG.). 352p. (J). (gr. 3-7). 2019. pap. 6.99 *(978-0-06-243784-6(4))*; 2017. 13.99 *(978-0-06-243783-9(6))* HarperCollins Pubs. (Tegen, Katherine Bks).
—A Babysitter's Guide to Monster Hunting #2: Beasts & Geeks. Ballarini, Joe. (Babysitter's Guide to Monsters Ser.: 2). (ENG.). 320p. (J). (gr. 3-7). 2020. pap. 7.99 *(978-0-06-243788-4(7))*; 2018. 13.99 *(978-0-06-243787-7(9))* HarperCollins Pubs. (Tegen, Katherine Bks).
—The Case of the Time-Capsule Bandit. Rhodes, O. K. & Spencer, Octavia. 2013. (Randi Rhodes, Ninja Detective Ser.: 1). (ENG.). 224p. (J). (gr. 3-7). 16.99 *(978-1-4424-7681-3(8),* Simon & Schuster Bks. For Young Readers) Simon & Schuster Bks. For Young Readers.
—Clawed! An Up2U Horror Adventure, 1 vol. Enderle, Dotti. 2013. (Up2U Adventures Ser.). (ENG.). 80p. (J). (gr. 2-5). lib. bdg. 29.93 *(978-1-61641-965-3(2),* 15213, Calico Chapter Bks.) ABDO Publishing Co.
—Hopper's Destiny. Fiedler, Lisa. 2016. (Mouseheart Ser.: 2). (ENG.). 368p. (J). (gr. 3-7). pap. 8.99 *(978-1-4814-2090-7(9),* McElderry, Margaret K. Bks.) McElderry, Margaret K. Bks.
—Mouseheart. Fiedler, Lisa. (Mouseheart Ser.: 1). (ENG.). (J). (gr. 3-7). 2015. 336p. pap. 8.99 *(978-1-4424-8783-6(8))*; 2014. 320p. 18.99 *(978-1-4424-8781-9(X))* McElderry, Margaret K. Bks. (McElderry, Margaret K. Bks.).
—Really New School: An Up2U Action Adventure, 1 vol. Fields, Jan. 2013. (Up2U Adventures Ser.). (ENG.). 80p. (J). (gr. 2-5). lib. bdg. 29.93 *(978-1-61641-969-1(5),* 15221, Calico Chapter Bks.) ABDO Publishing Co.
—Return of the Forgotten. Fiedler, Lisa. 2015. (Mouseheart Ser.: 3). (ENG.). 320p. (J). (gr. 3-7). 16.99 *(978-1-4814-2092-1(5),* McElderry, Margaret K. Bks.) McElderry, Margaret K. Bks.
—The Sloth Who Slowed Us Down. Wild, Margaret. 2018. (ENG.). 32p. (J). (gr. -1-2). 16.99 *(978-1-4197-3195-2(5),* Abrams Bks. for Young Readers) Abrams, Inc.
—Three Ways to Trap a Leprechaun. Lazar, Tara. 2020. (ENG.). 32p. (J). (gr. -1-3). 10.99 *(978-0-06-284128-5(9),* HarperCollins) HarperCollins Pubs. Ltd. GBR. Dist: HarperCollins Pubs.
—Zack & the Turkey Attack! Naylor, Phyllis Reynolds. 2018. (ENG.). 192p. (J). (gr. 2-6). pap. 7.99 *(978-1-4814-3780-6(1))* Simon & Schuster Children's Publishing.
Toader, Alex. The Day Dreamer. Rodriguez, Robert et al. 2005. (Shark Boy & Lava Girl Adventures Ser.: Bk. 1). 162p. (J). (gr. -1-7). per. *(978-1-933104-04-1(X))* Troublemaker Publishing, LP.
—Shark Boy & Lava Girl Adventures: Return to Planet Drool. Rodriguez, Robert & Roberson, Chris. 2005. (Shark Boy & Lava Girl Adventures Ser.: Book 2). 150p. (J). *(978-1-933104-05-8(8))* Troublemaker Publishing, LP.
—Shark Boy & Lava Girl Adventures: The Deep Sleep. Rodriguez, Robert & Roberson, Chris. 2005. 150p. (J). 10.95 *(978-1-933104-08-9(2))* Troublemaker Publishing, LP.
—Shark Boy & Lava Girl Adventures: The Knight Mare. Rodriguez, Robert & Roberson, Chris. 2005. 150p. (J). 10.95 *(978-1-933104-09-6(0))* Troublemaker Publishing, LP.
Tobar, Jorge. Cuaderno de la Rosa Tomo 4, 8 vols., Vol. 88. Tobar, Malena & Oyola, Milta, eds. 2011.Tr. of Roses-Student Manual. (SPA.). 74p. (J). 7.00 *(978-1-931984-86-7(7),* 7809-65S1) Faith & Action Team.
Tobar, Malena. Barnabas & His Great Mission for Christ. Jingling, Kathy, ed. 2011. (SPA.). 198p. (J). spiral bd. 7.00 *(978-1-931984-40-9(9),* 2002-00E1) Faith & Action Team.
—Bernabe y su Gran Mision por Cristo. Jingling, Kathy, ed. Oyola, Milta, tr. from ENG. 2011.Tr. of Barnabas & his Great Mission for Christ. (SPA.). 191p. (J). spiral bd. 7.00 *(978-1-931984-41-6(7),* 2002-00S1) Faith & Action Team.
—¡Vívelo al extremo! Nivel 1: Lecciones prácticas para aprender de Dios. Brannan, Dara, ed. 2011. 218p. (J).

T

ring bd. 20.00 *(978-1-931984-36-2(0))* Faith & Action Team.

Tobella, Montse. El Grito de la Botella. Albanell, Pep. 2004.Tr. of Scream from the Bottle. (SPA.). (J). pap. 7.99 *(978-84-236-6701-7(4))* Edebé ESP. Dist: Lectorum Pubns., Inc.

—Los Supermusicos. Navarro, Carlos. 2003.Tr. of Super Musicians. (SPA.). 45p. (J). 10.36 *(978-84-7901-701-9(5))* Oasis, Producciones Generales de Comunicacion, S.L. ESP. Dist: Lectorum Pubns., Inc.

Tobia, Lauren. Anna Hibiscus. Atinuke. 2010. (ENG.). 112p. (J). (gr. k-4). pap. 5.99 *(978-1-935279-73-0(4))* Kane Miller.

—Are You Sure, Mother Bear? Hest, Amy. 2016. (ENG.). 32p. (J). (-k). 15.99 *(978-0-7636-7207-2(6))* Candlewick Pr.

—Baby's Got the Blues. Shields, Carol Diggory. 2014. (ENG.). 32p. (J). (gr. -1-2). 16.99 *(978-0-7636-3260-1(0))* Candlewick Pr.

—Ciao, Baby! in the Park. Schaefer, Carole Lexa. 2018. 28p. (J). (— 1). bds. 7.99 *(978-0-7636-8398-6(1))* Candlewick Pr.

—Ciao, Baby! Ready for a Ride. Schaefer, Carole Lexa. 2018. 28p. (J). (— 1). bds. 7.99 *(978-0-7636-8397-9(3))* Candlewick Pr.

—Go Well, Anna Hibiscus! Atinuke. 2018. (ENG.). 112p. (J). pap. 5.99 *(978-1-61067-679-3(3))* Kane Miller.

—Good Luck Anna Hibiscus!, Bk. 3. Atinuke. ed. 2011. (ENG.). 112p. (J). (gr. k-4). pap. 5.99 *(978-1-61067-007-4(8))* Kane Miller.

—Happy in Our Skin. Manushkin, Fran. (ENG.). 32p. (J). 2018. (gr. -1-1). 7.99 *(978-0-7636-9972-7(1))*; 2015. (-k). 17.99 *(978-0-7636-7002-3(2))* Candlewick Pr.

—Have Fun Anna Hibiscus!, 4. Atinuke. 2011. (Anna Hibiscus! Chapter Bks.). (ENG.). 110p. (J). (gr. 1-3). 18.69 *(978-1-61067-008-1(6))* EDC Publishing.

—Hooray for Anna Hibiscus!, 2. Atinuke. 2010. (Anna Hibiscus! Chapter Bks.). (ENG.). 112p. (J). (gr. 1-3). 18.69 *(978-1-935279-74-7(2))* EDC Publishing.

—Let's Go to Playgroup. Hart, Caryl. 2017. (ENG.). 32p. (J). 11.99 *(978-1-61067-581-9(9))* Kane Miller.

—Let's Go to the Farm! Hart, Caryl. 2018. (ENG.). 32p. (J). 11.99 *(978-1-61067-630-4(0))* Kane Miller.

—Love from Anna Hibiscus! Atinuke. 2018. (ENG.). 112p. (J). pap. 5.99 *(978-1-61067-680-9(7))* Kane Miller.

—Welcome Home, Anna Hibiscus! Atinuke. 2018. (ENG.). 112p. (J). pap. 5.99 *(978-1-61067-678-6(5))* Kane Miller.

Tobias, Tom. Harry Meets a Bully. Tobias, Anne B. 2008. 16p. pap. 9.95 *(978-0-9822540-3-5(2))* Peppertree Pr., The.

—Harry's Problem First Loose Tooth. Tobias, Anne B. 2008. 16p. pap. 9.95 *(978-0-9818683-9-4(8))* Peppertree Pr., The.

Tobin, Jennifer, photos by. ABCs of the BWCAW: A Fun Guide to the Boundary Waters Canoe Area Wilderness. Tobin, Jennifer. Tobin, Adriana. 2003. 60p. (YA). bds. 17.95 *(978-0-9742555-0-7(5))* MyHandiwork.

Tobin, Marc. The Life & Times of Lilly the Lash: The Garden Gathering. Woik, Julie. 2009. (ENG.). 48p. (J). 19.95 *(978-0-9663335-7-2(8))* Snow In Sarasota Publishing.

Tocchini, Greg, et al. Eye for Eye, Vol. 2. Ciencin, Scott. 2004. 160p. (YA). pap. 12.95 *(978-1-59314-033-5(9))* CrossGeneration Comics, Inc.

Tocco, Douglas. Meet the Gizmos: The First Kids on the International Space Station. Tocco, John V. 2003. 32p. 16.95 *(978-0-9711665-2-3(8))*; per. 9.95 *(978-0-9711665-3-0(6))* Favorite Uncle Bks., LLC.

Toda, Yasunari. Mobile Suit Gundam Seed Astray R, Vol. 4. Chiba, Tomohiro. rev. ed. 2005. (Mobile Suit Gundam Seed (Novels) Ser.). 232p. per. 9.99 *(978-1-59532-997-4(8))*, Tokyopop Adult) TOKYOPOP, Inc.

—Scryed, 5 vols. Kuroda, Yosuke. 2003. Vol. 2. rev. ed. 192p. pap. 9.99 *(978-1-59182-229-5(7))*; Vol. 4. 4th rev. ed. 200p. pap. 9.99 *(978-1-59182-231-8(9))*; Vol. 5. rev. ed. 192p. pap. 9.99 *(978-1-59182-232-5(7))* TOKYOPOP, Inc.

Todd, Brandon. The Bear Must Go On. Petty, Dev. 2020. 40p. (J). (gr. -1-3). 17.99 *(978-1-9848-3747-9(8))*, Philomel Bks.) Penguin Young Readers Group.

Todd, Chuck. Is That a Skunk? Bogue, Gary. 2018. (ENG.). 40p. (J). 16.00 *(978-1-59714-399-8(5))* Heyday.

—The Raccoon Next Door: Getting along with Urban Wildlife. Bogue, Gary. 2016. (ENG.). 160p. pap. 16.95 *(978-1-890771-71-3(6))* Heyday.

—There's a Hummingbird in My Backyard. Bogue, Gary. 2010. 40p. (J). (gr. -1-3). 15.95 *(978-1-59714-131-4(3))* Heyday.

Todd, Justin. Treasure Island. Stevenson, Robert Louis. unabr. ed. 2003. (Chrysalis Childrens Classics Ser.). 208p. (YA). pap. *(978-1-84365-037-9(1)*, Pavilion Children's Books) Pavilion Bks.

Todd, Mark. My Monster Notebook. Harris, John. 2011. (ENG.). 48p. (J). (gr. 3-18). 16.95 *(978-1-60606-050-6(3)*, J. Paul Getty Museum) Getty Pubns.

—Whatcha Mean, What's a Zine? The Art of Making Zines & Mini-Comics. Watson, Esther Pearl. 2006. (ENG.). 112p. (YA). (gr. 7). pap. 13.99 *(978-0-618-56315-9(6)*, 496906) Houghton Mifflin Harcourt Publishing Co.

Todd, Michelle. The Littlest Reindeer. Dougherty, Brandi. 2017. (Littlest Ser.). (ENG.). 24p. (J). (gr. -1-k). pap. 3.99 *(978-1-338-15738-3(8)*, Cartwheel Bks.) Scholastic, Inc.

—The Littlest Valentine. Dougherty, Brandi. 2017. (J). *(978-1-338-20702-6(4))* Scholastic, Inc.

—The Littlest Valentine (Littlest Series) Dougherty, Brandi. 2017. (Littlest Ser.). (ENG.). 24p. (J). (gr. -1-k). pap. 3.99 *(978-1-338-15739-0(6)*, Cartwheel Bks.) Scholastic, Inc.

—Santa's Workshop. 2017. (ENG.). 12p. (J). (gr. -1-1). 13.99 *(978-1-4380-5007-2(0)*, B.E.S. Publishing) Peterson's.

—Time to Sleep, Puppy. Little Bee Books. 2017. (ENG.). 12p. (J). (gr. -1-k). bds. 8.99 *(978-1-4998-0551-2(9))* Little Bee Books Inc.

Todd, Michelle, jt. illus. see Chiacchiera, Moreno.

Todd, Mort, et al. Tales from the Crypt, 6. Van Lente, Fred et al. Lansdale, John L. et al. 2009. (Tales from the Crypt Ser.: 6). (ENG.). 96p. (J). (gr. 5-12). 22.44 *(978-1-59707-137-6(4)*, 900056070) Papercutz.

Todd, Sheri. Little Bent Cedar. Speed, Bryan W. 2007. (ENG.). 24p. (J). (gr. 2-4). per. *(978-1-933255-38-5(2))* DNA Pr.

Todd-Stanton, Joe. Bear. Queen, Ben. 2020. (ENG.). 160p. (J). 24.99 ***(978-1-68415-531-6(2)***, Archaia Entertainment) Boom! Studios.

Todd-Stanton, Joe. Everest: the Remarkable Story of Edmund Hillary & Tenzing Norgay. Stewart, Alexandra. 2020. (ENG.). 64p. (J). 21.99 *(978-1-5476-0159-2(0)*, 900200537, Bloomsbury Children's Bks.) Bloomsbury Publishing USA.

—The Story Pirates Present: Quest for the Crystal Crown. Bondor-Stone, Annabeth et al. 2020. (Story Pirates Ser.: 3). (ENG.). 288p. (J). (gr. 3-7). 13.99 *(978-0-593-12063-7(9)*, Random Hse. Bks. for Young Readers) Random Hse. Children's Bks.

Todd, Sue. An African Alphabet, 1 vol. Walters, Eric. 2017. (ENG.). 28p. (J). (gr. -1 — 1). bds. 9.95 *(978-1-4598-1070-9(8))* Orca Bk. Pubs. USA.

—Medio Pollito (Half-Chick) A Mexican Folktale. StJohn, Amanda. 2011. (Folktales from Around the World Ser.). (ENG.). 24p. (J). (gr. k-3). 28.50 *(978-1-60973-141-0(7)*, 201144) Child's World, Inc., The.

—Mira & the Big Story. Alary, Laura. 2012. (ENG.). 36p. (J). 12.00 *(978-1-55896-693-2(5)*, Skinner Hse. Bks.) Unitarian Universalist Assn.

—Steam! Taming the River Monster. Coleman, Wim & Perrin, Pat. 2015. (Setting the Stage for Fluency Ser.). (ENG.). 40p. (J). (gr. 3-5). lib. bdg. 27.99 *(978-1-939656-74-2(5))* Red Chair Pr.

Toddy, Irving. D Is for Drum: A Native American Alphabet. Shoulders, Michael & Shoulders, Debbie. rev. ed. 2006. (ENG.). 40p. (J). (gr. k-6). 16.95 *(978-1-58536-274-5(3))* Sleeping Bear Pr.

—Desert Digits: An Arizona Number Book. Gowan, Barbara. 2006. (Count Your Way Across the U. S. A. Ser.). (ENG.). 40p. (J). (gr. -1-3). 17.95 *(978-1-58536-162-5(3))* Sleeping Bear Pr.

—Little Woman Warrior Who Came Home. Yazzie, Evangeline Parsons. Ruffenach, Jessie, ed. 2005. (NAV & ENG.). 32p. (J). (gr. 4-7). 17.95 *(978-1-893354-55-5(5))* Salina Bookshelf Inc.

—A Summer's Trade/Shiigo Na'iini' Trotter, Deborah W. 2007. (ENG & NAV.). 32p. (J). (gr. -1-3). 17.95 *(978-1-893354-71-5(7))* Salina Bookshelf Inc.

Todo Color. Biblia Ilustrada para Ninos. Winkler, Jude. 2007. 172p. (J). (gr. -1-3). 12.99 *(978-0-89942-636-5(0))* Catholic Bk. Publishing Corp.

Toft, Kim Michelle. The World That We Want. Toft, Kim Michelle. 2005. 32p. (J). pap. *(978-0-7022-3482-8(6))* Univ. of Queensland Pr.

Toft, Lis. Gloria Rising. Cameron, Ann. 2004. (Julian's World Ser.). (ENG.). 112p. (J). (gr. 1-4). 5.99 *(978-0-440-41998-3(0)*, Random Hse. Bks. for Young Readers) Random Hse. Children's Bks.

Tofte, Mavis. Doogie Dork & the Storm. Tofte, Mavis. 2006. 64p. (J). per. 6.75 *(978-0-9709906-5-5(0))* Creative Quill Publishing, Inc.

—Doogie Dork's Wish. Tofte, Mavis. 2003. (J). per. 5.75 *(978-0-9709906-2-4(6))* Creative Quill Publishing, Inc.

Tofts, Hannah. One Cool Watermelon. Tofts, Hannah. 2008. (Things I Eat Ser.). (ENG.). 24p. (J). (gr. -1-k). *(978-1-84089-555-1(1))* Zero to Ten, Ltd.

Tognoni Miller, Christine, jt. illus. see Ozoude, Marie.

Togo, Narisa. Magnificent Birds. 2018. (ENG.). 32p. (J). (gr. 5-9). 20.00 *(978-1-5362-0169-7(3))* Candlewick Pr.

Tok, Stephanie. Kungfu for Kids. Eng, Paul. 2016. (Martial Arts for Kids Ser.). 48p. (J). (gr. k-3). 8.95 *(978-0-8048-4740-7(1))* Tuttle Publishing.

Tok, Stephanie. Karate for Kids. Tok, Stephanie. Rielly, Robin L. 2004. (Martial Arts for Kids Ser.). 48p. (J). (gr. k-3). 13.95 *(978-0-8048-3534-3(9))* Tuttle Publishing.

—Taekwondo for Kids. Tok, Stephanie. Park, Y. H. 2005. (Martial Arts for Kids Ser.). (ENG.). 48p. (J). (gr. k-3). 13.95 *(978-0-8048-3631-9(0))* Tuttle Publishing.

Toka, Yumie. Jimi's Book of Japanese: A Motivating Method to Learn Japanese (Extra Spicy Super Crunchy Edition) Takahashi, Peter X. ltd. ed. 2006. 172p. (J). pap. 34.95 *(978-0-9723247-1-7(2)*, PB&J OmniMedia) Takahashi & Black.

—Jimi's Book of Japanese: A Motivating Method to Learn Japanese (Hiragana) Takahashi, Peter X. 2003. (JPN & ENG.). 72p. reprint ed. pap. 18.95 *(978-0-9723247-0-0(4)*, PB&J OmniMedia) Takahashi & Black.

—Jimi's Book of Japanese: A Motivating Method to Learn Japanese (Kanji) Takahashi, Peter X. Moto, Mikki, ed. 2006. (J). pap. 24.95 *(978-0-9723247-5-5(5)*, PB&J OmniMedia) Takahashi & Black.

—Jimi's Book of Japanese: A Motivating Method to Learn Japanese (Katakana) Takahashi, Peter X. Moto, Mikki, ed. 2005. (JPN & ENG.). 76p. (J). pap. 18.95 *(978-0-9723247-2-4(0)*, PB&J OmniMedia) Takahashi & Black.

—Jimi's Book of Japanese: A Motivating Method to Learn Japanese (Some of My Best Friends Are Monkeys Edition), 2 vols. Takahashi, Peter X. Moto, Mikki, ed. ltd. ed. 2005. 146p. pap. 36.95 *(978-0-9723247-4-8(7)*, PB&J OmniMedia) Takahashi & Black.

—Jimi's Sumo Stack: A Motivating Method to Memorize Japanese. Takahashi, Peter X. 2006. pap. 19.95 *(978-0-9723247-8-6(X)*, PB&J OmniMedia) Takahashi & Black.

Tokareva, Anna. Margaret & Eleanor & the Unicorn. Tickner, Natalie. 2019. (ENG.). 38p. (J). pap. 9.95 ***(978-1-7063-2636-6(X))*** Independently Published.

Tokyopop Staff. Rave Master: The Sound of Thunder, Vol. 3. 2005. 96p. (J). pap. 7.99 *(978-1-59532-791-8(6))* TOKYOPOP, Inc.

Tokyopop Staff. Passion Fruit: Sweat & Honey, 3 vols., Vol. 1. Tokyopop Staff. ltd. ed. 2005. 208p. pap. 19.99 *(978-1-59182-796-2(5))* TOKYOPOP, Inc.

Tola, Olsi. The Bully Frog. West, Luthie M. 2018. (ENG.). 54p. 18.99 *(978-1-7322514-0-3(1))* Luthie M West.

Toland, Darrell. Edsel Mcfarlan's New Car. Holechek, Max. 2010. 52p. (J). *(978-1-935359-40-1(1))* Bk. Pubs. Network.

Toledano, Diana. Polly Diamond & the Magic Book. Kuipers, Alice. 2018. (Polly Diamond Ser.). (ENG.). 160p. (J). (gr. 1-4). 14.99 *(978-1-4521-5232-5(2))* Chronicle Bks. LLC.

—Polly Diamond & the Magic Book: Book 1. Kuipers, Alice. 2019. (ENG.). 112p. (J). (gr. 1-4). pap. 6.99 *(978-1-4521-8221-6(3))* Chronicle Bks. LLC.

—Polly Diamond & the Super, Stunning, Spectacular School Fair, Bk. 2. Kuipers, Alice. 2019. (ENG.). 112p. (J). (gr. 2-5). 14.99 *(978-1-4521-5233-2(0))* Chronicle Bks. LLC.

Toledano, Diana. Rocking Bed of Dreams. Meister, Cari. 2020. (New Books for Newborns Ser.). (ENG.). 16p. (J). (— 1). bds. 7.99 ***(978-1-5344-4174-3(3)***, Little Simon) Little Simon.

Toledano, Diane. One Snowy Day. Murray, Diana. 2018. (ENG.). 32p. (J). (-4). 17.99 *(978-1-4926-4586-3(9))* Sourcebooks, Inc.

Toledo, Aaron. Penelope Pinwheel & the Pink & Purple Palace. Wolf, Nancy. 2016. (ENG.). (J). 29.95 *(978-1-4787-8282-7(X))*; pap. 19.95 *(978-1-4787-8034-2(7))* Outskirts Pr., Inc.

Tolentino, Angela. A Whale Who Dreamt of a Snail / Traditional Chinese Edition: Babl Children's Books in Chinese & English. Heimbach, William. l.t. ed. 2016. (ENG.). (J). 14.99 *(978-1-68304-189-4(5))* Babl Books, Incorporated.

Tolford, Joshua. Blitz. Beatty, Hetty Burlingame. 2012. 124p. 40.95 *(978-1-258-25354-7(2))*; pap. 25.95 *(978-1-258-25430-8(1))* Literary Licensing, LLC.

Tolkien, J. R. R. The Hobbit. Tolkien, J. R. R. 70th anniv. ed. 2011. (ENG.). 400p. mass mkt. 8.99 *(978-0-261-10221-7(4))* HarperCollins Pubs. Ltd.

—The Hobbit. Tolkien, J. R. R. 75th anniv. ed. 2007. (ENG.). 320p. (gr. 7). 26.00 *(978-0-618-96863-3(6)*, 1022630) Houghton Mifflin Harcourt Publishing Co.

Tolland, Margaret. Go, Green Gecko! Hay, Gay. 2017. 40p. (J). (gr. 1-2). 17.95 *(978-1-76036-033-7(3)*, 6d1a72b0-c89a-49a8-8066-f192c0b154f0) Starfish Bay Publishing Pty Ltd. AUS. Dist: Baker & Taylor Publisher Services (BTPS).

—Seed Magic. McKinnon, Natalie. 2018. (Spider Ser.). 40p. (J). (gr. 1-2). 15.95 *(978-1-76036-031-3(7)*, 1ec2d89d-eb4c-41d0-91c6-e0c6833650fc) Starfish Bay Publishing Pty Ltd. AUS. Dist: Baker & Taylor Publisher Services (BTPS).

Tolle, Glenn. Funny Things Happened That Sunday Morning. Hranjec, Stephanie. 2018. (ENG.). 26p. (J). pap. 9.80 *(978-1-7908-6261-0(2))* Independently Published.

Tolman, Marije. Intercambio Magico. Heide, Iris van der. De Sterck, Goedele, tr. 2009. (Los Especiales de A la Orilla del Viento Ser.). (SPA.). 28p. (J). (gr. -1-3). *(978-968-16-8565-2(2))* Fondo de Cultura Economica.

—What Dog Knows. Heede, Sylvia Vanden. 2016. 128p. (J). pap. 19.99 *(978-1-77657-037-9(5))* Gecko Pr. NZL. Dist: Lerner Publishing Group.

—Wolf & Dog. Vanden Heede, Sylvia. 2013. (ENG.). 96p. (J). (gr. 1-4). 16.95 *(978-1-877579-47-9(5))* Gecko Pr. NZL. Dist: Lerner Publishing Group.

Tolman, Tom. Little One. Reid, Pamela Carrington. 2010. (J). *(978-1-59811-574-1(X))* Covenant Communications.

Tolson, Hannah. Ants. Williams, Susie. 2020. 32p. (J). ***(978-0-7787-7386-3(8))*** Crabtree Publishing Co.

Tolson, Hannah. Caterpillar & Bean: A First Science Storybook. Jenkins, Martin. 2019. (ENG.). 32p. (J). (-k). 16.99 *(978-1-5362-0170-3(7))* Candlewick Pr.

Tolson, Hannah. Centipedes & Millipedes. Williams, Susie. 2020. 32p. (J). ***(978-0-7787-7387-0(6))*** Crabtree Publishing Co.

Tolson, Hannah. I've Got a Tail! Murphy, Julie. 2020. (ENG.). 32p. (J). (gr. -1-1). 17.99 *(978-1-68152-501-3(1))* Amicus.

—I've Got Eyes! Exceptional Eyes of the Animal World. Murphy, Julie. 2018. 32p. (J). (gr. k-3). 17.99 *(978-1-68152-404-7(X))* Amicus.

—I've Got Feet!: Fantastical Feet of the Animal World. Murphy, Julie. 2017. 32p. (J). (gr. -1-1). 17.99 *(978-1-68152-195-4(4))* Amicus.

—My Mommy Is a Hero. 2018. 32p. 12.99 *(978-1-61067-721-9(8))* Kane Miller.

—Ossiri & the Bala Mengro. Quarmby, Katharine & O'Neill, Richard. 2017. (Child's Play Library). (ENG.). 32p. (J). *(978-1-84643-925-4(6))* Child's Play International Ltd.

Tolson, Hannah. Snails. Williams, Susie. 2020. 32p. (J). ***(978-0-7787-7388-7(4))*** Crabtree Publishing Co.

—Worms. Williams, Susie. 2020. 32p. (J). ***(978-0-7787-7389-4(2))*** Crabtree Publishing Co.

Tolson, Maria. Selah's Prayer. Khalfani, Natasha M. & Khalfani, Jabari N. 2015. (Selah's Prayer Ser.: Vol. 1). (ENG.). 30p. (J). (gr. k-6). 20.00 *(978-0-692-38558-6(4))* Khalfani, Natasha.

Tolson, Scott. If You Want My Advice- Owens, L. L. 2004. 25p. *(978-1-57021-030-3(6))* Comprehensive Health Education Foundation.

—The Longest Car Ride Ever. Owens, L. L. 2004. 28p. *(978-1-57021-032-7(2))* Comprehensive Health Education Foundation.

—The New Girl. Owens, L. L. 2004. 27p. *(978-1-57021-029-7(2))* Comprehensive Health Education Foundation.

Tolstikova, Daria & Tolstikova, Dasha. If a T. Rex Crashes Your Birthday Party. Esbaum, Jill. 2016. 40p. (J). (gr. -1-2). 14.95 *(978-1-4549-1550-8(1))* Sterling Publishing Co., Inc.

Tolstikova, Dasha. Friend or Foe?, 1 vol. Sobol, John. 2016. (ENG.). 32p. (J). (gr. -1-2). 18.95 *(978-1-55498-407-7(6))* Groundwood Bks. CAN. Dist: Publishers Group West (PGW).

—The Jacket. Hall, Kirsten. 2014. (ENG.). 48p. (J). (gr. -1-3). 17.95 *(978-1-59270-168-1(X))* Enchanted Lion Bks., LLC.

—Violet & the Woof. Grabill, Rebecca. 2018. (ENG.). 40p. (J). (gr. -1-3). 17.99 *(978-0-06-244110-2(8))* HarperCollins Pubs.

Tolstikova, Dasha, jt. illus. see Tolstikova, Daria.

Tolton, Laura. Grandpa's Lost Pin. Aboff, Marcie. 2016. (Spring Forward Ser.). (J). (gr. 1). *(978-1-4900-9373-4(7))* Benchmark Education Co.

Tolton, Laura. The Young Witch's Guide to Magick. Eason, Cassandra. 2020. (Young Witch's Guides: 2). 160p. (YA). (gr. 7-12). 16.95 ***(978-1-4549-3685-5(1))*** Sterling Publishing Co., Inc.

Tolutis, Vytenis, jt. illus. see Gil, Ismael.

Tom, Darcy. Advantage Reading Grade 3, Vol. 8114. Morss, Martha. Hamaguchi, Carla, ed. 2004. (Advantage Workbook Ser.). 112p. 8.99 *(978-1-59198-024-7(0)*, CTP 8114) Creative Teaching Pr., Inc.

—Down on the Farm. Jordano, Kimberly & Corcoran, Tebra. Fisch, Teri L., ed. 2003. (Stepping into Standards Theme Ser.). 64p. (J). (gr. k-2). pap. 10.99 *(978-1-57471-947-5(5)*, 2475) Creative Teaching Pr., Inc.

—Going Buggy! Jordano, Kimberly & Corcoran, Tebra. Fisch, Teri L., ed. 2003. (Stepping into Standards Theme Ser.). 64p. (J). (gr. k-2). pap. 10.99 *(978-1-57471-949-9(1)*, 2477) Creative Teaching Pr., Inc.

—Native American Peoples. Jennett, Pamela. Rous, Sheri, ed. 2003. (Stepping into Standards Theme Ser.). 64p. (J). (gr. 2-4). pap. 10.99 *(978-1-59198-003-2(8)*, CTP2485) Creative Teaching Pr., Inc.

—Rain Forest Adventures. Jordano, Kimberly & Corcoran, Tebra. Fisch, Teri L., ed. 2003. (Stepping into Standards Theme Ser.). 64p. (J). (gr. k-2). pap. 10.99 *(978-1-57471-945-1(9)*, 2473) Creative Teaching Pr., Inc.

—Reading First: Unlock the Secrets to Reading Success with Research-Based Strategies, Vol. 2259. Hults, Alaska. Hamaguchi, Carla, ed. 2003. 176p. per. 13.99 *(978-1-59198-009-4(7)*, CTP2259) Creative Teaching Pr., Inc.

—Rocks & Minerals. Shiotsu, Vicky. Rous, Sheri, ed. 2003. (Stepping into Standards Theme Ser.). 64p. (J). (gr. 2-4). pap. 10.99 *(978-1-59198-005-6(4)*, CTP2487) Creative Teaching Pr., Inc.

—Solar System. Cernek, Kim et al. Rous, Sheri & Hamaguchi, Carla, eds. 2003. (Stepping into Standards Theme Ser.). 64p. (J). (gr. 2-4). pap. 10.99 *(978-1-59198-001-8(1)*, 2483) Creative Teaching Pr., Inc.

—Super Senses. Jordano, Kimberly & Corcoran, Tebra. Fisch, Teri L., ed. 2003. (Stepping into Standards Theme Ser.). 64p. (J). (gr. k-2). pap. 10.99 *(978-1-57471-951-2(3)*, 2479) Creative Teaching Pr., Inc.

Tom, Darcy. Habitats. Tom, Darcy, ed. Phillips, Heather. Jennett, Pamela & Rous, Sheri, eds. 2003. (Stepping into Standards Theme Ser.). 64p. (J). (gr. 2-4). pap. 10.99 *(978-1-59198-007-0(0)*, CTP2489) Creative Teaching Pr., Inc.

Tom, Darcy & Grayson, Rick. Bookmaking Bonanza, Vol. 2234. Jordano, Kimberly & Adsit, Kim. Cernek, Kim, ed. 2004. 80p. (J). (gr. k-1). pap. 11.99 *(978-1-59198-049-0(6))* Creative Teaching Pr., Inc.

Tom, Darcy & Mathis, Teresa. Kid Concoctions, Creations & Contraptions. Eagan, Robynne. 2005. (ENG.). 224p. pap. 18.95 *(978-1-57310-455-5(8))* Teaching & Learning Co.

Tom, Darcy, jt. illus. see Campbell, Jenny.

Tom Jellett. The Besties Show & Smell. Arena, Felice. 2020. (Besties Ser.). (ENG.). 80p. (J). (gr. 1-3). 9.99 ***(978-1-76089-098-8(7)***, Puffin) Penguin Random Hse. AUS. Dist: Independent Pubs. Group.

Tom, Leonard. Under the Sea. Riggs, Kate. 2017. (ENG.). 14p. (J). (gr. -1 — 1). bds. 8.99 *(978-1-56846-302-5(2)*, Creative Editions) Creative Co., The.

Tomas, Nuria. Rain Cloud: A Story about the Water Cycle (and Plants, Too) Gagnon, Natalie. 2020. (ENG.). 30p. (J). pap. 9.49 ***(978-1-0904-1860-9(4))*** Independently Published.

Tomasek, Dean. The Christmas Tree That Cried. Marshall, Jane Garrett. 2013. 106p. pap. 24.99 *(978-0-9896247-0-1(6))* WRB Pub.

Tomasello, Sam. Gardening with Children. Hanneman, Monika et al. 2011. (BBG Guides for a Greener Planet Ser.). (ENG.). 120p. pap. 12.95 *(978-1-889538-78-5(7))* Brooklyn Botanic Garden.

Tomato Farm. Finders Keepers (DC Super Hero Girls) Carbone, Courtney. 2017. (Pictureback(R) Ser.). (ENG.). 16p. (J). (gr. -1-2). pap. 4.99 *(978-1-5247-6609-2(7)*, Random Hse. Bks. for Young Readers) Random Hse. Children's Bks.

Tomb, R. W. B. Revenge of the Goldfish: Upbeat, Fun Poems for 4 - 7 Year Olds. Griffey, A. F. B. 2016. (ENG.). 32p. (J). (gr. k-2). pap. *(978-0-9935564-0-1(X))* Louannvee Publishing.

Tombleson, Drew. A Tour Through Dragon Dreamland. Tombleson, Alan, ed. 2019. (Dragon Dreamland Ser.: Vol. 1). (ENG.). 36p. (J). (gr. k-4). 25.14 *(978-1-7336825-0-3(3))* ParaTomb Studios.

Tomes, Margot. Homesick: My Own Story. Fritz, Jean. 2007. (Puffin Modern Classics Ser.). (ENG.). 176p. (J). (gr. 3-7). 8.99 *(978-0-14-240761-5(5)*, Puffin Books) Penguin Young Readers Group.

Tomi, Doctor. Loving You Always. Tomi, Doctor. 2019. (ENG.). 26p. (J). pap. 10.00 *(978-1-0960-4135-1(9))* Independently Published.

Tomic, Tomislav. The Fairy Tale Handbook. Hamilton, Libby. 2014. (ENG.). 20p. (J). (gr. k-4). 22.99 *(978-0-7636-7130-3(4)*, Templar) Candlewick Pr.

—The Forbidden Expedition. Bell, Alex. 2019. (Polar Bear Explorers' Club Ser.: 2). (ENG.). 352p. (J). (gr. 3-7). 18.99 *(978-1-5344-0649-0(2)*, Simon & Schuster Bks. For Young Readers) Simon & Schuster Bks. For Young Readers.

—The Polar Bear Explorers' Club. Bell, Alex. 2018. (Polar Bear Explorers' Club Ser.: 1). (ENG.). 320p. (J). (gr. 3-7). 17.99 *(978-1-5344-0646-9(8)*, Simon & Schuster Bks. For Young Readers) Simon & Schuster Bks. For Young Readers.

Tomita, Sukehiro & Yazawa, Nao. Wedding Peach, Vol. 1. Tomita, Sukehiro. 2003. (Wedding Peach Ser.). (ENG.). 192p. (YA). pap. 9.95 *(978-1-59116-076-2(6))* Viz Media.

Tomizawa, Hitoshi. Alien Nine: Emulators. Tomizawa, Hitoshi. Pannone, Frank, ed. Jackson, Laura & Kobayashi, Yoko, trs. from JPN. 2004. 248p. pap. 9.99 (978-1-58664-924-1(8), CMX 65004G, CPM Manga) Central Park Media Corp.
—Alien Nine 1, Vol. 1. Tomizawa, Hitoshi. Pannone, Frank, ed. Jackson, Laura & Kobayashi, Yoko, trs. from JPN. 2003. 224p. (gr. 11-18). pap. 15.95 (978-1-58664-891-6(8), CMX 64201G, CPM Manga) Central Park Media Corp.
—Alien Nine 2, Vol. 2. Tomizawa, Hitoshi. Pannone, Frank, ed. Jackson, Laura & Kobayashi, Yoko, trs. from JPN. 2003. 224p. (gr. 11-18). pap. 15.95 (978-1-58664-892-3(6), CMX 64202G, CPM Manga) Central Park Media Corp.
—Treasure Hunter 1: Eternal Youth, 3 vols., Vol. 1. Tomizawa, Hitoshi. Pannone, Frank, ed. Kobayashi, Mayumi, tr. from JPN. 2004. Orig. Title: Hizenya Jyubei 2. 200p. pap. 9.99 (978-1-58664-921-0(3), CMX 65101G, CPM Manga) Central Park Media Corp.
—Treasure Hunter 2: Figurehead of Souls, 3 vols., Vol. 2. Tomizawa, Hitoshi. Pannone, Frank, ed. Kobayashi, Mayumi, tr. from JPN. 2004. Orig. Title: Hizenya Jyubei 2. 200p. pap. 9.99 (978-1-58664-922-7(1), CMX 65102G, CPM Manga) Central Park Media Corp.
—Treasure Hunter 3: The Last Crusade, 3 vols., Vol. 3. Tomizawa, Hitoshi. Pannone, Frank, ed. Kobayashi, Mayumi, tr. from JPN. 2004. Orig. Title: Hizenya Jyubei 2. 216p. pap. 9.99 (978-1-58664-923-4(X), CMX 65103G, CPM Manga) Central Park Media Corp.
Tomkinson, Tim. What Was the Gold Rush? Holub, Joan & Who HQ. 2013. (What Was? Ser.). 112p. (J). (gr. 3-7). pap. 5.99 (978-0-448-46289-9(3), Penguin Workshop) Penguin Young Readers Group.
—What Was the March on Washington? Krull, Kathleen & Who HQ. 2013. (What Was? Ser.). 112p. (J). (gr. 3-7). pap. 5.99 (978-0-448-46287-5(7), Penguin Workshop) Penguin Young Readers Group.
Tomlins, Karen. Winston Churchill. Daynes, Katie. 2006. (Usborne Famous Lives Gift Bks.). 64p. (J). (gr. 2-5). 8.99 (978-0-7945-1258-3(5), Usborne) EDC Publishing.
Tomlinson, Azure Chapman. The Three-Cornered Blanket. Chapman, Denalee Call & Call, Dennis Boyd. 2018. (ENG.). 50p. (J). pap. 5.99 (978-1-7238-4074-6(2)) Independently Published.
Tomlinson, Lauresa. Elaytay's Adventures in Space & Time: Part Two - We Meet at Last. Tomlinson, Laurea a. 2018. (We Meet at Last Ser.). (ENG.). 198p. (YA). (gr. 7-12). 17.99 **(978-1-950421-22-0(8))** Young of Heart Publishing.
—Elaytay's Adventures in Space & Time: We Came to Visit. Tomlinson, Lauresa A. 2018. (ENG.). 166p. (YA). (gr. 7-12). 17.99 **(978-1-950421-19-0(8))** Young of Heart Publishing.
—My Interview with a Fairy. Tomlinson, Lauresa A. 2018. (ENG.). 134p. (J). (gr. 2-6). 19.99 **(978-1-950421-21-3(X))** Young of Heart Publishing.
Tomlinson, Lauresa. Crazy Deja' Vu. Tomlinson, Lauresa. 2019. (ENG.). (YA). (gr. 7-12). 188p. pap. 16.99 (978-1-950421-09-1(0)); 282p. 24.99 **(978-1-950421-18-3(X))** Young of Heart Publishing.
Tomlinson, Lauresa. There's an Alien in My Cereal. Tomlinson, Lauresa. 2018. (ENG.). 72p. (J). (gr. 2-6). 16.99 **(978-1-950421-17-6(1))** Young of Heart Publishing.
Tomlinson, Lauresa. The Turning Stone. Tomlinson, Lauresa. 2nd ed. 2019. (ENG.). (J). (gr. 2-6). 104p. pap. 9.99 (978-1-950421-05-3(8)); 102p. 17.99 **(978-1-950421-20-6(1))** Young of Heart Publishing.
Tomlinson, Lauresa A. Crazy Deja Vu - Not Again. Tomlinson, Lauresa A. 2019. (ENG.). (YA). (gr. 7-12). 268p. 24.99 **(978-1-950421-16-9(3))**; 258p. pap. 16.99 **(978-1-950421-13-8(9))** Young of Heart Publishing.
Tomm, Nora. Who Believes What? Exploring the World's Major Religions. Wills, Anna. 2018. (ENG.). 40p. (J). (gr. 4-8). 18.95 (978-1-77147-333-0(9)) Owlkids Bks. Inc. CAN. Dist: Publishers Group West (PGW).
Tommer, Sarah. Sidney the Silly Who Only Eats 6. Penn, M. W. 2007. 32p. (J). (978-0-9784047-2-7(6)) Pays et Terroirs.
—Sidney the Silly Who Only Eats 6. Penn, Mw. 2013. 36p. pap. 13.95 (978-0-9840425-7-9(1)) MathWord Pr., LLC.
Tomos, Angharad. Rala Rwdins. Tomos, Angharad. 2005. (WEL.). 48p. pap. 1.95 (978-0-86243-065-8(8)) Y Lolfa GBR. Dist: Dufour Editions, Inc.
Tomos, Morgan. Welsh Folk Stories. Edwards, Meinir Wyn. 2012. (ENG.). 128p. (J). pap. 9.95 (978-1-84771-358-2(0)) Y Lolfa GBR. Dist: Casemate Pubs. & Bk. Distributors, LLC.
Tomova, Veselina. An Old Man's Winter Night: Ghostly Tales, 1 vol. Dawe, Tom. 2019. (ENG.). 60p. (J). (gr. 4-7). pap. 13.95 **(978-1-927917-23-7(9))** Running the Goat, Bks. & Broadsides CAN. Dist: Orca Bk. Pubs. USA.
—Spirited Away: Fairy Stories of Old Newfoundland, 1 vol. Dawe, Tom. (ENG.). 60p. (J). (gr. 4-7). 2019. pap. 13.95 **(978-1-927917-22-0(0))**; 2017. 22.99 **(978-1-927917-13-8(1))** Running the Goat, Bks. & Broadsides CAN. Dist: Orca Bk. Pubs. USA.
Tomova, Veselina & Tomova, Veselina. PB's Comet, 1 vol. Parsons, Marnie & Parsons, Marnie. 2018. (ENG.). 32p. (J). (gr. -1-3). pap. 12.95 **(978-1-927917-12-1(3))** Running the Goat, Bks. & Broadsides CAN. Dist: Orca Bk. Pubs. USA.
Tomova, Veselina, jt. illus. see Tomova, Veselina.
Tompkins, Abigail. Where's the Potty on This Ark? Olitzky, Kerry. 2018. (ENG.). 24p. (J). (gr. -1 — 1). 17.99 (978-1-5124-8370-3(2), Kar-Ben Publishing) Lerner Publishing Group.
Tompkins, Erle. The Adventures of Avery & Masa: Lost & Found on Java Island. Barrett, Steve. 2016. (ENG.). (J). pap. 8.99 (978-0-9982242-2-0(7)) Fauna Nirvana LLC.
Tonel. Drum, Chavi, Drum! Dole, Mayra L. 2013.Tr. of ¡Toca, Chavi, Toca!. (ENG & SPA.). 32p. (J). pap. 9.95 (978-0-89239-302-2(5), Children's Book Press) Lee & Low Bks., Inc.
—Toca, Chavi, Toca! Dole, Mayra L. 2003.Tr. of Drum, Chavi, Drum!. (ENG & SPA.). 32p. (J). 16.95 (978-0-89239-186-8(3)) Lee & Low Bks., Inc.
Tonel, jt. illus. see Pedlar, Elaine.

Tong, Andie. Batman Classic - The Joker's Ice Scream. Lemke, Donald. 2015. (I Can Read Level 2 Ser.). (ENG.). 32p. (J). (gr. -1-3). pap. 3.99 (978-0-06-234492-2(7)) HarperCollins Pubs.
—Batman Classic: Coin Toss. Black, Jake. 2016. 24p. (J). (gr. -1-3). pap. 3.99 (978-0-06-234491-5(9), HarperFestival) HarperCollins Pubs.
—Batman Classic: I Am Batman. Finnegan, Delphine. 2016. (I Can Read Level 2 Ser.). 32p. (J). (gr. -1-3). pap. 3.99 (978-0-06-236087-8(6)) HarperCollins Pubs.
—Batman Classic: Poison Ivy's Scare Fair. Lemke, Donald. 2017. 24p. (J). (gr. -1-3). pap. 3.99 (978-0-06-236077-9(9), HarperFestival) HarperCollins Pubs.
—Batman Versus Bane. Huelin, Jodi. 2012. (I Can Read Book 2 Ser.). (ENG.). 32p. (J). (gr. -1-3). pap. 3.99 (978-0-06-213224-6(5)) HarperCollins Pubs.
—Coin Toss. Black, Jake & Kane, Bob. 2016. (J). (978-1-4844-7564-5(X)) HarperCollins Pubs. Ltd.
—Day of the Undead. Sazaklis, John & Merkel, Joe F. 2013. (ENG.). 24p. (J). (gr. -1-3). pap. 3.99 (978-0-06-220999-3(X), HarperFestival) HarperCollins Pubs.
—Green Lantern: Legacy. Le, Minh. 2020. 144p. (J). (gr. 3-7). pap. 9.99 (978-1-4012-8355-1(1)) DC Comics.
—I Am Batman. Finnegan, Delphine et al. 2016. 32p. (J). (978-1-4844-9378-6(8)) Harper & Row Ltd.
—I Am Batman. Finnegan, Delphine. ed. 2016. (Batman Classic I Can Read Level 2 Ser.). (ENG.). 32p. (J). (gr. -1-3). 13.55 (978-0-606-39268-6(8)) Turtleback.
—Justice League Reading Collection. 2017. (I Can Read Level 2 Ser.). (ENG.). 160p. (J). (gr. -1-3). pap. 16.99 (978-0-06-229187-5(4)) HarperCollins Pubs.
—Nightmare in Gotham City. Lemke, Donald. 2015. (ENG.). 24p. (J). (gr. -1-3). pap. 3.99 (978-0-06-234486-1(2), HarperFestival) HarperCollins Pubs.
—Poison Ivy's Scare Fair. Lemke, Donald B. 2017. (J). (978-1-5182-3638-9(3)) HarperCollins Pubs. Ltd.
—Soldier Dogs #2: Attack on Pearl Harbor. Sutter, Marcus. 2018. (Soldier Dogs Ser.: 2). (ENG.). 176p. (J). (gr. 3-7). 12.99 (978-0-06-288854-9(4)); pap. 7.99 (978-0-06-284405-7(9)) HarperCollins Pubs. (HarperFestival).
—Soldier Dogs #3: Secret Mission: Guam. Sutter, Marcus. 2019. (Soldier Dogs Ser.: 3). (ENG.). 192p. (J). (gr. 3-7). pap. 7.99 (978-0-06-284407-1(5), HarperFestival) HarperCollins Pubs.
—Soldier Dogs #4: Victory at Normandy. Sutter, Marcus. 2019. (Soldier Dogs Ser.: 4). (ENG.). 192p. (J). (gr. 3-7). pap. 7.99 (978-0-06-284409-5(1), HarperFestival) HarperCollins Pubs.
—Soldier Dogs #5: Battle of the Bulge. Sutter, Marcus. 2019. (Soldier Dogs Ser.: 5). (ENG.). 192p. (J). (gr. 3-7). pap. 7.99 (978-0-06-295794-8(5), HarperFestival) HarperCollins Pubs.
—Soldier Dogs #6: Heroes on the Home Front. Sutter, Marcus. 2020. (Soldier Dogs Ser.: 6). (ENG.). 192p. (J). (gr. 3-7). pap. 7.99 (978-0-06-295797-9(X), HarperFestival) HarperCollins Pubs.
—Star Wars the Mighty Chewbacca in the Forest of Fear. Angleberger, Tom. 2018. (ENG.). 272p. (J). (gr. 4-7). 13.99 (978-1-368-01629-2(4), Disney Lucasfilm Press) Disney Publishing Worldwide.
—Superman's Superpowers. Rosen, Lucy. 2013. (I Can Read Level 2 Ser.). (ENG.). 32p. (J). (gr. -1-3). pap. 3.99 (978-0-06-223597-8(4)) HarperCollins Pubs.
—The Zodiac Legacy: Balance of Power. Lee, Stan & Moore, Stuart. (Zodiac Ser.). (ENG.). 448p. (J). (gr. 3-7). 2018. pap. 9.99 (978-1-4847-5250-0(3)); 2017. 16.99 (978-1-4847-1351-8(6)) Disney Pr.
—The Zodiac Legacy: Convergence. Lee, Stan & Moore, Stuart. 2015. (Zodiac Ser.). (ENG.). 488p. (J). (gr. 3-7). 16.99 (978-1-4231-8085-2(2)) Disney Pr.
—The Zodiac Legacy: the Dragon's Return. Lee, Stan. 2017. (Zodiac Ser.). (ENG.). 448p. (J). (gr. 3-7). pap. 9.99 (978-1-4847-5255-5(4)) Disney Pr.
—The Zodiac Legacy: the Dragon's Return. Lee, Stan & Moore, Stuart. 2016. (Zodiac Ser.: Bk. 2). (ENG.). 432p. (J). (gr. 3-7). 16.99 (978-1-4847-1352-5(4)) Disney Pr.
Tong, Kevin. The Earth Machine. Tong, Kevin. 2007. 32p. (J). (gr. -1-3). 15.95 (978-1-60108-001-1(8)) Red Cygnet Pr.
Tong, Paul. The Night of the Hurricane's Fury. Ransom, Candice. 2011. (On My Own History Ser.). 48p. (J). pap. 39.62 (978-0-7613-7621-7(6)); (ENG.). (gr. 2-4). pap. 7.99 (978-0-7613-3940-3(X)) Lerner Publishing Group. (First Avenue Editions).
—Pecos Bill. Krensky, Stephen. 2007. (On My Own Folklore Ser.). (ENG.). 48p. (J). (gr. 2-4). per. 7.99 (978-0-8225-6475-1(0), First Avenue Editions) Lerner Publishing Group.
—Pecos Bill. 2006. (On My Own Folklore Ser.). 48p. (J). (gr. -1-3). lib. bdg. 25.26 (978-1-57505-889-4(8), Millbrook Pr.) Lerner Publishing Group.
Tong Tong, Tong. I Can Do It: An Adaptation of Jack & the Beanstalk. Million, So. 2019. (ENG.). 36p. (J). pap. 25.01 **(978-1-5437-5411-7(2))** Partridge Pub.
Tong, Vivian. Finding Lost Stars. Curley, Grace H. 2019. (ENG.). 516p. (YA). (gr. 7-12). pap. 25.95 **(978-1-64633-215-1(6))** Independent Pub.
Toni, Alessandra. Where's My Mommy? Hao, K. T. 2008. (ENG.). 32p. (J). (gr. -1). 15.95 (978-1-933327-40-2(5)) Purple Bear Bks., Inc.
—Where's My Mommy? Hao, K. T. 2008. (ENG.). 32p. (J). (gr. -1). 16.50 (978-1-933327-41-9(3)) Purple Bear Bks., Inc.
Tonk, Ernest. Pirate of the North. McCracken, Harold. 2011. 224p. 44.95 (978-1-258-09631-1(5)) Literary Licensing, LLC.
Tontiuh, Duncan. Esquivel! Space-Age Sound Artist. Wood, Susan. 32p. (J). (gr. 1-4). 2020. pap. 8.99 (978-1-58089-674-0(X)); 2016. lib. bdg. 17.95 (978-1-58089-673-3(1)) Charlesbridge Publishing, Inc.
—¡Esquivel! un Artista Del Sonido de la Era Espacial. Wood, Susan. Calvo, Carlos E., tr. 2016. 32p. (J). (gr. 1-4). lib. bdg. 17.95 (978-1-58089-733-4(9)) Charlesbridge Publishing, Inc.

Tony Flowers. Small Town. Gwynne, Phillip. 2020. 32p. (J). (gr. k-2). 24.99 **(978-1-76089-348-4(X)**, Puffin) Penguin Random Hse. AUS. Dist: Independent Pubs. Group.
Toohey, Eileen N. 365 Knock-Knock Jokes. Myers, Robert. 2006. 128p. (J). (gr. 1-4). per. 5.95 (978-1-4027-4108-1(1)) Sterling Publishing Co., Inc.
Tooke, Susan. Brave Jack & the Unicorn. McNaughton, Janet. 2005. 32p. (J). (gr. k-3). 15.95 (978-0-88776-677-0(3), Tundra Bks.) Tundra Bks. CAN. Dist: Penguin Random Hse. LLC.
—F Is for Fiddlehead: A New Brunswick Alphabet. Lohnes, Marilyn. rev. ed. 2007. (Discover Canada Province by Province Ser.). (ENG.). 40p. (J). (gr. 1-7). 17.95 (978-1-58536-318-6(9)) Sleeping Bear Pr.
—A Fiddle for Angus. Wilson, Budge. 2006. 32p. (J). (gr. 1-4). pap. 13.95 (978-0-88776-785-2(0), Tundra Bks.) Tundra Bks. CAN. Dist: Penguin Random Hse. LLC.
—Free As the Wind, 1 vol. Bastedo, Jamie. 2010. (ENG.). 32p. (J). (gr. 2-4). pap. 10.95 (978-0-88995-446-5(1), 8a8c5d1c-bc3d-4068-96e0-d212019c3afc) Trifolium Bks., Inc. CAN. Dist: Firefly Bks., Ltd.
—Lasso the Wind: Aurelia's Verses & Other Poems, 1 vol. Clarke, George Elliott. 2013. (ENG.). 64p. (J). (gr. 1-3). 24.95 (978-1-77108-050-7(7), 9dd4bf5c-ee3f-4acb-a6f4-439b626bdd3f) Nimbus Publishing, Ltd. CAN. Dist: Baker & Taylor Publisher Services (BTPS).
—A Seaside Alphabet. Grassby, Donna. 2009. (ABC Our Country Ser.). 32p. (J). (gr. 1-4). pap. 7.95 (978-0-88776-938-2(1), Tundra Bks.) Tundra Bks. CAN. Dist: Penguin Random Hse. LLC.
—Up Home, 1 vol. Grant, Shauntay. ed. 2011. (ENG.). 32p. (J). (gr. -1-k). pap. 12.95 (978-1-55109-911-8(X), c4737853-47fc-4d51-a7cf-20e7ae676562) Nimbus Publishing, Ltd. CAN. Dist: Baker & Taylor Publisher Services (BTPS).
Tooke, Susan. B Is for Bluenose: A Nova Scotia Alphabet. Tooke, Susan. 2008. (Discover Canada Province by Province Ser.). (ENG.). 40p. (J). (gr. 1-3). 19.99 (978-1-58536-362-9(6), 202147) Sleeping Bear Pr.
Toothman, Lindsey. I'm Okay, Mommy. Toothman, Sherry. 2007. 20p. per. 24.95 (978-1-4241-8733-1(8)) America Star Bks.
Topaz, Ksenia. Jodie's Hanukkah Dig. Levine, Anna. 2008. (Hanukkah Ser.). (ENG.). 32p. (J). (gr. k-3). 17.95 (978-0-8225-7391-3(1), Kar-Ben Publishing) Lerner Publishing Group.
—Jodie's Shabbat Surprise. Levine, Anna. 2015. (ENG.). 32p. (J). (gr. k-3). lib. bdg. 17.95 (978-1-4677-3465-3(9), 9781467734653); E-Book 27.99 (978-1-4677-6204-5(0)) Lerner Publishing Group. (Kar-Ben Publishing).
—Zvuvi's Israel, Vol. Lehman-Wilzig, Tami. 2009. (Israel Ser.). (ENG.). 32p. (J). (gr. -1-2). pap. 7.95 (978-0-8225-8760-6(2), Kar-Ben Publishing) Lerner Publishing Group.
Topp, Reagan. Libby Logan: Alien Attack. Topp, Reagan. 2019. (Libby Logan Ser.: Vol. 1). (ENG.). 48p. (J). pap. 12.99 **(978-1-6898-8691-8(9))** Independently Published.
—Libby Logan: Crisis in Canada. Topp, Reagan. 2019. (Libby Logan (7 Years +) Ser.: Vol. 1). (ENG.). 70p. (J). pap. 14.99 **(978-1-6927-0878-8(3))** Independently Published.
—Libby Logan: Friends & Foes. Topp, Reagan. 2019. (Libby Logan & Lance Boyle Ser.: Vol. 2). (ENG.). 484p. (J). pap. 17.95 **(978-1-6927-0530-5(X))** Independently Published.
Toppenberg, Lily. Delta & Dawn: Mother & Baby Whales' Journey. Cruz, Stefanie. 2007. 32p. (J). lib. bdg. 15.95 (978-0-9791233-2-0(1)) Big Tomato Pr.
Toppi, Sergio. Pope John Paul II. Pagotto, Toni. 2006. (Comic Book Ser.). 64p. (J). pap. 7.95 (978-0-8198-5957-0(5)) Pauline Bks. & Media.
Torbergson, Paige B. That's One Odd Duck! Vines, Heather Glenn. 2018. (ENG.). 24p. (J). 22.95 (978-1-4808-6679-9(2)); pap. 12.45 (978-1-4808-6680-5(6)) Archway Publishing.
Torbert, Wayne E. Twelve for Thebes, a Tale of Ancient Greece. Torbert, Wayne E. 2009. 82p. pap. 8.95 (978-1-936051-73-1(7)) Peppertree Pr., The.
Torche, Jen, jt. illus. see Burke, Erin.
Torcida, María Luisa. 125 Refranes Infantiles. Herrera, J. Ignacio. (SPA.). (J). (gr. 3-5). 12.76 (978-84-305-9180-0(X), SU6580) Susaeta Ediciones, S.A. ESP. Dist: Lectorum Pubns., Inc.
Torcida, María Luisa. Poesías de Animales: La Selva en Verso. Torcida, María Luisa. Fuertes, Gloria. 2003. (SPA.). 126p. (978-84-305-7804-7(8), SU4856) Susaeta Ediciones, S.A. ESP. Dist: Lectorum Pubns., Inc.
Torgeson, Sarah. Hello, Cy! Delashmutt, Amy. 2007. 24p. (J). lib. bdg. 14.95 (978-1-932888-53-9(5)) Mascot Bks., Inc.
Toriyama, Akira. Dragon Ball, Vol. 6. Toriyama, Akira. 2010. (Dragon Ball Ser.: 6). (ENG.). 80p. (Orig.). (J). pap. 4.99 (978-1-4215-3122-9(4)) Viz Media.
—Dragon Ball: Chapter Book, Vol. 8: Fight to the Finish! Toriyama, Akira. 2010. (Dragon Ball Ser.: 8). (ENG.). 80p. (J). pap. 4.99 (978-1-4215-3124-3(0)) Viz Media.
—Dragon Ball: Chapter Book, Vol. 9. Toriyama, Akira. 2010. (ENG.). 80p. (J). pap. 4.99 (978-1-4215-3125-0(9)) Viz Media.
—Let the Tournament Begin! Toriyama, Akira. 2010. (Dragon Ball Ser.: 7). (ENG.). 80p. (J). pap. 4.99 (978-1-4215-3123-6(2)) Viz Media.
—One Enemy, One Goal. Toriyama, Akira. 2009. (Dragon Ball Ser.: 5). (ENG.). 80p. (J). pap. 4.99 (978-1-4215-3121-2(6)) Viz Media.
—Strongest under the Heavens. Toriyama, Akira. 2010. (Dragon Ball Ser.: 10). (ENG.). 80p. (J). pap. 4.99 (978-1-4215-3126-7(7)) Viz Media.
Torke, Barbara, jt. illus. see Torke, Kyle.
Torke, Kyle & Torke, Barbara. Ice Breaking: The Adventures of Clementine the Rescue Dog. 2018. 40p. (J). pap. (978-1-61599-379-6(7)) Loving Healing Pr., Inc.
Tormey, Carlotta. A Soldier in Disguise. McDonnell, Peter. 2005. 16p. (J). pap. (978-0-7367-2909-3(7)) Zaner-Bloser, Inc.

Tormo, Bea. The Secret of Shadow Lake (Creature Campers Book 1) McGee, Joe. 2019. (Creature Campers Ser.). (ENG.). 96p. (J). 12.99 (978-1-5248-5546-8(4)); pap. 6.99 (978-1-5248-5518-5(9)) Andrews McMeel Publishing.
—Surprise under the Stars (Creature Campers Book 2) McGee, Joe. 2020. (Creature Campers Ser.). (ENG.). 112p. (J). 12.99 (978-1-5248-5783-7(1)); pap. 6.99 (978-1-5248-5570-3(7)) Andrews McMeel Publishing.
Tormo, Bea. The Wall of Doom (Creature Campers Book 3) McGee, Joe. 2020. (Creature Campers Ser.: 3). (ENG.). 96p. (J). 12.99 **(978-1-5248-6143-8(X))**; pap. 6.99 **(978-1-5248-6090-5(5))** Andrews McMeel Publishing.
Tornatore, Carol. Earthquake Surprise: A Bailey Fish Adventure. Salisbury, Linda. 2012. 192p. (J). pap. 8.95 (978-1-881539-65-0(2)) Tabby Hse. Bks.
—Florida a to Z, Vol. Judson, Susan Ryan. 2014. (ENG.). 66p. (J). (gr. -1-12). pap. 18.95 (978-1-56164-610-4(5)) Pineapple Pr., Inc.
—Trouble in Contrary Woods: A Bailey Fish Adventure. Salisbury, Linda G. 2009. (J). 8.85 (978-1-881539-46-9(6)) Tabby Hse. Bks.
Tornqvist, Marit. A Calf for Christmas, 8 vols. Lindgren, Astrid. Lawson, Polly, tr. 2010. (ENG.). 36p. (J). (gr. -1-2). 17.95 (978-0-86315-785-1(8)) Floris Bks. GBR. Dist: Consortium Bk. Sales & Distribution.
—The Red Bird. Lindgren, Astrid & Crampton, Patricia. 2005. (J). 5.99 (978-0-439-62797-9(4), Levine, Arthur A. Bks.) Scholastic, Inc.
—Tom's Christmas Fish, 20 vols. Tornqvist-Verschuur, Rita. 2015. (ENG.). 32p. (J). 17.95 (978-1-78250-221-0(1)) Floris Bks. GBR. Dist: Consortium Bk. Sales & Distribution.
Toro, Valentina. Behind the Bookcase: Miep Gies, Anne Frank, & the Hiding Place. Lowell, Barbara. 2020. (ENG.). 40p. (J). (gr. 2-5). 17.99 (978-1-5415-5725-3(5), Kar-Ben Publishing) Lerner Publishing Group.
Torode, Justine. On the Farm Lift-the-Flap. Smith, Alastair. 2004. (Luxury Lift-the-Flap Ser.). 16p. (J). (gr. 1-18). 11.95 (978-0-7945-0508-0(2), Usborne) EDC Publishing.
Torode, Sam. Everyday Graces: Child's Book of Good Manners. Santorum, Karen. 2003. (Foundations Ser.). (ENG.). 407p. (J). 25.00 (978-1-932236-09-5(0)) ISI Bks.
Toron, Eli. Gifts to Treasure. Greenberger, Tehilla. 2007. (Fun to Read Book). 224p. (J). per. 10.95 (978-1-929628-32-2(3)) Hachai Publishing.
—Parsha with Rabbi Juravel: Bereishis. Juravel, Rabbi. 2005. (J). 26.95 (978-1-931681-83-4(X)) Israel Bookshop Pubns.
—Parsha with Rabbi Juravel: Shemos. Juravel, Rabbi. 2006. (J). 27.95 (978-1-60091-002-9(5)) Israel Bookshop Pubns.
Toron, Eli & Graybar, Shmuel. Eight Chanukah Tales. Mindel, Nissan. 2007. 78p. (J). 10.95 (978-0-8266-0039-4(5)) Kehot Pubn. Society.
Torralba, Enrique. Teotihuacanos, Toltecas y Tarascos. Pastrana, Miguel. 2019. (Historias de Verdad Ser.). (SPA.). 92p. (J). (gr. 4-7). pap. 12.00 (978-607-8469-58-1(4)) Nostra Ediciones MEX. Dist: Independent Pubs. Group.
Torre, Attilio. Blob's Odd Jobs. Patrick, B. 2006. (ENG.). 48p. (J). (gr. -1-3). 16.95 (978-0-9741319-3-1(8)) 4N Publishing LLC.
Torre, Beatriz Gonzalez. Emily Grows. Esposito, Kathleen Christina. 2019. (ENG.). 40p. (J). pap. 9.99 (978-1-7327815-2-8(4)) Centiramo Publishing.
Torre, Beatriz Gonzalez. Emily Crece. Torre, Beatriz Gonzalez, tr. Esposito, Kathleen Christina. 2019. (SPA.). 40p. (J). pap. 9.99 (978-1-7327815-4-2(0)) Centiramo Publishing.
Torrecilla, Pablo. I Kick the Ball: Pateo el Balón. Zepeda, Gwendolyn. Ventura, Gabriela Baeza, tr. 2011. (SPA & ENG.). 32p. (J). (gr. -1-3). 16.95 (978-1-55885-688-2(9), Piñata Books) Arte Publico Pr.
—Level up / Paso de Nivel. Zepeda, Gwendolyn. Baeza Ventura, Gabriela, tr. from ENG. 2012. (SPA & ENG.). (J). (gr. 5-9). 16.95 (978-1-55885-747-6(8), Piñata Books) Arte Publico Pr.
—The Road to Santiago. Figueredo, D. H. 2003. (ENG.). 32p. (J). 16.95 (978-1-58430-059-5(0)) Lee & Low Bks., Inc.
Torrecilla, Pablo, jt. illus. see Benatar, Raquel.
Torrecilla, Pablo, jt. illus. see Caraballo, Samuel.
Torrent, Dani. Folktales for Fearless Girls: The Stories We Were Never Told. Sayalero, Myriam. 2020. 224p. (J). (gr. 3-7). 24.99 (978-0-593-11522-0(8), Philomel Bks.) Penguin Young Readers Group.
—Goodnight Whispers. Leannah, Michael. 2018. (ENG.). 32p. (J). (gr. 3-5). 16.99 (978-1-64170-031-3(9), 550031) Familius LLC.
Torres, Ben. Kingpin: Born Against. 2017. (ENG.). 112p. (YA). (gr. 8-17). pap. 15.99 (978-1-302-90570-5(8)) Marvel Worldwide, Inc.
Torres, Diana. How Did Nonnie Get to Heaven? Bronstein, Arlene. 2013. (J). 48p. 19.95 (978-1-60131-158-0(3)); 54p. pap. 13.95 (978-1-60131-159-7(1)) Big Tent Bks. (Castlebridge Bks.).
Torres, Dottie. Jacob & His Magical Flying Bears. Sobel, Gerrie. 2009. 32p. pap. 12.95 (978-1-936051-16-8(8)) Peppertree Pr., The.
—Jacob & His Magical Flying Bears, a Halloween Story. Sobel, Gerrie. 2009. 32p. pap. 12.95 (978-1-936051-42-7(7)) Peppertree Pr., The.
Torres, Elena. Había una Vez una Princesa. Montes, Graciela. 2006. (Alfaguara Infantil Ser.). 26p. (J). 8.95 (978-1-59820-215-1(4), Alfaguara) Santillana USA Publishing Co., Inc.
Torres, German. The Werewolf Chase: A Mystery about Adaptations. Beauregard, Lynda. 2012. (Summer Camp Science Mysteries Ser.: 4). (ENG.). 48p. (gr. 3-6). pap. 39.62 (978-0-7613-9271-2(8), Graphic Universe™) Lerner Publishing Group.
—The Werewolf Chase No. 4: A Mystery about Adaptations. Beauregard, Lynda. 2012. (Summer Camp Science Mysteries Ser.: 4). (ENG.). 48p. (J). (gr. 3-6). pap. 6.95 (978-0-7613-8542-4(8), 9780761385424, Graphic Universe™) Lerner Publishing Group.

—The Yucky Duck Rescue No. 8: A Mystery about Pollution. Beauregard, Lynda. 2013. (Summer Camp Science Mysteries Ser.: 8). (ENG.). 48p. (J). (gr. 3-6). pap. 6.95 *(978-1-4677-0736-7(8)*, 9781467707367, Graphic Universe™) Lerner Publishing Group.

Torres, German, jt. illus. see Barón, Lara.

Torres, Irving. Matt the Rat & His Magic Cloud / Raton Mateo y Su Nube Magica: A Day at School / un Dia de Escuela. Liberto, Lorenzo. Gomez, Rocio, ed. 2003. (Matt the Rat Ser. / La Serie de Ratón Mateo). (ENG & SPA.). 32p. (J). lib. bdg. 20.00 *(978-0-9743668-0-7(3))* Harvest Sun Pr., LLC.

—Matt the Rat & His Sister Maggie (Raton Mateo y Su Hermana Maggie) When I Grow Up (Cuando Yo Crezca) Liberto, Lorenzo. Gomez, Rocio, ed. 2003. (Matt the Rat Ser. / La Serie de Ratón Mateo). (SPA & ENG.). 40p. (J). lib. bdg. 20.00 *(978-0-9743668-1-4(1))* Harvest Sun Pr., LLC.

—Matt the Rat Fights Back / Ratón Mateo se Defiende. Liberto, Lorenzo. Gomez, Rocio, tr. from ENG. 2005. (Matt the Rat Ser. / La Serie de Ratón Mateo). (ENG & SPA.). 32p. (J). lib. bdg. 20.00 *(978-0-9743668-4-5(6))* Harvest Sun Pr., LLC.

—Save the Planet / Salva el Planeta. Liberto, Lorenzo. Gomez, Rocio, tr. 2005. (Matt the Rat Ser. / La Serie de Ratón Mateo). (ENG & SPA.). 32p. (J). lib. bdg. 20.00 *(978-0-9743668-5-2(4))* Harvest Sun Pr., LLC.

Torres, Irving. Matt the Rat's Incredible Creations / Las Creaciones Increíbles de Ratón Mateo. Torres, Irving. Liberto, Lorenzo & Gomez, Rocio. 2004. (ENG & SPA.). 32p. (J). lib. bdg. 20.00 *(978-0-9743668-3-8(8))* Harvest Sun Pr., LLC.

—Practice Makes Perfect / la Práctica Hace al Maestro. Torres, Irving. Liberto, Lorenzo & Gomez, Rocio. 2004. (ENG & SPA.). 32p. (J). lib. bdg. 20.00 *(978-0-9743668-2-1(X))* Harvest Sun Pr., LLC.

Torres, Jickie. Watch Me Draw Robots. Walter Foster Publishing & Berry, Bob. 2014. (Watch Me Draw Ser.). (ENG.). 24p. (J). (gr. k-2). lib. bdg. 23.99 *(978-1-939581-38-9(9)*, Walter Foster Jr) Quarto Publishing Group USA.

Torres, Marina. El bibliobus Magico. Fernandez, Cesar. 2004. 88p. pap. 10.00 *(978-84-931888-1-8(6))* Editorial Brief ESP. Dist: Independent Pubs. Group.

Torres, Nora Estela. Travesuras del Tio Conejo. Espriella, Leopoldo Berdella De La. 2004. (Relato Ser.). (SPA.). 76p. (J). (gr. -1-7). per. *(978-958-30-0302-8(6))* Panamericana Editorial.

Torres, Nora Estela & Jaime, Daniel. Historia en Cuentos 3: Todo Por un Florero/el Cometa Llanero/el Zapatero Soldado. Caballero, Eduardo. 2004. (Literatura Juvenil (Panamericana Editorial) Ser.). (SPA.). 78p. (YA). (gr. -1-7). pap. *(978-958-30-0369-1(7))* Panamericana Editorial.

—Historia en Cuentos 4: El Almirante Nino/el Caballito de Bolivar/el Sargento de Doce Anos. Calderon, Eduardo Caballero. 2003. (Literatura Juvenil (Panamericana Editorial) Ser.). (SPA.). 75p. (YA). (gr. -1-7). per. *(978-958-30-0370-7(0))* Panamericana Editorial.

Torres, Raul Vazquez. Otra Vez Ese Tal Principito! Ordonez, Paulino. rev. ed. 2006. (Castillo de la Lectura Naranja Ser.). (SPA & ENG.). 152p. (J). (gr. 4-7). pap. 7.95 *(978-970-20-0178-2(1))* Castillo, Ediciones, S. A. de C. V. MEX. Dist: Macmillan.

Torres, Sebastián. Notebook: Luli at School: Cute Kawaii Notebook for Kids: 100 Pages of 8. 5 X11 Double Spaced Lined Paper for Writing, Journaling. Creatives, Luli & Friends. 2019. (Luli & Friends Ser.: Vol. 1). (ENG.). 102p. (J). pap. 6.99 *(978-1-0796-1744-3(2))* Independently Published.

Torres, Walter. Celebrate Christmas & Three Kings Day with Pablo & Carlitos. Flor Ada, Alma. 2006. (Cuentos para Celebrar / Stories to Celebrate Ser.). 30p. (J). (gr. k-6). per. 11.95 *(978-1-59820-136-9(0))* Santillana USA Publishing Co., Inc.

—El Pececito Magico. De Matos, Isabel Freire. 2004. (SPA.). 22p. (J). pap. 6.95 *(978-1-57581-578-7(8))* Santillana USA Publishing Co., Inc.

—Viaje a Isla de Mona. Montero, Mayra. 2009. (SPA.). 111p. (J). (gr. 4-7). pap. 8.95 *(978-1-934801-64-2(X))* Ediciones SM.

—¡Viva la Tortuga! León, Georgina Lázaro. (SPA.). 30p. (J). (gr. 3-5). 12.95 *(978-1-57581-605-0(9))* Santillana USA Publishing Co., Inc.

Torretta, Sara. The Direction Dance! Up, down, Left, & Right. Dahl, Michael. 2018. (Creative Movement Ser.). (ENG.). 24p. (J). (gr. -1-2). lib. bdg. 33.99 *(978-1-68410-246-4(4)*, 138432) Cantata Learning.

Torrey Balsara, Andrea. Jellybean Mouse. Roy, Philip. 2014. (ENG.). 32p. 11.95 *(978-1-55380-344-7(2))* Ronsdale Pr. CAN. Dist: SPD-Small Pr. Distribution.

—Mouse Tales. Roy, Philip. 2014. (ENG.). 32p. pap. 9.95 *(978-1-55380-262-4(4))* Ronsdale Pr. CAN. Dist: SPD-Small Pr. Distribution.

Torrey, Marjorie. Fairing Weather. Bragdon, Elspeth. 2018. (ENG.). 108p. (J). (gr. 3-6). pap. 9.99 *(978-1-4794-1686-8(X))* Wildside Pr., LLC.

Torrey, Michele & Newman, Barbara Johansen. The Case of the Gasping Garbage. Torrey, Michele. 2009. (Doyle & Fossey, Science Detectives Ser.: 1). 96p. (J). (gr. 4-7). pap. 6.95 *(978-1-4027-4960-5(0))* Sterling Publishing Co., Inc.

—The Case of the Mossy Lake Monster. Torrey, Michele. 2009. (Doyle & Fossey, Science Detectives Ser.: 2). 96p. (J). (gr. 4-7). pap. 6.95 *(978-1-4027-4962-9(7))* Sterling Publishing Co., Inc.

Torrey, Rich. The Almost Terrible Playdate. Torrey, Richard. 2016. (ENG.). 40p. (J). (gr. -1-2). 19.99 *(978-0-375-97430-4(X)*, Doubleday Bks. for Young Readers) Random Hse. Children's Bks.

—The Runaway Soccer Ball. Stiles, Amanda. 2010. 16p. (J). pap. *(978-0-545-24819-8(1))* Scholastic, Inc.

—Splat! Pérez-Mercado, Mary Margaret. 2011. (Rookie Ready to Learn Ser.). 40p. (J). pap. 5.95 *(978-0-531-26678-6(8))*; (gr. -1-k). lib. bdg. 23.00 *(978-0-531-26373-0(8))* Scholastic Library Publishing. (Children's Pr.).

Torrey, Richard. Almost. Torrey, Richard. 2009. (ENG.). 40p. (J). (gr. -1-3). 17.99 *(978-0-06-156166-5(5)*, Balzer & Bray) HarperCollins Pubs.

—Because. Torrey, Richard. 2011. (ENG.). 40p. (J). (gr. -1-3). 16.99 *(978-0-06-156173-3(8)*, Balzer & Bray) HarperCollins Pubs.

—My Dog, Bob. Torrey, Richard. 2016. (ENG.). 32p. (J). (gr. -1-3). 6.99 *(978-0-8234-3691-0(8))* Holiday Hse., Inc.

—Why? Torrey, Richard. 2010. (ENG.). 40p. (J). (gr. -1-3). 16.99 *(978-0-06-156170-2(3)*, Balzer & Bray) HarperCollins Pubs.

Torrey, Richard L. ¡Zas! Pérez-Mercado, Mary Margaret. 2011. (Rookie Ready to Learn Español Ser.). (SPA.). (J). 40p. pap. 5.95 *(978-0-531-26788-2(1))*; 32p. (gr. -1-1). lib. bdg. 23.00 *(978-0-531-26120-0(4))* Scholastic Library Publishing. (Children's Pr.).

Torrey, Richard L. Beans Baker's Best Shot. Torrey, Richard L. 2006. (Step into Reading Ser.: Vol. 3). 48p. (J). (gr. k-3). per. 3.99 *(978-0-375-82839-3(7)*, Random Hse. Bks. for Young Readers) Random Hse. Children's Bks.

Torrijos, Eduardo. Papalotes: Tecnicas de Armado y Vuelo. Torrijos, Eduardo. Garcia, Gretel. 2004. (SPA.). 157p. (J). pap. *(978-970-643-734-1(7))* Selector, S.A. de C.V. MEX. Dist: Spanish Pubs., LLC.

Torrisi, Gary. When Sammy Was a Puppy. Urmston, Kathleen. 2012. (ENG.). 12p. (gr. k-2). pap. 7.95 *(978-1-61181-242-8(9)*, Kaeden Bks.) Kaeden Corp.

Torseter, Oyvind. Brown. Ovreas, Hakon. Dickson, Kari, tr. 2019. (My Alter Ego Is a Superhero Ser.). (ENG.). 136p. (J). (gr. k-5). 16.95 *(978-1-59270-212-1(0))* Enchanted Lion Bks., LLC.

—Brown. Ovreas, Hakon. 2019. (My Alter Ego Is a Superhero Ser.). 136p. (J). (gr. k-5). pap. 9.95 *(978-1-59270-251-0(1))* Enchanted Lion Bks., LLC.

—My Father's Arms Are a Boat. Lunde, Stein Erik. Dickson, Kari, tr. 2013. (ENG.). 40p. (J). (gr. -1). 15.95 *(978-1-59270-124-7(8))* Enchanted Lion Bks., LLC.

Tortoise Dreaming Staff. Hook-Nosed Einiosaurus. Tortoise Dreaming Staff. 2017. (When Dinosaurs Ruled the Earth Ser.). (ENG.). 32p. (J). (gr. k-3). lib. bdg. 27.99 *(978-1-925235-21-0(1)*, Big and SMALL) ChoiceMaker Pty. Ltd., The AUS. Dist: Lerner Publishing Group.

—Suchomimus Smiles Like a Crocodile. Tortoise Dreaming Staff. 2017. (When Dinosaurs Ruled the Earth Ser.). (ENG.). 32p. (J). (gr. k-3). lib. bdg. 27.99 *(978-1-925235-23-4(8)*, Big and SMALL) ChoiceMaker Pty. Ltd., The AUS. Dist: Lerner Publishing Group.

—Three-Horned Triceratops. Tortoise Dreaming Staff. 2017. (When Dinosaurs Ruled the Earth Ser.). (ENG.). 32p. (J). (gr. k-3). lib. bdg. 27.99 *(978-1-925235-24-1(6)*, Big and SMALL) ChoiceMaker Pty. Ltd., The AUS. Dist: Lerner Publishing Group.

Tortop, Anil. The Leaky Story: A Fun-Filled Adventure into the Power of the Imagination & the Magic of Books! Sillett, Devon. 2017. (ENG.). 32p. (J). (gr. -1-3). 17.99 *(978-1-925335-39-2(9)*, 317168, EK Bks.) Exisle Publishing Pty Ltd. AUS. Dist: Hachette Bk. Group.

—Mary Bea Says Why Is for Yog. Hogan, Tamara Anne. 2013. 28p. pap. *(978-1-922204-06-6(4))* Vivid Publishing.

Tortosa, Wilson. Critical Strike. Bowen, Carl. 2014. (Shadow Squadron Ser.). (ENG.). 224p. (J). (gr. 4-8). pap. 8.95 *(978-1-62370-109-3(0)*, Capstone Young Readers) Capstone.

—Dark Agent, 1 vol. Bowen, Carl & Fuentes, Benny. 2014. (Shadow Squadron Ser.). (ENG.). 112p. (J). (gr. 4-8). 26.65 *(978-1-4342-9170-7(7)*, Stone Arch Bks.) Capstone.

—Dragon Teeth. Bowen, Carl & Fuentes, Benny. 2015. (Shadow Squadron Ser.). (ENG.). 112p. (J). (gr. 4-8). lib. bdg. 26.65 *(978-1-4965-0383-1(X)*, Stone Arch Bks.) Capstone.

—Eagle Down, 1 vol. Bowen, Carl & Fuentes, Benny. 2013. (Shadow Squadron Ser.). (ENG.). 112p. (J). (gr. 4-8). lib. bdg. 26.65 *(978-1-4342-4606-6(X)*, Stone Arch Bks.) Capstone.

—Elite Infantry. Bowen, Carl. 2013. (Shadow Squadron Ser.). (ENG.). 224p. (J). pap. 8.95 *(978-1-62370-032-4(9)*, Capstone Young Readers) Capstone.

—Guardian Angel. Bowen, Carl & Fuentes, Benny. 2015. (Shadow Squadron Ser.). (ENG.). 112p. (J). (gr. 4-8). lib. bdg. 26.65 *(978-1-4965-0382-4(1)*, Stone Arch Bks.) Capstone.

—Operación Águila. Bowen, Carl. 2019. (Escuadrón de la Sombra Ser.). (SPA.). 112p. (J). (gr. 4-8). lib. bdg. 26.65 *(978-1-4965-8549-3(6)*, 141298, Stone Arch Bks.) Capstone.

—Operación Demonio. Bowen, Carl. 2019. (Escuadrón de la Sombra Ser.). (SPA.). 112p. (J). (gr. 4-8). lib. bdg. 26.65 *(978-1-4965-8547-9(X)*, 141296, Stone Arch Bks.) Capstone.

—Operación Escudo. Bowen, Carl. 2019. (Escuadrón de la Sombra Ser.). (SPA.). 112p. (J). (gr. 4-8). lib. bdg. 26.65 *(978-1-4965-8550-9(X)*, 141299, Stone Arch Bks.) Capstone.

—Phantom Sun, 1 vol. Bowen, Carl & Fuentes, Benny. 2014. (Shadow Squadron Ser.). (ENG.). 112p. (J). (gr. 4-8). 26.65 *(978-1-4342-6399-5(1)*, Stone Arch Bks.) Capstone.

—Rogue Agent. Bowen, Carl. 2015. (Shadow Squadron Ser.). (ENG.). 224p. (J). (gr. 4-8). pap. 8.95 *(978-1-62370-296-0(8)*, Capstone Young Readers) Capstone.

—Sand Spider, 1 vol. Bowen, Carl. 2014. (Shadow Squadron Ser.). (ENG.). 112p. (J). (gr. 4-8). 26.65 *(978-1-4342-9169-1(3)*, Stone Arch Bks.) Capstone.

—Sea Demon, 1 vol. Bowen, Carl & Fuentes, Benny. 2013. (Shadow Squadron Ser.). (ENG.). 112p. (J). (gr. 4-8). lib. bdg. 26.65 *(978-1-4342-4604-2(3)*, Stone Arch Bks.) Capstone.

—Sniper Shield, 1 vol. Bowen, Carl & Fuentes, Benny. 2013. (Shadow Squadron Ser.). (ENG.). 112p. (J). (gr. 4-8). lib. bdg. 26.65 *(978-1-4342-4607-3(8)*, Stone Arch Bks.) Capstone.

—Steel Hammer. Bowen, Carl & Fuentes, Benny. 2015. (Shadow Squadron Ser.). (ENG.). 112p. (J). (gr. 4-8). lib. bdg. 26.65 *(978-1-4965-0385-5(6)*, Stone Arch Bks.) Capstone.

—White Needle, 1 vol. Bowen, Carl & Fuentes, Benny. 2014. (Shadow Squadron Ser.). (ENG.). 112p. (J). (gr. 4-8). 26.65 *(978-1-4342-6398-8(3)*, Stone Arch Bks.) Capstone.

Tortosa, Wilson & Bartolo, Michael. Death Camp Uprising: The Escape from Sobibor Concentration Camp. Yomtov, Nel. 2017. (Great Escapes of World War II Ser.). (ENG.). 32p. (J). (gr. 3-9). lib. bdg. 31.32 *(978-1-5157-3532-8(X)*, Capstone Pr.) Capstone.

Tortosa, Wilson & Fuentes, Benny. Black Anchor, 1 vol. Bowen, Carl. 2013. (Shadow Squadron Ser.). (ENG.). 112p. (J). (gr. 4-8). lib. bdg. 26.65 *(978-1-4342-4605-9(1)*, Stone Arch Bks.) Capstone.

Tortosa, Wilson, jt. illus. see Fuentes, Benny.

Tosolini, Nicola, et al. Uncle Scrooge: the Cursed Cell Phone. Savini, Alberto & Gilbert, Janet. 2020. (Uncle Scrooge Ser.). (ENG.). 96p. (J). (gr. 4-7). pap. 12.99 *(978-1-68405-626-2(8))* Idea & Design Works, LLC.

Toth, Dorothy. Crown the King #2, 1 vol. Weissman, D. S. 2016. (Deep Freeze Ser.). (ENG.). 216p. (YA). (gr. 6-12). lib. bdg. 28.56 *(978-1-68076-016-3(5)*, 21477, Epic Edge) EPIC Pr.

—Forever Royal #6, 1 vol. Weissman, D. S. 2016. (Deep Freeze Ser.). (ENG.). 216p. (YA). (gr. 6-12). lib. bdg. 28.56 *(978-1-68076-020-0(3)*, 21485, Epic Edge) EPIC Pr.

—Traitors Die #5, 1 vol. Weissman, D. S. 2016. (Deep Freeze Ser.). (ENG.). 216p. (YA). (gr. 6-12). lib. bdg. 28.56 *(978-1-68076-019-4(X)*, 21483, Epic Edge) EPIC Pr.

Toth, Shannon. Laika the Space Dog: First Hero in Outer Space, 1 vol. Wittrock, Jeni. 2014. (Animal Heroes Ser.). (ENG.). 32p. (J). (gr. k-2). 29.32 *(978-1-4795-5463-8(4))*; pap. 7.95 *(978-1-4795-5467-6(7))* Capstone. (Picture Window Bks.).

Totire, Valerie. Carla's New Glasses. Coulton, Mia. 2005. (ENG.). 16p. (gr. k-2). pap. 7.95 *(978-1-57874-092-5(4)*, Kaeden Bks.) Kaeden Corp.

—People Do Silly Things. Worthington, Lisa & Moon, Susan. 2003. (ENG.). 16p. (gr. k-2). pap. 7.95 *(978-1-57874-037-6(1)*, Kaeden Bks.) Kaeden Corp.

—There Goes Peanut Butter! Ketch, Ann. 2006. (ENG.). 12p. (gr. k-1). pap. 7.95 *(978-1-57874-036-9(3)*, 74-036-3, Kaeden Bks.) Kaeden Corp.

Tottisi, Gary. When Sammy Was a Puppy (6 Pack) Urmston, Kathleen. 2012. (ENG.). 12p. (gr. k-2). pap. *(978-1-61181-243-5(7)*, Kaeden Bks.) Kaeden Corp.

Tougas, Chris. Tinkle, Tinkle, Little Star. Tougas, Chris. 2018. (ENG.). 24p. (J). (gr. -1 — 1). bds. 9.99 *(978-1-77138-839-9(0))* Kids Can Pr., Ltd. CAN. Dist: Hachette Bk. Group.

Touliatou, Sophia. All about Anxiety. Lewis, Carrie. 2020. (ENG.). 88p. (J). (gr. 3-7). 14.99 *(978-1-5064-6320-9(7)*, Beaming Books) Augsburg Fortress, Pubs.

—Antonino's Impossible Dream, Vol. McGlen, Tim. 2019. (ENG.). 32p. (J). (gr. -1-3). 17.99 *(978-1-5064-4933-3(6)*, Beaming Books) Augsburg Fortress, Pubs.

—Cookie Blast Off! Welsh, Clare Helen. 2019. (Early Bird Readers — Purple (Early Bird Stories (tm)) Ser.). (ENG.). 32p. (J). (gr. k-3). 27.99 *(978-1-5415-4230-3(4)*, 9781541542303); pap. 7.99 *(978-1-5415-7416-8(8)*, 9781541574168) Lerner Publishing Group. (Lerner Pubns.).

—Flippy Floppy Farm Animals. Poitier, Anton. 2014. 10p. (J). 12.99 *(978-1-61067-310-5(7))* Kane Miller.

—Flippy Floppy Jungle Animals. Poitier, Anton. 2013. 16p. (J). 12.99 *(978-1-61067-169-9(4))* Kane Miller.

—Flippy Floppy Ocean Animals. Poitier, Anton. 2015. 10p. (J). 12.99 *(978-1-61067-346-4(8))* Kane Miller.

Toulmin-Rothe, Ann. Elizabeth Blackwell, the First Woman Doctor. Sabin, Francene & Macken, JoAnn Early. 2007. 53p. (J). *(978-0-439-66044-0(0))* Scholastic, Inc.

Toume, Kei. Lament of the Lamb, 7 vols., Vol. 7. Toume, Kei, creator. rev. ed. 2005. (Lament of the Lamb Ser.). (JPN & ENG.). 264p. pap. 9.99 *(978-1-59532-006-3(7))* TOKYOPOP, Inc.

Tour, Anat. A Is Not Only for Apple. Tseng, C. K. Thomas. 2016. (ENG.). (J). pap. 9.99 *(978-0-9978432-9-3(2))* Anat Tour.

Tour, Anat. Mama's Bag. Tour, Anat. 2016. (ENG.). (J). pap. 9.49 *(978-0-9978432-1-7(7))* Anat Tour.

Tourlonias, Joëlle. Elephantastic! Engler, Michael. 2014. (ENG.). 32p. (J). 16.99 *(978-1-4413-0841-2(5)*, 9781441308412) Peter Pauper Pr. Inc.

—A Tiger Like Me. Engler, Michael & Watkinson, Laura. 2019. 32p. (J). (gr. -1-1). 17.99 *(978-1-5420-4456-1(1)*, 9781542044561, AmazonCrossing) Amazon Publishing.

Tournier, Bertrand. Les Secrets de la Maison Abandonnee. Ferre, Gil. 2016. (FRE.). (J). pap. *(978-2-930821-40-5(X))* Plannum.

Tous, Mercè. Common Threads: Adam's Day at the Market. Essa, Huda. 2019. (ENG.). 32p. (J). (gr. -1-2). 16.99 *(978-1-5341-1010-6(0)*, 204760) Sleeping Bear Pr.

Tov, Basia. Attack of the Giant Stink Bugs. Bennett, Larry. 2015. (Ru-Lan Ser.: 2). (ENG.). 56p. (J). (gr. -1-3). pap. 10.95 *(978-1-940242-73-6(8))* Heritage Builders, LLC.

Tovahleh. Heldishkeyt inem Goldenem Land. Rotenberg, Yael. 2018. (YID.). 37p. (J). *(978-1-68091-255-5(0))* Kinder Shpiel USA, Inc.

Töwe, Nina. Jack & the Beanstalk: A Folktale. Töwe, Nina. 2017. (ENG.). 38p. (J). (gr. k-2). 18.99 *(978-988-8341-36-8(7)*, Minedition) Neugebauer, Michael (Publishing) Limited HKG. Dist: Penguin Random Hse. LLC.

Towle, Ben. Amelia Earhart: This Broad Ocean. Taylor, S. S. 2020. (Center for Cartoon Studies Presents Ser.). 96p. (J). (gr. 5-9). 17.99 *(978-1-368-02229-3(4))*; pap. 12.99 *(978-1-368-04287-1(2))* Hyperion Bks. for Children.

Townsend, F. H. The Brushwood Boy - Illustrated by F. H. Townsend. Kipling, Rudyard. 2016. (ENG.). (J). *(978-1-4733-3520-2(5))* Read Bks.

—A Child's History of England. Dickens, Charles. 2007. (ENG.). 420p. per. *(978-1-4065-5448-9(0))* Dodo Pr.

Townsend, Peter. Machine Mates. Whiting, Sue. 2003. 12p. (J). (gr. k-3). 22.00 *(978-0-7567-6650-4(8))* DIANE Publishing Co.

—Percival's Party. Turner, Jill. 2003. (J). pap. 12.95 *(978-1-74047-235-7(7))* Book Co. Publishing Pty, Ltd., The AUS. Dist: Penton Overseas, Inc.

Townsend, Shannon. Fire & Snow: A Tale of the Alaskan Gold Rush. Gunderson, J. 2007. (Historical Fiction Ser.). (ENG.). 56p. (J). (gr. 3-6). pap. 6.25 *(978-1-59889-405-9(6)*, Stone Arch Bks.) Capstone.

Townshend, Katie. Donkey Oatie's Christmas Pageant. Rath, Tom H. 2013. 24p. pap. *(978-0-9918033-6-1(1))* Wood Islands Prints.

Toy Box Staff. Who Lives Here? Wolfe, Jane. 2013. 8p. bds. 6.99 *(978-1-84322-651-2(0)*, Armadillo) Anness Publishing GBR. Dist: National Bk. Network.

—Who Says Moo? Wolfe, Jane. 2013. (ENG.). 8p. bds. 6.99 *(978-1-84322-679-6(0)*, Armadillo) Anness Publishing GBR. Dist: National Bk. Network.

—Who's Hiding? Wolfe, Jane. 2013. (ENG.). 8p. bds. 6.99 *(978-1-84322-657-4(X)*, Armadillo) Anness Publishing GBR. Dist: National Bk. Network.

Toye, Derek. Are Bowling Balls Bullies? Learning about Forces & Motion with the Garbage Gang. Troupe, Thomas Kingsley. 2015. (Garbage Gang's Super Science Questions Ser.). (ENG.). 24p. (J). (gr. k-2). lib. bdg. 27.32 *(978-1-4795-7057-7(5)*, Picture Window Bks.) Capstone.

—Do Ants Get Lost? Learning about Animal Communication with the Garbage Gang, 1 vol. Troupe, Thomas Kingsley. 2014. (Garbage Gang's Super Science Questions Ser.). (ENG.). 24p. (J). (gr. k-2). lib. bdg. 27.32 *(978-1-4795-5478-2(2)*, Picture Window Bks.) Capstone.

—Do Bees Poop? Learning about Living & Nonliving Things with the Garbage Gang, 1 vol. Troupe, Thomas Kingsley. 2014. (Garbage Gang's Super Science Questions Ser.). (ENG.). 24p. (J). (gr. k-2). lib. bdg. 27.32 *(978-1-4795-5477-5(4)*, Picture Window Bks.) Capstone.

—Do Plants Have Heads? Learning about Plant Parts with the Garbage Gang. Troupe, Thomas Kingsley. 2015. (Garbage Gang's Super Science Questions Ser.). (ENG.). 24p. (J). (gr. k-2). lib. bdg. 27.32 *(978-1-4795-7059-1(1)*, Picture Window Bks.) Capstone.

—The Garbage Gang's Super Science Questions, 4 vols. Troupe, Thomas Kingsley. 2015. (Garbage Gang's Super Science Questions Ser.). (ENG.). 24p. (J). (gr. k-2). 109.28 *(978-1-4795-8023-1(6)*, Picture Window Bks.) Capstone.

—Taj. Siegel, Elizabeth. 2007. 48p. (J). lib. bdg. 23.08 *(978-1-4242-1632-1(X))* Fitzgerald Bks.

—What's with the Long Naps, Bears? Learning about Hibernation with the Garbage Gang. Troupe, Thomas Kingsley. 2015. (Garbage Gang's Super Science Questions Ser.). (ENG.). 24p. (J). (gr. k-2). lib. bdg. 27.32 *(978-1-4795-7056-0(7)*, Picture Window Bks.) Capstone.

—Why Do Dead Fish Float? Learning about Matter with the Garbage Gang, 1 vol. Troupe, Thomas Kingsley. 2014. (Garbage Gang's Super Science Questions Ser.). (ENG.). 24p. (J). (gr. k-2). 27.32 *(978-1-4795-5479-9(0)*, Picture Window Bks.) Capstone.

—Why Does My Body Make Bubbles? Learning about the Digestive System with the Garbage Gang. Troupe, Thomas Kingsley. 2014. (Garbage Gang's Super Science Questions Ser.). (ENG.). 24p. (J). (gr. k-2). lib. bdg. 27.32 *(978-1-4795-5480-5(4)*, Picture Window Bks.) Capstone.

—You Call That a Nose? Learning about Human Senses with the Garbage Gang. Troupe, Thomas Kingsley. 2015. (Garbage Gang's Super Science Questions Ser.). (ENG.). 24p. (J). (gr. k-2). lib. bdg. 27.32 *(978-1-4795-7058-4(3)*, Picture Window Bks.) Capstone.

Trabalka, Pegy. Silent Voice. Rudner, Barry. I.t. ed. 2013. (ENG.). 30p. (J). 14.99 *(978-1-940775-00-5(0))* Nick Of Time Media, Inc.

Trabbold, Andrew. Siku's New Friend, 1 vol. Tremblay, Kaitlin. 2017. (Nunavummi Ser.). (ENG.). 32p. (J). (gr. 2-2). 7.95 ***(978-1-77266-560-4(6))*** Inhabit Education CAN. Dist: Consortium Bk. Sales & Distribution.

Trabbold, Andrew. Skraelings: Clashes in the Old Arctic, 1 vol. Qitsualik-Tinsley, Rachel & Qitsualik-Tinsley, Sean. 2014. (Arctic Moon Magick Ser.). (ENG.). 120p. (J). (gr. 7). pap. 10.95 *(978-1-927095-54-6(9))* Inhabit Media Inc. CAN. Dist: Consortium Bk. Sales & Distribution.

Trace, Casie. The Adventures of Edward the Baby Liraffe: Africa. Le Raff, Jack. 2019. (Adventures of Edward the Baby Liraffe Ser.: Vol. 1). (ENG.). 50p. (J). pap. 19.95 *(978-0-9922650-1-4(0))* Liraffe LLC.

Trace, Casie. The Adventures of Edward the Baby Liraffe: Europe. Le Raff, Jack. 2019. (Europe Ser.: Vol. 2). (ENG.). 68p. (J). pap. 19.95 ***(978-0-9922650-0-7(2))*** Liraffe LLC.

Trachock, Cathy. Black Bear Cub. Luther, Jacqueline & Lind, Alan. 2006. (ENG.). 32p. (J). pap. 3.95 *(978-1-59249-587-0(7))* Soundprints.

—Polar Bear Cub. Luther, Jacqueline. 2006. (ENG.). 32p. (J). pap. 3.95 *(978-1-59249-589-4(3))* Soundprints.

Trachok, Cathy. Raccoon at Clear Creek Road. Otto, Carolyn B. 2005. (Smithsonian's Backyard Ser.). 32p. (J). (gr. -1-3). pap. 8.95 incl. audio *(978-1-59249-490-3(0)*, SC5008); (ENG.). per. 6.95 *(978-1-59249-481-1(1)*, S5008) Soundprints.

Trachtman, Joseph. Kosher Tales: Not So Grim Stories for Children. Trachtman, Joseph, narrated by. 2007.Tr. of Kosher Tales. (ENG & YID.). 86p. (J). pap. 25.00 *(978-0-9795170-0-6(1))* Trachtman, Joseph.

Traini, Agostino. Jesus Is Risen! An Easter Pop-Up Book, Vol. 2018. (ENG.). 14p. (J). (gr. -1-3). 19.99 *(978-1-5064-3340-0(5)*, Sparkhouse Family) Augsburg Fortress, Pubs.

—The Lord Is My Shepherd: A Psalm 23 Pop-Up Book. 2020. (ENG.). 14p. (J). (gr. -1-5). 19.99 *(978-1-5064-5239-5(6)*, Beaming Books) Augsburg Fortress, Pubs.

Trammell, Brandon. Kody the Conservation Pup: Helps Tori Cross the Road. Birt, Michael. 2012. 58p. 27.95 *(978-0-578-11315-9(5))*; pap. 19.95 *(978-0-578-11306-7(6))* Birt Hse. Publishing.

Trammell, Jeremiah. The Cabin That Moose Built. Stihler, Cherie B. 2006. (Paws IV Ser.). 32p. (J). (gr. -1-2). pap. 10.99 *(978-1-57061-446-0(6)*, Little Bigfoot) Sasquatch Bks.
—The Giant Cabbage: An Alaska Folktale. Stihler, Cherie. 2003. (Paws IV Ser.). 32p. (J). (gr. -1-2). pap. 10.99 *(978-1-57061-357-9(5)*, Little Bigfoot) Sasquatch Bks.
—Little Red Riding Hood of the Pacific Northwest. Crews, Marcia. 2018. 32p. (J). (gr. -1-3). 17.99 *(978-1-63217-183-2(X)*, Little Bigfoot) Sasquatch Bks.
—My Name Isn't Oof! Warren the Warbler Takes Flight. Galligan, Michael. 2019. (Warren the Warbler Ser.). 32p. (J). (gr. -1-3). 17.99 *(978-1-63217-193-1(7)*, Little Bigfoot) Sasquatch Bks.
—Three Bears of the Pacific Northwest. Vaughan, Richard Lee & Vaughn, Marcia. 2011. (ENG.). 32p. (J). (gr. -1-2). 17.99 *(978-1-57061-684-6(1)*, Little Bigfoot) Sasquatch Bks.
—Three Bears of the Pacific Northwest. Vaughan, Richard & Crews, Marcia. 2016. (ENG.). 20p. (J). (— 1). bds. 9.99 *(978-1-63217-076-7(0)*, Little Bigfoot) Sasquatch Bks.
—Under Alaska's Midnight Sun. Vanasse, Deb. 2005. (Paws IV Ser.). 32p. (J). (gr. -1-2). pap. 10.99 *(978-1-57061-422-4(9)*, Little Bigfoot) Sasquatch Bks.
Trammell, Norma Jeanne. A Different Home: A New Foster Child's Story. DeGarmo, John & DeGarmo, Kelly. 2014. (ENG.). 48p. (J). 14.95 *(978-1-84905-987-9(X)*, 694315) Kingsley, Jessica Pubs. GBR. Dist: Hachette UK Distribution.
Tramontano, Priscilla, et al. Sonic the Hedgehog, Vol. 6: the Last Minute. Flynn, Ian. 2020. (Sonic the Hedgehog Ser.: 6). (ENG.). 96p. (J). (gr. 4-7). pap. 15.99 *(978-1-68405-672-9(1))* Idea & Design Works, LLC.
Tran, Aiki. Kai & His Magical Bobo. Tran, Kathy V. 2019. (Kai Panducorn Ser.: Vol. 2). (ENG.). 40p. (J). pap. 11.95 ***(978-1-7072-9856-3(4))*** Independently Published.
—This Christmas I Am Giving You. Pham, Havy & Tran, Kathy V. 2019. (ENG.). 36p. (J). pap. 9.95 ***(978-1-7124-4499-3(9))*** Independently Published.
Tran Art, Dahn. The Doctor's Disc-Eyes. Blom, Tracy & Sheridan, Scott. 2018. (ENG.). 40p. (J). 24.99 *(978-0-9906871-4-6(7))* Blom Pubns.
Tran Art, Danh. Everything on the Farm Poops. Culbreth, Kelly Lee. (ENG.). 26p. (J). (gr. k-4). 2019. pap. 9.99 *(978-0-578-49777-8(8))*; 2018. 17.99 *(978-0-578-43267-0(6))* Kelly Lee Culbreth.
Tran, Basia. My Footprints. Phi, Bao. 2019. (ENG.). 32p. (J). (gr. k-4). lib. bdg. 19.99 *(978-1-68446-000-7(X)*, 138466, Capstone Editions) Capstone.
—Two Parts of Me: I Am More Than My Body. Nicholas, Susan. Betz, Amy, ed. 2019. (Conscious Children's Bks.: Vol. 1). (ENG.). 38p. (J). (gr. k-4). 21.99 *(978-1-7324336-1-8(5))* Human Consciousness Consortium.
Tran, Danh. Get Real: An Adaptation of the Velveteen Rabbit. Jimerson, John. Jimerson, Rose, ed. 2019. (ENG.). 78p. (J). (gr. 1-4). pap. 14.99 *(978-0-578-44197-9(7))* John M. Jimerson.
Tran, Danh & Jimerson, Rose. Get Real: An Adaptation of the Velveteen Rabbit. 2018. (ENG.). 72p. (J). pap. 14.99 *(978-1-7210-4470-2(1))* CreateSpace Independent Publishing Platform.
Tran Phan, Aliosa. The Tale of Maude & Moody & the Giant Tomato. Blum, Ingo. 2019. (ENG.). 182p. (J). (gr. 2-5). pap. *(978-3-947410-10-1(7))* Blum, Ingo Planet-Oh Concepts.
Tran, Richard. Bella & the Blue Genie. Gould, Jonathan. Diamond, Lane, ed. 2018. (ENG.). 44p. (J). (gr. k-3). pap. 10.95 *(978-1-62253-088-5(8))* Evolved Publishing.
Tran, Turine. The Cursed Castle: an Escape Room in a Book: Use Your Wits to Survive & Decipher the Clues to Escape. Tracosas, L. J. 2020. (ENG.). 48p. (J). (gr. 3-17). 9.99 ***(978-0-7603-6893-0(7)***, 338461) becker&mayer! books.
Tran, Turine. Knit-Knotters. Hay, Sam. 2016. (Stella & the Night Sprites Ser.: 1). (ENG.). 96p. (J). (gr. 1-3). pap. 4.99 *(978-0-545-81998-5(9))* Scholastic, Inc.
Tranco, Miguel. The Story of Cyrano de Bergerac. Benni, Stefano & Curtis, Howard. 2017. (Save the Story Ser.: 9). (ENG.). 104p. (J). (gr. 3-7). 19.95 *(978-1-78269-021-4(2)*, Pushkin Children's Bks.) Steerforth Pr.
Trapani, Iza. Froggie Went A-Courtin' Trapani, Iza. 2006. (Iza Trapani's Extended Nursery Rhymes Ser.). 32p. (J). (gr. 2-k). pap. 7.95 *(978-1-58089-029-8(6))* Charlesbridge Publishing, Inc.
—Gabe & Goon. Trapani, Iza. 2016. 32p. (J). (gr. -1-1). lib. bdg. 16.95 *(978-1-58089-640-5(5))* Charlesbridge Publishing, Inc.
—Haunted Party. Trapani, Iza. 28p. (J). 2010. (gr. -1-2). pap. 7.95 *(978-1-58089-247-6(7))*; 2009. (ENG.). (gr. k-3). 22.44 *(978-1-58089-246-9(9))* Charlesbridge Publishing, Inc.
—Jingle Bells. Trapani, Iza. 2007. 32p. (J). (gr. -1-k). 7.95 *(978-1-58089-096-0(2))* Charlesbridge Publishing, Inc.
—Little Miss Muffet. Trapani, Iza. 2015. (ENG.). 32p. (J). (gr. -1-k). 6.95 *(978-1-62914-616-4(1)*, Sky Pony Pr.) Skyhorse Publishing Co., Inc.
—Mary Had a Little Lamb. Trapani, Iza. 2003. (Iza Trapani's Extended Nursery Rhymes Ser.). 32p. (J). (gr. -1-k). 7.95 *(978-1-58089-090-8(3))* Charlesbridge Publishing, Inc.
—Oh Where, Oh Where Has My Little Dog Gone? Trapani, Iza. 2008. (Iza Trapani's Extended Nursery Rhymes Ser.). 32p. (J). (gr. -1-k). pap. 7.99 *(978-1-58089-005-2(9))* Charlesbridge Publishing, Inc.
—Old King Cole. Trapani, Iza. 2015. (Iza Trapani's Extended Nursery Rhymes Ser.). 32p. (J). (-k). lib. bdg. 15.95 *(978-1-58089-632-0(4))* Charlesbridge Publishing, Inc.
—Old Macdonald Had a... Zoo? Trapani, Iza. 2017. (Iza Trapani's Extended Nursery Rhymes Ser.). 32p. (J). (-k). lib. bdg. 16.99 *(978-1-58089-729-7(0))* Charlesbridge Publishing, Inc.
—Rufus & Friends. Trapani, Iza. 2010. 36p. (J). (gr. -1-3). 16.95 *(978-1-58089-248-3(5))*; pap. 7.95 *(978-1-58089-249-0(3))* Charlesbridge Publishing, Inc.
—Rufus & Friends: Rhyme Time. Trapani, Iza. 2008. 40p. (J). (gr. -1-3). pap. 7.95 *(978-1-58089-207-0(8))* Charlesbridge Publishing, Inc.
—Shoo Fly! Trapani, Iza. 2007. (Iza Trapani's Extended Nursery Rhymes Ser.). 32p. (J). (gr. k-3). per. 7.95 *(978-1-58089-076-2(8))* Charlesbridge Publishing, Inc.
—Sing along with Iza & Friends: Row Row Row Your Boat. Trapani, Iza. 2004. 32p. (J). pap. 11.95 incl. audio compact disk *(978-1-58089-102-8(0))* Charlesbridge Publishing, Inc.
—Sing along with Iza & Friends: The Itsy Bitsy Spider. Trapani, Iza. 2004. 32p. (J). pap. 11.95 incl. audio compact disk *(978-1-58089-100-4(4))* Charlesbridge Publishing, Inc.
—Sing along with Iza & Friends: Twinkle, Twinkle Little Star. Trapani, Iza. 2004. 32p. (J). pap. 11.95 incl. audio compact disk *(978-1-58089-101-1(2))* Charlesbridge Publishing, Inc.
—Twinkle, Twinkle, Little Star. Trapani, Iza. 2008. (Iza Trapani's Extended Nursery Rhymes Ser.). (ENG.). 26p. (J). (gr. -1 — 1). bds. 7.95 *(978-1-58089-015-1(6))* Charlesbridge Publishing, Inc.
—Vole & Troll. Trapani, Iza. 2019. 32p. (J). (-k). lib. bdg. 15.99 *(978-1-58089-885-0(8))* Charlesbridge Publishing, Inc.
Trapani, Pam Taylor. Twinkleville Coloring Book: A Magical Fairy Coloring Adventure. Trapani, Pam Taylor. 2019. (ENG.). 52p. (J). pap. 6.95 *(978-1-7964-0370-1(9))* Independently Published.
Trapp, Karla. My Feelings Workbook. Wiemeier, Aaron. 2011. 104p. (J). pap. 19.95 *(978-1-59850-095-0(3))* Youthlight, Inc.
Trasler, Janee. Jesus Loves the Little Children, 1 vol. Zondervan Staff. 2008. (I Can Read! / Song Ser.). (ENG.). 32p. (J). (gr. -1-3). pap. 4.99 *(978-0-310-71620-4(9))* Zonderkidz.
—The Ruby Princess Runs Away (Jewel Kingdom #1) Malcolm, Jahnna N. 2020. (Jewel Kingdom Ser.: 1). (ENG.). 96p. (J). (gr. 2-5). pap. 6.99 *(978-1-338-56567-6(2)*, Scholastic Paperbacks) Scholastic, Inc.
—A Visit to the Farm. Feldman, Thea. 2006. 3p. (J). (gr. -1-3). bds. 5.99 *(978-1-932915-32-7(X))* Sandvik Publishing.
Trasler, Janee. Bathtime for Chickies. Trasler, Janee. 2015. (Chickies Ser.). (ENG.). 24p. (J). (gr. -1 — 1). bds. 8.99 *(978-0-06-234229-4(0)*, HarperFestival) HarperCollins Pubs.
—Bedtime for Chickies. Trasler, Janee. 2014. (Chickies Ser.). (ENG.). 24p. (J). (gr. -1 — 1). bds. 8.99 *(978-0-06-227468-7(6)*, HarperFestival) HarperCollins Pubs.
—Big Chickie, Little Chickie: A Book of Opposites. Trasler, Janee. 2016. (ENG.). 24p. (J). (gr. -1 — 1). bds. 8.99 *(978-0-06-234231-7(2)*, HarperFestival) HarperCollins Pubs.
—Dinnertime for Chickies. Trasler, Janee. 2014. (Chickies Ser.). (ENG.). 24p. (J). (gr. -1 — 1). bds. 8.99 *(978-0-06-227470-0(8)*, HarperFestival) HarperCollins Pubs.
—Goat in a Boat: an Acorn Book (a Frog & Dog Book #2) Trasler, Janee. 2020. (Frog & Dog Book Ser.: 2). (ENG.). 48p. (J). (gr. -1-1). pap. 4.99 *(978-1-338-54042-0(4))*; lib. bdg. 23.99 *(978-1-338-54045-1(9))* Scholastic, Inc.
—Mimi & Bear in the Snow. Trasler, Janee. 2015. (Mimi & Bear Ser.). (ENG.). 26p. (J). (gr. -1-k). bds. 7.99 *(978-0-374-30093-7(3)*, 9780374300937, Farrar, Straus & Giroux (BYR)) Farrar, Straus & Giroux.
—A New Chick for Chickies. Trasler, Janee. 2014. (Chickies Ser.). (ENG.). 24p. (J). (gr. -1 — 1). bds. 8.99 *(978-0-06-227471-7(6)*, HarperFestival) HarperCollins Pubs.
—Pottytime for Chickies. Trasler, Janee. 2014. (Chickies Ser.). (ENG.). 24p. (J). (gr. -1 — 1). bds. 8.99 *(978-0-06-227469-4(4)*, HarperFestival) HarperCollins Pubs.
Traverse, Jackie. Nikik & Wapus Save the People, 1 vol. McLellan, Joseph. 2015. (ENG.). 32p. (J). mass mkt. 10.95 *(978-1-894717-70-0(8)*, 4afc0c39-6c99-446c-876d-88e2b104bfc5) Pemmican Pubns., Inc. CAN. Dist: Firefly Bks., Ltd.
Travis, Caroline. French Quarter Tori & the Red Owl. Black, Cary & Schott, Gretchen Victoria. 2012. 38p. pap. 14.95 *(978-0-9754279-7-2(0))*; pap. 12.95 *(978-0-9754279-8-9(9))* Red Owl Pubns.
Travis, Stephanie. Bobby Beaver Learns a Lesson. Bowman, Andy. 26p. (J). (gr. k-5). pap. 6.95 *(978-1-931650-10-6(1))*; lib. bdg. 14.95 *(978-1-931650-11-3(X))* Coastal Publishing Carolina, Inc.
—Indian Slim. Bowman, Andy. 29p. (J). (gr. 1-6). pap. 6.95 *(978-1-931650-06-9(3))*; lib. bdg. 14.95 *(978-1-931650-07-6(1))* Coastal Publishing Carolina, Inc.
—Pokey's Garden. Bowman, Andy. 26p. (J). (gr. k-5). pap. 6.95 *(978-1-931650-08-3(X))*; lib. bdg. 14.95 *(978-1-931650-09-0(8))* Coastal Publishing Carolina, Inc.
—The Quilt. Bowman, Andy. 25p. (J). (gr. 1-6). pap. 6.95 *(978-1-931650-04-5(7))*; lib. bdg. 14.95 *(978-1-931650-05-2(5))* Coastal Publishing Carolina, Inc.
Travis, Tony. Victorianne Phoenix Is a Real Princess. Travis, Kinya Shakur. 2015. (Victorianne Phoenix - World of Discovery Ser.: Vol. 1). (ENG.). 30p. (J). (gr. k-5). pap. 10.99 *(978-0-9997754-9-3(9))* Through Their Eyes Bks.
Traxler, Bailey. The Winds of Happiness: Irie's Adventures. Fiedler-Buss, Teresa. 2018. (Winds of Happiness Ser.: Vol. 1). (ENG.). 50p. (J). (gr. 1-6). 24.99 *(978-1-7320905-0-7(5))* Winds of Happiness, LLC, The.
Traylor, Waverley, jt. illus. see Roberts, Curt.
Traynor, Daniel. Manda Panda Goes to Tea. Stacy, Lorraine. 2016. (ENG.). (J). (gr. k-2). pap. 16.99 *(978-0-9975539-3-2(6))* True Perspective Publishing Hse.
Traynor, Elizabeth. F Is for First State: A Delaware Alphabet. Crane, Carol. 2005. (State Ser.). (ENG.). 40p. (J). (gr. -1-3). 17.95 *(978-1-58536-154-0(2))* Sleeping Bear Pr.
—V Is for Venus Flytrap: A Plant Alphabet. Gagliano, Eugene. 2009. (Science Ser.). (ENG.). 40p. (J). (gr. k-8). 17.95 *(978-1-58536-350-6(2))* Sleeping Bear Pr.
Treacher, Dawn. Miss Pickle a Dizzy Witch. Wicks, Neelie. 2017. (Miss Pickle Stories Ser.: Vol. 1). (ENG.). 38p. (J). (gr. k-3). pap. *(978-0-9957721-0-6(X))* Skelwicks Arts.
Treatner, Meryl. We Both Read-The New Tribe. Carson, Jana. 2013. 44p. (J). pap. 4.99 *(978-1-60115-264-0(7))* Treasure Bay, Inc.
Treatner, Meryle. The Empty Pot: A Chinese Legend. Goldish, Meish. 2005. 14p. pap. 6.00 *(978-0-15-350582-9(6))* Harcourt Schl. Pubs.
Treffeisen, Brian, photos by. Freddy in the City: Memorable Monday. Bird, Janie. 2nd rev. ed. 2005.Tr. of Freddy en la Ciudad un Lunes Memorble. (SPA., 32p. (J). 10.95 *(978-1-59494-005-7(3))* CPCC Pr.
Treffry, Teresa. Playthings: 101 Used for Everyday Objects. Stagnitti, Karen. (J). (gr. k-3). pap. *(978-1-876367-61-9(X))* Wizard Bks.
Treg, Mccoy, jt. illus. see Thomas, Erika.
Trego Hill, Vicki. La Llorona - The Weeping Woman: An Hispanic Legend Told in Spanish & English. Hayes, Joe. 3rd ed. 2004. (SPA.). 32p. (J). (gr. 4-6). 16.95 *(978-0-938317-86-9(5))* Cinco Puntos Pr.
Treitler, Bennett. My Dad Is an Alcoholic, What about Me? A Pre-Teen Guide to Conquering Addictive Genes. Treitler, Marc & Treitler, Lianna. 2016. (ENG.). 148p. (J). pap. 9.99 *(978-0-9974263-0-4(6))* Do Good Pr.
Treitler, Bennett & Treitler, Rowena. Alcohol, Drugs & You: A Young Person's Guide to Avoiding Addiction. Treitler, Lianna. 2018. (ENG.). 196p. (J). pap. 9.99 ***(978-0-9974263-3-5(0))*** Silence Dogood Pr.
Treitler, Bennett and Rowena. Alcohol, Drugs & You: A Young Person's Guide to Avoiding Addiction. Treitler, Marc. 2018. (ENG.). 194p. (J). pap. 9.99 *(978-0-9974263-2-8(2))* Do Good Pr.
Treitler, Rowena, jt. illus. see Treitler, Bennett.
Trejo, Bladimir. Ecuador. Sojos, Catalina. 2015. (Serie Verde / Album Ilustrado Ser.). (SPA.). 24p. (J). pap. 12.95 *(978-9942-19-324-7(3))* Santillana USA Publishing Co., Inc.
Treleaven, Lou & Abey, Katie. Letter to Pluto. Treleaven, Lou. 2020. (Penpals on Pluto Ser.). (ENG.). 128p. (J). (gr. 2-5). lib. bdg. 15.99 *(978-1-84886-470-2(1))* Maverick Arts Publishing GBR. Dist: Lerner Publishing Group.
Treloar, Debi, photos by. Childrens Spaces: From Zero to Ten. Wilson, Judith. 2005. (ENG., 144p. pap. *(978-1-84172-871-1(3))* Ryland Peters & Small.
Tremaine, Michele. It's MY Future: Should I Be a Nurse Practitioner? Wick, Elaine. 2004. 64p. (J). lib. bdg. 12.95 *(978-0-9749769-0-7(3))* NAPNAP.
Tremblay, Danielle & Dupuis, Karina. Florida Monsters: A Search & Find Book. 2018. (ENG.). 22p. (J). (gr. -1). bds. 9.99 *(978-2-924734-15-5(0))* City Monsters Bks. CAN. Dist: Publishers Group West (PGW).
—Rocky Mountains Monsters: A Search & Find Book. 2018. (ENG.). 22p. (J). (gr. -1). bds. 9.99 *(978-2-924734-16-2(9))* City Monsters Bks. CAN. Dist: Publishers Group West (PGW).
Tremblay, Marie-Ève. Le Crapaud et Son Solo de Banjo: Les Grandes Chansons des Tout-Petits. 2019. (Grandes Chansons des Tout-Petits Ser.). (ENG.). 32p. (J). (gr. -1-k). pap. 7.95 *(978-2-924774-19-9(5))* La Montagne Secrete CAN. Dist: Independent Pubs. Group.
—Inside Your Insides: A Guide to the Microbes That Call You Home. Eamer, Claire. 2016. (ENG.). 36p. (J). (gr. 3-7). 17.95 *(978-1-77138-332-5(1))* Kids Can Pr., Ltd. CAN. Dist: Hachette Bk. Group.
—La Laine des Moutons: Les Grandes Chansons des Tout-Petits. 2019. (Grandes Chansons des Tout-Petits Ser.). (ENG.). 32p. (J). (gr. -1-k). pap. 7.95 *(978-2-924774-17-5(9))* La Montagne Secrete CAN. Dist: Independent Pubs. Group.
—Lines, Bars & Circles: How William Playfair Invented Graphs. Becker, Helaine. 2017. (ENG.). 36p. (J). (gr. 1-4). 17.95 *(978-1-77138-570-1(7))* Kids Can Pr., Ltd. CAN. Dist: Hachette Bk. Group.
—Le Roi, la Reine et le Petit Prince: Les Grandes Chansons des Tout-Petits. 2019. (Grandes Chansons des Tout-Petits Ser.). (ENG.). 32p. (J). (gr. -1-k). pap. 7.95 *(978-2-924774-18-2(7))* La Montagne Secrete CAN. Dist: Independent Pubs. Group.
—Under Pressure: The Science of Stress. Lloyd Kyi, Tanya. 2019. (ENG.). 76p. (YA). (gr. 6-9). 16.99 *(978-1-5253-0007-3(5))* Kids Can Pr., Ltd. CAN. Dist: Hachette Bk. Group.
Treml, Renee. One Very Tired Wombat. Treml, Renee. 2014. (ENG.). 32p. (J). (gr. -1-k). pap. 9.99 *(978-1-74275-579-3(8))* Random Hse. Australia AUS. Dist: Independent Pubs. Group.
Tremlin, Nathan. A Quilt of Wishes. Werner, Teresa O. l.t. ed. 2005. 21p. (J). per. 9.99 *(978-1-59879-037-5(4))* Lifevest Publishing, Inc.
—A Quilt of Wishes. Werner, Teresa Orem. l.t. ed. 2005. 26p. (J). 16.95 *(978-1-59879-147-1(8))* Lifevest Publishing, Inc.
Tremlin, Nathan & Chomiak, Joseph. Mookie: A Girl in Maximsubornia. Tremlin, Nathan & Chomiak, Joseph. Swanson, Matt. 2004. 48p. (J). (gr. 4-8). reprint ed. 18.00 *(978-0-7567-9081-3(6))* DIANE Publishing Co.
Tresilian, S. Behind the Ranges: Tales of Explorers, Pioneers & Travellers. Reynolds, E. E. 2011. (ENG.). 128p. pap. 15.99 *(978-0-521-13526-9(5))* Cambridge Univ. Pr.
—Unknown Ways: More Tales of Explorers, Pioneers & Travellers. Reynolds, E. E. 2011. (ENG.). 126p. pap. 20.99 *(978-1-107-60027-0(8))* Cambridge Univ. Pr.
Tresilian, Stuart. The Complete Jungle Book. Kipling, Rudyard. 2018. (ENG.). 480p. (J). 55.00 *(978-1-250-18912-7(8)*, 900192181, Holt, Henry & Co. Bks. For Young Readers) Holt, Henry & Co.
Tress, Arthur, photos by. Facing Up: Tress: Facing Up. ltd. ed. 2004. (ENG & FRE., 1250.00 *(978-0-9761396-7-6(7)*, Tress-LE1) Top Choice Pr., LLC.
Tretick, Stanley, photos by. Martin's Dream Day. Kelley, Kitty. 2017. (ENG., 40p. (J). (gr. k). 17.99 *(978-1-4814-6766-7(2))* Simon & Schuster Children's Publishing.
Trevas, Chris, jt. illus. see Reiff, Chris.
Trevinio, Juan. Dingbat: El Gato Voluntario. Johnson, Sandi. Johnson, Britt, ed. Short, Elizabeth, tr. from ENG. l.t. ed. 2003. Orig. Title: Dingbat the Wayward Cat. (SPA.). 14p. (J). (gr. k-5). spiral bd. 4.99 *(978-1-929063-85-7(7)*, 326) Moons & Stars Publishing For Children.
Trevino, Charity. Don't Judge a Bug by Its Color. Trevino, Renee. 2019. (ENG.). 26p. (J). pap. 9.25 *(978-1-0797-8890-7(5))* Independently Published.
Trevino, Juan. Dorp the Scottish Dragon - Book 1. Brundige, Britt & Durant, Sybrina, eds. 2019. (Dorp the Scottish Dragon Ser.: Vol. 1). (ENG.). 40p. (J). pap. 12.99 ***(978-1-6755-8107-0(X))*** Independently Published.
Trevino, Juan & Johnson, Jim. 1 - Dorp the Scottish Dragon: Scotland, 7 vols. Johnson, Sandi. Johnson, Britt & Durant, Sybrina, eds. 2nd rev. ed. 2014. (Lost from Loch Lomond Ser.: 1). 38p. (J). (gr. -1-6). pap. 12.99 *(978-1-929063-00-0(8)*, 101) Moons & Stars Publishing For Children.
Trevisan, Marco. Anything Is Possible. Belloni, Giulia. 2013. (ENG.). 32p. (J). (gr. -1-3). 16.95 *(978-1-926973-91-3(7)*, Owlkids) Owlkids Bks. Inc. CAN. Dist: Publishers Group West (PGW).
Trexler, Jennifer Suther. Zipper Finds a Job. Ritch, Catherine. 2014. (White Squirrel Parables Ser.: Vol. 2). (ENG.). 32p. (J). (gr. -1-3). 13.95 *(978-1-933341-40-8(8))* CRM.
Tribus, Theresa. Minnie & the Better Den. Noel, Carmel. 2020. (ENG.). 30p. (J). (gr. k-2). 11.99 ***(978-1-0878-6098-5(9))*** Indy Pub.
Trier, Walter. Emil & the Detectives. Kastner, Erich. 2014. (ENG.). 224p. (J). (gr. 4-9). pap. 13.99 *(978-1-4683-0829-7(7)*, 460829) Abrams, Inc.
Trier, Walter. The Jolly Steamship. Trier, Walter. Rowohlt, Harry. 2013. 32p. (J). (gr. -1-3). 17.95 *(978-0-7358-4127-7(6))* North-South Bks., Inc.
Trifia. Beware the Back of the Bus: A Florida Horror Story: Book Two. Lind, Stefan. 2019. (Beware the Back of the Bus Ser.: Vol. 2). (ENG.). 320p. (J). pap. 14.99 ***(978-1-7084-4535-5(8))*** Independently Published.
Trimarco, Peter. It's Just So. Trimarco, Peter. Faatz, Brenda. l.t. ed. 2016. (ENG.). 40p. (J). (gr. -1-2). 16.95 *(978-0-9970851-0-5(X))* Notable Kids Publishing.
Trimble, Anne M. The Crazy Adventure of Nicholas Mouse. Jeswald, Mary J. 2004. 32p. (J). 14.99 *(978-0-9760651-0-4(X))* OrangeFoot Publishing Co.
Trimmer, Tony. A Bill's Journey into Law, 1 vol. Slade, Suzanne. 2011. (Follow It! Ser.). (ENG.). 24p. (J). (gr. 1-3). pap. 7.49 *(978-1-4048-7027-7(X)*, Picture Window Bks.) Capstone.
—A Germ's Journey, 1 vol. Rooke, Thom. (Follow It! Ser.). (ENG.). 24p. (J). (gr. 1-3). 2011. pap. 7.49 *(978-1-4048-6710-9(4))*; 2010. lib. bdg. 27.32 *(978-1-4048-6268-5(4))* Capstone. (Picture Window Bks.).
—The Good Artist. Place, John. 2007. (ENG.). 36p. *(978-1-85345-424-0(9))* Crusade for World Revival.
Trimmer, Tony & Chatterton, Martin. A Joke a Day: 365 Guaranteed Giggles. Kingfisher Editors. 2007. (Sidesplitters Ser.). (ENG.). 64p. (J). (gr. 1-5). pap. 7.99 *(978-0-7534-6128-0(5)*, 900052965, Kingfisher) Roaring Brook Pr.
Trimpe, Herb, et al. Captain Britain: Legacy of a Legend. 2016. (ENG.). 208p. (YA). (gr. 8-17). pap. 19.99 *(978-1-302-90668-9(2))* Marvel Worldwide, Inc.
—Dinosaurs Attack. Gerani, Gary. 2014. 136p. pap. 19.99 *(978-1-61377-862-3(7)*, 9781613778623) Idea & Design Works, LLC.
—Wolverine Omnibus Vol. 1. 2020. 1056p. (YA). (gr. 8-17). 100.00 *(978-1-302-92267-2(X))* Marvel Worldwide, Inc.
Trimpe, Herb & Buscema, Sal. Incredible Hulk Epic Collection: in the Hands of Hydra. 2019. (ENG.). 440p. (YA). (gr. 4-17). pap. 39.99 *(978-1-302-91558-2(4))* Marvel Worldwide, Inc.
Trinh, Shelley Marie. Baby Paratrooper. Gum, Kayla June. Gum, Kayla June, ed. 2019. (Military Babies Ser.: Vol. 1). (ENG.). 26p. (J). pap. 12.99 ***(978-1-6908-7637-3(9))*** Independently Published.
Trinidad, Jose. Joseph's Coat of Many Colors- la Tunica de Muchos Colores de Jose. Swift, Grace Marie. 2017. (Sonship Ser.: Vol. 2). (ENG.). (J). 18.00 *(978-0-9703270-6-2(4))* Dimensions.
—Noah's Animals / Los Animales de Noe. Swift, Grace M. 2017. (Sonship Ser.: Vol. 3). (ENG.). (J). 18.00 *(978-0-9703270-7-9(2))* Dimensions.
Trinidad, Leo. Anxious Adam Braves the Test. Ventura, Marne. 2016. (Worry Warriors Ser.). (ENG.). 96p. (J). (gr. 2-4). pap. 5.95 *(978-1-4965-3650-1(9))*; lib. bdg. 25.99 *(978-1-4965-3611-2(8))* Capstone. (Stone Arch Bks.).
—Creepy Mazes. Potter, William. 2018. (Ultimate Finger Trace Mazes Ser.). 32p. (gr. 6-9). 28.50 *(978-1-5081-9724-9(5))*; pap. 11.75 *(978-1-5383-9000-9(0))* Rosen Publishing Group, Inc., The. (Windmill Bks.).
—Dangerous Mazes. Potter, William. 2018. (Ultimate Finger Trace Mazes Ser.). 32p. (gr. 6-9). 28.50 *(978-1-5081-9725-6(3))*; pap. 11.75 *(978-1-5383-9003-0(5))* Rosen Publishing Group, Inc., The. (Windmill Bks.).
—Edgy Estella Aces the Sleepover Party. Ventura, Marne. 2016. (Worry Warriors Ser.). (ENG.). 96p. (J). (gr. 2-4). lib. bdg. 25.99 *(978-1-4965-3610-5(X)*, Stone Arch Bks.) Capstone.
—Jittery Jake Conquers Stage Fright. Ventura, Marne. 2016. (Worry Warriors Ser.). (ENG.). 96p. (J). (gr. 2-4). lib. bdg. 25.99 *(978-1-4965-3612-9(6)*, Stone Arch Bks.) Capstone.
—Nervous Nellie Fights First-Day Frenzy. Ventura, Marne. 2016. (Worry Warriors Ser.). (ENG.). 96p. (J). (gr. 2-4). lib. bdg. 25.99 *(978-1-4965-3613-6(4)*, Stone Arch Bks.) Capstone.
—Scary Mazes. Potter, William. 2018. (Ultimate Finger Trace Mazes Ser.). 32p. (gr. 6-9). 28.50 *(978-1-5081-9726-3(1))*; pap. 11.75 *(978-1-5383-9006-1(X))* Rosen Publishing Group, Inc., The. (Windmill Bks.).
—Weird Mazes. Potter, William. 2018. (Ultimate Finger Trace Mazes Ser.). 32p. (gr. 6-9). 28.50

T

(978-1-5081-9727-0(X)); pap. 11.75 *(978-1-5383-9009-2(4))* Rosen Publishing Group, Inc., The. (Windmill Bks.).

—The Worry Warriors, 4 vols. Ventura, Marne. 2016. (Worry Warriors Ser.). (ENG.). 96p. (J). (gr. 2-4). lib. bdg., lib. bdg., lib. bdg. 103.96 *(978-1-4965-3665-5(7)*, Stone Arch Bks.) Capstone.

Trinity, Shaya & Julia, Hessler. From Heaven to Heaven. Kirkendol, Karin. 2018. (ENG.). 32p. (J). (gr. k-6). pap. 14.99 *(978-1-7325814-0-1(1))* Winfield Hse. Pr.

Trionfetti, Rossella. Weird & Wonderful Animals. 2019. (ENG.). 64p. (J). (gr. 2). 14.95 *(978-88-544-1527-0(8))* White Star ITA. Dist: Sterling Publishing Co., Inc.

Tripathi, Siddhartha. Milky Way. Nainy, Mamta. 2017. (ENG.). (J). (gr. k-1). 44p. 19.99 *(978-0-9890615-6-8(6))*; pap. 11.99 *(978-0-9890615-8-2(2))* Yali Publishing LLC.

Triplett, Chris Harper. Rocky the Sea Turtle. Kreitz, Tina. 2013. (ENG.). (J). 14.95 *(978-1-62086-132-5(1))* Mascot Bks., Inc.

Triplett, Gina & Call, Greg. The Sixty-Eight Rooms, 1. Malone, Marianne. 2011. (Sixty-Eight Rooms Adventures Ser.). (ENG.). 288p. (J). (gr. 4-6). lib. bdg. 22.44 *(978-0-375-95710-9(3))* Random House Publishing Group.

—The Sixty-Eight Rooms. Malone, Marianne. 2011. (Sixty-Eight Rooms Adventures Ser.: 1). (ENG.). 288p. (J). (gr. 3-7). pap. 7.99 *(978-0-375-85711-9(7)*, Yearling) Random Hse. Children's Bks.

Triplett, Ginger. Graylinger Grotto. Roark, Algernon Michael. 2011. (ENG.). 94p. (J). pap. 22.95 *(978-1-59299-631-5(0))* Inkwater Pr.

—Secret at the Zoo. James, Anne. 2019. (ENG.). 40p. (J). pap. 12.00 *(978-1-0745-8066-7(4))* Independently Published.

Tripodi, Pina. Sunny Finds Her Shine. Tripodi, Pina. 2019. (ENG.). 50p. (J). (gr. k-2). 17.99 ***(978-1-7342116-0-3(1))*** Tripodi, Pina.

Tripp, Christine. The Cool Coats. Brimner, Larry Dane. 2003. (Rookie Choices Ser.). 31p. (J). (gr. 1-2). 13.60 *(978-0-7569-3259-6(9))* Perfection Learning Corp.

—The Cool Coats. Brimner, Larry Dane. 2003. (Rookie Choices Ser.). (ENG.). 32p. (J). (gr. 1-2). pap. 5.95 *(978-0-516-27834-6(7))*; (J). 20.50 *(978-0-516-22545-6(6))* Scholastic Library Publishing. (Children's Pr.).

—Summer Fun. Brimner, Larry Dane. 2003. (Rookie Choices Ser.). (ENG.). 32p. (J). (gr. 1-2). 20.50 *(978-0-516-22548-7(0)*, Children's Pr.) Scholastic Library Publishing.

—Trash Trouble. Brimner, Larry Dane. 2003. (Rookie Choices Ser.). (ENG.). 32p. (J). (gr. 1-2). pap. 5.95 *(978-0-516-27837-7(1)*, Children's Pr.) Scholastic Library Publishing.

Tripp, Christine. Let's Talk about God. Tripp, Christine, tr. Kripke, Dorothy Karp. 2003. (J). 9.95 *(978-1-881283-34-8(8))* Alef Design Group.

Tripp, F. J. The Robber Hotzenplotz. Preussler, Otfried. Bell, Anthea, tr. 2016. (ENG.). 128p. (J). (gr. k-4). 17.95 *(978-1-59017-961-1(7)*, NYR Children's Collection) New York Review of Bks., Inc., The.

Tripp, Wallace. No Flying in the House. Brock, Betty. 2020. (Harper Trophy Bks.). (ENG.). 144p. (J). (gr. 3-7). pap. 6.99 *(978-0-06-440130-2(8)*, HarperCollins) HarperCollins Pubs. Ltd. GBR. Dist: HarperCollins Pubs.

Trippe, Dean. Power Lunch: First Course, Bk. 1. Torres, J. 2011. (Power Lunch Ser.: 1). (ENG.). 40p. (J). 12.99 *(978-1-934964-70-5(0)*, 9781934964705, Lion Forge) Oni Pr., Inc.

—Power Lunch Vol. 2 Bk. 2: Seconds. Torres, J. 2014. (Power Lunch Ser.: 2). (ENG.). 40p. (J). 12.99 *(978-1-62010-011-0(8)*, 9781620100110, Lion Forge) Oni Pr., Inc.

Trithart, Emma. Boo at the Zoo. Burton, Jeffrey. 2018. (ENG.). 14p. (J). (gr. -1-k). bds. 7.99 *(978-1-5344-2033-5(9)*, Little Simon) Little Simon.

—Crocodile's Burp. 2016. (Pardon Me! Ser.: 4). 14p. (J). spiral bd. *(978-1-84643-750-2(4))* Child's Play International Ltd.

—Friends Around the World Atlas: A Compassionate Approach to Seeing the World. Compassion International, Compassion. 2019. (ENG.). 72p. (J). 24.99 *(978-1-4964-2421-1(2)*, 20_29915) Tyndale Hse. Pubs.

—Goldilocks & the Three Bears: A Problem-Solving Story. Giroux, Lindsay Nina. 2016. (J). *(978-0-87659-707-1(X))* Gryphon Hse., Inc.

—Jingle Bells at the Zoo. Burton, Jeffrey. 2018. (ENG.). 14p. (J). (gr. -1 — 1). bds. 7.99 *(978-1-5344-2034-2(7)*, Little Simon) Little Simon.

—Leopard's Snore. 2016. (Pardon Me! Ser.: 4). 14p. (J). spiral bd. *(978-1-84643-752-6(0))* Child's Play International Ltd.

—Me & My Family Tree. Sweeney, Joan. 2nd ed. 2018. 32p. (J). (gr. -1-2). 12.99 *(978-1-5247-6848-5(0)*, Knopf Bks. for Young Readers); pap. 7.99 *(978-1-5247-6851-5(0)*, Dragonfly Bks.) Random Hse. Children's Bks.

—Myths & Legends. Lawrence, Sandra. 2017. (ENG.). (J). 72p. (gr. 1-4). 12.99 *(978-1-944530-11-2(8))*; 64p. *(978-1-84857-596-7(3))* Tiger Tales. (360 Degrees).

Trittin, Paul S. Mark's Story: An Introduction to the Gospel of Mark. Baker, Marvin G. 2nd ed. 2003. 136p. 16.95 *(978-0-9729256-1-7(9))*; pap. 9.95 *(978-0-9729256-0-0(0))* Baker Trittin Pr. (Innovative Christian Pubns.).

Triumph, Toby. You Are Awesome. Syed, Matthew. 2019. (ENG.). 160p. (J). 14.99 *(978-1-4926-8753-5(7)*, Sourcebooks Jabberwocky) Sourcebooks, Inc.

Trivas, Irene. Black, White, Just Right! Davol, Marguerite W. 2019. (ENG.). 32p. (J). (gr. -1-3). pap. 7.99 *(978-0-8075-0788-9(1)*, 807507881) Whitman, Albert & Co.

Trivedi, Ishan. Enny Penny's Valentine's Day Wish. Lee, Erin. 2018. (Enny Penny Ser.: 4). (ENG.). 24p. (J). (gr. k-2). pap. 9.95 *(978-0-9910907-3-0(X))* StoryBk. Genius, LLC.

Trobaugh, Scott, jt. illus. see Bersson, Robert.

Trochim, Linn. The Tall Trees: An Andrew & Feelo Eco Adventure. Vroom, Craig. 2019. (ENG.). 36p. (J). pap. 11.95 ***(978-1-6736-0669-0(5))*** Independently Published.

Trockstad, Marcy. Rat. Unger-Pengilly, Elaine. 2013. 120p. *(978-1-4602-2262-1(8))* FriesenPress.

Trod, Mariano, et al. The Brilliant Dr. Wogan. Montgomery, R. A. 2006. (Choose Your Own Adventure Ser.: No. 17). (ENG.). 144p. (J). (gr. 4-7). per. 6.99 *(978-1-933390-17-8(4)*, CHC17) Chooseco LLC.

—Trouble on Planet Earth. Montgomery, R. A. 2006. (Choose Your Own Adventure Ser.: No. 11). (ENG.). 144p. (J). (gr. 4-8). per. 6.99 *(978-1-933390-11-6(5)*, CHCL11) Chooseco LLC.

Trogdon, Kathryn. Tommy Hare & the Color Purple, 1 vol. DeVogt, Rindia M. 2009. (ENG.). 22p. pap. 24.95 *(978-1-61582-827-2(3))* America Star Bks.

Trolenberg, Karl. Play Day with Daddy. Kula, Cheryl. 2013. 20p. pap. 6.95 *(978-1-4575-2336-6(1))* Dog Ear Publishing, LLC.

Trondheim, Lewis. Mister O. Trondheim, Lewis. 2008. (ENG.). 48p. 13.95 *(978-1-56163-382-1(8))* NBM Publishing Co.

Trone, Jo. A Bee's Kiss. Glass, Graeme. 2012. 60p. pap. 21.50 *(978-1-61897-383-2(5)*, Strategic Bk. Publishing) Strategic Book Publishing & Rights Agency (SBPRA).

Trone, Melody. Barton the Bat's Pumpkin Patch. Beserra, Donna. 2016. (Creative Creatures Ser.: Vol. 2). (ENG.). (J). (gr. k-6). pap. 15.00 *(978-0-9982826-2-6(6))* Artistic Creations Bk. Publishing.

Trone, Melody Karns. Buffy the Butterfly's Apple Orchard. Beserra, Donna. 2016. (Creative Creatures Ser.: Vol. 1). (ENG.). (J). (gr. k-6). pap. 15.00 *(978-0-9982826-5-7(0))* Artistic Creations Bk. Publishing.

—Christopher James Mcabee & the Wonderful Tree. Davis, Lynda S. & Weisel, Kaitlyn E. 2013. 54p. pap. 6.99 *(978-0-9889907-0-8(9))* Sruvis Publishing.

—Twirly Shirley in Hurricane Shirley. Beserra, Donna. 2016. (Twirly Shirley Ser.: Vol. 3). (ENG.). (J). (gr. k-6). pap. 15.00 *(978-0-9982826-3-3(4))* Artistic Creations Bk. Publishing.

Trotta, Lee & Saemann, Kara. California Cheese. Trotta, Lee. 2019. (Cheesebook Ser.: Vol. 3). (ENG.). 24p. (J). (gr. k-4). pap. 6.00 ***(978-1-7923-0685-3(7))*** Globetrotta Productions.

Trotter, Stuart. All the Ways I Love You. Larkin, Susan. 2012. 16p. (J). *(978-1-4351-3857-5(0))* Barnes & Noble, Inc.

—The Big Carrot. Hawes, Alison. 2014. (Traditional Tales Ser.). (ENG.). 12p. (J). (gr. -1-k). pap. 5.95 *(978-1-62521-538-3(X)*, Capstone Classroom) Capstone.

—School Bus Bunny Bus. Williams, Sam. 2006. (ENG.). 10p. (J). (gr. -1-1). 12.95 *(978-1-905417-17-9(9))* Boxer Bks., Ltd. GBR. Dist: Sterling Publishing Co., Inc.

—What's under the Sea? Tahta, Sophie. rev. ed. 2006. (Starting Point Science Ser.). 24p. (J). (gr. 4-7). pap. 4.99 *(978-0-7945-1409-9(X)*, Usborne) EDC Publishing.

Trotter, Stuart, jt. illus. see Gray, Miranda.

Trotter, Stuart, jt. illus. see Rey, Luis.

Troughton, Guy. Whose Egg? Evans, Lynette. 2013. (ENG.). 36p. (J). (gr. -1). 16.99 *(978-1-60887-203-9(3))* Insight Editions.

—Whose Nest? Evans, Lynette. 2013. (ENG.). 40p. (J). (gr. -1). 16.99 *(978-1-60887-204-6(1)*, Earth Aware Editions) Mandala Publishing.

Troughton, Joanna. The Tiger Child: A Folk Tale from India. Troughton, Joanna. (ENG.). 32p. (J). pap. 11.95 *(978-0-14-038238-9(0))* Penguin Bks., Ltd. GBR. Dist: Trafalgar Square Publishing.

Trounce, Charlotte. Australia: A 3D Expanding Country Guide. Candlewick Press Staff. 2014. (Panorama Pops Ser.). (ENG.). 30p. (J). (gr. k-4). 8.99 *(978-0-7636-7505-9(9))* Candlewick Pr.

—Boston: Panorama Pops. Candlewick Press Staff. 2016. (Panorama Pops Ser.). (ENG.). 30p. (J). (gr. k-4). 8.99 *(978-0-7636-7863-0(5))* Candlewick Pr.

—Scratch & Learn World Atlas. Broom, Jenny. 2018. (Scratch & Learn Ser.). (ENG.). 16p. (J). (gr. -1-1). 17.99 *(978-1-78603-276-8(7)*, Wide Eyed Editions) Quarto Publishing Group UK GBR. Dist: Hachette Bk. Group.

Trounce, Charlotte. San Francisco: A 3D Keepsake Cityscape. Trounce, Charlotte. 2013. (Panorama Pops Ser.). (ENG.). 30p. (J). (gr. k-4). 8.99 *(978-0-7636-6471-8(5))* Candlewick Pr.

Trousdale, Taryn. My Name Is Mae. Pelz, Ramona. 2003. (J). per. 9.95 *(978-1-58597-190-9(1))* Leathers Publishing.

Trout Fishing in America Staff & Jorisch, Stéphane. Chicken Joe Forgets Something Important. 2011. (ENG.). 48p. (J). (gr. k-2). 16.95 *(978-2-923163-74-1(5))* La Montagne Secrete CAN. Dist: Independent Pubs. Group.

Trover, Zachary. Bulldozers, 1 vol. Tourville, Amanda Doering. 2009. (Mighty Machines Ser.). (ENG.). 32p. (J). (gr. k-4). 28.50 *(978-1-60270-621-7(2)*, 11428, Looking Glass Library) Magic Wagon.

—La Carta de Paula, 1 vol. Jones, Christianne C. Ruíz, Carlos, tr. 2006. (Read-It! Readers en Español: Story Collection).Tr. of Paula's Letter. (SPA.). 24p. (J). (gr. -1-3). 21.32 *(978-1-4048-1687-9(9)*, Picture Window Bks.) Capstone.

—¡Córrele, Córrele Ciempiés! Cuenta de Diez en Diez. Dahl, Michael. 2010. (Apréndete Tus Números/Know Your Numbers Ser.).Tr. of Speed, Speed Centipede! - Counting by Tens. (ENG.). 24p. (J). (gr. -1-2). lib. bdg. 27.32 *(978-1-4048-6299-9(4)*, Picture Window Bks.) Capstone.

—Cranes, 1 vol. Tourville, Amanda Doering. 2009. (Mighty Machines Ser.). (ENG.). 32p. (J). (gr. k-4). 28.50 *(978-1-60270-622-4(0)*, 11430, Looking Glass Library) Magic Wagon.

—Un Cuarto para Dos, 1 vol. Jones, Christianne C. Ruíz, Carlos, tr. 2006. (Read-It! Readers en Español: Story Collection).Tr. of Room to Share. (SPA.). 24p. (J). (gr. -1-3). 21.32 *(978-1-4048-1694-7(1)*, Picture Window Bks.) Capstone.

—Fire Trucks, 1 vol. Tourville, Amanda Doering. 2009. (Mighty Machines Ser.). (ENG.). 32p. (J). (gr. k-4). 28.50 *(978-1-60270-624-8(7)*, 11434, Looking Glass Library) Magic Wagon.

—Garbage Trucks, 1 vol. Tourville, Amanda Doering. 2009. (Mighty Machines Ser.). (ENG.). 32p. (J). (gr. k-4). 28.50 *(978-1-60270-625-5(5)*, 11436, Looking Glass Library) Magic Wagon.

—Guatemala ABCs: A Book about the People & Places of Guatemala, 1 vol. Aboff, Marcie. 2006. (Country ABCs Ser.). (ENG.). 32p. (J). (gr. k-5). 28.65 *(978-1-4048-1570-4(8)*, Picture Window Bks.) Capstone.

—Out & about at City Hall. Attebury, Nancy Garhan. 2005. (Field Trips Ser.). (ENG.). 24p. (J). (gr. -1-3). lib. bdg. 27.99 *(978-1-4048-1146-1(X)*, Picture Window Bks.) Capstone.

—The Top-Secret Adventure of John Darragh, Revolutionary War Spy. Roop, Peter & Roop, Connie. 2010. (History's Kid Heroes Ser.). (ENG.). 32p. (gr. 3-5). (J). pap. 8.99 *(978-0-7613-6193-0(6)*, 9780761361930, Graphic Universe™); lib. bdg. 26.60 *(978-0-7613-6174-9(X))* Lerner Publishing Group.

—Tractors, 1 vol. Tourville, Amanda Doering. 2009. (Mighty Machines Ser.). (ENG.). 32p. (J). (gr. k-4). 28.50 *(978-1-60270-626-2(3)*, 11438, Looking Glass Library) Magic Wagon.

Trover, Zachary, jt. illus. see Moore, Harry.

Trover, Zachary, jt. illus. see Random House Staff.

Troy, Andy, jt. illus. see Lim, Ronald.

Troy, Michael. The Quest for the Tellings. Morris, Elizabeth. 2012. 52p. (-18). pap. *(978-1-78222-055-8(0))* Paragon Publishing, Rothersthorpe.

Troy, Tony. Deas & Other Imaginings: Ten Spiritual Folktales for Children. Tarico, Valerie. 2011. (ENG.). 132p. (J). 25.95 *(978-0-9773929-4-0(5))* Oracle Institute Pr., LLC, The.

Troyer, Joy. La Semilla de Todo. Martignacco, Carole. 2018. (SPA.). 50p. (J). 17.99 *(978-0-9817244-5-4(0))* Dyeing Arts.

Trudeau, Scott. A Treasure to Share: Adventures in Social Skills. Trudeau, Scott. Holzbauer, David. 2003. 68p. (J). *(978-0-9743805-0-6(4))* Intellipop, LLC.

Trudell, Devin. 3 Stories. Trudell, Devin, . 2007. (YA). 10.00 *(978-0-9794004-0-7(6))* Art Night Bks.

Trueheart, Eric & Alexovich, Aaron. Invader ZIM Vol. 1: Deluxe Edition, Vol. 1. Vasquez, Jhonen. 2017. (Invader ZIM Ser.: 1). (ENG.). 328p. (J). 49.99 *(978-1-62010-413-2(X)*, 9781620104132, Lion Forge) Oni Pr., Inc.

Trueman, Matthew. Hippos Are Huge! London, Jonathan. (Read & Wonder Ser.). 32p. (J). (gr. k-3). 2017. 7.99 *(978-0-7636-7952-1(6))*; 2015. 16.99 *(978-0-7636-6592-0(4))* Candlewick Pr.

—If You Take Away the Otter. Buhrman-Deever, Susannah. 2020. 32p. (J). (gr. k-3). 16.99 *(978-0-7636-8934-6(3))* Candlewick Pr.

—In the Past. Elliott, David. 2018. 48p. (J). (gr. -1-2). 17.99 *(978-0-7636-6073-4(6))* Candlewick Pr.

—One Beetle Too Many. Lasky, Kathryn. 2014. (Candlewick Biographies Ser.). (ENG.). (J). (gr. 2-5). lib. bdg. 15.60 *(978-1-62765-401-2(1))* Perfection Learning Corp.

—One Beetle Too Many: The Extraordinary Adventures of Charles Darwin. Lasky, Kathryn. 2014. (Candlewick Biographies Ser.). (ENG.). 48p. (J). (gr. 2-5). 14.99 *(978-0-7636-6842-6(7))* Candlewick Pr.

—Simon & the Bear: A Hanukkah Tale. Kimmel, Eric A. (ENG.). 40p. (J). (gr. -1-3). 2020. 12.99 ***(978-1-368-04175-1(2))***; 2014. 16.99 *(978-1-4231-4355-0(8))* Hyperion Bks. for Children.

Trueman, Matthew & Phelan, Matt. Big George: How a Shy Boy Became President Washington. Rockwell, Anne. 2009. (ENG.). 48p. (J). (gr. 1-4). 17.99 *(978-0-15-216583-3(5)*, 1063324) Houghton Mifflin Harcourt Publishing Co.

Truemner-Caron, Lili. The Wildflower Bee & Bee. Goguen, Martha. 2020. (Dream, Believe, Achieve Ser.: Vol. 6). (ENG.). 36p. (J). pap. ***(978-1-927755-81-5(6))*** Agio Publishing Hse.

Truesdell, Sue. Chicken Said, "Cluck!" Grant, Judyann. 2008. (My First I Can Read Bks.). 32p. (J). (gr. -1-3). lib. bdg. 16.89 *(978-0-06-028724-5(1))* HarperCollins Pubs.

—Chicken Said, Cluck! Grant, Judyann Ackerman. 2008. (My First I Can Read Ser.). (ENG.). 32p. (J). (gr. -1-3). 16.99 *(978-0-06-028723-8(3))* HarperCollins Pubs.

—Chicken Said, Cluck! Grant, Judyann Ackerman. 2010. (My First I Can Read Ser.). (ENG.). 32p. (J). (gr. -1-3). pap. 4.99 *(978-0-06-444276-3(4))* HarperCollins Pubs.

—The Golly Sisters Go West. Byars, Betsy. 2003. (I Can Read Level 3 Ser.). (ENG.). 64p. (J). (gr. k-3). pap. 4.99 *(978-0-06-444132-2(6)*, HarperCollins) HarperCollins Pubs. Ltd. GBR. Dist: HarperCollins Pubs.

—Hey World, Here I Am! Little, Jean. 2015. 96p. pap. 6.00 *(978-1-61003-607-8(7))* Center for the Collaborative Classroom.

—How to Talk to Your Dog. George, Jean Craighead. 2003. (ENG.). 40p. (J). (gr. 1-4). pap. 7.99 *(978-0-06-000623-5(4))* HarperCollins Pubs.

—I Love Dogs. Stainton, Sue. 2010. (J). lib. bdg. 15.89 *(978-0-06-117058-4(5))* HarperCollins Pubs.

—A Moose That Says Moo. Hamburg, Jennifer. 2013. (ENG.). 32p. (J). (gr. -1 — 1). 16.99 *(978-0-374-35058-1(2)*, 900069451, Farrar, Straus & Giroux (BYR)) Farrar, Straus & Giroux.

Truffle. If It's for My Daughter, I'd Even Defeat a Demon Lord: Volume 1. CHIROLU. Warner, Matthew, tr. 2019. (If It's for My Daughter, I'd Even Defeat a Demon Lord (light Novel) Ser.). 188p. pap. 14.99 *(978-1-7183-5300-8(6))* J-Novel Club.

Trujillo, Robert. A Bean & Cheese Taco Birthday / un Cumpleaños con Tacos de Frijoles con Queso. Bertrand, Diane Gonzales & Ventura, Gabriela Baeza. 2015. (SPA & ENG.). 32p. (J). (gr. k-3). 17.95 *(978-1-55885-812-1(1))* Arte Publico Pr.

Trukhan, Ekaterina. ABCs of Kindness. Berger, Samantha. 2020. (Highlights Books of Kindness Ser.). (ENG.). 26p. (J). (-k). 12.99 *(978-1-68437-651-3(3)*, Highlights) Boyds Mills Pr.

—Apples for Little Fox. 2017. (ENG.). 32p. (J). (gr. -1-2). 17.99 *(978-0-399-55562-6(5))*; lib. bdg. 20.99 *(978-0-399-55563-3(3))* Random Hse. Children's Bks. (Random Hse. Bks. for Young Readers).

—Five Little Ducks. 2012. (J). *(978-1-58865-854-8(6))* Kidsbooks, LLC.

—Indestructibles: Baby, Find the Shapes! 2019. (Indestructibles Ser.). (ENG.). 12p. (J). pap. 5.95 *(978-1-5235-0624-8(5)*, 100624) Workman Publishing Co., Inc.

—Indestructibles: Baby, Let's Count! 2019. (Indestructibles Ser.). (ENG.). 12p. (J). (gr. k-k). pap. 5.95 *(978-1-5235-0622-4(9)*, 100622) Workman Publishing Co., Inc.

—Indestructibles: Baby, See the Colors! 2019. (Indestructibles Ser.). (ENG.). 12p. (J). pap. 5.95 *(978-1-5235-0623-1(7)*, 100623) Workman Publishing Co., Inc.

—Indestructibles: Hanukkah Baby. 2019. (Indestructibles Ser.). (ENG.). 12p. (J). pap. 5.95 *(978-1-5235-0804-4(3)*, 100804) Workman Publishing Co., Inc.

—Indestructibles: Let's Be Kind. 2020. (Indestructibles Ser.). (ENG.). 12p. (J). pap. 5.95 *(978-1-5235-0987-4(2)*, 100987) Workman Publishing Co., Inc.

—Indestructibles: Let's Go Outside! 2020. (Indestructibles Ser.). (ENG.). 12p. (J). (— 1). pap. 5.95 *(978-1-5235-0986-7(4)*, 100986) Workman Publishing Co., Inc.

—Kindness Counts 123. R.A. Strong, R. A. 2020. (Highlights Books of Kindness Ser.). (ENG.). 26p. (J). (-k). 12.99 *(978-1-68437-652-0(1)*, Highlights) Boyds Mills Pr.

—Little Fox & the Missing Moon. 2019. (ENG.). 32p. (J). (gr. -1-2). 17.99 *(978-0-399-55565-7(X))*; lib. bdg. 20.99 *(978-0-399-55566-4(8))* Random Hse. Children's Bks. (Random Hse. Bks. for Young Readers).

—10, 9, 8, Owl's up Late! Deutsch, Georgiana. 2018. (ENG.). 26p. (J). (gr. -1-k). 9.99 *(978-1-68412-184-7(1)*, Silver Dolphin Bks.) Printers Row Publishing Group.

Truman, Lucy. Braving the Deep. Teagan, Erin. 2018. (American Girl: Girl of the Year 2018 Ser.: 2). (SPA.). 192p. (J). (gr. 3-7). pap. 7.99 *(978-1-338-33125-7(6)*, Scholastic en Espanol) Scholastic, Inc.

—Luciana. Teagan, Erin. (J). 2018. 164p. *(978-1-5490-0282-3(1))*; 2017. (American Girl: Girl of the Year 2018 Ser.: 1). (SPA.). 192p. (gr. 3-7). pap. 7.99 *(978-1-338-26488-3(5))* Scholastic, Inc.

—Luciana: Braving the Deep. Teagan, Erin. 2017. (Girl of the Year Ser.: 1). (ENG.). 176p. (J). (gr. 3-7). Bk. 1. pap. 7.99 *(978-1-338-18648-2(5))*; Bk. 2. pap. 7.99 *(978-1-338-18650-5(7))* Scholastic, Inc.

—Unicorn Academy #1: Sophia & Rainbow. Sykes, Julie. 2019. (Unicorn Academy Ser.: 1). (ENG.). 128p. (J). (gr. 1-4). 5.99 *(978-1-9848-5082-9(2))*; lib. bdg. 12.99 *(978-1-9848-5083-6(0))* Random Hse. Children's Bks. (Random Hse. Bks. for Young Readers).

—Unicorn Academy #2: Scarlett & Blaze. Sykes, Julie. 2019. (Unicorn Academy Ser.: 2). (ENG.). 128p. (J). (gr. 1-4). 5.99 *(978-1-9848-5085-0(7))*; lib. bdg. 12.99 *(978-1-9848-5086-7(5))* Random Hse. Children's Bks. (Random Hse. Bks. for Young Readers).

—Unicorn Academy #3: Ava & Star. Sykes, Julie. 2019. (Unicorn Academy Ser.: 3). (ENG.). 128p. (J). (gr. 1-4). pap. 5.99 *(978-1-9848-5088-1(1)*, Random Hse. Bks. for Young Readers) Random Hse. Children's Bks.

—Unicorn Academy #4: Isabel & Cloud. Sykes, Julie. 2019. (Unicorn Academy Ser.: 4). (ENG.). 128p. (J). (gr. 1-4). pap. 5.99 *(978-1-9848-5091-1(1)*, Random Hse. Bks. for Young Readers) Random Hse. Children's Bks.

—Unicorn Academy #5: Layla & Dancer. Sykes, Julie. 2019. (Unicorn Academy Ser.: 5). (ENG.). 128p. (J). (gr. 1-4). 12.99 *(978-1-9848-5168-0(3)*, Random Hse. Bks. for Young Readers) Random Hse. Children's Bks.

—Unicorn Academy #6: Olivia & Snowflake. Sykes, Julie. 2019. (Unicorn Academy Ser.: 6). (ENG.). 128p. (J). (gr. 1-4). 12.99 *(978-1-9848-5171-0(3)*, Random Hse. Bks. for Young Readers) Random Hse. Children's Bks.

Truman, Lucy. Unicorn Academy #7: Rosa & Crystal. Sykes, Julie. 2020. (Unicorn Academy Ser.: 7). (ENG.). 128p. (J). (gr. 1-4). 5.99 ***(978-0-593-17945-1(5))***; lib. bdg. 12.99 ***(978-0-593-17946-8(3))*** Random Hse. Children's Bks. (Random Hse. Bks. for Young Readers).

—Unicorn Academy #8: Ariana & Whisper. Sykes, Julie. 2020. (Unicorn Academy Ser.: 8). (ENG.). 128p. (J). (gr. 1-4). 5.99 ***(978-0-593-17948-2(X))***; lib. bdg. 12.99 ***(978-0-593-17949-9(8))*** Random Hse. Children's Bks. (Random Hse. Bks. for Young Readers).

—Unicorn Academy: Magic of Friendship Boxed Set (Books 5-8), 4 vols. Sykes, Julie. 2020. (Unicorn Academy Ser.). (ENG.). 512p. (J). (gr. 1-4). 23.96 ***(978-0-593-37589-1(0)***, Random Hse. Bks. for Young Readers) Random Hse. Children's Bks.

—Unicorn Academy: Rainbow of Adventure Boxed Set (Books 1-4), 4 vols. Sykes, Julie. 2020. (Unicorn Academy Ser.). (ENG.). 512p. (J). (gr. 1-4). 23.96 ***(978-0-593-30151-7(X)***, Random Hse. Bks. for Young Readers) Random Hse. Children's Bks.

Truman, Timothy, et al. Airboy, Vol. 1. Dixon, Chuck. 2014. (Airboy Ser.: 1). 308p. pap. 29.99 *(978-1-61377-900-2(3)*, 9781613779002) Idea & Design Works, LLC.

Trumble, David. Enjella Uprooted: A Tooth Fairy Gets a New Job. Collen, Jane F. 2012. (ENG.). 260p. (J). pap. 14.49 *(978-0-9855732-0-1(1))* Streamline Brands.

Trunfio, Alessia. Ann Fights for Freedom: An Underground Railroad Survival Story. Smith, Nikki Shannon. 2019. (Girls Survive Ser.). (ENG.). 112p. (J). (gr. 3-7). lib. bdg. 25.99 *(978-1-4965-7853-2(8)*, 139371, Stone Arch Bks.) Capstone.

—Charlotte Spies for Justice: A Civil War Survival Story. Smith, Nikki Shannon. 2019. (Girls Survive Ser.). (ENG.). 112p. (J). (gr. 3-7). pap. 7.95 *(978-1-4965-8446-5(5)*, 140971); E-Book 4.95 *(978-1-4965-8389-5(2))* Capstone. (Stone Arch Bks.).

—Copyboy. Vawter, Vince. 2018. (ENG.). 240p. (YA). (gr. 6-9). 15.95 *(978-1-63079-105-6(9)*, 138669, Capstone Editions) Capstone.

—The Curse of Deadwood Hill: Book 2. Taddonio, Lea. 2017. (Lucky 8 Ser.). (ENG.). 48p. (J). (gr. 3-7). lib. bdg. 29.93 *(978-1-5321-3054-0(6)*, 27061, Spellbound) Magic Wagon.

—Deadwood Hill Strikes Back: Book 3. Taddonio, Lea. 2017. (Lucky 8 Ser.). (ENG.). 48p. (J). (gr. 3-7). lib. bdg. 29.93 *(978-1-5321-3055-7(4)*, 27062, Spellbound) Magic Wagon.

—The Deadwood Hill Trap: Book 4. Taddonio, Lea. 2017. (Lucky 8 Ser.). (ENG.). 48p. (J). (gr. 3-7). lib. bdg. 29.93 *(978-1-5321-3056-4(2)*, 27063, Spellbound) Magic Wagon.

—Emmi in the City: A Great Chicago Fire Survival Story. Alikhan, Salima. 2019. (Girls Survive Ser.). (ENG.). 112p. (J). (gr. 3-7). lib. bdg. 25.99 *(978-1-4965-7851-8(1)*, 139369, Stone Arch Bks.) Capstone.

—First Heroes of Flight. Feldman, Thea. Cottage Door Press, ed. 2019. (Smithsonian Kids Ser.). (ENG.). 12p. (J). (gr. -1-1). bds. 12.99 *(978-1-68052-604-2(9)*, 1004150) Cottage Door Pr.

—Lily & the Great Quake: A San Francisco Earthquake Survival Story. Bybee, Veeda. 2020. (Girls Survive Ser.). (ENG.). 112p. (J). (gr. 3-7). pap. 7.95 *(978-1-4965-9217-0(4)*, 142249); lib. bdg. 25.99 *(978-1-4965-8716-9(2)*, 141521) Capstone. (Stone Arch Bks.).

—Lucy Fights the Flames: A Triangle Shirtwaist Factory Survival Story. Gilbert, Julie Kathleen. 2019. (Girls Survive Ser.). (ENG.). 112p. (J). (gr. 3-7). pap. 7.95 *(978-1-4965-8448-9(1)*, 140973); lib. bdg. 25.99 *(978-1-4965-8386-4(8)*, 140682) Capstone. (Stone Arch Bks.).

—Sarah Journeys West: An Oregon Trail Survival Story. Smith, Nikki Shannon. 2020. (Girls Survive Ser.). (ENG.). 112p. (J). (gr. 3-7). pap. 7.95 *(978-1-4965-9218-7(2)*, 142250); lib. bdg. 25.99 *(978-1-4965-8718-3(9)*, 141522) Capstone. (Stone Arch Bks.).

—That Grand Easter Day! Lord, Jill Roman. 2018. (ENG.). 32p. (J). (gr. -1-2). 16.99 *(978-0-8249-5680-6(X))* Worthy Publishing.

—Welcome to Deadwood Hill: Book 1. Taddonio, Lea. 2017. (Lucky 8 Ser.). (ENG.). 48p. (J). (gr. 3-7). lib. bdg. 29.93 *(978-1-5321-3053-3(8)*, 27060, Spellbound) Magic Wagon.

Trunfio, Alessia & Forsyth, Matt. Alice on the Island: A Pearl Harbor Survival Story. Shimose Poe, Mayumi. 2019. (Girls Survive Ser.). (ENG.). 112p. (J). (gr. 3-7). pap. 7.95 *(978-1-4965-8012-2(5)*, 139979, Stone Arch Bks.) Capstone.

—Noelle at Sea: A Titanic Survival Story. Smith, Nikki Shannon. 2019. (Girls Survive Ser.). (ENG.). 112p. (J). (gr. 3-7). lib. bdg. 25.99 *(978-1-4965-7850-1(3)*, 139368, Stone Arch Bks.) Capstone.

Trunfio, Alessia, jt. illus. see Forsyth, Matt.

Truong, Marcelino. Descubrir la Biblia. Marchon, Benoit & Rosa, Jean-Pierre. (SPA.). 50p. (J). (gr. 3-5). 7.96 *(978-84-263-3188-5(2))* Vives, Luis Editorial (Edelvives) ESP. Dist: Lectorum Pubns., Inc.

Truong, Tom. Bear's Truck Is Stuck! Amazing Changing Pictures! Hegarty, Patricia. 2015. (ENG.). 14p. (J). (gr. -1-2). 12.99 *(978-1-68010-001-3(7))* Tiger Tales.

—Who's There? Beware! Amazing Changing Pictures! Hegarty, Patricia. 2015. (ENG.). 14p. (J). (gr. -1-2). 12.99 *(978-1-68010-000-6(9))* Tiger Tales.

Tryon, Leslie. Dear Peter Rabbit. Flor Ada, Alma. 2006. (Stories to Go! Ser.). (J). (gr. k-3). 12.65 *(978-0-7569-7322-3(8))* Perfection Learning Corp.

—Extra! Extra! Flor ADA, Alma. 2007. (SPA.). 32p. (J). pap. 13.95 *(978-1-63113-961-1(4))* Santillana USA Publishing Co., Inc.

—Extra! Extra! Fairy-Tale News from Hidden Forest. Flor Ada, Alma. 2007. (ENG.). 32p. (J). (gr. k-3). 17.99 *(978-0-689-82582-8(X)*, Atheneum Bks. for Young Readers) Simon & Schuster Children's Publishing.

—Pigs Can Fly! The Adventures of Harriet Pig & Friends. Chocolate, Debbi. 2004. 64p. (J). 15.95 *(978-0-8126-2706-0(7))* Cricket Bks.

—With Love, Little Red Hen. Flor Ada, Alma. 2004. (ENG.). 40p. (J). (gr. k-3). 7.99 *(978-0-689-87061-3(2)*, Atheneum Bks. for Young Readers) Simon & Schuster Children's Publishing.

Tsai, Dora. Karma: Reaping What We Sow. Young, Lena. 2005. 26p. (J). pap. *(978-1-933554-00-6(2))* Primordia.

—One World Healing. Young, Lena. 2005. 26p. (J). pap. *(978-1-933554-01-3(0))* Primordia.

Tsairis, Jeannie Brett, jt. illus. see Monroe, Michael Glenn.

Tsarfati, Einat. An after Bedtime Story. Smith, Shoham. 2016. (ENG.). 48p. (J). (gr. k-2). 16.95 *(978-1-4197-1873-1(8)*, Abrams Bks. for Young Readers) Abrams, Inc.

Tsarfati, Einat. Sandcastle. Tsarfati, Einat. 2020. (ENG.). 48p. (J). (gr. -1-1). 17.99 *(978-1-5362-1143-6(5))* Candlewick Pr.

Tseng, Jean, jt. illus. see Tseng, Mou-Sien.

Tseng, Mou-Sien & Tseng, Jean. Seesaw Girl. Park, Linda Sue. 2009. (ENG.). 96p. (J). (gr. 3-7). pap. 7.99 *(978-0-547-24888-2(1)*, 1100900) Houghton Mifflin Harcourt Publishing Co.

Tsilis, Thanos. The Iliad. Homer. 2013. (Greek Classics Ser.). (ENG.). 64p. pap. 6.95 *(978-1-906230-53-1(6))* Real Reads Ltd. GBR. Dist: Casemate Pubs. & Bk. Distributors, LLC.

—The Odyssey. Homer. 2013. (Greek Classics Ser.). (ENG.). 64p. pap. 6.95 *(978-1-906230-54-8(4))* Real Reads Ltd. GBR. Dist: Casemate Pubs. & Bk. Distributors, LLC.

Tsong, Jing Jing. Before We Met. Melmed, Laura Krauss. 2016. (ENG.). 32p. (J). (gr. -1-3). 17.99 *(978-1-4424-4156-9(9)*, Beach Lane Bks.) Beach Lane Bks.

—A Bucket of Blessings. Sehgal, Kabir & Sehgal, Surishtha. 2014. (ENG.). 32p. (J). (gr. -1-3). 18.99 *(978-1-4424-5870-3(4)*, Beach Lane Bks.) Beach Lane Bks.

—Feathers & Hair, What Animals Wear. Ward, Jennifer. 2017. (ENG.). 48p. (J). (gr. -1-3). 18.99 *(978-1-4814-3081-4(5)*, Beach Lane Bks.) Beach Lane Bks.

—Hiiaka Battles the Wind. Ahulii, Gabrielle. 2018. (ENG.). 16p. (J). bds. 7.95 *(978-1-933067-99-5(3))* Beachhouse Publishing, LLC.

—Maui Slows the Sun. Ahulii, Gabrielle. 2018. (ENG.). 16p. (J). bds. 7.95 *(978-1-933067-98-8(5))* Beachhouse Publishing, LLC.

—Shanghai Sukkah. Hyde, Heidi Smith. 2015. (ENG.). 32p. (J). (gr. k-4). 9.99 *(978-1-4677-3474-5(8)*, 9781467734745, Kar-Ben Publishing) Lerner Publishing Group.

—Trees. Hutchens, Verlie. 2019. (ENG.). 40p. (J). (gr. -1-3). 17.99 *(978-1-4814-4707-2(6)*, Beach Lane Bks.) Beach Lane Bks.

Tsosie, Dennison. Floating Around in the Middle. Alexander, Carmen. 2005. 30p. (J). (gr. -1-5). pap. 14.99 *(978-1-886383-76-0(6))* Blue Forge Pr.

Tsou, Page. Highest Mountain, Smallest Star: A Visual Compendium of Wonders. Baker, Kate. 2018. (ENG.). 80p. (J). (gr. 2-5). 22.00 *(978-1-5362-0405-6(6)*, Big Picture Press) Candlewick Pr.

Tsubomi No Yume. Rose et le Jardinier. Seigneur, Francoise. 2018. (FRE.). 32p. (J). pap. *(978-2-37011-629-1(3))* Editions Hélène Jacob.

Tsuchiya, Fujio. A Christmas Interview: Reporting Live from Bethlehem! Yoshiike, Yoshitaka. 2005. 32p. (J). (gr. -1-3). per. 7.95 *(978-0-8198-1572-9(1))* Pauline Bks. & Media.

Tsuda, Efrain Rodriguez. Murmullos de la Selva. Dubuvoy, Silvia et al. 2004. (Montana Encantada Ser.). (SPA.). 60p. (J). (gr. 3-5). pap. 9.99 *(978-84-241-8660-9(5))* Everest Editora ESP. Dist: Lectorum Pubns., Inc.

Tsuda, Masami. Kare Kano, Vol. 14. Kobayashi, Michelle, tr. from JPN. rev. ed. 2005. 200p. pap. 9.99 *(978-1-59532-588-4(3))* TOKYOPOP, Inc.

Tsuda, Masami. Kare Kano Vols. 1-3: His & Her Circumstances. Tsuda, Masami. rev. ed. 2004. 192p. pap. 9.99 *(978-1-59182-472-5(9))* TOKYOPOP, Inc.

—Kare Kano Vols. 1-3: His & Her Circumstances, 15 vols., Vol. 1. Tsuda, Masami. Niida, Jack, tr. from JPN. 2003. 192p. (gr. 6-13). pap. 9.99 *(978-1-931514-79-8(8))* TOKYOPOP, Inc.

—Kare Kano Vols. 1-3: His & Her Circumstances, 13 vols. Tsuda, Masami. rev. ed. Vol. 5. 2003. 192p. pap. 9.99 *(978-1-59182-180-9(0))*; Vol. 6. 2003. 192p. (YA). pap. 9.99 *(978-1-59182-181-6(9))*; Vol. 13. 2005. 208p. pap. 9.99 *(978-1-59532-587-7(5))* TOKYOPOP, Inc.

Tsuda, Masami. Kare Kano, Vol. 15. Tsuda, Masami, creator. rev. ed. 2005. 200p. pap. 9.99 *(978-1-59532-589-1(1))* TOKYOPOP, Inc.

Tsurumi, Andrea. Not Your Nest! Sterer, Gideon. 2019. (ENG.). 40p. (J). (gr. -1-2). 17.99 *(978-0-7352-2827-6(2)*, Dial Bks) Penguin Young Readers Group.

Tsurumi, Andrea. Sharko & Hippo. Kalan, Elliott. 2020. (ENG.). 40p. (J). (gr. -1-3). 17.99 ***(978-0-06-279109-2(5)***, Balzer & Bray) HarperCollins Pubs.

Tsurusaki, Takahiro. How NOT to Summon a Demon Lord: Volume 1. Murasaki, Yukiya. Denim, Garrison, tr. 2019. (How NOT to Summon a Demon Lord (light Novel) Ser.). 280p. pap. 14.99 *(978-1-7183-5200-1(X))* J-Novel Club.

—How NOT to Summon a Demon Lord: Volume 2. Murasaki, Yukiya. Denim, Garrison, tr. 2019. (How NOT to Summon a Demon Lord (light Novel) Ser.). (ENG.). 278p. pap. 14.99 *(978-1-7183-5201-8(8))* J-Novel Club.

—How NOT to Summon a Demon Lord: Volume 3. Murasaki, Yukiya. Denim, Garrison, tr. 2019. (How NOT to Summon a Demon Lord (light Novel) Ser.). (ENG.). 268p. pap. 14.99 *(978-1-7183-5202-5(6))* J-Novel Club.

—How NOT to Summon a Demon Lord: Volume 4. Murasaki, Yukiya. Denim, Garrison, tr. 2019. (How NOT to Summon a Demon Lord (light Novel) Ser.). 236p. pap. 14.99 *(978-1-7183-5203-2(4))* J-Novel Club.

—How NOT to Summon a Demon Lord: Volume 5. Murasaki, Yukiya. ZackZeal, tr. 2019. (How NOT to Summon a Demon Lord (light Novel) Ser.). (ENG.). 250p. pap. 14.99 *(978-1-7183-5204-9(2))* J-Novel Club.

—How NOT to Summon a Demon Lord: Volume 6. Murasaki, Yukiya. ZackZeal, tr. 2019. (How NOT to Summon a Demon Lord (light Novel) Ser.). 250p. pap. 14.99 *(978-1-7183-5205-6(0))* J-Novel Club.

Tsvetayeva, Elena. Where Birdie Lives: A Lift-The-Flap Book. Clever Publishing. 2019. (Clever Flaps Ser.). (ENG.). 14p. (J). (gr. -1 — 1). bds. 10.99 *(978-1-948418-00-3(2))* Clever Media Group.

Tu-Dean, Lorian. Dress Like a Girl. Toht, Patricia. 2019. (ENG.). 32p. (J). (gr. -1-3). 17.99 *(978-0-06-279892-3(8))* HarperCollins Pubs.

Tu, Lorian. May God Bless You & Keep You, Vol. Raymond Cunningham, Sarah. 2018. (ENG.). 32p. (J). 16.99 *(978-1-5064-4531-1(4)*, Beaming Books) Augsburg Fortress, Pubs.

—Stay Through the Storm, Vol. Rowland, Joanna. 2019. (ENG.). 32p. (J). (gr. -1-3). 16.99 *(978-1-5064-5058-2(X)*, Beaming Books) Augsburg Fortress, Pubs.

Tuason, Scott. Project Seahorse. Turner, Pamela S. 12th ed. 2010. (Scientists in the Field Ser.). (ENG.). 64p. (J). (gr. 5-7). 18.99 *(978-0-547-20713-1(1)*, 1059611) Houghton Mifflin Harcourt Publishing Co.

Tuason, Scott, photos by. The Dolphins of Shark Bay. Turner, Pamela S. 2013. (Scientists in the Field Ser.). (ENG., 80p. (J). (gr. 5-7). 18.99 *(978-0-547-71638-1(9)*, 1481807) Houghton Mifflin Harcourt Publishing Co.

Tuazon, Noel. A Good Day for Ducks. Whittingham, Jane. 2018. (ENG.). 24p. (J). (gr. -1-k). 16.95 *(978-1-77278-061-1(8))* Pajama Pr. CAN. Dist: Ingram Publisher Services.

—Wild One. Whittingham, Jane. 2018. (ENG.). 24p. (J). (gr. -1-k). 15.95 *(978-1-77278-036-9(7))* Pajama Pr. CAN. Dist: Ingram Publisher Services.

Tucci, Al. The Lonely Train. Kivel, Lee. 2005. 36p. (J). per. 14.95 *(978-0-9774999-0-8(1))* Kivel, Lee.

Tuchman, Mark. Blueberry Bonanza, 1 vol. Wohl, Lauren L. 2017. (Raccoon River Kids Adventures Ser.: 1). (ENG.). 72p. (J). (gr. 2-5). 14.95 *(978-1-943978-29-8(8)*, c1eca3e5-ea6f-4165-b02c-1828eb344c94) WunderMill, Inc.

—Extravaganza at the Plaza, 1 vol. Wohl, Lauren L. 2018. (Racoon River Kids Adventures Ser.: 2). (ENG.). 88p. (J). (gr. 2-5). 14.95 *(978-1-943978-31-1(X)*, 25bf8046-421f-460b-9533-46c7daf1fd81, Persnickety Pr.) WunderMill, Inc.

—Giraccula, 1 vol. Watkins, Caroline. 2019. (Bump in the Night Ser.: 1). (ENG.). 32p. (J). 16.95 *(978-1-943978-45-8(X)*, 4cd24c96-cf86-40f3-b2a7-ab98e997cdc1, Persnickety Pr.) WunderMill, Inc.

—Zooapalooza in the Park, 1 vol. Wohl, Lauren L. 2019. (Raccoon River Kids Adventures Ser.: 3). (ENG.). 88p. (J). 14.95 *(978-1-943978-43-4(3)*, 7409b1f6-e568-4b2c-9bd2-64ebea74fc49, Persnickety Pr.) WunderMill, Inc.

Tuck-Bernstein, Cheryl. Chicken Fingers, Mac & Cheese... Why Do You Always Have to Say Please? Rosen, Wendy & End, Jackie. 2005. 32p. (J). 14.99 *(978-0-7666-1986-9(9))* Modern Publishing.

Tuck, Beverly. Little Bianca. Webb, Mack Henry, Jr. 2006. 52p. (J). per. 15.95 *(978-0-9779576-0-6(8))* Pilinut Pr., Inc.

Tucker, Amanda. The Cutest Little Duckie. Valentine, Victoria. 2007. 80p. (J). per. 15.00 *(978-0-9723493-4-5(0)*, Water Forest Pr.) Skyline Pubn.

Tucker, Barclay. Fat Freddy. Holzer, Angela. 2009. 36p. (J). lib. bdg. 8.99 *(978-0-9821563-4-6(0))* Good Sound Publishing.

Tucker, Diane. The Proud Beech: A Long Island Folk Tale. Edelson, Madelyn. 2004. 48p. (J). pap. 14.95 *(978-0-9658920-7-0(7))* Edelson, Madelyn.

Tucker, E. Jake's Junction: Henry's Listening Ears. Hazlett, V. 2006. (ENG.). 28p. per. 11.95 *(978-1-59800-628-5(2))* Outskirts Pr., Inc.

Tucker, Eric. Finnius: The Tale of a Lost Little Elephant. Wundram, Bill. 2003. (J). *(978-1-59152-011-5(8)*, Sweetgrass Bks.) Farcountry Pr.

Tucker, Ezra. Kaymon: The Gorgon Hound. Blade, Adam. 2010. (Beast Quest Ser.: 16). (ENG.). 80p. (J). (gr. 2-5). 4.99 *(978-0-545-20034-9(2)*, Scholastic Paperbacks) Scholastic, Inc.

—Narga: The Sea Monster. Blade, Adam. 2010. (Beast Quest Ser.: 15). (ENG.). 80p. (J). (gr. 2-5). 4.99 *(978-0-545-20033-2(4)*, Scholastic Paperbacks) Scholastic, Inc.

Tucker, Hilary. Steadfast. Pirola, Isabella. 2016. (ENG.). 28p. (J). 19.99 *(978-1-63413-894-9(5))* Salem Author Services.

Tucker, Julie. Chasing the Spirit of Service. Zajac, Kristen. 2013. 24p. 19.95 *(978-1-61633-393-5(6))* Guardian Angel Publishing, Inc.

Tucker, Keith. The Apollo 13 Mission, 1 vol. Lemke, Donald & Lemke, Donald B. 2006. (Disasters in History Ser.). (ENG.). 32p. (J). (gr. 3-9). 31.32 *(978-0-7368-5476-4(2)*, Capstone Pr.) Capstone.

—George Washington Carver: Ingenious Inventor, 1 vol. Olson, Nathan. 2006. (Graphic Biographies Ser.). (ENG.). 32p. (J). (gr. 3-9). 31.32 *(978-0-7368-5484-9(3)*, Capstone Pr.) Capstone.

Tucker, Lewis R. & Mosher, Scott. The Dragon Who Lived Next Door. Gelber, Peter Frost. l.t. ed. 2003. 64p. (J). (gr. -1-6). pap. 12.00 *(978-0-9658920-4-9(2))* Fore Angels Pr.

Tucker, Marianne & Gilbert, Elizabeth T. Watch Me Draw Cinderella's Enchanted World. 2013. (Watch Me Draw Ser.). 24p. (J). (gr. -1-2). 25.65 *(978-1-936309-86-3(6))* Quarto Publishing Group USA.

Tucker, Marianne & Phillipson, Andy. Learn to Draw Plus Disney Pixar Cars. 2012. *(978-1-936309-70-2(X))* Quarto Publishing Group USA.

Tucker, Marianne, jt. illus. see Mosqueda, Olga T.

Tucker, Sian. Magic World of Learning. Young, Jay. 2003. 32p. *(978-1-903174-42-5(2)*, Pavilion Children's Books) Pavilion Bks.

Tucker, Sian. My Book of First Numbers. Tucker, Sian. 2003. (My Book of. . . Ser.). 48p. (YA). *(978-1-85602-482-2(2)*, Pavilion Children's Books) Pavilion Bks.

—My Book of First Words. Tucker, Sian. 2003. (My Book of. . . Ser.). 48p. (YA). *(978-1-85602-439-6(3)*, Pavilion Children's Books) Pavilion Bks.

Tucker, Tracey, et al. In Focus. Walden, Libby. 2016. (ENG.). 28p. (J). (gr. 2-6). 22.99 *(978-1-944530-02-0(9)*, 360 Degrees) Tiger Tales.

Tucker, Tracey. When I'm Big & Grown: When I'm Big & Grown: I Want to Be an Entrepreneur When I Grow Up. Black, Cassandra. 2012. (ENG.). 32p. (J). pap. *(978-0-9822503-7-2(1))* Stone Cottage Bks.

Tudor, Andy. Diggers Stencil Book. Stowell, Louie & Pearcey, Alice. Doherty, Gillian, ed. 2007. (Stencil Bks.). 14p. (J). bds. 12.99 *(978-0-7945-1576-8(2)*, Usborne) EDC Publishing.

—Usborne Tractors & Trucks Stencil Book. Pearcey, Alice. Milbourne, Anna, ed. 2006. 10p. (J). bds. 12.99 *(978-0-7945-1139-5(2)*, Usborne) EDC Publishing.

—Volcanoes. Turnbull, Stephanie. 2006. (Usborne Beginners Ser.). 32p. (J). (gr. 1). lib. bdg. 12.99 *(978-1-58086-949-2(1))*; 4.99 *(978-0-7945-1401-3(4))* EDC Publishing. (Usborne).

—Volcanoes. Turnbull, Stephanie. 2005. 32p. (J). pap. *(978-0-439-84610-3(2))* Scholastic, Inc.

—200 Paper Planes. ed. 2013. (200 Paper Planes Ser.). 402p. (J). pap. 13.99 *(978-0-7945-3371-7(X)*, Usborne) EDC Publishing.

Tudor, Andy & Haggerty, Tim. Planet Earth: Level 2. Pratt, Leonie. 2007. (Beginners Nature Ser.). 32p. (J). 4.99 *(978-0-7945-1707-6(2)*, Usborne) EDC Publishing.

Tudor, Tasha. Inside the Secret Garden: A Treasury of Crafts, Recipes, & Activities. Collins, Carolyn Strom & Eriksson, Christina Wyss. 2004. 130p. (J). (gr. 2-8). reprint ed. 25.00 *(978-0-7567-7630-5(9))* DIANE Publishing Co.

—The Night Before Christmas. Moore, Clement C. 10th anniv. ed. 2009. 32p. pap. 6.99 *(978-0-316-18947-7(2))* Hachette Bk. Group.

—The Secret Garden. Burnett, Frances Hodgson. 2020. (ENG.). 368p. (J). (gr. 3-7). 18.99 *(978-0-06-298195-0(1)*, HarperCollins) HarperCollins Pubs. Ltd. GBR. Dist: HarperCollins Pubs.

—The Secret Garden: Special Edition with Tasha Tudor Art & Bonus Materials. Burnett, Frances Hodgson. 100th anniv. ed. 2010. (Trophy Bk.). (ENG.). 384p. (J). (gr. 4-18). reprint ed. pap. 8.99 *(978-0-06-440188-3(X)*, HarperCollins) HarperCollins Pubs. Ltd. GBR. Dist: HarperCollins Pubs.

—The Secret Garden Book & Charm. Burnett, Frances Hodgson. deluxe ed. 2005. (Charming Classics). 368p. (J). 9.99 *(978-0-06-075771-7(X)*, HarperFestival) HarperCollins Pubs.

Tudor, Tasha. Around the Year. Tudor, Tasha. 2004. (ENG.). 64p. (J). (gr. -1-3). 7.99 *(978-0-689-87350-8(6)*, Aladdin) Simon & Schuster Children's Publishing.

—A Is for Annabelle: A Doll's Alphabet. Tudor, Tasha. 2004. (ENG.). 64p. (J). (gr. -1-3). reprint ed. 7.99 *(978-0-689-86996-9(7)*, Simon & Schuster/Paula Wiseman Bks.) Simon & Schuster/Paula Wiseman Bks.

—A Tale for Easter. Tudor, Tasha. 2014. (Classic Board Bks.). (ENG.). 34p. (J). (gr. -1 — 1). bds. 7.99 *(978-1-4424-8857-1(3)*, Little Simon) Little Simon.

—A Tale for Easter. Tudor, Tasha. 2004. (ENG.). 32p. (J). (gr. -1-3). 7.99 *(978-0-689-86694-4(1)*, Aladdin) Simon & Schuster Children's Publishing.

Tuell, Julia E., photos by. Women & Warriors of the Plains: The Pioneer Photography of Julia E. Tuell. Aadland, Dan & Michaelides, Marina. rev. ed. 182p. (J). (gr. 4). reprint ed. pap. *(978-0-87842-417-7(2)*, 660) Mountain Pr. Publishing Co., Inc.

Tufts, N. Jo. Wrinkly Socks Make Me Giggle. Wake, Shelley. 2005. (ENG.). 16p. (gr. k-2). pap. 7.95 *(978-1-57874-086-4(X)*, Kaeden Bks.) Kaeden Corp.

Tugeau, Jeremy. Always an Olivia: A Remarkable Family History. Herron, Carolivia. 2007. (Jewish Identity Ser.). 32p. (J). (gr. -1-3). 17.95 *(978-0-8225-7049-3(1)*, Kar-Ben Publishing) Lerner Publishing Group.

—The Buddy Files Bk. 4: The Case of the Fire Alarm. Butler, Dori Hillestad. 2011. (Buddy Files Ser.: 4). (ENG.). 144p. (J). (gr. 1-5). pap. 5.99 *(978-0-8075-0935-7(3)*, 807509353) Whitman, Albert & Co.

—Cars, Trucks, & Planes. 2010. (My World Ser.). (ENG.). 24p. (J). (gr. -1-1). pap. 8.15 *(978-1-61533-031-7(3))* Windmill Bks.

—Cars, Trucks & Planes/Carros, Camiones y Aviones. Rosa-Mendoza, Gladys. 2004. (English-Spanish Foundations Ser.). (SPA & ENG.). 20p. (J). (gr. -1). bds. 6.95 *(978-1-931398-14-5(3))* Me+Mi Publishing.

—The Case of the Fire Alarm, 4. Butler, Dori Hillestad. 2011. (Buddy Files Ser.: 4). (ENG.). 128p. (J). (gr. 1-3). 17.44 *(978-0-8075-0913-5(2))* Whitman, Albert & Co.

—The Case of the Library Monster. Butler, Dori Hillestad. ed. 2012. (Buddy Files Ser.: 5). (J). lib. bdg. 16.00 *(978-0-606-23839-7(5))* Turtleback.

—The Case of the Lost Boy, 1 vol., Bk. 1. Butler, Dori Hillestad. 2010. (Buddy Files Ser.: 1). (ENG.). 128p. (J). (gr. 1-5). pap. 5.99 *(978-0-8075-0932-6(9)*, 807509329) Whitman, Albert & Co.

—The Case of the Missing Family, 1 vol., Bk. 3. Butler, Dori Hillestad. 2010. (Buddy Files Ser.: 3). (ENG.). 144p. (J). (gr. 1-5). pap. 5.99 *(978-0-8075-0934-0(5)*, 807509345) Whitman, Albert & Co.

—The Case of the Mixed-Up Mutts Bk. 2, 1 vol., Bk. 2. Butler, Dori Hillestad. 2010. (Buddy Files Ser.: 2). (ENG.). 128p. (J). (gr. 1-5). pap. 5.99 *(978-0-8075-0933-3(7)*, 807509337) Whitman, Albert & Co.

—The Case of the School Ghost, Bk. 6. Butler, Dori Hillestad. 2013. (Buddy Files Ser.: Book 6). (ENG.). 144p. (J). (gr. 1-5). pap. 5.99 *(978-0-8075-0937-1(X)*, 080750937X) Whitman, Albert & Co.

—A Different Kind of Passover. Strauss, Linda Leopold. ed. 2017. (ENG.). 32p. (J). (gr. -1-3). E-Book 27.99 *(978-1-5124-2723-3(3)*, 9781512427233, Kar-Ben Publishing) Lerner Publishing Group.

—I Will Not Be Afraid. Adams, Michelle M. 2008. 32p. (J). (gr. -1-3). 14.99 *(978-0-7586-1335-6(0))* Concordia Publishing Hse.

—I Will Not Be Afraid. Medlock Adams, Michelle. 2017. (ENG.). (J). pap. 7.99 *(978-0-7586-6070-1(7))* Concordia Publishing Hse.

—Lizzie Newton & the San Francisco Earthquake. Krensky, Stephen. 2010. (History Speaks: Picture Books Plus Reader's Theater Ser.). (ENG.). 48p. (gr. 2-4). pap. 9.95 *(978-0-7613-3944-1(2))* Lerner Publishing Group.

—Making Friends with Mother Goose, 1 vol. 2011. (Mother Goose Nursery Rhymes Ser.). (ENG.). 32p. (J). (gr. k-4). 28.50 *(978-1-61641-145-9(7)*, 517, Looking Glass Library) Magic Wagon.

—Weather Fun with Mother Goose, 1 vol. 2011. (Mother Goose Nursery Rhymes Ser.). (ENG.). 32p. (J). (gr. k-4). 28.50 *(978-1-61641-147-3(3)*, 521, Looking Glass Library) Magic Wagon.

—Who Were the Beatles? Edgers, Geoff & Who HQ. 2006. (Who Was? Ser.). 112p. (J). (gr. 3-7). pap. 5.99 *(978-0-448-43906-8(9)*, Penguin Workshop) Penguin Young Readers Group.

—You Are So Wonderful. Lewis, Jacqueline J. 2020. (ENG.). 32p. (J). (gr. -1-2). 16.99 *(978-1-5064-6376-6(2)*, Beaming Books) Augsburg Fortress, Pubs.

Tugeau, Jeremy & Crisp, Dan. The Case of the Library Monster. Butler, Dori Hillestad. 2012. (Buddy Files Ser.: 5). (ENG.). 128p. (J). (gr. 1-5). pap. 5.99 *(978-0-8075-0936-4(1)*, 807509361) Whitman, Albert & Co.

Tukel, Onur. Little Friends, 0 vols. Tukel, Onur. 2012. (ENG.). 64p. (J). (gr. 1-4). 14.99 *(978-0-7614-6260-6(0)*, 9780761462606, Two Lions) Amazon Publishing.

Tulba, Rania M. Serena la Barquita: Un Libro Encantador para ni�os de 3 a 5 A�os. Young, Laura Thomae. 2019. (Puerto Alegre Ser.: Vol. 1). (SPA.). 30p. (J). pap. 9.99 ***(978-1-0866-8861-0(9))*** Independently Published.

Tulik, Alice, et al. Fishing Adventures. Tulik, Alice et al. 2006. (Adventure Story Collection Ser.). 36p. (J). (gr. 2-6). pap. 12.00 *(978-1-58084-248-8(8))* Lower Kuskokwim Schl. District.

Tulip, Jenny. Alphabet & First Words, Ages 6-7. Somerville, Louisa. 2016. 32p. (J). (gr. -1-12). pap. 6.99 *(978-1-86147-680-7(9)*, Armadillo) Anness Publishing GBR. Dist: National Bk. Network.

T

—Baby Jesus. Jeffs, Stephanie. 2004. (My First Find Out about Book Ser.). 24p. (gr. -1-18). pap. 3.95 (978-0-8294-1730-2(3)) Loyola Pr.

—Bywyd Iesu. Jeffs, Stephanie. Wyn, Delyth, tr. from ENG. 2005. (WEL.). 94p. (978-1-85994-496-7(5)) Cyhoeddiadau'r Gair.

—Fun Time Teddy Bear Stickers: Sticker & Colour-In Playbook with over 200 Reusable Stickers. Johnstone, Michael. 2017. (ENG.). 72p. (J). (gr. -1-12). pap. 8.99 (978-1-86147-771-2(6), Armadillo) Anness Publishing GBR. Dist: National Bk. Network.

—My Big Book of Words. Clark, Isobel. 2009. 48p. (J). (gr. 4-7). 9.99 (978-0-7548-1941-7(8)) Anness Publishing GBR. Dist: National Bk. Network.

—My Big Book of Words. Clarke, Isabel. 2014. 40p. (J). (gr. -1-k). 12.99 (978-1-86147-325-7(7), Armadillo) Anness Publishing GBR. Dist: National Bk. Network.

—My First French Word Book. 2004. (ENG & FRE.). 48p. (J). 5.99 (978-1-85854-237-9(5)) Brimax Books Ltd. GBR. Dist: Byeway Bks.

—My First Spanish Words. Vaamonde, Conchita, tr. 2004. (SPA.). 12p. (J). bds. 7.99 (978-1-85854-512-7(9)) Brimax Books Ltd. GBR. Dist: Byeway Bks.

—My First Word Book: Pictures & Words to Start Toddlers Reading & to Help Pre-Schoolers Develop Vocabulary Skills. Wotton, Joy. 2012. (ENG.). 200p. 9.99 (978-1-84322-617-8(0), Armadillo) Anness Publishing GBR. Dist: National Bk. Network.

—People Jesus Met. Jeffs, Stephanie. 2004. (My First Find Out about Book Ser.). 24p. (gr. -1-18). pap. 3.95 (978-0-8294-1731-9(1)) Loyola Pr.

—Phonics, Ages 6-7. Somerville, Louisa. 2016. 32p. (J). (gr. -1-12). pap. 6.99 (978-1-86147-684-5(1), Armadillo) Anness Publishing GBR. Dist: National Bk. Network.

—Sticker & Color-In Playbook: At Home. Clark, Isabel. 2016. (ENG.). 16p. (J). (gr. -1-12). pap. 4.99 (978-1-86147-720-0(1), Armadillo) Anness Publishing GBR. Dist: National Bk. Network.

—Sticker & Color-In Playbook: At the Shops. Clarke, Isabel. 2016. (ENG.). 16p. (J). (gr. -1-12). pap. 4.99 (978-1-86147-732-3(5), Armadillo) Anness Publishing GBR. Dist: National Bk. Network.

—Sticker & Color-In Playbook: Teddy Bear Colours. Johnstone, Michael. 2016. (ENG.). 16p. (J). (gr. -1-12). pap. 4.99 (978-1-86147-749-1(X), Armadillo) Anness Publishing GBR. Dist: National Bk. Network.

—Sticker & Color-In Playbook: Teddy Bear Counting. 2016. (ENG.). 16p. (J). (gr. -1-12). pap. 4.99 (978-1-86147-750-7(3), Armadillo) Anness Publishing GBR. Dist: National Bk. Network.

—Sticker & Color-In Playbook: Teddy Bear Opposites. Johnstone, Michael. 2016. (ENG.). 16p. (J). (gr. -1-12). pap. 4.99 (978-1-86147-721-7(X), Armadillo) Anness Publishing GBR. Dist: National Bk. Network.

—Sticker & Color-In Playbook: Teddy Bear Shapes. Johnstone, Michael. 2016. (ENG.). 16p. (J). (gr. -1-12). pap. 4.99 (978-1-86147-734-7(1), Armadillo) Anness Publishing GBR. Dist: National Bk. Network.

—Sticker & Color-In Playbook: The Teddy Bear Dance. 2016. (ENG.). 16p. (J). (gr. -1-12). pap. 4.99 (978-1-86147-751-4(1), Armadillo) Anness Publishing GBR. Dist: National Bk. Network.

—Sticker & Color-In Playbook: With over 50 Reusable Stickers: Playtime. Clarke, Isabel. 2016. (ENG.). 16p. (J). (gr. -1-12). pap. 4.99 (978-1-86147-733-0(3), Armadillo) Anness Publishing GBR. Dist: National Bk. Network.

—Sticker & Color-In Playbook: With over 50 Reusable Stickers: Teddy Bear Sizes. Clarke, Isabel. 2016. (ENG.). 16p. (J). (gr. -1-12). pap. 4.99 (978-1-86147-736-1(8), Armadillo) Anness Publishing GBR. Dist: National Bk. Network.

—Sticker & Colour- in Playbook: On the Farm. Clark, Isabel. 2016. (ENG.). 16p. (J). (gr. -1-12). pap. 4.99 (978-1-86147-748-4(1)) Anness Publishing, Inc.

—Sticker & Colour-In Playbook: With over 60 Reusable Stickers - Teddy Bear ABC. 2016. (ENG.). 16p. (J). (gr. -1-12). pap. 4.99 (978-1-86147-745-3(7), Armadillo) Anness Publishing GBR. Dist: National Bk. Network.

—Stories Jesus Told. Jeffs, Stephanie. 2004. (My First Find Out about Book Ser.). 24p. (gr. -1-18). pap. 3.95 (978-0-8294-1733-3(8)) Loyola Pr.

—Things Jesus Did. Jeffs, Stephanie. 2004. 24p. (gr. -1-18). pap. 3.95 (978-0-8294-1734-0(6)) Loyola Pr.

—Times Tables, Ages 6-7. Somerville, Louisa. 2016. 32p. pap. 6.99 (978-1-86147-688-3(4), Armadillo) Anness Publishing GBR. Dist: National Bk. Network.

—Who Lives Here? (Slide & Find). 10p. (J). bds. (978-1-57755-714-2(X)) Flying Frog Publishing, Inc.

—Who's Hiding in the Garden? 2008. 10p. (gr. -1-k). bds. 6.99 (978-1-57755-785-2(9)) Gardner Pubns.

—Who's Hiding in the Jungle? A Mystery Touch-and-Feel Flap Book! 2008. 10p. (gr. -1-k). bds. 6.99 (978-1-57755-784-5(0)) Flying Frog Publishing.

Tullet, Hervé. Help! We Need a Title! Tullet, Hervé. 2014. (ENG.). 64p. (J). (gr. -1-3). 18.99 (978-0-7636-7021-4(9)) Candlewick Pr.

Tulloch, Coral. Bouncing Back: An Eastern Barred Bandicoot Story. Cleave, Rohan. 2018. 32p. (J). (gr. 11-4). 18.95 (978-1-4863-0827-9(9)) CSIRO Publishing AUS. Dist: Stylus Publishing, LLC.

—Phasmid: Saving the Lord Howe Island Stick Insect. Cleave, Rohan. 2015. 32p. (J). (gr. 2-2). 19.95 (978-1-4863-0112-6(6)) CSIRO Publishing AUS. Dist: Stylus Publishing, LLC.

—Touch the Moon. Cummings, Phil. 2019. (ENG.). 32p. (J). (gr. 1). 19.99 (978-1-76052-365-7(8), A&U Children's) Allen & Unwin AUS. Dist: Independent Pubs. Group.

Tulloch, Scott. Willy's Dad. Tulloch, Scott. 2007. 32p. (978-1-86950-631-5(6)) HarperCollins Pubs. Australia.

Tuma, Tomás. Space Atlas. Dusek, Jiri & Pisala, Jan. 2014. (ENG.). 34p. (J). (gr. 1-3). 16.95 (978-1-4549-1237-8(5)) Sterling Publishing Co., Inc.

Tumblod, Gabriel. Brandon Begin Business School. Card, Simon & Johnson, DuJuan. 2019. (ENG.). 28p. (J). pap. 12.00 **(978-1-0831-3601-5(1))** Independently Published.

—Brandon Builds His Business. Card, Simon & Johnson, DuJuan. 2019. (ENG.). 32p. (J). pap. 12.00 **(978-1-0770-2953-8(5))** Independently Published.

—Suzanne Seeks Success. Johnson, DuJuan & Card, Simon. 2019. (ENG.). 30p. (J). pap. 12.00 **(978-1-7092-6851-9(4))** Independently Published.

—Tommy Stays Camera Ready. Card, Simon & Johnson, DuJuan. 2019. (ENG.). 32p. (J). pap. 12.00 **(978-1-7044-8344-3(1))** Independently Published.

Tumbold, Gabriel. Tommy's Taking Control. Card, Simon & Johnson, DuJuan. 2018. (You've Got Options Ser.: Vol. 3). (ENG.). 30p. (J). pap. 12.00 **(978-1-7904-7814-9(6))** Independently Published.

Tumminello, Giovanna, jt. illus. see Santitoro, Theresa.

Tummler, Claudia. The Adventures of Sweet Tea & Bela the Umbrella. Jorgensen, Shira. 2018. (ENG.). 34p. (J). pap. 9.95 (978-1-7905-7459-9(5)) Independently Published.

Tumulak, Ken. The Adventure of Friendship. Lim, Adele M. 2018. (ENG.). 42p. (J). pap. (978-1-912145-78-2(2)) Acorn Independent Pr.

Tunell, Ken. Comprehension Crosswords Grade 3, 6 vols. Shiotsu, Vicky. 2003. 32p. (J). 4.99 (978-1-56472-187-7(6)) Edupress, Inc.

—Selfus Esteemus Personalitus Low. Goss, Leon. 2005. (J). pap. (978-1-933156-08-8(2), VisionQuest Kids) GSVQ Publishing.

—Selfus Esteemus Personalitus Low. Goss, Leon, 3rd. ed. 2005. 32p. (J). per. 16.99 (978-1-933156-00-2(7), VisionQuest Kids) GSVQ Publishing.

Tung, Kadhima Ren. Grandma Lives with Us. Currim, Nazli. 2010. 46p. (J). 16.95 (978-0-9814629-5-0(2)) Acacia Publishing, Inc.

Tung, King. The King of Fighters 2003, Vol. 1. 2005. 128p. (YA). pap. 13.95 (978-1-58899-030-3(3)) DrMaster Pubns. Inc.

Tung, Nguyen the. Coloring Book: The Big Animals, Plants, Vehicles & Numbers Coloring Book for Toddlers, Preschoolers, Boys & Girls Aged 2-8. Hula, Hula. 2019. (ENG.). 140p. (J). pap. 8.50 **(978-1-6869-9361-9(7))** Independently Published.

—Libro para Colorear: Libro para Colorear Animales, Plantas, Veh&#65533;culos y N&#65533;meros para ni&#65533;os y ni&#65533;as de 1-4 a&#65533;os, 2-8 a&#65533;os y Preescolar. Hula, Hula. 2019. (SPA.). 140p. (J). pap. 8.50 **(978-1-6929-3287-9(X))** Independently Published.

Tung, Sam. How the Super Scrubs Saved Christmas. Beaulieu, Michael & Slovenski, Peter. 2019. (ENG.). 34p. (J). pap. 9.99 **(978-1-7093-7435-7(7))** Independently Published.

Túnica, Martín. The Picture of Dorian Gray. Morhain, Jorge C. & Túnica, Pablo. 2018. (Classic Fiction Ser.). (ENG.). 80p. (J). (gr. 5-9). lib. bdg. 27.32 (978-1-4965-6409-2(X), 138233, Stone Arch Bks.) Capstone.

Tunnicliffe, C. F. The Seasons & the Fisherman: A Book for Children. Darling, F. Fraser. 2011. (ENG.). 84p. pap. 23.99 (978-0-521-17594-4(1)) Cambridge Univ. Pr.

Tunstel Jr., Robert L. The Gift That Grandma Gave: Including Bloom's Leveled Questions Study Guide. Griffin, Ramona Rorie. 2011. 44p. pap. 24.95 (978-1-4560-1034-8(4)) America Star Bks.

—My Mind Looks Back & Wonders ... Griffin, Ramona Rorie. 2009. (ENG.). 28p. pap. 24.95 (978-1-60813-917-0(4)) America Star Bks.

Tuohy, Hannah. The Adventures of Bubba Jones: Time Traveling Through the Great Smoky Mountains. Alt, Jeff. 2015. (National Park Ser.: 1). (ENG.). 190p. (J). (gr. 3-7). pap. 9.99 (978-0-8253-0786-7(4)) Beaufort Bks., Inc.

—The Adventures of Bubba Jones (#3) Time Traveling Through Acadia National Park. Alt, Jeff. 2018. (National Park Ser.: 3). (ENG.). 200p. (J). (gr. 3-7). pap. 9.99 (978-0-8253-0882-6(8)) Beaufort Bks., Inc.

—The Adventures of Bubba Jones (#4) Alt, Jeff. 2020. (National Park Ser.: 4). (ENG.). 200p. (J). (gr. 4-7). pap. 9.99 (978-0-8253-0927-4(1)) Beaufort Bks., Inc.

Tuohy, Hannah. Oyster's Secret. Dunham, Traci. 2019. (ENG.). 34p. (J). (gr. -1-3). pap. 13.99 **(978-1-61254-388-8(X))** Brown Books Publishing Group.

Tupa, Christopher. The Monks Make Amends. Dorham, Sylvia. 2020. (ENG.). 24p. (J). (gr. -1-2). pap. 14.95 **(978-1-5051-1790-5(9)**, 2906) TAN Bks.

Turati, Valeria, jt. illus. see Tyminski, Lori.

Turchan, Monique. Courage. Roth, Irene. 2012. 24p. pap. 11.95 (978-1-61244-068-2(1)) Halo Publishing International.

—Leah's Voice. Demonia, Lori. 2012. 28p. pap. 12.95 (978-1-61244-089-7(4)) Halo Publishing International.

—Smarty Pig & the Test Taking Terror. Nero, Molly. 2012. 28p. pap. 12.95 (978-1-61244-055-2(X)) Halo Publishing International.

—What Am I Gonna Do? Wamsley, Jody. 2013. 24p. pap. 11.95 (978-1-61244-070-5(3)) Halo Publishing International.

Turchan, Monique. Mydoit. Turchan, Monique. 2013. 24p. pap. 11.95 (978-1-61244-144-3(0)) Halo Publishing International.

Turchyn, Sandie. The Girls' Guide to Dreams. Collier-Thompson, Kristi. 2006. 128p. (YA). (gr. 8-11). reprint ed. pap. 13.00 (978-0-7567-9899-4(X)) DIANE Publishing Co.

Turcios, Omar. David, Fish & Penguins... Turcios, Omar. Brokenbrow, Jon, tr. 2012. (ENG.). 36p. (J). (gr. -1-k). 14.95 (978-84-15241-94-2(1)) Cuento de Luz SL ESP. Dist: Publishers Group West (PGW).

—David, Peces, Pinguinos ... Turcios, Omar. 2012. (SPA.). 36p. (J). (gr. -1-k). 14.95 (978-84-15241-95-9(X)) Cuento de Luz SL ESP. Dist: Publishers Group West (PGW).

Turco, Laura Lo. The Great Pyramid: The Story of the Farmers, the God-King & the Most Astonding Structure Ever Built. Mann, Elizabeth. 2006. (Wonders of the World Book Ser.). (ENG.). 48p. (J). (gr. 4-8). pap. 12.95 (978-1-931414-11-1(4), 80e3405c-fa11-43b2-9c8a-06e85f79e420) Mikaya Pr.

Turconi, Stefano. The Crown of Venice, No. 7. Stevenson, Steve. 2014. (Agatha: Girl of Mystery Ser.: 7). (ENG.). 144p. (J). (gr. 2-5). 5.99 (978-0-448-46225-7(7), Grosset & Dunlap) Penguin Young Readers Group.

—The Curse of the Pharaoh #1, 1. Stevenson, Steve. 2013. (Agatha: Girl of Mystery Ser.: 1). (ENG.). 144p. (J). (gr. 2-4). 18.69 (978-0-448-46217-2(6)) Penguin Young Readers Group.

—Disney Treasure Island, Starring Mickey Mouse (Graphic Novel) Disney & Radice, Teresa. 2018. (ENG.). 104p. (J). (gr. 3-7). pap. 10.99 (978-1-5067-1158-4(8)) Dark Horse Comics.

—The King of Scotland's Sword. Stevenson, Steve. 2013. (Agatha: Girl of Mystery Ser.: 3). (ENG.). 144p. (J). (gr. 2-5). pap. 6.99 (978-0-448-46220-2(6), Grosset & Dunlap) Penguin Young Readers Group.

Turconi, Stefano, et al. Race for the Ultrapods, Vol. 2. Secchi, Richard & Salati, Giorgio. 2010. (Disney's Hero Squad Ser.). (ENG.). 128p. (J). (gr. 4-7). pap. 9.99 (978-1-60886-560-4(6)) Boom! Studios.

Turconi, Stefano. The Treasure of the Bermuda Triangle, No. 6. Stevenson, Steve. 2014. (Agatha: Girl of Mystery Ser.: 6). (ENG.). 144p. (J). (gr. 2-5). 6.99 (978-0-448-46224-0(9), Grosset & Dunlap) Penguin Young Readers Group.

—Violette Around the World, Vol. 1: My Head in the Clouds! Radice, Teresa. 2018. (Violette Around the World Ser.: 1). 48p. (J). (gr. 4-7). 12.99 (978-1-68405-188-5(6)) Idea & Design Works, LLC.

—Violette Around the World, Vol. 2: a New World Symphony!, Vol. 2. Radice, Teresa. 2019. (Violette Around the World Ser.: 2). 48p. (J). (gr. 4-7). 12.99 (978-1-68405-431-2(1)) Idea & Design Works, LLC.

Turcotte, Derek. Colours Made in Heaven, 1 vol. Turcotte, Michael. 2009. 13p. pap. 24.95 (978-1-60836-316-2(3)) America Star Bks.

Turdera, Cristian. Web Design for Kids. Vanden-Heuvel, John C., Sr. 2016. (ENG.). 14p. (J). (gr. -1-3). bds. 8.99 (978-1-4998-0311-2(7)) Little Bee Books Inc.

Turgeon, Stephane. Noah's Ark. 2007. 16p. (J). (gr. -1-3). (978-2-7641-0340-1(9)) Tormont Pubns.

Turk, Caron. Little Boys Bible Storybook for Fathers & Sons. Larsen, Carolyn. rev. ed. 2014. (ENG.). 288p. (J). 14.99 (978-0-8010-1548-9(0)) Baker Bks.

—Little Girls Bible Storybook for Fathers & Daughters. Larsen, Carolyn. rev. ed. 2014. (ENG.). 288p. (J). 14.99 (978-0-8010-1549-6(9)) Baker Bks.

—My 123 Bible Storybook. Larsen, Carolyn. 2008. (My Bible Storybooks Ser.). 30p. (J). (gr. -1-3). bds. (978-1-86920-925-4(7)) Christian Art Pubs.

—My ABC Bible Storybook. Larsen, Carolyn. 2008. (My Bible Storybooks Ser.). 30p. (J). (gr. -1-3). bds. (978-1-86920-926-1(5)) Christian Art Pubs.

—Prayers for Little Boys. Larsen, Carolyn. 2008. (Prayers For... Ser.). 131p. (J). (gr. -1-3). (978-1-86920-527-0(8)) Christian Art Pubs.

—Prayers for Little Girls. Larsen, Carolyn. 2008. (Prayers For... Ser.). 131p. (J). (gr. -1-3). (978-1-86920-526-3(X)) Christian Art Pubs.

Turk, Caron, jt. illus. see Elwell, Ellen Banks.

Turk, Cheri. Little Beth of the Forest. Turk, Cheri. 2015. (ENG.). 40p. (J). (gr. k-5). pap. 14.50 (978-0-9860024-8-9(8)) Specialty Greetings.

—The Stone Between Kings. Turk, Cheri. 2012. 36p. pap. 12.99 (978-0-9860024-0-3(2)) Specialty Greetings.

Turk, Evan. Be the Change: A Grandfather Gandhi Story. Gandhi, Arun & Hegedus, Bethany. 2016. (ENG.). 48p. (J). (gr. -1-3). 18.99 (978-1-4814-4265-7(1)) Simon & Schuster Children's Publishing.

—Grandfather Gandhi. Gandhi, Arun & Hegedus, Bethany. 2014. (ENG.). 48p. (J). (gr. -1-3). 18.99 (978-1-4424-2365-7(X)) Simon & Schuster Children's Publishing.

—Muddy: The Story of Blues Legend Muddy Waters. Mahin, Michael. 2017. (ENG.). 48p. (J). (gr. -1-3). 17.99 (978-1-4814-4349-4(6)) Simon & Schuster Children's Publishing.

Turk, Evan. Heartbeat. Turk, Evan. 2018. (ENG.). 56p. (J). (gr. -1-3). 17.99 (978-1-4814-3520-8(5), Atheneum Bks. for Young Readers) Simon & Schuster Children's Publishing.

—The Storyteller. Turk, Evan. 2016. (ENG.). 48p. (J). (gr. -1-3). 18.99 (978-1-4814-3518-5(3)) Simon & Schuster Children's Publishing.

—You Are Home: An Ode to the National Parks. Turk, Evan. 2019. (ENG.). 56p. (J). (gr. -1-3). 18.99 (978-1-5344-3282-6(5), Atheneum Bks. for Young Readers) Simon & Schuster Children's Publishing.

Turk, Hanne. The Secret House of Papa Mouse. Landa, Norbert. 2004. (Picture Books/Quality Time Ser.). 32p. (gr. k-3). lib. bdg. 26.00 (978-0-8368-4106-0(9), Gareth Stevens Learning Library) Stevens, Gareth Publishing LLLP.

Turkle, Brinton. Thy Friend, Obadiah. 2018. (J). pap. (978-1-893103-69-6(2)) Beautiful Feet Bks.

Turkle, Brinton. Obadiah the Bold. Turkle, Brinton, text. 2018. (J). pap. (978-1-893103-73-3(0)) Beautiful Feet Bks.

Turkowski, Einar. Houses Floating Home. 2016. 32p. (J). (gr. -1-3). 16.95 (978-1-59270-183-4(3)) Enchanted Lion Bks., LLC.

Turley, Gerry. A Bear's Year. Duval, Kathy. 2015. 40p. (J). (gr. -1-2). 17.99 (978-0-385-37011-0(3), Schwartz & Wade Bks.) Random Hse. Children's Bks.

—Lois Looks for Bob at Home. Nosy Crow. 2018. (Lois Looks for Bob Ser.). (ENG.). 12p. (J). (— 1). bds. 8.99 (978-1-5362-0254-0(1), Nosy Crow) Candlewick Pr.

—Lois Looks for Bob at the Beach. Nosy Crow. 2019. (Lois Looks for Bob Ser.). (ENG.). 12p. (J). (— 1). bds. 8.99 (978-1-5362-0588-6(5), Nosy Crow) Candlewick Pr.

—Lois Looks for Bob at the Museum. Nosy Crow. 2019. (Lois Looks for Bob Ser.). (ENG.). 12p. (J). (— 1). bds. 8.99 (978-1-5362-0589-3(3), Nosy Crow) Candlewick Pr.

—Lois Looks for Bob at the Park. Nosy Crow. 2018. (Lois Looks for Bob Ser.). (ENG.). 12p. (J). (— 1). bds. 8.99 (978-1-5362-0255-7(X), Nosy Crow) Candlewick Pr.

Turley, Joyce M. It's My Birthday. . . Finally! A Leap Year Story. Winfrey, Michelle Whitaker. 2003. 88p. (J). (gr. 3-7). per. 11.95 (978-0-9727179-0-8(0)) Hobby Hse. Publishing Group.

Turley, Joyce Mihran. The Autumn Calf, Vol. Haukos, Jill. 2016. (ENG.). 32p. (J). (gr. -1-12). 15.95 (978-1-63076-237-7(7)) Taylor Trade Publishing.

—Awesome Ospreys: Fishing Birds of the World, 1 vol. Love, Donna. rev. ed. 2005. (ENG.). 64p. (J). (gr. 3-7). pap. 12.00 (978-0-87842-512-9(8), 341) Mountain Pr. Publishing Co., Inc.

—One Night in the Everglades. Larsen, Laurel. 2012. (Long Term Ecological Research Ser.). (ENG.). 32p. (J). (gr. 3-7). 15.95 (978-0-9817700-4-8(5)) Taylor Trade Publishing.

Turley, Joyce Mihran. Loons: Diving Birds of the North, Vol. 1. Turley, Joyce Mihran, tr. Love, Donna. rev. ed. 64p. (J). (gr. 4). pap. 12.00 (978-0-87842-482-5(2), 340) Mountain Pr. Publishing Co., Inc.

Turman, Adam. J. B. 's Christmas Presents. Turman, Evelyn. I.t. ed. 2004. 28p. (J). 15.95 (978-0-9753042-0-4(8)) Turman, E.

Turnbloom, Lucas. Dragon & Captain. Allabach, P. R. 2015. (ENG.). 32p. (J). (gr. k-2). 17.95 (978-1-936261-33-8(2)) Flashlight Pr.

—Dream Jumper, Bk. 2. Grunberg, Greg. 2017. (Dream Jumper Ser.: 2). (ENG.). 224p. (J). (gr. 4-7). pap. 12.99 (978-0-545-82608-2(X), Graphix) Scholastic, Inc.

Turnbloom, Lucas. Curse of the Harvester. Turnbloom, Lucas. Grunberg, Greg. 2017. (Dream Jumper Ser.: 2). (ENG.). 224p. (J). (gr. 4-7). 24.99 (978-0-545-82607-5(1), Graphix) Scholastic, Inc.

Turnbull, Brian. Death or Victory: Tales of the Clan Maclean. Maclean, Fiona. 2011. 128p. (YA). pap. (978-2-930583-06-8(1)) White & MacLean Publishing BEL. Dist: Gardners Bks. Ltd.

Turnbull, E. G. What Are Little Boys Made Of? Francis, Wendy. 2019. (ENG.). 32p. (J). (978-1-925826-35-7(X)) Connor Court Publishing Pty Ltd.

Turnbull E G. What Are Little Girls Made Of? Francis, Wendy. 2019. (ENG.). 32p. (J). (978-1-925826-34-0(1)) Connor Court Publishing Pty Ltd.

Turnbull, Jesse. Hello Hairy Dawg. Aryal, Aimee. 2004. (J). (gr. -1-3). 19.95 (978-1-932888-04-1(7)) Mascot Bks., Inc.

Turnbull, Susan. The Mystery of the Pheasants. Meierhenry, Mark & Volk, David. 2012. 44p. (J). 14.95 (978-0-9845041-9-0(2)) South Dakota Historical Society Pr.

Turnbull, Victoria. The Sea Tiger. Turnbull, Victoria. 2015. (ENG.). 40p. (J). (gr. -1-2). 16.99 (978-0-7636-7986-6(0), Templar) Candlewick Pr.

Turner, Adam. The LoveBugs, Party Shoes Give Layla the Blues. Grady, Joanne. Rose, Naomi C., ed. 2019. (Lovebugs Ser.: Vol. 2). (ENG.). 34p. (J). 16.95 **(978-0-9990075-3-2(X))** Grady Bunch Bks., LLC.

Turner, Adam. Mystery at the Christmas Market. Diller, Janelle. Travis, Lisa, ed. 2014. 110p. (J). (gr. 1-4). pap. 5.99 (978-1-936376-18-6(0)) WorldTrek Publishing.

—Mystery of the Ballerina Ghost. Diller, Janelle. 2013. 104p. (J). pap. 5.99 (978-1-936376-00-1(8)) WorldTrek Publishing.

—Mystery of the Rusty Key: Australia 2. Diller, Janelle. Travis, Lisa, ed. 2018. (Pack-N-Go Girls Adventures Ser.: Vol. 11). (ENG.). 128p. (J). (gr. 1-3). pap. 5.99 (978-1-936376-58-2(X)) WorldTrek Publishing.

—Mystery of the Troubled Toucan. Travis, Lisa. Diller, Janelle, ed. 2015. (Pack-N-Go Girls Adventures - Brazil 1 Ser.). (ENG.). 128p. (J). (gr. 1-3). pap. 5.99 (978-1-936376-24-7(5)) WorldTrek Publishing.

Turner, Aubrey. Pity & the Princess. Crawford, Deborah Kay. 2013. 40p. pap. 24.95 (978-1-62709-695-9(7)) America Star Bks.

Turner, Cecilia. Davis & Pop Go Hiking. Wood, Cary D. 2014. (ENG.). (gr. -1-4). 30p. 34.95 (978-1-63047-217-7(4)); 32p. pap. 14.95 (978-1-63047-068-5(6)) Morgan James Publishing.

Turner, Cherie. Hope the Hip Hippo. Jay, Gina & Beattie, Julie. 2012. 48p. pap. (978-1-4602-0062-9(4)) FriesenPress.

Turner, Christina. Hello Santa! Turner, Christina. 2007. 16p. (J). (gr. -1). bds. 7.95 (978-0-9790347-0-1(1)) Mackenzie Smiles, LLC.

Turner-Deckert, Dianne. A Pillar of Pepper & Other Bible Rhymes. John Knapp, Ii. 2012. 130p. 29.99 (978-0-912290-34-8(X)) Ephemeron Pr.

Turner, Diane, jt. illus. see Tigue, Terry.

Turner, Dona. De Que Esta Hecho el Arco Iris? Schwartz, Betty Ann. 2005. (SPA & ENG.). 14p. (J). (gr. -1). 8.95 (978-1-58117-027-6(0), Intervisual/Piggy Toes) Bendon, Inc.

—What Makes a Rainbow? Schwartz, Betty Ann. 2006. (Magic Ribbon Books). (ENG.). 14p. (J). 4.95 (978-1-58117-220-1(6), Intervisual/Piggy Toes) Bendon, Inc.

—What Makes a Rainbow: (British Version) Schwartz, Betty Ann. 2004. 14p. (J). (978-1-58117-367-3(9), Intervisual/Piggy Toes) Bendon, Inc.

—What Makes Music? A Magic Ribbon Book. Schwartz, Betty Ann. 2005. (Stories to Share Ser.). 16p. (J). (gr. -1-3). act. bk. ed. 11.95 (978-1-58117-139-6(0), Intervisual/Piggy Toes) Bendon, Inc.

Turner, Dona. Ella Minnow Pea. Turner, Dona. 2008. (ENG.). 32p. (J). (978-1-59692-229-7(X)) MacAdam/Cage Publishing, Inc.

Turner, Dona & Brennan, Tim. Ella Minnow Pea. Turner, Dona & Dunn, Mark. gif. ed. 2009. (ENG.). 225p. (978-1-59692-299-0(0)) MacAdam/Cage Publishing, Inc.

Turner, Ginger. Abraham Lincoln: The Civil War President. Tiwari, Sarai. 2004. 48p. (J). pap. 17.95 (978-0-9742502-1-2(X)) Gossamer Bks., LLC.

Turner, Helen. Lucy & the Magic Crystal, 6. Shields, Gillian. 2008. (Mermaid S. O. S. Ser.: No. 6). (ENG.). 92p. (YA). (gr. k-3). 16.19 (978-1-59990-256-2(7), 9781599902562) Bloomsbury Publishing USA.

—Scarlett's New Friend, 5. Shields, Gillian. 2008. (Mermaid S. O. S. Ser.: 5). (ENG.). 91p. (YA). (gr. k-3). 16.19

(978-1-59990-255-5(9), 9781599902555) Bloomsbury Publishing USA.
—Skipper to the Rescue. Moss, Olivia. 2008. (Butterfly Meadow Ser.: 4). (ENG.). 80p. (J). (gr. k-3). 17.44 *(978-0-545-05459-1(1))* Scholastic, Inc.
—Sophie Makes a Splash. 3. Shields, Gillian. 2008. (Mermaid S. O. S. Ser.: 3). (ENG.). 96p. (J). (gr. k-3). pap. 16.19 *(978-1-59990-212-8(5)*, 9781599902128) Bloomsbury Publishing USA.
Turner, Ian. Biometrics: Your Body & the Science of Security. Birmingham, Maria. 2017. (ENG.). 48p. (J). (gr. 6-6). 16.95 *(978-1-77147-193-0(X))* Owlkids Bks. Inc. CAN. Dist: Publishers Group West (PGW).
Turner, Jeffrey. Who Am I? Turner, Jeffrey. 2017. (ENG.). 40p. (J). (gr. -1-3). 15.99 *(978-1-4814-5304-2(1)*, Aladdin) Simon & Schuster Children's Publishing.
Turner, Jennifer. A Jigger of Paint. Van Eyk, Cynthia. 2019. (ENG.). 20p. (J). *(978-1-5255-4258-9(3))*; pap. *(978-1-5255-4259-6(1))* FriesenPress.
—Richard Robert Raymond Roy: Very Small Boy. Van Eyk, Cynthia. 2018. (ENG.). 28p. (J). pap. *(978-1-5255-1294-0(3))* FriesenPress.
Turner, Michael W. Dear Old Granny's Nursery Rymes for the 21st Century. Goodnight, Rosemary. 2009. 64p. (J). 14.99 *(978-0-9816282-7-1(3))* Recipe Pubs.
Turner, Missy. Let's Draw Magical Unicorns: Create Beautiful Unicorns Step by Step! Turner, Missy. 2019. (ENG.). 96p. (J). pap. 9.99 *(978-1-78950-522-1(4)*, e57fd0e5-262f-405f-a9cb-71c62f11f9b2) Arcturus Publishing GBR. Dist: Baker & Taylor Publisher Services (BTPS).
Turner, Nadia. Hello Baby Animals! A First Book of Animals & the Sounds That They Make. Adam, Luisa. 2019. (ENG.). 24p. (J). (— 1). bds. *(978-0-6484095-5-7(4)*, Brolly Bks.) Borghesi & Adam Pubs. Pty Ltd.
—My Dinosaur ABC. Adam, Luisa. 2020. (ENG.). 28p. (J). (gr. -1-k). bds. *(978-0-6484571-4-5(1)*, Brolly Bks.) Borghesi & Adam Pubs. Pty Ltd.
Turner, Rich, photos by. Delta Skies Fine Art Folio, 2003. *(978-0-9762410-4-1(8))* Turner, Rich Photographs.
Turner, Sandy. Tales from Gizzard's Grill. Steig, Jeanne. 2004. 80p. (J). 17.89 *(978-0-06-000960-1(8)*, Cotler, Joanna Books) HarperCollins Pubs.
Turner, Suzette. Halloween Ooga-Ooga Ooum. Semple, Veronique & Semple, J. J. Semple, J. J., ed. 2011. (ENG.). 38p. (J). 9.95 *(978-0-9795331-5-0(5)*, Zardoz Pr.) Life Force Bks.
Turnham, Chris. Floors, Bk. 1. Carman, Patrick. 2013. (Floors Ser.: 1). (ENG.). 272p. (J). (gr. 4-7). pap. 7.99 *(978-0-545-46092-7(1)*, Scholastic Paperbacks) Scholastic, Inc.
—National Parks of the USA. Siber, Kate. 2018. (National Parks of the USA Ser.). (ENG.). 112p. (J). (gr. 1-4). 30.00 *(978-1-84780-976-6(6)*, 302819, Wide Eyed Editions) Quarto Publishing Group UK GBR. Dist: Hachette Bk. Group.
—National Parks of the USA: Activity Book: With More Than 15 Activities, a Fold-Out Poster & 50 Stickers! Siber, Kate & Grace, Claire. 2020. (National Parks of the USA Ser.). (ENG.). 32p. (J). (gr. 2-5). pap. 10.99 *(978-0-7112-5329-2(3)*, 335540, Wide Eyed Editions) Quarto Publishing Group UK GBR. Dist: Hachette Bk. Group.
Turnmyre, Dustin. Go, Bluey Go! McClean, Will. 2003. 32p. (J). 14.95 *(978-1-57072-252-3(8))* Overmountain Pr.
Turrill, Tiffany. The Journey of the Marmabill. Errico, Daniel. 2013. (ENG.). 32p. (J). (gr. -1-k). 16.95 *(978-1-62087-736-4(8)*, 620736, Sky Pony Pr.) Skyhorse Publishing Co., Inc.
—The Journey of the Noble Gnarble. Errico, Daniel. 2013. (ENG.). 32p. (J). (gr. -1-k). 16.95 *(978-1-62087-732-6(5)*, 620732, Sky Pony Pr.) Skyhorse Publishing Co., Inc.
Turu, Denise. Anito Reverbero & the Mystery of the Macabre Chickens. Knowles, James, ed. Giron, Alvaro, tr. 2018. (Tales of Anito Reverbero Ser.: Vol. 1). (ENG.). 34p. (J). pap. 9.99 *(978-1-7273-3853-9(7))* CreateSpace Independent Publishing Platform.
—Cuentos de Anito Reverbero: El Misterio de Los Pollos Macabros. Riol, Rubens. 2018. (Cuentos de Anito Reverbero Ser.: Vol. 1). (SPA.). 34p. (J). pap. 9.99 *(978-1-7273-3625-2(9))* CreateSpace Independent Publishing Platform.
—Dinosaur Devotions: 75 Dino Discoveries, Bible Truths, Fun Facts, & More!, 1 vol. Adams, Michelle Medlock. 2018. (ENG.). 160p. (J). 14.99 *(978-1-4002-0902-6(1))* Nelson, Thomas Inc.
—Who Is My Neighbor? Levine, Amy-Jill & Sasso, Sandy Eisenberg. 2019. (ENG.). 32p. (J). (gr. -1-2). 17.00 *(978-1-947888-07-4(2)*, 1947888072, Flyaway Bks.) Westminster John Knox Pr.
Turull, Dino. The Monstrous Alphabet: Volume 1. Fae, Nixie. ed. 2017. (ENG.). 36p. (YA). (gr. 7-12). 17.99 ***(978-1-64372-029-6(5))***; pap. 13.99 ***(978-1-64372-274-0(3))*** MacLaren-Cochrane Publishing, Inc. (Huskies Pub).
—The Monstrous Alphabet Dyslexic Edition: Dyslexic Font Volume 1. Fae, Nixie. ed. 2017. (ENG.). 36p. (YA). (gr. 7-12). 19.99 ***(978-1-64372-275-7(1))***; pap. 15.99 ***(978-1-64372-276-4(X))*** MacLaren-Cochrane Publishing, Inc.
Turvey, Raymond. Space. Morris, Ting & Morris, Neil. 2006. (Sticky Fingers Ser.). 32p. (J). lib. bdg. 27.10 *(978-1-59771-032-9(6))* Sea-To-Sea Pubns.
Tusa, Paola. MR Peter's Adventures in Siracusa, Sicily: Le Avventure Di Peter a Siracusa, Sicilia. Vaid, Michelle. 2017. (ENG.). 66p. (J). pap. *(978-1-9999194-0-5(8))* Life: Work In Progress.
Tusa, Tricia. The End of the Beginning: Being the Adventures of a Small Snail (and an Even Smaller Ant) Avi. 2008. (ENG.). 144p. (J). (gr. 3-7). pap. 6.95 *(978-0-15-205532-5(0)*, 1196636) Houghton Mifflin Harcourt Publishing Co.
—Fred Stays with Me! Coffelt, Nancy. 2011. (ENG.). 32p. (J). (gr. -1-3). pap. 8.99 *(978-0-316-07791-0(7))* Little, Brown Bks. for Young Readers.
—How to Make a Night. Ashman, Linda. Date not set. 32p. (J). (gr. -1-3). pap. 5.99 *(978-0-06-443699-1(3))* HarperCollins Pubs.
—It's Monday, Mrs. Jolly Bones! Hanson, Warren. 2013. (ENG.). 32p. (J). (gr. -1-1). 16.99 *(978-1-4424-1229-3(1)*, Beach Lane Bks.) Beach Lane Bks.
—Jan Has a Doll. Earl, Janice. 2005. (Green Light Readers Level 1 Ser.). (ENG.). 24p. (J). (gr. -1-3). pap. 3.95 *(978-0-15-205167-9(8)*, 1195586) Houghton Mifflin Harcourt Publishing Co.
—The Magic Hat. Fox, Mem. 2006. (ENG.). 32p. (J). (gr. -1-3). reprint ed. pap. 7.99 *(978-0-15-205715-2(3)*, 1197179) Houghton Mifflin Harcourt Publishing Co.
—Mrs. Spitzer's Garden. Pattou, Edith. gif. ed. 2007. (ENG.). 32p. (J). (gr. -1-3). 12.99 *(978-0-15-205802-9(8)*, 1197433) Houghton Mifflin Harcourt Publishing Co.
—The Problem with the Puddles. Feiffer, Kate. (ENG.). 208p. (J). (gr. 3-7). 2011. pap. 7.99 *(978-1-4424-2101-1(0))*; 2009. 16.99 *(978-1-4169-4961-9(5))* Simon & Schuster/Paula Wiseman Bks. (Simon & Schuster/Paula Wiseman Bks.).
—The Sandwich Swap. DiPucchio, Kelly. 2010. 32p. (J). (gr. -1-2). 16.99 *(978-1-4231-2484-9(7))* Hyperion Pr.
—Starring Prima! The Mouse of the Ballet Jolie. Mitchard, Jacquelyn. 2004. 160p. (J). (gr. 3-18). (ENG.). 15.99 *(978-0-06-057356-0(2))*; 16.89 *(978-0-06-057357-7(0))* HarperCollins Pubs.
—Treasure Map. Murphy, Stuart J. 2004. (MathStart 3 Ser.). (ENG.). 40p. (J). (gr. 2-18). pap. 5.99 *(978-0-06-446738-4(4))* HarperCollins Pubs.
—A Violin for Elva. Ray, Mary Lyn. 2015. (ENG.). 32p. (J). (gr. -1-3). 16.99 *(978-0-15-225483-4(8)*, 1202633, HMH Books For Young Readers) Houghton Mifflin Harcourt Publishing Co.
Tusa, Tricia. Is That You, Eleanor Sue? Tusa, Tricia. 2018. (ENG.). 32p. (J). 17.99 *(978-1-250-14323-5(3)*, 900180478) Roaring Brook Pr.
Tusan, Stan. African Giants. Prebeg, Rick, photos by. Knowlton, Laurie Lazzaro. 2005. (J). *(978-1-933248-08-0(4))* World Quest Learning.
Tuska, George & Craig, Johnny. Iron Man Epic Collection: the Man Who Killed Tony Stark. 2019. (ENG.). 496p. (J). (gr. 4-17). pap. 39.99 *(978-1-302-91630-5(0))* Marvel Worldwide, Inc.
Tuska, George & Ditko, Steve. Marvel Universe by John Byrne Omnibus Vol. 2, Vol. 2. 2018. (Marvel Universe by John Byrne Omnibus Ser.: 2). (ENG.). 1296p. (J). (gr. 4-17). 125.00 *(978-1-302-91401-1(4))* Marvel Worldwide, Inc.
Tust, Dorothea. Experimentos para Cada Dia del Otono. Van Saan, Anita. Bravo, J. A., tr. 2006. (SPA.). 89p. (J). pap. *(978-84-9754-221-0(5))* Ediciones Oniro S.A.
Tuttle, Todd. Spot. Tuttle, Todd. 2007. 20p. (J). 19.95 *(978-1-889829-16-6(1))* Window Bks.
Tuya, Jez. Daring Amelia. Lowell, Barbara. 2016. (J). *(978-0-451-53373-9(9)*, Warne, Frederick Pubs.) Penguin Bks., Ltd.
—Tales of a Fifth-Grade Knight. Gibson, Douglas. 2015. (Middle-Grade Novels Ser.). (ENG.). 160p. (J). (gr. 4-7). lib. bdg. 26.65 *(978-1-4965-0488-3(7)*, Stone Arch Bks.) Capstone.
—Thomas Edison & His Bright Idea. Demuth, Patricia Brennan. 2016. (Penguin Young Readers, Level 3 Ser.). 32p. (J). (gr. 1-3). pap. 4.99 *(978-0-448-48830-1(2)*, Penguin Young Readers) Penguin Young Readers Group.
—The Treasure of Pirate Frank. Peet, Mal & Graham, Elspeth. 2018. (ENG.). 32p. (J). (gr. -1-2). 15.99 *(978-0-7636-9644-3(7)*, Nosy Crow) Candlewick Pr.
—The William Hoy Story: How a Deaf Baseball Player Changed the Game. Churnin, Nancy. 2016. (ENG.). 32p. (J). (gr. -1-3). 16.99 *(978-0-8075-9192-5(0)*, 807591920) Whitman, Albert & Co.
Tweed, Sean, jt. illus. see Henkel, Vernon.
Tweed, Sean, jt. illus. see McInturff, Linda.
Twigg, Craig. A Special Bug Indeed, 1 vol. Rogers, Bryar Elizabeth. 2009. 41p. pap. 19.95 *(978-1-60749-750-9(6))* PublishAmerica, Inc.
Twinem, Neecy. E Is for Enchantment: A New Mexico Alphabet. James, Helen Foster. 2004. (State Ser.). (ENG.). 40p. (J). 17.95 *(978-1-58536-153-3(4)*, 1235984) Sleeping Bear Pr.
—I Love Mud! Williams, Rozanne Lanczak. 2005. (Reading for Fluency Ser.). 8p. (J). pap. 3.49 *(978-1-59198-141-1(7)*, 4241) Creative Teaching Pr., Inc.
—Three Hungry Spiders & One Fat Fly! Bentley, Dawn. 2010. (Stretchies Book Ser.). 16p. (J). (gr. -1-k). 8.99 *(978-0-8249-1460-8(0)*, Ideal Pubns.) Worthy Publishing.
Twinney, Dick. Brave Little Owl. Davies, Gill. 2006. (ENG.). 24p. (J). *(978-1-55168-279-2(6))* Fenn, H. B. & Co., Ltd.
Twins, Pope. Poke-A-Dot!: Who's in the Ocean? (30 Poke-able Poppin' Dots) 2012. (ENG.). 1p. (J). (gr. -1-1). 14.99 *(978-1-60169-270-2(6))* Innovative Kids.
Two Bulls, Marty Grant. The Mystery of the Maize. Meierhenry, Mark V. & Volk, David. 2010. 44p. (J). *(978-0-9822749-1-0(2)*, South Dakota State Historical Society Pr.) South Dakota Historical Society Pr.
Twohy, Mike. Mouse & Hippo. Twohy, Mike. 2017. (ENG.). 32p. (J). (gr. -1-3). 17.99 *(978-1-4814-5124-6(3)*, Simon & Schuster/Paula Wiseman Bks.) Simon & Schuster/Paula Wiseman Bks.
—Oops, Pounce, Quick, Run! An Alphabet Caper. Twohy, Mike. 2016. (ENG.). 32p. (J). (gr. -1-3). 17.99 *(978-0-06-237700-5(0))* HarperCollins Pubs.
—Outfoxed. Twohy, Mike. 2013. (ENG.). 40p. (J). (gr. -1-3). 16.99 *(978-1-4424-7392-8(4)*, Simon & Schuster Bks. For Young Readers) Simon & Schuster Bks. For Young Readers.
—Poindexter Makes a Friend. Twohy, Mike. 2011. (ENG.). 32p. (J). (gr. -1-3). 15.99 *(978-1-4424-0965-1(7)*, Simon & Schuster/Paula Wiseman Bks.) Simon & Schuster/Paula Wiseman Bks.
—Stop, Go, Yes, No! A Story of Opposites. Twohy, Mike. 2018. (ENG.). 32p. (J). (gr. -1-3). 17.99 *(978-0-06-246933-5(9)*, Balzer & Bray) HarperCollins Pubs.
—Wake up, Rupert! Twohy, Mike. 2014. (ENG.). 32p. (J). (gr. -1-3). 16.99 *(978-1-4424-5998-4(0)*, Simon & Schuster/Paula Wiseman Bks.) Simon & Schuster/Paula Wiseman Bks.
Twomey, Emily Golden. Buster's Brilliant Dot to Dot. Twomey, Emily Golden. 2014. (ENG.). 64p. (J). (gr. k-4). pap. 7.99 *(978-1-78055-201-9(7))* O'Mara, Michael Bks., Ltd. GBR. Dist: Independent Pubs. Group.
Twomey, Kevin, photos by. The Way I Used to Be. Smith, Amber. 2016. 384p. (YA). (gr. 9). 19.99 *(978-1-4814-4935-9(4)*, McElderry, Margaret K. Bks.) McElderry, Margaret K. Bks.
Twomey-Lange, Marianna, photos by. The True Legend of White Crow: Adventures of the Fudge Sisters. Halstead, Jayce N. 2004. 80p. (J). per. 7.95 *(978-0-9749046-3-4(5))* Aarow Pr.
Twork, Amanda J. O. & Twork, R. Cody, photos by. Rock! Answers to Questions of Faith. Twork, Carol Camp. 2004. 60p. (YA). 6.99 *(978-0-9707979-3-3(1))* Contemplation Corner Pr.
Twork, R. Cody, jt. photos by see Twork, Amanda J. O.
Tyczyńska, Miloslawa. Zoo the New Director. Tyczyńska, Miloslawa, tr. Judycki, Tomasz. 2019. (ENG.). 36p. (J). pap. 6.99 ***(978-1-7094-7814-7(4))*** Independently Published.
Tyger, Rory. Good Night, Sleep Tight! Freedman, Claire. 32p. (J). (gr. -1-2). 2013. (ENG.). pap. 4.99 *(978-1-58925-440-4(6))*; 2007. pap. 6.95 *(978-1-58925-405-3(8))* Tiger Tales.
—I Love You, Grandma. Tiger Tales. 2017. (ENG.). 28p. (J). (gr. -1-k). bds. 7.99 *(978-1-68010-524-7(8))* Tiger Tales.
—Maths Machine: A Fun New Way to Do Maths! Faulkner, Keith. 2004. (J). *(978-0-439-72174-5(1))* Scholastic, Inc.
Tyler, Craig. A Fine Kettle of Fish. adapted ed. 2005. 42p. (J). lib. bdg. 16.95 *(978-0-9761953-0-6(5))* Stairway Publishing.
Tyler, Gillian. The Bus Is for Us. Rosen, Michael. 2015. (ENG.). 32p. (J). (-k). 16.99 *(978-0-7636-6983-6(0))* Candlewick Pr.
—Hurry down to Derry Fair. Chaconas, Dori. 2011. (ENG.). 36p. (J). (gr. -1-2). 16.99 *(978-0-7636-3208-3(2))* Candlewick Pr.
Tyler Kazmier, Kit. Piece It Together Family Puzzle: Purrmaid Paradise. 2020. (ENG.). 24p. (J). (gr. -1-k). 14.99 ***(978-1-4521-7464-8(4))*** Chronicle Bks. LLC.
Tyler, Tim. Pizza Heart. Mazur, Cathy May. 2007. 20p. per. 24.95 *(978-1-4241-8747-8(8))* America Star Bks.
Tym, Kate. Princess Stories from Around the World. Williams, Sophy. 2004. 64p. (J). *(978-1-84458-142-9(X)*, Pavilion Children's Books) Pavilion Bks.
Tyminski, Lori & Turati, Valeria. Disney Bunnies: Thumper & the Egg. Vitale, Brooke. 2019. (World of Reading Level 1 Ser.). (ENG.). 32p. (J). (gr. -1-3). lib. bdg. 27.07 *(978-1-5321-4398-4(2)*, 33803) Spotlight.
—Thumper Finds an Egg. Driscoll, Laura & Disney Book Group. 2009. (ENG.). 24p. (J). (gr. -1-k). pap. 3.99 *(978-1-4231-1717-9(4))* Disney Pr.
—Thumper Finds an Egg / Tambor Encuentra un Huevito (English-Spanish) (Disney Bunnies) Driscoll, Laura. Collado Piriz, Laura, tr. 2019. (Disney Bilingual Ser.: 33). (ENG.). 24p. (J). (gr. -1-2). pap. 4.99 *(978-1-4998-0919-0(0)*, BuzzPop) Little Bee Books Inc.
Tyminski, Lori & Vallorani, Giorgio. Disney Bunnies Thumper's Fluffy Tail. Driscoll, Laura & Disney Books. rev. ed. 2008. (Touch-And-feel Book Ser.). (ENG.). 12p. (J). (gr. -1-k). bds. 6.99 *(978-1-4231-0443-8(9))* Disney Pr.
Tyminski, Lori & Ying, Victoria. Disney Princess Little Golden Book Favorites: Volume 3 (Disney Princess) Redbank, Tennant et al. 2014. (ENG.). 80p. (J). (-k). 6.99 *(978-0-7364-3098-2(9)*, Golden/Disney) Random Hse. Children's Bks.
Tyree, Mark, jt. illus. see Hargraves, Caitlin Rae.
Tyrell, Wes. I Met an Elkin Edson Once, 1 vol. Kelly, Dave. 2017. (ENG.). 32p. (J). 17.95 *(978-1-77276-031-6(5)*, f9cd624a-86d2-4619-90c1-fda6ad90c0fb) MacIntyre Purcell Publishing Inc. CAN. Dist: Baker & Taylor Publisher Services (BTPS).
Tyrol, Adelaide. A Child of God: Stories of Jesus & Stewardship Activities for Children. Caduto, Michael J. 2005. (ENG.). 48p. (J). 16.95 *(978-0-8091-6726-5(3)*, 6726-3) Paulist Pr.
Tyrrell, Frances. The Generous Fish. Jules, Jacqueline. 2020. (ENG.). 40p. (J). (gr. k-3). 16.95 *(978-1-937786-79-3(X)*, Wisdom Tales) World Wisdom, Inc.
—The Huron Carol. 2004. 32p. 16.00 *(978-0-8028-5263-2(7))* Eerdmans, William B. Publishing Co.
Tyrrell, Kayla. Froggy Kisses. Tyrrell, Kevin. 2008. 22p. pap. 24.95 *(978-1-60672-066-0(X))* America Star Bks.
Tyson, Liz. I Am a Monkey. Hevesi, Rachel. 2008. 44p. pap. *(978-1-906210-75-5(6))* Grosvenor Hse. Publishing Ltd.
Tyson, Tyshaun D. I Am Because He Is: A Book about God's Love. White, Adrianna. 2019. (ENG.). 28p. (J). pap. 12.95 ***(978-1-7946-9912-0(0))*** Independently Published.
Tzekov, Jack. Lily & Kayden's 1969 Woodstock Adventure. Soares, Valérie. 2014. (ENG.). 72p. (J). pap. *(978-1-927032-12-1(1))* Petra Bks.

U

Uderzo, Albert. Asterix Omnibus #1: Collects Asterix the Gaul, Asterix & the Golden Sickle, & Asterix & the Goths. Goscinny, René. 2020. (Asterix Ser.: 1). (ENG.). 152p. (J). 22.99 *(978-1-5458-0565-7(2)*, 900225739); pap. 14.99 *(978-1-5458-0566-4(0)*, 900225740) Papercutz.
—Asterix Omnibus #2: Collects Asterix the Gladiator, Asterix & the Banquet, & Asterix & Cleopatra. Goscinny, René. 2020. (Asterix Ser.: 2). (ENG.). 152p. (J). 22.99 *(978-1-5458-0567-1(9)*, 900225742); pap. 14.99 *(978-1-5458-0568-8(7)*, 900225743) Papercutz.
—Asterix Omnibus 3: Asterix & the Big Fight; Asterix in Britain; Asterix & the Normans. Goscinny, René. 2011. 144p. (J). (gr. 4-6). 29.99 *(978-1-4440-0427-4(1)*, Orion) Orion Publishing Group, Ltd. GBR. Dist: Hachette Bk. Group.
Uderzo, Albert. Asterix el Galo. Uderzo, Albert. Goscinny, René. 2009. (SPA.). 54p. 19.95 *(978-84-345-6719-1(9))* Grupo Anaya, S.A. ESP. Dist: Baker & Taylor Bks.
Uderzo, M. The Wright Brothers, Vol. 3. Lefèvre-Garros, J. P. 2012. (Cinebook Recounts Ser.: 3). (ENG.). 48p. (YA). (gr. 6-17). pap. 11.95 *(978-1-84918-100-6(4))* CineBook GBR. Dist: National Bk. Network.
Uderzo, M., jt. illus. see Chauvin, D.
Uderzo, Marcel, jt. illus. see Chauvin, Daniel.
Udon, jt. illus. see Stevens, Chris.
Udovic, David. Eight Wild Nights: A Family Hanukkah. Cleary, Brian P. 2006. 24p. (J). (gr. -1-3). lib. bdg. 16.95 *(978-1-58013-152-0(2)*, Kar-Ben Publishing) Lerner Publishing Group.
Ueda, Kumiko. The Magical Forest. Nelson, Brett Alan. 2003. 42p. (J). *(978-0-9655078-7-5(4))* Windsong Publishing Co.
Ueda, Miwa. Peach Girl Vol. 11: Change of Heart. Ueda, Miwa. 2004. (YA). pap. 9.99 *(978-1-59182-500-5(8))* TOKYOPOP, Inc.
Uehara, Sho. Bowhead Whale, 1 vol. Karpik, Joanasie. 2018. (Animals Illustrated Ser.). (ENG.). 28p. (J). (gr. k-2). 12.95 *(978-1-77227-162-1(4))* Inhabit Media Inc. CAN. Dist: Consortium Bk. Sales & Distribution.
Ueyama, Michiro. Chaotic Century. Ueyama, Michiro. (Zoids Ser.). (ENG.). Vol. 11. 2004. 82p. pap. 5.95 *(978-1-56931-858-4(1))*; Vol. 12. 2003. 72p. pap. 5.95 *(978-1-56931-867-6(0))*; Vol. 13. 2003. 81p. pap. 5.95 *(978-1-56931-813-3(1))*; Vol. 14. 2003. 96p. pap. 5.95 *(978-1-56931-898-0(0))* Viz Media.
Uff, Caroline. Pig on a Swing. Nimmo, Jenny. 2003. (ENG.). (J). 16.99 *(978-0-340-85241-5(0))* Hodder & Stoughton GBR. Dist: Trafalgar Square Publishing.
Ugalde Alcantara, Felipe. Mother Fox & Mr. Coyote / Mamá Zorra y Don Coyote. Villaseñor, Victor. Turcios, Guadalupe Vanessa, tr. (ENG & SPA.). 32p. (gr. 2-4). 16.95 *(978-1-55885-428-4(2)*, Piñata Books) Arte Publico Pr.
Ugalde, Felipe. Agua, Agüita / Water, Little Water. Argueta, Jorge. 2017. (ENG, SPA & NAH.). 32p. (J). (gr. 1-4). 17.95 *(978-1-55885-854-1(7))* Arte Publico Pr.
—La Hormiga de Sayil. Suarez, Carlos Ruiz. rev. ed. 2005. (Castillo de la Lectura Blanca Ser.). (SPA & ENG.). 68p. (J). (gr. -1-7). pap. 6.95 *(978-970-20-0334-2(2))* Castillo, Ediciones, S. A. de C. V. MEX. Dist: Macmillan.
—Zurdo el Que lo Lea! Gazquez, Juan Pablo Hernandez et al. rev. ed. 2007. (Castillo de la Lectura Roja Ser.). (SPA & ENG.). 206p. (YA). (gr. 7). pap. 8.95 *(978-970-20-0181-2(1))* Castillo, Ediciones, S. A. de C. V. MEX. Dist: Macmillan.
Ugalde, Felipe & Felipe, Ugalde Alcántara. Fuego, Fueguito. Argueta, Jorge et al. 2019. (ENG & SPA.). 32p. (J). (gr. 1-3). 17.95 *(978-1-55885-887-9(3))* Arte Publico Pr.
Ugawa, Hiroki. Shrine of the Morning Mist, Vol. 1. Ugawa, Hiroki. 2006. Orig. Title: Asagiri No Miko. 200p. per. 14.99 *(978-1-59816-343-8(4)*, Tokyopop Kids) TOKYOPOP, Inc.
Ugliano, Natascia. Abraham's Search for God. Vol. Jules, Jacqueline & Hechtkopf, Jacqueline. 2007. (Bible Ser.). (ENG.). 32p. (J). (gr. k-3). lib. bdg. 17.95 *(978-1-58013-243-5(X)*, Kar-Ben Publishing) Lerner Publishing Group.
—Benjamin & the Silver Goblet. Jules, Jacqueline. 2009. (Bible Ser.). (ENG.). 32p. (J). (gr. k-4). 17.95 *(978-0-8225-8757-6(2)*, Kar-Ben Publishing) Lerner Publishing Group.
—Netta & Her Plant. Gellman, Ellie B. 2014. (ENG.). 32p. (J). (gr. -1-2). 7.99 *(978-1-4677-0422-9(9)*, 9781467704229, Kar-Ben Publishing) Lerner Publishing Group.
—Sarah Laughs. Jules, Jacqueline. 2008. (Bible Ser.). 32p. (J). (gr. k-4). lib. bdg. 17.95 *(978-0-8225-7216-9(8)*, Kar-Ben Publishing) Lerner Publishing Group.
Uhelski, Casey. KeeKee's Big Adventures in London, England. Jones, Shannon. Pliscou, Lisa, ed. 2019. (KeeKee's Big Adventures Ser.). (ENG.). 40p. (J). (gr. k-2). 16.99 *(978-0-9990661-6-4(1))* Calithumpian Pr.
Uher, Brett. Dark Moon Diary, Vol. 1. 2007. (Dark Moon Diary Ser.). 192p. pap. 9.99 *(978-1-59532-844-1(0))* TOKYOPOP, Inc.
Uher, John, photos by. Kosher by Design Kids in the Kitchen. Fishbein, Susie. 2005. 192p. (J). (gr. 4-12). 22.99 *(978-1-57819-071-3(1))* Mesorah Pubns., Ltd.
Uhles, Mary. Beyond the Grave: An Up2U Mystery Adventure, 1 vol. Enderle, Dotti. 2013. (Up2U Adventures Ser.). (ENG.). 80p. (J). (gr. 2-5). 29.93 *(978-1-61641-964-6(4)*, 15211, Calico Chapter Bks.) ABDO Publishing Co.
—Kooky Crumbs: Poems in Praise of Dizzy Days. Lewis, J. Patrick. 2016. (ENG.). 32p. (J). 12.99 *(978-1-61067-371-6(9))* Kane Miller.
—The Little Kid's Table. Riehle, Mary Ann McCabe. 2015. (ENG.). 32p. (J). (gr. k-3). 16.99 *(978-1-58536-913-3(6)*, 203952) Sleeping Bear Pr.
—Mi Caida. Lindeen, Mary. 2016. (Early Rising Readers Ser.). (SPA.). 16p. (J). (gr. 1-1). 6.67 *(978-1-4788-3743-5(8))* Newmark Learning LLC.
Uhles, Mary Reaves. Levantate! McGillian, Jamie. 2016. (Early Rising Readers Ser.). (SPA.). 16p. (J). (gr. 1-1). 6.67 *(978-1-4788-3760-2(8))* Newmark Learning LLC.
—Mi Cuerpo. Lindeen, Mary. 2016. (Early Rising Readers Ser.). (SPA.). 16p. (J). (gr. 1-1). 6.67 *(978-1-4788-4197-5(4))* Newmark Learning LLC.
—A Tuba Christmas. Wilbur, Helen L. 2018. (ENG.). 32p. (J). (gr. k-2). 16.99 *(978-1-58536-384-1(7)*, 204580) Sleeping Bear Pr.
—The Twelve Days of Christmas in Tennessee. Duncan, Alice Faye. 2018. (Twelve Days of Christmas in America Ser.). (ENG.). (J). (gr. k). 40p. 12.95 *(978-1-4549-2859-1(X))*;

U

22p. bds. 7.95 *(978-1-4549-3090-7(X))* Sterling Publishing Co., Inc.

Uhlig, Elizabeth. Between the Shadows. Laub, Frima. 2007. (J). pap. 12.95 *(978-0-9786745-2-6(9))* Marble Hse. Editions.

—Clara Becomes a Citizen. Rothstein, Evelyn. 2009. (ENG.). 77p. (J). pap. 12.95 *(978-0-9786745-7-1(X))* Marble Hse. Editions.

—Clara's Great War. Rothstein, Evelyn. 2011. 88p. (J). pap. 12.95 *(978-0-9815345-9-6(7))* Marble Hse. Editions.

—Evelyn & the Two Evas. Rothstein, Evelyn. 2013. 63p. (YA). pap. 12.95 *(978-0-9834030-5-0(8))* Marble Hse. Editions.

—My Great Grandma Clara. Rothstein, Evelyn. 2006. 32p. (J). pap. 12.95 *(978-0-9677047-8-4(2))* Marble Hse. Editions.

—My Sandwich. Anderson, Lillian. 2012. 32p. (J). pap. 12.95 *(978-0-9834030-3-6(1))* Marble Hse. Editions.

Uhlig, Elizabeth. Children Just Like You. Uhlig, Elizabeth. 2007. (J). pap. 12.95 *(978-0-9786745-6-4(1))* Marble Hse. Editions.

—I See America! Uhlig, Elizabeth. 2009. (J). pap. 12.95 *(978-0-9815345-7-2(0))* Marble Hse. Editions.

—I Want to Be. Uhlig, Elizabeth. 2008. (ENG.). (J). pap. 12.95 *(978-0-9815345-1-0(1))* Marble Hse. Editions.

Uhlig, Elizabeth, jt. illus. see Laub, Frima.

Uhlman, Tom. Eruption! Volcanoes & the Science of Saving Lives. Rusch, Elizabeth. (Scientists in the Field Ser.). (ENG.). 80p. (J). (gr. 5-7). 2017. pap. 9.99 *(978-0-544-93245-6(5)*, 1657947, HMH Books For Young Readers); 2013. 18.99 *(978-0-547-50350-9(4)*, 1442756) Houghton Mifflin Harcourt Publishing Co.

Uhlman, Tom, photos by. The Bat Scientists. Carson, Mary Kay. (Scientists in the Field Ser.). (ENG., 80p. (J). (gr. 5-7). 2013. pap. 9.99 *(978-0-544-10493-8(5)*, 1540800); 2010. 18.99 *(978-0-547-19956-6(2)*, 1058461) Houghton Mifflin Harcourt Publishing Co.

—Emi & the Rhino Scientist. Carson, Mary Kay. 2010. (Scientists in the Field Ser.). 64p. (J). (gr. 6-8). 26.19 *(978-0-618-64639-5(6))*; (ENG., (gr. 5-7). pap. 9.99 *(978-0-547-40850-7(1)*, 1428813) Houghton Mifflin Harcourt Publishing Co.

—Inside Biosphere 2: Earth Science under Glass. Carson, Mary Kay. 2015. (Scientists in the Field Ser.). (ENG., 80p. (J). (gr. 5-7). 18.99 *(978-0-544-41664-2(3)*, 1594754, HMH Books For Young Readers) Houghton Mifflin Harcourt Publishing Co.

—The Mission to Pluto: The First Visit to an Ice Dwarf & the Kuiper Belt. Carson, Mary Kay. 2017. (Scientists in the Field Ser.). (ENG., 80p. (J). (gr. 5-7). 18.99 *(978-0-544-41671-0(6)*, 1594758, HMH Books For Young Readers) Houghton Mifflin Harcourt Publishing Co.

—Park Scientists: Gila Monsters, Geysers, & Grizzly Bears in America's Own Backyard. Carson, Mary Kay. 2017. (Scientists in the Field Ser.). (ENG., 80p. (J). (gr. 5-7). pap. 9.99 *(978-1-328-74090-8(0)*, 1677131, HMH Books For Young Readers) Houghton Mifflin Harcourt Publishing Co.

Uhouse, Debra. The Gift Within. Moss, Lucille. l.t. ed. 2005. 19p. (J). 14.95 *(978-1-59879-063-4(3))* Lifevest Publishing, Inc.

Uhre, Mark. Too. Nuttall, Susan. 2019. (ENG.). 48p. (J). *(978-1-5255-3371-6(1))*; pap. *(978-1-5255-3372-3(X))* FriesenPress.

Uhren, Anja. The Short Straw. Mathias, Irene. 2017. (ENG.). 30p. (J). (gr. -1-4). 14.99 *(978-1-941429-77-8(7))* Handersen Publishing.

Uhter, Kasey. Max & the Mystery of the Island. McMurray, Abraham. 2020. (ENG.). 136p. (J). pap. 6.25 ***(978-1-6760-6258-5(0))*** Independently Published.

Uihlein, Mary. Hello Little Owl. Uihlein, Mary. 2012. 24p. 22.95 *(978-1-61493-140-9(2))*; pap. 12.95 *(978-1-61493-139-3(9))* Peppertree Pr., The.

—Hello Little Owl, I Am Hermit Crab! Uihlein, Mary. 2013. 28p. 24.95 *(978-1-61493-159-1(3))*; pap. 12.95 *(978-1-61493-158-4(5))* Peppertree Pr., The.

Uitgeverij, Clavis. Encerrada: Anna's Tight Squeeze. De Smet, Marian & Meijer, Marja. Pacheco, Laura Emilia, tr. 2004. 28p. (J). 14.95 *(978-970-29-0665-0(2))* Santillana USA Publishing Co., Inc.

Ukazu, Ngozi. Check, Please! Book 2: Sticks & Scones. Ukazu, Ngozi. 2020. (Check, Please! Ser.: 2). (ENG.). 352p. (YA). 23.99 *(978-1-250-17949-4(1)*, 900189952); pap. 16.99 *(978-1-250-17950-0(5)*, 900189953) Roaring Brook Pr. (First Second Bks.).

Ukropina, Jovan & Orban, Jani. Overboard! Johnson, Terry Lynn. 2017. (Survivor Diaries). (ENG.). 112p. (J). (gr. 3-7). 9.99 *(978-0-544-97010-6(1)*, 1662447, HMH Books For Young Readers) Houghton Mifflin Harcourt Publishing Co.

Ulbricht, Juliet. Logos - in the Beginning. Rucker, Diana Lynn. 2018. (ENG.). 30p. (J). pap. 12.49 *(978-1-4984-4115-5(7))* Salem Author Services.

Uldal, Anne-Thea R. Abbiamo Mangiato il Nonno: [illustrato (in Bianco e Nero) Da Anne-Th�a R. Uldal]. Bjerregaard, Bjorn. Dzougov, Freja Vmskjold, tr. 2019. (ITA.). 28p. (J). pap. 5.50 ***(978-1-6926-9923-9(7))*** Independently Published.

—B. Bjerregaard und C. Lindhardts Beste Geschichten(Vicky und Die Apps, Damals Haben Wir Gro�vater Gegessen, Kuschelt und Die Veganen Werte) [Mit Sch�nen (S/W) Illustrationen Von Anne-Th�a R. Uldal]. Bjerregaard, Bjorn. Lindhardt, Claes, tr. 2019. (GER.). 86p. (J). pap. 8.00 ***(978-1-6546-0020-4(2))*** Independently Published.

—The Best Stories B. Bjerregaard Og C. Lindhardt(Vickey & Her Apps, Why We Ate Grandpa, Snuggles & the Vegan Values) [with Beautiful Illustrations(in Black/white) by Anne-Th�a R. Uldal]. Bjerregaard, Bjorn. Lindhardt, Claes, tr. 2019. (Children's Books for a Unique Audience Ser.: Vol. 3). (ENG.). 84p. (J). pap. 8.00 ***(978-1-0771-8439-8(5))*** Independently Published.

Uldal, Anne-Thea R. Entonces Comimos Abuelo/Why We Ate Grandpa: A Story for Bilingual Children/una Historia para niños Bilingües. Bjerregaard, Bjorn & Lindhardt, Claes. 2019. (ENG.). 28p. (J). pap. 5.50 *(978-1-0795-2936-4(5))* Independently Published.

—Snuggles & the Vegan Values: [Illustrated (in Black & White) by: Anne-Théa R. Uldal]. Bjerregaard, Bjorn. Lindhardt, Claes, tr. 2019. (Children's Books for a Unique Audience Ser.: Vol. 2). (ENG.). 30p. (J). pap. 6.00 *(978-1-0771-8619-4(3))* Independently Published.

Uldal, Anne-Thea R. Vicky & Her Apps: [5 Languages in One Book] Dansk/English/Deutsch/Italiano/Espa�ol/bilingual. Bjerregaard, Bjorn & Lindhardt, Claes. 2019. (Children's Books for a Unique Audience Ser.: Vol. 3). (ENG.). 38p. (J). pap. 6.00 ***(978-1-7040-5280-9(7))*** Independently Published.

Ulene, Nancy, jt. illus. see Guler, Greg.

Ulkutay & Co Ltd. Hey, Diddle, Diddle & Other Best-loved Rhymes. Gerlings, Rebecca, ed. 2009. (Nursery Rhymes Ser.). 32p. (J). (gr. -1-2). pap. 10.55 *(978-1-60754-126-4(2))* Windmill Bks.

—Itsy Bitsy Spider & Other Best-loved Rhymes. Gerlings, Rebecca, ed. 2009. (Nursery Rhymes Ser.). 32p. (J). (gr. -1-2). pap. 10.55 *(978-1-60754-129-5(7))* Windmill Bks.

—Little Miss Muffet & Other Best-loved Rhymes. Gerlings, Rebecca, ed. 2009. (Nursery Rhymes Ser.). 32p. (J). (gr. -1-2). pap. 10.55 *(978-1-60754-132-5(7))* Windmill Bks.

—Mary Had a Little Lamb & Other Best-loved Rhymes. Gerlings, Rebecca, ed. 2009. (Nursery Rhymes Ser.). 32p. (J). (gr. -1-2). pap. 10.55 *(978-1-60754-135-6(1))* Windmill Bks.

—Yankee Doodle & Other Best-loved Rhymes. Gerlings, Rebecca, ed. 2009. (Nursery Rhymes Ser.). 32p. (J). (gr. -1-2). pap. 10.55 *(978-1-60754-123-3(8))* Windmill Bks.

Ulkutay & Co Ltd & Ulkutay & Co Ltd. Wee Willie Winkie & Other Best-loved Rhymes. Gerlings, Rebecca, ed. 2009. (Nursery Rhymes Ser.). 32p. (J). (gr. -1-2). pap. 10.55 *(978-1-60754-138-7(6))* Windmill Bks.

Ulkutay & Co Ltd, jt. illus. see Ulkutay & Co Ltd.

Ulkutay Design Group & Choi, Allan. Thumbelina. Landolf, Diane Wright. ed. 2009. (Barbie Step into Reading Level 2 Ser.). 29p. lib. bdg. 13.55 *(978-1-4364-5096-6(9))* Turtleback.

Ulkutay Design Group Staff. Hey, Diddle, Diddle & Other Best-Loved Rhymes. Gerlings, Rebecca, ed. 2009. (Nursery Rhymes Ser.). 32p. (J). (gr. -1-2). lib. bdg. 25.60 *(978-1-60754-125-7(4))* Windmill Bks.

—Itsy Bitsy Spider & Other Best-Loved Rhymes. Gerlings, Rebecca, ed. 2009. (Nursery Rhymes Ser.). 32p. (J). (gr. -1-2). lib. bdg. 25.60 *(978-1-60754-128-8(9))* Windmill Bks.

—Little Miss Muffet & Other Best-Loved Rhymes. Gerlings, Rebecca, ed. 2009. (Nursery Rhymes Ser.). 32p. (J). (gr. -1-2). lib. bdg. 25.60 *(978-1-60754-131-8(9))* Windmill Bks.

—Mary Had a Little Lamb & Other Best-Loved Rhymes. Gerlings, Rebecca, ed. 2009. (Nursery Rhymes Ser.). 32p. (J). (gr. -1-2). lib. bdg. 25.60 *(978-1-60754-134-9(3))* Windmill Bks.

—Wee Willie Winkie & Other Best-Loved Rhymes. Gerlings, Rebecca, ed. 2009. (Nursery Rhymes Ser.). 32p. (J). (gr. -1-2). lib. bdg. 25.60 *(978-1-60754-137-0(8))* Windmill Bks.

—Yankee Doodle & Other Best-Loved Rhymes. Gerlings, Rebecca, ed. 2009. (Nursery Rhymes Ser.). 32p. (J). (gr. -1-2). lib. bdg. 25.60 *(978-1-60754-122-6(X))* Windmill Bks.

Ulmer, Louise. The Bible That Wouldn't Burn: William Tyndale's New Testament. Ulmer, Louise. 3rd ed. 2005. Orig. Title: The Bible That Wouldn't Burn: How the Tyndale English Version of the New Testament Came About. 34p. (YA). per., act. bk. ed. 8.95 *(978-0-941367-24-0(X))* Peach Blossom Pubns.

Ulrich, George. The Frog Prince/el Principe Rana: Spanish/English (We Both Read - Level 1-2) McKay, Sindy. 2016. (We Both Read - Level 1-2 Ser.). (ENG & SPA.). 44p. (J). pap. 4.99 *(978-1-60115-076-9(8))* Treasure Bay, Inc.

—The Hit-Away Kid. Christopher, Matt. 2009. (New Peach Street Mudders Sports Library). 64p. (J). (gr. 2-4). lib. bdg. 23.93 *(978-1-59953-318-6(9))* Norwood Hse. Pr.

—Simon Says. Willson, Sarah. 2006. (Step-By-Step Readers Ser.). (J). pap. *(978-1-59939-057-4(4)*, Reader's Digest Young Families, Inc.) Studio Fun International.

—The Spy on Third Base. Christopher, Matt. 2009. (New Peach Street Mudders Sports Library). 64p. (J). (gr. 2-4). lib. bdg. 23.93 *(978-1-59953-321-6(9))* Norwood Hse. Pr.

—What Do You See? Gikow, Louise. 2005. (My First Reader Ser.). (ENG.). 32p. (J). (gr. k-1). 18.50 *(978-0-516-25177-6(5)*, Children's Pr.) Scholastic Library Publishing.

—Who Was Daniel Boone? Kramer, Sydelle & Who HQ. 2006. (Who Was? Ser.). 112p. (J). (gr. 3-7). pap. 5.99 *(978-0-448-43902-0(6)*, Penguin Workshop) Penguin Young Readers Group.

—Who Was Daniel Boone? Kramer, Sydelle. 2006. (Who Was... ? Ser.). 108p. (gr. 2-6). 15.00 *(978-0-7569-6951-6(4))* Perfection Learning Corp.

Ulrich, George. Mrs. Picasso's Polliwog: A Mystery. Ulrich, George. 2003. 32p. pap. 7.95 *(978-1-891577-84-0(0))*; (J). (gr. -1-7). lib. bdg. 15.95 *(978-1-891577-83-3(2))* Images Pr.

Ulrich, Kelly. Carry Me to Kinshasa Our Adoption Journey. Yrjana, Colleen. 2012. 24p. pap. *(978-1-77097-655-9(8))* FriesenPress.

Ulrich, Kelly. Off the Beaten Path. Fedorowich, Mike. 2019. (ENG.). 60p. (J). ***(978-1-5255-4793-5(3))***; pap. ***(978-1-5255-4794-2(1))*** FriesenPress.

Ulrich, Kelly. Rusty Finds a Home: A Christmas Miracle. Griffiths, Allen & Godinez, Mary. 2012. 32p. pap. *(978-1-4602-0937-0(0))* FriesenPress.

Ultman, Suzy. Masha & Her Sisters. 2017. (ENG.). 10p. (J). bds. 9.99 *(978-1-4521-5159-5(8))* Chronicle Bks. LLC.

—Masha's World: Coloring & Activity Book. 2018. (ENG.). 48p. (J). (gr. -1-k). pap. 14.99 *(978-1-4521-6644-5(7))* Chronicle Bks. LLC.

—Tiny Farm. Chronicle Books Staff. 2017. (ENG.). 16p. (J). (gr. -1 — 1). bds. 7.99 *(978-1-4521-5158-8(X))* Chronicle Bks. LLC.

—Tiny Town. 2017. (ENG.). 16p. (J). (gr. -1 — 1). bds. 7.99 *(978-1-4521-5157-1(1))* Chronicle Bks. LLC.

—A to Z Menagerie. 2019. (ENG.). 28p. (J). (gr. -1 — 1). bds. 22.99 *(978-1-4521-7711-3(2))* Chronicle Bks. LLC.

Uman, Jennifer, jt. illus. see Vidali, Valerio.

Umana, Maria Gomez. Collie Rescue. Archer, Colleen Rutherford. 2004. 112p. (J). pap. *(978-1-894131-67-4(3)*, Virago Press) Penumbra Pr.

Umezu, Kazuo. The Drifting Classroom. Umezu, Kazuo. Roman, Annette, ed. 2007. (Drifting Classroom Ser.: 9). (ENG.). 192p. pap. 9.99 *(978-1-4215-0961-7(X))* Viz Media.

Umpierre, Migdalia. Sapo Sapito Sapote. Iturrondo, Angeles Molina. 2004. (Green Ser.). 24p. (J). *(978-1-57581-440-7(4))* Ediciones Santillana, Inc.

Umrikar, Sakharam. Max's Yoga Dream: If You Can Dream It, You Can Do It! Ludka, Richard. 2019. (Max's Dream Ser.: Vol. 2). (ENG.). 36p. (J). 14.99 ***(978-1-7328391-3-7(1))*** Positively Rich.

—Max's Yoga Dream: If You Can Dream It You Can Do It. Ludka, Richard. 2019. (Max's Dream Ser.: Vol. 2). (ENG.). 36p. (J). pap. 9.99 ***(978-1-7328391-2-0(3))*** Horn, Jonathan.

Umscheid, Kit. Pirate's Alphabet. Wigington, Patti. 2007. (ENG.). 32p. (J). (gr. -1-3). lib. bdg. 15.95 *(978-0-9766805-8-1(0))* Keene Publishing.

Unalp, Janet & Perry, Matt. Jacob's Promise: A Story about Faith. Banks, Celia. 2006. 32p. 14.99 *(978-0-9764460-6-4(5))* HonorNet.

Unbecomingname. The Legend of Zelda: A Sword in the Time of Guns: (EFC) Vol. 1. Row, J. Row, Natalia, ed. 2019. (Legend of Zelda: a Sword in the Time of Guns Ser.: Vol. 1). (ENG.). 76p. (J). pap. 5.99 ***(978-1-6919-2623-7(X))*** Independently Published.

Uncle Henry. Biode. Uncle Henry. 100th ed. 2004. 216p. pap. 7.99 *(978-1-932568-02-8(6)*, UHB003) Uncle Henry Bks.

—How the Tooth Fairy, of All People, Saved the Day. Uncle Henry. 100th ed. 2004. 64p. pap. 5.99 *(978-1-932568-00-4(X)*, UHB001) Uncle Henry Bks.

—The Vileburgers: With Friends Like This Who Needs Halloween? Uncle Henry. 100th ed. 2004. 88p. pap. 6.99 *(978-1-932568-01-1(8)*, UHB002) Uncle Henry Bks.

Undercuffler, Gary. The Boy Who Cried Wolf: A Tale about Telling the Truth. 2006. (Famous Fables Ser.). (J). 6.99 *(978-1-59939-026-0(4))* Cornerstone Pr.

—Francisco's Kites. Klepeis, Alicia & Ventura, Gabriela Baeza. 2015. (SPA & ENG.). (J). 17.95 *(978-1-55885-804-6(0)*, Piñata Books) Arte Publico Pr.

—Happy Birthday: The Story of the World's Most Popular Song, 1 vol. Allen, Nancy Kelly. 2010. (ENG.). 32p. (J). (gr. k-3). 16.99 *(978-1-58980-675-7(1)*, Pelican Publishing) Arcadia Publishing.

—Los Tres Osos. Hillert, Margaret. 2018. (BeginningtoRead Ser.). (SPA.). 32p. (J). (gr. -1-2). pap. 11.94 *(978-1-68404-242-5(9))* Norwood Hse. Pr.

—On the Wings of the Swan. Gulla, Rosemarie. 2008. (Treasury of the Lost Scrolls Ser.). (ENG.). 32p. (J). (gr. 1-4). 17.99 *(978-0-9793000-0-4(2)*, Alazar Pr.) Royal Swan Enterprises, Inc.

—The Three Bears. Hillert, Margaret. 2016. (BeginningtoRead Ser.). (ENG.). 32p. (J). (-2). lib. bdg. 22.60 *(978-1-59953-787-0(7))*; (gr. -1-2). pap. 11.94 *(978-1-60357-913-1(3))* Norwood Hse. Pr.

Undercuffler, Gary. Los Tres Osos. Undercuffler, Gary. Hillert, Margaret & Del Risco, Eida. 2018. (BeginningtoRead Ser.). (SPA.). 32p. (J). (gr. -1-2). lib. bdg. 22.60 *(978-1-59953-958-4(6))* Norwood Hse. Pr.

Undercuffler, Gary, jt. illus. see Jack Pullan.

Underhill, Alecia. For Horse-Crazy Girls Only: Everything You Want to Know about Horses. Wilsdon, Christina. 2010. (ENG.). 160p. (J). (gr. 3-6). 16.99 *(978-0-312-60323-6(1)*, 900064330) Feiwel & Friends.

Underwood, Edward. Big Box Little Box. Hart, Caryl. 2018. (ENG.). 32p. (J). 17.99 *(978-1-68119-786-9(3)*, 900186968, Bloomsbury Children's Bks.) Bloomsbury Publishing USA.

—One Shoe Two Shoes. Hart, Caryl. 2019. (ENG.). 32p. (J). 17.99 *(978-1-5476-0094-6(2)*, 900198463, Bloomsbury Children's Bks.) Bloomsbury Publishing USA.

—100 First Words. Nosy Crow. 2019. (ENG.). 14p. (J). (— 1). bds. 9.99 *(978-1-5362-0822-1(1)*, Nosy Crow) Candlewick Pr.

Underwood, Edward, jt. illus. see Jones, Lisa.

Underwood, Kay Povelite. Ferocious Fangs, Vol. Fleming, Sally. 2004. (It's Nature! Ser.). (ENG.). 32p. (J). (gr. 3-6). pap. 7.95 *(978-1-55971-587-4(1)*, NorthWord Bks. for Young Readers) T&N Children's Publishing.

—Rapid Runners, Vol. Fleming, Sally. 2004. (It's Nature! Ser.). (ENG.). 32p. (J). (gr. 3-6). pap. 7.95 *(978-1-55971-789-2(0)*, NorthWord Bks. for Young Readers) T&N Children's Publishing.

—Sharp Shooters, Vol. Feeney, Kathy. 2004. (It's Nature! Ser.). (ENG.). 32p. (J). (gr. 3-6). pap. 7.95 *(978-1-55971-794-6(7)*, NorthWord Bks. for Young Readers) T&N Children's Publishing.

Underwood, Lydia J. The Seventeen-Year Cicada. Penrod, Jill. 2020. (Terry's Garden Ser.: Vol. 6). (ENG.). 240p. (J). pap. 11.99 ***(978-1-6737-6003-3(1))*** Independently Published.

Underwood, Sandy. The Pony Tails Book of Colouring Fun & Horsey Facts. Alice the Pony. 2019. (ENG.). 104p. (J). ***(978-1-5255-5030-0(6))***; pap. ***(978-1-5255-5031-7(4))*** FriesenPress.

Unger, Erin. Memphis Learns the Hard Way. Gragg, Karla. 2013. 28p. pap. 6.95 *(978-0-9818396-7-7(3))* True Horizon Publishing.

Ungerer, Tomi. El Hombre de la Luna. Ungerer, Tomi. 2003. (Picture Books Collection). (SPA.). 40p. (J). (gr. k-3). pap. 10.95 *(978-968-19-0661-0(6))* Santillana USA Publishing Co., Inc.

—Rufus: The Bat Who Loved Colours. Ungerer, Tomi. 2003. (SPA.). 36p. (J). (gr. k-3). pap. 7.95 *(978-968-19-0746-4(9))* Aguilar, Altea, Taurus, Alfaguara, S.A. de C.V MEX. Dist: Santillana USA Publishing Co., Inc.

Ungermann Marshall, Yana. Gilda Gets Wise. Ungermann Marshall, Yana. 2008. 34p. (J). pap. *(978-0-9670982-6-5(2))* Yana's Kitchen.

Ungureanu, Dan. Nara & the Island. Ungureanu, Dan. 2016. (ENG.). 32p. (J). (gr. -1-3). 17.99 *(978-1-5124-1793-7(9)*, 9781512417937); E-Book 27.99 *(978-1-5124-1794-4(7)*, 9781512417944) Lerner Publishing Group.

Ungureanu, Dan Paul. A Tall Southern Tale. DeLong, Lucianne. l.t. ed. 2013. (Possum Squat Ser.). (ENG.). 40p. (J). 15.95 *(978-0-9833237-1-6(2))* Krullstone Publishing, LLC.

—Whiskers Takes a Walk: A Possum Squat Tale. DeLong, Lucianne. 2013. (Possum Squat Ser.). (ENG.). 40p. (J). 15.95 *(978-0-9833237-3-0(9))* Krullstone Publishing, LLC.

Unique Heritage Media. Cleopatra. Unique Heritage Media. 2018. (Pocket Bios Ser.). (ENG.). 32p. (J). 14.99 *(978-1-250-16621-0(7)*, 900187198) Roaring Brook Pr.

Unique Heritage Media & Berenger, Al. Blackbeard. Unique Heritage Media & Berenger, Al. 2018. (Pocket Bios Ser.). (ENG.). 32p. (J). 14.99 *(978-1-250-16605-0(5)*, 900187182) Roaring Brook Pr.

Unka, Vasanti. The Boring Book. 2016. (ENG.). 32p. (J). (gr. -1-k). 16.99 *(978-0-14-350575-4(0))* Penguin Group New Zealand, Ltd. NZL. Dist: Independent Pubs. Group.

—Hill & Hole Are Best Friends. Mewburn, Kyle. Roberto, Anna, ed. 2016. (ENG.). 40p. (J). 17.99 *(978-1-250-07637-3(4)*, 900152145) Feiwel & Friends.

Uno, Kat. Disney Princess: I See a Princess! Broderick, Kathy. 2020. (Look & Find Ser.). (ENG.). 14p. (J). *(978-1-5037-5266-5(6)*, 4ec2c83b-ffe2-44d1-9a80-7afd953b013c, p i kids) Phoenix International Publications, Inc.

—My First Day at School. Troupe, Thomas Kingsley. 2019. (School Rules Ser.). (ENG.). 24p. (J). (gr. k-2). pap. 8.95 *(978-1-5158-4062-6(X)*, 140056, Picture Window Bks.) Capstone.

—Staying Safe at School. Troupe, Thomas Kingsley. 2019. (School Rules Ser.). (ENG.). 24p. (J). (gr. k-2). pap. 8.95 *(978-1-5158-4065-7(4)*, 140059, Picture Window Bks.) Capstone.

—Sweet Little Unicorn: Sound Book Wood Module with Handle. Rose, Robin. Cottage Door Press, ed. 2017. (Early Bird Sound Bks.). (ENG.). 10p. (J). (gr. -1-k). bds. 9.99 *(978-1-68052-158-0(6)*, 1001560) Cottage Door Pr.

Unrau (), () Bernie. Alligator Alley. Unrau (), () Bernie. 2008. (ENG.). 314p. pap. *(978-0-9784552-5-5(8))* CalTex Pr.

—Confusion. Unrau (), () Bernie. 2008. (ENG.). 333p. pap. *(978-0-9784552-2-4(3))* CalTex Pr.

—Deadly Implant. Unrau (), () Bernie. 2008. (ENG.). 277p. pap. *(978-0-9781504-7-1(3))* CalTex Pr.

—Glazers. Unrau (), () Bernie. 2008. (ENG.). 303p. pap. *(978-0-9784552-3-1(1))* CalTex Pr.

—Golden Mask. Unrau (), () Bernie. 2008. (ENG.). 370p. pap. *(978-0-9781504-5-7(7))* CalTex Pr.

—Pulling Strings. Unrau (), () Bernie. 2008. (ENG.). 329p. pap. *(978-0-9782937-6-5(2))* CalTex Pr.

—Pulpit Fiction. Unrau (), () Bernie. 2008. (ENG.). 327p. pap. *(978-0-9784552-1-7(5))* CalTex Pr.

—Questa. Unrau (), () Bernie. 2008. (ENG.). 288p. pap. *(978-0-9781504-4-0(9))* CalTex Pr.

—Reflections. Unrau (), () Bernie. 2008. (ENG.). 336p. pap. *(978-0-9784552-0-0(7))* CalTex Pr.

—Sternwinder. Unrau (), () Bernie. 2008. (ENG.). 342p. pap. *(978-0-9781504-3-3(0))* CalTex Pr.

—Submarine Slide. Unrau (), () Bernie. 2008. (ENG.). 335p. pap. *(978-0-9781504-2-6(2))* CalTex Pr.

—Terra Vista. Unrau (), () Bernie. 2008. (ENG.). 325p. pap. *(978-0-9781504-8-8(1))* CalTex Pr.

Unrau (), () Bernie. Dentinator. Unrau (), () Bernie, photos by. 2008. (ENG.). 374p. pap. *(978-0-9781504-1-9(4))* CalTex Pr.

—Meltdown. Unrau (), () Bernie, photos by. 2008. (ENG.). 344p. pap. *(978-0-9782937-7-2(0))* CalTex Pr.

—Not a Drop. Unrau (), () Bernie, photos by. 2008. (ENG.). 339p. pap. *(978-0-9781504-6-4(5))* CalTex Pr.

—Ubar. Unrau (), () Bernie, photos by. 2008. (ENG.). 302p. pap. *(978-0-9781504-0-2(6))* CalTex Pr.

Unrau (), () Bernie, photos by. Big B. Unrau (), () Bernie. 2008. (ENG.). 331p. pap. *(978-0-9782937-5-8(4))* CalTex Pr.

—The Board. Unrau (), () Bernie. 2008. (ENG.). 340p. pap. *(978-0-9782937-1-0(1))* CalTex Pr.

—Hooked. Unrau (), () Bernie. 2008. (ENG.). 338p. pap. *(978-0-9782937-0-3(3))* CalTex Pr.

—The Rom. Unrau (), () Bernie. 2008. (ENG.). 365p. pap. *(978-0-9782937-3-4(8))* CalTex Pr.

Unruh, Charlotte Love. I Love You So Much. Sanchez, Gary. 2017. (ENG.). (J). 34.99 *(978-1-5456-2068-7(7))*; pap. 24.99 *(978-1-5456-1871-4(2))* Salem Author Services.

Unsplash Com, photos by. Alone in the Night. Stewart, Laurie. 2016. (ENG., (J). pap. *(978-0-9950101-4-7(5))* Corvid Moon Publishing.

Unten, Eren. Bubble Pirates! (Bubble Guppies) Golden Books. 2013. (Little Golden Book Ser.). (ENG.). 24p. (J). (-k). 4.99 *(978-0-449-81769-8(5)*, Golden Bks.) Random Hse. Children's Bks.

—The Doctor Is In! Golden Books. 2012. (Little Golden Book Ser.). (ENG.). 24p. (J). (gr. k-k). 4.99 *(978-0-307-97588-1(6)*, Golden Bks.) Random Hse. Children's Bks.

—I Am Brave. Capozzi, Suzy. 2018. (Rodale Kids Curious Readers/Level 2 Ser.: 4). 32p. (J). (gr. -1-1). pap. 4.99 *(978-1-62336-954-5(1)*, 9781623369545, Rodale Kids) Random Hse. Children's Bks.

—I Am Helpful: The Positive Power Series. Capozzi, Suzy. 2018. (Rodale Kids Curious Readers/Level 2 Ser.: 6). 32p. (J). (gr. -1-1). pap. 4.99 *(978-1-62336-960-6(6)*, 9781623369606, Rodale Kids) Random Hse. Children's Bks.

—I Am Smart. Capozzi, Suzy. 2018. (Rodale Kids Curious Readers/Level 2 Ser.: 5). 32p. (J). (gr. -1-1). pap. 4.99 *(978-1-62336-957-6(6)*, 9781623369576, Rodale Kids) Random Hse. Children's Bks.

—I Am Strong. Capozzi, Suzy. 2018. (Rodale Kids Curious Readers/Level 2 Ser.: 3). 32p. (J). (gr. -1-1). pap. 4.99

(978-1-62336-951-4(7), 9781623369514, Rodale Kids) Random Hse. Children's Bks.
—I Love My Tutu! Gilbert, Frances. 2019. (Step into Reading Ser.). 32p. (J). (gr. -1-1). pap. 4.99 *(978-0-525-64753-9(8)*, Random Hse. Bks. for Young Readers) Random Hse. Children's Bks.
—I Love Pink! Gilbert, Frances. 2017. (Step into Reading Ser.). 32p. (J). (gr. -1-1). 4.99 *(978-1-101-93737-2(8)*, Random Hse. Bks. for Young Readers) Random Hse. Children's Bks.
—I Love Pink. Gilbert, Frances. 2017. (Step into Reading Ser.). (ENG.). 32p. (J). (gr. -1-1). lib. bdg. 12.99 *(978-1-101-93738-9(6)*, Random Hse. Bks. for Young Readers) Random Hse. Children's Bks.
—Triple-Track Train Race! (Bubble Guppies) Tillworth, Mary. 2015. (Little Golden Book Ser.). (ENG.). 24p. (J). (-k). 4.99 *(978-0-553-49769-4(3)*, Golden Bks.) Random Hse. Children's Bks.
Unten, Eren & Unten, Eren. I Am Kind. Capozzi, Suzy. 2017. (Rodale Kids Curious Readers/Level 2 Ser.: 2). 32p. (J). (gr. -1-1). pap. 4.99 *(978-1-62336-878-4(2)*, 9781623368784, Rodale Kids) Random Hse. Children's Bks.
—I Am Thankful. Capozzi, Suzy. 2017. (Rodale Kids Curious Readers/Level 2 Ser.: 1). 32p. (J). (gr. -1-1). pap. 4.99 *(978-1-62336-876-0(6)*, 9781623368760, Rodale Kids) Random Hse. Children's Bks.
—I Am Thankful: The Positive Power Series. Capozzi, Suzy. 2017. (Rodale Kids Curious Readers/Level 2 Ser.: 1). 32p. (J). (gr. -1-1). 13.99 *(978-1-62336-920-0(7)*, 9781623369200, Rodale Kids) Random Hse. Children's Bks.
Unten, Eren, jt. illus. see Unten, Eren.
Unten, Eren Blanquet. I Am a Hero. Nicholas, Christopher. 2017. (J). *(978-1-5379-5736-4(8)*, Golden Bks.) Random Hse. Children's Bks.
—It's Time for Bubble Puppy! Golden Books Staff. 2012. (Little Golden Book Ser.). (ENG.). 24p. (J). (gr. -1-k). 4.99 *(978-0-307-93028-6(9)*, Golden Bks.) Random Hse. Children's Bks.
Unwin, Dave, jt. illus. see Capobianco, Danny.
Unwin, Mike. World of Animals: Internet-Linked. Davidson, Susanna. 2009. (Nature Encyclopedias Ser.). 144p. (YA). (gr. 3-18). pap. 16.99 *(978-0-7945-2033-5(2)*, Usborne) EDC Publishing.
Unzner, Christa. Leonardo Da Vinci. Dickins, Rosie & Ball, Karen. 2007. (Famous Lives Gift Bks). 63p. (J). (gr. 4-7). 8.99 *(978-0-7945-1594-2(0)*, Usborne) EDC Publishing.
—Princess Me. Wilson, Karma. 2007. (ENG.). 32p. (J). (gr. -1-3). 19.99 *(978-1-4169-4098-2(7)*, McElderry, Margaret K. Bks.) McElderry, Margaret K. Bks.
—The Tiptoe Guide to Tracking Fairies. Paquette, Ammi-Joan. 2009. (ENG.). 32p. (J). (gr. k-5). 15.95 *(978-1-933718-20-0(X))* Tanglewood Pr.
Unzueta, Ángel, jt. illus. see Broccardo, Andrea.
Unzueta, Ángel, jt. illus. see Virella, Nik.
Uon, Taraku & Gohda, Hiroaki. Mizuho & Kei's Diary. Zappa, Go. Hosaka, Toshi, tr. from JPN. 2005. 245p. pap. 7.95 *(978-1-58899-297-0(7))* ComicsOne Corp./Dr. Masters.
Upadhyay, Vikas. Can I Tell You about Friendship? A Helpful Introduction for Everyone. Knight, Bridget. 2019. (Can I Tell You About...? Ser.). (ENG.). 80p. 14.95 ***(978-1-78592-543-6(1)***, 696891) Kingsley, Jessica Pubs. GBR. Dist: Hachette UK Distribution.
—Can I Tell You about Nystagmus? A Guide for Friends, Family & Professionals. Neckles, Nadine. 2019. (Can I Tell You About...? Ser.). (ENG.). 80p. (J). 13.95 ***(978-1-78592-562-7(8)***, 696884) Kingsley, Jessica Pubs. GBR. Dist: Hachette UK Distribution.
Upama, Kata. Lucky, the Smiling Elephant's Best Friend Composition Notebook. The Smiling Elephant Notebooks. 2018. (ENG.). 118p. (J). pap. 5.99 *(978-1-7179-8251-3(4))* Independently Published.
Updegraff, Nicole. Black Girls, Brown Girls, What Could You Be? Anyabwele, Talitha. 2018. (ENG.). 30p. (J). pap. 12.99 *(978-0-9972861-0-6(5))* BGS Productions, Inc.
Updike, John & Hyman, Trina Schart. A Child's Calendar. Updike, John. 2004. (J). (gr. k-4). 28.95 incl. audio compact disk *(978-1-59112-932-5(X))* Live Oak Media.
Upham, Janice. Lou Battles Bullies. Jones, Donna. 2019. (ENG.). 26p. (J). (gr. 1-6). pap. 9.95 ***(978-0-9967744-5-1(9))*** Rowan Mountain Pr.
Upitis, Alvis, photos by. Amazing Grazing. Peterson, Cris. (ENG., 32p. 2011. (J). (gr. k-2). pap. 10.95 *(978-1-59078-868-4(0))*; 2003. (gr. 3-6). 26.19 *(978-1-56397-942-2(X))* Boyds Mills Pr.
—Century Farm: One Hundred Years on a Family Farm. Peterson, Cris. 2009. (ENG., 32p. (J). (gr. 2-k). pap. 12.99 *(978-1-59078-773-1(0))* Boyds Mills Pr.
—Cows, Cats, & Kids: A Veterinarian's Family at Work. Patrick, Jean L. S. 2003. (ENG., 48p. (gr. 2-1). 17.95 *(978-1-56397-111-2(9))* Boyds Mills Pr.
—Extra Cheese Please! Mozzarella's Journey from Cow to Pizza. Peterson, Cris. 2003. (ENG., 32p. (J). (gr. k-2). pap. 10.95 *(978-1-59078-246-0(1))* Boyds Mills Pr.
—Wild Horses: Black Hills Sanctuary. Peterson, Cris. 2009. (ENG., 32p. (J). (gr. 4-7). pap. 11.95 *(978-1-59078-799-1(4))* Boyds Mills Pr.
Uranas, Chuck, photos by. Custom Cars. Doeden, Matt. 2008. (Motor Mania Ser.). 48p. (J). (gr. 3-6). lib. bdg. 26.60 *(978-0-8225-7289-3(3))* Lerner Publishing Group.
Urasawa, Naoki. Herr Dr Tenma. Urasawa, Naoki. 2006. (Naoki Urasawa's Monster Ser.: Vol. 1). (ENG.). 224p. (gr. 11). pap. 9.99 *(978-1-59116-641-2(1))* Viz Media.
—Naoki Urasawa's 20th Century Boys, Vol. 11. Urasawa, Naoki. 2010. (20th Century Boys Ser.: 11). (ENG.). 232p. pap. 12.99 *(978-1-4215-2346-0(9))* Viz Media.
—Naoki Urasawa's 20th Century Boys, Vol. 12. Urasawa, Naoki. 2010. (20th Century Boys Ser.: 12). (ENG.). 232p. pap. 12.99 *(978-1-4215-2365-1(5))* Viz Media.
Urbain, Christophe, photos by. Emma in Paris. 2013. (ENG., 56p. (J). (gr. k). 17.95 *(978-1-59270-139-1(6))* Enchanted Lion Bks., LLC.
Urban, Chieu Anh. Color Wonder Winter Is Here! Urban, Chieu Anh. 2017. (Color Wonder Ser.). (ENG.). 14p. (J). (gr. -1 — 1). bds. 7.99 *(978-1-4814-8721-4(3)*, Little Simon) Little Simon.
—Hooray for Spring! Urban, Chieu Anh. 2016. (Color Wonder Ser.). (ENG.). 14p. (J). (gr. -1 — 1). bds. 7.99 *(978-1-4814-8720-7(5)*, Little Simon) Little Simon.
Urban, Helle. Little California. James, Helen Foster & Wilbur, Helen L. 2011. (My Little State Ser.). (ENG.). 22p. (J). 9.95 *(978-1-58536-538-8(6))* Sleeping Bear Pr.
—Little Colorado. Brennan-Nelson, Denise. 2011. (My Little State Ser.). (ENG.). 22p. (J). 9.95 *(978-1-58536-530-2(0))* Sleeping Bear Pr.
—Little Halloween. Brennan-Nelson, Denise. 2013. (Little Ser.). (ENG.). 20p. (J). (gr. -1-k). 8.99 *(978-1-58536-885-3(7)*, 202891) Sleeping Bear Pr.
—Little Minnesota. Wargin, Kathy-jo. 2011. (My Little State Ser.). (ENG.). 22p. (J). 9.95 *(978-1-58536-174-8(7))* Sleeping Bear Pr.
—Little Missouri. Young, Judy & Wargin, Kathy-jo. 2012. (My Little State Ser.). (ENG.). 22p. (J). 9.95 *(978-1-58536-206-6(9))* Sleeping Bear Pr.
—Little Wyoming. Gagliano, Eugene M. 2010. (My Little State Ser.). (ENG.). 22p. (J). 9.95 *(978-1-58536-544-9(0))* Sleeping Bear Pr.
—P Is for Pilgrim: A Thanksgiving Alphabet. Crane, Carol. rev. ed. 2007. (ENG.). 40p. (J). (gr. 1-4). 7.95 *(978-1-58536-353-7(7)*, 202306) Sleeping Bear Pr.
—Sonrieta. Brooks, Robert. 2008. 40p. (YA). 17.95 *(978-0-9792294-0-4(5))* Mystic Jaguar Publishing.
Urban, Keith. Teeny Tiny Tulula. Urban, Joyce. 2008. (ENG.). 38p. (J). pap. 9.95 *(978-0-9815370-0-9(6))* Urban, Keith Studios.
Urban, Suzanne. The Sounds of My Jewish Year, Vol. Gold-Vukson, Marji. 2003. (Very First Board Bks.). (ENG.). 12p. (J). bds. 4.95 *(978-1-58013-047-9(X)*, Kar-Ben Publishing) Lerner Publishing Group.
Urbano, Emilio, et al. Disney Fairies Graphic Novel #4: Tinker Bell to the Rescue. Mulazzi, Paola et al. 2010. (Disney Fairies Ser.: 4). (ENG.). 80p. (J). (gr. 1-6). 12.99 *(978-1-59707-230-4(3))* Papercutz.
—DuckTales: Imposters & Interns. Caramagna, Joe & Behling, Steve. 2020. (Duck Tales Ser.: 7). (ENG.). 72p. (J). (gr. 4-7). pap. 9.99 *(978-1-68405-613-2(6))* Idea & Design Works, LLC.
Urbano, Emilio, jt. illus. see Florio, Gianfranco.
Urbanovic, Jackie. The Bully Blockers Club. Bateman, Teresa. 2004. (ENG.). 32p. (J). (gr. -1-3). 6.99 *(978-0-8075-0919-7(1)*, 807509191) Whitman, Albert & Co.
—Don't Squeal Unless It's a Big Deal: A Tale of Tattletales. Ransom, Jeanie Franz. 2005. 32p. (J). 14.95 *(978-1-59147-239-1(3))*; (gr. -1-3). pap. 9.95 *(978-1-59147-240-7(7))* American Psychological Assn. (Magination Pr.).
—The Family (and Frog!) Haggadah. Isaacs, Ronald H. & Rostoker-Gruber, Karen. 2017. (J). *(978-0-87441-937-5(9))* Behrman Hse., Inc.
—Grandma Lena's Big Ol' Turnip. Hester, Denia Lewis. 2005. (ENG.). 32p. (J). (gr. -1-3). 6.99 *(978-0-8075-3023-8(9)*, 807530239) Whitman, Albert & Co.
—Grandma Lena's Big Ol'turnip. Hester, Denia Lewis. 2014. (AV2 Fiction Readalong Ser.: Vol. 138). (ENG.). 32p. (J). (gr. -1-3). lib. bdg. 34.28 *(978-1-4896-2329-4(9)*, AV2 by Weigl) Weigl Pubs., Inc.
—Horace the Horrible: A Knight Meets His Match, 1 vol. Koller, Jackie French & Köller. 2003. (ENG.). 32p. (J). 16.95 *(978-0-7614-5150-1(1))* Marshall Cavendish Corp.
—I Want Your Smile, Crocodile, 1 vol. Fretz, Denette. 2018. (ENG.). 32p. (J). 17.99 *(978-0-310-75890-7(4))* Zonderkidz.
—If You're Hoppy. Sayre, April Pulley. 2011. (ENG.). 40p. (J). (gr. -1-k). 16.99 *(978-0-06-156634-9(9)*, Greenwillow Bks.) HarperCollins Pubs.
—I've Lost My Hippopotamus. Prelutsky, Jack. 2012. (ENG.). 144p. (J). (gr. k-5). 18.99 *(978-0-06-201457-3(9))*; lib. bdg. 19.89 *(978-0-06-201458-0(7))* HarperCollins Pubs. (Greenwillow Bks.).
—Tell the Truth, Tyler. McConnaughhay, JoDee H. 2014. (Happy Day Ser.). (ENG.). 16p. (J). pap. 2.49 *(978-1-4143-9468-8(3)*, 4608458) Tyndale Hse. Pubs.
Urbanovic, Jackie. Duck & Cover. Urbanovic, Jackie. 2009. (Max the Duck Ser.: 3). (ENG.). 32p. (J). (gr. -1-2). 17.99 *(978-0-06-121444-8(2))* HarperCollins Pubs.
—Duck at the Door. Urbanovic, Jackie. (Max the Duck Ser.: 1). (ENG.). 32p. (J). (gr. -1-2). 2011. pap. 7.99 *(978-0-06-121440-0(X))*; 2007. 17.99 *(978-0-06-121438-7(8))* HarperCollins Pubs.
—Duck Soup. Urbanovic, Jackie. 2008. (Max the Duck Ser.: 2). (ENG.). 32p. (J). (gr. -1-2). 17.99 *(978-0-06-121441-7(8))* HarperCollins Pubs.
—Sitting Duck. Urbanovic, Jackie. 2010. (ENG.). 40p. (J). (gr. -1-2). 17.99 *(978-0-06-176583-4(X))* HarperCollins Pubs.
Urbanovic, Jackie & Mathieu, Joe. Ducks in a Row. Urbanovic, Jackie. 2011. (I Can Read Level 1 Ser.). (ENG.). 32p. (J). (gr. k-3). 16.99 *(978-0-06-186438-4(2))*; pap. 4.99 *(978-0-06-186437-7(4))* HarperCollins Pubs.
—Happy Go Ducky. Urbanovic, Jackie. 2012. (I Can Read Level 1 Ser.). (ENG.). 32p. (J). (gr. k-3). 16.99 *(978-0-06-186440-7(4))*; pap. 4.99 *(978-0-06-186439-1(0))* HarperCollins Pubs.
Urbanowich, Evelyn. Magnets. Feravolo, Rocco V. 2017. (ENG.). (J). pap. 12.95 *(978-0-692-83664-4(0))* Living Library Pr.
Urbanowicz, Kana. Magic Ramen: The Story of Momofuku Ando. Wang, Andrea. 2019. (ENG.). 40p. (J). (gr. -1-3). 17.99 *(978-1-4998-0703-5(1))* Little Bee Books Inc.
Urberuaga, Emilio. El Árbol de los Sueños. Alonso, Fernando. 2005. (Alfaguara Juvenil Ser.).Tr. of Dream Trees. (SPA.). 124p. (J). (gr. 5-8). pap. 10.95 *(978-968-19-0978-9(X))* Santillana USA Publishing Co., Inc.
—Cooper, Flying Dog. Ganges, Montse. 2009. (Cooper Ser.). 24p. (J). (gr. -1-3). 25.60 *(978-1-60754-239-1(0))*; pap. 8.15 *(978-1-60754-240-7(4))* Windmill Bks.
—Cooper, King of Cushion Island. Ganges, Montse. 2009. (Cooper Ser.). 24p. (J). (gr. -1-3). pap. 8.15 *(978-1-60754-243-8(9))* Windmill Bks.
—Fly Hunter. Ganges, Montse. 2009. (Cooper Ser.). 24p. (J). (gr. -1-3). pap. 8.15 *(978-1-60754-237-7(4))* Windmill Bks.
—King of Cushion Island. Ganges, Montse. 2009. (Cooper Ser.). 24p. (J). (gr. -1-3). lib. bdg. 25.60 *(978-1-60754-242-1(0))* Windmill Bks.
—Manolito Four-Eyes: the 2nd Volume of the Great Encyclopedia of My Life: The 2nd Volume of the Great Encyclopedia of My Life, 0 vols. Lindo, Elvira. unabr. ed. 2013. (Manolito Four-Eyes Ser.: 2). (ENG.). 162p. (J). (gr. 3-7). pap. 9.99 *(978-1-4778-1700-1(X)*, 9781477817001, Two Lions) Amazon Publishing.
—Manolito Gafotas, 0 vols. Lindo, Elvira. 2010. (SPA.). 192p. (J). (gr. 3-7). pap. 9.99 *(978-0-7614-5730-5(5)*, 9780761457305, Two Lions) Amazon Publishing.
—Meet Cooper. Ganges, Montse. 2009. (Cooper Ser.). 24p. (J). (gr. -1-3). pap. 8.15 *(978-1-60754-234-6(X))* Windmill Bks.
—Mi Laberinto. Guerrero, Pablo. 2004.Tr. of My Labyrinth. (SPA.). (J). 21.99 *(978-84-88342-42-3(X))* S.A. Kokinos ESP. Dist: Lectorum Pubns., Inc.
—Night Sounds, 1 vol. Sobrino, Javier. Amado, Elisa, tr. 2013. (ENG.). 36p. (J). (gr. -1-1). 16.95 *(978-1-55498-332-2(0))* Groundwood Bks. CAN. Dist: Publishers Group West (PGW).
Urberuaga, Emilio. Gilda, la Oveja Gigante. Urberuaga, Emilio. 2018. (SPA.). 44p. (J). 17.95 *(978-84-17123-23-9(7))* NubeOcho Ediciones ESP. Dist: Consortium Bk. Sales & Distribution.
—Gilda the Giant Sheep. Urberuaga, Emilio. Dawlatly, Ben, tr. 2018. (ENG.). 44p. (J). 17.95 *(978-84-17123-24-6(5))* NubeOcho Ediciones ESP. Dist: Consortium Bk. Sales & Distribution.
Urberuaga, Emilio, jt. illus. see Emilio, Urberuaga.
U'Ren, Andrea. The Bravest Woman in America. Moss, Marissa. 2011. (ENG.). 32p. (J). (gr. k-3). 16.99 *(978-1-58246-369-8(7)*, Tricycle Pr.) Random Hse. Children's Bks.
—One Potato, Two Potato. DeFelice, Cynthia. 2006. (ENG.). 32p. (J). (gr. -1-3). 19.99 *(978-0-374-35640-8(8)*, 900028331, Farrar, Straus & Giroux (BYR)) Farrar, Straus & Giroux.
U'Ren, Victoria & Wanner, Carole. The Dozen Dozens. Green, Tom. 2017. (ENG.). (J). *(978-1-5255-0926-1(8))*; pap. *(978-1-77097-056-4(8))* FriesenPress.
Urias, Abraham. Manuelito. Amado, Elisa. 2019. (ENG.). 96p. (YA). (gr. 7). 19.99 *(978-1-77321-266-1(4))* Annick Pr., Ltd. CAN. Dist: Publishers Group West (PGW).
—Manuelito (Spanish Edition) Amado, Elisa. 2019. (SPA.). 96p. (YA). (gr. 7). 19.99 *(978-1-77321-271-5(0))* Annick Pr., Ltd. CAN. Dist: Publishers Group West (PGW).
Uribe, Luisa. Anne of Green Gables. Montgomery, L. M. 2019. (ENG.). 256p. (J). 19.99 *(978-1-78888-383-2(7)*, 9b1de9e9-b77a-40f1-9a90-ad75acfc40a3) Arcturus Publishing GBR. Dist: Baker & Taylor Publisher Services (BTPS).
—Hand-Me-Down Magic #1: Stoop Sale Treasure. Haydu, Corey Ann. 2020. (Hand-Me-Down Magic Ser.: 1). 128p. (J). (gr. 1-5). 16.99 *(978-0-06-287825-0(5)*, Tegen, Katherine Bks) HarperCollins Pubs.
Uribe, Luisa. Hand-Me-Down Magic #2: Crystal Ball Fortunes. Haydu, Corey Ann. 2020. (Hand-Me-Down Magic Ser.: 2). 128p. (J). (gr. 1-5). 16.99 ***(978-0-06-287827-4(1)***, Tegen, Katherine Bks) HarperCollins Pubs.
Uribe, Luisa. I Love Us: a Book about Family (with Mirror & Fill-In Family Tree) Houghton Mifflin Harcourt, Houghton Mifflin. 2020. (ENG.). 24p. (J). (— 1). 8.99 *(978-0-358-19330-2(3)*, 1762430, HMH Books For Young Readers) Houghton Mifflin Harcourt Publishing Co.
—Operation Rescue Dog. Gianferrari, Maria. 2018. (ENG.). 40p. (J). 17.99 *(978-1-4998-0667-0(1))* Little Bee Books Inc.
Uribe, Luisa. Oro Salvaje. Perez de la Iglesia, Janina. 2019. (Torre Amarilla Ser.). (SPA.). 236p. (J). pap. ***(978-958-45-2456-0(9))*** Norma Ediciones, S.A.
Uribe, Luisa. The Queen & the First Christmas Tree: Queen Charlotte's Gift to England. Churnin, Nancy. 2018. (ENG.). 32p. (J). (gr. -1-3). 16.99 *(978-0-8075-6636-7(5)*, 807566365) Whitman, Albert & Co.
—The Secret Garden. Burnett, Frances Hodgson. 2018. (ENG.). 256p. (J). 19.99 *(978-1-78888-385-6(3)*, 29065476-3850-4e03-9870-1f89ce2aa775) Arcturus Publishing GBR. Dist: Baker & Taylor Publisher Services (BTPS).
—The Vast Wonder of the World: Biologist Ernest Everett Just. Mangal, Mélina. 2018. (ENG.). 40p. (J). (gr. 1-4). 19.99 *(978-1-5124-8375-8(3)*, Millbrook Pr.) Lerner Publishing Group.
Urosevic, Irena. Peter & the Parachute. Manning, James & Ridgeway, Nicola. 2020. (CBT Bks.: Vol. 81). (ENG.). 36p. (J). (gr. 1-4). pap. ***(978-1-80027-096-1(8))*** CBT Bks.
Urquia Linares, Natalia. Florecita Chang y Los Misterios Del Barrio Chino. Perez Diaz, Enrique. 2019. (Florecita Chang Ser.: Vol. 1). (SPA.). 28p. (J). pap. 22.50 ***(978-1-6992-5927-6(5))*** Independently Published.
Urru, Franco. Raphael, 1 vol. Lynch, Brian. 2015. (Teenage Mutant Ninja Turtles Ser.). (ENG.). 24p. (J). (gr. 3-7). 27.07 *(978-1-61479-341-0(7)*, 17341, Graphic Novels) Spotlight.
Ursell, Martin. Astonishing Art. Martineau, Susan. 2011. (Awesome Activities Ser.). (ENG.). 24p. (J). (gr. 3-6). pap. 10.60 *(978-1-61533-406-3(8))*; lib. bdg. 28.25 *(978-1-61533-369-1(X))* Windmill Bks.
—Chariot Race/La Carrera de Carrozas. Benton, Lynne. 2009. (Let's Read! Bks.). (FRE.). 32p. (J). (gr. 3-7). pap. 4.99 *(978-0-7641-4363-2(8)*, B.E.S. Publishing) Peterson's.
—Crazy Contraptions. Martineau, Susan. 2011. (Awesome Activities Ser.). (ENG.). 24p. (J). (gr. 3-6). pap. 10.60 *(978-1-61533-405-6(X))* Windmill Bks.
—Danny's Blog/El Blog de Daniel. Rabley, Stephen. Martin, Rosa Maria, tr. 2008. (Let's Read! Spanish-English Ser.).Tr. of El Blog de Daniel. (ENG.). 30p. (J). (gr. k-3). 17.44 *(978-0-7641-4047-1(7)*, B.E.S. Publishing) Peterson's.
—Dragon Boy. Goodhart, Pippa. 2nd ed. 2016. (Reading Ladder Ser.). (ENG.). 48p. (J). (gr. k-2). pap. 7.99 *(978-1-4052-8238-3(X))* Egmont Bks., Ltd. GBR. Dist: Independent Pubs. Group.
—Follow the Swallow. Julia, Donaldson. 2nd ed. 2016. (Reading Ladder Ser.). (ENG.). 48p. (J). (gr. k-2). pap. 7.99 *(978-1-4052-8200-0(2))* Egmont Bks., Ltd. GBR. Dist: Independent Pubs. Group.
—Marvelous Magic. Martineau, Susan. 2011. (Awesome Activities Ser.). (ENG.). 24p. (J). (gr. 3-6). pap. 10.60 *(978-1-61533-407-0(6))*; lib. bdg. 28.25 *(978-1-61533-368-4(1))* Windmill Bks.
—Where's Toto?/Donde esta Toto? Spanish/English Edition. Laird, Elizabeth. Martin, Rosa Maria, tr. 2009. (Let's Read! Spanish-English Ser.). (ENG.). 31p. (J). (gr. k-3). 17.44 *(978-0-7641-4218-5(6)*, B.E.S. Publishing) Peterson's.
Ursell, Martin, jt. illus. see Benton, Lynne.
Ursell, Martin, jt. illus. see Price, David.
Ursell, Martin, jt. illus. see Rabley, Stephen.
Ury, Laura. Arty's Long Day. Redmond, Mark L. 2003. 102p. pap. *(978-0-87398-042-5(5))* Sword of the Lord Pubs.
Us Now. The Story of Flight. Whitfield, Jakob. 2020. 48p. (J). (gr. 3-7). 18.99 ***(978-1-5263-6022-9(5)***, Wren & Rook) Hachette Children's Group GBR. Dist: Hachette Bk. Group.
Usai, Luca, et al. The Invisible Thief. Stilton, Geronimo & Schaffer, Andrea. 2015. 114p. (J). pap. *(978-0-545-92755-0(2))* Scholastic, Inc.
—The Perilous Plants. Stilton, Geronimo & Heim, Julia. 2016. 117p. (J). *(978-0-545-93092-5(8))* Scholastic, Inc.
Usai, Luca. Up. Ferrari, Alessandro. 2020. (Disney & Pixar Movies Ser.). (ENG.). 52p. (J). (gr. 2-6). lib. bdg. 28.50 ***(978-1-5321-4555-1(1)***, 35202, Graphic Novels) Spotlight.
Usai, Luca & Barbaro, Graziano. DuckTales: Mysteries & Mallards. Cavalieri, Joey & Caramagna, Joe. 2018. (Duck Tales Ser.: 2). 72p. (J). (gr. 2-5). pap. 9.99 *(978-1-68405-230-1(0))* Idea & Design Works, LLC.
Usai, Luca & Verzini, Daniele. Mice to the Rescue! Stilton, Geronimo & Schaffer, Andrea. 2014. 116p. (J). pap. *(978-0-545-86795-5(9))* Scholastic, Inc.
—Robot Attack. Stilton, Geronimo et al. 2015. 117p. (J). *(978-0-545-86796-2(7))* Scholastic, Inc.
Usai, Luca, jt. illus. see Melaranci, Elisabetta.
Usatsuka, Eiji. In Another World with My Smartphone: Volume 1. Fuyuhara, Patora. Hodgson, Andrew, tr. 2019. (In Another World with My Smartphone (light Novel) Ser.). 264p. pap. 14.99 *(978-1-7183-5000-7(7))* J-Novel Club.
—In Another World with My Smartphone: Volume 2. Fuyuhara, Patora. Hodgson, Andrew, tr. 2019. (In Another World with My Smartphone (light Novel) Ser.). 246p. pap. 14.99 *(978-1-7183-5001-4(5))* J-Novel Club.
—In Another World with My Smartphone: Volume 3. Fuyuhara, Patora. Hodgson, Andrew, tr. 2019. (In Another World with My Smartphone (light Novel) Ser.). (ENG.). 244p. pap. 14.99 *(978-1-7183-5002-1(3))* J-Novel Club.
—In Another World with My Smartphone: Volume 4. Fuyuhara, Patora. Hodgson, Andrew, tr. 2019. (In Another World with My Smartphone (light Novel) Ser.). 244p. pap. 14.99 *(978-1-7183-5003-8(1))* J-Novel Club.
—In Another World with My Smartphone: Volume 5. Fuyuhara, Patora. Hodgson, Andrew, tr. 2019. (In Another World with My Smartphone (light Novel) Ser.). 250p. pap. 14.99 *(978-1-7183-5004-5(X))* J-Novel Club.
—In Another World with My Smartphone: Volume 6. Fuyuhara, Patora. Hodgson, Andrew, tr. 2019. (In Another World with My Smartphone (light Novel) Ser.). 250p. pap. 14.99 *(978-1-7183-5005-2(8))* J-Novel Club.
Usher, Sam. All Aboard the London Bus. Toht, Patricia. 2017. (ENG.). 40p. (J). (gr. k-3). 18.99 *(978-1-84780-857-8(3)*, 316819, Frances Lincoln Children's Bks.) Quarto Publishing Group UK GBR. Dist: Hachette UK Distribution.
—Refuge. Booth, Anne. 2016. (ENG.). 32p. (J). (gr. -1-3). 15.99 *(978-0-316-36172-9(0))* Little, Brown Bks. for Young Readers.
—The Tin Snail. McAllister, Cameron. 2016. (ENG.). 288p. (J). (gr. 4-7). 16.99 *(978-0-553-53638-6(9)*, Delacorte Bks. for Young Readers) Random Hse. Children's Bks.
—What Will Danny Do Today? Goodhart, Pippa. 2016. (J). 11.99 *(978-1-61067-512-3(6))* Kane Miller.
Usher, Sam. Snow. Usher, Sam. 2015. (Seasons with Granddad Ser.). (ENG.). 40p. (J). (gr. -1-2). 16.99 *(978-0-7636-7958-3(5)*, Templar) Candlewick Pr.
—Storm. Usher, Sam. 2018. (Seasons with Granddad Ser.). (ENG.). 40p. (J). (gr. -1-2). 16.99 *(978-1-5362-0282-3(7)*, Templar) Candlewick Pr.
—Sun. Usher, Sam. 2018. (Seasons with Granddad Ser.). (ENG.). 40p. (J). (gr. -1-2). 16.99 *(978-0-7636-9949-9(7)*, Templar) Candlewick Pr.
Ushler, John. Roy Rogers' Favorite Western Stories. Snow, Dorothea J. 2011. 250p. 46.95 *(978-1-258-04169-4(3))* Literary Licensing, LLC.
—Walt Disney's Treasury of Classic Tales, Vol. 3. Reilly, Frank. 2018. (Treasury of Classic Tales Ser.: 3). (ENG.). 228p. (gr. 8-11). 49.99 *(978-1-68405-189-2(4))* Idea & Design Works, LLC.
Usova, Victoria. Red Boots & Assorted Things. Ross, Warren. 2016. (ENG.). 28p. (J). (gr. k-6). 12.95 *(978-0-9903086-2-1(6))* Ross, Warren K Jr.
Usui, Kanako. Fantastic Mr Wani. Usui, Kanako. 2006. 32p. (J). 15.95 *(978-1-58925-054-3(0))* Tiger Tales.
Utchenko, Olga. Holiday Cards: 25 Clever Cards to Color + Envelopes Included. Clever Publishing. 2018. (Clever Cards to Color Ser.). (ENG.). 54p. (J). (gr. -1-1). 10.99 *(978-1-948418-28-7(2))* Clever Media Group.

U

Uting, Justin. Sea Creature Creations: A Hand Print Discovery Book. Kidpressions!. 2008. 32p. pap. 24.95 *(978-1-60610-853-6(0))* America Star Bks.

Utley, David. Artic Skits. Ross, Kathryn & Pruitt, Kimberly. 2006. 88p. (J). per. 24.95 *(978-0-9725803-9-7(5))* Children's Publishing.

Utley, J. Stacy. What Mommy Does. Harvey Mph, Janera P. 2012. 24p. pap. 24.95 *(978-1-4560-4180-9(0))* America Star Bks.

Utomo, Gabhor. Blood Island. Windover, Liz. 2014. (ENG.). 144p. (J). (gr. 4-8). mass mkt. 6.99 *(978-1-937133-46-7(X))* Chooseco LLC.

—La Casa de Galletitas. Hillert, Margaret. 2018. (BeginningtoRead Ser.).Tr. of Cookie House. (SPA.). 32p. (J). (gr. -1-2). pap. 11.94 *(978-1-68404-237-1(2))* Norwood Hse. Pr.

—The Cookie House. Hillert, Margaret. 2016. (BeginningtoRead Ser.). (ENG.). 32p. (J). (-2). lib. bdg. 22.60 *(978-1-59953-779-5(6))*; (gr. -1-2). pap. 11.94 *(978-1-60357-905-6(2))* Norwood Hse. Pr.

—Eighth Grade Witch. Simpson, C. E. 2014. (ENG.). 144p. (J). (gr. 4-8). mass mkt. 6.99 *(978-1-937133-45-0(1))* Chooseco LLC.

Utomo, Gabhor. Joe. Lake, Joan. 2019. (ENG.). 40p. (J). 21.95 ***(978-1-64471-777-6(8))*** Covenant Bks.

Utomo, Gabhor. Lupita's First Dance / el Primer Baile de Lupita. Ruiz-Flores, Lupe. Baeza Ventura, Gabriela, tr. 2013. (SPA.). 32p. (J). 17.95 *(978-1-55885-772-8(9)*, Piñata Books) Arte Publico Pr.

—Mayanito's New Friends / Los Nuevos Amigos de Mayanito. Laviera, Tato. 2017. (ENG & SPA.). 32p. (J). (gr. 2-4). 17.95 *(978-1-55885-855-8(5)*, Piñata Books) Arte Publico Pr.

—Owl Tree. Montgomery, R. A. 2010. (ENG.). 80p. (Orig.). (J). pap. 7.99 *(978-1-933390-80-2(8))* Chooseco LLC.

—Pirate Treasure of the Onyx Dragon. Gilligan, Alison. 2011. (ENG.). 144p. (J). (gr. 4-8). pap. 6.99 *(978-1-933390-99-4(9))* Chooseco LLC.

—Simon of Cyrene & the Legend of the Easter Egg. DeGezelle, Terri. 2017. 25p. (J). pap. *(978-0-8198-9070-2(7))* Pauline Bks. & Media.

—Sir Wrinkles. Kalomas, Alice & Kerr, Lenora. 2005. (J). 14.95 *(978-0-9766639-0-4(2))* Sir Wrinkles Pr.

—Sir Wrinkles Goes to School. Kalomas, Alice & Kerr, Lenora. 2005. (J). 16.95 *(978-0-9766639-1-1(0))* Sir Wrinkles Pr.

—Surf Monkeys. Leibold, Jay. 2017. (ENG.). 144p. (J). (gr. 4-8). pap. 6.99 *(978-1-937133-24-5(9))* Chooseco LLC.

—The Tooth Collector Fairies: Batina's Best First Day. Ditto, Denise. 2016. (Tooth Collector Fairies Ser.: Vol. 1). (ENG.). (J). (gr. k-3). pap. 15.00 *(978-0-9967559-2-4(6))* Ditto Enterprises.

—The Tooth Collector Fairies: Home from Decay Valley. Ditto, Denise. 2018. (Tooth Collector Fairies Ser.: Vol. 2). (ENG.). 76p. (J). (gr. k-3). 22.99 *(978-0-9967559-6-2(9))* Ditto Enterprises.

Utomo, Gabhor. La Casa de Galletitas. Utomo, Gabhor. Hillert, Margaret & Del Risco, Eida. 2018. (BeginningtoRead Ser.).Tr. of Cookie House. (SPA.). 32p. (J). (gr. -1-2). lib. bdg. 22.60 *(978-1-59953-953-9(5))* Norwood Hse. Pr.

Utomo, Gabhor, jt. illus. see Jack Pullan.

Utopia. My Little Pony. Shears, William. 2005. (Look & Find Ser.). 18p. (J). (gr. -1-3). pap. 24.98 *(978-1-4127-3316-8(2)*, 7241700) Publications International, Ltd.

Utt, Mary Ann, jt. illus. see Rader, Laura.

Utton, Peter. It's the Troll: Lift-The-Flap Book. Grindley, Sally. 2018. (ENG.). 32p. (J). (gr. -1-k). 9.99 ***(978-1-4449-3784-8(7))*** Hachette Children's Group GBR. Dist: Hachette Bk. Group.

Utton, Peter. Let's Go on Safari!/Vamos de Safari! Anderson, Jill, ed. 2005. (Word Play/Juegos con Pala Ser.). (ENG.). 20p. (J). (gr. -1-17). bds. 6.95 *(978-1-58728-522-6(3))* Cooper Square Publishing Llc.

Uya, Nivola. Un Baño de Bosque (Bathing in the Forest) Ayats, Marc. 2020. (SPA.). 28p. (J). (gr. -1-3). 16.95 *(978-84-16733-57-6(0))* Cuento de Luz SL ESP. Dist: Publishers Group West (PGW).

—Bathing in the Forest. Ayats, Marc. 2020. 28p. (J). (gr. -1-3). 16.95 *(978-84-16733-58-3(9))* Cuento de Luz SL ESP. Dist: Publishers Group West (PGW).

—Life Is Beautiful! Eulate, Ana. Brokenbrow, Jon, tr. 2013. (ENG.). 28p. (J). (gr. -1-k). 16.95 *(978-84-15619-26-0(X))* Cuento de Luz SL ESP. Dist: Publishers Group West (PGW).

—A Very, Very Noisy Tractor. Pavon, Mar. Brokenbrow, Jon, tr. 2013. (ENG.). 28p. (J). (gr. -1-k). 15.95 *(978-84-15619-65-9(0))* Cuento de Luz SL ESP. Dist: Publishers Group West (PGW).

Uyetake, Neil & Breckel, Heather. My Little Pony: Friendship Is Magic. Cook, Katie & Nuhfer, Heather. 2015. (My Little Pony: Friendship Is Magic Ser.). (ENG.). 24p. (J). (gr. 2-5). lib. bdg. 27.07 *(978-1-61479-380-9(8)*, 18211, Graphic Novels) Spotlight.

Uyetake, Neil, jt. illus. see Garbowska, Agnes.

Uyetake, Neil, jt. illus. see Mebberson, Amy.

V

Vaca, Sally. Pete's Angel. Darden, Hunter. 2008. 44p. pap. 12.00 *(978-1-60693-264-3(0)*, Strategic Bk. Publishing) Strategic Book Publishing & Rights Agency (SBPRA).

Vaccaro Seeger, Laura. Snow Scene. Jackson, Richard. 2017. (ENG.). 40p. (J). 17.99 *(978-1-62672-680-2(9)*, 900170475) Roaring Brook Pr.

Vaccaro Seeger, Laura. Bully. Vaccaro Seeger, Laura. 2013. (ENG.). 40p. (J). (gr. -1-3). 18.99 *(978-1-59643-630-5(1)*, 900068271) Roaring Brook Pr.

Vachula, Monica. Noah Webster: Weaver of Words. Shea, Pegi Deitz. 2009. (ENG.). 40p. (J). (gr. 5-12). 18.99 *(978-1-59078-441-9(3)*, Calkins Creek) Boyds Mills Pr.

—Paul Revere's Ride. Longfellow, Henry & Boyds Mills Press Staff. 2011. (ENG.). 32p. (gr. 3-6). 26.19 *(978-1-56397-799-2(0))* Boyds Mills Pr.

—Paul Revere's Ride. Longfellow, Henry. 2011. (ENG.). 32p. (J). (gr. 4-7). pap. 11.95 *(978-1-59078-869-1(9))* Boyds Mills Pr.

Vachutinsky, Yuri. Daddy's Wardrobe. Boger, Yuval S. 2018. (HEB.). 36p. (J). pap. 9.95 *(978-1-936961-32-0(6)*, VRguy publishing) LINX Corp.

Vacura, Merri. Dogsled Molly. McAlpine, Janice. 2019. (ENG.). 44p. (J). *(978-1-5255-5168-0(X))*; pap. *(978-1-5255-5169-7(8))* FriesenPress.

—Molly Goes Camping: A Molly Mcpherson - 1st Lady Series Book. McAlpine, Janice. 2018. (Molly Mcpherson - 1st Lady Ser.). (ENG.). 32p. (J). *(978-1-5255-2456-1(9))* FriesenPress.

Vadalia, Hemali. Big Brother Little Brother. Graham, Rita Z. 2013. 42p. pap. 9.95 *(978-0-578-13165-8(X))* Graham, Rita.

Vaganos, Erin. Bonnwit Kabrit. Turnbull, Elizabeth. 2013. 36p. 17.95 *(978-1-61153-073-5(3))* Light Messages Publishing.

Vagharshyan, Lilit. You Are a Really Good Friend of Mine. Lilliom, Laura. 2007. 32p. (J). (POL & ENG.). pap. 16.95 *(978-1-60195-107-6(8))*; (ARA & ENG.). pap. 16.95 *(978-1-60195-310-0(0))* International Step by Step Assn.

Vagin, Vladimir. The Flying Witch. Yolen, Jane. 2003. 40p. (J). (gr. -1-1). 15.99 *(978-0-06-028536-4(2))* HarperCollins Pubs.

—Here Comes the Cat! Asch, Frank. 25th ed. 2011. (ENG.). 32p. (J). (gr. -1-3). 12.95 *(978-1-936365-41-8(3)*, bd29a1a7-7c04-4384-82e3-dd6e295f9305) McSweeney's Publishing.

—Here Comes the Cat! Asch, Frank. 2004. (Bookshelf Ser.). (J). pap. 5.99 *(978-0-439-66942-9(1))* Scholastic, Inc.

—Igual Al Rey. Paterson, Katherine. (Buenas Noches Ser.).Tr. of King's Equal. (SPA.). (J). (gr. 3-5). pap. 7.16 *(978-958-04-4167-0(7))* Norma S.A. COL. Dist: Lectorum Pubns., Inc.

Vagnozzi, Barbara. Five Little Mermaids. Scribens, Sunny. 2019. (ENG.). 32p. (J). *(978-1-78285-831-7(8))*; pap. *(978-1-78285-832-4(6))* Barefoot Bks., Inc.

—Honk, Honk, Vroom, Vroom: Sounds from the City. Shand, Jennifer. 2020. (Turn Without Tearing Ser.). (ENG.). 32p. (J). (gr. -1-1). 7.99 *(978-1-4867-1657-9(1)*, f7a73ab4-68f5-40ac-a98d-c1968b2de6fe) Flowerpot Pr.

—Jack & the Beanstalk. (Flip-Up Fairy Tales Ser.). 24p. (J). 2007. (gr. -1-2). audio compact disk *(978-1-84643-086-2(0))*; 2005. pap. *(978-1-904550-20-4(7))* Child's Play International Ltd.

—Jess & the Bean Root. Morgan, Ruth. 2005. (ENG.). 24p. (J). lib. bdg. 23.65 *(978-1-59646-732-3(0))* Dingles & Co.

—The Lion First Book of Parables, 1 vol. Rock, Lois. ed. 2014. (ENG.). 64p. (J). (gr. k-2). 14.99 *(978-0-7459-6409-6(5))* Lion Hudson PLC GBR. Dist: Independent Pubs. Group.

Vagnozzi, Barbara. Mi Primer Libro de Historias de la Biblia (My First Book of Bible Stories) Rock, Lois. 2013. (SPA.). 95p. (J). 15.99 ***(978-1-55883-103-2(7))*** Libros Desafio.

Vagnozzi, Barbara. Moo, Moo, Chew, Chew: Sounds from the Farm. Shand, Jennifer. 2019. (Turn Without Tearing Ser.). (ENG.). 32p. (J). (gr. -1-1). 7.99 *(978-1-4867-1583-1(4)*, c4918dfa-d44f-453f-81bd-35ce84a3f091) Flowerpot Pr.

—The Musicians of Bremen. 2007. (Flip-Up Fairy Tales Ser.). 24p. (J). (gr. 1-2). *(978-1-84643-115-9(8))* Child's Play International Ltd.

—Peck, Hen, Peck! & Ben's Pet. Atkins, Jill. 2019. (Early Bird Readers — Pink (Early Bird Stories (tm)) Ser.). (ENG.). 32p. (J). (gr. -1-2). pap. 7.99 *(978-1-5415-4623-3(7))* Lerner Publishing Group.

—Roar, Roar, Growl, Growl: Sounds from the Jungle. Shand, Jennifer. 2019. (Turn Without Tearing Ser.). (ENG.). 32p. (J). (gr. -1-1). 7.99 *(978-1-4867-1584-8(2)*, fcd43fae-3350-43ac-8897-6f3569663a1c) Flowerpot Pr.

—Rumble, Rumble, Grumble, Grumble: Sounds from the Sky. Shand, Jennifer. 2020. (Turn Without Tearing Ser.). (ENG.). 32p. (J). (gr. -1-1). 7.99 *(978-1-4867-1658-6(X)*, 28dfacbb-13b2-409a-9876-904dcbc2622e) Flowerpot Pr.

—Sleeping Beauty. 2007. (First Fairy Tales Ser.). 32p. (J). (gr. -1-3). lib. bdg. 28.50 *(978-1-59771-073-2(3))* Sea-To-Sea Pubns.

Vaillant, Tom. Pop-Up Volcano! Daugey, Fleur. 2020. (ENG.). 22p. (J). (gr. 1-3). 29.95 ***(978-0-500-65222-0(8)**, 565222)* Thames & Hudson.

Vaing, Jocelang. Trip Through Cambodia. Diep, Bridgette. 32p. (J). (gr. -1-3). 14.95 *(978-0-87592-054-2(3))* Scroll Pr., Inc.

Vainio, Pirkko. Little Bunny Finds Christmas. Vainio, Pirkko. 2008. 32p. (J). (gr. -1-3). 16.95 *(978-0-7358-2221-4(2))* North-South Bks., Inc.

Vainreb, M. Kligerovke: Aza Shtetele: Mesholim Fun Pirke Oves - in Bilder. Irenshtain, Hadas. 2017. (YID.). 73p. *(978-1-68091-168-8(6))* Kinder Shpiel USA, Inc.

Vaisberg, Diego. My Digital Community & Media. Hubbard, Ben. 2019. (Digital Citizens Ser.). (ENG.). 32p. (J). (gr. 2-5). 27.99 *(978-1-5415-3878-8(1)*, Lerner Pubns.) Lerner Publishing Group.

—My Digital Future. Hubbard, Ben. 2019. (Digital Citizens Ser.). (ENG.). 32p. (J). (gr. 2-5). 27.99 *(978-1-5415-3879-5(X)*, Lerner Pubns.) Lerner Publishing Group.

—My Digital Health & Wellness. Hubbard, Ben. 2019. (Digital Citizens Ser.). (ENG.). 32p. (J). (gr. 2-5). lib. bdg. 27.99 *(978-1-5415-3880-1(3)*, Lerner Pubns.) Lerner Publishing Group.

—My Digital Rights & Rules. Hubbard, Ben C. 2019. (Digital Citizens Ser.). (ENG.). 32p. (J). (gr. 2-5). 27.99 *(978-1-5415-3881-8(1)*, Lerner Pubns.) Lerner Publishing Group.

—My Digital Safety & Security. Hubbard, Ben. 2019. (Digital Citizens Ser.). (ENG.). 32p. (J). (gr. 2-5). 27.99 *(978-1-5415-3882-5(X)*, Lerner Pubns.) Lerner Publishing Group.

—My Digital World. Hubbard, Ben. 2019. (Digital Citizens Ser.). (ENG.). 32p. (J). (gr. 2-5). lib. bdg. 27.99 *(978-1-5415-3883-2(8)*, Lerner Pubns.) Lerner Publishing Group.

—101 Games to Play Before You Grow Up: Exciting & Fun Games to Play Anywhere. Walter Foster Jr. Creative Team. 2018. (101 Things Ser.). (ENG.). 144p. (J). (gr. 3-7). pap. 12.95 *(978-1-63322-337-0(X)*, Walter Foster Jr) Quarto Publishing Group USA.

Vaisberg, Diego & Beach, Bryan. The Science of Bridges & Tunnels: The Art of Engineering. Graham, Ian. 2019. (Science of Engineering Ser.). (ENG.). 32p. (J). (gr. 3-3). lib. bdg. 29.00 *(978-0-531-13199-2(8)*, Watts, Franklin) Scholastic Library Publishing.

Vaisberg, Diego & DGPH Stufio Staff. Dino. Vaisberg, Diego & DGPH Stufio Staff. 2018. (ENG.). 40p. (J). (gr. k-3). 15.99 *(978-1-5362-0280-9(0)*, Templar) Candlewick Pr.

Vakueva, Nina. Heavy Vinyl: Y2K-O! Usdin, Carly. 2020. (Heavy Vinyl Ser.). (ENG.). 112p. (YA). pap. 14.99 *(978-1-68415-495-1(2))* Boom! Studios.

—League of Legends: Ashe - Warmother. 2019. 144p. (YA). (gr. -1-17). pap. 15.99 *(978-1-302-91856-9(7))* Marvel Worldwide, Inc.

Valadi, Nashmin. Mouse & Frog & Rat Trap. Webster, William, ed. 2019. (ENG.). 40p. (J). (gr. k). pap. ***(978-0-6483864-4-5(9))*** Australian Self Publishing Group/ Inspiring Pubs.

—Painting Competition & Royal Hawk: Ancient Stories for Persia & Beyond. Webster, William, ed. 2019. (ENG.). 36p. (J). (gr. k-6). pap. ***(978-1-922327-02-4(6))*** Australian Self Publishing Group/ Inspiring Pubs.

—Painting Competition & Royal Hawk: Ancient Stories from Persia & Beyond. Webster, William, ed. 2019. (ENG.). 36p. (J). (gr. k-6). pap. ***(978-1-922327-03-1(4))*** Australian Self Publishing Group/ Inspiring Pubs.

—Sleeping Dragon & Spring of the Moon: Little Tales for Little Kids: Ancient Stories for Persia & Beyond. Webster, William, ed. 2019. (Book 4 Ser.). (ENG.). 36p. (J). (gr. 2-6). pap. ***(978-1-925908-82-4(8))*** Australian Self Publishing Group/ Inspiring Pubs.

—The Wise Pigeon & the Rustic & His Horse: Little Tales for Little Kids: Ancient Stories from Persia & Beyond. Webster, William, ed. 2019. (Book 3 Ser.). (ENG.). 42p. (J). (gr. 6). pap. ***(978-1-925908-80-0(1))*** Australian Self Publishing Group/ Inspiring Pubs.

Valan, photos by. It's a Good Thing There Are Insects. Fowler, Allan. 2006. (Rookie Read-About Science: Animals Ser.). (ENG., 32p. (J). (gr. 1-2). 4.95 *(978-0-516-44905-0(2))* Perfection Learning Corp.

Valat, Pierre-Marie. Inside the Body. Valat, Pierre-Marie. Houbre, Gilbert & Delafosse, Claude. Best, Clare, tr. 2012. (ENG.). 36p. (J). (gr. -1-k). spiral bd. 14.99 *(978-1-85103-412-3(9))* Moonlight Publishing, Ltd. GBR. Dist: Independent Pubs. Group.

—Water. Valat, Pierre-Marie. 2012. (ENG.). 36p. (J). (gr. -1-k). spiral bd. 13.99 *(978-1-85103-403-1(X))* Moonlight Publishing, Ltd. GBR. Dist: Independent Pubs. Group.

Valckx, Catharina. Zanzibar. Valckx, Catharina. 2019. (ENG.). 72p. (J). (gr. 1-3). 17.99 *(978-1-77657-255-7(6))* Gecko Pr. NZL. Dist: Lerner Publishing Group.

Valder, Justin. Henry the Honey Bee. Valder, Margret. 2010. 24p. pap. 11.50 *(978-1-60860-537-8(X)*, Eloquent Bks.) Strategic Book Publishing & Rights Agency (SBPRA).

Valderrama, Rosario. Ontario, la Mariposa Viajera. Pettersson, Aline. 2003. (SPA.). 72p. (gr. 3-5). pap. 8.95 *(978-968-19-0276-6(9))* Santillana USA Publishing Co., Inc.

Valdes, Ernesto R., jt. illus. see Ruano, Kelsy C.

Valdez Y Alanis, Erik. Snow White. Capstone Press Staff. 2009. (Graphic Spin Ser.). (ENG.). 40p. (J). (gr. 3-6). pap. 5.95 *(978-1-4342-1394-5(3)*, Stone Arch Bks.) Capstone.

Valdivia, Paloma. A Bailar: Let's Dance. Ortiz, Estrella. 2015. (ENG & SPA.). (J). *(978-0-545-85368-2(0))* Scholastic, Inc.

Valdivia, Paloma. Crack! Giménez de Ory, Beatriz. 2020. (ENG.). 28p. (J). bds. ***(978-1-64686-093-7(4))*** Barefoot Bks., Inc.

Valdivia, Paloma. De Paseo: Out & About. Ortiz, Estrella. 2015. (SPA & ENG.). (J). *(978-0-545-85369-9(9))* Scholastic, Inc.

Valdrighi, Alessandro. Could You Survive the Cretaceous Period? An Interactive Prehistoric Adventure. Braun, Eric Mark. 2020. (You Choose: Prehistoric Survival Ser.). (ENG.). 112p. (J). (gr. 3-7). pap. 6.95 *(978-1-4966-5807-4(8)*, 142239); lib. bdg. 32.65 *(978-1-5435-7401-2(7)*, 140692) Capstone.

—Could You Survive the Ice Age? An Interactive Prehistoric Adventure. Hoena, Blake. 2020. (You Choose: Prehistoric Survival Ser.). (ENG.). 112p. (J). (gr. 3-7). pap. 6.95 *(978-1-4966-5809-8(4)*, 142241); lib. bdg. 32.65 *(978-1-5435-7404-3(1)*, 140695) Capstone.

—EDGE: Sporting Heroes: Adam Peaty. Apps, Roy. ed. 2019. (EDGE: Sporting Heroes Ser.). 48p. (J). (gr. 2-7). 9.99 *(978-1-4451-5333-9(5)*, Franklin Watts) Hachette Children's Group GBR. Dist: Hachette Bk. Group.

—EDGE: Sporting Heroes: Cristiano Ronaldo. Apps, Roy. ed. 2019. (EDGE: Sporting Heroes Ser.). 48p. (J). (gr. 2-7). pap. 9.99 *(978-1-4451-5321-6(1)*, Franklin Watts) Hachette Children's Group GBR. Dist: Hachette Bk. Group.

—EDGE: Sporting Heroes: Fara Williams. Apps, Roy. ed. 2019. (EDGE: Sporting Heroes Ser.). (ENG.). 48p. (J). (gr. 2-7). 9.99 *(978-1-4451-5329-2(7)*, Franklin Watts) Hachette Children's Group GBR. Dist: Hachette Bk. Group.

—EDGE: Sporting Heroes: Greg Rutherford. Apps, Roy. ed. 2019. (EDGE: Sporting Heroes Ser.). (ENG.). 48p. (J). (gr. 2-7). 9.99 *(978-1-4451-5337-7(8)*, Franklin Watts) Hachette Children's Group GBR. Dist: Hachette Bk. Group.

—EDGE: Sporting Heroes: Harry Kane. Apps, Roy. ed. 2019. (EDGE: Sporting Heroes Ser.). 48p. (J). (gr. 2-7). 9.99 *(978-1-4451-5213-4(4)*, Franklin Watts) Hachette Children's Group GBR. Dist: Hachette Bk. Group.

—EDGE: Sporting Heroes: Neymar. Apps, Roy. ed. 2019. (EDGE: Sporting Heroes Ser.). 48p. (J). (gr. 2-7). 9.99 *(978-1-4451-5317-9(3)*, Franklin Watts) Hachette Children's Group GBR. Dist: Hachette Bk. Group.

—EDGE: Sporting Heroes: Serena Williams. Apps, Roy. ed. 2019. (EDGE: Sporting Heroes Ser.). (ENG.). 48p. (J). (gr. 2-7). 9.99 *(978-1-4451-5341-4(6)*, Franklin Watts) Hachette Children's Group GBR. Dist: Hachette Bk. Group.

—The Hadley Academy for the Improbably Gifted: A Novel, 1 vol. Grennan, Conor. 2019. (ENG.). 368p. (J). 16.99 *(978-1-4002-1534-8(X))* Nelson, Thomas Inc.

—Tunnelling to Freedom: The Great Escape from Stalag Luft III. Yomtov, Nel. 2017. (Great Escapes of World War II Ser.). (ENG.). 32p. (J). (gr. 3-9). pap. 7.95 *(978-1-5157-3536-6(2))*; lib. bdg. 31.32 *(978-1-5157-3531-1(1))* Capstone. (Capstone Pr.).

—U. S. Ghost Army: The Master Illusionists of World War II. Yomtov, Nel. 2019. (Amazing World War II Stories Ser.). (ENG.). 32p. (J). (gr. 3-9). pap. 7.95 *(978-1-5435-7551-4(X)*, 141083); lib. bdg. 34.65 *(978-1-5435-7316-9(9)*, 140621) Capstone.

—Writing History: Bronze Age. Ganeri, Anita. ed. 2019. (Writing History Ser.). 32p. (J). (gr. 5-7). 16.99 *(978-1-4451-5312-4(2)*, Franklin Watts) Hachette Children's Group GBR. Dist: Hachette Bk. Group.

—You Choose: Prehistoric Survival. Braun, Eric Mark et al. 2020. (You Choose: Prehistoric Survival Ser.). (ENG.). (J). (gr. 3-7). 130.60 *(978-1-5435-7410-4(6)*, 29359); pap., pap., pap. 27.80 *(978-1-4966-5834-0(5)*, 29945) Capstone.

Valencia, Esau Andrade. Un Tiempo Perfecto para Sonar. Sáenz, Benjamin Alire. 2008. (SPA.). 40p. (J). (gr. 1-4). 17.95 *(978-1-933693-01-9(0))* Cinco Puntos Pr.

Valente, Christa. A Giraffe for a Pet, 1 vol. Gray, Elizabeth. 2010. 16p. 24.95 *(978-1-4489-6515-1(2))* PublishAmerica, Inc.

Valente, Gianna Josephina & Valente, Peter Isaiah. Passed Away: Helping Young Children with Expressions of Family Loss - Adult Guide Included. Overstreet, Karen LaFaye. 2018. (ENG.). pap. 7.99 *(978-1-7324653-6-7(3))* Hom, Jonathan.

Valente, Peter Isaiah, jt. illus. see Valente, Gianna Josephina.

Valentin, Jeannette. The Frog That Went to the Moon. Guardado, Maria. 32p. (J). (gr. 3-18). 16.00 *(978-0-9710860-6-7(0))* Libros, Encouraging Cultural Literacy.

Valentina, Marina. Lost in the Roses. Valentina, Marina. 2007. 24p. (J). (gr. -1-1). 14.95 *(978-1-60108-014-1(X))* Red Cygnet Pr.

Valentine. Dina the Deaf Dinosaur. Addabbo, Carole. 2005. 32p. (J). pap. 19.95 *(978-1-889262-92-5(7))* Hannacroix Creek Bks., Inc.

Valentine, Allison. The Bubble Wrap Queen. Cook, Julia. 2008. (ENG.). 32p. (J). (gr. -1-3). pap. 9.95 *(978-1-931636-83-4(4))* National Ctr. For Youth Issues.

—Melvin the Magnificent Molar. Cook, Julia & Jana, Laura. 2010. (ENG.). 32p. (J). pap. 9.95 *(978-1-931636-74-2(5))* National Ctr. For Youth Issues.

—Soda Pop Head. Cook, Julia. 2011. (ENG.). (J). (gr. -1-3). pap. 9.95 *(978-1-931636-77-3(X))* National Ctr. For Youth Issues.

Valentine, Luke. Mary Margaret Mcmickle & the Fabulous Dragon. Sparer, E. G. 2019. (ENG.). 68p. (J). pap. 19.00 *(978-0-578-44135-1(7))* Hom, Jonathan.

Valentine, Luna. The Exceptional Maggie Chowder. Lute, Renee Beauregard. 2020. (ENG.). 256p. (J). (gr. 3-7). 16.99 ***(978-0-8075-3678-0(4)**,* 0807536784) Whitman, Albert & Co.

Valentine, M. K. Save the Sleepless Slumbernots! Fantastik, B. 2013. 32p. *(978-1-4602-2777-0(8))* FriesenPress.

Valentine, Madeline. A Day for Skating. Sullivan, Sarah. 2019. 32p. (J). (gr. -1-2). 16.99 *(978-0-7636-9686-3(2))* Candlewick Pr.

—Little Red Henry. Urban, Linda. 2015. 40p. (J). (gr. -1-3). 16.99 *(978-0-7636-6176-2(7))* Candlewick Pr.

—A Lullaby of Summer Things. Ziarnik, Natalie. 2018. 40p. (J). (gr. -1-3). 17.99 *(978-1-101-93552-1(9)*, Schwartz & Wade Bks.) Random Hse. Children's Bks.

—Teddy's Favorite Toy. Trimmer, Christian. 2018. (ENG.). 40p. (J). (gr. -1-3). 17.99 *(978-1-4814-8079-6(0)*, Atheneum Bks. for Young Readers) Simon & Schuster Children's Publishing.

—1, 2, 3, Jump! Detlefsen, Lisl H. 2019. (ENG.). 40p. (J). 17.99 *(978-1-62672-681-9(7)*, 900170543) Roaring Brook Pr.

Valenza, Bryan, jt. illus. see Silas, Thony.

Valenzuela, Jennifer. Una Balsa Milagrosa. Mendez Gatica, Patricia. Nunez, Miguel Angel, ed. 2019. (SPA.). 42p. (J). pap. 12.99 ***(978-1-0871-4767-3(0))*** Independently Published.

Valenzuela, Roger. Paulie Pick Finds Studioland. Valenzuela, Roger. Valenzuela, Raquel, tr. from ENG. 2003.Tr. of Paulie Pick encuentra Estudiolandia. (SPA.). 32p. 20.00 *(978-0-944551-69-1(6))* Bk. Pubs. of El Paso.

Valer, Frantisek. The Buffalo & the Boat: Thathánka na Wáta. 2004. (DAK, ENG & SIO.). 18p. (J). 9.95 *(978-0-9761082-3-8(2))* Lakota Language Consortium, Inc.

—Pispiza WAN Wayawa Iyaye/Prairie Dog Goes to School. 2006. (DAK, ENG & SIO.). 24p. (J). (gr. -1-3). pap. 9.95 *(978-0-9761082-4-5(0))* Lakota Language Consortium, Inc.

Valeria, Leonova. Two Doors of Love. Nicoloro-Tanner, Nancy. Temptest, Aishia, ed. 2019. (ENG.). 28p. (J). (gr. k-6). 24.99 ***(978-0-578-53037-6(6))*** nicoloro-tanner, nancy.

Valerio, Geraldo. All Aboard for Dreamland! Harby, Melanie. 2012. (ENG.). 32p. (J). (gr. -1-k). 16.99 *(978-1-4424-3091-4(5)*, Simon & Schuster Bks. For Young Readers) Simon & Schuster Bks. For Young Readers.

Valério, Geraldo. Conejito: A Folktale from Panama. MacDonald, Margaret Read. 2015. (ENG.). 32p. (J). (gr. -1-3). pap. 8.95 (978-1-939160-96-6(0)) August Hse. Pubs., Inc.
—Do You Have a Cat? Spinelli, Eileen. 2010. (ENG.). 32p. (J). (gr. -1-3). 16.00 (978-0-8028-5351-6(X), Eerdmans Bks For Young Readers) Eerdmans, William B. Publishing Co.
—Do You Have a Dog? Spinelli, Eileen. 2011. (ENG.). 26p. (J). 16.00 (978-0-8028-5387-5(0), Eerdmans Bks For Young Readers) Eerdmans, William B. Publishing Co.
—Do You Have a Hat? Spinelli, Eileen. 2004. (ENG.). 40p. (J). (gr. -1-3). 17.99 (978-0-689-86253-3(9), Simon & Schuster Bks. For Young Readers) Simon & Schuster Bks. For Young Readers.
—Go to Sleep, Gecko! A Balinese Folktale. 2015. (ENG.). 32p. (J). (gr. -1-3). pap. 8.95 (978-1-939160-92-8(8)) August Hse. Pubs., Inc.
—It's Moving Day! Hickman, Pamela. 2008. 32p. (J). (gr. -1-2). 17.95 (978-1-55453-074-8(1)) Kids Can Pr., Ltd. CAN. Dist: Hachette Bk. Group.
—Nannycatch Chronicles, 1 vol. Heneghan, James & McBay, Bruce. 2005. (ENG.). 96p. (J). (gr. 1-3). 16.95 (978-1-896580-56-2(4)) Tradewind Bks. CAN. Dist: Orca Bk. Pubs. USA.
—Surf War! A Folktale from the Marshall Islands. MacDonald, Margaret Read. 2009. (ENG.). 32p. (J). (gr. -1-3). 16.95 (978-0-87483-889-3(4)) August Hse. Pubs., Inc.
—When You Are Happy. Spinelli, Eileen. 2006. (ENG.). 40p. (J). (gr. -1-3). 19.99 (978-0-689-86251-9(2), Simon & Schuster Bks. For Young Readers) Simon & Schuster Bks. For Young Readers.
Valério, Geraldo & Valério, Geraldo. It's Moving Day! Hickman, Pamela. 2012. (ENG.). 32p. (J). (gr. -1-2). pap. 8.95 (978-1-55453-929-1(3)) Kids Can Pr., Ltd. CAN. Dist: Hachette Bk. Group.
Valério, Geraldo, jt. illus. see Valério, Geraldo.
Valero, Andrew. Snail. Gliane, Al. 2019. (ENG.). 32p. (J). pap. 9.99 (978-1-7132-9433-7(8)) Independently Published.
Vales, Chrissie. Sophie's Tales: Overcoming Obstacles. Paticoff, Melanie. 2012. 42p. 25.95 (978-0-9851575-6-2(9)) Sophie's Tales, LLC.
Valgeirsson, Helgi. Raven Saga. Valgeirsson, Helgi. 2019. (Yuletide Lads Ser.: Vol. 4). (ENG.). 58p. (J). pap. 14.99 (978-1-7111-7578-2(1)) Independently Published.
—The Yuletide Lads, Coloring Book: An Insight into the Universe of the Yuletide Lads. Valgeirsson, Helgi. 2020. (Yuletide Lads Ser.: Vol. 7). (ENG.). 50p. (J). pap. 9.99 (978-1-6611-3484-6(X)) Independently Published.
—The Yuletide Lads up to Their Neck. . A Summer Adventure. Valgeirsson, Helgi. 2019. (Yuletide Lads Ser.: Vol. 5). (ENG.). 50p. (J). pap. 14.99 (978-1-7091-5946-6(4)) Independently Published.
Valiant, Kristi. Be Brave, Willa Bean! Little Wings #2. Galante, Cecilia. 2011. (Little Wings Ser.: 2). 112p. (J). (gr. 1-4). 4.99 (978-0-375-86948-8(4), Random Hse. Bks. for Young Readers) Random Hse. Children's Bks.
—Cora Cooks Pancit. Lazo Gilmore, Dorina K. 2014. (ENG.). 32p. (J). pap. 10.95 (978-1-885008-48-0(1)); (gr. -1-3). 17.95 (978-1-885008-35-0(X)) Lee & Low Bks., Inc. (Shen's Bks.).
—Dancing Dreams. Ohrt, Kate. 2014. (ENG.). 18p. (J). bds. 8.99 (978-1-4494-3554-7(8)) Andrews McMeel Publishing.
—The Goodbye Cancer Garden, 1 vol. Matthies, Jana. 2011. (ENG.). 32p. (J). (gr. 1-3). 16.99 (978-0-8075-2994-2(X), 080752994X) Whitman, Albert & Co.
—The Goodbye Cancer Garden. Matthies, Janna. 2013. (AV2 Fiction Readalong Ser.). (ENG.). (J). (gr. k-3). 34.28 (978-1-62127-895-5(6), AV2 by Weigl) Weigl Pubs., Inc.
—Nelly Takes New York: A Little Girl's Adventures in the Big Apple. Pataki, Allison & Myers, Marya. 2019. (Big City Adventures Ser.). (ENG.). 48p. (J). (gr. -1-3). 17.99 (978-1-5344-2504-0(7), Simon & Schuster Bks. For Young Readers) Simon & Schuster Bks. For Young Readers.
—Oliver's First Christmas. Accord Publishing Staff. 2012. (ENG.). 14p. (J). (-k). bds. 5.99 (978-1-4494-2245-5(4)) Andrews McMeel Publishing.
—The One & Only Willa Bean, 4. Galante, Cecilia. 2013. (Little Wings Ser.: No. 4). (ENG.). 112p. (J). (gr. 1-3). lib. bdg. 17.44 (978-0-375-96950-8(0)) Random House Publishing Group.
—The One & Only Willa Bean. Galante, Cecilia. 2012. (Little Wings Ser.: 4). 112p. (J). (gr. 1-4). pap. 4.99 (978-0-375-86950-1(6), Random Hse. Bks. for Young Readers) Random Hse. Children's Bks.
—Pretty Minnie in Hollywood. Steel, Danielle. 2016. 32p. (J). (gr. -1-2). 17.99 (978-0-553-53755-0(5), Doubleday Bks. for Young Readers) Random Hse. Children's Bks.
—Pretty Minnie in Paris. Steel, Danielle. 2014. 32p. (J). (gr. -1-2). 17.99 (978-0-385-37000-4(8), Doubleday Bks. for Young Readers) Random Hse. Children's Bks.
Valko, Diane, et al. Biology: Overhead Transparencies - Student Reproducibles - Assessment Tools. Kupperstein, Joel. Hults, Alaska, ed. 2003. (Upper-Grade Science Transparency Ser.). 32p. (J). (gr. 5-8). pap. 9.99 (978-1-57471-977-2(7), 2799) Creative Teaching Pr., Inc.
Valko, Diane & Corbin, Hillam. Science Fair Projects & Activities: Creative Ideas Using Easy-to-Find Materials. McFarren, Kathleen & Graf, Mike. 2005. 144p. (J). pap. 18.99 (978-0-88160-376-7(7), LW407, Learning Works, The) Creative Teaching Pr., Inc.
Valko, Diane & Willardson, David. Leap into Literacy Winter. Geiser, Traci Ferguson & Boylan, Maureen McCourt. Cernek, Kim, ed. 2003. 160p. (J). (gr. k-2). pap. 17.99 (978-1-57471-958-1(0), 3374) Creative Teaching Pr., Inc.
Valla, Susanne. The Dog That Barked Bear. Ehnes, Tiffany. (ENG.). (J). 2018. 40p. pap. 14.95 (978-1-943419-66-1(3)); 2016. 19.95 (978-1-943419-38-8(8)) Prospective Pr.
Vallageas, Coralie. Shhh! the Farmer Is Sleeping! 22 Button Sound Book. Fowler, Cherry. 2017. (Early Bird Sound Bks.). (ENG.). 16p. (J). (gr. -1-k). bds. 16.99 (978-1-68052-240-2(X), 1002260) Cottage Door Pr.
Vallarino, Elisa & Sacco, Mauro. The Wall: A Timeless Tale. Macri, Giancarlo et al. 2019. (ENG.). 40p. (J). 16.99 (978-1-64124-038-3(5), 0383) Fox Chapel Publishing Co., Inc.
Vallarino, Sacco. Maps of the World: An Illustrated Children's Atlas of Adventure, Culture, & Discovery. Lavagno, Enrico. 2018. 136p. (J). (gr. 1-5). 24.99 (978-0-316-41770-9(X), Black Dog & Leventhal Pubs. Inc.) Hachette Bks.
Valle, Elizabeth. Daughters of the Sky. Lihn, Henry. 2018. (ENG.). 40p. (J). 19.99 (978-0-692-09239-2(0)) Hank of America Consulting LLC.
—The Joy Monster. Lihn, Henry. 2018. (ENG.). 42p. (J). 19.99 (978-0-692-15867-8(7)) Hank of America Consulting LLC.
Valleau, Gailon. Batchawana Silly Stuff. Hearn, Emily. 2011. (978-1-897475-70-6(5)) Hidden Brook Pr.
—Cool Blues. Daulby, Joan. 2018. (ENG.). 36p. (J). pap. (978-1-989322-03-1(4)) Pine Lake Bks.
Vallecchi, Alessandro, et al, photos by. Maddy's Amazing African Birthday, 1 vol. Williams, Megan K. 2009. (ENG., 32p. (J). (gr. 1-3). 12.95 (978-1-897187-47-0(5)) Second Story Pr. CAN. Dist: Orca Bk. Pubs. USA.
Vallejo, Esperanza. Cuentos de la Selva. Quiroga, Horacio. 2004.Tr. of Jungle Stories. (SPA.). 186p. (YA). (gr. -1-7). pap. (978-958-30-0458-2(8)) Panamericana Editorial.
—Mambro Se Fue a la Guerra. Arciniegas, Triunfo. 2004. (Primer Acto: Teatro Infantil y Juvenil Ser.). (SPA.). 66p. (J). (gr. -1-7). pap. (978-958-30-0434-6(0)) Panamericana Editorial.
—Memorias de Angola: Cuentos Africanos. Gomez, Luis Marcelino. 2004. (Letras Latinoamericanas Ser.). (SPA.). 131p. (YA). (gr. -1-7). per. (978-958-30-1257-0(2)) Panamericana Editorial.
—La Ventana y la Bruja. Arciniega, Triunfo. 2003. (Primer Acto: Teatro Infantil y Juvenil Ser.). (SPA.). 61p. (J). (gr. -1-7). pap. (978-958-30-0995-2(4)) Panamericana Editorial.
Vallejo, Francis. Jazz Day: The Making of a Famous Photograph. Orgill, Roxane. 2016. 66p. (J). (gr. 3-7). 18.99 (978-0-7636-6954-6(7)) Candlewick Pr.
Vallejo Franco, Beatriz. Ino y Samo. Vallejo Franco, Beatriz. 2019. (SPA.). 102p. (J). pap. 19.80 (978-1-7928-2252-0(9)) Independently Published.
Vallejo, Monse & Jiale, Kuang. Heung Bu & Nol Bu: Chinese & English. Smit, Fb. 2020. (ENG.). 54p. (J). (gr. 1-4). 17.95 (978-1-7327679-5-9(5)) Eeyagi Tales.
Vallejo, Monserratt & Kuang, Jiale. Heung Bu & Nol Bu: A Folktale in English & Korean. Smit, Fb. 2019. (ENG.). 54p. (J). pap. 12.95 (978-1-7327679-4-2(7)) Eeyagi Tales.
Valliant, Kristi. Ethan, a Soccer Player for Jesus. Cunningham, Elaine. 2010. 32p. (J). (978-0-8341-2486-8(6)) Beacon Hill Pr. of Kansas City.
Valliant, Regina & Lunzer, Lee. Judy Garland Cut-Out Dolls. Valliant, Regina. 2007. (ENG.). 16p. pap. 12.00 (978-0-9790668-9-4(1)) Paper Studio Pr.
Vallorani, Giorgio, jt. illus. see Tyminski, Lori.
Valter Ribeiro Pinto, Analizio. A Rainha. Dowgan, S. 2019. (Aventuras Heroicas: Uma Trilogia Infanto-Juvenil Ser.: Vol. 3). (POR.). 150p. (J). pap. 7.99 (978-1-6876-8779-1(X)) Independently Published.
Valverde, Mikel. The Adventures of Shola. Atxaga, Bernardo & Costa, Margaret Jull. 2014. (ENG.). 220p. (J). (gr. 4-7). 20.00 (978-1-78269-009-2(3), Pushkin Press) Steerforth Pr.
—El Juego del Cambia-Cambia. MacHado, Ana Maria & Machado, Ana María. 2004.Tr. of Change-Change Game. (SPA.). (J). 6.50 (978-84-348-8716-9(9)) SM Ediciones ESP. Dist: Lectorum Pubns., Inc.
—Mi Hermana Aixa. Torras, Meri. (SPA.). 120p. (J). (gr. 3-5). (978-84-246-5915-8(5), GL6491) La Galera, S.A. Editorial ESP. Dist: Lectorum Pubns., Inc.
—Shola & the Lions. Atxaga, Bernardo & Costa, Margaret Jull. 2016. (ENG.). 56p. (J). (gr. 2-5). pap. 9.99 (978-1-78269-064-1(6), Pushkin Children's Bks.) Steerforth Pr.
Vamos, Lesley. Best Ever Pranks (and More!) by Frankie Fish & Drew Bird. Helliar, Peter. 2017. (Frankie Fish Ser.). (ENG.). 128p. (J). (gr. 2-4). pap. 9.99 (978-1-76050-077-1(1)) Hardie Grant Egmont Pty, Ltd. AUS. Dist: Independent Pubs. Group.
—Frankie Fish & the Great Wall of Chaos, Volume 2. Helliar, Peter. 2018. (Frankie Fish Ser.: 2). (ENG.). 288p. (J). (gr. 2-4). pap. 11.99 (978-1-76050-082-5(8)) Hardie Grant Egmont Pty, Ltd. AUS. Dist: Independent Pubs. Group.
—Frankie Fish & the Viking Fiasco, Volume 3. Helliar, Peter. 2018. (Frankie Fish Ser.: 3). (ENG.). 288p. (J). (gr. 2-4). pap. 11.99 (978-1-76050-083-2(6)) Hardie Grant Egmont Pty, Ltd. AUS. Dist: Independent Pubs. Group.
—Frankie Fish & the Wild Wild Mess, Volume 5. Helliar, Peter. 2020. (Frankie Fish Ser.: 5). (ENG.). 272p. (J). (gr. 2-4). pap. 11.99 (978-1-76050-290-4(1)) Hardie Grant Egmont Pty, Ltd. AUS. Dist: Independent Pubs. Group.
Vamos, Lesley. Lou Lou & Pea & the Mural Mystery. Diamond, Jill. 2016. (Lou Lou & Pea Ser.). (ENG.). 272p. (J). 16.99 (978-0-374-30295-5(2), 900152881, Farrar, Straus & Giroux (BYR)) Farrar, Straus & Giroux.
—Lou Lou & Pea & the Mural Mystery. Diamond, Jill. 2018. (Lou Lou & Pea Ser.). (ENG.). 272p. (J). pap. 7.99 (978-1-250-14373-0(X), 900180548) Square Fish.
—My Dad Is a Superhero. Brown, Ruby. 2014. (J). (978-1-4351-5488-9(6)) Barnes & Noble, Inc.
—Punky Brewster: Punky Power. Sellner, Joelle. 2016. (ENG.). 256p. pap. 12.99 (978-1-941302-19-4(X), Lion Forge) Oni Pr., Inc.
Vampari, Ari. Nessie Feiert Weihnachten. Wynter, Isla. Kurz, Annette, tr. 2019. (GER.). 32p. (J). pap. 9.99 (978-1-7106-4823-2(6)) Independently Published.
Van Allsburg, Chris. Just a Dream. Van Allsburg, Chris. 2014. 48p. pap. 9.00 (978-1-61003-182-0(2)) Center for the Collaborative Classroom.
—The Polar Express Movie Shadowbook: An Interactive Shadow-Casting Bedtime Story. Van Allsburg, Chris. Zemeckis, Robert & Broyles, William, Jr. 2006. 12p. (J). (gr. 4-18). reprint ed. 13.00 (978-1-4223-5172-7(6)) DIANE Publishing Co.
van Amelsfort, Barbara. Yoga Exercises for Teens: Developing a Calmer Mind & a Stronger Body. Purperhart, Helen. Evans, Amina Marix, tr. from DUT. 2008. (SmartFun Activity Bks.). (ENG.). 160p. (J). (gr. 4). spiral bd. 19.95 (978-0-89793-504-3(7), Hunter Hse.) Turner Publishing Co.
—Yoga Exercises for Teens: Developing a Calmer Mind & a Stronger Body. Purperhart, Helen. Marix Evans, Amina, tr. 2008. (SmartFun Activity Bks.). (ENG.). 160p. (J). (gr. 4-12). pap. 14.95 (978-0-89793-503-6(9), Hunter Hse.) Turner Publishing Co.
—The Yoga Zoo Adventure: Animal Poses & Games for Little Kids. Purperhart, Helen. 2008. (SmartFun Activity Bks.). (ENG.). 160p. (J). (gr. k-2). pap. 14.95 (978-0-89793-505-0(5), Hunter Hse.) Turner Publishing Co.
Van, Annelies. Sheep Out of Water. Rabou, John. 2020. (ENG.). 32p. (J). (gr. k-2). 17.99 (978-988-8342-00-6(2), Minedition) Neugebauer, Michael (Publishing) Limited HKG. Dist: Penguin Random Hse. LLC.
Van Bakkum, Ramona. The Spider Who Was an Outsider. Harvey, Sarah. 2018. (ENG.). 44p. (J). pap. (978-0-9952045-4-6(3)) Tiny Tiger Publishing.
Van Buren, Nancy. Flash & Fancy an Otter Adventure on the Waccamaw River. Doran, Christine L. & Doran, Thomas P. 2015. (Flash & Fancy Ser.). (ENG.). 36p. (J). (gr. 1-5). 16.95 (978-0-692-04518-3(X)) Flash & Fancy Bks.
Van Buskirk, Steve. Dinosaurs. Van Buskirk, Steve. 2007. (Dinosaurs Pop-up Bks.). (J). (gr. -1-3). 4.99 (978-1-59340-379-9(8)) Grandreams Bks., Inc.
Van Campen, Elizabeth. Nope, No Lemons! Jajou, Rafee. 2018. (ENG.). 28p. (J). (gr. 2-4). pap. 13.45 (978-0-692-19219-1(0)) Jajou, Rafee.
Van Cleve, Barbara, photos by. Holding the Reins: A Ride Through Cowgirl Life. Talbert, Marc. 2003. 112p. (J). (gr. 3-7). 16.99 (978-0-06-029255-3(5)) HarperCollins Pubs.
van de Beek, Mariella. Go, Percy, Go! Priess, Brett. 2017. (ENG.). 24p. (J). (gr. -1-k). pap. (978-1-925386-90-5(2), Brolly Bks.) Borghesi & Adam Pubs. Pty Ltd.
van de Liejgraaf, Deborah. Anik & Yukon. Wehrmeijer, Annelien. 2015. (My Best Friend & Me Ser.). (ENG.). 10p. (J). (gr. k-1). bds. 6.99 (978-0-7641-6763-8(4), B.E.S. Publishing) Peterson's.
—Emma & Bo. Wejmeijer, Annelien. 2013. (My Best Friend & Me Ser.). (ENG.). 10p. (J). (gr. k-1). bds. 7.99 (978-0-7641-6635-8(2), B.E.S. Publishing) Peterson's.
—James & Cooper Finger Puppet Book. Vermeulen, Mariska. 2016. (My Best Friend & Me Ser.). (ENG.). 10p. (J). (gr. -1-k). bds. 6.99 (978-0-7641-6830-7(4), B.E.S. Publishing) Peterson's.
—Lily & Dolly. Wejmeijer, Annelien. 2013. (My Best Friend & Me Ser.). (ENG.). 10p. (J). (gr. k-1). bds. 6.99 (978-0-7641-6636-5(0), B.E.S. Publishing) Peterson's.
van Deelen, Fred. Dark Tracks. Gregory, Philippa. (Order of Darkness Ser.: 4). (ENG.). 320p. (YA). (gr. 9). 2019. pap. 12.99 (978-1-4424-7694-3(X)); 2018. 19.99 (978-1-4424-7693-6(1)) Simon Pulse. (Simon Pulse).
—Fools' Gold. Gregory, Philippa. 2014. (Order of Darkness Ser.: 3). (ENG.). 384p. (YA). (gr. 9). pap. 9.99 (978-1-4424-7691-2(5)); 19.99 (978-1-4424-7690-5(7)) Simon Pulse. (Simon Pulse).
—Stormbringers. Gregory, Philippa. 2013. (Order of Darkness Ser.: 2). (ENG.). 336p. (YA). (gr. 9). pap. 9.99 (978-1-4424-7688-2(5)); 17.99 (978-1-4424-7687-5(7)) Simon Pulse. (Simon Pulse).
van Deelen, Fred & Taylor, Sally. Changeling. Gregory, Philippa. 2013. (Order of Darkness Ser.: 1). (ENG.). 352p. (YA). (gr. 9). pap. 9.99 (978-1-4424-5345-6(1), Simon Pulse) Simon Pulse.
van Deelen, Fred, jt. illus. see Taylor, Sally.
Van Den Berg, Helen. Quake! Six Point Five: The Cat Survived. Veldkamp, Debby. 2004. (J). lib. bdg. 16.95 (978-1-930401-25-9(6)) Central Coast Bks./Pr.
van der Does, Ellis. Tabitha & Magoo Dress up Too. Tea, Michelle. 2020. (Drag Queen Story Hour Bks.). 48p. (J). 17.95 (978-1-936932-77-1(6)) Feminist Pr. at The City Univ. of New York.
van der Linde, Jori. Counting on Birds. Riggs, Kate. 2017. (ENG.). 14p. (J). (gr. -1 — 1). bds. 8.99 (978-1-56846-300-1(6), Creative Education) Creative Co., The.
van der Linde, Jori. Knowing the Name of a Bird. Yolen, Jane. 2020. (ENG.). 32p. (J). (gr. 1-3). 18.99 (978-1-56846-349-0(9), Creative Editions) Creative Co., The.
van der Linde, Jori. Phrases of the Moon: Lunar Poems. Lewis, J. Patrick. 2018. (ENG.). 32p. (J). (gr. 3-5). 18.99 (978-1-56846-311-7(1), Creative Editions) Creative Co., The.
van der Linde, Jori. Teatime. Stone, Tiffany. 2017. 32p. (J). 15.95 (978-1-927018-67-5(6)) Simply Read Bks. CAN. Dist: Ingram Publisher Services.
Van Der Linden, Gerdien. Monstersong. Stein, Mathilde. 2007. (ENG.). 32p. (J). (gr. -1-3). 15.95 (978-1-932425-90-1(X)) Lemniscaat USA.
Van Der Linden, Martijn. Hush Little Turtle. Rinck, Maranke. 2011. (ENG.). 24p. (J). (gr. -1). bds. 8.95 (978-1-935954-06-4(7), 9781935954064) Lemniscaat USA.
Van Der Meide, Shelley. Snap! Watson, Art. 2020. (ENG.). 30p. (J). pap. 13.95 (978-1-64670-500-9(9)) Covenant Bks.
Van Der Merwe, Stefan. ABC of All the Questions We Never Dare to Ask. 2010. (ENG.). 144p. per. (978-0-7957-0154-2(3)) NB Pubs. Ltd.
Van der Paardt, Melissa. Mimi & Shu in I'll Race You! Trimmer, Christian. 2015. (ENG.). 40p. (J). (gr. -1-3). 17.99 (978-1-4814-2330-4(4)) Simon & Schuster Children's Publishing.
van der Paardt, Melissa. Simon's New Bed. Trimmer, Christian. 2015. (ENG.). 32p. (J). (gr. -1-3). 17.99 (978-1-4814-3019-7(X)) Simon & Schuster Children's Publishing.
Van Der Put, Klaatje. Little Butterfly: Finger Puppet Book: (Finger Puppet Book for Toddlers & Babies, Baby Books for First Year, Animal Finger Puppets) Chronicle Books & ImageBooks. 2006. (Little Finger Puppet Board Bks.: FING). (ENG.). 12p. (J). (gr. -1 — 1). bds. 6.99 (978-0-8118-5645-4(3)) Chronicle Bks. LLC.
—Little Kitten: Finger Puppet Book: (Finger Puppet Book for Toddlers & Babies, Baby Books for First Year, Animal Finger Puppets) Chronicle Books & ImageBooks. 2007. (Little Finger Puppet Board Bks.: FING). (ENG.). 12p. (J). (gr. -1 — 1). bds. 6.99 (978-0-8118-5770-3(0)) Chronicle Bks. LLC.
—Little Puppy: Finger Puppet Book: (Puppet Book for Baby, Little Dog Board Book) Chronicle Books & ImageBooks. 2007. (Little Finger Puppet Board Bks.: FING). (ENG.). 12p. (J). (gr. -1 — 1). bds. 6.99 (978-0-8118-5771-0(9)) Chronicle Bks. LLC.
van der Sterre, Johanna. Feivel's Flying Horses. Hyde, Heidi Smith. 2010. (ENG.). 32p. (J). (gr. k-4). lib. bdg. 17.95 (978-0-7613-3957-1(4)); Vol. pap. 7.95 (978-0-7613-3959-5(0), 9780761339595) Lerner Publishing Group. (Kar-Ben Publishing).
—The First Christmas Present. Summerer, Marilyn. 2009. 32p. (J). (gr. -1). 14.99 (978-0-7586-1663-0(5)) Concordia Publishing Hse.
—Furniture Refinishing in A Class by Yourself. Van Slyke, Marge. Lambert, Barbara, ed. 2004. 91p. per. 9.95 (978-0-9755548-0-7(8)) Log Cabin Bks.
—Mendel's Accordion. Hyde, Heidi Smith. 2007. 30p. (J). (gr. 3-7). lib. bdg. 16.95 (978-1-58013-212-1(X), Kar-Ben Publishing) Lerner Publishing Group.
—The Parable of the Lost Sheep. Miller, Claire. 2008. (Arch Bks.). 16p. (J). (gr. k-4). pap. 1.99 (978-0-7586-1455-1(1)) Concordia Publishing Hse.
—Star of Wonder. Hinkle, Cynthia. 2005. (Arch Bks.). (ENG.). 16p. (J). 1.99 (978-0-7586-0724-9(5)) Concordia Publishing Hse.
Van Der Sterre, Johanna. W Is for Waterfall: An Alphabet of the Finger Lakes Region of New York State. Easterbrook, Aileen. 2018. (ENG.). 48p. (J). (gr. k-4). 24.95 (978-1-7321614-1-2(0)) Seneca Lake Pr.
van der Sterre, Johnanna. Why Do I Have to Make My Bed? Bradford, Wade. 2011. (ENG.). 32p. (J). (gr. -1-2). 16.99 (978-1-58246-327-8(1), Tricycle Pr.) Random Hse. Children's Bks.
Van Deun, Kim. The Black River Chronicles: Eye of the Observer. Fiction, Digital. Zanoni, Anne, ed. 2019. (Black River Academy Ser.: Vol. 3). (ENG.). 318p. (J). pap. (978-1-989414-12-5(5)) Digital Science Fiction.
Van Dijk, Jerianne. Emma Lea's First Tea Party. Donaldson, Babette. 2007. (ENG.). 32p. (J). 16.95 (978-0-9792612-0-6(1)) Blue Gate Bks.
—Emma Lea's Magic Teapot. Donaldson, Babette. 2007. 32p. (J). lib. bdg. 16.95 (978-0-9792612-1-3(X)) Blue Gate Bks.
—My Personal Story in ABCs. Alt, Susan. 2004. 32p. (J). pap. 15.95 (978-1-891846-27-4(2), TBPERSONAL, Twins Bks.) Sterling Investments I, LLC DBA Twins Magazine.
Van Doninck, Sebastiaan. Foreman Farley Has a Backhoe. Goebel, Jenny. 2014. (Penguin Core Concepts Ser.). 32p. (J). (gr. -1-k). 4.99 (978-0-448-46398-8(9), Grosset & Dunlap) Penguin Young Readers Group.
—It Started with a Big Bang: The Origin of Earth, You & Everything Else. Bal, Floor. 2019. (ENG.). 34p. (J). (gr. k-3). 17.99 (978-1-5253-0255-8(8)) Kids Can Pr., Ltd. CAN. Dist: Hachette Bk. Group.
van Doorn, Sandra. Sing to the Moon. Isdahl, Nansubuga Nagadya. 2018. 40p. (J). (gr. k-2). 17.99 (978-1-911373-39-1(0)) Lantana Publishing GBR. Dist: Lerner Publishing Group.
Van Draanen, Wendelin. Sammy Keyes & the Art of Deception. Van Draanen, Wendelin. 2004. (Sammy Keyes Ser.: Bk. 8). pap. 36.95 incl. audio (978-1-59519-001-7(5)); pap. 54.95 incl. audio compact disk (978-1-59519-003-1(1)) Live Oak Media.
—Sammy Keyes & the Search for Snake Eyes. Van Draanen, Wendelin. 2003. (Sammy Keyes Ser.: Bk. 7). pap. 36.95 incl. audio (978-1-59112-273-9(2)); pap. 54.95 incl. audio compact disk (978-1-59112-281-4(3)) Live Oak Media.
Van Dusen, Chris. Eugenia Lincoln & the Unexpected Package: Tales from Deckawoo Drive, Volume Four. Dicamillo, Kate. 2017. (Tales from Deckawoo Drive Ser.: 4). 112p. (J). (gr. 1-4). 14.99 (978-0-7636-7881-4(3)) Candlewick Pr.
—Eugenia Lincoln & the Unexpected Package: Tales from Deckawoo Drive, Volume Four. DiCamillo, Kate. 2018. (Tales from Deckawoo Drive Ser.: 4). 112p. (J). (gr. 1-4). pap. 5.99 (978-1-5362-0353-0(X)) Candlewick Pr.
—Even Monsters Go to School. Wheeler, Lisa. 2019. (ENG.). 32p. (J). (gr. -1-3). 17.99 (978-0-06-236642-9(4), Balzer & Bray) HarperCollins Pubs.
—Even Monsters Need to Sleep. Wheeler, Lisa. 2017. (ENG.). 32p. (J). (gr. -1-3). 17.99 (978-0-06-236640-5(8)) HarperCollins Pubs.
—Francine Poulet Meets the Ghost Raccoon. Dicamillo, Kate. ed. 2016. (Tales from Deckawoo Drive Ser.: 2). (ENG.). 112p. (J). (gr. 1-4). 16.00 (978-0-606-39088-0(X)) Turtleback.
—Francine Poulet Meets the Ghost Raccoon: Tales from Deckawoo Drive, Volume Two. DiCamillo, Kate. (Tales from Deckawoo Drive Ser.: 2). 112p. (J). (gr. 1-4). 2016. pap. 5.99 (978-0-7636-9088-5(0)); 2015. 12.99 (978-0-7636-6886-0(9)) Candlewick Pr.
—Leroy Ninker Saddles Up. Dicamillo, Kate. 2014. (Tales from Deckawoo Drive Ser.: Vol. 1). 96p. (J). (gr. 1-4). 12.99 (978-0-7636-6339-1(5)) Candlewick Pr.
—Leroy Ninker Saddles Up: Tales from Deckawoo Drive, Volume One. DiCamillo, Kate. 2015. (Tales from Deckawoo Drive Ser.: 1). 96p. (J). (gr. 1-4). pap. 5.99 (978-0-7636-8012-1(5)) Candlewick Pr.
—Mercy Watson Boxed Set: Adventures of a Porcine Wonder, 6 vols. DiCamillo, Kate. 2011. (Mercy Watson Ser.). (ENG.). (J). (gr. k-3). pap. 29.99 (978-0-7636-5709-3(3)) Candlewick Pr.

V

—Mercy Watson Fights Crime. DiCamillo, Kate. (Mercy Watson Ser.: 3). (ENG.). 80p. (J). 2010. (gr. 1-4). pap. 6.99 *(978-0-7636-4952-4(X))*; 2006. (gr. k-3). 15.99 *(978-0-7636-2590-0(6))* Candlewick Pr.

—Mercy Watson Goes for a Ride. Dicamillo, Kate. 2006. (Mercy Watson Ser.: 2). (ENG.). 80p. (J). (gr. k-4). 15.99 *(978-0-7636-2332-6(6))* Candlewick Pr.

—Mercy Watson Goes for a Ride. DiCamillo, Kate. 2009. (Mercy Watson Ser.: 2). (ENG.). 80p. (J). (gr. 1-4). pap. 6.99 *(978-0-7636-4505-2(2))* Candlewick Pr.

—Mercy Watson: Princess in Disguise. Dicamillo, Kate. 2007. (Mercy Watson Ser.: 4). (ENG.). 80p. (J). (gr. 1-4). 14.99 *(978-0-7636-3014-0(4))* Candlewick Pr.

—Mercy Watson: Princess in Disguise. DiCamillo, Kate. 2010. (Mercy Watson Ser.: 4). (ENG.). 80p. (J). (gr. 1-4). pap. 6.99 *(978-0-7636-4951-7(1))* Candlewick Pr.

—Mercy Watson: Something Wonky This Way Comes. DiCamillo, Kate. (Mercy Watson Ser.: 6). 96p. (J). (gr. 1-4). 2011. pap. 6.99 *(978-0-7636-5232-6(6))*; 2009. (ENG.). 15.99 *(978-0-7636-3644-9(4))* Candlewick Pr.

—Mercy Watson Thinks Like a Pig. DiCamillo, Kate. (Mercy Watson Ser.: 5). (ENG.). 80p. (J). (gr. 1-4). 2011. pap. 6.99 *(978-0-7636-5231-9(8))*; 2008. 15.99 *(978-0-7636-3265-6(1))* Candlewick Pr.

—Mercy Watson to the Rescue. DiCamillo, Kate. (Mercy Watson Ser.: 1). (ENG.). 80p. (J). 2009. (gr. 1-4). pap. 6.99 *(978-0-7636-4504-5(4))*; 2005. (gr. k-4). 15.99 *(978-0-7636-2270-1(2))* Candlewick Pr.

—A Piglet Named Mercy. Dicamillo, Kate. 2019. (ENG.). 32p. (J). (gr. -1-2). 18.99 *(978-0-7636-7753-4(1))* Candlewick Pr.

—President Taft Is Stuck in the Bath. Barnett, Mac. 2016. 32p. (J). (gr. -1-3). 7.99 *(978-0-7636-6556-2(8))* Candlewick Pr.

—Stella Endicott & the Anything-Is-Possible Poem: Tales from Deckawoo Drive, Volume Five. DiCamillo, Kate. 2020. (Tales from Deckawoo Drive Ser.). 96p. (J). (gr. 1-4). 14.99 *(978-1-5362-0180-2(4))* Candlewick Pr.

—Where Are You Going, Baby Lincoln? Tales from Deckawoo Drive, Volume Three. Dicamillo, Kate. (Tales from Deckawoo Drive Ser.: 3). 112p. (J). (gr. 1-4). 2017. pap. 5.99 *(978-0-7636-9758-7(3))*; 2016. 14.99 *(978-0-7636-7311-6(0))* Candlewick Pr.

—3 Adventures on Deckawoo Drive: 3 Books In 1. DiCamillo, Kate. 2019. (Tales from Deckawoo Drive Ser.). 304p. (J). (gr. 1-4). pap. 9.99 *(978-1-5362-0864-1(7))* Candlewick Pr.

Van Dusen, Chris. The Circus Ship. Van Dusen, Chris. 40p. (J). (gr. -1-3). 2015. 7.99 *(978-0-7636-5592-1(9))*; 2009. (ENG.). 17.99 *(978-0-7636-3090-4(X))* Candlewick Pr.

—Hattie & Hudson. Van Dusen, Chris. 2017. 40p. (J). (gr. -1-3). 16.99 *(978-0-7636-6545-6(2))* Candlewick Pr.

—If I Built a Car. Van Dusen, Chris. 2005. 32p. (J). (gr. -1-k). 17.99 *(978-0-525-47400-5(5))*, Dutton Books for Young Readers) Penguin Young Readers Group.

—If I Built a Car. Van Dusen, Chris. 2007. (gr. -1-3). lib. bdg. 17.00 *(978-0-7569-8149-5(2))* Perfection Learning Corp.

—If I Built a School. Van Dusen, Chris. 2019. (ENG.). 32p. (J). (gr. k-3). 17.99 *(978-0-525-55291-8(X)*, Dial Bks) Penguin Young Readers Group.

—Randy Riley's Really Big Hit. Van Dusen, Chris. 32p. (J). (gr. -1-3). 2016. 7.99 *(978-0-7636-8774-8(X))*; 2012. 16.99 *(978-0-7636-4946-3(5))* Candlewick Pr.

Van Dusen, Ross. Crocka Dog in the Evil Forest. 2015. (J). *(978-1-936744-54-1(6)*, Rio Grande Bks.) LPD Pr.

—How Crocka Dog Came to Be. 2015. (J). *(978-1-936744-39-8(2))* LPD Pr.

—Lyle Got Stuck in a Tree & Became an Honorary Fireman. 2015. (J). *(978-1-936744-45-9(7)*, Rio Grande Bks.) LPD Pr.

—What Makes a Rainbow? 2015. (J). *(978-1-936744-32-9(5)*, Rio Grande Bks.) LPD Pr.

—What Makes a Snowflake? 2015. (J). *(978-1-936744-48-0(1)*, Rio Grande Bks.) LPD Pr.

—What Makes the Lightning? 2016. (J). *(978-1-943681-03-7(1)*, Rio Grande Bks.) LPD Pr.

Van-Dyke-Hempenstall, Clare. Ryan the Gnome Adventures: The Garden Man & the Big Bang! Yeo, Julia. 2018. (ENG.). 34p. (J). pap. *(978-1-912021-89-5(7)*, Nightingale Books) Pegasus Elliot Mackenzie Pubs.

Van Eeden, Wesley. My ABC's. Ensley, John W., 2nd. 2017. (ENG.). (J). 16.99 *(978-1-62676-875-8(7)*, Melanin Origins, LLC) Grivante Pr.

Van Fleet, Mara. Little Color Fairies. Van Fleet, Mara. 2012. (ENG.). 16p. (J). (gr. -1-1). 15.99 *(978-1-4424-3434-9(1)*, Simon & Schuster/Paula Wiseman Bks.) Simon & Schuster/Paula Wiseman Bks.

—Mama's Pajamas. Van Fleet, Mara. 2017. (ENG.). 12p. (J). (gr. -1 — 1). 15.99 *(978-1-4814-7975-2(X)*, Simon & Schuster Bks. For Young Readers) Simon & Schuster Bks. For Young Readers.

—Night-Night, Princess. Van Fleet, Mara. 2014. (ENG.). 16p. (J). (gr. -1-1). 14.99 *(978-1-4424-8646-1(5)*, Simon & Schuster/Paula Wiseman Bks.) Simon & Schuster/Paula Wiseman Bks.

—Three Little Mermaids. Van Fleet, Mara. 2011. (ENG.). 16p. (J). (gr. -1-k). 17.99 *(978-1-4424-1286-6(0)*, Simon & Schuster/Paula Wiseman Bks.) Simon & Schuster/Paula Wiseman Bks.

Van Fleet, Matthew. Chomp Goes the Alligator. Van Fleet, Matthew. 2018. (ENG.). 26p. (J). (gr. -1). 19.99 *(978-1-5344-2677-1(9)*, Simon & Schuster/Paula Wiseman Bks.) Simon & Schuster/Paula Wiseman Bks.

—Dance. Van Fleet, Matthew. 2017. (ENG.). 16p. (J). (gr. -1). 19.99 *(978-1-4814-8707-8(8)*, Simon & Schuster/Paula Wiseman Bks.) Simon & Schuster/Paula Wiseman Bks.

—Heads. Van Fleet, Matthew. 2010. (ENG.). 18p. (J). (gr. -1-1). 19.99 *(978-1-4424-0379-6(9)*, Simon & Schuster/Paula Wiseman Bks.) Simon & Schuster/Paula Wiseman Bks.

—Lick! Van Fleet, Matthew. 2013. (ENG.). 14p. (J). (gr. -1-1). 9.99 *(978-1-4424-6049-2(0)*, Simon & Schuster/Paula Wiseman Bks.) Simon & Schuster/Paula Wiseman Bks.

—Monday the Bullfrog: A Huggable Puppet Concept Book about the Days of the Week. Van Fleet, Matthew. 2010. (ENG.). 20p. (J). (gr. -1). 24.99 *(978-1-4424-0958-3(4)*, Simon & Schuster/Paula Wiseman Bks.) Simon & Schuster/Paula Wiseman Bks.

—Munch! Van Fleet, Matthew. 2013. (ENG.). 14p. (J). (gr. -1-1). 9.99 *(978-1-4424-9425-1(5)*, Simon & Schuster/Paula Wiseman Bks.) Simon & Schuster/Paula Wiseman Bks.

—Oscar the Octopus: A Book about the Months of the Year. Van Fleet, Matthew. 2019. (ENG.). 14p. (J). (gr. -1-3). 17.99 *(978-1-5344-5237-4(0)*, Simon & Schuster/Paula Wiseman Bks.) Simon & Schuster/Paula Wiseman Bks.

—Sniff! Van Fleet, Matthew. 2012. (ENG.). 14p. (J). (gr. -1-1). 9.99 *(978-1-4424-6050-8(4)*, Simon & Schuster/Paula Wiseman Bks.) Simon & Schuster/Paula Wiseman Bks.

—Van Fleet Alphabet Heads: Alphabet; Heads. Van Fleet, Matthew. ed. 2013. (ENG.). 38p. (J). (gr. -1-2). 39.99 *(978-1-4424-8448-1(9)*, Simon & Schuster/Paula Wiseman Bks.) Simon & Schuster/Paula Wiseman Bks.

—Van Fleet Sniff! Lick! Munch! Sniff!; Lick!; Munch! Van Fleet, Matthew. ed. 2013. (ENG.). 42p. (J). (gr. -1-1). 29.99 *(978-1-4424-9509-8(X)*, Simon & Schuster/Paula Wiseman Bks.) Simon & Schuster/Paula Wiseman Bks.

van Frankenhuyzen, Gijsbert. Bambi's First Day. Salten, Felix. 2008. (ENG.). 32p. (J). (gr. k-6). 15.95 *(978-1-58536-422-0(3))* Sleeping Bear Pr.

—The Edmund Fitzgerald: The Song of the Bell. Wargin, Kathy-jo. 2003. (ENG.). 48p. (J). (gr. k-6). 17.95 *(978-1-58536-126-7(7))* Sleeping Bear Pr.

—F Is for Friendship: A Quilt Alphabet. Wilbur, Helen L. 2011. (Sleeping Bear Alphabets Ser.). (ENG.). 32p. (J). (gr. 1-4). lib. bdg. 16.95 *(978-1-58536-532-6(7)*, 202215) Sleeping Bear Pr.

—Friend on Freedom River. Whelan, Gloria. 2004. (Tales of Young Americans Ser.). (ENG.). 48p. (J). (gr. 1-4). 19.99 *(978-1-58536-222-6(0)*, 202052) Sleeping Bear Pr.

—Itsy Bitsy & Teeny Weeny. Van Frankenhuyzen, Robbyn Smith. 2009. (Hazel Ridge Farm Stories Ser.). (ENG.). 48p. (J). (gr. 1-4). 16.95 *(978-1-58536-417-6(7)*, 202152) Sleeping Bear Pr.

—Kelly of Hazel Ridge. Van Frankenhuyzen, Robbyn Smith. 3rd rev. ed. 2006. (Hazel Ridge Farm Stories Ser.). (ENG.). 32p. (J). (gr. k-5). 17.95 *(978-1-58536-268-4(9))* Sleeping Bear Pr.

—L Is for Lincoln: An Illinois Alphabet. Wargin, Kathy-jo. 2004. (Discover America State by State Ser.). (ENG.). 40p. (J). (gr. 1-3). pap. 7.95 *(978-1-58536-250-9(6)*, 202283) Sleeping Bear Pr.

—The Legend of Leelanau. Wargin, Kathy-jo. 2003. (Great Lakes Legend Ser.). (ENG.). 40p. (J). 17.95 *(978-1-58536-150-2(X))* Sleeping Bear Pr.

Van Frankenhuyzen, Gijsbert. The Legend of Michigan. Noble, Trinka Hakes. 2006. (Legend (Sleeping Bear) Ser.). (ENG.). 40p. (J). (gr. -1-3). 17.95 *(978-1-58536-278-3(6))* Sleeping Bear Pr.

van Frankenhuyzen, Gijsbert. The Legend of the Petoskey Stone. Wargin, Kathy-jo. 2004. (Great Lakes Legend Ser.). (ENG.). 40p. (J). 17.95 *(978-1-58536-217-2(4))* Sleeping Bear Pr.

—Mackinac Bridge: The Story of the Five-Mile Poem. Whelan, Gloria. 2006. (Tales of Young Americans Ser.). (ENG.). 40p. (J). (gr. 1-4). 17.95 *(978-1-58536-283-7(2)*, 202094) Sleeping Bear Pr.

—Saving Samantha: A True Story. Smith van Frankenhuyzen, Robbyn. 2004. (Hazel Ridge Farm Stories Ser.). (ENG.). 32p. (J). 17.95 *(978-1-58536-220-2(4))* Sleeping Bear Pr.

—T Is for Titanic: A Titanic Alphabet. Shoulders, Debbie & Shoulders, Michael. 2011. (ENG.). 32p. (gr. k-5). 17.95 *(978-1-58536-176-2(3))* Sleeping Bear Pr.

—W Is for Woof: A Dog Alphabet. Strother, Ruth. 2008. (ENG.). 40p. (J). (gr. k-6). 17.95 *(978-1-58536-343-8(X))* Sleeping Bear Pr.

Van Frankenhuyzen, Gijsbert, jt. illus. see Geister, David.

van Garderen, Ilse. A Beautiful Day. Pearce, Margaret. 2012. 24p. pap. 10.95 *(978-1-61633-251-8(4))* Guardian Angel Publishing, Inc.

van Genechten, Guido. Floppy's Friends. van Genechten, Guido. 2004. (ENG & POL.). 28p. (J). bds. *(978-1-84444-659-9(X))* Mantra Lingua.

—Kangaroo Christine. van Genechten, Guido. 2005. 24p. (J). (gr. 3-7). pap. 6.95 *(978-1-58925-396-4(5))* Tiger Tales.

—Snowy's Special Secret. van Genechten, Guido. 2005. 32p. (J). (gr. -1-2). 15.95 *(978-1-58925-049-9(4))* Tiger Tales.

Van Gool, A. A Child's Treasury of Bible Stories. Lefevre, A. M. et al. 2003. (ENG.). 124p. (J). (gr. 4-6). 16.95 *(978-1-58087-072-6(4))* Ignatius Pr.

van Haeringen, Annemarie. Leave a Message in the Sand: Poems about Giraffes, Bongos, & Other Creatures with Hooves. Dumon Tak, Bibi. 2020. 64p. (J). ***(978-0-8028-5548-0(2)***, Eerdmans Bks For Young Readers) Eerdmans, William B. Publishing Co.

Van Haeringen, Annemarie. 1 2 3 Little Donkey. Kromhout, Rindert. Nagelkerke, Bill, tr. from DUT. 2013. 24p. (J). (gr. -1-1). 14.95 *(978-1-877579-34-9(3))* Gecko Pr. NZL. Dist: Lerner Publishing Group.

van Haeringen, Annemarie. My Mama. van Haeringen, Annemarie. 2020. (ENG.). 32p. (J). (gr. -1-k). 17.99 *(978-1-77657-267-0(X))* Gecko Pr. NZL. Dist: Lerner Publishing Group.

van Heerden, Marjorie. Peter Pan & Laurie. Heese, Marié. 2019. (ENG.). (J). pap. 23.00 *(978-1-4853-1004-4(0))* Protea Boekhuis ZAF. Dist: Casemate Pubs. & Bk. Distributors, LLC.

van Hemeldonck, Tineke. Dragon Fire. De Kockere, Geert & Dom, An. 2015. 32p. (J). (gr. -1-k). 16.99 *(978-1-63220-599-5(8)*, Sky Pony Pr.) Skyhorse Publishing Co., Inc.

Van Hemeldonck, Tineke. Piglet Bo Can Do Anything! De Kockere, Geert. 2015. 32p. (J). (gr. -1-k). 16.99 *(978-1-63220-600-8(5)*, Sky Pony Pr.) Skyhorse Publishing Co., Inc.

—Piglet Bo Is Not Scared! De Kockere, Geert. 2015. 32p. (J). (gr. -1-k). 16.99 *(978-1-63450-182-8(9)*, Sky Pony Pr.) Skyhorse Publishing Co., Inc.

Van Hertbruggen, Anton. The Dog That Nino Didn't Have. Van de Vendel, Edward. 2015. 34p. (J). 17.00 *(978-0-8028-5451-3(6)*, Eerdmans Bks For Young Readers) Eerdmans, William B. Publishing Co.

Van Holle, Sarah. Folk Tales for Future Dreamers. Wibaux, Peter. Free, Ana, ed. 2018. (ENG.). 80p. (J). pap. 14.95 *(978-1-7326530-0-9(3))* Longline Imprints Ltd.

Van Hoorn, Aurea. An Open & Loving Heart: Gentle Words of Self-Endearment. Hirabayashi, Suzanne. 2003. 51p. 12.95 *(978-0-87516-701-5(2)*, Devorss Pubns.) DeVorss & Co.

Van Horn, William, jt. illus. see Gray, Jonathan.

Van Hout, Mies. Brave Ben. Stein, Mathilde. 2006. (ENG.). 32p. (J). (gr. 2-6). 15.95 *(978-1-932425-64-2(0))* Lemniscaat USA.

—The Child Cruncher. Stein, Mathilde. 2008. (ENG.). 32p. (J). (gr. -1-3). 16.95 *(978-1-59078-635-2(1))* Lemniscaat USA.

—Lovey & Dovey. Van Lieshout, Elle & Van Os, Erik. 2009. (ENG.). 32p. (J). (gr. k-2). 16.95 *(978-1-59078-660-4(2))* Lemniscaat USA.

—Mine! Stein, Mathilde. 2007. (ENG.). 26p. (J). (gr. -1-3). 16.95 *(978-1-59078-506-5(1))* Lemniscaat USA.

Van Kampen, Megan. Dedicated Dads: Stepfathers of Famous People. Hancock, Rusty. 2004. 138p. *(978-0-934981-12-5(4))* Lawells Publishing.

—Warm & Wonderful Stepmothers of Famous People. Wells, Sherry A. 2004. 131p. 20.00 *(978-0-934981-10-1(8))* Lawells Publishing.

van Kampen, Vlasta. Hip Hippos. Yolen, Jane. 2008. (ENG.). 18p. (J). bds. *(978-1-55470-009-7(4))* Me to We.

—Hoshmakaka. Thury, Fredrick H. 2003.Tr. of Last Straw. (SPA.). (J). (gr. 2-4). 13.56 *(978-84-8418-046-3(8))* Zendrera Zariquiey, Editorial ESP. Dist: Lectorum Pubns., Inc.

—One Hippo Hops. Yolen, Jane. 2008. (ENG.). 18p. (J). (gr. -1-k). bds. *(978-1-55470-007-3(8))* Me to We.

—Sad, Mad, Glad Hippos. Yolen, Jane. 2008. (ENG.). 18p. (J). (gr. -1-k). bds. *(978-1-55470-008-0(6))* Me to We.

—Under the Star: A Christmas Counting Story. Yolen, Jane. 2009. (ENG.). 24p. (J). (gr. -1-k). *(978-1-55470-201-5(1))* Me to We.

Van Kampen, Vlasta. Who Can?, 1 vol. Ghigna, Charles. 2018. (ENG.). 24p. (J). (gr. -1 — 1). bds. 9.95 *(978-1-4598-1369-4(3))* Orca Bk. Pubs. USA.

Van Leer, Brandon. Dream Girl, Dream! McCrary, Kayla T. 2018. (ENG.). 24p. (J). pap. 12.99 *(978-1-7246-7275-9(4))* CreateSpace Independent Publishing Platform.

Van Leeuwen, Corine. Stick Boy. Lewis, Elizabeth Connell. 2017. (ENG.). (J). (gr. k-5). 24.95 *(978-0-692-96815-4(6))* Nurturing Potential.

van Lieshout, Maria. Catching Kisses. Gibson, Amy. 2013. (ENG.). 32p. (J). (gr. -1-1). 16.99 *(978-0-312-37647-5(2)*, 900048480) Feiwel & Friends.

van Lindenhuizen, Eline. Good-Bye, Fish. Koppens, Judith. 2013. (Animal Square Ser.). 32p. (J). (gr. -1-k). 13.95 *(978-1-60537-153-5(X))* Clavis Publishing.

Van Lindenhuizen, Eline. My Body. Winters, Pierre. 2013. (Want to Know Ser.). (ENG.). 32p. (J). (gr. k-2). 16.95 *(978-1-60537-143-6(2))* Clavis Publishing.

van Lindenhuizen, Eline. Oops, I Dropped the Lemon Tart. Swerts, An. 2020. (ENG.). 48p. (J). (gr. 1). 17.95 ***(978-1-60537-579-3(9))*** Clavis Publishing.

van Lindenhuizen, Eline. Santa, Please Bring Me a Gnome. Swerts, An. 2017. 32p. (J). (gr. -1 — 1). 17.95 *(978-1-60537-275-4(7))* Clavis Publishing.

—Santa, Please Bring Me a Gnome. Swerts, An. 2017. (ENG.). 32p. (J). (gr. -1-2). pap. 9.95 *(978-1-60537-389-8(3))* Clavis ROM. Dist: Publishers Group West (PGW).

—The Seesaw. Koppens, Judith. 2013. (Animal Square Ser.). (ENG.). 32p. (J). (gr. -1-k). 13.95 *(978-1-60537-152-8(1))* Clavis Publishing.

—Sir Tim Has a Secret. Koppens, Judith. 2020. (Sir Tim Ser.). 32p. (J). (gr. -1). 17.95 *(978-1-60537-536-6(5))* Clavis Publishing.

—Sir Tim Is a Little Jealous. Koppens, Judith. 2019. (Sir Tim Ser.). 32p. (J). (ENG.). 17.95 *(978-1-60537-492-5(X))*; 9.95 *(978-1-60537-502-1(0))* Clavis Publishing.

Van Loon, Hendrik Willem & Price, Christine. Here & Now Story Book. Mitchell, Lucy Sprague. 2015. (ENG.). 256p. (J). (gr. k-3). pap. 7.99 *(978-0-486-79196-8(3))* Dover Pubns., Inc.

Van Norstrand, Kain. Dominic & the Secret Ingredient. Bonasia, Steve. 2012. (ENG.). 39p. (J). pap. 24.95 *(978-1-4327-9805-5(7))* Outskirts Pr., Inc.

Van Nutt, Robert. The Emperor & the Nightingale, 1 vol. Andersen, Hans. 2007. (Rabbit Ears-A Classic Tale Ser.).Tr. of Nattergalen. (ENG.). 44p. (J). (gr. 2-6). 28.50 *(978-1-59961-307-9(7)*, 12960, Picture Bk.) Spotlight.

—The Emperor's New Clothes, 1 vol. Andersen, Hans. 2005. (Rabbit Ears-A Classic Tale Ser.). (ENG.). 28p. (J). (gr. 2-6). 28.50 *(978-1-59197-746-9(0)*, 12937, Picture Bk.) Spotlight.

—The Firebird. Kessler, Brad. 2005. (Rabbit Ears-A Classic Tale Ser.). (ENG.). 36p. (J). (gr. 2-6). 28.50 *(978-1-59679-224-1(8)*, 12933, Picture Bk.) Spotlight.

—The Legend of Sleepy Hollow. Irving, Washington. 2005. (Rabbit Ears Ser.). 36p. (J). (gr. k-5). 25.65 *(978-1-59679-225-8(6))* Spotlight.

—The Ugly Duckling. Andersen, Hans. 2005. (Rabbit Ears-A Classic Tale Ser.). (ENG.). 42p. (J). (gr. 2-6). 28.50 *(978-1-59679-348-4(1)*, 12949, Picture Bk.) Spotlight.

Van Nutt, Robert & Bogdanovic, Toma. The Ugly Duckling. Van Nutt, Robert. 32p. (J). (gr. -1-3). 16.95 *(978-0-87592-055-9(1))* Scroll Pr., Inc.

Van Ommen, Sylvia. Sheep & Goat. Westera, Marleen. Forest-Flier, Nancy, tr. from DUT. 2006. (ENG.). 104p. (J). (gr. 2). 16.95 *(978-1-932425-81-9(0))* Lemniscaat USA.

Van Order, Laura & VonSeggen, Jon. Living Like a King's Kid. Van Dyke, Jan. rev. ed. 2003. 77p. (J). spiral bd. 30.00 *(978-1-58302-249-8(X))* Creative Ministry Solutions.

Van Patten, Bruce. Tales of Persia: Missionary Stories from Islamic Iran. Miller, William. 2005. 163p. per. 9.99 *(978-0-87552-615-7(2))* P & R Publishing.

Van Patter, Bruce. Grandpa's Box: Retelling the Biblical Story of Redemption. Meade, Starr. 2005. 286p. (J). (gr. 3-7). per. 13.99 *(978-0-87552-866-3(X))* P & R Publishing.

—Heidi. Spyri, Johanna. Hunsicker, Ranelda Mack, ed. 2006. (Classics for Young Readers Ser.). 287p. (J). (gr. 4-7). per. 11.99 *(978-0-87552-739-0(6))* P & R Publishing.

Van Rheenen, Barbara. Dinosaurs. Douglas, Jozua. 2012. (Want to Know Ser.). (ENG.). 30p. (J). (gr. -1-2). 16.95 *(978-1-60537-136-8(X))* Clavis Publishing.

Van Scott, Bethany. Boomer's Criss-Cross Christmas. Van Scott, Miriam. 2019. (ENG.). 26p. (J). pap. 9.69 ***(978-1-6861-8324-9(0))*** Independently Published.

Van Severen, Joe. The Fall into Sin: Genesis 2-3 for Children. Sanders, Nancy I. 2004. (Arch Bks.). (ENG.). 16p. (J). 1.99 *(978-0-7586-0618-1(4))* Concordia Publishing Hse.

Van Slyke, Rebecca, jt. illus. see Davis, Katheryn.

Van Stockum, Hilda. A Day on Skates: The Story of a Dutch Picnic. Van Stockum, Hilda. 2007. 40p. (J). (gr. 1). 19.95 *(978-1-932350-18-0(7))* Bethlehem Bks.

Van Tine, Laura. Captain Tristan Am I. Sharp, Michael. 2009. 20p. (J). pap. *(978-1-897455-10-4(0))* Avatar Pubns., Inc.

—Vayda Jane Bean - Chocolate. Sharp, Michael. 2007. 20p. pap. *(978-1-897455-70-8(4))* Avatar Pubns., Inc.

—Vayda Jayne Bean - Vanilla. Sharp, Michael. 2007. 20p. (J). (gr. -1-3). pap. *(978-0-9780969-5-3(9))* Avatar Pubns., Inc.

Van Vynckt, Virginia & Giblin, Sheri, photos by. Wok Every Day: From Fish & Chips to Chocolate Cake -Recipes & Techniques for Steaming, Grilling, Deep-Frying, Smoking, Braising, & Stir-Frying in the World's Most Versatile Pan. Grunes, Barbara. 2003. (ENG., 224p. (gr. 8-17). pap. 24.95 *(978-0-8118-3195-6(7))* Chronicle Bks. LLC.

Van Wagoner, Traci. Candy Canes in Bethlehem. Van Scott, Miriam. 2012. (J). 7.95 *(978-0-8198-1606-1(X))* Pauline Bks. & Media.

—Cody & Grandpa's Christmas Tradition, 1 vol. Metivier, Gary. 2016. (ENG.). 32p. (J). (gr. k-3). 16.99 *(978-1-4556-2170-5(6)*, Pelican Publishing) Arcadia Publishing.

—Global Citizenship: Engage in the Politics of a Changing World. Knutson, Julie. 2020. (Inquire & Investigate Ser.). (ENG.). 128p. (YA). (gr. 7-9). 22.95 *(978-1-61930-933-3(5)*, c4fe7807-0db4-4fe0-8b29-582eddd42cc6); pap. 17.95 *(978-1-61930-936-4(X)*, 80c886bc-25ff-461a-90f3-011dc3397f39) Nomad Pr.

—The Mermaid's Gift, 1 vol. McAdam, Claudia Cangilla. 2015. (ENG.). 32p. (J). (gr. k-3). 16.99 *(978-1-4556-2108-8(0)*, Pelican Publishing) Arcadia Publishing.

—Ruth Asawa: A Sculpting Life, 1 vol. Schoettler, Joan. 2018. (ENG.). 32p. (gr. 1-4). 16.99 *(978-1-4556-2397-6(0)*, Pelican Publishing) Arcadia Publishing.

Van Wijk, Bert. Jungle Tales: An English Translation of Horacio Quiroga's Cuentos de la Selva. Gibert, Jimena & Cornum, Lindsey, eds. Zorrilla, Jeff, tr. from SPA. 2012.Tr. of Cuentos de la Selva. (ENG.). 87p. (J). 14.00 *(978-0-615-70807-2(2))* Jungle Tales.

Van Wright, Cornelius. The Great Eggscape, 1 vol. Glass, Susan. 2011. 32p. (J). (gr. k-5). (ENG.). 16.95 *(978-1-59572-261-4(0))*; pap. 6.95 *(978-1-59572-253-9(X))* Star Bright Bks., Inc.

—Hoorade Day!, 1 vol. Day, Nancy Raines. 2018. (ENG.). 32p. (J). *(978-1-59572-807-4(4))* Star Bright Bks., Inc.

—How Do You Get a Mouse to Smile?, 1 vol. Grubman, Bonnie. 2009. (ENG.). 32p. (J). (gr. -1-3). pap. 6.50 *(978-1-59572-167-9(3))* Star Bright Bks., Inc.

—In the Promised Land: Lives of Jewish Americans. Rappaport, Doreen. 2005. 32p. (J). (gr. k-4). lib. bdg. 16.89 *(978-0-06-059395-7(4))* HarperCollins Pubs.

—Sam y el Dinero de la Suerte. Chinn, Karen. 2003.Tr. of Sam & the Lucky Money. (SPA.). (J). *(978-1-58430-167-7(8))* Lee & Low Bks., Inc.

—Zachary's Dinnertime, 1 vol. Levinson, Lara. 2012. (ENG.). 32p. (J). 16.95 *(978-1-59572-329-1(3))*; pap. 6.95 *(978-1-59572-330-7(7))* Star Bright Bks., Inc.

Van Wright, Cornelius & Ha, Ying-Hwa. Willie Covan Loved to Dance. Shahan, Sherry. Van Wright, Cornelius & Ha, Ying-Hwa, trs. 2004. (J). 15.95 *(978-1-59034-445-3(6))*; pap. *(978-1-59034-580-1(0))* Mondo Publishing.

Van Wright, Cornelius & Hu, Ying-Hwa. Alicia's Happy Day, 1 vol. Starr, Meg. 2003. (ENG.). 32p. (J). pap. 5.95 *(978-1-932065-06-0(7))* Star Bright Bks., Inc.

—Alicia's Happy Day (Spanish/English), 1 vol. Starr, Meg. Fiol, Maria, tr. from ENG. 2007. (SPA & ENG.). 32p. (J). (gr. k-3). pap. 6.95 *(978-1-59572-116-7(9))* Star Bright Bks., Inc.

—Alicia's Happy Day (Spanish/English), 1 vol. Starr, Meg. Fiol, Maria, tr. 2007. (ENG.). 32p. (J). (gr. -1-3). 15.95 *(978-1-59572-115-0(0))* Star Bright Bks., Inc.

—Baby Flo: Florence Mills Lights up the Stage. Schroeder, Alan. 2012. (ENG.). 40p. (J). 18.95 *(978-1-60060-410-2(2))* Lee & Low Bks., Inc.

—ColorFull: Celebrating the Colors God Gave Us. Williamson, Dorena. 2018. (ENG.). 32p. (J). (gr. -1-2). 14.99 *(978-1-4627-7764-8(3)*, 005799075, B&H Kids) B&H Publishing Group.

—El día más feliz de Alicia, 1 vol. Starr, Meg. Fiol, Maria A., tr. from ENG. 2003.Tr. of Alicia's Happy Day. (SPA.). 32p. (J). pap. 5.95 *(978-1-932065-03-9(2))* Star Bright Bks., Inc.

—I Told You I Can Play! 2006. (ENM.). 32p. (J). 16.95 *(978-1-933491-06-6(X))* Just Us Bks., Inc.

—Jumping the Broom. Black, Sonia W. 2004. 32p. (J). lib. bdg. 15.00 *(978-1-4242-0234-8(5))* Fitzgerald Bks.

—Let's Read About — Ruby Bridges. Bridges, Ruby & Maccarone, Grace. 2003. (Scholastic First Biographies Ser.). (J). *(978-0-439-51362-3(6))* Scholastic, Inc.

—Princess Grace. Hoffman, Mary. 2008. (ENG.). 32p. (J). (gr. -1-3). 18.99 *(978-0-8037-3260-5(0)*, Dial Bks) Penguin Young Readers Group.

—Sam y el Dinero de la Suerte. Chinn, Karen. 2003.Tr. of Sam & the Lucky Money. (SPA.). 32p. (J). pap. 10.95 *(978-1-58430-168-4(6))* Lee & Low Bks., Inc.

—Singing for Dr. King. Scholastic, Inc. Staff & Medearis, Angela Shelf. 2004. (Just for You Ser.). (ENG.). 32p. (gr.

k-3). pap. 3.99 *(978-0-439-56855-5(2)*, Teaching Resources) Scholastic, Inc.

Van Wright, Cornelius, jt. illus. see Hu, Ying-Hwa.

Van Wyk, Chris. Mr Hare Meets Mr Mandela. Bouma, Paddy. 2018. (ENG.). 32p. (J). pap. 11.95 *(978-1-4314-2438-2(2))* Jacana Media ZAF. Dist: Independent Pubs. Group.

Van Wyk, Hanri. First Picture Animals. Brooks, Felicity & Litchfield, Jo. 2008. (First Picture Board Bks.). 12p. (J). (gr. -1). bds. 11.99 *(978-0-7945-1831-8(1)*, Usborne) EDC Publishing.

—First Picture Dinosaurs. Taplin, Sam. 2007. (First Picture Board Bks.). 12p. (J). bds. 11.99 *(978-0-7945-1752-6(8)*, Usborne) EDC Publishing.

—Usborne Lift & Look Emergency Vehicles. Brooks, Felicity. 2007. (Lift & Look Board Bks.). 10p. (J). (gr. -1-k). bds. 9.99 *(978-0-7945-1596-6(7)*, Usborne) EDC Publishing.

—Usborne Lift & Look Tractors. Brooks, Felicity. 2007. (Lift & Look Board Bks.). 10p. (J). (gr. -1-k). bds. 9.99 *(978-0-7945-1597-3(5)*, Usborne) EDC Publishing.

Van Wyk, Hanri & Newell, Keith. First Picture Trucks. MMStudios, photos by. Helbrough, Emma & Brooks, Felicity. 2007. (First Picture Board Bks.). 16p. (J). (gr. -1-k). bds. 11.99 *(978-0-7945-1454-9(5)*, Usborne) EDC Publishing.

Van Wyk, Rupert. Arif Goes Shopping Pink a Band. al-Qadi, Charlotte. 2016. (Cambridge Reading Adventures Ser.). (ENG.). 16p. pap. 7.37 *(978-1-316-60810-4(7))* Cambridge Univ. Pr.

—Collins Big Cat Phonics for Letters & Sounds - Smart Gadgets: Band 06/Orange, Bd. 6. Nelson, Jo. 2018. (Collins Big Cat Phonics Ser.). (ENG.). 24p. (J). pap. 6.99 *(978-0-00-825177-2(0))* HarperCollins Pubs. Ltd. GBR. Dist: Independent Pubs. Group.

—The Pirate Pie Ship. Guillain, Adam et al. 2014. (Race Ahead with Reading Ser.). (ENG.). 32p. (J). (gr. 2-2). *(978-0-7787-1309-8(1))*; pap. *(978-0-7787-1368-5(7))* Crabtree Publishing Co.

—The Pirates on Holiday. Guillain, Adam et al. 2014. (Race Ahead with Reading Ser.). (ENG.). 32p. (J). (gr. 2-2). *(978-0-7787-1311-1(3))* Crabtree Publishing Co.

—Small, White Mice. Mackey, Cindy. 2018. (ENG.). 56p. (J). (gr. k-4). pap. 7.50 *(978-0-9990993-9-1(6))* Cyrano Bks.

van Wyk, Rupert. The Vanishing Rainforest. Platt, Richard. 2007. (ENG.). 32p. (J). pap. 16.95 *(978-0-7112-2170-3(7)*, White Lion Publishing) Quarto Publishing Group UK GBR. Dist: Hachette UK Distribution.

—The Vanishing Rainforest. Platt, Richard. 2003. (ENG.). 32p. (YA). *(978-0-7112-1960-1(5))* ReiseArt Buchhandlung GmbH.

van Zeyl, Marjan. Daisy the Hungry Duck, 30 vols. van Dort, Evelien. 2020. (ENG.). 12p. (J). 9.95 *(978-1-78250-634-8(9))* Floris Bks. GBR. Dist: Consortium Bk. Sales & Distribution.

Van Zeyl, Marjan. Goodnight. 2007. (ENG.). 10p. (J). (gr. -1-1). *(978-0-946206-61-2(9))* Wynestones Pr.

—Little Red Riding-Hood: A Grimm's Fairy Tale, 44 vols. Grimm, Wilhelm K. & Grimm, Jacob. Lawson, Polly, tr. 2008. (ENG.). 20p. (J). (gr. -1-3). *(978-0-86315-622-9(3))* Floris Bks.

Van Zyl, Lucius. My Dad Tried to Rob the Tooth Fairy. Van Zyl, Tertius. 2020. (ENG.). 26p. (J). pap. 6.00 ***(978-1-6540-0262-6(3))*** Independently Published.

Van Zyle, Daniel. Flight of the Golden Plover: The Amazing Migration Between Hawaii & Alaska. Miller, Debbie S. 2011. (ENG.). 32p. pap. 11.95 *(978-1-60223-151-1(6))* Univ. of Alaska Pr.

Van Zyle, Jon. Arctic Lights, Arctic Nights. Miller, Debbie S. 2007. (ENG.). 32p. (J). (gr. k-4). pap. 8.99 *(978-0-8027-9636-3(2)*, 900042471, Bloomsbury USA Childrens) Bloomsbury Publishing USA.

—Douggie: The Playful Pup Who Became a Sled Dog Hero. Flowers, Pam. 2008. (ENG.). 32p. (J). (gr. k-3). 15.95 *(978-0-88240-654-1(X))*; pap. 11.99 *(978-0-88240-655-8(8))* West Margin Pr. (Alaska Northwest Bks.).

—The Eyes of Gray Wolf. London, Jonathan. 2016. (ENG.). 32p. (J). (gr. k-3). pap. 10.99 *(978-1-943328-72-7(2)*, West Winds Pr.) West Margin Pr.

—Gone Again Ptarmigan. London, Jonathan. 2013. (ENG.). 32p. (J). pap. 12.95 *(978-1-60223-204-4(0))* Univ. of Alaska Pr.

—Honey Paw & Lightfoot. London, Jonathan. 2014. (ENG.). 32p. (J). 16.99 *(978-1-941821-10-7(3)*, Alaska Northwest Bks.) West Margin Pr.

—Kayuktuk: An Arctic Quest. Heinz, Brian J. 2004. (J). pap. 6.95 *(978-0-936335-09-4(2))*; 14.95 *(978-0-936335-08-7(4))* Ballyhoo BookWorks, Inc.

—A King Salmon Journey. Miller, Debbie S. & Eiler, John H. 2014. (ENG.). 44p. 15.95 *(978-1-60223-230-3(X))*; 32p. pap. 12.95 *(978-1-60223-231-0(8))* Univ. of Alaska Pr.

—Little Puffin's First Flight. London, Jonathan. 2016. (ENG.). 32p. (J). (gr. k-3). 10.99 *(978-0-88240-924-5(7)*, Alaska Northwest Bks.) West Margin Pr.

—Mardy Murie Did! Grandmother of Conservation. McDaniel, Jequita Potts. 2011. (J). *(978-1-58979-525-9(3))* Taylor Trade Publishing.

—Ollie's First Year. London, Jonathan. 2014. (ENG.). 32p. (J). 15.95 *(978-1-60223-228-0(8))* Univ. of Alaska Pr.

—A Polar Bear Journey. Miller, Debbie S. 2005. (ENG.). 32p. (J). (gr. 1-4). pap. 8.99 *(978-0-8027-7715-7(5)*, 9780802777157, Bloomsbury USA Childrens) Bloomsbury Publishing USA.

—Raven & River. Carlstrom, Nancy White. 2011. (ENG.). 32p. pap. 12.95 *(978-1-60223-150-4(8))* Univ. of Alaska Pr.

—The Seasons of Little Wolf. London, Jonathan. (ENG.). 32p. (J). (gr. k-3). 2016. pap. 11.99 *(978-1-941821-74-9(X))*; 2014. 16.99 *(978-1-941821-06-0(5))* West Margin Pr. (West Winds Pr.).

—Survival at 40 Below. Miller, Debbie S. 2012. (ENG.). 40p. (J). (gr. 2-5). lib. bdg. 24.94 *(978-0-8027-9816-9(0)*, 9780802798169) Walker & Co.

—What's a Shrew to You? Shields, Mary & Grace, Susan. 2008. (J). *(978-0-9618348-7-6(0))* Pyrola Publishing.

—A Woolly Mammoth Journey. Miller, Debbie S. 2010. (ENG.). 32p. (J). pap. 9.95 *(978-1-60223-098-9(6))* Univ. of Alaska Pr.

Van Zyle, Jon. The Great Serum Race: Blazing the Iditarod Trail. Van Zyle, Jon. Miller, Debbie S. 2006. (ENG.). 40p. (J). (gr. 2-7). pap. 9.99 *(978-0-8027-7723-2(6)*, 900036652, Bloomsbury USA Childrens) Bloomsbury Publishing USA.

VanArsdale, Anthony. The Boxcar Children Great Adventure 5-Book Set. 2017. (Boxcar Children Great Adventure Ser.). (ENG.). 768p. (J). (gr. 1-5). 34.95 *(978-0-8075-0693-6(1)*, 807506931) Whitman, Albert & Co.

—The Call of the Wild, 1 vol. London, Jack. 2010. (Calico Illustrated Classics Ser.). (ENG.). 112p. (J). (gr. 2-5). 29.93 *(978-1-60270-742-9(1)*, 3985, Calico Chapter Bks.) ABDO Publishing Co.

—The Clue in the Papyrus Scroll. 2017. (Boxcar Children Great Adventure Ser.: 2). (ENG.). 160p. (J). (gr. 1-5). 12.99 *(978-0-8075-0698-1(2)*, 807506982); 6.99 *(978-0-8075-0699-8(0)*, 807506990) Whitman, Albert & Co.

—The Detour of the Elephants. Warner, Gertrude Chandler. 2017. (Boxcar Children Great Adventure Ser.: 3). (ENG.). 144p. (J). (gr. 1-5). 6.99 *(978-0-8075-0685-1(0)*, 807506850); 12.99 *(978-0-8075-0684-4(2)*, 807506842) Whitman, Albert & Co.

—Journey on a Runaway Train. 2017. (Boxcar Children Great Adventure Ser.: 1). (ENG.). 160p. (J). (gr. 1-5). 6.99 *(978-0-8075-0696-7(6)*, 807506966); 12.99 *(978-0-8075-0695-0(8)*, 807506958) Whitman, Albert & Co.

—The Khipu & the Final Key. 2017. (Boxcar Children Great Adventure Ser.: 5). (ENG.). 144p. (J). (gr. 1-5). 6.99 *(978-0-8075-0682-0(6)*, 807506826); 12.99 *(978-0-8075-0681-3(8)*, 807506818) Whitman, Albert & Co.

—Last of the Mohicans, 1 vol. Cooper, James Fenimore. 2010. (Calico Illustrated Classics Ser.: No. 1). (ENG.). 112p. (J). (gr. 2-5). 29.93 *(978-1-60270-708-5(1)*, 3969, Calico Chapter Bks.) ABDO Publishing Co.

VanArsdale, Anthony. Mystery at Camp Survival. 2020. (Boxcar Children Mysteries Ser.). (ENG.). 128p. (J). (gr. 1-5). 12.99 ***(978-0-8075-0760-5(1)***, 807507601); pap. 6.99 ***(978-0-8075-0766-7(0)***, 807507660) Whitman, Albert & Co.

VanArsdale, Anthony. The Mystery at the Calgary Stampede. 2015. 104p. (J). *(978-1-4806-9406-4(1))* Whitman, Albert & Co.

VanArsdale, Anthony. The Mystery of the Forgotten Family. 2020. (Boxcar Children Mysteries Ser.). (ENG.). 128p. (J). (gr. 1-5). 12.99 ***(978-0-8075-0768-1(7)***, 807507687); pap. 6.99 ***(978-0-8075-0769-8(5)***, 807507695) Whitman, Albert & Co.

VanArsdale, Anthony. The Mystery of the Grinning Gargoyle. Warner, Gertrude Chandler. 2014. (Boxcar Children Mysteries Ser.: 137). (ENG.). 128p. (J). (gr. 1-5). pap. 5.99 *(978-0-8075-0893-0(4)*, 807508934) Whitman, Albert & Co.

—The Mystery of the Soccer Snitch. Warner, Gertrude Chandler. 2014. (Boxcar Children Mysteries Ser.: 136). (ENG.). 128p. (J). (gr. 1-5). pap. 5.99 *(978-0-8075-0896-1(9)*, 807508969) Whitman, Albert & Co.

—The Power down Mystery. Warner, Gertrude Chandler. 2019. (Boxcar Children Mysteries Ser.: 153). (ENG.). 128p. (J). (gr. 1-5). 12.99 *(978-0-8075-0757-5(1)*, 807507571); pap. 6.99 *(978-0-8075-0758-2(X)*, 080750758X) Whitman, Albert & Co.

Vanarsdale, Anthony. Sacajawea. Norwich, Grace. 2012. (I Am Ser.). (ENG.). 128p. (J). (gr. 3-7). pap. 5.99 *(978-0-545-40574-4(2)*, Scholastic Paperbacks) Scholastic, Inc.

VanArsdale, Anthony. Science Fair Sabotage. 2020. (Boxcar Children Mysteries Ser.). (ENG.). 128p. (J). (gr. 1-5). 12.99 ***(978-0-8075-0792-6(X)***, 080750792X); 6.99 ***(978-0-8075-0798-8(9)***, 0807507989) Whitman, Albert & Co.

VanArsdale, Anthony. Secret on the Thirteenth Floor. Warner, Gertrude Chandler. 2019. (Boxcar Children Mysteries Ser.: 152). (ENG.). 128p. (J). (gr. 1-5). 12.99 *(978-0-8075-0754-4(7)*, 807507547); pap. 6.99 *(978-0-8075-0755-1(5)*, 807507555) Whitman, Albert & Co.

—The Shackleton Sabotage. 2017. (Boxcar Children Great Adventure Ser.: 4). (ENG.). 160p. (J). (gr. 1-5). 12.99 *(978-0-8075-0687-5(7)*, 807506877); 6.99 *(978-0-8075-0688-2(5)*, 807506885) Whitman, Albert & Co.

VanArsdale, Anthony. The Skeleton Key Mystery. 2020. (Boxcar Children Mysteries Ser.). (ENG.). 128p. (J). (gr. 1-5). 6.99 ***(978-0-8075-0790-2(3)***, 0807507903); 12.99 ***(978-0-8075-0789-6(X)***, 080750789X) Whitman, Albert & Co.

VanArsdale, Anthony. The Sleepy Hollow Mystery. 2015. 111p. (J). *(978-1-4806-9407-1(X))* Whitman, Albert & Co.

—White Fang, 1 vol. London, Jack. 2011. (Calico Illustrated Classics Ser.: No. 3). (ENG.). 112p. (J). (gr. 2-5). 29.93 *(978-1-61641-112-1(0)*, 4031, Calico Chapter Bks.) ABDO Publishing Co.

VanBibber, Jodi. Bible Story Concepts for Fours & Fives: A Unique Blend of Bible Concepts & Preschool Skills. VanBibber, Jodi. 2004. 265p. (J). cd-rom 69.95 *(978-0-9755818-1-0(3)*, BSC-4s-5s) Sunny Hollow Pr.

—Bible Story Concepts for Twos & Threes: A Unique Blend of Bible Concepts & Preschool Skills. VanBibber, Jodi. 2004. 255p. (J). cd-rom 69.95 *(978-0-9755818-0-3(5)*, BSC-2s-3s) Sunny Hollow Pr.

Vance, Elsbet. Mistletoe Madness: A Short Story Collection. Vance, Elsbet, ed. 2004. (ENG.). 384p. (J). (gr. 1-5). pap. 8.95 *(978-0-9718348-2-8(2))* Blooming Tree Pr.

Vandegrift, April. We Live in Boise. McKetta, Elisabeth Sharp & Stead, James. 2019. (ENG.). 34p. (J). (gr. k-3). 13.99 *(978-0-9908323-5-5(X))* Frog Prince Pr.

Vanden Berg, Myra. Sparkle's Journey. Kreder Sr., Edward G. & Kreder, Mary Ellen DeLuca. 2013. 32p. pap. 5.99 *(978-0-9913232-0-3(3))* Kreder, Mary Ellen DeLuca.

Vanden Broeck, Fabricio. Perseo TS. Rincón García, Luis Antonio. 2015. (SPA.). 128p. (J). (gr. 4-7). pap. 7.95 *(978-607-8237-91-3(8))* Nostra Ediciones MEX. Dist: Independent Pubs. Group.

Vanden Broeck, Fabricio. My Shoes & I / Mis Zapatos y Yo: Crossing Three Borders / Cruzando Tres Fronteras. Vanden Broeck, Fabricio. Colato Laínez, René. 2019. (ENG & SPA.). 32p. (J). (gr. 1-3). 17.95 *(978-1-55885-884-8(9)*, Piñata Books) Arte Publico Pr.

Vandenberg, Kimberly. A Great Lakes Odyssey with Louis & Louise. Schram, Stephen T. 2018. (ENG.). 68p. (J). (gr. 2-6). pap. 14.99 *(978-1-937165-80-2(9))* Orange Hat Publishing.

Vandenberg, Kimberly. More Oomph: An ABC Book Celebrating Nature. Lingelbach, Anne. 2020. (ENG.). 56p. (J). (gr. 3-6). pap. 14.99 ***(978-1-64538-125-9(0))*** Orange Hat Publishing.

Vandenberg, Kimberly. The Pink Skeleton. Mackey, Madame. 2018. (ENG.). 20p. (J). (gr. k-3). pap. 10.00 *(978-1-948365-88-8(X))* Orange Hat Publishing.

Vandenberg, Kimberly. Silent Satisfaction. Schram, Stephen T. 2020. (Great Lakes Trilogy Ser.: Vol. 3). (ENG.). 60p. (J). (gr. 2-6). pap. 14.99 ***(978-1-64538-107-5(2))*** Orange Hat Publishing.

Vandenberg, Michael, photos by. My Train Book. Jacob, Ellen et al. 2007. (ENG., 16p. (J). (gr. -1-k). bds. 6.99 *(978-0-06-089970-7(0)*, Collins) HarperCollins Pubs.

Vandenbos, Scarlet. The Huggy Lady. Eernisse, Rachel. 2017. (ENG.). (J). (gr. k-1). 17.99 *(978-0-692-97874-0(7))* Eernisse, Rachel.

VandenBroeck, Fabricio. Thirsty, Thirsty Elephants. Markle, Sandra. 2017. 32p. (J). (gr. -1-2). lib. bdg. 16.99 *(978-1-58089-634-4(0))* Charlesbridge Publishing, Inc.

—Under the Mambo Moon. Durango, Julia. 2011. 48p. (J). (gr. 3-7). 12.95 *(978-1-57091-723-3(X))* Charlesbridge Publishing, Inc.

Vandenheede, Ruben, jt. illus. see Hockensmith, Laura.

Vander Pol, Matt. Super Ace & the Space Traffic Jam, 1 vol. Crouch, Cheryl. 2009. (I Can Read! Ser.). (ENG.). 32p. (J). pap. 4.99 *(978-0-310-71698-3(5))* Zonderkidz.

Vanderbeek, Don. Stormalong. Metaxas, Eric. 2004. (Rabbit Ears-A Classic Tale Ser.). (ENG.). 36p. (J). (gr. 2-6). 28.50 *(978-1-59197-772-8(X)*, 12928, Picture Bk.) Spotlight.

Vanderbilt, Amy. Negative Nine: Book 1 of the Early Math Series. Vanderbilt, Amy. Vanderbilt, Sabrina. 2008. 28p. (J). 14.99 *(978-0-7639-0719-8(7))* Trend Factor Pr.

Vanderhoop, Jannette. The Legend of Katama: The Creation Story of Dolphins, A Wampanoag Legend of Martha's Vineyard. 2004. 80p. (J). lib. bdg. 18.95 *(978-0-9755605-0-1(6))* Island Moon Pr.

VanderPloeg, Libby. Brooklyn Bailey, the Missing Dog. Sohn, Amy & Le Pape, Orna. 2020. 40p. (J). (gr. -1-3). 17.99 *(978-0-525-55273-4(1)*, Dial Bks) Penguin Young Readers Group.

—This Moment Is Your Life (and So Is This One) A Fun & Easy Guide to Mindfulness, Meditation, & Yoga. Gates, Mariam. 2018. 240p. (J). (gr. 5-9). 18.99 *(978-0-399-18662-2(X)*, Dial Bks) Penguin Young Readers Group.

Vanderstelt, Adrianna. A Calisbury Christmas. Porter, Marisa Grace. 2019. (ENG.). 30p. (J). (gr. k-5). 18.99 ***(978-0-578-60516-6(3))*** Porter, Marisa.

VanDerTuuk-Perkins, Jennifer E. & Perkins, Rodney R. Life with Gabriel. VanDerTuuk-Perkins, Jennifer E. l.t. ed. 2004. 22p. (J). per. 9.95 *(978-0-9749862-0-3(8))* Theragogy.com.

Vanderveen, Cary. Willy & Sherman: Battle of the Bulge. Devisser, Dave. 2019. (ENG.). (J). 116p. 22.95 ***(978-0-9996862-4-9(0))***; 118p. pap. 10.95 ***(978-0-9996862-3-2(2))*** School Forest Publishing LLC.

Vanderwier, Michelle. Beautiful Girl. Vanderwier, Michelle. 2019. (ENG.). 40p. (J). pap. 10.00 *(978-1-7934-4174-4(X))* Independently Published.

Vandevelde, Lucie. The House of Happy Spirits: A Children's Book Inspired by Friedensreich Hundertwasser. Elschner, Géraldine. 2020. (Children's Books Inspired by Famous Artworks Ser.). (ENG.). 32p. (J). (gr. -1-3). 14.95 ***(978-3-7913-7454-3(0))*** Prestel Verlag GmbH & Co KG. DEU. Dist: Penguin Random Hse. LLC.

Vandever, Daniel W. Fall in Line, Holden. Vandever, Daniel W. Frank, LaFrenda, ed. 2017. 32p. (J). *(978-1-893354-50-0(4))* Salina Bookshelf Inc.

Vandewater, Rena. The Nine Most Famous Reindeer of All. Sharp, Rhonda Winchell. 2004. 40p. (J). pap. 15.99 *(978-0-9748047-8-1(9))* Hickory Bark Productions.

VanDeWeghe, Lindsay & Bohnet, Christopher. Bur Bur & Friends 3 volume Set. Pastel, JoAnne & Fitzsimmons, Kakie. 2007. (J). lib. bdg. 39.95 *(978-0-9777121-5-1(X))* IGI Pr.

—Bur Bur Throws Out the First Pitch: An Exciting Baseball Experience. Fitzsimmons, Kakie. 2007. (Bur Bur & Friends Ser.). (ENG.). 30p. (J). (gr. -1-3). lib. bdg. *(978-0-9777121-4-4(1))* IGI Pr.

—Bur Bur's Fishing Adventure: An Exciting Fishing Adventure. Fitzsimmons, Kakie. 2007. (Bur Bur & Friends Ser.). 32p. (J). (gr. -1-3). lib. bdg. *(978-0-9777121-3-7(3))* IGI Pr.

Vandiver, Melissa. The Mermaids' Night Before Christmas. Asher, Sally. 2019. (J). ***(978-1-946160-55-3(5))*** Univ. of Louisiana at Lafayette Pr.

Vandiver, Melissa. Mermaids of New Orleans. Asher, Sally. 2018. (J). *(978-1-946160-28-7(8))* Univ. of Louisiana at Lafayette Pr.

Vane, Mitch. A Box Full of Phaeries, Phreddes & Fruit, 3 Vols. French, Jackie. 2003. (ENG.). 100p. *(978-0-207-19849-6(7))* HarperCollins Pubs. Australia.

—Crawfish Hunt. Arena, Felice & Kettle, Phil. 2004. (J). pap. *(978-1-59336-358-1(3))* Mondo Publishing.

—Fairy Bread. Dubosarsky, Ursula. 2019. (Puffin Nibbles Ser.). 80p. (J). (gr. k-2). pap. 9.99 *(978-0-14-131175-3(4)*, Puffin) Penguin Random Hse. AUS. Dist: Independent Pubs. Group.

—Hit the Beach. Arena, Felice & Kettle, Phil. 2004. (J). pap. *(978-1-59336-361-1(3))* Mondo Publishing.

—John Williamson's Christmas in Australia. Williamson, John. 2nd ed. 2018. 32p. (J). (gr. k-2). 13.99 *(978-0-14-350717-8(6))* Random Hse. Australia AUS. Dist: Independent Pubs. Group.

—Little Lunch Four. Katz, Danny. 2005. (Little Lunch Ser.). 64p. (J). pap. *(978-1-876372-84-2(2)*, Black Dog Books) Walker Bks. Australia Pty, Ltd.

—Little Lunch: Loads of Laughs. Katz, Danny. 2019. (ENG.). 128p. (J). (gr. 1-4). 15.99 *(978-1-5362-0914-3(7)*, Candlewick Entertainment) Candlewick Pr.

—Little Lunch: Triple Treats. Katz, Danny. 2019. (ENG.). 112p. (J). (gr. 1-4). 15.99 *(978-0-7636-9471-5(1)*, Candlewick Entertainment) Candlewick Pr.

—A Mountain of Mittens. Plourde, Lynn. 2009. 32p. (J). (gr. -1-3). pap. 7.95 *(978-1-57091-466-9(4))* Charlesbridge Publishing, Inc.

—Our Last Trip to the Market. Clarke, Lorin. 2017. (ENG.). 32p. (J). (-k). 18.99 *(978-1-925266-96-2(6))* Allen & Unwin AUS. Dist: Independent Pubs. Group.

—The Patch. Headley, Justina Chen. 2007. 32p. (J). (gr. k-3). pap. 7.95 *(978-1-58089-170-7(5))* Charlesbridge Publishing, Inc.

—A Phaery Named Phredde & Other Stories to Eat with a Banana. French, Jackie. 2004. 128p. (Orig.). *(978-0-207-20000-7(9))* HarperCollins Pubs. Australia.

—Phredde & a Frog Named Bruce & Other Stories to Eat with a Watermelon. French, Jackie. 2004. 128p. (Orig.). *(978-0-207-20001-4(7))* HarperCollins Pubs. Australia.

—Phredde & the Purple Pyramid: A Story to Eat with a Passionfruit. French, Jackie. 2003. (ENG.). 144p. (Orig.). *(978-0-207-19934-9(5))* HarperCollins Pubs. Australia.

—Phredde & the Zombie Librarian: And Other Stories to Eat with a BloodPlum. French, Jackie. 2004. 128p. (Orig.). *(978-0-207-20002-1(5))* HarperCollins Pubs. Australia.

—Poodle & Hound. Lasky, Kathryn. 2011. 48p. (J). (gr. k-3). pap. 6.95 *(978-1-58089-323-7(6))* Charlesbridge Publishing, Inc.

—Rotten School Day. Arena, Felice & Kettle, Phil. 2004. (J). pap. *(978-1-59336-364-2(8))* Mondo Publishing.

—Scratch Kitten Goes to Sea. Green, Jessica. 2009. (Scratch Kitten Ser.: 1). (ENG.). 96p. (J). (gr. 2-4). 8.99 *(978-1-921272-44-8(9))* Little Hare Bks. AUS. Dist: Independent Pubs. Group.

—Secret Agent Heroes. Arena, Felice & Kettle, Phil. 2004. (J). pap. *(978-1-59336-355-0(9))* Mondo Publishing.

—The Tree House. Arena, Felice & Kettle, Phil. 2004. (J). pap. *(978-1-59336-357-4(5))* Mondo Publishing.

—Wet World. Arena, Felice & Kettle, Phil. 2004. (J). pap. *(978-1-59336-356-7(7))* Mondo Publishing.

Vane, Mitch, jt. illus. see Gordon, Gus.

Vanessa, Balleza. ¡pero Es Que Aquí No Hay Palmeras! Kianny, Antigua N. 2018. (SPA.). 34p. (J). (gr. k-4). 18.99 *(978-1-949299-01-4(5))*; pap. 14.99 *(978-1-949299-00-7(7))* Jade Publishing.

vanFrankenhuyze, Gijsbert. H is for Horse: An Equestrian Alphabet. Ulmer, Michael. rev. ed. 2004. (Sports Alphabet Ser.). (ENG.). 40p. (J). (gr. 1-4). 19.99 *(978-1-58536-213-4(1)*, 202044) Sleeping Bear Pr.

Vang Nyman, Ingrid. Pippi Fhad-Stocainneach. Lindgren, Astrid. 2018. (GLA.). 192p. (J). pap. *(978-1-907165-31-3(2))* Akerbeltz.

—Pippi Longstocking. Lindgren, Astrid. Beard, Susan, tr. 2020. (ENG.). 144p. (J). (gr. 3-7). 8.99 *(978-0-593-11782-8(4)*, Puffin Books); 16.99 *(978-0-593-11781-1(6)*, Viking Books for Young Readers) Penguin Young Readers Group.

Vang, Richard. My Dad Is a Freemason. Vang, Richard. 2006. (Masonic Family Ser.). (ENG.). 31p. per. 16.95 *(978-0-9789066-0-3(8))* Square Circle Pr. LLC.

Vangsgard, Amy. Look Closer. Williams, Rozanne Lanczak. 2005. (Reading for Fluency Ser.). 8p. (J). pap. 3.49 *(978-1-59198-147-3(6)*, 4247) Creative Teaching Pr., Inc.

Vangsgard, Amy, jt. illus. see Hilliam, Corbin.

Vangsgard, Amy, jt. illus. see Hilliam, Corbin.

Vangsgard, Amy, jt. illus. see Rojas, Mary.

Vankirk Schue, Lori. Los Zanates de Valle Verde Protegen Sus Tierras. Giddan, Norman & Giddan, Jane. 2017. (SPA.). (J). pap. 9.99 *(978-0-9981068-0-9(1))* Cult Classics Pub.

—On Halloween Night. Schue, Lori. 2018. (ENG.). 36p. (J). (gr. k-6). 24.99 *(978-0-578-40063-1(4))* Schue, Lori.

Vanner, Chelsey & Andrews, Jazmine. Cookies & Milk. Mitchell, Mae. 2018. (ENG.). 54p. (J). 20.49 *(978-1-5456-4829-2(8))*; pap. 12.95 *(978-1-5456-4828-5(X))* Salem Author Services. (Mill City Press, Inc).

Vanoli, Flavia. El Autbús Turístico. (SPA.). 16p. 6.95 *(978-84-414-0553-0(0))* Editorial Edaf, S.L. ESP. Dist: Spanish Pubs., LLC.

—La Furgoneta de los Músicos. (SPA.). 16p. 6.95 *(978-84-414-0428-1(3))* Editorial Edaf, S.L. ESP. Dist: Spanish Pubs., LLC.

Vansant, Wayne. The Red Baron: The Graphic History of Richthofen's Flying Circus & the Air War in WWI. Vansant, Wayne. 2015. (Graphic Histories Ser.). (ENG.). 104p. (YA). (gr. 8-12). 34.65 *(978-1-939581-80-8(X)*, Zenith Pr.) Quarto Publishing Group USA.

Vanslette, Roxy. Poe the Crow. Devereux, Jan. Devereux, Jan, ed. 2004. 139p. (J). per. *(978-0-9749677-0-7(X))* Lakeview Pr.

Vant, Tim. The Witch's Cat. Vant, Jeanie. 2010. 24p. pap. 11.50 *(978-1-60976-051-9(4)*, Eloquent Bks.) Strategic Book Publishing & Rights Agency (SBPRA).

VanTuyle, David. Welcome to Wally's World! Golden Books Staff. 2015. (Pictureback(R) Ser.). (ENG.). 16p. (J). (gr. -1-2). 3.99 *(978-0-385-38764-4(4)*, Golden Bks.) Random Hse. Children's Bks.

VanTuyle, David, jt. illus. see Random House Editors.

Vanzet, Gaston. Bugs, 1 vol. Giulieri, Anne. 2012. (Engage Literacy Red Ser.). (ENG.). 32p. (gr. k-2). pap. 5.99 *(978-1-4296-8934-2(X)*, Capstone Pr.) Capstone.

—Clothing. Walker, Kate. 2011. (Recycling Ser.). 32p. (J). (gr. 1-1). 29.50 *(978-1-60870-128-5(X))* Cavendish Square Publishing LLC.

V

—Dinosaurs, 1 vol. Dale, Jay. 2012. (Engage Literacy Blue Ser.). (ENG.). 32p. (gr. k-2). pap. 5.99 *(978-1-4296-8974-8(9),* Capstone Pr.) Capstone.
—Food & Garden Waste. Walker, Kate. 2011. (Recycling Ser.). 32p. (J). (gr. 1-1). 29.50 *(978-1-60870-129-2(8))* Cavendish Square Publishing LLC.
—Glass. Walker, Kate. 2011. (Recycling Ser.). 32p. (J). (gr. 1-1). 29.50 *(978-1-60870-130-8(1))* Cavendish Square Publishing LLC.
—Metal Cans. Walker, Kate. 2011. (Recycling Ser.). 32p. (J). (gr. 1-1). 29.50 *(978-1-60870-131-5(X))* Cavendish Square Publishing LLC.
—Paper. Walker, Kate. 2011. (Recycling Ser.). 32p. (J). (gr. 1-1). 29.50 *(978-1-60870-132-2(8))* Cavendish Square Publishing LLC.
—Plastic Bottles & Bags. Walker, Kate. 2011. (Recycling Ser.). 32p. (J). (gr. 1-1). 29.50 *(978-1-60870-133-9(6))* Cavendish Square Publishing LLC.
Vanzo, Filippo. The Bug Girl: Maria Merian's Scientific Vision. Marsh, Sarah Glenn. 2019. (ENG.). 32p. (J). 16.99 *(978-0-8075-9257-1(9),* 807592579) Whitman, Albert & Co.
—Can You Survive a Supervolcano Eruption? An Interactive Doomsday Adventure. Hoena, Blake. 2016. (You Choose: Doomsday Ser.). (ENG.). 112p. (J). (gr. 3-7). lib. bdg. 32.65 *(978-1-4914-8108-0(0),* Capstone Pr.) Capstone.
Vaquero, Pilar, jt. illus. see Gonzalez de Echavarri, Jesus.
Vareberg, Gladys. Ryleigh's Little Bug Book, 1 vol. Burns, Helen Marie. 2009. 24p. pap. 24.95 *(978-1-60813-701-5(5))* America Star Bks.
Varela, Cecilia. Listen to the Birds: An Introduction to Classical Music. Gerhard, Ana. 2013. (ENG.). 48p. (J). (gr. 2-4). 16.95 *(978-2-923163-89-5(3))* La Montagne Secrete CAN. Dist: Independent Pubs. Group.
Varela, Juan D. Do Fish Kiss? Gummelt, Donna & Melchiorre, Dondino. Wall, Randy Hugh, ed. l.t. ed. 2006.Tr. of Los peces Besan. (SPA.). 32p. (J). 14.95 *(978-0-9764798-0-2(X))* Story Store Collection Publishing.
—Your Name Is Mud. Gummelt, Donna & Melchiorre, Dondino. Wall, Randy Hugh, ed. Varela, Carmen, tr. l.t. ed. 2006.Tr. of Tu nombre es Mud. 34p. (J). 14.95 *(978-0-9764798-3-3(4))* Story Store Collection Publishing.
Varela, Juan D. The Cookie Story. Varela, Juan D., tr. Sinclair, Nicholas et al. Wall, Randy Hugh, ed. l.t. ed. 2005.Tr. of Cuent de Galletas. (SPA.). 33p. (J). 14.95 *(978-0-9764798-1-9(8))* Story Store Collection Publishing.
—Cow Puppies. Varela, Juan D., tr. Gummelt, Donna & Melchiorre, Dondino. Wall, Randy Hugh, ed. 2006.Tr. of Cachorros Vaqueros. (SPA.). 32p. (J). 14.95 *(978-0-9764798-7-1(7))* Story Store Collection Publishing.
—Don't Get My Honey... . HONEY. Varela, Juan D., tr. Gummelt, Donna & Melchiorre, Dondino. Wall, Randy Hugh, ed. 2006. (SPA.). 34p. (J). 14.95 *(978-0-9764798-5-7(0))* Story Store Collection Publishing.
—I'm All Blown Up. Varela, Juan D., tr. Gummelt, Donna & Melchiorre, Dondino. Wall, Randy Hugh, ed. 2006.Tr. of Ya Creci. (SPA.). 34p. (J). 14.95 *(978-0-9764798-4-0(2))* Story Store Collection Publishing.
—Michelina the Magical Musical Good Witch of the Forest. Varela, Juan D., tr. Gummelt, Donna & Melchiorre, Dondino. Wall, Randy Hugh, ed. 2006. (SPA.). 34p. (J). 14.95 *(978-0-9764798-6-4(9))* Story Store Collection Publishing.
—My Sunshine Friend. Varela, Juan D., tr. Gummelt, Donna & Melchiorre, Dondino. Wall, Randy Hugh, ed. ed. 2006. (SPA.). 32p. (J). 14.95 *(978-0-9764798-2-6(6))* Story Store Collection Publishing.
Varga, Tunde. Anagrania's Challenge. Curic, Ina. 2018. (Whole Nutrition Ser.: Vol. 1). (ENG.). 34p. (J). (gr. k-5). 14.99 *(978-973-0-26102-8(4),* Imagine Creatively) Roseberg, Anders.
Vargas, Alexis. Give Me Love. Vargas, Alexis. Naranja, Editorial, ed. 2019. (SPA.). 300p. (J). pap. 16.19 *(978-1-0921-3478-1(6))* Independently Published.
Vargas, Marianella. The Best Time in Bahrain. Scott, Gretell M. 2019. (ENG.). 26p. (J). pap. 14.99 *(978-1-0761-3525-4(0))* Independently Published.
Vargas, Robert. Lottie Bright & the Starmaker's Universe. Grannis, Greg. 2006. (ENG.). 280p. (J). per. *(978-0-9778205-9-7(9))* Helm Publishing.
Vargas, Rodrigo. Ahora Abracadabra! Chapela Mendoza, Luz Maria Del Consuelo. 2016. (Cuentamelo Otra Vez Ser.). (SPA.). (J). 16.95 *(978-1-68165-262-7(5))* Trialtea USA, LLC.
Vargo, Joseph. Born of the Night: The Gothic Fantasy Artwork of Joseph Vargo. 2005. 182p. per. 24.99 *(978-0-9675756-6-7(4))* Monolith Graphics.
Vargo, Joseph, jt. illus. see Filipak, Christine.
Vargo, Kurt. The Tiger & the Brahmin. Gleeson, Brian. 2005. (Rabbit Ears-A Classic Tale Ser.). (ENG.). 36p. (J). (gr. 2-6). 28.50 *(978-1-59679-347-7(3),* 12948, Picture Bk.) Spotlight.
Vargo, Sharon. Monster & Dragon: Write Poems. Anderson, Shannon. 2018. (ENG.). 38p. (J). pap. 9.99 *(978-1-64071-016-0(7))* Burnett Young Books.
—Sugar & Shadow. 2012. 8p. (J). *(978-0-7367-2726-6(4))* Zaner-Bloser, Inc.
—A Wild & Woolly Night. Geiger, Lorraine Lynch. 2007. (J). (gr. -1-3). 15.95 *(978-1-891795-25-1(2))* RGU Group, The.
—The 15 Best Things about Being the New Kid. Copeland, Cynthia L. 2006. (Silly Millies Ser.). 32p. (J). (gr. -1-3). lib. bdg. 21.27 *(978-0-7613-2889-6(0),* Millbrook Pr.); (gr. 2). per. 5.95 *(978-0-8225-6473-7(4),* First Avenue Editions) Lerner Publishing Group.
Vargo, Sharon Hawkins. Words: A Computer Lesson. Haddon, Jean. 2003. (Silly Millies Ser.). 32p. (J). (gr. -1-1). pap. 4.99 *(978-0-7613-1797-5(X));* lib. bdg. 17.90 *(978-0-7613-2870-4(X))* Lerner Publishing Group. (Millbrook Pr.).
Varian, George & Clinedinst, B. West. Buccaneers & Pirates. Stockton, Frank Richard. 2007. (Dover Maritime Ser.). (ENG.). 335p. per. 12.95 *(978-0-486-45425-2(8))* Dover Pubns., Inc.
—Buccaneers & Pirates of Our Coasts. Stockton, Frank Richard. 2008. 364p. (gr. 4-7). 46.95 *(978-1-4369-8234-4(0));* pap. 31.95 *(978-1-4367-9391-9(2))* Kessinger Publishing, LLC.
Various. The Awesome Book of Monsters of the Deep. Paiva, Johannah Gilman, ed. 2013. (World of Wonder: the Awesome Book Of Ser.). (ENG.). 32p. (J). (gr. 3-7). 7.99 *(978-1-77093-777-2(X))* Flowerpot Pr.
—The Awesome Book of Prehistoric Animals. Paiva, Johannah Gilman, ed. 2013. (World of Wonder (Library) Ser.). (ENG.). 32p. (J). (gr. 3-7). 7.99 *(978-1-77093-780-2(3))* Flowerpot Pr.
—The Awesome Book of the Universe. Paiva, Johannah Gilman, ed. 2013. (ENG.). 32p. (J). (gr. 3-7). 7.99 *(978-1-77093-779-6(X))* Flowerpot Pr.
—The Awesome Book of Volcanoes. Paiva, Johannah Gilman, ed. 2013. (World of Wonder: the Awesome Book Of Ser.). (ENG.). 32p. (J). (gr. 3-7). 7.99 *(978-1-77093-778-9(1))* Flowerpot Pr.
—Brand New Readers Winter Fun! Box. 2010. (Brand New Readers Ser.). (ENG.). 80p. (J). (gr. -1-3). pap. 12.99 *(978-0-7636-5072-8(2))* Candlewick Pr.
—Cars Little Golden Book Favorites (Disney/Pixar Cars) 2017. (ENG.). 80p. (J). (-k). 7.99 *(978-0-7364-3679-3(0),* Golden/Disney) Random Hse. Children's Bks.
—Childhood of Famous Americans Ready-To-Read Value Pack: Abe Lincoln & the Muddy Pig; Albert Einstein; John Adams Speaks for Freedom; George Washington's First Victory; Ben Franklin & His First Kite; Thomas Jefferson & the Ghostriders. 2013. (Ready-To-read COFA Ser.). (ENG.). 208p. (J). (gr. k-2). pap. 17.96 *(978-1-4424-9440-4(9),* Simon Spotlight) Simon Spotlight.
—Dora's 10 Best Adventures. 2010. (Dora the Explorer Ser.). (ENG.). 248p. (J). 15.99 *(978-1-4424-0967-5(3),* Simon Spotlight/Nickelodeon) Simon Spotlight/Nickelodeon.
—Let's Read with Dora! 2010. (Dora the Explorer Ser.). (ENG.). 144p. (J). (gr. -1-1). pap. 7.99 *(978-1-4169-9742-9(3),* Simon Spotlight/Nickelodeon) Simon Spotlight/Nickelodeon.
—Looney Tunes Greatest Hits, Vol. 3. 2017. (ENG.). 128p. (gr. 3-7). pap. 12.99 *(978-1-4012-7160-2(X))* DC Comics.
—New Books for Newborns Collection: Good Night, My Darling Baby; Mama Loves You So; Blanket of Love; Welcome Home, Baby! ed. 2017. (New Books for Newborns Ser.). (ENG.). 64p. (J). (— 1). bds. 31.99 *(978-1-5344-1015-2(5),* Little Simon) Little Simon.
—The Really Big I Didn't Know That Book: Bugs, Sharks, Dinosaurs, Cars, & Trains. Aladdin Books. Paiva, Johannah Gilman, ed. 2014. (ENG.). 160p. (J). (gr. 2). 24.95 *(978-1-77093-927-1(X))* Flowerpot Children's Pr. Inc. CAN. Dist: Cardinal Pubs. Group.
—You Should Meet Collector's Set: Women Who Launched the Computer Age; Mae Jemison; Misty Copeland; Jesse Owens; Duke Kahanamoku; Katherine Johnson. ed. 2017. (You Should Meet Ser.). (ENG.). 288p. (J). (gr. 1-3). pap. 17.99 *(978-1-5344-0974-3(2),* Simon Spotlight) Simon Spotlight.
Various & Thompson, Ian. The Awesome Book of Planets & Their Moons. Farndon, John. Paiva, Johannah Gilman, ed. 2014. (ENG.). 32p. (J). (gr. 3-7). 7.99 *(978-1-4867-0342-5(9))* Flowerpot Children's Pr. Inc. CAN. Dist: Cardinal Pubs. Group.
Various Authors. Dora's Bedtime Adventures. 2005. (Dora the Explorer Ser.). (ENG.). 36p. (J). bds. 10.99 *(978-1-4169-0628-5(2),* Simon Spotlight/Nickelodeon) Simon Spotlight/Nickelodeon.
Various Authors, Chronicle. The Illustrated Treasury of Fairy Tales. Various Authors, Chronicle. 2003. (ENG.). 352p. (J). (gr. 1-3). 29.95 *(978-1-56846-144-1(5))* Creative Co., The.
Various Illustrators. Venganza Contra Las Moscas. McNicoll, Silvia. 2019. (Torre Amarilla Ser.). (SPA.). 288p. (J). pap. *(978-958-00-0282-6(7))* Norma Ediciones, S.A.
Varjotie, Claudia. A Er for Alfabet/ a Is for Alphabet. Gilbert, Tish. 2016. (NOR.). (J). pap. *(978-82-690472-0-2(1))* Mort Homme Bks.
Varkarotas, Heather. Surprise in Auntie's Garden! Morris, Ann. 2013. (ENG.). (J). (gr. -1-3). 14.95 *(978-1-62086-224-7(7))* Mascot Bks., Inc.
Varley, Susan. The Animals Grimm: a Treasury of Tales. Crossley-Holland, Kevin. 2019. 96p. (J). (gr. -1-2). 17.99 *(978-1-78344-747-3(8))* Penguin Random Hse. AUS. Dist: Independent Pubs. Group.
—Captain Small Pig, 1 vol. Waddell, Martin. (ENG.). 32p. (J). (gr. -1-3). 2017. pap. 7.95 *(978-1-56145-982-7(8));* 2010. 15.95 *(978-1-56145-519-5(9))* Peachtree Publishing Co. Inc.
—Jack y el Monstruo. Graham, Richard. (Cotton Cloud Ser.). (SPA.). 32p. (J). (gr. 1-3). *(978-84-7722-680-2(6))* Timun Mas, Editorial S.A. ESP. Dist: Lectorum Pubns., Inc.
—Lovely Old Lion. Jarman, Julia. 2015. (ENG.). 32p. (J). (gr. -1-3). 17.99 *(978-1-4677-9310-0(8),* 9781467793100); E-Book 27.99 *(978-1-4677-9543-2(7),* 9781467795432) Lerner Publishing Group.
—Sorrel & the Sleepover. Averiss Corrinne, Averiss. 2018. (ENG.). 32p. (J). (gr. -1-2). 12.99 *(978-1-4380-5056-0(9),* B.E.S. Publishing) Peterson's.
Varma, Ira. The Missing Jelly Beans: A Tale of Curiosity & Adventure. Varma, Sneh. 2019. (ENG.). 50p. (J). pap. 5.99 *(978-1-0748-5723-3(2))* Independently Published.
Varma, Ishan. The Quinceañera. Stamper, Judith Bauer. 2010. (J). *(978-1-60617-121-9(6))* Teaching Strategies, LLC.
Varnedoe, Catharine E. Whoa, Wiggle-Worm: A Little Lemon Book about an Overly Active Child, 1 bk. Lee, Betsy B. l.t. ed. 2003. 24p. (J). pap. 7.95 *(978-0-9720267-3-4(8))* Learning Abilities Bks.
Varol, Valentina. Elena the Paper Doll: ELENA Activity Book for Girls Ages 4-8. Varol, Valentina. 2019. (ENG.). 38p. (J). pap. 7.00 ***(978-1-7117-0117-2(3))*** Independently Published.
Varon, Sara. Odd Duck. Castellucci, Cecil. 2013. (ENG.). 96p. (J). (gr. 1-5). 16.99 *(978-1-59643-557-5(7),* 900062302, First Second Bks.) Roaring Brook Pr.
Varon, Sara. Bake Sale. Varon, Sara. 2011. (ENG.). 160p. (J). (gr. 3-7). 21.99 *(978-1-59643-740-1(5),* 900077688); pap. 17.99 *(978-1-59643-419-6(8),* 900053016) Roaring Brook Pr. (First Second Bks.).
—Robot Dreams. Varon, Sara. 2007. (ENG.). 208p. (J). (gr. 3-7). pap. 18.99 *(978-1-59643-108-9(3),* 9781596431089, First Second Bks.) Roaring Brook Pr.
—Robot Dreams. Varon, Sara. 2016. (ENG.). 224p. (J). pap. 12.99 *(978-1-250-07350-1(2),* 900150780) Square Fish.
Varona, German. 99 Bitcoins & an Elephant. Chen, Vincent. 2018. (ENG.). 38p. (J). (gr. k-3). pap. 10.99 *(978-1-7325577-1-0(3))* Vinny Tales.
Varona, German "wallok". 99 Bitcoins & an Elephant. Chen, Vincent. 2018. (ENG.). 38p. (J). (gr. k-3). 17.99 *(978-1-7325577-0-3(5))* Vinny Tales.
Vartan, Judy. Where's Grandma? Vartan, Judy. 2018. (ENG.). 38p. (J). (gr. k-5). 15.00 *(978-0-9986317-1-4(X))* Vartan, Judith A.
Vasconcellos, Dan. The Dog That Called the Pitch. Christopher, Matt. 2010. (Matt Christopher Sports Readers Ser.). 48p. (J). (gr. 1-3). lib. bdg. 23.93 *(978-1-59953-353-7(7))* Norwood Hse. Pr.
—The Dog That Pitched a No-Hitter. Christopher, Matt. 2010. (Matt Christopher Sports Readers Ser.). 48p. (J). (gr. 1-3). lib. bdg. 23.93 *(978-1-59953-351-3(0))* Norwood Hse. Pr.
—The Dog That Stole Home. Christopher, Matt. 2010. (Matt Christopher Sports Readers Ser.). 48p. (J). (gr. 1-3). lib. bdg. 23.93 *(978-1-59953-352-0(9))* Norwood Hse. Pr.
Vasconcellos, Daniel. All Keyed Up. Christopher, Matt. 7th ed. 2003. (ENG.). 64p. (J). (gr. 1-4). pap. 8.99 *(978-0-316-73821-7(2))* Little, Brown Bks. for Young Readers.
—Firsts. Cohn, Arlen. gif. ed. 2004. (ENG.). 28p. (J). bds. 9.99 *(978-1-57939-168-3(0))* Andrews McMeel Publishing.
—Heads Up. Christopher, Matt. 2003. (Soccer Cats Ser.: Bk. 6). 54p. (J). (gr. 1-4). 12.65 *(978-0-7569-3904-5(6))* Perfection Learning Corp.
—Kick It! Christopher, Matt. 2003. (ENG.). 64p. (J). (gr. 1-4). pap. 8.99 *(978-0-316-73808-8(5))* Little, Brown Bks. for Young Readers.
—Making the Save. Christopher, Matt. 11th ed. 2004. (ENG.). 64p. (J). (gr. 1-4). pap. 8.99 *(978-0-316-73745-6(3))* Little, Brown Bks. for Young Readers.
—Master of Disaster. Christopher, Matt. 2003. (ENG.). 64p. (J). (gr. 1-4). pap. 8.99 *(978-0-316-16498-6(4))* Little, Brown Bks. for Young Readers.
—Switch Play! Switch Play! Christopher, Matt. 9th ed. 2003. (ENG.). 64p. (J). (gr. 1-4). pap. 8.99 *(978-0-316-73807-1(7))* Little, Brown Bks. for Young Readers.
—You Lucky Dog. Christopher, Matt. 8th ed. 2003. (ENG.). 64p. (J). (gr. 1-4). pap. 8.99 *(978-0-316-73805-7(0))* Little, Brown Bks. for Young Readers.
—You Lucky Dog. Christopher, Matt. 2003. (Soccer Cats Ser.: Bk. 8). 49p. (J). (gr. 2-4). 12.65 *(978-0-7569-3907-6(0))* Perfection Learning Corp.
Vasilevsky, Marina. A Trixi, a Shmoop & a Monster. Dube, Tory. 2013. 32p. 19.99 *(978-0-9886193-1-9(8))* Dube, Tory.
Vasilkova, Yana. La Actitud de Agradecer: Libros de Accion de Gracias para Ninos, Cuentos Infantiles en Espa&#65533;ol para ni&#65533;os de 2 a 4, Books in Spanish for Kids. Gutierrez, Pedro & Winn, Melissa. 2019. (Oliver's Tips for Kids Ser.: Vol. 1). (SPA.). 42p. (J). pap. 9.99 ***(978-1-6771-0691-2(3))*** Independently Published.
—La Actitud de Agradecer: Libros de Accion de Gracias para Ninos, Cuentos Infantiles en Espa&#65533;ol para ni&#65533;os de 2 a 4, Books in Spanish for Kids. Winn, Melissa. 2019. (Oliver's Tips for Kids Ser.: Vol. 1). (SPA.). 40p. (J). pap. 9.99 ***(978-1-6777-4892-1(3))*** Independently Published.
—El Diente Flojo de Oliver: Diez Maneras para Sacar un Diente. Spanish Edition. Libros en Espa&#65533;ol para ni&#65533;os de 3-5 A&#65533;os. Winn, Melissa. Y&#65533;&#65533;ez, Alfonso, tr. 2020. (Consejos de Oliver para Ni&#65533;os Ser.: Vol. 2). (SPA.). 36p. (J). pap. 11.99 ***(978-1-6535-7266-3(3))*** Independently Published.
—Dino, the Potty Star: Potty Training Older Children, Stubborn Kids, & Baby Boys & Girls Who Refuse to Give up Their Diapers. the Funniest Dinosaurs Book for Children 3-5 Years-Old. Winn, Melissa. 2019. (ENG.). 40p. (J). pap. 11.99 ***(978-1-0992-5402-4(7))*** Independently Published.
—Help Your Angry Dragon: Self-Regulation Book for Kids, Children Books about Anger & Frustration Management, Picture Books Ages 3 5, Emotion & Feelings Books for Children. Rafailovic, Zorana & Winn, Melissa. 2019. (Oliver's Tips for Kids Ser.: Vol. 4). (ENG.). 38p. (J). pap. 11.99 ***(978-1-6716-8316-7(1))*** Independently Published.
—I Made My Fear Disappear: Help Kids Overcome a Fear of Monsters under the Bed, Bedtimes Story Fiction Children's Picture Book Ages 3 5, Emotions & Feelings Books. Winn, Melissa. 2019. (Oliver's Tips for Kids Ser.: Vol. 5). (ENG.). 40p. (J). pap. 9.99 ***(978-1-6786-5843-4(X))*** Independently Published.
Vasilovich, Guy. The 13 Nights of Halloween. Vasilovich, Guy. 2011. (ENG.). 40p. (J). (gr. -1-3). 16.99 *(978-0-06-180445-8(2))* HarperCollins Pubs.
Vasquez, Ivan & Redondo, Jesus. Spider-Man 2: Everyday Hero. Figueroa, Acton. movie tie-in ed. 2004. (Festival Reader Ser.). 32p. (J). (gr. -1-2). pap. 3.99 *(978-0-06-057363-8(5),* HarperFestival) HarperCollins Pubs.
Vasquez, Jay. Hawk. Robledo, Karla. 2020. (ENG.). 24p. (YA). pap. 20.99 ***(978-1-7283-6205-2(9))*** AuthorHouse.
Vásquez, Juan José. Times to Remember, the Fun & Easy Way to Memorize the Multiplication Tables. Warren, Sandra Jane. 2012. 86p. 24.95 *(978-0-9836580-0-9(5))* Joyful Learning Publications, LLC.
Vasquez, Juan Jose. Times to Remember, the Fun & Easy Way to Memorize the Multiplication Tables: Home & Classroom Resources. Warren, Sandra J. 2012. 246p. pap. 19.95 *(978-0-9836580-1-6(3))* Joyful Learning Publications, LLC.
Vasquez, Natalia. Carlos & Diego: A Tale from Peru. Mitchell, Sara. 2016. 24p. (J). pap. 9.95 *(978-1-927244-57-9(9))* Flying Start Bks. NZL. Dist: Flying Start Bks.
—Carlos & Diego (Big Book Edition) A Tale from Peru. Mitchell, Sara. 2016. 24p. (J). pap. *(978-1-927244-67-8(6))* Flying Start Bks.
—The Pied Piper of Hamelin. 2012. (Flip-Up Fairy Tales Ser.). 24p. (J). *(978-1-84643-480-8(7))* Child's Play International Ltd.
Vasquez, Natalie. The Pied Piper of Hamelin. 2012. (Flip-Up Fairy Tales Ser.). 24p. (J). *(978-1-84643-519-5(6))* Child's Play International Ltd.
Vasquez, Peter M. Lerts: Brink of Magic: Book One. Semer, Logan T. 2018. (Lerts: Brink of Magic Ser.: Vol. 1). (ENG.). 62p. (J). pap. 12.95 *(978-1-7294-7879-0(4))* Independently Published.
Vast, Émilie. From Father to Father. Vast, Émilie. 2018. (ENG.). 14p. (J). (— 1). bds. 7.99 *(978-1-58089-814-0(9))* Charlesbridge Publishing, Inc.
—From Mother to Mother. Vast, Émilie. 2018. (ENG.). 14p. (J). (— 1). bds. 7.99 *(978-1-58089-813-3(0))* Charlesbridge Publishing, Inc.
Vasudevan, Vidya. Lizzy Anne's Adventures, Vol. 1. Lizzy Anne's Adventures Staff & Zarrella, Sharon. 2011. 52p. (J). (gr. k-4). pap. 5.99 *(978-0-9845887-2-5(8))* Lizzy Anne's Adventures.
—Mbutu's Mangos. Free, Zaccai. 2006. 24p. (J). per. 12.95 *(978-0-9785326-0-4(0))* Solar Publishing LLC.
—My Mom Hugs Trees. Ringgold, Robyn. 2006. 24p. (J). per. 15.95 *(978-0-9785326-1-1(9))* Solar Publishing LLC.
Vaswani, Neela. This Is My Eye. Vaswani, Neela. 2018. 56p. (J). (gr. -1-3). 16.99 *(978-0-7636-7616-2(0))* Candlewick Pr.
Vasylenko, Veronica. Bedtime Bear. Conway, Sara. 2018. (Bedtime Board Bks.). (ENG.). 18p. (J). bds. 7.99 ***(978-1-926444-53-6(1))*** Rainstorm Pr.
Vasylenko, Veronica. The Best Snowman Ever. Stahl, Stephanie. 2013. (ENG.). 16p. (J). (gr. -1-k). bds. 8.95 *(978-1-58925-605-7(0))* Tiger Tales.
—God Is Always Good: Comfort for Kids Facing Grief, Fear, or Change, 1 vol. Fortner, Tama. 2014. (ENG.). 32p. (J). 12.99 *(978-0-7180-1145-1(7))* Nelson, Thomas Inc.
—Jingle Bells. 2007. (Padded Board Bks.). 18p. (J). (gr. -1-k). bds. 7.95 *(978-1-58925-821-1(5))* Tiger Tales.
—A Kiss Goodnight. Wright, Claire. 2017. (ENG.). 20p. (J). (gr. -1 — 1). bds. 6.99 *(978-1-68412-041-3(1),* Silver Dolphin Bks.) Printers Row Publishing Group.
—Panda-Monium! Platt, Cynthia. 2011. (ENG.). 32p. (J). (gr. -1-2). 15.95 *(978-1-58925-093-2(1));* pap. 7.95 *(978-1-58925-425-1(2))* Tiger Tales.
Vaugelade, Anais. The War. Vaugelade, Anais. Rouffiac, Marie-Christine & Streissguth, Thomas, trs. from FRE. 2005. (Picture Bks.). 32p. (J). (gr. k-2). 15.25 *(978-1-57505-562-6(7))* Lerner Publishing Group.
Vaughan, Brenna. All about Poop. Hayes, Kate. Garnsworthy, Marlo, ed. 2012. (ENG.). 38p. (J). pap. 14.95 *(978-0-9854248-0-0(X))* Pinwheel Bks.
—Code It! Create It! Ideas & Inspiration for Coding. Hutt, Sarah. 2017. (Girls Who Code Ser.). 144p. (J). (gr. 3-7). 8.99 *(978-0-399-54255-8(8),* Penguin Workshop) Penguin Young Readers Group.
—Crack the Code! Activities, Games, & Puzzles That Reveal the World of Coding! Hutt, Sarah. 2018. (Girls Who Code Ser.). 128p. (J). (gr. 3-7). pap. 12.99 *(978-0-399-54256-5(6),* Penguin Workshop) Penguin Young Readers Group.
—Just Breathe: Meditation, Mindfulness, Movement, & More. Chopra, Mallika. 2018. 112p. (J). (gr. 3-7). pap. 12.99 *(978-0-7624-9158-2(2),* Running Pr. Kids) Running Pr.
—Just Feel: How to Be Stronger, Happier, Healthier, & More. Chopra, Mallika. 2019. 128p. (J). (gr. 3-7). pap. 12.99 *(978-0-7624-9474-3(3),* Running Pr. Kids) Running Pr.
—Kisses. McFarlane, Sheryl. 2017. (ENG.). 40p. (J). (-4). 9.99 *(978-1-4926-5712-5(3),* Sourcebooks Jabberwocky) Sourcebooks, Inc.
Vaughan, Jack. Basic Concepts in Motion Fun Deck: Fd58. Parks, Amy. 2003. (J). *(978-1-58650-286-7(7))* Super Duper Pubns.
Vaughan, Jack, jt. illus. see Golliher, Bill.
Vaughan, Jeremy. Sandwich: Short Stories & Screenplays by Steven Coy. Coy, Steven. Saia, Karla, ed. 2003. 229p. (YA). per. 10.00 *(978-0-9743235-0-3(0))* Better Non Sequitur.
Vaughan, Karen H. Tangleweed & Brine. Sullivan, Deirdre. 2019. (ENG.). 180p. (YA). (gr. 9). 19.95 *(978-1-910411-92-6(2))* Little Island IRL. Dist: Independent Pubs. Group.
Vaughan, Ladonna. The Pedelkee Steamer: An S. W. Production. Vaughan, Christopher. 2016. (ENG.). (J). pap. 5.49 *(978-0-9863101-5-7(8))* Vaughan, Christopher.
Vaughn, Jenn. The Industrial Revolution: Investigate How Science & Technology Changed the World with 25 Projects. Mooney, Carla. 2011. (Build It Yourself Ser.). 128p. (J). (gr. 3-7). 21.95 *(978-1-936313-81-5(2),* 71319f6c-e7fb-4ede-a91d-9ff0baf540bf); pap. 15.95 *(978-1-936313-80-8(4),* 474945ea-1345-4a23-9d62-ab7d13a33646) Nomad Pr.
Vaughn, Lori. Our Journey to the Land of Flying Balloons. Dimitroff, Andrea and Ashley. 2019. (ENG.). 34p. (J). pap. 10.00 *(978-1-0793-1650-6(7))* Independently Published.
Vaughn, Royce. Seymour Bluffs & Robert Wadlow, the Tallest Man in the World: A Story about Diversity & Tolerance. 2007. 28p. (J). 12.95 *(978-0-9728538-4-2(7))* Amica Publishing.
—Seymour Bluffs & the Legend of the Piasa Bird. 2006. 24p. (J). pap. 9.95 *(978-0-9728538-2-8(0))* Amica Publishing.
Vaughns, Byron. The Legacy of Mr. Banjo! Tanguay, Dave. 2015. (Billy Batson & the Magic of Shazam! Ser.). (ENG.). 32p. (J). (gr. 3-6). lib. bdg. 22.60 *(978-1-4342-9746-4(2),* Stone Arch Bks.) Capstone.
—The Real Meaning of Christmas. Horton, Alice F. 2018. (ENG.). 40p. (J). pap. 15.00 *(978-1-7270-9607-1(X))* CreateSpace Independent Publishing Platform.

Vaux, Patricia. Five Minutes until Bed. Andrews McMeel Publishing Staff & Wang, Dorthea Deprisco. 2009. (ENG.). 14p. (J). (gr. 4-7). 14.99 (978-0-7407-8428-6(5)) Andrews McMeel Publishing.
—Five Minutes until Bed. Wang, Dorthea Deprisco. 2012. (ENG.). 14p. (J). (-k). bds. 5.99 (978-1-4494-2244-8(6)) Andrews McMeel Publishing.
Vavak, S. Dean. Calie's Gift. Arroyo, Madeline. 2003. 32p. (gr. 2-5). 16.95 (978-0-9740061-0-9(6), 1234106) Stairway Pubns.
—What Matthias Found. Arroyo, Madeline. 2005. 32p. (J). (gr. -1-3). 16.95 (978-0-9740061-1-6(4)) Stairway Pubns.
Vavouri, Elisa. Pavel & the Tree Army. Hyde, Heidi Smith. 2019. (ENG.). 32p. (J). (gr. k-3). 17.99 (978-1-5124-4446-9(4), Kar-Ben Publishing) Lerner Publishing Group.
Vaysset, Ghyslaine. El Cohete. Lindeen, Mary. 2016. (Early Rising Readers Ser.). (SPA.). 16p. (J). (gr. 1-1). 6.67 (978-1-4788-4190-6(7)) Newmark Learning LLC.
—Good As New. Mortensen, Lori. 2016. (Spring Forward Ser.). (J). (gr. 1). (978-1-4900-9375-8(3)) Benchmark Education Co.
—The Rocket. Lindeen, Mary. 2015. (Early Rising Readers Ser.). (J). (gr. -1-k). 5.83 (978-1-4788-2164-9(7)) Newmark Learning LLC.
—Yo Puedo. Craddock, Petra. 2016. (Early Rising Readers Ser.). (SPA.). 16p. (J). (gr. 1-1). 6.67 (978-1-4788-4207-1(5)) Newmark Learning LLC.
Vayssiere, Frederique. Katie: The Revolting Bridesmaid. Hooper, Mary. 2007. (Katie Ser.). 80p. (J). (gr. 2-4). per. 8.95 (978-0-7475-8611-1(X)) Bloomsbury Publishing Plc GBR. Dist: Independent Pubs. Group.
—The Revolting Baby. Hooper, Mary. 2008. (Katie Ser.). 96p. (J). (gr. 2-4). pap. 8.95 (978-0-7475-8613-5(6)) Bloomsbury Publishing Plc GBR. Dist: Independent Pubs. Group.
—The Revolting Holiday. Hooper, Mary. 2008. (Katie Ser.). 96p. (J). (gr. 2-4). pap. 8.95 (978-0-7475-8614-2(4)) Bloomsbury Publishing Plc GBR. Dist: Independent Pubs. Group.
—The Revolting Wedding. Hooper, Mary. 2007. (Katie Ser.). 96p. (J). (gr. 2-4). per. 8.95 (978-0-7475-8612-8(8)) Bloomsbury Publishing Plc GBR. Dist: Independent Pubs. Group.
Vaz De Carvalho, Joao. A Lovely Man. Pavón, Mar. 2019. (ENG.). 36p. (J). (gr. -1-k). 16.95 (978-84-16566-84-6(4)) Ediciones La Fragatina ESP. Dist: Independent Pubs. Group.
Vazan, Sandy. I Dreamed about a Hippopotamus in a Lipstick Factory. Braun, Anne. 2016. (ENG.). (J). pap. (978-1-4602-9267-9(7)) FriesenPress.
Vazquez, Joey. Ms. Marvel by Saladin Ahmed Vol. 2: Stormranger. 2020. 136p. (YA). (gr. 8-17). pap. 17.99 (978-1-302-91830-9(3)) Marvel Worldwide, Inc.
—Ms. Marvel Team-Up. 2019. (Marvel Team-Up Ser.: 1). 136p. (YA). (gr. 8-17). pap. 17.99 (978-1-302-91831-6(1)) Marvel Worldwide, Inc.
Veasey, Michele. Listening to the Mukies: And Their Character Building Adventures. Bohlken, Robert L. 2003. (ENG.). (J). (gr. 4-6). pap. 10.95 (978-0-930643-15-7(1)) Images Unlimited Publishing.
—Listening to the Mukies & Their Character Building Adventures. Bohlken, Robert L. 2003. (ENG.). (J). (gr. 2-7). 14.95 (978-0-930643-17-1(8)) Images Unlimited Publishing.
Vecchio, Luciano. Ares' Underworld Army. Simonson, Louise. 2018. (Wonder Woman the Amazing Amazon Ser.). (ENG.). 88p. (J). (gr. 2-7). lib. bdg. 24.65 (978-1-4965-6531-0(2), 138545, Stone Arch Bks.) Capstone.
—Attack of the Man-Bat! Black, Jake. 2015. (Batman: Comic Chapter Bks.). (ENG.). 88p. (J). (gr. 3-7). lib. bdg. 21.32 (978-1-4965-0513-2(1), Stone Arch Bks.) Capstone.
—Batman & the Flock of Fear. Manning, Matthew K. 2013. (Dark Knight Ser.). (ENG.). 88p. (J). (gr. 3-7). pap. 5.95 (978-1-4342-4217-4(X), Stone Arch Bks.) Capstone.
—Batman & the Killer Croc of Doom! Sutton, Laurie S. 2013. (Dark Knight Ser.). (ENG.). 88p. (J). (gr. 3-7). pap. 5.95 (978-1-4342-4215-0(3), Stone Arch Bks.) Capstone.
—Batman & the Villainous Voyage. Sonneborn, Scott. 2013. (Dark Knight Ser.). (ENG.). 88p. (J). (gr. 3-7). pap. 5.95 (978-1-4342-4216-7(1), Stone Arch Bks.) Capstone.
—Batman Crashes the Black Masquerade. Tulien, Sean. 2013. (Dark Knight Ser.). (ENG.). 88p. (J). (gr. 3-7). pap. 5.95 (978-1-4342-4824-4(0), Stone Arch Bks.) Capstone.
—Batman vs. the Cat Commander. Hult, Gene & Bright, J. E. 2013. (Dark Knight Ser.). (ENG.). 88p. (J). (gr. 3-7). pap. 5.95 (978-1-4342-4214-3(5), Stone Arch Bks.) Capstone.
—Batman vs. the Penguin. Sutton, Laurie S. 2013. (Dark Knight Ser.). (ENG.). 88p. (J). (gr. 3-7). pap. 5.95 (978-1-4342-4825-1(9), Stone Arch Bks.) Capstone.
—The Black Masquerade. Tulien, Sean. 2013. (Dark Knight Ser.). (ENG.). 88p. (J). (gr. 3-7). lib. bdg. 26.65 (978-1-4342-4486-4(5), Stone Arch Bks.) Capstone.
—Cat Commander. Hult, Gene & Bright, J. E. 2012. (Dark Knight Ser.). (ENG.). 88p. (J). (gr. 3-7). 26.65 (978-1-4342-4088-0(6), Stone Arch Bks.) Capstone.
—Catwoman's Nine Lives, 1 vol. Manning, Matthew K. 2014. (Batman: Comic Chapter Bks.). (ENG.). 88p. (J). (gr. 3-7). 21.32 (978-1-4342-9132-5(4), Stone Arch Bks.) Capstone.
—Catwoman's Purrfect Plot. Stephens, Sarah Hines. 2017. (Batman & Robin Adventures Ser.). (ENG.). 88p. (J). (gr. 2-6). lib. bdg. 26.65 (978-1-4965-5349-2(7), 136291, Stone Arch Bks.) Capstone.
—Cheetah Unleashed. Snider, Brandon T. 2018. (Wonder Woman the Amazing Amazon Ser.). (ENG.). 88p. (J). (gr. 2-7). lib. bdg. 24.65 (978-1-4965-6529-7(0), 138543, Stone Arch Bks.) Capstone.
—Circe's Dark Reign. Snider, Brandon T. 2018. (Wonder Woman the Amazing Amazon Ser.). (ENG.). 88p. (J). (gr. 2-7). lib. bdg. 24.65 (978-1-4965-6530-3(4), 138544, Stone Arch Bks.) Capstone.
—Clayface's Slime Spree. Sutton, Laurie S. 2016. (Batman & Robin Adventures Ser.). (ENG.). 88p. (J). (gr. 2-6). lib. bdg. 26.65 (978-1-4965-2536-9(1), Stone Arch Bks.) Capstone.
—The Clown Prince of Cards. Dahl, Michael. 2016. (Batman Tales of the Batcave Ser.). (ENG.). 40p. (J). (gr. 4-8). lib. bdg. 24.65 (978-1-4965-4013-3(1), Stone Arch Bks.) Capstone.
—The Crushing Coin. Dahl, Michael. 2016. (Batman Tales of the Batcave Ser.). (ENG.). 40p. (J). (gr. 4-8). lib. bdg. 24.65 (978-1-4965-4014-0(X), Stone Arch Bks.) Capstone.
—The Dark Knight: the Penguin's Crime Wave. Sutton, Laurie S. 2013. (ENG.). (J). (gr. 4-7). pap. 35.70 (978-1-4342-4872-5(0), Stone Arch Bks.) Capstone.
—The Dark Side of the Apokolips. Sutton, Laurie S. 2015. (Superman: Comic Chapter Bks.). (ENG.). 88p. (J). (gr. 3-7). lib. bdg. 21.32 (978-1-4965-0509-5(3), Stone Arch Bks.) Capstone.
—DC Super Hero Origins. Manning, Matthew K. & Sazaklis, John. 2015. (DC Super Heroes Origins Ser.). (ENG.). 48p. (J). (gr. k-2). lib. bdg., lib. bdg., lib. bdg. 95.96 (978-1-4965-0042-7(3), Stone Arch Bks.) Capstone.
—Demons of Deep Space. Sutton, Laurie S. 2012. (Man of Steel Ser.). (ENG.). 88p. (J). (gr. 3-7). lib. bdg. 26.65 (978-1-4342-4098-9(3)); pap. 5.95 (978-1-4342-4220-4(X)) Capstone. (Stone Arch Bks.).
—Dino Death-Trap. Dahl, Michael. 2016. (Batman Tales of the Batcave Ser.). (ENG.). 40p. (J). (gr. 4-8). lib. bdg. 24.65 (978-1-4965-4015-7(8), Stone Arch Bks.) Capstone.
—The Frozen Zone Freeze Ray. Dahl, Michael. 2018. (Batman Tales of the Batcave Ser.). (ENG.). 40p. (J). (gr. 4-8). lib. bdg. 24.65 (978-1-4965-5977-7(0), 137326, Stone Arch Bks.) Capstone.
—Giganta's Colossal Double-Cross. Simonson, Louise. 2018. (Wonder Woman the Amazing Amazon Ser.). (ENG.). 88p. (J). (gr. 2-7). lib. bdg. 24.65 (978-1-4965-6532-7(0), 138546, Stone Arch Bks.) Capstone.
—Harley Quinn's Crazy Creeper Caper. Simonson, Louise. 2017. (Batman & Robin Adventures Ser.). (ENG.). 88p. (J). (gr. 2-6). lib. bdg. 26.65 (978-1-4965-5347-8(0), 136289, Stone Arch Bks.) Capstone.
—Harley Quinn's Hat Trick. Dahl, Michael. 2018. (Batman Tales of the Batcave Ser.). (ENG.). 40p. (J). (gr. 4-8). lib. bdg. 24.65 (978-1-4965-5983-8(5), 137331, Stone Arch Bks.) Capstone.
—In the Mouth of the Whale. Beatty, Scott et al. 2015. (Beware the Batman Ser.). (ENG.). 32p. (J). (gr. 3-6). lib. bdg. 22.60 (978-1-4342-9740-2(3), Stone Arch Bks.) Capstone.
—The Jaguar's Jewel. Dahl, Michael. 2018. (Batman Tales of the Batcave Ser.). (ENG.). 40p. (J). (gr. 4-8). lib. bdg. 24.65 (978-1-4965-5984-5(3), 137333, Stone Arch Bks.) Capstone.
—The Joker's Magic Mayhem. Bright, J. E. 2016. (Batman & Robin Adventures Ser.). (ENG.). 88p. (J). (gr. 2-6). lib. bdg. 26.65 (978-1-4965-2538-3(8), Stone Arch Bks.) Capstone.
—Killer Croc of Doom! Sutton, Laurie S. 2012. (Dark Knight Ser.). (ENG.). 88p. (J). (gr. 3-7). 26.65 (978-1-4342-4097-2(5), Stone Arch Bks.) Capstone.
—Law & Disorder. Cohen, Ivan et al. 2015. (Beware the Batman Ser.). (ENG.). 32p. (J). (gr. 3-6). lib. bdg. 22.60 (978-1-4342-9738-9(1), Stone Arch Bks.) Capstone.
—Lex Luthor & the Kryptonite Caverns, 1 vol. Bright, J. E. 2012. (DC Super-Villains Ser.). (ENG.). 56p. (J). (gr. 3-6). pap. 5.95 (978-1-4342-3896-2(2), Stone Arch Bks.) Capstone.
—Lex Luthor's Power Grab! Simonson, Louise. 2015. (Superman: Comic Chapter Bks.). (ENG.). 88p. (J). (gr. 3-7). lib. bdg. 21.32 (978-1-4965-0508-8(5), Stone Arch Bks.) Capstone.
—Night of a Thousand Doomsdays, 1 vol. Sutton, Laurie S. 2013. (Man of Steel Ser.). (ENG.). 88p. (J). (gr. 3-7). 26.65 (978-1-4342-4487-1(3), Stone Arch Bks.) Capstone.
—Night of a Thousand Doomsdays. Sutton, Laurie S. 2013. (Man of Steel Ser.). (ENG.). 88p. (J). (gr. 3-7). pap. 5.95 (978-1-4342-4827-5(5), Stone Arch Bks.) Capstone.
—The Penguin's Crime Wave. Sutton, Laurie S. 2013. (Dark Knight Ser.). (ENG.). 88p. (J). (gr. 3-7). lib. bdg. 26.65 (978-1-4342-4485-7(7), Stone Arch Bks.) Capstone.
—The Penguin's Power Parasol. Dahl, Michael. 2016. (Batman Tales of the Batcave Ser.). (ENG.). 40p. (J). (gr. 4-8). lib. bdg. 24.65 (978-1-4965-4012-6(3), Stone Arch Bks.) Capstone.
—The Planet Collector, 1 vol. Sutton, Laurie S. 2014. (Superman: Comic Chapter Bks.). (ENG.). 88p. (J). (gr. 3-7). 21.32 (978-1-4342-9133-2(2), Stone Arch Bks.) Capstone.
—The Poisoned Planet, 1 vol. Manning, Matthew K. 2012. (Man of Steel Ser.). (ENG.). 88p. (J). (gr. 3-7). lib. bdg. 26.65 (978-1-4342-4091-0(6), Stone Arch Bks.) Capstone.
—Prisoner of the Penguin!, 1 vol. Sonneborn, Scott. 2014. (Batman: Comic Chapter Bks.). (ENG.). 88p. (J). (gr. 3-7). 21.32 (978-1-4342-9131-8(6), Stone Arch Bks.) Capstone.
—The Real Man of Steel, 1 vol. Sutton, Laurie S. 2014. (Superman: Comic Chapter Bks.). (ENG.). 88p. (J). (gr. 3-7). 21.32 (978-1-4342-9134-9(0), Stone Arch Bks.) Capstone.
—Scarecrow's Flock of Fear. Manning, Matthew K. 2012. (Dark Knight Ser.). (ENG.). 88p. (J). (gr. 3-7). lib. bdg. 26.65 (978-1-4342-4090-3(8), Stone Arch Bks.) Capstone.
—Scarecrow's Nightmare Maze. Bright, J. E. 2016. (Batman & Robin Adventures Ser.). (ENG.). 88p. (J). (gr. 2-6). lib. bdg. 26.65 (978-1-4965-2537-6(X), Stone Arch Bks.) Capstone.
—Scarecrow's Panic Plot. Beatty, Scott. 2015. (Batman: Comic Chapter Bks.). (ENG.). 88p. (J). (gr. 3-7). lib. bdg. 21.32 (978-1-4965-0512-5(3), Stone Arch Bks.) Capstone.
—Science Behind Batman. Biskup, Agnieszka & Enz, Tammy. 2016. (Science Behind Batman Ser.). (ENG.). 24p. (J). (gr. 1-3). pap., pap., pap. 20.85 (978-1-5157-2065-2(9), Stone Arch Bks.) Capstone.
—Science Behind Batman. Enz, Tammy & Biskup, Agnieszka. 2016. (Science Behind Batman Ser.). (ENG.). 24p. (J). (gr. 1-3). lib. bdg., lib. bdg., lib. bdg. 103.96 (978-1-5157-2062-1(4), Stone Arch Bks.) Capstone.
—The Science Behind Batman's Flying Machines. Enz, Tammy. 2016. (Science Behind Batman Ser.). (ENG.). 24p. (J). (gr. 1-3). lib. bdg. 25.99 (978-1-5157-2036-2(5), Stone Arch Bks.) Capstone.
—The Science Behind Batman's Ground Vehicles. Enz, Tammy. 2016. (Science Behind Batman Ser.). (ENG.). 24p. (J). (gr. 1-3). lib. bdg. 25.99 (978-1-5157-2034-8(9), Stone Arch Bks.) Capstone.
—The Science Behind Batman's Tools. Biskup, Agnieszka. 2016. (Science Behind Batman Ser.). (ENG.). 24p. (J). (gr. 1-3). lib. bdg. 25.99 (978-1-5157-2038-6(1), Stone Arch Bks.) Capstone.
—The Science Behind Batman's Uniform. Biskup, Agnieszka. 2016. (Science Behind Batman Ser.). (ENG.). 24p. (J). (gr. 1-3). lib. bdg. 25.99 (978-1-5157-2031-7(4), Stone Arch Bks.) Capstone.
—The Son of the Man-Bat. Cohen, Ivan et al. 2015. (Beware the Batman Ser.). (ENG.). 32p. (J). (gr. 3-6). lib. bdg. 22.60 (978-1-4342-9741-9(1), Stone Arch Bks.) Capstone.
—Supergirl vs. Brainiac, 1 vol. Sonneborn, Scott. 2013. (DC Super Heroes Ser.). (ENG.). 56p. (J). (gr. 3-6). lib. bdg. 26.65 (978-1-4342-6015-4(1), Stone Arch Bks.) Capstone.
—Superman & the Poisoned Planet. Manning, Matthew K. 2012. (Man of Steel Ser.). (ENG.). 88p. (J). (gr. 3-7). pap. 5.95 (978-1-4342-4224-2(2), Stone Arch Bks.) Capstone.
—Superman vs. Bizarro, 1 vol. Sazaklis, John. 2013. (DC Super Heroes Ser.). (ENG.). 56p. (J). (gr. 3-6). lib. bdg. 26.65 (978-1-4342-6012-3(7), Stone Arch Bks.) Capstone.
—Tattooed Man Trouble!, 1 vol. Cohen, Ivan & Eltaeb, Gabe. 2014. (Green Lantern: the Animated Ser.). (ENG.). 32p. (J). (gr. 2-5). 22.60 (978-1-4342-6480-0(7), Stone Arch Bks.) Capstone.
—Two-Face Face-Off. Sutton, Laurie S. 2016. (Batman & Robin Adventures Ser.). (ENG.). 88p. (J). (gr. 2-6). lib. bdg. 26.65 (978-1-4965-2535-2(3), Stone Arch Bks.) Capstone.
—The Villainous Venus Flytrap. Dahl, Michael. 2018. (Batman Tales of the Batcave Ser.). (ENG.). 40p. (J). (gr. 4-8). lib. bdg. 24.65 (978-1-4965-5978-4(9), 137327, Stone Arch Bks.) Capstone.
—Wonder Woman the Amazing Amazon. Snider, Brandon T. 2018. (Wonder Woman the Amazing Amazon Ser.). (ENG.). 88p. (J). (gr. 2-7). 98.60 (978-1-4965-6545-7(2), 28454, Stone Arch Bks.) Capstone.
—Wonder Woman vs. Circe, 1 vol. Bright, J. E. & Sutton, Laurie S. 2013. (DC Super Heroes Ser.). (ENG.). 56p. (J). (gr. 3-6). lib. bdg. 26.65 (978-1-4342-6014-7(3), Stone Arch Bks.) Capstone.
Vecchio, Luciano & Brizuela, Dario. Beware the Batman. Cohen, Ivan et al. 2015. (Beware the Batman Ser.). (ENG.). 32p. (J). (gr. 3-6). lib. bdg., lib. bdg., lib. bdg. 90.40 (978-1-4965-0302-2(3), Stone Arch Bks.) Capstone.
Vecchio, Luciano & DC Comics Staff. Danger on Deck! Sonneborn, Scott. 2013. (Dark Knight Ser.). (ENG.). 88p. (J). (gr. 3-7). 26.65 (978-1-4342-4092-7(4), Stone Arch Bks.) Capstone.
Vecchio, Luciano & Geoffrey, Beaulieu. Ironheart Vol. 2: Ten Rings. 2020. (Ironheart Ser.: 2). 112p. (YA). (gr. 4-17). pap. 17.99 (978-1-302-91509-4(6)) Marvel Worldwide, Inc.
Vecchio, Luciano, jt. illus. see Baltazar, Art.
Vecchio, Luciano, jt. illus. see Levins, Tim.
Vedder, Erik. Mad Mod Is in Vogue!, 1 vol. Beechen, Adam & Age, Heroic. 2014. (Teen Titans GO! Ser.). (ENG.). 32p. (J). (gr. 3-6). 22.60 (978-1-4342-9216-2(9), Stone Arch Bks.) Capstone.
Vega, Alison. Moon Tricks. Foster, Marilyn. 2012. 48p. pap. (978-1-77097-960-4(3)) FriesenPress.
Vega, Andrea. Before the Fear of Spiders. Orenshein, Jesse. 2019. (ENG.). 36p. (J). pap. 9.99 **(978-1-7023-4601-6(3))** Independently Published.
Vega, Anne. El Torneo de Trabalenguas / the Tongue Twister Tournament. Kanellos, Nicolás. 2016. (SPA & ENG.). 32p. (J). (gr. k-4). 17.95 (978-1-55885-832-9(6), Piñata Books) Arte Publico Pr.
Veiga, Dirceu. Rainbow Donuts. Cross, Shiloh. 2019. (ENG.). 24p. (J). (gr. k-3). 19.99 (978-0-578-42900-7(4)) Houstons Pr.
Veillé, Eric. Encyclopedia of Grannies. Veillé, Eric. 2019. (ENG.). 32p. (J). (gr. -1-2). 17.99 (978-1-77657-243-4(2)) Gecko Pr. NZL. Dist: Lerner Publishing Group.
—My Pictures after the Storm. Veillé, Eric. 2017. (ENG.). 32p. (J). (gr. -1-k). 16.99 (978-1-77657-104-8(5)) Gecko Pr. NZL. Dist: Lerner Publishing Group.
Veillette, Roseanne M. Buck & Ben Junior: Colors. Veillette, Roseanne M. 2016. (ENG.). (J). pap. 12.95 (978-0-9977504-0-9(5), Little Paws Pr.) Veillette, Roseanne.
Veilleux, Tam. You ROCK! Journal & Coloring Book: A Companion to the Award-Winning Children's Book, Crystal's Quest: an Adventure into the World of Gemstones. Fontanella, Lisa. 2019. (ENG.). 110p. (J). (gr. 3-6). pap. 8.99 **(978-0-578-55477-8(1))** Fontanella, Lisa Author, Designer, Coach.
Veinshtein, Debbie. Is God Sad? Daleski, Gil. Kaufman, Shirley, tr. from HEB. 2006. 40p. 14.95 (978-965-229-372-5(5)) Gefen Publishing Hse., Ltd ISR. Dist: Gefen Bks.
Veira, Michael. Excepcional. Domingues, Sarah Duque. 2018. (POR.). 84p. (J). pap. 7.00 (978-1-7198-6299-8(0)) Independently Published.
Vela, David, jt. illus. see Mori, Paula.
Velarde, Chase. When I Fall Asleep. Etherly, L. D. 2013. 36p. pap. 11.95 (978-0-9833877-6-3(1)) Inkspil Publishing.
Velasco, Francisco Ruiz. Shadows on Saplings. Kennedy, Mike. 2003. (Lone Wolf 2100 Ser.: 1). (ENG.). 104p. pap. 12.95 (978-1-56971-893-3(8)) Dark Horse Comics.
Velasco, Ruth. La Vuelta Al Mundo en 80 Días. Verne, Julio. 2016. (SPA.). 146p. (J). (gr. 4-7). pap. (978-9978-18-324-3(8)) Radmandi Editorial, Compania Ltd.
Velasquez, Eric. As Fast As Words Could Fly, 1 vol. Tuck, Pamela M. 2013. (ENG.). 40p. (J). 18.95 (978-1-60060-348-8(3)) Lee & Low Bks., Inc.
—Champion: The Story of Muhammad Ali. Haskins, Jim. 2018. 40p. (J). 17.99 (978-1-68119-588-9(7), 9781681195889, Bloomsbury USA Childrens) Bloomsbury Publishing USA.
—Emma's Escape: A Story of America's Underground Railroad. Gayle, Sharon Shavers. 3rd ed. 2003. (Soundprints' Read-and-Discover Ser.). (ENG.). 48p. (J). (gr. -1-3). pap. 3.95 (978-1-59249-021-9(2), S2009) Soundprints.
—Emma's Escape South: A Story of America's Underground Railroad. Gayle, Sharon Shavers. 2003. (Soundprints' Read-And-Discover: Level 3 Ser.). (ENG.). (J). (gr. -1-3). lib. bdg. 14.55 (978-0-7569-3360-9(9)) Perfection Learning Corp.
—Houdini: World's Greatest Mystery Man & Escape King. Krull, Kathleen. 2007. (ENG.). 32p. (J). (gr. 1-5). pap. 9.99 (978-0-8027-9646-2(X), 900044870, Bloomsbury USA Childrens) Bloomsbury Publishing USA.
—Journey to Jo'burg: A South African Story. Naidoo, Beverley. 2019. (ENG.). 112p. (J). (gr. 3-7). pap. 6.99 (978-0-06-288179-3(5), HarperCollins) HarperCollins Pubs. Ltd. GBR. Dist: HarperCollins Pubs.
—My Uncle Martin's Big Heart. Watkins, Angela Farris. 2010. (ENG.). 32p. (J). (gr. k-2). 19.95 (978-0-8109-8975-7(1), 670501, Abrams Bks. for Young Readers) Abrams, Inc.
—My Uncle Martin's Words for America: Martin Luther King Jr. 's Niece Tells How He Made a Difference. Watkins, Angela Farris. 2015. (ENG.). 40p. (J). (gr. 1-4). 9.95 (978-1-4197-1836-6(3), 1004703, Abrams Bks. for Young Readers) Abrams, Inc.
—New Shoes. Meyer, Susan Lynn. (ENG.). 32p. (J). (gr. 1-4). 2016. 7.99 (978-0-8234-3573-9(3)); 2015. 16.95 (978-0-8234-2528-0(2)) Holiday Hse., Inc.
—Ol' Clip-Clop: A Ghost Story. McKissack, Patricia C. 2013. (ENG.). 32p. (J). (gr. 1-4). 16.95 (978-0-8234-2265-4(8)) Holiday Hse., Inc.
—The Rain Stomper, 0 vols. Boswell, Addie. 2008. (ENG.). 32p. (J). (gr. -1-3). 16.99 (978-0-7614-5393-2(8), 9780761453932, Two Lions) Amazon Publishing.
Velasquez, Eric. Rosetta, Rosetta, Sit by Me! Walvoord, Linda. (ENG.). (J). (gr. 3-6). 2020. 98p. pap. 9.99 **(978-1-4778-1588-5(0)**, 9781477815885); 2004. 80p. 14.95 (978-0-7614-5171-6(4), 9780761451716) Amazon Publishing. (Two Lions).
—Ruth Objects: The Life of Ruth Bader Ginsburg. Rappaport, Doreen. 2020. (Big Words Book Ser.). 48p. (J). (gr. -1-3). 18.99 **(978-1-4847-4717-9(8))** Little, Brown Bks. for Young Readers.
Velasquez, Eric. Schomburg: el Hombre Que Creó una Biblioteca. Weatherford, Carole Boston. 2019. 48p. (J). (gr. 3-7). 9.99 (978-1-5362-0898-6(1)) Candlewick Pr.
—Schomburg: the Man Who Built a Library. Weatherford, Carole Boston. 48p. (J). 2019. (gr. 3-7). 9.99 (978-1-5362-0897-9(3)); 2017. (gr. 4-7). 17.99 (978-0-7636-8046-6(X)) Candlewick Pr.
—The Sound That Jazz Makes. Weatherford, Carole Boston. 2003. (ENG.). (J). (gr. 2-4). pap. 7.95 (978-0-8027-7674-7(4), 35a91a33-c050-4c11-bef9-7de72e534021) Fitzhenry & Whiteside, Ltd. CAN. Dist: Firefly Bks., Ltd.
—Strong Voices: Fifteen American Speeches Worth Knowing. Bolden, Tonya & Roberts, Cokie. 2020. (ENG.). 128p. (J). (gr. 3). 21.99 (978-0-06-257204-2(0), HarperCollins) HarperCollins Pubs. Ltd. GBR. Dist: HarperCollins Pubs.
—Swim!, 0 vols. Brigham, Marilyn. 2012. (ENG.). 24p. (J). (gr. -1-k). 7.99 (978-0-7614-6253-8(8), 9780761462538, Two Lions) Amazon Publishing.
—A Thirst for Home: A Story of Water Across the World. Ieronimo, Christine. 2014. (ENG.). 32p. (J). (gr. 1-4). 17.99 (978-0-8027-2307-9(1), 9780802723079, Bloomsbury USA Childrens) Bloomsbury Publishing USA.
—Touch the Sky. Malaspina, Ann. 2013. (AV2 Fiction Readalong Ser.: Vol. 99). (ENG.). (J). (gr. 1-4). 34.28 (978-1-62127-905-1(7), AV2 by Weigl) Weigl Pubs., Inc.
—Touch the Sky: Alice Coachman, Olympic High Jumper. Malaspina, Ann. 2012. (ENG.). 32p. (J). (gr. 1-3). 16.99 (978-0-8075-8035-6(X), 080758035X) Whitman, Albert & Co.
—Voices of Christmas, 1 vol. Grimes, Nikki. 2009. (ENG.). 32p. (J). (gr. -1-2). 16.99 (978-0-310-71192-6(4)) Zonderkidz.
Velasquez, Eric. Grandma's Gift. Velasquez, Eric. 2013. (ENG.). 32p. (J). (gr. k-1). pap. 9.99 (978-0-8027-3536-2(3), 900120816, Bloomsbury USA Childrens) Bloomsbury Publishing USA.
—Grandma's Records. Velasquez, Eric. 2004. (ENG.). 32p. (J). (gr. k-3). pap. 9.99 (978-0-8027-7660-0(4), 900032898, Bloomsbury USA Childrens) Bloomsbury Publishing USA.
—Looking for Bongo. Velasquez, Eric. 2016. (ENG.). 24p. (J). (gr. -1-k). 16.95 (978-0-8234-3565-4(2)) Holiday Hse., Inc.
Velasquez, Nicole. It's Okay to Be Different! (Esta Bien Ser Diferente!) Winner, Ramona Moreno. Date not set. (ENG & SPA.). 40p. (J). (gr. k-3). 9.95 (978-0-9651174-0-1(5)) BrainStorm 3000.
Velazquez, Eric. A Sweet Smell of Roses. Johnson, Angela. (ENG.). 32p. (J). 2007. (gr. k-3). 8.99 (978-1-4169-5361-6(2)); 2005. (gr. -1-3). 19.99 (978-0-689-83252-9(4)) Simon & Schuster Bks. For Young Readers. (Simon & Schuster Bks. For Young Readers).
Velazquez, Jaqueline. Los Maravidulces. Guczka Pacheco, Christel Rosemarie. 2016. (Cuentamelo Otra Vez Ser.). (SPA.). 24p. (J). 16.95 (978-1-68165-257-3(9)) Trialtea USA, LLC.

Velazquez, Jose Luis Reye, jt. illus. see Velazquez, Jose Luis Reyes.

Velazquez, Jose Luis Reyes & Velazquez, Jose Luis Reye. La Dulceria de Don Tono. Cohen, Milly. rev. ed. 2006. (Castillo de la Lectura Verde Ser.). (SPA & ENG.). 112p. (J). (gr. 2-4). pap. 7.95 *(978-970-20-0198-0(6))* Castillo, Ediciones, S. A. de C. V. MEX. Dist: Macmillan.

Veldhoven, Marijke, jt. illus. see Geeson, Andrew.

Velert, Miriam. El Libro del Abuelo: Un Mundo de Aventuras Entre la Realidad y la Fantasma. Garrido, Pedro Gelabert. 2003. (Ficcion Interactiva Ser.). (SPA.). 160p. pap. 14.95 *(978-84-89984-11-0(5))* Recursos, Ediciones ESP. Dist: Independent Pubs. Group.

Vélez, Gabriel J., jt. illus. see Barajas, Sal.

Velez, Jill Ondercin. In Your Seat, Mr. Pete! Goss, Leon. 2005. (J). pap. *(978-1-933156-11-8(2))*; per. 16.99 *(978-1-933156-04-0(X))* GSVQ Publishing. (VisionQuest Kids).

Velez, Walter. Black as a Bat. Dingles, Molly. 2005. (Community of Color Ser.). 32p. (J). pap. 10.95 *(978-1-59646-334-9(1))*; per. 10.95 *(978-1-59646-335-6(X))* Dingles & Co.

—Black as a Bat/Negro como un Murcielago. Dingles, Molly. (Community of Color Ser.). 32p. (J). 2005. (ENG & SPA.). pap. 10.95 *(978-1-59646-100-0(4))*; 2005. (ENG & SPA.). per. 10.95 *(978-1-59646-106-2(3))*; 2003. (SPA.). lib. bdg. 21.65 *(978-1-891997-33-4(5))* Dingles & Co.

—Blue as a Blueberry. Dingles, Molly. 2005. (Community of Color Ser.). 32p. (J). (ACO.). pap. 10.95 *(978-1-59646-328-8(7))*; per. 10.95 *(978-1-59646-329-5(5))* Dingles & Co.

—Blue as a Blueberry/Azul como un Arandano. Dingles, Molly. (Community of Color Ser.). 32p. (J). 2005. (ENG & SPA.). pap. 10.95 *(978-1-59646-097-3(0))*; 2005. (ENG & SPA.). per. 10.95 *(978-1-59646-103-1(9))*; 2003. (SPA.). lib. bdg. 21.65 *(978-1-891997-28-0(9))* Dingles & Co.

—Blue as a Blueberry/Bleu comme un Bleuet. Dingles, Molly. 2004. (Community of Color Ser.).Tr. of Bleu comme un Bleuet. (ENG & FRE.). 32p. (J). lib. bdg. 21.65 *(978-1-891997-72-3(6))* Dingles & Co.

—Brown as an Acorn. Dingles, Molly. (Community of Color Ser.). 32p. (J). 2005. per. 10.95 *(978-1-59646-347-9(3))*; 2004. pap. 10.95 *(978-1-59646-346-2(5))* Dingles & Co.

—Brown as an Acorn/Marrón como una Bellota. Dingles, Molly. (Community of Color Ser.).Tr. of Marrón como una Bellota. (ENG & SPA.). 32p. (J). 2005. per. 10.95 *(978-1-59646-109-3(8))*; 2004. lib. bdg. 21.65 *(978-1-891997-37-2(8))* Dingles & Co.

—Gray as a Dolphin. Dingles, Molly. (Community of Color Ser.). 32p. (J). 2005. per. 10.95 *(978-1-59646-343-1(0))*; 2004. pap. 10.95 *(978-1-59646-342-4(2))* Dingles & Co.

—Gray as a Dolphin/Gris como un Delfin. Dingles, Molly. 2004. (Community of Color Ser.).Tr. of Gris como un Delfin. (ENG & SPA.). 32p. (J). pap. 10.95 *(978-1-59646-092-8(X))*; lib. bdg. 21.65 *(978-1-891997-58-7(0))* Dingles & Co.

—Gray as a Dolphin/Gris como un Delfin. Dingles, Molly. 2005. (Community of Color Ser.). (ENG & SPA.). 32p. (J). per. 10.95 *(978-1-59646-110-9(1))* Dingles & Co.

—Green as a Frog. Dingles, Molly. 2005. (Community of Color Ser.). 32p. (J). pap. 10.95 *(978-1-59646-330-1(9))*; per. 10.95 *(978-1-59646-331-8(7))* Dingles & Co.

—Green as a Frog/Verde como una Rana. Dingles, Molly. (Community of Color Ser.). 32p. (J). 2005. (ENG & SPA.). pap. 10.95 *(978-1-59646-098-0(9))*; 2005. (ENG & SPA.). per. 10.95 *(978-1-59646-104-8(7))*; 2003. (SPA.). lib. bdg. 21.65 *(978-1-891997-29-7(7))* Dingles & Co.

—Green as a Frog/Vert comme une Grenouille. Dingles, Molly. 2004. (Community of Color Ser.).Tr. of Vert comme une Grenouille. (ENG & FRE.). 32p. (J). lib. bdg. 21.65 *(978-1-891997-71-6(8))* Dingles & Co.

—Little Red Riding Hood: A Tale about Staying Safe. 2006. (J). 6.99 *(978-1-59939-021-5(3))* Cornerstone Pr.

—Orange as a Pumpkin. Dingles, Molly. 2005. (Community of Color Ser.). 32p. (J). pap. 10.95 *(978-1-59646-332-5(5))*; per. 10.95 *(978-1-59646-333-2(3))* Dingles & Co.

—Orange as a Pumpkin/Anaranjado como una Calabaza. Dingles, Molly. (Community of Color Ser.).Tr. of Anaranjado como una Calabaza. 32p. (J). 2005. (ENG & SPA.). pap. 10.95 *(978-1-59646-099-7(7))*; 2005. (ENG & SPA.). per. 10.95 *(978-1-59646-105-5(5))*; 2003. lib. bdg. 21.65 *(978-1-891997-31-0(9))* Dingles & Co.

—Orange as a Pumpkin/Orange comme une Citrouille. Dingles, Molly. 2004. (Community of Color Ser.).Tr. of Orange comme une Citrouille. (ENG & FRE.). 32p. (J). lib. bdg. 21.65 *(978-1-891997-69-3(6))* Dingles & Co.

—Pink as a Piglet. Dingles, Molly. (Community of Color Ser.). 32p. (J). 2005. pap. 10.95 *(978-1-59646-336-3(8))*; 2005. per. 10.95 *(978-1-59646-337-0(6))*; 2004. lib. bdg. 21.65 *(978-1-891997-25-9(4))* Dingles & Co.

—Pink as a Piglet/Rosa como un Cerdito. Dingles, Molly. (Community of Color Ser.).Tr. of Rosa como un Cerdito. 32p. (J). 2005. (ENG & SPA.). pap. 10.95 *(978-1-59646-348-6(1))*; 2005. (ENG & SPA.). per. 10.95 *(978-1-59646-349-3(X))*; 2004. (SPA & ENG.). lib. bdg. 21.65 *(978-1-891997-34-1(3))* Dingles & Co.

—Purple as a Plum. Dingles, Molly. (Community of Color Ser.). 32p. (J). 2005. pap. 10.95 *(978-1-59646-338-7(4))*; 2005. per. 10.95 *(978-1-59646-339-4(2))*; 2004. lib. bdg. 21.65 *(978-1-891997-24-2(6))* Dingles & Co.

—Purple as a Plum/Morado como una Ciruela. Dingles, Molly. (Community of Color Ser.). 32p. (J). 2005. (ENG & SPA.). pap. 10.95 *(978-1-59646-350-9(3))*; 2005. (ENG & SPA.). per. 10.95 *(978-1-59646-351-6(1))*; 2004. lib. bdg. 21.65 *(978-1-891997-32-7(7))* Dingles & Co.

—Purple as a Plum/Violet comme une Prune. Dingles, Molly. 2004. (Community of Color Ser.).Tr. of Violet comme une Prune. (ENG & FRE.). 32p. (J). lib. bdg. 21.65 *(978-1-891997-68-6(8))* Dingles & Co.

—Red as a Fire Truck. Dingles, Molly. 2005. (Community of Color Ser.). 32p. (J). pap. 10.95 *(978-1-59646-324-0(4))*; per. 10.95 *(978-1-59646-325-7(2))* Dingles & Co.

—Red as a Fire Truck/Rojo como un camion de Bomberos. Dingles, Molly. (Community of Color Ser.).Tr. of Rojo Como un Camion de Bomberos. 32p. (J). 2005. (ENG & SPA.). pap. 10.95 *(978-1-59646-095-9(4))*; 2005. (ENG & SPA.). per. 10.95 *(978-1-59646-101-7(2))*; 2003. (SPA.). lib. bdg. 21.65 *(978-1-891997-27-3(0))* Dingles & Co.

—Red as a Firetruck/Rouge comme un camion de Pompiers. Dingles, Molly. 2004. (Community of Color Ser.).Tr. of Rouge comme un camion de Pompiers. (ENG & FRE.). 32p. (J). lib. bdg. 21.65 *(978-1-891997-73-0(4))* Dingles & Co.

—Turquoise as a Parakeet. Dingles, Molly. 2005. (Community of Color Ser.). (J). 32p. pap. 10.95 *(978-1-59646-344-8(9))*; 2005p. per. 10.95 *(978-1-59646-345-5(7))* Dingles & Co.

—Turquoise as a Parakeet/Turquesa como un Periquito. Dingles, Molly. (Community of Color Ser.).Tr. of Turquesa como un Periquito. (ENG & SPA.). 32p. (J). 2005. per. 10.95 *(978-1-59646-107-9(1))*; 2004. pap. 10.95 *(978-1-59646-094-2(6))*; 2004. lib. bdg. 21.65 *(978-1-891997-60-0(2))* Dingles & Co.

—Where Is Pig? Albee, Sarah. 2006. (Step-By-Step Readers Ser.). (J). pap. *(978-1-59939-056-7(6)*, Reader's Digest Young Families, Inc.) Studio Fun International.

—White as a Seashell. Dingles, Molly. 2005. (Community of Color Ser.). 32p. (J). pap. 10.95 *(978-1-59646-340-0(6))*; per. 10.95 *(978-1-59646-341-7(4))* Dingles & Co.

—White as a Seashell/Blanco como una concha Marina. Dingles, Molly. (Community of Color Ser.).Tr. of Blanco como una concha Marina. (ENG & SPA.). (J). 2005. 2005p. per. 10.95 *(978-1-59646-108-6(X))*; 2004. 32p. pap. 10.95 *(978-1-59646-091-1(1))*; 2004. 32p. lib. bdg. 21.65 *(978-1-891997-38-9(6))* Dingles & Co.

—Yellow as a Lemon. Dingles, Molly. 2005. (Community of Color Ser.). 32p. (J). pap. 10.95 *(978-1-59646-326-4(0))*; per. 10.95 *(978-1-59646-327-1(9))* Dingles & Co.

—Yellow as a Lemon/Amarillo como un Limon. Dingles, Molly. (Community of Color Ser.). 32p. (J). 2005. (ENG & SPA.). pap. 10.95 *(978-1-59646-096-6(2))*; 2005. (ENG & SPA.). per. 10.95 *(978-1-59646-102-4(0))*; 2003. (SPA.). lib. bdg. 21.65 *(978-1-891997-30-3(0))* Dingles & Co.

—Yellow as a Lemon/Jaune comme un Citron. Dingles, Molly. 2004. (Community of Color Ser.).Tr. of Jaune comme un Citron. (ENG & FRE.). 32p. (J). lib. bdg. 21.65 *(978-1-891997-70-9(X))* Dingles & Co.

Velica, Teodora. Carolee Sings in the Christmas Choir: A Christmas Story for Children of All Ages. Myers, Janice Limb. 2013. 48p. pap. 13.77 *(978-0-9897175-1-9(8))* LJM Publishing.

Velikan, Phil. Let's Make a Difference: Protecting Mountain Gorillas. Francine, Gabriella & Vayanian, Solara. 2013. (Save Coins for Causes Ser.). (ENG.). 32p. (J). 15.00 *(978-1-938504-02-0(X))* BBM Bks.

—Saint Theodora & Her Promise to God. Doyle, Mary K. 2013. 34p. 16.99 *(978-0-9897397-0-2(8))* Sisters of Providence.

Velitchenko, Olga. Beautiful Queen. Holman, Nedra. 2008. 40p. (J). *(978-1-4363-5461-5(7))* Xlibris Corp.

Velthuijs, Max. Frog in Love. Bell, Anthea. 2015. (J). *(978-1-4351-5750-7(8))* Barnes & Noble, Inc.

Venable, James. A Salute to Black Inventors Vol. 1: Coloring Learning Activities. Chandler, Ann. Chapman, Loring F., ed. 96p. (Orig.). (J). (gr. 3-8). pap. 6.95 *(978-1-877804-18-2(5))* Chandler/White Publishing Co.

Venditti, Maria Cristina. The Bright Light Inside. Kameneva, Aleksandra S. 2018. (ENG.). 36p. (J). 22.99 *(978-1-5456-4330-3(X))*; pap. 12.49 *(978-1-5456-4329-7(6))* Salem Author Services.

Vene, Alessandro. The Black Suitcase. Cervone, Shannon. 2013. (ENG.). 32p. (J). 15.99 *(978-1-938501-08-1(X))* Turn the Page Publishing.

—Gabi Babaroni on Broadway. Spergel, Heather. 2013. (ENG.). 32p. (J). 18.99 *(978-1-938501-29-6(2))* Turn the Page Publishing.

—The Misphits: Story of Snake. Schleuning, Todd & Schleuning, Cheryl. 2013. (ENG.). (J). (gr. -1-3). 15.95 *(978-1-62086-302-2(2))* Mascot Bks., Inc.

Venema, Lisa J. & Garland, Lynn Rockwell. Periwinkle Island. Coppage, Merry Ann. 2006. 86p. (J). (gr. -1-3). per. 36.99 *(978-1-4259-1931-3(6))* AuthorHouse.

Venezia, Mike. Eat Your Peas, Louise! Snow, Pegeen. 2011. 40p. (J). (gr. -1-k). (ENG.). pap. 5.95 *(978-0-531-26709-7(1))*; lib. bdg. 23.00 *(978-0-531-26527-7(7))* Scholastic Library Publishing. (Children's Pr.).

Venezia, Mike. Aaron Copland. Venezia, Mike. 2018. (ENG.). 40p. (J). (gr. 3-4). 29.00 *(978-0-531-22867-8(3))*; pap. 7.95 *(978-0-531-23370-2(7))* Scholastic Library Publishing. (Children's Pr.).

—Albert Einstein: Universal Genius. Venezia, Mike. (ENG.). 32p. (J). (gr. 3-4). 2009. pap. 6.95 *(978-0-531-22206-5(3))*; 2008. 28.00 *(978-0-531-14975-1(7))* Scholastic Library Publishing. (Children's Pr.).

—Alexander Graham Bell: Setting the Tone for Communication. Venezia, Mike. (ENG.). 32p. (J). (gr. 3-4). 2009. pap. 6.95 *(978-0-531-22207-2(1))*; 2008. 28.00 *(978-0-531-14976-8(5))* Scholastic Library Publishing. (Children's Pr.).

—Andrew Jackson. Venezia, Mike. 2005. (Getting to Know the U. S. Presidents Ser.). (ENG.). 32p. (J). (gr. 3-4). 28.00 *(978-0-516-22612-5(6)*, Children's Pr.) Scholastic Library Publishing.

—Andrew Jackson: Seventh President, 1829-1837. Venezia, Mike. 2005. (Getting to Know the U. S. Presidents Ser.). (ENG.). 32p. (J). (gr. 3-4). per. 7.95 *(978-0-516-27481-2(3)*, Children's Pr.) Scholastic Library Publishing.

—Andrew Johnson: Seventeenth President. Venezia, Mike. 2005. (Getting to Know the U. S. Presidents Ser.). (ENG.). 32p. (J). (gr. 3-7). lib. bdg. 28.00 *(978-0-516-22622-4(3)*, Children's Pr.) Scholastic Library Publishing.

—Beatles. Venezia, Mike. 2017. (ENG.). 40p. (J). (gr. 3-4). pap. 7.95 *(978-0-531-22243-0(8)*, Children's Pr.) Scholastic Library Publishing.

—Beatles, the (Revised Edition) Venezia, Mike. 2017. (ENG.). 40p. (J). (gr. 3-4). lib. bdg. 29.00 *(978-0-531-22061-0(3)*, Children's Pr.) Scholastic Library Publishing.

—Benjamin Franklin: Electrified the World with New Ideas. Venezia, Mike. 2009. (ENG.). 32p. (J). (gr. 3-4). 28.00 *(978-0-531-23701-4(X)*, Children's Pr.) Scholastic Library Publishing.

—Benjamin Harrison, 23. Venezia, Mike. 2006. (Getting to Know the U. S. Presidents Ser.). (ENG.). 32p. (J). (gr. 3-6). lib. bdg. 22.44 *(978-0-516-22628-6(2))* Scholastic Library Publishing.

—Bill Clinton: Forty-Second President, 1993-2001. Venezia, Mike. 2007. (Getting to Know the U. S. Presidents Ser.). (ENG.). 32p. (J). (gr. 3-4). 28.00 *(978-0-516-22646-0(0)*, Children's Pr.) Scholastic Library Publishing.

—Calvin Coolidge: Thirtieth President 1923-1929, 30. Venezia, Mike. 2007. (Getting to Know the U. S. Presidents Ser.). (ENG.). 32p. (J). (gr. 3-6). lib. bdg. 22.44 *(978-0-516-22634-7(7))* Scholastic Library Publishing.

—Camille Pissarro. Venezia, Mike. 2004. (Getting . Know Artists Ser.). (ENG.). 32p. (J). (gr. 3-4). pap. 6.95 *(978-0-516-26977-1(1)*, Children's Pr.) Scholastic Library Publishing.

—Charles Drew: Doctor Who Got the World Pumped up to Donate Blood. Venezia, Mike. 2009. (ENG.). 32p. (J). (gr. 3-4). pap. 6.95 *(978-0-531-21334-6(X)*, Children's Pr.); (gr. 2-5). 28.00 *(978-0-531-23725-0(7))* Scholastic Library Publishing.

—Chester A. Arthur. Venezia, Mike. 2006. (Getting to Know the U. S. Presidents Ser.). (ENG.). 32p. (J). (gr. 3-7). lib. bdg. 28.00 *(978-0-516-22626-2(6)*, Children's Pr.) Scholastic Library Publishing.

—Chester A. Arthur: Twenty-First President, 1881-1885. Venezia, Mike. 2006. (Getting to Know the U. S. Presidents Ser.). (ENG.). 32p. (J). (gr. 3-7). pap. 7.95 *(978-0-516-25401-2(4)*, Children's Pr.) Scholastic Library Publishing.

—Claude Monet. Venezia, Mike. rev. ed. 2014. (Getting to Know the World's Greatest Artists Ser.). (ENG.). 40p. (J). lib. bdg. 29.00 *(978-0-531-21979-9(8))* Scholastic Library Publishing.

—Diego Rivera. Venezia, Mike. 2015. (ENG.). 40p. (J). (gr. 3-4). lib. bdg. 29.00 *(978-0-531-21261-5(0)*, Children's Pr.) Scholastic Library Publishing.

—Diego Velázquez. Venezia, Mike. 2004. (Getting to Know the World's Greatest Artists Ser.). (ENG.). 32p. (J). (gr. 3-4). pap. 6.95 *(978-0-516-26980-1(1)*, Children's Pr.) Scholastic Library Publishing.

—Duke Ellington. Venezia, Mike. rev. ed. 2017. (ENG.). 40p. (J). (gr. 3-4). pap. 7.95 *(978-0-531-23036-7(8)*, Children's Pr.) Scholastic Library Publishing.

—Dwight D. Eisenhower: Thirty-Fourth President 1953-1961. Venezia, Mike. 2007. (Getting to Know the U. S. Presidents Ser.). (ENG.). 32p. (J). (gr. 3-4). 28.00 *(978-0-516-22638-5(X)*, Children's Pr.) Scholastic Library Publishing.

—Edgar Degas. Venezia, Mike. rev. ed. 2016. (ENG.). 40p. (J). (gr. 3-4). pap. 7.95 *(978-0-531-22087-0(7)*, Children's Pr.) Scholastic Library Publishing.

—Eugene Delacroix. Venezia, Mike. 2003. (Getting to Know World Artists Ser.). (ENG.). 32p. (J). 28.00 *(978-0-516-22576-0(6)*, Children's Pr.) Scholastic Library Publishing.

—Eugène Delacroix. Venezia, Mike. 2003. (Getting to Know the World's Greatest Artists Ser.). (ENG.). 32p. (J). pap. 6.95 *(978-0-516-26976-4(3)*, Children's Pr.) Scholastic Library Publishing.

—Faith Ringgold. Venezia, Mike. (ENG.). 32p. (J). (gr. 3-4). 2008. pap. 6.95 *(978-0-531-14757-3(6))*; 2007. 28.00 *(978-0-531-18526-1(5))* Scholastic Library Publishing. (Children's Pr.).

—Francisco Goya. Venezia, Mike. 2016. (ENG.). 40p. (J). (gr. 3-4). pap. 7.95 *(978-0-531-22106-8(7)*, Children's Pr.) Scholastic Library Publishing.

—Franklin D. Roosevelt: Thirty-Second President 1933-1945, 32. Venezia, Mike. 2007. (Getting to Know the U. S. Presidents Ser.). (ENG.). 32p. (J). (gr. 3-6). 22.44 *(978-0-516-22636-1(3))* Scholastic Library Publishing.

—Franklin Pierce: Fourteenth President. Venezia, Mike. 2005. (Getting to Know the U. S. Presidents Ser.). (ENG.). 32p. (J). (gr. 3-7). lib. bdg. 28.00 *(978-0-516-22619-4(3)*, Children's Pr.) Scholastic Library Publishing.

—Frederic Chopin. Venezia, Mike. rev. ed. 2017. (ENG.). 40p. (J). (gr. 3-4). pap. 7.95 *(978-0-531-23035-0(X)*, Children's Pr.) Scholastic Library Publishing.

—Frederic Remington. Venezia, Mike. 2003. (Getting to Know the World's Greatest Artists Ser.). (ENG.). 32p. (J). (gr. 3-4). pap. 6.95 *(978-0-516-27812-4(6)*, Children's Pr.) Scholastic Library Publishing.

—Frida Kahlo. Venezia, Mike. 2015. (ENG.). 40p. (J). (gr. 3-4). lib. bdg. 29.00 *(978-0-531-21259-2(9)*, Children's Pr.) Scholastic Library Publishing.

—George Bush. Venezia, Mike. 2008. (Getting to Know the U. S. Presidents Ser.). (ENG.). 32p. (J). (gr. 3-4). pap. 7.95 *(978-0-516-25536-1(3)*, Children's Pr.) Scholastic Library Publishing.

—George Gershwin. Venezia, Mike. rev. ed. 2017. (ENG.). 40p. (J). (gr. 3-4). pap. 7.95 *(978-0-531-23037-4(6)*, Children's Pr.) Scholastic Library Publishing.

—George Handel. Venezia, Mike. 2018. (ENG.). 40p. (J). (gr. 3-4). 29.00 *(978-0-531-22870-8(3))*; pap. 7.95 *(978-0-531-23373-3(1))* Scholastic Library Publishing. (Children's Pr.).

—George Washington. Venezia, Mike. 2005. (Getting to Know the U. S. Presidents Ser.). (ENG.). 32p. (J). (gr. 3-4). pap. 7.95 *(978-0-516-27475-1(9)*, Children's Pr.) Scholastic Library Publishing.

—Georges Seurat. Venezia, Mike. 2003. (ENG.). 32p. (J). (gr. 3-4). pap. 6.95 *(978-0-516-27813-1(4)*, Children's Pr.) Scholastic Library Publishing.

—Georgia O'Keefe. Venezia, Mike. 2015. (ENG.). 40p. (J). (gr. 3-4). pap. 7.95 *(978-0-531-21291-2(2)*, Children's Pr.) Scholastic Library Publishing.

—Georgia O'Keeffe. Venezia, Mike. 2005. (Getting to Know the World's Greatest Artists Ser.). (ENG.). (J). (gr. 1-4). lib. bdg. 17.55 *(978-1-62765-167-7(5))* Perfection Learning Corp.

—Gerald R. Ford: Thirty-Eighth President, 1974-1977. Venezia, Mike. (Getting to Know the U. S. Presidents Ser.). (ENG.). 32p. (J). (gr. 3-4). 2008. pap. 7.95 *(978-0-516-25597-2(5))*; 2007. 28.00 *(978-0-516-22642-2(8))* Scholastic Library Publishing. (Children's Pr.).

—Getting to Know the World's Greatest Artists - Titian. Venezia, Mike. 2003. (Getting to Know the World's Greatest Artists Ser.). (ENG.). 32p. (J). (gr. 3-4). pap. 6.95 *(978-0-516-26975-7(5)*, Children's Pr.) Scholastic Library Publishing.

—Grandma Moses. Venezia, Mike. 2004. (Getting to Know the World's Greatest Artists Ser.). (ENG.). 32p. (J). (gr. 3-4). pap. 6.95 *(978-0-516-27913-8(0)*, Children's Pr.) Scholastic Library Publishing.

—El Greco. Venezia, Mike. rev. ed. 2016. (ENG.). 40p. (J). (gr. 3-4). pap. 7.95 *(978-0-531-22088-7(5)*, Children's Pr.) Scholastic Library Publishing.

—Grover Cleveland: Twenty-Second & Twenty-Fourth President, 1885-1889, 1893-1897. Venezia, Mike. 2006. (Getting to Know the U. S. Presidents Ser.). (ENG.). 32p. (J). (gr. 3-7). pap. 7.95 *(978-0-516-25402-9(2))*; lib. bdg. 28.00 *(978-0-516-22627-9(4))* Scholastic Library Publishing. (Children's Pr.).

—Harry S. Truman: Thirty-Third President. Venezia, Mike. 2007. (Getting to Know the U. S. Presidents Ser.). 32p. (J). (gr. 3-4). 28.00 *(978-0-516-22637-8(1)*, Children's Pr.) Scholastic Library Publishing.

—Henry Ford: Big Wheel in the Auto Industry. Venezia, Mike. 2009. (ENG.). 32p. (J). (gr. 3-4). pap. 6.95 *(978-0-531-21335-3(8))*; 28.00 *(978-0-531-23726-7(5))* Scholastic Library Publishing. (Children's Pr.).

—Horace Pippin. Venezia, Mike. 2007. (Getting to Know the World's Greatest Artists Ser.). (ENG.). 32p. (J). (gr. 3-4). 28.00 *(978-0-531-18527-8(3)*, Children's Pr.) Scholastic Library Publishing.

—Jackson Pollock. Venezia, Mike. rev. ed. 2016. (ENG.). 40p. (J). (gr. 3-4). pap. 7.95 *(978-0-531-22089-4(3)*, Children's Pr.) Scholastic Library Publishing.

—James A. Garfield. Venezia, Mike. 2006. (Getting to Know the U. S. Presidents Ser.). (ENG.). 32p. (J). (gr. 3-7). lib. bdg. 28.00 *(978-0-516-22625-5(8)*, Children's Pr.) Scholastic Library Publishing.

—James Buchanan: Fifteenth President. Venezia, Mike. 2005. (Getting to Know the U. S. Presidents Ser.). (ENG.). 32p. (J). (gr. 3-7). lib. bdg. 28.00 *(978-0-516-22620-0(7)*, Children's Pr.) Scholastic Library Publishing.

—James K. Polk: Eleventh President, 1845-1849. Venezia, Mike. 2005. (Getting to Know the U. S. Presidents Ser.). (ENG.). 32p. (J). (gr. 3-4). 28.00 *(978-0-516-22616-3(9)*, Children's Pr.) Scholastic Library Publishing.

—James McNeill Whistler. Venezia, Mike. 2003. (Getting to Know World Artists Ser.). (ENG.). 32p. (J). 28.00 *(978-0-516-22578-4(2)*, Children's Pr.) Scholastic Library Publishing.

—James Monroe. Venezia, Mike. 2005. (Getting to Know the U. S. Presidents Ser.). (ENG.). 32p. (J). (gr. 3-4). pap. 7.95 *(978-0-516-27479-9(1)*, Children's Pr.) Scholastic Library Publishing.

—Jane Goodall: Researcher Who Champions Chimps. Venezia, Mike. 2010. (ENG.). 32p. (J). (gr. 3-4). 28.00 *(978-0-531-23731-1(1)*, Children's Pr.) Scholastic Library Publishing.

—Jimmy Carter: Thirty-Ninth President 1977-1981. Venezia, Mike. 2007. (Getting to Know the U. S. Presidents Ser.). (ENG.). 32p. (J). (gr. 3-4). 28.00 *(978-0-516-22643-9(6)*, Children's Pr.) Scholastic Library Publishing.

—Johann Sebastian Bach. Venezia, Mike. 2017. (ENG.). 40p. (J). (gr. 3-4). lib. bdg. 29.00 *(978-0-531-22060-3(5)*, Children's Pr.) Scholastic Library Publishing.

—John F. Kennedy: Thirty-Fifth President 1961-1963, 32. Venezia, Mike. 2007. (Getting to Know the U. S. Presidents Ser.). (ENG.). 32p. (J). (gr. 3-6). 22.44 *(978-0-516-22639-2(8))* Scholastic Library Publishing.

—John Philip Sousa. Venezia, Mike. 2018. (ENG.). 40p. (J). (gr. 3-4). 29.00 *(978-0-531-22869-2(X))*; pap. 7.95 *(978-0-531-23372-6(3))* Scholastic Library Publishing. (Children's Pr.).

—John Quincy Adams: Sixth President, 1825-1829. Venezia, Mike. 2005. (Getting to Know the U. S. Presidents Ser.). (ENG.). 32p. (J). (gr. 3-4). pap. 7.95 *(978-0-516-27480-5(5)*, Children's Pr.) Scholastic Library Publishing.

—John Tyler: Tenth President, 1841-1845. Venezia, Mike. 2005. (Getting to Know the U. S. Presidents Ser.). (ENG.). 32p. (J). (gr. 3-4). per. 7.95 *(978-0-516-27484-3(8))*; 28.00 *(978-0-516-22615-6(0))* Scholastic Library Publishing. (Children's Pr.).

—Leonard Bernstein. Venezia, Mike. 2017. (ENG.). 40p. (J). (gr. 3-4). lib. bdg. 29.00 *(978-0-531-22656-8(5))*; pap. 7.95 *(978-0-531-23034-3(1))* Scholastic Library Publishing. (Children's Pr.).

—Leonardo Davinci. Venezia, Mike. rev. ed. 2015. (ENG.). 40p. (J). (gr. 3-4). pap. 7.95 *(978-0-531-21289-9(0)*, Children's Pr.) Scholastic Library Publishing.

—Lise Meitner: Had the Right Vision about Nuclear Fission. Venezia, Mike. (Getting to Know the World's Greatest Inventors & Scientists Ser.). (ENG.). 32p. (J). 2010. (gr. 3-4). pap. 6.95 *(978-0-531-20776-5(5)*, Children's Pr.); 2009. (gr. 2-5). 28.00 *(978-0-531-23702-1(8))* Scholastic Library Publishing.

—Ludwig Van Beethoven. Venezia, Mike. 2017. (ENG.). 40p. (J). (gr. 3-4). lib. bdg. 29.00 *(978-0-531-22059-7(1)*, Children's Pr.) Scholastic Library Publishing.

—Luis Alvarez: Wild Idea Man. Venezia, Mike. (ENG.). 32p. (J). (gr. 3-4). 2010. pap. 6.95 *(978-0-531-20777-2(3))*; 2009. 28.00 *(978-0-531-23703-8(6))* Scholastic Library Publishing. (Children's Pr.).

—Lyndon B. Johnson: Thirty-Sixth President, 1963-1969. Venezia, Mike. 2007. (Getting to Know the U. S. Presidents Ser.). 32p. (J). (gr. 3-4). 28.00 *(978-0-516-22640-8(1)*, Children's Pr.) Scholastic Library Publishing.

—Marie Curie: Scientist Who Made Glowing Discoveries. Venezia, Mike. 2008. (ENG.). 32p. (J). (gr. 3-4). 28.00 *(978-0-531-14977-5(3)*, Children's Pr.) Scholastic Library Publishing.
—Martin Van Buren. Venezia, Mike. 2005. (Getting to Know the U. S. Presidents Ser.). (ENG.). 32p. (J). (gr. 3-4). 28.00 *(978-0-516-22613-2(4)*, Children's Pr.) Scholastic Library Publishing.
—Mary Cassatt. Venezia, Mike. rev. ed. 2015. (ENG.). 40p. (J). (gr. 3-4). pap. 7.95 *(978-0-531-21292-9(0)*, Children's Pr.) Scholastic Library Publishing.
—Mary Leakey - Archaeologist Who Really Dug Her Work. Venezia, Mike. 2009. (Getting to Know the World's Greatest Inventors & Scientists Ser.). (ENG.). 32p. (J). (gr. 2-5). 28.00 *(978-0-531-23727-4(3))* Scholastic Library Publishing.
—Michelangelo. Venezia, Mike. rev. ed. 2014. (ENG.). 40p. (J). (gr. 3-4). lib. bdg. 29.00 *(978-0-531-21977-5(1)*, Children's Pr.) Scholastic Library Publishing.
—Millard Fillmore: Thirteenth President. Venezia, Mike. 2005. (Getting to Know the U. S. Presidents Ser.). (ENG.). 32p. (J). (gr. 3-7). lib. bdg. 28.00 *(978-0-516-22618-7(5)*, Children's Pr.) Scholastic Library Publishing.
—Millard Fillmore: Thirteenth President, 1850-1853. Venezia, Mike. 2006. (Getting to Know the U. S. Presidents Ser.). (ENG.). 32p. (J). (gr. 3-7). per. 7.95 *(978-0-516-25487-6(1)*, Children's Pr.) Scholastic Library Publishing.
—Pablo Picasso. Venezia, Mike. 2014. (ENG.). 40p. (J). (gr. 3-4). pap. 7.95 *(978-0-531-22537-0(2))*; lib. bdg. 29.00 *(978-0-531-21976-8(3))* Scholastic Library Publishing. (Children's Pr.).
—Paul Cezanne. Venezia, Mike. 2016. (ENG.). 40p. (J). (gr. 3-4). pap. 7.95 *(978-0-531-22108-2(3)*, Children's Pr.) Scholastic Library Publishing.
—Peter Tchaikovsky. Venezia, Mike. 2018. (ENG.). 40p. (J). (gr. 3-4). pap. 7.95 *(978-0-531-23371-9(5)*, Children's Pr.) Scholastic Library Publishing.
—Peter Tchaikovsky (Revised Edition) Venezia, Mike. 2018. (ENG.). 40p. (J). (gr. 3-4). 29.00 *(978-0-531-22868-5(1)*, Children's Pr.) Scholastic Library Publishing.
—Pierre Auguste Renoir. Venezia, Mike. 2016. (ENG.). 40p. (J). (gr. 3-4). pap. 7.95 *(978-0-531-22107-5(5))*; lib. bdg. 29.00 *(978-0-531-21668-2(3))* Scholastic Library Publishing. (Children's Pr.).
—Rachel Carson: Clearing the Way for Environmental Protection. Venezia, Mike. (ENG.). 32p. (J). (gr. 3-4). 2010. pap. 6.95 *(978-0-531-20778-9(1))*; 2009. 28.00 *(978-0-531-23704-5(4))* Scholastic Library Publishing. (Children's Pr.).
—Rembrandt. Venezia, Mike. rev. ed. 2015. (ENG.). 40p. (J). (gr. 3-4). pap. 7.95 *(978-0-531-21290-5(4)*, Children's Pr.) Scholastic Library Publishing.
—René Magritte. Venezia, Mike. Magritte, Rene. 2003. (Getting to Know the World's Greatest Artists Ser.). (ENG.). 32p. (J). (gr. 3-4). pap. 6.95 *(978-0-516-27814-8(2)*, Children's Pr.) Scholastic Library Publishing.
—Richard M. Nixon: Thirty-Seventh President, 1969-1974. Venezia, Mike. 2007. (Getting to Know the U. S. Presidents Ser.). 32p. (J). (gr. 3-4). (ENG.). pap. 7.95 *(978-0-531-17949-9(4))*; 28.00 *(978-0-516-22641-5(X))* Scholastic Library Publishing. (Children's Pr.).
—Ronald Reagan: Fortieth President, 1981-1989. Venezia, Mike. 2007. (Getting to Know the U. S. Presidents Ser.). (ENG.). 32p. (J). (gr. 3-4). 28.00 *(978-0-516-22644-6(4)*, Children's Pr.) Scholastic Library Publishing.
—Rutherford B. Hayes: Nineteenth President, 1877-1881. Venezia, Mike. 2006. (Getting to Know the U. S. Presidents Ser.). 32p. (J). (gr. 3-7). pap. 7.95 *(978-0-516-25404-3(9))*; (ENG.). lib. bdg. 28.00 *(978-0-516-22624-8(X))* Scholastic Library Publishing. (Children's Pr.).
—Salvador Dali. Venezia, Mike. 2015. (ENG.). 40p. (J). (gr. 3-4). lib. bdg. 29.00 *(978-0-531-21262-2(9)*, Children's Pr.) Scholastic Library Publishing.
—Sandro Boticelli. Venezia, Mike. rev. ed. 2016. (ENG.). 40p. (J). (gr. 3-4). pap. 7.95 *(978-0-531-22086-3(9)*, Children's Pr.) Scholastic Library Publishing.
—Stephen Hawking: Cosmologist Who Gets a Big Bang Out of the Universe. Venezia, Mike. 2009. (ENG.). 32p. (J). (gr. 3-4). pap. 6.95 *(978-0-531-21337-7(4)*, Children's Pr.); (gr. 2-5). 28.00 *(978-0-531-23728-1(1))* Scholastic Library Publishing.
—Steve Jobs & Steve Wozniak: Geek Heroes Who Put the Personal in Computers. Venezia, Mike. 2010. (ENG.). 32p. (J). (gr. 3-4). pap. 6.95 *(978-0-531-22351-2(5)*, Children's Pr.) Scholastic Library Publishing.
—Thomas Edison: Inventor with a Lot of Bright Ideas. Venezia, Mike. (ENG.). 32p. (J). (gr. 3-4). 2009. pap. 6.95 *(978-0-531-22209-6(8))*; 2008. 28.00 *(978-0-531-14978-2(1))* Scholastic Library Publishing. (Children's Pr.).
—Thomas Jefferson: Third President, 1801-1809. Venezia, Mike. (Getting to Know the U. S. Presidents Ser.). (ENG.). 32p. (J). (gr. 3-4). 2005. pap. 7.95 *(978-0-516-27477-5(5)*, Children's Pr.); 3. 2004. 22.44 *(978-0-516-22608-8(8))* Scholastic Library Publishing.
—Titian. Venezia, Mike. 2003. (Getting to Know World Artists Ser.). (ENG.). 32p. (J). 28.00 *(978-0-516-22575-3(8)*, Children's Pr.) Scholastic Library Publishing.
—Ulysses S. Grant. Venezia, Mike. 2005. (Getting to Know the U. S. Presidents Ser.). (ENG.). 32p. (J). (gr. 3-7). lib. bdg. 28.00 *(978-0-516-22623-1(1)*, Children's Pr.) Scholastic Library Publishing.
—Vincent Van Gogh. Venezia, Mike. 2014. (ENG.). 40p. (J). (gr. 3-4). pap. 7.95 *(978-0-531-22539-4(9))*; lib. bdg. 29.00 *(978-0-531-21978-2(X))* Scholastic Library Publishing. (Children's Pr.).
—Warren G. Harding: Twenty-Ninth President, 1921-1923. Venezia, Mike. 2006. (Getting to Know the U. S. Presidents Ser.). (ENG.). 32p. (J). (gr. 3-7). lib. bdg. 28.00 *(978-0-516-22633-0(9))* Scholastic Library Publishing.
—William Henry Harrison. Venezia, Mike. 2005. (Getting to Know the U. S. Presidents Ser.). (ENG.). 32p. (J). (gr. 3-4). 28.00 *(978-0-516-22614-9(2)*, Children's Pr.) Scholastic Library Publishing.
—William Henry Harrison: Ninth President 1841. Venezia, Mike. 2005. (Getting to Know the U. S. Presidents Ser.). (ENG.). 32p. (J). (gr. 3-4). per. 7.95 *(978-0-516-27483-6(X)*, Children's Pr.) Scholastic Library Publishing.
—William Howard Taft: Twenty-Seventh President. Venezia, Mike. 2007. (Getting to Know the U. S. Presidents Ser.). 32p. (J). (gr. 3-7). pap. 7.95 *(978-0-516-25239-1(9)*, Children's Pr.) Scholastic Library Publishing.
—William McKinley. Venezia, Mike. 2006. (Getting to Know the U. S. Presidents Ser.). (ENG.). 32p. (J). (gr. 3-7). lib. bdg. 28.00 *(978-0-516-22629-3(0)*, Children's Pr.) Scholastic Library Publishing.
—Winslow Homer. Venezia, Mike. 2004. (Getting . Know Artists Ser.). (ENG.). 32p. (J). (gr. 3-4). pap. 6.95 *(978-0-516-26979-5(8)*, Children's Pr.) Scholastic Library Publishing.
—Woodrow Wilson: Twenty-Eighth President. Venezia, Mike. 2007. (Getting to Know the U. S. Presidents Ser.). 32p. (J). (gr. 3-7). pap. 7.95 *(978-0-516-25462-3(6)*, Children's Pr.) Scholastic Library Publishing.
—The Wright Brothers: Inventors Whose Ideas Really Took Flight. Venezia, Mike. 2010. (ENG.). 32p. (J). (gr. 3-4). pap. 6.95 *(978-0-531-22353-6(1)*, Children's Pr.); 28.00 *(978-0-531-23732-8(X))* Scholastic Library Publishing.
—Zachary Taylor: Twelfth President, 1849-1850. Venezia, Mike. 2005. (Getting to Know the U. S. Presidents Ser.). (ENG.). 32p. (J). (gr. 3-4). 28.00 *(978-0-516-22617-0(7)*, Children's Pr.) Scholastic Library Publishing.
Venkatakrishnan, Rames. Roadside Geology of Virginia. Frye, Keith. Alt, David & Hyndman, Donald W., eds. rev. ed. (Roadside Geology Ser.). 256p. (J). (gr. 4). pap. *(978-0-87842-199-2(8)*, 211) Mountain Pr. Publishing Co., Inc.
Veno, Joe. Count to Sleep America. Gamble, Adam & Jasper, Mark. 2015. (Count to Sleep Ser.). (ENG.). 20p. (J). (— 1). bds. 7.95 *(978-1-60219-231-7(6))* Good Night Bks.
—Count to Sleep California. Gamble, Adam & Jasper, Mark. 2014. (Count to Sleep Ser.). (ENG.). 20p. (J). (— 1). bds. 7.95 *(978-1-60219-200-3(6))* Good Night Bks.
—Count to Sleep Florida. Gamble, Adam & Jasper, Mark. 2014. (Count to Sleep Ser.). (ENG.). 20p. (J). (— 1). bds. 7.95 *(978-1-60219-202-7(2))* Good Night Bks.
—Count to Sleep Michigan. Gamble, Adam & Jasper, Mark. 2014. (Count to Sleep Ser.). (ENG.). 20p. (J). (— 1). bds. 7.95 *(978-1-60219-327-7(4))* Good Night Bks.
—Count to Sleep Minnesota. Gamble, Adam & Jasper, Mark. 2014. (Count to Sleep Ser.). (ENG.). 20p. (J). (— 1). bds. 7.95 *(978-1-60219-205-8(7))* Good Night Bks.
—Count to Sleep Texas. Gamble, Adam & Jasper, Mark. 2014. (Count to Sleep Ser.). (ENG.). 20p. (J). (— 1). bds. 7.95 *(978-1-60219-326-0(0))* Good Night Bks.
—Count to Sleep Wisconsin. Gamble, Adam & Jasper, Mark. 2014. (Count to Sleep Ser.). (ENG.). 20p. (J). (— 1). bds. 7.95 *(978-1-60219-328-4(2))* Good Night Bks.
—Good Night Alabama. Gamble, Adam & Jasper, Mark. 2015. (Good Night Our World Ser.). (ENG.). 20p. (J). (— 1). bds. 9.95 *(978-1-60219-220-1(0))* Good Night Bks.
—Good Night Arizona. Gamble, Adam. 2008. (Good Night Our World Ser.). (ENG.). 20p. (J). (gr. k — 1). bds. 9.95 *(978-1-60219-000-9(3))* Good Night Bks.
—Good Night Arkansas. Gamble, Adam & Jasper, Mark. 2019. (Good Night Our World Ser.). 20p. (J). (— 1). bds. 9.95 *(978-1-60219-778-7(4))* Good Night Bks.
—Good Night Atlanta. Gamble, Adam. 2007. (Good Night Our World Ser.). (ENG.). 20p. (J). (gr. k — 1). bds. 9.95 *(978-1-60219-001-6(1))* Good Night Bks.
—Good Night Boats. Gamble, Adam & Jasper, Mark. 2016. (Good Night Our World Ser.). (ENG.). 20p. (J). (— 1). bds. 9.95 *(978-1-60219-500-4(5))* Good Night Bks.
—Good Night Boston. Gamble, Adam. 2007. (Good Night Our World Ser.). (ENG.). 20p. (J). (gr. k — 1). bds. 9.95 *(978-1-60219-003-0(8))* Good Night Bks.
—Good Night Boston. Gamble, Adam. 2005. (J). bds. 9.95 *(978-0-9758502-4-4(5))* On Cape Pubns.
—Good Night Broadway. Gamble, Adam & Jasper, Mark. 2017. (Good Night Our World Ser.). 20p. (J). (gr. -1 — 1). bds. 9.95 *(978-1-60219-436-6(X))* Good Night Bks.
—Good Night Chicago. Gamble, Adam. 2006. (Good Night Our World Ser.). (ENG.). 20p. (J). (gr. k — 1). bds. 9.95 *(978-0-9777979-2-9(9))* Good Night Bks.
—Good Night Cowboys. Gamble, Adam & Jasper, Mark. 2017. (Good Night Our World Ser.). 20p. (J). (— 1). bds. 9.95 *(978-1-60219-509-7(9))* Good Night Bks.
—Good Night Dallas/Fort Worth. Gamble, Adam & Jasper, Mark. 2016. (Good Night Our World Ser.). (ENG.). 20p. (J). (— 1). bds. 9.95 *(978-1-60219-224-9(3))* Good Night Bks.
—Good Night Denver. Bouse, Susan. 2007. (Good Night Our World Ser.). (ENG.). 20p. (J). (gr. k — 1). bds. 9.95 *(978-1-60219-006-1(2))* Good Night Bks.
—Good Night Fire Engines. Gamble, Adam & Jasper, Mark. 2015. (Good Night Our World Ser.). (ENG.). 20p. (J). (— 1). bds. 9.95 *(978-1-60219-501-1(3))* Good Night Bks.
—Good Night Fish. Gamble, Adam & Jasper, Mark. 2016. (Good Night Our World Ser.). (ENG.). 20p. (J). (— 1). bds. 9.95 *(978-1-60219-502-8(1))* Good Night Bks.
—Good Night Florida. Gamble, Adam & Jasper, Mark. 2nd ed. 2010. (Good Night Our World Ser.). (ENG.). 20p. (J). (gr. k — 1). bds. 9.95 *(978-1-60219-045-0(3))* Good Night Bks.
—Good Night Hanukkah. Gamble, Adam & Jasper, Mark. 2019. (Good Night Our World Ser.). 20p. (J). (— 1). bds. 9.95 *(978-1-60219-801-2(2))* Good Night Bks.
—Good Night Hawaii. Gamble, Adam. 2007. (Good Night Our World Ser.). (ENG.). 20p. (J). (gr. k — 1). bds. 9.95 *(978-1-60219-007-8(0))* Good Night Bks.
—Good Night Honolulu. Gamble, Adam & Jasper, Mark. 2018. (Good Night Our World Ser.). 20p. (J). (— 1). bds. 9.95 *(978-1-60219-680-3(X))* Good Night Bks.
—Good Night Houston. Gamble, Adam & Jasper, Mark. 2016. (Good Night Our World Ser.). (ENG.). 20p. (J). (— 1). bds. 9.95 *(978-1-60219-504-2(8))* Good Night Bks.
—Good Night Idaho. Gamble, Adam & Jasper, Mark. 2018. (Good Night Our World Ser.). 20p. (J). (— 1). bds. 9.95 *(978-1-60219-410-6(6))* Good Night Bks.
—Good Night Kansas. Gamble, Adam & Jasper, Mark. 2017. (Good Night Our World Ser.). 20p. (J). (— 1). bds. 9.95 *(978-1-60219-223-2(5))* Good Night Bks.
—Good Night Minnesota. Gamble, Adam. 2009. (Good Night Our World Ser.). (ENG.). 20p. (J). (gr. k — 1). bds. 9.95 *(978-1-60219-034-4(8))* Good Night Bks.
—Good Night Mississippi. Gamble, Adam & Jasper, Mark. 2015. (Good Night Our World Ser.). (ENG.). 20p. (J). (— 1). bds. 9.95 *(978-1-60219-221-8(9))* Good Night Bks.
—Good Night Missouri. Gamble, Adam & Jasper, Mark. 2013. (Good Night Our World Ser.). (ENG.). 20p. (J). (— 1). bds. 9.95 *(978-1-60219-077-1(1))* Good Night Bks.
—Good Night New Jersey. Gamble, Adam & Clark, Dennis. 2008. (Good Night Our World Ser.). (ENG.). 20p. (J). (gr. k — 1). bds. 9.95 *(978-1-60219-025-2(9))* Good Night Bks.
—Good Night New York City. Gamble, Adam. 2006. (Good Night Our World Ser.). (ENG.). 24p. (J). (gr. k — 1). bds. 9.95 *(978-0-9777979-3-6(7))* Good Night Bks.
—Good Night Oklahoma. Gamble, Adam & Jasper, Mark. 2019. (Good Night Our World Ser.). 20p. (J). (— 1). bds. 9.95 *(978-1-60219-777-0(6))* Good Night Bks.
—Good Night Oregon. McCarthy, Dan. 2010. (Good Night Our World Ser.). (ENG.). 20p. (J). (gr. k — 1). bds. 9.95 *(978-1-60219-041-2(0))* Good Night Bks.
—Good Night Outer Banks. Gamble, Adam & Jasper, Mark. 2018. (Good Night Our World Ser.). (ENG.). 20p. (J). (— 1). bds. 9.95 *(978-1-60219-604-9(4))* Good Night Bks.
—Good Night Puerto Rico. Martinez, Lisa Bolivar & Martinez, Matthew. 2017. (Good Night Our World Ser.). 20p. (J). (— 1). bds. 9.95 *(978-1-60219-508-0(0))* Good Night Bks.
—Good Night Puppies. Gamble, Adam & Jasper, Mark. 2015. (Good Night Our World Ser.). (ENG.). 20p. (J). (— 1). bds. 9.95 *(978-1-60219-227-0(8))* Good Night Bks.
—Good Night Race Cars. Gamble, Adam & Jasper, Mark. 2015. (Good Night Our World Ser.). (ENG.). 20p. (J). (— 1). bds. 9.95 *(978-1-60219-228-7(6)*, 1396132) Good Night Bks.
—Good Night Seattle. Steere, Jay. 2007. (Good Night Our World Ser.). (ENG.). 20p. (J). (gr. k — 1). bds. 9.95 *(978-1-60219-014-6(3))* Good Night Bks.
—Good Night St Louis. Gamble, Adam & Jasper, Mark. 2017. (Good Night Our World Ser.). 20p. (J). (— 1). bds. 9.95 *(978-1-60219-467-0(X))* Good Night Bks.
—Good Night Tennessee. Gamble, Adam. 2007. (Good Night Our World Ser.). (ENG.). 20p. (J). (gr. k — 1). bds. 9.95 *(978-1-60219-019-1(4))* Good Night Bks.
—Good Night Virginia. Gamble, Adam. 2008. (Good Night Our World Ser.). (ENG.). 20p. (J). (gr. k — 1). bds. 9.95 *(978-1-60219-026-9(7))* Good Night Bks.
—Good Night Washington DC. Gamble, Adam. 2006. (Good Night Our World Ser.). (ENG.). 20p. (J). (gr. k — 1). bds. 9.95 *(978-0-9777979-1-2(0))* Good Night Bks.
—What's Eating You, Girls 'n Boysenberries? Hirschfield, Beth. 2009. 32p. (J). 16.95 *(978-0-9818126-3-2(5))* Ampersand, Inc.
Veno, Joe & Jasper, Mark. Buenas Noches, Nueva York. Gamble, Adam. 2013. (Buenas Noches Ser.). (SPA.). 24p. (J). (— 1). bds. 9.95 *(978-1-60219-091-7(7))* Good Night Bks.
Veno, Joe & Kelly, Cooper. Good Night Texas. Gamble, Adam. 2nd ed. 2011. (Good Night Our World Ser.). (ENG.). 20p. (J). (gr. k — 1). bds. 9.95 *(978-1-60219-053-5(4))* Good Night Bks.
Veno, Joe, jt. illus. see Holder, Jimmy.
Veno, Joe, jt. illus. see Lin, Arthur.
Veno, Joe, jt. illus. see Palmer, Ruth.
Veno, Joe, jt. illus. see Rosen, Anne.
Vent des Hove, Yaël. Mama, Me Cuentas un Cuento? Vent des Hove, Yaël. Vent des Hove, Yael. 2006. (SPA.). 32p. (J). (gr. -1-k). 20.99 *(978-84-261-3527-8(7))* Lectorum Pubns., Inc.
Vent, Le. The Lee Family. Paulson, Anna Caitlin. Paulson, Jacob Nathanael, ed. 2020. (ENG.). 26p. (J). pap. 12.00 ***(978-1-6547-2474-0(2))*** Independently Published.
Ventling, Elisabeth. Scoop. Cook, Julia. 2007. 32p. (J). 15.95 *(978-1-934073-07-0(5))* National Ctr. For Youth Issues.
Vento, Shawn. The Land of Noir: Book I: the Calling. Bobola, Frederick Lee. 2018. (ENG.). 448p. (YA). (gr. 7-12). 24.99 *(978-0-692-16136-4(8))* Bobola, Frederick.
Ventura, Marco. C Is for Ciao: An Italy Alphabet. Grodin, Elissa D. et al. 2008. (Discover the World Ser.). (ENG.). 40p. (J). (gr. 1-5). 17.95 *(978-1-58536-361-2(8))* Sleeping Bear Pr.
Ventura, Piero. Historia Ilustrada de la Humanidad: La Comunicación. Ventura, Piero. Piero, Ventura. (SPA.). 64p. (YA). (gr. 5-8). *(978-84-241-5902-3(0))* Everest Editora ESP. Dist: Lectorum Pubns., Inc.
Venturi-Pickett, Stacy. Jonah & the Fish: Based on Jonah 1-3:3. Pingry, Patricia A. 2005. (Stories from the Bible Ser.). (ENG.). 26p. (J). (gr. -1-k). bds. 6.95 *(978-0-8249-6626-3(0)*, Ideal Pubns.) Worthy Publishing.
—The Story of Loaves & Fishes. Pingry, Patricia A. 2003. 26p. (J). bds. 6.95 *(978-0-8249-6518-1(3)*, Ideal Pubns.) Worthy Publishing.
—The Story of Mary. Pingry, Patricia A. 2006. (ENG.). 32p. (J). (gr. -1-3). pap. 3.95 *(978-0-8249-5546-5(3)*, Ideal Pubns.) Worthy Publishing.
Venturi-Pickett, Stacy. The Story of Creation. Venturi-Pickett, Stacy, tr. Pingry, Patricia A., tr. 2003. 26p. (J). bds. 7.95 *(978-0-8249-6504-4(3)*, Ideal Pubns.) Worthy Publishing.
Venturini, Claudia. The Elves & the Trendy Shoes. Foster, Evelyn. 2015. (Tadpoles: Fairytale Twists Ser.). (ENG.). 32p. (J). (gr. 1-2). *(978-0-7787-1932-8(4))* Crabtree Publishing Co.
Venus, Joanna. Starting Fishing - Internet Linked. Patchett, Fiona. rev. ed. 2004. (First Skills Ser.). 32p. (J). pap. 4.95 *(978-0-7945-0672-8(0)*, Usborne) EDC Publishing.
Vera, Luisa. Ali Baba & the Forty Thieves. 2004. 63p. (J). *(978-1-84444-536-3(4))* Mantra Lingua.
Verano, Vladimir. Graveyard of a Queen. Xu, Lei. Mok, Kathy, tr. 2014. (Grave Robbers' Chronicles Ser.: 6). (ENG.). pap. 9.95 *(978-1-934159-36-1(0))* ThingsAsian Pr.
—The Prince, the Demon King, & the Monkey Warrior. 2011. (ENG.). 96p. (J). (gr. 3-6). pap. 9.95 *(978-1-934159-30-9(1))* ThingsAsian Pr.
Verbeck, Frank. Donegal Fairy Stories. MacManus, Seumas. 2012. (Dover Children's Classics Ser.). (ENG.). 256p. (J). (gr. 3-8). pap. 8.95 *(978-0-486-21971-4(2))* Dover Pubns., Inc.
Vercesi, Anthony. Plays to Play with in Class. Milgrim, Sally-Anne. 2003. (Plays & Play Collections). 216p. (YA). (gr. 8-12). pap. 11.00 *(978-0-89390-060-1(5))* Resource Pubns., Inc.
Verdon, Aurelie. Ultimate Spotlight: Savanna Animals. Dussausois, Sophie. 2019. (Ultimate Spotlight Ser.: 4). (ENG.). 14p. (J). (gr. k-3). 16.99 Editions Tourbillon FRA. Dist: Hachette Bk. Group.
Verdoux, Aurélia. Theo at the Beach. Crupi, Jaclyn. 2013. (J). *(978-1-4351-4722-5(7))* Barnes & Noble, Inc.
Vere, Ed. Too Noisy! Doyle, Malachy. 2012. (ENG.). 32p. (J). (gr. -1-2). 15.99 *(978-0-7636-6226-4(7))* Candlewick Pr.
Vere, Ed. Bedtime for Monsters. Vere, Ed. 2012. (ENG.). 32p. (J). (gr. -1-k). 14.99 *(978-0-8050-9509-8(8)*, 900080672, Holt, Henry & Co. Bks. For Young Readers) Holt, Henry & Co.
Verelst, Suana. Next Week When I'm Big. Guggenheim, Jaenet. l.t. ed. 2005. 32p. (J). (gr. -1-2). 19.95i *(978-1-929115-13-6(X))* Azro Pr., Inc.
—Razia's Ray of Hope: One Girl's Dream of an Education. Suneby, Elizabeth. 2020. (CitizenKid Ser.). (ENG.). 32p. (J). (gr. 3-7). pap. 10.99 *(978-1-77138-577-0(4))* Kids Can Pr., Ltd. CAN. Dist: Hachette Bk. Group.
—Razia's Ray of Hope: One Girl's Dream of an Education. Suneby, Liz. 2013. (CitizenKid Ser.). (ENG.). 32p. (J). (gr. 3-7). 18.99 *(978-1-55453-816-4(5))* Kids Can Pr., Ltd. CAN. Dist: Hachette Bk. Group.
Veres, Csongor. Chlo-Jo's Friends Around the World. Rawls, Linnea V. 2017. (ENG.). 26p. (J). (gr. k-3). 14.99 *(978-0-692-95364-8(7))* Adventure Ahead Pubn.
Veres, Laszlo. Charles Darwin & Alfred Russel Wallace: Band 18/Pearl (Collins Big Cat) Claybourne, Anna. 2014. (Collins Big Cat Ser.). (ENG.). 80p. (J). (gr. 5). pap. 11.99 *(978-0-00-753014-4(5))* HarperCollins Pubs. Ltd. GBR. Dist: Independent Pubs. Group.
—Collins Big Cat Phonics for Letters & Sounds - Animal Fun: Band 00/Lilac. Guille-Marrett, Emily & Raby, Charlotte. 2018. (Collins Big Cat Phonics Ser.). (ENG.). 16p. (J). pap. 6.99 *(978-0-00-825126-0(6))* HarperCollins Pubs. Ltd. GBR. Dist: Independent Pubs. Group.
Veres, Laszlo, jt. illus. see Keylock, Andy.
Verheijen, Jan. Mary's Little Donkey: And the Escape to Egypt, 40 vols. Sehlin, Gunhild. Latham, Hugh, tr. 3rd rev. ed. 2012. Orig. Title: Marias Lilla åsna. (ENG.). 144p. (J). pap. 12.95 *(978-0-86315-933-6(8))* Floris Bks. GBR. Dist: Consortium Bk. Sales & Distribution.
—Mary's Little Donkey: And the Flight to Egypt, 56 vols. Sehlin, Gunhild. Latham, Hugh & Maclean, Donald, trs. 2nd rev. ed. 2004. (ENG.). 160p. (J). (gr. 3-6). pap. 12.00 *(978-0-86315-064-7(0))* Floris Bks. GBR. Dist: SteinerBooks, Inc.
Verhille, Alexandre & Tavernier, Sarah. The Illustrated Atlas of Architecture & Marvelous Monuments. 2016. (ENG.). 48p. (J). (gr. 3-7). 27.95 *(978-3-89955-775-6(1))* Die Gestalten Verlag DEU. Dist: Ingram Publisher Services.
—Recordmania: Atlas of the Incredible. 2018. (ENG.). 48p. 24.95 *(978-3-89955-814-2(6))* Die Gestalten Verlag DEU. Dist: Ingram Publisher Services.
Verhoef, Sharon & Pinkham, Pamela. Something Wicked in the Land of Picatrix. Roland-James, Patricia & James, Robert L. Chidgey, Scarlett, ed. 2007. 281p. (J). pap. 12.95 *(978-0-9760789-9-9(6))* Aquila Ink Publishing.
Verhoeff, Nelleke. The Bread Pet: A Sourdough Story. DePalma, Kate. 2020. (ENG.). 32p. (J). pap. ***(978-1-64686-065-4(9))*** Barefoot Bks., Inc.
Verhoosky, Michele. Big Green Gorilla. Fonte, Mary Roessler & Hoppe, Jessica. 2013. 34p. 17.99 *(978-1-937260-92-7(5))* Sleepytown Pr.
Verhoosky, Michele. Molly Marie & the Amazing Jimmy. Verhoosky, Michele. 2012. 34p. pap. 10.95 *(978-1-937260-22-4(4))* Sleepytown Pr.
Verhoye, Annabelle. The Book of the Sword. Asai, Carrie. 2003. (Samurai Girl Ser.: 1). (ENG.). 224p. (YA). (gr. 11). pap. 11.99 *(978-0-689-85948-9(1)*, Simon Pulse) Simon Pulse.
Verkaik, Marcia. Casey the Container: And Her First Day in Port. Bowden, Kristina. 2019. (ENG.). 24p. (J). 17.99 *(978-1-7324014-0-2(3))*; pap. 8.99 *(978-1-7324014-1-9(1))* Twin 20 Publishing.
Verkruysse, Toni. A Gift from Grandma. Gould, Susan Lynn. 2013. 56p. pap. 20.50 *(978-1-61897-230-9(8)*, Strategic Bk. Publishing) Strategic Book Publishing & Rights Agency (SBPRA).
Verma, Dheeraj. The Battle of the Wilderness: Deadly Inferno. Abnett, Dan. 2007. (Graphic Battles of the Civil War Ser.). (ENG.). 48p. (YA). (gr. 4-7). lib. bdg. 35.45 *(978-1-4042-0780-6(5))* Rosen Publishing Group, Inc., The.
—Goblins. Jeffrey, Gary. 2012. (Graphic Mythical Creatures Ser.). (ENG.). 24p. (J). (gr. 3-5). pap. 8.15 *(978-1-4339-6761-0(8))*; lib. bdg. 24.95 *(978-1-4339-6759-7(6))* Stevens, Gareth Publishing LLLP. (Gareth Stevens Learning Library).
—The Monitor Versus the Merrimac: Ironclads at War. Abnett, Dan. 2007. (Graphic Battles of the Civil War Ser.). (ENG.). 48p. (J). (gr. 4-7). lib. bdg. 35.45 *(978-1-4042-0778-3(3))* Rosen Publishing Group, Inc., The.
—Unicorns. Jeffrey, Gary. 2012. (Graphic Mythical Creatures Ser.). (ENG.). 24p. (J). (gr. 3-5). pap. 8.15 *(978-1-4339-6769-6(3))*; lib. bdg. 24.95 *(978-1-4339-6767-2(7))* Stevens, Gareth Publishing LLLP. (Gareth Stevens Learning Library).
—Vampires. Jeffrey, Gary. 2012. (Graphic Mythical Creatures Ser.). (ENG.). 24p. (J). (gr. 3-5). pap. 8.15 *(978-1-4339-6773-3(1))*; lib. bdg. 24.95 *(978-1-4339-6771-9(5))* Stevens, Gareth Publishing LLLP. (Gareth Stevens Learning Library).

V

Verma, Prachand. Plate Tectonics. Luongo, Charlotte. 2010. (Big Ideas in Science Ser.). 48p. (gr. 5-5). 32.36 (978-0-7614-4397-1(5)) Cavendish Square Publishing LLC.

Vermillion, Danny. Ducky Bill's Great Race. McGhee, Patti Gray. 2013. 46p. 24.95 (978-1-63000-424-8(3)); 48p. pap. 24.95 (978-1-62709-522-8(5)) America Star Bks.

Vermillion, Veerle. The Old Man & the Fat Ginger Cat. Wijnberg, John. Balsdon, Lizette, ed. 2018. (ENG.). 64p. (J). pap. (978-0-620-80896-5(9)) Wijnberg, John.

—The Old Man & the Fat Ginger Cat. Wijnberg, John Paul. Balsdon, Lizette, ed. 2019. (978-0-620-82533-7 Ser.). (ENG.). 64p. (J). (978-0-620-82533-7(2)) Wijnberg, John.

Verne, Jules. Viaje al Centro de la Tierra. Orig. Title: Journey to the Center of the Earth. (SPA.). 160p. (YA). 11.95 (978-84-7281-084-6(4), AF1084) Auriga, Ediciones S.A. ESP. Dist: Continental Bk. Co., Inc.

—Viaje al Centro de la Tierra. 2003. (Advanced Reading Ser.). Orig. Title: Journey to the Center of the Earth. (SPA.). 246p. (J). pap. 11.95 (978-84-239-9063-4(X)) Espasa Calpe, S.A. ESP. Dist: Planeta Publishing Corp.

Verne, Jules, jt. illus. see Samartzi, Iris.

Vernell, Jerome. The Beauty in Me. Guerrero, Elsie. 2019. (ENG.). 28p. (J). (gr. 1-6). 19.99 (978-1-7327573-7-0(2)) Elsie Publishing Co.

—How Emily & Eli Created a Business. Guerrero, Elsie. 2019. (ENG.). 30p. (J). pap. 9.99 (978-1-0810-2882-4(3)) Independently Published.

—How Emily & Eli Created a Business. Guerrero, Elsie. 2019. (ENG.). 30p. (J). (gr. k-6). 19.99 (978-1-7327573-6-3(4)) Elsie Publishing Co.

Vernell Jr, Jerome. The Beauty in Me. Guerrero, Elsie. 2017. (ENG.). (J). pap. 9.95 (978-1-947825-83-3(6)) Yorkshire Publishing Group.

Vernon, Jeff. What Is Dreaming? Boritzer, Etan. 2007. 40p. (J). (gr. -1-3). 14.95 (978-0-9762743-7-7(X)); pap. 6.95 (978-0-9762743-6-0(1)) Lane, Veronica Bks.

—What Is True? Boritzer, Etan. 2010. (J). (978-0-9637597-0-2(1)) Lane, Veronica Bks.

Vernon, Rion. Sofa Boy. Langteau, Scott. 2008. (ENG.). 40p. (J). 16.95 (978-0-615-25125-7(0), 9780615251257) Shake the Moon Bks.

Verona Publishing. Lazy Robert. DeRosa, Nancy. 2006. (J). 5.95 (978-0-9769031-0-9(5)) Verona (Bk.) Publishing, Inc.

Verrall, Lisa. One Two, Baa Moo. Litton, Jonathan. 2015. (My Little World Ser.). (ENG.). 12p. (J). (-k). bds. 8.99 (978-1-68010-507-0(8)) Tiger Tales.

—Red Car, Blue Car. Litton, Jonathan. 2015. (My Little World Ser.). (ENG.). 12p. (J). (gr. -1-k). bds. 8.99 (978-1-68010-506-3(X)) Tiger Tales.

Verrept, Paul. El Pequeno Soldado. Verrept, Paul. Bourgeois, Elodie, tr. 2004. (SPA.). 26p. (J). (gr. -1-3). 17.99 (978-84-261-3306-9(1)) Juventud, Editorial ESP. Dist: Lectorum Pubns., Inc.

Verrett, Michael. Frizzy Frieda's Dye-Saster: Second Book in the Frizzy Frieda Series. Bankston, Pamela Cali. 2017. (Frizzy Frieda Ser.: Vol. 2). (ENG.). (J). (gr. 5-6). pap. 10.99 (978-1-942922-37-7(X)) Wee Creek Pr. LLC.

—LSU Night Before Christmas. Wilson, Janet. 2013. (ENG.). (J). 14.95 (978-1-62086-484-5(3)) Mascot Bks., Inc.

Verrett, Michael. Pontolong & Duckie. Verrett, Michael. 2nd ed. 2019. (Pontolong & Duckie Ser.: Vol. 1). (ENG.). 32p. (J). (gr. 1-6). 21.95 (978-1-0878-1954-9(7)) MVL/Imagine That.

Verrill, William. A Hero Named Mark. Puppel, Douglas. 2012. (J). lib. bdg. 25.00 (978-0-9788980-6-9(0)) Public Education Foundation, The.

Verseghy, Lauren a. A Rare Day. Miller, Michael A. Hogan, Stephanie F., ed. 2019. (ENG.). 40p. (J). (978-0-2288-2076-5(6)); pap. (978-0-2288-2075-8(8)) Tellwell Talent.

Verstegen, Jeska. The Gift for the Child, 50 vols. Wilkeshuis, Cornelius. (ENG.). 28p. (J). 16.95 (978-0-86315-349-5(6)) Floris Bks. GBR. Dist: SteinerBooks, Inc.

Verstraete, Elaine. Germ Hunter: A Story about Louis Pasteur. Alphin, Elaine Marie. 2003. (Creative Minds Biography Ser.). 64p. (J). lib. bdg. 22.60 (978-1-57505-179-6(6), Carolrhoda Bks.); (ENG.). (gr. 4-8). per. 9.99 (978-0-87614-929-4(8)) Lerner Publishing Group.

—Helen Keller. Sutcliffe, Jane. 2003. (On My Own Biographies Ser.). 48p. (J). (gr. 1-3). 6.95 (978-0-87614-903-4(4), Carolrhoda Bks.) Lerner Publishing Group.

—Many Ways to Be a Soldier. Pfeffer, Wendy. 2008. (On My Own History Ser.). (ENG.). 48p. (gr. 2-4). lib. bdg. 25.26 (978-0-8225-7279-4(6), Millbrook Pr.) Lerner Publishing Group.

—Shipwreck Search: Discovery of the H. L. Hunley. Walker, Sally M. (On My Own Science Ser.). (ENG.). 48p. (gr. 2-4). 2007. (J). per. 7.99 (978-0-8225-6449-2(1), First Avenue Editions); 2006. lib. bdg. 25.26 (978-1-57505-878-8(2), Millbrook Pr.) Lerner Publishing Group.

Vervoort, Sarah. It;s More Than A Game! Collar, Bill. 2007. (J). per. 6.95 (978-1-933556-81-9(1)) Publishers' Graphics, L.L.C.

Verwey, Amanda. Girl at the Bottom of the Sea. Tea, Michelle. 2015. 240p. (J). (gr. 6). 19.95 (978-1-940450-00-1(4), 01c89e20-c2e4-4b37-8c93-c206a5be0626) McSweeney's Publishing.

Verzini, Daniele, jt. illus. see Facciotto, Giuseppe.

Verzini, Daniele, jt. illus. see Usai, Luca.

Vess, Charles. Blueberry Girl. Gaiman, Neil. 2009. (ENG.). 32p. (J). (gr. -1-3). 17.99 (978-0-06-083808-9(6)) HarperCollins Pubs.

—Blueberry Girl. Gaiman, Neil. 2011. (ENG.). 32p. (J). (gr. -1-3). pap. 7.99 (978-0-06-083810-2(8), HarperCollins) HarperCollins Pubs. Ltd. GBR. Dist: HarperCollins Pubs.

—The Cats of Tanglewood Forest. De Lint, Charles. 304p. (J). (gr. 3-7). 2014. pap. 12.99 (978-0-316-05359-4(7)); 2013. 18.00 (978-0-316-05357-0(0)) Little, Brown Bks. for Young Readers.

—Driftwood Days. Lachenmeyer, Nathaniel. 2019. (ENG.). 48p. (J). (978-0-8028-5370-7(6), Eerdmans Bks For Young Readers) Eerdmans, William B. Publishing Co.

—Firebirds: An Anthology of Original Fantasy & Science Fiction. Alexander, Lloyd et al. Sharyn, November, ed. 2005. 432p. (YA). (gr. 7-11). 9.99 (978-0-14-240320-4(2), Firebird) Penguin Young Readers Group.

—Instructions. Gaiman, Neil. 2010. (ENG.). 40p. (J). (gr. -1-3). 16.99 (978-0-06-196030-7(6)); lib. bdg. 15.89 (978-0-06-196031-4(4)) HarperCollins Pubs. Ltd. GBR. (HarperCollins). Dist: HarperCollins Pubs.

—Instructions. Gaiman, Neil. 2015. (ENG.). 40p. (J). (gr. -1-3). 9.99 (978-0-06-196032-1(2), HarperCollins) HarperCollins Pubs. Ltd. GBR. Dist: HarperCollins Pubs.

—Rose. Smith, Jeff. 2009. (Bone Ser.). (ENG.). 144p. (J). (gr. 3-7). 26.99 (978-0-545-13542-9(7)); (gr. 4-8). pap. 12.99 (978-0-545-13543-6(5)) Scholastic, Inc. (Graphix).

—Seven Wild Sisters: A Modern Fairy Tale. De Lint, Charles. 272p. (J). (gr. 3-7). 2015. pap. 9.99 (978-0-316-05352-5(X)); 2014. (ENG.). 18.00 (978-0-316-05356-3(2)) Little, Brown Bks. for Young Readers.

Vest, Dianne. Miss Henn & Family. Lewis, Orane. I.t. ed. 2006. 27p. (J). per. 10.99 (978-1-59879-141-9(9)) Lifevest Publishing, Inc.

Vest, Sam. The Magic Hill. Bunt, Stephanie Marie. 2018. (ENG.). 34p. (J). pap. 11.00 (978-1-948863-04-9(9)) Bunt, Stephanie.

Vetere, Jenna. The House with Hundreds of Rooms. Beckwith, Allison. Lauerman, Kerry, ed. 2020. (ENG.). 32p. (J). pap. 12.99 (978-1-7187-7022-5(7)) CreateSpace Independent Publishing Platform.

Vetsch, Earnest. The Story of a Saucy Squirrel. Wright, Allan. Trust, The Gunston, ed. 2018. (ENG.). 44p. (J). pap. 7.99 (978-1-7286-1294-2(2)) Independently Published.

Viacava, Alejandra. Let's Go the Zoo! Castellanos, Graciela. 2019. (ENG.). 28p. (J). pap. 9.50 (978-1-6911-6842-2(4)) Independently Published.

—�Estoy Creciendo! Castellanos, Graciela. 2019. (SPA.). 24p. (J). pap. 9.50 (978-1-6922-3058-6(1)) Independently Published.

—�Vamos Al Zool�gico! Castellanos, Graciela. 2019. (SPA.). 28p. (J). pap. 9.50 (978-1-6911-8194-0(3)) Independently Published.

ViacomCBS, Arthur Desin. A Garfield ® Guide to Online Etiquette: Be Kind Online. Nickel, Scott et al. 2020. (Garfield's ® Guide to Digital Citizenship Ser.). (ENG.). 32p. (J). (gr. 2-5). pap. 8.99 (978-1-5415-8747-2(2), Lerner Pubns.) Lerner Publishing Group.

—A Garfield ® Guide to Online Friends: Not the Same As Real Friends! Nickel, Scott et al. 2020. (Garfield's ® Guide to Digital Citizenship Ser.). (ENG.). 32p. (J). (gr. 2-5). pap. 8.99 (978-1-5415-8749-6(9), Lerner Pubns.) Lerner Publishing Group.

—A Garfield ® Guide to Posting Online: Pause Before You Post. Nickel, Scott et al. 2020. (Garfield's ® Guide to Digital Citizenship Ser.). (ENG.). 32p. (J). (gr. 2-5). pap. 8.99 (978-1-5415-8750-2(2), Lerner Pubns.) Lerner Publishing Group.

—A Garfield ® Guide to Safe Downloading: Downloading Disaster! Nickel, Scott et al. 2020. (Garfield's ® Guide to Digital Citizenship Ser.). (ENG.). 32p. (J). (gr. 2-5). pap. 8.99 (978-1-5415-8748-9(0), Lerner Pubns.) Lerner Publishing Group.

Viall, Pauline. My Maize & Blue Day. Richards, Sonja. 2008. 32p. (J). 19.95 (978-0-9794935-1-5(X)) Olde Towne Publishing.

Vialva, Clivia & Francisco, David. The Story of the Little Candle: A Book of Inspiration. Meahjohn, Inshan. 2020. (ENG.). 30p. (J). (gr. -1-3). 13.95 (978-1-9822-4071-4(7), Balboa Pr.) Author Solutions, Inc.

Viana, Tatio. City on the Hill. Hall, Mark & West, Matthew. 2014. (ENG.). 32p. (gr. -1-3). 16.99 (978-1-4336-8231-5(1), 005603000, B&H Kids) B&H Publishing Group.

—Inside Battleships. Oxlade, Chris. 2017. (Inside Military Machines Ser.). (ENG.). 32p. (J). (gr. 3-6). lib. bdg. 27.99 (978-1-5124-3225-1(3), 9781512432251, Hungry Tomato ®) Lerner Publishing Group.

—Inside Submarines. Oxlade, Chris. 2017. (Inside Military Machines Ser.). (ENG.). 32p. (J). (gr. 3-6). lib. bdg. 27.99 (978-1-5124-3224-4(5), 9781512432244, Hungry Tomato ®) Lerner Publishing Group.

—Inside Tanks & Heavy Artillery. Oxlade, Chris. 2017. (Inside Military Machines Ser.). (ENG.). 32p. (J). (gr. 3-6). lib. bdg. 27.99 (978-1-5124-3226-8(1), 9781512432268, Hungry Tomato ®) Lerner Publishing Group.

Viana, Tatio, jt. illus. see Campidelli, Maurizio.

Vianney, M. John. Little Nellie of Holy God 1903-1908. Dominic, Sister M. 2009. (ENG.). 32p. (J). (gr. 2-2). pap. 12.95 (978-0-89555-834-3(3), 2120) TAN Bks.

Viano, Hannah. B Is for Bear: A Natural Alphabet. Viano, Hannah. 2015. (ENG.). 32p. (J). (-k). 16.99 (978-1-63217-039-2(6), Little Bigfoot) Sasquatch Bks.

—S Is for Salmon: A Pacific Northwest Alphabet. Viano, Hannah. 2014. 32p. (J). (-k). 16.99 (978-1-57061-873-4(9), Little Bigfoot) Sasquatch Bks.

Viator, Artifex. I'm So Cool. Waite, Victor H. 2019. (ENG.). 30p. (J). pap. 9.99 (978-1-7083-9518-6(0)) Independently Published.

Vicario, Evelyn. Mathematics for Life - Moses Meets the Triangles. Vicario, Evelyn. 2013. 48p. (J). pap. 7.99 (978-0-9826276-6-2(1), Bibia Publishing) Bibia, LLC.

Vicente, Fernando. Peter Pan. Barrie, J. M. Bustelo, Gabriela, tr. 2006. (Alfaguara Infantil y Juvenil Ser.). 229p. (J). (gr. 4-7). pap. (978-970-770-677-4(5)) Ediciones Alfaguara.

Vicente, Luise San. Lucila Se Llama Gabriela. Aguirre, Sonia Montecino. rev. ed. 2006. (Otra Escalera Ser.). (ENG.). 60p. (J). (gr. -1-k). pap. 12.95 (978-970-20-0828-6(X)) Castillo, Ediciones, S. A. de C. V. MEX. Dist: Macmillan.

Vick, Kari. Seven Ways to Trick a Troll. Lunge-Larsen, Lise. 2017. (ENG.). 96p. (J). 19.95 (978-0-8166-9977-3(1)) Univ. of Minnesota Pr.

—The Sock Goblin. Arrowsmith Decoux, Rose. 2018. (ENG.). 40p. (J). (gr. k-1). 16.95 (978-1-938237-26-3(9)) Skywater Publishing Co.

Vickers, Roy. If You Want to Visit a Sea Garden, 1 vol. Weisman, Kay. 2020. (ENG.). 32p. (J). (gr. k-3). 18.95 (978-1-55498-970-6(1)) Groundwood Bks. CAN. Dist: Publishers Group West (PGW).

Vickers, Roy Henry. The Elders Are Watching. Bouchard, David. 5th rev. deluxe ed. 2003. (ENG.). 56p. (J). 18.95 (978-1-55192-641-4(5)) Raincoast Bk. Distribution CAN. Dist: Publishers Group West (PGW).

Vickers, Roy Henry. Hello Humpback! Vickers, Roy Henry. Budd, Robert. 2017. (First West Coast Bks.: 1). (ENG.). 20p. (J). bds. (978-1-55017-799-2(0)) Harbour Publishing Co., Ltd.

—Raven Squawk, Orca Squeak. Vickers, Roy Henry. Budd, Robert. 2020. (First West Coast Bks.: 4). (ENG.). 20p. (J). bds. 9.95 (978-1-55017-904-0(7)) Harbour Publishing Co., Ltd. CAN. Dist: Publishers Group West (PGW).

—Sockeye Silver, Saltchuck Blue. Vickers, Roy Henry. Budd, Robert. 2019. (First West Coast Bks.: 3). (ENG.). 20p. (J). bds. (978-1-55017-870-8(9)) Harbour Publishing Co., Ltd.

Vickers, Stormi. My Beautiful Alone. Vickers, Stormi. 2004. (YA). per. 10.95 (978-1-888141-41-2(7)) Southeast Media.

Victoria, A. Katie, the Curious Kitty. Upton, J. 2017. (ENG.). (J). pap. 9.25 (978-0-9983202-0-5(X)) Heritage National Publishing.

Victoria Assanelli. You Can Control Your Voice: Loud or Quiet? Miller, Connie Colwell. 2017. (Making Good Choices Ser.). (ENG.). 24p. (J). (gr. 1-4). 20.95 (978-1-68151-167-2(3), Amicus Illustrated) Amicus Publishing.

—You Can Handle Conflict: Hands or Words? Miller, Connie Colwell. 2017. (Making Good Choices Ser.). (ENG.). 24p. (J). (gr. 1-4). 20.95 (978-1-68151-162-7(2), Amicus Illustrated) Amicus Publishing.

—You Can Listen to Directions: Stop or Go? Miller, Connie Colwell. 2017. (Making Good Choices Ser.). (ENG.). 24p. (J). (gr. 1-4). 20.95 (978-1-68151-166-5(5), Amicus Illustrated) Amicus Publishing.

—You Can Stay in Control: Wild or Calm? Miller, Connie Colwell. 2017. (Making Good Choices Ser.). (ENG.). 24p. (J). (gr. 1-4). 20.95 (978-1-68151-165-8(7), Amicus Illustrated) Amicus Publishing.

—You're Angry: Throw a Fit or Talk It Out? Miller, Connie Colwell. 2017. (Making Good Choices Ser.). (ENG.). 24p. (J). (gr. 1-4). 20.95 (978-1-68151-164-1(9), Amicus Illustrated) Amicus Publishing.

—You're in Trouble: Fib or Truth? Miller, Connie Colwell. 2017. (Making Good Choices Ser.). (ENG.). 24p. (J). (gr. 1-4). 20.95 (978-1-68151-163-4(0), Amicus Illustrated) Amicus Publishing.

Victoria, Danna. Adventures in the Pond: Bob & the Duck. Williams, Kay. 2nd ed. 2019. (ENG.). 30p. (J). pap. 7.91 (978-1-913165-10-9(8)) TinydragonBks.

—Adventures in the Pond: Fido the Fish at the Bottom of the Pond. Williams, Kay. 2nd ed. 2019. (ENG.). 30p. (J). pap. 7.91 (978-1-913165-01-7(9)) TinydragonBks.

—Adventures in the Pond: Gizmo Escapes. Williams, Kay. 2nd ed. 2019. (ENG.). 30p. (J). pap. 7.91 (978-1-913165-02-4(7)) TinydragonBks.

—Adventures in the Pond: Jaws Gets Toothache. Williams, Kay. 2nd ed. 2019. (ENG.). 30p. (J). pap. 7.91 (978-1-913165-04-8(3)) TinydragonBks.

—Adventures in the Pond: Snapper & the Hiccups. Williams, Kay. 2nd ed. 2019. (ENG.). 30p. (J). pap. 7.91 (978-1-913165-05-5(1)) TinydragonBks.

—Adventures in the Pond: The Big Move. Williams, Kay. 2nd ed. 2019. (ENG.). 32p. (J). pap. 7.91 (978-1-913165-07-9(8)) TinydragonBks.

—Adventures in the Pond: The Day the Fish Got a Shock. Williams, Kay. 2nd ed. 2019. (ENG.). 30p. (J). pap. 7.91 (978-1-913165-06-2(X)) TinydragonBks.

—Adventures in the Pond: Tiddles Caught in a Trap. Williams, Kay. 2nd ed. 2019. (ENG.). 30p. (J). pap. 7.91 (978-1-913165-03-1(5)) TinydragonBks.

—The Big Move. Williams, Kay. 2018. (Adventures in the Pond Ser.: Vol. 7). (ENG.). 32p. (J). pap. (978-1-9997416-9-3(2)) Cambria Bks.

—Bob & the Duck. Williams, Kay. 2016. (Adventures in the Pond Ser.: Vol. 6). (ENG.). 29p. (J). pap. (978-0-9955317-6-5(5)) Cambria Bks.

—The Dragon Who Lost His Fire. Williams, Kay. 2016. (ENG.). 29p. (J). pap. (978-0-9955317-7-2(3)) Cambria Bks.

—The Dragon Who Lost His Fire. Williams, Kay. 2nd ed. 2019. (ENG.). 30p. (J). pap. 7.91 (978-1-913165-09-3(4)) TinydragonBks.

—The House at the Bottom of the Garden. Williams, Kay. 2017. (ENG.). 37p. (J). (gr. 3-5). pap. (978-1-9997416-2-4(5)) Cambria Bks.

—The House at the Bottom of the Garden. Williams, Kay. 2nd ed. 2019. (ENG.). 36p. (J). pap. 7.91 (978-1-913165-08-6(6)) TinydragonBks.

—Snapper & the Hiccups. Williams, Kay. 2016. (Adventures in the Pond Ser.: Vol. 5). (ENG.). 29p. (J). (gr. 1-3). pap. (978-0-9955317-4-1(9)) Cambria Bks.

—The Talking Carrier Bag. Williams, Kay. 2018. (ENG.). 30p. (J). pap. (978-1-9164532-2-7(8)) Cambria Bks.

—The Talking Carrier Bag. Williams, Kay. 2nd ed. 2019. (ENG.). 30p. (J). pap. 7.82 (978-1-913165-00-0(0)) TinydragonBks.

Victoria, Dionne. Daddy's Favorites. Joy, Elissa. 2019. (ENG.). 40p. (J). pap. 10.99 (978-1-970133-01-1(5)) EduMatch.

Victoria, Kirton. Emma & the African Wishing Bead. Redmond, Valerie. 2013. 28p. pap. 13.95 (978-1-61244-115-3(7)) Halo Publishing International.

Victoria, Lisa. Clara's Gift from the Heart. 2006. (J). 17.95 (978-0-9674602-9-1(8)) Blue Marlin Pubns.

—A Simple Brown Leaf. Davis, L. J. 2006. (ENG.). 32p. (J). (gr. -1-3). 17.95 (978-0-9762007-8-9(3), 9780976200789) Abovo Publishing.

Vidal, Aleta. Romeo & Juliet: A Graphic Novel. Carreras, Hernan. 2018. (Classic Fiction Ser.). (ENG.). 80p. (J). (gr. 5-9). lib. bdg. 27.32 (978-1-4965-6112-1(0), 137709, Stone Arch Bks.) Capstone.

Vidal, Alexander. Los Angeles Is. Parhad, Elisa. 2018. (ENG.). 24p. (J). (gr. -1 — 1). bds. 12.95 (978-1-944903-23-7(2), Cameron Kids) Cameron + Co.

Vidal, Beatriz. Little Lek Longtail Learns to Sleep. Killion, Bette. 2016. 28p. (J). (gr. k-3). 17.95 (978-1-937786-63-2(3), Wisdom Tales) World Wisdom, Inc.

—Story of the Mongolian Tent House. Jamba, Dashdondog & Pellowski, Anne. 2020. (ENG.). 40p. (J). (gr. k-3). 16.95 (978-1-937786-81-6(1), Wisdom Tales) World Wisdom, Inc.

Vidal, Carla. One Unique Piece. Willey, Emily-Anne. 2019. (ENG.). 33p. (J). 25.95 (978-1-9772-0977-1(7)); pap. 15.95 (978-1-9772-0865-1(7)) Outskirts Pr., Inc.

Vidal, Francesca. Más Que Solo Amigos. Pollux, Violet. 2018. (No Me Dejes IR Ser.: Vol. 1). (SPA.). 224p. (J). pap. 10.00 (978-1-7201-0805-4(6)) Independently Published.

Vidal, Oriol. Bear Says Thank You. Dahl, Michael. 2011. (Hello Genius Ser.). (ENG.). 20p. (J). (gr. -1 — 1). bds. 7.99 (978-1-4048-6786-4(4), Picture Window Bks.) Capstone.

—Big Bed for Giraffe. Dahl, Michael. 2015. (Hello Genius Ser.). (ENG.). 20p. (J). (gr. -1 — 1). bds. 7.99 (978-1-4795-5791-2(9), Picture Window Bks.) Capstone.

—Build a Picture Monsters Sticker Book. 2013. (Build a Picture Sticker Bks.). (ENG.). (J). 6.99 (978-0-7945-2947-5(X), Usborne) EDC Publishing.

—Bunny Eats Lunch, 1 vol. Dahl, Michael. 2010. (Hello Genius Ser.). (ENG.). 20p. (J). (gr. -1 — 1). bds. 7.99 (978-1-4048-5728-5(1), Picture Window Bks.) Capstone.

—Bye-Bye Bottles, Zebra. Dahl, Michael. 2015. (Hello Genius Ser.). (ENG.). 20p. (J). (gr. -1 — 1). bds. 7.99 (978-1-4795-5792-9(7), Picture Window Bks.) Capstone.

—Dodging Dinosaurs. Mass, Wendy. 2019. (Time Jumpers Ser.: 4). (ENG.). 96p. (J). (gr. 1-3). pap. 4.99 (978-1-338-21745-2(3)) Scholastic, Inc.

—Duck, Duck, Dinosaur. George, Kallie. 2016. (ENG.). 40p. (J). (gr. -1-3). 17.99 (978-0-06-235308-5(X)) HarperCollins Pubs.

—Duck, Duck, Dinosaur: Bubble Blast. George, K. 2017. 32p. (J). (978-1-5364-1093-8(4)) Harper & Row Ltd.

—Duck, Duck, Dinosaur: Perfect Pumpkin. George, K. 2017. 32p. (J). (978-1-5182-4363-9(0)) Harper & Row Ltd.

—Duck, Duck, Dinosaur: Snowy Surprise. George, K. 2017. 32p. (J). (978-1-5364-2701-1(2)) Harper & Row Ltd.

—Duck, Duck, Dinosaur & the Noise at Night. George, Kallie. 2017. (ENG.). 40p. (J). (gr. -1-3). 17.99 (978-0-06-235317-7(9)) HarperCollins Pubs.

—Duck, Duck, Dinosaur: Bubble Blast. George, Kallie. 2017. (My First I Can Read Ser.). (ENG.). 32p. (J). (gr. -1-3). pap. 4.99 (978-0-06-235311-5(X)) HarperCollins Pubs.

—Duck, Duck, Dinosaur: Perfect Pumpkin. George, Kallie. 2017. (My First I Can Read Ser.). (ENG.). 32p. (J). (gr. -1-3). 16.99 (978-0-06-235315-3(2)); pap. 4.99 (978-0-06-235314-6(4)) HarperCollins Pubs.

—Duck, Duck, Dinosaur: Snowy Surprise. George, Kallie. 2017. (My First I Can Read Ser.). (ENG.). 32p. (J). (gr. -1-3). 16.99 (978-0-06-235319-1(5)); pap. 4.99 (978-0-06-235318-4(7)) HarperCollins Pubs.

—Duck, Duck, Dinosaur: Spring Smiles. George, Kallie. 2019. (My First I Can Read Ser.). (ENG.). 32p. (J). (gr. -1-3). 16.99 (978-0-06-235322-1(5)); pap. 4.99 (978-0-06-235321-4(7)) HarperCollins Pubs.

—Duck Goes Potty, 1 vol. Dahl, Michael. 2010. (Hello Genius Ser.). (ENG.). 20p. (J). (gr. -1 — 1). bds. 7.99 (978-1-4048-5726-1(5), Picture Window Bks.) Capstone.

—Escape from Egypt. Mass, Wendy. 2018. (Time Jumpers Ser.: 2). (ENG.). 96p. (J). (gr. 1-3). pap. 4.99 (978-1-338-21739-1(9)); lib. bdg. 15.99 (978-1-338-21740-7(2)) Scholastic, Inc.

—Fast-Forward to the Future. Mass, Wendy. 2019. (Time Jumpers Ser.: 3). (ENG.). 96p. (J). (gr. 1-3). pap. 4.99 (978-1-338-21742-1(9)); lib. bdg. 15.99 (978-1-338-21743-8(7)) Scholastic, Inc.

—Hello Genius. Dahl, Michael. (Hello Genius Ser.). (ENG.). 20p. 2016. (J). (gr. -1 — 1). bds., bds., bds. 199.75 (978-1-4795-8747-6(8)); 2015. (gr. 1-2). bds. 31.96 (978-1-4795-8062-0(7)) Capstone. (Picture Window Bks.).

—Hello Genius Milestone Box. Dahl, Michael. 2016. (Hello Genius Ser.). (ENG.). 24p. (J). (gr. 1-2). pap. 11.99 (978-1-4795-9838-0(0), Picture Window Bks.) Capstone.

—Hippo Says "Excuse Me" Dahl, Michael. 2011. (Hello Genius Ser.). (ENG.). 20p. (J). (gr. -1 — 1). bds. 7.99 (978-1-4048-6787-1(2), Picture Window Bks.) Capstone.

—Little Elephant Listens, 1 vol. Dahl, Michael. 2014. (Hello Genius Ser.). (ENG.). 20p. (J). (gr. -1 — 1). bds. 7.99 (978-1-4795-2289-7(9), Picture Window Bks.) Capstone.

—Little Lion Shares, 1 vol. Dahl, Michael. 2014. (Hello Genius Ser.). (ENG.). 20p. (J). (gr. -1 — 1). bds. 7.99 (978-1-4795-2287-3(2), Picture Window Bks.) Capstone.

—Little Monkey Calms Down, 1 vol. Dahl, Michael. 2014. (Hello Genius Ser.). (ENG.). 20p. (J). (gr. -1 — 1). bds. 7.99 (978-1-4795-2286-6(4), Picture Window Bks.) Capstone.

—Little Tiger Picks Up, 1 vol. Dahl, Michael. 2014. (Hello Genius Ser.). (ENG.). 20p. (J). (gr. -1 — 1). bds. 7.99 (978-1-4795-2288-0(0), Picture Window Bks.) Capstone.

—Lost in Space: An Up2U Action Adventure. Fields, Jan. 2017. (Up2U Adventures Set 3 Ser.). (ENG.). 80p. (J). (gr. 2-5). lib. bdg. 29.93 (978-1-5321-3030-4(9), 25508, Calico Chapter Bks.) ABDO Publishing Co.

—Mind Your Monsters. Bailey, Catherine. 2015. 40p. (J). (gr. -1-2). 14.95 (978-1-4549-1103-6(4)) Sterling Publishing Co., Inc.

—Mouse Says Sorry, 1 vol. Dahl, Michael. 2011. (Hello Genius Ser.). (ENG.). 20p. (J). (gr. -1 — 1). bds. 7.99 (978-1-4048-6789-5(9), Picture Window Bks.) Capstone.

—Nap Time for Kitty, 1 vol. Dahl, Michael. 2011. (Hello Genius Ser.). (ENG.). 20p. (J). (gr. -1 — 1). bds. 7.99 (978-1-4048-5216-7(6), Picture Window Bks.) Capstone.

—No More Pacifier, Duck. Dahl, Michael. 2015. (Hello Genius Ser.). (ENG.). 20p. (J). (gr. -1 — 1). bds. 7.99 (978-1-4795-5793-6(5), Picture Window Bks.) Capstone.

—One Little Lot: The 1-2-3s of an Urban Garden. Mullen, Diane C. 2020. 32p. (J). (gr. -1-2). lib. bdg. 16.99 *(978-1-58089-889-8(0))* Charlesbridge Publishing, Inc.

—Penguin Misses Mom. Dahl, Michael. 2016. (Hello Genius Ser.). (ENG.). 20p. (J). (gr. -1 — 1). bds. 7.99 *(978-1-4795-8739-1(7),* Picture Window Bks.) Capstone.

—Penguin Says Please, 1 vol. Dahl, Michael. 2011. (Hello Genius Ser.). (ENG.). 20p. (J). (gr. -1 — 1). bds. 7.99 *(978-1-4048-6788-8(0),* Picture Window Bks.) Capstone.

—Pig Takes a Bath, 1 vol. Dahl, Michael. 2010. (Hello Genius Ser.). (ENG.). 20p. (J). (gr. -1 — 1). bds. 7.99 *(978-1-4048-5729-2(X),* Picture Window Bks.) Capstone.

—Playdate for Panda. Dahl, Michael. 2016. (Hello Genius Ser.). (ENG.). 20p. (J). (gr. -1 — 1). bds. 7.99 *(978-1-4795-8741-4(9),* Picture Window Bks.) Capstone.

—Pony Brushes His Teeth, 1 vol. Dahl, Michael. 2010. (Hello Genius Ser.). (ENG.). 20p. (J). (gr. -1 — 1). bds. 7.99 *(978-1-4048-5727-8(3),* Picture Window Bks.) Capstone.

—Snack Time for Cow, 1 vol. Dahl, Michael. 2011. (Hello Genius Ser.). (ENG.). 20p. (J). (gr. -1 — 1). bds. 7.99 *(978-1-4048-6496-2(2),* Picture Window Bks.) Capstone.

—Stealing the Sword! Mass, Wendy. 2018. (Time Jumpers Ser.: 1). (ENG.). 96p. (J). (gr. 1-3). pap. 4.99 *(978-1-338-21736-0(4))* Scholastic, Inc.

—Story Time for Lamb, 1 vol. Dahl, Michael. 2011. (Hello Genius Ser.). (ENG.). 20p. (J). (gr. -1 — 1). bds. 7.99 *(978-1-4048-6495-5(4),* Picture Window Bks.) Capstone.

—Thumbs up, Brown Bear. Dahl, Michael. 2015. (Hello Genius Ser.). (ENG.). 20p. (J). (gr. -1 — 1). bds. 7.99 *(978-1-4795-5794-3(3),* Picture Window Bks.) Capstone.

Vidal, Sierra Mon Ann. Kitty Cat, Kitty Cat, Where Are You? Warner, Alexander J. S. 2019. (ENG.). 30p. (J). 26.99 *(978-1-5320-7880-4(3));* pap. 16.99 *(978-1-5320-7881-1(1))* iUniverse, Inc.

—Lady Meets Daisy. Harman-Pyers, Teagan. 2019. (ENG.). 28p. (J). pap. 24.14 *(978-1-7960-0325-3(5))* Xlibris Corp.

Vidali, Valerio. Telephone Tales. Rodari, Gianni. Shugaar, Anthony, tr. 2020. 212p. (J). 27.95 *(978-1-59270-284-8(8))* Enchanted Lion Bks., LLC.

Vidali, Valerio & Lopiz, Violeta. The Forest. Bozzi, Riccardo. 2018. 72p. (J). (gr. -1). pap. 29.95 *(978-1-59270-218-3(X))* Enchanted Lion Bks., LLC.

Vidali, Valerio & Uman, Jennifer. Jemmy Button. Vidali, Valerio & Uman, Jennifer. 2013. (ENG.). 48p. (J). (gr. k-12). 16.99 *(978-0-7636-6487-9(1),* Templar) Candlewick Pr.

VIDILI, Laura. Rebecca e le Janas. Zedda, Claudia. 2017. (Trenino Verde Ser.: Vol. 48). (ITA.). 114p. (J). pap. *(978-88-7356-318-1(X))* Condaghes.

Vidinhas, Catia. Being a Bear. Magalhaes, Álvaro. 2019. (ENG.). 36p. (J). (gr. -1-k). 16.95 *(978-84-16566-89-1(5))* Ediciones La Fragatina ESP. Dist: Independent Pubs. Group.

Vidro, Kenn. Square Pears Two: The Equal Sequel. Vidro, Kenn. 2004. (ENG.). 100p. (J). spiral bd. 9.95 *(978-0-9745308-1-9(6))* Gilbert Square Bks.

Vidyarthi, Abhinav. Tina the Purple Little Monster. Rojas, Angela. 2019. (ENG.). 52p. (J). pap. 12.00 *(978-1-0906-5069-6(8))* Independently Published.

Vieceli, Emma. Manga Shakespeare: Hamlet. Shakespeare, William. 2007. (ENG.). 204p. (J). (gr. 2-8). pap. 14.99 *(978-0-8109-9324-2(4))* Abrams, Inc.

—Manga Shakespeare: Much Ado about Nothing. Shakespeare, William. 2009. (Manga Shakespeare Ser.). (ENG.). 208p. (YA). (gr. 7-11). pap. 14.99 *(978-0-8109-4323-0(9),* Amulet Bks.) Abrams, Inc.

—Vampire Academy. Mead, Richelle. 2011. (Vampire Academy Ser.: 1). (ENG.). 144p. (YA). (gr. 7-18). pap. 12.99 *(978-1-59514-429-4(3),* Razorbill) Penguin Young Readers Group.

Vieceli, Emma & Brown, Kate. Scorpia: an Alex Rider Graphic Novel. Horowitz, Anthony & Johnston, Antony. 2017. (Alex Rider Ser.). (ENG.). 176p. (YA). (gr. 4-7). pap. 14.99 *(978-0-7636-9257-5(3))* Candlewick Pr.

Vieira, Andrei. Rahab's Promise. Gibbs, Noni & Kahrs, Christina. 2007. 32p. (J). (gr. -1-2). pap. 9.99 *(978-0-8127-0432-7(0))* Autumn Hse. Publishing Co.

Vieira, Eduardo. Mutant Bunny Island. Skye, Obert. 2017. (ENG.). 224p. (J). (gr. 3-7). 12.99 *(978-0-06-239912-0(8))* HarperCollins Pubs.

—Mutant Bunny Island #2: Bad Hare Day. Skye, Obert. 2018. (ENG.). 208p. (J). (gr. 3-7). 12.99 *(978-0-06-239915-1(2))* HarperCollins Pubs.

—Mutant Bunny Island #3: Buns of Steel. Skye, Obert. 2019. (ENG.). 208p. (J). (gr. 3-7). 12.99 *(978-0-06-239917-5(9))* HarperCollins Pubs.

Vieira, Gloria. Tiny the Mighty Eagle. Medina, Jennette. 2018. (ENG.). 44p. (J). pap. 14.95 *(978-1-64300-436-5(0))* Covenant Bks.

Vieira, Nuno Alexandre. The Dragon, the Whale & the Dolphin. Highley, Rainey Marie. 2019. (Dragon & the Whale Ser.: Vol. 3). (ENG.). 52p. (J). pap. 14.95 *(978-1-0986-4196-2(5))* Independently Published.

Vieira, Rayanne. Babysitting Nightmares: the Phantom Hour. Shepherd, Kat. 2019. (Babysitting Nightmares Ser.: 2). (ENG.). 224p. (J). 14.99 *(978-1-250-15699-0(8),* 900185128) Imprint IND. Dist: Macmillan.

—Babysitting Nightmares: the Shadow Hand. Shepherd, Kat. 2018. (Babysitting Nightmares Ser.: 1). (ENG.). 208p. (J). 13.99 *(978-1-250-15696-9(3),* 900185121) Imprint IND. Dist: Macmillan.

—Babysitting Nightmares: the Twilight Curse. Shepherd, Kat. 2019. (Babysitting Nightmares Ser.: 3). (ENG.). 224p. (J). 14.99 *(978-1-250-15701-0(3),* 900185131) Imprint IND. Dist: Macmillan.

—Math Adventures: Solve the Puzzles, Save the World! Virr, Paul & Potter, William. 2019. (ENG.). 128p. (J). pap. 9.99 *(978-1-78888-212-5(1),* 11924c36-4aa0-4390-8a7a-7ae2ef32c688) Arcturus Publishing GBR. Dist: Baker & Taylor Publisher Services (BTPS).

Vieira, Rayanne & Rodríguez, Geraldine. Science Adventures: Solve the Puzzles, Save the World! Woolf, Alex. 2020. (ENG.). 128p. (J). pap. 9.99 *(978-1-78950-597-9(6),* 98d68f2d-583b-4b11-8c48-e7e4bea886a2) Arcturus Publishing GBR. Dist: Baker & Taylor Publisher Services (BTPS).

Viel-Taschereau, Geneviève. Rhythm Rescue. Weber, Vicky. 2020. (ENG.). 44p. (J). pap. 12.99 ***(978-1-7342129-9-0(3))*** Trunk Up Bks.

Vieweg, Olivia. Ever After. Korth, Ines & Vom Baur, Adrian. 2020. 288p. (YA). (gr. 9-12). 33.32 ***(978-1-5415-8392-4(2),*** Graphic Universe™) Lerner Publishing Group.

Vieweg, Olivia. Ever After. Vieweg, Olivia. 2020. (ENG.). 288p. (YA). (gr. 9-12). pap. 16.99 ***(978-1-7284-1292-4(7),*** Graphic Universe™) Lerner Publishing Group.

Vigg, Vigg. Nothing Happens in This Book. Sadler, Judy Ann. 2018. (ENG.). 40p. (J). (gr. -1-2). 16.99 *(978-1-77138-737-8(8))* Kids Can Pr., Ltd. CAN. Dist: Hachette Bk. Group.

Vigil, Cristina. When Winston Wins. Fairchild-Lenyo, Mary. 2007. 36p. per. 14.95 *(978-1-59858-405-9(7))* Dog Ear Publishing, LLC.

Vigil, Luis Gerardo Sanchez & Broeck, Fabricio Vanden. The Flamingo's Legs. Romeu, Emma. 2004. (Colección Animales de América / Animals of the Americas Ser.). (SPA.). 32p. (gr. 3-5). pap. 11.95 *(978-1-59437-846-1(0))* Santillana USA Publishing Co., Inc.

—A Forest for the Monarch Butterfly. Romeu, Emma. 2005. (Colección Animales de América / Animals of the Americas Ser.). (SPA.). 48p. (gr. 3-5). pap. 11.95 *(978-1-59437-844-7(4))* Santillana USA Publishing Co., Inc.

—Here Comes the Grey Wolf. Romeu, Emma. 2004. (Colección Animales de América / Animals of the Americas Ser.). (SPA.). 32p. (gr. 3-5). pap. 11.95 *(978-1-59437-843-0(6))* Santillana USA Publishing Co., Inc.

—My Manatee Friend. Romeu, Emma. 2004. (Colección Animales de América / Animals of the Americas Ser.). (SPA.). 24p. (gr. 3-5). pap. 11.95 *(978-1-59437-845-4(2))* Santillana USA Publishing Co., Inc.

Vigla, Vincent. Being Me. Broski, Julie. 2011. (Rookie Ready to Learn Ser.). 40p. (J). (ENG.). pap. 5.95 *(978-0-531-26653-3(2));* (gr. -1-k). lib. bdg. 23.00 *(978-0-531-26428-7(9))* Scholastic Library Publishing. (Children's Pr.).

—My Magnetic Word Puzzles: Let's Make Words. 2006. (Magnix Learning Fun Ser.). 12p. (J). (gr. -1-3). 9.95 *(978-1-932915-19-8(2))* Sandvik Innovations, LLC.

Vignaga, Francesca Dafne. The Legend of UFOs, 1 vol. Troupe, Thomas Kingsley. 2012. (Legend Has It Ser.). (ENG.). 32p. (J). (gr. 2-4). lib. bdg. 27.99 *(978-1-4048-6657-7(4),* Picture Window Bks.) Capstone.

—The 10 Marys & the Little Gabriel. Magni, Aurora. 2011. (J). *(978-0-8091-6764-7(6))* Paulist Pr.

Vignoli, Daniella. El Lobo con Correa. Visconti, Guido. 2006. (Wolf on a Leash (Spanish) Ser.). (SPA.). 24p. (gr. k-3). lib. bdg. 25.00 *(978-0-8368-6262-1(7),* Gareth Stevens Learning Library) Stevens, Gareth Publishing LLLP.

—Wolf on a Leash. Visconti, Guido. 2006. (Wolf on a Leash Ser.). 24p. (gr. k-3). lib. bdg. 25.00 *(978-0-8368-6261-4(9),* Gareth Stevens Learning Library) Stevens, Gareth Publishing LLLP.

Vignolo, Enrique. Book 6 - Dorp the Scottish Dragon in a Lone Star Story. Johnson, Sandi. Durant, Sybrina, ed. 2019. (Dorp the Scottish Dragon Ser.: Vol. 6). (ENG.). 44p. (J). (gr. 3-6). pap. 12.99 ***(978-1-6712-9232-1(4))*** Independently Published.

Vignolo, Enrique. Catch of the Day! McMillan, Dawn. 2013. 25p. (gr. 3-3). pap. *(978-1-927197-70-7(8),* Red Rocket Readers) Flying Start Bks.

—Hopeless to Hopeful. Sommer, Carl. 2009. (Quest for Success Ser.). (ENG.). 56p. (YA). pap. 4.95 *(978-1-57537-278-5(9));* lib. bdg. 12.95 *(978-1-57537-253-2(3))* Advance Publishing, Inc.

Vignolo, Enrique. Lil' Metal Horn Unicorns. Durant, Sybrina & Johnson, Sandi. 2019. (ENG.). 38p. (J). pap. 14.99 ***(978-1-7070-0612-0(1))*** Independently Published.

Vignolo, Enrique. Miserable Millie. Sommer, Carl. (J). 2014. pap. *(978-1-57537-960-9(0));* 2007. (ENG.). 48p. 16.95 incl. audio compact disk *(978-1-57537-521-2(4));* 2007. (ENG.). 48p. (gr. -1-3). 9.95 *(978-1-57537-022-4(0));* 2007. (ENG.). 48p. (gr. -1-3). lib. bdg. 16.95 *(978-1-57537-071-2(9))* Advance Publishing, Inc.

—Miserable Millie(La Pobrecita Mili) Sommer, Carl. ed. 2009. (Another Sommer-Time Story Bilingual Ser.). (SPA & ENG.). 48p. (J). lib. bdg. 16.95 *(978-1-57537-160-3(X))* Advance Publishing, Inc.

—The Rebel. Sommer, Carl. 2009. (Quest for Success Ser.). (ENG.). 56p. (YA). pap. 4.95 *(978-1-57537-282-2(7));* lib. bdg. 12.95 *(978-1-57537-257-0(6))* Advance Publishing, Inc.

—The Rebel(El Rebelde) Sommer, Carl. ed. 2009. (Quest for Success Bilingual Ser.). (ENG & SPA.). 104p. (YA). lib. bdg. 14.95 *(978-1-57537-231-0(2))* Advance Publishing, Inc.

—The Runaway(La Escapada) Sommer, Carl. ed. 2009. (Quest for Success Bilingual Ser.). (SPA & ENG.). 104p. (YA). lib. bdg. 14.95 *(978-1-57537-234-1(7))* Advance Publishing, Inc.

Vignolo, Enrique. Santa's Sub: Making New Friends. Johnson, Sandi. Fisher, Sharon, ed. 2019. (ENG.). 34p. (J). pap. 12.99 ***(978-1-6717-0392-6(8))*** Independently Published.

Vignolo, Enrique. Spike the Rebel! Sommer, Carl. (J). 2014. pap. *(978-1-57537-967-8(8));* 2007. (ENG.). 48p. (gr. -1-3). lib. bdg. 16.95 *(978-1-57537-072-9(7));* 2007. (ENG.). 48p. 16.95 incl. audio compact disk *(978-1-57537-522-9(2));* 2007. (ENG.). 48p. 23.95 incl. audio compact disk *(978-1-57537-722-3(5));* 2007. (ENG.). 48p. (gr. -1-3). lib. bdg. 9.95 *(978-1-57537-023-1(9))* Advance Publishing, Inc.

—Spike the Rebel!(pua, el Rebelde!) Sommer, Carl. ed. 2009. (Another Sommer-Time Story Bilingual Ser.). (SPA & ENG.). 48p. (J). lib. bdg. 16.95 *(978-1-57537-167-2(7))* Advance Publishing, Inc.

Vignolo, Enrique. Steve the Cowboy in the Wild Wild West. Johnson, Sandi. Brundige, Britt, ed. 2019. (ENG.). 32p. (J). pap. 12.99 ***(978-1-6704-1862-3(6))*** Independently Published.

Vignolo, Enrique. The Tortoise & the Hare. Sommer, Carl. 2014. (Sommer-Time Story Classics Ser.). (ENG.). 32p. (J). (gr. k-4). 16.95 *(978-1-57537-086-6(7))* Advance Publishing, Inc.

Vignolo, Enrique, jt. illus. see Budwine, Greg.

Vignolo, Enrique, jt. illus. see Johnson, Jim.

Vigourt, Renaud. Skulk: A Lost Shadow's Puzzle Adventure. Etherington, Robin. 2020. (ENG.). 32p. (J). (gr. 2-6). 18.99 ***(978-1-78627-595-0(3),*** King, Laurence Publishing) Orion Publishing Group, Ltd. GBR. Dist: Hachette Bk. Group.

Vigovszky, Rita. Being Rosie. Zabel, Alanna. 2013. (ENG.). (J). pap. 14.95 *(978-0-9884449-6-6(8))* AZIAM Bks.

—The Only Way Out Is In. Zabel, Alanna. 2018. (ENG.). 34p. (J). pap. 16.95 *(978-0-9898077-6-0(2))* AZIAM Bks.

Vik, Lyn. Tuesdays with Henry: Making Moments with Grandma Ellen. Pentelechuk, Mariane. 2019. (ENG.). 48p. (J). *(978-1-5255-4459-0(4));* pap. *(978-1-5255-4460-6(8))* FriesenPress.

Vila, Alvaro F. Flood, 1 vol. Capstone Press Staff. 2013. (Fiction Picture Bks.). (ENG.). 32p. (J). (gr. 1-3). 22.60 *(978-1-4048-8006-1(2),* Picture Window Bks.) Capstone.

Vila Delclòs, Jordi. La Bella Durmiente. Bailer, Darice & Domínguez, Madelca. 2007. (SPA & ENG.). 28p. (J). *(978-0-545-03030-4(7))* Scholastic, Inc.

—El Flautista de Hamelín. Bailer, Darice & Domínguez, Madelca. 2007. (SPA & ENG.). 28p. (J). *(978-0-545-02961-2(9))* Scholastic, Inc.

Vilanova, Guiu, et al. Ruins of Ravencroft. 2020. (ENG.). 112p. (YA). (gr. 8-17). pap. 15.99 ***(978-1-302-92497-3(4))*** Marvel Worldwide, Inc.

Vilela, Caio, photos by. Goal! Taylor, Sean. 2014. (ENG., 40p. (J). (gr. -1-3). 17.99 *(978-1-62779-123-6(X),* 900135850, Holt, Henry & Co. Bks. For Young Readers) Holt, Henry & Co.

Vilela, Fernando. Arroz con Leche / Rice Pudding: Un Poema para Cocinar / a Cooking Poem, 1 vol. Argueta, Jorge. Amado, Elisa, tr. 2016. (Bilingual Cooking Poems Ser.). (SPA.). 32p. (J). (gr. -1-2). 8.95 *(978-1-55498-887-7(X))* Groundwood Bks. CAN. Dist: Publishers Group West (PGW).

Vilela, Fernando. Along the Tapajós. Vilela, Fernando. Hahn, Daniel, tr. 2019. (ENG.). 40p. (J). (gr. k-3). 17.99 *(978-1-5420-0868-6(9),* 9781542008686, AmazonCrossing) Amazon Publishing.

Vilela, Luiz, jt. illus. see Murdocca, Sal.

Villa, Alvaro F. Flood, 1 vol. 2013. (Fiction Picture Bks.). (ENG.). 32p. (J). (gr. 1-3). 15.95 *(978-1-62370-001-0(9),* Capstone Young Readers); 9.95 *(978-1-4795-2256-9(2),* Picture Window Bks.) Capstone.

Villa, Carlos. Shatterstar: Reality Star. 2019. (ENG.). 112p. (YA). (gr. 8-17). pap. 15.99 *(978-1-302-91522-3(3))* Marvel Worldwide, Inc.

Villa, Carlos & Gomez, Carlos. Secret Warps. 2019. (ENG.). 200p. (YA). (gr. 8-17). pap. 17.99 *(978-1-302-91776-0(5))* Marvel Worldwide, Inc.

Villa, Franscisco. Nos Importa un Comino el Rey Pepino. Nostlinger, Christine. 2019. (Torre Azul Ser.). (SPA.). 176p. (J). pap. ***(978-958-45-2904-6(8))*** Norma Ediciones, S.A.

Villagomez, Raul, jt. illus. see Gomez, Patricio.

Villalba, Ana. Seagull Red Band. Harper, Kathryn. 2016. (Cambridge Reading Adventures Ser.). (ENG.). 16p. pap. 7.37 *(978-1-316-50310-2(0))* Cambridge Univ. Pr.

Villalobos, Cinta. Polar Bear Island. Bonilla, Lindsay. 2018. (ENG.). 32p. (J). (gr. -1). 16.95 *(978-1-4549-2870-6(0))* Sterling Publishing Co., Inc.

Villalobos, Ethel M. Volcanoes A to Z Coloring Book. Pierce, Terry. 2003. 24p. pap. 4.95 *(978-1-57306-123-0(9))* Bess Pr., Inc.

Villalobos, Miguel. Hair Wars Coloring Book. Yellen, David. 2017. (ENG.). 32p. pap. 9.99 *(978-1-57687-846-0(5),* powerHouse Bks.) powerHse. Bks.

Villaloz, ChiChi & Etheridge, Katy. Do Dogs Dream? Villaloz, ChiChi & Etheridge, Katy. 2003. 32p. (J). lib. bdg. 16.95 *(978-0-9722180-5-4(X))* Malamute Pr.

—Do Dogs Vote? Villaloz, ChiChi & Etheridge, Katy. 2008. 32p. (J). lib. bdg. 24.95 *(978-0-9722180-0-9(9))* Malamute Pr.

Villalta, Ingrid. Mandy & Pandy Play Let's Count. Lin, Chris. 2008. 18p. (J). (gr. -1-3). bds. 9.99 *(978-0-9800156-5-2(0))* Mandy & Pandy Bks., LLC.

—Mandy & Pandy Play Sports. Lin, Chris. 2008. 20p. (J). (gr. -1-3). bds. 9.99 *(978-0-9800156-7-6(7))* Mandy & Pandy Bks., LLC.

—Mandy & Pandy Say Ni Hao Ma? Lin, Chris. 2007. 18p. (J). (gr. -1-3). bds. 9.95 *(978-0-9800156-4-5(2))* Mandy & Pandy Bks., LLC.

—Mandy & Pandy Visit China. Lin, Chris. 2008. 20p. (J). (gr. -1-3). bds. 9.99 *(978-0-9800156-6-9(9))* Mandy & Pandy Bks., LLC.

Villamuza, Noemi. Marc Just Couldn't Sleep. Keselman, Gabriela. 2007. (ENG.). 32p. (J). (gr. -1-k). pap. 5.99 *(978-1-929132-91-1(3))* Kane Miller.

—Pajaruli: Poemas para Seguir Andando. Plaza, José María & María, Plaza José. (SPA.). (J). *(978-84-392-8120-7(X),* EV0782) Gaviota Ediciones ESP. Dist: Lectorum Pubns., Inc.

Villamuza, Noemí. Me Gusta. Villamuza, Noemí, tr. Sobrino, Javier. (SPA.). 28p. 20.99 *(978-84-88342-35-5(7))* S.A. Kokinos ESP. Dist: Lectorum Pubns., Inc.

Villan, Oscar. Camilla the Zebra. Nunez, Marisa. 2003. 32p. (J). 14.95 *(978-84-95730-39-8(1))* Kalandraka Catalunya, Edicions, S.L. ESP. Dist: Independent Pubs. Group.

Villanelli, Paolo. Star Wars: Lando - Double or Nothing. 2018. (Star Wars: Lando - Double or Nothing (2018) Ser.: 1). (ENG.). 112p. (J). (gr. 4-17). pap. 15.99 *(978-1-302-91164-5(3))* Marvel Worldwide, Inc.

—Star Wars: Vader - Dark Visions. 2019. (ENG.). 112p. (YA). (gr. 4-17). pap. 15.99 *(978-1-302-91900-9(8))* Marvel Worldwide, Inc.

—Teenage Mutant Ninja Turtles. Random House. 2016. (Step into Reading Ser.). (ENG.). 24p. (J). (gr. -1-1). lib. bdg. 12.99 *(978-1-101-93856-0(0),* Random Hse. Bks. for Young Readers) Random Hse. Children's Bks.

—Teenage Mutant Ninja Turtles: Out of the Shadows Step into Reading. Random House. 2016. (Step into Reading Ser.). (ENG.). 24p. (J). (gr. -1-1). 4.99 *(978-1-101-93855-3(2),* Random Hse. Bks. for Young Readers) Random Hse. Children's Bks.

Villanelli, Paolo & Rosenberg, Rachelle. Rogue One: Volume 3. Houser, Jody. 2018. (Star Wars: Rogue One Ser.). (ENG.). 24p. (J). (gr. 6-12). lib. bdg. 27.07 *(978-1-5321-4170-6(X),* 28586, Graphic Novels) Spotlight.

Villanelli, Paolo, jt. illus. see Schiti, Valerio.

Villanueva, Catherine. The Amazing Adventure of Ava Appleby. Trainor, Marissa. 2017. (ENG.). (J). pap. 6.99 *(978-1-945169-12-0(5))* Orison Pubs.

Villanueva, Elisa. Letters to Nana. Cassady, Steve. 2019. (Solving Problems Through Literacy Ser.: Vol. 2). (ENG.). 34p. (J). pap. 10.00 ***(978-1-7934-9404-7(5))*** Independently Published.

Villari, Laura. Galaxy's Most Wanted. Pilgrim, Will Corona & Di Vito, Andrea. 2015. (Guardians of the Galaxy Ser.). (ENG.). 24p. (J). (gr. 3-6). 27.07 *(978-1-61479-391-5(3),* 18222, Marvel Age) Spotlight.

Villarreal, Francisco Javier. El Poeta. Calvo Merino, Diego. Nunez, Miguel Angel, ed. 2019. (Valores de Vida Ser.: Vol. 3). (SPA.). 46p. (J). pap. 13.99 *(978-1-7938-8676-7(8))* Independently Published.

Villarreal, Javier. Gelato Al Cioccolato. Violo Villalobos, Italo, ed. Cupertino, Lidia, tr. 2019. (ITA.). 62p. (J). pap. 12.99 ***(978-1-0867-2581-0(6))*** Independently Published.

Villarreal, Tanya E. Izzie's First Christmas, 1 vol. Villarreal, Tanya E. 2009. 28p. pap. 24.95 *(978-1-61546-093-9(4))* America Star Bks.

Villarrubia, Jose, jt. illus. see Futaki, Attila.

Villarrubia, Jose, jt. illus. see Pennington, Mark.

Villars, Melody. Lively Hope: An Advent Story. Asp, Jennifer. 2016. (ENG.). (J). pap. 23.95 *(978-1-5127-6204-4(0),* WestBow Pr.) Author Solutions, Inc.

Villavert, Armand, Jr. & Petersen, David. Muppet Robin Hood. Beedle, Tim. 2009. (Muppet Show Ser.). (ENG.). 112p. (J). (gr. 4-7). pap. 9.99 *(978-1-934506-79-0(6))* Boom! Studios.

Villegas, Teresa. Golemito. Stavans, Ilan. 2013. (ENG.). 32p. (J). 16.95 *(978-1-58838-292-4(3),* NewSouth Bks.) NewSouth, Inc.

Villella, Jessica. Myself, I & Me. Branda, Barnabus. 2013. 28p. pap. 24.95 *(978-1-63004-064-2(9))* America Star Bks.

Villeneuve, Anne. Loula & Mister the Monster. Villeneuve, Anne. 2015. (Loula Ser.). (ENG.). 32p. (J). (gr. -1-2). 16.95 *(978-1-77138-326-4(7))* Kids Can Pr., Ltd. CAN. Dist: Hachette Bk. Group.

—Loula Is Leaving for Africa. Villeneuve, Anne. 2013. (Loula Ser.). (ENG.). 32p. (J). (gr. -1-2). 16.95 *(978-1-55453-941-3(2))* Kids Can Pr., Ltd. CAN. Dist: Hachette Bk. Group.

Villeneuve, Mylène. Amy Has a Rash: Chickenpox. Audet, Nicole. 2017. (ENG.). 26p. (J). pap. 9.99 *(978-1-989041-07-9(8))* Nicole Publishing.

—Charles Hurt Himself Playing: Broken Arm. Audet, Nicole. 2017. (ENG.). 26p. (J). pap. 9.99 *(978-1-989041-03-1(5))* Nicole Publishing.

—Des Biscuits Spéciaux Pour Gabriel: Allergies. Audet, Dre Nicole. 2018. (FRE.). 30p. (J). pap. *(978-1-989041-16-1(7))* Dr. Nicole Publishing.

—Felix Is Curious about His Body: Human Body. Audet, Nicole. 2017. (ENG.). 26p. (J). pap. 9.99 *(978-1-989041-06-2(X))* Nicole Publishing.

—Joëlle Se Gratte la Tête: Poux. Audet, Nicole. 2018. (FRE.). 30p. (J). pap. *(978-1-989041-21-5(3))* Dr. Nicole Publishing.

—Léa a Mal Au Ventre: Gastro-Entérite. Audet, Nicole. 2018. (FRE.). 30p. (J). pap. *(978-1-989041-19-2(1))* Dr. Nicole Publishing.

—Lea Does Not Feel Well: Gastroenteritis. Audet, Nicole. 2017. (ENG.). 26p. (J). pap. 9.99 *(978-1-989041-00-0(0))* Nicole Publishing.

—Lucas Has an Earache: Otitis. Audet, Nicole. 2017. (ENG.). 26p. (J). pap. 9.99 *(978-1-989041-02-4(7))* Nicole Publishing.

—Maya' Head Is Itching: Lice. Audet, Nicole. 2017. (ENG.). 26p. (J). pap. 9.99 *(978-1-989041-05-5(1))* Nicole Publishing.

—Maya Visits Her Doctor: Vaccination. Audet, Nicole. 2017. (ENG.). 26p. (J). pap. 9.99 *(978-1-989041-01-7(9))* Nicole Publishing.

—Sabrina a des Boutons: Varicelle. Audet, Nicole. 2018. (FRE.). 30p. (J). pap. *(978-1-989041-23-9(X))* Dr. Nicole Publishing.

—Special Food for Sam: Allergies. Audet, Nicole. 2017. (ENG.). 26p. (J). pap. 9.99 *(978-1-989041-04-8(3))* Dr. Publishing.

Villet, Olivia. Monster Mess: Band 01B/Pink B (Collins Big Cat) Pym, Tasha. 2007. (Collins Big Cat Ser.). (ENG.). 16p. (J). (gr. -1-k). pap. 7.99 *(978-0-00-718650-1(9))* HarperCollins Pubs. Ltd. GBR. Dist: Independent Pubs. Group.

—Morris & the Cat Flap. French, Vivian. ed. 2011. (ENG.). 64p. (J). (gr. 2-4). pap. 5.99 *(978-0-00-714161-6(0),* HarperCollins Children's Bks.) HarperCollins Pubs. Ltd. GBR. Dist: HarperCollins Pubs.

—Morris in the Apple Tree. French, Vivian. ed. 2011. (ENG.). 64p. (J). pap. 5.99 *(978-0-00-718027-1(6),* HarperCollins Children's Bks.) HarperCollins Pubs. Ltd. GBR. Dist: HarperCollins Pubs.

—Morris the Mouse Hunter. French, Vivian. ed. 2011. (ENG.). 64p. (J). (gr. 2-4). pap. 5.99 *(978-0-00-714732-8(5),* HarperCollins Children's Bks.) HarperCollins Pubs. Ltd. GBR. Dist: HarperCollins Pubs.

V

Villeuve, Mylene. Charles S'Est Blessé en Jouant: Bras Cassé. Audet, Nicole. 2018. (FRE.). 30p. (J). pap. *(978-1-989041-17-8(5))* Dr. Nicole Publishing.

—Joëlle Va Chez le Docteur: Vaccination. Audet, Dre Nicole. 2018. (FRE.). 30p. (J). pap. *(978-1-989041-22-2(1))* Dr. Nicole Publishing.

—Lucas a Mal À L'Oreille: Otites. Audet, Nicole. 2018. (FRE.). 30p. (J). pap. *(978-1-989041-20-8(5))* Dr. Nicole Publishing.

Villim, Jim. I Love You Just Because. Heitritter, Laura. Date not set. 16p. (Orig.). (J). (gr. -1-18). pap. 6.95 *(978-1-885964-01-4(3))* P2 Educational Services, Inc.

Villines, Leo. Clean Your Room. Villines, Carol. 2008. 20p. pap. 24.95 *(978-1-60441-166-9(X))* America Star Bks.

Villnave, Erica. Sophie's Lovely Locks, 0 vols. Villnave, Erica. 2011. (ENG.). 32p. (J). (gr. k-3). 16.99 *(978-0-7614-5820-3(4)*, 9780761458203, Two Lions) Amazon Publishing.

Villnave, Erica Pelton. A Day at the Lake. Wallingford, Stephanie & Rynders, Dawn. 2013. (ENG.). 32p. (-k). pap. 10.95 *(978-1-938063-03-9(1)*, Mighty Media Kids) Mighty Media Pr.

—Nobody's Perfect: A Story for Children about Perfectionism. Burns, Ellen Flanagan. 2008. 48p. (J). (gr. 3-7). 14.95 *(978-1-4338-0379-6(8))*; pap. 9.95 *(978-1-4338-0380-2(1))* American Psychological Assn. (Magination Pr.).

—Oh Where, Oh Where Has My Little Dog Gone? Galvin, Laura. 2008. (ENG.). 32p. (J). (gr. -1-2). 9.95 *(978-1-59249-860-4(4))* Soundprints.

—Oh Where, Oh Where Has My Little Dog Gone? Galvin, Laura Gates. 2008. (ENG.). 32p. (J). (gr. -1-2). 17.95 *(978-1-59249-859-8(0))* Soundprints.

Vimislik, Matthew. Benji Franklin: Kid Zillionaire. Bean, Raymond. 2014. (Benji Franklin: Kid Zillionaire Ser.). (ENG.). 160p. (J). (gr. 2-5). 9.95 *(978-1-4342-6419-0(X)*, Stone Arch Bks.) Capstone.

—Benji Franklin: Kid Zillionaire: Money Troubles. Bean, Raymond. 2016. (Benji Franklin: Kid Zillionaire Ser.). (ENG.). 160p. (J). (gr. 2-5). pap. 6.95 *(978-1-4965-4137-6(5)*, Stone Arch Bks.) Capstone.

—Building Wealth (and Superpowered Rockets!), 1 vol. Bean, Raymond. 2014. (Benji Franklin: Kid Zillionaire Ser.). (ENG.). 88p. (J). (gr. 2-5). 22.65 *(978-1-4342-6418-3(1)*, Stone Arch Bks.) Capstone.

—Buying Stocks (and Solid Gold Submarines!) Bean, Raymond. 2015. (Benji Franklin: Kid Zillionaire Ser.). (ENG.). 88p. (J). (gr. 2-5). lib. bdg. 22.65 *(978-1-4965-0367-1(8)*, Stone Arch Bks.) Capstone.

—Investing Well (in Supersonic Spaceships!) Bean, Raymond. 2015. (Benji Franklin: Kid Zillionaire Ser.). (ENG.). 88p. (J). (gr. 2-5). lib. bdg. 22.65 *(978-1-4965-0368-8(6)*, Stone Arch Bks.) Capstone.

—Money Troubles. Bean, Raymond. 2015. (Benji Franklin: Kid Zillionaire Ser.). (ENG.). 160p. (J). (gr. 2-5). 9.95 *(978-1-4965-0369-5(4)*, Stone Arch Bks.) Capstone.

—Saving Money (and the World from Killer Dinos!), 1 vol. Bean, Raymond. 2014. (Benji Franklin: Kid Zillionaire Ser.). (ENG.). 88p. (J). (gr. 2-5). 22.65 *(978-1-4342-6417-6(3)*, Stone Arch Bks.) Capstone.

Vin, Lee. Crazy Love Story, Vol. 3. rev. ed. 2005. 208p. pap. 9.99 *(978-1-59182-949-2(6))* TOKYOPOP, Inc.

Vin, Lee. One, 11 vols. Vin, Lee. 192p. 9th rev. ed. 2006. (One Ser.: Vol. 9). per. 9.99 *(978-1-59532-013-1(X))*; 9th rev. ed. 2005. (One Ser.: Vol. 8). per. 9.99 *(978-1-59532-012-4(1))*; Vol. 6. 7th rev. ed. 2005. pap. 9.99 *(978-1-59532-010-0(5))* TOKYOPOP, Inc.

Vin, Lee. One, Vol. 7. Vin, Lee, creator. rev. ed. 2005. 192p. pap. 9.99 *(978-1-59532-011-7(3))* TOKYOPOP, Inc.

Vince, Charli. Heroes of Space: Who Changed the World. 2019. (Graphic Greats Ser.). (ENG.). 128p. (J). (gr. 4-7). pap. 12.99 *(978-1-4380-1201-8(2)*, B.E.S. Publishing) Peterson's.

Vince, Dawn. Emily & the Lamb. McAllister, Margaret. 2005. (ENG.). 24p. (J). lib. bdg. 23.65 *(978-1-59646-756-9(8))* Dingles & Co.

—Hero. Langford, Jane. 2005. (ENG.). 24p. (J). lib. bdg. 23.65 *(978-1-59646-720-0(7))* Dingles & Co.

Vince, Sarah. Boo! I See You! Make Believe Ideas Ltd. 2019. (ENG.). 22p. (J). (gr. -1-7). bds. *(978-1-78843-162-0(6))* Make Believe Ideas.

Vincent, Allison, jt. illus. see Cuthbert, R M.

Vincent, Andrew M. & Higgie, Will K. Washington D C , the Nation's Capital: Romance, Adventure, Achievement. Fox, Frances Margaret. 2012. 394p. 53.95 *(978-1-258-23323-5(1))*; pap. 38.95 *(978-1-258-24983-0(9))* Literary Licensing, LLC.

Vincent, Benjamin. Bluebonnet at the Alamo, 1 vol. Casad, Mary Brooke. 2013. (Bluebonnet Ser.). (ENG.). 32p. (J). (gr. k-3). 16.99 *(978-1-4556-1806-4(3)*, Pelican Publishing) Arcadia Publishing.

—Bluebonnet at the East Texas Oil Museum, 1 vol. Casad, Mary Brooke & Brooke Casad, Mary. 2005. (Bluebonnet Ser.). (ENG.). 32p. (J). (gr. k-3). 16.99 *(978-1-58980-358-9(2)*, Pelican Publishing) Arcadia Publishing.

—Bluebonnet at the Ocean Star Museum, 1 vol. Casad, Mary Brooke. 2012. (Bluebonnet Ser.). (ENG.). 32p. (J). (gr. k-3). 16.99 *(978-1-4556-1721-0(0)*, Pelican Publishing) Arcadia Publishing.

—Bluebonnet at the Texas State Capitol, 1 vol. Casad, Mary Brooke. 2017. (Bluebonnet Ser.). (ENG.). 32p. (gr. -1-3). 9.95 *(978-1-4556-2363-1(6)*, Pelican Publishing) Arcadia Publishing.

—Charlie the Horse. Abercrombie, Josephine. 2004. (J). 15.99 *(978-0-9769648-0-3(5))* J A Interests, Inc.

—Friends & Foes of Harry Potter: Names Decoded. Agarwal, Nikita & Agarwal, Chitra. 2006. 160p. (YA). pap. 15.95 *(978-1-59800-221-8(X))* Outskirts Pr., Inc.

Vincent, Kay. Bedtime Baby Cloth Book. 2020. (ENG.). 8p. (J). (— 1). 14.99 *(978-1-5290-0374-1(1)*, Campbell Bks.) Pan Macmillan GBR. Dist: Independent Pubs. Group.

—Playtime Baby Cloth Book. 2020. (ENG.). 6p. (J). (— 1). 13.99 *(978-1-5290-0373-4(3)*, Campbell Bks.) Pan Macmillan GBR. Dist: Independent Pubs. Group.

Vincent, Susan. Fantastic Fruits & Vivacious Vegetables: A. K. A. the ABCs of Happy Pooping. Vincent, Susan. 2019. (ENG.). 34p. (J). pap. 12.00 *(978-1-7307-1202-9(9))* Independently Published.

Vincenti, Antonio. The Beatitudes Explained. Vecchini, Silvia. 2017. 64p. (J). pap. *(978-0-8198-1238-4(2))* Pauline Bks. & Media.

—The Creed Explained. Vecchini, Silvia & Daughters of St. Paul Staff. 2015. (J). 6.95 *(978-0-8198-7519-8(8))* Pauline Bks. & Media.

—The 10 Commandments Explained. Vecchini, Silvia. 2015. (J). 6.95 *(978-0-8198-7523-5(6))* Pauline Bks. & Media.

Vincenti, Catherine. Pet Pals Grades 3-4: A Spanish-English Workbook. Vincenti, Catherine, ed. 2003.Tr. of Mascotas Companeros. (SPA.). 34p. wbk. ed. 3.00 *(978-0-941246-21-7(3)*, Humane Society Pr.) National Assn. for Humane & Environmental Education.

—Pet Pals Grades 5-6: A Spanish-English Workbook. Vincenti, Catherine, ed. 2003.Tr. of Mascotas Companeros. (SPA.). 34p. wbk. ed. 3.00 *(978-0-941246-22-4(1)*, Humane Society Pr.) National Assn. for Humane & Environmental Education.

—Pet Pals Grades K-2: A Spanish-English Workbook. Vincenti, Catherine, ed. 2003.Tr. of Mascotas Companeros. (SPA.). 34p. (J). wbk. ed. 3.00 *(978-0-941246-20-0(5)*, Humane Society Pr.) National Assn. for Humane & Environmental Education.

Vincentini, Federico. Absolute Carnage: Miles Morales. Ahmed, Saladin. 2020. (ENG.). 112p. (YA). (gr. 8-17). pap. 15.99 *(978-1-302-92014-2(6))* Marvel Worldwide, Inc.

Vincer, Carole. Beds & Bedding. Watson, Mary Gordon. 2nd rev. ed. 2006. (Threshold Picture Guides: 9). 24p. (Orig.). (gr. 3-18). pap. *(978-1-872082-69-1(6)*, J.A. Allen) The Crowood Press.

—Mounted Games. Webber, Toni. 2006. (Threshold Picture Guides: 30). 24p. pap. *(978-1-872082-60-8(2))* Kenilworth Pr., Ltd.

Vinci, Rosaria. Henrietta Owlsworth's Eyesight Plight! Jones, Sherry a. 2019. (ENG.). 42p. (J). 16.95 ***(978-1-951386-02-3(7))*** Dorry Pr.

Vine, Lucy. Germans Coming to America — Johnnie's Adventures: A Bilingual Book. Simon Dietz, Suzanne. Fetzner, Anika, tr. 2018. (ENG.). 42p. (J). pap. 10.99 *(978-0-9968870-6-9(7))* BeauDesigns.

Vine, Rachel Shana. Shekhinah. Sherman, Paulette Kouffman. 2013. 26p. pap. 10.95 *(978-0-9852469-5-2(2))* Parachute Jump Publishing.

Viner, Callie Lee, photos by. Pebbles Loves Counting. Viner, Callie Lee. 2013. 24p. pap. 12.95 *(978-1-61493-213-0(1))* Peppertree Pr., The.

Vines, Nandina. Watching Through the Day. Thorndyke, Julie. 2020. (ENG.). 32p. (J). (gr. k-3). ***(978-1-922332-07-3(0)***, IP Kidz) Interactive Pubns. Pty, Ltd.

Vints, Kostya. Ultimate Paper Airplanes for Kids: The Best Guide to Paper Airplanes - Complete Instructions + 48 Colorful Paper Planes! Dewar, Andrew. 2015. 160p. pap. 14.95 *(978-4-8053-1363-3(3))* Tuttle Publishing.

Viola, Karen. My Little Pony: Friendship Rocks! Froeb, Lori C. 2019. (ENG.). 32p. (J). (gr. 3-7). pap. 16.99 *(978-0-7944-4273-6(0)*, Studio Fun International) Printers Row Publishing Group.

—The Wand Chooses the Wizard. Pulles, Christina. 2018. (Harry Potter Ser.). 32p. (J). (gr. 1-1). 19.99 *(978-1-338-27600-8(X))* Scholastic, Inc.

Violet, Anna. How Anansi Got His Stories. Cooke, Trish. 2014. (Traditional Tales Ser.). (ENG.). 32p. (J). (gr. 1-2). pap. 7.95 *(978-1-62521-566-6(5)*, Capstone Classroom) Capstone.

—Mulan. Cooke, Trish. 2014. (Traditional Tales Ser.). (ENG.). 32p. (J). (gr. 2-3). pap. 7.95 *(978-1-62521-590-1(8)*, Capstone Classroom) Capstone.

Violet, Thao Nguyen. Princess Sariyah. Jean, Rose S. & Zaidan, Asim. 2018. (ENG.). 44p. (J). pap. *(978-1-7751760-0-8(2))* Jean, Rose Sharon.

Violi, Daniela. Del Tamaño Justo. MacHado, Ana Maria. Vasco, Irene, tr. 2019. (Torre de Papel Ser.). (SPA.). 90p. (J). (gr. 2-4). pap. 10.99 *(978-958-04-6265-1(8)*, Norma) Norma S.A. COL. Dist: Distribuidora Norma, Inc.

—El Niño y la Ballena. Scholes, Katherine. 2019. (SPA.). 78p. (J). (gr. 2-4). pap. 11.99 *(978-958-04-6020-6(5)*, Norma) Norma S.A. COL. Dist: Lectorum Pubns., Inc.

—Todo Sobre una Wafle. Horvath, Polly. Holguin, Magdalena, tr. 2006. (Coleccion Torre de Papel: Amarilla Ser.). (SPA.). 187p. (J). (gr. 4-7). per. 8.95 *(978-958-04-6495-2(2))* Norma S.A. COL. Dist: Distribuidora Norma, Inc.

—La Vaca de Octavio/la Arana Sube al Monte. Arciniegas, Triunfo. 2003. (Primer Acto: Teatro Infantil y Juvenil Ser.). (SPA.). 51p. (J). (gr. -1-7). pap. *(978-958-30-0312-7(3))* Panamericana Editorial.

Violi, Daniela. Una Voz para Jacinta y Otros Cuentos Infantiles. Lavin, Monica. 2019. (Torre Azul Ser.). (SPA.). 64p. (J). pap. ***(978-958-45-4134-5(X))*** Norma Ediciones, S.A.

Vipah Interactive. Margret & H. A. Rey's Curious George Goes Camping. Rey, Margret. 2015. 24p. pap. 4.00 *(978-1-61003-550-7(X))* Center for the Collaborative Classroom.

Vipah Interactive Staff. Curious George & the Hot Air Balloon, 1 vol. Rey, Margret & Rey, H. A. 2008. (Curious George Ser.). (ENG.). 24p. (J). (gr. k-3). lib. bdg. 27.07 *(978-1-59961-412-0(X)*, 5053, Picture Bk.) Spotlight.

—Curious George Feeds the Animals, 1 vol. Rey, Margret & Rey, H. A. 2008. (Curious George Ser.). (ENG.). 24p. (J). (gr. k-3). lib. bdg. 27.07 *(978-1-59961-413-7(8)*, 5054, Picture Bk.) Spotlight.

—Curious George in the Snow, 1 vol. Rey, H. A. & Rey, Margret. 2008. (Curious George Ser.). (ENG.). 24p. (J). (gr. k-3). lib. bdg. 27.07 *(978-1-59961-416-8(2)*, 5057, Picture Bk.) Spotlight.

—Curious George's Dream, 1 vol. Rey, H. A. & Rey, Margret. 2008. (Curious George Ser.). (ENG.). 24p. (J). (gr. k-3). lib. bdg. 27.07 *(978-1-59961-420-5(0)*, 5061, Picture Bk.) Spotlight.

—Curious George's First Day of School. Rey, Margret & Rey, H. A. 2005. (Curious George Ser.). (ENG.). 24p. (J). (gr. -1-3). 10.99 *(978-0-618-60565-1(7)*, 448943) Houghton Mifflin Harcourt Publishing Co.

—Feeds the Animals, 1 vol. Rey, Margret & Rey, H. A. 2005. (Curious George Ser.). (ENG.). 24p. (J). (gr. -1-3). 10.99 *(978-0-618-60387-9(5)*, 495928) Houghton Mifflin Harcourt Publishing Co.

—The New Adventures of Curious George. Rey, Margret & Rey, H. A. 2006. (Curious George Ser.). (ENG.). 208p. (J). (gr. -1-3). 10.99 *(978-0-618-66373-6(8)*, 589198) Houghton Mifflin Harcourt Publishing Co.

Vipah Interactive Staff, jt. illus. see Rey, Margret.

Virella, Nik & Unzueta, Angel. Star Wars: Poe Dameron Vol. 4: Legend Found. 2018. 160p. (J). (gr. 4-17). pap. 19.99 *(978-1-302-90743-3(3))* Marvel Worldwide, Inc.

Virgili, Marta Costa. My First Spot the Difference: Over 50 Fantastic Puzzles. Potter, Joe. 2018. (My First Activity Bks.). (ENG.). 64p. (J). (gr. -1-2). pap. 5.99 *(978-1-4380-1145-5(8)*, B.E.S. Publishing) Peterson's.

Virginia, Jennifer. Learn Phonics 'op' Story & Activities: A Princess & Paniyaram Series. V, Shyamala. 2018. (ENG.). 82p. (J). pap. 17.00 *(978-1-7198-2514-6(9))* Independently Published.

Virjan, Emma J. What This Story Needs Is a Bang & a Clang. Virjan, Emma J. 2017. (Pig in a Wig Book Ser.). (ENG.). 40p. (J). (gr. -1-3). 9.99 *(978-0-06-241530-1(1))* HarperCollins Pubs.

—What This Story Needs Is a Hush & a Shush. Virjan, Emma J. 2016. (Pig in a Wig Book Ser.). (ENG.). 40p. (J). (gr. -1-3). 9.99 *(978-0-06-241528-8(X))* HarperCollins Pubs.

—What This Story Needs Is a Munch & a Crunch. Virjan, Emma J. 2016. (Pig in a Wig Book Ser.). (ENG.). 40p. (J). (gr. -1-3). 9.99 *(978-0-06-241529-5(8))* HarperCollins Pubs.

—What This Story Needs Is a Pig in a Wig. Virjan, Emma J. 2015. (Pig in a Wig Book Ser.). (ENG.). 40p. (J). (gr. -1-3). 9.99 *(978-0-06-232724-6(0))* HarperCollins Pubs.

—What This Story Needs Is a Vroom & a Zoom. Virjan, Emma J. 2017. (Pig in a Wig Book Ser.). (ENG.). 40p. (J). (gr. -1-3). 9.99 *(978-0-06-249431-3(7))* HarperCollins Pubs.

Virta, Anni. Poika, Joka Unohti Nimens. Walsh, Tiina. 2018. (FIN.). (J). 38p. pap. 15.00 *(978-1-5425-4513-6(7))*; 34p. pap. 15.00 *(978-1-7274-1193-5(5))* CreateSpace Independent Publishing Platform.

—Poika, Joka Unohti Nimens. Walsh, Tiina. 2018. (FIN.). (J). 32p. pap. 15.00 *(978-1-7916-5447-4(9))*; 34p. pap. 22.50 *(978-1-7309-2424-8(7))*; 34p. pap. 22.50 *(978-1-7309-2476-7(X))*; 36p. pap. 22.50 *(978-1-7309-6064-2(2))*; 40p. pap. 22.50 *(978-1-7312-4191-7(7))*; 32p. pap. 22.50 *(978-1-7312-9558-3(8))*; 36p. pap. 22.50 *(978-1-7315-7334-6(0))*; 34p. pap. 25.00 *(978-1-7241-7109-2(7))*; 32p. pap. 22.50 *(978-1-7289-6664-9(7))*; 34p. pap. 22.50 *(978-1-7291-6116-6(2))*; 34p. pap. 22.50 *(978-1-7293-4069-1(5))*; 32p. pap. 22.50 *(978-1-7241-6514-5(3))* Independently Published.

—Poika, Joka Unohti Nimensä Aati. Walsh, Tiina. 2019. (FIN.). 32p. (J). pap. 22.50 *(978-1-0904-3390-9(5))* Independently Published.

—Poika, Joka Unohti Nimensä Daragh. Walsh, Tiina. 2019. (FIN.). 36p. (J). pap. 22.50 *(978-1-5425-0442-3(2))* CreateSpace Independent Publishing Platform.

—Poika, Joka Unohti Nimensä Denis. Walsh, Tiina. 2019. (FIN.). 34p. (J). pap. 22.50 *(978-1-7944-2854-6(2))* Independently Published.

—Poika, Joka Unohti Nimensä Jose. Walsh, Tiina. 2019. (FIN.). 32p. (J). pap. 22.50 *(978-1-7957-7134-4(8))* Independently Published.

—Poika, Joka Unohti Nimensä LEMMY. Walsh, Tiina. 2019. (FIN.). 34p. (J). pap. 22.50 *(978-1-0973-2386-9(2))* Independently Published.

—Poika, Joka Unohti Nimensä NICO. Walsh, Tiina. 2019. (FIN.). 32p. (J). pap. 22.50 *(978-1-0997-7019-7(X))* Independently Published.

—Poika, Joka Unohti Nimensä REMY. Walsh, Tiina. 2019. (FIN.). 32p. (J). pap. 22.50 *(978-1-0748-0580-7(1))* Independently Published.

Virta, Anni. Poika, Joka Unohti Nimens&#65533; ELVAR. Walsh, Tiina. 2019. (FIN.). 34p. (J). pap. 22.50 ***(978-1-6991-6534-8(3))*** Independently Published.

—Poika, Joka Unohti Nimens&#65533; EMIN. Walsh, Tiina. 2019. (FIN.). 32p. (J). pap. 22.50 ***(978-1-6934-0800-7(7))*** Independently Published.

—Poika, Joka Unohti Nimens&#65533; IMMANUEL. Walsh, Tiina. 2019. (FIN.). 40p. (J). pap. 22.50 ***(978-1-7078-8981-5(3))*** Independently Published.

—Poika, Joka Unohti Nimens&#65533; JONAEL. Walsh, Tiina. 2019. (FIN.). 36p. (J). pap. 22.50 ***(978-1-7078-9199-3(0))*** Independently Published.

—Poika, Joka Unohti Nimens&#65533; JOUKA. Walsh, Tiina. 2019. (FIN.). 34p. (J). pap. 22.50 ***(978-1-6965-7700-7(4))*** Independently Published.

—Poika, Joka Unohti Nimens&#65533; LEVI. Walsh, Tiina. 2019. (FIN.). 32p. (J). pap. 22.50 ***(978-1-5425-0938-1(6))*** CreateSpace Independent Publishing Platform.

Virta, Anni. Tytt. Walsh, Tiina. 2018. (FIN.). (J). 36p. pap. 22.50 *(978-1-5423-8879-5(1))*; 46p. pap. 15.00 *(978-1-7274-1263-5(X))* CreateSpace Independent Publishing Platform.

—Tytt. Walsh, Tiina. 2018. (J). (FIN.). 36p. pap. 22.50 *(978-1-7906-6214-2(1))*; (FIN.). 36p. pap. 22.50 *(978-1-7906-6251-7(6))*; (FIN.). 32p. pap. 22.50 *(978-1-7907-4903-4(4))*; (FIN.). 36p. pap. 22.50 *(978-1-7909-0823-3(X))*; (ENG.). 32p. pap. 22.50 *(978-1-7913-4096-4(2))*; (FIN.). 34p. pap. 22.50 *(978-1-7308-8365-1(6))*; (FIN.). 36p. pap. 22.50 *(978-1-7315-7356-8(1))*; (FIN.). 40p. pap. 22.50 *(978-1-7901-2455-8(7))*; (FIN.). 32p. pap. 22.50 *(978-1-7290-7923-2(7))* Independently Published.

Virta, Anni. Tytt&#65533;, Joka Unohti Nimens&#65533; ALINA. Walsh, Tiina. 2019. (FIN.). 34p. (J). pap. 22.50 ***(978-1-0886-7919-7(6))*** Independently Published.

—Tytt&#65533;, Joka Unohti Nimens&#65533; MIMMI. Walsh, Tiina. 2019. (FIN.). 34p. (J). pap. 22.50 ***(978-1-6949-9562-9(3))*** Independently Published.

—Tytt&#65533;, Joka Unohti Nimens&#65533; MY SOFIA. Walsh, Tiina. 2019. (FIN.). 38p. (J). pap. 22.50 ***(978-1-6867-2488-6(8))*** Independently Published.

—Tytt&#65533;, Joka Unohti Nimens&#65533; NADIA. Walsh, Tiina. 2019. (FIN.). 34p. (J). pap. 22.50 ***(978-1-7070-5420-6(7))*** Independently Published.

—Tytt&#65533;, Joka Unohti Nimens&#65533; NADIIRA. Walsh, Tiina. 2019. (FIN.). 38p. (J). pap. 22.50 ***(978-1-6950-1956-0(3))*** Independently Published.

—Tytt&#65533;, Joka Unohti Nimens&#65533; NAWAL. Walsh, Tiina. 2019. (FIN.). 34p. (J). pap. 22.50 ***(978-1-6950-1405-3(7))*** Independently Published.

—Tytt&#65533;, Joka Unohti Nimens&#65533; NILLA. Walsh, Tiina. 2019. (FIN.). 34p. (J). pap. 22.50 ***(978-1-7070-4181-7(4))*** Independently Published.

—Tytt&#65533;, Joka Unohti Nimens&#65533; VICTORIE. Walsh, Tiina. 2019. (FIN.). 40p. (J). pap. 22.50 ***(978-1-6716-3793-1(3))*** Independently Published.

Virta, Anni. Tyttö, Joka Unohti Nimensä ALFIINA. Walsh, Tiina. 2019. (FIN.). 38p. (J). pap. 22.50 *(978-1-0705-0939-6(6))* Independently Published.

—Tyttö, Joka Unohti Nimensä Elea. Walsh, Tiina. 2019. (FIN.). 32p. (J). pap. 22.50 *(978-1-7957-7996-8(9))* Independently Published.

—Tyttö, Joka Unohti Nimensä FIIA. Walsh, Tiina. 2019. (FIN.). 32p. (J). pap. 22.50 *(978-1-0968-3687-2(4))* Independently Published.

—Tyttö, Joka Unohti Nimensä Juulia. Walsh, Tiina. 2019. (FIN.). 36p. (J). pap. 22.50 *(978-1-7941-0798-4(3))* Independently Published.

—Tyttö, Joka Unohti Nimensä Lila. Walsh, Tiina. 2019. (FIN.). 32p. (J). pap. 22.50 *(978-1-5424-4456-9(X))* CreateSpace Independent Publishing Platform.

—Tyttö, Joka Unohti Nimensä Lotta. Walsh, Tiina. 2019. (FIN.). 34p. (J). pap. 22.50 *(978-1-7984-9149-2(4))* Independently Published.

—Tyttö, Joka Unohti Nimensä Maikki. Walsh, Tiina. 2019. (FIN.). 36p. (J). pap. 22.50 *(978-1-0913-3993-4(7))* Independently Published.

—Tyttö, Joka Unohti Nimensä Melissa. Walsh, Tiina. 2017. (FIN.). 38p. (J). pap. 22.50 *(978-1-5486-5988-2(6))* CreateSpace Independent Publishing Platform.

—Tyttö, Joka Unohti Nimensä Nella. Walsh, Tiina. 2018. (FIN.). 34p. (J). pap. 22.50 *(978-1-7929-7164-8(8))* Independently Published.

—Tyttö, Joka Unohti Nimensä Peppi. Walsh, Tiina. 2019. (FIN.). 34p. (J). pap. 22.50 *(978-1-5304-7894-1(4))* CreateSpace Independent Publishing Platform.

—Tyttö, Joka Unohti Nimensä Riona. Walsh, Tiina. 2019. (FIN.). 34p. (J). pap. 22.50 *(978-1-7944-3323-6(6))* Independently Published.

—Tyttö, Joka Unohti Nimensä Selina. Walsh, Tiina. 2019. (FIN.). 36p. (J). pap. 22.50 *(978-1-7932-5554-9(7))* Independently Published.

—What's My Name? Amanda Molly. Walsh, Tiina. 2018. (ENG.). 44p. (J). pap. 15.00 *(978-1-7274-1292-5(3))* CreateSpace Independent Publishing Platform.

—What's My Name? Anjelina. Walsh, Tiina. 2018. (ENG.). 38p. (J). pap. 15.00 *(978-1-7308-3609-1(7))* Independently Published.

Virta, Anni. What's My Name? BEA. Walsh, Tiina. 2019. (ENG.). 28p. (J). pap. 15.00 ***(978-1-6895-6548-6(9))*** Independently Published.

Virta, Anni. What's My Name? Blanca. Walsh, Tiina. 2018. (ENG.). 34p. (J). pap. 15.00 *(978-1-7909-0934-6(1))* Independently Published.

—What's My Name? Breanna. Walsh, Tiina. 2018. (ENG.). 36p. (J). pap. 15.00 *(978-1-7286-7197-0(3))* Independently Published.

Virta, Anni. What's My Name? CECIL. Walsh, Tiina. 2019. (ENG.). 32p. (J). pap. 15.00 ***(978-1-7106-9342-3(8))*** Independently Published.

—What's My Name? Cecilia. Walsh, Tiina. 2019. (ENG.). 36p. (J). pap. 15.00 ***(978-1-7962-2468-9(5))*** Independently Published.

Virta, Anni. What's My Name? Clelia. Walsh, Tiina. 2019. (ENG.). 34p. (J). pap. 15.00 *(978-1-7940-5450-9(2))* Independently Published.

Virta, Anni. What's My Name? DANANN. Walsh, Tiina. 2019. (ENG.). 34p. (J). pap. 15.00 ***(978-1-0891-8651-9(7))*** Independently Published.

—What's My Name? DESTANIE. Walsh, Tiina. 2019. (ENG.). 38p. (J). pap. 15.00 ***(978-1-6952-1282-4(7))*** Independently Published.

Virta, Anni. What's My Name? Dylan. Walsh, Tiina. 2018. (ENG.). 32p. (J). pap. 15.00 *(978-1-7903-1541-3(7))* Independently Published.

—What's My Name? Elizamae. Walsh, Tiina. 2018. (ENG.). 38p. (J). pap. 15.00 *(978-1-7238-6882-5(5))* Independently Published.

Virta, Anni. What's My Name? GENEVIEVE. Walsh, Tiina. 2019. (ENG.). 40p. (J). pap. 15.00 ***(978-1-6900-1776-9(7))*** Independently Published.

—What's My Name? GWENEVERE. Walsh, Tiina. 2019. (ENG.). 40p. (J). pap. 15.00 ***(978-1-6900-2251-0(5))*** Independently Published.

Virta, Anni. What's My Name? Henia. Walsh, Tiina. 2018. (ENG.). 32p. (J). pap. 15.00 *(978-1-7239-4015-6(1))* Independently Published.

—What's My Name? Ida. Walsh, Tiina. 2018. (ENG.). 28p. (J). pap. 15.00 *(978-1-7292-2127-3(0))* Independently Published.

—What's My Name? Idalia. Walsh, Tiina. 2018. (ENG.). 34p. (J). pap. 15.00 *(978-1-7292-2140-2(8))* Independently Published.

—What's My Name? Idalina. Walsh, Tiina. 2018. (ENG.). 36p. (J). pap. 15.00 *(978-1-7292-2178-5(5))* Independently Published.

—What's My Name? Ideashia. Walsh, Tiina. 2018. (ENG.). 38p. (J). pap. 15.00 *(978-1-7292-2198-3(X))* Independently Published.

—What's My Name? Idetta. Walsh, Tiina. 2018. (ENG.). 34p. (J). pap. 15.00 *(978-1-7292-2223-2(4))* Independently Published.
—What's My Name? Ileana. Walsh, Tiina. 2018. (ENG.). 34p. (J). pap. 15.00 *(978-1-7292-2250-8(1))* Independently Published.
—What's My Name? Ilia. Walsh, Tiina. 2018. (ENG.). 30p. (J). pap. 15.00 *(978-1-7292-2304-8(4))* Independently Published.
—What's My Name? Iliana. Walsh, Tiina. 2018. (ENG.). 34p. (J). pap. 15.00 *(978-1-7292-2281-2(1))* Independently Published.
—What's My Name? Ilka. Walsh, Tiina. 2018. (ENG.). 30p. (J). pap. 15.00 *(978-1-7292-6867-4(6))* Independently Published.
—What's My Name? Ilma. Walsh, Tiina. 2018. (ENG.). 30p. (J). pap. 15.00 *(978-1-7292-6896-4(X))* Independently Published.
—What's My Name? Ilona. Walsh, Tiina. 2018. (ENG.). 32p. (J). pap. 15.00 *(978-1-7292-6924-4(9))* Independently Published.
—What's My Name? Ilsa. Walsh, Tiina. 2018. (ENG.). 30p. (J). pap. 15.00 *(978-1-7292-6960-2(5))* Independently Published.
—What's My Name? Ilse. Walsh, Tiina. 2018. (ENG.). 30p. (J). pap. 15.00 *(978-1-7293-4119-3(5))* Independently Published.
—What's My Name? Ilyssa. Walsh, Tiina. 2018. (ENG.). 34p. (J). pap. 15.00 *(978-1-7293-4164-3(0))* Independently Published.
—What's My Name? Iman. Walsh, Tiina. 2018. (ENG.). 30p. (J). pap. 15.00 *(978-1-7293-4201-5(9))* Independently Published.
—What's My Name? Imelda. Walsh, Tiina. 2018. (ENG.). 34p. (J). pap. 15.00 *(978-1-7293-4216-9(7))* Independently Published.
—What's My Name? Inca. Walsh, Tiina. 2018. (ENG.). 30p. (J). pap. 15.00 *(978-1-7293-4242-8(6))* Independently Published.
—What's My Name? Indi. Walsh, Tiina. 2018. (ENG.). 30p. (J). pap. 15.00 *(978-1-7293-4270-1(1))* Independently Published.
—What's My Name? Indiana. Walsh, Tiina. 2018. (ENG.). 36p. (J). pap. 15.00 *(978-1-7293-4307-4(4))* Independently Published.
—What's My Name? Indigo. Walsh, Tiina. 2018. (ENG.). 34p. (J). pap. 15.00 *(978-1-7308-2352-7(1))* Independently Published.
—What's My Name? Indrajit. Walsh, Tiina. 2018. (ENG.). 38p. (J). pap. 15.00 *(978-1-7308-2642-9(3))* Independently Published.
—What's My Name? Indrani. Walsh, Tiina. 2018. (ENG.). 36p. (J). pap. 15.00 *(978-1-7308-2700-6(4))* Independently Published.
—What's My Name? Inez. Walsh, Tiina. 2018. (ENG.). 30p. (J). pap. 15.00 *(978-1-7308-2848-5(5))* Independently Published.
—What's My Name? Ingaborg. Walsh, Tiina. 2018. (ENG.). 38p. (J). pap. 15.00 *(978-1-7308-2884-3(1))* Independently Published.
—What's My Name? Inge. Walsh, Tiina. 2018. (ENG.). 30p. (J). pap. 15.00 *(978-1-7308-3425-7(6))* Independently Published.
—What's My Name? Ingrid. Walsh, Tiina. 2018. (ENG.). 34p. (J). pap. 15.00 *(978-1-7308-3474-5(4))* Independently Published.
—What's My Name? Iniko. Walsh, Tiina. 2018. (ENG.). 32p. (J). pap. 15.00 *(978-1-7308-3499-8(X))* Independently Published.
—What's My Name? Inis. Walsh, Tiina. 2018. (ENG.). 30p. (J). pap. 15.00 *(978-1-7308-3580-3(5))* Independently Published.
—What's My Name? Inka. Walsh, Tiina. 2018. (ENG.). 30p. (J). pap. 15.00 *(978-1-7308-3645-9(3))* Independently Published.
—What's My Name? Ino. Walsh, Tiina. 2018. (ENG.). 28p. (J). pap. 15.00 *(978-1-7308-8443-6(1))* Independently Published.
—What's My Name? Inola. Walsh, Tiina. 2018. (ENG.). 32p. (J). pap. 15.00 *(978-1-7308-8462-7(8))* Independently Published.
—What's My Name? Ioke. Walsh, Tiina. 2018. (ENG.). 30p. (J). pap. 15.00 *(978-1-7308-8551-8(9))* Independently Published.
—What's My Name? Iola. Walsh, Tiina. 2018. (ENG.). 30p. (J). pap. 15.00 *(978-1-7308-8682-9(5))* Independently Published.
—What's My Name? Iolana. Walsh, Tiina. 2018. (ENG.). 34p. (J). pap. 15.00 *(978-1-7308-8879-3(8))* Independently Published.
—What's My Name? Iona. Walsh, Tiina. 2018. (ENG.). 30p. (J). pap. 15.00 *(978-1-7309-2668-6(1))* Independently Published.
—What's My Name? Ionna. Walsh, Tiina. 2018. (ENG.). 32p. (J). pap. 15.00 *(978-1-7309-2745-4(9))* Independently Published.
—What's My Name? Irelyn. Walsh, Tiina. 2018. (ENG.). 36p. (J). pap. 15.00 *(978-1-7309-2816-1(1))* Independently Published.
—What's My Name? Irene. Walsh, Tiina. 2018. (ENG.). 34p. (J). pap. 15.00 *(978-1-7309-2870-3(6))* Independently Published.
—What's My Name? Irina. Walsh, Tiina. 2018. (ENG.). 32p. (J). pap. 15.00 *(978-1-7311-7935-7(9))* Independently Published.
—What's My Name? Iris. Walsh, Tiina. 2018. (ENG.). 30p. (J). pap. 15.00 *(978-1-7311-7962-3(6))* Independently Published.
—What's My Name? Irma. Walsh, Tiina. 2018. (ENG.). 30p. (J). pap. 15.00 *(978-1-7311-7989-0(8))* Independently Published.
—What's My Name? Irmina. Walsh, Tiina. 2018. (ENG.). 34p. (J). pap. 15.00 *(978-1-7311-8038-4(1))* Independently Published.
—What's My Name? Irmine. Walsh, Tiina. 2018. (ENG.). 34p. (J). pap. 15.00 *(978-1-7311-8910-3(9))* Independently Published.
—What's My Name? Irsia. Walsh, Tiina. 2018. (ENG.). 32p. (J). pap. 15.00 *(978-1-7311-8938-7(9))* Independently Published.
—What's My Name? Irvette. Walsh, Tiina. 2018. (ENG.). 36p. (J). pap. 15.00 *(978-1-7311-8979-0(6))* Independently Published.
—What's My Name? ISA. Walsh, Tiina. 2018. (ENG.). 28p. (J). pap. 15.00 *(978-1-7312-9520-0(0))* Independently Published.
—What's My Name? Isabela. Walsh, Tiina. 2018. (ENG.). 36p. (J). pap. 15.00 *(978-1-7313-4000-9(1))* Independently Published.
—What's My Name? Isadora. Walsh, Tiina. 2018. (ENG.). 36p. (J). pap. 15.00 *(978-1-7313-4800-5(2))* Independently Published.
—What's My Name? Isane. Walsh, Tiina. 2018. (ENG.). 32p. (J). pap. 15.00 *(978-1-7313-4986-6(6))* Independently Published.
—What's My Name? Ismene. Walsh, Tiina. 2018. (ENG.). 34p. (J). pap. 15.00 *(978-1-7313-5050-3(3))* Independently Published.
—What's My Name? Isolda. Walsh, Tiina. 2018. (ENG.). 34p. (J). pap. 15.00 *(978-1-7314-5966-4(1))* Independently Published.
—What's My Name? Isolde. Walsh, Tiina. 2018. (ENG.). 34p. (J). pap. 15.00 *(978-1-7314-6012-7(0))* Independently Published.
—What's My Name? Iva. Walsh, Tiina. 2018. (ENG.). 28p. (J). pap. 15.00 *(978-1-7314-9325-5(8))* Independently Published.
—What's My Name? Ivana. Walsh, Tiina. 2018. (ENG.). 32p. (J). pap. 15.00 *(978-1-7314-9386-6(X))* Independently Published.
—What's My Name? Ivanka. Walsh, Tiina. 2018. (ENG.). 34p. (J). pap. 15.00 *(978-1-7902-5417-0(5))* Independently Published.
—What's My Name? Ivanna. Walsh, Tiina. 2018. (ENG.). 34p. (J). pap. 15.00 *(978-1-7902-5450-7(7))* Independently Published.
—What's My Name? Ivonne. Walsh, Tiina. 2018. (ENG.). 34p. (J). pap. 15.00 *(978-1-7902-5504-7(X))* Independently Published.
—What's My Name? Ivory. Walsh, Tiina. 2018. (ENG.). 32p. (J). pap. 15.00 *(978-1-7902-5550-4(3))* Independently Published.
—What's My Name? Izabella. Walsh, Tiina. 2018. (ENG.). 38p. (J). pap. 15.00 *(978-1-7902-5655-6(0))* Independently Published.
—What's My Name? Jacalyn. Walsh, Tiina. 2018. (ENG.). 36p. (J). pap. 15.00 *(978-1-7902-5707-2(7))* Independently Published.
—What's My Name? Jacee. Walsh, Tiina. 2018. (ENG.). 32p. (J). pap. 15.00 *(978-1-7904-8894-0(X))* Independently Published.
—What's My Name? Jacelyn. Walsh, Tiina. 2018. (ENG.). 36p. (J). pap. 15.00 *(978-1-7902-5683-9(6))* Independently Published.
—What's My Name? Jacenia. Walsh, Tiina. 2018. (ENG.). 36p. (J). pap. 15.00 *(978-1-7904-8923-7(7))* Independently Published.
—What's My Name? Jacey. Walsh, Tiina. 2018. (ENG.). 32p. (J). pap. 15.00 *(978-1-7905-3832-4(7))* Independently Published.
—What's My Name? Jaci. Walsh, Tiina. 2018. (ENG.). 30p. (J). pap. 15.00 *(978-1-7905-3886-7(6))* Independently Published.
—What's My Name? Jacinta. Walsh, Tiina. 2018. (ENG.). 36p. (J). pap. 15.00 *(978-1-7905-3925-3(0))* Independently Published.
—What's My Name? Jacintha. Walsh, Tiina. 2018. (ENG.). 38p. (J). pap. 15.00 *(978-1-7905-3959-8(5))* Independently Published.
—What's My Name? Jackie. Walsh, Tiina. 2018. (ENG.). 34p. (J). pap. 15.00 *(978-1-7909-1782-2(4))* Independently Published.
—What's My Name? Jaclyn. Walsh, Tiina. 2018. (ENG.). 34p. (J). pap. 15.00 *(978-1-7909-1812-6(X))* Independently Published.
—What's My Name? Jacqualine. Walsh, Tiina. 2018. (ENG.). 42p. (J). pap. 15.00 *(978-1-7913-1703-4(0))* Independently Published.
—What's My Name? Jacquelyn. Walsh, Tiina. 2018. (ENG.). 40p. (J). pap. 15.00 *(978-1-7913-1763-8(4))* Independently Published.
—What's My Name? Jacquelyne. Walsh, Tiina. 2018. (ENG.). 42p. (J). pap. 15.00 *(978-1-7913-1809-3(6))* Independently Published.
—What's My Name? Jacy. Walsh, Tiina. 2018. (ENG.). 30p. (J). pap. 15.00 *(978-1-7913-9377-9(2))* Independently Published.
—What's My Name? Jaden. Walsh, Tiina. 2018. (ENG.). 32p. (J). pap. 15.00 *(978-1-7917-7692-3(2))* Independently Published.
—What's My Name? Jadira. Walsh, Tiina. 2018. (ENG.). 34p. (J). pap. 15.00 *(978-1-7917-7733-3(3))* Independently Published.
—What's My Name? Jady. Walsh, Tiina. 2018. (ENG.). 30p. (J). pap. 15.00 *(978-1-7918-1040-5(3))* Independently Published.
—What's My Name? Jae. Walsh, Tiina. 2018. (ENG.). 28p. (J). pap. 15.00 *(978-1-7918-1056-6(X))* Independently Published.
—What's My Name? Jael. Walsh, Tiina. 2018. (ENG.). 30p. (J). pap. 15.00 *(978-1-7918-1078-8(0))* Independently Published.
—What's My Name? Jaicee. Walsh, Tiina. 2018. (ENG.). 34p. (J). pap. 15.00 *(978-1-7918-1100-6(0))* Independently Published.
—What's My Name? Jaida. Walsh, Tiina. 2018. (ENG.). 32p. (J). pap. 15.00 *(978-1-7929-8309-2(3))* Independently Published.
—What's My Name? Jaime. Walsh, Tiina. 2018. (ENG.). 32p. (J). pap. 15.00 *(978-1-7929-8414-3(6))* Independently Published.
—What's My Name? Jaimee. Walsh, Tiina. 2019. (ENG.). 34p. (J). pap. 15.00 *(978-1-7929-8502-7(9))* Independently Published.
—What's My Name? Jaimelynn. Walsh, Tiina. 2019. (ENG.). 40p. (J). pap. 15.00 *(978-1-7929-8514-0(2))* Independently Published.
—What's My Name? Jaimi. Walsh, Tiina. 2019. (ENG.). 32p. (J). pap. 15.00 *(978-1-7929-9928-4(3))* Independently Published.
—What's My Name? Jaimie. Walsh, Tiina. 2019. (ENG.). 34p. (J). pap. 15.00 *(978-1-7930-0045-3(X))* Independently Published.
—What's My Name? Jaine. Walsh, Tiina. 2019. (ENG.). 32p. (J). pap. 15.00 *(978-1-7930-0935-7(X))* Independently Published.
—What's My Name? Jala. Walsh, Tiina. 2019. (ENG.). 30p. (J). pap. 15.00 *(978-1-7930-0993-7(7))* Independently Published.
—What's My Name? Jalen. Walsh, Tiina. 2019. (ENG.). 32p. (J). pap. 15.00 *(978-1-7930-1032-2(3))* Independently Published.
—What's My Name? Jamee. Walsh, Tiina. 2019. (ENG.). 32p. (J). pap. 15.00 *(978-1-7930-1436-8(1))* Independently Published.
—What's My Name? Jameelah. Walsh, Tiina. 2019. (ENG.). 38p. (J). pap. 15.00 *(978-1-7930-1466-5(3))* Independently Published.
—What's My Name? James. Walsh, Tiina. 2019. (ENG.). 32p. (J). pap. 15.00 *(978-1-7930-2103-8(1))* Independently Published.
—What's My Name? Jamesina. Walsh, Tiina. 2019. (ENG.). 38p. (J). pap. 15.00 *(978-1-7930-2137-3(6))* Independently Published.
—What's My Name? Jami. Walsh, Tiina. 2019. (ENG.). 30p. (J). pap. 15.00 *(978-1-7930-2184-7(8))* Independently Published.
—What's My Name? Jamia. Walsh, Tiina. 2019. (ENG.). 32p. (J). pap. 15.00 *(978-1-7930-2370-4(0))* Independently Published.
—What's My Name? Jamie. Walsh, Tiina. 2019. (ENG.). 32p. (J). pap. 15.00 *(978-1-7930-8012-7(7))* Independently Published.
—What's My Name? Jamielee. Walsh, Tiina. 2019. (ENG.). 38p. (J). pap. 15.00 *(978-1-7930-8043-1(7))* Independently Published.
—What's My Name? Jamila. Walsh, Tiina. 2019. (ENG.). 34p. (J). pap. 15.00 *(978-1-7932-0082-2(3))* Independently Published.
—What's My Name? Jamilah. Walsh, Tiina. 2019. (ENG.). 36p. (J). pap. 15.00 *(978-1-7932-0102-7(1))* Independently Published.
—What's My Name? Jamilia. Walsh, Tiina. 2019. (ENG.). 36p. (J). pap. 15.00 *(978-1-7932-0146-1(3))* Independently Published.
—What's My Name? Jamilla. Walsh, Tiina. 2019. (ENG.). 36p. (J). pap. 15.00 *(978-1-7932-4416-1(2))* Independently Published.
—What's My Name? Jamilyn. Walsh, Tiina. 2019. (ENG.). 36p. (J). pap. 15.00 *(978-1-7932-4543-4(6))* Independently Published.
—What's My Name? Jan. Walsh, Tiina. 2019. (ENG.). 28p. (J). pap. 15.00 *(978-1-7932-4627-1(0))* Independently Published.
—What's My Name? Jana. Walsh, Tiina. 2019. (ENG.). 30p. (J). pap. 15.00 *(978-1-7932-4660-8(2))* Independently Published.
—What's My Name? Janae. Walsh, Tiina. 2019. (ENG.). 32p. (J). pap. 15.00 *(978-1-7932-8225-5(0))* Independently Published.
—What's My Name? Janah. Walsh, Tiina. 2019. (ENG.). 32p. (J). pap. 15.00 *(978-1-7932-8324-5(9))* Independently Published.
—What's My Name? Janai. Walsh, Tiina. 2019. (ENG.). 32p. (J). pap. 15.00 *(978-1-7933-0477-3(7))* Independently Published.
—What's My Name? Janais. Walsh, Tiina. 2019. (ENG.). 34p. (J). pap. 15.00 *(978-1-7933-0520-6(X))* Independently Published.
—What's My Name? Janalee. Walsh, Tiina. 2019. (ENG.). 36p. (J). pap. 15.00 *(978-1-7933-0568-8(4))* Independently Published.
—What's My Name? Janalyn. Walsh, Tiina. 2019. (ENG.). 36p. (J). pap. 15.00 *(978-1-7933-0644-9(3))* Independently Published.
—What's My Name? Janaya. Walsh, Tiina. 2019. (ENG.). 34p. (J). pap. 15.00 *(978-1-7933-0757-6(1))* Independently Published.
—What's My Name? Janaye. Walsh, Tiina. 2019. (ENG.). 34p. (J). pap. 15.00 *(978-1-7933-1679-0(1))* Independently Published.
—What's My Name? Janee. Walsh, Tiina. 2019. (ENG.). 32p. (J). pap. 15.00 *(978-1-7934-3070-0(5))* Independently Published.
—What's My Name? Janell. Walsh, Tiina. 2019. (ENG.). 34p. (J). pap. 15.00 *(978-1-7934-3159-2(0))* Independently Published.
—What's My Name? Janella. Walsh, Tiina. 2019. (ENG.). 36p. (J). pap. 15.00 *(978-1-7934-3294-0(5))* Independently Published.
—What's My Name? Janey. Walsh, Tiina. 2019. (ENG.). 32p. (J). pap. 15.00 *(978-1-7934-4619-0(9))* Independently Published.
—What's My Name? Janicia. Walsh, Tiina. 2019. (ENG.). 36p. (J). pap. 15.00 *(978-1-7934-4673-2(3))* Independently Published.
—What's My Name? Janie. Walsh, Tiina. 2019. (ENG.). 32p. (J). pap. 15.00 *(978-1-7934-4826-2(4))* Independently Published.
—What's My Name? Janiece. Walsh, Tiina. 2019. (ENG.). 36p. (J). pap. 15.00 *(978-1-7938-8112-0(X))* Independently Published.
—What's My Name? Janine. Walsh, Tiina. 2019. (ENG.). 34p. (J). pap. 15.00 *(978-1-7938-8161-8(8))* Independently Published.
—What's My Name? Janis. Walsh, Tiina. 2019. (ENG.). 32p. (J). pap. 15.00 *(978-1-7939-3615-8(3))* Independently Published.
—What's My Name? Janise. Walsh, Tiina. 2019. (ENG.). 34p. (J). pap. 15.00 *(978-1-7939-3678-3(1))* Independently Published.
—What's My Name? Janka. Walsh, Tiina. 2019. (ENG.). 32p. (J). pap. 15.00 *(978-1-7939-3751-3(6))* Independently Published.
—What's My Name? Janna. Walsh, Tiina. 2019. (ENG.). 32p. (J). pap. 15.00 *(978-1-7939-3877-0(6))* Independently Published.
—What's My Name? Jannalee. Walsh, Tiina. 2019. (ENG.). 38p. (J). pap. 15.00 *(978-1-7939-5082-6(2))* Independently Published.
—What's My Name? Janneth. Walsh, Tiina. 2019. (ENG.). 36p. (J). pap. 15.00 *(978-1-7939-5151-9(9))* Independently Published.
—What's My Name? Jannie. Walsh, Tiina. 2019. (ENG.). 34p. (J). pap. 15.00 *(978-1-7939-5190-8(X))* Independently Published.
Virta, Anni. What's My Name? JANNINE. Walsh, Tiina. 2019. (ENG.). 36p. (J). pap. 15.00 ***(978-1-0894-0008-0(X))*** Independently Published.
Virta, Anni. What's My Name? Janny. Walsh, Tiina. 2019. (ENG.). 32p. (J). pap. 15.00 *(978-1-7939-7813-4(1))* Independently Published.
—What's My Name? Jans. Walsh, Tiina. 2019. (ENG.). 30p. (J). pap. 15.00 *(978-1-7939-7838-7(7))* Independently Published.
—What's My Name? Jaquelina. Walsh, Tiina. 2019. (ENG.). 40p. (J). pap. 15.00 *(978-1-7939-7851-6(4))* Independently Published.
—What's My Name? Jaqueline. Walsh, Tiina. 2019. (ENG.). 40p. (J). pap. 15.00 *(978-1-7939-7888-2(3))* Independently Published.
—What's My Name? Jasia. Walsh, Tiina. 2019. (ENG.). 32p. (J). pap. 15.00 *(978-1-7939-9453-0(6))* Independently Published.
—What's My Name? Jasmeen. Walsh, Tiina. 2019. (ENG.). 36p. (J). pap. 15.00 *(978-1-7939-9899-6(X))* Independently Published.
—What's My Name? Jasmin. Walsh, Tiina. 2019. (ENG.). 34p. (J). pap. 15.00 *(978-1-7940-0000-1(3))* Independently Published.
—What's My Name? Jaxine. Walsh, Tiina. 2019. (ENG.). 34p. (J). pap. 15.00 *(978-1-7940-0101-5(8))* Independently Published.
—What's My Name? Jaya. Walsh, Tiina. 2019. (ENG.). 30p. (J). pap. 15.00 *(978-1-7940-0141-1(7))* Independently Published.
—What's My Name? Jayane. Walsh, Tiina. 2019. (ENG.). 34p. (J). pap. 15.00 *(978-1-7940-0232-6(4))* Independently Published.
—What's My Name? Jayanti. Walsh, Tiina. 2019. (ENG.). 36p. (J). pap. 15.00 *(978-1-7940-5422-6(7))* Independently Published.
—What's My Name? Jaycee. Walsh, Tiina. 2019. (ENG.). 34p. (J). pap. 15.00 *(978-1-7940-5506-3(1))* Independently Published.
—What's My Name? Jaycie. Walsh, Tiina. 2019. (ENG.). 34p. (J). pap. 15.00 *(978-1-7940-5556-8(8))* Independently Published.
—What's My Name? Jayde. Walsh, Tiina. 2019. (ENG.). 32p. (J). pap. 15.00 *(978-1-7942-8139-4(8))* Independently Published.
—What's My Name? Jaymee. Walsh, Tiina. 2019. (ENG.). 34p. (J). pap. 15.00 *(978-1-7942-8098-4(7))* Independently Published.
—What's My Name? Jaymie. Walsh, Tiina. 2019. (ENG.). 34p. (J). pap. 15.00 *(978-1-7943-1488-7(1))* Independently Published.
—What's My Name? Jayna. Walsh, Tiina. 2019. (ENG.). 32p. (J). pap. 15.00 *(978-1-7943-1539-6(X))* Independently Published.
—What's My Name? Jayni. Walsh, Tiina. 2019. (ENG.). 32p. (J). pap. 15.00 *(978-1-7943-1668-3(X))* Independently Published.
—What's My Name? Jaynie. Walsh, Tiina. 2019. (ENG.). 34p. (J). pap. 15.00 *(978-1-7943-1744-4(9))* Independently Published.
Virta, Anni. What's My Name? JAYON. Walsh, Tiina. 2019. (ENG.). 32p. (J). pap. 15.00 ***(978-1-6952-0481-2(6))*** Independently Published.
Virta, Anni. What's My Name? Jazlyn. Walsh, Tiina. 2019. (ENG.). 34p. (J). pap. 15.00 *(978-1-7943-7295-5(4))* Independently Published.
—What's My Name? Jean. Walsh, Tiina. 2019. (ENG.). 30p. (J). pap. 15.00 *(978-1-7943-7397-6(7))* Independently Published.
—What's My Name? Jeana. Walsh, Tiina. 2019. (ENG.). 32p. (J). pap. 15.00 *(978-1-7944-9289-9(5))* Independently Published.
—What's My Name? Jeanay. Walsh, Tiina. 2019. (ENG.). 34p. (J). pap. 15.00 *(978-1-7944-9357-5(3))* Independently Published.
—What's My Name? Jeanelle. Walsh, Tiina. 2019. (ENG.). 38p. (J). pap. 15.00 *(978-1-7945-5804-5(7))* Independently Published.
—What's My Name? Jeanette. Walsh, Tiina. 2019. (ENG.). 38p. (J). pap. 15.00 *(978-1-7945-6236-3(2))* Independently Published.
—What's My Name? Jeanie. Walsh, Tiina. 2019. (ENG.). 34p. (J). pap. 15.00 *(978-1-7945-6321-6(0))* Independently Published.
—What's My Name? Jeanina. Walsh, Tiina. 2019. (ENG.). 36p. (J). pap. 15.00 *(978-1-7945-6376-6(8))* Independently Published.
—What's My Name? Jeanna. Walsh, Tiina. 2019. (ENG.). 34p. (J). pap. 15.00 *(978-1-7945-6412-1(8))* Independently Published.

—What's My Name? Jeanne. Walsh, Tiina. 2019. (ENG.). 34p. (J). pap. 15.00 *(978-1-7946-1995-1(X))* Independently Published.

—What's My Name? Jeannette. Walsh, Tiina. 2019. (ENG.). 40p. (J). pap. 15.00 *(978-1-7946-2562-4(3))* Independently Published.

—What's My Name? Jeena. Walsh, Tiina. 2019. (ENG.). 32p. (J). pap. 15.00 *(978-1-7950-7219-9(9))* Independently Published.

—What's My Name? Jemila. Walsh, Tiina. 2019. (ENG.). 34p. (J). pap. 15.00 *(978-1-7950-7292-2(X))* Independently Published.

—What's My Name? Jemima. Walsh, Tiina. 2019. (ENG.). 34p. (J). pap. 15.00 *(978-1-7952-2132-0(1))* Independently Published.

—What's My Name? Jemina. Walsh, Tiina. 2019. (ENG.). 34p. (J). pap. 15.00 *(978-1-7952-2178-8(X))* Independently Published.

—What's My Name? Jen. Walsh, Tiina. 2019. (ENG.). 28p. (J). pap. 15.00 *(978-1-7952-2270-9(0))* Independently Published.

—What's My Name? Jena. Walsh, Tiina. 2019. (ENG.). 30p. (J). pap. 15.00 *(978-1-7952-2307-2(3))* Independently Published.

—What's My Name? Jenae. Walsh, Tiina. 2019. (ENG.). 32p. (J). pap. 15.00 *(978-1-7952-2469-7(X))* Independently Published.

—What's My Name? Jenalyn. Walsh, Tiina. 2019. (ENG.). 36p. (J). pap. 15.00 *(978-1-7952-2503-8(3))* Independently Published.

—What's My Name? Jenarae. Walsh, Tiina. 2019. (ENG.). 36p. (J). pap. 15.00 *(978-1-7952-8355-7(6))* Independently Published.

—What's My Name? Jenavieve. Walsh, Tiina. 2019. (ENG.). 40p. (J). pap. 15.00 *(978-1-7952-8429-5(3))* Independently Published.

—What's My Name? Jenay. Walsh, Tiina. 2019. (ENG.). 32p. (J). pap. 15.00 *(978-1-7952-8489-9(7))* Independently Published.

—What's My Name? Jenaya. Walsh, Tiina. 2019. (ENG.). 34p. (J). pap. 15.00 *(978-1-7952-8526-1(5))* Independently Published.

—What's My Name? Jendayi. Walsh, Tiina. 2019. (ENG.). 36p. (J). pap. 15.00 *(978-1-7955-1761-4(1))* Independently Published.

—What's My Name? Jenee. Walsh, Tiina. 2019. (ENG.). 32p. (J). pap. 15.00 *(978-1-7955-1847-5(2))* Independently Published.

—What's My Name? Jenelle. Walsh, Tiina. 2019. (ENG.). 36p. (J). pap. 15.00 *(978-1-7958-4879-4(0))* Independently Published.

—What's My Name? Jenetta. Walsh, Tiina. 2019. (ENG.). 36p. (J). pap. 15.00 *(978-1-7958-5025-4(6))* Independently Published.

—What's My Name? Jenette. Walsh, Tiina. 2019. (ENG.). 36p. (J). pap. 15.00 *(978-1-7958-4955-5(X))* Independently Published.

—What's My Name? Jenica. Walsh, Tiina. 2019. (ENG.). 34p. (J). pap. 15.00 *(978-1-7962-3021-5(9))* Independently Published.

—What's My Name? Jenna. Walsh, Tiina. 2019. (ENG.). 32p. (J). pap. 15.00 *(978-1-7981-4354-4(2))* Independently Published.

—What's My Name? Jennabel. Walsh, Tiina. 2019. (ENG.). 38p. (J). pap. 15.00 *(978-1-0907-7274-9(2))* Independently Published.

—What's My Name? Jennah. Walsh, Tiina. 2019. (ENG.). 34p. (J). pap. 15.00 *(978-1-0907-7333-3(1))* Independently Published.

—What's My Name? Jennalee. Walsh, Tiina. 2019. (ENG.). 38p. (J). pap. 15.00 *(978-1-0907-7420-0(6))* Independently Published.

—What's My Name? Jennasee. Walsh, Tiina. 2019. (ENG.). 38p. (J). pap. 15.00 *(978-1-0907-7472-9(9))* Independently Published.

—What's My Name? Jennavieve. Walsh, Tiina. 2019. (ENG.). 42p. (J). pap. 15.00 *(978-1-0931-5625-6(2))* Independently Published.

—What's My Name? Jennelle. Walsh, Tiina. 2019. (ENG.). 38p. (J). pap. 15.00 *(978-1-0931-5728-4(3))* Independently Published.

—What's My Name? Jennessa. Walsh, Tiina. 2019. (ENG.). 38p. (J). pap. 15.00 *(978-1-0931-5809-0(3))* Independently Published.

—What's My Name? Jennie. Walsh, Tiina. 2019. (ENG.). 34p. (J). pap. 15.00 *(978-1-0931-5851-9(4))* Independently Published.

—What's My Name? JERILYN. Walsh, Tiina. 2019. (ENG.). 36p. (J). pap. 15.00 *(978-1-0971-9919-8(3))* Independently Published.

—What's My Name? JESARA. Walsh, Tiina. 2019. (ENG.). 34p. (J). pap. 15.00 *(978-1-0972-0098-6(1))* Independently Published.

—What's My Name? JESSAMINE. Walsh, Tiina. 2019. (ENG.). 40p. (J). pap. 15.00 *(978-1-0706-8470-3(8))* Independently Published.

—What's My Name? JESSAMYN. Walsh, Tiina. 2019. (ENG.). 38p. (J). pap. 15.00 *(978-1-0706-8614-1(X))* Independently Published.

—What's My Name? JETTA. Walsh, Tiina. 2019. (ENG.). 32p. (J). pap. 15.00 *(978-1-0714-2646-3(X))* Independently Published.

—What's My Name? JEWEL. Walsh, Tiina. 2019. (ENG.). 32p. (J). pap. 15.00 *(978-1-0714-2778-1(4))* Independently Published.

—What's My Name? JILIAN. Walsh, Tiina. 2019. (ENG.). 34p. (J). pap. 15.00 *(978-1-0714-2993-8(0))* Independently Published.

—What's My Name? JILL. Walsh, Tiina. 2019. (ENG.). 30p. (J). pap. 15.00 *(978-1-0723-7852-5(3))* Independently Published.

—What's My Name? JILLENE. Walsh, Tiina. 2019. (ENG.). 36p. (J). pap. 15.00 *(978-1-0723-8028-3(5))* Independently Published.

—What's My Name? JILLIANA. Walsh, Tiina. 2019. (ENG.). 38p. (J). pap. 15.00 *(978-1-0723-8150-1(8))* Independently Published.

—What's My Name? JILLIANE. Walsh, Tiina. 2019. (ENG.). 38p. (J). pap. 15.00 *(978-1-0723-9774-8(9))* Independently Published.

Virta, Anni. What's My Name? JILLIANNA. Walsh, Tiina. 2019. (ENG.). 40p. (J). pap. 15.00 ***(978-1-0870-6992-0(0))*** Independently Published.

—What's My Name? JILLY. Walsh, Tiina. 2019. (ENG.). 32p. (J). pap. 15.00 ***(978-1-0870-7095-7(3))*** Independently Published.

—What's My Name? JIMI. Walsh, Tiina. 2019. (ENG.). 30p. (J). pap. 15.00 ***(978-1-0870-7337-8(5))*** Independently Published.

—What's My Name? JINA. Walsh, Tiina. 2019. (ENG.). 30p. (J). pap. 15.00 ***(978-1-0870-7497-9(5))*** Independently Published.

—What's My Name? JINNI. Walsh, Tiina. 2019. (ENG.). 32p. (J). pap. 15.00 ***(978-1-0870-7682-9(X))*** Independently Published.

—What's My Name? JINNY. Walsh, Tiina. 2019. (ENG.). 32p. (J). pap. 15.00 ***(978-1-0870-7868-7(7))*** Independently Published.

—What's My Name? JISELLE. Walsh, Tiina. 2019. (ENG.). 36p. (J). pap. 15.00 ***(978-1-0870-8011-6(8))*** Independently Published.

—What's My Name? JO. Walsh, Tiina. 2019. (ENG.). 26p. (J). pap. 15.00 ***(978-1-0872-5414-2(0))*** Independently Published.

—What's My Name? JOANA. Walsh, Tiina. 2019. (ENG.). 32p. (J). pap. 15.00 ***(978-1-0872-5523-1(6))*** Independently Published.

—What's My Name? JOANN. Walsh, Tiina. 2019. (ENG.). 32p. (J). pap. 15.00 ***(978-1-0872-5690-0(9))*** Independently Published.

—What's My Name? JOANNE. Walsh, Tiina. 2019. (ENG.). 34p. (J). pap. 15.00 ***(978-1-0872-5837-9(5))*** Independently Published.

—What's My Name? JOCASTA. Walsh, Tiina. 2019. (ENG.). 36p. (J). pap. 15.00 ***(978-1-0872-6001-3(9))*** Independently Published.

—What's My Name? JOCELYNE. Walsh, Tiina. 2019. (ENG.). 38p. (J). pap. 15.00 ***(978-1-0872-6182-9(1))*** Independently Published.

—What's My Name? JOCELYNN. Walsh, Tiina. 2019. (ENG.). 38p. (J). pap. 15.00 ***(978-1-0872-6349-6(2))*** Independently Published.

—What's My Name? JOHNATHAN. Walsh, Tiina. 2019. (ENG.). 40p. (J). pap. 15.00 ***(978-1-6951-7224-1(8))*** Independently Published.

Virta, Anni. What's My Name? JULIUS. Walsh, Tiina. 2019. (ENG.). 34p. (J). pap. 15.00 *(978-1-0730-5671-2(6))* Independently Published.

—What's My Name? JUSTUS. Walsh, Tiina. 2019. (ENG.). 34p. (J). pap. 15.00 *(978-1-9759-1587-2(9))* CreateSpace Independent Publishing Platform.

—What's My Name? Kia. Walsh, Tiina. 2018. (ENG.). 28p. (J). pap. 15.00 *(978-1-7905-7286-1(X))* Independently Published.

Virta, Anni. What's My Name? LENNI. Walsh, Tiina. 2019. (ENG.). 32p. (J). pap. 15.00 ***(978-1-7078-9406-2(X))*** Independently Published.

Virta, Anni. What's My Name? Maci. Walsh, Tiina. 2018. (ENG.). 30p. (J). pap. 15.00 *(978-1-7915-5964-9(6))* Independently Published.

—What's My Name? Quinn. Walsh, Tiina. 2019. (ENG.). 32p. (J). pap. 15.00 *(978-1-7938-7151-0(5))* Independently Published.

—What's My Name? Riona. Walsh, Tiina. 2019. (ENG.). 32p. (J). pap. 15.00 *(978-1-7944-3363-2(5))* Independently Published.

—What's My Name? Selina. Walsh, Tiina. 2019. (ENG.). 34p. (J). pap. 15.00 *(978-1-7932-5511-2(3))* Independently Published.

Virta, Anni. What's My Name? SILAS. Walsh, Tiina. 2019. (ENG.). 32p. (J). pap. 15.00 ***(978-1-6952-0942-8(7))*** Independently Published.

Virta, Anni. What's My Name? URSULA. Walsh, Tiina. 2019. (ENG.). 34p. (J). pap. 15.00 *(978-1-0723-8263-8(6))* Independently Published.

Virta, Anni. What's My Name? VIOLETTE. Walsh, Tiina. 2019. (ENG.). 38p. (J). pap. 15.00 ***(978-1-6952-1587-0(7))*** Independently Published.

Visan, Raluca Alina. Unicorn Coloring Book for Kids Ages 4-8 8-12: Silly, Funny & Cute Ways Girls Can Be Magical Unicorns & Sparkle Their Way Through Life. Niculae, Anca. 2018. (Pony Coloring Bks.: Vol. 1). (ENG.). 54p. (J). pap. 5.99 *(978-1-7171-1914-8(X))* CreateSpace Independent Publishing Platform.

Visaya, Artemio. Paulina's Teddy Bear Journey. Schliewen, Richard. 2012. 104p. 24.95 *(978-1-62709-055-1(X))*; pap. 19.95 *(978-1-4626-9597-3(3))* America Star Bks.

Visca. Foldore de Chuteiras. Gomes, Alexandre de Castro. 2014. (POR.). 67p. (J). *(978-85-7596-341-8(4))* Fundacao Peiropolis Ltda.

Vischer, Frans. Fuddles. Vischer, Frans. (ENG.). 32p. (J). (gr. -1-3). 2019. 7.99 *(978-1-5344-3902-3(1))*; 2011. 18.99 *(978-1-4169-9155-7(7))* Simon & Schuster Children's Publishing. (Aladdin).

—Fuddles & Puddles. Vischer, Frans. 2016. (ENG.). 32p. (J). (gr. -1-3). 17.99 *(978-1-4814-3839-1(5)*, Aladdin) Simon & Schuster Children's Publishing.

—A Very Fuddles Christmas. Vischer, Frans. (ENG.). 32p. (J). (gr. -1-3). 2018. 7.99 *(978-1-5344-3357-1(0))*; 2013. 17.99 *(978-1-4169-9156-4(5))* Simon & Schuster Children's Publishing. (Aladdin).

Visco, Tamara. Let's Play Games in Chinese. Yao, Tao-Chung & McGinnis, Scott. rev. ed. 2005. (CHI & ENG.). 164p. (gr. k-18). pap. 25.95 *(978-0-88727-360-5(2))* Cheng & Tsui Co.

Vision, Mutiya Sahar. Daddy Loves His Baby Girl. Vision, Mutiya Sahar. Vision, David. 2009. 32p. 16.00 *(978-0-9659538-7-0(4))* Visor Bks.

Visions, Chris, jt. illus. see Rodriguez, Robbi.

Visitacion, Ayin. High in the Andes & Beyond the Valley. Herrera, James/H. 2020. (ENG.). 24p. (J). 22.95 ***(978-1-4808-8824-1(9))***; pap. 13.95 ***(978-1-4808-8823-4(0))*** Archway Publishing.

Visser, Annie. Tale of an Apple Tree. Visser, Shaina Elizabeth. 2016. (ENG.). (J). pap. 11.99 *(978-0-9983337-0-0(0))* Vister Bks.

Visser, Rino. David & Goliath. van Rijswijk, Cor. 2003. 43p. (J). *(978-1-894666-23-7(2))* Inheritance Pubns.

—Gideon Blows the Trumpet. van Rijswijk, Cor. 2003. 43p. (J). *(978-1-894666-22-0(4))* Inheritance Pubns.

Visuals, Roi. Drawmaster Robocar Poli: Super Stencil Kit: 4 Easy Steps to Draw Your Heroes. 2019. (Drawmaster Ser.). (ENG.). 24p. (J). (gr. k). 11.99 *(978-2-89802-093-3(1)*, CrackBoom! Bks.) Chouette Publishing CAN. Dist: Publishers Group West (PGW).

Vita, Ariela. The Donut Yogi. Kay, Sjoukje & Kay, Sjoukje. 2007. (ENG.). 32p. (J). 2.50 *(978-0-9789698-1-3(2))* Kay, Sjoukje.

Vitale, Raoul. The Cat Who Went to Heaven. Coatsworth, Elizabeth. 2008. (ENG.). 96p. (J). (gr. 3-7). pap. 6.99 *(978-1-4169-4973-2(9)*, Simon & Schuster/Paula Wiseman Bks.) Simon & Schuster/Paula Wiseman Bks.

—The Charm Bracelet. Rodda, Emily. 2003. (Fairy Realm Ser.). 128p. (J). (gr. 2-5). 8.99 *(978-0-06-009583-3(0))* HarperCollins Pubs.

—Fairy Realm #1: the Charm Bracelet Bk. 1. Rodda, Emily. 2009. (Fairy Realm Ser.: No. 1). (ENG.). 128p. (J). (gr. 2-5). pap. 4.99 *(978-0-06-009585-7(7))* HarperCollins Pubs.

—Fairy Realm #2: the Flower Fairies. Rodda, Emily. 2009. (Fairy Realm Ser.: No. 2). (ENG.). 128p. (J). (gr. 2-5). pap. 4.99 *(978-0-06-009588-8(1))* HarperCollins Pubs.

—The Flower Fairies. Rodda, Emily. 2003. (Fairy Realm Ser.). 128p. (J). 8.99 *(978-0-06-009586-4(5))* HarperCollins Pubs.

Vitale, Raoul & Tank, Daniel. Adam & Eve. 2005. (Family Bible Story Ser.). 93p. (J). pap. *(978-0-8280-1851-7(0))* Review & Herald Publishing Assn.

—Adam & Eve. Brand, Ruth R. 2005. (Family Bible Story Ser.). 95p. (J). (gr. -1-7). per. 19.99 *(978-0-8280-1850-0(2))* Review & Herald Publishing Assn.

Vitale, Stefano. Pond Circle. Franco, Betsy. 2009. (ENG.). 32p. (J). (gr. -1-3). 18.99 *(978-1-4169-4021-0(9)*, McElderry, Margaret K. Bks.) McElderry, Margaret K. Bks.

—There Is a Flower at the Tip of My Nose Smelling Me. Walker, Alice. 2006. (ENG.). 32p. (J). (gr. -1-3). 17.99 *(978-0-06-057080-4(6))* HarperCollins Pubs.

—Why War Is Never a Good Idea. Walker, Alice. 2007. 32p. (J). (gr. -1-3). lib. bdg. 17.89 *(978-0-06-075386-3(2))* HarperCollins Pubs.

Vitali, Daniela. Play with My Animals ABCs. 2003. 16p. (J). bds. 5.99 *(978-1-931722-34-6(X)*, Sixth Avenue Bks.) Grand Central Publishing.

Vitelli, Alessandra. Ligera Como un Pluma. Lavatelli, Anna. 2019. (Torre Roja Ser.). (SPA.). 56p. (J). pap. ***(978-958-776-650-9(4))*** Norma Ediciones, S.A.

Vito, Andrea Di & Rosenberg, Rachelle. Hawkeye: This Is Hawkeye. Wong, Clarissa. 2017. (World of Reading Level 1 Ser.). (ENG.). 32p. (J). (gr. -1-3). lib. bdg. 27.07 *(978-1-5321-4052-5(5)*, 25424) Spotlight.

Vitsky, Sally. Alphabet of Earth. Schwaeber, Barbie. 2009. (ENG.). 40p. 17.95 *(978-1-59249-996-0(1))* Soundprints.

—Alphabet of Earth. Schwaeber, Barbie Heit. 2009. (ENG.). 40p. (J). 9.95 *(978-1-59249-997-7(X))* Soundprints.

Vitt, Karren. Mike & a Lynx Named Kitty. Kerr, Mike. 2nd rev. ed. 2006. 112p. per. 13.50 *(978-1-931195-36-2(6))* KiwE Publishing, Ltd.

Vitulli, Miranda & Vitulli, Taliya. Raven Hoppersocks Iii & Granola's Bedtime. Zik- Grabow, Michelle. 2019. (ENG.). 166p. (J). 29.99 *(978-1-7960-3582-7(3))*; pap. 19.99 *(978-1-7960-3581-0(5))* Xlibris Corp.

Vitulli, Taliya, jt. illus. see Vitulli, Miranda.

Viva, Frank. Weekend Dad, 1 vol. Hrab, Naseem. 2020. (ENG.). 36p. (J). (gr. -1-2). 18.95 *(978-1-77306-108-5(9))* Groundwood Bks. CAN. Dist: Publishers Group West (PGW).

Viva, Frank. Sea Change. Viva, Frank. 2016. (ENG.). 120p. (J). (gr. 2-7). 18.95 *(978-1-935179-92-4(6))* TOON Books / RAW Junior, LLC.

Vivanco, Kelly. Snow White & Rose Red. Grimm, Brothers. 2014. 40p. (J). (gr. -1-4). 17.95 *(978-1-927018-34-7(X))* Simply Read Bks. CAN. Dist: Ingram Publisher Services.

—Thumbelina. Andersen, Hans Christian. 2017.Tr. of Tommelise. 48p. (J). (gr. k-4). 17.95 *(978-1-927018-73-6(0))* Simply Read Bks. CAN. Dist: Ingram Publisher Services.

Vivanco, Sylvia. Hermano Menor, Hermana Mayor. Lindeen, Mary. 2016. (Early Rising Readers Ser.). (SPA.). 16p. (J). (gr. 1-1). 6.67 *(978-1-4788-3723-7(3))* Newmark Learning LLC.

—Little Brother, Big Sister. Lindeen, Mary. 2015. (Early Rising Readers Ser.). (J). (gr. -1-k). 5.83 *(978-1-4788-2166-3(3))* Newmark Learning LLC.

—Look Up! Lindeen, Mary. 2015. (Early Rising Readers Ser.). (J). (gr. -1-k). 5.83 *(978-1-4788-1592-1(2))* Newmark Learning LLC.

—¡Mira Hacia Arriba! Lindeen, Mary. 2016. (Early Rising Readers Ser.). (SPA.). (J). (gr. -1). 6.67 *(978-1-4788-3704-6(7))* Newmark Learning LLC.

Vivas, Chad. I Wonder What Great Things You'll Do. Denton, Mitchell James. 2018. (ENG.). 26p. (J). (gr. k-2). *(978-0-646-99308-9(9))* Denton, Mitchell.

Vivas, Guadalupe. Flaqui y la Casa en El árbol. Vasquez, J. M. 2019. (Cuentos de Gatos y Perros Ser.: Vol. 3). (SPA.). 34p. (J). pap. 12.99 *(978-1-0735-8818-3(1))* Independently Published.

—El Gran Susto de Flaqui. Vasquez, J. M. 2019. (Cuentos de Gatos y Perros Ser.: Vol. 2). (SPA.). 36p. (J). pap. 12.99 *(978-1-0728-2021-5(8))* Independently Published.

Vivas, Julie. I Went Walking. Williams, Sue. 2014. 32p. pap. 27.00 *(978-1-61003-230-8(6))* Center for the Collaborative Classroom.

—I Went Walking. Williams, Sue. 2004. (J). (gr. -1-2). audio compact disk 28.95 *(978-1-59112-720-8(3))*; 2003. pap. 39.95 incl. audio compact disk *(978-1-59112-721-5(1))* Live Oak Media.

—Koala. Saxby, Claire. (Read & Wonder Ser.). (ENG.). 32p. (J). (gr. -1-3). 2019. 7.99 *(978-1-5362-0896-2(5))*; 2017. 16.99 *(978-0-7636-9481-4(9))* Candlewick Pr.

—Let the Celebrations Begin. Wild, Margaret. 2014. (ENG.). 40p. (J). (gr. 2-5). 16.99 *(978-0-7636-7013-9(8))* Candlewick Pr.

—Let's Go Visiting. Williams, Sue. 2003. (ENG.). 32p. (J). (gr. k — 1). bds. 6.95 *(978-0-15-204638-5(0)*, 1193973) Houghton Mifflin Harcourt Publishing Co.

—Let's Go Visiting. Williams, Sue. 2004. (ENG.). 32p. (gr. -1 — 1). pap. 7.99 *(978-0-15-202410-9(7)*, 1192726) Perfection Learning Corp.

—Noam Mechapes Zichronot. Fox, Mem. Dash Greenspan, Shari, tr. from ENG. 2005. Orig. Title: Wilfrid Gordon McDonald Partridge. (HEB.). 32p. 14.00 *(978-965-7108-43-7(8))* Urim Pubns. ISR. Dist: Coronet Bks.

—Samsara Dog. Manos, Helen. 2007. (ENG.). 40p. (J). (gr. 3-6). 10.99 *(978-1-933605-51-7(0))* Kane Miller.

Vivat, Booki. Frazzled: Everyday Disasters & Impending Doom. Vivat, Booki. 2016. (ENG.). 240p. (J). (gr. 3-7). 12.99 *(978-0-06-239879-6(2)*, HarperCollins) HarperCollins Pubs. Ltd. GBR. Dist: HarperCollins Pubs.

—Frazzled #2: Ordinary Mishaps & Inevitable Catastrophes. Vivat, Booki. 2017. (ENG.). 224p. (J). (gr. 3-7). 12.99 *(978-0-06-239881-9(4)*, HarperCollins) HarperCollins Pubs. Ltd. GBR. Dist: HarperCollins Pubs.

—Frazzled #3: Minor Incidents & Absolute Uncertainties. Vivat, Booki. 2019. (ENG.). 224p. (J). (gr. 3-7). 12.99 *(978-0-06-239883-3(0)*, HarperCollins) HarperCollins Pubs. Ltd. GBR. Dist: HarperCollins Pubs.

Vivian, Bart. Imagine. Vivian, Bart. 2013. (ENG.). 32p. (J). (gr. -1-3). 14.99 *(978-1-58270-329-9(9))* Aladdin/Beyond Words.

Vizcarra, Daniel. JJ Jellyfish Ashore. Peters, Tracy. 2019. (Many Adventures of Jj Jellyfish Ser.). (ENG.). 36p. (J). (gr. k-3). 14.00 ***(978-1-970079-71-5(1))*** Opportune Independent Publishing Co.

—JJ Jellyfish Heartless. Peters, Tracy. 2019. (Many Adventures of Jj Jellyfish Ser.). (ENG.). 32p. (J). (gr. k-3). 14.00 ***(978-1-970079-69-2(X))*** Opportune Independent Publishing Co.

—JJ Jellyfish Performs. Peters, Tracy. 2019. (Many Adventures of Jj Jellyfish Ser.). (ENG.). 32p. (J). (gr. k-3). 14.00 ***(978-1-970079-67-8(3))*** Opportune Independent Publishing Co.

Vizcarra, Marcelo. Scared Mouse: In a High Adventure. Sullivan, Rocio. 2017. (Scared Mouse Adventures Ser.: Vol. 1). (ENG.). 42p. (J). pap. 12.99 ***(978-1-9819-2490-5(6))*** CreateSpace Independent Publishing Platform.

Vo-Dinh, Mai. Tet: The New Year. Tran, Kim-Lan & Millar, Louise. 2005. (Multicultural Celebrations Ser.). 32p. (J). 4.95 *(978-1-59373-012-3(8))* Bunker Hill Publishing, Inc.

Voake, Charlotte. Bach, 1 vol. Khoury, Marielle D. & du Bouchet, Paule. 2012. (ENG.). 27p. (J). (gr. 2-6). 22.99 incl. audio compact disk *(978-1-85103-319-5(X))* Moonlight Publishing, Ltd. GBR. Dist: Independent Pubs. Group.

—Beatrix Potter & the Unfortunate Tale of a Borrowed Guinea Pig. Hopkinson, Deborah. 2016. (ENG.). 44p. (J). (gr. -1-3). 17.99 *(978-0-385-37325-8(2)*, Schwartz & Wade Bks.) Random Hse. Children's Bks.

—Caterpillar Caterpillar. French, Vivian. 2009. (Read & Wonder Ser.). (ENG.). (J). (gr. -1-3). lib. bdg. 17.60 *(978-1-68065-156-0(0))* Perfection Learning Corp.

—Caterpillar Caterpillar: Read & Wonder. French, Vivian. 2009. (Read & Wonder Ser.). (ENG.). 32p. (J). (gr. -1-3). pap. 7.99 *(978-0-7636-4263-1(0))* Candlewick Pr.

—Debussy, 1 vol. Babin, Pierre. 2012. (First Discovery Music Ser.). (ENG.). 28p. (J). (gr. 2-6). 19.99 *(978-1-85103-321-8(1))* Moonlight Publishing, Ltd. GBR. Dist: Independent Pubs. Group.

—Elsie Piddock Skips in Her Sleep. Farjeon, Eleanor. 2017. (ENG.). 96p. (J). (gr. 2-5). 12.00 *(978-0-7636-9055-7(4))* Candlewick Pr.

—Franz Schubert, 1 vol. Du Bouchet, Paule. 2013. (First Discovery Music Ser.). (ENG.). 26p. (J). (gr. 2-6). 19.99 incl. audio compact disk *(978-1-85103-312-6(2))* Moonlight Publishing, Ltd. GBR. Dist: Independent Pubs. Group.

—The Further Adventures of the Owl & the Pussy-Cat. Donaldson, Julia. 2017. (ENG.). 32p. (J). (gr. -1-2). 16.99 *(978-0-7636-9081-6(3))* Candlewick Pr.

—Insect Detective. Voake, Steve. (J). 2012. (ENG.). 32p. (gr. -1-k). 18.69 *(978-0-7636-4447-5(1))*; 2012. (ENG.). 32p. (gr. -1-3). pap. 7.99 *(978-0-7636-5816-8(2))*; 2010. 28p. *(978-1-4063-1051-1(4))* Candlewick Pr.

—Insect Detective. Voake, Steve. 2015. 32p. pap. 7.00 *(978-1-61003-407-4(4))* Center for the Collaborative Classroom.

—Ludwig Van Beethoven, 1 vol. Walcker, Yann. 2012. (First Discovery Music Ser.). (ENG.). 27p. (J). (gr. 2-6). 19.99 incl. audio compact disk *(978-1-85103-310-2(6))* Moonlight Publishing, Ltd. GBR. Dist: Independent Pubs. Group.

—Say It! Zolotow, Charlotte. 2015. (ENG.). 32p. (J). (-k). 15.99 *(978-0-7636-8115-9(6))* Candlewick Pr.

—Scholastic First Picture Dictionary. Scholastic, Inc. Staff & La Bretesche, Genevieve de. Manzanero, Paula, ed. rev. ed. 2009. (ENG.). 96p. (J). (gr. -1-1). 16.99 *(978-0-545-13769-0(1)*, Cartwheel Bks.) Scholastic, Inc.

—The Things That I Love about Trees. Butterworth, Chris. 2018. (ENG.). 32p. (J). (gr. k-3). 15.99 *(978-0-7636-9569-9(6))* Candlewick Pr.

Voake, Charlotte. Melissa's Octopus & Other Unsuitable Pets. Voake, Charlotte. 2015. (ENG.). 32p. (J). (gr. -1-2). 16.99 *(978-0-7636-7481-6(8))* Candlewick Pr.

Voake, Charlotte. Some Dinosaurs Are Small. Voake, Charlotte. 2020. (ENG.). 32p. (J). (gr. -1-2). 16.99 ***(978-1-5362-0936-5(8))*** Candlewick Pr.

Voake, Charlotte. Tweedle Dee Dee. Voake, Charlotte. 2008. (ENG.). 32p. (J). (gr. -1-2). 16.99 *(978-0-7636-3797-2(1))* Candlewick Pr.

Voerg, Kathy. Eat 'em Ups Apples. Tuchman, Gail. 2019. (ENG.). 12p. (J). (gr. -1-1). bds. 7.99 *(978-0-486-82508-3(6)*, 825086) Dover Pubns., Inc.

—Eat 'em Ups Bananas. Tuchman, Gail. 2019. (ENG.). 12p. (J). (gr. -1-1). pap. 7.99 *(978-0-486-82511-3(6)*, 825116) Dover Pubns., Inc.

—Eat 'em Ups Oranges. Tuchman, Gail. 2019. (ENG.). 12p. (J). (gr. -1-1). pap. 7.99 *(978-0-486-82509-0(4)*, 825094) Dover Pubns., Inc.

—Eat 'em Ups Pears. Tuchman, Gail. 2019. (ENG.). 12p. (J). (gr. -1-1). bds. 7.99 *(978-0-486-82510-6(8)*, 825108) Dover Pubns., Inc.

—I Don't Want to Go to School: Helping Children Cope with Separation Anxiety. Pando, Nancy. 2005. (Let's Talk Ser.). (ENG.). 48p. (J). (gr. -1-1). per. 9.95 *(978-0-88282-254-9(3))* New Horizon Pr. Pubs., Inc.

Vogel, Jarom. Boats: Fast & Slow. Volant, Iris. 2018. (ENG.). 48p. (J). (gr. k-4). 19.95 *(978-1-911171-92-8(5))* Flying Eye Bks. GBR. Dist: Penguin Random Hse. LLC.

—Horses: Wild & Tame. Volant, Iris. 2017. (ENG.). 48p. (J). (gr. k-4). 19.95 *(978-1-911171-80-5(1))* Flying Eye Bks. GBR. Dist: Penguin Random Hse. LLC.

Vogel, Naomi. The Happy Animal Alphabet! Vogel, Naomi. 2016. (ENG.). (J). pap. 9.95 *(978-0-692-81723-0(9))* Nay Vogel Photography & Design.

Vogel, Vin. Bob & Joss Get Lost! McCleery, Peter. 2017. (ENG.). 32p. (J). (gr. -1-3). 17.99 *(978-0-06-241531-8(X))* HarperCollins Pubs.

—Bob & Joss Take a Hike! McCleery, Peter. 2018. (ENG.). 32p. (J). (gr. -1-3). 17.99 *(978-0-06-241532-5(8))* HarperCollins Pubs.

—Maddi's Fridge. Brandt, Lois. 2014. (ENG.). 32p. (J). (gr. k-3). 17.95 *(978-1-936261-29-1(4))* Flashlight Pr.

—Music Class Today! Weinstone, David. 2015. (ENG.). 40p. (J). (gr. -1 — 1). 17.99 *(978-0-374-35131-1(7)*, 900138002, Farrar, Straus & Giroux (BYR)) Farrar, Straus & Giroux.

—Naughty Ninja Takes a Bath. Tarpley, Todd. 2020. 32p. (J). (gr. -1-2). 17.99 *(978-1-5420-9433-7(X)*, 9781542094337, Two Lions) Amazon Publishing.

—La Nevera de Maddi. Brandt, Lois. 2018. (SPA.). 32p. (J). (gr. k-2). 16.95 *(978-1-936261-97-0(9))* Flashlight Pr.

Vogt, Johannes. X-Ray Me! Look Inside Your Body. Horstschafer, Felicitas. 2019. (ENG.). 22p. (J). (gr. 1-5). bds. 12.99 *(978-0-06-288996-6(6)*, Greenwillow Bks.) HarperCollins Pubs.

Vohra, Sibi. The Three Billy Goats Gruff. Asbjømsen, Peter Christen. 2010. (J). *(978-1-60617-149-3(6))* Teaching Strategies, LLC.

Vohra, Subhash. The Little Red Hen. 2010. (J). *(978-1-60617-129-5(1))* Teaching Strategies, LLC.

Vohwinkel, Astrid. Nanuk Flies Home. Holtei, Christa. 2008. 26p. (J). (gr. 4-7). 16.00 *(978-0-8028-5342-4(0))* Eerdmans, William B. Publishing Co.

Voight, Lisa. Goodnight Cowtown. Drez, Jennifer & Bumstead, Robin. 2012. 40p. (J). 17.95 *(978-0-615-54492-2(4))* Petit Chou Chou, LLC.

Voiland, Adam, photos by. ABCs from Space: A Discovered Alphabet. Voiland, Adam. 2017. (ENG., 40p. (J). (gr. -1-3). 18.99 *(978-1-4814-9428-1(7)*, Simon & Schuster Bks. For Young Readers) Simon & Schuster Bks. For Young Readers.

Voje, Patty. Great Animal Escape Stories: True Adventures of Farm Animals. Cox, Barbara G. 2016. (ENG.). (J). (gr. k-6). pap. 9.99 *(978-0-9973745-3-7(5))* Windhorse Bks.

Vojtech, Anna. Friendly Beasts: An Old English Christmas Carol, 1 vol. St. James, Rebecca. 2012. (ENG.). 32p. (J). 16.99 *(978-0-310-72012-6(5))* Zonderkidz.

—Over in the Meadow. Wadsworth, Olive A. 2003. (Cheshire Studio Book Ser.). (ENG.). 32p. (J). pap. 7.95 *(978-0-7358-1871-2(1))* North-South Bks., Inc.

Volbeda, Ludwig. Tortot, the Cold Fish Who Lost His World & Found His Heart. Lindelauf, Benny. Watkinson, Laura, tr. 2018. (ENG.). 240p. (J). (gr. 7-9). 24.00 *(978-1-78269-154-9(5)*, Pushkin Children's Bks.) Steerforth Pr.

Volinski, Jessica, jt. illus. see DePrince, Erik.

Völk, Julie. The Dark & the Light. Völk, Julie. Hau, Kerstin. 2019. (ENG.). 40p. (J). (gr. -1-2). 17.95 *(978-0-7358-4385-1(6))* North-South Bks., Inc.

Volke, Gordon, et al. Panda Patrol Big Activity Book. 2004. 24p. 6.00 *(978-1-84161-111-2(5))* Ravette Publishing, Ltd. GBR. Dist: Parkwest Pubns., Inc.

—Panda Patrol Sticker, Story & Activitity Book, Vol. 2. 2004. 16p. pap., act. bk. ed. 6.00 *(978-1-84161-112-9(3))* Ravette Publishing, Ltd. GBR. Dist: Parkwest Pubns., Inc.

—Panda Patrol Sticker, Story & Activity Book. 2004. 16p. pap., act. bk. ed. 6.00 *(978-1-84161-072-6(0))* Ravette Publishing, Ltd. GBR. Dist: Parkwest Pubns., Inc.

—Panda Patrol Travel Games with Stickers. 2004. 16p. pap., act. bk. ed. 6.00 *(978-1-84161-110-5(7))* Ravette Publishing, Ltd. GBR. Dist: Parkwest Pubns., Inc.

Völker, Sven. There's a Little Black Spot on the Sun Today. Sting. 2015. 40p. (J). 19.95 *(978-0-7358-4238-0(8))* North-South Bks., Inc.

Volley, Will, et al. Romeo & Juliet. Shakespeare, William. Bryant, Clive, ed. Sanders, Joe Sutliff, tr. 2009. (ENG.). 176p. (gr. 4-18). pap. 16.95 *(978-1-906332-63-1(0)*, Classical Comics, Ltd.) Classical Comics GBR. Dist: Publishers Group West (PGW).

Volley, Will, jt. illus. see Sanchez, Alejandro.

Voloschuk, Myroslava. Bella the Butterfly Dog Goes to Work. Smith, Vicki. 2020. (Bella the Butterfly Dog Ser.: Vol. 1). (ENG.). 32p. (J). pap. 14.99 ***(978-1-948026-61-1(9))*** Write Integrity Pr.

Volpari, Daniela. A Deadly Fall. Wallace, Rich. 2016. (Haunted Ser.). (ENG.). 48p. (J). (gr. 3-7). 29.93 *(978-1-62402-147-3(6)*, 21571, Spellbound) Magic Wagon.

—Haunted, 4 vols. Wallace, Rich. 2016. (Haunted Ser.). 48p. (J). (gr. 3-7). lib. bdg. 114.00 *(978-1-62402-146-6(8)*, 21569, Spellbound) Magic Wagon.

—Lost in the Dark. Wallace, Rich. 2016. (Haunted Ser.). (ENG.). 48p. (J). (gr. 3-7). 29.93 *(978-1-62402-148-0(4)*, 21573, Spellbound) Magic Wagon.

—Phantom Flames. Wallace, Rich. 2016. (Haunted Ser.). (ENG.). 48p. (J). (gr. 3-7). 29.93 *(978-1-62402-150-3(6)*, 21577, Spellbound) Magic Wagon.

—When Bill Gates Memorized the Encyclopedia. Weakland, Mark. 2018. (Leaders Doing Headstands Ser.). (ENG.). 32p. (J). (gr. 1-4). pap. 7.95 *(978-1-5158-3048-1(9)*, 138683, Picture Window Bks.) Capstone.

—When Ruth Bader Ginsburg - Chewed 100 Sticks of Gum. Weakland, Mark. 2018. (Leaders Doing Headstands Ser.). (ENG.). 32p. (J). (gr. 1-4). lib. bdg. 28.65 *(978-1-5158-3039-9(X)*, 138676, Picture Window Bks.) Capstone.

Volpin, Lucy. We Love Dinosaurs. Volpin, Lucy. 2018. (ENG.). 32p. (J). (-k). 16.99 *(978-0-7636-9959-8(4)*, Nosy Crow) Candlewick Pr.

Voltaggio, Nicholas. Hippocrene Hindi Children's Picture Dictionary. Hippocrene Books Staff. Martin, Robert Stanly, ed. 2006. (ENG.). 112p. (J). pap. 14.95 *(978-0-7818-1129-3(5))* Hippocrene Bks., Inc.

—Vietnamese Children's Picture Dictionary: English-Vietnamese/Vietnamese-English. Martin, Robert, Jr. 2006. (ENG.). 112p. (J). (gr. 3-7). pap. 14.95 *(978-0-7818-1133-0(3))* Hippocrene Bks., Inc.

Voltz, Ralph. Bible for Me: 12 Favorite Stories, 1 vol. Holmes, Andy. 2003. (ENG.). 48p. 9.99 *(978-1-4003-0234-5(X))* Nelson, Thomas Inc.

—Junior Groovies: Trains (Storybook, Fun Facts & Toys) Ikids Staff. 2011. (ENG.). 10p. (J). (gr. -1-1). 12.99 *(978-1-60169-149-1(1))* Innovative Kids.

Voltz, Ralph. Manners & Me: An Easy-Peasy Guide for Kids & the Grown Ups Who Love Them. Dorrier, Nancy. 2019. (ENG.). 26p. (J). (gr. -1-2). pap. 9.99 ***(978-1-61254-378-9(2))*** Brown Books Publishing Group.

Volz, Katie. Tiggy Finds a Home. Volz, Carole A. 2013. 44p. (J). 18.95 *(978-1-62287-445-3(5))* First Edition Design eBook Publishing.

von Allmen, Tania. Ponders, Proverbs & Principles. Weckworth, Rodney R. 2005. 344p. pap. 14.95 *(978-1-929170-16-6(5)*, PDG) Publishers Design Group, Inc.

Von Amelsfort, Barbra. The Yoga Adventure for Children: Playing, Dancing, Moving, Breathing, Relaxing. Purperhart, Helen. 2007. (ENG.). 144p. (gr. -1-6). spiral bd. 19.95 *(978-0-89793-471-8(7))*; per. 14.95 *(978-0-89793-470-1(9))* Turner Publishing Co. (Hunter Hse.).

Von Braun, Jessica. Conquest of Greystone Valley. Brooks, Charlie. 2016. (Greystone Valley Ser.: Vol. 2). (ENG.). (YA). (gr. 7-12). 18.99 *(978-1-945760-16-7(8))*; pap. 9.99 *(978-1-945760-18-1(4))* Grey Gecko Pr.

von Buhler, Cynthia. Tell Us a Tale, Hans! The Life of Hans Christian Andersen. Fradin, Dennis Brindell. 2006. (J). *(978-1-59336-681-0(7))*; pap. *(978-1-59336-682-7(5))* Mondo Publishing.

—They Called Her Molly Pitcher. Rockwell, Anne. 2006. (ENG.). 40p. (J). (gr. -1-2). 7.99 *(978-0-553-11253-5(8)*, Dragonfly Bks.) Random Hse. Children's Bks.

von Buhler, Cynthia. Nicolaus Copernicus: The Earth Is a Planet. von Buhler, Cynthia, tr. Fradin, Dennis Brindell. 2003. 32p. (J). (gr. 2-6). 15.95 *(978-1-59336-006-1(1))*; pap. *(978-1-59336-007-8(X))* Mondo Publishing.

von der Sterre, Johanna. Moses & the Long Walk. Bader, Joanne. 2006. 16p. (J). 1.99 *(978-0-7586-0874-1(8))* Concordia Publishing Hse.

von Innerebner, Jessika. Banana Pants! (Miranda & Maude #2) Wunsch, Emma. 2019. (Miranda & Maude Ser.). (ENG.). (J). (gr. 2-5). 160p. pap. 6.99 *(978-1-4197-3695-7(7))*; 144p. 12.99 *(978-1-4197-3180-8(7))* Abrams, Inc. (Amulet Bks.).

—Be Brave Like Aquaman! (DC Super Friends) Hitchcock, Laura. 2019. (Pictureback(R) Ser.). (ENG.). 32p. (J). (gr. -1-2). pap. 5.99 *(978-1-9848-4831-4(3)*, Random Hse. Bks. for Young Readers) Random Hse. Children's Bks.

von Innerebner, Jessika. Les Cadeaux du Corbeau. Jaadee, Kung. Payette, Marie-Christine, tr. from ENG. 2020. Orig. Title: Gifts from Raven. (FRE.). 28p. (J). (gr. -1-k). 11.95 ***(978-1-989122-44-0(2))*** Medicine Wheel Education CAN. Dist: Orca Bk. Pubs. USA.

—Le Caillou de Guérison de Trudy. Spiller, Trudy. Payette, Marie-Christine, tr. from ENG. 2020. Orig. Title: Trudy's Healing Stone. (FRE.). 24p. (J). (gr. -1-k). 11.95 ***(978-1-989122-47-1(7))*** Medicine Wheel Education CAN. Dist: Orca Bk. Pubs. USA.

von Innerebner, Jessika. Camp Hero Double Trouble. Bellisario, Gina. 2018. (Ellie Ultra Ser.). (ENG.). 128p. (J). (gr. 1-3). pap. 6.95 *(978-1-4965-6517-4(7)*, 138521); lib. bdg. 25.99 *(978-1-4965-6513-6(4)*, 138519) Capstone. (Stone Arch Bks.).

von Innerebner, Jessika. Le Cercle d'aide et de Partage. Larsen-Jonasson, Theresa. Payette, Marie-Christine, tr. from ENG. 2020. Orig. Title: The Circle of Caring & Sharing. (FRE.). 24p. (J). (gr. -1-k). 11.95 ***(978-1-989122-45-7(0))*** Medicine Wheel Education CAN. Dist: Orca Bk. Pubs. USA.

—Les Enseignements du Danseur de Cerceaux. Anderson, Teddy. Payette, Marie-Christine, tr. from ENG. 2020. Orig. Title: The Hoop Dancer's Teachings. (FRE.). 24p. (J). (gr. -1-k). 11.95 ***(978-1-989122-49-5(3))*** Medicine Wheel Education CAN. Dist: Orca Bk. Pubs. USA.

Von Innerebner, Jessika. An Extra-Ordinary Girl. Bellisario, Gina. 2016. (Ellie Ultra Ser.). (ENG.). 128p. (J). (gr. 1-3). lib. bdg. 25.99 *(978-1-4965-3139-1(6)*, Stone Arch Bks.) Capstone.

—Grow up, Ant-Man! Snider, Brandon T. (ENG.). (J). (gr. -1-k). 2020. 30p. bds. 7.99 ***(978-1-368-05600-7(8))***; 2018. 32p. 12.99 *(978-1-368-02327-6(4))* Disney Publishing Worldwide. (Marvel Pr.).

von Innerebner, Jessika. Octo-Man & the Headless Monster #1. Kelley, Jane. 2017. (Escapades of Clint Mccool Ser.: 1). 96p. (J). (gr. 1-3). lib. bdg. 15.99 *(978-0-448-48754-0(3)*, Grosset & Dunlap) Penguin Young Readers Group.

von Innerebner, Jessika. La Plume D'aigle. Locke, Kevin. Payette, Marie-Christine, tr. from ENG. 2020. Orig. Title: The Eagle Feather. (FRE.). 24p. (J). (gr. -1-k). 11.95 ***(978-1-989122-46-4(9))*** Medicine Wheel Education CAN. Dist: Orca Bk. Pubs. USA.

von Innerebner, Jessika. The Princess & the Absolutely Not a Princess (Miranda & Maude #1) Wunsch, Emma. 2018. (Miranda & Maude Ser.). (ENG.). 144p. (J). (gr. 1-4). 12.99 *(978-1-4197-3179-2(3)*, Amulet Bks.) Abrams, Inc.

—The Princess & the Absolutely Not a Princess (Miranda & Maude #1) Wunsch, Emma. 2019. (ENG.). 160p. (J). (gr. 2-5). pap. 6.99 *(978-1-4197-3374-1(5))* Abrams, Inc.

Von Innerebner, Jessika. Queen of the Spelling Bee. Bellisario, Gina. 2016. (Ellie Ultra Ser.). (ENG.). 128p. (J). (gr. 1-3). lib. bdg. 25.99 *(978-1-4965-3141-4(8)*, Stone Arch Bks.) Capstone.

von Innerebner, Jessika. Recess Rebels (Miranda & Maude #3) Wunsch, Emma. (Miranda & Maude Ser.). (ENG.). 144p. (J). (gr. 2-5). 2020. pap. 6.99 *(978-1-4197-4088-6(1))*; 2019. 12.99 *(978-1-4197-3737-4(6))* Abrams, Inc. (Amulet Bks.).

—Rox's Secret Code. Archambault, Nathan & Lecocq, Mara. 2018. (ENG.). 40p. (J). (gr. -1-1). 17.99 *(978-1-57687-899-6(6)*, powerHouse Bks.) powerHse. Bks.

—Sol-Ray Man & the Freaky Flood #2. Kelley, Jane. 2017. (Escapades of Clint Mccool Ser.: 2). 96p. (J). (gr. 1-3). 5.99 *(978-0-451-53339-5(9)*, Grosset & Dunlap) Penguin Young Readers Group.

Von Innerebner, Jessika. Super Fluffy to the Rescue. Bellisario, Gina. 2016. (Ellie Ultra Ser.). (ENG.). 128p. (J). (gr. 1-3). lib. bdg. 25.99 *(978-1-4965-3142-1(6)*, Stone Arch Bks.) Capstone.

von Innerebner, Jessika. Super Spooked. Bellisario, Gina. 2018. (Ellie Ultra Ser.). (ENG.). 128p. (J). (gr. 1-3). lib. bdg. 25.99 *(978-1-4965-6512-9(6)*, 138517, Stone Arch Bks.) Capstone.

Von Innerebner, Jessika. Team Earth Takeover. Bellisario, Gina. 2016. (Ellie Ultra Ser.). (ENG.). 128p. (J). (gr. 1-3). lib. bdg. 25.99 *(978-1-4965-3143-8(4)*, Stone Arch Bks.) Capstone.

von Innerebner, Jessika. Team Earth Takeover. Bellisario, Gina. 2017. (Ellie Ultra Ser.). (ENG.). 128p. (J). (gr. 1-3). pap. 6.95 *(978-1-4965-3147-6(7)*, Stone Arch Bks.) Capstone.

von Innerebner, Jessika. Kevin the Unicorn: It's Not All Rainbows. von Innerebner, Jessika. 2019. (Kevin the Unicorn Ser.). (ENG.). 32p. (J). (gr. -1-2). 17.99 *(978-1-9848-1430-2(3)*, Dial Bks) Penguin Young Readers Group.

von Innerebner, Jessika. Kevin the Unicorn: Why Can't We Be Bestie-Corns? von Innerebner, Jessika. 2020. 32p. (J). (gr. -1-2). 17.99 ***(978-1-9848-1480-7(X)***, Dial Bks) Penguin Young Readers Group.

Von Kitzing, Constanze. Jack & the Beanstalk. Munton, Gill. 2014. (Traditional Tales Ser.). (ENG.). 24p. (J). (gr. k-1). pap. 6.95 *(978-1-62521-572-7(X)*, Capstone Classroom) Capstone.

von Königslöw, Andrea Wayne. Emily's Eighteen Aunts, 1 vol. Parkinson, Curtis. 2003. (ENG.). 30p. (J). *(978-0-7737-3336-7(1))* Fitzhenry & Whiteside, Ltd.

—Emily's Eighteen Aunts, 1 vol. Parkinson, Curtis. 2005. (ENG.). 32p. (J). (gr. k-2). pap. 5.95 *(978-1-55005-122-3(9)*, bc131fd8-d31d-47bb-9d50-e8ef216714b6) Trifolium Bks., Inc. CAN. Dist: Firefly Bks., Ltd.

Von Mungo, Mungo. Biscuit & Oscar Learn to Fly: Colour Version. Cheyne, Georgina. 2018. (ENG.). 34p. (J). pap. 9.99 *(978-1-7904-2493-1(3))* Independently Published.

Von Sperber, Annabelle. Where's the Architect: From Pyramids to Skyscrapers. an Architecture Look & Find Book. Rebscher, Susanne. 2018. (ENG.). 32p. (J). (gr. -1-3). 19.95 *(978-3-7913-7301-0(3))* Prestel Verlag GmbH & Co KG. DEU. Dist: Penguin Random Hse. LLC.

—Where's the Artist? From Cave Paintings to Modern Art - A Look & Find Book. 2015. (ENG.). 32p. (J). (gr. 3-7). 19.95 *(978-3-7913-7233-4(5))* Prestel Verlag GmbH & Co KG. DEU. Dist: Penguin Random Hse. LLC.

VonBokel, Jan. An Extra Ordinary Day. Fonner, Deborah K. 2012. 24p. 19.95 *(978-1-4327-8342-6(4))* Outskirts Pr., Inc.

Vondran, Elizabeth. My New Sister. Vondran, Kylee. 2019. (Life with Kylee Ser.: Vol. 1). (ENG.). 26p. (J). pap. 12.95 *(978-1-0932-7332-8(1))* Independently Published.

VonRecht. Raspus. Kay, Susan. 2009. 16p. pap. 8.99 *(978-1-4389-8380-6(8))* AuthorHouse.

VonSeggen, Jon, jt. illus. see Van Order, Laura.

Vonthron-Laver, Sarah. Harriet Can Carry It, 1 vol. Mueller, Kirk Jay. 2014. (ENG.). 32p. (J). 16.99 *(978-1-59572-675-9(6))* Star Bright Bks., Inc.

Voorheis, Tracy. Nibbles... a strawberry Tale. Voorheis, Tracy. 2007. 60p. (J). per. 19.00 *(978-0-9787113-0-6(0)*, Ithaca Pr.) Authors & Artists Publishers of New York, Inc.

Vorella2000. Laugh a Little. Tate, Singleton M. 2012. 24p. pap. 24.95 *(978-1-4560-9117-0(4))* America Star Bks.

Vorhand, Rachel. I Love You Gramma Nanna. Yerushalmi, Miriam. 2019. (ENG.). 40p. (J). 20.00 *(978-0-578-44232-7(9))* Sane.

Vorhees, D. Lawrey. Doorways of New Mexico. 2003. 154p. spiral bd. 29.95 *(978-0-9635589-7-8(8))* Elysian Hills.

Voronina, Natasha. How the Russian Snow Maiden Helped Santa Claus. Buyske, Gail. 2005. 32p. (J). 16.95 *(978-0-9725027-4-0(2))* Vernissage Pr., LLC.

Vosailagi, Jo. Pentapus. 2006. 120p. per. 12.56 *(978-1-4120-9272-2(8))* Trafford Publishing.

Vosburg, L. The Fighting Quaker: The Southern Campaigns of General Nathaniel Greene. Latham, Frank Brown. 2011. 194p. 42.95 *(978-1-258-00848-2(3))* Literary Licensing, LLC.

Vosburg, M. RIP, M. D. Schauer, M. 2010. (ENG.). 88p. pap. 12.99 *(978-1-60699-369-9(0)*, 699369) Fantagraphics Bks.

Vosburg, Mike, et al. What If? Classic: the Complete Collection Vol. 4. 2020. 488p. (J). (gr. 4-17). pap. 39.99 ***(978-1-302-92286-3(6))*** Marvel Worldwide, Inc.

Vosburg, Mike, jt. illus. see Infantino, Carmine.

Vosburg, Mike, jt. illus. see Kupperberg, Alan.

Vosburgh, Leonard. Davy Crockett. Ford, Anne. 2011. 48p. 35.95 *(978-1-258-06913-1(X))* Literary Licensing, LLC.

—Fear in the Forest. De Leeuw, Cateau. 2014. (ENG.). 123p. (J). pap. 14.95 *(978-1-932350-43-2(8))* Bethlehem Bks.

—A Flag for Lafitte: Story of the Battle of New Orleans. Lane, Frederick A. 2011. 192p. 42.95 *(978-1-258-06624-6(6))* Literary Licensing, LLC.

—The How & Why Wonder Book of Florence Nightingale. Webb, Robert N. 2011. 50p. 35.95 *(978-1-258-09107-1(0))* Literary Licensing, LLC.

—We Were There at the Battle of Gettysburg. Malkus, Alida Sims. 2013. (ENG.). 192p. (J). (gr. 3-8). pap. 6.99 *(978-0-486-49261-2(3))* Dover Pubns., Inc.

Voss, Jonathan. Whoo-Ku Haiku: a Great Horned Owl Story. Gianferrari, Maria. 2020. 32p. (J). (gr. -1-3). 16.99 *(978-0-399-54842-0(4)*, G.P. Putnam's Sons Books for Young Readers) Penguin Young Readers Group.

Voss, Jonathan D. Winnie: The True Story of the Bear Who Inspired Winnie-the-Pooh. Walker, Sally M. 2015. (ENG.). 40p. (J). (gr. -1-3). 17.99 *(978-0-8050-9715-3(5)*, 900097603, Holt, Henry & Co. Bks. For Young Readers) Holt, Henry & Co.

Voss, Jonathan D. Imagine That: A Hoot & Olive Story. Voss, Jonathan D. 2019. (Hoot & Olive Ser.: 2). (ENG.). 40p. (J). 17.99 *(978-1-250-31455-0(0)*, 900199538, Holt, Henry & Co. Bks. For Young Readers) Holt, Henry & Co.

Voute, Kathleen. The Magic Ball from Mars & Starboy. Biemiller, Carl L. 2003. 302p. (J). pap. 19.95 *(978-0-918736-09-3(9)*, Sense of Wonder Pr.) Rock, James A. & Co. Pubs.

—Magic Ball from Mars & Starboy. Biemiller, Carl L. 2003. 256p. (J). reprint ed. 26.95 *(978-0-918736-10-9(2)*, Sense of Wonder Pr.) Rock, James A. & Co. Pubs.

Voutila, Ritva. The Nutcracker. Lamond, Margrete. 2016. (ENG.). 32p. (J). (gr. k-3). 18.99 *(978-1-74297-778-2(2))* Little Hare Bks. AUS. Dist: Independent Pubs. Group.

—The Stone Lion. Wild, Margaret. 2015. (ENG.). 32p. (J). (gr. k-4). 17.99 *(978-1-921894-85-5(7))* Little Hare Bks. AUS. Dist: Independent Pubs. Group.

Vriesen, Giselle. The Moon in You: A Period Book for Girls. King, Alexandria. 2nd ed. 2019. (ENG.). 228p. (J). (gr. 4-6). pap. ***(978-0-9936624-8-5(X))*** Vriesen, Andrea.

—The Moon in You: A Period Love Book for Girls. King, Alexandria. 2020. (ENG.). 228p. (J). (gr. 4-6). pap. ***(978-0-9936624-9-2(8))*** Vriesen, Andrea.

Vroman, Dave. Jesse & His New Friends. Irwin, Esther. Puett, Gayle, ed. 2006. (J). spiral bd. 10.00 *(978-0-9778462-1-4(0))* Irwin, Esther L.

Vu, Thi. Dorp the Scottish Dragon - Book Three: Hollywood - the Movie. Brundige, Britt & Durant, Sybrina, eds. 2019. (Dorp the Scottish Dragon Ser.: Vol. 3). (ENG.). 28p. (J). pap. 12.00 ***(978-1-6790-9051-6(8))*** Independently Published.

—Red Hot Dot's Fire Safety Book. Johnson, Sandi. Durant, Sybrina, ed. 2019. (ENG.). 46p. (J). pap. 12.99 ***(978-1-6794-4382-4(8))*** Independently Published.

Vu, Thi. Red Hot Dot's Fire Safety Book: Fire Safety. Johnson, Sandi. Durant, Sybrina, ed. i.t. ed. 2014. 44p. (J). (gr. k-5). pap. 12.99 *(978-1-929063-86-4(5)*, 279) Moons & Stars Publishing For Children.

—3 - Dorp the Scottish Dragon Bk. 3: Book 3 - Hollywood - the Movie, 7 vols. Johnson, Sandi. Johnson, Britt & Durant, Sybrina, eds. 2004. (Little Choo-Choo Bks.). 28p. (J). (gr. -1-6). pap. 16.99 *(978-1-929063-02-4(4)*, 103) Moons & Stars Publishing For Children.

Vue, Tou. Burning Secrets, 1 vol. Brezenoff, Steve. (Vortex Bks.). (ENG.). 112p. (J). (gr. 5-9). 2008. pap. 7.19 *(978-1-59889-920-7(1))*; 2007. 26.65 *(978-1-59889-854-5(X))* Capstone. (Stone Arch Bks.).

—Claws in the Snow. Dahl, Michael. 2010. (Dragonblood Ser.). (ENG.). 40p. (J). (gr. 4-8). pap. 6.25 *(978-1-4342-2308-1(6)*, Stone Arch Bks.) Capstone.

—Dragon in the Desert. Dahl, Michael. (Dragonblood Ser.). (ENG.). 40p. (J). (gr. 4-8). 2010. pap. 6.25 *(978-1-4342-2309-8(4))*; 2009. 23.99 *(978-1-4342-1260-3(2))* Capstone. (Stone Arch Bks.).

Vue, Tou, jt. illus. see Evans, Mark.

Vuillamy, Clara. The Bear with Sticky Paws Won't Go to Bed. Vuillamy, Clara. 2010. (ENG.). 32p. (J). (gr. -1-2). 15.95 *(978-1-58925-087-1(7))* Tiger Tales.

Vuković, Elizabet. Be a Maker. Howes, Katey. 2019. (ENG.). 32p. (J). (gr. -1-3). 17.99 *(978-1-5124-9802-8(5)*, Carolrhoda Bks.) Lerner Publishing Group.

Vukovic, Elizabet. I Wanna Be a Cowgirl. Diterlizzi, Angela. 2017. (ENG.). 40p. (J). (gr. -1-3). 17.99 *(978-1-4814-5299-1(1)*, Beach Lane Bks.) Beach Lane Bks.

—Jasmine Toguchi, Drummer Girl. Michiko Florence, Debbi. 2018. (Jasmine Toguchi Ser.: 3). (ENG.). 128p. (J). pap. 5.99 *(978-0-374-30836-0(5)*, 900185579, Farrar, Straus & Giroux (BYR)) Farrar, Straus & Giroux.

—Jasmine Toguchi, Flamingo Keeper. Michiko Florence, Debbi. 2018. (Jasmine Toguchi Ser.: 4). (ENG.). 128p. (J). 15.99 *(978-0-374-30420-1(3)*, 900158919); pap. 5.99 *(978-0-374-30837-7(3)*, 900185590) Farrar, Straus & Giroux. (Farrar, Straus & Giroux (BYR)).

—Jasmine Toguchi, Mochi Queen. Michiko Florence, Debbi. 2017. (Jasmine Toguchi Ser.: 1). (ENG.). 128p. (J). 15.99 *(978-0-374-30410-2(6)*, 900158910, Farrar, Straus & Giroux (BYR)) Farrar, Straus & Giroux.

—Jasmine Toguchi, Mochi Queen. Michiko Florence, Debbi. 2017. (Jasmine Toguchi Ser.: 1). (ENG.). 128p. (J). pap. 5.99 *(978-0-374-30834-6(9)*, 900185577, Farrar, Straus & Giroux (BYR)) Farrar, Straus & Giroux.

—Jasmine Toguchi, Super Sleuth. Florence, Debbi Michiko. 2017. (J). pap. *(978-0-374-30414-0(9))* Farrar, Straus & Giroux.

—Jasmine Toguchi, Super Sleuth. Michiko Florence, Debbi. 2017. (Jasmine Toguchi Ser.: 2). (ENG.). 128p. (J). 16.99 *(978-0-374-30413-3(0)*, 900158913, Farrar, Straus & Giroux (BYR)) Farrar, Straus & Giroux.

—Jasmine Toguchi, Super Sleuth. Michiko Florence, Debbi. 2017. (Jasmine Toguchi Ser.: 2). (ENG.). 128p. (J). pap.

V

5.99 *(978-0-374-30835-3(7)*, 900185578, Farrar, Straus & Giroux (BYR)) Farrar, Straus & Giroux.

—Jesse Owens. Calkhoven, Laurie. 2017. (You Should Meet Ser.). (ENG.). 48p. (J). (gr. 1-3). pap. 4.99 *(978-1-4814-8095-6(2)*, Simon Spotlight) Simon Spotlight.

—An Ordinary Day. Arnold, Elana K. 2020. (ENG.). 40p. (J). (-3). 17.99 *(978-1-4814-7262-3(3)*, Beach Lane Bks.) Beach Lane Bks.

—Ruth Bader Ginsburg: Ready-To-Read Level 3. Calkhoven, Laurie. 2019. (You Should Meet Ser.). (ENG.). 48p. (J). (gr. 1-1). 17.99 *(978-1-5344-4858-2(6))*; pap. 4.99 *(978-1-5344-4857-5(8))* Simon Spotlight. (Simon Spotlight).

Vulliamy, Claire. The Bear with Sticky Paws. 2008. (Tiger Tales Ser.). 24p. (J). (gr. -1-2). 15.95 *(978-1-58925-070-3(2))* Tiger Tales.

Vulliamy, Clara. Bubble & Squeak. Mayhew, James. 2013. (J). *(978-1-4351-4770-6(7))* Barnes & Noble, Inc.

—Digby o'Day & the Great Diamond Robbery. Hughes, Shirley. 2015. (ENG.). 136p. (J). (gr. k-3). 12.99 *(978-0-7636-7445-8(1))* Candlewick Pr.

—Digby o'Day in the Fast Lane. Hughes, Shirley. 2014. (ENG.). 128p. (J). (gr. k-3). 12.99 *(978-0-7636-7369-7(2))* Candlewick Pr.

—Digby o'Day up, up, & Away. Hughes, Shirley. 2016. (ENG.). 136p. (J). (gr. k-3). 12.99 *(978-0-7636-7444-1(3))* Candlewick Pr.

—Keep Love in Your Heart, Little One. Andreae, Giles. 2007. 32p. (J). (gr. -1-3). 15.95 *(978-1-58925-066-6(4))* Tiger Tales.

—Mango & Bambang: The Not-a-Pig. Faber, Polly. 2016. 144p. (J). (gr. 1-4). 14.99 *(978-0-7636-8226-2(8))* Candlewick Pr.

—Mary in America. Rae, Gwynned. 2018. (Adventures of Mary Plain Ser.). (ENG.). 144p. (J). (gr. 1-3). 13.99 *(978-1-4052-8125-6(1))* Egmont Bks., Ltd. GBR. Dist: Independent Pubs. Group.

—Mary in London. Rae, Gwynned. 2018. (Adventures of Mary Plain Ser.). (ENG.). 160p. (J). (gr. 1-3). 13.99 *(978-1-4052-8124-9(3))* Egmont Bks., Ltd. GBR. Dist: Independent Pubs. Group.

Vulliamy, Clara. The Bear with Sticky Paws Goes to School. Vulliamy, Clara. 2009. 32p. (J). (gr. -1-2). 15.95 *(978-1-58925-081-9(8))* Tiger Tales.

—Bear with Sticky Paws Goes to School. Vulliamy, Clara. 2010. (ENG.). 32p. pap. 7.95 *(978-1-58925-424-4(4))* Tiger Tales.

Vulpas, Jennifer Cooney. The Grand Illusion: A Girl Soldier in the Civil War. Lipschutz, Caralyn Frooman. 2019. (ENG.). 210p. (YA). 26.99 *(978-1-5320-6756-3(9))*; pap. 13.99 *(978-1-5320-5375-7(4))* iUniverse, Inc.

Vuong, Ede. Mummy Wishes on a Star. Vuong, Vincent. 2018. (ENG.). 58p. (J). pap. 12.95 *(978-1-7307-9112-3(3))* Independently Published.

Vuong, Ernie. A Mochi Pirate's Courage. Vuong, Vincent. 2018. (ENG.). 60p. (J). pap. 12.95 *(978-1-7294-5922-5(6))* Independently Published.

Vyas, Bhavana. The Forbidden Temple: Stories from the Past. Padma, T. V. 2004. 95p. (J). *(978-81-8146-041-7(3))* Tulika Pubs.

W

W B, R. Dragons, Slime & Soggy Socks: Cool Poems to Inspire Positivity, Laughter & Discussion. Griffey, A. F. B. 2019. (ENG.). 34p. (J). (gr. k-4). pap. *(978-0-9935564-4-9(2))* Louannvee Publishing.

W, Chris, jt. illus. see Solomon, Kerita.

W., E., jt. illus. see Morgin, W. J.

W., Earl & Ridgell, Earl. I Like Birthdays! Interactive Book about Me. Bye, K. A. 2008. (ENG.). 30p. (J). (gr. -1-3). 13.95 *(978-1-934490-02-0(4))* Boys Town Pr.

Waananen, Lisa. The Solar System Through Infographics. Higgins, Nadia. 2013. (Super Science Infographics Ser.). (ENG.). 32p. (J). (gr. 3-5). pap. 8.99 *(978-1-4677-1594-2(8))*; lib. bdg. 26.65 *(978-1-4677-1289-7(2)*, Lerner Pubns.) Lerner Publishing Group.

Waber, Paulis. Lyle Walks the Dogs. Waber, Bernard. 2010. (ENG.). 24p. (J). (gr. -1-3). 17.99 *(978-0-547-22323-0(4)*, 1061787) Houghton Mifflin Harcourt Publishing Co.

Wabisabi. La Fiesta Sorpresa de Cumpleaños. Mira, Katish. 2017. (SPA.). 28p. (J). (gr. k-2). *(978-958-48-1979-6(8))* Restrepo, Ana.

Wach, Delia Bowman. Teddy Bear's Favorite Pictures: A Quiet Time Sharing Book. Wach, Delia Bowman. Cloyd, Nancy J. 2007. 32p. (J). (gr. -1). 15.95 *(978-0-929915-75-3(5))* Headline Bks., Inc.

Wachsmann, Carrie. Finding Christmas: A Mouse in Search of Christmas. Wachsmann, Carrie. 2018. (ENG.). 68p. (J). pap. *(978-1-895112-61-0(3))* Heartbeat Productions.

Wachter, Dave. Breath Of Bones: A Tale of the Golem. Niles, Steve & Santoro, Matt. Allie, Scott, ed. 2014. (ENG.). 80p. 14.99 *(978-1-61655-344-9(8))* Dark Horse Comics.

Wachter, Jill, photos by. The Museum of Heartbreak. Leder, Meg. 2016. (ENG., 288p. (YA). (gr. 9). 17.99 *(978-1-4814-3210-8(9)*, Simon Pulse) Simon Pulse.

—My First Day of School. Capucilli, Alyssa Satin. 2019. (My First Ser.). (ENG., 32p. (J). (gr. -1-k). 17.99 *(978-1-5344-2845-4(3))*; pap. 4.99 *(978-1-5344-2844-7(5))* Simon Spotlight. (Simon Spotlight).

—My First Puppy: Ready-To-Read Pre-Level 1. Capucilli, Alyssa Satin. 2019. (My First Ser.). (ENG., 32p. (J). (gr. -1-k). 17.99 *(978-1-5344-5380-7(6))*; pap. 4.99 *(978-1-5344-5379-1(2))* Simon Spotlight. (Simon Spotlight).

—My First Swim Class. Capucilli, Alyssa Satin. 2018. (My First Ser.). (ENG., 32p. (J). (gr. -1-k). 17.99 *(978-1-5344-0488-5(0))*; pap. 3.99 *(978-1-5344-0487-8(2))* Simon Spotlight. (Simon Spotlight).

—My First Yoga Class. Capucilli, Alyssa Satin. 2017. (My First Ser.). (ENG., 32p. (J). (gr. -1-k). 16.99 *(978-1-5344-0485-4(6))*; pap. 4.99 *(978-1-5344-0484-7(8))* Simon Spotlight. (Simon Spotlight).

Wacker, Ranae. God Made My Hands. Comley, Kathryn. 2004. (J). bds. 9.99 *(978-1-4183-0005-0(5))* Christ Inspired, Inc.

Wada, Rachel. The Phone Booth in Mr. Hirota's Garden, 1 vol. Smith, Heather. 2019. (ENG.). 32p. (J). (gr. 1-3). 19.95 *(978-1-4598-2103-3(3))* Orca Bk. Pubs. USA.

Waddington, Nicole. It's Good Sunday. Moore, Shahari. 2003. (J). *(978-0-9743394-0-5(7))* More Pr.

Waddy, F. Grammar-Land. Nesbitt, M. L. 2009. 124p. pap. 8.95 *(978-1-59915-332-2(7))* Yesterday's Classics.

Wade, Gini. Dic Penderyn. Edwards, Meinir Wyn. 2008. (Welsh Folk Tales in a Flash! Ser.). (ENG.). 24p. (J). pap. 4.95 *(978-1-84771-022-2(0))* Y Lolfa GBR. Dist: Casemate Pubs. & Bk. Distributors, LLC.

—Dragon & Mousie. Peters, Andrew Fusek. 2006. (ENG.). 32p. (J). pap. 5.95 *(978-0-86243-650-6(8))* Y Lolfa GBR. Dist: Casemate Pubs. & Bk. Distributors, LLC.

—Dragon & Mousie & the Snow Factory. Peters, Andrew Fusek. 2007. (ENG.). 32p. (J). pap. 7.95 *(978-0-86243-945-3(0))* Y Lolfa GBR. Dist: Casemate Pubs. & Bk. Distributors, LLC.

—Maelgwn, King of Gwynedd. Edwards, Meinir Wyn. 2008. (Welsh Folk Tales in a Flash! Ser.). (ENG.). 24p. (J). pap. 4.95 *(978-1-84771-024-6(7))* Y Lolfa GBR. Dist: Casemate Pubs. & Bk. Distributors, LLC.

—Red Bandits of Mawddwy. Edwards, Meinir Wyn. 2008. (Welsh Folk Tales in a Flash! Ser.). (ENG.). 24p. (J). pap. 4.95 *(978-1-84771-023-9(9))* Y Lolfa GBR. Dist: Casemate Pubs. & Bk. Distributors, LLC.

—Rhys & Meinir. Edwards, Meinir Wyn. 2007. (Welsh Folk Tales in a Flash! Ser.). (ENG.). 24p. (J). pap. 4.95 *(978-1-84771-020-8(4))* Y Lolfa GBR. Dist: Casemate Pubs. & Bk. Distributors, LLC.

Wade, Jerry. Fortitude: The Adventures of the Esteem Team. Sargent, Alan E. 2013. 84p. pap. 10.95 *(978-1-62516-984-6(1)*, Strategic Bk. Publishing) Strategic Book Publishing & Rights Agency (SBPRA).

Wade, Mervin, photos by. Prime Time Dimes in the Feds. Wade, Mervin. Wade, Mervin, ed. 2003. 80p. (YA). pap. *(978-0-9722738-0-0(8))* Melzee's Production.

Wademan, Spike. True Life Survival: Band 12/Copper (Collins Big Cat) Vale, Janice. 2007. (Collins Big Cat Ser.). (ENG.). 32p. (J). (gr. 2-4). pap. 9.99 *(978-0-00-723078-5(8))* HarperCollins Pubs. Ltd. GBR. Dist: Independent Pubs. Group.

Wadham, Anna. The Ant & the Big Bad Bully Goat. Fusek Peters, Andrew. (Traditional Tales with a Twist Ser.). 32p. (J). 2010. (gr. -1-2). *(978-1-84643-348-1(7))*; 2007. (gr. 2-2). pap. *(978-1-84643-079-4(8))* Child's Play International Ltd.

—Dingo Dog & the Billabong Storm. Fusek Peters, Andrew. (Traditional Tales with a Twist Ser.). 32p. (J). (gr. -1-2). 2010. audio compact disk *(978-1-84643-350-4(9))*; 2009. *(978-1-84643-247-7(2))* Child's Play International Ltd.

—When the Sun Shines on Antarctica: And Other Poems about the Frozen Continent. Latham, Irene. 2016. (ENG.). 32p. (J). (gr. 3-6). 19.99 *(978-1-4677-5216-9(9)*, 9781467752169); E-Book 30.65 *(978-1-4677-9729-0(4))* Lerner Publishing Group. (Millbrook Pr.).

Wadi, Nadirah. Let's Go to the Masjid. Wadi, Amatullah. 2020. (Islamic Adventure Ser.: Vol. 1). (ENG.). 36p. (J). pap. 9.99 ***(978-1-0955-7699-1(2))*** Independently Published.

Wadia, Niloufer. Sadiq Wants to Stitch. Nainy, Mamta. 2020. (ENG.). 40p. (J). (gr. -1-3). 13.95 ***(978-81-933889-1-4(7))*** Karadi Tales Co. Pvt, Ltd. IND. Dist: Consortium Bk. Sales & Distribution.

Wadkins, Fran. Resurrection Eggs Activity Book. Bradford, Amy L. & Larmoyeux, Mary. 2006. 58p. (J). (gr. 4-7). pap. 6.99 *(978-1-57229-790-6(5))* FamilyLife.

Wadsworth, Peter. Emily's Reindeer Christmas. Thomas, Toni. 2018. (ENG.). (J). 38p. *(978-0-9956652-2-4(2))*; 42p. pap. ***(978-0-9956652-5-5(7))*** Annalese Pr.

Wadsworth, Peter. Willy the Winsome Wallaby. Thomas, Toni. 2019. (ENG.). 24p. (J). ***(978-0-9956652-6-2(5))*** Annalese Pr.

Waechter, Philip. Bravo! Port, Moni. 2011. (Gecko Press Titles Ser.). 36p. 17.95 *(978-1-877467-71-4(5))* Gecko Pr. NZL. Dist: Lerner Publishing Group.

Waerea, James & Waerea, Mitch. Pukunui. Waerea, James. FireHydrant Creative Studios, ed. 2010. (ENG & MAO.). 26p. (J). pap. 14.95 *(978-0-9826066-0-5(5))* FireHydrant Creative Studios, Inc.

Waerea, Mitch, jt. illus. see Waerea, James.

Wagele, Elizabeth. Finding the Birthday Cake: Helping Children Raise Their Self-Esteem. 2007. (ENG.). 48p. (J). (gr. k-4). per. 8.95 *(978-0-88282-277-8(2))* New Horizon Pr. Pubs., Inc.

Waggoner, Sandy. Little Bible Jewels to Amaze Volume II. Hastings, Ronda. 2018. (Little Bible Jewels to Amaze Ser.: Vol. 2). (ENG.). 106p. (J). pap. 21.03 *(978-1-7195-2102-4(6))* CreateSpace Independent Publishing Platform.

Wagner, Connie. The Evil Mailbox & the Super Burrito, 1 vol. Wagner-Robertson, Garry. 2011. (ENG.). 96p. (gr. 3-6). 16.99 *(978-0-7643-3856-4(0)*, 9780764338564, Schiffer Publishing Ltd) Schiffer Publishing, Ltd.

Wagner, Gavin. The Mobile Monk: A Zen Tale. Cerpok, M. L. 2008. 73p. pap. 19.95 *(978-1-60610-138-4(2))* America Star Bks.

Wagner, Gerard. Three Grimms' Fairy Tales, 1 vol. Steiner, Rudolf. 2010. (ENG.). 88p. (J). 25.00 *(978-0-88010-716-7(2))* SteinerBooks, Inc.

Wagner, Jen. Old Don: A Heathen Tale. Heath, Josh. 2018. (ENG.). 40p. (J). pap. 15.95 *(978-1-7239-9517-0(7))* Independently Published.

Wagner, Justin & Wucinich, Warren. Pizzasaurus Rex. Wagner, Justin. 2018. (ENG.). 168p. (J). (gr. 6). pap. 14.99 *(978-1-62010-507-8(1)*, Lion Forge) Oni Pr., Inc.

Wagner, Ron, et al. Classic G. I. Joe, Vol. 8, 15 vols., Vol. 8. Hama, Larry. 2010. (Classic G. I. JOE Ser.: 8). (ENG.). 256p. pap. 24.99 *(978-1-60010-655-2(2)*, 9781600106552) Idea & Design Works, LLC.

Wagner, Sandra Glahn. The Ants Have Dyed. Wagner, Sandra Glahn. 2013. 20p. pap. 12.95 *(978-1-61493-171-3(2))* Peppertree Pr., The.

—Trickle, the Water Cycler. Wagner, Sandra Glahn. 2016. (ENG.). (J). pap. 14.95 *(978-1-61493-464-6(9))* Peppertree Pr., The.

Wagner, Steve. Socky, the Soft-Hearted Soccer Ball. Voigt, David & Voigt, Grady. 2011. pap. 12.00 *(978-0-9833310-6-3(5))* Aperture Pr., LLC.

Wagner, Zoey Abbott. Twindergarten. Ehrlich, Nikki. 2017. (ENG.). 32p. (J). (gr. -1-3). 15.99 *(978-0-06-256423-8(4))* HarperCollins Pubs.

Wagoner, Kim. The Mommy Mole. Medler, John, Jr. 2004. (J). pap. 15.00 *(978-0-8059-6664-0(1))* Dorrance Publishing Co., Inc.

Wahl, Phoebe. Paper Mice. Lloyd, Megan Wagner. 2019. (ENG.). 40p. (J). (gr. -1-3). 17.99 *(978-1-4814-8166-3(5)*, Simon & Schuster Bks. For Young Readers) Simon & Schuster Bks. For Young Readers.

Wahl, Valerie. Ayat Jamilah: Beautiful Signs: A Treasury of Islamic Wisdom for Children & Parents. 2010. (ENG.). 212p. (YA). pap. 19.95 *(978-1-55896-569-0(6)*, Skinner Hse. Bks.) Unitarian Universalist Assn.

—Kindness: A Treasury of Buddhist Wisdom for Children & Parents. Conover, Sarah. 2010. (ENG.). 184p. (YA). pap. 19.95 *(978-1-55896-568-3(8)*, Skinner Hse. Bks.) Unitarian Universalist Assn.

Wahman, Wendy. Don't Lick the Dog: Making Friends with Dogs. Wahman, Wendy. 2009. (ENG.). 32p. (J). (gr. -1-2). 18.99 *(978-0-8050-8733-8(8)*, 900049401, Holt, Henry & Co. Bks. For Young Readers) Holt, Henry & Co.

Wahyudi, Ardi. What Will Willabe Be? It's Better to Be a Willabe Than a Wannabe. Lightfoot, Leah Diamand. 2020. (ENG.). 44p. (J). 29.99 ***(978-1-7283-4894-0(3))***; pap. 16.99 ***(978-1-7283-4893-3(5))*** AuthorHouse.

Waid, Antoinette M., jt. illus. see Waid, Sara Joyce.

Waid, Antoinette M., jt. illus. see Waid, Sara J.

Waid, Sara J. & Waid, Antoinette M. The Fairy Seekers - the Sand Fairy, 1. Murphy, Breena. l.t. ed. 2006. 284p. (J). per. 14.95 *(978-0-9788010-0-7(8))* Edes Publishing Co.

Waid, Sara Joyce & Waid, Antoinette M. The Fairy Seekers - the Sand Fairy. Murphy, Breena. l.t. ed. 2006. 284p. (J). 24.95 *(978-0-9788010-1-4(6))* Edes Publishing Co.

Waipara, Zak. Maui - Sun Catcher. Tipene, Tim. Ruha, Rob, tr. 2016. (ENG.). 32p. (J). 19.00 *(978-0-947506-14-8(4)*, 13417, Oratia Bks.) Oratia Media NZL. Dist: Univ. of Hawaii Pr.

Waisman, Shirley. Yossi & the Monkeys: A Shavuot Story. MacLeod, Jennifer Tzivia. 2017. (ENG.). 32p. (J). (gr. -1-3). 17.99 *(978-1-4677-8932-5(1)*, 9781467789325, Kar-Ben Publishing) Lerner Publishing Group.

Waite, Donald E., jt. photos by see Calderwood, Damon.

Waite, Tyler. I May Not Be Like You but We Could Be Friends. Bishop, Sabrena. Butler-Likely, Tamira, ed. 2018. (ENG.). 26p. (J). (gr. 3-6). 19.99 *(978-1-948071-35-2(5))* Lauren Simone Publishing Hse.

Waites, Joan. An Artist's Night Before Christmas, 1 vol. 2017. (Night Before Christmas Ser.). (ENG.). 32p. (J). (gr. -1-3). 16.99 *(978-1-4556-2205-4(2)*, Pelican Publishing) Arcadia Publishing.

—Monsieur Durand's Grosse Affaire, 1 vol. St. Romain, Rose Anne. 2011. (ENG.). 32p. (J). (gr. k-3). 16.99 *(978-1-58980-808-9(8)*, Pelican Publishing) Arcadia Publishing.

—P Is for Police, 1 vol. Butler, Dori Hillestad. 2009. (ABC Ser.). (ENG.). 32p. (J). (gr. k-3). 16.99 *(978-1-58980-652-8(2)*, Pelican Publishing) Arcadia Publishing.

—Saint Faustina Kowalska: Messenger of Mercy. Wallace, Susan Helen. 2007. (Encounter the Saints Ser.: 23). (J). pap. 7.95 *(978-0-8198-7101-5(X))* Pauline Bks. & Media.

—What's the Difference? An Endangered Animal Subtraction Story, 1 vol. Slade, Suzanne. 2010. (Basic Math Operations Ser.). (ENG.). 32p. (J). (gr. -1-3). 16.95 *(978-1-60718-070-8(7))*; pap. 9.95 *(978-1-60718-081-4(2)*, 9781607180814) Arbordale Publishing.

Waites, Joan C. Daniel Boone: Trailblazer, 1 vol. Allen, Nancy Kelly. 2005. (ENG.). 32p. (J). (gr. k-3). 16.99 *(978-1-58980-212-4(8)*, Pelican Publishing) Arcadia Publishing.

—F Is for Firefighting, 1 vol. Butler, Dori Hillestad. 2007. (ABC Ser.). (ENG.). 32p. (J). (gr. k-3). 16.99 *(978-1-58980-420-3(1)*, Pelican Publishing) Arcadia Publishing.

—How-to Cowboy: 22 Secret, Magic How-to Fun Tricks. 2003. 96p. (J). pap. 5.95 *(978-0-9716911-1-7(8))* IM Pr.

—Moon's Cloud Blanket, 1 vol. St. Romain, Rose Anne. 2003. (ENG.). 32p. (J). (gr. k-3). 16.99 *(978-1-56554-922-7(8)*, Pelican Publishing) Arcadia Publishing.

—The Waving Girl, 1 vol. Nicholas, J. B. 2004. (ENG.). 32p. (J). (gr. k-3). pap. 8.99 *(978-1-58980-185-1(7)*, Pelican Publishing) Arcadia Publishing.

Wakageryu, et al. Ryu-Ki System: Sunserra. 2005. 234p. per. 29.95 *(978-0-9770121-0-7(7))* Ryu Cope.

Wake, Katherine. The Raven's Tale: & other Stories. Steven, Kenneth. 2007. (ENG.). 64p. pap. 13.99 *(978-0-7152-0846-5(2))* Saint Andrew Pr., Ltd. GBR. Dist: Westminster John Knox Pr.

Wake, Rich. The Tricks & Treats of Halloween! Murphy, Angela. 2014. (History of Fun Stuff Ser.). (ENG.). 48p. (J). (gr. 1-3). pap. 4.99 *(978-1-4814-0978-0(6)*, Simon Spotlight) Simon Spotlight.

—Way Past Bedtime. Lazar, Tara. 2017. (ENG.). 32p. (J). (gr. -1-2). 17.99 *(978-1-4814-4952-6(4)*, Simon & Schuster/Paula Wiseman Bks.) Simon & Schuster/Paula Wiseman Bks.

Wakefield, Scott. The Lion & the Mouse. Olmstead, Kathleen. 2014. (Silver Penny Stories Ser.). 48p. (J). (gr. -1-1). 4.95 *(978-1-4027-8347-0(7))* Sterling Publishing Co., Inc.

—The Three Little Pigs. Namm, Diane. 2012. (Silver Penny Stories Ser.). 48p. (J). (gr. -1-1). 4.95 *(978-1-4027-8434-7(1))* Sterling Publishing Co., Inc.

Wakefield, Scott J. The Gingerbread Boy. Namm, Diane. 2013. (J). *(978-1-4027-8431-6(7))* Sterling Publishing Co., Inc.

—God's Good News: More Than 60 Bible Stories & Devotions, 1 vol. Graham, Billy. 2018. 208p. (J). 17.99 *(978-1-4002-0989-7(7))* Nelson, Thomas Inc.

—Little Red Riding Hood. McFadden, Deanna. 2013. (Silver Penny Stories Ser.). 48p. (J). (gr. -1-1). 4.95 *(978-1-4027-8337-1(X))* Sterling Publishing Co., Inc.

Wakelin, Kirsti Anne. Catching Time, 1 vol. Gilmore, Rachna. 2010. (ENG.). 32p. (J). (gr. -1-1). 17.95 *(978-1-55455-162-0(5)*, 12473fa2-8ebe-4136-bca2-f435d45fb6f9) Trifolium Bks., Inc. CAN. Dist: Firefly Bks., Ltd.

—Dream Boats. Bar-el, Dan. 2013. 44p. (J). (gr. -1-3). 17.95 *(978-1-897476-87-1(6))* Simply Read Bks. CAN. Dist: Ingram Publisher Services.

—Looking for Loons. Lloyd, Jennifer. 2017. 32p. (J). (gr. -1-3). 8.99 *(978-1-77229-015-8(7))* Simply Read Bks. CAN. Dist: Ingram Publisher Services.

—A Pod of Orcas, 1 vol. McFarlane, Sheryl. 2006. (ENG.). 1p. (J). (gr. -1-k). per. 9.95 *(978-1-55041-722-7(3)*, 03a6ec1f-61cc-401f-b7c0-58faa8425aae) Trifolium Bks., Inc. CAN. Dist: Firefly Bks., Ltd.

—When They Are Up..., 1 vol. Thompson, Richard & Spicer, Maggee. (ENG.). 36p. (J). (gr. -1-k). 2007. per. 5.95 *(978-1-55041-709-8(6)*, 57612e99-3900-4438-9247-91b280f7d2c1); 2003. 9.95 *(978-1-55041-707-4(X)*, 6deb1948-567d-430a-ba26-b75805e12a2c) Trifolium Bks., Inc. CAN. Dist: Firefly Bks., Ltd.

Wakeman, Bill & Langley, Bill. Winnie the Pooh's A to ZZZZ. Ferguson, Don. 2009. 32p. (gr. -1-2). pap. 4.99 *(978-0-7868-4094-6(3))* Disney Pr.

Wakeman, Marion Freeman. The Curious Lobster. Hatch, Richard W. 2018. 352p. (J). (gr. 2-5). 14.99 *(978-1-68137-288-4(6)*, NYRB Kids) New York Review of Bks., Inc., The.

Wakeman, Peter, photos by. Simply Ball: With Pilates Principles. Pohlman, Jennifer & Searle, Rodney. 2005. 64p. (YA). reprint ed. 10.00 *(978-0-7567-9368-5(8))* DIANE Publishing Co.

Wakiyama, Hanako. Cat's Not-So-Perfect Sandcastle. Novesky, Amy. 2012. (ENG.). 28p. (J). (gr. -1-3). 14.95 *(978-0-9837668-2-7(7))* Plushy Feely Corp.

—From Dawn to Dreams: Poems for Busy Babies. Archer, Peggy. 2007. (ENG.). 32p. (J). (gr. k-k). 15.99 *(978-0-7636-2467-5(5))* Candlewick Pr.

—Goldie Locks Has Chicken Pox. Dealey, Erin. 2005. (ENG.). 40p. (J). (gr. -1-2). reprint ed. 8.99 *(978-0-689-87610-3(6)*, Aladdin) Simon & Schuster Children's Publishing.

—Little Bo Peep Can't Get to Sleep. Dealey, Erin. 2010. (ENG.). 40p. (J). (gr. -1-2). 13.99 *(978-1-4424-0935-4(5)*, Atheneum Bks. for Young Readers) Simon & Schuster Children's Publishing.

Wald, Christina. Anna Sewell's Black Beauty. East, Cathy. 2009. (Penguin Young Readers, Level 4 Ser.: No. 3). 48p. (J). (gr. 3-4). pap. 4.99 *(978-0-448-45190-9(5)*, Penguin Young Readers) Penguin Young Readers Group.

—Annie Jump Cannon, Astronomer, 1 vol. Gerber, Carole. 2011. (ENG.). 32p. (J). (gr. 1-5). 16.99 *(978-1-58980-911-6(4)*, Pelican Publishing) Arcadia Publishing.

—The Barnyard Read-And-Play Sticker Book. 2006. (ENG.). 12p. (J). (gr. -1). pap. 7.95 *(978-1-58017-640-8(2)*, 67640) Storey Publishing, LLC.

—Big Cats. Bowman, Donna H. 2008. (ENG.). 24p. (J). (gr. 3-18). 19.95 *(978-1-58117-781-7(X)*, Intervisual/Piggy Toes) Bendon, Inc.

—Camas & Sage: A Story of Bison Life on the Prairie, 1 vol. Patent, Dorothy Hinshaw. 2015. (ENG.). 48p. (J). pap. *(978-0-87842-641-6(8))* Mountain Pr. Publishing Co., Inc.

—Cash Kat, 1 vol. Singleton, Linda Joy. 2016. (ENG & SPA.). 32p. (J). (gr. k-3). 17.95 *(978-1-62855-728-2(1))* Arbordale Publishing.

—A Cool Summer Tail, 1 vol. Pearson, Carrie A. 2014. (ENG.). 32p. (J). (gr. -1-3). 17.95 *(978-1-62855-205-8(0))*; pap. 9.95 *(978-1-62855-214-0(X))* Arbordale Publishing.

—Denni-Jo & Pinto. Buchanan, Buck. 2017. (ENG.). 32p. (J). (gr. k-3). 16.99 *(978-1-943328-46-8(3)*, West Winds Pr.) West Margin Pr.

—Do Dolphins Really Smile? Driscoll, Laura. 2006. (Penguin Young Readers, Level 3 Ser.). 48p. (J). (gr. 1-3). mass mkt. 4.99 *(978-0-448-44341-6(4)*, Penguin Young Readers) Penguin Young Readers Group.

—Elena Efectivo, 1 vol. Singleton, Linda Joy. 2016.Tr. of Cash Kat. (SPA.). 32p. (J). (gr. k-3). pap. 11.95 *(978-1-62855-742-8(7))* Arbordale Publishing.

—Extreme Senses: Animals with Unusual Senses for Hunting Prey, 1 vol. Lay, Kathryn. 2012. (Sensing Their Prey Ser.). (ENG.). 32p. (J). (gr. -1-4). lib. bdg. 28.50 *(978-1-61641-865-6(6)*, 13277, Looking Glass Library) Magic Wagon.

—Extreme Senses: Animals with Unusual Senses for Hunting Prey: Animals with Unusual Senses for Hunting Prey. Lay, Kathryn. 2012. (Sensing Their Prey Ser.). (ENG.). 32p. (J). (gr. -1-4). E-Book 28.50 *(978-1-61478-860-7(X)*, 13278) ABDO Publishing Co.

—Fibonacci Zoo, 1 vol. Robinson, Tom. 2015. (ENG.). 32p. (J). (gr. 1-4). 17.95 *(978-1-62855-553-0(X))* Arbordale Publishing.

—The Fort on Fourth Street, 1 vol. Spangler, Lois. 2013. (ENG.). 32p. (J). (gr. 1-4). 17.95 *(978-1-60718-620-5(9))*; pap. 9.95 *(978-1-60718-632-8(2))* Arbordale Publishing.

—Habitat Spy, 1 vol. Kieber-King, Cynthia. 2011. (ENG.). 32p. (J). (gr. -1-3). 16.95 *(978-1-60718-122-4(3))*; pap. 8.95 *(978-1-60718-132-3(0))* Arbordale Publishing.

—Hearing Their Prey: Animals with an Amazing Sense of Hearing, 1 vol. Lay, Kathryn. 2012. (Sensing Their Prey Ser.). (ENG.). 32p. (J). (gr. -1-4). lib. bdg. 28.50 *(978-1-61641-866-3(4)*, 13279, Looking Glass Library) Magic Wagon.

—Henry the Impatient Heron, 1 vol. Love, Donna. 2009. (ENG.). 32p. (J). (gr. -1-3). 16.95 *(978-1-934359-90-7(4))*; pap. 8.95 *(978-1-60718-035-7(9))* Arbordale Publishing.

—I Want to Be a Crocodile. Troupe, Thomas Kingsley. 2015. (I Want to Be... Ser.). (ENG.). 24p. (J). (gr. k-3). lib. bdg. 27.32 (978-1-4795-6857-4(0), Picture Window Bks.) Capstone.

—Un Invierno Muy Abrigador, 1 vol. Pearson, Carrie A. 2012. (SPA & ENG.). 32p. (J). (gr. -1-3). 17.95 (978-1-60718-680-9(2)) Arbordale Publishing.

—Little Red Bat, 1 vol. Gerber, Carole. 2010. 32p. (J). (gr. -1-3). (ENG.). 16.95 (978-1-60718-069-2(3)); pap. 8.95 (978-1-60718-080-7(4)) Arbordale Publishing.

—Macarooned on a Dessert Island, 1 vol. Downing, Johnette. 2014. (ENG.). 32p. (J). (gr. k-3). 16.99 (978-1-4556-1936-8(1), Pelican Publishing) Arcadia Publishing.

—Seeing Their Prey: Animals with an Amazing Sense of Sight, 1 vol. Lay, Kathryn. 2012. (Sensing Their Prey Ser.). (ENG.). 32p. (J). (gr. -1-4). lib. bdg. 28.50 (978-1-61641-867-0(2), 13281, Looking Glass Library) Magic Wagon.

—Smelling Their Prey: Animals with an Amazing Sense of Smell, 1 vol. Lay, Kathryn. 2012. (Sensing Their Prey Ser.). (ENG.). 32p. (J). (gr. -1-4). lib. bdg. 28.50 (978-1-61641-868-7(0), 13283, Looking Glass Library) Magic Wagon.

—Tasting Their Prey: Animals with an Amazing Sense of Taste, 1 vol. Lay, Kathryn. 2012. (Sensing Their Prey Ser.). (ENG.). 32p. (J). (gr. -1-4). lib. bdg. 28.50 (978-1-61641-869-4(9), 13285, Looking Glass Library) Magic Wagon.

—Touching Their Prey: Animals with an Amazing Sense of Touch, 1 vol. Lay, Kathryn. 2012. (Sensing Their Prey Ser.). (ENG.). 32p. (J). (gr. -1-4). lib. bdg. 28.50 (978-1-61641-870-0(2), 13287, Looking Glass Library) Magic Wagon.

—A Warm Winter Tail, 1 vol. Pearson, Carrie A. 2012. 32p. (J). (gr. -1-3). (ENG.). 17.95 (978-1-60718-529-1(6)); (SPA & ENG.). pap. 9.95 (978-1-60718-538-3(5)) Arbordale Publishing.

—When Crabs Cross the Sand: The Christmas Island Crab Migration. Cooper, Sharon Katz. 2015. (Extraordinary Migrations Ser.). (ENG.). 24p. (J). (gr. k-3). lib. bdg. 27.32 (978-1-4795-6077-6(4), Picture Window Bks.) Capstone.

—Why the Possum Has a Large Grin, 1 vol. Downing, Johnette. 2012. (ENG.). 32p. (J). (gr. k-3). 16.99 (978-1-4556-1639-8(7), Pelican Publishing) Arcadia Publishing.

—The Wild Life of Elk. Love, Donna. 2011. (J). pap. (978-0-87842-579-2(9)) Mountain Pr. Publishing Co., Inc.

Wald, Christina. Un Fresco Cuento de Verano, 1 vol. Wald, Christina. Pearson, Carrie A. 2014.Tr. of Cool Summer Tail. (SPA & ENG.). 32p. (J). (gr. -1-3). pap. 11.95 (978-1-62855-223-2(9)) Arbordale Publishing.

Wald, Christina, jt. illus. see Keener, Anna.

Waldek, Kelly. The Big Purple Wonderbook. Richemont, Enid. 2009. (Go! Readers Ser.). 48p. (J). (gr. 2-5). pap. 12.85 (978-1-60754-279-7(X)); lib. bdg. 32.25 (978-1-60754-278-0(1)) Windmill Bks.

Walden, Tillie. Are You Listening? Walden, Tillie. 2019. (ENG.). 320p. (YA). 24.99 (978-1-62672-773-1(2), 900172912); pap. 17.99 (978-1-250-20756-2(8), 900201645) Roaring Brook Pr. (First Second Bks.).

Walder, Johan. I Love You Thiiiiiis Much! - Illustrated by Johan Walder. Richle, Urs. 2018. (I Love You Thiiiiiis Much! Ser.: Vol. 3). (ENG.). 38p. (J). (978-2-940636-02-0(8)) Coud9Pr., c/o Urs Richle.

Waldherr, Kris. Bless the Beasts: Children's Prayers & Poems about Animals. Cotner, June, ed. 2006. 63p. (J). (gr. 4-8). reprint ed. 13.00 (978-0-7567-9952-6(X)) DIANE Publishing Co.

Waldman, Bruce. Vampires, Werewolves, Zombies: From the papers of Herr Doktor Max Sturm & Baron Ludwig Von Drang. Peter Pauper Press Staff et al. 2010. 168p. 9.95 (978-1-59359-647-7(2)) Peter Pauper Pr. Inc.

Waldman, Maya. To-Do List. 2007. (ENG.). 48p. (J). (gr. k). 12.95 (978-0-9741319-5-5(4)) 4N Publishing LLC.

Waldman, Neil. A Land of Big Dreamers: Voices of Courage in America. Waldman, Neil. 2011. (Single Titles Ser.). (ENG.). 32p. (gr. 3-5). lib. bdg. 16.95 (978-0-8225-6810-0(1)) Lerner Publishing Group.

—The Snowflake: A Water Cycle Story. Waldman, Neil. 2003. 32p. lib. bdg. 23.90 (978-0-7613-1762-3(7), Millbrook Pr.) Lerner Publishing Group.

Waldorf, Tasha. A Letter to My Love: A Poetry Collection. Waldorf, Tasha. 2018. (ENG.). 28p. (J). pap. 7.50 (978-1-7170-1889-2(0)) CreateSpace Independent Publishing Platform.

Waldrep, Richard. Surfer of the Century. Crowe, Ellie. 2007. (ENG.). 48p. (J). pap. 12.95 (978-1-60060-461-4(7)) Lee & Low Bks., Inc.

Waldrod, Amy. Horace & Morris, but Mostly Dolores. Howe, James. 2003. pap. 39.95 incl. audio compact disk (978-1-59112-538-9(3)); 25.95 incl. audio (978-1-59112-242-5(2)); pap. 37.95 incl. audio (978-1-59112-243-2(0)) Live Oak Media.

Waldron, Kevin. Tiny Little Fly. Rosen, Michael. 2010. (ENG.). 32p. (J). (gr. 5-k). 16.99 (978-0-7636-4681-3(4)) Candlewick Pr.

Waldron, Kevin. Mr. Peek & the Misunderstanding at the Zoo. Waldron, Kevin. 2010. (ENG.). 48p. (J). (gr. k-12). 15.99 (978-0-7636-4549-6(4), Templar) Candlewick Pr.

—Panda-Monium at Peek Zoo. Waldron, Kevin. 2014. (ENG.). 40p. (J). (gr. -1-2). 16.99 (978-0-7636-6658-3(0), Templar) Candlewick Pr.

Wales, Johnny. Coyote Sings to the Moon. King, Thomas. 2008. (ENG.). 36p. (J). pap. (978-1-55263-868-2(5)) Magma.

—Coyote's New Suit. King, Tom. 2009. (ENG.). 40p. (J). (gr. k-3). pap. (978-1-55470-239-8(9)) Me to We.

Walke, Ted. Boating Safety Sidekicks Color a Fish: Freshwater Fish Coloring Book. Walke, Ted, compiled by. 2008. 28p. (J). (978-0-9718864-4-5(X)) Within Reach, Inc.

Walker, Anna. Collecting Seashells. Mitchell, Ainslie. 2005. (Science (Harcourt) Ser.). 14p. pap. 6.00 (978-0-15-349999-9(0)) Harcourt Schl. Pubs.

—Sadie & the Silver Shoes. Godwin, Jane. 2019. (ENG.). 32p. (J). (gr. -1-2). 16.99 (978-1-5362-0480-3(3)) Candlewick Pr.

—What Do You Wish For? Godwin, Jane. 2019. 32p. (J). (gr. -1-k). 15.99 (978-0-14-350624-9(2)) Random Hse. Australia AUS. Dist: Independent Pubs. Group.

Walker, Anna. I Love Birthdays. Walker, Anna. 2010. (ENG.). 32p. (J). (gr. -1-1). 9.99 (978-1-4169-8320-0(1), Simon & Schuster Bks. For Young Readers) Simon & Schuster Bks. For Young Readers.

—I Love Christmas. Walker, Anna. 2009. (ENG.). 32p. (J). (gr. -1-1). 9.99 (978-1-4169-8317-0(1), Simon & Schuster Bks. For Young Readers) Simon & Schuster Bks. For Young Readers.

—I Love My Dad. Walker, Anna. 2010. (ENG.). 32p. (J). (gr. -1-1). 9.99 (978-1-4169-8319-4(8), Simon & Schuster Bks. For Young Readers) Simon & Schuster Bks. For Young Readers.

—I Love My Mom. Walker, Anna. 2010. (ENG.). 32p. (J). (gr. -1-1). 9.99 (978-1-4169-8318-7(X), Simon & Schuster Bks. For Young Readers) Simon & Schuster Bks. For Young Readers.

—I Love to Dance. Walker, Anna. 2011. (ENG.). 32p. (J). (gr. -1-1). 9.99 (978-1-4169-8323-1(6), Simon & Schuster Bks. For Young Readers) Simon & Schuster Bks. For Young Readers.

—I Love to Sing. Walker, Anna. 2011. (ENG.). 32p. (J). (gr. -1-1). 9.99 (978-1-4169-8322-4(8), Simon & Schuster Bks. For Young Readers) Simon & Schuster Bks. For Young Readers.

—I Love Vacations. Walker, Anna. 2011. (ENG.). 32p. (J). (gr. -1-1). 9.99 (978-1-4169-8321-7(X), Simon & Schuster Bks. For Young Readers) Simon & Schuster Bks. For Young Readers.

Walker, Bobbie H. Abraham Lincoln. Pace, Betty. 2008. 32p. pap. 12.99 (978-1-4343-7969-6(8)) AuthorHouse.

Walker, Brad, et al. Heroes for Hire by Abnett & Lanning: the Complete Collection. 2017. (ENG.). 416p. (YA). (gr. 8-17). pap. 34.99 (978-1-302-90709-9(3)) Marvel Worldwide, Inc.

Walker, Brad. The Thanos Imperative. 2011. (ENG.). 200p. (YA). (gr. 8-17). pap. 19.99 (978-0-7851-4902-6(3)) Marvel Worldwide, Inc.

Walker, Bradley. The Adventures of Little Autumn. Schuette, Leslie Elaine. 2013. 24p. pap. 24.95 (978-1-4626-9778-6(X)) America Star Bks.

Walker, Bradley. The Adventures of Little Autumn. Schuette, Leslie Elaine. 2013. 24p. 24.95 (978-1-63004-507-4(1)) America Star Bks.

Walker, Brandy. The Mccory Chronicles: Katie Mccory & Destiny's Diamond. Collar, C. L. 2019. (Mccory Chronicles Ser.: Vol. 2). (ENG.). 200p. (J). pap. 12.99 (978-1-7091-4953-5(1)) Independently Published.

Walker, Chase. Jaadeh! Pailey, Robtel Neajai. Gbaa Sr, Amos W., tr. 2019. (ENG.). 58p. (J). (gr. 3-5). pap. 12.00 (978-1-7335161-0-5(7)) One Moore Bk.

Walker, Christine. Wooleycat's Musical Theater. Walker, Christine. Hysom, Dennis Joe. 2003. (ENG.). 32p. (J). (gr. -1-3). 18.95 (978-1-889910-25-3(2)); 11.95 (978-1-889910-26-0(0)) Tortuga Pr.

Walker, Cindy. Serenade of the Cricket. 2nd ed. 2004. (J). 12.95 (978-1-59655-000-1(7)) Cooper Publishing.

Walker, Cory, jt. illus. see Neves, Diogenes.

Walker, David. Baa! Oink! Moo! God Made the Animals, 1 vol. Greene, Rhonda Gowler. 2017. (ENG.). 26p. (J). bds. 9.99 (978-0-310-75227-1(2)) Zonderkidz.

—Bears & Blossoms. Parenteau, Shirley. 2018. (Bears on Chairs Ser.). 32p. (J). (-k). 15.99 (978-0-7636-9755-6(9)) Candlewick Pr.

Walker, David. Bears & Boos. Parenteau, Shirley. 2020. (Bears on Chairs Ser.). 32p. (J). (-k). 16.99 (978-1-5362-0837-5(X)) Candlewick Pr.

Walker, David. Bears in a Band. Parenteau Shirley, Shirley. 2016. (Bears on Chairs Ser.). 32p. (J). (-k). 15.99 (978-0-7636-8147-0(4)) Candlewick Pr.

—Bears in a Band. Parenteau, Shirley. 2018. (Bears on Chairs Ser.). 32p. (J). (— 1). bds. 6.99 (978-1-5362-0336-3(X)) Candlewick Pr.

—Bears in Beds. Parenteau, Shirley. 2012. (Bears on Chairs Ser.). (ENG.). 32p. (J). (-k). 15.99 (978-0-7636-5338-5(1)) Candlewick Pr.

—Bears in the Bath. Parenteau, Shirley. (Bears on Chairs Ser.). (J). (— 1). 2016. 30p. bds. 6.99 (978-0-7636-7946-0(1)); 2014. 32p. 15.99 (978-0-7636-6418-3(9)) Candlewick Pr.

—Bears in the Snow. Parenteau, Shirley. (Bears on Chairs Ser.). 32p. (J). (— 1). 2017. bds. 6.99 (978-0-7636-9521-7(1)); 2016. 15.99 (978-0-7636-8148-7(2)) Candlewick Pr.

—Bears on Chairs. Parenteau, Shirley. 2009. (Bears on Chairs Ser.). (ENG.). 32p. (J). (gr. -1-k). 15.99 (978-0-7636-3588-6(X)) Candlewick Pr.

—Bears on Chairs. Parenteau, Shirley. 2011. (Bears on Chairs Ser.). 32p. (J). (gr. -1 — 1). bds. 6.99 (978-0-7636-5092-6(7)) Candlewick Pr.

—Bears on Chairs: Book & Toy Gift Set. Parenteau, Shirley. 2016. (Bears on Chairs Ser.). (J). (— 1). 15.99 (978-0-7636-8878-3(9)) Candlewick Pr.

—Bears on Chairs/Osos en Sillas. Parenteau, Shirley. 2018. (Bears on Chairs Ser.). 32p. (J). (— 1). pap. 6.99 (978-0-7636-9965-9(9)) Candlewick Pr.

—Before You Were Mine. Boelts, Maribeth. 2008. (J). (gr. -1-3). 27.95 incl. audio (978-0-8045-6961-3(4)); 29.95 incl. audio compact disk (978-0-8045-4184-8(1)) Spoken Arts, Inc.

—The Great Easter Egg Scramble. Knapman, Timothy. 2013. (J). (978-1-4351-4594-8(1)) Barnes & Noble, Inc.

—If Animals Celebrated Christmas. Paul, Ann Whitford. (If Animals Kissed Good Night Ser.). (ENG.). (J). 2019. 24p. bds. 7.99 (978-0-374-31308-1(3), 900209754); 2018. 32p. 16.99 (978-0-374-30901-5(9), 900188209) Farrar, Straus & Giroux. (Farrar, Straus & Giroux (BYR)).

Walker, David. If Animals Gave Thanks. Paul, Ann Whitford. 2020. (If Animals Kissed Good Night Ser.). (ENG.). 32p. (J). 17.99 (978-0-374-31341-8(5), 900211525, Farrar, Straus & Giroux (BYR)) Farrar, Straus & Giroux.

Walker, David. If Animals Kissed Good Night. Paul, Ann Whitford. 2014. (If Animals Kissed Good Night Ser.). (ENG.). 34p. (J). (gr. -1-1). bds. 7.99 (978-0-374-30021-0(6), 900129088, Farrar, Straus & Giroux (BYR)) Farrar, Straus & Giroux.

—If Animals Said I Love You. Paul, Ann Whitford. 2017. (If Animals Kissed Good Night Ser.). (ENG.). 32p. (J). 16.99 (978-0-374-30602-1(8), 900173498, Farrar, Straus & Giroux (BYR)) Farrar, Straus & Giroux.

—If Animals Went to School. Paul, Ann Whitford. 2019. (If Animals Kissed Good Night Ser.). (ENG.). 32p. (J). 16.99 (978-0-374-30902-2(7), 900188210, Farrar, Straus & Giroux (BYR)) Farrar, Straus & Giroux.

Walker, David. Knock! Knock! Open the Door. Morgan, Michaela. 2020. (ENG.). 24p. (J). (gr. -1-k). pap. 10.99 (978-1-5290-2592-7(3), Macmillan Children's Bks.) Pan Macmillan GBR. Dist: Independent Pubs. Group.

Walker, David. Peep & Ducky. Martin, David. (Peep & Ducky Ser.). (J). (— 1). 2015. 24p. bds 6.99 (978-0-7636-7243-0(2)); 2013. 32p. 14.99 (978-0-7636-5039-1(0)) Candlewick Pr.

—Peep & Ducky It's Snowing! Martin, David. 2018. (Peep & Ducky Ser.). 32p. (J). (— 1). 14.99 (978-0-7636-9433-3(9)) Candlewick Pr.

—Peep & Ducky Rainy Day. Martin, David. 2015. (Peep & Ducky Ser.). 32p. (J). (— 1). 14.99 (978-0-7636-6884-6(2)) Candlewick Pr.

—The Shmoogly Boo. Wharton, Eileen. 2016. 24p. (J). (gr. -1-1). pap. 9.99 (978-1-907432-23-1(X)) Hogs Back Bks. GBR. Dist: Independent Pubs. Group.

—Time for a Hug. Gershator, Phillis & Green, Mim. 2013. (Snuggle Time Stories Ser.: 1). (ENG.). 22p. (J). (gr. -1-k). bds. 7.95 (978-1-4549-0856-2(4)) Sterling Publishing Co., Inc.

—Time for a Nap. Gershator, Phillis. 2018. (Snuggle Time Stories Ser.: 9). 22p. (J). (— 1). bds. 6.95 (978-1-4549-3130-0(2)) Sterling Publishing Co., Inc.

—Time for a Trip. Gershator, Phillis. 2018. (Snuggle Time Stories Ser.: 10). 22p. (J). (— 1). bds. 6.95 (978-1-4549-3016-7(0)) Sterling Publishing Co., Inc.

—Tiny Rabbit's Big Wish. Engle, Margarita. 2014. (ENG.). 32p. (J). (gr. -1-3). 16.99 (978-0-547-85286-7(X), 1501494, HMH Books For Young Readers) Houghton Mifflin Harcourt Publishing Co.

—You Mean the World to Me. Gibby, Bayne. 2013. (ENG.). 16p. (J). (gr. -1-k). bds. 8.99 (978-0-545-40570-6(X), Cartwheel Bks.) Scholastic, Inc.

Walker, David L. Best Friends. Cuyler, Margery. 2017. (Step into Reading Ser.). (ENG.). 32p. (J). (gr. -1-1). pap. 4.99 (978-0-399-55369-1(X), Random Hse. Bks. for Young Readers) Random Hse. Children's Bks.

Walker, David M. Before You Were Mine. Boelts, Maribeth. 2007. (ENG.). 32p. (J). (gr. -1-3). 17.99 (978-0-399-24526-8(X), G.P. Putnam's Sons Books for Young Readers) Penguin Young Readers Group.

—Flip, Flap, Fly! A Book for Babies Everywhere. Root, Phyllis. 2011. 32p. (J). (gr. -1 — 1). bds. 6.99 (978-0-7636-5325-5(X)) Candlewick Pr.

—How Do Giraffes Take Naps? Muldrow, Diane. 2016. (Little Golden Book Ser.). (ENG.). 24p. (J). (gr. -1-k). 4.99 (978-0-553-51333-2(8), Golden Bks.) Random Hse. Children's Bks.

—How Do Lions Say I Love You? Muldrow, Diane. 2013. (Little Golden Book Ser.). 24p. (J). (-k). 4.99 (978-0-449-81256-3(1), Golden Bks.) Random Hse. Children's Bks.

—How Do Penguins Play? Muldrow, Diane. 2011. (Little Golden Book Ser.). 32p. (J). (gr. -1-k). 4.99 (978-0-375-86501-5(2), Golden Bks.) Random Hse. Children's Bks.

—Peep & Ducky Rainy Day. Martin, David. 2018. (Peep & Ducky Ser.). 24p. (J). (— 1). bds. 6.99 (978-0-7636-9523-1(8)) Candlewick Pr.

Walker, Dugald Stewart. Fairy Tales from Hans Christian Andersen - Illustrated by Dugald Stewart Walker. Andersen, Hans. 2016. (ENG.). (J). (978-1-4733-3528-8(0)) Read Bks.

Walker, Jack. Tamla Bear & the Magic Goblin. Kelly, Diana. 2013. 30p. pap. (978-1-78148-182-0(2)) Grosvenor Hse. Publishing Ltd.

Walker, Jessica. Baby Feminists. Babbott-Klein, Libby. 2018. 24p. (J). (— 1). bds. 9.99 (978-0-451-48010-1(4), Viking Books for Young Readers) Penguin Young Readers Group.

Walker, Jessica. Baby Feminists: 25 Postcards for Change. Babbott-Klein, Libby. 2020. (ENG.). 27p. (J). (gr. -1-2). 9.99 (978-0-593-20221-0(X), Viking Books for Young Readers) Penguin Young Readers Group.

Walker, John. The Story of Christmas: The Birth of Jesus. 2008. (ENG.). 24p. (J). (gr. 2). 19.95 (978-1-58117-793-0(3), Intervisual/Piggy Toes) Bendon, Inc.

—Thank You for Thanksgiving. Mackall, Dandi Daley. 2008. 32p. (J). (gr. -1). 13.49 (978-0-7586-1500-8(0)) Concordia Publishing Hse.

—What God Wants for Christmas. Rainey, Barbara. 2011. (J). (gr. 4-7). 29.99 incl. audio compact disk (978-1-60200-428-3(5)) FamilyLife.

Walker, John, photos by. Ray Conka & the Sortian Jewell. van Gosen, Ryan O'Dell, IV. Maximilian Staff, ed. unabr. ed. 2004. 128p. (YA). lib. bdg. 12.50 (978-1-930211-55-1(4)) Maximilian Pr. Pubs.

Walker, John & Laiug, Naucie. Blake. Ashley, Jane, IV. Maximilian Press staff, ed. 2004. 32p. (gr. 1-5). pap. 10.00 (978-1-930211-57-5(0)) Maximilian Pr. Pubs.

Walker, Joni. Jesus Hears Me. 2008. 20p. (J). (gr. -1). bds. 6.49 (978-0-7586-1508-4(6)) Concordia Publishing Hse.

Walker, Joni. Apostles Creed. Walker, Joni. 2005. (Follow & Do Ser.). 32p. (J). 7.49 (978-0-7586-0802-4(0)) Concordia Publishing Hse.

—Follow & Do Books: The Lord's Prayer. Walker, Joni. 2004. (Follow & Do Ser.). 32p. (J). 7.49 (978-0-7586-0678-5(8)) Concordia Publishing Hse.

—Holy Baptism. Walker, Joni. 2005. (Follow & Do Ser.). 32p. (J). 7.49 (978-0-7586-0800-0(4)) Concordia Publishing Hse.

—Jesus Is with Me. Walker, Joni. 2004. 20p. (J). bds. 5.49 (978-0-7586-0628-0(1)) Concordia Publishing Hse.

—Jesus Knows Me. Walker, Joni. 2003. 14p. (J). (gr. -1-k). bds. 5.49 (978-0-7586-0507-8(2)) Concordia Publishing Hse.

—Lords Supper. Walker, Joni. 2005. (Follow & Do Ser.). 23p. (J). (gr. -1-3). 7.49 (978-0-7586-0801-7(2)) Concordia Publishing Hse.

—Tell Me the Christmas Story. Walker, Joni. 2003. 14p. (J). (gr. -1-k). bds. 5.49 (978-0-7586-0508-5(0)) Concordia Publishing Hse.

—Tell Me What God Made. Walker, Joni. 2007. 20p. (J). (gr. -1-3). bds. 6.49 (978-0-7586-1247-2(8)) Concordia Publishing Hse.

Walker, Joni. Tell Me the Easter Story. Walker, Joni, contrib. by. 2004. 14p. (J). bds. 5.49 (978-0-7586-0629-7(X)) Concordia Publishing Hse.

Walker, Karen. White Fang: With a Discussion of Resilience. London, Jack. 2003. (Values in Action Illustrated Classics Ser.). 191p. (J). (978-1-59203-038-5(6)) Learning Challenge, Inc.

Walker, Katherine. Hot Dog. Cottringer, Anne. 2005. (ENG.). 24p. (J). lib. bdg. 23.65 (978-1-59646-738-5(X)) Dingles & Co.

Walker, Kev, et al. Avengers Arena: the Complete Collection. 2018. (Avengers Arena: the Complete Collection: 1). (ENG.). 408p. (YA). (gr. 8-17). pap. 39.99 (978-1-302-91185-0(6)) Marvel Worldwide, Inc.

Walker, Kev. Black Panther Book 7: The Intergalactic Empire of Wakanda Part 2. 2019. 136p. (YA). (gr. 4-17). pap. 17.99 (978-1-302-91294-9(1)) Marvel Worldwide, Inc.

Walker, Kev, et al. Nova by Abnett & Lanning: the Complete Collection Vol. 1, Vol. 1. 2018. (ENG.). 504p. (YA). (gr. 8-17). pap. 39.99 (978-1-302-91134-8(1)) Marvel Worldwide, Inc.

Walker, Kev. Star Wars: Doctor Aphra Vol. 1: Aphra. 2017. 144p. (J). (gr. 4-17). pap. 17.99 (978-1-302-90677-1(1)) Marvel Worldwide, Inc.

Walker, Kev & Laming, Marc. Star Wars: Doctor Aphra Vol. 2: Doctor Aphra & the Enormous Profit. 2018. 168p. (J). (gr. 4-17). pap. 17.99 (978-1-302-90763-1(8)) Marvel Worldwide, Inc.

Walker, Madison. Mama's Heart Is Your Home. Serra, Emily. 2019. (ENG.). 24p. (J). pap. 11.00 (978-1-6792-0894-2(2)) Independently Published.

Walker, Mark Evan. Clovis Escapes! Bks. 3: Runt Farm. Lorenzo, Amanda. 2009. 136p. 12.95 (978-0-9800952-2-7(0)) BooktiMookti Pr.

Walker, Megan. Franny's Father Is a Feminist. Leet, Rhonda. 2018. (ENG.). 32p. (J). (gr. -1-2). 17.99 (978-1-57687-873-6(2), powerHouse Bks.) powerHse. Bks.

Walker, Patricia M. Andromed: Dream Believe Achieve Series. Goguen, Martha M. 2011. 36p. pap. (978-1-897435-35-9(5)) Agio Publishing Hse.

Walker, Peggy. My First Book of Buddhist Treasures. 2003. 38p. (J). 8.95 (978-0-915678-81-5(0)) World Tribune Pr.

Walker, Rory. Electricity! Graham, Ian. 2014. (You Wouldn't Want to Live Without... Ser.). (ENG.). 32p. (J). lib. bdg. 29.00 (978-0-531-21216-5(5), Watts, Franklin) Scholastic Library Publishing.

—You Wouldn't Want to Live Without Cell Phones! Pipe, Jim. 2014. (You Wouldn't Want to Live Without... Ser.). (ENG.). 32p. (J). lib. bdg. 29.00 (978-0-531-21217-2(3), Watts, Franklin) Scholastic Library Publishing.

Walker, Scott. Pants on Fire. Lloyd, Victoria. 2011. (ENG.). 64p. (J). pap. 5.99 (978-0-00-715525-5(5), HarperCollins Children's Bks.) HarperCollins Pubs. Ltd. GBR. Dist: HarperCollins Pubs.

Walker, Sherry & Gibbons, Myla. My Amazing Mom. Walker, Sherry. 2017. (ENG.). (J). pap. 9.13 (978-0-578-19687-9(5)) Walker, Sherry.

Walker, Sholto. Buzz & Bingo in the Starry Sky: Band 10/White (Collins Big Cat) Durant, Alan. 2005. (Collins Big Cat Ser.). (ENG.). 32p. (J). (gr. 1-3). pap. 9.99 (978-0-00-718630-3(4)) HarperCollins Pubs. Ltd. GBR. Dist: Independent Pubs. Group.

—Get the Rat! Lane, Alex. 2014. (Traditional Tales Ser.). (ENG.). 12p. (J). (gr. -1-k). pap. 5.95 (978-1-62521-562-8(2), Capstone Classroom) Capstone.

—Run, Three Blind Mice! Fuerst, Jeffrey B. 2009. (Reader's Theater Nursery Rhymes & Songs Set B Ser.). 48p. (J). pap. (978-1-60859-168-8(9)) Benchmark Education Co.

—Three Blind Mice. Fuerst, Jeffrey B. 2010. (Rising Readers Ser.). (J). 3.49 (978-1-60719-707-2(3)) Newmark Learning LLC.

Walker, Steven. Rosa's Bus: The Ride to Civil Rights. Kittinger, Jo S. (ENG.). 40p. (J). (gr. 2-4). 2017. pap. 7.99 (978-1-62979-848-6(7)); 2010. 17.99 (978-1-59078-722-9(6), Calkins Creek) Boyds Mills Pr.

Walker, Sylvia. I Am a Leader! Parker, David. 2005. (J). (978-0-439-73585-8(8)) Scholastic, Inc.

—I'm in Charge of Me! Parker, David. 2004. (Best Me I Can Be Ser.). (978-0-439-62810-5(5)) Scholastic, Inc.

—Three's a Crowd. Scholastic, Inc. Staff & Hooks, Gwendolyn. 2004. (Just for You Ser.). (ENG.). 32p. (gr. k-3). pap. 3.99 (978-0-439-56865-4(X), Teaching Resources) Scholastic, Inc.

—Three's a Crowd. Hooks, Gwendolyn. 2004. 32p. (J). lib. bdg. 15.00 (978-1-4242-0240-9(X)) Fitzgerald Bks.

Walker, Tigh, et al. Disney Kingdoms: Big Thunder Mountain Railroad #5. Hopeless, Dennis. 2016. (Disney Kingdoms: Big Thunder Mountain Railroad Ser.). (ENG.). 24p. (J). (gr. k-5). lib. bdg. 27.07 (978-1-61479-579-7(7), 24360, Graphic Novels) Spotlight.

—Disney Kingdoms: Big Thunder Mountain Railroad (Set), 5 vols. Hopeless, Dennis. 2016. (Disney Kingdoms: Big Thunder Mountain Railroad Ser.). (ENG.). 24p. (J). (gr. k-5). lib. bdg. 135.35 (978-1-61479-574-2(6), 24355, Graphic Novels) Spotlight.

W

Walker, Tigh & Bagley, Mark. Venom Vol. 4: The Nativity. 2018. (Venom (2017) Ser.: 4). (ENG.). 112p. (YA). (gr. 8-17). pap. 15.99 *(978-1-302-90983-3(5))* Marvel Worldwide, Inc.

Walker, Tigh & Beaulieu, Jean-François. Disney Kingdoms: Big Thunder Mountain Railroad #1. Hopeless, Dennis. 2016. (Disney Kingdoms: Big Thunder Mountain Railroad Ser.). (ENG.). 24p. (J). (gr. k-5). lib. bdg. 27.07 *(978-1-61479-575-9(4)*, 24356, Graphic Novels) Spotlight.

—Disney Kingdoms: Big Thunder Mountain Railroad #2. Hopeless, Dennis. 2016. (Disney Kingdoms: Big Thunder Mountain Railroad Ser.). (ENG.). 24p. (J). (gr. k-5). lib. bdg. 27.07 *(978-1-61479-576-6(2)*, 24357, Graphic Novels) Spotlight.

—Disney Kingdoms: Big Thunder Mountain Railroad #4. Hopeless, Dennis. 2016. (Disney Kingdoms: Big Thunder Mountain Railroad Ser.). (ENG.). 24p. (J). (gr. k-5). lib. bdg. 27.07 *(978-1-61479-578-0(9)*, 24359, Graphic Novels) Spotlight.

Walker, Tom, photos by. Wild Critters, 1 vol. Jones, Tim. 2nd ed. 2007. (ENG., 48p. (gr. -1-6). pap. 9.95 *(978-0-9790470-2-2(1))* Epicenter Pr., Inc.

Walker, Trenton & Price, Caleb. My Dad's in the Navy. Hughes, Annette. 2018. (ENG.). 26p. (J). pap. 12.00 *(978-1-948708-17-3(5))* HATCHBACK Publishing.

—My Mom's in the Army. Hughes, Annette. 2018. (ENG.). 26p. (J). pap. 12.00 *(978-1-948708-18-0(3))* HATCHBACK Publishing.

Walker, Vicki. Junkyard Umbrella. Thurston, Dorothy Dawn. 2017. (ENG.). 54p. (J). 22.99 *(978-0-692-97524-4(1))* Thurston, Dorothy Dawn.

Walker, Vik. First Class: Dragon Hunters, Book One. Walker, Vik. 2019. (Dragon Hunters Ser.: Vol. 1). (ENG.). 184p. (J). pap. 14.99 *(978-1-7939-6513-4(7))* Independently Published.

—The Ruby Dragon of Nital. Walker, Vik. 2019. (Dragons of Nital Ser.: Vol. 4). (ENG.). 138p. (J). pap. 12.99 *(978-1-7941-9891-3(1))* Independently Published.

Walkes, Irvin. Holy Cream Puff. Ardanaz, Nicolas. 2018. (ENG.). 144p. (YA). *(978-1-5255-1785-3(6))*; pap. *(978-1-5255-1786-0(4))* FriesenPress.

Walkley, Lizzie. The Bear Who Would Not Share. Graham, Oakley. 2015. (J). *(978-1-4351-6485-7(7))* Barnes & Noble, Inc.

—God Blesses Me. Ferreri, Della Ross. 2020. 16p. (J). (gr. -1 — 1). 8.99 *(978-1-5460-3377-6(7)*, Worthy Kids/Ideals) Worthy Publishing.

—Here Comes Peter Cottontail! Nelson, Steve & Rollins, Jack. 2020. (ENG.). (J). (gr. -1 — 1). 20p. bds. 7.99 *(978-1-5460-1430-0(6))*; 16p. bds. 13.99 *(978-1-5460-1431-7(4))* Worthy Publishing. (Worthy Kids/Ideals).

Walko, Bill. E'Steem: Goddess Of? James, Shawn. 2018. (ENG.). 50p. (J). pap. 7.99 *(978-1-9797-3216-1(7))* CreateSpace Independent Publishing Platform.

—E'Steem: The Sands of Time. James, Shawn. 2018. (ENG.). 110p. (J). pap. 12.00 *(978-1-9842-2375-3(5))* CreateSpace Independent Publishing Platform.

Walko, Bill. Isis: The Main Event. James, Shawn. 2020. (ENG.). 120p. (J). pap. 12.00 ***(978-1-6518-7158-4(2))*** Independently Published.

Wall, Beth. Special Growing Girl: A Guide to Puberty for Girls with Special Needs. Thayer, Jodi Wise. 2019. (ENG.). 62p. (J). pap. 17.95 ***(978-1-7218-8612-8(5))*** CreateSpace Independent Publishing Platform.

Wall Darby, Colleen. My Dog Harpo: The Biggest Kid I Know. Exelby, Kathy. 2007. (J). per. 20.00 *(978-1-932583-39-7(4))* Bates Jackson Engraving Co., Inc.

Wall, Karen. Time for Bed. Helmore, Jim. 2014. (Stripy Horse Ser.). (ENG.). 12p. (J). (gr. -1-k). bds. 7.99 *(978-1-4052-5302-4(9))* Egmont Bks., Ltd. GBR. Dist: Independent Pubs. Group.

Wall, Laura. Goose. Wall, Laura. 2015. (ENG.). 48p. (J). (gr. -1-3). 12.99 *(978-0-06-232435-1(7))* HarperCollins Pubs.

—Goose Goes to School. Wall, Laura. 2015. (ENG.). 48p. (J). (gr. -1-3). 12.99 *(978-0-06-232437-5(3))* HarperCollins Pubs.

—Goose Goes to the Zoo. Wall, Laura. 2016. (ENG.). 48p. (J). (gr. -1-3). 12.99 *(978-0-06-232441-2(1))* HarperCollins Pubs.

—Goose on the Farm. Wall, Laura. 2016. (ENG.). 48p. (J). (gr. -1-3). 12.99 *(978-0-06-232439-9(X))* HarperCollins Pubs.

—Goose on the Farm Board Book. Wall, Laura. 2017. (ENG.). 36p. (J). (gr. -1 — 1). bds. 7.99 *(978-0-06-232440-5(3)*, HarperFestival) HarperCollins Pubs.

Wall, Matthew. So You Want to Learn: Juggling. Wall, Matthew. 2017. 30p. (J). pap. 11.99 *(978-1-941429-57-0(2))* Handersen Publishing.

Wall, Mike. Christopher Robin: a Boy, a Bear, a Balloon. Rubiano, Brittany. 2018. (ENG.). 40p. (J). (gr. 1-3). 16.99 *(978-1-368-02588-1(9))* Disney Pr.

—Doc Is the Best Medicine! (Disney Junior: Doc Mcstuffins) Posner-Sanchez, Andrea. 2014. (Big Golden Book Ser.). (ENG.). 64p. (J). (gr. -1-2). 9.99 *(978-0-7364-3264-1(7)*, Golden/Disney) Random Hse. Children's Bks.

—Island of Youth (Disney Elena of Avalor) Katschke, Judy. 2018. (Little Golden Book Ser.). (ENG.). 24p. (J). (-k). 4.99 *(978-0-7364-3840-7(8)*, Golden/Disney) Random Hse. Children's Bks.

—Royal Vacation. Katschke, Judy. 2017. (Little Golden Book Ser.). (ENG.). 24p. (J). (-k). 4.99 *(978-0-7364-3743-1(6)*, Golden/Disney) Random Hse. Children's Bks.

Wall, Sheelagh. Sylvana & the Frog. Asheya. 2016. (ENG.). (J). pap. *(978-0-9949658-0-6(X))* Kassner, Asheya.

Wallace, Adam. Rhymes with Art: Learn Cartooning the Fun Way! Wallace, Adam. 2014. (ENG.). 166p. pap. *(978-0-9808282-6-9(0))* Krueger Wallace Pr.

Wallace, Andrea. Captain Benjamin Dale. Fox, Nita. 2008. 32p. (J). (gr. -1-3). pap. 5.99 *(978-0-9816107-0-2(6))* Fox's Den Publishing.

—Shining Star. Mcdonald, Megan. 2003. (Step into Reading Ser.). (ENG.). 48p. (J). (gr. k-3). pap. 4.99 *(978-0-307-26340-7(1)*, Random Hse. Bks. for Young Readers) Random Hse. Children's Bks.

Wallace, Benjamin. Danger Bear's Time Machine: An Illustrated Classic Coloring Book. Wallace, Benjamin. 2019. (ENG.). 56p. (J). pap. 6.99 ***(978-1-7063-1388-5(8))*** Independently Published.

Wallace, Brian. Daisy & the Dirty Dozen. Wallace, Brian. Wallace, Jessica, ed. 2018. (ENG.). 34p. (J). (gr. k-4). 17.99 *(978-0-692-09139-5(4))* Newport Pr.

Wallace, Chad. Earth Day Birthday. Schnetzler, Pattie. 2004. (Sharing Nature with Children Book Ser.). 32p. (J). 16.95 *(978-1-58469-053-5(4))*; 8.95 *(978-1-58469-054-2(2))* Dawn Pubns.

—Little Panda. Bowen, Sherry. 2003. (Books for Young Learners). (ENG.). 12p. (J). 5.75 net. *(978-1-57274-673-2(4)*, 2459, Bks. for Young Learners) Owen, Richard C. Pubs., Inc.

—Mighty Mole & Super Soil. Quattlebaum, Mary. 2015. (ENG.). 32p. (J). (gr. k-4). 16.95 *(978-1-58469-538-7(2)*, Dawn Pubns.) Sourcebooks, Inc.

—Pass the Energy, Please! McKinney, Barbara Shaw. 2004. (Sharing Nature with Children Book Ser.). 32p. (YA). (gr. 1-8). pap. 16.95 *(978-1-58469-001-6(1))* Dawn Pubns.

—Poetry for Young People: Henry Wadsworth Longfellow. Schoonmaker, Frances, ed. 2010. (Poetry for Young People Ser.: 6). 48p. (J). (gr. 3). pap. 6.95 *(978-1-4027-7292-4(0))* Sterling Publishing Co., Inc.

—Seahorses. Curtis, Jennifer Keats. 2012. (ENG.). 32p. (J). (gr. -1-3). 18.99 *(978-0-8050-9239-4(0)*, 900066643, Holt, Henry & Co. Bks. For Young Readers) Holt, Henry & Co.

—Tall Tall Tree, 1 vol. Fredericks, Anthony D. 2017. (ENG.). 32p. (J). (gr. -1-3). 16.99 *(978-1-58469-601-8(X))*; pap. 8.95 *(978-1-58469-602-5(8))* Sourcebooks, Inc. (Dawn Pubns.).

—Wake up, Bertha Bear! Mason, Chad. ed. 2006. (ENG.). 32p. (J). (gr. -1-3). 15.95 *(978-0-89272-655-4(5))* Down East Bks.

Wallace, Chad. The Mouse & the Meadow, 1 vol. Wallace, Chad. 2014. (ENG.). 32p. (J). (gr. k-4). 16.95 *(978-1-58469-481-6(5)*, Dawn Pubns.) Sourcebooks, Inc.

Wallace, Daggi. Katherine Stinson Otero: High Flyer, 1 vol. Petrick, Neila S. 2006. (ENG.). 32p. (J). (gr. k-3). 16.99 *(978-1-58980-368-8(X)*, Pelican Publishing) Arcadia Publishing.

Wallace, Donald. Thank You & Good Night. Gordon, Jon. 2016. (ENG.). 36p. (J). (gr. -1-4). 18.00 *(978-1-118-98691-2(1))* Wiley, John & Sons, Inc.

Wallace Harris, Whitney. Mama's Quilt & Blizzard the White River Otter: A Christmas Story. Harris, Don. 2016. (ENG.). (J). (gr. 1-6). 18.95 *(978-1-943258-25-3(2))* Warren Publishing, Inc.

Wallace, Ian. Canadian Railroad Trilogy, 1 vol. Lightfoot, Gordon. 2010. (ENG.). 56p. (gr. -1). 24.95 *(978-0-88899-953-5(4))* Groundwood Bks. CAN. Dist: Publishers Group West (PGW).

—Just So Stories, 1 vol., Vol. 1. Kipling, Rudyard. 2013. (ENG.). 64p. (J). (gr. k). 19.95 *(978-1-55498-212-7(X))* Groundwood Bks. CAN. Dist: Publishers Group West (PGW).

—The Mummer's Song, 1 vol. Davidge, Bud. 2009. (ENG.). 32p. (J). (gr. k). pap. 14.95 *(978-0-88899-960-3(7))* Groundwood Bks. CAN. Dist: Publishers Group West (PGW).

—Very Last First Time, 1 vol. Andrews, Jan. 2003. (ENG.). 32p. (J). 18.95 *(978-0-88899-043-3(X))* Groundwood Bks. CAN. Dist: Publishers Group West (PGW).

Wallace, Ian. Mr. Kneebone's New Digs. Wallace, Ian. (J). 16.95 *(978-0-88899-143-0(6))* Groundwood Bks. CAN. Dist: Publishers Group West (PGW).

Wallace, John. The Appalachian Trail. Bauer, Marion Dane. 2020. (Wonders of America Ser.). (ENG.). 32p. (J). (gr. -1-1). 17.99 ***(978-1-5344-6459-9(X))***; pap. 4.99 ***(978-1-5344-6458-2(1))*** Simon Spotlight. (Simon Spotlight).

Wallace, John. A Book Is Just Like You! All about the Parts of a Book. Fox, Kathleen. 2012. 32p. (J). 17.95 *(978-1-60213-060-9(4)*, Upstart Bks.) Highsmith Inc.

—Clouds. Bauer, Marion Dane. 2004. (Weather Ready-To-Reads Ser.). (ENG.). 32p. (J). (gr. -1-1). pap. 4.99 *(978-0-689-85441-5(2)*, Simon Spotlight) Simon Spotlight.

—Earthquake! Bauer, Marion Dane. (Natural Disasters Ser.). (ENG.). 32p. (J). (gr. -1-1). 2019. 17.99 *(978-1-5344-5561-0(2))*; 2009. pap. 4.99 *(978-1-4169-2551-4(1))* Simon Spotlight. (Simon Spotlight).

Wallace, John. Flood! Bauer, Marion Dane. (Natural Disasters Ser.). (ENG.). 32p. (J). (gr. -1-1). 2020. 17.99 ***(978-1-5344-6556-5(1))***; 2008. pap. 4.99 *(978-1-4169-2553-8(8))* Simon Spotlight. (Simon Spotlight).

Wallace, John. The Grand Canyon. Bauer, Marion Dane. (Wonders of America Ser.). (ENG.). 32p. (J). (gr. -1-1). 2019. 17.99 *(978-1-5344-4035-7(6))*; 2006. pap. 3.99 *(978-0-689-86946-4(0))* Simon Spotlight. (Simon Spotlight).

—The Mighty Mississippi. Bauer, Marion Dane. 2007. (Ready-To-Read Level 1 Ser.). (ENG.). 32p. (J). (gr. -1-1). lib. bdg. 16.19 *(978-0-689-86951-8(7))* Simon & Schuster, Inc.

—The Mighty Mississippi. Bauer, Marion Dane. (Wonders of America Ser.). (ENG.). 32p. (J). (gr. -1-1). 2019. 17.99 *(978-1-5344-5562-7(0))*; 2007. pap. 4.99 *(978-0-689-86950-1(9))* Simon Spotlight. (Simon Spotlight).

—Mother's Day Ribbons. Knudsen, Michelle. 2005. (ENG.). 12p. (J). bds. 6.99 *(978-0-689-86381-3(0)*, Little Simon) Little Simon.

—Mount Rushmore. Bauer, Marion Dane. 2007. (Ready-To-Read Level 1 Ser.). (ENG.). 32p. (J). (gr. -1-1). lib. bdg. 16.19 *(978-1-4169-3478-3(2)*, Aladdin) Simon & Schuster Children's Publishing.

—Mount Rushmore. Bauer, Marion Dane. (Wonders of America Ser.). (ENG.). 32p. (J). (gr. -1-1). 2018. 17.99 *(978-1-5344-3030-3(X))*; 2007. pap. 4.99 *(978-1-4169-3477-6(4))* Simon Spotlight. (Simon Spotlight).

—Niagara Falls. Bauer, Marion Dane. (Wonders of America Ser.). (ENG.). 32p. (J). (gr. -1-1). 2019. 17.99 *(978-1-5344-4540-6(4))*; 2006. pap. 4.99 *(978-0-689-86944-0(4))* Simon Spotlight. (Simon Spotlight).

—Rainbow. Bauer, Marion Dane. 2016. (Weather Ready-To-Reads Ser.). (ENG.). 32p. (J). (gr. -1-1). pap. 4.99 *(978-1-4814-6336-2(5)*, Simon Spotlight) Simon Spotlight.

—The Rocky Mountains. Bauer, Marion Dane. (Wonders of America Ser.). (ENG.). 32p. (J). (gr. -1-1). 2019. 17.99 *(978-1-5344-4539-0(0))*; 2006. pap. 4.99 *(978-0-689-86948-8(7))* Simon Spotlight. (Simon Spotlight).

—Snow. Bauer, Marion Dane. 2003. (Weather Ready-To-Reads Ser.). (ENG.). 32p. (J). (gr. -1-1). pap. 4.99 *(978-0-689-85437-8(4)*, Simon Spotlight) Simon Spotlight.

—Snow. Bauer, Dane. ed. 2005. 32p. (J). lib. bdg. 15.00 *(978-1-59054-934-6(1))* Fitzgerald Bks.

—The Statue of Liberty. Bauer, Marion Dane. 2007. (Ready-To-Read Level 1 Ser.). (ENG.). 32p. (J). (gr. -1-1). lib. bdg. 16.19 *(978-1-4169-3480-6(4)*, Aladdin) Simon & Schuster Children's Publishing.

—The Statue of Liberty. Bauer, Marion Dane. (Wonders of America Ser.). (ENG.). 32p. (J). (gr. -1-1). 2018. 17.99 *(978-1-5344-3031-0(8))*; 2007. pap. 4.99 *(978-1-4169-3479-0(0))* Simon Spotlight. (Simon Spotlight).

—Sun. Bauer, Marion Dane. 2016. (Weather Ready-To-Reads Ser.). (ENG.). 32p. (J). (gr. -1-1). pap. 3.99 *(978-1-4814-6339-3(X)*, Simon Spotlight) Simon Spotlight.

—Volcano! Bauer, Marion Dane. 2008. (Natural Disasters Ser.). (ENG.). 32p. (J). (gr. -1-1). pap. 4.99 *(978-1-4169-2549-1(X)*, Aladdin) Simon & Schuster Children's Publishing.

Wallace, John. Volcano! Bauer, Marion Dane. 2020. (Natural Disasters Ser.). (ENG.). 32p. (J). (gr. -1-1). 17.99 ***(978-1-5344-6555-8(3)***, Simon Spotlight) Simon Spotlight.

Wallace, John. We Love the Snow. Edwards, Richard. 2015. (ENG.). 32p. (J). (gr. -1-3). 7.99 *(978-1-85733-719-8(0))* Lerner Publishing Group.

—Wind. Bauer, Marion Dane. 2005. (Ready-to-Read Ser.). 32p. (gr. -1-1). 14.00 *(978-0-7569-5622-6(6))* Perfection Learning Corp.

—Wind. Bauer, Marion Dane. 2003. (Weather Ready-To-Reads Ser.). (ENG.). 32p. (J). (gr. -1-1). pap. 4.99 *(978-0-689-85443-9(9)*, Simon Spotlight) Simon Spotlight.

—Wonders of America Ready-To-Read Value Pack: The Grand Canyon; Niagara Falls; the Rocky Mountains; Mount Rushmore; the Statue of Liberty; Yellowstone. Bauer, Marion Dane. 2014. (Wonders of America Ser.). (ENG.). 192p. (J). (gr. -1-1). pap. 15.96 *(978-1-4814-2724-1(5)*, Simon Spotlight) Simon Spotlight.

—Yellowstone. Bauer, Marion Dane. 2008. (Ready-To-Read Level 1 Ser.). (ENG.). 32p. (J). (gr. -1-1). lib. bdg. 16.19 *(978-1-4169-5405-7(8)*, Aladdin) Simon & Schuster Children's Publishing.

—Yellowstone. Bauer, Marion Dane. (Wonders of America Ser.). (ENG.). 32p. (J). (gr. -1-1). 2019. 17.99 *(978-1-5344-4034-0(8))*; 2008. pap. 4.99 *(978-1-4169-5404-0(X))* Simon Spotlight. (Simon Spotlight).

Wallace, John. Rain. Wallace, John. Bauer, Marion Dane. 2004. (Weather Ready-To-Reads Ser.). (ENG.). 32p. (J). (gr. -1-1). pap. 4.99 *(978-0-689-85439-2(0)*, Simon Spotlight) Simon Spotlight.

Wallace, Joshua. The Life of Babe Didrikson: "Greatness Is Never Forgotten" Riley, Lehman & Austin, Megan. 2005. 47p. (J). pap. *(978-0-9760523-2-6(6))* Matter of Africa America Time.

Wallace, Leslie. Old Neb & the Ghost Ship, Vol. Swoboda, Lois. 2015. (Old Neb Ser.). (ENG.). 126p. (J). (gr. -1-12). pap. 10.95 *(978-1-56164-797-2(7))* Pineapple Pr., Inc.

—Old Neb & the Lighthouse Treasure. Swoboda, Lois. 2015. (Old Neb Ser.). (ENG.). 125p. pap. 10.95 *(978-1-56164-787-3(X))* Pineapple Pr., Inc.

Wallace, Loston. Race Against Crime. Black, Jake & Meredith Books Staff. 2008. 24p. (J). pap. 3.99 *(978-0-696-23958-8(2))* Meredith Bks.

Wallace, Marianne D. Earthsteps: A Rock's Journey Through Time. Spickert, Diane Nelson. 2010. (ENG.). 32p. (J). (gr. -1-3). pap. 13.95 *(978-1-55591-730-2(5))* Fulcrum Publishing.

Wallace, Morgana. Hedy & Her Amazing Invention. Wahl, Jan. 2019. (Amazing Women Ser.). 36p. (J). 16.95 *(978-0-9987999-9-5(8))* Penny Candy Bks., LLC.

Wallace, Nancy Elizabeth. Fly, Monarch! Fly!, 0 vols. Wallace, Nancy Elizabeth. 2013. (ENG.). 40p. (J). (gr. -1-1). 22.44 *(978-0-7614-6246-0(5)*, 9780761462460, Amazon Children's Publishing) Amazon Publishing.

—Pumpkin Day!, 0 vols. Wallace, Nancy Elizabeth. unabr. ed. 2012. (ENG.). 32p. (J). (gr. k-3). per. 9.99 *(978-0-7614-5327-7(X)*, 9780761453277, Two Lions) Amazon Publishing.

—Recycle Every Day, 0 vols. Wallace, Nancy Elizabeth. 2006. (ENG.). 41p. (J). (gr. -1-3). pap. 9.99 *(978-0-7614-5290-4(7)*, 9780761452904, Two Lions) Amazon Publishing.

—Rocks! Rocks! Rocks!, 0 vols. Wallace, Nancy Elizabeth. 2009. (ENG.). 48p. (J). (gr. -1-3). 17.99 *(978-0-7614-5528-8(0)*, 9780761455288, Two Lions) Amazon Publishing.

Wallace, Paula. Choose Your Days. 2016. (ENG.). 32p. (J). (gr. -1-2). 17.95 *(978-1-941026-37-3(0))* Cinco Puntos Pr.

Wallace, Robert E., photos by. The Adventures of Ichi, the Baby Deer Bk. 1: The Rescue. Wallace, Robert E. 2004. (Adventures of Ichi the Baby Deer Ser.: Bk. 1). (J). lib. bdg. 16.95 *(978-0-9755678-0-7(2))* Cirrus Publishing, LLC.

Wallace, Sam Amber. ABCs of Character. Miller, Dennis. 2003. 52p. (J). lib. bdg. 15.95 *(978-0-9722259-1-5(9))* Twin Peaks Publishing, Inc.

Waller, Diane Hardy, photos by. Does God Forgive Me? Gold, August. 2006. (ENG., 32p. (J). pap. 8.99 *(978-1-59473-142-6(X)*, 300d2eb7-64f9-4ccf-b080-20407e2c393e, Skylight Paths Publishing) LongHill Partners, Inc.

—Does God Hear My Prayer? Gold, August. 2005. (ENG., 32p. (J). pap. 8.99 *(978-1-59473-102-0(0)*, d5782d0a-b2cb-4f47-96fc-23e42ba4e9f4, Skylight Paths Publishing) LongHill Partners, Inc.

Waller, Joyce. The Lizard's Secret Door. Nelson, Connie. 2014. 32p. (J). 19.95 *(978-1-59298-933-1(0))* Beaver's Pond Pr., Inc.

Walles, Dwight. How, Why, When, Where: A Treasure Chest of Wonderful Bible Facts, Stories, Games! Coleman, William L. 2011. (J). pap. *(978-0-89191-717-5(9))* Cook, David C.

Walling, Sandy Seeley. Helga, the Hippopotamouse. Shimberg, Elaine Fantle. 2008. (ENG.). 36p. (J). 7.95 *(978-0-9741940-4-2(2))* Abernathy Hse. Publishing.

—Herman, the Hermit Crab. Shimberg, Elaine Fantle. I.t. ed. 2007. 28p. (J). 7.95 *(978-0-9741940-2-8(6))* Abernathy Hse. Publishing.

Walling, Sandy Seeley. A Day at the Beach: A Seaside Counting Book from One to Ten. Walling, Sandy Seeley. 2003. 28p. (J). 6.95 *(978-0-9741940-0-4(X))* Abernathy Hse. Publishing.

Walling, Sandy Seeley. ABC's at the Zoo! The Fun Way to Teach Your Child the Relationship between Upper Case & Lower Case Letters. Walling, Sandy Seeley, text. I.t. ed. 2004. 36p. (J). per. 7.95 *(978-0-9741940-1-1(8))* Abernathy Hse. Publishing.

Wallis, Angie. Ka-Lunk! Gallardo-Walker, Gloria. 2013. (ENG.). 21p. pap. *(978-0-9875296-5-7(X))* Aly's Bks.

Wallis, Becky. Three Stretchy Frogs. Bentley, Dawn. 2010. (Stretchies Book Ser.). 16p. (J). 8.99 *(978-0-8249-1459-2(7))* Hinkler Bks. Pty, Ltd. AUS. Dist: Ideals Pubns.

Wallis, Diz & Hardcastle, Nick. The Story of an Aviator. Calhoun, Marmaduke Randolph. Twist, Clint, ed. 2008. (Amazing Wonders Collection: 2). (ENG.). 16p. (J). (gr. 1-4). 19.99 *(978-0-7636-3906-8(0))* Candlewick Pr.

Wallis, Diz & Nicholls, Emma. Tyrannosaur. Twist, Clint & Fitzgibbon, Monty. 2008. (Amazing Wonders Collection: 1). (ENG.). 16p. (J). (gr. 1-4). 19.99 *(978-0-7636-3550-3(2))* Candlewick Pr.

Wallis, Emily. MR Snuffles' Birthday. Greaves, David. 2018. (ENG.). 32p. (J). *(978-1-912562-31-2(6))* Clink Street Publishing.

—Sparkling Jewel. Green, D. L. 2015. (Silver Pony Ranch Ser.: 1). (ENG.). 96p. (J). (gr. 1-3). pap. 4.99 *(978-0-545-79765-8(9))* Scholastic, Inc.

—Sweet Buttercup. Green, D. L. 2016. (Silver Pony Ranch Ser.: 2). (ENG.). 96p. (J). (gr. 1-3). 15.99 *(978-0-545-79770-2(5))* Scholastic, Inc.

Wallis, Rachel. Just One Child: Starting a Plastic-Free & Litter-free Journey. Bartlett, Debbie. 2019. (ENG.). 34p. (J). pap. ***(978-1-78623-619-7(2))*** Grosvenor Hse. Publishing Ltd.

Wallis, Rebbeca. On Thanksgiving Day. Zocchi, Judy. 2005. (Holiday Happenings Ser.). 32p. (J). pap. 10.95 *(978-1-59646-212-0(4))* Dingles & Co.

Wallis, Rebecca. Number 1 What Grows in the Sun? Zocchi, Judy. 2005. (Holiday Happenings Ser.). 32p. (J). per. 10.95 *(978-1-59646-273-1(6))* Dingles & Co.

—Number 1 What Grows in the Sun? 2005. (Community of Counting Ser.). 32p. (J). pap. 10.95 *(978-1-59646-272-4(8))* Dingles & Co.

—Number 1 What Grows in the Sun?/Número 1 Qué crece en el Sol? Dingles, Molly. 2005. (Community of Counting Ser.).Tr. of Número 1 Qué crece en el Sol?. (ENG & SPA.). 32p. (J). per. 10.95 *(978-1-59646-275-5(2))* Dingles & Co.

—Number 1 What Grows in the Sun?/Número 1 Qué crece en el Sol? 2005. (Community of Counting Ser.). (ENG & SPA.). 32p. (J). pap. 10.95 *(978-1-59646-274-8(4))*; lib. bdg. 21.65 *(978-1-891997-89-1(0))* Dingles & Co.

—Number 10 Where Is the Hen? Dingles, Molly. 2005. (Community of Counting Ser.). 32p. (J). (ENG.). lib. bdg. 21.65 *(978-1-891997-90-7(4))*; per. 10.95 *(978-1-59646-309-7(0))* Dingles & Co.

—Number 10 Where Is the Hen? 2005. (Community of Counting Ser.). 32p. (J). pap. 10.95 *(978-1-59646-308-0(2))* Dingles & Co.

—Number 10 Where Is the Hen?/Número 10 en dónde está la Gallina? Dingles, Molly. 2005. (Community of Counting Ser.). (ENG & SPA.). 32p. (J). per. 10.95 *(978-1-59646-311-0(2))* Dingles & Co.

—Number 10 Where Is the Hen?/Número 10 en dónde está la Gallina? 2005. (Community of Counting Ser.).Tr. of Número 10 en dónde está la Gallina?. (ENG & SPA.). 32p. (J). pap. 10.95 *(978-1-59646-310-3(4))*; lib. bdg. 21.65 *(978-1-891997-80-8(7))* Dingles & Co.

—Number 2 Let's Go to the Zoo! Dingles, Molly. 2005. (Community of Counting Ser.). 32p. (J). 10.95 *(978-1-59646-277-9(9))*; pap. 10.95 *(978-1-59646-276-2(0))* Dingles & Co.

—Number 2 Let's Go to the Zoo!/Número 2 Vamos al Zoologico! Dingles, Molly. 2005. (Community of Counting Ser.).Tr. of Número 2 Vamos al Zoologico!. (ENG & SPA.). 32p. (J). pap. 10.95 *(978-1-59646-278-6(7))*; lib. bdg. 21.65 *(978-1-891997-88-4(2))*; per. 10.95 *(978-1-59646-279-3(5))* Dingles & Co.

—Number 3 What's in the Sea? Dingles, Molly. 2005. (Community of Counting Ser.). 32p. (J). pap. 10.95 *(978-1-59646-280-9(9))*; per. 10.95 *(978-1-59646-281-6(7))* Dingles & Co.

—Number 3 What's in the Sea?/Número 3 Qué hay en el Mar? Dingles, Molly. 2005. (Community of Counting Ser.).Tr. of Número 3 Qué hay en el Mar?. (ENG & SPA.). 32p. (J). pap. 10.95 *(978-1-59646-282-3(5))*; lib. bdg. 21.65 *(978-1-891997-87-7(4))*; per. 10.95 *(978-1-59646-283-0(3))* Dingles & Co.

—Number 4 Shop at the Store! Dingles, Molly. (Community of Counting Ser.). (J). 2005. pap. 10.95 *(978-1-59646-284-7(1))*; 2005. per. 10.95

(978-1-59646-285-4(X)); 2004. (ENG.). lib. bdg. 21.65 *(978-1-891997-96-9(3))* Dingles & Co.

—Number 4 Shop at the Store!/Número 4 Vamos de compras a la Tienda! Dingles, Molly. 2005. (Community of Counting Ser.).Tr. of Número 4 Vamos de compras a la Tienda!. (ENG & SPA.). 32p. (J). pap. 10.95 *(978-1-59646-286-1(8))*; lib. bdg. 21.65 *(978-1-891997-86-0(6))*; per. 10.95 *(978-1-59646-287-8(6))* Dingles & Co.

—Number 5 Let's Go for a Drive! Dingles, Molly. 2005. (Community of Counting Ser.). 32p. (J). pap. 10.95 *(978-1-59646-288-5(4))*; (ENG.). lib. bdg. 21.65 *(978-1-891997-95-2(5))*; per. 10.95 *(978-1-59646-289-2(2))* Dingles & Co.

—Number 5 Let's Go for a Drive!/Número 5 Vamos a viajar en Coche! Dingles, Molly. 2005. (Community of Counting Ser.).Tr. of Número 5 Vamos a viajar en Coche!. (ENG & SPA.). 32p. (J). pap. 10.95 *(978-1-59646-290-8(6))*; lib. bdg. 21.65 *(978-1-891997-85-3(8))*; per. 10.95 *(978-1-59646-291-5(4))* Dingles & Co.

—Number 6 What Can We Mix? Dingles, Molly. 2005. (Community of Counting Ser.). 32p. (J). pap. 10.95 *(978-1-59646-292-2(2))*; per. 10.95 *(978-1-59646-293-9(0))* Dingles & Co.

—Number 6 What Can We Mix ? Dingles, Molly. 2005. (Community of Counting Ser.). 32p. (J). lib. bdg. 21.65 *(978-1-891997-94-5(7))* Dingles & Co.

—Number 6 What Can We Mix?/Número 6 Qué podemos Mezclar? Dingles, Molly. 2005. (Community of Counting Ser.).Tr. of Número 6 Qué podemos Mezclar?. (ENG & SPA.). 32p. (J). pap. 10.95 *(978-1-59646-294-6(9))*; lib. bdg. 21.65 *(978-1-891997-84-6(X))*; per. 10.95 *(978-1-59646-295-3(7))* Dingles & Co.

—Number 7 Stars in the Heaven. Dingles, Molly. (Community of Counting Ser.). 32p. (J). 2005. pap. 10.95 *(978-1-59646-296-0(5))*; 2005. per. 10.95 *(978-1-59646-297-7(3))*; 2004. lib. bdg. 21.65 *(978-1-891997-93-8(9))* Dingles & Co.

—Number 7 Stars in the Heaven/Número 7 Estrellas en el Cielo. Dingles, Molly. (Community of Counting Ser.).Tr. of Número 7 Estrellas en el Cielo. (ENG & SPA.). 32p. (J). 2005. pap. 10.95 *(978-1-59646-298-4(1))*; 2005. per. 10.95 *(978-1-59646-299-1(X))*; 2004. lib. bdg. 21.65 *(978-1-891997-83-9(1))* Dingles & Co.

—Number 8 Let's Stay up Late! Dingles, Molly. 2005. (Community of Counting Ser.). 32p. (J). pap. 10.95 *(978-1-59646-300-4(7))*; per. 10.95 *(978-1-59646-301-1(5))* Dingles & Co.

—Number 8 Let's Stay up Late!/Número 8 Vamos a quedarnos en vela hasta muy Noche! Dingles, Molly. (Community of Counting Ser.).Tr. of Número 8 Vamos a quedarnos en vela hasta muy Noche!. (ENG & SPA.). 32p. (J). 2005. pap. 10.95 *(978-1-59646-302-8(3))*; 2005. per. 10.95 *(978-1-59646-303-5(1))*; 2004. lib. bdg. 21.65 *(978-1-891997-82-2(3))* Dingles & Co.

—Number 9 Dress up to Dine! Dingles, Molly. (Community of Counting Ser.). 32p. (J). 2005. pap. 10.95 *(978-1-59646-304-2(X))*; 2005. per. 10.95 *(978-1-59646-305-9(8))*; 2004. lib. bdg. 21.65 *(978-1-891997-91-4(2))* Dingles & Co.

—Number 9 Dress up to Dine!/Número 9 Vestirse con elegancia para Cenar! Dingles, Molly. 2005. (Community of Counting Ser.).Tr. of Número 9 Vestirse con elegancia para Cenar!. (ENG & SPA.). 32p. (J). pap. 10.95 *(978-1-59646-306-6(6))*; lib. bdg. 21.65 *(978-1-891997-81-5(5))*; per. 10.95 *(978-1-59646-307-3(4))* Dingles & Co.

—On Chinese New Year. Zocchi, Judy. 2005. (Holiday Happenings Ser.). 32p. (J). pap. 10.95 *(978-1-59646-188-8(8))*; lib. bdg. 21.65 *(978-1-891997-55-6(6))*; per. 10.95 *(978-1-59646-189-5(6))* Dingles & Co.

—On Chinese New Year/el Año Nuevo Chino. Zocchi, Judy. 2005. (Holiday Happenings Ser.).Tr. of Año Nuevo Chino. (ENG & SPA.). 32p. (J). pap. 10.95 *(978-1-59646-190-1(X))*; lib. bdg. 21.65 *(978-1-891997-56-3(4))*; per. 10.95 *(978-1-59646-191-8(8))* Dingles & Co.

—On Christmas Eve. Zocchi, Judy. 2005. (Holiday Happenings Ser.). 32p. (J). pap. 10.95 *(978-1-59646-224-3(8))*; lib. bdg. 21.65 *(978-1-891997-47-1(5))* Dingles & Co.

—On Christmas Eve. Dingles, Molly. 2005. (Holiday Happenings Ser.). 32p. (J). per. 10.95 *(978-1-59646-225-0(6))* Dingles & Co.

—On Christmas Eve/la Nochebuena. Zocchi, Judy. 2005. (Holiday Happenings Ser.).Tr. of Nochebuena. 32p. (J). pap. 10.95 *(978-1-59646-226-7(4))*; (ENG & SPA.). lib. bdg. 21.65 *(978-1-891997-48-8(3))*; (ENG & SPA.). per. 10.95 *(978-1-59646-227-4(2))* Dingles & Co.

—On Easter Morning. Zocchi, Judy. 2005. (Holiday Happenings Ser.). 32p. (J). pap. 10.95 *(978-1-59646-192-5(6))*; (ENM.). lib. bdg. 21.65 *(978-1-891997-41-9(6))* Dingles & Co.

—On Easter Morning. Dingles, Molly. 2005. (Holiday Happenings Ser.). 32p. (J). per. 10.95 *(978-1-59646-193-2(4))* Dingles & Co.

—On Easter Morning/la mañana de Pascua. Zocchi, Judy. 2005. (Holiday Happenings Ser.).Tr. of mañana de Pascua. (ENG & SPA.). 32p. (J). pap. 10.95 *(978-1-59646-194-9(2))*; lib. bdg. 21.65 *(978-1-891997-42-6(4))*; per. 10.95 *(978-1-59646-195-6(0))* Dingles & Co.

—On Halloween Night. Zocchi, Judy. 2005. (Holiday Happenings Ser.). (J). 32p. pap. 10.95 *(978-1-59646-220-5(5))*; (ENG.). 32p. lib. bdg. 21.65 *(978-1-891997-77-8(7))*; per. 10.95 *(978-1-59646-221-2(3))* Dingles & Co.

—On Halloween Night/la noche de Halloween. Zocchi, Judy. 2005. (Holiday Happenings Ser.).Tr. of noche de Halloween. 32p. (J). pap. 10.95 *(978-1-59646-222-9(1))*; (ENG & SPA.). per. 10.95 *(978-1-59646-223-6(X))* Dingles & Co.

—On Halloween Night/la Noche de Halloween. Zocchi, Judy. 2005. (Holiday Happenings Ser.). (ENG & SPA.). 32p. (J). lib. bdg. 21.65 *(978-1-891997-76-1(9))* Dingles & Co.

—On Hanukkah. Zocchi, Judy. 2005. (Holiday Happenings Ser.). 32p. (J). pap. 10.95 *(978-1-59646-196-3(9))*; lib. bdg. 21.65 *(978-1-891997-45-7(9))*; per. 10.95 *(978-1-59646-197-0(7))* Dingles & Co.

—On Hanukkah/la Hanukkah. Zocchi, Judy. 2005. (Holiday Happenings Ser.).Tr. of Hanukkah. (ENG & SPA.). 32p. (J). pap. 10.95 *(978-1-59646-198-7(5))*; lib. bdg. 21.65 *(978-1-891997-46-4(7))*; per. 10.95 *(978-1-59646-199-4(3))* Dingles & Co.

—On Independence Day. Zocchi, Judy. 2005. (Holiday Happenings Ser.). 32p. (J). pap. 10.95 *(978-1-59646-208-3(6))*; lib. bdg. 21.65 *(978-1-891997-43-3(2))*; per. 10.95 *(978-1-59646-209-0(4))* Dingles & Co.

—On Independence Day/el día de la Independencia. Zocchi, Judy. 2005. (Holiday Happenings Ser.).Tr. of día de la Independencia. (ENG & SPA.). 32p. (J). pap. 10.95 *(978-1-59646-210-6(8))*; lib. bdg. 21.65 *(978-1-891997-44-0(0))*; per. 10.95 *(978-1-59646-211-3(6))* Dingles & Co.

—On Kwanzaa. Zocchi, Judy. 2006. (Global Adventures I Ser.). (J). pap. 10.95 *(978-1-59646-200-7(0))*; 32p. lib. bdg. 21.65 *(978-1-891997-49-5(1))*; 32p. per. 10.95 *(978-1-59646-201-4(9))* Dingles & Co.

—On Kwanzaa/la Kwanzaa. Zocchi, Judy. 2006. (Global Adventures I Ser.).Tr. of Kwanzaa. (ENG & SPA.). 32p. (J). pap. 10.95 *(978-1-59646-202-1(7))*; lib. bdg. 21.65 *(978-1-891997-50-1(5))*; per. 10.95 *(978-1-59646-203-8(5))* Dingles & Co.

—On New Year's Eve. Zocchi, Judy. 2005. (Holiday Happenings Ser.). 32p. (J). pap. 10.95 *(978-1-59646-216-8(7))*; lib. bdg. 21.65 *(978-1-891997-51-8(3))*; per. 10.95 *(978-1-59646-217-5(5))* Dingles & Co.

—On New Year's Eve/la Nochevieja. Zocchi, Judy. 2005. (Holiday Happenings Ser.).Tr. of Nochevieja. (ENG & SPA.). 32p. (J). pap. 10.95 *(978-1-59646-218-2(3))*; lib. bdg. 21.65 *(978-1-891997-52-5(1))*; per. 10.95 *(978-1-59646-219-9(1))* Dingles & Co.

—On Saint Patrick's Day. Zocchi, Judy. 2005. (Holiday Happenings Ser.). 32p. (J). pap. 10.95 *(978-1-59646-232-8(9))*; (ENG.). lib. bdg. 21.65 *(978-1-891997-39-6(4))*; per. 10.95 *(978-1-59646-233-5(7))* Dingles & Co.

—On Saint Patrick's Day/el día de San Patricio. Zocchi, Judy. 2005. (Holiday Happenings Ser.).Tr. of día de San Patricio. (ENG & SPA.). 32p. (J). pap. 10.95 *(978-1-59646-234-2(5))*; lib. bdg. 21.65 *(978-1-891997-40-2(8))*; per. 10.95 *(978-1-59646-235-9(3))* Dingles & Co.

—On Thanksgiving Day. Zocchi, Judy. (Holiday Happenings Ser.). 32p. (J). 2005. per. 10.95 *(978-1-59646-213-7(2))*; 2004. (ENM.). lib. bdg. 21.65 *(978-1-891997-74-7(2))* Dingles & Co.

—On Thanksgiving Day/el Día de Acción de Gracias. Zocchi, Judy. 2005. (Holiday Happenings Ser.).Tr. of Día de Acción de Gracias. (ENG & SPA.). 32p. (J). pap. 10.95 *(978-1-59646-214-4(0))*; lib. bdg. 21.65 *(978-1-891997-75-4(0))*; per. 10.95 *(978-1-59646-215-1(9))* Dingles & Co.

—On Three Kings Day. Zocchi, Judy. 2005. (Holiday Happenings Ser.). 32p. (J). pap. 10.95 *(978-1-59646-204-5(3))*; lib. bdg. 21.65 *(978-1-891997-53-2(X))*; per. 10.95 *(978-1-59646-205-2(1))* Dingles & Co.

—On Three Kings Day/el día de los tres Reyes Magos. Zocchi, Judy. 2005. (Holiday Happenings Ser.).Tr. of día de los tres Reyes Magos. (ENG & SPA.). 32p. (J). pap. 10.95 *(978-1-59646-206-9(X))*; lib. bdg. 21.65 *(978-1-891997-54-9(8))*; per. 10.95 *(978-1-59646-207-6(8))* Dingles & Co.

—On Valentine's Day. Zocchi, Judy. 2005. (Holiday Happenings Ser.). 32p. (J). lib. bdg. 21.65 *(978-1-891997-79-2(3))*; per. 10.95 *(978-1-59646-229-8(9))* Dingles & Co.

—On Valentine's Day/el día de San Valentín. Zocchi, Judy. 2005. (Holiday Happenings Ser.).Tr. of Día de San Valentín. (ENG & SPA.). 32p. (J). pap. 10.95 *(978-1-59646-230-4(2))*; lib. bdg. 21.65 *(978-1-891997-78-5(5))*; per. 10.95 *(978-1-59646-231-1(0))* Dingles & Co.

Wallner, Alexandra. Write on, Mercy! The Secret Life of Mercy Otis Warren. Woelfle, Gretchen. 2012. (ENG.). 40p. (J). (gr. 3-7). 16.95 *(978-1-59078-822-6(2))*, Calkins Creek) Boyds Mills Pr.

Wallner, Alexandra. Susan B. Anthony. Wallner, Alexandra. 2012. (ENG.). 32p. (J). (gr. 1-4). 16.95 *(978-0-8234-1953-1(3))* Holiday Hse., Inc.

Wallner, Alexandra & Wallner, John. A Picture Book of Thomas Jefferson. Adler, David A. 2018. (Picture Book Biography Ser.). 32p. (J). (gr. -1-3). 7.99 *(978-0-8234-4049-8(4))* Holiday Hse., Inc.

Wallner, Alexandra, jt. illus. see Wallner, John.

Wallner, John & Wallner, Alexandra. A Picture Book of Benjamin Franklin. Adler, David A. 2018. (Picture Book Biography Ser.). 32p. (J). (gr. -1-3). pap. 7.99 *(978-0-8234-4057-3(5))* Holiday Hse., Inc.

—A Picture Book of Benjamin Franklin. Adler, David A. 2008. (Picture Book Biography Ser.). (J). (gr. k-3). 28.95 incl. audio compact disk *(978-1-4301-0340-0(X))*;Set. pap. 37.95 incl. audio *(978-1-4301-0338-7(8))* Live Oak Media.

—A Picture Book of Florence Nightingale. Adler, David A. 2019. (Picture Book Biography Ser.). 32p. (J). (gr. -1-3). pap. 7.99 *(978-0-8234-4271-3(3))* Holiday Hse., Inc.

—A Picture Book of George Washington. Adler, David A. 2018. (Picture Book Biography Ser.). 32p. (J). (gr. -1-3). pap. 7.99 *(978-0-8234-4059-7(1))* Holiday Hse., Inc.

—A Picture Book of Louis Braille. Adler, David A. 2019. (Picture Book Biography Ser.). 32p. (J). (gr. -1-3). pap. 7.99 *(978-0-8234-4457-1(0))* Holiday Hse., Inc.

Wallner, John, jt. illus. see Wallner, Alexandra.

Walls, Eric. Addie Goes to Camp Mimi. Lipscomb, Joanna Dodd. 2018. (ENG.). 28p. (J). pap. 9.49 *(978-1-7315-7903-4(9))* Independently Published.

Walls, Ty. Rocket & the Magical Cosmic Candles. Sawler, Kimberly. 2006. 32p. (J). (gr. 4-7). 18.95 *(978-1-933285-51-1(6))* Brown Books Publishing Group.

Walluk, Wilbur. The Alaskan Ten-Footed Bear & Other Legends. 2013. 44p. pap. 9.95 *(978-1-61646-201-7(9))* Coachwhip Pubns.

Walmsley, Jane. The BFG. Dahl, Roald. 2008. 119p. 16.00 *(978-0-7569-8346-8(0))* Perfection Learning Corp.

Walrod, Amy. Horace & Morris but Mostly Dolores. Howe, James. 2003. 30p. (J). (gr. -1-3). 15.65 *(978-0-7569-2936-7(9))* Perfection Learning Corp.

—Horace & Morris Join the Chorus (but What about Dolores?) Howe, James. 2006. (J). pap. 44.95 incl. audio compact disk *(978-1-59112-909-7(5))*; pap. incl. audio *(978-1-59112-449-8(2))* Live Oak Media.

—Horace & Morris Join the Chorus (but What about Dolores?) Howe, James. 2005. (ENG.). 32p. (J). (gr. -1-3). 7.99 *(978-1-4169-0616-2(9))*, Atheneum Bks. for Young Readers) Simon & Schuster Children's Publishing.

—Horace & Morris Say Cheese (Which Makes Dolores Sneeze!) Howe, James. 2010. (ENG.). 32p. (J). (gr. -1-3). 7.99 *(978-0-689-87177-1(5))*, Atheneum Bks. for Young Readers) Simon & Schuster Children's Publishing.

—Horace & Morris Say Cheese (Which Makes Dolores Sneeze!) Howe, James. 2010. (ENG.). 32p. (J). (gr. -1-1). 21.19 *(978-0-689-83940-5(5))* Simon & Schuster, Inc.

Walrod, Amy. Horace & Morris but Mostly Dolores. Walrod, Amy. Howe, James. 2003. (ENG.). 32p. (J). (gr. -1-3). 7.99 *(978-0-689-85675-4(X))*, Atheneum Bks. for Young Readers) Simon & Schuster Children's Publishing.

Walrond, Beth. A Taste of the World: What People Eat & How They Celebrate Around the Globe. Little Gestalten, Little, ed. 2019. (ENG.). 80p. (J). 29.99 *(978-3-89955-818-0(9))* Die Gestalten Verlag DEU. Dist: Ingram Publisher Services.

Walsh, D. T. Counting with Mike the Tiger. Smith, Sherri. 2013. (ENG.). (J). (gr. -1-k). 14.95 *(978-1-62086-349-7(9))* Mascot Bks., Inc.

—Mike the Tiger Teaches the Alphabet. Smith, Sherri. 2013. (ENG.). (J). (gr. -1-k). 14.95 *(978-1-62086-348-0(0))* Mascot Bks., Inc.

—UGA Teaches the Alphabet. Smith, Sherri Graves. 2013. (ENG.). 28p. (J). (gr. -1-3). 14.95 *(978-1-62086-450-0(9))* Mascot Bks., Inc.

Walsh, Ellen Stoll. Balancing Act. Walsh, Ellen Stoll. 2010. (ENG.). 32p. (J). (gr. -1-3). 17.99 *(978-1-4424-0757-2(3))*, Beach Lane Bks.) Beach Lane Bks.

—Where Is Jumper? Walsh, Ellen Stoll. 2015. (ENG.). 32p. (J). (gr. -1-3). 17.99 *(978-1-4814-4508-5(1))*, Beach Lane Bks.) Beach Lane Bks.

Walsh, Illustrated by T. B. R. Cat in the Clouds. Pinder, Eric. 2017. (ENG.). 32p. (J). (gr. 1-3). 17.99 *(978-1-4671-3848-2(7))*, History Pr., The) Arcadia Publishing.

Walsh, Jennifer. Krickle Forest Adventures, Wizbet's Notebook. Yager, Karen & Williams, Kiersten. 2012. 60p. pap. 7.95 *(978-0-9855997-0-6(7))* Krickle Forest Adventures.

—Playing It Safe with Mr. See-More Safety Vol. 2: Let's Learn about Bicycle Safety. Rafael, Janis. Date not set. 24p. (J). (gr. -1-8). *(978-0-9655604-1-2(4))* Safeworld Publishing Co.

Walsh, Madeleine Riley. Deep in the Woods: A Benjamin Owl Book. Walsh, Becki. 2017. (ENG.). (J). *(978-1-5255-1279-7(X))*; pap. *(978-1-5255-1280-3(3))* FriesenPress.

Walsh, Marilyn. My Mum Says Blah Blah Blah. Walsh, Aly. 2012. 30p. pap. 15.97 *(978-1-61204-854-3(4))*, Strategic Bk. Publishing) Strategic Book Publishing & Rights Agency (SBPRA).

Walsh, Melanie. Isaac & His Amazing Asperger Superpowers! Walsh, Melanie. 2016. 32p. (J). (gr. -1-2). 16.99 *(978-0-7636-8121-0(0))* Candlewick Pr.

—Living with Mom & Living with Dad. Walsh, Melanie. 2012. (ENG.). 40p. (J). (gr. -1-2). 15.99 *(978-0-7636-5869-4(3))* Candlewick Pr.

—My Green Day: 10 Green Things I Can Do Today. Walsh, Melanie. 2020. (ENG.). 40p. (J). (gr. -1-2). 7.99 *(978-1-5362-1131-3(1))* Candlewick Pr.

—Trick or Treat? Walsh, Melanie. 2009. 16p. (J). (gr. -1-2). 6.99 *(978-0-7636-4295-2(9))* Candlewick Pr.

—10 Things I Can Do to Help My World. Walsh, Melanie. 2012. (ENG.). 40p. (J). (gr. -1-2). pap. 8.99 *(978-0-7636-5919-6(3))* Candlewick Pr.

Walsh, Michael, jt. illus. see Romero, Leonardo.

Walsh, Mike. ABC Kaleidoscope Book. Jackaman, Philippa. 16p. (J). bds. *(978-1-84322-126-5(8))* Alligator Bks. Ltd.

Walsh, Molly. Our World Is Relative. Sooy, Julia. 2019. (ENG.). 32p. (J). 17.99 *(978-1-250-29368-8(5))*, 900194904) Feiwel & Friends.

Walsh, Rebecca. The Girl Who Wanted to Dance. Ehrlich, Amy. 2009. 40p. (J). (gr. 1-4). 17.99 *(978-0-7636-1345-7(2))* Candlewick Pr.

Walsh, Richard H. Jayla the Number Navigator: Two Jumps To 100. Brennan, Lynda. 2018. (Math Milemarkers Ser.: Vol. 4). (ENG.). 52p. (J). pap. 12.95 *(978-1-7328503-0-9(5))* Math4Minors LLC.

Walsh, Sarah. Draw Bridge: A Draw-Your-Own Adventure (Interactive Children's Books, Kids Drawing Books, Creativity Books) Chronicle. 2017. (ENG.). 96p. (J). (gr. 1-17). pap. 14.99 *(978-1-4521-6097-9(X))* Chronicle Bks. LLC.

—Gift Boxes to Color & Make: Christmas. Nosy Crow Staff. 2017. (ENG.). 50p. (J). (gr. 3-7). pap. 15.99 *(978-0-7636-9637-5(4))*, Nosy Crow) Candlewick Pr.

—Hats of Faith. Cohan, Medeia. 2018. (ENG.). 12p. (J). (gr. -1 — 1). bds. 9.99 *(978-1-4521-7320-7(6))* Chronicle Bks. LLC.

—Herstory: 50 Women & Girls Who Shook up the World. Halligan, Katherine. 2018. (ENG.). 112p. (J). (gr. 3). 19.99 *(978-1-5344-3664-0(2))*, Simon & Schuster Bks. For Young Readers) Simon & Schuster Bks. For Young Readers.

—Tiny Blessings: for a Merry Christmas. Parker, Amy. 2016. 10p. (J). (gr. -1-1). 7.95 *(978-0-7624-6095-3(4))*, Running Pr. Kids) Running Pr.

—Tiny Blessings: for All Seasons. Parker, Amy. 2017. (ENG.). 10p. (J). (gr. -1 — 1). bds. 7.99 *(978-0-7624-6180-6(2))*, Running Pr. Kids) Running Pr.

—Tiny Blessings: for Mealtime. Parker, Amy. 2016. 10p. (J). (gr. -1 — 1). 7.95 *(978-0-7624-6096-0(2))*, Running Pr. Kids) Running Pr.

—Tiny Blessings: for My Family. Parker, Amy. 2017. 10p. (J). (gr. -1 — 1). bds. 7.99 *(978-0-7624-6178-3(0))*, Running Pr. Kids) Running Pr.

—True Colors. Steinberg, Billy & Kelly, Tom. 2018. (ENG.). 32p. (J). (gr. k-4). 9.99 *(978-1-5247-8780-6(9))*, Penguin Workshop) Penguin Young Readers Group.

—Truth & Daring: A Journal for the Thoughtful & Bold. Burningham, Sarah O'Leary. 2019. (ENG.). 120p. (gr. 5-17). 14.99 *(978-1-4521-7091-6(6))* Chronicle Bks. LLC.

—WildLives: 50 Extraordinary Animals That Made History. Lerwill, Ben. 2020. (ENG.). 112p. (J). (gr. 3). 21.99 *(978-1-5344-5484-2(5))*, Atheneum Bks. for Young Readers) Simon & Schuster Children's Publishing.

Walsh, Tina. Jude's Moon. Guettier, Nancy. (ENG.). 32p. (gr. -1-4). 2015. 19.95 *(978-1-63047-725-7(7))*; 2014. pap. 9.95 *(978-1-61448-964-1(5))* Morgan James Publishing.

Walsh, William. Grimsel: The Story of A Valiant Saint Bernard & Three Boys in the Swiss Alps. Zahn, Muriel. 2011. 178p. 42.95 *(978-1-258-07805-8(8))* Literary Licensing, LLC.

Walshaw, Sam. Little Giraffe at the Beach. Ackland, Nick. 2017. (Little Explorers Ser.). (ENG.). 10p. (J). (gr. -1 — 1). bds. 6.99 *(978-0-7641-6894-9(0))*, B.E.S. Publishing) Peterson's.

—Little Lion in the Garden. Ackland, Nick. 2017. (Little Explorers Ser.). (ENG.). 10p. (J). (gr. -1 — 1). bds. 6.99 *(978-0-7641-6895-6(9))*, B.E.S. Publishing) Peterson's.

Walshe, Dermot. The Fossil Hunters, 1 vol. Helmer, Marilyn. 2009. (Orca Echoes Ser.). (ENG.). 64p. (J). (gr. 1-3). pap. 6.95 *(978-1-55469-191-3(5))* Orca Bk. Pubs. USA.

Walstead, Curt. DJ's Allergies. Ormond, Jennifer. 2011. 16p. (gr. -1-k). bds. 8.95 *(978-0-9792010-1-1(2))* Ormond, Jennifer.

—No Treats for Bullies! Brill, Patricia Ann. 2018. (Dog Tales Collection: Vol. 5). (ENG.). 36p. (J). (gr. k-3). pap. 9.95 *(978-0-9995034-0-9(5))* Functional Fitness, LLC.

Walt Disney Company Staff & Golden Books Staff. Scamp. Bedford, Annie North & Golden Books Staff. 2004. (Little Golden Book Ser.). (ENG.). 24p. (J). (gr. -1-2). 4.99 *(978-0-7364-2311-3(7))*, Golden/Disney) Random Hse. Children's Bks.

Walt Disney Company Staff & Random House Disney Staff. Mother Goose. Random House Disney Staff. 2004. (Little Golden Book Ser.). (ENG.). 24p. (J). (gr. -1-2). 4.99 *(978-0-7364-2310-6(9))*, Golden/Disney) Random Hse. Children's Bks.

—Three Little Pigs. Golden Books Staff & Random House Disney Staff. 2004. (Little Golden Book Ser.). (ENG.). 24p. (J). (gr. -1-2). 4.99 *(978-0-7364-2312-0(5))*, Golden/Disney) Random Hse. Children's Bks.

Walt Disney Studio, et al. Lucky Puppy. Watson, Jane Werner. 2017. (Little Golden Book Ser.). (ENG.). 24p. (J). (-k). 4.99 *(978-0-7364-3686-1(3))*, Golden/Disney) Random Hse. Children's Bks.

Walt Disney Studio. Santa's Toy Shop (Disney) Dempster, Al. 2015. (Little Golden Book Ser.). (ENG.). 24p. (J). (-k). E-Book *(978-0-7364-3402-7(X))*, Golden/Disney) Random Hse. Children's Bks.

—Walt Disney's Classic Stories (Disney Classics) Walt Disney's Mickey Mouse & His Spaceship; Scamp; Cinderella's Friends; Little Man of Disneyland; the Lucky Puppy, 5 vols. Werner, Jane. 2017. (Little Golden Book Ser.). (ENG.). 120p. (J). (-k). 24.95 *(978-0-7364-3823-0(8))*, Golden/Disney) Random Hse. Children's Bks.

—Walt Disney's the Ugly Duckling (Disney Classic) North Bedford, Annie. 2017. (Little Golden Book Ser.). (ENG.). 24p. (J). (-k). 4.99 *(978-0-7364-3571-0(9))*, Golden/Disney) Random Hse. Children's Bks.

Walt Disney Studio & Marshall, Carol. Babes in Toyland (Disney Classic) Hazen, Barbara Shook. 2018. (Little Golden Book Ser.). (ENG.). 24p. (J). (-k). 4.99 *(978-0-7364-3879-7(3))*, Golden/Disney) Random Hse. Children's Bks.

Walt Disney Studio & Svendsen, Julius. Seven Dwarfs Find a House (Disney Classic) North Bedford, Annie. 2019. (Little Golden Book Ser.). (ENG.). 24p. (J). (-k). 4.99 *(978-0-7364-3975-6(7))*, Golden/Disney) Random Hse. Children's Bks.

Walt Disney Studios Staff. Little Man of Disneyland (Disney Classic) Random House Disney Staff. 2015. (Little Golden Book Ser.). (ENG.). 24p. (J). (-k). 4.99 *(978-0-7364-3485-0(2))*, Golden/Disney) Random Hse. Children's Bks.

Walt Disney Studios Staff & Random House Disney Staff. Grandpa Bunny. Werner, Janet et al. 2007. (Little Golden Book Ser.). (ENG.). 24p. (J). (gr. -1-2). 4.99 *(978-0-375-83930-6(5))*, Golden/Disney) Random Hse. Children's Bks.

Walt Disney Studios Staff, jt. illus. see Disney Storybook Artists Staff.

Walta, Gabriel Hernandez, et al. Doctor Strange by Donny Cates. 2019. 360p. (YA). (gr. 8-17). 34.99 *(978-1-302-91529-2(0))* Marvel Worldwide, Inc.

Walta, Gabriel Hernandez. Doctor Strange by Donny Cates Vol. 1: God of Magic, Vol. 1. 2018. (ENG.). 136p. (YA). (gr. 8-17). pap. 15.99 *(978-1-302-91064-8(7))* Marvel Worldwide, Inc.

—Vision. 2018. 488p. (YA). (gr. 8-17). 39.99 *(978-1-302-90853-9(7))* Marvel Worldwide, Inc.

—Vision: the Complete Collection. 2019. (ENG.). 272p. (YA). (gr. 8-17). pap. 29.99 *(978-1-302-92055-5(3))* Marvel Worldwide, Inc.

W

Waltch & Novy. Knights Club: the Alliance of Dragons: The Comic Book You Can Play. Shuky. 2020. (Comic Quests Ser.: 7). 104p. (J). (gr. 3-7). pap. 9.99 ***(978-1-68369-195-2(4))*** Quirk Bks.

Waltch & Novy. Knights Club: the Bands of Bravery: The Comic Book You Can Play. Shuky. 2018. (Comic Quests Ser.: 2). 184p. (J). (gr. 3-7). pap. 9.99 *(978-1-68369-055-9(9))* Quirk Bks.

—Knights Club: the Buried City: The Comic Book You Can Play. Shuky. 2020. (Comic Quests Ser.: 6). 104p. (J). (gr. 3-7). pap. 9.99 *(978-1-68369-147-1(4))* Quirk Bks.

Waltch, jt. illus. see Novy.

Walter, Alan. Bleak Trail. Pike, Diane. 2020. (ENG.). 94p. (YA). pap. ***(978-1-78222-760-1(1))*** Paragon Publishing, Rothersthorpe.

Walter, Debbie. Introducing Russell. Walter, Debbie. 2007. 68p. (J). per. 6.95 *(978-0-9766315-2-1(0))* Moose Run Productions.

Walter, Deborah. Teach a Child to READ in... 3 Simple Steps. Rigg, Diana. 2012. (J). (gr. -1-2). *(978-1-921560-88-0(6))* PLD Organisation Pty. Limited.

Walter Foster Jr. Creative Team. Frozen: Featuring Anna, Elsa, Olaf, & All Your Favorite Characters! Walter Foster Jr. Creative Team. 2015. (Learn to Draw Favorite Characters: Expanded Edition Ser.). (ENG.). 64p. (J). (gr. 3-5). 33.32 *(978-1-939581-64-8(8),* Walter Foster Jr) Quarto Publishing Group USA.

—Learn to Draw Military Machines: Step-By-Step Instructions for More Than 25 High-Powered Vehicles. Walter Foster Jr. Creative Team. 2016. (Learn to Draw: Expanded Edition Ser.). (ENG.). 64p. (J). (gr. 3-5). lib. bdg. 33.32 *(978-1-939581-98-3(2),* Walter Foster Jr) Quarto Publishing Group USA.

Walter Foster Jr. Creative Team, jt. illus. see Cuddy, Robbin.

Walter, J. Miss Callie Lallie's Mouse Tales. Frederick, Susan. 2006. 48p. pap. 16.95 *(978-1-4241-1431-3(4))* PublishAmerica, Inc.

Walter, Jayme. Slowman Snowman. Egleston, Philip. 2013. (ENG.). 34p. (J). pap. 9.25 *(978-0-9840777-2-4(3))* Ledford Publishing.

Walter, Lorin. Adding & Subtracting at the Lake. Rauen, Amy. 2008. (Getting Started with Math Ser.). 16p. (gr. -1-2). lib. bdg. 20.00 *(978-0-8368-8983-3(5),* Weekly Reader Leveled Readers) Stevens, Gareth Publishing LLLP.

—Contando Por la Ciudad. Sharp, Jean. 2007. (Matemáticas en Nuestro Mundo (Math in Our World) Ser.). (SPA.). 24p. (gr. 1-2). lib. bdg. 23.00 *(978-0-8368-8486-9(8),* Weekly Reader Leveled Readers) Stevens, Gareth Publishing LLLP.

—Counting in the City. Sharp, Jean. 2007. (Math in Our World Ser.). 24p. (gr. 1-2). pap. 8.15 *(978-0-8368-8477-7(9));* lib. bdg. 23.00 *(978-0-8368-8468-5(X))* Stevens, Gareth Publishing LLLP. (Weekly Reader Leveled Readers).

—Midiendo en la Exposcion de Perros. Rauen, Amy & Ayers, Amy. 2007. (Matemáticas en Nuestro Mundo (Math in Our World) Ser.). (SPA.). 24p. (gr. 1-2). lib. bdg. 23.00 *(978-0-8368-8492-0(2),* Weekly Reader Leveled Readers) Stevens, Gareth Publishing LLLP.

—Using Math Outdoors. Rauen, Amy. 2008. (Getting Started with Math Ser.). 16p. (gr. -1-2). pap. 5.30 *(978-0-8368-8989-5(4));* lib. bdg. 20.00 *(978-0-8368-8984-0(3))* Stevens, Gareth Publishing LLLP. (Weekly Reader Leveled Readers).

—Vamos a Sumar y Restar en el Lago. Rauen, Amy. 2008. (Matemáticas para Empezar (Getting Started with Math) Ser.). (SPA.). 16p. (gr. -1-2). lib. bdg. 20.00 *(978-0-8368-8993-2(2),* Weekly Reader Leveled Readers) Stevens, Gareth Publishing LLLP.

—Vamos a Usar las Matematicas al Aire Libre. Rauen, Amy. 2008. (Matemáticas para Empezar (Getting Started with Math) Ser.). (SPA.). 16p. (gr. -1-2). lib. bdg. 20.00 *(978-0-8368-8994-9(0),* Weekly Reader Leveled Readers) Stevens, Gareth Publishing LLLP.

Walter, Lorin, photos by. Measuring at the Dog Show. Rauen, Amy & Ayers, Amy. 2007. (Math in Our World Ser.). 24p. (gr. 1-2). lib. bdg. 23.00 *(978-0-8368-8474-6(4),* Weekly Reader Leveled Readers) Stevens, Gareth Publishing LLLP.

Walter, Wendy D. Return of the Duilaith: Ambril's Tale. Walter, Wendy D. 2012. 318p. (J). pap. 15.99 *(978-0-9857147-1-0(9),* Angry Bicycle) Walter, Wendy D.

Walters, Bob, jt. illus. see Fields, Laura.

Walters, Darryn, et al. The Christmas Surprise. 2012. (ENG.). 24p. (J). pap. 14.99 ***(978-1-6723-3976-6(6))*** Independently Published.

Walters, Kurt K. C. Chief Justice. Wetterer, Charles M. & Wetterer, Margaret K. 2005. 32p. (J). *(978-1-59336-306-2(0));* pap. *(978-1-59336-307-9(9))* Mondo Publishing.

Walters, Meg. Lucy Loves Sherman. Bailey, Catherine. 2017. (ENG.). 32p. (J). (gr. -1-k). 16.99 *(978-1-63450-705-9(3),* Sky Pony Pr.) Skyhorse Publishing Co., Inc.

Walters, Robert. Jurassic World Dinosaur Field Guide (Jurassic World) Holtz, Thomas R. & Brett-Surman, Michael. 2015. (ENG.). 160p. (J). (gr. 3-7). pap. 12.99 *(978-0-553-53685-0(0),* Random Hse. Bks. for Young Readers) Random Hse. Children's Bks.

—We Both Read-about Dinosaurs. McKay, Sindy. 2004. (We Both Read Ser.). 44p. (J). (gr. 1-2). 9.95 *(978-1-891327-53-7(4))* Treasure Bay, Inc.

—We Both Read-About Dinosaurs. McKay, Sindy. 2004. (We Both Read Ser.). 44p. (J). (gr. 1-2). pap. 4.99 *(978-1-891327-54-4(2))* Treasure Bay, Inc.

—We Both Read Bilingual Edition-About Dinosaurs/Acerca de Los Dinosaurios: Updated Cover, Information & Illustrations For 2020. McKay, Sindy. ed. 2011. (SPA.). 44p. (J). pap. 4.99 *(978-1-60115-050-9(4))* Treasure Bay, Inc.

Walters, Zoe. What Is God Mommy? Uyuklu, Leman. 2019. (All Things to Learn Ser.: Vol. 1). (ENG.). 26p. (J). pap. 9.50 ***(978-1-7097-5625-2(X))*** Independently Published.

Walther, Julia. Grandma & Me: A Kid's Guide for Alzheimer's & Dementia. Prior, Beatrice Tauber & Drummond, Mary Ann. 2017. (ENG.). 44p. (J). lib. bdg. 29.95 *(978-1-68350-701-7(0))* Morgan James Publishing.

Walthers, Don. The Fish Smuggler. Walthers, Joanie. 2013. (ENG.). 24p. (J). 19.95 *(978-1-4787-1167-4(1))* Outskirts Pr., Inc.

Walton, Alex. Billy Had to Move. Fraser, Theresa. 2009. (J). pap. 14.95 *(978-1-932690-87-3(5))* Loving Healing Pr., Inc.

—Billy Had to Move: A Foster Care Story. Fraser, Theresa. 2011. 32p. (gr. 3-7). 32.95 *(978-1-61599-118-1(2))* Loving Healing Pr., Inc.

—Gulf Islands Alphabet. Preece, Bronwyn. 2016. (ENG.). 56p. (J). (gr. k-3). 8.99 *(978-1-77229-011-0(4))* Simply Read Bks. CAN. Dist: Ingram Publisher Services.

—Little Library Mouse. Tara, Stephanie Lisa. 2006. 32p. (J). (gr. k). lib. bdg. 16.95 *(978-1-933285-39-9(7))* Brown Books Publishing Group.

—Snowy White World to Save. Tara, Stephanie Lisa. 2007. 32p. (J). (gr. -1-3). 16.95 *(978-1-933285-89-4(3))* Brown Books Publishing Group.

Walton, Haley. Elijah the Prophet: Volume 1. Walton, Tj. 2020. (ENG.). 28p. (J). 22.99 ***(978-1-63129-626-0(4));*** pap. 12.49 ***(978-1-63129-625-3(6))*** Salem Author Services.

Walton, J. Ambrose. A Master of Mysteries. Eustace, Robert & Meade, L. T. 2013. 106p. pap. 8.00 *(978-1-927558-41-6(7))* Birch Tree Publishing.

Walton, Jewell. B Is for Bossy. Rowe Mba, Tisha. 2019. (ENG.). 38p. (J). pap. 14.95 *(978-1-7979-7440-8(8))* Independently Published.

Walton, Jori. Will God Still Find Me? Walton, Vikki. 2019. (ENG.). 42p. (J). (gr. k-3). 19.99 *(978-1-950452-09-5(3))* Morewellson, Ltd.

Walton, Stephen. Counting Lions: Portraits from the Wild. Cotton, Katie. 2015. (ENG.). 40p. (J). (gr. k-12). 22.00 *(978-0-7636-8207-1(1))* Candlewick Pr.

Walton, Tony. Dumpy & the Firefighters. Andrews, Julie & Hamilton, Emma Walton. 2003. (Julie Andrews Collection). (ENG.). 32p. (J). (gr. -1-2). 15.99 *(978-0-06-052681-8(5),* Julie Andrews Collection) HarperCollins Pubs.

—Dumpy to the Rescue! Andrews, Julie & Hamilton, Emma Walton. 2004. 24p. (J). lib. bdg. 13.85 *(978-1-4242-0707-7(X))* Fitzgerald Bks.

—Dumpy's Apple Shop. Andrews, Julie. 2004. (My First I Can Read Bks.). 32p. (J). (gr. -1-18). lib. bdg. 15.89 *(978-0-06-052693-1(9))* HarperCollins Pubs.

—Dumpy's Happy Holiday. Andrews, Julie. 2005. (Julie Andrews Collection). 32p. (J). lib. bdg. 16.89 *(978-0-06-052685-6(8),* Julie Andrews Collection) HarperCollins Pubs.

—The Great American Mousical. Andrews, Julie & Hamilton, Emma Walton. 2006. (Julie Andrews Collection). (J). (gr. k-4). 160p. 15.99 *(978-0-06-057918-0(8),* Julie Andrews Collection); 147p. lib. bdg. 16.89 *(978-0-06-057919-7(6))* HarperCollins Pubs.

Walton, William J. Polly. Walton, William J. 2013. 88p. 20.00 *(978-0-615-79808-0(X))* Awkward Labs.

Waltrip, Mildred, jt. illus. see Fisher, Leonard Everett.

Walty, Margaret T. Rock-a-Bye Baby: Lullabies for Bedtime. 2005. 40p. (J). (gr. k-4). reprint ed. 15.00 *(978-0-7567-8555-0(3))* DIANE Publishing Co.

Waltz, Dan. Angelina Katrina: Bugs in My Backyard. Loper, Kathleen. l.t. ed. 2004. 24p. (J). 17.95 *(978-0-9741774-1-4(X))* D. W. Publishing.

—Angelina Katrina: Builds Troy Snowman. Loper, Kathleen. l.t. ed. 2004. 36p. (J). 17.95 *(978-0-9741774-5-8(8))* D. W. Publishing.

Waltz, Dan. Dragon Fly: A Gnome's Great Adventure. Waltz, Dan. 2007. 360p. (YA). per. 12.49 *(978-0-9741774-7-2(4))* D. W. Publishing.

—Kornstalkers: Corn Maze Massacre. Waltz, Dan. l.t. ed. 2005. (Chilled to the Bone! Ser.: No. 1). 120p. (J). per. 6.99 *(978-0-9741774-3-4(1))* D. W. Publishing.

Waltz, Dan Hall. Freckles the Frog: A Read-a-Long/Sing-a-Long Story Book. Waltz, Dan Hall. l.t. ed. 2003. 24p. (J). 19.95 *(978-0-9741774-0-3(7))* D. W. Publishing.

Waiz, Richard. Babe Ruth Saves Baseball! Murphy, Frank. 2005. (Step into Reading Ser.: Vol. 3). 48p. (J). (gr. k-3). pap. 4.99 *(978-0-375-83048-8(0),* Random Hse. Bks. for Young Readers) Random Hse. Children's Bks.

—Babe Ruth Saves Baseball. Murphy, Frank. 2005. (Step into Reading Ser.). 46p. (gr. -1-3). 14.00 *(978-0-7569-5161-0(5))* Perfection Learning Corp.

—Eat My Dust! Henry Ford's First Race. Kulling, Monica. 2004. (Step into Reading Ser.). 48p. (J). (gr. 1-3). 11.65 *(978-0-7569-3231-2(9))* Perfection Learning Corp.

—Eat My Dust! Henry Ford's First Race. Kulling, Monica. 2004. (Step into Reading Ser.). 48p. (J). (gr. k-3). pap. 4.99 *(978-0-375-81510-2(4),* Random Hse. Bks. for Young Readers) Random Hse. Children's Bks.

—Eat My Dust! Henry Ford's First Race. Kulling, Monica. 2004. (Step into Reading: Step 3 Ser.). (ENG.). 48p. (YA). (gr. k-2). lib. bdg. 16.19 *(978-0-375-91510-9(9))* Random Hse. Bks. for Young Readers.

—Francis Scott Key's Star-Spangled Banner. Kulling, Monica. 2012. (Step into Reading Ser.). (ENG.). 48p. (J). (gr. k-3). pap. 3.99 *(978-0-375-86725-5(2),* Random Hse. Bks. for Young Readers) Random Hse. Children's Bks.

—George Washington & the General's Dog. Murphy, Frank. 2015. 48p. pap. 5.00 *(978-1-61003-605-4(0))* Center for the Collaborative Classroom.

—Listen Up! Alexander Graham Bell's Talking Machine. Kulling, Monica. 2007. (Step into Reading Ser.). 48p. (J). (gr. k-3). per. 3.99 *(978-0-375-83115-7(0),* Random Hse. Bks. for Young Readers) Random Hse. Children's Bks.

—Thomas Jefferson's Feast. Murphy, Frank. 2004. (Step into Reading Ser.). 48p. 14.00 *(978-0-7569-3235-0(1))* Perfection Learning Corp.

—Thomas Jefferson's Feast. Murphy, Frank. 2003. (Step into Reading Ser.). (ENG.). 48p. (J). (gr. 2-4). pap. 4.99 *(978-0-375-82289-6(5),* Random Hse. Bks. for Young Readers) Random Hse. Children's Bks.

Wan, Joyce. Peep & Egg: I'm Not Hatching. Gehl, Laura. 2017. (Peep & Egg Ser.). (ENG.). 32p. (J). bds. 7.99 *(978-0-374-30542-0(0),* 9780374305420, Farrar, Straus & Giroux (BYR)) Farrar, Straus & Giroux.

—Pug & Pig Trick-Or-Treat. Gallion, Sue Lowell. 2017. (Pug & Pig Ser.). (ENG.). 40p. (J). (gr. -1-3). 17.99 *(978-1-4814-4977-9(X),* Beach Lane Bks.) Beach Lane Bks.

—Pug Meets Pig. Gallion, Sue Lowell. 2016. (Pug & Pig Ser.). (ENG.). 40p. (J). (gr. -1-3). 17.99 *(978-1-4814-2066-2(6),* Beach Lane Bks.) Beach Lane Bks.

—Sleepyheads. Howatt, Sandra J. 2014. (ENG.). 32p. (J). (gr. -1-3). 17.99 *(978-1-4424-2266-7(1),* Beach Lane Bks.) Beach Lane Bks.

Wan, Joyce. Are You My Mommy? Wan, Joyce. 2014. (ENG.). 18p. (J). (gr. -1 — 1). 6.99 *(978-0-545-54047-6(X),* Cartwheel Bks.) Scholastic, Inc.

—Good Night, Sweetie. Wan, Joyce. 2017. 14p. (J). (gr. -1-k). bds. 6.99 *(978-1-338-04534-5(2),* Cartwheel Bks.) Scholastic, Inc.

—Hug You, Kiss You, Love You. Wan, Joyce. 2013. 14p. (J). (— 1). bds. 6.99 *(978-0-545-54045-2(3),* Cartwheel Bks.) Scholastic, Inc.

—My Lucky Little Dragon. Wan, Joyce. 2014. 14p. (J). (— 1). bds. 6.99 *(978-0-545-54046-9(1),* Cartwheel Bks.) Scholastic, Inc.

—We Belong Together. Wan, Joyce. 2011. (ENG.). 14p. (J). (gr. k — 1). bds. 6.99 *(978-0-545-30740-6(6),* Cartwheel Bks.) Scholastic, Inc.

—You Are My Cupcake. Wan, Joyce. 2011. (ENG.). 14p. (J). (gr. k — 1). bds. 6.99 *(978-0-545-30741-3(4))* Scholastic, Inc.

—You Are My Cupcake: a Cloth Book. Wan, Joyce. 2016. (ENG.). 6p. (J). (— 1). 12.99 *(978-1-338-02921-5(5),* Cartwheel Bks.) Scholastic, Inc.

—You Are My Magical Unicorn. Wan, Joyce. 2018. 14p. (J). (gr. -1-k). bds. 6.99 *(978-1-338-33410-4(7),* Cartwheel Bks.) Scholastic, Inc.

—You Are My Merry Little Christmas. Wan, Joyce. 2016. 14p. (J). (— 1). 6.99 *(978-0-545-88093-0(9),* Cartwheel Bks.) Scholastic, Inc.

—You Are My Pumpkin. Wan, Joyce. 2016. (ENG.). 14p. (J). (— 1). 6.99 *(978-0-545-88092-3(0),* Cartwheel Bks.) Scholastic, Inc.

—You Are My Sweetheart. Wan, Joyce. 2018. (ENG.). 14p. (J). (gr. -1 — 1). 6.99 *(978-1-338-04536-9(9),* Cartwheel Bks.) Scholastic, Inc.

Wan, Stephanie. The Adventures of Hazar the Golden Canary. Wisma, Mare. 2020. (ENG.). 32p. (J). pap. 14.50 ***(978-1-7324576-4-5(6))*** Abdullah, Mary.

Wanardi, Jennifer. Romina's Rangoli. Iyengar, Malathi Michelle. 2007. (Romina's Rangoli Ser.). 32p. (J). (gr. -1-3). 16.95 *(978-1-885008-32-9(5),* Shen's Bks.) Lee & Low Bks., Inc.

Wandelmaier, Michael. Case Closed? Nine Mysteries Unlocked by Modern Science. Hughes, Susan. 2013. (ENG.). 88p. (J). (gr. 3-7). pap. 12.99 *(978-1-55453-363-3(5))* Kids Can Pr., Ltd. CAN. Dist: Hachette Bk. Group.

Wandulu, Timothy. Safari. Wandulu, Timothy. Warugaba, Christine. 2015. (ENG.). 26p. (J). pap. *(978-99977-771-0-2(7))* FURAHA Pubs. Ltd.

Wanecski, Erica Joan. Young Canaller. Stafford, Gerry. 2012. 60p. (J). pap. *(978-0-9667989-7-5(X))* Carlisle Pr.- Walnut Creek.

Wanert, Amandine. By the Sea: The Adventures of Jamie & Bella. Bonnewijn, Olivier. 2014. (ENG.). 44p. (J). (gr. 1-7). pap. 7.99 *(978-1-58617-924-3(1))* Ignatius Pr.

—Stories of Dolls. Davidson, Susanna. 2006. 48p. (J). (gr. 2-5). 8.99 *(978-0-7945-1327-6(1),* Usborne) EDC Publishing.

—Usborne Stories of Dolls & Fairies. Davidson, Susanna. 2007. (Usborne Ser.). 96p. (J). 9.99 *(978-0-7945-1779-3(X),* Usborne) EDC Publishing.

Wanert, Amandine, jt. illus. see Johnson, Elizabeth Crispina.

Wang, Amann. The Chief Cellist. Wang, Wenhua. Chen, Yu Yan, tr. 2015. (ENG.). (J). (gr. k-3). *(978-981-09-1803-3(8))* Balestier Pr.

—MR Horton's Violin. Wang, Wenhua. Chen, Yu Yan, tr. 2015. (ENG.). (J). (gr. k-4). *(978-981-09-1805-7(4))* Balestier Pr.

Wang, Annie. Christopher, Where's Kitty? Bozzo, Alessandro. 2019. (ENG.). 28p. (J). ***(978-1-5255-5523-7(5));*** pap. ***(978-1-5255-5524-4(3))*** FriesenPress.

Wang, Eva. Auntie Tigress & Other Favorite Chinese Folk Tales. Kung, Annie, tr. 2006. (ENG.). 48p. (J). (gr. -1). lib. bdg. 16.50 *(978-1-933327-29-7(4))* Purple Bear Bks., Inc.

—Auntie Tigress & Other Favorite Chinese Folk Tales. 2006. (ENG.). 48p. (J). 15.95 *(978-1-933327-28-0(6))* Purple Bear Bks., Inc.

Wang, Jacqueline. The Rescue of Nanoose, 1 vol. O'Loughlin, Chloe & Borrowman, Mary. 2004. (ENG.). 32p. (J). pap. *(978-1-894898-20-1(6))* TouchWood Editions.

Wang, Jen. In Real Life. Doctorow, Cory. 2014. (ENG.). 192p. (YA). (gr. 7). pap. 19.99 *(978-1-59643-658-9(1),* 900069549, First Second Bks.) Roaring Brook Pr.

—In Real Life. Doctorow, Cory. 2018. (ENG.). 208p. (YA). pap. 12.99 *(978-1-250-14428-7(0),* 900180628) Square Fish.

Wang, Jen. Stargazing. Wang, Jen. 2019. (ENG.). 224p. (J). 21.99 *(978-1-250-18387-3(1),* 900190966); pap. 12.99 *(978-1-250-18388-0(X),* 900190967) Roaring Brook Pr. (First Second Bks.).

Wang, Jue, jt. illus. see Yu, Chao.

Wang, Lei. Unicorns Are Real! Kindergarten Level Reading Book. Haag, Tiffany. 2019. (Kindergarten Ser.: Vol. 1). (ENG.). 26p. (J). (gr. k-1). pap. 6.99 ***(978-1-0878-0348-7(9))*** Indy Pub.

Wang, Lin. All about China: Stories, Songs, Crafts & Games for Kids. Branscombe, Allison. 64p. (J). (gr. 3-6). 2018. 14.99 *(978-0-8048-4849-7(1));* 2014. (ENG.). 16.95 *(978-0-8048-4121-4(7))* Tuttle Publishing.

—The Crane Girl: A Japanese Folktale, 1 vol. Manley, Curtis. 2017. (ENG.). 40p. (J). 19.95 *(978-1-885008-57-2(0),* 61e7ac74-aa8c-436c-99f4-91376447d387) Lee & Low Bks., Inc.

—Just Like You: Beautiful Babies Around the World, 1 vol. Konrad, Marla Stewart. 2010. (ENG.). 32p. (J). (gr. -1-2). 15.99 *(978-0-310-71478-1(8))* Zonderkidz.

—Little Sima & the Giant Bowl. Qu, Zhi. 2008. (On My Own Folklore Ser.). (ENG.). 48p. (gr. 2-4). lib. bdg. 25.26 *(978-0-8225-7620-4(1),* Millbrook Pr.) Lerner Publishing Group.

—Little Sima & the Giant Bowl: [a Chinese Folktale]. Qu, Zhi. 2009. (On My Own Folklore Ser.). (ENG.). 48p. (J). (gr. 2-4). pap. 7.99 *(978-1-58013-850-5(0),* First Avenue Editions) Lerner Publishing Group.

—The Story of Movie Star Anna May Wong, 1 vol. Yoo, Paula. 2019. (ENG.). 64p. (J). *(978-1-62014-853-2(6))* Lee & Low Bks., Inc.

Wang, Qi. Grand Old Flag. Schwaeber, Barbie H. Nussbaum, Ben, ed. 2006. (Smithsonian American Favorites Ser.). (ENG.). 32p. (J). (gr. 3-7). 14.95 *(978-1-59249-649-5(0))* Soundprints.

Wang, Qi, jt. illus. see Pamintuan, Macky.

Wang, Qi Z. El Día de los Veteranos. Brill, Marlene Targ. Fitzpatrick, Julia, tr. from ENG. 2005. (Yo Solo - Festividades (on My Own - Holidays) Ser.). (SPA.). 48p. (gr. 2-4). lib. bdg. 25.26 *(978-0-8225-3120-3(8))* Lerner Publishing Group.

—El Dia de Los Veteranos: Veterans Day. Brill, Marlene Targ. 2005. (Yo Solo Festividades Ser.). (SPA.). 48p. (J). (gr. 2-4). per. 5.95 *(978-0-8225-3121-0(6))* Lerner Publishing Group.

—Freedom's Fire. Falk, Elizabeth Sullivan. 2004. (J). *(978-1-59336-321-5(4));* pap. *(978-1-59336-322-2(2))* Mondo Publishing.

—Veterans Day. Brill, Marlene Targ. 2005. (On My Own Holidays Ser.). (J). (gr. 2-4). 43p. 25.26 *(978-1-57505-699-9(2));* (ENG.). 48p. pap. 7.99 *(978-1-57505-766-8(2),* First Avenue Editions) Lerner Publishing Group.

Wang, Qijun. The Kids Book of Black Canadian History. Sadlier, Rosemary. 2010. (Kids Book Of Ser.). (ENG.). 56p. (J). (gr. 3-7). 15.99 *(978-1-55453-587-3(5))* Kids Can Pr., Ltd. CAN. Dist: Hachette Bk. Group.

Wang, Sean. Carnival Capers! Esquivel, Eric. 2016. (LEGO DC Super Heroes Ser.). (ENG.). 32p. (J). (gr. -1-3). pap. 3.99 *(978-0-545-86815-0(7))* Scholastic, Inc.

—Carnival Capers! 2016. (J). *(978-1-4844-8682-5(X))* Scholastic, Inc.

—Catch That Crook! Steele, Michael Anthony. 2012. 23p. (J). *(978-1-4242-5333-0(3))* Scholastic, Inc.

—Mystery on the LEGO Express. King, Trey. 2014. 24p. (J). *(978-1-4242-6168-0(6))* Scholastic, Inc.

—Race Around the World! King, Trey. 2016. (J). *(978-1-4844-7160-9(1));* 24p. (gr. -1-3). pap. 3.99 *(978-0-545-86797-9(5))* Scholastic, Inc.

—Sidekick Showdown! King, Trey. 2016. (J). *(978-1-5182-2744-8(9))* Scholastic, Inc.

—Sidekick Showdown! King, Trey. ed. 2016. (LEGO DC Super Heroes 8X8 Ser.). (ENG.). 24p. (J). (gr. -1-3). 13.55 *(978-0-606-39149-8(5))* Turtleback.

—Space Justice. 2015. 32p. (J). *(978-0-545-82582-5(2))* Scholastic, Inc.

—La Vuelta Al Mundo! King, Trey. ed. 2016. (LEGO DC Super Heroes 8X8 Ser.). (SPA.). 24p. (J). (gr. -1-3). 13.55 *(978-0-606-39160-3(6))* Turtleback.

—Wrecking Valentine's Day! King, Trey. 2015. 24p. (J). *(978-1-4806-9662-4(5))* Scholastic, Inc.

Wang, Sean. Bad Goods. Wang, Sean. 2005. (Runners Ser.: 1). (ENG.). 168p. pap. 14.95 *(978-0-9768517-0-7(9))* Serve Man Pr.

Wang, Sean & Hyland, Greg. Deep-Sea Treasure Dive. King, Trey. 2016. 24p. (J). *(978-1-5182-0031-1(1))* Scholastic, Inc.

Wang, Shaoli. Chinese Fairy Tale Feasts: A Literary Cookbook. 2014. (ENG.). 160p. (J). 25.00 *(978-1-56656-993-4(1),* Crocodile Bks.) Interlink Publishing Group, Inc.

—Shu-Li & Diego, 1 vol. Yee, Paul. 2009. (ENG.). 85p. (J). (gr. 1-3). pap. 7.95 *(978-1-896580-53-1(X))* Tradewind Bks. CAN. Dist: Orca Bk. Pubs. USA.

—Shu-Li & Tamara, 1 vol. Yee, Paul. 2008. (ENG.). 72p. (J). (gr. 1-3). per. 7.95 *(978-1-896580-93-7(9))* Tradewind Bks. CAN. Dist: Orca Bk. Pubs. USA.

—ShuLi & the Magic Pear Tree, 1 vol. Yee, Paul. 2017. (Shu-Li Ser.). (ENG.). 72p. (J). (gr. 1-3). 8.95 *(978-1-926890-15-9(9))* Tradewind Bks. CAN. Dist: Orca Bk. Pubs. USA.

Wang, Suling. The Blue Ghost. Bauer, Marion Dane. 2006. (Stepping Stone Book(TM) Ser.). 96p. (J). (gr. 1-4). 4.99 *(978-0-375-83339-7(0),* Random Hse. Bks. for Young Readers) Random Hse. Children's Bks.

—The Magic Paintbrush. Yep, Laurence. 2003. (ENG.). 96p. (J). (gr. 3-7). pap. 6.99 *(978-0-06-440852-3(3))* HarperCollins Pubs.

—The Magic Paintbrush. Yep, Laurence. 2003. 89p. (J). (gr. 3-7). 12.65 *(978-0-7569-1444-8(2))* Perfection Learning Corp.

—When the Circus Came to Town. Yep, Laurence. 2004. 112p. (J). (gr. 3-5). 13.65 *(978-0-7569-2969-5(5))* Perfection Learning Corp.

Wang, Yujia. Over the Moon: Let Love In. Hosten, Colin & Dey, Sia. 2020. (Over the Moon Ser.). (ENG.). 32p. (J). (gr. -1-3). 15.99 ***(978-0-06-300241-8(8),*** HarperCollins) HarperCollins Pubs. Ltd. GBR. Dist: HarperCollins Pubs.

Wang, Zong-Zhou. D Is for Dancing Dragon: A China Alphabet. Crane, Carol. rev. ed. 2006. (Discover the World Ser.). (ENG.). 48p. (J). (gr. 1-3). 17.95 *(978-1-58536-273-8(5),* 202085) Sleeping Bear Pr.

Wannamaker, Joni Gruelle. Honest-to-Goodness Story of Raggedy Andy, 1 vol. Hall, Patricia. 2005. (ENG.). 32p. (J). (gr. k-3). 16.99 *(978-1-58980-251-3(9),* Pelican Publishing) Arcadia Publishing.

Wanner, Carole, jt. illus. see U'Ren, Victoria.

Wapahi, Robert. Dancing Hands: Signs of Learning. Hay, John & Harwich, Mary Belle. 2013. 78p. pap. 16.95 *(978-0-9888972-0-5(2))* Scotland Gate, Inc.

Warabe, Kimika. Joy to the World! Ebina, Hiro. 2006. (JPN.). 12p. (J). (gr. -1-k). bds. 9.95 *(978-0-8198-3985-5(X))* Pauline Bks. & Media.

Warburton, Sarah. Fairy Godmother Takes a Break. Bradman, Tony. 2014. (After Happily Ever After Ser.). (ENG.). 56p. (J). (gr. 3-6). pap. 4.95 *(978-1-4342-7961-3(8),* Stone Arch Bks.) Capstone.

—The Fairy Godmother Takes a Break. Bradman, Tony. 2009. (After Happily Ever After Ser.). (ENG.). 56p. (J). (gr. 3-6). 25.32 *(978-1-4342-1302-0(1),* Stone Arch Bks.) Capstone.

—The Frog Prince Hops to It, 1 vol. Bradman, Tony. (After Happily Ever After Ser.). (ENG.). 56p. (J). (gr. 3-6). 2014. pap. 5.05 *(978-1-4342-7962-0(6));* 2009. 25.32 *(978-1-4342-1303-7(X))* Capstone. (Stone Arch Bks.).

—Goldilocks & the Just Right Club. Bradman, Tony. (After Happily Ever After Ser.). (ENG.). 56p. (J). (gr. 3-6). 2014. pap. 5.05 *(978-1-4342-7963-7(4));* 2009. 25.32 *(978-1-4342-1304-4(8))* Capstone. (Stone Arch Bks.).

—Happy Ever After. Bradman, Tony. (After Happily Ever After Ser.). (ENG.). 56p. (J). (gr. 3-6). 2014. pap. 5.05 *(978-1-4342-7960-6(X));* 2009. lib. bdg. 25.32 *(978-1-4342-1301-3(3))* Capstone. (Stone Arch Bks.).

—Jack & the Bean Snacks, 1 vol. Bradman, Tony. (After Happily Ever After Ser.). (ENG.). 56p. (J). (gr. 3-6). 2014. pap. 5.05 *(978-1-4342-7964-4(2));* 2009. 25.32 *(978-1-4342-1305-1(6))* Capstone. (Stone Arch Bks.).

—Little Dragon. Magee, Wes. 2004. (ENG.). 24p. (J). lib. bdg. 23.65 *(978-1-59646-690-6(1))* Dingles & Co.

—Max & the Won't Go to Bed Show. Sperring, Mark. 2014. (ENG.). 32p. (J). (gr. -1-k). 16.99 *(978-0-545-70822-7(2),* Scholastic Pr.) Scholastic, Inc.

—Mr. Bear Gets Alarmed, 1 vol. Bradman, Tony. 2014. (After Happily Ever After Ser.). (ENG.). 56p. (J). (gr. 3-6). lib. bdg. 25.32 *(978-1-4342-7948-4(0),* Stone Arch Bks.) Capstone.

—Mr. Giant & the Beastly Baron, 1 vol. Bradman, Tony. 2014. (After Happily Ever After Ser.). (ENG.). 56p. (J). (gr. 3-6). lib. bdg. 25.32 *(978-1-4342-7949-1(9),* Stone Arch Bks.) Capstone.

—Mr. Wolf Bounces Back, 1 vol. Bradman, Tony. (After Happily Ever After Ser.). (ENG.). 56p. (J). (gr. 3-6). 2013. pap. 5.05 *(978-1-4342-6414-5(9));* 2009. 25.32 *(978-1-4342-1306-8(4))* Capstone. (Stone Arch Bks.).

—Mr. Wolf Bounces Back [Scholastic]. Bradman, Tony. 2009. (After Happily Ever After Ser.). (ENG.). 56p. (gr. 2-3). pap. 4.99 *(978-1-4342-1676-2(4),* Stone Arch Bks.) Capstone.

—The Princess & the Christmas Rescue. Hart, Caryl. 2017. (ENG.). 32p. (J). (gr. -1-2). 16.99 *(978-0-7636-9632-0(3),* Nosy Crow) Candlewick Pr.

—The Princess & the Giant. Hart, Caryl. 2015. (ENG.). 32p. (J). (gr. -1-2). 16.99 *(978-0-7636-8007-7(9),* Nosy Crow) Candlewick Pr.

—The Princess & the Presents. Hart, Caryl. 2014. (ENG.). 32p. (J). (gr. -1-2). 16.99 *(978-0-7636-7398-7(6),* Nosy Crow) Candlewick Pr.

—Rapunzel Lets Her Hair Down, 1 vol. Bradman, Tony. (After Happily Ever After Ser.). (ENG.). 56p. (J). (gr. 3-6). 2014. pap. 5.05 *(978-1-4342-7965-1(0));* 2009. lib. bdg. 25.32 *(978-1-4342-1307-5(2))* Capstone. (Stone Arch Bks.).

—Red Riding Hood Takes Charge, 1 vol. Bradman, Tony. (After Happily Ever After Ser.). (ENG.). 56p. (J). (gr. 3-6). 2013. pap. 5.05 *(978-1-4342-6413-8(0));* 2009. 25.32 *(978-1-4342-1308-2(0))* Capstone. (Stone Arch Bks.).

—Snow White & the Magic Mirror. Bradman, Tony. 2014. (After Happily Ever After Ser.). (ENG.). 56p. (J). (gr. 3-6). pap. 5.05 *(978-1-4342-7956-9(1));* lib. bdg. 25.32 *(978-1-4342-7950-7(2))* Capstone. (Stone Arch Bks.).

—The Three Little Pigs Go Camping, 1 vol. Bradman, Tony. 2014. (After Happily Ever After Ser.). (ENG.). 56p. (J). (gr. 3-6). lib. bdg. 25.32 *(978-1-4342-7952-1(9),* Stone Arch Bks.) Capstone.

—Twinkle. Holabird, Katharine. 2018. (Twinkle Ser.). (ENG.). 32p. (J). (gr. -1-2). 17.99 *(978-1-5344-2915-4(8),* Little Simon) Little Simon.

—Twinkle. Holabird, Katherine. 2014. (J). *(978-1-4351-5628-9(5))* Barnes & Noble, Inc.

—Twinkle Thinks Pink! Holabird, Katharine. 2020. (Twinkle Ser.). (ENG.). 32p. (J). (gr. -1-2). 17.99 *(978-1-5344-2917-8(4),* Little Simon) Little Simon.

—The Ugly Duckling Returns, 1 vol. Bradman, Tony. 2014. (After Happily Ever After Ser.). (ENG.). 56p. (J). (gr. 3-6). lib. bdg. 25.32 *(978-1-4342-7953-8(7),* Stone Arch Bks.) Capstone.

—The Wicked Stepmother Helps Out, 1 vol. Bradman, Tony. 2014. (After Happily Ever After Ser.). (ENG.). 56p. (J). (gr. 3-6). lib. bdg. 25.32 *(978-1-4342-7951-4(0),* Stone Arch Bks.) Capstone.

Warchocki, Tim. Have Your Cake & Eat It Too: The Family Plan for Lifelong Health & Fitness. 2004. *(978-0-9747008-0-9(0))* First Class Fitness Systems, Inc.

—My Fit Family. . . a Quick Start. 2004. cd-rom 9.95 *(978-0-9747008-2-3(7))* First Class Fitness Systems, Inc.

Ward, April. Adventure in the Park. Feldman, Thea. 2006. 20p. (J). *(978-0-696-23234-3(0))* Meredith Bks.

—Butterflies on Carmen Street/Mariposas en la Calle Carmen. Brown, Monica. 2007. (SPA & ENG.). 32p. (J). (gr. -1-2). 16.95 *(978-1-55885-484-0(3),* Piñata Books) Arte Publico Pr.

—Growing up with Tamales: Los Tamales de Ana. Zepeda, Gwendolyn & Ventura, Gabriela Baeza. 2008. (SPA & ENG.). 32p. (J). (gr. -1-2). 16.95 *(978-1-55885-493-2(2),* Piñata Books) Arte Publico Pr.

—Juan & the Chupacabras/Juan y el Chupacabras. Garza, Xavier. 2006. (ENG & SPA.). 32p. (J). (gr. -1-2). 16.95 *(978-1-55885-454-3(1),* Piñata Books) Arte Publico Pr.

Ward, Bonnie. Lights. Harvey, Patricia. 2018. (ENG.). 56p. (J). pap. 12.00 *(978-1-7309-6459-6(1))* Independently Published.

Ward, Cherise. Another Day. Mitchell, Carol. 2013. 206p. pap. 8.99 *(978-0-9899305-0-5(5))* CaribbeanReads.

—The Shark & the Parrotfish & Other Caribbean Fables. Picayo, Mario et al. 2014. 31p. (J). pap. *(978-1-934370-36-0(3))* Editorial Campana.

—With Grace: By Joanne C. Hillhouse. Hillhouse, Joanne C. 2017. (J). pap. *(978-1-934370-62-9(2))* Editorial Campana.

Ward, Christian, et al. Black Bolt. 2020. (ENG.). 288p. (YA). (gr. 8-17). 34.99 *(978-1-302-92140-8(1))* Marvel Worldwide, Inc.

Ward, Damian. Alphabet of Dance. Schwaeber, Barbie Heit. 2009. (Smithsonian Alphabet Books). (ENG.). 40p. (J). (gr. -1-k). 17.95 *(978-1-60727-110-9(9))* Soundprints.

—Everyone Feels Happy Sometimes, 1 vol. Meister, Cari. 2010. (Everyone Has Feelings Ser.). (ENG.). 24p. (J). (gr. k-2). lib. bdg. 26.65 *(978-1-4048-5754-4(0),* Picture Window Bks.) Capstone.

—Everyone Feels Sad Sometimes, 1 vol. Aboff, Marcie. 2010. (Everyone Has Feelings Ser.). (ENG.). 24p. (J). (gr. k-2). lib. bdg. 26.65 *(978-1-4048-5755-1(9),* Picture Window Bks.) Capstone.

—Everyone Feels Scared Sometimes, 1 vol. Aboff, Marcie. 2010. (Everyone Has Feelings Ser.). (ENG.). 24p. (J). (gr. k-2). lib. bdg. 26.65 *(978-1-4048-5756-8(7),* Picture Window Bks.) Capstone.

—It's a Thunderstorm!, 1 vol. Higgins, Nadia. 2010. (Weather Watchers Ser.). (ENG.). 32p. (J). (gr. -1-4). 28.50 *(978-1-60270-729-0(4),* 15239, Looking Glass Library) Magic Wagon.

—It's a Tornado!, 1 vol. Higgins, Nadia. 2010. (Weather Watchers Ser.). (ENG.). 32p. (J). (gr. k-4). 28.50 *(978-1-60270-730-6(8),* 15241, Looking Glass Library) Magic Wagon.

—It's a Tsunami!, 1 vol. Higgins, Nadia. 2010. (Weather Watchers Ser.). (ENG.). 32p. (J). (gr. -1-4). 28.50 *(978-1-60270-731-3(6),* 15243, Looking Glass Library) Magic Wagon.

—It's Hailing!, 1 vol. Higgins, Nadia. 2010. (Weather Watchers Ser.). (ENG.). 32p. (J). (gr. k-4). 28.50 *(978-1-60270-732-0(4),* 15245, Looking Glass Library) Magic Wagon.

—It's Raining!, 1 vol. Higgins, Nadia. 2010. (Weather Watchers Ser.). (ENG.). 32p. (J). (gr. -1-4). 28.50 *(978-1-60270-733-7(2),* 15247, Looking Glass Library) Magic Wagon.

—It's Snowing!, 1 vol. Higgins, Nadia. 2010. (Weather Watchers Ser.). (ENG.). 32p. (J). (gr. k-4). 28.50 *(978-1-60270-734-4(0),* 15249, Looking Glass Library) Magic Wagon.

—A Slave's Education in Courage: The Life of Frederick Douglass. Coleman, Wim & Perrin, Pat. 2014. (Setting the Stage for Fluency Ser.). (ENG.). 40p. (J). (gr. 3-5). pap. 8.99 *(978-1-939656-38-4(9))* Red Chair Pr.

Ward, Danielle. Saami & the White Wolf. Tapia-Bowes, Sally. 2016. (ENG.). (J). pap. *(978-0-9931919-6-1(7))* PurplePenguinPublishing.

Ward, E. F. We Were There at the Boston Tea Party. Webb, Robert N. 2013. (ENG.). 192p. (J). (gr. 3-8). pap. 6.99 *(978-0-486-49260-5(5),* 492605) Dover Pubns., Inc.

Ward, Fred, photos by. Gem Care. Ward, Charlotte, ed. 2nd ed. 2003. (Fred Ward Gem Book Ser.). 32p. pap. 9.95 *(978-1-887651-07-3(1))* Gem Bk. Pubs.

Ward, Helen. The King of Birds. Ward, Helen. 2018. (ENG.). 40p. (J). (gr. -1-3). 17.95 *(978-1-56792-625-5(8))* Godine, David R. Pub.

—The Town Mouse & the Country Mouse. Ward, Helen. 2012. (ENG.). 48p. (J). (gr. -1-3). 16.99 *(978-0-7636-6098-7(1),* Templar) Candlewick Pr.

Ward, Helen. The Rooster & the Fox. Ward, Helen, retold by. 2003. 40p. (J). (gr. k-3). 16.95 *(978-0-7613-1846-0(1),* First Avenue Editions) Lerner Publishing Group.

Ward, Jay Bryant. The Secret of the King. Nunes, Rachel Ann. 2005. 32p. (J). (gr. -1-3). 17.95 *(978-1-59038-241-7(2),* Shadow Mountain) Shadow Mountain Publishing.

Ward, John. The Bus Ride. Miller, William. 2013. (ENG.). 30p. (J). (gr. -1-18). reprint ed. pap. 10.95 *(978-1-58430-026-7(4))* Lee & Low Bks., Inc.

Ward, Juliana. Blackie's Day Out. Ward, Teresa. 2011. 32p. pap. *(978-1-77067-933-7(2))* FriesenPress.

Ward, Karen, jt. illus. see Yates, Bridget.

Ward, Keith. The Black Stallion. Farley, Walter. 2008. (Black Stallion Ser.). (ENG.). 288p. (J). (gr. 3-7). 15.99 *(978-0-375-85582-5(3),* Random Hse. Bks. for Young Readers) Random Hse. Children's Bks.

Ward, Kelly. The Fox & the Young Rooster. Kelly, Thomas E. 2011. 44p. pap. 24.95 *(978-1-4626-0343-5(2))* America Star Bks.

Ward, Lindsay. Let's Build! A Flip-And-Find-Out Book. Ward, Lindsay. 2020. (Wheels on the Go Ser.). 30p. (J). (gr. -1 — 1). bds. 8.99 *(978-0-06-286864-0(0),* HarperFestival) HarperCollins Pubs.

—Let's Go! A Flip-And-Find-Out Book. Ward, Lindsay. 2019. (Wheels on the Go Ser.). (ENG.). 30p. (J). (gr. -1-3). bds. 8.99 *(978-0-06-286863-3(2),* HarperFestival) HarperCollins Pubs.

—Pelly & Mr. Harrison Visit the Moon. Ward, Lindsay. ed. 2011. (ENG.). 36p. (J). (gr. -1-3). 11.99 *(978-1-935279-77-8(7))* Kane Miller.

—Rosco vs. the Baby. Ward, Lindsay. 2016. (ENG.). 32p. (J). (gr. -1-3). 17.99 *(978-1-4814-3657-1(0),* Simon & Schuster Bks. For Young Readers) Simon & Schuster Bks. For Young Readers.

—Vacation for Dexter! Ward, Lindsay. 2019. (Dexter T. Rexter Ser.: 3). 32p. (J). (gr. -1-2). 17.99 *(978-1-5420-4320-5(4),* 9781542043205, Two Lions) Amazon Publishing.

Ward, Lynd. Gaudenzia, Pride of the Palio. Henry, Marguerite. 2014. (ENG.). 304p. (J). (gr. 3-7). pap. 6.99 *(978-1-4814-0397-9(4),* Aladdin) Simon & Schuster Children's Publishing.

—Johnny Tremain. Forbes, Esther Hoskins. 2011. (Newbery Medal Ser.). (ENG.). 256p. (YA). (gr. 6-8). tchr. ed. 21.19 *(978-0-395-06766-6(9))* Houghton Mifflin Harcourt Publishing Co.

—The Little Red Lighthouse & the Great Gray Bridge: Restored Edition. Swift, Hildegarde H. 2003. (ENG.). 64p. (J). (gr. -1-3). pap. 8.99 *(978-0-15-204573-9(2),* 1193768) Houghton Mifflin Harcourt Publishing Co.

Ward, Matt. Dinosaur Rock: Band 01A/Pink a (Collins Big Cat) Harvey, Damien. 2005. (Collins Big Cat Ser.). (ENG.). 16p. (J). (gr. -1-k). pap. 7.99 *(978-0-00-718540-5(5))* HarperCollins Pubs. Ltd. GBR. Dist: Independent Pubs. Group.

Ward, Matthew, photos by. Learn Squash in a Weekend. Khan, Jahangir & Pratt, Kevin. 2005. 95p. (YA). reprint ed. pap. 15.00 *(978-0-7567-9415-6(3))* DIANE Publishing Co.

Ward, Megan. Emily Finds a Dog. Ward, Carla. 2007. (J). 15.95 *(978-0-9793124-0-3(X))* Tinkertown Museum.

Ward, Nancy. The Big X: A Community Comes Together. Nelson, S. M. & Lundy, Angela. 2018. (Kneehigh Pond Ser.: Vol. 1). (ENG.). 40p. (J). (gr. k-2). 24.99 *(978-1-948123-07-5(X));* pap. 14.99 *(978-1-948123-02-0(9))* Brainiac Bloomers, LLC.

—We're Going Traveling & You're My Ride Volume 1: What Are We Riding In? Nelson, S. M. Nelson, L. A., ed. 2018. (ENG.). 40p. (J). (gr. k-2). 24.99 *(978-1-948123-05-1(3))* Brainiac Bloomers, LLC.

Ward, Nancy, jt. illus. see Nelson, S. M.

Ward, Nick. Ada Lovelace (the First Names Series) Jeapes, Ben. 2020. (First Names Ser.). (ENG.). 144p. (J). (gr. 3-7). 9.99 *(978-1-4197-4075-6(X),* Abrams Bks. for Young Readers) Abrams, Inc.

—Deck the Walls: A Wacky Christmas Carol. Dealey, Erin. 2013. (ENG.). 32p. (J). (gr. 1-3). 14.99 *(978-1-58536-857-0(1),* 202892) Sleeping Bear Pr.

—Hans Christian Andersen. Fischel, Emma. 2010. (Famous People, Famous Lives Ser.). 38p. (J). *(978-89-491-8824-9(4))* Biryongso Publishing Co.

Ward, Nick. Another Rumpus. Ward, Nick. 2015. (ENG.). 24p. (J). (gr. -1-3). 7.99 *(978-1-85733-728-0(X))* Lerner Publishing Group.

Ward, Patricia R. & Pigford, Grady A. Maria Montessori. Sharpe, Paula A. 2010. 51p. (J). *(978-1-892142-47-4(3))* Cedar Tree Bks.

Ward, Rosanna Harrisson. Home for Snail. King, Jennifer. 2020. (ENG.). 34p. (J). pap. 9.99 ***(978-1-6938-8643-0(X))*** Independently Published.

Ward, Sarah. Baby Firsts: Record Cards for Baby's Important Milestones! Tiger Tales. 2016. (To Baby with Love Ser.). (ENG.). 20p. (J). (gr. k-12). 14.99 *(978-1-58925-235-6(7))* Tiger Tales.

—Baby's First Bear. Tiger Tales. 2016. (To Baby with Love Ser.). (ENG.). 10p. (J). (gr. -1 — 1). 14.99 *(978-1-58925-214-1(4))* Tiger Tales.

—Baby's First Bunny. Tiger Tales. 2016. (To Baby with Love Ser.). (ENG.). 10p. (J). (gr. -1 — 1). 14.99 *(978-1-58925-213-4(6))* Tiger Tales.

—Bedtime for Baby Sloth. McLean, Danielle. 2019. (ENG.). (J). 32p. (gr. -1-2). 17.99 *(978-1-68010-150-8(1));* 22p. (gr. 2-k). bds. 9.99 *(978-1-68010-600-8(7))* Tiger Tales.

—Cuddle Close, Little Koala. McLean, Danielle. 2020. (ENG.). 24p. (J). (gr. -1-2). 17.99 *(978-1-68010-187-4(0))* Tiger Tales.

—Good Night Baby! Tiger Tales. 2016. (To Baby with Love Ser.). (ENG.). 10p. (J). (gr. -1 — 1). bds. 9.99 *(978-1-58925-211-0(X))* Tiger Tales.

—Hello Baby! Tiger Tales. 2016. (To Baby with Love Ser.). (ENG.). 10p. (J). (gr. -1 — 1). bds. 9.99 *(978-1-58925-210-3(1))* Tiger Tales.

—I Love Mommy! Tiger Tales. 2018. (To Baby with Love Ser.). (ENG.). 12p. (J). (gr. -1 — 1). bds. 9.99 *(978-1-68010-545-2(0))* Tiger Tales.

—Love You, Baby! Tiger Tales. 2017. (To Baby with Love Ser.). (ENG.). 12p. (J). (gr. -1 — 1). bds. 9.99 *(978-1-68010-517-9(5))* Tiger Tales.

—My First Listen, Play, & Say! Tiger Tales. 2017. (To Baby with Love Ser.). (ENG.). 10p. (J). (gr. -1-k). bds. 14.99 *(978-1-68010-532-2(9))* Tiger Tales.

—My First Touch, Feel, & Play! Tiger Tales. 2017. (To Baby with Love Ser.). (ENG.). 10p. (J). (gr. -1 — 1). bds. 12.99 *(978-1-68010-533-9(7))* Tiger Tales.

—My Little Storybook: Little Duck Learns to Swim. 2016. (ENG.). 12p. (J). (gr. -1 — 1). bds. 4.99 *(978-1-4998-0190-3(4))* Little Bee Books Inc.

—Peekaboo Baby! Tiger Tales. 2016. (To Baby with Love Ser.). (ENG.). 10p. (J). (gr. -1 — 1). bds. 9.99 *(978-1-58925-212-7(8))* Tiger Tales.

WARD, Sarah. Say & Pray Bible Seek & Find: First Words, Stories, & Prayers, 1 vol. Stortz, Diane M. 2020. (ENG.). 12p. (J). bds. 12.99 ***(978-1-4002-1948-3(5))*** Nelson, Thomas Inc.

Ward, Sarah. Twinkle, Twinkle, Little Baby. Tiger Tales. 2017. (To Baby with Love Ser.). (ENG.). 12p. (J). (gr. -1 — 1). bds. 9.99 *(978-1-68010-515-5(9))* Tiger Tales.

Ward, Sarah G. Carry & Learn Numbers. Scholastic, Inc. Staff. 2015. (ENG.). 10p. (J). (— 1). 7.99 *(978-0-545-79790-0(X),* Cartwheel Bks.) Scholastic, Inc.

Ward, Scott. Comment les Teckels Sont Venus Au Monde (FR/en Bilingual Hardcover) Le Conte Fabuleux d'un Chien Court et Long. Jones, Kizzie. Cerven, Laura, tr. 2020. (FRE.). 82p. (J). 23.99 ***(978-1-947543-05-8(9))*** Tall Tales.

—Comment les Teckels Sont Venus Au Monde (FR/en Bilingual Softcover) Le Conte Fabuleux d'un Chien Court et Long. Jones, Kizzie. Cerven, Laura, tr. 2020. (FRE.). 82p. (J). pap. 14.99 ***(978-1-947543-06-5(7))*** Tall Tales.

Ward, Scott. Le Conte d'un Teckel et d'un Pelican: Comment une Amitie Se Formait (Hard Cvr French/English) Jones, Kizzie. Cerven, Laura, tr. 2017. (Tall Tales Ser.: Vol. 2). (FRE.). (J). (gr. k-4). 23.99 *(978-0-9979540-5-0(1))* Tall Tales.

—Le Conte d'un Teckel et d'un Pelican: Comment une Amitie Se Formait (Soft Cvr French/English) Jones, Kizzie. Cerven, Laura, tr. 2017. (Tall Tales Ser.: Vol. 2). (FRE.). (J). (gr. k-4). pap. 14.99 *(978-0-9979540-6-7(X))* Tall Tales.

Ward, Scott. Un Gran Cuento Acerca de Perros Salchicha y Disfraces: El Origen de Otras Razas. Jones, Kizzie Elizabeth. Winston, Alfonso, tr. 2019. (SPA.). 68p. (J). (gr. k-4). 23.99 ***(978-1-947543-04-1(0));*** pap. 15.99 ***(978-1-947543-02-7(4))*** Tall Tales.

Ward, Scott. Un Gran Cuento Acerca de un Perro Salchicha y un Pelicano Como una Amistad Llego a Ser. Jones, Kizzie. Winston, Alfonso, tr. 2017. (SPA.). (J). (gr. k-4). 23.99 *(978-0-9979540-1-2(9));* (Tall Tales Spanish/English Bi-Lingual Ser.: Vol. 2). pap. 14.99 *(978-0-9979540-2-9(7))* Tall Tales.

—Moon Beam Walking: Dream Space Books, 1 vol. Reynolds, D. G. 2009. 14p. pap. 19.95 *(978-1-61546-726-6(2))* PublishAmerica, Inc.

—El Origen de Los Perros Salchicha: Un Gran Cuento Acerca de un Perro Largo y Pequeno. Jones, Kizzie Elizabeth. Winston, Alfonso, tr. 2016. (Tall Tales Ser.: Vol. 1). (SPA.). (J). (gr. 2-6). 23.99 *(978-0-9973641-4-9(9));* pap. 14.99 *(978-0-9973641-3-2(0))* Tall Tales.

—A Tall Tale about a Dachshund & a Pelican: How a Friendship Came to Be. Jones, Kizzie. 2016. (Tall Tales Ser.: Vol. 2). (ENG.). (J). (gr. k-3). pap. 12.99 *(978-0-9973641-7-0(3))* Tall Tales.

Ward, Scott. A Tall Tale about Dachshunds in Costumes: How MORE Dogs Came to Be. Jones, Kizzie Elizabeth. 2019. (ENG.). 68p. (J). (gr. k-4). 23.99 ***(978-1-947543-00-3(8));*** pap. 15.99 ***(978-1-947543-01-0(6))*** Tall Tales.

Ward, Scott. A Tall Tale of a Dachshund & a Pelican: How a Friendship Came to Be. Jones, Kizzie. 2016. (Tall Tales Ser.: Vol. 2). (ENG.). 31p. (J). (gr. k-3). 21.99 *(978-0-9973641-6-3(5))* Tall Tales.

Ward, Sue Marshall. Sugar Lump's Night Before Christmas, 1 vol. Simmons, Lynn Sheffield. 2007. (Night Before Christmas Ser.). (ENG.). 48p. (J). (gr. k-5). 12.95 *(978-1-58980-439-5(2),* Pelican Publishing) Arcadia Publishing.

—Ten Redneck Babies: A Southern Counting Book, 1 vol. Davis, David. 2004. (ENG.). 32p. (J). (gr. k-k). 16.99 *(978-1-58980-232-2(2),* Pelican Publishing) Arcadia Publishing.

—Texas Aesop's Fables, 1 vol. Davis, David. 2008. (ENG.). 32p. (J). (gr. k-3). 16.99 *(978-1-58980-569-9(0),* Pelican Publishing) Arcadia Publishing.

—Texas Mother Goose, 1 vol. Davis, David. 2006. (ENG.). 40p. (J). (gr. k-3). 17.99 *(978-1-58980-369-5(8),* Pelican Publishing) Arcadia Publishing.

Warden, Gillian. The Cat on the Island. Crew, Gary. 2008. 32p. *(978-0-207-20070-0(X))* HarperCollins Pubs. Australia.

Warden, Jane. The Mystery of the Pink Bees. Warden, Jane. 2018. (ENG.). 34p. (J). pap. 9.00 *(978-1-7326741-0-3(8))* Warden, Chris.

Ware, Chelsey. Dave the Dragonfly. Scarborough, Ginger. 2016. (ENG.). (J). 22.95 *(978-1-63525-810-3(3))* Christian Faith Publishing.

Ware, Kate, jt. illus. see Aleksic, Vladimir.

Ware, Quinton. Joey & the Magic Dream Pillow. Vana, Dan. 2013. 20p. pap. 24.95 *(978-1-4626-7872-3(6))* America Star Bks.

Ware, Syrus Marcus. I Promise. 2019. 32p. (J). 16.95 *(978-1-55152-779-6(0))* Arsenal Pulp Pr. CAN. Dist: Consortium Bk. Sales & Distribution.

Waresak, Matt, jt. illus. see Skeesuck, Justin.

Warf, Gracie. No Peanuts for Me! Pangan, Catherine Hagerman. 2013. (ENG.). 30p. (J). (gr. -1-3). 14.95 *(978-1-62086-433-3(9))* Mascot Bks., Inc.

Warfield, D. L. Can't Hold Me Down. LeFlore, Lyah B. 2010. (Come Up Ser.). (ENG.). 272p. (J). (gr. 9-12). pap. 8.99 *(978-1-4169-7964-7(6))* Simon & Schuster, Inc.

—The World Is Mine. LeFlore, Lyah B. 2009. (Come Up Ser.). (ENG.). 304p. (YA). (gr. 9-18). pap. 8.99 *(978-1-4169-7963-0(8),* Simon Pulse) Simon Pulse.

Wargin, Ed, photos by. Minnesota. Wargin, Kathy-jo. 2008. (I Spy with My Little Eye Ser.). (ENG., 32p. (J). (gr. 1-4). 15.99 *(978-1-58536-359-9(6),* 202144) Sleeping Bear Pr.

Wargin, Kathy-jo & Bendall-Brunello, John. Scare a Bear. 2010. (ENG.). 32p. (J). (gr. -1-3). 15.95 *(978-1-58536-430-5(4))* Sleeping Bear Pr.

Warhola, James. If You're Happy & You Know It. Warhola, James. Scholastic, Inc. Staff. Geist, Ken, ed. 2007. (ENG.). 32p. (J). (gr. -1-k). 16.99 *(978-0-439-72766-2(9),* Orchard Bks.) Scholastic, Inc.

—Uncle Andy's: A Faabbbulous Visit with Andy Warhol. Warhola, James. 2005. (ENG.). 32p. (J). (gr. k-3). reprint ed. pap. 6.99 *(978-0-14-240347-1(4),* Puffin Books) Penguin Young Readers Group.

—Uncle Andy's Cats. Warhola, James. 2009. (ENG.). 32p. (J). (gr. k-3). 17.99 *(978-0-399-25180-1(4),* G.P. Putnam's Sons Books for Young Readers) Penguin Young Readers Group.

Waring, Geoff. Black Meets White. Fontes, Justine. 2005. (ENG.). 24p. (J). (— 1). 12.99 *(978-0-7636-1933-6(7))* Candlewick Pr.

Waring, Geoff. Oscar & the Bat: A Book about Sound. Waring, Geoff. 2009. (Start with Science Ser.). (ENG.). 32p. (J). (gr. -1-3). pap. 6.99 *(978-0-7636-4513-7(3))* Candlewick Pr.

—Oscar & the Bird: A Book about Electricity. Waring, Geoff. 2011. (Start with Science Ser.). (ENG.). 32p. (J). (gr. -1-3). pap. 6.99 *(978-0-7636-5302-6(0))* Candlewick Pr.

—Oscar & the Cricket: A Book about Moving & Rolling. Waring, Geoff. 2009. (Start with Science Ser.). (ENG.). 32p. (J). (gr. -1-3). pap. 6.99 *(978-0-7636-4512-0(5))* Candlewick Pr.

—Oscar & the Frog: A Book about Growing. Waring, Geoff. (Start with Science Ser.). (ENG.). (J). 2008. 32p. (gr. -1-3). pap. 6.99 *(978-0-7636-4030-9(1));* 2007. 27p. (gr. k-3). 18.69 *(978-0-7636-3558-9(8))* Candlewick Pr.

—Oscar & the Moth: A Book about Light & Dark. Waring, Geoff. 2008. (Start with Science Ser.). (ENG.). 32p. (J). (gr. -1-3). pap. 6.99 *(978-0-7636-4031-6(X))* Candlewick Pr.

—Oscar & the Snail: A Book about Things That We Use. Waring, Geoff. (Start with Science Ser.). (ENG.). 32p. (J). (gr. -1-3). 2011. pap. 6.99 *(978-0-7636-5303-3(9));* 2009. 14.99 *(978-0-7636-4039-2(5))* Candlewick Pr.

Waring, Zoe. Animal Bathtime. Conway, Sara. 2018. (Animal Time Ser.). (ENG.). 20p. (J). bds. 6.99 ***(978-1-77402-030-2(0))*** Rainstorm Pr.

W

—Animal School Time. Conway, Sara. 2019. (Animal Time Ser.). (ENG.). 20p. (J). (gr. -1 — 1). bds. 6.99 *(978-1-926444-52-9(3))* Rainstorm Pr.

Waring, Zoe. Arthur's Holiday Adventure. Jardine, Hannah & Clever Publishing. 2019. (Animal Adventures Ser.). (ENG.). 10p. (J). (gr. -1 — 1). bds. 7.99 *(978-1-949998-08-5(8))* Clever Media Group.

—Barks & Beeps (novelty Board Book) Houghton Mifflin Harcourt, Houghton Mifflin. 2020. (ENG.). 10p. (J). (— 1). 8.99 *(978-0-358-15657-4(2)*, 1757565, HMH Books For Young Readers) Houghton Mifflin Harcourt Publishing Co.

—Bella's Meadow Adventure. Jardine, Hannah & Clever Publishing. 2020. (Animal Adventures Ser.). (ENG.). 10p. (J). (gr. -1 — 1). bds. 7.99 *(978-1-949998-58-0(4))* Clever Media Group.

—Cat & Dog. Oswald, Helen. 2018. (Picture Bks.). (ENG.). 32p. (J). (gr. -1-k). 16.99 *(978-1-78700-455-9(4))* Willow Tree Bks. GBR. Dist: Independent Pubs. Group.

—Daisy's Big Adventure. Jardine, Hannah & Clever Publishing. 2019. (Animal Adventures Ser.). (ENG.). 10p. (J). (gr. -1 — 1). bds. 7.99 *(978-1-948418-76-8(2))* Clever Media Group.

—Danny's Pond Adventure. Jardine, Hannah & Clever Publishing. 2020. (Animal Adventures Ser.). (ENG.). 10p. (J). (gr. -1 — 1). bds. 7.99 *(978-1-949998-57-3(6))* Clever Media Group.

—Go Fish! Sauer, Tammi. 2018. (ENG.). 40p. (J). (gr. -1 — 1). 14.99 *(978-0-06-242155-5(7))* HarperCollins Pubs.

—Let's Build. Houghton Mifflin Harcourt, Houghton Mifflin & Gryta, Thomas. 2020. (ENG.). 56p. (J). (gr. -1-3). 14.99 *(978-1-328-60607-5(4)*, 1732506, HMH Books For Young Readers) Houghton Mifflin Harcourt Publishing Co.

—Let's Play Baseball: Chunky Lift-A-Flap Board Book. Swift, Ginger. Cottage Door Press, ed. 2019. (ENG.). 12p. (J). (gr. -1-k). bds. 7.99 *(978-1-68052-374-4(0)*, 1003390) Cottage Door Pr.

—Lily's Park Adventure. Jardine, Hannah & Clever Publishing. 2020. (Animal Adventures Ser.). (ENG.). 10p. (J). (gr. -1 — 1). bds. 7.99 *(978-1-948418-78-2(9))* Clever Media Group.

—Max's Rainforest Adventure. Jardine, Hannah & Clever Publishing. 2019. (Animal Adventures Ser.). (ENG.). 10p. (J). (gr. -1 — 1). bds. 7.99 *(978-1-948418-77-5(0))* Clever Media Group.

—Olivia's North Pole Adventure. Jardine, Hannah & Clever Publishing. 2019. (Animal Adventures Ser.). (ENG.). 10p. (J). (gr. -1 — 1). bds. 7.99 *(978-1-949998-07-8(X))* Clever Media Group.

—Peeping Beauty. Maier, Brenda. 2019. (ENG.). 32p. (J). (gr. -1-2). 17.99 *(978-1-4814-7272-2(0)*, Simon & Schuster/Paula Wiseman Bks.) Simon & Schuster/Paula Wiseman Bks.

—Pepper's Forest Adventure. Jardine, Hannah & Clever Publishing. 2020. (Animal Adventures Ser.). (ENG.). 10p. (J). (gr. -1 — 1). bds. 7.99 *(978-1-948418-75-1(4))* Clever Media Group.

—Truck, Truck, Goose! Sauer, Tammi. 2017. (ENG.). 40p. (J). (gr. -1 — 1). 14.99 *(978-0-06-242153-1(0))* HarperCollins Pubs.

—Truck, Truck, Goose! Board Book. Sauer, Tammi. 2018. (ENG.). 40p. (J). (gr. -1 — 1). bds. 7.99 *(978-0-06-242154-8(9)*, HarperFestival) HarperCollins Pubs.

—Twinkle, Twinkle, Dinosaur. Burton, Jeffrey. 2019. (Twinkle, Twinkle Ser.). (ENG.). 16p. (J). (gr. -1-k). bds. 5.99 *(978-1-5344-3975-7(7)*, Little Simon) Little Simon.

—Twinkle, Twinkle, Fairy Friend. Burton, Jeffrey. 2019. (Twinkle, Twinkle Ser.). (ENG.). 16p. (J). (gr. -1-k). bds. 5.99 *(978-1-5344-3977-1(3)*, Little Simon) Little Simon.

Waring, Zoe. Twinkle, Twinkle, Little Shark. Burton, Jeffrey. 2020. (Twinkle, Twinkle Ser.). (ENG.). 16p. (J). (-k). bds. 5.99 ***(978-1-5344-6010-2(1)**, Little Simon)* Little Simon.

—Twinkle, Twinkle, Mermaid Blue. Burton, Jeffrey. 2020. (Twinkle, Twinkle Ser.). (ENG.). 16p. (J). (-k). bds. 5.99 ***(978-1-5344-6011-9(X)**, Little Simon)* Little Simon.

Waring, Zoe. Twinkle, Twinkle, Robot Beep. Burton, Jeffrey. 2020. (Twinkle, Twinkle Ser.). (ENG.). 16p. (J). (-k). bds. 5.99 *(978-1-5344-6009-6(8)*, Little Simon) Little Simon.

—Twinkle, Twinkle, Unicorn. Burton, Jeffrey. 2019. (Twinkle, Twinkle Ser.). (ENG.). 16p. (J). (gr. -1-k). bds. 5.99 *(978-1-5344-3973-3(0)*, Little Simon) Little Simon.

Warm Day, Jonathan. Kiki's Journey. Orona-Ramirez, Kristy. (ENG.). 32p. (J). 2017. pap. 9.95 *(978-0-89239-410-4(2)*, Children's Book Press); 2013. 16.95 *(978-0-89239-214-8(2))* Lee & Low Bks., Inc.

Warmington, Amy. David & the Giant. Smith, Fiona Veitch. 2015. (ENG.). 32p. pap. 10.00 *(978-0-281-07457-0(7))* SPCK Publishing GBR. Dist: InterVarsity Pr.

—David & the Grumpy King. Smith, Fiona Veitch. 2015. (ENG.). 32p. pap. 10.00 *(978-0-281-07459-4(3))* SPCK Publishing GBR. Dist: InterVarsity Pr.

—David & the Kingmaker. Smith, Fiona Veitch. 2015. (ENG.). 32p. pap. 10.00 *(978-0-281-07456-3(9))* SPCK Publishing GBR. Dist: InterVarsity Pr.

—David & the Lonely Prince. Smith, Fiona Veitch. 2015. (ENG.). 32p. pap. 10.00 *(978-0-281-07458-7(5))* SPCK Publishing GBR. Dist: InterVarsity Pr.

—David & the Never-Ending Kingdom. Smith, Fiona Veitch. 2015. (ENG.). 32p. pap. 10.00 *(978-0-281-07460-0(7))* SPCK Publishing GBR. Dist: InterVarsity Pr.

Warms, Breanna. Baseball Bella & Ballerina Emma. Lavergne, Angele. 2018. (ENG.). 36p. (J). pap. *(978-1-5255-2204-8(3))* FriesenPress.

Warner Bros Staff. Hidden Creatures. 2018. (Harry Potter Ser.). (ENG.). 64p. (J). (gr. 1-1). 12.99 *(978-1-338-28094-4(5))* Scholastic, Inc.

Warner, Chalene, jt. illus. see Malekoff, Stephanie.

Warner, Danielle. Hidden Mickeys: A Mouse in the Land. Warner, Jeremy. 2012. 68p. pap. 5.95 *(978-0-9853555-2-4(2))* Portrait Health Publishing.

Warner, Darrell. Wuthering Heights. Brontë, Emily. 2004. (Paperback Classics Ser.). 158p. (J). (gr. 5). lib. bdg. 12.95 *(978-1-58086-604-0(2))* EDC Publishing.

Warner, Jessica. The Railroad Adventures of Chen Sing. Chiang, George. 2017. (ENG.). (J). *(978-1-4602-9939-5(6))*; pap. *(978-1-4602-9940-1(X))* FriesenPress.

Warner, Linda. Lighthouse Seeds. Love, Pamela. ed. 2004. (ENG.). 32p. (J). (gr. k-17). 15.95 *(978-0-89272-541-0(9))* Down East Bks.

Warner, Michael. Byron Carmichael Book One: The Human Corpse Trade. King, J. Eric & Graham, Greg. Mizer, Lindsay, ed. 2008. (ENG.). 408p. (gr. 8-12). 18.95 *(978-0-615-15770-2(X))* G & K Publishing.

Warner, Robert. Tales to Make You Scream for Your Momma. Warner, Michael N. 2018. 208p. (J). pap. 11.95 *(978-0-9963756-1-0(9))* All About Kids Publishing.

Warner, Susan Vandeventer. Wanda & Winky. McLean, Linda K. Fredericks, Mariah, ed. 2016. (ENG.). 38p. (J). (gr. k-5). pap. 12.00 *(978-0-9974810-0-6(5))* By The Creek Pubns.

Warnes, Tim. The Big Book Adventure. Ford, Emily. 2018. (ENG.). 32p. (J). (gr. 1-3). 17.99 *(978-1-68412-378-0(X)*, Silver Dolphin Bks.) Printers Row Publishing Group.

—Bless You, Santa! Sykes, Julie. 2004. 32p. (J). tchr. ed. 15.95 *(978-1-58925-041-3(9))* Tiger Tales.

—Bumbletum. Smallman, Steve. 2006. 24p. (J). (gr. -1-3). 15.95 *(978-1-58925-060-4(5))* Tiger Tales.

—Counting Leopard's Spots & other Stories. Oram, Hiawyn. 2005. 96p. (J). (gr. k-4). reprint ed. 17.00 *(978-0-7567-9252-7(5))* DIANE Publishing Co.

—Do You Have My Purr? West, Judy. 2014. (ENG.). 32p. (J). (gr. -1-2). 6.99 *(978-1-58925-511-1(9))* Tiger Tales.

—Don't Be So Nosy, Posy! Grant, Nicola. 2004. 32p. (J). tchr. ed. 15.95 *(978-1-58925-036-9(2))* Tiger Tales.

—God Is Watching over You, 1 vol. Lyons, P. J. 2016. (ENG.). 16p. (J). bds. 9.99 *(978-0-310-74881-6(X))* Zonderkidz.

—The Great Monster Hunt. Landa, Norbert. 2020. (Favorite Stories Ser.). (ENG.). 32p. (J). (gr. -1-2). 23.99 *(978-1-68010-197-3(8))* Tiger Tales.

—Hands off My Honey! Chapman, Jane. 2013. (ENG.). 32p. (J). (gr. -1-1). 12.95 *(978-1-58925-142-7(3))* Tiger Tales.

—I Don't Want to Go to Bed! Sykes, Julie. 2013. (ENG.). (J). (gr. -1-2). 32p. 14.99 *(978-1-58925-148-9(2))*; 26p. pap. 9.99 ***(978-1-58925-614-9(X))*** Tiger Tales.

Warnes, Tim. I Love School! Corderoy, Tracey. 2020. (ENG.). 32p. (J). (gr. -1-2). 17.99 ***(978-1-68010-230-7(3))*** Tiger Tales.

Warnes, Tim. I Love You As Big As the World. Van Buren, David. 2013. (ENG.). 22p. (J). (-k). bds. 8.95 *(978-1-58925-603-3(4))* Tiger Tales.

Warnes, Tim. I Love You More Than Christmas. Hattie, Ellie. 2020. (ENG.). 32p. (J). (gr. -1-2). 17.99 ***(978-1-68010-208-6(7))*** Tiger Tales.

Warnes, Tim. I Love You to the Moon & Back. Hepworth, Amelia. 2017. (ENG.). 24p. (J). (gr. -1-k). bds. 9.99 *(978-1-68010-522-3(1))* Tiger Tales.

—I'm Going to Give You a Bear Hug!, 1 vol. Cooney, Caroline B. (ENG.). 32p. (J). 2017. bds. 7.99 *(978-0-310-76440-3(8))*; 2016. 16.99 *(978-0-310-75473-2(9))* Zonderkidz.

—It's Christmas! Corderoy, Tracey. 2017. (ENG.). 32p. (J). (gr. -1-2). 16.99 *(978-1-68010-067-9(X))* Tiger Tales.

—I've Seen Santa! Bedford, David. 32p. 2008. pap. 6.95 *(978-1-58925-411-4(2))*; 2006. (J). (gr. -1-3). 15.95 *(978-1-58925-058-1(3))* Tiger Tales.

—Jesus Loves Me! 2008. (ENG.). 26p. (J). (gr. -1-k). bds. 7.99 *(978-1-4169-5367-8(1)*, Little Simon) Little Simon.

—Jesus Loves Me! 2006. (ENG.). 32p. (J). (gr. -1-3). 15.99 *(978-1-4169-0065-8(9)*, Simon & Schuster Bks. For Young Readers) Simon & Schuster Bks. For Young Readers.

—More! Corderoy, Tracey. 2015. (ENG.). 32p. (J). (gr. -1-2). 16.99 *(978-1-58925-193-9(8))* Tiger Tales.

Warnes, Tim, et al. My Favorite Bedtime Collection. Bright, Paul & Bedford, David. 2014. (J). *(978-1-4351-5722-4(2))* Little Tiger Pr.

Warnes, Tim. No! Corderoy, Tracey. (ENG.). (J). (gr. -1-k). 2015. 28p. bds. 7.99 *(978-1-58925-208-0(X))*; 2013. 32p. 14.99 *(978-1-58925-150-2(4))* Tiger Tales.

—Now! Corderoy, Tracey. 2018. (ENG.). 32p. (J). (gr. -1-2). 16.99 *(978-1-68010-033-4(5))* Tiger Tales.

—Only You Can Be You: What Makes You Different Makes You Great, 1 vol. Clarkson, Sally & Clarkson, Nathan. 2019. (ENG.). 32p. (J). 16.99 *(978-1-4002-1143-2(3))* Nelson, Thomas Inc.

—Only You Can Be You for Little Ones: What Makes You Different Makes You Great, 1 vol. Clarkson, Nathan & Clarkson, Sally. 2020. (ENG.). 20p. (J). bds. 12.99 *(978-1-4002-1144-9(1))* Nelson, Thomas Inc.

—Rise & Shine! Public Domain, Public. 2010. (ENG.). 26p. (J). (gr. -1-k). bds. 9.99 *(978-1-4424-0189-1(3)*, Little Simon) Little Simon.

—Say Boo to the Animals! Whybrow, Ian. 2017. (J). *(978-1-4351-6509-0(8))* Barnes & Noble, Inc.

—Say Hello to the Animals! Whybrow, Ian. 2017. 20p. (J). *(978-1-4351-6512-0(8))* Barnes & Noble, Inc.

—Scaredy Mouse. MacDonald, Alan. 2007. (Storytime Board Bks.). 16p. (J). (gr. -1-k). bds. 6.95 *(978-1-58925-827-3(4))* Tiger Tales.

—Scaredy Mouse. Macdonald, Alan. 2019. (Favorite Stories Ser.). (ENG.). 32p. (J). (gr. -1-2). lib. bdg. 23.99 *(978-1-68010-162-1(5))* Tiger Tales.

—Shhh! Sykes, Julie. 2006. (Storytime Board Bks.). 18p. (J). (gr. -1-1). bds. 6.95 *(978-1-58925-796-2(0))* Tiger Tales.

—Solo Tú Puedes Ser Tú - Bilingüe: Lo Que Te Hace Diferente Te Hace único, 1 vol. Clarkson, Sally & Clarkson, Nathan. ed. 2020. (SPA.). 32p. (J). 12.99 *(978-1-4002-1875-2(6))* Grupo Nelson.

—Sweet Dreams, Little Bear. 2013. (ENG.). 18p. (gr. -1). bds. 8.95 *(978-1-58925-604-0(2))* Tiger Tales.

—Thank You, Lord, for Everything, 1 vol. Lyons, P. J. 2015. (ENG.). 16p. (J). bds. 9.99 *(978-0-310-74812-0(7))* Zonderkidz.

Warnes, Tim. Tom's Tail. Jennings, Linda. 2020. (Favorite Stories Ser.). (ENG.). 32p. (J). (gr. -1-2). lib. bdg. 23.99 ***(978-1-68010-225-3(7))*** Tiger Tales.

Warnes, Tim. The Very Busy Farm. Grant, Nicola. 2019. (ENG.). 20p. (J). (— 1). bds. 6.99 *(978-1-68412-507-4(3)*, Silver Dolphin Bks.) Printers Row Publishing Group.

—A Very Special Hug. Smallman, Steve. 2008. (ENG.). 32p. (gr. -1-1). 18.69 *(978-1-58925-410-7(4))* Tiger Tales.

Warnes, Tim. Weasel Is Worried. Gavin, Ciara. 2020. (ENG.). 32p. (J). (gr. -1-2). 17.99 ***(978-1-68010-193-5(5))*** Tiger Tales.

Warnes, Tim. Bathtime, Little Tiger! Warnes, Tim. Sykes, Julie. 2003. (Little Tiger Lift-the-Flap Ser.). 12p. (J). 5.95 *(978-1-58925-693-4(X))* Tiger Tales.

—Can't You Sleep, Dotty? Warnes, Tim. 2003. 32p. (J). pap. 5.95 *(978-1-58925-376-6(0))* Tiger Tales.

—Can't You Sleep, Little Puppy? Warnes, Tim. 2014. (ENG.). 32p. (J). (gr. -1-2). 6.99 *(978-1-58925-508-1(9))* Tiger Tales.

—Chalk & Cheese. Warnes, Tim. 2008. (ENG.). 32p. (J). (gr. -1-3). 18.99 *(978-1-4169-1378-8(5)*, Simon & Schuster Bks. For Young Readers) Simon & Schuster Bks. For Young Readers.

—Happy Birthday, Dotty. Warnes, Tim. 2003. 32p. (J). tchr. ed. 15.95 *(978-1-58925-026-0(5))* Tiger Tales.

—Hide & Seek, Little Tiger. Warnes, Tim. Sykes, Julie. 2003. (Little Tiger Lift-the-Flap Ser.). 14p. (J). 5.95 *(978-1-58925-694-1(8))* Tiger Tales.

—Warning! Do Not Touch! Warnes, Tim. 2016. (ENG.). 32p. (J). (gr. -1-2). 16.99 *(978-1-68010-013-6(0))* Tiger Tales.

Warnes, Tim. Tom's Tail. Warnes, Tim, tr. Jennings, Linda. 2003. 32p. (J). pap. 6.95 *(978-1-58925-383-4(3))* Tiger Tales.

Warnes, Tim, jt. illus. see Mendez, Simon.

Warnham, Hayley. The Round the World Quiz Book, 1 vol. McMillan, Sue & Lonely Planet Kids. 2017. (ENG.). 160p. (J). (gr. 1-3). pap. 11.99 *(978-1-78657-432-9(2)*, 5370) Lonely Planet Global Ltd. IRL. Dist: Hachette Bk. Group.

Warnick, Elsa. Song for the Whooping Crane. Spinelli, Eileen. 2004. 32p. (J). (gr. 3-6). 16.00 *(978-0-8028-5172-7(X))* Eerdmans, William B. Publishing Co.

Warno, Kathleen. Timmy & Tammy: The Sea Turtles Adventures. Toliver, Karen. 2019. (Timmy & Tammy the Sea Turtles Adventures Ser.: Vol. 1). (ENG.). 26p. (J). pap. 9.13 ***(978-1-5136-4613-8(3))*** Independently Published.

Warpole, Ian. Dominican Republic. De Capua, Sarah. 2004. (Discovering Cultures Ser.). 48p. (gr. 3-4). lib. bdg. 29.50 *(978-0-7614-1722-4(2))* Cavendish Square Publishing LLC.

Warren, Beverly. Little Visits with Jesus. Simon, Mary Manz. 4th ed. 2006. (Little Visits Ser.). 266p. (J). (gr. -1-3). per. 13.49 *(978-0-7586-0846-8(2))* Concordia Publishing Hse.

—My Child, My Princess: A Parable about the King. Moore, Beth. 2014. (ENG.). 32p. (J). (gr. -1-3). 9.99 *(978-1-4336-8468-5(3)*, 005673928, B&H Kids) B&H Publishing Group.

Warren, David Michael. Starjumper Goes to the Moon. Deberry, Rev Jacqueline. 2018. (ENG.). 26p. (J). pap. 14.50 *(978-1-947514-10-2(5))* St. Clair Pubns.

Warren, David Michael & Hesselbein, Kent. Starjumper. Deberry Rev, Jacqueline. 2018. (ENG.). 26p. (J). pap. 14.50 *(978-1-947514-09-6(1))* St. Clair Pubns.

Warren, F. Don Winslow: Face to Face with the Scorpion. Martinek, Frank Victor. 2011. 224p. 44.95 *(978-1-258-07493-7(1))* Literary Licensing, LLC.

—Don Winslow Breaks the Spy Net. Martinek, Frank V. 2011. 226p. 44.95 *(978-1-258-07858-4(9))* Literary Licensing, LLC.

—Don Winslow Saves the Secret Formul. Martinek, Frank V. 2011. 226p. 44.95 *(978-1-258-07446-3(X))* Literary Licensing, LLC.

Warren, Henry. What Good Will Come. Hannigan, Jana. 2016. (ENG.). 25p. (J). (gr. 3-7). 14.00 *(978-1-61851-103-4(3))* Baha'i Publishing.

Warren, Joyce. Benny's Very Special Trip. Broughton, Theresa. 2008. 20p. pap. 24.95 *(978-1-60813-165-5(3))* America Star Bks.

Warren, Leonard. Penny Penguin: A Baby Penguin's Adventures on the Ice & Snow. Colby, Carolyn. 2011. 50p. 35.95 *(978-1-258-09986-2(1))* Literary Licensing, LLC.

Warren, Shari, et al. The Beach Box: Going to the Beach/Sand/Shells. Miller, Pam et al. 2008. (Rookie Reader Ser.). (ENG.). 88p. (J). (gr. k-3). pap. 9.95 *(978-0-516-29687-6(6)*, Children's Pr.) Scholastic Library Publishing.

Warren, Shari. Benny the Big Shot Goes to Camp. Bader, Bonnie. 2012. (Penguin Young Readers: Level 3 Ser.: No. 2). (ENG.). 48p. (J). (gr. 1-3). 16.19 *(978-0-448-42894-9(6))* Penguin Young Readers Group.

—Going to the Beach. Kittinger, Jo S. 2011. (Rookie Ready to Learn Ser.). 32p. (J). (ENG.). pap. 5.95 *(978-0-531-26801-8(2))*; (gr. -1-k). lib. bdg. 23.00 *(978-0-531-25641-1(3))* Scholastic Library Publishing. (Children's Pr.).

Warren, Steven Mathew. All about Charlie Horse: Charlie Horse & His Adventures. Warren, Tania Catherine. 2012. 26p. 24.95 *(978-1-4626-5442-0(8))* America Star Bks.

Warrick, Jessica. Alien in the Outfield. Houran, Lori Haskins. 2017. (How to Be an Earthling ® Ser.: 6). (ENG.). 64p. (J). (gr. 1-3). lib. bdg. 22.65 *(978-1-57565-844-5(5))* Astra Publishing Hse.

—Alien in the Outfield (Book 6) Perseverance. Houran, Lori Haskins. 2017. (How to Be an Earthling ® Ser.: 6). (ENG.). 64p. (J). (gr. 1-3). 6.99 *(978-1-57565-848-3(8))* Astra Publishing Hse.

—Alien in the Outfield (Book 6) Perseverance. Houran, Lori Haskins. ed. 2017. (How to Be an Earthling ® Ser.: 6). (ENG.). 64p. (J). (gr. 1-3). E-Book 34.65 *(978-1-57565-852-0(6))* Astra Publishing Hse.

—Bedtime for Sarah Sullivan. Paniagua, Kelly. 2012. 36p. (J). 13.95 *(978-1-60131-119-1(2))*; pap. 10.95 *(978-1-60131-120-7(6))* Big Tent Bks. (Castlebridge Bks.).

—Daddy Tries. Janosky, Brandon. 2017. (ENG.). (J). (gr. k-4). 18.95 *(978-0-692-83634-7(9))* Janosky, Brandon.

—Earth's Got Talent! Houran, Lori Haskins. 2016. (How to Be an Earthling ® Ser.: 4). (ENG.). 64p. (J). (gr. 1-3). lib. bdg. 22.65 *(978-1-57565-827-8(5))* Astra Publishing Hse.

—Earth's Got Talent! (Book 4) Courage. Houran, Lori Haskins. ed. 2016. (How to Be an Earthling ® Ser.: 4). (ENG.). 64p. (J). (gr. 1-3). E-Book 34.65 *(978-1-57565-829-2(1))* Astra Publishing Hse.

—Fish Finelli (Book 3), Volume 3. Farber, E. S. 2016. (Fish Finelli Ser.). (ENG.). 176p. (J). (gr. 3-7). 15.99 *(978-1-4521-3815-2(X))* Chronicle Bks. LLC.

—Greetings, Sharkling! Houran, Lori Haskins. 2016. (How to Be an Earthling ® Ser.: 2). (ENG.). 64p. (J). (gr. 1-3). 22.65 *(978-1-57565-821-6(6))* Astra Publishing Hse.

—Greetings, Sharkling! (Book 2) Honesty. Houran, Lori Haskins. ed. 2016. (How to Be an Earthling ® Ser.: 2). (ENG.). 64p. (J). (gr. 1-3). E-Book 34.65 *(978-1-57565-823-0(2))* Astra Publishing Hse.

—Hammer & Nails. Bledsoe, Josh. 2016. (ENG.). 32p. (J). (gr. k-2). 17.95 *(978-1-936261-36-9(7))* Flashlight Pr.

—Librarians of the Galaxy. Harkrader, Lisa. 2018. (How to Be an Earthling ® Ser.). (ENG.). 64p. (J). (gr. 1-3). 22.65 *(978-1-63592-023-9(X))* Astra Publishing Hse.

—Librarians of the Galaxy (Book 11) Acceptance. Harkrader, Lisa. 2018. (How to Be an Earthling ® Ser.). (ENG.). 64p. (J). (gr. 1-3). pap. 6.99 *(978-1-63592-024-6(8))* Astra Publishing Hse.

—The Lucky Tale of Two Dogs. Rosenthal, Cathy M. 2012. 40p. (J). pap. 12.95 *(978-0-9853752-0-1(5))* Pet Pundit Publishing.

—May the Votes Be with You (Book 7) Citizenship. Harkrader, Lisa. ed. 2017. (How to Be an Earthling ® Ser.: 7). (ENG.). 64p. (J). (gr. 1-3). E-Book 34.65 *(978-1-57565-853-7(4))* Astra Publishing Hse.

—Money Doesn't Grow on Mars. Houran, Lori Haskins. 2017. (How to Be an Earthling ® Ser.: 8). (ENG.). 64p. (J). (gr. 1-3). lib. bdg. 22.65 *(978-1-57565-846-9(1))* Astra Publishing Hse.

—Money Doesn't Grow on Mars (Book 8) Self-Control. Houran, Lori Haskins. 2017. (How to Be an Earthling ® Ser.: 8). (ENG.). 64p. (J). (gr. 1-3). 6.99 *(978-1-57565-850-6(X))* Astra Publishing Hse.

—Money Doesn't Grow on Mars (Book 8) Self-Control. Houran, Lori Haskins. ed. 2017. (How to Be an Earthling ® Ser.: 8). (ENG.). 64p. (J). (gr. 1-3). E-Book 34.65 *(978-1-57565-854-4(2))* Astra Publishing Hse.

—Monsters Monsters Go Away. Landgraf, James, Jr. 2008. 40p. (J). 8.99 *(978-0-9819283-0-2(7))* Makdan Publishing.

—No Place Like Space. Harkrader, Lisa. 2017. (How to Be an Earthling ® Ser.: 5). (ENG.). 64p. (J). (gr. 1-3). lib. bdg. 22.65 *(978-1-57565-843-8(7))* Astra Publishing Hse.

—No Place Like Space (Book 5) Kindness. Harkrader, Lisa. ed. 2017. (How to Be an Earthling ® Ser.: 5). (ENG.). 64p. (J). (gr. 1-3). E-Book 34.65 *(978-1-57565-851-3(8))* Astra Publishing Hse.

—One Small Step for Spork. Houran, Lori Haskins. 2018. (How to Be an Earthling ® Ser.). (ENG.). 64p. (J). (gr. 1-3). 22.65 *(978-1-63592-026-0(4))* Astra Publishing Hse.

—One Small Step for Spork (Book 12) Cooperation. Houran, Lori Haskins. 2018. (How to Be an Earthling ® Ser.). (ENG.). 64p. (J). (gr. 1-3). pap. 6.99 *(978-1-63592-027-7(2))* Astra Publishing Hse.

—Parks & Wrecks. Houran, Lori Haskins. 2018. (How to Be an Earthling ® Ser.). (ENG.). 64p. (J). (gr. 1-3). 22.65 *(978-1-63592-020-8(5))* Astra Publishing Hse.

—Parks & Wrecks (Book 10) Generosity. Houran, Lori Haskins. 2018. (How to Be an Earthling ® Ser.). (ENG.). 64p. (J). (gr. 1-3). pap. 6.99 *(978-1-63592-021-5(3))* Astra Publishing Hse.

—Planet of the Eggs. Harkrader, Lisa. 2018. (How to Be an Earthling ® Ser.). (ENG.). 64p. (J). (gr. 1-3). 22.65 *(978-1-63592-017-8(5))* Astra Publishing Hse.

—Planet of the Eggs (Book 9) Patience. Harkrader, Lisa. 2018. (How to Be an Earthling ® Ser.). (ENG.). 64p. (J). (gr. 1-3). pap. 6.99 *(978-1-63592-018-5(3))* Astra Publishing Hse.

—Spork Out of Orbit. Walker, Nan. 2016. (How to Be an Earthling ® Ser.: 1). (ENG.). 64p. (J). (gr. 1-3). 22.65 *(978-1-57565-818-6(6))* Astra Publishing Hse.

—Spork Out of Orbit (Book 1) Respect. Walker, Nan. ed. 2016. (How to Be an Earthling ® Ser.: 1). (ENG.). 64p. (J). (gr. 1-3). E-Book 34.65 *(978-1-57565-820-9(8))* Astra Publishing Hse.

—Take Me to Your Weeder. Morris, Kimberly. 2016. (How to Be an Earthling ® Ser.: 3). (ENG.). 64p. (J). (gr. 1-3). lib. bdg. 22.65 *(978-1-57565-824-7(0))* Astra Publishing Hse.

—Take Me to Your Weeder (Book 3) Responsibility. Morris, Kimberly. ed. 2016. (How to Be an Earthling ® Ser.: 3). (ENG.). 64p. (J). (gr. 1-3). E-Book 34.65 *(978-1-57565-826-1(7))* Astra Publishing Hse.

—The Wishmakers. Whitesides, Tyler. 2018. (Wishmakers Ser.: 1). (ENG.). (J). (gr. 3-7). 352p. pap. 6.99 *(978-0-06-256832-8(9))*; 336p. 16.99 *(978-0-06-256831-1(0))* HarperCollins Pubs.

Warter, Fred. Annie Oakley. Kunstler, James Howard. 2004. (Rabbit Ears-A Classic Tale Ser.). (ENG.). 36p. (J). (gr. 2-6). 28.50 *(978-1-59197-759-9(2)*, 12920, Picture Bk.) Spotlight.

Warwick, Anne. The Wood Scrogs. Hawk'sbee, Sylvia. 2017. (ENG.). 58p. (J). pap. *(978-1-911412-41-0(8))* Dolman Scott Ltd.

Warwick, Carrie. La Bandera de Estrellas Centelleantes: El Bimno Nacional. Welch, Catherine A. 2005. (Yo Solo - Historia (on My Own - History) Ser.). (SPA.). 48p. (J). (gr. 2-5). per. 6.95 *(978-0-8225-3115-9(1))* Lerner Publishing Group.

—The Star-Spangled Banner. Welch, Catherine A. 2004. (On My Own History Ser.). 48p. (J). (gr. 1-3). pap. 6.95 *(978-1-57505-697-5(6))*; (ENG.). (gr. 2-4). 25.26 *(978-1-57505-590-9(2))* Lerner Publishing Group.

Warwick, Carrie H. La Bandera de Estrellas Centelleantes: El Himno Nacional. Welch, Catherine A. Translations.com Staff, tr. 2005. (Yo Solo: Historia (on My Own History) Ser.).Tr. of Star-Spangled Banner. (SPA.). 48p. (J). (gr. 2-4). lib. bdg. 25.32 *(978-0-8225-3114-2(3)*, Ediciones Lerner) Lerner Publishing Group.

Warwick, Richard. Media Muscle: Body Image & the Media for Guys. Cox, Lisa. 2012. 40p. (gr. 8-12). pap. *(978-1-921633-62-1(X))* Wombat Bks.

Waryanto, Ian. Spotlight Soccer, 1 vol. Sanchez, Ricardo. 2014. (Sports Illustrated Kids Graphic Novels Ser.). (ENG.). 72p. (J). (gr. 3-8). 26.65 *(978-1-4342-4165-8(3),* Stone Arch Bks.) Capstone.

Wasden, Kevin. Hazzardous Universe. Wright, Julie. 2011. 242p. (J). pap. *(978-1-60861-206-2(6))* Covenant Communications.

Washburn, Calista, photos by. 20 Recipes Kids Should Know. Washburn, Esme. 2019. (ENG., 52p. (J). (gr. 5-9). 16.95 *(978-3-7913-8507-5(0))* Prestel Verlag GmbH & Co KG. DEU. Dist: Penguin Random Hse. LLC.

Washburn, Cecilia. Grateful Gracie: A Story about Gratitude. Tissot Lcsw, Jennifer. 2013. 34p. pap. 14.95 *(978-0-9882804-1-0(8))* Grateful Day Pr.

Washburn, Lucia. A Baby Panda Is Born. Ostby, Kristin. 2008. (All Aboard Science Reader Station Stop 2 Ser.). 48p. (J). (gr. 1-3). 16.19 *(978-0-448-44720-9(7))* Penguin Young Readers Group.

—Cheetah Cubs. Clarke, Ginjer L. 2007. (Penguin Young Readers, Level 3 Ser.). (ENG.). 48p. (J). (gr. 1-3). mass mkt. 4.99 *(978-0-448-44361-4(9),* Penguin Young Readers) Penguin Young Readers Group.

—Cheetah Cubs. Clarke, Ginjer L. 2007. (All Aboard Science Reader Ser.). 48p. (gr. 1-3). 14.00 *(978-0-7569-8169-3(7))* Perfection Learning Corp.

—Did Dinosaurs Have Feathers? Zoehfeld, Kathleen Weidner. (Let's-Read-and-Find-Out Science Ser.). 40p. (J). (gr. k-4). 2004. (ENG.). 15.99 *(978-0-06-029026-9(9));* 2004. lib. bdg. 16.89 *(978-0-06-029027-6(7));* 2003. (ENG.). pap. 5.99 *(978-0-06-445218-2(2))* HarperCollins Pubs.

—Dinosaur Tracks. Zoehfeld, Kathleen Weidner. 2007. (Let's-Read-And-Find-Out Science 2 Ser.). (ENG.). 40p. (J). (gr. k-4). pap. 6.99 *(978-0-06-445217-5(4))* HarperCollins Pubs.

—Where Did Dinosaurs Come From? Zoehfeld, Kathleen Weidner. 2010. (Let's-Read-And-Find-Out Science 2 Ser.). (ENG.). 40p. (J). (gr. k-4). pap. 5.99 *(978-0-06-445216-8(6))* HarperCollins Pubs.

Washington, C. E., jt. illus. see Smoak, I. W.

Washington, Christopher. High School Chronicles: Megan's Story. Sunflowerj. 2020. (High School Chronicles Ser.: Vol. 1). (ENG.). 306p. (J). pap. 12.00 ***(978-1-9739-4065-4(5))*** CreateSpace Independent Publishing Platform.

Washington, Joi. Penguin Baby. Lynch, Michelle. 2012. (1G Science Ser.). (ENG.). 28p. (J). pap. 8.00 *(978-1-61406-167-0(X))* American Reading Co.

—These Are Wolves. Fleischer, Jayson. 2016. (2G Predator Animals Ser.). (ENG.). 28p. (J). (gr. k-2). pap. 8.00 *(978-1-61541-508-3(4))* American Reading Co.

Washington, Joi. The Pink Book. Washington, Joi. 2014. (1-3Y Color My World Ser.). (ENG.). 20p. (J). (gr. k-2). pap. 8.00 *(978-1-61541-161-0(5))* American Reading Co.

—This Is a Savannah. Washington, Joi. Taylor, Trace & Zorzi, Gina. 2010. (1-3Y Ecosystems Ser.). (ENG.). 20p. (J). (gr. k-2). pap. 9.60 *(978-1-61541-226-6(3))* American Reading Co.

—This Is an Ocean. Washington, Joi. Taylor, Trace et al. 2010. (2G Ecosystems Ser.). (SPA & ENG.). 28p. (J). (gr. k-2). pap. 9.60 *(978-1-61541-224-2(7))* American Reading Co.

—Wolves. Washington, Joi. Dibble, Traci. 2010. (1-3Y Animals Ser.). (ENG.). 16p. (J). (gr. k-2). pap. 9.60 *(978-1-61541-363-8(4))* American Reading Co.

Washington, Jordan Caleb. Don't Get It Twisted!! Ag, Tarsha M. Washington Illustrations B. 2016. (ENG.). (J). pap. 10.99 *(978-1-4984-5860-3(2))* Salem Author Services.

Wasiak, Maria. Mango, the Scaredy Bat. Wasiak, Maria. 2016. (ENG.). 32p. (J). (gr. 1-3). pap. *(978-0-9946242-0-8(4))* Province Pr.

Wasielewski, Margaret. Mariam's Easter Parade. Markarian, Marianne. 2015. 32p. (J). 16.00 *(978-0-9767377-1-1(X))* Pomegranate Publishing.

Wasielewski, Margaret M. The Pesky Bird, Markarian, Marianne. l.t. ed. 2005. 32p. (J). 16.00 *(978-0-9767377-0-4(1))* Pomegranate Publishing.

Wasikhongo, Odalo Magruder. My First Book of Numbers. Wasikhongo, Odalo Magruder. 2012. 24p. pap. 5.00 *(978-0-9845203-2-9(5))* WasiWorks Studio LLC.

Wasowicz, Pawel. Tres Osos. Koons, Linda. 2016. (Early Rising Readers Ser.). (SPA.). (J). (gr. -1). 6.67 *(978-1-4788-3659-9(8))* Newmark Learning LLC.

Wass, Chip. Don't Feed the Bear. Doherty, Kathleen. 2018. 32p. (J). (gr. -1). 16.95 *(978-1-4549-1979-7(5))* Sterling Publishing Co., Inc.

—Monster Knows Math. Capote, Lori. 2013. (Monster Knows Math Ser.). (ENG.). 24p. (J). (gr. -1-3). lib. bdg., lib. bdg., lib. bdg. 75.96 *(978-1-4048-7950-8(1),* Picture Window Bks.) Capstone.

—Monster Knows More Than, Less Than, 1 vol. Capote, Lori. 2013. (Monster Knows Math Ser.). (ENG.). 24p. (J). (gr. -1-3). lib. bdg. 25.32 *(978-1-4048-7947-8(1),* Picture Window Bks.) Capstone.

—Monster Knows Numbers, 1 vol. Capote, Lori. 2013. (Monster Knows Math Ser.). (ENG.). 24p. (J). (gr. -1-3). lib. bdg. 25.32 *(978-1-4048-7946-1(3),* Picture Window Bks.) Capstone.

—Monster Knows Patterns, 1 vol. Capote, Lori. 2013. (Monster Knows Math Ser.). (ENG.). 24p. (J). (gr. -1-3). lib. bdg. 25.32 *(978-1-4048-7949-2(8),* Picture Window Bks.) Capstone.

Wasserman, Curt, et al. The Adventures of Ruff-N-Rescue: Adventures with the Heroes of New Barker Island. Wasserman, Shannon & Wasserman, Curt. 2006. 40p. (J). (gr. -1-3). 16.95 *(978-1-931643-87-0(3))* Seven Locks Pr.

Wassillie, Eliza, et al. Four Legged Adventures. Wassillie, Eliza et al. 2006. (Adventure Story Collection Ser.). 28p. (J). (gr. 2-6). pap. 10.00 *(978-1-58084-250-1(X))* Lower Kuskokwim Schl. District.

Wasson, Dave. The Big Ideas of Buster Bickles. Wasson, Dave. 2015. (ENG.). 40p. (J). (gr. -1-3). 17.99 *(978-0-06-229178-3(5))* HarperCollins Pubs.

Wasvary, Marcia. Mr G Clef & Friends. George, Francis. 2012. 32p. 24.95 *(978-1-4560-9642-7(7))* America Star Bks.

Watanabe, Bryce. Emma's Adventure: Mommy's Work Trip. Kapaona, Alyssa. 2019. (ENG.). 36p. (J). 14.99 *(978-1-58351-173-2(3),* 13632) Univ. of Hawaii Pr.

Watanabe, Kaori. Fairy Goodnight Kisses. Michalak, Jamie. 2008. 24p. (J). (gr. 4-7). bds. 7.95 *(978-1-58925-841-9(X))* Tiger Tales.

—Fairy Tea Party. Michalak, Jamie. 2008. 24p. (J). (gr. -1-3). bds. 7.95 *(978-1-58925-840-2(1))* Tiger Tales.

—Thank You Prayer. Grace, Will. Geist, Ken, ed. 2006. (My First Taggies Book Ser.). 10p. (J). (gr. k — 1). 12.99 *(978-0-439-87564-6(1),* Cartwheel Bks.) Scholastic, Inc.

Watanabe, Kaori. I Love You. Watanabe, Kaori. 2004. (My First Taggies Book Ser.). (ENG.). 3p. (J). (gr. -1 — 1). 12.99 *(978-0-439-64947-6(1),* Cartwheel Bks.) Scholastic, Inc.

Watanabe-Rocco, Sarah, jt. illus. see Rocco, Frank.

Watanabe, Rui. FAIRY TAIL Blue Mistral 4. Mashima, Hiro. 2018. (Fairy Tail: Blue Mistral Ser.: 4). (ENG.). 176p. (gr. 8-12). pap. 10.99 *(978-1-63236-530-9(8))* Kodansha America, Inc.

Watase, Yû. Bandit, 4. Watase, Yû. 2nd ed. 2004. (Fushigi Yugi Ser.). (ENG.). 200p. (YA). pap. 9.95 *(978-1-56931-993-2(6))* Viz Media.

Watase, Yuu. The Lost Word, 7 vols. Watase, Yuu. Caselman, Lance. 2004. (Alice 19th Ser.). (ENG.). 200p. pap. 9.99 *(978-1-59116-244-5(0))* Viz Media.

Watchorn, Sara. Sara Fay & the Elementals: Book 5: Quazzie & the Rock Kingdom. Watchorn, Sara. 2017. (Sara Fay & the Elementals Ser.: Vol. 5). (ENG.). (J). pap. 16.95 *(978-0-9990474-6-0(9))* Watchorn Motion.

—Sara Fay & the Elementals: Book 5: Quest & Meditation Journal. Watchorn, Sara. 2017. (ENG.). (J). pap. 10.95 *(978-0-9990474-7-7(7))* Watchorn Motion.

Water Raven, Sarah. The Five Demons You Meet in Hell. Carter, Timothy. 2013. (Boston Lefebvre Ser.: Vol. 1). (ENG.). 324p. (J). pap. 12.00 ***(978-1-0784-8305-6(1))*** Independently Published.

Watercolor Classes at Clark College Cont. I See You: In English & Amharic. Ready Set Go. Mulat, Worku L., tr. 2019. (ENG.). 38p. (J). pap. 9.99 *(978-1-7932-4613-4(0))* Independently Published.

Waterfield, Sarah. Rafi's Indian Dream - Hindi Version रफी का भारतीय सपना रफी का भारतीय सपना Gothard, Nicola. 2017. (HIN.). (J). (gr. 1-6). pap. *(978-1-9998608-1-3(0))* Generation 2050.

—Who Invited the Bees? Brown, Beatrice. Eaton, Shayla L., ed. 2018. (ENG.). 28p. (J). (gr. 1-3). 14.95 *(978-0-9983360-1-5(7))* Brown, Beatrice W.

Waterhouse, Stephen. My Pop-Up World Atlas. Ganeri, Anita. 2012. (ENG.). 16p. (J). (gr. k-3). 19.99 *(978-0-7636-6094-9(9),* Templar) Candlewick Pr.

—Raju's Ride. Mitchell, Pratima. 2005. (ENG.). 24p. (J). lib. bdg. 23.65 *(978-1-59646-726-2(6))* Dingles & Co.

Waterkeyn, Lana. Ask Mummy or Daddy. Vort, Carl. 2019. (ENG.). 100p. (J). pap. *(978-1-78623-517-6(X))* Grosvenor Hse. Publishing Ltd.

Watermark Rights Limited. Rainbow of Recipes (Butterbean's Cafe) Huntley, Tex. 2019. (ENG.). 128p. (J). (gr. -1-2). pap. 7.99 *(978-1-9848-4936-6(0),* Golden Bks.) Random Hse. Children's Bks.

—Sleepover Surprise (Sunny Day) Tillworth, Mary. 2019. (Little Golden Book Ser.). (ENG.). 24p. (J). (-k). 4.99 *(978-0-525-64737-9(6),* Golden Bks.) Random Hse. Children's Bks.

Waters, Alice. Into the Ocean. Coren, Giles. 2020. (ENG.). 10p. (J). (gr. -1-k). bds. 9.99 *(978-1-4197-3355-0(9),* 1259810, Abrams Appleseed) Abrams, Inc.

Waters, Beth. Child of St Kilda. Waters, Beth. 2019. (Child's Play Library). (ENG.). 64p. (J). *(978-1-78628-188-3(0))* Child's Play International Ltd.

Waters, Erica-Jane. Beach Bummer. Jakubowski, Michele. 2014. (Perfectly Poppy Ser.). (ENG.). 32p. (J). (gr. k-2). lib. bdg. 22.65 *(978-1-4795-2284-2(8),* Picture Window Bks.) Capstone.

—The Big Bike. Jakubowski, Michele. 2015. (Perfectly Poppy Ser.). (ENG.). 32p. (J). (gr. k-2). 22.65 *(978-1-4795-5801-8(X),* Picture Window Bks.) Capstone.

—Bubble Gum Rescue. Perelman, Helen. 2012. (Candy Fairies Ser.: 8). (ENG.). 128p. (J). (gr. 2-5). pap. 5.99 *(978-1-4424-2217-9(3),* Aladdin) Simon & Schuster Children's Publishing.

—Candy Fairies 3-Books-In-1! #2: Cool Mint; Magic Hearts; the Sugar Ball, 3 bks. in 1. Perelman, Helen. 2016. (Candy Fairies Ser.). (ENG.). 320p. (J). (gr. 2-5). pap. 8.99 *(978-1-4814-8566-1(0),* Simon & Schuster/Paula Wiseman Bks.) Simon & Schuster/Paula Wiseman Bks.

—A Candy Fairies Sweet Collection: Chocolate Dreams; Rainbow Swirl; Caramel Moon; Cool Mint. Perelman, Helen. ed. 2013. (Candy Fairies Ser.). (ENG.). 512p. (J). (gr. 2-5). pap. 23.99 *(978-1-4424-9390-2(9),* Aladdin) Simon & Schuster Children's Publishing.

—Candy Fairies Sweet-Tacular Collection Books 1-10: Chocolate Dreams; Rainbow Swirl; Caramel Moon; Cool Mint; Magic Hearts; the Sugar Ball; a Valentine's Surprise; Bubble Gum Rescue; Double Dip; Jelly Bean Jumble. Perelman, Helen. ed. 2019. (Candy Fairies Ser.). (ENG.). 1280p. (J). (gr. 2-5). pap. 59.99 *(978-1-5344-5572-6(8),* Aladdin) Simon & Schuster Children's Publishing.

—Caramel Moon. Perelman, Helen. 2010. (Candy Fairies Ser.: 3). (ENG.). 128p. (J). (gr. 2-5). pap. 5.99 *(978-1-4169-9456-5(4),* Aladdin) Simon & Schuster Children's Publishing.

—Caramel Moon. Perelman, Helen. 2013. (Candy Fairies Ser.: 3). (ENG.). 128p. (J). (gr. 2-5). 15.99 *(978-1-4424-5922-9(0),* Simon & Schuster/Paula Wiseman Bks.) Simon & Schuster/Paula Wiseman Bks.

—Chocolate Dreams. Perelman, Helen. 2010. (Candy Fairies Ser.: 1). (ENG.). 128p. (J). (gr. 2-5). pap. 5.99 *(978-1-4169-9454-1(8),* Aladdin) Simon & Schuster Children's Publishing.

—Chocolate Dreams. Perelman, Helen. 2012. (Candy Fairies Ser.: 1). (ENG.). 128p. (J). (gr. 2-5). 15.99 *(978-1-4424-5775-1(9),* Simon & Schuster/Paula Wiseman Bks.) Simon & Schuster/Paula Wiseman Bks.

—The Chocolate Rose. Perelman, Helen. 2013. (Candy Fairies Ser.: 11). (ENG.). 128p. (J). (gr. 2-5). pap. 5.99 *(978-1-4424-5299-2(4),* Aladdin) Simon & Schuster Children's Publishing.

—The Chocolate Rose. Perelman, Helen. 2013. (Candy Fairies Ser.: 11). (ENG.). 128p. (J). (gr. 2-5). 15.99 *(978-1-4424-6499-5(2),* Simon & Schuster/Paula Wiseman Bks.) Simon & Schuster/Paula Wiseman Bks.

—The Coconut Clue. Perelman, Helen. 2015. (Candy Fairies Ser.: 17). (ENG.). 128p. (J). (gr. 2-5). pap. 5.99 *(978-1-4814-0616-1(7),* Aladdin) Simon & Schuster Children's Publishing.

—Coconut Jack. Lewis, Jill & Blue Bananas. 2009. (Blue Bananas Ser.). (ENG.). 48p. (J). (gr. k-2). pap. 5.99 *(978-1-4052-4132-8(2))* Egmont Bks., Ltd. GBR. Dist: Independent Pubs. Group.

—Cool Mint. Perelman, Helen. 2010. (Candy Fairies Ser.: 4). (ENG.). 128p. (J). (gr. 2-5). pap. 5.99 *(978-1-4169-9457-2(2),* Aladdin) Simon & Schuster Children's Publishing.

—Double Dip. Perelman, Helen. 2012. (Candy Fairies Ser.: 9). (ENG.). 128p. (J). (gr. 2-5). pap. 5.99 *(978-1-4424-2219-3(X),* Aladdin) Simon & Schuster Children's Publishing.

—Double Dip. Perelman, Helen. 2012. (Candy Fairies Ser.: 9). (ENG.). 128p. (J). (gr. 2-5). 15.99 *(978-1-4424-5972-4(7),* Simon & Schuster/Paula Wiseman Bks.) Simon & Schuster/Paula Wiseman Bks.

—The Elves & the Shoemaker. Tiger Tales. 2017. (My First Fairy Tales Ser.). (ENG.). 32p. (J). (gr. -1-2). pap. 7.99 *(978-1-58925-496-1(1))* Tiger Tales.

—Emma Peror's New Clothes. Guillian, Adam et al. 2015. (Fairy Tales Today Ser.). (ENG.). 24p. (J). (gr. -1-2). 23.99 *(978-1-4795-8617-2(X),* Picture Window Bks.) Capstone.

—Frozen Treats. Perelman, Helen. 2014. (Candy Fairies Ser.: 13). (ENG.). 128p. (J). (gr. 2-5). pap. 5.99 *(978-1-4424-5303-6(6),* Aladdin) Simon & Schuster Children's Publishing.

—Gooey Goblins: Halloween Special. Perelman, Helen. 2011. (Candy Fairies Ser.). (ENG.). 176p. (J). (gr. 2-5). pap. 6.99 *(978-1-4424-2213-1(0),* Aladdin) Simon & Schuster Children's Publishing.

—Gooey Goblins: Halloween Special. Perelman, Helen. 2013. (Candy Fairies Ser.). (ENG.). 176p. (J). (gr. 2-5). 15.99 *(978-1-4424-6495-7(X),* Simon & Schuster/Paula Wiseman Bks.) Simon & Schuster/Paula Wiseman Bks.

—Jelly Bean Jumble. Perelman, Helen. 2013. (Candy Fairies Ser.: 10). (ENG.). 128p. (J). (gr. 2-5). pap. 5.99 *(978-1-4424-5297-8(8),* Aladdin) Simon & Schuster Children's Publishing.

—Jelly Bean Jumble. Perelman, Helen. 2013. (Candy Fairies Ser.: 10). (ENG.). 128p. (J). (gr. 2-5). 15.99 *(978-1-4424-6000-3(8),* Simon & Schuster/Paula Wiseman Bks.) Simon & Schuster/Paula Wiseman Bks.

—Magic Hearts, 5. Perelman, Helen. 2011. (Candy Fairies Ser.: 5). (ENG.). 128p. (J). (gr. 2-5). pap. 5.99 *(978-1-4424-0823-4(5),* Aladdin) Simon & Schuster Children's Publishing.

—Magic Hearts. Perelman, Helen. 2013. (Candy Fairies Ser.: 5). (ENG.). 128p. (J). (gr. 2-5). 15.99 *(978-1-4424-6494-0(1),* Simon & Schuster/Paula Wiseman Bks.) Simon & Schuster/Paula Wiseman Bks.

—Marshmallow Mystery. Perelman, Helen. 2014. (Candy Fairies Ser.: 12). (ENG.). 128p. (J). (gr. 2-5). 15.99 *(978-1-4424-6500-8(X));* pap. 5.99 *(978-1-4424-5301-2(X))* Simon & Schuster Children's Publishing. (Aladdin).

—Mini Sweets. Perelman, Helen. 2017. (Candy Fairies Ser.: 20). (ENG.). 128p. (J). (gr. 2-5). pap. 5.99 *(978-1-4814-4683-9(5),* Simon & Schuster/Paula Wiseman Bks.) Simon & Schuster/Paula Wiseman Bks.

—A Minty Mess. Perelman, Helen. 2016. (Candy Fairies Ser.: 19). (ENG.). 128p. (J). (gr. 2-5). pap. 5.99 *(978-1-4814-4680-8(0),* Aladdin) Simon & Schuster Children's Publishing.

—A Minty Mess. Perelman, Helen. 2016. (Candy Fairies Ser.: 19). (ENG.). 128p. (J). (gr. 2-5). 16.99 *(978-1-4814-4681-5(9),* Simon & Schuster/Paula Wiseman Bks.) Simon & Schuster/Paula Wiseman Bks.

—On the Seashore. Milbourne, Anna. 2006. 24p. (J). (gr. -1-3). 9.99 *(978-0-7945-1069-5(8),* Usborne) EDC Publishing.

—Outside Surprise. Jakubowski, Michele. 2015. (Perfectly Poppy Ser.). (ENG.). 32p. (J). (gr. k-2). 22.65 *(978-1-4795-5802-5(8),* Picture Window Bks.) Capstone.

—The Peppermint Princess: Super Special. Perelman, Helen. 2016. (Candy Fairies Ser.). (ENG.). 176p. (J). (gr. 2-5). pap. 6.99 *(978-1-4814-4686-0(X),* Aladdin) Simon & Schuster Children's Publishing.

—Pinky Bloom & the Case of the Missing Kiddush Cup. Press, Judy. 2018. (ENG.). 80p. (J). (gr. 3-6). 16.99 *(978-1-5415-4234-1(7),* Kar-Ben Publishing) Lerner Publishing Group.

—Poppy's Puppy. Jakubowski, Michele. 2015. (Perfectly Poppy Ser.). (ENG.). 32p. (J). (gr. k-2). 22.65 *(978-1-4795-5799-8(4),* Picture Window Bks.) Capstone.

—Rainbow Swirl, 2. Perelman, Helen. 2010. (Candy Fairies Ser.: 2). (ENG.). 128p. (J). (gr. 2-5). pap. 5.99 *(978-1-4169-9455-8(6),* Aladdin) Simon & Schuster Children's Publishing.

—Rainbow Swirl. Perelman, Helen. 2012. (Candy Fairies Ser.: 2). (ENG.). 128p. (J). (gr. 2-5). 15.99 *(978-1-4424-5776-8(7),* cvvc, Simon & Schuster/Paula Wiseman Bks.) Simon & Schuster/Paula Wiseman Bks.

—Rock Candy Treasure. Perelman, Helen. 2016. (Candy Fairies Ser.: 18). (ENG.). 128p. (J). (gr. 2-5). pap. 5.99 *(978-1-4814-4677-8(0),* Aladdin) Simon & Schuster Children's Publishing.

—A Royal Wedding: Super Special. Perelman, Helen. 2013. (Candy Fairies Ser.). (ENG.). 208p. (J). (gr. 2-5). pap. 5.99 *(978-1-4424-8898-4(0),* Aladdin) Simon & Schuster Children's Publishing.

—A Royal Wedding: Super Special. Perelman, Helen. 2013. (Candy Fairies Ser.). (ENG.). 208p. (J). (gr. 2-5). 15.99 *(978-1-4424-8899-1(9),* Simon & Schuster/Paula Wiseman Bks.) Simon & Schuster/Paula Wiseman Bks.

—Scholastic Reader Level 2: Flash Forward Fairy Tales: Snow White & the Seven Dogs. Meister, Cari. 2014. (Scholastic Reader Level 2 Ser.). (ENG.). 32p. (J). (gr. 1-2). pap. 3.99 *(978-0-545-56569-1(3))* Scholastic, Inc.

—Snowy Blast. Jakubowski, Michele. 2014. (Perfectly Poppy Ser.). (ENG.). 32p. (J). (gr. k-2). lib. bdg. 22.65 *(978-1-4795-2283-5(X),* Picture Window Bks.) Capstone.

—Soccer Star. Jakubowski, Michele. 2015. (Perfectly Poppy Ser.). (ENG.). 32p. (J). (gr. k-2). 22.65 *(978-1-4795-5800-1(1),* Picture Window Bks.) Capstone.

—The Sugar Ball. Perelman, Helen. 2011. (Candy Fairies Ser.: 6). (ENG.). 128p. (J). (gr. 2-5). pap. 5.99 *(978-1-4424-0825-8(1),* Aladdin) Simon & Schuster Children's Publishing.

—The Sugar Ball. Perelman, Helen. 2013. (Candy Fairies Ser.: 6). (ENG.). 128p. (J). (gr. 2-5). 15.99 *(978-1-4424-6498-8(4),* Simon & Schuster/Paula Wiseman Bks.) Simon & Schuster/Paula Wiseman Bks.

—Sweet Secrets. Perelman, Helen. 2015. (Candy Fairies Ser.: 15). (ENG.). 128p. (J). (gr. 2-5). pap. 5.99 *(978-1-4814-0610-9(8),* Aladdin) Simon & Schuster Children's Publishing.

—Taffy Trouble. Perelman, Helen. 2015. (Candy Fairies Ser.: 16). (ENG.). 128p. (J). (gr. -1-5). pap. 5.99 *(978-1-4814-0613-0(2),* Aladdin) Simon & Schuster Children's Publishing.

—Talent Trouble. Jakubowski, Michele. 2014. (Perfectly Poppy Ser.). (ENG.). 32p. (J). (gr. k-2). lib. bdg. 22.65 *(978-1-4795-2281-1(3),* Picture Window Bks.) Capstone.

—A Valentine's Surprise, 7. Perelman, Helen. 2011. (Candy Fairies Ser.: 7). (ENG.). 128p. (J). (gr. 2-5). pap. 5.99 *(978-1-4424-2215-5(7),* Aladdin) Simon & Schuster Children's Publishing.

Waters, Erica-Jane. If the Hat Fits. Waters, Erica-Jane. (Miss Bunsen's School for Brilliant Girls Ser.). (ENG.). 128p. (J). (gr. 1-5). 2020. pap. 5.99 ***(978-0-8075-5154-7(6),*** 807551546); 2019. 14.99 *(978-0-8075-5157-8(0),* 807551570) Whitman, Albert & Co.

—Light As a Feather. Waters, Erica-Jane. 2020. (Miss Bunsen's School for Brilliant Girls Ser.). (ENG.). 128p. (J). (gr. 1-5). pap. 5.99 ***(978-0-8075-5153-0(8),*** 807551538) Whitman, Albert & Co.

Waters, Erica-Jane. Light As a Feather. Waters, Erica-Jane. Waters, Erica-Jane. 2019. (Miss Bunsen's School for Brilliant Girls Ser.: 2). (ENG.). 128p. (J). (gr. 1-5). 14.99 *(978-0-8075-5158-5(9),* 807551589) Whitman, Albert & Co.

Waters, Erica-Jane. Penny for Your Thoughts. Waters, Erica-Jane. 2020. (Miss Bunsen's School for Brilliant Girls Ser.). (ENG.). 128p. (J). (gr. 1-5). pap. 5.99 ***(978-0-8075-5138-7(4),*** 0807551384); 14.99 ***(978-0-8075-5159-2(7),*** 807551597) Whitman, Albert & Co.

Waters, Fiona. Giant Tales from Around the World. Hall, Amanda. 2004. 96p. (J). 17.95 *(978-1-84458-143-6(8))* Avalon Publishing.

—The Princess & the Rainbow Coat. Negrin, Fabian. 2005. 32p. (J). *(978-1-84458-411-6(9),* Pavilion Children's Books) Pavilion Bks.

Waters, Galadriel. New Clues to Harry Potter: Hints from the Ultimate Unofficial Guide to the Mysteries of Harry Potter, Vol. 5. Waters, Galadriel. Mithrandir, Astre. 2003. (ENG.). 88p. (gr. 3-6). pap. 10.95 *(978-0-9723936-2-1(5),* 1230146) Wizarding World Pr.

Waters, Ruth. There's a Tiger Out There. Masson, Sophie. 2020. (ENG.). 32p. (J). (gr. -1-k). 18.99 ***(978-1-76050-144-0(1))*** Little Hare Bks. AUS. Dist: Independent Pubs. Group.

Waters, Susy Pilgrim. Mission: Sisterhood. Vander Pluym, Andrea. 2010. 80p. (YA). *(978-0-88441-753-8(0))* Girl Scouts of the USA.

Waters, Tony. Cinnamon's Busy Year. Waters, Tony. 2003. 32p. (J). (gr. -1-3). pap. 5.95 *(978-0-9710278-2-4(X))* All About Kids Publishing.

Waterton, Betty & Blades, Ann. Pettranella. Waterton, Betty. 2003. (J). pap. 5.95 *(978-0-88899-108-9(8))* Groundwood Bks. CAN. Dist: Publishers Group West (PGW).

Watjen, Laureen. Stowaways to Smith Island: Hayden & Chloe's Enchanted Journey with the Nurses to Maryland's Mysterious Smith Island. Davidson, Michele R. 2004. 128p. (J). pap. 8.95 *(978-0-9754170-1-0(0))* Smith Island Foundation.

Watkins, Abbey. The Blessed. Hurley, Tonya. 2012. (Blessed Ser.). (ENG.). 416p. (YA). (gr. 9). 17.99 *(978-1-4424-2951-2(8),* Simon & Schuster Bks. For Young Readers) Simon & Schuster Bks. For Young Readers.

—Precious Blood. Hurley, Tonya. 2013. (Blessed Ser.). (ENG.). 432p. (YA). (gr. 9). pap. 9.99 *(978-1-4424-2952-9(6),* Simon & Schuster Bks. For Young Readers) Simon & Schuster Bks. For Young Readers.

Watkins, Adam. Stubborn as a Mule & Other Silly Similes. Loewen, Nancy. (Ways to Say It Ser.). (ENG.). 24p. (J). (gr. 3-5). 2011. pap. 7.49 *(978-1-4048-6715-4(5));* 2010. lib. bdg. 28.65 *(978-1-4048-6271-5(4))* Capstone. (Picture Window Bks.).

Watkins, Adam F. R Is for Robot: A Noisy Alphabet. Watkins, Adam F. 2014. (ENG.). 32p. (J). (gr. -1-k). 16.99 *(978-0-8431-7237-9(1),* Price Stern Sloan) Penguin Young Readers Group.

—Raybot. Watkins, Adam F. 2016. (ENG.). 32p. (J). (-k). 17.99 *(978-0-8431-8300-9(4),* Price Stern Sloan) Penguin Young Readers Group.

Watkins, Amanda Lee. Runes & Gods for Kids. Hunter, Larisa C. & Haseleu, N. L. 2018. (ENG.). 166p. (J). pap. 38.00 *(978-1-989033-04-3(0))* Little Bird Bks.

W

Watkins, Christopher. Boyd-Friend: His Yippie-Skippie Journey to a Forever Home. Watkins, Patricia. l.t. ed. 2004. 44p. 10.95 (978-0-9753397-0-1(2)) Frayed Pages Publishing.

Watkins, Courtney. Backyard Wonders. MacCoon, Nancy. l.t. ed. 2003. 38p. (J). pap. 14.95 (978-0-9742495-0-6(5)) Vibatorium LLC.

Watkins, Greg. A Big Beaked, Big Bellied Bird Named Bill, 1 vol. Watkins, Greg. 2006. (Big Bill & Buddies Ser.). (ENG.). 32p. (J). (gr. k-3). 16.99 (978-1-58980-441-8(4), Pelican Publishing) Arcadia Publishing.

—A Big Beaked, Big Bellied Bird Named Bill. Watkins, Greg. 2005. 30p. 13.95 (978-0-9761318-1-6(1), 1239651) Cute & Cuddly Productions, Inc.

—Brendon Mouse's Big Idea to Save the Bad Bird Bunch, 1 vol. Watkins, Greg. 2007. (Big Bill & Buddies Ser.). (ENG.). 32p. (J). (gr. k-3). 16.99 (978-1-58980-449-4(X), Pelican Publishing) Arcadia Publishing.

Watkins, Laura. Bedtime in the Meadow. Shaw, Stephanie. 2013. (ENG.). 20p. (J). (gr. -1-k). bds. 8.95 (978-1-58925-628-6(X)) Tiger Tales.

—Can You Yawn Like a Fawn? A Help Your Child to Sleep Book. Sweeney, Monica & Yelvington, Lauren. 2016. (ENG.). 32p. (J). 15.99 (978-1-250-10416-8(5), 900163610) St. Martin's Pr.

—Hello, Mr. Moon. Gutierrez, Lorna. 2016. (J). (978-1-4351-6412-3(1)) Barnes & Noble, Inc.

Watkins, Laura. Oh No, Bobo! A Sweet Story with a Gentle Message about Personal Space. David, Donna. 2020. (Storytime Ser.). (ENG.). 24p. (J). (gr. -1-1). 17.95 **(978-0-7112-5111-3(8))** QEB Publishing Inc.

Watkins, Laura. Piper & Mabel: Two Very Wild but Very Good Dogs, 1 vol. Shankle, Melanie. 2020. (ENG.). 32p. (J). 17.99 (978-0-310-76086-3(0)) Zonderkidz.

Watkins, Liselotte. Life. Fredericks, Mariah. 2009. (In the Cards Ser.: No. 3). (ENG.). 272p. (J). pap. 5.99 (978-0-689-87659-2(9), Simon & Schuster/Paula Wiseman Bks.) Simon & Schuster/Paula Wiseman Bks.

—Love. Fredericks, Mariah. 2007. (In the Cards Ser.: No. 1). (ENG.). 288p. (YA). (gr. 4-8). pap. 5.99 (978-0-689-87655-4(6), Simon & Schuster/Paula Wiseman Bks.) Simon & Schuster/Paula Wiseman Bks.

Watkins Murrey, Denise Jaworowski. Reflections. Murray, Eleanor Jaworowski. 2017. (In Grandma's Eyes Ser.: Vol. 1). (ENG.). (J). 14.99 (978-0-692-93265-0(8)) Murray, Eleanor.

Watkins-Pitchford, Denys. The Little Grey Men: A Story for the Young in Heart. Andrews, Julie. 2004. 304p. (J). 17.89 (978-0-06-055449-1(5), Julie Andrews Collection) HarperCollins Pubs.

Watkins, Richard, photos by. Slavery: Bondage throughout History. Watkins, Richard. 2006. 136p. (J). (gr. 4-8). reprint ed. 18.00 (978-1-4223-5333-2(8)) DIANE Publishing Co.

Watkins, Tammy. The Magical Ballet Shoes: A Pinta & Polly Story, 1 vol. Franklin, Cathy. 2009. 25p. pap. 24.95 (978-1-4489-2007-5(8)) America Star Bks.

Watley, Ameera. We Love School! Watley, Marcia & Johnson, Eartha. 2012. (ENG.). 30p. pap. 21.99 (978-1-4691-7521-8(5)) Xlibris Corp.

Watley, Mitchell. I Would Tuck You In. Asper-Smith, Sarah. (J). 2014. 11p. (— 1). bds. 9.99 (978-1-57061-944-1(1)); 2012. 32p. (gr. -1-2). 16.99 (978-1-57061-844-4(5)) Sasquatch Bks. (Little Bigfoot).

—You Are Home with Me. Asper-Smith, Sarah. 2019. 32p. (J). (gr. -1-2). 16.99 (978-1-63217-224-2(0), Little Bigfoot) Sasquatch Bks.

Watling, James. Jehoshaphat: 2 Chronicles 20:1-30. 2005. (Little Learner Bible Story Books). 16p. (J). pap. 2.29 (978-0-7586-0945-8(0)) Concordia Publishing Hse.

—The Key to the Indian. Banks, Lynne Reid. 2004. (Indian in the Cupboard Ser.: No. 5). (ENG.). 288p. (J). (gr. 4-18). pap. 6.99 (978-0-380-80373-6(9), HarperCollins) HarperCollins Pubs. Ltd. GBR. Dist: HarperCollins Pubs.

—Samuel's Choice. Berleth, Richard. 2012. (ENG.). 40p. (J). (gr. -1-3). pap. 6.99 (978-0-8075-7219-1(5), 807572195) Whitman, Albert & Co.

—SeaMan: The Dog Who Explored the West with Lewis & Clark, 1 vol. Karwoski, Gail Langer. ed. 2003. (ENG.). 192p. (J). (gr. 3-7). 16.95 (978-1-56145-276-7(9), Q20194); pap. 9.99 (978-1-56145-190-6(8), Q20194) Peachtree Publishing Co. Inc.

Watson, Anne L. Skeeter & the Weasels. Shepard, Aaron. 2019. (ENG.). 50p. (J). (gr. k-3). 24.00 (978-1-62035-582-4(5)); pap. 12.00 (978-1-62035-581-7(7)) Shepard Pubns. (Skyhook Pr.).

Watson, Anne L. The Secret of Gingerbread Village: A Christmas Cookie Chronicle. Watson, Anne L. 2018. (ENG.). 36p. (J). (gr. k-3). 20.00 (978-1-62035-577-0(9)); pap. 10.00 (978-1-62035-576-3(0)) Shepard Pubns. (Skyhook Pr.).

Watson, Ben. The Caterbury Tails. Bush, Randall. 2013. 60p. pap. 13.99 (978-1-936670-75-8(5)) BorderStone Pr., LLC.

Watson-Dubisch, Carolyn. Night of the Armadillos, 1. Watson-Dubisch, Carolyn. l.t. ed. 2006. 32p. (J). per. 9.95 (978-0-9779295-2-8(3)) Medusa Road Pr.

Watson, Emily Grace. Keaton's Carrots. Pound, Sandra R. 2019. (ENG.). 24p. (J). 21.95 (978-1-64471-863-6(4)); pap. 12.95 (978-1-64471-862-9(6)) Covenant Bks.

Watson, Emmett. Mighty Maggie. Watson, James W. 2019. (ENG.). 46p. (J). pap. 15.00 (978-1-0935-1309-7(8)) Independently Published.

Watson, Esther Pearl. An ABC of What Art Can Be. McArthur, Meher. 2010. (ENG.). 32p. (J). (gr. -1-3). 17.95 (978-0-89236-999-7(X), J. Paul Getty Museum) Getty Pubns.

Watson, Jesse Joshua. The Backyard Animal Show. Draper, Sharon M. 2012. (Clubhouse Mysteries Ser.: 5). (ENG.). 128p. (J). (gr. 3-7). pap. 5.99 (978-1-4424-5022-6(3), Aladdin) Simon & Schuster Children's Publishing.

—The Backyard Animal Show. Draper, Sharon M. 2012. (Clubhouse Mysteries Ser.: 5). (ENG.). 128p. (J). (gr. 3-7). 15.99 (978-1-4424-5023-3(1), Simon & Schuster/Paula Wiseman Bks.) Simon & Schuster/Paula Wiseman Bks.

—Barfing in the Backseat: How I Survived My Family Road Trip. Winkler, Henry & Oliver, Lin. 2007. (Hank Zipzer Ser.: No. 12). 152p. (gr. 4-7). 15.00 (978-0-7569-8162-4(X)) Perfection Learning Corp.

—The Buried Bones Mystery. Draper, Sharon M. 2011. (Clubhouse Mysteries Ser.: 1). (ENG.). 112p. (J). (gr. 3-7). pap. 5.99 (978-1-4424-2709-9(4), Aladdin) Simon & Schuster Children's Publishing.

—The Buried Bones Mystery. Draper, Sharon M. 2011. (Clubhouse Mysteries Ser.: 1). (ENG.). 112p. (J). (gr. 3-7). lib. bdg. 15.99 (978-1-4424-2710-5(8), Simon & Schuster/Paula Wiseman Bks.) Simon & Schuster/Paula Wiseman Bks.

—Chess Rumble. Neri, G. 2007. (ENG.). 64p. (J). (gr. 3-7). 18.95 (978-1-58430-279-7(8)) Lee & Low Bks., Inc.

—Ghetto Cowboy. Neri, G. 2013. 224p. (J). (gr. 5). pap. 7.99 (978-0-7636-6453-4(7)) Candlewick Pr.

—I & I: Bob Marley. Medina, Tony. 2009. (ENG.). 48p. (J). (gr. 3-6). 19.95 (978-1-60060-257-3(6)) Lee & Low Bks., Inc.

—Lost in the Tunnel of Time. Draper, Sharon M. 2011. (Clubhouse Mysteries Ser.: 2). (ENG.). 112p. (J). (gr. 3-7). pap. 5.99 (978-1-4424-2704-4(3), Aladdin) Simon & Schuster Children's Publishing.

—Lost in the Tunnel of Time. Draper, Sharon M. 2011. (Clubhouse Mysteries Ser.: 2). (ENG.). 112p. (J). (gr. 3-7). lib. bdg. 15.99 (978-1-4424-2703-7(5), Simon & Schuster/Paula Wiseman Bks.) Simon & Schuster/Paula Wiseman Bks.

—Shadows of Caesar's Creek. Draper, Sharon M. 2011. (Clubhouse Mysteries Ser.: 3). (ENG.). 128p. (J). (gr. 3-7). 15.99 (978-1-4424-2712-9(4)); pap. 5.99 (978-1-4424-2711-2(6)) Simon & Schuster Children's Publishing. (Aladdin).

—The Soccer Fence: A Story of Friendship, Hope, & Apartheid in South Africa. Bildner, Phil. 2014. (ENG.). 40p. (J). (gr. 1-3). 17.99 (978-0-399-24790-3(4), G.P. Putnam's Sons Books for Young Readers) Penguin Young Readers Group.

—The Space Mission Adventure. Draper, Sharon M. 2012. (Clubhouse Mysteries Ser.: 4). (ENG.). 112p. (J). (gr. 3-7). 16.99 (978-1-4424-4225-2(5)); pap. 5.99 (978-1-4424-4226-9(3)) Simon & Schuster Children's Publishing. (Aladdin).

—Stars & Sparks on Stage. Draper, Sharon M. 2012. (Clubhouse Mysteries Ser.: 6). (ENG.). 144p. (J). (gr. 3-7). pap. 5.99 (978-1-4424-5457-6(1), Aladdin) Simon & Schuster Children's Publishing.

—Stars & Sparks on Stage. Draper, Sharon M. (Clubhouse Mysteries Ser.: 6). (ENG.). (J). 2012. 144p. (gr. 3-7). 15.99 (978-1-4424-5459-0(8)); 2007. 160p. pap. 4.99 (978-1-4169-0001-6(2)) Simon & Schuster/Paula Wiseman Bks. (Simon & Schuster/Paula Wiseman Bks.).

Watson, Judy. Extraordinary Ernie & Marvelous Maud. Watts, Frances. 2010. (ENG.). 80p. (J). (gr. 2-5). pap. 6.00 (978-0-8028-5363-9(3), Eerdmans Bks For Young Readers) Eerdmans, William B. Publishing Co.

—Goodnight, Mice! Watts, Frances. 24p. 2019. pap. 6.99 (978-0-7333-3176-3(9)); 2017. bds. 6.99 (978-0-7333-3530-3(6)) ABC Bks. AUS. Dist: HarperCollins Pubs.

—The Greatest Sheep in History. Watts, Frances. 2010. (ENG.). 88p. (YA). (gr. 2-5). pap. 6.00 (978-0-8028-5374-5(9), Eerdmans Bks For Young Readers) Eerdmans, William B. Publishing Co.

—Heroes of the Year. Watts, Frances. 2012. (ENG.). 84p. (J). pap. 6.00 (978-0-8028-5412-4(5), Eerdmans Bks For Young Readers) Eerdmans, William B. Publishing Co.

—The Middle Sheep. Watts, Fraces. 2010. (ENG.). 80p. (J). (gr. 2-5). pap. 6.00 (978-0-8028-5368-4(4)) Eerdmans, William B. Publishing Co.

—Tipper, Tipper! Bedford, David. 2008. 9p. bds. (978-1-921272-26-4(0)) Little Hare Bks. AUS. Dist: HarperCollins Pubs. Australia.

Watson, Laura. Big & Small, God Made Them All. Wilder, Ben. Carin, Siegfried, ed. 2016. (ENG.). 34p. (J). (gr. k-2). pap. 14.95 (978-0-9909865-7-7(8)) Thorpe, Betsy Literary Services.

—Hail to Spring! Ghigna, Charles. 2015. (Springtime Weather Wonders Ser.). (ENG.). 24p. (J). (gr. -1-2). lib. bdg. 22.65 (978-1-4795-6029-5(4), Picture Window Bks.) Capstone.

—Hello, Baby Pink B Band. Franklin, Glen & Bodman, Sue. 2017. (Cambridge Reading Adventures Ser.). (ENG.). 16p. (J). pap. 5.62 (978-1-108-43961-9(6)) Cambridge Univ. Pr.

—It's Much Too Early! Whybrow, Ian. 2016. (Cambridge Reading Adventures Ser.). (ENG.). 16p. pap. 7.37 (978-1-107-56032-1(2)) Cambridge Univ. Pr.

—My Big Evil Brother Packed My Lunch! Chronicle Books Staff. 2019. (ENG.). 12p. (J). (gr. -1-3). bds. 16.99 (978-1-4521-7089-3(4)) Chronicle Bks. LLC.

—Rain, Rain, Stay Today: Southwestern Nursery Rhymes. Profiri, Charline. 2014. (J). (978-1-933855-85-1(1)) Rio Nuevo Pubs.

—Raindrops Fall All Around. Ghigna, Charles. 2015. (Springtime Weather Wonders Ser.). (ENG.). 24p. (J). (gr. -1-2). lib. bdg. 22.65 (978-1-4795-6030-1(8), Picture Window Bks.) Capstone.

—So Many Babies, 1 vol. Crozier, Lorna. 2015. (ENG.). 24p. (J). (gr. -1 — 1). bds. 9.95 (978-1-4598-0831-7(2)) Orca Bk. Pubs. USA.

—A Windy Day in Spring. Ghigna, Charles. 2015. (Springtime Weather Wonders Ser.). (ENG.). 24p. (J). (gr. -1-2). lib. bdg. 22.65 (978-1-4795-6032-5(4), Picture Window Bks.) Capstone.

Watson, Mary. The Heart of the Lion. Watson, Peter. 2005. (ENG.). 32p. (J). (gr. 4-7). 15.95 (978-0-9726614-1-6(7)) Shenanigan Bks.

Watson, Mary. The Paper Dragonfly. Watson, Mary. 2007. (ENG.). 32p. (J). (gr. k-3). 15.95 (978-0-9726614-3-0(3)) Shenanigan Bks.

Watson, Mia & Burchell, Scott. A Wild Goose Chase. Stanley, Karen. 2017. (ENG.). 20p. (J). (gr. k-3). pap. (978-0-9934439-9-2(0)) Raven Crest Bks.

Watson, Nancy, jt. illus. see Miguel, Maridel Maddie.

Watson, Nathan. Return of Buzz Lightyear, 2. Snider, Jesse Blaze. 2010. (Kaboom! Graphic Novels Ser.). (ENG.). 112p. (J). (gr. 4-7). 26.19 (978-1-60886-557-4(6)) Boom! Studios.

—Return of Buzz Lightyear Vol. 2. Snider, Jesse Blaze. 2010. (Toy Story Ser.). (ENG.). 112p. (J). 24.99 (978-1-60886-558-1(4)) Boom! Studios.

—Toy Story: Some Assembly Required. Snider, Jesse Blaze. 2010. (Toy Story Ser.). 112p. (J). pap. 9.99 (978-1-60886-570-3(3)) Boom! Studios.

—Toy Story: Toy Overboard. Snider, Jesse Blaze. 2011. 128p. (J). pap. 9.99 (978-1-60886-605-2(X)) Boom! Studios.

Watson, Nick. Friendly Ness Sings the Friendly Ness Song: Sing along with the Ness Monsters. Tarrant, Marcus Adrian. 2019. (ENG.). 28p. (J). pap. (978-0-6484718-0-6(2)) M A Tarrant Nominees Pty Ltd.

Watson, Richar. My Book of Letters: For Ages 3+ 2016. (ENG.). (J). pap. (978-1-78209-799-0(6)) Miles Kelly Publishing, Ltd.

—Sticker Playbook Princess Carriage: A Fold-Out Story Activity Book for Toddlers. 2015. (Sticker Playbook Ser.). (ENG.). (J). (978-1-78209-575-0(6)) Miles Kelly Publishing, Ltd.

Watson, Richard. Crabby Pants, 1 vol. Gassman, Julie A. 2010. (Little Boost Ser.). (ENG.). 32p. (J). (gr. -1-1). lib. bdg. 23.99 (978-1-4048-6165-7(3), Picture Window Bks.) Capstone.

—Crabby Pants, 1 vol. Gassman, Julie. 2012. (Little Boost Ser.). (ENG.). 32p. (J). (gr. -1-1). 7.95 (978-1-4048-7416-9(X), Picture Window Bks.) Capstone.

—Diplodocus: The Dippy Idea, 1 vol. Bromage, Fran. 2019. (Dinosaur Adventures Ser.). (ENG.). 24p. (J). (gr. 1-2). 24.60 (978-1-7253-9513-8(4)); pap. 8.25 (978-1-7253-9511-4(8)) Rosen Publishing Group, Inc., The. (Windmill Bks.).

—Dog Diaries: A Middle School Story. Patterson, James. 2018. (Dog Diaries: 1). (ENG.). 208p. (J). (gr. 2-7). 9.99 (978-0-316-48748-1(1), Jimmy Patterson) Little Brown & Co.

—Dog Diaries: Mission Impawsible: A Middle School Story. Patterson, James & Butler, Steven. 2020. (Dog Diaries: 3). (ENG.). 208p. (J). (gr. 2-7). 9.99 (978-0-316-49447-2(X), Jimmy Patterson) Little Brown & Co.

—The Elves' Night Before Christmas. Kowitt, Holly & Manis, David. 2016. (J). pap. (978-1-338-08903-5(X)) Scholastic, Inc.

—The First Underwear. Lisle, Rebecca. 2019. (Early Bird Readers — Purple (Early Bird Stories (tm)) Ser.). (ENG.). 32p. (J). (gr. k-3). 27.99 (978-1-5415-4229-7(0), 9781541542297); pap. 7.99 (978-1-5415-7418-2(4), 9781541574182) Lerner Publishing Group. (Lerner Pubns.).

—Halloween. Platt, Richard. 2017. (Flip Flap Journeys Ser.). (ENG.). 14p. (J). (gr. k-2). bds. 13.99 (978-1-4052-7659-7(2)) Egmont Bks., Ltd. GBR. Dist: Independent Pubs. Group.

—I Saw an Invisible Lion Today: Quatrains. Cleary, Brian P. ed. 2016. (Poetry Adventures Ser.). (ENG.). 32p. (J). (gr. 2-5). E-Book 39.99 (978-1-4677-9732-0(4), Millbrook Pr.) Lerner Publishing Group.

—King Donal's Secret. Doyle, Malachy. 2005. (ENG.). 24p. (J). lib. bdg. 23.65 (978-1-59646-740-8(1)) Dingles & Co.

—Lacey Walker, Nonstop Talker, 1 vol. Jones, Christianne C. (Little Boost Ser.). (ENG.). 32p. (J). (gr. -1-1). 2013. 14.95 (978-1-4795-2156-2(6)); 2012. lib. bdg. 23.99 (978-1-4048-6796-3(1)) Capstone. (Picture Window Bks.).

Watson, Richard, et al. Little Boost. Gassman, Julie et al. 2018. (Little Boost Ser.). (ENG.). 32p. (J). (gr. -1-1). 287.88 (978-1-5158-3073-3(X), 28602, Picture Window Bks.) Capstone.

Watson, Richard. Lucía Villar Habla Sin Parar. Jones, Christianne C. (Pasito a Pasito Ser.).Tr. of Lacey Walker, Nonstop Talker. (SPA.). 32p. (J). (gr. -1-1). 2020. pap. 9.95 (978-1-5158-6083-9(3), 142361); 2019. lib. bdg. 23.99 (978-1-5158-4734-2(9), 141332) Capstone. (Picture Window Bks.).

—On the Trail of the Whale. De la Bédoyère, Camilla. Kelly, Richard, ed. 2017. (ENG.). 24p. (J). pap. 9.95 (978-1-78209-983-3(2)) Miles Kelly Publishing, Ltd. GBR. Dist: Parkwest Pubns., Inc.

—Pigeon Math. Citro, Asia. 2019. (ENG.). 40p. (J). (gr. k-5). 16.99 (978-1-943147-62-5(0), 31dc140c-9f39-44d6-b6b5-97bc1fbd5ec7) Innovation Pr., The.

—Pinocchio. Tiger Tales. 2019. (Fairy Tale Classics Ser.). (ENG.). 32p. (J). (gr. -1-2). lib. bdg. 23.99 (978-1-68010-160-7(9)) Tiger Tales.

Watson, Richard. Ramón el Gruñón. Gassman, Julie. 2020. (Pasito a Pasito Ser.).Tr. of Crabby Pants. (SPA.). 32p. (J). (gr. -1-1). 9.95 **(978-1-5158-7334-1(X)**, 201743); lib. bdg. 23.99 **(978-1-5158-7195-8(9)**, 200642) Capstone. (Picture Window Bks.).

Watson, Richard. Space Knights & Ice Dragons. Webster, Sheryl. 2017. (Reading Ladder Ser.). (ENG.). 48p. (J). (gr. k-2). pap. 7.99 (978-1-4052-7822-5(6)) Egmont Bks., Ltd. GBR. Dist: Independent Pubs. Group.

—Stone Underpants. Lisle, Rebecca. 2018. (ENG.). 32p. (J). (gr. -1-3). 17.99 (978-1-84886-311-8(X)) Maverick Arts Publishing GBR. Dist: Lerner Publishing Group.

—Terrible, Awful, Horrible Manners! Bracken, Beth. 2011. (Little Boost Ser.). (ENG.). 32p. (J). (gr. -1-1). lib. bdg. 23.99 (978-1-4048-6653-9(1), Picture Window Bks.) Capstone.

—Terrible, Awful, Horrible Manners, 1 vol. Bracken, Beth. 2012. (Little Boost Ser.). (ENG.). 32p. (J). (gr. -1-1). 7.95 (978-1-4048-7419-0(4), Picture Window Bks.) Capstone.

—Underneath My Bed: List Poems. Cleary, Brian P. ed. 2016. (Poetry Adventures Ser.). (ENG.). 32p. (J). (gr. 2-5). E-Book 39.99 (978-1-5124-1112-6(4), Millbrook Pr.) Lerner Publishing Group.

Watson, Richard, jt. illus. see Cooper, Jenny.

Watson, Richard J. The Legend of Saint Christopher. Hodges, Margaret. 2004. 32p. (J). (gr. 2-6). 18.00 (978-0-8028-5077-5(4)) Eerdmans, William B. Publishing Co.

Watson, Richard Jesse. The Legend of Saint Christopher. Hodges, Margaret. 2009. (ENG.). 32p. (J). (gr. k-5). 9.00 (978-0-8028-5360-8(9), Eerdmans Bks For Young Readers) Eerdmans, William B. Publishing Co.

—The Lord's Prayer: Words of Hope & Happiness, 1 vol. Warren, Rick. 2016. (ENG.). 32p. (J). 16.99 (978-0-310-75755-9(X)) Zonderkidz.

—The Night Before Christmas. Moore, Clement C. 2006. (ENG.). 40p. (J). (gr. -1-3). 16.99 (978-0-06-075741-0(8)) HarperCollins Pubs.

—The Night Before Christmas, Vol. Moore, Clement C. 2008. (ENG.). 40p. (J). (gr. -1-3). pap. 6.99 (978-0-06-075744-1(2)) HarperCollins Pubs.

Watson, Rob. I Can Do It: Help Raise Your Child's Self-Esteem. Lito, Dan E. 2008. (ENG.). 38p. (J). pap. (978-0-9784572-0-4(X)) Inspired Bks.

Watson, Tom & Long, Ethan. Stick Dog Dreams of Ice Cream. 2015. 216p. (J). (978-0-06-238092-0(3)) Harper & Row Ltd.

—Stick Dog Slurps Spaghetti. 2016. 238p. (J). (978-0-06-245857-5(4)) Harper & Row Ltd.

Watson, Travis & Lohr, Tyrel. Wars of the Boltians & Kuissians. Waschak, Jay et al. 2004. per. 25.00 (978-0-9764048-1-1(8)) Victory by Any Means Games.

Watt, Andy. What If... Thompson, Elisabeth C. 2018. (ENG.). 24p. (J). pap. (978-1-911596-91-2(8)) Spiderwize.

Watt, Coulter. Professor Angelicus Visits the Big Blue Ball. Ward, L. B. B. 2005. (J). lib. bdg. 19.95 (978-0-9759649-0-3(9)) Mumblefish Bks.

Watt, Fiona. Go to Sleep Little Baby. Watt, Fiona. 2009. (Baby Board Books w/CD Ser.). 12p. (J). (gr. -1). bds. 15.99 (978-0-7945-1936-0(9), Usborne) EDC Publishing.

Watt, Mélanie. Chester's Masterpiece. Watt, Mélanie. 2020. (Chester Ser.). (ENG.). 32p. (J). (gr. -1-3). pap. 8.99 **(978-1-55453-354-1(6))** Kids Can Pr., Ltd. CAN. Dist: Hachette Bk. Group.

Watt, Mélanie. Scaredy Squirrel at the Beach. Watt, Mélanie. 2012. (ENG.). 32p. (J). (gr. -1-3). pap. 7.95 (978-1-55453-462-3(3)) Kids Can Pr., Ltd. CAN. Dist: Hachette Bk. Group.

—Scaredy Squirrel at the Beach. Watt, Mélanie. 2008. (ENG.). 32p. (J). (gr. -1-3). 16.99 (978-1-55453-225-4(6)) Kids Can Pr., Ltd. CAN. Dist: Hachette Bk. Group.

Watt, Mélanie & Watt, Mélanie. The Alphabet. Watt, Mélanie & Watt, Mélanie. 2005. (Learning with Animals Ser.). (ENG.). 30p. (J). (gr. -1 — 1). bds. 5.95 (978-1-55337-829-7(6)) Kids Can Pr., Ltd. CAN. Dist: Hachette Bk. Group.

—Augustine. Watt, Mélanie & Watt, Mélanie. 2008. (ENG.). 32p. (J). (gr. -1-2). pap. 9.99 (978-1-55453-268-1(X)) Kids Can Pr., Ltd. CAN. Dist: Hachette Bk. Group.

—Chester. Watt, Mélanie & Watt, Mélanie. 2009. (Chester Ser.). (ENG.). 32p. (J). (gr. -1-3). pap. 8.99 (978-1-55453-460-9(7)) Kids Can Pr., Ltd. CAN. Dist: Hachette Bk. Group.

—Chester's Back! Watt, Mélanie & Watt, Mélanie. 2013. (Chester Ser.). (ENG.). 32p. (J). (gr. -1-3). 8.95 (978-1-55453-461-6(5)) Kids Can Pr., Ltd. CAN. Dist: Hachette Bk. Group.

—Chester's Masterpiece. Watt, Mélanie & Watt, Mélanie. 2010. (Chester Ser.). (ENG.). 32p. (J). (gr. -1-3). 18.95 (978-1-55453-566-8(2)) Kids Can Pr., Ltd. CAN. Dist: Hachette Bk. Group.

—Have I Got a Book for You! Watt, Mélanie & Watt, Mélanie. 2013. (ENG.). 32p. (J). (gr. k-4). pap. 9.99 (978-1-55453-483-8(6)) Kids Can Pr., Ltd. CAN. Dist: Hachette Bk. Group.

—Numbers. Watt, Mélanie & Watt, Mélanie. 2005. (Learning with Animals Ser.). (ENG.). 24p. (J). (gr. -1 — 1). bds. 5.95 (978-1-55337-831-0(8)) Kids Can Pr., Ltd. CAN. Dist: Hachette Bk. Group.

—Scaredy Squirrel. Watt, Mélanie & Watt, Mélanie. (ENG.). 40p. (J). (gr. -1-3). 2008. pap. 7.95 (978-1-55453-023-6(7)); 2006. 16.95 (978-1-55337-959-1(4)) Kids Can Pr., Ltd. CAN. Dist: Hachette Bk. Group.

—Scaredy Squirrel at Night. Watt, Mélanie & Watt, Mélanie. 2009. (ENG.). 32p. (J). (gr. -1-3). 16.95 (978-1-55453-288-9(4)) Kids Can Pr., Ltd. CAN. Dist: Hachette Bk. Group.

—Scaredy Squirrel Has a Birthday Party, 0 vols. Watt, Mélanie & Watt, Mélanie. (ENG.). 32p. (J). (gr. -1-3). 2014. pap. 7.99 (978-1-55453-716-7(9)); 2011. 16.95 (978-1-55453-468-5(2)) Kids Can Pr., Ltd. CAN. Dist: Hachette Bk. Group.

—Scaredy Squirrel Makes a Friend. Watt, Mélanie & Watt, Mélanie. 2007. (ENG.). 32p. (J). (gr. -1-3). 16.95 (978-1-55453-181-3(0)) Kids Can Pr., Ltd. CAN. Dist: Hachette Bk. Group.

Watt, Mélanie, jt. illus. see Watt, Mélanie.

Wattenberg, Jane. The Duck & the Kangaroo. Lear, Edward. 2009. (ENG.). 40p. (J). (gr. -1-k). 17.99 (978-0-06-136683-3(8), Greenwillow Bks.) HarperCollins Pubs.

Watters, Kristyn Mikayla. Savannah's Valentine. Little, Paul D. 2019. (ENG.). 52p. (J). pap. 12.99 (978-0-9988367-2-0(9)) King's Way Pr.

Watters, Timothy Teruo. When Piglets Fly. Watters, Timothy Teruo. 2019. (When Piglets Fly Ser.: Vol. 1). (ENG.). 70p. (J). (gr. 1-6). 19.99 (978-1-7337601-0-2(5)) Moon Lantern Studios.

Watton, Ross. Roman Myths. West, David. 2006. (Graphic Mythology Ser.). (ENG.). 48p. (J). (gr. 4-7). lib. bdg. 35.45 (978-1-4042-0803-2(8)) Rosen Publishing Group, Inc., The.

—Too Close to the Sun: The Story of Daedalus & Icarus: A Greek Legend. 2004. (ENG.). 20p. (J). (gr. 3-3). pap. 6.47 net. (978-0-7685-2121-4(1), Dominie Elementary) Savvas Learning Co.

Watton, Ross & Moore, Jo. The Encyclopedia of Awesome Machines. Petty, Kate. 2003. 112p. (J). (gr. 4-8). reprint ed. 15.00 *(978-0-7567-6963-5(9))* DIANE Publishing Co.

Watts, Bernadette. Bremen Town Musicians. Grimm, Brothers. 2020. (ENG.). 32p. (J). (gr. -1-2). 17.95 *(978-0-7358-4384-4(8))* North-South Bks., Inc.

—Hansel & Gretel. Grimm, Brothers. 2018. (ENG.). 32p. (J). (gr. -1-2). 17.95 *(978-0-7358-4327-1(9))* North-South Bks., Inc.

—The Little Gardener. Scheidl, Gerda Marie. 2019. (ENG.). 32p. (J). (gr. -1-2). 17.95 *(978-0-7358-4347-9(3))* North-South Bks., Inc.

Watts, Bernadette. The Little Mermaid. Andersen, Hans Christian. 2020. (ENG.). 48p. (J). (gr. -1-2). 17.95 ***(978-0-7358-4419-3(4))*** North-South Bks., Inc.

Watts, Bernadette. Little Red Riding Hood. Grimm, Brothers. 32p. (J). 2018. (ENG.). (gr. -1-3). 17.95 *(978-0-7358-4303-5(1))*; 2011. pap. 7.95 *(978-0-7358-4008-9(3))* North-South Bks., Inc.

—Mother Holly. Grimm, Brothers. 2016. (ENG.). 32p. 17.95 *(978-0-7358-4267-0(1))* North-South Bks., Inc.

—Shoemaker Martin. Tolstoy, Leo. 2018. (ENG.). 32p. (J). (gr. -1-3). 17.95 *(978-0-7358-4304-2(X))* North-South Bks., Inc.

—The Snow Queen. Andersen, Hans Christian. 2018. (ENG.). 32p. (J). (gr. -1-3). 17.95 *(978-0-7358-4302-8(3))* North-South Bks., Inc.

—Snow White. Grimm, Brothers. 2018. (ENG.). 32p. (J). (gr. -1-2). 17.95 *(978-1-55858-132-6(4))* North-South Bks., Inc.

—Ugly Duckling. Andersen, Hans Christian. 2008. 32p. (J). (gr. -1-3). pap. 7.95 *(978-0-7358-2146-0(1))* North-South Bks., Inc.

Watts, Bernadette. The Little Drummer Boy. Watts, Bernadette, adapted by. 2018. (ENG.). 32p. (J). (gr. -1-2). 17.95 *(978-0-7358-4325-7(2))* North-South Bks., Inc.

Watts, Bernadette. The Tortoise & the Hare. Watts, Bernadette, retold by. 2020. (ENG.). 32p. (J). (gr. -1-2). 8.95 ***(978-0-7358-4413-1(5))*** North-South Bks., Inc.

Watts, James. Hold up the Sky: And Other Native American Tales from Texas & The. Curry, Jane Louise. 2010. (ENG.). 176p. (J). (gr. 3-7). pap. 9.99 *(978-1-4424-2155-4(X)*, McElderry, Margaret K. Bks.) McElderry, Margaret K. Bks.

—Zack's Alligator & the First Snow. Mozelle, Shirley. 2011. (I Can Read Level 2 Ser.). (ENG.). 32p. (J). (gr. k-3). pap. 4.99 *(978-0-06-147372-2(3))* HarperCollins Pubs.

Watts, John. When Sea & Sky Are Blue. Parr, Letitia. 32p. (J). (gr. -1-3). 13.95 *(978-0-87592-059-7(4))* Scroll Pr., Inc.

Watts, Juliette. Why Would Anyone Cut a Tree Down? Burzynski, Roberta. Forest Service (U.S.), Northeastern Area State and Private Forestry, ed. 2013. (ENG.). 40p. (J). pap. 10.00 *(978-0-16-091626-7(7)*, Forest Service) United States Government Printing Office.

Watts, Leslie. If I Were the Moon: Twentieth - Anniversary Edition, 1 vol. Fitch, Sheree. 2nd ed. 2019. (ENG.). 32p. (J). 22.95 *(978-1-77108-739-1(0)*, b0e71718-b722-469a-892e-2d48f89c9c6b) Nimbus Publishing, Ltd. CAN. Dist: Baker & Taylor Publisher Services (BTPS).

Watts, Leslie Elizabeth. Making Grizzle Grow, 1 vol. Gilmore, Rachna. 2007. (ENG.). 32p. (J). (gr. -1-1). 14.95 *(978-1-55041-885-9(8)*, ad6fe766-ca84-4122-9f41-b950903ceebb) Fitzhenry & Whiteside, Ltd. CAN. Dist: Firefly Bks., Ltd.

—The Most Beautiful Kite in the World, 1 vol. Spalding, Andrea. 2005. (ENG.). 32p. (J). (gr. k-2). pap. 8.95 *(978-1-55041-805-7(X)*, 62e6e225-52d8-427f-9ad8-62b8184e8f61) Fitzhenry & Whiteside, Ltd. CAN. Dist: Firefly Bks., Ltd.

Watts, Leslie Elizabeth. The Baabaasheep Quartet. Watts, Leslie Elizabeth. 2005. (ENG.). 32p. (J). (gr. -1-1). 9.95 *(978-1-55041-890-3(4)*, ce1e69e6-da61-48ce-b1fa-6cde39445333) Fitzhenry & Whiteside, Ltd. CAN. Dist: Firefly Bks., Ltd.

Watts, Marjorie Anne & Bennett, Jill. The Complete Polly & the Wolf. Storr, Catherine. 2016. (ENG.). 304p. (J). (gr. 3-7). 17.95 *(978-1-68137-001-9(8)*, NYR Children's Collection) New York Review of Bks., Inc., The.

Watts, Sarah. The Alcatraz Escape. Chambliss Bertman, Jennifer. 2018. (Book Scavenger Ser.: 3). (ENG.). 368p. (J). 16.99 *(978-1-62779-963-8(X)*, 900164138, Holt, Henry & Co. Bks. For Young Readers) Holt, Henry & Co.

—The Alcatraz Escape. Chambliss Bertman, Jennifer. 2019. (Book Scavenger Ser.: 3). (ENG.). 272p. (J). pap. 7.99 *(978-1-250-30870-2(4)*, 900164139) Square Fish.

—The Cavendish Home for Boys & Girls. Legrand, Claire. (ENG.). (J). (gr. 5). 2013. 368p. pap. 8.99 *(978-1-4424-4292-4(1))*; 2012. 352p. 16.99 *(978-1-4424-4291-7(3))* Simon & Schuster Bks. For Young Readers. (Simon & Schuster Bks. For Young Readers).

—How Hippo Says Hello! Samoun, Abigail. 2014. (Little Traveler Ser.). (ENG.). 22p. (J). (gr. -1-k). bds. 6.95 *(978-1-4549-0820-3(3))* Sterling Publishing Co., Inc.

—How to Catch a Bogle. Jinks, Catherine. 2014. (How to Catch a Bogle Ser.: 1). (ENG.). 336p. (J). (gr. 5-7). pap. 7.99 *(978-0-544-33627-8(5)*, 1584173, HMH Books For Young Readers) Houghton Mifflin Harcourt Publishing Co.

—How to Catch a Bogle. Jinks, Catherine. 2014. (ENG.). (J). (gr. 5-7). lib. bdg. 17.60 *(978-1-62765-727-3(4))* Perfection Learning Corp.

—The Inn Between. Cohen, Marina. 2016. (ENG.). 208p. (J). 16.99 *(978-1-62672-202-6(1)*, 900145045) Roaring Brook Pr.

—Little Traveler's Library: Four Adventures in Eight Languages. Samoun, Abigail. 2016. (Little Traveler Ser.). 88p. (J). (gr. -1-k). 12.95 *(978-1-4549-2006-9(8))* Sterling Publishing Co., Inc.

Watts, Sharon. A Style All Her Own. Friedman, Laurie. 2005. 32p. (J). (gr. -1-3). lib. bdg. 15.95 *(978-1-57505-599-2(6))* Lerner Publishing Group.

—Teen Manners: From Malls to Meals to Messaging & Beyond. Post, Peggy & Senning, Cindy P. 2007. (ENG.). 144p. (YA). (gr. 8-12). 17.99 *(978-0-06-088198-6(4)*, HarperTeen) HarperCollins Pubs.

Watts, Suzanne. Bear Hugs: Romantically Ridiculous Animal Rhymes. Wilson, Karma. 2007. (ENG.). 32p. (J). (gr. -1-3). 7.99 *(978-1-4169-4958-9(5)*, McElderry, Margaret K. Bks.) McElderry, Margaret K. Bks.

—Hilda Must Be Dancing. Wilson, Karma. 2004. (ENG.). 32p. (J). (gr. -1-3). 18.99 *(978-0-689-84788-2(2)*, McElderry, Margaret K. Bks.) McElderry, Margaret K. Bks.

—Hilda Must Be Dancing. Wilson, Karma. 2008. (ENG.). 32p. (J). (gr. 1-3). 22.44 *(978-1-4169-5083-7(4))* Simon & Schuster, Inc.

—Ten Naughty Little Monkeys. Williams, Suzanne. 2007. 32p. (J). (gr. -1-3). lib. bdg. 17.89 *(978-0-06-059905-8(7))* HarperCollins Pubs.

Wax, John & Wax, Wendy. Oh, Baby! Krulik, Nancy. 2008. (Katie Kazoo, Switcheroo Ser.: No. 2). (ENG.). 80p. (J). (gr. 1-4). lib. bdg. 25.65 *(978-1-59961-453-3(7)*, 10944, Chapter Bks.) Spotlight.

Wax, Wendy, jt. illus. see Wax, John.

Waxman, Freesia & Smith, Jamie. Not Just a Toot. K J Bullock. 2017. (ENG.). (J). *(978-1-5255-1752-5(X))*; pap. *(978-1-5255-1753-2(8))* FriesenPress.

Way, MaryFaye. Ina the Octopus & Her Shipwreck Adventure. Anton, Amy Way. 2008. 28p. pap. 13.99 *(978-1-4389-2177-8(2))* AuthorHouse.

Waybright, Diane. Imagine If Thoughts Were Balloons. Vanvenutti, Rico. 2017. (ENG.). (J). pap. 12.99 *(978-0-9912614-2-0(9))* Hermes Hse. Pr.

Waycott, Flora. Hands to Heart: Breathe & Bend with Animal Friends. Bauermeister, Alex. 2019. (ENG.). 32p. (J). (gr. -1-3). 14.99 *(978-1-328-55041-5(9)*, 1724226, HMH Books For Young Readers) Houghton Mifflin Harcourt Publishing Co.

Waycott, Flora. Made with Love: Pancakes! Redmond, Lea. 2020. (ENG.). 20p. (J). (gr. -1 — 1). bds. 9.99 ***(978-1-4521-8026-7(1))*** Chronicle Bks. LLC.

Waycott, Flora. She Believed She Could, So She Did: A Journal of Powerful Quotes from Powerful Women. 2018. 208p. (J). (gr. 3-7). pap. 12.95 *(978-1-4549-2837-9(9))* Sterling Publishing Co., Inc.

Waycott, Flora. Winter Wonderland to Color: Coloring Book for Adults & Kids to Share. Waycott, Flora. 2016. (ENG.). 96p. (J). (gr. -1). pap. 15.99 *(978-0-06-256997-4(X))* HarperCollins Pubs.

Waygood, Adrian. Norm & Dig's Epic Adventure. Goodwin, John. 2018. (ENG.). 244p. (YA). (gr. 10-12). pap. *(978-1-9997204-7-6(4))* Anixe Publishing Ltd.

Waytula, Brian. Missions of Big Zach. Zachary, Ken. 2005. 36p. (J). (gr. -1-3). per. 9.95 *(978-1-59879-061-0(7))* Lifevest Publishing, Inc.

Waywell, Valerie J. Cookie Paws. Jorden, Edwin W. 2nd ed. 2007. (ENG.). 32p. (J). (gr. -1-3). 9.95 *(978-0-9793483-0-3(7))* Gilded Dog Enterprises LLC.

—Cookie Paws/Spreadin' the Sweetness. Jorden, Edwin W. 2008. 32p. (J). 12.95 *(978-0-9793483-1-0(5))* Gilded Dog Enterprises LLC.

Wazem, Pierre. Like a River. Wazem, Pierre. 2003. (Metal Hurlant Presents- Ser.: Vol. 1). 108p. pap. 9.95 *(978-1-930652-97-2(6))* Humanoids, Inc.

Weakley, Emma. Jonah. Nilsen, Lenie. 2018. (ENG.). 42p. (J). 19.99 *(978-1-940473-65-9(9))* Stonebridge Pubns.

Weale, Andrew. Magical Animals at Bedtime: Tales of Joy & Inspiration for You to Read with Your Child. Keunzler, Lou. 2013. (ENG.). 144p. (J). (gr. -1-3). pap. 24.95 *(978-1-78028-513-9(2)*, Watkins Publishing) Watkins Media Limited GBR. Dist: Penguin Random Hse. LLC.

Wealthall, Gracie-May. Norman Norty. Fuller, Scott. 2019. (ENG.). 66p. (J). pap. 6.18 ***(978-1-7094-0882-3(0))*** Independently Published.

Weatherford, Jeffery Boston. You Can Fly: The Tuskegee Airmen. Weatherford, Carole Boston. 2017. (ENG.). 96p. (J). (gr. 4-7). pap. 7.99 *(978-1-4814-4939-7(7))* Simon & Schuster Children's Publishing.

Weatherford, Robert. Desert Dog, 1 vol. Johnston, Tony. 2008. (ENG.). 32p. (J). (gr. 1-6). pap. 7.95 *(978-1-57805-133-5(9))* Sierra Club Bks. for Children.

Weatherwax, Barbara. Gaited Games: Activities for the Young Gaited Horse Fancier. Weatherwax, Barbara. 2004. 50p. (J). (gr. 1-8). 10.00 *(978-0-9740793-2-5(4))* Markwin Pr.

Weaver, Brandon, jt. illus. see Brandon, Dan.

Weaver, Brian M. & Numberman, Neil. Creepy Crawly Crime. Reynolds, Aaron. 2009. (Joey Fly, Private Eye Ser.: 1). (ENG.). 96p. (J). (gr. 2-4). pap. 15.99 *(978-0-8050-8786-4(9)*, 900050558) Square Fish.

Weaver, Dustin. S. H. I. E. L. D. by Hickman & Weaver: the Human Machine. 2019. (ENG.). 192p. (YA). (gr. 8-17). pap. 24.99 *(978-0-7851-5250-7(4))* Marvel Worldwide, Inc.

Weaver, Jo. A Story Like the Wind. Lewis, Gill. 2018. (ENG.). 80p. (J). 16.00 *(978-0-8028-5514-5(8)*, Eerdmans Bks For Young Readers) Eerdmans, William B. Publishing Co.

Weaver, Jo. Little Tigers. Weaver, Jo. 2019. (ENG.). 32p. (J). (gr. -1-2). 17.95 *(978-1-68263-110-2(9))* Peachtree Publishing Co. Inc.

—Little Whale, 1 vol. Weaver, Jo. 2018. (ENG.). 32p. (J). (gr. -1-2). 17.95 *(978-1-68263-049-5(8))* Peachtree Publishing Co. Inc.

Weaver, Lila Quintero. My Year in the Middle. Weaver, Lila Quintero. 2020. 288p. (J). (gr. 3-7). pap. 7.99 *(978-1-5362-1317-1(9))* Candlewick Pr.

Weaver, Lisa, jt. illus. see Yoder, Laura.

Weaver, Steve. Those Amazing Alligators, Vol. Feeney, Kathy. 2006. (Those Amazing Animals Ser.). (ENG.). 58p. (J). (gr. -1-12). per. 9.95 *(978-1-56164-356-1(4))* Pineapple Pr., Inc.

—Those Beautiful Butterflies, Vol. Cussen, Sarah. 2008. (Those Amazing Animals Ser.). (ENG.). (J). (gr. -1-12). 58p. pap. 9.95 *(978-1-56164-415-5(3))*; 55p. lib. bdg. 14.95 *(978-1-56164-414-8(5))* Pineapple Pr., Inc.

—Those Big Bears, Vol. Wicker, Jan Lee. 2011. (Those Amazing Animals Ser.). (ENG.). 56p. (J). (gr. -1-12). pap. 8.95 *(978-1-56164-492-6(7))*; lib. bdg. 14.95 *(978-1-56164-491-9(9))* Pineapple Pr., Inc.

—Those Colossal Cats, Vol. Magellan, Marta. 2009. (Those Amazing Animals Ser.). (ENG.). 55p. (J). (gr. -1-12). 14.95 *(978-1-56164-457-5(9))*; pap. 8.95 *(978-1-56164-458-2(7))* Pineapple Pr., Inc.

—Those Delightful Dolphins, Vol. Wicker, Jan Lee. 2007. (Those Amazing Animals Ser.). (ENG.). 58p. (J). (gr. -1-12). per. 9.95 *(978-1-56164-381-3(5))* Pineapple Pr., Inc.

—Those Enormous Elephants, Vol. Cussen, Sarah. 2012. (Those Amazing Animals Ser.). (ENG.). 56p. (J). (gr. -1-12). 14.95 *(978-1-56164-515-2(X))*; pap. 9.95 *(978-1-56164-516-9(8))* Pineapple Pr., Inc.

—Those Excellent Eagles, Vol. Wicker, Jan Lee. 2006. (Those Amazing Animals Ser.). (ENG.). 58p. (J). (gr. -1-12). pap. 9.95 *(978-1-56164-355-4(6))* Pineapple Pr., Inc.

—Those Excellent Eagles, Vol. Moore, H. G., photos by. Wicker, Jan Lee. 2006. (Those Amazing Animals Ser.). (ENG.). 55p. (J). (gr. -1-12). lib. bdg. 14.95 *(978-1-56164-360-8(2))* Pineapple Pr., Inc.

—Those Funny Flamingos, Vol. Wicker, Jan Lee. 2004. (Those Amazing Animals Ser.). (ENG.). 58p. (J). (gr. -1-12). pap. 9.95 *(978-1-56164-295-3(9))* Pineapple Pr., Inc.

—Those Giant Giraffes, Vol. Wicker, Jan Lee. 2015. (Those Amazing Animals Ser.). (ENG.). 56p. pap. 9.95 *(978-1-56164-788-0(8))* Pineapple Pr., Inc.

—Those Lively Lizards, Vol. Magellan, Marta. 2008. (Those Amazing Animals Ser.). (ENG.). 58p. (J). (gr. -1-12). pap. 9.95 *(978-1-56164-427-8(7))* Pineapple Pr., Inc.

—Those Magical Manatees, Vol. Wicker, Jan Lee. 2008. (Those Amazing Animals Ser.). (ENG.). 55p. (J). (gr. -1-12). lib. bdg. 14.95 *(978-1-56164-382-0(3))* Pineapple Pr., Inc.

—Those Magical Manatees, Vol. Wicker, Jan L. 2008. (Those Amazing Animals Ser.). (ENG.). 58p. (J). (gr. -1-12). pap. 9.95 *(978-1-56164-383-7(1))* Pineapple Pr., Inc.

—Those Mischievous Monkeys, Vol. Nickel, Bonnie. 2012. (Those Amazing Animals Ser.). (ENG.). 56p. (J). (gr. -1-12). pap. 9.95 *(978-1-56164-509-1(5))*; lib. bdg. 14.95 *(978-1-56164-510-7(9))* Pineapple Pr., Inc.

—Those Outrageous Owls, Vol. Moore, H. G., photos by. Wyatt, Laura. 2006. (Those Amazing Animals Ser.). (ENG.). (J). (gr. -1-12). 55p. 14.95 *(978-1-56164-365-3(3))*; 58p. per. 9.95 *(978-1-56164-366-0(1))* Pineapple Pr., Inc.

—Those Peculiar Pelicans, Vol. Cussen, Sarah. 2005. (Those Amazing Animals Ser.). (ENG.). 58p. (J). (gr. -1-12). per. 8.95 *(978-1-56164-340-0(8))* Pineapple Pr., Inc.

—Those Peculiar Pelicans, Vol. Hammond, Roger, photos by. Cussen, Sarah R. 2006. (Those Amazing Animals Ser.). (ENG.). 55p. (J). (gr. -1-12). lib. bdg. 14.95 *(978-1-56164-358-5(0))* Pineapple Pr., Inc.

—Those Perky Penguins, Vol. Cussen, Sarah. 2011. (Those Amazing Animals Ser.). (ENG.). 56p. (J). (gr. -1-12). 14.95 *(978-1-56164-504-6(4))*; pap. 9.95 *(978-1-56164-505-3(2))* Pineapple Pr., Inc.

—Those Terrific Turtles, Vol. Cussen, Sarah. 2006. (Those Amazing Animals Ser.). (ENG.). 55p. (J). (gr. -1-12). per. 9.95 *(978-1-56164-364-6(5))* Pineapple Pr., Inc.

Weaver, Steve, et al. Those Voracious Vultures, Vol. Magellan, Marta. 2008. (Those Amazing Animals Ser.). (ENG.). 55p. (J). (gr. -1-12). 14.95 *(978-1-56164-424-7(2))* Pineapple Pr., Inc.

Web, Ros. Pj & the Magical Starry Blanket. 2018. (Pj & the Magical Starry Blanket Ser.: Vol. 1). (ENG.). 60p. (J). pap. 12.99 *(978-1-7180-2463-2(0))* Independently Published.

Webb, Amanda. Legends of Aukera: The Ascendants - Volume One. Webb, Amanda. Webb, Rory. 2018. (Legends of Aukera Ser.). (ENG.). 116p. (YA). (gr. 7-12). pap. 18.99 *(978-1-63529-941-0(1))* Caliber Comics.

Webb, Amanda. Legends of Aukera: The Ascendants - Volume Three. Webb, Amanda. Webb, Rory. 2020. (Legends of Aukera Ser.). (ENG.). 104p. (YA). (gr. 7-12). pap. 19.99 ***(978-1-63529-861-1(X))*** Caliber Comics.

Webb, Amanda. Legends of Aukera: The Ascendants - Volume Two. Webb, Amanda. Webb, Rory. 2018. (Legends of Aukera Ser.). (ENG.). 104p. (YA). (gr. 7-12). pap. 18.99 *(978-1-63529-932-8(2))* Caliber Comics.

Webb, Arch. With Joffre at Verdun: A Story of the Western Front. Brereton, F. S. 2012. 240p. *(978-1-78139-196-9(3))* Benediction Classics.

Webb, Blair. The Education of Loosy Potts: Clean Your Room. Perry, Brien. 2018. (ENG.). 38p. (J). pap. 11.99 *(978-0-9980260-1-5(8))* Perry, Brien.

—The Education of Loosy Potts Clean Your Room. Perry, Brien. 2018. (Education of Loosy Potts Ser.: Vol. 1). (ENG.). 38p. (J). pap. 11.99 *(978-1-7307-2276-9(8))* Independently Published.

—Frog & Dog: Unlikely Friendships. Perry, Brien. 2019. (Frog & Dog Ser.: Vol. 1). (ENG.). 38p. (J). (gr. k-3). pap. 11.99 *(978-0-9980260-2-2(6))* Perry, Brien.

Webb, Celia. Webb's Wondrous Tales Book 1. Webb, Mack Henry, Jr. 2006. 184p. (YA). per. 14.95 *(978-0-9779576-1-3(6))* Pilinut Pr., Inc.

—Webb's Wondrous Tales Book 2. Webb, Mack H., Jr. 2007. 156p. (J). per. 14.95 *(978-0-9779576-3-7(2))* Pilinut Pr., Inc.

—Webb's Wondrous Tales Book 4. Webb, Mack H., Jr. 2019. (ENG.). 192p. (YA). (gr. 7-9). pap. 14.95 *(978-1-944390-03-7(0))* Pilinut Pr., Inc.

Webb, Jonathan. The Missing Sock: And Other Stories. Webb, Shirley. 2012. (ENG.). 36p. (J). pap. 21.99 ***(978-1-4771-5700-8(X))*** Xlibris Corp.

Webb-Jones, Darlene Y. a. K's Big Adventure. Munir, Jamilah. 2019. (ENG.). 36p. (J). 23.95 ***(978-1-64350-803-0(2))***; pap. 13.95 ***(978-1-64350-802-3(4))*** Page Publishing Inc.

Webb, Melissa. Fearsome Creatures. Farrer, Vashti. 2004. iv, 36p. (J). pap. *(978-0-7608-6744-0(5))* Sundance/Newbridge Educational Publishing.

—Luka's New Kite, 7 vols. Haydon, Julie. 2005. (ENG.). (J). (gr. 1). pap. 54.80 *(978-1-4189-1740-1(0))* Rigby Education.

—Tyrannosaurus Rex. Pryor, Kimberley Jane. 2012. (Discovering Dinosaurs Ser.). 32p. (gr. 3-3). 29.50 *(978-1-60870-539-9(0))* Cavendish Square Publishing LLC.

—Velociraptor. Pryor, Kimberley Jane. 2012. (Discovering Dinosaurs Ser.). 32p. (gr. 3-3). 29.50 *(978-1-60870-540-5(4))* Cavendish Square Publishing LLC.

Webb, Philip. Bee Alarm! Burslem, Diana & Freeman, Diana. 2013. 24p. (gr. 3-3). pap. *(978-1-77654-020-4(4)*, Red Rocket Readers) Flying Start Bks.

—Bubble Trouble: 3-in-1 Package. Eggleton, Jill. (Sails Literacy Ser.). 24p. (gr. k-18). 57.00 *(978-0-7578-8614-0(0))* Rigby Education.

—Bubble Trouble: 6 Small Books. Eggleton, Jill. (Sails Literacy Ser.). 24p. (gr. k-18). 25.00 *(978-0-7578-7726-1(5))* Rigby Education.

—Bubble Trouble: Big Book Only. Eggleton, Jill. (Sails Literacy Ser.). 24p. (gr. k-18). 27.00 *(978-0-7578-6197-0(0))* Rigby Education.

—Freddy Bear & the Big Bed. Cowley, Joy. 2017. (Freddy Bear Ser.). 20p. (J). (— 1). bds. 12.99 *(978-1-927262-96-2(8))* Upstart Pr. NZL. Dist: Independent Pubs. Group.

—Lazy Duck. Windsor, Jo. (Sails Literacy Ser.). 24p. (gr. k-18). 27.00 *(978-0-7635-6989-1(5))* Rigby Education.

—Lazy Duck: 3-in-1 Package. Windsor, Jo. (Sails Literacy Ser.). 24p. (gr. k-18). 57.00 *(978-0-7578-3199-7(0))* Rigby Education.

—Let's Play Ball, 6 pack. Holden, Pam. 2009. (Red Rocket Readers Ser.). 16p. (gr. -1-1). pap. *(978-1-877363-17-7(0)*, Red Rocket Readers) Flying Start Bks.

—Message from Camp, 6 pack. Holden, Pam. 2009. (Red Rocket Readers Ser.). 19p. (gr. 2-2). pap. *(978-1-877363-64-1(2)*, Red Rocket Readers) Flying Start Bks.

—Mrs. Mcfee. Eggleton, Jill. 2009. 39.95 *(978-0-7664-3147-8(9))* Abrams & Co. Pubs., Inc.

—So Fast, 6 pack. Holden, Pam. 2009. (Red Rocket Readers Ser.). 16p. (gr. -1-1). pap. *(978-1-877363-20-7(0)*, Red Rocket Readers) Flying Start Bks.

—Stories of Santa. Punter, Russell. 2006. (Young Reading Series 1 Gift Bks.). 48p. (J). 8.99 *(978-0-7945-1476-1(6)*, Usborne) EDC Publishing.

—Who is under There?, 1 vol. Dale, Jay. 2012. (Wonder Words Ser.). (ENG.). 32p. (gr. k-2). pap. 5.99 *(978-1-4296-8924-3(2)*, Capstone Pr.) Capstone.

Webb, Philip. Freddy Bear & the Toothpaste. Cowley, Joy. 2017. (Freddy Bear Ser.). 20p. (J). (— 1). bds. 12.99 *(978-1-927262-97-9(6))* Upstart Pr. NZL. Dist: Independent Pubs. Group.

Webb, Ray. Daily Life in Ancient & Modern Baghdad. Kotapish, Dawn. 2005. (Cities Through Time Ser.). 64p. (gr. 5-12). 25.26 *(978-0-8225-3219-4(0))* Lerner Publishing Group.

—Daily Life in Ancient & Modern Jerusalem. Slavik, Diane. (Cities Through Time Ser.). 64p. 2005. (gr. 5-12). 25.26 *(978-0-8225-3218-7(2))*; 2003. (J). 18.95 *(978-1-58013-075-2(5)*, Kar-Ben Publishing) Lerner Publishing Group.

Webb, Ros. Albert the Albatross: Attitude Equals Altitude. Redden IV, Oscar. 2019. (ENG.). 28p. (J). pap. 12.60 *(978-1-0956-7060-6(3))* Independently Published.

—El Amor de Los 10,000. Brown, Kecia. McManus, Makaila Imani, ed. 2019. (SPA.). 42p. (J). pap. 16.95 *(978-1-0734-0120-8(0))* Independently Published.

—The Cosmic Carrot: A Journey to Wellness, Clear Vision & Good Nutrition. Grand, Robert Alan. 2019. (ENG.). 40p. (gr. 3-7). pap. 10.95 *(978-1-64279-266-9(7))* Morgan James Publishing.

—Davey, Daisy & Pete: Pillow Fort Adventures. Hunter, T. E. 2019. (Imagine with Davey, Daisy & Pete Ser.: Vol. 3). (ENG.). 24p. (J). pap. 9.95 *(978-0-578-46097-0(1))* Hom, Jonathan.

—Davey, Daisy & Pete: The Things We Can Dream. Hunter, T. E. 2018. (Imagine with Davey, Daisy & Pete Ser.: Vol. 1). (ENG.). 24p. (J). pap. 9.95 *(978-0-578-40850-7(3))* Davey, Daisy & Pete - The Things We Can Dream.

Webb, Ros. Dreams of Zugunruhe. Kinsey, Michael C. 2020. (ENG.). 54p. (J). 21.99 ***(978-0-578-67223-6(5))*** Kinsey, Michael.

—Francesca Finds Her Father. Briseno, Kellie Ann. 2019. (Francesca Ser.). (ENG.). 34p. (J). (gr. k-5). 13.95 ***(978-0-578-57205-5(2))*** Kellie Ann Briseno.

Webb, Ros. Homestead Friends: Beatrice's Big Predicament! Levi, Sheli. 2019. (Homestead Friends Ser.: Vol. 5). (ENG.). 34p. (J). pap. 12.99 *(978-1-7330477-0-8(0))* Living Tree Pr.

—Homestead Friends: Leaping Leah's Big Trip to Town! Levi, Sheli. 2019. (Homestead Friends Ser.: Vol. 4). (ENG.). 32p. (J). pap. 12.99 *(978-1-7320355-9-1(8))* Living Tree Pr.

—I Can Do All Things! Samuel, Kenya. 2019. (ENG.). 26p. (J). pap. 9.99 *(978-1-7927-9704-0(4))* Independently Published.

Webb, Ros. I Love You More Than Christmas. McGinnis, Deborah. 2019. (ENG.). 24p. (J). 19.99 ***(978-0-578-51635-6(7))*** McGinnis, Deborah.

—I Love You More Than Christmas. McGinnis, Deborah Ann. 2019. (Christmas Softcover Ser.: 02). (ENG.). 24p. (J). pap. 14.99 ***(978-1-64667-006-2(X))*** McGinnis, Deborah.

Webb, Ros. The Love Of 10,000. Brown, Kecia. McManus, Makaila Imani, ed. 2019. (ENG.). 42p. (J). pap. 16.95 *(978-1-7232-5248-8(4))* CreateSpace Independent Publishing Platform.

—O Amor Dos 10. 000. Brown, Kecia. McManus, Makaila Imani, ed. 2019. (POR.). 42p. (J). pap. 16.95 *(978-1-0806-6269-2(3))* Independently Published.

Webb, Ross. The Cosmic Carrot: A Journey to Wellness, Clear Vision & Good Nutrition. Grand, Robert. I.t. ed. 2018. 34p. pap. 10.95 *(978-0-9967223-5-3(1))* COSMIC EDITIONS , LLC.

—Sophie & the Forest Bullies: Trouble in Sunshine Forest. Litscher Debruin, Kari. 2018. (Sunshine Forest Ser.: Vol. 2). (ENG.). 34p. (J). (gr. k-3). pap. 7.99 *(978-0-9995544-1-8(7))* Mabela Publishing.

W

Webb, Samantha. Glub. Webb, Samantha. 2019. (ENG.). 32p. (J). pap. *(978-1-9996577-1-0(3))* Little Goblins' Bks.

Webb, Sarah. You're Too Small, 1 vol. Claus, Fred J. 2009. 20p. pap. 24.95 *(978-1-60703-757-6(2))* America Star Bks.

Webb, Shamore. Mr Henry's Grass. Nicholson, Wanda. 2008. 76p. pap. 20.95 *(978-1-59800-665-0(7))* Outskirts Pr., Inc.

Webb, Stephanie. Huck & Finn, Bookstore Cats. Coolidge, Kevin. 2019. (ENG.). 32p. (J). (gr. -1-3). 8.99 *(978-1-64633-995-2(9))* From My Shelf Bks. & Gifts.

Webb, Terris. Tee & Tye Learn to Fly. Webb, Ramona. 2008. 20p. pap. 24.95 *(978-1-60703-729-3(7))* America Star Bks.

Webb, Trudi. There's a Bear in My Book! Graham, Cece. 2020. (Squishy in My Book Ser.). (ENG.). 10p. (J). (gr. -1-k). bds. 9.99 *(978-1-78958-423-3(X))* Top That! Publishing PLC GBR. Dist: Independent Pubs. Group.

—There's a Dinosaur in My Book! Graham, Cece. 2020. (Squishy in My Book Ser.). (ENG.). 10p. (J). (gr. -1-k). bds. 9.99 *(978-1-78958-424-0(8))* Top That! Publishing PLC GBR. Dist: Independent Pubs. Group.

—There's a Dragon in My Book! Graham, Cece. 2020. (Squishy in My Book Ser.). (ENG.). 10p. (J). (gr. -1-k). bds. 9.99 *(978-1-78958-417-2(5))* Top That! Publishing PLC GBR. Dist: Independent Pubs. Group.

—There's a Yeti in My Book! Graham, Cece. 2020. (Squishy in My Book Ser.). (ENG.). 10p. (J). (gr. -1-k). bds. 9.99 *(978-1-78958-416-5(7))* Top That! Publishing PLC GBR. Dist: Independent Pubs. Group.

Webber, B. Seriously, Kitty! Webber, B. 2018. (ENG.). 50p. (J). (gr. k-3). 22.00 *(978-1-7324597-0-0(3))* Open Water Pr.

Webber, Carol. Minnesota Moon. Polinski, Jo. 2007. 20p. per. 12.95 *(978-1-933482-60-6(5))* White Turtle Bks.

Webber-Feeney, Siri. Pearls of Wisdom: African & Caribbean Folktales:Text/2 CDs. Mama, Raouf & Romney, Mary. 2005. (gr. 4-12). pap., stu. ed. 28.00 incl. audio compact disk *(978-0-86647-218-0(5))* Pro Lingua Assocs., Inc.

Webber, Helen. No One Can Ever Steal Your Rainbow. Meislin, Barbara. 2005. 28p. 19.75 incl. audio compact disk *(978-0-9714506-0-8(9))* Purple Lady Productions.

Webber, Jennie. The Coral Kingdom. Knowles, Laura. 2018. (ENG.). 32p. (J). (gr. -1-2). 18.95 ***(978-1-910277-67-6(3)*** Words & Pictures) Quarto Publishing Group UK GBR. Dist: Hachette Bk. Group.

Webber, Jennie. It Starts with a Seed. Knowles, Laura. 2017. (ENG.). 32p. (J). (gr. 1-4). 18.95 *(978-1-910277-26-3(6),* Words & Pictures) Quarto Publishing Group UK GBR. Dist: Hachette Bk. Group.

Webber, John, et al. The Childhood of Jesus / la niñez de Jesús. 2007.Tr. of niñez de Jesús. (ENG & SPA.). 24p. (J). pap. 3.50 *(978-0-9801121-5-3(X))* Holy Heroes LLC.

Webber, John & Cohee, Ron. From an Angel in a Dream, the Story of Saint Joseph, Marys Husband: De un Angel en un Sueño, la Historia de San José, Esposo de Maria. Drake, Tim. Alvarado, Tomas, tr. 2nd ed. 2003. (SPA.). (J). 5.00 *(978-0-9747571-0-0(1))* Catholic World Mission.

Webber, Mike. Stranded in a Snowstorm! Wozniak, Paul. 2014. (ENG.). 82p. pap. 11.95 *(978-1-63047-173-6(9))* Morgan James Publishing.

Webber, Penny. Wow, What a Mama!! Njenga, Wamoro P. 2012. 58p. pap. 13.70 *(978-0-9827461-2-7(1))* Prop-Abilities Inc.

Weber, Andra. Red Rose & Blue Butterfly. Sirotzky, Sara. 2012. (ENG.). 32p. (J). (gr. -1-3). 17.95 *(978-1-4507-9594-4(3))* Ampersand, Inc.

Weber, Caressa. The Purple with Pink Polka Dot Ponies. Carithers, Rochelle. 2010. 102p. pap. 7.95 *(978-1-936107-31-5(7))* Salem Author Services.

Weber, Dennis. The Secret of Your Name. Bouchard, David. 2020. (ENG.). 32p. (J). (gr. 3-7). pap. 16.95 ***(978-0-88995-606-3(5),*** ec175ff2-fbd9-45cd-a6de-4794fe4ac357) Red Deer Pr. CAN. Dist: Firefly Bks., Ltd.

Weber, Dennis. The Secret of Your Name, 1 vol. Bouchard, David & Arcand, John. 2009. (ENG.). 32p. (J). (gr. 4-6). 24.95 *(978-0-88995-439-7(9),* 889d7b1b-b607-4b55-bc79-3564b105877c) Trifolium Bks., Inc. CAN. Dist: Firefly Bks., Ltd.

Weber, Jen Funk. Astounding Activities for Minecrafters: Puzzles & Games for Endless Fun. Sky Pony Press. 2019. (Activities for Minecrafters Ser.). 96p. (J). (gr. 1-5). pap. 11.99 *(978-1-5107-4102-7(X),* Sky Pony Pr.) Skyhorse Publishing Co., Inc.

Weber, Jill. Angel Bites the Bullet. Delton, Judy. 2003. (ENG.). 144p. (J). (gr. 3-7). pap. 10.95 *(978-0-618-36920-1(1),* 484409) Houghton Mifflin Harcourt Publishing Co.

—Angel's Mother's Baby. Judy Delton Family Trust Staff & Delton, Judy. 2003. (ENG.). 144p. (J). (gr. 3-7). pap. 10.95 *(978-0-618-36919-5(8),* 484426) Houghton Mifflin Harcourt Publishing Co.

—George Washington Carver: The Peanut Wizard. Driscoll, Laura. 2003. (Smart about History Ser.). 32p. (J). (gr. k-4). mass mkt. 6.99 *(978-0-448-43243-4(9),* Grosset & Dunlap) Penguin Young Readers Group.

—Goodnight Bubbala. Haft, Sheryl. 2019. (ENG.). 32p. (J). (gr. k-k). 17.99 *(978-0-525-55477-6(7),* Dial Bks) Penguin Young Readers Group.

—Pippa's Passover Plate. Kirkfield, Vivian. 2019. 40p. (J). (gr. -1-3). 17.99 *(978-0-8234-4162-4(8))* Holiday Hse., Inc.

—Smart about the Presidents. Cocca-Leffler, Maryann et al. 2004. (Smart about History Ser.). 64p. (J). (gr. k-4). mass mkt. 7.99 *(978-0-448-43372-1(9),* Grosset & Dunlap) Penguin Young Readers Group.

—The Story of Esther. Kimmel, Eric A. 2011. (ENG.). 32p. (J). (gr. -1-3). 16.95 *(978-0-8234-2223-4(2))* Holiday Hse., Inc.

—Story of Hanukkah. Adler, David A. 2011. (ENG.). 32p. (J). (gr. -1-3). 14.95 *(978-0-8234-2295-1(X))* Holiday Hse., Inc.

—The Story of Hanukkah. Adler, David A. (ENG.). (J). 2018. 24p. (— 1). bds. 7.99 *(978-0-8234-4032-0(X));* 2012. 32p. (gr. -1-3). pap. 7.99 *(978-0-8234-2547-1(9))* Holiday Hse., Inc.

—The Story of Passover. Adler, David A. (ENG.). 32p. (J). (gr. -1-3). 2015. 7.99 *(978-0-8234-3304-9(8));* 2014. 15.95 *(978-0-8234-2902-8(4))* Holiday Hse., Inc.

—What Is the Story of Hello Kitty? Anderson, Kirsten & Who HQ. 2019. (What Is the Story Of? Ser.). 112p. (J). (gr. 3-7). 6.99 *(978-1-5247-8839-1(2));* lib. bdg. 15.99 *(978-1-5247-8840-7(6))* Penguin Young Readers Group. (Penguin Workshop).

—Who Was John F. Kennedy? McDonough, Yona Zeldis & Who HQ. 2004. (Who Was? Ser.). 112p. (J). (gr. 3-7). pap. 5.99 *(978-0-448-43743-9(0),* Penguin Workshop) Penguin Young Readers Group.

Weber, Judy. A Cooper Tails Book: My First Snow. Sterling, B. K. 2019. (Cooper Tails Book Ser.: Vol. 2). (ENG.). 24p. (J). (gr. k-5). pap. 12.95 ***(978-0-578-54355-0(9))*** Sterling, Bridgette.

Weber, Judy. My New Family: A Cooper Tails Book. Sterling, B. K. 2019. (Cooper Tails Ser.: Vol. 1). (ENG.). 24p. (J). (gr. k-5). pap. 12.95 *(978-0-578-44760-5(6))* Sterling, Bridgette.

Weber, Lisa K. Annie's Adventures. Baratz-Logsted, Lauren. 2008. (Sisters Eight Ser.: 1). (J). (ENG.). 144p. (gr. 1-4). pap. 6.99 *(978-0-547-05338-7(X),* 1036248);1. 128p. (gr. 2-4). 21.19 *(978-0-547-13349-2(9))* Houghton Mifflin Harcourt Publishing Co.

—The Assistant Vanishes!, 1 vol. Dahl, Michael. 2013. (Hocus Pocus Hotel Ser.). (ENG.). 112p. (J). (gr. 3-6). lib. bdg. 25.32 *(978-1-4342-4101-6(7),* Stone Arch Bks.) Capstone.

—The Case of the Counterfeit Painting. Brezenoff, Steve. 2016. (Museum Mysteries Ser.). (ENG.). 128p. (J). (gr. 3-6). pap. 6.95 *(978-1-4965-2522-2(1));* lib. bdg. 26.65 *(978-1-4965-2518-5(3))* Capstone. (Stone Arch Bks.).

—Case of the Counterfeit Painting. Brezenoff, Steven. 2017. 118p. (J). pap. *(978-1-4965-2530-7(2),* Stone Arch Bks.) Capstone.

—The Case of the Haunted History Museum. Brezenoff, Steven. 2015. (Museum Mysteries Ser.). (ENG.). 128p. (J). (gr. 3-6). lib. bdg. 26.65 *(978-1-4342-9687-0(3),* Stone Arch Bks.) Capstone.

—The Case of the Missing Mom. Brezenoff, Steven. 2016. (Museum Mysteries Ser.). (ENG.). 128p. (J). (gr. 3-6). 26.65 *(978-1-4965-2517-8(5),* Stone Arch Bks.) Capstone.

—The Case of the Missing Museum Archives. Brezenoff, Steven. 2015. (Museum Mysteries Ser.). (ENG.). 128p. (J). (gr. 3-6). lib. bdg. 26.65 *(978-1-4342-9688-7(1),* Stone Arch Bks.) Capstone.

—The Case of the New Professor. Brezenoff, Steve. 2019. (Museum Mysteries Ser.). (ENG.). 128p. (J). (gr. 3-6). lib. bdg. 26.65 *(978-1-4965-7818-1(X),* 139246, Stone Arch Bks.) Capstone.

—The Case of the Portrait Vandal. Brezenoff, Steven. 2015. (Museum Mysteries Ser.). (ENG.). 128p. (J). (gr. 3-6). lib. bdg. 26.65 *(978-1-4342-9685-6(7),* Stone Arch Bks.) Capstone.

—The Case of the Soldier's Ghost. Brezenoff, Steve. 2016. (Museum Mysteries Ser.). (ENG.). 128p. (J). (gr. 3-6). pap. 6.95 *(978-1-4965-2523-9(X));* lib. bdg. 26.65 *(978-1-4965-2519-2(1))* Capstone. (Stone Arch Bks.).

—The Case of the Soldier's Ghost. Brezenoff, Steven. 2017. 120p. (J). pap. *(978-1-4965-2531-4(0),* Stone Arch Bks.) Capstone.

—The Case of the Stolen Sculpture. Brezenoff, Steven. 2015. (Museum Mysteries Ser.). (ENG.). 128p. (J). (gr. 3-6). lib. bdg. 26.65 *(978-1-4342-9686-3(5),* Stone Arch Bks.) Capstone.

—The Case of the Stolen Space Suit. Brezenoff, Steven. 2016. (Museum Mysteries Ser.). (ENG.). 128p. (J). (gr. 3-6). 26.65 *(978-1-4965-2516-1(7),* Stone Arch Bks.) Capstone.

—Drawing Princesses, Trolls, & Other Fairy-Tale Characters: 4D an Augmented Reading Drawing Experience. Cella, Clara. 2018. (Drawing With 4D Ser.). (ENG.). 32p. (J). (gr. 3-9). lib. bdg. 31.99 *(978-1-5435-3190-9(3),* 138816, Capstone Pr.) Capstone.

—Durinda's Dangers. Baratz-Logsted, Lauren. 2008. (Sisters Eight Ser.: 2). (J). (ENG.). 128p. (gr. 1-4). pap. 6.99 *(978-0-547-05339-4(8),* 1036249);2. 144p. (gr. 2-4). 18.69 *(978-0-547-13347-8(2))* Houghton Mifflin Harcourt Publishing Co.

—The Haunted Howl. Luper, Eric. 2016. (Key Hunters Ser.: 3). (ENG.). 128p. (J). (gr. 2-5). pap. 4.99 *(978-0-545-82211-4(4),* Scholastic Paperbacks) Scholastic, Inc.

—Marcia's Madness. Baratz-Logsted, Lauren et al. 2010. (Sisters Eight Ser.: 5). 128p. (J). (ENG.). (gr. 1-4). pap. 6.99 *(978-0-547-32864-5(8),* 1416978);5. (gr. 2-4). 18.69 *(978-0-547-33401-1(X))* Houghton Mifflin Harcourt Publishing Co.

—Out the Rear Window, 1 vol. Dahl, Michael. 2012. (Hocus Pocus Hotel Ser.). (ENG.). 112p. (J). (gr. 3-6). lib. bdg. 25.32 *(978-1-4342-4038-5(X),* Stone Arch Bks.) Capstone.

—Pecos Bill: Colossal Cowboy. Stone Arch Books Staff. 2010. (Graphic Spin Ser.). (ENG.). 40p. (J). (gr. 3-6). pap. 5.95 *(978-1-4342-2267-1(5),* Stone Arch Bks.) Capstone.

—Pecos Bill, Colossal Cowboy. Capstone Press Staff. 2010. (Graphic Spin Ser.). (ENG.). 40p. (J). (gr. 3-6). lib. bdg. 25.32 *(978-1-4342-1896-4(1),* Stone Arch Bks.) Capstone.

—Pecos Bill Tames a Colossal Cyclone, 1 vol. Braun, Eric & Bowman, James Cloyd. 2014. (American Folk Legends Ser.). (ENG.). 32p. (J). (gr. k-2). lib. bdg. 27.99 *(978-1-4795-5429-4(4),* Picture Window Bks.) Capstone.

—The Prisoners of the Thirteenth Floor, 1 vol. Dahl, Michael. 2014. (Hocus Pocus Hotel Ser.). (ENG.). 128p. (J). (gr. 3-6). 25.32 *(978-1-4342-6508-1(0),* Stone Arch Bks.) Capstone.

—The Return of Abracadabra. Dahl, Michael. (Hocus Pocus Hotel Ser.). (ENG.). 208p. (J). (gr. 3-6). 2015. pap. 7.95 *(978-1-4965-2486-7(1));* 2013. 10.95 *(978-1-4342-4721-6(X))* Capstone. (Stone Arch Bks.).

—The Thirteenth Mystery. Dahl, Michael. (Hocus Pocus Hotel Ser.). (ENG.). 224p. (J). (gr. 3-6). 2016. pap. 7.95 *(978-1-4965-0755-6(X));* 2014. 10.95 *(978-1-4342-6509-8(9))* Capstone. (Stone Arch Bks.).

—To Catch a Ghost, 1 vol. Dahl, Michael. 2012. (Hocus Pocus Hotel Ser.). (ENG.). 112p. (J). (gr. 3-6). lib. bdg. 25.32 *(978-1-4342-4100-9(9),* Stone Arch Bks.) Capstone.

—The Trouble with Abracadabra, 1 vol. Dahl, Michael. 2013. (Hocus Pocus Hotel Ser.). (ENG.). 112p. (J). (gr. 3-6). lib. bdg. 25.32 *(978-1-4342-4102-3(5),* Stone Arch Bks.) Capstone.

—Two Truths & a Lie: It's Alive! Paquette, Ammi-Joan & Thompson, Laurie Ann. (ENG.). 176p. (J). (gr. 3-7). 2018. pap. 10.99 *(978-0-06-241881-4(5));* 2017. 17.99 *(978-0-06-241879-1(3))* HarperCollins Pubs. (Walden Pond Pr.).

—The Wizard & the Wormhole, 1 vol. Dahl, Michael. 2014. (Hocus Pocus Hotel Ser.). (ENG.). 128p. (J). (gr. 3-6). 25.32 *(978-1-4342-6507-4(2),* Stone Arch Bks.) Capstone.

—You Decide, Ben Franklin! Hirschfeld, Leila & Hirschfeld, Tom. 2016. (J). pap. *(978-0-553-50952-6(7),* Salamander Bks.) Pavilion Bks.

Weber, M. S. Harry Goes to the Hospital: A Story for Children about What It's Like to Be in the Hospital. Bennett, Howard J. 2008. 32p. (J). (gr. -1-3). 14.95 *(978-1-4338-0319-2(4));* pap. 9.95 *(978-1-4338-0320-8(8))* American Psychological Assn. (Magination Pr.).

—It Hurts When I Poop! A Story for Children Who Are Scared to Use the Potty. Bennett, Howard J. 2007. 32p. (J). (gr. -1-1). 14.95 *(978-1-4338-0130-3(2),* 4418001); pap. 9.95 *(978-1-4338-0131-0(0),* 4418002) American Psychological Assn. (Magination Pr.).

—Lions Aren't Scared of Shots: A Story for Children about Visiting the Doctor. Bennett, Howard J. 2006. 32p. (J). (gr. -1-3). 14.95 *(978-1-59147-473-9(6),* 441A473); per. 9.95 *(978-1-59147-474-6(4),* 441A474) American Psychological Assn. (Magination Pr.).

Weber, Mark M. The Pirate Princess & Other Fairy Tales. Philip, Neil & Naohman. 2005. 88p. (J). 6.99 *(978-0-590-10856-0(5),* Levine, Arthur A. Bks.) Scholastic, Inc.

Weber, Penny. Amazingly Wonderful Things. Hohmeier, Maria. 2011. (ENG & SPA.). 32p. (J). (gr. -1-3). lib. bdg. 16.95 *(978-1-936299-10-2(0),* Raven Tree Pr.,Csi) Continental Sales, Inc.

—God's Love in Action: The Amazing Gift of Jesus. Kline, Tom. 2015. (ENG.). 62p. pap. 8.99 *(978-0-9863364-0-9(8))* Reality Check Pubns.

—Growing up with a Bucket Full of Happiness: Three Rules for a Happier Life. McCloud, Carol. 2010. 88p. (J). (gr. 4). pap. 9.95 *(978-1-933916-57-6(5))* Bucket Fillers, Inc.

—I Belong. Meiners, Cheri J. 2018. (Learning about Me & You Ser.). (ENG.). 24p. (J). (— 1). bds. 8.99 *(978-1-63198-214-9(1),* 82149) Free Spirit Publishing, Inc.

Weber, Penny. I Calm Down: A Book about Working Through Strong Emotions. Meiners, Cheri J. 2020. (Learning about Me & You Ser.). (ENG.). 24p. (J). (gr. -1-k). bds. 8.99 ***(978-1-63198-455-6(1),*** 84556) Free Spirit Publishing, Inc.

Weber, Penny. I Feel. Meiners, Cheri J. 2018. (Learning about Me & You Ser.). (ENG.). 24p. (J). (— 1). bds. 8.99 *(978-1-63198-217-0(6),* 82170) Free Spirit Publishing, Inc.

—I Help: A Book about Empathy & Kindness. Meiners, Cheri J. 2019. (Learning about Me & You Ser.). (ENG.). 24p. (J). bds. 8.99 *(978-1-63198-453-2(5),* 84532) Free Spirit Publishing, Inc.

—I Listen: A Book about Understanding & Connecting. Meiners, Cheri J. 2019. (Learning about Me & You Ser.). (ENG.). 24p. (J). (gr. -1 — 1). bds. 8.99 *(978-1-63198-380-1(6),* 83801) Free Spirit Publishing, Inc.

—I Play: A Board Book about Discovery & Cooperation. Meiners, Cheri J. 2018. (Learning about Me & You Ser.). (ENG.). 24p. (J). (-k). bds. 8.99 *(978-1-63198-220-0(6),* 82200) Free Spirit Publishing, Inc.

—I Share: A Board Book about Being Kind & Generous. Meiners, Cheri J. 2018. (Learning about Me & You Ser.). (ENG.). 24p. (J). (-k). bds. 8.99 *(978-1-63198-223-1(0),* 82231) Free Spirit Publishing, Inc.

—I Speak Up: A Book about Self-Expression & Communication. Meiners, Cheri J. 2019. (Learning about Me & You Ser.). (ENG.). 24p. (J). (gr. -1 — 1). bds. 8.99 *(978-1-63198-378-8(4),* 83788) Free Spirit Publishing, Inc.

—Je Suis Unique! Vassel, Jennifer D. 2018. (FRE.). 30p. (J). pap. 14.99 *(978-0-9915556-8-0(6))* BuddingRose Pubns.

—Jorge & the Lost Cookie Jar. Arroyo, Marta. 2017. (ENG.). (J). (gr. k-3). 14.99 *(978-0-9970032-4-6(3));* 34p. pap. 9.95 *(978-0-9970032-6-0(X))* Dayton Publishing.

—Jorge y el Jarro de Galletas Perdido. Arroyo, Marta. (SPA.). 34p. (J). (gr. k-3). 2019. pap. 9.95 *(978-0-9970032-7-7(8));* 2018. 14.99 *(978-0-9970032-9-1(4))* Dayton Publishing.

—On My Way to School. 2009. (J). pap. 13.95 *(978-0-9842146-0-0(7))* Concinnity Initiatives.

—Small but Mighty. Veech, Alyssa. 2018. (ENG.). 24p. (J). 19.99 *(978-0-578-41555-0(0))* Veech, Alyssa.

—Sophie & Spot. Byers, Amber. 2018. (Sophie & Spot Ser.: 1). (ENG.). 188p. (J). (gr. 1-5). pap. 9.99 *(978-1-7328286-0-5(1))* Tadpole Pr.

—Will You Fill My Bucket? Daily Acts of Love Around the World. McCloud, Carol & Wells, Karen. 2012. 32p. (J). (-4). pap. 9.95 *(978-1-933916-97-2(4))* Bucket Fillers, Inc.

Weber, Philip A., Jr. Mark & Dan Go West: Read Well Level K Unit 17 Storybook. Gunn, Barbara et al. 2003. (Read Well Level K Ser.). 20p. (J). *(978-1-57035-688-9(2),* 55571) Cambium Education, Inc.

—Traveling by Train: Read Well Level K Unit 19 Storybook. Gerald, Tom. 2003. (Read Well Level K Ser.). 20p. (J). *(978-1-57035-690-2(4),* 55597) Cambium Education, Inc.

Weber, Philip A., Jr. Amazing Insects: Read Well Level K Unit 4 Storybook. Sprick, Marilyn et al. 2003. (Read Well Level K Ser.). 20p. (J). *(978-1-57035-676-6(9))* Cambium Education, Inc.

Weber, Rich, jt. illus. see Lenehan, Mary.

Weber, Seth. It Is I. Weber, Seth. 2005. 32p. 10.00 *(978-0-9772447-0-6(9))* Ben Franklin Pr.

Webster, Carroll. Pebbles in the Wind. Baldner, Jean V. 52p. (Orig.). (YA). (gr. 7-18). pap. 5.95 *(978-0-9615317-0-6(3))* Baldner, Jean V.

Webster, Jean. Daddy-Long-Legs. Webster, Jean. 2018. 224p. pap. 9.95 *(978-1-84749-651-5(2),* 900200349, Alma Classics) Bloomsbury Publishing USA.

Webster, Kaitlyn. No One Owns a Tree. Melanson, Arlene Evelyn. 2016. (ENG.). (J). pap. *(978-1-4602-9186-3(7))* FriesenPress.

Webster, Sarah. Un Fantasma con Asma. Gil, Carmen. 2004. (Libros para Sonar Ser.). (SPA.). 40p. (J). 15.99 *(978-84-8464-186-5(4))* Kalandraka Editora, S.L. ESP. Dist: Lectorum Pubns., Inc.

Webster, Sean. The Black Dog. Lawrence, Tracey. 2018. (ENG.). 42p. (J). pap. *(978-0-9957323-1-5(0))* SRL Publishing Ltd.

—Where Is My Voice? Lawrence, Tracey. 2017. (ENG.). 50p. (J). pap. *(978-0-9957323-2-2(9))* SRL Publishing Ltd.

Wechsler, Doug, photos by. The Hidden Life of a Toad. Wechsler, Doug. 2017. 48p. (J). (gr. -1-3). lib. bdg. 17.99 *(978-1-58089-738-9(X))* Charlesbridge Publishing, Inc.

Wechsler, Nathalie. Once upon A Fly: The Adventures of Lamouche. Wechsler, Nathalie. 2005. 24p. (J). per. 7.99 *(978-0-9766998-1-1(8))* Finlay Prints, Inc.

—Once upon A Fly - Hardcover: The Adventures of Lamouche. Wechsler, Nathalie. 2005. 24p. (J). 10.95 *(978-0-9766998-0-4(X))* Finlay Prints, Inc.

Wedekind, Annie. Wild Blue: The Story of a Mustang Appaloosa. Wedekind, Annie. Haas, Jessie. 2009. (Breyer Horse Collection: 1). (ENG.). 128p. (J). (gr. 4-6). pap. 18.69 *(978-0-312-59917-1(X),* 900063858, Feiwel & Friends) Feiwel & Friends.

Wedelich, Sam. Chicken Little: the Real & Totally True Tale. Wedelich, Sam. 2020. (ENG.). 40p. (J). (gr. -1-3). 17.99 *(978-1-338-35901-5(0),* Scholastic Pr.) Scholastic, Inc.

Wedge, Chris. Bunny: A Picture Book Adapted from the Animated Film. Wedge, Chris. 2004. 30p. (J). (gr. k-4). reprint ed. 19.00 *(978-0-7567-7460-8(8))* DIANE Publishing Co.

Wedgeworth, Frederick & Ott, Steve. Nums of Shoreview: AC Epic Fantasy Adventures. Wedgeworth, Anthony Glenn. 2018. (ENG.). 294p. (J). pap. 19.98 *(978-0-9989650-3-1(0))* Wedgeworth, Anthony G.

Wedzin, James. How the Fox Got His Crossed Legs, 1 vol. Football, Virginia & Mantla, Rosa. Siemens, Mary, tr. ed. 2016. (ENG & DGR.). 32p. (J). (gr. 1-3). 20.95 *(978-1-894778-74-9(X))* Theytus Bks., Ltd. CAN. Dist: Orca Bk. Pubs. USA.

—How the Fox Saved the People. Football, Virginia. ed. 2009. (Fox Ser.). (ENG & DGR.). 56p. (gr. k-6). 26.95 *(978-1-894778-75-6(8))* Theytus Bks., Ltd. CAN. Dist: Univ. of Toronto Pr.

Weedn, Flavia. Angels, Vol. York Lumbard, Alexis. 2013. (ENG.). 28p. (J). (gr. -1-1). 14.95 *(978-1-937786-15-1(3),* Wisdom Tales) World Wisdom, Inc.

Weedon, Sandra. The Adventures of Humphrey the Guinea Pig: Humphrey Meets Father Christmas! Weedon, Christopher. 2019. (Adventures of Humphrey the Guinea Pig Ser.: Vol. 1). (ENG.). 34p. (J). pap. ***(978-1-78623-646-3(X))*** Grosvenor Hse. Publishing Ltd.

—The Adventures of Humphrey the Guinea Pig: Humphrey's Night Out. Weedon, Christopher. 2019. (Adventures of Humphrey the Guinea Pig Ser.: Vol. 1). (ENG.). 28p. (J). pap. ***(978-1-78623-634-0(6))*** Grosvenor Hse. Publishing Ltd.

Week, Jason. The Barftastic Life of Louie Burger. Meyerhoff, Jenny. 2013. (Barftastic Life of Louie Burger Ser.: 1). (ENG.). 240p. (J). (gr. 3-6). 13.99 *(978-0-374-30518-5(8),* 9780374305185, Farrar, Straus & Giroux (BYR)) Farrar, Straus & Giroux.

Weekly, Debbie. I Like Yellow. Schiller, Pamela Byrne. 2014. 15p. (J). *(978-1-60128-861-5(1))* Frog Street Pr.

Weeks, Jeanne G., jt. illus. see Weeks, Timothy A.

Weeks, Julie. E Is for Eagle. Russell M Ed, Katie. 2019. (ENG.). 32p. (J). pap. 14.99 ***(978-1-7916-6869-3(0))*** Independently Published.

Weeks, Mary. But Not Quite. Schneider, Judy. 2004. (J). 19.95 *(978-1-59404-005-4(2))* Peanut Butter Publishing.

Weeks, Timothy A. & Weeks, Jeanne G. Goldie's Search for Silver: The Wise Mullet Finale! Weeks, Timothy A. 2009. (ENG.). 48p. (J). pap. 14.99 *(978-0-9779928-2-9(9))* Foolosophy Media.

Weevers, Peter. Elf Night. Wahl, Jan. 2005. (Picture Bks.). 32p. (gr. k-2). 15.25 *(978-1-57505-512-1(0))* Lerner Publishing Group.

Wegener, Bill. The Bible Game - New Testament: The Bible Game - New Testament. Wegener, Bill, des. 2004. (YA). bds. 34.95 *(978-0-9753620-1-3(1))* IMAGINEX, LLC.

—The Bible Game - Old Testament: The Bible Game - Old Testament. Wegener, Bill, des. 2004. (YA). bds. 34.95 *(978-0-9753620-0-6(3),* Bible Game) IMAGINEX, LLC.

Wegener, Scott. Spy on History: Victor Dowd & the World War II Ghost Army. Alberti, Enigma. 2018. (Spy on History Ser.). (ENG.). 96p. (J). (gr. 5-8). 12.95 *(978-0-7611-9326-5(X),* 19326) Workman Publishing Co., Inc.

Wegman, Marcia. Lula Belle. Wegman, Marcia. 2012. 30p. pap. 16.00 *(978-1-932043-82-2(9))* Penfield Bks.

Wegman, William. Dress up Batty. Wegman, William. 2004. (ENG.). 18p. (gr. -1-17). 19.99 *(978-0-7868-1849-5(2))* Hyperion Bks. for Children.

Wegner, Fritz. Master Bun the Bakers' Boy. Ahlberg, Allan. 2017. (Happy Families Ser.). 24p. (J). (gr. k-2). pap. 12.99 *(978-0-14-137746-9(1))* Penguin Bks., Ltd. GBR. Dist: Independent Pubs. Group.

—Star Girl. Winterfeld, Henry. Schabert, Kyrill, tr. 2015. (ENG.). 192p. (J). (gr. 3-8). pap. 7.99 *(978-0-486-79468-6(7),* 794687) Dover Pubns., Inc.

Wehr, Julian. The Animated Bunny's Tail. Wehr, Paul. 2005. 20p. (J). 18.95 *(978-0-9748093-1-1(4))* Wehr Animations.

Wehrman, Richard. The Banyan Deer: A Parable of Courage & Compassion. Martin, Rafe. 2010. (ENG.). 48p. (J). (gr. 4). 15.00 *(978-0-86171-625-8(6))* Wisdom Pubns.

Wehrman, Vicki. Hanukkah Around the World. Lehman-Wilzig, Tami. 2009. (Hanukkah Ser.). 48p. (J). (gr. k-2). 16.95 *(978-0-8225-8761-3(0));* Vol. (ENG.). (gr. 3-5). pap. 7.95 *(978-0-8225-8762-0(9))* Lerner Publishing Group. (Kar-Ben Publishing).

—Night Catch. Ehrmantraut, Brenda. 2005. 32p. (J). lib. bdg. 15.95 *(978-0-9729833-9-6(2))* Bubble Gum Pr.
—Night Catch. Ehrmantraut, Brenda. 2014. (ENG.). 32p. (J). pap. 9.95 *(978-1-934617-28-1(8))* Elva Resa Publishing, LLC.
Wei, Miao. Chinese Fables & Folktales (II) Ma, Zheng & Li, Zheng. 2010. (ENG.). 48p. (J). (gr. -1-3). 16.95 *(978-1-60220-963-3(4))* Shanghai Translation Publishing Hse. CHN. Dist: Publishers Group West (PGW).
Wei, Valerie. The Owlets at Play. Krishnan, Laura. 2016. (ENG.). (J). 19.99 *(978-0-692-78397-9(0))* Krishnan, Laura.
Weida, Amanda. The Foxes at the Bay. Smith, Doris Aldrich. 2020. (ENG.). 38p. (J). pap. 16.00 ***(978-1-7258-7791-7(0))*** CreateSpace Independent Publishing Platform.
Weidemann, Linda. This Fleeting World: An Overview of Human History. Christian, David. 2004. (YA). pap. 8.00 *(978-0-9743091-4-9(1))* Berkshire Publishing Group.
Weidman, James. The Little Boy in a Dog Suit, 1 vol. Schombs, James. 2010. 28p. pap. 24.95 *(978-1-61582-053-5(1))* PublishAmerica, Inc.
Weidner, Brittany L. My Little Lola. Halloran, T. 2019. (ENG.). 32p. (J). pap. 9.99 ***(978-1-6873-9054-7(1))*** Independently Published.
Weidner, Teri. Baby Bear's Not Hibernating, Vol. Plourde, Lynn. 2016. (ENG.). 40p. 16.95 *(978-1-60893-622-9(8))* Down East Bks.
—Blue Corn Soup. Stutson, Caroline. 2017. (ENG.). 32p. (J). (gr. k-2). 16.99 *(978-1-58536-967-6(5)*, 204325) Sleeping Bear Pr.
—Give Yourself to the Rain: Poems for the Very Young. Brown, Margaret Wise. 2012. (ENG.). 32p. (J). (gr. -1-3). pap. 16.99 *(978-1-4424-6063-8(6)*, McElderry, Margaret K. Bks.) McElderry, Margaret K. Bks.
—Goodnight Baby Bear. Shoulders, Michael. 2010. (ENG.). 32p. (J). (gr. 1-4). 19.99 *(978-1-58536-471-8(1)*, 202190) Sleeping Bear Pr.
—Read Me a Story. Zimmerman, Brooke. 2003. (My First Treasury Ser.). 40p. (J). bds. 7.98 *(978-0-7853-8247-8(X)*, 7181900) Publications International, Ltd.
—Say Daddy! Shoulders, Michael. (ENG.). (J). 2013. 26p. (gr. -1-k). 8.99 *(978-1-58536-863-1(6)*, 202383); 2008. 32p. (gr. 1-4). 15.95 *(978-1-58536-354-4(5)*, 202140) Sleeping Bear Pr.
—Sleep, Baby, Sleep. 2009. 20p. (J). (gr. -1-k). 8.95 *(978-1-58925-843-3(6))* Tiger Tales.
Weidner, Teri. Always Twins. Weidner, Teri. 2015. (ENG.). 32p. (J). (gr. -1-k). 16.95 *(978-0-8234-3159-5(2))* Holiday Hse., Inc.
—Three Little Kittens. Weidner, Teri. 2011. (Favorite Mother Goose Rhymes Ser.). (ENG.). 16p. (J). (gr. -1-2). lib. bdg. 14.21 *(978-1-60954-285-6(1)*, 200237) Child's World, Inc., The.
Weigand, John, photos by. Beaching It! a Kid's Guide to la Jolla, California. Dyan, Penelope. 2013. 34p. pap. 11.95 *(978-1-61477-092-3(1))* Bellissima Publishing, LLC.
—The Comeback Kids — Book 10 — The American Bison. Dyan, Penelope. 2012. 34p. pap. 14.95 *(978-1-61477-063-3(8))* Bellissima Publishing, LLC.
—Cruisin' 4 Fun! a Kid's Guide to Santa Cruz, Californi. Dyan, Penelope. 2013. 34p. pap. 11.95 *(978-1-61477-082-4(4))* Bellissima Publishing, LLC.
—The Discovery in the Old Mine. Hillan, Pamela & Dyan, Penelope. 2013. 116p. pap. 8.95 *(978-1-61477-095-4(6))* Bellissima Publishing, LLC.
—The Jewels of the Crown. Hillan, Pamela & Dyan, Penelope. 2013. 128p. pap. 8.95 *(978-1-61477-111-1(1))* Bellissima Publishing, LLC.
—The Mummy's Secret. Hillan, Pamela & Dyan, Penelope. 2013. 112p. pap. 8.95 *(978-1-61477-099-2(9))* Bellissima Publishing, LLC.
—The Place of Tales — - a Kid's Guide to Canterbury, Kent, England. Dyan, Penelope. 2011. 40p. pap. 12.95 *(978-1-935630-66-1(0))* Bellissima Publishing, LLC.
—VanCouver's Song — - a Kid's Guide to Vancouver, Bc, Canada. Dyan, Penelope. 2013. 34p. pap. 11.95 *(978-1-61477-104-3(9))* Bellissima Publishing, LLC.
—When in Rome, a Kid's Guide to Rome. Dyan, Penelope. 2010. 50p. pap. 11.95 *(978-1-935630-00-5(8))* Bellissima Publishing, LLC.
Weigand, John D. It's Hot, Hot, Hot! a Kid's Guide to Hawaiian Volcanoes National Park. Dyan, Penelope. 2013. 34p. pap. 11.95 *(978-1-61477-118-0(9))* Bellissima Publishing, LLC.
—The Road to Hilo! a Kid's Guide to Hilo, Hawaii. Dyan, Penelope. 2013. 34p. pap. 11.95 *(978-1-61477-117-3(0))* Bellissima Publishing, LLC.
Weigand, John D., photos by. Abraham Lincoln Was Here! a Kid's Guide to Washington D C. Dyan, Penelope. 2009. 44p. pap. 11.95 *(978-1-935118-82-4(X))* Bellissima Publishing, LLC.
—Animal Rescue, Book 1, Seals, Sea Lions & Elephant Seals, Oh My! Dyan, Penelope. 2008. 60p. pap. 15.95 *(978-1-935118-21-3(8))* Bellissima Publishing, LLC.
—Animal Rescue, Book 2, Hanauma Bay, Hawaii. Dyan, Penelope. 2008. 56p. pap. 15.95 *(978-1-935118-43-5(9))* Bellissima Publishing, LLC.
—An Apple a Day! a Kid's Guide to Julian, Californi. Dyan, Penelope. 2010. 48p. pap. 11.95 *(978-1-935630-12-8(1))* Bellissima Publishing, LLC.
—Around Corners — -A Kid's Guide to Malaga, Spain. Dyan, Penelope. 2012. 34p. pap. 11.95 *(978-1-61477-032-9(8))* Bellissima Publishing, LLC.
—Beyond the Trees! a Kid's Guide to Lake Tahoe, Us. Dyan, Penelope. 2012. 34p. pap. 11.95 *(978-1-61477-027-5(1))* Bellissima Publishing, LLC.
—The Big Clock! a Kid's Guide to Munich, Germany. Dyan, Penelope. 2013. 34p. pap. 11.95 *(978-1-61477-080-0(8))* Bellissima Publishing, LLC.
—By the Bay! a Kid's Guide to San Diego, California. Dyan, Penelope. 2013. 34p. pap. 11.95 *(978-1-61477-087-9(5))* Bellissima Publishing, LLC.
—By the Sea — -A Kid's Guide to Valletta, Malt. Dyan, Penelope. 2011. 36p. pap. 11.95 *(978-1-935630-55-5(5))* Bellissima Publishing, LLC.
—Cabbages & Kings — A Kid's Guide to Tallinn, Estoni. Dyan, Penelope. 2011. 36p. pap. 11.95 *(978-1-61477-002-2(6))* Bellissima Publishing, LLC.
—The Cat Named Blake. Dyan, Penelope. 2013. 76p. pap. 8.95 *(978-1-61477-110-4(3))* Bellissima Publishing, LLC.
—Color Your Life! a Kid's Guide to Lisbon, Portugal. Dyan, Penelope. 2012. 34p. pap. 11.95 *(978-1-61477-030-5(1))* Bellissima Publishing, LLC.
—The Comeback Kids — Book 9 — the Barbary Macaques of Gibraltar. Dyan, Penelope. 2012. 36p. pap. 14.95 *(978-1-61477-036-7(0))* Bellissima Publishing, LLC.
—The Comeback Kids — Book 11 — The Wild Mustangs. Dyan, Penelope. 2013. 34p. pap. 14.95 *(978-1-61477-078-7(6))* Bellissima Publishing, LLC.
—The Comeback Kids, Book 12, the Redwood Forest. Dyan, Penelope. 2013. 34p. pap. 14.95 *(978-1-61477-081-7(6))* Bellissima Publishing, LLC.
—The Comeback Kids, Book 8, the Antioch Burrowing Owl. Dyan, Penelope. 2009. 60p. pap. 22.00 *(978-1-935118-86-2(2))* Bellissima Publishing, LLC.
—Do You Know Juneau? a Kid's Guide to Juneau, Alaska. Dyan, Penelope. 2013. 34p. pap. 11.95 *(978-1-61477-105-0(7))* Bellissima Publishing, LLC.
—Endangered — the Peninsular Bighorn Sheep. Dyan, Penelope. 2010. 44p. pap. 11.95 *(978-1-935630-10-4(5))* Bellissima Publishing, LLC.
—Flying High in the Sky — -for Boys Only. Dyan, Penelope. 2009. 42p. pap. 13.95 *(978-1-935118-66-4(8))* Bellissima Publishing, LLC.
—For the Matterhorn's Face, Zermatt Is the Place, a Kid's Guide to Zermatt, Switzerland. Dyan, Penelope. 2010. 50p. pap. 11.95 *(978-1-935630-04-3(0))* Bellissima Publishing, LLC.
—Fun in the Sun! a Kids' Guide to Santa Barbara, Californi. Dyan, Penelope. 2012. 34p. pap. 11.95 *(978-1-61477-051-0(4))* Bellissima Publishing, LLC.
—Gold Rush! a Kid's Guide to Techatticup Gold Mine, Eldorado Canyon, Nevad. Dyan, Penelope. 2010. 48p. pap. 11.95 *(978-1-935630-11-1(3))* Bellissima Publishing, LLC.
—Halfway to the Stars! a Kid's Guide to San Francisco. Dyan, Penelope. 2009. 44p. pap. 11.95 *(978-1-935118-88-6(9))* Bellissima Publishing, LLC.
—Hangin' Loose! a Kid's Guide to Oahu, Hawaii. Dyan, Penelope. 2009. 44p. pap. 11.95 *(978-1-935118-78-7(1))* Bellissima Publishing, LLC.
—High on a Hill! a Kid's Guide to Innsbruck, Austri. Dyan, Penelope. 2011. 40p. pap. 12.95 *(978-1-935630-76-0(8))* Bellissima Publishing, LLC.
—¡Hola Córdoba! a Kid's Guide to Córdoba, Spain. Dyan, Penelope. 2012. 34p. pap. 11.95 *(978-1-61477-035-0(2))* Bellissima Publishing, LLC.
—¡Hola Madrid! a Kid's Guide to Madrid, Spain. Dyan, Penelope. 2012. 34p. pap. 11.95 *(978-1-61477-031-2(X))* Bellissima Publishing, LLC.
—I Remember Still, a Kid's Guide to Seville, Spain. Dyan, Penelope. 2012. 34p. pap. 11.95 *(978-1-61477-034-3(4))* Bellissima Publishing, LLC.
—Island Style! a Kid's Guide to Coronado, California. Dyan, Penelope. 2013. 34p. pap. 11.95 *(978-1-61477-090-9(5))* Bellissima Publishing, LLC.
—It's Magic! a Kid's Guide to Monterey, California. Dyan, Penelope. 2013. 34p. pap. 11.95 *(978-1-61477-119-7(7))* Bellissima Publishing, LLC.
—It's Medieval! a Kid's Guide to Nuremberg, Germany. Dyan, Penelope. 2013. 34p. pap. 11.95 *(978-1-61477-079-4(4))* Bellissima Publishing, LLC.
—It's Nice to Be Gone When You're in Milan, a Kid's Guide to Milan, Italy. Dyan, Penelope. 2010. 50p. pap. 11.95 *(978-1-935630-03-6(2))* Bellissima Publishing, LLC.
—The Kingdom of York, a Kid's Guide to York, Uk. Dyan, Penelope. 2011. 34p. pap. 11.95 *(978-1-61477-004-6(2))* Bellissima Publishing, LLC.
—Kona Forevermore — A Kid's Guide to Kona Hawaii. Dyan, Penelope. 2013. 36p. pap. 11.95 *(978-1-61477-116-6(2))* Bellissima Publishing, LLC.
—Let It Snow! a Kid's Guide to Regensburg, Germany. Dyan, Penelope. 2013. 34p. pap. 11.95 *(978-1-61477-076-3(X))* Bellissima Publishing, LLC.
—A Lot o' Granada, a Kid's Guide to Granada, Spain. Dyan, Penelope. 2012. 34p. pap. 11.95 *(978-1-61477-033-6(6))* Bellissima Publishing, LLC.
—Marco Polo Was Here! a Kid's Guide to Venice, Italy. Dyan, Penelope. 2009. 42p. pap. 11.95 *(978-1-935118-69-5(2))* Bellissima Publishing, LLC.
—Movin' on! a Kid's Guide to Skagway, Alaska. Dyan, Penelope. 2013. 34p. pap. 11.95 *(978-1-61477-106-7(5))* Bellissima Publishing, LLC.
—New York! New York! a Kid's Guide to New York City. Dyan, Penelope. 2009. 44p. pap. 11.95 *(978-1-935118-79-4(X))* Bellissima Publishing, LLC.
—Oh Victoria! a Kid's Guide to Victoria, Bc. Canada. Dyan, Penelope. 2013. 34p. pap. 11.95 *(978-1-61477-108-1(1))* Bellissima Publishing, LLC.
—Oh Vienna! a Kid's Guide to Vienna, Austri. Dyan, Penelope. 2013. 34p. pap. 11.95 *(978-1-61477-073-2(5))* Bellissima Publishing, LLC.
—On the Hill! a Kid's Guide to Melk, Austri. Dyan, Penelope. 2013. 34p. pap. 11.95 *(978-1-61477-074-9(3))* Bellissima Publishing, LLC.
—On the Way to Rome — - a Kid's Guide to Civitavecchia , Italy. Dyan, Penelope. 2011. 34p. pap. 11.95 *(978-1-935630-59-3(8))* Bellissima Publishing, LLC.
—One Big Hole in the Ground, a Kid's Guide to Grand Canyon, Us. Dyan, Penelope. 2010. 50p. pap. 11.95 *(978-1-935630-02-9(4))* Bellissima Publishing, LLC.
—Over a Bridge! a Kid's Guide to Budapest, Hungary. Dyan, Penelope. 2013. 38p. pap. 11.95 *(978-1-61477-071-8(9))* Bellissima Publishing, LLC.
—Over Dover — -A Kid's Guide to Dover, Uk. Dyan, Penelope. 2011. 38p. pap. 11.95 *(978-1-61477-005-3(0))* Bellissima Publishing, LLC.
—Over the Edge, a Kid's Guide to Niagara Falls, Ontario, Canad. Dyan, Penelope. 2010. 48p. pap. 11.95 *(978-1-935630-07-4(5))* Bellissima Publishing, LLC.
—The Rain in Spain — -A Kid's Guide to Barcelona, Spain. Dyan, Penelope. 2011. 38p. pap. 12.95 *(978-1-935630-56-2(3))* Bellissima Publishing, LLC.
—Reindeer & Mermaids, a Kid's Guide to Helsinki Finland. Dyan, Penelope. 2011. 34p. pap. 11.95 *(978-1-61477-000-8(X))* Bellissima Publishing, LLC.
—The Ring of Evil. Hillan, Pamela & Dyan, Penelope. 2013. 124p. pap. 8.95 *(978-1-61477-114-2(6))* Bellissima Publishing, LLC.
—Rockin' the Rock, a Kid's Guide to the Rock of Gibraltar. Dyan, Penelope. 2012. 34p. pap. 11.95 *(978-1-61477-037-4(9))* Bellissima Publishing, LLC.
—A Royal Residence — A Kid's Guide to Windsor Castle. Dyan, Penelope. 2011. 40p. pap. 12.95 *(978-1-935630-65-4(2))* Bellissima Publishing, LLC.
—See You 2-Maui — -A Kid's Guide to Maui, Hawaii. Dyan, Penelope. 2012. 34p. pap. 11.95 *(978-1-61477-038-1(7))* Bellissima Publishing, LLC.
—Shoes & Ships & Sealing Wax — -A Kids's Guide to Warnemünde, Germany. Dyan, Penelope. 2011. 34p. pap. 11.95 *(978-1-935630-99-9(7))* Bellissima Publishing, LLC.
—Smile Seattle! a Kid's Guide to Seattle, Washington. Dyan, Penelope. 2013. 34p. pap. 11.95 *(978-1-61477-109-8(X))* Bellissima Publishing, LLC.
—Spend a Day in Old Pompeii, a Kid's Travel Guide to Ancient Pompeii, Italy. Dyan, Penelope. 2010. 50p. pap. 11.95 *(978-1-935630-01-2(6))* Bellissima Publishing, LLC.
—The Squeaky Wheel Gets to Greece — -A Kid's Guide to Athens, Greece. Dyan, Penelope. 2011. 36p. pap. 11.95 *(978-1-935630-58-6(X))* Bellissima Publishing, LLC.
—Steam Train! All the Way to Canterbury, England. Dyan, Penelope. 2011. 40p. pap. 11.95 *(978-1-935630-75-3(X))* Bellissima Publishing, LLC.
—A Step in Time — A Kid's Guide to Ephesus, Turkey. Dyan, Penelope. 2011. 40p. pap. 12.95 *(978-1-935630-57-9(1))* Bellissima Publishing, LLC.
—Take a Dam Tour! a Kid's Guide to Hoover Dam, Nevad. Dyan, Penelope. 2010. 50p. pap. 11.95 *(978-1-935630-05-0(9))* Bellissima Publishing, LLC.
—This Is Sweden — -A Kid's Guide to Stockholm, Swedem. Dyan, Penelope. 2011. 34p. pap. 11.95 *(978-1-61477-003-9(4))* Bellissima Publishing, LLC.
—This Is the House George Built! a Kid's Guide to Mount Vernon. Dyan, Penelope. 2009. 44p. pap. 11.95 *(978-1-935118-83-1(8))* Bellissima Publishing, LLC.
—Totems & More! a Kid's Guide to Ketchikan, Alaska. Dyan, Penelope. 2013. 34p. pap. 11.95 *(978-1-61477-107-4(3))* Bellissima Publishing, LLC.
—Turkish Delight — A Kid's Guide to Istanbul, Turkey. Dyan, Penelope. 2011. 44p. pap. 12.95 *(978-1-935630-54-8(7))* Bellissima Publishing, LLC.
—Walk the Renaissance Walk — -A Kid's Guide to Florence, Italy. Dyan, Penelope. 2009. 42p. pap. 11.95 *(978-1-935118-70-1(6))* Bellissima Publishing, LLC.
—Water & Blood — A Kid's Guide to St Petersburg, Russi. Dyan, Penelope. 2011. 34p. pap. 11.95 *(978-1-61477-001-5(8))* Bellissima Publishing, LLC.
—What Happens in Vegas a Kid's Guide to Las Vegas, Nevad. Dyan, Penelope. 2010. 48p. pap. 11.95 *(978-1-935630-06-7(7))* Bellissima Publishing, LLC.
—Where Is London Bridge? a Kid's Guide to London. Dyan, Penelope. 2009. 44p. pap. 11.95 *(978-1-935118-80-0(3))* Bellissima Publishing, LLC.
—Yesterday's Rain — - a Kid's Guide to Kauai, Hawaii. Dyan, Penelope. 2013. 34p. pap. 11.95 *(978-1-61477-100-5(6))* Bellissima Publishing, LLC.
—Yummy Solvang! a Kid's Guide to Solvang, Californi. Dyan, Penelope. 2012. 34p. pap. 11.95 *(978-1-61477-052-7(2))* Bellissima Publishing, LLC.
Weigel, Jeff. Jack & Jill Went up to Kill: A Book of Zombie Nursery Rhymes. Spradlin, Michael P. 2011. (ENG.). 96p. pap. 9.99 *(978-0-06-208359-3(7)*, William Morrow Paperbacks) HarperCollins Pubs.
—SMASH! Exploring the Mysteries of the Universe with the Large Hadron Collider. Latta, Sara L. 2017. 72p. (YA). (gr. 8-12). 33.32 *(978-1-4677-8551-8(2)*, 9781467785518, Graphic Universe™) Lerner Publishing Group.
—Smash! Exploring the Mysteries of the Universe with the Large Hadron Collider. Latta, Sara. ed. 2017. (ENG.). 72p. (YA). (gr. 8-12). E-Book 50.65 *(978-1-5124-3593-1(7)*, 9781512435931); E-Book 50.65 *(978-1-5124-2701-1(2)*, 9781512427011); E-Book 9.99 *(978-1-5124-3594-8(5)*, 9781512435948) Lerner Publishing Group. (Graphic Universe™).
Weigelt, Udo. Wild Wombat. Weigelt, Udo. 2019. (ENG.). 44p. (J). (gr. k-2). 17.99 *(978-988-8341-79-5(0)*, Minedition) Neugebauer, Michael (Publishing) Limited HKG. Dist: Penguin Random Hse. LLC.
Weighill, Damien. Cool Physics: Filled with Fantastic Facts for Kids of All Ages. Hutton, Sarah. 2017. 112p. (J). (gr. 5). 15.99 *(978-1-84365-324-0(9)*, Pavilion Children's Books) Pavilion Bks. GBR. Dist: Penguin Random Hse. LLC.
—Girl Talk. Cox, Lizzie. 2017. (Growing Up Ser.). (ENG.). 64p. (J). (gr. 3-6). pap. 14.95 *(978-1-68297-197-0(X))* QEB Publishing Inc.
—Guy Talk. Cox, Lizzie. 2017. (Growing Up Ser.). (ENG.). 64p. (J). (gr. 4-6). pap. 14.95 *(978-1-68297-196-3(1))* QEB Publishing Inc.
Weihs, Erika. Bar Mitzvah: A Jewish Boy's Coming of Age. Kimmel, Eric A. 2004. 143p. (J). (gr. 6-9). reprint ed. pap. 15.00 *(978-0-7567-7261-1(3))* DIANE Publishing Co.
—Menorahs, Mezuzas, & Other Jewish Symbols. Chaikin, Miriam. 2003. (ENG.). 112p. (J). (gr. 5-7). pap. 7.95 *(978-0-618-37835-7(9)*, 100323) Houghton Mifflin Harcourt Publishing Co.
Weikert, Dana, jt. illus. see O'Kane, George.
Weiler, Syd. The the Tinaja Tonight. Bissonette, Aim�e M. 2020. (Imagine This! Ser.). 32p. (J). (gr. -1-3). 17.99 ***(978-0-8075-7949-7(1)***, 0807579491) Whitman, Albert & Co.
Weiman, Jon. Beluga Passage. Lingemann, Linda. 2011. (Smithsonian Oceanic Collection Ser.). (ENG.). 32p. (J). (gr. -1-3). 19.95 *(978-1-60727-645-6(3))* Soundprints.
—Lobster's Secret. Hollenbeck, Kathleen M. 2011. (Smithsonian Oceanic Collection Ser.). (ENG.). 32p. (J). (gr. -1-3). 19.95 *(978-1-60727-653-1(4))*; 8.95 *(978-1-60727-654-8(2))* Soundprints.
Weinberg, Devorah. Gedalia the Goldfish Who Wanted Be Just Like the King. Yerushalmi, Miriam. 2007. 26p. (J). (gr. -1-3). 16.50 *(978-0-911643-36-7(2))* Aura Printing, Inc.
Weinberg, James. Straw House, Wood House, Brick House, Blow: Four Novellas by Daniel Nayeri. Nayeri, Daniel. 2011. (ENG.). 432p. (YA). (gr. 9). 19.99 *(978-0-7636-5526-6(0))* Candlewick Pr.
Weinberg, Steven. AstroNuts Mission One: the Plant Planet. Scieszka, Jon. 2019. (ENG.). 220p. (J). (gr. 3-7). 14.99 *(978-1-4521-7119-7(X))* Chronicle Bks. LLC.
—Great Ancient China Projects: You Can Build Yourself. Kramer, Lance. 2008. (Build It Yourself Ser.). 128p. (J). (gr. 3-7). pap. 21.95 *(978-1-934670-02-6(2)*, 06c2a185-19be-4f46-b61b-2d60b06c6382) Nomad Pr.
Weinberg, Steven. Fred & the Lumberjack. Weinberg, Steven. 2017. (ENG.). 40p. (J). (gr. -1-3). 17.99 *(978-1-4814-2983-2(3)*, McElderry, Margaret K. Bks.) McElderry, Margaret K. Bks.
—Rex Finds an Egg! Egg! Egg! Weinberg, Steven. 2015. (ENG.). 40p. (J). (gr. -1-3). 17.99 *(978-1-4814-0308-5(7)*, McElderry, Margaret K. Bks.) McElderry, Margaret K. Bks.
—You Must Be This Tall. Weinberg, Steven. 2016. (ENG.). 40p. (J). (gr. -1-3). 17.99 *(978-1-4814-2981-8(7)*, McElderry, Margaret K. Bks.) McElderry, Margaret K. Bks.
Weinbrenner, Jacquelyn. My Silly Willy Loose Tooth. Weinbrenner, Darlene. 2012. 24p. 24.95 *(978-1-4626-5180-1(1))* America Star Bks.
Weiner, Jonathan. Nadia's Hands. English, Karen. 2009. (ENG.). 32p. (J). (gr. k-2). pap. 9.99 *(978-1-59078-784-7(6))* Boyds Mills Pr.
Weingartner, Sara. Buffy Meets the Zoonicorns. Lubratt, Mark. 2015. 32p. (J). 16.95 *(978-1-59298-893-8(8))* Beaver's Pond Pr., Inc.
Weingartner, Sara J. Claire's Hair: A Tale of Hair, Heart, & Humor. Bleckwehl, Mary. 2017. (ENG.). 32p. (J). 16.95 *(978-1-59298-800-6(8))* Beaver's Pond Pr., Inc.
Weingast, Susana. Percepcion simbolica en el Arte. Weingast, Susana. 2004. 142p. (YA). pap. 19.00 *(978-1-931481-24-3(5))* LiArt-Literature & Art.
Weinheimer, Kim. The Bear Song. Weinheimer, Kim, as told by. 2012. 24p. pap. 9.95 *(978-1-935752-30-1(8))* Bryce Cullen Publishing.
Weinman, Brad. The Postman Always Brings Mice. Holm, Jennifer L. & Hamel, Jonathan. 2005. (Stink Files Ser.: No. 1). 129p. (J). 12.65 *(978-0-7569-6529-7(2))* Perfection Learning Corp.
—Tales from the Brothers Grimm & the Sisters Weird. Vande Velde, Vivian. 2005. (ENG.). 144p. (J). (gr. 5-7). reprint ed. pap. 7.99 *(978-0-15-205572-1(X)*, 1196759) Houghton Mifflin Harcourt Publishing Co.
—To Scratch a Thief. Holm, Jennifer L. & Hamel, Jonathan. (Stink Files Ser.: No. 2). 144p. 2005. pap. 4.99 *(978-0-06-052984-0(9)*, Harper Trophy); 2004. (J). 14.99 *(978-0-06-052982-6(2))*; 2004. (J). lib. bdg. 15.89 *(978-0-06-052983-3(0))* HarperCollins Pubs.
—Trouble Is My Beeswax. Hale, Bruce. 2003. (Chet Gecko Mystery Ser.: 8). (ENG.). 111p. (J). (gr. 4-6). 17.44 *(978-0-15-216718-9(8))* Houghton Mifflin Harcourt Publishing Co.
Weinmann, Julianne, jt. illus. see Weston, Andrea.
Weinstein, Ellen, jt. illus. see Kusama, Yayoi.
Weinstein, Holly. The Foodie Club. Shear, Dani. 2013. (ENG.). 50p. (J). 16.99 *(978-1-61053-027-9(6))* Blackbird Bks.
Weinstein, Holly. Potatoland & the Fable of Thunder & Lightning. Taylor, Neil. 2017. (ENG.). 34p. (J). (gr. -1-2). pap. 11.99 ***(978-1-61254-400-7(2))*** Brown Books Publishing Group.
Weinstock, Tony. Star of the Show. Ferreri, Della Ross. 2009. (ENG.). 36p. (J). (gr. -1-3). 15.95 *(978-1-934860-03-8(4))* Shenanigan Bks.
Weir, Carrie & Weir, Nolet. What Season Is It? Frigon, Kerry, photos by. Ferguson, Gloria. 2011. 28p. pap. 24.95 *(978-1-4626-4136-9(9))* America Star Bks.
Weir, Doffy. The Jealous Giant. Umansky, Kaye. 2005. 32p. (J). (gr. -1 — 1). pap. 6.95 *(978-1-903015-41-4(3))* Barn Owl Bks, London GBR. Dist: Independent Pubs. Group.
—The Romantic Giant. Umansky, Kaye. 2006. 29p. (J). (gr. k-2). pap. 6.95 *(978-1-903015-25-4(1))* Barn Owl Bks, London GBR. Dist: Independent Pubs. Group.
Weir, Nolet, jt. illus. see Weir, Carrie.
Weisenhoff, Rebecca. Gravity Will Always Pull You Down... A Child's Introduction to Gravity. Martin, Lawrence. 2016. (ENG.). 42p. (J). (gr. 1-6). pap. 9.99 *(978-1-879653-09-2(5))* Lakeside Pr.
Weiser, Florence. Cock-A-Doodle-Poo! Smallman, Steve. 2018. (ENG.). 32p. (J). (gr. -1-2). 16.99 *(978-1-68010-080-8(7))* Tiger Tales.
—Twinkle, Twinkle, Little Star: A Light-Up Bedtime Book. 2017. 20p. (J). (gr. -1 — 1). 10.99 *(978-0-7624-6182-0(9)*, Running Pr. Kids) Running Pr.
Weiser, Joey. Ghost Hog. Weiser, Joey. 2019. (ENG.). 168p. (J). 21.99 *(978-1-62010-654-9(X)*, Lion Forge) Oni Pr., Inc.
Weisgard, Leonard. The Golden Bunny. Brown, Margaret Wise. 2015. 32p. (J). (-k). 16.99 *(978-0-385-39274-7(5)*, Golden Bks.) Random Hse. Children's Bks.
—The Golden Egg Book. Brown, Margaret Wise. (J). 2018. 26p. (— 1). bds. 7.99 *(978-1-5247-6620-7(8))*; 2004. (ENG.). 32p. (gr. -1-2). 9.99 *(978-0-375-82717-4(X))* Random Hse. Children's Bks. (Golden Bks.).
—The Golden Egg Book. Brown, Margaret Wise. 2015. (Little Golden Book Ser.). 24p. (J). (-k). 4.99 *(978-0-385-38476-6(9)*, Golden Bks.) Random Hse. Children's Bks.
—The Little Island. Brown, Margaret Wise. 2003. (ENG.). 48p. (J). (gr. -1-2). 15.99 *(978-0-385-74640-3(7)*, Doubleday Bks. for Young Readers) Random Hse. Children's Bks.

—The Noisy Book Board Book. Brown, Margaret Wise. 2017. (ENG.). 36p. (J). (gr. -1 — 1). bds. 7.99 *(978-0-06-248465-9(6)*, HarperFestival) HarperCollins Pubs.

—The Noisy Book Treasury. Brown, Margaret Wise. 2014. (ENG.). 128p. (J). (gr. 2-4). pap. 14.99 *(978-0-486-78028-3(7)*, 780287) Dover Pubns., Inc.

—Penguin's Way. Johnston, Johanna. 2015. (ENG.). 48p. 20.00 *(978-1-85124-427-0(1))* Bodleian Library GBR. Dist: Chicago Distribution Ctr.

—The Quiet Noisy Book Board Book. Brown, Margaret Wise. 2017. (ENG.). 34p. (J). (gr. -1 — 1). bds. 7.99 *(978-0-06-248466-6(4)*, HarperFestival) HarperCollins Pubs.

—Whale's Way. Johnston, Johanna. 2015. (ENG.). 48p. 20.00 *(978-1-85124-428-7(X))* Bodleian Library GBR. Dist: Chicago Distribution Ctr.

Weishampel, Winifred Ann. Sparky the Firehouse Dog, 1 vol. Gibson, Steve. 2009. 20p. pap. 24.95 *(978-1-60836-254-7(X))* America Star Bks.

Weiskal, N. J. The Skittery Kitten & the Scaredy Cat. Weiskal, N. J. Weiskal, N. j. 2009. 36p. pap. 8.00 *(978-1-935125-59-4(1))* Robertson Publishing.

Weisner, David. Mr. Wuffles! Weisner, David. 2013. 14.99 *(978-0-9777098-8-5(4))*; 49.99 *(978-0-9777098-7-8(6))* Dreamscape Media, LLC.

Weiss, Alan, et al. Marvel Masterworks: the Avengers Vol. 20. 2020. (ENG.). 384p. (YA). (gr. 4-17). 75.00 *(978-1-302-92224-5(6))* Marvel Worldwide, Inc.

Weiss, Dan. My Favorite Word: Arcane. Rothe, Reagan. l.t. ed. 2016. (My Favorite Word Ser.: Vol. 1). (ENG.). (J). pap. 9.95 *(978-1-944715-10-6(X))* Black Rose Writing.

Weiss, Dave. Herald the Angel. Furches, Mike & Furches, Mary Jane. 2017. (ENG.). (J). 19.99 *(978-0-9995121-8-0(8))* Mindstir Media.

—Herald the Angel. Furches, Mike & Mary Jane, Furches. 2017. (ENG.). (J). pap. 12.99 *(978-0-9995121-0-4(2))* Mindstir Media.

Weiss, Ellen & Nelson, Marybeth. Dinosaur Rescue. Weiss, Ellen & Nelson, Marybeth. 2009. (J). *(978-1-59292-359-5(3))* SoftPlay, Inc.

—Elmo's Beautiful Day. Weiss, Ellen & Nelson, Marybeth. 2009. (J). *(978-1-59292-358-8(5))* SoftPlay, Inc.

Weiss, Emil. It's Like This, Cat. Neville, Emily Cheney. 2019. (Trophy Bk.). (ENG.). 176p. (J). (gr. 5-9). pap. 6.99 *(978-0-06-440073-2(5)*, HarperCollins) HarperCollins Pubs. Ltd. GBR. Dist: HarperCollins Pubs.

—It's Like This, Cat. Neville, Emily. 2017. (ENG.). 192p. (gr. 2-6). pap. 5.95 *(978-0-486-81478-0(5))* Dover Pubns., Inc.

—It's Like This, Cat. Neville, Emily. 2019. (ENG.). 190p. (J). (gr. 2-6). pap. 5.85 *(978-1-68422-363-3(6))* Martino Fine Bks.

Weiss, Harvey. Every Friday Night. Simon, Norma. (Festival Series of Picture Storybooks). (J). (gr. -1). spiral bd. 4.50 *(978-0-8381-0708-9(7))* United Synagogue of America Bk. Service.

Weiss, Lynn. I Like Company. Weiss, Lynn. Frazer, Adilia & Frazer, Charles, trs. 2011.Tr. of Me Gusta Compañía. (ENG & SPA.). 46p. (J). 17.95 *(978-0-9845424-6-8(9))* Koho Pono, LLC.

Weiss, Monica. Celebrate Martin Luther King, Jr. Day with Mrs. Park's Class. Flor Ada, Alma. 2006. (Stories to Celebrate Ser.). 30p. (J). (gr. k-6). per. 11.95 *(978-1-59820-125-3(5)*, Alfaguara) Santillana USA Publishing Co., Inc.

Weiss, Tracy. L D the Littlest Dragster. Mors, Peter D. & Mors, Terry M. 2009. 36p. pap. 16.99 *(978-1-4389-7445-3(0))* AuthorHouse.

Weissman, Bari. From Caterpillar to Butterfly. Heiligman, Deborah. 2015. (Let's-Read-And-Find-Out Science 1 Ser.). (ENG.). 32p. (J). (gr. -1-3). pap. 6.99 *(978-0-06-238183-5(0))* HarperCollins Pubs.

—From Caterpillar to Butterfly. Heiligman, Deborah. 2015. (Let's-Read-And-Find-Out Science 1 Ser.). (ENG.). (J). (gr. -1-3). lib. bdg. 17.60 *(978-1-62765-993-2(5))* Perfection Learning Corp.

—From Caterpillar to Butterfly Big Book. Heiligman, Deborah. 2008. (Let's-Read-And-Find-Out Science 1 Ser.). (ENG.). 32p. (J). (gr. -1-3). pap. 24.99 *(978-0-06-111975-0(X)*, HarperFestival) HarperCollins Pubs.

Weissmann, Joe. Can Hens Give Milk?, 1 vol. Stuchner, Joan Betty. 2013. (ENG.). 32p. (J). (gr. -1-k). 9.95 *(978-1-4598-0427-2(9))* Orca Bk. Pubs. USA.

—The Gingerbread Man. 2005. (J). 7.95 *(978-0-9770473-0-7(X))* Heersink, Roland.

—My Achy Body. Fromer, Liza & Gerstein, Francine. 2011. (Body Works). (ENG.). 24p. (J). (gr. 1-4). 12.95 *(978-1-77049-204-2(6)*, Tundra Bks.) Tundra Bks. CAN. Dist: Penguin Random Hse. LLC.

—My Itchy Body. Fromer, Liza & Gerstein, Francine. 2012. (Body Works). (ENG.). 24p. (J). (gr. 1-4). 12.95 *(978-1-77049-311-7(5)*, Tundra Bks.) Tundra Bks. CAN. Dist: Penguin Random Hse. LLC.

—My Messy Body. Fromer, Liza & Gerstein, Francine. 2011. (Body Works). (ENG.). 24p. (J). (gr. 1-4). 12.95 *(978-1-77049-202-8(X)*, Tundra Bks.) Tundra Bks. CAN. Dist: Penguin Random Hse. LLC.

—My Noisy Body. Fromer, Liza & Gerstein, Francine. 2011. (Body Works). (ENG.). 24p. (J). (gr. 1-4). 12.95 *(978-1-77049-201-1(1)*, Tundra Bks.) Tundra Bks. CAN. Dist: Penguin Random Hse. LLC.

—My Stretchy Body. Fromer, Liza & Gerstein, Francine. 2011. (Body Works). (ENG.). 24p. (J). (gr. 1-4). 12.95 *(978-1-77049-203-5(8)*, Tundra Bks.) Tundra Bks. CAN. Dist: Penguin Random Hse. LLC.

Weisz, Erica. Wrestling Dreams. Cabana, Colt. 2017. (ENG.). 40p. (J). (gr. k-2). 16.95 *(978-0-9888338-7-6(5))* Mrs. Weisz Bks.

Weitzel, Erica. Ben Dhere! Don Dhat! Tall Tales from the Island of Gullah. LaFer, Jenni. 2007. 96p. (J). per. 18.95 *(978-0-9800816-0-2(2))* Bread & Butter Bks.

Weitzman, David. Jenny: The Airplane That Taught America to Fly. Weitzman, David. 2006. 27p. (J). (gr. k-4). reprint ed. 19.00 *(978-1-4223-5582-4(9))* DIANE Publishing Co.

Welch, Chad. Adventures of the Elements Vol. 3: Dangerous Games. James, Richard E., III. Lyle, Maryann, ed. 2004. 169p. (YA). (gr. 3-12). pap. 5.95 *(978-0-9675901-2-7(4))* Alchemy Creative, Inc.

Welch, Gracie. The Deer from Ponchatoula, 1 vol. Wolfe, Susan Markle. 2009. 24p. pap. 24.95 *(978-1-60813-519-6(5))* America Star Bks.

Welch, Holly. Inside All, 1 vol. Mason, Margaret. 2008. (ENG.). 32p. (J). (gr. -1-3). 16.95 *(978-1-58469-111-2(5))*; pap. 8.95 *(978-1-58469-112-9(3))* Sourcebooks, Inc. (Dawn Pubns.).

Welch, Holly Felsen. Fever Heat. Felsen, Henry Gregor. 2013. 230p. pap. 15.00 *(978-1-62272-002-6(4))* Felsen Ink.

—Henry Gregor Felsen Street Rod Collection. Felsen, Henry Gregor. 2013. 75.00 *(978-1-62272-005-7(9))* Felsen Ink.

Welch, Jaime. Runes from the Woodpile: Runic Knowledge Revealed. 2004. 126p. 20.00 *(978-0-9749416-3-9(8))* Himminbjorg Publishing, Inc.

Welch, Jazmin. Finn & the Magic Backpack. Flynn, Julie. 2018. (ENG.). 30p. (J). pap. *(978-1-7753314-0-7(7))* Flynn, Julie.

—Finn & the Magic Backpack. Flynn, Julie. Van Vloten, Kristin, ed. 2018. (ENG.). 30p. (J). (gr. 4-5). *(978-1-7753314-1-4(5))* Flynn, Julie.

Welch, Jazmin & John, Cathryn. Finn & the Friends of the Forest. Flynn, Julie. 2020. (ENG.). 34p. (J). ***(978-1-7753314-3-8(1))***; pap. ***(978-1-7753314-2-1(3))*** Flynn, Julie.

Welch, Kathleen & McGillivray, Alan. Sometimes Even Elephants Forget: A Story about Alzheimer's Disease for Young Children, 1 vol. Welch, Kathleen & McGillivray, Alan. 2019. (ENG.). 32p. (J). (gr. -1-3). 16.99 *(978-1-4556-2469-0(1)*, Pelican Publishing) Arcadia Publishing.

Welch, Kelly. Ishi: The Last of His People. Collins, David R. et al. 2004. (Notable Americans Ser.). 96p. (YA). (gr. 6-12). 23.95 *(978-1-883846-54-1(4)*, First Biographies) Reynolds, Morgan Inc.

Welch, Mark. Counting with the Fairies of Willow Garden. Welch, Lance. 2012. 16p. pap. 24.95 *(978-1-62709-544-0(6))* America Star Bks.

Welch, Sheila Kelly. Sean's Quest. Anderson, Leone Castell. 2003. 162p. (J). 16.95 *(978-0-9638819-6-0(5))*; pap. 10.95 *(978-0-9638819-7-7(3))* ShadowPlay Pr.

—Something in the Air. Jones, Molly. 2005. (J). *(978-1-893516-03-8(2))* Our Child Pr.

Weldon, Andrew. Don't Look Now 3: Haircut & Just a Nibble. Jennings, Paul. 2015. (ENG.). 276p. (J). (gr. 2-6). pap. 9.99 *(978-1-74331-141-7(9))* Allen & Unwin AUS. Dist: Independent Pubs. Group.

—Don't Look Now 4: Hobby Farm & Seeing Red. Jennings, Paul. 2016. (ENG.). 276p. (J). (gr. 2-6). pap. 9.99 *(978-1-74331-142-4(7))* Allen & Unwin AUS. Dist: Independent Pubs. Group.

—The Extremely Weird Thing That Happened in Huggabie Falls. Cece, Adam. 2019. (Huggabie Falls Trilogy Ser.). (ENG.). 1p. (J). 8.99 *(978-1-925603-48-4(2))* Text Publishing Co. AUS. Dist: Consortium Bk. Sales & Distribution.

—Unbelievably Scary Thing That Happened in Huggabie Falls. Cece, Adam. 2019. (Huggabie Falls Trilogy Ser.). (ENG.). 224p. (J). 8.95 *(978-1-925773-01-9(9))* Text Publishing Co. AUS. Dist: Consortium Bk. Sales & Distribution.

—The Utterly Indescribable Thing That Happened in Huggabie Falls. Cece, Adam. 2019. (Huggabie Falls Trilogy Ser.). (ENG.). 1p. (J). 8.95 *(978-1-925773-45-3(0))* Text Publishing Co. AUS. Dist: Consortium Bk. Sales & Distribution.

Weldon, Andrew. Lazy Daisy, Cranky Frankie: Bedtime on the Farm. Weldon, Andrew. Jordan, Mary Ellen. 2013. (ENG.). 24p. (J). (gr. -1-3). 15.99 *(978-0-8075-4400-6(0)*, 807544000) Whitman, Albert & Co.

Welin, Raquel. Cuentos Golosos. Ortega, Ingrid. 2006. (SPA.). 64p. (J). mass mkt. 12.50 *(978-1-59835-012-8(9))* Cambridge BrickHouse, Inc.

Welker, Matthew S. Grand Poppa's Favorite Chair: No One Is As Special As You. Buckner, Andrew. 2011. 48p. pap. 24.95 *(978-1-4560-8294-9(9))* America Star Bks.

Wellborn, Morgan. Never Rub Noses with a Narwhal: An Alliterative Arctic ABC Book. Wellborn, Ruth. 2018. (ENG.). 64p. (J). pap. *(978-1-5255-2593-3(X))* FriesenPress.

Weller, Linda. Hands-on Math, Grades K-1: Manipulative Activities for the Classroom. Johnson, Virginia. Hamaguchi, Carla, ed. 2nd ed. 2006. 144p. (J). (gr. k-1). per. 19.99 *(978-1-59198-232-6(4)*, 2568) Creative Teaching Pr., Inc.

—Jumping into Journals: Guided Journaling for Beginning Readers & Writers. Jordano, Kimberly & Adsit, Kim. Cernek, Kim, ed. 2006. 112p. pap. 15.99 *(978-1-59198-227-2(8)*, 2229) Creative Teaching Pr., Inc.

—Writing Makeovers 5-6: Improving Skills - Adding Style. Jennett, Pamela. Rous, Sheri, ed. 2003. 96p. (YA). (gr. 6-8). pap. 11.99 *(978-1-57471-957-4(2)*, 2262) Creative Teaching Pr., Inc.

Weller, Ursula. Que? Como? Por Que?: Autos y Camiones. Caballero, D., tr. 2007. (Junior (Silver Dolphin) Ser.). 16p. (J). (gr. -1). *(978-970-718-490-9(6)*, Silver Dolphin en Español) Advanced Marketing, S. de R. L. de C. V.

Wellesley, Rosie. Moonlight Bear. Wellesley, Rosie. 2015. (ENG.). 32p. (J). (gr. -1-k). pap. 9.99 *(978-1-84365-292-2(7)*, Pavilion Children's Books) Pavilion Bks. GBR. Dist: Penguin Random Hse. LLC.

Welling, Peter. Back to School, Picky Little Witch!, 1 vol. Brokamp, Elizabeth. 2014. (Picky Little Witch Ser.). (ENG.). 32p. (J). (gr. k-3). 16.99 *(978-1-4556-1887-3(X)*, Pelican Publishing) Arcadia Publishing.

—What's up with This Chicken?, 1 vol. Sutton, Jane. 2015. (ENG.). 32p. (J). (gr. k-3). 16.99 *(978-1-4556-2085-2(8)*, Pelican Publishing) Arcadia Publishing.

Welling, Peter. Joe Van der Katt & the Great Picket Fence, 1 vol. Welling, Peter. 2005. (ENG.). 32p. (J). (gr. k-3). 16.99 *(978-1-58980-281-0(0)*, Pelican Publishing) Arcadia Publishing.

Welling, Peter J. The Kvetch Who Stole Hanukkah, 1 vol. Berlin, Bill & Berlin, Susan Isakoff. 2010. (ENG.). 32p. (J). (gr. k-3). 16.99 *(978-1-58980-798-3(7)*, Pelican Publishing) Arcadia Publishing.

Welling, Peter J. Darlene Halloween & the Great Chicago Fire, 1 vol. Welling, Peter J. 2007. (ENG.). 32p. (J). (gr. k-3). 16.99 *(978-1-58980-479-1(1)*, Pelican Publishing) Arcadia Publishing.

—Justin Potemkin & the 500-Mile Race, 1 vol. Welling, Peter J. 2004. (ENG.). 32p. (J). (gr. k-3). 16.99 *(978-1-58980-149-3(0)*, Pelican Publishing) Arcadia Publishing.

—Michael le Soufflé & the April Fool, 1 vol. Welling, Peter J. 2003. (ENG.). 32p. (J). (gr. k-3). 16.99 *(978-1-58980-105-9(9)*, Pelican Publishing) Arcadia Publishing.

Wellington, George. People, the World & I. Wellington, George, photos by. Date not set. viii, 94p. (YA). (gr. 7-18). mass mkt. 10.95 *(978-0-9670539-0-5(0))* Thomas, Sheldon Wade.

Wellington, Monica. The Little Snowflake. Metzger, Steve. 2003. (J). *(978-0-439-55656-9(2))* Scholastic, Inc.

Wellington, Monica. Apple Farmer Annie. Wellington, Monica. 2004. (ENG.). 32p. (J). (gr. -1-2). pap. 7.99 *(978-0-14-240124-8(2)*, Puffin Books) Penguin Young Readers Group.

—Apple Farmer Annie Board Book. Wellington, Monica. 2012. 24p. (J). (gr. -1 — 1). bds. 6.99 *(978-0-8037-3888-1(9)*, Dial Bks) Penguin Young Readers Group.

—Pizza at Sally's. Wellington, Monica. 2006. 32p. (J). (gr. -1-2). 16.99 *(978-0-525-47715-0(2)*, Dutton Books for Young Readers) Penguin Young Readers Group.

—Zinnia's Flower Garden. Wellington, Monica. 2007. (ENG.). 32p. (J). (gr. -1-2). pap. 6.99 *(978-0-14-240787-5(9)*, Puffin Books) Penguin Young Readers Group.

Wellman, Megan. Being Bella. Zuzo, Cheryl. 2008. (ENG.). 32p. pap. 9.95 *(978-1-933916-27-9(3))* Nelson Publishing & Marketing.

Wellman, Megan D. And That Is Why We Teach: A Celebration of Teachers. Graham, Patti. 2008. (ENG.). 32p. (J). (gr. 4-7). 17.95 *(978-1-933916-23-1(0))* Nelson Publishing & Marketing.

Wellner, Cathryn. Turkey Baby & the Hungry Hawk. Wellner, Cathryn. 2017. (Millie's Farm Family Ser.: Vol. 2). (ENG.). (J). (gr. k-3). *(978-0-9951653-9-7(4))* Espoir Pr.

—Turkey Baby Finds Her Magic. Wellner, Cathryn. 2017. (Millie's Farm Family Ser.: Vol. 3). (ENG.). (J). (gr. k-3). *(978-1-988760-00-1(3))* Espoir Pr.

Wells, Amanda M. Quincy the Quail & the Mysterious Egg. Renner, Barbara. 2019. (Quincy the Quail Ser.). (ENG.). 22p. (J). (gr. k-4). pap. 11.95 *(978-0-9990586-2-6(2))* Renner Writes.

Wells, Amanda M. Quincy the Quail Leads His Family on an Adventure. Renner, Barbara. 2019. (ENG.). 32p. (J). (gr. k-4). pap. 11.95 ***(978-0-9990586-4-0(9))*** Renner Writes.

Wells, Cynthia. Moonglow. Dickerson, Peggy. 2019. (ENG.). 48p. (J). (gr. k-5). 23.00 *(978-0-9981666-4-3(2))* Ice Wine Productions, Inc.

Wells, Daryl. Two Mrs. Gibsons. Igus, Toyomi. 2013. (ENG.). 32p. (J). (gr. 1-18). pap. 10.95 *(978-0-89239-170-7(7)*, Children's Book Press) Lee & Low Bks., Inc.

Wells, Emma. Sassy & the Vacuum Cleaner. Gill, Lesley. 2018. (ENG.). 22p. (J). (gr. k-1). pap. *(978-1-909465-71-8(2))* Cloister Hse. Pr., The.

Wells, Jack J. If Baby Bucking Bulls Could Talk. Shaw, Bill. 2010. 20p. 14.95 *(978-1-4269-3227-4(8))* Trafford Publishing.

Wells, Jenni. Happymerrythanksmas. Drews, Ann. 2018. (ENG.). 34p. (J). pap. 12.99 *(978-1-949609-70-7(7))* Pen It! Pubns., LLC.

Wells, Julie. Always Ours. Wopat, Christy. 2020. (ENG.). 36p. (J). (gr. k-4). 17.99 ***(978-1-64538-139-6(0))***; pap. 12.00 ***(978-1-64538-123-5(4))*** Orange Hat Publishing.

Wells, Lorraine. The Story of Easter. Pingry, Patricia A. 2006. (ENG.). 26p. (gr. -1-k). 12.95 *(978-0-8249-6649-2(X)*, Ideal Pubns.) Worthy Publishing.

Wells, Mark. Tommy's Lost Tooth. Wells, Mark. Wells, Meagan. 2011. 28p. pap. 11.99 *(978-1-61170-020-6(5))* Robertson Publishing.

Wells, Quierra LaQuelle. Trinny Bear & Dallas. Wells-Sanders, Glenora. 2012. 24p. pap. 11.50 *(978-1-61897-763-2(6)*, Strategic Bk. Publishing) Strategic Book Publishing & Rights Agency (SBPRA).

Wells, Rachel. Animales de la Granja. Watt, Fiona. 2004. (SPA.). 14p. (J). 9.95 *(978-0-7460-6113-8(7)*, Usborne) EDC Publishing.

—Animals. Watt, Fiona. 2006. 10p. (J). (gr. -1-k). bds. 9.99 *(978-0-7945-1227-9(5)*, Usborne) EDC Publishing.

—Baby Dinosaur Cloth Bk. Watt, Fiona. 2006. 10p. (J). 10.99 *(978-0-7945-1429-7(4)*, Usborne) EDC Publishing.

—Baby Monster Cloth Book. Watt, Fiona. 2007. (Usborne Cloth Bks.). 10p. (J). (gr. -1-k). 10.99 *(978-0-7945-1428-0(6)*, Usborne) EDC Publishing.

—Baby's Christmas. Brooks, Felicity & Allen, Francesca. 2005. (Baby's World (Usborne Board Books) Ser.). 10p. (J). (gr. -1-k). per., bds. 8.95 *(978-0-7945-1175-3(9)*, Usborne) EDC Publishing.

—Baby's Potty. Brooks, Felicity & Allen, Francesca. 2006. (Baby's Day Board Book Ser.). 10p. (J). (gr. -1). bds. 8.99 *(978-0-7945-1362-7(X)*, Usborne) EDC Publishing.

—Big Book of Sticker Math. Watt, Fiona. 2008. (Usborne Sticker Math Ser.). 151p. (J). (gr. -1-3). pap. 12.99 *(978-0-7945-1825-7(7)*, Usborne) EDC Publishing.

—Christmas Baby Jigsaw Book. Watt, Fiona. 2004. (Jigsaw Books Ser.). 14p. (J). 10.95 *(978-0-7945-0809-8(X)*, Usborne) EDC Publishing.

—Christmas Eve. Watt, Fiona. 2007. (Luxury Touchy-Feely Board Bks). 10p. (J). (gr. -1-k). bds. 11.99 *(978-0-7945-1478-5(2)*, Usborne) EDC Publishing.

—Esta No Es Mi Muneca. Watt, Fiona. 2005. (Titles in Spanish Ser.). (SPA.). 10p. (J). 7.95 *(978-0-7460-6102-2(1)*, Usborne) EDC Publishing.

—Farm. Watt, Fiona. 2008. (Usborne Touchy-Feely Board Bks.). 8p. (J). (gr. -1-k). bds. 15.99 *(978-0-7945-1959-9(8)*, Usborne) EDC Publishing.

—Mascotas. Watt, Fiona. 2004. (Titles in Spanish Ser.). (SPA.). 14p. (J). 9.95 *(978-0-7460-6112-1(9)*, Usborne) EDC Publishing.

—Muddy Hippo. Durber, Matt & Brooks, Felicity. 2007. (Play Bks). 10p. (J). (gr. -1-k). bds. 10.99 *(978-0-7945-1688-8(2)*, Usborne) EDC Publishing.

—The Nativity. Watt, Fiona. 2005. (Usborne Touchy-Feely Board Bks.). 10p. (J). (gr. -1-k). bds. 15.95 *(978-0-7945-1172-2(4)*, Usborne) EDC Publishing.

—Splish, Splash, Splosh Bath Bk. Cartwright, Mary. 2007. 8p. (J). 14.99 *(978-0-7945-1619-2(X)*, Usborne) EDC Publishing.

—That's Not My Bunny. Watt, Fiona. 2004. (Touchy-Feely Board Bks.). (SPA & ENG.). 1p. (J). (gr. -1-18). bds. 7.99 *(978-0-7460-4179-6(9))* EDC Publishing.

—That's Not My Car. Watt, Fiona. 2004. (Touchy-Feely Board Books Ser.). 10p. (J). 7.95 *(978-0-7945-0636-0(4)*, Usborne) EDC Publishing.

—That's Not My Donkey. Watt, Fiona. ed. 2011. (Touchy-Feely Board Books Ser.). 10p. (J). ring bd. 8.99 *(978-0-7945-3012-9(5)*, Usborne) EDC Publishing.

—That's Not My Dragon... Watt, Fiona. 2006. (Usborne Touchy-Feely Bks.). 10p. (J). (gr. -1-k). bds. 7.99 *(978-0-7945-1285-9(2)*, Usborne) EDC Publishing.

—That's Not My Duck... Watt, Fiona. 2014. (ENG.). (gr. -1). bds. 9.99 *(978-0-7945-3193-5(8)*, Usborne) EDC Publishing.

—That's Not My Elephant. Watt, Fiona. ed. 2012. (Touchy-Feely Board Bks). 10p. (J). ring bd. 8.99 *(978-0-7945-3167-6(9)*, Usborne) EDC Publishing.

—That's Not My Fairy. Watt, Fiona. 2004. 10p. (J). 9.99 *(978-0-7945-0793-0(X)*, Usborne) EDC Publishing.

—That's Not My Frog. Watt, Fiona. 2009. (Touchy-Feely Board Bks). 10p. (J). bds. 8.99 *(978-0-7945-2505-7(9)*, Usborne) EDC Publishing.

—That's Not My Kitten. Watt, Fiona. rev. ed. 2006. (Touchy-Feely Board Bks.). 10p. (J). (gr. -1-k). bds. 7.99 *(978-0-7945-1266-8(6)*, Usborne) EDC Publishing.

—That's Not My Mermaid: Her Hair Is Too Fluffy. Watt, Fiona. 2006. (Usborne Touchy-Feely Board Bks.). 10p. (J). (gr. -1-k). bds. 9.99 *(978-0-7945-1083-1(3)*, Usborne) EDC Publishing.

—That's Not My Monster. Watt, Fiona. (Usborne Touchy-Feely Bks.). 10p. (J). 2010. bds. 8.99 *(978-0-7945-2878-2(3))*; 2004. 7.99 *(978-0-7945-0818-0(9))* EDC Publishing. (Usborne).

—That's Not My Penguin. Watt, Fiona. 2007. (Usborne Touchy-Feely Board Bks.). 8p. (gr. -1-k). bds. 7.99 *(978-0-7945-1810-3(9)*, Usborne) EDC Publishing.

—That's Not My Pig... Its Nose Is Too Fuzzy. Watt, Fiona. 2014. (Usborne Touchy-Feely Board Bks.). (ENG.). 10p. (gr. -1). bds. 9.99 *(978-0-7945-2666-5(7)*, Usborne) EDC Publishing.

—That's Not My Pirate. Watt, Fiona. 2007. (Touchy-Feely Board Bks). 10p. (J). (gr. -1-k). bds. 8.99 *(978-0-7945-1702-1(1)*, Usborne) EDC Publishing.

—That's Not My Pony... Its Mane Is Too Fluffy. Watt, Fiona. 2007. (Usborne Touchy-Feely Board Bks.). 10p. (J). (gr. -1-k). bds. 7.99 *(978-0-7945-1630-7(0)*, Usborne) EDC Publishing.

—That's Not My Prince. Watt, Fiona. 2013. (Usborne Touchy-Feely Board Bks.). (ENG.). 10p. (J). 9.99 *(978-0-7945-2838-6(4)*, Usborne) EDC Publishing.

—That's Not My Princess. Watt, Fiona. 2006. (Usborne Touchy-Feely Board Bks.). 10p. (J). (gr. -1). bds. 9.99 *(978-0-7945-1325-2(5)*, Usborne) EDC Publishing.

—That's Not My Reindeer... Watt, Fiona. 2014. (Usborne Touchy-Feely Bks.). (ENG.). 10p. (gr. -1). bds. 9.99 *(978-0-7945-3390-8(6)*, Usborne) EDC Publishing.

—That's Not My Reindeer: Its Body Is Too Furry. Watt, Fiona. 2008. (Usborne Touchy-Feely Board Bks.). 10p. (J). (gr. -1-k). bds. 9.99 *(978-0-7945-1890-5(7)*, Usborne) EDC Publishing.

—That's Not My Robot... Watt, Fiona. 2005. (Usborne Touchy-Feely Board Bks.). 10p. (J). (gr. -1-k). bds. 7.95 *(978-0-7945-1169-2(4)*, Usborne) EDC Publishing.

—That's Not My Snowman. Watt, Fiona. 2006. (Usborne Touchy-Feely Board Bks.). 10p. (J). (gr. -1). bds. 9.99 *(978-0-7945-1414-3(6)*, Usborne) EDC Publishing.

—That's Not My Sticker Book Christmas. rev. ed. 2012. (That's Not My . . Sticker Bks). 28p. (J). pap. 4.99 *(978-0-7945-3318-2(3)*, Usborne) EDC Publishing.

—That's Not My Sticker Book Farm. 2012. (That's Not My Sticker Book Ser.). (ENG.). 24p. (J). (gr. -1-3). 4.99 *(978-0-7945-3204-8(7)*, Usborne) EDC Publishing.

—That's Not My Teddy... Watt, Fiona. 2008. (Usborne Touchy-Feely Board Bks.). 8p. (J). (gr. -1). bds. 7.99 *(978-0-7945-2026-7(X)*, Usborne) EDC Publishing.

—That's Not My Tiger. Watt, Fiona. 2010. (Touchy-Feely Board Bks.). 10p. (J). bds. 8.99 *(978-0-7945-2820-1(1))* EDC Publishing.

Wells, Rebekah. Wibber Dibber Doo, Merry Christmas to You. Pearse, Kaye Saoirse. 2016. (ENG.). (J). pap. 16.99 *(978-0-9963033-4-7(0))*; (gr. 3-6). 19.99 *(978-0-9963033-6-1(7))* Honeysuckle Acres.

Wells, Robert E. Can We Share the World with Tigers? Wells, Robert E. 2013. (AV2 Fiction Readalong Ser.: Vol. 51). (ENG.). (J). (gr. 1-4). 34.28 *(978-1-62127-873-3(5)*, AV2 by Weigl) Weigl Pubs., Inc.

—Can We Share the World with Tigers? Wells, Robert E. 2012. (Wells of Knowledge Science Ser.). (ENG.). 32p. (J). (gr. 1-3). 16.99 *(978-0-8075-1055-1(6)*, 807510556) Whitman, Albert & Co.

—Did a Dinosaur Drink This Water? Wells, Robert E. 2006. (Wells of Knowledge Science Ser.). (ENG.). 32p. (J). (gr. -1-3). 7.99 *(978-0-8075-8840-6(7)*, 807588407) Whitman, Albert & Co.

—How Do You Know What Time It Is? Wells, Robert E. 2013. (AV2 Fiction Readalong Ser.: Vol. 52). (ENG.). (J). (gr. -1-3). 34.28 *(978-1-62127-880-1(8)*, AV2 by Weigl) Weigl Pubs., Inc.

—Polar Bear, Why Is Your World Melting? Wells, Robert E. 2013. (AV2 Fiction Readalong Ser.: Vol. 53). (ENG.). (J). (gr. 2-4). 34.28 *(978-1-62127-888-7(3)*, AV2 by Weigl) Weigl Pubs., Inc.

—Polar Bear, Why Is Your World Melting? Wells, Robert E. 2008. (Wells of Knowledge Science Ser.). (ENG.). 32p. (J). (gr. 2-3). pap. 7.99 *(978-0-8075-6599-5(7),* 807565997) Whitman, Albert & Co.
—What's Older Than a Giant Tortoise? Wells, Robert E. 2013. (AV2 Fiction Readalong Ser.: Vol. 54). (ENG.). (J). (gr. -1-3). 34.28 *(978-1-62127-906-8(5),* AV2 by Weigl) Weigl Pubs., Inc.
—What's Older Than a Giant Tortoise? Wells, Robert E. 2004. (Wells of Knowledge Science Ser.). (ENG.). 32p. (J). (gr. -1-3). 7.99 *(978-0-8075-8832-1(6),* 807588326) Whitman, Albert & Co.
—What's So Special about Planet Earth? Wells, Robert E. 2010. (Wells of Knowledge Science Ser.). (ENG.). 32p. (J). (gr. 2-3). pap. 7.99 *(978-0-8075-8816-1(4),* 807588164) Whitman, Albert & Co.
—Why Do Elephants Need the Sun? Wells, Robert E. 2012. (Wells of Knowledge Science Ser.). (ENG.). 32p. (J). (gr. -1-3). pap. 7.99 *(978-0-8075-9082-9(7),* 807590827) Whitman, Albert & Co.
Wells, Robert G. The Tale of Mhoddy Dhoo. Jeffrey, Maggie. 2018. (ENG.). 50p. (J). pap. 6.48 *(978-1-7239-3805-4(X))* Independently Published.
Wells, Rosemary. I Love You! a Bushel & a Peck. Loesser, Frank. 2007. (ENG.). 32p. (J). (gr. -1-1). 7.99 *(978-0-06-443602-1(0))* HarperCollins Pubs.
—I Love You! A Bushel & A Peck. Loesser, Frank. 2004. 32p. (J). (gr. -1-1). lib. bdg. 16.89 *(978-0-06-028550-0(8))* HarperCollins Pubs.
—Mother Goose's Little Treasures. Opie, Iona. 2007. (My Very First Mother Goose Ser.). (ENG.). 56p. (J). (gr. -1-2). 17.99 *(978-0-7636-3655-5(X))* Candlewick Pr.
—My Very First Mother Goose. Opie, Iona. 2016. (My Very First Mother Goose Ser.). 108p. (J). (gr. k-12). 24.99 *(978-0-7636-8891-2(6))* Candlewick Pr.
—My Very First Mother Goose. Opie, Ian, ed. 2004. 107p. (J). reprint ed. 17.00 *(978-0-7567-8384-6(4))* DIANE Publishing Co.
—One, Two, Three, Mother Goose. Opie, Iona. 2016. (My Very First Mother Goose Ser.). 24p. (J). (— 1). bds. 8.99 *(978-0-7636-8766-3(9))* Candlewick Pr.
—Snuggle up with Mother Goose. Opie, Iona, ed. 2015. (My Very First Mother Goose Ser.). 26p. (J). (— 1). bds. 8.99 *(978-0-7636-7867-8(8))* Candlewick Pr.
—The Very Best Mother Goose Book Tower. Opie, Iona. 2010. (My Very First Mother Goose Ser.). (ENG.). 80p. (J). (gr. -1-k). pap. 9.99 *(978-0-7636-4983-8(X))* Candlewick Pr.
Wells, Rosemary. Bunny Cakes (Edición en Español) Wells, Rosemary. 2014. (Max & Ruby Ser.). (SPA.). 32p. (J). (gr. -1-k). 7.99 *(978-0-14-751586-5(6),* Puffin Books) Penguin Young Readers Group.
—Emily's First 100 Days of School. Wells, Rosemary. 2005. (ENG.). 64p. (J). (gr. -1-1). pap. 9.99 *(978-0-7868-1354-4(7))* Hyperion Pr.
—Felix Eats Up. Wells, Rosemary. 2019. (Felix & Fiona Ser.). 32p. (J). (gr. k-3). 14.99 *(978-0-7636-9548-4(3))* Candlewick Pr.
—Felix Stands Tall. Wells, Rosemary. (Felix & Fiona Ser.). 32p. (J). (gr. k-3). 2017. 5.99 *(978-0-7636-9418-0(5));* 2015. 14.99 *(978-0-7636-6111-3(2))* Candlewick Pr.
—Felix Stands Tall. Wells, Rosemary. ed. 2017. (Felix & Fiona Ser.). (ENG.). (J). (gr. k-3). lib. bdg. 14.75 *(978-0-606-39838-1(4))* Turtleback.
—Fiona's Little Accident. Wells, Rosemary. (Felix & Fiona Ser.). 32p. (J). (gr. k-3). 2019. 5.99 *(978-1-5362-0895-5(7));* 2018. 14.99 *(978-0-7636-8982-7(3))* Candlewick Pr.
—Fiona's Little Lie. Wells, Rosemary. (Felix & Fiona Ser.). 32p. (J). (gr. k-3). 2018. 5.99 *(978-1-5362-0300-4(9));* 2016. 14.99 *(978-0-7636-7312-3(9))* Candlewick Pr.
—Hand in Hand. Wells, Rosemary. 2016. (ENG.). 32p. (J). 17.99 *(978-1-62779-434-3(4),* 9781627794343, Holt, Henry & Co. Bks. For Young Readers) Holt, Henry & Co.
—Julieta, Estate Quieta! Wells, Rosemary. 2003. (SPA.). 38p. (J). (gr. k-3). 5.95 *(978-0-88272-433-1(9))* Santillana USA Publishing Co., Inc.
—Kindergators: Hands off, Harry! Wells, Rosemary. 2011. (ENG.). 40p. (J). (gr. -1-1). 14.99 *(978-0-06-192112-4(2),* Tegen, Katherine Bks) HarperCollins Pubs.
—Kindergators: Miracle Melts Down. Wells, Rosemary. 2012. (ENG.). 40p. (J). (gr. -1-3). 14.99 *(978-0-06-192115-5(7),* Tegen, Katherine Bks) HarperCollins Pubs.
—Love Waves. Wells, Rosemary. 2011. (ENG.). 32p. (J). (gr. -1-2). 15.99 *(978-0-7636-4989-0(9))* Candlewick Pr.
—Love Waves: Midi Edition. Wells, Rosemary. 2012. 32p. (J). (gr. k — 1). 8.99 *(978-0-7636-6224-0(0))* Candlewick Pr.
—Max & Ruby & Twin Trouble. Wells, Rosemary. 2019. (Max & Ruby Adventure Ser.). (ENG.). 32p. (J). (gr. -1-3). 17.99 *(978-1-5344-4365-5(7),* Simon & Schuster Bks. For Young Readers) Simon & Schuster Bks. For Young Readers.
—Max & Ruby at the Warthogs' Wedding. Wells, Rosemary. 2014. (Max & Ruby Ser.). 40p. (J). (gr. -1-k). 17.99 *(978-0-670-78461-5(3),* Viking Books for Young Readers) Penguin Young Readers Group.
—Noisy Nora. Wells, Rosemary. 2007. 28p. (gr. -1-2). 17.00 *(978-0-7569-7870-9(X))* Perfection Learning Corp.
—Otto Runs for President. Wells, Rosemary. 2011. (J). (gr. -1-4). 29.95 *(978-0-545-10690-0(7))* Weston Woods Studios, Inc.
—Read to Your Bunny. Wells, Rosemary. 2003. (ENG.). 12p. (J). bds. 7.99 *(978-0-439-54337-8(1),* Cartwheel Bks.) Scholastic, Inc.
—Ruby's Beauty Shop. Wells, Rosemary. 2004. (Max & Ruby Ser.). (ENG.). 32p. (J). (gr. -1-k). pap. 7.99 *(978-0-14-240194-1(3),* Puffin Books) Penguin Young Readers Group.
—Sleep, My Bunny. Wells, Rosemary. 2018. (ENG.). 24p. (J). (-k). 14.99 *(978-0-7636-9262-9(X))* Candlewick Pr.
—Stella's Starliner. Wells, Rosemary. 2014. (ENG.). 32p. (J). (gr. -1-3). 16.99 *(978-0-7636-1495-9(5))* Candlewick Pr.
—Time-Out for Sophie. Wells, Rosemary. 2013. (ENG.). 32p. (J). (gr. -1-k). 15.99 *(978-0-670-78511-7(3),* Viking Books for Young Readers) Penguin Young Readers Group.
—A Visit to Dr. Duck. Wells, Rosemary. 2014. 30p. (J). (-k). bds. 7.99 *(978-0-7636-7229-4(7))* Candlewick Pr.
—Yoko. Wells, Rosemary. Rosemary, Wells. Varela, Sandra Lopez, tr. 2003. (SPA.). 34p. (J). (gr. k-2). pap. 8.50 *(978-84-241-8034-8(8))* Everest Editora ESP. Dist: Lectorum Pubns., Inc.
—Yoko. Wells, Rosemary. 2009. (Yoko Book Ser.: 1). 32p. (J). (gr. -1-1). pap. 6.99 *(978-1-4231-1983-8(5))* Hyperion Pr.
Wells, Rosemary, jt. illus. see Williams, Garth.
Wells, Shan. And Dance with the Orange Cow. Mills, Nancy Libbey. 2003. 32p. (J). pap. 7.95 *(978-1-893815-10-0(2));* per. 12.95 *(978-1-893815-09-4(9))* Pie in the Sky Publishing, LLC.
—Never Eat Cabbage on Thursday. Mills, Nancy Libbey. ltd. ed. 2005. 32p. (J). 12.95 *(978-1-893815-08-7(0))* Pie in the Sky Publishing, LLC.
Wells-Smith, Abby. The Big Camping Adventure: Little Tommy Learns Lessons from the Great Outdoors. Toombs, Tom. 2013. 32p. pap. 12.95 *(978-1-61314-035-2(5))* Innovo Publishing, LLC.
Wells Smith, Abby. The Way to Be a Winner: Little Tommy Learns a Lesson in Working Together. Toombs, Tom. 2012. 32p. pap. 12.95 *(978-1-61314-034-5(7))* Innovo Publishing, LLC.
Welsh, Hayley. Gingerbread Aliens. Bennett, Sandra. 2012. (ENG.). 56p. (J). pap. *(978-0-9872356-4-0(8))* Australian Self Publishing Group/ Inspiring Pubs.
Welsh, Joey. The Gekkleberry Tree: A Humorous Tail about the Gekkards & One Legendary Tree. Welsh, Joey. 2005. (J). (gr. -1-3). 17.95 *(978-1-59247-244-4(3))* Scholargy Publishing, Inc.
Welsh, Mary Reddick. Sammy, the Little Green Snake Who Wanted to Fly. Welsh, Mary Reddick. 2011. 26p. pap. 11.95 *(978-1-936411-09-2(1))* YBK Pubs., Inc.
Weltevrede, Nona & Weltevrede, Pieter. Arjuna: The Gentle Warrior. Sperling, Vatsala. 2017. (ENG.). 32p. (J). (gr. -1-6). 15.95 *(978-1-59143-203-6(0),* Bear Cub Bks.) Bear & Co.
Weltevrede, Pieter, et al. Classic Tales from India: How Ganesh Got His Elephant Head & Other Stories. Sperling, Vatsala & Johari, Harish. 2020. (ENG.). 240p. (J). (gr. -1-6). pap. 18.99 *(978-1-59143-386-6(X),* Bear Cub Bks.) Bear & Co.
Weltevrede, Pieter. How Ganesh Got His Elephant Head. Johari, Harish & Sperling, Vatsala. 2003. (ENG.). 32p. (J). (gr. -1-6). 15.95 *(978-1-59143-021-6(6))* Bear & Co.
—The Magical Adventures of Krishna: How a Mischief Maker Saved the World. Sperling, Vatsala. 2nd ed. 2009. (ENG.). 32p. (J). (gr. -1-6). 15.95 *(978-1-59143-110-7(7),* Bear Cub Bks.) Bear & Co.
—Ram the Demon Slayer. Sperling, Vatsala. 2006. (ENG.). 32p. (J). (gr. -1-6). 15.95 *(978-1-59143-057-5(7),* Bear Cub Bks.) Bear & Co.
Weltevrede, Pieter, jt. illus. see Weltevrede, Nona.
Weltjens, Jochen, jt. photos by see Duhig, Lee.
Weltman, Relly. One Impeccable Ponytail. Martwick, Alica. 2019. (ENG.). 26p. (J). (gr. k-3). pap. 12.95 *(978-0-578-54890-6(9))* Alica C. Martwick.
Weltner, Dave. Canneh, the Reluctant Christmas Camel. Hanna, Margaret Leis. l.t. ed. 2003. 26p. (J). 7.95 *(978-0-9706654-7-8(4))* Sprite Pr.
—Quonby & the Tree Den. Chamberlain, Lyn. l.t. ed. 2004. 12p. (J). 7.95 *(978-0-9706654-8-5(2))* Sprite Pr.
—Summer Day. DuVall, Nell. l.t. ed. 2003. 13p. 7.95 *(978-0-9706654-6-1(6))* Sprite Pr.
Wenckebach, L. W. R., jt. illus. see Scheiner, A.
Wendel, Carie. Rock-A-Bye Baby. Everett, Melissa. 2013. 20p. (J). (gr. -1-3). bds. 8.99 *(978-1-77093-668-3(8))* Flowerpot Children's Pr. Inc. CAN. Dist: Cardinal Pubs. Group.
Wendel, Carrie. Rain, Rain, Go Away. Everett, Melissa. 2013. (ENG.). 20p. (J). (gr. -1-1). 8.99 *(978-1-77093-524-2(X))* Flowerpot Children's Pr. Inc. CAN. Dist: Cardinal Pubs. Group.
—Rock-A-Bye Baby. Everett, Melissa. 2013. (Record-A-Story Ser.). (ENG.). 18p. (J). (gr. -1). bds. *(978-1-77093-464-1(2))* Flowerpot Children's Pr. Inc.
Wendell, Jeremy. Archibald's Swiss Cheese Mountain. Lieberman, Sylvia. 2007. 44p. (J). (gr. k-2). 17.95 *(978-0-9795852-5-8(2))* Seven Locks Pr.
Wendell, Ulises. El Hombrecito Vestido de Gris. Alonso, Fernando. 2003. (SPA.). 94p. (J). (gr. 3-5). pap. 8.95 *(978-968-19-0439-5(7))* Santillana USA Publishing Co., Inc.
WendellDowling. Colorful Men & Women of the Mother Lode. Atkinson, Janet I. Atkinson, Janet I., ed. 2004. 253p. (YA). reprint ed. pap. 16.95 *(978-0-9653428-2-7(4))* Irene, Jan Pubns.
Wendland, Paula. El Bebé Raro. Hillert, Margaret. 2018. (BeginningtoRead Ser.).Tr. of Funny Baby. (SPA.). 32p. (J). (gr. -1-2). pap. 11.94 *(978-1-68404-235-7(6))* Norwood Hse. Pr.
—The Funny Baby. Hillert, Margaret. 2016. (BeginningtoRead Ser.). (ENG.). 32p. (J). (gr. -1-2). pap. 11.94 *(978-1-60357-907-0(9))* Norwood Hse. Pr.
—Guinea Fowl & Rabbit Get Justice: An African Folktale. Malaspina, Ann. 2013. (Folktales from Around the World Ser.). (ENG.). 24p. (J). (gr. k-3). 28.50 *(978-1-62323-614-4(2),* 206381) Child's World, Inc., The.
Wendland, Paula, jt. illus. see Jack Pullan.
Wendland, Paula Zinngrabe. The Funny Baby. Hillert, Margaret & Andersen, Hans. 2016. (BeginningtoRead Ser.). (ENG.). 32p. (J). (-2). lib. bdg. 22.60 *(978-1-59953-781-8(8))* Norwood Hse. Pr.
Wendland, Paula Zinngrabe. El Bebe Raro. Wendland, Paula Zinngrabe. Hillert, Margaret et al. 2018. (BeginningtoRead Ser.). (SPA.). 32p. (J). (gr. -1-2). lib. bdg. 22.60 *(978-1-59953-951-5(9))* Norwood Hse. Pr.
Wendt, Matt. Alien Incident on Planet J: Book 8. Jolley, Dan. 2008. (Twisted Journeys ® Ser.: 8). (ENG.). 112p. (J). (gr. 4-7). pap. 10.99 *(978-0-8225-8876-4(5),* Graphic Universe™) Lerner Publishing Group.
—Escape from Pyramid X. Jolley, Dan. 2007. (Twisted Journeys ® Ser.: 2). (ENG.). (J). (gr. 4-7). pap. 45.32 *(978-0-8225-9466-6(8))* Lerner Publishing Group.
—Escape from Pyramid X: Book 2. Jolley, Dan. 2007. (Twisted Journeys ® Ser.: 2). (ENG.). 112p. (J). (gr. 4-7). per. 10.99 *(978-0-8225-6779-0(2),* Graphic Universe™) Lerner Publishing Group.
—The Time Travel Trap. Jolley, Dan. 2008. (J). (gr. 4-7). (Twisted Journeys Ser.: Vol. 6). 111p. lib. bdg. 27.93 *(978-0-7613-9472-3(9),* Graphic Universe™); (Twisted Journeys ® Ser.: 6). (ENG.). pap. 45.32 *(978-0-8225-9470-3(6))* Lerner Publishing Group.
Wendt, Yohanna. The Bride's Price. Saint, Mimi. 2013. 16p. pap. 24.95 *(978-1-4241-4249-1(0))* America Star Bks.
Wendy, Watson, jt. illus. see Jodie, Dias.
Wenger, Amanda. Come & Play! Edwards, Aylan. 2018. (ENG.). 28p. (J). 22.95 *(978-1-64140-802-8(2))* Christian Faith Publishing.
Wenger-Smith, Amber. A Dead End & Burning Stone: The Last Wizard Books 3 And 4. Smith, Matthew. 2019. (Last Wizard Ser.: Vol. 2). (ENG.). 58p. (J). pap. 12.99 *(978-1-0742-1654-2(7))* Independently Published.
Wenisch, Tanja. Friends Always. 2014. 32p. (J). *(978-1-4338-1639-0(3),* Magination Pr.) American Psychological Assn.
Wennekes, Ron. If I Could Breathe Like Fishes Do, 11 vols. Stanley, Jan. 2006. 25p. (J). bds. 12.99 *(978-0-9776893-0-9(1))* Midwest Graphics, Inc.
Wensell, Ulises. Platero y Juan Ramon. Reviejo Hernandez, Carlos. 2006. (SPA.). 29p. (J). (gr. 6-8). 12.99 *(978-1-933032-10-8(3))* Lectorum Pubns., Inc.
—Ten Little Puppies/Diez Perritos: Bilingual Spanish-English Children's Book. Campoy, F. Isabel & Ada, Alma Flor. 2011. (ENG.). 32p. (J). (gr. -1-3). 16.99 *(978-0-06-147043-1(0),* HarperCollins Español) HarperCollins Christian Publishing.
Wensell, Ulises, jt. illus. see Boldt, Fabienne.
Wentzloff, Linden. Flo & Eddy's Water Adventure, 1 vol. Nunn, Lori. 2015. (ENG.). 48p. (J). (gr. 1-3). pap. 14.95 ***(978-1-926855-62-2(0))*** RMB Rocky Mountain Bks. CAN. Dist: Orca Bk. Pubs. USA.
Wenz-Vietor, Else. The Christmas Rose. Bauer, Sepp. 2008. 48p. (J). (gr. -1-3). 12.95 *(978-1-58089-232-2(9))* Charlesbridge Publishing, Inc.
Wenzel, Brendan. Beastly Babies. Jackson, Ellen. 2015. (ENG.). 32p. (J). (gr. -1-3). 17.99 *(978-1-4424-0834-0(0),* Beach Lane Bks.) Beach Lane Bks.
Wenzel, Brendan. Hello Hello. 2020. (ENG.). 40p. (J). (gr. -1 — 1). bds. 9.99 ***(978-1-7972-0265-5(0))*** Chronicle Bks. LLC.
Wenzel, Brendan. Hello Hello (Books for Preschool & Kindergarten, Poetry Books for Kids) 2018. (ENG.). 52p. (J). (gr. -1-k). 17.99 *(978-1-4521-5014-7(1))* Chronicle Bks. LLC.
—Life. Rylant, Cynthia. 2017. (ENG.). 48p. (J). (gr. -1). 17.99 *(978-1-4814-5162-8(6),* Beach Lane Bks.) Beach Lane Bks.
—One Day in the Eucalyptus, Eucalyptus Tree. Bernstrom, Daniel. 2016. (ENG.). 32p. (J). (gr. -1-3). 17.99 *(978-0-06-235485-3(X),* HarperCollins) HarperCollins Pubs. Ltd. GBR. Dist: HarperCollins Pubs.
—Some Bugs. DiTerlizzi, Angela. 2014. (ENG.). 32p. (J). (gr. -1-3). 17.99 *(978-1-4424-5880-2(1),* Beach Lane Bks.) Beach Lane Bks.
—Some Pets. DiTerlizzi, Angela. 2016. (ENG.). 32p. (J). (gr. -1-3). 18.99 *(978-1-4814-4402-6(6),* Beach Lane Bks.) Beach Lane Bks.
—A Stone Sat Still. 2019. (ENG.). 56p. (J). (gr. -1-k). 17.99 *(978-1-4521-7318-4(4))* Chronicle Bks. LLC.
—They All Saw a Cat (Cat Books for Kids, Beginning Reading Books, Preschool Prep Books) 2016. (ENG.). 44p. (J). (gr. -1-k). 16.99 *(978-1-4521-5013-0(3))* Chronicle Bks. LLC.
Wenzel, Brendan. They All Saw a Cat. Wenzel, Brendan. 2016. 44p. pap. 16.99 *(978-1-4521-8805-8(X))* Chronicle Bks. LLC.
Wenzel, David. Baby Loves You So Much! Spinelli, Eileen. 2008. (ENG.). 40p. (J). (gr. -1-3). 16.99 *(978-0-8249-5550-2(1),* Ideal Pubns.) Worthy Publishing.
—Bell's Breakthrough. Deutsch, Stacia & Cohon, Rhody. (Blast to the Past Ser.: 3). (ENG.). (J). (gr. 2-5). 2013. 128p. pap. 6.99 *(978-1-4424-9536-4(7));* 2005. 112p. pap. 6.99 *(978-0-689-87026-2(4))* Simon & Schuster/Paula Wiseman Bks. (Simon & Schuster/Paula Wiseman Bks.).
—Disney's Dream. Deutsch, Stacia & Cohon, Rhody. 2013. (Blast to the Past Ser.: 2). (ENG.). 128p. (J). (gr. 2-5). pap. 6.99 *(978-1-4424-9535-7(9),* Simon & Schuster/Paula Wiseman Bks.) Simon & Schuster/Paula Wiseman Bks.
—Disney's Dream. Deutsch/Cohon. 2005. 108p. (J). lib. bdg. 16.92 *(978-1-4242-1714-4(8))* Fitzgerald Bks.
—Frog Went A-Traveling: A Russian Folktale. StJohn, Amanda. 2011. (Folktales from Around the World Ser.). (ENG.). 24p. (J). (gr. k-3). 28.50 *(978-1-60973-136-6(0),* 201142) Child's World, Inc., The.
—A Hat for Ivan. Lucado, Max. ed. 2017. (ENG.). 32p. (J). 14.99 *(978-1-4335-5833-7(5))* Crossway.
—King's Courage. Deutsch, Stacia & Cohon, Rhody. (Blast to the Past Ser.: 4). (ENG.). (J). (gr. 2-5). 2013. 128p. pap. 5.99 *(978-1-4424-9537-1(5));* 2006. 112p. pap. 6.99 *(978-1-4169-1269-9(X))* Simon & Schuster/Paula Wiseman Bks. (Simon & Schuster/Paula Wiseman Bks.).
—Lincoln's Legacy. Deutsch, Stacia & Cohon, Rhody. 2005. (Blast to the Past Ser.: 1). (ENG.). 112p. (J). (gr. 2-5). pap. 6.99 *(978-0-689-87024-8(8),* Simon & Schuster/Paula Wiseman Bks.) Simon & Schuster/Paula Wiseman Bks.
—Lincoln's Legacy. Deutsch/Cohon. 2005. 104p. (J). lib. bdg. 16.92 *(978-1-4242-1716-8(4))* Fitzgerald Bks.
—Lincoln's Legacy. Deutsch, Stacia & Cohon, Rhody. 2013. (Blast to the Past Ser.: 1). (ENG.). 128p. (J). (gr. 2-5). pap. 6.99 *(978-1-4424-9534-0(0),* Simon & Schuster/Paula Wiseman Bks.) Simon & Schuster/Paula Wiseman Bks.
—Sacagawea's Strength. Deutsch, Stacia & Cohon, Rhody. 2006. (Blast to the Past Ser.: 5). (ENG.). 128p. (J). (gr. 2-5). pap. 6.99 *(978-1-4169-1270-5(3),* Simon & Schuster/Paula Wiseman Bks.) Simon & Schuster/Paula Wiseman Bks.
Wenzel, David, et al. Solomon Kane: the Original Marvel Years Omnibus. 2020. (ENG.). 624p. (gr. 13-17). 100.00 ***(978-1-302-92514-7(8))*** Marvel Worldwide, Inc.
Wenzel, David. To Build a Better Mouse. Sachs, Allan. 2017. (ENG.). (J). pap. 15.00 *(978-1-4575-5306-6(6))* Dog Ear Publishing, LLC.
—We Both Read-Soccer! Ross, Dev. 2010. 44p. (J). 9.95 *(978-1-60115-239-8(6));* pap. 4.99 *(978-1-60115-240-4(X))* Treasure Bay, Inc.
Wenzel, David, jt. illus. see Wenzel, David T.
Wenzel, David T. I Like to Eat Treats. Rothenberg, Annye. 2010. 48p. (J). pap. 9.95 *(978-0-9790420-2-7(X))* Perfecting Parenting Pr.
—The King of the Little Things, 1 vol. Lepp, Bil. 2013. (ENG.). 32p. (J). (gr. -1-3). 16.95 *(978-1-56145-708-3(6))* Peachtree Publishing Co. Inc.
—More or Less. Murphy, Stuart J. 2005. (MathStart 2 Ser.). (ENG.). 40p. (J). (gr. 1-18). pap. 6.99 *(978-0-06-053167-6(3))* HarperCollins Pubs.
—More or Less. Murphy, Stuart J. 2005. (Mathstart Ser.). 33p. (gr. 1-4). 16.00 *(978-0-7569-5225-9(5))* Perfection Learning Corp.
—Rodeo Time. Murphy, Stuart J. 2006. (MathStart 3 Ser.). (ENG.). 40p. (J). (gr. 2-5). pap. 5.99 *(978-0-06-055779-9(6))* HarperCollins Pubs.
—Sacagawea's Strength. Deutsch, Stacia & Cohon, Rhody. 2006. (Blast to the Past Ser.: Vol. 5). (ENG.). (J). (gr. 2-5). lib. bdg. 20.60 *(978-1-62765-942-0(0))* Perfection Learning Corp.
—Why Do I Have To? Rothenberg, Annye. 2009. 40p. (J). pap. 9.95 *(978-0-9790420-1-0(1))* Perfecting Parenting Pr.
Wenzel, David T. & Schories, Pat. Biscuit's ABC Adventure. Capucilli, Alyssa Satin. 2008. (Biscuit Ser.). 32p. (J). (gr. -1-2). pap. 3.99 *(978-0-06-112841-7(4),* HarperFestival) HarperCollins Pubs.
Wenzel, David T. & Wenzel, David. Your Special Gift. Lucado, Max et al. 2006. (Max Lucado's Wemmicks Ser.: 6). (ENG.). 32p. (J). (gr. -1-3). 16.99 *(978-1-58134-698-5(0))* Crossway.
Wenzel, Gregory. The Deep-Sea Floor. Collard, Sneed B., III. 2003. 32p. (J). (gr. 1-4). pap. 7.95 *(978-1-57091-403-4(6))* Charlesbridge Publishing, Inc.
—Loli the Leopard. Nussbaum, Ben. (ENG.). (J). (gr. -1-2). 2006. 32p. 9.95 *(978-1-59249-516-0(8),* PS6556); 2006. 36p. 8.95 *(978-1-59249-514-6(1),* SD6506); 2005. 36p. 14.95 *(978-1-59249-512-2(5),* H6506); 2005. 36p. pap. 6.95 *(978-1-59249-513-9(3),* S6506) Soundprints.
—Toko the Hippo. Nussbaum, Ben. 2006. (ENG.). 36p. (J). 14.99 *(978-1-59249-577-1(X));* 8.95 *(978-1-59249-580-1(X));* pap. 6.95 *(978-1-59249-578-8(8));* pap. 2.95 *(978-1-59249-579-5(6))* Soundprints.
Wenzel, Gregory. The Feathered Dinosaurs of China. Wenzel, Gregory. 2004. 32p. (J). (gr. 1-4). pap. 7.95 *(978-1-57091-562-8(8))* Charlesbridge Publishing, Inc.
Wenzel, Paul & Enik, Ted. Pooh's Halloween Parade. Gaines, Isabel & Milne, A. A. 2012. (J). *(978-1-4351-4175-9(X))* Disney Publishing Worldwide.
Werden's class. Nunamiut ABC: A Child's View of Life in an Alaska Village. Written & Illustrated by the 4th & 5th Graders of Anaktuvuk Pass, Alaska. Werden's class. 2003. 28p. (J). 3.95 *(978-0-930931-54-4(8))* Alaska Geographic Assn.
Wernert, Virginie. Enfants de L'océan. Verhoest, chris. 2019. (FRE.). 752p. (J). pap. 26.67 *(978-1-0802-0690-2(6))* Independently Published.
Wernicke, Maria. Candelaria. Galmez, Griselda. 2003. (SPA.). 38p. (J). (gr. k-3). pap. 9.95 *(978-968-19-0666-5(7))* Santillana USA Publishing Co., Inc.
Wernicke, María. Meet Jabron. White, Amy. 2008. (Fácil de Leer / Easy to Read Ser.). (ENG.). 16p. (J). pap. 5.99 ***(978-1-59820-567-1(6),*** Santillana Texto) Santillana USA Publishing Co., Inc.
Wernicke, Maria. Sol de los Amigos. Baranda, Maria. 2010. (SPA.). 56p. (J). (gr. 2-5). pap. *(978-607-7661-13-9(9))* Ediciones El Naranjo Sa De Cv.
—Te Presento a Jacobo. White, Amy. Kratky, Lada J., tr. 2009. (Colección Fácil de Leer Ser.). (SPA.). 16p. (gr. k-2). pap. 5.99 *(978-1-60396-415-9(0))* Ediciones Alfaguara ESP. Dist: Santillana USA Publishing Co., Inc.
Wernun, Anna. Ethan Is Caught Blue Faced! Pulchinski, Erin. 2013. 32p. pap. *(978-1-4602-2416-8(7))* FriesenPress.
Werth, Kurt. Alaska Harvest. Pedersen, Elsa. 2012. 194p. 42.95 *(978-1-258-23211-5(1));* pap. 27.95 *(978-1-258-23973-2(6))* Literary Licensing, LLC.
—Tales Merry & Wise. Minciell, Rose Laura & Ross, Rose Laura. 2011. 130p. 40.95 *(978-1-258-09714-1(1))* Literary Licensing, LLC.
—The Thing at the Foot of the Bed & Other Scary Tales. Leach, Maria. 2016. (ENG.). 128p. (J). (gr. 2-5). pap. 7.99 *(978-0-486-80786-7(X))* Dover Pubns., Inc.
Wertheim, Anne. Bottlenose Dolphin. Sherrow, Victoria. 2012. (ENG.). 24p. (J). pap. 3.95 *(978-1-60727-724-8(7))* Soundprints.
—Galapagos Fur Seal: At Home in the Tropics. Sherrow, Victoria. 2011. (ENG.). 32p. (J). pap. 8.95 *(978-1-60727-613-5(5))* Soundprints.
—Garter Snake at Willow Creek Lane. Halfmann, Janet. 2011. (ENG.). 32p. (J). (gr. k-4). 19.95 *(978-1-60727-206-9(7));* pap. 8.95 *(978-1-60727-208-3(3))* Soundprints.
—What Eats What in a Desert Food Chain, 1 vol. Slade, Suzanne. 2012. (Food Chains Ser.). (ENG.). 24p. (J). (gr. 2-4). 26.65 *(978-1-4048-7386-5(4));* pap. 8.95 *(978-1-4048-7690-3(1))* Capstone. (Picture Window Bks.).
—What Eats What in a Rain Forest Food Chain, 1 vol. Amstutz, Lisa J. 2012. (Food Chains Ser.). (ENG.). 24p. (J). (gr. 2-4). 26.65 *(978-1-4048-7387-2(2));* pap. 8.95 *(978-1-4048-7694-1(4))* Capstone. (Picture Window Bks.).

W

Wertz, Julia. The Emotionary: A Dictionary of Words That Don't Exist for Feelings That Do. Sher, Eden. 2017. (ENG.). 208p. (YA). (gr. 7). pap. 9.99 *(978-0-448-49384-8(5)*, Razorbill) Penguin Young Readers Group.

Wertz, Michael. ABCs of Golden Gate Park. Lindsey, Marta. 2020. (ENG.). 28p. (J). (gr. -1 — 1). bds. 12.99 *(978-1-5132-6303-8(X)*, West Margin Pr.) West Margin Pr.

—Golden Gate Park, an a to Z Adventure. Lindsey, Marta. 2020. (ENG.). 32p. (J). (gr. 1-3). 17.99 *(978-1-5132-6301-4(3)*, West Margin Pr.) West Margin Pr.

—A Spectacular Selection of Sea Critters: Concrete Poems. Franco, Betsy. 2015. (ENG.). 32p. (J). (gr. 2-5). 19.99 *(978-1-4677-2152-3(2)*, 9781467721523); E-Book 30.65 *(978-1-4677-8849-6(X))* Lerner Publishing Group. (Millbrook Pr.).

—Where's My Stuff? The Ultimate Teen Organizing Guide. Moss, Samantha. 2007. (ENG.). 96p. (YA). (gr. 8-12). pap. 16.95 *(978-0-9772660-5-0(2)*, Zest Bks.) Lerner Publishing Group.

—Where's My Stuff? 2nd Edition: The Ultimate Teen Organizing Guide. Moss, Samantha & Martin, Lesley. 2020. (ENG.). 120p. (YA). (gr. 6-12). lib. bdg. 37.32 *(978-1-5415-7894-4(5))*; 2nd ed. pap. 14.99 *(978-1-5415-7895-1(3))* Lerner Publishing Group. (Zest Bks.).

Wertz, Michael, jt. illus. see Starmer, Anika.

Werx, Art. Pippa Laurence, Creature Squisher (Black & White) English. Briley, Debra M. 2018. (ENG.). 58p. (J). pap. 6.00 *(978-1-7320290-9-5(1))* evangeline.

—Pippa Laurence, Criatura Squisher, (Spanish, Black & White) Briley, Deb M. 2018. (SPA.). 58p. (J). pap. 6.50 *(978-1-7320290-1-9(6))* evangeline.

Wes Wheeler. A Gator Took My Toothbrush. Frisby, Brandon. 2020. (ENG.). (J). pap. 16.99 ***(978-1-4621-3697-1(4)***, Horizon Pubs.) Cedar Fort, Inc./CFI Distribution.

Wesley, Omarr. Gusts & Gales: A Book about Wind, 1 vol. Sherman, Josepha. 2003. (Amazing Science: Weather Ser.). (ENG.). 24p. (J). (gr. -1-3). per. 8.95 *(978-1-4048-0338-1(6)*, Picture Window Bks.) Capstone.

—Gusts & Gales: A Book about Wind. Sherman, Josepha. 2003. (Amazing Science: Weather Ser.). (ENG.). 24p. (J). (gr. -1-3). 27.32 *(978-1-4048-0094-6(8)*, Picture Window Bks.) Capstone.

—Shapes in the Sky: A Book about Clouds, 1 vol. Sherman, Josepha. 2003. (Amazing Science: Weather Ser.). (ENG.). 24p. (J). (gr. -1-3). per. 8.95 *(978-1-4048-0341-1(6)*, Picture Window Bks.) Capstone.

—Sopla y Silba: Un Libro Sobre el Viento, 1 vol. Sherman, Josepha & Picture Window Books Staff. Robledo, Sol, tr. 2007. (Ciencia Asombrosa: el Tiempo Ser.). (SPA.). 24p. (J). (gr. -1-3). 27.32 *(978-1-4048-3217-6(3)*, Picture Window Bks.) Capstone.

Wess, Robert. Friends at Work & Play. Wess, Robert, photos by. Bunnett, Rochelle, photos by. 2003. 32p. (J). 14.95 *(978-0-9660884-2-7(5))*; pap. *(978-0-9660884-1-0(7))* Our Kids Pr.

Wesson, Andrea. Argus. Knudsen, Michelle. 2011. (ENG.). 32p. (J). (gr. -1-3). 17.99 *(978-0-7636-3790-3(4))* Candlewick Pr.

—Evangeline Mudd & the Golden-Haired Apes of the Ikkinasti Jungle. Elliott, David. 2004. 208p. pap. *(978-0-7445-8379-3(9))* Walker Bks., Ltd.

—Jack Quack, 1 vol. Nolan, Lucy. 2003. (ENG.). 32p. (J). (gr. k-3). pap. 5.95 *(978-0-7614-5153-2(6))* Marshall Cavendish Corp.

—A Pet for Miss Wright. Young, Judy. 2011. (ENG.). 40p. (J). (gr. 1-4). lib. bdg. 15.95 *(978-1-58536-509-8(2)*, 202202) Sleeping Bear Pr.

Wesson, Tim. Action Hero. Murtagh, Ciaran. 2017. (Fincredible Diary of Fin Spencer Ser.: 3). (ENG.). 224p. (J). (gr. 4-7). pap. 7.99 *(978-1-84812-532-2(1))* Bonnier Publishing GBR. Dist: Independent Pubs. Group.

—The Fincredible Diary of Fin Spencer: Stuntboy. Murtagh, Ciaran. 2016. (Fincredible Diary of Fin Spencer Ser.: 1). (ENG.). 224p. (J). (gr. 4-7). pap. 7.99 *(978-1-84812-434-9(1))* Bonnier Publishing GBR. Dist: Independent Pubs. Group.

Wesson, Tim. Kids Fight Plastic: How to Be A #2minutesuperhero. Dorey, Martin. 2020. (ENG.). 128p. (J). (gr. 2-5). 19.99 ***(978-1-5362-1277-8(6))***; pap. 9.99 ***(978-1-5362-1587-8(2))*** Candlewick Pr.

Wesson, Tim. Megastar. Murtagh, Ciaran. 2016. (Fincredible Diary of Fin Spencer Ser.: 2). (ENG.). 224p. (J). (gr. 4-7). pap. 7.99 *(978-1-84812-447-9(3))* Bonnier Publishing GBR. Dist: Independent Pubs. Group.

—Prom King. Murtagh, Ciaran. 2017. (Fincredible Diary of Fin Spencer Ser.: 4). (ENG.). 224p. (J). (gr. 4-7). pap. 8.99 *(978-1-84812-558-2(5))* Bonnier Publishing GBR. Dist: Independent Pubs. Group.

—Spies vs. Giant Slugs in the Jungle. Catlow, Nikalas. 2012. (Mega Mash-Up Ser.: 5). (ENG.). 96p. (J). (gr. 2-5). pap. 6.99 *(978-0-7636-5902-8(9)*, Nosy Crow) Candlewick Pr.

—Spy Toys: Out of Control. Powers, Mark. 2019. (Spy Toys Ser.). (ENG.). 208p. (J). 13.99 *(978-1-68119-960-3(2)*, 900194411, Bloomsbury Children's Bks.) Bloomsbury Publishing USA.

—Trolls vs. Cowboys in the Arctic. Catlow, Nikalas. 2012. (Mega Mash-Up Ser.: 6). (ENG.). 96p. (J). (gr. 2-5). pap. 6.99 *(978-0-7636-6271-4(2)*, Nosy Crow) Candlewick Pr.

Wesson, Tim, jt. illus. see Catlow, Nikalas.

West, Colin. Have You Seen the Crocodile? Read & Share. West, Colin. 2003. (Read & Share Ser.). (ENG.). 32p. (J). (gr. -1-3). pap. 3.99 *(978-0-7636-0862-0(9))* Candlewick Pr.

West, D. E. Ferdinand Uses the Potty. Tucker, Jason. 2009. (J). pap. 13.95 *(978-1-932690-82-8(4))* Loving Healing Pr., Inc.

West, David. Demons & Ghouls. Ganeri, Anita. 2010. (Dark Side Ser.). 32p. (J). pap. 10.50 *(978-1-4488-1564-7(9))*; lib. bdg. 28.50 *(978-1-61531-896-4(8))* Rosen Publishing Group, Inc., The. (PowerKids Pr.).

—Ghosts & Other Specters. Ganeri, Anita. 2010. (Dark Side Ser.). 32p. (J). pap. 10.50 *(978-1-4488-1566-1(5))*; (ENG.). lib. bdg. 28.50 *(978-1-61531-897-1(6))* Rosen Publishing Group, Inc., The. (PowerKids Pr.).

—The Illustrated Guide to Mythical Creatures. 2009. 48p. (J). (gr. 5-18). pap. 15.99 *(978-0-8437-1669-6(X))* Hammond World Atlas Corp.

—Looking Beyond. Parker, Steve. 2015. (Story of Space Ser.). (ENG.). 32p. (J). (gr. 3-6). 31.35 *(978-1-62588-076-5(6)*, 1389436) Black Rabbit Bks.

—On Water. Parker, Steven. 2012. (Future Transport Ser.). 32p. (gr. 5-5). 29.50 *(978-1-60870-780-5(6))* Cavendish Square Publishing LLC.

—Planes. 2017. (What's Inside? Ser.). 24p. (gr. k-3). lib. bdg. 28.50 *(978-1-62588-401-5(X))* Black Rabbit Bks.

—Probes to the Planets. Parker, Steve. 2015. (Story of Space Ser.). (ENG.). 32p. (J). (gr. 3-6). 31.35 *(978-1-62588-077-2(4))* Black Rabbit Bks.

—Race Cars. 2017. (What's Inside? Ser.). 24p. (gr. k-3). lib. bdg. 28.50 *(978-1-62588-403-9(6))* Black Rabbit Bks.

—Race to the Moon. Parker, Steve. 2015. (Story of Space Ser.). (ENG.). 32p. (J). (gr. 3-6). 31.35 *(978-1-62588-078-9(2))* Black Rabbit Bks.

—Satellites. Parker, Steve. 2015. (Story of Space Ser.). (ENG.). 32p. (J). (gr. 3-6). 31.35 *(978-1-62588-079-6(0))* Black Rabbit Bks.

—Space Pioneers. Parker, Steve. 2015. (Story of Space Ser.). (ENG.). 32p. (J). (gr. 3-6). 31.35 *(978-1-62588-080-2(4)*, 1389452) Black Rabbit Bks.

—Space Stations. Parker, Steve. 2015. (Story of Space Ser.). (ENG.). 32p. (J). (gr. 3-6). 31.35 *(978-1-62588-081-9(2))* Black Rabbit Bks.

—Tanks. 2017. (What's Inside? Ser.). 24p. (gr. k-3). lib. bdg. 28.50 *(978-1-62588-402-2(8))* Black Rabbit Bks.

West, David. Coelophysis & Other Dinosaurs & Reptiles from the Upper Triassic. West, David. 2012. (Dinosaurs! Ser.). (ENG.). 32p. (J). (gr. 3-6). pap. 10.50 *(978-1-4339-6713-9(8)*, Gareth Stevens Learning Library); lib. bdg. 27.60 *(978-1-4339-6711-5(1))* Stevens, Gareth Publishing LLLP.

—Combat Helicopters. West, David. 2019. (War Machines Ser.). (ENG.). 32p. (J). (gr. 5-6). pap. *(978-0-7787-6679-7(9)*, 91c2879e-11ce-476c-8571-32ba4cb4f1f6); lib. bdg. *(978-0-7787-6665-0(9)*, 98858c15-9e42-4909-b493-e7db24498fc7) Crabtree Publishing Co.

—Combat Planes. West, David. 2019. (War Machines Ser.). (ENG.). 32p. (J). (gr. 5-6). pap. *(978-0-7787-6680-3(2)*, b0f913c3-364a-444e-8934-15766fad132c); lib. bdg. *(978-0-7787-6666-7(7)*, ade46cb9-931b-4068-861d-f2c8b7eb540c) Crabtree Publishing Co.

—Lesothosaurus & Other Dinosaurs & Reptiles from the Lower Jurassic. West, David. 2012. (Dinosaurs! Ser.). (ENG.). 32p. (J). (gr. 3-6). pap. 10.50 *(978-1-4339-6717-7(0)*, Gareth Stevens Learning Library); lib. bdg. 27.60 *(978-1-4339-6715-3(4))* Stevens, Gareth Publishing LLLP.

—Pets in the Home. West, David. 2014. (Nora the Naturalist's Animals Ser.). 24p. (J). (gr. k-3). pap. 8.95 *(978-1-62588-052-9(9))* Black Rabbit Bks.

—Rockets & Missiles. West, David. 2019. (War Machines Ser.). (ENG.). 32p. (J). (gr. 5-6). pap. *(978-0-7787-6682-7(9)*, 3a13bc29-ab09-4f96-beb9-ec63250c2cb2); lib. bdg. *(978-0-7787-6667-4(5)*, 582de6be-be4d-48ae-8e72-d4a7e0ef7009) Crabtree Publishing Co.

—Spacecraft. West, David. 2017. (What's Inside? Ser.). 24p. (gr. k-3). 28.50 *(978-1-62588-404-6(4)*, Smart Apple Media) Black Rabbit Bks.

—Submarines. West, David. 2017. (What's Inside? Ser.). 24p. (gr. k-3). 28.50 *(978-1-62588-405-3(2)*, Smart Apple Media) Black Rabbit Bks.

—Submarines. West, David. 2019. (War Machines Ser.). (ENG.). 32p. (J). (gr. 5-6). pap. *(978-0-7787-6683-4(7)*, e2401d4c-7356-431e-8524-cfe7bc9870f8); lib. bdg. *(978-0-7787-6668-1(3)*, 3354c6de-69f0-4203-8467-4344c8b33dd3) Crabtree Publishing Co.

—Tanks. West, David. 2017. (What's Inside? Ser.). 24p. (J). (gr. k-3). 28.50 *(978-1-62588-406-0(0)*, Smart Apple Media) Black Rabbit Bks.

—Tanks. West, David. 2019. (War Machines Ser.). (ENG.). 32p. (J). (gr. 5-6). pap. *(978-0-7787-6684-1(5)*, 02674d78-310a-4f84-b7f0-dadef7336ce3); lib. bdg. *(978-0-7787-6669-8(1)*, c69f6e5e-e82d-415e-8f60-575babfdce9e) Crabtree Publishing Co.

—Ten of the Best Animal Myths. West, David. West, David. 2014. (Ten of the Best: Myths, Legends & Folk Stories Ser.). (ENG.). 24p. (J). (gr. 3-4). pap. *(978-0-7787-0807-0(1))* Crabtree Publishing Co.

—Ten of the Best Ghost Stories. West, David. West, David. 2014. (Ten of the Best: Myths, Legends & Folk Stories Ser.). (ENG.). 24p. (J). (gr. 3-4). pap. *(978-0-7787-0819-3(5))* Crabtree Publishing Co.

—Ten of the Best Giant Stories. West, David. West, David. 2014. (Ten of the Best: Myths, Legends & Folk Stories Ser.). (ENG.). 24p. (J). (gr. 3-4). pap. *(978-0-7787-0821-6(7))* Crabtree Publishing Co.

—Ten of the Best God & Goddess Stories. West, David. West, David. 2014. (Ten of the Best: Myths, Legends & Folk Stories Ser.). (ENG.). 24p. (J). (gr. 3-4). pap. *(978-0-7787-0823-0(3))* Crabtree Publishing Co.

—Ten of the Best Monster Stories. West, David. West, David. 2014. (Ten of the Best: Myths, Legends & Folk Stories Ser.). (ENG.). 24p. (J). (gr. 3-4). *(978-0-7787-0783-7(0))* Crabtree Publishing Co.

—Ten of the Best Mythical Hero Stories. West, David. West, David. 2014. (Ten of the Best: Myths, Legends & Folk Stories Ser.). (ENG.). 24p. (J). (gr. 3-4). *(978-0-7787-0785-1(7))* Crabtree Publishing Co.

—Ten of the Best Prince & Princess Stories. West, David. West, David. 2014. (Ten of the Best: Myths, Legends & Folk Stories Ser.). (ENG.). 24p. (J). (gr. 3-4). *(978-0-7787-0787-5(3))* Crabtree Publishing Co.

—Ten of the Best Witch & Sorcerer Stories. West, David. West, David. 2014. (Ten of the Best: Myths, Legends & Folk Stories Ser.). (ENG.). 24p. (J). (gr. 3-4). *(978-0-7787-0797-4(0))* Crabtree Publishing Co.

—Warships. West, David. 2019. (War Machines Ser.). (ENG.). 32p. (J). (gr. 5-6). pap. *(978-0-7787-6685-8(3)*, 7ceed681-b56c-4161-b08c-b4c7052b13ee); lib. bdg. *(978-0-7787-6678-0(0)*, ad024fd2-1862-41fb-aa20-de2e16f1906a) Crabtree Publishing Co.

West, David & Ganeri, Anita. Giants & Ogres. West, David & Ganeri, Anita. 2010. (Dark Side Ser.). 32p. (J). (ENG.). pap. 10.50 *(978-1-4488-1568-5(1))*; lib. bdg. 28.50 *(978-1-61531-898-8(4))* Rosen Publishing Group, Inc., The. (PowerKids Pr.).

—Vampires & the Undead. West, David & Ganeri, Anita. 2010. (Dark Side Ser.). 32p. (J). (ENG.). pap. 10.50 *(978-1-4488-1570-8(3))*; lib. bdg. 28.50 *(978-1-61531-899-5(2))* Rosen Publishing Group, Inc., The.

—Werewolves & Other Shape-Shifters. West, David & Ganeri, Anita. 2010. (Dark Side Ser.). (ENG.). 32p. (J). pap. 10.50 *(978-1-4488-1572-2(X))*; lib. bdg. 28.50 *(978-1-61531-900-8(X))* Rosen Publishing Group, Inc., The. (PowerKids Pr.).

—Witches & Warlocks. West, David & Ganeri, Anita. 2010. (Dark Side Ser.). 32p. (J). pap. 10.50 *(978-1-4488-1574-6(6))*; (ENG.). lib. bdg. 28.50 *(978-1-61531-901-5(8))* Rosen Publishing Group, Inc., The. (PowerKids Pr.).

West, David & Spender, Nik. Ankylosaurus: The Armored Dinosaur. West, David. 2009. (Graphic Dinosaurs Ser.). (ENG.). 32p. (J). pap. 12.30 *(978-1-4358-8596-7(1))*; (gr. 2-5). 28.50 *(978-1-4358-8590-5(2))* Rosen Publishing Group, Inc., The. (PowerKids Pr.).

West, Eddie, jt. illus. see Ilic, Nikolas.

West, Harold E. Old Ramon. Schaefer, Jack. 2016. (ENG.). 112p. (J). pap. 19.95 *(978-0-8263-5764-9(4))* Univ. of New Mexico Pr.

West, Jeff. The Acrobatic Empress ? The Story of Theodora. Phillips, Robin. 2006. (Who in the World Ser.: 0). (ENG.). 56p. (J). (gr. 2-4). per. 9.50 *(978-0-9728603-9-0(8)*, 86039) Well-Trained Mind Pr.

—The Story of the World: History for the Classical Child: Activity Book 3: Early Modern Times: from Elizabeth the First to the Forty-Niner S REVISED EDITION. Bauer, Susan Wise, ed. 2nd rev. ed. 2020. (Story of the World Ser.: 14). (ENG.). 418p. (J). (gr. 3-7). pap. 39.95 *(978-1-945841-47-7(8)*, 458447) Well-Trained Mind Pr.

—The Story of the World: History for the Classical Child: Volume 3, Early Modern Times: from Elizabeth the First to the Forty-Niners REVIS ED EDITION. Bauer, Susan Wise. 2nd rev. ed. 2020. (Story of the World Ser.: 11). (ENG.). 432p. (J). (gr. 3-7). pap. 19.95 *(978-1-945841-44-6(3)*, 458444); 24.95 *(978-1-945841-45-3(1)*, 458445) Well-Trained Mind Pr.

West, Jennifer. What Is Money? Boritzer, Etan. 2006. 40p. (J). pap. 6.95 *(978-0-9762743-3-9(7))* Lane, Veronica Bks.

West, Jeremy. Omni Presents the Universe. Conquistadore, H. I.t. ed. 2003. 51p. per. 8.99 *(978-1-932338-14-0(4))* Lifevest Publishing, Inc.

West, Joyce. The Drovers Road Collection: Three New Zealand Adventures, 3 vols. West, Joyce. 2003. (Bethlehem Budget Bks). (ENG.). 448p. (J). (gr. 7-9). pap. 16.95 *(978-1-883937-69-0(8))* Ignatius Pr.

West, June & Wright, Shannon. A Trip to the Cellar. West, Lily June Wolford. 2007. (J). (gr. -1-3). 16.99 *(978-1-59879-347-5(0))* Lifevest Publishing, Inc.

West, Karl. The Big Race Lace Case: Mack Rhino, Private Eye 1. Jacobs, Paul DuBois & Swender, Jennifer. 2020. (Quix Ser.). (ENG.). 80p. (J). (gr. k-3). 16.99 *(978-1-5344-4113-2(1))*; pap. 5.99 *(978-1-5344-4112-5(3))* Simon & Schuster Children's Publishing. (Aladdin).

West, Karl. The Candy Caper Case: Mack Rhino, Private Eye 2. Jacobs, Paul DuBois & Swender, Jennifer. 2020. (Quix Ser.). (ENG.). 80p. (J). (gr. k-3). 17.99 ***(978-1-5344-4116-3(6))***; pap. 5.99 ***(978-1-5344-4115-6(8))*** Simon & Schuster Children's Publishing. (Aladdin).

West, Karl. The Daring Prince Dashing. Reeder, Marilou. 2015. 32p. (J). (gr. -1-k). 16.99 *(978-1-63450-161-3(6)*, Sky Pony Pr.) Skyhorse Publishing Co., Inc.

—Red Riding Hood Meets the Three Bears. Guillain, Charlotte. 2016. (Fairy Tale Mix-Ups Ser.). (ENG.). 24p. (J). (gr. k-2). lib. bdg. 23.99 *(978-1-4109-8304-6(8)*, Raintree) Capstone.

West, Karl & Dunn, Robert. Pennsylvania Books for Kids Gift Set. Magsamen, Sandra et al. 2020. (ENG.). (J). (-3). 29.99 ***(978-1-7282-4190-6(1))*** Sourcebooks, Inc.

West Kinney, Troy and Margaret. The Thrall of Leif the Lucky: A Story of Viking Days. Liljencrantz, Ottilie A. 2017. (ENG.). (YA). (gr. 9-12). pap. 19.95 *(978-0-9976647-6-8(2))* Hillside Education.

West, Lorraine. I Like You but I Love Me. 2006. 36p. (J). pap. 12.95 *(978-0-9768674-1-8(9))* Hip Hop Schl. Hse.

—The Mirror & Me. 2005. 40p. (J). per. 12.95 *(978-0-9768674-0-1(0))* Hip Hop Schl. Hse.

West, Matthew. My Family, My Home. Skinner, Dawn. 2016. (Dysfunctional Piggies Ser.: Vol. 2). (ENG.). (J). pap. *(978-1-4602-7347-0(8))* FriesenPress.

West, Matthew M. Can't Help but Love Those Babies. Skinner, Dawn. 2018. (Dysfunctional Piggies Ser.). (ENG.). 48p. (J). pap. *(978-1-5255-1611-5(6))* FriesenPress.

—An Unforgettable Night at the Movies. Skinner, Dawn. 2018. (Dysfunctional Piggies Ser.). (ENG.). 48p. (J). pap. *(978-1-5255-2193-5(4))* FriesenPress.

Westbeld, Kristine. Everyone Called Her Sister Sarah. Bert, Ruth J. 2004. (ENG.). 32p. (J). (gr. -1-3). pap. 4.99 *(978-1-928915-62-1(0))* Evangel Publishing Hse.

Westberg, Jan. Bees to Trees: Reading, Writing, & Reciting Poems about Nature. Freese, Susan M., ed. 2008. (Poetry Power Ser.). (ENG.). 32p. (J). (gr. k-4). 29.93 *(978-1-60453-001-8(4)*, 12766, Super SandCastle) ABDO Publishing Co.

—Buses to Books: Reading, Writing, & Reciting Poems about School. Freese, Susan M. 2008. (Poetry Power Ser.). (ENG.). 32p. (J). (gr. k-4). 29.93 *(978-1-60453-002-5(2)*, 12768, Super SandCastle) ABDO Publishing Co.

—Nicknames to Nightmares: Reading, Writing, & Reciting Poems about Me. Freese, Susan M. 2008. (Poetry Power Ser.). (ENG.). 32p. (J). (gr. k-4). 29.93 *(978-1-60453-006-3(5)*, 12776, Super SandCastle) ABDO Publishing Co.

Westberg, Marijke De Roo. More about Vermont Gnomes. Westberg, Marijke De Roo. 2016. (ENG.). (J). 24.95 *(978-1-60571-310-6(4))* Northshire Pr.

Westbrook, Dick. The Great Royal Race. Sommer, Carl. (J). 2014. pap. *(978-1-57537-952-4(X))*; 2003. 48p. (gr. k-4). lib. bdg. 23.95 incl. audio compact disk *(978-1-57537-708-7(X))*; 2003. 48p. (gr. 1-4). 16.95 incl. audio compact disk *(978-1-57537-508-3(7))* Advance Publishing, Inc.

—The Great Royal Race(La Gran Carrera Real) Sommer, Carl. ed. 2009. (Another Sommer-Time Story Bilingual Ser.). (SPA & ENG.). 48p. (J). lib. bdg. 16.95 *(978-1-57537-152-8(9))* Advance Publishing, Inc.

—Mayor for a Day. Sommer, Carl. (J). 2014. pap. *(978-1-57537-959-3(7))*; 2003. (ENG.). 48p. (gr. k-4). lib. bdg. 23.95 incl. audio compact disk *(978-1-57537-713-1(6))*; 2003. (ENG.). 48p. (gr. 1-4). 16.95 incl. audio compact disk *(978-1-57537-513-7(3))* Advance Publishing, Inc.

—Mayor for a Day: Alcalde Por un Dia. Sommer, Carl. ed. 2009. (Another Sommer-Time Story Bilingual Ser.). (SPA & ENG.). 48p. (J). lib. bdg. 16.95 *(978-1-57537-159-7(6))* Advance Publishing, Inc.

—No One Will Ever Know. Sommer, Carl. 2003. (Another Sommer-Time Story Ser.). (ENG.). 48p. (J). (gr. 1-4). 16.95 incl. audio compact disk *(978-1-57537-506-9(0))* Advance Publishing, Inc.

—No One Will Ever Know Read-Along, 1 bk. Sommer, Carl. 2003. (Another Sommer-Time Story Ser.). (ENG.). 48p. (J). lib. bdg. 23.95 incl. audio compact disk *(978-1-57537-706-3(3))* Advance Publishing, Inc.

—No One Will Ever Know(Nadie Se Va a Enterar) Sommer, Carl. ed. 2009. (Another Sommer-Time Story Bilingual Ser.). (SPA & ENG.). 48p. (J). lib. bdg. 16.95 *(978-1-57537-163-4(4))* Advance Publishing, Inc.

Westcott, Nadine B. Who Has What? All about Girls' Bodies & Boys' Bodies. Harris, Robie H. 2011. (Let's Talk about You & Me Ser.). (ENG.). 32p. (J). (gr. -1-2). 16.99 *(978-0-7636-2931-1(6))* Candlewick Pr.

Westcott, Nadine Bernard. April Foolishness. Bateman, Teresa. 2004. (ENG.). 32p. (J). (gr. k-3). 6.99 *(978-0-8075-0405-5(X)*, 080750405X) Whitman, Albert & Co.

—Don't Forget Your Etiquette! The Essential Guide to Misbehavior. Greenberg, David. 2006. (ENG.). 40p. (J). (gr. 1-4). 18.99 *(978-0-374-34990-5(8)*, 900022649, Farrar, Straus & Giroux (BYR)) Farrar, Straus & Giroux.

—The Eensy-Weensy Spider. Hoberman, Mary Ann. (J). (gr. -1-1). 2004. (ENG.). 32p. pap. 7.99 *(978-0-316-73412-7(8))*; 2020. 22p. 7.99 *(978-0-316-53732-2(2))* Little, Brown Bks. for Young Readers.

—Even Little Kids Get Diabetes. Pirner, Connie White. 2012. (J). *(978-1-61913-145-3(5))* Weigl Pubs., Inc.

—I Know an Old Lady Who Swallowed a Fly, 3 vols. (J). (gr. -1 — 1). 2003. (ENG.). 11p. bds. 7.99 *(978-0-316-93084-0(9)*, Tingley, Megan Bks.); 2020. 22p. 7.99 *(978-0-316-53733-9(0))* Little, Brown Bks. for Young Readers.

—The Library Doors. Buzzeo, Toni. 2008. (J). (gr. -1-3). 17.95 *(978-1-60213-037-1(X))*; *(978-1-60213-027-2(2))* Highsmith Inc. (Upstart Bks.).

—The Lion Who Had Asthma. London, Jonathan. 2012. (J). *(978-1-61913-119-4(6))* Weigl Pubs., Inc.

—Miss Mary Mack. Hoberman, Mary Ann. (J). (gr. -1-1). 2003. 32p. pap. 7.99 *(978-0-316-07614-2(7))*; 2019. 24p. bds. 7.99 *(978-0-316-53734-6(9))* Little, Brown Bks. for Young Readers.

—Silly Milly. Lewison, Wendy Cheyette. 2010. (Scholastic Reader Level 1 Ser.). (ENG.). 32p. (J). (gr. -1-3). pap. 3.99 *(978-0-545-06859-8(2))* Scholastic, Inc.

—Todd's Box. Moran, Alex & Sullivan, Paula. 2004. (Green Light Readers Level 1 Ser.). (ENG.). 24p. (J). (gr. -1-3). pap. 4.99 *(978-0-15-205094-8(9)*, 1195382) Houghton Mifflin Harcourt Publishing Co.

—Todd's Box. Sullivan, Paula. 2004. (J). (gr. -1-1). 11.60 *(978-0-7569-5629-5(3))* Perfection Learning Corp.

—Up, down, & Around. Ayres, Katherine. 2008. 32p. (J). (-k). pap. 24.99 *(978-0-7636-4018-7(2))*; 6.99 *(978-0-7636-4017-0(4))* Candlewick Pr.

—What's So Yummy? All about Eating Well & Feeling Good. Harris, Robie H. 2014. (Let's Talk about You & Me Ser.). 40p. (J). (-k). 16.99 *(978-0-7636-3632-6(0))* Candlewick Pr.

—Who We Are! All about Being the Same & Being Different. Harris, Robie H. 2016. (Let's Talk about You & Me Ser.). 40p. (J). (-k). 16.99 *(978-0-7636-6903-4(2))* Candlewick Pr.

—Who's in My Family? All about Our Families. Harris, Robie H. 2012. (Let's Talk about You & Me Ser.). (ENG.). 40p. (J). (gr. -1-2). 16.99 *(978-0-7636-3631-9(2))* Candlewick Pr.

Westenbroek, Ken, jt. illus. see Krueger, Diane.

Westerfield, William Stephen. Saint Nick & the Space Nicks. Mears, Richard Chase. I.t. ed. 2004. 32p. (J). 16.95 *(978-0-9754056-0-4(8))* Tuxedo Blue, LLC.

Westerlund, Kate. Sharing Christmas. Thariet, Eve. 2019. (Minedition Classic Ser.). (ENG.). 32p. (J). (-k). 12.00 *(978-988-8341-91-7(X)*, Minedition) Neugebauer, Michael (Publishing) Limited HKG. Dist: Penguin Random Hse. LLC.

Westerman, Johanna. The Christmas Snowman. Cuyler, Margery. 2011. (ENG.). 32p. (J). (gr. k-3). 12.95 *(978-1-61608-483-7(9)*, 608483, Sky Pony Pr.) Skyhorse Publishing Co., Inc.

—We Both Read-The Boy Who Carried the Flag. Carson, Jana. 2010. (We Both Read Ser.). 44p. (J). (gr. 2-5). 9.95 *(978-1-60115-247-3(7))*; pap. 4.99 *(978-1-60115-248-0(5))* Treasure Bay, Inc.

Westerskov, Kim, photos by. Albatrosses. 2004. 32p. (J). pap. *(978-0-7685-2117-7(3))* Dominie Pr., Inc.

—Diving in Antarctica. 2004. 32p. (J). *(978-0-7685-2384-3(2))* Dominie Pr., Inc.

—Dolphins. 2004. 32p. (J). pap. *(978-0-7685-2110-8(6))* Dominie Pr., Inc.

—Forests in the Sea. 2004. 32p. (J). *(978-0-7685-2387-4(7))*; pap. *(978-0-7685-2116-0(5))* Dominie Pr., Inc.

—Friends in the Sea. 2004. 32p. (J). *(978-0-7685-2112-2(2))* Dominie Pr., Inc.

—Life in a Frozen Sea. 2004. 32p. (J). pap. *(978-0-7685-2114-6(9))* Dominie Pr., Inc.

—Ocean Travelers. 2004. (ENG., 32p. (J). (gr. 5-5). pap. 7.47 net. *(978-0-7685-2118-4(1)*, Dominie Elementary) Savvas Learning Co.

—Penguins. 2004. (ENG., 32p. (J). (gr. 4-4). pap. 7.47 net. *(978-0-7685-2111-5(4)*, Dominie Elementary) Savvas Learning Co.

—Whales. 2004. 32p. (J). *(978-0-7685-2109-2(2))* Dominie Pr., Inc.

Westgate, Alex. Coding, Bugs, & Fixes. Lyons, Heather & Tweedale, Elizabeth. 2016. (Kids Get Coding Ser.). (ENG.). 24p. (J). (gr. 1-4). 26.65 *(978-1-5124-1359-5(3)*, 9781512413595, Lerner Pubns.) Lerner Publishing Group.

—Coding in the Real World. Lyons, Heather. 2017. (Kids Get Coding Ser.). (ENG.). 24p. (J). (gr. 1-4). 26.65 *(978-1-5124-3943-4(6)*, Lerner Pubns.); pap. 7.99 *(978-1-5124-5586-1(5)*, 9781512455861) Lerner Publishing Group.

—Coding to Create & Communicate. Lyons, Heather. 2017. (Kids Get Coding Ser.). (ENG.). 24p. (J). (gr. 1-4). 26.65 *(978-1-5124-3944-1(4)*, 9781512439441, Lerner Pubns.); pap. 7.99 *(978-1-5124-5584-7(9))* Lerner Publishing Group.

—Follow That Bottle! A Plastic Recycling Journey. Heos, Bridget. 2016. (Keeping Cities Clean Ser.). (ENG.). 24p. (J). (gr. k-3). 20.95 *(978-1-60753-964-3(0))* Amicus Publishing.

—Follow That Garbage! A Journey to the Landfill. Heos, Bridget. 2016. (Keeping Cities Clean Ser.). (ENG.). 24p. (J). (gr. k-3). 20.95 *(978-1-60753-963-6(2))* Amicus Publishing.

—Follow That Paper! A Paper Recycling Journey. Heos, Bridget. 2016. (Keeping Cities Clean Ser.). (ENG.). 24p. (J). (gr. k-3). 20.95 *(978-1-60753-965-0(9))* Amicus Publishing.

—Learn to Program. Lyons, Heather & Tweedale, Elizabeth. 2016. (Kids Get Coding Ser.). (ENG.). 24p. (J). (gr. 1-4). 26.65 *(978-1-5124-1360-1(7)*, 9781512413601, Lerner Pubns.) Lerner Publishing Group.

—Online Safety for Coders. Lyons, Heather & Tweedale, Elizabeth. 2016. (Kids Get Coding Ser.). (ENG.). 24p. (J). (gr. 1-4). 26.65 *(978-1-5124-1361-8(5)*, 9781512413618, Lerner Pubns.) Lerner Publishing Group.

—Programming Awesome Apps. Lyons, Heather. 2017. (Kids Get Coding Ser.). (ENG.). 24p. (J). (gr. 1-4). 26.65 *(978-1-5124-3942-7(8)*, Lerner Pubns.) Lerner Publishing Group.

—Programming Games & Animation. Lyons, Heather. 2017. (Kids Get Coding Ser.). (ENG.). 24p. (J). (gr. 1-4). 26.65 *(978-1-5124-3941-0(X)*, Lerner Pubns.) Lerner Publishing Group.

—A World of Programming. Lyons, Heather & Tweedale, Elizabeth. 2016. (Kids Get Coding Ser.). (ENG.). 24p. (J). (gr. 1-4). 26.65 *(978-1-5124-1362-5(3)*, 9781512413625, Lerner Pubns.) Lerner Publishing Group.

Westlund, Laura. US History Through Infographics. Kenney, Karen Latchana. 2014. (Super Social Studies Infographics Ser.). (ENG.). 32p. (J). (gr. 3-5). lib. bdg. 26.65 *(978-1-4677-3459-2(4)*, Lerner Pubns.) Lerner Publishing Group.

—US History Through Infographics. Kenney, Karen Latchana. 2014. (Super Social Studies Infographics Ser.). (ENG.). 32p. (J). (gr. 3-5). pap. 8.99 *(978-1-4677-4568-0(5))* Lerner Publishing Group.

Westmaas, Julie. A Long Ago Place. Betten, Donna. 2019. (ENG.). 24p. (J). pap. 15.99 ***(978-1-7960-6546-6(3))*** Xlibris Corp.

Westmacott, Marion. The Australian Animal Atlas. Cronin, Leonard. 2018. (ENG.). 48p. (J). (gr. 1-7). 22.99 *(978-1-76029-414-4(4))* Allen & Unwin AUS. Dist: Independent Pubs. Group.

Westminster, School. Looking after Our Fascinating Earth. Westminster, School. 2019. (ENG.). 38p. (J). (gr. 1-3). pap. ***(978-0-9954086-7-8(X))*** Logorythm.

Weston, Andrea & Weinmann, Julianne. Journey to Everywhere. Weinmann, Julianne. 2020. (ENG.). 40p. (J). pap. 9.50 ***(978-1-0811-9021-7(3))*** Independently Published.

Weston, Laura. The Butterfly Garden. Weston, Laura. 2017. (ENG.). 12p. (J). (-k). bds. 14.99 *(978-0-7636-9317-6(0)*, Big Picture Press) Candlewick Pr.

Weston, Linda. Lua the Llama & the Mountain of Joy. Birks, Alison a. 2017. (ENG.). 28p. (J). (gr. k-6). pap. 12.95 *(978-0-9997208-0-6(5))* Birks, Alison.

Weston, Martha. Curious George & the Birthday Surprise. Rey, H. A. & Rey, Margret. 2003. (Curious George Ser.). (ENG.). 24p. (J). (gr. -1-3). pap. 4.99 *(978-0-618-34687-5(2)*, 494330) Houghton Mifflin Harcourt Publishing Co.

—Curious George Takes a Train, 1 vol. Rey, Margret & Rey, H. A. 2008. (Curious George Ser.). (ENG.). 24p. (J). (gr. k-3). lib. bdg. 27.07 *(978-1-59961-418-2(9)*, 5059, Picture Bk.) Spotlight.

—Curious George Visits the Library. Rey, H. A. & Rey, Margret. 2013. (Curious George Ser.). (ENG.). 24p. (J). (gr. -1-3). pap. 4.99 *(978-0-544-11450-0(7)*, 1541812) Houghton Mifflin Harcourt Publishing Co.

—Curious George's Neighborhood. Rey, H. A. & Rey, Margret. 2004. (Curious George Ser.). (ENG.). 10p. (J). (gr. -1 — 1). bds. 11.95 *(978-0-618-41203-7(4)*, 594270) Houghton Mifflin Harcourt Publishing Co.

—Did You See What I Saw? Winters, Kay. 2015. 32p. pap. 7.00 *(978-1-61003-529-3(1))* Center for the Collaborative Classroom.

—Do You Wanna Bet? Your Chance to Find Out about Probability. Cushman, Jean. 2007. (ENG.). 112p. (J). (gr. 5-7). pap. 7.99 *(978-0-618-82999-6(7)*, 100559) Houghton Mifflin Harcourt Publishing Co.

—Nate the Great & the Big Sniff. Sharmat, Marjorie Weinman & Sharmat, Mitchell. 2003. (Nate the Great Ser.: No. 23). (ENG.). 80p. (J). (gr. 1-4). pap. 5.99 *(978-0-440-41502-2(0)*, Yearling) Random Hse. Children's Bks.

—Nate the Great & the Big Sniff. Sharmat, Marjorie Weinman & Sharmat, Mitchell. ed. 2003. (Nate the Great Ser.: Bk. 23). 47p. (gr. -1-3). lib. bdg. 16.00 *(978-0-613-63966-8(9))* Turtleback.

—Owen Foote, Money Man. Greene, Stephanie & National Geographic Learning Staff. 2003. (ENG.). 96p. (J). (gr. -1-3). pap. 6.99 *(978-0-618-37837-1(5)*, 100325) Houghton Mifflin Harcourt Publishing Co.

—Owen Foote, Money Man. Greene, Stephanie. 2003. 88p. (gr. 2-4). 14.95 *(978-0-7569-1559-9(7))* Perfection Learning Corp.

—Owen Foote, Super Spy. Greene, Stephanie. 2005. (ENG.). 96p. (J). (gr. 1-4). pap. 8.95 *(978-0-618-55159-0(X)*, 100825) Houghton Mifflin Harcourt Publishing Co.

—Takes a Train. Rey, Margret & Rey, H. A. 2010. (Curious George Ser.). (ENG.). 24p. (J). (gr. -1-3). pap. 4.99 *(978-0-547-50424-7(1)*, 1442842) Houghton Mifflin Harcourt Publishing Co.

Weston, Martha, jt. illus. see Sharmat, Mitchell.

Weston, Paul. Storms & Hurricanes. Bone, Emily. ed. 2013. (Beginner's Science Ser.). 32p. (J). ring bd. 4.99 *(978-0-7945-3350-2(7)*, Usborne) EDC Publishing.

Weston, Steve. Dinosaur Canyon. Graf, Mike & Kaske, Anne. 2005. 40p. pap. 8.53 *(978-0-7578-9858-7(0))* Houghton Mifflin Harcourt Supplemental Pubs.

Weston, Steve & Field, James. Mahakala & Other Insect-Eating Dinosaurs, 1 vol. 2009. (Dinosaur Find Ser.). (ENG.). 24p. (J). (gr. k-3). lib. bdg. 27.32 *(978-1-4048-5177-1(1)*, Picture Window Bks.) Capstone.

—Sauropaganax & Other Meat-Eating Dinosaurs, 1 vol. 2009. (Dinosaur Find Ser.). (ENG.). 24p. (J). (gr. k-3). lib. bdg. 27.32 *(978-1-4048-5180-1(1)*, Picture Window Bks.) Capstone.

Weston, Steve, jt. illus. see Field, James.

Weston, Wendy J., jt. illus. see Dias, Jodie E.

Westwood, Jon. Drawing Aircraft, Ships, & High-Speed Vehicles: 4D an Augmented Reading Drawing Experience. Cella, Clara. 2018. (Drawing With 4D Ser.). (ENG.). 32p. (J). (gr. 3-9). lib. bdg. 31.99 *(978-1-5435-3188-6(1)*, 138814, Capstone Pr.) Capstone.

Westwood, Jon, et al. Drawing With 4D. Cella, Clara. 2018. (Drawing With 4D Ser.). (ENG.). 32p. (J). (gr. 3-9). 127.96 *(978-1-5435-3191-6(1)*, 28607, Capstone Classroom) Capstone.

Wethington, Julie & Wethington, Lang. Yes I Can! Have My Cake & Food Allergies Too. Wethington, Julie & Wethington, Lang. 2012. (J). *(978-0-9761444-1-0(7))* DragonWing Bks.

Wethington, Lang, jt. illus. see Wethington, Julie.

Wetmore, Barry. The Answer Is NO: Saying It & Sticking to It. Whitham, Cynthia. 2003. 224p. (J). pap. *(978-0-9622036-4-0(5))* Perspective Publishing, Inc.

—Good Friends Are Hard to Find: Help Your Child Find, Make, & Keep Friends. Frankel, Fred. 2003. 242p. (J). pap. 13.95 *(978-0-9622036-7-1(X))* Perspective Publishing, Inc.

—Win the Whining War & Other Skirmishes: A Family Peace Plan. Whitham, Cynthia. 2003. 198p. (J). pap. 13.95 *(978-0-9622036-3-3(7))* Perspective Publishing, Inc.

Wetterwald, Florence. Night-Night, Wooly (a Blabla Book) Wetterwald, Florence. 2016. (ENG.). 24p. (J). (— 1). bds. 7.99 *(978-0-553-52051-4(2)*, Random Hse. Bks. for Young Readers) Random Hse. Children's Bks.

—Peekaboo, Pierre (a Blabla Book) Wetterwald, Florence. 2016. 24p. (J). (— 1). bds. 7.99 *(978-0-553-51347-9(8)*, Random Hse. Bks. for Young Readers) Random Hse. Children's Bks.

Weyant, Christopher. Can I Tell You a Secret? Kang, Anna. 2016. (ENG.). 40p. (J). (gr. -1-3). 17.99 *(978-0-06-239684-6(6))* HarperCollins Pubs.

—Eraser. Kang, Anna. 2018. (ENG.). 40p. (J). (gr. -1-2). 17.99 *(978-1-5039-0258-9(7)*, 9781503902589, Two Lions) Amazon Publishing.

—I Am (Not) Scared. Kang, Anna. 2017. (You Are Not Small Ser.: 3). (ENG.). 32p. (J). (gr. -1-2). 17.99 *(978-1-5039-3745-1(3)*, 9781503937451, Two Lions) Amazon Publishing.

—It Is Not Perfect. Kang, Anna. 2020. (You Are Not Small Ser.: 5). (ENG.). 32p. (J). (gr. -1-2). 17.99 *(978-1-5420-1662-9(2)*, 9781542016629, Two Lions) Amazon Publishing.

—My Pillow Keeps Moving. Gehl, Laura. 2018. 40p. (J). (gr. -1-3). 17.99 *(978-0-425-28824-5(2)*, Viking Books for Young Readers) Penguin Young Readers Group.

—We Are Not Friends. Kang, Anna. 2019. (You Are Not Small Ser.: 4). (ENG.). 40p. (J). (gr. -1-2). 17.99 *(978-1-5420-4428-8(6)*, 9781542044288, Two Lions) Amazon Publishing.

—Will You Help Me Fall Asleep? Kang, Anna. 2018. (ENG.). 40p. (J). (gr. -1-3). 17.99 *(978-0-06-239685-3(4))* HarperCollins Pubs.

Weyant, Christopher. You Are Not Small Boxed Set. Kang, Anna. 2018. (You Are Not Small Ser.). (ENG.). 96p. (J). (gr. -1-2). 49.99 ***(978-1-5420-4023-5(X)***, 9781542040235, Two Lions) Amazon Publishing.

WFM Services. The Derby: A Timmy Wallings Story. Walsh, Patrick M., Jr. McGriff, Aaron C., ed. 2012. 188p. (J). *(978-0-9842929-4-3(2))* Daddy Bean Bks.

—Who Says Timmy Can't Play: The Derby: A Timmy Wallings Story. Walsh, Patrick M., Jr. McGriff, Aaron, ed. 2011. 135p. (J). *(978-0-9842929-3-6(4))* Daddy Bean Bks.

WGBH. FETCH! with Ruff Ruffman: Show's Over. Candlewick Press Staff. 2014. (Fetch! with Ruff Ruffman Ser.). (ENG.). 48p. (J). (gr. 1-4). pap. 4.99 *(978-0-7636-6809-9(5)*, Candlewick Entertainment) Candlewick Pr.

—Ruff Ruffman's 44 Favorite Science Activities. Candlewick Press Staff. 2015. (Fetch! with Ruff Ruffman Ser.). (ENG.). 132p. (J). (gr. 3-7). pap. 12.99 *(978-0-7636-7432-8(X)*, Candlewick Entertainment) Candlewick Pr.

WGBH Educational Foundation Staff. FETCH! with Ruff Ruffman: Doggie Duties. Candlewick Press Staff. 2014. (Fetch! with Ruff Ruffman Ser.). (ENG.). 48p. (J). (gr. 1-4). pap. 4.99 *(978-0-7636-6815-0(X)*, Candlewick Entertainment) Candlewick Pr.

WGBH Kids, Wgbh. Molly of Denali: a-Maze-ing Snow. WGBH Kids, Wgbh. 2019. (Molly of Denali Ser.). (ENG.). 24p. (J). (gr. -1-3). 4.99 *(978-0-06-295038-3(X)*, HarperCollins) HarperCollins Pubs. Ltd. GBR. Dist: HarperCollins Pubs.

—Molly of Denali: Berry Itchy Day. WGBH Kids, Wgbh. 2020. (I Can Read Level 1 Ser.). (ENG.). 32p. (J). (gr. -1-3). pap. 4.99 *(978-0-06-295044-4(4)*, HarperCollins) HarperCollins Pubs. Ltd. GBR. Dist: HarperCollins Pubs.

—Molly of Denali: Crane Song. WGBH Kids, Wgbh. 2020. (I Can Read Level 1 Ser.). (ENG.). 32p. (J). (gr. -1-3). pap. 4.99 *(978-0-06-295040-6(1)*, HarperCollins) HarperCollins Pubs. Ltd. GBR. Dist: HarperCollins Pubs.

—Molly of Denali: Little Dog Lost. WGBH Kids, Wgbh. 2019. (I Can Read Level 1 Ser.). (ENG.). 32p. (J). (gr. -1-3). pap. 4.99 *(978-0-06-295036-9(3)*, HarperCollins) HarperCollins Pubs. Ltd. GBR. Dist: HarperCollins Pubs.

—Molly of Denali: Molly's Awesome Alaska Guide. WGBH Kids, Wgbh. 2020. (Molly of Denali Ser.). (ENG.). 64p. (J). (gr. -1-3). pap. 6.99 *(978-0-06-295042-0(8)*, HarperCollins) HarperCollins Pubs. Ltd. GBR. Dist: HarperCollins Pubs.

—Molly of Denali: Party Moose. WGBH Kids, Wgbh. 2019. (I Can Read Level 1 Ser.). (ENG.). 32p. (J). (gr. -1-3). pap. 4.99 *(978-0-06-295034-5(7)*, HarperCollins) HarperCollins Pubs. Ltd. GBR. Dist: HarperCollins Pubs.

—Molly of Denali: Tubing Rocks! WGBH Kids, Wgbh. 2020. (Molly of Denali Ser.). (ENG.). 24p. (J). (gr. -1-3). 4.99 *(978-0-06-295046-8(0)*, HarperCollins) HarperCollins Pubs. Ltd. GBR. Dist: HarperCollins Pubs.

Whackink, Laura Lynn. Don't Be a Meaniehead. Anderson, Angelique S. 2018. (ENG.). 42p. (J). pap. 6.99 *(978-1-7901-9184-0(X))* Independently Published.

Whalen, Meg. Father Ben Gets Ready for Mass. Warner, Katie. 2019. (ENG.). 36p. (J). (gr. -1-k). 16.95 *(978-1-5051-1221-4(4)*, 2729) TAN Bks.

—I Went to Mass: What Did I See? Warner, Katie. 2018. (ENG.). 24p. (J). (gr. -1-1). 16.95 *(978-1-5051-1218-4(4))* TAN Bks.

—Let Us Pray: A Child's First Book of Prayers. Warner, Katie. 2019. (ENG.). 24p. (J). (gr. -1-1). bds. 9.95 *(978-1-5051-1222-1(2))* TAN Bks.

Whalen, Raymond J. Harriet's Big Adventure. Guiles, Glenn S. 2018. (ENG.). 32p. (J). *(978-1-5255-2688-6(X))*; pap. *(978-1-5255-2689-3(8))* FriesenPress.

—A Hug for Harriet. Guiles, Glenn S. 2017. (ENG.). (J). *(978-1-5255-0880-6(6))*; pap. *(978-1-5255-0881-3(4))* FriesenPress.

Whamond, Dave. Acting Wild: How We Behave Like Birds, Bugs, & Beasts. Birmingham, Maria. 2019. (ENG.). 32p. (J). (gr. 2-6). 16.95 *(978-1-77147-326-2(6))* Owlkids Bks. Inc. CAN. Dist: Publishers Group West (PGW).

—Bagels Come Home, 1 vol. Stuchner, Joan Betty. 2014. (Orca Echoes Ser.). (ENG.). 64p. (J). (gr. 1-3). pap. 6.95 *(978-1-4598-0346-6(9))* Orca Bk. Pubs. USA.

—Bagels on Board, 1 vol. Stuchner, Joan Betty. 2015. (Orca Echoes Ser.). (ENG.). 80p. (J). (gr. 1-3). pap. 6.95 *(978-1-4598-0695-5(6))* Orca Bk. Pubs. USA.

—Bagels the Brave, 1 vol. Stuchner, Joan Betty. 2015. (Orca Echoes Ser.). (ENG.). 64p. (J). (gr. 1-3). pap. 6.95 *(978-1-4598-0493-7(7))* Orca Bk. Pubs. USA.

—Boy Meets Dog: A Word Game Adventure. Wyatt, Valerie. 2013. (ENG.). 32p. (J). (gr. -1-3). 16.95 *(978-1-55453-824-9(6))* Kids Can Pr., Ltd. CAN. Dist: Hachette Bk. Group.

—Hot Dog & Bob Adventure 2: And the Particularly Pesky Attack of the Pencil People (Adventure #2) Rovetch, L. Bob. 2006. (Hot Dog & Bob Ser.: HOTD). (ENG.). 96p. (J). (gr. 1-5). pap. 4.95 *(978-0-8118-5322-4(5))* Chronicle Bks. LLC.

—Hot Dog & Bob Adventure 3: And the Dangerously Dizzy Attack of the Hypno Hamsters. Rovetch, L. Bob. 2007. (Hot Dog & Bob Ser.: HOTD). (ENG.). 96p. (J). (gr. 1-5). per. 4.95 *(978-0-8118-5602-7(X))* Chronicle Bks. LLC.

—Hot Dog & Bob: Adventure 5: And the Surprisingly Slobbery Attack of the Dog-Wash Doggies. Rovetch, L. Bob. 2007. (Hot Dog & Bob Ser.: HOTD). (ENG.). 96p. (J). (gr. 1-5). per. 4.95 *(978-0-8118-5746-8(8))* Chronicle Bks. LLC.

—Justine Mckeen & the Bird Nerd, 1 vol. Brouwer, Sigmund. 2013. (Orca Echoes Ser.). (ENG.). 64p. (J). (gr. 1-3). pap. 6.95 *(978-1-4598-0394-7(9))* Orca Bk. Pubs. USA.

—Justine Mckeen, Eat Your Beets, 1 vol. Brouwer, Sigmund. 2013. (Orca Echoes Ser.). (ENG.). 64p. (J). (gr. 1-3). pap. 6.95 *(978-1-55469-933-9(9))* Orca Bk. Pubs. USA.

—Justine Mckeen, Pooper Scooper, 1 vol. Brouwer, Sigmund. 2012. (Orca Echoes Ser.). (ENG.). 64p. (J). (gr. 1-3). pap. 6.95 *(978-1-55469-931-5(2))* Orca Bk. Pubs. USA.

—Justine Mckeen, Queen of Green, 1 vol. Brouwer, Sigmund. 2011. (Orca Echoes Ser.). (ENG.). 64p. (J). (gr. 1-3). pap. 6.95 *(978-1-55469-927-8(4))* Orca Bk. Pubs. USA.

—Justine McKeen vs. the Queen of Mean, 1 vol. Brouwer, Sigmund. 2014. (Orca Echoes Ser.). (ENG.). 64p. (J). (gr. 1-3). pap. 6.95 *(978-1-4598-0397-8(3))* Orca Bk. Pubs. USA.

—Justine McKeen, Walk the Talk, 1 vol. Brouwer, Sigmund. 2012. (Orca Echoes Ser.). (ENG.). 64p. (J). (gr. 1-3). pap. 6.95 *(978-1-55469-929-2(0))* Orca Bk. Pubs. USA.

—Messy Miranda, 1 vol. Szpirglas, Jeff & Saint-Onge, Danielle. 2013. (Orca Echoes Ser.). (ENG.). 64p. (J). (gr. 1-3). pap. 6.95 *(978-1-4598-0117-2(2))* Orca Bk. Pubs. USA.

Whamond, Dave. School Rules! Munsch, Robert. 2021. (ENG.). 32p. (J). (gr. -1-3). 7.99 ***(978-1-4431-8203-4(6))*** Scholastic Canada, Ltd. CAN. Dist: Publishers Group West (PGW).

Whamond, Dave. Alien Nate. Whamond, Dave. 2020. (ENG.). 64p. (J). (gr. 1-4). 14.99 *(978-1-5253-0209-1(4))* Kids Can Pr., Ltd. CAN. Dist: Hachette Bk. Group.

—Nick the Sidekick. Whamond, Dave. 2018. (ENG.). 48p. (J). (gr. 1-4). 14.99 *(978-1-77138-355-4(0))* Kids Can Pr., Ltd. CAN. Dist: Hachette Bk. Group.

—Rosie's Glasses. Whamond, Dave. 2018. (ENG.). 32p. (J). (gr. -1-2). 16.99 *(978-1-77138-991-4(5))* Kids Can Pr., Ltd. CAN. Dist: Hachette Bk. Group.

Wharry, Remy. Creative June. Lashe, Tyia. 2019. (ENG.). 34p. (J). pap. 12.00 *(978-1-7966-8258-8(6))* Independently Published.

—Melanin Beauty. Lashe, Tyia. 2018. (ENG.). 40p. (J). pap. 12.00 *(978-1-7277-2183-6(7))* CreateSpace Independent Publishing Platform.

Wharton, Jennifer Heyd. Broken Wings Will Fly, 1 vol. Blackistone, Mick. 2009. (ENG.). 32p. (J). (gr. 7-18). 10.95 *(978-0-87033-439-9(5)*, 9780870334399, Cornell Maritime Pr./Tidewater Pubs.) Schiffer Publishing, Ltd.

—First Sail, 1 vol. Henderson, Richard. 2009. (ENG.). 48p. (gr. 3-6). 15.95 *(978-0-87033-442-9(5)*, 3641, Cornell Maritime Pr./Tidewater Pubs.) Schiffer Publishing, Ltd.

—Like Me. Martelli, Dawn. 2004. (J). *(978-1-893516-01-4(6))* Our Child Pr.

Wharton, Sigrid, jt. illus. see Lundgren, Shai.

Whatley, Bruce. Christmas Wombat. French, Jackie. 2012. (ENG.). 32p. (J). (gr. -1-3). 17.99 *(978-0-547-86872-1(3)*, 1504335) Houghton Mifflin Harcourt Publishing Co.

—Diary of a Wombat. French, Jackie. 2007. 16p. (J). bds. *(978-0-7322-8662-0(X))* HarperCollins Pubs. Australia.

—Diary of a Wombat. French, Jackie. 2009. (ENG.). 32p. (J). (gr. -1-3). pap. 7.99 *(978-0-547-07669-0(X)*, 1042035) Houghton Mifflin Harcourt Publishing Co.

—Emily & the Big Bad Bunyip. French, Jackie. 2008. 32p. *(978-0-7322-8692-7(1))* HarperCollins Pubs. Australia.

—The Great Texas Hamster Drive, 0 vols. Kimmel, Eric A. & Korelitz, Jean Hanff. 2007. (ENG.). 40p. (J). (gr. k-3). 16.99 *(978-0-7614-5357-4(1)*, 9780761453574, Two Lions) Amazon Publishing.

—Here Comes Santa Claus. Autry, Gene & Haldeman, Dakley. 2004. 24p. (J). (gr. k-4). reprint ed. 17.00 *(978-0-7567-9048-6(4))* DIANE Publishing Co.

—How High Can a Kangaroo Hop? French, Jackie. 2008. 256p. pap. *(978-0-7322-8544-9(5))* HarperCollins Pubs. Australia.

—I Want a Hippopotamus for Christmas. Rox, John. 2005. (ENG.). 32p. (J). (gr. -1-3). 17.99 *(978-0-06-052942-0(3))* HarperCollins Pubs.

Whatley, Bruce. I Want a Hippopotamus for Christmas. Rox, John. 2020. (ENG.). 32p. (J). (gr. -1-3). 17.99 ***(978-0-06-304321-3(1)***, HarperCollins) HarperCollins Pubs. Ltd. GBR. Dist: HarperCollins Pubs.

Whatley, Bruce. Josephine Wants to Dance. French, Jackie. 32p. 2008. (J). pap. *(978-0-207-20080-9(7))*; 2006. *(978-0-207-20075-5(0))* HarperCollins Pubs. Australia.

—My Mom's the Best. Smith, Rosie. 2013. (J). *(978-0-545-60361-4(7))* Scholastic, Inc.

—The Night Before Christmas Board Book. Moore, Clement C. 2004. (ENG.). 32p. (J). (gr. -1 — 1). bds. 6.99 *(978-0-06-073917-1(7)*, HarperFestival) HarperCollins Pubs.

—On the First Day of Grade School. Brenner, Emily. 2004. 32p. (J). (gr. -1-1). lib. bdg. 16.89 *(978-0-06-051041-1(2))* HarperCollins Pubs.

—The Perfect Pet. Palatini, Margie. 2003. 32p. (J). (gr. -1-2). 16.99 *(978-0-06-000108-7(9))* HarperCollins Pubs.

—Pete the Sheep. French, Jackie. 2008. 30p. (J). bds. *(978-0-7322-8794-8(4))* HarperCollins Pubs. Australia.

—Pig on the Titanic: A True Story. Crew, Gary. 2005. 32p. (J). 15.99 *(978-0-06-052305-3(0))* HarperCollins Pubs.

—The Queen with the Wobbly Bottom. Gwynne, Phillip. 2013. (ENG.). 32p. (J). (gr. -1-2). 17.99 *(978-1-921714-59-7(X))* Little Hare Bks. AUS. Dist: Independent Pubs. Group.

—The Secret World of Wombats. French, Jackie. 2005. 176p. *(978-0-207-20031-1(9))* HarperCollins Pubs. Australia.

—Too Many Pears!, 1 vol. French, Jackie. (ENG.). 32p. (J). 2004. pap. 6.95 *(978-1-932065-48-0(2)*, 718-784-9112); 2003. 16.95 *(978-1-932065-47-3(4)*, 718-784-9112) Star Bright Bks., Inc.

—Too Many Pears! (Japanese/English), 1 vol. French, Jackie. 2007. (JPN & ENG.). 32p. (J). (gr. -1). pap. 5.95 *(978-1-59572-112-9(6))* Star Bright Bks., Inc.

—Too Many Pears! (Spanish/English), 1 vol. French, Jackie. 2005. 32p. (J). (ABK, SPA & ENG.). 16.95 *(978-1-59572-012-2(X))*; (SPA & ENG.). pap. 6.95 *(978-1-59572-013-9(8))* Star Bright Bks., Inc.

Whatley, Bruce. The Little Drummer Boy. Whatley, Bruce. 2011. (ENG.). 32p. (J). (gr. -1-k). pap. 10.99 *(978-1-86471-992-5(3))* Random Hse. Australia AUS. Dist: Independent Pubs. Group.

—Wait! No Paint! Whatley, Bruce. 2005. (ENG.). 32p. (J). (gr. -1-3). pap. 7.99 *(978-0-06-443546-8(6))* HarperCollins Pubs.

Whatmore, Candice. Easy Piano Classics. Marks, Anthony. Rogers, Kirsteen, ed. 2007. (Easy Piano Classics Ser.). 64p. (J). 18.99 *(978-0-7945-1273-6(9)*, Usborne) EDC Publishing.

—First Illustrated Science Dictionary. Khan, Sarah. Robson, Kirsteen, ed. 2013. (ENG.). 104p. (J). (gr. -1-3). 9.99 *(978-0-7945-3383-0(3)*, Usborne) EDC Publishing.

W

Whatmore, Candice & Barrance, Reuben. Mysteries & Marvels of Nature. Dalby, Elizabeth. Tatchell, Judy, ed. 2008. (Nature Encyclopedias Ser.). 128p. (J). (gr. 4-7). pap. 16.99 *(978-0-7945-1738-0(2)*, Usborne) EDC Publishing.
Whatmore, Candice, jt. illus. see Barrance, Reuben.
Wheatcroft, Ryan. We Are Family. Hegarty, Patricia. 2017. (ENG.). 32p. (J). (gr. -1-2). 16.99 *(978-1-68010-054-9(8))* Tiger Tales.
Wheatley, Doug. Episode III: Revenge of the Sith. Lane, Miles. 2009. (Star Wars Ser.: No. 2). (ENG.). 24p. (J). (gr. 6-12). 27.07 *(978-1-59961-617-9(3)*, 13773); 27.07 *(978-1-59961-618-6(1)*, 13774); 27.07 *(978-1-59961-620-9(3)*, 13776) Spotlight. (Graphic Novels).
—How to Train Your Dragon: the Serpent's Heir. DeBlois, Dean & Hamilton, Richard. 2017. (ENG.). 80p. (gr. 4-7). pap. 10.99 *(978-1-61655-931-1(4))* Dark Horse Comics.
Wheatley, Doug, jt. illus. see de la Fuente, Francisco.
Wheatley, Maria. How Do Your Senses Work? Tatchell, Judy. rev. ed. 2004. (Flip Flaps Ser.). 16p. (J). (gr. 2-18). pap. 7.95 *(978-0-7945-0642-1(9)*, Usborne) EDC Publishing.
—What Happens to Your Food. Smith, Alastair. 2003. 16p. (J). (gr. 2-18). pap. 7.95 *(978-0-7945-0643-8(7)*, Usborne) EDC Publishing.
Wheeler, David Cole. Scratch & Sketch Trace-Along Robots: An Art Activity Book for Artistic Inventors of All Ages. Nemmers, Lee. 2015. (ENG.). 64p. (J). 14.99 *(978-1-4413-1812-1(7)*, 9781441318121) Peter Pauper Pr. Inc.
Wheeler, Eliza. Cody & the Fountain of Happiness. Springstubb, Tricia. 2015. (Cody Ser.). 160p. (J). (gr. 2-5). 14.99 *(978-0-7636-5857-1(X))* Candlewick Pr.
—Cody & the Heart of a Champion. Springstubb, Tricia. (Cody Ser.). 160p. (J). (gr. 2-5). 2019. pap. 6.99 *(978-1-5362-0633-3(4))*; 2018. 14.99 *(978-0-7636-7921-7(6))* Candlewick Pr.
—Cody & the Mysteries of the Universe. Springstubb, Tricia. 2016. (Cody Ser.). 144p. (J). (gr. 2-5). 14.99 *(978-0-7636-5858-8(8))* Candlewick Pr.
—Cody & the Rules of Life. Springstubb, Tricia. (Cody Ser.). 176p. (J). (gr. 2-5). 2018. pap. 6.99 *(978-1-5362-0054-6(9))*; 2017. 14.99 *(978-0-7636-7920-0(8))* Candlewick Pr.
—Doll Bones. Black, Holly. 2013. (ENG.). 256p. (J). (gr. 5-9). 18.99 *(978-1-4169-6398-1(7)*, McElderry, Margaret K. Bks.) McElderry, Margaret K. Bks.
—Doll Bones. Black, Holly. 2015. (ENG.). (J). (gr. 5-9). lib. bdg. 18.60 *(978-1-62765-766-2(5))* Perfection Learning Corp.
—Fairy Spell: How Two Girls Convinced the World That Fairies Are Real. Nobleman, Marc Tyler. 2018. (ENG.). 40p. (J). (gr. -1-3). 17.99 *(978-0-544-69948-9(3)*, 1627718, Clarion Bks.) Houghton Mifflin Harcourt Trade & Reference Pubs.
—The Grudge Keeper, 1 vol. Rockliff, Mara. 2014. (ENG.). 32p. (J). (gr. -1-3). 16.95 *(978-1-56145-729-8(9))* Peachtree Publishing Co. Inc.
—The Incorrigible Children of Ashton Place: Book IV Bk. 4: The Interrupted Tale. Wood, Maryrose. 2015. (Incorrigible Children of Ashton Place Ser.: 4). (ENG.). 400p. (J). (gr. 3-7). pap. 6.99 *(978-0-06-179123-9(7)*, Balzer & Bray) HarperCollins Pubs.
—The Incorrigible Children of Ashton Place: Book IV Bk. IV: The Interrupted Tale. Wood, Maryrose. 2013. (Incorrigible Children of Ashton Place Ser.: 4). (ENG.). 400p. (J). (gr. 3-7). 16.99 *(978-0-06-179122-2(9)*, Balzer & Bray) HarperCollins Pubs.
—The Incorrigible Children of Ashton Place: Book V: The Unmapped Sea. Wood, Maryrose. 2016. (Incorrigible Children of Ashton Place Ser.: 5). (ENG.). 416p. (J). (gr. 3-7). pap. 7.99 *(978-0-06-211042-8(X)*, Balzer & Bray) HarperCollins Pubs.
—The Incorrigible Children of Ashton Place: Book V Bk. 5: The Unmapped Sea. Wood, Maryrose. 2015. (Incorrigible Children of Ashton Place Ser.: 5). (ENG.). 416p. (J). (gr. 3-7). 15.99 *(978-0-06-211041-1(1))* HarperCollins Pubs.
—The Incorrigible Children of Ashton Place: Book VI: The Long-Lost Home. Wood, Maryrose. (Incorrigible Children of Ashton Place Ser.: 6). (ENG.). 448p. (J). (gr. 3-7). 2019. pap. 7.99 *(978-0-06-211045-9(4))*; 2018. 15.99 *(978-0-06-211044-2(6))* HarperCollins Pubs. (Balzer & Bray).
—The Pomegranate Witch. Doyen, Denise. 2017. (ENG.). 40p. (J). (gr. k-3). 16.99 *(978-1-4521-4589-1(X))* Chronicle Bks. LLC.
—Tell Me a Tattoo Story. Mcghee, Alison. 2016. (ENG.). 32p. (J). (gr. -1-k). 16.99 *(978-1-4521-1937-3(6))* Chronicle Bks. LLC.
—This Is Our Baby, Born Today. Bajaj, Varsha. 2019. 28p. (J). (-k). bds. 7.99 *(978-1-9848-1413-5(3)*, Nancy Paulsen Books) Penguin Young Readers Group.
Wheeler, Eliza. What Does It Mean to Be Present? DiOrio, Rana. 2020. (What Does It Mean to Be... ? Ser.). 32p. (J). (-3). 8.99 ***(978-1-7282-2306-3(7)***, Little Pickle Pr.) Sourcebooks, Inc.
Wheeler, Eliza. When You Are Brave. Miller, Pat Zietlow. 2019. 40p. (J). (gr. -1-3). 17.99 *(978-0-316-39252-5(9))* Little Brown & Co.
—Wherever You Go. Miller, Pat Zietlow. 2019. 30p. (J). (gr. -1 — 1). 7.99 *(978-0-316-48794-8(5))* Little, Brown Bks. for Young Readers.
Wheeler, Eliza. Home in the Woods. Wheeler, Eliza. 2019. 40p. (J). (gr. k-3). 17.99 *(978-0-399-16290-9(9)*, Nancy Paulsen Books) Penguin Young Readers Group.
—Miss Maple's Seeds. Wheeler, Eliza. (ENG.). (J). 2017. 40p. (-k). pap. 8.99 *(978-0-425-28889-4(7)*, Puffin Books); 2013. 32p. (gr. -1-k). 17.99 *(978-0-399-25792-6(6)*, Nancy Paulsen Books) Penguin Young Readers Group.
—This Is Our Baby, Born Today. Wheeler, Eliza. Bajaj, Varsha. 2016. 32p. (J). (-k). 16.99 *(978-0-399-16684-6(X)*, Nancy Paulsen Books) Penguin Young Readers Group.
Wheeler, Elizabeth. Stories for Boys. Davis, Rebecca Harding. Cadwallader, Robin L., ed. 2019. (ENG.). 88p. (J). pap. 8.99 *(978-1-5176-2649-5(8))* CreateSpace Independent Publishing Platform.
Wheeler, Irvin. Justina's Dream. 2005. 30p. (J). *(978-1-887302-12-8(3))* Western Images Pubns., Inc.
Wheeler, Jody. A Cat's Tale, One Cat's Search for the Meaning of Life. Lindemann, Lindy. 2007. 28p. per. 12.95 *(978-1-934246-03-0(4))* Peppertree Pr., The.
—A Christmas Wish for Corduroy. Hennessy, B. G. 2017. (Corduroy Ser.). (ENG.). 32p. (J). (— 1). bds. 7.99 *(978-0-425-28875-7(7)*, Viking Books for Young Readers) Penguin Young Readers Group.
—Corduroy Lost & Found. Hennessy, B. G. 2006. (Corduroy Ser.). (ENG.). 32p. (J). (gr. -1-k). 16.99 *(978-0-670-06100-6(X)*, Viking Books for Young Readers) Penguin Young Readers Group.
—Corduroy Lost & Found. Hennessy, B. G. 2018. (Corduroy Ser.). (ENG.). 32p. (J). (-k). bds. 7.99 *(978-0-425-29085-9(9)*, Viking Books for Young Readers) Penguin Young Readers Group.
—Corduroy Takes a Bow. Davis, Viola. 2018. (Corduroy Ser.). 32p. (J). (-k). 17.99 *(978-0-425-29147-4(2)*, Viking Books for Young Readers) Penguin Young Readers Group.
—County Fair. Wilder, Laura Ingalls. 2003. (My First Little House Bks.). 17.00 *(978-0-7569-1727-2(1))* Perfection Learning Corp.
—Nate the Great & the Hungry Book Club. Sharmat, Marjorie Weinman & Sharmat, Mitchell. 2011. (Nate the Great Ser.: No. 26). 80p. (J). (gr. 1-4). 5.99 *(978-0-375-84548-2(8)*, Yearling) Random Hse. Children's Bks.
—Nate the Great & the Missing Birthday Snake. Sharmat, Andrew & Sharmat, Marjorie Weinman. (Nate the Great Ser.). (J). (gr. 1-4). 2018. 80p. 5.99 *(978-1-101-93470-8(0)*, Yearling); 2017. 48p. 12.99 *(978-1-101-93467-8(0)*, Delacorte Bks. for Young Readers); 2017. (ENG.). 64p. lib. bdg. 15.99 *(978-1-101-93469-2(7)*, Delacorte Bks. for Young Readers) Random Hse. Children's Bks.
—Nate the Great & the Wandering Word. Sharmat, Marjorie Weinman & Sharmat, Andrew. (Nate the Great Ser.: Bk. 27). (J). (gr. 1-4). 2019. 80p. 5.99 *(978-1-5247-6547-7(3)*, Yearling); 2018. 48p. 12.99 *(978-1-5247-6544-6(9)*, Delacorte Bks. for Young Readers); 2018. (ENG.). 64p. lib. bdg. 15.99 *(978-1-5247-6545-3(7)*, Delacorte Bks. for Young Readers) Random Hse. Children's Bks.
—Nate the Great Talks Turkey. Sharmat, Marjorie Weinman & Sharmat, Mitchell. 2007. (Nate the Great Ser.: No. 25). 96p. (J). (gr. 1-4). per. 5.99 *(978-0-440-42126-9(8)*, Yearling) Random Hse. Children's Bks.
—Nate the Great Talks Turkey: With Help from Olivia Sharp. Sharmat, Marjorie Weinman & Sharmat, Mitchell. ed. 2007. (Nate the Great Ser.: Bk. 25). (gr. -1-3). lib. bdg. 16.00 *(978-1-4177-9248-1(5))* Turtleback.
—Nate the Great, Where Are You? Sharmat, Marjorie Weinman & Sharmat, Mitchell. 2015. (Nate the Great Ser.). 64p. (J). (gr. 1-4). 5.99 *(978-0-449-81078-1(X)*, Yearling) Random Hse. Children's Bks.
—An Old-Fashioned Thanksgiving. Alcott, Louisa May. 2010. 40p. (J). (gr. -1-3). 14.99 *(978-0-8249-5620-2(6)*, Ideal Pubns.) Worthy Publishing.
Wheeler, Mary. Twirling & Dancing with Annie & Friends. Wheeler, Mary. 2016. (ENG.). (J). (gr. k-4). pap. 9.95 *(978-0-692-80814-6(0))*; 19.95 *(978-0-692-68048-3(9))* MC Wheeler Enterprises.
Wheeler, Ron. Exodus: Fun Bible Studies Using Puzzles & Stories. Woodman, Ros. 2005. (Activity Ser.). (ENG.). 64p. (J). (gr. 4-7). pap., act. bk. ed. 7.99 *(978-1-84550-067-2(9)*, 5598a3d5-20d8-4dfc-bb1d-76dc09fab922) Christian Focus Pubns. GBR. Dist: Baker & Taylor Publisher Services (BTPS).
—Four Square: A Companion to the Four Square Writing Method: Writing in the Content Areas for Grades 5-9. Gould, Judith S. & Gould, Evan Jay. Mitchell, Judy, ed. 2004. 112p. (J). pap. 11.95 *(978-1-57310-422-7(1))* Teaching & Learning Co.
—Four Square: The Personal Writing Coach, Grades 7-9. Gould, Judith S. & Burke, Mary F. 2005. 112p. (J). pap. 12.95 *(978-1-57310-448-7(5))* Teaching & Learning Co.
—Fun Bible Studies Using Puzzles & Stories. Woodman, Ros. 2006. (ENG.). 64p. (J). pap. 9.99 *(978-1-84550-223-2(X)*, 575e3ee2-10d7-4c58-be74-6b61c45b1eda) Christian Focus Pubns. GBR. Dist: Baker & Taylor Publisher Services (BTPS).
—Genesis: Fun Bible Studies Using Puzzles & Stories. Woodman, Ros. 2005. (Activity Ser.). (ENG.). 64p. (J). (gr. 4-7). pap., act. bk. ed. 9.99 *(978-1-84550-066-5(0)*, 17c1a715-2f57-40ae-8e43-0c81f258e5ea) Christian Focus Pubns. GBR. Dist: Baker & Taylor Publisher Services (BTPS).
—Great Scientists in Action. Shevick, Ed. 2004. (Science Action Labs Ser.). 64p. (J). pap. 9.95 *(978-1-57310-436-4(1)*, 1238118) Teaching & Learning Co.
—In the Lick of Time. Kumpe, Pam. 2019. (ENG.). 38p. (J). pap. 9.99 *(978-0-578-08096-3(6))* Hom, Jonathan.
—Math Phonics Pre-Algebra. Hein, Marilyn B. 2004. 96p. (J). pap. 10.65 *(978-1-57310-438-8(8))* Teaching & Learning Co.
—Matthew & Goliath. Davis, Brian. 2003. (Book of Matt Ser.: 3). 80p. (J). pap. 4.99 *(978-1-59269-058-9(0))* Mcruffy Pr.
—Matt's Birthday Blessing. Davis, Brian. 2003. (Book of Matt Ser.: Vol. 1). 80p. (J). pap. 4.99 *(978-1-59269-056-5(4))* Mcruffy Pr.
—My Shoes Got the Blues, Davis, Brian. 2003. (Book of Matt Ser.: 2). 80p. (J). pap. 4.99 *(978-1-59269-057-2(2))* Mcruffy Pr.
Wheeler, Samuel. Ten Chickens. Ecrivain, M. S. Belle. 2017. (ENG.). 28p. (J). pap. *(978-0-473-40651-6(9))* Nocturnal Customs Ltd.
Wheeler, Wesley. Searching for Christmas. Gardner, Holly. 2018. (ENG.). 32p. (J). (gr. k-3). 19.99 *(978-1-4621-2278-3(7))* Cedar Fort, Inc./CFI Distribution.
Wheelhouse, M. V. A Flat Iron for a Farthing. Ewing, Juliana Horatia. 2007. 212p. per. *(978-1-4065-2524-3(3))* Dodo Pr.
Whelan, Kat. One Little Blueberry. Salzano, Tammi. 2011. (ENG.). 22p. (J). (gr. -1-k). 12.95 *(978-1-58925-859-4(2))* Tiger Tales.
—'Twas the Night Before Christmas. Moore, Clement C. 2010. (ENG.). 24p. (J). (gr. -1-2). 12.95 *(978-1-58925-858-7(4))* Tiger Tales.
Whelan, Kevin. You Wouldn't Want to Sail on the Mayflower! A Trip That Took Entirely Too Long. Cook, Peter. rev. ed. 2013. (ENG.). 40p. (J). (gr. 3-12). pap. 9.95 *(978-0-531-23858-5(X)*, Watts, Franklin) Scholastic Library Publishing.
Whelan, Olwyn. The Barefoot Book of Blessings: From Many Faiths & Cultures. Dearborn, Sabrina. 2007. (ENG.). 40p. (J). (gr. -1-3). 18.99 *(978-1-84686-069-0(5))* Barefoot Bks., Inc.
—The Barefoot Book of Pirates. Walker, Richard. (Barefoot Bks.). 64p. (J). 2008. 19.99 *(978-1-84686-237-3(X))*; 2004. (gr. 3-6). 16.99 *(978-1-84148-131-9(9))* Barefoot Bks., Inc.
—The Barefoot Book of Princesses. Matthews, Caitlín. 2004. 64p. (J). (gr. k-4). 16.99 *(978-1-84148-172-2(6))* Barefoot Bks., Inc.
—Celtic Memories. Matthews, Caitlín. 2003. 80p. (J). 19.99 *(978-1-84148-097-8(5))* Barefoot Bks., Inc.
—Little Elephant. House, Catherine. 2007. 32p. pap. 11.95 *(978-1-59325-093-5(2))* Word Among Us Pr.
—Little Zebra. House, Catherine. 2007. 39p. (J). 11.95 *(978-1-59325-094-2(0))* Word Among Us Pr.
—Pirates Artist Card Portfolio. (J). 12.99 *(978-1-84148-485-3(7))* Barefoot Bks., Inc.
—Pirates Invitations. (J). 7.99 *(978-1-84148-486-0(5))* Barefoot Bks., Inc.
—Princesses Artist Card Portfolio. (J). 12.99 *(978-1-84148-484-6(9))* Barefoot Bks., Inc.
—Princesses Invitations. (J). 7.99 *(978-1-84148-470-9(9))* Barefoot Bks., Inc.
Whelan, Olwyn. The Barefoot Book of Princesses. Whelan, Olwyn. Matthews, Caitlín & Wolfson, Margaret. 2008. (Barefoot Bks.). 64p. (J). 19.99 *(978-1-84686-239-7(6))* Barefoot Bks., Inc.
—Tales from Celtic Lands. Whelan, Olwyn. Matthews, Caitlín & Cusack, Niamh. 2008. 80p. (J). (gr. -1-3). 21.99 *(978-1-84686-213-7(2))* Barefoot Bks., Inc.
Whelan, Olwyn. The Star Child. Whelan, Olwyn, tr. Maidment, Stella & Wilde, Oscar. gif. ed. 2003. 40p. (YA). *(978-1-84365-012-6(6)*, Pavilion Children's Books) Pavilion Bks.
Whelon, Chuck. Where's Santa? Jones, Bryony. 2015. (ENG.). 32p. (J). (gr. k-3). 12.99 *(978-1-4814-0619-2(1)*, Aladdin) Simon & Schuster Children's Publishing.
Whelon, Chuck. Where's the Princess? And Other Fairy Tale Searches. Whelon, Chuck. 2016. (ENG.). 32p. (J). (gr. k-3). 15.99 *(978-1-4814-4633-4(9)*, Aladdin) Simon & Schuster Children's Publishing.
Whelon, Chuck, jt. illus. see Clay, Adam.
Whigham, Rod. How to Draw Monster Trucks, 1 vol. Sautter, Aaron. 2007. (Drawing Cool Stuff Ser.). (ENG.). 32p. (J). (gr. 3-9). 28.65 *(978-1-4296-0079-8(9)*, Capstone Pr.) Capstone.
—Jim Thorpe: Greatest Athlete in the World, 1 vol. Fandel, Jennifer. 2008. (Graphic Biographies Ser.). (ENG.). 32p. (J). (gr. 3-9). per. 8.10 *(978-1-4296-1773-4(X))* Capstone.
—Samuel Morse & the Telegraph, 1 vol. Seidman, David. 2007. (Inventions & Discovery Ser.). (ENG.). 32p. (J). (gr. 3-9). pap. 8.10 *(978-0-7368-7898-2(X)*, Capstone Pr.) Capstone.
—Samuel Morse & the Telegraph, 1 vol. Seidman, David et al. 2007. (Inventions & Discovery Ser.). (ENG.). 32p. (J). (gr. 3-9). 31.32 *(978-0-7368-6846-4(1)*, Capstone Pr.) Capstone.
Whigham, Rod & Barnett, Charles, III. Christopher Columbus: Famous Explorer, 1 vol. Wade, Mary Dodson. 2007. (Graphic Biographies Ser.). (ENG.). 32p. (J). (gr. 3-9). pap. 8.10 *(978-0-7368-7905-7(6)*, 1264941, Capstone Pr.) Capstone.
Whild, Katharine. Marlowe the Great Detective. Whild, Katharine. l.t. ed. 2005. 36p. (J). 16.95 *(978-0-9712488-4-7(2))* Deerbrook Editions.
Whimp, Pauline. Bear Gets Stuck. Holden, Pam. 2015. 16p. (-1). pap. *(978-1-77654-127-0(8)*, Red Rocket Readers) Flying Start Bks.
—Greedy Gus the Pirate, 6 pack. Holden, Pam. 2009. (Red Rocket Readers Ser.). 18p. (gr. 2-2). pap. *(978-1-877363-74-0(X))* Flying Start Bks.
—Hunting for Treasure, 6 pack. Holden, Pam. 2009. (Red Rocket Readers Ser.). 17p. (gr. 2-2). pap. *(978-1-877363-65-8(0)*, Red Rocket Readers) Flying Start Bks.
—Paulo the Pilot, 6 pack. Holden, Pam. 2009. (Red Rocket Readers Ser.). 17p. (gr. 2-2). pap. *(978-1-877363-67-2(7)*, Red Rocket Readers) Flying Start Bks.
—The Rainbow Party, 6 pack. Holden, Pam. 2009. (Red Rocket Readers Ser.). 20p. pap. *(978-1-877363-82-5(0))* Flying Start Bks.
—Surprise from the Sky, 6 pack. Holden, Pam. 2009. (Red Rocket Readers Ser.). 21p. (gr. 2-1). pap. *(978-1-877363-68-9(5))* Flying Start Bks.
—Two Pirates, 6 pack. Holden, Pam. 2009. (Red Rocket Readers Ser.). 23p. (gr. 2-2). pap. *(978-1-877363-71-9(5))* Flying Start Bks.
—Watch the Ball, 6 pack. Holden, Pam. 2009. (Red Rocket Readers Ser.). 23p. (gr. 2-2). pap. *(978-1-877363-80-1(4))* Flying Start Bks.
Whipp, Katie. Otis & Baby Jean. Whipp, Jo. 2012. 26p. 24.95 *(978-1-4626-5049-1(X))* America Star Bks.
Whipple, Kevin. Woodford Brave. Jones, Marcia Thornton. 2015. (ENG.). 200p. (J). (gr. 4-7). 16.95 *(978-1-62979-305-4(1)*, Calkins Creek) Boyds Mills Pr.
Whipple, Rick. JoJo & Daddy Bake a Cake. O'Connor, Jane & Glasser, Robin Preiss. 2017. 32p. (J). *(978-1-5182-4989-1(2))* Harper & Row Ltd.
Whipple, Rick, jt. illus. see Cowdrey, Richard.
Whipple, Rick, jt. illus. see deGroat, Diane.
Whisker, Dan. Unicorns. Meister, Cari. 2019. (Mythical Creatures Ser.). (ENG.). 32p. (J). (gr. k-2). lib. bdg. 27.99 *(978-1-5158-4441-9(2)*, 140561, Picture Window Bks.) Capstone.
Whitaker, Margaret. Stacie's Geese at Goose Lake. Whitaker, Margaret. 2005. 36p. (J). pap. 12.00 *(978-0-9768051-0-6(3))* RoseFountain Pr., LLC.
Whitaker, Suzanne. Lilly & Zander: A Children's Story about Equine-Assisted Activities. Stamm, Linda J. 2014. (J). pap. *(978-1-938313-03-5(8))* Graphite Pr.
Whitaker, Tara Nicole. Bubble Kisses. Williams, Vanessa. 2020. 32p. (J). (gr. -1-3). 17.95 ***(978-1-4549-3834-7(X))*** Sterling Publishing Co., Inc.
Whitaker, Tara Nicole. Disney Princess: Ariel & the Sea Wolf (Younger Readers Graphic Novel) Marsham, Liz. 2019. (ENG.). 48p. (J). (gr. k-3). 7.99 *(978-1-5067-1203-1(7))* Dark Horse Comics.
—My Baby Loves Christmas. Asim, Jabari. 2019. (ENG.). 20p. (J). (gr. -1 — 1). bds. 7.99 *(978-0-06-288462-6(X)*, HarperFestival) HarperCollins Pubs.
Whitaker, Tara Nicole. My Baby Loves Halloween. Asim, Jabari. 2020. (ENG.). 20p. (J). (gr. -1 — 1). bds. 7.99 ***(978-0-06-288463-3(8)***, HarperFestival) HarperCollins Pubs.
Whitby, Charlotte. Dog in Danger! Black, Jess. 2013. (Animal Tales Ser.: 5). 96p. (J). (gr. 2-4). 7.99 *(978-1-74275-336-2(1))* Random Hse. Australia AUS. Dist: Independent Pubs. Group.
—Fright Night! Black, Jess. 2013. (Animal Tales Ser.: 6). 96p. (J). (gr. 2-4). 7.99 *(978-1-74275-338-6(8))* Random Hse. Australia AUS. Dist: Independent Pubs. Group.
—Lost in Translation: Buying This Book Helps the RSPCA Look after Animals! Kelly, Helen. 2013. (Animal Tales Ser.: 7). 96p. (J). (gr. 2-4). 7.99 *(978-1-74275-340-9(X))* Random Hse. Australia AUS. Dist: Independent Pubs. Group.
—Race to the Finish. Harding, David. 2013. (Animal Tales Ser.: 8). 96p. (J). (gr. 2-4). 7.99 *(978-1-74275-342-3(6))* Random Hse. Australia AUS. Dist: Independent Pubs. Group.
Whitchurch, Marilyn. Magic Moon Two Worlds: (Vol. 3), vol. 3. Moulton, Shirley. Dennis, Shilo, ed. 2017. (Magic Moon Ser.: 3). (ENG.). 146p. (gr. 3-5). pap. *(978-0-9983137-1-9(8))* Magic Moon Bks., LLC.
White, Annie. Be Careful of Strangers, 6 vols. McMillan, Dawn. 2005. (ENG.). (J). (gr. 2-3). pap., pap. 54.80 *(978-1-4189-1472-1(X))* Rigby Education.
—Who Am I? Yoga for Children of All Ages. Weisner, Jane Lee. 2006. 32p. (Orig.). (J). pap. 13.95 *(978-0-85572-341-5(6))* Warwick Publishing CAN. Dist: Two Rivers Distribution.
White, Ashley. A Moon of My Own, 1 vol. Rustgi, Jennifer. 2016. (ENG.). 32p. (J). (gr. k-4). 11.95 *(978-1-58469-572-1(2)*, Dawn Pubns.) Sourcebooks, Inc.
White, Charlotte. My Bed Is a Spaceship: The Globbus. Krasner, Nick. 2013. 122p. pap. *(978-1-909593-34-3(6))* Legend Pr.
White, Charlotte. My Bed Is a Spaceship: The Pirates of the Milky Way. Krasner, Nick. 2020. (ENG.). 124p. (J). pap. ***(978-1-78955-856-2(5))*** Authors OnLine, Ltd.
White, Charlotte L., jt. illus. see Heyer, Carol.
White, Christopher M. I Want to Go to Sleep. Daniels, Jaime S. 2019. (Sensory & Spectrum Ser.: Vol. 1). (ENG.). 26p. (J). pap. 12.97 *(978-1-0724-2676-9(5))* Independently Published.
White, Daniel, photos by. Your Safari: In Search of the Real Komodo Dragon. Truscott, Julia. 2005. 48p. (J). 11.95 *(978-1-59594-014-8(6)*, Wingspan Pr.) WingSpan Publishing.
White, Dave. Arctic Blast. Landers, Ace. 2012. 32p. (J). *(978-0-545-33455-6(1))* Scholastic, Inc.
—Cave Race! Landers, Ace. 2010. 32p. (J). *(978-0-545-20871-0(8))* Scholastic, Inc.
—The Force Awakens: Episode VII. Schaefer, Elizabeth. ed. 2016. (LEGO Star Wars 8X8 Ser.). (ENG.). 24p. (J). (gr. -1-3). 13.55 *(978-0-606-39117-7(7))* Turtleback.
—Hot Wheels: Wild Rides. Landers, Ace. 2009. 32p. (J). *(978-0-545-15347-8(6))* Scholastic, Inc.
—Race for Treasure. Landers, Ace. 2011. 32p. (J). pap. *(978-0-545-33454-9(3))* Scholastic, Inc.
—Revenge of the Sith. Landers, Ace. 2015. (LEGO Star Wars Ser.). (J). 24p. (gr. -1-3). pap. 3.99 *(978-0-545-78524-2(3))*; *(978-1-4806-9629-7(3))* Scholastic, Inc.
—Start Your Engines. Landers, Ace. 2007. (Scholastic Reader Ser.). (J). pap. *(978-0-545-02017-6(4))* Scholastic, Inc.
White, Dave. Emma & the Ice People: Special Dave White Tribute Edition. White, Dave. White, Barbi. 2018. (ENG.). 44p. (J). (gr. k-4). pap. 10.99 *(978-1-68160-632-3(1))* Crimson Cloak Publishing.
White, Dave, jt. illus. see Landers, Ace.
White, Dave, jt. illus. see Wisinski, Ed.
White, David. Body Bones. Rotner, Shelley, photos by. Rotner, Shelley. 2014. (ENG.). 32p. (J). (gr. 1-4). 16.95 *(978-0-8234-3162-5(2))* Holiday Hse., Inc.
—The Daughter of Dreams, a Fable of Destiny. Barna, Beverly. 2009. 28p. pap. 14.95 *(978-1-936051-09-0(5))* Peppertree Pr., The.
—Destiny's Wild Ride, a Tall Tale of the Legendary Hub Hubbell. Leipold, Judith. 2013. 32p. 24.95 *(978-1-61493-168-3(2))*; pap. 14.95 *(978-1-61493-167-6(4))* Peppertree Pr., The.
—Kicklighter Shadow & the Beeples. Lindemann, Lindy. 2009. 24p. pap. 12.95 *(978-0-9822540-9-7(1))* Peppertree Pr., The.
—A New Hope. Landers, Ace. 2015. (LEGO Star Wars Ser.). 24p. (J). (gr. -1-3). pap. 3.99 *(978-0-545-80135-5(4))* Scholastic, Inc.
—No Bones about It, Skeleton Jokes. Guess, Alison. 2008. 88p. pap. 9.95 *(978-0-9817572-4-7(3))* Peppertree Pr., The.
White, David A. Anakin: Space Pilot. Landers, Ace. 2011. (LEGO Star Wars Ser.). (ENG.). 16p. (J). (gr. -1-3). 12.99 *(978-0-545-30440-5(7))* Scholastic, Inc.

—Anakin to the Rescue! Landers, Ace. 2012. (LEGO Star Wars Ser.). 24p. (J). (gr. -1-3). pap. 3.99 *(978-0-545-47066-7(8))* Scholastic, Inc.

—Face Off. Kaplan, Arie. 2016. (LEGO Star Wars Ser.). 64p. (J). (gr. 2-5). pap. 8.99 *(978-0-545-92541-9(X))* Scholastic, Inc.

—The Force Awakens. Schaefer, Elizabeth. 2016. (LEGO Star Wars Ser.). 24p. (J). (gr. -1-3). pap. 3.99 *(978-0-545-94072-6(9))* Scholastic, Inc.

—Heroes! Cohen, Alana. 2011. (LEGO City Ser.). (ENG.). 16p. (J). (gr. -1-k). bds. 9.99 *(978-0-545-27439-5(7))* Scholastic, Inc.

White, Deborah. Little Visits with God. Jahsmann, Allan Hart & Simon, Martin P. 4th ed. 2006. (Little Visits Ser.). 413p. (J). (gr. 5-7). per. 13.49 *(978-0-7586-0847-5(0))* Concordia Publishing Hse.

—My Name Is Erica Montoya de la Cruz. Zirin, David. 2005. (ENG.). 16p. (J). 5.75 *(978-1-57274-732-6(3)*, 2779, Bks. for Young Learners) Owen, Richard C. Pubs., Inc.

White, Deborah J. Martin Luther. Grube, Edward C. 2012. (Hero of Faith Ser.). (ENG.). 58p. (J). pap. 7.99 *(978-0-7586-3075-9(1))* Concordia Publishing Hse.

White, Frances. Mary Jane: Her Visit. Judson, Clara Ingram. 2007. 108p. per. *(978-1-4065-4676-7(3))* Dodo Pr.

—Mary Jane - Her Book. Judson, Clara Ingram. 2007. 212p. 22.95 *(978-1-934671-13-9(4))*; per. 12.95 *(978-1-934671-14-6(2))* Salem Ridge Press LLC.

—Mary Jane - Her Visit. Judson, Clara Ingram. 2008. 220p. 22.95 *(978-1-934671-15-3(0))*; per. 12.95 *(978-1-934671-16-0(9))* Salem Ridge Press LLC.

White, Franicia. There Was a Bird. White, Franicia. White, Timothy, ed. 2016. (ENG.). (J). pap. 10.99 *(978-1-943449-21-7(X))* Wholesome Pr.

—There Was an Egg. White, Franicia. White, Timothy, ed. 2016. (ENG.). (J). pap. 11.99 *(978-1-943449-22-4(8))* Wholesome Pr.

White, Greg. Happy Root Beer. Swarbrick, David. 2017. (ENG.). (J). (gr. k-3). pap. 9.99 *(978-1-59095-047-0(X)*, ExamWise) Total Recall Learning, Inc.

White, Ian. Flash, Bang, Wheee! Clark, Karen. 2004. 24p. (J). *(978-1-85269-280-3(4))*; *(978-1-85269-350-3(9))*; *(978-1-85269-353-4(3))*; *(978-1-85269-355-8(X))*; *(978-1-85269-356-5(8))*; *(978-1-85269-374-9(6))*; *(978-1-85269-430-2(0))*; *(978-1-85269-432-6(7))*; *(978-1-85269-433-3(5))*; *(978-1-85269-434-0(3))*; *(978-1-85269-435-7(1))*; *(978-1-85269-437-1(8))*; *(978-1-85269-438-8(6))* Mantra Lingua.

—Flash Bang Wheee! Clark, Karen. 2004. (J). *(978-1-85269-678-8(8))* Mantra Lingua.

—Flash Bang Wheee! Clark, Karen. 2004. (ENG & VIE.). (J). pap. 12.95 *(978-1-85269-808-9(X))* Mantra Lingua GBR. Dist: Chinasprout, Inc.

White, Ian, jt. illus. see Clark, Karen.

White, Iris Weddell. Rose Colored Glasses. Radford, Ruby Lorraine. 2011. 46p. 35.95 *(978-1-258-03586-0(3))* Literary Licensing, LLC.

White, John, Jr. & Tank, Daniel. Abraham. Brand, Ruth Redding. 2004. (Family Bible Story Ser.). 109p. (J). 19.99 *(978-0-8280-1856-2(1)*, 010-570) Review & Herald Publishing Assn.

—Abraham. 2004. (Family Bible Story Ser.). 109p. (J). pap. *(978-0-8280-1857-9(X))* Review & Herald Publishing Assn.

White, Kathy. Mommy will always come Home. Summer, Laura LeClair. 2006. 35p. (J). per. 24.95 *(978-1-4276-0158-2(5))* Aardvark Global Publishing.

White, Keinyo. Dog Agility. Appleton-Smith, Laura. 2007. (ENG.). 19p. (J). pap. 8.95 *(978-1-60541-012-8(8)*, Books To Remember) Flyleaf Publishing.

White, Lee. Arctic White. Smith, Danna. 2016. (ENG.). 32p. (J). (gr. -1-3). 17.99 *(978-1-62779-104-5(3)*, 900135317, Holt, Henry & Co. Bks. For Young Readers) Holt, Henry & Co.

—Brewster the Rooster. Scillian, Devin. rev. ed. 2007. (ENG.). 32p. (J). (gr. 3-7). 16.95 *(978-1-58536-311-7(1))* Sleeping Bear Pr.

—A Crazy Day at the Critter Café. Odanaka, Barbara. 2009. (ENG.). 32p. (J). (gr. -1-3). 19.99 *(978-1-4169-3914-6(8)*, McElderry, Margaret K. Bks.) McElderry, Margaret K. Bks.

—Emma & the Whale. Case, Julie. 2017. 40p. (J). (gr. -1-3). 17.99 *(978-0-553-53847-2(0)*, Schwartz & Wade Bks.) Random Hse. Children's Bks.

—The House Takes a Vacation, 0 vols. Davies, Jacqueline. 2013. (ENG.). 34p. (J). (gr. -1-3). pap. 9.99 *(978-1-4778-1619-6(4)*, 9781477816196, Two Lions) Amazon Publishing.

—I Lived on Butterfly Hill. Agosin, Marjorie & Agosain, Marjorie. 2015. (ENG.). (J). (gr. 5-9). lib. bdg. 19.60 *(978-1-62765-652-8(9))* Perfection Learning Corp.

—I Lived on Butterfly Hill. Agosin, Marjorie. 2014. (Butterfly Hill Ser.). (ENG.). 464p. (J). (gr. 5-9). 19.99 *(978-1-4169-5344-9(2)*, Atheneum Bks. for Young Readers) Simon & Schuster Children's Publishing.

—I'll Do It Later. Ribke, Simone T. (Rookie Ready to Learn Ser.). (J). 2011. 40p. (gr. -1-k). pap. 5.95 *(978-0-531-26710-3(5))*; 2011. 40p. (gr. -1-k). lib. bdg. 23.00 *(978-0-531-26528-4(5))*; 2005. (ENG.). 32p. (gr. k-2). lib. bdg. 19.50 *(978-0-516-24861-5(8))* Scholastic Library Publishing. (Children's Pr.).

—Kate, Who Tamed the Wind. Scanlon, Liz Garton. 2018. 40p. (J). (gr. -1-3). 17.99 *(978-1-101-93479-1(4))*; (ENG.). lib. bdg. 20.99 *(978-1-101-93480-7(8))* Random Hse. Children's Bks. (Schwartz & Wade Bks.).

—The Library Ghost. Weatherford, Carole Boston. 2008. 22p. (J). (gr. -1-3). 17.95 *(978-1-60213-017-3(5)*, Upstart Bks.) Highsmith Inc.

—The Lost Track of Time. Britt, Paige. 2015. 324p. (J). (gr. 3-7). 17.99 *(978-0-545-53812-1(2)*, Scholastic Pr.) Scholastic, Inc.

—Love, Santa. Brockenbrough, Martha. 2017. (ENG.). 32p. (J). (gr. 4-7). 17.99 *(978-0-545-70030-6(2)*, Levine, Arthur A. Bks.) Scholastic, Inc.

—The Maine Coon's Haiku: And Other Poems for Cat Lovers. Rosen, Michael J. 2015. 56p. (J). (gr. 1-4). 17.99 *(978-0-7636-6492-3(8))* Candlewick Pr.

White, Lee. The Maps of Memory: Return to Butterfly Hill. Agosin, Marjorie. 2020. (Butterfly Hill Ser.). (ENG.). 368p. (J). (gr. 5-9). 18.99 ***(978-1-4814-6901-2(0)***, Atheneum/Caitlyn Dlouhy Books) Simon & Schuster Children's Publishing.

White, Lee. Stop That Nose!, 1 vol. Levine, Martha Peaslee. 2006. (ENG.). 32p. (J). (gr. -1-3). 14.95 *(978-0-7614-5280-5(X))* Marshall Cavendish Corp.

White, Lee, et al. Tales of Leafy Lane. White, Janet. 2007. 88p. per. *(978-1-84748-196-2(5))* Athena Pr.

White, Lee. What Are You Glad about? What Are You Mad About? Poems for When a Person Needs a Poem. Viorst, Judith. (ENG.). 112p. (J). (gr. 1-4). 2017. pap. 7.99 *(978-1-4814-2356-4(8))*; 2016. 17.99 *(978-1-4814-2355-7(X)*, Atheneum/Caitlyn Dlouhy Books) Simon & Schuster Children's Publishing.

White, Leslie. Disbelief 101: A Young Person's Guide to Atheism. Hitchcock, S. C. & Flynn, Tom. 2009. (ENG.). 112p. (gr. 9-18). pap. 9.95 *(978-1-884365-47-8(7))* See Sharp Pr.

White, Mack. Texas Tales Illustrated: The Revolution. Kearby, Mike. 2011. (Texas Tales Illustrated Ser.: 1). (ENG.). 32p. (J). (gr. k-7). pap. 6.95 *(978-0-87565-429-4(0))*; pap. 6.95 *(978-0-87565-439-3(8))* Texas Christian Univ. Pr.

—The Trail Drives, No. 2. Kearby, Mike. 2015. (Texas Tales Illustrated Ser.). (ENG.). 24p. pap. 5.95 *(978-0-87565-608-3(0))* Texas Christian Univ. Pr.

White, Marsha. Bear's New Classes. White, Marsha. 16p. (J). 10.95 *(978-1-58117-294-2(X)*, Intervisual/Piggy Toes) Bendon, Inc.

White, Mia. Careful- Not to HURT MY BABY, LOVE. White, Mia. 2007. per. 35.00 *(978-1-60361-714-7(0))* Belle Media International, Inc. Div of True News.

—CAREFUL, YOU Could HURT the DOLPHINS - Zoe's World Dr. Mia White. White, Mia. 2007. per. 24.00 *(978-1-60361-710-9(8))* Belle Media International, Inc. Div of True News.

—Femme FATALE - FAITH STORIES When Good Girls Are Caught in BAD Situations They Become Femme Fatales: Vamp. White, Mia. 2009. pap. 40.00 incl. DVD *(978-1-60361-203-6(3))* Belle Media International, Inc. Div of True News.

—VAMP -Chronicles - Pin up Heros don't become BaD: Vamp Series 2 the Golden Vessel. White, Mia. 2009. pap. *(978-1-60361-201-2(7))* Belle Media International, Inc. Div of True News.

—VAMP Courtesan - Beauties in Tough Spots an Historic Graphic Novel: Vamp's Adventures Time Travel Chronicles. White, Mia. 2009. pap. 35.00 *(978-1-60361-202-9(5)*, Holmes Bookshop) Belle Lumiere True News.

White, Michael. Sandy Claws & Chris Mouse. Shope, Ray & Shope, Lois. 2003. 32p. (J). 13.95 *(978-0-9714734-0-9(4))* Flutter-By Productions.

White, Michael P. Harriet's Horrible Hair Day, 1 vol. Stewart, Dawn Lesley. 2018. (ENG.). 32p. (J). (gr. -1-3). pap. 7.95 *(978-1-68263-035-8(8))* Peachtree Publishing Co. Inc.

—The Library Dragon, 1 vol. Deedy, Carmen Agra. 2012. (ENG.). 32p. (J). (gr. 1-5). 16.95 *(978-1-56145-091-6(X)*, Q06826); 19.95 *(978-1-56145-639-0(X))* Peachtree Publishing Co. Inc.

—Return of the Library Dragon, 1 vol. Deedy, Carmen Agra. 2012. (ENG.). 32p. (J). 16.95 *(978-1-56145-621-5(7))* Peachtree Publishing Co. Inc.

White, Michelle. Twinkle the Tooth Fairy. Ellsworth, Nick. 32p. (J). 5.98 *(978-0-7525-7628-2(3))* Parragon, Inc.

White, Mike. My Best Book of Early People. Hynes, Margaret. (Best Book Of Ser.). (ENG.). 32p. (J). 2019. pap. 7.99 *(978-0-7534-7499-0(9)*, 900198577); 2003. tchr. ed. 12.99 *(978-0-7534-5577-7(3)*, 900052548) Roaring Brook Pr. (Kingfisher).

White, Nick. Meet the Artist: Alberto Giacometti. 2018. (ENG.). 32p. (J). (gr. -1-3). pap. 12.95 *(978-1-84976-508-4(1))* Tate Publishing, Ltd. GBR. Dist: Hachette Bk. Group.

White, Nonie H. D. The Woodpecker Who Suffered from Headaches. White, Nonie H. D. 2006. (J). pap. 14.95 *(978-0-9786147-0-6(4))* Westside Studio.

White, Rachel. The Perfect Gift. Huppert, Susan. 2007. 24p. (J). per. *(978-0-9799635-0-6(8))* Homegrown Pubns.,LLC.

White, Rex. R.C. Duck, Private Eye. White, Kevin. 2016. 32p. (J). 15.95 *(978-0-9847122-2-9(4))* Chimeric Pr.

White, Sam. Empty Beaches: (Advanced: Vol 1) Fleishman, Brett. 2017. (ENG.). (J). (gr. 6-8). pap. 16.99 *(978-0-9993872-1-4(9))* Mindstir Media.

White, Sam O. Poor Pluto. Decesare, Jason F. 2019. (ENG.). 34p. (J). (gr. k-2). pap. 16.00 *(978-0-578-50578-7(9))* Decesare, Jason.

White, Samuel O. Poor Pluto. Decesare, Jason F. 2019. (ENG.). 34p. (J). (gr. k-2). 20.00 *(978-0-578-50579-4(7))* Decesare, Jason.

White, Siobhán. Chaya & the Spider Gem. Rankin, H. L. 2011. 152p. (YA). pap. 9.95 *(978-2-930583-10-5(X))* White & MacLean Publishing BEL. Dist: Gardners Bks. Ltd.

White, Tara B. A Wish for Little Tommy Turtle. Hughes, John P. 2011. 48p. pap. 24.95 *(978-1-4626-0011-3(5))* America Star Bks.

White, Teagan. Bunny Roo, I Love You. Marr, Melissa. 2015. 32p. (J). (gr. -1 — 1). 16.99 *(978-0-399-16742-3(0)*, Nancy Paulsen Books) Penguin Young Readers Group.

—Charles Darwin's on the Origin of Species. Darwin, Charles. 2018. 170p. (J). pap. *(978-1-4814-6250-1(4)*, Atheneum Bks. for Young Readers) Simon & Schuster Children's Publishing.

—Mice Skating. Silvestro, Annie. 2017. (Mice Skating Ser.: 1). 32p. (J). (gr. -1). 16.95 *(978-1-4549-1632-1(X))* Sterling Publishing Co., Inc.

—Perfect Ruin. DeStefano, Lauren. 2013. (Internment Chronicles Ser.: 1). (ENG.). 368p. (YA). (gr. 7). 18.99 *(978-1-4424-8061-2(0)*, Simon & Schuster Bks. For Young Readers) Simon & Schuster Bks. For Young Readers.

—Snow Sisters! Kokias, Kerri. 2018. 32p. (J). (gr. -1-2). 17.99 *(978-1-101-93883-6(8)*, Knopf Bks. for Young Readers) Random Hse. Children's Bks.

—That's Me Loving You. Rosenthal, Amy Krouse. 2016. (ENG.). 40p. (J). (gr. -1-2). 16.99 *(978-1-101-93238-4(4)*, Random Hse. Bks. for Young Readers) Random Hse. Children's Bks.

—That's Me Loving You. Rosenthal, Amy Krouse. 2018. (ENG.). 28p. (J). (— 1). bds. 8.99 *(978-1-9848-4773-7(2)*, Random Hse. Bks. for Young Readers) Random Hse. Children's Bks.

White, Teagan & Kaulitzki, Ramona. Stick Tac Toe: Magical Mash-Ups! Chronicle Books Staff. 2018. (ENG.). 60p. (J). (gr. -1-17). 7.99 *(978-1-4521-6401-4(0))* Chronicle Bks. LLC.

White, Teagan & Meyer, Jennifer L. Counting Sheep: Calpurnia Tate, Girl Vet. Kelly, Jacqueline. 2017. (Calpurnia Tate, Girl Vet Ser.: 2). (ENG.). 128p. (J). pap. 5.99 *(978-1-250-12945-1(1)*, 900161283) Square Fish.

—Skunked!: Calpurnia Tate, Girl Vet. Kelly, Jacqueline. 2016. (Calpurnia Tate, Girl Vet Ser.: 1). (ENG.). 112p. (J). 15.99 *(978-1-62779-868-6(4)*, 900161279, Holt, Henry & Co. Bks. For Young Readers) Holt, Henry & Co.

—Skunked!: Calpurnia Tate, Girl Vet. Kelly, Jacqueline. 2017. (Calpurnia Tate, Girl Vet Ser.: 1). (ENG.). 128p. (J). pap. 6.99 *(978-1-250-12944-4(3)*, 900161280) Square Fish.

White, Timothy. A Kayak Full of Ghosts. Millman, Lawrence. 2004. (International Folk Tales Ser.). (ENG.). 208p. pap. 13.95 *(978-1-56656-525-7(1))* Interlink Publishing Group, Inc.

White, Tina Jorgenson. Turtle's Journey, 1 vol. Briceno, Carole. 2009. 28p. pap. 24.95 *(978-1-60813-934-7(4))* America Star Bks.

White, Vicky. Ape. Jenkins, Martin. (ENG.). 48p. (J). (gr. -1-2). 2010. pap. 7.99 *(978-0-7636-4974-6(0))*; 2007. 16.99 *(978-0-7636-3471-1(9))* Candlewick Pr.

—Can We Save the Tiger? Jenkins, Martin. 2014. (ENG.). 56p. (J). (gr. k-3). 9.99 *(978-0-7636-7378-9(1))* Candlewick Pr.

—Can We Save the Tiger? Jenkins, Martin. 2014. (ENG.). (J). (gr. k-3). lib. bdg. 20.60 *(978-1-62765-705-1(3))* Perfection Learning Corp.

Whited, Susanne. Little Baby Poot-Poot. Whited, Susanne. 2016. (ENG.). (J). pap. 19.99 *(978-1-944701-00-0(1))* QuadMama Pr.

Whitehead, Brynne E. Unicorn Dreams Journal for Girls Blank & Lined Pages for Journaling & Drawing. Whitehead, Brynne. 2018. (Journals to Write In Ser.: Vol. 1). (ENG.). 102p. (J). pap. 9.97 *(978-1-7239-4440-6(8))* Independently Published.

Whitehead, Jenny. Punctuation Celebration. Bruno, Elsa Knight. 2012. (ENG.). 32p. (J). (gr. 1-4). pap. 8.99 *(978-1-250-00335-5(0)*, 900079869) Square Fish.

Whitehead, Jenny. You're a Crab! A Moody Day Book. Whitehead, Jenny. 2015. (ENG.). 32p. (J). (gr. -1-2). 16.99 *(978-0-8050-9361-2(3)*, 900073324, Holt, Henry & Co. Bks. For Young Readers) Holt, Henry & Co.

Whitehead, Kiki. Ollie under It. Kieta, Patricia. 2018. (ENG.). 30p. (J). pap. 13.00 *(978-1-9860-3116-5(0))* CreateSpace Independent Publishing Platform.

Whitehead, Paul. Where's the Chick? Counting Book. Auerbach, Annie. 2005. (J). bds. 14.99 *(978-0-9767325-5-6(6))* Toy Quest.

Whitehead, Pete. The Adventures of a Plastic Bottle: A Story about Recycling. Inches, Alison. 2009. (Little Green Bks.). (ENG.). 24p. (J). (gr. -1-1). pap. 4.99 *(978-1-4169-6788-0(5)*, Little Simon) Little Simon.

—Wack-A-Doodle School: 1,001 Grade-A Riddles, Jokes, & Tongue Twisters from Highlights. Highlights for Children Editorial Staff. 2015. (Highlights(TM) Laugh Attack! Joke Bks.). (ENG.). 256p. (J). (gr. 1-4). pap. 5.95 *(978-1-62979-427-3(9)*, Highlights) Boyds Mills Pr.

Whitehead, Rachael. How Blake Saved Fairy Land. Angman, Pauline Hagen. 2020. (ENG.). 44p. (J). ***(978-1-5255-6168-9(5))***; pap. ***(978-1-5255-6169-6(3))*** FriesenPress.

Whitehead, S. B. If Roast Beef Could Fly. Leno, Jay. 2005. 30p. (J). (gr. k-4). 18.00 *(978-0-7567-9365-4(3))* DIANE Publishing Co.

Whitehead, Vickie. Just Like Me. Whitehead, Vickie. 2018. (ENG.). 58p. (J). (gr. k-3). 24.95 *(978-1-63498-676-2(8))*; pap. 14.95 *(978-1-63498-675-5(X))* Bookstand Publishing.

Whitehead, Victoria E. & Shirk, Linda. Mary's Family Stories. Gerber, Mary Lichty. 2015. (ENG.). 124p. (J). (gr. -1). 8.50 *(978-0-7399-2512-6(1))* Rod & Staff Pubs., Inc.

Whitehouse, Ben. Adi Sorts with Variables. Karanja, Caroline. 2018. (Code Play Ser.). (ENG.). 24p. (J). (gr. k-3). pap. 7.95 *(978-1-5158-2750-4(X)*, 137952); lib. bdg. 27.99 *(978-1-5158-2746-7(1)*, 137948) Capstone. (Picture Window Bks.).

—Adi's Perfect Patterns & Loops. Karanja, Caroline. 2018. (Code Play Ser.). (ENG.). 24p. (J). (gr. k-3). pap. 7.95 *(978-1-5158-2748-1(8)*, 137950); lib. bdg. 27.99 *(978-1-5158-2744-3(5)*, 137946) Capstone. (Picture Window Bks.).

—The Big Bad Woof. Styles, Walker. 2017. (Rider Woofson Ser.: 8). (ENG.). 128p. (J). (gr. k-4). pap. 5.99 *(978-1-4814-9188-4(1)*, Little Simon) Little Simon.

—The Case of the Missing Tiger's Eye. Styles, Walker. 2016. (Rider Woofson Ser.: 1). (ENG.). 128p. (J). (gr. k-4). 16.99 *(978-1-4814-5738-5(1)*, Little Simon) Little Simon.

—Dinner for Dinos: Gulp, Guzzle, Chomp, Chew, 1 vol. 2018. (ENG.). 20p. (J). bds. 9.99 *(978-1-4003-1214-6(0))* Nelson, Thomas Inc.

—Gabi's Fabulous Functions. Karanja, Caroline. 2018. (Code Play Ser.). (ENG.). 24p. (J). (gr. k-3). lib. bdg. 27.99 *(978-1-5158-2743-6(7)*, 137945, Picture Window Bks.) Capstone.

—Gabi's If/Then Garden. Karanja, Caroline. 2018. (Code Play Ser.). (ENG.). 24p. (J). (gr. k-3). pap. 7.95 *(978-1-5158-2749-8(6)*, 137951); lib. bdg. 27.99 *(978-1-5158-2745-0(3)*, 137947) Capstone. (Picture Window Bks.).

—Ghosts & Goblins & Ninja, Oh My! Styles, Walker. 2016. (Rider Woofson Ser.: 4). (ENG.). 128p. (J). (gr. k-4). pap. 5.99 *(978-1-4814-6306-5(3)*, Little Simon) Little Simon.

—The Honest Woodcutter. Berne, Emma Carlson. 2019. (Classic Fables in Rhythm & Rhyme Ser.). (ENG.). 24p. (J). (gr. -1-2). lib. bdg. 33.99 *(978-1-68410-334-8(7)*, 140254) Cantata Learning.

—Labra-Cadabra-dor's Revenge. Styles, Walker. 2017. (Rider Woofson Ser.: 7). (ENG.). 128p. (J). (gr. k-4). 16.99 *(978-1-4814-8593-7(8)*, Little Simon) Little Simon.

—Labra-Cadabra-dor's Revenge. Styles, Walker. 2017. (Rider Woofson Ser.: 7). (ENG.). 128p. (J). (gr. k-4). pap. 5.99 *(978-1-4814-8592-0(X)*, Little Simon) Little Simon.

—Mystery Mountain Getaway. Styles, Walker. 2017. (Rider Woofson Ser.: 9). (ENG.). 128p. (J). (gr. k-4). 16.99 *(978-1-4814-9896-8(7))*; pap. 5.99 *(978-1-4814-9895-1(9))* Little Simon. (Little Simon).

—Old MacDino Had a Farm. Davies, Becky. 2017. (ENG.). 32p. (J). (gr. -1-2). 16.99 *(978-1-68010-063-1(7))* Tiger Tales.

—Pirates in Class 3. Donald, Alison. 2019. (ENG.). 32p. (J). (gr. -1-3). 17.99 *(978-1-84886-360-6(8))* Maverick Arts Publishing GBR. Dist: Lerner Publishing Group.

Whitehouse, Ben. Playing Wicked. Kahler, Alex R. 2020. (ENG.). 32p. (J). (gr. -1-3). 16.99 ***(978-0-8075-8739-3(7)***, 807587397) Whitman, Albert & Co.

Whitehouse, Ben. The Rival Detective. Styles, Walker. 2016. (Rider Woofson Ser.: 5). (ENG.). 128p. (J). (gr. k-4). pap. 5.99 *(978-1-4814-7107-7(4)*, Little Simon) Little Simon.

—Roar & Sparkles Go to School. Durst, Sarah Beth. 2017. 40p. (J). (gr. -1-1). 16.99 *(978-0-7624-5986-5(7)*, Running Pr. Kids) Running Pr.

—Sasha Sings: Understanding Parts of a Sentence. Meister, Cari. 2015. (Language on the Loose Ser.). (ENG.). 24p. (J). (gr. 2-4). pap. 7.95 *(978-1-4795-6968-7(2)*, Picture Window Bks.) Capstone.

—The Soccer Ball Monster Mystery. Styles, Walker. 2016. (Rider Woofson Ser.: 6). (ENG.). 128p. (J). (gr. k-4). pap. 5.99 *(978-1-4814-7110-7(4)*, Little Simon) Little Simon.

—Something Smells Fishy. Styles, Walker. 2016. (Rider Woofson Ser.: 2). (ENG.). 128p. (J). (gr. k-4). 16.99 *(978-1-4814-5742-2(X)*, Little Simon) Little Simon.

—Something Smells Fishy. Styles, Walker. 2016. (Rider Woofson Ser.: 2). (ENG.). 128p. (J). (gr. k-4). pap. 5.99 *(978-1-4814-5741-5(1)*, Little Simon) Little Simon.

—Undercover in the Bow-Wow Club. Styles, Walker. 2016. (Rider Woofson Ser.: 3). (ENG.). 128p. (J). (gr. k-4). pap. 5.99 *(978-1-4814-6303-4(9)*, Little Simon) Little Simon.

—The Very First Case. Styles, Walker. 2018. (Rider Woofson Ser.: 10). (ENG.). 128p. (J). (gr. k-4). 16.99 *(978-1-5344-1272-9(7))*; pap. 5.99 *(978-1-5344-1271-2(9))* Little Simon. (Little Simon).

—Where the Best Stories Hide. Yasiejko, Roman. 2020. (ENG.). 32p. (J). (gr. k-3). 17.99 *(978-1-5064-5401-6(1)*, Beaming Books) Augsburg Fortress, Pubs.

Whitehurst, John, et al. Bells Goes to the Fair. Knapp, Susan. l.t. ed. 2003. 40p. (J). (gr. -1-3). 12.95 *(978-1-888223-34-7(0))* McMillen Publishing.

Whitethorne, Bahe, Jr. The Day of Storms, 3 vols. Muller, Seth. Dubay, Tayloe, ed. 2010. (Keepers of the WindClaw Chronicles: Bk. 3). 224p. (J). pap. 12.95 *(978-1-893354-10-4(5))* Salina Bookshelf Inc.

—Learn along with Ashkii: First Grade Level 1. Ruffenach, Jessie E. et al. 2003. (NAV & ENG.). 16p. (J). (gr. -1-3). pap. 7.95 *(978-1-893354-41-8(5))* Salina Bookshelf Inc.

—Learn along with Ashkii: First Grade Level 2. Ruffenach, Jessie E. et al. 2003. (NAV & ENG.). 16p. (J). (gr. -1-3). pap. 7.95 *(978-1-893354-42-5(3))* Salina Bookshelf Inc.

—Learn along with Ashkii: Second Grade Level 1. Ruffenach, Jessie E. et al. 2003. (ENG & NAV.). 16p. (J). (gr. -1-3). pap. 7.95 *(978-1-893354-43-2(1))* Salina Bookshelf Inc.

—Learn along with Ashkii: Second Grade Level 2. Ruffenach, Jessie E. et al. 2003. (NAV & ENG.). 16p. (J). (gr. -1-3). pap. 7.95 *(978-1-893354-44-9(X))* Salina Bookshelf Inc.

—Learn along with Ashkii: Third Grade Level 1. Ruffenach, Jessie E. et al. 2003. (NAV & ENG.). 16p. (J). (gr. 4-7). pap. 7.95 *(978-1-893354-45-6(8))* Salina Bookshelf Inc.

—Learn along with Ashkii: Third Grade Level 2. Ruffenach, Jessie E. et al. 2003. (NAV & ENG.). 16p. (J). (gr. 4-7). pap. 7.95 *(978-1-893354-46-3(6))* Salina Bookshelf Inc.

—The Mockingbird's Manual. Muller, Seth. Tayloe, McConnell Dubay, ed. 2009. (Keepers of the WindClaw Chronicles: Bk. 1). (ENG.). 128p. (J). (gr. 4-7). pap. 12.95 *(978-1-893354-04-3(0))* Salina Bookshelf Inc.

Whitethorne, Bahe, Jr., jt. illus. see Whitethorne, Billy.

Whitethorne, Baje, Sr. Beauty Beside Me: Stories of My Grandmother's Skirts. Yazzie, Seraphine G. Ruffenach, Jessie Eve, ed. 2011. (NAV & ENG.). 32p. (J). (gr. -1-3). 17.95 *(978-1-893354-77-7(6))* Salina Bookshelf Inc.

Whitethorne, Baje. Little Black, a Pony: Liishzhiin Yazhi. Farley, Walter. Carr, Elsie, tr. 2006. (ENG & NAV.). 64p. (J). (gr. 4-7). 21.95 *(978-1-893354-90-6(3))* Salina Bookshelf Inc.

Whitethorne, Billy. The Navajo Year, Walk Through Many Seasons. Flood, Nancy Bo. 2006. (ENG.). 32p. (J). (gr. 4-7). 17.95 *(978-1-893354-06-7(7))* Salina Bookshelf Inc.

Whitethorne, Billy & Whitethorne, Bahe, Jr. The Navajo Year, Walk Through Many Seasons: Activities for Learning & Exploring. Flood, Nancy Bo. Ruffenach, Jessie E., ed. 2006. (ENG.). 48p. (J). (gr. 4-7). pap. 7.95 *(978-1-893354-98-2(9))* Salina Bookshelf Inc.

Whitfield, Christopher C. Khloe Can Be: A Police Officer. Auxier, Shannon. 2019. (Khloe Can Be Ser.: Vol. 1). (ENG.). 36p. (J). (gr. 1-3). pap. 10.99 *(978-1-7330602-0-2(0))* OZA.Inc.Co.

Whitfield, Eric. Sometimes, MS Is Yucky. Harrold, Kimberly. 2005. (ENG.). 40p. (J). pap. 12.95 *(978-1-59630-006-4(X)*, 1-59630-006-X) Science & Humanities Pr.

Whitfield, Eric T. Aunt Katie's Visit: A Child's First Book on Disabilities. Banister, Katie Rodriguez & Banister, Steve. 2003. (J). 16.99 *(978-0-9744908-0-9(6))* Access-4-All, Inc.

Whitfirld, Eric. Peggy: And Other Enchanting Character-Building Stories for Smar Boys Who Want to Grow up to Be Strong Men. Showstack, Richard. 2004. 200p. (YA). per. 14.95 *(978-1-888725-66-7(4)*, BeachHouse Bks.) Science & Humanities Pr.

W

Whiting, Sandra. Sir Waltie of Shoe. Shoemaker, Sharon. 2004. (J). per. 12.95 *(978-0-9759499-0-0(X))* Water Shoe Pr.

Whitlatch, Jessica A. A New Day - a New Beginning: All about a Day on the Farm. Dalton, Sherry A. 2011. 40p. pap. 24.95 *(978-1-4560-7462-3(8))* America Star Bks.

Whitler, Larry. The Chanteuse Sleigh Ride: Let Heaven & Nature Sing. Whitler, Larry. Macblane, Robin. 2019. (Robin & the Giant Ser.: Vol. 3). (ENG.). 32p. (J). (gr. k-4). 24.95 ***(978-0-578-55701-4(0))*** Robin & The Giant.

—The Chanteuse Sleigh Ride: Let Heaven & Nature Sing. Whitler, Larry. Macblane, Robin. 2019. (Robin & the Giant Ser.: Vol. 2). (ENG.). 32p. (J). pap. 9.95 ***(978-1-0887-4896-1(1))*** Independently Published.

Whitler, Larry. You Count, I Count: Your Life Has Purpose. Whitler, Larry. Macblane, Robin. 2019. (Robin & the Giant Ser.). (ENG.). (J). (gr. k-2). 64p. 29.95 *(978-0-578-46490-9(X))*; 66p. pap. 19.99 *(978-0-578-46579-1(5))* Robin & The Giant.

Whitley, Jason. The Kidzter Kids Meet Motown. Heyman, Bob. 2018. (ENG.). 98p. (J). pap. 8.99 *(978-1-7906-1988-7(2))* Independently Published.

Whitlock, Matt. Cranky Pants. Sanzo, Stephen. 2008. (ENG.). 32p. (J). 16.95 *(978-0-9759627-0-1(1))* Cranky Pants Publishing, LLC.

Whitlock, Matt. Punk 'n Patch. Whitlock, Matt. 2005. 32p. (J). (gr. -1-3). 16.95 *(978-0-9769057-0-7(1))* Little Hero.

—Punk's Christmas Carol: A Punk 'n Patch Book. Whitlock, Matt. 2006. 32p. (J). (gr. -1-3). 16.95 *(978-0-9769057-1-4(X))* Little Hero.

Whitlow, Stephen. Bedtime Prayers. Rainstorm Publishing, ed. 2018. (Tender Moments Ser.). (ENG.). 20p. (J). bds. 8.99 ***(978-1-926444-43-7(4))*** Rainstorm Pr.

Whitlow, Steve. God Bless My Boo Boo, 1 vol. Hall, Hannah C. 2015. (God Bless Book Ser.). (ENG.). 20p. (J). bds. 9.99 *(978-0-7180-3051-3(6))* Nelson, Thomas Inc.

—God Bless My Family, 1 vol. Hall, Hannah. 2017. (God Bless Book Ser.). (ENG.). 20p. (J). bds. 9.99 *(978-0-7180-9216-0(3))* Nelson, Thomas Inc.

—God Bless My Friends, 1 vol. Hall, Hannah. 2016. (God Bless Book Ser.). (ENG.). 20p. (J). bds. 9.99 *(978-0-7180-8953-5(7))* Nelson, Thomas Inc.

—God Bless My School, 1 vol. Hall, Hannah. 2017. (God Bless Book Ser.). (ENG.). 20p. (J). bds. 9.99 *(978-0-7180-1109-3(0))* Nelson, Thomas Inc.

—God Bless Our Baby, 1 vol. Hall, Hannah. 2017. (God Bless Book Ser.). (ENG.). 20p. (J). bds. 9.99 *(978-0-7180-8666-4(X))* Nelson, Thomas Inc.

—God Bless Our Bedtime Prayers, 1 vol. Hall, Hannah. 2018. (God Bless Book Ser.). (ENG.). 20p. (J). bds. 9.99 *(978-0-7180-9639-7(8))* Nelson, Thomas Inc.

—God Bless Our Country, 1 vol. Hall, Hannah. 2016. (God Bless Book Ser.). (ENG.). 20p. (J). bds. 9.99 *(978-0-7180-4017-8(1))* Nelson, Thomas Inc.

—God Bless Our Fall, 1 vol. Hall, Hannah C. 2015. (God Bless Book Ser.). (ENG.). 20p. (J). bds. 9.99 *(978-0-529-12333-6(9))* Nelson, Thomas Inc.

—God Bless You & Good Night, 1 vol. Hall, Hannah. 2018. (God Bless Book Ser.). (ENG.). 32p. (J). 16.99 *(978-1-4003-0897-2(6))* Nelson, Thomas Inc.

—God Bless You & Good Night Touch & Feel, 1 vol. Hall, Hannah. 2018. (God Bless Book Ser.). 18p. (J). bds. 9.99 *(978-1-4002-0923-1(4))* Nelson, Thomas Inc.

—Old MacDonald & Other Stories. 2011. (J). *(978-1-4508-2628-0(8))* Phoenix International Publications, Inc.

—The Story of Easter, 1 vol. Dowley, Tim & David, Juliet. ed. 2010. (ENG.). 24p. (J). (gr. k-2). bds. 7.99 *(978-1-85985-174-6(6)*, Candle Bks.) Lion Hudson PLC GBR. Dist: Kregel Pubns.

Whitman, Diana McManus. Finding Kyle Some Style, 1 vol. Guilmette, Patty. 2009. 32p. pap. 24.95 *(978-1-60703-962-4(1))* America Star Bks.

Whitman, Jennifer. Never Enough Frogs, 1 vol. Tessin, Kit Elaine. 2009. 19p. pap. 24.95 *(978-1-60836-185-4(3))* America Star Bks.

Whitman, Kailey. Under the Bodhi Tree: A Story of the Buddha. Hopkinson, Deborah. 2018. (ENG.). 32p. (J). 17.95 *(978-1-68364-153-7(1)*, 900220891) Sounds True, Inc.

Whitmire, Anna. Snowflake. Taylor, Clif. 2010. (J). *(978-1-886769-97-7(4))* Gold Leaf Pr.

Whitmore, Yvette. Dare to Be. . . Martin Luther King Jr. Alexander, Florence. 2003. (ENG & SPA.). 17p. (J). 3.99 *(978-0-915960-65-1(6))* Ebon Research Systems Publishing, LLC.

Whitney, Caffy. Small Talks on Big Questions Vol. 1: A Historical Companion to the Children's Catechism, 2 vols. Helms, Selah et al. 2003. 216p. 26.99 *(978-1-894400-02-2(X))* Joshua Pr., Inc. CAN. Dist: Gabriel Resources.

—Small Talks on Big Questions Vol. 2: A Historical Companion to the Children's Catechism, 2 vols. Helms, Selah & Thompson, Susan. 2003. 192p. 26.99 *(978-1-894400-05-3(4))* Joshua Pr., Inc. CAN. Dist: Gabriel Resources.

Whitney, Jennifer, photos by. Texas Hill Country Cuisine: Flavors from the Cabernet Grill Texas Wine Country Restaurant. Burtwell, Ross & Celeste Rosenfeld, Julia. 2014. (ENG., 196p. 34.95 *(978-0-9899450-0-4(6))* Creative Noggin.

Whitson, Andrew. Molly & the Stormy Sea. Doyle, Malachy. 2018. (ENG.). 36p. (J). (gr. -1-k). 21.99 *(978-1-912654-45-1(8))* Graffeg Limited GBR. Dist: Independent Pubs. Group.

—Molly & the Stormy Sea Postcard Pack. Doyle, Malachy. 2018. (ENG.). 36p. (J). (gr. k-2). 21.95 *(978-1-912654-52-9(0))* Graffeg Limited GBR. Dist: Independent Pubs. Group.

Whitson, Fred. My Beard. Thoolen, Jai D. 2018. (ENG.). 26p. (J). pap. *(978-0-6482030-3-2(4))* picklepoetry.

Whitt, Carlynn. Camp Wonderful Wild, 0 vols. Snyder, Laurel. 2013. (ENG.). 32p. (J). (gr. -1-3). 17.99 *(978-1-4778-1652-3(6)*, 9781477816523, Two Lions) Amazon Publishing.

—There's a Baby in There!, 0 vols. Mackall, Dandi Daley. 2012. (ENG.). 32p. (J). (gr. -1-3). 16.99 *(978-0-7614-6191-3(4)*, 9780761461913, Two Lions) Amazon Publishing.

Whitt, Shannon. Shakespeare's Seasons. Weiner, Miriam. 2012. (ENG.). 32p. (J). (gr. -1). 16.99 *(978-1-935703-57-0(9))* Downtown Bookworks.

Whittaker, Kay. The Imagineer (Fire Eye Edition) A Book of Miracles. Ashe, Gregory. 3rd ed. 2005. 198p. pap. *(978-1-905532-01-8(6))* Humdrumming, Ltd.

—The Imagineer (Snow Scene Edition) A Book of Miracles. Ashe, Gregory. 2nd ed. 2005. 198p. (YA). pap. *(978-1-905532-00-1(8))* Humdrumming, Ltd.

Whittaker, Stephen. The Crones. Blevins, James. 2008. 36p. pap. 24.95 *(978-1-60610-259-6(1))* America Star Bks.

Whittemore, Constance. The Lonesome Gnome. Hudson, Arthur K. 2011. 28p. pap. 35.95 *(978-1-258-09570-3(X))* Literary Licensing, LLC.

Whitten, Samantha & Lee, Jeannie. How to Draw Manga Chibis & Cute Critters. 2013. (Walter Foster Studio Ser.). 128p. (J). (gr. 3-8). 35.65 *(978-1-936309-93-1(9))* Quarto Publishing Group USA.

Whittingham, Kim. Six-Minute Nature Experiments. Brynie, Faith Hickman. 2006. 80p. (J). (gr. 4-8). reprint ed. pap. 11.00 *(978-1-4223-5105-5(X))* DIANE Publishing Co.

Whittingham, Wendy. Miss Wondergem's Dreadfully Dreadful Pie, 1 vol. Sherrard, Valerie. 2011. (ENG.). 32p. (J). (gr. k-5). pap. *(978-1-897174-81-4(0))* Breakwater Bks., Ltd.

Whittingham, Zane. Survivors of the Holocaust: True Stories of Six Extraordinary Children. Shackleton, Kath, ed. 2019. (ENG.). 96p. (J). (gr. 3-7). 19.99 *(978-1-4926-8892-1(4))*; pap. 14.99 *(978-1-4926-8893-8(2))* Sourcebooks, Inc. (Sourcebooks Jabberwocky).

Whittle, Jennifer. The Sling & the Stone. Babbage, Lisa Noel. Rhodes, Kim, ed. 2018. (Biblios Ser.: Vol. 1). (ENG.). 38p. (J). pap. 14.99 *(978-1-7200-3867-2(8))* Independently Published.

Whitty, Hannah. Little Bit of Love. Platt, Cynthia. 2011. (ENG.). 32p. (J). (gr. -1-2). pap. 7.95 *(978-1-58925-426-8(0))* Tiger Tales.

—A Little Bit of Love. Platt, Cynthia. 2011. (ENG.). 32p. (J). (gr. -1-2). 15.95 *(978-1-58925-095-6(8))* Tiger Tales.

Whitworth, Amber Harmon. Paddy o'Malley's Contrary Cow. Harmon, Coy Michie. 2019. (ENG.). 30p. (J). pap. 12.95 *(978-1-64300-868-4(4))* Covenant Bks.

Whitworth, Christy. Come Back, o Tiger! A Jataka Tale. 2012. *(978-1-60103-015-3(0))* Buddhist Text Translation Society.

Whitworth, John. Lizzy & Buster's Time for Fall. Whitworth, Melissa. 2019. (ENG.). 32p. (J). pap. 8.99 ***(978-0-578-59049-3(2))*** Brandrock Creative Co., The.

Who, Carrie Lou. Sean Michael K. Whistles the Wrong Way! Klitzner, Irene. 2011. (ENG.). 48p. 18.95 *(978-0-692-01275-8(3)*, 2f2eceb1-a00e-4f67-a99c-e6262ccfd9de) Attitude Pie Publishing.

Whyte, Alice. A Tree in the Garden: A New Vision. Oren, Miriam & Schram, Peninnah. 2004. vii, 55p. pap. *(978-0-9752958-0-9(2))* Nora Hse.

Whyte, Christen A., jt. illus. see Lopez, Daniela J.

Whyte, Hugh. Rock Steady: A Story of Noah's Ark. 2006. 28p. (J). (gr. k-4). reprint ed. 17.00 *(978-1-4223-5556-5(X))* DIANE Publishing Co.

Whyte, Mary. Chestnut, 1 vol. McGeorge, Constance W. 2004. (ENG.). 32p. (J). 16.95 *(978-1-56145-321-4(8))* Peachtree Publishing Co. Inc.

—I Love You the Purplest. Joosse, Barbara M. 2019. (ENG.). 24p. (J). (gr. -1 — 1). bds. 9.99 *(978-1-4521-7771-7(6))* Chronicle Bks. LLC.

Whytock, Cherry. My Cup Runneth Over: The Life of Angelica Cookson Potts. Whytock, Cherry. 2012. (ENG.). 192p. (YA). (gr. 7). pap. 9.99 *(978-1-4424-6055-3(5)*, Simon Pulse) Simon Pulse.

—My Scrumptious Scottish Dumplings: The Life of Angelica Cookson Potts. Whytock, Cherry. 2006. (ENG.). 192p. (YA). mass mkt. 5.99 *(978-0-689-86552-7(X)*, Simon Pulse) Simon Pulse.

Wiacek, Bob, et al. The Boston Massacre. Burgan, Michael & Hoena, Blake A. 2005. (Graphic History Ser.). (ENG.). 32p. (J). (gr. 3-9). 31.32 *(978-0-7368-4368-3(X)*, Capstone Pr.) Capstone.

Wiacek, Bob. More Simple Science Fair Projects: Grades 3-5. Tocci, Salvatore. 2006. (Scientific American Science Fair Projects Ser.). 48p. (J). (gr. 3-5). lib. bdg. 27.00 *(978-0-7910-9055-8(8))* Facts On File, Inc.

Wiberg, Harald. The Tomten, 30 vols. Lindgren, Astrid. 2nd rev. ed. (ENG.). 32p. (J). 17.95 *(978-0-86315-153-8(1))* Floris Bks. GBR. Dist: SteinerBooks, Inc.

Wichmann, Nadja. Am I Small? Li'ili'i Wau? English-Hawaiian: Children's Picture Book (Bilingual Edition) Winterberg, Philipp. Bezilla, Ku'ulei, tr. 2019. (GER.). 42p. (J). pap. 9.95 ***(978-1-7035-7047-2(2))*** Independently Published.

—Am I Small? Toho Do Ahu Geleng? English-Northern Batak/Pak-Pak Dairi: Children's Picture Book (Bilingual Edition) Winterberg, Philipp. Tampubolon, Marinaro, tr. 2019. (GER.). 42p. (J). pap. 9.95 ***(978-1-7035-7194-3(0))*** Independently Published.

—Bin Ich Klein? Amʊn Naa Saa Gʊŋɛ Aà? Deutsch-Anii/Gisida/Bassila/Baseca/Winji-Winji/Ouinji-Ouinji: Zweisprachiges Bilderbuch Zum Vorlesen F�r Kinder Ab 2 Jahren. Kiki, Castrio & Faith, Casty, trs. 2019. (GER.). 42p. (J). pap. 11.99 ***(978-1-7036-6637-3(2))*** Independently Published.

—Bin Ich Klein? انا زشعتا؟ Deutsch-Aram�isch/Ostaram�isch/Mand�isch: Zweisprachiges Bilderbuch Zum Vorlesen F�r Kinder Ab 2 Jahren. Winterberg, Philipp. Al-Saadi, Qais, tr. 2019. (GER.). 42p. (J). pap. 11.99 ***(978-1-7036-6634-2(8))*** Independently Published.

—Bin Ich Klein? ڪيا مئين ننڍڙي هان؟ Deutsch-Lahnda/Saraiki/Siraiki: Zweisprachiges Bilderbuch Zum Vorlesen F�r Kinder Ab 2 Jahren. Karachvi, Liaqat & Ahmad, Hafiz Shabbir, trs. 2019. (GER.). 42p. (J). pap. 11.99 ***(978-1-7036-6631-1(3))*** Independently Published.

—Bin Ich Klein? B�nn Ick L�dderk? Deutsch-Niederdeutsch/Plattdeutsch/Emsl�ndisches Platt: Zweisprachiges Bilderbuch Zum Vorlesen F�r Kinder Ab 2 Jahren. Winterberg, Philipp. Spiekermann, Helmut, tr. 2019. (GER.). 42p. (J). pap. 11.99 ***(978-1-7036-6630-4(5))*** Independently Published.

—Bin Ich Klein? Lau Be Maraki A? Deutsch-Hiri Motu/Police Motu/Motu Pidgin: Zweisprachiges Bilderbuch Zum Vorlesen F�r Kinder Ab 2 Jahren. Harper, Joshua & Rumbaoa, Voltaire, trs. 2019. (GER.). 42p. (J). pap. 11.99 ***(978-1-7036-6633-5(X))*** Independently Published.

—Bin Ich Klein? Li'ili'i Wau? Deutsch-Hawaiisch/Hawaiianisch: Zweisprachiges Bilderbuch Zum Vorlesen F�r Kinder Ab 2 Jahren. Winterberg, Philipp. Bezilla, Ku'ulei, tr. 2019. (GER.). 42p. (J). pap. 11.99 ***(978-1-7036-6635-9(6))*** Independently Published.

—Bin Ich Klein? Mi Liklik? Deutsch-Tok Pisin/Neuguinea-Pidgin: Zweisprachiges Bilderbuch Zum Vorlesen F�r Kinder Ab 2 Jahren. Sato, Naoyuki & Rupavele, Jimmy, trs. 2019. (GER.). 42p. (J). pap. 11.99 ***(978-1-7036-6627-4(5))*** Independently Published.

—Bin Ich Klein? Toho Do Ahu Geleng? Deutsch-N�rdliches Batak/Pak-Pak Dairi/Batak Dairi: Zweisprachiges Bilderbuch Zum Vorlesen F�r Kinder Ab 2 Jahren. Winterberg, Philipp. Tampubolon, Marinaro, tr. 2019. (GER.). 42p. (J). pap. 11.99 ***(978-1-7036-6628-1(3))*** Independently Published.

—Je Suis Petite, Moi ? Amʊn Naa Saa Gʊŋɛ Aà? Un Livre d'images Pour les Enfants (Edition Bilingue Fran�ais-Anii) Wuillemin, Laurence & Kiki, Castrio, trs. 2019. (FRE.). 42p. (J). pap. 11.99 ***(978-1-7037-5122-2(1))*** Independently Published.

—Je Suis Petite, Moi ? انا زشعتا؟ Un Livre d'images Pour les Enfants (Edition Bilingue Fran�ais-Aram�en) Wuillemin, Laurence & Al-Saadi, Qais, trs. 2019. (FRE.). 42p. (J). pap. 11.99 ***(978-1-7037-5124-6(8))*** Independently Published.

—Je Suis Petite, Moi ? ڪيا مئين ننڍڙي هان؟ Un Livre d'images Pour les Enfants (Edition Bilingue Fran�ais-Seraiki/saraiki/siraiki) Wuillemin, Laurence & Karachvi, Liaqat, trs. 2019. (FRE.). 42p. (J). pap. 11.99 ***(978-1-7037-5126-0(4))*** Independently Published.

—Je Suis Petite, Moi ? B�nn Ick L�dderk? Un Livre d'images Pour les Enfants (Edition Bilingue Fran�ais-Bas Allemand) Wuillemin, Laurence & Spiekermann, Helmut, trs. 2019. (FRE.). 42p. (J). pap. 11.99 ***(978-1-7037-5127-7(2))*** Independently Published.

—Je Suis Petite, Moi ? Lau Be Maraki A? Un Livre d'images Pour les Enfants (Edition Bilingue Fran�ais-Hiri Motu) Wuillemin, Laurence & Harper, Joshua, trs. 2019. (FRE.). 42p. (J). pap. 11.99 ***(978-1-7037-5125-3(6))*** Independently Published.

—Je Suis Petite, Moi ? Li'ili'i Wau? Un Livre d'images Pour les Enfants (Edition Bilingue Fran�ais-Hawa�en) Wuillemin, Laurence & Bezilla, Ku'ulei, trs. 2019. (FRE.). 42p. (J). pap. 11.99 ***(978-1-7037-5123-9(X))*** Independently Published.

—Je Suis Petite, Moi ? Toho Do Ahu Geleng? Un Livre d'images Pour les Enfants (Edition Bilingue Fran�ais-Batak/batak Dairi) Wuillemin, Laurence & Tampubolon, Marinaro, trs. 2019. (FRE.). 42p. (J). pap. 11.99 ***(978-1-7037-5128-4(0))*** Independently Published.

Wichterich, Joshua. Naseem's Journey. Farmay, Anjuli. 2019. (ENG.). 38p. (J). pap. 9.99 *(978-1-9861-1980-1(7))* CreateSpace Independent Publishing Platform.

Wicinas, Tami. Nathan Hale: America's First Spy. Derr, Aaron. 2018. (Hidden History — Spies Ser.). (ENG.). 32p. (J). (gr. 2-5). pap. 8.99 *(978-1-63440-296-5(0))*; lib. bdg. 26.65 *(978-1-63440-282-8(0))* Red Chair Pr.

Wick, Walter. A Christmas Tree. Marzollo, Jean. 2010. (I Spy Ser.). (ENG.). 24p. (J). (gr. -1-3). 9.99 *(978-0-545-22092-7(0)*, Cartwheel Bks.) Scholastic, Inc.

—Four Picture Riddle Books. Marzollo, Jean. 2005. (Scholastic Reader Level 1 Ser.). (ENG.). 128p. (J). (gr. -1-3). 6.99 *(978-0-439-76309-7(6)*, Cartwheel Bks.) Scholastic, Inc.

—I Spy A to Z. Marzollo, Jean. 2009. (I Spy Ser.). (ENG.). 56p. (J). (gr. -1-3). 13.99 *(978-0-545-10782-2(2)*, Cartwheel Bks.) Scholastic, Inc.

—I Spy Christmas: a Book of Picture Riddles. Marzollo, Jean. 2019. (I Spy Ser.). 40p. (J). (gr. -1-k). 14.99 *(978-1-338-33258-2(9)*, Cartwheel Bks.) Scholastic, Inc.

—I Spy Funny Teeth. Marzollo, Jean. 2003. (Scholastic Reader, Level 1 Ser.). (ENG.). 32p. (J). (gr. -1-3). pap. 3.99 *(978-0-439-52472-8(5)*, Cartwheel Bks.) Scholastic, Inc.

—I Spy Imagine That! Marzollo, Jean & Scholastic / LeapFrog. 2008. (J). 13.99 *(978-1-59319-933-3(3))* LeapFrog Enterprises, Inc.

—I Spy Lightning in the Sky. Marzollo, Jean. 2005. (Scholastic Reader Level 1 Ser.). 32p. (J). (gr. -1-3). pap. 3.99 *(978-0-439-68052-3(2)*, Cartwheel Bks.) Scholastic, Inc.

—I Spy Little Hearts. Marzollo, Jean. 2009. (I Spy Ser.). (ENG.). 26p. (J). (gr. -1-k). bds. 6.99 *(978-0-545-08917-3(4)*, Cartwheel Bks.) Scholastic, Inc.

—Little Bunnies. Marzollo, Jean. 2006. (I Spy Ser.). (ENG.). 24p. (J). (gr. k — 1). bds. 6.99 *(978-0-439-78535-8(9)*, Cartwheel Bks.) Scholastic, Inc.

—School Bus. Marzollo, Jean. 2003. (Scholastic Reader, Level 1 Ser.). (ENG.). 32p. (J). (gr. -1-3). pap. 3.99 *(978-0-439-52473-5(3)*, Cartwheel Bks.) Scholastic, Inc.

—Spooky Night: A Book of Picture Riddles. Marzollo, Jean. 2019. (I Spy Ser.). (ENG.). 40p. (J). (gr. -1-3). 14.99 *(978-1-338-35313-6(6)*, Cartwheel Bks.) Scholastic, Inc.

Wick, Walter. Can You See What I See? - Christmas. Wick, Walter. 2008. (Scholastic Reader Level 1 Ser.). (ENG.). 32p. (J). (gr. -1-3). pap. 3.99 *(978-0-545-07887-0(3))* Scholastic, Inc.

—Can You See What I See? Big Book of Search-and-Find Fun. Wick, Walter. 2016. (Can You See What I See? Ser.). (ENG.). 160p. (J). (gr. k-2). 12.99 *(978-0-545-83863-4(0)*, Cartwheel Bks.) Scholastic, Inc.

—Christmas Board Book (Can You See What I See?) Wick, Walter. 2015. (Can You See What I See? Ser.). (ENG.). 24p. (J). (gr. -1-k). bds. 6.99 *(978-0-545-83183-3(0)*, Cartwheel Bks.) Scholastic, Inc.

—On a Scary Scary Night: Picture Puzzles to Search & Solve. Wick, Walter. 2008. (Can You See What I See? Ser.). (ENG.). 40p. (J). (gr. -1-3). 13.99 *(978-0-439-70870-8(2))* Scholastic, Inc.

—Optical Tricks. Wick, Walter. 10th anniv. ed. 2008. (ENG.). 48p. (J). (gr. -1-3). 14.99 *(978-0-439-85520-4(9)*, Cartwheel Bks.) Scholastic, Inc.

—Picture Puzzles to Search & Solve. Wick, Walter. 2004. (Can You See What I See? Ser.). (ENG.). 40p. (J). (gr. -1-18). 13.99 *(978-0-439-61772-7(3)*, Cartwheel Bks.) Scholastic, Inc.

—A Ray of Light. Wick, Walter. 2019. (ENG.). 40p. (J). (gr. 1-3). 17.99 *(978-0-439-16587-7(3)*, Scholastic Pr.) Scholastic, Inc.

—Seymour & the Juice Box Boat. Wick, Walter. 2004. (Can You See What I See? Ser.). (ENG.). 32p. (J). (gr. -1-k). 10.99 *(978-0-439-61778-9(2)*, Cartwheel Bks.) Scholastic, Inc.

Wick, Walter. I Spy Adventure: 4 Picture Riddle Books. Wick, Walter, photos by. Marzollo, Jean. 2012. (J). *(978-1-4351-3984-8(4))* Scholastic, Inc.

—I Spy Little Toys. Wick, Walter, photos by. Marzollo, Jean. 2011. (I Spy Ser.). (ENG.). 26p. (J). (gr. -1-k). bds. 6.99 *(978-0-545-22096-5(3))* Scholastic, Inc.

Wick, Walter, photos by. C'est Moi l'Espion: Défis Suprêmes! Marzollo, Jean. Duchesne, Lucie, tr. (I Spy Bks.).Tr. of I Spy Fantasy. (FRE., 37p. (J). (gr. -1-3). pap. 16.99 *(978-0-590-24340-7(3))* Scholastic, Inc.

—C'est Moi l'Espion: Du Monde du Mystère. Marzollo, Jean. (I Spy Bks.).Tr. of I Spy Mystery: A Book of Picture Riddles. (FRE., 37p. (J). (gr. -1-3). pap. 16.99 *(978-0-590-24317-9(9))* Scholastic, Inc.

—I Spy: Interactive Sound Book of Picture Riddles. 2003. 30p. (J). 15.98 *(978-0-7853-8424-3(3))* Publications International, Ltd.

—I Spy a Candy Can. Marzollo, Jean. 2004. (Scholastic Reader Level 1 Ser.). (ENG., 32p. (J). (gr. -1-3). pap. 3.99 *(978-0-439-52474-2(1)*, Cartwheel Bks.) Scholastic, Inc.

—I Spy a Dinosaur's Eye. Marzollo, Jean. 2003. (Scholastic Reader Level 1 Ser.). (ENG., 32p. (J). (gr. -1-3). pap. 3.99 *(978-0-439-52471-1(7)*, Cartwheel Bks.) Scholastic, Inc.

—I Spy a Penguin. Marzollo, Jean. 2005. (Scholastic Reader, Level 1 Ser.). (ENG., 32p. (J). (gr. -1-3). pap. 3.99 *(978-0-439-73862-0(8)*, Cartwheel Bks.) Scholastic, Inc.

—I Spy a Pumpkin. Marzollo, Jean. 2006. (Scholastic Reader Level 1 Ser.). (ENG., 32p. (J). (gr. -1-3). pap. 3.99 *(978-0-439-73863-7(6)*, Cartwheel Bks.) Scholastic, Inc.

—I Spy a Scary Monster. Marzollo, Jean. 2005. (Scholastic Reader, Level 1 Ser.). (ENG., 32p. (J). (gr. -1-3). pap. 3.99 *(978-0-439-68054-7(9)*, Cartwheel Bks.) Scholastic, Inc.

—I Spy a Skeleton. Marzollo, Jean. 2010. (Scholastic Reader Level 1 Ser.). (ENG., 32p. (J). (gr. -1-1). pap. 3.99 *(978-0-545-17539-5(9))* Scholastic, Inc.

—I Spy an Egg in a Nest. Marzollo, Jean. 2011. (Scholastic Reader Level 1 Ser.). (ENG., 32p. (J). (gr. -1-2). pap. 3.99 *(978-0-545-22093-4(9)*, Cartwheel Bks.) Scholastic, Inc.

—I Spy Animals. Marzollo, Jean. 2012. (I Spy Ser.). (ENG., 32p. (J). (gr. -1-k). pap. 3.99 *(978-0-545-41583-5(7))* Scholastic, Inc.

—I Spy Letters. Marzollo, Jean. 2012. (I Spy Ser.). (ENG., 32p. (J). (gr. -1-k). pap. 3.99 *(978-0-545-41584-2(5))* Scholastic, Inc.

—I Spy Merry Christmas. Marzollo, Jean. 2007. (Scholastic Reader, Level 1 Ser.). (ENG., 64p. (J). (gr. -1-3). pap. 5.99 *(978-0-545-03945-1(2)*, Cartwheel Bks.) Scholastic, Inc.

—I Spy Nature. Marzollo, Jean. 2006. (J). *(978-0-439-80732-6(8))* Scholastic, Inc.

—I Spy Numbers. Marzollo, Jean. 2012. (I Spy Ser.). (ENG., 32p. (J). (gr. -1-k). pap. 3.99 *(978-0-545-41585-9(3))* Scholastic, Inc.

—I Spy Santa Claus. Marzollo, Jean. 2006. (Scholastic Reader, Level 1 Ser.). (ENG., 32p. (J). (gr. -1-3). per. 3.99 *(978-0-439-78414-6(X))* Scholastic, Inc.

—I Spy School. Marzollo, Jean. 2012. (Scholastic Reader Level 1 Ser.). (ENG., 32p. (J). (gr. -1-3). pap. 3.99 *(978-0-545-40281-1(6)*, Cartwheel Bks.) Scholastic, Inc.

—I Spy Spectacular: A Book of Picture Riddles. Marzollo, Jean. 2011. (I Spy Ser.). (ENG., 40p. (J). (gr. -1-3). 13.99 *(978-0-545-22278-5(8)*, Cartwheel Bks.) Scholastic, Inc.

—I Spy Thanksgiving. Marzollo, Jean. 2011. (Scholastic Reader Level 1 Ser.). (ENG., 32p. (J). (gr. -1-2). pap. 3.99 *(978-0-545-22094-1(7)*, Cartwheel Bks.) Scholastic, Inc.

—I Spy Ultimate Challenger! Marzollo, Jean. 2003. (I Spy Ser.). (ENG., 40p. (J). (gr. 2-5). pap. 13.99 *(978-0-439-45401-8(8)*, Cartwheel Bks.) Scholastic, Inc.

—Sticker Book & Picture Riddles. Marzollo, Jean. 2012. (I Spy Ser.). 400p. (J). (gr. -1-3). pap. 10.99 *(978-0-545-39074-3(5)*, Cartwheel Bks.) Scholastic, Inc.

Wick, Walter, photos by. Can You See What I See? 100 Fun Finds Read-and-Seek. Wick, Walter. 2009. (Scholastic Reader, Level 1 Ser.). (ENG., 32p. (J). (gr. -1-3). pap. 3.99 *(978-0-545-07888-7(1))* Scholastic, Inc.

—Can You See What I See? Animals. Wick, Walter. 2007. (Scholastic Reader Level 1 Ser.). (ENG., 32p. (J). (gr. -1-3). pap. 3.99 *(978-0-439-86227-1(2))* Scholastic, Inc.

—Can You See What I See? Night Before Christmas. Wick, Walter. 2005. (Can You See What I See? Ser.). (ENG., 40p. (J). (gr. k-3). 13.99 *(978-0-439-76927-3(2)*, Cartwheel Bks.) Scholastic, Inc.

—Once upon a Time: Picture Puzzles to Search & Solve. Wick, Walter. 2006. (Can You See What I See? Ser.). (ENG., 40p. (J). (gr. -1-3). 13.99 *(978-0-439-61777-2(4),* Cartwheel Bks.) Scholastic, Inc.

—Out of This World: Picture Puzzles to Search & Solve. Wick, Walter. 2013. (Can You See What I See? Ser.). (ENG., 40p. (J). (gr. -1-3). 13.99 *(978-0-545-24468-8(4),* Cartwheel Bks.) Scholastic, Inc.

—Toyland Express: Picture Puzzles to Search & Solve. Wick, Walter. 2011. (Can You See What I See? Ser.). (ENG., 40p. (J). (gr. 1-2). 13.99 *(978-0-545-24483-1(8))* Scholastic, Inc.

—Treasure Ship: Picture Puzzles to Search & Solve. Wick, Walter. 2010. (Can You See What I See? Ser.). (ENG., 40p. (J). (gr. -1-3). 13.99 *(978-0-439-02643-7(1),* Cartwheel Bks.) Scholastic, Inc.

Wickenden, Nadine. The Story of Jonah. 2006. 10p. (J). (gr. k-4). reprint ed. 8.00 *(978-0-7567-9923-6(6))* DIANE Publishing Co.

Wicker, Jo. Why Does God Pull Teeth? Owen, Denise. 2018. (ENG.). 28p. (J). (gr. k-5). pap. 8.95 *(978-1-945714-16-0(6))* Grateful Steps.

Wickham, Kimberly. Angels & Horses. 2007. 128p. per. 12.85 *(978-1-4251-0215-9(8))* Trafford Publishing.

—Summer of Magic Horses. 2007. 134p. 12.85 *(978-1-4251-3012-1(7))* Trafford Publishing.

Wicks, Maris. Astronauts: Women on the Final Frontier. Ottaviani, Jim. 2020. (ENG.). (J). 256p. pap. 19.99 *(978-1-62672-877-6(1),* 900176311); 176p. pap. 12.99 *(978-1-250-76003-6(8),* 900226992) Roaring Brook Pr. (First Second Bks.).

—Primates: The Fearless Science of Jane Goodall, Dian Fossey, & Biruté Galdikas. Ottaviani, Jim. 2013. (ENG.). 144p. (YA). (gr. 7). 22.99 *(978-1-59643-865-1(7),* 900098393, First Second Bks.) Roaring Brook Pr.

—Primates: The Fearless Science of Jane Goodall, Dian Fossey, & Biruté Galdikas. Ottaviani, Jim. 2015. (ENG.). 144p. (YA). (gr. 7). pap. 13.99 *(978-1-250-06293-2(4),* 900142635) Square Fish.

Wicks, Maris & Yan, Edison. Summer Brain Quest: Between Grades K And 1. Butler, Megan et al. 2017. (Summer Brain Quest Ser.). (ENG.). 160p. (J). (gr. k-1). pap. 12.95 *(978-0-7611-8916-9(5),* 18916) Workman Publishing Co., Inc.

Wicks, Maris, jt. illus. see Yan, Edison.

Wickstrom, Martin. Flying Test. Matson, Sara. 2020. (ENG.). 24p. (J). pap. ***(978-1-922374-98-1(9))*** Library For All Limited.

Wickstrom, Sylvie. Loose Tooth. Schaefer, Lola M. 2005. (My First I Can Read Ser.). (ENG.). 32p. (J). (gr. -1-3). pap. 4.99 *(978-0-06-052778-5(1))* HarperCollins Pubs.

Wickstrom, Sylvie K. Little Witch Learns to Read. Hautzig, Deborah. 2003. (Step into Reading Ser.). 48p. (J). (gr. k-3). pap. 4.99 *(978-0-375-82179-0(1),* Random Hse. Bks. for Young Readers) Random Hse. Children's Bks.

Wickstrom, Sylvie K. Loose Tooth. Wickstrom, Sylvie K., tr. Schaefer, Lola M. 2004. (My First I Can Read Bks.). 32p. (J). (gr. -1-18). 14.99 *(978-0-06-052776-1(5))* HarperCollins Pubs.

Wickstrom, Thor. Book Fair Day. Plourde, Lynn. 2006. (J). *(978-1-4156-8095-7(7),* Dutton Juvenile) Penguin Publishing Group.

Widdowson, Dan, et al. Fairy Tale Mix-Ups. Epelbaum, Mariano & Harrison, Paul. 2016. (Fairy Tale Mix-Ups Ser.). (ENG.). 24p. (J). (gr. k-2). lib. bdg., lib. bdg., lib. bdg. 95.96 *(978-1-4109-8325-1(0),* Raintree) Capstone.

Widdowson, Dan. The Frog Prince Saves Sleeping Beauty. Guillain, Charlotte. 2016. (Fairy Tale Mix-Ups Ser.). (ENG.). 24p. (J). (gr. k-2). lib. bdg. 23.99 *(978-1-4109-8302-2(1),* Raintree) Capstone.

Widdowson, Kay. Alpaca Bag. Howell, Mae Q. 2020. (Fun with Animals Ser.). (ENG.). 14p. (J). (gr. k-2). bds. 8.99 *(978-1-4867-1811-5(6),* b6e0130e-9600-4873-ad04-8b11e61c2fca) Flowerpot Pr.

—A Bear Hug at Bedtime. Novotny-Hunter, Jana. 2017. (Child's Play Library). 32p. (J). (ENG.). *(978-1-84643-987-2(6));* pap. *(978-1-84643-988-9(4))* Child's Play International Ltd.

—The Forest Man: The True Story of Jadav Payeng. Matheson, Anne. 2020. (ENG.). 40p. (J). (gr. k-2). 16.99 *(978-1-4867-1816-0(7),* a0838ba4-dd1d-47e8-bc0b-f9ed54b38475) Flowerpot Pr.

—Getting Dressed. Brooks, Felicity. 2010. (Sticker Bks). 16p. (J). pap. 6.99 *(978-0-7945-2668-9(3),* Usborne) EDC Publishing.

—Getting Dressed Magnet Book. Brooks, Felicity. 2009. (Magnet Bks). 10p. (J). bds. 19.99 *(978-0-7945-2356-5(0),* Usborne) EDC Publishing.

—I Can Go to School: An I-Can-Do-It Book. Segal, Douglas. 2007. (ENG.). 10p. (J). (gr. -1-k). bds. 10.95 *(978-1-58117-594-3(9),* Intervisual/Piggy Toes) Bendon, Inc.

—Journey Begins: A Journey Through the Bible with Caravan Bear & Friends. Rowlands, Avril. ed. 2018. (Animals' Caravan Ser.). (ENG.). 144p. (J). pap. 8.99 *(978-0-7459-7756-0(1))* Lion Hudson PLC GBR. Dist: Independent Pubs. Group.

—The Journey Continues: Adventures Through the Bible with Caravan Bear & Friends. Rowlands, Avril. ed. 2019. (Animals' Caravan Ser.). (ENG.). 144p. (J). (gr. 1-3). pap. 7.99 *(978-0-7459-7811-6(8))* Lion Hudson PLC GBR. Dist: Independent Pubs. Group.

—Panda Kisses. Capucilli, Alyssa Satin. 2008. (Step into Reading: Step 1 Ser.). (ENG.). 32p. (J). (gr. -1-1). lib. bdg. 16.19 *(978-0-375-94562-5(8))* Random House Publishing Group.

—Panda Kisses. Capucilli, Alyssa Satin. 2008. (Step into Reading Ser.). 48p. (J). (gr. -1-1). pap. 4.99 *(978-0-375-84562-8(3),* Random Hse. Bks. for Young Readers) Random Hse. Children's Bks.

—The Stories Jesus Told: Adventures Through the Bible with Caravan Bear & Friends. Rowlands, Avril. ed. 2018. (Animals' Caravan Ser.). (ENG.). 144p. (J). (gr. 2). pap. 7.99 *(978-0-7459-7757-7(X))* Lion Hudson PLC GBR. Dist: Independent Pubs. Group.

—Tiny Tots Bible. Rock, Lois. ed. 2013. (Tiny Tots Ser.). (ENG.). 128p. (J). (gr. -1-k). 12.99 *(978-0-7459-6383-9(8))* Lion Hudson PLC GBR. Dist: Independent Pubs. Group.

—Tiny Tots Easter, 1 vol. Rock, Lois. ed. 2015. (Tiny Tots Ser.). (ENG.). 32p. (J). (gr. -1 — 1). 7.99 *(978-0-7459-6456-0(7))* Lion Hudson PLC GBR. Dist: Independent Pubs. Group.

Widdowson, Kay. What Jesus Did: Adventures Through the Bible with Caravan Bear & Friends. Rowlands, Avril. ed. 2020. (Animals' Caravan Ser.). (ENG.). 144p. (J). (gr. 2). pap. 8.99 ***(978-0-7459-7815-4(0),*** Lion Children's) Lion Hudson PLC GBR. Dist: Independent Pubs. Group.

Widdowson, Kay. Who Jesus Was: Adventures Through the Bible with Caravan Bear & Friends. Rowlands, Avril. ed. 2020. (Animals' Caravan Ser.). (ENG.). 144p. (J). (gr. 2-4). pap. 8.99 *(978-0-7459-7813-0(4),* Lion Children's) Lion Hudson PLC GBR. Dist: Independent Pubs. Group.

Wideman, Logan. Bo Jackson Trades at a Yard Sale. Wideman, Logan. 2019. (Bo Jackson Chapter Bks.: Vol. 3). (ENG.). 36p. (J). pap. 5.99 ***(978-1-7084-9081-2(7))*** Independently Published.

Widener, Leslie Stall. Chukfi Rabbit's Big, Bad Bellyache: A Trickster Tale. 2014. (ENG.). 40p. (J). (gr. k-5). 16.95 *(978-1-935955-26-9(8))* Cinco Puntos Pr.

Widener, Terry. America's Champion Swimmer: Gertrude Ederle. Adler, David A. 2005. (ENG.). 32p. (J). (gr. -1-3). reprint ed. pap. 7.99 *(978-0-15-205251-5(8),* 1195820) Houghton Mifflin Harcourt Publishing Co.

—The Babe & I. Adler, David A. 2006. 28p. (gr. 1-4). 18.00 *(978-0-7569-6560-0(8))* Perfection Learning Corp.

—The Babe & I. Adler, David A. 2004. (ENG.). 32p. (J). (gr. -1-3). reprint ed. pap. 7.99 *(978-0-15-205026-9(4),* 1195179) Houghton Mifflin Harcourt Publishing Co.

—Girl Wonder. Hopkinson, Deborah. 2015. 40p. pap. 8.00 *(978-1-61003-606-1(9))* Center for the Collaborative Classroom.

—Girl Wonder: A Baseball Story in Nine Innings. Hopkinson, Deborah. 2006. (ENG.). 40p. (J). (gr. k-3). reprint ed. 7.99 *(978-1-4169-1393-1(9),* Aladdin) Simon & Schuster Children's Publishing.

—My Name Is James Madison Hemings. Winter, Jonah. 2016. (ENG.). 40p. (J). (gr. k-4). 17.99 *(978-0-385-38342-4(8),* Schwartz & Wade Bks.) Random Hse. Children's Bks.

—Steel Town. Winter, Jonah. 2008. (ENG.). 40p. (J). (gr. -1-3). 19.99 *(978-1-4169-4081-4(2),* Atheneum Bks. for Young Readers) Simon & Schuster Children's Publishing.

—The Streak: How Joe Dimaggio Became America's Hero. Rosenstock, Barb. 2014. (ENG.). 32p. (J). (gr. 3-7). 17.99 *(978-1-59078-992-6(X),* Calkins Creek) Boyds Mills Pr.

—The Twins & the Bird of Darkness: A Hero Tale from the Caribbean. San Souci, Robert D. ed. 2004. (J). (gr. k-3). spiral bd. *(978-0-616-14625-5(6))* Canadian National Institute for the Blind/Institut National Canadien pour les Aveugles.

—Yogi: The Life, Loves, & Language of Baseball Legend Yogi Berra. Rosenstock, Barb. 2019. (ENG.). 48p. (J). (gr. 2-5). 17.95 *(978-1-62979-824-0(X),* Calkins Creek) Boyds Mills Pr.

—You Never Heard of Willie Mays?! Winter, Jonah. 2016. 40p. (J). (gr. -1-3). 7.99 *(978-1-101-93421-0(2),* Dragonfly Bks.) Random Hse. Children's Bks.

Widermann, Eva. Arctic Giants, 1 vol. Christopher, Neil. 2011. (ENG.). 128p. (J). (gr. 3). 24.95 *(978-1-926569-09-3(1))* Inhabit Media Inc. CAN. Dist: Consortium Bk. Sales & Distribution.

—The Giant Bear: An Inuit Folktale. Angutinngurniq, Jose. 2020. 32p. (J). (gr. 4-6). 10.95 *(978-1-77227-271-0(X))* Inhabit Media Inc. CAN. Dist: Consortium Bk. Sales & Distribution.

—The Orphan & the Polar Bear. Qaunaq, Sakiasi. 2019. 32p. (J). 10.95 *(978-1-77227-229-1(9))* Inhabit Media Inc. CAN. Dist: Consortium Bk. Sales & Distribution.

Widermann, Eva & Kubina, Monica. Hera. Grayson, Devin. 2018. (Star Wars: Forces of Destiny Ser.). (ENG.). 24p. (J). (gr. 4-9). lib. bdg. 27.07 *(978-1-5321-4293-2(5),* 31119, Graphic Novels) Spotlight.

Widjaja, Keny. The Moving Trees & Little Thieves: A Boy Detective Story. St Benedict, Oswald. 2019. (ENG.). 68p. (J). (gr. k-5). 18.00 ***(978-1-63337-320-4(7))*** Roland Golf Services.

Widowati, Marini. Just a Swim? Norman, Donna Marie. 2008. 29p. pap. 24.95 *(978-1-60672-182-7(8))* America Star Bks.

Wiede, Matt. Star, Circle, Baylor: A Little Bear Shapes Book, 5460 vols. 2013. (Big Bear Bks.). (ENG.). 18p. (J). (gr. 17). bds. 9.95 *(978-1-60258-979-7(8))* Baylor Univ. Pr.

—1, 2, 3 Baylor: A Little Bear Counting Book. Big Bear Books Staff. 2012. (Big Bear Bks.). (ENG.). 18p. (gr. 17). bds. 9.95 *(978-1-60258-660-4(8))* Baylor Univ. Pr.

Wiedemann, Katy. Anatomicum: Welcome to the Museum. Paxton, Jennifer Z. 2020. (ENG.). 112p. (J). (gr. 3-7). 35.00 ***(978-1-5362-1506-9(6),*** Big Picture Press) Candlewick Pr.

Wiedemer, Leah. Adventures with Pawpaw: China. Scimone, Diana. 2003. 32p. (J). 8.95 *(978-0-9729507-0-1(2))* Peapod Publishing, Inc.

—Adventures with Pawpaw: Costa Rica. Scimone, Diana. 2003. 32p. (J). 8.95 *(978-0-9729507-2-5(9))* Peapod Publishing, Inc.

—Adventures with Pawpaw: France. Scimone, Diana. 2003. (Adventures with PawPaw Ser.). 32p. (J). 8.85 *(978-0-9729507-1-8(0))* Peapod Publishing, Inc.

Wiegle, Matt. Romeo & Juliet. SparkNotes Staff. 2008. (No Fear Shakespeare Illustrated Ser.: 3). 216p. (gr. 5-7). per. 9.95 *(978-1-4114-9874-7(7),* Spark Notes) Sterling Publishing Co., Inc.

Wiehle, Katrin. Children's Dinosaur Atlas. Malam, John. 2017. (ENG.). 32p. (J). (gr. k-3). 16.95 *(978-1-68297-198-7(8))* QEB Publishing Inc.

Wienke, Mason. In My Feet: Mason's Clubfoot Story. Wienke, Mason. 2018. (ENG.). 26p. (J). pap. 15.00 *(978-1-7212-6373-8(X))* CreateSpace Independent Publishing Platform.

Wiens, Carl. Wild Buildings & Bridges: Architecture Inspired by Nature. Kaner, Etta. 2018. (ENG.). 40p. (J). (gr. 3-7). 17.99 *(978-1-77138-781-1(5))* Kids Can Pr., Ltd. CAN. Dist: Hachette Bk. Group.

Wiens, Laura. Blue Moon Eletermary. Joyce, Nik. Arnold, Janelle, ed. 2018. (ENG.). 60p. (J). *(978-1-5255-3194-1(8));* pap. *(978-1-5255-3195-8(6))* FriesenPress.

Wieringo, Mike. Fantastic Four, Vol. 1. Waid, Mark. 2004. (Fantastic Four Ser.). 368p. (YA). 29.99 *(978-0-7851-1486-4(6))* Marvel Worldwide, Inc.

Wieringo, Mike, et al. Fantastic Four by Waid & Wieringo Omnibus. 2018. (Fantastic Four by Waid & Wieringo Omnibus Ser.: 1). 896p. (YA). (gr. 8-17). 100.00 *(978-1-302-91382-3(4))* Marvel Worldwide, Inc.

Wieringo, Mike. Imaginauts. Waid, Mark. 2003. (Fantastic Four Ser.: Vol. 1). 144p. (YA). pap. 12.99 *(978-0-7851-1063-7(1))* Marvel Worldwide, Inc.

Wieringo, Mike, et al. Spider-Man by Todd Dezago & Mike Wieringo Vol. 1. 2017. (ENG.). 456p. (J). (gr. 4-17). pap. 39.99 *(978-1-302-90699-3(2))* Marvel Worldwide, Inc.

Wieringo, Mike. Unthinkable, 3 vols., Vol. 2. Waid, Mark. 2003. (Fantastic Four Ser.). 192p. (YA). pap. 17.99 *(978-0-7851-1111-5(5))* Marvel Worldwide, Inc.

Wieringo, Mike, jt. illus. see Cruz, Roger.

Wiersma, Lisa. A Day in the Sky. Maas, Manja. 2017. (ENG.). (J). (gr. k-2). *(978-94-92593-10-8(6))* Graviant Educatieve Uitgaven.

Wiese, Kurt. The Blue Mittens. Reely, Mary Katharine. 2011. 164p. 41.95 *(978-1-258-10114-5(9))* Literary Licensing, LLC.

—Freddy Goes to Florida. Brooks, Walter R. 2012. (ENG.). 224p. (J). (gr. 4-9). 11.99 *(978-1-59020-741-3(6),* 902741, Amulet Bks.) Abrams, Inc.

—Freddy the Detective. Brooks, Walter R. 2010. (ENG.). 272p. (J). (gr. 4-9). 11.99 *(978-1-59020-418-4(2),* 902418, Amulet Bks.) Abrams, Inc.

—Silver Chief's Revenge. O'Brien, Jack. 2011. 222p. 44.95 *(978-1-258-09709-7(5))* Literary Licensing, LLC.

—Stories of Jesus. Smither, Ethel L. 2012. 82p. 37.95 *(978-1-258-23282-5(0));* pap. 22.95 *(978-1-258-24854-3(9))* Literary Licensing, LLC.

Wiesner, Al. The Bubble Flight. Stoltz, Donald R. 2008. 26p. pap. 24.95 *(978-1-60672-994-6(2))* America Star Bks.

Wiesner, David. Gonna Roll the Bones. Leiber, Fritz. 2004. 32p. (J). 16.95 *(978-0-689-03591-3(8));* *(978-0-689-03637-8(X))* ibooks, Inc. (Milk & Cookies).

—Night of the Gargoyles. Bunting, Eve. 2014. 32p. pap. 8.00 *(978-1-61003-176-9(8))* Center for the Collaborative Classroom.

Wiesner, David. Fish Girl. Wiesner, David. Napoli, Donna Jo. 2017. (ENG.). 192p. (J). (gr. 5-7). pap. 17.99 *(978-0-547-48393-1(7),* 1439924, Clarion Bks.) Houghton Mifflin Harcourt Trade & Reference Pubs.

—Free Fall. Wiesner, David. 2008. (ENG.). 32p. (J). (gr. -1-3). 17.99 *(978-0-06-156741-4(8))* HarperCollins Pubs.

—Hurricane, 1 vol. Wiesner, David. 2008. (ENG.). 32p. (J). (gr. -1-3). 10.99 *(978-0-547-06433-8(0),* 1040022) Houghton Mifflin Harcourt Publishing Co.

Wiesner, William. The Gunniwolf. fac. ed. 2017. 32p. reprint ed. 16.95 *(978-1-62654-326-3(7))* Echo Point Bks. and Media.

Wigal, Mike. Green Anole Meets Brown Anole, a Love Story. Escott, Maria. 2010. 28p. pap. 12.95 *(978-1-936051-82-3(6))* Peppertree Pr., The.

Wiggan, Desmond, jt. illus. see Bates, Lindsey E.

Wiggins, Claudia. Caw. Wiggins, Keith & Burke, Jennifer. 2019. (ENG.). 36p. (J). pap. 11.99 *(978-1-7982-0533-4(5))* Independently Published.

Wiggins, Claudia. Maxdog's Christmas Adventure. Burke, Jennifer. 2019. (ENG.). 36p. (J). pap. 11.99 ***(978-1-0897-7107-4(X))*** Independently Published.

Wiggins, Margaret W. My Neighbor Is Gone. Wiggins, Leah Holder. 2006. 28p. (J). per. 17.99 *(978-0-9768579-5-2(2))* eVision, LLC.

—What was Grandma Doing? Hopkins, Nicolia. 2007. (J). per. 9.99 *(978-0-9768579-8-3(7))* eVision, LLC.

Wiggins, Mick. Boats Float! Lyon, George Ella & Lyon, Benn. 2015. (ENG.). 40p. (J). (gr. -1-3). 17.99 *(978-1-4814-0380-1(X))* Simon & Schuster Children's Publishing.

—Planes Fly! Lyon, George Ella. 2013. (ENG.). 40p. (J). (gr. -1-2). 18.99 *(978-1-4424-5025-7(8))* Simon & Schuster Children's Publishing.

—Trains Run! Lyon, George Ella & Lyon, Benn. 2019. (ENG.). 40p. (J). (gr. -1-3). 17.99 *(978-1-4814-8202-8(5))* Simon & Schuster Children's Publishing.

Wiggs, Sue. Wee-Dolph, the Tiniest Reindeer. Lester, Vivian. 22p. (J). (gr. -1-3). pap. 4.00 *(978-1-929785-01-8(1))* Connexions Unlimited.

Wight, Eric. The Adventures of Caveboy. Bardhan-Quallen, Sudipta. (Caveboy Ser.). 80p. (J). 2019. pap. 6.99 *(978-1-61963-987-4(4),* 900154210, Bloomsbury Children's Bks.); 2017. (ENG.). 9.99 *(978-1-61963-986-7(6),* 900154185, Bloomsbury USA Childrens) Bloomsbury Publishing USA.

—Caveboy Is a Hit! Bardhan-Quallen, Sudipta. 2017. (Caveboy Ser.). 80p. (J). 9.99 *(978-1-68119-047-1(8),* 900156895, Bloomsbury USA Childrens) Bloomsbury Publishing USA.

—Caveboy Is Bored! Bardhan-Quallen, Sudipta. (Caveboy Ser.). 80p. (J). 2019. pap. 6.99 *(978-1-68119-046-4(X),* 900156897, Bloomsbury Children's Bks.); 2017. (ENG.). 9.99 *(978-1-68119-045-7(1),* 900156896, Bloomsbury USA Childrens) Bloomsbury Publishing USA.

—Everyone Loves Bacon. DiPucchio, Kelly. 2015. (ENG.). 40p. (J). (gr. -1-1). 17.99 *(978-0-374-30052-4(6),* 900133345, Farrar, Straus & Giroux (BYR)) Farrar, Straus & Giroux.

—Everyone Loves Cupcake. DiPucchio, Kelly. 2016. (ENG.). 40p. (J). 17.99 *(978-0-374-30293-1(6),* 900152736, Farrar, Straus & Giroux (BYR)) Farrar, Straus & Giroux.

—The Incredible Twisting Arm, Bk. 2. Egan, Kate & Lane, Mike. 2014. (Magic Shop Ser.: 2). (ENG.). 160p. (J). (gr. 2-4). pap. 7.99 *(978-1-250-04044-2(2),* 900123920) Feiwel & Friends.

—Jinxed!, 1. Scaletta, Kurtis. 2012. (Topps League Stories Ser.). (ENG.). 112p. (J). (gr. 2-4). 18.69 *(978-1-4197-0286-0(6),* Amulet Bks.) Abrams, Inc.

—A Topps League Story: Book Three: Zip It! Scaletta, Kurtis. 2012. (Topps League Story Ser.). (ENG.). 112p. (YA). (gr. 2-4). pap. 5.95 *(978-1-4197-0437-6(0),* Amulet Bks.) Abrams, Inc.

—The Vanishing Coin. Egan, Kate & Lane, Mike. 2014. (Magic Shop Ser.: 1). (ENG.). 160p. (J). (gr. 2-4). pap. 5.99 *(978-1-250-04043-5(4),* 9781250040435) Feiwel & Friends.

Wight, Eric. Frankie Pickle & the Closet of Doom. Wight, Eric. (Frankie Pickle Ser.). (ENG.). 96p. (J). (gr. 2-5). 2010. pap. 5.99 *(978-1-4424-1304-7(2));* 2009. 9.99 *(978-1-4169-6484-1(3))* Simon & Schuster Bks. For Young Readers. (Simon & Schuster Bks. For Young Readers).

—Frankie Pickle & the Mathematical Menace. Wight, Eric. 2011. (Frankie Pickle Ser.). (ENG.). 96p. (J). (gr. 2-5). 10.99 *(978-1-4169-8972-1(2),* Simon & Schuster Bks. For Young Readers) Simon & Schuster Bks. For Young Readers.

—Frankie Pickle & the Pine Run 3000. Wight, Eric. 2010. (Frankie Pickle Ser.). (ENG.). 96p. (J). (gr. 2-5). 10.99 *(978-1-4169-6485-8(1),* Simon & Schuster Bks. For Young Readers) Simon & Schuster Bks. For Young Readers.

Wight, Joseph & Espinosa, Rod. The Bombing of Pearl Harbor, 1 vol. Dunn, Joe. 2007. (Graphic History Ser.). (ENG.). 32p. (J). (gr. 3-8). 29.93 *(978-1-60270-074-1(5),* 9034, Graphic Planet - Fiction) Magic Wagon.

Wigley, Audrey Watson. The Boy & Girl Who Hated History. Igneri, David S. 2009. 44p. pap. 24.95 *(978-1-61546-828-7(5))* America Star Bks.

Wigmore, Kitty. James & the Pixie. Januarius & Botteley, Gerald. 2015. (ENG.). 50p. (J). (gr. 3-4). 24.95 *(978-1-78455-540-5(1),* 413e02d1-a62c-4c9a-8c6d-577ea252da53); pap. 13.95 *(978-1-78455-538-2(X),* 5266cc26-3339-496c-b472-7d85a8ea4888) Austin Macauley Pubs. Ltd. GBR. Dist: Baker & Taylor Publisher Services (BTPS).

Wigsby, Nick. The Truth (and Myths) about Creepy Places. Peacock, L. A. 2015. 96p. (J). *(978-0-545-83026-3(5))* Scholastic, Inc.

—The Truth (and Myths) about Sea Monsters. Peacock, L. A. 2015. 93p. (J). pap. *(978-0-545-70566-0(5))* Scholastic, Inc.

—The Truth (and Myths) about Thanksgiving. Peacock, L. A. 2013. 89p. (J). pap. *(978-0-545-56846-3(3))* Scholastic, Inc.

—The Truth (and Myths) about the Human Body. Peacock, L. A. 2016. 96p. (J). pap. *(978-0-545-93146-5(0))* Scholastic, Inc.

—The Truth (and Myths) about the Presidents. Peacock, L. A. 2014. 94p. (J). pap. *(978-0-545-56848-7(X))* Scholastic, Inc.

Wijesiri, Tina. Place in the Chase: A Nerdi Bunny Brief. Toombs, Aisha. 2019. (ENG.). 36p. (J). (gr. k-3). pap. 11.99 *(978-1-7337947-3-2(5),* Brown Brainy Brilliant Bks.) InkDrops Publishing.

Wijesiri, Tina. Wanda's Wand. Kupfer, Debbie Manber. 2019. (ENG.). 32p. (J). pap. 9.99 ***(978-1-6958-6993-6(1))*** Independently Published.

Wijngaard, Caspar. Star Wars: Doctor Aphra Vol. 7: A Rogue's End. 2020. (ENG.). 128p. (YA). (gr. 4-17). pap. 17.99 *(978-1-302-91909-2(1))* Marvel Worldwide, Inc.

Wijngaard, Caspar & Farrell, Triona. Assassin's Creed Last Descendants - Locus. Edginton, Ian. 2017. (Assassin's Creed Ser.). 112p. (gr. 7). pap. 16.99 *(978-1-78276-313-0(9))* Titan Bks. Ltd. GBR. Dist: Penguin Random Hse. LLC.

Wijngaard, Juan. Cloud Tea Monkeys. Peet, Mal & Graham, Elspeth. 2010. (ENG.). 56p. (J). (gr. -1-3). 17.99 *(978-0-7636-4453-6(6))* Candlewick Pr.

Wik, Jenny. Ellis Goes to the Doctor. Reuterstrand, Siri. 2012. (ENG.). 24p. (J). (gr. -1-k). 12.95 *(978-1-61608-662-6(9),* 608662, Sky Pony Pr.) Skyhorse Publishing Co., Inc.

—Ellis Is Scared of the Dark. Reuterstrand, Siri. 2012. 24p. (J). (gr. -1-k). 12.95 *(978-1-61608-667-1(X),* 608667, Sky Pony Pr.) Skyhorse Publishing Co., Inc.

Wikland, Ilon. The Brothers Lionheart. Lindgren, Astrid. Morgan, Jill, tr. from SWE. 2004. 231p. (J). 17.95 *(978-1-930900-24-0(4))* Purple Hse. Pr.

—The Holy Night, 32 vols. Lagerlöf, Selma. 2004. (ENG.). 40p. (J). 17.00 *(978-0-86315-467-6(0))* Floris Bks. GBR. Dist: SteinerBooks, Inc.

—Mio, My Son. Lindgren, Astrid. Morgan, Jill, tr. from SWE. 2015.Tr. of Mio, Min Mio. (ENG.). 184p. (J). (gr. 3-7). 16.95 *(978-1-59017-870-6(X),* NYR Children's Collection) New York Review of Bks., Inc., The.

—Mio, My Son. Lindgren, Astrid. 2003.Tr. of Mio, Min Mio. 179p. (J). 17.95 *(978-1-930900-23-3(6))* Purple Hse. Pr.

—Mio, My Son. Lindgren, Astrid. Morgan, Jill, tr. 2019. (ENG.). 184p. (J). (gr. 3-7). pap. 11.99 *(978-1-68137-350-8(5),* NYRB Kids) New York Review of Bks., Inc., The.

Wilburn, Kathy. Bunny, Bunny. Hall, Kirsten. 2003. (My First Reader Ser.). (ENG.). 32p. (J). 18.50 *(978-0-516-22923-2(0),* Children's Pr.) Scholastic Library Publishing.

Wilburn, Kathy. Scrooge. 2020. (ENG.). 10p. (J). bds. ***(978-1-64269-249-5(2),*** 27024a64-a5b1-42cf-9dbe-3f13164057ca, Sequoia Publishing & Media LLC) Phoenix International Publications, Inc.

Wilcox, Brian. Full Moon. Wilcox, Brian. David, Lawrence. 2004. 30p. (J). (gr. k-4). reprint ed. 16.00 *(978-0-7567-7762-3(3))* DIANE Publishing Co.

Wilcox, Cathy. Always Jack. Gervay, Susanne. 2013. 148p. (J). *(978-1-61067-226-9(7))* Kane Miller.

—Being Jack. Gervay, Susanne. 2015. 167p. (J). *(978-1-61067-455-3(3))* Kane Miller.

—Being Jack. Gervay, Susanne. 2016. (ENG.). 192p. (J). pap. 5.99 *(978-1-61067-379-2(4))* Kane Miller.

W

—Super Jack. Gervay, Susanne. 2003. 192p. (978-0-207-19918-9(3)) HarperCollins Pubs. Australia.
—SuperJack. Gervay, Susanne. 2013. (ENG.). 192p. (J). pap. 5.99 (978-1-61067-129-3(5)) Kane Miller.
Wilcox, Chelsea. One Sunny Day. McDermott, Karen. 2019. (ENG.). 24p. (J). (978-0-6485378-4-7(6)) Serenity Press.
—One Sunny Day. MC Dermott, Karen. 2019. (ENG.). 24p. (J). pap. (978-0-6485489-8-0(8)) Serenity Press.
Wild, Gill. Reading Your Bible: A Starter's Guide. Childress, Gavin & Dooley, Audrey. 2005. 101p. (J). (gr. -1-7). per. 9.00 (978-1-903087-41-1(4)) DayOne Pubns. GBR. Dist: Send The Light Distribution LLC.
Wilde, Carol. The Bells of Freedom. Butters, Dorothy Gilman. 2008. (J). (gr. 4-6). 21.00 (978-0-8446-6162-9(7)) Smith, Peter Pub., Inc.
Wilde, Cindy, et al. Color with Mom. 2016. (ENG.). 96p. (J). (gr. 1-6). pap. 12.95 (978-1-4549-1931-5(0)) Sterling Publishing Co., Inc.
Wilde, George. Silver Heels: A Story of Blackfeet Indians at Glacier National Park. Christie, Caroline. 2011. 162p. 41.95 (978-1-258-00441-5(0)) Literary Licensing, LLC.
Wilde, Irma. The Christmas Puppy. Wilde, Irma. dePaola, Tomie. 2015. (G&d Vintage Ser.). 24p. (J). (-k). bds. 9.99 (978-0-448-48765-6(9), Grosset & Dunlap) Penguin Young Readers Group.
Wilde, Kristie. It's a Jungle in Here. Wilde, Kristie. 2018. (Joyful Creation Ser.: Vol. 3). (ENG.). 28p. (J). pap. 12.99 (978-0-9974828-2-9(6)) Wilde Art.
—Made for a Purpose. Wilde, Kristie. 2016. (Joyful Creation Ser.: Vol. 1). (ENG.). 24p. (J). pap. 12.99 (978-0-9974828-0-5(X)) Wilde Art.
Wildgoose, Chris. Nightwalker. Lu, Marie. 2019. 208p. (J). (gr. 7-9). pap. 16.99 (978-1-4012-8004-8(8), DC Ink) DC Comics.
Wildish, Lee. All Better: A Touch-and-Heal Book. Wilcox, Leigh Attaway. 2007. (ENG.). 12p. (gr. -1). 12.95 (978-1-58117-591-2(4), Intervisual/Piggy Toes) Bendon, Inc.
—Bears, Bears, Bears! Waddell, Martin. 2013. (J). (978-1-4351-4999-1(8)) Barnes & Noble, Inc.
—The Boy Who Cried Wolf. 2008. (I'm Going to Read® Ser.). 32p. (J). (gr. 1-2). pap. 3.95 (978-1-4027-5546-0(5)) Sterling Publishing Co., Inc.
—Dancing with the Dinosaurs. Clarke, Jane. 2012. (ENG.). 32p. (J). (gr. -1-2). 12.95 (978-1-936140-67-1(5)) Charlesbridge Publishing, Inc.
—Doughnuts for a Dragon. Guillain, Adam & Guillain, Charlotte. 2nd ed. 2015. (George's Amazing Adventures Ser.). (ENG.). 32p. (J). (gr. -1-k). pap. 10.99 (978-1-4052-7054-0(3)) Egmont Bks., Ltd. GBR. Dist: Independent Pubs. Group.
—How to Babysit a Grandma. Reagan, Jean. (How to Ser.). (ENG.). (J). (— 1). 2018. 26p. bds. 8.99 (978-1-5247-7256-7(9)); 2014. 32p. 17.99 (978-0-385-75384-5(5)) Random Hse. Children's Bks. (Knopf Bks. for Young Readers).
—How to Babysit a Grandpa. Reagan, Jean. (How to Ser.). (ENG.). (J). (— 1). 2018. 24p. bds. 8.99 (978-1-5247-7255-0(0)); 2012. 32p. 17.99 (978-0-375-86713-2(9)) Random Hse. Children's Bks. (Knopf Bks. for Young Readers).
—How to Catch Santa. Reagan, Jean. (How to Ser.). (ENG.). (J). 2018. 26p. (— 1). bds. 8.99 (978-0-525-57991-5(5)); 2015. 32p. (gr. -1-3). 17.99 (978-0-553-49839-4(8)); 2015. 32p. (gr. -1-3). lib. bdg. 20.99 (978-0-553-49840-0(1)) Random Hse. Children's Bks. (Knopf Bks. for Young Readers).
—How to Get Your Teacher Ready. Reagan, Jean. 2017. (How to Ser.). (ENG.). 32p. (J). (gr. -1-3). 17.99 (978-0-553-53825-0(X), Knopf Bks. for Young Readers) Random Hse. Children's Bks.
—How to Raise a Mom. Reagan, Jean. 2017. (How to Ser.). (ENG.). 32p. (J). (gr. -1-3). 17.99 (978-0-553-53829-8(2), Knopf Bks. for Young Readers) Random Hse. Children's Bks.
Wildish, Lee. How to Read to a Grandma or Grandpa. Reagan, Jean. 2020. (How to Ser.). 32p. (J). (gr. -1-3). 17.99 (978-1-5247-0193-2(9)); (ENG.). lib. bdg. 20.99 (978-1-5247-0194-9(7)) Random Hse. Children's Bks. (Knopf Bks. for Young Readers).
Wildish, Lee. How to Scare a Ghost. Reagan, Jean. (How to Ser.). (ENG.). (J). 2019. 26p. (— 1). bds. 8.99 (978-1-9848-4868-0(2)); 2018. 32p. (gr. -1-3). 17.99 (978-1-5247-0190-1(4)); 2018. 32p. (gr. -1-3). lib. bdg. 20.99 (978-1-5247-0191-8(2)) Random Hse. Children's Bks. (Knopf Bks. for Young Readers).
—How to Surprise a Dad. Reagan, Jean. 2019. (How to Ser.). (ENG.). 26p. (J). (— 1). bds. 8.99 (978-1-9848-4959-5(X), Knopf Bks. for Young Readers) Random Hse. Children's Bks.
—Jellybeans for Giants. Guillain, Adam & Guillain, Charlotte. 2018. (George's Amazing Adventures Ser.). (ENG.). 32p. (J). (gr. -1-k). pap. 10.99 (978-1-4052-8524-7(9)) Egmont Bks., Ltd. GBR. Dist: Independent Pubs. Group.
—The KnitWits Make a Move! Frost, Michael, photos by. Tabby, Abigail. 2013. (ENG.). 32p. (J). (gr. -1-1). 14.99 (978-1-4424-5342-5(7), Little Simon) Little Simon.
—Leave Me Alone: A Tale of What Happens When You Stand up to a Bully. Gray, Kes. 2011. 32p. (J). (gr. k-2). pap. 8.99 (978-0-7641-4736-4(6), B.E.S. Publishing) Peterson's.
—Lizzy Mcdizzy & the Busy Dizzy Day. Weeks, Sarah. 2019. (ENG.). 32p. (J). (gr. -1-3). 17.99 (978-0-06-244205-5(8)) HarperCollins Pubs.
—Muffins for Mummies. Guillain, Charlotte & Guillain, Adam. 2017. (George's Amazing Adventures Ser.). (ENG.). 32p. (J). (gr. -1-k). pap. 10.99 (978-1-4052-7363-3(1)) Egmont Bks., Ltd. GBR. Dist: Independent Pubs. Group.
—Noisy Monsters. Greenwell, Jessica. 2010. (Busy Sounds Board Bks). 10p. (J). bds. 18.99 (978-0-7945-2769-3(8), Usborne) EDC Publishing.
—Noisy Zoo. Taplin, Sam. 2009. (Busy Sounds Board Book Ser.). 10p. (J). (gr. -1). bds. 18.99 (978-0-7945-2517-0(2), Usborne) EDC Publishing.
—Runaway Booger. Richtel, Matt. 2017. (ENG.). 32p. (J). (gr. -1-3). 14.99 (978-0-06-234984-2(8)) HarperCollins Pubs.
—Socks for Santa. Guillain, Adam & Guillain, Charlotte. 2nd ed. 2016. (George's Amazing Adventures Ser.). (ENG.). 32p. (J). (gr. -1-k). pap. 10.99 (978-1-4052-7055-7(1)) Egmont Bks., Ltd. GBR. Dist: Independent Pubs. Group.
—Sólo para Chicas: ¿Qué Me Está Pasando? Mi Pubertad. Delmege, Sarah. Paragon Books, ed. 2019. (SPA.). 96p. (YA). (gr. 4-9). 7.99 (978-1-68052-569-4(7), 2002110-SLA, Paragon Books) Cottage Door Pr.
—Spaghetti with the Yeti. Guillain, Charlotte & Guillain, Adam. 2nd ed. 2014. (George's Amazing Adventures Ser.). (ENG.). 32p. (J). (gr. -1-k). pap. 10.99 (978-1-4052-6351-1(2)) Egmont Bks., Ltd. GBR. Dist: Independent Pubs. Group.
—Thomas & the Dragon Queen. Crum, Shutta. 2013. (ENG.). 272p. (J). (gr. 4-6). 21.19 (978-0-375-85703-4(6)) Random House Publishing Group.
—Thomas & the Dragon Queen. Crum, Shutta. 2011. 272p. (J). (gr. 3-7). 6.99 (978-0-375-84634-2(4), Yearling) Random Hse. Children's Bks.
—Treats for a T. Rex. Adam, Guillain & Guillain, Charlotte. 2nd ed. 2016. (George's Amazing Adventures Ser.). (ENG.). 32p. (J). (gr. -1-k). pap. 10.99 (978-1-4052-7362-6(3)) Egmont Bks., Ltd. GBR. Dist: Independent Pubs. Group.
Wildish, Lee, jt. illus. see Guillain, Charlotte.
Wildlife Conservation Society, photos by. Amazing Sharks! Thomson, Sarah L. 2006. (I Can Read Bks.). 31p. (gr. -1-3). 14.00 (978-0-7569-6957-8(3)) Perfection Learning Corp.
—Amazing Whales! Thomson, Sarah L. 2006. (I Can Read Bks.). (gr. -1-3). 14.00 (978-0-7569-6665-2(5)) Perfection Learning Corp.
Wildman, Andrew, et al. Spider-Man 2099 vs. Venom 2099. 2019. (ENG.). 280p. (YA). (gr. 8-17). pap. 39.99 (978-1-302-91621-3(1)) Marvel Worldwide, Inc.
Wilds, Kazumi. All about Japan: Stories, Songs, Crafts & Games for Kids. Moore, Willamarie. 2017. 64p. (J). (gr. 3-6). 14.95 (978-4-8053-1440-1(0)) Tuttle Publishing.
—The Peace Tree from Hiroshima: A Little Japanese Bonsai with a Big Story. Moore, Sandra. 2015. 32p. (J). (gr. 2-6). 14.95 (978-4-8053-1347-3(1)) Tuttle Publishing.
—The Wakame Gatherers. Thompson, Holly. 2007. (Wakame Gatherers Ser.). 32p. (J). (gr. -1-3). 16.95 (978-1-885008-33-6(3), Shen's Bks.) Lee & Low Bks., Inc.
Wildsmith, Brian. Les Animaux de la Ferme. 2005. (FRE & ENG.). 16p. (J). (gr. -1 — 1). per., bds. 5.95 (978-1-59572-032-0(4)) Star Bright Bks., Inc.
—Brian Wildsmith's Amazing Animal Alphabet Book, 1 vol. 2008. (ENG.). 32p. (J). 17.95 (978-1-59572-104-4(5)) Star Bright Bks., Inc.
—Brian Wildsmith's Animal Colors. 16p. (J). 2004. (ARA.). bds. 4.95 (978-1-932065-44-2(X), 718-784-9112); 2004. (VIE.). bds. 4.95 (978-1-932065-51-0(2)); 2003. (POR.). bds. 4.95 (978-1-932065-27-5(X), 1-718-784-9112) Star Bright Bks., Inc.
—Brian Wildsmith's Animals to Count. 16p. (J). 2004. (ARA.). bds. 4.95 (978-1-932065-45-9(8), 718-784-9112); 2003. (VIE.). bds. 4.95 (978-1-932065-16-9(4), 17187849112) Star Bright Bks., Inc.
—Brian Wildsmith's Farm Animals. 2003. 16p. (J). (POR.). bds. 4.95 (978-1-932065-20-6(2), 1-718-784-9112); (VIE.). bds. 4.95 (978-1-932065-21-3(0)) Star Bright Bks., Inc.
—The Cherry Tree. Ikeda, Daisaku. McCraughrean, Geraldine, tr. from JPN. 2013. 6.95 (978-1-935523-57-4(0)) World Tribune Pr.
—A Child's Garden of Verses: A Collection of Scriptures, Prayers & Poems, 1 vol. Stevenson, Robert Louis. 2008. (ENG.). 32p. (J). 19.95 (978-1-59572-057-3(X)) Star Bright Bks., Inc.
—Les Couleurs des Animaux. 2005. (FRE & ENG.). 16p. (J). (gr. -1). per., bds. 5.95 (978-1-59572-031-3(6)) Star Bright Bks., Inc.
—Over the Deep Blue Sea. Ikeda, Daisaku. McCraughrean, Geraldine, tr. from JPN. 2013. 6.95 (978-1-935523-59-8(7)) World Tribune Pr.
—The Princess & the Moon. Ikeda, Daisaku. McCraughrean, Geraldine, tr. from JPN. 2013. 6.95 (978-1-935523-58-1(9)) World Tribune Pr.
—The Snow Country Prince. Ikeda, Daisaku. McCraughrean, Geraldine, tr. from JPN. 2013. 6.95 (978-1-935523-60-4(0)) World Tribune Pr.
Wildsmith, Brian. Brian Wildsmith's Animals to Count (Traditional Cantonese), 1 vol. Wildsmith, Brian, . 2003. (CHI & ENG.). 16p. (J). 4.99 (978-1-932065-18-3(0), 1-718-784-9112) Star Bright Bks., Inc.
Wildsmith, Brian. Animal Colors. Wildsmith, Brian. 2004. (PER.). 16p. (J). bds. 4.99 (978-1-932065-42-8(3)) Star Bright Bks., Inc.
—Animals to Count. Wildsmith, Brian. 16p. (J). 2004. (PER.). bds. 4.99 (978-1-932065-43-5(1)); 2003. (CHI.). bds. 4.99 (978-1-932065-17-6(2), 1718-784-9112) Star Bright Bks., Inc.
—Bear's Adventure, 1 vol. Wildsmith, Brian. 2018. (ENG.). 32p. (J). 17.99 (978-1-59572-805-0(8)) Star Bright Bks., Inc.
—Brian Wildsmith's Amazing Animal Alphabet Book. Wildsmith, Brian. 2007. 32p. (J). pap. 8.95 (978-1-59572-111-2(8)) Star Bright Bks., Inc.
—Brian Wildsmith's Animal Colors, 1 vol. Wildsmith, Brian. 16p. (J). 2004. (NAV.). 4.99 (978-1-932065-34-3(2), 718-784-9112); 2003. (KOR.). 4.99 (978-1-932065-28-2(8), 1-718-784-9112); 2003. (ENG.). 4.99 (978-1-932065-30-5(X), 1-718-784-9112) Star Bright Bks., Inc.
—Brian Wildsmith's Animal Colors (Simplified Mandarin) Wildsmith, Brian. 2004. (CHI.). 16p. (J). bds. 4.95 (978-1-932065-52-7(0), 7187849112) Star Bright Bks., Inc.
—Brian Wildsmith's Animal Colors (Traditional Cantonese) Wildsmith, Brian. 2004. (CHI.). 16p. (J). bds. 4.99 (978-1-932065-53-4(9)) Star Bright Bks., Inc.
—Brian Wildsmith's Animal Gallery. Wildsmith, Brian. 2020. (ENG.). 48p. (J). (gr. -1-3). 18.99 (978-1-5362-1235-8(0)) Candlewick Pr.
—Brian Wildsmith's Animals to Count, 1 vol. Wildsmith, Brian. (J). 2009. (ENG.). 32p. bds. 4.99 (978-1-59572-128-0(2)); 2003. (ENG.). 16p. 4.99 (978-1-932065-13-8(X), 1718-784-9112); 2003. (TAG.). 16p. 4.99 (978-1-932065-31-2(8), 1-718-784-9112); 2003. (POR.). 16p. bds. 4.95 (978-1-932065-15-2(6), 17187849112) Star Bright Bks., Inc.
—Brian Wildsmith's Farm Animals, 1 vol. Wildsmith, Brian. 2003. 16p. (J). (KOR.). 4.99 (978-1-932065-19-0(9), 1-718-784-9112); (TAG.). 4.99 (978-1-932065-29-9(6), 1-718-784-9112) Star Bright Bks., Inc.
—Daisy, 1 vol. Wildsmith, Brian. 2018. (ENG.). 48p. (J). (978-1-59572-803-6(1)) Star Bright Bks., Inc.
—The Easter Story. Wildsmith, Brian. 2004. 24p. (gr. -1-7). 18.00 (978-0-8028-5189-5(4)) Eerdmans, William B. Publishing Co.
—Farm Animals (Simplified Mandarin), 1 vol. Wildsmith, Brian. 2003. (CHI & ENG.). 16p. (J). 4.99 (978-1-932065-22-0(9), 1-718-784-9112) Star Bright Bks., Inc.
—Farm Animals (Traditional Cantonese) Wildsmith, Brian. 2003. (CHI.). 16p. (J). bds. 4.99 (978-1-932065-23-7(7), 1-718-784-9112) Star Bright Bks., Inc.
—Hunter & His Dog, 1 vol. Wildsmith, Brian. 2008. (ENG.). 32p. (J). 16.95 (978-1-59572-123-5(1)) Star Bright Bks., Inc.
—Jesus. Wildsmith, Brian. 2004. 24p. (gr. 3-7). 20.00 (978-0-8028-5212-0(2)) Eerdmans, William B. Publishing Co.
—Jungle Party, 1 vol. Wildsmith, Brian. 2006. (ENG.). 32p. (J). pap. 6.95 (978-1-59572-053-5(7)) Star Bright Bks., Inc.
—The Little Wood Duck, 1 vol. Wildsmith, Brian. 2006. (ENG.). 32p. (J). pap. 6.95 (978-1-59572-049-8(9)) Star Bright Bks., Inc.
—The Owl & the Woodpecker, 1 vol. Wildsmith, Brian. 2006. (ENG.). 32p. (J). (gr. -1-3). 16.95 (978-1-59572-043-6(X)); pap. 6.95 (978-1-59572-050-4(2)) Star Bright Bks., Inc.
—Professor Noah's Spaceship, 1 vol. Wildsmith, Brian. 2008. (ENG.). 32p. (J). 16.95 (978-1-59572-124-2(X)) Star Bright Bks., Inc.
Wilenius, Mikael. Ratkaiseva Muuttuja. Wilenius, Aleksi. Mattila, Matti, ed. 2018. (FIN.). 218p. (J). pap. 15.95 (978-1-7200-2548-1(7)) Independently Published.
Wiles, Frank. The First Fifth Form. Smith, Evelyn. 2013. 176p. pap. (978-1-909423-05-3(X)) Bks. to Treasure.
—The Small Sixth Form. Smith, Evelyn. 2013. 200p. pap. (978-1-909423-08-4(4)) Bks. to Treasure.
Wiles, Pat. Isabelle Lives a Dream. Sundberg, Peggy. l.t. ed. 2003. (ENG.). 32p. (J). 11.95 (978-0-9721057-1-2(9)) Cowgirl Peg Enterprises.
—Jazmine's Incredible Story. Sundberg, Peggy. 2006. 32p. (J). 16.95 (978-0-9721057-5-0(1), Cowgirl Peg Bks.) Cowgirl Peg Enterprises.
—Okey-Dokey Oakie. Sundberg, Peggy. 2008. (ENG.). 32p. (J). 17.95 (978-0-9721057-9-8(4)); pap. 11.95 (978-0-9721057-7-4(8)) Cowgirl Peg Enterprises. (Cowgirl Peg Bks.).
—Stepping Stones to the Sun. Nawashani. 2013. 68p. pap. 11.95 (978-1-4787-0445-4(4)) Outskirts Pr., Inc.
Wiley, Alvin R. American Independence: The Spanish Secret. Wiley, Barbara Middleton & Strassner, Liz Duffy. 2020. (ENG.). 134p. (J). pap. 6.99 (978-1-9742-3184-3(4)) CreateSpace Independent Publishing Platform.
Wiley, Bee. El Pequeno Dragon. Aiken, Joan. 2004.Tr. of Wooden Dragon. (SPA.). (J). 18.99 (978-84-88342-52-2(7)) S.A. Kokinos ESP. Dist: Lectorum Pubns., Inc.
Wiley, Lisa Manuzak. All Except Axle. Gallion, Sue Lowell. 2020. (ENG.). 48p. (J). (gr. -1-3). 17.99 (978-1-5344-4022-7(4), Aladdin) Simon & Schuster Children's Publishing.
Wiley, Nancy. Alice's Adventures in Wonderland. Carroll, Lewis. 2009. 88p. 35.00 (978-0-615-29492-6(8)) OBrien, Wiley Workspace.
Wilf. Help! I've Lost My Llama. Warbrook, Colette. 2018. (ENG.). 36p. (J). pap. 9.13 (978-1-5396-7000-1(7)) CreateSpace Independent Publishing Platform.
Wilharm, Sabine. The Story of the Little Pig Who Couldn't Say No. Ludwig, Sabine. 2013. 32p. (J). (gr. -1-1). 16.95 (978-1-62087-684-8(1), 620684, Sky Pony Pr.) Skyhorse Publishing Co., Inc.
Wilhelm, Doris L. It Is Me. Rogers, Leslie E. 2011. 24p. pap. 24.95 (978-1-4626-4596-1(8)) America Star Bks.
Wilhelm, Hans. A Monster Is Coming! Harrison, David L. 2011. (Step into Reading Ser.). 32p. (J). (gr. -1-1). pap. 4.99 (978-0-375-86677-7(9), Random Hse. Bks. for Young Readers) Random Hse. Children's Bks.
—Wake up, Sun! Harrison, David L. 2006. (Step into Reading Ser.: Vol. 2). 32p. (gr. -1-1). 4.99 (978-0-394-88256-7(3)) Perfection Learning Corp.
Wilhelm, Hans. Buddy for President. Wilhelm, Hans. 2016. (ENG.). 32p. (J). (gr. -1-3). 17.99 (978-0-06-240366-7(4)) HarperCollins Pubs.
—Hello, Sun! Wilhelm, Hans. 2005. 32p. (gr. k-2). 15.25 (978-1-57505-348-6(9)) Lerner Publishing Group.
—I Love Rainy Days! Wilhelm, Hans. 2011. (Scholastic Reader Level 1 Ser.). (ENG.). 32p. (J). (gr. -1-2). pap. 3.99 (978-0-545-24503-6(6), Cartwheel Bks.) Scholastic, Inc.
—I Love School! Wilhelm, Hans. 2010. (Scholastic Reader Level 1 Ser.). (ENG.). 32p. (J). (gr. -1-k). pap. 3.99 (978-0-545-13474-3(9), Cartwheel Bks.) Scholastic, Inc.
—I Won't Share! Wilhelm, Hans. 2010. (Scholastic Reader Level 1 Ser.). (ENG.). 32p. (J). (gr. -1-2). pap. 3.99 (978-0-439-77353-9(9)) Scholastic, Inc.
Wilhelm, Lauren. Love Has Many Faces. Merker, Patricia D. 2011. (Grand Master/Little Master Ser.: Bk. 3). (J). pap. (978-1-921883-09-5(X)) Pick-a-Woo Woo Pubs.
—Sink or Swim. Merker, Patricia D. 2011. (Grand Master/Little Master Ser.: Bk. 2). 28p. pap. (978-0-9806520-7-9(3)) Pick-a-Woo Woo Pubs.
Wilkerson, Teresa. Piddle Diddle's Lost Hat: Adventures of Piddle Diddle, the Widdle Penguin. Major, Wayne A. & Major, Ralphine. 2015. (ENG.). (J). pap. 9.95 (978-1-939289-63-6(7), Little Creek Bks.) Jan-Carol Publishing, INC.
Wilkes, Larry. Folktales of Eastern Europe: The Flying Ship & Other Traditional Stories. 2019. 128p. (J). (gr. -1-12). 16.00 (978-1-86147-863-4(1), Armadillo) Anness Publishing GBR. Dist: National Bk. Network.
Wilkie, Sue. There's a Rat In This City. Unger-Pengilly, Elaine. Pengilly, Gordon, ed. 2017. (ENG.). (J). (978-1-4602-9942-5(6)); pap. (978-1-4602-9943-2(4)) FriesenPress.
Wilkin, Corban. Grand Theft Horse: A Graphic Novel. Neri, Greg. 2016. (YA). (978-1-4677-9463-3(5), Graphic Universe™) Lerner Publishing Group.
Wilkin, Eloise. Baby Listens. Wilkin, Esther. 2012. (Little Golden Book Ser.). 24p. (J). (gr. k-k). 4.99 (978-0-307-93012-5(2), Golden Bks.) Random Hse. Children's Bks.
—Baby's Christmas. Wilkin, Esther. 2017. (Little Golden Book Ser.). 24p. (J). (-k). 4.99 (978-1-5247-2051-3(8), Golden Bks.) Random Hse. Children's Bks.
—Baby's Christmas. Wilkin, Esther. 2012. (Golden Baby Ser.). 26p. (J). (gr. k — 1). bds. 6.99 (978-0-375-87058-3(X), Golden Bks.) Random Hse. Children's Bks.
—The Christmas ABC. Johnson, Florence. (Big Golden Board Book Ser.). 24p. (J). (-k). 2015. bds. 10.99 (978-0-553-52225-9(6)); 2013. 4.99 (978-0-307-97891-2(5)) Random Hse. Children's Bks. (Golden Bks.).
—Eloise Wilkin Stories. Golden Books. 2005. (ENG.). 224p. (J). (gr. -1-2). 12.99 (978-0-375-82928-4(8), Golden Bks.) Random Hse. Children's Bks.
—Wonders of Nature. Watson, Jane Werner. 2010. (Little Golden Book Ser.). 32p. (J). (gr. -1-2). 4.99 (978-0-375-85486-6(X), Golden Bks.) Random Hse. Children's Bks.
Wilkin, Eloise & Meisel, Paul. Little Golden Book Mommy Stories. Cushman, Jean et al. 2015. 80p. (J). (-k). 7.99 (978-0-385-39273-0(7), Golden Bks.) Random Hse. Children's Bks.
Wilkin, Eloise, jt. illus. see Catusanu, Mircea.
Wilkin, Eloise, jt. illus. see Gergely, Tibor.
Wilkins, Cristina Luz. Sueve: El Valiente Asturcón. Trias Trueta, Katy. 2018. (SPA.). 44p. (J). pap. (978-0-6483467-0-8(6)) Wilkins, Cristina Luz.
Wilkins, Wendy H. Timber Howligan Secret Agent Cat. Frederick, H. J. 2015. (J). pap. 8.99 (978-0-9964246-9-1(5)) Lionheart Pr.
Wilkinson, Annie. The Art Lesson: A Shavuot Story. Marks, Allison & Marks, Wayne. 2017. (ENG.). 32p. (J). (gr. -1-2). 17.99 (978-1-4677-8172-5(X), 9781467781725); E-Book 27.99 (978-1-5124-2720-2(9), 9781512427202) Lerner Publishing Group. (Kar-Ben Publishing).
—My Valentine. Cooke, Brandy. 2010. (ENG.). 12p. (J). (gr. -1 — 1). bds. 6.99 (978-1-4424-0779-4(4), Little Simon) Little Simon.
—Peter Pan. Barrie, J. M. & Ladybird Books Staff. 2015. (Ladybird Classics Ser.). 72p. (J). (gr. k-3). 11.99 (978-1-4093-1222-2(4)) Penguin Bks., Ltd. GBR. Dist: Independent Pubs. Group.
Wilkinson, Kate. Finding Monkey Moon. Pulford, Elizabeth. 2015. (ENG.). 32p. (J). (gr. -1-2). 15.99 (978-0-7636-6777-1(3)) Candlewick Pr.
Wilkinson, Nancy. Tucson Charlie: Lost in the Desert. Verity, Art. 2018. (Tucson Charlie Ser.: Vol. 1). (ENG.). 88p. (J). pap. 11.55 (978-1-64204-244-3(7)) Primedia eLaunch LLC.
—Tucson Charlie: Lost in the Zoo. Verity, Art. 2018. (Tucson Charlie Ser.: Vol. 2). (ENG.). 104p. (J). pap. 12.95 (978-1-68454-937-5(X)) Primedia eLaunch LLC.
Wilkinson, Richard. Historium. Nelson, Jo. 2015. (Welcome to the Museum Ser.). (ENG.). 112p. (J). (gr. 3-7). 35.00 (978-0-7636-7984-2(4), Big Picture Press) Candlewick Pr.
Wilkinson, Ron. That Happiness Thing: A Hometown Fable. White, Ken. 2016. (ENG.). 32p. (J). (gr. k-5). pap. 14.99 (978-0-9979291-0-2(3)) Kenneth B. White.
Wilkon, Jozef. Bonko. Schnell, Robert W. 28p. (J). (gr. -1-3). 12.95 (978-0-87592-008-5(X)) Scroll Pr., Inc.
Wilkon, Józef. The Little Wolves. Herrmann, Svenja. 2020. (ENG.). 40p. (J). (gr. -1-2). 17.95 (978-0-7358-4397-4(X)) North-South Bks., Inc.
Wilkon, Jozef. Tim, the Peacemaker. Friesel, Uwe. 32p. (J). (gr. -1-3). 13.95 (978-0-87592-052-8(7)) Scroll Pr., Inc.
Wilks, Mike. The Weather Works. Wilks, Mike. 2016. (ENG.). 32p. (J). 17.95 (978-0-7649-7538-7(2)) Pomegranate Communications, Inc.
Wilks, Peter. It's Your Turn Now: Politeness. Wilks, Peter, tr. Leaney, Cindy. 2003. 31p. (J). 28.50 (978-1-58952-735-5(6)) Rourke Educational Media.
Wilks, Seth. The Hatmaker. Wilks, Seth. 2018. (ENG.). 310p. (J). (gr. 3-6). (978-0-9940674-0-1(2)) Wilks, Seth.
Will, Clark Moor. Aurora, Daughter of the Dawn: A Story of New Beginnings. Kopp, J. J. 2012. (ENG.). 72p. (YA). (gr. 6-12). pap. 12.95 (978-0-87071-671-3(9)) Oregon State Univ. Pr.
Will, Heidi. The Ghillie Girls: Irish Dance Pals. Will, Heidi. 2008. 24p. (J). pap. 9.99 (978-0-9821065-0-1(5)) Cinealta Pr.
Willan, Alex. Revver the Speedway Squirrel. Rinker, Sherri Duskey. 2020. (ENG.). 208p. (J). 16.99 (978-1-5476-0361-9(5), 900212586, Bloomsbury Children's Bks.) Bloomsbury Publishing USA.
Willard, Mary. Hugs Are for Every One... Willard, Baron And Mary. 2013. 54p. pap. 19.99 (978-0-9896257-0-8(2)) Blue Botte.
Willardson, David, jt. illus. see Mason, Mark.
Willardson, David, jt. illus. see Rojas, Mary.
Willardson, David, jt. illus. see Valko, Diane.
Willcox Smith, Jessie. Une VISITE de ST. NICOLAS / a VISIT from ST. NICHOLAS (Edition Bilingue Illustr�e) C'�tait la Nuit Avant No�l / Twas the Night Before Christmas. Clement C Moore. Barry, ed. 2019. (FRE.). 52p. (J). pap. 29.95 (978-1-6512-1748-1(3)) Independently Published.

Willcox Smith, Jessie & Nast, Thos. Twas the Night Before Christmas / a Visit from St. Nicholas (Illustrated) Barry, ed. 2019. (ENG.). 42p. (J). pap. 19.99 ***(978-1-6503-4705-9(7))*** Independently Published.

Willemin, Veronique. Te Tumu o Rapa Nui: El Arbolito de Rapa Nui. the Little Tree of Rapa Nui. le Petit Arbre de Rapa Nui. Orliac, Catherine. Haoa Cardinali, Viki et al, trs. 2005. (FRE, SPA & ENG.). 40p. (J). spiral bd. 12.00 *(978-1-880636-02-2(6))* Easter Island Foundation.

Willems, Mo. Don't Let the Pigeon Drive the Bus! 2005. 40p. (J). *(978-1-84428-013-1(6))* Walker Bks. Australia Pty, Ltd.

Willems, Mo. Are You Ready to Play Outside? (an Elephant & Piggie Book) Willems, Mo. 2008. (Elephant & Piggie Book Ser.: 7). (ENG.). 64p. (J). (gr. -1-k). 9.99 *(978-1-4231-1347-8(0))* Hyperion Pr.

—A Big Guy Took My Ball! (an Elephant & Piggie Book) Willems, Mo. 2013. (Elephant & Piggie Book Ser.: 19). (ENG.). 64p. (J). (gr. 1-3). 9.99 *(978-1-4231-7491-2(7))* Hyperion Bks. for Children.

—Can I Play Too? (an Elephant & Piggie Book) Willems, Mo. 2010. (Elephant & Piggie Book Ser.). (ENG.). 64p. (J). (gr. -1-k). 9.99 *(978-1-4231-1991-3(6))* Hyperion Pr.

—Cat the Cat, Who Is That? Willems, Mo. 2010. (ENG.). 32p. (J). (gr. -1-3). 10.99 *(978-0-06-172840-2(3))*; lib. bdg. 14.89 *(978-0-06-172841-9(1))* HarperCollins Pubs.

—A Cautionary Tale. Willems, Mo. ed. 2011. 40p. (gr. -1-1). 19.99 *(978-1-4231-4449-6(X))* Hyperion Pr.

—El Conjito Knuffle: Un Cuento Aleccionador. Willems, Mo. rev. ed. 2007. (Knuffle Bunny Ser.). (SPA.). 40p. (J). (gr. -1-k). pap. 7.99 *(978-1-4231-0567-1(2))* Hyperion Pr.

—¿Debo Compartir Mi Helado? (Spanish Edition) Willems, Mo. 2015. (Elephant & Piggie Book Ser.). (SPA.). 64p. (J). (gr. -1-k). 9.99 *(978-1-4847-2291-6(4))* Disney Publishing Worldwide.

—Don't Let the Pigeon Drive the Bus! Willems, Mo. 2003. (Pigeon Ser.). (ENG.). 40p. (J). (gr. -1-k). 16.99 *(978-0-7868-1988-1(X))* Hyperion Pr.

—Don't Let the Pigeon Drive the Bus! (Big Book Edition) (a Pigeon Series Book) Willems, Mo. 2012. (Pigeon Ser.). (ENG.). 40p. (J). (gr. -1-k). pap. 19.99 *(978-1-4231-4514-1(3))* Hyperion Pr.

—Don't Let the Pigeon Finish This Activity Book! (Pigeon Series) Willems, Mo. 2012. (Pigeon Ser.: 8). (ENG.). 272p. (J). (gr. -1 — 1). pap. 19.99 *(978-1-4231-3310-0(2))* Hyperion Pr.

—Don't Let the Pigeon Stay up Late! Willems, Mo. 2006. (Pigeon Ser.). (ENG.). 40p. (J). (gr. -1-k). 16.99 *(978-0-7868-3746-5(2))* Hyperion Pr.

—The Duckling Gets a Cookie!? (Pigeon Series) Willems, Mo. 2012. (ENG.). 40p. (J). (gr. -1-k). 16.99 *(978-1-4231-5128-9(3))* Hyperion Pr.

—Edwina, the Dinosaur Who Didn't Know She Was Extinct. Willems, Mo. 2006. (ENG.). 40p. (J). (gr. -1-k). 17.99 *(978-0-7868-3748-9(9))* Hyperion Pr.

—An Elephant & Piggie Biggie! Willems, Mo. 2017. (Elephant & Piggie Book Ser.). (ENG.). 320p. (J). (gr. 1-3). 16.99 *(978-1-4847-9967-3(4))* Hyperion Bks. for Children.

Willems, Mo. An Elephant & Piggie Biggie! Volume 3. Willems, Mo. 2020. (Elephant & Piggie Book Ser.). (ENG.). 320p. (J). (gr. -1-3). 16.99 ***(978-1-368-05715-8(2))*** Hyperion Bks. for Children.

Willems, Mo. Elephant & Piggie: the Complete Collection (an Elephant & Piggie Book) Willems, Mo. 2018. (Elephant & Piggie Book Ser.). (ENG.). 1600p. (J). (gr. 1-3). 150.00 *(978-1-368-02131-9(X))* Hyperion Bks. for Children.

—Elephants Cannot Dance! (an Elephant & Piggie Book) Willems, Mo. 2009. (Elephant & Piggie Book Ser.: 9). (ENG.). 64p. (J). (gr. -1-k). 9.99 *(978-1-4231-1410-9(8))* Hyperion Pr.

Willems, Mo. ¡Escucha Mi Trompeta! (an Elephant & Piggie Book, Spanish Edition) Willems, Mo. 2020. (Elephant & Piggie Book Ser.). (SPA.). 64p. (J). (gr. k-3). 9.99 ***(978-1-368-05613-7(X))*** Hyperion Bks. for Children.

Willems, Mo. ¡Esperar No Es Fácil! (Spanish Edition) Willems, Mo. 2017. (Elephant & Piggie Book Ser.). (ENG.). 64p. (J). (gr. 1-3). 9.99 *(978-1-4847-8698-7(X))* Hyperion Bks. for Children.

—¡Estamos en un Libro! (Spanish Edition) Willems, Mo. 2015. (Elephant & Piggie Book Ser.). (SPA.). 64p. (J). (gr. 1-3). 9.99 *(978-1-4847-2288-6(4))* Hyperion Bks. for Children.

—¿Estás Lista para Jugar Afuera? (an Elephant & Piggie Book, Spanish Edition) Willems, Mo. 2018. (Elephant & Piggie Book Ser.). (SPA.). 64p. (J). (gr. 1-3). 9.99 *(978-1-368-02133-3(6))* Hyperion Bks. for Children.

—Goldilocks & the Three Dinosaurs: As Retold by Mo Willems. Willems, Mo. 2012. (ENG.). 40p. (J). (gr. -1-2). 17.99 *(978-0-06-210418-2(7)*, Balzer & Bray) HarperCollins Pubs.

—Happy Pig Day! (an Elephant & Piggie Book) Willems, Mo. 2011. (Elephant & Piggie Book Ser.: 15). (ENG.). 64p. (J). (gr. -1-k). 9.99 *(978-1-4231-4342-0(6))* Hyperion Pr.

Willems, Mo. ¡He Perdido un Diente! (Spanish Edition) Willems, Mo. 2020. (Unlimited Squirrels Ser.). (SPA.). 96p. (J). (gr. k-3). 12.99 ***(978-1-368-05611-3(3))*** Hyperion Bks. for Children.

Willems, Mo. Hooray for Amanda & Her Alligator! Willems, Mo. 2011. (ENG.). 72p. (J). (gr. -1-3). 17.99 *(978-0-06-200400-0(X))* HarperCollins Pubs.

—¡Hoy Volaré! (Spanish Edition) Willems, Mo. 2015. (Elephant & Piggie Book Ser.). (SPA.). 64p. (J). (gr. 1-3). 9.99 *(978-1-4847-2287-9(6))* Disney Publishing Worldwide.

—I Am Going! (an Elephant & Piggie Book) Willems, Mo. 2010. (Elephant & Piggie Book Ser.: 11). (ENG.). 64p. (J). (gr. -1-k). 9.99 *(978-1-4231-1990-6(8))* Hyperion Pr.

—I Am Invited to a Party! (an Elephant & Piggie Book) Willems, Mo. rev. ed. 2007. (Elephant & Piggie Book Ser.). (ENG.). 64p. (J). (gr. -1-k). 9.99 *(978-1-4231-0687-6(3))* Hyperion Pr.

—I Broke My Trunk! (an Elephant & Piggie Book) Willems, Mo. 2011. (Elephant & Piggie Book Ser.). (ENG.). 64p. (J). (gr. -1-k). 9.99 *(978-1-4231-3309-4(9))* Hyperion Pr.

—I Lost My Tooth! (an Unlimited Squirrels Book) Willems, Mo. 2018. (Unlimited Squirrels Ser.: 1). (ENG.). 96p. (J). (gr. 1-3). 12.99 *(978-1-368-02457-0(2))* Hyperion Bks. for Children.

—I Love My New Toy! (an Elephant & Piggie Book) Willems, Mo. 2008. (Elephant & Piggie Book Ser.). (ENG.). 64p. (J). (gr. -1-k). 9.99 *(978-1-4231-0961-7(9))* Hyperion Pr.

—I Really Like Slop! (an Elephant & Piggie Book) Willems, Mo. 2015. (Elephant & Piggie Book Ser.: 24). (ENG.). 64p. (J). (gr. 1-3). 9.99 *(978-1-4847-2262-6(0))* Hyperion Bks. for Children.

—I Will Surprise My Friend! (an Elephant & Piggie Book) Willems, Mo. 2008. (Elephant & Piggie Book Ser.). (ENG.). 64p. (J). (gr. -1-k). 9.99 *(978-1-4231-0962-4(7))* Hyperion Pr.

—I Will Take a Nap! (an Elephant & Piggie Book) Willems, Mo. 2015. (Elephant & Piggie Book Ser.: 23). (ENG.). 64p. (J). (gr. 1-3). 9.99 *(978-1-4847-1630-4(2))* Hyperion Bks. for Children.

—I'm a Frog! (an Elephant & Piggie Book) Willems, Mo. 2013. (Elephant & Piggie Book Ser.: 20). (ENG.). 64p. (J). (gr. 1-3). 9.99 *(978-1-4231-8305-1(3))* Hyperion Pr.

—Knuffle Bunny: A Cautionary Tale. Willems, Mo. unabr. ed. 2006. (J). (gr. -1-1). 29.95 *(978-0-439-90583-1(4))* Weston Woods Studios, Inc.

—Knuffle Bunny: a Cautionary Tale. Willems, Mo. 2004. (Knuffle Bunny Ser.). (ENG.). 40p. (J). (gr. -1-k). 17.99 *(978-0-7868-1870-9(0))* Hyperion Pr.

—Knuffle Bunny Free: An Unexpected Diversion. Willems, Mo. 2010. (ENG.). 52p. (J). (gr. -1-3). 18.99 *(978-0-06-192957-1(3))* HarperCollins Pubs.

—Knuffle Bunny Free: Un Unexpected Diversion. Willems, Mo. 2010. (ENG.). 52p. (J). (gr. -1-3). lib. bdg. 18.89 *(978-0-06-192958-8(1))* HarperCollins Pubs.

—Knuffle Bunny Too: A Case of Mistaken Identity. Willems, Mo. rev. ed. 2007. (Knuffle Bunny Ser.). (ENG.). 48p. (J). (gr. -1-k). 17.99 *(978-1-4231-0299-1(1))* Hyperion Pr.

—¡la Paloma Encuentra un Perro Caliente! Willems, Mo. 2011. (SPA.). 40p. (J). (gr. -1-k). pap. 9.99 *(978-1-4231-4051-1(6))* Hyperion Pr.

—Leonardo, the Terrible Monster. Willems, Mo. 2005. (ENG.). 48p. (J). (gr. -1-k). 17.99 *(978-0-7868-5294-9(1))* Hyperion Pr.

—Let's Go for a Drive! (an Elephant & Piggie Book) Willems, Mo. 2012. (Elephant & Piggie Book Ser.: 18). (ENG.). 64p. (J). (gr. -1-k). 9.99 *(978-1-4231-6482-1(2))* Hyperion Pr.

—Let's Say Hi to Friends Who Fly! Willems, Mo. 2010. (ENG.). 32p. (J). (gr. -1-3). 10.99 *(978-0-06-172842-6(X))*; lib. bdg. 14.89 *(978-0-06-172846-4(2))* HarperCollins Pubs. (Balzer & Bray).

—Listen to My Trumpet! (an Elephant & Piggie Book) Willems, Mo. 2012. (Elephant & Piggie Book Ser.: 17). (ENG.). 64p. (J). (gr. -1-k). 9.99 *(978-1-4231-5404-4(5))* Hyperion Pr.

—My Friend Is Sad (an Elephant & Piggie Book) Willems, Mo. 2007. (Elephant & Piggie Book Ser.). (ENG.). 64p. (J). (gr. -1-k). 9.99 *(978-1-4231-0297-7(5))* Hyperion Pr.

—My New Friend Is So Fun! (an Elephant & Piggie Book) Willems, Mo. 2014. (Elephant & Piggie Book Ser.). (ENG.). 64p. (J). (gr. 1-3). 9.99 *(978-1-4231-7958-0(7))* Hyperion Bks. for Children.

—Naked Mole Rat Gets Dressed. Willems, Mo. 2009. (ENG.). 40p. (J). (gr. -1 — 1). 16.99 *(978-1-4231-1437-6(X))* Hyperion Pr.

—Nanette's Baguette. Willems, Mo. 2016. (ENG.). 40p. (J). (gr. -1-k). 17.99 *(978-1-4847-2286-2(8))* Disney Pr.

—¡No Dejes Que la Paloma Conduzca el Autobus! Willems, Mo. 2011.Tr. of Don't Let the Pigeon Drive the Bus. (SPA.). 40p. (J). (gr. -1-k). pap. 7.99 *(978-1-4231-4052-8(4))* Hyperion Pr.

—The Pigeon Finds a Hot Dog! Willems, Mo. 2004. (Pigeon Ser.). (ENG.). 40p. (J). (gr. -1-k). 16.99 *(978-0-7868-1869-3(7))* Hyperion Bks. for Children.

—The Pigeon Has Feelings, Too! Willems, Mo. 2005. (Pigeon Ser.). (ENG.). 12p. (J). (gr. -1-k). 6.99 *(978-0-7868-3650-5(4))* Hyperion Pr.

—The Pigeon Loves Things That Go! Willems, Mo. 2005. (Pigeon Ser.). (ENG.). 12p. (J). (gr. -1-k). 6.99 *(978-0-7868-3651-2(2))* Hyperion Pr.

—The Pigeon Needs a Bath! Willems, Mo. 2014. (Pigeon Ser.: 9). (ENG.). 40p. (J). (gr. -1-k). 16.99 *(978-1-4231-9087-5(4))* Hyperion Bks. for Children.

—The Pigeon Wants a Puppy! Willems, Mo. 2008. (Pigeon Ser.). (ENG.). 40p. (J). (gr. -1-k). 16.99 *(978-1-4231-0960-0(0))* Hyperion Pr.

—Pigs Make Me Sneeze! (an Elephant & Piggie Book) Willems, Mo. 2009. (Elephant & Piggie Book Ser.: 10). (ENG.). 64p. (J). (gr. -1-k). 9.99 *(978-1-4231-1411-6(6))* Hyperion Pr.

—¿Puedo Jugar Yo También? (an Elephant & Piggie Book, Spanish Edition) Willems, Mo. 2018. (Elephant & Piggie Book Ser.). (ENG.). 64p. (J). (gr. -1-k). 9.99 *(978-1-368-02134-0(4))* Hyperion Bks. for Children.

—Sam, the Most Scaredy-Cat Kid in the Whole World: A Leonardo, the Terrible Monster Companion. Willems, Mo. 2017. (ENG.). 48p. (J). (gr. -1-k). 17.99 *(978-1-368-00214-1(5))* Hyperion Bks. for Children.

—Should I Share My Ice Cream? (an Elephant & Piggie Book) Willems, Mo. 2011. (Elephant & Piggie Book Ser.). (ENG.). 64p. (J). (gr. -1-k). 9.99 *(978-1-4231-4343-7(4))* Hyperion Pr.

—The Thank You Book (an Elephant & Piggie Book) Willems, Mo. 2016. (Elephant & Piggie Book Ser.: 25). (ENG.). 64p. (J). (gr. 1-3). 9.99 *(978-1-4231-7828-6(9))* Hyperion Bks. for Children.

—That Is Not a Good Idea! Willems, Mo. 2013. (ENG.). 48p. (J). (gr. k-3). 17.99 *(978-0-06-220309-0(6)*, Balzer & Bray) HarperCollins Pubs.

—There Is a Bird on Your Head! (an Elephant & Piggie Book) Willems, Mo. rev. ed. 2007. (Elephant & Piggie Book Ser.). (ENG.). 64p. (J). (gr. -1-k). 9.99 *(978-1-4231-0686-9(5))* Hyperion Pr.

—¡Tienes un Pájaro en la Cabeza! (an Elephant & Piggie Book, Spanish Edition) Willems, Mo. 2017. (Elephant & Piggie Book Ser.). (ENG.). 64p. (J). (gr. 1-3). 9.99 *(978-1-4847-8697-0(1))* Hyperion Bks. for Children.

—Time to Pee! Willems, Mo. 2003. (ENG.). 40p. (J). (gr. -1-k). 16.99 *(978-0-7868-1868-6(9))* Hyperion Pr.

—Time to Say Please ! Willems, Mo. 2005. (ENG.). 40p. (J). (gr. -1-k). 16.99 *(978-0-7868-5293-2(3))* Hyperion Pr.

—Time to Sleep, Sheep the Sheep! Willems, Mo. 2010. (ENG.). 32p. (J). (gr. -1-3). 12.99 *(978-0-06-172847-1(0))*; lib. bdg. 14.89 *(978-0-06-172848-8(9))* HarperCollins Pubs.

—Today I Will Fly! (an Elephant & Piggie Book) Willems, Mo. 2007. (Elephant & Piggie Book Ser.). (ENG.). 64p. (J). (gr. -1-k). 9.99 *(978-1-4231-0295-3(9))* Hyperion Pr.

—¡un Tipo Grande Se Llevó Mi Pelota! (Spanish Edition) Willems, Mo. 2015. (Elephant & Piggie Book Ser.). (SPA.). 64p. (J). (gr. 1-3). 9.99 *(978-1-4847-2285-5(X))* Disney Publishing Worldwide.

Willems, Mo. ¡Vamos a Dar una Vuelta! (an Elephant & Piggie Book, Spanish Edition) Willems, Mo. 2020. (Elephant & Piggie Book Ser.). (SPA.). 64p. (J). (gr. k-3). 9.99 ***(978-1-368-05612-0(1))*** Hyperion Bks. for Children.

Willems, Mo. Waiting Is Not Easy! (an Elephant & Piggie Book) Willems, Mo. 2014. (Elephant & Piggie Book Ser.). (ENG.). 64p. (J). (gr. 1-3). 9.99 *(978-1-4231-9957-1(X))* Hyperion Bks. for Children.

—Watch Me Throw the Ball! (an Elephant & Piggie Book) Willems, Mo. 2009. (Elephant & Piggie Book Ser.: 8). (ENG.). 64p. (J). (gr. -1-k). 9.99 *(978-1-4231-1348-5(9))* Hyperion Pr.

—We Are in a Book! (an Elephant & Piggie Book) Willems, Mo. 2010. (Elephant & Piggie Book Ser.). (ENG.). 64p. (J). (gr. -1-k). 9.99 *(978-1-4231-3308-7(0))* Hyperion Pr.

—We Are in an ART-ivity Book! Willems, Mo. 2017. (Elephant & Piggie Book Ser.). (ENG.). 144p. (J). (gr. -1-3). pap. 14.99 *(978-1-4847-9816-4(3))* Hyperion Bks. for Children.

—Welcome: a Mo Willems Guide for New Arrivals. Willems, Mo. 2017. (ENG.). 32p. (J). (gr. -1 — 1). 15.99 *(978-1-4847-6746-7(2))* Disney Pr.

—What's Your Sound, Hound the Hound? Willems, Mo. 2010. (ENG.). 32p. (J). (gr. -1-3). 10.99 *(978-0-06-172844-0(6))*; lib. bdg. 14.89 *(978-0-06-172845-7(4))* HarperCollins Pubs.

—Who Flies, Cat the Cat? Willems, Mo. 2014. (ENG.). 22p. (J). (gr. -1 — 1). bds. 6.99 *(978-0-06-230652-4(9))* HarperCollins Pubs.

—Who Is That, Cat the Cat? Willems, Mo. 2014. (ENG.). 22p. (J). (gr. -1 — 1). bds. 6.99 *(978-0-06-230653-1(7))* HarperCollins Pubs.

—Who Says That, Cat the Cat? Willems, Mo. 2014. (ENG.). 22p. (J). (gr. -1 — 1). bds. 6.99 *(978-0-06-230654-8(5))* HarperCollins Pubs.

—Who Sleeps, Cat the Cat? Willems, Mo. 2014. (ENG.). 22p. (J). (gr. -1 — 1). bds. 7.99 *(978-0-06-230655-5(3))* HarperCollins Pubs.

—You Can Never Find a Rickshaw When It Monsoons: The World on One Cartoon a Day. Willems, Mo. 2006. (ENG.). 408p. (gr. 8-17). pap. 12.99 *(978-0-7868-3747-2(0))* Hyperion Pr.

Willems, Mo & Collier, Bryan. It's Shoe Time! Willems, Mo & Collier, Bryan. 2017. (Elephant & Piggie Like Reading! Ser.: 4). (ENG.). 64p. (J). (gr. -1-3). 9.99 *(978-1-4847-2647-1(2))* Hyperion Bks. for Children.

Willems, Mo & Harper, Charise Mericle. The Good for Nothing Button! Willems, Mo & Harper, Charise Mericle. 2017. (Elephant & Piggie Like Reading! Ser.: 3). (ENG.). 64p. (J). (gr. -1-3). 9.99 *(978-1-4847-2646-4(4))* Disney Pr.

Willems, Mo & Keller, Laurie. We Are Growing! Willems, Mo & Keller, Laurie. 2016. (Elephant & Piggie Like Reading! Ser.: 2). (ENG.). 64p. (J). (gr. -1-3). 9.99 *(978-1-4847-2635-8(9))* Hyperion Bks. for Children.

Willems, Mo & Pham, Leuyen. The Itchy Book! (Elephant & Piggie Like Reading!) Willems, Mo & Pham, Leuyen. 2018. (Elephant & Piggie Like Reading! Ser.: 5). (ENG.). 64p. (J). (gr. 1-3). 9.99 *(978-1-368-00564-7(0))* Hyperion Bks. for Children.

Willems, Mo, jt. illus. see Santat, Dan.

Willey, Bee. Indian Myths. Husain, Shahrukh. 2007. (Stories from Ancient Civilisations Ser.). 32p. (J). pap. 10.99 *(978-0-237-53376-2(6))* Evans Brothers, Ltd. GBR. Dist: Independent Pubs. Group.

—The Jesse Tree. McCaughrean, Geraldine. 2005. 93p. (J). (gr. k). 20.00 *(978-0-8028-5288-5(2)*, Eerdmans Bks For Young Readers) Eerdmans, William B. Publishing Co.

—El Ladron y la Bailarina. Matthews, Andrew. Rubio, Esther, tr. 2004. (SPA.). 30p. (J). 19.99 *(978-84-88342-39-3(X))* S.A. Kokinos ESP. Dist: Lectorum Pubns., Inc.

—The Mouse Who Saved Egypt. Alrawi, Karim. 2011. (ENG.). 32p. (J). (gr. -1-3). 16.95 *(978-1-56656-856-2(0)*, Crocodile Bks.) Interlink Publishing Group, Inc.

—Read with Me Snow White: Sticker Activity Book. Page, Nick & Page, Claire. 2006. (Read with Me (Make Believe Ideas) Ser.). 12p. (J). (gr. k-2). pap. *(978-1-84610-179-3(4))* Make Believe Ideas.

—River Story. Hooper, Meredith. 2015. (ENG.). 32p. (J). (gr. k-3). 6.99 *(978-0-7636-7646-9(2))* Candlewick Pr.

—River Story. Hooper, Meredith. 2015. (ENG.). (J). (gr. k-3). lib. bdg. 17.60 *(978-1-62765-758-7(4))* Perfection Learning Corp.

—Twelve Dancing Princesses. McCaughrean, Geraldine. 2014. (Traditional Tales Ser.). (ENG.). 32p. (J). (gr. 1-2). pap. 7.95 *(978-1-62521-606-9(8)*, Capstone Classroom) Capstone.

Willia, Sarah. Colors, Shapes & Sizes. Lafaye, Gwarmekia. 2019. (ENG.). 70p. (J). (gr. 2-4). 25.00 ***(978-0-692-18855-2(X))*** Gwarmekia.

William, Graf. Max Gets It!, 4 vols. Sparks, Candi. ed. 2008. (Can I Have Some Money? Ser.: Vol. 3). (ENG.). 32p. (J). pap. *(978-0-9789445-1-3(8))* Sparks Fly.

William, Harper. Racer Buddies-Opening Day at Daytona. Elliott, Craig. 2004. 40p. (J). per. 12.95 *(978-0-9746445-0-9(1)*, 1234022) Powerband, LLC.

William, Iceberg Dunbar. The Wacky Winter Witch. Williams, Guana Dunbar. 2003. (J). per. *(978-0-9740673-1-5(8))* Graphix Network.

William, Lorna, jt. illus. see Carroll, James Christopher.

William, Lorna, jt. illus. see Carroll, Jim.

Williams, Alexandra & Williams, David. Fairy Nyumbani. 2005. 24p. *(978-9966-956-41-5(7))* Jacaranda Designs Ltd.

Williams, Allen. Pan's Labyrinth: the Labyrinth of the Faun. del Toro, Guillermo & Funke, Cornelia. (ENG.). 272p. (YA). (gr. 9). 2020. pap. 12.99 ***(978-0-06-241447-2(X))***; 2019. 19.99 *(978-0-06-241446-5(1))* HarperCollins Pubs. (Tegen, Katherine Bks).

Williams, Angela. Kwanzaa: The Seven Principles. Terry, Rod. 2005. 64p. (J). (gr. 4-8). reprint ed. 8.00 *(978-0-7567-8635-9(5))* DIANE Publishing Co.

Williams, Angie, photos by. Daniel Keep Dreaming. Martin, Paige. Price, Ronnalda, ed. 2011. 48p. (J). pap. 15.00 *(978-0-578-08272-1(1))* Paige Martin Bks.

Williams, Anthony. Dracula, 1 vol. Stoker, Bram. 2019. (Graphic Novel Classics Ser.). (ENG.). 32p. (J). (gr. 4-4). 26.25 *(978-1-7253-0628-8(X))*; pap. 10.00 *(978-1-7253-0627-1(1))* Rosen Publishing Group, Inc., The. (PowerKids Pr.).

—Dracula: A Classic Pop-Up Tale. 2009. (ENG.). 16p. (J). 29.95 *(978-0-7893-2050-6(9))* Universe Publishing.

—Frankenstein, 1 vol. Shelley, Mary. 2019. (Graphic Novel Classics Ser.). (ENG.). 32p. (J). (gr. 4-4). 26.25 *(978-1-7253-0631-8(X))*; pap. 10.00 *(978-1-7253-0630-1(1))* Rosen Publishing Group, Inc., The. (PowerKids Pr.).

—The Hound of the Baskervilles, 1 vol. Doyle, Arthur Conan, ed. 2019. (Graphic Novel Classics Ser.). (ENG.). 32p. (J). (gr. 4-4). 26.25 *(978-1-7253-0634-9(4))*; pap. 10.00 *(978-1-7253-0633-2(6))* Rosen Publishing Group, Inc., The. (PowerKids Pr.).

—Scooby-Doo in Barnstormin' Banshee, 1 vol. Busch, Robbie. 2010. (Scooby-Doo Graphic Novels Ser.: No. 1). (ENG.). 24p. (J). (gr. 2-6). 27.07 *(978-1-59961-691-9(2)*, 559, Graphic Novels) Spotlight.

—This Ghost Is Toast! Abnett, Dan. 2007. (Real Ghostbusters Ser.). 96p. per. 8.95 *(978-1-84576-143-1(X)*, Titan Bks.) Titan Bks. Ltd. GBR. Dist: Penguin Random Hse. LLC.

Williams, Bill. Pirate Party. Lytle, Robert A. 2006. (Mackinac Passage Ser.). 258p. (J). (gr. 4-7). pap. 9.95 *(978-0-9749412-5-7(5))* EDCO Publishing, Inc.

Williams, Bob. Meet the Bukos. Williams, Bob. 2017. (ENG.). 44p. (J). (gr. 1-6). pap. 9.99 *(978-1-68160-386-5(1))* Crimson Cloak Publishing.

Williams, Bobbie Jo. Out the Big Door. Williams, Bobbie Jo. Williams, Margaret Louise. 2019. (Out the Big Door Ser.: Vol. 1). (ENG.). 28p. (J). pap. 9.99 *(978-1-0922-7906-2(7))* Independently Published.

Williams, Brian. Herkimer's Big Day: Herkimer the Police Horse Meets a Young Girl Named Sammy. Tyler, Sandy. 2012. (ENG.). 22p. (J). pap. 20.95 *(978-1-4327-9005-9(6))* Outskirts Pr., Inc.

Williams, Brian. The Tunnels. Williams, Brian. Gordon, Roderick. 2009. (Tunnels Ser.: 1). (ENG.). 496p. (J). (gr. 3-7). pap. 9.99 *(978-0-545-07881-8(4)*, Scholastic Paperbacks) Scholastic, Inc.

Williams, Brittney. Betty & Veronica: the Bond of Friendship. Rotante, Jamie Lee. 2020. (ENG.). 144p. (YA). (gr. 7). pap. 14.99 *(978-1-64576-985-9(2))* Archie Comic Pubns., Inc.

Williams, Brittney, et al. Goldie Vance Graphic Novel Gift Set. Larson, Hope & Ball, Jackie. 2019. (Goldie Vance Ser.). (ENG.). 448p. (J). pap. 39.99 *(978-1-68415-439-5(1))* Boom! Studios.

Williams, Brittney. Well My Teacher Said. Bodden, Michelle. 2007. 32p. (J). 14.95 *(978-0-9753089-2-9(0))* Water Daughter Publishing.

Williams, Brittney L. Lois Lane & the Friendship Challenge. Ellis, Grace. 2020. 160p. (J). (gr. 3-7). pap. 9.99 ***(978-1-4012-9637-7(8))*** DC Comics.

Williams, Brittney L. Patsy Walker, A. K. A. Hellcat! Vol. 3: Careless Whisker(s) 2017. (ENG.). 112p. (J). (gr. 4-17). pap. 15.99 *(978-1-302-90662-7(3))* Marvel Worldwide, Inc.

Williams, Carl Joseph. Mardi Gras Almost Didn't Come This Year. Price, Kathy. 2020. (J). *(978-1-5344-4425-6(4)*, Atheneum Bks. for Young Readers) Simon & Schuster Children's Publishing.

Williams, Carlene H. Santa's Stray. Basore, Polly M. 2004. 32p. (J). per. *(978-0-9771749-2-8(1))* AngelBooks.

—Santa's Stray in A Piano for Christmas. Basore, Polly M. 2005. 32p. (J). per. *(978-0-9771749-1-1(3))* AngelBooks.

Williams, Caroline. Baby's First Bible Stories: 12 Favorite Stories. Elliot, Rachel. Cottage Door Press, ed. 2018. (ENG.). 26p. (J). (gr. -1-1). bds. 9.99 *(978-1-68052-423-9(2)*, 2000220) Cottage Door Pr.

—Blessings for a Baby Boy. Piper, Sophie. ed. 2009. (ENG.). 48p. (J). (gr. k-k). 7.99 *(978-0-7459-6184-2(3))* Lion Hudson PLC GBR. Dist: Independent Pubs. Group.

—Blessings for a Baby Girl. Piper, Sophie. 11th ed. 2009. (ENG.). 48p. (J). (gr. k-k). 7.99 *(978-0-7459-6185-9(1))* Lion Hudson PLC GBR. Dist: Independent Pubs. Group.

—Everyone Needs a Friend. Piper, Sophie. 2010. (Everyone Needs Ser.). (ENG.). 6p. (J). (gr. k — 1). bds. 5.99 *(978-0-7459-6225-2(4))* Lion Hudson PLC GBR. Dist: Independent Pubs. Group.

Williams, Caspar. Pick Your Brains about Greece. Sanderson, Caroline. 2005. (Pick Your Brains Ser.). 128p. pap. 9.95 *(978-1-86011-220-1(X))* Cadogan Guides GBR. Dist: Globe Pequot Pr., The.

—Pick Your Brains about Ireland. O'Neill, Mary. 2005. (Pick Your Brains - Cadogan Ser.). (ENG.). 128p. pap. 9.95 *(978-1-86011-221-8(8))* Cadogan Guides GBR. Dist: Globe Pequot Pr., The.

—Pick Your Brains about Scotland. Kirkby, Mandy. 2005. (Pick Your Brains Ser.). 128p. pap. 9.95 *(978-1-86011-223-2(4))* Cadogan Guides GBR. Dist: Globe Pequot Pr., The.

—Pick Your Brains about the USA. Egginton, Jane. 2005. (Pick Your Brains - Cadogan Ser.). (ENG.). 128p. pap. 9.95 *(978-1-86011-222-5(6))* Cadogan Guides GBR. Dist: Globe Pequot Pr., The.

Williams, Christopher. Malcolm & the Money Tree. Esdaille-Richardson, Eudora. 2014. 31p. (J). pap. *(978-1-934370-49-0(5))* Editorial Campana.

W

Williams, David. My Mind Book. Williams, Fiona Maria. 2016. (ENG.). (J). (gr. 2-6). pap. *(978-0-9950415-0-9(4))* Williams, Fiona Maria.
Williams, David, jt. illus. see Williams, Alexandra.
Williams, Denny. Kelsie's Potty Adventure. Prater, Cindy. 2006. 40p. per. 19.95 *(978-1-59858-271-0(2))* Dog Ear Publishing, LLC.
Williams, Deshantren. The Adventures of Kyree & Kyere: The Basement. Sherry, Raymond. 2008. 24p. pap. 24.95 *(978-1-60703-288-5(0))* America Star Bks.
Williams, Don, et al. Disney Princess Little Golden Book Favorites, Vol. 2. Teitelbaum, Michael. 2010. (ENG.). 80p. (J). (gr. -1-2). 6.99 *(978-0-7364-2656-5(6)*, Golden/Disney) Random Hse. Children's Bks.
Williams, Don, jt. illus. see Cardona, Jose.
Williams, Don, jt. illus. see Russell, H. R.
Williams, E. Colin. The Battle for Camillo, 1 vol. Tate, Nikki. 2003. (Estorian Chronicles Ser.: 2). (ENG.). 322p. (J). (gr. 4-7). pap. 8.95 *(978-1-55039-127-5(5))* Sono Nis Pr. CAN. Dist: Orca Bk. Pubs. USA.
Williams-El, Belinda Irene. The King's Mascot. Singh, Rajinder. 2011. (ENG & ACO.). 28p. (J). (gr. -1-3). 10.00 *(978-0-918224-85-9(3))* Radiance Pubs.
williams, Emma Louise. What's That Smell Monkey? Williams, Emma Louise. 2012. 12p. pap. 7.99 *(978-1-939076-07-6(2))* Wiggies, Piggy.
Williams, Emma Louise. 30 Sheep & One Cow. Williams, Emma Louise. 2012. 24p. pap. 8.99 *(978-1-939076-05-2(6))* Wiggies, Piggy.
Williams, Eric L. Queen of the Dead. Drago, Ty. 2012. (ENG.). 432p. (J). (gr. 5-8). pap. 12.99 *(978-1-4022-7557-9(9)*, Sourcebooks Jabberwocky) Sourcebooks, Inc.
Williams, Florence White. Little Black Sambo. Bannerman, Helen. 2019. (ENG.). 32p. (J). (gr. k-5). pap. 5.99 ***(978-1-6951-4044-8(3))*** Independently Published.
Williams, Frederick C. Happiness Colouring Book. Williams, Frederick C. Chappell, Billie-Jean. 2012. 36p. pap. *(978-0-9566564-2-1(0))* Dreamality Bks.
Williams, G. L. The No Thank You Bite, 1 vol. Evans, Carol Wolfe. 2010. 16p. 24.95 *(978-1-4512-2132-9(0))* PublishAmerica, Inc.
Williams, Gail. The Abominog. Thomas, Amy A. 2013. 120p. pap. 6.99 *(978-0-9898579-0-1(5))* Passionate Purpose.
Williams, Garth. Animal Friends. Watson, Jane Werner. 2016. (Little Golden Book Ser.). 24p. (J). (gr. -1-k). 4.99 *(978-0-553-53642-3(7)*, Golden Bks.) Random Hse. Children's Bks.
—By the Shores of Silver Lake, 5. Wilder, Laura Ingalls. 2008. (Little House Ser.: 5). (ENG.). 304p. (J). (gr. 3-7). pap. 8.99 *(978-0-06-440005-3(0))* HarperCollins Pubs.
—By the Shores of Silver Lake: Full Color Edition. Wilder, Laura Ingalls. 2004. (Little House Ser.: 5). (ENG.). 304p. (J). (gr. 3-7). pap. 8.99 *(978-0-06-058184-8(0))* HarperCollins Pubs.
—Charlotte's Web. White, E. B. (Charming Classics). (J). 2005. 192p. pap. 7.99 *(978-0-06-084594-0(5)*, HarperFestival); 2006. 192p. mass mkt. 7.99 *(978-0-06-122874-2(5)*, Harper Trophy); Set. 2006. pap. 19.99 *(978-0-06-121502-5(3))* HarperCollins Pubs.
—Charlotte's Web. White, E. B. & DiCamillo, Kate. 2012. (ENG.). 192p. (J). (gr. 3-7). 16.99 *(978-0-06-026385-0(7))*; 9.99 *(978-0-06-112495-2(8))*; pap. 8.99 *(978-0-06-440055-8(7))* HarperCollins Pubs. Ltd. GBR. (HarperCollins). Dist: HarperCollins Pubs.
—Charlotte's Web. White, E. B. 2004. (CHI.). 158p. (YA). pap. *(978-957-08-2568-8(5))* Linking Publishing Co., Ltd.
—Charlotte's Web. White, E. B. 184p. (J). pap. 5.95 *(978-0-8072-8305-9(3)*, Listening Library) Random Hse. Audio Publishing Group.
—Charlotte's Web: a Harper Classic. White, E. B. & DiCamillo, Kate. 2017. (Harper Classic Ser.). (ENG.). 208p. (J). (gr. 3-7). 16.99 *(978-0-06-265875-3(1))* HarperCollins Pubs.
—Charlotte's Web Read-Aloud Edition. White, E. B. & DiCamillo, Kate. 2006. (ENG.). 192p. (J). (gr. 3-7). 16.99 *(978-0-06-088261-7(1))* HarperCollins Pubs.
—The Cricket in Times Square. Selden, George. (Chester Cricket Ser.). 151p. (J). (gr. 3-6). pap. 5.50 *(978-0-8072-8311-0(8)*, Listening Library) Random Hse. Audio Publishing Group.
—The Cricket in Times Square. Selden, George. 2008. (Chester Cricket & His Friends Ser.: 1). (ENG.). 144p. (J). (gr. 1-4). pap. 7.99 *(978-0-312-38003-8(8)*, 900050526) Square Fish.
—The Family under the Bridge. Carlson, Natalie Savage. 2019. (Trophy Bk.). (ENG.). 128p. (J). (gr. 3-7). pap. 6.99 *(978-0-06-440250-7(9)*, HarperCollins) HarperCollins Pubs. Ltd. GBR. Dist: HarperCollins Pubs.
—Farmer Boy. Wilder, Laura Ingalls. 2008. (Little House Ser.: 2). (ENG.). 384p. (J). (gr. 3-7). pap. 8.99 *(978-0-06-440003-9(4)*, HarperCollins) HarperCollins Pubs. Ltd. GBR. Dist: HarperCollins Pubs.
—Farmer Boy: Full Color Edition. Wilder, Laura Ingalls. 2004. (Little House Ser.: 2). (ENG.). 384p. (J). (gr. 3-7). pap. 8.99 *(978-0-06-058182-4(4))* HarperCollins Pubs.
—The First Four Years. Wilder, Laura Ingalls. 2008. (Little House Ser.: 9). (ENG.). 160p. (J). (gr. 3-7). pap. 8.99 *(978-0-06-440031-2(X)*, HarperCollins) HarperCollins Pubs. Ltd. GBR. Dist: HarperCollins Pubs.
—The First Four Years: Full Color Edition. Wilder, Laura Ingalls. 2004. (Little House Ser.: 9). (ENG.). 160p. (J). (gr. 3-7). pap. 9.99 *(978-0-06-058188-6(3))* HarperCollins Pubs.
—The Friendly Book. Brown, Margaret Wise. 2012. (Little Golden Book Ser.). 32p. (J). (gr. k-k). 4.99 *(978-0-307-92962-4(0)*, Golden Bks.) Random Hse. Children's Bks.
—Garth Williams's Furry Tales. 2016. 224p. (J). (-k). 12.99 *(978-1-101-93528-6(6)*, Golden Bks.) Random Hse. Children's Bks.
—The Giant Golden Book of Elves & Fairies. Werner, Janet. 2008. (Golden Classic Ser.). 80p. (J). (gr. -1-2). 16.99 *(978-0-375-84426-3(0)*, Golden Bks.) Random Hse. Children's Bks.
—Harry Kitten & Tucker Mouse / Chester Cricket's Pigeon Ride: Two Books in One. Selden, George. 2009. (Chester Cricket & His Friends Ser.). (ENG.). 144p. (J). (gr. 1-4). pap. 8.99 *(978-0-312-58248-7(X)*, 900062061) Square Fish.
—Home for a Bunny. Brown, Margaret Wise. (J). 2015. 26p. (-k). bds. 7.99 *(978-0-385-39093-4(9))*; 2012. 32p. (gr. k-k). 4.99 *(978-0-307-93009-5(2))*; 2003. 32p. (gr. -1-k). reprint ed. 9.99 *(978-0-307-10546-2(6))* Random Hse. Children's Bks. (Golden Bks.).
—The Kitten Who Thought He Was a Mouse. Norton, Miriam. 2008. (Little Golden Book Ser.). 32p. (J). (gr. -1-2). 4.99 *(978-0-375-84822-3(3)*, Golden Bks.) Random Hse. Children's Bks.
—Little Fur Family Board Book. Brown, Margaret Wise. 2005. (ENG.). 32p. (J). (gr. -1 — 1). bds. 7.99 *(978-0-06-075960-5(7)*, HarperFestival) HarperCollins Pubs.
—Little Fur Family Deluxe Edition in Keepsake Box. Brown, Margaret Wise. deluxe ed. 2003. (ENG.). 32p. (J). (gr. -1 — 1). pap. 17.99 *(978-0-06-051898-1(7)*, HarperFestival) HarperCollins Pubs.
Williams, Garth, et al. Little Golden Book Kitten Tales. Brown, Margaret Wise. 2017. (ENG.). 80p. (J). (-k). 7.99 *(978-0-399-55501-5(3)*, Golden Bks.) Random Hse. Children's Bks.
Williams, Garth. Little House 5-Book Full-Color Box Set: Books 1 To 5, Set. Wilder, Laura Ingalls. 2004. (Little House Ser.). (ENG.). 1648p. (J). (gr. 3-7). pap. 44.99 *(978-0-06-075428-0(1))* HarperCollins Pubs.
—A Little House Christmas Treasury: Festive Holiday Stories. Wilder, Laura Ingalls. 2005. (Little House Ser.). (ENG.). 144p. (J). (gr. 3-7). 14.99 *(978-0-06-076918-5(1))* HarperCollins Pubs.
—The Little House Cookbook. Walker, Barbara M. 2019. (ENG.). 256p. (J). (gr. 3). pap. 14.94 *(978-1-68411-711-6(9))* Melrovich, Igal.
—The Little House Cookbook: New Full-Color Edition: Frontier Foods from Laura Ingalls Wilder's Classic Stories. Walker, Barbara M. 2018. (Little House Nonfiction Ser.). (ENG.). 304p. (J). (gr. 3-7). 24.99 *(978-0-06-247079-9(5))* HarperCollins Pubs.
—Little House in the Big Woods. Wilder, Laura Ingalls. 2008. (Little House Ser.: 1). (ENG.). 256p. (J). (gr. 3-7). pap. 7.99 *(978-0-06-440001-5(8)*, HarperCollins) HarperCollins Pubs. Ltd. GBR. Dist: HarperCollins Pubs.
—Little House in the Big Woods: Full Color Edition. Wilder, Laura Ingalls. 2004. (Little House Ser.: 1). (ENG.). 256p. (J). (gr. 3-7). pap. 9.99 *(978-0-06-058180-0(8))* HarperCollins Pubs.
—Little House on the Prairie. Wilder, Laura Ingalls. 2008. (Little House Ser.: 3). (ENG.). 352p. (J). (gr. 3-7). pap. 8.99 *(978-0-06-440002-2(6)*, HarperCollins) HarperCollins Pubs. Ltd. GBR. Dist: HarperCollins Pubs.
—Little House on the Prairie. Wilder, Laura Ingalls & Videbeck, Sheila. 7th rev. ed. 2016. (Charming Classics). (ENG.). 544p. pap. 75.99 *(978-0-06-000046-2(5))* Lippincott Williams & Wilkins.
—Little House on the Prairie: Full Color Edition. Wilder, Laura Ingalls. (Little House Ser.: 3). (ENG.). (J). (gr. 3-7). 2004. 352p. pap. 9.99 *(978-0-06-058181-7(6))*; 75th anniv. ed. 2010. 368p. 16.99 *(978-0-06-195827-4(1))* HarperCollins Pubs.
—Little Silver House. Lindquist, Jennie D. 2008. (J). (gr. 2-6). 21.00 *(978-0-8446-6190-2(2))* Smith, Peter Pub., Inc.
—Little Town on the Prairie. Wilder, Laura Ingalls. 2003. (Little House Ser.). 320p. (J). pap. 5.99 *(978-0-06-052242-1(9))* HarperCollins Pubs.
—Little Town on the Prairie. Wilder, Laura Ingalls. 2008. (Little House Ser.: 7). (ENG.). 320p. (J). (gr. 3-7). pap. 8.99 *(978-0-06-440007-7(7)*, HarperCollins) HarperCollins Pubs. Ltd. GBR. Dist: HarperCollins Pubs.
—Little Town on the Prairie: Full Color Edition. Wilder, Laura Ingalls. 2004. (Little House Ser.: 7). (ENG.). 320p. (J). (gr. 3-7). pap. 9.99 *(978-0-06-058186-2(7))* HarperCollins Pubs.
—The Long Winter. Wilder, Laura Ingalls. 2008. (Little House Ser.: 6). (ENG.). 352p. (J). (gr. 3-7). pap. 8.99 *(978-0-06-440006-0(9)*, HarperCollins) HarperCollins Pubs. Ltd. GBR. Dist: HarperCollins Pubs.
—The Long Winter: Full Color Edition. Wilder, Laura Ingalls. 2004. (Little House Ser.: 6). (ENG.). 352p. (J). (gr. 3-7). pap. 9.99 *(978-0-06-058185-5(9))* HarperCollins Pubs.
—Mi Primer Libro de Contar. Moore, Lilian. 2017. (Little Golden Book Ser.). 24p. (J). (-k). 4.99 *(978-0-399-55361-5(4)*, Golden Bks.) Random Hse. Children's Bks.
—Mister Dog. Brown, Margaret Wise. 2003. (Little Golden Book Ser.). (ENG.). 24p. (J). (gr. -1-2). 4.99 *(978-0-307-10336-9(6)*, Golden Bks.) Random Hse. Children's Bks.
—My First Counting Book. Moore, Lilian. 2015. (Little Golden Board Book Ser.). 26p. (J). (-k). bds. 7.99 *(978-0-553-52223-5(X)*, Golden Bks.) Random Hse. Children's Bks.
—On the Banks of Plum Creek. Wilder, Laura Ingalls. 2008. (Little House Ser.: 4). (ENG.). 352p. (J). (gr. 3-7). pap. 8.99 *(978-0-06-440004-6(2)*, HarperCollins) HarperCollins Pubs. Ltd. GBR. Dist: HarperCollins Pubs.
—On the Banks of Plum Creek: Full Color Edition. Wilder, Laura Ingalls. 2004. (Little House Ser.: 4). (ENG.). 352p. (J). (gr. 3-7). pap. 9.99 *(978-0-06-058183-1(2))* HarperCollins Pubs.
—The Rescuers. Sharp, Margery. 2016. (ENG.). 160p. (J). (gr. 4-7). pap. 9.99 *(978-1-68137-007-1(7)*, NYRB Kids) New York Review of Bks., Inc., The.
—Stuart Little. White, E. B. 60th anniv. ed. (Trophy Bk.). (ENG.). 144p. (J). (gr. 3-7). 2020. pap. 7.99 *(978-0-06-440056-5(5))*; 2005. 16.99 *(978-0-06-026395-9(4))* HarperCollins Pubs. Ltd. GBR. (HarperCollins). Dist: HarperCollins Pubs.
—Stuart Little. White, E. B. 2004. (SPA.). 144p. (gr. 3-5). pap. 10.95 *(978-1-59437-554-5(2))* Santillana USA Publishing Co., Inc.
—Stuart Little Book & Charm. White, E. B. 2006. (Charming Classics). 144p. (J). (gr. 3-7). 6.99 *(978-0-06-082334-4(8)*, HarperFestival) HarperCollins Pubs.
—A Tale of Tails. MacPherson, Elizabeth. 2016. (Little Golden Book Ser.). 24p. (J). (gr. -1-k). 4.99 *(978-0-385-37863-5(7)*, Golden Bks.) Random Hse. Children's Bks.
—Telaraña de Carlota: Charlotte's Web (Spanish Edition), 1 vol. White, E. B. 2005. (SPA.). 224p. (J). (gr. 3-7). pap. 8.99 *(978-0-06-075740-3(X)*, HarperCollins Español) HarperCollins Christian Publishing.
—The Telarana of Carlota (La Telarana de Carlota) White, E. B. 2005. (Charlotte's Web Ser.). (SPA.). 224p. (J). 16.99 *(978-0-06-075739-7(6)*, Rayo) HarperCollins Pubs.
—The Telarana of Carlota (LaTelarana de Carlota) White, E. B. movie tie-in ed. 2006. (Charlotte's Web Ser.). (SPA.). 224p. (J). pap. 7.99 *(978-0-06-112522-5(9)*, Rayo) HarperCollins Pubs.
—These Happy Golden Years. Wilder, Laura Ingalls. rev. ed. 2008. (Little House Ser.: 8). (ENG.). 304p. (J). (gr. 3-7). pap. 8.99 *(978-0-06-440008-4(5)*, HarperCollins) HarperCollins Pubs. Ltd. GBR. Dist: HarperCollins Pubs.
—These Happy Golden Years: Full Color Edition. Wilder, Laura Ingalls. 2004. (Little House Ser.: 8). (ENG.). 304p. (J). (gr. 3-7). pap. 9.99 *(978-0-06-058187-9(5))* HarperCollins Pubs.
—Tucker's Countryside. Selden, George. 2012. (Chester Cricket & His Friends Ser.: 2). (ENG.). 192p. (J). (gr. 3-7). pap. 7.99 *(978-1-250-00256-3(7)*, 900079480) Square Fish.
Williams, Garth. Baby Animals. Williams, Garth. 2004. (Little Golden Book Ser.). 32p. (J). (gr. -1-2). 4.99 *(978-0-375-82933-8(4)*, Golden Bks.) Random Hse. Children's Bks.
—Baby's First Book. Williams, Garth. (Golden Baby Ser.). (J). 2011. 24p. (— 1). 6.99 *(978-0-375-85905-2(5))*; 2007. 32p. (gr. -1-2). 4.99 *(978-0-375-83916-0(X))* Random Hse. Children's Bks. (Golden Bks.).
—Bunnies' ABC. Williams, Garth. Golden Books. 2015. (Little Golden Book Ser.). 24p. (J). (-k). 4.99 *(978-0-385-39128-3(5)*, Golden Bks.) Random Hse. Children's Bks.
Williams, Garth & Wells, Rosemary. Stuart Little: Full Color Edition. White, E. B. 60th anniv. ed. 2005. (Stuart-Little Ser.). (ENG.). 144p. (J). (gr. 3-7). pap. 9.99 *(978-0-06-441092-2(7)*, HarperCollins) HarperCollins Pubs. Ltd. GBR. Dist: HarperCollins Pubs.
Williams, Garth, jt. illus. see Maze, Deborah.
Williams, George Alfred. Ten Girls from Dickens. Sweetser, Kate Dickinson. 2004. reprint ed. pap. 27.95 *(978-1-4179-3165-1(5))* Kessinger Publishing, LLC.
Williams, Glenn. Learning about Cows. Williams, Glenn, photos by. Lapsley, Sarah. 2008. 20p. (J). pap. *(978-1-935289-10-4(1))* Spalding Education International.
Williams, Harland. The Kid with Too Many Nightmares. 2004. (J). *(978-0-8431-1582-6(3)*, Price Stern Sloan) Penguin Publishing Group.
Williams, Jared T. Catie Copley. Kovacs, Deborah. 2007. (ENG.). 32p. (J). (gr. -1-3). 19.95 *(978-1-56792-332-2(1))* Godine, David R. Pub.
—Catie Copley's Great Escape. Kovacs, Deborah. 2009. (ENG.). 32p. (J). (gr. -1-3). 17.95 *(978-1-56792-379-7(8))* Godine, David R. Pub.
Williams, Jared T. Rabbit Ninja. Williams, Jared T. 2019. (ENG.). 32p. (J). 17.95 *(978-1-56792-628-6(2))* Godine, David R. Pub.
Williams, Jayne. Molly's Magic Smile. Cutrer, Elisabeth. Sexton, Jessa R., ed. 2013. 38p. 17.00 *(978-0-9860244-3-6(0))* O'More Publishing.
Williams, Jean. The Stork & the Birthday Stocking. Payne, Jackson. 2009. 24p. pap. 12.00 *(978-1-4389-8146-8(5))* AuthorHouse.
Williams, Jemima. Hibernate with Me. Scheuer, Benjamin. 2019. (ENG.). 40p. (J). (gr. -1-3). 17.99 *(978-1-5344-3217-8(5)*, Simon & Schuster Bks. For Young Readers) Simon & Schuster Bks. For Young Readers.
—Hundred Feet Tall. Scheuer, Benjamin. 2020. (ENG.). 40p. (J). (gr. -1-3). 17.99 *(978-1-5344-3219-2(1)*, Simon & Schuster Bks. For Young Readers) Simon & Schuster Bks. For Young Readers.
Williams, Jenny. A Lion in the Meadow. Mahy, Margaret. 2017. 57p. pap. *(978-1-897136-78-2(1)*, 73-W6781) Hachette New Zealand.
—Little Red Riding Hood. 2017. 24p. (J). (gr. -1-12). pap. 7.99 *(978-1-86147-818-4(6)*, Armadillo) Anness Publishing GBR. Dist: National Bk. Network.
—The Princess & the Wise Woman. Riley, Kana. 2012. (ENG.). 24p. (J). (gr. k-2). pap. 6.97 *(978-0-8136-2371-9(5)*, Modern Curriculum Pr.) Savvas Learning Co.
—A Storyteller Book - Red Riding Hood. Young, Lesley. 2013. (ENG.). 48p. (J). (gr. -1-12). pap. 7.99 *(978-1-84322-909-4(9)*, Armadillo) Anness Publishing GBR. Dist: National Bk. Network.
—25 Things to Do When Grandpa Passes Away, Mom & Dad Get Divorced, or the Dog Dies: Activities to Help Children Suffering Loss or Change. Kanyer, Laurie A. 2004. (ENG.). 80p. pap. 13.95 *(978-1-884734-53-3(7))* Parenting Pr., Inc.
Williams, Jessica. My Koala Doesn't Take Baths. Williams, Jessica. 2019. (ENG.). 20p. (J). pap. ***(978-1-9995397-5-7(3))*** All Write Here Publishing.
—Sleeping Brilliant. Williams, Jessica. 2020. (ENG.). 34p. (J). ***(978-1-9995397-8-8(8))*** All Write Here Publishing.
Williams, John. Runaways. Laybum, Joe. 2014. (ENG.). 144p. (J). (gr. 4-7). pap. 8.95 *(978-1-84780-080-0(7)*, Frances Lincoln Children's Bks.) Quarto Publishing Group UK GBR. Dist: Hachette Bk. Group.
Williams Jr., Anthony. Granny Says. Williams-Ashe, Marcella Norton. 2012. 46p. pap. 12.00 *(978-0-9764198-4-6(X))* Allecram Publishing.
Williams, Kareem Paul, jt. illus. see Thames, Leona.
Williams, Kristjana S. Into the Jungle: Stories for Mowgli. Rundell, Katherine. 2018. (ENG.). 240p. (J). (gr. 3-7). 24.99 *(978-1-5362-0527-5(3))* Candlewick Pr.
Williams, Larry. The League of Clique. Williams, Larry. 2007. (ENG.). 80p. per. 19.95 *(978-1-4241-5976-5(8))* America Star Bks.
Williams, Lily. Can You Crack the Code? A Fascinating History of Ciphers & Cryptography. Schwartz, Ella. 2019. (ENG.). 128p. (J). 21.99 *(978-1-68119-514-8(3)*, 900175603, Bloomsbury Children's Bks.) Bloomsbury Publishing USA.
Williams, Lily. If Elephants Disappeared. Williams, Lily. 2019. (If Animals Disappeared Ser.). (ENG.). 40p. (J). 18.99 *(978-1-250-14320-4(9)*, 900180477) Roaring Brook Pr.
—If Polar Bears Disappeared. Williams, Lily. 2018. (If Animals Disappeared Ser.). (ENG.). 40p. (J). 17.99 *(978-1-250-14319-8(5)*, 900180475) Roaring Brook Pr.
Williams, Lisa. Bad Luck, Lucy! Graves, Sue. 2008. (Tadpoles Ser.). (ENG.). 24p. (J). (gr. -1-3). pap. *(978-0-7787-3882-4(5))*; lib. bdg. *(978-0-7787-3851-0(5))* Crabtree Publishing Co.
—The Big Turnip: Band 00/Lilac (Collins Big Cat) Hughes, Mónica. 2006. (Collins Big Cat Ser.). (ENG.). 16p. (J). (gr. -1-k). pap. 7.99 *(978-0-00-718644-0(4))* HarperCollins Pubs. Ltd. GBR. Dist: Independent Pubs. Group.
—Cave-Baby & the Mammoth. French, Vivian. 2010. 32p. pap. *(978-1-84089-635-0(3))* Zero to Ten, Ltd.
Williams, Lisa. Finding Stones for Grandma. Griffiths, Sarah. 2020. (ENG.). 34p. (J). pap. ***(978-1-9999758-4-5(7))*** Team Author UK.
Williams, Lisa. If I Were an Alien. French, Vivian. 2009. (Get Set Readers Ser.). 32p. (J). (gr. -1-2). lib. bdg. 25.60 *(978-1-60754-267-4(6))* Windmill Bks.
—Sophie's Spectacles. Griffiths, Sarah. 2018. (ENG.). 38p. (J). pap. *(978-1-9999758-2-1(0))* Team Author UK.
Williams, Lisa. That's Our Home. Lennon, Jude. 2020. (ENG.). 34p. (J). (gr. k-1). pap. ***(978-1-9997959-6-2(2))*** Little Lamb Publishing.
Williams, Lorraine. Wave Goodbye, 1 vol. Reid, Rob. 2013. (ENG.). 24p. (J). pap. 10.95 *(978-1-60060-341-9(6))* Lee & Low Bks., Inc.
Williams, Mai'a. Meowoween. Williams, Jerry R. 2019. (ENG.). 34p. (J). pap. 9.99 *(978-1-7930-1367-5(5))* Independently Published.
Williams, Marcia. Archie's War: My Scrapbook of the First World War. Williams, Marcia. Yang, Belle. 2007. (ENG.). 48p. (J). (gr. 3-7). 18.99 *(978-0-7636-3532-9(4))* Candlewick Pr.
—The Elephant's Friend & Other Tales from Ancient India. Williams, Marcia. 2014. (ENG.). 40p. (J). (gr. 1-4). 8.99 *(978-0-7636-7055-9(3))* Candlewick Pr.
—The Elephant's Friend & Other Tales from Ancient India. Williams, Marcia. 2014. (ENG.). (J). (gr. 1-4). lib. bdg. 17.60 *(978-1-62765-387-9(2))* Perfection Learning Corp.
—Greek Myths. Williams, Marcia. 2011. (ENG.). 40p. (J). (gr. k-4). pap. 8.99 *(978-0-7636-5384-2(5))* Candlewick Pr.
—Hooray for Inventors! Williams, Marcia. 2013. (ENG.). 40p. (J). (gr. 3-7). pap. 7.99 *(978-0-7636-6749-8(8))* Candlewick Pr.
—Hooray for Women! Williams, Marcia. 2019. (ENG.). 48p. (J). (gr. 3-7). 17.99 *(978-1-5362-0111-6(1))* Candlewick Pr.
—Lizzy Bennet's Diary: Inspired by Jane Austen's Pride & Prejudice. Williams, Marcia. 2014. (ENG.). 112p. (J). (gr. 3-7). 16.99 *(978-0-7636-7030-6(8))* Candlewick Pr.
—The Romans: Gods, Emperors, & Dormice. Williams, Marcia. 2018. (ENG.). 40p. (J). (gr. 3-7). 11.99 *(978-0-7636-9978-9(0))* Candlewick Pr.
—Tales from Shakespeare. Williams, Marcia. Shakespeare, William. 2004. (ENG.). 40p. (J). (gr. 3-7). reprint ed. pap. 7.99 *(978-0-7636-2323-4(7))* Candlewick Pr.
—The Tudors: Kings, Queens, Scribes, & Ferrets! Williams, Marcia. 2016. (ENG.). 48p. (J). (gr. 3-7). 17.99 *(978-0-7636-8122-7(9))* Candlewick Pr.
Williams, Marisa A. The Peppermint Potties: A Twin Adventures Christmas Story. Williams, Tracey V. 2019. (ENG.). 60p. (J). pap. 7.99 ***(978-1-6715-0927-6(7))*** Independently Published.
Williams, Marquita. Mommy & Me. Abrams, Courtney. 2019. (Brown Girls Bks.: Vol. 1). (ENG.). 32p. (J). pap. 11.99 ***(978-1-7211-5147-9(8))*** CreateSpace Independent Publishing Platform.
Williams, Matt. I Think I Like You, Cat. Milan, Stefani. 2017. (ENG.). 44p. (J). pap. 9.99 *(978-0-9991251-6-8(8))* Starseed Universe Pr.
Williams, Nate. Classroom How-To: Giving a Presentation. Bodden, Valerie. 2015. (Classroom How-To Ser.). (ENG.). 48p. (J). (gr. 5-8). pap. 12.00 *(978-0-89812-986-1(9)*, Creative Paperbacks) Creative Co., The.
—Classroom How-To: Writing a Research Paper. Bodden, Valerie. 2015. (Classroom How-To Ser.). (ENG.). 48p. (J). (gr. 5-8). pap. 12.00 *(978-0-89812-989-2(3)*, Creative Paperbacks) Creative Co., The.
—How Fast Can You Go? Riggs, Kate. 2014. (ENG.). 14p. (J). (gr. -1-k). bds. 7.99 *(978-1-56846-253-0(0)*, Creative Editions) Creative Co., The.
—To the Rescue! Riggs, Kate. 2016. (ENG.). 14p. (J). (gr. -1 — 1). bds. 7.99 *(978-1-56846-288-2(3)*, Creative Editions) Creative Co., The.
Williams, Ocds Lorraine. Bambini una Meraviglia Stupenda! Una Prospettiva Cattolica Su Come e Perch� Dio Fa I Bambini (dall'et� Di 9 Anni in Su) Ruppersberger, Lester, ed. Marelli, Luca, tr. 2019. (ITA.). 52p. (J). pap. 10.88 ***(978-1-6994-1983-0(3))*** Independently Published.
Williams, Owen. Finding Ray's Key. Goddard, Sam. 2018. (ENG.). 42p. (J). pap. *(978-1-912635-00-9(3))* Filament Publishing.
Williams, Rachel. Princess Annabelle. Rogers, Debbie. 2017. (ENG.). (J). *(978-1-9997464-0-7(6))* Lioness Writing Ltd.
Williams, Raymond. The Unusual Pet Shop. Williams, Brenda May. 2012. 24p. pap. 11.50 *(978-1-61897-798-4(9)*, Strategic Bk. Publishing) Strategic Book Publishing & Rights Agency (SBPRA).

Williams, Rhonda, photos by. Mommy, Daddy, Where Do Babies Come From? Activity Book. Date not set. (Wonderful World of True Love Ser.). 16p. (J). (gr. k-4). pap. 3.95 *(978-0-9675068-0-7(8))* Media For Life.

Williams, Rob. Forever Fingerprints: An Amazing Discovery for Adopted Children. Eldridge, Sherrie. 2014. (ENG.). 32p. 15.95 *(978-1-84905-778-3(8)*, 694269) Kingsley, Jessica Pubs. GBR. Dist: Hachette UK Distribution.

—I Don't Have Your Eyes. Kitze, Carrie A. 2007. 32p. (J). (gr. -1-3). 16.95 *(978-0-9726244-2-8(2))* EMK Pr.

Williams, Ron. Dad's Falling Apart: Keeping It Together When a Family Member Has Multiple Sclerosis. Smith, Jennifer Crown. 2003. 32p. (J). per. 14.95 *(978-0-929173-36-8(8))* Health Press NA Incorporated.

Williams, Sam. Baby Cakes. Wilson, Karma. 2006. (ENG.). 32p. (J). (gr. -1 — 1). bds. 7.99 *(978-1-4169-0289-8(9)*, Little Simon) Little Simon.

—Baby, I Love You. Wilson, Karma. 2009. (ENG.). 30p. (J). (gr. -1 — 1). bds., bds. 7.99 *(978-1-4169-1910-0(4)*, Little Simon) Little Simon.

—Bathtime for Twins. Weiss, Ellen. 2012. (ENG.). 30p. (J). (gr. -1 — 1). bds. 7.99 *(978-1-4424-3026-6(5)*, Little Simon) Little Simon.

—¡Bienvenido a Casa, Bebé! (Welcome Home, Baby!) Tabby, Abigail. Romay, Alexis, tr. 2019. (New Books for Newborns Ser.). (SPA.). 16p. (J). (— 1). bds. 7.99 *(978-1-5344-5557-3(4)*, Libros Para Ninos) Libros Para Ninos.

—Frosty the Snowman. Rollins, Walter & Nelson, Steve. 2013. (ENG.). 16p. (J). (gr. -1-k). bds. 9.99 *(978-0-545-45005-8(5)*, Cartwheel Bks.) Scholastic, Inc.

—Little Red's Autumn Adventure. Ferguson, Sarah. 2009. (ENG.). 40p. (J). (gr. -1-1). 16.99 *(978-0-689-84341-9(0)*, Simon & Schuster/Paula Wiseman Bks.) Simon & Schuster/Paula Wiseman Bks.

—Little Red's Christmas Story. Ferguson, Sarah. 2011. (ENG.). 40p. (J). (gr. -1-2). pap. 19.99 *(978-1-4424-3076-1(1)*, Simon & Schuster/Paula Wiseman Bks.) Simon & Schuster/Paula Wiseman Bks.

—Little Red's Summer Adventure. Ferguson, Sarah & Duchess of York Staff. 2006. (ENG.). 40p. (J). (gr. -1-3). 17.99 *(978-0-689-85562-7(1)*, Simon & Schuster/Paula Wiseman Bks.) Simon & Schuster/Paula Wiseman Bks.

—No More Biting for Billy Goat! Ford, Bernette. 2013. (Ducky & Piggy Ser.). (ENG.). 32p. (J). (gr. -1-k). 14.95 *(978-1-907967-31-3(1))* Boxer Bks., Ltd. GBR. Dist: Sterling Publishing Co., Inc.

—No More Blanket for Lambkin! Ford, Bernette. 2010. (Ducky & Piggy Ser.). (ENG.). 26p. (J). (gr. k — 1). bds. 6.95 *(978-1-906250-47-8(2))* Boxer Bks., Ltd. GBR. Dist: Sterling Publishing Co., Inc.

—No More Diapers for Ducky! Ford, Bernette. 2007. (Ducky & Piggy Ser.). (ENG.). 26p. (J). (gr. -1 — 1). bds. 7.95 *(978-1-905417-38-4(1))* Boxer Bks., Ltd. GBR. Dist: Sterling Publishing Co., Inc.

—Playtime for Twins. Weiss, Ellen. 2012. (ENG.). 30p. (J). (gr. -1 — 1). bds. 7.99 *(978-1-4424-3027-3(3)*, Little Simon) Little Simon.

—Princess Puppy. Ford, Bernette G. 2013. (J). *(978-0-545-53967-8(6)*, Cartwheel Bks.) Scholastic, Inc.

—Twins in the Park. Weiss, Ellen. 2003. (Ready-To-Reads Ser.). (ENG.). 24p. (J). (gr. -1-k). pap. 4.99 *(978-0-689-85742-3(X)*, Simon Spotlight) Simon Spotlight.

—Welcome Home, Baby! Tabby, Abigail. 2017. (New Books for Newborns Ser.). (ENG.). 16p. (J). (— 1). bds. 8.99 *(978-1-5344-0103-7(2)*, Little Simon) Little Simon.

—Whatever You Do, I Love You. Weiss, Ellen. 2010. (ENG.). 16p. (J). (gr. -1 — 1). bds. 7.99 *(978-1-4424-0809-8(X)*, Little Simon) Little Simon.

—You're Getting a Baby Brother! Higginson, Sheila Sweeny. 2012. (ENG.). 24p. (J). (gr. -1-k). bds. 7.99 *(978-1-4424-2021-2(9)*, Little Simon) Little Simon.

—You're Getting a Baby Sister! Higginson, Sheila Sweeny. 2012. (ENG.). 24p. (J). (gr. -1-k). bds. 7.99 *(978-1-4424-2050-2(2)*, Little Simon) Little Simon.

Williams, Sam. Snack Time. Williams, Sam. 2016. (Noah's Park Ser.: 3). (ENG.). 14p. (J). (gr. -1-k). bds. 7.99 *(978-1-4814-4263-3(5)*, Little Simon) Little Simon.

Williams, Samantha. So, You Wanna Puppy?! Hirt, Jack. 2016. (ENG.). (J). 16.99 *(978-1-943331-27-7(8))* Orange Hat Publishing.

Williams, Samantha. What Is Wrong with Emma? When a Child's Friend or Relative Is Diagnosed with Juvenile Huntington's Disease. Patch, Ginnievive. Thomason, Sharon McClellan, ed. 2019. (Family Matters in Huntington's Disease Ser.: Vol. 1). (ENG.). 30p. (J). pap. 9.99 ***(978-1-7173-4395-6(3))*** CreateSpace Independent Publishing Platform.

Williams, Sanai. The ADVENTURES of Miss Polly: No More Bullying! Washington, Bianca L. 2020. (ENG.). 36p. (J). pap. 14.99 ***(978-1-6861-6432-3(7))*** Independently Published.

Williams, Sanai. The Adventures of Miss Polly: Overcoming Fear. Washington, Bianca L. 2019. (Adventures of Miss Polly Ser.: Vol. 1). (ENG.). 28p. (J). pap. 14.99 *(978-1-7946-3294-3(8))* Independently Published.

Williams, Sandra. God Knows Me: Pslam 139 for Little Hearts. Williams, Sandra. 2007. 24p. (J). 8.95 *(978-0-9789310-2-5(5))* Hardnett Publishing.

Williams, Scott & Sinclair, Alex. Superman for Tomorrow, Vol. 1. Azzarello, Brian & Loeb, Jeph. rev. ed. 2006. (Superman (DC Comics) Ser.). (ENG.). 160p. (YA). pap. 14.99 *(978-1-4012-0352-8(3))* DC Comics.

Williams, Sean. Teddy Is Ready: Second Edition. Spicer, Brad. 2018. 28p. (J). pap. 8.95 net. *(978-0-9975811-9-5(0))* SafePlans.

Williams, Shan. Quacker Meets His Dad the Squirrel: Tales from a Duck Named Quacker. Shelton, Ricky V. Date not set. (J). (gr. -1-1). pap. 7.00 *(978-0-9634257-3-7(0))* RVS Bks., Inc.

Williams, Sharon, jt. illus. see Demidova, Tania.

Williams, Shawnna L. My Two Dads. Buie, Alphonso. 2015. (ENG.). 18p. (J). pap. 9.95 *(978-0-692-09788-5(0))* Buie, Alphonso.

Williams, Sophy. The Abandoned Puppy. Webb, Holly. 2018. (Pet Rescue Adventures Ser.). (ENG.). 128p. (J). (gr. 1-4). 19.99 *(978-1-68010-091-4(2))* Tiger Tales.

—Alone in the Night. Webb, Holly. 2017. (Pet Rescue Adventures Ser.). (J). (ENG.). 128p. (gr. 1-4). 19.99 *(978-1-68010-060-0(2))*; 126p. *(978-1-5182-5346-1(6))* Tiger Tales.

—The Baby Firebird. Harrison, Paula. 2017. (Secret Rescuers Ser.: 3). (ENG.). 128p. (J). (gr. 2-5). pap. 5.99 *(978-1-4814-7613-3(0)*, Aladdin) Simon & Schuster Children's Publishing.

—The Brave Kitten. Webb, Holly. 2016. (Pet Rescue Adventures Ser.). (ENG.). 128p. (J). (gr. 1-3). 17.44 *(978-1-4844-7986-5(6))*; 4.99 *(978-1-58925-480-0(5))* Tiger Tales.

—The Curious Kitten. Webb, Holly. 2018. (Pet Rescue Adventures Ser.). (ENG.). 128p. (J). (gr. 1-4). 19.99 *(978-1-68010-090-7(4))* Tiger Tales.

—Grandpa's Boat. Catchpool, Michael. 2009. (ENG.). 32p. (J). (gr. k-k). pap. 11.99 *(978-1-84270-755-5(8))* Andersen Pr. GBR. Dist: Independent Pubs. Group.

—Harry the Homeless Puppy. Webb, Holly. 2015. (Pet Rescue Adventures Ser.). (ENG.). 128p. (J). (gr. 1-4). pap. 4.99 *(978-1-58925-474-9(0))*; lib. bdg. 19.99 *(978-1-68010-002-0(5))* Tiger Tales.

—A Home for Sandy. Webb, Holly. 2017. (Pet Rescue Adventures Ser.). (ENG.). 128p. (J). (gr. 1-4). 19.99 *(978-1-68010-059-4(9))* Tiger Tales.

—The Homeless Kitten. Webb, Holly. 2018. (Pet Rescue Adventures Ser.). (ENG.). 128p. (J). (gr. 1-4). 19.99 *(978-1-68010-092-1(0))* Tiger Tales.

—Jessie the Lonely Puppy. Webb, Holly. 2015. (Pet Rescue Adventures Ser.). (ENG.). 128p. (J). (gr. 1-4). pap. 4.99 *(978-1-58925-473-2(2))*; lib. bdg. 19.99 *(978-1-68010-003-7(3))* Tiger Tales.

—Kitten Nobody Wanted. Webb, Holly. 2015. (Pet Rescue Adventures Ser.). (ENG.). 128p. (J). (gr. 1-4). lib. bdg. 19.99 *(978-1-58925-182-3(2))* Tiger Tales.

—The Kitten Nobody Wanted & Other Tales. Webb, Holly. 2017. (Pet Rescue Adventures Ser.). (ENG.). 384p. (J). (gr. 1-4). pap. 10.99 *(978-1-68010-405-9(5))* Tiger Tales.

—Leo All Alone. Webb, Holly. 2016. (Pet Rescue Adventures Ser.). (ENG.). 128p. (J). (gr. 1-4). 4.99 *(978-1-58925-482-4(1))* Tiger Tales.

—The Loneliest Kitten. Webb, Holly. 2020. (Pet Rescue Adventures Ser.). (ENG.). 128p. (J). (gr. 1-4). 21.99 *(978-1-68010-184-3(6))*; pap. 5.99 *(978-1-68010-456-1(X))* Tiger Tales.

—Lost in the Snow. Webb, Holly. 2008. 96p. (J). (gr. 1-5). 3.99 *(978-1-56148-650-2(7)*, Good Bks.) Skyhorse Publishing Co., Inc.

—Lost in the Snow. Webb, Holly. 2015. (Pet Rescue Adventures Ser.). (ENG.). 128p. (J). (gr. 1-4). pap. 4.99 *(978-1-58925-472-5(4))*; lib. bdg. 19.99 *(978-1-68010-004-4(1))* Tiger Tales.

—The Lost Puppy. Webb, Holly. 2016. (Pet Rescue Adventures Ser.). (ENG.). 128p. (J). (gr. 1-3). 17.44 *(978-1-4844-9533-9(0))*; pap. 4.99 *(978-1-58925-491-6(0))* Tiger Tales.

—The Magic Fox. Harrison, Paula. 2017. (Secret Rescuers Ser.: 4). (ENG.). 112p. (J). (gr. 2-5). 16.99 *(978-1-4814-7620-1(3))*; pap. 5.99 *(978-1-4814-7619-5(X))* Simon & Schuster Children's Publishing. (Aladdin).

—The Missing Kitten. Webb, Holly. 2016. (Pet Rescue Adventures Ser.). (ENG.). 128p. (J). (gr. 1-3). 17.44 *(978-1-4844-9531-5(4))*; pap. 4.99 *(978-1-58925-488-6(0))* Tiger Tales.

—The Missing Kitten & Other Tales. Webb, Holly. 2018. (Pet Rescue Adventures Ser.). (ENG.). 384p. (J). (gr. 1-4). pap. 10.99 *(978-1-68010-415-8(2))* Tiger Tales.

—The Missing Puppy & Other Tales. Webb, Holly. 2017. (Pet Rescue Adventures Ser.). (ENG.). 384p. (J). (gr. 1-4). pap. 10.99 *(978-1-68010-404-2(7))* Tiger Tales.

—Misty the Abandoned Kitten. Webb, Holly. 2016. (Pet Rescue Adventures Ser.). (ENG.). 128p. (J). (gr. 1-3). 17.44 *(978-1-4844-9532-2(2))*; pap. 4.99 *(978-1-58925-489-3(9))* Tiger Tales.

Williams, Sophy. The Mystery Kitten. Webb, Holly. 2020. (Pet Rescue Adventures Ser.). (ENG.). 128p. (J). (gr. 1-4). pap. 5.99 ***(978-1-68010-475-2(6))***; lib. bdg. 14.99 ***(978-1-68010-222-2(2))*** Tiger Tales.

Williams, Sophy. The Nativity Story, 1 vol. McCaughrean, Geraldine. 2009. 48p. (J). 14.99 *(978-0-8254-7878-9(2)*, Lion Children's) Lion Hudson PLC GBR. Dist: Kregel Pubns.

—Oscar's Lonely Christmas. Webb, Holly. 2019. (Pet Rescue Adventures Ser.). (ENG.). 128p. (J). (gr. 1-4). 4.99 *(978-1-68010-448-6(9))*; lib. bdg. 19.99 *(978-1-68010-170-6(6))* Tiger Tales.

—The Perfect Kitten. Webb, Holly. 2019. (Pet Rescue Adventures Ser.). (ENG.). 128p. (J). (gr. 1-4). 4.99 *(978-1-68010-447-9(0))*; lib. bdg. 19.99 *(978-1-68010-169-0(2))* Tiger Tales.

—Prayers & Verses for a Child's Baptism. Piper, Sophie. ed. 2016. (ENG.). 64p. (J). (-k). 9.99 *(978-0-7459-7615-0(8))* Lion Hudson PLC GBR. Dist: Independent Pubs. Group.

—The Puppy Who Couldn't Sleep. Webb, Holly. 2020. (Pet Rescue Adventures Ser.). (ENG.). 128p. (J). (gr. 1-4). 21.99 *(978-1-68010-185-0(4))*; pap. 5.99 *(978-1-68010-457-8(8))* Tiger Tales.

—The Rescued Puppy. Webb, Holly. 2017. (Pet Rescue Adventures Ser.). (J). (ENG.). 128p. (gr. 1-4). 19.99 *(978-1-68010-051-8(3))*; 124p. *(978-1-5182-4904-4(3))* Tiger Tales.

—The Sad Puppy. Webb, Holly. 2018. (Pet Rescue Adventures Ser.). (ENG.). 128p. (J). (gr. 1-4). 19.99 *(978-1-68010-089-1(0))* Tiger Tales.

Williams, Sophy. Sam the Stolen Puppy. Webb, Holly. 2020. (Pet Rescue Adventures Ser.). (ENG.). 128p. (J). (gr. 1-4). pap. 5.99 ***(978-1-68010-476-9(4))***; lib. bdg. 14.99 ***(978-1-68010-223-9(0))*** Tiger Tales.

Williams, Sophy. Sammy the Shy Kitten. Webb, Holly. 2017. (Pet Rescue Adventures Ser.). (J). (ENG.). 128p. (gr. 1-4). 19.99 *(978-1-68010-050-1(5))*; 127p. *(978-1-5182-4902-0(7))* Tiger Tales.

—The Scruffy Puppy. Webb, Holly. 2016. (Pet Rescue Adventures Ser.). (ENG.). 128p. (J). (gr. 1-3). 17.44 *(978-1-4844-9534-6(9))*; pap. 4.99 *(978-1-58925-490-9(2))* Tiger Tales.

—The Sea Pony. Harrison, Paula. 2018. (Secret Rescuers Ser.: 6). (ENG.). 128p. (J). (gr. 2-5). 16.99 *(978-1-4814-7623-2(8))*; pap. 5.99 *(978-1-4814-7622-5(X))* Simon & Schuster Children's Publishing. (Aladdin).

—The Secret Kitten. Webb, Holly. 2017. (Pet Rescue Adventures Ser.). (ENG.). 128p. (J). (gr. 1-4). 19.99 *(978-1-68010-049-5(1))* Tiger Tales.

—The Secret Puppy. Webb, Holly. 2016. (Pet Rescue Adventures Ser.). (ENG.). 128p. (J). (gr. 1-3). 17.44 *(978-1-4844-7989-6(0))*; 4.99 *(978-1-58925-483-1(X))* Tiger Tales.

—The Secret Puppy & Other Tales. Webb, Holly. 2018. (Pet Rescue Adventures Ser.). (ENG.). 384p. (J). (gr. 1-4). pap. 10.99 *(978-1-68010-414-1(4))* Tiger Tales.

—The Secret Rescuers Magical Collection: The Storm Dragon; the Sky Unicorn; the Baby Firebird; the Magic Fox; the Star Wolf; the Sea Pony. Harrison, Paula. ed. 2018. (Secret Rescuers Ser.). (ENG.). 720p. (J). (gr. 2-5). pap. 35.99 *(978-1-5344-1961-2(6)*, Aladdin) Simon & Schuster Children's Publishing.

—Sky the Unwanted Kitten. Webb, Holly. 2016. (Pet Rescue Adventures Ser.). (J). (ENG.). 128p. (gr. 1-4). 4.99 *(978-1-58925-481-7(3))*; 122p. *(978-0-545-16624-9(1))* Tiger Tales.

—The Sky Unicorn. Harrison, Paula. 2017. (Secret Rescuers Ser.: 2). (ENG.). 112p. (J). (gr. 2-5). pap. 5.99 *(978-1-4814-7610-2(6)*, Simon & Schuster/Paula Wiseman Bks.) Simon & Schuster/Paula Wiseman Bks.

—The Star Wolf. Harrison, Paula. 2018. (Secret Rescuers Ser.: 5). (ENG.). 112p. (J). (gr. 2-5). 16.99 *(978-1-4814-7617-1(3))*; pap. 5.99 *(978-1-4814-7616-4(5))* Simon & Schuster Children's Publishing. (Aladdin).

—The Storm Dragon. Harrison, Paula. 2017. (Secret Rescuers Ser.: 1). (ENG.). 128p. (J). (gr. 2-5). pap. 5.99 *(978-1-4814-7607-2(6)*, Simon & Schuster/Paula Wiseman Bks.) Simon & Schuster/Paula Wiseman Bks.

—Teddy in Trouble. Webb, Holly. 2017. (Pet Rescue Adventures Ser.). (ENG.). 128p. (J). (gr. 1-4). 19.99 *(978-1-68010-062-4(9))* Tiger Tales.

—The Tiniest Puppy. Webb, Holly. 2017. (Pet Rescue Adventures Ser.). (J). (ENG.). 128p. (gr. 1-4). 19.99 *(978-1-68010-052-5(1))*; 126p. *(978-1-5182-4905-1(1))* Tiger Tales.

—The Unwanted Puppy. Webb, Holly. 2019. (Pet Rescue Adventures Ser.). (ENG.). 128p. (J). (gr. 1-4). 4.99 *(978-1-68010-449-3(7))*; lib. bdg. 19.99 *(978-1-68010-171-3(4))* Tiger Tales.

Williams, Steve. The Matt & the Monster Do to Mexico - la Mutt y la Monster Van a Mexi. Krakow, Amy. Knaus, Jill, tr. 2003.Tr. of La Mutt Y La Monster Van A Mexico. 32p. (J). (gr. 2-6). 15.00 *(978-0-9715224-1-1(3))* Wagging Tales Publishing.

—The Matt & the Monster 60 Sking & Snowboarding. Krakow, Amy. 2005. 32p. (J). (gr. k-6). 15.00 *(978-0-9715224-2-8(1))* Wagging Tales Publishing.

Williams, Sue. Fun in the Sun. Albee, Sarah. 2006. (Step-By-Step Readers Ser.). (J). pap. *(978-1-59939-058-1(2)*, Reader's Digest Young Families, Inc.) Studio Fun International.

—Under the Ramadan Moon. Whitman, Sylvia. 2012. (J). 32.71 *(978-1-61913-151-4(X))* Weigl Pubs., Inc.

—Under the Ramadan Moon, 1 vol. Whitman, Sylvia. 2011. (ENG.). 24p. (J). (gr. -1-3). 6.99 *(978-0-8075-8305-0(7)*, 807583057) Whitman, Albert & Co.

Williams, Ted. Curly Hare Gets It Straight. Douglas, Babette. 2006. (Kiss a Me Teacher Creature Stories Ser.). (J). (gr. -1-3). *(978-1-890343-35-4(8))* Kiss A Me Productions, Inc.

—My First Dictionary. Miller, Susan A. 2005. (My First Ser.). 160p. (J). 7.98 *(978-0-7853-8369-7(7)*, 7183800) Phoenix International Publications, Inc.

—Squirt: The Magic Cuddlefish. Douglas, Babette. 2006. (Kiss a Me Teacher Creature Stories Ser.). (J). (gr. -1-3). 9.99 *(978-1-890343-47-7(1))* Kiss A Me Productions, Inc.

Williams, Ted & Kaminski, Karol. My First English-Spanish Picture Dictionary. 2005. (ENG & SPA.). 96p. (gr. -1-3). 6.98 *(978-1-4127-1086-2(3)*, 7242100) Phoenix International Publications, Inc.

Williams, Tim. A Is for Alabama: Roll Tide Roll. Zangas, Sherri. 2009. (J). lib. bdg. 17.95 *(978-0-692-00093-9(3))* Mascot Bks., Inc.

—Gapper's Grand Tour: A Voyage Through Great American Ball Park. Altman, Joel. 2013. (ENG.). (J). (gr. -1-3). 14.95 *(978-1-62086-213-1(1))* Mascot Bks., Inc.

—Hello, Knightro! Callahan, Lauren & Callahan, Michael T. 2013. (ENG.). (J). (gr. 4-7). 14.95 *(978-1-62086-169-1(0))* Mascot Bks., Inc.

Williams, Timothy. Zoo See Me! Distler, Chris. 2019. (ENG.). 42p. (J). pap. 9.99 ***(978-1-6965-8917-8(7))*** Independently Published.

Williams, Toby. I Have a Question, Vol. 4. Martin, Tyler. I.t. ed. 2005. (Sadlier Phonics Reading Program). 8p. (gr. -1-1). 23.00 net. *(978-0-8215-7356-3(X))* Sadlier, William H. Inc.

Williams, Tracy. Princess & the Picnic That Never Happened. Holmes, Alecia. 2018. (ENG.). 24p. (J). pap. 7.00 *(978-1-7921-2781-6(2))* Independently Published.

Williams, True. The Adventures of Tom Sawyer: Novel, Illustrated. Twain, Mark. 2018. (ENG.). 256p. (YA). (gr. 7-13). pap. 11.99 *(978-1-7908-0608-9(9))* Independently Published.

Williams, Vera B. Amber Was Brave, Essie Was Smart. Williams, Vera B. 2004. (ENG.). 72p. (J). (gr. 2-7). reprint ed. pap. 7.99 *(978-0-06-057182-5(9)*, Greenwillow Bks.) HarperCollins Pubs.

—Amber Was Brave, Essie Was Smart. Williams, Vera B. 2003. (J). (gr. k-3). 25.95 incl. audio *(978-1-59112-186-2(8))* Live Oak Media.

—Amber Was Brave, Essie Was Smart. Williams, Vera B. 2004. 17.00 *(978-0-7569-3181-0(9))* Perfection Learning Corp.

—A Chair for Always. Williams, Vera B. 2009. (SPA.). 40p. (J). (gr. -1-3). 16.99 *(978-0-06-172279-0(0)*, Greenwillow Bks.) HarperCollins Pubs.

—A Chair for My Mother 25th Anniversary Edition. Williams, Vera B. 25th anniv. ed. 2007. (Reading Rainbow Bks.). (ENG.). 32p. (J). (gr. -1-3). pap. 7.99 *(978-0-688-04074-1(8)*, Greenwillow Bks.) HarperCollins Pubs.

—Un Sillón para Mi Mamá: A Chair for My Mother (Spanish Edition), 1 vol. Williams, Vera B. 25th anniv. ed. 2007. (SPA.). 32p. (J). (gr. -1-3). reprint ed. pap. 7.99 *(978-0-688-13200-2(6)*, MR5678) HarperCollins Español.

—Un Sillón para Siempre: A Chair for Always (Spanish Edition), 1 vol. Williams, Vera B. 2009.Tr. of Chair for Always. (SPA.). 40p. (J). (gr. -1-3). 17.99 *(978-0-06-172283-7(9)*, HarperCollins Español) HarperCollins Christian Publishing.

Williams, Vera B. & Raschka, Chris. Home at Last. Williams, Vera B. 2016. (ENG.). 40p. (J). (gr. -1-3). 17.99 *(978-0-06-134973-7(9)*, Greenwillow Bks.) HarperCollins Pubs.

Williams, Walter. A Monster for Tea. Williams, Walter. 2013. (ENG.). 32p. (J). (gr. -1-2). 17.99 *(978-0-9890698-3-0(4))* Fernwood & Hedges Bks.

Williams, Wilson. Ratón y León. Swain, Cynthia. 2016. (Jump into Genre Ser.). (SPA.). (J). (gr. 2). 5.25 *(978-1-4788-3610-0(5))* Newmark Learning LLC.

Williams, Wish. Good Night, Little Sea Otter, 1 vol. Halfmann, Janet. (ENG.). (J). 2012. 24p. 15.95 *(978-1-59572-277-5(7))*; 2010. 32p. (gr. -1-3). pap. 5.95 *(978-1-59572-254-6(8))* Star Bright Bks., Inc.

—Good Night, Little Sea Otter (Burmese Karen/English), 1 vol. Halfmann, Janet. 2012. (KAR & ENG.). 24p. (J). 5.95 *(978-1-59572-371-0(4))* Star Bright Bks., Inc.

—Good Night, Little Sea Otter (Burmese/English), 1 vol. Halfmann, Janet. 2012. (ENG.). 24p. (J). pap. 5.95 *(978-1-59572-370-3(6))* Star Bright Bks., Inc.

—Good Night, Little Sea Otter (Hmong/English), 1 vol. Halfmann, Janet. 2012. (ENG.). 24p. (J). pap. 5.95 *(978-1-59572-365-9(X))* Star Bright Bks., Inc.

—Good Night, Little Sea Otter (Portuguese/English), 1 vol. Halfmann, Janet. 2012. (ENG.). 24p. (J). pap. 5.95 *(978-1-59572-359-8(5))* Star Bright Bks., Inc.

—Witches, 1 vol. Christian, Cheryl. 2011. (ENG.). 32p. (J). pap. 5.95 *(978-1-59572-283-6(1))* Star Bright Bks., Inc.

Williams, Zac, photos by. Barbara Beery's Pink Princess Party Cookbook. Beery, Barbara. 2011. (ENG., 64p. (J). (gr. 2-7). spiral bd. 15.99 *(978-1-4424-1231-6(3)*, Simon & Schuster Bks. For Young Readers) Simon & Schuster Bks. For Young Readers.

Williamson, Ada C. Understood Betsy - Illustrated. Fisher, Dorothy Canfield. 2013. 112p. pap. 3.97 *(978-1-60386-582-1(9)*, Merchant Bks.) Rough Draft Printing.

Williamson, Ada Clendenin. The Sandman: More Farm Stories (Yesterday's Classics) Hopkins, William J. 2009. 150p. pap. 8.95 *(978-1-59915-301-8(7))* Yesterday's Classics.

Williamson, Al. Episode V Vol. 1: The Empire Strikes Back. Goodwin, Archie. 2010. (Star Wars Ser.: No. 3). (ENG.). 24p. (J). (gr. 6-12). 27.07 *(978-1-59961-701-5(3)*, 13782, Graphic Novels) Spotlight.

—Episode V Vol. 2: The Empire Strikes Back. Goodwin, Archie. 2010. (Star Wars Ser.: No. 3). (ENG.). 24p. (J). (gr. 6-12). 27.07 *(978-1-59961-702-2(1)*, 13783, Graphic Novels) Spotlight.

—Episode V Vol. 3: The Empire Strikes Back. Goodwin, Archie. 2010. (Star Wars Ser.: No. 3). (ENG.). 24p. (J). (gr. 6-12). 27.07 *(978-1-59961-703-9(X)*, 13784, Graphic Novels) Spotlight.

—Episode V Vol. 4: The Empire Strikes Back. Goodwin, Archie. 2010. (Star Wars Ser.: No. 3). (ENG.). 24p. (J). (gr. 6-12). 27.07 *(978-1-59961-704-6(8)*, 13785, Graphic Novels) Spotlight.

—Episode VI Vol. 1: Return of the Jedi Vol. 1, 1 vol. Goodwin, Archie. 2010. (Star Wars Ser.: No. 3). (ENG.). 24p. (J). (gr. 6-12). 27.07 *(978-1-59961-705-3(6)*, 13786, Graphic Novels) Spotlight.

—Episode VI Vol. 2: Return of the Jedi Vol. 2, 1 vol. Goodwin, Archie. 2010. (Star Wars Ser.: No. 3). (ENG.). 24p. (J). (gr. 6-12). 27.07 *(978-1-59961-706-0(4)*, 13787, Graphic Novels) Spotlight.

—Episode VI Vol. 3: Return of the Jedi Vol. 3, 1 vol. Goodwin, Archie. 2010. (Star Wars Ser.: No. 3). (ENG.). 24p. (J). (gr. 6-12). 27.07 *(978-1-59961-707-7(2)*, 13788, Graphic Novels) Spotlight.

—Episode VI Vol. 4: Return of the Jedi Vol. 4, 1 vol. Goodwin, Archie. 2010. (Star Wars Ser.: No. 3). (ENG.). 24p. (J). (gr. 6-12). 27.07 *(978-1-59961-708-4(0)*, 13789, Graphic Novels) Spotlight.

—Star Wars Legends Epic Collection: the Newspaper Strips Vol. 2. 2019. (ENG.). 504p. (YA). (gr. -1-17). pap. 39.99 *(978-1-302-91737-1(4))* Marvel Worldwide, Inc.

—X-9 Secret Agent Corrigan: 1977-1980, 5 vols., Vol. 5. Goodwin, Archie. 2013. (X-9 Ser.: 5). 288p. 49.99 *(978-1-61377-542-4(3)*, 9781613775424) Idea & Design Works, LLC.

Williamson, Al, jt. illus. see Davis, Jack.

Williamson, Alan, 8th. Timmy the Tow Truck, 6 vols. Williamson, Jennifer. 2005. 28p. (J). pap. *(978-0-9771678-1-4(X))* Theee Hole Punch Publishing.

Williamson, Alan, jt. illus. see Chaykin, Howard.

Williamson, Brian. The Secret Agent Training Manual: How to Make & Break Top Secret Messages: a Companion to the Secret Agents Jack & Max Stalwart Series. Hunt, Elizabeth Singer. 2017. (Secret Agents Jack & Max Stalwart Ser.: 1). 112p. (J). (gr. 2-7). pap. 9.99 *(978-1-60286-339-2(3)*, Running Pr. Kids) Running Pr.

W

—Secret Agents Jack & Max Stalwart: Book 1: the Battle for the Emerald Buddha: Thailand. Hunt, Elizabeth Singer. 2017. (Secret Agents Jack & Max Stalwart Ser.: 1). 144p. (J). (gr. 1-4). pap. 5.99 (978-1-60286-359-0(8), Running Pr. Kids) Running Pr.

—Secret Agents Jack & Max Stalwart: Book 2: the Adventure in the Amazon: Brazil. Hunt, Elizabeth Singer. 2017. (Secret Agents Jack & Max Stalwart Ser.: 2). 144p. (J). (gr. 1-4). pap. 5.99 (978-1-60286-361-3(X), Running Pr. Kids) Running Pr.

—Secret Agents Jack & Max Stalwart: Book 3: the Fate of the Irish Treasure: Ireland. Hunt, Elizabeth Singer. 2019. (Secret Agents Jack & Max Stalwart Ser.: 3). 144p. (J). (gr. 1-4). pap. 5.99 (978-1-60286-578-5(7), Running Pr. Kids) Running Pr.

—Secret Agents Jack & Max Stalwart: Book 4: the Race for Gold Rush Treasure: California, USA. Hunt, Elizabeth Singer. 2019. (Secret Agents Jack & Max Stalwart Ser.: 4). 128p. (J). (gr. 1-4). pap. 5.99 (978-1-60286-579-2(5), Running Pr. Kids) Running Pr.

Williamson, Brian, jt. illus. see Hansen, Jimmy.

Williamson, Fraser. Rata & the Waka: A Tale from New Zealand. Gibbs, Jephson. 2016. 24p. (J). pap. 9.95 (978-1-927244-55-5(2)) Flying Start Bks. NZL. Dist: Flying Start Bks.

—Rata & the Waka (Big Book Edition) A Tale from New Zealand. Gibbs, Jephson. 2016. 24p. (J). pap. (978-1-927244-65-4(X)) Flying Start Bks.

Williamson, Froser. My Clothes: Individual Title Six-Packs. (Sails Literacy Ser.). 16p. (gr. k-18). 27.00 (978-0-7635-4392-1(6)) Rigby Education.

Williamson, Gwyneth. Busy Ant Maths, Year 4, Bk. 4A. Mumford, Jeanette et al. 2014. (Busy Ant Maths Ser.). (ENG.). 72p. (J). (gr. 3). pap., stu. ed. 13.99 (978-0-00-756240-4(3)) HarperCollins Pubs. Ltd. GBR. Dist: Independent Pubs. Group.

Williamson, James. ELEMENOPEE, the Day I, M, N, O & P Left the Abc's. Hall, Pamela. 2005. 16p. (J). 12.95 (978-1-58117-209-6(5), Intervisual/Piggy Toes) Bendon, Inc.

Williamson, Jo. Petunia Paris's Parrot. Haworth, Katie. 2017. (ENG.). 40p. (J). (gr. -1-3). 17.99 (978-1-4998-0437-9(7)) Little Bee Books Inc.

Williamson, Katie, jt. photos by see Fletcher, Neil.

Williamson, Linda K. Veneti: Lake Michigan's Treasure. Birkholz, Gay Lyn. 2010. 52p. pap. 17.00 (978-1-60860-129-5(3), Strategic Bk. Publishing) Strategic Book Publishing & Rights Agency (SBPRA).

Williamson, Lisa Reid. My Friend Helga. Henderson, Rema Frazier. 2019. (ENG.). 42p. (J). pap. 10.00 **(978-1-6990-2219-1(4))** Independently Published.

Williamson, Melanie. Drift upon a Dream: Poems for Sleepy Babies. 2004. 32p. (J). 16.95 (978-1-57091-577-2(6)) Charlesbridge Publishing, Inc.

—The Great Fairy Tale Disaster. Conway, David. 2012. (ENG.). 32p. (J). (gr. -1-2). 12.95 (978-1-58925-111-3(3)) Tiger Tales.

—The Great Nursery Rhyme Disaster. Conway, David. 2009. (ENG.). 32p. (J). (gr. -1-1). 22.44 (978-1-58925-080-2(X)) Tiger Tales.

—Hound Dog. Bedford, David. 2006. (J). pap. 6.95 (978-1-58925-397-1(3)) Tiger Tales.

—The Hungry Wolf: A Story from North America. Don, Lari. 2013. (Animal Stories Ser.). 48p. (J). (gr. 1-4). pap. 8.99 (978-1-84686-872-6(6)) Barefoot Bks., Inc.

—Las Ruedas Del Autobús. 2017. (SPA.). 24p. (J). (gr. -1-1). 9.99 (978-1-84686-789-7(4)) Barefoot Bks., Inc.

—Masha & the Bear: A Story from Russia. Don, Lari. 2013. (Animal Stories Ser.). 48p. (J). (gr. 1-4). pap. 8.99 (978-1-84686-874-0(2)) Barefoot Bks., Inc.

—Never Trust a Tiger: A Story from Korea. Don, Lari. 2012. (Animal Stories Ser.). 48p. (J). (gr. 1-4). pap. 8.99 (978-1-84686-776-7(2)) Barefoot Bks., Inc.

—Sparrow, the Crow & the Pearl. Kerven, Rosalind. 2005. (ENG.). 24p. (J). lib. bdg. 23.65 (978-1-59646-754-5(1)) Dingles & Co.

—That Pesky Dragon. Sykes, Julie. 2007. 32p. (J). (gr. -1-3). 15.95 (978-1-58925-069-7(9)) Tiger Tales.

—The Tortoise's Gift: A Story from Zambia. Don, Lari. 2012. (Animal Stories Ser.). 48p. (J). (gr. 1-4). pap. 8.99 (978-1-84686-774-3(6)) Barefoot Bks., Inc.

—The Wheels on the Bus. Amador Family Staff & Barefoot Books Staff. 2014. 24p. (J). 16.99 (978-1-84686-787-3(8)) Barefoot Bks., Inc.

—The Wheels on the Bus. Barefoot Books Staff & Amador Family Staff. 2014. 24p. (J). (gr. -1-2). 9.99 (978-1-84686-788-0(6)) Barefoot Bks., Inc.

Williamson, Melanie. El magnífico plan de Lobo/ Wolf's Magnificent Plan. Williamson, Melanie. 2008. (SPA.). 29p. 20.95 (978-84-263-6837-9(9)) Vives, Luis Editorial (Edelvives) ESP. Dist: Baker & Taylor Bks.

Williamson, Pete. Dinkin Dings & the Double from Dimension 9. Bass, Guy. 2011. (Dinkin Dings Ser.). (ENG.). 128p. (J). (gr. 3-6). 17.44 (978-0-448-45434-4(3)) Penguin Young Readers Group.

—The Ghost of Grotteskew, 1 vol. Bass, Guy. 2014. (Stitch Head Ser.). (ENG.). 208p. (J). (gr. 3-6). 10.95 (978-1-62370-030-0(2), Capstone Young Readers) Capstone.

Williamson, Pete. Ma Famille: My Family. Davis, Mandie. Davis, Badger, ed. 2017. (FRE.). 68p. (J). pap. **(978-0-9954653-4-3(7))** Davis, Mandie.

—Ma Maison Est Mon Château: My Home Is My Castle. Davis, Mandie. Davis, Badger, ed. 2019. (FRE.). 74p. (J). pap. **(978-1-9164839-6-5(8))** Davis, Mandie.

Williamson, Pete. The Pirate's Eye, 1 vol. Bass, Guy. 2013. (Stitch Head Ser.). (ENG.). 208p. (J). (gr. 3-6). 10.95 (978-1-62370-008-9(6), Capstone Young Readers) Capstone.

—The Spider's Lair. Bass, Guy. 2015. (Stitch Head Ser.). (ENG.). 208p. (J). (gr. 3-6). 10.95 (978-1-62370-192-5(9), Capstone Young Readers) Capstone.

—Stitch Head, 1 vol. Bass, Guy. 2013. (Stitch Head Ser.). (ENG.). 192p. (J). (gr. 3-6). 10.95 (978-1-62370-007-2(8), Capstone Young Readers) Capstone.

Williamson, Pete. The the Strange Case of Dr Jekyll & Mr Hyde. Stevenson, Robert Louis. 2020. (ENG.). 128p. (J). (gr. 4-7). 16.99 **(978-1-78675-097-6(X))** Palazzo Editions, Ltd. GBR. Dist: Independent Pubs. Group.

Williamson, Sarah. Cactus & Flower: A Book about Life Cycles. Williamson, Sarah. 2020. (ENG.). 40p. (J). (gr. -1-3). 16.99 (978-1-4197-4337-5(6), Abrams Bks. for Young Readers) Abrams, Inc.

Willingham, Ellie. Wildwood. Willingham, Ellie. 2007. (ENG.). 136p. (J). (gr. -1-3). per. 10.00 (978-0-9792371-0-2(6)) Keene Publishing.

Willingham, Fred. Busy Fingers. Bowie, C. W. 2004. 28p. (J). (gr. -1 — 1). bds. 7.95 (978-1-58089-048-9(2)) Charlesbridge Publishing, Inc.

—Laboriosos deditos de las Manos. Bowie, C. W. Canetti, Yanitzia, tr. 2004.Tr. of Busy Fingers. 28p. (J). (gr. -1-1). 22.44 (978-1-58089-043-4(1)) Charlesbridge Publishing, Inc.

Willis, Caleb. Pajama Knights. Thayer, Kristi. 2010. 24p. pap. 11.50 (978-1-60860-669-6(4), Strategic Bk. Publishing) Strategic Book Publishing & Rights Agency (SBPRA).

Willis-Crowley, Kate. The Grand Goblin Ball. O'Connor, Jenny. 2018. (Goblin Princess Ser.). (ENG.). 112p. pap. 8.95 (978-0-571-31660-1(3), Faber & Faber Children's Bks.) Faber & Faber, Inc.

—Smoky the Dragon Baby. O'Connor, Jenny. 2018. (Goblin Princess Ser.). (ENG.). 96p. pap. 8.95 (978-0-571-31658-8(1), Faber & Faber Children's Bks.) Faber & Faber, Inc.

Willis, Drew. Crown of Earth. Bell, Hilari. 2010. (Shield, Sword, & Crown Ser.: 3). (ENG.). 272p. (J). (gr. 3-7). pap. 5.99 (978-1-4169-0599-8(5), Aladdin) Simon & Schuster Children's Publishing.

—The Forbidden Castle. Packard, Edward. 2013. (U-Ventures Ser.). (ENG.). 192p. (J). (gr. 3-7). pap. 6.99 (978-1-4424-3428-8(7), Simon & Schuster Bks. For Young Readers) Simon & Schuster Bks. For Young Readers.

—Hatchet. Paulsen, Gary. 20th anniv. ed. 2007. (ENG.). 192p. (J). (gr. 5-9). 19.99 (978-1-4169-2508-8(2), Simon & Schuster Bks. For Young Readers) Simon & Schuster Bks. For Young Readers.

—Hatchet: 30th Anniversary Edition. Paulsen, Gary. 30th ed. 2017. (ENG.). 224p. (J). (gr. 5-9). pap. 9.99 (978-1-4814-8629-3(2), Simon & Schuster Bks. For Young Readers) Simon & Schuster Bks. For Young Readers.

—Heroes of Olympus. Freeman, Philip. 2012. (ENG.). 352p. (J). (gr. 3-7). 17.99 (978-1-4424-1729-8(3), Simon & Schuster Bks. For Young Readers) Simon & Schuster Bks. For Young Readers.

—Heroes of Olympus. Freeman, Philip. 2013. (ENG.). 352p. (J). (gr. 3-7). pap. 10.99 (978-1-4424-1730-4(7), Simon & Schuster Bks. For Young Readers) Simon & Schuster Bks. For Young Readers.

—Nerd Camp 2. 0. Weissman, Elissa Brent. 2015. (ENG.). 304p. (J). (gr. 3-7). pap. 8.99 (978-1-4424-5295-4(1)) Simon & Schuster Children's Publishing.

—Nerd Camp 2.0. Weissman, Elissa Brent. 2014. (ENG.). 288p. (J). (gr. 3-7). 17.99 (978-1-4424-5294-7(3), Atheneum Bks. for Young Readers) Simon & Schuster Children's Publishing.

—Return to the Cave of Time. Packard, Edward. 2012. (U-Ventures Ser.). (ENG.). 160p. (Orig.). (J). (gr. 3-7). pap. 5.99 (978-1-4424-3427-1(9)) Simon & Schuster, Inc.

—Sword of Waters. Bell, Hilari. 2009. (Shield, Sword, & Crown Ser.: 2). (ENG.). 384p. (J). (gr. 3-7). pap. 6.99 (978-1-4169-0597-4(9), Aladdin) Simon & Schuster Children's Publishing.

—Sword of Waters, No. 2. Bell, Hilari. 2008. (Shield, Sword, & Crown Ser.: 2). (ENG.). 368p. (J). (gr. 3-7). 16.99 (978-1-4169-0596-7(0), Simon & Schuster/Paula Wiseman Bks.) Simon & Schuster/Paula Wiseman Bks.

—Through the Black Hole. Packard, Edward. 2012. (U-Ventures Ser.). (ENG.). 160p. (J). (gr. 3-7). pap. 5.99 (978-1-4424-3426-4(0)) Simon & Schuster, Inc.

Willis, Helena. The Diamond Mystery #1, No. 1. Widmark, Martin. 2014. (Whodunit Detective Agency Ser.: 1). (ENG.). 80p. (J). (gr. 2-4). 5.99 (978-0-448-48066-4(2), Grosset & Dunlap) Penguin Young Readers Group.

—The Movie Theater Mystery, 7. Widmark, Martin. 2016. (Whodunit Detective Agency Ser.). (ENG.). 80p. (J). (gr. 2-4). 18.69 (978-1-4844-6957-6(7)) Penguin Publishing Group.

—The Mummy Mystery. Widmark, Martin. 2015. 68p. (J). (978-1-4242-6332-5(8), Grosset & Dunlap) Penguin Publishing Group.

—The Swimming Pool Mystery. Widmark, Martin. 2015. 69p. (J). (978-1-4844-6770-1(1), Grosset & Dunlap) Penguin Publishing Group.

Willis, Janet. A Dad's Delight. 2006. (978-0-9785077-0-1(3)); pap. (978-0-9785077-1-8(1)) Khesed Foundation.

Willis, Michelle "Osawazhinkwaa-Ikwe. Kwezenhs Bimose. Willis, Michelle "Osawazhinkwaa-Ikwe. 2004. (OJI.). 8p. (J). per. (978-0-9758801-1-1(X)) Bay Mills Indian Community.

Willis, Peter. Erosion: How Hugh Bennett Saved America's Soil & Ended the Dust Bowl. Pattison, Darcy. 2020. (Moments in Science Ser.: 5). (ENG.). 34p. (J). (gr. 1-5). 23.99 **(978-1-62944-149-8(X))**; pap. 11.99 **(978-1-62944-150-4(3))** Mims Hse.

Willis, Sabien T. Lola Pitts' Green Eggs & Grits. Dumas, Dionne Blackmon. 2018. (ENG.). 34p. (J). 22.99 (978-1-5456-5113-1(2)); pap. 12.49 (978-1-5456-5112-4(4)) Salem Author Services.

Willis, Tania. Kidsgo! Hong Kong: Tell Your Parents Where to Go! Debram, Mio. 2011. (ENG.). 44p. pap. 10.00 (978-988-18967-5-9(4)) Haven Bks.

—Kidsgo London: Tell Your Parents Where to Go! Debram, Mio. 2011. (ENG.). 64p. pap. 10.00 (978-988-18967-4-2(6)) Haven Bks.

Willmore, Alex. AdoraBULL. Donald, Alison. 2019. (ENG.). 32p. (J). (gr. -1-3). 17.99 (978-1-84886-412-2(4)) Maverick Arts Publishing GBR. Dist: Lerner Publishing Group.

—The Christmas Truck, 1 vol. Thomas Nelson & Sons Staff. 2019. (ENG.). 12p. (J). bds. 8.99 (978-1-4002-1645-1(1)) Nelson, Thomas Inc.

Willmore, Alex. Cub Shrugs (Animal Time: Time to Read, Level 1) Houran, Lori Haskins. 2020. (Time to Read Ser.). (ENG.). 32p. (J). (gr. k-2). 12.99 **(978-0-8075-7197-2(0)**, 0807571970) Whitman, Albert & Co.

Willmore, Alex. Duck's Ditty. Grahame, Kenneth. (ENG.). (J). 2020. 36p. (gr. k-2). 16.99 (978-1-4867-1815-3(9), b2cdb2d2-66c9-49f2-bbe8-54cffb4fdd35); 2018. 20p. (gr. -1-1). bds. 12.99 (978-1-4867-1386-8(6), 5abdd1b0-7a17-42d2-b36f-10fc64c03555) Flowerpot Pr.

Willmore, Alex. Ghost Afraid of the Dark. Conway, Sara. 2019. (ENG.). 40p. (J). 16.99 **(978-1-989219-53-9(5))** Rainstorm Pr.

—Hide & Peek (Animal Time: Time to Read, Level 1) Houran, Lori Haskins. (Time to Read Ser.). (ENG.). 32p. (J). (gr. k-2). 2020. pap. 3.99 **(978-0-8075-7201-6(2)**, 807572012); 2019. 12.99 (978-0-8075-7208-5(X), 080757208X) Whitman, Albert & Co.

—Just Right Cat (Animal Time: Time to Read, Level 1) Houran, Lori Haskins. 2020. (Time to Read Ser.). (ENG.). 32p. (J). (gr. k-2). 12.99 **(978-0-8075-7196-5(2)**, 0807571962) Whitman, Albert & Co.

Willmore, Alex. Let's Find the Dinosaur. Tiger Tales. 2020. (ENG.). 12p. (J). (-k). bds. 9.99 (978-1-68010-599-5(X)) Tiger Tales.

Willmore, Alex. Let's Find the Kitten. Tiger Tales. 2020. (ENG.). 12p. (J). (-k). bds. 9.99 **(978-1-68010-628-2(7))** Tiger Tales.

Willmore, Alex. Let's Find the Mermaid. Tiger Tales. 2020. (ENG.). 12p. (J). (-k). bds. 9.99 (978-1-68010-608-4(2)) Tiger Tales.

—Let's Find the Penguin. Tiger Tales. 2019. (ENG.). 12p. (J). (gr. 2-k). bds. 9.99 (978-1-68010-582-7(5)) Tiger Tales.

Willmore, Alex. Let's Find the Puppy. Tiger Tales. 2020. (ENG.). 12p. (J). (-k). bds. 9.99 **(978-1-68010-629-9(5))** Tiger Tales.

Willmore, Alex. Let's Find the Tiger. Tiger Tales. 2019. (ENG.). 12p. (J). (gr. 2-k). bds. 9.99 (978-1-68010-583-4(3)) Tiger Tales.

—Me Counting Time: From Seconds to Centuries. Sweeney, Joan. 2019. 32p. (J). (gr. -1-2). 12.99 (978-0-525-64684-6(1), Knopf Bks. for Young Readers) Random Hse. Children's Bks.

—The New LiBEARian. Donald, Alison. 2018. (ENG.). 32p. (J). (gr. -1-3). 16.99 (978-0-544-97365-7(8), 1663219, Clarion Bks.) Houghton Mifflin Harcourt Trade & Reference Pubs.

—Potty Like a Superhero. Skwish, Emily. 2019. (ENG.). 22p. (J). (978-1-5037-4540-7(6), 3df80221-9617-4dbb-9961-8d27304fac98, p i kids) Phoenix International Publications, Inc.

Willmore, Alex. Stop, Fox! (Animal Time: Time to Read, Level 1) Houran, Lori Haskins. (Time to Read Ser.). (ENG.). 32p. (J). (gr. k-2). 2020. pap. 3.99 **(978-0-8075-7199-6(7)**, 807571997); 2019. 12.99 (978-0-8075-7209-2(8), 807572098) Whitman, Albert & Co.

—Things I Love by Bear. Linn, Susie. 2020. (5-Minute Stories Portrait Padded Board B Ser.). (ENG.). (J). 22p. (— 1). bds. 9.99 **(978-1-78958-636-7(4))**; 24p. (gr. -1-k). 12.99 **(978-1-78958-630-5(5))** Top That! Publishing PLC GBR. Dist: Independent Pubs. Group.

Willmore, Alex. The Wheels on The... Uh-Oh! Tarsky, Sue. 2018. (ENG.). 32p. (J). 16.99 (978-0-8075-8869-7(5), 807588695) Whitman, Albert & Co.

Willmore, Alex. It's MY Sausage. Willmore, Alex. 2020. (ENG.). 32p. (J). (gr. -1-3). 17.99 (978-1-84886-473-3(6)) Maverick Arts Publishing GBR. Dist: Lerner Publishing Group.

Willoughby, Yuko. Believers in Christ Volume 29: New Testament Volume 29 Ephesians: God's Workmanship. Lyster, R. Iona. 2011. (ENG.). 36p. (J). pap. (978-1-932381-26-9(0), 1029) Bible Visuals International, Inc.

—The Tabernacle, Part 1 a Picture of the Lord Jesus Vol. 09, Pt. 1: Old Testament Volume 9 Exodus Part 4. Piepgrass, Arlene & Hershey, Katherine. 2013. (ENG.). 36p. (J). pap. (978-1-932381-72-6(4), 2009) Bible Visuals International, Inc.

Willoughby, Yuko. The Tabernacle, Part 2 a Picture of the Lord Jesus Vol. 10, Pt. 2: Old Testament Volume 10 Exodus Part 5. Hershey, Katherine. 2013. (ENG.). 32p. (J). pap. (978-1-932381-73-3(2), 2010) Bible Visuals International, Inc.

Willoughby, Yuko, jt. illus. see Ober, Jonathan.

Willoughby, Yuko, jt. illus. see Olson, Ed.

WillowRaven, Aidana. Katie Bear: Fun Days at School. Sansone, V. K. 2007. 84p. pap. 16.95 (978-0-9798154-7-8(9)) Living Waters Publishing Co.

—Strangers in the Stable. Laughter, Jim. 2011. 24p. pap. 13.99 (978-0-9832740-3-2(7)) 4RV Pub.

Willowraven, Aidana. Walking Through Walls. Cioffi, Karen. 2020. (ENG.). 84p. (J). 21.99 **(978-1-950074-21-1(8))** 4RV Pub.

Wills, Fred. Just Stand by Me: Working Together in Groups. Wills, Fred. 2020. (Just Jessica's Life Lessons Ser.: Vol. 4). (ENG.). 32p. (J). (gr. k-6). 24.95 **(978-0-578-63563-7(1))** Just Jessica, L.L.C.

Wills, Sarah-Leigh. Atticus's Secret. Henwood, Jenny. 2017. (Rainbow Riding School Ser.: Vol. 1). (ENG.). 40p. (J). pap. **(978-1-912488-00-1(0))** Rainbow Riding Schl. Ltd., The.

Wills, Sarah-Leigh. The Dreamy Jeany Series: The Light. Bennett, Clayre. 2017. (Dreamy Jeany Ser.: Vol. 1). (ENG.). 42p. (J). (gr. 1-2). pap. (978-0-9957228-0-4(3)) Bennett, Clayre.

Willwerth, Maddy. Death & the Underhouse. Caniyo, Christina. 2017. (Book 1 of the Dream Walker Ser.: Vol. 1). (ENG.). 290p. (J). pap. 12.99 (978-1-7918-2013-8(1)) Independently Published.

Willy, April. Three Cups: Teaching Children How to Save, Spend & Be Charitable with Money Is As Easy As 1, 2, 3. St. Germain, Mark. 2007. (ENG.). 28p. (J). pap. 10.00 (978-0-9794563-0-5(4)) Three Cups, LLC.

—Tres Tazas. St. Germain, Mark. 2010.Tr. of Three Cups. (SPA.). 24p. (J). (978-0-9794563-1-2(2)) Three Cups, LLC.

Willy, Romont. En Tiempos Difíciles. Canetti, Yanitzia. 2010. (SPA & ENG.). 32p. (J). (gr. k-2). pap. 8.99 (978-1-59835-102-6(8), BrickHouse Education) Cambridge BrickHouse, Inc.

—When Times Are Tough. Canetti, Yanitzia. Keating, Alison, tr. 2009. 32p. (J). (gr. k-2). 8.99 (978-1-59835-103-3(6)) Cambridge BrickHouse, Inc.

Wilmink, Inga. Sticker Girl. Tashjian, Janet. 2016. (Sticker Girl Ser.: 1). (ENG.). 176p. (J). 13.99 (978-1-62779-335-3(6), 9781627793353, Holt, Henry & Co. Bks. For Young Readers) Holt, Henry & Co.

—Sticker Girl & the Cupcake Challenge, Vol. 3. Tashjian, Janet. 2018. (Sticker Girl Ser.: 3). (ENG.). 192p. (J). 14.99 (978-1-250-19647-7(7), 900194113, Holt, Henry & Co. Bks. For Young Readers) Holt, Henry & Co.

—Sticker Girl Rules the School. Tashjian, Janet. 2017. (Sticker Girl Ser.: 2). (ENG.). 192p. (J). 13.99 (978-1-62779-336-0(4), 9781627793360, Holt, Henry & Co. Bks. For Young Readers) Holt, Henry & Co.

—Sticker Girl Rules the School. Tashjian, Janet. 2018. (Sticker Girl Ser.: 2). (ENG.). 208p. (J). pap. 7.99 (978-1-250-18337-8(5), 900190817) Square Fish.

Wilmore, Alex. Hungry Puppy: Board Books with Plush Ears. 2019. (Snuggles Ser.). (ENG.). 10p. (J). (gr. -1 — 1). bds. 6.99 (978-1-4380-5072-0(0), B.E.S. Publishing) Peterson's.

—Sleepy Bunny: Board Books with Plush Ears. 2019. (Snuggles Ser.). (ENG.). 10p. (J). (gr. -1 — 1). bds. 6.99 (978-1-4380-5071-3(2), B.E.S. Publishing) Peterson's.

Wilmot, Anita. Bulkington. Neyer, Daniel. 2004. 136p. (YA). pap. 9.95 (978-0-9666701-1-0(6)) One Faithful Harp Publishing Co.

Wilsdorf, Anne. The Best Story. Spinelli, Eileen. 2008. 32p. (J). (gr. 1-3). 17.99 (978-0-8037-3055-7(1), Dial Bks) Penguin Young Readers Group.

—Five Funny Bunnies: Three Bouncing Tales, 0 vols. Van Leeuwen, Jean. 2012. (ENG.). 40p. (J). (gr. -1-3). 17.99 (978-0-7614-6114-2(0), 9780761461142, Two Lions) Amazon Publishing.

—A Hippy-Hoppy Toad. Archer, Peggy. 2018. 40p. (J). (gr. -1-2). 16.99 (978-0-399-55676-0(1)); (ENG.). lib. bdg. 19.99 (978-0-399-55677-7(X)) Random Hse. Children's Bks. (Schwartz & Wade Bks.).

—Homer: The Library Cat. Lindbergh, Reeve. 2011. (ENG.). 32p. (J). (gr. -1-3). 16.99 (978-0-7636-3448-3(4)) Candlewick Pr.

—My Dog's a Chicken. Montanari, Susan McElroy. 2016. 40p. (J). (gr. -1-3). 16.99 (978-0-385-38490-2(4), Schwartz & Wade Bks.) Random Hse. Children's Bks.

—Ruby Lu, Brave & True. Look, Lenore. 2006. (Ruby Lu Ser.). 105p. (J). (gr. 1-5). 11.65 (978-0-7569-6553-2(5)) Perfection Learning Corp.

—Ruby Lu, Brave & True. Look, Lenore. 2006. (ENG.). 112p. (J). (gr. 1-5). pap. 6.99 (978-1-4169-1389-4(0), Atheneum Bks. for Young Readers) Simon & Schuster Children's Publishing.

—Ruby Lu, Empress of Everything. Look, Lenore. 2007. 164p. (gr. 1-5). 16.00 (978-0-7569-8113-6(1)) Perfection Learning Corp.

—Ruby Lu, Empress of Everything. Look, Lenore. (ENG.). 176p. (J). (gr. 1-5). 2007. pap. 6.99 (978-1-4169-5003-5(6)); 2006. 16.99 (978-0-689-86460-5(4)) Simon & Schuster Children's Publishing. (Atheneum Bks. for Young Readers).

—Sophie's Squash. Miller, Pat Zietlow. 2013. (Sophie's Squash Ser.). 40p. (J). (gr. -1-2). 17.99 (978-0-307-97896-7(6), Schwartz & Wade Bks.) Random Hse. Children's Bks.

—Sophie's Squash Go to School. Miller, Pat Zietlow. 2016. (Sophie's Squash Ser.). (ENG.). 40p. (J). (gr. -1-2). 17.99 (978-0-553-50944-1(6), Schwartz & Wade Bks.) Random Hse. Children's Bks.

—There's Something about Sam. Barnaby, Hannah Rodgers. 2020. (ENG.). 32p. (J). (gr. -1-3). 17.99 (978-1-328-76680-9(2), 1680919, HMH Books For Young Readers) Houghton Mifflin Harcourt Publishing Co.

Wilson, Agy. From Heaven to Earth - Angel on My Shoulder. Wilson, Agy. 2004. (From Heaven to Earth Ser.). 150p. (J). (gr. 2-7). pap. 5.95 (978-0-9718348-1-1(4)) Blooming Tree Pr.

Wilson, Alex. Brujas y Magos. Hill, Douglas. 2003. (SPA.). 64p. (J). 14.95 (978-84-372-2321-6(0)) Altea, Ediciones, S.A. - Grupo Santillana ESP. Dist: Santillana USA Publishing Co., Inc.

Wilson, Alisha. Booklet Goes to the Doctor. Edman Lamote, Lisa. 2006. (Bookmann Family Presents Ser.). 32p. (J). (gr. k-3). 15.99 (978-1-933673-02-8(8), BookMann Pr.) Mann Publishing Group.

—A Day Out for Opus. Edman Lamote, Lisa. 2006. (Bookmann Family Presents Ser.). 32p. (J). (gr. k-3). 15.99 (978-1-933673-03-5(6), BookMann Pr.) Mann Publishing Group.

—Don't Judge a Book by Its Cover. Edman Lamote, Lisa. 2006. (Bookmann Family Presents Ser.). 32p. (J). (gr. k-3). 15.99 (978-1-933673-01-1(X), BookMann Pr.) Mann Publishing Group.

Wilson, Alonza S. The Living Ice Cream Guys. Renfroe, Ann. 2012. 34p. pap. 13.95 (978-0-9858398-9-5(9)) Mindstir Media.

Wilson, Ann. The Barefoot Book of Earth Tales. Casey, Dawn. 2013. 96p. (J). (gr. k-5). pap. 14.99 (978-1-84686-941-9(2)) Barefoot Bks., Inc.

Wilson, Anne. The Barefoot Book of Earth Tales. Casey, Dawn. 2009. 96p. (J). (gr. 1-5). 19.99 (978-1-84686-224-3(8)) Barefoot Bks., Inc.

—The Great Race: The Story of the Chinese Zodiac. Casey, Dawn. 32p. (J). (gr. -1-2). 2008. pap. 8.99 (978-1-84686-202-1(7)); 2006. (ENG.). 16.99 (978-1-905236-77-0(8)) Barefoot Bks., Inc.

—Masha & the Firebird. Bateson Hill, Margaret. 2005. (Folk Tales Ser.: 1). (RUS & ENG.). 32p. (J). pap. (978-1-84089-201-7(3)) Zero to Ten, Ltd.

—My First Box of Books: 1 2 3 Colours Animals, 3 vols. 2016. 72p. (J). (gr. -1-2). bds. 9.99 *(978-1-86147-416-2(4)*, Armadillo) Anness Publishing GBR. Dist: National Bk. Network.

—Prayers for Each & Every Day. Piper, Sophie. 2008. (ENG.). 64p. (J). (gr. -1-2). 14.95 *(978-1-55725-622-5(5))* Paraclete Pr., Inc.

—Red Alert! Endangered Animals Around the World. Barr, Catherine. 2018. (ENG.). 48p. (J). (gr. k-3). 17.99 *(978-1-58089-839-3(4))* Charlesbridge Publishing, Inc.

—Snakes & Ladders. Morpurgo, Michael. 2006. (Yellow Bananas Ser.). (ENG.). 48p. (J). (gr. -1-3). *(978-0-7787-0998-5(1))*; lib. bdg. *(978-0-7787-0952-7(3))* Crabtree Publishing Co.

—Storytime: First Tales for Sharing. Blackstone, Stella & Broadbent, Jim. 2008. (ENG.). 96p. (J). pap. 12.99 *(978-1-84686-165-9(9))* Barefoot Bks., Inc.

—Storytime: First Tales for Sharing. Blackstone, Stella. 2005. (ENG.). 96p. (J). (gr. -1-3). 19.99 *(978-1-84148-345-0(1))* Barefoot Bks., Inc.

—We're Roaming in the Rainforest. Krebs, Laurie. 2010. 40p. (J). (gr. k-5). pap. 8.99 *(978-1-84686-545-9(X))*; (gr. -1-5). 16.99 *(978-1-84686-331-8(7))* Barefoot Bks., Inc.

—We're Sailing down the Nile: A Journey Through Egypt. Krebs, Laurie. 2007. (ENG.). 44p. (J). (gr. -1-1). 22.44 *(978-1-84686-040-9(7))* Barefoot Bks., Ltd. GBR. Dist: Children's Plus, Inc.

Wilson, Anne. The Lord Is My Shepherd. Wilson, Anne. 2004. 32p. 16.00 *(978-0-8028-5250-2(5))* Eerdmans, William B. Publishing Co.

Wilson, Anne & Guay, Rebecca. The Barefoot Book of Ballet Stories. Casey, Dawn et al. 2009. 80p. (J). (gr. 2-6). 23.99 *(978-1-84686-262-5(0))* Barefoot Bks., Inc.

Wilson, Ava Blu. He Said My Name! Wilson, Ava Blu. 2019. (Abettermebook Ser.: Vol. 2). (ENG.). 38p. (J). pap. 10.99 *(978-1-0771-3039-5(2))* Independently Published.

—The Why, Oh Why's of Serena Dunson. Wilson, Ava Blu. 2019. (ENG.). 346p. (J). pap. 14.99 *(978-1-0937-9211-9(6))* Independently Published.

Wilson, Bill. Dorf's Art Lesson. Wilson, Bill. 2008. (ENG.). 16p. (J). spiral bd. 6.95 net. *(978-0-9818747-0-8(3))* Pippin & Maxx Arts & Entertain, LLC.

Wilson, Bob. Football Fred, Vol. 4. 2003. (ENG.). 80p. (J). pap. *(978-0-330-37091-2(X)*, Pan) Pan Macmillan.

Wilson, Bonnita. A Tale of Two Cookies: A Message of Kindness & Acceptance. Patterson, Trina Dawkins. 2011. (ENG.). 32p. (J). (gr. -1-3). pap. 10.99 *(978-0-9819860-9-8(9))* Amber Skye Publishing LLC.

Wilson, Cameron. Big Magnolia. Nesmith, Kimberly M. 2019. (ENG.). 30p. (J). 17.99 ***(978-1-7333696-0-2(0))*** Kimberly M. Nesmith.

Wilson, Cameron. Bullies Don't Phase Me! Hodges, Laurissa. 2019. (ENG.). 26p. (J). pap. 11.99 *(978-1-0756-2611-1(0))* Independently Published.

—The Good Book: A Kid's Guide to Becoming a Successful Student Leader. Wilmer, Da'nall. 2018. (ENG.). 30p. (J). pap. 12.99 *(978-0-692-15591-2(0))* Wilmer, Da'Nall.

—Is My Daddy Ok? A Story about PTSD for Kids. Floyd-White, Shatada. 2019. (ENG.). 34p. (J). pap. 12.99 *(978-1-0714-0301-3(X))* Independently Published.

Wilson, Charles Banks. The Story of Geronimo. Kjelgaard, Jim. Meadowcroft, Enid Lamonte, ed. 2011. 192p. 42.95 *(978-1-258-05298-0(9))* Literary Licensing, LLC.

—Whispering Wind: A Story of the Massacre at Sand Creek. Reeder, Red. 2011. 216p. 44.95 *(978-1-258-05996-5(7))* Literary Licensing, LLC.

Wilson, Clare. Animal Magnets. Edwards, Nicola & Hegarty, Patricia. 2018. (My First Ser.). (ENG.). 10p. (J). (gr. -1-k). bds. 12.99 *(978-1-68010-547-6(7))* Tiger Tales.

—Farm Magnets. Edwards, Nicola. 2019. (My First Ser.). (ENG.). 10p. (J). (gr. 2-k). bds. 12.99 *(978-1-68010-579-7(5))* Tiger Tales.

Wilson, Cristi. Just Because. Wilson, Cristi. l.t. ed. 2006. 24p. (J). (gr. -1-3). per. 10.99 *(978-1-59879-251-5(2))* Lifevest Publishing, Inc.

Wilson, Danny. Lots & Lots of Orange: A Trip to Neyland Stadium. Wilson, Danny. 2003. 24p. (J). 8.95 *(978-0-9743968-0-4(X))* Satellite Studio.

Wilson, Deborah. Zipporah's Farm. Perez, Ani. 2018. (ENG.). 230p. (J). 24.99 ***(978-1-936716-97-5(6)***, 45aaf972-28ee-4d7e-b742-44506a9e5185); pap. 19.99 ***(978-1-936716-96-8(8)***, c0bcc406-2a7a-4781-8812-acb1c1d35d64) Messianic Jewish Pubs.

Wilson, Drew. The Man in the Mist. 2014. 12p. (J). pap. ***(978-1-78369-242-2(1))*** Phonic Books, Ltd.

Wilson, Elisa & Shue, Linda Nicole. Grant the Ant: And Zeater the Sneaky Anteater. Shue, Alan. 2017. (ENG.). (J). pap. 12.00 *(978-0-9845687-6-5(X))* Bug Rhymes Bks.

Wilson, Elle. Silly Garden. Grimes, Jeff. 2020. (ENG.). 24p. (J). pap. 8.50 ***(978-1-0983-2490-2(0))*** BookBaby.

Wilson, Emily. Goober Man. Frazier, Peter. 2018. (ENG.). 32p. (J). (gr. k-6). 15.99 *(978-1-365-86104-8(X))*; pap. 11.99 *(978-1-365-86109-3(0))* Lulu Pr., Inc.

—Goober Man. Frazier, Peter. 2018. (ENG.). 32p. (J). (gr. k-6). pap. 13.99 *(978-1-64372-186-6(0)*, Huskies Pub) MacLaren-Cochrane Publishing, Inc.

—Goober Man Dyslexic Font. Frazier, Peter. 2018. (ENG.). 32p. (J). (gr. k-6). 21.99 *(978-1-365-86105-5(8))*; pap. 15.99 *(978-1-365-86110-9(4))* Lulu Pr., Inc.

Wilson-Gaber, Ashley J. Life Lessons from the Chapman Daily Adventures: Be a Mighty Warrior. Bauer, Chicaga A. 2017. (ENG.). 36p. (gr. -1-3). pap. 15.95 *(978-1-9736-0992-6(4)*, WestBow Pr.) Author Solutions, Inc.

Wilson, Gahan. Brains for Lunch: A Zombie Novel in Haiku?! Roy, Keri Anne & Holt, K. A. 2010. (ENG.). 96p. (J). (gr. 4-9). 22.99 *(978-1-59643-629-9(8)*, 900068270) Roaring Brook Pr.

Wilson, George, jt. illus. see Bolle, Frank.

Wilson, Gillian. The Girl Who Loved Cheese. Desautels, Bob & Barr, Ava Desautels. 2017. (ENG.). (J). *(978-1-5255-1615-3(9))*; pap. *(978-1-5255-1616-0(7))* FriesenPress.

—Killer Style: How Fashion Has Injured, Maimed, & Murdered Through History. McMahon, Serah-Marie & Matthews-David, Alison. 2019. (ENG.). 48p. (J). 17.95 *(978-1-77147-253-1(7))* Owlkids Bks. Inc. CAN. Dist: Publishers Group West (PGW).

Wilson, Helen Hughes. The Valiant Seven. Phelps, Netta Sheldon. 2004. (Classic Ser.). 222p. (gr. 4-7). pap. 15.95 *(978-0-87004-410-6(9))* Caxton Pr.

Wilson, Henrike. Brave Charlotte. Stohner, Anu. 2005. (ENG.). 32p. (J). (gr. -1-3). 17.99 *(978-1-58234-690-8(9)*, 900032321, Bloomsbury USA Childrens) Bloomsbury Publishing USA.

—Brave Charlotte. Stohner, Anu. 2014. 32p. pap. 8.00 *(978-1-61003-341-1(8))* Center for the Collaborative Classroom.

—I Am So Bored! 2016. 32p. (J). (gr. -1-k). 16.99 *(978-1-5107-0676-7(3)*, Sky Pony Pr.) Skyhorse Publishing Co., Inc.

Wilson, Jane Carol. Better Than a Homerun. Dehoff, Freda. 2016. (ENG.). 177p. (J). pap. 12.95 *(978-1-4787-7215-6(8))* Outskirts Pr., Inc.

Wilson, Janet. One Peace: True Stories of Young Activists, 1 vol. 2008. (ENG.). 52p. (J). (gr. 4-7). 19.95 *(978-1-55143-892-4(5))* Orca Bk. Pubs. USA.

—Solomon's Tree, 1 vol. Spalding, Andrea. 2005. (ENG.). 32p. (J). (gr. -1-k). 10.95 *(978-1-55143-380-6(X))* Orca Bk. Pubs. USA.

—Tiger Flowers, 1 vol. Quinlan, Patricia. 2005. (ENG.). 32p. (J). (gr. -1-1). per. 6.95 *(978-1-55005-139-1(3)*, 31c5cb1b-5066-438f-9834-51eba41853c9) Trifolium Bks., Inc. CAN. Dist: Firefly Bks., Ltd.

Wilson, John. Try: Building Confidence for Children, 1 vol. DiMare, Joseph S. 2019. (ENG.). 48p. (J). 16.99 *(978-0-7643-5778-7(6)*, 16321) Schiffer Publishing, Ltd.

Wilson, John, jt. illus. see Wilson, Whitleigh.

Wilson, Kate. Wesley Takes the Wrong Path. Bentley, Paula. 2018. (ENG.). 40p. (J). pap. *(978-1-78623-225-0(1))* Grosvenor Hse. Publishing Ltd.

Wilson, Katie. Numbers. 2017. (ENG.). 20p. (J). bds. *(978-1-4867-1304-2(1))* Flowerpot Children's Pr. Inc.

—Shapes. Flowerpot Press. 2017. (ENG.). 20p. (J). (gr. -1-1). bds. *(978-1-4867-1239-7(8))* Flowerpot Children's Pr. Inc.

Wilson, Kay. Penny's Big Day. Mika, Sharon Ann. 2003. (J). 8.95 *(978-0-9747836-0-4(9))* Button Flower Pr.

Wilson, Keith. Louis Pasteur & Pasteurization. Fandel, Jennifer & Barnett, Charles, III. 2007. (Inventions & Discovery Ser.). (ENG.). 32p. (J). (gr. 3-9). pap. 8.10 *(978-0-7368-7896-8(3)*, Capstone Pr.) Capstone.

Wilson, Kendell. Holding the Father's Hand. Wilson, Patsy Hobbs. 2019. (ENG.). 34p. (J). 25.95 *(978-1-4808-7074-1(9))*; pap. 16.95 *(978-1-4808-7075-8(7))* Archway Publishing.

Wilson, Lorna. Mr Tilly & the Christmas Lights. Leighton, Noreen. 2013. 38p. pap. *(978-0-9573315-7-0(6))* Tatterdemalion Blue.

—Mr Tilly & the Halloween Mystery. Leighton, Noreen. 2013. 42p. pap. *(978-0-9573315-6-3(8))* Tatterdemalion Blue.

—MR Tilly's Bake It Yourself Book. Leighton, Noreen. 2017. (ENG.). 69p. (J). pap. *(978-0-9933114-6-8(6))* Resonate and Blue.

Wilson, Lynda Farrington. A Is for Alligator. Velikanje, Kathryn. 2013. (ENG.). 34p. pap. 9.13 *(978-1-939896-04-9(5))* Levity Pr.

— A Is for Alligator. Shan Shan, Kathryn Velikanje. 2013. 34p. pap. 9.97 *(978-1-939896-13-1(4))* Levity Pr.

—B Is for Boys & Bees. Velikanje, Kathryn. 2013. 34p. pap. 9.13 *(978-1-939896-05-6(3))* Levity Pr.

—C Is for Crazy Cats. Velikanje, Kathryn. 2013. (ENG.). 40p. pap. 9.13 *(978-1-939896-06-3(1))* Levity Pr.

—D Is for Dragon. Velikanje, Kathryn. 2013. 34p. pap. 9.13 *(978-1-939896-07-0(X))* Levity Pr.

—E Is for Elephant. Velikanje, Kathryn. 2013. 36p. pap. 9.13 *(978-1-939896-08-7(8))* Levity Pr.

—E Is for Elephant. Shan Shan, Kathryn Velikanje. 2013. 36p. pap. 9.87 *(978-1-939896-17-9(7))* Levity Pr.

—Everyday Circus. Shan Shan, Kathryn. 2013. 48p. pap. 10.97 *(978-1-939896-01-8(0))* Levity Pr.

—F Is for Face. Velikanje, Kathryn. 2013. 40p. pap. 9.13 *(978-1-939896-09-4(6))* Levity Pr.

—G Is for Girly Girls. Velikanje, Kathryn. 2013. 36p. pap. 9.13 *(978-1-939896-10-0(X))* Levity Pr.

—H Is for Horse. Velikanje, Kathryn. 2013. 38p. pap. 9.13 *(978-1-939896-11-7(8))* Levity Pr.

—I Is for Ice Cream. Velikanje, Kathryn. 2013. (ENG.). 36p. pap. 9.13 *(978-1-939896-12-4(6))* Levity Pr.

—Temple Did It, & I Can, Too! Seven Simple Life Rules. Yacio, Jennifer Gilpin. 2015. (ENG.). 32p. (J). 14.95 *(978-1-935567-52-3(7))* Sensory Resources.

Wilson, Mark. Carpet of Dreams. Duder, Tessa. 2008. 32p. pap. *(978-0-207-19991-2(4))* HarperCollins Pubs. Australia.

—The Skunk with the Stinky Attitude. McLaughlin, Richard. 2013. 44p. (YA). pap. 13.75 *(978-1-939625-49-6(1))* Inkwell Books LLC.

Wilson, Mary Ann. Bucky: The Adventures of the Dinosaur Cowboy. Cunningham, Kay. 2004. 32p. (J). 18.99 *(978-1-57860-173-8(8)*, Clerisy Pr.) AdventureKEEN.

Wilson-Max, Ken. The Baby Goes Beep. O'Connell, Rebecca. 2010. (ENG.). 16p. (J). (gr. -1 — 1). bds. 7.99 *(978-0-8075-0508-3(0)*, 807505080) Whitman, Albert & Co.

—Baby Ruby Bawled. Stanley, Malaika Rose. 2010. (ENG.). 24p. (J). (gr. k-2). pap. 15.99 *(978-1-84853-017-1(X))* Transworld Publishers Ltd. GBR. Dist: Independent Pubs. Group.

—I Can Do It Too! Baicker, Karen. 2010. (ENG.). (J). (gr. -1 — 1). bds. 9.99 *(978-0-8118-7560-8(1))* Chronicle Bks. LLC.

—I Hate to Be Sick! Scholastic, Inc. Staff & Bermiss, Aamir Lee. 2004. (Just for You Ser.). (ENG.). 32p. (gr. k-3). pap. 3.99 *(978-0-439-56877-7(3)*, Teaching Resources) Scholastic, Inc.

Wilson-Max, Ken. Astro Girl. Wilson-Max, Ken. 2019. (ENG.). 32p. (J). (gr. -1-3). 16.99 *(978-1-5362-0946-4(5))* Candlewick Pr.

Wilson, Megan, jt. illus. see Charretier, Elsa.

Wilson, Meredith. My Dog, My Love, My Best Friend. Adcox, Norman. 2019. (ENG.). 34p. (J). (gr. 3-6). 24.99 ***(978-0-578-56496-8(3))*** Whippet Creative Works, Inc.

Wilson, Nay. Katie Helps a Turtle with Tummy Ache: A Glowstone Adventure. Lloyd-Davies, Nick. 2020. (Glowstone Adventures Ser.: Vol. 4). (ENG.). 50p. (J). pap. 10.99 ***(978-1-7985-6399-1(1))*** Independently Published.

Wilson, Olivia. Tree Fellas: Olly Oak. Gilbert, Jon. 2019. (ENG.). 36p. (J). pap. ***(978-1-78623-552-7(8))*** Grosvenor Hse. Publishing Ltd.

Wilson, Phil. After the Dinosaurs: Mammoths & Fossil Mammals. Brown, Charlotte Lewis. (I Can Read Level 2 Ser.). 32p. (J). (gr. -1-3). 2007. (ENG.). pap. 4.99 *(978-0-06-053055-6(3))*; 2006. lib. bdg. 17.89 *(978-0-06-053054-9(5))* HarperCollins Pubs.

—Baby Santa's Worldwide Christmas Adventure. DeLand, M. Maitland. 2010. 32p. (J). 14.95 *(978-1-60832-062-2(6))* Greenleaf Book Group.

—Beyond the Dinosaurs: Monsters of the Air & Sea. Brown, Charlotte Lewis. 2008. (I Can Read Level 2 Ser.). (ENG.). 32p. (J). (gr. -1-3). pap. 4.99 *(978-0-06-053058-7(8))* HarperCollins Pubs.

—Beyond the Dinosaurs: Monsters of the Air & Sea. Brown, Charlotte Lewis & Brown, Charlotte L. 2007. (I Can Read Bks.). (ENG.). 32p. (J). (gr. -1-3). 15.99 *(978-0-06-053056-3(1))* HarperCollins Pubs.

—The Day the Dinosaurs Died. Brown, Charlotte Lewis. 2007. (I Can Read Level 2 Ser.). (ENG.). 48p. (J). (gr. -1-3). pap. 4.99 *(978-0-06-000530-6(0))* HarperCollins Pubs.

—Medieval Castle: A Three Dimensional. 2004. (ENG.). (J). 22.00 *(978-1-58117-365-9(2)*, Intervisual/Piggy Toes) Bendon, Inc.

—Seven Little Brothers. Livshits, Larisa. 2012. 40p. pap. *(978-1-77097-322-0(2))* FriesenPress.

Wilson, Phil, jt. illus. see Rath, Robert.

Wilson, Raylene Jenee & Gibbons, Deanna. The Three Madelines. Whitmore, Hugh. 2012. 124p. pap. 15.95 *(978-0-9848314-4-9(4))* Sincerity Publishing.

Wilson, Rob. The Blank Page: How a Piece of Paper Connects to Everything. Blanco, Alberto. 2020. (ENG.). 32p. (J). (-k). 16.95 ***(978-1-946764-62-1(0)***, Plum Blossom Bks.) Parallax Pr.

Wilson, Roberta. The Quest: Adventure Story & Songs. Jacobson, John. 2005. (ENG.). 48p. (J). pap. 12.95 incl. audio compact disk *(978-1-4234-0019-6(4)*, 1423400194) Leonard, Hal Corp.

Wilson, Ron, et al. Master of Kung Fu Epic Collection: Weapon of the Soul. 2018. 480p. (YA). (gr. 8-17). pap. 39.99 *(978-1-302-90135-6(4))* Marvel Worldwide, Inc.

Wilson, Ron. Wolfpack: the Complete Collection. 2018. (ENG.). 392p. (YA). (gr. 8-17). pap. 39.99 *(978-1-302-91259-8(3))* Marvel Worldwide, Inc.

Wilson, Ron, jt. illus. see Kirby, Jack.

Wilson, Sam. The Familyman's Christmas Treasury. Wilson, Todd. 2017. (ENG.). 234p. (J). (gr. -1-2). pap. 29.99 ***(978-1-937639-29-7(0))*** Familyman Ministries.

Wilson Sanger, Amy. A Little Bit of Soul Food. Wilson Sanger, Amy. Sanger, Amy Wilson. 2004. (World Snacks Ser.). 20p. (J). (— 1). bds. 6.99 *(978-1-58246-109-0(0)*, Tricycle Pr.) Random Hse. Children's Bks.

—Yum Yum Dim Sum. Wilson Sanger, Amy. 2003. (World Snacks Ser.). 22p. (J). (gr. k — 1). bds. 6.99 *(978-1-58246-108-3(2)*, Knopf Bks. for Young Readers) Random Hse. Children's Bks.

Wilson, Spencer. Woodstock, Baby! A Far-Out Counting Book. 2019. 22p. (J). (— 1). bds. 7.99 *(978-0-525-58009-6(3)*, Doubleday Bks. for Young Readers) Random Hse. Children's Bks.

Wilson, Susie. A Kid's Herb Book: For Children of All Ages. Tierra, Lesley. 2018. (ENG.). 264p. (gr. -1-18). pap. 24.95 *(978-1-885003-36-2(6))* Reed, Robert D. Pubs.

Wilson, Teddy. Don't Cry but Smile & Remember. Brown, Ivorine. 2009. 20p. pap. 24.95 *(978-1-60836-808-2(4))* America Star Bks.

Wilson, Whitleigh & Wilson, John. Frog Makes a Friend. Wilson, Angela. 2013. 28p. pap. 24.95 *(978-1-63004-048-2(7))* America Star Bks.

Wilson, Yakira M. Mystical Meadows: The Fallen Meadow. Wilson, Yakira M. 2019. (Mystical Meadows Ser.: Vol. 1). (ENG.). 110p. (J). pap. 6.00 ***(978-1-6900-2689-1(8))*** Independently Published.

Wiltse, Kris, jt. illus. see Blackmore, Katherine.

Wiltshire, Sophie. Can I Tell You about Multiple Sclerosis? A Guide for Friends, Family & Professionals. Amos, Angela. 2016. (Can I Tell You About... ? Ser.). (ENG.). 48p. pap. 13.95 *(978-1-78592-146-9(0)*, 696320) Kingsley, Jessica Pubs. GBR. Dist: Hachette UK Distribution.

—Ollie & His Super Powers. Knowles, Alison. 2016. (Ollie & His Superpowers Ser.). (ENG.). 32p. (J). 15.95 *(978-1-78592-049-3(9)*, 694048) Kingsley, Jessica Pubs. GBR. Dist: Hachette UK Distribution.

—Ollie & the Silver Stripe. Knowles, Alison. 2017. (ENG.). 64p. (J). 17.95 *(978-1-78592-241-1(6)*, 696459) Kingsley, Jessica Pubs. GBR. Dist: Hachette UK Distribution.

Wilverding, Diane Agatha. Freddy the Adventurous Frog. Carella, Jane Anne. 2020. (ENG.). 46p. (J). pap. 11.95 ***(978-1-9819-9392-5(4))*** CreateSpace Independent Publishing Platform.

Wilx, Andy. Star Stories: Constellation Tales from Around the World. Ganeri, Anita. 2019. (ENG.). 96p. (J). (gr. 2-7). 19.99 *(978-0-7624-9505-4(7)*, Running Pr. Kids) Running Pr.

Wimberger, Zoe Jay. The Monster under Your Bed Is Just a Story in Your Head: Conquering Fear Through Neuroliteracy. Wimberger, Lisa. 2017. (ENG.). (J). pap. 9.99 *(978-0-692-80006-5(9))* Neurosculpting Institute.

Wimmer, Michael. A Taste of Blackberries. Smith, Doris Buchanan. 2004. (Trophy Bk.). (ENG.). 96p. (J). (gr. 3-7). reprint ed. pap. 5.99 *(978-0-06-440238-5(X)*, HarperCollins) HarperCollins Pubs. Ltd. GBR. Dist: HarperCollins Pubs.

Wimmer, Mike. Abraham. Keating, Frank. 2017. (Mount Rushmore Presidential Ser.). (ENG.). 32p. (J). (gr. 1-4). 17.99 *(978-1-4424-9319-3(4)*, Simon & Schuster/Paula Wiseman Bks.) Simon & Schuster/Paula Wiseman Bks.

—George: George Washington, Our Founding Father. Keating, Frank. 2012. (Mount Rushmore Presidential Ser.). (ENG.). 32p. (J). (gr. 1-4). 17.99 *(978-1-4169-5482-8(1)*, Simon & Schuster/Paula Wiseman Bks.) Simon & Schuster/Paula Wiseman Bks.

—Home Run: The Story of Babe Ruth. Burleigh, Robert. Plimpton, George, ed. 2003. (ENG.). 32p. (J). (gr. -1-3). pap. 7.99 *(978-0-15-204599-9(6)*, 1193849) Houghton Mifflin Harcourt Publishing Co.

—One Giant Leap. Burleigh, Robert. 2014. (ENG.). 40p. (J). (gr. 1-3). 8.99 *(978-0-14-751165-2(8)*, Puffin Books) Penguin Young Readers Group.

—Un Sabor a Moras. Smith, Doris Buchanan. Rioja, Alberto Jimenez, tr. (SPA.). (YA). (gr. 3-18). 14.95 *(978-1-930332-25-6(4)*, LC31160) Lectorum Pubns., Inc.

—Stealing Home: Jackie Robinson: Against the Odds. Burleigh, Robert. 2007. (ENG.). 32p. (J). (gr. 1-4). 18.99 *(978-0-689-86276-2(8)*, Simon & Schuster/Paula Wiseman Bks.) Simon & Schuster/Paula Wiseman Bks.

—Theodore. Keating, Frank. 2006. (Mount Rushmore Presidential Ser.). (ENG.). 32p. (J). (gr. 1-4). 17.99 *(978-0-689-86532-9(5)*, Simon & Schuster/Paula Wiseman Bks.) Simon & Schuster/Paula Wiseman Bks.

Wimmer, Sonja. Chelm for the Holidays. Frankel, Valerie Estelle. 2019. (ENG.). 72p. (J). (gr. 3-9). pap. 8.99 *(978-1-5415-5462-7(0)*, 9781541554627, Kar-Ben Publishing) Lerner Publishing Group.

—Could It Happen to Anyone? Pavon, Mar. Brokenbrow, Jon, tr. 2011. (ENG.). 32p. (J). (gr. k-2). 14.95 *(978-84-15241-03-4(8))* Cuento de Luz SL ESP. Dist: Publishers Group West (PGW).

—Hija. Andres Almada, Ariel. 2020. (Amor de Familia Ser.). (SPA.). 32p. (J). (gr. -1-3). 16.95 *(978-84-16733-71-2(6))* Cuento de Luz SL ESP. Dist: Publishers Group West (PGW).

—I Love My Purse. DeMont, Belle. 36p. (J). (gr. k-2). 2020. 9.95 *(978-1-55451-953-8(5))*; 2017. (ENG.). 18.95 *(978-1-55451-954-5(3))* Annick Pr., Ltd. CAN. Dist: Publishers Group West (PGW).

—Las Princesas Más Valientes. Brown, Dolores. 2018. (SPA.). 44p. (J). 17.95 *(978-84-17123-37-6(7))* NubeOcho Ediciones ESP. Dist: Consortium Bk. Sales & Distribution.

—Little One. Andres Almada, Ariel. Brokenbrow, Jon, tr. 2020. (Family Love Ser.). 32p. (J). (gr. -1-3). 16.95 *(978-84-16733-72-9(4))* Cuento de Luz SL ESP. Dist: Publishers Group West (PGW).

—A Night Time Story. Aliaga, Roberto. Brokenbrow, Jon, tr. 2012. (ENG.). 24p. (J). (gr. k-2). 14.95 *(978-84-15241-98-0(4))* Cuento de Luz SL ESP. Dist: Publishers Group West (PGW).

—La Ola de Estrellas. Brown, Dolores. 2020. (SPA.). 44p. (J). 15.95 *(978-84-17673-40-6(7))* NubeOcho Ediciones ESP. Dist: Consortium Bk. Sales & Distribution.

—The Sky of Afghanistan. Eulate, Ana. Brokenbrow, Jon, tr. 2012. 24p. (J). (gr. k-2). 15.95 *(978-84-15503-04-0(0))* Cuento de Luz SL ESP. Dist: Publishers Group West (PGW).

—Una Sorpresa para Tortuga. Merlan, Paula. 2017. (SPA.). 40p. (J). (gr. -1-3). 16.95 *(978-84-946333-5-5(X))* NubeOcho Ediciones ESP. Dist: Consortium Bk. Sales & Distribution.

—Story of a Cockroach. Gil, Carmen. Brokenbrow, Jon, tr. 2012. (Mini-Animalist Ser.). (ENG.). 32p. (J). (gr. -1-2). 14.95 *(978-84-15241-22-5(4))* Cuento de Luz SL ESP. Dist: Publishers Group West (PGW).

Wimmer, Sonja. Sugar & Snails. Tsiang, Sarah. 2018. (J). pap. ***(978-1-77321-004-9(1))*** Annick Pr., Ltd.

Wimmer, Sonja. Sugar & Snails. Tsiang, Sarah. 2018. (ENG.). 32p. (J). (gr. k-2). 18.95 *(978-1-77321-005-6(X))* Annick Pr., Ltd. CAN. Dist: Publishers Group West (PGW).

—A Surprise for Mrs. Tortoise. MerlAn, Paula. 2017. (ENG.). 40p. (J). (gr. -1-3). 16.95 *(978-84-946333-4-8(1))* NubeOcho Ediciones ESP. Dist: Consortium Bk. Sales & Distribution.

—The Truly Brave Princesses. Brown, Dolores. 2018. (ENG.). 44p. (J). 17.95 *(978-84-17123-38-3(5))* NubeOcho Ediciones ESP. Dist: Consortium Bk. Sales & Distribution.

—Walking Through a World of Aromas. Almada, Ariel Andres. Brokenbrow, Jon, tr. 2013. (ENG.). 24p. (J). (gr. k-2). 16.95 *(978-84-15619-48-2(0))* Cuento de Luz SL ESP. Dist: Publishers Group West (PGW).

—A Wave of Stars. Brown, Dolores. 2020. 44p. (J). 16.95 *(978-84-17673-41-3(5))* NubeOcho Ediciones ESP. Dist: Consortium Bk. Sales & Distribution.

Wimmer, Sonja. The Magic Hat Shop. Wimmer, Sonja. Brokenbrow, Jon, tr. 2019. (ENG.). 32p. (J). (gr. k). 11.95 *(978-84-16733-65-1(1))* Cuento de Luz SL ESP. Dist: Publishers Group West (PGW).

—The Word Collector. Wimmer, Sonja. Brokenbrow, Jon, tr. 2012. (ENG.). 32p. (J). (gr. k-2). 15.95 *(978-84-15241-34-8(8))* Cuento de Luz SL ESP. Dist: Publishers Group West (PGW).

Wimperis, Sarah. All Quiet on the Western Front. Remarque, Erich Maria. 2014. (World War I Ser.). (ENG.). 64p. pap. 6.95 *(978-1-906230-66-1(8))* Real Reads Ltd. GBR. Dist: Casemate Pubs. & Bk. Distributors, LLC.

Win, Zitkada Zi, jt. illus. see Duta, H'Upahu.

Winborn, Marsha. America's Promise. Powell, Alma. 2003. 32p. (J). (gr. -1-2). 16.89 *(978-0-06-052173-8(2))* HarperCollins Pubs.

—Digby & Kate & the Beautiful Day. Baker, Barbara. 2004. (Puffin Easy-to-Read Ser.). 48p. (J). (gr. 1-4). 11.65 *(978-0-7569-2959-6(8))* Perfection Learning Corp.

—Emma's Turtle. Bunting, Eve. (ENG.). 32p. (J). 2014. (gr. -1-3). pap. 6.95 *(978-1-62091-735-0(1))*; 2007. (gr. 2-k). 15.95 *(978-1-59078-350-4(6))* Boyds Mills Pr.

—Porky & Bess. Weiss, Ellen & Friedman, Mel. 2011. (Step into Reading Ser.). (ENG.). 48p. (J). (gr. 2-4). pap. 4.99 *(978-0-375-86113-0(0)*, Random Hse. Bks. for Young Readers) Random Hse. Children's Bks.

—A Winning Attitude. Daniel, Claire. 2007. 14p. pap. 4.75 *(978-0-15-377381-5(2))* Harcourt Schl. Pubs.

Winburn, Sean. The Barnyard Experience. Bauman, Melina J. 2019. (ENG.). 26p. (J). 22.95 ***(978-1-4808-7989-8(4))***; pap. 16.95 ***(978-1-4808-7991-1(6))*** Archway Publishing.

Winchel, Heidi. The Magic Potato - la Papa Magica: Story & coloring book in English & Spanish, 1. Romano, Elaine. Nielsen, Emily, tr. 2nd ed. 2004. (SPA.). 20p. (J). 3.00 *(978-0-9728225-3-4(4))* Mill Park Publishing.

Winchester, Elizabeth Siris. The Right Bite: Dentists As Detectives. Siris-Winchester, Elizabeth. 2007. (24/7 Science Behind the Scenes: Forensic Files Ser.). (ENG.). 64p. (YA). (gr. 5-8). 22.44 *(978-0-531-18734-0(9)*, Watts, Franklin) Scholastic Library Publishing.

Windfield, Chris. Spiffy, a Cat That Drinks Coffee. Draine, Doretha. 2018. (ENG.). 58p. (J). (gr. k-6). 24.95 *(978-1-63498-732-5(2))*; pap. 14.95 *(978-1-63498-731-8(4))* Bookstand Publishing.

Windle, Shayda. Eliana, Where Do Thoughts Come From? Wilson, Janice Marie. 2019. (ENG.). 44p. (J). pap. 9.95 ***(978-0-692-03668-6(7))*** Goodness Experience, The.

Windsor-Smith, Barry. Tower of the Elephant & Other Stories. Thomas, Roy & Howard, Robert E. 2003. (Conan Ser.: Vol. 1). (ENG.). 168p. pap. 15.99 *(978-1-59307-016-8(0))* Dark Horse Comics.

Windsor-Smith, Barry & Bright, Mark. Iron Man: Armor Wars. 2018. 208p. (J). (gr. 4-17). pap. 24.99 *(978-1-302-91391-5(3))* Marvel Worldwide, Inc.

Windsor-Smith, Barry & Kane, Gil. Conan the Barbarian Epic Collection: the Original Marvel Years - the Coming of Conan. 2020. (ENG.). 320p. (YA). (gr. 8-17). pap. 34.99 ***(978-1-302-92555-0(5))*** Marvel Worldwide, Inc.

Windsor, Susan. Animals by Design: Exploring Unique Creature Features. 2018. 125p. (J). pap. *(978-1-946246-12-7(3))* Institute for Creation Research.

—Dinosaurs: God's Mysterious Creatures. 2017. 121p. (J). pap. *(978-1-935587-93-4(5))* Institute for Creation Research.

—Space: God's Majestic Handiwork. 2017. 111p. (J). pap. *(978-1-946246-03-5(4))* Institute for Creation Research.

Wine, Rosene. This Is the Erie Canal. Newswanger, Rebecca. 2016. (ENG.). 48p. (J). 4.85 *(978-0-7399-2526-3(1))* Rod & Staff Pubs., Inc.

Winegar, Tony. Blue Ridge Moments: Blue Ridge Tenderpups Love the Seasons. Minton, Evelyn & Minton, Billie J. 2019. (Blue Ridge Tenderpups Ser.: Vol. 2). (ENG.). 26p. (J). pap. 12.95 *(978-1-0962-2215-6(9))* Independently Published.

Winfield, Alison. Old Friends, New Friends. Hall, Patricia. ed. 2005. (Ready-to-Read Ser.). 32p. (J). lib. bdg. 15.00 *(978-1-59054-930-8(9))* Fitzgerald Bks.

Winfield, Amy. Peppermint Pixie. Harvey, Natalie. 2013. 44p. pap. *(978-1-909202-10-8(X))* Little Acorns Publishing.

—The Plot Bunny. Jackson, Kristina. 2013. 24p. pap. *(978-1-909202-15-3(0))* Little Acorns Publishing.

Wingerter, Linda. Magic Hoofbeats: Horse Tales from Many Lands. Sherman, Josepha. 2004. (ENG.). 80p. (J). 19.99 *(978-1-84148-091-6(6))* Barefoot Bks., Inc.

—One Grain of Sand: A Lullaby. Seeger, Pete. 2005. 30p. (J). (gr. -1-4). reprint ed. 16.00 *(978-0-7567-8586-4(3))* DIANE Publishing Co.

Winget, Susan. Everyday Angels. Moulton, Mark Kimball. 2003. (ENG.). 32p. (J). 14.95 *(978-0-8249-5479-6(3)*, Ideal Pubns.) Worthy Publishing.

—The Visit: The Origin of the Night Before Christmas, 1 vol. Moulton, Mark Kimball. 2013. (ENG.). 56p. (gr. 3-6). 16.99 *(978-0-7643-4575-3(3)*, 4985) Schiffer Publishing, Ltd.

Winget, Susan. Tucker's Apple-Dandy Day. Winget, Susan. 2006. 40p. (J). (gr. -1-k). 13.89 *(978-0-06-054647-2(6))* HarperCollins Pubs.

—Tucker's Four-Carrot School Day. Winget, Susan. 2005. (ENG.). 40p. (J). (gr. -1-k). 12.99 *(978-0-06-054642-7(5))* HarperCollins Pubs.

Winget, Susan. The Visit. Winget, Susan, tr. Moulton, Mark Kimball. 2003. (ENG.). 56p. (J). 14.95 *(978-0-8249-5859-6(4)*, Ideal Pubns.) Worthy Publishing.

Winget, Susan, jt. illus. see Moore, Clement C.

Wingham, Peter. Pyramid Plot. Somper, Justin. 2004. (Puzzle Adventures Ser.). 48p. (J). pap. 4.95 *(978-0-7945-0139-6(7)*, Usborne) EDC Publishing.

Winick, Judd. Garfield Original Graphic Novel: Unreality TV: Unreality TV. Nickel, Scott & Evanier, Mark. 2017. (Garfield Ser.: 2). (ENG.). 96p. (J). (gr. 1-3). pap. 9.99 *(978-1-60886-975-6(X))* Boom! Studios.

Winicki, Danielle. Smoky: No Ordinary War Dog. Allsopp, Nigel. 2020. 32p. (J). (gr. k-2). 14.99 *(978-1-76079-153-7(9))* New Holland Pubs. Pty, Ltd. AUS. Dist: Independent Pubs. Group.

Winkowski, Jackie, photos by. Miki's Challenge: One sled dog's Story. Winkowski, Jackie. 2006. 44p. (J). 10.95 *(978-0-9791367-1-9(7))* Snowy Plains.

Winn, Anthony, et al. Star Wars Legends Epic Collection: Rise of the Sith Vol. 2. 2017. (ENG.). 496p. (J). (gr. 4-17). pap. 39.99 *(978-1-302-90790-7(5))* Marvel Worldwide, Inc.

Winn, Chris, jt. illus. see Galey, Chuck.

Winn, Christine M. Clover's Secret. Winn, Christine M. Walsh, David. 2004. 28p. (J). (gr. k-4). reprint ed. 15.00 *(978-0-7567-7653-4(8))* DIANE Publishing Co.

Winn, Christopher. The Sprite Sisters: Magic at Drysdale's School (Vol 7) Winn, Sheridan. 2013. 256p. pap. *(978-0-9574231-2-1(8))* Winn, Sheridan.

Winn, L. B. Butterpod Jerome & the Planet of Gabool. Winn, L. B. 2007. (J). pap. 18.95 *(978-0-9791884-0-4(7))* Winn, Lynnette.

Winnick, Karen B. Sybil's Night Ride. Winnick, Karen B. 2003. (ENG.). 32p. (gr. k-3). 28.69 *(978-1-56397-697-1(8))* Boyds Mills Pr.

Winship, Daniel. Friends (Parker) Parker, Theron. 2015. (ENG.). 36p. (J). pap. 14.99 *(978-0-9863552-2-6(4))* Savory Words.

—The Tortoise & the Hare: The Tortoise & the Hare. 2012. (SGN, ARA, BOS, CHI & FRE.). 32p. (J). pap. 19.95 incl. DVD *(978-0-9818139-2-9(5))* ASL Tales.

Winslow, Justin. El Perro y el Gato. Hines, Chrissie & Ferreras, Alberto. 2010.Tr. of Perro y el Gato: la Nieve. (SPA.). 28p. 3.99 *(978-0-9828167-1-4(5))* Home Box Office, Inc.

Winslow, Justin. El Perro y el Gato. Winslow, Justin, . 2010.Tr. of Perro y el Gato: la Nieve. (SPA.). 28p. 3.99 *(978-0-9828167-3-8(1))* Home Box Office, Inc.

Winslow, Tim. The Kingdom of Avalon. 2005. 48p. (J). *(978-0-9748505-0-4(0))* Winslow's Art.

Winstead, Leo. Weaver of Song: The Birth of Silent Night. Jackson, Mary Helene. l.t. ed. 2009. 40p. (J). 16.95 *(978-0-9825713-0-9(5))* Clifton Carriage House Pr.

Winstead, Rosie. Someday. Spinelli, Eileen. 2007. 32p. (J). (gr. -1-3). 17.99 *(978-0-8037-2941-4(3)*, Dial Bks) Penguin Young Readers Group.

Winston, David Lorenz. Life on a Chicken Farm. Winston, David Lorenz, photos by. Wolfman, Judy. 2004. (Life on a Farm Ser.). (ENG.). 48p. (gr. 2-5). lib. bdg. 23.93 *(978-1-57505-191-8(5))* Lerner Publishing Group.

—Life on a Dairy Farm. Winston, David Lorenz, photos by. Wolfman, Judy. 2004. (Life on a Farm Ser.). (ENG.). 48p. (gr. 2-5). lib. bdg. 23.93 *(978-1-57505-190-1(7))* Lerner Publishing Group.

—Life on a Sheep Farm. Winston, David Lorenz, photos by. Wolfman, Judy. 2004. (Life on a Farm Ser.). (ENG.). 48p. (gr. 2-5). lib. bdg. 23.93 *(978-1-57505-192-5(3))* Lerner Publishing Group.

—Life on an Apple Orchard. Winston, David Lorenz, photos by. Wolfman, Judy. 2004. (Life on a Farm Ser.). (ENG.). 48p. (gr. 2-5). lib. bdg. 23.93 *(978-1-57505-193-2(1))* Lerner Publishing Group.

Winston, David Lorenz, photos by. Life on a Cattle Farm. Wolfman, Judy. 2005. (Life on a Farm Ser.). 48p. (gr. 2-5). lib. bdg. 23.93 *(978-1-57505-516-9(3))* Lerner Publishing Group.

Winston, Dennis. Four-Hundred Meter Champion. Wooden, Thomas James, Jr. 2003. 103p. (J). mass mkt. 12.00 *(978-0-9740195-0-5(X))* New Castle Publishing Co.

Winston, Jeannie. Head, Shoulders, Knees, & Toes. ed. 2005. (Ready-to-Read Ser.). 24p. (J). lib. bdg. 15.00 *(978-1-59054-962-9(7))* Fitzgerald Bks.

—Trick or Treat! A Halloween Shapes Book. Imperato, Teresa. 2005. 12p. (J). 7.95 *(978-1-58117-325-3(3)*, Intervisual/Piggy Toes) Bendon, Inc.

—Whooo's That? Winters, Kay. 2009. (ENG.). 14p. (J). (gr. -1 — 1). 9.99 *(978-0-15-206480-8(X)*, 1199346) Houghton Mifflin Harcourt Publishing Co.

Winston, Sam, jt. illus. see Jeffers, Oliver.

Wint, Florence. Cowboy Ed. Grossman, Bill. 2004. 28p. (J). (gr. -1-3). reprint ed. *(978-0-7567-7851-4(4))* DIANE Publishing Co.

Winter, Janet. Cinderbear: Board Book & Puppet Theater. Brandon, Wendy. 2004. (J). *(978-1-883043-47-6(6))* Straight Edge Pr., The.

—Cinderbear: (Imagination in a Box) Brandon, Wendy. 2004. 10p. (J). bds. 17.99 *(978-1-883043-50-6(6)*, 6020) Straight Edge Pr., The.

—Little Red Riding Hood Story in a Box. O'Brien, Kristen. 2003. (Story in a Box Ser.). 12p. (J). (gr. -1-1). bds. 8.99 *(978-1-883043-41-4(7))* Straight Edge Pr., The.

Winter, Jeanette. Oil. Winter, Jonah. 2020. (ENG.). 40p. (J). (gr. -1-3). 17.99 *(978-1-5344-3077-8(6)*, Beach Lane Bks.) Beach Lane Bks.

—The Secret Project. Winter, Jonah. 2017. (ENG.). 40p. (J). (gr. k-3). 17.99 *(978-1-4814-6913-5(4)*, Beach Lane Bks.) Beach Lane Bks.

—The Secret World of Hildegard. Winter, Jonah. 2007. (J). *(978-0-439-50738-7(3)*, Levine, Arthur A. Bks.) Scholastic, Inc.

Winter, Jeanette. Biblioburro: A True Story from Colombia. Winter, Jeanette. 2010. (ENG.). 32p. (J). (gr. 1-4). 17.99 *(978-1-4169-9778-8(4)*, Beach Lane Bks.) Beach Lane Bks.

—Henri's Scissors. Winter, Jeanette. 2013. (ENG.). 40p. (J). (gr. k-3). 18.99 *(978-1-4424-6484-1(4)*, Beach Lane Bks.) Beach Lane Bks.

—The Librarian of Basra: A True Story from Iraq. Winter, Jeanette. 2005. (ENG.). 32p. (J). (gr. -1-3). 17.99 *(978-0-15-205445-8(6)*, 1196387) Houghton Mifflin Harcourt Publishing Co.

—Mr. Cornell's Dream Boxes. Winter, Jeanette. 2014. (ENG.). 40p. (J). (gr. -1-3). 19.99 *(978-1-4424-9900-3(1)*, Beach Lane Bks.) Beach Lane Bks.

—Nanuk the Ice Bear. Winter, Jeanette. 2016. (ENG.). 48p. (J). (gr. -1-3). 17.99 *(978-1-4814-4667-9(3)*, Beach Lane Bks.) Beach Lane Bks.

—Nasreen's Secret School: A True Story from Afghanistan. Winter, Jeanette. 2009. (ENG.). 40p. (J). (gr. 1-4). 17.99 *(978-1-4169-9437-4(8)*, Beach Lane Bks.) Beach Lane Bks.

—Our House Is on Fire: Greta Thunberg's Call to Save the Planet. Winter, Jeanette. 2019. (ENG.). 40p. (J). (gr. -1-3). 17.99 *(978-1-5344-6778-1(5)*, Beach Lane Bks.) Beach Lane Bks.

—Sisters: Venus & Serena Williams. Winter, Jeanette. 2019. (ENG.). 48p. (J). (gr. -1-3). 17.99 *(978-1-5344-3121-8(7)*, Beach Lane Bks.) Beach Lane Bks.

—Wangari's Trees of Peace: A True Story from Africa. Winter, Jeanette. 2008. (ENG.). 32p. (J). (gr. -1-3). 17.99 *(978-0-15-206545-4(8)*, 1199505) Houghton Mifflin Harcourt Publishing Co.

—The Watcher: Jane Goodall's Life with the Chimps. Winter, Jeanette. 2011. (ENG.). 48p. (J). (gr. -1-3). 17.99 *(978-0-375-86774-3(0)*, Schwartz & Wade Bks.) Random Hse. Children's Bks.

—The World Is Not a Rectangle: A Portrait of Architect Zaha Hadid. Winter, Jeanette. 2017. (ENG.). 56p. (J). (gr. k-5). 18.99 *(978-1-4814-4669-3(X)*, Beach Lane Bks.) Beach Lane Bks.

Winter, Milo. The Aesop for Children. Aesop, Aesop. 2013. 236p. pap. 9.97 *(978-1-60386-613-2(2))* Rough Draft Printing.

—Aesop's Fables. Aesop, Aesop. 2008. (J). *(978-1-934941-08-9(5))* Red & Black Pubs.

—Aesops Fables for Children. 2012. 294p. pap. *(978-1-907256-72-1(5))* Abela Publishing.

—Aesop's Favorite Fables: More Than 130 Classic Fables for Children! 2017. (Children's Classic Collections). (ENG.). 112p. (J). (gr. k-3). 12.99 *(978-1-944686-08-6(8)*, Racehorse Publishing) Skyhorse Publishing Co., Inc.

—Doctor Rabbit & Ki-Yi Coyote (Illustrated Edition) Hinkle, Thomas Clark. 2018. (ENG.). 56p. (J). pap. *(978-1-4068-1944-1(1))* Echo Library.

—The Illustrated Bible Story Book: New Testament. Loveland, Seymour. 2008. (Dover Read & Listen Ser.). (ENG.). 128p. (J). (gr. k-3). pap. 12.99 incl. cd-rom *(978-0-486-46835-8(6))* Dover Pubns., Inc.

—The Illustrated Bible Story Book - Old Testament. Loveland, Seymour. 2008. (Dover Read & Listen Ser.). (ENG.). 128p. (J). (gr. k-3). pap. 12.99 incl. cd-rom *(978-0-486-46844-0(5))* Dover Pubns., Inc.

—Tales from the Arabian Nights. 2017. (ENG.). 328p. (J). 14.99 *(978-1-63158-185-4(6)*, Racehorse Publishing) Skyhorse Publishing Co., Inc.

—The Three Little Kittens. Mother Goose, Mother. 2009. (Shape Bks.). (ENG.). 16p. (J). (gr. -1-1). pap. 9.95 *(978-1-59583-374-7(9)*, 9781595833747, Green Tiger Pr.) Laughing Elephant.

—The Three Little Pigs. 2008. (Shape Bks.). (ENG.). 16p. (J). (gr. -1-3). pap. 9.95 *(978-1-59583-265-8(3)*, 9781595832658, Green Tiger Pr.) Laughing Elephant.

Winter, Milo & Becker, Charlotte. The Gingerbread Boy: Fairy Tales from the World Over. Faulkner, Georgene. 2011. 98p. 38.95 *(978-1-258-09946-6(2))* Literary Licensing, LLC.

—The Little Red Hen & the Fox: Fairy Tales from the World Over. Faulkner, Georgene. 2011. 98p. 38.95 *(978-1-258-10173-2(4))* Literary Licensing, LLC.

Winter, Nilo. Aesop's Fables. Handford, S. A. l.t. ed. Date not set. (J). (gr. 1-12). lib. bdg. 22.95 *(978-0-88411-991-3(2))* Amereon Ltd.

Winter, P. K. Back at Eagle Lake: More Eagle Lake Giant Stories. Winter, P. K. 2009. 182p. pap. 18.50 *(978-1-4251-8831-3(1))* Trafford Publishing.

Winter, Shirley D. Emily in Netherworld: A Very Scary Day. Peters, Alan R. 2019. (Netherword Ser.: Vol. 4). (ENG.). 56p. (J). pap. 5.50 ***(978-1-7261-7028-4(4))*** CreateSpace Independent Publishing Platform.

Winter, Susan. Mommy's Best Kisses. Anastas, Margaret. 2003. (ENG.). 32p. (J). (gr. -1-1). 17.99 *(978-0-06-623601-8(0))* HarperCollins Pubs.

—Mommy's Best Kisses Board Book. Anastas, Margaret. 2008. (ENG.). 34p. (J). (gr. -1-k). bds. 7.99 *(978-0-06-124130-7(X)*, HarperFestival) HarperCollins Pubs.

—Sailing off to Sleep. Ashman, Linda. 2010. (ENG.). 32p. (J). (gr. -1-1). pap. 9.99 *(978-1-4424-1435-8(9)*, Simon & Schuster Bks. For Young Readers) Simon & Schuster Bks. For Young Readers.

Winter, Susan, photos by. A Hug for You. Anastas, Margaret. 2005. (ENG., 32p. (J). (gr. -1-1). 15.99 *(978-0-06-623613-1(4))* HarperCollins Pubs.

Winterhalt, Tara. Burton & Isabelle Pipistrelle: Out of the Bat Cave. Dias, Denise. 2010. (ENG.). 32p. 19.99 *(978-0-88854-485-8(5))* Royal Ontario Museum CAN. Dist: Univ. of Toronto Pr.

Winteringham, Claire. Claire Winteringham's Alphabet Parade. 2017. 24p. (J). bds. 10.95 *(978-0-7649-7659-9(1)*, POMEGRANATE KIDS) Pomegranate Communications, Inc.

Winters, Alexandria. Mommy is Sick. What Do You Do? Ashford, Marcia. 2019. (What Do You Do? Ser.: Vol. 1). (ENG.). 18p. (J). pap. 9.99 ***(978-0-578-53540-1(8))*** Heartstring Productions, LLD.

Winters, Nellie. Reflections from Them Days (English) A Residential School Memoir from Nunatsiavut. Oberndorfer, Erica, ed. 2020. (Qinuisaarniq Ser.). (ENG.). 26p. (J). pap. 10.95 ***(978-1-77450-207-5(0))*** Inhabit Education CAN. Dist: Consortium Bk. Sales & Distribution.

Winters, Ryan. Trouble in Toy Land. Rose, Emmaline. 2018. 180p. (J). pap. 6.99 *(978-1-7324073-4-3(7))* MacBeath, Emmaline.

Winthrop, Elizabeth. Franklin Delano Roosevelt: Letters from a Mill Town Girl. Winthrop, Elizabeth. unabr. ed. 2003. (J). (gr. 4-7). 25.95 incl. audio *(978-1-59112-213-5(9))* Live Oak Media.

Winton, Andrea Evans. Popoki, the Hawaiian Cat: An Amazing Adventure with the Whale. Gleasner, Diana C. 2004. (J). *(978-0-9651185-7-6(6))* Gleasner, Bill & Diana Inc.

Winton, Byron. The Stalker. Droney, Susan K. 2005. (ENG.). 272p. (YA). pap. 14.99 *(978-1-58124-277-5(8))* Fiction Works, The.

Wintor, Quinton. Stories for Boys Who Dare to Be Different: True Tales of Amazing Boys Who Changed the World Without Killing Dragons. Brooks, Ben. 2018. (ENG.). 160p. (J). (gr. 3-7). 16.99 *(978-0-7624-6592-7(1)*, Running Pr. Kids) Running Pr.

—Stories for Kids Who Dare to Be Different: True Tales of Amazing People Who Stood up & Stood Out. Brooks, Ben. 2019. (ENG.). 160p. (J). (gr. 3-7). 16.99 *(978-0-7624-6855-3(6)*, Running Pr. Kids) Running Pr.

Wintz-Litty, Julie. Silent Night: The Story of the Famous Carol. Weninger, Brigitte. 2018. (ENG.). 32p. (J). (gr. -1-2). 18.95 *(978-0-7358-4326-4(0))* North-South Bks., Inc.

Winward, Makenzie. The Sheep & the Chicken. Meyer, Lisa O. 2011. 16p. pap. 24.95 *(978-1-4626-0478-4(1))* America Star Bks.

Wippermann, Linda. Joayna: Hinter Den Schatten. Castle, Victoria M. 2016. (Joayna Ser.: Vol. 2). (GER.). 302p. (J). pap. 14.10 *(978-1-7200-8030-5(5))* Independently Published.

Wireman, Katharine R. The Birds' Christmas Carol. Wiggin, Kate Douglas. 2008. 76p. pap. 9.95 *(978-1-59915-239-4(8))* Yesterday's Classics.

Wirrenga, Shannon. Where Do Deacons Come From? Ficocelli, Elizabeth. 2011. 20p. (J). pap. 7.99 *(978-1-936453-03-0(7))* Bezalel Bks.

—Where Do Priests Come From? Ficocelli, Elizabeth. 2010. (J). pap. 7.99 *(978-0-9844864-0-3(2))* Bezalel Bks.

Wirsén, Stina. Hattie. Nilsson, Frida. 2020. (Hattie Ser.). (ENG.). 160p. (J). (gr. 2-5). 17.99 *(978-1-77657-270-0(X))* Gecko Pr. NZL. Dist: Lerner Publishing Group.

Wisa, Louis. Bawly & His Whistles: Book 16 - Uncle Wiggily. Garis, Howard R. Trust, The Gunston, ed. 2019. (ENG.). 28p. (J). pap. 6.99 *(978-1-0913-8597-9(1))* Independently Published.

—Bawly & the Church Steeple: Book 14 - Uncle Wiggily. Garis, Howard R. Trust, The Gunston, ed. 2019. (ENG.). 26p. (J). pap. 6.99 *(978-1-0913-6348-9(X))* Independently Published.

—Bawly & the Soldier Hat: Book 8 - Uncle Wiggily. Garis, Howard R. Trust, The Gunston, ed. 2019. (ENG.). 32p. (J). pap. 6.99 *(978-1-0907-4697-9(0))* Independently Published.

—Bawly & Uncle Wiggily: Book 3 - Garis, Howard R. Trust, The Gunston, ed. 2019. (ENG.). 26p. (J). pap. 6.99 *(978-1-0903-3431-2(1))* Independently Published.

—Bawly No-Tail & Jollie Longtail: Book 10 - Uncle Wiggily. Garis, Howard R. Trust, The Gunston, ed. 2019. (ITA.). 28p. (J). pap. 6.99 *(978-1-0909-8178-3(3))* Independently Published.

—Bed Time Stories: Uncle Wiggily in the Woods. Garis, Howard R. 2007. 160p. per. *(978-1-4065-2772-8(6))* Dodo Pr.

—Bed Time Stories: Uncle Wiggily's Adventures. Garis, Howard R. 2007. 140p. per. *(978-1-4065-2773-5(4))* Dodo Pr.

—Bed Time Stories: Uncle Wiggily's Travels. Garis, Howard R. 2007. 160p. per. *(978-1-4065-2774-2(2))* Dodo Pr.

—Bully & Bawly Go Swimming: Bully & Bawly No-Tail - Book 1. Garis, Howard R. Trust, The Gunston, ed. 2019. (ENG.). 30p. (J). pap. 5.99 *(978-1-0902-1861-2(3))* Independently Published.

—Bully & Bawly No-Tail: Uncle Wiggily. Garis, Howard R. Trust, The Gunston, ed. 2019. (ENG.). 286p. (J). pap. 12.99 *(978-1-0903-5487-7(8))* Independently Published.

—Bully & the Basket of Chips: Book 15 - Uncle Wiggily. Garis, Howard R. Trust, The Gunston, ed. 2019. (ENG.). 26p. (J). pap. 6.99 *(978-1-0913-6931-3(3))* Independently Published.

—Bully & the Water Bottle: Book 11 - Uncle Wiggily. Garis, Howard R. Trust, The Gunston, ed. 2019. (ENG.). 30p. (J). pap. 5.99 *(978-1-0909-9521-6(0))* Independently Published.

—Bully Makes a Water Wheel: Book 2. Garis, Howard R. Trust, The Gunston, ed. 2019. (ENG.). 26p. (J). pap. 5.99 *(978-1-0902-4784-1(2))* Independently Published.

—Bully No-Tail Plays Marbles: Book 7 Uncle Wiggily. Garis, Howard R. Trust, The Gunston, ed. 2019. (ENG.). 36p. (J). pap. 6.99 *(978-1-0907-1353-7(3))* Independently Published.

—Bully's & Bawly's Big Jump: Book 4 - Uncle Wiggily. Garis, Howard R. Trust, The Gunston, ed. 2019. (ENG.). 26p. (J). pap. 6.99 *(978-1-0903-6052-6(5))* Independently Published.

—Grandpa & Brighteyes Pigg: Book 21 - Uncle Wiggily. Garis, Howard R. Trust, The Gunston, ed. 2019. (ENG.). 26p. (J). pap. 6.99 *(978-1-0921-2470-6(5))* Independently Published.

—Grandpa Croaker & the Umbrella: Book 9 Uncle Wiggily. Garis, Howard R. Trust, The Gunston, ed. 2019. (ENG.). 32p. (J). pap. 6.99 *(978-1-0907-5731-9(X))* Independently Published.

—Grandpa Croaker & Uncle Wiggily: Book 17 - Uncle Wiggily. Garis, Howard R. Trust, The Gunston, ed. 2019. (ENG.). 26p. (J). pap. 6.99 *(978-1-0913-9064-5(9))* Independently Published.

—Grandpa Croaker Digs a Well: Book 5 - Uncle Wiggily. Garis, Howard R. Trust, The Gunston, ed. 2019. (ENG.). 28p. (J). pap. 6.99 *(978-1-0906-7179-0(2))* Independently Published.

—Mrs. No-Tail & Mrs. Longtail: Book 18 - Uncle Wiggily. Garis, Howard R. Trust, The Gunston, ed. 2019. (ENG.). 32p. (J). pap. 6.99 *(978-1-0914-0177-8(2))* Independently Published.

—Mrs. No-Tail & Nellie Chip-Chip: Book 23 - Uncle Wiggily. Garis, Howard R. Trust, The Gunston, ed. 2019. (ENG.). 26p. (J). pap. 6.99 *(978-1-0925-6918-7(9))* Independently Published.

—Papa No-Tail in Trouble: Book 6 - Uncle Wiggily. Garis, Howard R. Trust, The Gunston, ed. 2019. (ENG.). 34p. (J). pap. 6.99 *(978-1-0906-9990-9(5))* Independently Published.

—Sammie & Susie Littletail. Garis, Howard R. 2007. 120p. per. *(978-1-4065-2770-4(X))* Dodo Pr.

—Sammie & Susie Littletail: Uncle Wiggily. Garis, Howard R. Trust, The Gunston, ed. 2019. (ENG.). 162p. (J). pap. 7.99 *(978-1-7992-0413-8(8))* Independently Published.

Wisa, Louis. Sammie & Susie Littletail I, II, & III: Uncle Wiggily. Garis, Howard R. Trust, The Gunston, ed. 2019. (ENG.). 40p. (J). pap. 6.99 ***(978-1-7975-0233-5(6))*** Independently Published.

—Sammie & Susie Littletail. IV, V, & VI: Uncle Wiggily. Garis, Howard R. Trust, The Gunston, ed. 2019. (ENG.). 36p. (J). pap. 6.99 ***(978-1-7975-1478-9(4))*** Independently Published.

—Sammie & Susie Littletail X, XI & XII: Uncle Wiggily. Garis, Howard R. Trust, The Gunston, ed. 2019. (ENG.). 36p. (J). pap. 6.99 ***(978-1-7976-7394-3(7))*** Independently Published.

—Sammie & Susie Littletail XIX, XX & XXI: Uncle Wiggily. Garis, Howard R. Trust, The Gunston, ed. 2019. (ENG.). 38p. (J). pap. 6.99 ***(978-1-7979-1755-9(2))*** Independently Published.

—Sammie & Susie Littletail XVI, XVII & XVIII: Uncle Wiggily. Garis, Howard R. Trust, The Gunston, ed. 2019. (ENG.). 36p. (J). pap. 6.99 ***(978-1-7977-5684-4(2))*** Independently Published.

—Sammie & Susie Littletail XXII, XXIII & XXIV: Uncle Wiggily. Garis, Howard R. Trust, The Gunston, ed. 2019. (ENG.). 44p. (J). pap. 6.99 ***(978-1-7981-2699-8(0))*** Independently Published.

Wisa, Louis. Sammie & Susie Littletail XXV, XXVI, XXVII: Uncle Wiggily. Garis, Howard R. Trust, The Gunston, ed. 2019. (ENG.). 42p. (J). pap. 6.99 *(978-1-7981-9801-8(0))* Independently Published.

Wisa, Louis. Sammie & Sussie Littletail VII, VIII & IX: Uncle Wiggily. Garis, Howard R. Trust, The Gunston, ed. 2019. (ENG.). 36p. (J). pap. 6.99 *(978-1-7975-4678-0(3))* Independently Published.

Wisa, Louis. Uncle Wiggily's Adventures I & II - Uncle Wiggily. Garis, Howard. Trust, The Gunston, ed. 2019. (ENG.). 38p. (J). pap. 6.99 *(978-1-7962-5111-1(9))* Independently Published.

—Uncle Wiggily's Adventures III & IV: Uncle Wiggily. Garis, Howard R. Trust, The Gunston, ed. 2019. (ENG.). 36p. (J). pap. 6.99 *(978-1-7962-8461-4(0))* Independently Published.

—Uncle Wiggily's Adventures IX & X: Uncle Wiggily. Garis, Howard R. Trust, The Gunston, ed. 2019. (ENG.). 30p. (J). pap. 6.99 *(978-1-7965-0652-5(4))* Independently Published.

—Uncle Wiggily's Adventures V & VI: Uncle Wiggily. Garis, Howard R. Trust, The Gunston, ed. 2019. (ENG.). 28p. (J). pap. 6.99 *(978-1-7964-7753-5(2))* Independently Published.

—Uncle Wiggily's Adventures VII & VIII: Uncle Wiggily. Garis, Howard R. Trust, The Gunston, ed. 2019. (ENG.). 28p. (J). pap. 6.99 *(978-1-7964-7901-0(2))* Independently Published.

—Uncle Wiggily's Adventures XI & XII: Uncle Wiggily. Garis, Howard R. Trust, The Gunston, ed. 2019. (ENG.). 28p. (J). pap. 6.99 *(978-1-7965-4589-0(9))* Independently Published.

—Uncle Wiggily's Adventures XIII & XIV: Uncle Wiggily. Garis, Howard R. Trust, The Gunston, ed. 2019. (ENG.). 26p. (J). pap. 6.99 *(978-1-7966-0650-8(2))* Independently Published.

—Uncle Wiggily's Adventures XIX & XX: Uncle Wiggily. Garis, Howard R. Trust, The Gunston, ed. 2019. (ENG.). 32p. (J). pap. 6.99 *(978-1-7966-1850-1(0))* Independently Published.

—Uncle Wiggily's Adventures XVII & XVIII: Uncle Wiggily. Garis, Howard R. Trust, The Gunston, ed. 2019. (ENG.). 28p. (J). pap. 6.99 *(978-1-7966-1609-5(5))* Independently Published.

—Uncle Wiggily's Adventures XXI & XXII: Uncle Wiggily. Garis, Howard R. Trust, The Gunston, ed. 2019. (ENG.). 26p. (J). pap. 6.99 *(978-1-7966-8383-7(3))* Independently Published.

—Uncle Wiggily's Adventures XXIII & XXIV: Uncle Wiggily. Garis, Howard R. Trust, The Gunston, ed. 2019. (ENG.). 28p. (J). pap. 6.99 *(978-1-7967-3301-3(6))* Independently Published.

—Uncle Wiggily's Adventures XXIX & XXX & XXXI: Uncle Wiggily. Garis, Howard R. Trust, The Gunston, ed. 2019. (ENG.). 36p. (J). pap. 6.99 *(978-1-7970-6919-7(5))* Independently Published.

—Uncle Wiggily's Adventures XXV & XXVI: Uncle Wiggily. Garis, Howard R. Trust, The Gunston, ed. 2019. (ENG.). 30p. (J). pap. 6.99 *(978-1-7967-6007-1(2))* Independently Published.

—Uncle Wiggily's Adventures XXVII & XXVIII: Uncle Wiggily. Garis, Howard R. Trust, The Gunston, ed. 2019. (ENG.). 28p. (J). pap. 6.99 *(978-1-7967-6735-3(2))* Independently Published.

Wisa, Louis. Uncle Wiggily's Automobile. Garis, Howard R. 2019. (ENG.). 88p. (J). pap. 5.95 ***(978-1-6888-6205-0(6))*** Independently Published.

Wisbauer, Cortney. Rodney, the Ice Dragon. Wisbauer, Cortney. 2006. 48p. (J). 22.95 *(978-1-59879-215-7(6))* Lifevest Publishing, Inc.

Wise, Catlin. Ricky the Picky Koala. Tabernik, John. 2005. (J). 14.95 *(978-0-9773936-0-2(7))* Little Munchkin Bks.

Wise, Jesse D. Myrtle's True Friend. Wise, Alicia. 2008. 15p. pap. 24.95 *(978-1-60610-626-6(0))* America Star Bks.

Wise, Loveis. Say Her Name. Elliott, Zetta. 2020. 112p. (J). (gr. 7-17). 18.99 ***(978-1-368-04524-7(3))*** Little, Brown Bks. for Young Readers.

Wise, Terry. Zeke & Zak Fumble Through a Fairy Long Lesson. Rodgers, Lenora. Donovan, Yvette, ed. 2019. (ENG.). 22p. (J). (gr. 3-6). pap. 8.50 ***(978-1-942333-17-3(X))*** Performance Strategies.

Wiseman, Daniel. Baby Astronaut. Gehl, Laura. 2019. (Baby Scientist Ser.: 2). (ENG.). 22p. (J). (gr. -1 — 1). bds. 8.99 *(978-0-06-284134-6(3)*, HarperFestival) HarperCollins Pubs.

—Baby Botanist. Gehl, Laura. 2019. (Baby Scientist Ser.: 3). (ENG.). 22p. (J). (gr. -1 — 1). bds. 8.99 *(978-0-06-284132-2(7)*, HarperFestival) HarperCollins Pubs.

—Baby Oceanographer. Gehl, Laura. 2019. (Baby Scientist Ser.: 1). (ENG.). 22p. (J). (gr. -1 — 1). bds. 8.99 *(978-0-06-284133-9(5)*, HarperFestival) HarperCollins Pubs.

—Baby Paleontologist. Gehl, Laura. 2020. (Baby Scientist Ser.: 4). (ENG.). 22p. (J). (gr. -1 — 1). bds. 8.99 *(978-0-06-284135-3(1)*, HarperFestival) HarperCollins Pubs.

—Pet This Book. Young, Jessica. 2018. 32p. (J). 15.99 *(978-1-68119-507-0(0)*, 900175607, Bloomsbury Children's Bks.) Bloomsbury Publishing USA.

—Play This Book. Young, Jessica. 2018. 32p. (J). 15.99 *(978-1-68119-506-3(2)*, 900175599, Bloomsbury Children's Bks.) Bloomsbury Publishing USA.

—When Your Elephant Has the Sniffles. Hill, Susanna Leonard. 2017. (When Your... Ser.). (ENG.). 26p. (J). (gr. -1 — 1). bds. 7.99 *(978-1-4814-9504-2(6)*, Little Simon) Little Simon.

—When Your Lion Needs a Bath. Hill, Susanna Leonard. 2017. (When Your... Ser.). (ENG.). 26p. (J). (gr. -1 — 1). bds. 7.99 *(978-1-4814-9502-8(X)*, Little Simon) Little Simon.

—When Your Lion Needs a Bath & Other Stories: When Your Lion Needs a Bath; When Your Elephant Has the Sniffles; When Your Llama Needs a Haircut; When Your Monkeys Won't Go to Bed. Hill, Susanna Leonard. ed. 2019. (When Your... Ser.). (ENG.). 104p. (J). (gr. -1 — 1). bds. 31.99 *(978-1-5344-6283-0(X)*, Little Simon) Little Simon.

—When Your Llama Needs a Haircut. Hill, Susanna Leonard. 2018. (When Your... Ser.). (ENG.). 26p. (J). (gr. -1 — 1). bds. 7.99 *(978-1-5344-0563-9(1)*, Little Simon) Little Simon.

—When Your Monkeys Won't Go to Bed. Hill, Susanna Leonard. 2018. (When Your... Ser.). (ENG.). 26p. (J). (gr. -1 — 1). bds. 7.99 *(978-1-5344-0565-3(8)*, Little Simon) Little Simon.

Wiseman, Daniel. The World Needs More Purple People. Bell, Kristen & Hart, Benjamin. 2020. (ENG.). 40p. (J). (gr. -1-2). 17.99 ***(978-0-593-12196-2(1))***; lib. bdg. 20.99 ***(978-0-593-12197-9(X))*** Random Hse. Children's Bks. (Random Hse. Bks. for Young Readers).

Wisenfeld, Alison. Saint Francis: The Good Man of Assisi. Joslin, Mary. ed. 2014. (ENG.). 32p. (J). (gr. k-4). 9.99 *(978-0-7459-6492-8(3))* Lion Hudson PLC GBR. Dist: Independent Pubs. Group.

Wish, Katia. Is There an App for That? Smith, Bryan. 2015. (ENG.). 32p. (J). pap. 10.95 *(978-1-934490-74-7(1))* Boys Town Pr.

—Sophie's Animal Parade. Dixon, Amy. 2015. 32p. (J). (gr. -1-k). 16.99 *(978-1-63220-403-5(7)*, Sky Pony Pr.) Skyhorse Publishing Co., Inc.

Wisinski, Ed & White, Dave. Hot Wheels: To the Extreme. Harper, Benjamin. 2007. (Scholastic Reader Ser.). 30p. (J). pap. *(978-0-545-02019-0(0))* Scholastic, Inc.

Wisken, Steven. Kingfisher's Banquet. Beale, Alan. 2018. (ENG.). 42p. (J). pap. *(978-1-912021-54-3(4)*, Nightingale Books) Pegasus Elliot Mackenzie Pubs.

Wiskur, Darrell. Dragons of the Deep: Ocean Monsters Past & Present. Wieland, Carl. 2005. 78p. (J). 15.99 *(978-0-89051-424-5(0)*, Master Books) New Leaf Publishing Group.

Wisner, Luke. Say Cheese, God! Burciaga, David. l.t. ed. 2006. 24p. (J). (gr. -1-3). per. 11.99 *(978-1-59879-235-5(0))* Lifevest Publishing, Inc.

Wisnewski, Andrea. The Ink Garden of Brother Theophane. Millen, C. M. 2010. 32p. (J). (gr. k-3). 17.95 *(978-1-58089-179-0(9))* Charlesbridge Publishing, Inc.

—Little Old Farm Folk. 2017. (ENG.). 34p. (J). bds. 8.95 *(978-1-56792-594-4(4))* Godine, David R. Pub.

—Trio: The Tale of a Three-Legged Cat. 2017. (ENG.). 40p. (J). 17.95 *(978-1-56792-608-8(8))* Godine, David R. Pub.

Wisniewski, David. Ducky. Bunting, Eve. 2004. (ENG.). 32p. (J). (gr. k — 1). 6.99 *(978-0-618-43240-0(X)*, 100352) Houghton Mifflin Harcourt Publishing Co.

Wisniewski, David. Golem. Wisniewski, David. 2007. (ENG.). 32p. (J). (gr. 5-7). 7.99 *(978-0-618-89424-6(1)*, 100586) Houghton Mifflin Harcourt Publishing Co.

Wisniewski, Jim "Wiz". Amber & Sapphire: The Magic Spell. Walter, Ekaterina & Walter, Taya. 2017. (ENG.). (J). pap. 14.99 *(978-0-9994522-0-2(7))* Skazka Publishing.

Wister, T. F. Mystery in Hong Kong - the Case of the Disappeared Dumplings. Jefferson, W. C. 2018. (ENG.). 42p. (J). pap. *(978-988-78305-4-2(2))* Toucan Publishing, Incorporated.

—Mystery in London - the Case of the Strange Tourist. Jefferson, W. C. 2018. (ENG.). 42p. (J). pap. *(978-988-78305-7-3(7))* Toucan Publishing, Incorporated.

—Mystery in New York - the Case of the Missing Hot Dogs. Jefferson, W. C. 2018. (ENG.). 42p. (J). pap. *(978-988-78305-6-6(9))* Toucan Publishing, Incorporated.

—Mystery in Paris - the Case of the Vanished Baguettes. Jefferson, W. C. 2018. (ENG.). 42p. (J). pap. *(978-988-78305-5-9(0))* Toucan Publishing, Incorporated.

—The Zodiac Race - Dylan the Dog. Jefferson, W. C. 2017. (ENG.). (J). pap. *(978-988-78305-2-8(6))* Toucan Publishing, Incorporated.

—The Zodiac Race - Maxi the Monkey. Jefferson, W. C. 2017. (ENG.). (J). pap. *(978-988-78305-0-4(X))* Toucan Publishing, Incorporated.

—The Zodiac Race - Paolo the Pig. Jefferson, W. C. 2017. (ENG.). (J). pap. *(978-988-78305-3-5(4))* Toucan Publishing, Incorporated.

—The Zodiac Race - Rocky the Rooster. Jefferson, W. C. 2017. (ENG.). (J). pap. *(978-988-78305-1-1(8))* Toucan Publishing, Incorporated.

Witanto, Shiella. No Steps Behind: Beate Sirota Gordon's Battle for Women's Rights in Japan. Gottesfeld, Jeff. 2020. (ENG.). 44p. (J). (gr. 3-6). 18.99 *(978-1-939547-55-2(5))* Creston Bks.

Witbeck, Rylee. Stop Bullying: The Triple Stop-It Method & Six Other Techniques. Fackrell, Tamara A. 2019. (Character Education Heroes Ser.: Vol. 4). (ENG.). 78p. (J). pap. 15.99 ***(978-1-6864-2118-1(4))*** Independently Published.

Withrow, Lesley Breen. You're My Boo. Dopirak, Kate. 2016. (ENG.). 40p. (J). (gr. -1-3). 17.99 *(978-1-4424-4160-6(7)*, Beach Lane Bks.) Beach Lane Bks.

Witmer, Ruth. Talking with Hands. Martin, Mabel. 2007. (Little Jewel Book Ser.). 24p. (J). (gr. 2). pap. 2.70 *(978-0-7399-2394-8(3))* Rod & Staff Pubs., Inc.

Witnes, Vitus. Barau Barau. Baia, Edward. 2013. 24p. pap. *(978-9980-86-491-8(5))* Univ. of Papua New Guinea Pr.

Witschen, Kay. Clinker's Christmas Star. Witschen, Kay. 2004. 24p. (J). 6.95 *(978-0-9741352-1-2(6))* Dwitt Publishing.

Witschonke, Alan. The Brooklyn Bridge: The Story of the World's Most Famous Bridge & the Remarkable Family That Built It. Mann, Elizabeth. 2006. (Wonders of the World Book Ser.). (ENG.). 48p. (J). (gr. 4-8). pap. 14.95 *(978-1-931414-16-6(5)*, eda15294-d578-4888-887f-2c7cc98666f1) Mikaya Pr.

—Empire State Building: When New York Reached for the Skies. Hine, Lewis, photos by. Mann, Elizabeth. (Wonders of the World Book Ser.). 48p. (J). (gr. 4-8). 2006. pap. 12.95 *(978-1-931414-08-1(4)*, 2cad2ba0-06d7-471b-8932-2dc5c7f465ee); 2003. (ENG.). 19.95 *(978-1-931414-06-7(8)*, 6db0396f-e88b-4b68-ba9a-f74d8ff7c09b) Mikaya Pr.

—The Great Wall: The Story of Thousands of Miles of Earth & Stone That Turned a Nation into a Fortress. Mann, Elizabeth. 2006. (Wonders of the World Book Ser.). 48p. (J). (gr. 4-8). pap. 12.95 *(978-1-931414-12-8(2)*, e2db6e89-7588-4fe8-a65b-12999e9b0b56) Mikaya Pr.

—Hail to the Chief: The American Presidency. Robb, Don. rev. ed. 2010. 32p. (J). (gr. 1-4). 17.95 *(978-1-58089-285-8(X))*; pap. 7.95 *(978-1-58089-286-5(8))* Charlesbridge Publishing, Inc.

—The Hoover Dam: The Story of Hard Times, Tough People & the Taming of a Wild River. Mann, Elizabeth. 2006. (Wonders of the World Book Ser.). (ENG.). 48p. (J). (gr. 4-8). pap. 9.95 *(978-1-931414-13-5(0)*, f242a859-bfa7-4490-a001-0721c965e9de) Mikaya Pr.

Witt, David. Captured by Pirates: Book 1. Fontes, Ron & Fontes, Justine. 2007. (Twisted Journeys ® Ser.: 1). (ENG.). 112p. (J). (gr. 4-7). per. 10.99 *(978-0-8225-6202-3(2)*, Graphic Universe™) Lerner Publishing Group.

—The Hero Twins: Against the Lords of Death: A Mayan Myth. Jolley, Dan. 2008. (Graphic Myths & Legends Ser.). 48p. (J). (gr. 3-7). lib. bdg. 26.60 *(978-0-8225-7495-8(0))* Lerner Publishing Group.

—The Hero Twins: Against the Lords of Death [a Mayan Myth]. Jolley, Dan. 2009. (Graphic Myths & Legends Ser.). (ENG.). 48p. (J). (gr. 4-8). pap. 9.99 *(978-1-58013-892-5(6)*, Graphic Universe™) Lerner Publishing Group.

—Isis & Osiris: To the Ends of the Earth [an Egyptian Myth]. Limke, Jeff. 2007. (Graphic Myths & Legends Ser.). (ENG.). 48p. (J). (gr. 4-8). per. 9.99 *(978-0-8225-6482-9(3)*, Graphic Universe™) Lerner Publishing Group.

—Isis y Osiris: Hasta el Fin del Mundo: Un Mito Egipcio. Limke, Jeff. 2007. (Mitos y leyendas en viñetas (Graphic Myths & Legends) Ser.). (SPA & ENG.). 48p. (J). (gr. 4-7). per. 8.95 *(978-0-8225-7971-7(5)*, Ediciones Lerner) Lerner Publishing Group.

—Nightmare on Zombie Island. Storrie, Paul D. 2008. (Twisted Journeys ® Ser.: 5). (ENG.). (J). (gr. 4-7). pap. 45.32 *(978-0-8225-9469-7(2))* Lerner Publishing Group.

—Tricky Raven Tales. Schweizer, Chris. 2011. (Tricky Journeys Ser.: 4). (ENG.). (J). (gr. 2-4). pap. 39.62 *(978-0-7613-8628-5(9))* Lerner Publishing Group.

Witt, Eddie. Arvid & Hornschwatz Go Skunk Scoffing. Vil, Steve. 2011. 32p. pap. 24.95 *(978-1-4560-6043-5(0))* America Star Bks.

Witt, Rici. There's a Bear in my House. Rose, Alea. 2009. (ENG.). 24p. (J). reprint ed. 10.59 *(978-0-9803367-1-9(6))* Buttermoth Pr. AUS. Dist: Lulu Pr., Inc.

Witte, Anna. El Loro Tico Tango. Witte, Anna. (SPA.). 24p. (J). 2011. (gr. -1-1). 9.99 *(978-1-84686-670-8(7))*; 2005. pap. 6.99 *(978-1-84148-971-1(9))* Barefoot Bks., Inc.

—El Loro Tico Tango. Witte, Anna. 2019. (ENG.). 24p. (J). (gr. -1-2). pap. *(978-1-78285-423-4(1))* Barefoot Bks., Ltd.

—The Parrot Tico Tango. Witte, Anna. Amador, Brian. 2011. 24p. (J). (gr. -1-2). 9.99 *(978-1-84686-669-2(3))* Barefoot Bks., Inc.

—The Parrot Tico Tango. Witte, Anna. 2005. 24p. (J). (gr. k-3). 15.99 *(978-1-84148-243-9(9))* Barefoot Bks., Inc.

—Parrot Tico Tango. Witte, Anna. 2019. (ENG.). 24p. (J). (gr. -1-2). pap. *(978-1-78285-422-7(3))* Barefoot Bks., Ltd.

Witte, Iris. Samedo und der Glutblutstein. Witte, Iris. 2019. (Band Ser.: Vol. 2). (GER.). 42p. (J). pap. *(978-3-7487-0611-3(1))* BookRix GmbH & Co. KG.

Wittebrood, Menno. Where Is My Bear? Coxall, Darcy. 2015. 32p. (J). (gr. -1-1). pap. 8.99 *(978-1-907432-09-5(4))* Hogs Back Bks. GBR. Dist: Independent Pubs. Group.

Wittenberg, Stella. Norberto Nucagorda, Level 5.5. Ende, Michael. 2003. (SPA.). 32p. (J). (gr. 3-5). pap. 8.95 *(978-84-204-3719-4(0)*, AF1328) Santillana USA Publishing Co., Inc.

Wittkamp, Frantz. Konrad. Wittkamp, Frantz, tr. Nöstlinger, Christine. Ampudia, María Jesús, tr. 2nd ed. (SPA.). 148p. (J). 9.95 *(978-84-204-4781-0(1))* Ediciones Alfaguara ESP. Dist: Santillana USA Publishing Co., Inc.

Wittlinger, Laurie A., photos by. Crossing Paths: Living & Learning in China. Jin, Hong Gang et al. 2006. (CHI & ENG., 288p. (C). (gr. k-18). pap. 45.95 *(978-0-88727-370-4(X))* Cheng & Tsui Co.

—Shifting Tides: Culture in Contemporary China. Jin, Hong Gang et al. 2006. (Intermediate Chinese Course Ser.). (CHI & ENG., 272p. (C). (gr. k-18). pap. 45.95 *(978-0-88727-372-8(6))* Cheng & Tsui Co.

Wittmann, Patricia. Don't Wake up the Bear!, 0 vols. Murray, Marjorie Dennis. unabr. ed. 2006. (ENG.). 34p. (J). (gr. -1-2). per. 9.99 *(978-0-7614-5330-7(X)*, 9780761453307, Two Lions) Amazon Publishing.

Wittwer, Hala. Dragon Egg. Loehr, Mallory. 2007. (Step into Reading Ser.). 32p. (J). (gr. -1-1). pap. 4.99 *(978-0-375-84350-1(7)*, Random Hse. Bks. for Young Readers) Random Hse. Children's Bks.

Wittwer, Hala Swearingen. Spring Surprises. Hays, Anna Jane. 2010. (Step into Reading Ser.). 24p. (J). (gr. -1-1). pap. 4.99 *(978-0-375-85840-6(7)*, Random Hse. Bks. for Young Readers) Random Hse. Children's Bks.

Wittwer, Meg & Tillery, Paul, IV. Thundercluck! Chicken of Thor. Tillery, Paul, IV. 2019. (Thundercluck! Ser.). (ENG.). 256p. (J). pap. 7.99 *(978-1-250-21147-7(6)*, 900184616) Square Fish.

—Thundercluck! Chicken of Thor: Recipe for Revenge. Tillery, Paul, IV. 2019. (Thundercluck! Ser.). (ENG.). 256p. (J). 14.99 *(978-1-250-15530-6(4)*, 900184618) Roaring Brook Pr.

Wittwer, Meg, jt. illus. see Tillery, Paul, IV.

Wodin. Just Imagine. Thompson, John M. & Schultz, George M. 2006. 32p. (J). (gr. -1-3). 16.95 *(978-0-9740190-6-2(2))* Illumination Arts Publishing Co., Inc.

Woell, J. Fred. Gloucester: College Life Between Classes. Woell, J. Fred. 144p. (Orig.). (YA). pap. 15.00 *(978-0-9626935-2-6(9))* Turtle Gallery Editions.

Wohnoutka, Mike. Can't Sleep Without Sheep. Hill, Susanna Leonard. 2010. (ENG.). 40p. (J). (gr. -1-1). 17.99 *(978-0-8027-2066-5(6)*, 900063941, Bloomsbury USA Childrens) Bloomsbury Publishing USA.

—The Christmas Elf Countdown! Random House. 2017. 14p. (J). (— 1). bds. 7.99 *(978-1-101-94017-4(4)*, Random Hse. Bks. for Young Readers) Random Hse. Children's Bks.

Wohnoutka, Mike. Hanukkah Bear. Kimmel, Eric A. (J). 2020. 26p. (— 1). bds. 7.99 ***(978-0-8234-4750-3(2))***; 2014. (ENG.). 32p. (gr. -1-3). 7.99 *(978-0-8234-3169-4(X))*; 2013. (ENG.). 32p. (gr. -1-3). 17.99 *(978-0-8234-2855-7(9))* Holiday Hse., Inc.

Wohnoutka, Mike. Head, Shoulders, Knees, & Toes. 2009. (J). *(978-0-545-15604-2(1))* Scholastic, Inc.

—Jack's House. Bell, Karen Magnuson. 2009. (ENG.). 32p. (J). (gr. -1-3). pap. 8.99 *(978-0-8234-2242-5(9))* Holiday Hse., Inc.

—Moo! LaRochelle, David. (ENG.). (J). (gr. -1-3). 2014. 32p. bds. 7.99 *(978-0-8027-3802-8(8)*, 900139342); 2013. 40p. 17.99 *(978-0-8027-3409-9(X)*, 900085433) Bloomsbury Publishing USA. (Bloomsbury USA Childrens).

—Peekity Boo - What You Can Do! Roemer, Heidi Bee. 2019. (ENG.). 40p. (J). 17.99 *(978-1-250-12232-2(5)*, 900173592, Holt, Henry & Co. Bks. For Young Readers) Holt, Henry & Co.

Wohnoutka, Mike. See the Cat: Three Stories about a Dog. LaRochelle, David. 2020. (ENG.). 64p. (J). (gr. -1-3). 8.99 ***(978-1-5362-0427-8(7))*** Candlewick Pr.

Wohnoutka, Mike. Stay Close to Mama. Buzzeo, Toni. 2012. 32p. (J). (gr. -1-k). 15.99 *(978-1-4231-3482-4(6))* Hyperion Pr.

—A Teacher for Bear. Pace, Anne Marie. 2011. (J). *(978-0-545-37776-8(5))* Scholastic, Inc.

—This Is Not a Cat. LaRochelle, David. 2016. 40p. (J). (gr. -1). 14.95 *(978-1-4549-1574-4(9))* Sterling Publishing Co., Inc.

—This Little Piggy. 2005. (J). *(978-1-58987-106-9(5))* Kindermusik International.

—The Twelve Days of Christmas in Minnesota. Van Hoven, Constance. (Twelve Days of Christmas in America Ser.). (J). (-k). 2016. 22p. bds. 7.95 *(978-1-4549-2057-1(2))*; 2009. 40p. 12.95 *(978-1-4027-6395-3(6))* Sterling Publishing Co., Inc.

—When the Wizzy Foot Goes Walking. Schotter, Roni. 2007. (J). *(978-5-525-47791-9(2)*, Dutton Juvenile) Penguin Publishing Group.

Wohnoutka, Mike, jt. illus. see Francis, Guy.

Wojtko, Kimberlee. C Is for Carbon. Summers, Marilee. 2004. 61p. (J). per. 24.95 *(978-0-9753078-0-9(0))* MackStorm Productions, Inc.

Wojtowycz, David. ABC Animal Jamboree. Andreae, Giles. 2010. (ENG.). 32p. (J). (gr. -1-2). 16.95 *(978-1-58925-092-5(3))* Tiger Tales.

—Bustle in the Bushes. Andreae, Giles. 2012. (ENG.). 32p. (J). (gr. -1-2). 16.95 *(978-1-58925-109-0(1))* Tiger Tales.

—Cock-A-doodle-doo! Barnyard Hullabaloo. Andreae, Giles. 2004. (ENG.). 32p. (J). (gr. -1-2). reprint ed. pap. 9.99 *(978-1-58925-387-2(6))* Tiger Tales.

—Commotion in the Ocean. Andreae, Giles. 2011. (ENG.). 26p. (J). (-k). bds. 9.95 *(978-1-58925-863-1(0))* Tiger Tales.

—Dinosaurs Galore! Andreae, Giles. (ENG.). 32p. (J). (gr. -1-2). 2006. pap. 7.95 *(978-1-58925-399-5(X))*; 2005. 16.95 *(978-1-58925-044-4(3))* Tiger Tales.

—Elephant Joe, Brave Firefighter! 2015. (Step into Reading Ser.). (ENG.). 32p. (J). (gr. -1-1). 12.99 *(978-0-375-97203-4(X)*, Random Hse. Bks. for Young Readers) Random Hse. Children's Bks.

—The Pop-Up Dinosaurs Galore! Andreae, Giles. 2008. 14p. (J). (gr. 4-7). 15.95 *(978-1-58925-837-2(1))* Tiger Tales.

—Rumble in the Jungle. Andreae, Giles. 2011. (ENG.). 26p. (J). (-k). bds. 9.95 *(978-1-58925-864-8(9))* Tiger Tales.

—What Will You Wear, Claude? 2004. 10p. (J). (gr. -1-3). reprint ed. 8.00 *(978-0-7567-8259-7(7))* DIANE Publishing Co.

—Whatever the Weather, Clavde! 2004. 10p. (J). (gr. -1-2). reprint ed. 8.00 *(978-0-7567-8257-3(0))* DIANE Publishing Co.

Wolcott, Karen. Barbie. Gordh, Bill & Pugliano-Martin, Carol. 2006. (Step into Reading Ser.). (ENG.). 192p. (J). (gr. -1-1). pap. 8.99 *(978-0-375-84124-8(5)*, Random Hse. Bks. for Young Readers) Random Hse. Children's Bks.

—Barbie: On Your Toes. Jordan, Apple & RH Disney Staff. 2005. (Step into Reading Ser.: No. 1). (ENG.). 32p. (J). (gr. -1-1). pap. 4.99 *(978-0-375-83142-3(8)*, Random Hse. Bks. for Young Readers) Random Hse. Children's Bks.

—Barbie: Horse Show Champ (Barbie) Parker, Jessie. 2009. (Step into Reading Ser.). (ENG.). 32p. (J). (gr. -1-1). pap. 4.99 *(978-0-375-84701-1(4)*, Random Hse. Bks. for Young Readers) Random Hse. Children's Bks.

—Barbie Loves Ballet. Dias, Joe et al, photos by. Roberts, Angela. 2010. (Barbie Ser.). (J). 14.10 *(978-0-7569-7778-8(9))* Perfection Learning Corp.

—Curlee Girlee. Twersky, Atara. (Curlee Girlee Ser.).Tr. of Curlee Girlee. 32p. (J). (gr. -1-3). 2018. (SPA.). 14.99 *(978-0-9968438-3-6(3))*; 2016. (ENG.). 14.99 *(978-0-9968438-1-2(7))* Sandbox Publishing.

Wolek, Guy. A Brave New Mouse: Ellis Island Approved Immigrant, 1 vol. Horender, Philip M. 2013. (Maximilian P. Mouse, Time Traveler Ser.). (ENG.). 112p. (J). (gr. 3-6). lib. bdg. 29.93 *(978-1-61641-961-5(X)*, 11370, Calico Chapter Bks.) ABDO Publishing Co.

—Carson Chooses Forgiveness. Dungy, Tony & Dungy, Lauren. 2019. (Team Dungy Ser.). (ENG.). 32p. (J). (gr. 1-4). 16.99 *(978-0-7369-7322-9(2)*, 6973229) Harvest Hse. Pubs.

—Eleanor Roosevelt. Donnelly, Shannon. 2005. (Heroes of America Ser.). 236p. (gr. 3-8). lib. bdg. 27.07 *(978-1-59679-260-9(4)*, Abdo & Daughters) ABDO Publishing Co.

—Head West, Young Mouse: Transcontinental Railroad Traveler, 1 vol. Horender, Philip M. 2013. (Maximilian P. Mouse, Time Traveler Ser.). (ENG.). 112p. (J). (gr. 3-6). lib. bdg. 29.93 *(978-1-61641-959-2(8)*, 11366, Calico Chapter Bks.) ABDO Publishing Co.

—Homeward Bound: Civil Rights Mouse Leader, 1 vol. Horender, Philip M. 2013. (Maximilian P. Mouse, Time Traveler Ser.). (ENG.). 112p. (J). (gr. 3-6). lib. bdg. 29.93 *(978-1-61641-962-2(8)*, 11372, Calico Chapter Bks.) ABDO Publishing Co.

W

—The Jungle Book, 1 vol. Kipling, Rudyard. 2011. (Calico Illustrated Classics Ser.: No. 4). (ENG.). 112p. (J). (gr. 2-5). 29.93 *(978-1-61641-616-4(5)*, 4047, Calico Chapter Bks.) ABDO Publishing Co.

—The Mighty Maximilian: Samuel Clemens's Traveling Companion, 1 vol. Horender, Philip M. 2013. (Maximilian P. Mouse, Time Traveler Ser.). (ENG.). 112p. (J). (gr. 3-6). lib. bdg. 29.93 *(978-1-61641-960-8(1)*, 11368, Calico Chapter Bks.) ABDO Publishing Co.

—A Monster at School, 1 vol. Huneke, Amanda. 2013. (Monster on the Loose Ser.). (ENG.). 32p. (J). (gr. k-4). 28.50 *(978-1-61641-931-8(8)*, 11553, Looking Glass Library) Magic Wagon.

—A Monster in the Park, 1 vol. Huneke, Amanda. 2013. (Monster on the Loose Ser.). (ENG.). 32p. (J). (gr. k-4). 28.50 *(978-1-61641-932-5(6)*, 11555, Looking Glass Library) Magic Wagon.

—A Monster on the Bus, 1 vol. Huneke, Amanda. 2013. (Monster on the Loose Ser.). (ENG.). 32p. (J). (gr. k-4). 28.50 *(978-1-61641-933-2(4)*, 11557, Looking Glass Library) Magic Wagon.

—A Monster on the Loose, 1 vol. Huneke, Amanda. 2013. (Monster on the Loose Ser.). (ENG.). 32p. (J). (gr. k-4). 28.50 *(978-1-61641-934-9(2)*, 11559, Looking Glass Library) Magic Wagon.

—No More Noisy Nights. Niner, Holly L. 2017. (ENG.). 32p. (J). (gr. k-2). 17.95 *(978-1-936261-93-2(6))* Flashlight Pr.

—Ollie Outside: Screen-Free Fun. Oberschneider, Michael. 2016. (ENG.). 32p. (J). (gr. -1-2). pap. 9.99 *(978-1-63198-068-8(8))* Free Spirit Publishing, Inc.

—Patriotic Mouse: Boston Tea Party Participant, 1 vol. Horender, Philip M. 2013. (Maximilian P. Mouse, Time Traveler Ser.). (ENG.). 112p. (J). (gr. 3-6). lib. bdg. 29.93 *(978-1-61641-957-8(1)*, 11362, Calico Chapter Bks.) ABDO Publishing Co.

—Yankee Mouse: Gettysburg Address Observer. Horender, Philip M. 2013. (Maximilian P. Mouse, Time Traveler Ser.). (ENG.). 112p. (J). (gr. 3-6). lib. bdg. 29.93 *(978-1-61641-958-5(X)*, 11364, Calico Chapter Bks.) ABDO Publishing Co.

Wolf. The Bear Scare. Zaqen, Ra'ah. 2019. (ENG.). 26p. (J). pap. 9.13 *(978-1-7985-0810-7(9))* Independently Published.

Wolf, Bruce. Now I Eat My ABC's. Abrams, Pam. 2004. (ENG.). 14p. (J). (gr. k — 1). bds. 7.99 *(978-0-439-64942-1(0)*, Cartwheel Bks.) Scholastic, Inc.

Wolf, Bruce, photos by. The House That Mouse Built. Rudy, Maggie & Abrams, Pam. 2011. (ENG., 32p. (J). (gr. -1). 14.99 *(978-1-935703-25-9(0))* Downtown Bookworks.

Wolf, Carli Anne. One Big Light. Wolf, Carli Anne. 2019. (ENG.). 26p. (J). pap. 9.99 ***(978-1-6518-8035-7(2))*** Independently Published.

Wolf, Claudia. Bob's Great Escape, 1 vol. Mackall, Dandi Daley. 2011. (I Can Read! / a Horse Named Bob Ser.). (ENG.). 32p. (J). pap. 3.99 *(978-0-310-71784-3(1))* Zonderkidz.

—Double Trouble, 1 vol. Mackall, Dandi Daley. 2011. (I Can Read! / a Horse Named Bob Ser.). (ENG.). 32p. (J). pap. 4.99 *(978-0-310-71785-0(X))* Zonderkidz.

—Fighter Joe: The Fish of Which Dreams Are Made. Nicola, Robbin. 2006. 24p. (J). per. 2.99 *(978-1-59958-001-2(2))* Journey Stone Creations, LLC.

—A Horse Named Bob, 1 vol. Mackall, Dandi Daley. 2011. (I Can Read! / a Horse Named Bob Ser.). (ENG.). 32p. (J). pap. 4.99 *(978-0-310-71782-9(5))* Zonderkidz.

—Indigo's Gift: Does Indigo Have a Secret Gift? Van Oss, Laura. 2006. 24p. (J). per. 2.99 *(978-1-59958-003-6(9))* Journey Stone Creations, LLC.

—New Zealand ABCs: A Book about the People & Places of New Zealand. Schroeder, Holly. 2004. (Country ABCs Ser.). (ENG.). 32p. (J). (gr. k-5). 28.65 *(978-1-4048-0178-3(2)*, 1229507, Picture Window Bks.) Capstone.

—A Perfect Pony, 1 vol. Mackall, Dandi Daley. 2011. (I Can Read! / a Horse Named Bob Ser.). (ENG.). 32p. (J). pap. 4.99 *(978-0-310-71783-6(3))* Zonderkidz.

—100 Years Old with Baby Teeth: Will Caroline Ever Lose Her Tooth? Thompson, Deanna. 2006. 24p. (J). per. 2.99 *(978-1-59958-000-5(4))* Journey Stone Creations, LLC.

Wolf, Claudia. Grandma & Me. Wolf, Claudia. 2006. 24p. (J). per. 2.99 *(978-1-59958-024-1(1))* Journey Stone Creations, LLC.

Wolf, Elizabeth. Lettie's North Star. Falk, Elizabeth Sullivan. 2006. (J). *(978-1-59336-694-0(9))* Mondo Publishing.

—Passover Around the World, Vol. Lehman-Wilzig, Tami. 2007. (ENG.). 48p. (J). (gr. 3-5). per. 8.99 *(978-1-58013-215-2(4)*, Kar-Ben Publishing) Lerner Publishing Group.

—Who Was Eleanor Roosevelt? Thompson, Gare & Who HQ. 2004. (Who Was? Ser.). 112p. (J). (gr. 3-7). pap. 5.99 *(978-0-448-43509-1(8)*, Penguin Workshop) Penguin Young Readers Group.

—Who Was Eleanor Roosevelt? Thompson, Gare. 2004. (Who Was... ? Ser.). 106p. (gr. 3-7). 15.00 *(978-0-7569-2829-2(X))* Perfection Learning Corp.

—Who Was Ferdinand Magellan? Kramer, Sydelle. 2004. (Who Was... ? Ser.). 105p. (J). (gr. 3-7). 12.65 *(978-0-7569-4615-9(8))* Perfection Learning Corp.

—Who Was Martin Luther King, Jr. ? Bader, Bonnie & Who HQ. 2007. (Who Was? Ser.). (ENG.). 112p. (J). (gr. 3-7). pap. 5.99 *(978-0-448-44723-0(1)*, Penguin Workshop) Penguin Young Readers Group.

—Who Was Martin Luther King, Jr. ? Bader, Bonnie. 2008. (Who Was... ? Ser.). 105p. (J). (gr. 2-5). 12.65 *(978-0-7569-8935-4(3))* Perfection Learning Corp.

—Who Was Ronald Reagan? Milton, Joyce & Who HQ. 2004. (Who Was? Ser.). 112p. (J). (gr. 3-7). pap. 5.99 *(978-0-448-43344-8(3)*, Penguin Workshop) Penguin Young Readers Group.

Wolf, LeeHee. In, Out, Roundabout. Honey, Steve. Chang, Shinyoung, ed. 2018. (ENG.). 28p. (J). pap. 10.00 *(978-1-931166-86-7(2))* HSA Pubns.

Wolf, Matt. Geronimo Stilton 12-Copy Solid Self-Shipper. Stilton, Geronimo. 2004. (ENG.). (J). pap. 71.88 *(978-0-439-64099-2(7)*, Scholastic Paperbacks) Scholastic, Inc.

—Un granizado de moscas para el Conde. Stilton, Geronimo. (SPA.). 128p. (J). (gr. 3-5). pap. 7.95 *(978-1-59437-452-4(X))* Santillana USA Publishing Co., Inc.

—I'm Too Fond of My Fur! Stilton, Geronimo. 2004. (Geronimo Stilton Ser.: No. 4). 116p. (J). lib. bdg. 10.00 *(978-1-4242-0698-8(7))* Fitzgerald Bks.

—It's Halloween, You 'Fraidy Mouse! Stilton, Geronimo. 2004. 113p. (J). lib. bdg. 10.00 *(978-1-4242-0280-5(9))* Fitzgerald Bks.

—It's Halloween, You 'Fraidy Mouse! Stilton, Geronimo. 2004. (Geronimo Stilton Ser.: 11). 128p. (J). (gr. 2-5). pap. 7.99 *(978-0-439-55973-7(1)*, Scholastic Paperbacks) Scholastic, Inc.

—Lost Treasure of the Emerald Eye. Stilton, Geronimo. 2004. (Geronimo Stilton Ser.: No. 1). 116p. (J). lib. bdg. 10.00 *(978-1-4242-0695-7(2))* Fitzgerald Bks.

—Merry Christmas, Geronimo! Stilton, Geronimo. 2004. (Geronimo Stilton Ser.: No. 12). 113p. (J). lib. bdg. 10.00 *(978-1-4242-0281-2(7))* Fitzgerald Bks.

—The Mona Mousa Code. Stilton, Geronimo. 2005. (Geronimo Stilton Ser.: No. 15). 113p. (J). lib. bdg. 10.00 *(978-1-4242-0284-3(1))* Fitzgerald Bks.

—The Phantom of the Subway. Stilton, Geronimo. 2004. (Geronimo Stilton Ser.: No. 13). 112p. (J). lib. bdg. 10.00 *(978-1-4242-0282-9(5))* Fitzgerald Bks.

—The Search for Sunken Treasure. Stilton, Geronimo. 2006. (Geronimo Stilton Ser.: No. 25). 111p. (J). lib. bdg. 10.00 *(978-1-4242-1519-5(6))* Fitzgerald Bks.

—The Temple of the Ruby of Fire. Stilton, Geronimo. 2004. (Geronimo Stilton Ser.: No. 14). 109p. (J). lib. bdg. 10.00 *(978-1-4242-0283-6(3))* Fitzgerald Bks.

Wolf, Matt & Keys, Larry. Paws Off, Cheddarface! Stilton, Geronimo. 2004. (Geronimo Stilton Ser.: 6). 128p. (J). (gr. 2-5). pap. 7.99 *(978-0-439-55968-3(5))* Scholastic, Inc.

Wolf, Myron, photos by. Orange Fizz. Wolf, Clarissa. 2009. 32p. pap. 9.99 *(978-1-935105-39-8(6))* Avid Readers Publishing Group.

Wolfe, Alyce. Brian & the Storm: A Young Boy's First Hurricane. Chesnutt, Van. 2019. (ENG.). 36p. (J). (gr. 2-7). 19.95 ***(978-0-9995852-0-7(7))*** Means To An End.

Wolfe, Art, photos by. Northwest Animal Babies. Helman, Andrea. 2006. 32p. (J). (gr. -1-2). pap. 10.99 *(978-1-57061-462-0(8)*, Little Bigfoot) Sasquatch Bks.

—O Is for Orca. Helman, Andrea. 2016. 20p. (J). (— 1). bds. 9.99 *(978-1-63217-033-0(7)*, Little Bigfoot) Sasquatch Bks.

—O Is for Orca: An Alphabet Book. Helman, Andrea. 2003. 32p. (J). (gr. -1-2). pap. 10.99 *(978-1-57061-392-0(3)*, Little Bigfoot) Sasquatch Bks.

—1, 2, 3 Moose: An Animal Counting Book. Helman, Andrea. 2016. (ENG., 20p. (J). (— 1). bds. 9.99 *(978-1-63217-032-3(9)*, Little Bigfoot) Sasquatch Bks.

Wolfe, Bob & Wolfe, Diane, photos by. How It Happens at the ATV Plant. Anderson, Jenna. 2004. (How It Happens Ser.). 32p. (J). (gr. 2-5). lib. bdg. 19.95 *(978-1-881508-94-6(3))* Oliver Pr., Inc.

—How It Happens at the Building Site. Anderson, Jenna. 2004. (How It Happens Ser.). 32p. (J). (gr. 2-5). lib. bdg. 19.95 *(978-1-881508-95-3(1))* Oliver Pr., Inc.

—How It Happens at the Cereal Company. Rocker, Megan. 2004. (How It Happens Ser.). 32p. (J). (gr. 2-5). lib. bdg. 19.95 *(978-1-881508-96-0(X))* Oliver Pr., Inc.

—How It Happens at the Fireworks Factory. Rocker, Megan. 2004. (How It Happens Ser.). 32p. (J). (gr. 2-5). lib. bdg. 19.95 *(978-1-881508-97-7(8))* Oliver Pr., Inc.

—How It Happens at the Motorcycle Plant. Shofner, Shawndra. 2006. (How It Happens Ser.). 32p. (J). (gr. 2-5). lib. bdg. 19.95 *(978-1-881508-99-1(4))* Oliver Pr., Inc.

—How It Happens at the Pizza Company. Shofner, Shawndra. 2006. (How It Happens Ser.). 32p. (J). (gr. 2-5). lib. bdg. 19.95 *(978-1-881508-98-4(6))* Oliver Pr., Inc.

Wolfe, Diane, jt. illus. see Wolfe, Robert L.

Wolfe, Diane, jt. photos by see Wolfe, Bob.

Wolfe, Frances. The Little Toy Shop. Wolfe, Frances. 2008. 32p. (J). (gr. -1-2). 19.95 *(978-0-88776-865-1(2)*, Tundra Bks.) Tundra Bks. CAN. Dist: Penguin Random Hse. LLC.

Wolfe, Linda. Across the Road. 2008. 32p. (J). 10.00 *(978-0-937179-16-1(7))* Blue Scarab Pr.

Wolfe, Lynn. Viku & the Elephant: A Story from the Forests of India. Majumdar, Debu. 2011. (ENG.). 54p. (J). pap. 12.99 *(978-0-9832227-0-5(3))* Bo-Tree Hse.

Wolfe-Murray, Caroline. Dragons in Snow. Vol. Hayman, Judy. 2016. (Dragon Tales Ser.: Vol. 5). (ENG.). 216p. (J). (gr. 1-3). pap. *(978-1-910056-42-4(1))* Practical Inspiration Publishing.

Wolfe Murray, Caroline. Quest for Adventure. Hayman, Judy. 2015. (Dragon Tales Ser.: Vol. 3). (ENG.). 158p. (J). (gr. 3-5). pap. *(978-1-910056-22-6(7))* Practical Inspiration Publishing.

Wolfe, Robert L. & Wolfe, Diane. Holiday Cooking Around the World. Wolfe, Robert L. & Wolfe, Diane, photos by. Cornell, Kari A., ed. 2nd rev. exp. ed. 2003. (Easy Menu Ethnic Cookbooks). 72p. (J). (gr. 5-12). pap. 7.95 *(978-0-8225-4159-2(9))* Lerner Publishing Group.

Wolfenden, Heidi. If a Python Puts on Your PJ's What Should You Do? Wolfenden, Heidi. 2018. (What Should You Do? Ser.: Vol. 1). (ENG.). 30p. (J). (gr. k-2). pap. *(978-0-646-59824-6(4))* Wolfenden, Heidi.

Wolferman, Iris. I Am Who I Am. Hachler, Bruno. 2010. 16p. (J). (gr. -1 — 1). bds. 8.95 *(978-0-7358-2299-3(9))* North-South Bks., Inc.

—My Wish Tonight. Stalder, Päivi. 2010. 32p. (J). (gr. -1-3). 12.95 *(978-0-7358-2331-0(6))* North-South Bks., Inc.

Wolff, Ashley. Compost Stew: An A to Z Recipe for the Earth. Siddals, Mary McKenna. 2010. 40p. (J). (gr. -1-2). 15.99 *(978-1-58246-316-2(6)*, Tricycle Pr.) Random Hse. Children's Bks.

—Compost Stew: An a to Z Recipe for the Earth. Siddals, Mary McKenna. 2014. 40p. (J). (gr. -1-2). 7.99 *(978-0-385-75538-2(4)*, Dragonfly Bks.) Random Hse. Children's Bks.

—I Love My Daddy Because... Board Book. Gaylord, Laurel Porter. 2004. (ENG.). 11p. (J). (gr. -1 — 1). bds. 7.99 *(978-0-525-47250-6(9)*, Dutton Books for Young Readers) Penguin Young Readers Group.

—I Love My Mommy Because... Gaylord, Laurel Porter. 2004. (ENG.). 22p. (J). (gr. -1 — 1). bds. 7.99 *(978-0-525-47247-6(9)*, Dutton Books for Young Readers) Penguin Young Readers Group.

—In the Canyon. Scanlon, Liz Garton. 2015. (ENG.). 40p. (J). (gr. -1-3). 17.99 *(978-1-4814-0348-1(6)*, Beach Lane Bks.) Beach Lane Bks.

—Mama's Milk. Elsohn Ross, Michael. 2007. 32p. (J). (gr. -1-2). 12.95 *(978-1-58246-181-6(3)*, Tricycle Pr.) Random Hse. Children's Bks.

—Mama's Milk / Mamá Me Alimenta. Elsohn Ross, Michael. 2008. 32p. (J). (gr. -1-2). pap. 6.99 *(978-1-58246-245-5(3)*, Tricycle Pr.) Random Hse. Children's Bks.

—Mama's Milk / Mamá Me Alimenta. Elsohn Ross, Michael. 2016. 24p. (J). (-k). bds. 7.99 *(978-0-553-53874-8(8)*, Tricycle Pr.) Random Hse. Children's Bks.

—Miss Bindergarten & the Best Friends. Slate, Joseph. 2014. (Penguin Young Readers, Level 2 Ser.). 32p. (J). (gr. 1-2). pap. 3.99 *(978-0-448-48132-6(4)*, Penguin Young Readers) Penguin Young Readers Group.

—Miss Bindergarten & the Secret Bag. Slate, Joseph. 2013. (Penguin Young Readers, Level 2 Ser.). 32p. (J). (gr. 1-2). pap. 4.99 *(978-0-448-46803-7(4))*; 14.99 *(978-0-8037-3988-8(5))* Penguin Young Readers Group. (Penguin Young Readers).

—Miss Bindergarten & the Very Wet Day. Slate, Joseph. 2015. (Penguin Young Readers, Level 2 Ser.). 32p. (J). (gr. 1-2). 4.99 *(978-0-448-48700-7(4)*, Penguin Young Readers) Penguin Young Readers Group.

—Miss Bindergarten Celebrates the Last Day of Kindergarten. Slate, Joseph. 2008. (ENG.). 40p. (J). (gr. -1-k). pap. 7.99 *(978-0-14-241060-8(8)*, Puffin Books) Penguin Young Readers Group.

—Miss Bindergarten Has a Wild Day in Kindergarten. Slate, Joseph. 2006. 40p. (J). (gr. -1-k). reprint ed. pap. 7.99 *(978-0-14-240709-7(7)*, Puffin Books) Penguin Young Readers Group.

—Miss Bindergarten Stays Home from Kindergarten. Slate, Joseph. 2004. 40p. (J). (gr. -1-k). reprint ed. pap. 7.99 *(978-0-14-230127-2(2)*, Puffin Books) Penguin Young Readers Group.

—Miss Bindergarten Takes a Field Trip with Kindergarten. Slate, Joseph. 2004. 40p. (J). (gr. -1-k). pap. 7.99 *(978-0-14-240139-2(0)*, Puffin Books) Penguin Young Readers Group.

—Old MacDonald Had a Woodshop. Shulman, Lisa. 2004. 32p. (J). (gr. -1-k). reprint ed. pap. 7.99 *(978-0-14-240186-6(2)*, Puffin Books) Penguin Young Readers Group.

—Quiero a Mi Mama Porque (I Love My Mommy Because Eng/Span Ed) Gaylord, Laurel Porter. 2004.Tr. of I Love My Mommy Because. (ENG.). 22p. (J). (gr. -1 — 1). bds. 7.99 *(978-0-525-47248-3(7)*, Dutton Books for Young Readers) Penguin Young Readers Group.

—Quiero a Mi Papa Porque (I Love My Daddy Because English / Spanishedition) Gaylord, Laurel Porter. 2004. (ENG.). 22p. (J). (gr. -1 — 1). bds. 7.99 *(978-0-525-47251-3(7)*, Dutton Books for Young Readers) Penguin Young Readers Group.

Wolff, Ashley. Baby Bear Counts One. Wolff, Ashley. 2013. (Baby Bear Ser.). (ENG.). 40p. (J). (gr. -1-1). 16.99 *(978-1-4424-4158-3(5)*, Beach Lane Bks.) Beach Lane Bks.

—Baby Bear Sees Blue. Wolff, Ashley. 2012. (Baby Bear Ser.). (ENG.). 40p. (J). (gr. -1-1). 18.99 *(978-1-4424-1306-1(9)*, Beach Lane Bks.) Beach Lane Bks.

—The Baby Chicks Are Singing/Los Pollitos Dicen: Sing along in English & Spanish!/Vamos a Cantar Junto en Ingles y Espanol! Wolff, Ashley. ed. 2020. 22p. (J). (gr. -1 — 1). 7.99 *(978-0-316-49434-2(8))* Little, Brown Bks. for Young Readers.

—Where, Oh Where, Is Baby Bear? Wolff, Ashley. 2017. (Baby Bear Ser.). (ENG.). 32p. (J). (-3). 17.99 *(978-1-4814-9916-3(5)*, Beach Lane Bks.) Beach Lane Bks.

Wolff, Jason. Animals at the Farm/Animales de la Granja. Rosa-Mendoza, Gladys. 2004. (English-Spanish Foundations Ser.). (SPA & ENG.). 20p. (J). (gr. -1). bds. 6.95 *(978-1-931398-13-8(5))* Me+Mi Publishing.

—Attack of the Giant Flood, 1 vol., Vol. 5. Lay, Kathryn. 2010. (Wendy's Weather Warriors Ser.). (ENG.). 80p. (J). (gr. 2-5). 29.93 *(978-1-60270-758-0(8)*, 15261, Calico Chapter Bks.) ABDO Publishing Co.

—The Ball of Clay That Rolled Away, 0 vols. Lenhard, Elizabeth. 2012. (ENG.). 24p. (J). (gr. -1-k). 16.99 *(978-0-7614-6142-5(6)*, 9780761461425, Two Lions) Amazon Publishing.

—The Bird Who Ate Too Much. Gonzalez-Jensen, Margarita. 2003. (Rigby on Our Way to English Ser.). (ENG.). 24p. (gr. 3-3). pap. 50.70 *(978-0-7578-4208-5(9))* Rigby Education.

—Dinosaur Goes to Israel, Vol. Rauchwerger, Diane Levin. 2012. (ENG.). 24p. (J). (gr. -1-1). pap. 7.95 *(978-0-7613-5134-4(5)*, 9780761351344, Kar-Ben Publishing) Lerner Publishing Group.

—Dinosaur on Hanukkah. Rauchwerger, Diane Levin. 2005. (ENG.). 24p. (J). (gr. -1-1). 15.95 *(978-1-58013-145-2(X))*; Vol. per. 7.95 *(978-1-58013-143-8(3))* Lerner Publishing Group. (Kar-Ben Publishing).

—Dinosaur on Passover. Rauchwerger, Diane Levin. 2006. (ENG.). 24p. (J). (gr. -1-1). 15.95 *(978-1-58013-156-8(5))*; Vol. pap. 7.95 *(978-1-58013-161-2(1))* Lerner Publishing Group. (Kar-Ben Publishing).

—Dinosaur on Shabbat. Rauchwerger, Diane Levin & Levin, Diane. 2006. (ENG.). 24p. (J). (gr. -1-1). lib. bdg. 15.95 *(978-1-58013-159-9(X)*, Kar-Ben Publishing) Lerner Publishing Group.

—Dinosaur on Shabbat, Vol. Rauchwerger, Diane Levin. 2006. (ENG.). 24p. (J). (gr. -1-1). per. 7.99 *(978-1-58013-163-6(8)*, 9781580131636, Kar-Ben Publishing) Lerner Publishing Group.

—Hail to the King!, 1 vol., Vol. 4. Lay, Kathryn. 2010. (Wendy's Weather Warriors Ser.). (ENG.). 80p. (J). (gr. 2-5). 29.93 *(978-1-60270-757-3(X)*, 15259, Calico Chapter Bks.) ABDO Publishing Co.

—Hurricane Harry, 1 vol., Vol. 6. Lay, Kathryn. 2010. (Wendy's Weather Warriors Ser.). (ENG.). 80p. (J). (gr. 2-5). 29.93 *(978-1-60270-759-7(6)*, 15263, Calico Chapter Bks.) ABDO Publishing Co.

—Look Out for Lightning!, 1 vol., Vol. 2. Lay, Kathryn. 2010. (Wendy's Weather Warriors Ser.). (ENG.). 80p. (J). (gr. 2-5). 29.93 *(978-1-60270-755-9(3)*, 15255, Calico Chapter Bks.) ABDO Publishing Co.

—Sno-Vember!, 1 vol., Vol. 3. Lay, Kathryn. 2010. (Wendy's Weather Warriors Ser.). (ENG.). 80p. (J). (gr. 2-5). 29.93 *(978-1-60270-756-6(1)*, 15257, Calico Chapter Bks.) ABDO Publishing Co.

—Tornado Trouble, 1 vol., Vol. 1. Lay, Kathryn. 2010. (Wendy's Weather Warriors Ser.). (ENG.). 80p. (J). (gr. 2-5). 29.93 *(978-1-60270-754-2(5)*, 15253, Calico Chapter Bks.) ABDO Publishing Co.

Wolfhard, Steve. Stanley Will Probably Be Fine. Pla, Sally J. (ENG.). 288p. (J). (gr. 3-7). 2019. pap. 6.99 *(978-0-06-244580-3(4))*; 2018. 16.99 *(978-0-06-244579-7(0))* HarperCollins Pubs.

—The Zombie Chasers. Kloepfer, John. (Zombie Chasers Ser.: 1). (ENG.). 224p. (J). (gr. 3-7). 2011. pap. 6.99 *(978-0-06-185306-7(2))*; 2010. 16.99 *(978-0-06-185304-3(6))* HarperCollins Pubs.

—The Zombie Chasers #2: Undead Ahead. Kloepfer, John. 2011. (Zombie Chasers Ser.: 2). (ENG.). 224p. (J). (gr. 3-7). 16.99 *(978-0-06-185307-4(0))*; 2nd ed. pap. 6.99 *(978-0-06-185308-1(9))* HarperCollins Pubs.

—The Zombie Chasers #3: Sludgment Day. Kloepfer, John. 2012. (Zombie Chasers Ser.: 3). (ENG.). 224p. (J). (gr. 3-7). 16.99 *(978-0-06-185310-4(0))*; 3rd ed. pap. 5.99 *(978-0-06-185311-1(9))* HarperCollins Pubs.

Wolfsgruber, Linda. The Camel in the Sun, 1 vol. Ondaatje, Griffin. 2013. (ENG.). 40p. (J). (gr. k). 17.95 *(978-1-55498-381-0(9))* Groundwood Bks. CAN. Dist: Publishers Group West (PGW).

—I Am Not Little Red Riding Hood. Lecis, Alessandro & Shirtliffe, Leanne. 2013. 32p. (J). (gr. -1-1). 16.95 *(978-1-62087-985-6(9)*, 620985, Sky Pony Pr.) Skyhorse Publishing Co., Inc.

—Muddy: The Raccoon Who Stole Dishes. Ondaatje, Griffin. 2019. (ENG.). 32p. (J). (gr. -1-2). 17.95 *(978-0-7358-4337-0(6))* North-South Bks., Inc.

Wolfzorn, Gene, photos by. The Ducks of Park Place. Wolfzorn, Mary Ann. 2016. (ENG., (J). (gr. k-4). pap. 10.00 *(978-0-9848802-7-0(5))* Oak Hill Studios.

Wolk-Stanley, Jessica. Return to Earth. Geiger, Beth & Fuerst, Jeffrey B. ed. 2004. (Reader's Theater Ser.). (J). pap. *(978-1-4108-2306-9(7)*, A23067) Benchmark Education Co.

Wolos-Fonteno, Mary, et al. Tales with Tails: Animal Stories for Young People. Wolos-Fonteno, Mary et al. Salaam, Kiini Ibura, ed. 2006. 168p. (YA). pap. 15.95 *(978-0-940938-43-4(X)*, Pen & Rose Pr.) Harlin Jacque Pubns.

Woloszynek, Olivia. Maddie's Big Move. Young, Barbara E. 2019. (Life of Little Maddie Ser.: Vol. 1). (ENG.). 28p. (J). pap. 9.99 ***(978-1-7026-8419-4(9))*** Independently Published.

Wolsak-Frith, Wendy. Chester Bear, Where Are You?, 1 vol. Eyvindson, Peter. 2015. (ENG.). 32p. (J). (gr. -1-1). pap. 10.95 *(978-0-921827-08-5(3)*, d2562c9f-4755-4079-a7f6-93e83aa7f269) Pemmican Pubns., Inc. CAN. Dist: Firefly Bks., Ltd.

Wolsak, Wendy. Kyle's Bath, 1 vol. Eyvindson, Peter. 2016. (ENG.). 32p. (J). (gr. -1-2). mass mkt. 10.95 *(978-0-919143-05-0(9)*, 4c1e709c-2ae1-4447-a8bb-127d24501731) Pemmican Pubns., Inc. CAN. Dist: Firefly Bks., Ltd.

—Old Enough, 1 vol. Eyvindson, Peter. 2016. (ENG.). 32p. (J). pap. 5.95 *(978-0-919143-41-8(5)*, f1c78701-f5e6-4699-a516-e87679718428) Pemmican Pubns., Inc. CAN. Dist: Firefly Bks., Ltd.

—The Wish Wind, 1 vol. Eyvindson, Peter. 2015. (ENG.). 32p. (J). pap. 7.95 *(978-0-921827-03-0(2)*, 133ad96f-e78d-4ad8-b708-27c5d35b1767) Pemmican Pubns., Inc. CAN. Dist: Firefly Bks., Ltd.

Wolski, Bobbi, jt. illus. see Fisher, Bonnie.

Wolski, Igor & Godbey, Cory. Attack on Circuit City (Statistics) Poskitt, Kjartan & Casey, Catherine. 2017. (Mission Math Ser.). (ENG.). 48p. (J). (gr. 2-4). lib. bdg. 31.99 *(978-1-68297-190-1(2))* QEB Publishing Inc.

Wolski, Igor & Ledoyen, Sam. The Island of Tomorrow (Geometry) Poskitt, Kjartan & Litton, Jonathan. 2017. (Mission Math Ser.). (ENG.). 48p. (J). (gr. 2-4). lib. bdg. 31.99 *(978-1-68297-189-5(9))* QEB Publishing Inc.

—Lost in the Fourth Dimension (Measurement) Poskitt, Kjartan & Litton, Jonathan. 2017. (Mission Math Ser.). (ENG.). 48p. (J). (gr. 2-4). lib. bdg. 31.99 *(978-1-68297-191-8(0))* QEB Publishing Inc.

Womble, Louis. Have Yourself a Furry Little Christmas (Sesame Street) Kleinberg, Naomi. 2007. (ENG.). 12p. (J). (gr. k — 1). bds. 4.99 *(978-0-375-84133-0(4)*, Random Hse. Bks. for Young Readers) Random Hse. Children's Bks.

—My Fuzzy Valentine Deluxe Edition (Sesame Street) Kleinberg, Naomi. 2018. (ENG.). 12p. (J). (— 1). bds. 9.99 *(978-1-9848-5041-6(5)*, Random Hse. Bks. for Young Readers) Random Hse. Children's Bks.

Won, Annie. All Aboard the Moonlight Train. Crow, Kristyn. 2020. (ENG.). 32p. (J). (gr. -1-2). 20.99 *(978-0-525-64544-3(6)*, Doubleday Bks. for Young Readers) Random Hse. Children's Bks.

—The Elves & the Shoemaker. Suben, Eric. 2018. (Little Golden Book Ser.). 24p. (J). (-k). 4.99

(978-1-5247-7112-6(0), Golden Bks.) Random Hse. Children's Bks.

—In the Quiet, Noisy Woods. Rosen, Michael J. 2019. (ENG.). 40p. (J). (gr. -1-2). 17.99 *(978-1-5247-6665-8(8)*, Doubleday Bks. for Young Readers) Random Hse. Children's Bks.

—Margaret Wise Brown's the Whispering Rabbit. Brown, Margaret Wise. 2017. (J). *(978-1-5182-2278-8(1)*, Golden Bks.) Random Hse. Children's Bks.

Won, Brian. Cheerful Chick. Brockenbrough, Martha. 2019. (ENG.). 40p. (J). (gr. -1-3). 17.99 *(978-1-338-13418-6(3)*, Levine, Arthur A. Bks.) Scholastic, Inc.

—Eee-Moo! Dunklee, Annika. 2019. (ENG.). 40p. (J). (gr. -1-3). 17.99 *(978-1-5344-0174-7(1)*, Simon & Schuster/Paula Wiseman Bks.) Simon & Schuster/Paula Wiseman Bks.

—Good Night, Little Monsters. LaReau, Kara. 2018. (ENG.). 20p. (J). (gr. -1 — 1). 8.99 *(978-1-338-10559-9(0)*, Cartwheel Bks.) Scholastic, Inc.

—How to Tell a Story: 1 Book + 20 Story Blocks = a Million Adventures. Nayeri, Daniel. 2015. (ENG.). 144p. (J). (gr. 3-7). pap. 19.95 *(978-0-7611-8457-7(0)*, 18457) Workman Publishing Co., Inc.

—Secret Agent Man Goes Shopping for Shoes. Wynne-Jones, Tim. 2016. (ENG.). 32p. (J). (gr. -1-3). 16.99 *(978-0-7636-7119-8(3))* Candlewick Pr.

—Spunky Little Monkey. Martin, Bill & Sampson, Michael R. 2017. (ENG.). 32p. (J). (gr. -1-k). 17.99 *(978-0-545-77643-1(0)*, Scholastic Pr.) Scholastic, Inc.

Won, Kim Kang. The Queen's Knight, Vol. 2. Won, Kim Kang. rev. ed. 2005. 192p. pap. 9.99 *(978-1-59532-258-6(2))* TOKYOPOP, Inc.

Won, Soo Yon. Full House 3: Discord, Vol. 3. Won, Soo Yon. 2004. (Full House (CPM Media) Ser.). 208p. pap. 9.99 *(978-1-58664-972-2(8)*, CPM Manhwa) Central Park Media Corp.

Wonder, Tracey. Colors for Good Night: Beautiful Bedtime Stories. Strus-Vatovec, Maja. 2019. (ENG.). 26p. (J). pap. 9.95 *(978-1-0742-0867-7(6))* Independently Published.

Wong, Alice. Merry Christmas, Baby. Tabby, Abigail. 2019. (New Books for Newborns Ser.). (ENG.). 16p. (J). (— 1). bds. 7.99 *(978-1-5344-4554-3(4)*, Little Simon) Little Simon.

Wong, Angi Ma. Meet President Obama: America's 44th President. 2009. 32p. (J). *(978-1-928753-28-5(0))* Pacific Heritage Bks.

—My Story: Reggie: The L.A. Gator. 2007. 25p. *(978-1-928753-12-4(4))* Pacific Heritage Bks.

Wong, Benedict Norbert. Lo & Behold. Wong, Benedict Norbert. l.t. ed. 2003. 38p. (gr. 1-18). 16.95 *(978-0-9728192-0-6(7)*, LOBE) Taiji Arts Publishing.

—Lo & Behold: Good Enough to Eat. Wong, Benedict Norbert. l.t. ed. 2003. 40p. (J). (gr. 1-12). 16.95 *(978-0-9728192-1-3(5)*, 1002LB) Taiji Arts Publishing.

Wong, Gabriel. Patches the Beaver: Welcome to Harmony Woods. 2008. 36p. *(978-0-9783398-0-7(0))* Gauthier, Shane.

Wong, Justin. Yao Bai & the Egg Pirates. Myers, Tim. 2018. (J). *(978-1-5132-6102-7(9))* West Margin Pr.

Wong, Justine. Piece by Piece. Tan, Susan. 2019. (ENG.). 40p. (J). (gr. k-2). 19.95 *(978-0-87577-239-4(0))* Peabody Essex Museum.

Wong, Liz. Camp Secret. Mahle, Melissa & Dennis, Kathryn. 2013. (Junior Spies Ser.: 1). (ENG.). 268p. (J). pap. 10.99 *(978-0-9852273-4-0(6))* SpyGirls Pr.

—Pirate Queen: A Story of Zheng Yi Sao, 1 vol. Becker, Helaine. 2020. (ENG.). 36p. (J). (gr. 1-4). 17.95 *(978-1-77306-124-5(0))* Groundwood Bks. CAN. Dist: Publishers Group West (PGW).

Wong, Melissa Oliaivar. Double Rainbow Island: The Mauka Adventure. Ito, Jerilyn. 2013. 36p. pap. 10.95 *(978-1-937260-99-6(2))* Sleepytown Pr.

Wong, Michelle. Goosebumps: Download & Die! Vaughn, Jen. 2018. (Goosebumps Ser.). 80p. (J). (gr. 2-5). 12.99 *(978-1-68405-322-3(6))* Idea & Design Works, LLC.

Wong, Nichole. Ambrosia. Manalang, Dan. 2006. (ENG.). 32p. (J). (gr. k-2). 14.99 *(978-0-9769342-0-2(5))* Flip Publishing.

Wong, Nicole. Always My Grandpa: A Story for Children about Alzheimer's Disease. Scacco, Linda. 2005. 48p. (J). (gr. -1-3). 14.95 *(978-1-59147-311-4(X))*; per. 9.95 *(978-1-59147-312-1(8))* American Psychological Assn. (Magination Pr.).

—Baby in a Manger. Stiegemeyer, Julie. 2004. 32p. (J). (gr. k-4). 9.99 *(978-0-7586-0726-3(1))* Concordia Publishing Hse.

—Candy Shop. Wahl, Jan. 2005. 32p. (J). (gr. -1-3). pap. 7.95 *(978-1-57091-668-7(3))* Charlesbridge Publishing, Inc.

—Ferry Tail. Kenah, Katharine. 2014. (ENG.). 32p. (J). (gr. k-3). 16.99 *(978-1-58536-829-7(6)*, 203011) Sleeping Bear Pr.

—Flying Deep: Climb Inside Deep-Sea Submersible Alvin. Cusolito, Michelle. 2018. 32p. (J). (gr. k-4). 17.99 *(978-1-58089-811-9(4))*; pap. 7.99 *(978-1-58089-841-6(6))* Charlesbridge Publishing, Inc.

—The Hugging Tree: A Story about Resilience. Neimark, Jill. 2015. 32p. (J). *(978-1-4338-1907-0(4)*, Magination Pr.) American Psychological Assn.

—L Is for Library. Terry, Sonya. 2006. 32p. (J). (gr. -1-3). lib. bdg. 16.95 *(978-1-932146-44-8(X)*, Upstart Bks.) Highsmith Inc.

—My Grandpa Had a Stroke. Butler, Dori Hillestad. 2007. 32p. (J). (gr. 3-7). 14.95 *(978-1-59147-806-5(5))*; per. 9.95 *(978-1-59147-807-2(3))* American Psychological Assn. (Magination Pr.).

—No Monkeys, No Chocolate. Stewart, Melissa & Young, Allen. 2018. 32p. (J). (gr. k-3). pap. 7.99 *(978-1-58089-288-9(4))* Charlesbridge Publishing, Inc.

—No Monkeys, No Chocolate. Stewart, Melissa & Young, Allen M. 2013. 32p. (J). (gr. k-3). 16.95 *(978-1-58089-287-2(6))* Charlesbridge Publishing, Inc.

—Only One Year, 1 vol. Cheng, Andrea. 2013. (ENG.). 104p. (J). (gr. 2-5). 16.95 *(978-1-60060-252-8(5))* Lee & Low Bks., Inc.

—R Is for Research. Buzzeo, Toni. 2008. 17.95 *(978-1-60213-032-6(9))*; (J). (gr. 2-4). 17.95 *(978-1-60213-030-2(2))* Highsmith Inc. (Upstart Bks.).

—Sweet Dreaming. Rawlinson, Julia. 2018. 32p. (J). (-3). 17.99 *(978-1-4926-3442-3(5))* Sourcebooks, Inc.

—To the Stars! The First American Woman to Walk in Space. Van Vleet, Carmella & Sullivan, Kathy. 40p. (J). (gr. k-3). 2018. pap. 7.99 *(978-1-58089-645-0(6))*; 2016. lib. bdg. 16.95 *(978-1-58089-644-3(8))* Charlesbridge Publishing, Inc.

Wong, Nicole E. Candy Shop. Wahl, Jan. 2004. 32p. (J). (gr. -1-3). 15.95 *(978-1-57091-508-6(3))* Charlesbridge Publishing, Inc.

Wong, Priscilla. My Hometown. Griesmer, Russell. 2015. (Fiction Picture Bks.). (ENG.). 40p. (J). (gr. 1-4). 15.95 *(978-1-62370-174-1(0)*, Capstone Young Readers) Capstone.

—Trolls. Aventuras en Villa Troll (Trolls Little Golden Book) Man-Kong, Mary. 2016. (SPA.). 28p. (J). (gr. -1-k). pap. 6.95 *(978-607-31-4958-7(1)*, Altea) Penguin Random House Grupo Editorial ESP. Dist: Penguin Random Hse. LLC.

—Trolls Little Golden Book (DreamWorks Trolls) Man-Kong, Mary. 2016. (Little Golden Book Ser.). 24p. (J). (gr. -1-2). 4.99 *(978-0-399-55893-1(4)*, Golden Bks.) Random Hse. Children's Bks.

Wong, Scott. Power Play, 1 vol., 5. Rogers, Buddy & Avery, Ben. 2008. (TimeFlyz Ser.). (ENG.). 160p. (J). (gr. 4-6). 21.19 *(978-0-310-71365-4(X))* Zondervan.

—Time Trap, 1 vol., 6. Avery, Ben & Zondervan Staff. 2009. (TimeFlyz Ser.). (ENG.). 160p. (J). (gr. 4-6). 21.19 *(978-0-310-71366-1(8))* Zonderkidz.

Wong, Scott & Merced, Eric. Battle Between, 1 vol. Avery, Ben. 2012. (Z Graphic Novels / TimeFlyz Ser.). (ENG.). 160p. (J). pap. 6.99 *(978-0-310-71367-8(6))* Zondervan.

Wong, Stanley. The River. Hathorn, Libby. 2003. 40p. 28.95 *(978-1-86366-516-2(1))* Education Services Australia Ltd. AUS. Dist: Cheng & Tsui Co.

Wong, Tony. The Legendary Couple, Vol. 4. Cha, Louis. 2003. 120p. (YA). (gr. 8-18). pap. 13.95 *(978-1-58899-233-8(0))* ComicsOne Corp./Dr. Masters.

Wong, Walden, jt. illus. see Barberi, Carlo.

Wong, Walden, jt. illus. see Ng, Leandro.

Woo. Rebirth, 11 vols., Vol. 4. Lee, Kang-Woo. Ryu, Youngju, tr. from JPN. rev. ed. 2003. 176p. pap. 9.99 *(978-1-59182-219-6(X))* TOKYOPOP, Inc.

WOO. Rebirth, Vol. 13. Yi, Kang-u. rev. ed. 2005. 200p. pap. 9.99 *(978-1-59532-028-5(8))* TOKYOPOP, Inc.

Woo. Rebirth, 11 vols. Woo. rev. ed. 192p. Vol. 6. 2004. pap. 9.99 *(978-1-59182-524-1(5))*; Vol. 12. 2005. pap. 9.99 *(978-1-59532-027-8(X))* TOKYOPOP, Inc.

—RebirthTM, Vol. 10. Woo. Hahm, Jennifer, tr. from KOR. rev. ed. 2004. 192p. (YA). pap. 9.99 *(978-1-59182-528-9(8))* TOKYOPOP, Inc.

Woo, Howie. Who Discovered America? Wyatt, Valerie. 2008. 40p. (J). (gr. 3-7). 17.95 *(978-1-55453-128-8(4))* Kids Can Pr., Ltd. CAN. Dist: Hachette Bk. Group.

Woo Kim, Jin. Snow White & the Seven Dwarfs. McFadden, Deanna. 2012. (Silver Penny Stories Ser.). 48p. (J). (gr. -1-1). 4.95 *(978-1-4027-8342-5(6))* Sterling Publishing Co., Inc.

Woo, Samantha. A Doll for Grandma: A Story about Alzheimer's Disease. Sharkey, Paulette Bochnig. 2020. (ENG.). 32p. (J). (gr. k-3). 17.99 *(978-1-5064-5738-3(X)*, Beaming Books) Augsburg Fortress, Pubs.

—Krit Dreams of Dragon Fruit: A Story of Leaving & Finding Home. Becher, Natalie & France, Emily. 2020. 32p. (J). (gr. -1-3). 17.95 *(978-1-61180-775-2(1)*, Bala Kids) Shambhala Pubns., Inc.

Wood, Alison. The Big-Crowned Princess. Marfani, Ayesha. 2018. (ENG.). 36p. (J). (gr. 1-4). pap. 9.99 *(978-1-68160-638-5(0))* Crimson Cloak Publishing.

Wood, Alix. Body Snatching. 2013. (Why'd They Do That? Strange Customs of the Past Ser.). 32p. (J). (gr. 4-6). pap. 63.00 *(978-1-4339-9574-3(3))* Stevens, Gareth Publishing LLLP.

Wood, Alix. Body Snatching. Wood, Alix. 2013. (Why'd They Do That? Strange Customs of the Past Ser.). 32p. (J). (gr. 4-6). pap. 10.50 *(978-1-4339-9573-6(5))* Stevens, Gareth Publishing LLLP.

—Dueling. Wood, Alix. 2013. (Why'd They Do That? Strange Customs of the Past Ser.). 32p. (J). (gr. 4-6). pap. 10.50 *(978-1-4339-9577-4(8))*; pap. 63.00 *(978-1-4339-9578-1(6))* Stevens, Gareth Publishing LLLP.

—Gladiators: Fighting to the Death. Wood, Alix. 2013. 32p. (J). (gr. 4-6). 26.60 *(978-1-4339-9580-4(8))*; pap. 10.50 *(978-1-4339-9581-1(6))*; pap. 63.00 *(978-1-4339-9582-8(4))* Stevens, Gareth Publishing LLLP.

—Human Sacrifice. Wood, Alix. 2013. (Why'd They Do That? Strange Customs of the Past Ser.). 32p. (J). (gr. 4-6). pap. 63.00 *(978-1-4339-9586-6(7))*; pap. 10.50 *(978-1-4339-9585-9(9))* Stevens, Gareth Publishing LLLP.

—Mummification. Wood, Alix. 2013. 32p. (J). (gr. 4-6). 26.60 *(978-1-4339-9588-0(3))*; pap. 10.50 *(978-1-4339-9589-7(1))*; pap. 63.00 *(978-1-4339-9590-3(5))* Stevens, Gareth Publishing LLLP.

—Witch Trials. Wood, Alix. 2013. 32p. (J). (gr. 4-6). 26.60 *(978-1-4339-9592-7(1))*; pap. 10.50 *(978-1-4339-9593-4(X))*; pap. 63.00 *(978-1-4339-9594-1(8))* Stevens, Gareth Publishing LLLP.

Wood, Amanda. Why Can't They See the Real Me? Ratcliff, Danielle. 2019. (ENG.). 40p. (J). pap. 12.49 *(978-1-0756-2326-4(X))* Independently Published.

Wood, Audrey & Wood, Bruce Robert. Alphabet Rescue. 2006. (J). *(978-0-439-88927-8(8))* Scholastic, Inc.

Wood, Audrey & Wood, Don. The Napping House. Wood, Audrey. 25th ed. 2009. (ENG.). 32p. (J). (gr. -1-3). 18.99 *(978-0-15-256708-8(9)*, 1099017) Houghton Mifflin Harcourt Publishing Co.

Wood, Ben. Meet... the Flying Doctors. Ivanoff, George. 2017. 36p. (J). (gr. 2). 15.99 *(978-0-14-378067-0(0))* Random Hse. Australia AUS. Dist: Independent Pubs. Group.

Wood, Ben. Real Pigeons Eat Danger (Book 2) McDonald, Andrew. 2020. (Real Pigeons Ser.: 2). (ENG.). 224p. (J). (gr. 3-7). 13.99 ***(978-0-593-11946-4(0))***; lib. bdg. 16.99 ***(978-0-593-11947-1(9))*** Random Hse. Children's Bks. (Random Hse. Bks. for Young Readers).

Wood, Ben. Real Pigeons Fight Crime (Book 1) McDonald, Andrew. 2020. (Real Pigeons Ser.: 1). (ENG.). 208p. (J). (gr. 3-7). 13.99 *(978-0-593-11942-6(8))*; lib. bdg. 16.99 *(978-0-593-11943-3(6))* Random Hse. Children's Bks. (Random Hse. Bks. for Young Readers).

Wood, Ben. Real Pigeons Nest Hard (Book 3) McDonald, Andrew. 2020. (Real Pigeons Ser.: 3). (ENG.). 224p. (J). (gr. 3-7). 13.99 ***(978-0-593-11950-1(9))***; lib. bdg. 16.99 ***(978-0-593-11951-8(7))*** Random Hse. Children's Bks. (Random Hse. Bks. for Young Readers).

Wood, Ben. Squishy Taylor, 4 vols. Wild, Alisa. 2017. (Squishy Taylor Ser.). (ENG.). 128p. (J). (gr. 2-4). 98.60 *(978-1-5158-1991-2(4)*, 27343, Picture Window Bks.) Capstone.

—Squishy Taylor, 2 vols. Wild, Ailsa. 2018. (Squishy Taylor Ser.). (ENG.). 128p. (J). (gr. 2-4). pap., pap. 13.90 *(978-1-5158-1995-0(7)*, 27347); pap., pap., pap. 41.70 *(978-1-5158-1996-7(5)*, 27348) Capstone. (Picture Window Bks.).

—Squishy Taylor & a Question of Trust. Wild, Alisa. 2017. (Squishy Taylor Ser.). (ENG.). 128p. (J). (gr. 2-4). lib. bdg. 25.32 *(978-1-5158-1955-4(8)*, 136638, Picture Window Bks.) Capstone.

—Squishy Taylor & the Bonus Sisters. Wild, Alisa. 2017. (Squishy Taylor Ser.). (ENG.). 128p. (J). (gr. 2-4). lib. bdg. 25.32 *(978-1-5158-1956-1(6)*, 136639, Picture Window Bks.) Capstone.

—Squishy Taylor & the Mess-Makers. Wild, Alisa. 2017. (Squishy Taylor Ser.). (ENG.). 128p. (J). (gr. 2-4). lib. bdg. 25.32 *(978-1-5158-1957-8(4)*, 136640, Picture Window Bks.) Capstone.

—Squishy Taylor & the Vase That Wasn't. Wild, Alisa. 2017. (Squishy Taylor Ser.). (ENG.). 128p. (J). (gr. 2-4). lib. bdg. 25.32 *(978-1-5158-1958-5(2)*, 136641, Picture Window Bks.) Capstone.

Wood, Bruce. Alphabet Mystery. Wood, Audrey. 2003. (ENG.). 40p. (J). (gr. -1 — 1). 17.99 *(978-0-439-44337-1(7)*, Blue Sky Pr., The) Scholastic, Inc.

—Ten Little Fish. Wood, Audrey. 2004. (ENG.). 40p. (J). (gr. -1-k). 17.99 *(978-0-439-63569-1(1)*, Blue Sky Pr., The) Scholastic, Inc.

Wood, Bruce. Alphabet Rescue. Wood, Bruce. Wood, Audrey. 2006. (ENG.). 40p. (J). (gr. -1-k). 17.99 *(978-0-439-85316-3(8)*, Blue Sky Pr., The) Scholastic, Inc.

Wood, Bruce Robert, jt. illus. see Wood, Audrey.

Wood, Chaz. A Hare's Tale 2 - the Golden Hare. Auty, Rob. 2013. 102p. pap. *(978-1-908098-90-0(2))* 2QT, Ltd. (Publishing).

Wood, Clifford. A Great Adventure in the Woods. Paris, Glen. 2019. (ENG.). 36p. (J). pap. 9.99 *(978-1-0936-5213-0(6))* Independently Published.

Wood, Colleen. Lessons from Mother Earth, 1 vol. McLeod, Elaine. 2010. (ENG.). 24p. (J). (gr. k-k). pap. 8.95 *(978-0-88899-832-3(5))* Groundwood Bks. CAN. Dist: Publishers Group West (PGW).

Wood, Damian. Alphabet of Dance. Schwaeber, Barbie Heit. 2009. (Smithsonian Alphabet Books). (ENG.). 40p. (J). (gr. -1-k). 9.95 *(978-1-60727-111-6(7))* Soundprints.

—If Cookie Had a Cookie. Galvin, Laura Gates. 2009. (Sesame Street Read, Play & Go Ser.). 20p. (J). (gr. -1). 9.99 incl. audio compact disk *(978-1-59069-867-9(3))* Studio Mouse LLC.

Wood, Don. The Birthday Queen. Wood, Audrey. 2013. (ENG.). 32p. (J). (gr. -1-3). 17.99 *(978-0-545-41474-6(1)*, Blue Sky Pr., The) Scholastic, Inc.

—The Full Moon at the Napping House. Wood, Audrey. 2015. (ENG.). 32p. (J). (gr. -1-3). 17.99 *(978-0-544-30832-9(8)*, 1581566, HMH Books For Young Readers) Houghton Mifflin Harcourt Publishing Co.

—The Full Moon at the Napping House (padded Board Book) Wood, Audrey. 2019. (ENG.). 30p. (J). (— 1). bds. 8.99 *(978-1-328-58515-8(8)*, 1729331, HMH Books For Young Readers) Houghton Mifflin Harcourt Publishing Co.

—King Bidgood's in the Bathtub. Wood, Audrey. 2010. (ENG.). 32p. (J). (gr. -1-3). pap. 7.99 *(978-0-15-205435-9(9)*, 1196356) Houghton Mifflin Harcourt Publishing Co.

—The Napping House. Wood, Audrey. (ENG.). (J). (gr. k — 1). 2010. 34p. bds. 8.99 *(978-0-547-48147-0(0)*, 1439512); 2005. 16p. bds. 11.99 *(978-0-15-205620-9(3)*, 1196904) Houghton Mifflin Harcourt Publishing Co.

—Napping House / La Casa Adormecida. Wood, Audrey. 2012. (ENG.). 32p. (J). (gr. -1 — 1). bds. 6.99 *(978-0-547-71920-7(5)*, 1481835) Houghton Mifflin Harcourt Publishing Co.

—The Napping House Board Book. Wood, Audrey. 2015. (ENG.). 32p. (J). (— 1). bds. 7.99 *(978-0-544-60225-0(0)*, 1616872, HMH Books For Young Readers) Houghton Mifflin Harcourt Publishing Co.

—Piggy Pie Po. Wood, Audrey. (ENG.). (J). 2016. 30p. (— 1). bds. 7.99 *(978-0-544-79113-8(4)*, 1639280, HMH Books For Young Readers); 2010. 32p. (gr. -1-3). 17.99 *(978-0-15-202494-9(8)*, 1192966) Houghton Mifflin Harcourt Publishing Co.

—Piggy Pie Po. Wood, Audrey. 2018. (ENG.). 32p. (J). (gr. -1-3). pap. 7.99 *(978-1-328-88612-5(3)*, 1698482, HMH Books For Young Readers) Houghton Mifflin Harcourt Publishing Co.

Wood, Don. Quick As a Cricket. Wood, Audrey. 2020. (ENG.). 32p. (J). (— 1). bds. 8.99 ***(978-0-358-36264-7(4)***, 1784601); (gr. -1-3). 16.99 ***(978-0-358-36262-3(8)***, 1784599); (gr. -1-3). pap. 8.99 ***(978-0-358-36263-0(6)***, 1784600) Houghton Mifflin Harcourt Publishing Co. (HMH Books For Young Readers).

Wood, Don. The Little Mouse, the Red Ripe Strawberry & the Big Hungry Bear. Wood, Don. Wood, Audrey. 2007. (Child's Play Library). (ENG.). 32p. (J). audio compact disk *(978-1-84643-050-3(X))* Child's Play International Ltd.

Wood, Don, jt. illus. see Wood, Audrey.

Wood, Dorreya. Pick-a-WooWoo - Bliss: A breathtaking story of transformation that reveals 'we are never Alone', 16 vols., Vol. 5. Wood, Dorreya. 2009. 32p. pap. *(978-0-9803669-4-5(1))* Pick-a-Woo Woo Pubs.

Wood, Douglas. Wally the Warthog. Tinsley, Jillian. 2012. 24p. (J). pap. 10.99 *(978-1-61254-782-4(6))* Small Pr., The.

Wood, Ethan. Junior Paleontologist Activity Book: Ages 5 to 12: Explore, Learn, Protect. National Park Service Staff, ed. rev. ed. 2012. (ENG.). 22p. (gr. k-6). 6.00 *(978-0-16-090846-0(9))* National Park Service Div. of Pubns.

Wood, Evelyn. The Busy World of Bees. Wood, Evelyn. Wood, Aselle, ed. 2016. (Exploring with Too Woo Ser.). (ENG.). 40p. (J). (gr. 4-6). pap. *(978-0-9934145-2-7(4))* too-woo.com.

Wood, Gerald. Music Theory for Beginners. Danes, Emma. 2006. (Music Theory Ser.). 48p. (J). (gr. 4). lib. bdg. 16.95 *(978-1-58086-562-3(3))* EDC Publishing.

—Viking World. Wingate, Philippa & Millard, Anne. 2004. (Illustrated World History Ser.). 64p. (J). (gr. 6). lib. bdg. 19.95 *(978-1-58086-628-6(X)*, Usborne) EDC Publishing.

—Who Were the First People? Cox, Phil Roxbee & Reid, Struan. rev. ed. 2006. (Starting Point History Ser.). 32p. (J). (gr. 1). lib. bdg. 12.95 *(978-1-58086-499-2(6))* EDC Publishing.

Wood, Gerald, jt. illus. see Jackson, Ian.

Wood, Hannah. Bible Favorites. Sanders, Nancy I. 2015. (One Sentence Storybooks Ser.). (ENG.). 120p. (J). pap. 15.99 *(978-1-58997-799-0(8)*, 4622221) Focus on the Family Publishing.

—Bible Stories, 1 vol. David, Juliet & Williamson, Karen. ed. 2016. (ENG.). 104p. (J). 7.99 *(978-1-78128-305-9(2)*, Candle Bks.) Lion Hudson PLC GBR. Dist: Independent Pubs. Group.

—Café Cosmos. Scott, Janine. 2009. (Treasure Chest Readers Ser.). 24p. (J). (gr. -1-2). pap. 8.15 *(978-1-60754-674-0(4))*; lib. bdg. 25.60 *(978-1-60754-673-3(6))* Windmill Bks.

—Dino Pop-up Faces: A Let's Pretend Pop-up Book. 2007. (ENG.). 12p. (J). (gr. -1-3). 14.95 *(978-1-58117-596-7(5)*, Intervisual/Piggy Toes) Bendon, Inc.

—Dino-School - Alphabet. Junor, Amy. 2014. (Dino-School Ser.). (ENG.). 22p. (J). (— 1). bds. 7.99 *(978-1-74297-657-0(3))* Hardie Grant Egmont Pty, Ltd. AUS. Dist: Independent Pubs. Group.

—The Dog & the Fox. Jinks, Jenny. 2019. (Early Bird Readers — Yellow (Early Bird Stories (tm)) Ser.). (ENG.). 32p. (J). (gr. -1-2). 27.99 *(978-1-5415-4171-9(5)*, Lerner Pubns.) Lerner Publishing Group.

—Dog Hair EVERYWHERE! Set Of 6. Parkes, Brenda. 2014. (Shared Reading Foundations Ser.). (J). (gr. 1). 36.00 net. *(978-1-4900-0046-6(1))* Benchmark Education Co.

—Dog Hair EVERYWHERE! Book Set. Parkes, Brenda. 2014. (Shared Reading Foundations Ser.). (J). (gr. 1). 72.00 net. *(978-1-4900-0016-9(X))* Benchmark Education Co.

—Enough to Go Around: A Story of Generosity. Johnson, Kristin F. 2018. (Cloverleaf Books (tm) — Stories with Character Ser.). (ENG.). 24p. (J). (gr. k-2). 25.32 *(978-1-5124-8648-3(5)*, Millbrook Pr.) Lerner Publishing Group.

—Enough to Go Around: A Story of Generosity. Johnson, Kristin. 2018. (Cloverleaf Books (tm) — Stories with Character Ser.). (ENG.). 24p. (J). (gr. k-2). pap. 8.99 *(978-1-5415-1067-8(4)*, Millbrook Pr.) Lerner Publishing Group.

—Hey, Diddle, Diddle: And Other Favorite Nursery Rhymes. Tiger Tales. 2012. (ENG.). 22p. (J). (-k). bds. 8.95 *(978-1-58925-870-9(3))* Tiger Tales.

—Mars Mouse. Scott, Janine. 2009. (Treasure Chest Readers Ser.). 24p. (J). (gr. -1-2). pap. 8.15 *(978-1-60754-677-1(9))*; lib. bdg. 25.60 *(978-1-60754-676-4(0))* Windmill Bks.

—Monsters Dance. Hodgman, Ann. 2013. (ENG.). 16p. (J). (gr. -1). bds. 8.95 *(978-1-58925-627-9(1))* Tiger Tales.

—Old MacDonald Had a Farm: And Other Favorite Children's Songs. Tiger Tales. 2012. (ENG.). 22p. (J). (-k). bds. 8.95 *(978-1-58925-874-7(6))* Tiger Tales.

—One Snowy Day. Salzano, Tammi. 2010. (ENG.). 24p. (J). (gr. -1-k). bds. 8.95 *(978-1-58925-857-0(6))* Tiger Tales.

—One Sunny Day. Salzano, Tammi. 2012. (ENG.). 22p. (J). (-k). bds. 8.95 *(978-1-58925-871-6(1))* Tiger Tales.

—One Windy Day. Salzano, Tammi. 2012. (ENG.). 22p. (J). (-k). bds. 8.95 *(978-1-58925-875-4(4))* Tiger Tales.

—Quack! Ribbit! Roar! Wooden Slider Book with Sound. Byrd, Ruby. Cottage Door Press, ed. 2017. (Slide & Sound Ser.). (ENG.). 16p. (J). (gr. -1-1). bds. 18.99 *(978-1-68052-184-9(5)*, 1001821) Cottage Door Pr.

—Sam the Star & Clown Fun! Dale, Elizabeth. 2019. (Early Bird Readers — Red (Early Bird Stories (tm)) Ser.). (ENG.). 32p. (J). (gr. -1-2). pap. 7.99 *(978-1-5415-4627-1(X))* Lerner Publishing Group.

—This Little Piggy: And Other Favorite Action Rhymes. Tiger Tales. 2010. (ENG.). 22p. (J). (gr. -1-k). bds. 8.95 *(978-1-58925-849-5(5))* Tiger Tales.

—Truck Party. Salzano, Tammi. 2011. (ENG.). 20p. bds. 7.95 *(978-1-58925-865-5(7))* Tiger Tales.

—The Wise Men, 1 vol. David, Juliet. 2009. (Christmas Trio Ser.). 18p. (J). bds. 4.99 *(978-0-8254-7407-1(8)*, Candle Bks.) Lion Hudson PLC GBR. Dist: Kregel Pubns.

Wood, Hannah & Mahoney, Daniel J. Rainforest Wonders. Ranson, Erin. 2007. (Sparkling Slide Nature Bks.). (ENG.). 12p. (J). (gr. -1-k). 9.99 *(978-1-84666-356-7(3)*, Tide Mill Pr.) Top That! Publishing PLC GBR. Dist: Independent Pubs. Group.

Wood, Hannah, jt. illus. see Jarzabek, Ela.

Wood, Hannah, jt. illus. see Mahoney, Daniel.

Wood, Jennifer. The Year of the Horse: Tales from the Chinese Zodiac. Chin, Oliver. 2013. (Tales from the Chinese Zodiac Ser.: 8). (ENG.). 36p. (J). (gr. -1-3). 15.95 *(978-1-59702-080-0(X))* Immedium.

—The Year of the Snake: Tales from the Chinese Zodiac. Chin, Oliver, ed. 2012. (Tales from the Chinese Zodiac Ser.: 8). (ENG.). 36p. (J). (gr. -1-3). 15.95 *(978-1-59702-038-1(9))* Immedium.

W

Wood, Joe. Everybody Has a Daddy. Williams, Vicki & Williams, Kathy. 2003. 16p. (J). 7.95 *(978-0-9747597-0-8(8))* Self-Esteem Adventures Pr.

Wood, Judith V. Hillary Clinton: An American Journey. Driscoll, Laura. 2008. (ENG.). 48p. (J). (gr. 3-6). 16.19 *(978-0-448-44787-2(8))* Penguin Young Readers Group.

Wood, Karen. This Loving Light of Mine. Scott, Amber. 2020. (ENG.). 23p. (J). pap. 13.95 ***(978-1-4787-8069-4(X))*** Outskirts Pr., Inc.

Wood, Katie. Balance Beam Boss. Maddox, Jake. 2019. (Jake Maddox Girl Sports Stories Ser.). (ENG.). 72p. (J). (gr. 3-6). 25.32 *(978-1-4965-8325-3(6)*, 140496); pap. 5.95 *(978-1-4965-8451-9(1)*, 140976) Capstone. (Stone Arch Bks.).

—Cake Pops with Rosa Parks. Steinkraus, Kyla. 2017. (Time Hop Sweets Shop Ser.). (ENG.). 32p. (gr. 1-3). pap. 7.95 *(978-1-68342-427-7(1)*, 9781683424277) Rourke Educational Media.

—Cheer Choice, 1 vol. Maddox, Jake. 2014. (Jake Maddox Girl Sports Stories Ser.). (ENG.). 72p. (J). (gr. 3-6). 25.32 *(978-1-4342-4143-6(2)*, Stone Arch Bks.) Capstone.

—Cora's Decision. Gurtler, Janet. 2015. (Mermaid Kingdom Ser.). (ENG.). 96p. (J). (gr. 3-5). 23.99 *(978-1-4342-9695-5(4)*, Stone Arch Bks.) Capstone.

—Cowgirl Grit. Maddox, Jake. 2018. (Jake Maddox Girl Sports Stories Ser.). (ENG.). 72p. (J). (gr. 3-6). lib. bdg. 25.32 *(978-1-4965-5847-3(2)*, 136932, Stone Arch Bks.) Capstone.

—The Creepy Cathedral. Canasi, Brittany. 2017. (G. H. O. S. T. Squad Ser.). (ENG.). 48p. (gr. 3-5). pap. 8.95 *(978-1-68342-438-3(7)*, 9781683424383) Rourke Educational Media.

—Cupcakes with Sally Ride. Steinkraus, Kyla. 2017. (Time Hop Sweets Shop Ser.). (ENG.). 32p. (gr. 1-3). 24.22 *(978-1-68342-333-1(X)*, 9781683423331); pap. 7.95 *(978-1-68342-429-1(8)*, 9781683424291) Rourke Educational Media.

—Dance Team Dilemma, 1 vol. Maddox, Jake. 2013. (Jake Maddox Girl Sports Stories Ser.). (ENG.). 72p. (J). (gr. 3-6). pap. 5.95 *(978-1-4342-4201-3(3))*; lib. bdg. 25.32 *(978-1-4342-4014-9(2))* Capstone. (Stone Arch Bks.).

—Dancing Solo, 1 vol. Maddox, Jake. 2014. (Jake Maddox Girl Sports Stories Ser.). (ENG.). 72p. (J). (gr. 3-6). 25.32 *(978-1-4342-4142-9(4)*, Stone Arch Bks.) Capstone.

—Digging Deep. Maddox, Jake. 2018. (Jake Maddox Girl Sports Stories Ser.). (ENG.). 72p. (J). (gr. 3-6). lib. bdg. 25.32 *(978-1-4965-6356-9(5)*, 138075, Stone Arch Bks.) Capstone.

—Fairy Color-In Locked Diary. Mudpuppy. 2017. (ENG.). 192p. (J). (gr. -1-7). 10.99 *(978-0-7353-5214-8(3))* Mudpuppy Pr.

—Fright at the Museum. Robertson, K. A. 2017. (G. H. O. S. T. Squad Ser.). (ENG.). 48p. (gr. 3-5). pap. 8.95 *(978-1-68342-437-6(9)*, 9781683424376) Rourke Educational Media.

—Gymnastics Jitters, 1 vol. Maddox, Jake. 2012. (Jake Maddox Girl Sports Stories Ser.). (ENG.). 72p. (J). (gr. 3-6). pap. 5.95 *(978-1-4342-3908-2(X))*; lib. bdg. 25.32 *(978-1-4342-3293-9(X))* Capstone. (Stone Arch Bks.).

—Horseback Hurdles, 1 vol. Maddox, Jake & Berne, Emma Carlson. 2012. (Jake Maddox Girl Sports Stories Ser.). (ENG.). 72p. (J). (gr. 3-6). pap. 5.95 *(978-1-4342-3905-1(5))*; lib. bdg. 25.32 *(978-1-4342-3294-6(8))* Capstone. (Stone Arch Bks.).

—Ice Rink Rookie. Maddox, Jake & Brandes, Wendy L. 2018. (Jake Maddox Girl Sports Stories Ser.). (ENG.). 72p. (J). (gr. 3-6). lib. bdg. 25.32 *(978-1-4965-5848-0(0)*, 136933, Stone Arch Bks.) Capstone.

Wood, Katie. Jake Maddox Girl Sports Stories. Maddox, Jake. (Jake Maddox Girl Sports Stories Ser.). (ENG.). (J). (gr. 3-6). 2020. 1114.08 ***(978-1-4965-9771-7(0)***, 199576); 2020. pap., pap., pap. 160.60 ***(978-1-4965-9931-5(4)***, 201365); 2019. 1063.44 *(978-1-4965-8328-4(0)*, 29316); 2019. pap., pap., pap. 154.70 *(978-1-4965-8496-0(1)*, 29572) Capstone. (Stone Arch Bks.).

Wood, Katie. Longboard Let Down. Maddox, Jake. 2017. (Jake Maddox Girl Sports Stories Ser.). (ENG.). 72p. (J). (gr. 3-6). lib. bdg. 25.32 *(978-1-4965-4972-3(4)*, 135864, Stone Arch Bks.) Capstone.

—Pastries with Pocahontas. Steinkraus, Kyla. 2017. (Time Hop Sweets Shop Ser.). (ENG.). 32p. (gr. 1-3). 24.22 *(978-1-68342-330-0(5)*, 9781683423300) Rourke Educational Media.

—Phantom at the Funhouse. Canasi, Brittany. 2017. (G. H. O. S. T. Squad Ser.). (ENG.). 48p. (gr. 3-5). pap. 8.95 *(978-1-68342-439-0(5)*, 9781683424390) Rourke Educational Media.

—Pool Panic. Maddox, Jake. 2016. (Jake Maddox Girl Sports Stories Ser.). (ENG.). 72p. (J). (gr. 3-6). lib. bdg. 25.32 *(978-1-4965-2618-2(X)*, Stone Arch Bks.) Capstone.

—Rachel's Secret. Gurtler, Janet. 2015. (Mermaid Kingdom Ser.). (ENG.). 96p. (J). (gr. 3-5). 23.99 *(978-1-4342-9694-8(6)*, Stone Arch Bks.) Capstone.

—Rachel's Worry. Gurtler, Janet. 2016. (Mermaid Kingdom Ser.). (ENG.). 96p. (J). (gr. 3-5). 23.99 *(978-1-4965-2607-6(4)*, Stone Arch Bks.) Capstone.

—Rebound Time, 1 vol. Maddox, Jake & Berne, Emma Carlson. 2013. (Jake Maddox Girl Sports Stories Ser.). (ENG.). 72p. (J). (gr. 3-6). pap. 5.95 *(978-1-4342-4202-0(1))*; lib. bdg. 25.32 *(978-1-4342-4013-2(4))* Capstone. (Stone Arch Bks.).

—Running Scared, 1 vol. Maddox, Jake & Berne, Emma Carlson. 2013. (Jake Maddox Girl Sports Stories Ser.). (ENG.). 72p. (J). (gr. 3-6). pap. 5.95 *(978-1-4342-4203-7(X))*; lib. bdg. 25.32 *(978-1-4342-4015-6(0))* Capstone. (Stone Arch Bks.).

—Shyanna's Song. Gurtler, Janet. 2015. (Mermaid Kingdom Ser.). (ENG.). 96p. (J). (gr. 3-5). lib. bdg. 23.99 *(978-1-4342-9693-1(8)*, Stone Arch Bks.) Capstone.

—Shyanna's Wish. Gurtler, Janet. 2015. (Mermaid Kingdom Ser.). (ENG.). 96p. (J). (gr. 3-5). 23.99 *(978-1-4342-9696-2(2)*, Stone Arch Bks.) Capstone.

—Skating Showdown, 1 vol. Maddox, Jake. 2013. (Jake Maddox Girl Sports Stories Ser.). (ENG.). 72p. (J). (gr. 3-6). pap. 5.95 *(978-1-4342-4204-4(8))*; lib. bdg. 25.32 *(978-1-4342-4012-5(6))* Capstone. (Stone Arch Bks.).

—Soccer Show-Off, 1 vol. Maddox, Jake. 2014. (Jake Maddox Girl Sports Stories Ser.). (ENG.). 72p. (J). (gr. 3-6). 25.32 *(978-1-4342-4144-3(0)*, Stone Arch Bks.) Capstone.

—Soccer Surprise, 1 vol. Maddox, Jake & Berne, Emma Carlson. 2012. (Jake Maddox Girl Sports Stories Ser.). (ENG.). 72p. (J). (gr. 3-6). pap. 5.95 *(978-1-4342-3906-8(3))*; lib. bdg. 25.32 *(978-1-4342-3291-5(3))* Capstone. (Stone Arch Bks.).

—Softball Surprise, 1 vol. Maddox, Jake. 2014. (Jake Maddox Girl Sports Stories Ser.). (ENG.). 72p. (J). (gr. 3-6). 25.32 *(978-1-4342-4141-2(6)*, Stone Arch Bks.) Capstone.

—Softball Switch-Up. Maddox, Jake. 2019. (Jake Maddox Girl Sports Stories Ser.). (ENG.). 72p. (J). (gr. 3-6). pap. 5.95 *(978-1-4965-8450-2(3)*, 140975, Stone Arch Bks.) Capstone.

—Spook in the Stacks. Robertson, K. A. 2017. (G. H. O. S. T. Squad Ser.). (ENG.). 48p. (gr. 3-5). pap. 8.95 *(978-1-68342-436-9(0)*, 9781683424369) Rourke Educational Media.

—Squad Struggles. Maddox, Jake. 2017. (Jake Maddox Girl Sports Stories Ser.). (ENG.). 72p. (J). (gr. 3-6). lib. bdg. 25.32 *(978-1-4965-4971-6(6)*, 135859, Stone Arch Bks.) Capstone.

—Striker's Sister. Maddox, Jake. 2018. (Jake Maddox Girl Sports Stories Ser.). (ENG.). 72p. (J). (gr. 3-6). lib. bdg. 25.32 *(978-1-4965-6355-2(7)*, 138071, Stone Arch Bks.) Capstone.

—Strudels with Susan B. Anthony. Steinkraus, Kyla. 2017. (Time Hop Sweets Shop Ser.). (ENG.). 32p. (gr. 1-3). 24.22 *(978-1-68342-332-4(1)*, 9781683423324); pap. 7.95 *(978-1-68342-428-4(X)*, 9781683424284) Rourke Educational Media.

—Volleyball Dreams, 1 vol. Maddox, Jake. 2012. (Jake Maddox Girl Sports Stories Ser.). (ENG.). 72p. (J). (gr. 3-6). pap. 5.95 *(978-1-4342-3907-5(1))*; lib. bdg. 25.32 *(978-1-4342-3292-2(1))* Capstone. (Stone Arch Bks.).

—Volleyball Victory. Maddox, Jake. 2016. (Jake Maddox Girl Sports Stories Ser.). (ENG.). 72p. (J). (gr. 3-6). lib. bdg. 25.32 *(978-1-4965-2619-9(8)*, Stone Arch Bks.) Capstone.

Wood, Laura. Camilla, Cartographer. Dillemuth, Julie. 2019. (J). *(978-1-4338-3033-4(7)*, Magination Pr.) American Psychological Assn.

—If an Armadillo Went to a Restaurant. Fischer, Ellen. 2014. (ENG.). 32p. (J). (-2). 14.95 *(978-1-938063-39-8(2)*, Mighty Media Kids) Mighty Media Pr.

—If an Elephant Went to School. Fischer, Ellen. 2015. (ENG.). 32p. (J). (-2). 14.95 *(978-1-938063-61-9(9)*, Mighty Media Kids) Mighty Media Pr.

—Lucy in the City: A Story about Spatial Thinking. Dillemuth, Julie. 2015. 40p. (J). pap. *(978-1-4338-1928-5(7)*, Magination Pr.) American Psychological Assn.

—Mapping My Day. Dillemuth, Julie. 2017. 40p. (J). *(978-1-4338-2333-6(0)*, Magination Pr.) American Psychological Assn.

Wood, Laura. The Princess & the Fowl One. Preston, Ian. 2nd ed. 2020. (Imago Ser.: Vol. 1). (ENG.). 216p. (J). pap. ***(978-1-78132-989-4(3))*** SilverWood Bks.

—Relly, Ogi Ogi & the Secret of Dragon's Teeth Cave. Preston, Ian. 2020. (Imago Ser.: Vol. 2). (ENG.). 216p. (J). pap. ***(978-1-78132-924-5(9))*** SilverWood Bks.

Wood, Laura. Second Grade, Here I Come! Steinberg, D. J. 2017. (Here I Come! Ser.). (ENG.). 32p. (J). (gr. k-2). pap. 5.99 *(978-0-515-15808-3(9)*, Grosset & Dunlap) Penguin Young Readers Group.

Wood, Madeline. It Happened in Maine. Schmidt, Mollie. 2013. (ENG.). 56p. (J). pap. 10.95 *(978-1-59713-137-7(7))* Goose River Pr.

Wood, Michele. Born to Swing: Lil Hardin Armstrong's Life in Jazz. Rockliff, Mara. 2018. (ENG.). 32p. (J). (gr. 2-5). 17.95 *(978-1-62979-555-3(0)*, Calkins Creek) Boyds Mills Pr.

—BOX: Henry Brown Mails Himself to Freedom. Weatherford, Carole Boston. 2020. 56p. (J). (gr. 5). 17.99 *(978-0-7636-9156-1(9))* Candlewick Pr.

—Chasing Freedom: The Life Journeys of Harriet Tubman & Susan B. Anthony, Inspired by Historical Facts. Grimes, Nikki. 2015. (ENG.). 56p. (J). (gr. 1-5). 21.99 *(978-0-439-79338-4(6)*, Orchard Bks.) Scholastic, Inc.

—Clap Your Hands: A Celebration of Gospel, 1 vol. Igus, Toyomi. 2019. (ENG.). 40p. (J). 16.99 *(978-0-310-76947-7(7))* Zonderkidz.

—Going Back Home: An Artist Returns to the South. Igus, Toyomi. 2013. (ENG.). 32p. (J). (gr. 1-18). pap. 9.95 *(978-0-89239-197-4(9)*, Children's Book Press) Lee & Low Bks., Inc.

—I Lay My Stitches Down. Grady, Cynthia. 2012. (ENG.). 34p. (YA). 17.00 *(978-0-8028-5386-8(2)*, Eerdmans Bks For Young Readers) Eerdmans, William B. Publishing Co.

—I See the Rhythm. Igus, Toyomi. 2013. (ENG.). 32p. (J). (gr. 1). pap. 10.95 *(978-0-89239-212-4(6))* Lee & Low Bks., Inc.

—Like a Bird: The Art of the American Slave Song. Grady, Cynthia. 2016. (ENG.). 40p. (J). (gr. 3-6). 19.99 *(978-1-4677-8550-1(4)*, 9781467785501); E-Book 30.65 *(978-1-5124-0889-8(1))* Lerner Publishing Group. (Millbrook Pr.).

Wood, Morgan. Adventures in the Forest. Sackanay, Kathleen. 2007. 24p. (J). pap. 8.45 *(978-0-9791276-2-5(9))* Athanatos Publishing Group.

Wood, Muriel. Aram's Choice, 1 vol. Skrypuch, Marsha Forchuk. 2006. (New Beginnings Ser.). (ENG.). 84p. (J). (gr. 1-2). per. 10.95 *(978-1-55041-354-0(6)*, e18a7b6e-d67d-4b7e-9fe6-27994b354303) Trifolium Bks., Inc. CAN. Dist: Firefly Bks., Ltd.

—Call Me Aram, 1 vol. Skrypuch, Marsha Forchuk. 2008. (New Beginnings Ser.). (ENG.). 86p. (J). (gr. 4-6). 16.95 *(978-1-55455-000-5(9)*, 9d969868-ceca-4d81-a659-c37dd5e413a7) Fitzhenry & Whiteside, Ltd. CAN. Dist: Firefly Bks., Ltd.

—Call Me Aram, 1 vol. Skrypuch, Marsha Forchuk. 2008. (New Beginnings Ser.). (ENG.). 86p. (J). (gr. 4-6). pap. 9.95 *(978-1-55455-001-2(7)*, d98b4fad-6949-4768-ac52-e1ce9e2d0dec) Trifolium Bks., Inc. CAN. Dist: Firefly Bks., Ltd.

—Light & Color: I Wonder Why. Lowery, Lawrence F. 2014. (I Wonder Why Ser.). (ENG.). 36p. (J). (gr. k-3). pap. 11.95 *(978-1-938946-51-6(0))* National Science Teachers Assn.

—Lizzie's Storm, 1 vol. Fitz-Gibbon, Sally. 2004. (ENG.). 64p. (J). (gr. 3-4). pap. 7.95 *(978-1-55041-795-1(9)*, b353ce02-1c4d-4d41-a62f-6ab128847d94) Trifolium Bks., Inc. CAN. Dist: Firefly Bks., Ltd.

—Old Bird, 1 vol. Morck, Irene. 2005. (ENG.). 32p. (J). (gr. 1-2). pap. 7.95 *(978-1-55041-697-8(9)*, 39dfb4c1-507d-4fe0-aa1d-b49666b29acb) Fitzhenry & Whiteside, Ltd. CAN. Dist: Firefly Bks., Ltd.

—The Olden Days Coat. Laurence, Margaret. 2004. (ENG.). 32p. (J). (gr. 2-5). pap. 8.99 *(978-0-88776-704-3(4)*, Tundra Bks.) Tundra Bks. CAN. Dist: Penguin Random Hse. LLC.

Wood, Ryan. The Worst Twelve Days of Christmas. Bardhan-Quallen, Sudipta. 2011. (ENG.). 32p. (J). (gr. -1-3). 15.95 *(978-1-4197-0033-0(2)*, Abrams Bks. for Young Readers) Abrams, Inc.

Wood, Steve. Butterfly Magic. Hillyer, Rhonda. 2013. 84p. pap. 12.00 *(978-1-62212-306-3(9)*, Strategic Bk. Publishing) Strategic Book Publishing & Rights Agency (SBPRA).

Wood, Steven. ABC on the Farm. Winget, Rosie. Cottage Door Press, ed. 2019. (Large Lift-A-Flap Board Book Ser.). (ENG.). 10p. (J). (gr. -1-k). bds. 12.99 *(978-1-68052-309-6(0)*, 1002841) Cottage Door Pr.

—Brain Boosters: Memory Puzzles. Regan, Lisa. 2018. (Brain Boosters Ser.: 5). (ENG.). 96p. (J). pap. 9.99 *(978-1-78888-340-5(3)*, e27e047b-229a-49bc-aabc-d7f5cfbaff16) Arcturus Publishing GBR. Dist: Baker & Taylor Publisher Services (BTPS).

—My Secret Alien. Dale, Elizabeth. 2nd ed. 2016. (Reading Ladder Ser.). (ENG.). 48p. (J). (gr. k-2). pap. 7.99 *(978-1-4052-8231-4(2))* Egmont Bks., Ltd. GBR. Dist: Independent Pubs. Group.

—Peeking under Your Skin. Kenney, Karen Latchana. 2016. (What's Beneath Ser.). (ENG.). 32p. (J). (gr. -1-3). lib. bdg. 27.99 *(978-1-4795-8668-4(4)*, Picture Window Bks.) Capstone.

—Peeking Underground. Kenney, Karen Latchana. 2016. (What's Beneath Ser.). (ENG.). 32p. (J). (gr. -1-3). lib. bdg. 27.99 *(978-1-4795-8666-0(8)*, Picture Window Bks.) Capstone.

Wood, Steven, jt. illus. see Nasner, Alyssa.

Wood, Tracey. See What You Can Be: Explore Careers That Could Be for You! Heiman, Diane & Suneby, Liz. 2009. (ENG.). 108p. (gr. 4-7). spiral bd. 9.95 *(978-1-59369-277-3(3))* American Girl Publishing, Inc.

Wood, Will. The Day Robby the Rat Became a Hero Maker. Wood, Robert. 2018. (ENG.). 32p. (J). pap. 13.95 *(978-1-64300-589-8(8))* Covenant Bks.

Woodard, Brad. Oh No, Astro! Roeser, Matt. 2016. (ENG.). 40p. (J). (gr. -1-3). 17.99 *(978-1-4814-3976-3(6)*, Simon & Schuster Bks. For Young Readers) Simon & Schuster Bks. For Young Readers.

Woodard, Dana. The Little Pig That Was Afraid of the Mud. Galloway, Shannon. 2007. (J). (gr. -1-3). per. 12.99 *(978-1-59879-244-7(X))* Lifevest Publishing, Inc.

Woodard, Sorah Junkin. Come on Down. Murdock, Bob E. unabr. ed. 2003. 97p. (J). spiral bd. *(978-0-9754363-0-1(9))* Murdock, Bob E.

Woodbury et al, Charles H., jt. illus. see Fuert, L. A.

Woodcock, Fiona. The Unbudgeable Curmudgeon. Burgess, Matthew. 2019. (ENG.). 32p. (J). (gr. -1-3). 17.99 *(978-0-399-55662-3(1))*; lib. bdg. 20.99 *(978-0-399-55663-0(X))* Random Hse. Children's Bks. (Knopf Bks. for Young Readers).

Woodcock, Fiona. Hello. Woodcock, Fiona. 2019. (ENG.). 40p. (J). (gr. -1-3). 17.99 *(978-0-06-264456-5(4)*, Greenwillow Bks.) HarperCollins Pubs.

—Look. Woodcock, Fiona. 2018. (ENG.). 40p. (J). (gr. -1-3). 17.99 *(978-0-06-264455-8(6)*, Greenwillow Bks.) HarperCollins Pubs.

Woodcock, John. Color & Doodle Your Way Across the USA. 2013. 108p. *(978-1-78157-023-4(X)*, Ilex Pr.) Octopus Publishing Group.

—Ride by Moonlight. Bates, Michelle. Leigh, Susannah, ed. rev. ed. 2004. (Sandy Lane Stables Ser.). (ENG.). 118p. (J). pap. 4.95 *(978-0-7945-0547-9(3)*, Usborne) EDC Publishing.

—True Desert Adventures. Harvey, Gill. 2004. (True Adventure Stories Ser.). 144p. (J). pap. 4.95 *(978-0-7945-0381-9(0)*, Usborne) EDC Publishing.

—True Everest Adventures. Dowswell, Paul. 2004. (True Adventure Stories Ser.). 144p. (J). pap. 4.95 *(978-0-7945-0373-4(X)*, Usborne) EDC Publishing.

—True Polar Adventures. Dowswell, Paul. 2004. (True Adventure Stories Ser.). 144p. (J). pap. 4.95 *(978-0-7945-0404-5(3)*, Usborne) EDC Publishing.

—Whales & Dolphins. Davidson, Susannah et al. 2003. (Usborne Discovery Ser.). 48p. (J). pap. *(978-0-439-56060-3(8))*; pap. *(978-0-439-57780-9(2))* Scholastic, Inc.

Woodcock, John, jt. illus. see Hancock, David.

Woodcock, Marcy. A Grateful Heart under My Bed. Bloom, Janice Stitziel. 2007. 36p. (J). per. 15.99 *(978-1-934643-06-8(8))* Villager Bk. Publishing.

—Wonderfully Made under My Bed. Bloom, Janice Stitziel. 2007. 36p. (J). per. 15.99 *(978-1-934643-00-6(9))* Villager Bk. Publishing.

Wooden, Lenny. Sojourner Truth. Kudlinski, Kathleen. 2003. (Childhood of Famous Americans Ser.). (ENG.). 160p. (J). (gr. 3-7). mass mkt. 7.99 *(978-0-689-85274-9(6)*, Simon & Schuster/Paula Wiseman Bks.) Simon & Schuster/Paula Wiseman Bks.

Woodford-Robinson, Rieko. Shoo! Shoo! Shoo! Trussell-Cullen, Alan. 2010. (ENG.). 16p. (J). (gr. k-1). pap. 7.95 *(978-1-61181-035-6(3)*, Kaeden Bks.) Kaeden Corp.

Woodland, Bette. A Walk in Pirate's Cove, 1 vol. Hochman, Marisa. 2012. (ENG.). 32p. (J). *(978-0-9865679-0-2(6))* Fitzhenry & Whiteside, Ltd.

Woodman, Ned. Mission 3: In Deep. Zucker, Jonny. 2013. (Max Flash Ser.: 3). (ENG.). 144p. (J). (gr. 2-5). lib. bdg. 27.99 *(978-1-4677-1209-5(4)*, 9781467712095, Darby Creek) Lerner Publishing Group.

—Mission 3: in Deep. Zucker, Jonny. 2013. (Max Flash Ser.: 3). (ENG.). 144p. (J). (gr. 2-5). pap. 7.95 *(978-1-4677-1473-0(9)*, 9781467714730, Darby Creek) Lerner Publishing Group.

—Mission 5: Subzero. Zucker, Jonny. 2013. (Max Flash Ser.: 5). (ENG.). 144p. (J). (gr. 2-5). pap. 7.95 *(978-1-4677-1481-5(X)*, 9781467714815, Darby Creek) Lerner Publishing Group.

—Mission 6: Short Circuit. Zucker, Jonny. 2013. (Max Flash Ser.: 6). (ENG.). 144p. (J). (gr. 2-5). pap. 7.95 *(978-1-4677-1480-8(1)*, 9781467714808, Darby Creek) Lerner Publishing Group.

Woodman, Ned, jt. illus. see Ruiz, Jose Alfonso Ocampo.

Woodroffe, David. The Grandpas' Book: For the Grandpa Who's Best at Everything. Gribble, John. 2010. (Best at Everything Ser.). (ENG.). 144p. (J). (gr. 3-7). 9.99 *(978-0-545-13396-8(3)*, Scholastic Nonfiction) Scholastic, Inc.

Woodrome, Glenn D. Mitzi: Tale of a Dog. West, Dennis. Wickwire, Carolyn, ed. 2016. (ENG.). (J). (gr. 1-6). pap. 9.99 *(978-0-9978774-2-7(1))* Dennis West.

Woodrow, Tammy. Sunny Honeybee Is Lost. Woodrow, Tammy. 2019. (ENG.). 30p. (J). pap. ***(978-1-989322-15-4(8))*** Pine Lake Bks.

Woodruff, Liza. The Big Scoop, 1 vol. Cirrone, Dorian. 2006. (Marshall Cavendish Chapter Book Ser.). (ENG.). 74p. (J). (gr. 2-5). 14.99 *(978-0-7614-5323-9(7))* Marshall Cavendish Corp.

—The Biggest Pumpkin Ever! Woodhouse, Emma. 2007. (J). pap. *(978-0-545-00232-5(X))* Scholastic, Inc.

—If It's Snowy & You Know It, Clap Your Paws! Norman, Kim. abr. ed. 2015. 26p. (J). (— 1). bds. 6.95 *(978-1-4549-1692-5(3))* Sterling Publishing Co., Inc.

—The Long Wait: Estimation. Cobb, Annie. 2006. (Math Matters ® Ser.). (ENG.). 32p. (J). (gr. k-3). pap. 5.95 *(978-1-57565-094-4(0))* Astra Publishing Hse.

—The Missing Silver Dollar, 1 vol. Cirrone, Dorian. 2006. (Lindy Blues Ser.). (ENG.). 32p. (J). (gr. -1-3). 14.95 *(978-0-7614-5284-3(2))* Marshall Cavendish Corp.

—Montones de Problemas (Stacks of Trouble) Multiplication. Brenner, Martha F. 2007. (Math Matters en Español Ser.). (SPA.). 32p. (J). (gr. 1-3). pap. 5.95 *(978-1-57565-252-8(8))* Astra Publishing Hse.

—She'll Be Coming up the Mountain. Norman, Kim. 2016. (ENG.). 32p. (J). (gr. -1). 14.95 *(978-1-4549-1610-9(9))* Sterling Publishing Co., Inc.

—Stacks of Trouble: Multiplication. Brenner, Martha F. 2006. (Math Matters ® Ser.). (ENG.). 32p. (J). (gr. k-3). pap. 5.95 *(978-1-57565-098-2(3))* Astra Publishing Hse.

—Ten on the Sled. Norman, Kimberly. 2010. 26p. (J). (gr. -1). 14.95 *(978-1-4027-7076-0(6))* Sterling Publishing Co., Inc.

—Ten on the Sled. Norman, Kim. (J). 2015. 32p. (gr. -1). pap. 6.95 *(978-1-4549-1683-3(4))*; 2014. 24p. (— 1). bds. 6.95 *(978-1-4549-1191-3(3))* Sterling Publishing Co., Inc.

—Too-Tall Tina: Comparing Measurements. Pitino, Donna Marie. 2006. (Math Matters ® Ser.). (ENG.). 32p. (J). (gr. k-2). pap. 5.95 *(978-1-57565-150-7(5))* Astra Publishing Hse.

—The Twelve Days of Christmas in New England. Buzzeo, Toni. (Twelve Days of Christmas in America Ser.). (J). (-k). 2018. 22p. bds. 7.95 *(978-1-4549-2996-3(0))*; 2015. 40p. 12.95 *(978-1-4549-1492-1(0))* Sterling Publishing Co., Inc.

—What Time Is It? 2005. (My First Reader Ser.). (ENG.). 32p. (J). (gr. k-4). per. 3.95 *(978-0-516-25279-7(8)*, Children's Pr.) Scholastic Library Publishing.

Woodruff, Liza. Mary Had a Little Lamb. Woodruff, Liza. 2011. (Favorite Mother Goose Rhymes Ser.). (ENG.). 16p. (J). (gr. -1-2). lib. bdg. 14.21 *(978-1-60954-281-8(9)*, 200233) Child's World, Inc., The.

—What Time Is It? Woodruff, Liza. Demar, Regier. 2005. (My First Reader Ser.). (ENG.). 32p. (J). (gr. k-1). 18.50 *(978-0-516-25180-6(5)*, Children's Pr.) Scholastic Library Publishing.

Woodruff, Paul. M. Monsters, Myths, & Mysteries: A Tangled Tour Maze Book. Woodruff, Paul. M. 2005. 52p. (J). 8.95 *(978-0-9764327-0-8(6))* Woodruff, Paul.

Woodrum, Larry. The Christmas Tree Fort. Woodrum, Margaret. 2010. 32p. pap. 13.00 *(978-1-60911-329-2(2)*, Eloquent Bks.) Strategic Book Publishing & Rights Agency (SBPRA).

Woods, Chelsea M. Gabry Finds the Love of Her Life. Woods, Chelsea M. 2018. (ENG.). 36p. (J). pap. 17.00 *(978-1-7907-5147-1(0))* Independently Published.

Woods, Christopher & McClintic, Ben. Where's Hanuman? 2009. (ENG.). 32p. (J). (gr. 3-18). 9.95 *(978-0-9779785-8-8(3)*, d6880c06-8af8-4892-9a7d-ab6fb30eb25e) Torchlight Publishing.

Woods, Lisa. Mabel & the Queen of Dreams, 1 vol. Herz, Henry et al. 2016. (ENG.). 32p. (J). 16.99 *(978-0-7643-5137-2(0)*, 7522) Schiffer Publishing, Ltd.

Woods, Michael. Butterfly. Johnson, Jinny. 2010. (J). 28.50 *(978-1-59920-352-2(9))* Black Rabbit Bks.

—Duck. Johnson, Jinny. 2010. (J). 28.50 *(978-1-59920-353-9(7))* Black Rabbit Bks.

—Parrot. Johnson, Jinny. 2007. (Zoo Animals in the Wild Ser.). 32p. (J). (gr. -1-3). lib. bdg. 28.50 *(978-1-58340-904-6(1))* Black Rabbit Bks.

Woods, Michele. The Hungry Little Cat. Fotso, Serge. 2011. 32p. pap. 24.95 *(978-1-4626-1805-7(7))* America Star Bks.

—The Little Girl & the Lost Bag. Fotso, Serge. 2011. 20p. pap. 24.95 *(978-1-4626-1741-8(7))* America Star Bks.

Woods, Muriel. Tooga: The Story of a Polar Bear, 1 vol. Woods, Shirley. 2004. 32p. (J). (gr. 3-4). pap. 7.95 *(978-1-55041-900-9(5),* 1c57e31c-2367-4c68-ba23-de18d616c273) Clockwise Pr. CAN. Dist: Firefly Bks., Ltd.

Woods, Rosemary. On My Way to a Happy Life. Chopra, Deepak & Tracy, Kristina. 2010. (ENG.). 32p. (J). (gr. -1-2). 15.99 ***(978-1-4019-2575-8(8))*** Hay Hse., Inc.

Woods, Rosemary. One Well: The Story of Water on Earth. Strauss, Rochelle. 2007. (CitizenKid Ser.). (ENG.). 32p. (J). (gr. 3-7). 18.95 *(978-1-55337-954-6(3))* Kids Can Pr., Ltd. CAN. Dist: Hachette Bk. Group.

Woods, Rosie. Full Moon Night in Silk Cotton Tree Village: a Collection of Caribbean Folk Tales: Band 15/Emerald (Collins Big Cat) Agard, John & Nichols, Grace. 2016. (Collins Big Cat Ser.). (ENG.). 48p. (J). pap. 10.99 *(978-0-00-814724-2(8))* HarperCollins Pubs. Ltd. GBR. Dist: Independent Pubs. Group.

Woods, Tom. Lizzie Reaches the Rainbow. Woods, Lara. 2016. (ENG.). (J). *(978-0-9953976-2-0(7));* pap. *(978-0-9953976-0-6(0))* Serenity Press.

Woods, Vanessa. The Breakaway Kid. Atkins, Ben. 2nd rev. ed. 2005. (ENG.). 32p. (J). per. 8.00 *(978-0-9768653-0-8(0))* Summer Day Publishing, LLC.

Woods, Vashti. Walk It Out, Zola! Holmes, Pinkie A. & La Chelle Dupree, Debra. 2017. (ENG.). 38p. (J). 22.99 *(978-1-5456-1443-3(1));* pap. 12.49 *(978-1-5456-1441-9(5))* Salem Author Services.

Woodward, Alice B. The Peter Pan Picture Book. O'Connor, Daniel & Barrie, J. M. 2015. (ENG.). 96p. (J). (gr. k-3). pap. 12.99 *(978-0-486-79430-3(X))* Dover Pubns., Inc.

—The Story of Peter Pan. Barrie, J. M. unabr. ed. 2011. (Dover Children's Thrift Classics Ser.). (ENG.). 96p. (J). (gr. 3-8). reprint ed. pap. 3.50 *(978-0-486-27294-8(X))* Dover Pubns., Inc.

Woodward, Antonia. Bible Promises for Baby's Baptism, 1 vol. Piper, Sophie. ed. 2015. (ENG.). 32p. (J). (— 1). 8.99 *(978-0-7459-6554-3(7))* Lion Hudson PLC GBR. Dist: Independent Pubs. Group.

—Bible Promises for Baby's Christening, 1 vol. Piper, Sophie. ed. 2015. (ENG.). 32p. (J). (— 1). 8.99 *(978-0-7459-7620-4(4))* Lion Hudson PLC GBR. Dist: Independent Pubs. Group.

—Bible Promises for Baby's Dedication, 1 vol. Piper, Sophie. ed. 2015. (ENG.). 32p. (J). (— 1). 9.99 *(978-0-7459-7606-8(9))* Lion Hudson PLC GBR. Dist: Kregel Pubns.

—Jesus Calling for Little Ones, 1 vol. Young, Sarah. 2015. (Jesus Calling® Ser.). (ENG.). 26p. (J). bds. 8.99 *(978-0-7180-3384-2(1))* Nelson, Thomas Inc.

—Our New Baby Memory Book. ed. 2017. (ENG.). 48p. 16.99 *(978-0-7459-7723-2(5))* Lion Hudson PLC GBR. Dist: Independent Pubs. Group.

Woodward, Antonia. The Extra Special Baby: The Story of the Christmas Promise. Woodward, Antonia. ed. 2018. (ENG.). 32p. (J). pap. 8.99 *(978-0-7459-7678-5(6))* Lion Hudson PLC GBR. Dist: Independent Pubs. Group.

—Noah & the Great Big Boat. Woodward, Antonia. ed. 2019. (ENG.). 32p. (J). (gr. -1-k). pap. 9.99 *(978-0-7459-7681-5(6))* Lion Hudson PLC GBR. Dist: Independent Pubs. Group.

—The Not-So-Very Lost Lamb. Woodward, Antonia. ed. 2019. (ENG.). 32p. (J). (gr. -1-k). pap. 9.99 *(978-0-7459-7680-8(8))* Lion Hudson PLC GBR. Dist: Independent Pubs. Group.

—The Promised One: The Wonderful Story of Easter. Woodward, Antonia. ed. 2017. (ENG.). 32p. (J). pap. 8.99 *(978-0-7459-7679-2(4))* Lion Hudson PLC GBR. Dist: Independent Pubs. Group.

Woodward, Elaine. Young Billy: A New Beginning!, Vol. 2. Sargent, Dave & Sargent, Pat. 2003. (Young Animal Pride Ser.: 2). 24p. (J). pap. 10.95 *(978-1-56763-866-0(X));* lib. bdg. 20.95 *(978-1-56763-865-3(1))* Ozark Publishing.

—Young Dike: Teamwork! Sargent, Dave & Sargent, Pat. 2003. (Young Animal Pride Ser.: 5). 24p. (J). 5. pap. 6.95 *(978-1-56763-872-1(4));* Vol. 5. lib. bdg. 20.95 *(978-1-56763-871-4(6))* Ozark Publishing.

—Young Redi: Friendship!, Vol. 3. Sargent, Dave & Sargent, Pat. 2003. (Young Animal Pride Ser.: 3). 24p. (J). pap. 10.95 *(978-1-56763-868-4(6));* lib. bdg. 20.95 *(978-1-56763-867-7(8))* Ozark Publishing.

Woodward, Emilie. Once upon a Blueberry. Woodward, Emilie. 2020. (ENG.). 42p. (J). pap. 13.56 ***(978-1-6613-6923-1(5))*** Independently Published.

Woodward II, Ed. The Ferry Boat. Francis, JennaKay. 2013. 12p. pap. 8.95 *(978-1-61633-426-0(6))* Guardian Angel Publishing, Inc.

Woodward, Joanie. Seven Little Monkeys. Woodward, Joanie. 2005. 40p. (J). per. *(978-0-9754676-4-0(6))* Yeoman Hse.

Woodward, Jonathan. A Day in the Life of T. Rex. Brooks, Susie. 2016. (Reading Ladder Ser.). (ENG.). 32p. (J). (gr. 1-3). pap. 7.99 *(978-1-4052-8040-2(9))* Egmont Bks., Ltd. GBR. Dist: Independent Pubs. Group.

—Fluttering Minibeast Adventures. French, Jess. 2016. (ENG.). 32p. (J). (gr. -1-k). 10.99 *(978-1-4052-7755-6(6))* Egmont Bks., Ltd. GBR. Dist: Independent Pubs. Group.

—Sounds of the Sky. Butterfield, Moira. 2020. (ENG.). 24p. (J). (gr. k-3). 19.99 *(978-1-944530-27-3(4),* 360 Degrees) Tiger Tales.

—Tickly Minibeast Adventures. French, Jess. 2016. (ENG.). 32p. (J). (gr. -1-k). 10.99 *(978-1-4052-7756-3(4))* Egmont Bks., Ltd. GBR. Dist: Independent Pubs. Group.

Woodward, Jonathan, photos by. Cut in Half: An Inside Look at Everyday Objects. Warren, Mike. 2018. (ENG.). 144p. (J). 29.95 *(978-1-4521-6862-3(8))* Chronicle Bks. LLC.

Woodward, Ryan. The Invincible Ed. Woodward, Ryan. 2004. (ENG.). 112p. pap. 13.95 *(978-1-59307-194-3(9))* Dark Horse Comics.

Woodward, Sarah. Planet Splooch. Thiveos, Maria, tr. 2003.Tr. of Planeta Splooch. (ENG & SPA.). 59p. (J). pap. 12.99 *(978-0-9728041-0-3(2))* Garcia, Cezanne.

Woodword, Elaine. Young Dawn: Friends Care! Sargent, Dave & Sargent, Pat. 2005. (Young Animal Pride Ser.: 8). 24p. (J). 8. pap. 6.95 *(978-1-56763-878-3(3));* Vol. 8. lib. bdg. 20.95 *(978-1-56763-877-6(5))* Ozark Publishing.

—Young Sammy: I'm a Little Stinker!, Vol. 9. Sargent, Dave & Sargent, Pat. 2005. (Young Animal Pride Ser.). 24p. (J). pap. 10.95 *(978-1-56763-880-6(5))* Ozark Publishing.

—Young White Thunder: I'm a Leader!, Vol. 6. Sargent, Dave & Sargent, Pat. 2005. (Young Animal Pride Ser.). 24p. (J). pap. 10.95 *(978-1-56763-874-5(0))* Ozark Publishing.

Woodworth, Viki. Who Goes to School? Hillert, Margaret. 2016. (BeginningtoRead Ser.). (ENG.). 32p. (J). (gr. -1-2). pap. 11.94 *(978-1-60357-949-0(4));* (gr. k-2). 22.60 *(978-1-59953-808-2(3))* Norwood Hse. Pr.

Woody. Tortoise & the Baboon. Howell, Gill. 2004. (ENG.). 16p. (J). lib. bdg. 23.65 *(978-1-59646-686-9(3))* Dingles & Co.

Woodyard, Benjamin & Jeaurond, Paul. Madison Saves the Day. Green, Stella. 2017. (ENG.). (J). pap. *(978-0-9937118-5-5(5))* Green, Stella Mary.

Woodyard, Sandy Lilly. Cathy, the Castaway Cat. Young, Norene. 2012. 34p. 24.95 *(978-1-4626-6111-4(4))* America Star Bks.

Woolf, Catherine Maria. My First Hike. Woolf, Catherine Maria. 2008. (ENG.). 22p. (J). (gr. -1). bds. 7.95 *(978-1-58469-113-6(1),* Dawn Pubns.) Sourcebooks, Inc.

Woolf, Julia. All Gone. North, Merry. 2005. (J). *(978-1-57151-753-1(7))* Playhouse Publishing.

—Black, 1 vol. Stockland, Patricia M. 2008. (Colors Ser.). (ENG.). 24p. (J). (gr. -1-2). 27.07 *(978-1-60270-255-4(1),* 4413, Looking Glass Library) Magic Wagon.

—Blue, 1 vol. Stockland, Patricia M. 2008. (Colors Ser.). (ENG.). 24p. (J). (gr. -1-2). 27.07 *(978-1-60270-256-1(X),* 4415, Looking Glass Library) Magic Wagon.

—Brown, 1 vol. Stockland, Patricia M. 2011. (Colors Ser.). (ENG.). 24p. (J). (gr. -1-2). 27.07 *(978-1-61641-135-0(X),* 4427, Looking Glass Library) Magic Wagon.

—Calm down, Zebra. Kuenzler, Lou. 2020. (ENG.). 32p. (J). (gr. 3-7). 16.95 *(978-0-571-35170-1(0))* Faber & Faber, Inc.

—Five Black Cats. Hegarty, Patricia. (ENG.). 22p. (J). (gr. -1-k). 2016. bds. 6.99 *(978-1-58925-239-4(X));* 2013. bds. 8.95 *(978-1-58925-611-8(5))* Tiger Tales.

—Five Busy Elves. Hegarty, Patricia. 2014. (ENG.). 22p. (J). (gr. -1-k). bds. 8.99 *(978-1-58925-561-6(5))* Tiger Tales.

—Five Little Ghosts. Hegarty, Patricia. 2014. (ENG.). 22p. (J). (gr. -1-k). bds. 8.99 *(978-1-58925-587-6(9))* Tiger Tales.

—Gingerbread Joy. 2008. (ENG.). 10p. (J). bds. 4.95 *(978-1-58117-814-2(X),* Intervisual/Piggy Toes) Bendon, Inc.

—Gray, 1 vol. Stockland, Patricia M. 2011. (Colors Ser.). (ENG.). 24p. (J). (gr. -1-2). 27.07 *(978-1-61641-136-7(8),* 4429, Looking Glass Library) Magic Wagon.

—Green, 1 vol. Stockland, Patricia M. 2008. (Colors Ser.). (ENG.). 24p. (J). (gr. -1-2). 27.07 *(978-1-60270-257-8(8),* 4417, Looking Glass Library) Magic Wagon.

—Halloween ABC. Albee, Sarah. (J). 2015. 26p. (-k). bds. 7.99 *(978-0-553-52422-2(4),* Random Hse. Bks. for Young Readers); 2009. 32p. (gr. -1-k). 4.99 *(978-0-375-84823-0(1),* Golden Bks.) Random Hse. Children's Bks.

—Not yet Zebra. Kuenzler, Lou. 2018. (ENG.). 32p. (J). (gr. -1-1). 16.95 *(978-0-571-34288-4(4),* Faber & Faber Children's Bks.) Faber & Faber, Inc.

—One Hug. Moore, Katrina. 2019. (ENG.). 32p. (J). (gr. -1 — 1). 14.99 *(978-0-06-284954-0(9),* Tegen, Katherine Bks) HarperCollins Pubs.

—Red, 1 vol. Stockland, Patricia M. 2008. (Colors Ser.). (ENG.). 24p. (J). (gr. -1-2). 27.07 *(978-1-60270-258-5(6),* 4419, Looking Glass Library) Magic Wagon.

—Reindeer Run. 2008. (ENG.). 10p. (J). bds. 4.95 *(978-1-58117-813-5(1),* Intervisual/Piggy Toes) Bendon, Inc.

—Snow Wonder. Ghigna, Charles. 2008. (Step into Reading Ser.: Vol. 2). 24p. (J). (gr. -1-1). 4.99 *(978-0-375-85586-3(6),* Random Hse. Bks. for Young Readers) Random Hse. Children's Bks.

—Snowman Surprise. 2008. (ENG.). 10p. (J). bds. 4.95 *(978-1-58117-812-8(3),* Intervisual/Piggy Toes) Bendon, Inc.

—Special Star. 2008. (ENG.). 10p. (J). bds. 4.95 *(978-1-58117-815-9(8),* Intervisual/Piggy Toes) Bendon, Inc.

—Tan, 1 vol. Stockland, Patricia M. 2011. (Colors Ser.). (ENG.). 24p. (J). (gr. -1-2). 27.07 *(978-1-61641-140-4(6),* 4437, Looking Glass Library) Magic Wagon.

—White, 1 vol. Stockland, Patricia M. 2008. (Colors Ser.). (ENG.). 24p. (J). (gr. -1-2). 27.07 *(978-1-60270-259-2(4),* 4421, Looking Glass Library) Magic Wagon.

—Yellow, 1 vol. Stockland, Patricia M. 2008. (Colors Ser.). (ENG.). 24p. (J). (gr. -1-2). 27.07 *(978-1-60270-260-8(8),* 4423, Looking Glass Library) Magic Wagon.

Woolf, Julia. Duck & Penguin Are NOT Friends. Woolf, Julia. 2019. (ENG.). 32p. (J). (gr. -1-3). 16.95 *(978-1-68263-132-4(X))* Peachtree Publishing Co. Inc.

Woollatt, Sue. A Cool Kid's Field Guide to Global Warming. Farrington, Karen. 2009. (Cool Kid's Field Guide Ser.). 26p. (J). (gr. 1-3). spiral bd. 6.99 *(978-0-8416-7146-1(X))* Hammond World Atlas Corp.

Woolley, Kim. Getting to Know Italy & Italian. Sansone, Emma. 2005. 33p. (J). reprint ed. pap. 13.00 *(978-0-7567-9579-5(6))* DIANE Publishing Co.

Woolley, Patricia. The Thrift Store Bears. Evans, Olive. 2004. (ENG.). 41p. (J). 18.97 *(978-0-9748954-0-6(7))* Teddy Traveler Co.

Woolley, Sara. Charlotte & the Quiet Place. Sosin, Deborah. 2015. 40p. (J). (gr. -1-2). 16.95 *(978-1-941529-02-7(X),* Plum Blossom Bks.) Parallax Pr.

Woolley, Tom. Living in ... Around the World Collection: Living in ... Brazil; Living in ... China; Living in ... India; Living in ... Italy; Living in ... Mexico; Living in ... South Africa. Perkins, Chloe. ed. 2017. (Living In... Ser.). (ENG.). 192p. (J). (gr. k-2). pap. 17.99 *(978-1-5344-0199-0(7),* Simon Spotlight) Simon Spotlight.

—Living in ... Australia. Perkins, Chloe. 2017. (Living In... Ser.). (ENG.). 32p. (J). (gr. k-2). pap. 4.99 *(978-1-4814-8092-5(8),* Simon Spotlight) Simon Spotlight.

—Living in ... Brazil. Perkins, Chloe & Silva, Reg. 2016. (Living In... Ser.). (ENG.). 32p. (J). (gr. k-2). pap. 4.99 *(978-1-4814-5203-8(7))* Simon & Schuster, Inc.

—Living in ... China. Perkins, Chloe. 2016. (Living In... Ser.). (ENG.). 32p. (J). (gr. k-2). pap. 4.99 *(978-1-4814-6047-7(1),* Simon Spotlight) Simon Spotlight.

—Living in ... India. Perkins, Chloe. 2016. (Living In... Ser.). (ENG.). 32p. (J). (gr. k-2). pap. 4.99 *(978-1-4814-7089-6(2))* Simon & Schuster.

—Living in ... Mexico. Perkins, Chloe. 2016. (Living In... Ser.). (ENG.). 32p. (J). (gr. k-2). pap. 4.99 *(978-1-4814-6050-7(1),* Simon Spotlight) Simon Spotlight.

—Living in ... Russia. Burton, Jesse. 2018. (Living In... Ser.). (ENG.). 32p. (J). (gr. k-2). 17.99 *(978-1-5344-1766-3(4));* pap. 4.99 *(978-1-5344-1765-6(6))* Simon Spotlight. (Simon Spotlight).

—Living in ... South Africa. Perkins, Chloe. 2016. (Living In... Ser.). (ENG.). 32p. (J). (gr. k-2). pap. 4.99 *(978-1-4814-7092-6(2),* Simon Spotlight) Simon Spotlight.

—Living in ... South Korea. Perkins, Chloe. 2017. (Living In... Ser.). (ENG.). 32p. (J). (gr. k-2). 17.99 *(978-1-5344-0143-3(1));* pap. 4.99 *(978-1-5344-0142-6(3))* Simon Spotlight. (Simon Spotlight).

Woolley, Tom, jt. illus. see Silva, Reg.

Woollvin, Bethan. The Button Book. Nicholls, Sally. 2020. (ENG.). 32p. (J). (gr. -1-2). 16.99 *(978-0-7352-6715-2(4),* Tundra Bks.) Tundra Bks. CAN. Dist: Penguin Random Hse. LLC.

Woollvin, Bethan. Bo the Brave. Woollvin, Bethan. 2020. (ENG.). 32p. (J). (gr. k-4). 17.99 *(978-1-68263-182-9(6))* Peachtree Publishing Co. Inc.

—Hansel & Gretel. Woollvin, Bethan. 2018. (ENG.). 32p. (J). (gr. k-4). 16.95 *(978-1-68263-073-0(0))* Peachtree Publishing Co. Inc.

Woollvin, Bethan. Little Red. Woollvin, Bethan. (ENG.). 32p. (J). (gr. k-4). 2020. 8.99 ***(978-1-68263-217-8(2));*** 2016. 16.95 *(978-1-56145-917-9(8))* Peachtree Publishing Co. Inc.

Woollvin, Bethan. Rapunzel, 1 vol. Woollvin, Bethan. 2017. (ENG.). 32p. (J). (gr. k-4). 16.95 *(978-1-68263-003-7(X))* Peachtree Publishing Co. Inc.

Woolmer, Nancy. A Christmas Surprise. Gregory, Larry. 2004. 24p. pap. 24.95 *(978-1-4137-3014-2(0))* PublishAmerica, Inc.

Wools, Katie. Sun & Moon Take Turns, 1 vol. DeBarbieri, Lili. 2019. (ENG.). 32p. (J). (gr. -1-3). 14.99 *(978-0-7643-5695-7(X),* 16112) Schiffer Publishing, Ltd.

Wooten, Jason. A Boy with a Sling. Carver, Dale. 2017. (ENG.). 22p. (J). pap. 9.99 *(978-0-692-04738-5(7))* Brikwoo Creative Group.

Wooten, Neal. Benny the Brave. McKelvey, Lonnie. 2008. 28p. (J). pap. 7.99 *(978-0-9817521-3-6(6))* Mirror Publishing.

—Freddy Freckles: Friends, Flags, Facts & Fun. Skerwarski, N. D. 2007. 52p. (J). pap. 16.99 *(978-0-9800675-3-8(7))* Mirror Publishing.

Wooten, Neal, jt. illus. see Austin, Antoinette.

Wooten, Neal, jt. illus. see Schandy, Rosita.

Wooten, Vernon Lee. Mattie & Percy: The Story of a Chicken & a Duck. Briggs-Anderson, Naomi. 2011. 32p. pap. 24.95 *(978-1-4560-5319-2(1))* America Star Bks.

Wopschall, Kayla. Jungle Air: Based on a True Story. Petitt, Karlene. 2018. (ENG.). 98p. (J). (gr. 3-6). pap. 11.99 *(978-1-944738-06-8(1))* BLLE Creative.

Worcester, Retta. Christmas in the Country. Collyer, Barbara & Foley, John R. 2020. (Little Golden Book Ser.). 24p. (J). (-k). 4.99 ***(978-0-593-11995-2(9),*** Golden Bks.) Random Hse. Children's Bks.

Word, Amanda, jt. illus. see Iadonisi, Carmin.

Wordwindow. Shakespeare for Children Picture Book. 2007. 32p. (J). 14.95 *(978-0-9774484-8-7(7))* Wordwindow LLC.

Workman, Dan. Gossip: Before Word Gets Around, 1 vol. Rondina, Catherine. 2016. (Lorimer Deal with It Ser.). (ENG.). 32p. (J). (gr. 4-9). 24.95 *(978-1-55277-499-1(6),* 8e054487-16e7-4baa-8b55-e3e5ec4d91f5) James Lorimer & Co. Ltd., Pubs. CAN. Dist: Lerner Publishing Group.

—Gossip: Deal with It Before Word Gets Around, 1 vol. Rondina, Catherine. 2004. (Lorimer Deal with It Ser.). (ENG.). 32p. (J). (gr. 4-8). pap. 12.95 *(978-1-55028-821-6(0),* 9781550288216) James Lorimer & Co. Ltd., Pubs. CAN. Dist: Orca Bk. Pubs. USA.

—Lying: Deal with It Straight Up, 1 vol. Rondina, Catherine. 2016. (Lorimer Deal with It Ser.). (ENG.). 32p. (J). (gr. 4-9). pap. 12.95 *(978-1-55028-906-0(3),* 906) James Lorimer & Co. Ltd., Pubs. CAN. Dist: Lerner Publishing Group.

—Rudeness: Deal with It If You Please, 1 vol. Rondina, Catherine. 2016. (Lorimer Deal with It Ser.). (ENG.). 32p. (J). (gr. 4-9). 12.95 *(978-1-55028-870-4(9),* 9c890129-5c5e-4c06-9a75-ae83e198f12a) James Lorimer & Co. Ltd., Pubs. CAN. Dist: Lerner Publishing Group.

Workman, Heather. The Adventures of la Mike & Otis. Ray, Ray. 2019. (ENG.). 30p. (J). 14.99 ***(978-1-7331631-0-1(7));*** pap. 7.99 ***(978-1-7331631-2-5(3))*** Fun Family Publishing.

—Catch My Kiss: The Forever Ride. Smith, Kimberly Divita. 2019. (Catch My Kiss Ser.: Vol. 3). (ENG.). 34p. (J). (gr. k-4). pap. 12.99 ***(978-0-578-59896-3(5))*** Kimberly DiVita Smith.

Workman, Heather. Women Who March. Raub Dershowitz, Adena. 2018. (ENG.). 28p. (J). pap. 14.95 *(978-0-692-05378-2(6))* Dershowitz, Adena.

Workman, Lisa. Color Your World! (Sunny Day) Chlebowski, Rachel. 2018. (ENG.). 128p. (J). (gr. -1-2). pap. 7.99 *(978-0-525-57770-6(X),* Golden Bks.) Random Hse. Children's Bks.

—Merry-Go-Round: El Carrusel. Schiller, Pamela Byrne. 2015. (SPA & ENG.). 11p. (J). *(978-1-63237-039-6(5))* Frog Street Pr.

Workman, Lisa & Workman, Terry. ¿Por Qué el Colibrí Bebe Néctar? 2016. (Jump into Genre Ser.). (SPA.). (J). (gr. 3). 5.25 *(978-1-4788-3618-6(0))* Newmark Learning LLC.

Workman, Lisa, jt. illus. see Workman, Terry.

Workman, Lisa A. Keep Styling! (Sunny Day) Golden Books. 2018. (ENG.). 128p. (J). (gr. -1-2). pap. 7.99 *(978-1-5247-6854-6(5),* Golden Bks.) Random Hse. Children's Bks.

Workman, Paula J. Our Gang & the Shrinking Machine. Stamps, Sarah. 2008. 33p. pap. 24.95 *(978-1-60610-953-3(7))* PublishAmerica, Inc.

Workman, Terry. Miss Mary Mack & the Jumping Elephants. Fuerst, Jeffrey B. 2009. (Reader's Theater Nursery Rhymes & Songs Set B Ser.). 48p. (J). pap. *(978-1-60859-161-9(1))* Benchmark Education Co.

Workman, Terry & Workman, Lisa. Cartoon How-To. Bellen-Berthézène, Cyndie. 2005. 48p. (J). *(978-0-439-81332-7(8))* Scholastic, Inc.

Workman, Terry, jt. illus. see Workman, Lisa.

Workshop, Sesame, et al. Sesame: Stories to Grow On. Wage, Erin Rose & Winslow, Claire. 2019. (Me Reader Jr Ser.). (ENG.). 80p. (J). bds. *(978-1-5037-4570-4(8),* 07f6cb7f-2b90-4773-b0ab-517d89f70106, p i kids) Phoenix International Publications, Inc.

—Sesame Street: Stories to Grow On. Wage, Erin Rose & Winslow, Claire. 2019. (Me Reader Jr Ser.). (ENG.). 80p. (J). bds. *(978-1-5037-4997-9(5),* 5e7d3d06-f5f6-4d6f-8698-5d8a13a156e3, p i kids) Phoenix International Publications, Inc.

World-Famous San Diego Zoo Staff, photos by. Little Panda: The World Welcomes Hua Mei at the San Diego Zoo. Ryder, Joanne. 2004. (ENG.). 32p. (J). (gr. k-3). 7.99 *(978-0-689-86616-6(X),* Simon & Schuster Bks. For Young Readers) Simon & Schuster Bks. For Young Readers.

Worlds Beyond Art. Puanani & the Volcano: Hawaiian Island Adventures. Jeffries, Jo Ann. Tabor, Sierra, ed. 2020. (Hawaiian Island Adventures Ser.: Vol. 1). (HAW.). 68p. (J). (gr. 2-4). pap. 16.95 ***(978-1-949711-05-9(6))*** Bluewater Pubns.

Wormell, Chris. Dinosaurium: Welcome to the Museum. Mangus, Lily. 2018. (Welcome to the Museum Ser.). (ENG.). 112p. (J). (gr. 3-7). 35.00 *(978-0-7636-9900-0(4),* Big Picture Press) Candlewick Pr.

—Planetarium. Prinja, Raman. 2019. (Welcome to the Museum Ser.). (ENG.). 112p. (J). (gr. 3-7). 35.00 *(978-1-5362-0623-4(7),* Big Picture Press) Candlewick Pr.

—Swan Song. Lewis, J. Patrick. 2005. 32p. (J). reprint ed. 17.00 *(978-0-7567-8662-5(2))* DIANE Publishing Co.

Wormell, Chris. Molly & the Night Monster. Wormell, Chris. 2011. (ENG.). 32p. (J). (gr. -1-k). pap. 9.99 *(978-1-86230-185-6(9),* Red Fox) Random House Children's Books GBR. Dist: Independent Pubs. Group.

—The Wild Girl. Wormell, Chris. 2006. 32p. (J). (gr. -1). 17.00 *(978-0-8028-5311-0(0),* Eerdmans Bks For Young Readers) Eerdmans, William B. Publishing Co.

Wormell, Christopher. A Number of Animals. Green, Kate. 2012. (ENG.). 32p. (J). (gr. -1-k). 15.99 *(978-1-56846-222-6(0),* Creative Editions) Creative Co., The.

—A Number of Animals Nesting Blocks. Green, Kate. 2013. (ENG.). (J). (gr. -1-k). 24.99 *(978-1-56846-248-6(4),* Creative Editions) Creative Co., The.

—Swan Song. Lewis, J. Patrick. 2003. (ENG.). 32p. (J). (gr. 3-17). 18.95 *(978-1-56846-175-5(5),* Creative Editions) Creative Co., The.

Worms, Ina. Langenscheidt Grundschulwoerterbuch Deutsch - Primary School Dictionary German (monolingual) Hoppenstedt, Gila & Richardson, Karen. 3rd ed. 2019. (GER.). 240p. (J). 19.99 *(978-3-468-20613-9(5))* Langenscheidt Publishing Group.

Worrall, Linda. Snow White & the Seven Dwarfs: A Story about Vanity. 2006. (J). 6.99 *(978-1-59939-025-3(6))* Cornerstone Pr.

Worrell, Nicole. One Day I Will Grow Up. Fraley, Patty. 2013. 18p. pap. 7.75 *(978-1-4575-2142-3(3))* Dog Ear Publishing, LLC.

Worsley, Belinda. Henry & the Hand-Me-Downs. Powell, Jillian. 2005. 32p. (J). lib. bdg. 9.00 *(978-1-4242-0886-9(6))* Fitzgerald Bks.

—Sally Sets Sail. Gurney, Stella. 2009. (Get Ready (Windmill Books) Ser.). 32p. (J). (gr. k-2). lib. bdg. 25.60 *(978-1-60754-261-2(7))* Windmill Bks.

—Yummy in My Tummy! Harrison, Paul. 2009. (Get Ready (Windmill Books) Ser.). 32p. (J). (gr. k-2). lib. bdg. 25.60 *(978-1-60754-263-6(3))* Windmill Bks.

Worsley, Belinda & Adamson, Gareth. Topsy & Tim Go for Gold. Adamson, Jean. 2016. (Topsy & Tim Ser.). (ENG.). 32p. (J). (gr. -1-1). pap. 9.99 *(978-1-4093-0946-8(0))* Penguin Bks., Ltd. GBR. Dist: Independent Pubs. Group.

Worsley, John, Ill. Painkillers: Book One. Worsley, John, III, text. 2004. 48p. (YA). per. 5.00 *(978-0-9764033-0-2(7))* Openvein.

Worthen, Alex. Sheppard's Last Lamb. Hall, Annalisa. 2016. (ENG.). 32p. (J). (gr. -1-3). 14.99 *(978-1-4621-1853-3(4),* Bonneville Bks.) Cedar Fort, Inc./CFI Distribution.

Worthington, Jennifer & Shoals, Melinda. The Gift That Saved Christmas. 2008. 40p. (J). 17.00 *(978-0-9773460-1-1(3))* Spritelee Enterprises.

Worthington, Leonie. Bath Time. Bedford, David. 2010. (Lift-The-Flap Book Ser.). (ENG.). 16p. (gr. -1-k). 9.99 *(978-1-921541-13-1(X))* Little Hare Bks. AUS. Dist: Independent Pubs. Group.

—Follow an Elf. McLean, Wendy & Book Company Staff. 2003. (Sparkle Bks.). 10p. (J). bds. 8.95 *(978-1-74047-314-9(0))* Book Co. Publishing Pty, Ltd., The AUS. Dist: Penton Overseas, Inc.

—Whose Knickers? Munro, Maisie. 2008. *(978-1-921272-20-2(1))* Little Hare Bks. AUS. Dist: HarperCollins Pubs. Australia.

—Whose Pyjamas? A Flip the Flap Book. Munro, Maisie. 2008. (ENG.). *(978-1-921272-21-9(X))* Little Hare Bks. AUS. Dist: HarperCollins Pubs. Australia.

W

Wotton, Jon. Rosie & Her Formidable Bark, Indomitable Nose & Rambunctious Tail! Williams, Vivienne. 2017. (ENG.). 30p. (J). pap. *(978-0-9957545-0-8(0))* Conscious Publishing.
—Rosie & Her Formidable Bark, Indomitable Nose & Rambunctioustail. Williams, Vivienne. 2013. 46p. pap. *(978-0-9576680-4-1(X))* Williams, Vivienne.
Woupio, Amy. Making Faces. Woupio, Isaac Jay. 2008. 20p. per. 24.95 *(978-1-4241-9865-8(8))* America Star Bks.
Wozniak, Erin. The You Rock! Coloring Book. Miletsky, Jay. 2019. (You Rock! Group Ser.: Vol. 1). (ENG.). 56p. (J). pap. 6.95 ***(978-0-578-53808-2(3))*** New Paige Pr., LLC.
Wozniak, Lana. Rockin' Coloring & Activity Book. Miletsky, Jay. 2019. (You Rock Group Ser.: Vol. 1). (ENG.). 32p. (J). pap. 9.95 ***(978-0-578-53533-3(5))*** New Paige Pr., LLC.
Wozniak, Patricia A. McGooster & Mcgyman Begin Their Adventures. Rochkind, Pat. 2008. 144p. (J). (gr. 4-7). per. 12.95 *(978-0-9792430-1-1(7))* Wing Lane Pr.
Wragg, Nate. Elwood Bigfoot: Wanted: Birdie Friends! Esbaum, Jill. 2015. 32p. (J). (gr. -1-2). 14.95 *(978-1-4549-0879-1(3)*, 1394145) Sterling Publishing Co., Inc.
—Go Go Gorillas: A Romping Bedtime Tale. Wensink, Patrick. 2017. (ENG.). 32p. (J). (gr. -1-3). 17.99 *(978-0-06-238118-7(0))* HarperCollins Pubs.
—Goldi Rocks & the Three Bears. Schwartz, Corey Rosen & Coulton, Beth. 2014. (ENG.). 32p. (J). (gr. k-3). 17.99 *(978-0-399-25685-1(7)*, G.P. Putnam's Sons Books for Young Readers) Penguin Young Readers Group.
—Gorillas Go Bananas. Wensink, Patrick. 2018. (ENG.). 32p. (J). (gr. -1-3). 17.99 *(978-0-06-238120-0(2))* HarperCollins Pubs.
—Monster Trucks. Denise, Anika. 2016. (ENG.). 32p. (J). (gr. -1-3). 17.99 *(978-0-06-234522-6(2))* HarperCollins Pubs.
—Monster Trucks Board Book. Denise, Anika. 2018. (ENG.). 32p. (J). (gr. -1 — 1). bds. 7.99 *(978-0-06-274162-2(4)*, HarperFestival) HarperCollins Pubs.
—Pumpkin Magic. Masessa, Ed. 2020. (ENG.). 32p. (J). (gr. -1-k). pap. 6.99 *(978-1-338-56332-0(7)*, Cartwheel Bks.) Scholastic, Inc.
—Rosie the Dragon & Charlie Make Waves. Kerstein, Lauren H. 2019. (ENG.). 40p. (J). (gr. -1-2). 17.99 *(978-1-5420-4292-5(5)*, 9781542042925, Two Lions) Amazon Publishing.
Wragg, Nate. Rosie the Dragon & Charlie Say Good Night. Kerstein, Lauren H. 2020. (Rosie the Dragon & Charlie Ser.). (ENG.). 40p. (J). (gr. k-2). 17.99 ***(978-1-5420-1848-7(X)***, 9781542018487, Two Lions) Amazon Publishing.
Wragg, Nate. 10 Little Ninjas. Paul, Miranda. (J). (-k). 2018. 26p. bds. 7.99 *(978-1-5247-7071-6(X))*; 2016. 32p. 16.99 *(978-0-553-53497-9(1))* Random Hse. Children's Bks. (Knopf Bks. for Young Readers).
Wray, Jordan. My Cat Needs Me. Cottrell, Jane. 2017. (ENG.). 20p. (J). (gr. -1-1). bds. *(978-1-4867-1309-7(2))* Flowerpot Children's Pr. Inc.
—My Christmas ABCs (an Alphabet Book), 1 vol. 2018. (ENG.). 20p. (J). bds. 9.99 *(978-1-4002-0981-1(1))* Nelson, Thomas Inc.
—My Dog Needs Me. Cottrell, Jane. 2017. (Pet Needs Ser.). (ENG.). 20p. (J). (gr. -1-k). bds. 7.99 *(978-1-4867-1308-0(4)*, 2a86569b-90ae-4f37-9bb5-15c4aa1808ff) Flowerpot Pr.
—Ned in Bed & Fun at the Park. Atkins, Jill. 2019. (Early Bird Readers — Pink (Early Bird Stories (tm)) Ser.). (ENG.). 32p. (J). (gr. -1-2). 27.99 *(978-1-5415-4160-3(X)*, Lerner Pubns.) Lerner Publishing Group.
Wray, Zoe & Fox, Christyan. Living in Space. Daynes, Katie. 2006. (Beginners Nature: Level 2 Ser.). 32p. (J). (gr. 1-3). 4.99 *(978-0-7945-1339-9(5)*, Usborne) EDC Publishing.
Wray, Zoe & Kushii, Tetsuo. Dinosaurs. Turnbull, Stephanie. 2006. (Beginners Nature: Level 2 Ser.). 32p. (J). (gr. 1-3). 4.99 *(978-0-7945-1334-4(4)*, Usborne) EDC Publishing.
Wray, Zoe, jt. illus. see Donaera, Patrizia.
Wray, Zoe, jt. illus. see Kushii, Tetsuo.
Wreford, Polly, photos by. Baking with Kids. Collister, Linda. 2006. (ENG., 128p. (J). (gr. 3-7). *(978-1-84597-220-2(1))* Ryland Peters & Small.
—Christmas Crafting with Kids. Woram, Catherine. 2011. (ENG., 128p. pap. *(978-1-84975-141-4(2))* Ryland Peters & Small.
—Gardening with Kids. Cox, Martyn & Woram, Catherine. 2008. (ENG., 128p. *(978-1-84597-590-6(1)*, CICO Books) Ryland Peters & Small.
Wren, Jenny. In the Jungle. 2017. (First Explorers Ser.). (ENG.). 10p. (J). (— 1). bds. 8.95 *(978-1-4549-2656-6(2))* Sterling Publishing Co., Inc.
—Night Animals. 2017. (First Explorers Ser.). (ENG.). 10p. (J). (— 1). bds. 8.95 *(978-1-4549-2657-3(0))* Sterling Publishing Co., Inc.
—Now You Are One: Keepsake Greeting Card Board Book. Birdsong, Minnie. Cottage Door Press, ed. ed. 2017. (Little Bird Greetings Ser.). (ENG.). 8p. (J). (gr. -1-k). bds. 6.99 *(978-1-68052-206-8(X)*, 1000471) Cottage Door Pr.
—Princess Snow & the Unicorn. 2017. (ENG.). 24p. (J). 9.99 *(978-1-78810-551-4(6))* Igloo Bks. GBR. Dist: Simon & Schuster, Inc.
—We See a Cloud: Band 11/Lime (Collins Big Cat) Crebbin, June et al. 2015. (Collins Big Cat Ser.). (ENG.). 32p. (J). (gr. 2-2). pap. 9.95 *(978-0-00-759125-1(X))* HarperCollins Pubs. Ltd. GBR. Dist: Independent Pubs. Group.
—Wilderness: An Interactive Atlas of Animals. Pang, Hannah. 2016. (ENG.). 28p. (J). (gr. 2-6). 22.99 *(978-1-944530-03-7(7)*, 360 Degrees) Tiger Tales.
Wrenn, Charles. The Guns of Europe. Altsheler, Joseph A. (World War I Ser.: Vol. 1). (J). reprint ed. 2010. 338p. (gr. 4-7). 36.76 *(978-1-164-35775-9(1))*; 2010. 338p. (gr. 4-7). pap. 24.76 *(978-1-163-97980-8(5))*; 2008. 336p. 45.95 *(978-0-548-98692-9(4))*; 2007. 340p. per. 30.95 *(978-0-548-66038-6(7))* Kessinger Publishing, LLC.
—The Hosts of the Air: The Story of a Quest in the Great War. Altsheler, Joseph A. (World War I Ser.: Vol. 2). (J). reprint ed. 2010. 346p. (gr. 4-7). 37.56 *(978-1-164-36346-0(8))*; 2010. 346p. (gr. 4-7). pap. 25.56 *(978-1-163-98051-4(X))*; 2008. 344p. 46.95 *(978-0-548-98763-6(7))*; 2007. 348p. per. 31.95 *(978-0-548-65961-8(3))* Kessinger Publishing, LLC.
Wrenn, Charles L. The Great Sioux Trail: A Story of Mountain & Plain. Altsheler, Joseph A. 2009. 258p. (YA). pap. *(978-1-4099-7085-9(X))* Dodo Pr.
—The Sun of Quebec: A Story of a Great Crisis. Altsheler, Joseph A. (French & Indian War Ser.: Vol. 6). 356p. (J). reprint ed. 2010. (gr. 4-7). pap. 25.56 *(978-1-163-19471-3(9))*; 2008. 46.95 *(978-1-4366-7287-0(2))*; 2007. per. 31.95 *(978-1-4325-9779-5(5))* Kessinger Publishing, LLC.
—The Tree of Appomattox: A Story of the Civil War's Close. Altsheler, Joseph A. (Civil War Ser.: Vol. 8). 332p. (J). reprint ed. 2011. (gr. 4-7). 45.95 *(978-1-169-88135-8(1))*; 2010. (gr. 4-7). 36.76 *(978-1-163-21361-2(6))*; 2010. (gr. 4-7). pap. 24.76 *(978-1-162-78752-7(X))*; 2005. 45.95 *(978-1-4326-1333-4(2))* Kessinger Publishing, LLC.
Wrenn, Tom. The Clever Monkey Rides Again. 2007. (Story Cove Ser.). (ENG.). 32p. (J). (gr. -1-3). pap. 3.95 *(978-0-87483-828-2(2))* August Hse. Pubs., Inc.
—The Drum: A Folktale from India. Cleveland, Rob. 2006. (Story Cove Ser.). (ENG.). 32p. (J). (gr. -1-3). pap. 4.95 *(978-0-87483-802-2(9))* August Hse. Pubs., Inc.
—Juan Bobo Sends the Pig to Mass. Acevedo, Ari. 2008. (Story Cove Ser.). (SPA & ENG.). 24p. (J). (gr. -1-3). pap. 4.95 *(978-0-87483-883-1(5))* August Hse. Pubs., Inc.
—The Magic Pot: Story Cove. DeSpain, Pleasant. 2007. (Story Cove Ser.). (ENG.). 32p. (J). (gr. -1-3). pap. 3.95 *(978-0-87483-827-5(4))* August Hse. Pubs., Inc.
—The Stolen Smell. Hamilton, Martha & Weiss, Mitch. 2007. (Story Cove Ser.). (ENG.). 32p. (J). (gr. -1-3). 4.95 *(978-0-87483-838-1(X))* August Hse. Pubs., Inc.
—A Tale of Two Frogs. Hamilton, Martha & Weiss, Mitch. 2006. (Story Cove Ser.). (ENG.). 32p. (J). (gr. -1-3). pap. 4.95 *(978-0-87483-812-1(6))* August Hse. Pubs., Inc.
—The Well of Truth: A Folktale from Egypt. Hamilton, Martha & Weiss, Mitch. 2008. (Story Cove Ser.). (ENG.). 32p. (J). (gr. -1-3). pap. 4.95 *(978-0-87483-880-0(0))* August Hse. Pubs., Inc.
—Why Koala Has a Stumpy Tail. Hamilton, Martha & Weiss, Mitch. 2007. (Story Cove Ser.). (ENG.). 24p. (J). (gr. -1-3). pap. 4.95 *(978-0-87483-879-4(7))* August Hse. Pubs., Inc.
Wright, Alex. Birnbaum's Walt Disney World. Birnbaum Travel Guides Staff. Lefkon, Wendy et al, eds. rev. ed. 2007. (ENG.). 272p. (J). (gr. -1-17). pap. 16.95 *(978-1-4231-0392-9(0)*, Disney Editions) Disney Pr.
—Disney Cruise Line 2008. Safro, Jill, ed. rev. ed. 2007. (ENG.). 224p. (gr. -1-17). pap. 13.95 *(978-1-4231-0389-9(0)*, Disney Editions) Disney Pr.
Wright, Alison. Joey's Pets: I'll Take the Zoo. Croskey II, Joseph Perry & Ellwood, Kathleen Marie, eds. 2019. (ENG.). 36p. (J). pap. 11.17 *(978-1-7977-4443-8(7))* Independently Published.
Wright, Alison H. Uniquely you. Lazurek, Michelle S. 2018. pap. 9.99 *(978-1-946638-70-0(6))* Elk Lake Publishing, Inc.
—Uniquely You. Lazurek, Michelle S. 2018. pap. 9.99 *(978-1-946638-69-4(2))* Elk Lake Publishing, Inc.
Wright, Alson. God Made Us Special. Wells, Sharon D. 2004. 20p. pap. 19.99 *(978-1-4120-3166-0(4))* Trafford Publishing.
Wright, Anna. A Tower of Giraffes: Animal Bunches. Wright, Anna. 2015. (ENG.). 32p. (J). (gr. -1-2). lib. bdg. 17.95 *(978-1-58089-707-5(X))* Charlesbridge Publishing, Inc.
Wright, Annabel. The Lion Who Stole My Arm. Davies, Nicola. 2014. (Heroes of the Wild Ser.). (ENG.). 96p. (J). (gr. 2-5). 14.99 *(978-0-7636-6620-0(3))* Candlewick Pr.
—Manatee Rescue. Davies, Nicola. 2016. (Heroes of the Wild Ser.). (ENG.). 112p. (J). (gr. 2-5). 14.99 *(978-0-7636-7830-2(9))* Candlewick Pr.
Wright, Bambi. Alligators Don't Peep: The Adventures of Ellen & Eric. Huffman, Dayle. 2018. (ENG.). 26p. (J). (gr. k-4). pap. 9.95 *(978-0-692-06796-3(5))* Grateful Abundance Publishing.
Wright, Blanche Fisher. The Real Mother Goose. 2017. (J). pap. *(978-1-5124-2602-1(4))*; (ENG.). 214p. (gr. -1-4). E-Book 19.99 *(978-1-5124-2603-8(2)*, First Avenue Editions); (ENG.). 214p. (gr. -1-4). E-Book 19.99 *(978-1-5124-6673-7(5)*, 9781512466737, First Avenue Editions) Lerner Publishing Group.
—Real Mother Goose Clock Book. 22p. (J). (gr. -1-2). 6.95 *(978-1-56288-095-8(0))* Checkerboard Pr., Inc.
—The Real Mother Goose Coloring Book. Gache, Stephen Vance. 2009. (Dover Classic Stories Coloring Book Ser.). (ENG.). 32p. (J). (gr. k-5). pap. 3.99 *(978-0-486-46991-1(3))* Dover Pubns., Inc.
Wright, Bradley. A Mindfulness Planner: For Tweens & Teens. Wright, Angelique. 2020. (Version 1 Ser.: Vol. 1). (ENG.). 206p. (J). pap. 11.00 ***(978-1-6741-1358-6(7))*** Independently Published.
Wright, Brent A. Hank the Honking Goose Learns to Listen. Keith, Patty J., photos by. Keith, Patty J. 2013. 36p. pap. 12.95 *(978-0-9893303-1-2(1))* Patty's Blooming Words.
Wright, Carol. It Came from Outer Space. Bradman, Tony. 2004. 25p. (J). *(978-1-85269-336-7(3))*; *(978-1-85269-393-0(2))* Mantra Lingua.
Wright, Chris. Nature Boy Nature Strikes Back. Patterson, Eric. 2008. 108p. pap. 6.95 *(978-1-935105-15-2(9))* Avid Readers Publishing Group.
Wright, Christopher. Carl Nose the Truth. Patterson, Eric. 2007. 104p. (J). pap. 6.95 *(978-0-9797106-6-7(9))* Avid Readers Publishing Group.
—Have You Seen My Pencil? Poems & Musings. Brock, Justin. 2007. (J). pap. *(978-0-9796210-0-0(3))* OPUS II Bks.
—Nature Boy. Patterson, Eric. 2007. 112p. (J). pap. 6.95 *(978-0-9797106-0-5(X))* Avid Readers Publishing Group.
Wright, Cornelius Van & Hu, Ying-Hwa. Baby Flo: Florence Mills Lights up the Stage, 1 vol. Schroeder, Alan. 2019. (ENG.). 1p. (J). (gr. 1-6). pap. 11.95 ***(978-1-64379-086-2(2)***, ac8f54b6-73af-49a1-8708-39e1768b3146) Lee & Low Bks., Inc.
Wright, Cornelius Van, jt. illus. see Hu, Ying-Hwa.
Wright, David, jt. illus. see Kushii, Tetsuo.
Wright, Diane Beem. An Earth Child's Book of the Year. Camden, Marian Louise. 2011. 32p. pap. *(978-1-77067-742-5(9))* FriesenPress.
—An Earth Child's Book of Verse. Camden, Marian Louise. 2011. 32p. pap. *(978-1-77067-695-4(3))* FriesenPress.
Wright, Douglas. La Funcion de Teatro. Lopez, Horacio. 2003. (SPA.). 38p. (J). (gr. k-3). pap. 8.95 *(978-950-511-622-5(5))* Santillana USA Publishing Co., Inc.
Wright, Freire. Noah's Ark. Hayward, Linda. 2018. (Step into Reading Ser.). (ENG.). 32p. (J). (gr. -1-1). pap. 4.99 *(978-0-394-88716-6(6)*, Random Hse. Bks. for Young Readers) Random Hse. Children's Bks.
Wright, Gordy. Strange but True: 10 of the World's Greatest Mysteries Explained. Hulick, Kathryn. ed. 2019. (ENG.). 128p. (J). (gr. 5-9). ***(978-1-78603-784-8(X))*** Frances Lincoln Childrens Bks.
Wright, Hawley. I Miss You! A Military Kid's Book about Deployment, Vol. Andrews, Beth. 2007. (ENG.). 56p. (-k). per. 12.99 *(978-1-59102-534-4(6))* Prometheus Bks., Pubs.
Wright, Jay. Anorak Vol. 3: The Happy Mag for Kids. Anorak Press Staff. 2013. (ENG.). 68p. (J). pap. 9.99 *(978-1-4236-3389-1(X)*, Anorak Pr.) Gibbs Smith, Publisher.
Wright, Johanna. Clover Twig & the Perilous Path. Umansky, Kaye. 2013. (ENG.). 272p. (J). (gr. 3-7). pap. 15.99 *(978-1-250-02727-6(6)*, 9781250027276) Square Fish.
—Everything's Changed. Sternberg, Julie. (Top-Secret Diary of Celie Valentine Ser.). (ENG.). (J). (gr. 3-7). 2020. 176p. pap. 9.99 *(978-1-68437-706-0(4))*; 2017. 160p. 16.95 *(978-1-62979-672-7(7))* Boyds Mills Pr.
—Friendship Over. Sternberg, Julie. (Top-Secret Diary of Celie Valentine Ser.). (ENG.). 160p. (J). (gr. 3-7). 2014. 15.95 *(978-1-59078-993-3(8))*; Bk. 1. 2015. pap. 9.99 *(978-1-62979-405-1(8))* Boyds Mills Pr.
—Keep a Pocket in Your Poem: Classic Poems & Playful Parodies. Lewis, J. Patrick. 2017. (ENG.). 32p. (J). (gr. k-4). 17.95 *(978-1-59078-921-6(0)*, Wordsong) Boyds Mills Pr.
—Secrets Out! Sternberg, Julie. (Top-Secret Diary of Celie Valentine Ser.). 176p. (J). (gr. 3-7). 2018. pap. 9.99 *(978-1-62979-891-2(6))*; Bk. 2. 2015. (ENG.). 15.95 *(978-1-62091-777-0(7))* Boyds Mills Pr.
Wright, Johanna. Bunnies on Ice. Wright, Johanna. 2013. (ENG.). 32p. (J). (gr. -1-1). 16.99 *(978-1-59643-404-2(X)*, 9781596434042) Roaring Brook Pr.
Wright, John R. Steps to Liberty. Marsh, Laura F. 2007. 32p. (J). 17.95 *(978-0-615-16563-9(X))* Junior League of Central Westchester.
Wright, Jonathan. Wild Eggs: A Tale of Arctic Egg Collecting, 1 vol. Napayok-Short, Suzie. 2018. (ENG.). 36p. (J). (gr. k-2). 11.95 *(978-1-77227-149-2(7))* Inhabit Media Inc. CAN. Dist: Consortium Bk. Sales & Distribution.
Wright Jr, Robert. Mummy in the Museum. Wright Jr, Robert. 2019. (ENG.). 78p. (J). pap. 5.99 *(978-1-0929-7114-0(9))* Independently Published.
Wright, Lana. Do Pebbles Eat Chili? & Other Outlandish Poems: Featuring the Cast of the You Rock! Group! Jay. 2019. (ENG.). 40p. (J). pap. 11.95 ***(978-0-578-59464-4(1))*** New Paige Pr., LLC.
Wright, Louise. Awesome Women Activity Book. Regan, Lisa. 2020. (ENG.). 48p. (J). pap. 6.99 *(978-1-83857-629-5(0)*, 62789a73-dba5-480c-bede-8e6788156d0a) Arcturus Publishing GBR. Dist: Baker & Taylor Publisher Services (BTPS).
—101 Awesome Women Who Changed Our World. Adams, Julia. 2018. (101 Awesome Women Ser.). (ENG.). 128p. (J). pap. 9.99 *(978-1-78888-377-1(2)*, e24f15d7-282a-4285-bac4-22290a617e8f) Arcturus Publishing GBR. Dist: Baker & Taylor Publisher Services (BTPS).
Wright, Louise & Muñoz, Isabel. World-Changing Women: 101 Super Scientists. Adams, Julia & Philip, Claire. 2020. (101 Awesome Women Ser.). (ENG.). 128p. (J). pap. 9.99 *(978-1-78950-594-8(1)*, 5a38ece8-e420-4cbb-8ded-23a9b5298028) Arcturus Publishing GBR. Dist: Baker & Taylor Publisher Services (BTPS).
Wright, Lucy. Alices Journey Beyond Moon, 1 vol. Carter, R. J. 2004. (ENG.). 98p. *(978-1-903889-76-3(6))* Telos Publishing, Ltd. GBR. Dist: Fitzhenry & Whiteside, Ltd.
—Alice's Journey Beyond the Moon, 1 vol. Carter, R J. ltd. num. ed. (ENG.). 98p. 59.95 *(978-1-903889-77-0(4))* Telos Publishing, Ltd. GBR. Dist: Fitzhenry & Whiteside, Ltd.
Wright, Marguerite. A'Marie the Azar. Yisrael, Naamee. Editing Services, Apple of His Eye, ed. 2019. (ENG.). 48p. (J). pap. 19.99 *(978-1-7986-9342-1(9))* Independently Published.
Wright, Michael. Jake Starts School. Wright, Michael. 2010. (ENG.). 48p. (J). (gr. -1-1). 21.19 *(978-0-312-60884-2(5)*, 900065180) Square Fish.
Wright, Mike. Jokelopedia: The Biggest, Best, Silliest, Dumbest Joke Book Ever! Blank, Eva et al. 3rd ed. 2016. (ENG.). 288p. (J). (gr. 2-7). pap. 9.95 *(978-0-7611-8997-8(1)*, 18997) Workman Publishing Co., Inc.
—Li'l Book O' Big Laughs. 2004. 96p. (J). pap. *(978-0-439-68983-0(X))* Scholastic, Inc.
Wright, Nathan T. Harriet Wants to Vote. Wright, Karla. 2020. (ENG.). 26p. (J). pap. 15.00 ***(978-1-6602-3297-0(X))*** Independently Published.
Wright, Patricia. West African Folk Tales. Vernon-Jackson, Hugh. 2003. (African American Ser.). (ENG.). 144p. pap. 8.95 *(978-0-486-42764-5(1))* Dover Pubns., Inc.
Wright, Petrina. A Lizard Got into the Paint Pots. Pickering, Jill. 2003. (ENG.). 220p. (J). (gr. -1-3). 14.95 *(978-0-333-98858-9(2))* Macmillan Caribbean GBR. Dist: Interlink Publishing Group, Inc.
Wright, Robert. Monster in the Morning. McDonnell, Thomas. 2018. (ENG.). 38p. (J). (gr. k-3). pap. 10.95 *(978-0-9995330-9-3(6))* Primedia eLaunch LLC.
Wright, Robert A. Monster in the Morning. McDonnell, Tom. 2019. (ENG.). 38p. (J). (gr. k-2). 16.95 *(978-1-7326830-9-9(3))* Primedia eLaunch LLC.
Wright, Samantha. The Coronado Kid. Belkin, Dick. 2018. (ENG.). 26p. (J). 22.99 *(978-1-5456-5631-0(2))*; pap. 12.49 *(978-1-5456-5630-3(4))* Salem Author Services.
Wright, Sara Ann. Max Makes a Visit. Morimoto, Diana. 2011. 28p. pap. 24.95 *(978-1-4512-4545-5(9))* America Star Bks.
Wright, Sarah Jane. A Christmas Goodnight. Buck, Nola. 2011. (ENG.). 24p. (J). (gr. -1-k). 12.99 *(978-0-06-166491-5(X)*, Tegen, Katherine Bks) HarperCollins Pubs.
—I Heart You. Fleming, Meg. 2016. (ENG.). 40p. (J). (gr. -1-3). 17.99 *(978-1-4424-8895-3(6)*, Beach Lane Bks.) Beach Lane Bks.
—I Heart You. Fleming, Meg. 2019. (Classic Board Bks.). (ENG.). 36p. (J). (gr. -1-3). bds. 7.99 *(978-1-5344-5130-8(7)*, Little Simon) Little Simon.
—Lola Dutch. Wright, Kenneth. 2018. (Lola Dutch Ser.). 40p. (J). 17.99 *(978-1-68119-551-3(8)*, 900177320, Bloomsbury USA Childrens) Bloomsbury Publishing USA.
—Lola Dutch I Love You So Much. Wright, Kenneth. 2019. (Lola Dutch Ser.). 40p. (J). 17.99 *(978-1-5476-0117-2(5)*, 900199129, Bloomsbury Children's Bks.) Bloomsbury Publishing USA.
—Lola Dutch When I Grow Up. Wright, Kenneth. 2019. (Lola Dutch Ser.). 200p. (J). 17.99 *(978-1-68119-554-4(2)*, 900177318, Bloomsbury Children's Bks.) Bloomsbury Publishing USA.
—The Secrets of Eastcliff-By-the-Sea: The Story of Annaliese Easterling & Throckmorton, Her Simply Remarkable Sock Monkey. Beha, Eileen. 2015. (ENG.). 288p. (J). (gr. 3-7). pap. 8.99 *(978-1-4424-9841-9(2)*, Beach Lane Bks.) Beach Lane Bks.
Wright, Shannon. I'm Gonna Push Through! Wright, Jasmyn. 2020. (ENG.). 40p. (J). (gr. -1-3). 17.99 *(978-1-5344-3965-8(X)*, Atheneum Bks. for Young Readers) Simon & Schuster Children's Publishing.
—My Mommy Medicine. Danticat, Edwidge. 2019. (ENG.). 32p. (J). 17.99 *(978-1-250-14091-3(9)*, 900179769) Roaring Brook Pr.
Wright, Shannon, jt. illus. see West, June.
Wright Sisters Staff. Thank You. Warburton, Olivia. ed. 2004. (ENG.). 32p. 7.99 *(978-0-7459-5149-2(X))* Lion Hudson PLC GBR. Dist: Independent Pubs. Group.
Wright, Spencer. Little Ant A, 1 vol. Sanborn, Perry F. 2010. 20p. pap. 24.95 *(978-1-4489-6159-7(9))* PublishAmerica, Inc.
Wright, Tanner. Amy & Kate vs. the Frog. Palmer, Bobbie. 2020. (ENG.). 26p. (J). pap. 9.50 ***(978-1-7091-4046-4(1))*** Independently Published.
Wright, Wendy L. The Adventures of Giggles & Owen: Adventure Two - Pawsistance Pays Off. Terrill Holdman, Shirley. 2011. 46p. pap. 17.95 *(978-1-4575-0568-3(1))* Dog Ear Publishing, LLC.
Wrightson, Bernie. Secret of the Swamp Thing. Wein, Len. 2005. 232p. (YA). (gr. 7-18). pap. 9.99 *(978-1-4012-0798-4(7))* DC Comics.
Wrightson, Bernie & Lee, Pat. Marvel Knights Punisher by Golden, Sniegoski, & Wrightson: Purgatory. 2019. (ENG.). 200p. (YA). (gr. 8-17). pap. 24.99 *(978-1-302-91608-4(4))* Marvel Worldwide, Inc.
Wrike, Jessica. The Greener Pond. Blake, Nyron. 2019. (ENG.). 32p. (J). pap. 8.95 ***(978-0-578-52946-2(7))*** Blake, Nyron.
Written by Elli Matthews; Illustrated by. Surprising Katie on Halloween. Matthews, Elli. 2011. 24p. pap. 24.95 *(978-1-4560-7486-9(5))* America Star Bks.
Written by Shelia West; Illustrated by D. Porky Porcupine Tackles Football. West, Shelia. 2011. 20p. pap. 24.95 *(978-1-4560-5528-8(3))* America Star Bks.
Wroblewski, Nick. Hush Hush, Forest. Casanova, Mary. 2018. 40p. (J). (gr. -1). 16.95 *(978-0-8166-9425-9(7))* Univ. of Minnesota Pr.
—Wake up, Island. Casanova, Mary. 2016. (J). 40p. 14.95 *(978-0-8166-8935-4(0))*; pap. *(978-0-8166-8936-1(9))* Univ. of Minnesota Pr.
Wroth, Dean. Charles & David. Chamberlin, Kate. 2010. 32p. (J). pap. 9.95 *(978-0-944727-37-9(9))*; lib. bdg. 15.95 *(978-0-944727-36-2(0))* Jason & Nordic Pubs. (Turtle Bks.).
—Chef Philip Has Autism. Feuerbach, Jennifer. 2014. 32p. (J). pap. 10.49 *(978-0-944727-61-4(1)*, Turtle Bks.) Jason & Nordic Pubs.
—Two Hands to Hold. Castro, Anita. 2013. 32p. (J). pap. 10.49 *(978-0-944727-57-7(3))*; lib. bdg. 16.95 *(978-0-944727-58-4(1))* Jason & Nordic Pubs. (Turtle Bks.).
Wu, Aiden. A Body's Battle: The Immune System. Wu, Aiden. 2019. (ENG.). 26p. (J). (gr. -1-3). pap. 12.99 *(978-1-7926-7210-1(1))* Independently Published.
Wu, Annie. Star Wars: Join the Resistance Attack on Starkiller Base: Book 3. Acker, Ben & Blacker, Ben. 2018. (Join the Resistance Ser.). (ENG.). 208p. (J). (gr. 3-7). 12.99 *(978-1-368-02141-8(7)*, Disney Lucasfilm Press) Disney Publishing Worldwide.
—Star Wars: Lando's Luck. Ireland, Justina. 2018. (ENG.). 176p. (J). (gr. 3-7). 12.99 *(978-1-368-04150-8(7)*, Disney Lucasfilm Press) Disney Publishing Worldwide.
Wu, Donald. Dogerella. Boelts, Maribeth. 2008. (Step into Reading Ser.). (ENG.). 48p. (J). (gr. k-3). pap. 4.99 *(978-0-375-83393-9(5)*, Random Hse. Bks. for Young Readers) Random Hse. Children's Bks.
—A Dog's Life, 0 vols. Sherman, Caroline. 2012. (ENG.). 24p. (J). (gr. -1-2). 12.99 *(978-0-7614-6200-2(7)*, 9780761462002, Two Lions) Amazon Publishing.
—J Is for Jack-O'-Lantern: A Halloween Alphabet. Brennan-Nelson, Denise. 2009. (Holiday Ser.). (ENG.). 40p. (J). (gr. -1-3). 14.95 *(978-1-58536-443-5(6))* Sleeping Bear Pr.
—Shaggy Dogs, Waggy Dogs, 0 vols. Hubbell, Patricia. 2011. (ENG.). 32p. (J). (gr. -1-3). 17.99 *(978-0-7614-5957-6(X)*, 9780761459576, Two Lions) Amazon Publishing.
—She Sells Seashells & Other Tricky Tongue Twisters, 1 vol. Loewen, Nancy. 2010. (Ways to Say It Ser.). (ENG.). 24p.

(J). (gr. 3-5). lib. bdg. 28.65 *(978-1-4048-6273-9(0)*, Picture Window Bks.) Capstone.

—You're Toast & Other Metaphors We Adore, 1 vol. Loewen, Nancy. (Ways to Say It Ser.). (ENG.). 24p. (J). (gr. 3-5). 2011. pap. 7.49 *(978-1-4048-6717-8(1))*; 2010. lib. bdg. 28.65 *(978-1-4048-6270-8(6))* Capstone. (Picture Window Bks.).

Wu, Helen. How to Get on the Naughty List. Rock, Nic. 2016. (ENG.). (J). pap. *(978-976-8205-47-6(4))* Author-Pubs. (miscellaneous).

Wu, Helen H. Chevy, the Perfect Pet. Patrick, Jill O. 2018. (ENG.). 62p. (J). 20.95 *(978-1-947656-61-1(9))* Butterfly Typeface, The.

Wu, Julie. Go to Sleep, Hide & Seek. Crowe, Ellie. 2009. 10p. (J). bds. 11.95 *(978-1-59700-759-7(5))* Island Heritage Publishing.

Wu, Junyi. Beatrix Potter, Scientist. Metcalf, Lindsay H. 2020. (She Made History Ser.). 32p. (J). (gr. -1-3). 16.99 ***(978-0-8075-5175-2(9)***, 0807551759) Whitman, Albert & Co.

Wu, Junyi. Scary Stories for Young Foxes. Heidicker, Christian McKay. 2019. (ENG.). 320p. (J). 16.99 *(978-1-250-18142-8(9)*, 900190382, Holt, Henry & Co. Bks. For Young Readers) Holt, Henry & Co.

Wu, Junyi. Two Bicycles in Beijing. Robeson, Teresa. 2020. (ENG.). 32p. (J). (gr. -1-3). 16.99 ***(978-0-8075-0764-3(4)***, 0807507644) Whitman, Albert & Co.

Wu, Katy. Born Curious: 20 Girls Who Grew up to Be Awesome Scientists. Freeman, Martha. 2020. (ENG.). 128p. (J). (gr. 2-7). 19.99 *(978-1-5344-2153-0(X)*, Simon & Schuster Bks. For Young Readers) Simon & Schuster Bks. For Young Readers.

—Dumpling Dreams: How Joyce Chen Brought the Dumpling from Beijing to Cambridge. Clickard, Carrie. 2017. (ENG.). 48p. (J). (gr. -1-3). 17.99 *(978-1-4814-6707-0(7)*, Simon & Schuster Bks. For Young Readers) Simon & Schuster Bks. For Young Readers.

—Grace Hopper: Queen of Computer Code. Wallmark, Laurie. 2017. (People Who Shaped Our World Ser.: 1). 48p. (J). (gr. k). 16.95 *(978-1-4549-2000-7(9))* Sterling Publishing Co., Inc.

—Hedy Lamarr's Double Life: Hollywood Legend & Brilliant Inventor. Wallmark, Laurie. 2019. (People Who Shaped Our World Ser.: 4). 48p. (J). (gr. k). 16.95 *(978-1-4549-2691-7(0))* Sterling Publishing Co., Inc.

—The Little Red Stroller. Furst, Joshua. 2019. 40p. (J). (gr. -1-3). 17.99 *(978-0-7352-2880-1(9)*, Dial Bks) Penguin Young Readers Group.

—Sylvia's Bookshop: The Story of Paris's Beloved Bookstore & Its Founder (As Told by the Bookstore Itself!) Burleigh, Robert. 2018. (ENG.). 32p. (J). (gr. -1-3). 17.99 *(978-1-4814-7245-6(3)*, Simon & Schuster/Paula Wiseman Bks.) Simon & Schuster/Paula Wiseman Bks.

Wu, Leslie. Butterfly Tree, 1 vol. Markle, Sandra. 2011. (ENG.). 32p. (J). (gr. -1-3). 16.95 *(978-1-56145-539-3(3))* Peachtree Publishing Co. Inc.

—The Very Best Daddy of All. Bauer, Marion Dane. 2011. (Classic Board Bks.). (ENG.). 34p. (J). (gr. -1 — 1). bds. 7.99 *(978-1-4169-8517-4(4)*, Little Simon) Little Simon.

—The Very Best Daddy of All. Bauer, Marion Dane. 2007. (ENG.). 40p. (J). (gr. -1-3). 6.99 *(978-1-4169-2736-5(0)*, Simon & Schuster Bks. For Young Readers) Simon & Schuster Bks. For Young Readers.

Wu, Mike. Oona Finds an Egg. Griffin, Adele. 2016. (Oodlethunks Ser.: 1). (ENG.). 160p. (J). (gr. 3-7). 12.99 *(978-0-545-73279-6(4)*, Scholastic Pr.) Scholastic, Inc.

—Steg-O-Normous. Griffin, Adele. 2016. (Oodlethunks Ser.: 2). (ENG.). 160p. (J). (gr. 3-7). 12.99 *(978-0-545-73284-0(0)*, Scholastic Pr.) Scholastic, Inc.

—Welcome to Camp Woggle. Griffin, Adele. 2017. (Oodlethunks Ser.: 3). (ENG.). 144p. (J). (gr. 3-7). 12.99 *(978-0-545-73291-8(3)*, Scholastic Pr.) Scholastic, Inc.

Wu, Mike. Ellie. Wu, Mike. 2015. 40p. (J). (gr. -1-k). 16.99 *(978-1-4847-1239-9(0))* Disney Publishing Worldwide.

—Ellie in Concert. Wu, Mike. 2017. (ENG.). 40p. (J). (gr. -1-k). 16.99 *(978-1-4847-1238-2(2))* Hyperion Bks. for Children.

—Ellie Makes a Friend. Wu, Mike. 2020. 40p. (J). (gr. -1-k). 16.99 *(978-1-368-01000-9(8))* Hyperion Bks. for Children.

—Henri's Hats: Pixar Animation Studios Artist Showcase. Wu, Mike. 2018. (Artist Showcase Ser.). (ENG.). 48p. (J). (gr. -1-k). 16.99 *(978-1-4847-0903-0(9))* Disney Pr.

WU, Stacie, jt. illus. see Lee, Hanlim.

Wu, Stacie, jt. illus. see Lee, Han.

Wu, Vivien. Cars 3 Little Golden Book (Disney/Pixar Cars 3) Saxon, Victoria. 2017. (Little Golden Book Ser.). (ENG.). 24p. (J). (-k). 4.99 *(978-0-7364-3730-1(4)*, Golden/Disney) Random Hse. Children's Bks.

Wu, Vivien. A Guide to the Universe. Sutherland, Kari & L'Engle, Madeleine. 2018. 192p. (J). ***(978-1-74299-442-0(3))*** Disney Publishing Worldwide.

Wu, Vivien. Purrmaids - A Star Purr-Formance. Bardhan-Quallen, Sudipta. 2019. (Purrmaids Ser.: 5). (ENG.). 96p. (J). (gr. 1-4). 12.99 *(978-0-525-64635-8(3)*, Random Hse. Bks. for Young Readers) Random Hse. Children's Bks.

—Purrmaids #5: a Star Purr-Formance. Bardhan-Quallen, Sudipta. 2019. (Purrmaids Ser.: 5). (ENG.). 96p. (J). (gr. 1-4). 4.99 *(978-0-525-64634-1(5)*, Random Hse. Bks. for Young Readers) Random Hse. Children's Bks.

—Tutu Terrific! (Disney Palace Pets: Whisker Haven Tales) RH Disney Staff. 2016. (Little Golden Book Ser.). (ENG.). 24p. (J). (-k). 4.99 *(978-0-7364-3504-8(2)*, Golden/Disney) Random Hse. Children's Bks.

—Zootopia. Giuliani, Alfred. 2016. (J). *(978-1-4806-9720-1(6)*, Golden Bks.) Random Hse. Children's Bks.

Wu, Yi-Hsaun. Sing & Slide: Old MacDonald Had a Farm. 2017. (Sing & Slide Ser.). (ENG.). 12p. (J). (gr. -1 — 1). bds. 12.99 *(978-1-68412-123-6(X)*, Silver Dolphin Bks.) Printers Row Publishing Group.

—Sing & Slide: the Itsy Bitsy Spider. 2017. (Sing & Slide Ser.). (ENG.). 12p. (J). (gr. -1 — 1). bds. 12.99 *(978-1-68412-124-3(8)*, Silver Dolphin Bks.) Printers Row Publishing Group.

—Sing & Slide: the Wheels on the Bus. 2017. (Sing & Slide Ser.). (ENG.). 12p. (J). (gr. -1 — 1). bds. 12.99 *(978-1-68412-125-0(6)*, Silver Dolphin Bks.) Printers Row Publishing Group.

Wu, Yi-Hsuan. Busy Noisy Ocean. Crowe, Carmen. Cottage Door Press, ed. 2020. (Interactive Early Bird Children's Song Book with 10 Sing-Along Tunes Ser.). (ENG.). 10p. (J). (gr. -1-1). bds. 18.99 ***(978-1-68052-895-2(4)***, 1006120) Cottage Door Pr.

Wu, Yi-Hsuan. Happy & Hoppy: Easter Basket Flip-A-Flap Board Book. Redd, R. I. Cottage Door Press, ed. 2017. (Flip a Flap Ser.). (ENG.). 10p. (J). (gr. -1-k). bds. 8.99 *(978-1-68052-287-7(6)*, 1002720) Cottage Door Pr.

—Laugh & Sing: Silly Animal Songs. Wing, Scarlett. Cottage Door Press, ed. 2019. (Early Bird Song Bks.). (ENG.). 10p. (J). (gr. -1-2). bds. 18.99 *(978-1-68052-709-4(6)*, 1004420) Cottage Door Pr.

—Mommy's Big Helper: Touch & Feel Multi Activity Book. Downy, Rufus. Cottage Door Press, ed. 2018. (Early Bird Learning Ser.). (ENG.). 10p. (J). (gr. -1-k). bds. 9.99 *(978-1-68052-242-6(6)*, 1002280) Cottage Door Pr.

—My Peekaboo Things That Go. Marx, Jonny. 2019. (ENG.). 12p. (J). (gr. 2-k). bds. 10.99 *(978-1-68010-593-3(0))* Tiger Tales.

—My Very First Christmas. Amiot, Karine-Marie. 2018. (ENG.). 16p. (J). (gr. -1-k). bds. 8.99 *(978-1-64060-107-9(4))* Paraclete Pr., Inc.

—Sing & Slide: Twinkle Twinkle Little Star. Editors of Silver Dolphin Books. 2019. (Sing & Slide Ser.). (ENG.). 12p. (J). (gr. -1-k). bds. 12.99 *(978-1-68412-667-5(3)*, Silver Dolphin Bks.) Printers Row Publishing Group.

Wu, Yi-Hsuan. Who Said Boo? 2020. (Who Said? Ser.). (ENG.). 10p. (J). (— 1). bds. 8.99 ***(978-1-64517-363-2(1)***, Silver Dolphin Bks.) Printers Row Publishing Group.

Wu, Yi-Hsuan. Who Said Moo? 2020. (Who Said? Ser.). (ENG.). 10p. (J). (— 1). bds. 8.99 *(978-1-68412-981-2(8)*, Silver Dolphin Bks.) Printers Row Publishing Group.

Wucinich, Warren. Courtney Crumrin Vol. 1 Vol. 1: The Night Things. Naifeh, Ted. 2017. (Courtney Crumrin Ser.: 1). (ENG.). 136p. (J). pap. 10.00 *(978-1-62010-419-4(9)*, 9781620104194, Lion Forge) Oni Pr., Inc.

—Courtney Crumrin Vol. 4: Monstrous Holiday. Naifeh, Ted. 2019. (Courtney Crumrin Ser.: 4). (ENG.). 136p. (YA). pap. 12.99 *(978-1-62010-569-6(1)*, Lion Forge) Oni Pr., Inc.

—Courtney Crumrin Vol. 5. Naifeh, Ted. 2019. (Courtney Crumrin Ser.: 5). (ENG.). 144p. (J). pap. 12.99 *(978-1-62010-640-2(X)*, Lion Forge) Oni Pr., Inc.

—Invader ZIM Vol. 3, Vol. 3. Trueheart, Eric & Vasquez, Jhonen. 2016. (Invader ZIM Ser.: 3). (ENG.). 136p. (J). pap. 19.99 *(978-1-62010-371-5(0)*, 9781620103715, Lion Forge) Oni Pr., Inc.

Wucinich, Warren & Stresing, Fred C. Invader ZIM Vol. 9. Logan, Sam. 2020. (Invader ZIM Ser.: 9). (ENG.). 128p. (J). pap. 19.99 *(978-1-62010-692-1(2)*, Lion Forge) Oni Pr., Inc.

Wucinich, Warren, jt. illus. see Naifeh, Ted.

Wucinich, Warren, jt. illus. see Wagner, Justin.

Wujcik, Holly. Sam & Alex; the Tale of Two Searching Hearts. Butler, Thom. 2019. (ENG.). 104p. (J). pap. 7.95 ***(978-1-6716-7661-9(0))*** Independently Published.

Wulfekotte, Dana. Cilla Lee-Jenkins: Future Author Extraordinaire. Tan, Susan. 2018. (Cilla Lee-Jenkins Ser.: 1). (ENG.). 272p. (J). pap. 7.99 *(978-1-250-14400-3(0)*, 900160969) Square Fish.

—Cilla Lee-Jenkins: the Epic Story. Tan, Susan. 2019. (Cilla Lee-Jenkins Ser.: 3). (ENG.). 272p. (J). 16.99 *(978-1-250-18363-7(4)*, 900190936) Roaring Brook Pr.

—Cilla Lee-Jenkins: the Epic Story. Tan, Susan. 2020. (Cilla Lee-Jenkins Ser.: 3). (ENG.). 272p. (J). pap. 7.99 *(978-1-250-23342-4(9)*, 900190937) Square Fish.

—Cilla Lee-Jenkins: This Book Is a Classic. Tan, Susan. 2018. (Cilla Lee-Jenkins Ser.: 2). (ENG.). 272p. (J). 16.99 *(978-1-62672-553-9(5)*, 900160971) Roaring Brook Pr.

—Cilla Lee-Jenkins: This Book Is a Classic. Tan, Susan. 2019. (Cilla Lee-Jenkins Ser.: 2). (ENG.). 288p. (J). pap. 7.99 *(978-1-250-29435-7(5)*, 900160972) Square Fish.

—One Snowy Morning. Tseng, Kevin. 2019. (ENG.). 32p. (J). (-k). 16.99 *(978-0-7352-3041-5(2)*, Dial Bks) Penguin Young Readers Group.

—The Remember Balloons. Oliveros, Jessie. 2018. (ENG.). 48p. (J). (gr. k-4). 18.99 *(978-1-4814-8915-7(1)*, Simon & Schuster Bks. For Young Readers) Simon & Schuster Bks. For Young Readers.

Wulfekotte, Dana. Rabbit & Possum. Wulfekotte, Dana. 2018. (ENG.). 40p. (J). (gr. -1-3). 17.99 *(978-0-06-245581-9(8)*, Greenwillow Bks.) HarperCollins Pubs.

Wulfing, Amy J. A Train Ride to Grandma's (with NO Chocolate Donut!) Shortle, Stacy & Mooney, Dean J. M. 2009. 48p. (J). 18.95 *(978-0-9759850-5-2(1))* Maple Leaf Ctr.

—You Would Be Surprised. Baretz, Susie. 2010. (ENG.). 32p. (J). 16.95 *(978-0-9759850-9-0(4))* Maple Leaf Ctr.

Wulfing, Sulamith. Fairy Tales. 2004. 58p. (gr. -1-3). 9.95 *(978-1-885394-40-8(3))* Bluestar Communications Corp.

Wummer, Amy. Adventure Annie Goes to Kindergarten. Buzzeo, Toni. 2013. 32p. (J). (gr. -1-k). mass mkt. 7.99 *(978-0-14-242695-1(4)*, Puffin Books) Penguin Young Readers Group.

—The Bay School Blogger: Spread of Ideas. Walker, Nan. 2008. (Social Studies Connects ® Ser.). (ENG.). 32p. (J). (gr. 1-3). pap. 5.95 *(978-1-57565-258-0(7))* Astra Publishing Hse.

—The Case of the Amazing Zelda, Vol. 4. Montgomery, Lewis B. 2009. (Milo & Jazz Mysteries Ser.). 96p. (J). (gr. k-3). 22.60 *(978-1-57565-298-6(6))* Astra Publishing Hse.

—The Case of the Amazing Zelda. Montgomery, Lewis B. 2012. (Milo & Jazz Mysteries Ser.: Vol. 4). (ENG.). (J). (gr. 2-4). pap. 20.95 incl. audio compact disk *(978-1-4301-1209-9(3))* Live Oak Media.

—The Case of the Amazing Zelda (Book 4) Montgomery, Lewis B. 2009. (Milo & Jazz Mysteries ® Ser.). (ENG.). 96p. (J). (gr. 2-5). pap. 6.95 *(978-1-57565-296-2(X)*, 9781575652962) Astra Publishing Hse.

—The Case of the Buried Bones. Montgomery, Lewis B. 2014. (Milo & Jazz Mysteries ® Ser.: 12). 112p. (J). (gr. 2-5). lib. bdg. 22.60 *(978-1-57565-640-3(X))* Astra Publishing Hse.

—The Case of the Crooked Campaign. Montgomery, Lewis B. 2012. (Milo & Jazz Mysteries ® Ser.: 9). (ENG.). 112p. (J). (gr. 2-5). lib. bdg. 22.60 *(978-1-57565-435-5(0))* Astra Publishing Hse.

—The Case of the Crooked Campaign (Book 9), No. 9. Montgomery, Lewis B. 2012. (Milo & Jazz Mysteries ® Ser.: 9). (ENG.). 112p. (J). (gr. 2-5). pap. 6.95 *(978-1-57565-436-2(9)*, 9781575654362) Astra Publishing Hse.

—The Case of the Diamonds in the Desk. Montgomery, Lewis B. 2012. (Milo & Jazz Mysteries Ser.). 96p. (J). (gr. 2-5). pap. 39.62 *(978-0-7613-9207-1(6))*; lib. bdg. 22.60 *(978-1-57565-392-1(3))* Astra Publishing Hse.

—The Case of the Diamonds in the Desk (Book 8), No. 8. Montgomery, Lewis B. 2012. (Milo & Jazz Mysteries ® Ser.). (ENG.). 96p. (J). (gr. 2-5). pap. 6.95 *(978-1-57565-391-4(5)*, 9781575653914) Astra Publishing Hse.

—The Case of the Haunted Haunted House, Vol. 3. Montgomery, Lewis B. 2009. (Milo & Jazz Mysteries Ser.). 96p. (J). (gr. k-3). 22.60 *(978-1-57565-297-9(8))* Astra Publishing Hse.

—The Case of the Haunted Haunted House. Montgomery, Lewis B. 2012. (Milo & Jazz Mysteries Ser.: Vol. 3). (ENG.). (J). (gr. 2-4). pap. 20.95 incl. audio compact disk *(978-1-4301-1206-8(9))* Live Oak Media.

—The Case of the Haunted Haunted House (Book 3), Vol. 3. Montgomery, Lewis B. 2009. (Milo & Jazz Mysteries ® Ser.). (ENG.). 96p. (J). (gr. 2-5). pap. 6.95 *(978-1-57565-295-5(1)*, 9781575652955) Astra Publishing Hse.

—The Case of the July 4th Jinx, 5. Montgomery, Lewis B. 2010. (Milo & Jazz Mysteries ® Ser.). (ENG.). 96p. (J). (gr. 2-5). lib. bdg. 22.65 *(978-1-57565-315-0(X)*, 9781575653150) Astra Publishing Hse.

—The Case of the July 4th Jinx (Book 5), No. 5. Montgomery, Lewis B. 2010. (Milo & Jazz Mysteries ® Ser.). (ENG.). 96p. (J). (gr. 2-5). pap. 6.95 *(978-1-57565-308-2(7)*, 9781575653082) Astra Publishing Hse.

—The Case of the Locked Box. Montgomery, Lewis B. 2013. (Milo & Jazz Mysteries Ser.: Vol. 11). (ENG.). 106p. (J). (gr. 2-4). lib. bdg. 22.60 *(978-1-57565-625-0(6))* Astra Publishing Hse.

—The Case of the Locked Box (Book 11), No. 11. Montgomery, Lewis B. 2013. (Milo & Jazz Mysteries ® Ser.: 11). (ENG.). 112p. (J). (gr. 2-5). pap. 6.95 *(978-1-57565-626-7(4)*, 9781575656267) Astra Publishing Hse.

—The Case of the Missing Moose. Montgomery, Lewis B. 2011. (Milo & Jazz Mysteries Ser.). 96p. (J). 22.60 *(978-1-57565-331-0(1))*; pap. 39.62 *(978-0-7613-7607-1(0))* Astra Publishing Hse.

—The Case of the Missing Moose (Book 6), No. 6. Montgomery, Lewis B. 2011. (Milo & Jazz Mysteries ® Ser.: No. 6). (ENG.). 96p. (J). (gr. 2-5). pap. 6.95 *(978-1-57565-322-8(2)*, 9781575653228) Astra Publishing Hse.

—The Case of the Poisoned Pig (Book 2), No. 2. Montgomery, Lewis B. 2009. (Milo & Jazz Mysteries ® Ser.). (ENG.). 96p. (J). (gr. 2-5). pap. 6.95 *(978-1-57565-286-3(2)*, 9781575652863) Astra Publishing Hse.

—The Case of the Purple Pool. Montgomery, Lewis B. 2011. (Milo & Jazz Mysteries Ser.). pap. 39.62 *(978-0-7613-8358-1(1))*;No. 7. 96p. (J). lib. bdg. 22.60 *(978-1-57565-343-3(5))* Astra Publishing Hse.

—The Case of the Purple Pool (Book 7), No. 7. Montgomery, Lewis B. 2011. (Milo & Jazz Mysteries ® Ser.). (ENG.). 96p. (J). (gr. 2-5). pap. 6.95 *(978-1-57565-342-6(7)*, 9781575653426) Astra Publishing Hse.

—The Case of the Stinky Socks (Book 1), No. 1. Montgomery, Lewis B. 2009. (Milo & Jazz Mysteries ® Ser.). (ENG.). 96p. (J). (gr. 2-5). pap. 6.95 *(978-1-57565-285-6(4)*, 9781575652856) Astra Publishing Hse.

—The Case of the Superstar Scam. Montgomery, Lewis B. 2013. (Milo & Jazz Mysteries ® Ser.). 112p. (J). (gr. 2-5). 22.60 *(978-1-57565-518-5(7))* Astra Publishing Hse.

—The Case of the Superstar Scam (Book 10), No. 10. Montgomery, Lewis B. 2013. (Milo & Jazz Mysteries ® Ser.). (ENG.). 112p. (J). (gr. 2-5). pap. 6.95 *(978-1-57565-519-2(5)*, 9781575655192) Astra Publishing Hse.

—The Case of Vampire Vivian: Bats. Knudsen, Michelle. 2006. (Science Solves It! ® Ser.). (ENG.). 32p. (J). (gr. 1-3). pap. 5.95 *(978-1-57565-127-9(0))* Astra Publishing Hse.

—El Caso de Vivian la Vampira. Knudsen, Michelle. 2008. (Science Solves It! en Espanol Ser.). (SPA.). 32p. (J). (gr. -1-3). pap. 5.95 *(978-1-57565-277-1(3))* Astra Publishing Hse.

—El Caso de Vivian la Vampira (the Case of Vampire Vivian) Knudsen, Michelle. 2009. (Science Solves It! ® en Espanol Ser.). (SPA.). (gr. 1-3). pap. 33.92 *(978-0-7613-4800-9(X))* Lerner Publishing Group.

—Dear God, Let's Talk about YOU. Moore, Karen. 2006. 128p. (J). pap. 8.99 *(978-0-7847-1247-4(6)*, 42174) Standard Publishing.

—Early Birdy Gets the Worm. Lansky, Bruce. 2010. 10p. (J). bds. 6.99 *(978-1-4169-9316-2(9))* Meadowbrook Pr.

—God Made You Just Right. Lord, Jill Roman. 2016. 22p. (J). bds. 7.99 *(978-0-8249-1976-4(9))* Worthy Publishing.

—Hi God, Let's Talk about My Life. Moore, Karen. 2006. 128p. (YA). pap. 8.99 *(978-0-7847-1246-7(8)*, 42173) Standard Publishing.

—Hocus Focus: Vision. Willson, Sarah. 2006. (Science Solves It! ® Ser.). (ENG.). 32p. (J). (gr. 1-3). pap. 5.95 *(978-1-57565-136-1(X))* Astra Publishing Hse.

—Horrible Harry & the Field Day Revenge! Kline, Suzy. 2018. (Horrible Harry Ser.: 36). (ENG.). 80p. (J). (gr. 2-5). 4.99 *(978-0-425-29038-5(7)*, Puffin Books) Penguin Young Readers Group.

—Horrible Harry & the Hallway Bully. Kline, Suzy. 2015. (Horrible Harry Ser.: 31). 80p. (J). (gr. 1-3). 4.99 *(978-0-14-750967-3(X)*, Puffin Books) Penguin Young Readers Group.

—Horrible Harry & the June Box. Kline, Suzy. 2012. (Horrible Harry Ser.: 27). 80p. (J). (gr. 2-4). pap. 4.99 *(978-0-14-242185-7(5)*, Puffin Books) Penguin Young Readers Group.

—Horrible Harry & the Missing Diamond. Kline, Suzy. 2014. (Horrible Harry Ser.: 30). 80p. (J). (gr. 2-4). pap. 4.99 *(978-0-14-242228-1(2)*, Puffin Books) Penguin Young Readers Group.

—Horrible Harry & the Scarlet Scissors. Kline, Suzy. 2013. (Horrible Harry Ser.). 80p. (J). (gr. 2-4). pap. 4.99 *(978-0-14-242671-5(7)*, Puffin Books) Penguin Young Readers Group.

—Horrible Harry & the Secret Treasure. Kline, Suzy. 2012. (Horrible Harry Ser.: 26). (ENG.). 80p. (J). (gr. 2-4). 4.99 *(978-0-14-242021-8(2)*, Puffin Books) Penguin Young Readers Group.

—Horrible Harry & the Wedding Spies. Kline, Suzy. 2016. (Horrible Harry Ser.: 32). (ENG.). 80p. (J). (gr. 2-5). 4.99 *(978-0-14-750968-0(8)*, Puffin Books) Penguin Young Readers Group.

—Horrible Harry Goes Cuckoo. Kline, Suzy. 2011. (Horrible Harry Ser.: 25). 80p. (J). (gr. 2-4). 4.99 *(978-0-14-241876-5(5)*, Puffin Books) Penguin Young Readers Group.

—Horrible Harry Says Goodbye. Kline, Suzy. (Horrible Harry Ser.: 37). 80p. (J). (gr. 2-5). 2019. 4.99 *(978-0-451-47964-8(5)*, Puffin Books); 2018. 14.99 *(978-0-451-47963-1(7)*, Viking Books for Young Readers) Penguin Young Readers Group.

—Jesus Must Be Really Special. Bishop, Jennie. 2006. (Heritage Builders Ser.). 32p. (J). 14.99 *(978-0-7847-1379-2(0)*, 04029) Standard Publishing.

—Keesha's Bright Idea. May, Eleanor. 2009. (Social Studies Connects ® Ser.). (ENG.). (gr. 1-3). pap. 33.92 *(978-0-7613-4806-1(9))* Lerner Publishing Group.

—Keesha's Bright Idea: Saving Energy. May, Eleanor. 2008. (Social Studies Connects ® Ser.). (ENG.). 32p. (J). (gr. 1-3). pap. 5.95 *(978-1-57565-273-3(0))* Astra Publishing Hse.

—Monkey See, Monkey Do at the Zoo. Lansky, Bruce. 2010. 10p. (J). bds. 6.99 *(978-1-4169-9317-9(7))* Meadowbrook Pr.

—More Five-Minute Devotions for Children: Celebrating God's World As a Family. Kennedy, Pamela & Kennedy, Douglas. 2005. (ENG.). 48p. (J). 14.95 *(978-0-8249-5502-1(1)*, Ideal Pubns.) Worthy Publishing.

—Movin' on In! Patriotic Symbols. Jordan, Taylor. 2006. (Social Studies Connects ® Ser.). (ENG.). 32p. (J). (gr. 1-3). pap. 5.95 *(978-1-57565-159-0(9))* Astra Publishing Hse.

—The Night Before Class Picture Day. Wing, Natasha. 2016. (Night Before Ser.). (ENG.). 32p. (J). (-k). pap. 4.99 *(978-0-448-48902-5(3)*, Grosset & Dunlap) Penguin Young Readers Group.

—The Night Before Election Day. Wing, Natasha. 2020. (Night Before Ser.). 32p. (J). (-k). pap. 5.99 *(978-0-593-09567-6(7)*, Grosset & Dunlap) Penguin Young Readers Group.

—The Night Before Father's Day. Wing, Natasha. 2012. (Night Before Ser.). 32p. (J). (gr. -1-k). pap. 4.99 *(978-0-448-45871-7(3)*, Grosset & Dunlap) Penguin Young Readers Group.

—The Night Before Groundhog Day. Wing, Natasha. 2019. (Night Before Ser.). 32p. (J). (gr. -1-3). pap. 4.99 *(978-1-5247-9325-8(6)*, Grosset & Dunlap) Penguin Young Readers Group.

—The Night Before Hanukkah, Vol. Wing, Natasha. 2014. (Night Before Ser.). 32p. (J). (gr. -1-k). 4.99 *(978-0-448-48140-1(5)*, Grosset & Dunlap) Penguin Young Readers Group.

—The Night Before Kindergarten Graduation. Wing, Natasha. 2019. (Night Before Ser.). 32p. (J). (gr. -1-1). pap. 4.99 *(978-1-5247-9001-1(X)*, Grosset & Dunlap) Penguin Young Readers Group.

—The Night Before Mother's Day. Wing, Natasha. 2010. (Night Before Ser.). 32p. (J). (gr. -1-1). 17.44 *(978-0-448-45213-5(8))* Penguin Young Readers Group.

—The Night Before My Birthday. Wing, Natasha. 2014. (Night Before Ser.). (ENG.). 32p. (J). (gr. -1-k). 4.99 *(978-0-448-48000-8(X)*, Grosset & Dunlap) Penguin Young Readers Group.

—The Night Before My Dance Recital. Wing, Natasha. 2015. (J). *(978-1-4806-9186-5(0)*, Grosset & Dunlap) Penguin Publishing Group.

—The Night Before My Dance Recital. Wing, Natasha. 2015. (Night Before Ser.). lib. bdg. 14.75 *(978-0-606-37543-6(0))* Turtleback.

—The Night Before My First Communion. Wing, Natasha. 2018. (Night Before Ser.). (ENG.). 32p. (J). (-k). pap. 4.99 *(978-1-5247-8619-9(5)*, Grosset & Dunlap) Penguin Young Readers Group.

—The Night Before New Year's. Wing, Natasha. 2009. (Night Before Ser.). 32p. (J). (gr. -1-k). pap. 4.99 *(978-0-448-45212-8(X)*, Grosset & Dunlap) Penguin Young Readers Group.

—The Night Before Preschool. Wing, Natasha. (Night Before Ser.). (ENG.). 32p. (J). (gr. -1-k). 2014. 12.99 *(978-0-448-48254-5(1))*; 2011. pap. 4.99 *(978-0-448-45451-1(3))* Penguin Young Readers Group. (Grosset & Dunlap).

—The Night Before St. Patrick's Day. Wing, Natasha. 2009. (Night Before Ser.). 32p. (J). (gr. -1-3). pap. 4.99 *(978-0-448-44852-7(1)*, Grosset & Dunlap) Penguin Young Readers Group.

—The Night Before the Fourth of July. Wing, Natasha. 2015. (Night Before Ser.). 32p. (J). (gr. -1-k). bds. 4.99 *(978-0-448-48712-0(8)*, Grosset & Dunlap) Penguin Young Readers Group.

—The Night Before the New Pet. Wing, Natasha. 2016. (Night Before Ser.). 32p. (J). (-k). pap. 4.99 *(978-0-448-48903-2(1)*, Grosset & Dunlap) Penguin Young Readers Group.

—The Night Before the Snow Day. Wing, Natasha. 2016. (Night Before Ser.). 32p. (J). (-k). pap. 4.99

W

(978-0-399-53942-8(5), Grosset & Dunlap) Penguin Young Readers Group.
—The Night Before the Snow Day. Wing, Natasha. ed. 2016. (Night Before Ser.). (ENG.). 32p. (J). (gr. -1-1). 14.75 *(978-0-606-39315-7(3))* Turtleback.
—Otto & the New Girl: Symmetry. Walker, Nan. 2017. (Math Matters ® Ser.). (ENG.). 32p. (J). (gr. k-3). 5.95 *(978-1-57565-864-3(X))* Astra Publishing Hse.
—Otto & the New Girl: Symmetry. Walker, Nan. ed. 2017. (Math Matters ® Ser.). (ENG.). 32p. (J). (gr. k-3). E-Book 23.99 *(978-1-57565-867-4(4))* Astra Publishing Hse.
—Polar BRRR Delivers. Lansky, Bruce. 2010. 10p. (J). bds. 6.99 *(978-1-4169-9318-6(5))* Meadowbrook Pr.
—Real Heroes Don't Wear Capes: Heroes. Driscoll, Laura. 2007. (Social Studies Connects ® Ser.). (ENG.). 32p. (J). (gr. 1-3). pap. 5.95 *(978-1-57565-245-0(5))* Astra Publishing Hse.
—Ruby Makes It Even! Odd/Even Numbers. Harkrader, Lisa. 2015. (Math Matters ® Ser.). (ENG.). 32p. (J). (gr. k-3). pap. 5.95 *(978-1-57565-805-6(4))*; E-Book 23.99 *(978-1-57565-806-3(2))* Astra Publishing Hse.
—Sally's Big Save: Spending & Saving. Driscoll, Laura. 2006. (Social Studies Connects ® Ser.). (ENG.). 32p. (J). (gr. 1-3). pap. 5.95 *(978-1-57565-164-4(5))* Astra Publishing Hse.
—Stressbusters: Producers & Consumers. Walker, Nan. 2006. (Social Studies Connects ® Ser.). (ENG.). 32p. (J). (gr. 1-3). pap. 5.95 *(978-1-57565-185-9(8))* Astra Publishing Hse.
—This Is the Challah. Hepker, Sue. 2012. (J). *(978-0-87441-522-3(5))*; *(978-0-87441-922-1(0))* Behrman Hse., Inc.
—Tiger Turcotte Takes on the Know-It-All. Flood, Pansie Hart. 2005. 72p. (J). (gr. 1-4). pap. 6.95 *(978-1-57505-900-6(2))* Lerner Publishing Group.
—Tiger's Trouble with Donut Head. Flood, Pansie Hart. 2005. 71p. (J). lib. bdg. 19.93 *(978-1-57505-814-6(6)*, Carolrhoda Bks.) Lerner Publishing Group.
—Two Homes for Tyler: A Story about Understanding Divorce. Kennedy, Pamela. 2008. (ENG.). 32p. (J). (gr. -1). 8.99 *(978-0-8249-5582-3(X)*, Ideal Pubns.) Worthy Publishing.
—Ty's Triple Trouble: Volunteering. May, Eleanor. 2007. (Social Studies Connects ® Ser.). (ENG.). 32p. (J). (gr. k-2). pap. 5.95 *(978-1-57565-237-5(4))* Astra Publishing Hse.
—Valentines Are for Saying I Love You. Sutherland, Margaret. 2007. (ENG.). 24p. (J). (gr. -1-k). mass mkt. 4.99 *(978-0-448-44702-5(9)*, Grosset & Dunlap) Penguin Young Readers Group.
—What Is America? Adams, Michelle Medlock. 2019. (What Is... ? Ser.). 22p. (J). (gr. -1-1). bds. 6.99 *(978-0-8249-1695-4(6)*, Worthy Kids/Ideals) Worthy Publishing.
—What Is Halloween? Adams, Michelle Medlock. 2019. 22p. (J). bds. 6.99 *(978-0-8249-1699-2(9)*, Worthy Kids/Ideals) Worthy Publishing.
—Whatcha Got? Scarcity & Value. Dussling, Jennifer. 2006. (Social Studies Connects ® Ser.). (ENG.). 32p. (J). (gr. 1-3). pap. 5.95 *(978-1-57565-143-9(2))* Astra Publishing Hse.
Wummer, Amy. It's Test Day, Tiger Turcotte. Wummer, Amy, tr. Flood, Pansie Hart. 2004. (Young Reader Fiction Ser.). 72p. (J). (gr. 1-4). pap. 6.95 *(978-1-57505-670-8(4))*; lib. bdg. 19.93 *(978-1-57505-056-0(0)*, Carolrhoda Bks.) Lerner Publishing Group.
Wummer, Amy, jt. illus. see Cuddy, Robin.
Wummer, Amy, jt. illus. see Montgomery, Lewis B.
Wummer, Amy, jt. illus. see Remkiewicz, Frank.
Wurst, Thomas Scott. Pearl's Christmas Present. Wurst, Thomas Scott. 2006. 40p. (J). 20.00 *(978-0-9772441-1-9(3))* Pearl & Dotty.
Wurster, Laurie. Some of Us Want Wrinkles. Roman, Stacey. 2005. (J). per. 16.95 *(978-1-59858-033-4(7))* Dog Ear Publishing, LLC.
Wuthrich, Belle. Choosing to Live, Choosing to Die: The Complexities of Assisted Dying, 1 vol. Tate, Nikki. 2019. (Orca Issues Ser.: 3). (ENG.). 176p. (YA). (gr. 8-12). pap. 19.95 *(978-1-4598-1889-7(X))* Orca Bk. Pubs. USA.
—Eat Up! An Infographic Exploration of Food. Ayer, Paula & Banyard, Antonia. 2017. (Visual Exploration Ser.). (ENG.). 72p. (gr. 3-7). 22.95 *(978-1-55451-884-5(9))* Annick Pr., Ltd. CAN. Dist: Publishers Group West (PGW).
—Eat Up! An Inforgraphic Exploration of Food. Ayer, Paula & Banyard, Antonia. 2017. (Visual Exploration Ser.). (ENG.). 72p. (gr. 3-7). pap. 12.95 *(978-1-55451-883-8(0))* Annick Pr., Ltd. CAN. Dist: Publishers Group West (PGW).
Wuthrich, Belle. Heads Up: Changing Minds on Mental Health. Siebert, Melanie. 2020. (Orca Issues Ser.: 4). (ENG.). 192p. (YA). (gr. 8-12). pap. 24.95 ***(978-1-4598-1911-5(X))*** Orca Bk. Pubs. USA.
Wuthrich, Belle. Water Wow! A Visual Exploration. Banyard, Antonia & Ayer, Paula. 2016. (Visual Exploration Ser.). (ENG.). 64p. (J). (gr. 3-7). pap. 12.95 *(978-1-55451-821-0(0))* Annick Pr., Ltd. CAN. Dist: Publishers Group West (PGW).
Wyatt, David. The Beasts of Grimheart. Larwood, Kieran. 2019. (Five Realms Podkin One Ear Ser.). (ENG.). 320p. (J). (gr. 3-5). 15.95 *(978-0-571-32844-4(X)*, Faber & Faber Children's Bks.) Faber & Faber, Inc.
—The Beasts of Grimheart. Larwood, Kieran. (Longburrow Ser.). (ENG.). 272p. (J). (gr. 5-7). 2020. pap. 7.99 *(978-0-358-20692-7(8)*, 1763861); 2019. 16.99 *(978-1-328-69602-1(2)*, 1671320) Houghton Mifflin Harcourt Trade & Reference Pubs. (Clarion Bks.).
—The Emerald Throne. Baldry, Cherith. 2003. (Eaglesmount Ser.). (J). 144p. 15.95 *(978-1-59034-584-9(3))*; 141p. pap. *(978-1-59034-585-6(1))* Mondo Publishing.
—The Gift of Dark Hollow. Larwood, Kieran. 2019. (Longburrow Ser.). (ENG.). 288p. (J). (gr. 5-7). pap. 7.99 *(978-1-328-54993-8(3)*, 1724301, HMH Books For Young Readers) Houghton Mifflin Harcourt Publishing Co.
—The Gift of Dark Hollow. Larwood, Kieran. 2018. (Longburrow Ser.). (ENG.). 272p. (J). (gr. 5-7). 16.99 *(978-1-328-69601-4(4)*, 1671318, Clarion Bks.) Houghton Mifflin Harcourt Trade & Reference Pubs.
—The Lake of Darkness. Baldry, Cherith. 2004. (Eaglesmount Ser.). 144p. (J). 15.95 *(978-1-59034-586-3(X))*; pap. *(978-1-59034-587-0(8))* Mondo Publishing.
Wyatt, David, et al. A Miscellany of Magical Beasts. Holland, Simon. 2016. (ENG.). 48p. (J). 17.99 *(978-1-68119-430-1(9)*, 9781681194301, Bloomsbury USA Childrens) Bloomsbury Publishing USA.
Wyatt, David. Peter Pan de Rojo Escarlata. McCaughrean, Geraldine. Gonzalez-Gallarza, Isabel, tr. 2006. 296p. (J). (gr. 5-8). 17.95 *(978-958-704-467-6(3))* Ediciones Alfaguara ESP. Dist: Santillana USA Publishing Co., Inc.
—Podkin One-Ear. Larwood, Kieran. (Longburrow Ser.). (ENG.). (J). (gr. 5-7). 2018. 272p. pap. 7.99 *(978-1-328-49803-8(4)*, 1717863, HMH Books For Young Readers); 2017. 256p. 16.99 *(978-1-328-69582-6(4)*, 1671494) Houghton Mifflin Harcourt Publishing Co.
—Stealaway. Peyton, K. M. 2004. (ENG.). 96p. (J). 12.95 *(978-0-8126-2722-0(9))* Cricket Bks.
Wyatt, David & Pinfold, Levi. Illusionology: The Secret Science of Magic. Schafer, Albert. 2012. (Ologies Ser.). (ENG.). 30p. (J). (gr. 3-7). 24.99 *(978-0-7636-5588-4(0))* Candlewick Pr.
Wyatt, David, jt. illus. see Stevens, Tim.
Wyatt, Jacob, et al. Ms. Marvel Meets the Marvel Universe. 2020. (ENG.). 248p. (J). (gr. 5-9). pap. 12.99 ***(978-1-302-92362-4(5))*** Marvel Worldwide, Inc.
Wyatt, Michael. The Night Wanderer: A Graphic Novel. Taylor, Drew Hayden. 2013. (ENG.). 104p. (YA). (gr. 7-12). pap. 14.95 *(978-1-55451-572-1(6)*, 9781554515721) Annick Pr., Ltd. CAN. Dist: Publishers Group West (PGW).
Wyatt, Sue. The Legend of the Seven Sisters: A Traditional Aboriginal Story from Western Australia. O'Brien, May L. 2nd ed. 2010. 18p. (J). (gr. k-5). pap. 17.95 *(978-0-85575-699-4(3))* Aboriginal Studies Pr. AUS. Dist: Independent Pubs. Group.
—Wunambi the Water Snake. O'Brien, May L. 2nd ed. 2005. 32p. (J). (gr. k-5). pap. 17.95 *(978-0-85575-500-3(8))* Aboriginal Studies Pr. AUS. Dist: Independent Pubs. Group.
Wyckoff, Helene Waldner. The Christmas Kitty. Eakin, June Deas. 2005. (ENG.). 30p. pap. 15.50 *(978-1-4120-6864-2(9))* Trafford Publishing.
Wyeth, Andrew N. & Kuerner, Karl J. The Land of Truth & Phantasy: Life & Painting at Ring Farm USA. McLellan, Richard A. gif. ed. 2005. (ENG.). 187p. 24.00 *(978-0-9747536-0-7(2))* McLellan Bks.
Wyeth, Jamie. Sammy in the Sky. Walsh, Barbara. 2011. (ENG.). 32p. (J). (gr. -1-3). 16.99 *(978-0-7636-4927-2(9))* Candlewick Pr.
Wyeth, N. C. King Arthur: Sir Thomas Malory's History of King Arthur & His Knights of the Round Table. 2018. (Scribner Classics Ser.). (ENG.). 288p. (J). (gr. 5). 29.99 *(978-1-5344-2841-6(0)*, Atheneum Bks. for Young Readers) Simon & Schuster Children's Publishing.
—The Last of the Mohicans. Cooper, James Fenimore. 2013. (Scribner Classics Ser.). (ENG.). 368p. (J). (gr. 5). 24.99 *(978-1-4424-8130-5(7)*, Atheneum Bks. for Young Readers) Simon & Schuster Children's Publishing.
—Rip Van Winkle: The Wonderland Edition. Irving, Washington. 2016. 96p. pap. 13.95 *(978-1-883789-85-5(0))* Black Dome Pr. Corp.
—The Yearling. Rawlings, Marjorie Kinnan. 2013. (Scribner Classics Ser.). (ENG.). 416p. (J). (gr. 5-9). 29.99 *(978-1-4424-8209-8(5)*, Atheneum Bks. for Young Readers) Simon & Schuster Children's Publishing.
Wyeth, N. C. Kidnapped. Wyeth, N. C. Stevenson, Robert Louis. 2004. (Scribner Storybook Classics Ser.). (ENG.). 64p. (J). (gr. 3-7). 19.99 *(978-0-689-86542-8(2)*, Atheneum Bks. for Young Readers) Simon & Schuster Children's Publishing.
Wyeth, N. C. & Rhead, Louis. Treasure Island (Illustrated) With Artwork by N. C. Wyeth & Louis Rhead. Stevenson, Robert Louis. 2019. (Top Five Classics Ser.: Vol. 9). (ENG.). 272p. (J). (gr. 2-6). 34.99 *(978-1-938938-40-5(2))* Top Five Bks.
Wyhoff, Mark, photos by. Wildlife & Trees in British Columbia, 1 vol. Guy, Stewart et al. rev. ed. 2006. (ENG., 336p. (gr. 4). pap. 29.95 *(978-1-55105-071-3(4)*, 664b8141-2c62-42eb-9420-9ab271b35250) Lone Pine Publishing USA.
Wyk, Hanri van, jt. illus. see Meredith, Samantha.
Wyk, Rupert Van. Future Fashion. Ivy, Darlene. 2020. (ENG.). 28p. (J). pap. ***(978-1-922374-96-7(2))*** Library For All Limited.
Wyland Studios Staff. Wyland's Spouty And Friends. 2004. 37p. 20.95 *(978-1-884840-59-3(0))* Wyland Worldwide, LLC.
Wyles, Betty. Jorge, the Gift. Eichler, Darlene. 2016. (ENG.). (J). 16.95 *(978-1-941069-63-9(0))*; pap. 10.95 *(978-1-941069-62-2(2))* ProsePress.
—Where's the Kitty. Eichler, Darlene. 2013. 52p. pap. 18.95 *(978-0-9893063-1-7(3))* ProsePress.
Wylie, T. J. The Goodenoughs Get in Sync: A Story for Kids about the Tough Day When Filibuster Grabbed Darwin's Rabbit's Foot... Kranowitz, Carol Stock. 2004. 86p. (J). 14.95 *(978-1-931615-17-4(9)*, 978-1-931615-17-4) Sensory Resources.
Wyly, Kim. When Fur & Feather Get Together. Margrave, David R. 2018. (ENG.). 32p. (J). 11.99 *(978-1-945507-72-4(1))* Carpenter's Son Publishing.
Wyman, David, photos by. Young Man with Camera. Sher, Emil. 2015. (ENG., 240p. (YA). (gr. 7). 17.99 *(978-0-545-54131-2(X)*, Levine, Arthur A. Bks.) Scholastic, Inc.
Wyman, Deborah. The Adventures of Petey the Chiweenie: Learning Patience. Minks, Carla Tucker. 2020. (Learning Ser.: Vol. 2). (ENG.). 40p. (J). 20.95 ***(978-1-5136-5895-7(6))*** Morgan James Publishing.
Wyman, M. C., et al. S. H. I. E. L. D.: Hydra Reborn. 2017. 352p. (J). (gr. 4-17). pap. 34.99 *(978-1-302-90684-9(4))* Marvel Worldwide, Inc.
Wyman, M. C. & Anderson, Bill. Prince, the Future King: A Father's Example. Harris, Kandi. 2005. 32p. (J). bds. 19.95 *(978-0-9770331-0-2(4))* Harris, K Publishing, Inc.
Wyman, M. C., jt. illus. see Campos, Marc.
Wynn, Kim. Paws & Claws. Stranex, Glenn. 2017. (ENG.). 128p. (J). pap. *(978-1-78623-200-7(6))* Grosvenor Hse. Publishing Ltd.
—Paws & Claws 2. Stranex, Glenn. 2018. (Paws & Claws Ser.: Vol. 2). (ENG.). 150p. (J). pap. *(978-1-78623-328-8(2))* Grosvenor Hse. Publishing Ltd.
Wynn, Marcy. Do You Know Hank the Hippo? Wynn, Marcy. l.t. ed. 2016. (ENG.). (J). pap. 12.95 *(978-0-692-77545-5(5))* Simply Hooked.
Wynne, Patricia. Brain: A 21st Century Look at a 400 Million Year Old Organ. DeSalle, Rob. 2010. (Wallace & Darwin Ser.: 2). (ENG.). 40p. (J). (gr. 3-7). 18.95 *(978-1-59373-085-7(3))* Bunker Hill Publishing, Inc.
—Dinosaur Days. Chaikin, Andrew. 2012. 32p. (J). pap. *(978-0-7166-1650-4(5))* World Bk., Inc.
—When Dinosaurs Walked. Chaikin, Andrew. 2004. (Treasure Tree Ser.). 32p. (J). *(978-0-7166-1607-8(6))* World Bk., Inc.
Wynne, Patricia J. Birds: Nature's Magnificent Flying Machines. Arnold, Caroline. 2003. (ENG.). 32p. (J). (gr. 1-4). pap. 7.95 *(978-1-57091-572-7(5))* Charlesbridge Publishing, Inc.
—The Bumblebee Queen. Sayre, April Pulley. 2006. 32p. (J). (gr. -1-3). pap. 7.95 *(978-1-57091-363-1(3))* Charlesbridge Publishing, Inc.
—The Bumblebee Queen. Sayre, April Pulley. 2006. (gr. -1-3). lib. bdg. 17.95 *(978-0-7569-6968-4(9))* Perfection Learning Corp.
—Hello, Baby Beluga. Lunde, Darrin P. 2016. 14p. (J). (— 1). bds. 6.95 *(978-1-58089-525-5(5))* Charlesbridge Publishing, Inc.
—Hello, Baby Beluga. Lunde, Darrin P. & Stock, Catherine. 2011. 32p. (J). (gr. -1-2). pap. 6.95 *(978-1-57091-740-0(X))* Charlesbridge Publishing, Inc.
—Hello, Bumblebee Bat. Lunde, Darrin. 2016. 14p. (J). (— 1). bds. 6.95 *(978-1-58089-526-2(3))* Charlesbridge Publishing, Inc.
—Hello, Bumblebee Bat. Lunde, Darrin. 2007. (J). (gr. -1-1). 14.60 *(978-0-7569-8048-1(8))* Perfection Learning Corp.
—Hello, Mama Wallaroo. Lunde, Darrin. 2013. 32p. (J). (gr. -1-2). pap. 6.95 *(978-1-57091-797-4(3))*; lib. bdg. 15.95 *(978-1-57091-796-7(5))* Charlesbridge Publishing, Inc.
—Meet the Meerkat. Lunde, Darrin. 2007. (ENG.). 32p. (J). (gr. -1-2). pap. 7.95 *(978-1-58089-154-7(3))* Charlesbridge Publishing, Inc.
—Meet the Meerkat. Lunde, Darrin. 2007. (gr. -1-1). 17.95 *(978-0-7569-8047-4(X))* Perfection Learning Corp.
—Monkey Colors. Lunde, Darrin. 2012. 32p. (J). (gr. -1-2). 22.44 *(978-1-57091-741-7(8))*; pap. 7.99 *(978-1-57091-742-4(6))* Charlesbridge Publishing, Inc.
—What the Dog Knows Young Readers Edition: Scent, Science, & the Amazing Ways Dogs Perceive the World. Warren, Cat. 2019. (ENG.). 336p. (J). (gr. 3-7). 17.99 *(978-1-5344-2814-0(3)*, Simon & Schuster Bks. For Young Readers) Simon & Schuster Bks. For Young Readers.
Wyrick, Monica. A. D. D. Not B. A. D. Penn, Audrey. 2003. (New Child & Family Press Titles Ser.). 32p. pap. 9.95 *(978-0-87868-849-4(8)*, 8498, Child & Family Pr.) Child Welfare League of America, Inc.
—Art Smart, Science Detective: The Case of the Sliding Spaceship Illustrated by Monica Wyrick. Melinda, Long. 2018. (Young Palmetto Bks.). (ENG.). 64p. (J). pap. 12.99 *(978-1-61117-935-4(1))* Univ. of South Carolina Pr.
—The Brown Mountain Lights: A North Carolina Legend. Crane, Carol. 2012. 36p. (J). pap. 11.99 *(978-1-935711-19-3(9))* Peak City Publishing, LLC.
—Crabbing. Balsley, Tilda. 2016. (Young Palmetto Bks.). (ENG.). 32p. (J). 18.99 *(978-1-61117-640-7(9))* Univ. of South Carolina Pr.
—Dreaming with Animals: Anna Hyatt Huntington & Brookgreen Gardens. Dunn, L. Kerr. 2017. (Young Palmetto Bks.). (ENG.). 40p. (J). 18.99 *(978-1-61117-820-3(7))* Univ. of South Carolina Pr.
Wysong, Ryan. William's in a Wheelchair. Swaney, Kathleen M. 2008. 24p. pap. 24.95 *(978-1-60703-447-6(6))* America Star Bks.
Wysotski, Chrissie. This is the Dog, 1 vol. McFarlane, Sheryl. 2003. (ENG.). 32p. *(978-1-55041-551-3(4))* Fitzhenry & Whiteside, Ltd.
Wyss, Johann David. The Swiss Family Robinson. Kingston, William Henry Giles, tr. 2005. 188p. per. 6.95 *(978-1-4209-2269-1(6))* Digireads.com Publishing.
—The Swiss Family Robinson. 2004. reprint ed. pap. 30.95 *(978-1-4191-5012-8(X))*; pap. 1.99 *(978-1-4192-5012-5(4))* Kessinger Publishing, LLC.
Wyss, Manspeter. King for One Day. Brenner, Peter. 36p. (J). (gr. -1-3). 12.95 *(978-0-87592-027-6(6))* Scroll Pr., Inc.

X

Xanthos, Carol. How Does the Holy Ghost Make Me Feel? Camesecca, Michele. 2010. 44p. *(978-1-60641-245-9(0))* Deseret Bk. Co.
Xerox. The Secret Adventures of Pickle Boy. Bee, Jack. 2019. (Secret Adventures of Pickle Boy Ser.: Vol. 1). (ENG.). 244p. (J). pap. 9.95 *(978-1-7984-3743-8(0))* Independently Published.
Xian Nu Studio, jt. illus. see Ota, Yuko Geneviev.
Xian Nu Studio Staff. Challenge, 2. Marr, Melissa. 2010. (Wicked Lovely: Desert Tales Ser.: 2). (ENG.). 176p. (YA). (gr. 8-12). 26.19 *(978-0-06-149349-2(X))* HarperCollins Pubs.
Xian Nu Studio Staff & Ota, Yuko Geneviev. A Match Made in Heaven, No. 8. Robbins, Trina. 2013. (My Boyfriend Is a Monster Ser.: 8). (ENG.). 128p. (YA). (gr. 7-12). lib. bdg. 29.32 *(978-0-7613-6857-1(4)*, 9780761368571, Graphic Universe™) Lerner Publishing Group.
Xian Nu Studio Staff, jt. illus. see Diaz, Irene.
Xian Nu Studio, Xian Nu. Vampire Kisses: Graveyard Games, No. 1. Schreiber, Ellen. 2011. (Vampire Kisses: Blood Relatives Ser.). (ENG.). 192p. (YA). (gr. 8). pap. 10.99 *(978-0-06-202672-9(0)*, Tegen, Katherine Bks) HarperCollins Pubs.
—Wicked Lovely: Desert Tales, Volume 3: Resolve. Marr, Melissa. 2011. (Wicked Lovely: Desert Tales Ser.: 3). (ENG.). 176p. (YA). (gr. 8-18). pap. 9.99 *(978-0-06-149350-8(3))* HarperCollins Pubs.
Xiao, Yao. How to Solve a Problem: The Rise (and Falls) of a Rock-Climbing Champion. Shiraishi, Ashima. 2020. (ENG.). 40p. (J). (gr. -1-3). 17.99 *(978-1-5247-7327-4(1))*; lib. bdg. 20.99 *(978-1-5247-7328-1(X))* Random Hse. Children's Bks.
Xin, Lin. I Can Eat with Chopsticks: A Tale of Chopsticks & How They Became a Pair. a Story in English & Chinese. ed. 2018. 42p. (J). (gr. k-4). 16.95 *(978-1-60220-452-2(7))* Shanghai Translation Publishing Hse. CHN. Dist: Publishers Group West (PGW).
Xin, Xiao. Earth Day Every Day. Bullard, Lisa. 2011. (Planet Protectors Ser.). pap. 39.62 *(978-0-7613-8652-0(1)*, Millbrook Pr.) Lerner Publishing Group.
—Look Out for Litter. Bullard, Lisa. 2011. (Planet Protectors Ser.). pap. 39.62 *(978-0-7613-8654-4(8)*, Millbrook Pr.) Lerner Publishing Group.
—Mary's Garden: How Does it Grow? Harris, Brooke. 2009. (Reader's Theater Nursery Rhymes & Songs Set B Ser.). 48p. (J). pap. *(978-1-60859-160-2(3))* Benchmark Education Co.
—Watch over Our Water. Bullard, Lisa. 2011. (Planet Protectors Ser.). pap. 39.62 *(978-0-7613-8657-5(2)*, Millbrook Pr.) Lerner Publishing Group.
Xin, Xiao & Zheng, Xin. Go Green for Earth Day. Bullard, Lisa. 2018. (Go Green (Early Bird Stories (tm)) Ser.). (ENG.). 24p. (J). (gr. k-2). 27.99 *(978-1-5415-2014-1(9)*, Lerner Pubns.) Lerner Publishing Group.
Xinxin, Xia. Moon Messenger: A Story Told in English & Chinese. Jie, Wei. Wert, Yinin, tr. 2020. 42p. (J). (gr. -1-3). 14.95 *(978-1-60220-462-1(4))* Shanghai Translation Publishing Hse. CHN. Dist: Publishers Group West (PGW).
Xiong, Kim. The Clay General. 2008. (J). 18.95 *(978-1-60603-002-8(7))* Better Chinese LLC.
—The Dragon Tribe. 2008. (ENG & CHI.). 33p. (J). 18.95 *(978-1-60603-000-4(0))* Better Chinese LLC.
—Kitchen God. 2008. 32p. (J). 18.95 *(978-1-60603-001-1(9))* Better Chinese LLC.
—Paper Horse. 2008. (ENG & CHI.). 37p. (J). 18.95 *(978-1-60603-003-5(5))* Better Chinese LLC.
Xiong, Tou Yia. Pickles + Ocho. Wellik, Dan. 2017. (ENG.). (J). 17.95 *(978-1-59298-780-1(X))* Beaver's Pond Pr., Inc.
Xist, Publishing. Cats All Dressed Up. Xist Publishing. 2015. (Discover Ser.). (ENG.). 28p. (J). (gr. -1-k). pap. 9.99 *(978-1-5324-0533-4(2))* Xist Publishing.
—Horses. Xist Publishing. 2012. (Discover Ser.). (ENG.). 28p. (J). (gr. -1-k). pap. 9.99 *(978-1-62395-056-9(2))* Xist Publishing.
—House. Xist Publishing. 2012. (Discover Ser.). (ENG.). 28p. (J). (gr. -1-k). pap. 9.99 *(978-1-62395-057-6(0))* Xist Publishing.
—The Twelve Days of Christmas: A Christmas Counting Book. Brighton, Bridget. 2015. 36p. (J). (gr. -1-2). pap. 9.99 *(978-1-5324-0933-2(8))* Xist Publishing.
Xu, Lis. When Molly Drew Dogs. Kerbel, Deborah. 2019. (ENG.). 32p. (J). (gr. 2-5). 16.95 *(978-1-77147-338-5(X))* Owlkids Bks. Inc. CAN. Dist: Publishers Group West (PGW).
Xu, Nicole. All of a Sudden & Forever: Help & Healing after the Oklahoma City Bombing. Barton, Chris. 2020. (ENG.). 40p. (J). (gr. 2-5). 19.99 *(978-1-5415-2669-3(4)*, Carolrhoda Bks.) Lerner Publishing Group.
Xu, Ru. Endgames. Xu, Ru. 2019. (NewsPrints Ser.: 2). (ENG.). 208p. (J). (gr. 3-7). pap. 12.99 *(978-0-545-80317-5(9)*, Graphix) Scholastic, Inc.
Xu, Wei & Zheng, Xiaoyan. To Share One Moon. Wang, Ruowen. 2008. 32p. (J). (gr. 2-4). *(978-0-9738799-5-7(5))* Kevin & Robin Bks., Ltd.
Xu, Wendy. Mooncakes. Walker, Suzanne. 2019. (ENG.). 256p. (YA). (gr. 8). pap. 14.99 *(978-1-5493-0304-3(X)*, 6d8f8499-ed34-4175-aece-4b5a301353ec, Lion Forge) Oni Pr., Inc.
Xuan, Xuan Loc. Snowy the Leopard of the High Mountains. Petkovic, Milisava. 2018. (ENG.). 38p. (J). 14.99 *(978-1-64124-015-4(6)*, 0154) Fox Chapel Publishing Co., Inc.
Xuan, YongSheng. D Is for Dragon Dance. Compestine, Ying Chang. 2018. 32p. (J). (gr. -1-3). 18.99 *(978-0-8234-4029-0(X))* Holiday Hse., Inc.
—The Story of Chopsticks: Amazing Chinese Inventions. Compestine, Ying Chang. 2016. (Amazing Chinese Inventions Ser.). (ENG.). 40p. (J). (gr. -1-3). 15.95 *(978-1-59702-120-3(2))* Immedium.
—The Story of Kites: Amazing Chinese Inventions. Compestine, Ying Chang. 2016. (Amazing Chinese Inventions Ser.). (ENG.). 40p. (J). (gr. -1-3). 15.95 *(978-1-59702-122-7(9))* Immedium.
—The Story of Noodles: Amazing Chinese Inventions. Compestine, Ying Chang. 2016. (Amazing Chinese Inventions Ser.). (ENG.). 40p. (J). (gr. -1-3). 15.95 *(978-1-59702-121-0(0))* Immedium.
—The Story of Paper: Amazing Chinese Inventions. Compestine, Ying Chang. 2016. (Amazing Chinese Inventions Ser.). (ENG.). 40p. (J). (gr. -1-3). 15.95 *(978-1-59702-123-4(7))* Immedium.

Y

Y, Helen. Los Suenos de Brianna: Solamente Quisiera Saber. Williams, Iris M. Narvaez, Maria, tr. 2018. (Los Suenos de Brianna Ser.: Vol. 1). (SPA.). 34p. (J). pap. 15.95 *(978-1-947656-88-8(0))* Butterfly Typeface, The.

Yabuki, Go. Scrapped Princess, 3 vols., Vol. 1. 2005. (Scrapped Princess Ser.). 184p. pap. 14.99 *(978-1-59532-981-3(1),* Tokyopop Adult) TOKYOPOP, Inc.

—Scrapped Princess, 3 vols., Vol. 2. Yubuki, Go & Azumi, Yukinobu. 2nd rev. ed. 2006. (Scrapped Princess Ser.). 192p. per. 14.99 *(978-1-59532-982-0(X),* Tokyopop Adult) TOKYOPOP, Inc.

Yaccarino, Dan. Boy & Bot. Dyckman, Ame. (J). (-k). 2016. 24p. bds. 7.99 *(978-1-101-93688-7(6));* 2012. 32p. 16.99 *(978-0-375-86756-9(2))* Random Hse. Children's Bks. (Knopf Bks. for Young Readers).

—Count on the Subway. Jacobs, Paul DuBois & Swender, Jennifer. 2014. (ENG.). 32p. (J). (-k). 14.99 *(978-0-307-97923-0(7));* lib. bdg. 17.99 *(978-0-307-97924-7(5))* Random Hse. Children's Bks. (Knopf Bks. for Young Readers).

—Five Little Ducks. Churchill, Jill. 2005. 26p. (J). (gr. -1 — 1). bds. 5.99 *(978-0-06-073465-7(5),* HarperFestival) HarperCollins Pubs.

—Five Little Elves. Public Domain, Public. 2016. (ENG.). 16p. (J). (gr. -1 — 1). bds. 6.99 *(978-0-06-225338-5(7),* HarperFestival) HarperCollins Pubs.

—Five Little Pumpkins. Public Domain, Public. 2003. (ENG.). 16p. (J). (gr. -1-k). bds. 6.99 *(978-0-694-01177-3(0),* HarperFestival) HarperCollins Pubs.

—Girl + Bot. Dyckman, Ame. 2017. (J). *(978-1-5247-0072-0(X))* Knopf, Alfred A. Inc.

—I Love Going Through This Book. Burleigh, Robert. Date not set. 40p. (J). (gr. -1-3). pap. 5.99 *(978-0-06-443647-2(0))* HarperCollins Pubs.

—Smashy Town. Zimmerman, Andrea & Clemesha, David. 2020. 32p. (J). (gr. -1-3). 17.99 *(978-0-06-291037-0(X),* HarperCollins) HarperCollins Pubs. Ltd. GBR. Dist: HarperCollins Pubs.

—Trashy Town Board Book. Zimmerman, Andrea & Clemesha, David. 2018. (ENG.). 26p. (J). (gr. -1 — 1). bds. 7.99 *(978-0-06-249103-9(2),* HarperFestival) HarperCollins Pubs.

Yaccarino, Dan. Dan Yaccarino's Mother Goose. Yaccarino, Dan. 2003. (Little Golden Book Ser.). 32p. (J). (gr. -1-2). 4.99 *(978-0-375-82571-2(1),* Golden Bks.) Random Hse. Children's Bks.

—Every Friday. Yaccarino, Dan. 2012. (ENG.). 32p. (J). (gr. -1-2). pap. 7.99 *(978-1-250-00473-4(X),* 900080725) Square Fish.

—Five Little Bunnies. Yaccarino, Dan. 2016. (ENG.). 16p. (J). (gr. -1 — 1). bds. 6.99 *(978-0-06-225339-2(5))* HarperCollins Pubs.

—Five Little Pumpkins Came Back Board Book. Yaccarino, Dan. 2018. (ENG.). 16p. (J). (gr. -1 — 1). bds. 6.99 *(978-0-06-284021-9(5),* HarperFestival) HarperCollins Pubs.

—Giant Tess. Yaccarino, Dan. 2019. (ENG.). 40p. (J). (gr. -1-3). 17.99 *(978-0-06-267027-4(1))* HarperCollins Pubs.

—I Am a Story. Yaccarino, Dan. 2016. (ENG.). 40p. (J). (gr. -1-3). 17.99 *(978-0-06-241106-8(3))* HarperCollins Pubs.

—Morris Mole. Yaccarino, Dan. 2017. (ENG.). 40p. (J). (gr. -1-3). 17.99 *(978-0-06-241107-5(1))* HarperCollins Pubs.

—New Pet. Yaccarino, Dan. 2003. (ENG.). 40p. (gr. -1-2). pap. 4.99 *(978-0-7868-1429-9(2))* Hyperion Pr.

—Unlovable. Yaccarino, Dan. rev. ed. 2004. (ENG.). 32p. (J). (gr. -1-1). reprint ed. pap. 8.99 *(978-0-8050-7532-8(1),* 900021844) Square Fish.

—Where the Four Winds Blow. Yaccarino, Dan. 2003. 104p. (J). 17.89 *(978-0-06-623627-8(4),* Cotler, Joanna Books) HarperCollins Pubs.

—Zorgoochi Intergalactic Pizza: Delivery of Doom. Yaccarino, Dan. 2014. (ENG.). 336p. (J). (gr. 3-7). 16.99 *(978-1-250-00844-2(1),* 9781250008442) Feiwel & Friends.

Yaciuk, Donovan, jt. illus. see Henderson, Scott B.

Yaeger, Mark. Nathaniel's Journey: The King's Armory. Kelby, Tom. 2003. (J). per. *(978-1-930914-04-9(0))* Hands to the Plow, Inc.

Yaffe, Denise. Earth Kids: Environmental Superheroes: Story 21: the Meeting. Yaffe, Denise. Murdock, Lisa. 2019. (Environmental Superheroes Ser.: Vol. 1). (ENG.). 40p. (J). pap. 10.00 *(978-1-0705-4402-1(7))* Independently Published.

Yagmin, Daniel, Jr. Norton B. Nice. 2009. (J). *(978-1-60108-018-9(2))* Red Cygnet Pr.

Yahathugoda, Chethanika & Yahathugoda, Thissarika. The Space Master. Udumalagala, Daphni. 2019. (ENG.). 44p. (J). ***(978-1-5255-5198-7(1))****;* pap. ***(978-1-5255-5199-4(X))*** FriesenPress.

Yahathugoda, Thissarika, jt. illus. see Yahathugoda, Chethanika.

Yahuan, Yuan. The Bamboo & Me: Exploring Bamboo's Many Uses in Daily Life. Bin, Xu. ed. 2018. 42p. (J). (gr. -1-3). 16.95 *(978-1-60220-454-6(3))* Shanghai Translation Publishing Hse. CHN. Dist: Publishers Group West (PGW).

Yahya, Daan. Sammy Saves for a Birthday Gift. Kelly, Angela. 2019. (ENG.). 24p. (J). pap. 12.95 *(978-1-0957-8981-0(3))* Independently Published.

Yak, Patricia. What Color Are Kisses? Yak, Patricia. 2019. (ENG.). 28p. (J). pap. 14.95 ***(978-1-6755-5058-8(1))*** Independently Published.

Yakubivska, Marina. Bitcoin Money: A Tale of Bitville Discovering Good Money. Caras, Michael. 2019. (ENG.). 28p. (J). (gr. -1-3). 14.99 ***(978-0-578-49067-0(6))*** Caras, Michael.

—Bitcoin-Raha: Tarina Bittil�n Lapsista Ja Kest�v�n Rahan L�ytymisest� Caras, Michael. 2019. (FIN.). 28p. (J). (gr. 1-6). pap. 14.99 ***(978-0-578-54888-3(7))*** Caras, Michael.

—El Dinero Bitcoin: El Cuento de Bitvilla Descubriendo el Buen Dinero. Caras, Michael. 2019. (SPA.). 28p. (J). (gr. 1-6). pap. 14.99 ***(978-0-578-51921-0(6))*** Caras, Michael.

—La Moneta Bitcoin: La Storia Della Città Di Bitville Alla Scoperta Della Buona Moneta. Caras, Michael. 2019. (ITA.). 28p. (J). (gr. k-6). pap. 14.99 ***(978-0-578-52844-1(4))*** Caras, Michael.

—La Monnaie Bitcoin: L'histoire de Bitville découvrant la Bonne Monnaie. Caras, Michael. 2019. (FRE.). 28p. (J). (gr. k-6). pap. 14.99 ***(978-0-578-52834-2(7))*** Caras, Michael.

—ビットコインのビット村が良い; Caras, Michael. 2019. (JPN.). 28p. (J). (gr. k-6). pap. 14.99 ***(978-0-578-53704-7(4))*** Caras, Michael.

Yalcin, Elena. Pumpkin Head. Keiffer, Ebriana. 2018. (ENG.). 28p. (J). pap. 12.95 *(978-0-578-19966-5(1))* Mystical Publishing.

—VALENTINA, the Paper Doll Activity Book for Girls Ages 4-8: Paper Doll with the Dresses for Coloring & Cutting Out, Mazes, Color by Numbers, Find the Differences, Match the Pictures, Trace the Pictures & More! 2019. (ENG.). 48p. (J). (gr. k-4). pap. 8.00 *(978-1-7261-9950-6(9))* CreateSpace Independent Publishing Platform.

Yalowitz, Paul. Boy, Can He Dance! Spinelli, Eileen. 2012. (ENG.). 32p. (J). (gr. -1-3). 16.99 *(978-1-4424-7441-3(6),* Simon & Schuster Bks. For Young Readers) Simon & Schuster Bks. For Young Readers.

Yamada, Jane. Character Education Resource Guide. Burch, Regina G. Fisch, Teri L., ed. 2003. 80p. (J). (gr. k-4). pap. 13.99 *(978-1-57471-982-6(3),* 3109) Creative Teaching Pr., Inc.

—Developing Reading Fluency, Grade 3: Using Modeled Reading, Phrasing, & Repeated Oral Reading. Callella, Trisha. Fisch, Teri L., ed. 2003. (Developing Reading Fluency Ser.). 96p. (J). (gr. 3-4). pap. 14.99 *(978-1-57471-996-3(3),* 2240) Creative Teaching Pr., Inc.

—Discover Air. Vogel, Julia. 2014. (Science Around Us Ser.). (ENG.). 24p. (J). (gr. -1-2). 25.64 *(978-1-62687-300-1(3),* 207141) Child's World, Inc., The.

—Discover Dirt. Hall, Pamela. 2014. (Science Around Us Ser.). (ENG.). 24p. (J). (gr. -1-2). 25.64 *(978-1-62687-301-8(1),* 207142) Child's World, Inc., The.

—Discover Electricity. Vogel, Julia. 2014. (Science Around Us Ser.). (ENG.). 24p. (J). (gr. -1-2). 25.64 *(978-1-62687-302-5(X),* 207143) Child's World, Inc., The.

—Discover Energy. Vogel, Julia. 2014. (Science Around Us Ser.). (ENG.). 24p. (J). (gr. -1-2). 25.64 *(978-1-62687-303-2(8),* 207144) Child's World, Inc., The.

—Discover Shadows. Hall, Pamela. 2014. (Science Around Us Ser.). (ENG.). 24p. (J). (gr. -1-2). 25.64 *(978-1-62687-305-6(4),* 207146) Child's World, Inc., The.

—Interactive Projects & Displays: Ideas for a Student-Created Learning Environment. Groeneweg, Nicole. F, Stacey, ed. 2006. (J). pap. 13.99 *(978-1-59198-315-6(0))* Creative Teaching Pr., Inc.

—5 Steps to Drawing Aircraft. Hall, Pamela. 2018. (5 Steps to Drawing Ser.). (ENG.). 32p. (J). (gr. k-3). 29.93 *(978-1-5038-2475-1(6),* 212235) Child's World, Inc., The.

Yamada, Jane & Ember, Kathi. Catch 'Em Being Good!, Burch, Regina G. Hamaguchi, Carla & Fisch, Teri, eds. 2003. 80p. (J). pap. 10.99 *(978-1-57471-992-5(0))* Creative Teaching Pr., Inc.

Yamada, Kana. Feel the Summer. Thomson, Sarah L. 2006. (ENG.). 32p. (J). (gr. -1-3). 14.95 *(978-1-59687-174-8(1))* iBks., Inc.

Yamada, Kazuaki. My Little Chick. Elschner, Géraldine. 2019. (ENG.). 32p. (J). (gr. -1-k). 17.99 *(978-988-8341-74-0(X),* Minedition) Neugebauer, Michael (Publishing) Limited HKG. Dist: Penguin Random Hse. LLC.

Yamada, Kazuaki. A Concert in the Park. Yamada, Kazuaki. 2018. (ENG.). 32p. (J). (gr. -1-k). 18.99 *(978-988-8341-48-1(0),* Minedition) Neugebauer, Michael (Publishing) Limited HKG. Dist: Penguin Random Hse. LLC.

Yamada, Mika. Sleepy Steve: Modeling Healthy Sleep for Children, One Night at a Time. Day, Samantha. 2019. (ENG.). 30p. (J). pap. 9.99 *(978-1-0722-2976-6(5))* Independently Published.

Yamada, Mike. Bad Guy. Barnaby, Hannah. 2017. (ENG.). 32p. (J). (gr. -1-3). 17.99 *(978-1-4814-6010-1(2),* Simon & Schuster Bks. For Young Readers) Simon & Schuster Bks. For Young Readers.

—Bedtime Blast-Off! Reynolds, Luke. 2016. (ENG.). 40p. (J). (gr. -1-1). 16.99 *(978-0-545-77855-8(7),* Orchard Bks.) Scholastic, Inc.

—Choo-Choo School. Rosenthal, Amy Krouse. 2020. (ENG.). 40p. (J). (gr. -1-2). 14.99 *(978-0-7636-9742-6(7))* Candlewick Pr.

—Go, Go, Cars! Liberts, Jennifer. 2018. (Step into Reading Ser.). (J). (gr. -1-1). 24p. 4.99 *(978-0-399-55461-2(0));* (ENG.). 32p. lib. bdg. 12.99 *(978-0-399-55462-9(9))* Random Hse. Children's Bks. (Random Hse. Bks. for Young Readers).

—Go, Go, Trucks! Liberts, Jennifer. 2017. (Step into Reading Ser.). 32p. (J). (gr. -1-1). 4.99 *(978-0-399-54951-9(X));* (ENG.). lib. bdg. 12.99 *(978-0-399-54952-6(8))* Random Hse. Children's Bks. (Random Hse. Bks. for Young Readers).

—I Love You for Miles & Miles. Goldberg, Alison. (ENG.). (J). 2018. 24p. bds. 7.99 *(978-0-374-31211-4(7),* 900198873); 2017. 32p. 17.99 *(978-0-374-30443-0(2),* 900159321) Farrar, Straus & Giroux. (Farrar, Straus & Giroux (BYR)).

—Kai to the Rescue. Penn, Audrey. 2016. (ENG.). 40p. (J). (gr. -1-k). 17.99 *(978-0-545-81636-6(X))* Scholastic, Inc.

Yamaguchi, Keika. Puddle Pug. Norman, Kim. (J). 2018. 30p. (— 1). bds. 7.95 *(978-1-4549-2715-0(1));* 2014. 40p. (gr. -1). 14.95 *(978-1-4549-0436-6(4))* Sterling Publishing Co., Inc.

—Teeny Tiny Toady. Esbaum, Jill. 2016. (ENG.). 40p. (J). (gr. -1-2). 14.95 *(978-1-4549-1454-9(8))* Sterling Publishing Co., Inc.

—Thunder Pug. Norman, Kim. 2019. (ENG.). 40p. (J). (gr. -1). 16.95 *(978-1-4549-2358-9(X))* Sterling Publishing Co., Inc.

—What about Moose? Schwartz, Corey Rosen & Gomez, Rebecca J. 2015. (ENG.). 40p. (J). (gr. -1-3). 18.99 *(978-1-4814-0496-9(2),* Atheneum Bks. for Young Readers) Simon & Schuster Children's Publishing.

Yamamoto, Lani. Albert. Yamamoto, Lani. 2004. (ENG.). 32p. (J). 10.95 *(978-1-58536-251-6(4))* Sleeping Bear Pr.

Yamamoto, Matsuko. Ding Dong. Shimizu, Michio. McLaughlin, Sako, tr. 2009. 32p. 14.95 *(978-1-74126-440-1(5))* R.I.C. Pubns. AUS. Dist: SCB Distributors.

Yamamoto, Satoshi. Pokémon. Miyaki, Tetsuichiro. 2013. (J). *(978-1-4844-1630-3(9))* Viz Media.

—Pokémon Adventures: Black 2 & White 2, Vol. 1. Kusaka, Hidenori. 2017. (Pokémon Adventures: Black 2 & White 2 Ser.: 1). (ENG.). 200p. (J). pap. 9.99 *(978-1-4215-8437-9(9))* Viz Media.

—Pokémon Adventures: Black 2 & White 2, Vol. 2. Kusaka, Hidenori. 2018. (Pokémon Adventures: Black 2 & White 2 Ser.: 2). (ENG.). 208p. (J). pap. 9.99 *(978-1-4215-8438-6(7))* Viz Media.

—Pokémon Adventures Diamond & Pearl / Platinum Box Set: Includes Volumes 1-11. Kusaka, Hidenori. 2014. (Pokémon Manga Box Sets Ser.). (ENG.). 2304p. (J). pap. 89.99 *(978-1-4215-7777-7(1))* Viz Media.

—Pokémon Adventures (Emerald), Vol. 26. Kusaka, Hidenori. 2015. (Pokemon Ser.: 26). (ENG.). 144p. (J). pap. 9.99 *(978-1-4215-3560-9(2))* Viz Media.

—Pokémon Adventures (Emerald), Vol. 27. Kusaka, Hidenori. 2015. (Pokemon Ser.: 27). (ENG.). 208p. (J). pap. 9.99 *(978-1-4215-3561-6(0))* Viz Media.

—Pokémon Adventures (Emerald), Vol. 28. Kusaka, Hidenori. 2015. (Pokemon Ser.: 28). (ENG.). 208p. (J). pap. 9.99 *(978-1-4215-3562-3(9))* Viz Media.

—Pokémon Adventures (Emerald), Vol. 29. Kusaka, Hidenori. 2015. (Pokemon Ser.: 29). (ENG.). 224p. (J). pap. 9.99 *(978-1-4215-3563-0(7))* Viz Media.

—Pokémon Adventures FireRed & LeafGreen / Emerald Box Set: Includes Vols. 23-29. Kusaka, Hidenori. 2015. (Pokémon Manga Box Sets Ser.). (ENG.). 1576p. (J). pap. 54.99 *(978-1-4215-8278-8(3))* Viz Media.

—Pokémon Adventures (FireRed & LeafGreen), Vol. 24. 2014. (Pokemon Ser.: 24). (ENG.). 216p. (J). pap. 9.99 *(978-1-4215-3558-6(0))* Viz Media.

—Pokémon Adventures (Gold & Silver), Vol. 12. Kusaka, Hidenori. 2011. (Pokemon Ser.: 12). (ENG.). 208p. (J). pap. 9.99 *(978-1-4215-3546-3(7))* Viz Media.

—Pokémon Adventures (Gold & Silver), Vol. 13. Kusaka, Hidenori. 2011. (Pokemon Ser.: 13). (ENG.). 208p. (J). pap. 9.99 *(978-1-4215-3547-0(5))* Viz Media.

—Pokémon Adventures (Gold & Silver), Vol. 14. Kusaka, Hidenori. 2011. (Pokemon Ser.: 14). (ENG.). 208p. (J). pap. 9.99 *(978-1-4215-3548-7(3))* Viz Media.

—Pokémon Adventures Ruby & Sapphire Box Set: Includes Volumes 15-22. Kusaka, Hidenori. 2014. (Pokémon Manga Box Sets Ser.). (ENG.). 1576p. (J). pap. 59.99 *(978-1-4215-7776-0(3))* Viz Media.

—Pokémon Black & White, Vol. 7. Kusaka, Hidenori. 2012. (Pokemon: Black & White Ser.). (ENG.). 96p. (J). (gr. 3-6). 17.44 *(978-1-4215-4282-9(X))* Viz Media.

—Pokémon Omega Ruby Alpha Sapphire, Vol. 3. 2017. (Pokemon Ser.: 3). (ENG.). 96p. (J). pap. 4.99 *(978-1-4215-9156-8(1))* Viz Media.

—Pokémon Omega Ruby Alpha Sapphire, Vol. 1, Vol. 1. 2016. (Pokemon Ser.: 1). (ENG.). 96p. (J). pap. 4.99 *(978-1-4215-9070-7(0))* Viz Media.

—Pokémon Omega Ruby Alpha Sapphire, Vol. 2, Vol. 2. 2016. (Pokemon Ser.: 2). (ENG.). 112p. (J). pap. 4.99 *(978-1-4215-9016-5(6))* Viz Media.

—Pokémon Omega Ruby Alpha Sapphire, Vol. 5. 2017. (Pokemon Ser.: 5). (ENG.). 88p. (J). pap. 4.99 *(978-1-4215-9626-6(1))* Viz Media.

—Pokemon Omega Ruby & Alpha Sapphire, Vol. 4. 2017. (Pokemon Ser.: 4). (ENG.). 96p. (J). pap. 4.99 *(978-1-4215-9223-7(1))* Viz Media.

—Pokémon Omega Ruby & Alpha Sapphire, Vol. 6. 2018. (Pokemon Ser.: 6). (ENG.). 120p. (J). pap. 4.99 *(978-1-4215-9738-6(1))* Viz Media.

—Pokémon: Sun & Moon, Vol. 1. Kusaka, Hidenori. 2018. (Pokémon: Sun & Moon Ser.: 1). (ENG.). 80p. (J). pap. 4.99 *(978-1-9747-0075-2(5))* Viz Media.

—Pokémon: Sun & Moon, Vol. 2. Kusaka, Hidenori. 2018. (Pokémon: Sun & Moon Ser.: 2). (ENG.). 120p. (J). pap. 4.99 *(978-1-9747-0130-8(1))* Viz Media.

—Pokémon: Sun & Moon, Vol. 3. Kusaka, Hidenori. 2019. (Pokémon: Sun & Moon Ser.: 3). (ENG.). 88p. (J). pap. 4.99 *(978-1-9747-0260-2(X))* Viz Media.

—Pokémon: Sun & Moon, Vol. 4. Kusaka, Hidenori. 2019. (Pokémon: Sun & Moon Ser.: 4). (ENG.). 88p. (J). pap. 4.99 *(978-1-9747-0305-0(3))* Viz Media.

Yamamoto, Satoshi. Pokémon: Sun & Moon, Vol. 7. Kusaka, Hidenori. 2020. (Pokémon: Sun & Moon Ser.: 7). (ENG.). 88p. (J). pap. 4.99 ***(978-1-9747-1115-4(3))*** Viz Media.

—Pokémon: Sun & Moon, Vol. 8. Kusaka, Hidenori. 2020. (Pokémon: Sun & Moon Ser.: 8). (ENG.). 96p. (J). pap. 4.99 ***(978-1-9747-1116-1(1))*** Viz Media.

Yamamoto, Satoshi. Pokémon X Y, Vol. 5. Kusaka, Hidenori. 2015. 96p. (J). pap. 4.99 *(978-1-4215-8250-4(3))* Viz Media.

—Pokémon X Y, Vol. 6. Kusaka, Hidenori. 2016. 96p. (J). pap. 4.99 *(978-1-4215-8335-8(6))* Viz Media.

—Pokémon X*y Complete Box Set: Includes Vols. 1-12. Kusaka, Hidenori. 2017. (Pokémon Manga Box Sets Ser.). (ENG.). 1216p. (J). pap. 54.99 *(978-1-4215-9849-9(3))* Viz Media.

—Pokémon X*y, Vol. 1, Vol. 1. Kusaka, Hidenori. 2014. (Pokemon Ser.: 1). (ENG.). 96p. (J). pap. 4.99 *(978-1-4215-7980-1(4))* Viz Media.

—Pokémon X*y, Vol. 10. 2017. (Pokemon Ser.: 10). (ENG.). 112p. (J). pap. 4.99 *(978-1-4215-9164-3(2))* Viz Media.

—Pokémon X*y, Vol. 11. 2017. (Pokemon Ser.: 11). (ENG.). 96p. (J). pap. 4.99 *(978-1-4215-9066-0(2))* Viz Media.

—Pokémon X*y, Vol. 12. 2017. (Pokemon Ser.: 12). (ENG.). 112p. (J). pap. 4.99 *(978-1-4215-9625-9(3))* Viz Media.

—Pokémon X*y, Vol. 2, Vol. 2. Kusaka, Hidenori. 2015. (Pokemon Ser.: 2). (ENG.). 112p. (J). pap. 4.99 *(978-1-4215-7834-7(4))* Viz Media.

—Pokémon X*y, Vol. 8, Vol. 8. 2016. (Pokemon Ser.: 8). (ENG.). 96p. (J). pap. 4.99 *(978-1-4215-8779-0(3))* Viz Media.

—Pokémon X*y, Vol. 9. 2017. (Pokemon Ser.: 9). (ENG.). 96p. (J). pap. 4.99 *(978-1-4215-9155-1(3))* Viz Media.

Yamamoto, Tadayoshi. Jeeper the Fire Engine. Watanabe, Shigeo. 2005. 28p. (J). 11.95 *(978-4-902216-14-1(0))* R.I.C. Publications Asia Co., Inc. JPN. Dist: Continental Enterprises Group, Inc. (CEG).

Yamamura, Hajime. Rebirth of the Demonslayer. Yamamura, Hajime. 192p. (YA). Vol. 1. 2004. pap. 9.99 *(978-1-58655-540-5(5));* Vol. 3. 2005. pap. 9.99 *(978-1-58655-689-1(4),* AWNOV-0554) Media Blasters, Inc.

Yamasaki, James. Boy Dumplings. Compestine, Ying Chang. 2009. (ENG.). 32p. (J). (gr. -1-3). 16.95 *(978-0-8234-1955-5(X))* Holiday Hse., Inc.

—Christmas Chaos: Hidden Picture Puzzles, 1 vol. Kalz, Jill. 2012. (Seek It Out Ser.). (ENG.). 32p. (J). (gr. k-3). 9.95 *(978-1-4048-7724-5(X));* lib. bdg. 27.32 *(978-1-4048-7494-7(1))* Capstone. (Picture Window Bks.).

Yamasaki, Katie. God's Big Plan. Caldwell, Elizabeth F. & Hiebert, Theodore. 2019. (ENG.). 40p. (J). (gr. -1-2). 17.00 *(978-1-947888-06-7(4),* 1947888064, Flyaway Bks.) Westminster John Knox Pr.

—Pockets. Lynch, Joseph. l.t. ed. (J). pap. 16.98 *(978-0-932970-83-1(4))* Prinit Pr.

Yamasaki, Katie. Fish for Jimmy. Yamasaki, Katie. 2013. (ENG.). 32p. (J). (gr. 1-4). 16.95 *(978-0-8234-2375-0(1))* Holiday Hse., Inc.

Yamaski, James. Boy Dumplings: A Chinese Food Tale. Compestine, Ying Chang. 2016. (ENG.). 40p. (J). (gr. -1-3). 15.95 *(978-1-59702-119-7(9))* Immedium.

Yamate, Sandra S. & Yao, Carolina. Char Siu Bao Boy. 2004. 32p. (J). (gr. k-3). pap. 15.95 *(978-1-879965-19-5(4))* Polychrome Publishing Corp.

Yamawaki, Yuriko. Dr. Mouse's Mission. Nakagawa, Masafumi. Perry, Mia Lynn, tr. 2007. (R. I. C. Story Chest Ser.). 27p. (J). (gr. -1-1). 14.95 incl. audio compact disk *(978-1-74126-051-9(5))* R.I.C. Pubns. AUS. Dist: SCB Distributors.

Yan, Edison. Summer Brain Quest: Between Grades 3 And 4. Walker, Persephone et al. 2017. (Summer Brain Quest Ser.). (ENG.). 160p. (J). (gr. 4-5). pap. 12.95 *(978-0-7611-8919-0(X),* 18919) Workman Publishing Co., Inc.

Yan, Edison & Wicks, Maris. Summer Brain Quest: Between Grades Pre-K & K. Heos, Bridget & Workman Publishing. 2018. (Summer Brain Quest Ser.). (ENG.). 160p. (gr. -1-k). pap. 12.95 *(978-1-5235-0299-8(1),* 100299) Workman Publishing Co., Inc.

Yan, Edison, jt. illus. see Cummings, Matt.

Yan, Edison, jt. illus. see Dukes, Rachel.

Yan, Edison, jt. illus. see Pietch, Carey.

Yan, Edison, jt. illus. see Thomas, Chad.

Yan, Edison, jt. illus. see Wicks, Maris.

Yan, Stan. 1 Block Down. Carew, Kieran. 2004. 24p. (YA). 2.95 *(978-0-9755041-2-3(6))* Squid Works.

Yan, Xindi. Best Buds Forever. Maker, Martha. 2020. (Craftily Ever After Ser.: 7). (ENG.). 128p. (J). (gr. k-4). 17.99 ***(978-1-5344-6355-4(0))****;* pap. 5.99 ***(978-1-5344-6354-7(2))*** Little Simon. (Little Simon).

Yan, Xindi. Breaking the Piggy Bank. Maker, Martha. 2019. (Craftily Ever After Ser.: 6). (ENG.). 128p. (J). (gr. k-4). 16.99 *(978-1-5344-2903-1(4));* pap. 5.99 *(978-1-5344-2902-4(6))* Little Simon. (Little Simon).

—Craftily Ever after 4 Books In 1! The un-Friendship Bracelet; Making the Band; Tie-Dye Disaster; Dream Machine. Maker, Martha. 2019. (Craftily Ever After Ser.). (ENG.). 512p. (J). (gr. k-4). 14.99 *(978-1-5344-5634-1(1),* Little Simon) Little Simon.

—The Craftily Ever after Collection: The un-Friendship Bracelet; Making the Band; Tie-Dye Disaster; Dream Machine. Maker, Martha. ed. 2018. (Craftily Ever After Ser.). (ENG.). 512p. (J). (gr. k-4). pap. 23.99 *(978-1-5344-3221-5(3),* Little Simon) Little Simon.

—DIY Pet Shop. Maker, Martha. 2018. (Craftily Ever After Ser.: 5). (ENG.). 128p. (J). (gr. k-4). 16.99 *(978-1-5344-2900-0(X));* pap. 5.99 *(978-1-5344-2899-7(2))* Little Simon. (Little Simon).

—Dream Machine. Maker, Martha. 2018. (Craftily Ever After Ser.: 4). (ENG.). 128p. (J). (gr. k-4). 16.99 *(978-1-5344-1731-1(1));* pap. 5.99 *(978-1-5344-1730-4(3))* Little Simon. (Little Simon).

—Grandpa Grumps. Moore, Katrina. 2020. (ENG.). 40p. (J). (gr. -1-3). 17.99 *(978-1-4998-0886-5(0))* Little Bee Books Inc.

—The Itty Bitty Witch. Speed Shaskan, Trisha. 2019. 32p. (J). (gr. -1-2). 17.99 *(978-1-5420-4123-2(6),* 9781542041232, Two Lions) Amazon Publishing.

—Making the Band. Maker, Martha. 2018. (Craftily Ever After Ser.: 2). (ENG.). 128p. (J). (gr. k-4). 16.99 *(978-1-5344-0911-8(4));* pap. 5.99 *(978-1-5344-0910-1(6))* Little Simon. (Little Simon).

—Sylvia Rose & the Cherry Tree, 1 vol. Shapiro-Hurt, Sandy. 2018. (ENG.). 36p. (J). (gr. k-3). 17.95 *(978-0-88448-527-8(7),* 884527) Tilbury Hse. Pubs.

—Tie-Dye Disaster. Maker, Martha. 2018. (Craftily Ever After Ser.: 3). (ENG.). 128p. (J). (gr. k-4). 16.99 *(978-1-5344-1728-1(1));* pap. 5.99 *(978-1-5344-1727-4(3))* Little Simon. (Little Simon).

—The un-Friendship Bracelet. Maker, Martha. 2018. (Craftily Ever After Ser.: 1). (ENG.). 128p. (J). (gr. k-4). 17.99 *(978-1-5344-0908-8(4));* pap. 5.99 *(978-1-5344-0907-1(6))* Little Simon. (Little Simon).

Yanagisawa, Kazuaki. The Guin Saga Manga. Kurimoto, Kaoru. (Guin Saga Ser.: 1). (ENG.). 200p. Vol. 1. 2007. (J). (gr. 8-12). per. 12.95 (978-1-932234-80-0(2)); Vol. 2. 2008. (gr. 11). per. 12.95 (978-1-934287-07-1(5)) Kodansha America, Inc. (Vertical).

—The Seven Magi, Vol. 3. Kurimoto, Kaoru. 2008. (Guin Saga Ser.: 3). (ENG.). 200p. (gr. 11). per. 12.95 (978-1-934287-08-8(3), Vertical) Kodansha America, Inc.

Yanez, Francisca. Anne: An Imagining of the Life of Anne Frank. Agosin, Marjorie. Nanfito, Jacqueline, tr. from SPA. 2017. (ENG.). 66p. (YA). (gr. 7-12). (978-1-910146-26-2(9)) Solis Pr.

Yang, Aboo. Remembering Barkley. Frankel, Erin. 2020. (ENG.). 32p. (J). (gr. -1-3). 16.99 (978-0-8075-9448-3(2), 0807594482) Whitman, Albert & Co.

Yang, Belle. Always Come Home to Me. Yang, Belle. 2007. (ENG.). 32p. (J). (gr. -1-3). 16.99 (978-0-7636-2899-4(9)) Candlewick Pr.

—Angel in Beijing. Yang, Belle. 2018. 32p. (J). (gr. -1-3). 16.99 (978-0-7636-9270-4(0)) Candlewick Pr.

—Foo, the Flying Frog of Washtub Pond. Yang, Belle. 2009. (ENG.). 32p. (J). (gr. -1-2). 16.99 (978-0-7636-3615-9(0)) Candlewick Pr.

—Hannah Is My Name. Yang, Belle. 2007. (J). (gr. k-4). 14.65 (978-0-7569-8124-2(7)) Perfection Learning Corp.

—Hannah Is My Name: A Young Immigrant's Story. Yang, Belle. 2007. (ENG.). 32p. (J). (gr. k-4). pap. 6.99 (978-0-7636-3521-3(9)) Candlewick Pr.

—A Nest in Springtime: A Bilingual Book of Numbers. Yang, Belle. ed. 2012. (ENG.). 24p. (J). (gr. k — 1). bds. 6.99 (978-0-7636-5279-1(2)) Candlewick Pr.

—Summertime Rainbow: A Mandarin Chinese-English Bilingual Book of Colors. Yang, Belle. 2012. 22p. (J). (gr. k — 1). bds. 6.99 (978-0-7636-5280-7(6)) Candlewick Pr.

Yang, Dorothy. Elliot HATES His Lunch! Yang, Adalia. 2020. (ENG.). 28p. (J). (978-0-2288-2722-1(1)); pap. (978-0-2288-2720-7(5)) Tellwell Talent.

Yang, Gene Luen. The Rosary Comic Book. Plen, Lark. 2003. 56p. (J). mass mkt. 5.95 (978-0-8198-6479-6(X), 332-312) Pauline Bks. & Media.

Yang, Gene Luen. American Born Chinese. Yang, Gene Luen. (ENG.). 240p. (YA). (gr. 7-18). 2007. 24.99 (978-1-59643-373-1(6), 900050139); 2006. pap. 18.99 (978-1-59643-152-2(0), 900037739) Roaring Brook Pr. (First Second Bks.).

—Boxers. Yang, Gene Luen. 2013. (Boxers & Saints Ser.: 1). (ENG.). 336p. (YA). (gr. 7-12). pap. 18.99 (978-1-59643-359-5(0), 900049329, First Second Bks.) Roaring Brook Pr.

—Boxers & Saints Boxed Set. Yang, Gene Luen. Plen, Lark. 2013. (Boxers & Saints Ser.: 1). (ENG.). 512p. (YA). (gr. 7). 34.99 (978-1-59643-924-5(6), 900121625, First Second Bks.) Roaring Brook Pr.

—Saints. Yang, Gene Luen. Plen, Lark. 2013. (Boxers & Saints Ser.: Vol. 2). (ENG.). (YA). (gr. 7). lib. bdg. 26.60 (978-1-62765-516-3(6)) Perfection Learning Corp.

—Saints. Yang, Gene Luen. 2013. (Boxers & Saints Ser.: 2). (ENG.). 176p. (YA). (gr. 7). pap. 15.99 (978-1-59643-689-3(1), 900072232, First Second Bks.) Roaring Brook Pr.

Yang, HyeWon. Green River. Lee, WonKyeong. 2014. (MySELF Bookshelf Ser.). (ENG.). 32p. (J). (gr. k-2). pap. 11.94 (978-1-60357-695-6(9)); lib. bdg. 25.27 (978-1-59953-660-6(9)) Norwood Hse. Pr.

Yang, James. Stop! Bot! 2019. 40p. (J). (-k). 17.99 (978-0-425-28881-8(1), Viking Books for Young Readers) Penguin Young Readers Group.

Yang, James. Bus! Stop! Yang, James. 2018. 32p. (J). (-k). 17.99 (978-0-425-28877-1(3), Viking Books for Young Readers) Penguin Young Readers Group.

—Joey & Jet: Book 1 of Their Adventures. Yang, James. 2012. (ENG.). 32p. (J). (gr. -1-k). pap. 16.99 (978-1-4424-5930-4(1), Atheneum Bks. for Young Readers) Simon & Schuster Children's Publishing.

—Joey & Jet in Space. Yang, James. 2006. (ENG.). 32p. (J). (gr. -1-k). 19.99 (978-0-689-86927-3(4), Atheneum/Richard Jackson Bks.) Simon & Schuster Children's Publishing.

—Puzzlehead. Yang, James. 2015. (ENG.). 32p. (J). (gr. -1-1). 13.99 (978-1-4814-7507-5(X), Atheneum Bks. for Young Readers) Simon & Schuster Children's Publishing.

Yang, Joy. Spirit Day: A Book about Spreading Joy. Little Bee Books. 2019. (ENG.). 22p. (J). (— 1). bds. 6.99 (978-1-4998-0969-5(7)) Little Bee Books Inc.

Yang, Kyung-Il. Blade of Heaven, Vol. 2. rev. ed. 2005. 288p. pap. 14.99 (978-1-59532-328-6(7), Tokyopop Adult) TOKYOPOP, Inc.

—Blade of Heaven, Vol. 3. rev. ed. 2005. 280p. pap. 14.99 (978-1-59532-329-3(5), Tokyopop Adult) TOKYOPOP, Inc.

—Blade of Heaven, Vol. 7. 2005. 296p. pap. 14.99 (978-1-59532-327-9(9), Tokyopop Adult) TOKYOPOP, Inc.

Yang, Lei. Unicorns Are Real! Using All130 Kindergarten Level Sight Words! Haag, Tiffany. 2019. (K Ser.: Vol. 1). (ENG.). 26p. (J). pap. 9.99 (978-1-6932-6237-1(1)) Independently Published.

Yang, Peng. The Secret Birthday Present. Chen, Ju. 2020. (Little Jack's Secret Adventures in China Ser.). (ENG.). 32p. (J). 5.99 (978-1-912268-41-2(8), 88412e78-205e-4b50-842e-5e85b242a48b) Design Media Publishing Ltd. HKG. Dist: Baker & Taylor Publisher Services (BTPS).

—Secrets of the Terracotta Army. Wei, Chen. 2020. (Little Jack's Secret Adventures in China Ser.). (ENG.). 32p. (J). 5.99 (978-1-912268-40-5(X), 29137b35-e589-451b-b414-70a0998264e4) Design Media Publishing Ltd. HKG. Dist: Baker & Taylor Publisher Services (BTPS).

Yang, Stella. My Family: Individual Title Six-Packs. (Sails Literacy Ser.). 16p. (gr. k-18). 27.00 (978-0-7635-4393-8(4)) Rigby Education.

—The Snowman, 6 vols., Pack. (Sails Literacy Ser.). 16p. (gr. k-18). 27.00 (978-0-7635-4439-3(6)) Rigby Education.

Yang, Yeng. My Community. Howell, Raven. 2018. (ENG.). 30p. (J). (gr. k-6). 21.99 (978-1-387-02119-2(2)); pap. 15.99 (978-1-387-02122-2(2)) Lulu Pr., Inc.

—My Community Dyslexic Edition: Dyslexic Font. Howell, Raven. ed. 2018. (ENG.). 30p. (J). (gr. k-6). 19.99 (978-1-64372-060-9(0)) MacLaren-Cochrane Publishing, Inc.

—A New Book for Jack. Lunsford, Lois. ed. 2017. (ENG.). 32p. (J). (gr. k-6). pap. 13.99 (978-1-64372-222-1(0)) MacLaren-Cochrane Publishing, Inc.

—A New Book for Jack Dyslexic Edition: Dyslexic Font. Lunsford, Lois. ed. 2017. (ENG.). 32p. (J). (gr. k-6). pap. 15.99 (978-1-64372-224-5(7)); 19.99 (978-1-64372-223-8(9)) MacLaren-Cochrane Publishing, Inc.

Yang, Yi. You Are My Everything: Determined Little Maghara!!! Peterson, M. E. 2008. 43p. pap. 24.95 (978-1-60610-807-9(7)) America Star Bks.

Yanish, Brian. ScrapKins: Junk Re-Thunk: Amazing Creations You Can Make from Junk! Yanish, Brian. 2016. (ENG.). 80p. (J). pap. 12.99 (978-1-62779-133-5(7), 900136753, Holt, Henry & Co. Bks. For Young Readers) Holt, Henry & Co.

Yankey, Lindsey. My Grandma & Me. Javaherbin, Mina. 2019. (ENG.). 32p. (J). (gr. -1-3). 16.99 (978-0-7636-9494-4(0)) Candlewick Pr.

Yao, Carolina, jt. illus. see Yamate, Sandra S.

Yap, Weda. Rain, Hail, Sleet & Snow. Larrick, Nancy. 2011. 68p. 36.95 (978-1-258-08878-1(9)) Literary Licensing, LLC.

—Rain, Hail, Sleet & Snow. Larrick, Nancy. 2016. (ENG.). (J). (gr. 3-6). pap. 12.95 (978-0-692-81047-7(1)) Living Library Pr.

Yapo Yapo, Martial. Tiwa et la Pierre Miroir. Bilé, Serge & Bernabé, Joby. 2017. (FRE.). 34p. (978-2-916868-43-1(7)) Cercle éditions.

Yapsangco, Kenn. The St John's Cross Spider. Whincup, Sara. 2015. (ENG.). 28p. (J). pap. 28.22 (978-1-5035-0985-6(0)) Xlibris Corp.

Yarbrough, Kim. Frannie & the Big Birthday Wish. Yarbrough, Kim. Williams, Iris M., ed. 2018. (ENG.). 52p. (J). pap. 20.95 (978-1-947656-79-6(1)) Butterfly Typeface, The.

Yarbrough, Mark. The Legend of Jake, the Salty Dog. Gossett, Robert A. 2007. (J). 8.95 (978-0-9793560-0-1(8)) Salty Dog, Inc., The.

Yarbusova, Francesca. Hedgehog in the Fog. Norstein, Yuri & Kozlov, Sergey. Golburt, Luba, tr. from RUS. 2013. (ENG.). 48p. (J). 17.95 (978-0-9845867-0-7(9)) Rovakada, LLC.

Yarchi, Jacky. The Gang of Four Kung-Fooey to the Rescue. Petersell, Yaacov. 2005. 192p. (J). pap. 7.95 (978-0-943706-51-1(3), Devora Publishing) Simcha Media Group.

Yardin, David, jt. illus. see Larroca, Salvador.

Yardley, Joanna. B Is for Big Sky Country. Collard, Sneed B., III. 2003. (Discover America State by State Ser.). (ENG.). 40p. (J). 17.95 (978-1-58536-098-7(8)) Sleeping Bear Pr.

—P Is for Peace Garden: A North Dakota Alphabet. Salonen, Roxane B. 2005. (Discover America State by State Ser.). (ENG.). 40p. (J). (gr. -1-7). 17.95 (978-1-58536-142-7(9)) Sleeping Bear Pr.

—Shep: Our Most Loyal Dog. Collard, Sneed B., III. 2006. (ENG.). 32p. (J). (gr. 1-4). 19.99 (978-1-58536-259-2(X), 202074) Sleeping Bear Pr.

Yardley, Liz. The Firefly Legacy - Book VI. Yardley, Liz. 2013. 336p. pap. (978-0-9872013-1-7(X)) BlueFlower Bks.

—The Firefly Legacy - Book VII. Yardley, Liz. 2013. 314p. pap. (978-0-9872013-2-4(8)) BlueFlower Bks.

Yardley, Tracy. Cosmo Vol. 1. Flynn, Ian. 2018. (ENG.). 128p. (J). (gr. 4-7). pap. 12.99 (978-1-68255-865-2(7)) Archie Comic Pubns., Inc.

Yardley, Tracy, et al. Fallout Part 1. Flynn, Ian. 2019. (Sonic the Hedgehog Ser.). (ENG.). 24p. (J). (gr. 2-8). lib. bdg. 27.07 (978-1-5321-4433-2(4), 33838, Graphic Novels) Spotlight.

—The Fate of Dr. Eggman Part 1. Flynn, Ian. 2019. (Sonic the Hedgehog Ser.). (ENG.). 24p. (J). (gr. 2-8). lib. bdg. 27.07 (978-1-5321-4437-0(7), 33842, Graphic Novels) Spotlight.

—The Fate of Dr. Eggman Part 2. Flynn, Ian. 2019. (Sonic the Hedgehog Ser.). (ENG.). 24p. (J). (gr. 2-8). lib. bdg. 27.07 (978-1-5321-4438-7(5), 33843, Graphic Novels) Spotlight.

Yardley, Tracy, et al. Sonic the Hedgehog, Vol. 1: ¡Consecuencias! (Sonic the Hedgehog, Vol 1: Fallout! Spanish Edition) Flynn, Ian. 2020. (Sonic the Hedgehog Spanish Ser.: 1). 104p. (J). (gr. 4-7). pap. 15.99 (978-1-68405-749-8(3)) Idea & Design Works, LLC.

Yardley, Tracy & Lawrence, Jack. Sonic the Hedgehog, Vol. 5: Crisis City. Flynn, Ian. 2020. (Sonic the Hedgehog Ser.: 5). 96p. (J). (gr. 4-7). pap. 15.99 (978-1-68405-617-0(9)) Idea & Design Works, LLC.

Yardley, Tracy & Stanley, Evan. Sonic the Hedgehog, Vol. 3: Battle for Angel Island. Flynn, Ian. 2019. (Sonic the Hedgehog Ser.: 3). 96p. (J). (gr. 4-7). pap. 15.99 (978-1-68405-498-5(2)) Idea & Design Works, LLC.

Yarlett, Emma. Crinkle, Crinkle, Little Star: Trace the Stars. Hear Them Crinkle. Krasner, Justin. 2017. (ENG.). 16p. (J). 12.95 (978-1-5235-0120-5(0), 100120) Workman Publishing Co., Inc.

—Nibbles: The Book Monster. 2016. (J). (978-1-61067-467-6(7)) Kane Miller.

—Penguinaut. Colleen, Marcie. 2018. (ENG.). 32p. (J). (gr. -1-k). 17.99 (978-0-545-84884-8(9)) Scholastic, Inc.

Yarlett, Emma. Sidney, Stella, & the Moon. Yarlett, Emma. 2013. (ENG.). 44p. (J). (gr. k-3). 16.99 (978-0-7636-6623-1(8), Templar) Candlewick Pr.

Yarnall, Karen Sturdy. Along the Chesapeake & Delaware Canal. Maxson, H. A. & Young, Claudia H. 2005. 64p. (J). per. 9.95 (978-0-9741713-2-6(8)) Bay Oak Pubs., Ltd.

Yaron, Sophie. The Promise: The Moving Story of a Family in the Holocaust. Schloss, Eva & Powers, Barbara. 2006. 160p. (J). (gr. 13-18). 12.99 (978-0-14-132081-6(8)) Penguin Bks., Ltd. GBR. Dist: Independent Pubs. Group.

Yashima, Taro. Crow Boy. Yashima, Taro. 2004. 34p. (J). (gr. k-3). reprint ed. pap. 14.00 (978-0-7567-7102-7(1)) DIANE Publishing Co.

—Crow Boy. Yashima, Taro. pap. 35.95 incl. audio compact disk (978-1-59112-803-8(X)) Live Oak Media.

Yaskina, Valentina. I Love You Cards: 25 Clever Cards to Color + Envelopes Included. Clever Publishing. 2018. (Clever Cards to Color Ser.). (ENG.). 54p. (J). (gr. -1-1). 10.99 (978-1-948418-27-0(4)) Clever Media Group.

Yasser, Noura. My Parents Taught Me Good Manners - Carol Receives the Humanitarian Award. Russell, Cathy Prather. Bharol, Kashika, ed. 2019. (My Parents Taught Me Good Manners Ser.: Vol. 5). (ENG.). 28p. (J). pap. 19.99 (978-1-7055-3156-3(3)) Independently Published.

Yasu. Toradora! (Light Novel) Vol. 1. Takemiya, Yuyuko. 2018. (Toradora! (Light Novel) Ser.: 1). (ENG.). 240p. (YA). pap. 13.99 (978-1-62692-795-7(2), 900192512) Seven Seas Entertainment, LLC.

—Toradora! (Light Novel) Vol. 2. Takemiya, Yuyuko. 2018. (Toradora! (Light Novel) Ser.: 2). (ENG.). 240p. (YA). pap. 13.99 (978-1-62692-861-9(4), 900192645) Seven Seas Entertainment, LLC.

—Toradora! (Light Novel) Vol. 3. Takemiya, Yuyuko. 2018. (Toradora! (Light Novel) Ser.: 3). (ENG.). 240p. (YA). pap. 13.99 (978-1-62692-938-8(6), 900195635) Seven Seas Entertainment, LLC.

—Toradora! (Light Novel) Vol. 4. Takemiya, Yuyuko. 2019. (Toradora! (Light Novel) Ser.: 4). (ENG.). 240p. (YA). pap. 13.99 (978-1-62692-989-0(0), 900198017) Seven Seas Entertainment, LLC.

Yasui, Koji. The King Who Saved the Dove. Kato, Etsuo. 2014. (J). 8.95 (978-1-935523-68-0(6)) World Tribune Pr.

Yasunari, Toda. Scryed, 5 vols., Vol. 1. Kuroda, Yosuke. 2003. 192p. (YA). pap. 9.99 (978-1-59182-228-8(9)) TOKYOPOP, Inc.

—Scryed, Vol. 3. Yosuke, Kuroda. rev. ed. 2003. 192p. pap. 9.99 (978-1-59182-230-1(0)) TOKYOPOP, Inc.

Yates, Beth. The Terrific Trip of Douglas Drip. Mace, Carol. Hardcastle, E., ed. 2019. (ENG.). 26p. (J). pap. 8.99 (978-1-5272-5243-1(4), Curious Cat Bks.) Legacy Bound.

Yates, Bridget & Ward, Karen. The Jumping Orie Story. Clough, Paige. 2015. (J). (978-1-942945-24-6(8)) Night Heron Media.

—The Jumping Orie Story. Clough, Paige. 2015. (J). (978-0-9915511-2-5(5)) Rule 2 Bks.

Yates, Gene. The Chameleon Colors Book. 2006. (J). (978-1-58865-361-1(7)) Kidsbooks, LLC.

—The Dragon Opposites Book. 2006. (J). (978-1-58865-362-8(5)) Kidsbooks, LLC.

—The Elephant Alphabet Book. 2006. (J). (978-1-58865-363-5(3)) Kidsbooks, LLC.

—The Giraffe Numbers Book. 2006. (J). (978-1-58865-364-2(1)) Kidsbooks, LLC.

—The Snake Shapes Book. 2006. (J). (978-1-58865-365-9(X)) Kidsbooks, LLC.

Yates, Gene. What Can Simon Be? Yates, Gene. Frank, Thomas. 2006. (J). (978-1-58865-366-6(8)) Kidsbooks, LLC.

Yates, Kelly. Venomous. Krovatin, Christopher. 2011. (ENG.). 336p. (YA). (gr. 8). pap. 8.99 (978-1-4424-1298-9(4), Atheneum Bks. for Young Readers) Simon & Schuster Children's Publishing.

Yates, Louise. Young Fredle. Voigt, Cynthia. 2012. 240p. (J). (gr. 4-6). 21.19 (978-0-375-86457-5(1), Knopf Bks. for Young Readers); (gr. 3-7). 7.99 (978-0-375-85787-4(7), Yearling) Random Hse. Children's Bks.

Yates, Wyeth. The Castoffs Vol. 2: Into the Wastelands. Reed, M. K. & Smith, Brian "Smitty". 2017. (ENG.). 144p. (J). pap. 12.99 (978-1-941302-32-3(7), dceb3c67-8be6-4d46-8fff-224e0e7b9db1, Lion Forge) Oni Pr., Inc.

—The Castoffs Vol. 3: Rise of the Machines. Reed, M. K. & Smith, Brian "Smitty". 2018. (ENG.). 136p. (YA). pap. 12.99 (978-1-941302-73-6(4), 07e3e1de-d3fd-4b4f-ad0a-9855b730c0ed, Lion Forge) Oni Pr., Inc.

—The Mars Challenge: The Past, Present, & Future of Human Spaceflight. Wilgus, Alison. 2020. (ENG.). (YA). 40p. 24.99 (978-1-250-25825-0(1), 900219781); 208p. pap. 17.99 (978-1-62672-083-1(5), 900134907) Roaring Brook Pr. (First Second Bks.).

Yatsunenko, Anastasia. Zafira e Rubi Ogni Strega Ha il Suo Stregone. de Las Cuevas, Fernanda. 2018. (ITA.). 26p. (J). pap. 9.95 (978-1-7180-0155-8(X)) Independently Published.

Yaweera, Sasiprapa, jt. illus. see Pornkerd, Vorrarit.

Yayo. If I Had a Million Onions, 1 vol. Fitch, Sheree. 2005. (ENG.). 64p. (J). (gr. 1-3). 15.95 (978-1-896580-78-4(5)) Tradewind Bks. CAN. Dist: Orca Bk. Pubs. USA.

—Night Sky Wheel Ride, 1 vol. Fitch, Sheree. 2013. (ENG.). 32p. (J). (gr. -1-k). 16.95 (978-1-896580-67-8(X)) Tradewind Bks. CAN. Dist: Orca Bk. Pubs. USA.

—Sam Swallow & the Riddleworld League, 1 vol. New, William. 2013. (ENG.). 144p. (J). (gr. 4-7). pap. 12.95 (978-1-896580-98-2(X)) Tradewind Bks. CAN. Dist: Orca Bk. Pubs. USA.

—Where Are You Little Red Ball?, 1 vol. McMaster, Juliet & Cote, Patricia. Reva, Maria, tr. 2016. (ENG.). 12p. (J). (gr. -1 — 1). bds. 8.95 (978-1-926890-12-8(4)) Tradewind Bks. CAN. Dist: Orca Bk. Pubs. USA.

Yazawa, Nao. Wedding Peach. Tomita, Sukehiro. 2004. (Wedding Peach Ser.). (ENG.). Vol. 4. 192p. pap. 9.95 (978-1-59116-132-5(0)); Vol. 5. 200p. pap. 9.95 (978-1-59116-257-5(2)) Viz Media.

—Young Love, Vol. 7. Tomita, Sukehiro. 2004. (Wedding Peach Ser.). (ENG.). 200p. pap. 9.95 (978-1-59116-450-0(8)) Viz Media.

Yazawa, Nao, jt. illus. see Tomita, Sukehiro.

Yazdani, Ashley Benham. A Green Place to Be: the Creation of Central Park. Yazdani, Ashley Benham. 2019. 40p. (J). (gr. 2-5). 17.99 (978-0-7636-9695-5(1)) Candlewick Pr.

Yazzie, Benton. The Shaman & the Water Serpent. Dewey, Jennifer Owings. 2007. (ENG.). 40p. (J). 19.95 (978-0-8263-4211-9(6)) Univ. of New Mexico Pr.

Yazzie, Johnson, jt. illus. see Brycelea, Clifford.

Yazzie, Peterson. The Hogan That Great-Grandfather Built. Flood, Nancy Bo. 2012. (ENG & NAV.). 32p. (J). (gr. -1-3). 17.95 (978-1-893354-97-5(0)) Salina Bookshelf Inc.

Ybáñez, Terry. That's Not Fair! - ¡No es Justo! Emma Tenayuca's Struggle for Justice - La Lucha de Emma Tenayuca Por la Justicia. Tafolla, Carmen & Teneyuca, Sharyll. 2008. (SPA & ENG.). 40p. (J). (gr. k-2). 19.95 (978-0-916727-33-8(5)) Wings Pr.

Ycaza, Roger. Hay Palabras Que Los Peces No Entienden. Fernanda Heredia, Maria. 2016. (Serie Azul Ser.). (SPA.). 168p. (J). (gr. 5-8). pap. 12.95 (978-1-64101-196-9(3)) Santillana USA Publishing Co., Inc.

Yeagle, Dean. The Cow in Apple Time. Frost, Robert. 2005. 32p. (J). 15.95 (978-0-9758970-1-0(2)) Beekman & Hathaway.

Yeates, Thomas. Arthur & Lancelot: The Fight for Camelot. Limke, Jeff. 2008. (Graphic Myths & Legends Ser.). (ENG.). 48p. (gr. 4-8). pap. 8.95 (978-0-8225-8513-8(8)) Lerner Publishing Group.

—Arthur & Lancelot: The Fight for Camelot - An English Legend. Limke, Jeff. 2007. (Graphic Myths & Legends Ser.). (ENG.). 48p. (J). (gr. 4-8). lib. bdg. 27.93 (978-0-8225-6296-2(0), Graphic Universe™) Lerner Publishing Group.

—Arthur & Lancelot: The Fight for Camelot [an English Legend]. Limke, Jeff. 2015. (Graphic Myths & Legends Ser.). (ENG.). 48p. (gr. 4-8). 21.32 (978-1-4677-5979-3(1), Lerner Digital) Lerner Publishing Group.

—Atalanta: The Race Against Destiny. Fontes, Justine & Fontes, Ron. 2007. (Graphic Myths & Legends Ser.). (ENG.). 48p. (J). (gr. 4-8). lib. bdg. 27.99 (978-0-8225-5965-8(X), Graphic Universe™) Lerner Publishing Group.

—Atalanta: The Race Against Destiny [a Greek Myth]. Fontes, Justine & Fontes, Ron. 2008. (Graphic Myths & Legends Ser.). (ENG.). 48p. (J). (gr. 4-8). per. 9.99 (978-0-8225-6569-7(2), Graphic Universe™) Lerner Publishing Group.

—King Arthur: Excalibur Unsheathed [an English Legend]. Limke, Jeff. 2007. (Graphic Myths & Legends Ser.). (ENG.). 48p. (J). (gr. 4-8). per. 9.99 (978-0-8225-6483-6(1), Graphic Universe™) Lerner Publishing Group.

—Odysseus: Escaping Poseidon's Curse. Jolley, Dan. 2007. (Graphic Myths & Legends Ser.). (ENG.). 48p. (J). (gr. 4-8). lib. bdg. 27.99 (978-0-8225-6208-5(1), 9780822562085, Graphic Universe™) Lerner Publishing Group.

—Odysseus: Escaping Poseidon's Curse [a Greek Legend]. Jolley, Dan. (Graphic Myths & Legends Ser.). (ENG.). 48p. (gr. 4-8). 2015. 21.32 (978-1-4677-5983-0(X), Lerner Digital); 2008. (J). pap. 9.99 (978-0-8225-8515-2(4), Graphic Universe™) Lerner Publishing Group.

—Perseus: The Hunt for Medusa's Head [a Greek Myth]. Storrie, Paul D. (Graphic Myths & Legends Ser.). (ENG.). 48p. (gr. 4-8). 2015. 21.32 (978-1-4677-5984-7(8), Lerner Digital); 2009. (J). pap. 9.99 (978-1-58013-888-8(8), Graphic Universe™) Lerner Publishing Group.

—El Rey Arturo: La Espada Excalibur Desenvainada: Una Leyenda Inglesa. Limke, Jeff. Translations.com Staff, tr. from ENG. 2007. (Mitos y leyendas en viñetas (Graphic Myths & Legends) Ser.).Tr. of King Arthur - Excalibur Unsheathed [An English Legend. (SPA.). 48p. (J). (gr. 4-8). per. 8.95 (978-0-8225-7968-7(5)) Lerner Publishing Group.

—Robin Hood: Outlaw of Sherwood Forest, an English Legend. Storrie, Paul D. 2008. (Graphic Myths & Legends Ser.). 48p. (J). (gr. 3-7). per. 8.95 (978-0-8225-6572-7(2)) Lerner Publishing Group.

—William Tell: One Against an Empire [a Swiss Legend]. Storrie, Paul D. 2009. (Graphic Myths & Legends Ser.). (ENG.). 48p. (J). (gr. 4-8). pap. 9.99 (978-1-58013-828-4(4), Graphic Universe™) Lerner Publishing Group.

Yee, Jeanne. The Saga of Simon the Skinny Pig: Simon Saves the Day. Oshiro, Kimberley. 2012. 38p. pap. 12.50 (978-1-61170-089-3(2)) Robertson Publishing.

Yee, Josie. Drip, Drop! the Rain Won't Stop! Your Turn, My Turn Reader. Higginson, Sheila Sweeny. 2010. (Playskool Ser.). (ENG.). 24p. (J). (gr. -1-k). pap. 3.99 (978-1-4169-9046-8(1), Simon Spotlight) Simon Spotlight.

—The Peculiar Possum. Hecht, Tracey. 2018. (Grow & Read Early Reader, Level 2 Ser.: 3). (ENG.). 64p. (J). (gr. k-2). 12.99 (978-1-944020-19-4(5), Fabled Films Pr. LLC) Fabled Films LLC.

—The Slithery Shakedown. Hecht, Tracey. 2018. (Grow & Read Early Reader, Level 2 Ser.: 2). (ENG.). 64p. (J). (gr. k-2). pap. 5.99 (978-1-944020-16-3(0), Fabled Films Pr. LLC) Fabled Films LLC.

—A Surprise Party. Silverhardt, Lauryn. 2003. (Dora the Explorer Ser.). (ENG.). 22p. (J). bds. 4.99 (978-0-689-85483-5(8), Simon Spotlight/Nickelodeon) Simon Spotlight/Nickelodeon.

Yee, Nong. Little Red Dot Here I Come. Low, Lk. 2020. (ENG.). 28p. (J). pap. 19.91 (978-1-5437-5567-1(4)) Partridge Pub.

Yee, Patrick. Asian Children's Favorite Stories: Folktales from China, Japan, Korea, India, the Philippines & Other Asian Lands. Conger, David & Romulo, Liana. 2019. 64p. (J). (gr. k-8). 14.99 (978-0-8048-5023-0(2)) Tuttle Publishing.

—Chinese Myths & Legends: The Monkey King & Other Adventures. Fu, Shelley. 2018. 128p. (J). (gr. k-8). 17.99 (978-0-8048-5027-8(5)) Tuttle Publishing.

Yee, Rebecca. The Adventures of Little Korra Jane: Ant Trouble. Linn, Lory. 2019. (ENG.). 28p. (J). pap. 12.99 (978-1-6989-5312-0(7)) Independently Published.

Yee, Reimena. The Very Short, Entirely True History of Mermaids. Laskow, Sarah. 2020. (ENG.). 96p. (J). (gr. 3-7). 12.99 (978-1-5247-9275-6(6), Penguin Workshop) Penguin Young Readers Group.

Yee, Tammy. A Is for Aloha: A Hawaii Alphabet. Goldsberry, U'ilani. 2005. (Discover America State by State Ser.). (ENG.). 40p. (J). (gr. k-5). 17.95 (978-1-58536-146-5(1)) Sleeping Bear Pr.

—Shark Patrol: A Discovery Adventure in Hawaii. Hirschi, Ron. 2019. (ENG.). 32p. (J). (gr. 1-5). 12.95 (978-1-949307-00-9(X)) Mutual Publishing LLC.

—Swimming with Humuhumu: A Young Snorkeler's First Guide to Hawaiian Sea Life. Hirschi, Ron. 32p. (J). 14.99 *(978-0-931548-67-3(5)*, 25098-000) Island Heritage Publishing.

—A True Princess of Hawai'i. Greenway, Beth. 2017. (ENG & SPA.). 32p. (J). (gr. k-3). 17.95 *(978-1-62855-948-4(9))* Arbordale Publishing.

—The Tsunami Quilt: Grandfather's Story. Fredericks, Anthony D. rev. ed. 2007. (Tales of Young Americans Ser.). (ENG.). 32p. (J). (gr. 1-4). 17.95 *(978-1-58536-313-1(8)*, 202117) Sleeping Bear Pr.

—Una Verdadera Princesa de Hawái. Greenway, Beth. 2017. (SPA.). 32p. (J). (gr. k-3). pap. 9.95 *(978-1-62855-950-7(0))* Arbordale Publishing.

Yee, Tammy. Rescate en el Río: (River Rescue) [Spanish Edition]. Yee, Tammy. Curtis, Jennifer Keats. 2019. (SPA.). 32p. (J). pap. 11.95 *(978-1-60718-875-9(9))* Arbordale Publishing.

Yee, Wong Herbert. Eddie the Raccoon: (Brand New Readers. Friend, Catherine. 2004. (Brand New Readers Ser.). (ENG.). 32p. (J). (gr. -1-3). pap. 5.99 *(978-0-7636-2334-0(2))* Candlewick Pr.

—Get That Pest! Douglas, Erin. 2003. (Green Light Readers Level 2 Ser.). (ENG.). 24p. (J). (gr. -1-3). pap. 3.95 *(978-0-15-204833-4(2)*, 1194595) Houghton Mifflin Harcourt Publishing Co.

—Get That Pest! / ¡Agarren a Ése! Douglas, Erin. Campoy, F. Isabel & Flor Ada, Alma, trs. ed. 2008. (Green Light Readers Level 2 Ser.). (ENG.). 28p. (J). (gr. k-2). pap. 4.99 *(978-0-15-206269-9(6)*, 1198790) Houghton Mifflin Harcourt Publishing Co.

—Moving Day. Brandon, Anthony G. 2005. (Green Light Readers Level 2 Ser.). (ENG.). 32p. (J). (gr. -1-3). pap. 4.99 *(978-0-15-205652-0(1)*, 1196995) Houghton Mifflin Harcourt Publishing Co.

Yee, Wong Herbert. Mummies at the Museum. 2018. 107p. (J). ***(978-1-5490-1900-5(7))*** Holt, Henry & Co.

Yee, Wong Herbert. Fine Feathered Friends. Yee, Wong Herbert. 2011. (Mouse & Mole Story Ser.). (ENG.). 48p. (J). (gr. 1-4). pap. 4.99 *(978-0-547-51977-7(X)*, 1445276, HMH Books For Young Readers) Houghton Mifflin Harcourt Publishing Co.

—Mouse & Mole, a Winter Wonderland. Yee, Wong Herbert. 2011. (Mouse & Mole Story Ser.). (ENG.). 48p. (J). (gr. 1-4). pap. 4.99 *(978-0-547-57697-8(8)*, 1458451) Houghton Mifflin Harcourt Publishing Co.

—My Autumn Book. Yee, Wong Herbert. 2015. (ENG.). 32p. (J). (gr. -1-1). 14.99 *(978-0-8050-9922-5(0)*, 900125962, Holt, Henry & Co. Bks. For Young Readers) Holt, Henry & Co.

—Secret Valentine. Yee, Wong Herbert. 2013. (Mouse & Mole Story Ser.). (ENG.). 48p. (J). (gr. 1-4). 15.99 *(978-0-547-88719-7(1)*, 1507662) Houghton Mifflin Harcourt Publishing Co.

—Summer Days & Nights. Yee, Wong Herbert. 2012. (ENG.). 32p. (J). (gr. -1-1). 18.99 *(978-0-8050-9078-9(9)*, 900061501, Holt, Henry & Co. Bks. For Young Readers) Holt, Henry & Co.

—Tracks in the Snow. Yee, Wong Herbert. 2007. (ENG.). 32p. (J). (gr. -1-1). per. 7.99 *(978-0-312-37134-0(9)*, 900044662) Square Fish.

Yeesman, Vinit, jt. illus. see Meesukhon, Patcharee.

Yeh, Alicia. Buddha's Wisdom. Hsuan Hua. 2004. (ENG & CHI.). (J). *(978-0-88139-867-0(5))* Buddhist Text Translation Society.

Yelchin, Eugene. The Assassination of Brangwain Spurge. Anderson, M. T. 2020. 544p. (J). (gr. 5-9). pap. 14.99 *(978-1-5362-1309-6(8))* Candlewick Pr.

—Crybaby. Beaumont, Karen. 2015. (ENG.). 40p. (J). (gr. -1-1). 17.99 *(978-0-8050-8974-5(8)*, 9780805089745, Holt, Henry & Co. Bks. For Young Readers) Holt, Henry & Co.

—Elephant in the Dark. Javaherbin, Mina & Jalal al-Din Rumi. 2015. 32p. (J). (gr. -1-3). 17.99 *(978-0-545-63670-4(1)*, Scholastic Pr.) Scholastic, Inc.

—The Rooster Who Would Not Be Quiet! Deedy, Carmen Agra. 2017. (ENG.). 48p. (J). (gr. -1-3). 17.99 *(978-0-545-72288-9(8)*, Scholastic Pr.) Scholastic, Inc.

—Seeds, Bees, Butterflies, & More! Poems for Two Voices. Gerber, Carole. 2013. (ENG.). 32p. (J). (gr. -1-3). 18.99 *(978-0-8050-9211-0(0)*, 900066058, Holt, Henry & Co. Bks. For Young Readers) Holt, Henry & Co.

—Seven Hungry Babies. Fleming, Candace. 2010. (ENG.). 40p. (J). (gr. -1-2). 16.99 *(978-1-4169-5402-6(3)*, Atheneum Bks. for Young Readers) Simon & Schuster Children's Publishing.

—Who Ate All the Cookie Dough? Beaumont, Karen. 2008. (ENG.). 32p. (J). (gr. -1-k). 18.99 *(978-0-8050-8267-8(0)*, 900042144, Holt, Henry & Co. Bks. For Young Readers) Holt, Henry & Co.

—Won Ton: A Cat Tale Told in Haiku. Wardlaw, Lee. 2011. (ENG.). 40p. (J). (gr. -1-3). 18.99 *(978-0-8050-8995-0(0)*, 900058840, Holt, Henry & Co. Bks. For Young Readers) Holt, Henry & Co.

—Won Ton & Chopstick. Wardlaw, Lee. 2015. (ENG.). 40p. (J). (gr. -1-3). 17.99 *(978-0-8050-9987-4(5)*, 9780805099874, Holt, Henry & Co. Bks. For Young Readers) Holt, Henry & Co.

Yelchin, Eugene. Arcady's Goal. Yelchin, Eugene. 2015. (ENG.). 256p. (J). (gr. 4-7). pap. 7.99 *(978-1-250-06814-9(2)*, 900147082) Square Fish.

—The Assassination of Brangwain Spurge. Yelchin, Eugene. Anderson, M. T. 2018. 544p. (J). (gr. 5-9). 24.99 *(978-0-7636-9822-5(9))* Candlewick Pr.

—Breaking Stalin's Nose. Yelchin, Eugene. 2013. (ENG.). (J). (gr. 4-7). lib. bdg. 18.60 *(978-1-62765-141-7(1))* Perfection Learning Corp.

—Breaking Stalin's Nose. Yelchin, Eugene. 2013. (ENG.). 176p. (J). (gr. 4-7). pap. 8.99 *(978-1-250-03410-6(8)*, 900120580) Square Fish.

—Spring Hare. Yelchin, Eugene. 2017. (ENG.). 32p. (J). 16.99 *(978-1-62779-392-6(5)*, 900148914, Holt, Henry & Co. Bks. For Young Readers) Holt, Henry & Co.

—Spy Runner. Yelchin, Eugene. 2019. (ENG.). 352p. (J). 17.99 *(978-1-250-12081-6(0)*, 900173090, Holt, Henry & Co. Bks. For Young Readers) Holt, Henry & Co.

Yelchin, Eugene & Kuryla, Mary. The Next Door Bear. Yelchin, Eugene & Kuryla, Mary. 2011. (ENG.). 40p. (J). (gr. -1-3). 16.99 *(978-0-06-125925-8(X))* HarperCollins Pubs.

Yelenak, Andy. Run, Dad, Run! Blackett, Dulcibella. 2004. (ENG.). 32p. (J). 15.00 *(978-1-891369-44-5(X))* Breakaway Bks.

Yellowhale s.r.l. Rudolph the Red-Nosed Reindeer Read-Along Book & CD. 2019. (ENG.). 32p. (J). (gr. -1-k). 9.99 incl. audio compact disk *(978-1-68412-005-5(5)*, Silver Dolphin Bks.) Printers Row Publishing Group.

Yellowhawk, James Mark. In the Footsteps of Crazy Horse. Marshall, Joseph, III & Marshall, Joseph. 2015. (ENG.). 176p. (J). (gr. 5-9). 16.95 *(978-1-4197-0785-8(X)*, 1059701, Amulet Bks.) Abrams, Inc.

Yeo, Miranda. The Birthday Wish List! (Sunny Day) Matheis, Mickie. 2018. (Pictureback(R) Ser.). (ENG.). 24p. (J). (gr. -1-2). pap. 5.99 *(978-1-5247-6852-2(9)*, Random Hse. Bks. for Young Readers) Random Hse. Children's Bks.

—Nickelodeon Sunny Day: Time to Style! Acampora, Courtney. 2019. (ENG.). 10p. (J). (gr. -1-k). 10.99 *(978-0-7944-4311-5(7)*, Studio Fun International) Printers Row Publishing Group.

Yeo, Miranda, jt. illus. see Random House.

Yeowell, Peter. Charlie & His Marvellous Mind. Yeowell, Peter. 2019. (ENG.). 30p. (J). pap. 9.99 *(978-1-7944-9565-4(7))* Independently Published.

Yerbey, Lindsey Blake. Worms Like to Wiggle. Peters, Elizabeth Anne. 2007. (J). *(978-0-9769737-1-3(5))* Creative Minds Pubns.

Yeretskaya, Yevgeniya. Flurry: A Mini Snowflakes Pop-Up Book. Preston Chushcoff, Jennifer. 2019. 7p. (J). 14.99 *(978-1-62348-653-2(X))* Jumping Jack Pr.

—The Snow Queen: A Pop-Up Adaption of a Classic Fairytale. 2013. (ENG.). 7p. 29.95 *(978-1-60580-955-7(1)*, 9781605809557) Jumping Jack Pr.

Yerkes, Lane. Goldilocks & the Three Bears: Pop-up Storybook Theater. Slater, Teddy. 2004. 10p. (J). (gr. k-4). reprint ed. 17.00 *(978-0-7567-8224-5(4))* DIANE Publishing Co.

—Let's Discover the Bible, Vol. 1. Rose, Shirley. 64p. (J). (gr. k-2). pap. 4.75 *(978-0-87441-538-4(1))* Behrman Hse., Inc.

—The Sounds of Music. Casterline, L. C. 2004. (Picture Books/Quality Time Ser.). 16p. (gr. k-3). lib. bdg. 21.00 *(978-0-8368-4100-8(X)*, Gareth Stevens Learning Library) Stevens, Gareth Publishing LLLP.

Yerko, Vladyslav. The Tinderbox. Andersen, Hans. 2016.Tr. of ???????. (ENG.). 24p. (J). 17.95 *(978-0-9965606-4-1(5)*, 9780996560641) A-BA-BA HAUS.

Yerrill, Gail. Exactly Like Me. Moss, Stephanie. 2018. (ENG.). 26p. (J). bds. 8.99 *(978-1-4998-8013-7(8))* Igloo Bks. GBR. Dist: Simon & Schuster, Inc.

Yerrill, Gail. Grandma Snuggles, 1 vol. Nellist, Glenys. 2020. (ENG.). 18p. (J). bds. 9.99 ***(978-0-310-77074-9(2))*** Zonderkidz.

Yerrill, Gail. How Popcorn the Bear Found His Name! Howard, Debbie. 2016. (ENG.). 31p. (J). pap. *(978-0-9575804-9-7(5))* Bright Star Characters.

—A Magical Christmas. Freedman, Claire. 2016. (ENG.). 22p. (J). (gr. -1-k). bds. 6.99 *(978-1-58925-236-3(5))* Tiger Tales.

—The Stable Cat's Christmas. Vrba, Christina. 2017. 32p. (J). (gr. -1-2). 16.99 *(978-0-8249-5683-7(4))* Worthy Publishing.

—Starry Night, Sleep Tight. 2009. 24p. (J). (gr. -1-1). 12.95 *(978-1-58925-844-0(4))* Tiger Tales.

—Time for Bed, Sleepyhead: The Falling Asleep Book, 1 vol. Amen, Daniel. 2016. (ENG.). 32p. (J). 16.99 *(978-0-310-75822-8(X))* Zonderkidz.

Yerrill, Gail & Over, John. Popcorn the Bear & Biscuit's Odd Ears! Howard, Debbie. 2016. (ENG.). 31p. (J). pap. *(978-0-9575804-7-3(9))* Bright Star Characters.

—Popcorn the Bear & the Mysterious Snowman. Howard, Debbie. 2016. (ENG.). 31p. (J). pap. *(978-0-9575804-8-0(7))* Bright Star Characters.

Yerxa, Leo. Last Leaf First Snowflake to Fall. Yerxa, Leo. (J). 16.95 *(978-0-88899-183-6(5))* Groundwood Bks. CAN. Dist: Publishers Group West (PGW).

Yesh, Jeff. Benjamin Franklin: Writer, Inventor, Statesman, 1 vol. Nettleton, Pamela Hill. 2003. (Biographies Ser.). (ENG.). 24p. (J). (gr. k-3). per. 8.95 *(978-1-4048-0459-3(5)*, Picture Window Bks.) Capstone.

—Evening Meals Around the World, 1 vol. Zurakowski, Michele. 2004. (Meals Around the World Ser.). (ENG.). 24p. (J). (gr. k-4). per. 8.95 *(978-1-4048-1132-4(X)*, Picture Window Bks.) Capstone.

—Flakes & Flurries: A Book about Snow, 1 vol. Sherman, Josepha. 2003. (Amazing Science: Weather Ser.). (ENG.). 24p. (J). (gr. -1-3). per. 8.95 *(978-1-4048-0342-8(4)*, Picture Window Bks.) Capstone.

—Morning Meals Around the World, 1 vol. Gregoire, Maryellen. 2004. (Meals Around the World Ser.). (ENG.). 24p. (J). (gr. k-4). per. 8.95 *(978-1-4048-1130-0(3)*, Picture Window Bks.) Capstone.

—Nearest to the Sun: The Planet Mercury, 1 vol. Loewen, Nancy. 2008. (Amazing Science: Planets Ser.). (ENG.). 24p. (J). (gr. k-4). lib. bdg. 27.32 *(978-1-4048-3954-0(2)*, 1278902, Picture Window Bks.) Capstone.

—Our Home Planet: Earth, 1 vol. Loewen, Nancy. 2008. (Amazing Science: Planets Ser.). (ENG.). 24p. (J). (gr. k-4). lib. bdg. 27.32 *(978-1-4048-3951-9(8)*, 1278903, Picture Window Bks.) Capstone.

—Pocahontas: Peacemaker & Friend to the Colonists. Nettleton, Pamela Hill. 2003. (Biographies Ser.). (ENG.). 24p. (J). (gr. k-3). 27.32 *(978-1-4048-0187-5(1)*, Picture Window Bks.) Capstone.

—Splish! Splash! A Book about Rain, 1 vol. Sherman, Josepha. 2003. (Amazing Science: Weather Ser.). (ENG.). 24p. (J). (gr. -1-3). per. 8.95 *(978-1-4048-0339-8(4)*, Picture Window Bks.) Capstone.

—Temperate Deciduous Forests: Lands of Falling Leaves, 1 vol. Salas, Laura Purdie. 2007. (Amazing Science: Ecosystems Ser.). (ENG.). 24p. (J). (gr. k-3). lib. bdg. 25.99 *(978-1-4048-3099-8(5)*, Picture Window Bks.) Capstone.

—The United States ABCs: A Book about the People & Places of the United States. Schroeder, Holly. 2004. (Country ABCs Ser.). (ENG.). 32p. (J). (gr. k-5). 28.65 *(978-1-4048-0181-3(2)*, 1229509, Picture Window Bks.) Capstone.

Yesh, Jeff & Nichols, Garry. Sally Ride: Astronaut, Scientist, Teacher. Nettleton, Pamela Hill. 2003. (Biographies Ser.). (ENG.). 24p. (J). (gr. k-3). 27.32 *(978-1-4048-0189-9(8)*, Picture Window Bks.) Capstone.

Yezerski, Thomas F. Pinch & Dash & the Terrible Couch. Daley, Michael J. 2013. 48p. (J). (gr. k-3). pap. 5.95 *(978-1-58089-380-0(5))*; 18.69 *(978-1-58089-379-4(1))* Charlesbridge Publishing, Inc.

—Pinch & Dash Make Soup. Daley, Michael J. 2012. (Adventures of Pinch & Dash Ser.). 48p. (J). (gr. k-3). 12.95 *(978-1-58089-346-6(5))*; pap. 5.95 *(978-1-58089-347-3(3))* Charlesbridge Publishing, Inc.

—Pinch & Dash Make Soup. Daley, Michael J. 2012. (Pinch & Dash Ser.). (ENG.). (J). (gr. k-3). lib. bdg. 16.55 *(978-1-61383-336-0(9))* Perfection Learning Corp.

Yi, A. Ivanhoe Swift Left Home at Six. Godwin, Jane. 2020. (ENG.). 32p. (J). (gr. -1-k). 18.99 *(978-1-76063-186-4(8)*, A&U Children's) Allen & Unwin AUS. Dist: Independent Pubs. Group.

Yi, Anny. What Is Hip-Hop? Morse, Eric. 2017. (ENG.). 40p. (J). (gr. -1-2). 15.95 *(978-1-61775-584-2(2)*, Black Sheep) Akashic Bks.

—What Is Punk? Morse, Eric. 2015. (ENG.). 32p. (J). 15.95 *(978-1-61775-392-3(0)*, Black Sheep) Akashic Bks.

Yi, Hye Won. Pruebalo, 1 vol. Jones, Christianne C. Ruíz, Carlos, tr. 2006. (Read-It! Readers en Español: Story Collection).Tr. of Just Try It. (SPA.). 24p. (J). (gr. -1-3). 21.32 *(978-1-4048-1692-3(5)*, Picture Window Bks.) Capstone.

Yi, J. Clementine Rose & the Famous Friend. Harvey, Jacqueline. 2015. 160p. (J). (gr. 2-4). 9.99 *(978-1-74275-755-1(3))* Random Hse. Australia AUS. Dist: Independent Pubs. Group.

—Clementine Rose & the Farm Fiasco, 4. Harvey, Jacqueline. 2015. (Clementine Rose Ser.: 4). (ENG.). 160p. (J). (gr. 2-4). 8.99 *(978-1-74275-547-2(X))* Random Hse. Australia AUS. Dist: Independent Pubs. Group.

—Clementine Rose & the Pet Day Disaster. Harvey, Jacqueline. 2015. (Clementine Rose Ser.: 2). (ENG.). 160p. (J). (gr. 2-4). 9.99 *(978-1-74275-543-4(7))* Random Hse. Australia AUS. Dist: Independent Pubs. Group.

—Clementine Rose & the Surprise Visitor, Vol. 1. Harvey, Jacqueline. 2015. (Clementine Rose Ser.: 1). (ENG.). 144p. (J). (gr. 2-4). 8.99 *(978-1-74275-541-0(0))* Random Hse. Australia AUS. Dist: Independent Pubs. Group.

Yia Xiong, Tou. Pickles + Ocho. Wellik, Dan. 2019. (SPA.). 32p. (J). 17.95 *(978-1-64343-963-1(4))* Beaver's Pond Pr., Inc.

Yianolatos, Michael, jt. illus. see Flannery, Alex.

Yice, Lett. Pride & Prejudice: A Kinderguides Illustrated Learning Guide. Colting, Fredrik & Medina, Melissa. 2017. (KinderGuides Early Learning Guide to Culture Classics Ser.). 45p. (J). 16.95 *(978-0-9977145-5-5(7))* Moppet Bks.

Yilmaz, Necdet. The Christmas Stick: A Children's Story. Myers, Tim J. 2014. (ENG.). 32p. (J). pap. 13.99 *(978-1-61261-571-4(6))* Paraclete Pr., Inc.

—Robin Hood & the Golden Arrow, 1 vol. Picture Window Books Staff. 2008. (Read-It! Readers: Legends Ser.). (ENG.). 32p. (J). (gr. k-3). 21.32 *(978-1-4048-4843-6(6)*, Picture Window Bks.) Capstone.

—The Truth about Unicorns, 1 vol. Blaisdell, Molly. 2010. (Fairy-Tale Superstars Ser.). (ENG.). 32p. (J). (gr. 1-3). lib. bdg. 27.99 *(978-1-4048-5748-3(6)*, Picture Window Bks.) Capstone.

Yim, Gyeong-mi. The Emperor's New Clothes. Andersen, Hans. Cowley, Joy, ed. 2015. (World Classics Ser.). (ENG.). 32p. (J). (gr. k-4). 10.00 *(978-1-925186-10-9(5)*, Big and SMALL) ChoiceMaker Pty. Ltd., The AUS. Dist: Lerner Publishing Group.

—The Emperor's New Clothes. Andersen, Hans Christian. 2015. (World Classics Ser.). (ENG.). 32p. (J). (gr. k-4). 5.00 *(978-1-925186-04-8(0)*, Big and SMALL) ChoiceMaker Pty. Ltd., The AUS. Dist: Lerner Publishing Group.

Yin, Leah. Zona & the Big Buzzzy Secret. Yin, Leah. 2013. 54p. *(978-0-9918396-0-5(9))* Leah Yin Studio.

Yin, Robert. Seashells. Yin, Robert, photos by. 2004. (ENG.). 24p. (J). (gr. 1-2). pap. 6.50 *(978-0-7685-0355-5(8)*, Dominie Elementary) Savvas Learning Co.

—Sharks & Rays. Yin, Robert, photos by. 2004. (ENG.). 24p. (J). (gr. 1-2). pap. 7.47 net. *(978-0-7685-0357-9(4)*, Dominie Elementary) Savvas Learning Co.

Yinfoo, Anne. Alice-Miranda Holds the Key: Alice-Miranda is home for the holidays! Harvey, Jacqueline. 2017. (Alice-Miranda Ser.: 15). (ENG.). 384p. (J). (gr. 3-7). 9.99 *(978-0-14-378070-0(0))* Random Hse. Australia AUS. Dist: Independent Pubs. Group.

Ying, Victoria. Baby Unicorn: Finger Puppet Book: (Unicorn Puppet Book, Unicorn Book for Babies, Tiny Finger Puppet Books) Chronicle Books. 2018. (ENG.). 12p. (J). (gr. -1 — 1). bds. 7.99 *(978-1-4521-7076-3(2))* Chronicle Bks. LLC.

—Bella's Birthday Unicorn. Burkhart, Jessica. 2014. (Unicorn Magic Ser.: 1). (ENG.). 144p. (J). (gr. 1-4). pap. 6.99 *(978-1-4424-9822-8(6)*, Aladdin) Simon & Schuster Children's Publishing.

—Diana: Princess of the Amazons. Hale, Shannon & Hale, Dean. 2020. 144p. (J). (gr. 3-7). pap. 9.99 *(978-1-4012-9111-2(2))* DC Comics.

—Don't Chicken Out. Stout, Shawn K. 2013. (Not-So-Ordinary Girl Ser.: 3). (ENG.). 176p. (J). (gr. 1-5). pap. 5.99 *(978-1-4169-7111-5(4)*, Aladdin) Simon & Schuster Children's Publishing.

—Don't Chicken Out. Stout, Shawn K. 2013. (Not-So-Ordinary Girl Ser.: 3). (ENG.). 176p. (J). (gr. 1-5). 15.99 *(978-1-4169-7929-6(8)*, Simon & Schuster/Paula Wiseman Bks.) Simon & Schuster/Paula Wiseman Bks.

—An Egg to Crack (a Hanazuki Chapter Book) (a Hanazuki Chapter Book) Davidowitz, Stacy. 2018. (ENG.). 128p. (J). (gr. 1-4). 12.99 *(978-1-4197-2951-5(9)*, Amulet Bks.) Abrams, Inc.

—Hanazuki: a Spark in the Dark: (a Hanazuki Chapter Book) Davidowitz, Stacy. 2019. (Hanazuki Chapter Bks.). (ENG.). 160p. (J). (gr. 1-4). pap. 6.99 *(978-1-4197-3433-5(4)*, Amulet Bks.) Abrams, Inc.

—Hanazuki: Dazzle & Dance: (a Hanazuki Chapter Book) Davidowitz, Stacy. 2019. (Hanazuki Chapter Bks.). (ENG.). 160p. (J). (gr. 1-4). 12.99 *(978-1-4197-3129-7(7)*, Amulet Bks.) Abrams, Inc.

—The Hidden Treasure. Burkhart, Jessica. 2015. (Unicorn Magic Ser.: 4). (ENG.). 112p. (J). (gr. 1-4). pap. 6.99 *(978-1-4424-9829-7(3)*, Aladdin) Simon & Schuster Children's Publishing.

—Lost & Found, What's That Sound? Ying, Jonathan. 2017. (ENG.). 32p. (J). (gr. -1-3). 14.99 *(978-0-06-238068-5(0))* HarperCollins Pubs.

—Lost & Found, What's That Sound? Board Book. Ying, Jonathan. 2018. (ENG.). 28p. (J). (gr. -1 — 1). bds. 7.99 *(978-0-06-238069-2(9)*, HarperFestival) HarperCollins Pubs.

—Not Quite Black & White. Ying, Jonathan. 2016. (ENG.). 32p. (J). (gr. -1-3). 14.99 *(978-0-06-238066-1(4))* HarperCollins Pubs.

—Not Quite Black & White Board Book. Ying, Jonathan. 2017. (ENG.). 28p. (J). (gr. -1 — 1). bds. 7.99 *(978-0-06-238067-8(2)*, HarperFestival) HarperCollins Pubs.

—Take a Ride by My Side. Ying, Jonathan. 2018. (ENG.). 32p. (J). (gr. -1-3). 14.99 *(978-0-06-238070-8(2))* HarperCollins Pubs.

—Tangled (Disney Tangled) Smiley, Ben. 2010. (Little Golden Book Ser.). (ENG.). 24p. (J). (gr. -1-2). 4.99 *(978-0-7364-2684-8(1)*, Golden/Disney) Random Hse. Children's Bks.

—Unicorn Magic the Royal Collection Books 1-4: Bella's Birthday Unicorn; Where's Glimmer?; Green with Envy; the Hidden Treasure. Burkhart, Jessica. ed. 2017. (Unicorn Magic Ser.). (ENG.). 544p. (J). (gr. 1-4). pap. 27.99 *(978-1-5344-0618-6(2)*, Aladdin) Simon & Schuster Children's Publishing.

—Where's Glimmer? Burkhart, Jessica. 2014. (Unicorn Magic Ser.: 2). (ENG.). 144p. (J). (gr. 1-4). pap. 6.99 *(978-1-4424-9824-2(2)*, Aladdin) Simon & Schuster Children's Publishing.

Ying, Victoria. Meow! Ying, Victoria. 2017. (ENG.). 32p. (J). (gr. -1-3). 15.99 *(978-0-06-244096-9(9))* HarperCollins Pubs.

Ying, Victoria, jt. illus. see Tyminski, Lori.

Yip, Mingmei. Chinese Children's Favorite Stories: Fables, Myths & Fairy Tales. Yip, Mingmei. 2018. (ENG.). 96p. (J). (gr. k-8). 12.99 *(978-0-8048-5017-9(8))* Tuttle Publishing.

Yishan, Li. The Assassination of John F. Kennedy: November 22 1963, 1 vol. Collins, Terry. 2014. (24-Hour History Ser.). (ENG.). 48p. (J). (gr. 3-9). pap. 8.95 *(978-1-4329-9300-9(3)*, Heinemann) Capstone.

Yiwing, Vivian. Bee a Dreamer. Toft, Ryen. 2018. (ENG.). 32p. (J). pap. 9.95 *(978-0-9968906-0-1(2)*, Social Motion Publishing) Social Motion Publishing.

Yiwing, Vivian. Bee a Dreamer. Toft, Ryen. 2019. (ENG.). 32p. (J). (gr. 2-5). 14.95 ***(978-0-9968906-1-8(0)***, Social Motion Publishing) Social Motion Publishing.

Ynion, Bryan Jason. Kramer the Gamer. Margaret, McArthur. 2019. (Rob the Robot Ser.: Vol. 3). (ENG.). 34p. (J). (gr. 2-6). *(978-0-6484449-5-4(3))*; pap. *(978-0-6484449-4-7(5))* McArthur, Margaret.

—Pat's Online Chat. Margaret, McArthur. 2019. (Rob the Robot Ser.: Vol. 2). (ENG.). 32p. (J). (gr. 2-6). *(978-0-6484449-3-0(7))*; pap. *(978-0-6484449-7-8(X))* McArthur, Margaret.

—Rob's New Smartpad. Margaret, McArthur. 2018. (Rob the Robot Ser.: Vol. 1). (ENG.). 34p. (J). (gr. 2-6). *(978-0-6484449-1-6(0))*; pap. *(978-0-6484449-0-9(2))* McArthur, Margaret.

Yo, Yuen Wong. Digimon: Digital Monsters, 5 vols., Vol. 5. rev. ed. 2003. 164p. pap. 9.99 *(978-1-59182-160-1(6))* TOKYOPOP, Inc.

Yockteng, Rafael. Jimmy the Greatest!, 1 vol. Buitrago, Jairo. Amado, Elisa, tr. 2012. (ENG.). 52p. (J). (gr. -1-2). 18.95 *(978-1-55498-178-6(6))* Groundwood Bks. CAN. Dist: Publishers Group West (PGW).

—Lion & Mouse, 1 vol. Buitrago, Jairo. Amado Ramírez, Elizabeth del Pilar & Amado, Elisa, trs. 2019. (ENG.). 32p. (J). (gr. k-2). 18.95 *(978-1-77306-224-2(7))* Groundwood Bks. CAN. Dist: Publishers Group West (PGW).

—On the Other Side of the Garden. Amado, Elisa & Buitrago, Jairo. 2018. (ENG.). 56p. E-Book *(978-1-55498-984-3(1))* Groundwood Bks.

—Sopa de Frijoles / Bean Soup, 1 vol. Argueta, Jorge. 2017. (SPA.). 32p. (J). (gr. -1-2). 8.95 *(978-1-77306-002-6(3))* Groundwood Bks. CAN. Dist: Publishers Group West (PGW).

—Two White Rabbits, 1 vol. Buitrago, Jairo. Amado, Elisa, tr. 2015. (ENG.). 32p. (J). (gr. -1-2). 18.95 *(978-1-55498-741-2(5))* Groundwood Bks. CAN. Dist: Publishers Group West (PGW).

—Walk with Me, 1 vol. Buitrago, Jairo. Amado, Elisa, tr. 2017. (ENG.). 32p. (J). (gr. -1-2). 18.95 *(978-1-55498-857-0(8))* Groundwood Bks. CAN. Dist: Publishers Group West (PGW).

Yockteng, Rafael. Gabriel García Márquez: Gabito. Yockteng, Rafael. Lázaro León, Georgina. 2014. (SPA.). (J). 14.99 *(978-1-933032-85-6(5))* Lectorum Pubns., Inc.

Yocum, Sam, 2nd, photos by. Cowpie Corgi: A Dog's Tale. Yocum, Randi. 2007. 32p. (J). lib. bdg. 16.98 *(978-0-9663629-3-0(4))* By Grace Enterprises.

Yoder, Greg. The Swing: A Storybook to Color. 2003. (J). 4.00 *(978-1-930353-88-6(X))* Masthof Pr.

Yoder, Laura & Weaver, Lisa. Joanna's Journey. Martin, Rebecca. 2006. 168p. (YA). pap. 9.99 *(978-1-933753-01-0(3))* Carlisle Pr.- Walnut Creek.

Yoe, Craig. Knock-Knock! Who's There? A Load of Laughs & Jokes for Kids. Yoe, Craig. 2018. (ENG.). 288p. (J). (gr. k-4). pap. 5.99 *(978-1-4814-7820-5(6),* Little Simon) Little Simon.
—Lol: A Load of Laughs & Jokes for Kids. Yoe, Craig. 2017. (ENG.). 288p. (J). (gr. k-4). pap. 5.99 *(978-1-4814-7818-2(4),* Little Simon) Little Simon.
Yoe! Studio Staff. Hello, Friends! Ciminera, Siobhan & Rao, Lisa. 2009. (Yo Gabba Gabba! Ser.). (ENG.). 64p. (J). 4.99 *(978-1-4169-7460-4(1),* Simon Scribbles) Simon Scribbles.
Yoga, Afrianas Dwi, jt. illus. see Alcomendas, Jp.
Yokococo. Matilda & Hans. Yokococo. 2013. (ENG.). 32p. (J). (gr. -1-2). 16.99 *(978-0-7636-6434-3(0),* Templar) Candlewick Pr.
Yokota, Hiromitsu. The Tale of the Oki Islands: A Tale from Japan. Barchers, Suzanne I. 2013. (Tales of Honor Ser.). (ENG.). 32p. (J). (gr. 1-3). lib. bdg. 26.65 *(978-1-937529-78-9(9))* Red Chair Pr.
—The Tale of the Oki Islands: A Tale from Japan. Barchers, Suzanne. 2013. (Tales of Honor Ser.). (ENG.). 32p. (J). (gr. 1-3). pap. 8.99 *(978-1-937529-62-8(2))* Red Chair Pr.
Yomtob, Andrea. Dr. Duncan Dog on Duty! Dunn-Dern, Lisa. 2007. (J). (gr. -1-3). per. 16.99 *(978-1-933156-20-0(1),* Visikid Bks.) GSVQ Publishing.
Yoneyama, Natsuko. What I Can Learn from the Incredible & Fantastic Life of Steve Jobs. Medina, Melissa & Colting, Fredrik. 2017. 32p. (J). 14.95 *(978-0-9977145-9-3(X))* Moppet Bks.
Yonezu, Yusuke. Seek & Count. Yonezu, Yusuke. 2019. (Yonezu Board Book Ser.). (ENG.). 20p. (J). (gr. -1-k). bds. 11.99 *(978-988-8341-39-9(1),* Minedition) Neugebauer, Michael (Publishing) Limited HKG. Dist: Penguin Random Hse. LLC.
—We Love Each Other. Yonezu, Yusuke. 2013. (Yonezu Board Book Ser.). (ENG.). 28p. (J). (— 1). bds. 9.95 *(978-988-8240-56-2(0),* Minedition) Neugebauer, Michael (Publishing) Limited HKG. Dist: Penguin Random Hse. LLC.
Yong, Billy. Book 1: Vision of Gold. Scott, Jenny. 2019. (Clairvoyant Claire Ser.). (ENG.). 48p. (J). (gr. 3-7). lib. bdg. 29.93 *(978-1-5321-3656-6(0),* 33758, Spellbound) Magic Wagon.
—Book 2: Vision of Flames. Scott, Jenny. 2019. (Clairvoyant Claire Ser.). (ENG.). 48p. (J). (gr. 3-7). lib. bdg. 29.93 *(978-1-5321-3657-3(9),* 33760, Spellbound) Magic Wagon.
—Book 3: Vision of a Star. Scott, Jenny. 2019. (Clairvoyant Claire Ser.). (ENG.). 48p. (J). (gr. 3-7). lib. bdg. 29.93 *(978-1-5321-3658-0(7),* 33762, Spellbound) Magic Wagon.
—Book 4: Vision of Pearls. Scott, Jenny. 2019. (Clairvoyant Claire Ser.). (ENG.). 48p. (J). (gr. 3-7). lib. bdg. 29.93 *(978-1-5321-3659-7(5),* 33764, Spellbound) Magic Wagon.
—Clairvoyant Claire (Set), 4 vols. Scott, Jenny. 2019. (Clairvoyant Claire Ser.). (ENG.). 48p. (J). (gr. 3-7). lib. bdg. 119.72 *(978-1-5321-3655-9(2),* 33756, Spellbound) Magic Wagon.
Yongco, Rumar. The Bird Who Couldn't Fly. Butler, Brenda Davies. 2019. (ENG.). 24p. (J). pap. 15.99 ***(978-1-7960-5354-8(6))*** Xlibris Corp.
—Hi, I Love You. Stewart, Artney. 2020. (ENG.). 24p. (J). 22.95 ***(978-1-4808-8923-1(7))***; pap. 12.95 ***(978-1-4808-8922-4(9))*** Archway Publishing.
—A Mother's Advice to Her Child. Layne, M. 2019. (ENG.). 30p. (J). pap. 16.95 ***(978-1-9736-6575-5(1),*** WestBow Pr.) Author Solutions, Inc.
—Zoe's Gospel Hope. Smith, Amelia. 2020. (ENG.). 24p. (J). pap. 10.95 ***(978-1-6642-0250-4(1),*** WestBow Pr.) Author Solutions, Inc.
Yonge, J. D. Molly Mouse & the Sleepless Nights. Bell, Madeline. 2019. (ENG.). 44p. (J). pap. 9.49 *(978-1-7325905-8-8(3))* Dancing With Bear Publishing.
Yonts, Barbara, photos by. Catering to Children: With Recipes for Memorable Tea Parties. Hawkins, Linda J. 2003. 56p. (J). (gr. k-5). 19.99 *(978-0-9742806-0-8(7))* Heart to Heart Publishing, Inc.
Yoo, Taeeun. Kitten & the Night Watchman. Sullivan, John. 2018. (ENG.). 40p. (J). (gr. -1-3). 17.99 *(978-1-4814-6191-7(5),* Simon & Schuster/Paula Wiseman Bks.) Simon & Schuster/Paula Wiseman Bks.
—Round. Sidman, Joyce. 2017. (ENG.). 32p. (J). (gr. -1-3). 17.99 *(978-0-544-38761-4(9),* 1592445, HMH Books For Young Readers) Houghton Mifflin Harcourt Publishing Co.
—So Many Days. McGhee, Alison. 2010. (ENG.). 40p. (J). (gr. k-2). 15.99 *(978-1-4169-5857-4(6),* Atheneum Bks. for Young Readers) Simon & Schuster Children's Publishing.
—Strictly No Elephants. Mantchev, Lisa. 2015. (ENG.). 32p. (J). (gr. -1-3). 17.99 *(978-1-4814-1647-4(2),* Simon & Schuster Bks. For Young Readers) Simon & Schuster Bks. For Young Readers.
—The Umbrella Queen. Bridges, Shirin. 2008. (ENG.). 40p. (J). (gr. k-3). 16.99 *(978-0-06-075040-4(5),* Greenwillow Bks.) HarperCollins Pubs.
—When the Storm Comes. Ashman, Linda. 2020. 32p. (J). (gr. -1-2). 17.99 *(978-0-399-54609-9(X),* Nancy Paulsen Books) Penguin Young Readers Group.
Yoo, Taeeun. You Are a Lion! And Other Fun Yoga Poses. Yoo, Taeeun. (ENG.). (J). 2018. 30p. (— 1). bds. 8.99 *(978-0-525-51512-8(7))*; 2012. 40p. (gr. -1-k). 17.99 *(978-0-399-25602-8(4))* Penguin Young Readers Group. (Nancy Paulsen Books).
Yoon, Helen. Ball & Balloon. Sanders, Rob. 2019. (ENG.). 40p. (J). (gr. -1-3). 17.99 *(978-1-5344-2562-0(4),* McElderry, Margaret K. Bks.) McElderry, Margaret K. Bks.
Yoon, Jae-Ho. In Dream World, Vol. 3. Yoon, Jae-Ho. 3rd rev. ed. 2005. (In Dream World Ser.). 208p. per. 9.99 *(978-1-59532-518-1(2))* TOKYOPOP, Inc.
Yoon, Jae-Ho. In Dream World, Vol. 2. Yoon, Jae-Ho, creator. rev. ed. 2005. 192p. (YA). pap. 9.99 *(978-1-59532-517-4(4))* TOKYOPOP, Inc.
Yoon, Jenny. Gnome, Sweet Gnome. 2018. (Sherlock Gnomes Ser.). (ENG.). 24p. (J). (gr. -1-2). pap. 3.99 *(978-1-5344-1054-1(6),* Simon Spotlight) Simon Spotlight.
Yoon, JooHee. Beastly Verse. 2015. (ENG.). 48p. (J). (gr. -1-3). 18.95 *(978-1-59270-166-7(3))* Enchanted Lion Bks., LLC.
—The Tiger Who Would Be King. Thurber, James. 2015. (ENG.). 40p. (J). (gr. k-4). 18.95 *(978-1-59270-182-7(5))* Enchanted Lion Bks., LLC.
Yoon, Salina. My Shimmery Christmas Book. 2005. 10p. (J). bds. 8.95 *(978-1-58117-045-0(9),* Intervisual/Piggy Toes) Bendon, Inc.
—Peek-a-Boo Farm Animals. 2005. (Peek-a-Boo Guess Who Book Ser.: Vol. 2). 10p. (J). 7.95 *(978-1-58117-158-7(7),* Intervisual/Piggy Toes) Bendon, Inc.
—Peek-a-Boo Wild Animals. 2005. (Peek-a-Boo Guess Who Book Ser.: Vol. 1). 10p. (J). (gr. -1-k). 7.95 *(978-1-58117-157-0(9),* Intervisual/Piggy Toes) Bendon, Inc.
—Ziggy the Zebra. Ellis, Libby. 2005. 14p. (J). (gr. k-3). 9.95 *(978-1-58117-104-4(8),* Intervisual/Piggy Toes) Bendon, Inc.
Yoon, Salina. Busy Little Bee. Yoon, Salina. 2020. (on-The-Go Book Ser.). (ENG.). 12p. (J). (— 1). bds. 7.99 ***(978-1-5344-5994-6(4),*** Little Simon) Little Simon.
—Busy Little Fishy. Yoon, Salina. 2020. (on-The-Go Book Ser.). (ENG.). 12p. (J). (— 1). bds. 7.99 ***(978-1-5344-5995-3(2),*** Little Simon) Little Simon.
Yoon, Salina. Christmas Puppy: A Wag My Tail Book. Yoon, Salina. 2019. (Wag My Tail Book Ser.). (ENG.). 12p. (J). (gr. -1). bds. 7.99 *(978-1-5344-4343-3(6),* Little Simon) Little Simon.
—Easter Bunny: A Wag My Tail Book. Yoon, Salina. 2020. (Wag My Tail Book Ser.). (ENG.). 12p. (J). (gr. -1). bds. 7.99 *(978-1-5344-4344-0(4),* Little Simon) Little Simon.
—Five Silly Turkeys. Yoon, Salina. 2005. 10p. (J). (gr. -1-k). bds. 7.99 *(978-0-8431-1416-4(9),* Price Stern Sloan) Penguin Young Readers Group.
—Found. Yoon, Salina. 2014. (ENG.). 40p. (J). (gr. -1-1). 14.99 *(978-0-8027-3559-1(2),* 900121351, Bloomsbury USA Childrens) Bloomsbury Publishing USA.
—Halloween Kitty. Yoon, Salina. 2019. (Wag My Tail Book Ser.). (ENG.). 12p. (J). (gr. -1). bds. 7.99 *(978-1-5344-4342-6(8),* Little Simon) Little Simon.
—Humpty Dumpty. Yoon, Salina. 2012. (ENG.). 18p. (J). (gr. -1 — 1). bds. 5.99 *(978-1-4424-1411-2(1),* Little Simon) Little Simon.
—Jack & Jill: A Halloween Nursery Rhyme. Yoon, Salina. 2012. (ENG.). 18p. (J). (gr. -1 — 1). bds. 5.99 *(978-1-4424-1410-5(3),* Little Simon) Little Simon.
—Kiki & Jax: The Life-Changing Magic of Friendship. Yoon, Salina. Kondo, Marie. 2019. (ENG.). 40p. (J). (gr. -1-2). 17.99 *(978-0-525-64626-6(4))*; lib. bdg. 20.99 *(978-0-525-64627-3(2))* Random Hse. Children's Bks. (Crown Books For Young Readers).
—Kiki & Jax: la Magia de la Amistad / Kiki & Jax: the Life-Changing Magic of Friendship. Yoon, Salina. Kondo, Marie. 2019. (SPA.). 40p. (J). (gr. k-3). 17.95 *(978-1-64473-126-0(6),* Beascoa) Penguin Random House Grupo Editorial ESP. Dist: Penguin Random Hse. LLC.
—My Chanukah Playbook. Yoon, Salina. 2009. (ENG.). 10p. (J). (gr. -1-k). 10.99 *(978-1-4169-8957-8(9),* Little Simon) Little Simon.
—My First Menorah. Yoon, Salina. 2005. (ENG.). 20p. (J). (gr. -1-2). bds. 7.99 *(978-0-689-87746-9(3),* Little Simon) Little Simon.
—Opposnakes: A Lift-the-Flap Book about Opposites. Yoon, Salina. 2009. (ENG.). 16p. (J). (gr. -1-1). 12.99 *(978-1-4169-7875-6(5),* Little Simon) Little Simon.
—Peek-A-Love. Yoon, Salina. 2010. (ENG.). 14p. (J). (gr. -1 — 1). 6.99 *(978-1-4424-0655-1(0),* Little Simon) Little Simon.
—Penguin & Pinecone. Yoon, Salina. 2012. (Penguin Ser.). (ENG.). 40p. (J). (gr. -1-6). 14.99 *(978-0-8027-2843-2(X),* 900084711, Bloomsbury USA Childrens) Bloomsbury Publishing USA.
—Penguin Gets Dressed! Yoon, Salina. 2010. 10p. bds. 7.95 *(978-1-60747-750-1(5),* Pickwick Pr.) Phoenix Bks., Inc.
—Penguin Gets Ready for Bed! Yoon, Salina. 2010. 10p. bds. 7.95 *(978-1-60747-751-8(3),* Pickwick Pr.) Phoenix Bks., Inc.
—Penguin Goes to the Farm! Yoon, Salina. 2010. 10p. bds. 7.95 *(978-1-60747-752-5(1),* Pickwick Pr.) Phoenix Bks., Inc.
—Penguin in Love. Yoon, Salina. (Penguin Ser.). (J). (gr. -1-1). 2014. 30p. bds. 7.99 *(978-0-8027-3758-8(7),* 900135684); 2013. (ENG.). 40p. 14.99 *(978-0-8027-3600-0(9),* 900123419) Bloomsbury Publishing USA. (Bloomsbury USA Childrens).
—Penguin on Vacation. Yoon, Salina. 2013. (Penguin Ser.). (ENG.). 40p. (J). (gr. -1-1). 14.99 *(978-0-8027-3397-9(2),* 900084821, Bloomsbury USA Childrens) Bloomsbury Publishing USA.
—Wings: A Book to Touch & Feel. Yoon, Salina. 2010. (ENG.). 14p. (J). (gr. -1 — 1). bds. 8.99 *(978-1-4169-8958-5(7),* Little Simon) Little Simon.
Yorinks, Adrienne. Hummingbirds: Facts & Folklore from the Americas. Yorinks, Adrienne. Larson, Jeanette. 2011. 64p. (J). (gr. 4-7). pap. 8.95 *(978-1-58089-333-6(3))* Charlesbridge Publishing, Inc.
York, Deborah Ward. Calvin C. Waxwing. Ward, Eva D. I.t. ed. 2006. 34p. (J). per. 14.00 *(978-0-9776514-5-0(2))* Beech River Bks.
York, Janell & Young Illustrators Club, Leading Edge Ac. Song of the Earth. Barton, Sandy. 2019. (ENG.). 60p. (J). pap. 12.99 *(978-1-0912-6049-8(4))* Independently Published.
York, Shane. Dexter the Duck Gets His Quack. Witte, Jessica Pierce. 2012. 30p. 24.95 *(978-1-4626-6592-1(6))* America Star Bks.
York, Susanne, photos by. Carousel Kids. Kendall, Diane & Marsh, Merle. 2004. (J). *(978-0-9762385-0-8(0))* Houston Zoo, Inc.
Yorobe, Rolly. Be You-Nique. Watson, M. Rhea. 2019. (ENG.). 26p. (J). pap. 11.99 ***(978-1-6790-8551-2(4))*** Independently Published.
Yoshchenko, Yaroslava. My Little Dragon Goes to Sleep: Humorous Picture Rhyming Book for Kids Age 3-8, Cute & Funny Bedtime Story about a Naughty Dragon & Her Patient Mother Full of Love & Acceptance. Swan, Anna. 2019. (ENG.). 46p. (J). pap. 10.99 *(978-1-7985-7287-0(7))* Independently Published.
Yoshi. Big Al. Clements, Andrew. 2015. 32p. pap. 8.00 *(978-1-61003-598-9(4))* Center for the Collaborative Classroom.
—The First Story Ever Told. Jendresen, Erik & Villoldo, Alberto. 2008. (ENG.). 36p. (J). (gr. -1-2). 12.99 *(978-1-4169-8961-5(7),* Simon & Schuster Bks. For Young Readers) Simon & Schuster Bks. For Young Readers.
—Making the World. Wood, Douglas. 2008. (ENG.). 44p. (J). (gr. -1-2). 13.99 *(978-1-4169-8596-9(4),* Simon & Schuster Bks. For Young Readers) Simon & Schuster Bks. For Young Readers.
Yoshida, Reiko. Tokyo Mew Mew, 10 vols., Vol. 7. Ikumi, Mia. 7th rev. ed. 2004. 208p. pap. 9.99 *(978-1-59182-550-0(4),* Tokyopop Kids) TOKYOPOP, Inc.
—Tokyo Mew-Mew: Volume 5, Vol. 5. Ikumi, Mia. 2006. (Tokyo Mew-Mew (Spanish) Ser.). (SPA.). 184p. reprint ed. pap. 10.95 *(978-1-59497-173-0(0))* Public Square Bks.
—Tokyo Mew Mew Volume 2, Vol. 2. Ikumi, Mia. 2006. (SPA.). 176p. reprint ed. pap. 10.95 *(978-1-59497-170-9(6))* Public Square Bks.
—Tokyo Mew Mew Volume 7, Vol. 7. Ikumi, Mia. 2006. (SPA.). 185p. reprint ed. pap. 10.95 *(978-1-59497-198-3(6))* Public Square Bks.
Yoshikawa, Eiji. Vagabond. Yoshikawa, Eiji. 2004. (Vagabond Ser.). (ENG.). (YA). 200p. pap. 9.95 *(978-1-59116-454-8(0))*; Vol. 17. 192p. pap. 9.95 *(978-1-59116-455-5(9))* Viz Media.
—Vagabond, Vol. 7. Yoshikawa, Eiji. 2003. (ENG.). 200p. (YA). pap. 9.95 *(978-1-59116-073-1(1))* Viz Media.
Yoshikawa, Eiji & Inoue, Takehiko. Vagabond. Yoshikawa, Eiji & Inoue, Takehiko. 2004. (Vagabond Ser.). (ENG.). Vol. 9. 208p. pap. 9.95 *(978-1-59116-256-8(4))*; Vol. 10. 224p. pap. 9.95 *(978-1-59116-340-4(4))*; Vol. 11. 224p. pap. 9.95 *(978-1-59116-396-1(X))*; Vol. 15. 200p. pap. 9.95 *(978-1-59116-453-1(2))* Viz Media.
—Vagabond, Vol. 12. Yoshikawa, Eiji & Inoue, Takehiko. 2004. (ENG.). 200p. pap. 9.95 *(978-1-59116-434-0(6))* Viz Media.
Yoshikawa, Sachiko. The Boy from the Dragon Palace. MacDonald, Margaret Read. 2018. (ENG.). 32p. (J). (-3). pap. 7.99 *(978-0-8075-7514-7(3),* 807575143) Whitman, Albert & Co.
—The Boy from the Dragon Palace. 2011. (ENG.). 32p. (J). (gr. -1-3). 16.99 *(978-0-8075-7513-0(5),* 807575135) Whitman, Albert & Co.
—The Boy from the Dragon Palace: A Folktale from Japan. 2012. (J). *(978-1-61913-110-1(2))* Weigl Pubs., Inc.
—But I Read It on the Internet! Buzzeo, Toni. 2013. 32p. (J). 17.95 *(978-1-60213-062-3(0),* Upstart Bks.) Highsmith Inc.
—Fire up with Reading! Buzzeo, Toni. 2007. 32p. 17.95 *(978-1-60213-019-7(1))*; (J). (gr. -1-3). 17.95 *(978-1-932146-91-2(1))* Highsmith Inc. (Upstart Bks.).
—The Great Dewey Hunt. Buzzeo, Toni. 2009. (Mrs. Skorupski Story Ser.). (J). 36p. (gr. -1-3). 17.95 *(978-1-60213-041-8(8))*; *(978-1-60213-029-6(9))* Highsmith Inc. (Upstart Bks.).
—Hamsters, Shells, & Spelling Bees: School Poems. Hopkins, Lee Bennett. 2008. (I Can Read Bks.). 48p. (J). (gr. -1-3). lib. bdg. 17.89 *(978-0-06-074113-6(9))* HarperCollins Pubs.
—Kindness Is Cooler, Mrs. Ruler. Cuyler, Margery. 2007. (ENG.). 48p. (J). (gr. k-5). 18.99 *(978-0-689-87344-7(1),* Simon & Schuster Bks. For Young Readers) Simon & Schuster Bks. For Young Readers.
—Kitty Up! Wojtusik, Elizabeth. 2008. (J). *(978-0-8037-3045-8(4),* Dial) Penguin Publishing Group.
—The Last Day of Kindergarten, 0 vols. Loewen, Nancy. 2011. (ENG.). 32p. (J). (gr. -1-1). 16.99 *(978-0-7614-5807-4(7),* 9780761458074, Two Lions) Amazon Publishing.
—No T. Rex in the Library. Buzzeo, Toni. 2010. (ENG.). 32p. (J). (gr. -1-3). 18.99 *(978-1-4169-3927-6(X),* McElderry, Margaret K. Bks.) McElderry, Margaret K. Bks.
—Our Librarian Won't Tell Us Anything! Buzzeo, Toni. 2006. 32p. (J). (gr. -1-k). lib. bdg. 17.95 *(978-1-932146-73-8(3),* Upstart Bks.) Highsmith Inc.
—Shout! Little Poems That Roar. Bagert, Brod. 2007. 32p. (J). (gr. -1-3). 17.99 *(978-0-8037-2972-8(3),* Dial Bks) Penguin Young Readers Group.
Yoshikawa, Sachiko. Razzamadaddy, 1 vol. Yoshikawa, Sachiko, tr. Walvoord, Linda. 2004. (ENG.). 32p. (J). 14.95 *(978-0-7614-5158-7(7))* Marshall Cavendish Corp.
Yoshimura, Takumi. Neon Genesis Evangelion: the Shinji Ikari Detective Diary Volume 1: The Shinji Ikari Detective Diary Volume 1. Yoshimura, Takumi. Horn, Carl Gustav, ed. 2013. (Neon Genesis Evangelion: the Shinji Ikari Detective Diary Ser.). (ENG.). 184p. pap. 9.99 *(978-1-61655-225-1(5))* Dark Horse Comics.
Yoshitani, Yoshi. Zatanna & the House of Secrets. Cody, Matthew. 2020. 152p. (J). (gr. 3-7). pap. 9.99 *(978-1-4012-9070-2(1))* DC Comics.
Yoshiyasu. Zen Scratch Art: Magical Woodlands. 2018. (ENG.). 6p. (YA). (gr. 6). 15.99 *(978-4-05-621076-7(4))* Gakken Plus Co., Ltd. JPN. Dist: Simon & Schuster, Inc.
Yoshizaki, Mine. Sgt. Frog. Yoshizaki, Mine. 2005. 10th rev. ed. (Sgt. Frog Ser.: Vol. 10). 184p. pap. 9.99 *(978-1-59182-344-5(7))*; Vol. 6. 6th rev. ed. 192p. pap. 9.99 *(978-1-59182-708-5(6))* TOKYOPOP, Inc.
Yoshizaki, Mine. Sgt. Frog. Yoshizaki, Mine, creator. rev. ed. 2005. 192p. Vol. 7. pap. 9.99 *(978-1-59532-448-1(8))*; Vol. 8. pap. 9.99 *(978-1-59532-449-8(6))* TOKYOPOP, Inc.
Yoshizumi, Carol. Girls Love Gymnastics. American Girl Editors. 2007. 64p. (J). (gr. 4-7). pap. 8.95 *(978-1-59369-283-4(8))* American Girl Publishing, Inc.
—Leela Can Skate Pink B Band. Hawes, Alison. 2016. (Cambridge Reading Adventures Ser.). (ENG.). 16p. pap. 7.37 *(978-1-107-57582-0(6))* Cambridge Univ. Pr.
—Real Beauty: 101 Ways to Feel Great about You. Kauchak, Therese. 2008. (American Girl Library). (ENG.). 120p. (J). pap. 9.95 *(978-1-58485-908-6(3))* American Girl Publishing, Inc.
Yotter, Tate. Anne Bonny: Pirate Queen of the Caribbean. Leaf, Christina. 2020. (Pirate Tales Ser.). (ENG.). 24p. (J). (gr. 3-8). pap. 7.99 ***(978-1-68103-839-1(0))***; lib. bdg. 29.95 ***(978-1-64487-300-7(1))*** Bellwether Media. (Black Sheep).
—Blackbeard: Captain of the Queen Anne's Revenge. Hoena, Blake. 2020. (Pirate Tales Ser.). (ENG.). 24p. (J). (gr. 3-8). pap. 7.99 ***(978-1-68103-840-7(4))***; lib. bdg. 29.95 ***(978-1-64487-301-4(X))*** Bellwether Media. (Black Sheep).
—Ching Shih: The World's Most Successful Pirate. Leaf, Christina. 2020. (Pirate Tales Ser.). (ENG.). 24p. (J). (gr. 3-8). pap. 7.99 ***(978-1-68103-841-4(2))***; lib. bdg. 29.95 ***(978-1-64487-302-1(8))*** Bellwether Media. (Black Sheep).
Yotter, Tate. Flight 19: Lost in the Bermuda Triangle. Bowman, Chris. 2019. (Paranormal Mysteries Ser.). (ENG.). 24p. (J). (gr. 3-8). lib. bdg. 22.95 *(978-1-64487-094-5(0),* Black Sheep) Bellwether Media.
Yotter, Tate. Henry Morgan: Feared Buccaneer of the New World. Hoena, Blake. 2020. (Pirate Tales Ser.). (ENG.). 24p. (J). (gr. 3-8). pap. 7.99 ***(978-1-68103-842-1(0))***; lib. bdg. 29.95 ***(978-1-64487-303-8(6))*** Bellwether Media. (Black Sheep).
—Mary Read: Pirate in Disguise. Leaf, Christina. 2020. (Pirate Tales Ser.). (ENG.). 24p. (J). (gr. 3-8). pap. 7.99 ***(978-1-68103-843-8(9))***; lib. bdg. 29.95 ***(978-1-64487-304-5(4))*** Bellwether Media. (Black Sheep).
Yotter, Tate. The Roswell UFO Incident. Hoena, Blake. 2019. (Paranormal Mysteries Ser.). (ENG.). 24p. (J). (gr. 3-8). lib. bdg. 22.95 *(978-1-64487-097-6(5),* Black Sheep) Bellwether Media.
Yotter, Tate. Sir Francis Drake & the Trip Around the World. Hoena, Blake. 2020. (Pirate Tales Ser.). (ENG.). 24p. (J). (gr. 3-8). pap. 7.99 ***(978-1-68103-844-5(7))***; lib. bdg. 29.95 ***(978-1-64487-305-2(2))*** Bellwether Media. (Black Sheep).
YouDae, Kim. Handy Mr. Hippo. InSeon, Chae. rev. ed. 2014. (MySELF Bookshelf Ser.). (ENG.). 32p. (J). (gr. k-2). pap. 11.94 *(978-1-60357-661-1(4))*; lib. bdg. 25.27 *(978-1-59953-652-1(8))* Norwood Hse. Pr.
YouNeek Studios. Martin Luther King Jr.: Voice for Equality! Buckley, James, Jr. 2019. (Show Me History! Ser.). (ENG.). 96p. (J). (gr. 3-7). 12.99 *(978-1-68412-546-3(4),* Portable Pr.) Printers Row Publishing Group.
Young, Adam. Wendy the Whitebark Pine. O'Hearn, Darcee. 2018. (ENG.). 56p. (J). pap. *(978-1-5255-1055-7(X))* FriesenPress.
Young, Alicia. Hush, Mouse. Benishek, Becky. 2018. (ENG.). 24p. (J). (gr. k-6). 17.99 *(978-1-387-83056-5(2))* Lulu Pr., Inc.
—Scarlett's Journey: The Adventures of a Runner Duck. Dembowski, Becky. 2017. (ENG.). 34p. (J). (gr. k-4). 18.00 *(978-0-9992689-0-2(2))* DNA2Market.
Young, Amy. A Unicorn Named Sparkle. Young, Amy. (Unicorn Named Sparkle Ser.: 1). (ENG.). (J). 2018. 32p. bds. 7.99 *(978-0-374-30872-8(1),* 900187523); 2016. 40p. 16.99 *(978-0-374-30185-9(9),* 900140948) Farrar, Straus & Giroux. (Farrar, Straus & Giroux (BYR)).
—A Unicorn Named Sparkle & the Pumpkin Monster. Young, Amy. 2020. (Unicorn Named Sparkle Ser.). (ENG.). 40p. (J). 17.99 *(978-0-374-30850-6(0),* 900186734, Farrar, Straus & Giroux (BYR)) Farrar, Straus & Giroux.
—A Unicorn Named Sparkle's First Christmas. Young, Amy. (Unicorn Named Sparkle Ser.). (ENG.). (J). 2019. 32p. bds. 7.99 *(978-0-374-31210-7(9),* 900198838); 2018. 40p. 16.99 *(978-0-374-30813-1(6),* 900184776) Farrar, Straus & Giroux. (Farrar, Straus & Giroux (BYR)).
Young, Aviance. Pinksta & the Polka Dotted-Pinstriped-Pants-Wearing Princess. Alexander, Sy. 2005. (J). per. 9.00 *(978-0-9655726-2-0(5))* Proud 2-B Me Publishing!.
Young, Beverley. How Plants & Trees Work: A Hands-On Guide to the Natural World. Dorion, Christiane. 2017. (Explore the Earth Ser.). (ENG.). 18p. (J). (gr. 2-5). 19.99 *(978-0-7636-9298-8(0),* Templar) Candlewick Pr.
—How the Weather Works: A Hands-On Guide to Our Changing Climate. Dorion, Christiane. 2011. (Explore the Earth Ser.). (ENG.). 20p. (J). (gr. 2-5). 19.99 *(978-0-7636-5262-3(8),* Templar) Candlewick Pr.
—How the World Works: A Hands-On Guide to Our Amazing Planet. Dorion, Christian. 2010. (Explore the Earth Ser.). (ENG.). 18p. (J). (gr. 2-5). 21.99 *(978-0-7636-4801-5(9),* Templar) Candlewick Pr.
Young, Bill. Copters. Paul, John. 2012. 36p. 24.95 *(978-1-4626-9458-7(6))* America Star Bks.
—Dinner with a Dinosaur. Austin, Laurie. 2016. (ENG.). (J). pap. 9.99 *(978-0-578-18226-1(2))* Austin, Laurie .
Young, Bill, jt. illus. see Margolis, Al.
Young, Bruce & Young, Jennifer Law, photos by. Rockbridge: A Photographic Essay. Young, Bruce & Young, Jennifer Law. Wolfe, Andrew, ed. 2005. 124p. 34.95 *(978-0-9768238-4-1(5))* Mariner Publishing.
Young, Courtny. Los Sue�os de Corey. M, Aziza. 2016. (SPA.). 26p. (J). pap. 12.50 ***(978-1-7931-3755-5(2))*** Independently Published.
Young, Craig. The Adventures of Imhotep. Akinje, Wale. 2006. (J). *(978-0-9768485-0-9(3))* Nile Publishing.
Young, Cybele. Jack Pine, 1 vol. Patton, Christopher. 2007. (ENG.). 32p. (J). (gr. 1-7). 18.95 *(978-0-88899-780-7(9))* Groundwood Bks. CAN. Dist: Publishers Group West (PGW).
Young, Cybèle. Nancy Knows. 2017. 32p. (J). (— 1). bds. 8.99 *(978-1-101-91892-0(6),* Tundra Bks.) Tundra Bks. CAN. Dist: Penguin Random Hse. LLC.
Young, Cybèle & Kloepper, Madeline. Little Blue Chair. Fagan, Cary. 2017. (ENG.). 40p. (J). (gr. -1-2). 16.99 *(978-1-77049-755-9(2),* Tundra Bks.) Tundra Bks. CAN. Dist: Penguin Random Hse. LLC.
Young, Cybèle & Young, Cybèle. The Queen's Shadow: A Story about How Animals See. Young, Cybèle & Young, Cybèle. 2015. (ENG.). 40p. (J). (gr. 2-6). 16.95 *(978-1-894786-60-7(2))* Kids Can Pr., Ltd. CAN. Dist: Hachette Bk. Group.

Young, Cybèle, jt. illus. see Young, Cybèle.
Young, Dalandra. Noonimals: First Day of School. Young, Dalandra. 2019. (ENG.). 42p. (J). pap. ***(978-1-989161-97-5(9))*** Hasmark Services Publishing.
Young, Dot. Where Are My Christmas Presents? Rives, J. G. 2007. 44p. (J). 17.95 *(978-0-9790014-0-6(4))* Sterli Publishing.
Young, Ed. Bird & Diz. Golio, Gary. 2015. 26p. (J). (gr. -1-3). 19.99 *(978-0-7636-6660-6(2))* Candlewick Pr.
—Catastrophe by the Sea. 2019. (ENG.). 32p. (J). (gr. 1-4). 16.99 *(978-1-5132-6234-5(3),* West Margin Pr.) West Margin Pr.
—The Emperor & the Kite. Yolen, Jane. 2015. 32p. pap. 7.00 *(978-1-61003-535-4(6))* Center for the Collaborative Classroom.
—I Bliss: An Islamic Tale. Oppenheim, Shulamith. 2004. 29p. (J). (gr. k-4). reprint ed. 16.00 *(978-0-7567-7575-9(2))* DIANE Publishing Co.
—Moon Bear. Guiberson, Brenda Z. 2010. (ENG.). 40p. (J). pap. 7.99 *(978-0-8050-9258-5(7))* Holt, Henry & Co.
—Shanghai Messenger, 1 vol. Cheng, Andrea. 2005. (ENG.). 40p. (J). (gr. 3-7). 17.95 *(978-1-58430-238-4(0))* Lee & Low Bks., Inc.
—Smile: How Young Charlie Chaplin Taught the World to Laugh (and Cry) Golio, Gary. 2019. 48p. (J). (gr. 3-7). 17.99 *(978-0-7636-9761-7(3))* Candlewick Pr.
—A Strange Place to Call Home: The World's Most Dangerous Habitats & the Animals That Call Them Home. Singer, Marilyn. 2015. (ENG.). 44p. (J). (gr. k-3). 7.99 *(978-1-4521-4125-1(8))* Chronicle Bks. LLC.
—Tai Chi Morning: Snapshots of China. Grimes, Nikki. 2004. (ENG.). 64p. (J). 15.95 *(978-0-8126-2707-7(5))* Cricket Bks.
—Tiger of the Snows: Tenzing Norgay: the Boy Whose Dream Was Everest. Burleigh, Robert. 2010. (ENG.). 40p. (J). (gr. 2-5). 16.99 *(978-1-4424-2192-9(4),* Atheneum Bks. for Young Readers) Simon & Schuster Children's Publishing.
—Tsunami! Kajikawa, Kimiko. 2009. (ENG.). 32p. (J). (gr. -1-k). 17.99 *(978-0-399-25006-4(9),* Philomel Bks.) Penguin Young Readers Group.
—Wabi Sabi. Reibstein, Mark. 2008. 48p. (J). (gr. -1-3). 19.99 *(978-0-316-11825-5(7))* Little Brown & Co.
—Yugen. Reibstein, Mark. 2019. 32p. (J). (gr. -1-2). 17.95 *(978-1-60980-865-5(7),* Triangle Square) Seven Stories Pr.
Young, Ed. The Cat from Hunger Mountain. Young, Ed. 2016. (ENG.). 32p. (J). (gr. -1-3). 17.99 *(978-0-399-17278-6(5),* Philomel Bks.) Penguin Young Readers Group.
—Seven Blind Mice. Young, Ed. 2012. (ENG.). 36p. (J). (gr. -1 — 1). bds. 8.99 *(978-0-399-25742-1(X),* Philomel Bks.) Penguin Young Readers Group.
—Seven Blind Mice. Young, Ed. 2007. pap. 14.95 incl. audio *(978-0-439-02784-7(5));* (J). 24.95 incl. audio *(978-0-439-02782-3(9))* Scholastic, Inc.
—Seven Blind Mice. Young, Ed. 2011. 18.95 *(978-0-439-02785-4(3));* (J). 29.95 *(978-0-439-02783-0(7))* Weston Woods Studios, Inc.
—The Sons of the Dragon King: A Chinese Legend. Young, Ed. 2004. (ENG.). 32p. (J). (gr. -1-3). 19.99 *(978-0-689-85184-1(7),* Atheneum Bks. for Young Readers) Simon & Schuster Children's Publishing.
—Voices of the Heart. Young, Ed. 2019. 32p. (J). (gr. k-4). 9.95 *(978-1-60980-867-9(3),* Triangle Square) Seven Stories Pr.
—The Weather's Bet. Young, Ed. 2020. (ENG.). 32p. (J). (gr. -1-3). 18.99 *(978-0-525-51382-7(5),* Philomel Bks.) Penguin Young Readers Group.
Young, Elijah. Adorable Dori: The Mean Queen. Cook, Nancy Lynn. 2018. (ENG.). 34p. (J). pap. 9.25 *(978-1-7202-5379-2(X))* Independently Published.
Young, Ellsworth. More Jataka Tales. Babbitt, Ellen C. 2006. pap. *(978-1-4065-0347-0(9))* Dodo Pr.
—More Jataka Tales. Babbitt, Ellen C. 2008. 92p. pap. 7.95 *(978-1-59915-310-0(6))* Yesterday's Classics.
Young, Emma. Arts & Crafts of Ancient China. Morris, Ting. 2006. (Arts & Crafts of Ser.). 32p. (J). lib. bdg. 27.10 *(978-1-58340-914-5(9),* 1262690) Black Rabbit Bks.
—Arts & Crafts of Ancient Greece. Morris, Ting. 2006. (Arts & Crafts of Ser.). 32p. (J). lib. bdg. 28.50 *(978-1-58340-912-1(2),* 1262692) Black Rabbit Bks.
—Arts & Crafts of Ancient Rome. Morris, Ting. 2006. (Arts & Crafts of Ser.). 32p. (J). lib. bdg. 28.50 *(978-1-58340-913-8(0),* 1262693) Black Rabbit Bks.
—Arts & Crafts of the Aztecs & Maya. Morris, Ting. 2006. (Arts & Crafts of the Ancient World Ser.). 32p. (J). lib. bdg. 28.50 *(978-1-58340-915-2(7),* 1262694) Black Rabbit Bks.
—Arts & Crafts of the Native Americans. Morris, Ting. 2006. (Arts & Crafts of the Ancient World Ser.). 32p. (J). lib. bdg. 28.50 *(978-1-58340-916-9(5))* Black Rabbit Bks.
Young, Eric. Cupid: God of Love. Temple, Teri & Temple, Emily. 2015. (Roman Mythology Ser.). (ENG.). 32p. (J). (gr. 2-5). 29.93 *(978-1-63143-715-1(1),* 208558) Child's World, Inc., The.
—Diana: Goddess of Hunting & Protector of Animals. Temple, Teri & Temple, Emily. 2015. (Roman Mythology Ser.). (ENG.). 32p. (J). (gr. 2-5). 29.93 *(978-1-63143-716-8(X),* 208559) Child's World, Inc., The.
—Juno: Queen of the Gods, Goddess of Marriage. Temple, Teri & Temple, Emily. 2015. (Roman Mythology Ser.). (ENG.). 32p. (J). (gr. 2-5). 29.93 *(978-1-63143-717-5(8),* 208560) Child's World, Inc., The.
—Jupiter: King of the Gods, God of Sky & Storms. Temple, Teri & Temple, Emily. 2015. (Roman Mythology Ser.). (ENG.). 32p. (J). (gr. 2-5). 29.93 *(978-1-63143-718-2(6),* 208561) Child's World, Inc., The.
—Mars: God of War. Temple, Teri & Temple, Emily. 2015. (Roman Mythology Ser.). (ENG.). 32p. (J). (gr. 2-5). 29.93 *(978-1-63143-719-9(4),* 208562) Child's World, Inc., The.
—Mercury: God of Travels & Trade. Temple, Teri & Temple, Emily. 2015. (Roman Mythology Ser.). (ENG.). 32p. (J). (gr. 2-5). 29.93 *(978-1-63143-720-5(8),* 208563) Child's World, Inc., The.
—Minerva: Goddess of Wisdom, War, & Crafts. Temple, Teri & Temple, Emily. 2015. (Roman Mythology Ser.). (ENG.). 32p. (J). (gr. 2-5). 29.93 *(978-1-63143-721-2(6),* 208564) Child's World, Inc., The.
—Neptune: God of the Sea & Earthquakes. Temple, Teri & Temple, Emily. 2015. (Roman Mythology Ser.). (ENG.). 32p. (J). (gr. 2-5). 29.93 *(978-1-63143-722-9(4),* 208565) Child's World, Inc., The.
—Pluto: God of the Underworld. Temple, Teri & Temple, Emily. 2015. (Roman Mythology Ser.). (ENG.). 32p. (J). (gr. 2-5). 29.93 *(978-1-63143-723-6(2),* 208566) Child's World, Inc., The.
—Saturn: God of Sowing & Seeds. Temple, Teri & Temple, Emily. 2015. (Roman Mythology Ser.). (ENG.). 32p. (J). (gr. 2-5). 29.93 *(978-1-63143-724-3(0),* 208567) Child's World, Inc., The.
—Venus: Goddess of Love & Beauty. Temple, Teri & Temple, Emily. 2015. (Roman Mythology Ser.). (ENG.). 32p. (J). (gr. 2-5). 29.93 *(978-1-63143-725-0(9),* 208568) Child's World, Inc., The.
Young, Eugene Randolph. The Food Convention. Young, Eugene Randolph, des. l.t. ed. 2006. 32p. (J). 16.95 *(978-0-9792000-0-7(8))* Les Lum Pubs.
Young, Heather. The Great Expedition: Dog the Dragon, Book 3. Lasterday, J. 2017. (ENG.). (J). pap. 5.99 *(978-0-9981054-2-0(2))* Walker Hammond Pubs.
Young Illustrators Club, Leading Edge Ac, jt. illus. see York, Janell.
Young, James. Jack & the Giants. Salsi, Lynn. 2012. (ENG.). 32p. (J). 16.95 *(978-0-938467-52-6(2))* Headline Bks., Inc.
Young, Jasmine. Eve of the Moon. Marshall, Tj. 2019. (ENG.). 198p. (J). pap. 8.99 *(978-1-7250-6836-0(2))* CreateSpace Independent Publishing Platform.
Young, Jennifer Law, jt. photos by see Young, Bruce.
Young, Karen L. Princess Penelope: Snowflakes, Handprints, & Play-Dates. Bronstein, Christine. 2018. (Stewie BOOM! Ser.). (ENG.). 46p. (J). (gr. -1-3). pap. 9.99 *(978-0-9972962-7-3(5))* Nothing But The Truth, LLC.
—Princess Penelope: The Case of the Eweey, Gooey, Gross & Very Stinky Experiment: Bronstein, Christine. 2016. (Stewie BOOM! Ser.). (ENG.). 58p. (J). (gr. -1-3). 17.99 *(978-0-9963074-8-2(6))* Nothing But The Truth, LLC.
—Princess Penelope: The Case of the Eweey, Gooey, Gross & Very Stinky Experiment. Bronstein, Christine. 2016. (Stewie BOOM! Ser.). (ENG.). 58p. (J). (gr. -1-3). pap. 9.99 *(978-0-9963074-9-9(4))* Nothing But The Truth, LLC.
—Starts School. Bronstein, Christine. 2014. (Stewie BOOM! Ser.). (ENG.). 48p. (J). (gr. -1-3). 17.99 *(978-0-9904652-0-1(9))* Nothing But The Truth, LLC.
—Stewie BOOM! & Princess Penelope: Handprints, Snowflakes & Playdates. Bronstein, Christine. 2018. (Stewie BOOM! Ser.). (ENG.). 36p. (J). (gr. -1-3). 22.50 *(978-0-9972962-8-0(3))* Nothing But The Truth, LLC.
—Stewie BOOM! Boss of the Big Boy Bed: Boss of the Big Boy Bed. Bronstein, Christine. 2015. (Stewie BOOM! Ser.). (ENG.). 60p. (gr. -1-2). 17.99 *(978-0-9904652-9-4(2));* pap. 11.99 *(978-0-9963074-0-6(0))* Nothing But The Truth, LLC.
—Stewie BOOM! Starts School. Bronstein, Christine. 2014. (Stewie BOOM! Ser.). (ENG.). 48p. (gr. -1-3). pap. 9.99 *(978-0-9883754-9-9(4))* Nothing But The Truth, LLC.
Young, Mary. Caminando Bajo la Nieve. Wetterer, Margaret K. & Wetterer, Charles M. 2007. (Yo Solo - Historia (on My Own - History) Ser.). (SPA.). 48p. (gr. 2-4). lib. bdg. 25.26 *(978-0-8225-7786-7(0))* Lerner Publishing Group.
Young, Mary O'Keefe. Merry Christmas, Curious George (with Stickers) Rey, H. A. & Hapka, Catherine. 2017. (Curious George Ser.). (ENG.). 24p. (J). (gr. -1-3). pap. 5.99 *(978-1-328-69558-1(1),* 1671221, HMH Books For Young Readers) Houghton Mifflin Harcourt Publishing Co.
Young, Mary O'Keefe. Caminando Bajo la Nieve. Wetterer, Margaret K. & Wetterer, Charles M. 2007. (Yo Solo Historia Ser.). 48p. (J). (gr. 4-7). per. 6.95 *(978-0-8225-7789-8(5))* Lerner Publishing Group.
—Feliz Navidad, Jorge el Curioso. Rey, H. A. ed. 2012. (Curious George Ser.).Tr. of Merry Christmas, Curious George. (ENG.). 32p. (J). (gr. -1-3). 10.99 *(978-0-547-74503-9(6),* 1486266) Houghton Mifflin Harcourt Publishing Co.
—Hanukkah. Fishman, Cathy Goldberg. 2004. (On My Own Holidays Ser.). 48p. (J). (gr. 2-4). lib. bdg. 25.26 *(978-1-57505-195-6(8))* Lerner Publishing Group.
—Happy Easter, Curious George. Anderson, R. P. et al. 2010. (Curious George Ser.). (ENG.). 24p. (J). (gr. -1-3). 9.99 *(978-0-547-04825-3(4),* 1035143) Houghton Mifflin Harcourt Publishing Co.
—Happy Valentine's Day. Rey, H. A. 2011. (Curious George Ser.). (ENG.). 14p. (J). (gr. -1-3). 8.99 *(978-0-547-13107-8(0),* 1048361) Houghton Mifflin Harcourt Publishing Co.
—Merry Christmas, Curious George. Rey, H. A. et al. 2012. (Curious George Ser.). (ENG.). 32p. (J). (gr. -1-3). 9.99 *(978-0-547-76054-4(X),* 1488729) Houghton Mifflin Harcourt Publishing Co.
—The Snow Walker. Wetterer, Margaret K. & Wetterer, Charles M. unabr. ed. (Historical Fiction Ser.). (J). (gr. 1-6). 24.95 incl. audio *(978-0-87499-394-3(6))* Live Oak Media.
Young, Mary O'Keefe, jt. illus. see Schories, Pat.
Young, Ned. Big Rig. Swenson, Jamie A. 2014. (ENG.). 32p. (J). (gr. -1-k). 16.99 *(978-1-4231-6330-5(3))* Hyperion Bks. for Children.
—Super Saurus & the Egg. Underwood, Deborah. 2018. (Super Saurus Ser.: 1). (ENG.). 40p. (J). (gr. -1-k). 16.99 *(978-1-4231-7569-8(7))* Hyperion Bks. for Children.
—Super Saurus Saves Kindergarten. Underwood, Deborah. 2017. (ENG.). 40p. (J). (gr. -1-k). 16.99 *(978-1-4231-7568-1(9))* Disney Pr.
Young, Ned. Zoomer. Young, Ned. 2010. (ENG.). 32p. (J). (gr. -1-2). 16.99 *(978-0-06-170088-0(6))* HarperCollins Pubs.
—Zoomer's Out-Of-This-World Christmas. Young, Ned. 2013. (ENG.). 32p. (J). (gr. -1-3). 17.99 *(978-0-06-199959-8(8))* HarperCollins Pubs.
Young Noh, Mi. Threads of Time, Vol. 5. Hong, Jihae, tr. rev. ed. 2005. 192p. pap. 9.99 *(978-1-59532-036-0(9))* TOKYOPOP, Inc.
Young Noh, Mi. Threads of Time, Vol. 4. Young Noh, Mi, creator. rev. ed. 2005. 192p. pap. 9.99 *(978-1-59532-035-3(0))* TOKYOPOP, Inc.
Young, Norman. Bible Stories. Amery, Heather. gif. ed. 2004. (Bible Tales Readers Ser.). (ENG.). 1p. (J). (gr. -1-3). 24.95 *(978-0-7460-4145-1(4))* EDC Publishing.
—The Christmas Story. rev. ed. 2006. (Usborne Bible Tales Ser.). 16p. (J). (gr. -1-3). pap. 4.99 *(978-0-7945-1286-6(0),* Usborne) EDC Publishing.
—The Incredible Present. Castor, Harriet. 2004. (Usborne Young Reading: Series Two Ser.). 64p. (J). (gr. k-4). 8.99 *(978-0-7945-1785-4(4),* Usborne) EDC Publishing.
—Starting Soccer. Edom, Helen & Osborne, Mike. 2006. (First Skills Ser.). 32p. (J). (gr. k-3). lib. bdg. 12.99 *(978-1-58086-907-2(6),* Usborne) EDC Publishing.
—The Story of Jesus for Young Children. 2005. (Usborne Bible Tales Ser.). 98p. (J). (gr. -1-k). 14.99 incl. audio compact disk *(978-0-7945-0831-9(6),* Usborne) EDC Publishing.
Young, Norman & Ablett, Barry. Horse & Pony Treasury. Dickins, Rosie & Pratt, Leonie. Sims, Lesley, ed. 2006. (Horse & Pony Treasury Ser.). 93p. (J). 19.99 *(978-0-7945-1431-0(6),* Usborne) EDC Publishing.
Young, Patricia A. The Holy Monks of Mt. Athos. Young, Patricia A. l.t. ed. 2005. 28p. (J). 20.00 *(978-0-913026-24-3(7));* 10.00 *(978-0-913026-49-6(2))* St. Nectarios Pr.
Young, Paul. Colm's Lambs. McQuinn, Anna. 2013. (Glenmore Valley Ser.: 1). (ENG.). 32p. (J). pap. 13.95 *(978-1-84717-339-3(X))* O'Brien Pr., Ltd., The IRL. Dist: Casemate Pubs. & Bk. Distributors, LLC.
—A Rosette for Maeve? McQuinn, Anna. 2013. (Glenmore Valley Ser.: 2). (ENG.). 32p. (J). pap. 13.95 *(978-1-84717-340-9(3))* O'Brien Pr., Ltd., The IRL. Dist: Casemate Pubs. & Bk. Distributors, LLC.
Young, Pauline. I Lost My Talk, 1 vol. Joe, Rita. 2019. (ENG.). 32p. (J). 18.95 *(978-1-77108-810-7(9),* 0f672eba-5495-4b43-964e-a342f609f323) Nimbus Publishing, Ltd. CAN. Dist: Baker & Taylor Publisher Services (BTPS).
—I'm Finding My Talk, 1 vol. Thomas, Rebecca. 2019. (ENG.). 32p. (J). 18.95 *(978-1-77108-811-4(7),* 8f5c35ba-0b88-4023-90db-31b9f76d9022) Nimbus Publishing, Ltd. CAN. Dist: Baker & Taylor Publisher Services (BTPS).
Young, Pippa. On the Farm. (Match & Twist Ser.). (J). 11.99 *(978-0-525-47054-0(9),* Dutton Juvenile) Penguin Publishing Group.
Young, Ross. Show Me the Number: A Missouri Number Book. Young, Judy. rev. ed. 2007. (State Counting Ser.). (ENG.). 40p. (J). (gr. 1-7). 17.95 *(978-1-58536-156-4(9))* Sleeping Bear Pr.
Young, Sarah. Greek Myths. Turnbull, Ann. 2010. 168p. (J). (gr. 5). 21.99 *(978-0-7636-5111-4(7))* Candlewick Pr.
Young, Sarah. Endangered Animals: a 3D Pocket Guide. Young, Sarah. Candlewick Press Staff. 2014. (Panorama Pops Ser.). (ENG.). 30p. (J). (gr. k-4). 8.99 *(978-0-7636-6985-0(7))* Candlewick Pr.
Young, Selina. The Kitten with No Name. French, Vivian. 2010. (ENG.). 112p. 14.99 *(978-1-4440-0077-1(2))* Orion Publishing Group, Ltd. GBR. Dist: Hachette Bk. Group.
—Ladybird Ladybird. French, Vivian. 2003. (ENG.). 32p. pap. *(978-1-84255-284-1(8),* Orion Children's Bks.) Hachette Children's Group.
Young, Shane, photos by. Princess Zelda & the Frog. Gardner, Carol. 2011. (ENG., 40p. (J). (gr. -1-3). 16.99 *(978-0-312-60325-0(8),* 9780312603250) Feiwel & Friends.
Young, Shelley. Doc Broc's Cave Adventure. Young, Shelley. 2005. 44p. 19.95 *(978-1-58054-406-1(1))* Woodland Publishing, Inc.
Young, Skott. Spider-Man Legend of the Spider-Clan, 3 vols. Andrews, Kaare. 2003. (Mangaverse Ser.: Vol. 3). 128p. (YA). pap. 11.99 *(978-0-7851-1114-6(X))* Marvel Worldwide, Inc.
Young, Skottie. Fortunately, the Milk. Gaiman, Neil. 2013. (ENG.). 128p. (J). (gr. 3-7). 14.99 *(978-0-06-222407-1(7),* HarperCollins) HarperCollins Pubs.
—Fortunately, the Milk. Gaiman, Neil. 2014. (ENG.). 128p. (J). (gr. 3-7). pap. 6.99 *(978-0-06-222408-8(5),* HarperCollins) HarperCollins Pubs. Ltd. GBR. Dist: HarperCollins Pubs.
—Human Torch: Burn. Kesel, Karl. 2004. (Fantastic Four Ser.). 144p. (YA). pap. 14.99 *(978-0-7851-1236-5(7))* Marvel Worldwide, Inc.
Young, Skottie, et al. Marvelous Land of Oz, 8 vols. Shanower, Eric. Horwitz, Michael, ed. 2014. (Marvelous Land of Oz Ser.: Vol. 8). (ENG.). 24p. (J). (gr. 3-8). 216.56 *(978-1-61479-234-5(8),* 11346) ABDO Publishing Co.
Young, Skottie. The Marvelous Land of Oz: Adapted from the Novel by L. Frank Baum. Shanower, Eric & Baum, L. Frank. 2014. (Marvelous Land of Oz Ser.). (ENG.). 24p. (J). (gr. 3-8). 27.07 *(978-1-61479-238-3(0),* 11350) ABDO Publishing Co.
—Marvelous Land of Oz: Vol. 1, 1 vol. Shanower, Eric. 2014. (Marvelous Land of Oz Ser.). (ENG.). 24p. (J). (gr. 3-8). 27.07 *(978-1-61479-235-2(6),* 11347) ABDO Publishing Co.
—Marvelous Land of Oz: Vol. 2, 1 vol. Shanower, Eric. 2014. (Marvelous Land of Oz Ser.). (ENG.). 24p. (J). (gr. 3-8). 27.07 *(978-1-61479-236-9(4),* 11348) ABDO Publishing Co.
—Marvelous Land of Oz: Vol. 3, 1 vol. Shanower, Eric. 2014. (Marvelous Land of Oz Ser.). (ENG.). 24p. (J). (gr. 3-8). 27.07 *(978-1-61479-237-6(2),* 11349) ABDO Publishing Co.
—Monstrous. Connolly, MarcyKate. (ENG.). (J). (gr. 3-7). 2016. 448p. pap. 7.99 *(978-0-06-227272-0(1));* 2015. 432p. 16.99 *(978-0-06-227271-3(3))* HarperCollins Pubs.
Young, Skottie. Oz: the Complete Collection - Ozma/Dorothy & the Wizard. 2020. (ENG.). 368p. (J). (gr. -1-17). pap. 15.99 ***(978-1-302-92121-7(5))*** Marvel Worldwide, Inc.
Young, Skottie. Oz: the Complete Collection - Wonderful Wizard/Marvelous Land. 2020. (ENG.). 416p. (J). (gr. 4-7). pap. 15.99 *(978-1-302-92120-0(7))* Marvel Worldwide, Inc.
Young, Skottie, et al. Rocket Raccoon #5: Storytailer. Young, Skottie. 2017. (Guardians of the Galaxy: Rocket Raccoon Ser.). (ENG.). 24p. (J). (gr. 6-12). lib. bdg. 27.07 *(978-1-5321-4088-4(6),* 25493, Marvel Age) Spotlight.
—Rocket Raccoon #6: Misfit Mechs. Young, Skottie. 2017. (Guardians of the Galaxy: Rocket Raccoon Ser.). (ENG.). 24p. (J). (gr. 6-12). lib. bdg. 27.07 *(978-1-5321-4089-1(4),* 25494, Marvel Age) Spotlight.
Young, Skottie. Wonderful Wizard of Oz. Shanower, Eric. 2014. (Wonderful Wizard of Oz Ser.). (ENG.). 24p. (J). (gr. 3-8). 27.07 *(978-1-61479-227-7(5),* 15346) ABDO Publishing Co.
—Wonderful Wizard of Oz, 8 vols., Set. Shanower, Eric. 2014. (Wonderful Wizard of Oz Ser.: Vol. 8). (ENG.). 24p. (J). (gr. 3-8). 216.56 *(978-1-61479-225-3(9),* 15344) ABDO Publishing Co.
—The Wonderful Wizard of Oz, Vol. 4. Shanower, Eric & Baum, L. Frank. 2014. (Wonderful Wizard of Oz Ser.). (ENG.). 24p. (J). (gr. 3-8). 27.07 *(978-1-61479-229-1(1),* 15348) ABDO Publishing Co.
—Wonderful Wizard of Oz: Vol. 3, 1 vol. Shanower, Eric. 2014. (Wonderful Wizard of Oz Ser.). (ENG.). 24p. (J). (gr. 3-8). 27.07 *(978-1-61479-228-4(3),* 15347) ABDO Publishing Co.
Young, Skottie & Beaulieu, Jean-François. Rocket Raccoon #1: a Chasing Tale Part One. Young, Skottie. 2017. (Guardians of the Galaxy: Rocket Raccoon Ser.). (ENG.). 24p. (J). (gr. 6-12). lib. bdg. 27.07 *(978-1-5321-4084-6(3),* 25489, Marvel Age) Spotlight.
—Rocket Raccoon #2: a Chasing Tale Part Two. Young, Skottie. 2017. (Guardians of the Galaxy: Rocket Raccoon Ser.). (ENG.). 24p. (J). (gr. 6-12). lib. bdg. 27.07 *(978-1-5321-4085-3(1),* 25490, Marvel Age) Spotlight.
—Rocket Raccoon #3: a Chasing Tale Part Three. Young, Skottie. 2017. (Guardians of the Galaxy: Rocket Raccoon Ser.). (ENG.). 24p. (J). (gr. 6-12). lib. bdg. 27.07 *(978-1-5321-4086-0(X),* 25491, Marvel Age) Spotlight.
—Rocket Raccoon #4: a Chasing Tale Part Four. Young, Skottie. 2017. (Guardians of the Galaxy: Rocket Raccoon Ser.). (ENG.). 24p. (J). (gr. 6-12). lib. bdg. 27.07 *(978-1-5321-4087-7(8),* 25492, Marvel Age) Spotlight.
Young, Stephanie & Smith, Tim. The Blue Forest, 1 vol. Fischer, Luke. 2015. (ENG.). 48p. (J). *(978-1-58420-147-2(9),* Lindisfarne Bks.) SteinerBooks, Inc.
Young, Sue. Tommy Tractor Goes to the City, 1 vol. Ayers, Sanda. 2009. 29p. pap. 19.95 *(978-1-61582-054-2(X))* PublishAmerica, Inc.
Young, Susan. Jody & the Monsters. Mackey, Cindy. 2019. (ENG.). 42p. (J). (gr. k-3). pap. 11.99 *(978-1-7322739-1-7(X))* Cyrano Bks.
—Piper & Pickle: Smile. Barton, Brittney B. 2013. 68p. 18.99 *(978-0-9856336-0-8(3))* P2 Publishing.
Young, Susan G. Kai & Ty Go to Hawaii. Newman, Adam T. 2018. (ENG.). 46p. (J). pap. 14.95 *(978-0-9910909-6-9(9))* MiLo Ink Bks.
Young, Tim. Hellie & the Sensational Magic Carpet. Young, Helen Ann. 2013. 106p. pap. *(978-1-908353-02-3(3))* Young Editions.
Young, Tim Blair. Hello to Hellie's World. Young, Helen Ann. 2013. 46p. pap. *(978-1-908353-00-9(7))* Young Editions.
—Your World Discovery Scrapbook. Young, Helen Ann. 2013. 40p. pap. *(978-1-908353-03-0(1))* Young Editions.
Young, Timothy. Am I Big Enough? A Fun Little Book on Manners, 1 vol. Pinckney, Julia. 2016. (ENG.). 32p. (J). 16.99 *(978-0-7643-5053-5(6),* 6857) Schiffer Publishing, Ltd.
—Beauty & Bernice, 1 vol. Viau, Nancy. 2018. (ENG.). 144p. (gr. 3-6). 12.99 *(978-0-7643-5580-6(5),* 9951) Schiffer Publishing, Ltd.
—Do Not Open the Box, 1 vol. 2016. (ENG.). 32p. (J). 16.99 *(978-0-7643-5043-6(9),* 6805) Schiffer Publishing, Ltd.
—Just One Thing!, 1 vol. Viau, Nancy. 2016. (ENG.). 144p. (gr. 3-6). 12.99 *(978-0-7643-5162-4(1),* 7556) Schiffer Publishing, Ltd.
Youngblood, Carol. Vacation Paws. Payne, Helen. 2006. 50p. per. 10.00 *(978-0-9786276-6-9(0))* Mentzer Printing Ink.
Youngblood, David W. Dr. Jim & the Special Stethoscope. Nicol, Scott Thomas. 2010. (Adventures of Dr. Jim Ser.). 32p. (J). pap. 12.95 *(978-0-9830355-7-2(1),* Creative Hse. Kids Pr.) Bourgeois Media & Consulting.
Youngbluth, Chris. The South Overlook Oaks. Reardon, John. 2006. 119p. (J). (gr. 4-7). 16.95 *(978-1-931643-91-7(1))* Seven Locks Pr.
Younger, Nathan C. Pewp. Blythe, Kenton. 2019. (Pewp Ser.: Vol. 1). (ENG.). 34p. (J). (gr. k-3). 15.00 ***(978-1-7770402-0-8(5))*** Mr. Cal Cumin.
Youngsuk, Ratchanee. Let's Imagine. Wing, Scarlett. Cottage Door Press, ed. 2020. (Mirror & Me Children's Interactive Mirrored Board Book Ser.). (ENG.). 10p. (J). (gr. -1 — 1). bds. 8.99 ***(978-1-68052-982-1(X),*** 1006100) Cottage Door Pr.
Yourell, Pam. Anya's Gift: A Tale of Two Christmases, 1 vol. Jones, Sandy. 2009. 48p. pap. 24.95 *(978-1-61546-129-5(9))* America Star Bks.
Yourell, Pamela. The Adventures of Dan & Sam. Weber, Suzon Babitt & Yingling, Phyllis S. 2019. (Steps to Success Ser.: Vol. 1). (ENG.). 40p. (J). pap. 8.95 ***(978-1-882788-18-7(4))*** Vangar Pubs./Baltimore.
Youso, Justin & Kaino, Kim. The Twined Basket: A Story & Activity Book for Ages 10 - 12. McNutt, Nan & Miller, Bruce ""subiyay"". 2011. (Native American Art Activity Book Ser.). (ENG.). 56p. (J). (gr. 5-7). pap. 9.95 *(978-0-88240-760-9(0),* West Winds Pr.) West Margin Pr.
Youth of the Achuar Tribe of Ecuador. Nantu & Auju: How the Moon & the Potoo Bird Came to Be. Mayaprua, Alejandro Taish. 2005. (J). 15.95 *(978-0-9745477-0-1(0))* Arutam Pr.
Youtsey, Scott, jt. illus. see McCorkindale, Bruce.

Y

Youzhi, He. Stories Behind Chinese Idioms (II) Ma, Zheng & Li, Zheng. 2010. (ENG.). 48p. (J). (gr. 3-6). 16.95 (978-1-60220-966-4(9)) Shanghai Translation Publishing Hse. CHN. Dist: Publishers Group West (PGW).

YoYo. The Warriors' Trial, 5. YoYo. 2011. (Vermonia Ser.). (ENG.). 208p. (J). (gr. 5-8). 22.44 (978-0-7636-5610-2(0)) Candlewick Pr.

Yu, Brenna Burns. Hazel & Twig: the Birthday Fortune. Yu, Brenna Burns. 2018. (Hazel & Twig Ser.). 40p. (J). (gr. -1-2). 15.99 (978-0-7636-8970-4(X)) Candlewick Pr.

Yu, Chao & Wang, Jue. Where the Buffalo Jump. Cook, Gerri. 2003. (Dinosaur Soup Ser.). 120p. (YA). (gr. 3-5). pap. 9.95 (978-1-895836-95-0(6)) River Bks. CAN. Dist: Fitzhenry & Whiteside, Ltd.

Yu, Chao, jt. illus. see Bennett, Lorna.

Yu, Jennifer. Texas Animal Ranch: Ricky's Secret Friends Series, vols. 6, vol. 2. Yu, Jennifer. 2018. (Ricky's Secret Friends Picturebook Ser.: 6). (ENG & CHI.). (gr. 1-4). 49.95 (978-0-9787591-2-4(5)) Direct World Publishing.

Yu, Jennifer & Yu, Jennifer. Talking Flower Garden: A Series of Ricky's Secret Friends, vols. 6, vol. 5. 2018. (Ricky's Secret Friends Picturebook Ser.). (ENG & CHI.). (gr. 1-6). 49.95 (978-0-9787591-1-7(7)) Direct World Publishing.

Yu, Jennifer, jt. illus. see Yu, Jennifer.

Yu, Ji. A Dachshund's Wish. Tavano, Joe. 2006. (ENG.). 80p. (J). (gr. 2-4). pap. 16.99 (978-0-9744287-1-0(X)) Minted Prose, LLC.

Yu, Leinil Francis. Captain America by Ta-Nehisi Coates Vol. 1: Winter in America. 2019. (Captain America by Ta-Nehisi Coates Ser.: 1). 152p. (YA). (gr. 8-17). pap. 17.99 (978-1-302-91194-2(5)) Marvel Worldwide, Inc.

Yu, Leinil Francis, et al. Indestructible Hulk by Mark Waid: the Complete Collection. 2017. (ENG.). 504p. (YA). (gr. 8-17). pap. 39.99 (978-1-302-90800-3(6)) Marvel Worldwide, Inc.

Yu, Leinil Francis. Phoenix Resurrection: the Return of Jean Grey. 2018. (ENG.). 136p. (YA). (gr. 8-17). pap. 17.99 (978-1-302-91163-8(5)) Marvel Worldwide, Inc.

—Rebel Jail: Volume 4. Aaron, Jason. 2017. (Star Wars: Rebel Jail Ser.). (ENG.). 24p. (J). (gr. 6-12). lib. bdg. 27.07 (978-1-5321-4144-7(0), 27017, Graphic Novels) Spotlight.

Yu, Leinil Francis, et al. The Shu-Torun War: Volume 1. Gillen, Kieron. 2018. (Star Wars: Darth Vader Ser.). (ENG.). 32p. (J). (gr. 6-12). lib. bdg. 27.07 (978-1-5321-4162-1(9), 28578, Graphic Novels) Spotlight.

—Star Wars Vol. 2. 2017. 280p. (J). (gr. 4-17). 34.99 (978-1-302-90374-9(8)) Marvel Worldwide, Inc.

—War of the Realms: Strikeforce. 2019. (ENG.). 112p. (YA). (gr. 8-17). pap. 15.99 (978-1-302-91855-2(9)) Marvel Worldwide, Inc.

Yu, Leinil Francis. X-Men by Jonathan Hickman Vol. 1. 2020. 176p. (YA). (gr. 8-17). pap. 17.99 (978-1-302-91981-8(4)) Marvel Worldwide, Inc.

Yu, Leinil Francis & Kubert, Adam. Captain America by Ta-Nehisi Coates Vol. 1. 2020. 288p. (YA). (gr. 8-17). 34.99 (978-1-302-92322-8(6)) Marvel Worldwide, Inc.

Yu, Leinil Francis & Rocafort, Kenneth. Inhumans vs. X-Men. 2017. (ENG.). 208p. (YA). (gr. 8-17). 50.00 (978-1-302-90653-5(4)) Marvel Worldwide, Inc.

Yu, Seung-Beom. Patterns from Nature: The Art of Klimt. Yu, Myeong-Hwa. 2017. (Stories of Art Ser.). (ENG.). 36p. (J). (gr. 3-5). lib. bdg. 10.00 (978-1-925235-30-2(0), Big and SMALL) ChoiceMaker Pty. Ltd., The AUS. Dist: Lerner Publishing Group.

Yu, Sue Mi. Animal Paradise, 3 vols., Vol. 3. Yu, Sue Mi. 2007. (Animal Paradise Ser.: Vol. 3). 232p. pap. 9.95 (978-1-59697-073-1(1)) Infinity Studios LLC.

Yu, Tae-Won. TinkerActive Workbooks: 2nd Grade Science. Butler, Megan Hewes & Odd Dot. 2019. (TinkerActive Workbooks Ser.: 6). (ENG.). 128p. (J). pap. 12.99 (978-1-250-30726-2(0), 900197989, Odd Dot) St. Martin's Pr.

Yuan, Yidan. Cub's Wish. Flores, Angie. 2017. (ENG.). (J). (gr. k-2). 18.00 (978-0-9979738-0-8(3)) Flores, Angie.

Yudetamago. The Kinnikuman LegacyTM. Yudetamago. Yamazaki, Joe, tr. 2005. (Ultimate Muscle Ser.: Vol. 5). (ENG.). 232p. (YA). pap. 7.95 (978-1-59116-426-5(5)) Viz Media.

Yue, Emily. Round 'Bout Midnight. McDonald, Trevy A. 2018. pap. 15.00 (978-0-9670712-5-1(9)) zReyomi Publishing.

Yue, Stephanie. And Then There Were Gnomes: Book 2, No. 2. Venable, Colleen Af. 2010. (Guinea PIG, Pet Shop Private Eye Ser.: 2). (ENG.). 48p. (J). (gr. 2-5). pap. 6.99 (978-0-7613-5480-2(8), 9780761354802, Graphic Universe™) Lerner Publishing Group.

—The Ferret's a Foot, 3 vols., No. 3. Venable, Colleen A. F. 2011. (Guinea PIG, Pet Shop Private Eye Ser.: 3). (ENG.). 48p. (J). (gr. 2-5). 27.99 (978-0-7613-5223-5(6), 9780761352235, Graphic Universe™) Lerner Publishing Group.

—The Ferret's a Foot: Book 3, No. 3. Venable, Colleen Af. 2011. (Guinea PIG, Pet Shop Private Eye Ser.: 3). (ENG.). 48p. (J). (gr. 2-5). pap. 6.99 (978-0-7613-5629-5(0), 9780761356295, Graphic Universe™) Lerner Publishing Group.

—Fish You Were Here, 4 vols., No. 4. Venable, Colleen A. F. 2011. (Guinea PIG, Pet Shop Private Eye Ser.: 4). (ENG.). 48p. (J). (gr. 2-5). lib. bdg. 27.99 (978-0-7613-5224-2(4), 9780761352242, Graphic Universe™) Lerner Publishing Group.

—Fish You Were Here: Book 4, No. 4. Venable, Colleen Af. 2011. (Guinea PIG, Pet Shop Private Eye Ser.: 4). (ENG.). 48p. (J). (gr. 2-5). pap. 6.99 (978-0-7613-5630-1(4), 9780761356301, Graphic Universe™) Lerner Publishing Group.

—Going, Going, Dragon! Venable, Colleen A. F. ed. 2013. (Guinea Pig, Pet Shop Private Eye Ser.: 6). (ENG.). 46p. lib. bdg. 17.15 (978-0-606-33994-0(9)) Turtleback.

—Going, Going, Dragon! Book 6. Venable, Colleen Af. ed. 2013. (Guinea PIG, Pet Shop Private Eye Ser.). (ENG.). 48p. (J). (gr. 2-5). E-Book 42.65 (978-1-4677-0973-6(5), Graphic Universe™) Lerner Publishing Group.

—Good Night, Bunny. Thompson, Lauren. 2018. (ENG.). 32p. (J). (gr. -1-k). 16.99 (978-0-545-60335-5(8), Orchard Bks.) Scholastic, Inc.

—Hamster & Cheese: Book 1, No. 1. Venable, Colleen Af. 2010. (Guinea PIG, Pet Shop Private Eye Ser.: 1). (ENG.). 48p. (J). (gr. 2-5). pap. 6.99 (978-0-7613-5479-6(4), 9780761354796, Graphic Universe™) Lerner Publishing Group.

—Raining Cats & Detectives. Venable, Colleen A. F. ed. 2012. (Guinea Pig, Pet Shop Private Eye Ser.: 5). lib. bdg. 17.15 (978-0-606-26631-4(3)) Turtleback.

—Raining Cats & Detectives: Book 5, No. 5. Venable, Colleen Af. 2012. (Guinea PIG, Pet Shop Private Eye Ser.: 5). (ENG.). 48p. (J). (gr. 2-5). pap. 6.99 (978-0-7613-8541-7(X), 9780761385417, Graphic Universe™) Lerner Publishing Group.

—Such a Little Mouse. Schertle, Alice. 2015. (ENG.). 32p. (J). (gr. -1-k). 16.99 (978-0-545-64929-2(3)) Scholastic, Inc.

Yuen, Charles. Emeril's There's a Chef in My Soup! Recipes for the Kid in Everyone. Lagasse, Emeril. 2005. (ENG.). 256p. (J). 28.99 (978-0-688-17706-5(9), HarperCollins) HarperCollins Pubs. Ltd. GBR. Dist: HarperCollins Pubs.

Yuen, Sammy, Jr. Expedition to Pine Hollow. Decter, Ed. 2007. (Outriders Ser.: 3). (ENG.). 240p. (J). (gr. 3-7). pap. 11.99 (978-1-4169-1307-8(6), Simon & Schuster/Paula Wiseman Bks.) Simon & Schuster/Paula Wiseman Bks.

Yuen, Sammy. Incarceron. Fisher, Catherine. November, S., ed. 2011. (ENG.). 464p. (YA). (gr. 7-18). pap. 10.99 (978-0-14-241852-9(8), Firebird) Penguin Young Readers Group.

Yuen Wong Yu. Digimon, 5 vols., Vol. 1. Hongo, Akiyoshi. 2003. 164p. (gr. 2-18). pap. 9.99 (978-1-59182-076-5(6)) TOKYOPOP, Inc.

Yuichi, Kimura. Hot Hot Pancakes! 2020. 32p. (J). (gr. -1). 17.95 (978-2-89802-161-9(X), CrackBoom! Bks.) Chouette Publishing CAN. Dist: Publishers Group West (PGW).

Yuichi, Kimura, jt. illus. see Nelvana Ltd., Staff.

Yuichi, Kimura, jt. illus. see Nelvana Ltd.

Yuio. Iron Magicians: the Search for the Magic Crystals: The Comic Book You Can Play. Cetrix. 2019. (Comic Quests Ser.: 5). 176p. (J). (gr. 3-7). pap. 9.99 (978-1-68369-129-7(6)) Quirk Bks.

Yuji, Iwahara. Quest. Watson, Andi. 2004. (Marvel Heroes Ser.). 120p. (YA). pap. 13.99 (978-0-7851-1298-3(7)) Marvel Worldwide, Inc.

Yulia, Lushnikova. Moush Wants to Get Lost. Baghdasaryan, Rouzanna. 2010. 32p. (J). (POL & ENG.). pap. 16.95 (978-1-60195-103-8(5)); (ARA.). pap. 16.95 (978-1-60195-091-8(8)) International Step by Step Assn.

Yuliana, Yuffie. Being Mindful. Morris, Hannah. Duncan, Kit, ed. 2017. (Contented Kids Ser.: Vol. 2). (ENG.). 28p. (J). pap. (978-1-912274-15-4(9)) ActiveMindCare Publishing.

—Being Stressed. Morris, Hannah. Duncan, Kit, ed. 2017. (Contented Kids Ser.: Vol. 1). (ENG.). 38p. (J). pap. (978-1-912274-12-3(4)) ActiveMindCare Publishing.

—In That Very Spot: With Little Marcus Aurelius. Rothman, Suzanne. 2018. (ENG.). 32p. (J). pap. 10.00 (978-0-692-15187-7(7)) Rothman Editions.

—Will You Play with Me? Kenney, Alexis. Taylor, Tamara, ed. 2018. (Autism Project Ser.: Vol. 1). (ENG.). 28p. (J). (gr. k-3). 18.99 (978-0-9970313-2-4(8)); pap. 9.49 (978-0-9970313-3-1(6)) Tamara Taylor Edu Publishing LLC.

Yuly, Toni. Early Bird. Yuly, Toni. 2014. (ENG.). 40p. (J). (— 1). 15.99 (978-1-250-04327-6(1), 9781250043276) Feiwel & Friends.

—Play Day School Day. Yuly, Toni. 2020. 32p. (J). (gr. -1-3). 16.99 (978-1-5362-0283-0(5)) Candlewick Pr.

—Thank You, Bees. Yuly, Toni. (J). (-k). 2020. 28p. bds. 8.99 (978-1-5362-1168-9(0)); 2017. 32p. 15.99 (978-0-7636-9261-2(1)) Candlewick Pr.

Yum, Heekyoung. Leah's Dream Dollhouse (Shimmer & Shine) Tillworth, Mary. 2016. (Pictureback(R) Ser.). (ENG.). 16p. (J). (gr. -1-2). 4.99 (978-1-101-93249-0(X), Random Hse. Bks. for Young Readers) Random Hse. Children's Bks.

Yum, Hyewon. Bark in the Park! Poems for Dog Lovers. Corman, Avery. 2019. (ENG.). 48p. (J). (gr. -1-k). 17.99 (978-1-338-11839-1(0), Orchard Bks.) Scholastic, Inc.

—Clever Little Witch. Van, Muon Thi. 2019. (ENG.). 40p. (J). (gr. -1-1). 17.99 (978-1-4814-8171-7(1)); E-Book (978-1-4814-8172-4(X)) McElderry, Margaret K. Bks. (McElderry, Margaret K. Bks.).

—A Piece of Home. Watts, Jeri. 2016. 32p. (J). (gr. k-3). 16.99 (978-0-7636-6971-3(7)) Candlewick Pr.

—Someday, Narwhal. Mantchev, Lisa. 2017. (ENG.). 40p. (J). (gr. -1-3). 17.99 (978-1-4814-7970-7(9), Simon & Schuster/Paula Wiseman Bks.) Simon & Schuster/Paula Wiseman Bks.

Yum, Hyewon. Mom, It's My First Day of Kindergarten!, 1 vol. Yum, Hyewon. 2012. (ENG.). 40p. (J). (gr. -1-2). 18.99 (978-0-374-35004-8(3), 900077454, Farrar, Straus & Giroux (BYR)) Farrar, Straus & Giroux.

—Saturday Is Swimming Day. Yum, Hyewon. 2018. 40p. (J). (gr. -1-1). 16.99 (978-0-7636-9117-2(8)) Candlewick Pr.

—The Twins' Blanket. Yum, Hyewon. 2011. (ENG.). 40p. (J). (gr. -1-1). 18.99 (978-0-374-37972-8(6), 900068267, Farrar, Straus & Giroux (BYR)) Farrar, Straus & Giroux.

—The Twins' Little Sister. Yum, Hyewon. 2014. (ENG.). 40p. (J). (gr. -1-1). 17.99 (978-0-374-37973-5(4), 900121865, Farrar, Straus & Giroux (BYR)) Farrar, Straus & Giroux.

Yum, Hyewon & Yum, Hyewon. Lion Needs a Haircut. 2020. (ENG.). 40p. (J). (gr. -1-2). 16.99 (978-1-4197-4224-8(8), 1680001, Abrams Bks. for Young Readers) Abrams, Inc.

Yum, Hyewon, jt. illus. see Yum, Hyewon.

Yumenokaori. Bugs of the World: 250 Creepy-Crawly Creatures from Around Planet Earth. Tomasinelli, Francesco. 2020. 192p. (J). (gr. 1-5). 24.99 (978-0-7624-6896-6(3), Black Dog & Leventhal Pubs. Inc.) Running Pr.

Yun, Gong-Joo. Welcome to the Seashore: Seashore Creatures. Yun, Hui-Jeong. 2017. (Science Storybooks Ser.). (ENG.). 32p. (J). (gr. k-4). lib. bdg. 27.99 (978-1-925235-17-3(3), Big and SMALL) ChoiceMaker Pty. Ltd., The AUS. Dist: Lerner Publishing Group.

Yun, Yeji. The Odyssey. Medina, Melissa & Colting, Fredrik. 2017. (KinderGuides Early Learning Guide to Culture Classics Ser.). 48p. (J). 16.95 (978-0-9988205-1-4(2)) Moppet Bks.

Yung Yoo, Sun. The Red Shoes. Andersen, Hans & Fowler, Gloria. 2008. (ENG.). 32p. (J). (gr. -1-3). 16.95 (978-1-934429-06-8(6)) AMMO Bks., LLC.

Yunger, Joshua. Wobar & the Quest for the Magic Calumet. Homeyer, Henry. 2012. (ENG.). 144p. (YA). (gr. 3-9). 19.95 (978-1-59373-108-3(6)) Bunker Hill Publishing, Inc.

Yuricich, Jillian Grace. What did Grandma See? 2006. (J). lib. bdg. 15.99 (978-0-9774696-0-4(3)) Gilboy Publishing.

Yurksaitis, Stephanie. Genevieve the Singing Ladybug. Yurksaitis, Anne. 2013. 28p. pap. 24.95 (978-1-63000-927-4(X)) America Star Bks.

—The Ingle Bingle. Yurksaitis, Anne. 2012. 16p. pap. 24.95 (978-1-4626-7687-3(1)) America Star Bks.

Yuste, Patricia. Los Diamantes Del Cielo. Canetti, Yanitzia. 2017. (Rising Readers Ser.). (SPA.). (J). (gr. 1). 5.83 (978-1-4788-2718-4(1)) Newmark Learning LLC.

Yustiadi, A. Best Mommy Ever. Nelson, Richard. 2018. (ENG.). 40p. (J). (gr. k-2). (978-1-7752839-5-9(X)); pap. (978-1-7752839-3-5(3)) Nelson, Richard.

—My Little Big Brother. Nelson, Richard. 2018. (ENG.). (J). (gr. k). 26p. (978-1-7752839-8-0(4)); 28p. pap. (978-1-7752839-7-3(6)) Nelson, Richard.

Yutenji, Ako. Liling Po, Vol. 1. Yutenji, Ako. 2005. 208p. pap. 14.99 (978-1-59532-519-8(0), Tokyopop Adult) TOKYOPOP, Inc.

—Liling-Po, Vol. 3. Yutenji, Ako. 3rd rev. ed. 2005. (Liling-Po Ser.). 192p. per. 14.99 (978-1-59532-521-1(2), Tokyopop Adult) TOKYOPOP, Inc.

Yutenji, Ako. Liling-PO, Vol. 2. Yutenji, Ako, creator. rev. ed. 2005. 200p. pap. 14.99 (978-1-59532-520-4(4), Tokyopop Adult) TOKYOPOP, Inc.

Yuu, Lee Young. Kill Me, Kiss Me, 5 vols., Vol. 5. Yuu, Lee Young. rev. ed. 2005. 184p. pap. 9.99 (978-1-59532-420-7(8)) TOKYOPOP, Inc.

Yuu, Shiina. A Little Princess. Burnett, Frances Hodgson. 2017. (Illustrated Classics Ser.). (ENG.). 400p. (J). pap. 11.99 (978-1-62692-611-0(5), 9781626926110) Seven Seas Entertainment, LLC.

Yuzuru & Kanako. Point Blank: the Graphic Novel. Horowitz, Anthony & Johnston, Antony. 2007. (Alex Rider Ser.). (ENG.). 176p. (J). (gr. 5-18). 16.99 (978-0-399-25026-2(3), Philomel Bks.) Penguin Young Readers Group.

—Stormbreaker: the Graphic Novel. Horowitz, Anthony. 2006. (Alex Rider Ser.). (ENG.). 144p. (J). (gr. 5-18). pap. 14.99 (978-0-399-24633-3(9), Philomel Bks.) Penguin Young Readers Group.

Yuzuru, jt. illus. see Kanako.

Yvonne, Symank. Chave's Memories / Los Recuerdos de Chave. Isabel, Delgado Maria. 2008. 32p. (J). pap. 7.95 (978-1-55885-244-0(1), Piñata Books) Arte Publico Pr.

Z

Zabarylo-Duma, Ewa. Teddy's Christmas Wish. deVet, L. J. 2013. (J). (ENG.). 48p. (978-0-9873686-0-7(5)); (ENG.). 48p. pap. (978-0-9873686-1-4(3)); 46p. pap. (978-0-9873686-5-2(6)) Print-Rite Publishers.

Zabel, Anna. The Most Ungrateful Girl in the World. James, Petra. 2019. (ENG.). 288p. (J). (gr. 3-5). 16.99 (978-0-14-379367-0(5), Puffin) Penguin Random Hse. AUS. Dist: Independent Pubs. Group.

Zabel, Randy & Broesch, Valerie. Al-the-Gator & Freddy Frog. 2007. 48p. (J). per. 18.99 (978-0-9797513-0-1(6)) 4RV Pub.

Zabib, Fadwa. Al-Firqah Al-Musiqiyah. Al-Bandawi, Jalil Khazal. 2018. (ARA.). 19p. (J). (978-9953-37-256-3(X)) Academia.

Zaboski, Dave. The Squirrel Manifesto. Edelman, Ric & Edelman, Jean. 2018. (ENG.). 40p. (J). (gr. -1-3). 17.99 (978-1-5344-4166-8(2), Aladdin) Simon & Schuster Children's Publishing.

Zaboski, Dave. Gideon's Dream: A Tale of New Beginnings. Zaboski, Dave. Dychtwald, Ken et al. 2008. 40p. (J). (gr. -1-3). lib. bdg. 17.89 (978-0-06-143498-3(1)) HarperCollins Pubs.

Zabriskie, Judy Mehn. Freckles: The Mystery of the Little White Dog in the Desert. Howey, Paul M. 2003. 72p. (gr. 2-5). lib. bdg. 14.95 (978-0-9677292-1-3(1)) AZTexts Publishing, Inc.

Zacarias, Betania. Abrazo de Oso. Isern, Susanna. 2017. (SPA.). 36p. (J). (gr. -1-3). 14.95 (978-84-946333-6-2(8)) NubeOcho Ediciones ESP. Dist: Consortium Bk. Sales & Distribution.

—Bear Hug. Isern, Susanna. 2017. (ENG.). 36p. (J). (gr. -1-3). 14.95 (978-84-946333-3-1(3)) NubeOcho Ediciones ESP. Dist: Consortium Bk. Sales & Distribution.

Zacarias, Betania. The More We Get Together. Cortright, Celeste. 2020. (ENG.). (J). pap. (978-1-78285-933-8(0)) Barefoot Bks., Inc.

—The More We Get Together. Cortright, Celeste et al. 2020. (J). (978-1-78285-932-1(2)) Barefoot Bks., Inc.

Zacchi, Lucia. El Himno de las Ranas. Cross, Elsa. 2005. (SPA.). (J). (gr. k-2). pap. 10.95 (978-968-494-052-9(1), CI2003) Centro de Informacion y Desarrollo de la Comunicacion y la Literatura MEX. Dist: Iaconi, Mariuccia Bk. Imports, Lectorum Pubns., Inc.

Zach, William. Bedtime Nature Tails: Baby Spider. Zach. 2019. (Bedtime Nature Tails Ser.: Vol. 3). (ENG.). 36p. (J). 16.95 (978-0-578-58877-3(3)) Mr Nick Productions.

Zach, William. Bedtime Nature Tails: Dumpy the Caterpillar. Zach. 2019. (Bedtime Nature Tails Ser.: Vol. 2). (ENG.). 36p. (J). 16.95 (978-0-578-54782-4(1)) Mr Nick Productions.

—Bedtime Nature Tails: Mr. Sowbug & Friends. Zach, Nicholas. 2019. (Bedtime Nature Tails Ser.: Vol. 1). (ENG.). 36p. (J). 16.95 (978-0-578-50645-6(9)) Mr Nick Productions.

Zach, William. Bedtime Nature Tails: Slithery the Snake. Zach, Nicholas. 2020. (Bedtime Nature Tails Ser.: Vol. 4). (ENG.). 36p. (J). 16.95 (978-0-578-63692-4(1)) Mr Nick Productions.

Zacker, Sandi. The Adventures of Saleiah & Emm: Book 1. Alvarado, I. J. 2009. 16p. pap. 11.99 (978-1-4490-0515-3(2)) AuthorHouse.

Zaffo, George J. The How & Why Wonder Book of MacHines. Gulkin, Sidney & Notkin, Jerome J. 2011. 48p. pap. 35.95 (978-1-258-10533-4(0)) Literary Licensing, LLC.

Zagarenski, Pamela. ¿Dónde Me Escondo? American Heritage Dictionary Editors, ed. 2005.Tr. of Where Am I Hiding?. (ENG.). 8p. (J). (gr. -1 — 1). bds. 4.99 (978-0-618-51176-1(8), J02902) Houghton Mifflin Harcourt Publishing Co.

—The Fabled Life of Aesop: The Extraordinary Journey & Collected Tales of the World's Greatest Storyteller. Lendler, Ian. 2020. (ENG.). 64p. (J). (gr. -1-3). 18.99 (978-1-328-58552-3(2), 1729191, HMH Books For Young Readers) Houghton Mifflin Harcourt Publishing Co.

—Qué Día Es? American Heritage Dictionary Editors. 2005.Tr. of What Day Is It?. (SPA.). 8p. (J). (— 1). bds. 3.95 (978-0-618-44874-6(8), J02802) Houghton Mifflin Harcourt Publishing Co.

—Qué Juego? American Heritage Dictionary Editors, ed. 2004. (Good Beginnings Ser.).Tr. of What Am I Playing?. (SPA.). 8p. (J). (gr. k — 1). bds. 3.95 (978-0-618-44375-8(4), J02602) Houghton Mifflin Harcourt Publishing Co.

—Red Sings from Treetops: A Year in Colors. Sidman, Joyce. 2009. (ENG.). 32p. (J). (gr. -1-3). 18.99 (978-0-547-01494-4(5), 1031109) Houghton Mifflin Harcourt Publishing Co.

—Sleep Like a Tiger. Logue, Mary. 2012. (ENG.). 40p. (J). (gr. -1-3). 17.99 (978-0-547-64102-7(8), 1469620) Houghton Mifflin Harcourt Publishing Co.

—This Is Just to Say: Poems of Apology & Forgiveness. Sidman, Joyce. 2007. (ENG.). 48p. (J). (gr. 5-7). 17.99 (978-0-618-61680-0(2), 546941) Houghton Mifflin Harcourt Publishing Co.

—What Can I Do When It Rains? (Qué Puedo Hacer Cuando Llueve?) American Heritage Dictionary Editors, ed. ed. 2004. (Good Beginnings Ser.). (SPA.). 8p. (J). (gr. k — 1). bds. 4.99 (978-0-618-44376-5(2), J02702) Houghton Mifflin Harcourt Publishing Co.

—What the Heart Knows: Chants, Charms, & Blessings. Sidman, Joyce. 2013. (ENG.). 80p. (YA). (gr. 7). 17.99 (978-0-544-10616-1(4), 1540739) Houghton Mifflin Harcourt Publishing Co.

—Zola's Elephant. de Sève, Randall. 2018. (ENG.). 40p. (J). (gr. -1-3). 17.99 (978-1-328-88629-3(8), 1698512, HMH Books For Young Readers) Houghton Mifflin Harcourt Publishing Co.

Zager, Ellen Kahan. And There Was Evening, & There Was Morning. Zager, Ellen Kahan. Helfand, Harriet Cohen. 2018. (ENG.). 24p. (J). (gr. -1-3). 17.99 (978-1-5124-8364-2(8), Kar-Ben Publishing) Lerner Publishing Group.

Zagnoli, Olimpia. Mister Horizontal & Miss Vertical. Revah, Noemie. 2014. 48p. (J). (gr. -1-3). 17.95 (978-1-59270-161-2(2)) Enchanted Lion Bks., LLC.

Zahares, Wade. Frosty the Snowman. 2013. (ENG.). 28p. (J). (gr. -1-3). 17.95 (978-1-62354-012-8(7)) Charlesbridge Publishing, Inc.

—Liberty Rising: The Story of the Statue of Liberty. Shea, Pegi Deitz. 2013. (ENG.). 44p. (J). (gr. k-4). 10.99 (978-1-250-02720-7(9), 900098291) Square Fish.

—Red Are the Apples. Harshman, Marc & Ryan, Cheryl. 2007. (ENG.). 32p. (J). (gr. -1-3). pap. 7.99 (978-0-15-206065-7(0), 1198217) Houghton Mifflin Harcourt Publishing Co.

Zaharias, Terrilynn. The Duckie Walk. Hoercher, Donald F. 2011. 28p. pap. 12.50 (978-1-60976-912-3(0), Eloquent Bks.) Strategic Book Publishing & Rights Agency (SBPRA).

Zaharopoulos, Spyros. Zeus Og Zoe Er Fra Norge. Andersen, Sofie. 2019. (NOR.). 36p. (J). (978-618-5318-75-8(X)) Fylatos, Ekdoseis.

Zahedi, Morteza. Good Night, Commander, 1 vol. Akbarpour, Ahmad. Eskandani, Shadi & Mixter, Helen, trs. 2010. (ENG.). 24p. (J). (gr. 1). 17.95 (978-0-88899-989-4(5)) Groundwood Bks. CAN. Dist: Publishers Group West (PGW).

Zahler, Thom, jt. illus. see Colombo, Alexandra.

Zahler, Thomas. Twilight Sparkle, 1 vol. Zahler, Thomas. 2015. (My Little Pony Ser.). (ENG.). 24p. (J). (gr. 1-8). 27.07 (978-1-61479-336-6(0), 17158, Graphic Novels) Spotlight.

Zahn, Ellsworth E. Dudley. Zahn, Ellsworth E. 2012. 44p. (J). (gr. -1-k). 15.95 (978-0-9637308-1-7(9)) Marion Street Pr., LLC.

Zahnd, Mark. Ridiculous Knock-Knocks. Tait, Chris. 2010. (Jokes & Riddles Ser.). (ENG.). 96p. (J). (gr. k-3). 17.44 (978-1-4027-7852-0(X)) Sterling Publishing Co., Inc.

Zahova, Borislava. Alex & Maya Love to Surf. Coulter, Chrys. 2016. (ENG.). 20p. (J). pap. 8.99 (978-0-692-12942-5(1)) Cloudbreak Media Inc.

Zahradka, Miroslav. The Un-Terrible Tiger. Zahradka, Miroslav. 32p. (J). (gr. -1-3). 12.95 (978-0-87592-056-6(X)) Scroll Pr., Inc.

Zaidi, Ishan. Keep Counting. 2010. (J). (978-1-60617-145-5(3)) Teaching Strategies, LLC.

Zaidi, Nadeem. Agua Por Todas Partes. Del Moral, Susana. 2006. (SPA.). 8p. (J). (gr. -1). (978-970-718-452-7(3), Silver Dolphin en Español) Advanced Marketing, S. de R. L. de C. V.

—Animales a Tu Alrededor. Singer, Marilyn. 2004. (Baby Einstein Ser.). (SPA.). 16p. (J). bds. (978-970-718-152-6(4), Silver Dolphin en Español) Advanced Marketing, S. de R. L. de C. V.

—Asomate y Ve Las Figuras. Aigner-Clark, Julie. 2004. (Baby Einstein Ser.). (SPA.). 16p. (J). bds. *(978-970-718-151-9(6),* Silver Dolphin en Español) Advanced Marketing, S. de R. L. de C. V.

—Asomate Y Ve Los Numeros. Aigner-Clark, Julie. 2004. (Baby Einstein Ser.). (SPA.). 16p. (J). bds. *(978-970-718-150-2(8),* Silver Dolphin en Español) Advanced Marketing, S. de R. L. de C. V.

—Baby Da Vinci, Mi Cuerpo. Del Moral, Susana. 2006. (Baby Einstein Ser.). (SPA.). 6p. (J). (gr. -1-k). bds. *(978-970-718-455-8(8),* Silver Dolphin en Español) Advanced Marketing, S. de R. L. de C. V.

—Baby Einstein Colores: Libro con Ventanas. Aigner-Clark, Julie. 2007. (Baby Einstein Ser.). 5p. (J). (gr. -1). *(978-970-718-469-5(8),* Silver Dolphin en Español) Advanced Marketing, S. de R. L. de C. V.

—Baby Einstein: on the Farm. Aigner-Clark, Julie. 2007. (Baby Einstein Ser.). (ENG.). *(978-0-7634-2150-2(2))* Walt Disney Records.

—Baby Einstein Poemas Preciosos: Pretty Poems & Wonderful Words. Aigner-Clark, Julie. 2004. (SPA.). 10p. (J). 9.95 *(978-970-718-210-3(5),* Silver Dolphin Bks.) Readerlink Distribution Services, LLC.

—Baby Mozart: Musica Por Todas Partes. 2005. (Baby Einstein: Libros de Carton Ser.). (SPA.). 16p. (J). (gr. -1). bds. *(978-970-718-309-4(8),* Silver Dolphin en Español) Advanced Marketing, S. de R. L. de C. V.

—La Casa de Violet. Del Moral, Susana. 2005. (Baby Einstein: Libros de Carton Ser.). (SPA.). 10p. (J). (gr. -1). bds. *(978-970-718-305-6(5),* Silver Dolphin en Español) Advanced Marketing, S. de R. L. de C. V.

—Como Me Siento. Del Moral, Susana. 2005. (Baby Einstein: Libros de Carton Ser.). (SPA.). 14p. (J). (gr. -1). bds. *(978-970-718-308-7(X),* Silver Dolphin en Español) Advanced Marketing, S. de R. L. de C. V.

—Formas: Libro con Ventanas. 2007. (Baby Einstein Ser.). 5p. (J). (gr. -1). *(978-970-718-468-8(X),* Silver Dolphin en Español) Advanced Marketing, S. de R. L. de C. V.

—Fun with Animals Friendship Box. Singer, Marilyn. 2009. (J). *(978-1-4231-2797-0(8)); (978-1-4231-2798-7(6)); (978-1-4231-2799-4(4))* Disney Pr.

—El Juego de las Formas. Del Moral, Susana. 2005. (Baby Einstein: Libros de Carton Ser.). (SPA.). 6p. (J). (gr. -1). bds. *(978-970-718-303-2(9),* Silver Dolphin en Español) Advanced Marketing, S. de R. L. de C. V.

—Las Rimas de Bard: Un Libro con Ventanas. Del Moral, Susana. 2005. (Baby Einstein: Libros de Carton Ser.). (SPA.). 16p. (J). (gr. -1). bds. *(978-970-718-304-9(7),* Silver Dolphin en Español) Advanced Marketing, S. de R. L. de C. V.

—Master Pieces. Aigner-Clark, Julie. 2004. (SPA.). 10p. (J). 9.95 *(978-970-718-211-0(3),* Silver Dolphin Bks.) Readerlink Distribution Services, LLC.

—El Mundo A Mi Alrededor: El Cielo. Del Moral, Susana. 2005. (Baby Einstein: Libros de Carton Ser.). (SPA.). 12p. (J). (gr. -1). bds. *(978-970-718-312-4(8),* Silver Dolphin en Español) Advanced Marketing, S. de R. L. de C. V.

—El Mundo a Mi Alrededor: El Oceano. Silver Dolphin en Español Editors. 2007. (Baby Einstein Ser.). (SPA.). 12p. (J). (gr. -1). bds. *(978-970-718-457-2(4),* Silver Dolphin en Español) Advanced Marketing, S. de R. L. de C. V.

—Un Paseo Por la Selva. Del Moral, Susana. 2005. (Baby Einstein: Libros de Carton Ser.). (SPA.). 10p. (J). (gr. -1). bds. *(978-970-718-306-3(3),* Silver Dolphin en Español) Advanced Marketing, S. de R. L. de C. V.

—Que Flota? Un Libro para Banarse y Disfrutar. Del Moral, Susana. 2006. (Baby Einstein Ser.). (SPA.). 8p. (J). (gr. -1). *(978-970-718-453-4(1),* Silver Dolphin en Español) Advanced Marketing, S. de R. L. de C. V.

—Una Ventana Al Color. Aigner-Clark, Julie. 2007. (Baby Einstein Ser.). 10p. (J). (gr. -1-k). *(978-970-718-454-1(X),* Silver Dolphin en Español) Advanced Marketing, S. de R. L. de C. V.

Zaiken, Beth. Mega Rex: A Tyrannosaurus Named Scotty. Persons, W. Scott. 2020. (ENG.). 128p. (J). pap. 13.95 *(978-1-55017-905-7(5))* Harbour Publishing Co., Ltd. CAN. Dist: Publishers Group West (PGW).

Zaikina, Maria. The Greedy Sparrow: An Armenian Tale, 0 vols. Kasbarian, Lucine. 2011. (ENG.). 32p. (J). (gr. -1-3). 17.99 *(978-0-7614-5821-0(2),* 9780761458210, Two Lions) Amazon Publishing.

Zain, Damian. Kids in History: Albert Einstein. Canavan, Roger. ed. 2020. (Kids in History Ser.). 140p. (J). (gr. 3). pap. 8.95 *(978-1-912904-77-8(2))* Book Hse. GBR. Dist: Sterling Publishing Co., Inc.

—Kids in History: Helen Keller. Catchpole, Barbara. ed. 2020. (Kids in History Ser.). 152p. (J). (gr. 3). pap. 8.95 *(978-1-912904-76-1(4))* Book Hse. GBR. Dist: Sterling Publishing Co., Inc.

—Kids in History: Mary, Queen of Scots. Macdonald, Fiona. ed. 2020. (Kids in History Ser.). (ENG.). 128p. (J). (gr. 3). pap. 8.95 *(978-1-912537-97-6(4))* Book Hse. GBR. Dist: Sterling Publishing Co., Inc.

—Kids in History: Wolfgang Amadeus Mozart. Catchpole, Barbara. ed. 2020. (Kids in History Ser.). 128p. (J). (gr. 3). pap. 8.95 *(978-1-912537-98-3(2))* Book Hse. GBR. Dist: Sterling Publishing Co., Inc.

—Kirby Mccook & the Jesus Chronicles. ED., Stephen Arterburn M. & Brotherton, M. N. 2019. (ENG.). 224p. (J). 17.99 *(978-1-4964-2977-3(X),* 20_30075) Tyndale Hse. Pubs.

Zak, Drahos. The Pied Piper of Hamelin. Holden, Robert. 2004. 28p. (J). (gr. k-4). reprint ed. 15.00 *(978-0-7567-7686-2(4))* DIANE Publishing Co.

Zakanitch, Robert Rahway. Good Dog. Gottfried, Maya. 2005. (ENG.). 40p. (J). (gr. k-4). 21.19 *(978-0-375-83049-5(9))* Random House Publishing Group.

—Our Farm: By the Animals of Farm Sanctuary. Gottfried, Maya. 2010. 40p. (J). (gr. k-3). 17.99 *(978-0-375-86118-5(1),* Knopf Bks. for Young Readers) Random Hse. Children's Bks.

Zakimi, Paola. The Christmas Tree Who Loved Trains. Silvestro, Annie. 2018. (ENG.). 32p. (J). (gr. -1-3). 17.99 *(978-0-06-256168-8(5))* HarperCollins Pubs.

Zakimi, Paola. Here Comes Ocean. Fleming, Meg. 2020. (ENG.). 40p. (J). (gr. -1-3). 17.99 *(978-1-5344-2883-6(6),* Beach Lane Bks.) Beach Lane Bks.

Zakimi, Paola. Ruby's Sword. Veissid, Jacqueline. 2019. (ENG.). 40p. (J). (gr. -1-k). 16.99 *(978-1-4521-6391-8(X))* Chronicle Bks. LLC.

—Secrets I Know. George, Kallie. 2017. 32p. (J). (gr. -1-2). 17.99 *(978-1-101-93893-5(5));* (ENG.). lib. bdg. 20.99 *(978-1-101-93894-2(3))* Random Hse. Children's Bks. (Schwartz & Wade Bks.).

—Teddy & Co. Voigt, Cynthia. (ENG.). 192p. (J). (gr. 2-5). 2018. 7.99 *(978-0-553-51163-5(7),* Yearling); 2016. 16.99 *(978-0-553-51160-4(2),* Knopf Bks. for Young Readers) Random Hse. Children's Bks.

Zalben, Jane Breskin. Light. 2018. (J). *(978-1-68115-533-3(8),* Apples & Honey Pr.) Behrman Hse., Inc.

Zalben, Jane Breskin. Pearl's Eight Days of Chanukah: With a Story & Activity for Each Night. Zalben, Jane Breskin. 2012. (ENG.). 48p. (J). (gr. -1-3). 22.99 *(978-1-4424-7294-5(4),* Simon & Schuster Bks. For Young Readers) Simon & Schuster Bks. For Young Readers.

—Saturday Night at the Beastro. Zalben, Jane Breskin. 2004. 40p. (J). (gr. 2-4). lib. bdg. 16.89 *(978-0-06-029228-7(8))* HarperCollins Pubs.

Zalevskaya, Anastacia. Real Girls' Guide to Everything: That Makes It Awesome to Be a Girl! Brereton, Erin. 2011. (ENG.). 192p. (J). pap. 12.95 *(978-1-60078-561-0(1))* Triumph Bks.

Zalewski, Todd. Woolly Mammoths. Wadsworth, Ginger. (On My Own Science Ser.). (ENG.). 48p. (gr. 2-4). 2007. (J). per. 7.99 *(978-0-8225-6447-8(5),* First Avenue Editions); 2006. lib. bdg. 25.26 *(978-1-57505-879-5(0),* Millbrook Pr.) Lerner Publishing Group.

Zalme, Ron. Diego's Buzzing Bee Adventure. Inches, Alison. 2008. (Go, Diego, Go! Ser.: 7). (ENG.). 24p. (J). (gr. -1-1). pap. 3.99 *(978-1-4169-4776-9(0),* Simon Spotlight/Nickelodeon) Simon Spotlight/Nickelodeon.

—Double Team, 2. Teitelbaum, Michael. 2008. (Backyard Sports Ser.: 2). (ENG.). 74p. (J). (gr. k-3). 16.19 *(978-0-448-44712-4(6))* Penguin Young Readers Group.

Zalme, Ron. Garfield's ® Guide to Drawing the World's Best-Looking Cat (and His Friends) Nickel, Scott. 2020. (ENG.). 32p. (J). (gr. 2-5). pap. 8.99 ***(978-1-7284-1373-0(7),*** Lerner Pubns.) Lerner Publishing Group.

—Garfield's Guide to Drawing the World's Best-Looking Cat (and His Friends) Nickel, Scott. 2020. (ENG.). 32p. (J). (gr. 2-5). 27.99 ***(978-1-5415-8986-5(6),*** Lerner Pubns.) Lerner Publishing Group.

Zalme, Ron. How to Draw. Barbo, Maria S. & West, Tracey. 2018. (Pokémon Ser.). (ENG.). 144p. (J). (gr. 2-5). pap. 11.99 *(978-1-338-28381-5(2))* Scholastic, Inc.

—How to Draw Nintendo Greatest Heroes & Villains. 2007. *(978-0-439-91324-9(1))* Scholastic, Inc.

—How to Draw Sinnoh Superstars. 2010. 32p. (J). pap. *(978-0-545-22625-7(2))* Scholastic, Inc.

—A Humpback Whale Tale. 2006. (Go, Diego, Go! Ser.: Vol. 2). (ENG.). 24p. (J). (gr. -1-2). pap. 3.99 *(978-1-4169-1511-9(7),* Simon Spotlight/Nickelodeon) Simon Spotlight/Nickelodeon.

—It's Sharing Day! Larsen, Kirsten. 2007. (SPA & ENG.). (J). pap. *(978-0-439-92237-1(2),* Scholastic) Scholastic, Inc.

—It's Sharing Day! Larsen, Kirsten. 2007. (Dora the Explorer Ser.: 22). (ENG & SPA.). 24p. (J). pap. 3.99 *(978-1-4169-1575-1(3),* Simon Spotlight/Nickelodeon) Simon Spotlight/Nickelodeon.

—Pokémon: How to Draw Unova Heroes. 2011. 31p. (J). pap. *(978-0-545-35086-0(7))* Scholastic, Inc.

—Rainy Day Tales. 2009. (J). *(978-1-59078-734-2(X))* Highlights for Children.

—Sunny Day Tales. 2009. (J). *(978-1-59078-735-9(8))* Highlights for Children.

—Tricked Out, 6 vols., 6. Teitelbaum, Michael. 2009. (Backyard Sports Ser.: 6). (ENG.). 80p. (J). (gr. k-3). 16.19 *(978-0-448-45072-8(0))* Penguin Young Readers Group.

Zaman, Farida. Count Your Way Through Iran. Haskins, James & Benson, Kathleen. 2006. (Count Your Way Ser.). 40p. (J). (gr. -1-3). lib. bdg. 19.93 *(978-1-57505-881-8(2),* Millbrook Pr.) Lerner Publishing Group.

—Los Frijoles Mágicos. Hillert, Margaret. 2018. (BeginningtoRead Ser.).Tr. of Magic Beans. (SPA.). 32p. (J). (gr. -1-2). pap. 11.94 *(978-1-68404-239-5(9))* Norwood Hse. Pr.

—Korean Celebrations: Games, Crafts, Recipes & More for Kids. Cho, Tina. 2019. 48p. (J). (gr. 3-7). 14.99 *(978-0-8048-4694-3(4))* Tuttle Publishing.

—The Magic Beans. Hillert, Margaret. 2016. (BeginningtoRead Ser.). (ENG.). 32p. (J). (gr. -1-2). pap. 11.94 *(978-1-60357-910-0(9))* Norwood Hse. Pr.

—The Magic Braid. Singh, Rina. Date not set. 134p. (J). pap. *(978-0-920813-25-6(9))* Sister Vision Pr.

—My First Book of Hindi Words: An ABC Rhyming Book of Hindi Language & Indian Culture. Singh, Rina. 2016. 32p. (J). (gr. -1-3). 12.95 *(978-0-8048-4562-5(X))* Tuttle Publishing.

—Nearly Nonsense: Hoja Tales from Turkey. Singh, Rina. 2011. 48p. (J). (gr. k-3). 17.95 *(978-0-88776-974-0(8),* Tundra Bks.) Tundra Bks. CAN. Dist: Penguin Random Hse. LLC.

—The Remarkable Journey of Josh's Kippah, Vol. Elissa, Barbara. 2010. (ENG.). (J). (gr. -1-2). 24p. lib. bdg. 7.95 *(978-0-8225-9911-1(2));* 32p. pap. 7.95 *(978-0-8225-9933-3(3))* Lerner Publishing Group. (Kar-Ben Publishing).

—Two Shoes, Blue Shoes, New Shoes!, 1 vol. Fitz-Gibbon, Sally. 2005. (ENG.). 32p. (J). (gr. k-3). pap. 7.95 *(978-1-55041-731-9(2),* 0ddac64c-35f6-48a0-9f50-f5c847a5efef) Trifolium Bks., Inc. CAN. Dist: Firefly Bks., Ltd.

—The Yoga Game. Beliveau, Kathy. 2012. 42p. (J). (gr. -1-2). pap. 9.95 *(978-1-897476-72-7(8))* Simply Read Bks. CAN. Dist: Ingram Publisher Services.

Zaman, Farida, jt. illus. see Jack Pullan.

Zaman, Farida, jt. illus. see Jamana, Pharida.

Zamanian, Marjan. Celebrating Norouz (Persian New Year) Jalali, Yassaman. 2003. 28p. (J). (gr. -1-6). pap. 12.99 *(978-0-9728020-0-0(2))* Saman Publishing.

Zamazing, Cherie. Birthdays Around the World, 1 vol. Dale, Jay. 2012. (Engage Literacy Yellow Ser.). (ENG.). 32p. (gr. k-2). pap. 5.99 *(978-1-4296-8966-3(8),* Capstone Pr.) Capstone.

Zamazing, Cherie. I'm Calm: A Book to Help Kids Overcome Anxiety & Stressful Situations. Sanders, Jayneen. 2020. (ENG.). 34p. (J). ***(978-1-925089-81-3(9)); (978-1-925089-84-4(3));*** pap. ***(978-1-925089-80-6(0));*** pap. ***(978-1-925089-82-0(7))*** UpLoad Publishing Pty, Ltd.

Zamazing, Cherie. Let's Make a Boat, 1 vol. Dale, Jay. 2012. (Wonder Words Ser.). (ENG.). 32p. (gr. k-2). pap. 5.99 *(978-1-4296-8916-8(1),* Capstone Pr.) Capstone.

—Letter to Sam, 1 vol. Dale, Jay. 2012. (Engage Literacy Green Ser.). (ENG.). 32p. (gr. k-2). pap. 5.99 *(978-1-4296-9033-1(X),* Capstone Pr.) Capstone.

—No Means No! Teaching Personal Boundaries, Consent; Empowering Children by Respecting Their Choices & Right to Say 'no!' Sanders, Jayneen. 2017. (ENG.). 32p. (J). (gr. k-3). *(978-1-925089-14-1(2),* Educate2Empower Publishing) UpLoad Publishing Pty, Ltd.

—Off You Go!, 1 vol. Dale, Jay. 2012. (Wonder Words Ser.). (ENG.). 32p. (gr. k-2). pap. 5.99 *(978-1-4296-8910-6(2),* Capstone Pr.) Capstone.

—Talking about Feelings: A Book to Assist Adults in Helping Children Unpack, Understand & Manage Their Feelings & Emotions. Sanders, Jayneen. 2018. (ENG.). 42p. (J). (gr. k-4). *(978-1-925089-30-1(4));* pap. *(978-1-925089-07-3(X))* UpLoad Publishing Pty, Ltd.

Zamazing, Cherie, jt. illus. see Shephard, David.

Zambarano, Richard. Wilbur & Wilma's Colorful Campus Tour - University of Arizona A-Z. 2004. (J). 9.99 *(978-1-933069-02-9(3))* Odd Duck Ink, Inc.

Zamboni, David. Balloon Blessing. Marie, Jill Jana. 2008. 28p. pap. 12.95 *(978-0-9820479-7-2(5))* Peppertree Pr., The.

—The Enchanted Tree. Heller, Donna & Payne, James. 2007. 44p. per. 14.95 *(978-1-934246-72-6(7))* Peppertree Pr., The.

—Finnigan the Dragon. Howell, Julie Ann. 2009. 24p. pap. 12.95 *(978-1-936051-61-8(3))* Peppertree Pr., The.

—Finnigan the Dragon. James, Julie Ann. 2018. (ENG.). 24p. (J). (gr. k-3). pap. 12.95 *(978-1-61493-605-3(6))* Peppertree Pr., The.

—The True Meaning of Christmas, the Greatest Gift of All. Alpert, Barbara. 2009. 24p. pap. 12.95 *(978-1-936051-18-2(4))* Peppertree Pr., The.

—Zoo Rendezvous. Marie, Jill Jana. 2008. 24p. pap. 12.95 *(978-0-9817572-9-2(4))* Peppertree Pr., The.

Zammit, Jeanelle, jt. illus. see Micallef, Bernard.

Zamora, J. I Want a Pet Turkey. Sides, Matthew. 2019. (ENG.). 32p. (J). 19.95 *(978-0-578-48781-6(0))* Moose Egg Productions.

Zamora, Marcelo, et al. Classic Fiction. Agrimbau, Diego et al. 2017. (Classic Fiction Ser.). (ENG.). 80p. (J). (gr. 5-9). 163.92 *(978-1-4965-5603-5(8),* 27325, Stone Arch Bks.) Capstone.

Zampino, Phil. Brush Beats: Different Brush Beats Rhythms & Sounds on the Drum Set. Zampino, Phil. 2004. 25p. (YA). (gr. 5-18). pap. 11.50 *(978-0-942253-29-0(9))* PAZ Publishing.

Zamudio, David. Hello There, Big Brother! Howard, Brooke Leigh. 2018. (ENG.). 40p. (J). *(978-1-5255-1954-3(9));* pap. *(978-1-5255-1955-0(7))* FriesenPress.

—Hello There, Big Sister! Howard, Brooke Leigh. 2018. (ENG.). 40p. (J). *(978-1-5255-1951-2(4));* pap. *(978-1-5255-1952-9(2))* FriesenPress.

Zamyslov, Ivan, jt. illus. see Fajardo, Ruben Carral.

Zanchettin, Gianfranco. Maurice's Soap Bubbles. Zanchettin, Olindo. Saba, Andrew Michael, ed. 2020. (ENG.). 26p. (J). pap. 12.95 ***(978-1-6901-6210-0(4))*** Independently Published.

Zanella, Susy. My Magic Wand: A Magical Sound Book! 2019. (ENG.). 14p. (J). (gr. -1-1). bds. 14.95 *(978-88-544-1553-9(7))* White Star ITA. Dist: Sterling Publishing Co., Inc.

—My Wild Orchestra: A Magical Sound Book! 2019. (ENG.). 14p. (J). (gr. -1-1). bds. 14.95 *(978-88-544-1554-6(5))* White Star ITA. Dist: Sterling Publishing Co., Inc.

Zangara, Orion. Breaking Out the Devil: Book 3. Yolen, Jane & Stemple, Adam. 2019. (Stone Man Mysteries Ser.). 88p. (YA). (gr. 7-12). (ENG.). pap. 8.99 *(978-1-5415-7288-1(2));* lib. bdg. 29.32 *(978-1-4677-4198-9(1))* Lerner Publishing Group. (Graphic Universe™).

—Sanctuary, No. 2. Yolen, Jane & Stemple, Adam. 2018. (Stone Man Mysteries Ser.). 88p. (YA). (gr. 7-12). 29.32 *(978-1-4677-4197-2(3),* 9781467741972, Graphic Universe™) Lerner Publishing Group.

—Sanctuary: Book 2. Yolen, Jane & Stemple, Adam. 2018. (Stone Man Mysteries Ser.). (ENG.). 88p. (YA). (gr. 7-12). pap. 8.99 *(978-1-5415-1043-2(7),* 9781541510432, Graphic Universe™) Lerner Publishing Group.

—Stone Cold, No. 1. Yolen, Jane & Stemple, Adam. 2016. (Stone Man Mysteries Ser.: 1). (ENG.). 80p. (YA). (gr. 7-12). lib. bdg. 29.32 *(978-1-4677-4196-5(5),* f40113d8-bc38-43af-8eb4-83fa1cb9553c, Graphic Universe™) Lerner Publishing Group.

—Stone Cold: Book 1. Yolen, Jane & Stemple, Adam. ed. 2016. (Stone Man Mysteries Ser.: 1). (ENG.). 80p. (gr. 7-12). (J). E-Book 43.99 *(978-1-5124-0903-1(0),* 9781512409031);No. 1. (YA). pap. 8.99 *(978-1-5124-1155-3(8),* 9781512411553) Lerner Publishing Group. (Graphic Universe™).

Zanni, Roger. If You Were a Kid on the Mayflower. Son, John. 2018. (If You Were a Kid Ser.). (ENG.). 32p. (J). (gr. 2-4). lib. bdg. 26.00 *(978-0-531-23216-3(6),* Children's Pr.) Scholastic Library Publishing.

Zapata, Jeff & Simko, Joe. Welcome to Smellville (Garbage Pail Kids Book 1) (B&N Signed Edition) Stine, R.l. 2020. (ENG.). (J). (gr. 3-7). 14.99 ***(978-1-4197-5309-1(6))*** Abrams, Inc.

Zapata, Jeff, jt. illus. see Simko, Joe.

Zapater Oliva, Carlos & Depew, Robert. Bathtime with Bubbles. Friden, Chris. 2008. (J). *(978-0-9801849-2-1(4))* Haydenburri Lane.

Zapater Oliva, Carlos & Glazier, Garth. Pajamatime with P.J. Friden, Chris. 2008. (J). *(978-0-9758785-9-0(X)); (978-0-9801849-5-2(9))* Haydenburri Lane.

—Sleepytime with Rory. Friden, Chris. 2008. (J). *(978-0-9801849-1-4(6))* Haydenburri Lane.

Zaper, Monika. Amelia & Camelia Make a Great Team. Pennington, Kate. 2019. (Beyond a Joke Ser.: Vol. 1). (ENG.). 36p. (J). pap. ***(978-0-6483910-1-2(9))*** Beyond A Joke Inc.

—Bullies Need Friends Too. Pennington, Kate. 2019. (Beyond a Joke Ser.: Vol. 3). (ENG.). 32p. (J). pap. ***(978-0-6483910-3-6(5))*** Beyond A Joke Inc.

—Don't Stare at My Underwear - It's Rude. Pennington, Kate. 2019. (Beyond a Joke Ser.: Vol. 2). (ENG.). 32p. (J). pap. ***(978-0-6483910-0-5(0))*** Beyond A Joke Inc.

—Please Don't Tease. Pennington, Kate. 2019. (Beyond a Joke Ser.: Vol. 4). (ENG.). 32p. (J). pap. ***(978-0-6483910-2-9(7))*** Beyond A Joke Inc.

Zappia, Francesca. Now Entering Addamsville. Zappia, Francesca. 2019. (ENG.). 368p. (YA). (gr. 9). 17.99 *(978-0-06-293527-4(5),* Greenwillow Bks.) HarperCollins Pubs.

Zapple, Elias & Etorma, Crisanto. Amo a Mi Hermano Mayor. Terán, Camila Ayala, tr. 2020. (Cuentos para Dormir Ser.: Vol. 2). (SPA.). 32p. (J). pap. ***(978-1-912704-45-3(5))*** Heads or Tales Pr.

Zarate, Jesus. Mi Familia Calaca / My Skeleton Family. Weill, Cynthia. 2016. (First Concepts in Mexican Folk Art Ser.). (ENG.). 32p. (J). (gr. -1-2). pap. 7.95 *(978-1-941026-34-2(6))* Cinco Puntos Pr.

—My Skeleton Family. Weill, Cynthia. 2013. (First Concepts in Mexican Folk Art Ser.). (ENG.). 32p. (J). (-k). 14.95 *(978-1-935955-50-4(0))* Cinco Puntos Pr.

Zarb, Mike. Mr. Da Vinci's Time Machine. Gold, Robin. 2010. (Belmont & the Dragon Ser.: 3). (ENG.). 48p. (J). (gr. 2-4). pap. 6.99 *(978-1-74166-442-3(X))* Random Hse. Australia AUS. Dist: Independent Pubs. Group.

—Pearlie & Opal. Harmer, Wendy. 2014. (Pearlie Ser.: 3). 48p. (Orig.). (J). (gr. 2-4). pap. 7.99 *(978-1-74051-890-1(X))* Random Hse. Australia AUS. Dist: Independent Pubs. Group.

—Pearlie & the Big Doll. Harmer, Wendy. 2014. (Pearlie Ser.: 2). 48p. (Orig.). (J). (gr. 2-4). pap. 7.99 *(978-1-74051-889-5(6))* Random Hse. Australia AUS. Dist: Independent Pubs. Group.

—Pearlie & the Lost Handbag. Harmer, Wendy. 2014. (Pearlie Ser.: 4). 48p. (Orig.). (J). (gr. 2-4). pap. 7.99 *(978-1-74166-102-6(1))* Random Hse. Australia AUS. Dist: Independent Pubs. Group.

—Pearlie in the Park. Harmer, Wendy. 10th anniv. ed. 2014. (Pearlie Ser.: 1). 48p. (Orig.). (J). (gr. 2-4). pap. 7.99 *(978-1-74275-938-8(6))* Random Hse. Australia AUS. Dist: Independent Pubs. Group.

Zarco Villarosa, Jorge. Animalitos de la Granja (1) / Little Farm Animals. Book 1. Abad Ros, Irena. 2020. (Animalitos Ser.). (SPA.). 48p. (J). (-k). 14.95 ***(978-84-488-5495-9(0),*** Beascoa) Penguin Random House Grupo Editorial ESP. Dist: Penguin Random Hse. LLC.

—Animalitos Del Mar (2) /Little Sea Animals. Book 2. Abad Ros, Irena. 2020. (Animalitos Ser.). (SPA.). 48p. (J). (-k). 14.95 ***(978-84-488-5496-6(9),*** Beascoa) Penguin Random House Grupo Editorial ESP. Dist: Penguin Random Hse. LLC.

Zarcone, Marley. Earth Girl Made Easy. Castellucci, Cecil. 2017. (Young Animal Ser.). (ENG.). 144p. pap. 16.99 *(978-1-4012-7099-5(9))* DC Comics.

Zareba, Lukasz. Where Do My Prayers Go? Lee, Stephi. 2013. (ENG.). 32p. (J). 14.95 *(978-0-578-11938-0(2))* Stephi Lee.

Zarraonandia, Thomas. Johnny Jingle. Zarraonandia, Thomas. 2nd ed. 2003. 30p. (J). (gr. -1-7). per. 20.00 *(978-0-9741070-0-4(X))* Zarraonandia, Anne.

Zarrin, Laura. The Best Baker. Manushkin, Fran. 2020. (Katie Woo's Neighborhood Ser.). (ENG.). 32p. (J). (gr. k-2). pap. 5.95 *(978-1-5158-5873-7(1),* 142129); lib. bdg. 21.32 *(978-1-5158-4813-4(2),* 141497) Capstone. (Picture Window Bks.).

—Best Neighborhood Ever. Manushkin, Fran. ed. 2020. (Katie Woo's Neighborhood Ser.). (ENG.). 96p. (J). (gr. k-2). pap. 5.95 *(978-1-5158-6092-1(2),* 142368, Picture Window Bks.) Capstone.

—Friends in the Mall. Manushkin, Fran. 2019. (Katie Woo's Neighborhood Ser.). (ENG.). 32p. (J). (gr. k-2). pap. 5.95 *(978-1-5158-4558-4(3),* 141146); lib. bdg. 21.32 *(978-1-5158-4458-7(7),* 140570) Capstone. (Picture Window Bks.).

—Good Morning, Farmer Carmen! Manushkin, Fran. 2020. (Katie Woo's Neighborhood Ser.). (ENG.). 32p. (J). (gr. k-2). pap. 5.95 *(978-1-5158-5875-1(8),* 142131); lib. bdg. 21.32 *(978-1-5158-4815-8(9),* 141499) Capstone. (Picture Window Bks.).

—Helping Mayor Patty. Manushkin, Fran. 2019. (Katie Woo's Neighborhood Ser.). (ENG.). 32p. (J). (gr. k-2). 21.32 *(978-1-5158-4457-0(9),* 140569, Picture Window Bks.) Capstone.

—In All Colors. Pope, Elodie. 2018. (ENG & SPA.). 16p. (J). (gr. -1-k). bds. 7.99 *(978-1-338-26902-4(X),* Scholastic en Espanol) Scholastic, Inc.

—Katie Woo's Neighborhood. Manushkin, Fran. 2020. (Katie Woo's Neighborhood Ser.). (ENG.). (J). (gr. k-2). 170.56 *(978-1-5158-4821-9(3),* 29788); pap., pap., pap. 47.60 *(978-1-5158-6036-5(1),* 29984) Capstone. (Picture Window Bks.).

—Katie's Vet Loves Pets. Manushkin, Fran. 2020. (Katie Woo's Neighborhood Ser.). (ENG.). 32p. (J). (gr. k-2). pap. 5.95 *(978-1-5158-5876-8(6),* 142132); lib. bdg. 21.32 *(978-1-5158-4816-5(7),* 141500) Capstone. (Picture Window Bks.).

Z

—Mi Oso. Craddock, Petra. 2016. (Early Rising Readers Ser.). (SPA.). 16p. (J). (gr. 1-1). 6.67 (978-1-4788-3742-8(X)) Newmark Learning LLC.

—Open Wide, Katie! Manushkin, Fran. 2020. (Katie Woo's Neighborhood Ser.). (ENG.). 32p. (J). (gr. k-2). pap. 5.95 (978-1-5158-5874-4(X), 142130); lib. bdg. 21.32 (978-1-5158-4814-1(0), 141498) Capstone. (Picture Window Bks.).

—Stocking up for the Storm. Manushkin, Fran. 2019. (Katie Woo's Neighborhood Ser.). (ENG.). 32p. (J). (gr. k-2). 21.32 (978-1-5158-4455-6(2), 140567, Picture Window Bks.) Capstone.

—Super Paramedic! Manushkin, Fran. 2019. (Katie Woo's Neighborhood Ser.). (ENG.). 32p. (J). (gr. k-2). pap. 5.95 (978-1-5158-4557-7(5), 141145); lib. bdg. 21.32 (978-1-5158-4456-3(0), 140568) Capstone. (Picture Window Bks.).

—Wallace & Grace & the Cupcake Caper. Alexander, Heather. (Wallace & Grace Ser.). 80p. (J). 2018. pap. 6.99 (978-1-68119-011-2(7), 900154812, Bloomsbury Children's Bks.); 2017. 9.99 (978-1-68119-010-5(9), 900154813, Bloomsbury USA Childrens) Bloomsbury Publishing USA.

—Wallace & Grace & the Lost Puppy. Alexander, Heather. 2017. (Wallace & Grace Ser.). (ENG.). 80p. (J). 9.99 (978-1-68119-012-9(5), 900154800, Bloomsbury USA Childrens) Bloomsbury Publishing USA.

—Wallace & Grace Take the Case. Alexander, Heather. (Wallace & Grace Ser.). 80p. (J). 2018. pap. 6.99 (978-1-61963-989-8(0), 900154238, Bloomsbury Children's Bks.); 2017. 9.99 (978-1-61963-988-1(2), 900154265, Bloomsbury USA Childrens) Bloomsbury Publishing USA.

—The Wheels on the Bus. 2018. (ENG & SPA.). 14p. (J). (gr. -1-k). bds. 7.99 (978-1-338-26903-1(8), Scholastic en Espanol) Scholastic, Inc.

Zarvatski, Derek. The Fisherman & His Wife. Boyd, Roland. Wright, Carol, ed. rev. ed. 20p. (J). (gr. 1-2). pap. 6.95 (978-0-9701573-0-0(4)) Chameleon Designs.

Zater, Valeria. Easter the Bunny. Arlan, Joni. 2018. (ENG.). 22p. (J). pap. 10.99 (978-1-5456-5352-4(6), Mill City Press, Inc) Salem Author Services.

Zau. Hazelnut Days. Bourdier, Emmanuel. 2018. (ENG.). 40p. (J). (gr. k-2). 17.99 (978-988-8341-54-2(5), Minedition) Neugebauer, Michael (Publishing) Limited HKG. Dist: Penguin Random Hse. LLC.

Zaü. The Two Doves: A Children's Book Inspired by Pablo Picasso. Elschner, Géraldine. 2017. (Children's Books Inspired by Famous Artworks Ser.). (ENG.). 32p. (J). (gr. -1-3). 14.95 (978-3-7913-7330-0(7)) Prestel Verlag GmbH & Co KG. DEU. Dist: Penguin Random Hse. LLC.

Zaun, Paris, jt. illus. see Zaun, Sarah.

Zaun, Sarah & Zaun, Paris. My Name Is Destiny. Zaun, Sarah. 2018. (ENG.). 20p. (J). (gr. k-6). pap. 12.95 (978-0-692-05388-1(3)) Courage Publishing.

Zavadskyi, Sergii. Once upon a Time: Bedtime with a Smile Picture Books. Mazor, Sarah. 2019. (Bedtime Stories with Uncle Willy Ser.: Vol. 1). (ENG.). 42p. (J). pap. 12.98 (978-1-0911-2613-8(5)) Independently Published.

Zavala, Paola. Mariko Takashi & the Case of the Gremlin Horde. Bair, Christopher. 2nd ed. 2018. (Mariko Takashi Ser.: Vol. 1). (ENG.). 168p. (YA). pap. 9.95 (978-0-9992311-0-4(3)) Elfen Media.

Zavrel, Stepan. Vodnik. Zavrel, Stepan. 32p. (J). (gr. -1-3). 14.95 (978-0-87592-058-0(6)) Scroll Pr., Inc.

Zawlocka, Aleksandra. The Secret Laboratory 1: Gravity Gone! Bottger, Kristen. 2018. (Secret Laboratory Ser.: Vol. 1). (ENG.). 102p. (J). pap. 5.99 (978-1-7177-7467-5(9)) Independently Published.

Zayatz, Corey. My Name Is Rocky. Donnelly, Mark D. 2016. (ENG.). (J). (gr. k-4). 16.95 (978-0-9977996-0-6(9)) Primedia eLaunch LLC.

—Theresa's Sock. Donnelly, Mark. 2017. (ENG.). (J). (gr. k-4). 16.95 (978-0-9995330-5-5(3)) Primedia eLaunch LLC.

Zayatz, Corey. Twenty-Five Cents. Donnelly, Mark D. 2019. (ENG.). 38p. (J). (gr. k-3). 20.00 (978-1-7340139-0-0(7)) Primedia eLaunch LLC.

Zayatz, Cory. Captain Draggin's Unstoppable Flying Machine. Chimera, Paul. 2019. (ENG.). 26p. (J). (gr. k-3). 19.95 (978-1-7340139-4-8(X)) Primedia eLaunch LLC.

Zayatz, Cory. Max Finds a Rainbow. Glaser, Judie. 2019. (ENG.). 30p. (J). (gr. k-3). 16.95 (978-1-7326830-5-1(0)) Primedia eLaunch LLC.

Zazo. Monica Adventures #2: We Fought Each Other As Kids... Now We're in Love?! Sousa, Mauricio de. 2019. (Monica Adventures Ser.). (ENG.). 128p. (J). 13.99 (978-1-5458-0217-5(3), 900198834) Papercutz.

—We Fought Each Other As Kids... Now We're in Love?! Sousa, Mauricio de. 2019. (Monica Adventures Ser.). (ENG.). 128p. (J). pap. 8.99 (978-1-5458-0216-8(5), 900198762) Papercutz.

Zazo, jt. illus. see Gladfelter, Allen.

Zdinak, Zackery. The Little Pine Tree: A Brothers Grimm Fairytale. Green, Dorothy Clare. 2018. (ENG.). 44p. (J). (gr. k-6). pap. 12.95 (978-1-59713-201-5(2)) Goose River Pr.

Zecca, Katherine. Down in Mississippi, 1 vol. Downing, Johnette. 2016. (ENG.). 32p. (J). 16.99 (978-1-4556-2098-2(X), Pelican Publishing) Arcadia Publishing.

—In My Backyard, 1 vol. Giogas, Valarie. 2007. (ENG.). 32p. (J). (gr. -1-3). 15.95 (978-0-9777423-1-8(8)); pap. 8.95 (978-1-934359-17-4(3)) Arbordale Publishing.

—In My Backyard in Chinese. Giogas, Valarie. Shuqi, Yang, tr. 2019. (CHI.). 32p. (J). (gr. -1-2). pap. 11.95 (978-1-60718-394-5(3)) Arbordale Publishing.

—River Song: With the Banana Slug String Band. Van Zandt, Steve. 2007. (ENG.). 32p. (J). (gr. -1-5). 9.99 (978-1-58469-094-8(1), 1268621, Dawn Pubns.) Sourcebooks, Inc.

—River Song: With the Banana Slug String Band (Includes Music CD) Van Zandt, Steve. 2007. (ENG.). 32p. (J). (gr. k-4). 17.99 (978-1-58469-093-1(3), 1268621, Dawn Pubns.) Sourcebooks, Inc.

—The Tree That Came Home: An IslandWood Story Inspired by the True Story of a 92-Foot Beam That Returned to Bainbridge Island, Washington. Brainerd, Debbi. 2008. 63p. (J). pap. (978-0-9821633-0-6(4)) IslandWood.

Zechel, Elizabeth. The Colossal Fossil Fiasco: Lucy's Lab #3. Houts, Michelle. 2018. (Lucy's Lab Ser.: 3). (ENG.). 112p. (J). (gr. 1-3). 13.99 (978-1-5107-1070-2(1)); pap. 4.99 (978-1-5107-1071-9(X)) Skyhorse Publishing Co., Inc. (Sky Pony Pr.).

—The Little General & the Giant Snowflake. Harvey, Matthea. 2009. (ENG.). 64p. (J). (gr. 3-5). 10.95 (978-0-9820539-1-1(6), 982391) Tin Hse. Bks., LLC.

—Nuts about Science: Lucy's Lab #1. Houts, Michelle. 2017. (Lucy?s Lab Ser.). (ENG.). 112p. (J). (gr. 1-4). 13.99 (978-1-5107-1064-1(7), Sky Pony Pr.) Skyhorse Publishing Co., Inc.

—Scampers & the Scientific Method. Allegra, Mike. 2019. (ENG.). 32p. (J). (gr. -1-3). 16.95 (978-1-58469-642-1(7), Dawn Pubns.) Sourcebooks, Inc.

—Solids, Liquids, Guess Who's Got Gas? Lucy's Lab #2. Houts, Michelle. 2017. (Lucy's Lab Ser.: 2). (ENG.). 104p. (J). (gr. 1-4). 13.99 (978-1-5107-1067-2(1), Sky Pony Pr.) Skyhorse Publishing Co., Inc.

Zechman, Abby. Dragonfly Farms: The Old Dog. Ortiz, Jennifer Anne. 2020. (Dragonfly Farms Ser.: Vol. 2). (ENG.). 30p. (J). pap. 9.15 (978-1-6547-3262-2(1)) Independently Published.

Zeck, Mike & Layton, Bob. Marvel Super-Heroes Secret Wars. 2011. 376p. (J). (gr. 4-17). pap. 34.99 (978-0-7851-5868-4(5)) Marvel Worldwide, Inc.

Zeger, James G. Squirrels Can't Burp: And Other Fun Facts about God's Creatures! Zeger, Mary. 2018. (ENG.). 28p. (J). pap. 12.95 (978-1-64140-825-7(1)) Christian Faith Publishing.

Zeineshev, Aidar. Sammy the Station Wagon. Nuriel, Tal. 2017. (ENG.). 36p. (J). pap. 9.95 (978-0-9997262-0-4(X)); 14.95 (978-0-692-96604-4(8)) Nuriel, Tal.

Zeiroth, Emily. Candma Goes to Heaven. Burch, Monica. 2019. (ENG.). 34p. (J). (gr. k-2). pap. 14.99 (978-0-578-51460-4(5)) Impresa Bk. Group.

Zela, Richard. Iroqueses, Cheroquís y Sioux. Navarrete, Federico. 2015. (SPA.). 76p. (J). (gr. 4-7). pap. 11.95 (978-607-8237-51-7(9)) Nostra Ediciones MEX. Dist: Independent Pubs. Group.

Zelenka, Yvonne. Aprendamos con Tito sobre la Epilepsia. Zelenka, Yvonne. 2007. (SPA.). 24p. (J). 6.95 (978-0-9787727-1-0(7)) Medicus Pr., Inc.

Zelinsky, Paul O. All-Of-a-Kind Family Hanukkah. Jenkins, Emily. 2018. 40p. (J). (gr. -1-2). 17.99 (978-0-399-55419-3(X)); (ENG.). 20.99 (978-0-399-55420-9(3)) Random Hse. Children's Bks. (Schwartz & Wade Bks.).

—Awful Ogre Running Wild. Prelutsky, Jack. 2008. 40p. (J). (gr. -1-3). lib. bdg. 18.89 (978-0-06-623867-8(6), Greenwillow Bks.) HarperCollins Pubs.

—Awful Ogre's Awful Day. Prelutsky, Jack. 2005. (ENG.). 40p. (J). (gr. k-5). reprint ed. pap. 7.99 (978-0-06-077459-2(2), Greenwillow Bks.) HarperCollins Pubs.

—Circle, Square, Moose. Bingham, Kelly. 2014. (ENG.). 48p. (J). (gr. -1-3). 17.99 (978-0-06-229003-8(7), Greenwillow Bks.) HarperCollins Pubs.

—Earwig & the Witch. Jones, Diana Wynne. 2012. (ENG.). 128p. (J). (gr. 3-7). 15.99 (978-0-06-207511-6(X), Greenwillow Bks.) HarperCollins Pubs.

—The Story of Mrs. Lovewright & Purrless Her Cat. Segal, Lore. 2005. (ENG.). 40p. (J). (gr. -1-3). reprint ed. 17.99 (978-0-689-87327-0(1), Atheneum/Anne Schwartz Bks.) Simon & Schuster Children's Publishing.

—Toy Dance Party. Jenkins, Emily. 2008. (Toys Go Out Ser.: 2). (ENG.). 176p. (J). (gr. 1-4). 16.99 (978-0-375-83935-1(6), Schwartz & Wade Bks.) Random Hse. Children's Bks.

—Toy Dance Party: Being the Further Adventures of a Bossyboots Stingray, a Courageous Buffalo, & a Hopeful Round Someone Called Plastic. Jenkins, Emily. 2010. (Toys Go Out Ser.: 2). (ENG.). 176p. (J). (gr. 1-4). 6.99 (978-0-375-85525-2(4), Schwartz & Wade Bks.) Random Hse. Children's Bks.

—Toys Come Home: Being the Early Experiences of an Intelligent Stingray, a Brave Buffalo, & a Brand-New Someone Called Plastic. Jenkins, Emily. (Toys Go Out Ser.: 3). 144p. (J). (gr. 1-4). 2016. 6.99 (978-0-449-81592-2(7)); 2011. 16.99 (978-0-375-86200-7(5)) Random Hse. Children's Bks. (Schwartz & Wade Bks.).

—Toys Go Out: Being the Adventures of a Knowledgeable Stingray, a Toughy Little Buffalo, & Someone Called Plastic. Jenkins, Emily. 2008. (Toys Go Out Ser.: 1). (ENG.). 144p. (J). (gr. 1-4). 6.99 (978-0-385-73661-9(4), Yearling) Random Hse. Children's Bks.

—Toys Meet Snow: Being the Wintertime Adventures of a Curious Stuffed Buffalo, a Sensitive Plush Stingray, & a Book-Loving Rubber Ball. Jenkins, Emily. 2015. 40p. (J). (gr. -1-2). 17.99 (978-0-385-37330-2(9), Schwartz & Wade Bks.) Random Hse. Children's Bks.

—Z Is for Moose. Bingham, Kelly. 2012. (ENG.). 32p. (J). (gr. -1-2). 16.99 (978-0-06-079984-7(6)); lib. bdg. 17.89 (978-0-06-079985-4(4)) HarperCollins Pubs. (Greenwillow Bks.).

Zeltner, Tim. Little Boo. Wunderli, Stephen. 2014. (ENG.). 32p. (J). (gr. -1-2). 16.99 (978-0-8050-9708-5(2), 900097295, Holt, Henry & Co. Bks. For Young Readers) Holt, Henry & Co.

Zelz, Eric. Pass the Pandowdy, Please: Chewing on History with Famous Folks & Their Fabulous Foods, 1 vol. Zelz, Abigail. 2016. (ENG.). 40p. (J). (gr. 2-6). 17.95 (978-0-88448-468-4(8), 884468) Tilbury Hse. Pubs.

Zemach, Kaethe, jt. illus. see Zemach, Margot.

Zemach, Margot & Zemach, Kaethe. Eating up Gladys. 2005. (J). (978-0-439-66491-2(8), Levine, Arthur A. Bks.) Scholastic, Inc.

Zeman, Ludmila. Gilgamesh. Zeman, Ludmila, narrated by. 2005. (SPA.). (J). 29.95 (978-968-7381-51-0(5)); pap. 21.95 (978-968-7381-47-3(7)) Tecolote, Ediciones, S.A. de C.V. MEX. Dist: Iaconi, Mariuccia Bk. Imports.

Zembrowski, Sunni. Why Ducks Waddle & Geese Don't. Wachob, Chuck. (978-0-578-15467-1(6)) Wachob, Chuck.

Zemke, Deborah. The Absolutely, Positively No Princesses Book. Lendler, Ian. 2019. (ENG.). 36p. (J). (gr. 1-5). 16.99 (978-1-939547-51-4(2)) Creston Bks.

Zemke, Deborah. The Case of the Bad Apples: A Wilcox & Griswold Mystery. Newman, Robin. 2020. (Wilcox & Griswold Mysteries Ser.). (ENG.). 48p. (J). (gr. k-3). 18.99 (978-1-939547-76-7(8)) Creston Bks.

Zemke, Deborah. The Case of the Missing Carrot Cake: A Wilcox & Griswold Mystery. Newman, Robin. 2015. (Wilcox & Griswold Mysteries Ser.). (ENG.). 40p. (J). (gr. k-5). 18.99 (978-1-939547-17-0(2)) Creston Bks.

—The Case of the Poached Egg: A Wilcox & Griswold Mystery. Newman, Robin. 2017. (Wilcox & Griswold Mysteries Ser.). (ENG.). 48p. (J). (gr. k-5). 15.95 (978-1-939547-30-9(X)) Creston Bks.

—Cock-A-Doodle-Oops! Degman, Lori. 2014. (ENG.). 36p. (J). (gr. -1-3). 16.99 (978-1-939547-07-1(5)) Creston Bks.

—Jasper. Galloway, Ginger. 2003. (Books for Young Learners). (ENG.). 16p. (J). 5.75 net. (978-1-57274-539-1(8), 2457, Bks. for Young Learners) Owen, Richard C. Pubs., Inc.

—The Night Before First Grade. Wing, Natasha. 2005. (Night Before Ser.). (ENG.). 32p. (J). (gr. k-1). pap. 4.99 (978-0-448-43747-7(3), Grosset & Dunlap) Penguin Young Readers Group.

—Sky-High Sukkah, Vol. Packer, Rachel Ornstein. 2016. (ENG.). (J). (978-1-68115-513-5(3)) Behrman Hse., Inc.

—Wise Acres. Shannon, George. 2004. (ENG.). 40p. (J). (gr. -1-7). 15.95 (978-1-59354-041-8(8), Handprint Bks.) Chronicle Bks. LLC.

Zengin-Karaian, Alex & Fach, Gernot. The Last Word in Astronomy. Feigin, Misha. Zengin-Karaian, Victoria & Zengin-Karaian, Alex, eds. 2004. 86p. per. 11.95 (978-0-9741277-1-2(X), Fleur Publishing) Fleur Art Productions.

Zenko, Karda. A Hug for Grandma. MacGregor, Cynthia. 2017. (ENG.). 34p. (J). (gr. k-5). pap. 9.99 (978-1-68160-512-8(0)) Crimson Cloak Publishing.

—The Night I Rode on Santa's Sleigh. MacGregor, Cynthia. 2017. (ENG.). 30p. (J). (gr. 1-6). pap. 9.99 (978-1-68160-498-5(1)) Crimson Cloak Publishing.

Zenou, Izak. My Two Dads & Me. Joosten, Michael. 2019. (ENG.). 22p. (J). (— 1). bds. 8.99 (978-0-525-58010-2(7), Doubleday Bks. for Young Readers) Random Hse. Children's Bks.

—My Two Moms & Me. Joosten, Michael. 2019. (ENG.). 22p. (J). (— 1). bds. 8.99 (978-0-525-58012-6(3), Doubleday Bks. for Young Readers) Random Hse. Children's Bks.

Zenz, Aaron. Biggety Bat: Chow down, Biggety! Ingalls, Ann. 2015. (Scholastic Reader, Level 1 Ser.). (ENG.). 32p. (J). (gr. -1-1). pap. 3.99 (978-0-545-66264-2(8)) Scholastic, Inc.

—Howie Finds a Hug, 1 vol. Henderson, Sara. 2008. (I Can Read! / Howie Ser.). (ENG.). 32p. (J). (gr. -1-3). pap. 4.99 (978-0-310-71607-5(1)) Zonderkidz.

—Howie Goes Shopping, 1 vol. Henderson, Sara. 2008. (I Can Read! / Howie Ser.). (ENG.). 32p. (J). (gr. -1-3). pap. 4.99 (978-0-310-71606-8(3)) Zonderkidz.

—Howie Wants to Play, 1 vol. Henderson, Sara. 2008. (I Can Read! / Howie Ser.). (ENG.). 32p. (J). (gr. -1-3). pap. 4.99 (978-0-310-71604-4(7)) Zonderkidz.

—Howie's Tea Party, 1 vol. Henderson, Sara. 2008. (I Can Read! / Howie Ser.). (ENG.). 32p. (J). (gr. -1-3). pap. 4.99 (978-0-310-71605-1(5)) Zonderkidz.

—Porcupine Valentine. 2016. (J). (978-0-545-90155-0(3)) Scholastic, Inc.

—The Runaway Mitten. Lewis, Anne Margaret. 2015. 40p. (J). (gr. -1-k). 15.99 (978-1-63450-213-9(2), Sky Pony Pr.) Skyhorse Publishing Co., Inc.

—The Runaway Pumpkin. Lewis, Anne Margaret. 2015. 40p. (J). (gr. -1-k). 15.99 (978-1-63450-214-6(0), Sky Pony Pr.) Skyhorse Publishing Co., Inc.

—The Runaway Pumpkin. Lewis, Anne. 2018. (ENG.). 22p. (J). (gr. -1-2). bds. 5.99 (978-1-5107-2764-9(7), Sky Pony Pr.) Skyhorse Publishing Co., Inc.

—The Runaway Santa. Lewis, Anne Margaret. 2015. 40p. (J). (gr. -1-k). 15.99 (978-1-63450-589-5(1), Sky Pony Pr.) Skyhorse Publishing Co., Inc.

—The Runaway Santa: A Christmas Adventure Story. Lewis, Anne. 2017. (ENG.). 20p. (J). bds. 5.99 (978-1-5107-2765-6(5), Sky Pony Pr.) Skyhorse Publishing Co., Inc.

—Skeleton Meets the Mummy. Metzger, Steve. 2011. (ENG.). 32p. (J). (gr. -1-3). pap. 6.99 (978-0-545-23032-2(2), Cartwheel Bks.) Scholastic, Inc.

—The Spaghetti-Slurping Sewer Serpent, 0 vols. Ripes, Laura. 2012. (ENG.). 32p. (J). (gr. k-3). 16.99 (978-0-7614-6101-2(9), 9780761461012, Two Lions) Amazon Publishing.

Zenz, Aaron. I Love Ewe: An Ode to Animal Moms. Zenz, Aaron. 2015. (ENG.). 22p. (J). (gr. -1-1). bds. 7.99 (978-1-61963-666-8(2), 9781619636668, Bloomsbury USA Childrens) Bloomsbury Publishing USA.

Zenz, Aaron, jt. illus. see Henderson, Sara.

Zephyr, Jay, jt. illus. see Aronson, Jeff.

Zerbetz, Evon. Aleutian Sparrow. Hesse, Karen. 2005. (ENG.). 160p. (J). (gr. 4-9). reprint ed. pap. 7.99 (978-1-4169-0327-7(5), McElderry, Margaret K. Bks.) McElderry, Margaret K. Bks.

—Aleutian Sparrow. Hesse, Karen. 2005. 156p. (J). (gr. 5-9). 13.65 (978-0-7569-5589-2(0)) Perfection Learning Corp.

—Dream Flights on Arctic Nights. Hartman, Brooke. 2019. (ENG.). 32p. (J). (gr. k-2). 16.99 (978-1-5132-6189-8(4), Alaska Northwest Bks.) West Margin Pr.

—Lucky Hares & Itchy Bears: And Other Alaskan Animals. Ewing, Susan. Blessing, Marlene, ed. 2012. (ENG.). 32p. (J). 16.95 (978-0-9858506-0-9(4)) Octopoda Pr.

—Ten Rowdy Ravens. Ewing, Susan. 2005. (ENG.). 32p. (J). (gr. -1-1). per. 11.99 (978-0-88240-610-7(8), Alaska Northwest Bks.) West Margin Pr.

Zerga, Susan A., photos by. Autumn Rescue. Wilson, Karen Collett. 2004. (Deer Tales Ser.). (J). (gr. k-6). 15.95 (978-0-9722570-1-5(2)) Snowbound Bks.

Zeringue, Dona. I Am I. Zeringue, Dona. 32p. (Orig.). (YA). (gr. 6-12). pap. 7.50 (978-1-882913-02-2(7)) Thornton Publishing.

Zermeño, Gaby. Boo: Chunky Peek a Flap Board Book. VonFeder, Rosa. Cottage Door Press, ed. 2017. (Peek a Flap Ser.). (ENG.). 12p. (J). (gr. -1-k). bds. 8.99 (978-1-68052-189-4(6), 1001870) Cottage Door Pr.

Zerner, Jesse. Christmas Stories. Hanft, Joshua E. 2005. (Great Illustrated Classics Ser.). (ENG.). 240p. (J). (gr. 3-8). lib. bdg. 25.65 (978-1-59679-238-8(8), 9282) Spotlight.

Zetsuboupuppet. IAmMoshow the Cat Rapper Official Coloring Book: Meowliday Edition. The Cat Rapper, IamMoshow. 2019. (ENG.). 48p. (J). pap. 14.95 (978-1-6946-7188-2(7)) Independently Published.

Zettler, Andrew. The Teeniest Tiniest Yawn. Zettler, Andrew. I.t. ed. 2014. (ENG.). 36p. (J). 17.99 (978-0-9912370-0-5(5)) Royal Penny Pr., The.

Zevgolis, Irene. The Dreamer & the Moon: An Inspirational Story with a Ballet Theme. 2008. (J). (978-0-615-17590-4(2)) E-City Publishing.

Zezelj, Danijel, jt. illus. see Mandrake, Tom.

Zgud, Alex. Beverlee Beaz the Brown Burmese. Macaulay, Regan W. H. 2nd ed. 2019. (ENG.). 48p. (J). pap. (978-1-987976-52-6(5)) Mirror World Publishing.

—Merry Myrrh the Christmas Bat. Macaulay, Regan. 2019. (ENG.). 24p. (J). (gr. k-3). 19.95 (978-1-61633-937-1(3)) Guardian Angel Publishing, Inc.

—Merry Myrrh, the Christmas Bat. Macaulay, Regan W. H. I.t. ed. 2018. (ENG.). 24p. (J). (gr. k-2). pap. 10.95 (978-1-61633-935-7(7)) Guardian Angel Publishing, Inc.

Zhai, Rea. On My Way to School. Weakland, Mark. 2019. (School Rules Ser.). (ENG.). 24p. (J). (gr. k-2). pap. 8.95 (978-1-5158-4063-3(8), 140057, Picture Window Bks.) Capstone.

—Parker Bell & the Science of Friendship. Platt, Cynthia. 2019. (ENG.). 160p. (J). (gr. 3-7). 16.99 (978-1-328-97347-4(6), 1708149, Clarion Bks.) Houghton Mifflin Harcourt Trade & Reference Pubs.

—Schools Have Rules. Troupe, Thomas Kingsley. 2019. (School Rules Ser.). (ENG.). 24p. (J). (gr. k-2). pap. 8.95 (978-1-5158-4064-0(6), 140058, Picture Window Bks.) Capstone.

Zhai, Rea. A Super Sticky Mistake: The Story of How Harry Coover Accidentally Invented Super Glue! Donald, Alison. 2020. (ENG.). 32p. (J). (gr. -1-3). 17.99 (978-1-84886-647-8(X)) Maverick Arts Publishing GBR. Dist: Lerner Publishing Group.

Zhan, Qi. The Case of the Missing Moustache. Lazzaro, Fernanda. 2019. (Tillsonbugger Adventures Ser.). (ENG.). 28p. (J). (978-1-5255-5556-5(1)); pap. (978-1-5255-5557-2(X)) FriesenPress.

Zhan, Qi. Tillsonbugger Adventures: The Swarm That Swarmed. Lazzaro, Fernanda. 2018. (ENG.). 24p. (J). (978-1-5255-2694-7(4)); pap. (978-1-5255-2695-4(2)) FriesenPress.

Zhang, Alice X. Marvel Powers of a Girl. Cink, Lorraine. 2019. (ENG.). 144p. (YA). (gr. 7-17). 16.99 (978-1-368-02526-3(9), Marvel Pr.) Disney Publishing Worldwide.

Zhang, Annie. A Frog Named Waldor. Rankine-Van Wassenhoven, Jacqueline. 2008. 20p. per. 24.95 (978-1-4241-9926-6(3)) America Star Bks.

Zhang, Nancy. Clothes Minded. Taylor, Chloë. 2015. (Sew Zoey Ser.: 11). (ENG.). 160p. (J). (gr. 3-7). pap. 6.99 (978-1-4814-2927-6(2), Simon Spotlight) Simon Spotlight.

—Cut from the Same Cloth. Taylor, Chloë. 2016. (Sew Zoey Ser.: 14). (ENG.). 176p. (J). (gr. 3-7). 17.99 (978-1-4814-5297-7(5), Simon Spotlight) Simon Spotlight.

—Cute As a Button. Taylor, Chloë. 2014. (Sew Zoey Ser.: 5). (ENG.). 176p. (J). (gr. 3-7). pap. 5.99 (978-1-4814-0248-4(X), Simon Spotlight) Simon Spotlight.

—Dressed to Frill. Taylor, Chloë. 2015. (Sew Zoey Ser.: 12). (ENG.). 160p. (J). (gr. 3-7). pap. 6.99 (978-1-4814-2930-6(2), Simon Spotlight) Simon Spotlight.

—Knot Too Shabby! Taylor, Chloe. 2014. (Sew Zoey Ser.: 7). (ENG.). 176p. (J). (gr. 3-7). pap. 5.99 (978-1-4814-1398-5(8), Simon Spotlight) Simon Spotlight.

—Lights, Camera, Fashion! Taylor, Chloe. 2013. (Sew Zoey Ser.: 3). (ENG.). 176p. (J). (gr. 3-7). pap. 5.99 (978-1-4424-8979-0(0), Simon Spotlight) Simon Spotlight.

—Miss Paul & the President: The Creative Campaign for Women's Right to Vote. Robbins, Dean. 2016. 40p. (J). (gr. -1-3). 17.99 (978-1-101-93720-4(3), Knopf Bks. for Young Readers) Random Hse. Children's Bks.

—No Truth Without Ruth: the Life of Ruth Bader Ginsburg. Krull, Kathleen. 2018. (ENG.). 48p. (J). (gr. -1-3). 17.99 (978-0-06-256011-7(5)) HarperCollins Pubs.

—On Pins & Needles. Taylor, Chloe. 2013. (Sew Zoey Ser.: 2). (ENG.). 160p. (J). (gr. 3-7). pap. 6.99 (978-1-4424-7936-4(1), Simon Spotlight) Simon Spotlight.

—Ready to Wear. Taylor, Chloe. 2013. (Sew Zoey Ser.: 1). (ENG.). 176p. (J). (gr. 3-7). pap. 6.99 (978-1-4424-7933-3(7), Simon Spotlight) Simon Spotlight.

—Sewing in Circles. Taylor, Chloë. 2015. (Sew Zoey Ser.: 13). (ENG.). 176p. (J). (gr. 3-7). pap. 6.99 (978-1-4814-4032-5(2), Simon Spotlight) Simon Spotlight.

—Stitches & Stones. Taylor, Chloe. 2013. (Sew Zoey Ser.: 4). (ENG.). 176p. (J). (gr. 3-7). 16.99 (978-1-4424-9803-7(X));Bk. 4. pap. 5.99 (978-1-4424-9802-0(1)) Simon Spotlight. (Simon Spotlight).

—Swatch Out! Taylor, Chloe. 2014. (Sew Zoey Ser.: 8). (ENG.). 176p. (J). (gr. 3-7). pap. 5.99 (978-1-4814-1535-4(2), Simon Spotlight) Simon Spotlight.

—A Tangled Thread. Taylor, Chloë. 2014. (Sew Zoey Ser.: 6). (ENG.). 176p. (J). (gr. 3-7). 16.99 (978-1-4814-0444-0(X), Simon Spotlight) Simon Spotlight.

—A Tangled Thread. Taylor, Chloe. 2014. (Sew Zoey Ser.: 6). (ENG.). 176p. (J). (gr. 3-7). pap. 5.99 (978-1-4814-0443-3(1), Simon Spotlight) Simon Spotlight.

Zhang, Nancy, jt. illus. see Christy, Jana.

Zhang, Song Nan. Awakening the Dragon: The Dragon Boat Festival. Chan, Arlene. 2007. 24p. (J). (gr. 1-4). pap. 10.95 *(978-0-88776-805-7(9)*, Tundra Bks.) Tundra Bks. CAN. Dist: Penguin Random Hse. LLC.

—The Day I Became a Canadian: A Citizenship Scrapbook. Bannatyne-Cugnet, Jo. 2008. 24p. (J). (gr. 2-4). pap. 10.95 *(978-0-88776-892-7(X)*, Tundra Bks.) Tundra Bks. CAN. Dist: Penguin Random Hse. LLC.

—Emma's Story. Hodge, Deborah. 2003. 24p. (J). (gr. k-3). 17.95 *(978-0-88776-632-9(3)*, Tundra Bks.) Tundra Bks. CAN. Dist: Penguin Random Hse. LLC.

—Lady White Snake: A Tale from Chinese Opera: Bilingual - Simplified Chinese & English. Shepard, Aaron. 2016. (ENG.). (J). pap. 12.95 *(978-1-57227-131-9(0))* Pan Asian Pubns. (U S A), Inc.

—Lady White Snake: A Tale from Chinese Opera: Bilingual - Traditional Chinese & English. Shepard, Aaron. Chen, Isabella, tr. 2016. (ENG.). (J). pap. 12.95 *(978-1-57227-128-9(0))* Pan Asian Pubns. (U S A), Inc.

—The Man Who Made Parks: The Story of Parkbuilder Frederick Law Olmsted. Wishinsky, Frieda. 2009. 32p. (J). (gr. k-4). pap. 10.95 *(978-0-88776-902-3(0)*, Tundra Bks.) Tundra Bks. CAN. Dist: Penguin Random Hse. LLC.

Zhang, Song Nan. The Great Voyages of Zheng He. Zhang, Song Nan. Zhang, Hao Yu. 2005. 32p. (J). 16.95 *(978-1-57227-088-6(8))*; (ENG & CHI.). 16.95 *(978-1-57227-090-9(X))* Pan Asia Pubns. (USA), Inc.

—The Great Voyages of Zheng He: English/Vietnamese. Zhang, Song Nan. Zhang, Hao Yu. Do, Kim-Thu, tr. from ENG. 2005. (ENG & VIE.). 32p. (J). 16.95 *(978-1-57227-091-6(8))* Pan Asia Pubns. (USA), Inc.

—A Time of Golden Dragons. Zhang, Song Nan. Zhang, Hao Yu. 2006. 24p. (J). (gr. 4-7). pap. 11.95 *(978-0-88776-791-3(5)*, Tundra Bks.) Tundra Bks. CAN. Dist: Penguin Random Hse. LLC.

Zhao, Amei. Painted Skies. Mallory, Carolyn. (ENG.). 36p. (J). (gr. k-2). 2018. pap. 10.95 *(978-1-77227-219-2(1))*; 2015. 16.95 *(978-1-77227-004-4(0))* Inhabit Media Inc. CAN. Dist: Consortium Bk. Sales & Distribution.

Zhao, Amei & McLeod, Kagan. Muskox, 1 vol. Flaherty, William & Niptanatiak, Allen. 2016. (Animals Illustrated Ser.). (ENG.). 24p. (J). (gr. k-2). 12.95 *(978-1-77227-122-5(5))* Inhabit Media Inc. CAN. Dist: Consortium Bk. Sales & Distribution.

Zheng, Wen. Star & Cloud: Venerable Master Hsing Yun. Wheeler-Gibb, Madelon, tr. from CHI. 2003. (Buddhist Legends of Adventure & Courage Ser.). 148p. (J). pap. 10.00 *(978-0-9715612-4-3(9))* Buddha's Light Publications USA Corp.

Zheng, Xiaoyan, jt. illus. see Xu, Wei.

Zheng, Xin. Earth Day Every Day. Bullard, Lisa. 2011. (Cloverleaf Books (tm) — Planet Protectors Ser.). (ENG.). 24p. (J). (gr. k-2). pap. 8.99 *(978-0-7613-8512-7(6)*, 9780761385127, Millbrook Pr.) Lerner Publishing Group.

—Go Green by Caring for Water. Bullard, Lisa. 2018. (Go Green (Early Bird Stories (tm)) Ser.). (ENG.). 24p. (J). (gr. k-2). pap. 7.99 *(978-1-5415-2711-9(9))*; lib. bdg. 27.99 *(978-1-5415-2017-2(3)*, Lerner Pubns.) Lerner Publishing Group.

—Look Out for Litter. Bullard, Lisa. 2011. (Cloverleaf Books (tm) — Planet Protectors Ser.). (ENG.). 24p. (J). (gr. k-2). pap. 8.99 *(978-0-7613-8514-1(2)*, 9780761385141, Millbrook Pr.) Lerner Publishing Group.

—Watch over Our Water. Bullard, Lisa. 2011. (Cloverleaf Books (tm) — Planet Protectors Ser.). (ENG.). 24p. (J). (gr. k-2). pap. 8.99 *(978-0-7613-8517-2(7)*, 9780761385172, Millbrook Pr.) Lerner Publishing Group.

Zheng, Xin, jt. illus. see Xin, Xiao.

Zhihong, He. Long-Long's New Year. Zhihong, He. Gower, Catherine. 2005. (ENG.). 32p. (J). (gr. k-3). 16.95 *(978-0-8048-3666-1(3))* Tuttle Publishing.

Zhing, Amy, jt. illus. see Zito, Francesco.

Zhiying, Yu. Ode to the Goddess of the Luo River. Luying, Ye. 2020. (ENG.). 78p. (J). (gr. 4-7). 35.00 *(978-988-8341-94-8(4)*, Minedition) Neugebauer, Michael (Publishing) Limited HKG. Dist: Penguin Random Hse. LLC.

Zhou, Dahuang, jt. illus. see Zhou, ShanZuo.

Zhou, ShanZuo & Zhou, Dahuang. Flying Paintings: the Zhou Brothers: a Story of Revolution & Art. Alznauer, Amy. 2020. 48p. (J). (gr. k-4). 17.99 ***(978-1-5362-0428-5(5))*** Candlewick Pr.

Zhu, Ping. The Strange Birds of Flannery O'Connor. Alznauer, Amy. 2020. 64p. (J). 18.95 *(978-1-59270-295-4(3))* Enchanted Lion Bks., LLC.

Zhuang, Qing. How Long Is Forever? Carey, Kelly. 2020. 32p. (J). (gr. -1-2). lib. bdg. 16.99 *(978-1-58089-578-1(6))* Charlesbridge Publishing, Inc.

Zhuravlova, Olga. Cheeky Charlie: Bugs & Bananas. Waugh, Mat. 2018. (ENG.). 150p. (J). (gr. 2-4). pap. *(978-1-912883-07-3(4))* Big Red Button Bks.

—Cheeky Charlie: He Didn't Mean It. Waugh, Mat. 2018. (Cheeky Charlie Ser.: Vol. 4). (ENG.). 140p. (J). (gr. 2-4). pap. *(978-1-912883-09-7(0))* Big Red Button Bks.

—Cheeky Charlie: King of Chaos. Waugh, Mat. 2018. (ENG.). 156p. (J). (gr. 2-4). pap. *(978-1-912883-08-0(2))* Big Red Button Bks.

Ziborova, Dasha. En Ingles, por Supuesto. Nobisso, Josephine. 2003. Orig. Title: In English, of Course. (SPA.). 32p. (J). (gr. k-2). 16.95 *(978-0-940112-14-8(0))* Gingerbread Hse.

—En ingles, por Supuesto. Nobisso, Josephine. 2003. Orig. Title: In English, of Course. (SPA.). 32p. (J). (gr. k-2). pap. 8.95 *(978-0-940112-16-2(7))* Gingerbread Hse.

—In English, of Course. Nobisso, Josephine. 2003.Tr. of En Ingles, Por Supuesto. (ENG.). 32p. (J). (gr. -1). 16.95 *(978-0-940112-07-0(8))*; pap. 8.95 *(978-0-940112-08-7(6))* Gingerbread Hse.

—The Numbers Dance: A Counting Comedy. Nobisso, Josephine. 2005. (ENG.). 32p. (J). (gr. k-2). 16.95 *(978-0-940112-11-7(6))*; pap. 8.95 *(978-0-940112-12-4(4))* Gingerbread Hse.

Ziegler, Michael. The Friendship Alphabet. Ziegler, Michael, photos by. Bramwell, Wendie et al. 2003. 32p. (J). pap. *(978-0-9741388-3-1(5))* Committee for Children.

Zielinski, Dave, photos by. The ABC's of Motocross. Louck, Cheryl. 2003. 24p. (J). per. 14.95 *(978-0-9744230-0-5(9))* Louck, Cheryl.

Ziermann, Stefanie. The Battle of the Books. Harings, Audrey. Lammers, Martina, tr. 2019. (ENG.). 238p. (J). pap. 9.99 ***(978-1-7058-5836-3(8))*** Independently Published.

Zieroth, Emily. Allen Linn's Children's Bible Book: Creation & the Life of Jesus. Linn, Allen. 2020. (ENG.). 36p. (J). pap. 8.95 ***(978-0-9982014-8-1(0))*** Pyramid Pubs.

Zieroth, Emily. Emily & Daniel's First Dollar. Eshet, Amit. 2017. (ENG.). 40p. (J). (gr. k-3). *(978-965-92633-5-6(X))*; pap. *(978-965-92633-6-3(8))* Simple Story.

—La Foret Magique. Souhila. La Liseuse, Editions, ed. 2016. (FRE.). (J). pap. *(978-2-37108-039-3(X))* L@ Liseuse.

—Journey to Jazzland. De Saulnier, Gia Volterra. 2013. 44p. 14.99 *(978-0-9851492-8-4(0))* Flying Turtle Publishing.

—Maya & Daniel's First Dollar (Hebrew Edition) מאיה ודניאל עושים עסקים Eshet, Amit. 2019. (HEB.). 42p. (J). (gr. k-3). *(978-965-92633-7-0(6))* Simple Story.

—Patient Penelope. Joseph, Terrica. 2017. (ENG.). (J). (gr. k-3). pap. 9.99 *(978-1-970016-10-9(8))*; (gr. 1-4). 14.99 *(978-1-970016-09-3(4))* Fruit Springs, LLC.

Zieroth, Emily, jt. illus. see Cliette, Emanuel.

Ziersch, Nahum. Chip & Chase. Loughlin, Patrick. 2015. 144p. (J). (gr. 2-4). 9.99 *(978-0-85798-270-4(2))* Random Hse. Australia AUS. Dist: Independent Pubs. Group.

—Show & Go. 2015. 144p. (J). (gr. 2-4). 9.99 *(978-0-85798-268-1(0))* Random Hse. Australia AUS. Dist: Independent Pubs. Group.

Zilber, Denis. Get to Work, Hercules!, 1 vol. McMullan, Kate. 2011. (Myth-O-Mania Ser.: Bk. 7). (ENG.). 208p. (J). (gr. 4-8). pap. 5.95 *(978-1-4342-3440-7(1)*, Stone Arch Bks.) Capstone.

—Go for the Gold, Atalanta!, 1 vol. McMullan, Kate. 2011. (Myth-O-Mania Ser.: Bk. 8). (ENG.). 192p. (J). (gr. 4-8). pap. 5.95 *(978-1-4342-3441-4(X)*, Stone Arch Bks.) Capstone.

—Have a Hot Time, Hades!, 1 vol. McMullan, Kate. 2011. (Myth-O-Mania Ser.: Bk. 1). (ENG.). 176p. (J). (gr. 4-8). pap. 5.95 *(978-1-4342-3437-7(1)*, Stone Arch Bks.) Capstone.

—Keep a Lid on It, Pandora!, 1 vol. McMullan, Kate. 2011. (Myth-O-Mania Ser.: Bk. 6). (ENG.). 192p. (J). (gr. 4-8). pap. 5.95 *(978-1-4342-3439-1(8)*, Stone Arch Bks.) Capstone.

—Nice Shot, Cupid!, 1 vol. McMullan, Kate. 2011. (Myth-O-Mania Ser.: Bk. 4). (ENG.). 208p. (J). (gr. 4-8). pap. 5.95 *(978-1-4342-3435-3(5)*, Stone Arch Bks.) Capstone.

—Phone Home, Persephone!, 1 vol. McMullan, Kate. 2011. (Myth-O-Mania Ser.: Bk. 2). (ENG.). 176p. (J). (gr. 4-8). pap. 5.95 *(978-1-4342-3436-0(3)*, Stone Arch Bks.) Capstone.

—Puss in Boots. Namm, Diane. 2012. (Silver Penny Stories Ser.). 48p. (J). (gr. -1-1). 4.95 *(978-1-4027-8435-4(X))* Sterling Publishing Co., Inc.

—Say Cheese, Medusa!, 1 vol. McMullan, Kate. 2011. (Myth-O-Mania Ser.: Bk. 3). (ENG.). 208p. (J). (gr. 4-8). pap. 5.95 *(978-1-4342-3442-1(8)*, Stone Arch Bks.) Capstone.

—Stop That Bull, Theseus!, 1 vol. McMullan, Kate. 2011. (Myth-O-Mania Ser.: Bk. 5). (ENG.). 192p. (J). (gr. 4-8). pap. 5.95 *(978-1-4342-3438-4(X)*, Stone Arch Bks.) Capstone.

Zilber, Denis & Olafsdottir, Linda. The Princess & the Pea. Namm, Diane & Andersen, Hans. 2013. (Silver Penny Stories Ser.). 48p. (J). (gr. -1-1). 4.95 *(978-1-4027-8436-1(8))* Sterling Publishing Co., Inc.

Zilber, Denis, jt. illus. see Altmann, Scott.

Zilis, Tom. Cats: Read Well Level K Unit 12 Storybook. Sprick, Marilyn et al. 2003. (Read Well Level K Ser.). 20p. (J). *(978-1-57035-683-4(1)*, 55520) Cambium Education, Inc.

—The Little Red Hen: Read Well Level K Unit 20 Storybook. 2003. (Read Well Level K Ser.). 20p. (J). *(978-1-57035-691-9(2)*, 55600) Cambium Education, Inc.

—Man's Best Friend: Read Well Level K Unit 5 Storybook. Sprick, Marilyn et al. 2003. (Read Well Level K Ser.). 20p. (J). *(978-1-57035-677-3(7))* Cambium Education, Inc.

—Rescue Workers: Read Well Level K Unit 11 Storybook. Sprick, Marilyn et al. 2003. (Read Well Level K Ser.). 20p. (J). *(978-1-57035-682-7(3)*, 55511) Cambium Education, Inc.

Zima, Gordon & Zima, Paula. Sun Birds & Evergreens: The Nuk-Chuk Stories. 2005. (J). *(978-0-9742894-3-4(4))* Hutton Electronic Publishing.

Zima, Paula, jt. illus. see Zima, Gordon.

Zima, Siegfried, jt. illus. see Benchimol, Brigitte.

Zimanski, Anne. Babbling Beth the Story Chef: And the Berry Awesome Recipe. Freckles, Lauren. 2019. (Babbling Beth the Story Chef Ser.: Vol. 2). (ENG.). 34p. (J). (gr. k-3). 24.99 ***(978-0-9972386-0-0(7))*** Franklin, Lauren.

Zimanski, Anne. Babbling Beth the Story Chef: Superhero Recipe. Freckles, Lauren. 2017. (Babbling Beth the Story Chef Ser.). (ENG.). (J). (gr. k-3). 21.99 *(978-0-9972386-2-4(3))*; pap. 17.99 *(978-0-9972386-1-7(5))* Franklin, Lauren.

Zimdars, Jason. Prince Martin & the Cave Bear: Two Kids, Colossal Courage, & a Classic Quest. Hale, Brandon. 2019. (Prince Martin Epic Ser.: Vol. 4). (ENG.). 174p. (J). (gr. 2-4). 29.99 *(978-1-7321278-6-9(7))*; pap. 11.99 *(978-1-7321278-7-6(5))* Band of Brothers Bks.

—Prince Martin & the Dragons: A Classic Adventure Book about a Boy, a Knight, & the True Meaning of Loyalty. Hale, Brandon. 2018. (Prince Martin Epic Ser.: Vol. 3). (ENG.). 100p. (J). (gr. 1-4). 21.99 *(978-1-7321278-3-8(2))*; pap. 9.99 *(978-1-7321278-2-1(4))* Band of Brothers Bks.

Zimdars, Jason. Prince Martin & the Last Centaur: A Tale of Two Brothers, a Courageous Kid, & the Duel for the Desert. Hale, Brandon. 2020. (Prince Martin Epic Ser.: Vol. 5). (ENG.). 194p. (J). (gr. 3-5). 28.99 ***(978-1-7321278-9-0(1))***; pap. 13.99 ***(978-1-7321278-8-3(3))*** Band of Brothers Bks.

Zimdars, Jason. Prince Martin & the Thieves: A Brave Boy, a Valiant Knight, & a Timeless Tale of Courage & Compassion. Hale, Brandon. 2018. (Prince Martin Epic Ser.: Vol. 2). (ENG.). 94p. (J). (gr. 1-3). 21.99 *(978-1-7321278-5-2(9))* Band of Brothers Bks.

—Prince Martin & the Thieves: A Brave Boy, a Valiant Knight, & a Timeless Tale of Courage & Compassion (Grayscale Art Edition) Hale, Brandon. 2018. (ENG.). 94p. (J). pap. 7.99 *(978-1-7321278-1-4(6))* Band of Brothers Bks.

—Prince Martin Wins His Sword: A Classic Tale about a Boy Who Discovers the True Meaning of Courage, Grit, & Friendship. Hale, Brandon. 2018. (Prince Martin Epic Ser.: Vol. 1). (ENG.). 56p. (J). (gr. k-3). 21.79 *(978-1-7321278-4-5(0))* Band of Brothers Bks.

—Prince Martin Wins His Sword: A Classic Tale about a Boy Who Discovers the True Meaning of Courage, Grit, & Friendship (Grayscale Art Edition) Hale, Brandon. 2018. (ENG.). 56p. (J). (gr. 3-7). pap. 7.99 *(978-1-7321278-0-7(8))* Band of Brothers Bks.

Zimenka, Leila. The Bedtime Battle. Nelson, M. R. 2018. (ENG.). 32p. (J). (gr. -1-3). pap. 9.99 *(978-1-5324-0820-5(X))* Xist Publishing.

Zimmer, Dirk. An I Can Read Halloween Treat, Set. HarperCollins Publishers Ltd. Staff et al. 2004. (I Can Read Bks.). (J). (gr. k-3). pap. 11.99 *(978-0-06-054237-5(3)*, Harper Trophy) HarperCollins Pubs.

—Jaap de Tuinman. Aardvark, Esperanza. 2006. (DUT.). 14.95 *(978-0-9766859-9-9(X))* Macaronic Pr.

Zimmer, Glenn. Baby's Bucket Book. McCloud, Carol. 2014. 16p. (J). (— 1). bds. 7.95 *(978-0-9960999-2-9(1))* Bucket Fillers, Inc.

—Bucket Filling from A to Z: The Key to Being Happy. McCloud, Carol & Butzke, Caryn. 2017. 32p. (J). (gr. -1-4). pap. 9.95 *(978-0-9974864-3-8(0))* Bucket Fillers, Inc.

—Buckets, Dippers, & Lids: Secrets to Your Happiness. McCloud, Carol. 2018. (ENG.). 48p. (J). (gr. 2-8). pap. 10.95 *(978-1-945369-01-8(9))* Bucket Fillers, Inc.

—Dollars & Sense. Deutsch, Tehilla. 2012. 36p. (J). 12.95 *(978-1-929628-65-0(X))* Hachai Publishing.

—There Is a Reason Why. Soban Biniashvili, Freidele Galya. 2016. (ENG.). 38p. (J). 12.95 *(978-1-929628-90-2(0))* Hachai Publishing.

Zimmer, Kevin. Buster the Little Garbage Truck. Berneger, Marcia. 2015. (ENG.). 32p. (J). (gr. -1-1). 14.99 *(978-1-58536-894-5(6)*, 203814) Sleeping Bear Pr.

—Mr. Goat's Valentine. Bunting, Eve. 2016. (ENG.). 32p. (J). (gr. k-2). 16.99 *(978-1-58536-944-7(6)*, 204024) Sleeping Bear Pr.

—Troo Makes a Big Splash, 1 vol. Crouch, Cheryl. 2011. (I Can Read! / Rainforest Friends Ser.). (ENG.). 32p. (J). (gr. -1-2). pap. 4.99 *(978-0-310-71810-9(4))* Zonderkidz.

—Troo's Big Climb, 1 vol. Crouch, Cheryl. 2011. (I Can Read! / Rainforest Friends Ser.). (ENG.). 32p. (J). (gr. -1-2). pap. 4.99 *(978-0-310-71808-6(2))* Zonderkidz.

—Troo's Secret Clubhouse, 1 vol. Crouch, Cheryl. 2011. (I Can Read! / Rainforest Friends Ser.). (ENG.). 32p. (J). (gr. -1-2). pap. 4.99 *(978-0-310-71809-3(0))* Zonderkidz.

Zimmer, Kevin J. Otter & Owl & the Big Ah-Choo!, 1 vol. Zondervan Staff & Bowman, Crystal. 2008. (I Can Read! / Otter & Owl Ser.). (ENG.). 32p. (J). pap. 4.99 *(978-0-310-71705-8(1))* Zonderkidz.

—Otter & Owl Say I'm Sorry, 1 vol. Bowman, Crystal. 2008. (I Can Read! / Otter & Owl Ser.). (ENG.). 32p. (J). pap. 4.99 *(978-0-310-71707-2(8))* Zonderkidz.

—Otter & Owl's Helpful Hike, 1 vol. Bowman, Crystal. 2008. (I Can Read! / Otter & Owl Ser.). (ENG.). 32p. (J). pap. 4.99 *(978-0-310-71704-1(3))*; pap. 4.99 *(978-0-310-71706-5(X))* Zonderkidz.

Zimmerman, Andrea & Clemesha, David. All Buckled Up. Zimmerman, Andrea. 2019. (ENG.). 28p. (J). (gr. -1-k). bds. 8.99 *(978-1-5344-3868-2(8)*, Little Simon) Little Simon.

—Digger Man. Zimmerman, Andrea & Clemesha, David. 2016. (Digger Man Ser.: 1). (ENG.). 32p. (J). bds. 7.99 *(978-1-62779-444-2(1)*, 900150728, Holt, Henry & Co. Bks. For Young Readers) Holt, Henry & Co.

—Digger Man. Zimmerman, Andrea & Clemesha, David. 2007. (Digger Man Ser.: 1). (ENG.). 32p. (J). (gr. -1-k). pap. 7.99 *(978-0-8050-8203-6(4)*, 900040876) Square Fish.

—Train Man. Zimmerman, Andrea & Clemesha, David. 2017. (Digger Man Ser.: 3). (ENG.). 32p. (J). bds. 8.99 *(978-1-62779-504-3(9)*, 900152958, Holt, Henry & Co. Bks. For Young Readers) Holt, Henry & Co.

Zimmerman, Andrea, jt. illus. see Clemesha, David.

Zimmerman, Edith Fay Martin & Kanagy, Audrey Ann Zimmerman. Little Bear Builds a Wigwam. Stoltzfus, Sherman Matthew. 2010. 32p. (J). *(978-0-9646590-2-5(6))* J&M Publishing.

Zimmerman, Kadie. Have You Ever Seen a Bear with a Purple Smile? Budds, Laura. 2013. 16p. (J). 16.95 *(978-1-59152-114-3(9))* Farcountry Pr.

Zimmerman, Louis. That's Bingzy! Busy Building Self-Esteem. Richards, Arlene. 2007. 32p. (J). (gr. -1-3). 19.95 incl. audio compact disk *(978-0-9794323-4-7(0))* Bing Note, Inc.

Zimmerman, Rusty. Thunder Rolling down the Mountain: The Story of Chief Joseph & the Nez Perce, 1 vol. Biskup, Agnieszka. (American Graphic Ser.). (ENG.). 32p. (gr. 3-9). 2011. (J). pap. 8.10 *(978-1-4296-6270-3(0))*; 2011. pap. 47.70 *(978-1-4296-6437-0(1)*, Capstone Pr.); 2010. (J). lib. bdg. 31.32 *(978-1-4296-5472-2(4))* Capstone.

Zimmerman, Suzanne. God's Precious Gift. Mast, Dorcas R. 2011. 107p. (J). pap. *(978-0-7399-2429-7(X))* Rod & Staff Pubs., Inc.

Zimmerman, T. W. The Day the Horse Was Free. Dodgson, Y. K. rev. ed. 2005. 24p. (J). 11.95 *(978-0-9748091-1-3(X))* Alaska Avenue Pr.

Ziner, Amie. There Once Was a Sky Full of Stars. Crelin, Bob. 2005. 36p. pap. 12.95 *(978-1-931559-04-1(X))* Sky Publishing.

Zinn, Alarna. Ruby Who? Bartholomew, Andrew & Bartholomew, Hailey. 2012. 40p. pap. *(978-0-9876653-0-0(8))* Pause for Effect Ltd.

Zinsmeister, Elke. Ten Fat Sausages. 2006. (Classic Books with Holes Big Book Ser.). 16p. (J). (gr. -1-3). spiral bd. *(978-1-84643-008-4(9))* Child's Play International Ltd.

Ziolkowski, Ania. Goodnight, Boone. Collins, Yozette Yogi & Jennings, Marlis. 2012. 24p. pap. 11.95 *(978-1-937376-18-5(4))* All Star Pr.

Zipperer, Susan Johnson. Esmerelda the Silly Goose. Childress, Mildred Tickfer. 2004. 52p. (J). (gr. -1-3). 11.95 *(978-1-887774-17-8(3)*, Wynden) Canmore Pr.

Zircher, Patrick, et al. Secret Avengers by Rick Remender: the Complete Collection. 2019. (ENG.). 384p. (YA). (gr. 8-17). pap. 34.99 *(978-1-302-91643-5(2))* Marvel Worldwide, Inc.

Ziss, Debra. Be Healthy! It's a Girl Thing: Food, Fitness, & Feeling Great. Jukes, Mavis et al. 2003. (ENG.). 128p. (J). (gr. 3-7). pap. 12.99 *(978-0-679-89029-4(7)*, Knopf Bks. for Young Readers) Random Hse. Children's Bks.

—Dolphin's Big Leap. Weinberger, Kimberly. 2003. (Hello Reader! Ser.). 30p. (J). *(978-0-439-44159-9(5))* Scholastic, Inc.

Zitnak, Allison Day. The Happiness of Being Me: An A-Z Owners Manual, 1 vol. DuBois, Juli. 2009. 47p. pap. 24.95 *(978-1-60749-613-7(5))* America Star Bks.

Zito, Francesco. Leaves. Lawrence, Carol. 2018. (Baby Explorer Ser.). (ENG.). 24p. (J). bds. 6.99 *(978-0-8075-0516-8(1)*, 807505161) Whitman, Albert & Co.

—Santa's Workshop: Chunky Lift a Flap Board Book. Berry Byrd, Holly. Cottage Door Press, ed. 2017. (Chunky Lift-A-Flap Board Book Ser.). (ENG.). 12p. (J). (gr. -1-k). bds. 7.99 *(978-1-68052-229-7(9)*, 1002150) Cottage Door Pr.

—Water. Lawrence, Carol. 2018. (Baby Explorer Ser.). (ENG.). 24p. (J). bds. 6.99 *(978-0-8075-0517-5(X)*, 080750517X) Whitman, Albert & Co.

Zito, Francesco & Zhing, Amy. Bugs. Lawrence, Carol. 2019. (Baby Explorer Ser.). (ENG.). 24p. (J). (gr. -1 — 1). bds. 6.99 *(978-0-8075-0522-9(6)*, 807505226) Whitman, Albert & Co.

—Rocks. Lawrence, Carol. 2019. (Baby Explorer Ser.). (ENG.). 24p. (J). (gr. -1 — 1). bds. 6.99 *(978-0-8075-0523-6(4)*, 807505234) Whitman, Albert & Co.

Zittel, Michael. The Philistine: Anthology/Chronology, 1 book. Mongillo, Michael. 2003. 216p. (YA). pap. 24.95 *(978-0-9743086-0-9(9))* United Comics.

Zivoin, Jennifer. Ahoy, Ghost Ship Ahead! James, Brian. 2007. (Pirate School Ser.: 2). 64p. (J). (gr. 1-3). pap. 3.99 *(978-0-448-44625-7(1)*, Grosset & Dunlap) Penguin Young Readers Group.

—Ahoy, Ghost Ship Ahead! James, Brian. 2009. (Pirate School Ser.: No. 2). (ENG.). 64p. (J). (gr. 2-4). 27.07 *(978-1-59961-583-7(5)*, 12626, Chapter Bks.) Spotlight.

Zivoin, Jennifer. Algo Pasa en Mi Ciudad: Un Relato Sobre la Injusticia y el Racismo. Celano, Marianne et al. 2020. (SPA.). 32p. (J). (gr. k-2). 18.95 ***(978-84-16470-03-7(0))*** Fineo Editorial, S.L. ESP. Dist: Independent Pubs. Group.

Zivoin, Jennifer. All My Stripes: A Story for Children with Autism. Rudolph, Shaina & Royer, Danielle. 2014. (J). pap. *(978-1-4338-1917-9(1)*, Magination Pr.) American Psychological Assn.

—Attack on the High Seas! #3, No. 3. James, Brian. 2007. (Pirate School Ser.: 3). 64p. (J). (gr. 1-3). pap. 3.99 *(978-0-448-44645-5(6)*, Grosset & Dunlap) Penguin Young Readers Group.

—Big Red & the Little Bitty Wolf: A Tale about Bullies. Ransom, Jeanie Franz. 2016. 32p. (J). *(978-1-4338-2048-9(X)*, Magination Pr.) American Psychological Assn.

—Camp Buccaneer. James, Brian. 2009. (Pirate School Ser.: No. 6). (ENG.). 64p. (J). (gr. 2-4). 27.07 *(978-1-59961-587-5(8)*, 12630, Chapter Bks.) Spotlight.

—The Curse of Snake Island. James, Brian. 2007. (Pirate School Ser.: 1). 64p. (J). (gr. 1-3). pap. 3.99 *(978-0-448-44574-8(3)*, Grosset & Dunlap) Penguin Young Readers Group.

—Did You Hear? A Story about Gossip. Sileo, Frank J. 2017. 32p. (J). *(978-1-4338-2720-4(4)*, Magination Pr.) American Psychological Assn.

—Fantastic You. Dufayet, Danielle. 2019. (J). *(978-1-4338-3028-0(0)*, Magination Pr.) American Psychological Assn.

—Port of Spies. James, Brian. 2007. (Pirate School Ser.: 4). 64p. (J). (gr. 1-3). pap. 3.99 *(978-0-448-44646-2(4)*, Grosset & Dunlap) Penguin Young Readers Group.

—Port of Spies. James, Brian. 2009. (Pirate School Ser.: No. 4). (ENG.). 64p. (J). (gr. 2-4). 27.07 *(978-1-59961-585-1(1)*, 12628, Chapter Bks.) Spotlight.

—Something Happened in Our Town: A Child's Story about Racial Injustice. Celano, Marianne et al. 2018. 32p. (J). *(978-1-4338-2854-6(5)*, Magination Pr.) American Psychological Assn.

—Treasure Trouble. James, Brian. 2009. (Pirate School Ser.: No. 5). (ENG.). 64p. (J). (gr. 2-4). 27.07 *(978-1-59961-586-8(X)*, 12629, Chapter Bks.) Spotlight.

—We Both Read-Jack & the Toddler. McKay, Sindy. 2011. (ENG.). 44p. (J). 9.95 *(978-1-60115-249-7(3))*; pap. 4.99 *(978-1-60115-250-3(7))* Treasure Bay, Inc.

—A World of Pausabilities: An Exercise in Mindfulness. Sileo, Frank J. 2017. 32p. (J). *(978-1-4338-2323-7(3)*, Magination Pr.) American Psychological Assn.

—You Are Your Strong: Coping with Big Emotions. Dufayet, Danielle. 2019. (J). *(978-1-4338-2939-0(8)*, Magination Pr.) American Psychological Assn.

Zlatic, Tomislav. Little Bears Go Shopping. Maisner, Heather. 2015. (J). *(978-1-4351-6516-8(0))* Barnes & Noble, Inc.

—Runny Honey. Clarke, Jane. 2008. (Tadpoles Ser.). (ENG.). 24p. (J). (gr. -1-3). pap. *(978-0-7787-3893-0(0))*; lib. bdg. *(978-0-7787-3862-6(0))* Crabtree Publishing Co.

—The Three Little Pigs & the New Neighbor. Blackford, Andy. 2014. (Tadpoles: Fairytale Twists Ser.). (ENG.). 32p. (J). (gr. 1-2). (978-0-7787-0447-8(5)); pap. (978-0-7787-0482-9(3)) Crabtree Publishing Co.

Zmiycharova, Gergana. Is Heaven Boring? Lowery, Allison P. Tate, Angela R., ed. 2017. (ENG.). 26p. (J). pap. 6.99 (978-1-5481-0409-2(4)) CreateSpace Independent Publishing Platform.

Zmora, Avram. Shabbos, Shabbos I Love You. Lieberman, Naomi. Rosenfeld, D. L., ed. 2013. (ENG.). 32p. (J). 10.95 (978-1-929628-70-4(6)) Hachai Publishing.

Zoavo, Giulia. Experiment with Outdoor Science. Arnold, Nick. 2020. (STEAM Ahead Ser.). (ENG.). 80p. (J). (gr. 3-4). pap. 14.95 **(978-0-7112-4397-2(2)**, 328364, QED Publishing) Quarto Publishing Group UK GBR. Dist: Hachette UK Distribution.

Zoells, Darcy Day. When God Gave Us Words. Sasso, Sandy Eisenberg. 2018. (ENG.). 40p. (J). (gr. -1-3). 16.00 (978-1-947888-01-2(3), Flyaway Bks.) Westminster John Knox Pr.

Zollars, Jaime. Cakes & Miracles: A Purim Tale, 0 vols. Goldin, Barbara Diamond. 2010. (ENG.). 32p. (J). (gr. 1-3). 17.99 (978-0-7614-5701-5(1), 9780761457015, Two Lions) Amazon Publishing.

—Enter a Glossy Web. Ruebush, McKenna. 2016. (ENG.). 400p. (YA). 16.99 (978-1-62779-370-4(4), 900148126, Holt, Henry & Co. Bks. For Young Readers) Holt, Henry & Co.

—Foxheart. Legrand, Claire. 2016. (ENG.). 480p. (J). (gr. 3-7). 16.99 (978-0-06-242773-1(3), Greenwillow Bks.) HarperCollins Pubs.

—Greenglass House. Milford, Kate. (Greenglass House Ser.). (ENG.). (J). (gr. 5-7). 2016. 400p. pap. 7.99 (978-0-544-54028-6(X), 1608839, HMH Books For Young Readers); 2014. 384p. 18.99 (978-0-544-05270-3(6), 1533148) Houghton Mifflin Harcourt Publishing Co.

—Not in Room 204: Breaking the Silence of Abuse. Riggs, Shannon. 2017. (ENG.). 32p. (J). (-3). pap. 7.99 (978-0-8075-5766-2(8), 807557668) Whitman, Albert & Co.

—The Shabbat Puppy, 0 vols. Kimmelman, Leslie. 2012. (ENG.). 32p. (J). (gr. -1-3). 17.99 (978-0-7614-6145-6(0), 9780761461456, Two Lions) Amazon Publishing.

—Tom's Midnight Garden. Pearce, Philippa. 2018. (ENG.). 320p. (J). (gr. 3-7). pap. 7.99 (978-0-06-269658-8(0), Greenwillow Bks.) HarperCollins Pubs.

—The Truth about Dragons. 2019. (J). (978-0-316-48147-2(5)) Little Brown & Co.

—Wicked Nix. Coakley, Lena. (ENG.). (J). (gr. 3-7). 2019. 176p. pap. 8.99 (978-1-4197-3703-9(1)); 2018. 160p. 16.99 (978-1-4197-2869-3(5)) Abrams, Inc. (Amulet Bks.).

Zoller, Jayson D. The Best Pet. Seagreaves, Kelly E. l.t. ed. 2004. 29p. (J). lib. bdg. 14.95 (978-1-932338-56-0(X)); per. 8.99 (978-1-932338-53-9(5)) Lifevest Publishing, Inc.

Zolotić, Aleksandar. Pleased to Eat You: Book 3. Gohmann, Johanna. 2018. (Electric Zombie Ser.). (ENG.). 112p. (J). (gr. 2-5). lib. bdg. 29.93 (978-1-5321-3363-3(4), 31149, Calico Chapter Bks.) ABDO Publishing Co.

Zolotic, Aleksandar. Collins Big Cat Phonics for Letters & Sounds - Watch Out, Nebit!: Band 06/Orange, Bd. 6. Dale, Katie. 2018. (Collins Big Cat Phonics Ser.). (ENG.). 24p. (J). (gr. 1-2). pap. 6.99 (978-0-00-825172-7(X)) HarperCollins Pubs. Ltd. GBR. Dist: Independent Pubs. Group.

—The Creepy Doll: An Up2U Horror Adventure. Varlow, Scarlet. 2017. (Up2U Adventures Set 3 Ser.). (ENG.). 80p. (J). (gr. 2-5). lib. bdg. 29.93 (978-1-5321-3029-8(5), 25506, Calico Chapter Bks.) ABDO Publishing Co.

—Shazam!: a Shazam Showdown. West, Alexandra. 2019. (I Can Read Level 3 Ser.). (ENG.). 32p. (J). (gr. -1-3). pap. 4.99 (978-0-06-289863-0(9)) HarperCollins Pubs.

—Way Too Many Latkes: A Hanukkah in Chelm. Glaser, Linda. 2017. (ENG.). 32p. (J). (gr. -1-2). 17.99 (978-1-5124-2092-0(1), 9781512420920, Kar-Ben Publishing) Lerner Publishing Group.

Zolotic, Aleksander. George & Grace Find an Egg. Jenkins, Amanda. 2017. (Text Connections Guided Close Reading Ser.). (J). (gr. 2). (978-1-4900-1846-1(8)) Benchmark Education Co.

—Mama Kisses, Papa Hugs. Bergren, Lisa Tawn. 2020. (ENG.). 40p. (J). (gr. -1-2). 11.99 (978-0-525-65409-4(7), WaterBrook Pr.) Crown Publishing Group, The.

—Saving Squirt. Freed, Kira. 2017. (Text Connections Guided Close Reading Ser.). (J). (gr. 2). (978-1-4900-1834-8(4)) Benchmark Education Co.

Zoloti¿, Aleksandar. Knock 'Em Dead, Bk. 4. Gohmann, Johanna. 2018. (Electric Zombie Ser.). (ENG.). 112p. (J). (gr. 2-5). lib. bdg. 29.93 (978-1-5321-3364-0(2), 31151, Calico Chapter Bks.) ABDO Publishing Co.

—Lurching to the Beat, Bk. 1. Gohmann, Johanna. 2018. (Electric Zombie Ser.). (ENG.). 112p. (J). (gr. 2-5). lib. bdg. 29.93 (978-1-5321-3361-9(8), 31145, Calico Chapter Bks.) ABDO Publishing Co.

—Shock & Roll, Bk. 2. Gohmann, Johanna. 2018. (Electric Zombie Ser.). (ENG.). 112p. (J). (gr. 2-5). lib. bdg. 29.93 (978-1-5321-3362-6(6), 31147, Calico Chapter Bks.) ABDO Publishing Co.

Zommer, Yuval. The Skies above My Eyes. Guillain, Charlotte. 2018. (Look Closer Ser.). (ENG.). 20p. (J). (gr. -1-2). 24.95 **(978-1-910277-69-0(X)**, Words & Pictures) Quarto Publishing Group UK GBR. Dist: Hachette Bk. Group.

—The Street Beneath My Feet. Guillain, Charlotte. 2017. (Look Closer Ser.). (ENG.). 20p. (J). (gr. k-3). 24.95 **(978-1-68297-136-9(8)**, Words & Pictures) Quarto Publishing Group UK GBR. Dist: Hachette Bk. Group.

Zommer, Yuval. The Big Blue Thing on the Hill. Zommer, Yuval. 2015. (ENG.). 32p. (J). (gr. -1-2). 16.99 (978-0-7636-7403-8(6), Templar) Candlewick Pr.

—Big Brown Bear's Cave. Zommer, Yuval. 2018. (ENG.). 32p. (J). (gr. -1-2). 16.99 (978-0-7636-9646-7(3), Templar) Candlewick Pr.

—One Hundred Bones. Zommer, Yuval. 2016. (ENG.). 32p. (J). (gr. -1-2). 16.99 (978-0-7636-8183-8(0), Templar) Candlewick Pr.

Zong, Grace. Four Peppy Puppies. Diesen, Deborah. 2018. (ENG.). 32p. (J). (gr. -1-2). 16.99 (978-1-58536-386-5(3), 204408) Sleeping Bear Pr.

—Goldy Luck & the Three Pandas. Yim, Natasha. 32p. (J). (gr. -1-3). 2015. pap. 7.95 (978-1-58089-653-5(7)); 2014. lib. bdg. 16.95 (978-1-58089-652-8(9)) Charlesbridge Publishing, Inc.

—Mrs. Mcbee Leaves Room 3, 1 vol. McLellan, Gretchen Brandenberg. 2017. (ENG.). 32p. (J). (gr. -1-2). 16.95 (978-1-56145-944-5(5)) Peachtree Publishing Co. Inc.

—Nixie Ness: Cooking Star. Mills, Claudia. 2019. (After-School Superstars Ser.: 1). 144p. (J). (gr. 2-5). 15.99 (978-0-8234-4093-1(1), Margaret Ferguson Books) Holiday Hse., Inc.

—Our Food. Lin, Grace & McKneally, Ranida T. 2016. 40p. (J). (gr. k-3). lib. bdg. 16.95 (978-1-58089-590-3(5)) Charlesbridge Publishing, Inc.

—Our Food: A Healthy Serving of Science & Poems. Lin, Grace & McKneally, Ranida T. 2018. 40p. (J). (gr. k-3). pap. 7.99 (978-1-58089-591-0(3)) Charlesbridge Publishing, Inc.

—Vera Vance: Comics Star. Mills, Claudia. 2020. (After-School Superstars Ser.: 2). 128p. (J). (gr. 2-5). 15.99 (978-0-8234-4094-8(X), Margaret Ferguson Books) Holiday Hse., Inc.

Zong, Louie. Test This Book! A Laugh-Out-loud Picture Book about Experiments & Science! Zong, Louie. 2020. (ENG.). 32p. (J). 17.99 (978-1-250-22580-1(9), 900208639) Imprint IND. Dist: Macmillan.

Zonneveld, Famke. Waldorf Alphabet Book, 1 vol. 2005. (ENG.). 54p. (J). (gr. 4-7). per. 12.95 (978-0-88010-559-0(3), Bell Pond Bks.) SteinerBooks, Inc.

—What Julianna Could See, 1 vol. Margulies, Paul. 2004. (ENG.). 32p. (J). pap. 11.95 (978-0-88010-515-6(1)) SteinerBooks, Inc.

Zonta, Rose. The Greenhouse Kids: Dan Dellon's Secret. Awad, Shelley. 2009. 127p. (J). pap. (978-0-88887-379-8(4)) Borealis Pr.

Zoo, Keith. Code This Game! Make Your Game Using Python, Then Break Your Game to Create a New One! Ray, Meg & Odd Dot. 2019. (ENG.). 320p. (J). 24.99 (978-1-250-30669-2(8), 900197844, Odd Dot) St. Martin's Pr.

Zoo, Keith. Show-How Guides: Friendship Bracelets: The 10 Essential Bracelets Everyone Should Know! Zoo, Keith. Odd Dot. 2020. (Show-How Guides). (ENG.). 48p. (J). pap. 5.99 (978-1-250-24996-8(1), 900215057, Odd Dot) St. Martin's Pr.

—Show-How Guides: Hair Braiding: The 9 Essential Braids Everyone Should Know! Zoo, Keith. Odd Dot. 2020. (Show-How Guides). (ENG.). 48p. (J). pap. 5.99 (978-1-250-24997-5(X), 900215058, Odd Dot) St. Martin's Pr.

—Show-How Guides: Knots: The 20 Essential Knots Everyone Should Know! Zoo, Keith. Odd Dot. 2020. (Show-How Guides). (ENG.). 48p. (J). pap. 5.99 (978-1-250-24995-1(3), 900215056, Odd Dot) St. Martin's Pr.

—Show-How Guides: Paper Airplanes: The 11 Essential Planes Everyone Should Know! Zoo, Keith. Odd Dot. 2020. (Show-How Guides). (ENG.). 48p. (J). pap. 5.99 (978-1-250-24994-4(5), 900215055, Odd Dot) St. Martin's Pr.

—Tiny World: Pins! Zoo, Keith. Odd Dot. 2019. (Tiny World Ser.: 2). (ENG.). 32p. (J). pap. 14.99 (978-1-250-20384-7(8), 900200607, Odd Dot) St. Martin's Pr.

Zorat, Maurizio. Checked. Kadohata, Cynthia. 2018. (ENG.). 416p. (J). (gr. 5-9). 17.99 (978-1-4814-4661-7(4), Atheneum/Caitlyn Dlouhy Books) Simon & Schuster Children's Publishing.

Zornow, Jeff. Werewolf, 1 vol. Zornow, Jeff. 2007. (Graphic Horror Ser.). (ENG.). 32p. (J). (gr. 3-6). 29.93 (978-1-60270-062-8(1), 9078, Graphic Planet - Fiction) Magic Wagon.

Zoromski, Ariel & Zoromski, Leia. Do You Know Bailey? Strojny, Shelley. 2016. (ENG.). (J). (gr. 1-6). pap. 11.00 (978-1-943331-42-0(1)) Orange Hat Publishing.

Zoromski, Leia, jt. illus. see Zoromski, Ariel.

Zorvoc, Karen. Adaya Solves the Case of the Missing Easter Rabbit: A Saskatchewan Fairy Tale. 4 Paws Games and Publishing, ed. 2019. (Adaya Ser.: Vol. 1). (ENG.). 42p. (J). pap. (978-1-988345-92-5(8)) Caswell, Vickianne.

Zosienka. The Moon Keeper. Zosienka. 2020. (ENG.). 40p. (J). (gr. -1-3). 17.99 (978-0-06-295952-2(2), HarperCollins) HarperCollins Pubs. Ltd. GBR. Dist: HarperCollins Pubs.

Zoto, Gabriel Q., jt. illus. see Zoto, Maximus B.

Zoto, Maximus B. & Zoto, Gabriel Q. The Gauntlet. Zoto, Sandra D. C. 2020. (ENG.). 20p. (J). **(978-1-5255-7417-7(5))**; pap. **(978-1-5255-7418-4(3))** FriesenPress.

Zou, Bridgette. Norman & the Nom Nom Factory. Zou, Bridgette. 2018. (ENG.). 32p. (J). (gr. -1-3). 18.99 (978-1-63592-032-1(9), StarBerry) Astra Publishing Hse.

Zourelias, Diana. A First Sudoku Book. Pazzelli, John. 2006. (Dover Children's Activity Bks.). (ENG.). 64p. (J). (gr. 3-8). per. 3.95 (978-0-486-45074-2(0), 450740) Dover Pubns., Inc.

—Kids' Kakuro. Pazzelli, John. 2006. (Dover Children's Activity Bks.). (ENG.). 62p. (J). (gr. 3). per. 5.95 (978-0-486-45344-6(8)) Dover Pubns., Inc.

Zourelias-Noro, Diane. The 1, 2, 3 Bees: A Counting Book. Wheldon, Nicole. 2005. 24p. (J). (gr. -1-7). 17.95 (978-0-9744792-1-7(7)) Acmon Blue Publishing.

Zowada, Timmy. Block Bad Sportsmanship: Short Stories on Becoming a Good Sport & Overcoming Bad Sportsmanship. Day, Sophia & Pearson, Kayla. 2019. (Help Me Become Ser.: 10). 76p. (J). (ENG.). 14.99 (978-1-64370-744-0(2), 1fe58256-a12b-4db6-baf8-a0bf042f39a4); pap. 9.99 (978-1-64370-745-7(0), f7a54c40-96fa-47a2-8926-cf88f3edcc42) MVP Kids Media.

—Limit Laziness: Short Stories on Becoming Diligent & Overcoming Laziness. Day, Sophia & Pearson, Kayla. 2019. (Help Me Become Ser.: 11). 76p. (J). 14.99 (978-1-64370-746-4(9), 1438b397-8930-4f42-b069-a51b9842cc47); (ENG.). pap. 9.99 (978-1-64370-747-1(7), 510614c8-e1dc-4552-af64-35a4c542c085) MVP Kids Media.

—Phase Out Forgetfulness: Short Stories on Becoming Responsible & Overcoming Forgetfulness. Day, Sophia & Pearson, Kayla. 2019. (Help Me Become Ser.: 9). 76p. (J). 14.99 (978-1-64370-742-6(6), a33f284c-80eb-46fa-82ce-e9672db3b480); pap. 9.99 (978-1-64370-743-3(4), 7b6548b5-dbbc-4e5e-849f-a5a09d182fbf) MVP Kids Media.

—Pick Your Promises: Short Stories on Becoming Dependable & Overcoming Breaking Promises. Day, Sophia & Pearson, Kayla. 2019. (Help Me Become Ser.: 12). 76p. (J). (ENG.). 14.99 (978-1-64370-748-8(5), 009d1993-929f-499f-a6f7-c6f5b6e502b7); pap. 9.99 (978-1-64370-749-5(3), cb60e884-24df-4d91-9f10-d30da5adb60d) MVP Kids Media.

—Stand down, Bullies. Day, Sophia & Pearson, Kayla. 2018. (Help Me Become Ser.: 6). (ENG.). 72p. (J). 14.99 (978-1-64255-233-1(X), 90936b2e-d32b-4891-83a1-9b9207b9bc9e) MVP Kids Media.

—Stand Together Against Bullying: Becoming a Hero & Overcoming Bullying Together. Day, Sophia & Pearson, Kayla. 2018. (Help Me Become Ser.: 5). (ENG.). 72p. (J). 14.99 (978-1-64255-232-4(1), 101b1088-1f5f-48b2-abb5-c528b4c0969e) MVP Kids Media.

—Stomp Out Selfishness: Short Stories on Becoming Considerate & Overcoming Selfishness. Day, Sophia & Pearson, Kayla. 2019. (Help Me Become Ser.: 1). 72p. (J). pap. 9.99 (978-1-64370-759-4(0), 86e77604-0f74-4db1-aa58-066d224c3f67) MVP Kids Media.

Zowada, Timothy. Lock up Lying: Short Stories on Becoming Honest & Overcoming Lying. Day, Sophia & Pearson, Kayla. 2020. (Help Me Become Ser.: 3). (ENG.). 76p. (J). pap. 9.99 (978-1-64204-796-7(1), c925b3e0-7afa-48b1-936f-a90a1d1ec26d) MVP Kids Media.

—Stand up to Bullies: Short Stories on Becoming Brave & Overcoming Being Bullied. Day, Sophia & Pearson, Kayla. 2019. (Help Me Become Ser.: 4). (ENG.). 76p. (J). pap. 9.99 (978-1-64204-795-0(3), f63a5db4-7a9b-4cf5-97d2-e070d8a8ce99) MVP Kids Media.

Zowada, Timothy, jt. illus. see Strouse, Stephanie.

Zraick, Robert, jt. illus. see Noon, Connie.

Zschock, Martha Day. Butterflies & Friends: An Art Activity Book for Adventurous Artists of All Ages. Conlon, Mara. 2009. (Scratch & Sketch Ser.). 64p. (J). (gr. 1). spiral bd., act. bk. ed. 12.99 (978-1-59359-841-9(6)) Peter Pauper Pr. Inc.

—Circus Scratch & Sketch: An Art Activity Book. Paulding, Barbara. 2009. (Scratch & Sketch Ser.). 64p. (J). (gr. -1). spiral bd. 14.99 (978-1-59359-832-7(7)) Peter Pauper Pr. Inc.

—Monsters: An Art Activity Book for Creative Kids of All Ages. Nemmers, Lee. 2013. (Scratch & Sketch Ser.). (ENG.). 64p. (J). (gr. k). spiral bd. 12.99 (978-1-4413-1154-2(8)) Peter Pauper Pr. Inc.

—The Night Sky: Stories of the Stars (Bedtime Shadow Book) Tunnell, Amber. 2014. (ENG.). 7p. (J). 12.99 (978-1-4413-1581-6(0), 9781441315816) Peter Pauper Pr. Inc.

—No Monsters Here! A Bedtime Shadow Book. Nemmers, Lee. 2015. (ENG.). 7p. (J). 12.99 (978-1-4413-1833-6(X), 9781441318336) Peter Pauper Pr. Inc.

—Pirates Scratch & Sketch: For Adventurous Artists & Explorers of All Ages. Nemmers, Tom. 2007. 64p. (J). 12.99 (978-1-59359-871-6(8)) Peter Pauper Pr. Inc.

—Scratch & Sketch Trace-Along Constellations: An Art Activity Book for Artistic Stargazers of All Ages. Nemmers, Lee. 2014. (ENG.). (J). (gr. k). 14.99 (978-1-4413-1726-1(0), 9781441317261) Peter Pauper Pr. Inc.

—Scratch & Sketch Trace-Along Doodle Mania: An Art Activity Book for Imaginative Artists of All Ages. Levy, Talia. 2014. (ENG.). (J). (gr. k). 14.99 (978-1-4413-1727-8(9), 9781441317278) Peter Pauper Pr. Inc.

—Scratch & Sketch Vikings: An Art Activity Book for Legendary Artists & Explorers of All Ages. Gandolfi, Claudine. 2015. (ENG.). 64p. (J). 12.99 (978-1-4413-1813-8(5), 9781441318138) Peter Pauper Pr. Inc.

—Spooky Scratch & Sketch: For Spooky Artists & Trick-or-Treaters of All Ages. 2007. (Scratch & Sketch sER.). 80p. (J). 12.99 (978-1-59359-881-5(5)) Peter Pauper Pr. Inc.

—Whoo's There? A Bedtime Shadow Book. Zschock, Heather. 2005. (Activity Book Ser.). 16p. (J). (gr. -1-4). 12.99 (978-1-59359-904-1(8)) Peter Pauper Pr. Inc.

Zschock, Martha Day. Journey Around Nantucket from A to Z. Zschock, Martha Day. 2008. (Journey Around... Ser.). 32p. (J). (gr. 1-6). 17.95 (978-1-933212-82-1(9), Commonwealth Editions) Applewood Bks.

Zubal, Lynn. Sonoran Desert Frog. Zubal, Lynn. 2011. (ENG.). 22p. (J). pap. 16.95 (978-1-59299-600-1(0)) Inkwater Pr.

Zubiat, Gabriel. De Mis Poemas Vividos. González Reyes, Amaury. Hernández, René Mario, ed. l.t. ed. 2003. (SPA.). 100p. (YA). pap. (978-1-931481-20-5(2)) LiArt-Literature & Art.

Zuckerberg, J. R. A Quick & Easy Guide to Queer & Trans Identities. G., Mady. 2019. (ENG.). 96p. (YA). pap. 9.99 (978-1-62010-586-3(1), Lion Forge) Oni Pr., Inc.

Zuckerman, Andrew, photos by. Creature Baby Animals. 2014. (ENG., 20p. (J). (gr. -1 — 1). bds. 7.99 (978-1-4521-1721-8(7)) Chronicle Bks. LLC.

—Creature Colors. 2014. (ENG., 20p. (J). (gr. -1 — 1). bds. 7.99 (978-1-4521-1668-6(7)) Chronicle Bks. LLC.

—Creature Sounds. 2014. (ENG., 20p. (J). (gr. -1 — 1). bds. 7.99 (978-1-4521-1722-5(5)) Chronicle Bks. LLC.

Zug, Mark. Darke. Sage, Angie. ed. 2012. (Septimus Heap Ser.: 6). (J). lib. bdg. 18.40 (978-0-606-26264-4(4)) Turtleback.

—Flyte. Sage, Angie. ed. 2007. (Septimus Heap Ser.: 2). 532p. (J). (gr. 4-7). lib. bdg. 18.40 (978-1-4178-1566-1(3)) Turtleback.

—Fyre. Sage, Angie. 2013. 702p. (J). (978-0-06-224697-4(6)) HarperCollins Pubs.

—Magyk. Sage, Angie. 2007. (Septimus Heap Ser.: Bk. 1). 564p. (gr. 4-7). 18.00 (978-0-7569-7760-3(6)) Perfection Learning Corp.

—Queste. Sage, Angie. ed. 2009. (Septimus Heap Ser.: 4). 596p. (J). lib. bdg. 18.40 (978-0-606-02607-9(X)) Turtleback.

—Septimus Heap, Set. Sage, Angie. 2007. (Septimus Heap Ser.: Bks. 1-2). (J). (gr. 4). pap. 15.99 (978-0-06-136195-1(X), Tegen, Katherine Bks) HarperCollins Pubs.

—Septimus Heap, Book Five: Syren. Sage, Angie. (Septimus Heap Ser.: 5). (ENG.). (J). (gr. 4). 2011. 656p. pap. 7.99 (978-0-06-088212-9(3)); 2009. 640p. lib. bdg. 18.89 (978-0-06-088211-2(5)); 2009. 640p. 17.99 (978-0-06-088210-5(7)) HarperCollins Pubs. (Tegen, Katherine Bks).

—Septimus Heap, Book Four: Queste. Sage, Angie. (Septimus Heap Ser.: 4). (ENG.). (J). (gr. 4). 2009. 624p. pap. 8.99 (978-0-06-088209-9(3)); 2008. 608p. 18.99 (978-0-06-088207-5(7)) HarperCollins Pubs. (Tegen, Katherine Bks).

—Septimus Heap, Book One: Magyk. Sage, Angie. (Septimus Heap Ser.: 1). (ENG.). (J). (gr. 4-18). 2005. 576p. 18.99 (978-0-06-057731-5(2)); 2005. 576p. lib. bdg. 18.89 (978-0-06-057732-2(0)); 2006. 608p. reprint ed. pap. 7.99 (978-0-06-057733-9(9)) HarperCollins Pubs. (Tegen, Katherine Bks).

—Septimus Heap, Book Seven: Fyre. Sage, Angie. 2013. (Septimus Heap Ser.: 7). (ENG.). 720p. (J). (gr. 3-7). 17.99 (978-0-06-124245-8(4), Tegen, Katherine Bks) HarperCollins Pubs.

—Septimus Heap, Book Six: Darke. Sage, Angie. (Septimus Heap Ser.: 6). (ENG.). 656p. (J). (gr. 4). 2012. pap. 7.99 (978-0-06-124244-1(6)); Bk. 6. 2011. 17.99 (978-0-06-124242-7(X)) HarperCollins Pubs. (Tegen, Katherine Bks).

—Septimus Heap, Book Three: Physik. Sage, Angie. (Septimus Heap Ser.: 3). (ENG.). (J). (gr. 4-7). 2007. 560p. 17.99 (978-0-06-057737-7(1)); Bk. 3. 2008. 576p. pap. 7.99 (978-0-06-057739-1(8)) HarperCollins Pubs. (Tegen, Katherine Bks).

—Septimus Heap, Book Two: Flyte. Sage, Angie. (Septimus Heap Ser.: 2). (ENG.). 544p. (J). (gr. 4-7). 2007. pap. 7.99 (978-0-06-057736-0(3)); 2006. 17.99 (978-0-06-057734-6(7)) HarperCollins Pubs. (Tegen, Katherine Bks).

—Septimus Heap: the Magykal Papers. Sage, Angie. 2009. (Septimus Heap Ser.). (ENG.). 176p. (J). (gr. 3-7). 17.99 (978-0-06-170416-1(4), Tegen, Katherine Bks) HarperCollins Pubs.

—The Seven Keys of Balabad. Haven, Paul. 2010. (ENG.). 288p. (J). (gr. 4-6). lib. bdg. 21.19 (978-0-375-93350-9(6)) Random House Publishing Group.

—Swordbird. Fan, Nancy Yi. 2008. (Swordbird Ser.: 1). (ENG.). 256p. (J). (gr. 3-7). pap. 6.99 (978-0-06-113101-1(6)) HarperCollins Pubs.

—Swordbird. Fan, Nancy Yi. 2007. (Swordbird Ser.). (J). (gr. 3-7). 219p. 15.99 (978-0-06-113099-1(0), HarperCollins); 217p. lib. bdg. 16.89 (978-0-06-113100-4(8)) HarperCollins Pubs.

—Todhunter Moon: Sandrider. Sage, Angie. ed. 2016. (Septimus Heap: TodHunter Moon Ser.: 2). (ENG.). 496p. (J). (gr. 3-7). 18.40 (978-0-606-39255-6(6)) Turtleback.

—TodHunter Moon, Book One: PathFinder. Sage, Angie. (World of Septimus Heap Ser.: 1). (ENG.). (J). (gr. 3-7). 2015. 496p. pap. 7.99 (978-0-06-227246-1(2)); 2014. 480p. 17.99 (978-0-06-227245-4(4)) HarperCollins Pubs. (Tegen, Katherine Bks).

—TodHunter Moon, Book Three: StarChaser. Sage, Angie. (World of Septimus Heap Ser.: 3). (ENG.). 496p. (J). (gr. 3-7). 2017. pap. 7.99 (978-0-06-227252-2(7)); 2016. 17.99 (978-0-06-227251-5(9)) HarperCollins Pubs. (Tegen, Katherine Bks).

—TodHunter Moon, Book Two: SandRider. Sage, Angie. 2015. (World of Septimus Heap Ser.: 2). (ENG.). 480p. (J). (gr. 3-7). 17.99 (978-0-06-227248-5(9), Tegen, Katherine Bks) HarperCollins Pubs.

Zuill, Andrea. Cat Dog Dog: The Story of a Blended Family. Buchet, Nelly. 2020. (ENG.). 40p. (J). (gr. -1-2). 17.99 (978-1-9848-4899-4(2)); lib. bdg. 20.99 (978-1-9848-4900-7(X)) Random Hse. Children's Bks. (Schwartz & Wade Bks.).

Zuill, Andrea. Wolf Camp. Zuill, Andrea. 40p. (J). (gr. -1-3). 2018. (ENG.). pap. 7.99 (978-1-9848-5165-9(9)); 2016. 17.99 (978-0-553-50912-0(8)) Random Hse. Children's Bks. (Schwartz & Wade Bks.).

Zulewski, Timothy. Four Friends Find Fun. Doyle, V. L. & Rohm, Robert. 2005. 32p. (J). 18.95 (978-0-9651672-4-6(0)) Eklektika Pr., Inc.

Zulkifli, Azhari. Islamic Manners. D'Oyen, Fatima. 2012. (ENG.). 64p. (J). (gr. -1-2). pap., act. bk. ed. 5.95 (978-0-86037-463-3(7)) Kube Publishing Ltd. GBR. Dist: Consortium Bk. Sales & Distribution.

Numeric

PUBLISHER NAME INDEX

Volume 3

10 Finger Pr., (*978-0-9728131; 978-1-933174*) 8435 Belize Pl., Wellington, FL 33414 USA Tel 561-434-9044; Toll Free: 866-7-author
E-mail: mahesh@10fingerspress.com
Web site: http://www.10fingerspress.com
Dist(s): **Independent Pubs. Group**
Midpoint Trade Bks., Inc.

10 To 2 Children's Bks., (*978-0-9849487; 978-0-615-74608-1; 978-0-615-74627-2; 978-0-615-79610-9; 978-0-615-79632-1; 978-0-615-84753-5; 978-0-615-87923-9*) P.O. Box 5173, Clinton, NJ 08809 USA Tel 610-570-4196
E-mail: darylkcobb@yahoo.com
Web site: http://www.darylcobb.com
Dist(s): **CreateSpace Independent Publishing Platform.**

100 Book Challenge *See* **American Reading Co.**

101 Bk. *Imprint of* **Michaelson Entertainment**

1105 West House, (*978-0-9976172*) P.O. Box 1835, McKinney, TX 75070 USA Tel 214-606-7735
E-mail: hello@knookerdoodle.com.

114th Aviation Co. Assn., (*978-0-9742465*) 15151 Berry Trail, Suite 403, Dallas, TX 75248-6319 USA
E-mail: steve@stibbens.com.

11th Hour Productions *See* **Twilight Tales, Inc.**

121 Pubns., (*978-0-9841931; 978-0-692-58320-3; 978-1-949356*) 13200 Shadow Mountain Dr., Saratoga, CA 95070 USA (SAN 858-690X)
E-mail: mattweber11@yahoo.com
Web site: http://www.121publications.com
Dist(s): **CreateSpace Independent Publishing Platform**
Independent Pubs. Group.

1212 Pr., (*978-0-9764985*) 1212 Beverley Rd., Brooklyn, NY 11218 USA Tel 718-462-4004
E-mail: rgistudio@earthlink.net.

12-Story Library *Imprint of* **Bookstaves, LLC**

12th Media Services, (*978-1-68092*) 3651 Peachtree Pkwy. Suite E275, Suwanee, GA 30024 USA
E-mail: tony.darnell@12thmedia.com.

13 Hands Pubns., (*978-0-9767260*) Div. Crooked Roads Productions, LLC, Orders Addr.: 914 Westwood Blvd., #518, Los Angeles, CA 90024 USA Fax: 310-388-6012
E-mail: mnaughton@earthlink.net
Web site: http://www.13handsonline.com; http://www.gildedhearse.com.

1-315-820-1714 *See* **Liber Publishing Hse.**

13th & Joan, (*978-0-9916015; 978-0-9985210; 978-0-9989702; 978-1-7322479; 978-1-7324712; 978-1-7326464; 978-1-7335154; 978-1-7331313; 978-1-7342346; 978-1-953156*) 205 N. Michigan Ave. Suite No. 810, Chicago, IL 60601 USA Tel 770-609-9833
E-mail: info@13thandjoan.com
Web site: www.13thandjoan.com.

1517 Publishing, (*978-1-945500; 978-1-945978; 978-1-948969*) Orders Addr.: 24701 Raymond Way, Spc 225, Lake Forest, CA 92630 USA (SAN 990-638X) Tel 949-748-0616
E-mail: ted@1517legacy.com; steve@1517legacy.com
Web site: http://www.1517legacy.com.

153 Fish Publishing, (*978-0-9747918*) 230 SW Railroad St., Sheridan, OR 97378-1745 USA.

1537 Pr., (*978-0-692-81624-0; 978-0-578-50588-6*) 1537 1/2 N Commonwealth Ave, Los Angeles, CA 90027 USA Tel 559-991-6031
E-mail: beckmedina@gmail.com
Web site: http://beckmedina.com.

1610 Media, LLC *See* **Appointed Media Group, LLC**

16th Avenue Pr., (*978-0-9742854*) P.O. Box 166, Portage, MI 49081 USA Fax: 269-372-6970
E-mail: theawrites@sbcglobal.net
Web site: http://www.fearnoflame.com.

16th Place Publishing, (*978-0-9745152*) 171 S. 16th Pl., Pocatello, ID 83201 USA
E-mail: brobergbook@yahoo.com
Web site: http://www.stoleninnocencebook.com.

1776 Pr., (*978-0-9825243*) 19 Coleman Rd., Wethersfield, CT 06109 USA.

1-800 ProColor, Incorporated *See* **Robertson Publishing**

1948, (*978-0-692-73934-1; 978-0-692-74533-5; 978-0-692-75287-6; 978-0-692-77028-3*) 333 jones Lester Rd., ROXBORO, NC 27574 USA Tel 336-599-8006.

1988 *See* **Sofija Zlatanova**

1989, (*978-0-578-45545-7*) 3333 Port Royale Dr. S., Ft. Lauderdale, FL 33308 USA Tel 954-591-6614
E-mail: bunnytrailseries@gmail.com.

1996, (*978-0-9998071*) Miramar RWay, BLDG 5112, San Diego, CA 92145 USA Tel 619-813-1254; Fax: 619-813-1254
E-mail: carloocaya15@yahoo.com.

1Ellipsis Press *See* **Ellipsis Pr.**

1st Impression Publishing, (*978-0-9763365*) P.O. Box 10339, Burbank, CA 91510-0339 USA Tel 818-843-1300; Fax: 818-846-5657
E-mail: sahysen@earthlink.net
Web site: http://www.1stimpressionpublishing.com.

1st World Library *See* **Groundbreaking Pr.**

1st World Library - Literary Society *Imprint of* **1st World Publishing, Inc.**

1st World Publishing *Imprint of* **1st World Publishing, Inc.**

1st World Publishing, Inc., (*978-0-9638502; 978-1-887472; 978-1-59540; 978-1-4218*) Orders Addr.: 1100 N. 4th St., Suite 9, Fairfield, IA 52556-2169 USA Toll Free: 877-209-5004; *Imprints:* 1st World Publishing (Frst Wrld Pub); 1st World Library - Literary Society (1st Wrld); Sunstar Publishing (SunstarPub)
E-mail: ed@1stworldpublishing.com; order@1stworldpublishing.com; info@1stworldpublishing.com; rodney@1stworldlibrary.org
Web site: http://www.1stworldpublishing.com
Dist(s): **Follett School Solutions**
Ingram Content Group
New Leaf Distributing Co., Inc.

1stBooks Library *See* **AuthorHouse**

1stWorld Library, Limited *See* **1st World Publishing, Inc.**

2 Donn Bks., (*978-0-9770893*) 11354 Links Dr., Reston, VA 20190-4807 USA (SAN 256-7407)
Web site: http://www.2donnbooks.com.

2018, (*978-1-7328064*) 4642 Rowell Point, Colorado Springs, CO 80923 USA Tel 719-491-0963
E-mail: batprime3986@gmail.com.

20/20 Publishing, (*978-0-9668718*) Orders Addr.: 3941 S. Bristol Suite D520, Santa Ana, CA 92704 USA Tel 800-991-3296
E-mail: dawn@dawnmartin.com
Web site: http://www.dawnmartin.com
Dist(s): **Distributors, The.**

2020 Vision Pr., (*978-0-9710675*) 2744 Crown Point, Las Cruces, NM 88011 USA Tel 505-532-9693; Fax: 505-532-9694
E-mail: josh@joshhunt.com
Web site: http://www.joshhunt.com.

20th Maine, Inc., (*978-0-9704408*) 859 Lawrence Rd., Pownal, ME 04069-6118 USA
E-mail: pat@20thmaine.com
Web site: http://www.20thmaine.com.

21st Century Pr., (*978-0-9660906; 978-0-9700639; 978-0-9717009; 978-0-9725719; 978-0-9728899; 978-0-9749811; 978-0-9766243; 978-0-9771964; 978-0-9779535; 978-0-9817769; 978-0-9824428; 978-0-9827616; 978-0-9838359; 978-0-9894317; 978-0-9911004; 978-0-9863864; 978-0-9981392; 978-1-951774) 3308 S. Meadowlark Ave., Springfield, MO 65807 USA Tel 417-889-4803; Fax: 417-889-2210; Toll Free: 800-658-0284; Imprints:* Sonship Press (Sonship Pr) Do not confuse with 21st Century Press in Southlake, TX
E-mail: lee@21stcenturypress.com
Web site: https://www.21stcenturypress.com
Dist(s): **Anchor Distributors**
Baker & Taylor Publisher Services (BTPS)
CreateSpace Independent Publishing Platform
Send The Light Distribution LLC
Two Rivers Distribution.

21st Century Pubs., (*978-0-9607298*) 1320 Curt Gowdy Dr., Cheyenne, WY 82009 USA (SAN 239-1740) Tel 307-638-2254
E-mail: chismaturi@prodigy.net
Web site: http://www.triplecrownwinnerearlsande.com
Dist(s): **Emery-Pratt Co.**
Blackwell.

21st Century Publishing Hse. (CHN) (*978-7-5391; 978-7-88861; 978-7-900386; 978-7-5568) Dist. by* **Chinasprout.**

22 West Bks., (*978-0-9767788*) Orders Addr.: P.O. Box 155, Sheldonville, MA 02070-0155 USA
E-mail: chris@22wb.com
Web site: http://www.22wb.com.

23andMe, (*978-0-9891537*) 1390 Shorebird Way, Mountain View, CA 94043 USA Tel 650-963-8948
E-mail: sryan@23andme.com
Web site: www.23andme.com
Dist(s): **Abrams, Inc.**
Hachette Bk. Group
Publishers Group West (PGW).

23rd St. Publishing, (*978-0-9800821*) Orders Addr.: P.O. Box 863734, Plano, TX 75086-3734 USA (SAN 855-1421) Tel 214-717-7244
E-mail: stacy@23rdstpublishing.com
Web site: http://23rdStPublishing.com
Dist(s): **Follett School Solutions.**

25 Dreams Educational Media, (*978-0-9768019*) 8622 Bellanca Ave., Suite J, Los Angeles, CA 90045 USA.

2B Pr., (*978-0-9765430*) 206 Clear Springs, Peachtree City, GA 30269 USA Tel 770-487-1348
E-mail: tami@2bpress.com
Web site: http://www.2bpress.com.

2D Cloud *See* **2dcloud**

2dcloud, (*978-0-615-25380-0; 978-0-578-01983-3; 978-1-937541*) 3364 S. Lituanica Ave. No. 1R, Chicago, IL 60608 USA Tel 773-715-9551
Web site: http://www.2dcloud.com
Dist(s): **Consortium Bk. Sales & Distribution.**

2DHse. Publishing, (*978-0-615-75181-8; 978-0-615-76647-8; 978-0-9895256*) 2075 Clover Dr., Monterey Park, CA 91735 USA Tel 818-793-9252
E-mail: 2dhouse@earthlink.net.

2Giggles, (*978-0-9801020*) 25811 Mill Pond Ln., Spring, TX 77373 USA
E-mail: vineandfig@gmail.com.

2Lakes Publishing, (*978-0-9722400; 978-0-578-52353-8*) Orders Addr.: 3661 Natalie Way, Bandon, OR 97411 USA
E-mail: heidi2lakes@2lakespublishing.com
Web site: http://www.2lakespublishing.com.

2MPower, (*978-0-9767046*) 25231 Grissom Rd., Laguna Hills, CA 92653-5237 USA Tel 949-837-1268; Fax: 949-470-0659
E-mail: arnovigen@yahoo.com
Web site: http://www.2mpwr.com.

3 Fates Pr., (*978-1-940938*) 2025 Bell Rd., Morgantown, IN 46160 USA Tel 269-235-4737; *Imprints:* Line By Lion Publications (LineByLion)
E-mail: admin@3fatespress.com
Web site: www.3fatespress.com.

3 Pals Media, LLC, (*978-0-9770960*) 424 Greenleaf Ave., Burlington, WA 98233 USA Tel 360-755-2299; Fax: 360-755-8010
Web site: http://www.pumpkinpatchpals.com.

3,000 Letters, (*978-0-9983577*) 240 e. Connecticut Ave., southern pines, NC 28387 USA Tel 910-690-3190
E-mail: gayvinpowers07@gmail.com
Web site: www.gayvinpowers.com.

302 Publishing, (*978-0-9790165*) 9139 SW Excalibur Pl., Portland, OR 97219-9721 USA Tel 503-246-2499 (phone/fax).

333 Publishing, (*978-0-578-23196-9*) 2020, 412 VIsta Cove, Victoria, TX 77904 USA.

353rd Regimental History Project, (*978-0-9748916*) 2650 N. 64th, Wavnatusa, WI 53213-1407 USA Tel 414-444-7120
E-mail: suzannb@wyoming.com.

360 Degrees *Imprint of* **Tiger Tales**

360 Marketing, LLC, (*978-0-9702654*) 6 Trumbull St., Saintnington, CT 06378 USA Tel 860-535-2240; Fax: 860-535-3243 (call first)
E-mail: three60mrk@aol.com; claudia@chasem2.com.

3-C Institute for Social Development, (*978-0-9779290; 978-0-9789871; 978-1-934409*) 1903 N. Harrison Ave., Suite 101, Cary, NC 27513 USA Tel 919-677-0101; Fax: 919-677-0112
E-mail: info@3cisd.com
Web site: http://www.3cisd.com.

3cs Publishing, The, (*978-0-9773341*) P.O. Box 8096, Silver Spring, MD 20907 USA
Web site: http://www.the3cs.com.

3D Alley, Inc., (*978-0-9776845*) 4525 Harding Rd., Suite 317, Nashville, TN 37205 USA.

3DTotal.com (GBR) (*978-0-9551530) Dist. by* **Consort Bk Sales.**

3G Publishing, Inc., (*978-0-9833544; 978-0-9854968; 978-1-941247*) 3508 Pk. Lake Ln., Norcross, GA 30092 USA Tel 404-553-1566; Fax: 770-676-0626 Do not confuse with 3G Publishing, Inc in New Berlin, WI
E-mail: myrna.gale@gmail.com
Web site: 3gpublishinginc.com.

3H Dowsing International LLC, (*978-0-9656653; 978-1-932229*) W10160 Cty. Rd. C, Wautoma, WI 54982 USA Tel 920-787-4747; Fax: 920-787-2006
E-mail: ilovedowsing@hotmail.com
Web site: http://store.yahoo.com/dowsing.

3N Media Group, (*978-0-9741686*) P.O. Box 705, Morris Plains, NJ 07950 USA Fax: 240-220-0500
E-mail: 3nmediagrp@optonline.net.

3perfections, (*978-0-9759909*) 833 Great Oaks Trail, Eagan, MN 55123 USA Tel 651-905-1098
E-mail: perfections3@aol.com
Web site: http://www.3perfections.com.

4 Childrens Sake Pubns., (*978-0-9752982*) Orders Addr.: P.O. Box 594, Moosup, CT 06354 USA; Edit Addr.: 357 N. Main St., Moosup, CT 06354 USA.

4 Sonkist Angels *See* **Four Sonkist Angels**

4000 Years of Writing History, (*978-0-9748786*) P.O. Box 484, Redondo Beach, CA 90277-0484 USA
Web site: http://www.lmlk.com.

405 Pubns., (*978-0-9790832; 978-0-692-91923-1; 978-0-692-08339-0*) Orders Addr.: 10026 S. Linn Ave, Oklahoma City, OK 73159 USA (SAN 852-3754); *Imprints:* Three Ring Circus Publishing House, Inc. (MYID_I_THREE R)
E-mail: quimbysneet@gmail.com
Web site: http://www.quimbysneet.com
Dist(s): **Ingram Content Group.**

423-508-9642 *See* **Noble Success Publishing**

43 Degrees North LLC, (*978-0-9744444*) P.O. Box 781, Wilson, NY 14172 USA Tel 716-751-3604; Fax: 716-751-0105
E-mail: jeff@tailgatetrivia.com
Web site: http://www.tailgatetrivia.com.

44 Enterprises, (*978-0-615-22510-4; 978-0-615-24951-3*) 820A W. 47th St., Savannah, GA 31405 USA.

45th Parallel Concepts Limited *See* **Level 603 LLC**

45th Parallel Press *Imprint of* **Cherry Lake Publishing**

47North *Imprint of* **Amazon Publishing**

499, *(978-1-7335569)* 500 Westover Dr., No. 13616, Sanford, NC 27330 USA Tel 336-917-9783; *Imprints:* Evolved Teacher Press (MYID_D_EVOLVED)
E-mail: gahmya@evolvedteacher.com
Web site: www.evolvedteacher.com.

4All Ages LLC, *(978-0-9787986)* 5 Murdock Rd., Suite 100, East Rockaway, NY 11518 USA (SAN 851-643X) Tel 516-561-3146
E-mail: laws123@aol.com
Web site: http://www.colorpets.com.

4Elliott Publishing, Inc., *(978-0-9846963)* 6829 NW 15th Ave., Miami, FL 33142 USA Tel 786-277-2693
E-mail: sxye320@yahoo.comtees.

4mPr., *(978-0-9896681)* 2639 Sherrie Ln., Thompsons Stn, TN 37179 USA Tel 615-473-1469
E-mail: jpmarrs@gmail.com.

4N Publishing LLC, *(978-0-9741319; 978-0-9798841)* Orders Addr.: 44-73 21st St., D-6, Long Island City, NY 11101 USA Tel 718-482-1135
E-mail: brendan@4npublishing.com; erin@4npublishing.com; ij@4npublishing.com
Web site: http://www.4npublishing.com.

4RV Pub, *(978-0-9797513; 978-0-9818685; 978-0-9840708; 978-0-9825886; 978-0-9826423; 978-0-9826594; 978-0-9828346; 978-0-9832740; 978-0-9838018; 978-0-9852661; 978-0-9889617; 978-1-940310; 978-1-950074)* 2912 Rankin Terr., Edmond, OK 73013 USA Tel 405-225-6851
E-mail: president@4rvpublishingllc.com
Web site: http://www.4rvpublishingllc.com
Dist(s): **Follett School Solutions.**

4th Dimension Enterprises, Inc., *(978-0-9819088)* 40 Memorial Hwy. Apt. 27N, New Rochelle, NY 10801-8340 USA
E-mail: info@4thdimensionpublishing.com
Web site: http://www.4thdimensionpublishing.com.

4th Division Pr. *Imprint of* **Kurdyla, E L Publishing LLC**

5 Fold Media LLC *See* **Andy Sanders**

5 Muses Publishing, *(978-0-9786180)* 100 Andover Pk. Ste 150-108, TUKWILA, WA 98188 USA
E-mail: rlpolhill@5musespublishing.com
Web site: http://www.5MusesPublishing.com.

5 Prince Publishing, *(978-0-615-46134-2; 978-0-615-52891-5; 978-0-9848529; 978-0-9853345; 978-0-615-64941-2; 978-0-615-65268-9; 978-0-615-65747-9; 978-0-615-66869-7; 978-0-615-68734-6; 978-0-615-68919-7; 978-1-939217; 978-1-63112)* Orders Addr.: P.O. Box 16507, Denver, CO 80216 USA Tel 303-257-0389
E-mail: books@5princebooks.com
Web site: www.5princebooks.com
Dist(s): **CreateSpace Independent Publishing Platform**
Ingram Content Group
Smashwords.

5 Spot *Imprint of* **Grand Central Publishing**

5 Star Pubns., LLC, *(978-0-9843881; 978-0-9832473; 978-0-9854386)* c/o Tlj Bookstore, Llc, 9134 Piscataway Rd. No. 805, Clinton, MD 20735 USA
E-mail: shawn5star@yahoo.com; shawncvalentine@yahoo.com
Web site: http://www.5starpublications.net
Dist(s): **Icon Distribution.**

5 Star Stories, Inc., *(978-0-9659470)* Orders Addr.: 14625 Greenville St., Houston, TX 77015-4711 USA Tel 713-455-1073; Fax: 713-583-7017
E-mail: isellfantasy@hotmail.com
Web site: http://www.TexasSecedes.com.

50/50 Publishing *See* **Soulo Communications**

5,6 Pickup Sticks Publishing, *(978-0-9762145)* 2493 Sunridge Ave., SE, Atlanta, GA 30315 USA Tel 404-627-9132
E-mail: tcmac1@bellsouth.net.

5am Pr., LLC, *(978-0-692-81057-6)* 27034 Glenside Ln., OLMSTED TWP, OH 44138 USA Tel 216-262-7725
E-mail: keith@messypopup.com
Web site: http://www.messypopup.com.

5m Publishing (GBR) *(978-0-9530150; 978-0-9555011; 978-1-910455) Dist. by* **IPG Chicago.**

671 Press *See* **Octane Pr.**

6-mile Roots, *(978-0-9771255)* 1469 260th, Marion, KS 66861 USA Tel 620-924-5254
E-mail: joel@hillsborofreepress.com.

7 Robots, Inc., *(978-0-9778454)* 714 Washington Ave., Suite No. 9, New York, NY 11238 USA
Web site: http://www.7robots.com
Dist(s): **Diamond Comic Distributors, Inc.**

711Press *Imprint of* **Vendera Publishing**

716 Productions, *(978-0-9795529)* 3200 Airport Ave., Suite 16, Santa Monica, CA 90405 USA
Web site: http://learningwhoweare.com.

7th Generation *Imprint of* **Book Publishing Co.**

80 West Publishing, Inc., *(978-0-9763417)* 2222 Ponce de Leon Blvd., 6th Flr., Coral Gables, FL 33134 USA Tel 305-448-8117; Fax: 305-448-8453
E-mail: joellen@adkinsadv.com.

826 Valencia, *(978-0-9768467; 978-0-9770844; 978-0-9779289; 978-0-9790073; 978-1-934750; 978-1-948644)* 44 Gough St., San Francisco, CA 94103 USA
E-mail: field.ops@826national.org
Web site: www.826national.org
Dist(s): **Publishers Group West (PGW).**

826michigan, *(978-0-9779289; 978-0-9827293; 978-0-9966315)* 115 E. Liberty St., Ann Arbor, MI 48104-2109 USA
Web site: http://www.826michigan.org.

8-Ball Express, Inc., *(978-0-9747273)* 316 California, Suite 529, Reno, NV 89509-1650 USA Tel 415-776-1596 (for wholesale orders); Toll Free: 877-368-2255 (for retail sales only)
E-mail: rgivens@toast.net
Web site: http://www.8-ballbible.com.

8N Publishing, LLC, *(978-0-9992523)* P.O. Box 972364, Ypsilanti, MI 48197 USA Tel 734-985-8519
E-mail: SJLomas9@gmail.com.

978-0-8283Branden Books *See* **Branden Bks.**

A & B Books *See* **A & B Distributors & Pubs. Group**

A & B Distributors & Pubs. Group, *(978-1-881316; 978-1-886433)* Div. of A&B Distributors, 1000 Atlantic Ave., Brooklyn, NY 11238 USA (SAN 630-9216) Tel 718-783-7808; Fax: 718-783-7267; Toll Free: 877-542-6657; 146 Lawrence St., Brooklyn, NY 11201 (SAN 631-385X)
E-mail: maxtay@webspan.net
Dist(s): **D & J Bk. Distributors**
Red Sea Pr.

A & D Bks., *(978-0-9743294)* 3708 E. 45th St., Tulsa, OK 74135 USA Tel 918-748-4348 (phone/fax)
E-mail: a_dbooks@live.com.

A & E Children's Pr., *(978-0-9728134)* 6107 S. Jericho Way, Centennial, CO 80016 USA
E-mail: maked4@aol.com.

A & E Sivells Pubns. *Imprint of* **Word For Word Publishing Co.**

A & L Communications, Inc., *(978-0-9714320)* 1946 Magnolia Crest Ln., Sugar Land, TX 77478 USA
E-mail: allysoncward@yahoo.com
Web site: http://www.algiershistory.com
Dist(s): **Forest Sales & Distributing Co.**

A & M Writing and Publishing,, *(978-0-9764824; 978-0-9861841; 978-1-7330228)* 141 Saratoga Avenue, No. 1317, Santa Clara, CA 95051 USA Tel 408-244-8053; Fax: 408-244-8098
E-mail: ctillson@amwriting.com
Web site: http://www.amwriting.com
Dist(s): **Partners Bk. Distributing, Inc.**

A & P Publishing and Games, LLC, *(978-0-578-41366-2; 978-0-578-46505-0; 978-0-578-46506-7)* 1714 Ave. C, Danbury, TX 77534 USA Tel 713-817-1267
E-mail: willabel01@yahoo.com
Dist(s): **Independent Pub.**

A & W Enterprises, *(978-0-9617896)* P.O. Box 8133, Roanoke, VA 24014 USA (SAN 665-603X) Tel 540-427-1154; Toll Free: 800-484-1492 (ext. 4267)
E-mail: gwalker@interlink.com.

A B C-123 Publishing, *(978-0-9711474; 978-0-578-16435-9)* Orders Addr.: P.O. Box 100145, Staten Island, NY 10310 USA Fax: 718-980-4416; 718-351-4863; Toll Free: 866-339-3936; Edit Addr.: 159 New Dorp Plaza, 2nd Flr., Staten Island, NY 10306 USA; P.O. Box 30096, Staten Island, NY 30096
E-mail: thomas@deweydoes.com; contact@deweydoes.com
Web site: http://www.deweydoes.com.

A B C-Clio Information Services *See* **ABC-CLIO, LLC**

A B Publishing, *(978-1-881545; 978-1-59765)* P.O. Box 83, North Star, MI 48862-0083 USA Toll Free: 800-882-6443
E-mail: abpub@hotmail.com; joabpub@hotmail.com
Web site: http://www.abpub.com
Dist(s): **Send The Light Distribution LLC**
Spring Arbor Distributors, Inc.

A Beautiful, Wonderful Me LLC, *(978-0-9986624)* 1503 Main St No. 172, Grandview, MO 64030 USA Tel 816-277-7467
E-mail: abeautifulwonderfulme@gmail.com.

A Blessed Heritage Educational Resources, *(978-0-9759320; 978-0-9767866; 978-1-7326022)* 10602 Redwood Dr., Baytown, TX 77520 USA
E-mail: belinda.bullard@blessedheritage.com
Web site: http://www.blessedheritage.com.

A+ Bk. Publishing, *(978-1-929819)* Orders Addr.: P.O. Box 250165, Franklin, MI 48025-0165 USA Tel 248-223-9322; Fax: 248-223-9161; Edit Addr.: 29233 Wellington Ct., No. 61, Southfield, MI 48034 USA; *Imprints:* Capstone Press (Capstone)
E-mail: kpcartwright@ameritech.net
Dist(s): **Capstone.**

A. Borough Bks., *(978-0-9640606; 978-1-893597)* Orders Addr.: 3901 Silver Bell Dr., Charlotte, NC 28211 USA Tel 704-364-1788; Fax: 704-366-9079; Toll Free: 800-843-8490
E-mail: humorbooks@aol.com
Dist(s): **Parnassus Bk. Distributors.**

A Boy Named Jack, *(978-0-9987153)* 6383 W Conestoga St, Beverly Hills, FL 34465 USA Tel 813-727-5551
E-mail: aboynamedjack@yahoo.com
Web site: aboynamedjack.us.

A Buen Paso S.C.P. (ESP) *(978-84-937211; 978-84-938036; 978-84-939414; 978-84-940533; 978-84-941579; 978-84-942854) Dist. by* **Lectorum Pubns.**

A Cappela Publishing, *(978-0-9656309; 978-0-9724979; 978-0-9779139; 978-0-9818933; 978-0-9846177; 978-0-9850202)* P.O. Box 3691, Sarasota, FL 34230-3691 USA (SAN 253-567X) Tel 941-351-2050; Fax: 941-351-4735; *Imprints:* Advocate House (Advoca Hse) Do not confuse with A Cappella Publishing, Los Angeles, CA
E-mail: acappub@aol.com
Web site: http://www.acappela.com; http://www.lillythelash.com.

A Cappella Bks., *(978-1-55652)* 814 N. Franklin, Chicago, IL 60610 USA Tel 312-337-0747; Fax: 312-640-0542; Toll Free: 800-888-4741
E-mail: publish@ipgbook.com; orders@ipgbook.com
Web site: http://www.ipgbook.com.

Caribbean Experience Con Amor, LLC, A, *(978-0-9797641)* P.O. Box 1155, Avondale, PA 19311 USA Tel 610-806-2013 Alternate #610-806-2013
Web site: http://www.marisadejesus.com.

A Cupcake & Giggles Publishing, *(978-0-9963847)* 902 Greenhouse Patio Dr. NW, Kennesaw , GA 30144 USA Tel 4047881379
Dist(s): **CreateSpace Independent Publishing Platform.**

A Different Kind of Safari LLC, *(978-0-9890134; 978-1-7350061)* 39 Skunk Hollow Rd., Jericho, VT 05495 USA Tel 802-238-0822
E-mail: hchipp@comcast.net
Web site: www.adifferentkindofsafari.com.

AEVAC, Inc., *(978-0-913356)* 7 Silver Lake Dr., Summit, NJ 07901-3233 USA (SAN 204-5567).

A H W Publishing, *(978-0-9741434)* 1124 W. 19th Ave., Spokane, WA 99203 USA (SAN 255-4070)
E-mail: annifrommainz@dc4pc.net.

A I G A / Art With Heart *See* **Art With Heart Press**

AIMS International Bks., Inc., *(978-0-922852)* 7709 Hamilton Ave., Cincinnati, OH 45231-3103 USA (SAN 630-270X) Tel 513-521-5590; Fax: 513-521-5592; Toll Free: 800-733-2067
E-mail: aimsbooks@fuse.net
Web site: http://www.aimsbooks.com
Dist(s): **Shen's Bks.**

A i T/Planet Lar, *(978-0-9676847; 978-0-9709360; 978-1-932051)* 2034 47th Ave., San Francisco, CA 94116 USA Tel 415-504-7516 (phone/fax)
E-mail: larry@ait-planetlar.com
Web site: http://www.ait-planetlar.com
Dist(s): **Diamond Comic Distributors, Inc.**
Diamond Bk. Distributors
L P C Group.

A JuneOne Production *Imprint of* **JuneOne Publishing Hub**

AK Peters, Ltd., *(978-1-56881; 978-1-138-05124-9)* 5 Commonwealth Rd. Suite 2c, Natick, MA 01760 USA (SAN 299-1810) Tel 508-651-0887 All inquiries; Fax: 508-651-0889; 7625 Empire Dr., Florence, KY 41042
E-mail: service@akpeters.com
Web site: http://www.akpeters.com
Dist(s): **Follett School Solutions**
MyiLibrary
Taylor & Francis Group.

A K Peters/CRC Pr. *Imprint of* **CRC Pr. LLC**

A Kidz World *Imprint of* **ABUAA, Inc.**

ALPI International, Ltd., *(978-1-886647)* 1685 34th St., Oakland, CA 94608 USA Tel 510-655-6456; Fax: 510-655-2093; Toll Free: 800-678-2574
E-mail: becky@alpi.net.

AMG Pubs., *(978-0-89957; 978-1-61715; 978-1-63070)* Subs. of AMG Publishing Inc., Orders Addr.: P.O. Box 22000, Chattanooga, TN 37422 USA Tel 423-894-6060; Fax: 423-894-9511; Toll Free Fax: 800-265-6690; Toll Free: 800-266-4977; Edit Addr.: 6815 Shallowford Rd., Chattanooga, TN 37421 USA (SAN 211-3074) Toll Free Fax: 800-266-4577; 800-265-6690; *Imprints:* Living Ink Books (Liv Ink Bks)
E-mail: trevor@amgpublishers.com; sales@AMGpublishers.com
Web site: http://www.amgpublishers.com; http://www.livinginkbooks.com
Dist(s): **Anchor Distributors**
Spring Arbor Distributors, Inc.

AMICA Publishing Hse., *(978-1-884187)* Div. of AMICA International, 844 Industry Dr., No. 20, Seattle, WA 98188-3410 USA Tel 206-467-1035; Fax: 206-467-1522
E-mail: amica@ix.netcom.com
Web site: http://www.amicaint.com.

AMSC, Adventures in Math & Social Studies for Children, *(978-1-889639)* Orders Addr.: 818 W. Grover St., Lynden, WA 98264 USA Tel 360-354-4412; Toll Free: 800-306-1772
E-mail: math1@earthlink.net.

A N A D E M, Incorporated *See* **Anadem Publishing, Inc.**

A Neat Read Publishing LLC, *(978-0-578-19321-2; 978-0-692-93443-2; 978-1-7321596; 978-1-7330555; 978-1-7357612)* 3018 Brush St NE, Canton, OH 44705 USA Tel 330-452-1522
E-mail: clarknoveltysign@aol.com
Web site: http://aneatreadpublishing.com.

A New Day..A New Way!, *(978-0-9749177)* 5525B Via La Mesa, Laguna Woods, CA 92637 USA Tel 949-340-0615; Fax: 949-723-0030
E-mail: kathleenscott@anewday-anewway.com; kathleen_scott@sbcglobal.net
Web site: http://www.anewday-anewway.com
Dist(s): **New Leaf Distributing Co., Inc.**

APTE, Inc., *(978-1-889651; 978-1-931872; 978-1-932736; 978-1-933229)* 820 Church St., Suite 300, Evanston, IL 60201 USA Toll Free: 800-494-1112
E-mail: pierred@apte.com; sally@apte.com
Web site: http://www.apte.com
Dist(s): **Brodart Co.**
Educational Resources
Follett School Solutions
Learning Services.

A PAR Educational, LLC, *(978-0-578-12712-5; 978-0-9973365)* 300 Adams Dr. Apt 301, McKees Rocks , PA 15136 USA.

ARO Publishing Co., *(978-0-89868)* Box 193, 398 S. 1100 W., Provo, UT 84601 USA (SAN 212-6370) Tel 801-377-8218; Fax: 801-818-0616
E-mail: arobook@yahoo.com
Dist(s): **Forest Hse. Publishing Co., Inc.**

A Road to Discovery Series Guide *Imprint of* **Perry Heights Pr.**

A. Rose *See* **Rose, A.**

ASDA Publishing, Inc., *(978-0-9632319)* 904 Forest Lake Dr., Lakeland, FL 33809 USA Tel 841-859-2194.

A Story Plus Children Bks., *(978-0-9778477)* Div. of Top Award, Inc., P.O. Box 1174, Pine Lake, GA 30072-1174 USA (SAN 850-3907) Tel 404-667-2619
E-mail: astoryplu@comcast.net
Web site: http://www.astoryplus.com.

A StoryPlus *See* **A Story Plus Children Bks.**

A to Z Publishing, LLC *See* **Summer Storm Publishing, LLC**

A. V. P., Incorporated *See* **IBE, Inc.**

A. W. Ink, Inc., *(978-0-9820932)* P.O. Box 1184, Kamas, UT 84036-1184 USA
E-mail: lesliesaunders@kw.com.

A2Z Bks. Publishing, *(978-1-943284)* 1990 Young Rd, Lithonia, GA 30058 USA Tel 770-808-4478
E-mail: sdoverharris@gmail.com
Web site: www.A2ZBooksPublishing.com.

A3 Publishing *See* **Burnett Young Books**

A3D Impressions, *(978-0-578-19392-2; 978-0-578-19453-0; 978-0-578-20193-1; 978-0-578-20194-8; 978-1-7320677; 978-1-7327285; 978-1-7344724)* 4335 E Whitman St., Tucson, AZ 85711 USA
Web site: www.a3dimpressions.com.

A4J Publishing, *(978-0-9831372)* P.O. Box 1101, Orlando, FL 32802 USA Tel 678-358-9820; Fax: 407-237-0135
E-mail: vikki@a4jpublishing.com
Web site: www.a4jpublishing.com.

AAA POP, *(978-0-9762282)* 4147 S. Tenmile Lake, Lakeside, OR 97449 USA
Web site: http://www.aaapop.com.

AAA Reality Games LLC, *(978-0-9837264)* 11693 San Vicente Blvd. Suite 380, Los Angeles, CA 90049 USA Tel 310-696-1045
E-mail: hartgetzen@hotmail.com
Dist(s): **Smashwords.**

Aaduna, *(978-0-9768626)* 2021 Del Norte Ave., Saint Louis, MO 63117 USA Tel 314-647-3437
E-mail: mroach@thecollegeschool.org
Web site: http://www.senecorps.com.

Aakenbaaken & Kent, *(978-1-938436)* 2206 White Oak Dr., Valdosta, GA 31602 USA Tel 917-607-8263
E-mail: akeditor@inbox.com.

Açedrex Publishing *See* **Acedrex Publishing**

A&D Xtreme *Imprint of* **ABDO Publishing Co.**

A&J Publishing LLC, *(978-1-943346)* 3266 Hartwell St., Johns Island, SC 29455 USA Tel 843-670-2642
E-mail: geoffcollins66@hotmail.com
Web site: theajadventures.com
Dist(s): **INscribe Digital**
Independent Pubs. Group.

A&M Moonlight Creations, *(978-1-938783)* 5848 Birchwood Dr, Mentor, OH 44060 USA Tel 440-257-5008
E-mail: comboj2@yahoo.com
Web site: www.mortalrealmwitch.com.

AAO Publishing, *(978-0-9786431)* a/o Melody Farloe, P.O. Box 6208, Beverly Hills, CA 90212 USA
E-mail: puffybuffy1@yahoo.com
Web site: http://www.puffybuffy.com.

Aardvark Global Publishing, *(978-0-9770328; 978-1-933570; 978-1-59971; 978-1-4276)* 9587 S. Grandview Dr., Sandy, UT 84092 USA Do not confuse with Aardvark Global Publishing, Atlanta, GA
E-mail: info@eckohousepublishing.com
Web site: http://eckohousepublishing.com/; http://aardvarkglobalpublishing.com/; http://eckobooks.com
Dist(s): **AK Pr. Distribution**
Follett School Solutions
Lulu Pr., Inc.
SPD-Small Pr. Distribution.

Aardvark Pubs., *(978-0-615-13532-8; 978-0-615-13673-8; 978-0-615-14219-7; 978-0-615-17808-0)* 1615 Shannon Rd., Girard, OH 44420 USA
E-mail: info@aardvarkpublishers.com
Web site: http://www.aardvarkpublishers.com
Dist(s): **Lulu Pr., Inc.**

Aardvark's Weedpatch Pr., *(978-0-9755567)* P.O. Box 1841, Rogue River, OR 97537-1841 USA
Web site: http://www.aardvarksweedpatch.com.

AARO Publishing, *(978-1-893563)* Orders Addr.: P.O. Box 1281, Palisade, CO 81526 USA; Edit Addr.: PO Box 1281 Palisade, Co 81526, Palisade, CO 81526 USA (SAN 255-7185) Tel 970-314-7690 (phone/fax)970 985 4018
E-mail: carwe@earthlink.net
Web site: http://www.snowff.com
Dist(s): **Follett School Solutions.**

Aaron Bk. Publishing, *(978-0-9819195)* 1093 Bristol Caverns Hwy., Bristol, TN 37620 USA (SAN 856-924X) Tel 423-212-1208
E-mail: info@aaronbookpublishing.com
Web site: http://www.aaronbookpublishing.com.

Aaron C Ministries, *(978-1-933519)* 1005 Pine Oak Dr., Edmond, OK 73034-5139 USA Tel 405-348-3410
E-mail: bible@jpdawson.com
Web site: http://www.jpdawson.com.

Aaron Levy Pubns., LLC, *(978-1-931463)* 1760 Stumpf Blvd., Gretna, LA 70056 USA Tel 504-258-4332
E-mail: aaronlevy1@aol.com; kelleylevy12@gmail.com
Web site: http://www.goodlifemedialic.com.

Aaron Press *See* **Publishing Assocs., Inc.**

Aaron-Barrada, Inc., *(978-0-9768671; 978-0-615-12767-5)* 79 Valley High, Ruffs Dale, PA 15679 USA Tel 724-696-4332; Fax: 612-545-3210
E-mail: aaronbarradainc@aol.com
Web site: http://www.pottiestickers.com.

Aarow Pr., *(978-0-9749046)* 3215 Buckingham Ave., Lakeland, FL 33803 USA (SAN 255-8653) Tel 863-709-8882 (phone/fax)
E-mail: aarowpress@yahoo.com.

AB Film Publishing, *(978-0-9897068)* 290 W. 12 Street, Apt. A, New York, NY 10014 USA Tel 212-741-1441
E-mail: abaxter@ramapo.edu
Web site: http://abfilmpublishing9.wordpress.com
Dist(s): **Lulu Pr., Inc.**

AB Rolle Publications *See* **ABR Pubns.**

A-BA-BA HAUS, *(978-0-9965606)* 227 W. 149th Street, Apt. No. 6F, NEW YORK, NY 10039 USA Tel 347-951-6263
E-mail: tmalkovych@gmail.com.

A-BA-BA-HA-LA-MA-HA Pubs. *Imprint of* **Windy Press International Publishing Hse., LLC**

Abacus Bks., Inc., *(978-0-9716292)* Div. of Abacus Bks.com, 1420 58th Ave. N, Saint Petersburg, FL 33703 USA Tel 727-742-3889; Fax: 727-522-0606
E-mail: necole@abacusbooks.com; info@abacusbooks.com
Web site: http://www.abacusbooks.com.

Abadaba Reading LLC, *(978-0-9789473)* P.O. Box 80, Charlottesville, VA 22902-5335 USA (SAN 852-0240)
Web site: http://www.adabadaalphabet.com.

aBASK Publishing, *(978-0-9843855; 978-0-9962399)* 320 National Pl., Apt 5, Longmont, CO 80501-3326 USA
E-mail: Publisher@AbaskPublishing.com; kathygode@yahoo.com
Web site: http://abaskpublishing.com.

Abba's Hse. International Publishing, *(978-0-692-37641-6; 978-0-692-39156-3; 978-0-9971037)* 3015 W. Maplewood Ave, Bellingham, WA 98225 USA Tel 360-201-5574
E-mail: gatheringtheharvest@yahoo.com
Web site: www.anthonyecclesiastes.com.

†ABBE Pubs. Assn. of Washington, D.C., *(978-0-7883; 978-0-88164; 978-0-941864; 978-1-55914)* Orders Addr.: 4111 Gallows Rd., Virginia Div., Annandale, VA 22003 USA (SAN 239-1430)
E-mail: abbe.publishers@verizon.net; vze3hcqz@verizon.net; *CIP.*

Abbeville Kids *Imprint of* **Abbeville Pr., Inc.**

†Abbeville Pr., Inc., *(978-0-7892; 978-0-89659; 978-1-55859)* 137 Varick St., 5th Flr., New York, NY 10013 USA (SAN 211-4755) Tel 212-366-5585; Fax: 212-366-6966; Toll Free: 800-278-2665; 1094 Flex Dr., Jackson, TN 38301; *Imprints:* Abbeville Kids (Abbeville Kids)
E-mail: abbeville@abbeville.com
Web site: http://www.abbeville.com
Dist(s): **Follett School Solutions**
Ingram Publisher Services
MyiLibrary
Norton, W. W. & Co., Inc.
Penguin Random Hse. Distribution
Penguin Random Hse. LLC
Two Rivers Distribution
ebrary, Inc.; *CIP.*

Abbey Pr., *(978-0-87029)* 1 Hill Dr., Saint Meinrad, IN 47577-0128 USA (SAN 201-2057) Tel 812-357-8215; Fax: 812-357-8388; Toll Free: 800-325-2511
E-mail: customerservice@abbeypress.com
Web site: http://www.abbeypress.com/
Dist(s): **Open Road Integrated Media, Inc.**
Open Road Distribution.

Abbott Avenue Pr., *(978-0-9767514)* 859 Hollywood Way, Suite 258, Burbank, CA 91505 USA
E-mail: info@abbottavenuepress.com
Web site: http://www.abbottavenuepress.com.

Abbott Pr. *Imprint of* **Author Solutions, Inc.**

ABC *Imprint of* **DC Comics**

ABC Bk. *Imprint of* **Michaelson Entertainment**

ABC Bks. (AUS) *(978-0-7333; 978-1-74086; 978-0-646-51687-5) Dist. by* **HarperCollins Pubs.**

ABC Bks., *(978-0-9785108)* P.O. Box 2246, Sunnyvale, CA 94087-2246 USA Do not confuse with ABC Books in Plano, TX.

ABC Children's Bks. (AUS) *(978-0-9577218) Dist. by* **HarperCollins Pubs.**

ABC Development, Inc., *(978-0-9767179)* 6869 Stapoint Ct., Suite 107, Winter Park, FL 32792 USA Tel 407-671-6000; Fax: 407-671-6602; Toll Free: 800-222-3053
E-mail: sales@abc-development.com
Web site: http://www.abc-development.com.

ABC for Girls Like Me, *(978-0-692-14101-4; 978-0-692-14664-4; 978-0-692-14714-6; 978-0-692-16271-2; 978-0-578-45811-3; 978-1-7336910)* 530 W Stocker St Apt 206, GLENDALE, CA 91202 USA Tel 404-345-1312
E-mail: goolsbymelanie@gmail.com
Dist(s): **Ingram Content Group.**

ABC Pr., *(978-0-9758622)* 550 Iron Mountain Rd., El Dorado, AR 71730 USA Tel 870-863-5779 Do not confuse with ABC Pr. in Walnut Creek, CA
E-mail: srwood@suddenlink.net
Web site: http://RamonaWoodBooks.com.

ABC Pubs., *(978-0-9772685)* 32 Meadowlark Ln., Willingboro, NJ 08046-2108 USA Tel 609-880-0897
E-mail: fg@abc-advantage.com
Web site: http://www.abc-advantage.com.

ABC Schermerhorn Walters Company *See* **Schermerhorn, Walters Co.**

†ABC-CLIO, LLC, *(978-0-275; 978-0-313; 978-0-8371; 978-0-86569; 978-0-87287; 978-0-87436; 978-0-89789; 978-0-89930; 978-0-903450; 978-0-938865; 978-1-56308; 978-1-56720; 978-1-57607; 978-1-85109; 978-1-58683; 978-1-59158; 978-0-9742537; 978-1-59884; 978-1-4408; 978-1-61069) 130 Cremona Dr., Santa Barbara, CA 93117 USA (SAN 301-5467) Tel 805-968-1911; Fax: 805-685-9685; Toll Free: 800-368-6868; P.O. Box 93116, Goleta, CA 93116 (SAN 857-7099); Imprints:* Praeger (Praeger Pubs); Greenwood (GreenWABC); Libraries Unlimited (LibdUnltd); Linworth Publishing, Incorporated (Linworth)
E-mail: customerservice@abc-clio.com; service@abc-clio.com; salesuk@abc-clio.com
Web site: http://www.abc-clio.com
Dist(s): **Bookhouse, The**
Casemate Academic
Ebsco Publishing
Follett School Solutions
MyiLibrary
ebrary, Inc.; *CIP.*

Abccurate Business Ventures, *(978-0-9755341)* P.O. Box 2236, Smyrna, TN 37167 USA Tel 615-831-7100
E-mail: editor@abccurate.com
Web site: http://www.abccurate.com.

ABCDE Academic Bks. for Children's Development Through Education, *(978-0-9754008)* P.O. Box 374, Shrub Oak, NY 10588 USA.

ABCDMoon *See* **ABCDMoon Publishing**

ABCDMoon Publishing, *(978-0-9729216)* P.O. Box 910732, Lexington, KY 40591-0732 USA Tel 859-873-5031
E-mail: tex@charliethemonkey.com; amy@charliethemonkey.com
Web site: http://www.charliethemonkey.com.

ABCs Connection, Inc., *(978-0-9755475)* 1209 Caribou Crossing, Suite 101, Durham, NC 27713 USA Tel 919-451-4991; Fax: 919-484-1980
E-mail: casey_wallace@yahoo.com
Web site: http://www.abcsconnection.com.

ABCS OF GOD, *(978-0-578-44895-4)* 704 Blossom Ln., Lincoln, CA 95648 USA Tel 916-203-8112
E-mail: 704@att.net
Dist(s): **Ingram Content Group.**

ABC's Unlimited *See* **See abc's LC**

Abdelsalam Corp., *(978-0-9755975)* 2499 Trewigtown Rd., Colmar, PA 18915 USA.

Abdiel Productions, *(978-0-9768088)* 4802 Nassau Ave., NE, No. 31, Tacoma, WA 98422-4632 USA.

Abdo & Daughters *Imprint of* **ABDO Publishing Co.**

Abdo & Daughters Publishing *See* **ABDO Publishing Co.**

Abdo Kids *Imprint of* **ABDO Publishing Co.**

Abdo Kids-Jumbo *Imprint of* **ABDO Publishing Co.**

Abdo Kids-Junior *Imprint of* **ABDO Publishing Co.**

†ABDO Publishing Co., *(978-0-939179; 978-1-56239; 978-1-57765; 978-1-59197; 978-1-59679; 978-1-59928; 978-1-59961; 978-1-60270; 978-1-60453; 978-1-61613; 978-1-61714; 978-1-61758; 978-1-61783; 978-1-61784; 978-1-61785; 978-1-61786; 978-1-61787; 978-1-61478; 978-1-61479; 978-1-61480; 978-1-62401; 978-1-62402; 978-1-62403; 978-1-62968; 978-1-62969; 978-1-62970; 978-1-68076; 978-1-68077; 978-1-68078; 978-1-68079; 978-1-68080; 978-1-5321; 978-1-0982) Div. of ABDO Publishing Group, Orders Addr.: 8000 W. 78th St. Suite 310, Edina, MN 55439 USA (SAN 662-9172) Tel 952-831-2120; Fax: 952-831-1632; Toll Free Fax: 800-862-3480; Toll Free: 800-800-1312; Imprints:* Abdo & Daughters (Abdo & Dghtrs); Checkerboard Library (Checkerboard Library); SandCastle (SndCastle); Buddy Books (Buddy Bks); Super SandCastle (SuperSandcastle); Essential Library (EssentialLibrary); A&D Xtreme (A&DXtreme); SportsZone (SportsZone); Big Buddy Books (BigBuddy); Core Library (CoreLibrary); Calico Chapter Books (CalicoChapter); Abdo Kids (AbdoKids); EPIC Press (EPICPress); Abdo Zoom-Dash (AbdoZDash); Abdo Zoom-Launch (AbdoZLaunch); Abdo Kids-Junior (AbdoKidsJr); Abdo Kids-Jumbo (AKJumbo); Abdo Zoom-Fly (AbdoZFly); Calico Kid (CalicoKid)
E-mail: info@abdopublishing.com
Web site: http://www.abdopublishing.com
Dist(s): **Ebsco Publishing**
Follett School Solutions
MyiLibrary
North Star Editions; *CIP.*

Abdo Zoom-Dash *Imprint of* **ABDO Publishing Co.**

Abdo Zoom-Fly *Imprint of* **ABDO Publishing Co.**

Abdo Zoom-Launch *Imprint of* **ABDO Publishing Co.**

Abdullah, Mary, *(978-1-7324576)* 131 Purchase Street, Apt. No. C24, Rye, NY 10580 USA Tel 917-355-6467
E-mail: gremi5@icloud.com.

Abecedarian Bks., *(978-0-9763106; 978-0-9791401; 978-0-9822985; 978-0-9915275)* 2817 Forest Glen Dr., Baldwin, MD 21013-9574 USA Tel 410-692-6777; 877-782-2221; Fax: 410-692-9125 Do not confuse with Abecedarian Books in Portland, OR
E-mail: books@abeced.com
Web site: http://www.abeced.com
Dist(s): **Book Clearing Hse.**

Abedus Pr., *(978-0-9763091)* P.O. Box 8018, La Crescenta, CA 91224-0018 USA (SAN 256-2936)
E-mail: jadams@usc.edu.

Abegg Press *See* **Milner Crest Publishing, LLC**

Abelard Bks. (GBR) *(978-0-9558483) Dist. by* **LuluCom.**

Abelson Pr., *(978-0-9830421)* Orders Addr.: 8334 E. 133rd St., GRANDVIEW, MO 64030 USA Tel 816-398-5859
E-mail: jabelson27@gmail.com.

Abernathy Hse. Publishing, *(978-0-9741940)* Orders Addr.: P.O. Box 1109, Yarmouth, ME 04096-1109 USA (SAN 255-4380) Tel 207-838-6170
E-mail: info@abernathyhousepub.com; abernathyhp@aol.com
Web site: http://www.abernathyhousepub.com
Dist(s): **Brodart Co.**
Follett School Solutions.

Aberon Pubns., *(978-0-9641959; 978-0-9963210)* 549 W. 123rd St., Suite 2b, New York, NY 10027 USA Tel 212-663-9228; Fax: 212-961-9515
E-mail: aberonp@aol.com.

Abidenme Bks., *(978-0-9714515)* P.O. Box 144, Island Heights, NJ 08732-0144 USA (SAN 254-1203) Fax: 732-573-0551; Toll Free: 888-540-8022
E-mail: angela@booksformilitarykids.com
Web site: http://booksformilitarykids.com.

Abiding Life Ministries International, *(978-0-9670843; 978-0-9819546)* Orders Addr.: P.O. Box 620998, Littleton, CO 80162-0998 USA (SAN 299-8629) Tel 303-972-0859; 719-485-5558; Fax: 303-973-2682; Edit Addr.: 8191 Southpark Ln. Unit 102, Littleton, CO 80120-4639 USA; *Imprints:* Abiding Life Press (Abiding Life Pr)
E-mail: AbideLife@aol.com
Web site: http://www.abidinglife.com.

Abiding Life Pr. *Imprint of* **Abiding Life Ministries International**

Abiding Life Press *See* **Abiding Life Ministries International**

Abilene Christian Univ. Pr., *(978-0-89112; 978-0-915547; 978-1-68426)* ACU Box 29138, Abilene, TX 79699-9138 USA (SAN 207-1681) Tel 325-674-2720; Fax: 325-674-6471; Toll Free: 800-444-4228; *Imprints:* Leafwood Publishers (LeafwoodPubs)
E-mail: lettie.morrow@acu.edu
Web site: http://www.acupressbooks.com/; http://www.leafwoodpublishers.com
Dist(s): **Anchor Distributors**
INscribe Digital
Independent Pubs. Group
Send The Light Distribution LLC
ebrary, Inc.

†Abingdon Pr., *(978-0-687; 978-1-4267; 978-1-63088; 978-1-5018; 978-1-7910)* Div. of United Methodist Publishing House, Orders Addr.: 2222 Rosa L. Parks Blvd., Nashville, TN 37228 USA Tel 615-749-6409; 615-749-6000; Fax: 615-749-6056; Toll Free: 800-627-1789; Edit Addr.: 201 Eighth Ave., S., Nashville, TN 37202 USA (SAN 699-9956) Tel 615-749-6000; Toll Free Fax: 800-445-8189; Toll Free: 800-672-1789; *Imprints:* Cokesbury (Cokesbury)
E-mail: rburgoyne@umpublishing.org; cokes_serv@cokesbury.com
Web site: http://www.abingdonpress.com/; http://www.umph.org
Dist(s): **Church Publishing, Inc.**
Follett School Solutions
Ingram Publisher Services
Simon & Schuster, Inc.
United Methodist Publishing Hse.
ebrary, Inc.; *CIP.*

Abingdon Square Publishing, Ltd., *(978-0-9823480; 978-0-9830762; 978-1-7349849)* 463 W. St., Suite G-122, New York, NY 10014-2029 USA Tel 212-691-2543
Web site: http://www.abingdonsquarepublishing.com.

Abique, Incorporated *See* **Abique Pub**

Abique Pub, *(978-1-892298)* Orders Addr.: 50 Haystack Pl., Pagosa Springs, CO 81147 USA Tel 970-731-2513 during spring and summer; 214-466-1074 during winter; Edit Addr.: 1512 Country Ln., Allen, TX 75002 USA Tel 972-359-0136 Fall and winter
E-mail: abique@gmail.com.

Able Journey Pr., *(978-1-934249)* P.O. Box 5517, Trenton, NJ 08638-9998 USA Toll Free Fax: 877-650-3610; Toll Free: 877-650-3610
E-mail: ivanwright@ablejourneypress.com
Web site: http://ablejourneypress.com.

AbleNet, Inc., *(978-0-9666667; 978-0-9764246; 978-0-9819934; 978-0-9825180; 978-1-935696; 978-1-62744)* 2625 Patton Rd., Roseville, MN 55113 USA Tel 651-294-2200; Toll Free: 800-322-0956; 1081 Tenth Ave./Southeast, Minneapolis, MN 55414
E-mail: kbrown@ablenetinc.com; customerservice@ablenetinc.com
Web site: http://www.ablenetinc.com
Dist(s): **Follett School Solutions.**

Abligio Bks., *(978-1-934437)* 1330 E Scorpio Pl, Chandler, AZ 85249-2136 USA (SAN 853-2362) Tel 480-272-6063
E-mail: publisher@abligio.com
Web site: http://abligio.com.

ABM Enterprises, Inc., *(978-0-9656688)* Orders Addr.: P.O. Box 123, Amelia Court House, VA 23002-0123 USA Tel 804-561-3655; Fax: 804-561-2065; Edit Addr.: 16311 Goodesbridge Rd., Amelia Court House, VA 23002 USA
E-mail: LarryDavies@SowingSeedsofFaith.com
Web site: http://www.SowingSeedsofFaith.com.

Abolet Publishing, *(978-0-9774555; 978-0-9818984)* 1348 East Capitol St., NE, Washington, DC 20003 USA (SAN 856-8618)
Web site: http://www.ronkoshes.com.

Aboriginal Studies Pr. (AUS) *(978-0-85575; 978-0-908097; 978-0-9871353; 978-0-646-33600-8; 978-1-922059; 978-1-922102; 978-1-925302) Dist. by* **IPG Chicago.**

Abounding Love Ministries, Inc., *(978-0-9678519)* Orders Addr.: P.O. Box 425, Jackson, CA 95642 USA Tel 209-296-7264 (phone/fax); Edit Addr.: 225 Endicott Ave., Jackson, CA 95642-2512 USA
E-mail: alms@aboundinglove.org
Web site: http://www.aboundinglove.org.

About Comics, *(978-0-9716338; 978-0-9753958; 978-0-9790750; 978-0-9819563; 978-1-936404; 978-1-949996)* 1569 Edgemont Dr., Camarillo, CA 93010-3130 USA
E-mail: questions@aboutcomics.com
Web site: http://www.Combustoica.com; http://www.aboutcomics.com
Dist(s): **Diamond Comic Distributors, Inc.**
Diamond Bk. Distributors.

About Time Publishing, *(978-0-9791550; 978-0-9821214; 978-0-9847928; 978-0-9983133; 978-1-7349133)* 29792 Harper Rd., Junction City, OR 97448 USA Tel 541-954-6724
E-mail: mfaris1950@gmail.com
Web site: http://www.abouttimepublishing.com; http://www.judeco.net.

About Your Time LLC, *(978-0-9744768; 978-0-9799737; 978-0-9844266)* P.O. Box 582, S. Orange, NJ 07079 USA Tel 646-232-3212; Fax: 973-766-1019
E-mail: ayt1@busybodybook.com
Web site: http://www.busybodybook.com
Dist(s): **Publishers Storage & Shipping.**

Above Any Odds Enterainment, *(978-0-578-40081-5; 978-0-578-67440-7)* 20 Blum St., Newark, NJ 07103 USA Tel 917-573-9236
E-mail: vineldaa85@gmail.com.

Above the Clouds Publishing, *(978-1-60227)* P.O. Box 313, Stanhope, NJ 07874 USA (SAN 852-1328) Fax: 973-448-7789; Toll Free: 800-936-2319
E-mail: publisher@abovethecloudspublishing.com
Web site: http://abovethecloudspublishing.com
Dist(s): **Follett School Solutions.**

Abovo Publishing, *(978-0-9762007)* P.O. Box 1231, Bonita, CA 91908 USA
E-mail: abovo@cox.net
Dist(s): **Quality Bks., Inc.**

ABR Pubns., *(978-0-9742367)* Orders Addr.: 1945 Cliff Valley Way, Ste. 250b, Atlanta, GA 30329 USA Tel 404-510-3131; Fax: 404-371-1838
E-mail: roll6128@bellsouth.net
Web site: http://www.drboydpublications.com
Dist(s): **Follett School Solutions.**

Abrams & Co. Pubs., Inc.,
Dist(s): **Abrams Learning Trends.**

Abrams Appleseed *Imprint of* **Abrams, Inc.**

Abrams Bks. for Young Readers *Imprint of* **Abrams, Inc.**

Abrams ComicArts *Imprint of* **Abrams, Inc.**

Abrams, Harry N. Incorporated *See* **Abrams, Inc.**

Abrams Image *Imprint of* **Abrams, Inc.**

Abrams, Inc., *(978-0-8109; 978-1-4197; 978-1-61769; 978-1-61312; 978-1-68335)* A Subsidiary of La Martinière Groupe, Orders Addr.: The Market Building Third Floor, 72-82 Rosebery Ave., London, EC1R 4RW GBR Tel 020 7713 2060; Fax: 020 7713 2061; Edit Addr.: 115 West 18th St., New York, NY 10011 USA (SAN 200-2434) Tel 212-206-7715; Fax: 212-519-1210; *Imprints:* Amulet Books (Amulet Bks); Abrams Books for Young Readers (ABYR); Abrams Image (Abrams Image); Abrams ComicArts (Abram ComicArts); Abrams Appleseed (AbramsAppleseed); Abrams Noterie (Abrams Noterie); Abrams Press (Abrams Pr); Overlook Press, The (OvrlkPr)
E-mail: webmaster@abramsbooks.com
Web site: http://www.abramsbooks.com
Dist(s): **Andrews McMeel Publishing**
Children's Plus, Inc.
Ediciones Universal
Follett School Solutions
Hachette Bk. Group
Norton, W. W. & Co., Inc.
Open Road Integrated Media, Inc.

Abrams Noterie *Imprint of* **Abrams, Inc.**

Abrams Pr. *Imprint of* **Abrams, Inc.**

ABREN (A Bk. to Read Empowers Nicaraguans), *(978-1-937314)* 1310 Mercy St., Mountain View, CA 94041 USA Tel 415-637-4243
E-mail: kmundera@yahoo.com.

Abril BookStore & Publishing, *(978-0-9704131; 978-0-9772265; 978-0-9796842; 978-1-949618)* 415 E. Broadway, Suite 102, Glendale, CA 91205 USA Tel 818-243-4112; Fax: 818-243-4158
E-mail: noor@abrilbooks.com; abrilbooks@earthlink.net
Web site: http://www.abrilbooks.com
Dist(s): **Follett School Solutions.**

Absalon Pr., *(978-0-9846687)* 34192 Capistrano by the Sea, Dana Point, CA 92629 USA (SAN 920-1335) Tel 949-493-6953 (phone/fax)
E-mail: jody.payne@cox.net
Web site: www.absalonpress.com.

Absecon Lighthouse, *(978-0-9779988)* 31 S. Rhode Island Ave., Atlantic City, NJ 08401 USA Tel 609-441-1360; Fax: 609-449-1919
E-mail: abseconlighthouse@verizon.net
Web site: http://www.abseconlighthouse.org.

Absey & Co., *(978-1-888842)* 23011 Northcrest, Spring, TX 77389 USA Tel 281-257-2340; Fax: 281-251-4676; Toll Free: 888-412-2739
E-mail: Abseyandco@aol.com
Web site: http://www.absey.biz
Dist(s): **Bibliotech, Inc.**
Brodart Co.
Follett School Solutions.

Absolutely Perfect!, *(978-0-9970546)* 139 Summer St., Kennebunk, ME 04043 USA Tel 207-985-8888
E-mail: danie.connolly@yahoo.com.

ABTA Pubns. & Products, *(978-0-9761517; 978-0-9844660)* P.O. Box 492123, Redding, CA 96049 USA Fax: 530-221-0917
E-mail: info@abtaproducts.com
Web site: http://www.autismandbehavior.com.

ABUAA, Inc., *(978-0-9760406)* Orders Addr.: P.O. Box 1542, Whitefish, MT 59937 USA Fax: 406-362-3407; Edit Addr.: 7347 Farm to Market Rd., Whitefish, MT 59937 USA; *Imprints:* A Kidz World (Kidz Wrld)
Web site: http://www.akidzworld.com.

Abundant Harvest Publishing, *(978-1-7327173; 978-1-7349949)* 35145 Oak Glen Rd, Yucaipa, CA 92399 USA Tel 909-222-5338
E-mail: eriksahakian@gmail.com
Web site: www.abundantharvestpublishing.com.

Abuzz Bks., *(978-0-9715865)* P.O. Box 15753, Scottsdale, AZ 85267 USA
E-mail: author@20umbrellas.com
Dist(s): **Quality Bks., Inc.**

Abuzz Press *Imprint of* **Booklocker.com, Inc.**

Abysso Bks., (*978-0-9747228*) 817 E. Mackinac Ave., Oak Creek, WI 53154 USA
E-mail: asala@mac.com
Web site: http://www.pottersfield.posthaven.com; pottersfield.posthaven.com.

AC Pubns. Group LLC, (*978-1-933302*) P.O. Box 260543, Lakewood, CO 80226 USA
E-mail: dksimoneau@acpublicationsgroup.com
Web site: http://www.acpublicationsgroup.com.

AC Writings, (*978-0-9796780; 978-0-578-50055-3; 978-0-578-68252-5*) 322 PUNTA BAJA Dr., Solana Beach, CA 92075 USA (SAN 854-0896).

Acacia Publishing, Inc., (*978-0-9666572; 978-0-9671187; 978-0-9762224; 978-0-9774306; 978-0-9788283; 978-0-9790826; 978-0-9792531; 978-0-9793273; 978-0-9814629; 978-1-935089*) 770 N. Monterey St. Ste. C, Gilbert, AZ 85233-3821 USA Toll Free: 866-265-4553
E-mail: jason@hiredpen.com; editor@acaiapublishing.com; kgray@acaciapublishing.com
Web site: http://www.acaciapublishing.com
Dist(s): **Book Clearing Hse.**
Follett School Solutions.

Academic Edge, Inc., (*978-0-9754754; 978-0-9814537*) Orders Addr.: P.O. Box 23605, Lexington, KY 40523-3605 USA Tel 859-224-3000; Fax: 812-331-8021; Edit Addr.: 216 E. Allen St., Suite 143, Bloomington, IN 47402 USA
E-mail: george@academicedge.com
Web site: http://www.academicedge.com.

Academic Internet Publishers Incorporated *See* **Cram101 Inc.**

Academic Media Solutions *See* **Putnam Productions**

Academic Solutions, Inc., (*978-0-9635364; 978-0-9740200*) Orders Addr.: P.O. Box 102, Harvard, MA 01451 USA Tel 978-456-6829; Fax: 978-456-3053; Toll Free: 877-222-3765 (877-ACADSOL)
E-mail: asibooks@acadsol.com
Web site: http://www.acadsol.com.

Academic Systems Corp., (*978-1-928962*) 2933 Bunker Hill Ln. Ste. 107, Santa Clara, CA 95054-1124 USA Toll Free: 800-694-6830
E-mail: info@academic.com
Web site: http://www.academic.com.

Academic Therapy Pubns., Inc., (*978-0-87879; 978-1-57128; 978-1-63402*) 20 Leveroni Ct., Novato, CA 94949-5746 USA (SAN 201-2111) Tel 415-883-3314; Fax: 415-883-3720; Toll Free: 800-422-7249
E-mail: sales@academictherapy.com; customerservice@academictherapy.com
Web site: http://www.academictherapy.com; http://www.highnoonbooks.com
Dist(s): **Cambium Education, Inc.**
Follett School Solutions
P C I Education
PRO-ED, Inc.

Academy Chicago Pubs., Ltd. *Imprint of* **Chicago Review Pr., Inc.**

†Academy of American Franciscan History, (*978-0-88382*) 1712 Euclid Ave., Berkeley, CA 94709 USA (SAN 201-1964) Tel 510-548-1755; Fax: 510-549-9466
E-mail: acadafh@fst.edu
Web site: http://www.aafh.org
Dist(s): **Johns Hopkins Univ. Pr.**
Univ. Pr. of Florida; *CIP.*

Academy Park Pr. *Imprint of* **Williamson County Public Library**

Acadian Hse. Publishing, (*978-0-925417; 978-0-9995884; 978-1-7352641*) Orders Addr.: P.O. Box 52247, Lafayette, LA 70505 USA Tel 337-235-8851; Fax: 337-235-9925; Toll Free: 800-850-8851; Edit Addr.: 100 Asma Blvd., Suite 365, Lafayette, LA 70508 USA (SAN 253-1305)
E-mail: info@acadianhouse.com
Web site: http://www.acadianhouse.com
Dist(s): **Follett School Solutions**
Forest Sales & Distributing Co.

ACC Children's Classics (GBR) (*978-1-85149*) *Dist. by* **Natl Bk Netwk.**

Accelarated Christian Education, Inc., (*978-1-56265*) P.O. Box 1438, Lewisville, TX 75067-1438 USA Tel 972-315-1776; Fax: 972-315-8681.

Accelerator Bks., (*978-0-9815245; 978-0-9841399; 978-0-9838940; 978-0-9848966; 978-0-692-79234-6*) P.O. Box 1241, Princeton, NJ 08542 USA Tel 732-642-9721
E-mail: gemma@acceleratorbooks.com
Web site: http://www.acceleratorbooks.com.

Accend Pr., (*978-0-692-09336-8; 978-0-578-43344-8*) 39 Evergreen St., Mount Holly, NJ 08060 USA Tel 609-744-5078
E-mail: kristlokan@gmail.com.

Accent On Success, (*978-0-9743700*) 29 Benton Pl., Saint Louis, MO 63104 USA Tel 314-664-6110; Fax: 314-664-6577
E-mail: jbishop@accentonsuccess.com
Web site: http://www.TeachingMoments.com.

Accent Pubns. *Imprint of* **Ajoyin Publishing, Inc.**

Access for Disabled Americans, (*978-1-928616*) 301 Village Sq., Orinda, CA 94563-2505 USA
E-mail: PSmither@aol.com
Web site: http://maxpages.com/disabledaccess; http://www.accessfordisabled.com.

Access-4-All, Inc., (*978-0-9744908*) P.O. Box 220751, Sain Louis, MO 63122-0751 USA Tel 314-821-7011; Fax: 314-909-8086
E-mail: steve@access-4-all.com
Web site: http://www.access-4-all.com.

Accessibilities, (*978-0-9774546*) 1131 E. Spruce St., Sault Ste. Marie, MI 49783 USA
E-mail: geri.taeckens@isahealthfund.org
Web site: http://www.isahealthfund.org.

Acclaim Pr., Inc., (*978-0-9773198; 978-0-9790025; 978-0-9798802; 978-1-935001; 978-1-938905; 978-1-942613; 978-1-948901*) Orders Addr.: P.O. Box 238, Morley, MO 63767 USA (SAN 991-0980) Tel 573-472-9800; Fax: 573-472-1608; Toll Free: 877-427-2665; Edit Addr.: 171 Co. Hwy. 430, Oran, MO 63771 USA; *Imprints:* Joey Books (Joey Bks)
Web site: http://www.acclaimpress.com
Dist(s): **Follett School Solutions**
Partners Bk. Distributing, Inc.

Acclimated Spooks, Light, & Power, (*978-0-615-25755-6*) 1106 W. 2nd, Tahlequah, OK 74464 USA
E-mail: graclandwest@gmail.com
Web site: http://www.acclimatedspooks.com
Dist(s): **Lulu Pr., Inc.**

Accordian Bks., (*978-0-9754098*) Orders Addr.: P.O. Box 69912, West Hollywood, CA 90069 USA (SAN 256-0046); Edit Addr.: 69912 W. Hollywood, Hollywood, CA 90069 USA
E-mail: crystalilluminations@msn.com.

Ace *Imprint of* **Penguin Publishing Group**

Ace Academics, Inc., (*978-1-57633; 978-1-881374*) 69 Tulip St., Bergenfield, NJ 07621 USA Tel 201-784-0001; Fax: 201-784-7704; *Imprints:* Exambusters (Exambusters)
E-mail: highself@aol.com; info@exambusters.com; exambusters@gmail.com
Web site: http://www.exambusters.com
Dist(s): **INscribe Digital**
Independent Pubs. Group
eBookit.com
.

Ace Reid Enterprises *See* **Cowpokes Cartoon Bks.**

Acedrex Publishing, (*978-1-937291*) 550 N. Harrison Rd. No. 5101, Tucson, AZ 85748 USA Tel 401-743-0052
E-mail: acedrexpublishing@yahoo.com
Web site: acedrex.com.

Acen Press *See* **DNA Pr.**

ACER Pr. (AUS) (*978-0-85563; 978-0-86431; 978-1-74286*) *Dist. by* **IPG Chicago.**

Acey, Mary J., (*978-0-9771920*) 178-39 147th Ave., Springfield Gardens, NY 11434 USA Tel 718-949-2670; Fax: 718-949-7464
E-mail: jestac1@aol.com.

Aceybee Publishing, (*978-0-9763958*) 285 W. Kootenai, No. 7, Richfield, ID 23349-5344 USA.

Achiev *See* **Achieve Pubns.**

Achieve Pubns., (*978-0-9727762; 978-0-615-12053-9*) Orders Addr.: 1216 Scobee Dr., Lansdale, PA 19446 USA Fax: 215-368-1431 (fax orders)
E-mail: achievepub@verizon.net
Web site: http://www.achievepublications.com
Dist(s): **Book Clearing Hse.**
Follett School Solutions.

Achieve3000, (*978-1-932166; 978-0-615-12027-0; 978-1-935675; 978-1-938916; 978-1-63256*) 1091 River Ave., Lakewood, NJ 08701 USA Tel 732-367-5505; Fax: 732-367-2313; Toll Free: 877-803-6505
E-mail: kelly.tanko@achieve3000.com
Web site: http://www.achieve3000.com.

Achievers Technology Resource, Inc., (*978-0-9716113*) PMB No. 455, 442 Rte. 202-206 N., Bedminster, NJ 07921-1522 USA (SAN 254-2811)
Web site: http://www.achieversrus.com.

Achieving Corporate Excellence, Inc., (*978-0-9746262*) Orders Addr.: P.O. Box 651119, Vero Beach, FL 32965-1119 USA Toll Free: 877-656-8313; Edit Addr.: 8003 Kenwood Rd., Fort Pierce, FL 34951 USA
Web site: http://www.acespeaks.com.

ACME Pr., (*978-0-9629880*) Orders Addr.: P.O. Box 1702, Westminster, MD 21158 USA Tel 410-848-7577; Edit Addr.: 1116 E. Deep Run Rd., Westminster, MD 21158 USA
Dist(s): **Follett School Solutions.**

Acmon Blue Publishing, (*978-0-9744792*) P.O. Box 475, Tujunga, CA 91043-0475 USA (SAN 255-5638) Tel 818-352-2551 (phone/fax)
E-mail: info@acmonblue.com
Web site: http://www.acmonblue.com.

Acorn *Imprint of* **Oak Tree Publishing**

Acorn Bks., (*978-0-9664470; 978-1-930472*) 7337 Terrace, Kansas City, MO 64114-1256 USA Tel 816-523-8321; Fax: 816-333-3843; Toll Free: 888-422-0320 Do not confuse with companies with the same or similar name in Springfield, IL, Bloomington, IN, St. Albans, VT
E-mail: jami.parkison@micro.com
Web site: http://www.acornbks.com.

Acorn Bks., (*978-0-9648957; 978-0-9837299*) P.O. Box 7348, Springfield, IL 62791-7348 USA Tel 217-525-8202; Fax: 217-525-8212 Do not confuse with companies iwth the same or similar name in Kansas, MO, Bloomington, IN, St. Albans, VT
E-mail: amy@afterabortion.org; elliotinstitute@gmail.com
Web site: http://www.afterabortion.org
Dist(s): **Ingram Content Group**
MyiLibrary.

Acorn Guild Press, LLC *See* **Marion Street Pr., LLC**

Acorn Hill Pr., (*978-0-9788889*) 155 Parkhurst Dr., Jackson, MS 39202 USA Tel 601-668-3533.

Acorn Pr., The (CAN) (*978-0-9698606; 978-1-894838; 978-1-77366*) *Dist. by* **BTPS.**

Acorn Publishing, (*978-0-937921*) Div. of Vitesse Pr., PMB 367, 45 State St., Montpelier, VT 05601 USA (SAN 659-4840) Tel 802-229-4243; Fax: 802-229-6939 Do not confuse with companies with the same or similar name in Midvale, UT, Broomfield, CO, Battle Creek, MI, Sisters, OR, Suffern, NY,Saltlake City, UT, Portland, OR, Sping Lake, MI
E-mail: dick@vitessepress.com
Web site: http://www.vitessepress.com
Dist(s): **Hood, Alan C. & Co., Inc.**

Acorn Publishing, (*978-0-9678801; 978-0-9710988; 978-0-9728969; 978-0-9774449*) Div. of Development Initiatives, 186 N. 23rd St., Battle Creek, MI 49015-1711 USA (SAN 854-6258) Tel 269-962-8184 (phone\fax); Toll Free: 877-700-2219 (phone\fax) Do not confuse with companies with the same or similar name in Broomfield, CO, Midvale, UT, Montpelier, VT, Sisters, OR, Suffern, NY, Salt Lake City, UT, Portland, OR, Sping Lake, MI
E-mail: editor@acornpublishing.com
Web site: http://www.acornpublishing.com.

Acoustic Learning Inc., (*978-0-9761435; 978-0-9800581; 978-1-936412*) 215 Prospect Ave., Highland Park, IL 60035-3357 USA
E-mail: eartraining@aruffo.com
Web site: http://www.acousticlearning.com.

Acres Publishing, (*978-0-9741081*) 311 Prospect St., Alton, IL 62002 USA.

Acrobatic Cats Publishing *See* **MJ Brooks Co.**

Across Ocean Bks., (*978-0-944176*) 1309 Redwood Ln., Davis, CA 95616 USA (SAN 242-8741) Tel 530-304-9927 Do not confuse with Terra Nova Press in Pacifica, CA .

ACS, LLC Arnica Creative Services, (*978-0-9726535; 978-0-9745686; 978-0-9794771; 978-0-9801942; 978-0-9816822; 978-0-9822482; 978-0-9826401*) 41206 wood Haven Dr., Palm Desert, CA 92211 USA (SAN 255-0091) Tel 503-593-2618
E-mail: ross@ideasbyacs.com
Web site: http://www.ideasbyacs.com
Dist(s): **American West Bks.**

ACTA Pubns., (*978-0-87946; 978-0-914070; 978-0-915388*) 5559 Howard St., Skokie, IL 60077-2621 USA (SAN 204-7489) Toll Free Fax: 800-397-0079; Toll Free: 800-397-2282; 4848 N. Clark St., Chicago, IL 60640
E-mail: actapublications@aol.com
Web site: http://www.actapublications.com
Dist(s): **BookMobile**
INscribe Digital
Independent Pubs. Group
Spring Arbor Distributors, Inc.

Actar D, (*978-0-9893317; 978-1-940291; 978-1-945150; 978-1-948765*) 440 Pk. Ave. South, 17th FL, New York, NY 10016 USA Tel 212-966-2207; Fax: 212-966-2214
E-mail: brian@actar-d.com; ricardo.devesa@actar-d.com
Web site: www.actar-d.com
Dist(s): **Ingram Publisher Services.**

Action Bks., (*978-0-900575; 978-0-9765692; 978-0-9799755; 978-0-9831480; 978-0-9898048*) Dept Of English, U. Of Notre Dame 356 O'shaughnessy Hall, Notre Dame, IN 46556 USA
Web site: http://www.actionbooks.org
Dist(s): **SPD-Small Pr. Distribution.**

Action Factor, Inc., (*978-0-9720763; 978-0-9754618*) PMB 218, 3195 Dayton-Xenia Rd., Suite 900, Beavercreek, OH 45434-6390 USA Tel 937-426-4364 (phone/fax)
E-mail: cgifford@actionfactor.com
Web site: http://www.actionfactor.com.

Action Lab Entertainment, (*978-0-9854952; 978-0-9859652; 978-1-939352; 978-1-63229*) 306 Bridlewood Ct., Canonsburg, PA 15317 USA Tel 513-313-7612
E-mail: spryor@actionlabcomics.com
Web site: http://www.actionlabcomics.com
Dist(s): **Diamond Comic Distributors, Inc.**
Diamond Bk. Distributors
MyiLibrary.

Action Organizing, (*978-0-9721964*) Div. of Successful Organizing Solutions, Orders Addr.: 406 Shato Ln., Madison, WI 53716 USA Tel 608-441-6767; Edit Addr.: P.O. Box 202, Milton, WI 53563 USA Tel 608-868-4079; Toll Free: 888-577-6655
E-mail: info@SOSorganize.net; sales@SOSorganize.net
Web site: http://www.actionorganizing.com.

Action Publishing, Inc., (*978-1-882210*) Div. of Action Products International, Inc., 344 Cypress Rd., Ocala, FL 34472-3108 USA Tel 352-687-2202; Fax: 352-687-4961; Toll Free: 800-772-2846 Do not confuse with companies with the same or similar name in Newport Beach, CA, Burlingame, CA, West Los Angeles, CA, Houstin, TX, Chicago, IL, Glendale, CA, Austin, TX.

Actionopolis *Imprint of* **Komikwerks, LLC**

Active Images, (*978-0-9740567; 978-0-9766761*) Orders Addr.: 8910 Rayford Dr., Los Angeles, CA 90045 USA Tel 310-215-0362; Fax: 775-890-5787 do not confuse with Active Images, Incorporated in Sterling, VA
E-mail: richard@comicraft.com
Web site: http://www.activeimages.com
Dist(s): **Ingram Content Group**
Partners Pubs. Group, Inc.

Active Learning Corp., (*978-0-912813*) P.O. Box 254, New Paltz, NY 12561 USA (SAN 282-7794) Tel 845-255-0844; Fax: 845-255-8796
E-mail: panmans@newpaltz.edu; info@activelearning.com
Web site: http://www.activelearningcorp.com.

Active Learning Systems, LLC, (*978-1-57652*) P.O. Box 254, Epping, NH 03042 USA Tel 603-679-3332; Fax: 603-679-2611; Toll Free: 800-644-5059
E-mail: info@iimresearch.com
Web site: http://www.iimresearch.com.

Active Media Publishing, LLC, (*978-0-9745645; 978-0-9848808; 978-1-940367*) Orders Addr.: 614 E. Hwy 50 No. 235, Clermont, FL 34711 USA (SAN 255-6545); 614 E. Hwy 50 No. 235, Clermont, FL 34711 (SAN 255-6545); *Imprints:* Red Giant Entertainment (RedGiant)
E-mail: wizbenny@aol.com
Web site: http://redgiantentertainment.com
Dist(s): **Diamond Comic Distributors, Inc.**
Diamond Bk. Distributors
Elsevier.

Active Parenting Pubs., (*978-0-9618020; 978-1-880283; 978-1-59723*) 1955 Vaughn Rd. NW, Suite 108, Kennesaw, GA 30144-7808 USA (SAN 666-301X) Tel 770-429-0565; Fax: 770-429-0334; Toll Free: 800-825-0060
E-mail: cservice@activeparenting.com; ckeller@activeparenting.com
Web site: http://www.activeparenting.com
Dist(s): **Follett School Solutions**
National Bk. Network.

Active Spud Pr., (*978-0-9845388*) 324 E. 13th St., No. 3, New York, NY 10003 USA Tel 818-518-7381
E-mail: steve@activespudpress.com
Web site: http://www.activespudpress.com.

Active Synapse, (*978-0-9677255*) Orders Addr.: 5336 Park Lane Dr., Columbus, OH 43231-4072 USA
E-mail: Daryn@ActiveSynapse.com
Web site: http://www.activesynapse.com
Dist(s): **Brodart Co.**
Cold Cut Comics Distribution
Diamond Distributors, Inc.
Emery-Pratt Co.
Follett School Solutions
Midwest Library Service.

Activity Resources Co., Inc., (*978-0-918932; 978-1-882293*) Orders Addr.: P.O. Box 4875, Hayward, CA 94540 USA (SAN 209-0201) Tel 510-782-1300; Fax: 510-782-8172; Edit Addr.: 20655 Hathaway Ave., Hayward, CA 94541 USA
E-mail: info@activityresources.com
Web site: http://www.activityresources.com
Dist(s): **Delta Education, LLC**
Follett School Solutions
Seymour, Dale Pubns.

ACTNew Bks., (*978-0-9762326*) 12687 Blue Star Memorial Hwy., South Haven, MI 49090 USA
E-mail: actnewbooks@yahoo.com
Web site: http://www.actnewbooks.com.

Acts of Kindness, (*978-1-7333535*) 3103 S. 115th E. Ave., Tulsa, OK 74146 USA Tel 918-812-5181
E-mail: godwinchishala@yahoo.com
Web site: HEAVENSHEARTBEAT.CO.

ACTS Pr., (*978-0-9721698; 978-0-9800065; 978-1-940661*) Div. of Coptic Orthodox Church - Diocese of Los Angeles, 1617 W. La Palma Ave., Anaheim, CA 92801 USA
E-mail: office@actslibrary.org
Web site: www.actslibrary.org.

Actual Magic Enterprises, LLC, (*978-0-9891807; 978-1-7353558*) 17606 N. 17th Pl., Unit 1106, Phoenix, AZ 85022 USA Tel 602-992-5552
E-mail: debmctiernan@centurylink.net
Web site: www.deborahmctiernan.com.

Ad Center, The *See* **Leathers Publishing**

Ad Stellae Bks., (*978-0-615-31487-7; 978-0-615-31488-4; 978-0-615-34834-6; 978-0-615-62523-2; 978-0-615-64517-9; 978-0-615-80434-7; 978-0-692-29376-8*) 3088 Delta Pines Dr., Eugene, OR 97408 USA Fax: 866-302-3827
Web site: http://www.adstellaebooks.com
Dist(s): **CreateSpace Independent Publishing Platform**
Smashwords.

Adam Enterprises *See* **Amberwood Pr.**

Adam Hill Pubns., (*978-0-9769360*) Orders Addr.: 9001 SW 55 Ct., Fort Lauderdale, FL 33328 USA
E-mail: adamhilldesign@gmail.com
Web site: http://www.adamhilldesign.us
Dist(s): **Baker & Taylor Publisher Services (BTPS)**
BWI
Follett School Solutions.

Adams & Perkins *See* **Rocket City Publishing**

Adams, Anne Marie Rea, (*978-0-9742782*) 9 Terraza Dr., Newport Coast, CA 92657-1510 USA.

Adams, Carl M, (*978-0-9899710*) 1207 Honu Loop, Aiea, HI 96701 USA Tel 309-696-7636
E-mail: cmadams6@yahoo.com.

Adams, Clint *See* **Credo Italia**

Adam's Creations Publishing, LLC, (*978-0-9785695*) Div. of JAH Innovations, Inc., 550 Fossett Rd., Zebulon, GA 30295 USA (SAN 851-0091) Tel 404-909-1025
E-mail: info@adamscreationspublishing.com
Web site: http://www.adamscreationspublishing.com
Dist(s): **BCH Fulfillment & Distribution.**

Adams, Evelyn, (*978-0-9761102*) 727 Virginia Ave., Midland, PA 15059-1429 USA Tel 724-643-9968; Fax: 724-775-8648
E-mail: rjb@timesnet.net
Web site: http://www.storiesfromvic.com.

Adams, Jeanette *See* **Camelot Tales**

†Adams Media Corp., (*978-0-937860; 978-1-55850; 978-1-58062; 978-1-59337; 978-1-59869; 978-1-60550; 978-1-4405; 978-1-5072*) Div.of Simon & Schuster, Inc., Orders Addr.: Simon and Schuster, Inc. Ordering Processing Dept. 100 Front St., Riverside, NJ 08075-1197 USA (SAN 215-2886) Toll Free Fax: 800-943-9831; Toll Free: 800-223-2336; Edit Addr.: Adams Media 57 Littlefield St., Avon, MA 02322 USA Tel 508-427-7100; *Imprints:* Everything (EverythingUSA)
E-mail: Khelsea.Purvis@simonandschuster.com; Purchaseorders@simonandschuster.com
Web site: http://www.simonandschuster.com
Dist(s): **Cranbury International**
CreateSpace Independent Publishing Platform

Ebsco Publishing
Follett School Solutions
Curreri, Michelle Morrow
MyiLibrary
Simon & Schuster, Inc.
Univ. Pr. of Kentucky
ebrary, Inc.; *CIP.*

Adams Publishing *See* **Adams Media Corp.**

Adams Publishing, (*978-0-9729189*) 320 Lincoln Rd., Branchland, WV 25506 USA Tel 304-824-2504 (phone/fax) Do not confuse with companies with the same or similar name in Topanga, CA, Rainier, WA, Boston, MA
E-mail: Adamspublisher@zoominternet.net
Web site: http://www.geocities.com/daycarebook/index.html.

Adamson, Mac, (*978-0-9779369*) P.O. Box 690, Midway, UT 84049 USA Tel 801-318-8544
E-mail: madamson@kids4fitkids.org
Web site: http://kids4fitkids.org.

Adams-Pomeroy Pr., (*978-0-9661009; 978-0-9967921*) Orders Addr.: P.O. Box 189, Albany, WI 53502 USA Tel 608-862-3645; Fax: 608-862-3647; Toll Free: 877-862-3645; Edit Addr.: 103 N. Jackson St., Albany, WI 53502 USA
E-mail: adamspomeroy@ckhnet.com
Dist(s): **Follett School Solutions.**

Adaptive Studios, (*978-0-9960666; 978-0-9864484; 978-0-9964887; 978-1-945293*) 3733 Motor Ave 3rd Flr., Los Angeles, CA 90034 USA Tel 310-876-1675
E-mail: tj@adaptivestudios.com
Web site: adaptivestudios.com
Dist(s): **Ingram Publisher Services**
MyiLibrary.

ADB Artist Publishing, (*978-0-9798580*) Div. of Fusion Group, Inc., Orders Addr.: P.O. Box 490965, Lawrenceville, GA 30049 USA (SAN 854-5774).

Addassa Prendergast Pubs., (*978-0-9715016; 978-0-9716264; 978-0-9722239; 978-0-9723202*) Div. of Dawkins Project, The, 1531 Palmer Dr., Fayetteville, NC 28303 USA Tel 910-488-3953 (phone/fax); 910 488 3953
E-mail: bookman1531@yahoo.com; paulandrewdawkins@yahoo.com
Web site: http://www.thedawkinsproject.com.

Added Upon, Inc., (*978-0-9740319*) Orders Addr.: P.O. Box 65327, Vancouver, WA 98665 USA
E-mail: dunnjessel@msn.com.

Addi-Boo Bks., (*978-0-9911410*) 78 Ryerson St., Brooklyn, NY 11205 USA Tel 347-512-7882
E-mail: stephen.epps@eppsscholars.org.

Addison Wesley, (*978-0-06; 978-0-13; 978-0-201; 978-0-321; 978-0-582; 978-0-673; 978-0-8053*) 75 Arlington St., Suite 300, Boston, MA 02116 USA Tel 617-848-7500
Web site: http://www.aw-bc.com
Dist(s): **Pearson Education**
Pearson Technology Group.

Addison Wesley Schl., Orders Addr.: a/o Order Dept., 200 Old Tappan Rd., Old Tappan, NJ 07675 USA Toll Free Fax: 800-445-6991; Toll Free: 800-922-0579; Edit Addr.: 75 Arlington St., Boston, MA 02116 USA Tel 617-848-7500; *Imprints:* Scott Foresman (S-Foresman)
Web site: http://www.aw-bc.com.

Addison-Wesley Educational Pubs., Inc., (*978-0-321; 978-0-328; 978-0-673*) Div. of Addison Wesley Longman, Inc., 75 Arlington St., Boston, MA 02116 USA Tel 617-848-7500; Toll Free: 800-447-2226; *Imprints:* Scott Foresman (Scott Frsmn); Scott Foresman (S-Foresman)
Web site: http://www.awl.com.

†**Addison-Wesley Longman, Inc.,** (*978-0-201; 978-0-321; 978-0-582; 978-0-673; 978-0-8013; 978-0-8053; 978-0-9654123*) Orders Addr.: 200 Old Tappan Rd., Old Tappan, NJ 07675 USA (SAN 299-4739) Toll Free: 800-922-0579; Edit Addr.: 75 Arlington St., Suite 300, Boston, MA 02116 USA (SAN 200-2000) Tel 617-848-7500; Toll Free: 800-447-2226
E-mail: pearsoned@eds.com; orderdeptnj@pearsoned.com
Web site: http://www.awl.com
Dist(s): **Continental Bk. Co., Inc.**
MyiLibrary
Pearson Education
Trans-Atlantic Pubns., Inc.; *CIP.*

Addison-Wesley Longman, Ltd. (GBR) (*978-0-582*) *Dist. by* **Trans-Atl Phila.**

Addison-Wesley Publishing Company, Incorporated *See* **Addison-Wesley Longman, Inc.**

Addy's Rescue Fund, (*978-0-692-75867-0; 978-0-692-87784-5; 978-0-692-90384-1; 978-0-692-10251-0*) 642 Tamarack Ln, LEMOORE, CA 93245 USA Tel 559-904-1705.

Adelante Productions, Inc., (*978-0-9748017*) 600 Columbus Ave., 8G, New York, NY 10024 USA
E-mail: info@adelantepro.com
Web site: http://www.adelantepro.com.

Adelphi Pr., (*978-0-9610796*) 324 Hammonton Pl., Silver Spring, MD 20904-6344 USA (SAN 265-0541) Do not confuse with Adelphi Pr., Wyomissing, PA.

Adhemar Pr. USA, (*978-0-578-06275-4*) 7440 S. Black Hawk, No. 15-102, Englewood, CO 80112 USA
E-mail: jtbeiser@gmail.com.

AdHouse Bks., (*978-0-9721794; 978-0-9770304; 978-1-935233*) 3905 Brook Road., Richmond, VA 23227 USA
Dist(s): **Diamond Comic Distributors, Inc.**
Diamond Bk. Distributors.

Adibooks.com, (*978-0-9728909; 978-0-9743872; 978-0-9748753; 978-0-9758993; 978-0-9760575; 978-0-9763465; 978-0-9764322; 978-0-9767424; 978-0-9772505; 978-0-9776044; 978-0-9778606; 978-0-9779682; 978-0-9787515; 978-0-9789741; 978-0-9791289; 978-0-9794769; 978-0-9797885; 978-0-9801635; 978-0-9815594; 978-0-9817447; 978-0-9821073; 978-0-9823972; 978-0-9841294; 978-0-9843390; 978-0-9845852; 978-0-9846346; 978-0-9852824; 978-0-9887395; 978-0-9899978; 978-0-9914043; 978-0-9960318; 978-0-9904151; 978-0-9908554;) 181 Industrial Ave., Lowell, MA 01852 USA Fax: 978-458-3026*
E-mail: tcampbell@kingprinting.com
Web site: http://www.adibooks.com
Dist(s): **Cardinal Pubs. Group.**

Adirondack Kids Pr., (*978-0-9707044; 978-0-9826250; 978-1-7346509*) 39 Second St., Camden, NY 13316 USA Tel 315-245-2437
E-mail: info@adirondackkids.com
Web site: http://www.adirondackkids.com.

†**Adirondack Mountain Club, Inc.,** (*978-0-935272; 978-1-931951; 978-0-9896073; 978-0-9961168; 978-0-9986371; 978-1-7332240*) 814 Goggins Rd., Lake George, NY 12845-4117 USA (SAN 204-7691) Tel 518-668-4447 (customer service); Fax: 518-668-3746; Toll Free: 800-395-8080 (orders only)
E-mail: pubs@adk.org; adkinfo@adk.org
Web site: http://www.adk.org
Dist(s): **Alpenbooks Pr. LLC**
Equinox, Ltd.
North Country Bks., Inc.
Peregrine Outfitters; *CIP.*

Adisoft, Inc., (*978-0-9674897*) Orders Addr.: P.O. Box 2094, San Leandro, CA 94577-2094 USA Tel 510-483-3556; Fax: 510-483-3885; Edit Addr.: 664 Joaquin Ave., San Leandro, CA 94577 USA; *Imprints:* Wawa Press (Wawa)
E-mail: information@adisoft-inc.com
Web site: http://www.adisoft-inc.com.

Adiva, Incorporated *See* **TEG Publishing**

Adjust Communications, (*978-0-9765973*) 905 Hwy. 321 NW, Suite No. 364, Hickory, NC 28601 USA Tel 828-850-3237; Fax: 866-334-4360
Web site: http://www.victoryafterhighschool.com.

Adler, Karen, (*978-0-9679772*) 34738 McDaniel Dr., Northfork, CA 93643 USA Tel 559-877-2033.

Admirable Publishing LLC, (*978-0-9986891*) P.O. Box 881821, Port St. Lucie, FL 34988 USA Tel 772-332-5822
E-mail: debrasweeting@icloud.com.

Adonoke Inc., (*978-0-9773180*) 8354 Craine Dr., Manlius, NY 13104-9421 USA
E-mail: info@adonokebooks.com
Web site: http://www.adonokebooks.com.

Adoption Tribe Publishing *See* **MMB Enterprises, LLC**

ADR BookPrint *See* **ADR Inc.**

ADR Inc., (*978-0-9742743; 978-0-9761513; 978-0-9795033; 978-0-9802452; 978-0-9819864; 978-0-9908488; 978-0-578-76765-9*) 2012 Northern Ave., Wichita, KS 67216 USA Tel 316-522-5599; Fax: 316-522-5445; Toll Free: 800-767-6066
E-mail: bcatron@adr.biz
Web site: http://www.adr.biz.

Adrema Pr., (*978-0-9717290; 978-1-59611*) Orders Addr.: P.O. Box 14592, North Palm Beach, FL 33408 USA; Edit Addr.: P.O. Box 14157, North Palm Beach, FL 33408-2368 USA
E-mail: media@melissaa.com
Web site: http://adremapress.com
Dist(s): **CreateSpace Independent Publishing Platform**
Ingram Content Group.

ADV Manga, (*978-1-57813*) Div. of A. D. Vision, Inc., 5750 Bintliff, Suite 200, Houston, TX 77036 USA
Web site: http://www.ADVFilms.com
Dist(s): **Diamond Comic Distributors, Inc.**
Diamond Bk. Distributors.

Advance Cal Tech, Inc., (*978-0-943759*) 210 Clary Ave., San Gabriel, CA 91776-1375 USA (SAN 242-2603).

Advance Materials Ltd. (GBR) (*978-0-9532440; 978-0-9559265; 978-0-9547695; 978-0-9565431; 978-0-9576012; 978-0-9927056*) *Dist. by* **Cambridge U Pr.**

Advance Publishers, Incorporated *See* **Advance Pubs. LLC**

Advance Pubs. LLC, (*978-0-9619525; 978-1-57973; 978-1-885222*) 1060 Maitland Center Cmns Blvd. Ste. 365, Maitland, FL 32751-7499 USA (SAN 244-9226) Toll Free: 800-777-2041
E-mail: advpublish@aol.com; questions@adv-pub.com
Web site: http://www.advancepublishers.com.

Advance Publishing, Inc., (*978-0-9610810; 978-1-57537; 978-1-64206*) 6950 Fulton St., Houston, TX 77022 USA (SAN 263-9572) Tel 713-695-0600; Fax: 713-695-8585; Toll Free: 800-917-9630; *Imprints:* Another Sommer-Time Story (Another Sommer) Do not confuse with Advance Publishing, Brownburg, IN
E-mail: info@advancepublishing.com
Web site: http://www.advancepublishing.com
Dist(s): **Follett School Solutions.**

Advanced Marketing, S. de R. L. de C. V. (MEX) (*978-970-718*) *Dist. by* **Bilingual Pubns.**

Advanced Publishing LLC, (*978-0-9857367; 978-1-63132*) 3200 A Danville Blvd. Suite 204, Alamo, CA 94507 USA Tel 925-837-7303
E-mail: eric@aliveeastbay.com
Web site: www.alivebookpublishing.com.

Advantage BibleStudy *Imprint of* **Advantage Bks.**

Advantage Books *See* **Advantage Bks., LLC**

Advantage Bks., (*978-0-9754332; 978-1-59755*) Div. of Advantage Pr., Inc., Orders Addr.: P.O. Box 160847, Altamonte Springs, FL 32716 USA; *Imprints:* Advantage Childrens (Advan Childrens); Advantage BibleStudy (Adv BibleStudy) Do not confuse with companies with the same or similar name in Newoport Beach, CA, Silver Spring, MD
E-mail: mike@advbooks.com
Web site: http://advbookstore.com
Dist(s): **National Bk. Network.**

Advantage Bks., LLC, (*978-0-9660366; 978-0-9714609; 978-0-9823326*) 3268 Arcadia Pl.NW, Washington, DC 20015-2330 USA (SAN 253-8237) Tel 202-966-4044; Fax: 2002-966-1561; Toll Free: 888-238-8588 Do not confuse with companies with the same or similar name in New Port Beach, CA, Longwood, FL
E-mail: advantagebooksdc@aol.com
Web site: http://www.addvance.com
Dist(s): **National Bk. Network.**

Advantage Childrens *Imprint of* **Advantage Bks.**

Advantage World Pr., (*978-1-932450*) Div. of TheMoneyCoach.net, LLC, P.O. Box 1307, Mountainside, NJ 07092 USA (SAN 255-7452) Fax: 866-494-2461; Toll Free: 866-494-2461
Web site: http://www.themoneycoach.net
Dist(s): **Ingram Content Group**
Smashwords.

Advent Truth Ministries, (*978-0-9749490*) P.O. Box 307, Forsyth, GA 31029 USA Tel 404-322-5683
E-mail: adventtruth@yahoo.com
Web site: www.adventtruth.org; www.thesabbathtruth.org.

Adventure Ahead Pubn., (*978-0-692-15189-1*) P.O. Box 842, Shaw Island, WA 98286 USA Tel 360-317-6238
E-mail: adventureahead@outlook.com
Dist(s): **CreateSpace Independent Publishing Platform.**

Adventure & Discovery Pr., (*978-0-9744672*) P.O. Box 11631, Syracuse, NY 13218 USA Toll Free: 800-682-2662.

Adventure Beyond The Horizon *See* **Omega Pr.**

Adventure Bks. of Seattle, (*978-0-9823271; 978-0-692-32193-5*) 2415 I St. NE, No. D, Auburn, WA 98002 USA (SAN 857-8664) Tel 253-929-6259
Web site: http://www.adventurebooksofseattle.com
Dist(s): **Ingram Content Group.**

Adventure Boys Inc., (*978-0-9791922; 978-0-9791952; 978-0-9796392*) 11005 35th Ave. NE, Seattle, WA 98119-6809 USA (SAN 852-727X) 11/20/06: Do not be confused with Madison Park Greetings & Front Porch Classics, Inc.
Web site: http://www.adventureboys.com.

Adventure Experience *See* **Adventure Experience Pr.**

Adventure Experience Pr., (*978-1-7322694*) 7010 Streamwood Pt, Colorado Springs, CO 80922 USA Tel 719-322-6992
E-mail: eric@adventureexperience.net
Web site: www.adventureexperience.net; www.adventuredevos.com.

Adventure Hse., (*978-1-886937; 978-1-59798*) 914 Laredo Rd., Silver Spring, MD 20901-1867 USA Tel 301-754-1589; Fax: 978-215-7412
E-mail: sales@adventurehouse.com
Web site: http://www.adventurehouse.com
Dist(s): **Diamond Comic Distributors, Inc.**
Diamond Bk. Distributors.

Adventure in Discovery, (*978-0-9743414; 978-0-578-62668-0*) 18011 N. Hwy. A1A, Jupiter, FL 33477 USA Tel 561-746-8410
E-mail: info@adventureindiscovery.com
Web site: http://adventureindiscovery.com/
Dist(s): **Follett School Solutions**
Southern Bk. Service
Sunburst Bks., Inc., Distributor of Florida Bks.

Adventure Pr., (*978-0-9758654*) Orders Addr.: P.O. Box 1778, Canon City, CO 81215 USA Tel 208-880-7899; P.O. Box 1778, Canon City, CO 81215 Tel 208-880-7899
E-mail: antelope85@hotmail.com
Web site: http://www.kingsventures.com.

Adventure Productions, Inc., (*978-0-9614904*) 3404 Terry Lake Rd., Fort Collins, CO 80524 USA (SAN 693-3955) Tel 970-493-8776; Fax: 970-484-5825 Do not confuse with Adventure Productions, Reno, NV.
E-mail: cjansen@wild-west.com.

Adventure Pubns. *Imprint of* **AdventureKEEN**

AdventureKEEN, (*978-0-89732; 978-0-89997; 978-0-911824; 978-0-934860; 978-0-9617367; 978-0-9647083; 978-1-57860; 978-1-878208; 978-1-885061; 978-1-59193; 978-0-9777651; 978-1-939324; 978-1-62809; 978-0-9903716; 978-1-63404; 978-1-64359; 978-1-64755; 978-1-64901) 2204 First Ave. S. Suite 102, Birmingham, AL 35233 USA Tel 205-322-0439; Fax: 205-326-1012; Imprints:* Adventure Publications (AdvntrPubns); Wilderness Press (WildrnssPr); Clerisy Press (ClerisyPress)
E-mail: molly@adventurewithkeen.com
Web site: www.theunofficialguides.com; www.adventurewithkeen.com; www.adventurepublications.net; www.clerisypress.com; www.wildernesspress.com; www.menasharidge.com
Dist(s): **MyiLibrary**
Publishers Group West (PGW).

Adventures Galore, (*978-0-9759542*) Orders Addr.: P.O. Box 748, Lake George, CO 80827 USA Tel 719-748-8458; Fax: 719-748-8459; Edit Addr.: 35100 Hwy. 24, Lake George, CO 80827 USA
Web site: http://www.adventuresgalore.com.

Adventures in Print, (*978-0-615-37286-0; 978-0-9908487; 978-0-9972665; 978-0-9974036*) 55 Greenview Dr. Apt 6, Manchester, NH 03102 USA Tel 603-728-7701
E-mail: i.message99@live.com.

Adventures of Everyday Geniuses, The *Imprint of* **Mainstream Connections Publishing**

Adventures of Henry, LLC, (*978-1-936813*) 627 Evans St., Oshkosh, WI 54901 USA Tel 920-252-3578
E-mail: Darrin.Anderson@gmail.com
Web site: Www.adventuresofhenry.com.

Adventures of Hillary, The *Imprint of* **Nelson Publishing, LLC**

Adventures of Lady LLC, The, (*978-0-9789984*) 4907 White Bud Ct., Windermere, FL 34786 USA (SAN 852-1360).

Adventures of Pookie, The, (*978-0-692-16062-6; 978-0-578-58257-3*) 86027 Albermarle Ct., Fernandina Beach, FL 32034 USA Tel 330-844-7602
E-mail: theadventuresofpookie@gmail.com
Dist(s): **Ingram Content Group.**

Adventures Unlimited Pr., (*978-0-932813; 978-1-931882; 978-1-935487; 978-1-939149; 978-1-948803*) Orders Addr.: P.O. Box 74, Kempton, IL 60946 USA (SAN 630-1126) Tel 815-253-6390; Fax: 815-253-6300; Edit Addr.: 303 Main St., Kempton, IL 60946 USA (SAN 250-3484)
E-mail: auphq@frontiernet.net
Web site: http://www.adventuresunlimitedpress.com
Dist(s): **Hancock Hse. Pubs.**
New Leaf Distributing Co., Inc.
SCB Distributors.

Advocate Hse. *Imprint of* **A Cappela Publishing**

AE Pubns. (GBR) (*978-1-906672; 978-1-907708*) *Dist. by* **IPG Chicago.**

Aea Media, LLC, (*978-0-9862908*) 500 Umstead Dr., Chapel Hill, NC 27516 USA Tel 919-357-6948
E-mail: atkinsae@gmail.com
Web site: terrowintrilogy.com.

Aegaeon Publishing, (*978-1-934810*) Div. of Aegaeon Group International, One Penn Plaza 250 W. 34th St., 36th Flr., New York, NY 10119 USA Tel 212-835-1629
Web site: http://www.aegaeonpublishing.com.

Aegean Design, (*978-0-9758803*) 5009 20th Ave., NW, Seattle, WA 98107 USA Tel 206-612-9698
E-mail: bdarling@handofzeus.com
Web site: http://www.aegeandesign.net.

Aegypan, (*978-1-59818; 978-1-60312*) Div. of Alan Rodgers Bks., 4750 Lincoln Blvd., No. 360, Marina del Rey, CA 90292-9303 USA.

Aenor Trust, The, (*978-0-9724251; 978-0-9766401; 978-0-9768128*) Orders Addr.: P.O. Box 1410, Silverton, OR 97381 USA; Edit Addr.: 1286 Pressler Court S., Salem, OR 97306 USA
Web site: http://www.aenortrust.org; http://www.stellarlane.org.

Aeon Publishing Inc., (*978-0-9713099; 978-0-9718509; 978-1-932047; 978-1-932303; 978-1-932560; 978-1-59526; 978-1-933626; 978-1-60594*) Orders Addr.: 7580 NW 5th St. #16535, Fort Lauderdale, FL 33318 USA Tel 954-726-0902; Fax: 954-726-0903; Toll Free: 866-229-9244; *Imprints:* Llumina Christian Books (LluminaChrist); Llumina Press (Llumina Pr); Llumina Kids (Llumina Kids)
E-mail: diane@llumina.com
Web site: http://www.llumina.com.

Aeon Publishing, Incorporated *See* **Breezeway Books**

AequiLibris Publishing LLC, (*978-0-9816446*) Orders Addr.: P.O. Box 1542, New London, NH 03257 USA
Web site: http://www.AequiLibrisPublishing.com.

Aerial Photography Services, Inc., (*978-0-936672; 978-1-880970; 978-0-9789603; 978-0-9815804; 978-0-9836193; 978-0-9916287*) 2511 S. Tryon St., Charlotte, NC 28203 USA (SAN 214-2791) Tel 704-333-5143; Fax: 704-333-4911
E-mail: aps@aps-1.com; gregg@aps-1.com
Web site: http://www.aps-1.com.

Aerilyn Bks., (*978-0-9997830*) 1545 Edgefield Ln., Hoffman Estates, IL 60169 USA
E-mail: info@aerilynbooks.com
Web site: www.aerilynbooks.com
Dist(s): **Independent Pubs. Group.**

Aerospace 1 Pubns., (*978-0-9705150*) 8 Brookstone Ct., Streamwood, IL 60107 USA
E-mail: aerospace1@aol.com.

Aesop Pubs., LLC, (*978-0-9725218*) 11153 Powder Horn Dr., Potomac, MD 20854 USA
E-mail: plastcfigs@aol.com.

AFCHRON, (*978-1-892824; 978-1-938976*) Orders Addr.: 1692 Golf Link Dr., Atlanta, GA 30088 USA
E-mail: afchron5@aol.com
Web site: http://www.afchron.com
Dist(s): **Copyright Clearance Ctr., Inc.**
EBSCO Media.

Affirming Faith, (*978-0-9798627; 978-0-9897373; 978-1-7335517*) 1181 Whispering Knoll Ln., Rochester Hills, MI 48306 USA (SAN 854-591X) Tel 248-909-5735; Fax: 248-608-1756
E-mail: loriwagner@affirmingfaith.com
Web site: http://www.affirmingfaith.com
Dist(s): **Pentecostal Publishing Hse.**

Africa World Pr., (*978-0-86543; 978-1-59221*) 541 W. Ingham Ave., Suite B, Trenton, NJ 08638 USA (SAN 692-3925) Tel 609-695-3200; Fax: 609-695-6466
E-mail: customerservice@africaworldpressbooks.com
Web site: http://www.africaworldpressbooks.com.

African American Chronicle Software Publishing Corporation *See* **AFCHRON**

African American Images, (*978-0-913543; 978-0-9749000; 978-1-934155*) P.O. Box 1799, Chicago Hts, IL 60412-1799 USA Toll Free: 800-552-1991
E-mail: aai@africanamericanimages.com; customer@africanamericanimages.com
Web site: http://AfricanAmericanImages.com
Dist(s): **Ebsco Publishing**
Follett School Solutions
Independent Pubs. Group
MyiLibrary
ebrary, Inc.

African Christian Pr. (GHA) *(978-9964-87) Dist. by* **Mich St U Pr.**

Africana Homestead Legacy Pubs., Inc., *(978-0-9653308; 978-0-9770904; 978-0-9799537; 978-0-9818939; 978-0-9825842; 978-0-9831151; 978-1-937622)* Orders Addr.: 926 Haddonfield Rd., Suite E. #329, Cherry Hill, NJ 08002 USA (SAN 914-4811) Tel 856-673-0363; *Imprints:* Nefu Books (Nefu Bks)
E-mail: sales@ahlpub.com; customer-service@ahlpub.com
Web site: http://www.ahlpub.com.

Afrolez Productions, LLC, *(978-0-615-16123-5)* P.O. Box 58085, Philadelphia, PA 19102-8085 USA Tel 215-701-6150
E-mail: contact@notherapedocumentary.org
Web site: http://www.notherapedocumentary.org.

AfterShock Comics, *(978-0-9795939; 978-0-9801479; 978-1-935002; 978-0-692-94590-2; 978-1-949028)* 15300 Ventura Blvd Suite 507, Sherman Oaks, CA 91403 USA
E-mail: christinaharrington@aftershock.ninja; mikemarts@aftershock.ninja
Web site: www.aftershockcomics.com
Dist(s): **Diamond Comic Distributors, Inc.**

Afton Historical Society Pr., *(978-0-9639338; 978-1-890434; 978-0-9976296)* Orders Addr.: 165 Western Ave. N., Suite 15, St. Paul, MN 55102 USA Tel 651-436-8443
E-mail: aftonpress@gmail.com
Web site: http://www.aftonpress.com
Dist(s): **Bookmen, Inc.**
Brodart Co.
Coutts Information Services
Eastern Bk. Co.
Follett School Solutions
Galda Library Services, Inc.

Afton Publishing, *(978-0-89359)* Orders Addr.: P.O. Box 1399, Andover, NJ 07821-1399 USA (SAN 692-2570) Tel 973-579-2442; Fax: 973-579-2842; Toll Free: 888-238-6665
E-mail: info3@aftonpublishing.com
Web site: http://www.aftonpublishing.com.

Against All Oddz Publishing, *(978-0-9913040; 978-0-9961916)* 2500 Chamberlayne Ave., Richmond, VA 23222 USA Tel 804-347-2590
E-mail: lbking73@gmail.com.

Agape Inc, *(978-0-9994012; 978-1-950320)* 15600 E Caley Pl, Centennial, CO 80016 USA Tel 720-988-0850; *Imprints:* Lighthouse Press (MYID_F_LIGHTHO)
E-mail: agapeinc2@gmail.com
Web site: www.thelighthousebooks.com.

Agapy LLC *See* **Agapy Publishing**

Agapy Publishing, *(978-0-9721328; 978-1-938522)* a/o Agapy Publishing, 1608 Sun Prairie Dr., St. Joseph, MI 49085 USA Tel 321-345-8297
E-mail: info@agapy.com; president@agapy.com
Web site: http://www.agapy.com
Dist(s): **Ingram Content Group.**

Agate Publishing, Inc., *(978-0-940625; 978-0-9609516; 978-1-57284; 978-0-9724562; 978-1-932841)* 1501 Madison St., Evanston, IL 60202 USA
Web site: http://www.agatepublishing.com
Dist(s): **MyiLibrary**
Publishers Group West (PGW)
ebrary, Inc.

A-Gator Publishing,

AGB Publishing, *(978-1-930908)* Div. of Mini Enterprises - M.E., 19425 Bankers House Dr., Katy, TX 77449-0243 USA; *Imprints:* AGB/me (AGB-me)
E-mail: minienterprises@msn.com; minitaylr@msn.com.

AGB/me *Imprint of* **AGB Publishing**

AGC Outreach Ministry, *(978-0-9774115)* 801 WHITEHEAD RD, GREENSBURG, PA 15658 USA Tel 724-219-3858
E-mail: stevenjsmith799@gmail.com
Web site: www.hisgreatworks.com.

Ageless Treasures, *(978-0-9705726)* Orders Addr.: 3536 Saint Andrews Village Cir., Louisville, KY 40241-2664 USA (SAN 253-794X) Tel 502-412-5940; Fax: 502-327-6233
E-mail: dcw0810@insightbb.com; carlawebb@agelesstreasures.net.

Agent of Danger *Imprint of* **Komikwerks, LLC**

Agents of Change, *(978-1-928992)* Div. of Granite Publishing, LLC, P.O. Box 1429, Columbus, NC 28722-1429 USA Tel 828-894-3088; Fax: 828-894-8454; Toll Free: 800-366-0264
E-mail: brian@5thworld.com
Web site: http://5thworld.com
Dist(s): **New Leaf Distributing Co., Inc.**

Age-Trotters Press *See* **Cameltrotters Publishing**

Agile Pr., *(978-0-9718239)* P.O. Box 1939, Chicago, IL 60690-1939 USA
E-mail: agilepress@agileresearch.com.

AGL Editions, *(978-0-9745629)* 1000 Bay Dr., No. 524, Niceville, FL 32578 USA.

Aglob Publishing, *(978-0-9708560; 978-1-59427)* P.O. Box 4036, Hallandale, FL 33008 USA Tel 954-456-1476; Fax: 954-456-3903
E-mail: info@aglobpublishing.com; info@aglob.com
Web site: http://www.aglobpublishing.com.

AGM Communications, *(978-0-9985807)* P.O. Box 52772, Baton Rouge, LA 70892 USA; *Imprints:* Muscle Books (MYID_A_MUSCLE)
E-mail: mvgray2000@yahoo.com.

Agnes, Bella Bks., *(978-1-7321975)* 2250 NW Thorncroft Dr, Apt 332, Hillsboro, OR 97124 USA Tel 404-713-5605
E-mail: arlynesimonphd@gmail.com
Web site: www.arlynesimon.com.

Agora Pubns., Inc., *(978-1-887250; 978-0-9904599)* 17 Dean St., Millis, MA 02054 USA (SAN 851-8521) Tel 508-376-1073 (phone/fax)
E-mail: agorapub@verizon.net; info@agorapublication.com
Web site: http://www.agorapublications.com
Dist(s): **Philosophy Documentation Ctr.**

Agreka Bks., LLC, *(978-1-888106; 978-0-9777072; 978-1-934243)* P.O. Box 14405, Scottsdale, AZ 85267-14405 USA Tel 480-767-1774; Toll Free Fax: 888-771-7758; Toll Free: 800-360-5284
E-mail: info@agreka.com
Web site: http://www.agreka.com; http://www.utahbooks.com; http://www.historypreserved.com
Dist(s): **Ingram Content Group**
Quality Bks., Inc.

AGS Secondary *Imprint of* **Savvas Learning Co.**

Agua Caliente Pr., *(978-0-9768275)* 4352 Riley Rd., Gladwin, MI 48624 USA Tel 989-426-8400
E-mail: maryhansen4@hotmail.com.

Aguilar *Imprint of* **Penguin Random Hse. Grupo Editorial (USA) LLC**

Aguilar, Altea, Taurus, Alfaguara, S.A. de C.V (MEX) *(978-968-19) Dist. by* **Santillana.**

Aguilar Chilena de Ediciones, Ltd. (CHL) *(978-956-239; 978-956-347) Dist. by* **Santillana.**

Aguilar Chilena de Ediciones, Ltd. (CHL) *(978-956-239; 978-956-347) Dist. by* **Ediciones.**

Aguilar Editorial (MEX) *Dist. by* **Santillana.**

Aguirre Cox, Vicki & Ernest, *(978-0-9767994)* 10810 Lake Path Dr., San Antonio, TX 78217 USA Tel 210-364-8590; Fax: 210-653-3089
E-mail: vacemas@aol.com.

Aha! Elora Danan Productions, *(978-0-9786729)* P.O. Box 428, Estero, FL 33928 USA
Dist(s): **Follett School Solutions.**

aha! Process, Inc., *(978-0-9647437; 978-1-929229; 978-1-934583; 978-1-938248; 978-1-948244)* P.O. Box 727, Highlands, TX 77562-0727 USA Tel 281-426-5300; Fax: 281-426-5600; Toll Free: 800-424-9484
Web site: http://www.ahaprocess.com
Dist(s): **Follett School Solutions**
Greenleaf Book Group.

Aharon, Sara *See* **Enterprise Leaf Pr.**

A-Head Publishing, *(978-0-9816283)* 41 Via Del Sol, Nicasio, CA 94946 USA (SAN 856-0862)
E-mail: aheadpublishing@gmail.com
Web site: http://www.a-headpublishing.com.

Ahlman Publishing, *(978-0-9712906)* Div. of KODIAK Publishing, 9525 W. 230 St., Morristown, MN 55052 USA Tel 507-685-4247; Fax: 507-685-4280
E-mail: larryahlman@hotmail.com
Web site: http://www.ahlmans.com/mittens.html
Dist(s): **Partners Bk. Distributing, Inc.**

Ahmed, *(978-0-692-69940-9)* 2600 Gramercy St apt 447, houston, TX 77030 USA Tel 713-470-8000.

Ahoy Comics, *(978-0-9980442; 978-1-952090)* 101 Enderberry Cir., Syracuse, NY 13224 USA Tel 410-683-7080
E-mail: info@comicsahoy.com
Web site: www.comicsahoy.com
Dist(s): **Diamond Comic Distributors, Inc.**

Ahzar's Bk. Co. Publishing, *(978-0-9746130)* 3675 So. Rainbow Blvd No. 107, Las Vegas, NV 89103 USA Tel 702-391-1914; Fax: 702-871-8777
E-mail: croesus@joimail.com.

AIC Publications, *(978-0-9799464)* P.O. Box 152672, Arlington, TX 76015-8672 USA
E-mail: president@aicpublications.com.

Aidan's Butterfly Pubns., *(978-0-9787341)* 4946 W. Laurie Ln., Glendale, AZ 85302 USA Fax: 623-776-9921
E-mail: eetagt@aol.com.

Ailam Publishing LLC, *(978-0-9837759)* 12900 S. May, Calumet Park, IL 60827 USA (SAN 860-2859)
E-mail: ailampublishing@aol.com.

A.I.M. Enterprises, *(978-0-9772303)* 507 Grace - Stockham, Aurora, NE 68818-7019 USA
Web site: http://www.aim4theheart.com.

Aim Higher Bks., *(978-0-9713292)* 10556 Combie Rd., Suite 6242, Auburn, CA 95602 USA
E-mail: sales@aimhigherbooks.com
Web site: http://www.AimHigherBooks.com.

Aim Higher Publishing *See* **Aim Higher Bks.**

AIMS Education Foundation, *(978-1-881431; 978-1-932093; 978-1-60519)* Orders Addr.: 1595 S. Chestnut Ave., Fresno, CA 93702-4706 USA Tel 559-255-4094; Fax: 559-255-6396; Toll Free: 888-733-2467
E-mail: aimsed@aimsedu.org
Web site: http://www.aimsedu.org.

AIMS Multimedia, *(978-0-8068)* 1 Discovery Pl., Silver Spring, MD 20910-3354 USA (SAN 687-3464) Toll Free: 800-367-2467
Web site: http://www.aimsmultimedia.com/
Dist(s): **Follett School Solutions**
Weston Woods Studios, Inc.

Ain't No Joke Bks., *(978-0-9778342)* 118 Lyman Pl., West Palm Beach, FL 33409 USA Tel 305-757-0318; 419-5895100
E-mail: keithgwright@yahoo.com
Dist(s): **BookBaby.**

Aint No Jokes Books Incorporated *See* **Ain't No Joke Bks.**

Air & Nothingness Pr., *(978-0-9679429; 978-0-9991953; 978-1-7358356)* 2224 Delaware Ave., Pittsburgh, PA 15218 USA
E-mail: info@aanpress.com
Web site: http://www.aanpress.com.

airjam.com, *(978-0-9786478)* 3379 C1/2 Road, Palisade, CO 81526 USA.

Airplane Reader Publishing, *(978-0-9702405; 978-0-9765485)* Div. of Pro Leisure Tour, Inc., 9260 E. Lake Pl., Greenwood Village, CO 80111 USA (SAN 253-6935) Fax: 303-221-2766 24-hour dedicated fax line; Toll Free: 877-611-6222 voice mail, 24 hours
E-mail: theo@12milestoparadise.com; tedsimendinger@comcast.net; ted@funnyted.com
Web site: http://www.proleisuretour.com; http://www.piggychurch.com; http://www.12milestoparadise.com; http://www.richwithoutmoney.org; http://www.jurassictrout.com; http://www.tukibanjo.com.

Airways International, Inc., *(978-0-9653993)* Orders Addr.: P.O. Box 1109, Sandpoint, ID 83864 USA Tel 208-263-2098; Fax: 208-263-5906; Edit Addr.: P.O. Box 1109, Sandpoint, ID 83864 USA
E-mail: airways@airwaysmag.com
Web site: http://www.airwaysmag.com.

AJL Publishers, *(978-0-9794618)* 25 Auvergne, Newport Coast, CA 92657 USA (SAN 853-5116) Tel 949-887-9073; Fax: 949-640-0339
E-mail: bachas@cox.net.

AJM Bks., *(978-0-9896211)* 11121 W. Amelia Ave, Avondale, AZ 85392 USA Tel 623-877-9114
E-mail: ajohnsonmccurdy@yahoo.com.

Ajoyin Publishing, Inc., *(978-0-9787472; 978-0-9792739; 978-0-9818488; 978-1-60920)* Orders Addr.: P.O. Box 342, Three Rivers, MI 49093 USA; Edit Addr.: 55919 Buckhorn Rd., Three Rivers, MI 49093 USA (SAN 852-9817) Toll Free: 888-273-4569; *Imprints:* Accent Publications (Acent)
E-mail: pam@ajoyin.com
Web site: http://www.ajoyin.com.

AJS Pubns., Inc., *(978-0-931298; 978-1-892291; 978-0-9904772)* 229 Brier Ct., Island Lake, IL 60042 USA (SAN 223-5846) Tel 847-526-5027; Fax: 847-487-5229 Do not confuse with AJS Publishing, Inc., Los Angeles, CA
Web site: http://www.ajspublications.com.

AK Classics, LLC, *(978-0-9814945; 978-0-692-92223-1; 978-1-7320482; 978-1-7357964)* P.O. Box 77023, Charlotte, NC 28271-7003 USA
E-mail: marcuskimbrough@aol.com
Web site: www.akclassicstories.com.

AK Pr. (GBR) *(978-1-873176; 978-1-902593; 978-1-904859; 978-1-84935) Dist. by* **Consort Bk Sales.**

AKA Wendy Wonder, *(978-0-9967904)* 3020 SW 15th Ct, Gresham, OR 97080 USA Tel 541-771-3711
E-mail: mssveen@aol.com.

Akasha Classics *Imprint of* **Akasha Publishing, LLC**

Akasha Publishing, LLC, *(978-1-60512)* Orders Addr.: 2050 Emerald Ln., Fairfield, IA 52556 USA Fax: 866-485-5727; Toll Free: 877-745-7317; *Imprints:* Akasha Classics (Akasha Classics)
E-mail: registrar@akashapublishing.com
Web site: http://www.akashapublishing.com
Dist(s): **Follett School Solutions**
Ingram Content Group.

Akashic Bks., *(978-1-888451; 978-0-9719206; 978-1-933354; 978-1-936070; 978-1-61775)* 232 Third St., No. B404, Brooklyn, NY 11215 USA Tel 718-643-9193; Fax: 718-643-9195; *Imprints:* Black Sheep (BlckSheep); Jones, Kaylie Books (KJones Bks)
E-mail: info@akashicbooks.com
Web site: http://www.akashicbooks.com
Dist(s): **Consortium Bk. Sales & Distribution**
Follett School Solutions
MyiLibrary
Open Road Integrated Media, Inc.
SPD-Small Pr. Distribution
ebrary, Inc.

AKA:yoLa, *(978-0-9842288; 978-1-936688; 978-1-942168; 978-1-951960)* 315 Bernadette Dr. Ste 3, Columbia, MO 65203 USA Tel 573-864-1479; *Imprints:* Compass Flower Press (CompassFlower)
Web site: http://www.akayola.com; www.compassflowerpress.com; www.aka-publishing.com
Dist(s): **eBookit.com.**

AKB Design, *(978-0-9748702)* Orders Addr.: 17640 Corkill Rd., #27, Desert Hot Springs, CA 92241 USA Tel 760-329-3233; 760-895-6646
Web site: www.akbdesign.com.

Akiara Bks. (ESP) *(978-84-17440) Dist. by* **IPG Chicago.**

Akimbo Bks., *(978-0-9990787)* P.O. Box 944, New York, NY 10002 USA Tel 917-530-6611
E-mail: adjowii@yahoo.com.

Akinleye, Titilope, *(978-0-9983312)* 3410 whispering hills Pl., Laurel, MD 20724 USA Tel 301-317-3924
E-mail: Titiakinleye@yahoo.com.

Akins, ShaKera, *(978-0-692-98411-6; 978-0-578-47467-0)* P.O. Box 616815, Orlando, FL 32861 USA Tel 407-970-7480
E-mail: shakera.akins@gmail.com.

Akmaeon Publishing, LLC, *(978-0-9850410; 978-0-9988827)* 309 Pirkle Ferry Rd. Suite C200, Cumming, GA 30040 USA Tel 404-402-3793
E-mail: free3055@bellsouth.net.

AKMO Pubs., *(978-0-9745952)* P.O. Box 669, Odessa, FL 33556-9998 USA.

Akom Publishing Hse., *(978-0-9799134)* 244 Madison Ave., No. 745, New York, NY 10016 USA
E-mail: Akom2000@aol.com
Web site: http://www.akompublishinghouse.com.

Alaafia Kids Co., *(978-0-9788737)* 1020 Stonebrook Rd. Unit B, Sykesville, MD 21784-6173 USA.

Alabama Folklife Assn., *(978-0-9672672; 978-0-9772132)* Orders Addr.: c/o Alabama Center for Traditional Culture, 410 N. Hull St, Montgomery, AL 36104 USA Tel 334-242-3601; Fax: 334-269-9098
E-mail: joycecauthen@bellsouth.net
Web site: http://www.alabamafolklife.org.

Alabaster Bk. Pub., *(978-0-9725031; 978-0-9768108; 978-0-9790949; 978-0-9796866; 978-0-9815763; 978-0-9823005; 978-0-9846137; 978-0-9846320; 978-0-9840004; 978-0-9860300; 978-0-9912660; 978-0-9861790; 978-0-9982352; 978-1-7346763)* Orders Addr.: P.O. Box 401, Kernersville, NC 27285 USA Tel 336-295-4322; Fax: 336-996-2011; P.O. Box 401, Kernersville, NC 27285 Fax: 336-996-2011; Edit Addr.: 324 Lakeside Dr., Kernersville, NC 27284 USA
E-mail: pblshralabaster@aol.com; ljdixie@aol.com
Web site: http://www.publisheralabaster.org; http://www.PublisherAlabaster.biz.

Alabaster Books *See* **Alabaster Bk. Pub.**

Aladdin *Imprint of* **Simon & Schuster Children's Publishing**

Aladdin Library *Imprint of* **Simon & Schuster Children's Publishing**

Aladdin Paperbacks *Imprint of* **Simon & Schuster Children's Publishing**

Aladdin/Beyond Words,
Dist(s): **Simon & Schuster, Inc.**

Alarie, Shirley, *(978-0-9968087; 978-1-7334983)* 10423 Hallmark Blvd, Riverview, FL 33578 USA Tel 413-441-9769
E-mail: shirleyalarie@gmail.com
Web site: https://findinggodamongus.com.

Alaska Avenue Pr., *(978-0-9748091)* 5770 Alaska Ave., Alto, MI 49302-9714 USA Tel 616-868-0308
E-mail: stonehillis47657@aol.com.

Alaska Geographic Assn., *(978-0-930931; 978-0-9602876; 978-0-9825765; 978-1-938494)* 241 N. C St., Anchorage, AK 99501 USA (SAN 223-5269) Tel 907-274-8440; Fax: 907-274-8343
E-mail: dwhitecar@alaskageographic.org
Web site: http://www.alaskageographic.org.

Alaska Independent Pubs., *(978-0-9743369; 978-0-9797442; 978-0-9883390)* Orders Addr.: P.O. Box 1125, Homer, AK 99603 USA Toll Free: 877-210-2665
E-mail: wizardworksak@gmail.com
Dist(s): **Wizard Works.**

Alaska Native Language Ctr., *(978-0-933769; 978-1-55500)* Univ. of Alaska, P.O. Box 757680, Fairbanks, AK 99775-7680 USA (SAN 692-9796) Tel 907-474-7874; Fax: 907-474-6586
E-mail: fntla@uaf.edu
Web site: http://www.uaf.edu/anlc
Dist(s): **Chicago Distribution Ctr.**
Todd Communications
Wizard Works.

Alaska Natural History Association *See* **Alaska Geographic Assn.**

Alaska Northwest Bks. *Imprint of* **West Margin Pr.**

Alaska Zoo, The, *(978-0-9673915)* 4731 O'Malley Rd., Anchorage, AK 99516 USA.

Alazar Pr. *Imprint of* **Royal Swan Enterprises, Inc.**

Alba House *See* **St Pauls/Alba Hse. Pubs.**

Alban Lake Publishing, *(978-0-9915767; 978-0-578-43514-5; 978-0-578-50253-3; 978-0-578-52502-0)* P.O. Box 782, Cedar Rapids, IA 52406-0782 USA Tel 319-431-5206
E-mail: albanlake@yahoo.com
Web site: www.albanlake.com.

Albatros (ARG) *(978-950-24) Dist. by* **Lectorum Pubns.**

Albatross FunnyBks., *(978-0-9983792; 978-1-949889)* 2701 A Meadow Rose Dr., Nashville, TN 37206 USA Tel 615-430-1647
E-mail: ericpwl@icloud.com
Web site: www.thegoon.com
Dist(s): **Diamond Comic Distributors, Inc.**

Albatross Pubs., *(978-0-615-45506-8; 978-1-946963)* Orders Addr.: Corso Europa 382, Villaricca Napoli , 80010 ITA Tel 406-219-4006; Edit Addr.: 54-3853 Akoni Pule Hwy, Kapaau, HI 96755 USA
E-mail: albatrosspublishers@gmail.com.

Albee, Michael, *(978-0-9745405)* 1575 W. Mable, Anaheim, CA 92802 USA Tel 714-863-2149
E-mail: malbee@fairmontschools.net.

Albers, Christine, *(978-0-615-19666-4)* 6924 Brookview Dr., Urbandale, IA 50322 USA Tel 515-270-4606
E-mail: albears5@msn.com.

Albin-Michel, Editions (FRA) *(978-2-226) Dist. by* **Distribks Inc.**

Albright Creative, LLC, *(978-0-578-44332-4; 978-0-578-45680-5; 978-0-578-45681-2; 978-0-578-68069-9)* P.O. Box 2381, Lee's Summit, MO 64063 USA Tel 816-875-6416
E-mail: erin@albrightcreative.us
Web site: albrightcreative.us.

Album Publishing Company, Incorporated *See* **RJI Publishing**

ALCAPS, LLC, *(978-0-9769769)* 4004 Cibola Village Dr., NE, Albuquerque, NM 87111 USA
Web site: http://www.heartstohearts.net.

Alchemist's Almanac *See* **Pseudepigrapha Publishing**

Alchemy Bks., *(978-0-931290)* 1029 Solano Ave., No. E, Albany, CA 94706-1680 USA (SAN 111-3119).

Alchemy Creative, Inc., *(978-0-9675901)* 4650 Cardinal Dr., Beaumont, TX 77705 USA Tel 409-842-5240 ext 18
Web site: http://www.ecpadventures.com; http://www.adventuresoftheelements.com/.

Alchemy Hero Publishing, *(978-0-9975433)* 10442 s artesian, Chicago, IL 60655 USA Tel 773-732-7722
E-mail: luisr124@gmail.com.

Alchemy Ranch Books *See* **BRYN WILLIAMS LLC**

ALCJR Enterprises, *(978-0-9752760; 978-0-692-60956-9)* P.O. Box 4067, Midlothian, VA 23112-0001 USA Tel 804-677-4557; Fax: 804-744-0100
E-mail: alcjr@verizon.net
Web site: http://www.alcjr.com.

Aldelo Systems Inc., *(978-0-9765992)* 4641 Spyres Way Ste. 4, Modesto, CA 95356-9802 USA
E-mail: sales@aldelo.com
Web site: http://www.aldelo.com.

Alderac Entertainment Group, *(978-1-887953; 978-1-59472)* 4045 Guasti Rd., No. 210, Ontario, CA 91761 USA
E-mail: kcarpenter@alderac.com; dlepore@alderac.com
Web site: http://www.alderac.com
Dist(s): **PSI (Publisher Services, Inc.).**

Alef Design Group, *(978-1-881283)* 4423 Fruitland Ave., Los Angeles, CA 90058 USA Tel 323-582-1200; Fax: 323-585-0327; Toll Free: 800-845-0662
E-mail: jane@torahaura.com
Web site: http://www.torahaura.com
Dist(s): **Follett School Solutions.**

Alegria Hispana Pubns., *(978-0-944356)* Orders Addr.: P.O. Box 3765, Ventura, CA 93003 USA (SAN 243-4695) Tel 805-642-3969; Edit Addr.: 958 Scenic Way Dr., Ventura, CA 93003-1435 USA (SAN 243-4709).

Alegro Publishing, *(978-0-9799740; 978-0-615-63638-2; 978-0-578-43831-3; 978-0-578-43833-7)* 10644 Marine View Dr. SW, Seattle, WA 98146 USA Tel 206-999-8824
E-mail: joycemajor1@hotmail.com; info@alegropublishing.com
Web site: http://www.alegropublishing.com; http://www.smilingattheworld.com
Dist(s): **Partners/West Book Distributors.**

Aleixo, James, *(978-0-692-19030-2; 978-0-578-41294-8)* 196 Galloping Hill Rd., Roselle Park, NJ 07204 USA Tel 908-380-3903
E-mail: anna_aleixo@yahoo.com.

Alenick, Chaya, *(978-0-692-05225-9; 978-0-692-06592-1)* 3347 Forrest Dr., Hollywood, FL 33021 USA Tel 786-426-8611
E-mail: chaya.alenick@yahoo.com
Dist(s): **Ingram Content Group.**

Alethea In Heart, *(978-0-9719805; 978-1-932370)* PO Box 127, Charlotte, MI 48813 USA
E-mail: truthinheart@hotmail.com
Web site: http://www.truthinheart.com.

Alex Joseph Publishing, *(978-0-9988744)* 2120 N Pass Ave, Burbank, CA 91505 USA
E-mail: leadintoink@gmail.com.

Alexander Art L.P., *(978-1-883576)* P.O. Box 1417, Beaverton, OR 97075-1417 USA Tel 503-362-7939; Fax: 503-361-7401; Toll Free: 800-896-4630
E-mail: sales@alexanderart.com
Web site: http://www.alexanderart.com.

Alexander, John, *(978-0-692-15209-6; 978-0-692-15211-9; 978-0-578-40682-4)* 8548 Markham Dr., FRISCO, TX 75035 USA Tel 214-762-5945
E-mail: john@alexandernovels.com
Dist(s): **Ingram Content Group.**

Alexander, Lorraine *See* **Alexander, Raine**

Alexander Pubns., *(978-0-9623078)* Orders Addr.: P.O. Box 518, Forney, TX 75126 USA Tel 972-552-9519; Edit Addr.: 806 E. Buffalo St., Forney, TX 75126 USA.

Alexander, Raine, *(978-0-9816301)* 2356 Peeler Rd., Dunwoody, GA 30338 USA
E-mail: 2raine@gmail.com
Web site: www.EdoSchool.org.

Alexander Stoll Templeton, *(978-0-9982464)* 3513 W. Howe St., Seattle, WA 98199 USA Tel 206-669-9536
E-mail: templetonas@gmail.com.

Alexander-Marcus Publishing, *(978-0-9760944)* 1115 Tunnel Rd., Santa Barbara, CA 93105 USA
E-mail: andreamarcuslaw@cox.net.

Alexie Bks., *(978-0-9679416)* Div. of Alexie Enterprises, Inc., P.O. Box 3843, Carmel, IN 46082 USA Tel 317-844-5638; Fax: 317-846-0788
E-mail: BusJobs@aol.com; alexie8@aol.com; sales@alexiebooks.com
Web site: http://www.alexieenterprises.com
Dist(s): **Distributors, The.**

AlexMax Publishing Inc., *(978-0-9796643)* Orders Addr.: 4919 Flat Shoals Pkwy Suite 107B-137, Decatur, GA 30034 USA Tel 404-981-4442
E-mail: isbninfo@alexmaxpublishing.com
Web site: http://www.alexmaxpublishing.com.

ALEXZUS Bks., *(978-0-9724733)* 244 Fifth Ave., Suite B260, New York, NY 10001 USA
E-mail: jenbvic@aol.com.

Alfaguara *Imprint of* **Santillana USA Publishing Co., Inc.**

Alfaguara S.A. de Ediciones (ARG) *(978-950-511; 978-987-04) Dist. by* **Santillana.**

Alfranpedoc, *(978-1-930502)* 4100 W. Coyote Ridge Tr., Tucson, AZ 85746 USA Tel 213-926-0762
E-mail: Waylandhi@aol.com
Web site: http://www.books-by-doc.com.

Alfred Publishing Co., Inc., *(978-0-7390; 978-0-87487; 978-0-88284; 978-1-58951; 978-1-4574; 978-1-4706)* Orders Addr.: P.O. Box 10003, Van Nuys, CA 91410-0003 USA; Edit Addr.: 123 Dry Rd., Oriskany, NY 13424 USA Tel 315-736-1572; Fax: 315-736-7281; *Imprints:* Warner Bros. Publications (Warner Bro); Suzuki (Szuki)
E-mail: customerservice@alfred.com; permissions@alfred.com; submissions@alfred.com
Web site: http://www.alfred.com
Dist(s): **Follett School Solutions**
Leonard, Hal Corp.

Algar Editorial, Feditres, S.L. (ESP) *(978-84-923853; 978-84-931382; 978-84-95722; 978-84-96514) Dist. by* **Lectorum Pubns.**

†Algonquin Bks. of Chapel Hill, *(978-0-7611; 978-0-912697; 978-0-945575; 978-1-56512; 978-1-61620; 978-1-64375; 978-1-64904)* Div. of Workman Publishing Co., Inc., Orders Addr.: 225 Varick St. Flr. 9, New York, NY 10014-4381 USA Toll Free Fax: 800-521-1832 (fax orders, customer service); Toll Free: 800-722-7202 (orders, customer service); Edit Addr.: P.O. Box 2225, Chapel Hill, NC 27515-2225 USA (SAN 282-7506) Tel 919-967-0108 (editorial, publicity, marketing); Fax: 919-933-0272 (editorial, publicity, marketing)
E-mail: dialogue@algonquin.com; inquiring@algonquin.com; brunson@algonquin.com
Web site: http://www.algonquin.com; http://www.booksellerscorner.com
Dist(s): **Open Road Integrated Media, Inc.**
Workman Publishing Co., Inc.; *CIP.*

ALHsiccesslines, *(978-0-615-62527-0)* 13737 Dunbar Terr., Germantown, MD 20874 USA Tel 301-540-2928
E-mail: ALHpromo@aol.com.

Ali Gator (AUS) *(978-1-921772) Dist. by* **Consort Bk Sales.**

ALI Pictures *See* **Bks. That Will Enhance Your Life**

Alianza Editorial, S. A. (ESP) *(978-84-206; 978-84-605; 978-84-9104; 978-84-9181) Dist. by* **AIMS Intl.**

Alianza Editorial, S. A. (ESP) *(978-84-206; 978-84-605; 978-84-9104; 978-84-9181) Dist. by* **Distribks Inc.**

Alianza Editorial, S. A. (ESP) *(978-84-206; 978-84-605; 978-84-9104; 978-84-9181) Dist. by* **Continental Bk.**

Alianza Editorial, S. A. (ESP) *(978-84-206; 978-84-605; 978-84-9104; 978-84-9181) Dist. by* **Lectorum Pubns.**

Alianza Editorial, S. A. (ESP) *(978-84-206; 978-84-605; 978-84-9104; 978-84-9181) Dist. by* **Libros in Spanish, LLC.**

Alias Enterprises LLC *See* **Lamp Post Inc.**

Alien Time Treasure, *(978-0-9727309)* P.O. Box 2665, Newport, RI 02840 USA
E-mail: webmaster@alientimetreasure.com
Web site: http://alientimetreasure.com.

ALife Media, LLC, *(978-1-7321425)* 65 W. 73rd St., New York, NY 10023 USA Tel 347-721-0479
E-mail: alfie.writes@gmail.com.

Alisa Hope Wagner *See* **Marked Writers Publishing**

Aliso Street Productions, *(978-0-9840120)* P.O. Box 36422, Albuquerque, NM 87176 USA Tel 505-414-6366
E-mail: AlisoStreet@aol.com.

All About Kids Publishing, *(978-0-9700863; 978-0-9710278; 978-0-9744446; 978-0-9801468; 978-0-615-11427-9; 978-0-9963756; 978-1-7330468)* Orders Addr.: P.O. Box 159, Gilroy, CA 95021 USA (SAN 253-8601) Tel 408-337-1152
E-mail: lguevara@allaboutkidspub.com
Web site: www.oliverbrightside.com; www.allaboutkidspub.com
Dist(s): **Ingram Content Group**
Pathway Bk. Service.

All About Learning Pr., *(978-1-935197)* 2038 E. Anvil Lake Rd., Eagle River, WI 54521 USA (SAN 856-8812) Tel 715-477-1976; Toll Free Fax: 877-774-8006
E-mail: mr@all-about-spelling.com
Web site: http://www.all-about-learning-press.com.

All Around Our World Publishing Co., Inc., *(978-0-9799050)* 629 Park Ave., Beloit, WI 53511 USA Tel 608-207-9777; Fax: 608-207-9888
E-mail: brendaaaow@charter.net.

All For One Pr., *(978-0-9745951)* 29193 Northwestern Hwy, No. 658, Southfield, MI 48034 USA (SAN 255-6804) Tel 313-617-4012
E-mail: allforonepress@hotmail.com.

All Gold Publishing Co., *(978-0-9701519)* Orders Addr.: P.O. Box 13504, Dayton, OH 45413-0504 USA Tel 937-586-9804; Edit Addr.: 907 Reist, Dayton, OH 45408-1350 USA
E-mail: allgoldceo@netzero.net
Web site: http://www.allgoldpublishing.com.

All Hallows Eve Press *See* **HallowStyle, LLC**

All Health Chiropractic Ctrs. Inc., *(978-0-9770527)* 567 Church St., Royersford, PA 19468 USA (SAN 256-6443) Tel 610-948-4161
E-mail: susiequsie6@aol.com
Web site: http://www.drsnappy.com.

All Kidding Aside, *(978-0-9794317)* 2829 S. Cypress, Sioux City, IA 51106 USA Tel 712-276-4315
E-mail: bestma34@cableone.net
Web site: http://www.allkiddingaside.biz.

All Nations Pr., *(978-0-9725110; 978-0-9777954; 978-0-9912721)* P.O. Box 10821, Tallahassee, FL 32302 USA Do not confuse with companies with the same or similar name in Colorado Springs, CO, Southlake, TX
E-mail: rcamp427@gmail.com; allnationseditors@gmail.com
Web site: http://http:/allnationseditors.wix.com/books-seller
Dist(s): **Follett School Solutions**
Itasca Bks.

All Over Creation, *(978-0-9788950)* P.O. Box 382, Madera, CA 93639 USA
E-mail: astorybytory@yahoo.com.

All Points Pr., *(978-0-9850827; 978-1-7339161)* 103 Chestnut Ridge Rd., Latrobe, PA 15650 USA (SAN 920-2501) Tel 724-539-4591; Fax: 724-539-3417
E-mail: edward.t62@gmail.com.

All Star Pr., *(978-0-9767816; 978-1-937376)* 944 Oakview Rd., Tarpon Springs, FL 34689 USA Tel 502-713-3149
E-mail: allstarpress@verizon.net
Web site: www.allstarpress.com
Dist(s): **Smashwords.**

All Systems Grow, *(978-0-578-41284-9)* 6721 SW 64th Ave., Miami, FL 33143 USA Tel 305-298-8026
E-mail: patdonovanauthor@yahoo.com
Dist(s): **Ingram Content Group.**

All That Productions, Inc., *(978-0-9679441; 978-0-9903422; 978-1-7339510)* Orders Addr.: P.O. Box 1594, Humble, TX 77347 USA Tel 281-878-2062
E-mail: allthat3@peoplepc.com.

All Things Liz Loves, *(978-1-949142)* 84 Davis Boulsvard Apt. 303, Tampa, FL 33606 USA Tel 804-405-3705
E-mail: allthingslizloves@gmail.com
Web site: www.allthingslizloves.com.

All Things That Matter Pr., *(978-0-9822056; 978-0-9822722; 978-0-9840984; 978-0-9842594; 978-0-9844219; 978-0-9846154; 978-0-9846216; 978-0-9846297; 978-0-9846392; 978-0-9846517; 978-0-9847215; 978-0-9850066; 978-0-9857789; 978-0-9885427; 978-0-9894032; 978-0-9960413; 978-0-9907158; 978-0-9966634; 978-0-9980717; 978-0-9995243; 978-1-7327237; 978-1-7334448; 978-1-7346855)* 79 Jones Rd., Somerville, ME 04348 USA
E-mail: allthingsthatmatterpress@gmail.com
Web site: http://www.allthingsthatmatterpress.com.

Allaf, Mashhad Al, *(978-0-9722722)* P.O. Box 2063, Chester, VA 23831-8440 USA.

Allecram Publishing, *(978-0-9764198)* P.O. Box 6003, Dayton, OH 45405 USA Tel 937-278-6630
E-mail: marcellaashe@sbcglobal.net
Web site: http://www.allecrampublishing.com.

Allegheny Pr., *(978-0-910042)* 19323 Elgin Rd., Corry, PA 16407 USA (SAN 201-2456) Tel 814-664-8504
E-mail: hjohn@tbscc.com
Dist(s): **Follett School Solutions.**

Allegiant Publishing Group, *(978-1-945737)* 171 Durham Rd., Dover, NH 03820 USA Tel 603-343-8107
E-mail: info@allegiantpublishing.com
Web site: www.allegiantpublishing.com.

Allen & Unwin (AUS) *(978-0-04; 978-0-86861; 978-1-86373; 978-1-86448; 978-1-875680; 978-0-7299; 978-1-86508; 978-1-74114; 978-1-74115; 978-1-74175; 978-1-74176; 978-1-74237; 978-1-74269; 978-1-877505; 978-0-7316-7153-3; 978-0-646-24696-3; 978-1-74331; 978-1-74343;-1-76011; 978-1-925266; 978-1-925267; 978-1-925268; 978-1-76029; 978-1-925393; 978-1-925394; 978-1-925395; 978-1-76052; 978-1-925575; 978-1-925576; 978-1-925577; 978-1-76063; 978-1-76087; 978-1-922351; 978-1-76106) Dist. by* **IPG Chicago.**

Allen, Edward Publishing, LLC, *(978-0-9853123; 978-0-9967663; 978-0-9983730)* 73 Terri Sue Ct., Hampton, VA 23666 USA Tel 757-768-5544
E-mail: jscottprice@gmail.com; leahdprice@gmail.com
Web site: http://www.edwardallenpublishing.com
Dist(s): **BookBaby.**

Allen, Jeffrey S. & Roger J. Klein *See* **Inner Coaching**

Allen Publishing, USA *See* **ALEXZUS Bks.**

Allen, Toi Operations, *(978-0-9753787)* 11300 E. 85th Terr., Raytown, MO 64138 USA Tel 816-737-5293; Fax: 816-923-2634
E-mail: itasca2001@aol.com.

Allen-Ayers Bks., *(978-0-9658702)* 4621 S. Atlantic Ave., No. 7603, Ponce Inlet, PA 32127 USA Tel 386-761-3956
E-mail: allen-ayers@cfl.rr.com.

AllensRusk Pr., *(978-0-9672246)* P.O. Box 100213, Nashville, TN 38134 USA Tel 615-365-0993
E-mail: allensrusk@aol.com.

Allergic Child Publishing Group, *(978-1-58628)* 6660 Delmonico Dr., Suite D249, Colorado Springs, CO 80919 USA Tel 719-338-0202; Fax: 719-633-0375
E-mail: nicole@allergicchild.com
Web site: http://www.allergicchild.com
Dist(s): **Follett School Solutions.**

Alli Kat Publishing, *(978-0-9788725)* 2353 Alexandria Dr., Suite 201, Lexington, KY 40504 USA Tel 859-264-7700; Fax: 859-264-7744
E-mail: eyemanjlh@aol.com.

Allied Publishing *See* **Flying Frog Publishing, Inc.**

Alligator Boogaloo, *(978-0-9721416)* 2531 San Jose Ave, Alameda, CA 94501 USA
E-mail: jerroldconnors@gmail.com; business@alligatorboogaloo.com
Web site: http://www.alligatorboogaloo.com.

Alligator Pr., *(978-0-9675658; 978-0-9884057; 978-0-9914334)* Orders Addr.: P.O. Box 526368, Salt Lake City, UT 84152 USA Tel 512-762-5427 Do not confuse with Alligator Press, Carson City, NV
E-mail: k.kimball333@gmail.com
Web site: http://www.alligatorpress.com
Dist(s): **BookBaby.**

Allium Pr. of Chicago, *(978-0-9840676; 978-0-9831938; 978-0-9890535; 978-0-9967558; 978-0-9996982; 978-1-7348017)* 1530 Elgin Ave., Forest Park, IL 60130 USA (SAN 858-3331)
Web site: http://www.alliumpress.com/
Dist(s): **Follett School Solutions**
INscribe Digital
Ingram Content Group
Smashwords.

Allocca Biotechnology, LLC, *(978-0-9659987; 978-0-9769213)* 19 Lorraine Ct., Northport, NY 11768 USA Tel 631-757-3919; Fax: 631-757-3918
E-mail: john@allocca.com
Web site: http://www.allocca.com.

Allocca, Christine A., *(978-0-615-21480-1)* 3940 Laurel Canyon Blvd., No. 399, Studio City, CA 91604 USA Tel 818-486-2730
Web site: http://www.little-green-giants.com.

Allocca Technology & Healthcare Research *See* **Allocca Biotechnology, LLC**

Allosaurus Pubs., *(978-0-9620900; 978-1-888325)* Div. of North Carolina Learning Institute for Fitness & Education, Orders Addr.: P.O. Box 10245, Greensboro, NC 27404 USA (SAN 250-0906) Tel 336-292-6999
E-mail: ally@infionline.net
Web site: http://www.allosauruspublishers.com
Dist(s): **Follett School Solutions.**

Allpony, *(978-1-7323871)* 106 Laurel Hill Rd, Chapel Hill, NC 27514 USA Tel 919-818-3734
E-mail: susan@allpony.com.

Allured Business Media, *(978-0-931710; 978-1-932633)* 336 Gundersen Dr. Ste. A, Carol Stream, IL 60188-2403 USA (SAN 222-4933)
Web site: http://www.alluredbooks.com/
Dist(s): **ebrary, Inc.**

Allured Publishing Corporation *See* **Allured Business Media**

Allworth Pr. *Imprint of* **Skyhorse Publishing Co., Inc.**

AllWrite Advertising & Publishing *See* **Allwrite Publishing**

Allwrite Publishing, *(978-0-9744935; 978-0-9844931; 978-0-9887332; 978-1-941716)* Orders Addr.: 3300 Buckeye Rd. Suite 264, Atlanta, GA 30341 USA Tel 770-284-8983; Fax: 770-284-8986; Edit Addr.: P.O. Box 1071, Atlanta, GA 30301 USA Tel 404-221-0703
E-mail: info@allwritepublishing.com; annette@allwritepublishing.com
Web site: http://www.allwritepublishing.com; http://www.e-allwrite.com
Dist(s): **Ingram Content Group.**

Alma Bks. (GBR) *(978-0-9517497; 978-1-84688; 978-1-84749) Dist. by* **Macmillan.**

Alma Classics *Imprint of* **Bloomsbury Publishing USA**

Alma Little *Imprint of* **Elva Resa Publishing, LLC**

Alma Pr., *(978-0-9746333)* 1204 Abbot Kinney Blvd., Venice, CA 90291 USA (SAN 255-6723) Fax: 310-314-3883
E-mail: info@almapress.com
Web site: http://www.almapress.com.

Almadraba Infantil y Juvenil (ESP) *(978-84-92702; 978-84-15207) Dist. by* **Lectorum Pubns.**

Almanac Publishing Co., *(978-1-928720)* Mt. Hope Ave., Lewiston, ME 04240 USA Tel 207-755-2246; Fax: 207-755-2422
Web site: http://www.farmersalmanac.com
Dist(s): **Sterling Publishing Co., Inc.**

Almond Publishing, *(978-0-9777314)* P.O. Box 573, Petaluma, CA 94953 USA (SAN 850-0673)
E-mail: contact@almondpublishing.com
Web site: http://www.almondpublishing.com.

Almuzara, Editorial (ESP) *(978-84-607; 978-84-933378; 978-84-933901; 978-84-96416; 978-84-88586; 978-84-96968) Dist. by* **Spanish.**

Aloha Publications *See* **catBOX Entertainment, Inc.**

Aloha Wellness Pubs., *(978-0-9727548)* 2333 Kapiolani Blvd., Suite 2108, Honolulu, HI 96826 USA (SAN 255-0539) Tel 808-941-8253; Fax: 808-925-4233; Toll Free: 866-233-6941
E-mail: crites@hawaii.rr.com
Web site: http://www.alohawellnesstravel.com
Dist(s): **Booklines Hawaii, Ltd.**

Alouette Enterprises, Inc., *(978-0-9797577; 978-0-9799922)* 7307 E. Solano Dr., Scottsdale, AZ 85250 USA
E-mail: DonnaFridrych@aol.com.

Alpenrose Pr., *(978-0-9603624; 978-1-889385)* Orders Addr.: P.O. Box 4245, Frisco, CO 80443 USA (SAN 222-2612) Tel 970-409-1479
E-mail: alpenrosepress@msn.com
Web site: http://www.alpenrosepress.com
Dist(s): **Alpenbooks Pr. LLC.**

Alpha *Imprint of* **Dorling Kindersley Publishing, Inc.**

Alpha Academic Pr., *(978-0-9660943)* 321 College Dr., Edison, NJ 08817 USA Tel 732-248-6582
E-mail: alpha-academic@usa.net
Web site: http://www.alpha-academic.com.

Alpha & Omega Publishing, *(978-0-9767778)* 3409 Daniel Place Dr., Charlotte, NC 28213 USA Tel 704-724-1683; Fax: 270-721-6019 Do not confuse iwth companies with the same name in Fremont, NE, Springfield, OR
E-mail: alphaomega@carolina.rr.com.

Alpha Behavior Consultants, *(978-0-9758755)* 12740 NW 11th St., Miami, FL 33172 USA
E-mail: info@alphbehc.com
Web site: http://www.alphabehc.com.

Alpha Bible Pubns., *(978-1-877917)* P.O. Box 155, Hood River, OR 97031 USA; P.O. Box 157, Morton, WA 98356 Tel 541-386-6634
Dist(s): **Pentecostal Publishing Hse.**
eBookit.com.

Alpha Buddies Inc., *(978-0-692-68521-1; 978-0-578-46331-5; 978-0-578-48867-7)* 711 Linda Terr., Wheeling, IL 60090 USA Tel 847-971-3788
E-mail: donnarink@alphabuddies.com.

Alpha Business Development Advisors LLC *See* **En Prose Pubns.**

Alpha Connections, *(978-0-9715779; 978-0-9747610; 978-1-936933)* 530 W. Idaho Blvd., Emmett, ID 83617 USA
E-mail: contact@dragonsfuryseries.com
Web site: http://www.dragonsfuryseries.com
Dist(s): **Ingram Content Group**
Smashwords.

Alpha Heartland Press *See* **Heartland Foundation, Inc.**

Alpha Ink, LLC, The, *(978-1-7334090)* 1603 Capitol Ave., No. 310 A247, Cheyenne, WY 82001 USA Tel 307-222-2976
E-mail: marketing@thealphaink.com
Web site: www.thealphaink.com.

Alpha Learning World, Inc., *(978-0-9791680)* 1064 Mohegan Rd., Venice, FL 34293 USA (SAN 852-6362)
E-mail: trisley1@verizon.net
Web site: http://alphalearningworld.com.

Alpha Media & Publishing - AM & P, LLC, 2851 S. Ocean Blvd. Ste 6-V, BOCA RATON, FL 33432 USA Tel 561-613-7770
E-mail: Editor@AlphaMediaAndPublishing.com
Dist(s): **Ingram Content Group.**

Alpha Omega Pubns., Inc., *(978-0-7403; 978-0-86717; 978-1-58095)* 300 N. McKemy Ave., Chandler, AZ 85226-2618 USA Tel 602-438-2717; Fax: 480-785-8034; Toll Free: 800-682-7391; 804 N. 2nd

Publisher Name Index

Ave. E., Rock Rapids, IA 51246 (SAN 853-2826) Tel 800-622-3070; Fax: 712-472-4856; *Imprints:* Lifepac (Lifepac); Horizons (Hrnzns AZ); Weaver (Weaver)
E-mail: cpatterson@aop.com
Web site: http://www.aop.com
Dist(s): **Follett School Solutions**
Send The Light Distribution LLC
Spring Arbor Distributors, Inc.

Alpha OmeGa Publishing, *(978-0-9658073)* 1217 Cape Coral Pkwy., Cape Coral, FL 33904 USA Tel 941-542-3666; Fax: 941-945-7963; Toll Free: 800-542-3666; 4219 SE First Ct., Cape Coral, FL 33904
E-mail: GPMueller@aol.com
Web site: http://www.Floridawest.com/Liestorm.

Alpha Run Pr., LLC, *(978-0-9761182; 978-1-933289)* Orders Addr.: P.O. Box 15079, Silver Spring, MD 20914-5079 USA Tel 202-508-3392; Edit Addr.: 1717 K St. NW, Suite 600, Washington, DC 20036 USA
E-mail: alpharp@aol.com
Web site: http://www.alpharunpress.com.

Alpha Shade, Inc., *(978-0-9768705)* 11850 85th Pl., N., Maple Grove, MN 55369 USA Tel 763-424-9316
E-mail: alphashade1@aol.com
Web site: http://www.alpha-shade.com.

Alpha Writers Ltd., *(978-0-9772018)* Orders Addr.: P.O. Box 561262, The Colony, TX 75056 USA (SAN 256-9256) Fax: 425-955-0859; Toll Free: 866-751-4340 Outside of Dallas
E-mail: source@alphawritersltd.com
Web site: http://www.alphawritersltd.com.

Alpha-kidZ, *(978-0-9749220; 978-0-9823534)* P.O. Box 1552, West Monroe, LA 71294-1552 USA Tel 318-651-0833; Fax: 318-396-4073
Web site: http://www.alphakidz.com.

AlphaLove Publishing, *(978-0-9764307)* P.O. Box 248, South Orange, NJ 07079 USA Fax: 973-275-3973.

Alpine Archaeological Consultants, Inc., *(978-0-9743137)* P.O. Box 2075, Montrose, CO 81402-2075 USA Tel 970-249-6761; Fax: 970-249-8482
E-mail: susan_chandler@alpinearchaeology.com
Web site: http://www.alpinearchaeology.com.

†Alpine Pubns., Inc., *(978-0-931866; 978-1-57779)* Orders Addr.: 38262 Linman Rd., Crawford, CO 81415 USA (SAN 255-2094) Tel 970-921-5005; Fax: 970-921-5081; Toll Free: 800-777-7257
E-mail: customerservice@alpinepub.com; alpinepublishing@aol.com
Web site: http://www.alpinepub.com
Dist(s): **Follett School Solutions**; *CIP.*

Alpine River Pr., *(978-0-9891471)* 660 Haley LN, Red Bluff, CA 96080 USA Tel 530-200-2745
E-mail: alpineriverpress@gmail.com.

Alta Omnimedia, *(978-0-9726360)* 2 Valley View Ave., Ste. 116, San Jose, CA 95127 USA
Web site: http://www.altaomnimedia.com.

Alta Publishing LLC, *(978-0-9767120)* P.O. Box 108, Bellvue, CO 80512 USA (SAN 256-4874) Do not confuse with companies with the same name in Sandy, UT, Midvale, UT.

Alta Retreat Ctr., *(978-0-9746151)* 20 Alta School Rd., Alta, WY 83414 USA Tel 307-353-8200; Fax: 208-354-4002
E-mail: altacp@ida.net.

Altar of Influence, *(978-0-692-25456-1; 978-0-9996797)* 370 E Silver Hawk Ct, Washington, UT 84780 USA Tel 619.884.9718
E-mail: Jacob@circleofreign.com.

Altea, Ediciones, S.A. - Grupo Santillana (ESP) *(978-84-372) Dist. by* **Santillana.**

Altea, Ediciones, S.A. - Grupo Santillana (ESP) *(978-84-372) Dist. by* **Lectorum Pubns.**

Alterna Comics, *(978-0-9797874; 978-1-934985; 978-1-945762)* Div. of Alterna Comics, Inc., Orders Addr.: 23 Trumpet Ln., Levittown, NY 11756 USA Tel 516-304-6733; Fax: 516-644-2386
E-mail: publisher@alternacomics.com
Web site: http://www.alternacomics.com
Dist(s): **Diamond Comic Distributors, Inc.**
Independent Pubs. Group
MyiLibrary.

Alternative Comics, *(978-1-891867; 978-1-934460; 978-1-68148)* 21607B Stevens Creek Blvd., Cupertino, CA 95014 USA Do not confuse with companies with the same or similar name in Goleta, GA, Billerica, MA
E-mail: marc@wowcool.com
Web site: http://www.indyworld.com
Dist(s): **Consortium Bk. Sales & Distribution**
Diamond Comic Distributors, Inc.
Diamond Bk. Distributors
Last Gasp of San Francisco.

Alternative Press, Incorporated *See* **Alternative Comics**

AlterNet Bks., *(978-0-9633687; 978-0-9752724)* 77 Federal St., 2nd Flr., San Francisco, CA 94107 USA Tel 415-284-1420; Fax: 415-284-1414
E-mail: valrie@alternet.org
Web site: http://www.alternet.org.

Althos *See* **DiscoverNet**

Altrusa Club of Baton /Rouge, Inc., *(978-0-692-04117-8; 978-0-578-55199-9)* 16246 Shenandoah Dr., Baton Rouge, LA 70817 USA Tel 225-753-9307
E-mail: carmels@cox.net
Dist(s): **Ingram Content Group.**

Altschuler, Richard & Assocs., Inc., *(978-1-884092)* 100 W. 57th St., No. 2M, New York, NY 10019 USA (SAN 299-2949) Tel 212-397-7233; Fax: 212-397-6090; *Imprints:* Chaucer Press (Chaucer Pr)
E-mail: lcra@aol.com; raltschuler@rcn.com
Web site: http://www.richardaltschuler.com
Dist(s): **BookBaby**
Ingram Content Group
Longleaf Services
Syracuse Univ. Pr.
Univ. Pr. of New England.

A-Lu Publishing, *(978-0-9817092)* 4257 Holiday Rd., Traverse City, MI 49686 USA
Dist(s): **BookBaby.**

Alvarado, Rudolph *See* **Caballo Pr. of Ann Arbor**

ALVARADOPLUS, *(978-0-9791782)* 315 Luna St., Apt 1B, San Juan, PR 00901-1488 USA (SAN 852-6710)
E-mail: ALVARADOPlus@aol.com.

Alvarez, Jesus, *(978-0-9792507)* 254 San Diego Ave., Brownsville, TX 78526 USA Tel 956-542-2722
E-mail: alvarcorp@msn.com.

Alway, Bruce, *(978-0-692-93718-1; 978-0-692-94868-2; 978-0-692-06155-8)* 2714 Regway Ave., Long Beach, CA 90810 USA Tel 540-877-7482
E-mail: BruceAlway23@gmail.com.

A.M. Green Publishing, *(978-1-935479)* P.O. Box 1085, Amston, CT 06231 USA Tel 617-391-7350
E-mail: JSmith@amgreenpublishing.com
Web site: http://www.amgreenpublishing.com.

AM Ink Publishing, *(978-0-9845801; 978-0-9852146; 978-0-9884468; 978-0-9910330; 978-1-943201)* PO Box 194, Southwick, MA 01077 USA (SAN 859-8142) Tel 413-222-1143
E-mail: Mike@AuthorMike.com
Web site: http://www.AMInkPublishing.com; https://aminkpublishing.com/dark-ink.

Ama Deus Energy Pr., *(978-0-9962780; 978-0-9987414; 978-0-9998412; 978-1-7348359)* 1065 Alden Nash, Lowell, MI 49331 USA Tel 616-340-7892
E-mail: bcomos@sbcglobal.net
Web site: www.ama-deus-international.com.

AMA Verlag GmbH (DEU) *(978-3-89922; 978-3-927190; 978-3-932587) Dist. by* **Mel Bay.**

†AMACOM, *(978-0-7612; 978-0-8144)* Div. of Harpercollins Leadership, P.O. Box 141000, Nashville, TN 37214 USA (SAN 201-1670) Toll Free: 800-250-5308
E-mail: pubservice@amanet.org
Web site: http://www.amacombooks.org
Dist(s): **Ebsco Publishing**
Follett School Solutions
HarperCollins Christian Publishing
HarperCollins Pubs.
MyiLibrary
Nelson, Thomas Inc.
Productivity Pr.
Wybel Marketing Group
ebrary, Inc.; *CIP.*

Amadeus Press *Imprint of* **Leonard, Hal Corp.**

Amagi Bks. *Imprint of* **Liberty Fund, Inc.**

Amalgamated Story *Imprint of* **Santore, Marcia**

Amalgamated Widgets Unlimited, *(978-0-615-54280-5; 978-0-692-74884-8; 978-0-692-76379-7)* 2995 Woodside Rd., Suite 400-166, Woodside, CA 94062 USA Tel 650-780-9288; 425-298-6552
E-mail: ng@awun.net
Web site: dandelom.com
Dist(s): **CreateSpace Independent Publishing Platform**
Dummy Record Do Not USE!!!!.

amana pubns., *(978-0-915957; 978-1-59008)* Div. of amana corp., 10710 Tucker St., Beltsville, MD 20705-2223 USA (SAN 630-9798) Tel 301-595-5999; Fax: 301-595-5888; Toll Free: 800-660-1777
E-mail: amana@igprinting.com
Web site: http://www.amana-publications.com.

Amanda Lowney Bks. LLC, *(978-0-578-47290-4; 978-0-578-47451-9; 978-1-7348460)* 2729 W Woodfield Dr, Mequon, WI 53092 USA Tel 414-467-3456
E-mail: amandalowneybooks@gmail.com
Web site: www.amandalowneybooks.com.

Amani Publishing, LLC, *(978-0-9752851; 978-0-9788937; 978-0-9815847; 978-0-9833666)* P.O. Box 12045, Tallahassee, FL 32317 USA Tel 850-264-3341 Do not confuse with Amani Publishing in Pineville, LA
E-mail: amanipublishing@aol.com
Web site: http://www.barbarajoewilliams.com
Dist(s): **Ingram Content Group.**

Amaquemecan, Editorial (MEX) *(978-968-7205) Dist. by* **AIMS Intl.**

Amaquemecan, Editorial (MEX) *(978-968-7205) Dist. by* **Continental Bk.**

AMARA Entertainment, *(978-0-9760745)* 1024 Frans Rd., Westfield, NC 27053 USA Tel 336-351-3437 (phone/fax)
E-mail: rpitt@charlesthechef.com
Web site: http://www.charlesthechef.com.

Amato, G. J., *(978-0-615-38545-7; 978-0-9829962; 978-0-9894561; 978-1-7338936)* 5 Westview Ct., Avon, CT 06001-4540 USA Tel 860-675-6712
E-mail: gaetanoja@aol.com
Web site: getkidsmovingnow.com.

AmazeBk. Pr., *(978-0-9986360)* 5729 SE 50th Ave, Portland, OR 97206 USA Tel 503-961-2656
E-mail: clubchris@gmail.com.

Amazement Square, *(978-0-9815308)* 27 Ninth St., Lynchburg, VA 24504 USA
Web site: http://www.amazementsquare.org.

Amazing Drama Anointed Voices Original Music, *(978-0-9725827)* 1256 Cranwood Square N., Columbus, OH 43229-1341 USA Tel 614-431-5311
E-mail: kfd43229@aol.com
Web site: http://www.keys.decisivenet.com.

Amazing Dreams Publishing, *(978-0-9719628)* P.O. Box 1811, Asheville, NC 28802 USA
E-mail: contact@amazingdreamspublishing.com
Web site: http://www.amazingdreamspublishing.com
Dist(s): **ASP Wholesale**
CreateSpace Independent Publishing Platform.

Amazing Factory, The, *(978-0-9776282; 978-0-9788469; 978-0-9790302)* 5527 San Gabriel Way, Orlando, FL 32837 USA
E-mail: theamazingfactory@hotmail.com
Web site: http://www.theamazingfactory.com.

Amazing Herbs Pr., *(978-0-9742962)* 545 8th Ave., Suite 401, New York, NY 10018 USA Tel 770-982-0107; Fax: 770-982-0273; Toll Free: 800-241-9138 (orders)
E-mail: tnc100@bellsouth.net
Web site: http://www.amazingherbspress.com.

AMazing Pubns., *(978-0-9763434)* 337 W. Napa St., Sonoma, CA 95476 USA.

Amazing Publishing Company, A *See* **Rhymeglow LLC**

Amazon Children's Publishing *Imprint of* **Amazon Publishing**

Amazon Creations, *(978-1-7336818)* 14107 Chartley Falls Dr, Houston, TX 77044 USA Tel 214-455-3808
E-mail: gyw1954@gmail.com.

Amazon Encore *Imprint of* **Amazon Publishing**

Amazon Publishing, *(978-0-8034; 978-1-61109; 978-1-4778; 978-1-5039; 978-1-5420; 978-1-6625)* 2021 7th Ave., Seattle, WA 98121 USA; *Imprints:* AmazonCrossing (AmazonCross); Amazon Children's Publishing (AmazonChldns); Thomas & Mercer (Thomas&MercerA); Montlake Romance (Montlake); 47North (FortySevN); Amazon Encore (Amazon Encore); Little A (LittleA); Jet City Comics (JetCityComics); Two Lions (TwoLions); Skyscape (Skyscape); AmazonClassics (AmazonClass)
E-mail: Customerservice@brilliancepublishing.com
Web site: http://www.amazon.com/amazoncrossing; http://www.apub.com/; http://www.amazon.com/amazonpublishing
Dist(s): **Brilliance Publishing, Inc.**
Children's Plus, Inc.
CreateSpace Independent Publishing Platform
MyiLibrary.

AmazonClassics *Imprint of* **Amazon Publishing**

AmazonCrossing *See* **Amazon Publishing**

AmazonCrossing *Imprint of* **Amazon Publishing**

Ambassador Bks. *Imprint of* **Paulist Pr.**

Ambassador Bks., Inc., *(978-0-9646439; 978-1-929039)* 446 Main St. Ste. 19, Worcester, MA 01608-2368 USA Toll Free: 800-577-0909
E-mail: info@ambassadorbooks.com
Web site: http://www.ambassadorbooks.com
Dist(s): **Christian Bk. Distributors**
Spring Arbor Distributors, Inc.

Ambassador International *Imprint of* **Emerald Hse. Group, Inc.**

Ambassador Pubns., *(978-1-58572)* 3110 E. Medicine Lake Blvd., Plymouth, MN 55441 USA Tel 763-545-5631; Fax: 763-545-0079
E-mail: parished@aflc.org
Web site: http://www.aflc.org.

Ambassador-Emerald, International *Imprint of* **Emerald Hse. Group, Inc.**

Amber Bks. (GBR) *(978-1-904687; 978-0-9544356; 978-1-905704; 978-1-906626; 978-1-909160; 978-1-908696; 978-1-907446; 978-1-78274) Dist. by* **Sterling.**

Amber Bks., *(978-0-9655064; 978-0-9702224; 978-0-9727519; 978-0-9749779; 978-0-9767735; 978-0-9790976; 978-0-9824922; 978-1-937269)* Div. of Amber Communications Group, Inc., Orders Addr.: 1334 E. Chandler Blvd., Suite 5-D67, Phoenix, AZ 85048 USA Tel 602-743-7211; 602-743-7426; Fax: 480-283-0991; *Imprints:* Colossus Books (Colossus)
E-mail: amberbks@aol.com
Web site: http://www.amberbooks.com
Dist(s): **A & B Distributors & Pubs. Group**
African World Bks.
Book Wholesalers, Inc.
Brodart Co.
D & J Bk. Distributors
Follett School Solutions
Independent Pubs. Group
Midwest Library Service
Quality Bks., Inc.
Unique Bks., Inc.

Amber Communications Group, Inc., 1334 East Chandler Blvd., Suite 5-D67, Phoenix, AZ 85048 USA.

Amber Marie Publishing, *(978-0-9771981)* 10413 Coffee Grinder Ct., Las Vegas, NV 89129 USA (SAN 256-9744) Tel 702-238-3846.

Amber Skye Publishing LLC, *(978-0-9819860; 978-0-9831839; 978-0-9894003; 978-0-692-47081-7; 978-0-9977266)* 1935 Berkshire Dr., Eagan, MN 55122 USA
E-mail: publisher@amberskyepublishing.com
Web site: http://www.amberskyepublishing.com; www.itascabooks.com
Dist(s): **CreateSpace Independent Publishing Platform**
Itasca Bks.

Amber Trust, The *See* **Aenor Trust, The**

Amber Victoria LLC, *(978-1-7335285)* 18436 N. 92 St., Scottsdale, AZ 85255 USA Tel 480-430-7777
E-mail: ambervictoria360@gmail.com.

Amber Woods Publishing, *(978-0-9743717)* P.O. Box 280, Excelsior, MN 55331 USA Tel 952-476-1670
Web site: http://www.amberwoodspublishing.com.

Amberjack Publishing Co., *(978-0-692-30068-8; 978-0-692-30154-8; 978-0-692-33339-6; 978-0-692-33341-9; 978-0-692-39045-0; 978-0-692-40203-0; 978-0-692-42948-8; 978-0-692-42951-8; 978-0-692-44642-3; 978-0-692-44646-1; 978-0-692-46743-5; 978-0-692-48712-9; 978-0-692-50148-1; 978-0-692-51719-2; 978-0-692-51720-8; 978-0-692-53639-1; 978-0-692-53640-7; 978-0-692-58289-3; 978-0-692-58297-8; 978-0-692-58721-8; 978-0-9972377; 978-1-944995; 978-1-948705; 978-1-950064) P.O. Box 4668 #89611, New York, NY 10163 USA; Imprints:* Little Adventures (Little Advent)
Dist(s): **Independent Pubs. Group**
Midpoint Trade Bks., Inc.

Amberley Publishing (GBR) *(978-1-84868; 978-1-4456) Dist. by* **IPG Chicago.**

Amberock Pubns., *(978-0-9754636)* P.O. Box 491, Dallas, NC 28034 USA
Web site: http://www.meandmybassguitar.com.

Amberwaves, *(978-0-9708913)* P.O. Box 487, Becket, MA 01223 USA (SAN 256-4254) Tel 413-623-0012; 413-623-6042 (phone/fax); 305 Brooker Hill Rd., Becket, MA 01223 Tel 413-623-0012; Fax: 413-623-6042
E-mail: shenwa@bcn.net
Web site: http://www.amberwaves.org.

Amberwood Pr., *(978-0-9630243; 978-0-9776445; 978-0-615-95885-9)* 509 Albany Post Rd., New Paltz, NY 12561-3629 USA Do not confuse with Amberwood Pr., in Ventura, CA
E-mail: nava@vegkitchen.com
Web site: http://www.vegkitchen.com
Dist(s): **CreateSpace Independent Publishing Platform.**

Ambitious Abbey, LLC, *(978-0-692-10005-9)* 1105 Howard St., Bridgeport, OH 43219 USA Tel 304-951-0221
E-mail: ambitiousabbeybooks@gmail.com
Web site: www.AmbitiousAbbey.com.

Ambrosia Press LLC, *(978-0-9729346; 978-0-9778656; 978-0-9525344; 978-0-9862590)* 2 Waban Rd., Timberlake, OH 44095 USA Tel 440-951-7780; Fax: 440-951-0565
E-mail: willowhse@yahoo.com
Web site: http://www.ruthfawcettbooks.com.

Ameeramac Bks. *Imprint of* **Ameeramac Bks. Inc.**

Ameeramac Bks. Inc., *(978-0-9762911)* Div. of Ameeramac Reporting, Inc., 168 Putnam Ave., Brooklyn, NY 11216-1606 USA Tel 917-353-1644; Fax: 718-636-8210; *Imprints:* Ameeramac Books (AmeeraBks)
E-mail: ameeramac@optonline.com.

Ameeramac Reporting, Incorporated *See* **Ameeramac Bks. Inc.**

Amelia Street Press *See* **Prytania Pr.**

Amereon Ltd., *(978-0-8488; 978-0-88411; 978-0-89190; 978-1-59683)* Orders Addr.: P.O. Box 1200, Mattituck, NY 11952 USA (SAN 201-2413) Tel 631-298-5100; Fax: 631-298-5631; *Imprints:* Rivercity Press (Rivercity Pr); American Reprint Company (Am Repr)
E-mail: info@amereon.net
Dist(s): **Follett School Solutions**
Ingram Publisher Services.

America Hispanic Consulting Group Inc., *(978-0-9978819)* P.O. Box 1709, Fresno, CA 93717 USA Tel 559-392-3710
E-mail: susan@cottoncandybooks.com
Web site: www.cottoncandybooks.com.

America Sports Publishing, *(978-0-9721199)* Orders Addr.: P.O. Box 132, Brookfield, OH 44403 USA Tel 330-448-0866; Toll Free: 866-255-2267; Edit Addr.: 6881 Stewart Rd., Brookfield, OH 44403 USA Fax: 330-448-0936
E-mail: Info@AthleticScholarshipBook.com
Web site: http://www.AthleticScholarshipBook.com
Dist(s): **Cardinal Pubs. Group**
Quality Bks., Inc.
Unique Bks., Inc.

America Star Bks., *(978-1-61102; 978-1-63249; 978-1-63382; 978-1-63448; 978-1-68090; 978-1-68122; 978-1-68176; 978-1-68229; 978-1-63508; 978-1-68290; 978-1-68394)* 550 Highland St. Ste 105, Frederick, MD 21701 USA Tel 301-228-2595; Fax: 301-228-2596; P.O. Box 151, Frederick, MD 21705
Web site: www.americastarbooks.pub
Dist(s): **Independent Pubs. Group.**

American Academy of Pediatrics, *(978-0-910761; 978-1-58110; 978-0-578-04930-4; 978-0-578-05484-1; 978-1-61002)* 141 NW Point Blvd., Elk Grove Village, IL 60007-1098 USA (SAN 265-3540) Tel 847-434-4000; Fax: 847-434-8000; Toll Free: 888-227-1770; 387 Park Ave., S., New York, NY 10016
E-mail: pubs@aap.org
Web site: http://www.aap.org/bookstore
Dist(s): **Caldwell Letter Service**
Ebsco Publishing
Follett School Solutions
Independent Pubs. Group
Ingram Publisher Services
Majors, J. A. Co.
MyiLibrary
Rittenhouse Bk. Distributors
Two Rivers Distribution
ebrary, Inc.

American Animal Hospital Assn. Pr., *(978-0-941451; 978-0-9616498; 978-1-58326)* Orders Addr.: 12575 W. Bayaud Ave., Lakewood, CO 80228 USA (SAN 224-4799) Tel 303-986-2800; Fax: 303-986-1700; Toll Free: 800-252-2242
E-mail: msc@aahanet.org
Web site: http://press.aahanet.org
Dist(s): **Matthews Medical Bk. Co.**

American Antiquarian Society, *(978-0-912296; 978-0-944026; 978-1-929545)* 185 Salisbury St., Worcester, MA 01609 USA (SAN 206-474X) Tel 508-752-5221; Fax: 508-754-9069
E-mail: library@mwa.org
Web site: http://www.americanantiquarian.org
Dist(s): **Oak Knoll Pr.**

American Assn. of Veterinary Parasitologists, *(978-0-9770942)* 3915 S. 48th St. Terr., Saint Joseph, MO 64503 USA
Web site: http://www.aavp.org.

American Atheist Pr., (*978-0-910309; 978-0-911826; 978-1-57884; 978-0-9981819*) Subs. of Charles E. Stevens, P.O. Box 5733, Parsippany, NJ 07054-6733 USA (SAN 206-7188) Tel 908-276-7300; Fax: 908-276-7402
E-mail: editor@atheists.org; info@atheists.org
Web site: http://www.atheists.org.

American Bar Assn., (*978-0-89707; 978-1-57073; 978-1-59031; 978-1-60442; 978-1-61632; 978-0-615-36849-8; 978-0-615-36850-4; 978-1-61438; 978-1-62722; 978-1-63425; 978-0-578-55688-8*) 321 N Clark St, 20th FL, Chicago, IL 60654 USA (SAN 211-4798) Tel 312-988-6011 Toll Free: 800-285-2221
E-mail: natalie.cirar@americanbar.org
Web site: http://www.americanbar.org
Dist(s): **MyiLibrary**
National Bk. Network.

American Bible Society, (*978-0-8267; 978-1-58516; 978-1-937628; 978-1-941448; 978-1-941449*) Orders Addr.: 6201 E. 43rd St., Tulsa, OK 74135-6562 USA (SAN 662-7129) Toll Free Fax: 866-570-2877; Edit Addr.: 1865 Broadway, New York, NY 10023-9980 USA (SAN 203-5189) Tel 212-408-1200; Fax: 212-408-1305; 700 Plaza Dr., 2nd Flr., Secaucus, NJ 07094
E-mail: info@americanbible.org
Web site: http://www.bibles.org; http://www.americanbible.org
Dist(s): **Anchor Distributors.**

American Bk. Co., (*978-1-932410; 978-1-59807; 978-1-62800; 978-1-64117*) 103 Executive Dr., Woodstock, GA 30188 USA Tel 770-928-2834 Toll Free: 888-254-5877 Do not confuse with companies with the same name in Chesterfield, VA, Knoxville, TN, Florence, AL
E-mail: dpintozzi@americanbookcompany.com
Web site: http://www.americanbookcompany.com.

American Book Publishing *See* **American Bk. Publishing Group**

American Bk. Publishing Group, (*978-1-930586; 978-1-58982; 978-0-615-54716-9*) P.O. Box 65624, Salt Lake City, UT 84165 USA (SAN 254-4725) Fax: 801-382-0881; Toll Free: 888-288-7413; *Imprints*: Bedside Books (Bedside Bks); Millennial Mind Publishing (Millennial Mind)
E-mail: orders@american-book.com; info@american-book.com; operations@american-book.com
Web site: http://www.american-book.com
Dist(s): **Seven Locks Pr.**

American Bookworks Corp., (*978-0-9622813; 978-1-884965*) 309 Florida Hill Rd., Ridgefield, CT 06877 USA Tel 203-438-0345; Fax: 203-438-0379
E-mail: info@abwcorporation.com
Web site: http://www.abwcorporation.com.

†**American Camping Assn.**, (*978-0-87603*) 5000 State Rd. 67, N., Martinsville, IN 46151-7902 USA (SAN 201-2596) Tel 765-342-8456 (General Info.); Fax: 765-349-6357 (orders); Toll Free: 800-428-2267 (orders)
E-mail: bookstore@aca-camps.org
Web site: http://www.acacamps.org; *CIP.*

American Cancer Society, Inc., (*978-0-944235; 978-1-60443*) 250 Williams St., Atlanta, GA 30303-1002 USA (SAN 227-6941) Tel 404-320-3333; Fax: 404-325-9341; Toll Free: 800-ACS-2345
Web site: http://www.cancer.org
Dist(s): **Independent Pubs. Group**
McGraw-Hill Cos., The
McGraw-Hill Professional Publishing
MyiLibrary
Wiley-Blackwell.

American Carriage Hse. Publishing, (*978-0-9705734; 978-1-935176*) P.O. Box 1778, Penn Valley, CA 95946 USA Tel 530-432-8860; Fax: 530-265-9650 Do not confuse with Carraige House Publishing in Middleton, CA
E-mail: info@americancarriagehousepublishing.com; editor@americancarriagehousepublishing.com; research@americancarriagehousepublishing.com; assistant@americancarriagehousepublishing.com
Web site: http://www.americancarriagehousepublishing.com
Dist(s): **Send The Light Distribution LLC**
Smashwords.

†**American Chemical Society**, (*978-0-8412; 978-0-692-96437-8; 978-0-692-96439-2; 978-0-578-62767-0; 978-0-578-62768-7*) 1155 16th St., NW, Washington, DC 20036 USA (SAN 201-2626) Tel 202-872-4600; Toll Free: 800-227-5558; 2001 Evans Rd., Cary, NC 27513
E-mail: service@acs.org; help@acs.org
Web site: http://www.acs.org; http://www.ChemCenter.org
Dist(s): **Follett School Solutions**
Oxford Univ. Pr., Inc.; *CIP.*

American Classical League, The, (*978-0-939507*) Orders Addr.: 860 NW Washington Blvd. Suite A, Hamilton, OH 45013 USA (SAN 225-8358) Tel 513-529-7741; Fax: 513-529-7742
E-mail: info@aclclassics.org
Web site: http://www.aclclassics.org.

American Correctional Assn., (*978-0-929310; 978-0-942974; 978-1-56991*) 206 N. Washington St. Ste. 200, Alexandria, VA 22314-2528 USA (SAN 204-8051) Toll Free: 800-222-5646 (ext. 1860)
Web site: http://www.aca.org.

American Dental Assn., (*978-0-910074; 978-1-932305; 978-1-60122; 978-1-935201; 978-0-9860279; 978-1-941807; 978-1-68447*) 211 E. Chicago Ave., Chicago, IL 60611 USA (SAN 202-4519) Tel 312-440-2568; 312-440-2500; Fax: 312-440-7461
E-mail: survey@ada.org
Web site: http://www.ada.org.

American Diabetes Assn., (*978-0-945448; 978-1-58040*) Orders Addr.: 1701 N. Beauregard St., Alexandria, VA 22311 USA Toll Free Fax: 800-998-3103 (orders); Toll Free: 800-323-4900 (orders)
E-mail: lboswell@diabetes.org
Web site: http://www.diabetes.org
Dist(s): **McGraw-Hill Cos., The**
McGraw-Hill Professional Publishing
McGraw-Hill Trade
MyiLibrary
Publishers Group West (PGW).

American Dog *Imprint of* **Ideate Prairie**

American Driving Society, (*978-0-9727292*) P.O. Box 278, Cross Plains, WI 53528-0278 USA Do not confuse with American Driving Society in Lakeville, CT
E-mail: ann@americandrivingsociety.org
Web site: http://www.americandrivingsociety.org.

American Education Publishing *Imprint of* **Carson-Dellosa Publishing, LLC**

American Fisheries Society, (*978-0-913235; 978-1-888569; 978-1-934874*) 5410 Grosvenor Ln., Suite 110, Bethesda, MD 20814-2199 USA (SAN 284-964X) Tel 301-897-8616; Fax: 301-897-5080
E-mail: main@fisheries.org; afspubs@pbd.com
Web site: http://www.fisheries.org
Dist(s): **PBD, Inc.**

American French Genealogical Society, (*978-1-929920; 978-1-932749; 978-1-60305*) Orders Addr.: P.O. Box 830, Woonsocket, RI 02895 USA; Edit Addr.: 78 Earle St., Woonsocket, RI 02895 USA
E-mail: RDBeaudry@afgs.org
Web site: http://www.afgs.org.

American Girl *Imprint of* **American Girl Publishing, Inc.**

†**American Girl Publishing, Inc.**, (*978-0-937295; 978-1-56247; 978-1-58485; 978-1-59369; 978-1-60958; 978-1-68337*) Subs. of Mattel, Inc., Orders Addr.: P.O. Box 620991, Middleton, WI 53562-0991 USA Tel 608-836-4848; Toll Free Fax: 800-257-3865; Toll Free: 800-233-0264; Edit Addr.: 8400 Fairway Pl., Middleton, WI 53562 USA (SAN 298-6337) Tel 608-836-4848; Fax: 608-831-7089; *Imprints*: American Girl (Amer Girl)
E-mail: pub.orders@americangirl.com
Web site: http://www.americangirlpublishing.com
Dist(s): **Children's Plus, Inc.**
Follett School Solutions; *CIP.*

American Gramaphone LLC *See* **Mannheim Steamroller L.L.C.**

American Ground Water Trust, (*978-0-9641186*) Orders Addr.: 16 Centre St., Concord, NH 03301 USA Tel 603-228-5444; Fax: 603-228-6557
E-mail: trustinfo@agwt.org
Web site: http://www.agwt.org.

American Health Publishing, (*978-0-9754443*) Orders Addr.: P.O. Box 282, Clarence, NY 14031 USA Tel 716-741-0177 Do not confuse with Americanhealth Publishing Company in Dallas, TX
E-mail: americahealthpub@aol.com
Web site: http://www.growingahealthyfamily.com.

American Heritage *See* **Forbes Custom Publishing**

American Heritage Publishing, (*978-0-9754859; 978-0-578-12953-2*) 5710 Mt. Repose Ln. NW, Peachtree Corners, GA 30092-1428 USA Tel 404-495-3720 (phone/fax)
E-mail: tomross01@gmail.com
Web site: http://www.privilegesofwar.com
Dist(s): **BookBaby.**

American Historical Pr., (*978-0-9654754; 978-1-892724*) 10755 Sherman Way, Suite 2, Sun Valley, CA 91352 USA Tel 818-503-0133; Fax: 818-503-9081; Toll Free: 800-550-5750
E-mail: ahp@amhistpress.com
Web site: http://www.amhistpress.com/
Dist(s): **Chicago Distribution Ctr.**

American Home-School Publishing, LLC, (*978-0-9667067; 978-0-9779000*) Orders Addr.: 6102 SE. State Rte. C, Cameron, MO 64429 USA (SAN 254-7244) Tel 816-632-1503; Fax: 816-632-1448; Toll Free Fax: 800-557-0234; Toll Free: 800-684-2121
E-mail: booklovers@ahsp.com
Web site: http://www.ahsp.com.

American Humanist Assn., (*978-0-931779*) 1821 Jefferson Pl. NW, Washington, 20036 SUN (SAN 266-9412) Tel 202-238-9088; Fax: 202-238-9047; Toll Free: 800-837-3792; *Imprints*: Humanist Press (Humanist Press)
E-mail: publishing@americanhumanist.org
Web site: http://www.thehumanist.org; http://www.americanhumanist.org; http://humanistpress.com
Dist(s): **Ingram Content Group.**

American Institute For CPCU, (*978-0-89462; 978-0-89463*) 720 Providence Rd., Malvern, PA 19355 USA (SAN 210-1629) Tel 610-644-2100; Fax: 610-640-9576; Toll Free: 800-644-2101
E-mail: cserv@cpcuiia.org
Web site: http://www.aicpcu.org.

American Institute for Property & Liability Underwriters, Incorporated *See* **American Institute For CPCU**

American International Distribution Corp., Orders Addr.: 82 Winter Sport Ln., Williston, VT 05495 USA (SAN 631-1083) Tel 802-488-2665; Edit Addr.: 82 Winter Sport Ln., Williston, VT 05495 USA (SAN 630-2238) Toll Free: 800-488-2665
E-mail: jmacon@aidcvt.com
Web site: http://www.aidcvt.com/Specialty/Home.asp.

American International Printing & Marketing *See* **Graphix Network**

American LaserTechnic, (*978-0-9741805*) 1300 NE Miami Gardens Dr. Apt. 407, Miami, FL 33179-4731 USA
E-mail: dan-gregory@attbi.com
Web site: http://www.americanlasertechnic.com.

American Law Institute, (*978-0-8318*) 4025 Chestnut St., Philadelphia, PA 19104-3099 USA (SAN 204-756X) Tel 215-243-1656 Director of Books; 215-245-1654 (Library); 215-243-1700 (Customer Service); Fax: 215-243-0319; Toll Free: 800-253-6397
E-mail: mcarroll@ali-cle.org; namster@ali.org
Web site: http://www.ali-cle.org; http://www.ali.org.

†**American Library Assn.**, (*978-0-8389; 978-1-937589*) 50 E. Huron St., Chicago, IL 60611 USA (SAN 201-0062) Tel 312-280-2425; 312-944-8085; Fax: 770-280-4155 (Orders); Toll Free: 800-545-2433; 866-746-7252 (Orders); P.O. Box 932501, Atlanta, GA 31193-2501
E-mail: EditionsMarketing@ala.org
Web site: http://www.ala.org; http://www.alastore.ala.org
Dist(s): **Ebsco Publishing**
Follett School Solutions
Independent Pubs. Group
MyiLibrary
ebrary, Inc.; *CIP.*

American Literary Pr., (*978-1-56167; 978-1-934696*) Orders Addr.: 8019 Belair Rd., Suite 10, Baltimore, MD 21236 USA Tel 410-882-7700; Fax: 410-882-7703; Toll Free: 800-873-2003; *Imprints*: Shooting Star Edition (SSE)
E-mail: americanliterarypress@comcast.net
Web site: http://www.my-new-publisher.com
Dist(s): **MyiLibrary.**

American Literary Publishing *Imprint of* **LifeReloaded Specialty Publishing LLC**

American Map Corp., (*978-0-8416*) Div. of Langenscheidt Pubs., Inc., P.O. Box 780010, Maspeth, NY 11378-0010 USA (SAN 202-4624) Toll Free: 800-432-6277
E-mail: customerservice@americanmap.com
Web site: http://www.americanmap.com
Dist(s): **Fujii Assocs.**
Langenscheidt Publishing Group.

†**American Mathematical Society**, (*978-0-8218; 978-0-8284; 978-0-88385; 978-0-9835005; 978-1-61444; 978-1-4704; 978-1-939512*) Orders Addr.: 201 Charles St., Providence, RI 02904 USA (SAN 250-3263) Tel 401-455-4000; Fax: 401-331-3842; Toll Free: 800-321-4267; *Imprints*: Chelsea Publishing Company, Incorporated (Chelsea Pub Co); MAA Press (MAAPress)
E-mail: las@ams.org
Web site: http://www.ams.org
Dist(s): **Cambridge Univ. Pr.**
Ebsco Publishing
ProQuest LLC; *CIP.*

American Meteorological Society, (*978-0-933876; 978-1-878220; 978-1-935704; 978-1-940033; 978-1-944970; 978-0-578-59598-6*) 45 Beacon St, Boston, MA 02108-3693 USA (SAN 225-2139) Tel 617-227-2425; Fax: 617-742-8718
E-mail: mfriedman@ametsoc.org
Web site: http://www.ametsoc.org/ams
Dist(s): **Chicago Distribution Ctr.**
MyiLibrary
Springer
ebrary, Inc.

American Mythology Productions, (*978-1-945205*) P.O. Box 325, Bel Air, MD 21014 USA Tel 410-652-7008
E-mail: james.kuhoric@americanmythology.net
Web site: www.americanmythology.net
Dist(s): **Diamond Comic Distributors, Inc.**
Diamond Bk. Distributors.

American Poets Society *Imprint of* **Gem Printing**

†**American Psychological Assn.**, (*978-0-912704; 978-0-945354; 978-1-55798; 978-1-59147; 978-0-9792125; 978-1-4338*) Orders Addr.: P.O. Box 92984, Washington, DC 20090-2984 USA (SAN 685-3137) Tel 202-336-6123; 202-336-5510 202-336-5502 (orders); Toll Free: 800-374-2721; Edit Addr.: 750 First St., NE, Washington, DC 20002-4242 USA (SAN 255-5921) Tel 202-336-5500; P.O. Box 77318, Washington, DC 20013-8318 Toll Free: 800-374-2721; *Imprints*: Magination Press (Magination Press)
E-mail: ghughes@spa.org; jmacomber@apa.org; books@apa.org
Web site: http://www.apa.org
Dist(s): **Follett School Solutions**
Oxford Univ. Pr., Inc.; *CIP.*

American Quilter's Society *Imprint of* **Collector Bks.**

American Reading Co., (*978-1-59301; 978-1-61541; 978-1-61406; 978-1-63437; 978-1-64053; 978-1-64851*) 201 S. Gulph Rd., King Of Prussia, PA 19406 USA (SAN 930-3553) Tel 610-992-4150; Toll Free: 866-810-2665; *Imprints*: ARC Press Books (MYID_M_ARC PRE); ARC Press Comics (MYID_J_ARC PRE); Bird, Bunny & Bear (MYID_H_BIRD, B); Pajarito, Conjeo y Oso (MYID_K_PAJARIT)
E-mail: robbie.byerly@americanreading.com
Web site: http://www.americanreading.com.

American Reprint Co. *Imprint of* **Amereon Ltd.**

American Retrospects, LLC, (*978-0-9747666*) Orders Addr.: P.O. Box 352576, Toledo, OH 43635-2576 USA Tel 419-824-4500; Fax: 419-885-4255
E-mail: jkw@americanretro.net; jkw@bex.net; mds@bex.net; mds@americanretro.net
Web site: http://www.americanretro.net.

American Revolution Publishing, (*978-0-9760948*) 12514 Mustang Dr., Poway, CA 92064 USA Tel 858-513-7864
E-mail: marc-m@cox.net; marciceman@cox.net; amrevpub@cox.net
Web site: http://www.amrevpub.com
Dist(s): **Book Clearing Hse.**
Quality Bks., Inc.

American Schl. of Classical Studies at Athens, (*978-0-87661; 978-1-62139*) 6-8 Charlton St., Princeton, NJ 08540-5232 USA (SAN 201-1697) Tel 609-683-0800; Fax: 609-924-0578
E-mail: castein@ascsa.org
Web site: http://www.ascsa.edu.gr/publications
Dist(s): **Casemate Pubs. & Bk. Distributors, LLC**
Casemate Academic
Firebrand Technologies
MyiLibrary
ebrary, Inc.

American Society for Microbiology *See* **ASM Pr.**

American Society of Mechanical Engineers, The, (*978-0-7918*) 22 Law Dr.., Fairfield, NJ 07007-2300 USA (SAN 201-1379) Tel 973-882-1176; Fax: 973-882-1717; Toll Free: 800-843-2763
E-mail: pruskil@asme.org
Web site: http://www.asme.org.

American Society of Plant BIOLOGISTS, (*978-0-943088*) 15501 Monona Dr., Rockville, MD 20855-2768 USA (SAN 240-3366) Tel 301-251-0560; Fax: 301-279-2996
E-mail: education@aspb.org
Web site: http://aspp.org.

American Society of Plant Physiologists *See* **American Society of Plant BIOLOGISTS**

American Success Institute, Inc., (*978-1-884864*) 31 Central St. #5, Wellesley, MA 02482 USA Tel 781-237-7368
E-mail: info@Success.org
Web site: http://www.success.org
Dist(s): **BookBaby.**

American Swedish Historical Museum, (*978-0-9800761*) 1900 Pattison Ave., Philadelphia, PA 19145-5901 USA Tel 215-389-1776; Fax: 215-389-9901
E-mail: info@americanswedish.org
Web site: http://www.americanswedish.org.

American Technical Pubs., Inc., (*978-0-8269*) 10100 Orland Pkwy., Orland Park, IL 60467-5756 USA (SAN 206-8141) Toll Free: 800-323-3471
E-mail: service@americantech.net
Web site: http://www.americantech.net
Dist(s): **Follett School Solutions.**

American Traveler Pr., (*978-0-914846; 978-0-935810; 978-0-939650; 978-1-55838; 978-1-885590; 978-1-58581; 978-1-55838-153-7*) Orders Addr.: 5738 N. Central Ave., Phoenix, AZ 85012 USA (SAN 220-0864) Tel 602-234-1574; Fax: 602-234-3062; Toll Free: 800-521-9221; *Imprints*: Golden West Publishers (GoldenWest)
E-mail: info@AmericanTravelerPress.com
Web site: http://www.PrimerPublishers.com; http://www.RenaissanceHousePublishers.com; http://www.AmericanTravelerPress.com; http://www.ClayThompsonBooks.com; http://www.GoldenWestPublishers.com; www.GoldenWestCookbooks.com
Dist(s): **Chicago Distribution Ctr.**
Follett School Solutions
INscribe Digital.

American Trek Bks., (*978-0-9815221; 978-0-9821178*) 1371 Morley Ave., Rochester Hills, MI 48307 USA (SAN 855-7748).

American Trust Pubns., (*978-0-89259*) 745 Mcclintock Dr., Suite 314, Burr Ridge, IL 60527 USA (SAN 664-6158)
Dist(s): **Halalco Bks.**
Meta Co., LLC.

American Univ. in Cairo Pr., (*978-977-424; 978-1-936190; 978-977-416; 978-1-936481; 978-1-61797; 978-1-64903*) 113 Kasr el Aini St., Cairo, 11511 EGY Tel 909-223-3530; One Rockefeller Plaza, NEW YORK, NY 10020 Tel 212-730-8800; Fax: 212-730-1600
E-mail: aucpress@aucegypt.edu
Web site: http://www.aucegypt.edu
Dist(s): **Books International, Inc.**
Casemate Academic
MyiLibrary
Oxford Univ. Pr., Inc.
Oxford University Press USA - OSO
Two Rivers Distribution
ebrary, Inc.

American Water Works Assn., (*978-0-89867; 978-1-58321; 978-1-61300; 978-1-62576; 978-1-64717*) 6666 W. Quincy Ave., Denver, CO 80235-3098 USA (SAN 212-8241) Tel 303-347-6266; Fax: 303-794-7310; Toll Free: 800-926-7337 (customer service/orders)
E-mail: mramey@awwa.org
Web site: http://www.awwa.org
Dist(s): **Follett School Solutions**
ebrary, Inc.

American Wind Power Ctr., (*978-0-9679480*) Div. of National Windmill Project, Inc., 1501 Canyon Lake Dr., Lubbock, TX 79403 USA Tel 806-747-8734; Fax: 806-740-0668
E-mail: charris@windmill.com
Web site: http://www.windmill.com.

American World Publishing, (*978-0-615-16443-4; 978-0-615-16444-1; 978-0-615-16701-5*) P.O. Box 534, Union City, GA 30291 USA
E-mail: andrewhitmore@yahoo.com
Dist(s): **Lulu Pr., Inc.**

Americana Souvenirs & Gifts, (*978-1-890541*) 206 Hanover St., Gettysburg, PA 17325-1911 USA (SAN 169-7366) Toll Free: 800-692-7436.

America's Great Stories, (*978-0-615-34265-8*) 10100 Yankee Hill Rd., Lincoln, NE 68526 USA Tel 402-486-1776
E-mail: terrificteam@aol.com.

Americas Group, The, (*978-0-935047*) Subs. of Harris/Ragan Management Group, 654 N. Sepulveda Blvd. Ste. 1, Los Angeles, CA 90049-2170 USA (SAN 694-4698) Toll Free: 800-966-7716
E-mail: hrmg@aol.com
Web site: http://www.americasgroup.com
Dist(s): **Penton Overseas, Inc.**

America's Test Kitchen, *(978-0-936184; 978-1-933615; 978-1-936493; 978-1-940352; 978-1-945256; 978-1-948703)* 17 Station St., Brookline, MA 02445 USA (SAN 221-1939) Tel 617-232-1000; Fax: 617-232-1572; *Imprints:* America's Test Ktichen Kids (Am Test Kit Kids) Do not confuse with Cook's Illustrated, Lubbock, TX
Web site: http://www.cooksillustrated.com; http://www.americastestkitchentv.com; http://www.cookscountrytv.com; http://www.cookscountry.com; http://www.americastestkitchen.com
Dist(s): **Penguin Random Hse. Distribution**
Penguin Random Hse. LLC
Random Hse., Inc.

America's Test Kitchen Kids *Imprint of* **America's Test Kitchen**

Amerisearch, Inc., *(978-0-9653557; 978-0-9753455; 978-0-9778085; 978-0-9827101; 978-0-9896491)* Orders Addr.: P.O. Box 20163, Saint Louis, MO 63123 USA (SAN 254-6426) Tel 314-487-4395; Fax: 314-487-4489; Toll Free: 888-872-9673 (888-USA-WORD); Edit Addr.: 4346 Southview Way Dr., Saint Louis, MO 63129 USA
E-mail: wjfederer@gmail.com
Web site: http://www.amerisearch.net.

AmeriTales Entertainment, LLC, *(978-0-9798739)* 3525 Del Mar Heights Rd., Suite 623, San Diego, CA 92130 USA Tel 858-449-6900; Fax: 425-795-6026
E-mail: tcarter@ameritales.com
Dist(s): **Follett School Solutions.**

Amerotica *Imprint of* **NBM Publishing Co.**

Amethyst Moon *See* **Amethyst Moon Publishing and Services**

Amethyst Moon Publishing and Services, *(978-0-9792426; 978-1-935354; 978-1-938714)* Orders Addr.: P.O. Box 87885, Tucson, AZ 85754 USA
Web site: http://www.ampubbooks.com.

Amharic Kids, *(978-0-9797481)* 7201 88th Ave., Brooklyn Park, MN 55445 USA Tel 612-636-7878
E-mail: hamish@bellward.com
Web site: http://www.amharickids.com
Dist(s): **Follett School Solutions.**

Amherst Pr., *(978-0-910122; 978-0-942495; 978-1-930596)* Div. of The Guest Cottage, Inc., Orders Addr.: P.O. Box 774, Saint Germain, WI 54558 USA (SAN 213-9820) Tel 715-477-0424; Fax: 715-477-0405; Toll Free: 800-333-8122; Edit Addr.: P.O. Box 774, Saint Germain, WI 54558 USA (SAN 666-6450) Do not confuse with companies with the same name in Amherst, NY, North Hampton, NH
E-mail: sales@theguestcottage.com
Web site: http://www.theguestcottage.com
Dist(s): **Partners Bk. Distributing, Inc.**

Amiaya Entertainment, *(978-0-9745075; 978-0-9777544)* 1154 E. 229 St., Apt. 12C, Bronx, NY 10466 USA.

Amichai Charnoff, *(978-0-692-81729-2; 978-0-692-82098-8)* 11812 Smoketree Rd., POTOMAC, MD 20854 USA Tel 301-706-7385
E-mail: amicharnoff@gmail.com; amicharnoff@gmail.com
Dist(s): **CreateSpace Independent Publishing Platform.**

Amicus, *(978-1-68152)* P.O. Box 1329, Mankato, MN 56002 USA Tel 507-388-9357
E-mail: rglaser@amicuspublishing.us; anna.erickson@amicuspublishing.us; info@amicuspublishing.us
Web site: www.amicuspublishing.us
Dist(s): **Chronicle Bks. LLC**
Hachette Bk. Group.

Amicus Educational *See* **Amicus Publishing**

Amicus High Interest *Imprint of* **Amicus Publishing**

Amicus Illustrated *Imprint of* **Amicus Publishing**

Amicus Pr., *(978-0-914861)* 4201 Underwood Rd., Baltimore, MD 21218 USA (SAN 289-0518) Tel 301-889-5056.

Amicus Publishing, *(978-1-60753; 978-1-68151; 978-1-64549)* P.O. Box 1329, Mankato, MN 56002 USA Tel 507-388-9357; Fax: 507-388-2746; *Imprints:* Amicus High Interest (High Interest); Amicus Illustrated (Illustrate); Amicus Readers (Readers)
E-mail: anna.erickson@amicuspublishing.us; rglaser@amicuspublishing.us; info@amicuspublishing.us
Web site: http://www.amicuspublishing.us
Dist(s): **Follett School Solutions**
MyiLibrary.

Amicus Readers *Imprint of* **Amicus Publishing**

AMIDEAST, *(978-0-913957)* 1730 M. St. NW, Suite 1100, Washington, DC 20036-4505 USA (SAN 286-7184) Tel 202-776-9600; Fax: 202-776-7000
E-mail: inquiries@amideast.org
Web site: http://www.amideast.org.

Amigo Pubns., Inc., *(978-0-9658533)* Orders Addr.: P.O. Box 666, Los Olivos, CA 93441-0666 USA Tel 805-686-4616; Fax: 805-688-3427; Toll Free: 888-502-6446; Edit Addr.: 3029 W. Hwy. 154, Los Olivos, CA 93441-0666 USA
E-mail: Amigo@Conquistador.com
Web site: http://www.conquistador.com; http://www.equibooks.com.

Aminov, Iskander, *(978-0-692-11432-2)* 7055 Forest Glen Dr. K, Rockford, IL 61114 USA Tel 217-721-8483
E-mail: iskander.aminov@gmail.com
Dist(s): **Ingram Content Group.**

Amira Rock Publishing, *(978-0-9821075; 978-0-9828007; 978-0-9833354)* 31 High St., Felton, PA 17322 USA (SAN 857-2844).

Amistad *Imprint of* **HarperCollins Pubs.**

AMMO Bks., LLC, *(978-0-9786076; 978-1-934429; 978-1-62326; 978-0-9976536)* 300 S Raymond Ave Suite 3, Pasadena, CA 91105 USA (SAN 851-1128) Tel 323-223-2666; Fax: 323-978-4200; 1 Ingram Blvd., La Vergne, TN 37086
E-mail: contact@ammobooks.com; paul@ammobooks.com
Web site: http://www.ammobooks.com
Dist(s): **Follett School Solutions**
Ingram Publisher Services.

Ammons Communications, Ltd., *(978-0-9651232; 978-0-9753023; 978-0-9815702; 978-0-9824099; 978-0-9827611; 978-0-9837382; 978-0-9853728; 978-0-9892169; 978-0-9895694; 978-0-9913803; 978-0-9908766; 978-0-9965199; 978-0-9971647; 978-0-9987359; 978-1-7338640; 978-1-7351316)* 1025 Milford Church Rd., Taylors,, SC 29687 USA (SAN 851-0881) Tel 828-226-0640; *Imprints:* Catch the Spirit of Appalachia (CSA)
E-mail: amyammonsgarza@gmail.com
Web site: http://www.spiritofappalachia.org; http://www.catchthespiritofappalachia.com; http://www.storiesofmountainfolk.com; http://www.csabooks.com.

AMN Publishing, *(978-0-9728129)* P.O. Box 323, Massapequa, NY 11758 USA
E-mail: AMNPub@aol.com
Web site: http://amnpub.tripod.com.

Amoeba Bks., *(978-0-9786473)* 5260 Rogers Rd., G-6, Hamburg, NY 14075 USA
E-mail: marketing@amoebabooks.com
Web site: http://www.amoebabooks.com
Dist(s): **Follett School Solutions.**

Ampdzine, *(978-0-9980332)* 435 N. Andrews Ave., Loft 404, Fort Lauderdale, FL 33301 USA Tel 954-525-2624; Fax: 954-525-2634
E-mail: info@ampdzine.com
Web site: ampdzine.com.

Amped Media, *(978-0-9742287)* 22 Shaw Pl., Walla Walla, WA 99362 USA.

Ampelon Publishing, LLC, *(978-0-9748825; 978-0-9786394; 978-0-9798104; 978-0-9817705; 978-0-9823286; 978-0-9840095; 978-0-9893419; 978-0-9982617; 978-0-9990527; 978-1-7323117; 978-1-7336206)* P.O. Box 140675, Boise, ID 83714 USA
E-mail: info@ampelonpublishing.com
Web site: http://www.ampelonpublishing.com
Dist(s): **Smashwords.**

Ampersand, Inc., *(978-0-9745932; 978-0-9761235; 978-0-9818126; 978-0-9905603; 978-0-9962525; 978-0-9974493; 978-0-9985222; 978-0-9994775; 978-1-7340708)* Orders Addr.: 515 Madison St., New Orleans, LA 70116 USA
Web site: http://www.ampersandworks.com
Dist(s): **Follett School Solutions.**

Ampersand Media LLC, *(978-1-950107)* 34 Buckingham Dr, Colchester, VT 05446 USA Tel 802-249-4983
E-mail: danielholtz802@gmail.com; katrina@ampersandmedia.rocks
Web site: http://stinkleberrypie.com; http://danielmholtz.com; http://ampersandmedia.rocks.

Amphorae Publishing Group,; *Imprints:* Goldminds Publishing (MYID_F_GOLDMIN)
E-mail: info@amphoraepublishing.com
Web site: www.amphoraepublishing.com
Dist(s): **Independent Pubs. Group**
Midpoint Trade Bks., Inc.

Amsco Music *Imprint of* **Music Sales Corp.**

AMSCO Schl. Pubns., Inc., *(978-0-87720; 978-1-56765)* 315 Hudson St., Suite 501, New York, NY 10013-1085 USA (SAN 201-1751) Toll Free: 866-902-6726 all orders
Web site: http://www.amscopub.com
Dist(s): **Bolchazy-Carducci Pubs.**

AMSI Venture, Incorporated *See* **Sleep Garden, Inc.**

Amulet Bks. *Imprint of* **Abrams, Inc.**

Amuzed Art, *(978-0-9996978)* 4389 S. Carson St., Carson City, NV 89701 USA Tel 775-232-1282; Fax: 775-232-1282
E-mail: amuzedart@yahoo.com
Web site: amuzedart.com.

Amy Misch, *(978-0-692-92249-1)* 21522A Marine Dr, Stanwood, WA 98292 USA Tel 937-308-1345; Fax: 937-308-1345
E-mail: amymisch27@gmail.com
Web site: www.amymisch.com.

Anachel Communications, *(978-0-615-62081-7)* 2008 Waterstone Dr., Franklin, TN 37069 USA Tel 615-370-8450
E-mail: carrie@anachel.com
Web site: www.carriegerlachcecil.com.

Anadem Publishing, Inc., *(978-0-9646891; 978-1-890018)* 3620 N. High St., Suite 201, Columbus, OH 43214 USA Tel 614-262-2539; Fax: 614-262-6630; Toll Free: 800-633-0055
E-mail: anadem@erinet.com
Web site: http://www.anadem.com.

Anaiah, Ruth, *(978-0-9769675)* P.O. Box 2142, Brandon, FL 33509-2142 USA
E-mail: dozministry2001@yahoo.com.

Anamchara Bks. *Imprint of* **Harding Hse. Publishing Sebice Inc.**

Anancy Bks. LLC, *(978-0-9753297; 978-1-941553)* Div. of Anancy Enterprise LLC, P.O. Box 28677, San Jose, CA 95159-8677 USA Tel 408-286-0726 Call Anytime; Fax: 408-947-0668 Fax Anytime
Web site: http://www.Anancybooks.com.

Anancybooks.com *See* **Anancy Bks. LLC**

Ananse Pr., *(978-0-9605670; 978-0-9749437)* Orders Addr.: P.O. Box 22565, Seattle, WA 98122-0565 USA (SAN 216-3292) Tel 206-325-8205; Fax: 206-328-4371; 1504 32nd Ave. S., Seattle, WA 98144-3918 (SAN 241-6123)
E-mail: gumbomedia@earthlink.net; gumbomedia@yahoo.com
Web site: http://home.usaa.net/~gumbomedia/ananse/index.htm.

AnaPlinaPub-Dallas *See* **Phebe Phillips, Inc.**

Anar Bks. LLC, *(978-0-9748285)* 10266 Virginia Swan Pl., Cupertino, CA 95014-2025 USA
E-mail: anoopbusiness@yahoo.com
Web site: http://www.anarbooks.com.

Anat Tour, *(978-0-9978432; 978-1-7341648)* 6340 Raydel Ct., San Diego, CA 92120 USA Tel 619-920-1213
Dist(s): **CreateSpace Independent Publishing Platform.**

Anaya Multimedia, S.A. (ESP) *(978-84-415; 978-84-7614) Dist. by* **Continental Bk.**

Anbeyond Pr., *(978-0-9744014)* 10420 NE 190th St., Bothell, WA 98011 USA (SAN 255-7886) Tel 425-483-9943; 22833 Bothell Everett Hwy. No. 102, PMB 1227, Bothell, WA 98021
E-mail: rm@anbeyond.com
Web site: http://www.anbeyond.com.

Ancestral Light Publishing, *(978-0-9718530)* 1969 S. Alafaya Trail, No. 322, Orlando, FL 32828 USA Tel 407-382-1707; Fax: 509-356-6971
E-mail: gigante@uaia.org.

Ancestral Tracks, *(978-0-9701266; 978-0-9754161)* P.O. Box 1064, Hillsboro, OR 97123-1064 USA
E-mail: books@ancestraltracks.com; cbeattie@ancestraltracks.com; ginger@ancestraltracks.com
Web site: http://www.ancestraltracks.com.

Anchor *Imprint of* **Knopf Doubleday Publishing Group**

Anchor Group, *(978-0-9852663; 978-0-9855385; 978-0-9882707; 978-0-615-71893-4; 978-0-9886334; 978-0-9888476; 978-0-9891753; 978-0-9897073; 978-0-615-91474-9; 978-0-9915174)* 225 Brookside Dr., FLUSHING, MI 48433 USA Tel 810-964-3767 (Tel/Fax)
E-mail: rourkewrites@gmail.com
Dist(s): **CreateSpace Independent Publishing Platform.**

Anchorage Foundation Pr., *(978-0-9795266)* 1518 Mohle Dr., Austin, TX 78703 USA
Dist(s): **Greenleaf Book Group.**

Ancient Days Pubs., *(978-0-9741405)* P.O. Box 356, Landisville, PA 17538 USA
E-mail: abrdl@ptd.net.

Ancient Faith Publishing, *(978-0-9622713; 978-1-888212; 978-0-9822770; 978-1-936270; 978-1-944967)* Orders Addr.: P.O. Box 748, Chesterton, IN 46304 USA Tel 831-336-5118; Fax: 831-336-8882; Toll Free: 800-967-7377; Edit Addr.: 1550 Birdie Way, Chesterton, IN 46304 USA (SAN 175-8624) Tel 831-336-5118; Fax: 831-336-8682; Toll Free: 800-967-7377
Web site: store.ancientfaith.com
Dist(s): **Midpoint Trade Bks., Inc.**
Spring Arbor Distributors, Inc.

Ancient Golf Publishing *See* **LuckySports**

Ancient Studios, *(978-0-9744216; 978-0-692-95854-4)* 13 Pine St., Winooski, VT 05404 USA Tel 8023389293
E-mail: janivescampbell@aol.com
Dist(s): **CreateSpace Independent Publishing Platform.**

Ancient Wisdom Publications *See* **Murine Pubns. LLC**

& P PUBLISHING & GAMES, A *See* **A & P Publishing and Games, LLC**

Andana Editorial (ESP) *Dist. by* **Lectorum Pubns.**

Andehem Publishing, LLC, *(978-1-946813)* 1643 Heatherwood Trail, Xenia, OH 45385 USA Tel 937-912-9063
E-mail: dawn30fl@hotmail.com.

Andersen Pr. (GBR) *(978-0-86264; 978-0-905478; 978-1-84270; 978-1-84939; 978-1-78344) Dist. by* **IPG Chicago.**

Andersen Pr. (GBR) *(978-0-86264; 978-0-905478; 978-1-84270; 978-1-84939; 978-1-78344) Dist. by* **Trafalgar.**

Andersen Pr. (GBR) *(978-0-86264; 978-0-905478; 978-1-84270; 978-1-84939; 978-1-78344) Dist. by* **Lerner Pub.**

Anderson, Christine F. Publishing & Media, *(978-0-692-21124-3; 978-0-692-22045-0; 978-0-692-23961-2; 978-0-692-24772-3; 978-0-692-26421-8; 978-0-692-26422-5; 978-0-692-26423-2; 978-0-692-26424-9; 978-0-692-27096-7; 978-0-692-27363-0; 978-0-692-27912-0; 978-0-692-27914-4; 978-0-692-28210-6; 978-0-692-28212-0; 978-0-692-28750-7; 978-0-692-29483-3; 978-0-692-29484-0; 978-0-692-29949-4; 978-0-692-30398-6; 978-0-692-30399-3; 978-0-692-30415-0; 978-0-692-30814-1; 978-0-692-31267-4; 978-0-692-32217-8; 978-0-692-32992-4; 978-0-692-33385-3;) P.O. Box 1492, Madison, VA 22727 USA Tel 5409484973*
Dist(s): **CreateSpace Independent Publishing Platform.**

Anderson, Frost, *(978-0-692-85913-1)* 733 Ash St., Twin Falls, ID 83301 USA Tel 208-360-6707
E-mail: jeffwcrawford5+LVP0003482@gmail.com; jeffwcrawford5+LVP0003482@gmail.com.

Anderson, George, *(978-0-9743682; 978-0-9819004)* 12301 Wilshire Blvd., Suite 418, Los Angeles, CA 90025 USA Tel 310-207-3591; Fax: 310-207-6234
E-mail: georgeandereson@aol.com
Web site: http://www.andersonservices.com.

Anderson House Foundation *See* **Windy Press International Publishing Hse., LLC**

Anderson Law Group, *(978-0-9728128; 978-0-9797860)* 3225 Mcleod Dr., Las Vegas, NV 89121 USA; 3225 Mcleod Dr., Las Vegas, NV 89121
E-mail: tmathis@alglaw.com
Web site: http://www.andersonadvisors.com.

Anderson, Mariya, *(978-0-692-07564-7; 978-0-692-08373-4; 978-0-578-66904-5; 978-0-578-67012-6; 978-0-578-70551-4; 978-0-578-75159-7; 978-0-578-76132-9)* 2 Camino Por Los Arboles, ATHERTON, CA 94027 USA Tel 650-276-5368
E-mail: mariyanikiforova@gmail.com
Dist(s): **Ingram Content Group.**

Anderson, Marshall, *(978-0-578-43586-2)* 23916 S Stoney Path Dr, Sun Lakes, AZ 85248 USA Tel 602-622-9696
E-mail: marshalla17@hotmail.com.

Anderson Publishing, *(978-0-9718249)* Orders Addr.: P.O. Box 5544, Douglasville, GA 30154 USA Toll Free: 866-942-0790 (phone/fax); Edit Addr.: 5178 Holly Springs Dr., Douglasville, GA 30135 USA Do not confuse with companies with the same or similar name in Navato, CA, Saginawi, MI, Burley, ID, Cincinnati, MO, Anacortes, WA, Indio, CA
E-mail: canderson@andersonpub.com
Web site: http://www.andersonpub.com
Dist(s): **ACW Pr.**

Anderson, Sara *See* **Sara Anderson Children's Bks.**

ANDInternational, *(978-0-9762291)* 74 Woodcleft Ave., Freeport, NY 11520 USA Tel 516-546-2025; Fax: 516-546-6010; Toll Free: 800-229-2634
E-mail: orders@andihq.com; andihq@aol.com
Web site: http://www.andihq.com.

Andre Deutsch (GBR) *(978-0-233; 978-1-78097) Dist. by* **Trans-Atl Phila.**

Andre Deutsch (GBR) *(978-0-233; 978-1-78097) Dist. by* **Trafalgar.**

Andres & Blanton, *(978-0-9830318; 978-0-9966721)* 42 Corey Ln., Niantic, CT 06357 USA Tel 860-941-9258
E-mail: sscheyder@sbcglobal.net.

†Andrews McMeel Publishing, *(978-0-8362; 978-0-939251; 978-1-57939; 978-0-7407; 978-1-4494; 978-1-5248)* Orders Addr.: c/o Simon & Schuster, Inc., 100 Front St., Riverside, NJ 08075 USA Toll Free Fax: 800-943-9831; Toll Free: 800-943-9839 (Customer Service); 800-897-7650 (Credit Dept.); Edit Addr.: 1130 Walnut St., Kansas City, MO 64106-2109 USA (SAN 202-540X) Toll Free: 800-851-8923
Web site: http://www.AndrewsMcMeel.com
Dist(s): **Children's Plus, Inc.**
Follett School Solutions
Simon & Schuster, Inc.; *CIP.*

Andromeda Pr. *Imprint of* **Oyebanji, Adam**

Andromeda Pr., Inc., *(978-0-9820649; 978-1-938503)* 2600 Birdie Thompson Dr., Pocatello, ID 83201 USA Tel 208-406-1220
E-mail: Andromedapress@gmail.com; strialbe@gmail.com.

Andrus, Ashley, *(978-0-9772000)* 104 Kempton Dr., Lafayette, LA 70508-6547 USA
E-mail: ala@andrus.com.

Andy Sanders, *(978-0-9825775; 978-0-9827980; 978-1-936578; 978-1-942056)* 5701 East Cir. Dr. No. 338, Cicero, NY 13039 USA
E-mail: cathysanders.design@gmail.com
Dist(s): **Whitaker Hse.**

ANEKO Pr. *Imprint of* **Life Sentence Publishing, Inc.**

Anela Publishing *See* **Abidenme Bks.**

Anemone Publishing, *(978-0-9759264)* 16 Rope Ferry Rd, Hanover, NH 03755 USA Tel 603-643-0922
E-mail: carolynne.krusi.99@alum.dartmouth.org.

AnewPr., Inc. *Imprint of* **AnewPr., Inc.**

AnewPress *See* **AnewPr., Inc.**

AnewPr., Inc., *(978-1-7324371; 978-1-970109)* P.O. Box 5958, Philadelphia, PA 19137 USA; *Imprints:* AnewPress, Inc. (MYID_K_ANEWPRE)
E-mail: operations@2nimble.com
Web site: www.anewpress.com.

AnEx Pubns., *(978-0-9711774)* 9 Bartlet St., Suite 131, Andover, MA 01810 USA Toll Free: 866-616-4400
E-mail: rich_hewett@yahoo.com
Web site: http://www.anexx.com.

Angel Applications, *(978-0-615-18904-8)* 1624 Yorktown Dr., Charlottesville, VA 22901 USA Tel 434-293-2819 (phone/fax)
E-mail: kgarstang@cstone.net
Dist(s): **R J Communications, LLC.**

Angel Avenue Press *See* **Candlelight Bay Publishing**

Angel Eyes Publishing, *(978-0-9755346)* 1914 Hollywood Rd., Atlanta, GA 30318 USA (SAN 256-0542) Tel 404-566-0598
E-mail: dawnettelounds@yahoo.com
Web site: http://www.angeleyespublishing.com.

Angel Fingers Foundation *See* **Mullins Pubns. & Apparel, LLC**

Angel Heart Children's Pr., *(978-0-9712124)* Orders Addr.: P.O. Box 63, East Enterprise, IN 47019 USA Tel 812-594-2438; Fax: 812-594-2438
E-mail: dianemccarty@hotmail.com
Web site: http://www.geocities.com/hs_mom2000.

Angel Insights Press *See* **Stop N Go Fitness**

Angel Island Assoc., *(978-0-9667352)* P.O. Box 866, Tiburon, CA 94920 USA Tel 415-435-3522; Fax: 415-435-2950
E-mail: valaia@att.net
Web site: http://www.angelisland.org
Dist(s): **Follett School Solutions.**

Angel Island Productions, *(978-0-578-19637-4; 978-0-578-19799-9)* 28 Great Hill Dr, Bethel, CT 06801 USA.

Angel Mind, *(978-0-9729866)* 5776-D Lindero Canyon Dr. #123, Westlake Village, CA 91362 USA Tel 818-424-2619; Fax: 818-780-8880
E-mail: bill@angelmind.net
Web site: http://www.angelmind.net.

Angel Pr., *(978-0-9716590)* Div. of The Angelic Light Research Institute, Orders Addr.: P.O. Box 1375, Sedona, AZ 86339 USA Tel 928-451-1222; 928-853-5753 Do not confuse with companies with the same or similar names in Tiburon, CA, Pell City, AL, Concord, NC, Rancho Santa Margarita, CA, St. Thomas, VI, TraversAFB, CA. Monterey, CA
E-mail: angelpress@angelsangelsangels.org; angels@angelsangelsangels.org
Web site: http://www.angelsangelsangels.org; http://www.angelsangelsangels.com; http://www.angelsangelsangels.net; http://www.angellightfeather.com.

Angela Ritacca-Lovenguth, *(978-0-692-97659-3)* 4660 NE Belknap Ct. Suite No. 101 G, HILLSBORO, OR 97124 USA Tel 503-539-7459
E-mail: ImpressionsbyACRL@gmail.com
Dist(s): **Ingram Content Group.**

AngelaCstyles Holdngs LLC, *(978-0-9974495)* 13055 Moorpark, Studio City, CA 91604 USA Tel 312-927-5786
E-mail: angelacstyles@me.com
Web site: www.prettycurlsclub.com.

Angela's Bookshelf *See* **A B Publishing**

AngelBooks, *(978-0-9771749)* 4340 Janesville, Bel Aire, KS 67220 USA
Web site: http://www.thesecretofpink.com.

Angel's BBQ, *(978-0-578-16633-9)* 21 W. Oglethorpe Ln, Savannah, GA 314019 USA.

Angel's Boy Enterprises, *(978-0-9755352)* 8306 Wilshire Blvd., No. 3004, Beverly Hills, CA 90211 USA
Web site: http://www.angelboi.com.

Angel's Diary, *(978-0-615-31217-0; 978-0-9860041)* 6321 Thunder Blitz Ave., Las Vegas, NV 89131 USA.

Angels Landing, *(978-0-9899141)* 347 Butterfly Ln., Hermitage, PA 16148 USA Tel 724-977-0847
E-mail: trpags@roadrunner.com
Web site: https://sites.google.com/site/littlelambs20/.

Angels of Agape, *(978-0-615-25466-1)* 211 Shawnee Valley, East Stroudsburg, PA 18302 USA Tel 973-460-3882
E-mail: angelsofagape@yahoo.com
Web site: http://www.angelsofagape.com.

Angelus Pr., *(978-0-935952; 978-0-9639032; 978-1-892331; 978-1-930959; 978-1-937843; 978-1-949124)* Div. of Society of Saint Pius X, 2915 Forest Ave., Kansas City, MO 64109 USA (SAN 222-769X) Tel 816-753-3150; Fax: 816-753-3557; Toll Free Fax: 888-855-9022; Toll Free: 800-966-7337 (orders)
E-mail: info@angeluspress.org; stownshend@angeluspress.org; bklaske@angeluspress.org; vtan@angeluspress.org
Web site: http://www.angeluspress.org.

Angelworks Pr., *(978-0-578-00741-0; 978-0-578-12854-2)* 901 Brutscher St., No.D144, Newberg, OR 97132 USA Tel 503-830-0741; 17884 Kelok Rd., Lake Oswego, OR 97034
E-mail: susan@susanmarek.com
Dist(s): **Lulu Pr., Inc.**

ANGI PERRETTI *Imprint of* **MCrc Industries, LLC**

Angie Blue Bks., LLC, *(978-0-9677547)* 376 County Road 2740., Mico, TX 78056-5353 USA
E-mail: info@AngieBlue.com
Web site: http://www.AngieBlue.com.

Angiesink, *(978-0-615-17415-0)* P.O. Box 323, Tuskegee Institute, AL 36087 USA
E-mail: angiesink@bellsouth.net
Dist(s): **Lulu Pr., Inc.**

Angle Press *See* **Angle Valley Pr.**

Angle Valley Pr., *(978-0-9711950)* P.O. Box 4098, Winchester, VA 22604 USA (SAN 255-8629) Tel 540-539-1260
E-mail: anglevalleypress@yahoo.com
Web site: http://www.AngleValleyPress.com
Dist(s): **Ingram Content Group.**

Anglican Bk. Ctr. (CAN) *(978-0-919030; 978-0-919891; 978-0-921846; 978-1-55126) Dist. by* **Forward Movement.**

Anglo-American Book Company, Limited (UK) *See* **Crown Hse. Publishing LLC**

Angry Bicycle *Imprint of* **Walter, Wendy D.**

Animal Band Productions, Inc., The, *(978-0-9752619)* P.O. Box 392, Mount Juliet, TN 37121 USA Tel 615-754-8701
E-mail: info@theanimalband.com
Web site: http://www.theanimalband.com.

Animal Crackers Publishing, LLC, *(978-0-9798343)* 1143 Auraria Pkwy. No. A-201, Denver, CO 80204 USA (SAN 854-5170)
Web site: www.animalcrackerspublishing.com.

Animal Hero Kids, *(978-0-615-99522-9; 978-0-578-67171-0; 978-1-7357399)* 13782 151 Ln. N., Jupiter, FL 33478 USA Tel 561-236-8843
E-mail: Susanh@animalherokids.org
Web site: AnimalHeroKids.org.

Animal Teachers Enterprises, *(978-0-9788858)* 5902G Queenston St., Springfield, VA 22152 USA
E-mail: snork5902g@yahoo.com
Web site: http://funkman.org/animal/services/catalog.html.

Animal Tracks Pr., *(978-0-9760342)* P.O. Box 432, Cotah, CA 94931 USA (SAN 256-1808) Tel 707-776-8019; Fax: 707-795-2919
Web site: http://www.animaltrackspress.com.

Animalations, *(978-0-9776628; 978-1-933818)* 4186 Melodia Songo Ct., Las Vegas, NV 89135 USA (SAN 257-9111) Fax: 702-804-4220; Toll Free Fax: 866-670-8337; Toll Free: 866-670-8337
E-mail: info@animalations.com
Web site: http://Animalations.com.

AnimeVillage.com *See* **Bandai Entertainment, Inc.**

Animus Ferrum Publishing, *(978-0-692-49790-6; 978-0-9974906; 978-0-578-67684-5)* 1525 BENNINGTON DR, MISHAWAKA, IN 46544 USA Tel 574-261-8317
E-mail: tracykorn@comcast.net.

Anita, *(978-0-615-52716-1)* 6639 E. Broadway 165, Tucson, AZ 85710 USA Tel 520-370-8998
E-mail: its4u@aneatlook.com
Web site: www.yourstoryyourtalent.com.

Anjana Publishing (HKG) *(978-988-12394; 978-988-12395; 978-988-15028) Dist. by* **BTPS.**

ANKA, *(978-0-615-73378-4)* 3165 Nostrand Ave., 6B, Brooklyn, NY 11229 USA Tel 917-294-2939
E-mail: anna.kaplun@gmail.com.

Ankh Bks. (CAN) *(978-0-9738036) Dist. by* **Mtn Bk Co.**

Ann Arbor District Library, *(978-0-9749589; 978-1-947989)* 343 S. 5th Ave., Ann Arbor, MI 48104 USA Tel 734-327-4200; Fax: 734-327-8324; *Imprints:* Fifth Avenue Press (FifthAvePr)
E-mail: PURCHASING@AADL.ORG; grimest@aadl.org
Web site: http://www.aadl.org.

Ann Arbor Editions LLC, *(978-1-58726)* 2500 S. State St., Ann Arbor, MI 48104 USA Tel 734-913-1302; Fax: 734-913-1249; 1094 Flex Dr., Jackson, TN 38301; *Imprints:* Mitten Press (Mitten Pr)
E-mail: ljohnson@aaeditions.com
Web site: http://www.annarbormediagroup.com; http://www.mittenpress.com; http://www.aaeditions.com
Dist(s): **Follett School Solutions**
Independent Pubs. Group
Two Rivers Distribution.

Ann Arbor Media Group, LLC *See* **Ann Arbor Editions LLC**

Anna Stilianessis, *(978-0-692-18047-1)* 54 Chandler Dr., Wayne, NJ 07470 USA Tel 973-879-9320
E-mail: astilly1208@gmail.com
Web site: www.themomof4.com.

Annadale Comics, *(978-0-9972562; 978-1-945582)* 72 Lorrain Avenu, Staten Island, NY 10312 USA Tel 718-967-1470
E-mail: johnrap316@gmail.com.

Annade Publishing, *(978-0-9761740)* 18964 Lauder, Detroit, MI 48235 USA
Web site: www.annade.com.

Annapolis Publishing Co., *(978-1-884878)* Orders Addr.: 3430 2nd St. # 400, Brooklyn, MD 21225-1603 USA (SAN 631-4414) Toll Free: 800-536-1414
E-mail: Katherine@AnnapolisPublishing.com
Web site: http://www.AnnapolisPublishing.com; http://www.mewarren.com; http://www.AnnapolisBooks.com.

AnnArt Pr., *(978-0-9769719)* R R 1, Box 621, Richards, MO 64778 USA.

Anna's Friends, *(978-0-692-63196-6; 978-0-692-63197-3; 978-0-692-63198-0; 978-0-692-65763-8; 978-0-692-65851-2; 978-0-692-69324-7; 978-0-692-71370-9; 978-0-692-74368-3; 978-1-7325002)* 243 E. Savoy St., Lecanto, FL 34461 USA Tel 615-815-7068
E-mail: yvonne@annasfriends.com
Web site: www.annasfriends.com
Dist(s): **CreateSpace Independent Publishing Platform.**

Annedawn Publishing, *(978-0-9632793; 978-0-9755153; 978-1-7342967)*
E-mail: annedawn@aol.com.

Anness Publishing (GBR) *(978-1-85967; 978-1-86147; 978-1-901289; 978-1-901688; 978-1-84038; 978-0-7548; 978-1-84090; 978-1-903141; 978-1-84215; 978-1-84309; 978-1-84322; 978-1-84476; 978-1-84477; 978-1-84681; 978-0-85723; 978-1-78019) Dist. by* **Natl Bk Netwk.**

Anness Publishing, Inc., *(978-1-886890)* 39 Sandy Ln., Eatontown, NJ 07724-2445 USA (SAN 299-0563) Toll Free: 800-354-9657
E-mail: AFioravanti@anness.com
Dist(s): **National Bk. Network.**

Annick Pr., Ltd. (CAN) *(978-0-920236; 978-0-920303; 978-1-55037; 978-1-55451) Dist. by* **PerseuPGW.**

Annick Pr., Ltd. (CAN) *(978-0-920236; 978-0-920303; 978-1-55037; 978-1-55451) Dist. by* **Children Plus.**

Annie Mouse Bks., *(978-0-9793379; 978-0-9914094)* P.O. Box 142, Harrisville, PA 16038 USA (SAN 853-1676)
E-mail: anniemousebooks@gmail.com; anniemousebooks@yahoo.com
Web site: http://www.anniemousebooks.com.

annie tillery mysteries, *(978-0-692-85719-9; 978-0-9989714)* 283 Grand Blvd., Massapequa Park, NY 11762 USA Tel 516-798-0341; Fax: 516-798-0341
E-mail: lmf217@hotmail.com
Web site: lindamariafrank.com.

Annie's *Imprint of* **Annie's Publishing, LLC**

Annie's Media, LLC *See* **Annie's Publishing, LLC**

Annie's Publishing, LLC, *(978-0-88195; 978-0-9638031; 978-0-9655269; 978-1-57367; 978-1-882138; 978-1-931171; 978-1-59012; 978-1-59217; 978-0-9748217; 978-1-59635; 978-1-933802; 978-1-64025)* 111 Corporate Dr., Big Sandy, TX 75755 USA Fax: 260-589-8093 (Clothilde); *Imprints:* Annie's (Annies)
Web site: http://www.drgnetwork.com
Dist(s): **Follett School Solutions**
Independent Pubs. Group
MyiLibrary
ebrary, Inc.

Annika Pubns., *(978-0-9670516)* Orders Addr.: P.O. Box 264, Fergus Falls, MN 56537 USA Tel 218-736-7735; Edit Addr.: R.R. 4, Box 50, Fergus Falls, MN 56537 USA.

Anno Domini, *(978-0-9792145; 978-1-939689)* 584 Ironwood Terr., Woodburn, OR 97071 USA (SAN 852-7946) Tel 971-226-4356.

†Annual Reviews, Inc., *(978-0-8243)* 4139 El Camino Way, P.O. Box 10139, Palo Alto, CA 94303-0139 USA (SAN 201-1816) Tel 650-493-4400; Fax: 650-424-0910; Toll Free: 800-523-8635 (including California, Alaska, Hawaii & Canada)
E-mail: service@annualreviews.org
Web site: http://www.AnnualReviews.org; *CIP.*

Anointed Pubs., *(978-0-9763841)* Orders Addr.: 1227-40 Seaton Rd., Durham, NC 27713 USA Tel 919-806-0651; Edit Addr.: 1227-40 seaton Rd., Durham, NC 27713 USA
E-mail: jainjie@msn.com
Web site: http://www.joanjai.com
Dist(s): **Brown Enterprises, Inc.**

Anointed Publishing Co., *(978-0-615-19205-5; 978-0-615-25069-4; 978-0-615-36490-2; 978-0-615-37865-7; 978-0-615-78457-1)* 8123 Winter Blue Ct., Springfield, VA 22153 USA Tel 321-947-0706
Web site: http://www.cheniselytrelle.com.

Anointed Word Pubns., *(978-0-9744024)* 611 N. Pennsylvania Ave., Lansing, MI 48912 USA Tel 517-372-3407.

Anomaly Publishing, *(978-0-9800123)* 3700 Ceres Dr., Salt Lake City, UT 84124 USA Tel 801-278-3245
Dist(s): **Smashwords.**

Anorak Pr. *Imprint of* **Gibbs Smith, Publisher**

Another Ep Publishing, *(978-0-9740685; 978-0-615-11795-9)* Div. of Episodes By Wroe, P.O. Box 300, Walnut, CA 91788-0300 USA (SAN 253-2530) Tel 909-448-5356.

Another Language Pr., *(978-0-922852)* 7709 Hamilton Ave., Cincinnati, OH 45231-3103 USA Tel 513-521-5590; Fax: 513-521-5592; Toll Free: 800-733-2067
E-mail: aimsbooks@juno.com
Dist(s): **AIMS International Bks., Inc.**

Another Sommer-Time Story *Imprint of* **Advance Publishing, Inc.**

Another World Pr., *(978-0-615-98065-2)* 326 W. Liberty St., Reno, NV 89501 USA Tel 775-324-3333
E-mail: rbl@robertbrucelindsay.com.

AnotherThinkComing Pr., *(978-0-692-82443-6; 978-0-9987767)* 19830 WALLFLOWER LN, APPLE VALLEY, CA 92308-3643 USA Tel 760-553-1644
E-mail: d_thompson@hotmail.com; d_thompson@hotmail.com; d_thompson@hotmail.com
Dist(s): **CreateSpace Independent Publishing Platform.**

Answers In Genesis, *(978-1-893345; 978-1-60092; 978-1-62691; 978-1-9844)* Orders Addr.: P.O. Box 510, Hebron, KY 41048 USA Fax: 859-727-2299; Toll Free: 800-778-3390
E-mail: dzordel@answersingenesis.org
Web site: http://www.answersingenesis.org
Dist(s): **Master Bks.**
New Leaf Publishing Group
Send The Light Distribution LLC.

Answers in Genesis Ministries *See* **Answers In Genesis**

ANT Bank$ *See* **VIP INK Publishing Group, Inc.**

Antarctic Pr., Inc., *(978-0-930655; 978-0-9663588; 978-0-9728978; 978-1-932453; 978-0-9768043; 978-0-9776424; 978-0-9787725; 978-0-9792723; 978-0-9797719; 978-0-9801255; 978-0-9816647; 978-0-9822253; 978-0-9823742; 978-0-9841107; 978-0-9843375; 978-0-9844879; 978-0-9831823; 978-0-9837934; 978-0-9850925; 978-1-939364) Div. of Ben Dunn Corp., 7272 Wurzbach Rd., Suite 204, San Antonio, TX 78240 USA Tel 210-614-0396; Fax: 210-614-5029 Do not confuse with Antarctic Pr., Bellevue, WA*
E-mail: apcog1@gmail.com
Web site: http://www.antarctic-press.com
Dist(s): **Diamond Comic Distributors, Inc.**
Diamond Bk. Distributors
MyiLibrary.

Anthem Pr. (GBR) *(978-1-898855; 978-1-84331; 978-0-85728; 978-1-78308) Dist. by* **Bks Intl VA.**

Anthem Pr. (GBR) *(978-1-898855; 978-1-84331; 978-0-85728; 978-1-78308) Dist. by* **Bolchazy-Carducci.**

AntHill Publishing, *(978-0-9718544)* 5315 Clarendon Rd., Brooklyn, NY 11203 USA Tel 718-629-0294 (phone/fax) Do not confuse with Ant Hill Publishing in Gorman, TX
E-mail: anthillpublishing@hotmail.com.

Anthology of Poetry, Inc., *(978-1-883931)* Orders Addr.: P.O. Box 698, Asheboro, NC 27204-0698 USA Tel 336-626-7762; Fax: 336-626-2622; Edit Addr.: 307 E. Salisbury St., Asheboro, NC 27203 USA
E-mail: poetry@anthologyofpoetry.com
Web site: http://www.anthologyofpoetry.com.

Anthro Co., The, *(978-1-878464)* 200 Carroll St., No. 21, Susanville, CA 96130 USA Tel 530-251-5712
E-mail: devajan@earthlink.net
Web site: http://www.ishifacts.com
Dist(s): **Social Studies Schl. Service.**

Anthroposophic Press, Incorporated *See* **SteinerBooks, Inc.**

Anticipation Pr., *(978-0-9754046)* 3563 Sueldo St. Ste. Q, Sn Luis Obisp, CA 93401-7332 USA Do not confuse with Anticipation Press in Cheyenne, WY
E-mail: doingbigbiz@aol.com
Web site: http://www.anticipationpress.com; http://www.zacacreekdevelopment.com.

Antioch Publishing Co., *(978-0-7824; 978-0-89954; 978-1-4017)* Div. of Trends International, 5188 W. 74th St., Indianapolis, IN 46268 USA Tel 317-388-4060; 317-388-1414; Toll Free: 800-315-2110 Do not confuse with Antioch Publishing Co., Torrance, CA
Web site: http://www.antioch.com.

Antipodes Bks. & Beyond, 9707 Fairway Ave., Silver Spring, MD 20901-3001 USA Tel 301-602-9519; Fax: 301-565-0160
E-mail: Antipode@antipodesbooks.com
Web site: http://www.antipodesbooks.com.

Antique Collectors' Club, *(978-0-902028; 978-0-907462; 978-1-85149)* Orders Addr.: Eastworks, 116 Pleasant St., Easthampton, MA 01027 USA (SAN 630-7787) Tel 413-529-0861; Fax: 413-529-0862; Toll Free: 800-252-5231 (orders)
E-mail: info@antiquecc.com; sales@antiquecc.com
Web site: http://www.antiquecollectorsclub.com
Dist(s): **National Bk. Network.**

Antiques, Incorporated *See* **Kovels Antiques, Inc.**

Antiquity Publishing, *(978-0-9793284)* 4127 McLaughlin Ave., No. 15, Los Angeles, CA 90066-5445 USA Tel 310-390-9093 (phone/fax)
E-mail: Randwulf@humnet.ucla.edu.

Antlers & Fins LLC, *(978-0-9800643)* P.O. Box 82, Henefer, UT 84033 USA
E-mail: info@billygoeshunting.com
Web site: http://www.BillyGoesHunting.com.

Anton Berkshire Publishing, *(978-0-9746330)* Orders Addr.: P.O. Box 372, Markle, IN 46770 USA (SAN 255-6618); Edit Addr.: 9374 N. Marzane Rd., Markle, IN 46770 USA
Web site: http://www.antonberkshirepublishing.com.

Antoniades, Basil, *(978-0-615-24661-1)* 9 Belden Ct., Timonium, MD 21093 USA Tel 410-560-9911
E-mail: basilantoniades@earthlink.net
Web site: http://www.havingfunwithgreekmythology.com
Dist(s): **Lulu Pr., Inc.**

Antonucci, Jason, *(978-0-692-11302-8; 978-0-578-66897-0)* 126 JOSIAH NORTON RD, CAPE NEDDICK, ME 03902 USA Tel 603-988-4935
E-mail: jasonm.antonucci@gmail.com
Dist(s): **Ingram Content Group.**

Antrim Hse., *(978-0-9662783; 978-0-9762091; 978-0-9770633; 978-0-9792226; 978-0-9798451; 978-0-9817883; 978-0-9823970; 978-0-9843418; 978-1-936482; 978-1-943826)* 21 Goodrich Rd., Simsbury, CT 06070-1804 USA; P.O. Box 111, Tariffville, CT 06081
Web site: http://www.antrimhousebooks.com
Dist(s): **BookBaby**
Distributors, The.

Antroll Publishing Co., *(978-1-877656)* 2616 Elmont St., Wheaton, MD 20902 USA Tel 301-942-0492.

Anvil Bks., Ltd. (IRL) *(978-0-900068; 978-0-947962; 978-1-901737) Dist. by* **Dufour.**

Anyone Can Write bks., *(978-0-9771470)* 2890 N. Hills Dr., NE, Atlanta, GA 30305-3210 USA Tel 404-261-1616
Web site: http://www.anyonecanwrite.com.

Anystar Publishing *See* **Nolia Crown Prods.**

Anythings Possible, Inc., *(978-1-892186)* Orders Addr.: 1863 N. Farwell Ave., Milwaukee, WI 53202 USA Fax: 414-226-4901; Toll Free: 800-543-7153
E-mail: info@special-kids.com
Web site: http://www.special-kids.com.

Anzalone, Frank, *(978-0-9770788)* P.O. Box 110422, Campbell, CA 95011 USA Tel 408-247-7572; Fax: 408-984-1519
E-mail: info@mckyfoto.com
Web site: http://www.mckyfoto.com.

AoPS Inc., *(978-0-9773045; 978-1-934124)* Orders Addr.: 10865 Rancho Bernardo Rd Ste 100, San Diego, CA 92127 USA Tel 858-675-4555; Fax: 855-430-9531; Toll Free Fax: 855-430-9531
E-mail: orders@artofproblemsolving.com
Web site: http://www.artofproblemsolving.com; http://www.beastacademy.com.

Aoyama Publishing *See* **Marble Hse. Editions**

AP Bks., *(978-0-9841927)* P.O. Box 799, Pennington, NJ 08534 USA Fax: 609-730-1286
Dist(s): **Cardinal Pubs. Group.**

AP Publishing, *(978-0-9722906)* Orders Addr.: P.O. Box 160, Merrimac, WI 53561 USA
Web site: http://www.wildlife-trails.com
Dist(s): **Ingram Content Group.**

Apage4You Bk. Publishing, *(978-0-9723616)* 2025 Balla Way, Suite 200, Grand Prairie, TX 75051-3907 USA Tel 972-264-2892; Fax: 214-722-1254; Toll Free: 800-519-7323
E-mail: apage4you@starband.net
Web site: http://www.publishfast.com; http://www.apage4youpublishing.com.

APCWriter & Pub. *Imprint of* **Cox, Audrey Phillips**

Ape Entertainment, *(978-0-9741398; 978-0-9791050; 978-0-9801314; 978-1-934944; 978-1-936340; 978-1-937676; 978-1-62782)* P.O. Box 7100, San Diego, CA 92167 USA
Dist(s): **Diamond Comic Distributors, Inc.**
Diamond Bk. Distributors.

Ape Pen Publishing *See* **Ballard, Donald W.**

Aperturas Foundation, *(978-0-9745220)* P.O. Box 25163, Chicago, IL 60625 USA Tel 773-478-7973
E-mail: aperturas@yahoo.com
Web site: http://www.aperturas.info.

Aperture *Imprint of* **Aperture Foundation, Inc.**

†Aperture Foundation, Inc., *(978-0-89381; 978-0-912334; 978-0-900406; 978-1-931788; 978-1-59711; 978-1-68395)* 547 West 27th St., 4th Flr., New York, NY 10001 USA (SAN 201-1832); *Imprints:* Aperture (Aper)
E-mail: alang@aperture.org
Dist(s): **D.A.P./Distributed Art Pubs.**
Farrar, Straus & Giroux
Ingram Publisher Services; *CIP.*

Aperture Pr., LLC, *(978-0-615-40395-3; 978-0-615-41313-6; 978-0-615-41888-9;*

978-0-9833310; 978-0-9836878; 978-0-9850026; 978-0-9889351; 978-0-9910962; 978-0-9909302; 978-0-9973020; 978-0-9995158; 978-1-7329329) PO Box 6485, Reading, PA 19610 USA
E-mail: steve@aperturepress.net
Web site: http://www.aperturepress.net
Dist(s): **Lulu Pr., Inc.**

Apex Performance Solutions, LLC, (*978-0-9824519*) 467 Springdale Rd., Westfield, MA 01085 USA Tel 413-562-2299; Fax: 413-562-2289; 113 Ne Carleston Oaks Dr., Port St.Lucie, FL 34983
E-mail: jwojcik@apexperformancesolutions.com
Web site: http://www.apexperformancesolutions.com
Dist(s): **Follett School Solutions**
Partners Pubs. Group, Inc.

APG Sales & Distribution Services, Div. of Warehousing and Fulfillment Specialists, LLC (WFS, LLC), 7344 Cockrill Bend Blvd., Nashville, TN 37209-1043 USA (SAN 630-818X) Toll Free: 800-327-5113
E-mail: sswift@agpbooks.com
Web site: http://www.apgbooks.com.

APG Sales & Fulfillment *See* **APG Sales & Distribution Services**

APILA Ediciones (ESP) (*978-84-937102; 978-84-937896; 978-84-939736*) *Dist. by* **Lectorum Pubns.**

Aplastic Anemia + MDS International Foundation, (*978-0-9755572*) Orders Addr.: P.O. Box 613, Annapolis, MD 21404-0613 USA Tel 410-867-0242; Fax: 410-867-0240; Toll Free: 800-747-2820; Edit Addr.: P.O. Box 310, Churchton, MD 20733-0310 USA
E-mail: help@aamds.org
Web site: http://www.aamds.org.

Apocalyptic Tangerine Pr., (*978-0-9821138; 978-0-9897496*) Orders Addr.: 1969 Laurel Ave., No. 5, Saint Paul, MN 55104-5820 USA Tel 304-942-4912.

Apodixis Press *See* **Read Well Publishing Inc.**

Apollo Computer Systems, Inc., (*978-0-9610582*) 616 14th St., Arcata, CA 95521 USA (SAN 264-651X) Tel 707-822-0318.

Apollo Pubs., (*978-0-9718532; 978-0-9721368; 978-1-932832; 978-1-946599*) P.O. Box 9, Santa Cruz, CA 95063 USA Tel 831 479 9626 (phone/fax); 800-881-0181
E-mail: michael@apollopub.com
Web site: http://www.apollopub.com
Dist(s): **TNT Media Group, Inc.**

Apollo Science Pubs., LLC, (*978-0-9814551*) P.O. Box 26671, San Diego, CA 92196 USA Tel 858-635-6558
E-mail: zhibo.zhang@ieee.org
Web site: http://www.aspublishers.com.

Apologetics Pr., Inc., (*978-0-932859; 978-1-60063*) 230 Landmark Dr., Montgomery, AL 36117-2752 USA (SAN 688-9190) Tel 334-272-8558; Fax: 334-270-2002; Toll Free: 800-234-8558 (orders only)
E-mail: mail@apologeticspress.org
Web site: http://www.apologeticspress.org
Dist(s): **Send The Light Distribution LLC.**

Apologia Educational Ministries, Inc., (*978-0-9656294; 978-1-932012; 978-1-935495; 978-1-940110; 978-1-946506*) 1106 Meridian Plaza Ste 220/340, Anderson, IN 46016 USA Tel 765-608-3280; Fax: 765-608-3290; Toll Free: 888-524-4724
E-mail: patti@apologia.com
Web site: http://www.apologia.com.

Apologue Entertainment, LLC, (*978-0-9819825*) Orders Addr.: 1075 Meghan Ave., Algonquin, IL 60102 USA
E-mail: gary.mack@apologueentertainment.com
Web site: http://www.apologueentertainment.com.

Appalachian Hse., (*978-0-9662800*) Orders Addr.: P.O. Box 627, Boiling Springs, PA 17007 USA (SAN 299-5328) Tel 717-609-6234
E-mail: apphouse@pa.net.

Appalachian Log Publishing Co., The, (*978-1-885935*) Orders Addr.: P.O. Box 20297, Charleston, WV 25362-1297 USA Tel 304-342-5789; Edit Addr.: 878 Anaconda Ave., Charleston, WV 25302 USA
E-mail: gregory@newwave.net.

†Appalachian Mountain Club Bks., (*978-0-910146; 978-1-878239; 978-1-929173; 978-1-934028; 978-1-62842*) 5 Joy St., Boston, MA 02108 USA (SAN 203-4808) Tel 617-523-0655; Fax: 617-523-0722; Toll Free: 800-262-4455
E-mail: kbreunig@outdoors.org; alakri@outdoors.org
Web site: http://www.outdoors.org
Dist(s): **Globe Pequot Pr., The**
National Bk. Network; *CIP.*

Applause Theatre & Cinema *Imprint of* **Leonard, Hal Corp.**

Apple Corps Pubs., (*978-0-9619484; 978-1-934397*) 1600 Sunset Ln., Oklahoma City, OK 73127 USA (SAN 245-0461) Fax: 888-375-7017; Toll Free: 800-335-9208
E-mail: tom@tomquaid.com
Dist(s): **Univ. of Oklahoma Pr.**

Apple Cover Books *See* **New Monic Bks.**

Apple House Publishing, (*978-0-9966954*) 8 Orchard Blossom Rd, Windham, NH 03087 USA Tel 301-717-3034
E-mail: jennifersmithwriter@outlook.com
Web site: www.jenniferwsmith.com.

Apple of the Eye Publishing, (*978-0-615-38892-2; 978-0-9829289*) 2800 Neilson Way, No. 614, Santa Monica, CA 90405 USA Tel 818-486-0904
Web site: http://www.thealmightybible.com
Dist(s): **Casscom Media.**

Apple Pie Pubs., (*978-0-9675123*) 5745 SW 75th St., PMB 325, Gainesville, FL 32608 USA Tel 352-472-2833 (phone/fax); Fax: 352-335-9080
E-mail: applepienow@aol.com
Web site: http://www.applepienow.com.

Appleby, Linda *See* **Seeds of Imagination**

AppleNobb Books *See* **Happy Apple Bks.**

Apples & Honey Pr. *Imprint of* **Behrman Hse., Inc.**

Applesauce Pr. *Imprint of* **Cider Mill Pr. Bk. Pubs., LLC**

Appleseed Pr. Bk. Pub. LLC, (*978-1-60464*) Orders Addr.: 12 Port Farm Rd., Kennebunkport, ME 04046-0404 USA (SAN 854-5405) Tel 207-641-3489; Fax: 207-967-8233
E-mail: appleseedgiftbooks@mac.com
Web site: http://www.appleseedpress.com.

Appleton, Brian H., (*978-0-692-84690-2; 978-0-692-86873-7; 978-0-692-86890-4; 978-0-692-87342-7; 978-0-692-88335-8; 978-0-692-90690-3; 978-0-692-97720-0; 978-0-692-98035-4; 978-0-692-99289-0; 978-0-692-19972-5; 978-0-692-04293-9; 978-0-578-40299-4; 978-0-578-57697-8; 978-0-578-57839-2) 5669 Snell Ave # 126, SAN JOSE, CA 95123 USA Tel 408 363 1721*
E-mail: iranianb@sbcglobal.net; iranianb@sbcglobal.net.

†Applewood Bks., (*978-0-918222; 978-1-55709; 978-1-889833; 978-1-933212; 978-1-4290; 978-0-9819430; 978-1-60889; 978-0-9844156; 978-0-9836416; 978-1-938700; 978-0-9882885; 978-1-941216; 978-1-5162; 978-1-944038; 978-1-945187; 978-1-64194*) 1 River Rd., Carlisle, MA 01741-1820 USA (SAN 210-3419) Toll Free: 800-277-5312; 1 Ingram Blvd., La Vergne, TN 37086; *Imprints:* Commonwealth Editions (CommonwealthEd)
E-mail: applewood@awb.com; svec@awb.com
Web site: http://www.awb.com
Dist(s): **Follett School Solutions**
Ingram Publisher Services; *CIP.*

Applied Database Technology, Inc., (*978-0-9742610*) 715 E. Sprague Ave. Suite 125, Spokane, WA 99202 USA
Web site: http://www.applieddatabase.com.

Appointed Media Group, LLC, (*978-0-9984148*) 1425 Battlefield Blvd. No. 1934, Chesapeake, VA 23327 USA Tel 757-935-7180
E-mail: roy@appointedpictures.org.

Apprentice Hse., (*978-1-934074; 978-1-62720*) Dept. Communication/Loyola College in MD, 4501 N. Charles St., Baltimore, MD 21210 USA.

Apprentice Shop Bks., LLC, (*978-0-9723410; 978-0-9842549; 978-0-9850144*) P.O. Box 375, Amherst, NH 03031 USA Fax: 603-472-2588
E-mail: apprenticeshpbks@aol.com
Web site: http://www.apprenticeshopbooks.com
Dist(s): **Follett School Solutions.**

Appropriate Solutions Press *See* **Echo Point Bks. and Media**

Apricot Pr., (*978-1-885027*) P.O. Box 98, Nephi, UT 84648 USA Toll Free: 800-731-6145
E-mail: books@apricotpress.com
Web site: http://www.apricotpress.com.

April Arts Press & Productions, (*978-0-9650918*) P.O. Box 64, Morgan Hill, CA 95038-0064 USA
E-mail: books@aprilartspress.com
Web site: http://www.aprilartspress.com
Dist(s): **Follett School Solutions.**

April Fool Publishing, (*978-0-692-16938-4; 978-0-578-52314-9; 978-0-578-53203-5; 978-0-578-66786-7*) 352 Home Pl. Dr., Easley, SC 29640 USA Tel 864-770-5986
E-mail: mattpelicano@icloud.com
Dist(s): **Ingram Content Group.**

April Press *See* **April Arts Press & Productions**

April Tale Bks., Radunska 8/13 app.10, Kyiv, 02034 UKR
E-mail: april4tale@gmail.com

APS Publishing, (*978-0-9906361; 978-1-945145*) 5739 S. Calumet Ave Unit 1s, Chicago, IL 60637 USA Tel 773-440-2004; 847-942-6135
E-mail: authorspromotingsuccess@gmail.com
Web site: www.weareaps.com.

AP's Travels *See* **Aunt Patty's Travels-London**

Apte, Stu, (*978-0-615-20409-3; 978-0-9821227*) 133 Plantation Dr., Tavernier, FL 33070 USA Tel 305-852-7440 (phone/fax)
E-mail: stuwho@bellsouth.net
Dist(s): **Emerald Bk. Co.**

Aquafire Sulis, (*978-0-9826321*) 216 Seventh Ave., 5E, New York, NY 10011 USA Tel 212-691-7288
E-mail: info@aquafiresulis.com.

Aquarian Age Publishing, Inc., (*978-0-9767530*) 250, 56th St., Fort Lauderdale, FL 33334 USA
E-mail: info@aquarianagepublishing.com
Web site: http://www.lawsofhealing.com; http://www.aquarianagepublishing.com.

Aquarius Pr., (*978-0-9718214; 978-0-9819208; 978-0-9846212; 978-0-9852877; 978-0-9857357; 978-0-9961390; 978-0-9971996; 978-0-9985278; 978-0-9992232; 978-1-7322091; 978-1-7330898; 978-1-7348273; 978-1-7357408*) Orders Addr.: P.O. Box 23096, Detroit, MI 48223 USA Tel 313-515-8122; Toll Free Fax: 877-979-3639 Do not confuse with companies with the same or similar names in Santa Fe, NM, Baltimore, MD, Watchung, NJ
E-mail: aquariuspress@sbcglobal.net; aquariuspress@gmail.com
Web site: http://www.AUXmedia.studio; http://www.AquariusPress.net; http://www.WillowLit.net
Dist(s): **Ingram Publisher Services**
SPD-Small Pr. Distribution.

Aqueduct Pr., (*978-0-9746559; 978-1-933500; 978-1-61976*) P.O. Box 95787, Seattle, WA 98145-2787 USA (SAN 256-131X); 4 White Brook Rd., Gilsum, NH 6448
Web site: http://www.aqueductpress.com
Dist(s): **Follett School Solutions**
Pathway Bk. Service.

Aquila Ink Publishing, (*978-0-9760789*) P.O. Box 160, Rio Nido, CA 95471 USA (SAN 850-9050) Tel 707-799-5981; 707-887-9090; Fax: 707-869-2973
E-mail: aquila@aquilaink.com
Web site: http://www.aquilaink.com.

Aquinas & Krone Publishing, LLC, (*978-0-9800448; 978-0-9843526; 978-0-9849505*) P.O. Box 1304, Merchantville, NJ 08109 USA (SAN 855-0751) Tel 856-665-3999.

A.R. Harding Publishing Co., (*978-0-936622*) 2878 E. Main St., Columbus, OH 43209 USA (SAN 206-4936) Tel 614-231-9585
E-mail: erics@furfishgame.com.

AR Thomas Publishing, (*978-0-692-12809-1*) 25222 NW Fwy 141, Cypress, TX 77429 USA Tel 832-914-7510
E-mail: lbhawi@yahoo.com.

Aradiance Publishing, (*978-0-9715737*) P.O. Box 13855, Mill Creek, WA 98082 USA.

Arago Publishing, LLC, (*978-0-9742698; 978-0-9788457*) 90087 Cape Arago Hwy., Coos Bay, OR 97420 USA (SAN 255-4607)
E-mail: surfdance@iceinternet.com.

Arango-Duque, J. F. *See* **Arango's Publishing**

Arango's Publishing, (*978-0-9655750*) 1776 Polk St., No. 3K-032, Hollywood, FL 33020 USA (SAN 299-2078)
E-mail: arangoduke@aol.com
Dist(s): **Hispanic Bks. Distributors & Pubs., Inc.**
Lectorum Pubns., Inc.
Libros Sin Fronteras
Quality Bks., Inc.

Aranjo, Karl, (*978-0-9770667*) 16 Greenwood, Irvine, CA 92604 USA Tel 949-786-8765
E-mail: karlaranjo@yahoo.com
Web site: http://guitaru.com.

Arbiter Pr., (*978-0-9621385; 978-0-615-35216-9; 978-0-615-35859-8*) 1732 N. Lakemont Ave., Winter Park, FL 32792 USA (SAN 251-1282); 1732 Arbor Pk. Dr., Winter Park, FL 32789 Tel 407-647-2606
E-mail: chsblackwell@gmail.com
Dist(s): **Bookazine Co., Inc.**

Arbor Bks., (*978-0-9771870; 978-0-9777764; 978-0-9786107; 978-0-9790469; 978-0-9794118; 978-0-9800582; 978-0-9818658; 978-0-9841992*) 244 Madison Ave., No. 254, New York, NY 10016 USA; 19 Apero Rd., Suite 301, Ramsey, NJ 7446 Do not confuse with Arbor Books in Media, PA
Web site: http://www.arborbooks.com
Dist(s): **Follett School Solutions.**

Arbordale Publishing, (*978-0-9764943; 978-0-9768823; 978-0-9777423; 978-1-934359; 978-1-60718; 978-1-62855; 978-1-64351*) 612 Johnnie Dodds Blvd., Suite A2, Mount Pleasant, SC 29464 USA (SAN 256-6109) Tel 843-971-6722; Fax: 843-216-3804
E-mail: leegerman@arbordalepublishing.com
Web site: http://www.arbordalepublishing.com
Dist(s): **BWI**
Baker & Taylor Bks.
Brodart Co.
Children's Plus, Inc.
Ediciones Enlace de PR, Inc.
Follett School Solutions
Ingram Publisher Services.

Arborville Bks., (*978-0-9886988*) 2115 Nature Cove Ct. No. 203, Ann Arbor, MI 48104 USA Tel 734-663-8175
E-mail: arborvillebooks@gmail.com
Dist(s): **Lulu Pr., Inc.**

Arborwoodgen LLC, (*978-0-9973686*) 23500 Cristo Rey Dr. Unit 107D, Cupertino, CA 95014-6520 USA Tel 650-967-3008
E-mail: wualan@labmed2.ucsf.edu.

Arbutus Pr., (*978-0-9665316; 978-0-9766104; 978-1-933926*) Orders Addr.: 2364 Pinehurst Trail, Traverse City, MI 49686 USA Tel 231-946-7240
E-mail: editor@arbutuspress.com
Web site: http://www.arbutuspress.com
Dist(s): **Follett School Solutions.**

Arc Manor, (*978-0-9786536; 978-0-9794154; 978-1-60450; 978-1-61242; 978-1-64710; 978-1-64973*) P.O. Box 10339, Rockville, MD 20849 USA Tel 240-645-2214; Fax: 310-388-8449; *Imprints:* TARK Classic Fiction (TARK Classic Fiction); Serenity Publishers (Serentiy Pubs)
E-mail: admin@arcmanor.com
Web site: http://www.HeartsKiss.com; http://www.ArcManor.com; http://www.PhoenixPick.com; http://www.PhoenixRider.com; http://http://www.ManorWodehouse.com; http://www.galaxysedge.com/
Dist(s): **Follett School Solutions**
Ingram Publisher Services
Smashwords.

ARC Pr. Bks. *Imprint of* **American Reading Co.**

ARC Pr. Comics *Imprint of* **American Reading Co.**

ARC Pr., Div. of American Reading Co., 201 S. Gulph Rd., King of Prussia, PA 19406 USA.

Arcade Publishing *Imprint of* **Skyhorse Publishing Co., Inc.**

Arcadia Bks. Ltd. (GBR) (*978-1-900850; 978-1-905147; 978-1-906413; 978-1-908129; 978-1-910050; 978-1-911350*) *Dist. by* **BTPS.**

Arcadia Publications *See* **Linden Hill Publishing**

Arcadia Publishing, (*978-0-88289; 978-0-910462; 978-0-911116; 978-1-56554; 978-0-7385; 978-1-58973; 978-1-58980; 978-1-59629; 978-1-4396; 978-1-60949; 978-1-4556; 978-1-61423; 978-1-4671; 978-0-578-11080-6; 978-1-62584; 978-1-62585; 978-1-62619; 978-0-578-12310-3;-0-615-91258-5; 978-0-9903765; 978-1-944313; 978-1-5316; 978-1-5402; 978-0-578-19068-6; 978-0-578-59417-0; 978-0-578-59418-7) Orders Addr.: 420 Wando Pk. Blvd., Mount Pleasant, SC 29464 USA (SAN 255-268X) Tel 843-853-2070; Fax: 843-853-0044; Toll Free: 888-313-2665; Imprints:* History Press, The (HistoryPress); Pelican Publishing (PelicanPub) Do not confuse with Arcadia Publishing in Greenwood Village, CO
E-mail: sales@arcadiapublishing.com
Web site: http://www.arcadiapublishing.com
Dist(s): **INscribe Digital**
MyiLibrary
Open Road Integrated Media, Inc.

Arcadiam Games, (*978-0-9769951*) 3106 NE 83rd Ave., Portland, OR 97220 USA
E-mail: travisbrown@crossroads-rpg.com
Web site: http://www.crossroads-rpg.com.

Arcadian Hse., (*978-0-9766666*) 3040 Rightmire Blvd., Columbus, OH 43221 USA
E-mail: lyn@arcadianhouse.com
Web site: http://www.arcadianhouse.com.

Arcana Studio, Inc., (*978-0-9763095; 978-0-9809204; 978-1-926914; 978-1-927424; 978-1-927421*) 930 Winthrop Ln., Rockford, IL 61107 USA
Web site: http://www.arcanastudio.com
Dist(s): **Diamond Comic Distributors, Inc.**
Diamond Bk. Distributors.

Archaeopress (GBR) (*978-0-9539923; 978-1-905739; 978-1-78491; 978-1-78969*) *Dist. by* **CasemateAcad.**

Archaia Entertainment *Imprint of* **Boom! Studios**

Archangel Studios, LLC, (*978-0-9714714*) 507 S. Parish Pl., Burbank, CA 91506-2951 USA
E-mail: thredstar_hq@hotmail.com
Web site: http://www.theredstar.com
Dist(s): **Diamond Comic Distributors, Inc.**
Diamond Bk. Distributors.

Archbury Pr., (*978-0-615-44224-2; 978-0-615-56552-1; 978-0-615-60617-0; 978-0-615-81067-6; 978-0-615-90212-8; 978-0-692-23243-9*) P.O. Box 20668, Boulder, CO 80308 USA Tel 303-516-9694
E-mail: archburypress@aol.com
Web site: cafedion.com.

Archdeacon Bks., (*978-0-692-20966-0; 978-0-692-24065-6; 978-0-692-43443-7; 978-0-692-53166-2; 978-0-692-55279-7; 978-0-692-75684-3; 978-0-692-91562-2; 978-0-692-96824-6; 978-0-692-07939-3; 978-1-949422*) 1713 Strawberry Ln, Birmingham, AL 35244 USA Tel 205-424-2255
E-mail: woody@woodynorman-llc.com; woody.norman@gmail.com
Web site: https://www.facebook.com/ArchdeaconBooks/; http://www.woodynorman-llc.com
Dist(s): **CreateSpace Independent Publishing Platform**
Ingram Bk. Co.

ArcheBooks *Imprint of* **ArcheBooks Publishing, Inc.**

ArcheBooks Publishing, Inc., (*978-1-59507*) 6081 Silver King Blvd. Unit 903, Cape Coral, FL 33914 USA Tel 239-542-7595; 9101 W. Sahara Ave., Las Vegas, NV 89117; *Imprints:* ArcheBooks (ArchBks)
E-mail: publisher@archebooks.com
Web site: http://www.archebooks.com
Dist(s): **Follett School Solutions**
ISD.

Archeion Press, LLC *See* **Akasha Publishing, LLC**

Archeological Assessments, Inc., (*978-0-9638956; 978-0-9794044*) P.O. Box 1631, Nashville, AR 71852 USA
E-mail: aaimjb@aol.com
Web site: http://www.arkansasstories.com.

Archer Fields, Inc., (*978-0-9627767; 978-1-56466*) 155 Sixth Ave., New York, NY 10013 USA Tel 212-627-1999; Fax: 212-627-9484; Toll Free: 800-338-2665
Dist(s): **D.A.P./Distributed Art Pubs.**

Archer's Pr., (*978-0-615-68449-9; 978-0-615-70040-3; 978-0-615-70731-0; 978-0-9894749; 978-0-692-23029-9; 978-0-692-41131-5; 978-0-692-47473-0; 978-0-692-61477-8; 978-0-692-62625-2*) 2795 Parker Rd., Florissant, MO 63033 USA Tel 3146168101
Web site: www.archerspress.com
Dist(s): **CreateSpace Independent Publishing Platform.**

Archeworks, (*978-0-9753405*) 625 N. Kingsbury St., Chicago, IL 60610 USA Tel 312-867-7254; Fax: 312-867-7260
E-mail: info@archeworks.org
Web site: http://www.archeworks.org.

Archie Comic Pubns., Inc., (*978-1-879794; 978-1-936975; 978-1-61988; 978-1-62738; 978-1-68183; 978-1-68255; 978-1-64576*) 629 Fifth Ave, Suite 100, Pelham, NY 10803-1242 USA Tel 914-381-5155; Fax: 914-381-2335; *Imprints:* Archie Comics (Archie Comics); Dark Circle Comics (Dark Circle)
E-mail: haroldb@archiecomics.com
Web site: http://www.archiecomics.com
Dist(s): **Diamond Comic Distributors, Inc.**
Diamond Bk. Distributors
Follett School Solutions
Penguin Random Hse. Distribution
Penguin Random Hse. LLC
Random Hse., Inc.

Archie Comics *Imprint of* **Archie Comic Pubns., Inc.**

Archie Publishing, (*978-0-9779064*) P.O. Box 521732, Salt Lake City, UT 84152-1732 USA (SAN 850-5616) Tel 801-232-3840
E-mail: mcf@archiepublishing.com
Web site: http://www.archiepublishing.com
Dist(s): **American West Bks.**

Archimede Editions (FRA) (*978-2-211*) *Dist. by* **Distribks Inc.**

Archipelago Pr., (*978-1-893335*) Orders Addr.: P.O. Box 1540, Los Gatos, CA 95031 USA (SAN 299-7541) Tel 408-354-5587 (phone/fax) Do not confuse with

companies with the same name in Saint Thomas, VI, Friday Harbor, WA
E-mail: pelago2000@aol.com
Web site: http://www.rosswell.com.

Archival Services, Incorporated *See* **Red River Pr.**

Archives Pr. *Imprint of* **Media Assocs.**

Archives Press, The *See* **Media Assocs.**

Archus Pr., LLC, *(978-0-9648564; 978-1-893047; 978-0-9852248)* 620 Miller St., Rochester, MI 48307 USA Tel 248-218-0356; Toll Free: 888-275-5639
E-mail: leigharrathoon@gmail.com.

Archway Publishing, *(978-1-4808; 978-1-6657)* Div. of Author Solutions, Inc., 1663 Liberty Dr., Bloomington, IN 47403 USA Fax: 317-454-0544 Toll Free: 888-242-5904
E-mail: sfurr@authorsolutions.com
Web site: http://www.archwaypublishing.com
Dist(s): **Author Solutions, Inc.**
Baker & Taylor Publisher Services (BTPS).

Arco *Imprint of* **Peterson's**

Arcoiris Records, Inc., *(978-1-57417)* P.O. Box 7428, Berkeley, CA 94707 USA Tel 510-527-5539
Dist(s): **Follett School Solutions**
Lectorum Pubns., Inc.

Arctos Pr., *(978-0-9657015; 978-0-9725384; 978-0-9897847)* 116 Cloud View Rd., Sausalito, CA 94965 USA Tel 415 331 2503
Web site: http://www.members.aol.com/runes/index.html
Dist(s): **Quality Bks., Inc.**
SPD-Small Pr. Distribution.

Arcturus Pubs., Inc., *(978-0-916877)* P.O. Box 606, Cherry Hill, NJ 08003 USA (SAN 653-9718) Tel 609-428-3863.

Arcturus Publishing (GBR) *(978-1-900032; 978-1-84193; 978-1-84837; 978-1-84858; 978-1-78212; 978-1-78404; 978-1-78428; 978-1-78599; 978-1-78828) Dist. by* **BTPS.**

Arcturus Publishing (GBR) *(978-1-900032; 978-1-84193; 978-1-84837; 978-1-84858; 978-1-78212; 978-1-78404; 978-1-78428; 978-1-78599; 978-1-78828) Dist. by* **Black Rab.**

Ardden Entertainment (GBR) *(978-0-9561259) Dist. by* **Diamond Book Dists.**

Arden Pr., Inc., *(978-0-912869)* Orders Addr.: P.O. Box 418, Denver, CO 80201 USA (SAN 277-6553) Tel 303-697-6766; Fax: 303-697-3443; Edit Addr.: 20723 Seminole Rd., Indian Hills, CO 80454 USA Do not confuse with Arden Pr. Inc., Cleveland, OH
E-mail: ardenpress@msn.com
Dist(s): **Follett School Solutions.**

Ardent Writer Pr., LLC, The, *(978-1-938667; 978-1-64066)* 1014 Stone Dr., Brownsboro, AL 35741 USA Tel 256-694-6744
E-mail: gierhartsteve@att.net.

ARDI Research Pr., *(978-0-9640600)* 13571 Millpond Way, San Diego, CA 92129 USA (SAN 298-1866) Fax: 619-484-0377
E-mail: roger@rdooley.com.

Area Fifty One Productions *See* **Media Blasters, Inc.**

Areteem Institute, *(978-1-944863)* 15707 Rockfield Blvd, Irvine, CA 92618 USA Tel 949-679-8989
E-mail: kren@areteem.org
Web site: www.areteem.org.

Argami Productions, LLC, *(978-0-9798324)* 774 Verona Lake Dr., Weston, FL 33326 USA; 4501 Forbes Blvd, Lanham, MD 20706
E-mail: ellenwv@aol.com
Dist(s): **Follett School Solutions**
New Leaf Publishing Group.

Argee Pubs., *(978-0-917961)* 4453 Manitou, Okemos, MI 48864 USA (SAN 247-7858) Tel 517-349-1254.

Argon Pr., *(978-0-9910554; 978-0-9908831; 978-1-944815)* 3442 Pigeon Hill, Muskegon, MI 49441 USA Tel 231-224-6468
E-mail: steve@argonpress.com
Web site: http://www.argonpress.com.

Argonaut Publishing Co., *(978-0-9635118)* 284 Clearview Rd., Chuluota, FL 32766 USA (SAN 297-8199) Tel 407-977-5207 (phone) Do not confuse with companies with the same or similar name in Los Angeles, CA, Santa Barbara, CA
E-mail: spottedtail@spottedtail.com
Web site: http://www.spottedtail.com.

Argonauts, The, *(978-0-615-23045-0; 978-0-615-33914-6; 978-0-9827842)* Orders Addr.: 929 Canterbury Ln., Waukesha, WI 53188 USA
E-mail: smkstoll@yahoo.com
Web site: http://www.theArgonauts.com.

Argonne Bks. LLC, *(978-0-692-18284-0; 978-0-578-60012-3)* 542 Argonne Dr. NW, Atlanta, GA 30305 USA Tel 404-852-7919
E-mail: lissa.webber@gmail.com
Dist(s): **Ingram Content Group.**

Argos Gameware *See* **H&M Systems Software, Inc.**

Argot Pr., *(978-1-64489)* 206 Cherry St., Muscatine, IA 52761 USA Tel 563-299-3362
E-mail: spostr@gmail.com.

Argus Enterprises International, Inc., *(978-0-9801555; 978-0-9819075; 978-0-9823050; 978-0-9841342; 978-0-9842596; 978-0-9845142; 978-0-9846195; 978-0-9846348; 978-0-9846439; 978-0-615-50768-2; 978-0-615-50816-0; 978-0-615-50820-7; 978-0-615-51728-5; 978-0-615-51733-9; 978-0-615-51734-6; 978-0-615-52229-6; 978-0-615-52387-3; 978-0-615-52392-7; 978-0-615-52688-1; 978-0-615-53228-8; 978-0-615-53320-9; 978-0-615-53503-6; 978-0-615-53629-3; 978-0-615-54552-3; 978-0-615-55032-9; 978-0-615-55098-5; 978-0-615-55127-2; 978-0-615-55238-5) Orders Addr.: P.O. Box 914, Kernersville, NC 27285 USA Tel 336-354-7173; Fax: 336-993-2497; Edit Addr.: 9001 Ridge Hill St., Kernersville, NC 27284 USA*
Web site: http://www.a-argusbooks.com; http://www.abetterbewrite.com; http://abook4you.com
Dist(s): **CreateSpace Independent Publishing Platform**
Follett School Solutions.

Ariella Publishing, *(978-0-9861106)* 320 Kearney Dr., Owings Mills, MD 21117 USA Tel 410-654-3822
E-mail: izya50@yahoo.com.

Arise Foundation, *(978-1-58614)* P.O. Box 2147, Jupiter, FL 33468-2147 USA (SAN 253-4835) Toll Free: 888-680-6100
E-mail: yisaacs@ariselife-skills.org
Web site: http://www.ariseife-skills.org
Dist(s): **Follett School Solutions.**

Aristata Publishing, *(978-0-9754912)* 16429 Lost Canyon Rd., Santa Clarita, CA 91387 USA (SAN 256-6508) Tel 661-299-9478 (phone/fax)
E-mail: aristata@craigelliottgallery.com; celliott@socal.rr.com
Web site: http://www.craigelliottgallery.com
Dist(s): **APG Sales & Distribution Services.**

ARIVA Publishing, *(978-0-9822952; 978-1-938056)* 244 Madison Ave, Suite 7100, New York, NY 10016-2817 USA Tel 646-706-7129
E-mail: info@arivapublishing.com
Dist(s): **Greenleaf Book Group.**

Arizona Blueberry Studios, *(978-0-9727894)* P.O. Box 5, Pasadena, CA 91102 USA Toll Free: 800-767-7186
E-mail: books@rossanthony.com
Web site: http://www.rossanthony.com/books.

Arizona Elk Society, *(978-0-9825181)* P.O. Box 190, Peoria, AZ 85380 USA.

Arizona Highways, *(978-0-916179; 978-1-893860; 978-1-932082; 978-0-9822788; 978-0-9845709; 978-0-9837132; 978-0-9887875; 978-0-9916228; 978-0-9971247; 978-0-9987893; 978-0-9989812; 978-0-9989813)* Div. of Arizona Dept. of Transportation, 2039 W. Lewis Ave., Phoenix, AZ 85009 USA (SAN 294-8974)
E-mail: mbianchi@azdot.gov; aphares@azdot.gov; kmero@azdot.gov
Web site: http://www.arizonahighways.com.

†Arizona Historical Society, *(978-0-910037)* 949 E. Second St., Tucson, AZ 85719 USA (SAN 201-6982) Tel 520-628-5774; Fax: 520-628-5695
Dist(s): **University of Arizona Pr.**; *CIP.*

Arizona Sonora Desert Museum Pr., *(978-1-886679)* Arizona Sonora Desert Museum, 2021 N. Kinney Rd., Tucson, AZ 85743 USA Tel 520-883-3061; Fax: 520-883-3048
E-mail: asdmpress@desertmuseum.org; info@desertmuseum.org
Web site: http://www.desertmuseum.org
Dist(s): **Rio Nuevo Pubs.**

Ark Hse. Pr. (AUS) *(978-0-9752044; 978-0-9757986; 978-0-9775671; 978-0-9803458; 978-0-9804523; 978-0-9805414; 978-1-921589; 978-0-9873888; 978-0-9875839; 978-0-9875932; 978-0-9922699; 978-0-9923452; 978-0-9925192; 978-0-9925726; 978-0-9941941; 978-0-9942832; 978-0-9943675; 978-0-9944299; 978-0-9945516; 978-0-9945968; 978-0-9953917; 978-0-9954215; 978-0-6480451; 978-0-6480508; 978-0-6480845; 978-0-6481016; 978-0-6481734; 978-0-6482639; 978-0-6482914; 978-0-6483719; 978-0-6483905; 978-0-6484410; 978-0-6484585;) Dist. by* **STL Dist.**

Ark Watch Holdings LLC, *(978-0-9765358; 978-0-615-25019-9; 978-0-615-25020-5; 978-0-615-25021-2; 978-0-578-05938-9; 978-0-615-99015-6; 978-0-692-39260-7; 978-0-692-57098-2; 978-0-692-57589-5; 978-0-692-58048-6; 978-0-692-59038-6; 978-0-692-59199-4)* Div. of Serpentauria Media LLC, 4766 E. Eden Dr., Cave Creek, AZ 85331-3870 USA
E-mail: erikauthor@aol.com; arkwatchholdingsllc@hotmail.com
Web site: http://www.arkwatch.com
Dist(s): **CreateSpace Independent Publishing Platform.**

Arlen Hse. (IRL) *(978-1-903631) Dist. by* **LongleafServ.**

Arlene, Carmen Hibbs, *(978-0-9762567)* 584 Choctaw Dr., Madisonville, KY 42431 USA Tel 270-821-1968
E-mail: arlenehibbs@yahoo.com
Web site: http://www.heavenlyharborbooks.com.

Arlington & Amelia, *(978-1-886541)* Orders Addr.: 1830 Lee Rd., Winter Park, FL 32789 USA Tel 407-293-1132; Toll Free Fax: 1-866-618-0540 Do not confuse with Priority Press in Dallas, TX & Yardley, PA
E-mail: nbaa@cfl.rr.com
Web site: http://www.weddingsurvivalguide.net
Dist(s): **Southern Bk. Service.**

Arlington Pubns., *(978-0-9753611)* 2205 Manera St., Odessa, TX 79763 USA Tel 432-582-0272; Fax: 432-332-2499 Do not confuse with Arlington Publications Incorporated in Arlington, TX
E-mail: tommwhite@cableone.net.

Armadillo Bks., *(978-0-9786132)* 4735 NE 24th Ave., Portland, OR 97211 USA (SAN 851-0865) Do not confuse with Armadillo Books in Houston, TX
E-mail: phtdoyle@yahoo.com
Web site: http://www.edgarfont.com; http://www.nextreststopearth.com
Dist(s): **Follett School Solutions.**

Armchair Pr., LLC, *(978-0-9744627)* P.O. Box 215, Ross, CA 94957-0215 USA Tel 415-460-9750; Fax: 415-460-0850
E-mail: ozzie@armchairpress.com.

Armen, Rose Maiolo, *(978-0-692-06994-3)* 12 N. Ledge Rock Rd., Niantic, CT 06357 USA Tel 860-514-3027
E-mail: rarmen@sbcglobal.net.

Arment Biological Press *See* **Coachwhip Pubns.**

Armina Pr. *Imprint of* **Polis Bks.**

Armor of Hope Writing & Publishing Services, LLC, *(978-0-692-05841-1; 978-0-692-16932-2; 978-1-7336134)*
E-mail: armorofhope121@gmail.com
Web site: www.armorofhopewritingservices.com.

Armour of Light Publishing, *(978-0-9620604; 978-0-9788590; 978-0-9817120; 978-0-9825476; 978-0-9857539)* P.O. Box 778, Chapel Hill, NC 27514 USA (SAN 249-4337)
E-mail: publisher@armouroflight.org
Web site: http://www.armouroflight.org.

Armstrong, Greg, *(978-0-578-11703-4; 978-0-578-12191-8; 978-0-578-12368-4)* 27082 O Neill Dr., Unit 325, Ladera Ranch, CA 92694 USA Tel 949-701-7190.

Armstrong Valley Publishing Co., *(978-1-928798)* Orders Addr.: P.O. Box 1275, Murfreesboro, TN 37133-1275 USA Tel 615-895-5445; Fax: 615-893-2688; Edit Addr.: 2568 Armstrong Valley Rd., Murfreesboro, TN 37128 USA
E-mail: rsanders@raider.net.

Arnica Publishing, *(978-0-9728538)* Orders Addr.: P.O. Box 543, Choteau, MT 59422 USA; Edit Addr.: 3961 Hwy 89 S., Choteau, MT 59422 USA
E-mail: arnica@3rivers.net; pbechtold1@gmail.com.

Arnica Publishing, Incorporated *See* **ACS, LLC Arnica Creative Services**

Arnold, Patricia *See* **www.margaretmouse.com publishing co.**

Arnstein, Bennett, *(978-0-9620058)* 3049 W. Eighth St., No. 535, Los Angeles, CA 90005 USA (SAN 247-5162) Tel 213-388-3517
E-mail: b_arnstein@hotmail.com.

ARose Bks. *Imprint of* **ARose Books Publishing, LLC**

ARose Books Publishing, LLC, *(978-0-9723970; 978-0-9740636; 978-0-9819298; 978-0-9846081; 978-0-692-37550-1; 978-1-945986)* 310 Fox Rd., Havre De Grace, MD 21078 USA Fax: 888-889-6945 (phone/fax); *Imprints:* ARose Books (ARoseBks)
Web site: http://www.arosebooks.com
Dist(s): **CreateSpace Independent Publishing Platform.**

Around The Globe Pr., *(978-0-9760573)* 11505 E. Calle Javelina, Tucson, AZ 85748-6339 USA Tel 520-290-8915
E-mail: aroundtheglobepress@earthlink.net
Web site: http://www.aroundtheglobepress.com.

Around the Way Book Publishers *See* **Around the Way Books**

Around the Way Books, *(978-0-9755342)* P.O. Box 1497, Waterbury, CT 06721 USA Toll Free: 888-610-5969
E-mail: htaylor@AroundTheWayBooks.com; info@aroundthewaybooks.com
Web site: http://www.AroundTheWayBooks.com
Dist(s): **Lushena Bks.**

Around The World Pubns., LLC, *(978-0-9772591)* P.O. Box 1024, Franktown, CO 80116-1024 USA Do not confuse with Around The World Publications in Seattle, WA
E-mail: bbrasier@etsgroup.com
Web site: http://www.worldthroughchildseyes.com.

Arquilla Pr., *(978-0-692-14751-1)* 1801 Paddington Ave., Naperville, IL 60563 USA Tel 630-369-2169
E-mail: carmelamartino@gmail.com
Dist(s): **Ingram Content Group.**

Arrest Me Not Publishing *See* **As Seen on the Internet / Arrest Me Not**

Arrinton Pubns., *(978-0-9754540)* Orders Addr.: P.O. Box 2573, Chesapeake, VA 23327 USA Tel 757-450-6068; Fax: 757-410-4215; Edit Addr.: 1601 Orchard Grove Dr., Chesapeake, VA 23320-1411 USA
E-mail: gobooks@cox.net.

Arrow Pubns., *(978-0-9715514; 978-0-9765849)* Orders Addr.: 16653 E. Kingstree Blvd., Fountain Hills, AZ 85268-5439 USA Do not confuse with companies with the same or similar names in Cedar Rapids, IA, Kensington, MD
E-mail: arrowpublications@cox.net
Web site: http://www.arrowpublications.net.

Arrowhead Publishing, *(978-0-9640056)* 1238 Riva Rose Cir., Castle Rock, CO 80104-9650 USA Tel 303-663-9415 Do not confuse with companies with the same name in Lake Arrowhead, CA, Carlsbad, CA.

Arruzza, Richard *See* **Three Spots Productions**

Arsenal Pulp Pr. (CAN) *(978-0-88978; 978-1-55152) Dist. by* **Consort Bk Sales.**

Arseya, LLC, *(978-0-9745185; 978-1-935093)* 10 Pleasantville Rd., New Vernon, NJ 07976 USA (SAN 255-6588) Tel 973-993-1504; Fax: 973-993-9182; *Imprints:* Arseya Publishing (Arseya Pub)
E-mail: arseya@arseya.com
Web site: http://www.arseya.com.

Arseya Publishing *Imprint of* **Arseya, LLC**

Art & Creativity For Healing, Inc., *(978-0-9748462)* 26079 Getty Dr., Laguna Niguel, CA 92677 USA Tel 949-367-1902; Fax: 949-367-1904
E-mail: laurie@art4healing.org
Web site: http://www.art4healing.org.

Art & Soul Expressions, *(978-0-9729192)* P.O. Box 957, Mount Shasta, CA 96067 USA.

Art as Responsar *See* **Art as Responsa LLC**

Art as Responsa LLC, *(978-0-578-05270-0; 978-0-9845456)* 2550 Southshore Blvd., Lake Oswego, OR 97034 USA (SAN 859-631X) Tel 503-344-6065 (phone/fax); Fax: 503-344-6065; ART AS RESPONSA LLC 2550 Southshore Blvd., Lake Oswego, OR 97034
E-mail: marsha@art-responsa.com
Web site: http://www.artasresponsa.com; http://www.art-responsa.com; www.marshaplafkin.com.

A.R.T Bks. 4Kids, *(978-0-9968775)* 6256 Hillandale Dr. Apt 106, Lithonia, GA 30058 USA Tel 404-821-1726
E-mail: Reading_Is_Golden@yahoo.com.

Art Deco Dog Publishing, *(978-1-7323827)* P.O. Box 193, Moss Beach, CA 94038 USA Tel 650-728-8400; Fax: 650-728-5400
E-mail: artdecodog@gmail.com
Web site: https://longnoselegacy.com; houndbeautiful.com; artdecodog.com.

Art In The Heartland, *(978-0-9725461; 978-0-9752839; 978-0-9762103; 978-0-9766587; 978-0-9778450)* P.O. Box 1785, Columbus, IN 47202-1785 USA
E-mail: sbreeding@artintheheartland.com
Web site: http://www.breedingbooks.com; http://www.artintheheartlandbooks.com.

Art Night Bks., *(978-0-9794004)* 3348 N. Dousman St., Milwaukee, WI 53212 USA Tel 414-213-7443
E-mail: devintrudell@mac.com; angievasquez13@sbcglobal.net
Web site: http://artnightbooks.com.

Art Of Essex Fine Art, The, *(978-0-615-31464-8)* 3007 Lakewood Ct., Jefferson City, MO 65109 USA
Web site: www.essexgarner.com.

Art of War Plus Bks. *Imprint of* **Clearbridge Publishing**

Art Official Media LLC, *(978-0-9768061; 978-0-9834874; 978-0-9883825)* Orders Addr.: P.O. Box 532532, Baltimore, MD 21212 SUN Tel 443-693-7622; Edit Addr.: 1044 Radnor Ave., Indianapolis, IN 46253-2532 USA
Web site: http://www.artofficialmedia.com; http://www.UrbaniaMag.com
Dist(s): **Afrikan World Bk. Distributor.**

Art With Heart Press, *(978-0-9715240; 978-0-9841365)* Div. of Art with Heart, Orders Addr.: P.O. Box 94402, Seattle, WA 98124-6702 USA (SAN 850-2676)
E-mail: info@artwithheart.org
Web site: http://www.artwithheart.org
Dist(s): **Partners/West Book Distributors.**

Art&Media Communications LLC, *(978-0-9778932)* P.O. Box 7743, Bloomfield Hills, MI 48302-4830 USA (SAN 850-4520)
E-mail: lrtucci@artemediacomm.com
Web site: http://www.artineraries.com; http://www.touringtracks.com.

ArtAnswer, *(978-0-9755413; 978-0-9771520)* P.O. Box 50387, Billings, MT 59105 USA Tel 406-672-8482
E-mail: artanswer@artanswer.com
Web site: http://www.artanswer.com.

†Arte Publico Pr., *(978-0-934770; 978-1-55885; 978-1-61192; 978-1-5185)* Univ. of Houston 4902 Gulf Fwy, Bldg. 19, Rm. 100, Houston, TX 77204-2004 USA (SAN 213-4594) Tel 713-743-2998; 713-743-3080; Fax: 713-743-2847; Toll Free: 800-633-2783; Univ. of Houston 4902 Gulf Freeway, Rm. 100, Houston, TX 77023; *Imprints:* Piñata Books (Pinata Bks)
E-mail: bkorders@uh.edu; appinfo@uh.edu
Web site: http://www.artepublicopress.com
Dist(s): **Book Wholesalers, Inc.**
Booksource, The
Bound to Stay Bound Bks.
Brodart Co.
Children's Plus, Inc.
Follett School Solutions
Keystone Bks. & Media LLC
Lectorum Pubns., Inc.
Mackin Educational Resources
Midwest Library Service
Perfection Learning Corp.
Perma-Bound Bks.
Quality Bks., Inc.
Rainbow Bk. Co.
Unique Bks., Inc.
Yankee Bk. Peddler, Inc.
ebrary, Inc.; *CIP.*

Artemesia Publishing, LLC, *(978-1-932926; 978-1-951122)* Orders Addr.: 9 Mockingbird Hill Rd., Tijeras, NM 87059 USA Tel 505-286-0892; *Imprints:* Kinkajou Press (Kinkajou Pr)
E-mail: info@artemesiapublishing.com; g.habiger@artemesiapublishing.com
Web site: http://www.apbooks.net; http://www.artemesiapublishing.com; http://www.tangent-games.com; http://www.kinkajoupress.com/
Dist(s): **Bks. West**
Follett School Solutions
Hachette Bk. Group
Independent Pubs. Group
Midpoint Trade Bks., Inc.

Artemisia Enterprises, *(978-0-9755416)* P.O. Box 3106 Mosshall Way, San Jose, CA 95135 USA
E-mail: sales@amazonheart.org
Web site: http://www.amazonheart.org.

Artesian Pr., *(978-1-58659)* 372 South 900 W., Provo, UT 84601 USA (SAN 253-1259) Tel 801-375-0800; Fax: 801-222-9199; Toll Free Fax: 888-326-3125; Toll Free: 888-734-9355; 20 Commercial Blvd., Novato, CA 94949
E-mail: info@artesianpress.com
Web site: http://www.artesianpress.com
Dist(s): **Follett School Solutions.**

Arthritis Foundation, *(978-0-912423; 978-0-692-63011-2)* 1330 W. Peachtree St., Atlanta, GA 30309 USA (SAN 267-677X) Tel 404-965-7622; Fax: 404-872-9559; Toll Free: 800-283-7800 Do not confuse with Arthritis Foundation, Southfield, MI
E-mail: sbernstein@arthritis.org
Web site: http://www.arthritis.org.

Article One *See* **Marsh Creek Pr.**

Artisan, *(978-1-57965; 978-1-885183; 978-1-64829)* Div. of Workman Publishing Co., Inc., 225 Varick St. Flr. 9, New York, NY 10014-4381 USA Toll Free: 800-967-5630 Do not confuse with Artisan, Wheaton, IL
E-mail: artisan@workman.com
Dist(s): **Open Road Integrated Media, Inc.**
Workman Publishing Co., Inc.

Artisan Bookworks, *(978-0-9898692; 978-0-9911747; 978-0-9979578; 978-0-9991200; 978-1-7357891)* PO Box 1972, Sequim, WA 98382 USA Tel 425-954-5277 E-mail: books@artisanbookworks.com Web site: http://www.artisanbookworks.com.

Artisan House *See* **Artisan**

Artisan Pubs., *(978-0-934666)* P.O. Box 1529, Muskogee, OK 74402 USA (SAN 211-8408) Tel 918-682-8341; Fax: 918-682-1263.

Artisan Sales *See* **Artisan Pubs.**

Artist Designs, *(978-0-9760409)* P.O. Box 548, Webster, WI 54893 USA Tel 715-222-2362.

Artist Studios, Ltd., *(978-1-931037; 978-1-59487; 978-1-61562)* 444 Spear St. Ste. 101, San Francisco, CA 94105-1693 USA.

Artistic Angels Corp., *(978-0-9890410)* 535 Valley View Rd. Apt. D301, Branson, MO 65616 USA Tel 417-544-1766; Fax: 417-544-1766 E-mail: artisticangels4you@yahoo.com.

Artistic Creations Bk. Publishing, *(978-0-9796843; 978-0-692-76837-2; 978-0-9982826)* 2215 6th Ave., Apt. D, Moline, IL 61265 USA E-mail: bookwoman1110@hotmail.com Web site: http://beserrashomebasedbiz.blogspot; http://artisticcreationsbookpublishing.books.officelive.com/default.aspx; http:///site/discoveryourtalentshow/; http:///site/fairytalekidssite/ *Dist(s):* **Partners Bk. Distributing, Inc.**

Artistic Ventures LLC, *(978-0-9771495)* Orders Addr.: 3 Glade Mallow Rd., Malta, NY 12020 USA; Edit Addr.: 3 Glade Mallow Rd., Malta, NY 12020-4326 USA; *Imprints:* Artistic Ventures Publishing (Artistic Ventures) E-mail: dawn@artistic-ventures.com Web site: http://www.artistic-ventures.com *Dist(s):* **Follett School Solutions.**

Artistic Ventures Publishing *Imprint of* **Artistic Ventures LLC**

Artists On Video, LLC / (d/b/a) MN Productions, *(978-0-9799440; 978-1-937106)* 84 Chaumont Sq. NW, Atlanta, GA 30327 USA.

Artists' Orchard, LLC, The, *(978-0-9843166; 978-0-9857014; 978-0-9964752)* P.O. Box 113317, Pittsburgh, PA 15241 USA (SAN 859-0389) Tel 724-255-6408 E-mail: sales@theartistsorchard.com; publish@theartistsorchard.com Web site: http://theartistsorchard.com.

Artist's Pr., *(978-0-924556)* P.O. Box 16087, Minneapolis, MN 55416-0087 USA Tel 952-486-8353 E-mail: artistspress@aim.com Web site: http://www.artistspress.com.

ArtMar Productions, *(978-0-9799089)* 60 W. 71st St., No. 1B, New York, NY 10023 USA (SAN 854-7416) E-mail: mihorowitz@aol.com Web site: http://www.marlynhorowitz.com.

Art-Medium, *(978-0-9817971)* P.O. Box 390739, Mountain View, CA 94039-0739 USA (SAN 856-5848) E-mail: tangobelly@yahoo.com Web site: http://www.AKPhotography.net.

Artos Press Enterprises *See* **Creative Cranium Concept, The**

Artpacks, *(978-0-9790247; 978-0-9834637)* 535 22nd St., NE, Rochester, MN 55906 USA (SAN 852-2227) Tel 507-273-2529 E-mail: storymatters@charter.net.

Artpress Publishing, Inc. *See* **Cheesy Bread Publishing**

Artrum Media, *(978-0-9840574; 978-0-9841957; 978-0-9845352; 978-0-9837050; 978-1-938107)* 627 Brickle Ridge Rd., Decatur, TN 37322 USA (SAN 858-3080) E-mail: info@artrummedia.com Web site: http://www.artrummedia.com *Dist(s):* **New Tradition Bks.**

Arts and Minds Studio Inc., *(978-0-9767048)* Div. of Brian Alan Lane & Donna Cohen Lane, 19655 NW Stavis Bay Rd., Seabeck, WA 98380-9797 USA Tel 360-830-2614 (phonefax) E-mail: bal@brianalanlane.com; dc@donnacohen.com Web site: http://www.artsandminds.studio/; http://www.atinytale.com/; http://www.mindgameswithaserialkiller.com/.

Arts Love Expression, *(978-0-9998515)* 11319 Palisades Dr., Pacific Palisades, CA 90272 USA Tel 310-461-8647; *Imprints:* Bahoo Tide, LLC (Bahoo Tide) E-mail: ajahd@bahootide.com.

Arts Pubns., *(978-0-9766590)* P.O. Box 3006, Evansdale, IA 50707-0006 USA (SAN 256-4963) Tel 319-287-5901 (phone/fax) Do not confuse with Arts Publications in Corte Madera, CA E-mail: ceremonypress@mchsi.com; infoartspublications@mchsi.com Web site: http://www.artspublicationsbooks.com.

ArtScroll Series *Imprint of* **Mesorah Pubns., Ltd.**

ArtsKindred, *(978-1-7321862; 978-1-951183)* 11 4th Ave., East Northport, NY 11731 USA Tel 347-615-0784 E-mail: anetta4music@gmail.com.

Artstreet LLC, *(978-0-9758971)* 10 Crestmont Rd. Apt. 7P, Montclair, NJ 07042-1936 USA Toll Free: 866-543-7878 E-mail: sjimenez@brandstreetllc.com Web site: http://www.brandstreetllc.com.

Artsy Bee, LLC, *(978-0-615-75521-2; 978-0-692-48443-2; 978-0-692-58845-1)* 133 Naperville Dr., Cary, NC 27519-5409 USA Tel 919-274-6155 E-mail: rtbliss@gmail.com.

Artust Nasus Publishing, *(978-0-9763260)* 500 Rosita Ave., PO Box 1515, Westcliffe, CO 81252 USA Web site: http://www.naturallybalancedhealth.com.

Artworks International, *(978-1-57938)* Orders Addr.: 3101 Clairmont Rd., Suite C, Atlanta, GA 30329 USA (SAN 255-6456) Tel 404-214-4331; Fax: 404-214-4390 E-mail: derek.adams@andersonpress.com Web site: http://www.andersonpress.com.

ArtWrite Productions, *(978-0-9777693; 978-1-939846)* 1555 Gardena Ave. NE, Fridley, MN 55432-5848 USA (SAN 850-1432) Tel 763-572-8740 E-mail: artwrite@bitstream.net Web site: http://artwriteproductions.com; http://adaptedclassics.com *Dist(s):* **Follett School Solutions.**

Arundel Press *See* **Arundel Publishing**

Arundel Publishing, *(978-1-933608)* 36 Crystal Farm Rd., Warwick, NY 10990 USA Do not confuse with Arundel Press in Seattle, WA E-mail: Sharon@SharonLinnea.com *Dist(s):* **Follett School Solutions Ingram Publisher Services.**

Arutam Pr., *(978-0-9745477)* 62 Ave Maria, Monterey, CA 93940 USA Tel 831-375-6005 E-mail: emurray@sacredsite.com Web site: http://www.elizabethmurray.com.

Arzana, Inc., *(978-0-9770475)* Orders Addr.: P.O. Box 60473, Potomac, MD 20859 USA Tel 301-437-0017 E-mail: balance@arzanaworld.com Web site: http://www.arzanaworld.com.

As Sabr Pubns. *Imprint of* **Imago Pr.**

As Seen on the Internet / Arrest Me Not, *(978-0-9640336)* P.O. Box 608685, Cleveland, OH 44108-0685 USA Tel 440-487-8413; Fax: 425-963-3821 Web site: http://www.asseenontheinternet.tv.

As Simple As That Publishing, *(978-0-9728666)* Orders Addr.: P.O. Box 25 Fern Road, Southampton, NY 11968 USA Web site: http://www.simpleasthat.com.

As Sparkle Speaks & Informs/ASSI, *(978-0-9706187)* Orders Addr.: P.O. Box 1313, Madison, TN 37116-1313 USA Tel 615-860-9762; Fax: 615-870-0959; Edit Addr.: 1672 Liberty Hill Dr., Madison, TN 37115 USA E-mail: searlessparkle@aol.com.

ASA Publishing Company *See* **ASA Publishing Corp.**

ASA Publishing Corp., *(978-1-886528; 978-0-615-13671-4; 978-0-615-14056-8; 978-0-615-14611-9; 978-0-615-15185-4; 978-0-615-15682-8; 978-0-615-17383-2; 978-0-615-18613-9; 978-0-615-18894-2; 978-0-615-21769-7; 978-0-615-21856-4; 978-0-615-25705-1; 978-0-615-26064-8; 978-0-615-26127-0; 978-0-615-27139-2; 978-0-615-27323-5; 978-0-9819570; 978-0-9841442; 978-0-9826490; 978-0-9828135; 978-0-615-44821-3; 978-0-615-46081-9; 978-0-615-46083-3; 978-0-615-46622-4; 978-0-615-46780-1; 978-0-615-47496-0; 978-0-615-47775-6; 97) 105 E. Front St., Suite 101, Monroe, MI 48161 USA Tel 734-230-7174; Fax: 734-230-7176* E-mail: asapublishingcorporation@gmail.com; asapublisher@gmail.com Web site: http://www.asapublishingcorporation.com/ *Dist(s):* **CreateSpace Independent Publishing Platform Ingram Content Group.**

ASA-CSSA-SSSA, *(978-0-89118)* 5585 Guilford Rd., Madison, WI 53711 USA (SAN 206-2879) Tel 608-268-4960; Fax: 608-273-2021 E-mail: books@agronomy.org; books@crops.org; books@soils.org Web site: http://www.soils.org; http://www.crops.org; http://www.agronomy.org.

Asbury Heritage Publishing, *(978-0-9859132)* 4601 Abercorne Terr., Louisville, KY 40241 USA Tel 502-897-3241; Fax: 502-897-3241 E-mail: bakerbutterfly@gmail.com.

Ascend Bks., LLC, *(978-0-9817166; 978-0-9841130; 978-0-9830619; 978-0-9836952; 978-0-9856314; 978-0-9889964; 978-0-9893095; 978-0-9912756; 978-0-9904375; 978-0-9961944; 978-0-9966742; 978-0-9989224; 978-1-7323447; 978-1-7344637)* 7221 W. 79th St. Suite 206, Overland Park, KS 66204 USA (SAN 856-3454) Tel 913-948-5500 E-mail: bsnodgrass@ascendbooks.com; mgore@ascendbooks.com Web site: http://www.ascendbooks.com *Dist(s):* **APG Sales & Distribution Services American West Bks.**

Ascend Media, LLC *See* **Ascend Bks., LLC**

Ascend Pr., *(978-0-9998571)* 67 Magnolia Farms Dr., Asheville, NC 28806 USA Tel 828-260-2645 E-mail: richardaab@gmail.com.

Ascended Ideas, *(978-0-9795103; 978-0-692-00063-2; 978-0-9823969)* P.O. Box 120, Coldiron, KY 40819-0120 USA Web site: http://www.ascendedideas.com.

Ascending Realm Publishing, *(978-0-9762135)* P.O. Box 2223, Centennial, CO 80161-2223 USA E-mail: brandon@ascendingrealm.com Web site: http://www.ascendingrealm.com.

Ascension Education, *(978-0-9640837)* Orders Addr.: P.O. Box 504, Venice, CA 90294 USA Tel 310-254-4092; Edit Addr.: 1814 Pacific Ave., No. 17, Venice, CA 90291 USA E-mail: ascension2020@comcast.net Web site: http://www.ascension-education.com.

Ascension Lutheran Church, *(978-0-9715472)* 314 W. Main St., Danville, VA 24541 USA Tel 434-792-5795; Fax: 434-799-3900 E-mail: chrismonsministry@gmail.com Web site: http://www.chrismon.org.

Ascension Pr., *(978-0-9659228; 978-0-9742238; 978-0-9744451; 978-1-932631; 978-1-932645; 978-1-932927; 978-1-934217; 978-1-935940; 978-1-945179; 978-1-950784)* Orders Addr.: W5180 Jefferson St., Necedah, WI 54646 USA (SAN 256-0224) Tel 608-565-2024; Fax: 608-565-2025; Toll Free: 800-376-0520; Edit Addr.: P.O. Box 1990, West Chester, PA 19341 USA Tel 610-696-7795; Fax: 610-696-7796; Toll Free: 800-376-0520; 20 Hagerty Blvd., Suite 3, West Chester, PA 19341 E-mail: mflickinger@ascensionpress.com Web site: http://www.ascensionpress.com *Dist(s):* **Follett School Solutions.**

Ascent Pubns., *(978-0-9815302)* P.O. Box 928, Warrenton, MO 63383 USA E-mail: michael@ascentpublications.com; info@ascentpublications.com Web site: http://www.ascentpublications.com.

Ascribed *Imprint of* **dg ink**

ASD Publishing, *(978-0-9836049; 978-0-9853441; 978-0-9961029)* 102 Arlington Ave., Hawthorne, NJ 07506 USA Tel 973-280-0145 E-mail: bbscout@hotmail.com *Dist(s):* **BookBaby.**

ASE Media, *(978-0-9768890)* 5777 Crowntree Ln. Apt 208, ORLANDO, FL 32829 USA E-mail: anne@easterlingfamily.com Web site: http://www.asemedia.com.

Ashay by the Bay, *(978-0-9704048)* Orders Addr.: P.O. Box 2394, Union City, CA 94587 USA Tel 510-477-0967; Edit Addr.: P.O. Box 2394, Union City, CA 94587-7394 USA E-mail: poetashay@aol.com Web site: http://www.ashaybythebay.com.

Ashberry Lane, *(978-0-9893967; 978-1-941720)* P.O. Box 665, Gaston, OR 97119 USA Tel 503-860-5069 E-mail: christina@ashberrylane.net Web site: www.ashberrylane.net.

Ashcroft, Yoko, *(978-0-9993077)* 9946 Clyde Cir., LITTLETON, CO 80129 USA Tel 720-308-8172 E-mail: yokoashcroft@yahoo.com.

Ashland Creek Pr. *Imprint of* **Byte Level Research**

Ashley & Taylor Publishing, Co., *(978-0-9745469)* P.O. Box 2793, Huntsville, AL 35804 USA Tel 256-430-1889 E-mail: AshleyTaylor4God@comcast.net.

AshleyAlan Enterprises, *(978-0-9702171; 978-0-9710145)* Orders Addr.: P.O. Box 1510, Kyle, TX 78640-1510 USA Tel 512-405-3065; Fax: 512-405-3066; Edit Addr.: 115 Hogan, Kyle, TX 78640 USA E-mail: celestem@kyle-tx.com Web site: http://www.ashleyanlan.com.

Ashlye V. Enterprises, LLC, *(978-0-9792934)* P.O. Box 3301, Columbia, SC 29230 USA Tel 803-361-1161; Fax: 803-772-2878; Toll Free: 866-382-3558 E-mail: ashlyev@gmail.com Web site: http://www.ashlyev.com.

Ashmolean Museum (GBR) *(978-0-900090; 978-0-907849; 978-1-85444) Dist. by* **Natl Bk Netwk.**

Ashtabula County Genealogical Society, *(978-1-888851)* 860 Sherman St., Geneva, OH 44041-9101 USA Tel 440-466-4521; Fax: 440-466-0162 E-mail: acgs@ashtabulagen.org Web site: http://www.ashtabulagen.org.

Ashtastical, *(978-0-9914211)* 1601 Pleasant Run Rd., Carrollton, TX 75006 USA Tel 214-893-4011 E-mail: Ash2b_me@hotmail.com.

Ashway Pr., *(978-0-9754575)* Div. of Ashway, 5624 Double Tree Cir., Birmingham, AL 35242 USA Tel 205-995-8482 E-mail: janetpeine@aol.com Web site: http://www.givingmeaway.com.

ASI, *(978-0-9759271)* 12 Brandywine Dr., Warwick, NY 10990 USA Web site: www.asipublishing.com.

Asia for Kids *Imprint of* **Infini Pr., LLC**

Asiana Media, *(978-0-9778944)* Orders Addr.: P.O. Box 13693, Tempe, AZ 85284-0062 USA Tel 602-743-7155; *Imprints:* Juice & Berries, The (The Juice & Ber) E-mail: info@asianamedia.com; info@thejuiceandberries.com Web site: http://www.asianamedia.com; http://www.thejuiceandberries.com; http://www.faithittomakeit.com.

Asimow, Dyanne, *(978-0-9859522)* 8071 Willow Glen Rd., Los Angeles, CA 90046 USA Tel 323-654-3075 E-mail: dyanne8071@sbcglobal.net.

ASJA Pr. *Imprint of* **iUniverse, Inc.**

ASK Publishing, L.L.C., *(978-0-9742967)* 34046 Jefferson Ave., St Clr Shores, MI 48082-1162 USA (SAN 255-4976) E-mail: admin@askpublishingllc.net Web site: http://www.askpublishingllc.net *Dist(s):* **Quality Bks., Inc.**

ASL Tales, *(978-0-9818139)* Orders Addr.: P.O. Box 80354, Portland, OR 97210 USA E-mail: info@asltales.net Web site: http://www.asltales.net *Dist(s):* **Follett School Solutions.**

Aslan Publishing, *(978-0-944031)* Owned by Renaissance Book Services Corp., 2490 Black Rock Tpke., No. 342, Fairfield, CT 06432 USA (SAN 242-6129) Fax: 203-374-4766; Toll Free: 800-786-5427 E-mail: information@AslanPublishing.com; harold@aslanpublishing.com; aslan@sevenlive.net Web site: http://www.AslanPublishing.com *Dist(s):* **APG Sales & Distribution Services.**

ASM Pr., *(978-0-914826; 978-1-55581; 978-1-68367; 978-0-578-19314-4)* Div. of American Society For Microbiology, 1752 N St., NW, Washington, DC 20036 USA (SAN 202-1153) Toll Free Fax: 1-800-546-1503; P.O. Box 605, Herndon, VA 20172 E-mail: books@asmusa.org Web site: http://www.asmpress.org; www.asmscience.org *Dist(s):* **Follett School Solutions MyiLibrary Rittenhouse Bk. Distributors Wiley, John & Sons, Inc. ebrary, Inc.**

ASMedia Publishing, *(978-0-9743407)* 299 Swanville Rd., Frankfort, ME 04438 USA Fax: 207-223-5241 E-mail: asmedia2002@aol.com.

Asmodee North America, Inc., *(978-1-887911; 978-1-58994; 978-1-61661; 978-1-63344)* 1995 Cty. Rd. B2 W, Roseville, MN 55113-2725 USA Web site: http://www.fantasyflightgames.com *Dist(s):* **Diamond Comic Distributors, Inc. Diamond Bk. Distributors.**

ASP Corp. Entertainment Group, Inc., *(978-0-9754147)* 3695 F Cascade Rd., Suite 229, Atlanta, GA 30331 USA Tel 404-344-7700; Fax: 404-344-7700 Web site: http://www.hannibaltrilogy.com.

Aspect *Imprint of* **Grand Central Publishing**

Aspect Bk. *Imprint of* **TEACH Services, Inc.**

Aspen Bks., *(978-1-56236)* Div. of Worldwide Pubs., Inc., P.O. Box 1271, Bountiful, UT 84011-1271 USA Toll Free: 800-748-4850 E-mail: jasay@qwest.net; prawlins@aspenbook.com *Dist(s):* **Cedar Fort, Inc./CFI Distribution Independent Pubs. Group Origin Bk. Sales, Inc.**

Aspen Light Publishing, *(978-0-9743620; 978-0-9834896; 978-0-9913920)* Orders Addr.: 13506 Summerport Village Pkwy. Suite #155, Windermere, FL 34786 USA Fax: 407-910-2453; Toll Free: 800-437-1695 E-mail: orders@aspenlightpublishing.com *Dist(s):* **DeVorss & Co.**

Aspen MLT, Inc., *(978-0-9774821; 978-0-9823628; 978-0-9854473; 978-1-941511; 978-1-944902; 978-1-946960)* 5855 Green Valley Cir. Suite 111, Culver City, CA 90230-9023 USA (SAN 257-6260) Fax: 310-348-9731 Web site: www.aspencomics.com *Dist(s):* **Diamond Comic Distributors, Inc. Diamond Bk. Distributors.**

Aspirations Media, Inc., *(978-0-9776043; 978-0-9800034)* 7755 Lakeview Ln., Spring Lake Park, MN 55432 USA (SAN 257-7305) Web site: http://www.aspirationsmediainc.com.

Aspire Publishing, *(978-0-9799021)* 30081 Canyon Creek, Trabuco Canyon, CA 92679 USA Web site: 4aspirebooks.com.

Aspiring Author's Ink., *(978-0-692-84269-0; 978-0-692-85975-9; 978-0-692-85976-6; 978-0-692-89859-8; 978-0-692-91465-6; 978-0-692-92876-9; 978-0-692-93998-7; 978-0-692-94523-0; 978-0-9994400; 978-0-692-97461-2; 978-1-7335709)* 6400 NW 106th PL, Alachua, FL 32615 USA Tel 352-363-4944 E-mail: kandraalbury@gmail.com Web site: kandraalbury.org.

Aspiring Families Press, *(978-0-9961941)* 12625 High Bluff Drive, Suite 104, Dan Diego, CA 92130 USA Tel 858-531-1122 E-mail: azmairamaker@gmail.com; j@monkeycmedia.com Web site: www.aspiringfamiliespress.com.

ASQ Quality Press *See* **Quality Pr.**

Associated Arts Pub., *(978-0-9840358)* 536 Tiara Dr., Grand Junction, CO 81507 USA Tel 970-241-8024 E-mail: suehughey@optimum.net Web site: http://SCStrange.com; HerbysSecretFormula.com *Dist(s):* **CreateSpace Independent Publishing Platform Follett School Solutions.**

Association for Supervision & Curriculum Development, *(978-0-87120; 978-1-4166)* 1703 N. Beauregaurd St., Alexandria, VA 22311 USA (SAN 201-1352) Tel 703-578-9600; Fax: 703-575-5400; Toll Free: 800-933-2723 E-mail: member@ascd.org; books@ascd.org; acquisitions@ascd.org Web site: http://www.ascd.org *Dist(s):* **Ebsco Publishing Follett School Solutions Ingram Content Group MyiLibrary ebrary, Inc.**

Assn. of Asthma Educators, *(978-0-9821228)* 1215 Anthony Ave., Columbia, SC 29201-1701 USA Tel 803-540-7530; Fax: 803-254-3773; Toll Free: 888-988-7747 E-mail: marie.queen@queencommunicationsllc.com Web site: http://www.asthmaeducators.org.

Assn. of Christian Schls. International, *(978-1-58331)* Orders Addr.: P.O. Box 65130, Colorado Springs, CO 80962-5130 USA; Edit Addr.: 731 Chapel Hills Dr., Colorado Springs, CO 80920 USA (SAN 689-5751) Tel 719-528-6906; Fax: 719-531-0631; Toll Free: 800-367-0798 (orders only) E-mail: webmaster@acsi.org; info@acsi.org Web site: http://www.acsi.org.

Association of Jewish Libraries, *(978-0-929262)* P.O. Box 1118, Teaneck, NJ 07666 USA E-mail: ajlibs@osu.edu; publications@jewishlibaries.org Web site: http://www.jewishlibraries.org.

Assouline (FRA) *(978-2-84323; 978-2-908228; 978-2-7594) Dist. by* **TwoRivers.**

AS-Sunnah Foundation of America *See* **Islamic Supreme Council of America**

Asta Publications, LLC, *(978-0-9777060; 978-1-934947)* Orders Addr.: 112 Black Oak Ct., Saintckbridge, GA 30281 USA Fax: 678-814-1370; Toll Free: 800-482-4190 E-mail: acollins@astapublications.com; astapubl@gmail.com; ahoward@astapublications.com Web site: http://www.astapublications.com *Dist(s):* **A & B Distributors & Pubs. Group.**

Astakos Publishing, (*978-0-9792991*) P.O. Box 227, Roscoe, IL 61073-9330 USA Tel 815-623-6616
E-mail: astakospublishing@charter.net
Web site: http://www.astakospublishing.com
Dist(s): **Follett School Solutions**
Quality Bks., Inc.

A-Star*, (*978-0-9858935*) 13 W. St. Apt. 2, Greenfield, MA 01301 USA Tel 415-505-5873
E-mail: info@adriennenunez.net
Web site: www.adriennenunez.net.

Asteroid Publishing, (*978-0-9841187*) 251 Middle Rd., Boxborough, MA 01719 USA Tel 978-549-0464
Dist(s): **Smashwords.**

Aston & James Publications *See* **Aston & James Publishing, LLC**

Aston & James Publishing, LLC, (*978-1-946745*) 500 N. Michigan Ave., Chicago, IL 60611 USA Tel 773-412-6212
Dist(s): **CreateSpace Independent Publishing Platform.**

Astonish Comics, (*978-0-9721259*) 10061 Riverside Dr., Suite No. 785, Toluca Lake, CA 91602 USA
Web site: http://www.theastonishfactory.com
Dist(s): **Diamond Comic Distributors, Inc.**
Diamond Bk. Distributors.

Astor Pr., (*978-0-9764119; 978-0-615-14497-9; 978-0-615-18601-6; 978-0-615-21360-6; 978-0-615-26465-3; 978-0-578-00527-0; 978-0-578-01799-0; 978-0-578-02611-4; 978-0-578-02667-1; 978-0-9899257; 978-1-949464*) 6 Prospect St., Maynard, MA 01754 USA
E-mail: mail@shanddaramon.com; klangerdude@gmail.com
Web site: http://www.astorpress.com; http://brassbellbooks.com
Dist(s): **Lulu Pr., Inc.**
Smashwords.

Astor-Honor, Inc., (*978-0-8392*) 16 E. 40th St., Third Flr., New York, NY 10016 USA (SAN 203-5022) Tel 212-840-8800; Fax: 212-840-7246.

Astra Publishing Hse., (*978-1-57565; 978-0-9819697; 978-1-940947; 978-1-63592; 978-1-6626*) 19 W 21st St, New York, NY 10177 USA; *Imprints:* StarBerry (StarBerry)
E-mail: tgonzalez@astrapublishinghouse.com; atrager@astrapublishinghouse.com
Web site: https://boydsmillsandkane.com/
Dist(s): **Children's Plus, Inc.**
Follett School Solutions
Lerner Publishing Group
MyiLibrary
Penguin Random Hse. Distribution
Penguin Random Hse. LLC.

Astral Publishing Co., (*978-0-9645867*) Orders Addr.: P.O. Box 3955, Santa Barbara, CA 93130-3955 USA (SAN 298-5705) Tel 805-967-7667; Edit Addr.: 333 Old Mill Rd., No. 324, Santa Barbara, CA 93110 USA
E-mail: wveigele@aol.com
Web site: http://www.astralpublishing.com
Dist(s): **Quality Bks., Inc.**

Astri My Astri Publishing, (*978-0-9760541; 978-0-9859712*) 602 3rd Ave. SW, Waukon, IA 52172 USA Tel 563-568-6229; Fax: 563-568-5377
E-mail: gourleyd@mchsi.com; deb@astrimyastri.com; gourleydeb@gmail.com
Web site: http://www.astrimyastri.com.

Astronaut Ink, (*978-0-9772727*) Orders Addr.: 180 Newbury St. 4106, Danvers, MA 01923 USA
E-mail: joe@popartproperties.com
Web site: http://www.popartproperties.com.

ASunnyDay Publishing, (*978-0-9818366*) 17 Hillside Ave., Suite 102, Rockville Centre, NY 11570 USA Tel 516-884-7661
E-mail: dariarosebooks@gmail.com
Web site: http://www.dariarosebooks.com.

At Ease Pr., (*978-0-917921*) Div. of Be at Ease School of Etiquette, 1212 W. Ben White Blvd., #214, Austin, TX 78704-7197 USA (SAN 656-9900)
E-mail: haroldalmon@gmail.com; schoolofetiquette@ateasepress.com
Web site: http://ateasepress.com; http://baeschoolofetiquette.blogspot.com/; http://baesoe.com
Dist(s): **Lulu Pr., Inc.**

At Home With Cristin *Imprint of* **Mill Creek Pr.**

At Peace Media, LLC, (*978-0-9742002*) 1117 E. Putnam Ave., No. 345, Riverside, CT 06878 USA Tel 203-698-2688; Fax: 203-698-3441; Toll Free: 800-575-7715
E-mail: john@atpeacemedia.com
Web site: http://www.atpeacemedia.com.

At Your Service of St. Louis County, LLC, (*978-0-9856611*) 73 Clermont Ln., St. Louis, MO 63124 USA Tel 314-994-1382; Fax: 314-997-6227
E-mail: katec1112@gmail.com
Web site: www.atyourservicestlcounty.com.

Atelier Finwhale, (*978-0-9882561*) P.O. Box 60608, Palo Alto, CA 94306-9991 USA Tel 650-787-2198
E-mail: 3marjorie14@gmail.com.

Atelier Mythologie, (*978-0-9899905; 978-1-945308*) 3815 E Pike, Seattle, WA 98122 USA Tel 206-724-4144
E-mail: publisher@ateliermythologie.com.

Atelier19, (*978-1-7325495*) 1570 26th Ave., San Francisco, CA 94122 USA Tel 415-205-4994
E-mail: info@bizibots.com
Web site: www.bizibots.com.

ATF Pr. (AUS) (*978-0-9586399; 978-1-920691; 978-1-921511; 978-1-921816; 978-0-646-29485-8; 978-0-646-35334-0; 978-1-922239; 978-1-925232; 978-1-925309; 978-1-925371; 978-1-925438; 978-1-925486; 978-1-925612; 978-1-925643; 978-1-925679; 978-1-925872*) *Dist. by* **ISD USA.**

Athanata Arts, Ltd., (*978-0-9727993*) P.O. Box 321, Garden City, NY 11530 USA (SAN 255-5018) Tel 516-742-8735
E-mail: info@athanata.com
Web site: http://www.athanata.com.

Athanatos Publishing Group, (*978-0-9791276; 978-0-9822776; 978-1-936830; 978-1-947844; 978-1-64594*) PO Box 57, Greenwood, WI 54437 USA (SAN 852-5234); *Imprints:* Suzeteo Enterprises (SuzeteoEnt)
E-mail: publisher@suzeteo.com
Web site: http://www.suzeteo.com.

Athenaeum Music & Arts Library *Imprint of* **Library Assn. of La Jolla**

Atheneum Bks. for Young Readers *Imprint of* **Simon & Schuster Children's Publishing**

Atheneum/Anne Schwartz Bks. *Imprint of* **Simon & Schuster Children's Publishing**

Atheneum/Caitlyn Dlouhy Books *Imprint of* **Simon & Schuster Children's Publishing**

Atheneum/Richard Jackson Bks. *Imprint of* **Simon & Schuster Children's Publishing**

Atherton Haight, (*978-0-9840678*) 2021 NW 65th St., No. 3, Seattle, WA 09117 USA (SAN 858-3358)
E-mail: info@athertonhaight.com
Web site: http://www.athertonhaight.com.

AthertonCustoms, (*978-0-578-00865-3; 978-0-615-33485-1; 978-0-9827167*) 6536 Aldergate Ln., Las Vegas, NV 89110 USA Tel 702-438-6596
E-mail: jim@athertoncustoms.com
Web site: http://www.athertoncustoms.com
Dist(s): **Lulu Pr., Inc.**

ATInternational Pubs., (*978-0-9773816*) 227 Sunflower Ln., West Windsor, NJ 08550-2439 USA
E-mail: atinetus@yahoo.com.

Atkinson, Janet Irene *See* **Irene, Jan Pubns.**

Atlantic Bks., Ltd. (GBR) (*978-1-903809; 978-1-84354; 978-1-84887; 978-0-85789; 978-0-85740; 978-1-78239; 978-1-78649*) *Dist. by* **IPG Chicago.**

Atlantic Bridge Publishing, (*978-0-9700930; 978-0-9706913; 978-1-931761; 978-1-59578; 978-1-62210*) 10509 Sedgegrass Dr., Indianapolis, IN 46235 USA Tel 317-826-8059 Do not confuse with Bridge Works Publishing Company, Inc. in Bridgehampton, NY
E-mail: linda@atlanticbridge.net
Web site: http://www.liquidsilverbooks.com; http://www.atlanticbridge.net
Dist(s): **INscribe Digital**
Independent Pubs. Group.

Atlantic Publishing Company *See* **Atlantic Publishing Group, Inc.**

Atlantic Publishing Group, Inc., (*978-0-910627; 978-1-60138; 978-1-62023*) 1405 SW. 6th Ave., Ocala, FL 34471-0640 USA (SAN 268-1250) Toll Free: 800-814-1132 Do not confuse with companies with the same or similar name in Tabor City, NC , Aurora, IL , Lakeland, FL , Combs, KY , Neosho, MO
E-mail: info@atlantic-pub.com; sales@atlantic-pub.com
Web site: http://www.atlantic-pub.com
Dist(s): **MyiLibrary.**

Atlantida (ARG) (*978-950-08*) *Dist. by* **AIMS Intl.**

Atlas Games *Imprint of* **Trident, Inc.**

Atlas Publishing *Imprint of* **Atlas Publishing LLC**

Atlas Publishing LLC, (*978-0-9969679; 978-1-945033*) 42072 5th St Suite 103, Temecula, CA 92590 USA Tel 858-222-3747; *Imprints:* Atlas Publishing (AtlasP)
E-mail: permissions@atlaspublishing.biz; brent@atlaspublishing.biz
Web site: http://www.atlaspublishing.biz
Dist(s): **Ingram Publisher Services.**

Atma Global Knowledge Media, Inc., (*978-0-9905459; 978-1-943967*) 41 W. 25th St., New York, NY 10010 USA Tel 212-254-0083; *Imprints:* Full Circle Media, Inc. (FullCircleMedia)
E-mail: spdunung@msn.com; sdunung@atmaglobal.com; sarora@atmaglobal.com
Web site: www.maddieandsayara.com; www.fcmediainc.com; www.atmaglobal.com.

Atom Pr., 926 Flemington St., Pittsburgh, PA 15217 USA Tel 951-801-0391
E-mail: atomtitan@hotmail.com.

Atombank Bks., (*978-0-9905160*) 111 Pheasant Walk, Guilderland, NY 12303 USA Tel 518-421-5962
E-mail: atombankbooks@gmail.com
Web site: atombankbooks.com.

Atomic Basement, 1222 N. Commonwealth Ave. Apt. No. 4, Los Angeles, CA 90029-2058 USA Tel 386-679-9106
E-mail: oilerhggns@aol.com.

Atomic Fruit Pr., (*978-0-9753225*) 404 13th Ave., Huntington, WV 25701 USA
Web site: http://www.apocalyptictangerine.com.

Atria Bks. *Imprint of* **Simon & Schuster**

Atria Bks *Imprint of* **Atria Bks.**

Atria Bks., Div. of Simon & Schuster, 1230 Avenue of the Americas, 13th Flr., New York, NY 10020 USA; *Imprints:* Beyond Words/Atria Books (AtriaBks); Atria Books (AtriBksimp); Keywords Press (Keywords Press)
Dist(s): **Follett School Solutions**
MyiLibrary
Simon & Schuster, Inc.

Atria/Emily Bestler Bks. *Imprint of* **Atria/Emily Bestler Bks.**

Atria/Emily Bestler Bks., 1230 Avenue of the Americas, New York, NY 10020 USA; *Imprints:* Atria/Emily Bestler Books (AEBB)
Dist(s): **Simon & Schuster, Inc.**

Atrium Publishing, Incorporated *See* **mTrellis Publishing, Inc.**

Attack The Text / Magedo Publishing *See* **Attack The Text Publishing**

Attack The Text Publishing, (*978-0-9755923; 978-0-9842882*) 905 N. Pacific St., No. C, Oceanside, CA 92831 USA
Web site: http://www.attackthetext.com; http://www.magedo.com.

Attainment Co., Inc., (*978-0-934731; 978-1-57861; 978-1-943148; 978-1-944315; 978-1-64856*) Orders Addr.: P.O. Box 930160, Verona, WI 53593 USA (SAN 694-1656) Tel 608-845-7880; Fax: 608-845-8040; Toll Free: 800-327-4269; Edit Addr.: 504 Commerce Pkwy., Verona, WI 53953 USA (SAN 631-6174); *Imprints:* IEP Resources (IEP Res)
E-mail: info@attainmentcompany.com; sue@attainmentcompany.com; ameyer@attainmentcompany.com
Web site: http://www.attainmentcompany.com/
Dist(s): **Follett School Solutions**
Linx Educational Publishing, Inc.
Sunburst Communications, Inc.

Attic Studio Pr. *Imprint of* **Attic Studio Publishing Hse.**

Attic Studio Publishing Hse., (*978-1-883551*) Orders Addr.: P.O. Box 75, Clinton Corners, NY 12514 USA (SAN 298-2838) Tel 845-266-8100; Edit Addr.: 564 Schultzville Rd., Clinton Corners, NY 12514 USA (SAN 298-2846); *Imprints:* Attic Studio Press (Attic Studio); Maple Corners Press (Maple Corners Pr)
E-mail: collegeavepress@aol.com; atticstudiopress@aol.com
Dist(s): **BookBaby**
Emerald Bk. Co.
Spring Arbor Distributors, Inc.

Atticus, C. J., (*978-0-9887780*) 41 Radford Ct. Sw, Marietta, GA 30060 USA Tel 770-805-9422
E-mail: atticus@cjatticus.com.

Attitude Pie Publishing, (*978-0-692-01275-8; 978-0-692-90265-3*) 2100 NE 214th St., North Miami Beach, FL 33179 USA Tel 305-725-0446; 419-281-5100 (x 1151)
E-mail: MPYANOWSKI@BOOKMASTERS.COM
Dist(s): **Baker & Taylor Publisher Services (BTPS).**

Attitude Pr. Inc.,

Attitudes in Dressing, Inc., (*978-0-9766640*) 1350 Broadway, New York, NY 10018 USA Tel 212-279-3492; Fax: 212-564-3426; Toll Free: 800-899-0503
Web site: http://www.bodywrappers.com.

ATU Golden Pubns., (*978-0-9753119*) 8283 Main St., Bokeelia, FL 33922 USA
E-mail: chrissydl@aol.com
Web site: http://www.pgaa.com.

Auckland Univ. Pr. (NZL) (*978-1-86940; 978-1-77558; 978-0-9941465-0-2*) *Dist. by* **IPG Chicago.**

Auctus Pubs., (*978-0-9979607; 978-1-7327882; 978-1-7334456*) 606 Merion Avenue, First Flr., Havertown, PA 19083 USA Tel 267-736-3003; Fax: 267-736-3003
E-mail: info@auctuspublishers.com
Web site: Auctuspublishers.com.

Audeamus LLC, (*978-0-615-29498-8; 978-0-615-53342-1; 978-0-615-58386-0; 978-0-9855110; 978-0-9890362; 978-0-9969259*) 3652 YOUNG WOLF Dr., Simi Valley, CA 93065 USA.

Audible Studios on Brilliance Audio *Imprint of* **Brilliance Publishing, Inc.**

Audio Bookshelf, (*978-1-883332; 978-0-9741711; 978-0-9761932; 978-0-9814890; 978-1-935430*) Orders Addr.: 44 Ocean View Dr., Middletown, RI 02842 USA Tel 401-849-2333; Fax: 401-842-0440; Toll Free: 800-234-1713; Edit Addr.: P.O. Box 83, Belfast, ME 04915-0083 USA
E-mail: dd@audiobookshelf.com
Web site: http://www.audiobookshelf.com
Dist(s): **AudioGO**
Follett School Solutions
Landmark Audiobooks
Professional Media Service Corp.

Audio Craft Press *See* **AudioCraft Publishing, Inc.**

Audio Holdings, LLC, (*978-1-60136*) P.O. Box 119, Franklin Park, NJ 08823 USA (SAN 851-0776) Tel 732-940-4286; Fax: 732-940-0534
E-mail: mgladishev@gmail.com
Dist(s): **Ebsco Publishing.**

Audio Partners, Incorporated *See* **Audio Partners Publishing Corp.**

Audio Partners Publishing Corp., (*978-0-88690; 978-0-945353; 978-1-57270*) 42 Whitecap Dr., North Kingstown, RI 02852-7445 USA (SAN 253-4622) Toll Free Fax: 877-492-0873; Toll Free: 800-621-0182
E-mail: info@audiopartners.com
Dist(s): **Follett School Solutions**
Landmark Audiobooks
Two Rivers Distribution.

Audio Renaissance *See* **Macmillan Audio**

AudioCraft Publishing, Inc., (*978-1-893699; 978-1-942950*) Orders Addr.: P.O. Box 281, Topinabee, MI 49791 USA Tel 231-238-0338; Fax: 231-238-0339; Toll Free: 888-420-4244; Edit Addr.: P.O. Box 281, Topinabee, MI 49791 USA
E-mail: ck@americanchillers.com; store@americanchillers.com; shawn@americanchillers.com
Web site: http://www.audiocraftpublishing.com; http://www.michiganchillers.com; http://www.americanchillers.com
Dist(s): **Follett School Solutions**
Partners Bk. Distributing, Inc.

†AudioGO, (*978-0-563; 978-0-7540; 978-0-7927; 978-0-89340; 978-1-55504; 978-1-60283; 978-1-60998; 978-1-62064; 978-1-62460; 978-1-4815; 978-1-4821*) Orders Addr.: c/o Perseus, 1094 Flex Dr., Jackson, TN 38301 USA; Edit Addr.: 42 Whitecap Dr., North Kingstown, RI 02852-7445 USA (SAN 858-7701) Toll Free: 800-621-0182; *Imprints:* Sound Library (SoundLib)
E-mail: laura.almeida@audiogo.com
Web site: http://www.audiogo.com/us/
Dist(s): **Ebsco Publishing**
Findaway World, LLC
Follett School Solutions
INscribe Digital
Two Rivers Distribution; *CIP.*

Audioscope, (*978-1-57375*) Div. of K-tel International (USA), Inc., 2605 Fernbrook Ln., N., No. H-O, Plymouth, MN 55447 USA Tel 612-559-6888; Fax: 612-559-6848; Toll Free: 800-328-6640
Web site: http://www.ktel.com
Dist(s): **Follett School Solutions.**

Audisee Sound & Music, (*978-0-9666910; 978-1-930827; 978-0-9980365*) 6736 38th, SW, Seattle, WA 98126 USA Tel 206-938-2347; Fax: 206-938-0163
E-mail: audisee@audisee.com
Web site: http://www.CarTours.org.

Auditors of God, The (GBR) (*978-0-9561587; 978-0-9572919*) *Dist. by* **LuluCom.**

Audrey Pr., (*978-1-936426*) P.O. Box 6113, Maryville, TN 37802 USA Tel 865-254-4463
E-mail: valarie@audreypress.com
Web site: www.audreypress.com.

Audrey Productions, (*978-0-9722673*) 7809 Paper Flower Ct., Las Vegas, NV 89128 USA Tel 702-228-4803 (phone/fax)
Dist(s): **Follett School Solutions.**

Audubon Pr. & Christian Bk. Service, (*978-0-9652883; 978-0-9742365; 978-0-9820731*) Orders Addr.: P.O. Box 8055, Laurel, MS 39441 USA Tel 601-649-8572; Fax: 601-649-8571; Toll Free: 800-405-3788; Edit Addr.: 2601 Audubon Dr., Laurel, MS 39440 USA
E-mail: buybooks@audubonpress.com
Web site: http://www.audubonpress.com.

Augsburg Bks. *Imprint of* **Augsburg Fortress, Pubs.**

†Augsburg Fortress, Pubs., (*978-0-8006; 978-0-8066; 978-1-4514; 978-1-5064*) Orders Addr.: P.O. Box 1209, Minneapolis, MN 55440-1209 USA (SAN 169-4081) Toll Free Fax: 800-722-7766; Toll Free: 800-328-4648 (orders only); Edit Addr.: 510 Marquette 8th Fl., Minneapolis, MN 55402 USA Tel 800-328-4648 800-722-7766; *Imprints:* Fortress Press (Fortress Pr); Augsburg Books (Augsburg Bks); Sparkhouse Family (Sparkhse); Beaming Books (Beaming Bks)
E-mail: customerservice@augsburgfortress.org; info@augsburgfortress.org; subscriptions@augsburgfortress.org; copyright@augsburgfortress.org; international@augsburgfortress.org
Web site: http://www.augsburgfortress.org
Dist(s): **National Bk. Network**
ebrary, Inc.; *CIP.*

Augsburg Fortress Publishers, Publishing House of The Evangelical Lutheran Church in America *See* **Augsburg Fortress, Pubs.**

†August Hse. Pubs., Inc., (*978-0-87483; 978-0-935304; 978-1-939160; 978-1-941459; 978-1-941460; 978-1-947301*) 3500 Piedmont Rd. NE, Suite 310, Atlanta, GA 30305 USA (SAN 223-7288) Tel 404-442-4425; Fax: 404-442-4435; Toll Free: 800-284-8784; 3500 Piedmont Rd. Suite 310, Atlanta, GA 30305; *Imprints:* August House Story Cove (August Hse Story Cove)
E-mail: ahinfo@augusthouse.com; order@augusthouse.com
Web site: http://www.augusthouse.com
Dist(s): **Findaway World, LLC**
Follett School Solutions; *CIP.*

August House Story Cove *Imprint of* **August Hse. Pubs., Inc.**

August in Au Train Press, (*978-0-9904124*) P.O. Box 6, Au Train, MI 49806 USA Tel 810-516-1434
E-mail: kwujciak@stadiumadventureseries.com
Web site: stadiumadventureseries.com.

August Too Publishing, (*978-0-9767103*) 1346 E. Poinsettia St., Long Beach, CA 90805-3128 USA
E-mail: writeme@paulcarhart.com.

Augusta Win Publishing, (*978-0-9766597*) Orders Addr.: P.O. Box 53, Turin, NY 13473 USA; Edit Addr.: 6159 W. Main, Turin, NY 13473 USA
E-mail: augustawinpub@yahoo.com
Web site: http://www.augustawinpublishing.com.

Augustana College Geology Dept. Pr., (*978-0-9797015*) 639 38th St., Rock Island, IL 61201-2296 USA Tel 309-794-7318; Fax: 309-794-7564
Web site: http://www.augustana.edu.

Augustine Pr., (*978-0-9626431*) 900 Old Koenig Ln., No. 135, Austin, TX 78756 USA Tel 512-459-5194; Fax: 512-451-0755
E-mail: morganp@flash.net.

Augustinians of the Assumption *See* **Ambassador Bks., Inc.**

Augustus Publishing, (*978-0-9759453; 978-0-9792816; 978-0-9825415; 978-1-935883; 978-0-578-50932-7; 978-0-578-58774-5*) Div. of Augustus Productions, 600 W. 218 St., Suite 3K, New York, NY 10034 USA Tel 646-526-7998
E-mail: jc@augustuspublishing.com; gfhood1@aol.com; aw@augustuspublishing.com
Web site: http://www.augustuspublishing.com
Dist(s): **A & B Distributors & Pubs. Group**
Follett School Solutions
MyiLibrary
Publishers Group West (PGW).

Aunt Patty's Travels-London, (*978-0-9659668*) 4811 Wesleyan Woods Dr., Macon, GA 31210 USA.

Aunt Strawberry Bks., *(978-0-9669988)* Orders Addr.: P.O. Box 819, Boulder, CO 80306-0819 USA (SAN 299-9811) Tel 303-449-3574; Fax: 303-444-9221
E-mail: readasbs@hotmail.com
Dist(s): **Brodart Co.**
Follett School Solutions.

Auntielynny Publications *See* **Chanticlair Publishing**

Aunty Ems Boutique, *(978-0-9742122)* P.O. Box 1963, Havasu Lake Landing, CA 92363 USA.

Aura Printing, Inc., *(978-0-911643)* 88 Parkville Ave., Brooklyn, NY 11230 USA (SAN 237-9317) Tel 718-435-9103; Fax: 718-871-9488
Dist(s): **Bookazine Co., Inc.**

Aura Productions LLC *See* **Simple Ink, LLC**

Aurandt, Paul H II, *(978-0-9887774)* 1035 Pk. Ave., River Forest, IL 60305 USA Tel 708-366-5371; Fax: 708-366-9184
E-mail: paul@paulharvey.com
Web site: http://www.paulharvey.com.

Auricle Ink Pubs., *(978-0-9661826; 978-0-9825785)* P.O. Box 20607, Sedona, AZ 86341 USA Tel 928-284-0860
E-mail: rcarmen27@yahoo.com
Web site: http://www.hearingproblems.com
Dist(s): **Academic Bk. Ctr., Inc.**
Bk. Hse., Inc., The
Brodart Co.
Coutts Information Services
Emery-Pratt Co.
Follett School Solutions
Franklin Bk. Co., Inc.
Majors, J. A. Co.
Matthews Medical Bk. Co.
Midwest Library Service
Yankee Bk. Peddler, Inc.

Auriga, Ediciones S.A. (ESP) *(978-84-7281) Dist. by* **Continental Bk.**

Aurora Books *Imprint of* **Eco-Justice Pr., LLC**

Aurora Bks., *(978-0-9753508)* 512 Willow Branch Rd., Norman, OK 73072 USA
E-mail: aurorabooks@netzero.net.

Aurora Libris Corp., *(978-1-932233)* 40 E. 83rd St., Apt. 35, New York, NY 10028 USA Toll Free: 866-763-8411
E-mail: lavinia@laviniasworld.com
Web site: http://www.laviniasworld.com.

Aurora Metro Pubns. Ltd. (GBR) *(978-0-9515877; 978-0-9536757; 978-0-9542330; 978-0-9546912; 978-0-9551566; 978-1-906582; 978-0-9566329) Dist. by* **Consort Bk Sales.**

Aurora Metro Pubns. Ltd. (GBR) *(978-0-9515877; 978-0-9536757; 978-0-9542330; 978-0-9546912; 978-0-9551566; 978-1-906582; 978-0-9566329) Dist. by* **PerseuPGW.**

Aurora Pubs., Inc., *(978-0-9791758)* Orders Addr.: 5970 S.W. 18th St., No. 117, Boca Raton, FL 33433-7197 USA; Edit Addr.: 814 N. Franklin St., Chicago, IL 60610 USA; *Imprints:* Kids' Library (Kids Lib)
E-mail: aurorapublishers@aol.com
Web site: http://www.aurorapublishers.com
Dist(s): **Ebsco Publishing**
Follett School Solutions
Independent Pubs. Group
MyiLibrary.

Aurora Publishing, Incor[porated *See* **Aurora Publishing, Inc.**

Aurora Publishing, Inc., *(978-1-934496)* 3655 Torrance Blvd., Suite 430, Torrance, CA 90503 USA; *Imprints:* Deux (Deux); LuvLuv (LuvLuv) Do not confuse with companies with the same or similar name in Arljgton, VA, College Grove, TN,, West Palm Beach, FL, Eagle River, AK, West Hartford, CT, Fort Lauderdale, FL
E-mail: info@aurora-publishing.com
Web site: http://www.aurora-publishing.com; http://www.deux-press.com; http://www.luvluv-press.com
Dist(s): **Diamond Comic Distributors, Inc.**
Diamond Bk. Distributors.

Austin & Charlie Adventures *Imprint of* **Paw Print Pubns.**

Austin & Company, Inc., *(978-0-9657153)* 104 S. Union St., Suite 202, Traverse City, MI 49684 USA (SAN 631-1466) Tel 231-933-4649; Fax: 231-933-4659
E-mail: aandn@aol.com
Web site: http://www.austinandcompanyinc.com.

Austin & Nelson Publishing *See* **Austin & Company, Inc.**

Austin Christopher Swift, *(978-0-9764208)* 154 Golden Autumn Pl., Woodlands, TX 77384 USA Tel 956-421-5750; Fax: 956-421-5721
E-mail: john@toppmarketing.com.

Austin, Dorothy, *(978-0-578-40192-8)* 4948 S. Forrestville Garden unit, Chicago, IL 60615 USA Tel 312-835-0403
E-mail: DorithyAustin4948@gmail.com
Dist(s): **Independent Pub.**

Austin Energy Green Building Program, *(978-0-9679069)* Orders Addr.: P.O. Box 1088, Austin, TX 78767 USA Tel 512-322-6172; Fax: 512-505-3711; Edit Addr.: 721 Barton Springs Rd., Austin, TX 78704 USA
E-mail: dick.peterson@austinenergy.com
Web site: http://www.austinenergy.com.

Austin, Laurie , *(978-0-578-18226-1)* 15627 158th Ave SE, Renton, WA 98058 USA.

Austin Macauley Pubs. Ltd. (GBR) *(978-1-905609; 978-1-84963; 978-1-78455; 978-1-78554; 978-1-78629; 978-1-78612; 978-1-78823; 978-1-78693; 978-1-78710; 978-1-78848; 978-1-78878; 978-1-5289) Dist. by* **LightSource CS.**

Austin, Nanette, *(978-0-9600409)* 540 Strathaven Ct., Turlock, CA 95382 USA Tel 209-613-1622
E-mail: nan@nanaustinink.com
Web site: www.nanaustinink.com.

Austin, Stephen F. State Univ. Pr., *(978-1-936205; 978-1-62288)* Orders Addr.: P.O. Box 13002, Nacogdoches, TX 75962 USA Tel 936-468-1078; Fax: 936-468-2614; Edit Addr.: 1936 North St. Liberal Arts N., 203 English, Nacogdoches, TX 75962 USA
Dist(s): **MyiLibrary**
Texas A&M Univ. Pr.
ebrary, Inc.

Australian Academic Pr. (AUS) *(978-1-875378; 978-1-921513; 978-1-922117; 978-1-925644) Dist. by* **IngramPubServ.**

Australian Fishing Network (AUS) *(978-0-9587143; 978-1-86513; 978-1-86252-412-5; 978-0-646-00117-3; 978-0-646-15871-6; 978-0-646-19310-6; 978-0-646-20528-1; 978-0-646-20908-1; 978-0-646-21731-4; 978-0-646-24873-8; 978-0-646-25433-3; 978-0-646-25434-0; 978-0-646-30130-3; 978-0-646-31918-6) Dist. by* **Cardinal.**

Authentic Media (GBR) *(978-0-8499; 978-0-85009; 978-1-86024; 978-1-78078) Dist. by* **EMI CMG Dist.**

Autherine Publishing, *(978-0-9912000)* 306 Burleigh Ct., Winter Springs, FL 32708 USA Tel 407-542-5002
E-mail: JanetAutherine@GrowIntoGreatness.com; Autherine@aol.com
Web site: www.GrowintoGreatness.com; www.janetautherine.com.

Author Academy Elite, *(978-0-692-31830-0; 978-1-943526; 978-1-946114; 978-0-692-85391-7; 978-1-64085; 978-0-692-88922-0; 978-0-578-57522-3; 978-1-64746)* P.O. Box 43, Powell, OH 43065 USA Tel 740-272-0093
Dist(s): **CreateSpace Independent Publishing Platform.**

Author at Work *Imprint of* **Owen, Richard C. Pubs., Inc.**

Author Pubns., *(978-0-9724987)* P.O. Box 927, Turlock, CA 95381-0927 USA
E-mail: ochoa_f@msn.com
Web site: http://www.gonzostation.org.

Author Solutions, Inc., Div. of Penguin Group (USA) Inc., 1663 Liberty Dr., Bloomington, IN 47403 USA Tel 812-334-5223; Toll Free: 877-655-1722; *Imprints:* WestBow Press (WestBowPr); Balboa Press (BalboaPr); Inspiring Voices (InspVoices); Abbott Press (AbbottPr); PartridgeIndia (PARTRIDGEINDIA)
E-mail: sfurr@authorsolutions
Web site: http://www.authorsolutions.com
Dist(s): **Baker & Taylor Publisher Services (BTPS)**
CreateSpace Independent Publishing Platform
Xlibris Corp.
Zondervan.

AuthorHouse, *(978-1-58500; 978-0-9675669; 978-1-58721; 978-1-58820; 978-0-7596; 978-1-4033; 978-1-4107; 978-1-4140; 978-1-4184; 978-1-4208; 978-1-4259; 978-1-4343; 978-1-4389; 978-1-4490; 978-1-4520; 978-1-61764; 978-1-4567; 978-1-4582; 978-1-4624; 978-1-4633; 978-1-4634; 978-0-9846457; 978-1-4670; 978-1-4678; 978-1-4685; 978-1-4772; 978-1-4817; 978-1-4918; 978-1-4969; 978-1-5049; 978-1-5065; 978-1-5246; 978-1-5462; 978-1-7283; 978-1-6655) Div. of Author Solutions, Inc., 1663 Liberty Dr., Suite 200, Bloomington, IN 47403 USA (SAN 253-7605) Fax: 812-336-5449; Toll Free: 888-519-5121; Imprints:* Life Rich Publishing (Life Rich Pub)
E-mail: authorsupport@authorhouse.com; sfurr@authorsolutions.com
Web site: http://www.authorhouse.com
Dist(s): **Author Solutions, Inc.**
Baker & Taylor Publisher Services (BTPS)
BookBaby
CreateSpace Independent Publishing Platform
Follett School Solutions
Ingram Publisher Services
Lulu Pr., Inc.
MyiLibrary
Smashwords.

AuthorMike Ink *See* **AM Ink Publishing**

Authors & Artists Publishers of New York, Inc., *(978-0-9708053; 978-0-9724922; 978-0-9740683; 978-0-9754298; 978-0-9763993; 978-0-9766716; 978-0-9771482; 978-0-9786211; 978-0-9787113; 978-0-9819746; 978-0-9825971; 978-0-9839121; 978-0-9850947)* 21 Sta. Rd. Suite 211, Wilton, CT 06897 USA; *Imprints:* Ithaca Press (IthacaPress)
Web site: http://www.ithacapress.com
Dist(s): **Follett School Solutions.**

Authors Choice Pr. *Imprint of* **iUniverse, Inc.**

Author's Connection Pr., *(978-0-927206)* 777 College Pk. Dr., SW No. 60, Albany, OR 97322-8430 USA
Web site: http://www.acpublish.com.

Authors' Discovery Cooperation, Inc., *(978-0-9794443; 978-0-9800854; 978-0-9844730)* 165 Cherry Ln., Robert Lee, TX 76945 USA (SAN 853-4276) Tel 325-453-4595
E-mail: ldudney@nwol.net
Web site: http://www.authorsdiscovery.com.

Authors Pen, LLC, The, *(978-0-9906711; 978-1-948248)* 16415 Lynn Crest, Houston, TX 77083 USA Tel 904-613-6299
E-mail: info@tapwriting.com
Web site: www.tapwriting.com.

Authors Pr., *(978-1-947995; 978-1-948653; 978-1-64314)* Orders Addr.: 1321 Buchanan Rd, Pittsburg, 94565 SUN; Edit Addr.: 1321 Buchanan Rd, Pittsburg, CA 94565 USA Tel 925-698-2619.

Authors' Press, The *See* **Quantum Manifestations Publishing**

Author's Publishing, LLC, *(978-0-9728902; 978-1-60415)* 104 Lake June Rd. NW, Lake Placid, FL 33852 USA
E-mail: debono@strato.net
Web site: http://www.fantasyreaders.com.

Autism & Behavior Training Associates *See* **ABTA Pubns. & Products**

Autism Asperger Publishing Co., *(978-0-9672514; 978-1-931282; 978-1-934575; 978-1-937473; 978-1-942197)* Orders Addr.: P.O. Box 23173, Overland Park, KS 66283-0173 USA Tel 913-599-3311; Fax: 913-492-2546; 11209 Strang Line Rd, Lenexa, KS 66215 (SAN 920-9220); Edit Addr.: 15490 Qunvira, Overland Park, KS 66221 USA
E-mail: kmcbr41457@aol.com
Web site: http://www.asperger.net
Dist(s): **Follett School Solutions**
Independent Pubs. Group.

Autism Research Institute, *(978-0-9740360)* 4182 Adams Ave., San Diego, CA 92116 USA Fax: 619-563-6840
E-mail: salt97302@yahoo.com
Web site: http://www.autismresearchinstitute.com.

Automatic Pictures Publishing, *(978-0-9818737; 978-0-9892221; 978-0-9912729)* 5721 Valley Oak Dr., Los Angeles, CA 90068 USA Tel 323-935-1800; Fax: 323-935-8040
E-mail: automaticstudio@gmail.com
Web site: http://www.lookingglasswars.com
Dist(s): **Diamond Comic Distributors, Inc.**
Diamond Bk. Distributors
Publishers Group West (PGW).

Automatic Publishing *See* **Automatic Pictures Publishing**

Automobile Assn. (GBR) *(978-0-7495; 978-0-86145; 978-0-901088; 978-1-872163) Dist. by* **IPG Chicago.**

Automobile Assn. (GBR) *(978-0-7495; 978-0-86145; 978-0-901088; 978-1-872163) Dist. by* **Trafalgar.**

Automobiles-Memory Lane Publishing, *(978-0-9746667)* Orders Addr.: P.O. Box 228, Vicksburg, MI 49097 USA (SAN 255-7118) Tel 269-649-3614 (phone/fax); Edit Addr.: 2294 E. VW Ave., Vicksburg, MI 49097 USA.

Autonomedia, *(978-0-936756; 978-1-57027)* Orders Addr.: P.O. Box 568, Brooklyn, NY 11211-0568 USA; Edit Addr.: 55 S. Eleventh St., #4b, Brooklyn, NY 11211-0568 USA (SAN 221-3869) Tel 718-963-2603
E-mail: info@autonomedia.org
Web site: http://www.autonomedia.org
Dist(s): **AK Pr. Distribution**
Lulu Pr., Inc.
SPD-Small Pr. Distribution.

Autumn Arch Publishing, *(978-0-9904504; 978-0-9992026; 978-1-7338095)* 3115 Blue Ridge Ct NE, Cedar Rapids, IA 52402 USA Tel 319-200-6398
E-mail: aaron@aaronbunce.com
Web site: autumnarchpublishing.com.

Autumn Gold Pr., *(978-0-9972158)* 5374 Dunwoody Club Creek, ATLANTA, GA 30360 USA Tel 770-396-7001
E-mail: geliad@bellsouth.net
Web site: geliawrites.com.

Autumn Hill Bks., Inc., *(978-0-9754444; 978-0-9843036; 978-0-9827466; 978-0-9987400)* P.O. Box 22, Iowa City, IA 52244 USA Tel 319-354-2456; 814 N. Franklin St., Chicago, IL 60610
E-mail: info@autumnhillbooks.com
Web site: http://www.autumnhillbooks.com
Dist(s): **Ebsco Publishing**
Follett School Solutions
Independent Pubs. Group
MyiLibrary.

Autumn Hse. Publishing, *(978-0-9637825)* Orders Addr.: P.O. Box 763833, Dallas, TX 75376 USA; Edit Addr.: 1535 Acapulco Dr., Dallas, TX 75232 USA Tel 214-376-8959 Do not confuse with the same or similar name in Lexington, KY, Hagerstown, MD
E-mail: millijp@earthlink.net.

Autumn Hse. Publishing Co., *(978-0-8127; 978-1-878951)* Div. of Review & Herald Publishing Assn., 55 W. Oakridge Dr., Hagerstown, MD 21740 USA Do not confuse with companies with the same name in Lexington, KY, Dallas, TX.

Autumn Publishing Group, LLC, *(978-1-890877)* Orders Addr.: P.O. Box 71604, Madison Heights, MI 48071 USA Tel 248-589-5249; Fax: 248-585-5715; Toll Free: 888-876-4114; Edit Addr.: 30755 Barrington Ave., Madison Heights, MI 48071 USA
Web site: http://www.wiredin.net/childcare
Dist(s): **Unique Bks., Inc.**

Autumn's End Pr., *(978-0-9984076)* P.O. Box 999, Tacoma, WA 98401 USA Tel 253-225-0702
E-mail: contact@byjenn.com
Web site: www.byjenn.com.

Auzou, Philippe Editions (FRA) *(978-2-7338) Dist. by* **Consort Bk Sales.**

AV2 by Weigl *Imprint of* **Weigl Pubs., Inc.**

Avalerion Bks., Inc., *(978-0-9834119)* 190 Beagle Rd., Bethel, PA 19507 USA Tel 717-933-9999
E-mail: avalerionbooks@yahoo.com.

Avalon Publishing, *(978-0-7867; 978-0-912528; 978-0-918373; 978-0-929654; 978-0-931188; 978-0-935701; 978-0-941423; 978-0-945465; 978-0-9603322; 978-1-56025; 978-1-56201; 978-1-56261; 978-1-56691; 978-1-56858; 978-1-56924; 978-1-57354; 978-1-58005; 978-1-878067; 978-1-59880; 978-1-60094; 978-1-61237; 978-1-61238; 978-1-63121; 978-1-64049; 978-1-64171) Div. of Perseus Books Group, 1700 4th St., Berkeley, CA 94710-1711 USA (SAN 221-7406); Imprints:* Westview Press (WstvwPr)
Web site: http://www.avalonpub.com
Dist(s): **Bilingual Pubns. Co., The**
CreateSpace Independent Publishing Platform
Ebsco Publishing
Follett School Solutions
Hachette Bk. Group
MyiLibrary
Publishers Group West (PGW)
ebrary, Inc.

Avant Garde Publishing *See* **The Publishing Place LLC**

Avant-garde Bks., *(978-0-9743676; 978-0-9908992; 978-0-9977566; 978-1-946753)* Orders Addr.: P.O. Box 566, Mableton, GA 30126 USA Tel 770-739-4039 Do not confuse with Avant garde Publishing in Norman, OK
E-mail: brightsmile.hardy@live.com
Web site: www.avantgardebooks.net.

Avant-garde Publishing Company *See* **Avant-garde Bks.**

Avari Pr., *(978-1-933770)* 2198 Old Philadelphia Pk., Lancaster, PA 17602 USA (SAN 257-9413)
E-mail: av42@antham.net.

Avatar Pr., Inc., *(978-0-9706784; 978-1-59291)* 9 Triumph Dr., Urbana, IL 61802 USA Tel 217-384-2211; Fax: 217-384-2216 Do not confuse with companies with the same or similar name in Sunnyside, NY, Atlanta, GA, Brick, NJ
E-mail: william@avatarpress.net
Web site: http://www.avatarpress.com
Dist(s): **Diamond Comic Distributors, Inc.**
Diamond Bk. Distributors
Simon & Schuster
Simon & Schuster, Inc.

Avatar Pubns., Inc. (CAN) *(978-0-9735379; 978-0-9738442; 978-0-9737401; 978-0-9738555; 978-1-897455) Dist. by* **indiCo.**

Ave Maria Pr., *(978-0-87061; 978-0-87793; 978-0-88347; 978-0-939516; 978-1-893732; 978-1-932057; 978-1-59471; 978-1-933495; 978-0-9972710; 978-1-64680)* P.O. Box 428, Notre Dame, IN 46556-0428 USA (SAN 201-1255) Tel 574-287-2831; Fax: 574-239-2904; Toll Free Fax: 800-282-5681; Toll Free: 800-282-1865
E-mail: avemariapress.1@nd.edu
Web site: http://www.forestofpeace.com; http://www.avemariapress.com; http://www.sorinbooks.com
Dist(s): **MyiLibrary.**

Aventine Pr, *(978-0-9719382; 978-0-9722932; 978-1-59330)* 750 State St. Unit 319, San Diego, CA 92101-6073 USA Toll Free: 866-246-6142
E-mail: info@aventinepress.com
Web site: http://www.aventinepress.com
Dist(s): **Ingram Publisher Services.**

Average Dog Publishing, *(978-1-7337590)* 802 N Kaufman Dr, Deer Park, TX 77536 USA Tel 281-785-1572
E-mail: lhcattle@yahoo.com.

AverHill Pr., *(978-0-9766107)* 2545 SW Terwilliger Blvd., No. 807, Portland, OR 97201 USA.

Avery *Imprint of* **Penguin Publishing Group**

Avery Color Studios, Inc., *(978-0-932212; 978-1-892384)* 511 D Ave., Gwinn, MI 49841 USA (SAN 211-1470) Tel 906-346-3908; Fax: 906-346-3015; Toll Free: 800-722-9925
E-mail: avery@portup.com
Dist(s): **Partners Bk. Distributing, Inc.**
Hale, Robert & Co., Inc.

Avery Goode-Reid Pubs., *(978-0-9766620)* P.O. Box 702, Ormond Beach, FL 32175-0702 USA Tel 386-615-0493
E-mail: marianstomblin@aol.com
Web site: http://www.mariantomblin.com.

Avery's, Tom Totally Tennis, *(978-0-9727444)* 5771 12th Ave., NW, Naples, FL 34119 USA
Web site: http://tomavery.com.

AveryToday, Inc., *(978-0-692-84145-7; 978-0-692-89846-8; 978-0-692-91908-8)* P.O. Box 1516, ENGLEWOOD, CO 80150 USA Tel 409-200-4774
E-mail: jeffwcrawford5+LVP0003232@gmail.com; jeffwcrawford5+LVP0003232@gmail.com.

Avian Welfare Coalition, Inc., *(978-0-615-19395-3)* 1923 Ashland Ave., Saint Paul, MN 55104 USA
E-mail: info@avianwelfare.org
Web site: http://www.avianwelfare.org.

Aviation Supplies & Academics, Inc., *(978-0-940732; 978-1-56027; 978-1-61954; 978-1-63134; 978-1-64425)* 7005 132nd Pl., SE, Newcastle, WA 98059-3153 USA (SAN 219-709X) Tel 425-235-1500; Fax: 425-235-0128; Toll Free: 800-272-2359
E-mail: asa@asa2fly.com
Web site: http://www.asa2fly.com
Dist(s): **Aviation Bk. Co.**
Baker & Taylor Publisher Services (BTPS)
Follett School Solutions
Legato Pubs. Group
MyiLibrary
Publishers Group West (PGW)
Wing Aero
ebrary, Inc.

Avid Readers Publishing Group, *(978-0-9797106; 978-0-9801438; 978-1-935105; 978-1-61286)* 2802 Belshire Ave., Lakewood, CA 90715 USA Tel 562-243-5918; Toll Free: 888-966-6835
E-mail: arpg@ericpatterson.name
Web site: http://www.avidreaderspg.com.

Avisson Pr., Inc., *(978-1-888105)* Orders Addr.: P.O. Box 38816, Greensboro, NC 27438-8816 USA (SAN 298-8127) Tel 336-288-6989; Fax: 336-288-6989; Edit Addr.: 3007 Taliaferro Rd., Greensboro, NC 27408 USA (SAN 298-8097)
Dist(s): **Follett School Solutions.**

Avista Products, *(978-0-9798741)* 2411 NE Loop 410. Ste. 108, San Antonio, TX 78217-6600 USA
E-mail: cbooker@avistaproducts.com
Web site: http://www.avistaproducts.com.

Avitable Publisher *See* **Avitable Pub.**

Aviva Gittle Publishing, *(978-0-692-35568-8; 978-1-942736)* 330 Rayford Rd. 177, Spring, TX 77386 USA Tel 619-577-0126
Web site: http://gotogittle.com/
Dist(s): **CreateSpace Independent Publishing Platform.**

Aviva Publishing *See* **Aviva Publishing**

Aviva Publishing, *(978-1-890427; 978-0-9841497; 978-1-935586; 978-1-938686; 978-1-940984; 978-0-692-40228-3; 978-1-943164; 978-1-944335; 978-1-947937; 978-0-692-06101-5; 978-0-578-43916-7; 978-1-950241;*

978-0-578-66763-8; 978-1-63618) 2301 Saranac Ave., Suite 101, Lake Placid, NY 12946-1139 USA Tel 518-523-1320
E-mail: susan@avivapubs.com
Web site: http://www.avivapubs.com
Dist(s): **BookBaby**
Lulu Pr., Inc.
Midpoint Trade Bks., Inc.

Avocus Publishing, Inc., *(978-0-9627671; 978-1-890765)* 4 White Brook Rd., Gilsum, NH 03448 USA (SAN 248-2223) Tel 603-357-0236; Fax: 603-357-2073; Toll Free: 800-345-6665
E-mail: info@avocus.com
Web site: http://www.avocus.com
Dist(s): **Pathway Bk. Service.**

Avon Bks. *Imprint of* **HarperCollins Pubs.**

Avon Impulse *Imprint of* **HarperCollins Pubs.**

AW Teen *Imprint of* **Whitman, Albert & Co.**

AW2 Visions, *(978-0-615-41407-2; 978-0-692-29349-2; 978-0-692-50071-2)* 15323 Ensenada Dr., Houston, TX 77083 USA Tel 281-561-7714; Fax: 281-561-7070
E-mail: awashington88@comcast.net.

A.W.A. Gang *Imprint of* **Journey Stone Creations, LLC**

Awa Pr. (NZL) *(978-0-9582509; 978-0-9582538; 978-0-9582629; 978-0-9582750; 978-0-9582916; 978-1-877551; 978-1-927249; 978-1-927249-13-0; 978-1-927249-14-7)* *Dist. by* **IPG Chicago.**

Awaken Publishing *See* **Now Age Knowledge**

Awaken Specialty Pr., *(978-0-9794713)* P.O. Box 491, Centerton, AR 72719 USA (SAN 853-5248) Tel 479-586-2574
E-mail: celeste@awakenspecialtypress.com
Web site: http://www.awakenspecialtypress.com
Dist(s): **Follett School Solutions.**

Awakened Path Bks., LLC, *(978-0-578-21111-4; 978-1-7329486)* 18 Maple Ave., No. 279, Barrington, RI 02806 USA
Dist(s): **Ingram Content Group.**

Award Pubns. Ltd. (GBR) *(978-0-86163; 978-1-84135; 978-0-9537785; 978-1-904618; 978-1-905503; 978-1-907604; 978-1-906572; 978-1-78270; 978-1-909763)* *Dist. by* **Parkwest Pubns.**

Awareness Pubns., *(978-0-9744163)* 310-A S. Alu Rd., Wailuku, HI 96793 USA Tel 808-244-3782 Do not confuse with companies with the same name in Greenfield, WI, Santa Maria, CA, Houston, TX, Pocomoke City, MD
E-mail: awarep@mauigateway.com
Web site: http://www.awarenesspublications.org
Dist(s): **New Leaf Distributing Co., Inc.**

Awen Hse. Publishing, *(978-0-9826670)* 8949 Bellcove Cir., Colorado Springs, CO 80920 USA Tel 719-287-7074
E-mail: dunning.rebecca@gmail.com
Web site: http://www.rebeccadunning.com.

Awesome Bk. Publishing, *(978-0-9840538; 978-0-9895194)* P.O. Box 1157, Roseland, FL 32957 USA Tel 321-632-0177.

Awesome Guides, Inc., *(978-0-9703694; 978-0-9723218)* 127 W. Fairbanks Ave., Suite No. 421, Winter Park, FL 32789 USA Fax: 407-678-4337
E-mail: sales@awesomeguides.com; cl@awesomeguides.com
Web site: http://www.awesomeguides.com.

Awe-Struck E-Books, Incorporated *See* **Awe-Struck Publishing**

Awe-Struck Publishing, *(978-1-928670; 978-1-58749)* Div. of Mundania Pr., LLC, 6470a Glenway Ave. #109, Cincinnati, OH 45211 USA (SAN 854-4980); *Imprints*: Byte/Me Teen Book (Byte Me Teen); Earthling Press (Earthling Prss)
E-mail: dan@mundania.com
Web site: http://www.awe-struck.net.

Awkward Labs, *(978-0-615-79808-0)* P.O. Box 398, Felton, DE 19943 USA Tel 302-430-6077
E-mail: wjwalton@yahoo.com.

AWOC.COM, *(978-0-9707507; 978-1-62016)* P.O. Box 2819, Denton, TX 76202 USA
E-mail: editor@awoc.com
Web site: http://www.awoc.com.

A-Works New York, Incorporated *See* **One Peace Bks., Inc.**

Axiom Hse., *(978-0-9760237)* P.O. Box 2901, Fairfax, VA 22031 USA
E-mail: orders@axiomhouse.com
Web site: http://www.axiomhouse.com/index.htm
Dist(s): **Baker & Taylor Publisher Services (BTPS)**
Follett School Solutions.

Axiom Pr. *Imprint of* **Genesis Communications, Inc.**

Axios Pr., *(978-0-9661908; 978-0-9753662; 978-1-60419)* P.O. Box 118, Mount Jackson, VA 22842 USA Tel 540-984-3829; Fax: 540-984-3843; Toll Free: 888-542-9467 (orders only); 4501 Forbes Blvd., Lanham, MD 20706 Do not confuse with Axios Publishing Corporation, Seattle, WA
E-mail: info@axiosinstitute.org
Web site: http://www.axiosinstitute.org
Dist(s): **Follett School Solutions**
MyiLibrary
National Bk. Network.

Axle Publishing Co., Inc., *(978-0-9755895)* Orders Addr.: P.O. Box 269, Rockdale, TX 76567 USA (SAN 256-3746) Tel 800-866-2685 (Toll-Free); 512-446-0644 (Jody"s Direct Line); Fax: 512-446-2686 Fax Line; Edit Addr.: 1506 O'Kelley Rd., Rockdale, TX 76567 USA Tel 512-446-0644; Toll Free: 800-866-2685
E-mail: jody@axlegalench.com; jody@laid-back.com; roosterrdz@aol.com
Web site: http://www.axlegalench.com; http://www.laid-back.com; http://www.roostermorris.com
Dist(s): **Follett School Solutions.**

Aylen Publishing, *(978-0-9708623; 978-0-9765040; 978-0-9857708; 978-0-9910084; 978-0-9862848)* Subs. of Master Planning Group International, 7830 E. Camelback Re No. 711, Scottsdale, AZ 85251 USA Toll Free: 800-443-1976
Web site: http://www.masterplanninggroup.com; http://www.Aylen.com.

AZ Bks. LLC, *(978-1-61889)* 9330 LBJ Freeway, Dallas, TX 74243 USA Tel 214-438-3922; Fax: 214-561-6795; 245 8Th Ave., #180, New York, NY 10011
E-mail: anastasia.lobynko@az-books.com; support@booksonix.com
Dist(s): **Follett School Solutions.**

AZ Group Publishing House *See* **AZ Bks. LLC**

Azaida Media, LLC, *(978-0-9864405)* 7726 Gunston Plaza No. 1648, Lorton, VA 22199 USA Tel 571-303-1800
E-mail: info@azaidamedia.com
Web site: http://www.azaidamedia.com.

Azalea Creek Publishing, *(978-0-9677934)* c/o Tom Kendrick, 308 Bloomfield Rd., Sebastopol, CA 95472 USA Tel 707-823-2911 (phone/fax)
E-mail: azalea@sonic.net
Web site: http://www.sonic.net/dragonfly/azaleaforth.html; http://www.sonic.net/dragonfly/adhtml.html; http://southwestdragonflies.net/Order_Form.html; http://southwestdragonflies.net/ColoringBook.html
Dist(s): **American West Bks.**
Bored Feet Pr.
Rio Nuevo Pubs.

AZIAM Bks., *(978-0-9884449; 978-0-9898077; 978-0-9862075)* P.O. Box 267, Santa Monica, CA 90406 USA Tel 310-913-1315
E-mail: info@aziam.com.

AZIAM Yoga *See* **AZIAM Bks.**

Azimuth Media *Imprint of* **Hopkins Publishing**

Azimuth Pr., *(978-0-9632074; 978-1-886218)* 4041 Bowman Blvd., Suite 211, Macon, GA 31210 USA Tel 770-994-9449; Fax: 770-996-6928 Do not confuse with companies with the same or similar name in Alexander, NC, Arnold, MD.

Azoka Co., The, *(978-0-9745560)* P.O. Box Box 323, Greenland, NH 03885 USA Tel 603-772-0181; Fax: 603-772-0550
Web site: http://www.seacoastcenter.com.

Azreal Publishing Co., *(978-0-9755566)* Orders Addr.: P.O. Box 21139, Tallahassee, FL 32312 USA; Edit Addr.: 1937 Saxon St., Tallahassee, FL 32310 USA
Web site: http://.

Azrec Book Publishing *See* **Aztec Bk. Publishing**

Azro Pr., Inc., *(978-0-9660239; 978-1-929115)* Orders Addr.: 1704 Llano St., Suite B, PMB 342, Sante Fe, NM 87505 USA Tel 505-989-3272; Fax: 505-989-3832
E-mail: books@azropress.com
Web site: http://www.azropress.com
Dist(s): **Follett School Solutions**
SCB Distributors.

Aztec 5 Publishing, *(978-0-9769478)* Orders Addr.: P.O. Box 11693, Glendale, AZ 85318 USA Tel 623-537-4567 (phone/fax)
E-mail: aztec5publishing@aol.com.

Aztec Bk. Publishing, *(978-0-9787674; 978-0-9801258; 978-0-9838916; 978-0-9905293)* 1606 Delaware Ave., Wilmington, DE 19806 USA Tel 302-575-1993; Fax: 302-575-1977
Web site: http://www.azteccopies.com.

Aztex Corp., *(978-0-89404)* P.O. Box 50046, Tucson, AZ 85703-1046 USA (SAN 210-0371) Tel 520-882-4656; Fax: 520-792-8501
E-mail: ac@aztexcorp.com
Web site: http://www.aztexcorp.com.

AZTexts Publishing, Inc., *(978-0-9677292)* P.O. Box 93487, Phoenix, AZ 85070-3487 USA Tel 480-283-0994 (phone/fax); 1043 E. Amberwood Dr., Phoenix, AZ 85048
E-mail: aztexts@cox.net
Web site: http://FrecklesFriends.org; http://www.aztexts.com
Dist(s): **Quality Bks., Inc.**

Azure Coast Pr., *(978-0-578-42189-6)* 1600 Ctr. Ave. Suite 1A, Fort Lee, NJ 07024 USA Tel 201-486-1377
E-mail: rarrechea@aol.com
Dist(s): **Independent Pub.**

Azure Communications, *(978-0-9618741)* Orders Addr.: P.O. Box 23387, New Orleans, LA 70183 USA (SAN 668-7695); Edit Addr.: 37383 Overland Trail, Prairieville, LA 70769 USA (SAN 668-7709) Tel 225-744-4094
E-mail: gszczurek@eatel.net.

Azuria Bks., *(978-0-9796444)* P.O. Box 535, Clyde, NC 28721 USA Tel 828-627-9685
E-mail: timbramlett@charter.net.

Azzurri Publishing, *(978-0-692-30257-6; 978-0-692-42035-5; 978-0-9967298)* 2355 Westwood Blvd. No. 647, Los Angeles, CA 90064 USA Tel 206-683-1718
E-mail: peterawick@gmail.com
Web site: www.peter-wick.com.

B & B Educational Advancement & Pubns., Inc., *(978-1-937065)* 1407 Ford St., Golden, CO 80401 USA (SAN 860-1801) Tel 303-279-8659; Fax: 303-648-5135
E-mail: lmrpc@aol.com.

B&B Publishing, *(978-1-885813)* 63418 Everett Rd., Coos Bay, OR 97420 USA Tel 541-269-9277 Do not confuse with companies with the same or similar name in Fort Collins, CO, Westminster, CO, Walworth, WI, Greenfield, IN
Dist(s): **Partners/West Book Distributors.**

B B Y Publications *See* **bby Publications at The University of West Alabama**

BF Publishing, *(978-0-9653327)* 17503 Brushy River Ct., Houston, TX 77095-6905 USA Tel 281-256-1213 Do not confuse with B.F. Publishing, Huntington Beach, CA
E-mail: BFPub1@aol.com
Dist(s): **Origin Bk. Sales, Inc.**

B F Q Press, Incorporated *See* **TotalRecall Pubns.**

B G R Publishing *See* **EMG Networks**

B. L. Moore, *(978-0-578-43796-5)* 310 N. Broad St. S7, Carneys Point, NJ 08069 USA Tel 609-805-7330
E-mail: BLMooreAuthor@gmail.com
Dist(s): **Ingram Content Group.**

B.R. Publishing Co., *(978-0-9625593; 978-1-884538)* 1725 Pinebrook Dr., Knoxville, TN 37909 USA Tel 423-691-1990.

B Small Publishing (GBR) *(978-1-874735; 978-1-902915; 978-1-905710; 978-1-908164; 978-1-909767; 978-1-911509)* *Dist. by* **IPG Chicago.**

B. T. Brooks, *(978-0-9772282)* Orders Addr.: 7015 Crabapple Ln., Kansas City, MO 64129 USA Tel 816-810-1277; 7015 Crabapple Ln., Kansas City, MO 64129 Tel 816-810-1277
E-mail: btbrookspublish@aol.com.

B V Wespat, *(978-0-9713342; 978-0-9788934; 978-0-9819699)* 1641 N. Memorial Dr., Lancaster, OH 43130 USA
Dist(s): **Brodart Co.**
Partners Bk. Distributing, Inc.

B2Z Publishing, Inc., *(978-0-9712070)* Orders Addr.: P.O. Box 307, Severna Park, MD 21146 USA (SAN 254-1068) Tel 410-431-8890; Fax: 410-431-5236
E-mail: towardcure@aol.com
Web site: http://www.mabcie.com.

B3 Publishing, *(978-0-9767849)* Div. of Dream Believer Factory, Inc., Orders Addr.: P.O. Box 360170, Strongsville, OH 44136 USA; Edit Addr.: 19428 Bennington Dr., Strongsville, OH 44136 USA
E-mail: dbfiest@roadrunner.com.

BABAIAN, Edward, *(978-1-7331068)* 2386 E. Del Mar Blvd. No. 104, Pasadena, CA 91107 USA Tel 909-208-5182
E-mail: Eddiewritescopy@gmail.com
Dist(s): **Ingram Content Group.**

Babb, James, *(978-0-9914921)* P.O. Box 547, De Queen, AR 71832 USA Tel 870-584-6131
E-mail: JASUB1017@YAHOO.COM.

Babbling Bks., *(978-0-9798609)* 3849 Prado Dr., Sarasota, FL 34235-3528 USA
E-mail: babblingbooks@yahoo.com.

Babel Books, Inc *See* **Pintos, Yoselem G.**

Babel Libros (COL) *(978-958-8445; 978-958-97602; 978-958-98273)* *Dist. by* **Lectorum Pubns.**

Babl Books, Incorporated, *(978-1-68304)* 510 Crestwood Rd, Kaysville, UT 84606 USA Toll Free: 844-311-9649
E-mail: contact@bablbooks.com
Web site: http://www.bablbooks.com.

Baboosic Enterprises, LLC, *(978-0-9787660)* P.O. Box 6102, Bloomington, IN 47408-9990 USA
Web site: http://www.bunnyrabbitonthemoon.com.

Babulinka Libros (ESP) *Dist. by* **Lectorum Pubns.**

Baby Abuelita Productions, Inc., *(978-0-9788379; 978-0-615-19145-4)* 6619 S. Dixie Hwy. No. 139, Miami, FL 33143 USA (SAN 851-7207) Toll Free: 877-722-8352
E-mail: cfenster@babyabuelita.com
Web site: http://www.babyabuelita.com.

Baby Einstein Co., LLC, The, *(978-1-892309; 978-1-931580)* Subs. of Walt Disney Productions, 1233 Flower St., Glendale, CA 91201 USA Tel 818-544-4842
E-mail: ellen.portantino@disney.com
Web site: http://www.babyeinstein.com
Dist(s): **Disney Publishing Worldwide**
Penton Overseas, Inc.
Right Start, Inc.
Rounder Kids Music Distribution.

Baby Faye Bks. *Imprint of* **Northstar Entertainment Group, LLC**

Baby Music Boom, Inc., *(978-0-9647786)* Orders Addr.: P.O. Box 62188, Minneapolis, MN 55426 USA Tel 612-470-1667; Fax: 612-474-1297; Toll Free: 888-470-1667; Edit Addr.: 19000 Maple Ln., Deephaven, MN 55331 USA
E-mail: babyboomms@aol.com
Web site: http://www.babymusicboom.com.

Baby Professor (Education Kids) *Imprint of* **Speedy Publishing LLC**

Baby Shadows, *(978-0-9744928)* 150 W. 56th St., Suite 4410, New York, NY 10019 USA (SAN 255-6367)
Web site: http://www.babyshadows.com.

Baby Shark Productions, *(978-0-9765125)* 15338 Roberts Ave., Jacksonville, FL 32218-1833 USA Tel 904-751-1564
E-mail: jackbradford90@aol.com
Web site: http://www.gregmoutafis.com.

Baby Tattoo Bks., *(978-0-9729388; 978-0-9778949; 978-0-9793307; 978-0-9845210; 978-1-61404)* 6045 Longridge Ave., Van Nuys, CA 91401 USA (SAN 255-2159) Tel 818-416-5314
E-mail: info@babytatto.com
Web site: http://www.babytattoo.com
Dist(s): **SCB Distributors.**

Babypie Publishing, *(978-0-9753668; 978-0-9884471; 978-1-945446)* 151 Mansfield Rd., Waitsfield, VT 05673 USA Tel 310-823-2661
E-mail: info@relationship-masters.com
Web site: http://www.babypiepublishing.com.

Bacchus Bks., *(978-0-9717952)* Div. of Petmida, Incorporated, P.O. Box 1801, Pacific Palisades, CA 90272 USA Fax: 310-459-4233; Toll Free: 877-604-6522
E-mail: customerservice@domdeluise.com
Web site: http://www.domdeluise.com.

Back Bay Bks. *Imprint of* **Little Brown & Co.**

Back Channel Pr., *(978-0-9767590; 978-0-9789546; 978-1-934582)* 170 Mechanic St., Portsmouth, NH 03801 USA Tel 603-436-9485
E-mail: ngstudio@comcast.net
Web site: http://www.nancygrossmanbooks.com
Dist(s): **Ingram Content Group.**

Back Home Industries, *(978-1-880045)* Orders Addr.: P.O. Box 22495, Milwaukie, OR 97269 USA Tel 503-654-2300; Fax: 503-659-9351; Edit Addr.: 8431 SE 36th Ave., Portland, OR 97222 USA
E-mail: backhome@integrity.com
Web site: http://webs.integrity.com/backhome.

Back In THE BRONX, *(978-0-9657221)* Orders Addr.: P.O. Box 141H, Scarsdale, NY 10583 USA Tel 914-592-1647; Fax: 914-592-4893; Toll Free: 800-727-6695; Edit Addr.: 40 Herkimer Rd., Scarsdale, NY 10583 USA
E-mail: info@backinthebronx.com
Web site: http://www.backinthebronx.com.

Back River Company, The, LLC, *(978-0-9672882)* 238 Robinson St. # 13, Wakefield, RI 02879-3549 USA.

Back Yard Pub., *(978-0-9707560; 978-1-931934)* Div. of Wensel Enterprises, 7720 N. Moonwind Terr., Dunnellon, FL 34433 USA Tel 352-795-0844; Fax: 352-795-0813
E-mail: wwensel@backyardpublisher.com; wwensel@hughes.net; wensel@hughes.net
Web site: http://www.backyardpublisher.com.

Back2Life, Inc., *(978-0-9760151)* 8608 N. Richmond Ave., 1st Flr., Kansas City, MO 64157 USA Tel 816-835-4477; Fax: 816-891-7789
E-mail: ckehoe@back2life.us
Web site: http://www.back2life.us.

Back2Life Ministries *See* **Back2Life, Inc.**

Backinprint.com *Imprint of* **iUniverse, Inc.**

Backintyme *Imprint of* **Backintyme Publishing**

Backintyme Publishing, *(978-0-939479)* 1341 Grapevine Rd., Crofton, KY 42217 USA (SAN 663-2726) Tel 270-985-8568; *Imprints*: Backintyme (Backintyme FL)
E-mail: backintyme@mehrapublishing.com
Web site: http://www.backintyme.biz.

Backpack Bowie *See* **Educational Expertise, LLC**

Backpack Pubs., *(978-0-9854439)* Orders Addr.: P.O. Box 31, South Webster, OH 45682 USA Tel 740-778-3110
E-mail: itsthedoc@yahoo.com
Web site: http://www.backpackpublishers.com.

Backroads Pr., *(978-0-9642371; 978-0-9724033)* Orders Addr.: P.O. Box 651, Mooresville, IN 46158 USA Tel 317-831-2815 (phone/fax); Edit Addr.: 452 Tulip Dr., Mooresville, IN 46158 USA
E-mail: wend@iquest.net
Web site: http://www.publishershomepages.com/php/Backroads_Press.

Backwaters Pr., The, *(978-0-9677149; 978-0-9726187; 978-0-9765231; 978-0-9785782; 978-0-9793934; 978-0-9816936; 978-1-935218)* 3502 N. 52nd St., Omaha, NE 68104-3506 USA Tel 402-451-4052
E-mail: thebackwaterspress@gmail.com
Web site: http://www.thebackwaterspress.org
Dist(s): **SPD-Small Pr. Distribution**
Univ. of Nebraska Pr.

Backwoods Publishing Co., *(978-0-9722501)* Rte. 1, Box 270, Boswell, OK 74727 USA Do not confuse with Backwoods Publishing in Logan, OH.

Backyard Ambassador Reader Publishing Co., *(978-0-9793808)* 2 New Grant Ct., Columbia, SC 29209 USA
E-mail: caroline.bennett@att.com
Web site: http://www.bareader.com.

Backyard Scientist, Inc., *(978-0-9618663; 978-1-888427)* P.O. Box 16966, Irvine, CA 92623 USA (SAN 219-1725) Tel 714-551-2392; Fax: 714-552-5351
E-mail: backyrdsci@aol.com.

Bad Choices Media, *(978-0-9721327)* P.O. Box 827, Chincoteague Island, VA 23336 USA
E-mail: acanfld@gmail.com; andrea@studio4264.com; andrea@badchoicesmedia.com.

Bad Frog Art/SMG Bks, *(978-0-9795361)* Orders Addr.: 14931 251st Pl. SE, Issaquah, WA 98027 USA
E-mail: steve@stevegritton.info
Web site: www.stevegritton.info.

B.A.D Mouse Publishing, *(978-0-615-40313-7; 978-0-9905353)* 234 Ryder Rd., Manhasset, NY 11030 USA
E-mail: charlotte.lee@lhh.com
Web site: http://www.bringadeadmouse.com.

Bad Publishing, *(978-0-9765414)* 21522 5th Pl. S., DeMoines, WA 98198 USA Tel 206-824-6106
E-mail: edwardhl@hsd401.org.

Badalamenti, Andrew, *(978-0-615-25180-6)* 206 Franklin Rd., Denville, NJ 07834 USA
Dist(s): **Lulu Pr., Inc.**

badalato, *(978-0-692-80076-8)*
Dist(s): **CreateSpace Independent Publishing Platform.**

BadCoaches, Incorporated *See* **Tony Franklin Cos., The**

Badgerland Bks. LLC, *(978-0-9765510)* Orders Addr.: 5407 Marsh Woods Dr., McFarland, WI 53558 USA
E-mail: sales@badgerlandbooks.com; joe_martino@uwbucky.com
Web site: http://www.badgerlandbooks.com; http://www.uwbucky.com
Dist(s): **Follett School Solutions.**

Badgley Publishing Co., *(978-0-615-16452-6; 978-0-615-18086-1; 978-0-615-22382-7; 978-0-615-48336-8; 978-0-615-48533-1; 978-0-615-49470-8; 978-0-615-50189-5; 978-0-615-51007-1; 978-0-615-52884-7; 978-0-615-53929-4; 978-0-615-55272-9; 978-0-615-56181-3; 978-0-615-56748-8; 978-0-615-58055-5; 978-0-615-60373-5; 978-0-615-62091-6; 978-0-9854403; 978-0-615-75840-4; 978-0-615-76440-5; 978-0-615-78594-3; 978-0-615-80762-1; 978-0-615-80981-6; 978-0-615-81198-7; 978-0-615-84531-9; 978-0-615-86207-1;*

Publisher Name Index

978-0-615-88046-4; 978-) 5570 Sherrick Dr., Canal Winchester, OH 43110 USA Tel 614-893-1612
Web site: http://www.badgleypublishingcompany.com/
Dist(s): **CreateSpace Independent Publishing Platform**
Ingram Content Group
Lulu Pr., Inc.
Dummy Record Do Not USE!!!!.

Badi Publishing Corporation *See* **Changing-Times.net**

Badiru, Adedeji, *(978-0-9768100)* P.O. Box 341441, Beavercreek, OH 45434 USA
E-mail: deji@badiru.com
Web site: abicspublications.com.

Baen Bks., *(978-0-671; 978-1-55594; 978-0-7434)* Orders Addr.: c/o Simon & Schuster, 200 Old Tappan Rd., Old Tappan, NJ 07675 USA Fax: 800-445-6991; Toll Free: 800-223-2336; Edit Addr.: c/o Simon & Schuster, 1230 Ave. of the Americas, New York, NY 10020 USA (SAN 658-8417) Tel 212-698-7000; Toll Free: 800-223-2348 (customer service)
Web site: http://www.simonsays.com/
Dist(s): **Children's Plus, Inc.**
Diamond Comic Distributors, Inc.
Diamond Bk. Distributors
Simon & Schuster
Simon & Schuster, Inc.

Baetzel, Jeff, *(978-0-692-97869-6)* 4531 N. Krueger Rd., Long Grove, IL 60047 USA Tel 847-438-3370
E-mail: jjbaetzel@hotmail.com
Dist(s): **Ingram Content Group.**

Baha'i Publishing, *(978-1-931847; 978-1-61851)* Orders Addr.: 2427 Bond St., University Park, IL 60466-3101 USA Toll Free Fax: 800-705-4923; Toll Free: 800-705-4925; Edit Addr.: 415 Linden Ave., Wilmete, IL 60091-2886 USA Tel 847-425-7950; Fax: 847-425-7951
Web site: http://www.bahaibooksusa.com/
Dist(s): **Follett School Solutions**
Independent Pubs. Group.

Baha'i Publishing Trust, U.S., *(978-0-87743)* 415 Linden Ave., Wilmette, IL 60091 USA
Dist(s): **Baha'i Distribution Service.**

BaHar Publishing, L.C., *(978-0-9718939; 978-0-9818219; 978-0-9837742)* 1429 Commercial St., Waterloo, IA 50702 USA Toll Free: 888-600-6033
E-mail: chaveevahdread@yahoo.com
Web site: http://www.baharpublishing.com.

BaHart Publications / Eight Legs Publishing *See* **Bh Pubns.**

Bahoo Tide, LLC *Imprint of* **Arts Love Expression**

Bailey, Martha, *(978-0-9786448)* 6882 S. Peaceful Hills Rd., Morrison, CO 80465 USA Tel 303-697-4591 (phone/fax)
E-mail: nebjr@earthlink.net.

Bailie, Julene, *(978-0-692-81857-2; 978-0-692-90946-1; 978-0-692-13157-2; 978-0-578-59084-4)*
E-mail: juleneba@yahoo.com; juleneba@yahoo.com; juleneba@yahoo.com
Dist(s): **CreateSpace Independent Publishing Platform.**

Bailiwick Pr., *(978-1-934649)* 3836 Tradition St., Fort Collins, CO 80526-3107 USA; 250 W. 57Th St. 15Th Flr., New York, NY 10016
Web site: http://bailiwickpress.com
Dist(s): **Follett School Solutions**
Legato Pubs. Group
MyiLibrary
Publishers Group West (PGW)
ebrary, Inc.

Baird, Jeri, *(978-0-692-07599-9)* 1120 Phillips Ct., Apt D, Montrose, CO 81401 USA Tel 217-512-9074
E-mail: jeribaird11@gmail.com
Dist(s): **Ingram Content Group.**

Baird, Robert Kade, *(978-0-692-99142-8; 978-0-692-99542-6)* 6453 Amanda Michelle Ln., NORTH LAS VEGAS, NV 89086 USA Tel 702-498-7275
E-mail: rafaandthemistbook@gmail.com
Dist(s): **Ingram Content Group.**

Baker Academic, *(978-0-8010)* Div. of Baker Publishing Group, Orders Addr.: P.O. Box 6287, Grand Rapids, MI 49516-6287 USA Toll Free Fax: 800-398-3111 (orders only); Toll Free: 800-877-2665 (orders only); Edit Addr.: 6030 Fulton Ave., Ada, MI 49301 USA Tel 616-676-9185; Fax: 616-676-9573
Web site: http://www.bakerpublishinggroup.com
Dist(s): **Baker Publishing Group**
ebrary, Inc.

Baker & Taylor Bks., *(978-0-8480; 978-1-222; 978-1-223)* A Follett Company, Orders Addr.: Commerce Service Ctr., 251 Mt. Olive Church Rd., Commerce, GA 30599 USA (SAN 169-1503) Tel 404-335-5000; Toll Free: 800-775-1200 (customer service); 800-775-1800 (orders); Reno Service Ctr., 1160 Trademark Dr., Suite 111, Reno, NV 89511 (SAN 169-4464) Tel 775-850-3800; Fax: 775-850-3826 (customer service); Toll Free Fax: 800-775-1700 (orders); Edit Addr.: Bridgewater Service Ctr. 1120 US Hwy. 22, E., Bridgewater, NJ 08807 USA (SAN 169-4901) Toll Free: 800-775-1500 (customer service); Momence Service Ctr., 501W. Gladiolus St., Momence, IL 60954-1799 (SAN 169-2100) Tel 815-472-2444 (international customers); Fax: 815-472-9886 (international customers); Toll Free: 800-775-2300 (customer service, academic libraries)
E-mail: btinfo@btol.com
Web site: http://www.btol.com.

Baker & Taylor, CATS, *(978-1-4352; 978-1-4395; 978-1-4420; 978-1-4487; 978-1-4517; 978-1-4806; 978-1-5182)* 1120 Rte. 22 E., Bridgewater, NJ 08807 USA Toll Free: 800-775-1500; *Imprints:* Paw Prints (Paw Prints USA)
Web site: http://www.baker-taylor.com/pawprints
Dist(s): **Baker & Taylor Bks.**
Follett School Solutions.

Baker & Taylor Publisher Services (BTPS), A Follett Company, Orders Addr.: 30 Amberwood Pkwy., Ashland, OH 44805 USA (SAN 631-936X) Fax: 419-281-6883; Toll Free: 800-537-6727; 30 Amberwood Pkwy., Ashland, OH 44805 (SAN 760-9264) Fax: 419-281-6883; Toll Free: 800-537-6727
E-mail: orders@atlasbooks.com
Web site: http://www.bookmasters.com/.

Baker & Taylor Publishing Group *See* **Readerlink Distribution Services, LLC**

Baker Book House, Incorporated *See* **Baker Publishing Group**

Baker Bks., *(978-0-8010; 978-0-913686)* Div. of Baker Publishing Group, Orders Addr.: P.O. Box 6287, Grand Rapids, MI 49516-6287 USA (SAN 299-1500) Toll Free Fax: 800-398-3111 (orders only); Toll Free: 800-877-2665 (orders only); Edit Addr.: 6030 E. Fulton, Ada, MI 49301 USA (SAN 201-4041) Tel 616-676-9185; Fax: 616-676-9573
Web site: http://www.bakerpublishinggroup.com
Dist(s): **Baker Publishing Group**
Faith Alive Christian Resources
Follett School Solutions
Twentieth Century Christian Bks.
ebrary, Inc.

Baker, Carol Robinson, *(978-0-692-07947-8; 978-0-692-07962-1; 978-0-692-07967-6)* 9009 Buckingham Ct., Woodway, TX 76712 USA Tel 254-644-6123
E-mail: carolsbaker@gmail.com
Dist(s): **Ingram Content Group.**

Baker College Publishing Co., *(978-1-885545)* Div. of Baker College, 1050 W. Bristol Rd., Flint, MI 48507 USA Toll Free: 800-339-9879
Dist(s): **Follett School Solutions.**

Baker, Debbie, *(978-0-692-04498-8)* 611 N Johnson St., Tallassee, AL 36078 USA Tel 334-415-3553
E-mail: debbiebaker095@gmail.com
Dist(s): **Ingram Content Group.**

Baker, Elizabeth, *(978-0-578-45052-0)* 7091 Webster Rd., Creston, CA 93432 USA Tel 805-400-4357
E-mail: Ed@biochem3d.com
Dist(s): **Ingram Content Group.**

Baker, Helen Interiors, Inc., *(978-0-9743511)* Orders Addr.: P.O. Box 367, West Harwich, MA 02671 USA Tel 508-432-0287; Fax: 508-430-7744; Edit Addr.: 94 Main St., West Harwich, MA 02671 USA
E-mail: hbunce@attbi.com
Web site: http://www.shoppingthecape.com.

Baker Publishing Group, *(978-0-8007; 978-0-8010; 978-1-58743; 978-1-4412; 978-1-4934; 978-1-68196; 978-1-5409)* Orders Addr.: P.O. Box 6287, Grand Rapids, MI 49516-6287 USA Tel 616-676-9573; Toll Free Fax: 800-398-3111 (orders only); Toll Free: 800-877-2665 (orders only); Edit Addr.: 6030 E. Fulton, Ada, MI 49301 USA Tel 616-676-9185; Fax: 616-676-9573; Toll Free Fax: 800-398-3111; Toll Free: 800-877-2665
E-mail: webmaster@bakerpublishinggroup.com
Web site: http://www.bakerbooks.com; http://www.bakerpublishinggroup.com
Dist(s): **Follett School Solutions**
Twentieth Century Christian Bks.
christianaudio
ebrary, Inc.

Baker Trittin Concepts *See* **Baker Trittin Pr.**

Baker Trittin Pr., *(978-0-9729256; 978-0-9752880; 978-0-9787316; 978-0-9814893)* P.O. Box 277, Winona Lake, IN 46590-0277 USA Fax: 574-269-6100; Toll Free: 1-888-741-4386; *Imprints:* Innovative Christian Publications (Innov Chris Pubns); Tweener Press (Tweener Pr)
E-mail: paul@btconcepts.com
Web site: http://www.bakertrittinpress.com; http://www.gospelstoryteller.com.

Baker, Walter H. Company *See* **Baker's Plays**

Baker's Plays, *(978-0-87440)* Div. of Samuel French, Inc., 45 W. 25th St., New York, NY 10010 USA (SAN 202-3717) Tel 212-255-8085; Fax: 212-627-7754
E-mail: info@bakersplays.com
Web site: http://www.bakersplays.com.

Bala Kids *Imprint of* **Shambhala Pubns., Inc.**

Balaam Books LLC, *(978-0-9785585)* 1825 W. Ave., Unit 11, Miami Beach, FL 33139-1441 USA (SAN 850-9972) Tel 305-531-9351; Fax: 305-531-9348
E-mail: Info@BalaamBooks.com
Web site: http://www.BalaamBooks.com.

Balance Bks., Inc., *(978-0-9743908)* P.O. Box 86, Des Plaines, IL 60016-0086 USA
Web site: http://www.balance-books.com
Dist(s): **Distributors, The.**

Balanced Families, *(978-0-9759468)* 432 N. 750 E., Lindon, UT 84042 USA Tel 801-380-3247; Fax: 801-785-3938
E-mail: info@starsofthesky.com.

Balanced Systems, Inc., *(978-0-9760037)* 995 Artdale, White Lake, MI 48383 USA.

Balboa Pr. *Imprint of* **Author Solutions, Inc.**

Balboa Pr., Div. of Hay House, Inc., 1663 Liberty Dr., Bloomington, IN 47403 USA Tel 877-407-4847
E-mail: customersupport@balboapress.com
Web site: http://www.balboapress.com
Dist(s): **Author Solutions, Inc.**
Baker & Taylor Publisher Services (BTPS)
Zondervan.

Balcony Bks., *(978-0-615-46893-8; 978-0-9879732-4-5)* 1606 Willow Ln., McKinney, TX 75070 USA Tel 214-790-4686; 469-879-8696
Dist(s): **CreateSpace Independent Publishing Platform**
Dummy Record Do Not USE!!!!.

Bald Eagle Books *See* **Who Would Win?**

Baldner, Jean V., *(978-0-9615317)* 1618 Burnett Ave., Ames, IA 50010-5337 USA (SAN 694-6526).

Baldwin, Christopher John, *(978-1-938384)* P.O. Box 1141, Northhampton, MA 01061 USA Tel 360-705-2742
E-mail: chrisjohnbaldwin@gmail.com.

Balhund Entertainment, LLC, *(978-0-9743277)* 3018 Paulcrest Dr., Los Angeles, CA 90046 USA Tel 323-848-8778
Web site: http://www.magusgame.com.

Baliko, Janelle A., *(978-0-9799012)* 45486 Locust Grove Dr., Valley Lee, MD 20692-3217 USA
E-mail: itdoesnthavetobepink@yahoo.com
Web site: http://www.itdoesnthavetobepink.com.

Ball, Jennifer, *(978-0-692-35516-9; 978-0-692-35517-6; 978-0-692-56522-3; 978-0-692-13935-6)* 15170 Copeland Way, SPRING HILL, FL 34604 USA Tel 352-650-2717.

Ball, Michael, *(978-0-9765750)* 2000 Bradley Ln., Russellville, AR 72801-4627 USA.

Ball Publishing, *(978-0-9626796; 978-1-883052; 978-1-7332541)* Orders Addr.: 622 Town Rd., West Chicago, IL 60185 USA Tel 630-588-3352; Fax: 630-562-7984; Toll Free: 888-888-0013 (U.S. & Canada only); Edit Addr.: P.O. Box 1660, West Chicago, IL 60186-1660 USA
E-mail: info@ballpublishing.com
Web site: http://www.ballbookshelf.com
Dist(s): **Independent Pubs. Group.**

Ball, Rulon Jay *See* **JBall Publishing**

Ballad Productions, *(978-0-9753663)* Orders Addr.: P.O. Box 4, North Miami Beach, FL 33164 USA Tel 786-285-3619; Edit Addr.: 163rd St., Suite No. 4, North Miami Beach, FL 33164 USA
E-mail: drlaz770@aol.com
Web site: http://www.drlaz.com.

Ballantine Bks. *Imprint of* **Random House Publishing Group**

Ballantine, Robert *See* **P.F.B. Publishing**

Ballard & Tighe Pubs., *(978-0-937270; 978-1-55501; 978-1-59989)* Div. of Educational Ideas, Inc., 471 Atlas St., Brea, CA 92821 USA (SAN 200-7991) Tel 714-990-4332; Fax: 714-255-9828; Toll Free: 800-321-4332
Web site: http://www.ballard-tighe.com.

Ballard, Donald W., *(978-0-9768779)* Orders Addr.: 37823 Menard Ct., Fremont, CA 94536 USA Toll Free: 800-506-7401
E-mail: donballard@comcast.net
Web site: http://www.magicalhotel.com.

Ballard Publishing Group, LLC, *(978-1-7324067; 978-1-7332980)* 434 NW 20 Ave., Fort Lauderdale, FL 33311 USA Tel 954-303-8789
E-mail: ballardpublishinggroup@gmail.com.

BalletMet Dance Centre, *(978-0-692-01667-1)* 322 Mount Vernon Ave., Columbus, OH 43235 USA Tel 614-586-8635
E-mail: education@balletmet.org
Web site: http://www.balletmet.org
Dist(s): **BookMasters.**

Ballinger Printing & Graphics, *(978-0-9754957; 978-0-615-20730-8)* 906 Hutchings Ave., Ballinger, TX 76821 USA Tel 325-365-8206; Fax: 325-365-2209; Toll Free: 888-915-8206
E-mail: michael.o.white@att.net; ballingerprinting@verizon.net
Dist(s): **Publishers Services.**

Balloon Bks. *Imprint of* **Sterling Publishing Co., Inc.**

Balloon Magic, *(978-1-931084)* 928 W. 20 N., Orem, UT 84057-1918 USA; *Imprints:* Penny's Publishing (Pennys Pubng)
E-mail: mlh@balloonmagic.com
Web site: http://www.balloonmagic.com.

Ballybunnion Bks., *(978-0-9726340)* Orders Addr.: P.O. Box 6357, Virginia Beach, VA 23456 USA; Edit Addr.: 833 Maitland Dr., Virginia Beach, VA 23454 USA
E-mail: brian@wbrianmurphy.com
Web site: http://www.warrenmurphy.com.

Ballyhoo Books *See* **Ballyhoo BookWorks, Inc.**

Ballyhoo BookWorks, Inc., *(978-0-936335)* Orders Addr.: P.O. Box 534, Shoreham, NY 11786 USA (SAN 697-8487); Edit Addr.: 1 Sylvan Dr., Wading River, NY 11792 USA (SAN 698-2239) Tel 631-929-8148
E-mail: ballyhoo@optonline.net.

Ballyhoo Printing, *(978-0-9742792; 978-0-9800580; 978-0-9976224)* 187 W. Frontage Rd., Lewistown, MT 59457 USA Tel 406-538-7988
E-mail: ballyhoo@ballyhooprinting.com
Web site: http://www.ballyhooprinting.com.

Ballylongford Bks., *(978-0-9753612; 978-0-9961943)* 2588 Welsford Rd., Suite 100, Columbus, OH 43221 USA Tel 614-774-0300.

Balona Bks., *(978-0-9765479; 978-1-934376)* P.O. Box 690106, Stockton, CA 95269-0106 USA
E-mail: author@balona.com; jonathan@balona.com
Web site: http://www.balona.com.

Balticbard Publishing *Imprint of* **Leyva, Barbara**

Baltov, Deanna, *(978-0-692-78706-9)* 909 Agate St, San Diego, CA 92109 USA Tel 973-296-7331
E-mail: dpost24@gmail.com.

Balue Fox Publishing Company *See* **McWilliams Mediation Group Ltd.**

Balzer & Bray *Imprint of* **HarperCollins Pubs.**

Bamboo River Pr., *(978-0-9798173)* 12565 SE Callahan Rd., Portland, OR 97086-9708 USA (SAN 854-4484) Tel 503-761-4360
Web site: http://www.bambooriverpress.com.

Bamboo Zoo, LLC, *(978-0-9774493)* 1637 Dahlia St., Denver, CO 80220 USA (SAN 257-5965) Tel 720-323-4955
E-mail: kim@bamboo-zoo.com
Web site: http://www.bamboo-zoo.com.

Banana Bunch Publishing, *(978-0-9761763)* 2260 Banana St., Saint James City, FL 33956 USA Tel 239-283-9306.

Banana Luna Bks., *(978-0-692-52556-2; 978-0-578-40270-3)* 18400 SW Boones Ferry Rd. G206, TIGARD, OR 97224 USA Tel 503-443-5638.

Banana Oil Bks. *Imprint of* **Cyberwizard Productions**

Banana Patch Pr., *(978-0-9715333; 978-0-9800063)* Orders Addr.: P.O. Box 950, Hanapepe, HI 96716 USA (SAN 254-3087) Tel 808-335-5944; Fax: 808-335-3830; Toll Free: 800-914-5944
E-mail: carolan@aloha.net
Web site: http://www.bananapatchpress.com
Dist(s): **Booklines Hawaii, Ltd.**
Islander Group.

Banana Pr., *(978-0-9799065)* 2935 S. Fish Hatchery Rd., No. 3, Suite 254, Fitchburg, WI 53711 USA Tel 608-658-0023
E-mail: info@bananalady.com
Web site: http://www.bananalady.com.

Banana Tree Publishing, *(978-1-7327484)* 4936 SE 114th Ave, Portland, OR 97266 USA Tel 971-865-6415
E-mail: melinda.m.tran@outlook.com
Web site: www.bananatreepublishing.com.

Bancroft Pr., *(978-0-9631246; 978-0-9635376; 978-1-890862; 978-1-61088)* P.O. Box 65360, Baltimore, MD 21209-9945 USA Tel 410-358-0658; Fax: 410-764-1967; Toll Free: 800-637-7377 Do not confuse with Bancroft Pr., San Rafael, CA
E-mail: bruceb@bancroftpress.com
Web site: http://www.bancroftpress.com
Dist(s): **Academic Bk. Ctr., Inc.**
Baker & Taylor Publisher Services (BTPS)
Book Wholesalers, Inc.
Bk. Hse., Inc., The
Brodart Co.
Coutts Information Services
Emery-Pratt Co.
Follett School Solutions
Mackin Library Media
Midwest Library Service
Smashwords
Yankee Bk. Peddler, Inc.

Band of Brothers Bks., *(978-1-7321278)* 13000 Green Valley Dr., Oklahoma City, OK 73120 USA Tel 405-210-5336
E-mail: bhale1978@gmail.com.

Banda Pr. International, Inc., *(978-0-9773175)* 6050 Stetson Hills Blvd., No. 313, Colorado Springs, CO 80922 USA
Web site: http://www.bandapress.com.

Bandai Entertainment, Inc., *(978-1-58354; 978-1-59409; 978-1-60496)* Div. of Bandai Entertainment, Inc., 5551 Katella Ave., Cypress, CA 90630 USA Tel 714-816-9760; Fax: 714-816-6708; Toll Free: 877-772-6463
Web site: http://www.bandai-ent.com
Dist(s): **Diamond Comic Distributors, Inc.**
Diamond Bk. Distributors
Follett School Solutions.

B&B Publishing, *(978-0-9894693; 978-0-9907476)* 1970 N. Leslie St. No. 560, Pahrump, NV 89060 USA Tel 641-424-0367
E-mail: bvos98@gmail.com.

B&H Bks. *Imprint of* **B&H Publishing Group**

B&H Kids *Imprint of* **B&H Publishing Group**

B&H Publishing Group *See* **B&H Publishing Group**

†B&H Publishing Group, *(978-0-8054; 978-0-87981; 978-1-55819; 978-1-58640; 978-0-8400; 978-1-4336)* Div. of LifeWay Christian Resources of the Southern Baptist Convention, One LifeWay Plaza MSN 114, Nashville, TN 37234-0114 USA (SAN 201-937X) Tel 615-251-2520; Fax: 615-251-5026 (Books Only); 615-251-2036 (Bibles Only); 615-251-2413 (Gifts/Supplies Only); Toll Free: 800-725-5416; 800-251-3225 (retailers); 800-296-4036 (orders/returns); 800-448-8032 (consumers); 800-458-2772 (churches); *Imprints:* Holman Bible Publishers (Holman Bible); B&H Books (B&H Bks.); B&H Kids (B&H Kids)
E-mail: broadmanholman@lifeway.com; heather.counsellor@bhpublishinggroup.com; wes.banks@bhpublishinggroup.com; laurene.martin@lifeway.com; tom.gilbert@lifeway.com
Web site: http://www.bhpublishinggroup.com; http://www.lifeway.com
Dist(s): **Follett School Solutions**
Simon & Schuster, Inc.
christianaudio; *CIP.*

B&J Marketing LLC, *(978-0-9774606)* 17 Robbins Wilks Rd., Bassfield, MS 39421 USA Tel 601-731-2447
E-mail: wastvedt@bellsouth.net.

Bangzoom Pubs., *(978-0-9728646; 978-0-9772927; 978-0-9779099)* Div. of Bangzoom Software, Inc., 14 Storrs Ave., Braintree, MA 02184 USA (SAN 256-6923) Toll Free: 800-589-7333
Web site: http://www.bangzoom.com
Dist(s): **Partners Pubs. Group, Inc.**

Bangzoom Software, Incorporated *See* **Bangzoom Pubs.**

Banis & Associates *See* **Science & Humanities Pr.**

Banks, A J & Associates, Incorporated *See* **BaHar Publishing, L.C.**

Banner of Truth, The, *(978-0-85151)* Orders Addr.: P.O. Box 621, Carlisle, PA 17013 USA Tel 717-249-5747; Fax:

717-249-0604; Toll Free: 800-263-8085; Edit Addr.: 63 E. Louther St., Carlisle, PA 17013 USA (SAN 112-1553)
E-mail: info@banneroftruth.org
Web site: http://www.banneroftruth.co.uk
Dist(s): **Spring Arbor Distributors, Inc.**

Banta, Sandra, *(978-0-9799729)* 16849A Willow Glen Rd., Brownsville, CA 95919 USA Tel 530-675-2010
E-mail: sfbanta@aol.com
Web site: http://www.lilonesbooks.com.

Bantam *Imprint of* **Random House Publishing Group**

Bantam Bks. for Young Readers *Imprint of* **Random Hse. Children's Bks.**

Bantam Doubleday Dell Large Print Group, Inc., *(978-0-385)* Orders Addr.: 2451 S. Wolf Rd., Des Plaines, IL 60018 USA Toll Free: 800-323-9872 (orders); 800-258-4233 (EDI ordering); Edit Addr.: 1540 Broadway, New York, NY 10036-4094 USA
Dist(s): **Penguin Random Hse. Distribution**
Penguin Random Hse. LLC
Beeler, Thomas T. Pub.

Banyan Bks., *(978-0-615-63108-0)* 251 Bethany Farms Dr., Ball Ground, GA 30107 USA Tel 770-315-1244 Do not confuse with Banyan Books in Miami, FL, Santa Barabara, CA
Web site: www.juliekorzenko.com
Dist(s): **CreateSpace Independent Publishing Platform.**

Banyan Hypnosis Center for Training & Services, Inc., *(978-0-9712290)* 1431 Warner Ave. Ste. E, Tustin, CA 92780-6444 USA (SAN 253-9381)
E-mail: Maureen@hypnosiscenter.com.

Banyan Publishing, Incorporated *See* **Banyan Hypnosis Center for Training & Services, Inc.**

Banyon Publishing, Inc., *(978-0-9747960)* 235 W Brandon Blvd., Suite 223, Brandon, FL 33511 USA Fax: 813-243-0701
E-mail: banyonpublishing@aol.com
Web site: http://www.banyonpublishing.com.

Baobab Pr., *(978-1-936097)* 121 California Ave., Reno, NV 89509 USA (SAN 858-298X) Tel 775-786-1188
Dist(s): **Publishers Group West (PGW).**

Baobab Publishing, *(978-0-692-52890-7; 978-0-692-52959-1; 978-0-692-52981-2; 978-0-692-52993-5; 978-0-692-54987-2; 978-0-692-55392-3; 978-0-692-59517-6; 978-0-692-59520-6; 978-0-692-63252-9; 978-0-692-66153-6; 978-0-692-68957-8; 978-0-692-72627-3; 978-0-9982231; 978-1-947045) 7421 Penland Dr., Riverdale, GA 30296 USA Tel 770-376-5243*
Dist(s): **CreateSpace Independent Publishing Platform.**

Baptist Publishing Hse., *(978-0-89114)* Div. of Baptist Missionary Assn. of America, P.O. Box 7270, Texarkana, TX 75505-7270 USA (SAN 183-6544) Tel 870-772-4550; Fax: 870-772-5451; Toll Free: 800-333-1442
E-mail: info@bph.org; pathway@bph.org
Web site: http://www.bph.org.

Baptist Spanish Publishing Hse./Casa Bavtista de Publicaciones: Mundo Hispano, *(978-0-311)* 7000 Alabama St., El Paso, TX 79914 USA (SAN 299-920X) Tel 916-566-9656; Fax: 916-562-6502; Toll Free: 800-755-5958
E-mail: cbpsales1@juno.com
Web site: http://casabautista.org.

Bar charts Publishing, Inc. *See* **BarCharts Publishing, Inc.**

Bara Publishing, *(978-0-9842517)* 131 Gilbert Dr., Beaufort, NC 28516 USA Tel 252-838-1803
Dist(s): **Follett School Solutions**
ebrary, Inc.

Barabara Pr., *(978-0-9719097)* 5929 S. Kolmar Ave., Chicago, IL 60629 USA Tel 773-735-1176 (phone/fax)
E-mail: captsma@comcast.net
Web site: http://www.barabarapress.com.

Barach Publishing, *(978-0-9767453)* 900 N. Walnut Creek, Suite 100, No. 280, Mansfield, TX 76063 USA
E-mail: lgonzalez@barachpublishing.com
Web site: http://www.barachpublishing.com.

Baraka Bks. (CAN) *(978-0-9812405; 978-1-926824; 978-1-77186) Dist. by* **IPG Chicago.**

Barany Publishing, *(978-0-9832960; 978-0-9895004; 978-1-944841)* 771 Kingston Ave. No. 108, Oakland, CA 94611 USA Tel 510-333-7320
E-mail: BETH@BETHBARANY.COM
Web site: http://www.bethbarany.com
Dist(s): **Smashwords.**

Barbary Coast Books *See* **Gold Street Pr.**

Barbour & Company, Incorporated *See* **Barbour Publishing, Inc.**

Barbour Bks. *Imprint of* **Barbour Publishing, Inc.**

Barbour Publishing, Inc., *(978-0-916441; 978-1-55748; 978-1-57748; 978-1-58660; 978-1-59310; 978-1-59789; 978-1-60260; 978-1-60742; 978-1-61626; 978-1-62029; 978-1-62416; 978-1-62836; 978-1-63058; 978-1-63409; 978-1-944836; 978-1-68322; 978-1-64352; 978-1-63609)* Orders Addr.: P.O. Box 719, Uhrichsville, OH 44683 USA (SAN 295-7094) Fax: 740-922-5948; Toll Free Fax: 800-220-5948; Toll Free: 800-852-8010; *Imprints:* Barbour Books (Barbour Bks); Casa Promesa (Casa Promesa); Shiloh Kidz (Shiloh Kidz); GoTandem (GoTandem); 'Shiloh Run Studios (Shiloh Run)
E-mail: info@barbourbooks.com
Web site: http://www.barbourbooks.com
Dist(s): **Anchor Distributors**
Follett School Solutions
Spring Arbor Distributors, Inc.

Barcelona Pubs., *(978-0-9624080; 978-1-891278; 978-1-937440; 978-1-945411)* Orders Addr.: 10231 Plano Rd., Dallas, TX 78132 USA (SAN 298-6299) Tel 214-553-9795; Toll Free: 866-620-6943
E-mail: barcelonapublishers@gvtc.com; warehouse@barcelonapublishers.com
Web site: http://www.barcelonapublishers.com
Dist(s): **MyiLibrary**
Ware-Pak, Inc.
ebrary, Inc.

BarCharts Publishing, Inc., *(978-1-57222; 978-1-4232)* 6000 Pk. of Commerce Blvd. Suite D, Boca Raton, FL 33487-8230 USA (SAN 299-5026) Tel 561-989-3666 ext.3054; Fax: 561-989-3722; Toll Free: 800-226-7799
E-mail: jmijares@barcharts.com
Web site: http://www.quickstudy.com; http://www.barcharts.com
Dist(s): **Follett School Solutions.**

Bard College Pubns. Office, *(978-0-941276; 978-1-931493; 978-1-936192)* P.O. Box 5000, Annandale-on-Hudson, NY 12504-5000 USA Tel 845-758-7872 (7418); Fax: 845-758-7554; *Imprints:* Center for Curatorial Studies (Ctr Curatorial Studies)
E-mail: admission@bard.edu; info@levy.org
Web site: http://www.levy.org; http://www.bard.edu
Dist(s): **D.A.P./Distributed Art Pubs.**

Bard, Frank, *(978-0-9767098)* Orders Addr.: 3801 Corbett Rd., North Lewisburg, OH 43060-9616 USA Tel 937-869-0235
E-mail: fbard@ctcn.net
Web site: http://www.ctcn.net/~febard.

Bardic Pr., *(978-0-9745667)* P.O. Box 761, Oregon House, CA 95962-0761 USA Tel 539-692-1180
E-mail: info@bardic-press.com; andrew@bardic-press.com
Web site: http://www.bardic-press.com.

Bardin & Marsee Publishing, *(978-0-9770169; 978-0-9792394; 978-0-9840857; 978-1-60969)* po box 190351, Birmingham, AL 35219 USA (SAN 854-6215) Toll Free: 866-846-4338
E-mail: bobby@bardinmarsee.com
Web site: http://www.bardinmarsee.com.

Bare Bones Training & Consulting Company *See* **Straus, Jane**

BareBones Publishing, *(978-0-9779601)* P.O. Box 8, McDonough, NY 13801 USA
Web site: http://www.dustinwarburton.com; http://www.bonfed.com; http://www.BareBonespublishing.com
Dist(s): **BCH Fulfillment & Distribution.**

Barefoot Bks., Ltd. (GBR) *(978-1-84148; 978-1-898000; 978-1-901223; 978-1-902283; 978-1-905236; 978-1-84686; 978-1-78285) Dist. by* **Children Plus.**

Barefoot Bks., Inc., *(978-1-84148; 978-1-898000; 978-1-901223; 978-1-902283; 978-1-905236; 978-1-84686; 978-1-64686)* Orders Addr.: 2067 Massachusetts Ave., 5th Fl., Cambridge, MA 02140 USA Tel 866-417-2369; Fax: 888-346-9138
E-mail: ussales@barefootbooks.com
Web site: http://www.barefootbooks.com
Dist(s): **Banta Packaging & Fulfillment.**

Barefoot Pr., *(978-1-882133)* Orders Addr.: P.O. Box 28514, Raleigh, NC 27611 USA (SAN 248-5656) Tel 919-834-1164; Edit Addr.: 700 W. Morgan St., Raleigh, NC 27603 USA (SAN 248-5664).

Barker, Lesley, *(978-0-9763211)* 1630 Rathford Dr., Saint Louis, MO 63146-3911 USA
E-mail: asklesley@teamlesley.com
Web site: http://www.teamlesley.com.

Barker, Thomas Bks., Photography, & Films, 1223 Lake Point Dr., Webster, NY 14580 USA Tel 585-265-4015
E-mail: tbbeqa@mac.com
Web site: tombarker.net.

Barksdale, Colleen, *(978-0-578-50447-6)* 21155 Fondant Ave. N., Forest Lake, MN 55025 USA Tel 651-464-0094
E-mail: 2019authoroflife@gmail.com.

Barmarle Pubns., *(978-0-9619463)* 735 Nardo Rd., Encinitas, CA 92024 USA (SAN 245-0070) Tel 760-753-6950.

Barnaby & Co., *(978-0-9642836; 978-0-615-74648-7)* 30 W. Chester St., Nantucket, MA 02554 USA Tel 508-901-1793
E-mail: barnaby@nantucket.net.

Barnaby Bks., Inc., *(978-0-940350)* 3290 Pacific Heights Rd., Honolulu, HI 96813 USA (SAN 217-5010) Fax: 808-531-0089
E-mail: barnaby@lava.net; publisher@barnabybooks.com
Web site: http://www.barnabybooks.com
Dist(s): **Bess Pr., Inc.**

Barner, Oren , *(978-0-578-19413-4)* 5534 Charlotte Dr., New Orleans, LA 70122 USA.

Barnes & Noble Bks.-Imports, *(978-0-389)* 4720 Boston Way, Lanham, MD 20706 USA (SAN 206-7803) Tel 301-459-3366; Toll Free: 800-462-6420
Dist(s): **Rowman & Littlefield Publishers, Inc.**

Barnes & Noble, Inc., *(978-0-7607; 978-0-88029; 978-1-4028; 978-1-4114; 978-1-4351; 978-1-61551; 978-1-61552; 978-1-61553; 978-1-61554; 978-1-61555; 978-1-61556; 978-1-61557; 978-1-61558; 978-1-61559; 978-1-61560; 978-1-61679; 978-1-61680; 978-1-61681; 978-1-61682; 978-1-61683; 978-1-61684; 978-1-61685; 978-1-61686; 978-1-61687; 978-1-61688; 978-1-970008) 76 Ninth Ave., 9th Flr., New York, NY 10011 USA (SAN 141-3651) Tel 212-414-6385; 122 Fifth Ave., New York, NY 10011; Imprints:* Blackbirch Press, Incorporated (Blackbirch Pr); SparkNotes (SparkNotes)
E-mail: smcculloch@bn.com
Dist(s): **Bookazine Co., Inc.**
Dover Pubns., Inc.
Sterling Publishing Co., Inc.

Barnes & Noble Pr., *(978-1-68101; 978-1-5380; 978-1-9870; 978-1-0787; 978-1-6635)* 76 Ninth Ave, New York, NY 10011 USA; 1166 Avenue of the Americas 18th Flr., New York, NY 10036
Web site: print.nookpress.com; press.barnesandnobel.com.

BARNES, DONNA, *(978-1-7337993)* 122 Nelson St., Durham, NC 27707 USA Tel 919-680-0805
E-mail: quasifree@msn.com
Dist(s): **Ingram Content Group.**

Barnes Printing, *(978-0-9658838; 978-0-9863483; 978-1-948254)* 1076 Klopman Mill Rd., Denton, NC 27239-7305 USA Tel 336-859-1964; Fax: 336-859-4923
E-mail: elizabeth@barnesprinting.com
Web site: www.barnesprinting.com.

Barnesyard Bks., *(978-0-9674681)* P.O. Box 254, Sergeantsville, NJ 08557 USA Tel 609-397-6600; Fax: 609-397-3262
E-mail: info@barnesyardbooks.com
Web site: http://www.barnesyardbooks.com
Dist(s): **Follett School Solutions.**

Barnette, Donald, *(978-0-9747816)* 591 Mira Vista Ave., Oakland, CA 94610-1928 USA.

Barnhardt & Ashe Publishing, Inc., *(978-0-9715402; 978-0-9801744)* 444 Brickell Ave., Suite 51, PMB 432, Miami, FL 33131 USA Toll Free: 800-283-6360
E-mail: barnhardtashe@aol.com
Web site: http://www.barnhardtashepublishing.com.

Barnsley Ink *Imprint of* **Write Way Publishing Co. LLC**

Baron Ridge Productions, *(978-0-692-02990-9; 978-0-692-03128-5)* 7703 W. Shady Ln., Wichita, KS 67205 USA Tel 316-409-6498
E-mail: mindycook@cox.net; mindy@baronridgeproductions.com
Web site: http://www.baronridgeproductions.org.

Barr, Tricia, *(978-0-9989777; 978-1-7337494)* P.O. Box 1224, SAHUARITA, AZ 85629 USA Tel 520-954-4422
Dist(s): **Ingram Content Group.**

Barranca Pr., *(978-1-939604)* 1450 Couse St. (No. 10), Taos, NM 87571 USA Tel 575-613-1026
E-mail: lisa@barrancapress.com
Web site: www.barrancapress.com.

Barren Hill Bks., *(978-0-9769896)* 646 Highland Ave., South Portland, ME 04106 USA Tel 207-767-3268
E-mail: info@BarrenHillBooks.com
Web site: http://www.barrenhillbooks.com/.

Barrera, Elizabeth Paige, *(978-0-9984620; 978-0-578-51830-5)* 4025 Burke Rd., Pasadena, TX 77504 USA Tel 713-550-7220; *Imprints:* Infinity Flower Publishing, LLC (MYID_A_INFINIT)
E-mail: epaigeburks.book@gmail.com
Web site: http://www.epaigeburks.com/.

Barrett, Dave, *(978-0-578-21461-0; 978-0-578-21462-7; 978-0-578-60756-6; 978-0-578-60757-3)* 5 Independence Ave., Hampden, ME 04444 USA.

Barrett's Bookshelf, *(978-0-9728731)* 16165 SW Inverurie Rd., Lake Oswego, OR 97035 USA Tel 503-697-4208.

†Barricade Bks., Inc., *(978-0-934878; 978-0-942637; 978-0-9623032; 978-1-56980)* 2037 Lemoine Ave., Suite 362, Fort Lee, NJ 07024 USA (SAN 299-1780) Tel 201-944-7600; Toll Free: 800-592-6657; 4501 Forbes Blvd., Lanham, MD 20706
E-mail: customerservice@barricadebooks.com
Web site: http://www.barricadebooks.com
Dist(s): **Follett School Solutions**
MyiLibrary
National Bk. Network
Partners Bk. Distributing, Inc.
ebrary, Inc.; *CIP.*

Barricks, Jeri Ministry, *(978-0-9743512)* P.O. Box 347, Buffalo, NY 14225 USA Fax: 716-685-6839
E-mail: jeribar37@hotmail.com
Web site: http://www.jeribarricks.net.

Barrier Breaker Publishing Inc., *(978-0-9823078)* 4131 Planters Watch Dr., Charlotte, NC 28278 USA
E-mail: ave@barrierbreakeronline.com
Web site: http://www.barrierbreakeronline.com.

Barringer Publishing, *(978-0-9825109; 978-0-9828425; 978-0-9831989; 978-0-9833088; 978-0-9839050; 978-0-9851184; 978-0-9882034; 978-0-9891694; 978-0-9896338; 978-0-9903935; 978-0-9908209; 978-0-9961973; 978-0-9989069; 978-1-7339837; 978-1-7352525)* 2317 Harrier Run, Naples, FL 34105 USA
Web site: barringerpublishing.com
Dist(s): **Follett School Solutions.**

Barron's Educational Series, Inc. *Imprint of* **Kaplan Publishing**

Barrow, Shelley *See* **Mikenzi's Kardz & Bks. Llc.**

Barsotti Bks., *(978-0-9642112; 978-0-9818188)* 2239 Hidden Valley Ln., Camino, CA 95709-9722 USA Tel 530-642-8341; Fax: 530-642-9703
E-mail: jb@barsottibooks.com
Web site: http://www.barsottibooks.com.

Bartleby Pr., *(978-0-910155; 978-0-935437)* 8600 Foundry St. Savage Mill Box 2043, Savage, MD 20763 USA (SAN 241-2098) Tel 301-949-2443; Fax: 301-949-2205; Toll Free: 800-953-9929
E-mail: Inquiries@bartlebythepublisher.com
Web site: http://www.BartlebythePublisher.com
Dist(s): **Casemate Pubs. & Bk. Distributors, LLC**
MyiLibrary.

Barton Bks., *(978-0-615-69695-9; 978-0-615-78343-7)* Orders Addr.: 4505 Sentinel Ct., Rocklin, CA 95677 USA Tel 916-787-0962; *Imprints:* Flickerfawn (Flickerfawn)
E-mail: dredsovrn@me.com; dredsovrn@wavecable.com
Web site: www.flickerfawn.com; www.FionaThornBook.com; www.jbartonbooks.com.

Barton, Carol, *(978-1-7330134)* 165 Lost River Ln., Bowling Green, KY 42104 USA Tel 270-779-5563
E-mail: noel10new2@twc.com.

Barton, D.C. Publishing, *(978-0-9759426)* P.O. Box 3057, Lakeland, FL 33801-6602 USA Tel 863-665-5986
E-mail: dfcbible@aol.com.

Barton Publications, *(978-0-9778455)* Orders Addr.: 1613 Sunrise Ln., Eau Claire, WI 54703-2574 USA
E-mail: bartonpub@ymail.com
Web site: http://www.westmusic.com/1002410-print-music-books/m1090-music-therapy-books/m1090i-texts/biomedical-foundations-of-music-as-therapy-838708.htm
Dist(s): **West Music Co.**

Barton-Veerman Co., *(978-0-9724616; 978-0-9978516)* 205 N Washington St, Wheaton, IL 60187 USA Tel 630-871-1212
E-mail: accounting@livingstonecorp.com
Web site: http://www.livingstonecorp.com
Dist(s): **BookBaby.**

Bartram Team, The, *(978-0-615-31220-0)* 1251 Pine Valley Dr., New Bern , NC 28562 USA.

Bas Relief, LLC, *(978-0-9657472)* Orders Addr.: P.O. Box 645, Union, WV 24983 USA Tel 304-832-6647
E-mail: Barea@basrelief.org
Web site: http://www.basrelief.org
Dist(s): **Follett School Solutions.**

Bas Relief Publishing *See* **Bas Relief, LLC**

Bases Loaded Bks. *Imprint of* **ChildrenzBks.**

Basic Black Publishing, *(978-0-9801320)* Orders Addr.: 8584 W. Appleton Ave., Unit X, Milwaukee, WI 53225 USA.

†Basic Bks., *(978-0-201; 978-0-465; 978-0-7382; 978-0-7867; 978-0-8133; 978-0-86531; 978-0-931188; 978-0-938410; 978-0-941423; 978-1-56025; 978-1-56858; 978-1-56924; 978-1-58005; 978-1-58243; 978-1-878067; 978-1-887178; 978-1-4789; 978-1-5416)* A Member of Perseus Books Group, Orders Addr.: 5500 Central Ave., Boulder, CO 80301-2877 USA Fax: 303-449-3356 (customer service); Toll Free: 800-371-1669 (customer service); Edit Addr.: 387 Park Ave., S., New York, NY 10016 USA (SAN 201-4521) Tel 212-340-8100; Fax: 212-340-8135; 1290 Avenue of the Americas, New York, NY 10104; *Imprints:* Seal Press (SealPrHBG)
E-mail: perseus.orders@perseusbooks.com
Web site: http://www.perseusbooksgroup.com; http://www.perseusbooksgroup.com/basic/home.jsp
Dist(s): **Blackstone Audio, Inc.**
Follett School Solutions
Hachette Bk. Group
MyiLibrary
ebrary, Inc.; *CIP.*

Basic Distribution, Inc., 360 Hurst St., Linden, NJ 07036 USA Tel 908-523-0555; Fax: 908-523-0373
E-mail: ssullivan@basicdistributioninc.com
Web site: http://www.basicdistributioninc.com.

Basic ESL *Imprint of* **Bilingual Dictionaries, Inc.**

Basic Health Pubns., Inc., *(978-1-59120)* 28812 Top of the World Dr., Laguna Beach, CA 92651 USA (SAN 858-4893) Tel 949-715-7327; Fax: 949-415-7328; Toll Free: 800-575-8890 (orders only)
E-mail: ngoldfind@basicmediagroup.com
Web site: http://www.basichealthpub.com
Dist(s): **Follett School Solutions**
Ingram Publisher Services.

Basic Knowledge Publishing Co., *(978-1-885501)* 1024 Debbie Ln., Maryville, MO 64468 USA Tel 816-562-2665.

Basic Skills Assessment & Educational Services, *(978-1-888786)* 19146 S. Molalla Ave., Oregon City, OR 97045-8975 USA Tel 503-650-5282; Fax: 503-557-2953
E-mail: basicsk@MSN.COM
Web site: http://www.basicskills.net.

Basketball Fundamentals *See* **SportAmerica**

Basm Bks., *(978-1-7322337)* 4610 Chattahoochee Xing SE, Marietta, GA 30067 USA Tel 770-547-5215
E-mail: bailabooks@gmail.com.

Bass Cove Bks., *(978-0-9630074)* 57 North St., Kennebunkport, ME 04046 USA Tel 207-967-4152
E-mail: amabee@adelphia.net.

Bass, Robert Enterprises, *(978-0-692-09813-4; 978-0-578-52952-3)* 67 Stratford Dr., Penrose, NC 28766 USA Tel 828-553-8741
E-mail: adalynelliott@gmail.com
Dist(s): **Ingram Content Group.**

Bass, Sheila, *(978-0-9766366)* 23 Conn. St., Woodsville, NH 03785 USA
E-mail: a_15bass@yahoo.com.

Bassan, Malca, *(978-0-9744039; 978-0-692-25535-3)* 9801 Collins Ave., Apt. 15Q, Bal Harbor, FL 33154 USA Tel 305-868-0365; Fax: 305-865-6992
E-mail: mabassan27@gmail.com.

Bassett, Maurice, *(978-0-9760402; 978-0-9762653; 978-1-60025)* Orders Addr.: P.O. Box 839, Anna Maria, FL 34216-0839 USA Tel 919-423-2460
E-mail: reinventingyourself@gmail.com
Web site: http://www.abrahammaslow.com; http://www.stevechandler.com; http://www.mauricebassett.com.

Bastion Pr., Inc., *(978-0-9714392; 978-1-59263)* Orders Addr.: P.O. Box 46753, Seattle, WA 98146 USA; Edit Addr.: 8405 16th Ave., SW., Seattle, WA 98106-2365 USA Tel 206-763-3368; Fax: 206-763-3370 Do not confuse with Bastion Pr., Los Angeles, CA
E-mail: jim@bastionpress.com
Web site: http://www.bastionpress.com
Dist(s): **Studio 2 Publishing, Inc.**

Bat Wing Pr *Imprint of* **Harbor Hse.**

Batchelor, Leyetta, *(978-0-578-44012-5)* 6193 Aurelian Springs Rd, Halifax, NC 27839 USA Tel 252-326-3341
E-mail: leyetta13@gmail.com.

Bat-El Publishing, *(978-0-9832025)* 3400 Colville Pl., Encino, CA 91436 USA Tel 818-461-9294
E-mail: talyanai7@gmail.com.

Publisher Name Index

Batelier Publishing, *(978-0-9789429)* 3140 Bourbon St. Cir., Rockwall, TX 75032 USA
E-mail: batelierpublishing@yahoo.com
Web site: http://www.batelier.bravehost.com.

Bates Jackson Engraving Co., Inc., *(978-1-932583; 978-0-9831157; 978-0-9885895)* 17-21 Elm St., Buffalo, NY 14203 USA Tel 716-854-3000; Fax: 716-847-1965
E-mail: ed@batesjackson.com
Web site: http://www.batesjackson.com.

Batfish Bks., *(978-0-9728653)* Div. of O'Neill, Michael P. Photography, Inc., P.O. Box 32909, Palm Beach Gardens, FL 33420-2909 USA (SAN 255-1780) Tel 305-333-7166; Fax: 561-840-1939
E-mail: mpo@msn.com
Web site: http://www.batfishbooks.com
Dist(s): **Follett School Solutions**
Southern Bk. Service.

†**Bathtub Row Pr.,** *(978-0-941232)* Orders Addr.: P.O. Box 43, Los Alamos, NM 87544 USA (SAN 276-9603) Tel 505-662-2660; Fax: 505-662-6312; Edit Addr.: 1050 Bathtub Row, Los Alamos, NM 87544 USA (SAN 241-9025)
E-mail: shar5992@gmail.com
Web site: http://losalamoshistory.org; *CIP.*

Battat, Inc., *(978-0-9794542; 978-0-9843722; 978-0-9844904; 978-0-9883165; 978-0-9891839; 978-0-9963272; 978-0-692-81454-3; 978-0-692-82334-7; 978-0-692-82578-5; 978-0-692-82579-2; 978-0-692-89111-7; 978-0-692-96027-1; 978-0-692-98872-5; 978-0-692-04479-7; 978-0-692-07793-1; 978-0-692-08323-9; 978-0-692-10296-1; 978-0-692-13583-9; 978-0-578-40814-9; 978-0-578-46375-9; 978-0-578-50767-5; 978-0-578-50822-1; 978-0-578-51878-7; 978-0-578-53553-1; 978-0-578-54717-6; 978-0-578-62758-8; 978-0-578-63262-9; 978-0) 1560 Military Tpke., Plattsburgh, NY 12901-7458 USA (SAN 853-4683).*

Battle Creek Area Mathematics & Science Ctr., *(978-1-933281)* 765 Upton Ave., Battle Creek, MI 49015 USA Tel 269-965-9440
Web site: http://bcmsc.k12.mi.us.

Batyah & Assocs. Publishing, *(978-0-9749571)* 141 California St, Highland Park, MI 48203 USA
E-mail: baroberts07@yahoo.com
Web site: http://www.batasspub.com.

Batyah Productions, Inc., *(978-0-9649608)* 6434 Saxet St., Houston, TX 77055-5317 USA.

BAU Publishing Group, *(978-0-9766770)* 1808 Strawberry Dr NE, Rio Rancho, NM 87144 USA
E-mail: tizeclark2000@yahoo.com; admin@baupublishing.com
Web site: http://www.baupublishing.com.

Bauer, Linda, *(978-0-9798146)* Orders Addr.: P.O. Box 308, Eastford, CT 06242 USA
Dist(s): **CreateSpace Independent Publishing Platform.**

Bauer Media Bks. (AUS) *(978-0-949128; 978-0-949892; 978-1-86396; 978-1-74245; 978-0-646-36336-3; 978-1-906312) Dist. by* **HachBkGrp.**

Bauhan Publishing LLC, *(978-0-87233)* Orders Addr.: P.O. Box 117, Peterborough, NH 03458 USA (SAN 204-384X) Tel 603-567-4430
E-mail: sales@bauhanpublishing.com; sbauhan@bauhanpublishing.com
Web site: http://www.bauhanpublishing.com
Dist(s): **Casemate Pubs. & Bk. Distributors, LLC**
East-West Export Bks.

Bauhan, William L. Incorporated *See* **Bauhan Publishing LLC**

Baum & Baum, LLC, *(978-0-9839373)* 14196 Cranston St., Livonia, MI 48154-4251 USA Tel 734-422-0546
E-mail: lbaum@mi.rr.com.

Bauman, Chris *See* **Blynbeek Publishing**

Baumbach, Laura *See* **MLR Pr., LLC**

Baxter Pr., *(978-1-888237; 978-0-9907879; 978-0-9973372; 978-1-947505)* 700 S. Friendswood Dr., Suite C, Friendswood, TX 77546 USA Tel 281-992-0628; Fax: 815-572-5115
E-mail: baxter2@flash.net
Web site: http://baxterpress.com
Dist(s): **Greenleaf Book Group**
Spirit Rising.

Baxter The Dog Bks., *(978-1-7321588; 978-1-7344749)* 9850 S. Maryland Pkwy. Ste A-5 336, Las Vegas, NV 89183 USA Tel 702-518-9213
E-mail: hi@baxterthedogbooks.com
Web site: baxterthedogbooks.com.

Bay Company Books, Inc. *See* **Bay Co. Bks., Inc.**

Bay Co. Bks., Inc., *(978-1-7324647; 978-0-692-15964-4)* 825 Front St., Santa Cruz, CA 95060 USA Tel 831-460-3258.

Bay Horse Creations LLC, *(978-0-9749320)* 508 W. Irvine Rd., Phoenix, AZ 85086 USA Tel 602-818-7879
Web site: http://www.bayhorsecreations.com.

Bay Light Publishing, *(978-0-9670280; 978-0-9741817)* P.O. Box 3032, Mooresville, NC 28117 USA (SAN 299-9196) Tel 704-664-7541; Fax: 704-664-2712; Toll Free: 866-541-3895
E-mail: baylightpub@compuserve.com
Web site: http://www.baylightpub.com.

Bay Media, Inc., *(978-0-9665239; 978-0-9717047; 978-0-9823354)* Orders Addr.: 550m Ritchie Hwy., #271 Severna Pk., Severna Park, MD 21146 USA Tel 410-647-8402; Fax: 410-544-4640
Web site: http://www.baymed.com.

Bay Mills Indian Community, *(978-0-9758801)* 12140 W. Lakeshore Dr., Brimley, MI 49715 USA
Web site: http://www.bmic.net.

Bay Oak Pubs., Ltd., *(978-0-9704692; 978-0-9741713; 978-0-9800874)* 34 Wimbledon Dr., Dover, DE 19904 USA
E-mail: bayoakpublishers@aol.com
Web site: http://www.bayoakpublishers.com
Dist(s): **Follett School Solutions**
Washington Bk. Distributors.

Bay Publishing, *(978-0-9822046)* P.O. Box 4569, Santa Rosa, CA 95402-4569 USA (SAN 857-5401)
E-mail: ron@bayyellow.com.

Bay Villager, The, *(978-0-9769742)* 4923 43rd. St., Dickinson, TX 77539 USA
E-mail: lindalou36@hotmail.com.

Bay, William Music, *(978-0-9859227; 978-0-9888327; 978-0-9983842; 978-0-9996980; 978-1-7327088; 978-1-7337169)* 4 Denny Ln., St. Louis, MO 63131 USA Tel 314-707-7366
E-mail: bill@melbay.com
Dist(s): **Mel Bay Pubns., Inc.**

BAYADA Publishing Hse., LLC, *(978-0-692-92260-6)* 9012 Kinsale Cir., Richmond, VA 23228 USA Tel 804-218-3110; Fax: 804-218-3110
E-mail: jackiehunter.11@juno.com.

Bayard Editions (FRA) *(978-2-227; 978-2-7009; 978-2-7470; 978-2-915480; 978-2-9518356) Dist. by* **Distribks Inc.**

Bayberry Cottage Gallery, *(978-0-615-61021-4; 978-0-615-89363-1)* 9074 Highland St., Mauricetown, NJ 08329 USA Tel 856-785-9927
E-mail: nanptidy@yahoo.com
Web site: http://nancy-patterson.artistwebsites.com.

Bayeux Arts, Inc. (CAN) *(978-1-896209; 978-1-897411; 978-1-988440) Dist. by* **Chicago Distribution Ctr.**

Bayliss, Erin, *(978-0-9778471)* 320 Roan Dr., Grants Pass, OR 97526 USA
E-mail: rise4him@q.com.

Baylor College of Medicine, *(978-1-888997; 978-1-944035)* Div. of Center for Educational Outreach, Orders Addr.: Center For Educational Outreach Baylor College Of Medicine One Baylor Plaza, Bcm411, Houston, TX 77030 USA Tel 713-798-8200; Fax: 713-798-8201; Toll Free: 800-798-8244; *Imprints:* BioEd (BioEd)
E-mail: edoutreach@bcm.edu; nmoreno@bcm.edu; marthay@bcm.edu; mslopez@bcm.edu
Web site: http://www.bcm.edu/edoutreach; http://www.bioedonline.org; http://www.bcm.edu.

Baylor Univ. Pr., *(978-0-918954; 978-1-878804; 978-1-932792; 978-1-60258; 978-1-4813)* 1920 S. Fourth St., Waco, TX 76706 USA Tel 254-710-3164; Fax: 254-710-3440
E-mail: Diane_Smith@baylor.edu
Web site: http://www.baylorpress.com
Dist(s): **Longleaf Services**
MyiLibrary
ebrary, Inc.

Bayou Publishing, *(978-1-886298)* Div. of Bayou Publishing, LLC, Orders Addr.: 2524 Nottingham, Houston, TX 77005 USA (SAN 859-2810) Tel 713-526-4558; Fax: 713-526-4342; Toll Free: 800-340-2034 Do not confuse with Bayou Publishing, Longboat Key, FL
E-mail: info@bayoupublishing.com; orders@bayoupublishing.com; vloos@bayoupublishing.com
Web site: http://www.bayoupublishing.com
Dist(s): **Baker & Taylor Publisher Services (BTPS)**
Quality Bks., Inc.
Unique Bks., Inc.

Bayou Publishing, *(978-0-9643441)* 700 John Ringling Blvd., No. T1810, Sarasota, FL 34236-1542 USA Do not confuse with Bayou Publishing, Houston, TX
E-mail: mnecht7725@aol.com
Web site: http://members.aol.com/mnecht7725/FORDVCE/index.html
Dist(s): **Distributors, The**
North Country Bks., Inc.

Bayport Pr. *Imprint of* **Wellness Pubn.**

BaySidePr., *(978-0-9988034)* 330 Mission Bay Blvd. N., San Francisco, CA 94158 USA Tel 415-621-8937
E-mail: fahnestk@sbcglobal.net
Web site: www.jacksonfahnestock.com.

Baysmore Bks., *(978-0-9857160; 978-0-692-78985-8)* P.O. Box 21402, Long Beach, CA 90801 USA Tel 562-208-3646
E-mail: baysmorebooks@gmail.com.

Bazow, Thomas, *(978-0-9777725)* 4845 Romaine Spring Dr., Fenton, MO 63026-5840 USA
Web site: http://www.inhistimepublishing.com.

Bazuji Publishing LLC, *(978-0-9761555)* 3843 53rd St., SE, Tappen, ND 58487 USA (SAN 256-2626) Toll Free: 800-615-7606
Web site: http://www.bazuji.com.

BB International Productions, Inc., *(978-0-9754329)* 1200 W. Ave., Suite 707, Miami Beach, FL 33139-4316 USA
Web site: http://www.bibiadventures.com.

BBC Audiobooks America *See* **AudioGO**

BBI Incorporated *See* **Bush Brothers & Co.**

BBM Bks., *(978-1-938504)* 21 Harbor Pointe Dr., Corona del Mar, CA 92625 USA Tel 949-302-5849
E-mail: inspiredcreationsca@gmail.com.

BBR *Imprint of* **BBR: Books for Brilliance & Resilience**

BBR: Books for Brilliance & Resilience, *(978-0-9753245)* P.O. Box 5236, Takoma Park, MD 20913-5236 USA Toll Free: 888-898-2322; *Imprints:* BBR (B B R)
Web site: http://www.letscommunicate.org.

BBRACK Productions, Inc., *(978-0-9728837)* 1345-B Triad Ctr. Dr., No. 181, Saint Peters, MO 63376 USA Tel 636-936-2311
E-mail: 1stB@bbrack.com
Web site: http://www.bbrack.com.

B-Bright publishing, *(978-1-943417)* 16210 tahoe dr, Jersey Village, TX 77040 USA Tel 281-606-5820
E-mail: gdbanks@gmail.com.

bby Publications at The University of West Alabama, *(978-1-885775)* Div. of College of Education, Orders Addr.: UWA Station 60, Livingston, AL 35470 USA Tel 205-652-5406; Fax: 205-652-5400
E-mail: tpartridge@uwa.edu; dknight@uwa.edu
Web site: http://www.bbypublications.com.

BC Publishing, *(978-0-9740511)* 633-1 Elk Ct., Fayetteville, NC 28301 USA Tel 910-578-2621; *Imprints:* Kids1st Books (Kids1st Bks) Do not confuse with BC Publishing in Tampa, FL
E-mail: dbradleyclarke@yahoo.com.

BCB Productions, 180 church st, whitinsville, MA 01588 USA Tel 508-372-9151
Dist(s): **CreateSpace Independent Publishing Platform.**

BCM International Inc., *(978-0-86508)* 201 Granite Run Dr., Suite 260, Lancaster, PA 17601 USA (SAN 211-7762) Tel 717-560-9601 Main Phone Number; Toll Free: 888-226-4685
E-mail: info@bcmintl.org
Web site: http://www.bcmintl.org
Dist(s): **CLC Pubns.**
Send The Light Distribution LLC.

BCM Publications, Incorporated *See* **BCM International Inc.**

BCP Pubns., *(978-0-615-20692-9; 978-0-615-21056-8; 978-0-578-02129-4)* 3215 E. 17th St., Vancouver, WA 98661 USA
E-mail: bcpwriter2000@yahoo.com
Web site: http://www.authortree.com/bcpwriter2000
Dist(s): **AuthorHouse.**

BDA Publishing, *(978-0-9794716)* P.O. Box 541715, Dallas, TX 75354-1715 USA Tel 972-532-8805; Fax: 214-350-9275; 3163 Citation Dr., Dallas, TX 75229-5840
E-mail: bbd@sbcglobal.net
Web site: http://www.evanbrain.com; http://barrybdoyle.com/.

Be Heard Publishing, *(978-0-692-93977-2; 978-1-7342949)* 939 Dalkeith, St Louis, MO 63132 USA Tel 314-323-2737
E-mail: rebeccatclark@yahoo.com
Web site: www.wittykidsclub.com.

Be Naturally Curious, *(978-1-942403)* 160 W 85th St., New York, NY 10024 USA Tel 347-229-5559
E-mail: valerie@benaturallycurious.com
Web site: www.benaturallycurious.com.

Be There Bedtime Stories LLC, *(978-0-692-74330-0)* 35 Giovanni Aisle, IRVINE, CA 92614 USA Tel 949-394-1714.

Bea is for Business, *(978-0-9893403)* P.O. Box 3009, Charlotte, NC 28230 USA Tel 704-325-9232
E-mail: jamieabrown@hotmail.com
Web site: www.beaisforbusiness.com.

Beach Bks., *(978-0-9763052; 978-0-615-57831-6)* 430 Noe St., San Francisco, CA 94114 USA Tel 415-251-3845
E-mail: gyaltsen@yahoo.com
Web site: http://www.jefferybeach.com
Dist(s): **CreateSpace Independent Publishing Platform.**

Beach Front Bks., *(978-0-9651281)* P.O. Box 545, East Bridgewater, MA 02333 USA Tel 508-378-9319; Fax: 508-378-7621 Do not confuse with Beach Front Books in East Bridgewater, MA
E-mail: beachfrontbooks@aol.com.

Beach Lane Bks. *Imprint of* **Beach Lane Bks.**

Beach Lane Bks., Div. of Simon & Schuster Children's Publishing, 1230 Ave. of the Americas, New York, NY 10020 USA; *Imprints:* Beach Lane Books (BeachLane)
Dist(s): **Children's Plus, Inc.**
Follett School Solutions
Simon & Schuster, Inc.

Beach Lloyd Pubs., LLC, *(978-0-9743158; 978-0-9792778; 978-0-9819417)* Orders Addr.: P.O. Box 2183, Southeastern, PA 19399-2183 USA (SAN 255-4992) Tel 610-407-0130; Fax: 775-254-0633; Toll Free: 866-218-3253; Edit Addr.: 40 Cabot Dr., Wayne, PA 19087-5619 USA
E-mail: beachlloyd@erols.com
Web site: http://www.beachlloyd.com
Dist(s): **MBS Textbook Exchange, Inc.**

Beachcomber Press.com, *(978-0-9800630)* 33021 Adelante St., Temecula, CA 92592 USA Tel 951-699-2932
E-mail: ashleyludwig@verizon.net.

Beachfront Bks., *(978-0-9768816)* Orders Addr.: P.O. Box 16-287, Seattle, WA 98116 USA; Edit Addr.: 5641 Beach Dr. SW, Seattle, WA 98116 USA
Web site: http://www.beachfront books.org
Dist(s): **Follett School Solutions.**

Beachfront Publishing, *(978-1-892339)* Div. of Words, Words, Words, Inc., Orders Addr.: P.O. Box 811922, Boca Raton, FL 33481 USA; 4705 Brook Top Ct., Raleigh, NC 27606
E-mail: info@beachfrontentertainment.com
Web site: http://www.beachfrontentertainment.com
Dist(s): **Follett School Solutions.**

BeachHouse Bks. *Imprint of* **Science & Humanities Pr.**

Beachhouse Publishing, LLC, *(978-0-9729905; 978-1-933067; 978-1-949000)* P.O. Box 5464, Kaneohe, HI 96744 USA
E-mail: info@beachhousepublishing.com
Web site: www.beachhousepublishing.com
Dist(s): **Booklines Hawaii, Ltd.**
Islander Group.

BeachWalk Bks. Inc., *(978-0-9770158)* P.O. Box 446, Glenview, IL 60025 USA Tel 847-729-2222; Fax: 847-729-5215; Toll Free Fax: 866-720-3222; 2136 Fir St., Glenview, IL 60025
E-mail: amcdonald@beachwalkbooks.com
Web site: http://www.beachwalkbooks.com.

Beachwalker Pr., *(978-0-9727639)* 5557 SW Village Pl., Beaverton, OR 97007 USA Tel 503-799-6061; Fax: 503-644-9335
E-mail: beachwalkerpress@aol.com
Web site: http://www.beachwalkerpress.com.

Beacon Hill Press of Kansas City *See* **Beacon Hill Pr. of Kansas City**

Beacon Pr. *Imprint of* **Beacon Pr.**

Beacon Pr., *(978-0-8070)* Orders Addr.: 25 Beacon St., Boston, MA 02108-2892 USA (SAN 201-4483) Tel 617-742-2110; Fax: 617-723-3097; *Imprints:* Beacon Press (BeaconPress)
E-mail: marketing@beacon.org
Web site: http://www.beacon.org
Dist(s): **Ebsco Publishing**
Houghton Mifflin Harcourt Publishing Co.
Houghton Mifflin Harcourt Trade & Reference Pubs.
MyiLibrary
Penguin Random Hse. Distribution
Penguin Random Hse. LLC
Random Hse., Inc.
Simon & Schuster, Inc.

Beacon Publishing *See* **Blue Sparrow Bks.**

Beacon Street Girls *Imprint of* **B*tween Productions, Inc.**

BeActive Publishing Co., *(978-0-9722714)* 29834 N. Cave Creek Rd., S118, PMB 142, Cave Creek, AZ 85331-7831 USA Tel 480-563-0315; Fax: 480-502-0664
Web site: http://www.beactivesportsmarketing.com.

Beagle Bay Bks., *(978-0-9679591; 978-0-9749610)* Div. of Beagle Bay, Inc., 2325 Homestead Pl., Reno, NV 89509-3657 USA
E-mail: info@beaglebay.com
Web site: http://www.beaglebay.com
Dist(s): **Brodart Co.**

Beagle Bks. Publishing, LLC, *(978-0-9841813)* 43 Highridge Rd., Westport, MA 02790 USA (SAN 858-6519).

Beak Star Bks., *(978-1-944724)* 10620 Belmont Pl., Powell, OH 43065 USA Tel 614-307-2663
E-mail: jdmilligan@columbus.rr.com
Web site: beakstarbooks.com.

BeaLu Bks., *(978-0-9990924; 978-1-7333092; 978-1-7341065; 978-1-7353641; 978-1-7356455)* 10401 N Oregon Ave, Tampa, FL 33612 USA Tel 813-390-5467
E-mail: luana@bealubooks.com
Web site: www.bealubooks.com.

Beaming Books *Imprint of* **Augsburg Fortress, Pubs.**

Bean Bk. Publishing, *(978-0-9761990)* 9246 E. Havasupai Dr., Scottsdale, AZ 85255 USA Tel 480-502-1257 (phone/fax)
E-mail: dawn.crichton@dcranch.com; Juliecrichton@cox.net
Web site: http://www.stringbeansorjellybeans.com; http://www.bean-books.com.

Bean Bks., *(978-0-9825601)* 416 W. Ave. B, Newberry, MI 49868 USA.

Bean Sprouts *Imprint of* **Standard Publishing**

Beaner Bks., *(978-0-9849293)* 541 Redford Pl. Dr., Rolesville, NC 27571 USA Tel 855-286-9687
E-mail: alphabetownusa@gmail.com
Web site: http://www.alphabetownusa.com.

BeanPole Bks. *Imprint of* **Harren Communications, LLC**

BeanSprout Bks., *(978-0-692-25923-8; 978-1-7322049; 978-1-950471)* 6151 White Tip Rd., Jacksonville, FL 32258 USA Tel 407-234-1837
E-mail: thesecretartgallery@gmail.com; tgrant5625@gmail.com
Dist(s): **Ingram Content Group.**

Beanstalk Pubns, *(978-0-9785302)* 4762 Camino del Rey, Santa Barbara, CA 93110 USA Tel 805-448-0898
E-mail: mjmckechnie@beanstalkpublications.com
Web site: http://www.beanstalkpublications.com.

Bear & Company *See* **Boyds Collection Ltd., The**

†**Bear & Co.,** *(978-0-939680; 978-1-879181; 978-1-59143)* Orders Addr.: P.O. Box 388, Rochester, VT 05767-0388 USA; Edit Addr.: One Park St., Rochester, VT 05767 USA (SAN 216-7174) Tel 802-767-3174; Fax: 802-767-3726; Toll Free: 800-246-8648; *Imprints:* Bear Cub Books (Bear Cub Books)
E-mail: customerservice@innertraditions.com; info@innertraditions.com
Web site: http://www.innertraditions.com
Dist(s): **Book Wholesalers, Inc.**
Bookazine Co., Inc.
Brodart Co.
Inner Traditions International, Ltd.
Integral Yoga Pubns.
MyiLibrary
New Leaf Distributing Co., Inc.
Nutri-Bks. Corp.
Partners Bk. Distributing, Inc.
Partners/West Book Distributors
Phoenix Distributors
Quality Bks., Inc.
Simon & Schuster
Simon & Schuster, Inc.; *CIP.*

Bear Cub Bks. *Imprint of* **Bear & Co.**

Bear State Bks., *(978-1-892622)* Orders Addr.: P.O. Box 96, Exeter, CA 93221 USA Tel 559-280-8547; Fax: 559-594-5383; Edit Addr.: 199 E. Pine St., Exeter, CA 93221 USA Tel 559-280-8547
E-mail: cdbrewer@gmx.com
Web site: bearstatebooks.com.

Bearhead Publishing, LLC, *(978-0-9776260; 978-0-9799153; 978-0-9824373; 978-0-9829307; 978-1-937508)* P.O. Box 16539, Louisville, KY 40256

USA (SAN 257-7798); 2217 Mary Catherine Dr., Louisville, KY 40216
E-mail: garyd@sissymarlyn.com; garydbhp@insightbb.com
Web site: http://www.sissymarlyn.com; http://www.bearheadpublishing.com.

Bearing Bks. *Imprint of* **Red Cygnet Pr.**

Bearly Cooking *Imprint of* **Mountain n' Air Bks.**

BearManor Media, *(978-0-9714570; 978-1-59393; 978-1-62933)* P.O. Box 71426, Albany, GA 31708 USA Tel 580-252-3547
E-mail: benohmart@gmail.com
Web site: http://www.bearmanormedia.com.

Bearport Publishing Co., Inc., *(978-1-59716; 978-1-936087; 978-1-936088; 978-1-936089; 978-1-936090; 978-0-9824758; 978-0-9824759; 978-0-9824760; 978-0-9824761; 978-0-9824762; 978-0-9824763; 978-0-9824764; 978-1-61772; 978-1-62724; 978-1-943074; 978-1-943553; 978-1-944102; 978-1-944997; 978-1-944998; 978-1-68402; 978-1-64280; 978-1-64747) 45 W. 21st St., Ste. 3B, New York, NY 10010 USA (SAN 256-2103) Toll Free: 877-337-8577 (and fax); 5357 Penn Ave. S., Minneapolis, MN 55419 Tel 877-337-8577; Fax: 866-337-8557*
E-mail: kenngoin@earthlink.net; marketing@bearportpublishing.com; info@bearportpublishing.com; vyaw@bearportpublishing.com
Web site: http://www.bearportpublishing.com
Dist(s): **Follett School Solutions**
Independent Pubs. Group
MyiLibrary.

Bear's Designs Unlimited, *(978-0-9638473)* 7505 320th St., W., Northfield, MN 55057 USA Tel 507-645-9050; Toll Free: 800-497-8757.

Bear's Place Publishing, *(978-1-7328112; 978-1-7342675)* 584 Horse Ferry Rd, Lawrenceville, GA 30044 USA Tel 770-845-8130
E-mail: doctorsdl@yahoo.com
Web site: doctordiane.com.

Bearwallow Blessings Ministries, *(978-0-9768514)* HC 63 Box 77A-1 Rte. 637, Jewell Ridge, VA 24622 USA
Web site: http://www.bearwallowblessings.com.

Beascoa, Ediciones S.A. (ESP) *(978-84-488; 978-84-7546) Dist. by* **Distribks Inc.**

Beascoa, Ediciones S.A. (ESP) *(978-84-488; 978-84-7546) Dist. by* **Lectorum Pubns.**

Beatin' Path Pubns., LLC, *(978-0-9795470; 978-0-9797522; 978-0-9825839; 978-0-9832648; 978-0-9882814; 978-0-9894773; 978-0-9861795; 978-0-9963591; 978-1-7333455)* Orders Addr.: 302 E. College St., Bridgewater, VA 22812-1509 USA (SAN 853-7003) Tel 540-478-4833; Fax: 540-237-4684
E-mail: beatinpath@mac.com
Web site: http://www.beatinpathpublications.com
Dist(s): **Music is Elementary**
Plank Road Publishing
Music in Motion
West Music Co.

Beatto, Sabat, *(978-1-7337532)* 550 W. 125th St., New York, NY 10472 USA Tel 347-641-5754
Dist(s): **CreateSpace Independent Publishing Platform.**

Beau Francis Pr., *(978-0-9792147)* 4100 Newport Pl., Suite 400, Newport Beach, CA 92660 USA Tel 949-499-0679.

BeauDesigns, *(978-0-9841395; 978-0-9968870)* P.O. Box 496, Youngstown, NY 14174 USA Tel 716-745-7328
Dist(s): **Niagara Collectibles.**

Beaufort Bks., Inc., *(978-0-8253; 978-0-9852135)* 27 W. 20th St., Suite 1102, New York, NY 10011 USA (SAN 215-2304) Tel 212-727-0190; Fax: 212-727-0195
E-mail: midpointny@aol.com
Dist(s): **Follett School Solutions**
Independent Pubs. Group
Midpoint Trade Bks., Inc.

Beautiful America Publishing Co., *(978-0-89802)* Orders Addr.: P.O. Box 244, Woodburn, OR 97071-0244 USA (SAN 251-2548) Tel 503-982-4616; Fax: 503-982-2825; Toll Free: 800-874-1233; Edit Addr.: 2600 Progress Way, Woodburn, OR 97071 USA (SAN 211-4623)
E-mail: bapco@beautifulamericapub.com
Web site: http://www.beautifulamericapub.com
Dist(s): **Follett School Solutions**
Koen Pacific
Partners/West Book Distributors.

Beautiful Feet Bks., *(978-0-9643803; 978-1-893103)* 1306 Mill St., San Luis Obispo, CA 93401-2817 USA Toll Free: 800-889-1978
E-mail: russell@bfbooks.com
Web site: http://www.bfbooks.com
Dist(s): **Follett School Solutions.**

Beautiful Zion Baptist Church *See* **A & L Communications, Inc.**

Beauty Beneath the Rubble, *(978-0-692-11094-2; 978-0-578-46205-9; 978-0-578-46226-4)* 256 W. Pebble Creek Ln., Orange, CA 92865 USA Tel 909-702-4052
E-mail: nushinalloo@gmail.com.

Beaver Island Arts, *(978-0-9708575)* P.O. Box 40, Bay City, MI 49708-0040 USA (SAN 253-8385) Tel 517-894-5925
E-mail: mblocksma@yahoo.com
Web site: http://beaverislandarts.com
Dist(s): **Follett School Solutions**
Indiana Univ. Pr.
Ingram Publisher Services
Partners Bk. Distributing, Inc.
Two Rivers Distribution.

Beaver Meadow Publishing, *(978-0-9742085)* 11 Clarence Russell Rd., Thurman, NY 12885 USA Tel 518-623-9305; 352-463-3089
E-mail: PerkinFL@aol.com
Web site: http://www.persisgranger.com.

Beaver's Pond Pr., Inc., *(978-1-890676; 978-1-931646; 978-1-59298; 978-1-64343)* 939 Seventh St. W., Saint Paul, MN 55102 USA Tel 952-829-8818
E-mail: mack@beaverspondpress.com
Web site: http://www.beaverspondpress.com
Dist(s): **Itasca Bks.**

Because Time Flies, Inc., *(978-0-9652652; 978-0-9754073)* 155 N. Harbor Dr., Concourse Suite 2, Chicago, IL 60601-7364 USA Tel 312-938-0938; Fax: 312-938-0029; Toll Free: 800-694-4786
E-mail: journals@covad.net
Web site: http://www.becausetimeflies.com.

Beck Global Publishing, *(978-0-9816942)* 10600 E. Rte. Y, Ashland, MO 65010 USA
Web site: http://www.beckpillowtalk.com.

Beck Publishing *See* **Beck Global Publishing**

Becker, Christie, *(978-0-9728116)* 7 Whispering Pines Ct., Hilton Head, SC 29926-2542 USA
E-mail: beachbeckers@msn.com
Web site: http://www.cbeckerbooks.com.

Becker Doyle & Associates *See* **BDA Publishing**

Becker, Frank *See* **Greenbush Pr.**

Becker, Savan C., *(978-0-615-23554-7)* 1521 Farlow Ave., Crofton, MD 21114 USA Tel 443-292-8098; Fax: 443-603-2998
E-mail: savan@psinerspace.net
Dist(s): **Lulu Pr., Inc.**

becker&mayer! books, *(978-0-9700346; 978-0-9748486; 978-1-932855; 978-1-60380)* 11120 NE 33rd Pl. No. 101, Bellevue, WA 98004-1448 USA (SAN 760-7792) Toll Free: 866-319-5900; *Imprints:* SmartLab (SmartLab)
E-mail: cindyd@beckermayer.com; info@beckermayer.com
Web site: http://www.beckermayer.com; http://www.everydaywisdom.net
Dist(s): **Bks. Are Fun, Ltd.**
Chronicle Bks. LLC
Hachette Bk. Group
INscribe Digital
Independent Pubs. Group
Midpoint Trade Bks., Inc.
Quarto Publishing Group USA.

Becket, *(978-0-9898785; 978-1-941240)* 78665 Villeta Dr, La Quinta, CA 92253 USA Tel 760-413-0031
E-mail: ibecket7@gmail.com.

Beckham Pubns. Co, *(978-0-931761; 978-0-9802380; 978-0-9816505; 978-0-9823876; 978-0-9841991; 978-0-9827943; 978-0-9833402; 978-0-9848243; 978-0-9905904; 978-0-9984870)* Orders Addr.: 13619 Cedar Creek Ln., SILVER SPRING, MD 20904 USA (SAN 683-2237) Tel 240-643-9284; Fax: 866-659-3306; Toll Free Fax: 866-659-3306; Edit Addr.: 13619 Cedar Creek Ln., Silver Spring, MD 20904-5308 USA
E-mail: barry@beckhamhouse.com
Web site: http://www.beckhamhouse.com
Dist(s): **BCH Fulfillment & Distribution.**

Beckham Publications Group, Incorporated *See* **Beckham Pubns. Co**

Becklyns, LLC, *(978-0-9860222)* 23 Bob White Way, Weatogue, CT 06089 USA.

Beckon Bks. *Imprint of* **Southwestern Publishing Hse., Inc.**

Become a Millionaire *See* **Grampa Jones's Publishing Co.**

Becoming Hero, *(978-0-9990022)* Urb. Los Caobos, Ponce, PR 00716 USA Tel 540-287-7629; Fax: 540-287-7629
E-mail: jen.finelli.veldhuyzen@gmail.com
Web site: byjenfinelli.com.

Bed Bks., *(978-1-933652)* 101 Westgate Dr., Trinidad, CA 95570 USA
Web site: http://www.readinginbed.com; http://www.bedbooks.NET.

Bed of Angels, Inc., *(978-0-9909751)* 9663 Santa Monica Blvd. Suite 559, Beverly Hills, CA 90210 USA Tel 310-734-8542
E-mail: h@eworldmedia.com
Web site: www.eworldmedia.com.

Bedazzled Ink Publishing Co., *(978-0-9759555; 978-1-934452; 978-1-939562; 978-1-943837; 978-1-945805; 978-1-949290)* 2137 Pennsylvania Ave., Fairfield, CA 94533 USA; *Imprints:* Dragonfeather Books (Dragonfeather Bks)
E-mail: publisher@bedazzledink.com
Web site: http://www.bedazzledink.com
Dist(s): **Follett School Solutions**
Independent Pubs. Group.

Bedbug Bks., *(978-0-692-04504-6)* 4044 Carmel Brooks Way, SAN DIEGO, CA 92130 USA Tel 858-922-9554
E-mail: rachelmarie.rm@gmail.com
Dist(s): **Ingram Content Group.**

Bedell, Barbara F., *(978-0-9743731)* 74 Hidden Bay Dr., S Dartmouth, MA 02748-3089 USA
E-mail: bb280z@yahoo.com.

Bedell, Lashundra, *(978-0-615-58737-0; 978-0-9896672)* P.O. Box 33552, Decatur, GA 30033 USA Tel 678-755-3270
E-mail: lashundrabedell@yahoo.com.

Bedford Hse. Bks., *(978-0-9960916)* 93 hancock St., brooklyn, NY 11216 USA Tel 917-815-5969
E-mail: dave@bedfordhousebooks.com.

Bedford/Saint Martin's, *(978-0-312; 978-1-4576)* Div. of Holtzbrinck Publishers, Orders Addr.: 16365 James Madison Hwy., Gordonsville, VA 22942 USA Tel 540-672-7600; Toll Free Fax: 800-672-2054; Toll Free: 888-330-8477; Edit Addr.: 33 Irving Pl., New York, NY 10003 USA Tel 212-375-7000; Fax: 212-614-1885; Toll Free: 800-223-1715; 75 Arlington St., Boston, MA 02116 Tel 617-399-4000; Fax: 617-426-8582; Toll Free: 800-779-7440
E-mail: permissionsdept@bedfordstmartins.com; communication@bedfordstmartins.com
Web site: http://www.bfwpub.com
Dist(s): **Follett School Solutions**
Macmillan
Springer.

Bednark, Sara, *(978-0-615-18545-3)* 10013 SE Eastmont Dr., Damascus, OR 97089 USA
E-mail: rbednark@gmail.com
Web site: http://www.sara.bednark.com
Dist(s): **Lulu Pr., Inc.**

Bedrock Books, Incorporated *See* **Dry, Paul Bks., Inc.**

Bedside Bks. *Imprint of* **American Bk. Publishing Group**

Bedside Pr. (CAN) *(978-0-9939970; 978-1-988715) Dist. by* **D C D.**

Bee at Ease Press *See* **At Ease Pr.**

Bee Creative, LLC, *(978-0-615-75686-8; 978-0-615-94698-6; 978-0-615-98240-3; 978-0-9975745)* 2704 NW 119th, Oklahoma City, OK 73120 USA Tel 405-924-9265
E-mail: callie.belinda@gmail.com
Web site: www.beecreativeinc.com.

Bee Instinctive, *(978-0-692-17262-9)* 547 Blue Hill Ave., BOSTON, MA 02121 USA Tel 617-861-7520
E-mail: ssenat2@gmail.com
Dist(s): **Ingram Content Group.**

Beech, Michael, *(978-0-9817741)* 8603 W. 84th Cir., Arvada, CO 80005 USA Tel 303-456-5350
Web site: http://www.ebookselfpublishing.com; http://www.digital3dstereo.com.

Beech River Bks., *(978-1-930149; 978-0-9776514; 978-0-9793778; 978-0-9825214; 978-0-9839367; 978-0-9905814)* P.O. Box 62, Center Ossipee, NH 03814 USA Tel 603-539-3537; *Imprints:* Writer's Publishing Cooperative (Writ Pub Coop)
E-mail: banddmarion@roadrunner.com
Web site: http://www.beechriverbooks.com
Dist(s): **Enfield Publishing & Distribution Co., Inc.**

Beech Seal Press, Incorporated *See* **Images from the Past, Inc.**

Beecher Scott, *(978-0-9763077)* 1925 Westchester Rd. Apt. 214, Waterloo, IA 50701-4522 USA.

Beecroft Publishing (GBR) *(978-0-9546186) Dist. by* **LightSource CS.**

BeeHappi, *(978-0-9993343)* P.O. Box 81042, Austin, TX 78728 USA Tel 855-445-9556
E-mail: Maribel.Valls@beehappi.com
Web site: www.beehappi.com.

Beehive Bks., *(978-1-948886)* 4701 Chester Ave suite 1B, Philadelphia, PA 19143 USA Tel 609-468-8659
E-mail: joshuaon@gmail.com
Web site: beehivebooks.com
Dist(s): **Consortium Bk. Sales & Distribution.**

Beehive Inc., *(978-0-692-77210-2)* 9213 camptown Ct., MECHANICSVILLE, VA 23116 USA Tel 804-299-3772.

Beekman & Hathaway, *(978-0-9758970)* P.O. Box 2355, Amherst, MA 01004-2355 USA
E-mail: cdc@beekmanandhathaway.com
Web site: http://www.beekmanandhathaway.com.

Beekman Bks., Inc., *(978-0-8464)* 300 Old All Angels Hill Rd., Wappingers Falls, NY 12590 USA (SAN 170-1622) Tel 845-297-2690; Fax: 845-297-1002
E-mail: manager@beekmanbooks.com
Web site: http://www.beekmanbooks.com
Dist(s): **Follett School Solutions.**

BeeLine Bks., *(978-0-9903368)* 2 Fallgreen Ct., Santa Rosa, CA 95409 USA Tel 414-686-4777
E-mail: bonjourdwd@comcast.net.

Beeman Jorgensen, Inc., *(978-0-929758)* 7510 Allisonville Rd., Indianapolis, IN 46250 USA (SAN 250-1279) Tel 317-841-7677; Fax: 317-849-2001; Toll Free: 800-553-5319
Dist(s): **Hachette Bk. Group**
MBI Distribution Services/Quayside Distribution
Practice Ring.

BeerBooks.com, *(978-0-9662084; 978-0-9819282; 978-0-9904513)* P.O. Box 771012, Cleveland, OH 44107 USA
E-mail: email@beerbooks.com
Web site: http://www.beerbooks.com.

Bee's Ink Publishing, *(978-0-615-57799-9; 978-0-615-63296-4)* 15800 Hwy. 3 No. 113, Webster, TX 77598 USA Tel 713-876-3222
E-mail: bwilsonent@aol.com.

Beeson, Jan, *(978-0-9890482)* 232 E. 52nd St., San Bernardino, CA 92404 USA Tel 714-936-1390
E-mail: rotcmpj@charter.net.

Beetle Bug Bks., *(978-0-9658365)* Orders Addr.: P.O. Box 4636, San Clemente, CA 92674 USA (SAN 299-3864) Tel 949-498-0162; Fax: 949-498-2531; Edit Addr.: 1504 Avenida Hacienda, San Clemente, CA 92672 USA (SAN 299-3872)
E-mail: BookOrders@BeetleBugBooks.com
Web site: http://www.BeetleBugBooks.com
Dist(s): **Follett School Solutions**
Unique Bks., Inc.

Beevinwood, Inc., *(978-0-9652902)* Orders Addr.: 5748 Clark Rd., West Manchester, OH 45382 USA Tel 937-678-9910; Fax: 937-678-7715
E-mail: C1C2C3@aol.com.

Beex Art Bks., *(978-0-9724358)* P.O. Box 9143, Fountain Valley, CA 92728-9143 USA.

Before Christmas Pr., *(978-0-9759902)* Orders Addr.: 15170 State Rte. 550, Athens, OH 45701 USA
Web site: http://www.beforechristmaspress.com.

Before Someday Publishing, *(978-0-9850659; 978-1-943598)* P.O. Box 371, Apex, NC 27502-9998 USA
E-mail: beforesomeday@gmail.com.

Beggs, Christina, *(978-0-692-18086-0)* 4824 Washington St., Lake Wales, FL 33859 USA Tel 863-241-1632
E-mail: christinab1589@gmail.com
Dist(s): **Ingram Content Group.**

Begin Smart LLC, *(978-1-934618; 978-1-60906)* 515 Valley St., Suite 180, Maplewood, NJ 07040 USA (SAN 854-0497) Tel 973-763-8191; Fax: 973-763-5944
E-mail: info@beginsmartbooks.com
Dist(s): **Sterling Publishing Co., Inc.**

Beginner Method Series *Imprint of* **Brass in Color**

Begoo Bks., LLC, *(978-0-9884922)* 48 N. Clover Dr., Great Neck, NY 11021 USA Tel 516-314-4808
E-mail: cuilly@aol.com.

Behave'n Kids Pr., *(978-0-9714405)* 8922 Cuming St., Omaha, NE 68114 USA Tel 402-926-4373; Fax: 402-926-3898
E-mail: janiep@behavenkids.com
Web site: http://www.behavenkids.com/
Dist(s): **Book Clearing Hse.**

Behavenkids Press *See* **Behave'n Kids Pr.**

Behavioral Health & Human Development Ctr., *(978-0-9777672)* 4517 Lorino St., Suite 1, Metairie, LA 70006 USA Tel 504-454-3015
E-mail: carlos@littleduckyjr.com
Web site: http://littleduckyjr.com.

Behind the Scenes Bks., *(978-0-9770879)* 90 Windsor Dr., Pine Brook, NJ 07058 USA Tel 973-274-9472; Fax: 973-274-9272
E-mail: ma@behindthescenesmarketing.com.

Behrman Hse., Inc., *(978-0-87441; 978-1-68115)* 11 Edison Pl., Springfield, NJ 07081 USA (SAN 201-4459) Tel 973-379-7200; Fax: 973-379-7280; Toll Free: 800-221-2755; *Imprints:* Apples & Honey Press (ApplesandHoney)
E-mail: webmaster@behrmanhouse.com; orders@behrmanhouse.com; customersupport@behrmanhouse.com
Web site: http://www.behrmanhouse.com; http://www.arepublish.com
Dist(s): **Follett School Solutions.**

Beijing Language & Culture Univ. Pr., China (CHN) *(978-7-5619) Dist. by* **China Bks.**

Beil, Frederic C. Pub., Inc., *(978-0-913720; 978-1-929490)* Orders Addr.: 609 Whitaker St., Savannah, GA 31401 USA (SAN 240-9909) Tel 912-233-2446
Web site: http://www.beil.com.

Belgrave Hse., *(978-0-9660643; 978-0-9741068; 978-0-9801778; 978-0-9821717; 978-0-9844144; 978-1-61084; 978-1-947812)* 190 Belgrave Ave., San Francisco, CA 94117-4228 USA Tel 415-661-5025; Fax: 415-661-5703
E-mail: neff@belgravehouse.com
Web site: http://www.belgravehouse.com.

Believer's Dream Publishing, *(978-0-9832273; 978-0-9905951)* 9650 Strickland Rd. Suite 103 - 255, Raleigh, NC 27615 USA Tel 919-847-3884
E-mail: believersdreampublishing@gmail.com
Web site: believersdreampublishing.com.

Believers Publishing, *(978-0-9795680)* 2245 N. Green Valley Pkwy., Suite 282, Henderson, NV 89014 USA
E-mail: believerspublishing@gmail.com
Web site: http://believerspublishing.com
Dist(s): **Send The Light Distribution LLC.**

Belisarian Bks., *(978-0-9658481)* Div. of Iconoclast, 6513 NW 30th Terr., Bethany, OK 73008 USA Tel 405-789-1030
E-mail: belisarianbooks@yahoo.com
Web site: http://www.belisarianbooks.tk/.

Belknap Digital Archives, *(978-0-9747471)* Orders Addr.: P.O. Box 1487, Meredith, NH 03253 USA Tel 603-279-8358; Edit Addr.: 20 True Rd., Unit No. 86, Meredith, NH 03253 USA
E-mail: apollock@worldpath.net
Web site: http://www.belknapdigital.com.

Belknap Pr. *Imprint of* **Harvard Univ. Pr.**

Belknap Publishing & Design, *(978-0-9723420; 978-0-9816403)* P.O. Box 22387, Honolulu, HI 96823-2387 USA; *Imprints:* Calabash Books (Calabash Bks)
Web site: http://belknappublishing.com
Dist(s): **Booklines Hawaii, Ltd.**
Follett School Solutions.

Bell, Albert, *(978-0-9979288)* 22 W. 12th St., Holland, MI 49423 USA Tel 616-395-7558
E-mail: bell@hope.edu
Web site: www.albertbell.com.

Bell & Murry, *(978-0-9987995)* P.O. Box 164, Walnut Creek, CA 94597 USA Tel 925-708-2350
E-mail: Dot@bellandmurry.com
Web site: bellandmurry.com.

Bell Bridge Bks. *Imprint of* **BelleBks., Inc.**

Bell, Danny, *(978-0-692-99739-0)* 11853 Lindblade St., Culver City, CA 90230 USA Tel 310-896-6904
E-mail: elanaruthblack@gmail.com
Dist(s): **Ingram Content Group.**

Bell, Keith, *(978-0-9995720)* 1613 N. Federal Hwy., LAKE WORTH, FL 33460 USA Tel 561-582-1881
E-mail: kbellrpi@gmail.com
Dist(s): **Ingram Content Group.**

Bell, Megan, *(978-0-9889775)* 5710 Fox Chase Trail, Galena, OH 43021 USA Tel 740-548-6550
E-mail: meganericbell@gmail.com.

Bell Pond Bks. *Imprint of* **SteinerBooks, Inc.**

Bella & Bruno Bks., *(978-0-9894402)* 34-08 30th St. Apt A22, Astoria, NY 11106 USA Tel 585-746-2696
E-mail: aneeck@rochester.rr.com
Web site: bellaandbrunobooks.com.

Bella & Harry, LLC, *(978-0-9837092; 978-1-937616; 978-1-946768)* 15057 Sweetgum St., Delray Beach, FL

Publisher Name Index

33446 USA (SAN 920-3052) Tel 561-350-3649; 1 Ingram Rd., La Vergne, TN 37086
E-mail: BellaAndHarryGo@aol.com
Web site: www.BellaAndHarry.com
Dist(s): **Follett School Solutions**
Ingram Publisher Services.

Bella Bks., Inc., *(978-0-930044; 978-0-941483; 978-1-56280; 978-0-9677753; 978-1-931513; 978-1-59493; 978-1-64247)* Orders Addr.: P.O. Box 10543, Tallahassee, FL 32302 USA Tel 850-576-2370; Fax: 850-576-3498; Toll Free: 800-729-4992
E-mail: Linda@BellaBooks.com
Web site: http://www.bellabooks.com
Dist(s): **Bella Distribution**
Ingram Publisher Services
Two Rivers Distribution.

Bella International, Limited *See* **Wanderlust Publishing**

Bella Publishing *See* **Bellissima Publishing, LLC**

Bella Rosa Bks., *(978-0-9747685; 978-1-933523; 978-1-62268)* P.O. Box 4251, Rock Hill, SC 29732 USA
E-mail: info@bellarosabooks.com
Web site: http://www.bellarosabooks.com
Dist(s): **Follett School Solutions.**

Bellaboozle Books, Inc., *(978-0-9765398)* 104 Lariat Dr., Canonsburg, PA 15317-3284 USA
E-mail: lkravec@adelphia.net.

Bellagio Pr. *Imprint of* **Taj Bks. International LLC**

Bellamy, Christopher Daniel, *(978-0-9979039)* 301 Cassidy Rd. Ext., Thomasville, GA 31792 USA Tel 254-498-1559
E-mail: danbellamy@yahoo.com
Web site: www.inflatablestories.com.

Bellamy, Kaitlin, *(978-0-692-19572-7; 978-0-578-44576-2; 978-0-578-59663-1; 978-0-578-77205-9)* 8741 McCormack McRae Way, Orlando, FL 32836 USA Tel 540-570-0727
E-mail: ExecutiveGeekVO@gmail.com
Dist(s): **Ingram Content Group.**

Bellastoria Pr., *(978-0-615-40644-2; 978-0-9910861; 978-1-942209)* 100 Hilltop Rd., Longmeadow, MA 01106 USA Tel 413-567-3278
E-mail: lcardilloplatzer@hotmail.com
Web site: http://www.lindacardillo.com/.

Belle, Alec John, *(978-0-692-94771-5)* 1175 Airport Rd., CARSON CITY, NV 89701 USA Tel 775-430-3186
E-mail: bellealec@gmail.com
Dist(s): **Ingram Content Group.**

Belle Isle Bks. *Imprint of* **Brandylane Pubs., Inc.**

Belle Lumiere True News, 2525 Squaw Ct., Antioch, CA 94531-8003 USA Toll Free: 888-473-1555; *Imprints:* Holmes Bookshop (Holmes Bkshop).

Belle Media International, Incorporated *See* **Belle Media International, Inc. Div of True News**

Belle Media International, Inc. Div of True News, *(978-0-9703419; 978-1-60361)* Div. of Belle Lumiere True News, Orders Addr.: P.O. Box 191024, San Francisco, CA 94119 USA Tel 949-813-5343
E-mail: holmesbookshop@yahoo.com; BelleBusiness@yahoo.com; dr.miawhite@yahoo.com.

Belle Publishing, *(978-0-578-11303-6; 978-0-578-11304-3; 978-0-9909986)* 18000 S. Park Blvd., Shaker Heights, OH 44120 USA Tel 216-543-7671
E-mail: lleya1@yahoo.com
Web site: www.thecupcakejones.com
Dist(s): **Independent Pubs. Group.**

BelleAire Pr., *(978-0-9640138; 978-0-9765234)* 5707 NW 50th Pl., Gainesville, FL 32653-4079 USA Tel 352-377-1870
E-mail: belleairepress@earthlink.net
Dist(s): **Atlas Bks.**
Baker & Taylor Publisher Services (BTPS)
Follett School Solutions
MyiLibrary.

BelleBks., Inc., *(978-1-893896; 978-0-9673035; 978-0-9759653; 978-1-933417; 978-0-9768760; 978-0-9802453; 978-0-9821756; 978-0-9841258; 978-0-9843256; 978-1-935661; 978-1-61026; 978-1-61194)* 4513 Ernie Dr., Memphis, TN 38116 USA Tel 901-344-9024; Fax: 901-344-9068; *Imprints:* Bell Bridge Books (Bell Bridge); ImaJinn Books (ImaJinnBooks)
E-mail: bellebooks@bellebooks.com; debbsmith@aol.com; production@bellebooks.com
Web site: http://www.BelleBooks.com; http://www.BellBridgeBooks.com
Dist(s): **MyiLibrary.**

Bellerophon Bks., *(978-0-88388)* Orders Addr.: P.O. Box 21307, Santa Barbara, CA 93121-1307 USA (SAN 254-7856) Tel 805-965-7034; Fax: 805-965-8286; Toll Free: 800-253-9943
E-mail: bellerophonbooks@bellerophonbooks.com
Web site: http://www.bellerophonbooks.com
Dist(s): **Follett School Solutions.**

Bellissima Publishing, LLC, *(978-0-9768417; 978-0-9771916; 978-0-9776993; 978-0-9790449; 978-0-9793358; 978-0-9794006; 978-0-9794815; 978-1-935118; 978-1-935630; 978-1-61477)* Orders Addr.: P.O. Box 650, Jamul, CA 91935 USA
E-mail: pdweigandjd@aol.com; admin@bellissimapublishing.com
Web site: http://www.bellissimapublishing.com; http://www.surfergirlsummer.com; http://bellissimapublishing.viewwork.com/bellissima_publishing_llc/selfolio.html.

Bello, Andres (CHL) *(978-956-13) Dist. by* **Continental Bk.**

Bellreh Publishing, *(978-0-9966102)* 2501 Ohio Dr, No. 214, Plano, TX 75093 USA Tel 716-946-7308
E-mail: sheriabell@gmail.com
Web site: www.sheriabell.com.

Bellwether Media, *(978-1-60014; 978-1-61211; 978-1-61891; 978-1-62617; 978-1-68103; 978-1-64487; 978-1-64834)* Orders Addr.: 6012 Blue Circle Dr., Minnetonka, MN 55343 USA (SAN 920-8135) Tel 612-825-2545; Fax: 612-825-2544; Toll Free Fax: 800-675-6679; Toll Free: 800-679-8068; Edit Addr.: 6012 Blue Circle Dr., Minnetonka, MN 55343 USA; *Imprints:* Blastoff! Readers (Blastoff Rdrs); Torque Books (Torque Bks); Pilot Books (PilotBks); Epic Books (EpicBks); Express Books (Express Bks); Black Sheep (BlackSheepUSA); Blastoff! Discovery (MYID_O_BLASTOF)
E-mail: marketing@bellwethermedia.com; tom@bellwethermedia.com; dzobel@bellwethermedia.com; knewell@bellwethermedia.com
Web site: http://www.bellwethermedia.com
Dist(s): **Follett Media Distribution**
Follett School Solutions
Independent Pubs. Group.

Belmar Pubns., *(978-0-9746366; 978-1-7335191)* 504 - 17th Ave., South Belmar, NJ 07719 USA Fax: 212-737-5211
E-mail: arthurpaone@aol.com.

Belshe, Judy *See* **Snuggle Up Bks.**

Beluga-Duga Pr., *(978-1-932176)* Orders Addr.: P.O. Box 893, Rio Vista, CA 94571 USA.

Ben Franklin Pr., *(978-0-9772447; 978-0-615-64586-5)* 910 S. Hohokam Dr., Suite 104, Tempe, AZ 85281 USA Tel 480-968-7959; Fax: 480-966-3694
E-mail: rickburress@benfranklinpress.net.

Benavides, Griselda, *(978-0-692-77556-1; 978-0-692-15691-9)* 13063 Magnolia Ave, Chino, CA 91710 USA Tel 917-473-5144
E-mail: g_benavides@aol.com
Web site: griseldabenavides.com.

BenBella Bks., *(978-1-932100; 978-1-933771; 978-0-9792331; 978-1-935251; 978-1-935618; 978-1-936661; 978-1-937856; 978-1-939529; 978-1-940363; 978-1-941631; 978-1-942952; 978-1-944648; 978-1-946885; 978-1-948836; 978-1-950665; 978-1-953295)* 10300 N Central Expy Suite 400, Dallas, TX 75231 USA Tel 214-750-3600; Fax: 214-750-3645; 387 Park Ave. St., New York, NY 10016; *Imprints:* SmartPop (SmartPop)
E-mail: brittney@benbellabooks.com
Web site: http://www.benbellabooks.com
Dist(s): **Follett School Solutions**
Ingram Publisher Services
MyiLibrary
Open Road Integrated Media, Inc.
Two Rivers Distribution
ebrary, Inc.

Bench Press *See* **Gallant Hse. Publishing**

Benchland Publishing, *(978-0-615-89563-5; 978-0-615-99890-9; 978-0-692-33103-3; 978-0-692-50463-5; 978-0-692-74329-4; 978-1-7321915)* 1525 Treehouse Ln S, Keller, TX 76262 USA Tel 8174319899
E-mail: jay.hosler@gmail.com; paul@treent.com
Dist(s): **CreateSpace Independent Publishing Platform.**

Benchmark Book Craft, *(978-0-9744015)* P.O. Box 19583, Colorado City, CO 81019 USA Tel 719-676-3009.

Benchmark Education Co., *(978-1-58344; 978-1-892393; 978-1-59000; 978-1-4108; 978-1-60437; 978-1-60634; 978-1-935440; 978-1-935441; 978-1-60859; 978-1-935469; 978-1-935470; 978-1-935471; 978-1-935472; 978-1-935473; 978-1-61672; 978-1-936254; 978-1-936255; 978-1-936256;-1-936257; 978-1-936258; 978-1-4509; 978-1-4900; 978-1-5021; 978-1-5125; 978-1-5322; 978-1-9873; 978-1-0786) 145 Huguenot St 8th Flr, New Rochelle, NY 10801 USA Tel 914-637-7200; Toll Free Fax: 877-732-8273; Toll Free: 877-236-2465*
E-mail: bhaggerty@benchmarkeducation.com
Web site: http://www.benchmarkeducation.com.

Bendon, Inc., *(978-1-57759; 978-1-58117; 978-1-888443; 978-1-888567; 978-1-4037; 978-1-932209; 978-1-59394; 978-1-60139; 978-1-61568; 978-1-4530; 978-1-61405; 978-1-62191; 978-1-62615; 978-1-63109; 978-1-63346; 978-1-5050; 978-1-6902)* 1840 Baney Rd. South, Ashland, OH 44805 USA (SAN 803-317X); *Imprints:* Spirit Press (SpiritPr); Intervisual/Piggy Toes (IntervisPiggy)
Web site: http://www.bendonpub.com.

Bendon Publishing International *See* **Bendon, Inc.**

Bendt Family Ministries *See* **Valerie Bendt**

Bene Factum Publishing, Ltd. (GBR) *(978-0-9522754; 978-1-903071; 978-1-909657) Dist. by* **IPG Chicago.**

Benedetti, Jef, *(978-0-9801372)* 4242 Johnstown Rd., Gahanna, OH 43230 USA (SAN 855-2991).

Benefactory, Inc., The, *(978-1-58021; 978-1-882728)* 3 Baneberry Ln., Riverwoods, IL 60015-3534 USA Toll Free: 800-729-7251
E-mail: benefactry@aol.com.

Benicia Literary Arts, *(978-0-9703737; 978-0-578-43134-5)* P.O. Box 763, Benicia, CA 94510 USA Tel 707-745-5540 (phone/fax)
E-mail: editor@carquinezreview.com
Web site: http://www.carquinezreview.com.

Benitez Productions, *(978-0-9966030; 978-1-949328)* P.O. Box 16101, Encino, CA 91416 USA Tel 818-343-5159
E-mail: art@joebenitez.com
Web site: joebenitez.com
Dist(s): **Diamond Comic Distributors, Inc.**

Benjamin Franklin Pr., *(978-0-9789827; 978-0-9795257; 978-0-9799941; 978-0-692-98402-4; 978-0-692-06064-3; 978-0-578-43090-4; 978-0-578-50901-3; 978-0-578-50902-0)* P.O. Box 51936, Pacific Grove, CA 93950 USA Fax: 831-626-3734; *Imprints:* Osanto University Press (OsantoUniv)
E-mail: loye@benjaminfranklinpress.com
Web site: http://www.benjaminfranklinpress.com
Dist(s): **BookBaby.**

Benjamin Pr., *(978-0-9663478; 978-0-9793431; 978-0-9836106; 978-1-7334047)* Div. of Elmwood Inn Fine Teas, 135 N. 2nd St., Danville, KY 40422 USA Tel 859-236-6641; Toll Free Fax: 888-879-0467; Toll Free: 800-765-2139 Do not confuse with Benjamin Pr., Northampton, MA
E-mail: BR@benjaminpress.com
Web site: http://www.benjaminpress.com
Dist(s): **Independent Pubs. Group**
Midpoint Trade Bks., Inc.
Partners Pubs. Group, Inc.

Benjey Media *See* **Tuxedo Pr.**

Bennett Day Schl., Inc., *(978-0-578-47162-4; 978-1-7333606)* 955 W Grand Ave, Chicago, IL 60642 USA Tel 312-870-0286
E-mail: cameron.smith@bennettday.org
Web site: www.bennettday.org.

Bennett, Krista, *(978-1-7347045)* 3271 E Sweetwater Springs Dr, Washington, UT 84780 USA Tel 4357604258
E-mail: bennett.krista.l@gmail.com
Dist(s): **Ingram Content Group.**

Bennett, Robert *See* **Archeological Assessments, Inc.**

Bennett/Novak & Co., Inc., *(978-0-9713454)* 8500 Holloway Dr., Los Angeles, CA 90069 USA Tel 310-657-2975; Fax: 310-657-4006
Dist(s): **National Bk. Network.**

Bennovations Publishing Services, *(978-0-9721066)* P.O. Box 28906, San Diego, CA 92198 USA Tel 858-663-5302; Fax: 858-777-5779
E-mail: info@bennovations.com
Web site: http://www.bennovations.com.

Benny's Bks., *(978-0-692-13602-7; 978-0-692-13997-4)* 9116 Jason Dr., FORT WORTH, TX 76108 USA Tel 940-765-1818
E-mail: jose.a.robles@hotmail.com
Dist(s): **Ingram Content Group.**

Benoy Publishing, *(978-0-9720809; 978-1-932162)* 735 Bragg Dr., Unit H, Wilmington, NC 28412 USA Tel 910-796-0424 (phone/fax)
E-mail: bbppdodo@aol.com
Web site: http://www.benoypublishing.com.

Bensley, Ann-Mari, *(978-0-9995242)* 12307 NE 68th Pl, Kirkland, WA 98033 USA Tel 425-443-6940
E-mail: sbens@outlook.com.

Benson, Lyn, *(978-0-615-13524-3)* 7063 E. Briarwood Dr., Centennial, CO 80112 USA Fax: 303-736-4075
E-mail: lynbenson@msn.com.

Benson, Queen M., *(978-0-615-12716-3)* 106 James River Dr., Newport News, VA 23601 USA
E-mail: dbbenson@verizon.net
Web site: http://www.lactose-limited.com.

Bent Branch Press, *(978-0-9990363)* 108 Crestwood Dr., Tullahoma, TN 37388 USA Tel 615-517-0545
E-mail: ibprayin@hotmail.com.

Bent Castle Workshops, *(978-0-9768848)* P.O. Box 10551, Rochester, NY 14610-0551 USA
E-mail: knot@enchantedglyph.com
Web site: http://www.bentcastle.com.

BentDaiSha, LLC, *(978-0-9749465)* 11020 E. Indigo Bush Pl., Tucson, AZ 85748-3558 USA
E-mail: bentdaisha@cox.net.

Bentivegna, Fred, *(978-0-9766228)* 445 W. 27th St., Chicago, IL 60616 USA Tel 312-225-5514 (phone/fax)
E-mail: fbentivegna@sbcglobal.net.

Bentle Bks., *(978-0-9746904)* Orders Addr.: P.O. Box 2274, Oakhurst, CA 93644 USA Fax: 559-683-6206; Edit Addr.: 42564 Buckeye Rd., Oakhurst, CA 93644 USA
E-mail: terrahulse@sierratel.com
Web site: http://www.bentlebooks.com
Dist(s): **Follett School Solutions.**

Bentley, Trish, *(978-0-9774752)* 347 E. 6th St., Apt. 2B, New York, NY 10002 USA.

Benton, John Bks., *(978-0-9635411)* 127 S. El Molino Ave., Pasadena, CA 91101-2510 USA Tel 626-405-0950; Fax: 818-564-0952
Dist(s): **Spring Arbor Distributors, Inc.**

Benzie, Andrew Bks., *(978-0-9852229; 978-0-9897584; 978-1-941713; 978-1-950562)* 2982 Santos Ln. APT No. 306, Walnut Creek, CA 94597 USA Tel 925-253-7790
E-mail: andrew@andrewbenzie.com
Web site: http://www.andrewbenziebooks.com.

Berbay Publishing (AUS) *(978-0-9806711; 978-0-9942895; 978-0-9943841; 978-0-6483973; 978-0-6485291; 978-0-6487851; 978-0-6489533) Dist. by* **IPG Chicago.**

Berens, David F., *(978-0-692-07272-1; 978-0-692-09037-4; 978-0-578-51034-7)* 1013 Cross Meadow Rd., KNOXVILLE, TN 37934 USA Tel 865-382-7773
E-mail: david.f.berens@gmail.com
Dist(s): **Ingram Content Group.**

Beres, Nancy, *(978-0-9752801)* 2025 Willow Glen Ln., Columbus, OH 43229-1550 USA.

Berg, Jeremy, *(978-0-9791700; 978-0-9837422; 978-1-939790)* 2204 E. Grand Ave., Everett, WA 98201-3339 USA
Web site: http://www.lorian.org.

Bergli Bks. (CHE) *(978-3-9520002; 978-3-905252; 978-2-88407; 978-3-03869) Dist. by* **ISD USA.**

Bergner, Bobby, *(978-0-615-21301-9; 978-0-615-22870-9)* 237 Sycamore Ln., Phoenixville, PA 19460 USA
Web site: http://www.moofax.com.

Bergstrom Bks., *(978-0-9787648)* 521 12th Ave. NE., Devils Lake, ND 58301 USA Tel 701-662-3320
E-mail: Candace@lakechevy.com.

Berkeley Major Publishing, *(978-0-9720691)* 8282 Skyline Cir., Oakland, CA 94605-4230 USA Fax: 419-791-7109
E-mail: dallon@progidy.net; BMP@berkeleymp.com
Web site: http://www.berkeleymp.com.

Berkeley Science Bks., *(978-0-9764138)* 529 Bonnie Dr., El Cerrito, CA 94530 USA Tel 510-524-8094
E-mail: wdflannery@aol.com.

Berkley *Imprint of* **Penguin Publishing Group**

Berkshire Publishing Group, *(978-0-9743091; 978-0-9770159; 978-1-933782; 978-1-61472)* 120 Castle St., Great Barrington, MA 01230 USA Tel 413-528-0206; Fax: 413-541-0076
E-mail: info@berkshirepublishing.com; cservice@berkshirepublishing.com
Web site: http://www.berkshirepublishing.com
Dist(s): **Follett School Solutions**
MyiLibrary.

Berlin, Stuart, *(978-0-615-22518-0; 978-0-615-48240-8; 978-0-9914128)* 1910 Larch St., Simi Valley, CA 93065 USA
E-mail: westwing1910@yahoo.com.

Berlin, Theodore *See* **Theodore Berlin Publishing**

Berlitz Languages, Inc. *Imprint of* **Berlitz Publishing**

Berlitz Publishing, 46-35 54th Rd., Maspeth, NY 11378 USA; *Imprints:* Berlitz Languages, Incorporated (Berlitz Lang)
E-mail: customerservice@langenscheidt.com
Web site: http://www.berlitzbooks.com
Dist(s): **Ingram Publisher Services**
Langenscheidt Publishing Group.

Bernard Design *See* **Elmdale Park Books**

Bernie's Bks., *(978-0-692-19119-4; 978-0-692-19120-0; 978-0-578-40480-6)* 5452 Trumpet Vine Trl. SE, Mableton, GA 30126-5650 USA Tel 443-825-5954
E-mail: karimi.faith@gmail.com.

Bernson Pr., *(978-0-9720509)* Orders Addr.: P.O. Box 55563, Sherman Oaks, CA 91413 USA Tel 818-268-3660; Edit Addr.: 5530 Allot Ave., Sherman Oaks, CA 91401 USA
E-mail: janet.bernson@gmail.com; thehealingartist@mac.com
Web site: http://www.thehealingartist.com; www.janetbernson.com.

Bernstein, Susan, *(978-0-9706596)* 31100 Northwestern Hwy., Farmington Hills, MI 48334-2519 USA Tel 248-737-8400; Fax: 248-737-4392; Toll Free: 800-225-5726
E-mail: les380414744@aol.com
Web site: http://www.epominonousepstein.com.

Berry, Joy Enterprises, *(978-1-60577)* 146 W. 29th St., Suite 11RW, New York, NY 10001 USA Tel 212-868-8282; Fax: 212-868-4110
Web site: http://www.joyberrymedia.com
Dist(s): **Two Rivers Distribution.**

Bertelsman, Verlagsgruppe C. GmbH (DEU) *(978-3-570) Dist. by* **Distribks Inc.**

Bertrand Brasil Editora SA (BRA) *(978-85-286) Dist. by* **Distribks Inc.**

Berube, Stacey, *(978-0-578-41461-4; 978-1-7334109)* 14 Howard Ave., Bourne, MA 02532 USA Tel 508-265-6717
E-mail: TaylynSenec@gmail.com
Dist(s): **Ingram Content Group.**

Berwick Court Publishing, *(978-0-615-34122-4; 978-0-615-35191-9; 978-0-9838846; 978-0-9889540; 978-0-9909515; 978-1-944376)* 4057 Enfield Ave., Skokie, IL 60076 USA Tel 312-772-3799
E-mail: matt@berwickcourt.com
Web site: http://berwickcourt.com.

Beryl Bks., *(978-1-7321747)* 7412 Madison St., Forest Park, IL 60130 USA Tel 216-403-8561
E-mail: jaymontville@gmail.com.

B.E.S. Publishing *Imprint of* **Peterson's**

Beshqoy, Nisreen, *(978-0-9759181)* P.O. Box 3846, Costa Mesa, CA 92628-3846 USA
E-mail: nisreenbeshqoy@hotmail.com
Web site: http://www.arabicandislamicbooksbynisreen.com.

Bess Pr., Inc., *(978-0-935848; 978-1-57306; 978-1-880188; 978-0-615-50460-5; 978-0-615-56510-1)* 3565 Harding Ave., Honolulu, HI 96816 USA (SAN 239-4111) Tel 808-734-7159; Fax: 808-732-3627
E-mail: kelly@besspress.com
Web site: http://www.besspress.com
Dist(s): **China Books & Periodicals, Inc.**
Follett School Solutions
Univ. of Hawaii Pr.

Best Books *See* **Library Reprints, Inc.**

Best eWay Pubns., Inc., *(978-0-9910062; 978-1-944084)* 3233 NE 34th St., Fort Lauderdale, FL 33308 USA Tel 847-612-7866
E-mail: barbaragoodheart@hotmail.com; cgoodheart847@hotmail.com
Web site: BesteWay.com.

Best Fairy Bks., *(978-0-9632524; 978-0-9786791)* 739 San Joaquin Rd, Poinciana, FL 34759 USA (SAN 851-2930) Tel 410-371-1855
E-mail: fairybooklady@gmail.com
Web site: http://bestfairybooks.com
Dist(s): **Follett School Solutions.**

Best Friends Books *See* **Children's Kindness Network**

Best Friends Productions, *(978-0-9765140)* 131 Bank St., New York, NY 10014-2177 USA
Web site: http://www.bestfriendsproductions.com.

Best of East Texas Pubs., *(978-1-878096)* Div. of Bob Bowman & Assocs., 515 S. First, Lufkin, TX 75901 USA Tel 409-634-7444; Fax: 409-634-7750.

Best Publishing Co., *(978-0-941332; 978-1-930536; 978-1-947239)* Div. of WCHMedia Group, Orders Addr.: 631 U.S. Hwy. 1, Ste 307, North Palm Beach, FL 33408 USA (SAN 238-9509) Tel 561-776-6066; Fax: 561-776-7476
E-mail: lorraine@bestpub.com
Web site: http://www.bestpub.com
Dist(s): **Rittenhouse Bk. Distributors.**

BEST VARIETY SHOP *See* **FASTLANE LLC**

Beth Detjens, Author, *(978-0-578-44327-0; 978-0-578-49724-2; 978-1-7340742)* 1134 Collinsville

Crossing Boulevard, Suite 111, Collinsville, IL 62234 USA Tel 618-975-3141
E-mail: beth.detjens@gmail.com.

Bethany Claire Bks., *(978-0-9899502; 978-0-9960037; 978-0-9961136; 978-0-9978610; 978-1-947731; 978-1-970110)* P.O. Box 278, Clarendon, TX 79226 USA Tel 806-662-7201
E-mail: bclaire@bethanyclaire.com
Web site: www.bethanyclaire.com
Dist(s): **BookBaby.**

†**Bethany Hse. Pubs.**, *(978-0-7642; 978-0-87123; 978-1-55661; 978-1-56179; 978-1-57778; 978-1-880089; 978-1-59066)* Div. of Baker Publishing Group, Orders Addr.: P.O. Box 6287, Grand Rapids, MI 49516-6287 USA Toll Free Fax: 800-398-3111 (orders); Toll Free: 800-877-2665 (orders); Edit Addr.: 11400 Hampshire Ave., S., Bloomington, MN 55438-2455 USA (SAN 201-4416) Tel 952-829-2500; Fax: 952-996-1393
E-mail: orders@bakerbooks.com
Web site: http://www.bethanyhouse.com
Dist(s): **Anchor Distributors**
Appalachian Bible Co.
Baker Publishing Group
Brodart Co.
Cambridge Univ. Pr.
Faith Alive Christian Resources
Follett School Solutions
Send The Light Distribution LLC
Spring Arbor Distributors, Inc.
Beeler, Thomas T. Pub.; *CIP.*

Bethlehem Bks., *(978-1-883937; 978-1-932350)* Div. of Bethlehem Community, Orders Addr.: 10194 Garfield St. S., Bathgate, ND 58216-4031 USA Tel 701-265-3725; Fax: 701-265-3716; Toll Free: 800-757-6831 Do not confuse with bethlehem Books in Richmond, VA
E-mail: contact@bethlehembooks.com
Web site: http://www.bethlehembooks.com
Dist(s): **Follett School Solutions**
Ignatius Pr.
Spring Arbor Distributors, Inc.

Bethstewartministries, *(978-0-9909447)* 510 Knob hill ct, Ft Wright, KY 41011 USA Tel 859-391-6656
E-mail: Bethstewartky@gmail.com
Web site: Www.bethstewartministries.com.

Betrock Information Systems, Inc., *(978-0-9629761)* 7770 Davie Rd. Ext., Hollywood, FL 33024 USA Tel 954-981-2821; Fax: 954-981-2823
E-mail: Lori@betrock.com
Web site: http://www.hortworld.com.

Bettenhausen, Jo Anne *See* **CBM Publishing**

Better Be Write Publisher, A *See* **W & B Pubs.**

Better Chinese LLC, *(978-1-60603; 978-1-68194)* P.O. Box 695, Palo Alto, CA 94303 USA Tel 650-384-0902; 2479 E Bayshore Rd., Suite 110, Palo Alto, CA 94303 Tel 650-384-0902; Fax: 702-442-7968
E-mail: usa@betterchinese.com
Web site: http://www.BetterChinese.com.

Better Comics, *(978-0-9728070)* P.O. Box 541924, Dallas, TX 75354-1924 USA
E-mail: JESmith@bettercomics.com
Web site: http://www.bettercomics.com.

Better Homes & Gardens Books *See* **Meredith Bks.**

Better Karma, LLC, *(978-0-9824329; 978-0-9828426; 978-0-9847753; 978-0-9962897)* 6018 Goldenrod Ct., Alexandria, VA 22310 USA (SAN 858-1495) Tel 703-971-1072
E-mail: publisher@betterkarmapublishing.com
Web site: http://www.BetterKarmaPublishing.com
Dist(s): **Smashwords.**

Better Me Bks., Inc., *(978-0-9770294)* P.O. Box 834, Marlton, NJ 08053 USA Tel 609-206-6318; Fax: 856-489-0234
E-mail: bettermebooks@aol.Com
Web site: http://www.bettermebooks.com.

Better Non Sequitur, *(978-0-9743235)* 11925 Via Zapata, El Cajon, CA 92019 USA Tel 619-246-5190
E-mail: steven@betternonsequitur.com
Web site: http://www.betternonsequitur.com.

Better Than One Publishing, *(978-0-9758958)* 27582 120th St., Staples, MN 56479 USA
Web site: http://www.creatingedumaterials.com.

Better Tomorrow Publishing, A, *(978-0-9795768)* P.O. Box 2975, Upper Marlboro, MD 20773-2975 USA Fax: 301-576-8070
E-mail: andy@abettertomorrowpublishing.net; sandy@abtpub.com
Web site: http://abettertomorrowpublishing.net.

BetterLink Pr., Inc., *(978-1-60220)* 99 Pk. Ave., R.R. Donnelley, New York, NY 10016 USA
Dist(s): **Penguin Publishing Group**
Simon & Schuster, Inc.
Tuttle Publishing
Univ. of Hawaii Pr.

BetterNot Enterprises, *(978-0-692-47105-0; 978-0-692-69079-6; 978-0-692-93150-9)* 200 E Del Mar Blvd Suite 304, PASADENA, CA 91105 USA Tel 661-287-9995.

Bettino, Teresa Adele, *(978-0-9742842)* 8403 Cosby Ln., Mechanicsville, VA 23116 USA Tel 804-779-2672
E-mail: tbettino@msn.com.

Betts, Linda, *(978-0-9767802)* Orders Addr.: 6050 Pagenkopf Rd., Maple Plain, MN 55359 USA Tel 763-479-2789; Fax: 763-476-6508
E-mail: lynrae@hotmail.com.

Betty Crocker *Imprint of* **Houghton Mifflin Harcourt Publishing Co.**

Between the Lakes Group, LLC, *(978-0-9727403; 978-0-9766342; 978-0-9791000; 978-0-9826073)* Orders Addr.: P.O. Box 13, Taconic, CT 06079-0013 USA Tel 860-824-0640
E-mail: geoff@betweenthelakes.com
Web site: http://www.betweenthelakes.com.

Between the Lines Publishing, *(978-0-9979395; 978-0-9996556; 978-1-7321723; 978-1-950502)* 410 caribou trail, lutsen, MN 55612 USA (SAN 990-6533) Tel 910-331-8171; *Imprints:* Willow River Press (MYID_N_WILLOW)
E-mail: inquiries@btwnthelines.com
Web site: www.btwnthelines.com.

Beverly Hills Publishing, *(978-0-9758870; 978-0-9777074; 978-0-9791967)* 291 S. La Cienega Blvd., Suites 107/108, Beverly Hills, CA 90211-3325 USA (SAN 850-0029) Tel 310-854-0705; Fax: 310-854-1840; Toll Free: 800-521-5669
E-mail: silvers@bevhillspub.com
Web site: http://www.bevhillspub.com.

Beyer, Jenna, *(978-0-692-99946-2; 978-1-7320529; 978-0-692-12203-7; 978-0-692-19882-7)* 218 N Madison St., Monroe, WA 98272 USA Tel 425-870-7179
E-mail: GoldenBeyer@gmail.com
Dist(s): **Ingram Content Group.**

BEYOND PUBLISHING, *(978-0-9961486; 978-0-692-82269-2; 978-0-9987292; 978-1-947256; 978-1-7326299; 978-1-949873; 978-1-952884)* 7722 Liberty Dr. Suite C, Huntington Beach, CA 92647 USA Tel 918-955-3227
E-mail: michael@beyondpublishing.net
Web site: www.Beyondpublishing.net.

Beyond the Stars, Incorporated *See* **Beyond the Stars Pubns.**

Beyond the Stars Pubns., *(978-0-9763635)* 14902 Preston Rd., Suite 404-764, Dallas, TX 75254 USA
E-mail: rjohnson@beyondthestarsbooks.com
Web site: http://www.beyondthestarsbooks.com.

Beyond Words *Imprint of* **Simon & Schuster**

Beyond Words Publishing, Inc., *(978-0-941831; 978-1-58270; 978-1-885223)* 20827 NW Cornell Rd., Suite 500, Hillsboro, OR 97124-9808 USA (SAN 666-4210) Tel 503-531-8700; Fax: 503-531-8773; Toll Free: 800-284-9673
E-mail: info@beyondword.com; sales@beyondword.com
Web site: http://www.beyondword.com
Dist(s): **Follett School Solutions**
Simon & Schuster, Inc.

Beyond Words/Atria Bks. *Imprint of* **Atria Bks.**

Beyond Your Words, *(978-0-9788789)* P.O. Box 5842, Newport Beach, CA 92662-9266 USA
Web site: http://www.beyondyourwords.com.

Bezalel Bks., *(978-0-9792258; 978-0-9794976; 978-0-9800483; 978-0-9818854; 978-0-9821222; 978-0-9823388; 978-0-9844864; 978-1-936453)* P.O. Box 300427, Waterford, MI 48330 USA
E-mail: bezalelbooks@gmail.com
Web site: http://www.bezalelbooks.com.

BFG Pr., LLC, *(978-0-9820307)* Div. of The PIE Group, P.O. Box 2269, Ewa Beach, HI 96706 USA (SAN 857-0590) Tel 808-428-0733
Web site: http://www.bfgpress.com/.

BFI Publishing (GBR) *(978-0-85170; 978-0-900212; 978-1-903786; 978-1-84457) Dist. by* **Macmillan.**

BGA Stories, *(978-0-9724806)* 3414 Forest Hills Cir., Garland, TX 75044-2000 USA (SAN 254-878X) Tel 972-496-0416
E-mail: bga@bgastories.com
Web site: http://www.bgastories.com.

BGS Productions, Inc., *(978-0-9972861)* 17798 SW 36th St., MIRAMAR, FL 33029 USA Tel 404-594-4962
E-mail: info.blackgirlspeaks@gmail.com; tanyabwele@gmail.com
Web site: www.blackgirlspeaks.com.

Bh Pubns., *(978-0-9760348)*
Web site: http://www.octopusrex.com; www.iammyhair.com.

Bhakta Program Institute *See* **Rupanuga Vedic College**

Bharat Babies, *(978-0-692-96283-1)* 31 Perry St., Somerville, MA 02143 USA Tel 508-369-6853
E-mail: namaste@bharatbabies.com
Web site: www.bharatbabies.com.

BHB International, Incorporated *See* **Continental Enterprises Group, Inc. (CEG)**

BHF Publishing, *(978-0-9801913; 978-0-615-13143-6)* 7139 Hwy. 85, Suite 274, Riverdale, GA 30274 USA Tel 678-925-4175
E-mail: melissabowan@hotmail.com; stdennis@highly-favored.net
Web site: http://www.highly-favored.net.

Biabe Publishing, *(978-0-9825944; 978-0-9984926)* 401 E Las Olas Blvd. Ste 130 Box 412, Fort Lauderdale, FL 33301 USA
E-mail: lissee@gmail.com.

Bibia, LLC, *(978-0-9826276; 978-0-615-74924-2; 978-1-940760)* PMB206 2880 Bicentennial Pkwy., Suite 100, Henderson, NV 89044 USA Tel 702-896-0967; *Imprints:* Bibia Publishing (Bibia)
E-mail: bibiapublishing@gmail.com
Web site: www.bibiapublishing.com.

Bibia Publishing *Imprint of* **Bibia, LLC**

Bible Based Studies, *(978-0-9797786)* 1134 SE 3rd St., Crystal River, FL 34429 USA Tel 352-795-5128
E-mail: info@biblebasedstudies.org
Web site: http://www.biblebasedstudies.org.

Bible Facts Pr., *(978-0-9762892; 978-0-9772942)* 631 Martin Ave. Suite 1, Rohnert Park, CA 94928 USA
Web site: http://www.biblefactspress.com.

Bible Game *Imprint of* **IMAGINEX, LLC**

Bible League, *(978-1-882536; 978-1-61825; 978-1-61870; 978-1-62826)*
E-mail: info@bibleleagueusa.com
Web site: http://www.bibleleagueusa.com.

Bible Pathway Ministries, *(978-1-879595)* Orders Addr.: P.O. Box 20123, Murfreesboro, TN 37133 USA Tel 615-896-4243; Fax: 615-893-1744; Toll Free: 800-598-7884; Edit Addr.: P.O. Box 20123, Murfreesboro, TN 37129-0123 USA
E-mail: mail@biblepathway.org
Web site: http://www.biblepathway.org
Dist(s): **Send The Light Distribution LLC.**

Bible Visuals International, Inc., *(978-1-932381; 978-1-933206; 978-1-64104)* Orders Addr.: P.O. Box 153, Akron, PA 17501-0153 USA
Web site: http://www.biblevisuals.org.

Bible-4-Life.com *See* **SundaySchoolNetwork.com**

BibleByte Books *See* **Kidware Software, LLC**

Bibleco, Inc., *(978-0-9746058; 978-0-9754978)* 153 Pinehurst Dr., Easton, PA 18042 USA (SAN 256-0801) Fax: 610-438-3964; *Imprints:* Biblemania (Bibleman)
E-mail: biblemania@aol.com
Web site: http://www.biblemania.com.

Biblemania *Imprint of* **Bibleco, Inc.**

BibleRhymes *Imprint of* **BibleRhymes Publishing, L.L.C.**

BibleRhymes Publishing, L.L.C., *(978-0-9790605; 978-1-947049)* Orders Addr.: 54211 Horizon Dr., Shelby Township, MI 48316 USA (SAN 852-3207); *Imprints:* BibleRhymes (BibleRhymes USA)
E-mail: CustomerService@BibleRhymes.com
Web site: http://www.BibleRhymes.com.

Biblesoft, Inc., *(978-1-56514)* 22030 Seventh Ave., S., Suite 204, Seattle, WA 98198-6235 USA (SAN 298-7473) Tel 206-824-0547; Fax: 206-824-2729
Web site: http://www.biblesoft.com
Dist(s): **Anchor Distributors**
Spring Arbor Distributors, Inc.

BiblesPlus, *(978-0-9769109)* 13741 Annandale Dr., No. 20D, Seal Beach, CA 90740 USA Toll Free: 866-924-2537
E-mail: biblesplus7@yahoo.com
Web site: http://www.biblesplus.com.

Biblical Counseling Institute *See* **Skinner, Kerry L.**

Biblical Standards Pubns., *(978-0-9678798)* 287 Caldwell Dr., Maggie Valley, NC 28751 USA Tel 828-926-0606
E-mail: waltdot@primeline.com.

Biblio Bks. International, *(978-0-9729545; 978-0-9741190; 978-0-9748524; 978-0-9766681; 978-0-9785565; 978-0-9833352)* Kendall Tamiami Executive Airport 14005 SW 127th St., Miami, FL 33186 USA Tel 786 573 3999; Fax: 786 573 2090
E-mail: info@bibliobooks.com
Web site: http://www.bibliobooks.com.

Biblio Resource Pubns., Inc., *(978-1-934185)* 108 1/2 S. Moore St., Bessemer, MI 49911 USA Tel 906-364-2190
E-mail: info@BiblioResource.com
Web site: http://www.BiblioResource.com
Dist(s): **Follett School Solutions.**

Biblio Services, Inc., *(978-1-59608; 978-1-61887; 978-1-64131)* 399 Ave. Munoz Rivera, San Juan, PR 00918 USA Tel 787-753-1231; Fax: 787-753-1222
E-mail: ventas@biblioservices.com; vale@biblioservices.com; anthony@biblioservices.com
Web site: http://www.biblioservices.com.

Biblioasis (CAN) *(978-0-9735881; 978-0-9735971; 978-1-897231; 978-0-9738184; 978-1-926845) Dist. by* **Consort Bk Sales.**

BiblioBazaar *See* **Creative Media Partners, LLC**

Bibliograf, S.A. (ESP) *(978-84-7153; 978-84-8332) Dist. by* **Distribks Inc.**

Bibliograf, S.A. (ESP) *(978-84-7153; 978-84-8332) Dist. by* **Continental Bk.**

Bibliographisches Institut & F. A. Brockhaus AG (DEU) *(978-3-411) Dist. by* **IBD Ltd.**

Bibliographisches Institut & F. A. Brockhaus AG (DEU) *(978-3-411) Dist. by* **Intl Bk Import.**

Bibliographisches Institut & F. A. Brockhaus AG (DEU) *(978-3-411) Dist. by* **Distribks Inc.**

Bibliographisches Institut & F. A. Brockhaus AG (DEU) *(978-3-411) Dist. by* **Continental Bk.**

BiblioLife *Imprint of* **Creative Media Partners, LLC**

Bibliotech Pr., *(978-1-61895; 978-1-64799; 978-1-63637)* 8559 GLEN CREST DR, SUN VALLEY, CA 91352 USA Tel 818-546-1554
E-mail: BibliotechPress@gmail.com.

Biblo & Tannen Booksellers & Pubs., Inc., *(978-0-8196)* P.O. Box 302, Cheshire, CT 06410 USA (SAN 202-4071) Tel 203-250-1647 (phone/fax); Toll Free: 800-272-8778
E-mail: biblo.moser@gte.net.

BIC Alliance, *(978-0-9768310)* Orders Addr.: P.O. Box 40166, Baton Rouge, LA 70835 USA Fax: 225-751-9993; Toll Free: 800-460-4242; Edit Addr.: 6378 Quinn Dr., Baton Rouge, LA 70817 USA
E-mail: brady@bicalliance.com
Web site: http://www.bicpublishing.com.

Bicast, Inc., *(978-0-9638258; 978-0-9701008; 978-0-9766753)* Orders Addr.: P.O. Box 2676, Williamsburg, VA 23187 USA Tel 757-229-3276; Fax: 757-253-2273; Toll Free: 800-767-8273; Edit Addr.: 231 K Parkway Dr., Williamsburg, VA 23185 USA
E-mail: bicastpub@aol.com; jogaertner@hughes.net
Web site: http://www.lighthousesusa.com.

Bick Publishing Hse., *(978-1-884158)* 307 Neck Rd., Madison, CT 06443 USA Tel 203-245-0073; 203 245 0073; Fax: 203-245-5990; 30 Amberwood Pkwy., Ashland, OH 44805
E-mail: bickpubhse@aol.com
Web site: http://www.bickpubhouse.com
Dist(s): **Follett School Solutions**
Quality Bks., Inc.

Bickering Owls Publishing *Imprint of* **Maracle, Derek**

Bickico Enterprises, Inc., *(978-0-9746508; 978-0-9834081)* 19W042 Ave. Normandy E., Oak Brook, IL 60523 USA
E-mail: bickico@aol.com.

BICs Pr., *(978-0-9764253)* 1866 John F. Kennedy Blvd., No. B1, Jersey City, NJ 07305 USA.

Bicycle Bell Bks., *(978-0-9981468; 978-1-7358172)* 10808 NW 75th St., KANSAS CITY, MO 64152 USA Tel 816-659-5268
E-mail: j.ballou@sbcglobal.net
Web site: BicycleBellBooks.com.

Bienna Bks., *(978-0-9815075)* 21310 Poplar Way, Brier, WA 98036 USA Tel 206-774-3649.

Bienvenue Pr., *(978-0-692-08164-8; 978-0-692-11737-8; 978-0-692-12191-7; 978-0-692-14427-5; 978-0-692-15533-2; 978-0-692-18524-7; 978-0-578-41249-8; 978-0-578-42335-7; 978-0-578-43970-9; 978-0-578-46164-9; 978-0-578-47234-8; 978-0-578-49555-2; 978-0-578-52069-8; 978-0-578-57088-4; 978-0-578-60544-9; 978-0-578-61817-3; 978-0-578-67611-1; 978-1-7350454) 112 Sapphire Springs Rd., Youngsville, LA 70592 USA Tel 337-230-4097*
E-mail: alvincent@bienvenuepress.com
Web site: www.bienvenuepress.com
Dist(s): **CreateSpace Independent Publishing Platform.**

Bier Brothers, Inc., *(978-0-9677238)* 147 Wild Dunes Way, Jackson, NJ 08527-4050 USA (SAN) Fax: 810-815-2979; *Imprints:* Sweet Dreams Press (Sweet Press)
E-mail: Dsb342@aol.com; contactus@nightsprytes.com
Web site: http://www.newbreedcomics.com; http://www.nightsprytes.com.

Big Bear Publishing U.S., *(978-0-9801215)* P.O. Box 191, Ronks, PA 17572-9611 USA (SAN 855-2517) Tel 717-768-4644
E-mail: lonniebrinkley@yahoo.com
Web site: http://www.ibelievesanta.com.

Big Belly Bks., *(978-0-9749554; 978-0-692-37003-2; 978-0-9961792)* Orders Addr.: 2778 W. Schuss Mtn. Dr., Bellaire, MI 49615 USA; Edit Addr.: 2778 W. Schuss Mtn. Dr., Bellaire, MI 49615 USA
E-mail: sc@bigbellybooks.com
Web site: http://www.bigbellybooks.com.

Big Bks. for Little People *Imprint of* **Friendly Planet**

Big Blue World Bks. *Imprint of* **Gumdrop Pr.**

Big Book Pr., LLC, *(978-0-9793219; 978-0-9848920)* Orders Addr.: 47774 Scots Borough Sq., Potomac Falls, VA 20165 USA Tel 240-355-3465
E-mail: frankchawkins@gmail.com; books@boysguidebooks.com; books@bigbookpress.com; books@girlsguidebooks.net; books@boysandgirlsguidebooks.com
Web site: http://www.boysguidebooks.blogspot.com; http://www.boysguidebooks.com; http://www.girlsguidebooks.net; http://www.bigbookpress.com; http://www.boysandgirlsguidebooks.com
Dist(s): **Independent Pubs. Group**
MyiLibrary
Small Pr. United.

Big Bk. Pubns., *(978-0-615-17074-9; 978-0-615-21065-0)* P.O. Box 7867, Largo, MD 20792 USA
E-mail: nicole@bigbookpublications.com
Web site: http://www.nigbookpublications.com.

Big Books, by George!, *(978-1-59246)* Orders Addr.: P.O. Box 1018, Keller, TX 76244 USA; Edit Addr.: 901 Briar Ridge Dr., Keller, TX 76244 USA
Dist(s): **Follett School Solutions.**

Big Brown Box, Inc., The, *(978-0-9764647)* 443 Hill Rd., Douglassville, PA 19518-9530 USA Tel 610-385-7587
Web site: http://www.thebigbrownbox.com
Dist(s): **Book Clearing Hse.**

Big Buddy Bks. *Imprint of* **ABDO Publishing Co.**

Big City Publishing, *(978-0-9762071; 978-0-9845873)* 230 Central St., Auburndale, MA 02492 USA Fax: 617-795-1650
E-mail: mellisa@bigcitypublishing.com
Web site: http://www.anglesfromtheattic.com.

Big Company, LLC, The, *(978-0-9800752)* 4790 Irvine Blvd., Suite 105-176, Irvine, CA 92620 USA (SAN 855-1383)
E-mail: info@thebigcompanyllc.com.

Big Country Publishing, LLC, *(978-0-9845088; 978-0-9847831; 978-1-938487)* 7691 Shaffer Pkwy., Suite C, Littleton, CO 80127 USA.

Big Creek Publishing, *(978-0-9742021)* Orders Addr.: P.O. Box 884, Sunberry, OH 43074 USA Tel 740-965-4127; Fax: 740-965-9541; Edit Addr.: 930 Joe Walker Rd., Sunbury, OH 43074 USA (SAN 255-4054) Tel 740-965-4127
E-mail: bigcreekpublishing@msn.com.

Big Dreams Publishing, *(978-0-9771868)* 8180 S. Allison Ct., Littleton, CO 80128 USA.

Big Earth Publishing *See* **Bower Hse.**

Big Entertainment, Inc., *(978-0-9645175; 978-1-57780)* 2255 Glades Rd., Suite 237W, Boca Raton, FL 33431-7395 USA Tel 407-998-8000; Fax: 407-998-2974
Dist(s): **Kable Media Services.**

Big Eyes Publishing, *(978-1-943574)* 1221 Inverness Ct., Schererville, IN 46375 USA Tel 219-515-2565
E-mail: Thomasconti@yahoo.com.

Big Guy Bks., Inc, *(978-1-929945)* 6866 Embarcadero Ln., Carlsbad, CA 92011 USA (SAN 253-0392) Toll Free: 800-536-3030
E-mail: robert@bigguybooks.com
Web site: http://www.timesoldiers.com; http://www.bigguybooks.com;

http://www.freedinosaurbook.com; https://GreatBooksForBoys.com
Dist(s): **Follett School Solutions.**

Big Guy Books, Incorporated *See* **Big Guy Bks., Inc**

Big H Bks. *Imprint of* **Harvey, Alan**

Big Head Pr., *(978-0-9743814; 978-0-9853167)* P.O. Box 1853, Round Rock, TX 78680 USA
E-mail: contact@bigheadpress.com
Web site: http://www.bigheadpress.com
Dist(s): **Diamond Comic Distributors, Inc.**

Big Idea Productions, P.O. Box 189, Lombard, IL 60148 USA Tel 630-652-6000; Fax: 630-652-6001
Dist(s): **Vision Video**
Word Entertainment.

Big Ideas Learning, LLC, *(978-1-60840; 978-1-68033; 978-1-63598; 978-1-64208; 978-1-64245; 978-1-64312; 978-1-64432; 978-1-64727)* 1762 Norcross Rd., Erie, PA 16510 USA (SAN 857-751X) Tel 814-824-6365; 814-824-6370; Fax: 814-824-6377; Toll Free Fax: 888-432-9245; Toll Free: 877-552-7766
E-mail: eforish@larsontexts.com
Web site: http://bigideaslearning.com
Dist(s): **Houghton Mifflin Harcourt Publishing Co.**
Macmillan.

Big Kid Bks., *(978-0-9771990)* 6671 Sunset Blvd., No. 1585-101, Los Angeles, CA 90028 USA.

Big Kid Science, *(978-0-9721819; 978-1-937548; 978-1-944161)* 680 Iris Ave., Boulder, CO 80304 USA; 814 N. Franklin St., Chicago, IL 60610
E-mail: jeff@bigkidscience.com
Web site: http://www.jeffreybennett.com
Dist(s): **Follett School Solutions**
Independent Pubs. Group
MyiLibrary
ebrary, Inc.

Big Kids Productions (Publishing), *(978-0-930249)* 15 Marco Ln., Rochester, NY 14622-3228 USA (SAN 670-8617)
E-mail: pattiup@rochester.rr.com
Web site: http://www.rochesternyeats.com
Dist(s): **North Country Bks., Inc.**

Big Kids Publishing, Incorporated *See* **Big Kids Productions (Publishing)**

Big Lil' Bks., *(978-0-9749041)* Div. of ShadeTree Publishing, 3625 Tallman SE, Grand Rapids, MI 49508 USA
E-mail: janiceintheshade@msn.com.

Big Mouth Hse. *Imprint of* **Small Beer Pr.**

Big Picture Press *Imprint of* **Candlewick Pr.**

Big Picture, The, *(978-0-9794304; 978-0-9882125; 978-0-9996724)* 5976 Leland, Ann Arbor, MI 48105-9309 USA Tel 734-223-4933
E-mail: kmaclean@kjmaclean.com
Web site: http://www.kjmaclean.com/.

Big Ransom Studio, *(978-0-9754728; 978-1-933732)* P.O. Box 489, Georgetown, TX 78627-0489 USA
E-mail: sales@bigransom.com
Web site: http://www.mindtrippress.com
Dist(s): **Mind Trip Pr.**

Big Rig LLC, *(978-0-692-79625-2; 978-0-9997696)* 2820 Selwyn Ave Suite 847, Charlotte, NC 28209 USA Tel 704-585-7609
E-mail: thebigrigkids@gmail.com
Web site: www.thebigrigkids.org.

Big River Distribution, *(978-0-9795944; 978-0-9823575; 978-0-9845519)* Orders Addr.: 8214 Exchange Way, Saint Louis, MO 63144 USA (SAN 631-9114) Tel 314-918-9800; Fax: 314-918-9804
E-mail: info@bigriverdist.com; randy@bigriverdist.com
Web site: http://www.bigriverdist.com
Dist(s): **Follett School Solutions.**

Big Secret, The, *(978-0-9724924)* P.O. Box 1994, Slidell, LA 70459 USA Tel 985-781-8704 (phone/fax)
Web site: http://www.thebigsecret.org.

Big Sil LLC., *(978-0-9967352; 978-0-9983357)* P.O. Box 1755, Hoboken, NJ 07030 USA Tel 201-615-9601
E-mail: bigsiladventures@gmail.com.

Big Sky Stories Publishing *See* **Arnica Publishing**

Big Smile, Inc., *(978-0-9761891)* P.O. Box 1042, Stroudsburg, PA 18360 USA Fax: 646-542-5319
E-mail: marcjohnjefferies@yahoo.com
Web site: http://www.marcjohnonline.com.

Big Smile Pr., LLC, *(978-0-9888462)* 180 Hollow Way, Ingleside, IL 60041 USA Tel 847-973-9084
E-mail: kellyp123@comcast.net.

Big Table Publishing Co., *(978-0-9753211; 978-0-9824955; 978-0-9842473; 978-0-9845733; 978-0-9830666; 978-0-9849567; 978-0-9886191; 978-0-9904872; 978-0-9908413; 978-0-9965405; 978-0-9969887; 978-1-945917)* 289 Elliot St., Newton Upper Falls, MA 02464 USA Tel 617-592-5805
Web site: http://www.bigtablepublishing.com.

Big Tent Bks., *(978-1-60131; 978-0-578-47138-9; 978-0-578-66280-0)* 115 Bluebill Dr., Savannah, GA 31419 USA (SAN 851-1136); *Imprints:* Parents Publishing Group (Parents Pub); Castlebridge Books (Castlebridge Bks)
E-mail: admin@dragonpencil.com; admin@bigtentbooks.com
Web site: http://www.bigtentbooks.com
Dist(s): **Castlebridge Distribution**
Music, Bks. & Business, Inc.

Big Tent Entertainment, Inc., *(978-1-59226)* 216 W. 18th St., New York, NY 10011 USA Tel 212-604-0064
Dist(s): **Independent Pubs. Group**
Midpoint Trade Bks., Inc.

Big Tomato Pr., *(978-0-9791233)* Orders Addr.: 1480 Sutterville Rd., Sacramento, CA 95822 USA Tel 916-798-2125
E-mail: jocelyn@bigtomatopress.com
Web site: http://www.bigtomatopress.com
Dist(s): **Follett School Solutions.**

Big Valley Pr., *(978-0-9765372)* 401 E. Holum St, Deforest, WI 53532 USA Tel 608-513-0724
E-mail: stuart@stotts.com
Web site: http://www.bigvalleypress.com
Dist(s): **Follett School Solutions.**

Big Valley Publishing, *(978-0-9726004)* 516 N. Chinowth, Visalia, CA 93291 USA Do not confuse with company with similar name in Northridge, CA
E-mail: erkna@aol.com.

Big Wave Bks., *(978-0-9754979)* P.O. Box 108, Charlestown, RI 02813 USA Tel 401-322-8711
Web site: http://www.bigwavebooks.com.

Big World Little Om *See* **Sahtva**

Bigfoot Bks. (GBR) *(978-0-9554555) Dist. by* **NStarEdit.**

Biggaloo Bks., *(978-0-9818145)* 660 Fairway Terr., Naples, FL 34103 USA (SAN 856-6267)
Dist(s): **Music, Bks. & Business, Inc.**

Kat Biggie Pr., *(978-0-9899347; 978-0-9861969; 978-0-9987779; 978-0-9994377; 978-1-948604)* P.O. Box 290041, Columbia, SC 29229 USA Tel 803-608-5138; *Imprints:* Purple Butterfly Press (MYID_M_PURPLE)
E-mail: info@writepublishsell.co
Web site: http://writepublishsell.co; http://katbiggiepress.com.

Big-head fish, *(978-0-9765007)*
E-mail: info@bigheadfish.com/.

BigKids Bilingual Bks., *(978-0-9844310)* P.O. Box 537, Glendale, CA 91209 USA (SAN 859-385X) Tel 626-407-8886
E-mail: jalexan@alumni.usc.edu
Web site: http://www.bigkidsbilingualbooks.com.

Bigwarfe, Alexa *See* **Kat Biggie Pr.**

Bilal, Nabeeh, *(978-0-615-95158-4; 978-0-692-57311-2; 978-0-692-62252-0; 978-0-692-75743-7; 978-0-692-81373-7; 978-0-692-91555-4; 978-0-692-08756-5; 978-0-692-13045-2)* Orders Addr.: 1888 Savannah Pl SE, washington, DC 20020 USA Tel 202-421-8241; 700 S. Berendo St. Apt. 403, Los Angeles, CA 90005
E-mail: mtcanady@gmail.com; nabeeh_bilal@hotmail.com
Web site: http://www.callaloothebook.com.

Bilbo Bks., *(978-0-9800108; 978-0-9981627; 978-1-7326180)* 1384 W. Peachtree St., NW, No. C-4, Atlanta, GA 30309-2913 USA
E-mail: bilbobookspublishing@gmail.com.

Bilingual Dictionaries, Inc., *(978-0-933146; 978-1-946986)* Orders Addr.: P.O. Box 1154, Murrieta, CA 92564 USA (SAN 221-9697) Tel 951-296-2445; Fax: 951-296-9911; 42225 Remington Ave, A4, Temecula, CA 92590 (SAN 990-4972) Tel 951-296-2445; Fax: 951-296-9911; *Imprints:* Basic ESL (MYID_H_BASIC E)
E-mail: manager@bilingualdictionaries.com; support@bilingualdictionaries.com
Web site: http://www.bilingualdictionaries.com
Dist(s): **Booksource, The**
Follett School Solutions.

Bilingual Educational Services, Inc., *(978-0-86624; 978-0-89075)* 2514 S. Grand Ave., Los Angeles, CA 90007 USA (SAN 218-4680) Tel 213-749-6213; Fax: 213-749-1820; Toll Free: 800-448-6032
E-mail: sales@besbooks.com
Web site: http://www.besbooks.com
Dist(s): **Follett School Solutions.**

Bilingual Language Materials *See* **MAAT Resources, Inc.**

Bilingual Language Materials *Imprint of* **MAAT Resources, Inc.**

Bilingual Pr./Editorial Bilingue, *(978-0-916950; 978-0-927534; 978-1-931010; 978-1-939743)* Orders Addr.: Hispanic Research Ctr. Arizona State Univ. P.O. Box 875303, Tempe, AZ 85287-5303 USA (SAN 208-5526) Fax: 480-965-8309; Toll Free: 800-965-2280; Edit Addr.: Bilingual Review Pr. Administration Bldg. Rm. B-255 Arizona State Univ., Tempe, AZ 85281 USA
E-mail: brp@asu.edu
Web site: http://www.asu.edu/brp
Dist(s): **Libros Sin Fronteras**
SPD-Small Pr. Distribution.

Bilingual Pubns., *(978-0-9644678)* P.O. Box 12678, Denver, CO 80212 USA Tel 303-433-0979 Do not confuse with Bilingual Pubns. Co., New York, NY.

Bilingual Pubns. Co., The, 270 Lafayette St., New York, NY 10012 USA (SAN 164-8993) Tel 212-431-3500; Fax: 212-431-3567 Do not confuse with Bilingual Pubns., in Denver, CO
E-mail: lindagoodman@juno.com; spanishbks@aol.com.

Bill of Rights Institute, The, *(978-1-932785; 978-0-692-23022-0; 978-0-692-89225-1)* 200 N. Glebe Rd. Ste. 200, Arlington, VA 22203-3756 USA Toll Free: 800-838-7870
E-mail: sales@billofrightsinstitute.org; mwong@billofrightsinstitute.org; wneal@billofrightsinstitute.org
Web site: http://www.billofrightsinstitute.org
Dist(s): **CLEARVUE/eav, Inc.**
Social Studies Schl. Service
Teacher's Discovery.

Billiard Congress of America, *(978-1-878493)* 5 Piedmont Ctr NE Ste. 435, Atlanta, GA 30305-1509 USA
E-mail: amy@bca-pool.com; marketing@bca-pool.com
Web site: http://www.bca-pool.com.

Billings, David J., *(978-0-9789036)* 12441 SE Lusted Rd., Sandy, OR 97055-7556 USA
E-mail: david@davidjbillings.com; david@roadtripbook.com
Web site: http://www.roadtripbook.com.

Billings Worldwide Brain, *(978-0-9654169)* P.O. Box 701, Addison, TX 75001 USA (SAN 299-2426)
E-mail: dave@hamr.com
Web site: http://www.hamr.com
Dist(s): **Distributors, The.**

Billion $ Baby Pubns., *(978-0-9707945)* 22817 Ventura Blvd., Suite 408, Woodland Hills, CA 91364 USA (SAN 254-3265) Toll Free Fax: 888-232-9022; Toll Free: 800-499-2771
E-mail: Diedra@BabyPublications.com; dottie@babypublications.com
Web site: http://www.BabyPublication.com.

Billionaire Butterfly, LLC, *(978-0-9852262; 978-0-692-81697-4; 978-0-692-81764-3)* 109-15 Queens Blvd. Apt. 2C, Forest Hills, NY 11375 USA Tel 718-810-8700
E-mail: lenaure@gmail.com.

Billiot, Wendy Wilson, *(978-0-9762592)* 2715 Bayou DuLarge Rd., Theriot, LA 70397 USA
E-mail: wwbilliot@gmail.com
Web site: http://www.wetlandbooks.com.

Billy Jo Bks., *(978-0-9765088)* 9111 Oat Ave., Gerber, CA 96035-9723 USA Tel 530-385-1820
E-mail: biljoho@earthlink.net.

Billy the Bear & His Friends, Inc., *(978-0-9641338)* 1909 Munster Ave., Saint Paul, MN 55116 USA Tel 651-699-7636; Fax: 651-690-4815.

BillyFish Bks. LLC, *(978-0-9849155)* 518 E. Datura Ct., Pueblo West, CO 81007 USA Tel 719-464-1126
E-mail: jason@expedition360.com
Dist(s): **Ingram Content Group.**

Bimini Bks., *(978-0-9753118)* 9553 SW 189 Terr., Suite 200, Miami, FL 33157 USA Tel 305-256-0638
E-mail: biminibooks@aol.com.

Bindlestick Bks., *(978-0-578-16673-5; 978-0-578-16732-9; 978-0-692-59737-8; 978-0-692-70921-4; 978-0-692-70929-0; 978-0-692-77061-0; 978-0-578-42172-8; 978-0-578-43023-2; 978-0-578-44968-5)* 616 1/2 Canyon Rd., Santa Fe, NM 87501 USA Tel 917-679-8080
E-mail: jeffreyschweitzer01@gmail.com
Web site: www.bindlestickbooks.com.

Bindu Bks. *Imprint of* **Inner Traditions International, Ltd.**

Binet International, *(978-0-942787)* P.O. Box 1429, Carlsbad, CA 92008 USA (SAN 667-7088) Tel 760-941-7929.

Bing Note, Inc., *(978-0-9794323)* 300 Caldecott Ln., No. 215, Oakland, CA 94618 USA
E-mail: lisa@bingnote.com
Web site: http://www.bingnote.com.

Bingham Putnam Publishing, *(978-0-9760504)* 326 Newport Dr., No. 1710, Naples, FL 34114 USA.

Bingo Bks., Inc., *(978-1-933530)* P.O. Box 3355, Austin, TX 78763-3355 USA Toll Free: 877-246-4644
Web site: http://www.bingobooks.com.

Binney & Smith, Inc., *(978-0-86696)* P.O. Box 431, Easton, PA 18042 USA (SAN 216-5899).

Binx Bks., *(978-0-9801796)* 33 W. Delaware Pl. Apt. 9F, Chicago, IL 60610-7361 USA.

Bio Rx, *(978-0-9772977)* 10828 Kenwood Rd., Cincinnati, OH 45242-2812 USA
E-mail: info@biorx.net
Web site: http://www.biorx.net.

Bio-Dynamic Farming & Gardening Assn., Inc., *(978-0-938250)* 25844 Butler Rd., Junction City, OR 97448 USA (SAN 224-9871) Tel 541-998-0105; Fax: 541-998-0406; Toll Free: 888-516-7797
E-mail: info@biodynamics.com
Web site: http://www.biodynamics.com
Dist(s): **New Leaf Distributing Co., Inc.**
Small Changes, Inc.
SteinerBooks, Inc.

BioEd *Imprint of* **Baylor College of Medicine**

Biographical Publishing Co., *(978-0-9637240; 978-1-929882; 978-0-9913521; 978-0-9976028; 978-1-7338120)* 95 Sycamore Dr., Prospect, CT 06712-1493 USA (SAN 298-2692) Tel 203-758-3661; Fax: 253-793-2618
E-mail: biopub@aol.com
Web site: http://www.biopub.us
Dist(s): **Pathway Bk. Service.**

BIONIC Pr., *(978-0-9892448)* 8612 S. Terra Pointe Way, West Jordan, UT 84088 USA Tel 801-231-1969
E-mail: r.harkness@hsc.utah.edu
Web site: www.bionicpressbooks.com.

Bios for Kids *Imprint of* **Panda Publishing, L.L.C.**

Birch Brook Pr., *(978-0-913559; 978-0-9789974; 978-0-9842003; 978-0-9915777)* P.O. Box 81, Delhi, NY 13753 USA (SAN 631-5321) Fax: 607-746-7453 (phone/fax)
E-mail: birchbrook@copper.net
Web site: http://www.birchbrookpress.info.

Birch Island, *(978-0-9772692; 978-0-9818668; 978-0-615-96113-2)* P.O. Box 988 27 Dillingham Rd., Manchester, VT 05254 USA (SAN 257-1625) Tel 802-362-0074; 802-342-7844
E-mail: historicalpages@yahoo.com
Web site: http://www.historicalpages.com
Dist(s): **CreateSpace Independent Publishing Platform**
Independent Pubs. Group.

Birch Tree Publishing, *(978-0-615-60274-5; 978-0-9894487)* 3830 Valley Centre Dr. Suite 705-432, San Diego, CA 92130 USA Tel 858-212-6111 Do not confuse with Birch Tree Publishing in Miami, FL, Southbury, CT
E-mail: nimpentoad@gmail.com
Dist(s): **CreateSpace Independent Publishing Platform.**

Birchall Publishing, *(978-0-9857816)* P.O. Box 92054, Oceanside, CA 92054 USA Tel 720-347-0771
E-mail: lorrielbirchall@gmail.com.

Bird, Bunny & Bear *Imprint of* **American Reading Co.**

Birdcage Books *See* **Birdcage Pr.**

Birdcage Pr., *(978-1-889613; 978-1-59960)* 853 Alma St., Palo Alto, CA 94301 USA Tel 650-462-6300; Fax: 650-462-6305; Toll Free: 800-247-6553
E-mail: info@birdcagepress.com
Web site: http://www.birdcagepress.com.

Birdsall, Bonnie Thomas, *(978-0-9762679)* 3421 Lacewood Rd., Tampa, FL 33618 USA
E-mail: swimtaichibon@juno.com.

Birdseed Bks., *(978-0-9774142)* 520 17th St., Dallas, WI 54733 USA; *Imprints:* Birdseed Books for Kids (Birdseed Books for Kids)
Web site: http://www.birdseedbooksforkids.com.

Birdseed Books for Kids *Imprint of* **Birdseed Bks.**

Birdsong Bks., *(978-0-9662761; 978-0-9833406)* Orders Addr.: 1322 Bayview Rd., Middletown, DE 19709 USA Tel 302-378-7274; Fax: 302-378-0339; Edit Addr.: 814 N. Franklin St, Chicago, IL 60610 USA
E-mail: birdsongbooks@delaware.net
Web site: http://www.birdsongbooks.com
Dist(s): **Common Ground Distributors, Inc.**
Follett School Solutions
Independent Pubs. Group
MyiLibrary.

Birkhauser Boston *See* **Birkhäuser Boston**

Birkhäuser Boston, *(978-0-8176)* Div. of Springer-Verlag GmbH & Co. KG, Orders Addr.: P.O. Box 2485, Secaucus, NJ 07094 USA (SAN 241-6344) Tel 201-348-4033; Edit Addr.: 675 Massachusetts Ave., Cambridge, MA 02139 USA (SAN 213-2869) Tel 617-876-2333; Toll Free: 800-777-4643 (customer service)
Web site: http://www.birkhauser.com
Dist(s): **Follett School Solutions**
Metapress
MyiLibrary
Palgrave Macmillan
Springer
ebrary, Inc.

Birks, Alison, *(978-0-9997208)* 100 Blueberry Hill Rd., Bridgewater, CT 06752 USA Tel 860-733-5191
E-mail: Alison.Birks@gmail.com.

Birlinn, Ltd. (GBR) *(978-1-874744; 978-1-84158; 978-1-84341; 978-1-84697; 978-0-85790; 978-1-78027; 978-1-912476; 978-1-78885; 978-1-78886; 978-1-83983) Dist. by* **Casemate Pubs.**

Birt Hse. Publishing, *(978-0-578-11306-7; 978-0-578-11315-9)* 100 Bluebonnet St., Apt. 108, Stephenville, TX 76401 USA.

Bis B.V., Uitgeverij (BIS Publishers) (NLD) *(978-90-72007; 978-90-6369) Dist. by* **HachBkGrp.**

Bisham Hill Bks., *(978-0-9744281)* Orders Addr.: 25 Old Kings Hwy. N. Ste. 13, #192, Darien, CT 06820 USA
E-mail: designtospec@gmail.com
Web site: http://www.bishamhill.com.

Bishop Museum Pr., *(978-0-910240; 978-0-930897; 978-1-58178)* Orders Addr.: 1525 Bernice St., Honolulu, HI 96817-2704 USA (SAN 202-408X) Tel 808-847-8260; 808-848-4135; *Imprints:* Kamahoi Press (Kamahoi Pr)
E-mail: press@bishopmuseum.org
Web site: http://www.bishopmuseum.org
Dist(s): **Booklines Hawaii, Ltd.**
Islander Group.

Bishop, Susan Lynn, *(978-0-9772878)* Orders Addr.: P.O. Box 13, Onley, IL 62450 USA Tel 618-392-4011; Edit Addr.: P.O. Box 13, Olney, IL 62450-0013 USA
E-mail: suzyb@wabash.net.

Bisiar Music Publishing, *(978-0-9753091)* Orders Addr.: P.O. Box 424, Evergreen, CO 80437-0424 USA (SAN 256-0356) Tel 303-670-0752 (phone/fax); Edit Addr.: 3661 A Evergreen Pkwy., Evergreen, CO 80437-0424 USA
E-mail: bisiar@earthlink.net
Web site: http://www.eddiespaghettiusa.com.

Bison Bks. *Imprint of* **Univ. of Nebraska Pr.**

Bit of Boston Bks., A, *(978-0-9788637)* Orders Addr.: 208 Commonwealth Ave., Boston, MA 02116 USA; Edit Addr.: P.O. Box 990208, Boston, MA 02116 USA
E-mail: jamesrholland@mindspring.com.

Bitingduck Pr., *(978-1-938463)* 1262 Sunnyoaks Cir., Altadena, CA 91001 USA Tel 626-507-8033
E-mail: jay@bitingduckpress.com
Web site: http://www.bitingduckpress.com
Dist(s): **Follett School Solutions**
Independent Pubs. Group
Midpoint Trade Bks., Inc.
SPD-Small Pr. Distribution.

Bitter Oleander Pr., The, *(978-0-9664358; 978-0-9786335; 978-0-9883525; 978-0-9862049; 978-0-9993279; 978-1-7346535)* 4983 Tall Oaks Dr., Fayetteville, NY 13066-9776 USA (SAN 855-9686)
E-mail: info@bitteroleander.com
Web site: http://www.bitteroleander.com
Dist(s): **SPD-Small Pr. Distribution.**

Bitterroot Mountain Publishing, *(978-0-9817874; 978-0-9852784; 978-1-940025)* P.O. Box 3508, Hayden, ID 83835-3508 USA.

Bitty Book Pr., *(978-1-887270)* 851 Mt. Vernon Ct., Naperville, IL 60563 USA Tel 630-420-1887; Fax: 630-963-0341; Toll Free: 800-750-6649; 2736 Maple Ave., Downers Grove, IL 60515
E-mail: maryannako@aol.com
Web site: http://www.namepower101.com.

Bixie Gate Publishing, *(978-0-9773433)* 22694 SW Lincoln St., Sherwood, OR 97140 USA (SAN 257-3474)
E-mail: shannonk23@comcast.net
Web site: http://www.bixiegatepublishing.com; http://www.shannonkeegan.com.

Biz Hub (Business & Investing) *Imprint of* **Speedy Publishing LLC**

Biz4Kids *Imprint of* **Round Cow Media Group**

For full information on wholesalers and distributors, refer to the Wholesaler and Distributor Name Index

Bizzy Girls Publishing, *(978-0-9833532)* 1508 Veteran Ave. No. 205, Los Angeles, CA 90024 USA Tel 310-467-7300
E-mail: dekanafani@yahoo.com
Web site: Www.bizzygirls.com.

Bjelkier Pr., *(978-0-9828217)* 1620 Louis Ln., Hastings, MN 55033 USA (SAN 859-9025) Tel 651-437-8244
E-mail: toysammy@embarqmail.com.

Bjelopetrovich, Beba Foundation, *(978-0-9745724)* 5555 W. Howard St., Skokie, IL 60077-2621 USA Tel 847-679-6710; Fax: 847-679-6717.

†BJU Pr., *(978-0-89084; 978-1-57924; 978-1-59166; 978-1-60682; 978-1-62856; 978-1-64626)* 1700 Wade Hampton Blvd., Greenville, SC 29614 USA (SAN 223-7512) Tel 864-242-5731; 864-370-1800 (ext. 4397; Fax: 864-298-0268; Toll Free Fax: 800-525-8398; Toll Free: 800-845-5731; *Imprints:* JourneyForth (JmyForth); Bloomsbury Visual Arts (BloomsVisual)
E-mail: bjup@bjup.com
Web site: http://www.bjupress.com
Dist(s): **Follett School Solutions**; *CIP.*

Bk. Jungle *Imprint of* **Standard Publications, Inc.**

BKB Group, Inc., The, *(978-0-9747628)* Orders Addr.: 11146 Harbour Springs Cr., Boca Raton, FL 33428 USA Tel 561-218-1215; Fax: 561-218-1214; Toll Free: 888-321-7664; Edit Addr.: 11146 HARBOUR SPRINGS CR., 11146 HARBOUR SPRINGS CR., BOCA RATON, FL 33428 USA
E-mail: rfproductions@adelphia.net
Web site: http://www.billybutterfly.com.

Bk.barn Publishing *Imprint of* **Compass Productions Inc.**

Bk.ify by Sanitaryum *Imprint of* **Sanitaryum**

Bks. for Young Learners *Imprint of* **Owen, Richard C. Pubs., Inc.**

Black Academy Pr., Inc., *(978-0-87831)* Orders Addr.: 4011 Old Court Rd., Pikesville, MD 21208-2808 USA (SAN 218-6489)
E-mail: bapress@aol.com; info@blackacademypress.com
Web site: http://www.blackacademypress.com.

Black, Amy Jackson, *(978-0-615-16743-5)* 107 Southglen, Terre Haute, IN 47802 USA
E-mail: godzgrl4evr@msn.com
Dist(s): **Lulu Pr., Inc.**

Black and White Publishing Ltd. (GBR) *(978-1-873631; 978-0-9515151; 978-1-902927; 978-1-903265; 978-1-84502; 978-1-910230; 978-1-78530) Dist. by* **IPG Chicago.**

Black Bart Bks., *(978-0-615-20238-9; 978-0-615-23723-7; 978-0-578-01524-8; 978-0-578-02511-7; 978-0-578-08320-9)* 3447 Little Carpenter Creek Rd., Fernwood, ID 83830 USA
Web site: http://www.blackbaradventures.com
Dist(s): **Lulu Pr., Inc.**

Black Bed Sheet Bks., *(978-0-9822530; 978-0-9842136; 978-0-9833773; 978-0-9858829; 978-0-9886590; 978-0-615-88139-3; 978-0-615-90327-9; 978-0-615-90623-2; 978-0-615-90684-3; 978-0-615-94207-0; 978-0-615-94575-0; 978-0-615-94689-4; 978-0-615-94893-5; 978-0-615-99827-5; 978-0-692-21851-8; 978-0-692-23039-8; 978-0-692-23974-2; 978-0-692-24044-1; 978-0-692-24087-8; 978-0-692-25565-0; 978-0-692-25829-3; 978-0-692-26626-7; 978-0-692-26983-1; 978-0-692-27830-7; 978-0-692-31231-5; 978-0-692-31456-2; 978-0-692-31673-3; 9) 7865 Valley Quail Ct., Antelope, CA 95843-2031 USA (SAN 857-6785)*
E-mail: bbsadmin@downwarden.com
Web site: http://www.downwarden.com/blackbedsheet; https://www.downwarden.com/blackbedsheetdigital
Dist(s): **CreateSpace Independent Publishing Platform.**

Black Belt Training, *(978-0-9759744)* 9109 Cochran Heights, Dallas, TX 75220 USA Tel 214-351-2234 (phone/fax)
E-mail: drted@wwwin.com
Web site: http://www.wwwin.com.

Black Bird Bks., *(978-0-9763238)* Orders Addr.: P.O. Box 901, Ankeny, IA 50021 USA; Edit Addr.: P.O. Box 901, Ankeny, IA 50021-0901 USA
E-mail: lizzie3blackbird@hotmail.com.

Black Cat *Imprint of* **Grove/Atlantic, Inc.**

Black Chook Bks. (NZL) *(978-0-473-40332-4) Dist. by* **IPG Chicago.**

Black, Clinton L., *(978-0-9620180)* Orders Addr.: P.O. Box 9096, Fort Lauderdale, FL 33310 USA Tel 954-722-0415; Fax: 954-720-7674
E-mail: thepurposeofhumanlife@yahoo.com
Dist(s): **Southern Bk. Service.**

Black Coat Pr. *Imprint of* **HollywoodComics.com, LLC**

Black Coffee Publishing, *(978-0-9745238)* Orders Addr.: 5543 Edmondson Pike, No. 213, Nashville, TN 37211-5808 USA Tel 615-969-5516
E-mail: Jenniferwiseblack@gmail.com; bcpubl@aol.com
Web site: Http://www.MediaTrauma.com; http://www.blackcoffeepublishing.com.

Black Creek Publishing Group, *(978-0-9895323; 978-0-9904596; 978-0-9962919; 978-0-9978983)* 2102 Kimberton Rd. No. 266, Kimberton, PA 19460 USA Tel 832-350-3029
E-mail: jchenry@blackcreekpublishinggroup.com
Web site: www.blackcreekpublishinggroup.com.

Black Diamond Publishing, *(978-0-9715139)* 415 E. 32nd St., Indianapolis, IN 46205 USA Do not confuse with Black Diamond Publishing in Brooklyn,NY
E-mail: LWatk82805@aol.com; BDPub@aol.com; Linda@lindawatkins.org
Web site: http://www.lindawatkins.org.

Black Dog & Leventhal Pubs. Inc. *Imprint of* **Hachette Bks.**

Black Dog & Leventhal Pubs. Inc. *Imprint of* **Running Pr.**

Black Dog Books, *(978-1-884449; 978-1-928619)* 1115 Pine Meadows Ct., Normal, IL 61761 USA Tel 309-310-6984
E-mail: info@blackdogbooks.net; blackdogbooks_tomroberts@yahoo.com
Web site: http://www.blackdogbooks.net.

Black Dog Publishing Ltd. (GBR) *(978-0-9521773; 978-1-901033; 978-1-904772; 978-1-906155; 978-1-907317; 978-1-908966; 978-1-910433) Dist. by* **Consort Bk Sales.**

Black Dog Publishing/Tuscany Bay Bks., *(978-1-7335103)* 3005 Candice Ct., Simi Valley, CA 93063 USA Tel 805-795-3165
E-mail: JIMCHRISTINA@YAHOO.COM
Web site: www.blackdogpublishing.co.

Black Dolphin Diving, *(978-0-9646281)* 5022 Two Harbors, Avalon, CA 90704-5022 USA Tel 310-510-2109
E-mail: bkdolphin@aol.com
Web site: http://www.divecatalina.com.

Black Dome Pr. Corp., *(978-0-9628523; 978-1-883789)* 1011 Rte. 296, Hensonville, NY 12439 USA (SAN 257-6996) Tel 518-734-6357; Fax: 518-734-5802; Toll Free: 800-513-9013; 649 Delaware Ave., Delmar, NY 12054
E-mail: blackdomep@aol.com
Web site: http://www.blackdomepress.com
Dist(s): **Follett School Solutions**
North Country Bks., Inc.

Black Dot Pubns., *(978-0-9649740)* Orders Addr.: P.O. Box 1068, Ojai, CA 93024 USA Tel 805-640-8825; Edit Addr.: 1208 Gregory St., Ojai, CA 93023 USA
E-mail: blackdotpubs@yahoo.com
Web site: http://www.backdotpubs.com; http://www.chuckhillig.com
Dist(s): **New Leaf Distributing Co., Inc.**

Black Falcon Publications *See* **LMW Works**

Black Forest Pr., *(978-1-58275; 978-1-881116)* Div. of Black Forest Enterprises, Orders Addr.: P.O. Box 6342, Chula Vista, CA 91909-6342 USA Fax: 619-482-8704; Toll Free: 800-451-9404 (General Information, Submission Inquiries and Acquisitions); 888-808-5440 (Book Sales, Marketing and Promotion); Edit Addr.: 1075 Hayuco Plz., Chula Vista, CA 91910-7006 USA (SAN 298-8445); *Imprints:* Sonnenschein Books (Sonnenschein Bks)
E-mail: bfp@blackforestpress.com
Web site: http://www.blackforestpress.com.

Black Forge, *(978-0-615-55725-0; 978-0-615-58405-8; 978-1-938083)* 304 S. Jones Blvd. No. 3593, Las Vegas, NV 89107 USA
E-mail: aya@ayaknight.com
Web site: http://www.ayaknight.com
Dist(s): **CreateSpace Independent Publishing Platform**
Independently Published.

Black Garnet Pr., *(978-0-9832383; 978-0-9911790)* 1313 St. Helena Ave., Santa Rosa, CA 95404 USA Tel 707-526-3331
E-mail: sandybaker131@gmail.com
Web site: sandybakerwriter.com.

Black Girl Speaks *See* **BGS Productions, Inc.**

Black Hat Pr., *(978-0-9614462; 978-1-887649)* Orders Addr.: P.O. Box 12, Goodhue, MN 55027-0012 USA (SAN 689-4259) Tel 651-923-4590; Edit Addr.: 508 Second Ave., Goodhue, MN 55027-0012 USA
E-mail: blackhatpress@yahoo.com.

Black Hawk Pr., Inc., The, *(978-0-9778731; 978-0-9817613)* 803 Charter Pl., Charlotte, NC 28211 USA Tel 704-364-1164
E-mail: info@blackhawkpress.com
Web site: http://www.blackhawkpress.com
Dist(s): **Blu Sky Media Group.**

Black Heart, Inc., *(978-0-9701879)* Orders Addr.: P.O. Box 3856, Rock Island, IL 61201 USA Tel 319-355-8223; Fax: 801-991-6950; Toll Free: 877-839-5115; Edit Addr.: 935 17th St., Bettenforf, IA 52722 USA
E-mail: jbryson@black-heart.net
Web site: http://www.black-heart.net.

Black Heron Pr., *(978-0-930773; 978-1-936364)* Orders Addr.: P.O. Box 13396, Mill Creek, WA 98145 USA (SAN 677-623X) Fax: 425-355-4929; Edit Addr.: 27 West 20Th St., New York, NY 10011 USA
E-mail: Jgoldberon@aol.com
Web site: http://www.blackheronpress.com
Dist(s): **Follett School Solutions**
Independent Pubs. Group
Midpoint Trade Bks., Inc.
ebrary, Inc.

Black Jasmine, *(978-0-9788802)* 46 Pleasant St., Sharon, MA 02067 USA
E-mail: deemajoan@yahoo.com
Web site: http://www.deemasglass.com.

Black, Judith Storyteller, *(978-0-9701073)* 33 Prospect St., Marblehead, MA 01941 USA Tel 781-631-4417
E-mail: jb@storiesalive.com
Web site: http://www.storiesalive.com.

Black Kite Publishing, *(978-0-9906795; 978-0-9957215-3-1)* 3 Buckeye, Galena, IL 61036 USA Tel 815-776-0285
E-mail: kathleen@ewtravel.com
Dist(s): **Lulu Pr., Inc.**

Black Lab Publishing LLC, *(978-0-9742815)* Orders Addr.: P.O. Box 6244, Laconia, NH 03247 USA Tel 603-714-8023; 606-524-1114
E-mail: loni@bearandkatie.com
Web site: http://www.bearandkatie.com; http://www.blacklabpublishing.com.

BLACK LACQUER Pr. & MARKETING INC., *(978-1-948288; 978-1-951313)* 3225 McLEOD Dr. SUITE100, LAS VEGAS, NV 89121 USA Tel 855-505-5640
E-mail: gulia.alba@blacklacquerpress.com
Web site: www.blacklacquerpress.com.

Black Library, The (GBR) *(978-1-84154; 978-1-84416; 978-1-84970; 978-0-85787; 978-1-78030; 978-1-78193; 978-1-78251; 978-1-78496) Dist. by* **S and S Inc.**

Black Literary, Inc., *(978-0-615-22609-5; 978-0-615-30323-9; 978-0-615-37753-7)* P.O. Box 492, Catlett, VA 20119 USA Tel 540-788-4992
E-mail: CHancasky@aol.com.

Black Mask Studios, ., Los Angeles, CA 90232 USA
E-mail: hitusup@blackmaskstudios.com
Web site: http://www.http://blackmaskstudios.com
Dist(s): **Diamond Comic Distributors, Inc.**

Black Oak Media, Inc., *(978-0-9790401; 978-1-61876)* P.O. Box 122, Cherry Valley, IL 61016 USA Do not confuse with companies with a similar name in Lincoln, NE, Lambertville, NJ, Springfield, MO
E-mail: info@blackoakmedia.org
Web site: http://www.blackoakmedia.org
Dist(s): **Follett School Solutions.**

Black Oak Press, Illinois *See* **Black Oak Media, Inc.**

Black Orb *See* **Angie Blue Bks., LLC**

Black Pearl Bks., *(978-0-9728005; 978-0-9766007; 978-0-9773438)* Orders Addr.: 3653-F Flakes Mill Road, PMB 306, Atlanta, GA 30034 USA Do not
E-mail: hurst@blackpearlbooks.com
Web site: http://www.blackpearlbooks.com
Dist(s): **African World Bks.**
American Wholesale Bk. Co.
Bookazine Co., Inc.
Brodart Co.
Quality Bks., Inc.

Black Plum Bks., *(978-0-9785317)* Orders Addr.: 1302 Abby Ct., Juneau, AK 99801-9599 USA
Web site: http://www.blackplumebooks.com
Dist(s): **Follett School Solutions.**

Black Rabbit Bks., *(978-1-58340; 978-1-887068; 978-1-59920; 978-1-77092; 978-1-62310; 978-1-62588; 978-1-68071; 978-1-68072; 978-1-64466)* Orders Addr.: P.O. Box 3263, Mankato, MN 56002 USA (SAN 925-4862); Edit Addr.: 123 S. Broad St., Mankato, MN 56001 USA (SAN 858-902X); *Imprints:* Smart Apple Media (SmartAppleMed); Bolt (Bolt); Hi Jinx (HiJinx)
E-mail: jbesel@blackrabbitbooks.com; info@blackrabbitbooks.com
Web site: http://www.blackrabbitbooks.com
Dist(s): **Follett School Solutions**
Hachette Bk. Group
INscribe Digital
Independent Pubs. Group
RiverStream Publishing
Scholastic, Inc.
myON.

Black River Trading Co., *(978-0-9649083; 978-0-9797492)* P.O. Box 7, Oxford, MI 48371 USA (SAN 854-2724) Tel 248-628-5150; Fax: 248-628-6422
E-mail: jane@whoopforjoy.com
Web site: http://www.whoopforjoy.com
Dist(s): **Bookmen, Inc.**

Black Rose Bks. (CAN) *(978-0-919618; 978-0-919619; 978-0-920057; 978-0-921689; 978-1-55164; 978-1-895431) Dist. by* **Chicago Distribution Ctr.**

Black Rose Writing, *(978-0-615-20158-0; 978-0-615-20274-7; 978-0-615-20494-9; 978-0-615-20616-5; 978-0-9821012; 978-0-9819742; 978-0-9825542; 978-0-9825823; 978-1-935605; 978-1-61296; 978-1-944715; 978-1-68433)* P.O. Box 1540, Castroville, TX 78009 USA
E-mail: creator@blackrosewriting.com; sales@blackrosewriting.com
Web site: http://www.blackrosewritiing.com; http://www.blackrosewriting.com/books
Dist(s): **Ingram Content Group**
Lulu Pr., Inc.

Black Sheep *Imprint of* **Bellwether Media**

Black Sheep *Imprint of* **Akashic Bks.**

Black Ship Publishing, *(978-0-9851969; 978-0-9914484; 978-0-9905469)* 1767 12th St. Suite 378, Hood River, OR 97031 USA Tel 310-696-9515
E-mail: smartcookie1@mac.com
Dist(s): **BookBaby**
Legato Pubs. Group
Ingram Content Group
MyiLibrary
Publishers Group West (PGW).

Black Society Pages, Inc., *(978-0-9758611)* 228 S. Washington St., Alexandria, VA 22314 USA.

Black Squirrel Bks. *Imprint of* **Kent State Univ. Pr.**

Black Sugar Pr., *(978-0-9976010)* 13518 L St., Omaha, NE 68137 USA Tel 402-884-5995
E-mail: blacksugar@conciergemarketing.com.

Black Threads Pr., *(978-0-9824796)* 3037 S. Buchanan St., Arlington, VA 22206-1512 USA
Web site: http://www.BlackThreads.com
Dist(s): **CreateSpace Independent Publishing Platform**
Ingram Content Group.

Blackberry Hill Pr., *(978-0-9792947)* Orders Addr.: 2860 Mohawk St., Sauquoit, NY 13456-3322 USA Tel 315-737-5147
Web site: http://www.dorothystacy.com
Dist(s): **North Country Bks., Inc.**

Blackberry Maine, *(978-0-942396; 978-0-615-15951-5; 978-0-9824389)* 617 E. Neck Rd., Nobleboro, ME 04555 USA (SAN 207-7949) Tel 207-729-5083; Fax: 207-729-6783
E-mail: chimfarm@gwi.net
Web site: http://www.blackberrybooksme.com
Dist(s): **SPD-Small Pr. Distribution.**

Blackberry Pubns., *(978-0-9776987; 978-0-9972260)* 3915 11th Street, Ecorse, MI 48229 USA Tel 313-297-7809; 313-627-1520
E-mail: blackberrybooks@yahoo.com.

Blackberry Pubs., *(978-0-615-12702-6)* 2545 Hwy. 76, Portland, TN 37148 USA Tel 615-325-3970
E-mail: fussellb@comcast.net
Web site: http://www.blackberrypublishers.com
Dist(s): **Sadler, Dale.**

Blackberry: Salted in the Shell *See* **Blackberry Maine**

Blackbirch Pr., Inc. *Imprint of* **Peel Productions, Inc.**

Blackbirch Pr., Inc. *Imprint of* **Cengage Gale**

Blackbirch Pr., Inc. *Imprint of* **Soundprints**

Blackbirch Pr., Inc. *Imprint of* **Barnes & Noble, Inc.**

Blackbirch Pr., Inc. *Imprint of* **Mardick Pr.**

Blackbirch Pr., Inc. *Imprint of* **Sunstone Pr.**

Blackbirch Pr., Inc. *Imprint of* **Cherry Lake Publishing**

Blackbirch Pr., Inc. *Imprint of* **Seacoast Publishing, Inc.**

Blackbird Bks., *(978-1-61053)* 1012 3rd Street, Suite 301, Santa Monica, CA 90403 USA Tel 310-422-7098
E-mail: editor@bbirdbooks.com
Web site: http://www.bbirdbooks.com.

Blackbird's World Publishing Co., *(978-0-9789798)* Orders Addr.: P.O. Box 475, Clyde, TX 79510 USA Tel 325-201-2495; Edit Addr.: Box 475 212 Hunt St., Clyde, TX 79510 USA
E-mail: blackbird@blackbirdsworldpublishingcompany.net
Web site: http://blackbirdsworldpublishingcompany.net.

Blackcurrant Pr. Co., *(978-0-9817111; 978-0-9840379; 978-0-9903781)* 116-35 194th St., Saint Albans, NY 11412 USA (SAN 856-3128)
Web site: http://www.blackcurrantpress.com.

Blackfoot Burkino Cherokee Publishing, *(978-0-9722724)* Orders Addr.: P.O. Box 58074, Houston, TX 77258 USA Tel 832-504-1331; Edit Addr.: 1912 Trentwood Pl., Charlotte, NC 28216 USA
E-mail: bbcpublishin80@gmail.com.

BlacknBlue Pr. UK *Imprint of* **Blacknblue Pr.**

Blacknblue Pr., *(978-0-9677652; 978-0-9840718)* 108 Benarr Ave., Fort Walton Beach, FL 32548 USA Tel 850-862-2874 (phone/fax); 13 Dellands Overton, Basingstoke, RG25 3LD Tel 1256 770736 (phone/fax); *Imprints:* BlacknBlue Press UK (BlacknBlue Pr UK)
E-mail: edddwicke@hotmail.com
Web site: http://www.blacknbluepress.info
Dist(s): **Ingram Content Group.**

Blackside Publishing, *(978-1-943630; 978-1-68355)* 5209 Del Paz Dr., Colorado Springs, CO 80918 USA
E-mail: publishing@blacksideconcepts.com; blacksidepublishing@gmail.com
Web site: www.blacksidepublishing.com.

Blacksmith Bks. (HKG) *(978-962-86732; 978-988-17742; 978-988-99799; 978-988-19003; 978-988-16139; 978-988-13765) Dist. by* **Natl Bk Netwk.**

Blacksmith Bks., LLC, *(978-0-9772515)* P.O. Box 4228, Lisle, IL 60532-9228 USA; 6141 Dixon Dr., Lisle, IL 60532-4151
E-mail: maboone1@comcast.net
Dist(s): **National Bk. Network.**

Black-Smith Enterprises, *(978-0-9762720)* 31536 Avondale, Westland, MI 48186 USA
E-mail: blacksmithenterprises@yahoo.com; janaya_black@yahoo.com
Web site: http://www.black-smithenterprises.com
Dist(s): **Ingram Content Group.**

Blackstaff Pr., Ltd. (GBR) *(978-0-85640) Dist. by* **Casemate Pubs.**

Blackstone Audio Books, Incorporated *See* **Blackstone Audio, Inc.**

Blackstone Audio, Inc., *(978-0-7861; 978-1-4332; 978-1-4417; 978-1-4551; 978-1-4708; 978-1-4829; 978-1-4830; 978-1-5046; 978-1-5047; 978-1-5384; 978-1-5385; 978-1-9824; 978-1-9825; 978-1-9826; 978-1-7999; 978-1-0940; 978-1-0941; 978-1-6644; 978-1-6645; 978-1-6646; 978-1-6647; 978-1-6650; 978-1-6651; 978-1-6652) 31 Mistletoe Rd., Ashland, OR 97520 USA (SAN 173-2811) Fax: 800-482-9294; Toll Free Fax: 800-482-9294; Toll Free: 800-729-2665*
E-mail: Orders@blackstoneaudio.com; megan.wahrenbrock@blackstoneaudio.com
Web site: http://www.blackstoneaudio.com
Dist(s): **Ebsco Publishing**
Findaway World, LLC
Follett School Solutions
Hachette Bk. Group
INscribe Digital
Independent Pubs. Group
Listen & Live Audio, Inc.
MyiLibrary
OverDrive, Inc.
Penguin Publishing Group
Recorded Bks., Inc.
Simon & Schuster, Inc.
Zondervan.

Blackstone Editions, *(978-0-9725017; 978-0-9816402)* 312-24 Wellesley St. W., Toronto, ON M4Y 2X6 CAN Tel 647-344-2206
Web site: http://www.blackstoneeditions.com.

Blacktastic.net, *(978-0-9834275; 978-0-9961146)* 7945 Fincastle Ct., Sacramento, CA 95829 USA Tel 916-525-1703
E-mail: brotherhypnotic@hotmail.com.

Blacktypewriter Pr. *Imprint of* **Pittsburgh Literary Arts Network LLC**

BlackWords Press *See* **KA Productions, LLC**

Blade Publishing, *(978-1-929409)* 110 W. C St. Ste. 1300, San Diego, CA 92101-3978 USA (SAN 254-7678)
E-mail: bladeinternational@yahoo.com.

BladeRunner Publishing, *(978-0-9785477)* P.O. Box 4298, Greenville, SC 29608 USA Tel 864-313-6182
E-mail: bladerunnerpublishing@charter.net.

Publisher Name Index

Bladestar Publishing, *(978-0-9787931)* Orders Addr.: 1499 N. 950 W., Orem, UT 84057 USA Fax: 484-414-1674
E-mail: Promotion@BladestarPublishing.com
Web site: http://www.bladestarpublishing.com
Dist(s): **Brodart Co.**

Blaft Pubns., ., ., CA 1 USA
Web site: http://www.blaft.com/
Dist(s): **SPD-Small Pr. Distribution**
Smashwords.

Blair *Imprint of* **Carolina Wren Pr.**

Blair, *(978-0-89587; 978-0-910244)* Orders Addr.: 120 Morris St., Durham, NC 27701 USA (SAN 201-4319) Tel 919-560-2738
E-mail: sutton@blairpub.com
Web site: http://www.blairpub.com
Dist(s): **Chicago Distribution Ctr.**
Smashwords.

Blair, John F. Pub. *See* **Blair**

Blair, Rebecca E, *(978-0-692-17683-2)* 214 SW 9th St., Ogden, IA 50212 USA Tel 515-230-0014
E-mail: rebl@netins.net
Dist(s): **Ingram Content Group.**

Blake, Edna, *(978-0-9668906)* 7 Babble Creek Ct., O Fallon, MO 63368-8321 USA.

Blake, John Publishing, Ltd. (GBR) *(978-0-905846; 978-1-85782; 978-1-903402; 978-1-904034; 978-1-84358; 978-1-84454; 978-1-78219; 978-1-78418; 978-1-78606) Dist. by* **IPG Chicago.**

Blake, Monica, *(978-0-9764155)* P.O. Box 475233, San Francisco, CA 94147 USA Tel 415-995-2515; Fax: 415-876-1002
E-mail: blakesfo@yahoo.com.

Blake, Nyron, *(978-0-578-52946-2)* 2132 Houston st, Norman, OK 73073 USA Tel 718-687-7541
E-mail: nyronblake@yahoo.com.

Blake-Virostko, Pamela, *(978-0-9801975)* 7546 S. Virostko Rd., Rockville, IN 47872 USA Tel 765-548-2635
E-mail: PVirostko@aol.com.

Blanchard, Graham, *(978-0-9854090; 978-0-9897949; 978-0-692-85033-6)* P.O. Box 300235, Austin, TX 78703 USA Tel 512-647-2099
E-mail: callie@grahamblanchard.com
Web site: http://www.grahamblanchard.com
Dist(s): **Ingram Publisher Services**
Send The Light Distribution LLC.

Blancmange Publishing LLC, *(978-0-9779488)* P.O. Box 17184, Memphis, TN 38187-7184 USA (SAN 850-7023).

Blanket Street Publishing, *(978-0-9760929)* 17278 Summit Hills Dr., Santa Clarita, CA 91387 USA
E-mail: kstrauss@socal.rr.com.

Blast Cafe, *(978-1-948750)* 21381 Pinetree Ln, Huntington Beach, CA 92646 USA Tel 310-625-9141
E-mail: stephenhcook@gmail.com
Web site: www.BlastCafe.com.

Blastoff! Discovery *Imprint of* **Bellwether Media**

Blastoff! Readers *Imprint of* **Bellwether Media**

Blatant Times, *(978-0-9744376)* 608 Patton Rd., Great Bend, KS 67530 USA
Web site: http://www.cpcis.net.

Blaumond Pr., *(978-0-9789031)* 740 SE. Greenville Blvd., Suite 400, Box 283, Greenville, NC 27858 USA (SAN 851-9021) Tel 252-754-4837; Fax: 252-353-0732
E-mail: info@blaumondpress.com
Web site: http://www.blaumondpress.com.

Blaze Publishing, LLC, *(978-0-9970104; 978-1-945519)* 64 Melvin Dr., Fredericksburg, VA 22406 USA Tel 703-470-8323
E-mail: kdehaba@blazepub.com; etilton@blazepub.com
Web site: www.blazepub.com.

Blaze, Ronan *See* **Medal Bks.**

Blazing Ideas Ltd., *(978-0-9801243; 978-0-9856029; 978-0-9992828; 978-0-9997030; 978-1-948518)* 11141 Blackforest way, Gaithersburg, MD 20879 USA Tel 301-476-0778
E-mail: lotit2000@yahoo.com; ookubena@gmail.com; ololade@blazing-ideas.com; olayemi@blazing-ideas.com
Web site: www.blazing-ideas.com.

BLD Enterprises *See* **Innovo Publishing, LLC**

Blessed and Highly Favored *See* **BHF Publishing**

Blessed Beginnings Publishing, *(978-0-9727201)* P.O. Box 241282, Milwaukee, WI 53223 USA Tel 414-351-6467
E-mail: pinksolitaire97@yahoo.com.

Blessed Bk. Publishing, *(978-0-692-90686-6; 978-0-692-94964-1; 978-1-7350881)* 936 B 7th St. PMB 180, Novato, CA 94945 USA Tel 415-612-0401
E-mail: laurie@beatingtheoddsnow.com
Dist(s): **Independent Pub.**

Blessings Unlimited, LLC, *(978-0-9742796)* P.O. Box 186, Highland Springs, VA 23075 USA Tel 804-640-7137 Do not confuse with Blessings Unlimited in Bloomington, MN
Web site: http://www.blessingsunlimited.info.

Blind Ferret Entertainment (CAN) *(978-0-9736946) Dist. by* **Diamond Book Dists.**

Blind Wolf Studios, *(978-0-9749941)* P.O. Box 465, Cross River, NY 10518 USA
Web site: http://www.blindwolfstudios.com.

Blink,
Dist(s): **Zondervan.**

Bliss Group, *(978-0-9885359; 978-1-940021)* 725 River Rd. No. 32-215, Edgewater, NJ 07020 USA Tel 551-333-9409
E-mail: alansrbradshaw@gmail.com
Dist(s): **Ingram Content Group**
MyiLibrary.

Bliss on Tap, *(978-0-9763768; 978-0-9825098; 978-0-9896143)* 28326 Wellfleet Ln., Saugus, CA 91350 USA
E-mail: pephillipson@aol.com
Web site: http://www.godthedyslexicdog.com
Dist(s): **MyiLibrary.**

Bliss Publishing, *(978-0-9910996)* 3127 176th St., Lansing, IL 60438 USA Tel 708-474-6702
E-mail: blisswoods@comcast.net.

Blissful Light Pr., *(978-0-692-89247-3; 978-0-578-49714-3)* 1334 W. 21st. St., Houston, TX 77008 USA Tel 832-654-4831
E-mail: sandirhea@yahoo.com.

Blister Books LLC *See* **Mother Lode Pr. LLC**

BLLE Creative, *(978-0-692-96918-2)* 1453 NW Davenport Ave, BEND, OR 97703 USA Tel 206-947-0576
E-mail: kayla@jetstarpublishing.com
Dist(s): **Ingram Content Group.**

Bloated Toe Publishing, *(978-0-9795741; 978-0-9836925; 978-1-939216)* P.O. Box 324, Peru, NY 12972 USA Tel 518-563-9469 (phone/fax)
E-mail: sales@bloatedtoe.com; jcj@bloatedtoe.com
Web site: http://www.bloatedtoe.com.

Bloch Publishing Co., *(978-0-8197)* 5875 Mining Ter. Ste. 104, Jacksonville, FL 32257-3225 USA (SAN 214-204X)
E-mail: BlochPub@worldnet.att.net
Web site: http://www.blochpub.com/
Dist(s): **Follett School Solutions.**

Block Publishing, *(978-0-9761625)* 1120 Forest Ave., No. 306, Pacific Grove, CA 93950 USA Fax: 831-655-4830
E-mail: blockpub@sbcglobal.net
Web site: http://www.blockpublishing.com
Dist(s): **Baker & Taylor Publisher Services (BTPS)**
Follett School Solutions.

Block System, The *See* **Block System, The**

Block System, The, *(978-0-9665545; 978-0-9800875)* 3824 Brookhaven Cir., Fort Worth, TX 76109 USA Tel 817-732-2633; Fax: 817-732-0836
E-mail: andblock@gmail.com
Web site: http://www.blockcenter.com.

BlogIntoBook.com *Imprint of* **Gatekeeper Pr.**

Blom Pubns., *(978-0-9906871; 978-0-692-18818-7; 978-0-578-40953-5; 978-0-578-41236-8; 978-1-7336349; 978-1-7345901)* 2280 Braumiller Rd., Delaware, OH 43015 USA Tel 503-939-7627
E-mail: TracyBlom@hotmail.com
Web site: theblomdotcom.com.

Blondvic Enterprises, *(978-0-692-81633-2)* 141 E. 4th St., # 420, Saint Paul, MN 55101 USA Tel 651-295-4033
E-mail: stacybecker@comcast.net; stacybecker@comcast.net.

Blood-Horse, Inc., The, *(978-0-936032; 978-0-939049; 978-1-58150)* Div. of The Blood-Horse, Inc., 3101 Beaumont Centre Cir., Lexington, KY 40513 USA (SAN 203-5294) Tel 859-278-2361 (Retailers); Fax: 859-276-6868; Toll Free: 800-866-2361 (Retailers); *Imprints:* Eclipse Press (Eclip Press)
E-mail: info@eclipsepress.com
Web site: http://www.eclipsepress.com
Dist(s): **Smashwords**
Western International, Inc.

Bloodletting Pr., *(978-0-9720859; 978-0-9768531; 978-1-935006)* 25222 E Welches Rd Unit 29 USA, Welches, OR 97067 USA Tel 503-298-4811
Web site: http://www.miskatonicbooks.com.

Bloom & Grow Bks., *(978-1-931969)* Div. of Bloom & Grow, Inc., Orders Addr.: 149 S. Barrington Ave., #363, Los Angeles, CA 90049 USA Tel 310-472-0505
E-mail: stephanie@bloomandogrow.com; info@bloomandgrow.com
Web site: http://www.bloomandgrow.com; http://www.placetogrow.com
Dist(s): **Beyda for Bks., LLC.**

Bloom & Grow, Incorporated *See* **Bloom & Grow Bks.**

Bloom, Barbara, *(978-0-615-64982-5; 978-0-9883351)* 11907 Oakcroft Dr., Houston, TX 77070 USA Tel 832-717-7818
Web site: www.smartscarlet.com
Dist(s): **CreateSpace Independent Publishing Platform.**

Bloomer's Bks. Llc., *(978-0-9840295; 978-0-692-24835-5; 978-0-9997244)* 272 Prospect St., Willimantic, CT 06226 USA Tel 860-423-0901
E-mail: rhbloomer@pobox.com
Web site: Bloomer'sBooks.com.

Blooming Tree Pr., *(978-0-9718348; 978-0-9769417; 978-1-933831)* Div. of Hees Enterprises, LLC, Orders Addr.: P.O. Box 140934, Austin, TX 78714-0934 USA Tel 512-921-8846; Fax: 512-873-7710; Edit Addr.: 10703 Jonwood Way, Austin, TX 78753 USA Tel 512-921-8846; Fax: 512-873-7710; *Imprints:* Ready Blade (Ready Blade)
E-mail: email@bloomingtreepress.com; bloomingtree@gmail.com
Web site: http://www.bloomingtreepress.com.

Blooming Twig Books LLC, *(978-0-9777736; 978-1-933918; 978-1-61343; 978-1-937753)* Orders Addr.: 228 Pk. Ave., S. No. 66675, NEW YORK, NY 10003 USA Tel 866-389-1482; Fax: 866-298-7260; Edit Addr.: 228 Pk. Ave., S. No. 66675, NEW YORK, NY 10003 USA (SAN 991-1693) Tel 866-389-1482; Fax: 866-298-7260
Web site: http://www.bloomingtwig.com
Dist(s): **Cardinal Pubs. Group.**

BloomingFields, *(978-0-9645971)* 44 Voyagers Ln., Ashland, MA 01721 USA; *Imprints:* Wisdom Audio-Books (Wisdom Aud-Bks)
E-mail: markpoetry@hotmail.com.

BloominThyme Pr., *(978-0-9832464; 978-0-9884871; 978-0-9911182; 978-0-9964391; 978-0-9977738)* P.O. Box 491345, Leesburg, FL 34749 USA Tel 352-638-3121
E-mail: dsvenetta@gmail.com
Dist(s): **Follett School Solutions.**

Bloom's Literary Criticism *Imprint of* **Facts On File, Inc.**

Bloomsbury Academic & Professional *See* **Bloomsbury Academic & Professional**

Bloomsbury Academic & Professional, *(978-1-4411; 978-1-62892)* 175 Fifth Ave., New York, NY 10010 USA; *Imprints:* Continuum (Continu); Fairchild Books (Fairchild Bks)
E-mail: AskAcademic@BloomsburyUSA.com
Web site: http://www.bloomsburyacademicusa.com/html/
Dist(s): **Bloomsbury Publishing USA**
Casemate Academic
Independent Pubs. Group
Macmillan
MyiLibrary
National Bk. Network.

Bloomsbury Activity Bks. *Imprint of* **Bloomsbury Publishing USA**

Bloomsbury Children's Bks. *Imprint of* **Bloomsbury Publishing USA**

Bloomsbury Paperbacks *Imprint of* **Bloomsbury Publishing USA**

Bloomsbury Pr., *(978-0-9667039)* 4340 Anza St., No. 6, San Francisco, CA 94121 USA Do not confuse with Bloomsberry Pr., New York, NY
Dist(s): **Macmillan.**

Bloomsbury Publishing Plc (GBR) *(978-0-225; 978-0-245; 978-0-264; 978-0-333; 978-0-485; 978-0-510; 978-0-540; 978-0-567; 978-0-7136; 978-0-7470; 978-0-7475; 978-0-7478; 978-0-85045; 978-0-85177; 978-0-85263; 978-0-85314; 978-0-85496; 978-0-86292; 978-0-906515; 978-0-907582; 978-0-948230; 978-1-85399; 978-1-85532; 978-1-85973; 978-1-899791; 978-1-901362; 978-0-212; 978-0-85146; 978-0-85147; 978-0-85317; 978-0-86019; 978-0-946716; 978-0-9507160; 978-1-902579; 978-1-84113; 978-1-85691; 978-1-897737; 978-0-9506785; 978-1-8735) Dist. by* **Consort Bk Sales.**

Bloomsbury Publishing Plc (GBR) *(978-0-225; 978-0-245; 978-0-264; 978-0-333; 978-0-485; 978-0-510; 978-0-540; 978-0-567; 978-0-7136; 978-0-7470; 978-0-7475; 978-0-7478; 978-0-85045; 978-0-85177; 978-0-85263; 978-0-85314; 978-0-85496; 978-0-86292; 978-0-906515; 978-0-907582; 978-0-948230; 978-1-85399; 978-1-85532; 978-1-85973; 978-1-899791; 978-1-901362; 978-0-212; 978-0-85146; 978-0-85147; 978-0-85317; 978-0-86019; 978-0-946716; 978-0-9507160; 978-1-902579; 978-1-84113; 978-1-85691; 978-1-897737; 978-0-9506785; 978-1-8735) Dist. by* **Natl Bk Netwk.**

Bloomsbury Publishing Plc (GBR) *(978-0-225; 978-0-245; 978-0-264; 978-0-333; 978-0-485; 978-0-510; 978-0-540; 978-0-567; 978-0-7136; 978-0-7470; 978-0-7475; 978-0-7478; 978-0-85045; 978-0-85177; 978-0-85263; 978-0-85314; 978-0-85496; 978-0-86292; 978-0-906515; 978-0-907582; 978-0-948230; 978-1-85399; 978-1-85532; 978-1-85973; 978-1-899791; 978-1-901362; 978-0-212; 978-0-85146; 978-0-85147; 978-0-85317; 978-0-86019; 978-0-946716; 978-0-9507160; 978-1-902579; 978-1-84113; 978-1-85691; 978-1-897737; 978-0-9506785; 978-1-8735) Dist. by* **Macmillan.**

Bloomsbury Publishing Plc (GBR) *(978-0-225; 978-0-245; 978-0-264; 978-0-333; 978-0-485; 978-0-510; 978-0-540; 978-0-567; 978-0-7136; 978-0-7470; 978-0-7475; 978-0-7478; 978-0-85045; 978-0-85177; 978-0-85263; 978-0-85314; 978-0-85496; 978-0-86292; 978-0-906515; 978-0-907582; 978-0-948230; 978-1-85399; 978-1-85532; 978-1-85973; 978-1-899791; 978-1-901362; 978-0-212; 978-0-85146; 978-0-85147; 978-0-85317; 978-0-86019; 978-0-946716; 978-0-9507160; 978-1-902579; 978-1-84113; 978-1-85691; 978-1-897737; 978-0-9506785; 978-1-8735) Dist. by* **IPG Chicago.**

Bloomsbury Publishing Plc (GBR) *(978-0-225; 978-0-245; 978-0-264; 978-0-333; 978-0-485; 978-0-510; 978-0-540; 978-0-567; 978-0-7136; 978-0-7470; 978-0-7475; 978-0-7478; 978-0-85045; 978-0-85177; 978-0-85263; 978-0-85314; 978-0-85496; 978-0-86292; 978-0-906515; 978-0-907582; 978-0-948230; 978-1-85399; 978-1-85532; 978-1-85973; 978-1-899791; 978-1-901362; 978-0-212; 978-0-85146; 978-0-85147; 978-0-85317; 978-0-86019; 978-0-946716; 978-0-9507160; 978-1-902579; 978-1-84113; 978-1-85691; 978-1-897737; 978-0-9506785; 978-1-8735) Dist. by* **Players Pr.**

Bloomsbury Publishing Plc (GBR) *(978-0-225; 978-0-245; 978-0-264; 978-0-333; 978-0-485; 978-0-510; 978-0-540; 978-0-567; 978-0-7136; 978-0-7470; 978-0-7475; 978-0-7478; 978-0-85045; 978-0-85177; 978-0-85263; 978-0-85314; 978-0-85496; 978-0-86292; 978-0-906515; 978-0-907582; 978-0-948230; 978-1-85399; 978-1-85532; 978-1-85973; 978-1-899791; 978-1-901362; 978-0-212; 978-0-85146; 978-0-85147; 978-0-85317; 978-0-86019; 978-0-946716; 978-0-9507160; 978-1-902579; 978-1-84113; 978-1-85691; 978-1-897737; 978-0-9506785; 978-1-8735) Dist. by* **Trafalgar.**

Bloomsbury Publishing USA, *(978-1-58234; 978-1-59691; 978-1-59990; 978-1-60819; 978-1-84706; 978-1-61963; 978-1-62040; 978-1-62356; 978-1-62892; 978-1-63286; 978-1-5013; 978-1-68119; 978-1-63557; 978-1-5476)* Orders Addr.: 16365 James Madison Hwy., Gordonsville, VA 22942-8501 USA Tel 888-330-8477; Toll Free: 888-330-8477; Edit Addr.: 175 Fifth Ave., Suite 300, New York, NY 10010 USA Toll Free: 888-330-8477; 1385 Broadway, New York, NY 10018 Tel 212-419-5300; *Imprints:* Bloomsbury USA Childrens (Bloom Child); Bloomsbury Paperbacks (BloomsPap); Bloomsbury USA (BloomsburyUSA); Bloomsbury Sigma (BloomsSigma); Alma Classics (AlmaClassics); Osprey (OspreyUSA); Bloomsbury Sport (BloomSport); Bloomsbury Activity Books (BloomActivity); Shire (Shire); The Arden Shakespeare (ArdenUSA); Bloomsbury Children's Books (BloomsChildren); Bloomsbury Young Adult (BlmsburyYA)
E-mail: bloomsbury.kids@bloomsburyusa.com; nathaniel.knaebel@bloomsbury.com; mike.o'connor@bloomsbury.com
Web site: http://www.bloomsburyusa.com
Dist(s): **Bloomsbury Publishing US Trade**
Casemate Academic
Children's Plus, Inc.
INscribe Digital
Macmillan
MyiLibrary
Penguin Random Hse. Distribution
Penguin Random Hse. LLC
St. Martin's Pr.

Bloomsbury Sigma *Imprint of* **Bloomsbury Publishing USA**

Bloomsbury Sport *Imprint of* **Bloomsbury Publishing USA**

Bloomsbury USA *Imprint of* **Bloomsbury Publishing USA**

Bloomsbury USA Childrens *Imprint of* **Bloomsbury Publishing USA**

Bloomsbury USA Childrens *Imprint of* **Walker & Co.**

Bloomsbury Visual Arts *Imprint of* **BJU Pr.**

Bloomsbury Young Adult *Imprint of* **Bloomsbury Publishing USA**

Blow's Innovation to Art - (BIA), *(978-0-9820772)* 8090 Atlantic Blvd, E-160, Jacksonville, FL 32211 USA Tel 904-469-1169 business number
E-mail: biabizz@aol.com; blows.art@gmail.com
Web site: http://www.myspace.com/biabizz1
Dist(s): **Ingram Content Group.**

BLPH, Inc., *(978-0-9759158; 978-0-9772425; 978-0-9791099)* P.O. Box 764, Springfield, OR 97477-0132 USA
E-mail: printing@bestlittleprinthouse.com
Web site: http://www.bestlittleprinthouse.com.

BLR Bks., *(978-0-9721839)* 94 Circle Dr., Waltham, MA 02452 USA
Dist(s): **Pathway Bk. Service.**

Blu Phi'er Publishing, LLC, *(978-0-9772034; 978-0-9799884; 978-0-9823845; 978-0-9858378)* 2400 W. Grand Ave., Marshall, TX 75670 USA Tel 903-935-4223
E-mail: phierstarter@bluphier.com
Web site: http://www.bluphier.com.

Blue Apple Bks., *(978-1-934706; 978-1-60905)* 515 Valley St., Suite 180, Maplewood, NJ 07040 USA (SAN 854-4727) Fax: 973-763-5944
E-mail: info@blueapplebooks.com
Web site: http://www.blueapplebooks.com
Dist(s): **Chronicle Bks. LLC**
Consortium Bk. Sales & Distribution
Hachette Bk. Group
Learning Connection, The
Penguin Random Hse. Distribution
Penguin Random Hse. LLC
Random Hse., Inc.

Blue Bark Pr., *(978-0-615-18110-3)* 7 View South Ave., Jamaica Plain, MA 02130 USA Tel 617-840-3418.

Blue Barn, Inc., *(978-0-692-84662-9; 978-0-692-84810-4; 978-0-692-84855-5)* 4313 Bluebell Ave., STUDIO CITY, CA 91604 USA Tel 310-625-2837
E-mail: jeffwcrawford5+LVP0003368@gmail.com; jeffwcrawford5+LVP0003368@gmail.com.

Blue Bear Publishing *See* **Beach Front Bks.**

Blue Begonia Pr., *(978-0-911287)* 311 Hillcrest Dr, Selah, WA 98942 USA (SAN 268-3652) Tel 509-452-9748
E-mail: adpeters@charter.net
Web site: http://bluebegoniapress.com
Dist(s): **Partners/West Book Distributors.**

Blue Bike Bks. (CAN) *(978-0-9739116; 978-1-897278; 978-1-926700) Dist. by* **Lone Pine.**

Blue Blanket Publishing, *(978-0-9903623)* 16 Poland Spring Rd., Auburn, ME 04210 USA Tel 207-402-0954
E-mail: cjiadonisi@gmail.com.

Blue Bk. Pubns., Inc., *(978-0-9625943; 978-1-886768; 978-1-936120; 978-1-947314)* 8009 34th Ave. S., Suite 250, Minneapolis, MN 55425 USA (SAN 860-4452) Tel 952-854-5229; Fax: 952-853-1486; Toll Free: 800-877-4867 Do not confuse with Blue Book Pubs., Inc. in La Jolla, CA
E-mail: bluebook@bluebookinc.com; clints@bluebookinc.com; support@bluebookinc.com
Web site: bluebookofgunvalues.com; bluebookofguitarvalues.com
Dist(s): **Alfred Publishing Co., Inc.**
Follett School Solutions
Music Sales Corp.
Omnibus Pr.

Blue Botte, *(978-0-9896257)* 14907 W. Autumn Ln., Nine Mile Falls, WA 99026 USA Tel 509-465-4534
E-mail: willarda2z@msn.com.

Blue Boy Publishing Co., *(978-0-9742632)* P.O. Box 691, Camillus, NY 13031-0691 USA.

Blue Brush Media, *(978-0-9777382)* 851 Monroe Ave., NE, Renton, WA 98056 USA (SAN 850-0878) Tel 425-818-8850 Do not confuse with Dolphin Media LLC in Huntsville, AL
E-mail: kunle@mamaAfricana.com
Web site: http://www.bluebrushmedia.com
Dist(s): **Follett School Solutions**
NewLife Bk. Distributors.

Blue Cat (GBR) *(978-0-9559851) Dist. by* **LuluCom.**

Blue Cat Bks, *(978-0-9779763)* P.O. Box 2818, Covina, CA 91722 USA Tel 626-339-1223
E-mail: info@bluecatpublishers.com
Web site: http://bluecatpublishers.com.

Blue Chip Publishing, (*978-0-9673970*) Orders Addr.: P.O. Box 26657, Austin, TX 78755 USA Tel 512-345-3021; Fax: 512-345-0181; Edit Addr.: 4119 Circletree Loop, Austin, TX 78731 USA Do not confuse with Blue Chip Publishing Corp., Keizer, OR
E-mail: MAMA19@aol.com.

Blue Cove Publishing, (*978-1-945595*) P.O. Box 1828, Dunnellon, FL 34430 USA Tel 352-489-0436
E-mail: mbatesd@aol.com
Web site: www.bluecovepublishing.com.

Blue Crown Pr., (*978-0-615-52468-9; 978-0-9839308; 978-0-9855874*) P.O. Box 871826, Canton, MI 48187 USA Tel 734-905-0068
E-mail: author@emlynchand.com
Web site: www.novelpublicity.com.

Blue Cubicle Pr., LLC, (*978-0-9745900; 978-0-9827136; 978-1-938583*) P.O. Box 250382, Plano, TX 75025-0382 USA Tel 972-824-0646; *Imprints:* Castle Builder Press (Castle Builder)
Web site: http://www.bluecubiclepress.com.

Blue Devil Games, (*978-0-9763795*) P.O. Box 19359, Plantation, FL 33318 USA Tel 954-315-0920
Web site: http://www.bluedevilgames.com.

Blue Dog Pr., (*978-0-615-70122-6; 978-0-615-70260-5; 978-0-615-75677-6; 978-0-9893053; 978-0-692-29258-7; 978-0-692-30477-8; 978-0-692-35353-0; 978-0-692-37687-4; 978-0-692-39537-0; 978-0-692-50934-0; 978-0-692-53397-0; 978-1-7353218*) 324 Martin Ave, Maple Shade, NJ 08056 USA Tel 8567184621
E-mail: accounts@ebbrown.net
Dist(s): **Ingram Bk. Co.**

Blue Dolphin Publishing, Inc., (*978-0-931892; 978-1-57733*) Orders Addr.: P.O. Box 8, Nevada City, CA 95959 USA (SAN 223-2480) Tel 530-477-1503; Fax: 530-477-8342; Toll Free: 800-643-0765; Edit Addr.: 13340-d Grass Valley Ave., Grass Valley, CA 95945 USA (SAN 696-009X); *Imprints:* Papillon Publishing (Papillon Pubng)
E-mail: bdolphin@bluedolphinpublishing.com; clemens@bluedolphinpublishing.com
Web site: http://www.bluedolphinpublishing.com
Dist(s): **Follett School Solutions**
New Leaf Distributing Co., Inc.

Blue Dome, Inc., (*978-0-9720654; 978-1-932099; 978-1-59784; 978-1-935295; 978-1-68206; 978-1-68236*) 335 Clifton Ave, Clifton, NJ 07011 USA Tel 646-415-9331; Fax: 646-827-6228; *Imprints:* Tughra Books (TughraBks)
E-mail: info@bluedomepress.com
Web site: http://www.tughrabooks.com; http://www.bluedomepress.com
Dist(s): **National Bk. Network.**

Blue Dome Press *See* **Blue Dome, Inc.**

Blue Dot Pubns. LLC, (*978-1-7331212; 978-1-7350005*) 819 Greenberry Ln., San Rafael, CA 94903 USA Tel 415-205-4884
E-mail: hello@bluedotkidspress.com
Web site: https://www.bluedotkidspress.com/
Dist(s): **Consortium Bk. Sales & Distribution.**

Blue Dragon Publishing, (*978-0-9832454; 978-1-939696*) P.O. Box 247, Lightfoot, VA 23090 USA Tel 757-941-5007
E-mail: BlueDragonPub@cox.net
Web site: http://www.blue-dragon-publishing.com
Dist(s): **Ingram Bk. Co.**

Blue Dream Studios, (*978-0-9789168*) 1133 Cedarview Ln., Franklin, TN 37067-4075 USA
Web site: http://www.bluedreamstudios.com
Dist(s): **Diamond Comic Distributors, Inc.**
Diamond Bk. Distributors
Diamond Distributors, Inc.

Blue Eagle Bks., Inc., (*978-0-9794655*) 5773 Woodway, PMB 190, Houston, TX 77057 USA Tel 713-789-1516 (phone/fax)
E-mail: sjones@blueeaglebooks.com
Web site: http://blueeaglebooks.com.

Blue Eyed Mayhem Publishing, (*978-0-9794545*) 6 Hopemont Dr., Mount Laurel, NJ 08054 USA Tel 609-781-0291
Dist(s): **Smashwords.**

Blue Forge Pr., (*978-1-883573; 978-1-886383; 978-1-59092*) Div. of Blue Forge Group, Orders Addr.: 7419 Ebbert Dr., SE, Port Orchard, WA 98367 USA (SAN 299-1330) Tel 360-769-7174 phone
E-mail: blueforgepress@gmail.com
Web site: http://www.blueforgepress.com.

Blue Fox Pr., (*978-0-9763119*) Pierce Arrow Bldg., 1685 Elmwood Ave., Suite 315, Buffalo, NY 14207-2407 USA Tel 716-447-1590; Fax: 716-837-7066
E-mail: bluefoxpress@yahoo.com
Web site: http://www.bluefoxpress.com.

Blue Fuji Pubs., (*978-0-9843647*) 14 Cambridge Rd., East Hanover, NJ 07936 USA
E-mail: kevin@kevinkato.com
Web site: http://www.kevinkato.com
Dist(s): **Smashwords.**

Blue Fyre Pr., (*978-1-7327701; 978-1-951009*) 6172 S Crestview St, Littleton, CO 80120 USA Tel 720-235-2087
E-mail: kendramerritt85@gmail.com.

Blue Gate Bks., (*978-0-9792612*) P.O. Box 2137, Nevada City, CA 95959 USA (SAN 852-923X) Tel 530-263-4501
E-mail: babette@babettedonaldson.com; info@emmaleabooks.com
Web site: http://www.bluegatebooks.com; http://www.sidecarscooter.com; http://www.emmaleabooks.com; http://www.Fun-With-Tea.com.

Blue Horizon Publishing Co., (*978-0-9658786; 978-0-9955738-0-2*) 25012 S. Harmony Rd., Cheney, WA 99004-9798 USA Tel 509-235-8547.

Blue Horse Books *Imprint of* **Great Lakes Literary, LLC**

Blue Ink Press *See* **Blue Ink Pr.**

Blue Ink Pr., (*978-0-9817234*) 1246 Heart Ave., Amherst, OH 44001 USA Tel 440-823-8320
E-mail: dougk@icehorseadventures.com
Web site: http://www.icehorseadventures.com
Dist(s): **Blu Sky Media Group.**

Blue Ink Pr., (*978-0-692-35368-4; 978-0-9968673; 978-0-692-63512-4; 978-0-692-71762-2; 978-0-692-72745-4; 978-1-948449*) 2621 Hiking Trail, Raleigh, NC 27615 USA Tel 919-418-8746 Do not confuse with Blue Ink Press in Amherst, OH
Web site: www.blueinkpress.com; www.sherrytorgent.com
Dist(s): **CreateSpace Independent Publishing Platform**
Ingram Content Group.

Blue Jay Bks. *Imprint of* **Crooked River Pr.**

Blue Jay Pr., (*978-0-9913000*) 1020 se 22 ave, Portland, OR 97214 USA Tel 503-679-7652
E-mail: ktboyer@spiretech.com.

Blue Kitty, The, (*978-0-9796814*) P.O. Box 254, Syracuse, NY 13214 USA
E-mail: info@thebluekitty.com.

Blue Lantern Books *See* **Laughing Elephant**

Blue Lion Productions, Ltd, (*978-0-9761132*) 302 Smith St., Freeport, NY 11520 USA Tel 516-546-4611
E-mail: info@bluelionproductions.com
Web site: http://www.bluelionproductions.com.

Blue Lobster Pr., (*978-0-9709569*) Orders Addr.: 3919 Union St., Levant, ME 04456-4358 USA
E-mail: books@bluelobsterpress.com; poet@robertpottle.com
Web site: http://www.bluelobsterpress.com.

Blue Logic Publishing, (*978-0-9860669*) P.O. Box 797492, Dallas, TX 75379 USA Tel 972-380-1467
E-mail: contact@bluelogicpublishing.com
Web site: www.bluelogicpublishing.com.

Blue Lotus Wave, (*978-0-9789624*) Orders Addr.: 15 Surrey Dr., Riverside, CT 06878-1516 USA (SAN 852-0631) Tel 203-344-1344 Do not confuse with Blue Lotus Press in Palmyra, MA.

blue manatee children's Bookstore *See* **Blue Manatee Press**

Blue Manatee Press, (*978-1-936669*) 3054 Madison Rd., Cincinnati, OH 45209 USA (SAN 920-4601) Tel 513-731-2665
E-mail: press@bluemanateebooks.com; johnsandy@bluemanateebooks.com
Web site: www.bluemanateepress.com
Dist(s): **Independent Pubs. Group.**

Blue Marble Bks. *Imprint of* **Sphinx Publishing**

Blue Marlin Pubns., (*978-0-9674602; 978-0-9792918; 978-0-9885295; 978-1-7321097; 978-1-7345734*) 823 Aberdeen Rd., West Bay Shore, NY 11706 USA Tel 631-666-0353 (phone/fax)
E-mail: jude@bluemarlinpubs.com
Web site: http://www.BlueMarlinPubs.com
Dist(s): **Follett School Solutions.**

Blue Morpho Bks., (*978-1-7321165*) 455 Pernello Rd., Ferrum, VA 24088 USA Tel 540-365-2151
E-mail: janefenton.books@gmail.com.

Blue Mountain Arts Inc., (*978-0-88396; 978-1-58786; 978-1-59842; 978-1-68088*) Orders Addr.: P.O. Box 4549, Boulder, CO 80306 USA (SAN 299-9609) Tel 303-449-0536; Fax: 303-417-6434; 303-417-6496; Toll Free Fax: 800-943-6666; 800-545-8573; Toll Free: 800-525-0642; *Imprints:* Blue Mountain Press (Blue Mntn Pr); Rabbit's Foot Press (Rabb Ft Pr)
Web site: http://www.sps.com/.

Blue Mountain Arts (R) by SPS Studios, Incorporated *See* **Blue Mountain Arts Inc.**

Blue Mountain Pr. *Imprint of* **Blue Mountain Arts Inc.**

Blue Mustang Pr., (*978-0-9759737; 978-1-935199*) 175B Mansfield Ave., Suite 240, Norton, MA 02766 USA Tel 206-350-2823 (phone/fax)
E-mail: info@bluemustangpress.com
Web site: http://www.bluemustangpress.com.

Blue Note Bks. *Imprint of* **Blue Note Pubns.**

Blue Note Pubns., (*978-1-878398; 978-0-9830758; 978-0-9855562; 978-0-9895563; 978-0-9903068; 978-0-9963066; 978-0-9977638; 978-1-7338019*) Orders Addr.: 721 N. Dr. Ste. D, Melbourne, FL 32934 USA Toll Free: 800-624-0401 (order number); *Imprints:* Blue Note Books (Blue Note Bks)
E-mail: bluenotepress@gmail.com
Web site: http://www.bluenotebooks.com.

Blue Owl Editions, (*978-0-9672793*) 6254 Girvin Dr., Oakland, CA 94611 USA Tel 510-482-3038 (phone/fax)
E-mail: edanti@ispwest.com; enricoanti@yahoo.com
Dist(s): **Independent Pubs. Group**
Smashwords.

Blue Peach Publishing, (*978-0-615-15922-5*) 2 Wyeth Cir., Southborough, MA 01772 USA
Dist(s): **Lulu Pr., Inc.**

Blue Pig Productions, (*978-1-932545*) P.O. Box 691779, Orlando, FL 32869-1779 USA (SAN 255-4763) Tel 407-854-5679 (phone/fax)
E-mail: bluepigprod@aol.com
Web site: http://www.repunzal.com.

Blue Planet Press *See* **Ninth Planet Pr.**

Blue Portal Pr. LLC, (*978-0-9893963*) 2400 Wilderness Way, Marietta, GA 30066 USA Tel 404-372-1530
E-mail: red170@yahoo.com
Web site: http://blueportalpressllc.weebly.com/.

Blue River Pr., (*978-0-9718959; 978-0-9763361; 978-0-9799240; 978-0-9819289; 978-1-935628; 978-1-68157; 978-0-9963247*) Orders Addr.: 2402 N. Shadeland Ave., Suite A, Indianapolis, IN 46219 USA Tel 317-352-8200; Fax: 317-352-8202; Toll Free: 800-296-0481 Do not confuse with Blue River Press in Bloomingdale, IL
E-mail: tdoherty@cardinalpub.com
Web site: http://www.cardinalpub.com; www.brpressbooks.com
Dist(s): **Cardinal Pubs. Group**
MyiLibrary.

Blue Room Bks. *Imprint of* **WRITER for HIRE!**

Blue Scarab Pr., (*978-0-937179*) Orders Addr.: 811 Normandie Blvd., Bowling Green, OH 43402 USA (SAN 658-4640) Tel 419-819-4506
E-mail: haraldwyndham@gmail.com.

Blue Scribbles Publishing, (*978-0-615-24897-4*) P.O. Box 2054, Centreville, VA 20120 USA
E-mail: bluescribbles@gmail.com
Web site: http://www.bluescribbles.com.

Blue Shoe Publishing, (*978-0-9725552*) c/o Christine Merser, 38 W. 74th St., 3A, New York, NY 10023 USA Tel 212-579-0310
E-mail: inquiry@blueshoestrategy.com; inquiry@blueshoepublishing.com; LLim@BlueShoeStrategy.com
Web site: http://www.blueshoepublishing.com.

Blue Shutter Bks., (*978-0-9729379*) Orders Addr.: 5125 Schultz Bridge Rd., Zionsville, PA 18092-2543 USA Tel 215-541-3362; Fax: 425-491-4282
E-mail: rworthington@blueshutterbooks.com
Web site: http://www.blueshutterbooks.com.

Blue Skies Above Texas Co., (*978-0-9800019*) 14781 Memorial Dr., No. 399, Houston, TX 77079 USA Tel 281-920-0043
E-mail: BlueSkiesAboveTexas@yahoo.com.

Blue Sky at Night Publishing, (*978-0-9768623*) 25679 360th Ave., Hillman, MN 56338-2431 USA
E-mail: Jill@JournalBuddies.com
Web site: http://www.JournalBuddies.com.

Blue Sky Daisies, (*978-0-9905529; 978-1-944435*) 1907 N. Valleyview, Wichita, KS 67212 USA Tel 316-573-9733
E-mail: blueskydaisies@gmail.com
Web site: www.blueskydaisies.wordpress.com.

Blue Sky Ink, (*978-1-59475*) P.O. Box 1067, Brentwood, TN 37024-1067 USA (SAN 255-7401) Tel 805-677-6815
Dist(s): **Send The Light Distribution LLC.**

Blue Sky Pr., The *Imprint of* **Scholastic, Inc.**

Blue Sky Pr., (*978-0-9746896*) P.O. Box 6192, Malibu, CA 90264-6192 USA Tel 818-706-9814; 557 Broadway., New York, NY 10012 Do not confuse with Blue Sky Press in San Jose CA, Placerville CO, Silver Spring MD, Berkeley CA, Dallas TX
E-mail: laura@lauralarsen.com
Web site: http://www.lauralarsen.com
Dist(s): **Follett School Solutions.**

Blue Socks Media LLC, (*978-0-692-80162-8; 978-0-692-80714-9*) 2108 S. Bloulevard, Suite 108, Charlotte, NC 28203 USA Tel 704-562-4502
E-mail: tsteedman@raggs.com
Web site: http://www.raggs.com.

Blue Sparrow Bks., (*978-1-929266; 978-0-9841318; 978-1-937509; 978-1-942611; 978-1-63582*) 631 U.S. Hwy. 1 Suite 201, North Palm Beach, FL 33408 USA (SAN 858-5024) Tel 888-618-5253; 2330 Kemper Ln., Cincinnati, OH 45206; *Imprints:* Little Sparrow (MYD_D_LITTLE) Do not confuse with Beacon Publishing in Theodore, AL, Brimfield, MA
E-mail: admin@bluesparrowbooks.org
Web site: http://www.matthewkelly.org; http://www.beaconpublishinginc.com/
Dist(s): **BookBaby**
Follett School Solutions
Smashwords.

Blue State Pr., (*978-0-9773674*) 17771 Plumtree Ln., Yorba Linda, CA 92886 USA.

Blue Suit Bks., (*978-0-9748563*) P.O. Box 840057, New Orleans, LA 70184 USA (SAN 255-8998) Tel 504-450-4334
E-mail: bluesuit@imaginationmovers.com
Web site: http://www.imaginationmovers.com.

Blue Thistle Pr., (*978-0-9760505; 978-0-9786302*) 6187 FM 314, Ben Wheeler, TX 75754-4030 USA Tel 903-539-2500
E-mail: lkayers@hotmail.com
Web site: http://www.lindaayersbooks.com.

Blue Thunder Bks., (*978-0-9673000; 978-0-9839454*) 16717 Van Owens St., Lake Balboa, CA 91406 USA //Do not confuse with Blue Thunder Bks in Grand Rapids, MI
E-mail: d@savage1.com
Web site: http://SAVAGE1.com; http://www.CoolCatLovesYou.com.

Blue Thunder One, Inc., (*978-0-9719284*) P.O. Box 2435, Riverview, MI 48192 USA.

Blue Tie Publishing, (*978-0-9777972*) 1 Hale Rd., East Hampton, CT 06424 USA Tel 860-267-0432
E-mail: tanner@sbcglobal.net.

Blue Tiger Publishing, (*978-0-9759903*) P.O. Box 3776, Glendale, CA 91221-0776 USA Tel 310-497-9291
E-mail: travis_english@charter.net.

Blue Tree LLC, (*978-0-9711321; 978-0-9792014; 978-0-9802245; 978-0-9893088*) Orders Addr.: P.O. Box 148, Portsmouth, NH 03802 USA Tel 603-436-0831; Fax: 603-686-5054
E-mail: contact@thebluetree.com
Web site: http://www.thebluetree.com.

Blue Unicorn Edition, LLC, (*978-1-891355; 978-1-58396*) 12300 NW 56th Ave., Gainesville, FL 32653 USA Toll Free Fax: 866-334-1497 (orders)
E-mail: tienda1@instabook.net
Web site: http://www.instabookpublisher.com.

Blue Vase Productions, (*978-0-9770125*) 2455 Otay Ctr. Dr. Apt 118 Ste 252, San Diego, CA 92154 USA (SAN 257-4454) Fax: 619-819-6311
E-mail: legal@eljarronazul.com; ventas@eljarronazul.com
Web site: http://www.eljarronazul.com.

Blue Water Pr., LLC, (*978-0-9796046*) 8814 Sir Barton Ln., Waxhaw, NC 28173 USA Tel 704-551-9051
E-mail: Tonibranner@aol.com; jmacgregor@cadencemarketinggroup.com.

Blue Water Publishing, (*978-0-9796160*) 805 N. Orange Ave., Fallbrook, CA 92028-1525 USA
E-mail: bluewaterpub@sbcglobal.net.

Blue Willow Pr., (*978-0-9767473*) 197 Lamplight Ln., Bozeman, MT 59718 USA Tel 406-388-0272; Fax: 423-318-2329
E-mail: bluewillowpress@yahoo.com; obachs@juno.com
Web site: http://www.bluewillowpress.com
Dist(s): **Canyonlands Pubns.**

Blue Wing Pubns., Workshops & Lectures, (*978-0-9795663; 978-0-692-73942-6*) 11985 N. Cayce Ln, Casa Grande, AZ 85194 USA Toll Free: 877-591-4156
E-mail: sdk@bluewingworkshops.com
Web site: http://www.bluewingworkshops.com
Dist(s): **CreateSpace Independent Publishing Platform.**

Blue Zebra Entertainment, Incorporated *See* **Murphey, Hiromi**

Blueberry Illustrations, (*978-0-692-75274-6*) 104 Overlook Bend, Kingsland, GA 31548 USA Tel 912-409-7343
E-mail: SLCarrollauthor@gmail.com.

Bluebonnets, Boots & Bks. Pr., (*978-0-9645493; 978-0-9800061*) 11010 Hanning Ln., Houston, TX 77041-5006 USA; P.O. Box 19632, Houston, TX 77224-9632
E-mail: rita@bookconnectiononline.com
Web site: http://www.ABCsPress.com
Dist(s): **Complete Book & Media Supply**
Follett School Solutions
News Group
Partners Pubs. Group, Inc.

BlueBoreas Press *See* **PM Moon Pub., LLC**

Bluechip Publishers *See* **BlueChip Pubs.**

BlueChip Pubs., (*978-0-930251*) Orders Addr.: P.O. Box 4204, Jackson, WY 83001 USA
E-mail: info@bluechippublishers.com
Dist(s): **Ingram Content Group.**

BlueCougar Studios, (*978-0-615-16770-1; 978-0-615-17434-1*) 3805 Grandview Ave., NW No. 4, Roanoke, VA 24012 USA
E-mail: info@bluecougarsrufios.com
Dist(s): **Lulu Pr., Inc.**

Bluedoor, llc, (*978-1-59984; 978-1-68135; 978-1-64386*) 10949 Bren Rd., E., Minneapolis, MN 55343 USA Tel 952-934-1624; Fax: 952-934-4269; Toll Free: 800-979-1624
E-mail: mary@bluedoorpublishing.com
Web site: http://bluedoorpublishing.com.

Blue-Eyed Star Creations, LLC, (*978-0-9994409*) 2 Old Forest St., Middleton, MA 01949 USA Tel 617-592-9958
E-mail: blueeyedstarcreations@gmail.com
Web site: blue-eyedstarcreations.com.

Bluefire *Imprint of* **Random Hse. Children's Bks.**

Bluefish River Pr., (*978-0-9714701*) P.O. Box 1398, Duxbury, MA 02332 USA
E-mail: dpallai@bluefishriverpress.com
Web site: http://www.bluefishriverspress.com.

BlueLine Book Publishers *See* **Great American Pubs.**

Blueline Publishing, (*978-0-9776906*) P.O. Box 11569, Denver, CO 80211 USA (SAN 856-2539) Tel 303-477-5272; Fax: 866-876-2915
Web site: http://www.bluelinepub.com
Dist(s): **Follett School Solutions.**

BlueMoonGreenLake, (*978-0-9968237*) 700 N. Colorado Blvd, Denver, CO 80206 USA Tel 303-548-8507
E-mail: Kellymcondon66@gmail.com
Web site: www.BlueMoonGreenLake.com.

BlueSky Publishing, (*978-0-9724386*) Div. of BlueSky Medical Group, Inc., 6965 El Camino Real Suite 105-602, Carlsbad, CA 92009 USA Tel 760-603-8130; 760-603-8331 (phone/fax)
E-mail: publishingdivision@blueskymedical.com
Web site: http://www.boypresident.com.

Bluestar Communications Corp., (*978-1-885394*) c/o Words Distributing Company, 7900 Edgewater Dr., Oakland, CA 94621 USA; Edit Addr.: 7080 Norfolk Rd., Berkeley, CA 94705 USA.

Bluestocking Pr., (*978-0-942617*) Orders Addr.: P.O. Box 1014, Placerville, CA 95667 USA (SAN 667-2981) Tel 530-622-8586; Fax: 530-642-9222; Toll Free: 800-959-8586 (orders); Edit Addr.: 3333 Gold Country Dr., El Dorado, CA 95623 USA (SAN 667-299X)
E-mail: annmarie@bluestockingpress.com
Web site: http://www.bluestockingpress.com.

Bluestone Bks., (*978-0-9720046*) P.O. Box 761, Edmonds, WA 98020 USA
Web site: http://www.cmc.net/~jlwrig.

Bluewater Productions, Inc., (*978-0-9792751*) 2950 Newmarket Pl., Suite 101, Bellingham, WA 98226 USA Tel 360-778-1033
Web site: http://www.bluewaterprod.com/
Dist(s): **Diamond Comic Distributors, Inc.**
Diamond Bk. Distributors
MyiLibrary
SCB Distributors.

Bluewater Pubns., (*978-0-9719946; 978-1-934610; 978-1-949711*) 1812 Cty. Rd. 111, Killen, AL 35645 USA

Tel 256-762-7153 Do not confuse with Heart Of Dixie Publishing Corporation in Foley, AL
E-mail: angela.broyles@gmail.com; malcolm.broyles@gmail.com
Web site: http://www.bwpublications.com
Dist(s): **Follett School Solutions.**

Bluewood Bks., *(978-0-912517)* Div. of The Siyeh Group, Inc., P.O. Box 689, San Mateo, CA 94010 USA (SAN 265-3214) Tel 650-548-0754; Fax: 650-548-0654
E-mail: Bluewoodb@aol.com
Dist(s): **Follett School Solutions**
L P C Group
SCB Distributors.

Bluffton Bks., *(978-0-89986; 978-0-9702635)* Orders Addr.: 714b Kodiak Trail, Cedar Park, TX 78613 USA
E-mail: ethno777@mac.com.

Blume (ESP) *(978-84-89396; 978-84-932442; 978-84-95939; 978-84-9801)* *Dist. by* **IPG Chicago.**

Blumont Company, The, *(978-0-9776024)* 161 Great Rd., Littleton, MA 01460 USA (SAN 257-702X) Tel 781-899-6468
E-mail: slblu@netway.com.

Blurb, Inc., *(978-0-464; 978-1-4579; 978-1-320; 978-1-5184; 978-1-364; 978-1-366; 978-1-367; 978-1-388; 978-1-389; 978-0-368; 978-0-578-46536-4; 978-1-714; 978-1-715)* Orders Addr.: 580 California St. #300, San Francisco, CA 94104 USA (SAN 860-0813)
Web site: http://www.blurb.com
Dist(s): **Lulu Pr., Inc.**

Blushing Rose Publishing, *(978-1-884807)* Orders Addr.: P.O. Box 2238, San Anselmo, CA 94979-2238 USA Tel 415-407-0170 Toll Free: 800-898-2263
E-mail: nancya555@yahoo.com
Web site: http://www.blushingrose.com.

Blynbeek Publishing, *(978-0-9996633)* 1117 Phyllis Ave., Mountain View, CA 94040 USA Tel 408-431-9467
E-mail: jchristianb@gmail.com.

BMC Advertising, Incorporated *See* **BMCFerrell**

BMCFerrell, *(978-0-9764460; 978-0-9788242)* 6450 S. Lewis Ave. Ste. 300, Tulsa, OK 74136-1068 USA
Web site: http://www.bmcferrell.com.

BMI Educational Services, *(978-0-922443; 978-1-60884; 978-1-60933; 978-1-63071; 978-1-5367)* Orders Addr.: 26 Haypress Rd., Cranbury, NJ 08512 USA (SAN 760-7032); Edit Addr.: P.O. Box 800, Dayton, NJ 08810-0800 USA (SAN 169-4669) Tel 732-329-6991; Fax: 732-329-6994; Toll Free Fax: 800-986-9393 (orders only); Toll Free: 800-222-8100 (orders only)
E-mail: info@bmionline.com
Web site: http://www.bmionline.com/.

BN Publishing, *(978-1-68411)* 3503 Jack Northrup Ave., Ste. # Z2741, Hawthorne, CA 90250 USA
E-mail: info@bnpublishing.com
Web site: http://www.bnpublishing.com.

Boarding House Publishing, *(978-0-9725365; 978-0-9774432)* 3896 Miramonte Ave., Loveland, CO 80538 USA
Web site: http://www.rdeducation.home.att.net.

Boardwalk Bks., *(978-0-9976078)* 5 Sweetwater Ave., Bedford, MA 01730 USA Tel 781-910-9129
E-mail: Jimpetipas@me.com
Web site: www.boardwalkbooks.net.

Boathouse Press *See* **BoathouseBooks**

BoathouseBooks, *(978-0-9776469)* P.O. Box 244, Tiburon, CA 94920 USA
Web site: http://boathousebooks.com
Dist(s): **Follett School Solutions.**

Boatman Pr., LLC, *(978-0-9909025; 978-0-578-59915-1; 978-1-7355514)* 545 Tucker Hill Rd., Thetford Center, VT 05075 USA Tel 802-785-2012
E-mail: boatman@deanwhitlock.com
Web site: deanwhitlock.com.

Bob Thomas Bks., *(978-0-9717682)* Orders Addr.: P.O. Box 853, Black Mountain, NC 28711 USA; Edit Addr.: P.O. Box 815, Kure Beach, NC 28449 USA Toll Free Fax: 866-615-0417.

Bobcat Publishing, *(978-0-9776419)* 5105 Cascabel Rd., Atascadero, CA 93422 USA (SAN 852-9051)
E-mail: llyn@llynsplace.com; llyntroy@sbcglobal.net
Web site: http://www.llynsplace.com.

Bobola, Frederick, *(978-0-692-16136-4; 978-1-7331094)* 22521, Santa Clarita, CA 91350 USA Tel 661-860-0818
E-mail: flbobola@gmail.com.

Bobrich Publishing *See* **Wollaston Pr.**

Boca Raton Museum of Art, *(978-0-936859)* 501 Plaza Real, Mizner Park, Boca Raton, FL 33432 USA (SAN 278-2251) Tel 561-392-2500; Fax: 561-391-6410
E-mail: amodine@bocamuseum.org; lford@bocamuseum.org
Web site: http://www.bocamuseum.org
Dist(s): **Antique Collectors' Club**
RAM Pubns. & Distribution
Univ. Pr. of Florida.

Bocelli Production, *(978-0-9908444)* 3924 Song Sparrow Dr., Wake Forest, NC 27587 USA Tel 919-247-6198
E-mail: bocelliproduction@gmail.com.

BOCH Publishing, L.L.C., *(978-1-949350)* 41620 Pheasant Creek Dr., Canton, MI 48188 USA Tel 734-718-2973
E-mail: BOCHpublishing@gmail.com
Web site: www.bochpub.com.

BoCook Publishing, *(978-0-9848791)* 12702 SE 222nd Dr., Damascus, OR 97089 USA Tel 503-853-1362
E-mail: janet_l_carlson@yahoo.com.

Bodkin Pointe Pr., *(978-0-9752684)* Orders Addr.: P.O. Box 654, Gibson Island, MD 21056 USA; 116 Tim Mara Dr., Jupiter, FL 33477 Tel 561-629-2528
E-mail: cathy@bodkinpointepress.com
Web site: http://www.bodkinpointepress.com.

Bodleian Library (GBR) *(978-1-85124; 978-0-900177)* *Dist. by* **Chicago Distribution Ctr.**

Body & Mind Productions, Inc., *(978-0-9742569; 978-0-9752648; 978-0-9771609; 978-0-9792177; 978-0-9820889; 978-0-9828370; 978-0-9830885; 978-0-9855550; 978-0-9904468)* 9429 Cedar Heights Ave., Las Vegas, NV 89134-0194 USA Tel 949-263-4676
E-mail: bodymindheal@aol.com
Web site: http://www.healingreiki.com
Dist(s): **Follett School Solutions**
New Leaf Distributing Co., Inc.
Quality Bks., Inc.

Body by Bella, LLC, *(978-0-9993882)* 3400 Duveneck Dr, Raleigh, NC 27616 USA Tel 919-561-3111
E-mail: bodybybelladotcom@gmail.com
Dist(s): **Ingram Content Group.**

Body Tone Multimedia, *(978-0-9760650)* P.O. Box 580691, Elk Grove, CA 95758-0012 USA
E-mail: body_tone_multimedia@mac.com
Web site: http://www.bodytonemultimedia.com.

Bodycrafting Systems, Inc., *(978-0-9745265)* Orders Addr.: P.O. Box 1512, Nokomis, FL 34274 USA Fax: 941-484-9650
Web site: http://www.kidpowerfitness.com.

BodyLife Publishers *See* **Windblown Media**

Boettcher, Ashley L., *(978-0-9768123)* Orders Addr.: P.O. Box 997, Southwick, MA 01077-0997 USA (SAN 256-5811) Tel 413-569-9492 available from 10am to 5pm m-f and 11am to 4pm sat; Edit Addr.: 45 Powder Mill Rd., Southwick, MA 01077 USA
E-mail: ljabphil413@juno.com
Web site: http://www.ALBbooks.com.

Bohemian Trash Studios, *(978-0-9767540)* 3322 Clearview, San Angelo, TX 76904 USA Tel 325-944-3282; *Imprints:* Star Cross'd Destiny (Star Cross)
Web site: http://www.bohemiantrash.com.

Boho Bks., *(978-0-9814709; 978-0-9891181; 978-0-9907073; 978-0-9988455)* 36179 S. Sawtell Rd, Molalla, OR 97038 USA Tel 503-807-8908; 503-829-3630
E-mail: leeglbeagl@bohobooks.com
Web site: http://www.bohobooks.com.

Bohobza Music, *(978-0-9744943)* P.O. Box 745, Teaneck, NJ 07666-0745 USA Tel 201-862-1692 (phone/fax)
E-mail: wetalkjazz@aol.com
Web site: http://www.ronibenhur.com.

Bois Pubns., *(978-0-9727967; 978-0-9971403)* 5411 Colfax Pl., Oklahoma City, OK 73112 USA Tel 405-947-7988 Evening; 405-713-4757 Daytime
E-mail: au444@cox.net; athomas14@cox.net
Web site: http://au4444.blogspot.com/.

Boland, Janie M., *(978-0-692-78147-0; 978-0-692-83475-6; 978-0-692-86491-3; 978-0-692-93936-9)* 4128 Abbott Dr., BAKERSFIELD, CA 93312 USA Tel 559-936-9838.

†Bolchazy-Carducci Pubs., *(978-0-86516; 978-1-61041)* 1570 Baskin Rd., Mundelein, IL 60060-4474 USA (SAN 219-7685) Toll Free: 800-392-6453
E-mail: jcull@bolchazy.com
Web site: http://www.bolchazy.com
Dist(s): **Follett School Solutions**
MyiLibrary; *CIP.*

Bold Illustrations *Imprint of* **FASTLANE LLC**

Bold Strokes Bks., *(978-1-933110; 978-1-60282; 978-1-62639; 978-1-63555; 978-1-63679)* 648 S Cambridge Rd, Johnsonville, NY 12094 USA Tel 518-753-6642; Fax: 518-753-6648
E-mail: bsb@boldstrokesbooks.com; publisher@boldstrokesbooks.com
Web site: http://www.boldstrokesbooks.com
Dist(s): **Abraham Assocs. Inc.**
Bella Distribution
Bookazine Co., Inc.
Two Rivers Distribution.

Bold Venture Pr., *(978-0-9712246)* 2726 NW 104th Avenue, No. 105, Sunrise, FL 33322 USA Tel 609-346-4184
E-mail: boldventurepress@aol.com
Web site: http://www.boldventurepress.com.

Bold Vision Bks., *(978-0-9853563; 978-0-615-66644-0; 978-0-615-83824-3; 978-0-615-89134-7; 978-0-615-90206-7; 978-0-9912842; 978-0-692-29107-8; 978-0-692-29972-2; 978-0-692-33303-7; 978-0-692-33924-4; 978-0-692-36096-5; 978-0-692-38991-1; 978-0-692-42912-9; 978-0-692-43536-6; 978-0-692-43641-7; 978-0-692-43701-8; 978-0-692-43876-3; 978-0-692-43904-3; 978-0-692-65630-3; 978-0-692-65946-5; 978-0-692-65959-5; 978-0-692-68050-6; 978-0-692-74301-0; 978-0-692-74695-0; 978-0-9978514; 978-1-946708) P.O. Box 2011, Friendswood, TX 77549 USA Tel 281-797-3920 (Tel/Fax)*
E-mail: kaeporter@gmail.com
Web site: www.boldvisionbooks.com
Dist(s): **CreateSpace Independent Publishing Platform.**

Bold Visions Consulting, LLC, *(978-0-692-73996-9; 978-1-7330563)* 2350 W. Galbraith, Apt 8, Cincinnati, OH 45239 USA Tel 513-317-9553
Web site: www.boldvisionsconsulting.com
Dist(s): **CreateSpace Independent Publishing Platform.**

Bolden, Christian, *(978-0-692-96171-1)* 70 I St. ST APT 130, Washington, DC 20003 USA Tel 202-294-2747; Fax: 202-294-2747
E-mail: chris93047@yahoo.com.

Boll Weevil Pr., *(978-0-9889568; 978-0-692-93440-1; 978-0-692-96596-2; 978-0-578-46887-7; 978-1-7334670)* 2 Camphor Dr., Newnan, GA 30265 USA Tel 404-594-6278
E-mail: wjeffbishop@yahoo.com
Web site: www.bollweevilpress.com.

Bollix Bks., *(978-1-932188)* 1609 W. Callender Ave., Peoria, IL 61606 USA
E-mail: staley.krause@insightbb.com
Web site: http://www.bollixbooks.com
Dist(s): **Follett School Solutions**
PSI (Publisher Services, Inc.).

Bollywood Groove, *(978-1-945792)* 1304 N Wood St., Unit 1, Chicago, IL 60622 USA Tel 312-772-6559
E-mail: info@bollygroove.com.

Bolt *Imprint of* **Black Rabbit Bks.**

Bolton Publishing LLC, *(978-0-9855312)* Orders Addr.: 7255 N. US Hwy. 377, Rochelle, TX 76872-3019 USA
E-mail: ghbolton51@gmail.com.

Bon Tiki Bks., *(978-0-9747072)* 8100 Thomas Dr., Panama City Beach, FL 32408 USA
E-mail: bontiki@knology.net
Web site: http://www.sparkythorne.com.

Bond, Troy, *(978-0-615-45092-6; 978-0-692-68481-8)* 800 45Th St, West Des Moines, IA 50265 USA Tel 515-326-4025
E-mail: troydonovanbond@yahoo.com
Dist(s): **Lulu Pr., Inc.**

Bondcliff Bks., *(978-0-9657475; 978-1-931271)* Orders Addr.: P.O. Box 385, Littleton, NH 03561 USA Toll Free: 800-859-7581; Edit Addr.: 8 Bluejay Ln., Littleton, NH 03561 USA
E-mail: bondclif@ncia.net
Dist(s): **Peregrine Outfitters.**

Bongiorno Bks., *(978-0-9715819)* P.O. Box 83-2345, Richardson, TX 75083 USA Tel 972-671-6117; Fax: 972-671-0601
E-mail: info@bongiornobooks.com
Web site: http://www.tangledhearts.com; http://www.bongiornobooks.com
Dist(s): **Nonetheless Pr.**

Bongo Comics Group *Imprint of* **Bongo Entertainment, Inc.**

Bongo Entertainment, Inc., *(978-0-9642999; 978-1-892849; 978-1-940293)* 1440 S. Sepulveda, 3rd Flr., Los Angeles, CA 90025 USA Tel 310-966-6168; Fax: 310-966-6181; *Imprints:* Bongo Comics Group (Bongo Comics Grp).

Bonita and Hodge Publishing Group, *(978-0-9838935; 978-1-7355432)* 1553 Emporia St. Bldg 21 Unit 101, Aurora, CO 80010 USA; *Imprints:* Seraphina (Seraphina)
E-mail: bandhpublishing@gmail.com; booknerd436@gmail.com; sheliawritesbooks@yahoo.com
Web site: http://www.sheliawritesbooks.com; http://www.sheliaebell.net.

Bonita & Hodge Publishing Group *See* **Bonita and Hodge Publishing Group**

Bonne Amie Publishing *See* **Chantilly Books**

Bonner, Larry, *(978-0-9747855)* 305 Chapwith Rd., Garner, NC 27529-4882 USA
Web site: http://www.bigrawhidebutte.com.

Bonneville Bks. *Imprint of* **Cedar Fort, Inc./CFI Distribution**

Bonneville B.V. (NLD) *(978-90-73304)* *Dist. by* **CFI Dist.**

Bonnier Publishing (GBR) *(978-1-78576)* *Dist. by* **IPG Chicago.**

Bonnier Publishing USA, Div. of Bonnier Publishing, 251 Park Ave. S., 12th Flr., New York, NY 10010 USA; *Imprints:* Yellow Jacket (YellowJack)
Web site: http://bonnierpublishingusa.com/
Dist(s): **Simon & Schuster, Inc.**

Bonnier Zaffre (GBR) *(978-1-78696; 978-1-83877)* *Dist. by* **IPG Chicago.**

Bonsai Bks., *(978-0-9998338)* 3595 Conton Rd. Ste. 116-141, Marietta, GA 30066 USA Tel 678-358-5182
E-mail: MuCompAd@gmail.com.

Bonus Bks., Inc., *(978-0-929387; 978-0-931028; 978-0-933893; 978-1-56625)* 875 N. Michigan Ave., Suite 1416, Chicago, IL 60611 USA (SAN 630-0804) Tel 312-467-0580; Fax: 312-467-9271
E-mail: amanda@bonusbooks.com
Web site: http://www.bonusbooks.com
Dist(s): **National Bk. Network**
Send The Light Distribution LLC.

Boo Bks., Inc., *(978-1-887864)* 7628 S. Paulina, Chicago, IL 60620 USA Tel 312-873-1584; Toll Free: 800-205-1140.

Booger Red's Bks., Inc., *(978-0-9650751)* P.O. Drawer G, Clifton, CO 81520 USA Tel 970-434-4140
E-mail: booger-gj@att.net.

Bk. Bench, The, *(978-1-891142)* 617 Herschler Ave., Evanston, WY 82930 USA Tel 307-789-3642
E-mail: atterol@allwest.net.

Bk. Club of America, *(978-1-59384)* 1812 Front St., Scotch Plains, NJ 07076-1103 USA (SAN 255-3279) Do not confuse with Book Club of America in Mechanicsburg, PA
E-mail: dcarey@bookclubusa.com.

Bk. Club of California, The, *(978-0-9819597; 978-0-692-05342-3; 978-0-692-06779-6; 978-1-7325482)* 312 Sutter St., Suite 500, San Francisco, CA 94108 USA.

Book Co. Publishing Pty, Ltd., The (AUS) *(978-1-74047; 978-1-86309; 978-1-74202)* *Dist. by* **Penton Overseas.**

Book Couple LLC, The, *(978-0-9908458; 978-1-7331571)* 21161 Via Ventura, BOCA RATON, FL 33433 USA Tel 561-218-4237
E-mail: gary@thebookcouple.com
Web site: www.thebookcouple.com.

Bk. Cravers Publishing, LLC, *(978-1-945375)* 1750 Delta Waters Rd. No 102-263, Medford, OR 97504 USA Tel 541-944-8982
E-mail: john.bcpublishing@gmail.com.

Bk. Ends, *(978-0-9677817)* 2001 N. Halsted St. Ste. 201, Chicago, IL 60614-4365 USA
E-mail: sacredflight@yahoo.com
Web site: http://www.sacredflight.com.

Bk. Entree(TM), *(978-0-9725311; 978-1-59819; 978-0-9771365)* Orders Addr.: P.O. Box 9177, Rochester, MN 55903 USA (SAN 256-8969); *Imprints:* Pickled Eggs Press (TM) (P E P); Waiting Room to Heaven (Wait Room Hvn)
E-mail: publisher@bookentree.com
Web site: http://bowwowdetectives.com; http://meowmeowdetectives.com; bookentree.com
Dist(s): **Ecompass Business Ctr.**

Bk. Garden Publishing, *(978-0-9818614)* Orders Addr.: 147 Roesch Ave., Oreland, PA 19075 USA
E-mail: JDHoliday51@gmail.com; JDHoliday51@outlook.com; jangen51@verizon.net
Web site: http://jdholiday.blogspot.com; https://www.barnesandnoble.com/s/%22J.D.+Holiday%22?_requestid=793356; http://jdswritersblog.blogspot.com.

Book Guild, Ltd. (GBR) *(978-1-85776; 978-0-86332; 978-1-84624; 978-1-909716; 978-1-910878; 978-1-912083; 978-1-911320; 978-1-910508; 978-1-910298; 978-1-909984; 978-1-912362; 978-1-912575)* *Dist. by* **Trans-Atl Phila.**

Book Her Publications *Imprint of* **Lyrically Korrect Publishing**

Book Hse. (GBR) *(978-1-904194; 978-1-904642; 978-1-905087; 978-1-906714; 978-1-907184; 978-1-910184; 978-1-911242)* *Dist. by* **Sterling.**

Book Hse. (GBR) *(978-1-904194; 978-1-904642; 978-1-905087; 978-1-906714; 978-1-907184; 978-1-910184; 978-1-911242)* *Dist. by* **Black Rab.**

Book M Publishing, *(978-0-9829502; 978-0-9913761)* 10925 Briar Forest No. 2016, Houston, TX 77042 USA Tel 713-962-0754
E-mail: bmeg@sbcglobal.net.

Bk. Nook Productions, *(978-0-9748990)* P.O. Box 101, Richmond, TX 77406 USA Tel 832-721-7655
E-mail: stephiemara@aol.com
Dist(s): **Follett School Solutions.**

Book of Hope International *See* **OneHope**

Bk. of Signs Foundation, *(978-0-9773009)* 444 E. Roosevelt Rd., Suite 173, Lombard, IL 60148 USA Tel 630-914-5015.

Book Peddlers, *(978-0-916773; 978-1-931863)* 2828 Hedberg Dr., Hopkins, MN 55305-3403 USA (SAN 653-9548) Toll Free: 800-255-3379
E-mail: vlansky@bookpeddlers.com
Web site: http://www.practicalparenting.com; http://www.bookpeddlers.com
Dist(s): **Gryphon Hse., Inc.**
MyiLibrary
Publishers Group West (PGW)
Skandisk, Inc.

Bk. Pubs. Network, *(978-1-887542; 978-0-9755407; 978-1-935359; 978-1-937454; 978-1-940598; 978-1-945271; 978-1-948963)* P.O. Box 2256, Bothell, WA 98041 USA Tel 425-483-3040; Fax: 425-483-3098
E-mail: sherynhara@earthlink.net
Web site: http://www.bookpublishersnetwork.com
Dist(s): **BookBaby**
Danforth Bk. Distribution
Epicenter Pr., Inc.
Follett School Solutions
Greenleaf Book Group
Independent Pubs. Group
Midpoint Trade Bks., Inc.
MyiLibrary
Partners Bk. Distributing, Inc.
Smashwords.

Bk. Pubs. of El Paso, *(978-0-944551; 978-0-9836455; 978-0-9916296; 978-0-9979247; 978-0-9992117; 978-1-7345223)* a/o Book Publishers of El Paso, 2200 San Jose Ave., El Paso, TX 79930 USA Tel 915-778-6670 (phone/fax) Do not confuse with Sundance Pr., Glen Carbon, IL
E-mail: bpep2@sbcglobal.net
Web site: bookpublishersofelpaso.com.

†Book Publishing Co., *(978-0-913990; 978-1-57067; 978-0-9669317; 978-0-9673108; 978-0-9779183; 978-1-939053)* P.O. Box 99, Summertown, TN 38483 USA (SAN 202-439X) Tel 931-964-3571; Fax: 931-964-3518; Toll Free: 888-260-8458; *Imprints:* Native Voices (Native Voices); 7th Generation (SeventhGen)
E-mail: info@bookpubco.com
Web site: http://www.bookpubco.com
Dist(s): **Children's Plus, Inc.**
CreateSpace Independent Publishing Platform
Follett School Solutions
Four Winds Trading Co.
Integral Yoga Pubns.
New Leaf Distributing Co., Inc.
Nutri-Bks. Corp.
Orca Bk. Pubs. USA
Partners Bk. Distributing, Inc.
Rio Nuevo Pubs.
Smashwords; *CIP.*

Book Sales, Inc., *(978-0-7628; 978-0-7858; 978-0-89009; 978-1-55521; 978-1-57715; 978-1-4161)* Orders Addr.: 400 1st Ave N. Ste. 300, Minneapolis, MN 55401-1721 USA (SAN 169-488X) Toll Free: 800-526-7257; Edit Addr.: 276 Fifth Ave., Suite 206, New York, NY 10001 USA (SAN 299-4062) Tel 212-779-4972; Fax: 212-779-6058; *Imprints:* Chartwell (Chrtwell)
E-mail: sales@booksalesusa.com
Web site: http://www.booksalesusa.com/
Dist(s): **Continental Bk. Co., Inc.**
Hachette Bk. Group
MyiLibrary
Quarto Publishing Group USA.

For full information on wholesalers and distributors, refer to the Wholesaler and Distributor Name Index

Bk. Shelf, *(978-0-9714160; 978-0-9913845)* Orders Addr.: P.O. Box 320804, Fairfield, CT 06825 USA Tel 203-257-0158
E-mail: service@bookshelf123.com; michellespraybooks@gmail.com
Web site: http://www.bookshelf123.com; http://www.myabcsbook.com/; http://www.havingscoliosis.com/.

Book Shop, Ltd., The, *(978-1-936199)* 35 E. 9th St., No. 74, New York, NY 10003 USA Tel 917-388-2493; Fax: 917-534-1304
E-mail: nancy@thebookshopltd.com
Web site: http://thebookshopltd.com.

Book Smugglers Publishing, *(978-1-942302)* 99 Kingsland Ave. No. 302, Brooklyn, NY 11222 USA Tel 310-795-7394
E-mail: contact@thebooksmugglers.com
Web site: www.thebooksmugglers.com.

Book Star Pub., *(978-0-615-21005-6; 978-0-578-02827-9; 978-0-615-30612-4; 978-0-692-00622-1; 978-0-9843033)* 3748 S.em Light Dr., Las Vegas, NV 89115 USA (SAN 924-5243) Fax: 702-644-2909
Web site: http://www.bookstarpublisher.com.

Bk. Stops Here, *(978-0-9631612)* 1108 Rocky Point Ct., NE, Albuquerque, NM 87123 USA Tel 505-296-9047 (phone/fax)
E-mail: gldjvb@home.com
Web site: http://www.bookstopshere.com.

Book Tree, The, *(978-1-885395; 978-1-58509)* Orders Addr.: P.O. Box 16476, San Diego, CA 92176 USA Tel 619-280-1263; Fax: 619-280-1285; Toll Free: 800-700-8733
E-mail: orders@thebooktree.com
Web site: http://www.thebooktree.com
Dist(s): **New Leaf Distributing Co., Inc.**

Bk. Vine Pr., *(978-1-949574; 978-1-950955; 978-1-951886; 978-1-952835; 978-1-953699)* 505 W. Lancaster Ct., Inverness, IL 60010 USA Tel 847-382-9090
E-mail: admin@bookvinepress.com
Web site: www.bookvinepress.com.

Book Web Publishing, Limited, *(978-0-9716567; 978-0-9795733)* P.O. Box 81, Bellmore, NY 11710 USA
E-mail: jeri@jerifink.com; donna@bookwebpublishing.com
Web site: http://www.bookwebpublishing.com.

Book Wholesalers, Inc., *(978-0-7587; 978-1-4046; 978-1-4131; 978-1-4155; 978-1-4156; 978-1-4287)* 1847 Mercer Rd., Lexington, KY 40511-1001 USA (SAN 135-5449) Toll Free: 800-888-4478
E-mail: jcarrico@bwibooks.com; lison@bwibooks.com
Web site: http://www.bwibooks.com
Dist(s): **Follett School Solutions.**

Bk. Writing Inc, *(978-0-9994657; 978-1-950088; 978-1-951630; 978-1-952263)* 1111 Wilshire Blvd, Los Angeles, CA 90017 USA Tel 888-588-5175
E-mail: irene.pearson@bookwritinginc.com
Web site: https://www.bookwritinginc.com/.

Bookaroos Publishing, Inc., *(978-0-9678167)* Orders Addr.: P.O. Box 8518, Fayetteville, AR 72703 USA Tel 479-443-0339; Fax: 479-443-0339; Edit Addr.: 484 E. Pharris Dr., Fayetteville, AR 72703 USA
E-mail: books@bookaroos.com; tammybronson@bookaroos.com
Web site: http://www.bookaroos.com; http://www.seahorserun.com; http://www.tammybronson.com; http://www.tinysnail.com
Dist(s): **Follett School Solutions.**

Book-Art Press Solutions LLC *See* **INFORMA INC**

Bookateer Publishing, *(978-0-9819368; 978-1-936476)* 4 Park Ave., Uncasville, CT 06382 USA
E-mail: mj@denicalisdragonchronicles.com; grizlegirl@sbcglobal.net
Web site: www.grizlegirlproductions.com; www.bookateerpublishing.com; www.denicalisdragonchronicles.com
Dist(s): **Smashwords.**

BookBaby, *(978-1-60984; 978-1-61792; 978-1-61842; 978-1-61927; 978-1-62095; 978-1-62309; 978-1-62488; 978-1-62675; 978-1-4835; 978-1-63192; 978-1-943612; 978-1-68222; 978-1-5439; 978-0-692-95466-9; 978-0-692-11235-9; 978-0-692-11236-6; 978-0-578-41517-8;-1-0983) 7905 N. Rt 130, Pennsauken, NJ 08110 USA Toll Free: 877-961-6878; 7905 N Crescent Blvd, Pennsauken, NJ 08110 Toll Free: 877-961-6878*
E-mail: info@bookbaby.com; support@bookbaby.com; jburton@bookbaby.com; jfoley@bookbaby.com
Web site: http://www.bookbaby.com
Dist(s): **Amazon Digital Services Inc.**
Independent Pubs. Group.

BookBound Publishing, *(978-1-932367)* Orders Addr.: 26500 W. Agoura Rd., Suite 102-593, Calabasas, CA 91302 USA (SAN 256-3177) Toll Free: 866-985-2665
E-mail: stacyquest@bookbound.net
Web site: http://www.bookbound.net; http://bookboundpublishing.com.

BookChamp LLC., *(978-0-9760111)* c/o Winter & Company P.C, 605 King Georges Post Rd., Fords, NJ 08863 USA
E-mail: info@bookchamp.net
Web site: http://www.bookchamp.net
Dist(s): **Chicago Review Pr., Inc.**

Bookcraft, Inc. *Imprint of* **Deseret Bk. Co.**

BookCrafters, *(978-0-9845194; 978-0-9832819; 978-0-9837470; 978-1-937862; 978-1-943650; 978-1-950647)* Orders Addr.: 12056 Ridgeview Ln., Parker, CO 80138-7141 USA (SAN 859-6352) Tel 720-851-0397
E-mail: bookcrafterscolorado@gmail.com
Web site: http://bookcrafters.net
Dist(s): **Advocate Distribution Solutions**
BookPartners, Inc.
Ingram Content Group
Send The Light Distribution LLC
Smashwords.

Bookends Pr., *(978-0-9724926; 978-0-9740922; 978-1-932667; 978-1-938315; 978-1-950125; 978-1-953166)* Orders Addr.: 4130 NW 16th Blvd., Gainesville, FL 32604 USA Fax: 352-373-6905; Toll Free: 800-881-3208; P.O. Box 14513, Gainsville, FL 32604
E-mail: copyright@renaissance-printing.com
Web site: http://www.bookendspress.com
Dist(s): **Freeman Family Ministries**
Rosewood Foundation, The
StarCrossed Productions
Truth Pubns.

Booker Lane Press *See* **Punta Gorda Pr.**

BOOKGEMSFORKIDS, *(978-0-9763596)* 111 Primrose Ln., Wyomissing, PA 19610 USA
E-mail: sukumar@idreampublications.com
Web site: http://www.idreampublications.com.

BookLife Publishing Ltd. (GBR) *(978-1-78637; 978-1-910512; 978-1-78998; 978-1-83927) Dist. by* **IPG Chicago.**

BookLight Pr., *(978-0-9841307; 978-0-615-73688-4)* Orders Addr.: 5994 S. Holly St. #118, Greenwood Village, CO 80111 USA (SAN 858-5164) Tel 303-916-8124; Edit Addr.: P.O. Box 380161, Cambridge, MA 02139-0161 USA
E-mail: jmarsh@booklightpress.com
Web site: www.booklightpress.com
Dist(s): **Follett School Solutions.**

Booklight Publishing, *(978-1-7337407)* 12429 Madrone Forest Dr., Nevada City, CA 95959 USA Tel 530-913-9608
E-mail: lila@lilareyna.com.

Booklines Hawaii, Ltd., *(978-1-929844; 978-1-58849; 978-1-60274)* Div. of Islander Group, 269 Pali'i St., Mililani, HI 96789 USA (SAN 630-6624) Tel 808-676-0116; Fax: 808-676-0634
E-mail: customerservice@booklines.com
Web site: http://www.booklineshawaii.com
Dist(s): **Follett School Solutions**
Islander Group.

Booklocker.com, Inc., *(978-1-929072; 978-1-931391; 978-1-59113; 978-1-60145; 978-1-60910; 978-1-61434; 978-1-62141; 978-1-62646; 978-1-63263; 978-1-63490; 978-1-63491; 978-1-63492; 978-1-64438; 978-1-64718; 978-1-64719)* 200 2nd Ave. S. #526, Saint Petersburg, FL 33701 USA (SAN 254-363X) Fax: 305-768-0261; *Imprints:* Abuzz Press (AbuzzPr)
E-mail: booklocker@booklocker.com; angela@writersweekly.com
Web site: http://www.booklocker.com; http://www.writersweekly.com.

BookLogix, *(978-0-615-18278-0; 978-0-615-18390-9; 978-0-615-25890-4; 978-1-61005; 978-1-63183; 978-0-9978038; 978-1-6653)* 1264 Old Alpharetta Rd., Alpharetta, GA 30005 USA (SAN 860-0376) Tel 470-239-8547; Fax: 888-564-7890
E-mail: Angela@booklogix.com; Ahmad@booklogix.com
Web site: http://www.booklogix.com.

Booklogix Publishing Services *See* **BookLogix**

BookMann Pr. *Imprint of* **Mann Publishing Group**

Bookmark Bks., LLC, *(978-0-9764163)* P.O. Box 2996, Chester, VA 23831 USA Tel 804-706-6399 (phone/fax)
E-mail: bookmarkbooks@verizon.net.

Bookmark, The, *(978-0-930227)* Orders Addr.: 29021 Ave. Sherman, Unit 109, Santa Clarita, CA 91355 USA (SAN 694-6410) Tel 661-294-8022; Fax: 661-294-8027; Toll Free: 800-220-7767 Do not confuse with other companies with the same name in Marietta, GA, Knightstown, IN
E-mail: thebookmark@earthlink.net
Web site: http://www.thebookmark.com.

Bookmasters Distribution *See* **Baker & Taylor Publisher Services (BTPS)**

Bookmates *Imprint of* **Penny Laine Papers, Inc.**

BookMobile *See* **Syren Bk. Co.**

BookPartners, LLC, *(978-1-936495)* 725 3rd St. P.O. Box 790, Cedar Key, FL 32625-0790 USA Tel 352-543-9307; Fax: 407-287-6002
E-mail: jpdwyer@dwyerogrady.com
Web site: www.bookpartners.org.

BookPatch LLC, The, *(978-1-62030; 978-1-63318; 978-1-68273; 978-1-946447; 978-1-946634; 978-1-946812; 978-1-946982; 978-1-947136; 978-1-947289; 978-1-947519; 978-1-947778; 978-1-947962; 978-1-948186; 978-1-948339; 978-1-64254; 978-1-64550; 978-1-64858; 978-0-578-68064-4) 4400 N. Scottsdale Rd., Scottsdale, AZ 85251 USA Tel 602-403-5600*
E-mail: victor@thebookpatch.com
Web site: http://www.thebookpatch.com
Dist(s): **BookBaby**
Ingram Content Group
Lulu Pr., Inc.

BookPatch.com, The *See* **BookPatch LLC, The**

Bookpublisher.com *See* **Wheatmark, Inc.**

Bks. Are Fun, Ltd., *(978-0-9649777; 978-1-58209; 978-1-890409; 978-1-59795; 978-1-60626)* 1 Readers Digest Rd., Pleasantville, NY 10570-7000 USA
E-mail: msmall@booksarefun.com
Web site: http://www.booksarefun.com
Dist(s): **Sandvik Publishing.**

Bks. By Aleena, *(978-0-692-12283-9)* 4163 Bowen Way, VALDOSTA, GA 31605 USA Tel 912-398-0365
E-mail: hector.m.rodriguezortiz@gmail.com
Dist(s): **Ingram Content Group.**

Books by Bookends *See* **Long Dash Publishing**

Bks. by Elle, Inc., *(978-0-692-72108-7; 978-0-692-78400-6; 978-0-9982709; 978-0-9992504; 978-1-951017)* 225 College Dr. #65504, Orange Park, FL 32065 USA Tel 904-962-8587
Web site: www.elleklass.weebly.com
Dist(s): **CreateSpace Independent Publishing Platform.**

Books by Kids LLC, *(978-0-615-19963-4; 978-0-9830954)* 1021 Oak St., Jacksonville, FL 32204 USA Tel 904-376-7029; Fax: 904-355-1832
Web site: http://www.booksbykids.com
Dist(s): **Chicago Distribution Ctr.**

Bks. by Matt, *(978-0-9727660)* 33 Stoddard Way, Berkeley, CA 94708 USA Tel 510-849-2986; Fax: 510-849-1012
E-mail: mylamby@hotmail.com.

Bks. del Sur, *(978-0-9973280; 978-1-7339785)* 1375 Heron Dr., Antioch, IL 60002 USA Tel 608-217-0758
E-mail: heather@booksdelsur.org
Web site: www.booksdelsurstore.org.

Books for Brats *Imprint of* **Little Redhaired Girl Publishing, Inc.**

Bks. for Children of the World, *(978-0-9661186; 978-0-9762078)* 6701 N. Bryant Ave., Oklahoma City, OK 73121 USA Tel 405-721-7417; Fax: 405-478-4352; Toll Free: 888-838-0003.

Books for Children Publishing *See* **Guiffre Bk. Publishing**

Books International, Inc., *(978-1-891078)* Orders Addr.: P.O. Box 605, Herndon, VA 20172-0605 USA (SAN 131-761X) Tel 703-661-1500; Fax: 703-661-1501
E-mail: bimail@presswarehouse.com.

Bks. on Demand, *(978-0-608; 978-0-7837; 978-0-8357; 978-0-598)* Div. of UMI, 300 N. Zeeb Rd., Ann Arbor, MI 48106-1346 USA.

Bks. on the Path, *(978-0-9743390)* P.O. Box 436, Barker, TX 77413-0436 USA Tel 281-492-6050; Fax: 832-201-7620; Toll Free: 866-875-7284
E-mail: info@patriarchspath.org
Web site: http://www.booksonthepath.com.

Bks. That Will Enhance Your Life, *(978-0-615-20297-6; 978-0-615-38405-4; 978-0-9831419; 978-0-9838457; 978-0-9848980; 978-0-692-68079-7)* Div. of Andrews Leadership International, 8816 Ave. M New St., Brooklyn, NY 11236 USA Tel 917-327-1029; *Imprints:* BTWEYL (BTWEYL)
E-mail: production@alipictures.com; john@johnaandrews.com
Web site: http://www.alipictures.com.

Books To Believe In *Imprint of* **Thornton Publishing, Inc.**

Books To Remember *Imprint of* **Flyleaf Publishing**

Bks. Unbound E-Publishing Co., *(978-1-59201)* 1110 Kerwin St., Piscataway, NJ 08854-3323 USA
Web site: http://www.booksunbound.com.

Bks. with a Porpoise, LLC, *(978-1-7327454)* 1807 Doris Dr., Menlo Park, CA 94025 USA Tel 312-622-4593
E-mail: rglass2222@gmail.com.

Bks. With Purpose LLC., *(978-1-7326422; 978-1-7330313)* 989 Riverpoint Ct., POWELL, OH 43065 USA Tel 614-595-2045
E-mail: laurenkelleybooks@gmail.com.

Bks. With Soul, *(978-1-949325)* 12653 N 17th Pl., Phoenix, AZ 85022 USA Tel 602-758-9189
E-mail: aksmithbook@gmail.com
Web site: www.bookswithsoul.com.

Books2Go, *(978-1-59590)* 780 Reservoir Ave., Suite 243, Cranston, RI 02910 USA Tel 401-537-9175
E-mail: books2go@writerscollective.net
Web site: http://www.mybooks2go.com.

Books-A-Million, Inc., *(978-1-63111; 978-1-5325)* 402 Industrial Dr., Birmingham, AL 35211 USA Tel 205-942-3737
E-mail: Publishing@BooksAMillion.com
Web site: www.booksamillion.com.

BooksbyDave Inc., *(978-0-9768867)* Orders Addr.: 5010 James loop, Killeen, TX 76542 USA Tel 254-628-1961
E-mail: project17us@yahoo.com
Web site: http://www.geocities.com/oilsbydave.

Booksforboys, *(978-0-9761440)* 8 Marigold Ct., Holtsville, NY 11742 USA
Web site: http://booksforboys.com.

Bookshelf Global Publishing, *(978-0-9755395; 978-0-9766954; 978-0-9779012; 978-0-9800430; 978-0-9850656)* 503 Second Ave., Destin, FL 32541 USA (SAN 850-4652) Tel 770-560-8016
E-mail: office@bookshelfglobal.com
Web site: http://www.bookshelfglobal.com.

Bookshelf, The *See* **Open Door Publishers, Inc.**

Booksmart Pubns., *(978-0-9790896)* Orders Addr.: P.O. Box 4774, Mission Viejo, CA 92690 USA (SAN 852-4211) Tel 949-462-0076; Edit Addr.: 19 Bolero, Mission Viejo, CA 92692 USA
E-mail: b_smart@cox.net
Web site: http://www.booksmartpublications.com.

booksonnet.com, *(978-1-888562; 978-0-9675540)* Div. of Shoestring Productions, P.O. Box 36, Saint Augustine, FL 32085 USA Tel 904-829-3812 Do not confuse with companies with the same name in Prather CA, Santa Barbara CA, Aptos CA, Belvedere CA, Albion CA, Pensacola, FL
E-mail: billbooks@bellsouth.net
Dist(s): **Ingram Content Group.**

Booksource, The, *(978-0-7383; 978-0-8335; 978-0-911891; 978-0-9641084; 978-1-886379; 978-1-890760; 978-0-7568; 978-1-4117; 978-1-4178; 978-1-60446; 978-1-4364)* Div. of GL group, Inc., Orders Addr.: 1230 Macklind Ave., Saint Louis, MO 63110-1432 USA (SAN 169-4324) Tel 314-647-0600 Toll Free Fax: 800-647-1923; Toll Free: 800-444-0435
E-mail: khostman@booksource.com; shankins@glgrp.com; gbonebrake@glgrp.com; shankins@booksource.com
Web site: http://www.booksource.com; http://www.goodluckgroup.com/.

Bookstand Publishing, *(978-1-58909; 978-1-61863; 978-1-63498; 978-1-953710)* 305 Vineyard Town Ctr., Suite 302, Morgan Hill, CA 95037 USA Tel 408-852-1832; Fax: 408-852-1812
E-mail: orders@bookstandpublishing.com
Web site: http://www.BookstandPublishing.com.

Bookstaves, LLC, *(978-1-63235; 978-1-64582)* P.O. Box 727, Mankato, MN 56002 USA Tel 651-242-3066; *Imprints:* 12-Story Library (12StryLib)
E-mail: tsnow@bookstaves.net
Web site: http://www.12storylibrary.com.

Bookstrand-Siren Publishing, Incorporated *See* **Siren-BookStrand, Inc.**

Booksville, U.S.A., *(978-0-9630887; 978-0-9720041)* P.O. Box 710352, Houston, TX 77271-0352 USA Tel 713-726-8115 (phone/fax); *Imprints:* Circle of Friends (CirFriends)
E-mail: elkewat@aol.com; lindawatersbooks@aol.com; ethnicbooks@aol.com
Web site: http://lindawaters.com.

BooktiMookti Pr., *(978-0-9800952)* P.O. Box 17520, Seattle, WA 98127 USA
E-mail: helen@booktimookti.com
Web site: http://www.BooktiMookti.com; http://www.RuntFarm.com
Dist(s): **Itasca Bks.**

Booktrope, *(978-0-9841786; 978-1-935961; 978-1-62015; 978-1-5137)* Div. of Libertary Co., 1219 Sixteenth Ave East, Seattle, WA 98112 USA (SAN 858-639X) Tel 206-235-3384; *Imprints:* Booktrope Editions (Booktrope Edtns); Vox Dei (VoxDei)
E-mail: publisher@booktrope.com; production@booktrope.com; info@booktrope.com; accounting@booktrope.com
Web site: http://www.booktrope.com.

Booktrope Editions *Imprint of* **Booktrope**

Bookwhip, *(978-1-948801; 978-1-949723; 978-1-950580; 978-1-951469; 978-1-953537)* Orders Addr.: 1545 S Harbor Blvd No. 2100, FULLERTON, CA 92832 USA Tel 855-339-3589; Edit Addr.: 1545 S Harbor Blvd No. 2100, FULLERTON, CA 92832 USA Tel 855-339-3589
E-mail: brandon@bookwhip.com
Web site: www.bookwhip.com.

BookWise Publishing, *(978-1-60645; 978-0-615-15370-4; 978-0-578-42434-7)* Orders Addr.: 12707 S. City Pk. Way, Riverton, UT 84065 USA Tel 801-635-4821
E-mail: chrisbizzz@comcast.net; karenkchristoffersen@gmail.com
Web site: http://www.bookwisepublishing.com
Dist(s): **CreateSpace Independent Publishing Platform.**

Bookworks, LLC, *(978-0-615-98953-2; 978-0-692-21126-7; 978-0-9906156; 978-1-942407; 978-0-9993556)* 78 Beech St., Trumbull, CT 06611 USA
E-mail: w.thorpe@bookworksllc.com.

Bk.worm, *(978-1-949808)* P.O. Box 90101, Alexandria, VA 22309 USA Tel 703-799-6666
E-mail: peacedrama@gmail.com.

Bookworm Bks., *(978-0-9749423)* P.O. Box 77277, Washington, DC 20013 USA (SAN 255-8874) Fax: 202-387-5127; Toll Free: 877-302-0067
E-mail: info@bookwormbooks.biz
Web site: http://www.bookwormbooks.biz.

Boom Entertainment, Inc., 5670 Wilshire Blvd., Ste 450, Los Angeles, CA 90036 USA
Dist(s): **Diamond Comic Distributors, Inc.**
Diamond Bk. Distributors
Follett School Solutions
Simon & Schuster, Inc.

Boom! Studios, *(978-1-932386; 978-1-934506; 978-1-60886; 978-1-936393; 978-1-61398; 978-1-939867; 978-1-68159; 978-1-68415; 978-1-64144; 978-1-64668)* 1800 Century Pk. E., Suite 200, Los Angeles, CA 90067 USA Tel 310-895-7746; 5670 Wilshire Blvd., Suite No. 400, Los Angeles, CA 90036; *Imprints:* Archaia Entertainment (ArchaiaEnt)
E-mail: khenning@boom-studios.com
Web site: http://www.boom-studios.com
Dist(s): **Children's Plus, Inc.**
INscribe Digital
Independent Pubs. Group
MyiLibrary
Simon & Schuster, Inc.
Simon & Schuster Children's Publishing.

Boomer Bks. *Imprint of* **Editorium, The**

Boone Bks., *(978-0-9765294)* P.O. Box 262147, Plano, TX 75026-2147 USA Toll Free: 800-755-6628
E-mail: cadprof@boonebooks.com
Web site: http://www.boonebooks.com.

Boosey & Hawkes, Inc., 229 W. 28th St. Flr. 11, New York, NY 10001-5915 USA
E-mail: bhsales@ny.boosey.com
Web site: http://www.boosey.com
Dist(s): **Leonard, Hal Corp.**

Boot in the Door Pubns., *(978-0-9788183; 978-1-7340231)* P.O. Box 132031, Spring, TX 77393 USA
E-mail: lesaboutin@gmail.com; lesakhoward@gmail.com
Web site: https://www.bootinthedoor.com/.

Booth, Jesse, *(978-0-692-19470-6; 978-0-578-48160-9)* 294 W. 680 N., Centerville, UT 84014 USA Tel 385-290-2081
E-mail: jtulkas2@hotmail.com
Dist(s): **Ingram Content Group.**

Booth, John Harvey, *(978-0-9754291)* 246 Schilling St., West Lafayette, IN 47906 USA Tel 765-743-8728
E-mail: jhbooth2003@yahoo.com.

Boothroyd & Allnut, *(978-0-578-11204-6; 978-0-9904207)* 5115 68th Ave. NE, Marysville, WA 98270 USA.

Borah Pr., *(978-0-9657879)* 1100 Rd. M, Redwood Valley, CA 95470 USA Tel 707-485-0922; Fax: 707-485-7071
E-mail: JPack@pacific.net.

Border Pr., *(978-0-9650977; 978-0-9843150; 978-0-9848915; 978-0-9898641; 978-0-9862801; 978-0-9968737; 978-0-9997804; 978-1-7346802)*

Orders Addr.: P.O. Box 3124, Sewanee, TN 37375 USA Tel 337-577-1762; Toll Free Fax: 866-669-3207
E-mail: borderpress@gmail.com
Web site: http://borderpressbooks.com.

Borders Group, Inc., *(978-0-681)* 100 Phoenix Dr., Ann Arbor, MI 48108 USA Tel 734-477-1100
Web site: http://www.borders.com.

Borders Personal Publishing, *(978-1-4134)* a/o Pam Durant, 2 International Plaza, Suite 340, Philadelphia, PA 19113 USA Tel 610-915-5214; Fax: 610-915-0294; Toll Free: 888-795-4274
E-mail: dave@xlibris.com
Dist(s): **Xlibris Corp.**

Borders Pr., *(978-0-681)* Div. of Borders Group, Inc., 100 Phoenix Dr., Ann Arbor, MI 48108 USA; *Imprints:* State Street Press (State St Pr)
Web site: http://www.bordersstores.com; http://www.bordersgroupinc.com; http://www.borders.com.

BorderStone Pr., LLC, *(978-0-9842284; 978-1-936670)* Orders Addr.: P.O. Box 1383, Mountain Home, AR 72653 USA Tel 870-405-1146; 436 Olympic Dr., MOUNTAIN HOME, 72654 Tel 870-405-1146
E-mail: borderstonepress@gmail.com
Web site: http://www.borderstonepress.com; http://www.facebook.com/pages/BorderStone-Press-LLC/137970880138?ref=ts.

Bordighera Incorporated, *(978-1-884419; 978-1-59954)* Orders Addr.: P.O. Box 1374, Lafayette, IN 47902-1374 USA; Edit Addr.: John D. Calandra Italian American Institute 25 W. 43rd St., 17th Flr., New York, NY 10036 USA Tel 212-642-2005
E-mail: dstarewich@verizon.net; anthony.tamburri@qc.cuny.edu
Dist(s): **SPD-Small Pr. Distribution.**

Borealis Bk. *Imprint of* **Minnesota Historical Society Pr.**

Borealis Pr., *(978-0-9632651; 978-0-9819950)* P.O. Box 230, Surry, ME 04684 USA Tel 207-667-3700; Fax: 207-667-9649; Toll Free: 800-669-6845.

Borghesi & Adam Pubs. Pty Ltd (AUS) *(978-0-9577403; 978-1-877035; 978-0-9775720; 978-0-9802892; 978-1-921346; 978-0-9806308; 978-0-9807307; 978-1-921756; 978-0-9871404; 978-0-9871986; 978-0-9872735; 978-0-9873068; 978-0-9873895; 978-0-9925668; 978-0-9942634; 978-1-925386; 978-0-6484095; 978-0-6484571; 978-0-6485557; 978-0-6486918; 978-1-922418) Dist. by* **IPG Chicago.**

Borgo Press *See* **Borgo Publishing**

Borgo Publishing, *(978-0-9843979; 978-0-9883893; 978-0-9905431; 978-0-9968783; 978-0-9984606; 978-0-9993830; 978-1-7339165; 978-1-7345730)* 3811 Derby Downs Dr., Tuscaloosa, AL 35405 USA Tel 205-454-4256
E-mail: borgogirl@bellsouth.net.

BoriBoricha INC *See* **Starry Forest Bks., Inc.**

Born to Blaze Ministries, *(978-0-9762910)* 2131 20th St SE, Buffalo, MN 55313-4813 USA Tel 612-207-5682
E-mail: info@borntoblaze.com
Web site: http://www.borntoblaze.com.

borntalking.com, *(978-0-9720892)* 34116 Blue Heron Dr., Solon, OH 44139-5641 USA
E-mail: david@borntalking.com
Web site: http://www.borntalking.com.

Borromeo Bks., *(978-0-9763098)* Orders Addr.: P.O. Box 7273, Saint Paul, MN 55107 USA.

Boshu Pr., *(978-0-9755624)* 3 Dogwood Ct., Greenville, NC 27858 USA
E-mail: boshucelli@earthlink.net.

BOSS Business Services *See* **Anderson Law Group**

Boss Paws Publishing, *(978-0-9769058)* 2536 Ridgewood Ave., Louisville, KY 40217 USA Tel 502-649-6864
E-mail: ag@animalgambill.org.

Bosse, Andre Ctr., *(978-0-9786128)* 302 Hanson St., Hart, MI 49420-1385 USA Tel 231-873-1707; Fax: 231-873-1456
E-mail: maltbie7@charter.net
Web site: http://www.andrebossecenter.org.

Boston Common Press *See* **America's Test Kitchen**

BOT Publishing, LLC, *(978-0-9759493)* P.O. Box 62, Mount Pleasant, SC 29465 USA
Web site: http://thebeautyoftruth.com.

BotDM, *(978-0-692-15315-4; 978-1-7327353)* 14895 W. 54th Ave, Golden, CO 80403 USA Tel 303-808-5881
E-mail: kate.b.marshall@gmail.com.

Botero de Borrero, Beatriz & Martha Olga Botero de Gomez (COL) *(978-958-33) Dist. by* **Lectorum Pubns.**

Bothwell Pr., *(978-0-9855353)* 664 H St., Salt Lake City, UT 84103 USA (SAN 920-3397) Tel 801-532-2204 Do not confuse with Bothwell Pr. in Athens, GA
E-mail: Bothwellpress@gmail.com.

Bo-Tree Hse., *(978-0-9832227; 978-0-9968516)* 1749 Del Mar Dr., Idaho Falls, ID 83404 USA Tel 650-701-4645 (cell)
E-mail: Debu.majumdar@botreehouse.com
Web site: http://www. botreehouse.com
Dist(s): **CreateSpace Independent Publishing Platform**
Follett School Solutions
Ingram Content Group
Smashwords.

Bottom Line Media, *(978-0-9759997; 978-0-9852192; 978-0-9899545; 978-1-7352345)* 10123 William Carey Dr., Orlando, FL 32832 USA Tel 407-382-6000; Fax: 407-382-1008
E-mail: bottomline@orlandoteam.com
Web site: www.pioneers.org/books.

Bottom of the Hill Publishing, *(978-1-935785; 978-1-61203; 978-1-4837)* 200 Terry Rd., Somerville, TN 38068 USA Tel 901-465-8497
E-mail: info@bottomofthehillpublishing.com
Web site: bottomofthehillpublishing.com
Dist(s): **MyiLibrary.**

Bottom-Up Media, *(978-0-9765337)* 5413 Nueces Bay Dr., Rowlett, TX 75089 USA (SAN 854-7440) Tel 214-550-2563
E-mail: steve@bottomupmedia.com
Web site: http://www.bottomupmedia.com
Dist(s): **Ingram Content Group.**

Bouje Publishing, LLC, *(978-0-9779265)* Orders Addr.: 17659 Montebello Rd, Cupertino, CA 95014 USA.

Boulden Publishing, *(978-1-878076; 978-1-892421)* Div. of Turtle Pine, Inc., Orders Addr.: P.O. Box 1186, Weaverville, CA 96093-1186 USA Tel 530-623-5399; Fax: 530-623-5525; Toll Free: 800-238-8433
E-mail: ken@bouldenpublishing.com
Web site: http://www.bouldenpublishing.com
Dist(s): **Follett School Solutions**
MAR*CO Products, Inc.
Social Studies Schl. Service
Sunburst Communications, Inc.

Boulder Street Bks. LLC, *(978-0-578-06778-0)* P.O. Box 380, Green Mountain Falls, CO 80819 USA
E-mail: editor@boulderstreetbooks.com
Web site: http://www.boulderstreetbooks.com
Dist(s): **Outskirts Pr., Inc.**

Bouncing Ball Bks., Inc., *(978-1-934138)* P.O. Box 6509, Spring Hill, FL 34611-6509 USA (SAN 851-6073)
E-mail: bouncingballbooks@yahoo.com
Web site: http://www.bouncingballbooks.com.

Bound & Determined Pubs., *(978-0-9704006)* Orders Addr.: 18116 Woodrow Rd., Brainerd, MN 56401 USA
E-mail: adamrmarcotte@yahoo.com
Web site: http://www.sover.net/~niliacus/a&h/; http://www.adamandheidi.net.

Bound by Grace Pr., LLC, *(978-0-9787087)* Orders Addr.: 924 Campbell Ct., Batavia, IL 60510 USA Tel 630-772-7172
E-mail: denise@boundbygracepress.com
Web site: http://www.boundbygracepress.com
Dist(s): **Theological Bk. Service.**

Bound Publishing *See* **Spellbound River Pr.**

Bounty Project, The, *(978-0-9665861)* 6310 Georgetown Pike, McLean, VA 22101 USA Tel 703-442-7557
E-mail: kjackson@1771.org.

Bourgeois Media & Consulting, *(978-0-9796288; 978-0-9827877; 978-0-9830355; 978-0-9831971; 978-0-9834868; 978-0-9840281; 978-0-9854244; 978-0-9967348; 978-1-7323679)* 1712 E. Riverside Dr. 124, Austin, TX 78741 USA; *Imprints:* Creative House Kids Press (CreatHseKids)
E-mail: chpress@live.com
Web site: http://bourgeoismedia.com.

Boutin, Lesa *See* **Boot in the Door Pubns.**

Boutique Natural Health Solutions, LLC, *(978-0-9982234)* 4410 Wood Creek Dr, Marietta, GA 30062 USA Tel 404-200-6851; Fax: 404-200-6851
E-mail: birgit@birgitscoaching.com.

Boutique of Quality Books Publishing Co., Inc., *(978-0-60808; 978-0-9828689; 978-0-9831699; 978-1-937084; 978-1-939371; 978-1-945448; 978-1-952782)* 960 Oaktree Blvd., Christiansburg, VA 24073 USA Tel 678-316-4150; Fax: 678-999-3738; *Imprints:* BQB Publishing (BQBPubng); WriteLife Publishing (WriteLifePub)
E-mail: writelife@boutiqueofqualitybooks.com
Web site: http://www.bqbpublishing.com
Dist(s): **INscribe Digital**
Independent Pubs. Group
New Leaf Distributing Co., Inc.

Boutte, Sarah, *(978-0-692-96434-7; 978-0-578-52568-6)* 300 Copperfield Way, YOUNGSVILLE, LA 70592 USA Tel 858-699-5437
E-mail: sneels_44@yahoo.com
Dist(s): **Ingram Content Group.**

Bow Historical Bks.,
Dist(s): **Oxford Univ. Pr., Inc.**

Bowden Music Co., *(978-0-9702219)* 1511 Grand Ave., Fort Worth, TX 76106 USA Tel 817-624-1547 (phone/fax)
E-mail: essieb@mindspring.com.

Bower Bks. *Imprint of* **Storybook Meadow Publishing**

†Bower Hse., *(978-0-915024; 978-0-917895; 978-0-929969; 978-0-933472; 978-0-942394; 978-0-9634607; 978-0-9643161; 978-0-9653751; 978-0-9657159; 978-1-55566; 978-1-56579; 978-1-879483; 978-1-889593; 978-1-890768; 978-0-9704098; 978-1-931599; 978-0-9713678; 978-0-9718378; 978-1-932557; 978-1-934553; 978-1-60648; 978-1-942280; 978-1-917895) P.O. Box 7459, Denver, CO 80207 USA (SAN 209-2425) Toll Free Fax: 800-217-7104; Toll Free: 800-217-7104; Imprints:* Trails Books (Trails Bks); Johnson Books (JohnsonBks); Westcliffe Publishers (WestcliffePubs)
E-mail: books@bowerhousebooks.com; margaret@bowerhousebooks.com
Web site: http://www.bowerhousebooks.com
Dist(s): **Baker & Taylor Publisher Services (BTPS);** *CIP.*

Bowers, Renata *See* **Frieda B.**

Bowles, Sharon, *(978-0-692-67659-2)* 9 Wellington Ct., Little Rock, AR 72227 USA Tel 501-517-6084
E-mail: sharon@aristotle.net.

Bowman, Rosanne, *(978-0-578-41245-0)* 1612 Karen Ave., Lima, OH 45801 USA Tel 419-516-6149
E-mail: writer@rosannebowman.com
Dist(s): **Ingram Content Group.**

Bowman's Pr., LLC, *(978-1-933142)* 9321 226th St. SE, Woodinville, WA 98077 USA
E-mail: info@bowmanspress.com
Web site: http://www.bowmanspress.com.

Bowmar/Noble Pubs., *(978-0-8107; 978-0-8372)* 220 E. Danieldale Dr., De Soto, TX 75115-2490 USA (SAN 201-4157).

Bowrider Pr., *(978-0-9825663)* 1451 Fairbanks Pl., Los Angeles, CA 90026 USA Tel 310-497-1789
Dist(s): **Follett School Solutions.**

Box Girls, The, *(978-0-9769908)* 149 S. Barrington Ave, No. 126, Los Angeles, CA 90049 USA Fax: 310-440-0145
Web site: http://www.theboxgirls.com.

Boxer Bks., Ltd. (GBR) *(978-0-9547373; 978-1-905417; 978-1-910126) Dist. by* **Sterling.**

Boxes & Arrows, Incorporated *See* **Backintyme Publishing**

Boyars, Marion Pubs., Inc., *(978-0-7145; 978-0-905223)* 237 E. 39th St., No. 1A, New York, NY 10016-2110 USA (SAN 284-981X) Tel 212-697-1599; Fax: 212-808-0664; Toll Free: 800-283-3572 (orders only)
Dist(s): **Consortium Bk. Sales & Distribution**
MyiLibrary.

Boyars, Marion Pubs., Ltd. (GBR) *(978-0-7145; 978-1-84230) Dist. by* **Consort Bk Sales.**

Boyce, S. M. *See* **Wispvine Publishing**

Boyce, Tami Design, *(978-0-692-78511-9; 978-0-692-97044-7; 978-0-692-99539-6)* 1772 Orange Grove Shores Dr., Charleston, SC 29407 USA Tel 843-814-4664
Web site: http://www.tamiboyce.com
Dist(s): **CreateSpace Independent Publishing Platform.**

Boyd Bks., *(978-0-692-18983-2; 978-1-7339390)* 7510 Burdette Way, Beltsville, MD 20705 USA Tel 215-983-6366
E-mail: melimunro.boyd@yahoo.com.

Boyd, Charlisa Dunning, *(978-0-692-96963-2)* 1421 Beacon Valley Dr., Raleigh, NC 27604 USA Tel 919-890-5773
E-mail: Charlisa.boyd@outlook.com.

Boyd, Melissa *See* **Boyd Bks.**

Boydell & Brewer, Inc., *(978-0-85115; 978-0-85991; 978-0-907239; 978-0-938100; 978-1-57113; 978-1-58046; 978-1-85566; 978-1-870252; 978-1-878822; 978-1-879751; 978-1-900639; 978-1-84384; 978-1-84383; 978-1-64014; 978-1-64825)* Div. of Boydell & Brewer Group, Ltd., Orders Addr.: 668 Mount Hope Ave., Rochester, NY 14620-2731 USA (SAN 013-8479) Tel 585-275-0419; Fax: 585-271-8778
E-mail: boydell@boydellusa.net; boydell@boydell.co.uk
Web site: http://www.boydellandbrewer.com
Dist(s): **Casemate Pubs. & Bk. Distributors, LLC**
Casemate Academic
MyiLibrary
ebrary, Inc.

Boyds Collection Ltd., The, *(978-0-9712840; 978-0-9713174)* 75 Cunningham Rd., Gettysburg, PA 17325-7142 USA
E-mail: alana@boydsstuff.com
Web site: http://www.boydsstuff.com.

Boyds Mills & Kane *See* **Astra Publishing Hse.**

Boyds Mills Pr., *(978-1-56397; 978-1-878093; 978-1-886910; 978-1-59078; 978-1-932425; 978-1-62091; 978-1-62979; 978-0-9961172; 978-0-9961173; 978-1-943283; 978-1-68238; 978-1-68329; 978-1-68437; 978-1-64472; 978-1-7922)* Div. of Highlights For Children, Inc., 815 Church St., Honesdale, PA 18431 USA (SAN 852-3177) Tel 570-251-4513; 570-251-4592 Toll Free: 800-490-5111 Admin line; 877-512-8366; 800-874-8817 Cust Svc Columbus, OH; *Imprints:* Wordsong (Wordsong); Calkins Creek (Calkins Creek); Front Street (FrtSt); Lemniscaat (Lemnisca); Highlights (Highlights)
E-mail: admin@boydsmillspress.com; marketing@boydsmillspress.com
Web site: http://www.boydsmillspress.com; http://www.wordsongpoetry.com; http://www.calkinscreekbooks.com; http://www.frontstreetbooks.com
Dist(s): **Children's Plus, Inc.**
Follett School Solutions
INscribe Digital
Lectorum Pubns., Inc.
Penguin Random Hse. Distribution
Penguin Random Hse. LLC
Perfection Learning Corp.
Ingram Academic
Two Rivers Distribution.

Boyle & Dalton *Imprint of* **Columbus Pr.**

Boynton, Colin (GBR) *(978-0-9559931) Dist. by* **LuluCom.**

Boys Read Bks., *(978-0-9801224)* 3211 NW 75th St., Seattle, WA 98117 USA Tel 206-321-5500
E-mail: john@boysread.org.

Boys Town, Nebraska Center, Public Service Division *See* **Boys Town Pr.**

Boys Town Pr., *(978-0-938510; 978-1-889322; 978-1-934490; 978-1-936734; 978-1-944882)* Div. of Father Flanagan's Boys' Home, 13603 Flanagan Blvd, Boys Town, NE 68010 USA (SAN 215-8477) Tel 531-355-1320; Fax: 531-355-1310; Toll Free: 800-282-6657
E-mail: btpress@boystown.org
Web site: http://www.boystownpress.org
Dist(s): **Brodart Co.**
Quality Bks., Inc.

bPlus Bks. *Imprint of* **Bumble Bee Publishing**

BPM Research LLC, *(978-0-9829224)* 939 Bloomfield St., Hoboken, NJ 07030 USA Tel 551-226-9372
E-mail: michael@bpm-research.com
Web site: http://www.bpm-research.com.

BPT Media, *(978-0-9772126)* P.O. Box 28663, Philadelphia, PA 19151-0663 USA
E-mail: vharris52@gmail.com.

BQB Publishing *Imprint of* **Boutique of Quality Books Publishing Co., Inc.**

Bradbury, Heidi, *(978-0-692-90149-6; 978-0-692-98968-5; 978-0-692-19591-8)* 2244 E. Ojai Ave., OJAI, CA 93023 USA Tel 805-701-4945
E-mail: heidi@heidibradburyfineart.com
Dist(s): **Ingram Content Group.**

Bradford, Elizabeth, *(978-0-692-18388-5)* 36 Bird Ln., Garrison, NY 10524 USA Tel 845-736-4029
E-mail: bradford.eliz11@gmail.com
Dist(s): **Ingram Content Group.**

Bradford Pr., Inc., *(978-0-9705618; 978-0-9801563)* Orders Addr.: P.O. Box 6802, South Bend, IN 46660-6802 USA Tel 574-876-3601; Fax: 574-255-9358 Do not confuse with companies with same name in Bradford, MA, Palm Beach, FL, Chicago, IL
E-mail: BradfordPress@comcast.net; Info@Bradford-Press.com
Web site: http://www.Bradford-Press.com.

Bradford-Franklin, *(978-0-9767676)* P.O. Box 495, Hartsville, TN 37074 USA Tel 615-374-3712; Fax: 615-374-4649
E-mail: bradfordfranklin@bellsouth.net
Web site: http://www.jackmccall.com.

Bradley, Judy & Assocs., LLC, *(978-0-615-57032-7)* 230 E. 45th St., Savannah, GA 31405 USA Tel 912-232-7636
E-mail: judybee58@gmail.com.

BradyBooks *See* **Nature Works Press**

Bradybooks.biz, *(978-0-9754169)* 1888 County Road 72., Bailey, CO 80421-2175 USA
E-mail: readbradybooks@aol.com
Web site: http://bradybooks.biz.

Braided Image, *(978-0-9725170)* 3064 Old New Cut Rd., Springfield, TN 37172 USA
E-mail: masterbraider@mindspring.com
Web site: http://www.braidedimage.com.

BrailleInk, *(978-0-9769313)* 1704 Holly St., Austin, TX 78702-5424 USA Toll Free: 800-324-2919
E-mail: info@brailleink.org
Web site: http://www.brailleink.org.

Brainbow Pr., *(978-0-9796715; 978-0-9825867)* 7914 N. Roundstone Dr., Tucson, AZ 85741 USA (SAN 854-0594) Tel 520-481-1919
E-mail: 19@19.org; edipyuksel@gmail.com; brainbowpress@gmail.com
Web site: http://www.brainbowpress.com; http://www.islamicreform.org; http://www.yuksel.org; http://www.19.org
Dist(s): **Ingram Content Group.**

BrainBox, Limited *See* **Gray Jay Bks.**

Brainchild Publishing *See* **Mindfull Publishing**

Brainerd Enterprises, *(978-0-9747441)* 419 Old Clyde Pk. Rd., Livingston, MT 59047 USA Tel 406-222-8273; Fax: 406-222-3769
E-mail: sally@heirofkingmeldh.com
Web site: http://www.heirofkingmeldh.com.

BrainFriendly Learning, *(978-0-9759226)* 6801 6th St., NW, Washington, DC 20012-1911 USA Tel 202-723-7337; Fax: 202-726-6117
E-mail: stevecarroll@speakeasy.net
Web site: http://www.kathleencarroll.com.

Brainiac Bloomers, LLC, *(978-1-948123)* 7155 Country Oaks Dr, Memphis, TN 38125 USA Tel 901-273-4202
E-mail: la@brainiacbloomers.com
Web site: brainiacbloomers.com.

Brainstorm Co., The, *(978-0-9728354)* Orders Addr.: 11684 Ventura Blvd., No. 970, Studio City, CA 91604 USA (SAN 255-5174) Tel 818-763-2674
E-mail: weddinggames@hotmail.com
Web site: http://www.TheBrainstormCompany.com
Dist(s): **Independent Pubs. Group.**

Brainstorm Pubns., Inc., *(978-0-9723429)* 24 NE 24th Ave., Pompano Beach, FL 33062 USA Tel 954-941-3329; Fax: 954-943-7708 Do not confuse with Brainstorm Publications in Lake Oswego, OR
E-mail: tditocco@brainstormpublications.com
Web site: http://www.brainstormpublications.com.

BrainStorm 3000, *(978-0-9651174)* P.O. Box 80513, Goleta, CA 93118 USA Tel 805-448-7149; 805-448-7149
Dist(s): **Educational Bk. Distributors.**

BrainStream, *(978-0-9785892)* 21307 Park Valley Dr., Katy, TX 77450-4811 USA
E-mail: bvogt@brainstream.com.

Braintext, Inc., *(978-0-9816270)* 3660 Wilshire Blvd. Ste. 400, Los Angeles, CA 90010-2753 USA
E-mail: info@braintext.com
Web site: http://www.braintext.com.

BrainX, Inc., *(978-0-9741604)* 45 Rincon Dr. Unit 1033B, Camarillo, CA 93012-8424 USA
E-mail: info@brainx.com
Web site: http://www.brainx.com
Dist(s): **Majors, J. A. Co.**
Rittenhouse Bk. Distributors.

Braley & Thompson, Inc., *(978-1-883239)* P.O. Box 1396, Saint Albans, WV 25177-1396 USA Tel 304-722-1704; Fax: 304-722-1709; Toll Free: 800-258-5453.

Bran Nue Productions, *(978-0-615-44662-2; 978-0-9851574)* 7878 LaSalle Ave. No. 231, Baton Rouge, LA 70806 USA Tel 225-678-6631
E-mail: brannuepro@gmail.com.

Branch Springs Publishing, *(978-0-9727622)* Orders Addr.: 500 Watts Dr., Huntsville, AL 35801 USA Tel 256 539 1064; Edit Addr.: 500 Watts Dr., Huntsville, AL 35801 USA
E-mail: fchap10220@aol.com.

Branching Plot Bks., *(978-0-9860166; 978-0-9891840)* 700 Sleater Kinney Rd SE Ste B-137, Lacey, WA 98503 USA Tel 800-454-8529
E-mail: arthurmills@branchingplotbooks.com
Web site: http://www.branchingplotbooks.com.

Brand New Happy moon Pub., *(978-0-692-19898-8)* 2332 Rambo Ct., Santa Clara, CA 95054 USA Tel 475-449-3971
E-mail: bnhm.publishing@gmail.com
Web site: http://www.brandnewhappymoonpublishing.com.

Brand, Shoshana, *(978-0-9978213)* 44633 31st St. W, Lancaster, CA 93536 USA Tel 818-217-6060; Fax: 818-217-6060
E-mail: creativerosh@gmail.com.

Branded Black Publishing, *(978-0-9746913)* P.O. Box 950781, Oklahoma City, OK 73195 USA Web site: http://www.ebonymarshal.com; http://www.brandedblackpublishing.com; http://www.gospelofthegun.com; http://www.seanchandler.com.

Branded Pros., *(978-0-578-19793-7; 978-0-578-57190-4)* 2040 S. Alma School Rd. #1-171, Chandler, AZ 85286 USA.

Brandeis Univ., Rose Art Museum, *(978-0-9726641; 978-0-9761593)* 415 South St., Waltham, MA 02254 USA (SAN 278-243X) Tel 781-736-3434; Fax: 781-736-3439 E-mail: tjking@brandeis.edu Web site: http://www.brandeis.edu/rose *Dist(s):* **D.A.P./Distributed Art Pubs.**

Branden Bks., *(978-0-8283)* Div. of Branden Publishing Co., P.O. Box 812094, Wellesley, MA 02482 USA (SAN 201-4106) Tel 781-235-3634; Fax: 781-790-1056 E-mail: branden@brandenbooks.com; danteu@danteuniversity.org Web site: http://www.brandenbooks.com; http://www.danteuniversity.org; http://www.adolphcaso.com *Dist(s):* **Brodart Co.**
Follett School Solutions
eBookit.com.

Brandrock Creative Co., The, *(978-0-692-13056-8; 978-0-578-59049-3)* 1034 Grider Dr., Gallatin, TN 37066 USA Tel 281-818-8188 E-mail: jwhit243@gmail.com.

Brandylane Pubs., Inc., *(978-0-9627635; 978-1-883911; 978-0-9838264; 978-0-9849588; 978-0-9859358; 978-1-939930; 978-1-947860; 978-1-951565; 978-1-953021)* Orders Addr.: 5 S. 1st St., Richmond, VA 23219-3716 USA; *Imprints:* Belle Isle Books (Belleisle) E-mail: rhpruett@brandylanepublishers.com Web site: http://www.brandylanepublishers.com *Dist(s):* **Baker & Taylor International**
Follett School Solutions
Ingram Content Group
Smashwords.

Brass in Color, *(978-1-7320252; 978-1-949670; 978-1-952680)* Orders Addr.: P.O. Box PO Box 5701, Bloomington IN, IN 47407 USA; Edit Addr.: PO Box 5701, Bloomington IN, IN 47407 USA; *Imprints:* Beginner Method Series (MYID_I_BEGINNE) E-mail: brassincolor@gmail.com Web site: www.brassincolor.com.

Brass, Robin Studio, Inc. (CAN) *(978-1-896941) Dist. by* **IPG Chicago.**

BrassHeart Music, *(978-0-9673762; 978-0-9721478; 978-0-9826278)* 256 S. Robertson Blvd., Suite 2288, Beverly Hills, CA 90211 USA Tel 323-932-0534; Fax: 323-937-6884; 323-933-4209; *Imprints:* Kid's Creative Classics (Kids Creative Classics); Dream A World (Dream A World) E-mail: bunny@dreamaworld.com; brassheartmusic@aol.com Web site: http://www.brassheartmusic.com; http://www.dreamaworld.com *Dist(s):* **DeVorss & Co.**
Music Design, Inc.
New Leaf Distributing Co., Inc.

Bratcher Publishing *Imprint of* **Write Place**

Braughler Bks. LLC, *(978-0-9822187; 978-0-9971375; 978-1-945091; 978-1-970063)* 251 W Central Ave No. 163, Springboro, OH 45066 USA Tel 937-582-6657 E-mail: david.braughler@braughlerbooks.com Web site: http://www.braughlerbooks.com.

Braun Pubns., *(978-0-9774302)* 150 Clinton Ln., Spring Valley, NY 10977 USA.

Brave Knight Media, LLC, *(978-0-9997141)* 13451 Columbine Cir, Thornton, CO 80241 USA Tel 508-667-0367 E-mail: peter@braveknightmedia.com Web site: braveknightmedia.com.

Brave Ulysses Bks., *(978-0-9700125; 978-0-615-16272-0; 978-0-615-18969-7; 978-0-615-22032-1; 978-0-615-26030-3)* P.O. Box 1877, Asheville, NC 28802 USA E-mail: cecil@braveulysses.com; info@braveulysses.com *Dist(s):* **Lulu Pr., Inc.**
Parnassus Bk. Distributors.

Braveheart Pr., LLC, *(978-0-9763935)* 23852 Pacific Coast Hwy., Suite 572, Malibu, CA 90265 USA Tel 310-770-7831; Fax: 310-456-5109 do not confuse with BraveHeart Press in Woodland Park, CO E-mail: showrunnerbrv@aol.com Web site: http://www.braveheartpressllc.com.

Braxton, Theresa, *(978-0-692-95780-6)* 1 Gloucester ct, GLYNDON, MD 21136 USA Tel 443-240-5948 E-mail: lilbraxton23@gmail.com *Dist(s):* **Ingram Content Group.**

Braziller, George Inc., *(978-0-8076)* 171 Madison Ave., Suite 1103, New York, NY 10016 USA (SAN 201-9310) Tel 212-889-0909; Fax: 212-689-5405 *Dist(s):* **Norton, W. W. & Co., Inc.**
Penguin Random Hse. Distribution
Penguin Random Hse. LLC.

Brazos Valley Pr., *(978-0-9726822)* Orders Addr.: P.O. Box 215, Calvert, TX 77837-0215 USA Tel 979-364-2439; Fax: 800-881-2032; Edit Addr.: 508 E. Texas, Calvert, TX 77837 USA (SAN 858-2947) E-mail: jkennedy@brazosvalleypress.com Web site: http://www.brazosvalleypress.com.

BRAZZLE, *(978-0-692-93528-6; 978-1-7324015)* 1777 LARIMER ST, Denver, CO 80202 USA Tel 303-888-6288; Fax: 303-888-6288 E-mail: jensalimi@yahoo.com.

Brda, Tracy, *(978-0-9742355)* P.O. Box 510065, Saint Louis, MO 63129 USA Tel 314-293-0015; Fax: 636-343-0564 E-mail: info@power-twins.com.

Bread & Butter Bks., *(978-0-9800816)* 229 E. Ct. St., Cincinnati, OH 45202 USA Tel 513-884-0468 E-mail: jkiddielit@cinci.rr.com.

Breadcrumbs LLC, *(978-0-692-85182-1; 978-0-692-94143-0; 978-0-692-14348-3; 978-0-578-64399-1)* 862 Longmeadow St., Longmeadow, MA 01106 USA Tel 413-567-8019 E-mail: cropsey@comcast.net.

Break-A-Leg Bks., *(978-0-9668522)* 12332 Laurel Terr., Studio City, CA 91604 USA Tel 818-508-5585; Fax: 818-752-0682.

Breakaway Bks., *(978-1-55821; 978-1-891369; 978-1-62124)* P.O. Box 24, Halcottsville, NY 12438 USA Tel 607-326-4805; Fax: 212-898-0408; Toll Free: 800-548-4348 (voicemail) Do not confuse with Breakaway Bks., Albany, TX E-mail: breakawaybooks@gmail.com Web site: http://www.breakawaybooks.com *Dist(s):* **Consortium Bk. Sales & Distribution.**

Breaking Cycles Bks., *(978-0-9741202)* Orders Addr.: P.O. Box 402, Severn, MD 21144-0402 USA Tel 410-519-6787 E-mail: BrCyBks@msn.com Web site: http://www.breaking-cycles-visions-of-hope.com.

Breaking the Barrier, Inc., *(978-0-9712817; 978-0-9728570; 978-0-9758573; 978-0-9777987; 978-0-9817961; 978-0-9846477; 978-0-9846490; 978-0-9903122; 978-0-9963192; 978-0-9976527)* 63 Shirley Rd., Groton, MA 01450 USA Fax: 978-448-1237; Toll Free: 866-862-7325 Do not confuse with Breaking the Barrier Ministry, Inc. in Pennsauken, NJ E-mail: info@tobreak.com; john@tobreak.com Web site: http://www.tobreak.com.

Breaklight Pubns., *(978-0-9974421)* 380 Red Bay Ln., Marco Island, FL 34145 USA Tel 516-680-4494 E-mail: dr.dolores.burton@gmail.com Web site: www.breaklightpublications.com.

Breakneck Bks. *Imprint of* **Variance Author Services**

Breakneck Books *See* **Breakneck Media**

Breakneck Media, *(978-0-9786551; 978-0-9796929; 978-0-9836017; 978-0-9840423; 978-0-9886725; 978-1-941539)* 20 Sampson Rd., Rochester, NH 03867 USA E-mail: info@jeremyrobinsononline.com Web site: http://www.jeremyrobinsononline.com.

Brealey, Nicholas Publishing, *(978-0-9839558; 978-1-941176)* 20 Park Plaza, Suite 1115A, Boston, MA 02116 USA *Dist(s):* **Consortium Bk. Sales & Distribution**
Hachette Bk. Group
MyiLibrary.

Breath & Shadows Productions, *(978-0-9720176; 978-0-9821029)* P.O. Box 10557, Tampa, FL 33679 USA Tel 813-251-8187 Web site: http://www.breathandshadows.com.

Breathless Vintage Enterprises, *(978-0-9842053)* Orders Addr.: PO Box 28168, Portland, OR 97228 USA (SAN 858-7221) E-mail: morgan@breathlessvintage.com.

Breckling Pr., *(978-0-9721218; 978-1-933308)* 283 Michigan Ave., Elmhurst, IL 60126 USA Web site: http://www.brecklingpress.com *Dist(s):* **Independent Pubs. Group.**

Bree's Gift Publishing, *(978-0-9748512)* 3840 Listerman Rd., Howell, MI 48855 USA Tel 517-552-9184 E-mail: kimmie67@sbcglobal.net.

Breezeway Books, *(978-1-62550)* 7101 W. Commercial Blvd. No. 4E, Tamarac, FL 33319 USA Tel 954-726-0902; Fax: 954-726-0903 E-mail: dgreenspan@llumina.com Web site: www.llumina.com.

Breezy Reads, *(978-0-9759784; 978-1-938327)* Orders Addr.: 2800 N Bogus Basin Rd APT C103, Boise, ID 83702 USA (SAN 256-3762) E-mail: breezyreads@gmail.com Web site: http://www.breezyreads.com.

Breezy Way Publishing *Imprint of* **Gatekeeper Pr.**

Bremer Press *See* **Zachmeyer, Mary L.**

Brenden, Sally, *(978-0-9898918; 978-0-9972957)* 831 2nd Ave. N., Sauk Rapids, MN 56379 USA Tel 320-250-5245 E-mail: brendenbooks@gmail.com Web site: brendenbooks.com.

BrenMar Communications, *(978-0-9903034)* 17313 Hialeah Dr., Odessa, FL 33556 USA Tel 813-920-9761 E-mail: authorbrendamartin@gmail.com Web site: http://www.brendamartin.net.

Brennan, Laura, *(978-1-7323846)* P.O. Box 4956, West Hills, CA 91308 USA Tel 818-264-8379 E-mail: Laura@LauraBrennanWrites.com.

Brennan, Matt, *(978-0-692-12587-8; 978-0-578-72366-2)* 1719 Grismer Ave. Apt. 11, BURBANK, CA 91504 USA Tel 818-469-5661 E-mail: mattarama.mb@gmail.com *Dist(s):* **Ingram Content Group.**

Brenneman, Lynette, *(978-0-9859737)* 260 Brenneman Rd., Lancaster, PA 17603 USA Tel 717-872-4815 E-mail: lleaman@verizon.net.

Brenner Publishing, LLC, *(978-0-9777203)* P.O. Box 584, Hicksville, NY 11802-0584 USA Tel 516-433-0804.

Brent Darnell International, *(978-0-9799258; 978-0-9836709; 978-0-9889330; 978-0-9862965; 978-0-9962646; 978-0-9970445; 978-1-946637)* 1940 The Exchange Suite 100, Atlanta, GA 30339 USA.

Brentwood Christian Pr. *Imprint of* **Brentwood Communications Group**

Brentwood Communications Group, *(978-0-916573; 978-1-55630; 978-1-59581)* 4000 Beallwood Ave., Columbus, GA 31904 USA (SAN 297-1895) Tel 706-576-5787 Toll Free: 800-334-8861; *Imprints:* Brentwood Christian Press (BrtwdChrist Pr) Do not confuse with Brentwood Communications Group in Vista, CA E-mail: brentwood@knology.net Web site: http://www.brentwoodbooks.com; http://www.brentwoodreview.com; http://www.newchristianbooks.com *Dist(s):* **Ingram Publisher Services.**

Brentwood Home Video, *(978-0-7378; 978-0-924739; 978-1-57119; 978-1-879902)* Div. of Brentwood Communications, Inc., 810 Lawrence Dr., Suite 100, Newbury Park, CA 91320 USA Toll Free: 888-335-0528 E-mail: brentcom@earthlink.net Web site: http://www.ssetsites.com/e-bci/default.htm *Dist(s):* **Follett School Solutions.**

Brentwood Kids Co. *Imprint of* **Brentwood Music, Inc.**

Brentwood Music, Inc., *(978-0-7601; 978-1-55897)* 2555 Meridian Blvd. Ste. 100, Franklin, TN 37067-6364 USA Toll Free: 800-333-9000 (audio & video orders); 800-846-7664 (book orders); *Imprints:* Brentwood Kids Company (Brentwood Kids) Web site: http://www.providentmusic.com *Dist(s):* **Appalachian Bible Co.**
Central South Christian Distribution
Leonard, Hal Corp.
New Day Christian Distributors Gifts, Inc.
Provident Music Distribution
Spring Arbor Distributors, Inc.

Brentwood Publishing Group *See* **Writing for the Lord Ministries**

Brentwood-Benson Music Publishing, *(978-1-59802; 978-0-9830602)* Orders Addr.: 101 Winners Cir., Brentwood, TN 37027 USA (SAN 256-9574) Toll Free: 800-846-7664 E-mail: sales@brentwoodbenson.com; jroher@brentwoodbenson.net Web site: http://www.brentwoodbenson.com *Dist(s):* **Leonard, Hal Corp.**

†Brethren Pr., *(978-0-87178)* Div. of Church of the Brethren, 1451 Dundee Ave., Elgin, IL 60120-1694 USA (SAN 201-9329) Tel 847-742-5100; 800-441-3712; Fax: 847-742-1407; Toll Free: 800-441-3712 E-mail: brethren_press_gb@brethren.org Web site: http://www.brethrenpress.com *Dist(s):* **Follett School Solutions**; *CIP.*

Brethren Revival Fellowship, *(978-0-9745027; 978-0-9777766; 978-0-9828895; 978-1-946688)* 26 United Zion Cir., Lititz, PA 17543-7956 USA Fax: 717-625-0511 E-mail: harpri@dejazzd.com; brf@brfwitness.org Web site: http://www.brfwitness.org.

Brewer Bear Bks., *(978-0-692-19549-9; 978-0-9600441)* 27 Pinewood Cir., Safety Harbor, FL 34695 USA Tel 352-514-1351 E-mail: caseyh181@gmail.com *Dist(s):* **CreateSpace Independent Publishing Platform.**

Brewer, Neil, *(978-0-9771807)* 5290 Cedar Way Dr., NE, Corydon, IN 47112 USA Tel 812-952-3482 E-mail: 8oclock@aye.net Web site: http://www.booksbybrewer.com *Dist(s):* **BookBaby.**

Brewer Technologies, *(978-0-9774748)* P.O. Box 141, Cornwall, PA 17016 USA Tel 717-228-1708; Fax: 717-228-1709; Toll Free: 877-449-2556 E-mail: nicholelmoore@comcast.net Web site: http://www.tonybrewer.com.

Brewer's Historical Publications *See* **Bear State Bks.**

Brewster Moon, *(978-0-9854423)* 13940 Cedar Rd. Suite 386, University Heights, OH 44118 USA Tel 216-408-1616 E-mail: tbrown@brewstermoon.com.

Brewster, Robert, *(978-0-615-37153-5)* 185 NE 4th Ave. Apt 317, Delray Beach, FL 33483 USA Tel 561-400-7799 *Dist(s):* **Outskirts Pr., Inc.**

Brian A. Griffen, *(978-0-578-42024-0)* 4021 Jefferson Woods Dr., Powhatan, VA 23139 USA Tel 804-598-3092 E-mail: brianagriffen@gmail.com *Dist(s):* **Ingram Content Group.**

Brian J. Publishing, Incorporated *See* **Holography Sells**

Briarcliffe Press *See* **Sunny Palms Pr.**

Brickey E-Publishing, *(978-0-9758964)* 1029E Salisbury St., Kernersville, NC 27284-3063 USA E-mail: mainoffice@brickey-epublishing.com Web site: http://www.brickey-epublishing.com.

BrickHouse Bks., Inc., *(978-0-932616; 978-1-935916; 978-1-938144)* 306 Suffolk Rd., Baltimore, MD 21218 USA (SAN 209-4622) Tel 410-235 7690 E-mail: charriss@towson.edu; clarindaharriss13@gmail.com Web site: http://www.brickhousebooks.com *Dist(s):* **INscribe Digital**
Itasca Bks.

BrickHouse Education *Imprint of* **Cambridge BrickHouse, Inc.**

Bridge Ink, *(978-0-9641963)* 32580 SW Arbor Lake Dr., Wilsonville, OR 97070-8471 USA E-mail: bob@bridgeink.com Web site: http://www.bridgeink.com *Dist(s):* **Far West Bk. Service**
Follett School Solutions
Partners/West Book Distributors.

Bridge Pubns., Inc., *(978-0-88404; 978-1-57318; 978-1-4031; 978-1-61177; 978-1-4572; 978-1-0789)* Orders Addr.: 5600 E. Olympic Blvd., Commerce, CA 90022 USA (SAN 208-3884) Tel 323-888-6200; Fax: 323-888-6210; Toll Free: 800-722-1733; 800-334-5433; Edit Addr.: 4751_Fountain Ave., Los Angeles, CA 90029 USA E-mail: annarnow@bridgepub.com; daniellem@bridgepub.com; donarnow@bridgepub.com; purchaser@bridgepub.com Web site: http://www.bridgepub.com; http://www.clearbodyclearmind.com; http://www.scientology.org; http://www.dianetics.org *Dist(s):* **Bookazine Co., Inc.**
Brodart Co.
Follett School Solutions
Landmark Audiobooks.

Bridge Publishing Group, *(978-0-9728439)* P.O. Box 1673, Walnut, CA 91788-1673 USA Tel 909-444-9088; Fax: 909-595-9526 E-mail: dafangzeng@yahoo.com.

Bridge To Life Ministries, Incorporated *See* **Advent Truth Ministries**

Bridge-Logos Foundation *See* **Bridge-Logos, Inc.**

Bridge-Logos, Inc., *(978-0-88270; 978-0-912106; 978-0-9841034; 978-1-61036)* Orders Addr.: 14260 W. Newberry Rd, Newberry, FL 32669 USA (SAN 253-5254) Tel 352-727-9324; Toll Free: 800-935-6467 (orders only); 800-631-5802 (orders only) E-mail: SWooldridge@bridgelogos.com Web site: http://www.bridgelogos.com *Dist(s):* **Anchor Distributors**
Destiny Image Pubs.
Send The Light Distribution LLC
Spring Arbor Distributors, Inc.
Whitaker Hse.

Bridges, Joseph (AUS) *(978-0-646-19404-2) Dist. by* **Carson Dellos.**

Bridges to Better Learning, *(978-0-9970558)* 3201 NE 183 St. Apt. 508, Aventura, FL 33160 USA Tel 954-849-1157; Fax: 305-682-0032 E-mail: dwander6@gmail.com.

Bridget Maloy Steber, *(978-0-578-45211-1)* 7790 Lake Blvd., Spanish Fort, AL 36527 USA Tel 251-979-5622 E-mail: steberb1@gmail.com *Dist(s):* **Ingram Content Group.**

Bridgeway Bks., *(978-1-933538; 978-1-934454)* Div. of BookPros, LLC, 2100 Kramer Ln., Suite 300, Austin, TX 78758 USA Tel 512-478-2028 Web site: http://www.bridgewaybooks.net.

BR:IEFing Assocs. of New England, *(978-0-9706105)* Orders Addr.: P.O. Box 3159, Kingston, NY 12402-3159 USA Tel 845-339-0998; Edit Addr.: 289 Fair St., Suite 2A, Kingston, NY 12401-3844 USA.

Briggs & Schuster, *(978-0-9835120; 978-1-7321916)* 520 Ashford Dr., Coppell, TX 75019 USA Tel 214-810-2443; Fax: 443-797-1909 E-mail: douglas@donascimento.com; nicoledonascimento@gmail.com Web site: http://www.bsa.im.

Briggs, Mark, *(978-1-7343345)* 10303 E.150th Ave, Brighton, CO 80602 USA Tel 817-798-4893 E-mail: mbriggswriting@gmail.com.

Briggs, Sharon, *(978-0-615-13051-4)* 109 Hope Way, Auburn, KY 42206 USA E-mail: sharondeneice109@yahoo.com.

Brigham Young Univ., *(978-0-8425)* 205 UPB, Provo, UT 84602 USA (SAN 201-9337) Tel 801-422-2809; Fax: 801-422-0591; *Imprints:* BYU Creative Works (BYUCreative) E-mail: diane_foerster@byu.edu Web site: http://www.upb.byu.edu *Dist(s):* **Brigham Young Univ. Print Services**
Chicago Distribution Ctr.
Follett School Solutions
Indiana Univ. Pr.
Univ. of Chicago Pr.

Brighid Publishing, *(978-0-9965974)* 20735 SW 90th Ave, Tualatin, OR 97062 USA Tel 503-691-0349 E-mail: abuenzli_pdx@hotmail.com Web site: http://skyegenaro.com.

Bright & Morning Star Bks., *(978-0-9986879)* 19506 Whitewood Dr., Spring, TX 77373 USA E-mail: sharon47@embarqmail.com.

Bright Cloud Publishing, *(978-0-9770727)* E-mail: brightcloud@verizon.net Web site: http://www.brightcloudpublishing.com.

Bright Connections Media, *(978-1-62267)* 233 N. Michigan Ave. Suite 2000, Chicago, IL 60601 USA Tel 312-729-5800 E-mail: orders@innlog.net Web site: www.brightconnectionsmedia.com *Dist(s):* **Continental Sales.**

Bright Eyes Pr., *(978-0-9728019)* 862 Congressional Rd., Simi Valley, CA 93065 USA Tel 805-579-0027 E-mail: kassie@kgraves.com Web site: http://www.brighteyespress.com.

Bright Hse. Publishing, LLC, *(978-0-9981891)* 1303 Clover Valley Way, Edgewood, MD 21040 USA Tel 443-819-8919 E-mail: yvannabright@gmail.com.

Bright Ideas! Educational Resources, *(978-1-892427)* P.O. Box 333, Cheswold, DE 19936 USA Toll Free: 877-492-8081 E-mail: hogan@inet.net.

BRIGHT IDEAS GRAPHICS, *(978-0-692-79823-2; 978-0-692-83463-3; 978-0-692-87847-7; 978-0-692-93004-5; 978-0-692-93084-7; 978-0-692-04911-2; 978-0-692-14946-1; 978-0-692-15729-9)* 1105 S. OLMSTED PARKWAY, MIDDLETOWN, DE 19709 USA Tel 609-481-7089.

Bright of America, *(978-1-930355)* 300 Greenbrier Rd., Summersville, WV 26651 USA Tel 304-872-3000; Fax: 304-872-3033; Toll Free: 800-917-2368.

Bright Sky Publishing *See* **Night Heron Media**

Bright Solutions for Dyslexia, LLC, *(978-0-9744343; 978-0-9755871)* 2059 Camden Ave., Suite 186, San

Publisher Name Index

Jose, CA 95124-2024 USA Tel 408-559-3652; Fax: 408-377-0503
E-mail: susan@brightsolutions.us
Web site: http://www.brightsolutions.us.

Bright Spots, (978-0-9769150) P.O. Box 3868, Rancho Santa Fe, CA 92067 USA Toll Free: 888-301-8880
E-mail: lmarneson@msn.com
Web site: http://www.brightspotsgames.com.

Bright Tyke Creations LLC, (978-0-615-33119-5; 978-0-615-63721-1) 217 Sassafras St., New Florence, PA 15944 USA
Web site: http://www.brighttykecreations.info.

BrightBerry Pr., (978-0-9720924) 4262 Kennebec Rd., Dixmont, ME 04932 USA Tel 207-234-4225
E-mail: jeanhay@brightberrypress.com; dbright@brightberrypress.com
Web site: http://www.brightberrypress.com
Dist(s): **CreateSpace Independent Publishing Platform.**

Bright-Brights Media Co., The, (978-0-9752553) 1059 Briar Ave., Provo, UT 84604 USA Tel 801-375-3455.

Brighter Child *Imprint of* **Carson-Dellosa Publishing, LLC**

Brighter Day Publishing, (978-0-615-26080-8; 978-0-9841855) P.O. Box 505, Washington Township, MI 48094 USA
Web site: http://www.publishinganswers.com.

Brighter Horizons Publishing, (978-1-929662) P.O. Box 448, Littleton, CO 80160 USA Tel 303-347-2904; Fax: 303-795-5951
E-mail: brighterhorizons@earthlink.net
Web site: http://home.earthlink.net/~brighterhorizons
Dist(s): **Book Wholesalers, Inc.**

Brighter Minds Children's Publishing, (978-1-57791) Div. of Brighter Child Interactive, LLC, 600 D Lakeview Plaza Blvd., Worthington, OH 43085 USA Tel 614-430-3021; Fax: 614-430-3152; *Imprints:* Little Melody Press (Little Melody Pr); Penny Candy Press (Penny Candy Pr)
E-mail: ranf@brightermindsmedia.com; books@Brightermindspublishing.com
Web site: http://www.brightermindspublishing.com
Dist(s): **Two Rivers Distribution.**

Brightline Publishing *See* **Rainbow Reach**

Brighton Publishing LLC, (978-1-936587; 978-1-62183) 501 W. Ray Rd. Suite No. 4, Chandler, AZ 85225 USA Tel 602-487-2964
E-mail: donald@brightonpublishing.com
Web site: brightonpublishing.com.

BrightPoint Pr. *Imprint of* **ReferencePoint Pr., Inc.**

BrightShadow Publishing, (978-0-9914513) 2131 Five Mile Line Rd., Penfield, NY 14526 USA Tel 585-764-3493
E-mail: penfieldartscenter@gmail.com.

Brightside Co., (978-0-9743720) 5040 S. Elmira St., Greenwood Village, CO 80111-3608 USA (SAN 255-5573) Tel 303-694-6065; Fax: 303-694-1009
E-mail: cynthiadormer@msn.com.

Brightwell Publishing, LLC, (978-0-9776033) 7151 Delmar Blvd., Saint Louis, MO 63130-4304 USA (SAN 257-7046) Tel 314-662-2736
E-mail: publisher@brightwellpublishing.net
Web site: http://www.brightwellpublishing.net; http://maryedwardswertsch.net.

Brikwoo Creative Group, (978-0-615-77571-5; 978-0-615-88374-8; 978-0-692-46476-2; 978-0-692-93834-8; 978-0-692-04738-5) 224 Poplar Ave., Trenton, GA 30752 USA Tel 423-618-9178
E-mail: brian@brikwoo.com
Web site: www.brikwoo.com.

Briley & Baxter Publications, (978-1-7331536; 978-1-7350168) 1 Chapel Hill Dr., Plymouth, MA 02360 USA Tel 781-389-7299
E-mail: stacy.ohalloran@brileybaxterbooks.com
Web site: brileybaxterbooks.com.

Brilliance Publishing *See* **Brilliance Publishing, Inc.**

Brilliance Publishing, Inc., (978-0-930435; 978-1-56100; 978-1-56740; 978-1-58788; 978-1-59086; 978-1-59355; 978-1-59600; 978-1-59710; 978-1-59737; 978-1-4233; 978-1-4418; 978-1-61106; 978-1-4558; 978-1-4692; 978-1-4805; 978-1-4915; 978-1-5012; 978-1-5113; 978-1-5226; 978-1-5318; 978-1-5366; 978-1-5436; 978-1-9786; 978-1-7213; 978-1-7997; 978-1-7135; 978-1-7136; 979-8-9850001) *Orders Addr.: P.O. Box 887, Grand Haven, MI 49417 USA (SAN 690-1395) Tel 616-846-5256; Fax: 616-846-0630; Toll Free: 800-648-2312 x330 (phone/fax, retail & library orders); Edit Addr.: 1704 Eaton Dr., Grand Haven, MI 49417 USA (SAN 858-138X) Toll Free: 800-648-2312 x330;* *Imprints:* Audible Studios on Brilliance Audio (AudibleStudios); Candlewick on Brilliance Audio (Candlewick)
E-mail: sales@brillianceaudio.com; customerservice@brillianceaudio.com; jcraig@brilliancepublishing.com
Web site: http://www.brilliancepublishing.com
Dist(s): **Bolinda Publishing, Inc.**
Bookazine Co., Inc.
Diamond Bk. Distributors
Findaway World, LLC
Follett School Solutions
Readerlink Distribution Services, LLC.

Brimax Books Ltd. (GBR) (978-0-86112; 978-0-900195; 978-0-904494; 978-1-85854; 978-1-904952; 978-1-905279; 978-1-84656) *Dist. by* **Byeway Bks.**

Brimming Cup, The, (978-0-9991525) 2266 Broadwater Dr., Jacksonville, FL 32225 USA Tel 904-707-7914
E-mail: brimmingcup@gmail.com
Web site: www.thebrimmingcup.com.

BriMoral Stories, (978-0-578-41528-4; 978-0-578-43173-4; 978-0-578-43530-5; 978-0-578-45825-0; 978-1-7332425; 978-1-953581) 1977 S. Saint Michael Dr., Tucson, AZ 85713 USA Tel 520-891-1149
E-mail: brian.determined.morales.8@gmail.com
Dist(s): **Ingram Content Group.**

Brimstone Fiction *Imprint of* **LPC**

BrimWood Pr., (978-0-9770704) 1941 Larsen Dr., Camino, CA 95709 USA Tel 530-644-7538; Fax: 530-647-9208; *Imprints:* Tools For Young Historians (Tools YngHist)
E-mail: marcia@brimwoodpress.com
Web site: http://www.brimwoodpress.com.

Brindle Pr., (978-0-9749080; 978-0-692-99148-0) 14121 Cardinal Ln., Houston, TX 77079 USA
Web site: http://www.brindlepress.com.

Brinkley Bks., Inc., (978-0-9793288) P.O. Box 1753, Healdsburg, CA 95448 USA
E-mail: laura@brinkleybooks.com
Web site: http://www.brinkleybooks.com
Dist(s): **BCH Fulfillment & Distribution.**

Brinsights, LLC, (978-0-9799454; 978-0-615-31228-6; 978-0-615-36380-6) 141 E. 88th St., New York, NY 10128-2248 USA (SAN 854-848X)
E-mail: geri@brinsights.net; linaperl@gmail.com
Web site: http://www.mygreensanta.com.

BRIO Pr., (978-0-9817830; 978-0-9819290; 978-0-9826687; 978-1-937061) 12 S. Sixth St., No.1250, Minneapolis, MN 55402 USA (SAN 856-5376) Tel 612-746-8800; Fax: 612-746-8811; Toll Free: 888-333-7979
E-mail: tmiller@briobooks.com
Web site: http://www.briobooks.com.

BRIO Publishing *See* **BRIO Pr.**

Briona Glen Publishing, LLC *See* **Grey Gate Media, LLC**

Briscoe, Nicole , (978-0-578-17838-7) 8302 Widgeon Place, Laurel, MD 20724 USA.

Brisk Pr., (978-0-9770885; 978-0-9799254; 978-0-9832758; 978-0-9899895; 978-0-9966774; 978-0-9987907; 978-1-7343038) 13 Chestnut Ct. Unit D, Brielle, NJ 08730-1371 USA
E-mail: brisk.press@gmail.com
Web site: http://www.briskpress.com
Dist(s): **Bella Distribution**
Two Rivers Distribution.

Bristol Hse., Ltd., (978-0-917851; 978-1-885224) P.O. Box 4020, Anderson, IN 46013 USA (SAN 225-4638) Tel 765-644-0856; Fax: 765-622-1045; Toll Free: 800-451-7323.

Bristol Publishing Co., (978-0-9755667) P.O. Box 3103, San Angelo, TX 76902-3103 USA Do not confuse with Bristal Publishing Company in San Jacinto, CA
E-mail: bristolpublishing@sbcglobal.net
Dist(s): **Alliance Bk. Co.**

Britannica Educational Publishing *Imprint of* **Rosen Publishing Group, Inc., The**

Brite Bks., (978-0-9726363) Orders Addr.: P.O. Box 801, Ortonville, MI 48462 USA; Edit Addr.: 1580 Duck Creek Ln., Ortonville, MI 48462 USA
E-mail: twebb@britebooks.org; twebb@tawglobal.com
Web site: http://www.britebooks.org; http://www.tawglobal.com; http://www.promises-for-life.com.

Brite International *See* **Brite Music, Inc.**

Brite Music, Inc., (978-0-944803) Orders Addr.: P.O. Box 65688-0688, Salt Lake City, UT 84165 USA (SAN 244-948X) Tel 801-263-9191; Fax: 801-263-9198; Edit Addr.: P.O. Box 171076, Salt Lake Cty, UT 84117-1076 USA (SAN 244-9498)
Web site: http://www.britemusic.com.

Brite Pr., (978-0-9743185) 3447 Countyline Rd., Chalfont, PA 18914-3625 USA Tel 215-822-1659; Fax: 305-402-8163
E-mail: tntdns@aol.com.

Britfield *Imprint of* **Devonfield**

British Library, Historical Print Editions *Imprint of* **Creative Media Partners, LLC**

British Library, The (GBR) (978-0-7123) *Dist. by* **IPG Chicago.**

Britt Allcroft Productions, (978-0-9743690; 978-0-9767139; 978-0-9793343) 133 Wadsworth Ave., Santa Monica, CA 90405 USA Tel 310-428-4033; Fax: 310 392 9769
E-mail: holly_wright@verizon.net
Web site: http://www.brittallcroftproductions.com.

Brittany's Bks, (978-0-9778796) 1736 Crest Pl., Colorado Spgs, CO 80911-1110 USA
E-mail: admin@brittanysbooks.com
Web site: http://www.brittanysbooks.com.

Britton & Case Prs., (978-0-9980066) 10871 S. Durand Rd, Durand, MI 48429 USA.

Broad Creek Pr., (978-0-9837148; 978-0-9904662) P.O. Box 43, Mount Airy, NC 27030 USA Tel 336-473-7256
Dist(s): **BookBaby.**

Broad View Publishing, (978-0-9815384) P.O. Box 2726, Bristol, CT 06011-2726 USA Tel 860-793-7618
E-mail: info@broadviewpublishing.com; publicity@painisnotadisease.com
Web site: http://www.broadviewpublishing.com; http://www.painisnotadisease.com.

Broadcast Quality Productions, Inc., (978-0-9716136) 3199 Nottaway Ct., Atlanta, GA 30341 USA Tel 404-292-7777 (phone/fax)
Web site: http://www.bqproductions.com.

Broader Horizon Books *See* **Littletonhouse Publishing**

Broadnax, Cassandra A.L., (978-0-9771608) 295 Pannel Rd., Reidsville, NC 27320 USA.

BroadStreet Publishing, (978-1-4245) Orders Addr.: 2745 Chicory Rd., Racine, WI 53403 USA (SAN 990-2635); Edit Addr.: 8646 Eagle Creek Cir. Suite 210, Savage, MN 55378 USA (SAN 256-8535) Tel 952-300-6250
E-mail: michelle.winger@broadstreetpublishing.com
Web site: http://www.BROADSTREETPUBLISHING.COM.

BroadSword Comics/ Jim Balent Studios, (978-0-9745367) P.O. Box 596, Brodheadsville, PA 18322 USA
E-mail: tarot@jimbalent.com
Web site: http://www.jimbalent.com.

Broadway Bks. *Imprint of* **Crown/Archetype**

Broadway Cares, (978-0-9754840) 165 W. 46th St., 13th Flr., New York, NY 10036 USA Tel 212-840-0770; Fax: 212-840-0551
E-mail: viola@bcefa.org.

Broadway Play Publishing, Inc., (978-0-88145) P.O. Box 1901, New York, NY 10021-0049 USA (SAN 260-1699)
E-mail: BroadwayPl@aol.com; bppi@broadwayplaypubl.com
Web site: http://www.BroadwayPlayPubl.com
Dist(s): **Follett School Solutions**
MyiLibrary.

Broccoli Bks. *Imprint of* **Broccoli International USA, Inc.**

Broccoli International USA, Inc., (978-1-932480; 978-1-59741) Orders Addr.: P.O. Box 66078, Los Angeles, CA 90066 USA Tel 310-815-0600; Fax: 310-815-0660; Edit Addr.: 11806 Gorham Ave. Apt. 4, Los Angeles, CA 90049-5446 USA; *Imprints:* Broccoli Books (Broccoli Bks)
E-mail: info@broccolibooks.com; ardith@bro-usa.com; wholesale@broccolibooks.com; books@animegamers.com; wholesale@bro-usa.com
Web site: http://www.bro-usa.com; http://www.broccolibooks.com; http://www.synch-point.com; http://www.boysenberrybooks.com
Dist(s): **Diamond Bk. Distributors**
Simon & Schuster, Inc.

Brockhaus, F. A., GmbH (DEU) (978-3-325; 978-3-7653) *Dist. by* **Intl Bk Import.**

Brodie, Richard *See* **Firebreak Publishing Co.**

Brogan, Kelly MD, (978-0-692-17060-1) 3975 Crawford Ave., Miami, FL 33133 USA Tel 646-418-4934
E-mail: drbrogan@kellybroganmd.com.

Broken Bread Publishing, (978-0-9769464) 6417 S. Iris Way, Littleton, CO 80123-3135 USA
E-mail: books@brokenbreadpublishing.com
Web site: http://www.brokenbreadpublishing.com
Dist(s): **Spring Arbor Distributors, Inc.**

Broken Leg Bks., (978-0-692-45627-9) 10021 Briley Way, Villa Park, CA 92861 USA Tel 1-714-872-7969
Dist(s): **CreateSpace Independent Publishing Platform.**

Broken Oak Publishing, (978-0-9795020) P.O. Box 255, Ridgetop, TN 37152 USA.

Broken Shackle Publishing, International, (978-0-9759908) P.O. Box 20312, Piedmont, CA 94620 USA
E-mail: jstickmon@msn.com.

Bromwell Bks., (978-0-9753345) 2500 E. Fourth Ave., Denver, CO 80206 USA Tel 303-388-5969; Fax: 303-764-7544
E-mail: steven_replogle@dpsk12.org
Web site: http://bromwell.dpsk12.org.

Bronwen Publishing, (978-0-9779267) 4 Colchester Pl., Suite 4A, Newtown, PA 18940 USA (SAN 850-6426) Tel 215-968-2204
Web site: http://www.bronwenpublishing.com
Dist(s): **Follett School Solutions.**

Bronwynn Pr., LLC, (978-0-9821404; 978-0-9848487) P.O. Box 297, Troy, NY 12182 USA Tel 518-328-7891
E-mail: bell@bronwynnpress.com
Web site: http://www.bronwynnpress.com; http://www.gappy.tv.

Bronx Originals Books *See* **Daylight Bks.**

Brook Farm Bks., (978-0-919761) 479 U.S. Hwy. 1, P.O. Box 246, Bridgewater, ME 04735 USA (SAN 133-9095) Tel 506-375-4680 (phone/fax); Toll Free: 877-375-4680
E-mail: jean@brookfarmbook.com; jean@brookfarmbooks.com
Dist(s): **Brodart Co.**
ebrary, Inc.

Brooke, Karen L., (978-0-692-35518-3; 978-0-692-35520-6; 978-0-692-38746-7; 978-0-692-57377-8; 978-0-692-59152-9; 978-0-692-62381-7; 978-0-692-81452-9; 978-0-692-94837-8; 978-0-692-95735-6; 978-0-578-45818-2; 978-0-578-53755-9) 214 Waterloo St., Warrenton, VA 20186 USA Tel 5402167969
Web site: http://katlynnbrooke.com/
Dist(s): **CreateSpace Independent Publishing Platform.**

BrookeBubble, (978-0-692-11628-9) 1310 W. Huron St., Ann Arbor, MI 48103 USA Tel 219-508-0352
E-mail: i.am.brandon.patterson@gmail.com
Web site: www.BrookeBubble.com.

Brookehaven Publishing, (978-0-9844867; 978-1-940905) P.O. Box 352, Rocklin, CA 95677 USA
E-mail: info@brookehavenpublishing.com
Web site: http://www.brookehavenpublishing.com
Dist(s): **Lulu Pr., Inc.**
Smashwords.

Brookes, Paul H. Publishing Company Incorporated *See* **Brookes Publishing**

Brookes Publishing, (978-0-933716; 978-1-55766; 978-1-59857; 978-1-68125) Orders Addr.: P.O. Box 10624, Baltimore, MD 21285-0624 USA (SAN 212-730X) Tel 410-337-9580; Fax: 410-337-8539; Toll Free: 800-638-3775 (customer service/ordering/billing/fulfillment); Edit Addr.: 409 Washington Ave., Suite 500, Baltimore, MD 21204 USA (SAN 666-6485)
E-mail: custserv@brookespublishing.com
Web site: http://www.brookespublishing.com
Dist(s): **Follett School Solutions.**

Brookfield Reader, Inc., The, (978-0-9660172; 978-1-930093) 137 Peyton Rd., Sterling, VA 20165-5605 USA (SAN 299-4445)
Dist(s): **Book Wholesalers, Inc.**
Brodart Co.
Quality Bks., Inc.

Brooklyn Botanic Garden, (978-0-945352; 978-1-889538) 1000 Washington Ave., Brooklyn, NY 11225-1099 USA (SAN 203-1094) Tel 718-623-7200; 718-625-5838; Fax: 718-622-7839; 718-857-2430
E-mail: ripodell@bbg.org
Web site: http://www.bbg.org
Dist(s): **Sterling Publishing Co., Inc.**

Brooklyn Pubs., (978-1-930961; 978-1-931000; 978-1-931805; 978-1-932404; 978-1-60003; 978-1-64479) Orders Addr.: P.O. Box 248, Cedar Rapids, IA 52406 USA
E-mail: orders@brookpub.com; customerservice@brookpub.com
Web site: http://https://www.brookpub.com
Dist(s): **Follett School Solutions.**

Brooklyn Publishing, (978-0-692-96601-3; 978-0-692-12500-7; 978-0-578-49099-1; 978-0-578-60438-1; 978-0-578-69347-7) 20510 Colonial Isle Dr., TAMPA, FL 33647 USA Tel 646-529-9300
E-mail: karlin@brooklynpublishing.com
Dist(s): **Ingram Content Group.**

Brooklyn Publishing Company *See* **Brooklyn Pubs.**

Brooks & Brooks, (978-0-9682530) 5510 Owensmouth Ave. Apt. 102, Woodland Hls, CA 91367-7011 USA
E-mail: runningbrooks@hotmail.com.

Brooks, Andree Aelion, (978-0-9702700) 15 Hitchcock Rd., Westport, CT 06880 USA Tel 203-226-9834; Fax: 203-226-0814
E-mail: andreebrooks@hotmail.com.

†Brooks/Cole, (978-0-12; 978-0-15; 978-0-314; 978-0-534; 978-0-8185; 978-1-56527; 978-0-495) Div. of Thomson Learning, Orders Addr.: 7625 Empire Dr., Florence, KY 41042-2978 USA Tel 606-525-2230; Toll Free: 800-354-9706 (orders); Edit Addr.: 511 Forest Lodge Rd., Pacific Grove, CA 93950 USA (SAN 202-3369) Tel 831-373-0728; Fax: 831-375-6414; 10 Davis Dr., Belmont, CA 94002 Tel 650-595-2350
E-mail: info@brookscole.com
Web site: http://www.brookscole.com; http://www.duxbury.com
Dist(s): **CENGAGE Learning**
Houghton Mifflin Harcourt Trade & Reference Pubs.; *CIP.*

Brooks/Cole Publishing Company *See* **Brooks/Cole**

Brookshire Pubns., Inc., (978-1-880976) 200 Hazel St., Lancaster, PA 17603 USA Tel 717-392-1321; Fax: 717-392-2078
E-mail: carla@brookshireprinting.com.

Brookteam Corp., (978-0-9745864) P.O. Box 276225, Boca Raton, FL 33427 USA Fax: 561-367-9976; Toll Free: 866-571-7878; *Imprints:* Shirt Tales (Shirt Tales)
E-mail: brookteam@worldnet.att.net
Web site: http://www.brookteam.com.

Broomstick Engine LLC, (978-0-692-82451-1) 850 Morning Sun Dr., Encinitas, CA 92024 USA Tel 604-671-5252
E-mail: spencer@broomstickengine.com
Web site: www.alittleradical.com.

Brophy, Doris Anne, (978-0-9745232) 90 Bingham Ave., Rumson, NJ 07760 USA Tel 732-345-7276
E-mail: dambrophy@yahoo.com.

Broqueville Publishing, Inc., (978-0-9669024; 978-0-9719413) 1260 Logan Ave., Suite B3, Costa Mesa, CA 92626 USA (SAN 255-0083) Tel 714-624-6441; Fax: 714-668-9972
E-mail: bookorders@broqueville.com
Web site: http://www.broqueville.com.

Brosen Bks., (978-0-9830359) 124 Wave, Laguna Beach, CA 92651 USA Tel 949-374-4127
E-mail: bryan@brosencreative.com
Web site: www.brosenbooks.com
Dist(s): **Follett School Solutions.**

Brosquil Edicions, S.L. (ESP) (978-84-95620; 978-84-96154; 978-84-9795) *Dist. by* **Lectorum Pubns.**

Bross Publishing, (978-0-9763561) 168 Island Pond Rd., No. 1, Manchester, NH 03109 USA (SAN 256-355X) Tel 603-623-2503 (phone/fax)
E-mail: brosspublishing@sunnyfla.us.

Brother Maynard Publishing, (978-0-615-55017-6; 978-0-578-40603-9) 6879 Blue Ridge Dr., Belmont, MI 49306 USA Do not confuse with Brother Maynard Publishing in Crystal River, FL
Dist(s): **CreateSpace Independent Publishing Platform**
Dummy Record Do Not USE!!!!.

BrotherBiz Publishing, (978-0-615-47658-2) 96 School St., Lexington, MA 02421 USA Tel 781-862-3962
E-mail: BrotherBiz@earthlink.net.

Brothers Epps, The, (978-0-578-42197-1; 978-1-7334189) 4844 Tanner Oaks Dr., Evans, GA 30809 USA Tel 434-489-7684
E-mail: info@thebrothersepps.com
Dist(s): **Independent Pub.**

Brothers N Publishing Corp., (978-0-9886272) 565 S. Mason Rd. No. 204, Katy, TX 77450 USA Tel 832-472-8200
E-mail: brothersnbooks@gmail.com.

Brotman-Marshfield Curriculums, (978-0-9762568) 22 Howard St., Newton, MA 02458 USA Tel 617-332-5616; Fax: 617-332-9679
E-mail: brotmanco@aol.com.

Broviak Publishing, (978-0-9897522) 10203 holly berry Cir., fishers, IN 46038 USA Tel 317-776-0421
E-mail: broviak@evilteacher.com.

Brown, Ana, (978-0-692-84467-0; 978-0-692-07004-8; 978-1-7320214) 868 Pk. View No. 5, Mountain view, CA 95054 USA Tel 305-772-0671; Fax: 305-772-0671
E-mail: anadvbrown@gmail.com.

Brown & Lowe Bks., (978-1-7322303; 978-1-7355048) 6564 Loisdale Ct No. 600, Springfield, VA 22150 USA (SAN 991-4943) Tel 703-408-0485
E-mail: denise@brownlowebooks.com; info@brownlowebooks.com
Web site: www.brownlowebooks.com.

Brown Barn Bks., *(978-0-9746481; 978-0-9768126; 978-0-9798824)* Div. of Pictures of Record, Inc., Orders Addr.: Editorial@brownbarnbooks.com 119 Kettle Creek Rd., Weston, CT 06883 USA Tel 203-227-3387; Fax: 203-222-9673
E-mail: editorial@brownbarnbooks.com
Web site: http://www.brownbarnbooks.com
Dist(s): **BookBaby**
Follett School Solutions.

Brown Bear Books, *(978-0-9670861)* 325 High St., Santa Cruz, CA 95060 USA Tel 831-457-1135
E-mail: brwnbear@sasquatch.com.

Brown Bear Bks., *(978-1-933834; 978-1-936333)* PMB 20, 6890 E. Sunrise Dr., Suite 120, Tucson, AZ 85750-0739 USA
E-mail: info@brownreference.com
Dist(s): **Black Rabbit Bks.**

Brown, Beatrice W, *(978-0-9983360)* 4664 Clifden Ave, Grovetown, GA 30813 USA Tel 706-350-5400
E-mail: beabrown2580@gmail.com.

Brown Bks. *Imprint of* **Olivo, Andy**

Brown, Bonnie M., *(978-0-9624705)* 548 Saint Johns Pl., Franklin, TN 37064-8901 USA
E-mail: bonnibear@aol.com.

Brown Books Publishing Group, *(978-0-9713265; 978-0-9744597; 978-0-9753907; 978-1-933285; 978-1-934812; 978-1-61254; 978-1-948307)* 16250 Knoll Trail Dr. Ste 205, Dallas, TX 75248 USA Tel 972-381-0009; Fax: 972-248-4336
E-mail: auburn.layman@brownbooks.com
Web site: http://www.brownbooks.com; http://www.thep3press.com
Dist(s): **BookBaby**
Follett School Solutions
Open Road Integrated Media, Inc.

Brown Books Small Press *See* **Small Pr., The**

Brown Brainy Brilliant Bks. *Imprint of* **InkDrops Publishing**

Brown County Historical Society, *(978-0-9765095; 978-0-9964029)* 2 N. Broadway, New Ulm, MN 56073 USA Fax: 507-354-1068 Do not confuse with Brown County Historical Society in Green Bay, WI
E-mail: director@browncountyhistorymn.org.

Brown County Historical Society, *(978-0-9641499)* Orders Addr.: P.O. Box 1411, Green Bay, WI 54305-1411 USA Tel 920-437-1840; Fax: 920-455-4518; Edit Addr.: 1008 S. Monroe Ave., Green Bay, WI 54301-3206 USA Do not confuse with Brown County Historical Society, Nashville, IN, New Ulm, MN
E-mail: bchs@netnet.net
Web site: http://www.browncohistoricalsoc.org.

Brown, David Book Company, The *See* **Casemate Academic**

Brown Dog Bks., *(978-0-9721967)* P.O. Box 2196, Flemington, NJ 08822 USA
E-mail: darhosta@mac.com
Web site: http://www.browndogbooks.com
Dist(s): **Book Wholesalers, Inc.**
Brodart Co.
Follett Media Distribution
Follett School Solutions.

Brown, Donald R., *(978-1-7326542)* 2345 185th Ct. Apt. 17, Lansing, IL 60438 USA Tel 708-953-2815
E-mail: Donnieb1087@gmail.com.

Brown Girls Bks., LLC, *(978-1-944359)* 107 Terrell Dr., Rolesville, NC 27571 USA Tel 919-909-8038
E-mail: jacquelinthomas@gmail.com
Dist(s): **INscribe Digital.**

Brown Girls Publishing *Imprint of* **INscribe Digital**

Brown, Harold *See* **Brown&Matthews**

Brown, Kathleen, *(978-0-9796063)* P.O. Box 1920, Clemmons, NC 27012 USA (SAN 853-8719) Tel 336-778-0699
E-mail: rbrown20221@bellsouth.net.

Brown, Kawani, *(978-0-9971763)* 1017 Chestnut ave., Long Beach, CA 90813 USA Tel 909-913-0260
E-mail: nahbexpo@gmail.com.

Brown, Keith, *(978-0-578-47285-0; 978-0-578-47852-4; 978-0-578-48877-6; 978-0-578-69989-9; 978-0-578-69990-5)* 24196 Andover, Dearborn Heights, MI 48125 USA Tel 313-418-6932
E-mail: keith@keithperrybrown.com
Dist(s): **Ingram Content Group.**

Brown, Linda P., *(978-0-9989128)* 481 Guilford Ave, Claremont CA, CA 91711 USA Tel 310-701-7409
E-mail: info@lindapbrown.com
Web site: lindapbrown.com.

Brown, Nielsen, *(978-0-9725581)* Orders Addr.: P.O. Box 4174 , Estes Park, CO 80517 USA
E-mail: kristinnielsen@msn.com.

Brown, P.C., *(978-0-578-52176-3; 978-0-578-23087-0)* 30 N Gould St Suite R, Sheridan, WY 82801 USA Tel 757-618-0712
E-mail: moonrisingauthor@gmail.com
Web site: http://pcbrownauthor.com.

Brown, Samuel E., *(978-0-9770372)* P.O. Box 7009, Jackson, MS 39282 USA Tel 601-540-5470
E-mail: pcsandc@hotmail.com.

Brown Spotted Dog Publishing, *(978-1-7321250)* 6327 N. 126th St., Enid, OK 73701 USA Tel 580-554-5995
E-mail: lbenkendorf@gmail.com.

Brown, William N. Jr., *(978-0-692-96477-4)* 8728 Potomac Blvd, Charlotte, NC 28216 USA Tel 704-779-8342; Fax: 704-779-8342
E-mail: wnbcreative@yahoo.com.

Brown&Matthews, *(978-0-9759370)* 2923 E. Michigan St., Orlando, FL 32806 USA (SAN 256-2030)
E-mail: jkmatthews@cfl.rr.com
Web site: http://www.cafepress.com/sitm; http://www.janetmatthews.com.

Brownell, F. & Son, Pubs., *(978-0-9767409; 978-0-9789127)* P.O. Box 76, Montezuma, IA 50171 USA
Web site: http://www.brownells.com.

Brownian Bee Pr., *(978-0-9789688)* 37574 Dew Drop Rd., Lanesboro, MN 55949 USA
E-mail: info@brownianbee.com
Web site: http://www.brownianbee.com
Dist(s): **Unique Bks., Inc.**

Brownstone Monkey Productions, Inc., *(978-0-9785773)* 55 W. 84th St., No. 9, New York, NY 10024-1002 USA Tel 212-933-4168; Fax: 212-228-6149
E-mail: nicole@brownstonemonkey.com; kfiore@nyc.rr.com
Web site: http://brownstonemonkey.com; http://lenithepug.com.

BRP Publishing Group, *(978-0-9801506; 978-1-935460; 978-1-941295)* P.O. Box 822674, Vancouver, WA 98682 USA
E-mail: publisher@nitisbooks.com; publisher@barkingrainpress.org
Web site: http://www.nitisbooks.com; http://www.barkingrainpress.org
Dist(s): **CreateSpace Independent Publishing Platform**
Ingram Content Group
Mackin Educational Resources
OverDrive, Inc.

Brujo Film Production *See* **Pascualina Producciones S.A.**

Bruno & Brown Pr., *(978-1-7321238)* 8949 Clairton Ct., Las Vegas, NV 89117 USA Tel 702-504-6354
E-mail: sunshinegbruno@gmail.com.

Bruno, Elizabeth *See* **Uitti, Daniel**

Brunson Publishing, *(978-0-9758614)* Orders Addr.: P.O. Box 1133, Alamogordo, NM 88310 USA Tel 706-367-1334
E-mail: oldmaid4jesus@yahoo.com; tim@teenpact.com
Web site: http://www.oldmaidministries.com; http://www.teenpact.com.

Brunswick Publishing Corp., *(978-0-931494; 978-1-55618)* 593 Southlake Blvd., Richmond, VA 23236-3092 USA (SAN 211-6332)
E-mail: brunswickbooks@verizon.net; info@brunswickbooks.com
Web site: http://www.brunswickbooks.com/.

Bruño, Editorial (ESP) *(978-84-216) Dist. by* **Dist Plaza Mayor.**

Bruño, Editorial (ESP) *(978-84-216) Dist. by* **Lectorum Pubns.**

Brush Creek Publishing, *(978-0-692-75888-5)* 6690 Little Galilee Rd., CLINTON, IL 61727 USA Tel 217-219-0323.

Bryan House Publishers, Incorporated *See* **ECS Learning Systems, Inc.**

Bryan, Tracy Publishing, *(978-0-692-70088-4; 978-0-692-70091-4; 978-0-692-71069-2; 978-0-692-81614-1; 978-0-692-83014-7; 978-0-692-83153-3; 978-0-578-41015-9; 978-0-578-41016-6; 978-0-578-41017-3)* 2886 rickenbacker trail, PORT ORANGE, FL 32128 USA Tel 386-299-5310.

Bryan-Kennedy Entertainment, LLC, *(978-0-615-34098-2; 978-0-615-34699-1; 978-0-9885358)* PO Box 1561, Santa Rosa Beach, FL 32459 USA Tel 615-405-9939
E-mail: mackennedy@mac.com
Web site: http://www.Bryan-Kennedy.com.

Bryars, Bart, *(978-0-692-82963-9)* 2521 Piedmont Rd. NE #2432, ATLANTA, GA 30324 USA Tel 917-251-0463
E-mail: jeffwcrawford5+LVP0003234@gmail.com; jeffwcrawford5+LVP0003234@gmail.com.

Bryce Cullen Publishing, *(978-1-935752)* 510 MONROE ST STE 201, HOBOKEN, NJ 07030 USA Tel 201-888-8570
E-mail: davidgettis@brycecullen.com
Web site: http://www.brycecullen.com
Dist(s): **Ingram Content Group.**

BRYN WILLIAMS LLC, *(978-0-9881814; 978-0-9909461)* Orders Addr.: 655 Orville Rd. E., Eatonville, WA 98328 USA
E-mail: cb@cbwilliams.us
Web site: www.cbwilliams.us.

Brynestad, Lea, *(978-0-692-10001-1)* 906 Sawyer Pl., Stillwater, MN 55082 USA Tel 651-275-1345
E-mail: dlbrynestad@gmail.com
Dist(s): **Ingram Content Group.**

Bryson Taylor Press *See* **Bryson Taylor Publishing**

Bryson Taylor Publishing, *(978-0-9773738; 978-0-9841934; 978-0-9882940; 978-0-9983867)* Div. of Bryson Taylor Inc., 199 New County Rd., Saco, ME 04072 USA (SAN 257-4403) Tel 207-838-2146
E-mail: deb@brysontaylor.com
Web site: http://www.brysontaylorpublishing.com.

Brzamo Publishing, *(978-0-9743580)* 887 Richart Ln., Greenwood, IN 46142 USA.

B'Squeak Productions, *(978-0-9746782)* P.O. Box 151, Menlo Park, CA 94026-0151 USA
E-mail: rights@bsqueak.com
Web site: http://www.bsqueak.com.

BTH CREATIONS, LLC, *(978-0-9995736)* 3539 MULBERRY WAY, Duluth, GA 30096 USA Tel 678-665-2225
E-mail: drkelahenry@gmail.com.

BTSena Pubns., *(978-0-692-20521-1; 978-0-692-78537-9; 978-0-692-79943-7; 978-0-692-90381-0; 978-0-692-91765-7)* 2703 N Northacres Dr., Hobbs, NM 88240 USA Tel 5754411649
Dist(s): **CreateSpace Independent Publishing Platform.**

B*tween Productions, Inc., *(978-0-9746587; 978-0-9758511; 978-1-933566)* 1666 Massachusetts Ave., Suite 17, Lexington, MA 02420 USA Tel 781-863-8228; Fax: 781-863-8338; *Imprints:* Beacon Street Girls (B Street Girls)
E-mail: kblais@btweenproductions.com
Web site: http://www.beaconstreetgirls.com.

BTWEYL *Imprint of* **Bks. That Will Enhance Your Life**

Bubble Gum Pr., *(978-0-9729833; 978-0-9839907)* 1420 N. State St., Aberdeen, SD 57401-2167 USA
E-mail: bmehrmantraut@msn.com
Web site: http://www.bubblegumpress.com
Dist(s): **Follett School Solutions.**

Buchbinder, Leonardo, *(978-0-9774044; 978-0-615-34717-2)* 8001 NW 84 Terr., Tamarac, FL 33321 USA Tel 954-261-9488
E-mail: mstenn5031@aol.com.

Bucher, Maryleigh, *(978-0-9908752)* 149 Whites Point Dr., Cookeville, TN 38506 USA Tel 931-349-0808
E-mail: mlkbucher@hotmail.com.

Buck Engineering Company, Incorporated, Lab-Volt Systems Division *See* **Lab-Volt Systems, Inc.**

Buck Publishing, *(978-0-9725912)* Orders Addr.: P.O. Box 12231, Roanoke, VA 24023-2231 USA Tel 540-985-0618 (phone/fax); Edit Addr.: 710 Ferdinand Ave., No. 9, Roanoke, VA 24016 USA Do not confuse with companies with the same or similar name in Birmingham, AL, Fairbanks, AK.

Buckbeech Studios, *(978-0-9771494)* Orders Addr.: P.O. Box 430, Stanford, IN 47463-0430 USA Tel 812-369-6061; Edit Addr.: 30 Amberwood Pkwy., Ashland, OH 44805 USA
E-mail: publisher@buckbeech.com
Web site: http://www.buckbeech.com
Dist(s): **Follett School Solutions.**

Bucket Fillers, Inc., *(978-0-9960999; 978-0-9974864; 978-1-945369)* P.O. Box 255, Brighton, MI 48116 USA Tel 810-229-5468; Fax: 810-588-6782
E-mail: info@bucketfillers101.com
Web site: http://www.bucketfillers101.com
Dist(s): **Independent Pubs. Group.**

Bucket Fillosophy *See* **Bucket Fillers, Inc.**

Bucket of Books *See* **Bimini Bks.**

Bucking Horse Bks., *(978-0-9844460; 978-1-7328753)* P.O. Box 8507, Missoula, MT 59807 USA
E-mail: collard@bigsky.net
Web site: http://www.buckinghorsebooks.com
Dist(s): **Mountain Pr. Publishing Co., Inc.**

Buckley, Barbara, *(978-0-692-89591-7; 978-0-578-74166-6)* 3416 Pebble Beach Dr., LAKE WORTH, FL 33467 USA Tel 561-868-5699
E-mail: babfla@aol.com
Dist(s): **Ingram Content Group.**

Bucknell Univ. Pr., *(978-0-8387; 978-1-68448)* 6 Taylor Hall, Lewisburg, PA 17837 USA
E-mail: esm102@rutgers.edu
Web site: http://www.bucjnell.edu/UniversityPress
Dist(s): **Associated Univ. Presses**
Baker & Taylor International
Chicago Distribution Ctr.
MyiLibrary
Rowman & Littlefield Publishers, Inc.
Rutgers Univ. Pr.
TextStream
ebrary, Inc.

Bucks Enterprises — Services and Training Inc., *(978-0-692-62430-2; 978-0-692-70595-7; 978-0-692-82321-7; 978-0-692-88137-8; 978-0-692-88658-8; 978-0-692-92634-5; 978-0-578-51066-8)* 90444 Cty. Rd. H, Mitchell, NE 69357 USA Tel 308-641-4835; Toll Free: 308-641-4835
Dist(s): **CreateSpace Independent Publishing Platform.**

Buddha Baby Bks., *(978-0-9968660)* 113 Norfolk Ave SW No. 8, Roanoke, VA 24011 USA Tel 919-536-8715
E-mail: buddhababybooks@gmail.com.

Buddha's Light Publications USA Corp, *(978-0-9715612; 978-0-9717495; 978-1-932293; 978-1-939596)* 3456 S. Glenmark Dr., Hacienda Heights, CA 91745 USA Tel 626-961-9697; 84 Margaret St., London, w1w 8td Tel 020-7636-8394; Fax: 020-7580-6220
E-mail: blpusacorp@gmail.com
Web site: http://www.blpusa.com
Dist(s): **Follett School Solutions.**

Buddha's Light Publishing *See* **Buddha's Light Publications USA Corp**

Buddhi Pubns., *(978-0-9644226)* Orders Addr.: P.O. Box 208, Canyon, CA 94516 USA Tel 510-376-7796; Fax: 510-376-3503; Edit Addr.: 35 Pinehurst Rd., Canyon, CA 94516 USA.

Buddhist Text Translation Society, *(978-0-88139; 978-0-917512; 978-1-60103; 978-0-88139-767-3; 978-1-64217)* Affil. of Dharma Realm Buddhist Assoc., Orders Addr.: 4951 Bodhi Way, Ukiah, CA 95482 USA Tel 707-462-0939; Fax: 707-462-0949; Edit Addr.: 4951 Bodhi Way,, Ukiah, CA 95482 USA (SAN 281-3556) Tel 707-463-4977 (phone/fax)
E-mail: vajrawheel@gmail.com; heng.yin@drbu.edu; bttsonline@snetworking.com; jinjingshih@gmail.com; katherine.lam-hansard@drba.org
Web site: http://www.bttsonline.org; http://buddhisttexts.org
Dist(s): **Follett School Solutions.**

Buddies Publishing, LLC, *(978-1-946719)* 37263 Charter Oaks Blvd., Clinton Township, MI 48036 USA Tel 586-855-6400
E-mail: philpirkola@gmail.com
Web site: http://www.buddiespublishing.com.

Budding Artists, Inc., *(978-1-888108)* 222 Palisades Ave., Santa Monica, CA 90402-2734 USA.

Budding Biologist, *(978-0-9855481)* 2939 NE 11TH Terr., Gainesville, FL 32609 USA Tel 919-621-5725
E-mail: kcallis@ufl.edu
Dist(s): **Independent Pubs. Group.**

Budding Family Publishing, *(978-0-9741882)* P.O. Box 2078, Manhattan Beach, CA 90267-2078 USA Fax: 310-374-1030
E-mail: renee@buddingfamily.com
Web site: http://www.buddingfamily.com.

BuddingRose Pubns., *(978-0-9915556)* 15061 Calle Verano, Chino Hills, CA 91709 USA Tel 909-636-3448
E-mail: buddingrose.publications@gmail.com.

Buddy Bks. *Imprint of* **ABDO Publishing Co.**

Buddy Bks. Publishing, *(978-0-9799980; 978-1-934887)* P.O. Box 3354, Pinehurst, NC 28374 USA Tel 910-295-2876
E-mail: admin@buddybookspublishing.com
Web site: http://www.buddybookspublishing.com.

Buenaventura Pr., *(978-0-9766848; 978-0-9800039; 978-1-935443)* P.O. Box 23661, Oakland, CA 94623 USA
Web site: http://www.buenaventurapress.com
Dist(s): **D.A.P./Distributed Art Pubs.**

Buffalo Arts Publishing, *(978-0-9839170; 978-0-615-93179-1; 978-0-692-38985-0; 978-0-692-43404-8; 978-0-692-46782-4; 978-0-692-53862-3; 978-0-692-72347-0; 978-0-9978741; 978-1-950006)* 179 Greenfield Dr., Tonawanda, NY 14150 USA Tel 716-692-1042
E-mail: lkagelmacher@gmail.com; sales@buffaloartspublishing.com
Web site: http://www.buffaloartspublishing.com.

Buffalo Fine Arts Academy *See* **Buffalo Fine Arts/Albright-Knox Art Gallery**

†Buffalo Fine Arts/Albright-Knox Art Gallery, *(978-0-914782; 978-1-887457)* Albright-Knox Art Gallery, 1285 Elmwood Ave., Buffalo, NY 14222 USA (SAN 202-4845) Tel 716-882-8700; Fax: 716-882-1958
Dist(s): **D.A.P./Distributed Art Pubs.**; *CIP.*

Bug Boy Bks., *(978-0-615-19036-5)* 2085 Kenneth St., Burton, MI 48529 USA
E-mail: nativeamericanandrew@yahoo.com; andrew@bugboyandy.com
Dist(s): **Lulu Pr., Inc.**

Bug Boy Publishing *See* **Bug Boy Bks.**

Bug Rhymes Bks., *(978-0-9845687)* P.O. Box 211, East Olympia, WA 98540 USA
E-mail: bugrhymesbooks@comcast.net
Web site: http://bugrhymesbooks.com
Dist(s): **Partners/West Book Distributors.**

BugaBk. llc, *(978-0-9888974)* 7667 Cahill Rd. Suite 100, Edina, MN 55439 USA Tel 952-943-1441
E-mail: dustinh@bugabook.com
Web site: www.bugabook.com.

BugBear Bks., *(978-0-9978669)* 2203 E 51st Ln, Spokane, WA 99223 USA Tel 206-240-9961
E-mail: guypace@me.com
Web site: guypace.com.

Bugeye Bks., *(978-0-9722249)* 10645 N. Tatum Blvd., Suite 200-246, Phoenix, AZ 85028 USA Tel 602-980-7101; Fax: 480-483-3460
E-mail: insightstudios@cox.net
Web site: http://www.bugeyebooks.com.

Buggs Books *See* **Mogul Comics**

Buhman, Ron, *(978-0-9747961)* Orders Addr.: ., Aransas Pass, TX 78335 USA; Edit Addr.: P.O. Box P O Box 634, Aransas Pass, TX 78335 USA Tel 361-944-0671; Fax: 361-944-0671
E-mail: rkb919@juno.com
Web site: http://jam-packed-action.com.

Buie, Alphonso, *(978-0-692-09788-5; 978-1-7342183)* 42426 S. Marsuerite Way, Lancaster, CA 93536 USA Tel 573-353-0279
E-mail: alphonsoabuie@gmail.com.

Build Your Story, *(978-0-9748416)* Orders Addr.: P.O. Box 6003, Midlothian, VA 23112 USA Fax: 810-592-2479; Toll Free: 866-807-8679; Edit Addr.: 2212 Water Horse Ct., Midlothian, VA 23112 USA
E-mail: oscar@buildyourstory.com
Web site: http://www.buildyourstory.com.

Builders' Stone Publishing, LLC, *(978-0-9791504)* 6932 Sylvan Woods Dr., Sanford, FL 32771 USA (SAN 852-5994) Tel 407-549-5066
E-mail: pschoemann@broadandcassel.com
Web site: http://www.buildersstonepublishing.com.

Building Blocks, LLC, *(978-0-943452)* 38 W. 567 Brindlewood Ln., Elgin, IL 60123 USA (SAN 240-6063) Tel 847-742-1013; Fax: 847-742-1054 (orders); Toll Free: 800-233-2448 Do not confuse with companies with similar and same name in Madison,NJ, Westbury NY
E-mail: dick@bblocksonline.com
Web site: http://www.bblocksonline.com
Dist(s): **Gryphon Hse., Inc.**

Bukowski, Katie Lynn, *(978-0-692-97225-0; 978-0-692-98878-7; 978-0-692-07032-1; 978-0-692-15675-9)* 261 S Walnut St, Manteno, IL 60950 USA Tel 815-953-5073
E-mail: katie_bukowski@yahoo.com
Dist(s): **Ingram Content Group.**

Bulfinch *Imprint of* **Little Brown & Co.**

Bull & Brain Creative, *(978-1-7341119)* P.O. Box 507, Erie, CO 80516 USA Tel 206-779-6957
E-mail: seancarney@gmail.com
Web site: wedivided.us.

Bull, David Publishing, Inc., *(978-0-9649722; 978-1-893618; 978-1-935007)* 4250 E. Camelback Rd., Suite K150, Phoenix, AZ 85018 USA Tel 602-852-9500; Fax: 602-852-9503; Toll Free: 800-831-1758
E-mail: dbull@bullpublishing.com; info@bullpublishing.com; tmoore@bullpublishing.com
Web site: http://www.bullpublishing.com.

Bullard, Belinda *See* **A Blessed Heritage Educational Resources**

Bulldog Pr., *(978-0-9672710)* P.O. Box 620358, Woodside, CA 94062-0358 USA Tel 650-851-8218; Fax:

Publisher Name Index

650-851-1753 Do not confuse with companies with the same name in Frankfort, IN, Whittier, CA
E-mail: dputnam555@aol.com
Web site: http://www.americanbulldogger.com.

Bullfrog Bks. *Imprint of* **Jump! Inc.**

BullsEye, LLC *See* **Hargrave Pr.**

Bumble Bee Bks., *(978-0-9914701)* 1804 Benodot St., Champaign, IL 61822 USA Tel 217-898-7835
E-mail: storytym@comcast.net.

Bumble Bee Publishing, *(978-0-9754342; 978-1-933982)* Div. of Bumble Bee Productions, Inc., Orders Addr.: 725 Watch Island Reach, Chesapeake, VA 23320 USA (SAN 256-1611) Tel 757-410-9409 (phone/fax); Toll Free: 866-782-9533 (phone/fax); Edit Addr.: P.O. Box 1757, Chesapeake, VA 23327-1757 USA (SAN 256-162X) Tel 747-410-9409; 5721 M St., Lincoln, NE 68510 (SAN 256-1638); *Imprints:* bPlus Books (bPlus Bks)
E-mail: buzz707@bbpmail.com
Web site: http://www.yesterdaywehadahurricane.com; http://www.bumblebeepublishing.com; http://www.rubyleethebumblebee.com; http://www.bumblebeeproductions.com; http://www.bplusbooks.com.

Bumples, *(978-0-9700952)* 676 Post Rd., Darien, CT 06820-4717 USA
E-mail: bumples@aol.com; Bumples@aol.com.

Bumpy Pumpkin, *(978-0-9754696)* 3405 Heather Dr., Augusta, GA 30909 USA
Web site: http://www.bumpypumpkin.com.

Bundoran Pr. (CAN) *(978-0-9782052; 978-0-9877352; 978-1-927881; 978-0-9880674) Dist. by* **D C D.**

Bunim and Bannigan Ltd., *(978-1-933480)* PMB 157, 111 E. 14th St., New York, NY 10003-4103 USA
Web site: http://www.bunim&bannigan.com; http://www.bunimbannigan.com
Dist(s): **Itasca Bks.**

Bunker Hill Publishing, Inc., *(978-1-59373)* 285 River Rd., Piermont, NH 03779-3009 USA; 27 W. 20th St., New York, NY 10011
E-mail: mail@bunkerhillpublishing.com
Web site: http://www.bunkerhillpublishing.com
Dist(s): **Follett School Solutions**
Independent Pubs. Group
Midpoint Trade Bks., Inc.

Bunny & The Crocodile Pr., The, *(978-0-938572)* 1821 Glade Ct., Annapolis, MD 21403-1945 USA Tel 410-267-7432 (phone/fax); *Imprints:* Forest Woods Media Productions (Forest Woods Media)
E-mail: gracecav@comcast.net
Web site: http://www.members.aol.com/grace7623/grace.htm.

Bunnyone Bks., *(978-0-692-11454-4; 978-0-578-41518-5)* 48 Boclair rd, Grenada, MS 38901 USA Tel 662-614-0309
E-mail: Janiehouston51@gmail.com.

Bunster, Alejandra, *(978-0-692-40506-2; 978-0-692-73515-2; 978-0-692-19115-6)* 254 San Sebastian Ave., Coral Gables, FL 33134 USA Tel 305-446-5673
E-mail: abunster@carrollton.org.

Bunt, Stephanie, *(978-0-692-08504-2; 978-1-948863)* 4454 Vista Del Monte No. 5, Sherman Oaks, CA 91403 USA Tel 310-592-9844
E-mail: stephanie_bunt@yahoo.com
Dist(s): **Ingram Content Group.**

Buo Books LLC. *See* **Buño Bks. LLC.**

Buño Bks. LLC., *(978-1-7331687)* 815 Thermal View Dr, Tryon, NC 28782 USA Tel 864-607-0038
E-mail: Optimum.perf@gmail.com
Web site: Bunobooks.com
Dist(s): **Consortium Bk. Sales & Distribution.**

Burden-Evans, Patricia, *(978-0-615-15120-5)* 1814 Palmyra Dr., Greenville, MS 38701 USA
E-mail: pevan6@aol.com
Dist(s): **Lulu Pr., Inc.**

BurgYoung Publishing, *(978-0-9716511)* 4105 E. Florida Ave., No. 300, Denver, CO 80222 USA Tel 303-757-5406
E-mail: tmcco@msn.com; infoby@burgyoungpublishing.com
Web site: http://www.burgyoungpublishing.com; http://www.gettingtoknowgod.com.

Buried Treasure Publishing, *(978-0-9800993; 978-0-615-14018-6)* 2813 NW Westbrooke Cir., Blue Springs, MO 64015 USA
E-mail: sales@buriedtreasurepublishing.com; duaneporter@yahoo.com
Web site: http://buriedtreasurepublishing.com
Dist(s): **Lulu Pr., Inc.**

Burkhardt The Artist, *(978-0-9762996)* P.O. Box 35, Alexandria, KY 41001 USA Tel 859-694-6000
E-mail: rockyburk@hotmail.com
Web site: http://www.rockyburkhardt.com.

Burkhart Bks. *Imprint of* **Taylor, Tim P.**

Burkhart Bks., *(978-0-9790975)* 4000 N. Meridian St., Suite 17G, Indianapolis, IN 46208 USA (SAN 852-4270)
E-mail: l.burkhart@sbcglobal.net
Web site: http://www.burkhartnetwork.com
Dist(s): **Distributors, The**
Partners Bk. Distributing, Inc.

Burleigh Dodds Science Publishing Ltd. (GBR) *(978-1-78676) Dist. by* **IngramPubServ.**

Burley Creek Studio *See* **White Dog Studio**

Burlington, David, *(978-0-9772136)* 16723 Basin Oak., San Antonio, TX 78247-6220 USA
E-mail: dave@bassfishingaskdave.com
Web site: http://www.bassfishingaskdave.com.

Burlington National, Inc., *(978-1-57706)* Orders Addr.: P.O. Box 841, Mandeville, LA 70470 USA Tel 504-250-7228; Edit Addr.: 6301 Perrier, New Orleans, LA 70118 USA
E-mail: books@burlingtonnational.com.

Burman Books, Inc. (CAN) *(978-0-9736632; 978-0-9737166; 978-0-9739097; 978-1-897404; 978-0-9781380; 978-1-927005) Dist. by* **InnovativeLog.**

Burnett Young Books, *(978-1-64071)* P.O. Box 1, Clarklake, MI 49234 USA Tel 330-651-1604
E-mail: cyleyoung61@yahoo.com
Web site: www.burnettyoungbooks.com.

Burney Enterprises Unlimited, *(978-0-9745360)* P.O. Box 401402, Redford, MI 48240-9402 USA.

BurnhillWolf, *(978-0-9645655)* 321 Prospect St., NW, Lenoir, NC 28645 USA Tel 704-754-0287
E-mail: Burnwolf@charter.net
Web site: http://www.burnhillwolf.com
Dist(s): **CreateSpace Independent Publishing Platform.**

Burning Bush Creation, *(978-0-9768680; 978-1-60390)* 2114 Queen Ave. N., Minneapolis, MN 55411-2435 USA Tel 612-529-0198; Fax: 612-529-0199
E-mail: ron@mcconico.com
Web site: http://www.burningbushcreation.com.

Burns, Hazlette H., *(978-0-692-10725-6)* 5 WHITE BIRCH Ln., Pinehurst, NC 28374 USA Tel 704-322-0969
E-mail: hazburns@yahoo.com
Dist(s): **Ingram Content Group.**

Burns, Phillys, *(978-0-9620065)* 7450 Olivetas Ave., No. 230, La Jolla, CA 92037 USA (SAN 247-526X).

BurnsBooks, *(978-0-9726099)* 50 Joe's Hill Rd., Danbury, CT 06811 USA Tel 203-744-0232
E-mail: burnsbookspub@aol.com
Web site: http://www.burnsbookspublishing.com.

Burt Creations *See* **Burt, Steven E.**

Burt, Steven E., *(978-0-9649283; 978-0-9741407; 978-0-9856188)* Orders Addr.: 17101 SE. 94th Berrien Ct., The Villages, FL 32162 USA (SAN 253-925X) Tel 352-391-8293
E-mail: passtev@aol.com
Web site: http://www.SteveBurtBooks.com.

Burton, Kenneth Hugh, *(978-0-9747043)* Orders Addr.: P.O. Box 38142, Atlanta, GA 30334 USA Tel 404-799-1908; Edit Addr.: 406 Collier Ridge Dr. NW, Atlanta, GA 30318-7312 USA
E-mail: notrub18@bellsouth.net.

Bury Your Inner Weapons Publishing Co., *(978-0-692-13367-5; 978-0-692-13810-6)* 5355 Tartan Hill Ave, LAS VEGAS, NV 89141 USA Tel 321-298-2212
E-mail: stewartmarriott@gmail.com
Web site: www.buryyourinnerweapons4peace.com
Dist(s): **CreateSpace Independent Publishing Platform**
Ingram Content Group.

Busch, Melinda K., *(978-0-692-99192-3)* 8724 Avalon St., Rancho Cucamonga, CA 91701 USA Tel 909-319-0962
E-mail: melikay.busch@gmail.com
Dist(s): **Ingram Content Group.**

Buscher, Julie W., *(978-0-9786352)* Orders Addr.: P.O. Box 627, Brighton, CO 80601-0627 USA (SAN 851-1802) Tel 303-659-7354
E-mail: julobush2@q.com
Web site: http://www.homerthehelicopter.com.

Bush, Bill *See* **Bush Publishing Inc.**

Bush Brothers & Co., *(978-0-9779308)* 1016 E. Weisgarber Rd., Knoxville, TN 37909-2683 USA.

Bush Publishing Inc., *(978-0-9723102; 978-0-9778728; 978-0-9798113; 978-0-9824391; 978-0-9836109)* 5427 S. 94th E. Ave., Tulsa, OK 74104 USA
Web site: http://www.bushpublishing.com.

Bushel & Peck Bks., *(978-1-7336335; 978-1-952239)* 7675 N First St, Apt 206, Fresno, CA 93720 USA Tel 717-318-5003; *Imprints:* You Are Here Books (URHereBks)
E-mail: bushelandpeckbooks@gmail.com
Web site: https://bushelandpeckbooks.com/
Dist(s): **Baker & Taylor Publisher Services (BTPS).**

Bushweller, Ellie, *(978-0-615-24478-5)* 9 Worth St., South Burlington, VT 05403 USA
Dist(s): **Lulu Pr., Inc.**

Business Angel Pr., *(978-0-9798909)* 174 W. Foothill Blvd., No. 327, Monrovia, CA 91016 USA (SAN 854-6738) Tel 626-357-1922; Fax: 818-475-1474; Toll Free: 800-705-6545
E-mail: contact@businessangelpress.com
Web site: http://www.businessangelpress.com.

Business Bks. International, *(978-0-916673)* P.O. Box 1587, New Canaan, CT 06840 USA (SAN 297-1860) Tel 203-966-9645; Fax: 203-966-6018
E-mail: lesdv@businessbooksusa.com
Web site: http://www.businessbooksusa.com.

Business Bks., LLC, *(978-0-9723714)* 2709 Washington Ave., 21A, Evansville, IN 47714 USA
E-mail: mbussingbu@aol.com
Web site: http://www.bussinessbooksllc.com.

Business Jobs *See* **Alexie Bks.**

Business Plus *Imprint of* **Grand Central Publishing**

Business Word, The *See* **Sterling Investments I, LLC DBA Twins Magazine**

Buster B.B. Publishing, *(978-0-9726691)* 1530 Indian Springs Rd., Pine Beach, NY 12566 USA
E-mail: mirror38@aol.com
Web site: http://www.reflectionsseminars.com.

Busy Bee Bks., *(978-0-9759281)* 2160 110th St., SE, Delano, MN 55328 USA Tel 952-237-7218
E-mail: debbyanderson@juno.com.

Butler Book Publishing *See* **Butler Bks.**

Butler Bks., *(978-0-9627459; 978-1-884532; 978-1-935497; 978-1-941953; 978-1-953058)* Orders Addr.: 608 Briar Hill Rd., Louisville, KY 40206 USA (SAN 990-0667) Tel 502-897-9393; Fax: 502-897-9797
E-mail: ckbutler@aol.com; eric@butlerbooks.com; billy@butlerbooks.com
Web site: https://www.butlerbooks.com
Dist(s): **Follett School Solutions.**

Butler Ctr. for Arkansas Studies, *(978-0-9708574; 978-0-9800897; 978-1-935106; 978-1-945624)* c/o Central Arkansas Library System, 100 Rock St., Little Rock, AR 72201 USA
Web site: http://www.cals.org; http://www.butlercenter.org
Dist(s): **Chicago Distribution Ctr.**
MyiLibrary
Univ. of Arkansas Pr.

Butler, Kate Bks., *(978-0-9993600; 978-1-948927; 978-1-952725)* 157 Bridgeton Pike, Mullica Hill, NJ 08062 USA Tel 714-401-1371
E-mail: katebutlerbooks@gmail.com
Web site: www.katebutlerbooks.com.

BuTo, Ltd. Co., *(978-0-9729569)* P.O. Box 9018, Austin, TX 78766 USA (SAN 255-4321) Fax: 512-450-0372
E-mail: butoltdco@aol.com
Web site: http://www.buto.biz.

Buttar, Deborah *See* **GMEC Publishing**

Buttercup Media, *(978-0-9768152)* Orders Addr.: P.O. Box 222003, Dallas, TX 75222 USA Tel 214-890-6833
E-mail: michael.p.collins1@gmail.com
Dist(s): **BookBaby.**

Butterfly Bk. Makers, *(978-0-9754117)* 1450 W. 800 N., Orem, UT 84057 USA
E-mail: hatfiron@aol.com.

Butterfly Books *See* **Black Garnet Pr.**

Butterfly Garden Bks., *(978-0-692-26847-6; 978-0-692-29926-5; 978-1-7321166)* 723 Euel Dr., McDonough, GA 30252 USA Tel 770-713-9735
E-mail: sabrina30054@yahoo.com
Web site: www.sabrinasargent.com.

Butterfly Ink Publishing, *(978-0-9745423)* 20637 Skouras Dr., Winnetka, CA 91306 USA
E-mail: butterflyinkpub@aol.com; kim@butterflyinkpublishing.com
Web site: http://www.butterflyinkpublishing.com.

Butterfly Park Educational Materials, Inc., *(978-0-9744575)* 3126 Elmira Ct., Denver, CO 80238-2929 USA
E-mail: butterflypark@comcast.net
Web site: http://www.butterflyparkphonics.com.

Butterfly Pavilion, *(978-0-9729000)* 6252 W. 104th Ave., Westminster, CO 80020 USA Tel 303-469-5441; Fax: 303-657-5944
E-mail: ptennyson@butterflies.org
Web site: http://www.butterflies.org.

Butterfly Press *See* **Butterfly Productions, LLC**

Butterfly Productions, LLC, *(978-0-9752936)* 165 Shadow Rock Dr., Sedona, AZ 86336 USA Tel 928-204-2811; Fax: 928-204-9118 Do not confuse with companies with the same or similar name in New York, NY, Worcester, MA, Houston, TX, Old Town, ME, Dayton, OH, Cochranville, PA, Princeton, NJ , Amherst, MA, Charston, WV, Pheonix, AZ
E-mail: butterfly@sedona.net
Web site: http://www.butterflyproductions.info.

Butterfly Typeface, The, *(978-1-942022; 978-0-9909919; 978-0-692-48438-8; 978-1-947656; 978-1-951883)* 8509 W Markham St No. 56193, Little Rock, AR 72215 USA Tel 501-681-0080
E-mail: butterflytypeface.imw@gmail.com
Web site: www.butterflytypeface.com.

Butterhouse Publishing, *(978-0-9763971)* 12251 N. 32nd St., Suite 4, Phoenix, AZ 85032 USA
E-mail: financialstories@juno.com.

Buttermilk Bks., *(978-0-9978909; 978-1-7331576)* 1482 Highland Cir., Myrtle Beach, SC 29575 USA Tel 843-655-5377
E-mail: tomwinn@sc.rr.com.

Buttermoth Pr. (AUS) *(978-0-9803367) Dist. by* **LuluCom.**

Butters Pr., *(978-0-9754960)* 2047 Gale Rd., Eaton Rapids, MI 48827 USA
Web site: http://www.throughtheears.com.

Button Bks. (GBR) *(978-1-908985) Dist. by* **PerseuPGW.**

Button Bucket Bks., *(978-0-615-91505-0; 978-0-615-95000-6; 978-0-692-11232-8)* 2715 N. Ocean Boulevard, 14-F, Fort Lauderdale, FL 33308 USA Tel 954554-3153
Dist(s): **CreateSpace Independent Publishing Platform.**

Button Flower Pr., *(978-0-9747836)* 7422 Westview Dr., Boardman, OH 44512 USA.

Button Poetry, *(978-0-9896415; 978-1-943735)* 5118 42nd Ave No. 1, Minneapolis, MN 55408 USA Tel 303-517-0784
E-mail: sam@buttonpoetry.com
Web site: ButtonPoetry.com
Dist(s): **SCB Distributors**
SPD-Small Pr. Distribution.

Buttonberry Bks., *(978-0-9768227)* 29 Sawmill Rd., Lebanon, NJ 08833 USA
Web site: http://www.buttonberrybooks.com
Dist(s): **Follett School Solutions.**

Buttonweed Pr., L.L.C., *(978-0-9755675)* 204 7th St W. # 125, Northfield, MN 55057-2419 USA (SAN 256-1700)
E-mail: info@buttonweedpress.com
Web site: http://www.buttonweedpress.com
Dist(s): **Follett School Solutions**
Partners Bk. Distributing, Inc.

Buttonwood Pr., *(978-0-9660685; 978-0-9742920; 978-0-9823351; 978-0-9891462; 978-0-9965562; 978-0-9972464; 978-0-9998096)* Orders Addr.: P.O. Box 716, Haslett, MI 48840 USA Tel 517-339-9871; Fax: 517-339-5908; Edit Addr.: 5951 Buttonwood Dr., Haslett, MI 48840 USA Do not confuse with companies with the same name Champaign, IL, Potomac, MD, New York, NY, Solvang, CA
E-mail: rlbald@aol.com
Web site: http://www.buttonwoodpress.com
Dist(s): **Partners Bk. Distributing, Inc.**

Buy Books on the Web.Com *See* **Infinity Publishing**

Buy Rite, *(978-0-9723744; 978-1-60421)* 88 Vanderveer Rd., Freehold, NJ 07728 USA Tel 732-294-9000; Fax: 732-294-9363; Toll Free: 888-777-7952
Web site: http://www.buyriteinc.com.

Buz-Land Presentations, Inc., *(978-0-9766990)* 73 Harding Rd., Wyckoff, NJ 07481 USA Tel 201-848-0595; 73 Harding Rd., Wyckoff, NJ 07481-2730 (SAN 256-5692)
E-mail: buzi.bee@verizon.net
Web site: http://www.buz-land.com; www.WWRT.org.

Buzzard Pr. International, *(978-0-9648488)* 506 W. Donna Dr., Merced, CA 95348 USA Tel 209-723-6738; Fax: 209-723-6253
E-mail: buzzard@buzzardpress.com
Dist(s): **Sunbelt Pubns., Inc.**

BuzzPop *Imprint of* **Little Bee Books Inc.**

Buzzy's Bks., *(978-0-9719054)* P.O. Box 566, Grafton, MA 01519 USA Tel 508-839-2442; Fax: 508-839-7396
E-mail: buzzy@buzzysbooks.org
Web site: http://www.buzzysbooks.org.

B.W. Van Alstyne, *(978-0-692-94898-9; 978-0-692-97327-1; 978-0-578-42650-1; 978-0-578-42651-8)* 602 W 28th St., Bryan, TX 77803 USA Tel 979-777-6094
E-mail: b.w.vanalstyne@gmail.com
Dist(s): **Ingram Content Group.**

By Grace Enterprises, *(978-0-9663629; 978-1-940591)* 9515 Twin Oaks Dr., Manvel, TX 77578-5307 USA
E-mail: hulettepl@aol.com; pamlv@aol.com
Web site: http://www.bygraceent.com
Dist(s): **Follett School Solutions.**

By His Grace Publishing, *(978-0-9991835)* 1189 East Hwy. C, Lamar, MO 64759 USA Tel 417-214-1847; Fax: 417-214-1847
E-mail: rebecca.emery@gmail.com
Web site: byhisgracepublishing.com.

by shayne, *(978-0-9725593)* P.O. Box 221474, Santa Clarita, CA 91322 USA
Web site: http://www.byshayne.com.

By The Creek Pubns., *(978-0-9974810)* 238 Shore Brook Ln., Commerce Twp., MI 48390 USA Tel 248-390-3906
E-mail: lindakmclean@yahoo.com.

By the Light of the Moon Pr., *(978-0-9992614)* 27071 Catamaran Dr., Tega Cay, SC 29708 USA Tel 720-326-2502
E-mail: maryjane.capps@gmail.com.

ByD Pr., *(978-0-9721035)* 1424 33rd St., NW, Washington, DC 20007 USA Tel 202-342-9189 (phone/fax)
E-mail: bydpress@erols.com
Dist(s): **Independent Pubs. Group.**

BYE Publishing Services, *(978-0-9656739)* Orders Addr.: P.O. BOX 582016, Elk Grove, CA 95758 USA Tel 916-529-3119 Corporate Hq; Fax: 916-683-1476; Edit Addr.: PO BOX 582016, Elk Grove, CA 95758 USA Tel 916-529-3119
E-mail: byepublishing@comcast.net
Web site: http://www.byepublishing.com; http://www.nationalbyesociety.org.

Byeway *Imprint of* **Byeway Bks.**

Byeway Bks., *(978-1-85997; 978-1-904586; 978-1-933581; 978-1-934004; 978-1-60176)* 15941 W. 65th St., Shawnee, KS 66217-9342 USA Toll Free Fax: 866-426-3929; Toll Free: 866-429-3929; *Imprints:* Byeway (Byeway)
E-mail: customerservice@byewaybooks.com
Web site: http://www.byewaybooks.com/how_to_order.html.

Byrd, Fay T., *(978-0-9776805)* 9325 Pan Ridge Rd., Baltimore, MD 21234 USA (SAN 257-9898) Tel 410-661-0295
E-mail: faysangelharp@aol.com
Web site: www.faysangelharp.com.

Byrd, Jesse Jr, *(978-0-692-90925-6; 978-0-692-90926-3; 978-0-9997050)* 1630 Kabel Dr., New Orleans, LA 70131 USA Tel 510-205-8711
E-mail: marybmorrison@aol.com; 87byrd@gmail.com
Web site: www.MaryMorrison.com; www.JesseBCreative.com
Dist(s): **Ingram Content Group.**

Byrne, Robert, *(978-0-692-14366-7)* 1854 Ringsted Dr., Solvang, CA 93463 USA Tel 805-886-9321
E-mail: robert@robertbyrne.com
Web site: www.robertbyrne.com.

Byte Level Research, *(978-0-9796475; 978-1-61822)* 2305 Ashland St. No. C417, Ashland, OR 97520 USA (SAN 853-9847); *Imprints:* Ashland Creek Press (AshlandCreek)
Web site: https://www.bytelevelbooks.com; https://www.ashlandcreekpress.com
Dist(s): **Follett School Solutions**
INscribe Digital.

Byte Me! Inc., *(978-0-9798611; 978-0-615-14953-0)* P.O. Box 60705, Reno, NV 89506 USA (SAN 854-5863) Tel 775-772-6378; 775-972-3322; Fax: 775-972-3323 Never after 5p.m. pst
E-mail: saraw1@clearwire.net; alma_corazon12@yahoo.com
Web site: http://www.cdebooksbyteme.org; http://www.stores.lulu.com/georgiahedrick; http://www.stores.lulu.com/georgiahedrick; http://www.stores.lulu.com/georgiahedrick
Dist(s): **Lulu Pr., Inc.**

Byte/Me Teen Bk. *Imprint of* **Awe-Struck Publishing**

BYU Creative Works *Imprint of* **Brigham Young Univ.**

Bywater Bks., *(978-1-932859; 978-1-61294)* P.O. Box 3671, Ann Arbor, MI 48106-3671 USA Tel 734-662-8815 Do not confuse with Bywater Books in Honaunau, HI
E-mail: salemwestbywater@gmail.com; ann.mcman@gmail.com
Web site: http://www.bywaterbooks.com
Dist(s): **Consortium Bk. Sales & Distribution**
MyiLibrary.

Bywater Bks., *(978-0-9653017)* P.O. Box 133, Honaunau, HI 96726-0133 USA; 387 Pk. Ave. S., New York, NY 10016 Do not confuse with Bywater Books in Ann Arbor, MI
Dist(s): **Consortium Bk. Sales & Distribution.**

C A Filius *See* **Charwood Pubns.**

C & C Educational Materials, LLC, *(978-0-9640524; 978-0-9747205; 978-0-9963509)* 12514 Dermott Dr., Houston, TX 77065 USA
E-mail: barbara.cobaugh@att.net
Web site: www.strategiesforstaar.com.

C & C Productions, *(978-0-9753273)* PMB 254, 330 SW 43rd St., No. K, Renton, WA 98055 USA.

C&D Enterprises, *(978-0-9633231; 978-0-9765938)* P.O. Box 7201, Arlington, VA 22207-7201 USA Fax: 703-276-3033
E-mail: harryfp@comcast.net.

C&D International, *(978-0-937347)* 111 Ferguson Ct., Suite 105, Irving, TX 75062-7014 USA (SAN 659-1523) Toll Free: 800-231-0442.

C & H Pubns., *(978-0-9740882)* 31201 S. 596 Ln., Grove, OK 74344 USA.

†C & T Publishing, *(978-0-914881; 978-1-57120; 978-1-60705; 978-1-61745; 978-1-64403)* Orders Addr.: 1651 Challenge Dr., Concord, CA 94520 USA (SAN 289-0720) Tel 925-677-0377; Fax: 925-617-0374; Toll Free: 800-284-1114; *Imprints:* Stash Books (StashBks); FunStitch Studio (FunStitch Stu)
E-mail: ctinfo@ctpub.com
Web site: http://www.ctpub.com
Dist(s): **Follett School Solutions**
MyiLibrary
National Bk. Network
Open Road Integrated Media, Inc.
ebrary, Inc.; *CIP.*

CBI Pr., *(978-0-9705812)* 6 Jeffrey Cir., Bedford, MA 01730 USA Do not confuse with C B I Press, Arlington, VA
E-mail: nancy_nugent@comcast.net
Web site: http://www.cbipress.com.

C. B. Publishing House, Incorporated *See* **Cubbie Blue Publishing**

C C L S Publishing Hse., *(978-1-928882; 978-0-7428)* 3191 Coral Way, Suite 114, Miami, FL 33145-3209 USA (SAN 254-4695) Tel 305-529-2257; Fax: 305-443-8538; Toll Free: 800-704-8181
E-mail: info@cclscorp.com
Web site: http://www.cclscorp.com
Dist(s): **Continental Bk. Co., Inc.**

CEF Pr., *(978-1-55976)* Div.of Child Evangelism Fellowship, Orders Addr.: P.O. Box 348, Warrenton, MO 63383 USA Tel 636-456-4321; Fax: 636-456-2078; Toll Free: 800-748-7710; Edit Addr.: 2300 E. Hwy. M, Warrenton, MO 63383 USA (SAN 211-7789)
E-mail: custserv@cefonline.com
Web site: http://www.cefonline.com; http://www.cefpress.com.

CES Industries, Inc., *(978-0-86711)* 2023 New Hwy., Farmingdale, NY 11735-1103 USA (SAN 237-9864)
E-mail: m.nesenoff@cesindustries.com
Web site: http://www.cesindustries.com.

CFKR Career Materials, Inc., *(978-0-934783; 978-1-887481)* P.O. Box 99, Meadow Vista, CA 95722-0099 USA (SAN 694-2547) Toll Free Fax: 800-770-0433; Toll Free: 800-525-5626
E-mail: requestinfo@cfkr.com; cfkr@cfkr.com; order@cfkr.com
Web site: http://www.cfkr.com.

C I S Communications, Inc., *(978-0-935063; 978-1-56062)* 180 Park Ave., Lakewood, NJ 08701 USA (SAN 694-5953) Tel 732-905-3000; Fax: 732-367-6666.

C. LaVielle, *(978-0-9983260)* 2313 NE Alameda St., Portland, OR 97212 USA Tel 503-287-0511; Fax: 503-287-0511
E-mail: clavielle@hotmail.com
Web site: www.clavielle.com.

C. Lee McKenzie *Imprint of* **McKenzie, Cheryl**

CMSP Projects, *(978-0-942851)* School of Engineering, 51 Astor Pl., New York, NY 10003 USA (SAN 667-6731) Tel 212-228-0950.

CPI Pubs., *(978-0-9648363)* Div. of Christopher Productions, Inc., 1115 David Ave., Pacific Grove, CA 93950 USA Tel 818-831-9268; Fax: 818-845-2128
Dist(s): **Austin & Company, Inc.**

CPI Publishing, Inc., 311 E. 51st St., New York, NY 10022 USA (SAN 218-6896) Tel 212-753-3800
Dist(s): **Modern Curriculum Pr.**

CPM Educational Program, *(978-1-885145; 978-1-931287; 978-1-60328)* 1233 Noonan Dr., Sacramento, CA 95822 USA Tel 916-446-9936; Fax: 916-444-5263
E-mail: cpm@cpm.org; bradley@cpm.org
Web site: http://www.cpm.org.

C R C Publications *See* **Faith Alive Christian Resources**

C R C World Literature Ministries *See* **C R C World Literature Ministries/Libros Desafio**

C R C World Literature Ministries/Libros Desafio, *(978-0-939125; 978-1-55883; 978-1-55955)* Subs. of CRC Pubns., 2850 Kalamazoo Ave., SE, Grand Rapids, MI 49560 USA (SAN 251-3269) Tel 616-224-0785 (customer service); Fax: 616-224-0834; Toll Free: 800-333-8300
E-mail: info@worldliterature.org
Web site: http://www.worldliterature.org/
Dist(s): **Faith Alive Christian Resources.**

CRM, *(978-0-9713534; 978-1-933341)* Orders Addr.: P.O. Box 2124, Hendersonville, NC 28793 USA Tel 828-877-3356; Fax: 828-890-1511; Edit Addr.: 1916 Reasonover Rd., Cedar Mountain, NC 28218 USA
E-mail: crm@ciridmus.com
Web site: http://www.ciridmus.com
Dist(s): **Send The Light Distribution LLC.**

C R Pubns., *(978-0-615-15964-5; 978-0-615-15981-2; 978-0-615-16029-0; 978-0-615-16673-5)* 415 E. 15th, Kearny, NE 68847-6959 USA
Web site: http://www.IDealinHope.com/author
Dist(s): **Lulu Pr., Inc.**

†CSS Publishing Co., *(978-0-7880; 978-0-89536; 978-1-55673; 978-0-615-84860-0)* Orders Addr.: 5450 N. Dixie Hwy., Lima, OH 45807-9559 USA Tel 800-241-4056; 419-227-1818; Fax: 419-228-9184; Toll Free: 800-241-4056 Customer Service); 800-537-1030 Orders; Edit Addr.: P.O. Box 4503, Lima, OH 45802-4503 USA (SAN 207-0707) Tel 419-227-1818; Fax: 419-228-9184; Toll Free: 800-537-1030 (Orders); 800-241-4056 (Customer Service); *Imprints:* Fairway Press (Fairway Pr) Do not confuse with CSS Publishing in Tularosa, NM
E-mail: editor@csspub.com; csr@csspub.com; info@csspub.com; orders@csspub.com
Web site: http://www.csspub.com
Dist(s): **Spring Arbor Distributors, Inc.**; *CIP.*

C T A, Inc., *(978-0-9712618; 978-0-9718985; 978-0-9728816; 978-0-9744640; 978-0-9747923; 978-0-9754499; 978-0-9759330; 978-1-933234; 978-1-935404; 978-1-943216; 978-1-947699; 978-1-951094)* P.O. Box 1205, Fenton, MO 63026-1205 USA Tel 636-305-3100; Toll Free: 800-999-1874
Web site: http://www.ctainc.com.

C Turtle Publishing, *(978-0-9979656)* 30 N. Gould St. Suite 5467, Sheridan, WY 82801 USA Tel 812-786-5594
E-mail: kylelbmorey@gmail.com
Web site: www.cturtlepublishing.com.

C. W. Historicals, LLC, *(978-0-9637745)* Orders Addr.: P.O. Box 113, Collingswood, NJ 08108 USA Tel 856-854-1290; Fax: 856-854-1290 (*69); Edit Addr.: 901 Lakeshore Dr., Westmont, NJ 08108 USA
E-mail: cwhist@erols.com.

C Z M Press *See* **Touchstones Discussion Project**

C2 (C squared) Publishing, *(978-0-9773115)* P.O. Box 5269, Vienna, WV 26105 USA
E-mail: noelclntn@yahoo.com; princeofwarwood@gmail.com.

Caballito Children's Bks. *Imprint of* **Caballo Pr. of Ann Arbor**

Caballo Pr. of Ann Arbor, *(978-0-615-18757-0; 978-0-9824766; 978-0-615-44366-9; 978-0-9840418; 978-0-692-39908-8; 978-0-692-50604-2; 978-0-692-82464-1)* Orders Addr.: 24 Frank Lloyd Wright Dr. P.O. Box 415, Ann Arbor, MI 48106-0445 USA Tel 734-972-5790; *Imprints:* Caballito Children's Books (Caballito)
E-mail: admin@caballopress.com
Web site: http://www.caballopress.com
Dist(s): **CreateSpace Independent Publishing Platform**
Ingram Content Group.

Cabat Studio Pubns., *(978-0-913521)* 627 N. Fourth Ave., Tucson, AZ 85705 USA (SAN 285-1539) Tel 520-622-6362
E-mail: junecabat@hotmail.com.

Cabbage Patch Pr., *(978-0-9729044)* 2255 Orange Grove Rd. No. 23205, Tucson, AZ 85741 USA Tel 520-241-2680
E-mail: cabbagepatchpress@hotmail.com
Web site: http://www.cabbagepatchpress.com.

CABI (GBR) *(978-0-85198; 978-0-85199) Dist. by* **Stylus Pub VA.**

Cable Publishing, *(978-0-9799494; 978-1-934980)* 14090 E. Keinenen Rd., Brule, WI 54820 USA Tel 715-372-8497; Fax: 715-372-8448
Web site: http://www.cablepublishing.com
Dist(s): **Follett School Solutions.**

Caboandcoral.com, *(978-0-615-17598-0; 978-0-692-00269-8; 978-0-692-01170-6; 978-0-9833841)* 1227 Stratford Ct., Del Mar, CA 92014 USA
E-mail: udo@caboandcoral.com
Web site: http://www.caboandcoral.com.

Cacoethes Publishing Hse., LLC, *(978-0-9799015; 978-0-9802447; 978-0-9816190; 978-0-9817733; 978-0-9818208; 978-1-60695)* 14715 Pacific Ave. S., Suite 604, Tacoma, WA 98444 USA (SAN 854-7122) Tel 253-536-3747; Fax: 253-537-3117
E-mail: cacoethespublishing@comcast.net
Web site: http://www.cacoethespublishing.com; http://www.loticmagazine.com
Dist(s): **Ingram Content Group.**

Cactus Publishing, LLC, *(978-0-9766674)* 1235 S. Gilbert Rd., Suite 3-62, Mesa, AZ 85204 USA Do not confuse with companies iwht the same or similar name in East Perth, WA, Atlanta, GA, Peoria, AZ
E-mail: glsweetaz@msn.com.

CaDaVa Publishing, *(978-0-9997814)* 906 Oscar Cross Ave., PADUCAH, KY 42003 USA Tel 270-845-1304
E-mail: cadavapublishing@gmail.com
Dist(s): **Ingram Content Group.**

Cadcim Technologies, *(978-0-9663537; 978-1-932709; 978-1-936646; 978-1-942689; 978-1-64057)* 525 St. Andrews Dr., Schererville, IN 46375 USA Tel 219-614-7235; 219-228-4908; Fax: 270-717-0185
E-mail: cadcim@yahoo.com; sales@cadcim.com
Web site: https://www.cadcim.com.

Cadence Group, The *See* **New Shelves Bks.**

Cadogan Guides (GBR) *(978-0-946313; 978-0-947754; 978-1-85744; 978-1-86011; 978-1-78194) Dist. by* **Globe Pequot.**

Cafe Lango *See* **Pavilion Pubs.**

Caged Dragon Publishing, *(978-1-7321659)* 2036 E. Cuming St., Fremont, NE 68025 USA Tel 530-315-8144
E-mail: j.d.campbell.author@gmail.com.

Cahill Publishing, *(978-0-9744027)* 1016-F Brentwood Way, Atlanta, GA 30350 USA
E-mail: e-diane@hotmail.com.

Cahill Publishing Company *See* **Advance Publishing, Inc.**

Cahokia Mounds Museum Society, *(978-1-881563)* 30 Ramey St., Collinsville, IL 62234 USA Tel 618-344-7316; Fax: 618-346-5162
E-mail: cmms@ezl.com; giftshop@ezl.com
Web site: http://www.cahokiamounds.com.

CAI Publishing, *(978-0-9787766; 978-0-9971381)* Orders Addr.: 807 Black Duck Dr., Port Orange, FL 32127-4726 USA (SAN 851-6006) Tel 386-383-5198
E-mail: wacummins@clearwire.net
Web site: http://www.caipublishing.net
Dist(s): **Ingram Content Group.**

Caillouet, Gerry, *(978-0-578-05418-6; 978-2-89718)* 8193 Emerick Rd., West Milton, OH 45383 USA Tel 937-698-3656
E-mail: ggoutdoors@aol.com
Web site: http://www.godsgreatoutdoors.org
Dist(s): **Publishers Group West (PGW)**
Perseus Bks. Group.

Cairns, Mary C., *(978-0-692-98477-2)* P.O. Box 34, Altenburg, MO 63732 USA Tel 573-768-4814
E-mail: mchriscairns@gmail.com
Dist(s): **Ingram Content Group.**

Caitboo LLC, *(978-0-9818717)* 2474 Walnut St., No. 260, Cary, NC 27518-9212 USA (SAN 856-7948) Tel 919-851-8646
E-mail: caitboo@gmail.com
Web site: http://www.caitboo.com.

Caitlin Pr., Inc. (CAN) *(978-0-920576; 978-1-894759; 978-1-927575; 978-1-987915) Dist. by* **IPG Chicago.**

Calabash Bks. *Imprint of* **Belknap Publishing & Design**

Calabrese, Christine, *(978-0-9995220)* 10 Marlboro Dr., Huntington, NY 11743 USA Tel 516-312-2078
E-mail: chrissykcalabrese@gmail.com
Web site: www.christinecalabrese.com.

Calaca Pr., *(978-0-9660773; 978-0-9717035; 978-0-9843359)* Orders Addr.: P.O. Box 2309, National City, CA 91951 USA Tel 619-434-9036 (phone/fax); Edit Addr.: 502 Rose Dr., National City, CA 91950 USA; *Imprints:* Red CalacArts Publications (Red CalacArts)
E-mail: calacapress@cox.net
Web site: http://calacapress.com; http://redcalacartscollective.org; http://www.myspace.com/calacalandia
Dist(s): **BookMobile**
SPD-Small Pr. Distribution.

Calaroga Publishing, *(978-0-9815793)* 619 Madison St., Suite 110, Oregon City, OR 97045 USA
Web site: www.slimsaneandsexy.com.

Caldwell, Judy, *(978-0-9774463)* 11216 Windy Peak Rdg., Sandy, UT 84094 USA Fax: 801-571-1422
E-mail: jlynncaldwell@msn.com.

Caleb's Pr., *(978-0-9729568)* 421 Seminole Ct., High Point, NC 27265-8631 USA Tel 336-887-6846; Fax: 888-726-9304
E-mail: calebspress@aol.com
Web site: http://www.calebspress.com.

Caledonia Pr., LLC, *(978-0-9890975)* P.O. Box 436166, Louisville, KY 40253 USA Tel 502-773-5874
E-mail: gbgodby@insightbb.com
Web site: http://giovannagodby.com.

Calfee, Susan S. *See* **Wordwhittler Bks.**

Cali Publishing, *(978-0-9793004)* 2875 NE 191st St., Suite 511, Aventua, FL 33180 USA Tel 786-200-9374; Fax: 305-937-4161
E-mail: lallouz@glmace.com
Web site: http://www.calipublishing.com.

Caliber Comics, *(978-0-941613; 978-0-9826549; 978-0-9836307; 978-0-9857493; 978-0-9960306; 978-1-942351; 978-1-63529)* P.O. Box 44114 Parkside, Canton, MI 48187 USA (SAN 666-1777) Tel 734-453-8346; 734-812-8733
E-mail: calcomic@aol.com
Web site: http://www.calibercomics.com
Dist(s): **Diamond Comic Distributors, Inc.**
MyiLibrary.

Caliber Pubns., *(978-0-9673696)* 1295 Lincoln Dr., Marion, IA 52302 USA Tel 319-294-9468; Fax: 319-373-1370; Toll Free: 877-480-5790
E-mail: larson1965@aol.com
Web site: http://www.calpubs.com.

Caliburn Bks. *Imprint of* **MQuills Publishing**

Calico Chapter Bks. *Imprint of* **ABDO Publishing Co.**

Calico Chapter Bks *Imprint of* **Magic Wagon**

Calico Connection, Inc., The, *(978-0-9767658)* 300 N. David Ln., Muskogee, OK 74403 USA Tel 918-687-6577 Do not confuse with Calico Publishing in Seabrook, TX
E-mail: calicoasay@cox.net.

Calico Kid *Imprint of* **ABDO Publishing Co.**

Calico Publishing *See* **Calico Connection, Inc., The**

California Foundation for Agriculture in the Classroom, *(978-0-615-26927-6; 978-0-615-34893-3; 978-0-615-44052-1; 978-0-9850855)* 2300 River Plaza Dr., Sacramento, CA 95833 USA
Web site: LearnAboutAg.org.

California Is Me, *(978-0-9742010)* P.O. Box 23841, Alexandria, VA 22304 USA Tel 202-321-1425
E-mail: QueenC@caliisme.com
Web site: http://www.calisme.com.

California Street *Imprint of* **Firefall Editions**

Calithumpian Pr., *(978-0-9886341; 978-0-9990661; 978-1-7357353)* 2355 Waldemere St, Sarasota, FL 34239-2440 USA Tel 571-344-2591
E-mail: Shannon@KeeKeesBigAdventures.com; info@calithumpianpress.com
Web site: http://www.KeeKeesBigAdventures.com; http://calithumpianpress.com
Dist(s): **Independent Pubs. Group**
MyiLibrary
Small Pr. United.

Calkins Creek *Imprint of* **Boyds Mills Pr.**

Callahan, Sheila, *(978-1-936934)* 901 Iystra Ln., Chapel Hill, NC 27517 USA Tel 919-968-8909
E-mail: sheilacallaham@gmail.com
Web site: sheilacallaham.com.

Callaway Arts & Entertainment, 19 Fulton St., 5th Flr., New York, NY 10038 USA
E-mail: info@callaway.com
Web site: http://www.callaaway.com
Dist(s): **Ingram Publisher Services**
Macmillan
National Bk. Network.

Callaway Editions, Inc., *(978-0-935112; 978-1-7345377)* Div. of Callaway Arts & Entertainment, 41 Union Sq. West, Suite 1101, New York, NY 10003 USA (SAN 213-2931) Tel 646-465-4667
E-mail: ivan@callaway.com
Web site: http://www.callaway.com
Dist(s): **Abrams, Inc.**
Holt, Henry & Co.
Hachette Bk. Group
National Bk. Network
Penguin Random Hse. Distribution
Penguin Random Hse. LLC
Penguin Publishing Group
Simon & Schuster Children's Publishing.

Calliope Publications *See* **Sounds Devine**

Callirobics, *(978-0-9630478)* Orders Addr.: P.O. Box 6634, Charlottesville, VA 22906 USA Tel 804-293-7055; Fax: 804-293-9008; Toll Free: 800-769-2891; Edit Addr.: 1616 King Mountain Rd., Charlottesville, VA 22901 USA
E-mail: cal-avir@cfw.com
Web site: http://www.callirobics.com.

Callis Editora Ltda (BRA) *(978-85-7416; 978-85-85642) Dist. by* **IPG Chicago.**

Callison, J.L., *(978-0-9987771)* 407 Hinman St, Aurora, IL 60505 USA Tel 630-978-2093; Fax: 630-978-2093
E-mail: authorjlcallison@gmail.com
Web site: www.jlcallison.com.

Callisto Media Inc., *(978-0-615-59880-2; 978-1-62315; 978-1-939754; 978-1-64152; 978-1-64611; 978-1-64739; 978-1-64876)* 918 Parker St #A-12, Berkeley, CA 94710 USA
E-mail: moesterle@callistomedia.com; production@callistomedia.com
Web site: www.rockridgeuniversity.com; http://www.callistomedia.com
Dist(s): **CreateSpace Independent Publishing Platform**
Ingram Publisher Services
Ingram Content Group.

Callout Pr., *(978-0-9971911)* PO Box 250, Olalla, WA 98359 USA Tel 844-344-4374
E-mail: robert@calloutpress.com.

Cally Pr., *(978-0-9766199)* 3964 Loftlands Dr., Earlysville, VA 22936 USA
E-mail: callypress@aol.com.

Calm & Colorful, *(978-1-7321831)* 2224 Wetstone Dr., Thousand Oaks, CA 91362 USA Tel 805-657-1884
E-mail: accounts@calmandcolorful.com
Web site: www.calmandcolorful.com.

Calm Flame Publishing Co., *(978-0-9745263)* 10745 Gilespie St., Las Vegas, NV 89123 USA.

Calm Unity Books *See* **Calm Unity Pr.**

Calm Unity Pr., *(978-1-882260)* 3922 23rd St., San Francisco, CA 94114-3303 USA Fax: 415-821-5389 (Call before faxing); *Imprints:* Pelagia Press (Pelagia Pr)
E-mail: rabar@mindspring.com.

Calvary Chapel Church, Inc., *(978-0-9708600; 978-1-932283)* 2401 W. Cypress Creek Rd., Fort Lauderdale, FL 33309 USA
E-mail: snt@thecalebgroup.com; kirk@calvaryftl.org
Dist(s): **Send The Light Distribution LLC.**

Calvary Productions Fresh Media *See* **Word Productions LLC**

Calvin Partnership, LLC, *(978-1-891533)* 40 Ardmore Rd., Ho-Ho-Kus, NJ 07443-1008 USA Tel 201-670-8412; Fax: 201-670-0464
E-mail: jahelka@attglobal.net.

Calychio Publishing, *(978-0-9649156; 978-0-9964126)* 4138 Kildare St., Eugene, OR 97404 USA Tel 501-653-8990
E-mail: tshionyim@yahoo.com.

Camas Pr., *(978-0-9856698)* 2219 240th Ave. SE, Sammamish, WA 98075 USA Tel 425-922-5064
E-mail: info@camaspress.com.

Camber Pr., *(978-0-9727455)* 807 Central Ave. # 2, Peekskill, NY 10566-2039 USA
Web site: http://www.camberpress.com.

Cambium Education, Inc., *(978-0-944584; 978-1-57035; 978-1-59318; 978-1-932282; 978-1-4168; 978-1-60218; 978-1-60697)* 4093 Specialty Pl., Longmont, CO 80504 USA (SAN 243-945X) Tel 303-651-2829; Fax: 303-907-8694; Toll Free: 800-547-6747 (orders only)
E-mail: publishing@sopriswest.com; customerservice@cambiumlearning.com
Web site: http://www.sopriswest.com.

Cambria Creations, LLC, *(978-0-9770916)* 515 Main St., Johnston, PA 15901 USA Tel 814-535-5571; Fax: 814-535-1079
E-mail: djwlaw@wvdsl.net.

Cambridge Bks. *Imprint of* **Write Words, Inc.**

Cambridge Bk. Co., *(978-0-8428)* Div. of Simon & Schuster, Inc., 4350 Equity Dr., Box 249, Columbus, OH 43216 USA (SAN 169-5703) Toll Free: 800-238-5833
Web site: http://www.simonsays.com/.

Cambridge BrickHouse, Inc., *(978-1-58018; 978-1-59835)* 60 Island St. Suite 102 E., Lawrence, MA 01844 USA; *Imprints:* CBH Books (CBH Bks); BrickHouse Education (BrickHse)
E-mail: edelgado@cambridgebh.com; ycanetti@cambridgebh.com; mkamelle@cambridgebh.com
Web site: http://www.cambridgebh.com; http://www.brickhouseeducation.com
Dist(s): **Ediciones Universal**
Follett School Solutions
Lectorum Pubns., Inc.

Cambridge Educational Services, Inc., *(978-1-58894)* 2860 S River Rd, Des Plaines, IL 60018 USA Tel 847-299-2930; Fax: 847-299-2933 Do not confuse with Cambridge Educational in Charleston, WV
Web site: http://www.cambridgeed.com.

Cambridge House Pr. *Imprint of* **Sterling & Ross Pubs.**

Cambridge Hse. Publishing Co., LLC, *(978-0-9711359)* P.O. Box 383, Saddle River, NJ 07458 USA Fax: 973-777-8075
E-mail: cambridgehouse@verizon.net
Web site: http://www.cezanneismissing.com; http://www.cambridgehousepublishing.com.

Cambridge Univ. Pr. (GBR) *(978-0-521; 978-1-108; 978-1-107; 978-1-139; 978-1-316) Dist. by* **Cambridge U Pr.**

†Cambridge Univ. Pr., *(978-0-521; 978-0-511)* Orders Addr.: 100 Brook Hill Dr., West Nyack, NY 10994-2133 USA (SAN 281-3769) Tel 845-353-7500; Fax: 845-353-4141; Toll Free: 800-872-7423 (orders, returns, credit & accounting); 800-937-9600; Edit Addr.: 32 Avenue of the Americas, New York, NY 10013-2473 USA (SAN 200-206X) Tel 212-924-3900; Fax: 212-691-3239
E-mail: customer_service@cup.org; orders@cup.org; information@cup.org
Web site: http://www.cambridge.org/
Dist(s): **Baker Bks.**
Boydell & Brewer, Inc.
Casemate Academic
CreateSpace Independent Publishing Platform
Ebsco Publishing
Cengage Gale
ISD
Ingram Publisher Services
Ingram Content Group
Rittenhouse Bk. Distributors
Savvas Learning Co.
Two Rivers Distribution
ebrary, Inc.; *CIP.*

Cambridge Way Publishing, *(978-0-9746976)* 149 Cambridge Way, Macon, GA 31220-8736 USA (SAN 255-8041) Tel 478-475-1763
E-mail: whwatson2@cox.net.

Cambridge-Hitachi (GBR) *(978-1-84565) Dist. by* **Cambridge U Pr.**

CamCat Publishing, *(978-1-929017; 978-0-7443; 978-0-9702385; 978-1-931540)* Orders Addr.: 101 Creekside Crossing Ste 280, Brentwood, TN 37027 USA (SAN 254-4962) Tel 833-782-5747; Edit Addr.: 101 Creekside Crossing Ste 280, Brentwood, TN 37027 USA Tel 833-782-5747
E-mail: sue@camcatpublishing.com; staff@camcatpublishing.com; dayna@camcatpublishing.com
Web site: http://www.synergebooks.com; https://camcatpublishing.com/; http://camcatbooks.com/.

Camelot Publishing, *(978-0-9754063)* Orders Addr.: P.O. Box 500057, Lake Los Angeles, CA 93535 USA (SAN 256-0666)
E-mail: camelotpublishing@hotmail.com
Web site: http://www.camelotpublishing.com.

Camelot Tales, *(978-0-9672375)*
E-mail: jeanette.adams@hotmail.com
Web site: http://www.bellowinghills.com.

Cameltrotters Publishing, *(978-0-9666110; 978-0-9764475)* Orders Addr.: P.O. Box 3026, Pinedale, CA 93650-3526 USA Tel 559-447-9393 (phone/fax)
E-mail: ted@atborgeas.com
Web site: http://www.atborgeas.com.

Cameo Pubns., LLC, *(978-0-9715739; 978-0-9744149; 978-0-9744966; 978-0-9774659)* Orders Addr.: 2175 Deer Run Trl., Jacksonville, FL 32246-1068 USA
E-mail: info@cameopublications.com; publisher@cameopublications.com
Web site: http://www.cameopublications.com
Dist(s): **Bookazine Co., Inc.**
CreateSpace Independent Publishing Platform
Distributors, The
New Leaf Publishing Group
Scholastic, Inc.
Shenanigan Bks.

Cameron + Co., *(978-0-918684; 978-1-937359; 978-1-944903; 978-1-949480; 978-1-951836)* 149 Kentucky St., Suite 7, Petaluma, CA 94952 USA Tel 707-769-1617; Fax: 415-223-8520; *Imprints:* Roundtree Press (RoundtreePr); Cameron Kids (CameronKids); Cameron Books (Cameron Bks)
E-mail: orders@cameronbooks.com; info@cameronbooks.com
Web site: http://www.cameronbooks.com
Dist(s): **Abrams, Inc.**
Abrams & Co. Pubs., Inc.
Andrews McMeel Publishing
Follett School Solutions
Hachette Bk. Group
Ingram Publisher Services
MyiLibrary
Publishers Group West (PGW).

Cameron Books *Imprint of* **Cameron + Co.**

Cameron Kids *Imprint of* **Cameron + Co.**

Camino Bks., Inc., *(978-0-940159; 978-1-933822; 978-1-68098)* P.O. Box 59026, Philadelphia, PA 19102 USA (SAN 664-225X) Tel 215-413-1917; Fax: 215-413-3255
E-mail: camino@caminobooks.com
Web site: http://www.caminobooks.com
Dist(s): **Follett School Solutions**
INscribe Digital
Independent Pubs. Group
Partners Pubs. Group, Inc.

Camino E.E. & Bk. Co., *(978-0-940808; 978-1-55893)* Orders Addr.: a/o Jan Linzy, P.O. Box 6400, Incline Village, NV 89450 USA (SAN 219-841X) Tel 775-831-3078 (phone/fax); Fax: 775-831-3078 (phone/fax)
E-mail: info@camino-books.com
Web site: http://www.camino-books.com.

Camino Real Calendar LLC, *(978-0-9743501)* P.O. Box 17667, Anaheim, CA 92817 USA Toll Free: 800-200-6331
E-mail: support@caminosports.com
Web site: http://www.caminosports.com.

Camino Real Sports Marketing *See* **Camino Real Calendar LLC**

Cammilleri Productions, *(978-0-615-25933-8)* 2565 San Clemente Dr., Unit 206, Corta Mesa, CA 92626 USA (SAN 857-507X) Tel 714-486-1318
E-mail: jcammilleri@ca.rr.com.

Camozzi, Victor, *(978-0-692-58132-2; 978-0-692-75176-3)* 7220 Lapin Cove, AUSTIN, TX 78739 USA Tel 512-468-7188.

Camp Pope Publishing, *(978-0-9628936; 978-1-929919)* Orders Addr.: P.O. Box 2232, Iowa City, IA 52244 USA Tel 319-351-2407; Fax: 319-339-5964; Toll Free: 800-204-2407; Edit Addr.: 1117 E. Davenport, Iowa City, IA 52245 USA
E-mail: mail@camppope.com
Web site: http://www.camppope.com
Dist(s): **Ingram Content Group.**

Campanita Bks. *Imprint of* **Editorial Campana**

CampCrest Publishing, *(978-0-9763257)* 385 Hidden Hollow Ln., Chickamauga, GA 30707 USA
E-mail: sallyworland@mindspring.com.

Campfire *Imprint of* **Steerforth Pr.**

Camping Guideposts *See* **Wordshed**

Campus Crusade for Christ, *(978-1-56399)* Affil. of Campus Crusade for Christ International, Orders Addr.: 375 Hwy. 74 S., Suite A, Peachtree City, GA 30269 USA Tel 770-631-9940; Fax: 770-631-9916; Toll Free: 800-827-2788
E-mail: customerservice@campuscrusade.org
Web site: http://www.campuscrusade.com.

Can Do Duck Publishing, *(978-0-9768384)* P.O. Box 1045, Voorhees, NJ 08043 USA Tel 856-816-5255; Fax: 856-429-0094
E-mail: ducktormorty@thecandoduck.com
Web site: http://www.thecandoduck.com.

Canadian Geographic Enterprises (CAN) *(978-0-9685821; 978-1-894524) Dist. by* **HachBkGrp.**

Canal History & Technology Pr. *Imprint of* **Delaware &Lehigh National Heritage Corridor, Inc.**

Canary Connect Pubns., *(978-0-9643462)* Div. of SOBOLE, Inc., 605 Holiday Rd., Coralville, IA 52241-1016 USA Tel 319-338-3827; Fax: 612-435-3340; *Imprints:* Just Think Books (Just Think Bks)
E-mail: sondrak@canaryconnect.com
Web site: http://www.canaryconnect.com; http://www.justthinkbooks.com; http://www.simplechoicesforhealthiereating.com; http://www.transitionstobetterliving.com
Dist(s): **Follett School Solutions**
Integral Yoga Pubns.
Nutri-Bks. Corp.

Candalyse Publishing, *(978-0-9798217; 978-0-9802275; 978-0-9817112)* Orders Addr.: P.O. Box 783, Smallwood, NY 12778 USA; Edit Addr.: 57 Karl Ave., Smallwood, NY 12778-0783 USA; *Imprints:* Chaklet Coffee Books (ChakletCoffee)
E-mail: candalysepublishing@gmail.com; chakletcoffee@gmail.com
Web site: http://www.candalysepublishing.com; http://www.chakletbooks.com
Dist(s): **Ingram Content Group.**

C&C Educational Materials, LLC *See* **C & C Educational Materials, LLC**

Candid Liv, *(978-0-9600373)* P.O. Box 335690, North Las Vegas, NV 89033 USA
Web site: www.candidliv.com.

C&K Publishing Co., *(978-0-9844342)* Orders Addr.: P.O. Box 291162, Columbia, SC 29229 USA Tel 803-414-0180; Fax: 803-462-1188; Edit Addr.: 320 Whitehurst Way, Columbia, SC 29229 USA
E-mail: candkpub@bellsouth.net.

Candle Light Pr., *(978-0-9743147; 978-0-9766053; 978-0-9895371; 978-0-9966176)* 1470 Walker Way, Coralville, IA 52242 USA Do not confuse with Candle Light Press in Martinez, CA.
E-mail: ding@candlelightpress.com
Web site: http://www.candlelightpress.com
Dist(s): **Follett School Solutions.**

CandleHill Publishing Co., *(978-1-945383)* 40 Pinehurst Ln., Half Moon Bay, CA 94019 USA Tel 415-350-6020
E-mail: tkirkhillyard@gmail.com.

Candlelight Bay Publishing, *(978-1-7326633)* 351 Riverview Dr., Grafton, WI 53024 USA Tel 414-573-7899
E-mail: Kidsdorool@gmail.com.

Candlelight Stories, Inc., *(978-0-615-14024-7)* 9909 Topanga Canyon Blvd., Chatsworth, CA 91311 USA
E-mail: orders@candlelightstories.com
Web site: http://www.candlelightstories.com
Dist(s): **Lulu Pr., Inc.**

Candleshoe Bks., *(978-0-9825089)* 3122 N. California Ave., Suite 3L, Chicago, IL 60618 USA
E-mail: info@candleshoebooks.com
Web site: http://www.candleshoebooks.com
Dist(s): **Music, Bks. & Business, Inc.**

Candleshoe Press, Inc. *See* **Candleshoe Bks.**

Candlewick Entertainment *Imprint of* **Candlewick Pr.**

Candlewick on Brilliance Audio *Imprint of* **Brilliance Publishing, Inc.**

†Candlewick Pr., *(978-0-7636; 978-1-56402; 978-1-5362)* Div. of Walker Bks., London, England, 99 Dover St., Somerville, MA 02144 USA Tel 617-661-3330; Fax: 617-661-0565; *Imprints:* Templar (Templar); Nosy Crow (NosyCrow); Big Picture Press (Big Picture Pr); Candlewick Entertainment (Candlewick Entmt) Do not confuse with Candlewick Pr., Crystal Lake, IL
E-mail: bigbear@candlewick.com; salesinfo@candlewick.com
Web site: http://www.candlewick.com/
Dist(s): **Children's Plus, Inc.**
Follett School Solutions
Penguin Random Hse. Distribution
Penguin Random Hse. LLC
Perfection Learning Corp.
Random Hse., Inc.; *CIP.*

Candlewood Pr. *Imprint of* **Harding Hse. Publishing Sebice Inc.**

C&V 4 Seasons Publishing, *(978-0-692-26548-2; 978-0-9864036; 978-1-7358388)* P.O. Box 683, Mayflower, AR 72106 USA Tel 501-336-4726
E-mail: mariahoskins50@yahoo.com
Web site: www.seasons2dream.com.

Candy Cane Bks. *Imprint of* **Sunlight Publishing**

Candy Wrapper, *(978-1-940556)* 2885 Sanford Ave SW No. 26878, Grandville, MI 49418 USA
E-mail: winintl@gmail.com; cynthealiu@gmail.com; cynthealiu2@gmail.com.

Candy Wrapper Inc. *See* **Candy Wrapper**

Candy's Creations *See* **Fruitbearer Publishing, LLC**

Cane River Trading Co., Inc., *(978-0-9744189)* 1473 Cty. Rte. 26, Climax, NY 12042-2211 USA Tel 518-731-8598
E-mail: ny5kmagi@aol.com
Web site: http://members.aol.com/CaneR71456/.

Canh Nam Pubs., *(978-0-9749097; 978-0-9772129; 978-0-9799345; 978-0-9883504)* 2607 Military Rd., Arlington, VA 22207 USA
E-mail: canhnam@dc.net.

Canis Lupus Productions, *(978-0-9661789)* Orders Addr.: P.O. Box 128262, San Diego, CA 92102-8262 USA; Edit Addr.: 1940 Third Ave., Unit 406, San Diego, CA 92101-2622 USA Tel 310-873-3232 (phone/fax)
E-mail: jlbrooks@email.com.

Canmore Pr., *(978-1-887774)* Orders Addr.: P.O. Box 510794, Melbourne Beach, FL 32951-0794 USA Tel 321-729-0078; Fax: 321-724-1162; *Imprints:* Wynden (Wynden)
E-mail: publish@canmorepress.com
Web site: http://www.canmorepress.com.

Cannady, John, *(978-0-9754345)* 6126 Dunwoody Ct., Montgomery, AL 36117-5012 USA
E-mail: katphishe@starband.net
Web site: http://www.hopetkd.com.

Cannon, K. L., *(978-0-9675594)* 9412 Meadow Vale, Austin, TX 78758 USA Tel 512-837-6281; Fax: 512-837-7205
E-mail: cankl@msn.com.

Cannon Publishing Group, *(978-0-9766291)* 230 Merrill Rd., Walla Walla, WA 99362 USA
Web site: http://www.cannonpublishinggroup.com.

Canoed Sun Publishing, LLC, *(978-0-9836081)* 902 Franklin Ave., Council Bluffs, IA 51503 USA Tel 402-541-6452.

Canon Pr., *(978-1-885767; 978-1-930443; 978-1-59128; 978-1-935000; 978-1-944503; 978-1-947644; 978-1-952410)* Div. of Credenda Agenda, Orders Addr.: P.O. Box 8729, Moscow, ID 83843 USA (SAN 257-3792); 207 N Main St, Moscow, ID 83843 (SAN 990-1671) Tel 208-596-3867; *Imprints:* Canonball Books (Canonball) Do not confuse with companies with the same or similar names in Grand Rapids, MI, Centerville, UT
E-mail: brian@canonpress.org
Web site: http://www.canonpress.com; http://www.canonballbooks.com; http://www.logospressonline.com
Dist(s): **Follett School Solutions.**

Canon Pubs., *(978-0-9889696)* 10 Canon Cir., Greenwood Village, CO 80111 USA Tel 303-721-8266; Fax: 303-721-8266
E-mail: Debra@DebraFine.com
Dist(s): **Independent Pubs. Group**
Midpoint Trade Bks., Inc.
ebrary, Inc.

Canonball Bks. *Imprint of* **Canon Pr.**

Canongate Bks. (GBR) *(978-0-86241; 978-0-903937; 978-1-84195; 978-1-84767; 978-0-85786; 978-1-78211; 978-1-78689) Dist. by* **PerseuPGW.**

Cantab Publishing, *(978-0-9745150)* P.O. Box 381591, Cambridge, MA 02238-1591 USA.

Cantata Learning, *(978-1-63290; 978-1-68410)* 1710 Roe Crest Dr., North Mankato, MN 56003 USA Tel 952-224-0518
E-mail: info@cantatalearning.com
Web site: cantatalearning.com
Dist(s): **Capstone.**

Cantemos-bilingual bks. and music, *(978-0-9623930; 978-1-892306)* Orders Addr.: 15696 Altamira Dr., Chino Hills, CA 91709 USA Tel 909-239-2735
E-mail: jarjetb@writeme.com; bakergeorgette@yahoo.com
Web site: http://www.cantemosco.com; http://www.simplespanishsongs.com
Dist(s): **Continental Bk. Co., Inc.**
Follett School Solutions
Midwest Library Service.

Canterbury Classics *Imprint of* **Printers Row Publishing Group**

Canterbury Hse. Publishing, Ltd. *Imprint of* **Dudley Court Press**

Canterwine Pr., *(978-0-9764184)* 608 Longview Ave., Anacortes, WA 98221 USA Tel 360-941-4692
E-mail: jordanmcmakin@hotmail.com
Web site: http://www.canterwinepress.com.

Cantrell, Wendy, *(978-1-7325057)* 45 Allison Rd., Mills River, NC 28759 USA Tel 828-891-2750
E-mail: cantrellfarm@yahoo.com.

Cantu, Ricardo, *(978-0-615-14898-4; 978-0-615-15149-6; 978-0-615-18600-9)* 2389 Tobello Blvd., Indianapolis, IN 46234 USA
E-mail: ricardocantu6908@sbcglobal.net
Dist(s): **Lulu Pr., Inc.**

Canyon Beach Visual Communications, *(978-0-9754221)* PMB 108, 10 St. Francis Way, Unit 9, Cranberry Township, PA 16066 USA Tel 724-612-5784
E-mail: info@canyonbeach.com
Web site: http://www.canyonbeach.com.

Canyon Hawk Bks., *(978-0-578-10507-9)* 1750 El Paso Real, La Jolla, CA 92037 USA Tel 858-454-2475
E-mail: hobbes@san.rr.com.

Cap & Compass, LLC, *(978-0-9717366)* 132 Chestnut St., Branford, CT 06405 USA Tel 203-483-7005
E-mail: jesse@capandcompass.com
Web site: http://www.capandcompass.com
Dist(s): **Baker & Taylor Publisher Services (BTPS).**

Capercaillie Bks., Ltd (GBR) *(978-0-9542905; 978-0-9545206; 978-0-9549625; 978-0-9551246; 978-1-909305) Dist. by* **MYID_F_GATEWOO.**

Capital Apple Pr., *(978-0-9830686)* 742 Front St. No. 1, Catasauqua, PA 18032 USA Tel 610-596-0266.

Capital City Bks. LLC, *(978-0-9842881; 978-0-9835788)* c/o Hartwood Publishing, 1 N. 5th St., Suite 511, Richmond, VA 23219 USA Tel 804-836-6870; Fax: 804-644-3092
E-mail: capitalcitybooks@gmail.com
Web site: http://www.capitalcitybooks.com.

Capital Communications, Inc., *(978-0-9647700)* P.O. Box 10338, Sarasota, FL 34278-0338 USA Tel 941-342-9088; Fax: 941-377-3120; Toll Free: 800-546-8378
E-mail: capital@investors.org
Web site: http://www.investors.org.

Capital Publishing, *(978-0-9773016)* 6311 10th Ave., Brooklyn, NY 11219 USA Tel 718-921-6400; Fax: 718-921-0160
E-mail: pommedia@pommedia.com.

Capital Station Bks., LLC, *(978-0-9980452; 978-1-7334428; 978-1-7347587)* 5115 Hildreth Ln., Stockton, CA 95212 USA
E-mail: s.adelle.s@gmail.com.

Capitol Advantage Publishing *See* **Congress At Your Fingertips**

Cappella Publishing, A, *(978-0-9760271)* 20505 Yorba Linda Blvd., Suite 505, Yorba Linda, CA 92886 USA Tel 714-336-2350; Fax: 714-685-7773
E-mail: cgriffiths@acappellapublishing.com
Web site: http://www.acappellapublishing.com.

Capraro Press *See* **Leaders Pr.**

Capri Publishing, *(978-0-9769132; 978-0-9788612)* 4401 NW 39th St., #518, Midwest City, OK 73112 USA Tel 405-623-7619
E-mail: capripub@aol.com
Web site: http://www.capripublishing.net.

Capriccio Publishing, *(978-0-9770076)* 11100 SW 93rd Ct. Rd., Suite 10-405, Ocala, FL 34481 USA Tel 352-873-1403.

Capricorn Hse. Publishing, *(978-0-9791702; 978-1-60466)* 5122 Annesway Dr., Nashville, TN 37205 USA
E-mail: pclif@comcast.net.

Capricorn Publishing, *(978-0-9753970; 978-0-9774757)* 706 E. Brewster St., Appleton, WI 54911 USA Tel 920-475-0674; Fax: 920-954-9533
E-mail: getovd@yahoo.com
Web site: http://www.CapricornPublishing.com.

Capricorn Publishing, Incorporated *See* **Capricorn Publishing**

CAPS, LLC *See* **ALCAPS, LLC**

Capstone *Imprint of* **Wiley, John & Sons, Inc.**

Capstone, *(978-0-7368; 978-0-929895; 978-1-56065; 978-0-7565; 978-1-4048; 978-1-59889; 978-1-4296; 978-1-934338; 978-1-4342; 978-1-936700; 978-1-937412; 978-1-62065; 978-1-4765; 978-1-62370; 978-1-4795; 978-1-62521; 978-1-4914; 978-1-63079; 978-1-4965; 978-1-4966; 978-1-5157; 978-1-5158; 978-1-68436; 978-1-5435; 978-1-9771; 978-1-68446; 978-1-6639) Div. of Coughlan Companies. LLC, 1905 Lookout Dr., North Mankato, MN 55003 USA Tel 507-385-8215; Fax: 507-388-3752; Orders Addr.: 1710 Roe Crest Dr., North Mankato, MN 56003 USA (SAN 254-1815) Toll Free Fax: 888-262-0705; Toll Free: 800-747-4992; Edit Addr.: 5050 Lincoln Dr Suite 200, Edina, MN 55436 USA Fax: 952-933-2410; Toll Free: 888-517-8977; Imprints:* Pebble (Pebble Bks); Capstone Press (Capstone); Capstone Classroom (Cpstone Class); Capstone Editions (Caps Editions); Capstone Young Readers (Cap Young Rea); Compass Point Books (Compass Pt); Heinemann (Heinemn); Maupin House Publishing (Maupin Pub); Picture Window Books (Pic Window); Raintree (RaintreeCap);

Red Brick Learning (Red BrickL); Switch Press (Switch Pr); Stone Arch Books (Stone Arch); NA-h (NA-h); NA-r (NA-r) Do not confuse with Capstone Pr., Inc. in Decatur, IL
E-mail: customerservice@capstonepub.com
Web site: http://www.capstone-press.com; http://www.capstonepub.com; http://www.capstoneclassroom.com
Dist(s): **Casemate Pubs. & Bk. Distributors, LLC**
Continental Bk. Co., Inc.
Ebsco Publishing
Follett School Solutions
Lectorum Pubns., Inc.
MyiLibrary
SPD-Small Pr. Distribution.

Capstone Academics LLC, (*978-1-933557*) 3815 N. Brookfield Rd., Suite No. 104-122, Brookfield, WI 53045 USA (SAN 256-6761) Tel 262-754-4699; Toll Free: 888-922-7786
E-mail: contact@capstoneacademics.com
Web site: http://www.capstoneacademics.com.

Capstone Bks., (*978-0-9752843*) P.O. Box 7025, Greenwood, IN 46142 USA Tel 317-414-4770; 1710 Roe Crest Drive, N. Mankato, MN 56003
Web site: http://www.capstonebooks.com
Dist(s): **Follett School Solutions.**

Capstone Classroom *Imprint of* **Capstone**

Capstone Editions *Imprint of* **Capstone**

Capstone Media Services, (*978-0-578-42014-1; 978-0-578-42394-4; 978-0-578-42414-9; 978-0-578-42644-0; 978-0-578-43104-8; 978-0-578-43108-6; 978-0-578-43109-3; 978-0-578-43110-9; 978-0-578-43112-3; 978-0-578-43113-0; 978-0-578-43115-4; 978-0-578-43176-5; 978-0-578-43350-9; 978-0-578-43399-8; 978-0-578-43400-1; 978-0-578-43522-0; 978-0-578-43529-9; 978-0-578-43630-2; 978-0-578-43738-5; 978-0-578-43894-8; 978-0-578-43896-2; 978-0-578-43950-1; 978-0-578-43951-8; 978-0-578-43952-5; 978-0-578-43988-4; 978-0-578-44038-5;) 14 Wall St., NEW YORK, NY 10005 USA Tel 347-748-1480*
E-mail: Support@capstonemediaservice.com
Dist(s): **Ingram Content Group.**

Capstone Pr. *Imprint of* **Capstone**

Capstone Pr. *Imprint of* **A+ Bk. Publishing**

Capstone Press, Incorporated *See* **Capstone**

Capstone Pr., Inc., (*978-0-9667204*) 172 Dipper Ln., No. 6, Decatur, IL 62522 USA Tel 217-422-6033 Do not confuse with Capstone Pr., Inc., Mankato, MN
E-mail: jsjcj@fgi.net.

Capstone Young Readers *Imprint of* **Capstone**

Captain & Harry LLC, The, (*978-0-9724777*) 8875 Section Line Rd., Harbor Beach, MI 48441-9616 USA
E-mail: janlangley5@gmail.com
Web site: http://www.michiganghoststories.net; http://www.thecaptainandharry.com.

Captain Caleb Communications, (*978-0-9703021*) 1250 Cynder Ct., Annapolis, MD 21401-7504 USA Tel 410 626 8904; 410-626-8904
E-mail: jcurtis@toad.net
Web site: http://www.oysterbook.com.

Captain Fiddle Pubns., (*978-0-931877*) 4 Elm Ct., Newmarket, NH 03857 USA (SAN 686-0508) Tel 603-659-2658
E-mail: cFiddle@tiac.net
Web site: http://www.captainfiddle.com.

Captain McFinn and Friends LLC, McFinn Pr., (*978-0-9799283; 978-0-9859482*) 2445 Belmont Ave., Youungstown, OH 44504-0186 USA Tel 330-747-2661; Fax: 330-743-2719
E-mail: kbaker@cafarocompany.com.

Captain, Tamira R. *See* **Stories From Four Publishing Co.**

Captain the Big Dog Pr., (*978-0-9995096*) P.O. Box 1135, Pentwater, MI 49449 USA Tel 231-869-5896
E-mail: ordoobadifamily@gmail.com.

Captio Corp., (*978-0-9766614*) 2230 Tioga Dr., Menlo Park, CA 94025-6640 USA
Web site: http://www.captio.com.

Capture Bks., (*978-0-9798664*) 12331 Checkerboard Cir., Norman, OK 73026 USA (SAN 854-6207) Tel 405-485-8131
Web site: http://capturebooks.com.

Capturing Memories, (*978-0-9727759*) 9228 SW 209th St, Vashon, WA 98070 USA Tel 206-463-5652
E-mail: roger@capturingmemories.com; stories@capturingmemories.com
Web site: http://www.capturingmemories.com.

Captus, LLC, (*978-0-9776627*) 32725 Ledge Hill Dr., Solon, OH 44139 USA Tel 440-498-9178; Fax: 440-238-2967
E-mail: czlance@yahoo.com
Web site: http://www.babyalmamater.com.

Capybara Madness, (*978-0-9899847*) 700 Jerrys Ln., Buda, TX 78610 USA Tel 512-751-6667
E-mail: typaldos@gmail.com
Web site: www.capybaramadness.com.

Carapetian, Chris, (*978-1-7324264*) 44509 Palo Verde st, Lancaster, CA 93536 USA Tel 818-216-3302
E-mail: hirisedesign@gmail.com.

Caravan of Dreams Productions, (*978-0-929856*) Div. of Caravan of Dreams, 512 Main St. Ste. 1500, Fort Worth, TX 76102-3922 USA (SAN 250-4855).

Carazona Creations LLC, (*978-0-9753724*) PO Box 635, Clarkdale, AZ 86324 USA Toll Free: 888-328-3300
E-mail: carazona@carazonacreations.com
Web site: http://www.carazonacreations.com.

Carbon Publishing *See* **Parallel Vortex**

Carden Jennings Publishing Co., Ltd., (*978-1-891524*) 375 Greenbrier Dr., Suite 100, Charlottesvle, VA 22901-1618 USA
Web site: http://www.cjp.com.

Cardigras.com *See* **airjam.com**

Cardinal Brands, Inc., (*978-1-932435*) 1251 SW Arrowhead Rd. Ste. A, Topeka, KS 66604-4061 USA Toll Free: 800-444-0038
Web site: http://www.witty-one.com; http://www.cardinalbrands.com.

Cardinal Pr., (*978-0-9779518*) 19 W. 76th St. Suite 1be, New York, NY 10023 USA
Web site: http://www.cardinal-press.com.

Cardinal Pubs. Group, 2402 N. Shadeland Ave. Ste. A, Indianapolis, IN 46219-1746 USA (SAN 631-7936)
E-mail: tdoherty@in.net.

Cardinal Rule Pr. *Imprint of* **Dismondy, Maria Inc.**

Cardlings, (*978-0-9760108*) Orders Addr.: P.O. Box 931, Pueblo, CO 81002 USA; Edit Addr.: 815 W. 14th St., Pueblo, CO 81003 USA
E-mail: gnome@cardlings.com
Web site: http://www.cardlings.com.

Cardwell, Robert K, (*978-1-7323433; 978-1-7338348*) 1 Warwick Rd., Ocean City, NJ 08226 USA Tel 609-334-3777
E-mail: kdrc4@aol.com.

Career Pr. *Imprint of* **Red Wheel/Weiser**

Carefree Publishing *Imprint of* **Milano, Jacque & Assocs.**

Carey III, John, (*978-0-9799876*) 5510 NE. Antioch Suite 133, Gladstone, MO 64118 USA (SAN 854-9222)
E-mail: ecarey1222@yahoo.com.

Carey, Nicole, (*978-0-578-46245-5; 978-1-7331945; 978-1-7354788*) 3801 14th Ave., Kearney, NE 68845 USA Tel 308-240-0142
E-mail: ronicki@yahoo.com.

Carey, Rebecca, (*978-0-9791331*) 1035 S. 43rd St., Wilmington, NC 28403-4369 USA
E-mail: because@aol.com
Web site: http://www.bigarthouse.com.

Carey, William Library Publishers *See* **Carey, William Publishing**

Carey, William Publishing, (*978-0-87808; 978-1-64508*) 10 W. Dry Creek Cir., Littleton, CO 80120 USA (SAN 208-2101)
E-mail: publishing@wclbooks.com
Web site: https://missionbooks.org/
Dist(s): **Anchor Distributors**
Ingram Content Group
Whitaker Hse.

Cargill Consulting, Inc., (*978-0-9743780; 978-1-7333428*) 19836 Linda Ln., Harrah, OK 73045-9351 USA
Web site: http://www.cargillconsulting.com.

Caribbean Publishing *See* **Coconut Pr., LLC**

Caribbean Scene, (*978-0-9678030*) 5 Walnut Ave., East Norwich, NY 11732 USA.

CaribbeanReads, (*978-0-615-22865-5; 978-0-9832978; 978-0-9899305; 978-0-9908659; 978-0-9964358; 978-0-9978900; 978-0-9992372; 978-1-7338299; 978-1-953747*) 10314 Collingham Dr., Fairfax, VA 22032 USA Tel 202-683-0611
E-mail: carol.mitchell@caribbeanreads.com
Web site: www.caribbeanreads.com.

Caritas Communications, (*978-0-9668228; 978-0-9753259; 978-0-9799390; 978-0-615-76666-9; 978-0-615-87196-7*) 216 N. Green Bay Road, No. 208, Thiensville, WI 53092-2010 USA Tel 414-531-0503; Fax: 262-238-9039 Do not confuse with Caritas Communications Incorporated in New York, NY, Rhinebeck, NY
E-mail: dgawlik@wi.rr.com
Dist(s): **CreateSpace Independent Publishing Platform.**

Carleton Bks., (*978-0-9759738*) 335 N. Main Ave., Tucson, AZ 85701 USA.

Carlisle Pr.- Walnut Creek, (*978-0-9642548; 978-1-890050; 978-1-933753*) 2673 Township Rd., No. 421, Sugarcreek, OH 44681 USA Tel 330-852-1900; Fax: 330-852-3285; Toll Free: 800-852-4482 Do not confuse with companies with the same name in Mechanicsburg, PA, Sedona, AZ, Benbrook, TX.

CarLou Interactive Media & Publishing, (*978-0-9759325*) 12439 Magnolia Blvd., No. 170, Valley Village, CA 91607 USA
E-mail: tess@worldtrust.org
Web site: http://www.carloumedia.com.

Carlsbad Caverns Guadalupe Mountains Assn., (*978-0-916907*) P.O. Box 1417, Carlsbad, NM 88221-1417 USA (SAN 268-6627) Tel 505-785-2485.

Carlsbad Caverns Natural History Association *See* **Carlsbad Caverns Guadalupe Mountains Assn.**

Carlsen Verlag (DEU) (*978-3-551*) *Dist. by* **Distribks Inc.**

Carlson, Debra R., (*978-0-9765950*) 1705 N. 160th St., Omaha, NE 68118-2408 USA
Web site: http://www.cozykidspress.com.

Carlson Pr., (*978-0-9972220*) 614 BRADBURY RD, MONROVIA, CA 91016 USA Tel 951-541-7944
E-mail: carlsonlighthouse@hotmail.com.

Carlton Bks., Ltd. (GBR) (*978-1-85868; 978-1-84222; 978-1-84442; 978-1-84732; 978-1-78097; 978-1-78739; 978-1-911610*) *Dist. by* **TwoRivers.**

Carlton Kids (GBR) (*978-1-78312*) *Dist. by* **TwoRivers.**

Carmean Productions LLC, (*978-0-9839799*) 1905 NW 37th Blvd., Gainesville, FL 32605 USA Tel 352-514-5625
E-mail: John@johncarmean.com
Web site: www.carmeanproductions.com.

Carmel Concepts, Ltd., (*978-0-9646285*) 50 Mt. Tiburon Rd., Tiburon, CA 94920 USA Tel 415-435-8066; Fax: 415-435-3750.

Carnegie Learning Incorporated *See* **Carnegie Learning Inc.**

Carnegie Learning Inc., (*978-1-930804; 978-1-932409; 978-1-934239; 978-1-934800; 978-1-935162; 978-1-936152; 978-1-60972; 978-1-949240; 978-1-68459*) 501 Grant St., Suite 1075, Pittsburgh, PA 15219 USA Tel 412-690-2442 Toll Free: 888-851-7094
Web site: http://carnegielearning.com.

Carney Educational Services, (*978-1-930288*) 1150 Foothill Blvd., Ste B, La Canada, CA 91011 USA Toll Free: 888-511-7737
E-mail: michellecarroll67@gmail.com
Web site: http://www.thebrightmind.com
Dist(s): **Sunbelt Pubns., Inc.**

Carney, Sean Creative LLC *See* **Bull & Brain Creative**

Carnifex Pr., (*978-0-9759727; 978-0-9789583*) P.O. Box 1686, Ormond Beach, FL 32175 USA Tel 386-677-2980
E-mail: carnifexpress@hotmail.com
Web site: http://www.carnifexpress.net.

Carnivore Games, (*978-0-9749150; 978-1-7339749*) Orders Addr.: P.O. Box 846, Londonderry, NH 03053-0846 USA; Edit Addr.: 12 Emerald Dr., Derry, NH 03038 USA
E-mail: brad@carnivoregames.com
Web site: http://www.carnivoregames.com/.

Carol J. Pierre, LLC, (*978-0-578-19829-3*) 2045 Mt. Zion Rd., Suite 366, Morrow, GA 30260 USA Tel 678-615-5965; *Imprints:* Pierre Publishing (PierrePub)
E-mail: millonesinc@yahoo.com; moneymindbook@gmail.com
Web site: www.moneymindbooks.com.

Carol Kalhagen-Tamanaha, (*978-0-9799493*) 36020 Big Trout Rd., Hebo, OR 97122 USA
E-mail: beartotem@earthlink.net
Web site: http://www.CarolKalhagenWildlifeart.com.

Carole "Lisa Lynn" Gilbert, (*978-0-692-98458-1; 978-0-692-11031-7; 978-0-692-19521-5; 978-0-692-19793-6; 978-1-7329447; 978-1-7346873*) 1708 Quail Valley Rd., Iowa Park, TX 76367 USA Tel 940-592-1136; Fax: 940-592-1136
E-mail: mamagilbert@aol.com
Web site: carolelgilbert.com.

Carolina Academic Pr., (*978-0-89089; 978-1-59460; 978-1-61163; 978-1-5310*) 700 Kent St., Durham, NC 27701 USA (SAN 210-7848) Tel 919-489-7486; Fax: 919-493-5668
E-mail: tim@cap-press.com; css@cap-press.com
Dist(s): **Follett School Solutions.**

Carolina Biological Supply Co., (*978-0-89278; 978-1-4350*) 2700 York Rd., Burlington, NC 27215-3398 USA (SAN 249-2784) Tel 336-584-0381; Fax: 910-584-3399; Toll Free Fax: 800-222-7112; Toll Free: 800-334-5551
E-mail: carolina@carolina.com
Web site: http://www.carolina.com
Dist(s): **Follett School Solutions.**

Carolina Canines for Service Inc., (*978-0-9800070*) P.O. Box 12643, Wilmington, NC 28405-1823 USA Tel 910-362-8181; Fax: 910-362-8184; Toll Free: 866-910-3647
Web site: http://www.carolinacanines.org.

Carolina Children, (*978-0-9794580*) P.O. Box 862, Mauldin, SC 29662 USA
Web site: http://carolinachildren.net.

†Carolina Wren Pr., (*978-0-932112; 978-1-949467*) 905 W. Main St. Suite 19 D-1, Durham, NC 27701 USA (SAN 213-0327) Tel 919-682-0555; *Imprints:* Blair (MYID_W_BLAIR)
E-mail: ops@blairpubl.com
Dist(s): **Consortium Bk. Sales & Distribution**
Follett School Solutions
MyiLibrary; *CIP.*

Carolrhoda Bks. *Imprint of* **Lerner Publishing Group**

Carolrhoda Lab™ *Imprint of* **Lerner Publishing Group**

Carolyn & Kristina's Bookshelf, (*978-0-615-18357-2*) 550 Brittany Ct., North Huntingdon, PA 15642 USA
E-mail: prin66@aol.com; cnkbkshelf@aim.com
Dist(s): **Lulu Pr., Inc.**

Carolyn Clare Givens Writing & Editing, (*978-0-9988454; 978-978-099-884-4*) 7412 Shadowstone Dr., Charlotte, NC 28270 USA Tel 734-837-3436; Fax: 734-837-3436
E-mail: carolynclaregivens@gmail.com
Web site: http://carolyncgivens.com.

Carousel Pubns., Inc., (*978-0-9759382*) P.O. Box 225, Springfield, NJ 07081 USA
Web site: http://www.net2infinity/aplaceinthesky.

Carp Cove Pr., (*978-0-9703752*) Orders Addr.: 9099 Oneida River Pk. Dr., Clay, NY 13041 USA Tel 315-652-4964
E-mail: carpcovepress@holisticanimal.com; Colleen@holisticanimal.com
Web site: http://www.holisticanimal.com/.

Carp Hse. Pr., (*978-0-9860663; 978-0-9860663-0-6*) 4403-B Catlin Cir., Carp interim, CA 93013 USA Tel 805-684-0691
E-mail: Gold2@cox.com.

Carpe Noctem Publishing LLC, (*978-0-9965756; 978-1-950032*) P.O. Box 7949, Little Rock, AR 72217 USA Tel 501-993-2080
E-mail: authorjencrane@gmail.com
Web site: www.JenCraneBooks.com.

Carpe Viam Productions, LLC, (*978-0-9892949*) Orders Addr.: 3217 E. Shea Blvd. No. 305, Phoenix, AZ 85028 USA (SAN 920-8356) Tel 602-762-1473
E-mail: dwight@theLittleRedRacingCar.com
Web site: www.theLittleRedRacingCar.com.

Carpenter's Son Publishing, (*978-0-9832846; 978-0-9835571; 978-0-9839876; 978-0-9849771; 978-0-9849772; 978-0-9851085; 978-0-9883043; 978-0-9883962; 978-0-9885931; 978-0-9889403; 978-0-9893722; 978-1-940262; 978-1-942557; 978-1-942587; 978-1-945507; 978-1-946889; 978-1-948484; 978-1-949572; 978-1-950892; 978-1-7340850; 978-1-952025) 307 Verde Meadow Dr., Franklin, TN 37067 USA Tel 615-472-1128*
E-mail: larry@christianbookservices.com
Dist(s): **Ingram Publisher Services**
MyiLibrary
Send The Light Distribution LLC
Smashwords.

Carradice Collection, (*978-0-9985385; 978-0-578-41138-5; 978-0-578-53389-6; 978-0-578-60087-1*) 3925 Ivy St. Apt. 1 Front, East Chicago, IN 46312 USA Tel 219-718-6894; 3925 Ivy St. Apt. 1front, East Chicago, IN 46312
E-mail: ihadadream44@gmail.com; mikey_talbot@hotmail.com
Web site: http://carradicecollection.com.

Carriage House Publishing *See* **American Carriage Hse. Publishing**

Carrier, Therese, (*978-0-9797648*) 2020 Fieldstone Pkwy., Suite 900 PMB 121, Franklin, TN 37069 USA
Web site: http://hwbdproductions.com.

Carrington Bks., (*978-0-9787143; 978-0-9820003; 978-0-9819656*) P.O. Box 451399, Los Angeles, CA 90045 USA Tel 310-628-5557; 12975 Agustin Pl., No. A-109, Playa Vista, CA 90094
Web site: http://www.StudentSafetyTips.com.

Carroll Pr., (*978-0-9986187*) 1510 Grand Ave, Seattle, WA 98122 USA Tel 206-328-5218
E-mail: mccormick.mj@comcast.net
Web site: susanmccormickbooks.com.

Carroll, Sherry, (*978-0-9752994*) P.O. Box 34603, Washington, DC 20774 USA
E-mail: carrollcom01@aol.com.

Carson, Tracy, (*978-0-9767077*) 1998 66th St., SE, Bismarck, ND 58504-3835 USA
Web site: http://www.grandmaisnowabutterfly.com.

Carson-Dellosa Christian *Imprint of* **Carson-Dellosa Publishing, LLC**

Carson-Dellosa Publishing Company, Incorporated *See* **Carson-Dellosa Publishing, LLC**

Carson-Dellosa Publishing, LLC, (*978-0-88724; 978-1-57156; 978-1-57332; 978-1-59441; 978-1-60022; 978-1-60418; 978-1-936022; 978-1-936023; 978-1-936024; 978-0-9823625; 978-0-9823626; 978-0-9823627; 978-0-692-00200-1; 978-1-60996; 978-1-62057; 978-1-62223; 978-1-62399; 978-1-62442; 978-1-62648; 978-1-4838) Orders Addr.: P.O. Box 35665, Greensboro, NC 27425 USA Tel 336-632-0084; Fax: 336-808-3249; Toll Free: 800-321-0943; Imprints:* Carson-Dellosa Christian (CDChristian); DJ Inkers (DJInk); HighReach Learning, Incorporated (HghRchLrn); Brighter Child (BrighterChild); Spectrum (Spectrum Dell); American Education Publishing (AEP); Frank Schaffer Publications (FS Pubns); Instructional Fair (InstFair); Thinking Kids (ThinkKids)
Web site: http://www.carsondellosa.com
Dist(s): **Follett School Solutions.**

Carsume, (*978-0-9883927*) 16509 Old Forest Rd., Hacienda Heights, CA 91745 USA Tel 626-968-2192
E-mail: sumeta@verizon.net.

Carter, Deborah, (*978-0-692-56254-3*) 380 Clocks Blvd., Massapequa, NY 11758 USA Tel 516-557-9562
E-mail: jobmagic@aol.com.

CarterPr. LLC, (*978-1-950596*) 725 River Rd., Suite 32-174, Edgewater, NJ 07020 USA Tel 866-233-7307
E-mail: zac@carterpress.com
Web site: www.carterpress.com.

Cartoon Connections Pr., (*978-0-9657136*) P.O. Box 10889, White Bear Lake, MN 55110 USA (SAN 299-352X) Tel 651-429-1244; 651-429-7660; 24145 435Th Ave., Aitkin, MN 56431
E-mail: CartoonC@aol.com
Web site: http://www.cartooningbasics.com; http://www.cartoonconnections.com
Dist(s): **Follett School Solutions**
F&W Media, Inc.

Cartoonmario.com, (*978-0-9766755*) 5084 S. 65th St., Greenfield, WI 53220-4504 USA Tel 414-541-9221 (phone/fax)
E-mail: mdm@cartoonmario.com
Web site: http://www.cartoonmario.com.

Cartoons & Caricatures *See* **Drawing From History**

Cartwheel Bks. *Imprint of* **Scholastic, Inc.**

Cartwright Publishing, (*978-0-9861613; 978-1-7321736*) P.O. Box 145, Corte Madera, CA 94925 USA Tel 415-354-2388
E-mail: mark@datagroup.com.

Caruso, Kevin M. *See* **Aerospace 1 Pubns.**

Caryn Solutions, LLC, (*978-0-9791046*) Orders Addr.: P.O. Box 635, Naples, FL 34106 USA (SAN 852-4726) Tel 239-404-5820
E-mail: caryn@carynsolutions.com
Web site: http://www.carynsolutions.com.

CaryPress *See* **CaryPr. International Bks.**

CaryPr. International Bks., (*978-0-615-86265-1; 978-1-63103*) 8263 NC HWY 86 N, Providence, NC 27315 USA Tel 3363880248
Web site: http://www.write-a-book.org/; http://memoirtherapist.com/; www.CaryPress.com; ghostwriters-for-hire.com; saleattraction.com
Dist(s): **CreateSpace Independent Publishing Platform.**

Casa Bautista de Publicaciones, (*978-0-311*) Div. of Southern Baptist Convention, Orders Addr.: P.O. Box 4255, El Paso, TX 79914 USA (SAN 220-0139) Tel 915-566-9656; Fax: 915-562-6502; Toll Free: 800-755-5958; *Imprints:* Editorial Mundo Hispano (Edit Mundo)
E-mail: epena@casabautista.org
Web site: http://www.casabautista.org
Dist(s): **Smashwords.**

Casa Creacion *Imprint of* **Charisma Media**

Casa de Estudios de Literatura y Talleres Artisticos Amaquemecan A.C. (MEX) (*978-968-6465*) *Dist. by* **Lectorum Pubns.**

Casa de Periodistas Editorial, (*978-0-9743102*) Orders Addr.: P.O. Box 9021787, San Juan, PR 00902-1787

Publisher Name Index

USA; Edit Addr.: Calle de la Luna, Esq. Calle de San José, San Juan, PR 00902-1787 USA
E-mail: muitiser@coqui.net
Web site: http://www.asppro.org.

Casa de Snapdragon LLC, *(978-0-9793075; 978-0-9840530; 978-0-9845681; 978-1-937240)* Orders Addr.: 12901 Bryce Ave., NE, Albuquerque, NM 87112 USA Tel 505-508-5513
E-mail: sales@casadesnapdragon.com; managingeditor@casadesnapdragon.com
Web site: http://www.casadesnapdragon.com
Dist(s): **Smashwords.**

Casa Nazarena de Publicacions, *(978-1-56344)* 6401 The Paseo, Kansas City, MO 64131 USA Tel 816-333-7000; Fax: 816-333-1748; Toll Free: 800-462-8711
E-mail: donnie@nph.com
Dist(s): **The Foundry Publishing.**

Casa Promesa *Imprint of* **Barbour Publishing, Inc.**

Cascade Design Publishing *See* **Cascade, Inc.**

Cascade, Inc., *(978-0-9726173)* 1085 Commonwealth Ave., PMB 253, Boston, MA 02215 USA Tel 617-558-1038; *Imprints:* Philograph (Philograph)
E-mail: info@philograph.com
Web site: http://www.philograph.com.

Cascade Pass, Inc., *(978-1-880599; 978-0-615-39461-9; 978-1-935999)* Orders Addr.: 4223 Glencoe Ave., Suite C-105, Marina del Rey, CA 90292 USA Tel 310-305-0210; Fax: 310-305-7850; Toll Free: 888-837-0704
E-mail: jlc@cascadepass.com
Web site: http://www.cascadepass.com
Dist(s): **Follett School Solutions.**

Cascade Pr., *(978-0-692-83243-1)* 3411 Greenacres Rd, Mesa, WA 99343 USA Tel 509-430-3390
E-mail: lovewillfindu2@gmail.com
Dist(s): **Independent Pub.**

Cascade Publishing Incorporated *See* **Compass Productions Inc.**

Cascade Writing, *(978-0-9767519)* 1808 Lake Dr., Camano Island, WA 98282 USA Tel 360-387-8023
E-mail: dennisc@whidbey.net.

Cascadia Publishing Hse., LLC, *(978-0-9665021; 978-1-931038; 978-1-68027)* Orders Addr.: 126 Klingerman Rd., Telford, PA 18969 USA Tel 215-723-9125; Fax: 215-721-2312
E-mail: editor@cascadiapublishinghouse; mking@cascadiapublishinghouse.com; contact@cascadiapublishinghouse.com
Web site: http://www.pandorapressus.com; http://www.cascadiapublishinghouse.com
Dist(s): **Follett School Solutions**
Herald Pr.

Cascarano, John *See* **Lock & Mane**

Case, Darrell, *(978-0-615-60186-1; 978-0-692-78774-8; 978-0-692-88205-4)* 4118 W Co Rd 975 N, Farmersburg, IN 47850 USA Tel 812-394-2219 (phone/fax)
Web site: darrellcase.com
Dist(s): **CreateSpace Independent Publishing Platform.**

Casemate Academic, *(978-0-9774094; 978-1-935488)* Orders Addr.: P.O. Box 511, Oakville, CT 06779 USA (SAN 630-9461) Tel 860-945-9329; Fax: 860-945-9468; Toll Free: 800-791-9354; Edit Addr.: 20 Main St., Oakville, CT 06779 USA
E-mail: queries@dbbconline.com
Web site: http://www.oxbowbooks.com
Dist(s): **Casemate Pubs. & Bk. Distributors, LLC.**

Casemate Pubs. & Bk. Distributors, LLC, *(978-0-9711709; 978-1-932033; 978-1-935149; 978-1-61200; 978-1-952715; 978-1-63624)* Orders Addr.: 1950 Lawrence Rd., Havertown, PA 19083 USA; 22883 Quicksilver Dr., Herndon, VA 20166 (SAN 631-9386) Tel 703-661-1500; Edit Addr.: 180 Varick St. Suite 816, New York, NY 10014 USA
E-mail: casemate@casematepublishing.com
Web site: http://www.casematepublishing.com
Dist(s): **MyiLibrary**
Open Road Integrated Media, Inc.
ebrary, Inc.

Casey Joy Bks., *(978-0-692-96067-7)* 4053 Rivertown Ln, Wyoming, MI 49418 USA Tel 616-293-9908
E-mail: caseyjoybergman@att.net
Dist(s): **Independent Pub.**

Caseys World Bks., *(978-0-9765872)* Orders Addr.: 1998 Skyline Dr., Saintughton, WI 53589 USA Tel 608-335-0401 Please call with any questions. Leave a voice message if no answer.
E-mail: kate@caseysworld.net
Web site: http://www.caseysworld.net.

Caslon Books *See* **Slangman Publishing**

Caslon Pr., *(978-0-9728144)* 315 Richards Ave., Portsmouth, NH 03801-5239 USA Tel 603-431-6823
E-mail: jbf@fergus.com
Web site: http://www.jbf.fergus.com.

Caso, George R., *(978-0-9719290)* 2445 Babylon Tpke., Merrick, NY 11566 USA Tel 516-379-9397.

Cassandra Armstrong *See* **Storm Moon Pr., LLC**

Cassava Republic Pr. (GBR) *(978-1-911115) Dist. by* **Consort Bk Sales.**

Casscom Media, *(978-1-930034; 978-1-936081; 978-1-62758)* 6000 Industrial Dr., Greenville, TX 75402 USA Tel 903-455-2555; Fax: 903-455-4448; Toll Free: 800-974-1555
E-mail: sue@casscommedia.com; kathy@casscomedia.com
Web site: http://www.casscommedia.com
Dist(s): **Destiny Image Pubs.**
Follett School Solutions.

Cassette & Video Learning Systems *See* **Watch & Learn, Inc.**

Cassette Communications, Incorporated *See* **Casscom Media**

Castadream LLC, *(978-0-692-47520-1)* 69 Shaker CT, GUILFORD, CT 06437 USA Tel 203-361-6300.

Castaneda, Kay, *(978-0-578-43935-8; 978-0-578-43936-5)* 12155 Pebble St. Unit 200, Fishers, IN 46038 USA Tel 317-737-6993
E-mail: kay@whiteriverwriters.com
Dist(s): **Ingram Content Group.**

Castellated Pr., *(978-0-9746416)* 21325 NE 130th Ave., Fort McCoy, FL 32134 USA
E-mail: shzamek@gmail.com
Web site: http://www.castellatedpress.com.

Casterman, Editions (FRA) *(978-2-203; 978-2-542) Dist. by* **Distribks Inc.**

Castillo, Ediciones, S. A. de C. V. (MEX) *(978-968-6635; 978-968-7415; 978-970-20) Dist. by* **Mariuccia Iaconi Bk Imports.**

Castillo, Ediciones, S. A. de C. V. (MEX) *(978-968-6635; 978-968-7415; 978-970-20) Dist. by* **Macmillan.**

Castillo, Ediciones, S. A. de C. V. (MEX) *(978-968-6635; 978-968-7415; 978-970-20) Dist. by* **Lectorum Pubns.**

Castle Builder Pr. *Imprint of* **Blue Cubicle Pr., LLC**

Castle Creative, *(978-0-692-99043-8; 978-0-692-99044-5)* P.O. Box 391, Mount Hood Parkdale, OR 97041 USA Tel 541-490-2324
E-mail: teamc2g2@gmail.com
Dist(s): **Ingram Content Group.**

Castle Keep Pr. *Imprint of* **Rock, James A. & Co. Pubs.**

Castle Pacific Publishing, *(978-0-9653869; 978-0-9749305; 978-0-9774168)* P.O. Box 77089, Seattle, WA 98177 USA Tel 206-839-0984; Toll Free: 888-756-2665 (888-756-BOOK)
Web site: http://www.castlepacific.com.

Castle Pr., *(978-0-9669263; 978-0-9835012)* 1222 N. Fair Oaks Ave., Pasadena, CA 91103 USA Fax: 626-789-7385
E-mail: george@castlepress.com.

Castle Rock Creative, Inc., *(978-0-9820544; 978-1-939445; 978-1-943754; 978-0-9982107)* 212 Grey Ave., Evanston, IL 60202 USA (SAN 857-1023) Tel 847-328-2561 (phone/fax)
Web site: http://www.daveneta.com; www.Trailblazerbooks.com.

Castlebay, Inc., *(978-0-9748145)* P.O. Box 168, Round Pond, ME 04564-0168 USA Tel 207-529-5438
E-mail: castlebay@castlebay.net.

Castleberry Farms Pr., *(978-1-891907)* Orders Addr.: P.O. Box 337, Poplar, WI 54864 USA Tel 715-364-8404
E-mail: cbfarmpr@centurytel.net
Web site: http://www.castleberryfarmspress.com; http://www.cbfarmpr.com.

Castlebridge Bks. *Imprint of* **Big Tent Bks.**

Castlebrook Pubns., *(978-0-9641697; 978-0-9798242; 978-0-615-99230-3; 978-0-692-53831-9; 978-0-692-61641-3)* Orders Addr.: P.O. Box 132, Camp Meeker, CA 95419 USA; 1535 Farmers Ln., Pmb #237, Santa Rosa, CA 95405
E-mail: castlebrookpublications@aol.com
Web site: http://www.youdrawitbooks.com; http://www.printanddraw.com
Dist(s): **CreateSpace Independent Publishing Platform**
Follett School Solutions.

Castleconal Pr., *(978-0-9677348)* 1517 National Ave., Madison, WI 53716 USA Tel 608-222-6051; Fax: 608-221-5264
E-mail: dfleming@madison.k12.wi.us.

Castlegate Pr., *(978-0-9743588)* 457 Terraces Ct., Mesquite, NV 89027 USA Tel 303-550-3360; Fax: 702-346-2058.

Castleton, Julia J, *(978-0-578-06109-2)* P.O. Box 880371, Pukalani, HI 96788 USA.

Castro, Shirley, *(978-0-9790307; 978-0-578-62659-8)* 9917 Stockholm Pl., Bakersfield, CA 93306 USA Tel 661-331-9546
Web site: http://www.pelicanfamily.com.

Cat Marcs Publishing, *(978-0-9843899; 978-1-943786)* P.O. Box 54, Silverdale, WA 98383 USA Tel 360-271-4448
E-mail: crysmm307@aol.com; info@catmarcs.com
Web site: http://crystalmarcos.com/; http://catmarcs.com/.

Catalpa Pr., *(978-0-9745665; 978-0-9763810; 978-0-615-56579-8)* P.O. Box 27303, Oakland, CA 94602-0303 USA (SAN 256-4068)
E-mail: jack@jackschroder.com; staff@catalpapress.com
Web site: http://www.jackschroder.com; http://www.malpracticebooks.com.

Catalyst Bk. Pr., *(978-0-9802081; 978-1-946395; 978-1-946498; 978-1-7335474)* 2941 Kelly St., Livermore, CA 94551-5921 USA (SAN 855-4803); *Imprints:* Story Press Africa (MYID_O_STORY P)
E-mail: jlpowers@evaporites.com; jlpowers@catalystbookpress.com
Web site: http://www.catalystpress.org
Dist(s): **Consortium Bk. Sales & Distribution.**

Catalyst Game Labs *Imprint of* **InMediaRes Productions**

Catamount Publishing LLC, *(978-0-9752922)* P.O. Box 30015, Denver, CO 80218 USA Tel 303-839-1687 Do not confuse with Catamount Publishing LLC in Allenstown, NH.

Catapulta Pr., *(978-0-9762986)* 2242 Hemingway Dr., Suite H, Fort Myers, FL 33912 USA
Dist(s): **Hachette Bk. Group.**

Catawba Publishing Co., *(978-1-59712)* 5945 Orr Rd. Ste. F, Charlotte, NC 28213-7314 USA
E-mail: info@catawbapublishing.com
Web site: http://www.catawbapublishing.com.

catBOX Entertainment, Inc., *(978-0-9706062)* Orders Addr.: P.O. Box 1077, Oklahoma City, OK 73101 USA Tel 405-232-1400; Edit Addr.: P.O. Box 1077, Oklahoma City, OK 73101 USA
E-mail: alohapublishing@aol.com
Web site: http://www.catdetectives.com; http://www.catboxentertainment.com.

Catch 22 Publishing, *(978-0-9759691)* 1228 Tennyson Ln., Naperville, IL 60540 USA
E-mail: kthomaschicago@gmail.com
Web site: http://www.livinglifesociety.com.

Catch 22 Publishing Incorporated *See* **Catch 22 Publishing**

Catch the Spirit of Appalachia *Imprint of* **Ammons Communications, Ltd.**

Catch-A-Winner Publishing, *(978-0-9845630; 978-0-9985254; 978-1-7340800; 978-1-7344586; 978-1-7347381)* P.O. Box 160125, San Antonio, TX 78280 USA Tel 210-387-8189
E-mail: jamestaylor22@live.com.

Catechesis of the Good Shepherd *Imprint of* **Liturgy Training Pubns.**

Caterpillar & Gypsy Moth Pr. *Imprint of* **Reynoso, Michelle**

Cates, Jr., Richard L, *(978-0-692-93813-3)* 5992 Cty. Rd T, Spring Green, WI 53588 USA Tel 608-588-2836; Fax: 608-588-2836
E-mail: richardlcates@gmail.com.

Cathal Entertainment *Imprint of* **Cathal Entertainment**

Cathal Entertainment, *(978-0-9822656; 978-0-615-77486-2; 978-0-615-77543-2)* 11381 SW 17th Ct., Miramar, FL 33025 USA Tel 305-206-3699; *Imprints:* Cathal Entertainment (MYID_S_CATHAL)
E-mail: phil.mccalli@gmail.com
Web site: cathalclub.com
Dist(s): **CreateSpace Independent Publishing Platform**
INscribe Digital.

Cathedral of the Holy Spirit, *(978-0-917595)* Div. of Chapel Hill Harvester Church, 4650 Flat Shoals Rd., Decatur, GA 30034 USA (SAN 657-1484) Tel 404-243-5020; Fax: 404-243-5927; Toll Free: 800-241-4702.

Cathedrall Pr./Encycloware, *(978-0-9626554)* 2703 Townes Dr., Greenville, NC 27858 USA Tel 252-341-8906
E-mail: encycloware@suddenlink.net
Web site: http://www.KabalyonKey.com.

Catherine Fenquist, *(978-0-692-19381-5; 978-0-692-19382-2; 978-0-578-67052-2)* 7413 10th Hole Dr., Windsor, CA 95492 USA Tel 707-483-9957
E-mail: Catherine.Fenquist@gmail.com
Dist(s): **Ingram Content Group.**

Cathier Pr., *(978-0-9720445)* 156 Gates Rd., Lizella, GA 31052 USA.

Catholic Answers, Inc., *(978-1-888992; 978-1-933919; 978-1-938983; 978-1-941663; 978-1-68357)* 2020 Gillespie Way, El Cajon, CA 92020-0908 USA Tel 619-387-7200; Fax: 619-387-0042; Toll Free: 888-291-8000 (orders)
E-mail: mobrien@catholic.com
Web site: http://www.catholic.com.

Catholic Authors Pr., *(978-0-9776168; 978-0-9789432)* 203 Fairfield Ave., Hartford, CT 06114 USA
E-mail: books@catholicauthors.org
Web site: http://www.catholicauthors.org.

Catholic Bk. Publishing Corp., *(978-0-89942; 978-0-9623410; 978-1-878718; 978-1-933066; 978-1-937913; 978-1-941243; 978-1-947070; 978-1-948843; 978-1-948844; 978-1-953152)* 77 West End Rd., Totowa, NJ 07512-1405 USA (SAN 204-3432) Tel 973-890-2400; Fax: 973-890-2410; Toll Free: 800-892-6657; *Imprints:* Resurrection Press (Resurrection Pr)
E-mail: resurpress@aol.com
Web site: http://www.catholicbkpub.com
Dist(s): **ACTA Pubns.**
Moshy Brothers, Inc.
Spring Arbor Distributors, Inc.

Catholic Heritage Curricula *See* **Little Way Pr.**

Catholic Heritage Curricula, *(978-0-9788376; 978-0-9824585; 978-0-9836832; 978-0-9851642; 978-0-9858343; 978-0-9883797; 978-0-9913264; 978-1-946207)*
Web site: https://www.chcweb.com.

Catholic World Mission, *(978-0-9747571; 978-0-9765180; 978-1-933643)* 33 Rossotto Dr., Hamden, CT 06514 USA Tel 203-848-3323; Fax: 203-407-4823
E-mail: george.sirois@catholicworldmission.org
Web site: http://www.catholicworldmission.org.

Catronaut Bks., *(978-0-9893522)* 203 Beaver Ct, No. 11, Colorado Springs, CO 80905 USA Tel 719-575-9355
E-mail: thelastlaunch@hotmail.com.

Cats Corner Publishing, *(978-1-7334195; 978-1-7340097; 978-1-7343502; 978-1-953147)* 615 Lakeridge St, Kingsport, TN 37663 USA Tel 423-366-1234
E-mail: claysproles books@gmail.com
Web site: http://claysproles.com/.

Cats Ink, *(978-0-9763441)* P.O. Box 387, Chagrin Falls, OH 44022 USA Tel 440-247-6486
Web site: http://www.lillieandrose.com.

CatsCurious Pr., *(978-0-9790889)* 5312 Dillon Cir., Haltom City, TX 76137 USA (SAN 852-4084) Tel 210-326-8239; Toll Free Fax: 866-372-2490
E-mail: sonyamshannon@charter.net
Web site: http://www.catscratchbooks.com; http://www.catscuriouspress.com
Dist(s): **Follett School Solutions.**

Catskill Ctr. for Conservation & Development, Inc., *(978-0-9616712)* General Delivery, Arkville, NY 12406 USA (SAN 660-9953) Tel 914-586-2611; Fax: 914-586-3044; Rte. 28, Arkville, NY 12406 (SAN 660-9961)
E-mail: cccd@catskill.net
Web site: http://catshillcenter.org.

Catslip Arts, LLC, *(978-0-9729414)* 668 Cook St., Suite 200, Denver, CO 80206 USA Tel 303-322-9483; Fax: 303-758-6388
E-mail: books@catsliparts.com
Web site: http://www.catsliparts.com.

Catterfly Pr., *(978-0-9741074)* 122 Eagle Ridge Rd., Lake Orion, MI 48360-2612 USA Tel 248-789-2227; Fax: 248-393-2535
E-mail: frejen111@aol.com
Web site: http://www.catterflypress.com.

CattLeLogos Brand Management Systems, *(978-0-9745612)* 2522 Lombard St., Suite 300, Philadelphia, PA 19146-1025 USA Fax: 215-827-5578
E-mail: info@cattlelogos.com
Web site: http://www.cattlelogos.com.

Catto Creations, LLC, *(978-0-9702633; 978-1-938078)* 3125 Crusade Ln., Green Bay, WI 54313 USA Tel 920-494-4237; 920 494 4237
E-mail: cattocreations@gmail.com
Web site: http://www.cattocreations.com.

Catton Communications, *(978-0-615-76872-4; 978-0-578-55240-8; 978-0-578-63310-7)* 301 Farmbrook Pass, Canton, GA 30115 USA Tel 918-853-4682
Web site: http://www.cattoncommunications.com
Dist(s): **CreateSpace Independent Publishing Platform.**

Caution Bks., *(978-0-9754148)* P.O. Box 2235, Newport Beach, CA 92659 USA
Web site: http://www.cautionbooks.com.

Cave Hollow Pr., *(978-0-9713497; 978-1-7342678)* 304 Grover St., Warrensburg, MO 64093-2439 USA
E-mail: rmkinder@sprintmail.com
Web site: http://www.cavehollowpress.com.

Caveat Press, Incorporated *See* **White Cloud Pr.**

Cavendish Children's Bks. *Imprint of* **Marshall Cavendish Corp.**

Cavendish Square *See* **Cavendish Square Publishing LLC**

Cavendish Square *Imprint of* **Cavendish Square Publishing LLC**

Cavendish Square Publishing LLC, *(978-0-7614; 978-1-60870; 978-1-62712; 978-1-5026)* 303 Pk. Ave. S. Suite 1247, New York, NY 10010 USA (SAN 760-9639) Tel 646-205-7426; *Imprints:* Cavendish Square (CavendishSq)
E-mail: hollyc@rosenpub.com; csq_cs@csqpub.com
Web site: http://www.cavendishsq.com
Dist(s): **Follett School Solutions**
MyiLibrary.

Cavizzana Press *See* **21st Century Pubs.**

†Caxton Pr., *(978-0-87004)* Div. of Caxton Printers. Ltd., 312 Main St., Caldwell, ID 83605-3299 USA (SAN 201-9698) Tel 208-459-7421; Fax: 208-459-7450; Toll Free: 800-657-6465
E-mail: publish@caxtonprinters.com; sgipson@caxtonpress.com
Web site: http://www.caxtonpress.com
Dist(s): **MyiLibrary**
Univ. of Nebraska Pr.; *CIP.*

Caxton Printers, Limited *See* **Caxton Pr.**

Caxton, Wm Ltd., *(978-0-940473)* P.O. Box 220, Ellison Bay, WI 54210-0220 USA (SAN 135-1303) Tel 920-854-2955.

CB Publishing & Design *Imprint of* **UBUS Communications Systems**

CBAY Bks., 4501 Forbes Blvd., Lanham, MD 20706 USA
Dist(s): **Follett School Solutions**
Independent Pubs. Group.

CBE READERS, 11306 SAGECREEK DR, HOUSTON, TX 77089 USA Tel 832-775-3721.

CBH Bks. *Imprint of* **Cambridge BrickHouse, Inc.**

CBJ Entertainment, *(978-0-9997551)* 7457 Easterly Ln., Memphis, TN 38125 USA Tel 901-690-1956
E-mail: cbjentertainment1@yahoo.com.

CBM Publishing, *(978-0-9743988)* P.O. Box 6938, Lincoln, NE 68506 USA
E-mail: mvbettenhausen@alltel.net.

CC Conglomerate LLC, *(978-0-9998853)* 1430 Seagirt Blvd., Far Rockaway, NY 11691 USA Tel 917-663-0125
E-mail: cynthia@cynthiacordero.com
Web site: cynthiacordero.com.

CCA & B, LLC, *(978-0-9769907; 978-0-9843651; 978-0-9887032; 978-0-9970920; 978-0-9988109; 978-0-9600665; 978-1-7336905)* Orders Addr.: 3350 Riverwood Pkwy. Suite 300, Atlanta, GA 30339 USA Fax: 678-990-1182; Toll Free: 877-919-4105
E-mail: sales@elfontheshelf.com; christa@elfontheshelf.com
Web site: http://elfontheshelf.com; http://www.ccaandb.com; http://alightinthenight.com.

CCC of America, *(978-1-56814)* P.O. Box 166349, Irving, TX 75016-6349 USA (SAN 298-7546) Toll Free: 800-935-2222
E-mail: customerservice@cccofamerica.com
Web site: http://www.cccofamerica.com
Dist(s): **Liguori Pubns.**

CCH Services, Inc., *(978-0-9768383)* 8862 Earhart Ave., Los Angeles, CA 90045 USA Tel 562-895-0682
Web site: http://www.realworldrecovery.com.

CCP Publishing & Entertainment, *(978-0-9677385; 978-0-9800655; 978-0-9801265)* 9602 Glenwood Rd., No. 362, Brooklyn, NY 11236 USA
E-mail: brillionaireone@gmail.com
Web site: www.ccppublishing.com; http://www.thecccowanshow.com; http://www.cccowan.com.

CCRiddles, *(978-0-9785118; 978-0-9819833; 978-1-941747)* 878 Laramie Ct., Newbury Park, CA 91320 USA Tel 805-338-4170; Fax: 805-498-2901
E-mail: ccriddles@gmail.com
Web site: http://www.ccriddles.com.

CD Publishing, *(978-0-9859042)* 38041 Manzanita St., Newark, CA 94560 USA Tel 510-709-7459
E-mail: caseydevargas@yahoo.com.

CDS Books *See* **Vanguard Pr.**

CE Bilingual Bks. LLC, *(978-0-9801305)* P.O. Box 31848, Philadelphia, PA 19104-1848 USA (SAN 855-2819) Fax: 215-352-0409; 28 Eight St., Hicksville, NY 11801
E-mail: cebilingualbooks@gmail.com
Web site: http://www.cebilingualbooks.com
Dist(s): **Follett School Solutions.**

Ce Code Efficiency, Inc., *(978-0-9769931)* Orders Addr.: P.O. Box 1184, State College, PA 16804-1184 USA; Edit Addr.: 120 E. Beaver Ave., #208, State College, PA 16801 USA
E-mail: rlp188@psu.edu
Web site: http://www.personal.psu.edu/rlp188.

Cebrano Publishing, *(978-0-9761366)* P.O. Box 27236, Barrigada, GU 96921 USA
E-mail: billyb1937@yahoo.com.

Cedar Bay Pr., L.L.C., *(978-1-57555)* P.O. Box 230084, Portland, OR 97281-0084 USA (SAN 298-6361)
E-mail: cedarbay@hotmail.com.

Cedar Creek Publishing, *(978-0-9790205; 978-0-9842449; 978-0-9839192; 978-0-9891465; 978-1-942882)* P.O. Box 115, Bremo Bluff, VA 23022 USA (SAN 857-1368) Tel 434-842-6203
E-mail: cedarcreekbooks@aol.com
Web site: http://www.cedarcreekauthors.com
Dist(s): **BCH Fulfillment & Distribution.**

Cedar Creek Publishing Service, *(978-0-9659419)* P.O. Box 115, Bremo Bluff, VA 23022 USA Tel 434-842-6203 Do not confuse with companies with same or similar names in Hayward, CA, Anderson, IN, Indianapolis, IN
E-mail: cedarcreekbooks@aol.com.

Cedar Crest Bks., *(978-0-910291)* 17 Lookout Ave., Natick, MA 01760 USA (SAN 241-2837) Tel 508-653-8839
E-mail: davidrottenberg@yahoo.com; publisher@cedarcrestbooks.com
Web site: http://www.cedarcrestbooks.com
Dist(s): **Follett School Solutions.**

Cedar Fort, Inc. *Imprint of* **Cedar Fort, Inc./CFI Distribution**

Cedar Fort, Inc./CFI Distribution, *(978-0-88290; 978-0-934126; 978-1-55517; 978-1-59955; 978-1-4621)* 2373 West 700 South, Springville, UT 84663 USA (SAN 170-2858) Tel 801-489-4084; Fax: 801-489-1097; Toll Free: 800-759-2665; *Imprints:* Bonneville Books (Bonneville Bks); Horizon Publishers (HorPubs); Cedar Fort, Incorporated (Cedar Fort); Sweetwater Books (Sweetwater Bks)
E-mail: skybook@cedarfort.com
Web site: http://www.cedarfort.com
Dist(s): **Casemate Pubs. & Bk. Distributors, LLC**
Follett School Solutions
Todd Communications.

Cedar Grove Bks., *(978-0-9740212; 978-0-9835077; 978-1-941958)* 3205 Elmhurst St., Rowlett, TX 75088 USA (SAN 255-3732) Tel 415-364-8292
E-mail: rperry@cedargrovebooks.com
Web site: http://www.cedargrovebooks.com
Dist(s): **Independent Pubs. Group**
Small Pr. United.

Cedar Hse. Pubs., *(978-0-9676289)* Orders Addr.: P.O. Box 399, Monroe, VA 24574 USA Tel 434-929-8002 (phone/fax); Fax: 434-929-1059; Edit Addr.: 407 Eastview Dr., Madison Heights, VA 24572 USA
E-mail: info@cedarhousepublishers.com
Web site: http://www.cedarhousepublishers.com
Dist(s): **Send The Light Distribution LLC.**

Cedar Kroft Studios, *(978-1-7323936)* 3365 Springplace Rd., Lewisburg, TN 37091 USA Tel 931-637-8518
E-mail: wishuwell4ever@yahoo.com.

Cedar Loft Productions *See* **Cedar Loft Publishing**

Cedar Loft Publishing, *(978-0-615-95768-5; 978-0-692-22011-5; 978-0-9907449; 978-0-692-31333-6; 978-0-692-43060-6; 978-0-692-44612-6; 978-0-692-54041-1; 978-0-692-62473-9; 978-0-692-65781-2; 978-0-692-66121-5; 978-0-692-68130-5; 978-0-692-70082-2; 978-0-692-73427-8; 978-0-9979156) P.O. Box 1125, Petersburg, WV 26847 USA Tel 304-470-0189*
E-mail: jennymckinney23@gmail.com
Web site: http://clpublishing.net
Dist(s): **CreateSpace Independent Publishing Platform.**

Cedar Shamrock Publishing, *(978-0-9760680)* P.O. Box 70775, Madison, WI 53707 USA
Web site: http://www.wyattwalker.com
Dist(s): **Partners Bk. Distributing, Inc.**

Cedar Tree Bks., *(978-0-9657328; 978-1-892142)* P.O. Box 4256, Wilmington, DE 19807-0256 USA
E-mail: books@ctpress.com
Web site: http://www.cedartreebooks.com.

Cedar Tree Publishing, *(978-0-9658075)* 201 Matilda St NE Ste. B, Grand Rapids, MI 49503-1593 USA Do not confuse with Cedar Tree Publishing, Cedaredge, CO
E-mail: georan@tapshoe,com
Web site: http://www.cedartreepublishing.com; www.johnnietuitel.com
Dist(s): **Austin & Company, Inc.**

Cedar Valley Publishing, *(978-1-933476)* N6854 Cedar Valley Rd., Fredonia, WI 53021 USA Tel 920-994-9906 Do not confuse with Cedar Valley Publishing in Cascade, WI, Jesup, IA
E-mail: stacey@cedarvalleypublishing.com
Web site: http://www.cedarvalleypublishing.com
Dist(s): **Follett School Solutions.**

Cedar Valley Publishing, *(978-0-615-12024-9)* P.O. Box 621, Jesup, IA 50648 USA Do not confuse with Cedar Valley Publishing in Cascade, WI.

Cedartip Co., The, *(978-0-9771844)* Orders Addr.: P.O. Box 231, Manhattan, KS 66505-0231 USA; Edit Addr.: 3004 Pawnee Cir., Manhattan, KS 66502-1973 USA
E-mail: orders@cedartip.com
Web site: http://www.cedartip.com.

Celebration Media, *(978-0-692-18742-5)* 4600 E. Moody Blvd. 3P, Bunnell, FL 32110 USA Tel 386-517-4523
E-mail: smckenney66@gmail.com
Dist(s): **Ingram Content Group.**

Celebration Pr. *Imprint of* **Savvas Learning Co.**

Celebration Pr., Orders Addr.: 135 South Mount Zion Rd. P.O. Box 2500, Lebanon, IN 46052 USA Toll Free Fax: 800-393-3156; Toll Free: 800-526-9907; *Imprints:* Good Year Books (GYB) Do not confuse with Celebration Press in Onalaska WI, Denver CO
Web site: http://www.aw-bc.com; http://www.pearsonlearning.com/rightsPerm.rtf.

Celeste Ediciones, S.A. (ESP) *(978-84-8211; 978-84-87553) Dist. by* **Lectorum Pubns.**

Celestial Arts *Imprint of* **Ten Speed Pr.**

Celestine Pr., *(978-0-9749382; 978-0-578-08538-8)* 25 Ashland St., Rochester, NY 14620 USA (SAN 255-9927)
E-mail: hellerest@earthlink.net
Web site: http://www.celestinepress.com
Dist(s): **Lulu Pr., Inc.**

Cellar Door Publishing, *(978-0-9766831)* 3439 NE Sandy Blvd, Suite 309, Portland, OR 97232 USA
Web site: http://www.cellardoorpublishing.com.

Celltrition, *(978-0-9746378)* 13472 Vidalia Rd., Pass Christian, MS 39571 USA Tel 228-586-2455.

Cellular Publishing, *(978-1-886358)* Div. of Lakeshore Business Services, P.O. Box 119, Sedona, AZ 86339-0119 USA Tel 520-300-7711; Fax: 413-825-8356.

Celo Valley Bks., *(978-0-923687)* 160 Ohle Rd., Burnsville, NC 28714 USA (SAN 251-7973) Tel 828-675-5918
E-mail: diatoday@msn.com.

Celstumo Publishing, *(978-0-9761041)* A Subs. of Celebration Studios of Missouri, Orders Addr.: P.O. Box 201, Glencoe, MO 63038 USA Tel 636-458-1819 (phone/fax)
E-mail: celstumo@celstumo.com
Web site: http://www.celstumo.com.

Celtic Cat Publishing, *(978-0-9658950; 978-0-9819238; 978-0-9847836; 978-0-9891380; 978-0-9905945; 978-1-947020)* Orders Addr.: 5111 Green Valley Dr, Knoxville, TN 37914 USA Tel 865-541-7130; Edit Addr.: 5111 Green Valley Dr, Knoxville, TN 37901 USA Tel 865-248-3133
E-mail: info@celticcatpublishing.com
Web site: http://www.celticcatpublishing.com.

Celtic Chicago Inc. *See* **Celtic Chicago Inc.**

Celtic Chicago Inc., *(978-0-9777135)* 8120 N. Lehigh Ave. Suite 100, Morton Grove, IL 60053 USA (SAN 853-0688) Tel 773-405-3748
E-mail: MARLENEB@CELTICCHICAGO.COM
Web site: www.projectplaybooks.com; www.musichaslegs.com.

Celtic Cross Communications, *(978-0-9740981; 978-0-9887271)* 5114 Canyon Oaks Dr., Brighton, MI 48114 USA
Web site: http://www.celticcrosscommunications.com
Dist(s): **Send The Light Distribution LLC.**

Celtic Hearts Pr., *(978-1-949575)* 1723 Mapleleaf Blvd., Oldsmar, FL 34677 USA Tel 727-686-0998
E-mail: cassidyoconnorauthor@gmail.com
Web site: www.cassidykoconnor.com.

Celtic Sunrise, *(978-0-9840893)* P.O. Box 174, New Ringgold, PA 17960 USA (SAN 858-3900) Fax: 570-943-2102
Web site: http://www.celticsunrise.com.

CEM Ventures, Ltd., *(978-0-9760072)* P.O. Box 1713, Harwich, MA 02645 USA Tel 508-896-4988; Fax: 508-896-2586; Toll Free: 866-246 — 7800; 112 Griffith's Pond Rd., Brewster, MA 02631
E-mail: cemventures@yahoo.com
Web site: http://www.jaysonthebluejay.com.

Cemetery Dance Pubns., *(978-1-881475; 978-1-58767)* Orders Addr.: 132-B Industry Ln., Unit 7, Forest Hills, MD 21050 USA Tel 410-588-5901; Fax: 410-588-5904
E-mail: cdancepub@aol.com; info@cemeterydance.com
Web site: http://www.cemeterydance.com.

†**Cengage Gale,** *(978-0-13; 978-0-7876; 978-0-8103; 978-0-936474; 978-1-57302; 978-1-878623; 978-1-59413; 978-1-59414; 978-1-59415; 978-1-4144; 978-1-4205; 978-1-59722; 978-1-4328; 978-1-5358)* Subs. of Cengage Learning, Orders Addr.: P.O. Box 9187, Farmington Hills, MI 48333-9187 USA Toll Free Fax: 800 414 5043; Toll Free: 800 877 4253; Edit Addr.: 27500 Drake Rd., Farmington Hills, MI 48331 USA (SAN 213-4373) Tel 248-699-8495 Toll Free: 800-877-4253; a/o Wheeler Publishing, 295 Kennedy Memorial Dr., Waterville, ME 04901 Toll Free: 800 223 1244; *Imprints:* UXL (UXL); Macmillan Reference USA (Macmillan Ref); Charles Scribner's Sons (C Scribners Sons); Kidhaven (Kidhaven); Blackbirch Press, Incorporated (Blackbirch Pr); Lucent Books (Lucent Books); Greenhaven Press, Incorporated (Greenhaven Pr); Five Star (Five Star ME); Wheeler Publishing, Incorporated (Wheel); Walker Large Print (Walker Large Pt); Five Star Trade (Five Star Trade); Kennebec Large Print (Kennebec Lrg); KidHaven Publishing (KidHaven Publ); Greenhaven Publishing (GreenHav)
E-mail: gale.salesassistance@thomson.com
Web site: http://www.gale.com
Dist(s): **Follett School Solutions**
Send The Light Distribution LLC
Smashwords
Thorndike Pr.; *CIP.*

†**Cengage Heinle,** *(978-0-8384; 978-0-88377; 978-0-912066; 978-1-4130)* Div. of Cengage Learning, Orders Addr.: 10650 Toebben Dr., Independence, KY 41051 USA Toll Free Fax: 800 487 8488
E-mail: reply@heinle.com
Web site: http://www.heinle.com
Dist(s): **CENGAGE Learning**; *CIP.*

Cengage Learning *Imprint of* **CENGAGE Learning**

CENGAGE Learning, Orders Addr.: 10650 Toebben Dr., Independence, KY 41051 USA (SAN 200-2213) Tel 859-525-6620; Fax: 859-525-0978; Toll Free Fax: 800-487-8488; Toll Free: 800-354-9706; *Imprints:* Cengage Learning (CengLearning); National Geographic Learning (Nat Geo Learn)
Web site: http://www.cengage.com/
Dist(s): **Amazon Digital Services Inc.**
Delmar Cengage Learning
Follett School Solutions
Johns Hopkins Univ. Pr.
OptumInsight, Inc.

Cengage Learning Australia (AUS) *(978-0-17; 978-0-646-20862-6; 978-0-646-20863-3; 978-0-646-22565-4; 978-0-646-22598-2; 978-0-646-24330-6; 978-0-646-26850-7; 978-0-646-26853-8; 978-0-646-26854-5; 978-0-646-26855-2; 978-0-646-47716-9) Dist. by* **Cheng Tsui.**

CENGAGE Learning Custom Publishing, *(978-0-87393; 978-0-931920; 978-0-7593; 978-1-4266; 978-0-357; 978-1-4390; 978-1-111; 978-1-133; 978-1-285; 978-1-305; 978-1-337)* 5191 Natrop Blvd., Mason, OH 45240 USA Toll Free: 800-543-0487
E-mail: debbie.stowell@cengage.com
Web site: http://www.thomsoncustom.com
Dist(s): **CENGAGE Learning**
Follett School Solutions.

†**Cengage South-Western,** *(978-0-03; 978-0-324; 978-0-538)* Div. of Cengage Learning, 5191 Natorp Blvd., Mason, OH 45040 USA (SAN 202-7518) Tel 513 229 1000; Toll Free Fax: 800-437-8488; Toll Free: 800-354-9706 (orders only); 800-543-0487
Web site: http://www.thomsonedu.com/
Dist(s): **CENGAGE Learning**
International Thomson Computer Pr.; *CIP.*

Cenozoic Pr., *(978-0-615-38180-0; 978-0-615-52278-4)* 354 Via La Canada No. 7, Orange, CA 92869 USA Tel 714-928-6648
E-mail: arajic@gmail.com.

Ctr. for Appalachian Trail Studies, *(978-0-9636342; 978-0-9707916)* Orders Addr.: 17 S. Meadow Dr., Sudbury, MA 01776 USA Tel 781-752-6100 (phone/fax)
E-mail: orders@trailplace.com
Web site: http://trailplace.com/orders.html.

Center for Applications of Psychological Type, Inc., *(978-0-935652)* 2815 NW 13th St., Suite 401, Gainesville, FL 32609 USA (SAN 213-9162) Tel 352-375-0160; Fax: 352-378-0503; Toll Free: 800-777-2278
E-mail: rob@capt.org
Web site: http://www.capt.org.

Center for Applied Psychology, Incorporated *See* **Childswork/Childsplay**

Ctr. for Basque Studies, *(978-1-877802; 978-1-935709; 978-1-949805)* 1664 N. Virginia St., MS 2322, Reno, NV 89557-2322 USA Tel 775-784-4854; Fax: 775-784-1355
E-mail: basque@unr.edu
Web site: http://basquebooks.myshopify.com/
Dist(s): **University of Nevada Pr.**

Ctr. For Cultural Leadership, *(978-0-9745948)* P.O. Box 70, La Grange, CA 95239 USA
Web site: http://www.christianculture.com.

Center for Economic Research & Social Change *See* **Haymarket Bks.**

Ctr. for Educational Policy Research, *(978-0-9729538)* 720 E. 13th Ave., Suite 201, Eugene, OR 97401 USA Tel 541-346-6153; Fax: 541-346-6154; Toll Free: 877-766-2279
E-mail: Terri_Heath@s4s.org
Web site: http://www.s4s.org.

Center for Labor Research and Education, Univ. of California, Los Angeles, *(978-0-89215; 978-0-615-12275-5; 978-0-9836289)* Orders Addr.: 675 S. Pk. View St., Los Angeles, CA 90057 USA Tel 213-780-4155 x205
E-mail: jamonroe@ucla.edu
Web site: http://www.labor.ucla.edu.

Center for Learning, The, *(978-1-56077)* Orders Addr.: 590 E. Western Reserve Rd. Unit 10-h, Youngstown, OH 44514 USA Tel 800-767-9090; Toll Free Fax: 888-767-8080; Toll Free: 800-767-9090 (ordering); Edit Addr.: 29313 Clemens Rd. Ste. 2E, Westlake, OH 44145-1052 USA (SAN 248-2029)
E-mail: ahollis@centerforlearning.org
Web site: http://www.centerforlearning.org.

Center for Loss & Life Transition *See* **Companion Pr.**

Ctr. for Safe & Responsible Internet Use, *(978-0-9724236)* 474 W. 29th Ave., Eugene, OR 97405-2729 USA Tel 541-344-9125
E-mail: info@responsiblenetizen.org
Web site: http://www.responsiblenetizen.org.

Center for Self-Actualization, Incorporated, The, *(978-0-9758799; 978-0-9788389; 978-0-9823847; 978-0-615-38102-2; 978-0-9846266; 978-0-9851608)* P.O. Box 98466, Atlanta, GA 30359-2166 USA Tel 770-623-4133; Fax: 770-623-3853
E-mail: centerforself@yahoo.com
Web site: http://www.selfactualized.org.

†**Ctr. for Strategic & International Studies,** *(978-0-89206; 978-0-615-19961-0)* 1800 K St., NW, Washington, DC 20006 USA (SAN 281-4021) Tel 202-887-0200; Fax: 202-775-3199; 4501 Forbes Blvd., Lanhan, MD 20706
E-mail: books@csis.org
Web site: http://www.csis.org; http://www.csisbookstore.org
Dist(s): **Books International, Inc.**
Follett School Solutions
MyiLibrary
Rowman & Littlefield Publishers, Inc.; *CIP.*

Ctr. for the Affirmation of Responsible Education, *(978-0-9740071)* 496 Gold Ct., San Andreas, CA 95249 USA Tel 209-754-9218
E-mail: jnorton2@earthlink.net.

Center for the Collaborative Classroom, *(978-1-57621; 978-1-885603; 978-1-59892; 978-1-61003; 978-1-68246; 978-1-64940)* 1001 Marina Village Pkwy Suite 110, ALAMEDA, CA 94501 USA Tel 510-533-0213; Fax: 510-464-3670; Toll Free: 800-666-7270
E-mail: pubs@devstu.org; brandon_holroyd@devstu.org; bholroyd@collaborativeclassroom.org
Web site: http://www.devstu.org; http://www.collaborativeclassroom.org
Dist(s): **Booksource, The.**

Ctr. for Victims of Torture, The, *(978-0-9759789)* 717 E. River Rd., Minneapolis, MN 55455 USA Tel 612-436-4800.

Ctr. for Western Studies, *(978-0-931170)* Div. of Augustana University, Orders Addr.: Augustana Univ. 2001 S. Summit Ave., Sioux Falls, SD 57197 USA (SAN 211-4844) Tel 605-274-4007; Fax: 605-274-4999
E-mail: harry.thompson@augie.edu; cws@augie.edu
Web site: http://augie.edu/cws
Dist(s): **Dakota West Bks.**

Center For Youth Issues, Incorporated *See* **National Ctr. For Youth Issues**

Ctr. of SW Studies, Fort Lewis College, *(978-0-9727664)* 1000 Rim Dr., Durango, CO 81301 USA
E-mail: gulliford_a@fortlewis.edu
Web site: http://www.swcenter.fortlewis.edu.

Ctr. Stage Puppets, *(978-0-9795087)* P.O. Box 8279, Bend, OR 97708 USA Tel 541-420-7943
E-mail: info@centerstagepuppets.com
Web site: http://www.centerstagepuppets.com.

Centering Corp., *(978-1-56123)* 6406 Maple St, Omaha, NE 68104-0600 USA (SAN 298-1815) Tel 402-553-1200; Fax: 402-553-0507
E-mail: j1200@aol.com
Web site: http://www.centering.org
Dist(s): **Follett School Solutions.**

CenterLine Media, *(978-0-9754212; 978-0-9814896)* 115 Greenwood Ave., Ambler, PA 19002-5709 USA Tel 215-646-4591; Fax: 215-933-6819
E-mail: info@centerlinemedia.com
Web site: http://www.centerlinemedia.com.

Centerpunch Pr., *(978-0-9724882)* P.O. Box 43151, Cincinnati, OH 45243 USA Tel 513-561-3392 (phone/fax)
E-mail: info@centerpunchpress.com
Web site: http://www.centerpunchpress.com.

Centerstream Publishing, *(978-0-931759; 978-1-57424)* Orders Addr.: P.O. Box 17878, Anaheim Hills, CA 92817 USA (SAN 683-8022) Tel 714-779-9390 (phone/fax)
E-mail: centerstrm@aol.com
Web site: http://www.pma-online.org
Dist(s): **Booklines Hawaii, Ltd.**
Leonard, Hal Corp.
MyiLibrary.

Centipede Dragon A Benevolent Creature, *(978-0-692-23349-8; 978-0-692-33306-8; 978-0-692-84099-3; 978-0-692-88976-3)* 7002 Memorial Heights Dr., Alexandria, VA 22306 USA Tel 703-975-0993
Dist(s): **CreateSpace Independent Publishing Platform.**

Centiramo Publishing, *(978-0-692-98500-7; 978-0-692-14219-6; 978-1-7327815; 978-1-7347256)* 11 Minker Pl, Belleville, NJ 07109-1732 USA Tel 201-674-0274; Fax: 201-674-0274
E-mail: pierceram@gmail.com
Web site: www.centiramopublishing.com
Dist(s): **CreateSpace Independent Publishing Platform.**

Central Ave. Pr, *(978-0-9715344; 978-0-9798452)* 8400 Menaul Blvd. NE, Suite A No. 211, Albuquerque, NM 87112 USA
E-mail: oelfkej@aol.com
Web site: http://www.centralavepress.com
Dist(s): **Quality Bks., Inc.**

Central Avenue Publishing (CAN) *(978-1-926760; 978-0-9812737; 978-1-77168) Dist. by* **IPG Chicago.**

Central Coast Bks./Pr., *(978-0-9658776; 978-1-930401)* Orders Addr.: P.O. Box 3654, San Luis Obispo, CA 93403 USA (SAN 631-1547) Tel 805-534-0307 (phone/fax); Edit Addr.: 831 a Via Esteban, Samn Luis, Obispo, CA 94301 USA (SAN 631-1539)
E-mail: ccbooks@surfari.net.

Central Coast Press *See* **Central Coast Bks./Pr.**

Central Conference of American Rabbis/CCAR Pr., *(978-0-88123; 978-0-916694)* 355 Lexington Ave., 18th Flr., New York, NY 10017-6603 USA (SAN 204-3262) Tel 212-972-3636; Fax: 212-692-0819; Toll Free: 800-935-2227
E-mail: ccarpress@ccarnet.org; info@ccarnet.org
Web site: http://ccarpress.org.

Central Orb Publishing, *(978-0-9818818)* P.O. Box 830, Orem, UT 84059-0830 USA
E-mail: Thesoulalliance@Hotmail.com
Web site: http://www.createspace.com/3347335; http://www.lulu.com/thesoulalliance; http://www.createspace.com/3351702.

Central Park Media Corp., *(978-1-56219; 978-1-57800; 978-1-887692; 978-1-58664)* 250 W. 57th St. Ste. 1723, New York, NY 10107-1708 USA (SAN 631-3191) Toll Free: 800-833-7456; *Imprints:* CPM Manga (CPM Manga); CPM Comics (CPM Comics); Manga 18 (Manga Eighteen); CPM Manhwa (CPM Manhwa)
E-mail: info@teamcpm.com
Web site: http://www.centralparkmedia.com/; http://www.cpmpress.com/
Dist(s): **Hobbies Hawaii Distributors.**

Central Park Tutors Bks., *(978-0-692-76743-6; 978-0-9988340)* 244 Fifth Avenue, Suite 2231, New York, NY 10001 USA Tel 917-502-9108; Fax: 917-502-9108
E-mail: michaelawallach@yahoo.com
Web site: http://centralparktutors.com/subject/books/
Dist(s): **Independent Pubs. Group**
Midpoint Trade Bks., Inc.

Central Recovery Pr., *(978-0-9799869; 978-0-9818482; 978-1-936290; 978-1-937612; 978-1-942094; 978-1-949481)* 3321 N. Buffalo Dr. Suite 275, Las Vegas, NV 89129 USA (SAN 854-9532) Tel 702-868-5830; Fax: 702-868-5831
E-mail: phughes@centralrecovery.com; vkilleen@centralrecovery.com
Web site: http://www.centralrecoverypress.com
Dist(s): **Consortium Bk. Sales & Distribution**
Elsevier
Follett School Solutions
Health Communications, Inc.
MyiLibrary.

Centro Bks., LLC, *(978-1-933572)* 3636 Fieldston Rd. Apt. 6P, Bronx, NY 10463-2041 USA (SAN 256-7229)
Web site: http://www.centrobooks.com.

Centro de Informacion y Desarrollo de la Comunicacion y la Literatura (MEX) *(978-968-494) Dist. by* **Mariuccia Iaconi Bk Imports.**

Centro de Informacion y Desarrollo de la Comunicacion y la Literatura (MEX) *(978-968-494) Dist. by* **AIMS Intl.**

Centro de Informacion y Desarrollo de la Comunicacion y la Literatura (MEX) *(978-968-494) Dist. by* **Continental Bk.**

Centro de Informacion y Desarrollo de la Comunicacion y la Literatura (MEX) *(978-968-494) Dist. by* **Lectorum Pubns.**

Centurion Bks., *(978-0-692-37166-4; 978-0-692-86932-1; 978-0-692-90093-2)* 8001 Magnolia Ridge Ct, Louisville, KY 40291 USA Tel 502-494-2890
Web site: http://jessicaminyard.com
Dist(s): **CreateSpace Independent Publishing Platform.**

Centurion Pr., *(978-0-9800805)* 740 Breeze Hill Rd., #171, Vista, CA 92081 USA Fax: 760-631-3607
E-mail: fedthought@gmail.com
Web site: http://www.centurionpress.com.

Cepia LLC., *(978-0-9777241)* 121 Hunter Ave., Suite 103, Saint Louis, MO 63124 USA Tel 314-725-4900; Fax: 314-725-4919
E-mail: support@cepiallc.com
Web site: http://www.cepiallc.com.

Ceravolo Maret, Anita, *(978-0-692-92214-9; 978-0-692-93666-5)* 202 Broad St., Bloomfield, NJ 07003 USA Tel 973-747-7697
E-mail: ceravolo_maret@live.com
Dist(s): **CreateSpace Independent Publishing Platform.**

Cerebellum Corp., *(978-1-58198; 978-1-886156; 978-1-59626; 978-1-61867)* 145 Corte Madera Town Ctr, Ste 406, rte Madera, CA 94925 USA (SAN 299-240X) Tel 415-541-9901; Fax: 805-426-8136; Toll Free: 800-238-9669
E-mail: customerservice@cerebellum.com; cerebell@mindspring.com; admin@cerebellum.com
Web site: www.cerebellum.com; http://www.standarddeviants.com
Dist(s): **Follett School Solutions.**

Cerebral Press International, *(978-0-916309)* HC-71 Box 121-1, Thornfield, MO 65762 USA (SAN 295-9461) Tel 417-679-4748
E-mail: lagunapress@braintypes.com
Web site: http://www.braintypes.com.

Ceres Pr., *(978-0-9606138; 978-1-886101)* P.O. Box 87, Woodstock, NY 12498 USA (SAN 217-0949) Tel 845-679-5573; Toll Free: 888-804-8848 Do not confuse with Ceres Pr., Stamford, CT
E-mail: cem620@aol.com
Web site: http://www.heathyhighways.com
Dist(s): **Integral Yoga Pubns.**
New Leaf Distributing Co., Inc.
Nutri-Bks. Corp.
Partners Bk. Distributing, Inc.

Ceres Software, Incorporated *See* **Inspiration Software, Inc.**

Cernunnos (FRA) *(978-2-37495) Dist. by* **HachBkGrp.**

Certified Firearms Instructors, LLC, *(978-0-9741480)* P.O. Box 131254, Saint Paul, MN 55113-1254 USA Tel 952-935-2414; Fax: 952-935-4122
E-mail: jolson@gw.hamline.edu
Web site: http://www.aacfi.com.

Cervena Barva Pr., *(978-0-615-17167-8; 978-0-615-20097-2; 978-0-615-25796-9; 978-0-615-25797-6; 978-0-615-25983-3; 978-0-615-26369-4; 978-0-578-00416-7; 978-0-692-00181-3; 978-0-578-02262-8; 978-0-578-02491-2; 978-0-578-04084-4; 978-0-692-00642-9; 978-0-578-04207-7; 978-0-9844732; 978-0-9831041; 978-0-578-08091-8; 978-0-9883713; 978-0-9910091; 978-0-692-28317-2; 978-0-692-30231-6; 978-0-692-33628-1; 978-0-9861111; 978-0-9966894; 978-0-9981027; 978-0-9984253; 978-0-692-08026-9; 978-0-692-13790-1; 978-1-950063) P.O. Box 440357, West Somerville, MA 02144-3222 USA Tel 617-764-2229*
E-mail: editor@cervenabarvapress.com
Web site: http://www.cervenabarvapress.com
Dist(s): **Instant Pub.**
SPD-Small Pr. Distribution.

CET *Imprint of* **Greater Cincinnati TV Educational Foundation**

C E V Multimedia, Ltd., *(978-1-57078; 978-1-59535; 978-1-60333; 978-1-61459)* Orders Addr.: P.O. Box 65265, Lubbock, TX 79464 USA Tel 806-745-8820; Fax: 806-745-5300; Toll Free Fax: 800-243-6398; Toll Free: 800-922-9965; Edit Addr.: 1020 SE Loop 289, Lubbock, TX 79404 USA
E-mail: cev@cevmultimedia.com
Web site: http://www.cevmultimedia.com
Dist(s): **Follett School Solutions.**

CFM, *(978-0-9728620; 978-0-9769071; 978-0-9908661)* 112 Greene St., New York City, NY 10012 USA Tel 212-966-3864; Fax: 212-226-1041
E-mail: info@cfmgallery.com
Web site: http://www.cfmgallery.com.

CG Star, L.L.C. *See* **C-It Entertainment Group, LLC**

C.G.S. Pr., *(978-0-9660726)* P.O. Box 1394, Mountainside, NJ 07092 USA Tel 908-233-8293 (phone/fax)
E-mail: Gwynnic2000@aol.com.

Chacmool Pr., *(978-0-9789391)* 849 W. University Pkwy., Baltimore, MD 21210 USA
E-mail: publisher@chacmoolpress.com
Web site: http://www.chacmoolpress.com.

Chafie Pr., LLC, *(978-0-9833190; 978-0-9903532)* 7557 Rambler Rd. Suite 626, Dallas, TX 75231 USA Tel 214-628-8600
E-mail: trish.jones@chafiehds.com
Web site: http://www.chafiepress.com
Dist(s): **Follett School Solutions**
Pathway Bk. Service.

Chagrin River Publishing Co., *(978-1-929821; 978-0-615-32246-9)* Orders Addr.: P.O. Box 173, Chagrin Falls, OH 44022 USA Tel 440-893-9250; Edit Addr.: 21 E. Summit St., Chargrin Falls, OH 44022 USA
Dist(s): **Follett School Solutions.**

Chai Yo Maui Pr., *(978-0-615-31840-0; 978-0-9855804)* P.O. Box 331, Kihei, HI 96753 USA.

Chaklet Coffee Bks *Imprint of* **Candalyse Publishing**

Chamberlain Hart Enterprises, Inc., *(978-0-9749756)* P.O. Box 1600, Fairfield, IA 52556 USA Tel 641-469-3717; Fax: 641-469-6647
E-mail: che@iowatelecom.net
Web site: http://www.chamberlainhart.com.

Chambers Kingfisher Graham Publishers, Incorporated *See* **Larousse Kingfisher Chambers, Inc.**

Chambers, Ta'mara, *(978-0-692-11886-3)* 8503 Bridgeway Dr., Fort Wayne, IN 46816 USA Tel 260-210-2642
E-mail: amaralove721@gmail.com.

Chameleon Designs, *(978-0-9701573)* P.O. Box 61855, North Charleston, SC 29419 USA Tel 843-761-7426
E-mail: yeleth@aol.com.

Chamike Pubs., *(978-1-884876)* 9000 Doris Dr., Fort Washington, MD 20744 USA Tel 301-248-4034.

CHAMPEAU, BRANDY *See* **Exploring ExPr.ion LLC**

Champion Athlete Publishing Company *See* **National Assn. of Speed & Explosion**

Championship Chess, *(978-0-9729456; 978-0-9772489)* Div. of Teachable Tech, Inc., Orders Addr.: 3565 Evans Rd., Atlanta, GA 30340 USA Toll Free: 888-328-7373
E-mail: dj@championshipchess.net
Web site: http://www.championshipchess.net.

Champlain Avenue Bks., Inc., *(978-0-9855008; 978-0-9896347; 978-0-9908256; 978-1-943063)* 2360 Corporate Cir. Suite 400, Henderson, NV 89074-7722 USA Tel 760-684-5861
E-mail: champlainavenuebooks@hotmail.com
Web site: champlainavenuebooks@hotmail.com
Dist(s): **Smashwords.**

Chan, David, *(978-0-9754302)* 12511 Fox Trace Ln., Houston, TX 77066-4029 USA Tel 281-580-7042
E-mail: david@chancomputerhelp.com.

Chandiramani, Riya, *(978-0-692-05362-1; 978-0-692-05363-8)* 4047 Irving St., Philadelphia, PA 19104 USA Tel (+852) 68089894
E-mail: riya.chandiramani@gmail.com
Dist(s): **Ingram Content Group.**

Chandler Hse. Pr., *(978-0-9636277; 978-1-886284)* P.O. Box 20126, Worcester, MA 01602 USA Fax: 508-753-7419
E-mail: chandlerhousepress@yahoo.com
Web site: http://www.chandlerhousebooks.com
Dist(s): **Follett School Solutions.**

Chandler Publishing, *(978-1-7326823)* 49 Ctr. Ct., Roslyn Heights, NY 11577 USA Tel 310-909-3571
E-mail: whitney@sleepeezkidz.com.

Chandler/White Publishing Co., *(978-1-877804)* 517 W. Midvale Ave., Philadelphia, PA 19144-4617 USA
Dist(s): **Alliance Hse., Inc.**

Chaney, Denise Ann, *(978-0-692-10888-8; 978-0-692-12992-0; 978-0-692-19846-9)* 166 Arrowhead Dr., PAGOSA SPRINGS, CO 81147 USA Tel 719-588-9202
E-mail: neisly@hotmail.com
Dist(s): **Ingram Content Group.**

Change Is Strange, Inc., *(978-0-9755902)* 3630 21st St., Boulder, CO 80304-1608 USA
E-mail: info@changeisstrange.com
Web site: http://www.changeisstrange.com
Dist(s): **Follett School Solutions.**

Changing Lives Changing The World, Incorporated *See* **Changing Lives Publishing**

Changing Lives Pr., *(978-0-9850248; 978-0-9882476; 978-0-9894529; 978-0-9904396; 978-0-9909424)* 91-18 159th Ave., Howard Beach, NY 11414 USA Tel 347-304-0625
E-mail: anminerva727@gmail.com; aminerva727@aol.com
Web site: http://www.changinglivespress.com
Dist(s): **BookBaby**
Follett School Solutions
Independent Pubs. Group
Midpoint Trade Bks., Inc.
ebrary, Inc.

Changing Lives Publishing, *(978-0-9653700; 978-0-9774513; 978-0-9798553)* Div. of Changing Lives Changing The World, Inc., P.O. Box 132, Sharpes, FL 32959 USA Tel 321-637-1128; Toll Free: 866-578-1900
E-mail: print2publish@gmail.com
Web site: http://www.print2publish.com.

Changing World Publishing, *(978-0-9829274)* 7224 E. Jenan Dr., Scottsdale, AZ 85260 USA Tel 480-945-8855
E-mail: east@cox.net.

Changing-Times.net, *(978-0-9741930)* Orders Addr.: P.O. Box 39651, Phoenix, AZ 85069-9651 USA
Web site: http://www.changing-times.net.

Channel Publishing, Ltd., *(978-0-945501; 978-1-933053; 978-1-946729)* 4750 Longley Ln., Suite 209, Reno, NV 89502 USA (SAN 247-1256) Tel 775-825-0880; Fax: 775-825-5633; Toll Free: 800-248-2882
E-mail: info@channelpublishing.com
Web site: http://www.channelpublishing.com.

Chanticlair Publishing, *(978-0-692-22416-8; 978-0-692-80319-6; 978-0-692-07326-1; 978-0-578-51383-6; 978-0-578-51928-9)* P.O. Box 74672, San Clemente, CA 92673 USA Tel 949-378-0287
E-mail: Auntielynny@gmail.com.

Chantilly Books, *(978-0-9841960)* Div. of Boone Amie Publishing, Orders Addr.: 14240-A Sullyfield Cir., Chantilly, VA 20151 USA (SAN 858-6853) Fax: 703-830-7100
E-mail: sue@a-childs-book.com
Web site: http://www.a-childs-book.com.

Chapel Hill Press, Inc., *(978-1-880849; 978-1-59715)* 11312 US 15-501 N Ste 107-223, Chapel Hill, NC 27517 USA Tel 919-929-8389
E-mail: edwina.woodbury@chapelhillpress.com
Web site: http://www.chapelhillpress.com
Dist(s): **Blair**
Follett School Solutions
Univ. of North Carolina Pr.

Chapel Song Publishing *See* **Wild Willow Pr.**

Chapin Hse. Bks. *Imprint of* **Florida Historical Society**

Chapman, Chris & Eric P. Hvolboll, *(978-0-9765061)* 2741 Cuerta Rd., Santa Barbara, CA 93105 USA Fax: 805-882-9897.

Chapman Pr., LLC, *(978-0-9725420)* 949 S. Josephine St., Denver, CO 80209 USA
E-mail: taylor@babsonfarms.com; taylor@babsonfarms.com
Web site: http://www.chapmanpress.com.

Chapter & Verse Pr., *(978-0-9724549)* 7350 Detrick Jordan Pike, Springfield, OH 45502-9660 USA Tel 937-964-0294
E-mail: nashvila@bright.net.

Chapter Bks. *Imprint of* **Spotlight**

Chapterhouse Comics (CAN) *(978-0-9947386; 978-0-9950098; 978-1-988247) Dist. by* **D C D.**

Chara Pr., *(978-0-9862513; 978-1-944705)* 74 Brandywine Rd., Fords, NJ 08863-1320 USA Tel 732-225-5046
E-mail: jamiebee.banta@gmail.com.

Character Arts, *(978-0-9772259)* 37 Pond Rd., Bldg. 2, Wilton, CT 06897 USA Tel 203-834-0323.

Character Development Group, Inc,, *(978-0-9653163; 978-1-892056)* Div. of Character Development Group, Inc., Orders Addr.: P.O. Box 35136, Greensboro, NC 27425-5136 USA Tel 336-668-9373; Fax: 336-668-9375; Edit Addr.: 8646 W. Market St. Suite 102, Greensboro, NC 27409 USA
E-mail: info@charactereducation.com
Web site: http://www.charactereducation.com
Dist(s): **Follett School Solutions.**

Character Development Publishing *See* **Character Development Group, Inc,**

Character-in-Action *Imprint of* **Quiet Impact, Inc.**

Charbonneau, Bradley, *(978-1-7322434)* 15129 Killion St., Sherman Oaks, CA 91411 USA Tel 415-558-8400
E-mail: ingram@likomaisland.com
Dist(s): **Ingram Content Group.**

CharFaye Publishing, Incorporated *See* **FayeHouse. Pr. International**

Charisma Hse. *Imprint of* **Charisma Media**

Charisma Kids *Imprint of* **Charisma Media**

Charisma Media, *(978-0-88419; 978-0-930525; 978-1-59185; 978-1-59979; 978-1-61638; 978-1-62136; 978-1-62998; 978-1-62999; 978-1-63641)* Div. of Creation House Pr., 600 Rinehart Rd., Lake Mary, FL 32746 USA (SAN 677-5640) Tel 407-333-0600; Fax: 407-333-7100; Toll Free: 800-283-8494; *Imprints:* Charisma House (Charisma Hse); Casa Creacion (Casa Cre); Creation House (CreatHse); Siloam Press (Siloam Pr); Charisma Kids (Charisma Kids); Realms (Realms); Frontline (Frontline FLA)
Web site: http://www.charismamedia.com/
Dist(s): **Dake Publishing**
Follett School Solutions
INscribe Digital
Independent Pubs. Group
Lulu Pr., Inc.
Pura Vida Bks., Inc.
SPD-Small Pr. Distribution
Send The Light Distribution LLC.

Charlene Adler, *(978-0-692-94597-1; 978-0-9994165)* 510 E. Washington, DELAVAN, WI 53115 USA Tel 816-813-1708
E-mail: mmmuffin4@gmail.com
Dist(s): **Ingram Content Group.**

Charles River Media, *(978-1-886801; 978-1-58450)* Orders Addr.: P.O. Box 960, Herndon, VA 20172 USA (SAN 254-1564) Fax: 703-996-1010; Toll Free: 800-382-8505; Edit Addr.: 25 Thomson Pl., Boston, MA 02210-1202 USA
E-mail: info@charlesriver.com
Web site: http://www.charlesriver.com
Dist(s): **CENGAGE Learning**
Delmar Cengage Learning
ebrary, Inc.

Charles River Pr., *(978-0-9754913; 978-0-9791304; 978-0-9793844; 978-0-9820946; 978-1-936185; 978-1-940676)* 37 Evergreen Rd., Norton, MA 02766 USA Fax: 508-297-3628; P.O. Box 1122, Mansfield, MA 02048 (SAN 256-2251); *Imprints:* Gap Tooth Publishing (Gap Tooth Pubng) Do not confuse with Charles River Pr. in Alexandria, VA
E-mail: jwomack@charlesriverpress.com; customerservice@charlesriverpress.com
Web site: http://www.charlesriverpress.com.

Charles Scribner's Sons *Imprint of* **Cengage Gale**

Charlesbridge Publishing, Inc., *(978-0-88106; 978-0-935508; 978-1-57091; 978-1-58089; 978-1-879085; 978-1-60734; 978-0-9822939; 978-0-9823064; 978-1-936140; 978-1-63289; 978-1-64537)* Orders Addr.: c/o Penguin Random House, 400 Hahn Rd., Westminster, MD 21157 USA Toll Free Fax: 800-669-1536; Toll Free: 800-733-3000; Edit Addr.: 85 Main St., Watertown, MA 02472 USA (SAN 240-5474) Tel 617-926-0329; Fax: 617-926-5720; Toll Free Fax: 800-926-5775; Toll Free: 800-225-3214; *Imprints:* Mackinac Island Press, Incorporated (Mackinac); Imagine Publishing (ImaginePub); Charlesbridge Teen (CharlesbridgeT)
E-mail: orders@charlesbridge.com
Web site: http://www.charlesbridge.com
Dist(s): **Children's Plus, Inc.**
Continental Bk. Co., Inc.
Follett School Solutions
Lectorum Pubns., Inc.
MyiLibrary
Penguin Random Hse. Distribution
Penguin Random Hse. LLC
Random Hse., Inc.

Charlesbridge Teen *Imprint of* **Charlesbridge Publishing, Inc.**

Charlie & Albert, *(978-0-9801329)* 2920 Applewood Ct., Suite 192, Atlanta, GA 30345-1401 USA Tel 770-938-8863.

Charlie Co., *(978-0-578-42731-7)* 1561 East Ave., Rochester, NY 14610 USA Tel 585-303-6121
E-mail: johns@exhibitsandmore.com.

Charlie's Gift, *(978-0-9786795)* 920 York Rd., Suite 350, Hinsdale, IL 60521 USA Tel 630-399-8164.

Charlie's Port, *(978-0-692-90898-3; 978-0-9997510; 978-0-692-03537-5)* 9305 Bluejack Ln., Roswell, GA 30076 USA Tel 678-800-8787
E-mail: mc@charliesport.org
Web site: www.charliesport.org.

Charming Pubns., *(978-0-9773531)* Orders Addr.: P.O. Box 90792, Austin, TX 78709-0792 USA Tel 512-288-4803
E-mail: minia.lopez@gmail.com
Web site: http://www.happychildrenbooks.com.

Chartwell *Imprint of* **Book Sales, Inc.**

Charwood Pubns., *(978-0-615-58076-0; 978-0-615-66672-3; 978-0-9910347; 978-0-692-79990-1; 978-0-692-80308-0; 978-0-9986914)* Orders Addr.: P.O. Box 14881, Long Beach, CA 90853 USA Tel 562-810-7176
E-mail: charlesflius@gmail.com
Web site: www.charlesflius.com; www.charwoodpublications.com.

Chaser Media LLC, *(978-0-9747447)* P.O. Box 99, Dorset, VT 05251 USA
Web site: http://www.chasermedia.com.

Chateau Thierry Pr., *(978-0-935046)* Div. of Joan Thiry Enterprises, Ltd., 2100 W. Estes, Chicago, IL 60645 USA (SAN 281-4056) Tel 773-262-2234; Fax: 773-262-2235
E-mail: percival6390@sbcglobal.net.

Chatelain, Linda, *(978-1-938669)* Orders Addr.: 4106 S. Middlepark Ln., West Valley City, UT 84119 USA Tel 801-654-7793
E-mail: lchat1950@hotmail.com.

Chatoyant, *(978-0-9661452)* P.O. Box 832, Aptos, CA 95001 USA (SAN 253-9454) Tel 831-662-2723
E-mail: books@chatoyant.com
Web site: http://www.chatoyant.com.

Chatting Timmy, 845 16Th St unit 28, San Diego, CA 92101 USA Tel 678-862-2178
E-mail: iracanada@bellsouth.net
Dist(s): **Ingram Content Group.**

Chaucer Pr. *Imprint of* **Altschuler, Richard & Assocs., Inc.**

Chauncey Park Pr., *(978-0-9667808)* Div. of Charles Chauncey Wells, Inc., 735 N. Grove Ave., Oak Park, IL 60302-1551 USA Tel 708-524-0695; Fax: 708-524-0742
E-mail: chauncey@wells1.com
Web site: http://www.wells1.com.

CHB Media, *(978-0-9822819; 978-0-9851507; 978-0-9886315; 978-0-9911189; 978-0-9863842)* Div. of Christian Heartbeat, Inc., 3039 Needle Palm Dr., Edgewater, FL 32141 USA Tel 386-690-9295
E-mail: christianheartbeat@gmail.com
Web site: http://www.chbmediaonline.com.

Checker Book Publishing Group *See* **Devil's Due Digital, Inc. - A Checker Digital Co.**

Checkerboard Library *Imprint of* **ABDO Publishing Co.**

†**Checkerboard Pr., Inc.,** *(978-1-56288)* 1560 Revere Rd., Yardley, PA 19067-4351 USA; *CIP.*

Checkmark Bks. *Imprint of* **Facts On File, Inc.**

Cheerful Cherub, *(978-0-9753417)* Orders Addr.: 10071 S. Maples Ln., Highlands Ranch, CO 80129 USA Tel 303-471-8472; Edit Addr.: 10071 S. Maples Ln., Highlands Ranch, CO 80129 USA
E-mail: coloradodonna@q.com
Web site: http://www.cheerfulcherub.com.

Cheesy Bread Publishing, *(978-1-7323816)* 510 Wallace, Chicago Heights, IL 60411 USA Tel 708-491-6382
E-mail: art.pressley@yahoo.com.

CheeTrann Creations LLC, *(978-0-9834761; 978-1-7320332)* 203 Airport Dr. Unit A5, Sitka, AK 99835 USA Tel 907-738-4303
E-mail: Tom@SKRandolph.com
Web site: www.skrandolph.com.

Chelsea Clubhouse *Imprint of* **Facts On File, Inc.**

Chelsea Green Publishing, *(978-0-930031; 978-1-890132; 978-1-931498; 978-1-933392; 978-1-60358; 978-1-64502)* 85 N. Main St., Suite 120, White River Junction, VT 05001 USA
E-mail: info@chelseagreen.com
Web site: http://www.chelseagreen.com
Dist(s): **Follett School Solutions**
Independent Pubs. Group.

Chelsea Hse. *Imprint of* **Facts On File, Inc.**

Chelsea lagrange, *(978-0-692-15625-4; 978-0-692-17382-4; 978-0-578-40438-7)* 9078 Blackhawk trl., Lucerne Valley, CA 92356 USA Tel 760-646-2660
E-mail: Chelsealagrange@gmail.com
Dist(s): **Ingram Content Group.**

Chelsea Media *See* **Chelsea Multimedia**

Chelsea Multimedia, *(978-0-9822348)* P.O. Box 4668 19830, New York, NY 10163-4668 USA Tel 203-853-0540; *Imprints:* Chelsea Press (Chelsea Press)
Web site: http://www.chelseapress.com
Dist(s): **CreateSpace Independent Publishing Platform.**

Chelsea Pr. *Imprint of* **Chelsea Multimedia**

Chelsea Publishing Co., Inc. *Imprint of* **American Mathematical Society**

Chemical Heritage Foundation, *(978-0-941901)* 315 Chestnut St., Philadelphia, PA 19106-2702 USA (SAN 666-0193) Tel 215-925-2222; Fax: 215-925-1954; Toll Free: 888-224-6006
E-mail: booksales@chemheritage.org
Web site: http://www.chemheritage.org.

Chen, Stephen, *(978-0-692-14249-3)* 5106 E. Palo Brea Ln., Cave Creek, AZ 85331 USA Tel 602-284-6501
E-mail: schendesigns@gmail.com
Dist(s): **Ingram Content Group.**

Cheng & Tsui Co., *(978-0-88727; 978-0-917056; 978-1-62291)* 25 W. St., Boston, MA 02111-1213 USA (SAN 169-3387)
E-mail: service@cheng-tsui.com
Web site: http://www.cheng-tsui.com
Dist(s): **Chinasprout, Inc.**
Follett School Solutions.

Cheng Chung Bk. Co., Ltd. (TWN) *(978-957-09) Dist. by* **Cheng Tsui.**

Cheniere Pr., *(978-0-9725146; 978-0-9786260)* 151 La Jolla Dr., Santa Barbara, CA 93109 USA
E-mail: webmaster@cheniere.org.

Cherakota Books *See* **Cherakota Publishing**

Cherakota Publishing, *(978-0-9795678)* Orders Addr.: P.O. Box 603, Two Harbors, MN 55616 USA
E-mail: info@cherakotapublishing.com
Web site: http://www.cherakotapublishing.com.

Cherish the Children *See* **Chris A. Zeigler Dendy Consulting LLC**

Cherokee Bks., *(978-0-9640458; 978-1-930052)* Orders Addr.: 24 Meadow Ridge Pkwy. Dover, De 19904, Dover, DE 19904-5800 USA Tel 302-734-8782; Fax: 302-734-3198 Do not confuse with Cherokee Bks., Ponca City, OK
E-mail: milthanna@aol.com
Web site: http://www.cherokeebooks.com
Dist(s): **Washington Bk. Distributors.**

Cherokee Publishing Company *See* **Cherokee Bks.**

Cherokee Rose Publishing, LLC, *(978-0-9968902; 978-0-9994622)* 2367 Barrett Cottage Pl., Marietta, GA 30066 USA Tel 678-403-2272
E-mail: margeryphelps@msn.com
Web site: www.margeryphelps.com; www.findingmargaret.com; www.cherokeerosepublishing.com.

Cherry Blossom Press *Imprint of* **Cherry Lake Publishing**

Cherry Lake Publishing, *(978-1-60279; 978-1-61080; 978-1-62431; 978-1-62753; 978-1-63137; 978-1-63188; 978-1-63362; 978-1-63470; 978-1-63471; 978-1-63472; 978-1-5341)* 1215 Overidgeview Ct., Ann Arbor, MI 48103 USA Tel 248-705-2045; 1750 Northway Dr., Suite 101, North Mankato, MN 56003 (SAN 858-9275) Tel 866-918-3956; Toll Free Fax: 866-489-6490; *Imprints:* Blackbirch Press, Incorporated (Blackbirch Pr); 45th Parallel Press (45 Parallel); Cherry Blossom Press (Cherry Bloss Pr)
E-mail: customerservice@cherrylakepublishing.com; benmondloch@me.com; lois.hume@sleepingbearpress.com
Web site: http://cherrylakepublishing.com; www.sleepingbearpress.com
Dist(s): **Follett School Solutions**
MyiLibrary.

Cherry Lane Books *See* **Cherry Lane Music Co.**

†**Cherry Lane Music Co.,** *(978-0-89524; 978-1-57560; 978-1-60378)* 6 E. 32nd St., 11th Flr., New York, NY 10016 USA (SAN 219-0788) Tel 212-561-3000; Fax: 212-251-0822
E-mail: print@cherrylane.com
Web site: http://www.cherrylane.com
Dist(s): **Leonard, Hal Corp.**
MyiLibrary
National Bk. Network; *CIP.*

Cherry Red Bks. (GBR) *(978-0-9517206; 978-1-901447) Dist. by* **IPG Chicago.**

Cherry Street Pr., *(978-0-9764921)* 139A N. 22nd St., Philadelphia, PA 19103 USA Fax: 215-568-4329
Dist(s): **Follett School Solutions.**

Cherry, Tasha *See* **Pop Academy of Music**

Cherry Tree Bks., *(978-0-9666832; 978-0-9774665)* 433 Perkins Rd., Weybridge, VT 05753 USA Tel 802-545-2474
E-mail: idahw@pshift.com; lmwash@together.net
Web site: http://www.cherrytreebooks.net.

Cherry Tree Lane Publishing, *(978-0-9771858)* 125 Cobblestone Ct., Berea, OH 44017-1079 USA
E-mail: sharesom@wowway.com.

Cherry Tree Pr. LLC, *(978-0-9772771)* Orders Addr.: 525 W. 14th St., #185, Traverse City, MI 49684-4968 USA Tel 231-421-1012; Edit Addr.: 526 W. 14th St., No. 185, Traverse City, MI 49684-4968 USA Do not confuse with Cherry Tree Press in Palo Alto, CA
E-mail: info@cherrytreepress.com
Web site: http://www.CherryTreePress.com; http://www.AmlaColorToo.com
Dist(s): **Partners Bk. Distributing, Inc.**

Cherrytree Bks. (GBR) *(978-0-7451; 978-0-7540; 978-1-84234) Dist. by* **IPG Chicago.**

Cherrytree Pubns., Inc., *(978-0-9677757)* 881 Ocean Dr., No. 18B, Biscayne, FL 33149 USA Tel 305-361-1828.

Chesed Avraham Temple, *(978-0-9801799)* Orders Addr.: P.O. Box 35456, Los Angeles, CA 90035 USA (SAN 855-4137) Tel 310-654-0303
E-mail: meissany@ca.rr.com
Web site: http://www.EbrahimNeissany.com.

Cheshire House Bks., *(978-0-9675073)* P.O. Box 2484, New York, NY 10021 USA Tel 212-861-5404 (phone/fax)
E-mail: Chershirehouse@webtv.net
Web site: http://www.samthecat.com
Dist(s): **Brodart Co.**
Follet Higher Education Grp
Follett School Solutions.

Chess Detective Pr., *(978-0-9761962)* 1 Red Fox Ln., Englewood, CO 80111 USA Tel 303-770-6696 (phone/fax)
Web site: http://www.coloradomasterchess.com
Dist(s): **Follett School Solutions.**

Chess Library, The, *(978-0-9661889)* 12615 SW 297th Way, Vashon, WA 98070 USA
E-mail: pkmccready@netscape.net; admin@thechesslibrary.com
Web site: http://www.thechesslibrary.com.

Chessmore Publishing *See* **Eusebian Publishing**

Chester Comix, LLC, *(978-0-9729616; 978-1-933122; 978-0-692-95704-2; 978-1-7323612)* P.O. Box 5653, Williamsburg, VA 23188 USA
E-mail: chestercomix@yahoo.com
Web site: http://www.chestercomix.com
Dist(s): **Follett School Solutions.**

Chester Music *Imprint of* **Music Sales Corp.**

Chester Music (GBR) *(978-0-7119) Dist. by* **H Leonard.**

Cheval International, *(978-0-9640610; 978-1-885351)* P.O. Box 706, Black Hawk, SD 57718-0706 USA
E-mail: cheval@rapidnet.com
Web site: http://www.chevalinternational.com
Dist(s): **Barnes & Noble Bks.-Imports.**

Cheveux Roux LLC *See* **Gray & Gold Publishing**

Chi Chi Rodriguez Books *See* **Caribbean Experience Con Amor, LLC, A**

Chiang Mai Bks., *(978-0-578-19214-7)* 1006 Marley Manor Dr. Apt 103, Salisbury, MD 21804 USA.

Chiappini, Lydia , *(978-0-9669355)* 60 Gaisler Rd., Blairstown, NJ 07825 USA Tel 908-362-5604
E-mail: lydiachiappini@yahoo.com.

Chiaramonti, Gregory, *(978-0-615-13848-0)* 825 Cherry St., Trenton, NJ 08638-3322 USA
E-mail: gcmonti@yahoo.com
Web site: http://www.probie-thespaceprobe.com
Dist(s): **Lulu Pr., Inc.**

Chicago Children's Museum, *(978-0-9759580)* Navy Pier, 700 E. Grand Ave., Chicago, IL 60611 USA Tel 312-527-1000; Fax: 312-527-9082
Web site: http://www.chichildrensmuseum.org
Dist(s): **Follett School Solutions**
Independent Pubs. Group
ebrary, Inc.

Chicago Distribution Ctr., Orders Addr.: 11030 S. Langley Ave., Chicago, IL 60628 USA (SAN 630-6047) Tel 773-702-7000 (International); Fax: 773-702-7212 (International); Toll Free Fax: 800-621-8476 (USA/Canada); Toll Free: 800-621-2736 (USA/Canada); 800-621-8471 (credit & collections)
E-mail: custserv@press.uchicago.edu; orders@press.uchicago.edu
Web site: http://www.press.uchicago.edu; http://www.press.uchicago.edu/presswide/cdc/.

†**Chicago Review Pr., Inc.,** *(978-0-89733; 978-0-912777; 978-0-913705; 978-0-914090; 978-0-914091; 978-0-915864; 978-1-55652; 978-1-56976; 978-1-61373; 978-1-61374; 978-1-64160)* 814 N. Franklin St., Chicago, IL 60610 USA (SAN 213-5744) Tel 312-337-0747; Toll Free: 800-888-4741 (orders only); *Imprints:* Hill, Lawrence Books (Lawrence Hill); Zephyr Press (ZephPr); Academy Chicago Publishers, Limited (AcadChicagoPubs)
E-mail: frontdesk@chicagoreviewpress.com; orders@ipgbook.com
Web site: http://www.ipgbook.com; http://www.chicagoreviewpress.com
Dist(s): **AK Pr. Distribution**
Cobblestone Publishing Co.
Ebsco Publishing
Follett School Solutions
Gryphon Hse., Inc.
Independent Pubs. Group
Lulu Pr., Inc.
MyiLibrary
SAGE Pubns., Inc.
ebrary, Inc.; *CIP.*

Chicago Spectrum Pr., *(978-1-58374; 978-1-886094)* Div. of Evanston Publishing Inc., Orders Addr.: 6611 Foxcroft Rd., Prospect, KY 40059 USA Tel 502-899-1919; Toll Free: 800-594-5190; 888-266-5780 (888-BOOKS-80)
E-mail: dorothykavka@twc.com
Web site: www.fineartbykavka.com.

Chicago Unzipped, *(978-0-9771699; 978-0-9817538)* 633 Clark St., No. 2-634, Evanston, IL 60208 USA (SAN 856-4558) Tel 847-491-8757
Web site: http://www.chicagounzipped.com.

Chick Light Publishing, *(978-0-9769198)* 845 Monticello Ct., Cape Coral, FL 33904 USA Tel 239-945-1939 (phone/fax)
E-mail: vince@chicklight.com
Web site: http://chicklight.com.

Chick Pubns., Inc., *(978-0-937958; 978-0-7589)* P.O. Box 3500, Ontario, CA 91761-1019 USA (SAN 211-7770) Tel 909-987-0771; Fax: 909-941-8128; Toll Free: 800-932-3050
E-mail: orderdesk@chick.com
Web site: http://www.chick.com.

Chickadee Words *Imprint of* **Chickadee Words, LLC**

Chickadee Words, LLC, *(978-0-9981291; 978-0-9998315; 978-1-7357338)* 5220 N. Randolph Rd, Kansas City, MO 64119 USA Tel 816-807-7025; *Imprints:* Chickadee Words (MYID_S_CHICKAD)
E-mail: kathy@chickadeewords.com
Web site: chickadeewords.com
Dist(s): **BookBaby**
Ingram Bk. Co.

Chickaloon Village Publishing, *(978-0-9767217)* Orders Addr.: P.O. Box 1105, Chickaloon, AK 99674 USA Tel 907-745-0707; Fax: 907-745-0709
E-mail: cvadmin@chickaloon.org
Web site: http://www.chickaloon.org.

Chicken Hse., The *Imprint of* **Scholastic, Inc.**

Chicken Socks *Imprint of* **Klutz**

Chicken Soup for the Soul Publishing, LLC, *(978-1-935096; 978-1-61159)* 132 E. Putnam Ave., Cos Cob, CT 06807 USA; 180 Varick St. Suite 816, New York, NY 10014; *Imprints:* CSS Backlist (CSSBacklist)
E-mail: evergreenstables@hotmail.com
Dist(s): **Follett School Solutions**
Leonard, Hal Corp.
MyiLibrary
Open Road Integrated Media, Inc.
Simon & Schuster
Simon & Schuster, Inc.

Chickering-Moller Project, *(978-0-9860799)* 414 W. 16th Street, Traverse City, MI 49684 USA.

Chicory Pr., *(978-0-9785886)* 49 Maple Ave., Morgantown, WV 26501 USA Tel 304-292-1115
E-mail: efaulkes@mail.wvu.edu.

Chien, Paris *See* **La Librairie Parisienne**

Chihuly Workshop, Inc., *(978-0-9608382; 978-1-57684)* Orders Addr.: P.O. Box 70856, Seattle, WA 98127 USA (SAN 240-3579) Tel 206-297-1304; Fax: 206-297-6207; Toll Free: 800-574-7272 (trade orders) Do not confuse with Portland Pr., Inc., Chapel Hill, NC
E-mail: jacobb@portlandpress.net
Web site: http://www.chihuly.com; http://www.portlandpress.net; http://www.chihulyworkshop.com
Dist(s): **Follett School Solutions.**

ChikChatr Ink, *(978-0-9766634)* P.O. Box 3302, Brentwood, TN 37024-3302 USA Tel 615-731-7422.

Child Advocates, Inc., *(978-0-9754953)* 2401 Portsmouth, Suite 210, Houston, TX 77098 USA Tel 713-529-1396; Fax: 713-529-1390
Web site: http://www.childadvocates.org
Dist(s): **Follett School Solutions.**

Child & Family Pr. *Imprint of* **Child Welfare League of America, Inc.**

Child Life Bks., LLC, *(978-0-9771143; 978-0-9791687)* 22303 Charlotte Dr., Torrance, CA 90505-2118 USA
E-mail: liana@mannersicare.com.

Child Like Faith Children's Bks. LLC, *(978-1-7328586; 978-1-7331584; 978-1-7348268; 978-1-7355149)* 2012 Wages Way, Jacksonville, FL 32218 USA Tel 904-207-5044
E-mail: lsg19596@gmail.com; kim@abcbookpublishers.com; clfcbs@gmail.com
Web site: https://childlikefaithchildrensbooks.com/.

Child Scope Productions, *(978-0-9678778)* Div. of Moschea Promotions, 5016 N. Lydell Ave., White Fish Bay, WI 53217 USA Tel 414-332-1897; Fax: 414-332-1609
E-mail: mosch@execpc.com.

Child Sensitive Communication, LLC, *(978-0-9743197; 978-1-933803; 978-0-9979174; 978-0-9986292)* P.O. Box 150806, Nashville, TN 37215-0806 USA; *Imprints:* Karyn Henley Resources (Krayn Henley)
Web site: http://www.karynhenley.com; http://throatofthenight.com
Dist(s): **Brown Bks.**

†**Child Welfare League of America, Inc.,** *(978-0-87868; 978-1-58760)* Orders Addr.: P.O. Box 932831, Atlanta, GA 31193-2831 USA Tel 770-280-4164; Toll Free: 800-407-6273; Edit Addr.: 2345 Crystal Dr., Suite 250, Arlington, VA 22202 USA (SAN 201-9876) Tel 703-412-2400; Fax: 703-412-2401 (orders only); PBD 420 Eagleview Blvd., Exton, PA 19341 (SAN 851-2558) Tel 202-638-2952; Fax: 202-638-4004; *Imprints:* C W L A Press (CWLA Pr); Child & Family Press (Child-Family Pr)
E-mail: order@cwla.org
Web site: http://www.cwla.org/pubs
Dist(s): **Lectorum Pubns., Inc.**; *CIP.*

Child1st Pubns., LLC, *(978-0-9844972; 978-0-9829873; 978-1-936981; 978-1-947484)* Orders Addr.: PO Box 150226, Grand Rapids, MI 49515 USA
Web site: http://www.child1st.com
Dist(s): **Follett School Solutions.**

Childcraft Education Corp., *(978-1-890275; 978-1-58669)* Div. of School Speciality, 2920 Old Tree Dr., Lancaster, PA 17603 USA Tel 717-391-4027; Fax: 717-397-7436; Toll Free: 800-631-5652
E-mail: kmyers@childcrafteducation.com
Web site: http://www.childcrafteducation.com/.

Childhood Anxiety Network *See* **Selective Mutism Anxiety Research & Treatment Ctr.**

Children *Imprint of* **Star Light Pr.**

Children Concept Publishing, *(978-0-9745219)* Orders Addr.: P.O. Box 1179, Highland, MI 48357 USA; Edit Addr.: 1651 S. Milford Rd., Highland, MI 48357 USA.

Children Learning Awareness, Safety & Self-Defense, *(978-0-9768273)* Orders Addr.: 16815 Gault St., Lake Balboa, CA 91406 USA Tel 818-990-9909 (phone/fax); *Imprints:* CLASS Publications (CLASS Pubns)
E-mail: janet@classeducation.org; janet@classpublications.com
Web site: http://www.classeducation.org; http://www.classpublications.com
Dist(s): **Class Pubns., Inc.**

Children Left Behind, *(978-0-9829203)* P.O. Box 129, Berryville, AR 72616 USA Tel 870-654-3207
E-mail: LKHudd@yahoo.com
Web site: http://childrenleftbehind.org.

Children of Color/The Indra Collection, *(978-0-9746779)* P.O. Box 992, Great Falls, VA 22066 USA
Web site: http://www.childrenofcolor.com.

Children's Author, *(978-0-692-96975-5; 978-0-692-13151-0)* 12425 Hastings Rd, Midwest City, OK 73130 USA Tel 405-816-4011
E-mail: roxiemcbride@sbcglobal.net
Web site: roxiemcbride.com.

Children's Better Health Institute, *(978-1-885453)* Div. of Benjamin Franklin Literary & Medical Society, Inc., 1100 Waterway Blvd., Indianapolis, IN 46202 USA Tel 317-636-8881; Fax: 317-684-8094; Toll Free: 800-558-2376.

Childrens Bible Society, *(978-0-9777446)* Orders Addr.: P.O. Box 96, Hemet, CA 92546 USA Tel 951-652-9456; Edit Addr.: 1123 W. Acacia Ave., Hemet, CA 92543 USA
E-mail: kristy@actstracts.com
Web site: http://www.childrensbiblesociety.org/.

Children's Book Press *Imprint of* **Lee & Low Bks., Inc.**

Children's Bk. Publishing, *(978-0-692-18457-8; 978-0-692-18724-1; 978-0-692-04436-0)* 1523 Moore St., Huntingdon, PA 16652 USA Tel 814-644-9883
E-mail: JandCbooks18@gmail.com
Dist(s): **Ingram Content Group.**

Children's Bookshoppe Stop, The, *(978-0-9728393)* 7719 James Monroe Way, Gloucester, VA 23061 USA Tel 804-601-0707 (phone/fax)
E-mail: jacquelinesbooksforkids@yahoo.com
Web site: http://www.surftcbs.com.

Children's Classic Book Pubs., *(978-0-9794753)* Orders Addr.: 103 Josh Ln., Poolville, TX 76487 USA (SAN 853-5280)
E-mail: orders@snerfycat.com; misterfish@snerfycat.com; ccbp@snerfycat.com
Web site: www.SnerfyCat.com.

Children's Creative Writing Institute, The, *(978-0-692-24484-5; 978-0-692-24485-2; 978-0-692-24486-9; 978-0-692-24487-6; 978-0-692-24488-3; 978-0-692-24489-0)* 17610 Weddington St., Encino, CA 91316 USA Tel 8185158712
Web site: www.ccwi.net
Dist(s): **CreateSpace Independent Publishing Platform.**

Children's Express Foundation, Inc., *(978-0-9621641)* 1331 H St, NW, Suite 900, Washington, DC 20005 USA (SAN 251-6993) Tel 202-737-7377; Fax: 202-737-0193
E-mail: s1@dc.ce.org
Web site: http://www.ce.org.

Children's Illustrated Classics,

Children's Insight *Imprint of* **Insight Services, Inc**

Children's Kindness Network, *(978-0-9662268; 978-0-9745184)* Orders Addr.: 1323 Barkleigh Ln., Franklin, TN 37064 USA Tel 970-453-0410; Fax: 970-453-7375; Toll Free: 800-699-4541
E-mail: ted@moozie.com
Dist(s): **Bibliotech, Inc.**

Children's Legacy, *(978-0-9629365)* Orders Addr.: P.O. Box 300305, Denver, CO 80203 USA; Edit Addr.: 2553 Dexter St., Denver, CO 80207 USA Tel 303-830-7595.

Children's Literacy Pubns., *(978-0-9710432)* P.O. Box 5581, Sun City Center, FL 33571 USA Toll Free Fax: 1-866-350-4502; Toll Free: 1-800-585-1893
E-mail: janet@makereadingfirst.com
Web site: http://www.makereadingfirst.com.

Children's Plus, Inc., 1387 Dutch Ameican, Beecher, IL 60401 USA Tel 708-946-4100; Fax: 709-946-4199
E-mail: danw@childrensplusinc.com
Web site: http://www.childrensplusinc.com
Dist(s): **Stevens, Gareth Publishing LLLP.**

Children's Poetic Pr., *(978-0-692-64574-1; 978-0-692-80728-6; 978-0-578-63313-8; 978-0-578-65781-3; 978-0-578-71497-4)* 415 S. Lombard Ave. Apt No. 305, Oak Park, IL 60302 USA Tel 708-548-7191
Dist(s): **CreateSpace Independent Publishing Platform.**

Children's Pr. *Imprint of* **Scholastic Library Publishing**

Children's Psychological Health Ctr., Inc., The, *(978-0-9790846)* 2105 Divisadero St., San Francisco, CA 94115 USA Tel 415-292-7119; Fax: 415-749-2802
E-mail: gil.kliman@cphc-sf.org
Web site: http://www.cphc-sf.org.

Children's Publishing, *(978-0-9725803; 978-0-9789347)* Orders Addr.: 101 Crepe Myrtle Ln., Georgetown, TX 78633-4724 USA (SAN 254-9328) Toll Free: 877-864-7364
E-mail: carlson@childrenspublishing.com
Web site: http://www.childrenspublishing.com
Dist(s): **Quality Bks., Inc.**
Speech Bin, Inc., The.

Children's Success Unlimited LLC, *(978-0-9829613)* 160 Greentree Dr., Suite 101, Dover, DE 19904 USA Tel 917-208-7785
E-mail: bolbrys@ion-partners.com
Dist(s): **Emerald Bk. Co.**
Greenleaf Book Group.

Children's Village Foundation, Inc., *(978-0-9740481)* 1350 W. Hanley Ave., Coeur d'Alene, ID 83815 USA Tel 208-667-1189; Fax: 208-664-5735
E-mail: tinka@thechildrensvillage.org
Web site: http://www.thechildrensvillage.org.

ChildrenzBks., *(978-0-9748989)* P.O. Box 1431, Tucson, AZ 85702-1431 USA; *Imprints:* Bases Loaded Books (Bases Loaded Bks)
E-mail: sales@childrenzbooks.com
Web site: http://www.childrenzbooks.com.

Child's Play International Ltd. (GBR) *(978-0-85953; 978-1-904550; 978-1-84643) Dist. by* **Children Plus.**

†Child's World, Inc., The, *(978-0-89565; 978-0-913778; 978-1-56766; 978-1-59296; 978-1-60253; 978-1-60954; 978-1-60973; 978-1-61473; 978-1-62323; 978-1-62687; 978-1-63143; 978-1-63407; 978-1-5038)* 1980 Lookout Dr., Mankato, MN 56003 USA (SAN 858-5385) Tel 507-385-1044; Fax: 888-320-2329; Toll Free Fax: 800-599-7323; *Imprints:* Spirit of Americar (Spirit of Am); MOMENTUM (MOMENTUMMN)
E-mail: info@childsworld.com; mary.berendes@childsworld.com; mike.peterson@childsworld.com
Web site: http://www.childsworld.com
Dist(s): **Peterson Publishing Co., Inc.**; *CIP.*

Childswork/Childsplay, *(978-1-882732; 978-1-58815; 978-1-931704)* Div. of The Guidance Channel, Orders Addr.: P.O. Box 760, Plainview, NY 11803-0760 USA Tel 516-349-5520; Fax: 516-349-5521; Toll Free Fax: 800-262-1886; Toll Free: 800-962-1141; 45 Executive Dr. Ste. 201, Plainview, NY 11803-1738
E-mail: karens@at-risk.com; info@childswork.com
Web site: http://www.childswork.com.

Chiliric Pubns., *(978-0-9755253)* 1423 6th St., Eureka, CA 95501 USA Tel 707-443-4046
Web site: http://www.geocities.com/harleysgreatadventures/; http://www.Geocities.com/harleys_great_adventures.

Chimera Pubns. (GBR) *(978-1-901388; 978-1-903931) Dist. by* **PerseuPGW.**

Chimeric Pr., *(978-0-9847122)* 5299 Rau Rd., West Branch, MI 48661 USA Tel 989-343-9953
E-mail: info@chimericpress.com
Web site: www.chimericpress.com.

Chin & A Pr., *(978-0-9746341)* 2809 79th Ave., Brooklyn Park, MN 55444 USA Tel 763-549-8821
E-mail: jlodien@earthlink.net; ChinAndAPress@earthlink.net
Web site: http://www.allbeethere.com.

Chin Music Pr., *(978-0-9741995; 978-0-9844576; 978-0-9850416; 978-0-9887693; 978-1-63405)* 2621 24th Ave. W., Seattle, WA 98199 USA Tel 206-380-1947 (phone/fax)
E-mail: bruce@chinmusicpress.com
Web site: http://www.chinmusicpress.com
Dist(s): **Consortium Bk. Sales & Distribution**
Follett School Solutions
MyiLibrary.

†China Books & Periodicals, Inc., *(978-0-8351)* 360 Swift Ave., Suite 48, South San Francisco, CA 94080 USA (SAN 145-0557) Tel 650-872-7718; 650-872-7076; Fax: 650-872-7808
E-mail: chris@chinabooks.com
Web site: http://www.chinabooks.com
Dist(s): **Follett School Solutions**
SPD-Small Pr. Distribution; *CIP.*

China Language University Pr. (CHN) *(978-7-88703) Dist. by* **China Bks.**

Chinasoft (AUS) *(978-1-876739; 978-0-646-06656-1; 978-0-646-06657-8; 978-0-646-06658-5; 978-0-646-13326-3; 978-0-646-13327-0; 978-0-646-13328-7; 978-0-646-22328-5; 978-0-646-22329-2; 978-0-646-22330-8; 978-0-646-25096-0; 978-0-646-25097-7) Dist. by* **Cheng Tsui.**

Chinasprout, Inc., *(978-0-9707332; 978-0-9747302; 978-0-9820227; 978-1-945947)* 110 W. 32nd St., Flr. 6, New York, NY 10001-3205 USA Toll Free: 800-644-2611
E-mail: info@chinasprout.com
Web site: http://www.chinasprout.com
Dist(s): **China Books & Periodicals, Inc.**
Follett School Solutions.

Chipman, Marilyn, *(978-0-9745857)* P.O. Box 441233, Aurora, CO 80044-1233 USA
E-mail: chipman@mscd.edu
Web site: http://www.marilynchipman.com.

Chipotle Publishing, LLC, *(978-0-9823918; 978-0-9965218)* 631 N. Stephanie St., Suite 282, Henderson, NV 89014 USA Tel 702-565-0746
E-mail: megan@chipotlepublishing.com
Web site: www.chipotlepublishing.com.

Chippewa Valley Museum, *(978-0-9636191; 978-1-7334036)* Orders Addr.: P.O. Box 1204, Eau Claire, WI 54702 USA Tel 715-834-7871; Fax: 715-834-6624; Edit Addr.: Carson Park Dr., Eau Claire, WI 54702 USA
E-mail: info@cvmuseum.com
Web site: http://www.cvmuseum.com
Dist(s): **Chicago Distribution Ctr.**
Univ. of Wisconsin Pr.

Chiron Pubns., *(978-0-933029; 978-1-888602; 978-1-63051)* 932 Hendersonville Rd.; STE 104, Asheville, NC 28803 USA (SAN 689-1659) Tel 828-333-5245; Fax: 828-333-4787; Toll Free: 800-397-8109
E-mail: stevebuser@gmail.com
Web site: http://www.chironpublications.com.

ChironBooks *Imprint of* **Coleman/Perrin**

Chisholm, Juan Phillip *See* **Green Light Bks. and Publishing, LLC**

Chock-Lit Pubns., *(978-0-9742344)* 26 Douvaine Ct., The Woodlands, TX 77382 USA
E-mail: publisher@chocklitpublications.com
Web site: http://www.chocklitpublications.com.

Chocolate Sauce, *(978-0-9740268; 978-0-9911314)* 211 E. 60th street, sweet C3, New York, NY 10022 USA
Web site: http://www.chocolatesaucebooks.com
Dist(s): **SPI Bks.**

Choi, Sophia, *(978-0-692-41049-3; 978-0-692-07768-9)* 1226 Golden Vale Dr., Riverside, CA 92506 USA Tel 951-756-8883.

Choice PH, *(978-0-9841910; 978-0-9887595; 978-0-9991517)* 412 Olive Ave., Suite 305, Huntington Beach, CA 92648 USA (SAN 858-6829)
E-mail: choiceph@aol.com
Dist(s): **eBookit.com.**

Choice Point Editions, *(978-0-9778774)* 7883 N. Pershing AVE., Stockton, CA 95207 USA Tel 209-952-7108; Fax: 209-951-3216
E-mail: choicepointeditions@inreach.com
Web site: http://www.choicepointeditions.com.

Choice Publishing House *See* **Choice PH**

ChoiceMaker Pty. Ltd., The (AUS) *(978-0-9805673; 978-1-921790; 978-1-925186; 978-1-925233; 978-1-925234; 978-1-925235; 978-1-925246; 978-1-925247; 978-1-925248; 978-1-925249; 978-1-925250; 978-1-925251; 978-1-925252) Dist. by* **Lerner Pub.**

Choices Education Program, Watson Institute, Brown University *See* **Choices Program, Watson Institute, Brown Univ.**

Choices For Tomorrow, *(978-0-9748689)* 43H Meadow Pond Dr., Leominster, MA 01453 USA
E-mail: moniquehoude@yahoo.com.

Choices International, *(978-0-9768530)* Orders Addr.: P.O. Box 408, Berries Springs, MI 49103 USA Tel 269-471-9718 (phone/fax); Edit Addr.: P.O. Box 408, Berrien Sprgs, MI 49103-0408 USA
E-mail: pennyturner@sbcglobal.net; yourchoices@choicesinternational.info.

Choices Program, Watson Institute, Brown Univ., *(978-1-891306; 978-1-60123)* The Choices Program-Brown Univ. Box 1948, Providence, RI 02912 USA Tel 401-863-3155; Fax: 401-863-1247
E-mail: choices@brown.edu
Web site: http://www.choices.edu.

Cholita Prints & Pub. Co., *(978-0-9742956; 978-0-692-16734-2)* Orders Addr.: P.O. Box 8018, Sante Fe, NM 87504 USA; Edit Addr.: 655 W. San Francisco St., Sante Fe, NM 87501 USA
E-mail: cholitaprints@comcast.net
Dist(s): **Follett School Solutions.**

Choltus, Rebekah L., *(978-0-692-27186-5)* 3260 SW Evergreen Ter, Portland, OR 97205 USA Tel 503-475-1458
E-mail: choltus@msn.com.

Chong, Lisa, *(978-0-9997557)* 208 8th St., Huntington Beach, CA 92648 USA Tel 714-323-0924
E-mail: LisaKLChong@gmail.com.

Choo Choo Clan, *(978-0-9788670)* 1616 Brockton Ave., Apt. 104, Los Angeles, CA 90025 USA Tel 626-715-3342
E-mail: joey0724@hotmail.com
Web site: http://www.choochooclan.com.

Choose Joy Enterprise *See* **Choose Joy Publishing**

Choose Joy Publishing, *(978-0-692-14977-5)* 4533 Ravenwood Pl, Union city, GA 30291 USA Tel 404-786-1846
E-mail: Miriammuhammad1908@yahoo.com.

Chooseco LLC, *(978-0-9745356; 978-1-933390; 978-1-937133)* Orders Addr.: P.O. Box 46, Waitsfield, VT 05673 USA (SAN 852-1131); Edit Addr.: 340 Mad River Pk., Waitsfield, VT 05673 USA (SAN 852-1158) Tel 802-496-2595
E-mail: mbounty@chooseco.com; webmail@chooseco.com
Web site: http://www.cyoa.com; http://www.chooseco.com
Dist(s): **Follett School Solutions.**

Choosing The Best Publishing, *(978-0-9724890; 978-0-9819748; 978-0-9819759; 978-0-9974442; 978-1-7334174)* 2625 Cumberland Pkwy., Suite 200, Atlanta, GA 30339 USA Tel 770-803-3100; Fax: 770-803-3110; Toll Free: 800-774-2378
E-mail: bcook@ctbpublishing.com; book@ctbpublishing.com
Web site: http://www.choosingthebest.org.

Choristers Guild, *(978-1-929187)* 2834 W. Kingsley Rd., Garland, TX 75041-2498 USA (SAN 689-9188) Tel 972-271-1521; Fax: 972-840-3113
E-mail: choristers@choristersguild.org
Web site: http://www.choristersguild.org
Dist(s): **Faith Alive Christian Resources**
Lorenz Corp., The.

Chosen Bks., *(978-0-8007)* Div. of Baker Publishing Group, Orders Addr.: P.O. Box 6287, Grand Rapids, MI 49516-6287 USA Toll Free Fax: 800-398-3111 (orders only); Toll Free: 800-877-2665 (orders only); Edit Addr.: 6030 E. Fulton, Ada, MI 49301 USA Tel 616-676-9185; Fax: 616-676-9573
Web site: http://www.bakerpublishinggroup.com
Dist(s): **Baker Publishing Group**
Faith Alive Christian Resources.

Chosen Word Publishing, *(978-0-9707536; 978-0-9748056; 978-0-9754779)* P.O. Box 481886, Charlotte, NC 28269 USA Tel 704-527-2177; Fax: 704-527-1677
E-mail: jeannette@chosenwordpublishing.com
Web site: http://www.chosenwordpublishing.com.

ChosenButterfly Publishing, *(978-0-9831637; 978-0-9915202; 978-1-945377)* 10 Fernwood Dr, Lancaster, NY 14086 USA Tel 856-357-3801
Web site: http://www.cb-publishing.com
Dist(s): **Smashwords.**

Chou Chou Pr., *(978-0-9606140; 978-0-9716605; 978-0-9789152)* 4 Whimbrel Ct., Okatie, SC 29909 USA (SAN 220-2379) Tel 631-744-5784
E-mail: chouchou@hargray.com; info@bilingualkids.com
Web site: http://www.bilingualkids.com
Dist(s): **Follett School Solutions.**

Chouette Publishing (CAN) *(978-2-9815807; 978-2-924786; 978-2-89802) Dist. by* **PerseuPGW.**

Chowder Bay Bks., *(978-0-9795364)* P.O. Box 5542, Lake Worth, FL 33466-5542 USA (SAN 853-7119)
Web site: http://www.chowderbaybooks.com.

CHPublishing, Incorporated *See* **Triumphant Living Enterprises, Inc.**

Chris A. Zeigler Dendy Consulting LLC, *(978-0-9679911)* P.O. Box 189, Cedar Bluff, AL 35959 USA Fax: 256-779-5203
E-mail: chrisdendy@mindspring.com
Web site: http://www.chrisdendy.com
Dist(s): **Follett School Solutions.**

Chris Six Group, The, *(978-0-9899182)* P.O. Box 1829, New York, NY 10159-1829 USA Tel 718-514-0452
E-mail: thechrissixgroup@msn.com.

Christ Inspired, Inc., *(978-1-4183)* 2263 Dicey Rd., Weatherford, TX 76085-3619 USA
Web site: http://www.christinspired.com.

Christian Aid Ministries, *(978-1-885270)* Orders Addr.: P.O. Box 360, Berlin, OH 44610 USA Tel 330-893-2428; Fax: 330-893-2305; Edit Addr.: 4464 S.R. 39 E., Berlin, OH 44610 USA Tel 216-893-2428.

Christian Bible Studies, *(978-0-9763357)* P.O. Box 11155, Lansing, MI 48911 USA Tel 517-272-9076
E-mail: verseyawilliams@sbcglobal.net
Web site: http://www.christianstudies7.com.

Christian Courier Pubns., *(978-0-9678044; 978-1-932723)* P.O. Box 11746, Jackson, TN 38308 USA Tel 731-256-7280
E-mail: david@christiancourier.com
Web site: http://www.christiancourier.com.

Christian Cowgirl *See* **Sonrise Stable Bks.**

Christian Education Resources, *(978-1-933479)* P.O. Box 320099, Cocoa Beach, FL 32932 USA.

Christian Faith Publishing, *(978-1-68197; 978-1-63525; 978-1-63575; 978-1-64028; 978-1-64079; 978-1-64114; 978-1-64140; 978-1-64191; 978-1-64258; 978-1-64299; 978-1-64349; 978-1-64416; 978-1-64458; 978-1-64492; 978-1-64515; 978-1-64569; 978-1-0980)* 296 Chestnut St., Meadville, PA 16335 USA Tel 646-503-4906; 832 Park Ave., Meadville, PA 16335 Tel 814-253-6442; Toll Free: 866-554-0919
E-mail: dustin@christianfaithpublishing.com
Web site: www.christianfaithpublishing.com; ChristianFaithPublishing.com.

Christian Focus Pubns. (GBR) *(978-0-906731; 978-1-85792; 978-1-871676; 978-1-84550; 978-1-78191) Dist. by* **BTPS.**

Christian Focus Pubns. (GBR) *(978-0-906731; 978-1-85792; 978-1-871676; 978-1-84550; 978-1-78191) Dist. by* **Spring Arbor Dist.**

Christian Focus Pubns. (GBR) *(978-0-906731; 978-1-85792; 978-1-871676; 978-1-84550; 978-1-78191) Dist. by* **STL Dist.**

Christian, Harvey Pubs. Inc., *(978-1-932774)* 3107 Hwy. 321, Hampton, TN 37658 USA Tel 423-768-2297
E-mail: books@harveycp.com
Web site: http://www.harveycp.com.

Christian Heartbeat Incorporated *See* **CHB Media**

Christian Liberty Pr., *(978-1-930092; 978-1-930367; 978-1-932971; 978-1-935796; 978-1-62982)* Div. of Church of Christian Liberty, 502 W. Euclid Ave., Arlington Heights, IL 60004 USA
E-mail: e.shewan@christianlibertypress.com; linak@christianlibertypress.com; larsj@christianlibertypress.com
Web site: http://www.christianlibertypress.com.

Christian Life Bks., *(978-0-9646289; 978-1-931393)* Subs. of River Revival Ministries, Inc., Orders Addr.: P.O. Box 36355, Pensacola, FL 32516-6355 USA Tel 850-457-7057; Fax: 850-458-9339
E-mail: mail@drlarrymartin.org
Web site: http://www.rrmi.org.

Christian Life Workshops *See* **Noble Publishing Assocs.**

Christian Light Pubns., Inc., *(978-0-87813)* 1066 Chicago Ave., Harrisonburg, VA 22802 USA (SAN 206-7315) Tel 540-434-0768; Fax: 540-433-8896
E-mail: johnh@clp.org.

Christian Living Books, Inc. *Imprint of* **Pneuma Life Publishing, Inc.**

Christian Logic, *(978-0-9745315; 978-1-7330826)* PO Box 1381, Durango, CO 81302 USA Tel 563-505-5258
E-mail: hansbluedorn@gmail.com
Web site: http://www.fallacydetective.com.

Christian Novel Studies, *(978-0-9707712)* 5208 E. Lake Rd., Saginaw, MN 55779 USA Tel 218-729-9733; Fax: 509-271-8614
E-mail: cnsroe@aol.com; chsroe@aol.com
Web site: http://www.christiannovelstudies.homestead.com.

Christian Publishing Corp., *(978-0-9770320)* 19530 E. Dickenson Pl., Aurora, CO 80013 USA Tel 303-752-0845
E-mail: carterpattillo@aol.com.

Christian Science Publishing Society, The *See* **Eddy, The Writings of Mary Baker**

Christian Services Publishing, *(978-1-879854)* Div. of Christian Services Network, 1975 Janich Ranch Ct., El Cajon, CA 92019 USA Tel 619-334-0706; Fax: 619-579-0685; Toll Free: 800-484-6184 Do not confuse with Christian Services, Damascus, MD
E-mail: tim@csnbooks.com
Web site: http://csnbooks.com.

Christian Visionary Communications, *(978-0-9746867)* P.O. Box 63, Sharon Center, OH 44274-0063 USA
E-mail: lorshir3@verizon.net
Web site: http://www.christianary.org.

Christian Visual Arts of California, *(978-0-9766584)* 64969 Pine St., Hume, CA 93628-9619 USA Tel 559-335-2797; Fax: 559-335-2107
E-mail: dajohnson@spiralcomm.net.

Christian Voice Publishing, A, *(978-0-9776747; 978-0-9786580; 978-1-934327)* 2031 W. Superior St. Ste. 1, Duluth, MN 55806-2036 USA.

Christiangela Productions, *(978-0-9720773)* 3340 SE. Federal Hwy., #310, Saintart, FL 34997 USA.

Christianstar.Me *See* **Fomenky Publishing**

Christine S White, *(978-0-9998133)* 315 W. st N., Ahoskie, NC 27910 USA Tel 252-287-8896
E-mail: destinedtosoar63@yahoo.com
Web site: www.soaringhigh.net.

Christine, Yates, *(978-0-9741210)* 13165 Oak Farm Dr., Woodbridge, VA 22192 USA
Web site: http://www.freekidcrafts.com.

Christine's Closet, *(978-0-9713405)* 10300 Grand Oak Dr., Austin, TX 78750 USA Tel 512-918-9255; Fax: 512-873-9818; Toll Free: 800-591-1165
E-mail: chrissy@chrissy.com
Web site: http://www.chrissy.com.

Christopher Arnold Hill, *(978-0-692-19611-3)* 117 6253 Lankershim Blvd., N. Hollywood, CA 91606 USA Tel 323-632-2510
E-mail: chriswisegamgee@yahoo.com
Dist(s): **Ingram Content Group.**

Christopher Davis, Jr., *(978-0-578-43937-2; 978-0-578-45747-5)* CMR 415, APO, AE 09114 USA Tel 803-350-0503
E-mail: bookingchristopher@gmail.com
Dist(s): **Ingram Content Group.**

Christopher Winkle Products *See* **First Stage Concepts**

Chronicle Bks. *Imprint of* **Chronicle Bks. LLC**

†Chronicle Bks. LLC, *(978-0-8118; 978-0-87701; 978-0-938491; 978-1-4521; 978-1-7972)* Div. of The McEvoy Group, Orders Addr.: 680 Second St., San Francisco, CA 94107 USA (SAN 202-165X) Tel 415-537-4200; Fax: 415-537-4460; Toll Free Fax: 800-286-9471; Toll Free: 800-759-0190 (orders only); Edit Addr.: 3 Center Plaza, Boston, MA 2108 USA; *Imprints:* SeaStar Books (SeaStar Chronic); Handprint Books (HandprintBks); Chronicle Books (ChronBks)
E-mail: order.desk@hbgusa.com; customer.service@hbgusa.com
Web site: http://www.chroniclebooks.com
Dist(s): **Children's Plus, Inc.**
Diamond Bk. Distributors
Follett School Solutions
Leonard, Hal Corp.
Hachette Bk. Group
Ingram Publisher Services
Music Sales Corp.; *CIP.*

Chronicle Guidance Pubns., Inc., *(978-0-912578; 978-1-55631)* Orders Addr.: 66 Aurora St., Moravia, NY 13118-3569 USA Tel 315-497-0330; 315-497-3359; Toll Free: 800-622-7284
E-mail: CustomerService@ChronicleGuidance.com
Web site: http://www.chronicleguidance.com
Dist(s): **Follett School Solutions.**

Chronicles *See* **Life Chronicles Publishing**

Chronos Press *See* **WingSpan Publishing**

Chrysalis Education, *(978-1-929298; 978-1-930643; 978-1-931983; 978-1-932333; 978-1-59389)* Div. of The Creative Company, 1980 Lookout Dr., North Mankato, MN 56003 USA Tel 507-388-6273; Fax: 507-388-2746; Toll Free: 800-445-6209
E-mail: schlichted@aol.com; info@thecreativecompany.us
Dist(s): **Creative Co., The.**

Chrysalis Pr., *(978-0-9795933)* Orders Addr.: P.O. Box 13129, Newport Beach, CA 92658 USA (SAN 853-8514)
E-mail: amber@chrysalispress.com
Web site: http://www.Chrysalispress.com
Dist(s): **Follett School Solutions.**

Chubasco Publishing Company *See* **Perelandra Publishing Co.**

Chucklebks. Publishing, *(978-0-9702730)* 27 Brown St., Andover, MA 01810 USA Tel 978-749-0674
E-mail: jeff@chucklebooks.com
Web site: http://www.chucklebooks.com; http://www.incredibleassemblies.com
Dist(s): **Partners Bk. Distributing, Inc.**

Chun, Anthony, *(978-0-9994539)* 855 1/2 N. Alexandria Ave., Los Angeles, CA 90029 USA Tel 323-383-2034
E-mail: anthonychun72@gmail.com.

Chung, Jo Anne *See* **Vision Unlimited Pr.**

Church at Cane Creek *See* **No Greater Joy Ministries, Inc.**

Church Hse. Publishing (GBR) *(978-0-7151; 978-0-9562821; 978-1-78140) Dist. by* **Westminster John Knox.**

Church Hymnal Corporation *See* **Church Publishing, Inc.**

Church Publishing, Inc., *(978-0-89869; 978-1-59627; 978-1-59628; 978-1-64065)* Orders Addr.: 19 E. 34th St., New York, NY 10016 USA (SAN 857-0140) Tel 212-592-1800; Fax: 212-779-3392; Toll Free: 800-242-1918; Edit Addr.: 19 East 34th st, New York, NY 10016 USA; *Imprints:* Seabury Books (Seabury Bks); Morehouse Publishing (MoreHse Pubng); Living the Good News (LTGN)
E-mail: rmasteller@cpg.org; churchpublishingorders@pbd.com; lort@cpg.org; lsimonello@cpg.org
Web site: http://www.churchpublishing.org
Dist(s): **Abingdon Pr.**
Macmillan
MyiLibrary
Open Road Integrated Media, Inc.

Church Without Walls Publications, USA *See* **Masha, Segun Inc.**

CHUTE,, PHILLIP B. EA, *(978-0-692-06056-8; 978-1-7328855)* 45506 BAYBERRY Pl., TEMECULA, CA 92592 USA Tel 951-302-2285; Fax: 951-719-1853
E-mail: phillipchute1@verizon.net
Web site: temeculataxservice.net; www.silverthreadoflife.com; wwww.phillipbchute.com.

Chuttani, Kabir, *(978-0-9749364)* 8 Nameloc Rd., Plymouth, MA 02360-1418 USA.

CI Publishing Group, *(978-0-692-08310-9; 978-0-692-08313-0; 978-0-578-51677-6)* 3113 Ruhl Ave Apt 11B, Columbus, OH 43209 USA Tel 614-209-4393
E-mail: cipubgroup@gmail.com
Dist(s): **Ingram Content Group.**

Cicada Bks. (GBR) *(978-0-9562053; 978-1-908714) Dist. by* **Consort Bk Sales.**

CicadaSun, *(978-0-9779808)* P.O. Box 90834, Austin, TX 78709-0834 USA
E-mail: service@cicadasun.com
Web site: http://www.cicadasun.com.

CIFC Pr., *(978-0-615-18435-7)* 65 Bayard St., New York, NY 10013 USA
E-mail: christinaseid@chinatownicecreamfactory.com
Web site: http://www.chinatownicecreamfactory.com
Dist(s): **Lulu Pr., Inc.**

Cideb (ITA) *(978-88-7754; 978-88-530) Dist. by* **Distribks Inc.**

Cider Mill Pr. Bk. Pubs., LLC, *(978-1-933662; 978-1-60433; 978-1-941868; 978-1-64643; 978-1-64785)* PO Box 454 12 Spring St., Kennebunkport, ME 04046 USA (SAN 257-1927) Tel 207-967-8232; Fax: 207-967-8233; *Imprints:* Applesauce Press (Applesauce Pr)
E-mail: johnwhalen@cidermillpress.com
Web site: http://www.cidermillpress.com
Dist(s): **Simon & Schuster**
Simon & Schuster, Inc.
Sterling Publishing Co., Inc.

Cidermill Bks., *(978-0-9748483)* P.O. Box 32250, San Jose, CA 95152-2250 USA
E-mail: info@cidermillbooks.com
Web site: http://www.cidermillbooks.com.

CiDuMos, *(978-0-692-77143-3; 978-0-692-77666-7; 978-0-692-80223-6; 978-0-692-80597-8; 978-0-692-05074-3; 978-0-692-05076-7)* 405 Woodway Ln., Longview, TX 75605 USA Tel 903-240-6959
Web site: www.cimowrites.com
Dist(s): **CreateSpace Independent Publishing Platform.**

Ciletti Publishing Group, Inc., The, *(978-0-917665; 978-0-9768655)* 2421 Redwood Ct., Longmont, CO 80503 USA Tel 720-494-1473; Fax: 720-494-1471
E-mail: barbaraj@odysseybooks.net
Dist(s): **Follett School Solutions.**

CILLYart4U, *(978-0-9985955)* 236 E. Fairmont DR, Tempe, AZ 85282 USA Tel 480-543-9352
Web site: www.cillyart4u.wix.com/cillyart4u
Dist(s): **CreateSpace Independent Publishing Platform.**

Cinco Puntos Pr., *(978-0-938317; 978-1-933693; 978-1-935955; 978-1-941026; 978-1-947627)* 701 Texas Ave., El Paso, TX 79901 USA (SAN 661-0080) Tel 915-838-1625; Fax: 915-838-1635; Toll Free: 800-566-9072
E-mail: leebyrd@cincopuntos.com
Web site: http://www.cincopuntos.com
Dist(s): **Children's Plus, Inc.**
Consortium Bk. Sales & Distribution
Follett School Solutions
Lectorum Pubns., Inc.
MyiLibrary.

Cinealta Pr., *(978-0-9821065)* 2060 W. Mulberry Dr., Chandler, AZ 85286-6771 USA
Web site: http://www.cinealtapress.com.

CineBook (GBR) *(978-1-905460; 978-1-84918) Dist. by* **Natl Bk Netwk.**

Cinnamon Bay Entertainment Group, *(978-0-9727116)* 1300 W. Menlo Ave No. 113, Hemet, CA 92543 USA
E-mail: rsdan4043@yahoo.com.

Cinnamon Ridge Publishing, *(978-0-9800762)* 7121 W. Craig Rd., Suite 113, No. 284, Las Vegas, NV 89129 USA.

Circelli, Kristina, *(978-0-9763728; 978-0-615-40270-3)* 9655 Crotty Ave., Hastings, FL 32145 USA Tel 386-290-7294
E-mail: kristinacircelli@gmail.com
Web site: www.kristinacircelli.com.

Circle Journey, Ltd., *(978-0-9741104)* 22 East Gay St., Suite 801, Columbus, OH 43215 USA Fax: 614-564-7795; Toll Free: 877-247-2534
E-mail: connections@circlejourney.com
Web site: http://www.circlejourney.com.

Circle of Friends *Imprint of* **Booksville, U.S.A.**

Circle Pr., *(978-0-9651601; 978-0-9743661; 978-1-933271)* Div. of Circle Media, Inc., Orders Addr.: 33 Rossotto Dr., Hamden, CT 06514 USA Tel 203-230-3805; Fax: 203-230-3838; Toll Free: 888-881-0729; Edit Addr.: 432 Washington Ave., North Haven, CT 06473 USA Do not confuse with companies with the same name in Huntington Beach, CA, New York, NY, Itasca, IL
E-mail: victor@catholicformation.com.

Circle Studios, *(978-0-9768022)* 200 Medicine Way, Eureka Springs, AR 72632 USA Tel 479-253-5826
Dist(s): **Follett School Solutions.**

Circles Legacy Publishing, LLC, *(978-0-692-94613-8; 978-0-692-95206-1; 978-0-692-95797-4; 978-0-692-95798-1; 978-0-692-95799-8; 978-0-692-95990-9; 978-0-692-96184-1; 978-0-692-05662-2; 978-0-692-09424-2; 978-0-578-42821-5; 978-0-578-50152-9; 978-0-578-55604-8; 978-0-578-61652-0; 978-0-578-66442-2; 978-0-578-70287-2; 978-0-578-74888-7) 84 Liberty Lakes Dr, Valparaiso, IN 46385 USA Tel 281-682-7327*
E-mail: jjoslin3@att.net
Dist(s): **CreateSpace Independent Publishing Platform.**

Circling Rivers, *(978-1-939530)* Orders Addr.: P.O. Box 8291, Richmond, VA 23226 USA Tel 804-272-4625; *Imprints:* Gertrude M Books (MYID_ M)
Web site: http://www.circlingrivers.com.

Circumpolar Pr., *(978-1-878051)* Subs. of Wizard Works, P.O. Box 1125, Homer, AK 99603 USA Tel 907-235-8757 (phone/fax); Toll Free: 877-210-2665
E-mail: wizard@xyz.net
Web site: http://www.xyz.net/~wizard.

Ciro's Bks., *(978-0-9676643; 978-1-934499)* 4152 Meridian St., No. 6, Bellingham, WA 98226 USA
E-mail: info@cirosbooks.com
Web site: http://www.cirosbooks.com; http://www.howwouldyouvote.us; http://www.onepersononevoteonline.com
Dist(s): **BCH Fulfillment & Distribution**
Smashwords.

Cirrus Publishing, LLC, *(978-0-9755678)* Orders Addr.: P.O. Box 291724, Davie, FL 33329-1724 USA Fax: 954-965-2643
E-mail: cirruspublish@aol.com
Web site: http://www.yessy.com/wildimages.

C-It Entertainment Group, LLC, *(978-0-9718151)* 230 S. Hamilton Dr. Unit 204, Beverly Hills, CA 90211 USA Tel 213-925-1535; Fax: 213-291-1473
E-mail: dennischristen@hotmail.com
Web site: http://www.booksnflicks.com.

Citified Pubns., *(978-0-9832174)* 1310 Valley Lake Dr., Schaumburg, IL 60195 USA Tel 708-308-2854
E-mail: djsbchi@gmail.com.

Citizen Pr, *(978-0-9779100)* P.O. Box 1369, Glendale, CA 91209-1369 USA Tel 310-497-7419; Fax: 818-450-0518
E-mail: citizen@citizenpress.net
Web site: http://www.citizenpress.net.

Citizens Publishing, *(978-0-9755597)* 17636 W. Neuberry Ridge Dr., Lockport, IL 60441 USA
Web site: http://www.citizenspublishing.com.

Citizens Rising, *(978-0-9997645)* P.O. Box 1118, Tryon, NC 28782 USA Tel 707-845-5499
E-mail: dhoffman@internews.org.

Citrus Roots - Preserving Citrus Heritage Foundation, *(978-0-9669508)* Orders Addr.: P.O. Box 4038, BALBOA, CA 92661 USA Tel 949-673-7877
Web site: http://www.citrusroots.com.

City Castles Publishing, *(978-0-615-22213-4; 978-0-615-26743-2; 978-0-615-56258-2)* 12160 E. Iowa Dr., Aurora, CO 80012 USA
Web site: http://www.citycastles.com.

City Creek Pr., Inc., *(978-1-883841)* P.O. Box 8415, Minneapolis, MN 55408-0415 USA
E-mail: orders@citycreek.com
Web site: http://www.citycreek.com
Dist(s): **Follett School Solutions.**

City Girl Gone Country, *(978-0-9904469)* 1983 Hwy. NN Box 344, Hermann, MO 65041 USA Tel 573-486-3091
E-mail: djweingarth@ktis.net.

†City Lights Bks., *(978-0-87286)* 261 Columbus Ave., San Francisco, CA 94133 USA (SAN 202-1684) Tel 415-362-1901; Fax: 415-362-4921
E-mail: staff@citylights.com
Web site: http://www.citylights.com
Dist(s): **Consortium Bk. Sales & Distribution**
MyiLibrary
SPD-Small Pr. Distribution; *CIP.*

City Lights Pr. *Imprint of* **Wolfpack Publishing**

City Monsters Bks. (CAN) *(978-2-924734) Dist. by* **PerseuPGW.**

City of Elmhurst, *(978-0-9708003)* 209 N. York St., Elmhurst, IL 60126 USA Tel 630-530-3000; Fax: 630-530-3014
E-mail: nancy.wilson@elmhurst.org
Web site: http://www.elmhurst.org.

City of God, St. Joseph's Hill of Hope, *(978-1-892957)* Orders Addr.: P.O. Box 1055, Brea, CA 92822 USA Tel 714-528-6962; Fax: 714-528-0707; Edit Addr.: 7351 Carbon Canyon Rd., Brea, CA 92823 USA
E-mail: mail@themiracleofstjoseph.org
Web site: http://www.themiracleofstjoseph.org.

City of Manassas Department of Social Services, *(978-0-9747385)* 9324 West St. Ste. 201, Manassas, VA 20110-5198 USA.

City of Oaks Publishing *See* **Meder, Julia**

City on a Hill, Inc., *(978-0-9779521)* 4085 Hancock Bridge Pkwy., Suite 111-269, North Fort Myers, FL 33903 USA Tel 614-488-6953
E-mail: info@cityonahillinc.org
Web site: http://www.cityonahillinc.org.

City Point Bks., *(978-0-615-27021-0)* P.O. Box 221, Yulee, FL 32041 USA
Dist(s): **Simon & Schuster, Inc.**

City Salvage Records, *(978-0-9713865)* 195 St. Marks Ave., No. 4, Brooklyn, NY 11238 USA Tel 718-857-6822
E-mail: andy@citysalvagerecords.com
Web site: http://citysalvagerecords.com.

CityLit Pr., *(978-1-936328)* c/o CityLit Project, 120 S. Curley St., Baltimore, MD 21224-2235 USA Tel 410-274-5691
E-mail: info@citylitproject.org
Web site: http://www.citylitprojet.org.

CityWeb Corp., *(978-0-9719803)* P.O. Box 702216, Tulsa, OK 74170-2216 USA Tel 918-369-0544
E-mail: citywebcorporation@acken.com
Web site: http://www.citywebbooks.com.

Civitas:Institute for the Study of Civil Society (GBR) *(978-1-903386) Dist. by* **Coronet Bks.**

CJ Publishing Co., *(978-0-9655777)* Div. of McPhaul, Inc, 1370 electric ave apt 404, lincoln park, MI 48146 USA
E-mail: johnmcphaul@live.com.

CJK Publishing, *(978-0-9889100; 978-1-7353967)* 120 N. Denver St., Dallas, TX 75203 USA Tel 469-914-1089
E-mail: quineka@demarcusjones.com
Web site: www.demarcusjones.com.

CJR, *(978-0-9796411; 978-1-941607; 978-1-943764)* 8079 Barcarole Ct., Springfield, VA 22153-2945 USA Tel 571-481-5396
E-mail: books.kiteb@gmail.com
Web site: http://www.go2melik.org/NewBridgesTextbooks.lsp.

CJT Publishing, *(978-0-692-83362-9)* 500 Veterans Memorial Pkwy., East Providence, RI 02914 USA Tel 843-469-4417
E-mail: cjtalbert@pga.com.

CK Books *See* **CK Books Publishing**

CK Bks., *(978-0-9797580)* 395A S. Hwy. 65, No. 324, Lincoln, CA 95648 USA.

CK Books Publishing, *(978-0-9800529; 978-0-9832984; 978-0-9881993; 978-0-9892152; 978-1-949085)* P.O. Box 214, New Glarus, WI 53574 USA Tel 608-220-1885
Web site: http://ckbookspublishing.com
Dist(s): **Follett School Solutions.**

CKE Pubns., *(978-0-935133; 978-1-932327)* Div. of Carolyn Kyle Enterprises, Orders Addr.: P.O. Box 12869, Olympia, WA 98508-2869 USA (SAN 695-197X) Toll Free: 800-428-7402; Edit Addr.: P.O. Box 12869, Olympia, WA 98508-2869 USA
E-mail: ckepubs@aol.com
Web site: http://www.ckepublications.com.

CKK Educational, LLC., *(978-0-9743499; 978-0-9963087)* 17 W. 8th St., Ocean City, NJ 08226-3430 USA Tel 609-398-1949; Toll Free: 866-543-5463
Web site: http://www.tannersmanners.com.

CKNY Paw Productions, *(978-0-692-92176-0)* 1280 Fifth Ave. Unit 15E, New York, NY 10029 USA Tel 212-810-6105
E-mail: hanakodesignstudio@gmail.com.

cky *See* **Congregation Kehilas Yaakov (CKY)**

CLADACH Publishing, *(978-0-9670386; 978-0-9759619; 978-0-9818929; 978-0-9891014; 978-1-945099)* P.O. Box 336144, Greeley, CO 80633 USA Tel 970-371-9530
E-mail: office@cladach.com
Web site: http://www.cladach.com.

Claim Stake Productions *See* **Claim Stake Publishing, LLC**

Claim Stake Publishing, LLC, *(978-1-936284)* P.O. Box 1586, Aspen, CO 81612 USA
E-mail: pfioravante@tmwent.com
Web site: http://www.travelswithgannonandwyatt.com
Dist(s): **Baker & Taylor Publisher Services (BTPS).**

Clair, Aspen, *(978-0-578-20089-7; 978-0-578-20118-4)* 1022 N Anthony Ave, Anthony, KS 67003 USA.

Claire Luana, *(978-0-9977018; 978-1-948947)* 11923 NE Sumner St STE 681096, Portland, OR 97220 USA
E-mail: claire.luana.author@gmail.com
Web site: http://www.liveedgepublishing.com; http://www.claireluana.com.

Claire Pubns. (GBR) *(978-1-871098; 978-1-904572) Dist. by* **Parkwest Pubns.**

Clairmont Pr., Inc., *(978-0-9623319; 978-1-56733)* Orders Addr.: P.O. Box 11743, Montgomery, AL 36111 USA Tel 334-874-8638; Edit Addr.: Rte. 2, Box 191, Selma, AL 36701 USA.

Clandestine Pr., The, *(978-0-9766261)* 314 Taylor Pl., Ithaca, NY 14850-3135 USA Tel 607-273-8036
E-mail: dohertyprint@juno.com.

Clapper Publishing Co., *(978-0-930184)* Div. of Clapper Publishing Co., Inc., 2400 E. Devon, Suite 375, Des Plaines, IL 60018 USA (SAN 210-7104) Tel 847-635-5800; Fax: 847-635-6311.

Clara Publishing, *(978-0-9706347; 978-0-692-45828-0; 978-1-7342900)* Orders Addr.: 680 Napa Ct., Claremont, CA 91711-1553 USA (SAN 254-7236)
E-mail: clarapub@ca.rr.com
Web site: http://www.magicunion.com.

Clarence-Henry Bks., *(978-0-615-19572-8; 978-0-578-05235-9; 978-0-615-42297-8; 978-0-9882909)* 4135 Teton Pl., Alexandria, VA 22312 USA
Web site: http://www.c-hbooks.com.

Claretian Pubns., *(978-0-89570)* 205 W. Monroe St., 9th Flr., Chicago, IL 60606 USA (SAN 207-5598) Tel 312-236-7782
E-mail: schneiderc@claretians.org.

Clarion Bks. *Imprint of* **Houghton Mifflin Harcourt Publishing Co.**

Clarion Bks. *Imprint of* **Houghton Mifflin Harcourt Trade & Reference Pubs.**

Clarionton Press *See* **Twelve Star Pr.**

Clarissa C. Foster, *(978-0-578-46127-4)* 62 Old Agua Fria Rd. W., Santa Fe, NM 87508 USA Tel 505-470-7019
E-mail: clarissa.caldwell@gmail.com
Dist(s): **Ingram Content Group.**

Clark Bks., *(978-0-9741677; 978-0-615-11591-7; 978-0-615-11769-0)* 599 Shapleigh Corner Rd., Shapleigh, ME 04076 USA (SAN 630-2017) Tel 207-636-1769 Do not confuse with Clark Books in Baton Rouge, LA
E-mail: clarkbooks@metrocast.net
Web site: http://www.clarkbooksmaine.com.

Clark, I. E. Publications *See* **Family Plays**

Clark, N. Laurie *See* **Clark Pubs.**

Clark Productions Ltd. Inc., *(978-0-9777289)* P.O. Box 583, Little Rock, AR 72203 USA Tel 501-280-9424
E-mail: ouida-clark56@yahoo.com.

Clark Pubs., *(978-0-9641197)* 133 Chestnut St., Amherst, MA 01002 USA Tel 413-549-0575; 941-255-0431
E-mail: ellusmith@aol.com
Dist(s): **Brodart Co.**
North Country Bks., Inc.
Quality Bks., Inc.

Clark Publishing, Inc., *(978-1-883589; 978-0-9822201; 978-0-9825057; 978-0-9827453; 978-0-9832639)* Orders Addr.: P.O. Box 34102, Lexington, KY 40588 USA Toll Free: 800-944-3995; Edit Addr.: 250 E. Short St., Lexington, KY 40507 USA Toll Free: 859-944-3995 Do not confuse with companies with same or similar names in Tacoma, WA, Topeka, KS, Annapolis, MD
E-mail: bclark@theclarkgroupinfo.com
Web site: http://www.theclarkgroupinfo.com; http://www.kyalmanac.com; http://www.clarkpublishing.com; http://www.clarklegacies.com
Dist(s): **Follett School Solutions.**

Clarkson Potter *Imprint of* **Crown Publishing Group, The**

CLASS Publications *Imprint of* **Children Learning Awareness, Safety & Self-Defense**

Classic Bks. Library *Imprint of* **Editorium, The**

Classic Bks., *(978-1-58201; 978-0-7426)* Orders Addr.: P.O. Box 130, Murrieta, CA 92564-0130 USA Tel 951-767-1803; Fax: 951-767-0133
Dist(s): **Reprint Services Corp.**

Classic Bookwrights *Imprint of* **Lindaloo Enterprises**

Classic Comic Store, Ltd. (GBR) *(978-1-906814; 978-1-910619; 978-1-911238) Dist. by* **Casemate Pubs.**

Classic Textbooks, *(978-1-4047)* Div of Classic Books, Orders Addr.: P.O. Box 130, Murrieta, CA 92564-0130 USA
E-mail: newbookorders@gmail.com.

Classical Academic Pr., *(978-1-60051)* 3920 Market St., Camp Hill, PA 17011-4202 USA
Web site: http://www.classicalacademicpress.com.

Classical Comics (GBR) *(978-1-906332; 978-1-907127) Dist. by* **PerseuPGW.**

Classical Conversations, Inc., *(978-0-9727197; 978-0-9798333; 978-0-692-00116-5; 978-0-9829845; 978-0-9851701; 978-0-9884965; 978-0-9904720; 978-0-9965660; 978-0-9972442; 978-0-9984373; 978-0-9995748; 978-0-9996995; 978-0-9996996; 978-1-7329639; 978-1-7329640; 978-1-951571)* Orders Addr.: 255 Air Tool Dr., Southern Pines, NC 28387 USA (SAN 854-5065) Tel 910-687-0288
E-mail: bortins@yahoo.com; info@classicalconversations.com; cwidman@classicalconversations.com
Web site: http://www.classicalconversations.com.

Classical Home Education *See* **Pandia Pr.**

Classical Learning Universe, LLC, *(978-0-9721733; 978-0-9763376; 978-0-9793021)* 305 W. Broadway, Suite 184, New York, NY 10013 USA Tel 718-357-2431; Fax: 718-357-2432; Toll Free: 888-684-5922
E-mail: lindsay@classicallearning.com
Web site: http://www.classicallearning.com.

Classical Magic, Inc., *(978-0-9675997; 978-0-9794947)* P.O. Box 1809, Banner Elk, NC 28604 USA Tel 828-898-7764 (phone/fax); 828-898-9571
E-mail: comapers@skybest.com
Web site: http://www.classicalmagic.net
Dist(s): **Book Clearing Hse.**

Classics International Entertainment, Inc., *(978-1-57209)* 324 Main Ave., Suite 183, Norwalk, CT 06851 USA Tel 203-849-8977; Fax: 203-847-5746.

Classroom Complete Pr. *Imprint of* **Rainbow Horizons Publishing, Inc.**

Classroom Library Company *See* **Classroom Library Co.**

Classroom Library Co., *(978-1-56137; 978-1-58130; 978-1-60878; 978-1-4569; 978-1-5020)* Div. of Conn Education Inc., Orders Addr.: 3901 Union Blvd., Suite 157, Saint Louis, MO 63115 USA (SAN 991-0573) Tel

Publisher Name Index

888-318-2665; Fax: 877-716-7272; 3901 Union Blvd, suite 159, St Louis, MO 63115 (SAN 991-0581) Tel 888-318-2665; Fax: 877-716-7272; *Imprints:* Novel Units, Inc. (NvlUnitsI)
E-mail: ben@classroomlibrary.com
Web site: http://www.classroomlibrarycompany.com.

Clavis (ROM) *(978-973-97411) Dist. by* **PerseuPGW.**

Clavis Publishing, *(978-1-60537)* 814 N. Franklin St., Chicago, IL 60610 USA; 250 West 57Th St. 15Th Flr., New York, NY 10016
E-mail: info@clavis.be
Web site: http://www.clavis.be
Dist(s): **Follett School Solutions**
Legato Pubs. Group
Publishers Group West (PGW).

Clawfoot Publishing, *(978-0-9747881)* 1236 S. Pekin Rd., Woodland, WA 98674 USA Tel 360-901-9932; Fax: 360-225-1311
E-mail: bobsbooks@zerfing.com
Web site: http://www.zerfing.com/bobsbooks.

Claxton, Sarah, *(978-0-692-10369-2; 978-0-692-16261-3)* 27 W. Durham St., Philadelphia, PA 19119 USA Tel 240-938-1562
E-mail: sarah.adler.claxton@gmail.com
Dist(s): **Ingram Content Group.**

Clay Jars Publishing, *(978-0-9843369)* 2232 Ralph Ave., 1st Flr., Brooklyn, NY 11234-5610 USA (SAN 859-1156) Tel 718-502-7935
E-mail: clayjarspublishing@gmail.com; justgottawrite@aol.com
Web site: http://www.clayjarspublishing.com.

Claybar Publishing, *(978-0-9787918)* 4007 Greenbriar Dr., Suite E, Stafford, TX 77477-3923 USA (SAN 851-5778) Tel 281-491-4009; Fax: 281-491-4024; Toll Free: 888-491-9533
E-mail: cbarclay@qdiinc.com
Web site: http://www.qdiinc.com.

Clayro Corp., *(978-0-9709523)* P.O. Box 270605, Oklahoma City, OK 73137-0605 USA Tel 405-373-2347; Fax: 405-373-0923
E-mail: waderoddy@yahoo.com
Web site: http://tcpublishers.com.

Clayton, Mike, *(978-0-9772622)* 639 Howard Rd., West Point, NY 10996-1510 USA
Web site: http://www.session6wrestling.com.

Clean Teen Publishing, *(978-0-9894701; 978-1-940534; 978-1-63422)* 1107, Kettlewood Dr., Justin, TX 76247 USA Tel 469-583-8737; *Imprints:* Crimson Tree Publishing (Crimson Tree)
E-mail: submissions@cleanteenpublishing.com
Web site: http://www.cleanteenpublishing.com; www.crimsontreepublishing.com; www.changingtidespublishing.com
Dist(s): **Independent Pubs. Group**
Ingram Content Group
Midpoint Trade Bks., Inc.

Clear Braces L.L.C., *(978-0-9790682)* 1530 Palisade Ave., Fort Lee, NJ 07024 USA Tel 201-947-6453
E-mail: drjfortlee@aol.com
Web site: http://www.pediatric-dentistry.com.

Clear Creek Pubs., *(978-0-9653543; 978-0-9975839)* Orders Addr.: 115 Clear Creek Ct., Fayetteville, GA 30215 USA Tel 770-461-9460
E-mail: patcruzan@aol.com.

Clear Fork Publishing, *(978-0-9899568; 978-0-9974370; 978-1-946101; 978-1-950169)* 102 S. Swenson, Stamford, TX 79553 USA Tel 325-773-5550; *Imprints:* Spork (Spork)
E-mail: callie@clearforkmediagroup.com
Web site: clearforkpublishing.com.

Clear Horizon, *(978-0-9773569; 978-1-936187)* 605 Silverthorn Rd., Gulf Breeze, FL 32561 USA Tel 850-934-0819; Fax: 850-934-9981
E-mail: info@maxpress.com; ginac@maxpress.com
Web site: http://www.maxpress.com.

Clear Light Pubs., *(978-0-940666; 978-1-57416)* 823 Don Diego, Santa Fe, NM 87501 USA (SAN 219-7758) Tel 505-989-9590; Fax: 505-989-9519; Toll Free: 800-253-2747; 823 Don Diego, Sante Fe, CA 87501 Do not confuse with Clear Light Pub., Seattle, WA
E-mail: service@clearlightbooks.com; janet@clearlightbooks.com
Web site: http://www.clearlightbooks.com
Dist(s): **Follett School Solutions.**

Clear Water Pr., *(978-0-9742972; 978-0-9828995)* 1909 S. Stagecoach Dr., Olathe, KS 66062 USA Do not confuse with Clear Water Press in Reno, NV
E-mail: editor@clearwaterpress.com
Web site: http://www.clearwaterpress.com
Dist(s): **Send The Light Distribution LLC.**

Clear Wind Publishing, *(978-0-578-42570-2; 978-0-578-42571-9; 978-0-578-48868-4; 978-0-578-51065-1; 978-0-578-59180-3; 978-0-578-77212-7; 978-0-578-77215-8)* 4300 Elmgreen Dr., Roanoke, TX 76262 USA Tel 817-333-7060
E-mail: aaronwronko@gmail.com
Dist(s): **Ingram Content Group.**

Clearbridge Publishing, *(978-1-929194)* Div. of Science of Strategy Institute, Orders Addr.: Science Of Strategy Institute 2829 Linkview Dr., Las Vegas, NV 89134 USA (SAN 857-8524) Tel 702-721-9631; *Imprints:* Art of War Plus Books (Art War Plus)
E-mail: gagliardi.gary@gmail.com
Web site: http://www.scienceofstrategy.org.

Clearwater Publishing *See* **Clearwater Publishing, LLC**

Clearwater Publishing, LLC, *(978-0-9769465)* 1101 Waterfall Ln., Lakeland, FL 33803 USA.

ClearWaters Publishing, *(978-0-9841439)* 7539 Parkview Dr., Columbia, SC 29223 USA Tel 803-404-8893
E-mail: clearwatersllc@yahoo.com; thomashuntersjr@yahoo.com
Web site: http://www.tjhunteronline.com.

Cleis Pr. *Imprint of* **Start Publishing LLC**

Clem Publishing, *(978-0-9772225)* P.O. Box 246, Danvers, IL 61732 USA Tel 309-530-0710; 116 W. North St., Danvers, IL 61732
E-mail: josephclem@hotmail.com.

Clements, J. S. Corporation *See* **Clements, Jehan**

Clements, Jehan, *(978-0-9622500)* Orders Addr.: P.O. Box 543, Tarrytown, NY 10591 USA Tel 914-293-7884
E-mail: storyteller1@optonline.net
Web site: http://www.flipoverpicturebooks.com.

Clemson University Digital Press *See* **Clemson Univ. Pr.**

Clemson Univ. Pr., *(978-0-9741516; 978-0-9771263; 978-0-9796066; 978-0-9842598; 978-0-9835339; 978-0-9890826; 978-0-9908958; 978-1-942954; 978-1-78694; 978-1-949979)* c/o Ctr. for Electronic & Digital Publishing, 611 Strode Tower, Clemson Univ., Clemson, SC 29634-0522 USA
E-mail: amero@clemson.edu
Web site: https://www.clemson.edu/centers-institutes/press/
Dist(s): **Oxford Univ. Pr., Inc.**

Clendenin Fine Art Concepts, *(978-0-9897662)* 8160 Manitoba St., No. 104, Playa del Rey, CA 90293 USA Tel 310-821-3941; Fax: 310-821-2282
E-mail: aclendenin@verizon.net
Web site: www.clendeninfineart.com.

Cleo and Olive, *(978-0-692-75647-8)* 44 Buckelew Bridge Rd., ANNISTON, AL 36207 USA Tel 256-239-3135.

Clerisy Pr. *Imprint of* **AdventureKEEN**

Cleveland Clinic Pr., *(978-1-59624)* c/o Lawrence D. Chilnick, 9500 Euclid Ave., NA32, Cleveland, OH 44195 USA Tel 216-444-1158; Fax: 216-444-9385
E-mail: chilnil@ccf.org
Web site: http://www.clevelandclinicpress.org
Dist(s): **Ingram Publisher Services.**

†Cleveland Museum of Art, *(978-0-910386; 978-0-940717; 978-1-935294)* 11150 East Blvd., Cleveland, OH 44106-1797 USA (SAN 278-4572) Tel 216-421-7340; Fax: 216-421-9409; Toll Free: 1-877-262-4748
E-mail: bbradley@clevelnadart.org
Web site: http://www.clevelandart.org
Dist(s): **Art Media Resources, Inc.**
Chicago Distribution Ctr.
D.A.P./Distributed Art Pubs.
Hopkins Fulfillment Services
Hudson Hills Pr. LLC
Indiana Univ. Pr.
Ohio Univ. Pr.
Univ. of Washington Pr.; *CIP.*

Cleveland Stock Images, *(978-0-9617637; 978-0-692-86770-9; 978-1-7338131)* 7124 Baker Ln., Chagrin Falls, OH 44023 USA (SAN 664-8533) Tel 216-548-4484; Fax: 216-249-5828
E-mail: jsjidc@aol.com.

Clever Factory, The, *(978-1-59277; 978-1-64038)* 545 Mainstream Dr., Suite 406, Nashville, TN 37228 USA.

Clever Girl Publishing, *(978-0-692-95655-7; 978-0-692-14357-5; 978-0-692-14362-9; 978-0-692-14619-4; 978-0-578-67317-2)* 33 A St., Bonne Terre, MO 63628 USA Tel 573-631-9284
E-mail: missyannlang@gmail.com.

Clever Media Group, *(978-1-948418; 978-1-949998; 978-1-951100)* 90 State St., Albany, NY 12207 USA Tel 541-255-3815
E-mail: n.vorobyeva@clever-publishing.com
Dist(s): **Hachette Bk. Group**
Quarto Publishing Group USA.

CleverKits,LLC, *(978-0-9778771)* 12 Brinckerhoff Ave, Stamford, CT 06905-3201 USA Fax: 267-821-7523
E-mail: cleverkits@yahoo.com
Web site: http://www.cleverkits.com.

CLF Publishing, *(978-0-9857372; 978-0-9884237; 978-0-9892358; 978-0-9899408; 978-0-9960815; 978-0-9961971; 978-1-945102)* 10063 Maple Ave., Hesperia, CA 92345 USA Tel 760-669-8149
E-mail: DRCWE@YAHOO.COM
Dist(s): **Lulu Pr., Inc.**

Cliff House, *(978-1-68320)* 1600 Cliff Rd E, Burnsville, MN 55337 USA
Dist(s): **RiverStream Publishing.**

Cliff Road Bks., *(978-1-60261)* 3437 Cliff Rd., Birmingham, AL 35222 USA (SAN 857-409X)
E-mail: holly@cliffroadbooks.com.

Cliffhanger Bks., *(978-0-615-49921-5; 978-0-615-78254-6)* 2756 Vista Bluff Blvd., Lewisville, TX 75067 USA Tel 972-743-0736
E-mail: khosey@gmail.com; kevin@cliffhangerbooks.com
Web site: http://www.cliffhangerbooks.com
Dist(s): **CreateSpace Independent Publishing Platform.**

Clifton Carriage House Pr., *(978-0-9825713)* 12 S. Sixth St., No. 1250, Minneapolis, MN 55402 USA Fax: 612-746-8811
E-mail: wreynolds@briobooks.com
Web site: http://www.briobooks.com.

Climb Your Moutain Publishing, *(978-1-7338162)* P.O. Box 245, Sequim, WA 98382 USA Tel 907-942-7563
E-mail: akfishwoman@hotmail.com.

Clinch, David *See* **Clinch Media**

Clinch Media, *(978-0-9800835)* 1339 Mill Glen Dr., Atlanta, GA 30338 USA (SAN 855-1588) Tel 770-730-1721
E-mail: clinch@bellsouth.net
Web site: http://www.theleprechauntrap.com.

Clockroot Bks. *Imprint of* **Interlink Publishing Group, Inc.**

Clocktower Bks., *(978-0-7433)* P.O. Box 600973, San Diego, CA 92160-0973 USA
E-mail: publishers@cox.net; johntcullen@cox.net
Web site: http://www.clocktowerbooks.com; http://www.johntcullen.com
Dist(s): **CreateSpace Independent Publishing Platform**
Smashwords.

Clocktower Fiction *See* **Clocktower Bks.**

Clocktower Hill Research & Publishing Group, LLC, *(978-0-9832130)* 23 Oakfield Dr., Rome, GA 30161 USA Tel 706-936-0254; Fax: 973-201-1755; *Imprints:* Lucas Violet (LucasViolet)
E-mail: davidehrler@clocktowerhill.com
Web site: http://www.clocktowerhill.com.

ClockTower Pubns., *(978-0-9704280)* 203 Skyland Dr., Dept. I, Staunton, VA 24401-2358 USA Tel 540-885-6614
E-mail: trgww@ntelos.net.

Clockwise Pr. (CAN) *(978-0-9939351; 978-1-988347) Dist. by* **Firefly Bks Limited.**

CLOJ Publishing, *(978-0-9767711)* 544 Rialto Ave., Venice, CA 90291-4248 USA (SAN 256-5129) Tel 310-399-6126
E-mail: publisher@clojpublishing.com
Web site: http://www.clojpublishing.com.

Cloonfad Pr., *(978-0-9744744; 978-0-9769404; 978-0-9797772)* Orders Addr.: P.O. Box 106, Cassville, NJ 08527 USA Tel 732-833-9800 (phone/fax)
E-mail: cloonfad@optonline.net
Web site: http://www.cloonfadpress.com
Dist(s): **Gatewood Pr.**

Cloquet River Pr., *(978-0-9720050; 978-0-9792175; 978-1-7324434)* 5353 Knudsen Rd, Duluth, MN 55803 USA Tel 218-721-3213; Fax: 218-725-5074
E-mail: cloquetriverpress@yahoo.com
Web site: http://www.cloquetriverpress.com
Dist(s): **Partners Bk. Distributing, Inc.**

Closer Looks Bks., *(978-0-9763593)* 864 Horns Corners Rd., Cedarburg, WI 53012 USA
E-mail: sggk@wi.rr.com
Web site: http://home.wi.rr.com/acloserlookbooks.

Clotho Pr., *(978-0-9821271)* 13205 Bluhill Rd., Silver Spring, MD 20910 USA Tel 301-962-8984
E-mail: polka.dot@verizon.net
Web site: http://www.womenmakingamerica.com
Dist(s): **Independent Pubs. Group**
Midpoint Trade Bks., Inc.

Cloud 9 Ranch, *(978-0-9767690)* 231 Jung Blvd., E, Naples, FL 34120 USA Tel 239-353-6877; Fax: 239-353-7579
E-mail: nsfcloud9@aol.com
Web site: http://www.cloud9ranch.info.

Cloud, Kat Creations, *(978-0-692-88310-5; 978-0-692-88311-2)* 903 E Constitution Dr., Chandler, AZ 85225 USA Tel 480-748-0826
Dist(s): **Ingram Content Group.**

Cloud Lake Publications *See* **Cloud Lake Publishing**

Cloud Lake Publishing, *(978-0-9787054)* 1440 Beaumont Avenue, Ste 2-198, Beaumont, CA 92223 USA Tel 707-239-4060
E-mail: mlarchibald@mac.com
Web site: http://www.winecountrywriter.com.

Cloud Mountain Publishing *See* **Easter Island Foundation**

Cloudbreak Media Inc., *(978-0-692-12942-5)* 4817 Katherine Ave, Sherman Oaks, CA 91423 USA Tel 323-243-2909
E-mail: chrys@chryscoulter.com
Dist(s): **Ingram Content Group.**

Cloudland.net Publishing, *(978-1-882906)* Orders Addr.: HC 33, Box 50-A, Pettigrew, AR 72752-9501 USA Tel 870-861-5536; Fax: 870-861-5736; Toll Free: 800-838-4453
E-mail: tim@timernst.com
Web site: http://www.TimErnst.com
Dist(s): **Chicago Distribution Ctr.**
Univ. of Arkansas Pr.

Cloudless Sky, *(978-0-9978443)* P.O. Box 32992, Santa Fe, NM 87594 USA Tel 505-670-3177
E-mail: derekfis@yahoo.com.

Cloudmaker Entertainment, *(978-0-9743989)* 7654 195th Ave. Ct. E., Bonney Lake, WA 98390 USA Tel 253-862-1490 (phone/fax)
E-mail: trox@cloudmakerentertainment.com
Web site: http://www.cloudmakerentertainment.com.

Cloudstone, *(978-1-879846)* 10 Patchin Pl., New York, NY 10011 USA Tel 212-929-6871.

Cloudwalker Publications *See* **Working Title Publishing**

Clouser, Lisa M., *(978-0-692-53171-6; 978-0-692-63828-6; 978-0-9977202)* 11 Countryside Ct., Camp Hill, PA 17011 USA Tel 717-737-3334
Dist(s): **CreateSpace Independent Publishing Platform.**

Clovercroft Publishing, 307 Verde Meadow Dr., Franklin, TN 37067 USA Tel 615-472-1128
E-mail: larry@christianbookservices.com
Dist(s): **Ingram Publisher Services.**

Club Pro Products, *(978-0-9725721)* 153 Raquet Club Dr., Rancho Mirage, CA 92270 USA
E-mail: info@robstanger.com
Web site: http://www.robstanger.com.

Club4Girls *Imprint of* **Club4Girls Publishing Co.**

Club4Girls Publishing Co., *(978-0-9712297)* 4017 Dutch Harbor Ct., Raleigh, NC 27606-8604 USA Tel 919-387-9939; *Imprints:* Club4Girls (ClubFourGirls)
E-mail: bob@sas.com.

ClueSearchPuzzles.com, *(978-0-9753879)* 7645 N. Union Blvd. #175, Colorado Springs, CO 80920-3863 USA Tel 719-659-9034
E-mail: books@cluesearchpuzzles.com
Web site: http://www.cluesearchpuzzles.com.

Cluster Storm Publishing, *(978-1-56998)* Orders Addr.: 507 E. 3750 N., Provo, UT 84604 USA Tel 801-623-9101
E-mail: cjmartell@gmail.com.

Clydesdale Pr., LLC, *(978-0-9729606)* P.O. Box 2375, Kesington, MD 20891 USA
Dist(s): **Simon & Schuster, Inc.**
Two Rivers Distribution.

CMB Publishing Co., *(978-0-9722969)* 24 Appleton St., Suite 1, Boston, MA 02116 USA Tel 617-306-5581; Fax: 617-451-0168
E-mail: info@cmbpublishing.com
Web site: http://www.cmbpublishing.com/.

CMC Publishing, *(978-0-9787336)* 1 Heritage Pl., Nesconset, NY 11767 USA
E-mail: colleenssite@yahoo.com.

CMK Pubs. LLC, *(978-0-9743159)* .

CMS Enterprises, *(978-0-9768170)* Orders Addr.: P.O. Box 8039, Van Nuys, CA 91409 USA (SAN 256-5226); Edit Addr.: 6429 Whitman Ave., Van Nuys, CA 91406 USA
E-mail: cms55@hotmail.com.

CNL Publishing, *(978-0-9766921)* 105 Wedgewood Dr., Fairfield, AL 35064 USA Tel 205-835-5444; Fax: 205-923-3218.

CNPIECSB, 332 W Cermak Rd., Apt. 2D, Chicago, IL 60616 USA.

CNT Robotics LLC, *(978-0-9993918)*
E-mail: roboteer@comcast.net
Web site: www.cntrobotics.com.

Coach Enterprises, *(978-0-9636706)* 616 Munntown Rd., Finleyville, PA 15332 USA Tel 724-348-4843; Fax: 724-348-5549.

Coach Hse. Bks. (CAN) *(978-1-55245; 978-1-77056) Dist. by* **Consort Bk Sales.**

coach speak & serve, *(978-0-9987829; 978-0-9990044)* 1219 N Classen blvd, oklahoma city, OK 73106 USA Tel 405-246-0077; Fax: 405-246-0077
E-mail: support@coachspeakserve.com
Web site: coachspeakserve.com.

Coachwhip Pubns., *(978-1-930585; 978-1-61646)* 1505 English Brook Dr., Landisville, PA 17538 USA
E-mail: chadarment@verizon.net
Web site: http://www.coachwhipbooks.com.

Coal City Stories, *(978-0-9849028)* 1101 Cole Dr., Lilburn, GA 30047 USA Tel 678-896-9493 (Tel/Fax)
E-mail: emilie.bush@gmail.com; machineseat@hotmail.com
Web site: CoalCitySteam.com.

Coal Hole Productions, *(978-0-9709630)* 207 Hemlock Ln., Bloomsburg, PA 17815 USA Tel 570-784-4561
E-mail: ceo@coalhole.com
Web site: http://www.coalhole.com
Dist(s): **Partners Bk. Distributing, Inc.**

Coal Under Pr.ure, LLC, *(978-0-9763400; 978-0-9913704; 978-1-7326303)* Div. of Coal Under Pressure, LLC, Orders Addr.: 109 Ambersweet Way No. 280, Davenport, FL 33897 USA
E-mail: coalunderpressurepubs@gmail.com
Web site: http://www.coalunderpressure.com.

Coal Under Pressure Publications *See* **Coal Under Pr.ure, LLC**

Coast View Publishing, *(978-0-9849732)* 638 Camino De Los Mares Suite H130-157, San Clemente, CA 92673 USA Tel 949-388-7996
E-mail: coastviewpublishing@yahoo.com.

Coastal Carolina Pr., *(978-1-928556)* Orders Addr.: P.O. Box 9111, Chapel Hill, NC 27515-9111 USA
E-mail: books@coastalcarolinapress.org
Web site: http://www.coastalcarolinapress.org
Dist(s): **Blair**
Parnassus Bk. Distributors.

Coastal Publishing Carolina, Inc., *(978-0-9705727; 978-1-931650)* 504 Amberjack Way, Summerville, SC 29485 USA Tel 843-821-6168; Fax: 843-851-6949
E-mail: coastalpublishing@earthlink.net
Web site: http://coastalpublishing.net/.

Coastal Publishing, LLC, *(978-0-9755573)* No. 226, 1133 Bal Harbor Blvd., Suite 1139, Punta Gorda, FL 33950-6574 USA Tel 941-505-5547.

Cobalt Pr., *(978-0-9747805)* P.O. Box 5393, Hauppauge, NY 11788 USA Do not confuse with Cobalt Pr. in Minneapolis, MN
Web site: http://www.geocities.com/corrinedzwil/index.html.

Cobblestone Pr., *(978-0-9649021)* 7340 Cobblestone Dr. W, Indianapolis, IN 46236 USA Tel 317-253-7476; Fax: 317-475-9578; Toll Free: 800-420-6655 Do not confuse with companies with the same or similar name in Midland, MI, Huntsville, AL
Dist(s): **Publishers Group West (PGW).**

Cobblestone Publishing Co., *(978-0-382; 978-0-942389; 978-0-9607638)* Div. of Cricket Magazine Group, 30 Grove St., Suite C, Peterborough, NH 03458 USA (SAN 237-9937) Tel 603-924-7209; Fax: 603-924-7380; Toll Free: 800-821-0115; P.O. Box 487, Effingham, IL 62401
E-mail: custsvc@cobblestone.mv.com
Web site: http://www.cobblestonepub.com
Dist(s): **Americana Publishing, Inc.**
Follett School Solutions.

Cobblesworth Studio, *(978-0-692-91147-1)* Orders Addr.: 1261 Bistre St, Longmont, CO 80501 USA Tel 720-467-3119; Edit Addr.: 1261 Bistre St, Longmont, CO 80501 USA Tel 720-467-3119
E-mail: cobblesworth@gmail.com; travisrueckert88@gmail.com
Web site: https://www.facebook.com/Cobblesworth
Dist(s): **Independent Pub.**

Cobbs Creations, *(978-0-692-75070-4; 978-0-692-96368-5; 978-0-692-98749-0; 978-0-692-14642-2; 978-0-692-14643-9; 978-0-692-17740-2)* 1861 Holly Point Rd., PROSPERITY, SC 29127 USA Tel 803-924-1947.

Cochise County Juvenile Detention Ctr., *(978-0-9771011)* P.O. Box 208, Bisbee, AZ 85603 USA Fax: 520-432-7136
Web site: http://www.co.cochise.az.us/schools.

Cochran, Russ Co., The, *(978-0-939947; 978-0-9816923)* P.O. Box 469, West Plains, MO 65775 USA (SAN 663-8236) Fax: 417-256-6666
E-mail: russcochran333@gmail.com
Web site: http://www.russcochran.com.

For full information on wholesalers and distributors, refer to the Wholesaler and Distributor Name Index

Cochrane Farms, (*978-0-9992841*) 13220 Lowell unit c, Broomfield, CO 80020 USA Tel 720-244-8148
E-mail: cottagesimplicity@gmail.com.

Cockburn Publishing, (*978-1-887461*) 1504 Mithra St., New Orleans, LA 70122-2018 USA.

Cockey, EJ & Company *See* **The Painted Word, Ltd.**

Cockney Kid Publishing, (*978-0-9903710*) 986 Woodstock Ln., Ventura, CA 93001 USA Tel 805-258-6325
E-mail: davisivor@yahoo.com
Web site: ivordavisbeatles.com.

Coconut Info, (*978-1-929317*) Orders Addr.: P.O. Box 75460, Honolulu, HI 96836 USA Tel 808-947-6543; Fax: 808-923-6544
E-mail: sales@coconutinfo.com; info@coconutinfo.com
Web site: http://www.coconutinfo.com
Dist(s): **Booklines Hawaii, Ltd.**

Coconut Pr., LLC, (*978-0-9702168; 978-0-9778913; 978-0-578-44083-5*) Div. of Puerto Rico Postcard Co., Inc, Orders Addr.: P.O. Box 309540, Saint Thomas, VI 00803 USA Tel 787-248-3774; Fax: 787-253-8449; Edit Addr.: P.O. Box 79170, Carolina, PR 00984 USA Do not confuse with companies with same or similar names in Coral Gables, FL, Missouri City, TX
E-mail: Angelaspenceley1@msn.com
Dist(s): **Puerto Rico Postcard.**

Coda Grove Publishing, (*978-0-9889113*) P.O. Box 275, Fairfax, VT 05454 USA Tel 802-849-2777
E-mail: codagrovepub@gmail.com.

Cody Roach Enterprises, (*978-1-7322370*) 5 W Winter Pk. St., Orlando, FL 32804 USA Tel 407-579-6453
E-mail: codyroachenterprizes@gmail.com.

Cody's Guide, (*978-0-9755305*) 3855 Humbug Creek Rd., Applegate, OR 97530 USA
Web site: http://www.codysguide.com.

Coffee Hse. Ink, (*978-0-9663176*) 32370 SE Judd Rd., Eagle Creek, OR 97022 USA Tel 503-637-3277; Fax: 503-423-7980
E-mail: donmillll@aol.com
Web site: http://www.coffeehouseink.com.

Coffee Hse. Pr., (*978-0-918273; 978-1-56689*) 79 13th Ave NE Ste. 110, Minneapolis, MN 55413-1073 USA (SAN 206-3883); 387 Pk. Ave. S., New York, NY 10016
Web site: http://www.coffeehousepress.org
Dist(s): **BookMobile**
Consortium Bk. Sales & Distribution
Follett School Solutions
MyiLibrary
Open Road Integrated Media, Inc.
SPD-Small Pr. Distribution.

Coffragants (CAN) (*978-2-921997; 978-2-89517; 978-2-89558*) *Dist. by* **Penton Overseas.**

Coghlan Group, The *See* **Phoenix International, Inc.**

Cogi Garden Bks., (*978-0-692-83770-2; 978-0-692-85083-1*) 811 Lyon St NE, Grand Rapids, MI 49503 USA Tel 301-367-2830
E-mail: dirmeyer@gmail.com
Dist(s): **CreateSpace Independent Publishing Platform.**

Cognella Academic Publishing *Imprint of* **Cognella, Inc.**

Cognella, Inc., (*978-0-9763162; 978-1-934269; 978-1-935551; 978-1-60927; 978-1-62131; 978-1-62661; 978-1-63189; 978-1-63487; 978-1-5165; 978-1-7935*) 3970 Sorrento Valley Blvd. Suite 500, San Diego, CA 92121 USA (SAN 990-1701) Toll Free: 800-200-3908; *Imprints:* Cognella Academic Publishing (CognellaAcad)
E-mail: accounting@universityreaders.com; ap@cognella.com
Web site: http://www.universityreaders.com; http://www.cognella.com
Dist(s): **Independent Pubs. Group.**

Cognisaya, (*978-0-615-60544-9; 978-0-9852568; 978-0-9980759*) 3104 SE Misty Ct, Port Orchard, WA 98367 USA Tel 360-602-1913
Web site: cognisaya.com
Dist(s): **CreateSpace Independent Publishing Platform.**

Cohen, Deanna Moreau, 1626a Garden St., Santa Barbara, CA 93101-1110 USA
E-mail: liftveil2@cs.com.

Cohen, Sonia *See* **Gigi Enterprises**

Cohn, Tricia, (*978-0-9743847*) 16158 Highgate Dr., Riverside, CA 92503-8718 USA Tel 714-272-6972
E-mail: triciacohn@beobi.com
Web site: http://www.beobi.com.

Coho Press *See* **Dot Dot Bks.**

Cokesbury *Imprint of* **Abingdon Pr.**

Cola, Arthur, (*978-0-9789423*) 425 Robins Run, Papa Adventures, Burlington, WI 53105 USA
E-mail: arthurcola@yahoo.com
Dist(s): **Partners Bk. Distributing, Inc.**

Colbert Hse., LLC, The, (*978-1-887399*) Orders Addr.: P.O. Box 786, Mustang, OK 73064-0786 USA Tel 405-204-0043
E-mail: customerservice@colberthouse.com
Web site: http://www.colberthouse.com.

Colbert House, The *See* **Colbert Hse., LLC, The**

Colby Studio, (*978-0-9976198*) P.O. Box 681, Castine, ME 04421 USA Tel 207-322-0432
E-mail: kasey@eternav.com
Web site: ivystories.com.

Cold River Pubns., (*978-0-9712867; 978-0-692-52577-7*) P.O. Box 606, Long Lake, NY 12847-0606 USA Tel 518-624-3581
E-mail: criver@telenet.net; criver@telenent.net
Web site: http://www.coldriverwoodworks.com
Dist(s): **Smashwords.**

Cole, Mark, (*978-0-615-86154-8; 978-0-615-92911-8; 978-0-692-02398-3; 978-0-692-23967-4; 978-0-692-25816-3*) 112 Ash Ridge Pl., Pearl, MS 39208 USA Tel 601-540-5125
E-mail: wnxaz@hotmail.com
Dist(s): **CreateSpace Independent Publishing Platform.**

Cole Publishing, (*978-0-9678779; 978-0-9773973; 978-0-9787317*) 13428 Maxella Ave., Suite 701, Marina Del Rey, CA 90292 USA (SAN 256-856X) Fax: 310-209-2448
E-mail: candace@candacecole.com; ccpprod@aol.com
Web site: http://candacecole.com/.

Cole, Reginald, (*978-0-692-81245-7*) 1705 Inverness Ave., Dundalk, MD 21222 USA Tel 301-502-2964
E-mail: reggie.cole@outlook.com.

Cole-Dai, Phyllis, (*978-0-615-24350-4*) 712 6th St., Brookings, SD 57006 USA Tel 605-692-7001
E-mail: phyllis@phylliscoledai.com; coledai@brookings.net
Web site: http://www.phylliscoledai.com.

Coleman, CJ, (*978-0-9773651*) 2191 Craig Springs Rd., Sturgis, MS 39769 USA Tel 662-312-4383
E-mail: cillycreations@hotmail.com
Web site: http://www.cillycreations.com.

Coleman Ranch Pr., (*978-0-9677069*) Orders Addr.: P.O. Box 1496, Sacramento, CA 95812 USA Tel 916-393-9032; Toll Free Fax: 888-532-4190; Toll Free: 877-765-3225
E-mail: colemanranch@comcast.net
Web site: http://www.CRPRESS.com.

Coleman, Wim *See* **Coleman/Perrin**

Coleman/Perrin, (*978-1-935178*) 405 Walnut St., Chapel Hill, NC 27517 USA Tel 919-338-8119; *Imprints:* ChironBooks (ChironBooks)
E-mail: wim-pat@gmail.com; info@chironbooks.com
Web site: http://www.playsonideas.com; http://www.chironbooks.com; http://www.madeirapress.com
Dist(s): **BookBaby**
Pathway Bk. Service.

Colibri Children's Adventures *See* **Leaning Rock Pr.**

Colihue (ARG) (*978-950-581*) *Dist. by* **AIMS Intl.**

Collector Bks., (*978-0-89145; 978-1-57432; 978-1-60460*) Div. of Schroeder Publishing Co., Inc., Orders Addr.: P.O. Box 3009, Paducah, KY 42003 USA (SAN 157-5368) Tel 270-898-6211; 270-898-7903; Fax: 270-898-8890; 270-898-1173; Toll Free: 800-626-5420 (orders only); Edit Addr.: 5801 Kentucky Dam Rd., Paducah, KY 42003 USA (SAN 200-7479); *Imprints:* American Quilter's Society (Am Quilters Soc)
E-mail: Info@collectorbooks.com; info@AQSquilt.com
Web site: http://www.collectorbooks.com; http://www.americanquilter.com/.

Collectors Pr., Inc., (*978-0-9635202; 978-1-888054; 978-1-933112*) Orders Addr.: P.O. Box 230986, Portland, OR 97281 USA Tel 503-684-3030; Fax: 503-684-3777; Toll Free: 800-423-1848; Edit Addr.: P.O. Box 230986, Portland, OR 97281-0986 USA
E-mail: lperry@collectorspress.com; rperry@collectorspress.com
Web site: http://www.collectorspress.com
Dist(s): **Universe Publishing**
Worldwide Media Service, Inc.

College & Career Pr., LLC, (*978-0-9745251; 978-0-9829210*) P.O. Box 300484, Chicago, IL 60630 USA Tel 773-718-0366; Fax: 777-777-7777; P.O. Box 300484, Chicago, IL 60630
E-mail: andymorkes@gmail.com
Web site: http://www.collegeandcareerpress.com; http://www.ccpnewsletters.com
Dist(s): **Brodart Co.**
Follett School Solutions.

College Assistance & Scholarship Help, Incorporated *See* **College Assistance, Inc.**

College Assistance, Inc., (*978-0-9760251*) Orders Addr.: 7235 Promenade Dr. Apt. J401, Boca Raton, FL 33433-6982 USA Toll Free: 866-346-7890
E-mail: llbrodereecy@aol.com; thecollegebook@aol.com
Web site: http://www.librodelauniversidad.com; http://www.thecollegebook.com; http://www.reecysbook.com.

College Hse. Enterprises, LLC, (*978-0-9655911; 978-0-9700675; 978-0-9723567; 978-0-9762413; 978-0-9792581; 978-1-935673*) 5713 Glen Cove Dr., Knoxville, TN 37919-8611 USA (SAN 253-5831) Tel 865-558-6111 (phone/fax)
Web site: http://www.collegehousebooks.com.

College of DuPage Pr., (*978-1-932514*) Orders Addr.: 425 Fawell Blvd., Glen Ellyn, IL 60137 USA Fax: 630-942-3333; Toll Free: 800-290-4474
E-mail: software@cod.edu
Web site: http://www.dupagepress.com.

College Planning Network, (*978-1-880344*) 914 E. Jefferson, Campion Tower, Seattle, WA 98122 USA Tel 206-323-0624; Fax: 206-323-0623
E-mail: seaspn@collegeplan.org
Web site: http://www.collegeplan.org.

College Prowler, Inc., (*978-1-932215; 978-1-59658; 978-1-4274*) 5001 Baum Blvd. Ste. 750, Pittsburgh, PA 15213-1856 USA Toll Free Fax: 800-772-4972; Toll Free: 800-290-2682; *Imprints:* Off The Record (Off The Rcd)
E-mail: joey@collegeprowler.com; luke@collegeprowler.com
Web site: http://www.collegeprowler.com.

Collegiate Kids Bks., LLC, (*978-0-9836211; 978-0-692-01848-4; 978-0-9886542*) 3956 2nd St. Dr. NW, Hickory, NC 28601 USA Tel 828-773-5398
E-mail: bryan@collegiatekidsbooks.com
Web site: http://www.collegiatekidsbooks.com.

Collins *Imprint of* **HarperCollins Pubs.**

Collins Christian Co., The, (*978-0-692-66059-1*) 1043 Myrtle Ln, Cocoa, FL 32922 USA Tel 321-208-1538
E-mail: zlcinc2015@gmail.com.

Collins Pr., The (IRL) (*978-0-9516306; 978-1-898256; 978-1-903464; 978-1-905172; 978-1-84889*) *Dist. by* **Dufour.**

Collins, Robert, (*978-0-9766426*) 865 Helke Rd., Vandalia, OH 45377 USA; *Imprints:* Peregrine Communications (Peregrine Comm)
E-mail: adaglo@gemair.com
Web site: http://www.ufoconspiracy.com/.

Colonel Davenport Historical Foundation, (*978-0-9755934*) P.O. Box 4703, Rock Island, IL 61204 USA
Web site: http://www.davenporthouse.org.

†Colonial Williamsburg Foundation, (*978-0-87935; 978-0-910412*) P.O. Box 3532, Williamsburg, VA 23187-3532 USA (SAN 128-4630) Fax: 757-565-8999 (orders only); Toll Free: 800-446-9240 (orders only)
Web site: http://www.colonialwilliamsburg.com
Dist(s): **Antique Collectors' Club**
National Bk. Network
University of Virginia Pr.; *CIP.*

Color & Learn, (*978-0-9795190*) P.O. Box 1592, Saint Augustine, FL 32085-1592 USA (SAN 853-6023)
Web site: http://www.colorandlearn.com.

Color & Light Editions, (*978-0-9671527; 978-0-9835239*) 371 Drakes View Dr., Inverness, CA 94937 USA Tel 415-663-1616
E-mail: kathleenpgoodwin@gmail.com
Web site: http://BlairGoodwin.com
Dist(s): **Partners Bk. Distributing, Inc.**

Color Loco *See* **Color Loco, LLC**

Color Loco, LLC, (*978-0-9770652; 978-0-9788778*) 213 Woodland Dr., Downingtown, PA 19335-9335 USA
Web site: http://www.ColorLoco.com.

Colorado Associated University Press *See* **Univ. Pr. of Colorado**

Colorfield Creative, LLC, (*978-1-948227*) 2324 NW 113th St, Oklahoma City, OK 73120 USA Tel 405-249-4254
E-mail: colorfieldcreative@gmail.com.

Colorful Bks. Pr., (*978-0-9746152*) 935 Ottawa Ave., Ypsilanti, MI 48198 USA.

Colorful Crayons For Kids Publishing, LLC *See* **Jeb Cool Kids Entertainment, Inc**

Colossus Bks. *Imprint of* **Amber Bks.**

Colourpoint Bks. (GBR) (*978-1-898392; 978-1-904242; 978-1-906578; 978-1-78073*) *Dist. by* **Casemate Pubs.**

Columba Pr. (IRL) (*978-0-948183; 978-1-85607; 978-1-78218*) *Dist. by* **Casemate Pubs.**

Columba Pr. (IRL) (*978-0-948183; 978-1-85607; 978-1-78218*) *Dist. by* **Dufour.**

†Columbia Univ. Pr., (*978-0-231*) Orders Addr.: 61 W. 62nd St., New York, NY 10023-7015 USA (SAN 212-2480) Toll Free Fax: 800-944-1844; Toll Free: 800-944-8648 x 6240 (orders); Edit Addr.: 61 W. 62nd St., New York, NY 10023 USA (SAN 212-2472) Tel 212-459-0600; Fax: 212-459-3678; 387 Pk. Ave., S., New York, NY 10016
E-mail: cupbooks@columbia.edu
Web site: http://www.columbia.edu/cu/cup
Dist(s): **Cambridge Univ. Pr.**
Casemate Academic
CreateSpace Independent Publishing Platform
De Gruyter, Inc.
Ebsco Publishing
Follett School Solutions
ISD
MyiLibrary
Open Road Integrated Media, Inc.
Ingram Academic
Wiley, John & Sons, Inc.
ebrary, Inc.; *CIP.*

Columbine Pr., (*978-0-9651272; 978-0-9768570; 978-0-9965407*) Orders Addr.: P.O. Box 1950, Cripple Creek, CO 80813 USA Tel 719-689-2141; Edit Addr.: 340 Colorado Ave., Cripple Creek, CO 80813 USA Do not confuse with companies with the same name in Bainbridge Island, WA, East Hampton, NY
E-mail: pkmacv@earthlink.net.

Columbine Publishing Group, LLC, (*978-0-615-47989-7; 978-1-945422; 978-1-64914*) P.O. Box 416, Angel Fire, NM 87710 USA Tel 480-639-3700; *Imprints:* Secret Staircase Books, an imprint of Columbine Publishing Group, LLC (MYID_O_SECRET)
Dist(s): **CreateSpace Independent Publishing Platform**
Dummy Record Do Not USE!!!!.

Columbus Pr., (*978-0-9891737; 978-1-63337*) 1658 Harvard Ave., Columbus, OH 43203 USA Tel 614-441-9777; *Imprints:* Boyle & Dalton (Boyle n Dalton)
E-mail: info@columbuspressbooks.com
Web site: www.ColumbusPressBooks.com
Dist(s): **BookBaby.**

Columbus Zoo & Aquarium, The, (*978-0-9841554*) 4850 W. Powell Rd., P.O. Box 400, Powell, OH 43065 USA (SAN 858-589X) Tel 614-645-3400; Fax: 614-645-3465
E-mail: fran.baby@columbuszoo.org
Web site: http://www.columbuszoo.org.

Column Hall Concepts, LLC, (*978-0-9786584*) 217 - 82nd St., Brooklyn, NY 11209 USA Tel 718-836-1072
Web site: http://www.heydadthebook.com
Dist(s): **Follett School Solutions.**

Combel Editorial, S.A. (ESP) (*978-84-7864; 978-84-9825*) *Dist. by* **IPG Chicago.**

Combs-Hulme Publishing, (*978-0-9769854*) 1720 Eldridge Ave. W., Saint Paul, MN 55113 USA Tel 651-631-2173 Do not confuse with Combs Publishing in Winston-Salem, NC
E-mail: lvhulme@aol.com.

Come & Get It Publishing, (*978-0-9653042; 978-0-9753883; 978-0-692-64839-1*) Orders Addr.: P.O. Box 1562, Madison, VA 22727 USA Tel 540-829-0516 Toll Free: 800-825-9008; Edit Addr.: 214 E. Spencer St., No. 1, Culpeper, VA 22701 USA
E-mail: comeandgetproducts@gmail.com
Dist(s): **Publishers Group West (PGW).**

Come As A Child, (*978-1-7338134*) 135 Joinda, Vass, NC 28394 USA Tel 910-691-4001
E-mail: debigatlyn@gmail.com.

Comfort Tales, LLC, (*978-0-9741586*) Orders Addr.: 47 Watsons Way, Medford, NJ 08055 USA (SAN 255-464X) Tel 856-988-0884; Fax: 856-988-8499
E-mail: comforttales@aol.com.

Comic Library International, (*978-1-929515*) 2049 Alfred St., Pittsburgh, PA 15212-1426 USA; *Imprints:* Solovisions (Solovisions)
E-mail: gbstudios@comcast.net
Web site: http://www.geocities.com/SoHo/Cafe/9669/clipage.html
Dist(s): **Diamond Comic Distributors, Inc.**

ComicMix, (*978-1-939888*) 71 Hauxhurst Ave., Weehawken, NJ 07086 USA Tel 551-265-9059
E-mail: glenn@comicmix.com
Web site: http://www.comicmix.com
Dist(s): **Diamond Comic Distributors, Inc.**

Comics Lit *Imprint of* **NBM Publishing Co.**

Comics Workshop, (*978-0-9824153; 978-1-7343869*) 93 Bennett Rd., Henniker, NH 03242 USA
Web site: http://www.marekbennett.com.

ComicsOne Corp./Dr. Masters, (*978-1-58899*) P.O. Box 14232, Fremont, CA 94539-1532 USA
Dist(s): **Diamond Comic Distributors, Inc.**
Diamond Bk. Distributors
L P C Group.

Command Performance Language Institute, (*978-0-929724*) 25 Hopkins Ct., Berkeley, CA 94706 USA (SAN 250-1694) Tel 510-524-1191; Fax: 510-527-9880
E-mail: consee@aol.com
Web site: http://www.hometown.aol.com/commandperform1/myhomepage/business.html
Dist(s): **Alta English Publishers**
Applause Learning Resources
Athelstan Pubns.
Betty Segal, Inc.
BookLink
Calliope Bks.
Carlex
Continental Bk. Co., Inc.
Delta Systems Company, Inc.
Educational Showcase
Edumate-Educational Materials, Inc.
European Bk. Co., Inc.
Follett School Solutions
Gessler Publishing Co., Inc.
International Bk. Ctr., Inc.
Midwest European Pubns.
Miller Educational Materials
Multi-Cultural Bks. & Videos, Inc.
Sky Oaks Productions, Inc.
SpeakWare
Teacher's Discovery
Tempo Bookstore
2Learn-English
World of Reading, Ltd.

Command Publishing, LLC, (*978-0-9778356*) 43311 Joy Rd. Suite 201, Canton, MI 48187-2075 USA (SAN 850-2706).

Commercial Communications Incorporated *See* **Great Lakes Design**

Commission on Culture and Tourism, (*978-0-9759389*) 1 Constitution Plz., Hartford, CT 06103-1803 USA
E-mail: kazkozlowski@snet.net.

Committed 2 Win, LLC, (*978-0-578-22353-7*) P.O. Box 22087, Waco, TX 76702 USA Tel 888-926-6648
E-mail: darryl@committed2win.com
Web site: http://darryl.mykajabi.com/.

Committee for Children, (*978-0-9741388*) 568 First Ave. S., Suite 600, Seattle, WA 98104-2804 USA Toll Free: 800-634-4449
Web site: http://www.cfchildren.org.

Common Courtesy, (*978-0-9746148*) 709 Uwharrie St., Asheboro, NC 27203 USA Tel 336-629-5274
E-mail: jjdortch@earthlink.net.

Common Deer Pr. (CAN) (*978-0-9950729; 978-1-988761*) *Dist. by* **Natl Bk Netwk.**

Commonwealth Books, LLC *See* **Commonwealth Books of Virginia, LLC**

Commonwealth Books of Virginia, LLC, (*978-0-9825922; 978-0-9854863; 978-0-9904018; 978-0-9909592; 978-0-9961368; 978-1-943642*) 50 Willway Ave., Richmond, VA 23226 USA Tel 703-307-7715
E-mail: jct@commonwealthbooks.org; info@commonwealthbooks.org
Web site: http://www.commonwealthbooks.org; http://www.commonwealthbooks.org; www.thomasjeffersonsenlightenment.org; www.bayardtberndt.org
Dist(s): **MyiLibrary**
Small Pr. United
ebrary, Inc.

Commonwealth Bks.,Black Widow,
Dist(s): **National Bk. Network.**

Commonwealth Editions *Imprint of* **Applewood Bks.**

Communication Service Corporation *See* **Gryphon Hse., Inc.**

Community Bks. (CAN) (*978-0-9694180; 978-0-9698407; 978-1-896496*) *Dist. by* **Col U Pr.**

Community Voice Media, LLC, (*978-0-9776613; 978-0-9885741*) P.O. Box 564, Round Hill, VA

Publisher Name Index

20142-5640 USA Tel 540-751-2214; Fax: 540-751-2215
E-mail: bobbicarducci@communityvoicemedia.com
Web site: http://www.communityvoicemedia.com.

Community Works!, *(978-0-9742213)* 13313 Country Way Cir., Fredericksburg, VA 22404 USA
E-mail: arayu1@comcast.net; carol@carolynnfitzpatrick.com
Web site: http://www.carolynnfitzpatrick.com
Dist(s): **New Leaf Distributing Co., Inc.**

Companhia das Letras (BRA) *(978-85-7164; 978-85-85095; 978-85-85466; 978-85-359) Dist. by* **Distribks Inc.**

Companhia Melhoramentos de Sao Paulo Industrias de Papel (BRA) *(978-85-06) Dist. by* **Lectorum Pubns.**

Companion Pr., *(978-1-879651; 978-1-61722)* Div. of Ctr. for Loss & Life Transition, 3735 Broken Bow Rd., Fort Collins, CO 80526 USA Tel 970-226-6050; Fax: 970-226-6051; Toll Free Fax: 800-922-6051 (orders only) Do not confuse with companies with the same name in Santa Barbara, CA, Aliso Viejo, CA
E-mail: wolfelt@centerforloss.com
Web site: http://www.centerforloss.com
Dist(s): **Ebsco Publishing**
Independent Pubs. Group
MyiLibrary
ebrary, Inc.

CompanionHouse Bks. *Imprint of* **Fox Chapel Publishing Co., Inc.**

Company's Coming Publishing, Ltd. (CAN) *(978-0-9690695; 978-0-9693322; 978-1-895455; 978-1-896891; 978-1-897069; 978-1-897477; 978-1-927126; 978-1-77207) Dist. by* **Lone Pine.**

Compass *Imprint of* **Raphel Marketing, Inc.**

Compass Books *See* **Lake Street Pubs.**

Compass Flower Pr. *Imprint of* **AKA:yoLa**

Compass Point Bks. *Imprint of* **Capstone**

Compass Productions Inc., *(978-1-63264)* 9316 Lakeview Ave SW Ste B-1, Lakewood, WA 98499 USA Tel 206-430-6021; *Imprints:* Bookbarn Publishing (MYID_Z_BKBARN)
E-mail: mark@cascade-publishing.com
Dist(s): **Atlas Bks.**
Baker & Taylor Publisher Services (BTPS).

Compass Publishing *See* **Sunesis Publishing Co.**

Compass Publishing, *(978-0-9753102)* Orders Addr.: P.O. Box 280188, Lakewood, CO 80228-0188 USA (SAN 256-0186) Tel 818-264-9606 (phone/fax); Fax: 818-433-7445; Edit Addr.: 1912 Rivera Rd., Santa Fe Spring, CA 90670 USA
E-mail: billhowey@actorsmenu.com
Web site: http://www.actorsmenu.com
Dist(s): **Follett School Solutions**
Independent Pubs. Group.

Compassion Outreach Ministry *See* **Stott, Darrel Ministry**

Compassion Pets Publishing, *(978-0-615-13428-4; 978-0-615-30968-2)* 34672 Hardtack Ln., Shingletown, CA 96088 USA (SAN 858-5954) Tel 530-474-1038
E-mail: compassionpet.pub@frontiernet.net
Web site: http://www.compassionpets.com.

Compendium, Inc., Publishing & Communications, *(978-0-9640178; 978-1-888387; 978-1-932319; 978-1-935414; 978-1-938298; 978-1-943200; 978-1-946873; 978-1-970147)* Orders Addr.: P.O. Box 5308, Lynnwood, WA 98046-5308 USA (SAN 253-7109) Tel 425-673-2238; Fax: 425-673-6949; Toll Free: 800-914-3327; Edit Addr.: 600 N. 36th St. Ste. 400, Seattle, WA 98103-8699 USA; 2100 N. Pacific St., Seattle, WA 98103
E-mail: kobi@compendiuminc.com; connie@compendiuminc.com; carolanne@compendiuminc.com
Web site: http://www.compendiuminc.com; http://www.live-inspired.com
Dist(s): **APG Sales & Distribution Services.**

Competitor Creeds *See* **Moon Chaser Publishing**

Complete in Christ Ministries, Inc., *(978-0-9795007)* P.O. Box 42027, Baton Rouge, LA 70835 USA
E-mail: completeinchrist@cox.net
Web site: http://www.cicmblog.com.

Comprecom, *(978-0-9772809)* 411 Hess Ave., Golden, CO 80401 USA.

Comprehensive Health Education Foundation, *(978-0-935529; 978-1-57021)* 159 S. Jackson St. Ste. 510, Seattle, WA 98104-4416 USA (SAN 696-3668) Toll Free: 800-323-2433
E-mail: chefstaff@chef.org
Web site: http://www.chef.org/.

Compsych Systems, Inc., Pubns. Div., *(978-0-929948)* Div. of Compsych Systems, Inc., P.O. Box 1568, Pacific Palisades, CA 90272 USA (SAN 250-8281) Tel 310-454-6426 (phone/fax)
Web site: http://www.jeanettegriver.com
Dist(s): **Follett School Solutions.**

Compton, Tyler, *(978-0-9893845)* 1627 N. Laurel Ave. No. 5, Los Angeles, CA 90046 USA Tel 323-350-2120
E-mail: ts_compton@yahoo.com.

Computer Age Education *See* **Learning Net, The**

Computer Athlete Media, *(978-0-9820447)* P.O. Box 687, Princeton Junction, NJ 08550 USA
E-mail: support@computerathlete.net
Web site: http://www.computerathlete.net.

Computer Classics (R), *(978-0-9721216; 978-0-9748870; 978-0-9836019; 978-0-9899265)* 5036 Suter Dr., Nashville, TN 37211-5155 USA
E-mail: computerclassics@mindspring.com
Web site: http://www.computer-classics.com.

ComQwest, LLC, *(978-0-9753454)* 1350 E. Flamingo Rd., Suite No. 265, Las Vegas, NV 89119 USA
Web site: http://www.comqwest.com.

Comstock Publishing Assocs. *Imprint of* **Cornell Univ. Pr.**

ComteQ Publishing, *(978-0-9674074; 978-0-9766889; 978-0-9793771; 978-1-935232; 978-1-941501)* Div. of ComteQ Communications, LLC, Orders Addr.: 7806 Marshall Ave., Margate, NJ 08402 USA Tel 609-487-9000
E-mail: publisher@comteqpublishing.com
Web site: http://www.comteqpublishing.com
Dist(s): **BookBaby.**

Comunicadora Koine, Inc., *(978-0-9794682; 978-0-9834966)* Orders Addr.: P.O. Box RR3 Box 3801, San Juan, PR 00926 USA Tel 787-642-2053; Fax: 787-753-7077; Edit Addr.: 1118 Calle Padres Capuchinos, Rio Piedras, PR 00925 USA
E-mail: comunicadorakoine@gmail.com
Web site: http://www.comunicadorakoine.com.

Conari Press *Imprint of* **Mango Media**

ConArtistE Pubng., *(978-0-9755386)* 6084 Churn Creek Rd., Redding, CA 96002 USA Tel 530-209-4338
E-mail: conartiste@msn.com
Web site: www.conartiste.com.

Concepcion, Jorge, *(978-0-9761779)* 9125 SW 56th Ter., Miami, FL 33173-1605 USA
E-mail: jconcepcion1@msn.com.

Concept Media Group, LLC, The, *(978-0-9864191)* 1408 N. Riverfront Blvd., No. 134, Dallas, TX 75207 USA Tel 214-854-2150
E-mail: sherilyn@theconceptmediagroup.com
Web site: www.TheConceptMediaGroup.com.

Concepts *See* **Developmental Vision Concepts**

Concepts 'N' Publishing, *(978-1-879940)* Orders Addr.: P.O. Box 10413, College Station, TX 77842 USA
Web site: http://www.ethaemm.homestead.com.

Concepts Redefined, *(978-0-692-83922-5; 978-0-692-83939-3; 978-0-9986630; 978-1-7330938)* 11739 Mango cross ct., Seffner, FL 33584 USA Tel 813-598-9481
E-mail: creynolds70@verizon.net; creynolds70@verizon.net; creynolds70@verizon.net
Web site: www.jaycethebee.com
Dist(s): **CreateSpace Independent Publishing Platform.**

Concerned Christians, *(978-0-9768352)* P.O. Box 18, Mesa, AZ 85211 USA Tel 480-833-2537; Fax: 480-833-4116
E-mail: jim@concernedchristians.org
Web site: http://www.concernedchristians.org.

Concerned Communications, *(978-0-936785; 978-1-58938)* Orders Addr.: P.O. Box 1000, Siloam Springs, AR 72761-1000 USA (SAN 699-8623) Tel 501-594-9000; Fax: 501-549-4002; Toll Free: 800-447-4332; Edit Addr.: 700 E. Granite St., Siloam Springs, AR 72761 USA (SAN 699-8631)
E-mail: lustwrt@areasonfor.com
Web site: http://www.areasonfor.com
Dist(s): **Project Patch.**

Conciliar Press *See* **Ancient Faith Publishing**

Concinnity Initiatives, *(978-0-9842146; 978-0-615-49009-0; 978-0-615-53946-1)* 2733 Meade St., Denver, CO 80211-4076 USA
E-mail: kevin.mccaffrey@firstpersonpublishing.com; jeffrey.fugate@navy.mil
Web site: http://www.firstpersonpublishing.com.

Concord Theatricals, *(978-0-573)* 235 Pk. Ave. S., 5th Fl., New York, NY 10003 USA; *Imprints:* French, Samuel, Inc. (SamFrnchUSA); French, Samuel , Ltd. (SamFrnchUK)
Web site: www.concord.com; www.concordtheatricals.com.

Concordia Publishing Hse., *(978-0-570; 978-0-7586)* Subs. of Lutheran Church Missouri Synod, 3558 S. Jefferson Ave., Saint Louis, MO 63118-3968 USA (SAN 202-1781) Tel 314-268-1000; Fax: 314-268-1360; Toll Free Fax: 800-490-9889 (orders only); Toll Free: 800-325-3040 (orders only); 800-325-0191
E-mail: cphorder@cph.org
Web site: http://www.cph.org.

Concordis Publishing, *(978-0-578-41781-3)* 28160 McBean Pkwy. Unit 25201, VALENCIA, CA 91354 USA Tel 310-650-0213
E-mail: concordispublishing@gmail.com
Dist(s): **Ingram Content Group.**

Concourse Pr., *(978-0-911323)* Subs. of East-West Fine Arts Corp., Orders Addr.: 14 Ridgeview Rd., Newtown Sq, PA 19073-3002 USA (SAN 269-249X); Edit Addr.: P.O. Box 8265, Philadelphia, PA 19101 USA
E-mail: site.concoursepress@gmail.com
Web site: http://www.ConcoursePress.com
Dist(s): **Brodart Co.**

Concrete Jungle Pr., *(978-0-9749048; 978-1-945610)* 47-04 168th St., Flushing, NY 11358 USA
E-mail: dw@dwaynedworsky.com
Web site: http://www.dwaynedworsky.com; www.alphacentauriandbeyond.com.

Condor Designs, *(978-0-692-80859-7; 978-0-692-80933-4)* P.O. Box 155, FISH CAMP, CA 93623 USA Tel 559-341-8854
E-mail: mscondor@gmail.com; mscondor@gmail.com.

Conerly, Lawrence, *(978-0-9765669)* 85 Mt. Canaan Rd., Tylertown, MS 39667 USA
E-mail: augsept@bellsouth.net.

Conexion Educativa, *(978-0-9702021)* 900 Alameda St., Villa Granada, San Juan, PR 00923 USA Tel 787-766-4448; Fax: 787-250-8709
E-mail: conexion@coqui.net
Web site: http://home.coqui.net/conexion.

Conflict Games, LLC, *(978-0-9824507; 978-1-7331144)* Orders Addr.: 15 Green Hill Ct., Nanuet, NY 10954 USA Tel 845-689-9014
E-mail: mscott@conflictroleplaying.com
Web site: http://www.conflictbooks.com/.

Cong Bais Tziporah, *(978-0-9728849; 978-0-9767166; 978-1-934098)* 3 Harrison Ave., Spring Valley, NY 10977 USA.

Congregation Agudat Achim, *(978-0-9770172)* 2117 Union St., Schenectady, NY 12309 USA
Web site: http://www.divinekosher.com.

Congregation Kehilas Yaakov (CKY), *(978-0-9770352; 978-0-9847019)* 2 Omni Ct., Lakewood, NJ 08701 USA Tel 732-942-8374.

Congress At Your Fingertips, *(978-1-879617; 978-0-9969346; 978-0-9994368; 978-1-7340022)* Div. of Capitol Advantage, LLC, Orders Addr.: P.O. Box 309, Newington, VA 22122 USA Tel 703-550-9500; Fax: 703-550-0406; Toll Free: 877-827-3321
Web site: http://congressatyourfingertips.com.

Congressional Publishing, Inc., *(978-0-9762916)* P.O. Box 1318, Leesburg, VA 20177 USA Tel 703-777-6737; Fax: 703-777-6272
E-mail: congressionalpub@verizon.net
Web site: http://www.congressionalpublishing.com.

Coniston Designs (AUS) *(978-0-86435) Dist. by* **IPG Chicago.**

Conley, Connie, *(978-0-9800898)* 4555 SW Willow St., Seattle, WA 98136 USA (SAN 855-1731)
E-mail: puppyluck@comcast.net.

Connect With Your Kid Bks., *(978-0-9746094)* 106 Central Park Sq., No.150, Los Alamos, NV 87544 USA Toll Free: 888-388-5437
E-mail: DrSillyScience@comcast.net
Web site: http://www.DrSillyScience.com.

Connected 2 The Father Publishing *See* **Urban Advocacy**

Connecticut Pr., The, *(978-0-9825468; 978-0-9977907)* 36 Wildlife Ct., Cheshire, CT 06410 USA Tel 203-257-6020
E-mail: pjmalia@connecticutpress.com; celestemalia@connecticutpress.com
Web site: http://www.connecticutpress.com
Dist(s): **Ingram Bk. Co.**
Ingram Content Group.

Connection, *(978-0-9743687)* 601 Daniel Ct., Nashville, TN 37221-6512 USA.

Connelly Pr., The, *(978-0-9797415; 978-1-7341309)* 243 Abrahams Ln., Villanova, PA 19085 USA Tel 610-316-1997
Dist(s): **eBookit.com.**

Connexions Unlimited, *(978-1-929785)* 1021 Silver Lake Blvd., Frankfort, KY 40601 USA Tel 502-695-5181.

Connors, E. W. Publishing Co., *(978-0-9635587)* P.O. Box 691, Buffalo, NY 14205-0691 USA Tel 716-851-1343.

Conquistador Pubns., *(978-0-9978732)* 36 Alcira Ct., St. Augustine, FL 32086 USA Tel 904-834-4160
E-mail: kathleen.caulfield@yahoo.com.

Conscience Studio, *(978-0-9828492; 978-1-7356337)* 90 W. Univ. St., Alfred, NY 14802-1134 USA (SAN 859-9203) Tel 607-587-9111
E-mail: ConscienceStudio@gmail.com
Web site: http://www.consciencestudio.com.

Conscious Culture Publishing, *(978-1-7322051)* 450 Leland Ave., San Francisco, CA 94134 USA Tel 415-902-0557
E-mail: marlon@artnomad.com
Web site: https://www.consciousculturepublishing.com/.

Conscious Living Pubns., *(978-1-890580)* Lake St N No. 403, WAYZATA, MN 55391 USA Tel 831-566-4998; 831-247-5155
E-mail: info@leonardjacobson.com
Dist(s): **New Leaf Distributing Co., Inc.**

Consciousness-Based Education Association, *(978-0-9727877)* 1100 Univ. Manor Dr., B-24, Fairfield, IA 52556 USA Tel 641-472-1663; Fax: 641-472-3116; Toll Free: 888-472-1677
E-mail: info@cbeprograms.org
Web site: http://www.cbeprograms.org.

Consejo Estatal Electoral (MEX) *(978-970-58) Dist. by* **Santillana.**

Consilient Pubns., *(978-0-9746242)* 8176 S. Centaur Dr., Evergreen, CO 80439 USA Tel 303-679-1538
E-mail: stephanie@cost-benefit-jr.com
Web site: http://www.cost-benefit-jr.com.

Consortium Bk. Sales & Distribution, Div. of Ingram Content Group, Orders Addr.: 1094 Flex Dr., Jackson, TN 38301-5070 USA; Edit Addr.: 34 13th Ave NE, Suite 100, Minneapolis, MN 55413-1007 USA (SAN 200-6049) Toll Free: 800-283-3572 (orders)
E-mail: info@cbsd.com
Web site: http://www.cbsd.com/
Dist(s): **Follett School Solutions.**

Consortium Publishing Co., *(978-0-9644681; 978-0-9707173; 978-0-9748830; 978-1-7320567)* Div. of Creative Ideas, Inc., Orders Addr.: P.O. Box 998, Jacksonville, IL 62651 USA; Edit Addr.: P.O. Box 1535, Jacksonville, IL 62651-1535 USA Tel 217-243-7628 (phone/fax); Toll Free: 800-419-8698; 888-456-7235; 4 Sunnydale Ave., Jacksonville, IL 62650
E-mail: consortm@aol.com
Web site: http://www.creativeideas.com.

Consortium, The *See* **Consortium Publishing Co.**

Constitutional Rights Foundation *Imprint of* **Constitutional Rights Foundation**

Constitutional Rights Foundation, *(978-1-886253)* 601 S. Kingsley Dr., Los Angeles, CA 90005 USA (SAN 225-6401) Tel 213-487-5590; Fax: 213-386-0459; Toll Free: 800-488-4273; *Imprints:* Constitutional Rights Foundation (MYID_C_CONSTIT) Do not confuse with Constitutional Rights Foundation Chicago in Chicago, IL
E-mail: crf@crf.usa
Web site: http://www.crf-usa.org.

Consultant's Unlimited *See* **Schwarz Pauper Pr.**

Consumer Pr., The, *(978-0-9717119)* 6 Berkley Rd., Glenville, NY 12302 USA (SAN 254-5446)
E-mail: richesq@mindspring.com
Web site: http://www.theconsumerpress.com.

†Consumer Reports Bks., *(978-0-89043)* Div. of Consumers Union of U. S., Inc., 101 Truman Ave., Yonkers, NY 10703 USA (SAN 224-1048) Tel 914-378-2000; Fax: 914-378-2925; Toll Free: 800-500-9760 (book dept.)
Web site: http://www.consumerreports.org/
Dist(s): **Ingram Publisher Services**; *CIP.*

Consumers Union of U. S., Inc., *(978-0-89043; 978-0-9755388; 978-1-933524)* Orders Addr.: 540 Barnum Ave., Bridgeport, CT 06608 USA (SAN 661-9800); Edit Addr.: 101 Truman Ave., Yonkers, NY 10703 USA (SAN 269-3518) Tel 914-378-2000; Fax: 914-378-2925
Web site: http://ConsumersReports.org
Dist(s): **Ingram Publisher Services**
Macmillan.

Contemplation Corner Pr., *(978-0-9707979; 978-0-9758748)* 1229 Randy Rd., Ashland City, TN 37015 USA Tel 615-746-8220; Fax: 615-746-3697
E-mail: ccpress1@bellsouth.net
Web site: http://www.contemplationcornerpress.com.

Contemporary Fiction *Imprint of* **Noel, Jaren**

Context Productions, *(978-0-578-42159-9; 978-1-7329913; 978-1-7345055; 978-1-7351151)* 1 Eastwood Dr., East Windsor, NJ 08520 USA Tel 609-578-8202
E-mail: kristie@contextproductions.com
Dist(s): **Independent Pubs. Group**
Ingram Content Group.

Continental Bk. Co., Inc., *(978-0-9626800)* Eastern Div., 80-00 Cooper Ave., Bldg. No. 29, Glendale, NY 11385 USA (SAN 169-5436) Tel 718-326-0560; Fax: 718-326-4276; Toll Free: 800-364-0350; Western Div., 625 E. 70th Ave., No. 5, Denver, CO 80229 (SAN 630-2882) Tel 303-289-1761; Fax: 303-289-1764
E-mail: hola@continentalbook.com; esl@continentalbook.com; bonjour@continentalbook.com; tag@continentalbook.com
Web site: http://www.continentalbook.com
Dist(s): **Follett School Solutions.**

Continental Enterprises Group, Inc. (CEG), Orders Addr.: 108 Red Row St., Easley, SC 29640-2820 USA (SAN 631-0915)
E-mail: ContactUs@centerprisesgrp.com.

Continental Pr., Inc., *(978-0-8454; 978-1-5240)* Orders Addr.: 520 E. Bainbridge St., Elizabethtown, PA 17022 USA (SAN 202-182X) Tel 717-367-1836; Fax: 717-367-5660; Toll Free: 800-233-0759; *Imprints:* Seedling Publications (Seedlg Pubns)
E-mail: educationsales@continentalpress.com
Web site: http://www.continentalpress.com.

Continental Sales, Inc.,; *Imprints:* New in Chess (New Chess); Raven Tree Press,Csi (RAVEN TREE PRE); New In Chess,Csi (NEW IN CHESS,C)
Dist(s): **National Bk. Network.**

Continuum *Imprint of* **Bloomsbury Academic & Professional**

Contmedia Inc,

Conundrum Pr. (CAN) *(978-0-9685161; 978-0-9680364; 978-0-9689496; 978-1-894994; 978-1-77262) Dist. by* **Consort Bk Sales.**

Convergent Bks. *Imprint of* **Crown Publishing Group, The**

CONVERPAGE, *(978-0-9728155; 978-0-9815720; 978-0-9820733; 978-0-9825854; 978-0-9835784; 978-0-9851721; 978-0-9858282; 978-0-615-84393-3; 978-0-9910923)* 23 Acorn St., Scituate, MA 02066-3324 USA
E-mail: pmccallum@comcast.net
Web site: www.converpage.com.

Conversations for Action and Listening Pubn., *(978-0-692-43550-2; 978-0-9977110)* 95 Westminster Dr., Oakland , CA 94618 USA Tel 5102203334
Dist(s): **CreateSpace Independent Publishing Platform.**

Conway, Kathleen R., *(978-0-9897763; 978-0-9973737)* 5 Camelot Ln., Bourne, MA 02532 USA Tel 508-415-1295
E-mail: capecodscribe@yahoo.com
Web site: http://www.capecodscribe.com; https://wickedwhalepublishing.wordpress.com
Dist(s): **BookBaby**
Cape Cod Scribe.

Cook, Cheryl *See* **Heavenly C. Publishing**

Cook Communication, *(978-0-9726996)* Orders Addr.: 6086 Dunes Dr., Sanford, NC 27332 USA Tel 312-859-8090; 919-498-6421; Fax: 866-652-8493
E-mail: cookcomm@gte.net; cookcomm@ameritech.net
Web site: http://www.author-me.com; http://www.reservebooks.com.

Cook, David, *(978-0-9741629)* P.O. Box 657, Albemarle, NC 28001 USA Do not confuse with companies with the same name in Chapel Hill, NC, Boerne, TX
E-mail: info@dac-and.com
Web site: http://www.dac-and.com.

Cook, David C., *(978-0-7814; 978-0-88207; 978-0-89191; 978-0-89693; 978-0-912692; 978-1-55513; 978-1-56476; 978-1-4347)* 4050 Lee Vance View, Colorado Springs, CO 80918 USA (SAN 206-0981) Tel 719-536-0100; Fax: 719-536-3244; Toll Free: 800-708-5550; 800-323-7543 (Customer Service)
E-mail: wendi.lord@davidccook.com
Web site: http://www.davidccook.com
Dist(s): **Follett School Solutions.**

Cook, David C. Publishing Company *See* **Cook, David C.**

Cook, Jahde, *(978-0-9991510)* 973 E. Well Springs Rd., Midvale, UT 84047 USA Tel 801-628-9226
E-mail: jahdeofelia@gmail.com
Web site: www.jahdethewriter.com.

Cook, Ken Co., *(978-0-9652491)* 2855 S Calhoun Rd, New Berlin, WI 53151 USA Tel 414-466-6060; Fax: 414-466-0840
E-mail: nics@kencook.com
Web site: http://www.kencook.com.

Cookbook Resources, LLC, *(978-0-9677932; 978-1-931294; 978-1-59769)* 541 Doubletree Dr., Highland Village, TX 75077 USA (SAN 253-5262) Tel

972-317-0245; Fax: 972-317-6404; Toll Free: 866-229-2665
E-mail: lauren@cookbookresources.com
Web site: http://www.cookbookresourses.com
Dist(s): **Bk. Marketing Plus.**

Cookie Bear Pr., Inc., (*978-0-9701155*) Orders Addr.: P.O. Box 5074, Buffalo Grove, IL 60089 USA (SAN 253-6579) Tel 847-955-0001; 847-478-9202; Fax: 847-955-0002; Edit Addr.: 205 Thompson Blvd., Buffalo Grove, IL 60089 USA
E-mail: info@cookiebearpress.com
Web site: http://www.cookiebearpress.com
Dist(s): **Distributors, The.**

Cookie Jar, (*978-1-933799; 978-1-60095*) Cookie Jar Entertainment, Inc., P.O. Box 35665, Greensboro, NC 27425 USA Fax: 336-808-3249; Toll Free: 800-321-0903; *Imprints:* Doodlebops (Doodlebops)
Web site: http://www.cinar.com/EN/
Dist(s): **Carson-Dellosa Publishing, LLC.**

Cookie O'Gorman, (*978-0-9978174*) 105 Carver Ct., Warner Robins, GA 31088 USA Tel 478-218-0166
E-mail: aireeahna@cox.net.

Cool Kids Create, (*978-0-9797297*) 48 Beach 217 St., Breezy Point, NY 11697 USA
Web site: http://www.coolkidscreate.com
Dist(s): **BCH Fulfillment & Distribution.**

Cool, Kim @ Historic Venice Pr., (*978-0-9721655*) 312 Shore Rd., Venice, FL 34285 USA
Web site: http://www.historicvenicepress.com
Dist(s): **American Wholesale Bk. Co.**
Bk. Warehouse
Southern Bk. Service.

Cool Springs Pr. *Imprint of* **Quarto Publishing Group USA**

Cool Things Pr., (*978-0-615-20795-7; 978-0-615-20796-4; 978-0-615-78176-1; 978-0-692-45762-7*) P.O. Box 3852, Concord, NH 03302-3952 USA Tel 6037157852
Dist(s): **CreateSpace Independent Publishing Platform**
Lulu Pr., Inc.

Coolbular Inc, (*978-0-578-15459-6; 978-0-9980946*) PO Box 1764, Evergreen, CO 80439 USA
E-mail: author.adir.rondack@gmail.com
Web site: http://to-kill-a-predator.com/.

Coolidge Corner Pr., (*978-1-7338376*) 28 Oak Sq. Ave., Boston, MA 02135 USA Tel 857-264-0674
E-mail: editor@coolidge-corner-press.com.

Coolmath.com, Inc., (*978-0-9791628*) P.O. Box 4386, Costa Mesa, CA 92628-4386 USA
Web site: http://Coolmath.com.

CoolSpeak Publishing Co., (*978-0-615-75939-5; 978-0-615-76596-9; 978-0-615-83196-1; 978-0-615-96867-4; 978-0-692-23542-3; 978-0-692-42448-3; 978-0-692-48950-5; 978-0-692-52130-4; 978-0-692-52792-4; 978-0-692-72682-2; 978-0-692-76203-5; 978-0-692-77684-1; 978-0-692-87782-1; 978-0-692-05795-7; 978-0-692-18688-6; 978-0-578-52470-2; 978-0-578-61637-7; 978-0-578-73290-9*) *148 Stone Hill Dr., Pottstown, PA 19464 USA Tel 888-300-1880; Fax: 888-300-1860*
E-mail: info@coolspeak.net
Dist(s): **CreateSpace Independent Publishing Platform.**

Coon, Kathy, (*978-0-9741300*) P.O. Box 14267, Baton Rouge, LA 70898 USA
Web site: http://www.dogintelligencetest.com.

Cooper, Gene, (*978-0-615-85312-3*) 6 Peter Cooper Rd. Apt. 3C, New York, NY 10010 USA Tel 212-228-5083
E-mail: cooper.gene82@gmail.com.

Cooper Publishing, (*978-1-59655*) Orders Addr.: P.O. Box 1974, Englewood, FL 34295 USA Tel 941-587-0396
E-mail: cooper.publishing@yahoo.com.

Cooper, Robbi, (*978-0-9749643*) 9 Scott Crescent, Austin, TX 78703 USA
Web site: http://www.everythingfromthegarden.com.

Cooper Square Publishing Llc,
Dist(s): **National Bk. Network**
Rowman & Littlefield Publishers, Inc.

Cooperative Kids, (*978-0-9821121*) P.O. Box 432, Enfield, CT 06083-0432 USA (SAN 857-2917) Tel 860-265-2272
E-mail: info@cooperativekids.com
Web site: http://www.cooperativekids.com.

Cooperfly Books *See* **Cooperfly Creative Arts, Inc.**

Cooperfly Creative Arts, Inc., (*978-0-9669504; 978-0-9970476*) 3184 Plainfield NE PMB 248, Grand Rapids, MI 49525 USA Tel 616-364-5870
E-mail: kevin@tomatocollection.com
Web site: http://www.tomatocollection.com
Dist(s): **Indig, Stanley M. Specialty Pubn.**

Cooper's Pack, (*978-0-9794882*) Div. of Cooper's Pack Publishing, Orders Addr.: 1900 W. Nickerson St., Suite 116-130, Seattle, WA 98119 USA (SAN 853-5825) Tel 206-235-1886 Toll Free: 877-278-3278
E-mail: brandon@cooperspack.com
Web site: http://www.CoopersPack.com.

Copano Bay Pr., (*978-0-9767799; 978-0-9822467; 978-0-9829828; 978-0-9847372; 978-0-9884357; 978-1-941324*) Orders Addr.: P.O. Box 1992, Fulton, TX 78358-1992 USA Tel 361-776-1836; P.O. Box 1992, Fulton, TX 78358
E-mail: orders@booksontexas.com
Web site: http://www.booksontexas.com.

Copeland, Kenneth Pubns., (*978-0-88114; 978-0-938458; 978-1-57562; 978-1-60463*) Subs. of Eagle Mountain International Church, Kenneth Copeland Ministries, Fort Worth, TX 76192 USA Tel 817-252-2700; Toll Free: 800-600-7395
E-mail: mjohnson@kcm.org
Web site: http://www.kcm.org.contact.html
Dist(s): **Anchor Distributors**
Appalachian Bible Co.
Central South Christian Distribution
Harrison House Pubs.
New Day Christian Distributors Gifts, Inc.
Spring Arbor Distributors, Inc.

Copernicus Pr., (*978-0-9741638*) 933 Dwyer Ave., Saint Louis, MO 63122 USA Tel 314-822-8597 Do not confuse with Copernicus Pr. in Atlanta, GA
E-mail: nikolom@slu.edu
Web site: http://www.Copernicuspress.com
Dist(s): **Unique Bks., Inc.**

Copley Custom Textbooks, (*978-0-87411; 978-1-58152; 978-1-58390*) Div. of XanEdu Publishing Inc., 530 Great Rd., Acton, MA 01720 USA (SAN 687-4959) Tel 978-263-9090; Fax: 978-263-9190; Toll Free: 800-562-2147; *Imprints:* Copley Publishing Group (Copley Pub Grp)
E-mail: textbook@copleypublishing.com; publish@copleycustom.com
Web site: http://www.xanedu.com.

Copley Publishing Group *See* **Copley Custom Textbooks**

Copley Publishing Group *Imprint of* **Copley Custom Textbooks**

Coppenrath, F. Verlag KG (DEU) (*978-3-88547; 978-3-920192; 978-3-8157*) *Dist. by* **Distribks Inc.**

Copper Moon Press *See* **TangleTown Media Inc.**

Copyright Office *Imprint of* **United States Government Printing Office**

Coram Deo Pr., (*978-0-9769054*) One Nelson Pkwy., 2400 FM 407, Highland Village, TX 75077 USA Tel 972-318-5222; Fax: 972-692-5140
E-mail: press@coramdeoacademy.org
Web site: http://www.coramdeopress.com.

Corbett Features, (*978-0-9762294*) Div. of Corbett Features, 100 Cummings Ctr. Suite 432-a, Beverly, MA 01915 USA Tel 978-232-1124; Fax: 978-232-1124; *Imprints:* Griffin Comics (Griffin Comics)
E-mail: cdesign.ma.ultranet@rcn.com
Web site: http://www.corbettfeatures.com.

Corbus Systems, (*978-0-9742347*) 20368 Forestwood, Southfield, MI 48076 USA Tel 248-356-9427
E-mail: info@corbus-systems.com
Web site: http://www.corbus-systems.com.

Corby Books, (*978-0-9776458; 978-0-9819605; 978-0-9827846; 978-0-9833586; 978-0-9859377; 978-0-9890731; 978-0-9912451; 978-0-9961362; 978-1-7321150; 978-1-7352702*) 51760 Whitestable Ln, South Bend, IN 46637 USA
E-mail: prestonward1@aol.com; jimtach@aol.com.

CORD Communications, (*978-1-55502; 978-1-57837*) Subs. of Ctr. for Occupational Research & Development, Orders Addr.: P.O. Box 21206, Waco, TX 76702-1206 USA Tel 254-776-1822; Fax: 254-776-3906; Toll Free: 800-231-3015; Edit Addr.: 324 Kelly Dr., Waco, TX 76710 USA
E-mail: webmaster@cord.org
Web site: http://www.cord.org/index.cfm.

Cordon Pubns., (*978-0-9822083; 978-0-9826984; 978-0-615-39009-3; 978-0-9829049; 978-0-9834908; 978-0-9839858; 978-1-937912*) 5161 Great Lakes Dr. So., Evansville, IN 47715 USA (SAN 857-5460) Tel 812-303-9070
E-mail: coraseaman@hotmail.com
Web site: http://www.Cordon Publications.com.

Cordoves, Barbara & Gladys M., (*978-0-9637252*) 2800 SW 106th Ave., Miami, FL 33165-2748 USA.

Core Knowledge Foundation, (*978-1-890517; 978-1-933486; 978-1-68380*) Orders Addr.: 801 E. High St., Charlottesville, VA 22902 USA Tel 434-977-7550; Fax: 434-977-0021; Toll Free: 800-238-3233
E-mail: mjones@coreknowledge.org; coreknow@coreknowledge.org
Web site: http://www.coreknowledge.org.

Core Library *Imprint of* **ABDO Publishing Co.**

Core Publishing & Consulting, Inc., (*978-1-933079*) 13016 Bee St., Suite 208, Dallas, TX 75234 USA (SAN 256-1514) Tel 214-926-4742; Fax: 972-243-5854
E-mail: stan.peterson@sbcglobal.net
Web site: www.core-publishing.com.

Corelink Solution, The, (*978-0-578-40812-5; 978-0-578-44515-1; 978-1-7336346*) 2207 Concord Pike, Wilmington, DE 19803 USA Tel 610-505-6043
E-mail: jamesrosseau@thecorelinksolution.com
Web site: www.thecorelinksolution.com.

CoreyJF Publishing, (*978-0-9895101*) 12299 Greenleaf Ave., Potomac, MD 20854 USA Tel 301-564-3058
E-mail: corey@coreyjf.com
Web site: http://www.coreyjf.com; www.egrettheelephant.com.

Corgi Tales Publishing, (*978-0-615-26492-9*) 57715 Hwy. 58, McKittrick, CA 93251 USA
Dist(s): **Lulu Pr., Inc.**

Corimbo, Editorial S.L. (ESP) (*978-84-8470; 978-84-95150*) *Dist. by* **Mariuccia Iaconi Bk Imports.**

Corimbo, Editorial S.L. (ESP) (*978-84-8470; 978-84-95150*) *Dist. by* **Distribks Inc.**

Corimbo, Editorial S.L. (ESP) (*978-84-8470; 978-84-95150*) *Dist. by* **Lectorum Pubns.**

Cork Hill Pr., (*978-1-59408*) P.O. Box 117, Carmel, IN 46082-0117 USA
Web site: http://www.corkhillpress.com
Dist(s): **CreateSpace Independent Publishing Platform.**

Corman Productions, (*978-0-9655749*) 6729 Dume Dr., Malibu, CA 90265 USA Tel 310-457-7524; Fax: 310-457-5941
E-mail: Dikkybird@aol.com.

Cormier, Shawn *See* **Pine View Pr.**

Cormorant Bks. Inc. (CAN) (*978-0-920953; 978-1-896951; 978-1-897151; 978-1-77086*) *Dist. by* **Orca Bk Pub.**

Corn Crib Publishing, (*978-0-9907688; 978-1-7353663*) 18988 Point Lookout Rd., Lexington Park, MD 20653 USA Tel 301-862-3421
E-mail: Christina@CornCribStudio.com
Web site: corncribstudio.com.

Corn, Richard LLC, (*978-0-9985849*) 8 Colonial Ct., New Canaan, CT 06840 USA Tel 203-561-0865
E-mail: mathtutorct@yahoo.com.

Corn Tassel Pr., (*978-0-9752597*) 9655 Corn Tassel Ct., Columbia, MD 21046 USA Fax: 301-776-6538.

Cornell, A.J. Pubns., (*978-0-9727439; 978-0-9850501*) 18-74 Corporal Kennedy St., Bayside, NY 11360 USA Tel 718-423-4082.

Cornell Lab Publishing Group, The *Imprint of* **WunderMill, Inc.**

Cornell Maritime Pr./Tidewater Pubs. *Imprint of* **Schiffer Publishing, Ltd.**

†Cornell Univ. Pr., (*978-0-8014; 978-0-87546; 978-1-5017*) Orders Addr.: P.O. Box 6525, Ithaca, NY 14851 USA (SAN 281-5680) Tel 607-277-2211; Toll Free Fax: 800-688-2877; Toll Free: 800-666-2211; Edit Addr.: Sage House, 512 E. State St., Ithaca, NY 14851 USA (SAN 202-1862) Tel 607-277-2338; *Imprints:* Comstock Publishing Associates (Comstock Pub); Northern Illinois University Press (NorthIUPr)
E-mail: cupressinfo@cornell.edu; orders@nbninternational.com; cupress-sales@cornell.edu
Web site: http://www.cornellpress.cornell.edu
Dist(s): **CUP Services**
Casemate Academic
De Gruyter, Inc.
Follett School Solutions
Hachette Bk. Group
Longleaf Services
MyiLibrary
Oxford Univ. Pr., Inc.
ebrary, Inc.; *CIP.*

Corner Publishing Group, (*978-0-692-92074-9; 978-0-692-92076-3; 978-0-9993730*) PO Box 1518, Dawsonville, GA 30534 USA Tel 770-815-9494
E-mail: corey.parson@cornerpublishinggroup.com
Web site: cornerpublishinggroup.com.

Corner To Learn Ltd. (GBR) (*978-0-9545353; 978-1-905434; 978-1-908702*) *Dist. by* **Parkwest Pubns.**

Cornerstone Bk. Publishers *Imprint of* **Cornerstone Bk. Pubs.**

Cornerstone Bk. Pubs., (*978-1-887560; 978-1-934935; 978-1-61342*) Orders Addr.: P.O. Box 24652, New Orleans, LA 70184 USA; *Imprints:* Cornerstone Book Publishers (Cstone Bk Pubs)
E-mail: 1cornerstonebooks@gmail.com
Web site: http://www.cornerstonepublishers.com.

Cornerstone Family Ministries/Lamplighter Publishing, (*978-1-58474*) Orders Addr.: P.O. Box 777, Waverly, PA 18471 USA Tel 717-585-1314; Fax: 717-587-4246; Toll Free: 888-246-7735; Edit Addr.: Waverly Community Ctr., Main St., S. Wing, 2nd Flr., Waverly, PA 18471 USA
E-mail: cfm@epix.net
Web site: http://www.agospel.com
Dist(s): **Follett School Solutions.**

Cornerstone Pr., (*978-0-9668488; 978-0-9774802; 978-0-9846739; 978-1-7333086*) c/o Univ. of Wisconsin, Dept. of English, 325 Collins Classroom Center, Univ. of Wisconsin-Stevens Point 1801 Fourth Ave, Stevens Point, WI 54481-3897 USA Tel 715-346-4532; Fax: 715-346-2849 Do not confuse with companies with the same name in Kents Hill, ME, Arnold, MO
E-mail: ross.tangedal@uwsp.edu.

Cornerstone Pr., (*978-0-918476*) 1825 Bender Ln., Arnold, MO 63010-0388 USA (SAN 210-0584) Tel 636-296-9662 Do not confuse with companies with the same name in Edison, NJ, Kents Hill, ME, Pearland, TX, Stevens Point, WI
E-mail: anthsum@sbcglobal.net.

Cornerstone Pr. Chicago, (*978-0-940895*) 939 W. Willson, Chicago, IL 60640 USA (SAN 664-7200) Tel 773-561-2450; 773-989-4920; Fax: 773-989-2076; Toll Free: 888-407-7377
E-mail: cspress@jpusa.org
Web site: http://www.cornerstonepress.com.

Cornerstone Publishing, Inc., (*978-1-882185*) Orders Addr.: P.O. Box 23015, Evansville, IN 47724 USA (SAN 298-735X) Tel 812-470-3971 Do not confuse with companies with the same name in Decatur, GA, Altamonte Springs, FL, Wichita, KS
E-mail: cornerstonepublishinghouse@gmail.com
Web site: http://www.cornerstonepublishinghouse.com
Dist(s): **Book Clearing Hse.**
Ingram Content Group.

Cornerstonia, (*978-0-9828588*) 9457 Venezia Plantation Dr., Orlando, FL 32829 USA Tel 407-222-4287
E-mail: author@cornerstonia.com
Web site: http://www.cornerstonia.com.

CornerWind Media, L.L.C., (*978-0-9741072*) Orders Addr.: 2635 Whitehall Ct., Rock Hill, SC 29732 USA Tel 803-329-7140; Fax: 803-329-7145
Web site: http://www.twiggyleaf.com; http://www.cornerwind.com.

Corning Museum of Glass, (*978-0-87290*) One Museum Way, Corning, NY 14830 USA (SAN 202-1897) Fax: 607-974-7365; Toll Free: 800-732-6845
E-mail: cmg@cmog.org; pr@cmog.org
Web site: http://www.cmog.org
Dist(s): **Associated Univ. Presses**
Casemate Academic
Hudson Hills Pr. LLC
National Bk. Network.

Cornsilk Pr., (*978-0-9989337*) 5020 Dory Way, Fair Oaks, CA 95628 USA Tel 916-342-2390
E-mail: ssnavarro22@gmail.com.

Corolishine Bks., (*978-0-692-05498-7; 978-0-692-08080-1*) P.O. Box 394, Forest Knolls, CA 94933 USA Tel 415-419-9390
E-mail: marlenemar1@yahoo.com
Web site: www.marlenesusan.com.

Corona Pr., (*978-1-891619*) 4535 Palmer Ct., Niwot, CO 80503 USA Tel 303-247-1455; Fax: 303-417-0355; Toll Free: 888-648-3877 Do not confuse with Corona Pr., Brooklandville, MD
E-mail: coronapress@aol.com.

Coronet Bks., (*978-0-89563*) 33 Ashley Dr., Schwenksville, PA 19473 USA (SAN 210-6043) Tel 484-919-6486; Fax: 215-717-4655 Do not confuse with Coronet Bks. & Pubns., Eagle Point, OR
E-mail: ronsmolin@earthlink.net; order@coronetbooks.com
Web site: http://www.coronetbooks.com
Dist(s): **ISD**
MyiLibrary.

Corpus Communications *See* **Caritas Communications**

Corraini (ITA) (*978-88-86250; 978-88-87942; 978-88-7570*) *Dist. by* **Dist Art Pubs.**

Corroluna Pr., (*978-0-9986661*) 904 Queenstown Rd., Lancaster, VA 22503 USA Tel 804-387-3653; Fax: 804-387-3653
E-mail: mjbeswickart@gmail.com
Web site: maryjobeswick.com.

Corrugated Sky, LLC, (*978-0-9982605; 978-1-950903*) 11215 Kings Hwy., Montross, VA 22520 USA
E-mail: publisher@corrugatedsky.com
Web site: http://www.corrugatedsky.com.

Cortright Fellowship Pr., (*978-0-9706684*) P.O. Box 434, Allegan, MI 49010 USA
E-mail: ekklesia@accn.org
Web site: http://www.redbay.com/ekklesia.

Corunda, Ediciones, S.A. de C.V. (MEX) (*978-968-6044; 978-968-7444*) *Dist. by* **AIMS Intl.**

Corwin Pr., (*978-0-7619; 978-0-8039; 978-1-57517; 978-1-879179; 978-1-4129*) Affil. of Sage Pubns., Inc., 2455 Teller Rd., Thousand Oaks, CA 91320-2218 USA Tel 805-499-9734; 805-499-9774 (customer service); Fax: 805-499-0871; 805-499-5323
E-mail: info@sagepub.com
Web site: http://www.corwinpress.com
Dist(s): **Follett School Solutions**
MyiLibrary
SAGE Pubns., Inc.
ebrary, Inc.

Corwin Press, Incorporated *See* **Corwin Pr.**

Coryell, Skip *See* **White Feather Press, LLC**

Coscia, Alexandra, (*978-1-7335291*) 138 Thornbury Rd. E., Scarsdale, NY 10583 USA Tel 248-835-6617
E-mail: alexandratracey@gmail.com.

Cosimo Classics *Imprint of* **Cosimo, Inc.**

Cosimo, Inc., (*978-1-59605; 978-1-60206; 978-1-60520; 978-1-61640; 978-1-944529; 978-1-945934; 978-1-64679*) 116 W. 23rd Street, 5th Fl, New York, NY 10011-1818 USA Tel 212-989-3616; Fax: 212-989-3662; *Imprints:* Cosimo Classics (CosClassics)
E-mail: adake@cosimobooks.com; info@cosimobooks.com
Web site: http://www.cosimobooks.com
Dist(s): **Follett School Solutions**
INscribe Digital
Independent Pubs. Group.

COSMIC EDITIONS , LLC, (*978-0-9967223*) P.O. Box 348491, Miami, FL 33234 USA Tel 305-951-6571
E-mail: cosmiceditions@gmail.com
Web site: WWW.COSMICEDITIONS.COM.

Cosmic Gargoyle Creative Solutions, (*978-0-9835843*) 3883 Turtle Creek Blvd. No. 1202, Dallas, TX 75219 USA Tel 214-679-4725; *Imprints:* Lonely Swan Books (Lonely Swan)
E-mail: cosmicgargoyle@gmail.com
Dist(s): **Smashwords.**

Cosmic Media Group, The *See* **COSMIC EDITIONS , LLC**

COSMIC VORTEX, (*978-0-9719580*) Div. of TETRA XII Inc., Orders Addr.: P.O. Box 322, Paia, HI 96779 USA
E-mail: atlantis@archaeologist.com; aloha@mauivortex.com
Web site: http://www.atlantistoday.com; http://atlantis-motherland.com.

Cosmographia Pubns., (*978-0-615-60710-8*) 6 1/2 W. 3rd St., Spencer, IA 51301 USA Tel 712-580-3271
E-mail: hnewgard@gmail.com.

Cosmos Books *See* **Prime**

Cosmos Publishing, (*978-0-9660449; 978-1-932455*) 262 River Vale Rd., River Vale, NJ 07675 USA (SAN 631-0486) Tel 201-664-3494; Fax: 201-664-3402 Do not confuse with companies with the same in Bellevue, WA, Saint Louis, MO
E-mail: info@greeceinprint.com
Web site: http://www.greeceinprint.com.

Cosmos Publishing Company, Incorporated *See* **Cosmos Publishing**

Costa, Adriane Photography, (*978-1-7323726*) 54 Mustang Ct., DANVILLE, CA 94526 USA Tel 925-768-5001
E-mail: adriane.e.costa@gmail.com
Dist(s): **Ingram Content Group.**

Costello, Katelyn, (*978-0-578-40352-6*) 1260 Lehigh Sta. Rd. Apt. 705, Henrietta, NY 14467 USA Tel 585-397-4347
E-mail: scripturient101@gmail.com
Dist(s): **Ingram Content Group.**

Costley, Jennifer, (*978-0-692-18888-0*) 607 S. Main St., Pendleton, OR 97801 USA Tel 541-248-0672
E-mail: author@mflorson.com
Dist(s): **Ingram Content Group.**

Publisher Name Index

Costume & Fashion Pr. *Imprint of* **Quite Specific Media Group, Ltd.**

Cosulich, Charlotte, *(978-0-692-18860-6)* 306 E. Ranch Rd., Sacramento, CA 95825 USA Tel 916-485-3915
E-mail: charlotte11@comcast.net.

Cote Literary Group, The, *(978-1-929175)* 483 Old Carolina Ct., Mount Pleasant, SC 29464 USA (SAN 850-4881) Tel 843-881-6080; Fax: 843-278-8456
E-mail: editor@corinthianbooks.com; dickcote@earthlink.net
Web site: http://www.corinthianbooks.com
Dist(s): **Brodart Co.**
Follett School Solutions
Quality Bks., Inc.
eBookit.com.

Coteau Bks. (CAN) *(978-0-919926; 978-1-55050; 978-0-9780316) Dist. by* **Orca Bk Pub.**

Cotler, Joanna Books *Imprint of* **HarperCollins Pubs.**

Cotsen Occasional Pr., *(978-0-9666084; 978-0-9745168; 978-0-9971510)* Div. of Cotsen Family Foundation, 12100 Wilshire Blvd. Suite 905, Los Angeles, CA 90025 USA Tel 310-826-9113
E-mail: jolie@cotsenfamilyoffice.com
Web site: http://www.hesdegraaf.com/hes/.

Cottage Door Pr., *(978-1-68052; 978-1-64638)* 218 James St., Barrington, IL 60010 USA (SAN 990-1051) Tel 224-228-6000; *Imprints:* Parragon Books (Parragon Bks)
E-mail: kfinnamore@cottagedoorpress.com; contactus@cottagedoorpress.com; ksholly@cottagedoorpress.com
Web site: http://www.cottagedoorpress.com.

cottage in the woods Pr., *(978-0-9971552)* 3917 Lyman Rd, oakland, CA 94602 USA Tel 510-316-7182
E-mail: yosgurl@yahoo.com.

Cotton Candy Pr. *Imprint of* **Unveiled Media, LLC**

Cotton, Karen O., *(978-0-692-25813-2; 978-0-692-27344-9; 978-0-692-85154-8; 978-0-692-04453-7; 978-0-578-40033-4)* 5006 Foxen Ct., Cheyenne, WY 82001 USA Tel 307-214-0277
E-mail: cotton.karen@gmail.com
Web site: karencotton.net.

Cottonwood Graphics, Incorporated *See* **Cottonwood Publishing, Inc.**

Cottonwood Pr., Inc., *(978-1-877673; 978-1-936162)* 109-B Cameron Dr., Fort Collins, CO 80525 USA Tel 970-204-0715; Fax: 970-204-0761; Toll Free: 800-864-4297 Do not confuse with companies with same name in Novato, CA, Lawrence, KS, Wilsonville, OR
E-mail: cottonwood@cottonwoodpress.com
Web site: http://www.cottonwoodpress.com
Dist(s): **ebrary, Inc.**

CottonWood Publishing Co., *(978-0-9766804)* 840 W. Washington St., Ann Arbor, MI 48103 USA Do not confuse with Cottonwood Publishing Company in Saint George, UT Helena MT.

Cottonwood Publishing, Inc., *(978-0-9626999; 978-1-886370)* 296 Willowbrook Dr., Helena, MT 59602-7764 USA Toll Free: 800-937-6343 Do not confuse with Cottonwood Publishing in Saint George, UT Ann Arbor MI
E-mail: oldmt@mt.net
Web site: http://www.oldmontana.com
Dist(s): **CreateSpace Independent Publishing Platform**
Mountain Pr. Publishing Co., Inc.

Coulee Region Pubns., Inc., *(978-0-9650629)* 307 Twin Oak Dr., Altoona, WI 54720-1383 USA.

Counce, Paula, *(978-0-9762776)* 1628 Bob O Link Dr., Venice, FL 34293 USA
Web site: http://www.ajourneyremembered.com.

†Council for Agricultural Science & Technology (CAST), *(978-1-887383)* 4420 W. Lincoln Way, Ames, IA 50014-3347 USA (SAN 225-7416) Tel 515-292-2125; Fax: 515-292-4512; Toll Free Fax: 800-375-2278; Toll Free: 800-762-4232
E-mail: cast@cast-science.org
Web site: http://www.cast-science.org; *CIP.*

Council for Indian Education, *(978-0-89992)* Orders Addr.: 1240 Burlington Ave., Billings, MT 59102-4224 USA Tel 406-248-3465; Fax: 406-248-1297
E-mail: cie@cie-mt.org
Web site: http://www.cie-mt.org
Dist(s): **Follett School Solutions.**

Council Oak Bks., *(978-0-933031; 978-1-57178)* Orders Addr.: 2822 Van Ness Ave., San Francisco, CA 94109 USA (SAN 689-5522) Tel 415-931-7700; Fax: 415-931-9911; Toll Free: 800-247-8850 (orders only)
E-mail: order@counciloakbooks.com; publicity@counciloakbooks.com
Web site: http://www.counciloakbooks.com
Dist(s): **Independent Pubs. Group**
New Leaf Distributing Co., Inc.
Univ. of Oklahoma Pr.

Count On Learning, *(978-0-9771472)* 1406 Arlington Ave., Baton Rouge, LA 70808 USA
E-mail: admin@countonlearning.com
Web site: http://www.countonlearning.com.

Counterbalance Bks., *(978-0-9774906; 978-0-9799592; 978-0-9989923)* P.O. Box 876, Duvall, WA 98019-0876 USA
E-mail: admin@counterbalancebooks.com; publisher@counterbalancebooks.com
Web site: http://www.counterbalancebooks.com.

Counterpath Pr., *(978-1-933996)* P.O. Box 18351, Denver, CO 80218 USA
E-mail: tr@counterpathpress.org
Web site: http://www.counterpathpress.org
Dist(s): **SPD-Small Pr. Distribution.**

Counterpoint *Imprint of* **Counterpoint Pr.**

Counterpoint LLC *See* **Counterpoint Pr.**

Counterpoint Pr., *(978-1-58243; 978-1-887178; 978-1-59376; 978-1-61902; 978-1-944869; 978-1-64009; 978-1-949017)* 2560 Ninth St., Suite 318, Berkeley, CA 94710-2205 USA Fax: 510-704-0268; *Imprints:* Soft Skull Press (Soft); Counterpoint (Countpt)
E-mail: info@counterpointpress.com
Web site: http://www.counterpointpress.com
Dist(s): **Lulu Pr., Inc.**
MyiLibrary
Open Road Integrated Media, Inc.
Penguin Random Hse. Distribution
Penguin Random Hse. LLC
Publishers Group West (PGW).

Counting Pup Pr., *(978-0-9969452; 978-0-9986572; 978-1-948246)* 3616 Harden Blvd, No. 315, Lakeland, FL 33803 USA Tel 863-255-5438
E-mail: countingpup@gmail.com
Web site: countingpup.com.

Countinghouse Pr., Inc., *(978-0-9664732; 978-0-9786191; 978-0-9911102)* 6632 Telegraph Rd., Suite 311, Bloomfield Hills, MI 48301 USA Tel 248-642-7191; Fax: 248-642-7192
E-mail: lcharla@comcast.net
Web site: http://www.countinghousepress.com.

Country Bookshop, The, *(978-0-9991317)* 140 NW Broad St., Southern Pines, NC 28387 USA Tel 910-692-3211
E-mail: kimberlyddaniels@gmail.com.

Country Boy Publishing Co., *(978-0-9795574)* Orders Addr.: 300 Collier Dr., Winter Haven, FL 33884 USA
E-mail: dgreenl2@tampabay.rr.com
Web site: http://www.countryboypublishing.com.

Country Bumpkin Pubns. USA, *(978-0-9677938)* 212 California Ave., Watertown, NY 13601 USA Tel 315-782-0941
E-mail: bsteve3@twcny.rr.com.

Country Girl Publishing, *(978-0-615-26902-3)* 5537 Shallowriver Rd., Clinton, MD 20735 USA.

Country Kid Publishing LLC, *(978-0-9754624; 978-0-9963649)* 951 Canyon Tr Ct., Yorkville, IL 60560 USA
E-mail: michaelwaguespack@gmail.com
Web site: http://www.countrykidpublishing.com
Dist(s): **Angler's Bk. Supply**
Follett School Solutions.

Country Messenger Pr. Publishing Group, LLC, *(978-0-9619407; 978-0-9801554; 978-1-937162)* 27657 Hwy. 97, Okanogan, WA 98840 USA (SAN 244-5638) Tel 253-216-6364
E-mail: kfreel@cmppg.org; edna@cmppg.org
Web site: http://www.cmppg.com.

Country Side Pr., The, *(978-0-9746360)* Orders Addr.: 49850 Miller Rd., North Powder, OR 97867 USA Tel 541-856-3239
E-mail: debbys@rconnects.com
Web site: http://www.thecountrysidepress.com.

Courage Publishing, *(978-0-692-05388-1; 978-0-692-16578-2)* 813 12th Ave W., West Fargo, ND 58078 USA Tel 701-200-8480
E-mail: sarahzaun@hotmail.com.

Courage to Change *See* **CTC Publishing**

Courier Publications *See* **Christian Courier Pubns.**

Course Technology, *(978-0-534; 978-0-619; 978-0-7600; 978-0-7895; 978-0-87709; 978-0-87835; 978-0-89426; 978-0-928763; 978-1-56527; 978-1-878748; 978-1-4188; 978-1-59863; 978-1-4239; 978-1-60334)* Div. of Cengage Learning, Orders Addr.: 20 Channel Ctr St., Boston, MA 02210-3402 USA Toll Free Fax: 800-881-8922
E-mail: Esales@thomsonlearning.com; stacy.hiquet@thomson.com; cheryl.mondillo@thomson.com
Web site: http://www.course.com/
Dist(s): **Alfred Publishing Co., Inc.**
CENGAGE Learning
Delmar Cengage Learning
Ebsco Publishing
Leonard, Hal Corp.
ebrary, Inc.

Courtyard Publishing, LLC, *(978-0-9795260)* Div. of Alchemical Courtyard, LLC, 1688 Meridian Ave., 10th Flr., Miami Beach, FL 33139 USA Tel 305-695-9380
E-mail: info@courtyardpublishing.com
Web site: http://www.courtyardpublishing.com.

Covenant Bks., *(978-0-615-42722-5; 978-0-692-58739-3)* 4200 Kensington High St., Naples, FL 34105 USA Tel 239-643-0887 Do not confuse with Covenant Books in Fort Wayne, IN
E-mail: robertpetterson@msn.com
Dist(s): **CreateSpace Independent Publishing Platform.**

†Covenant Communications, *(978-0-9649122)* 1009 Jones St., Old Hickory, TN 37138 USA Tel 615-847-2066; Fax: 615-860-3601; Toll Free: 800-979-3882 Do nt oconfuse with Covenant Communications in Old Hickory, TN
Dist(s): **Quality Bks., Inc.**; *CIP.*

Covenant Communications, Inc., *(978-1-55503; 978-1-57734; 978-1-59156; 978-1-59811; 978-1-60861; 978-1-62108; 978-1-68047; 978-1-5244)* Orders Addr.: 920 E State Rd Ste F, American Fork, UT 84003-0416 USA (SAN 169-8540) Tel 801-756-9966; 801-756-1041; Fax: 801-756-1049; Toll Free: 800-662-9545; Edit Addr.: 920 E. State Rd., Suite F, American Fork, UT 84003 USA Toll Free: 800-662-9545 Do not confuse with Covenant Communications in American Fork, UT
E-mail: verls@covenant-lds.com
Web site: http://www.covenant-lds.com
Dist(s): **Follett School Solutions.**

Covenant Support Network *See* **The 101 Group, Inc.**

Coventry Pool & Garden Houses *See* **Manor Hse. Publishing Co., Inc.**

Covercraft *Imprint of* **Perfection Learning Corp.**

Covered Bridge Bks., *(978-0-9722027)* 336 Covered Bridge Rd., Cherry Hill, NJ 08034-2949 USA.

Covered Bridge Children's Books *See* **Covered Bridge Bks.**

Covered Wagon Publishing LLC, *(978-0-9723259)* P.O. Box 473038, Aurora, CO 80047 USA (SAN 254-7813) Tel 303-751-0992; Fax: 303-632-6794
E-mail: CoveredWagon@comcast.net
Web site: http://www.RockyMountainMysteries.com.

Covert & Sergiacomi Publishing, *(978-0-578-41850-6)* 10 Saint Augustine Dr., Charleston, SC 29407 USA Tel 843-670-6645
E-mail: covertj1986@gmail.com
Dist(s): **CreateSpace Independent Publishing Platform.**

Cow Heard Records, *(978-0-9763012)* 3622 Altura Ave., La Crescenta, CA 91214 USA
Web site: http://www.thesunflowers.com.

Cowan, Pricilla J., *(978-0-9822542; 978-0-9841194; 978-0-9840083; 978-0-9891159; 978-0-9896988)* 11594 SW 135th Ave., Tigard, OR 97223 USA
Web site: http://www.storiesbypj.com.

Cowboy Collector Pubns., *(978-0-9628078)* Orders Addr.: P.O. Box 7486, Long Beach, CA 90807 USA Tel 714-840-3942; Edit Addr.: 4677 Rio Ave., Long Beach, CA 90805 USA Tel 213-428-6972
Dist(s): **Hervey's Booklink & Cookbook Warehouse.**

Cowboy Magazine, *(978-0-9765969)* Orders Addr.: P.O. Box 126, La Veta, CO 81055 USA Tel 719-742-5250; Fax: 719-742-3034; Edit Addr.: 124 N. Main St., La Veta, CO 81055 USA
E-mail: workincowboy@amigo.net
Web site: http://www.cowboymagazine.com.

COWCATCHER Pubns., *(978-0-9821521; 978-0-9960533; 978-0-9975172)* 2 Village North Dr. #25, Hilton Head Island, SC 29926 USA Tel 843-816-7883
Web site: http://www.do-the-write-thing.com.

Cowcatcher Pubns. *See* **COWCATCHER Pubns.**

Cowgirl Peg Bks. *Imprint of* **Cowgirl Peg Enterprises**

Cowgirl Peg Enterprises, *(978-0-9721057; 978-0-615-59075-2; 978-0-692-95998-5)* Orders Addr.: P.O. Box 293055, Kerrville, TX 78029 USA; *Imprints:* Cowgirl Peg Books (Cowgirl Peg Books)
E-mail: cowgirlpeg2@gmail.com
Web site: http://www.cowgirlpeg.com
Dist(s): **Bks. West**
Follett School Solutions.

Cowpokes Cartoon Bks., *(978-0-917207)* P.O. Box 290868, Kerrville, TX 78029-0868 USA (SAN 656-089X) Tel 830-257-7446 (phone/fax); Toll Free: 800-257-7441 (phone/fax)
E-mail: cartoons@cowpokes.com
Web site: http://www.cowpokes.com.

Cox & Castelluccio, 7637 Lauppe Ln., Citrus Heights, CA 95621 USA Tel 530-605-9272
E-mail: amyreneecox@gmail.com
Dist(s): **Ingram Content Group.**

Cox, Audrey Phillips, *(978-0-692-11181-9; 978-0-692-11183-3; 978-1-7324065)* P.O. Box 348 1616 Cadillac Ave, DAUPHIN ISLAND, AL 36528 USA Tel 251-391-6557; *Imprints:* APCWriter & Publisher (APCWriter Pub)
E-mail: apcoxmail@gmail.com; bookinfo@apcwriterpublisher.com; audrey@apcwriterpublisher.com
Web site: http://www.apc-writter-blogger.com; http://www.apc-writer-publisher.com; http://www.audreyphillipscox.com
Dist(s): **Ingram Content Group.**

Cox, Donald, *(978-0-692-07527-2; 978-0-692-13808-3; 978-0-692-16885-1)* 945 San Ildefonso Rd., TRLR 53, Los Alamos, NM 87544 USA Tel 505-426-5410
E-mail: 3times10tothe8th@live.com
Dist(s): **Ingram Content Group.**

Cox, Gene, *(978-0-9669672)* 2309 Limerick Dr., Tallahassee, FL 32308 USA Tel 850-893-1789
E-mail: gccox@mail.istal.com.

Cox, Julie, *(978-0-9742118)* P.O. Box 77966, Fort Worth, TX 76177 USA
E-mail: info@facereadingacademy.com
Web site: http://www.facereadingacademy.com.

Cox, Mark Design *See* **Sympathetic Pr.**

Coyote Canyon Pr., *(978-0-9796607; 978-0-9821298; 978-0-9890080; 978-1-7321903)* 693 Black Hills Dr., Claremont, CA 91711-2928 USA Toll Free Fax: 800-319-4707
E-mail: tom@coyotecanyonpress.com
Web site: http://www.coyotecanyonpress.com.

Coyote Cowboy Co., *(978-0-939343)* Orders Addr.: P.O. Box 2190, Benson, AZ 85602 USA (SAN 663-0820) Tel 520-586-1077; Toll Free: 800-654-2550; Edit Addr.: 1251 S. Red Chile Rd., Benson, AZ 85602 USA
E-mail: cindylou@baxterblack.com
Web site: http://www.baxterblack.com
Dist(s): **Follett School Solutions.**

Coyote Moon Publishing *See* **Cowgirl Peg Enterprises**

CoyWolf Entertainment (TM) *See* **Bk. Entree(TM)**

CoZi Publishing LLC, *(978-0-9749151)* P.O. Box 211, Rutland, VT 05702-0211 USA
E-mail: publish@cozi.com
Web site: http://www.cozi.com.

Cozy Graphics Corp., *(978-1-932002; 978-1-59343)* 61-20 G.C.P., Apt. B1204, Forest Hills, NY 11375 USA Tel 718-592-9782 (phone/fax); *Imprints:* Cozy Publishing House (Cozy Pub Hse)
E-mail: publisher@cozygraphics.com
Web site: http://www.cozygraphics.com.

Cozy Publishing Hse. *Imprint of* **Cozy Graphics Corp.**

CP Production Studios Publishing Co., P.O. Box 64551, Phoenix, AZ 85082 USA Tel 630-788-7839
E-mail: cpprostudios3@gmail.com
Dist(s): **CreateSpace Independent Publishing Platform.**

CPCC Pr., *(978-1-59494)* P.O. Box 35009, Charlotte, NC 28235-5009 USA Tel 704-330-6789
E-mail: cpccpress@cpcc.edu; melissa.wilson@cpcc.edu; amy.rogers@cpcc.edu; emma.reynolds@cpcc.edu
Web site: http://www.cpccservicescorp.com; http://https://cpccpress.com/.

CPM Comics *Imprint of* **Central Park Media Corp.**

CPM Manga *Imprint of* **Central Park Media Corp.**

CPM Manhwa *Imprint of* **Central Park Media Corp.**

CPR Pubng, *(978-0-9778597)* 740 13th St., Fennimore, WI 53809 USA.

CQ Pr. Library Reference *Imprint of* **CQ Pr.**

†CQ Pr., *(978-0-7401; 978-0-87187; 978-0-9625531; 978-1-56692; 978-1-56802; 978-1-933116; 978-1-60426; 978-0-9823537; 978-1-60871)* Div. of SAGE Pubns., Inc., Orders Addr.: a/o Order Dept., 2300 N. St. NW, Suite 800, Washington, DC 20037 USA (SAN 256-470X) Toll Free: 866-427-7737 (customer service - orders); *Imprints:* C Q Press Library Reference (CQ Pr Lib Ref)
E-mail: customerservice@cqpress.com
Web site: http://www.cqpress.com
Dist(s): **MyiLibrary**
SAGE Pubns., Inc.
ebrary, Inc.; *CIP.*

CR Publishing, *(978-0-9982115)* 947 W. 5950 S., Spanish Fork, UT 84660 USA Tel 801-376-5982; Fax: 801-376-5982
E-mail: christina.utah@gmail.com.

Crabtree Publishing Co. (CAN) *(978-0-7787; 978-0-86505; 978-1-4271) Dist. by* **Children Plus.**

Cracker the Crab LLC, *(978-0-9725560)* P.O. Box 80475, Simpsonville, SC 29680-0475 USA Do not confuse with Two Bear Publishing Company in Alpine, CA
E-mail: jillkcogdill@twobearproducts.com; jcogdill@crackerthecrab.com; jkcogdill@msn.com
Web site: http://www.crackerthecrab.com.

Crafterina, *(978-0-9886652; 978-0-9886653; 978-0-692-58583-2; 978-0-692-93016-8)* 206 Warren St. No. 4R, Jersey City, NJ 07302 USA Tel 443-235-1436
E-mail: VanessaEstelleSalgado@gmail.com.

Craig, Frankye, *(978-0-9794904)* 1735 Caughlin Creek Rd., Reno, NV 89519 USA Tel 775-747-1138; Fax: 775-747-1138
E-mail: FrankyeEBD@aol.com.

Crain, Suzanne, *(978-0-9763254)* 10423 Brickey Rd., Red Bud, IL 62278-3519 USA
E-mail: slcrain@hcis.net.

Cram101 Inc., *(978-1-4288; 978-1-61654; 978-1-61698; 978-1-61744; 978-1-61461; 978-1-61490; 978-1-61812; 978-1-61830; 978-1-61905; 978-1-61906; 978-1-4672; 978-1-4784; 978-1-4902; 978-1-4970; 978-1-5388)* 40 W. Easy St., Suite 1, Simi Valley, CA 93021 USA (SAN 851-2175); 6593 Collins Dr., Ste. D18, Moorpark, CA 93021
E-mail: www.palitt.com
Web site: http://www.cram101.com.

Cranberry Quill Publishing Co., *(978-0-9741406; 978-0-9884899; 978-0-9914246; 978-0-9965986)* P.O. Box 26227, Fayetteville, NC 28301-4901 USA Tel 910-257-5109
E-mail: writearlybooks@gmail.com
Web site: http://www.cranberryquill.com.

Crane Bks., *(978-0-9647924)* Div. of Math in Motion, 668 Stony Hill Rd., No. 233, Yardley, PA 19067 USA Tel 215-321-5556; Fax: 215-310-9412
E-mail: info@mathinmotion.com
Web site: http://www.mathinmotion.com.

†Crane Hill Pubs., *(978-0-9621455; 978-1-57587; 978-1-881548)* 3608 Clairmont Ave., Birmingham, AL 35222-3508 USA Tel 205-714-3007; Fax: 205-714-3008
E-mail: cranemail@cranehill.com
Web site: http://www.cranehill.com; *CIP.*

Crane Institute of America, Inc., *(978-0-9744279; 978-0-9855502; 978-1-946269)* 3880 Saint Johns Pkwy., Sanford, FL 32771 USA Tel 407-322-6800; Fax: 407-330-0660; Toll Free: 800-832-2726
E-mail: annc@craneinstitute.com; info@craneinstitute.com
Web site: http://www.craneinstitute.com.

Crane Publishing, *(978-0-9753608)* 308 Trinity Rd., Venice, FL 34293 USA Do not confuse with companies with the same name in Paramus, New Jersey.
E-mail: jborza@cranepublishing.net
Web site: http://www.cranepublishing.net.

Cranky Pants Publishing, LLC, *(978-0-9759627)* 2 Upland Rd., W., Arlington, MA 02474 USA
E-mail: ssanzo@yahoo.com.

Crary Pubns., *(978-0-9743438; 978-0-9980887)* 5233 Painted Pebble St., North Las Vegas, NV 89081 USA
E-mail: tabrown@crarypublications.com
Web site: http://www.CraryPublications.com
Dist(s): **Ingram Content Group.**

Craven Street Bks. *Imprint of* **Linden Publishing Co., Inc.**

Crawford, Dana, *(978-0-9742362)* 921 N. Chaparral, Suite 208, Corpus Christi, TX 78401-0208 USA
E-mail: wt.loss@ccinternet.net
Web site: http://www.naturalweight.net.

Crawford, Quinton Douglass, *(978-0-615-14879-3)* 225 Santa Ana Ct., Fairfield, CA 94533 USA
Web site: http://www.knowledgefortomorrow.com
Dist(s): **Lulu Pr., Inc.**

Crayens *See* **Coolidge Corner Pr.**

Crazy 8 Pr., *(978-0-615-56701-3; 978-0-615-75884-8; 978-0-692-20450-4; 978-0-9969275)* 8 Davis Rd., Port Washington, NY 11050 USA Tel 516-883-8079
Dist(s): **CreateSpace Independent Publishing Platform.**

Crazy A, *(978-0-578-45787-1)* 514 Country Club Dr., Stockbridge, GA 30281 USA Tel 770-507-4538
E-mail: thecrazyablogger@gmail.com
Dist(s): **Independent Pub.**

Crazy Dream Publishing, LLC *See* **Waltham Publishing, LLC**

Crazy Man Press, LLC, *(978-0-9743553)* 33 University Sq., Suite 254, Madison, WI 53715-1042 USA Tel 608-215-0532
E-mail: info@crazymanpress.com
Web site: http://www.crazymanpress.com.

Crazy Pet Pr., The, *(978-0-9744749)* 655 N. Azusa Ave., No. 104, Azusa, CA 91708 USA Tel 831-438-2730; Fax: 831-438-2764; Toll Free: 877-860-2100
E-mail: kpbooks@calcentral.com
Web site: http://www.crazydog.com; http://www.crazypetpress.com; http://www.kidoodlepetpress.com.

Crazy Red Head Publishing, *(978-0-692-71498-0; 978-0-692-76622-4; 978-0-692-76623-1; 978-0-9992968)* 3900 Walnut Lake rd, West Bloomfield, MI 48323 USA Tel 248-227-5508
Dist(s): **Independent Pub.**

†CRC Pr. LLC, *(978-0-8493; 978-0-87762; 978-0-87819; 978-0-935184; 978-1-56676; 978-1-57491; 978-1-58488; 978-1-58716; 978-1-4200; 978-1-4398; 978-1-4665; 978-1-4822; 978-1-4987; 978-1-351)* Subs. of Taylor & Francis, Inc., Orders Addr.: 6000 Broken Sound Pkwy., NW, Ste. 300, Boca Raton, FL 33487 USA Tel 800-272-7737 Toll Free Fax: 800-374-3401; Edit Addr.: 270 Madison Ave., New York, NY 10016 USA; *Imprints:* A K Peters/CRC Press (AKPetersCRCPr)
E-mail: orders@crcpress.com; Theresa.Gutierrez@taylorandfrancis.com
Web site: http://www.crcpress.com; http://www.taylorandfrancis.com
Dist(s): **Ebsco Publishing**
Follett School Solutions
MyiLibrary
Oxford Univ. Pr., Inc.
Rittenhouse Bk. Distributors
Taylor & Francis Group
Thieme Medical Pubs., Inc.
ebrary, Inc.; *CIP.*

CRE Lease Talk, Incorporated, *(978-0-9820726)* Orders Addr.: P.O. Box 341594, Memphis, TN 38134-1084 USA Tel 901-399-0967
E-mail: valencia.mackie@comcast.net; valencia@creleasetalk.com
Web site: http://www.CRELeaseTalk.com.

Create & Blossom, LLC, *(978-0-615-76536-5; 978-0-9890039; 978-0-615-83176-3; 978-0-9910489; 978-0-9915412; 978-0-9903486; 978-0-9906662; 978-0-9909652; 978-0-9860866; 978-0-9969105; 978-0-9972921; 978-1-945304; 978-0-692-07007-9; 978-0-692-15731-2; 978-0-692-19174-3*
E-mail: createandblossomllc@gmail.com
Web site: www.kennishagriffin.com.

Create Loving Kindness, *(978-0-9977115)* 1313 N. Ritchie Ct., Chicago, IL 60610 USA Tel 310-220-7733
E-mail: debsmazor@gmail.com.

Create Noise Publishing, *(978-0-9961346; 978-1-945109)* 1233 W. 74th St., Los Angeles, CA 90044 USA Tel 323-365-9239
E-mail: drealashon@gmail.com; createnoise1@gmail.com
Web site: www.createnoise.org.

Created For You, *(978-0-615-17773-1; 978-0-615-17775-5; 978-0-9819968)* Orders Addr.: P.O. Box 4448, Horseshoe Bay, TX 78657 USA; Edit Addr.: 305 Sunspot, Horseshoe Bay, TX 78657-4448 USA Tel 830-596-2726
Dist(s): **Publishers Services.**

CreateSpace Independent Publishing Platform, *(978-1-58898; 978-1-5423; 978-1-59109; 978-1-59456; 978-1-59457; 978-1-4196; 978-1-4348; 978-1-4382; 978-1-4392; 978-1-4404; 978-1-4414; 978-1-4421; 978-1-61550; 978-1-4486; 978-1-4495; 978-1-4499; 978-1-4505; 978-1-4515; 978-1-4528; 978-1-4536; 978-1-4537; 978-1-4538; 978-1-4563; 978-1-4564; 978-1-4565; 978-1-61789; 978-1-4609; 978-1-4610; 978-1-4611; 978-1-61396; 978-1-61397; 978-1-4635; 978-1-4636; 978-1-4637; 978-1-4662; 978-1-4663; 978-1-4664; 978-1-61914; 978-1-61915; 978-1-61916; 978) Orders Addr.: 4900 LaCross Rd., North Charleston, SC 29406 USA (SAN 255-2132) Tel 843-225-4700 (Ask for ordering department); Fax: 843-577-7506; Toll Free: 866-308-6235; 4900 LaCross Rd., North Charleston, SC 29406*
E-mail: info@createspace.com
Web site: http://www.createspace.com
Dist(s): **Amazon Digital Services Inc.**
Independently Published.

Creating Worlds with Words, LLC, *(978-1-7320589)* 7972 Crescent Moon Pl., Anchorage, AK 99507 USA Tel 907-354-7413
E-mail: k.t.munson1@gmail.com
Dist(s): **Ingram Content Group.**

Creation By Design, *(978-0-9828077; 978-1-936532)* 95 Bennett Rd., Teaneck, NJ 07666 USA Tel 914-714-3300
E-mail: CrtnByDsgn@aol.com
Dist(s): **Send The Light Distribution LLC.**

Creation Hse. *Imprint of* **Charisma Media**

Creation Instruction Publishing, *(978-1-928765)* Orders Addr.: P.O. Box 304, Plentywood, MT 59254 USA Tel 406-895-2689; Edit Addr.: 1770 S. Overland, Juniata, NE 68955 USA
E-mail: creation1@juno.com
Web site: http://www.creationinstruction.org/.

Creation Resource Foundation, *(978-0-9672713)* P.O. Box 570, El Dorado, CA 95667 USA Tel 530-626-4447; Fax: 530-626-5215; Toll Free: 800-497-1454
E-mail: info@creationresource.org
Web site: http://www.awesomeworks.com; http://www.creationresource.org/
Dist(s): **Send The Light Distribution LLC.**

Creative 3, LLC, *(978-1-933815)* 2236 E Spring Hill Rd., Springfield, MO 65804 USA Tel 417-882-2145; Fax: 417-882-2145; Toll Free Fax: 800-866-1360; Toll Free: 800-866-1360; *Imprints:* Quirkles, The (The Quirkles)
E-mail: info@quirkles.com; thequirkles@aol.com
Web site: http://www.quirkles.com.

Creative Attic, Inc., The, *(978-0-9653955)* P.O. Box 187, Canterbury, NH 03224 USA Tel 603-783-9103; Fax: 603-783-0118; Toll Free: 888-566-6539
E-mail: the5kids@aol.com.

Creative Avenues Media, *(978-1-7327161)* 3736 SW 10th, 4, Portland, OR 97239 USA Tel 503-754-5831
E-mail: natepjensen@gmail.com
Web site: http://portlandchildrensbookillustrator.com/.

Creative Bk. Pubs., *(978-0-9754818; 978-0-9763093; 978-0-9765467; 978-0-9779662; 978-0-9795460)* 1912 Falcon Dr., Ridgefield, WA 98642 USA
Web site: http://www.creativebookpublishers.com.

Creative Chapps, *(978-1-947997)* 25 River Rock Way, Franklinton, NC 27525 USA Tel 919-400-9935
E-mail: sixchapps@gmail.com.

Creative Communication, *(978-1-60050)* Orders Addr.: P.O. Box 303, Smithfield, UT 84335 USA Tel 435-713-4411; Fax: 435-713-4422; Edit Addr.: 1488 . 200 W., Logan, UT 84341 USA Do not confuse with companies with the same or similar name in Forest Grove, OR, Seattle, WA, Trabuco Canyon, CA, Nixa, MO, Chelan, WA, La Mesa, CA, Kalamazoo, MI
E-mail: drtom@poeticpower.com
Web site: http://www.poeticpower.com
Dist(s): **Independent Pubs. Group.**

Creative Co., The, *(978-0-87191; 978-0-88682; 978-0-89812; 978-1-56660; 978-1-56846; 978-1-58341; 978-1-60818; 978-1-62832; 978-1-68277; 978-1-64000; 978-1-64026)* 123 S. Broad St., Mankato, MN 56001 USA Tel 507-388-6273; Fax: 507-388-4797; Toll Free: 800-445-6209; *Imprints:* Creative Editions (Creative Eds); Creative Education (Creat Educ); Creative Paperbacks (Creative Paperbks) Do not confuse with The Creative Co., Lawrenceburg, IN
E-mail: info@thecreativecompany.us; kate.riggs@thecreativecompany.us
Web site: http://www.thecreativecompany.us
Dist(s): **Abraham Assocs. Inc.**
Children's Plus, Inc.
Hachette Bk. Group
RiverStream Publishing.

Creative Continuum, Inc., *(978-0-9713804; 978-1-932252; 978-1-62192)* 2910 E. La Palma Ave. Ste. C, Anaheim, CA 92806-2618 USA
E-mail: info@creativecontinuum.com
Web site: http://www.creativecontinuum.com.

Creative Conversations, *(978-0-9768235)* 11767 W. Coal Mine Dr., Littleton, CO 80127 USA Tel 303-437-8533.

Creative Cranium Concept, The, *(978-0-9741009)* Orders Addr.: 2560 Reed Ave, Marshalltown, IA 50158 USA Tel 303-875-8742; Edit Addr.: 2560 Reed Ave, Marshalltown, IA 50158 USA Tel 303-875-8742
E-mail: Rhonda@RhondaSpellman.com
Web site: http://www.rhondaspellman.com; http://AutismWithRhonda.com.

Creative Creature Publishing, *(978-0-9964983; 978-1-7353083)* 53 Chadwick Ln., Westcliffe, CO 81252 USA Tel 719-285-5650
E-mail: creativecreaturepublishing@gmail.com
Web site: http://www.creativecreaturepublishing.com/.

Creative Curriculum Initiatives *See* **Curriculum Concepts International**

Creative Dragon Pr., *(978-0-9831996)* 208A Oxhead Rd., Centereach, NY 11720 USA Tel 631-738-9082
E-mail: cheryl_orlassino@hotmail.com.

Creative Dreaming Ltd., *(978-0-615-14010-0; 978-0-615-14725-3; 978-0-615-15431-2; 978-0-615-15487-9; 978-0-615-15521-0; 978-0-615-16439-7; 978-0-615-17664-2; 978-0-615-18006-9; 978-0-615-18260-5; 978-0-615-18340-4; 978-0-615-18424-1; 978-0-615-18654-2; 978-0-615-18886-7; 978-0-615-23631-5) 6433 Topanga Canyon Blvd., No. 120, Woodland Hills, CA 91303 USA*
Dist(s): **Lulu Pr., Inc.**

Creative Editions *Imprint of* **Creative Co., The**

Creative Education *Imprint of* **Creative Co., The**

Creative Education & Publishing, *(978-0-9824964; 978-0-9825969; 978-0-9835315; 978-0-9859066; 978-0-9903851)* 3339 Ardley Ct., Falls Church, VA 22041 USA Tel 703-856-7005
E-mail: alameddine_kaddoura@yahoo.com; info@creativeeducationandpublishing.com
Web site: http://www.creativeeducationandpublishing.com.

Creative Educational Video *See* **C E V Multimedia, Ltd.**

Creative Energy, LLC, *(978-0-9821062; 978-0-9829825; 978-1-945372)* 20322 Sequoia Trace, Spring, TX 77379 USA (SAN 857-2771)
E-mail: drkmcleod@yahoo.com.

Creative Enterprises, *(978-1-880675)* 1040 Harvard Blvd., Dayton, OH 45406-5047 USA (SAN 253-5491) Tel 937-278-7159; Toll Free: 888-266-5777 Do not confuse with companies with the same or similar name in Mattapoisett, MA, Cordova, TN, Brooklyn, NY, Kittery, ME, Montgomery Village, MD
E-mail: allen45406@aol.com
Web site: http://creative-enterprises.org.

Creative Home & Family Endeavors, *(978-0-9747306)* 1555 Main St., Suite A-3-287, Windsor, CO 80550 USA Tel 970-221-0737
E-mail: endeavors4@aol.com.

†Creative Homeowner, *(978-0-932944; 978-1-58011; 978-1-880029)* Div. of Courier Corporation, 24 Park Way, Upper Saddle River, NJ 07458-9960 USA (SAN 213-6627) Tel 201-934-7100; Fax: 201-934-8971; Toll Free: 800-631-7795
E-mail: info@creativehomeowner.com
Web site: http://www.creativehomeowner.com
Dist(s): **Dover Pubns., Inc.**
Follett School Solutions
Independent Pubs. Group
MyiLibrary; *CIP.*

Creative House Press *See* **Bourgeois Media & Consulting**

Creative Hse. Kids Pr. *Imprint of* **Bourgeois Media & Consulting**

Creative Image Pubs., *(978-0-9742667)* 102 E. Main, Georgetown, KY 40324 USA
E-mail: Kathy@creativeimagepublishers.com
Web site: http://www.creativeimagepublishers.com.

Creative Learning Books *See* **Aradiance Publishing**

Creative Learning Consultants, Incorporated *See* **Pieces of Learning**

Creative Learning Exchange, *(978-0-9753169; 978-0-9960128)* 27 Central St., Acton, MA 01720-3522 USA (SAN 850-8836) Tel 978-287-0070; Fax: 978-287-0080
E-mail: stuntzln@clexchange.org
Web site: http://www.clexchange.org.

Creative Life Publishing, *(978-0-9779072)* 210 Indian Oak Dr., No. 1163, Waleska, GA 30183 USA Tel 770-720-1975
E-mail: affiliate@caroleoconnell.com
Web site: http://www.caroleoconnell.com.

Creative Marketing Concepts, Inc., *(978-0-9761408)* 2775 Jade St., Mora, MN 55051 USA Tel 320-679-4105; Fax: 320-679-3349; Toll Free: 800-605-4280 Do not confuse with companies with the same name in Saint Louis, MO, Los Angeles, CA
E-mail: cmc@creativemk.com
Web site: http://www.creativemk.com.

Creative Media Partners, LLC, *(978-1-115; 978-1-4264; 978-1-4346; 978-1-4375; 978-0-554; 978-0-559; 978-0-526; 978-0-341; 978-0-469; 978-0-699; 978-1-103; 978-1-110; 978-1-113; 978-1-116; 978-1-117; 978-1-140; 978-1-141; 978-1-142; 978-1-143; 978-1-144; 978-1-145; 978-1-146; 978-1-147; 978-1-148; 978-1-149; 978-1-170; 978-1-171; 978-1-172; 978-1-173; 978-1-174; 978-1-175; 978-1-176; 978-1-177; 978-1-178; 978-1-179; 978-1-240; 978-1-241; 978-1-242; 978-1-243; 978-1-244; 978-1-245; 978-1-246; 978-1-247; 978-1-248; 978-1-2) P.O. Box 21206, Charleston, SC 29413 USA Tel 843-696-0416; Fax: 843-853-9251; 33 Cannon St., Charleston, SC 29403 Tel 843-408-2303; Imprints:* BiblioLife (Bibliolife); Nabu Press (Nabu Pr); Gale ECCO, Print Editions (GECCO); British Library, Historical Print Editions (BritLibrary); Wentworth Press (Wentworth Pr); Gale, Study Guides (GaleStudy) 11/15/05 Owner also owns Indigo, Inc. of Charleston, SC but the two companies are not connected. LT
E-mail: jason@creativmedia.io; info@bibliolife.com; info@bibliolabs.com
Web site: support.creativemedia.io; http://www.bibliobazaar.com; www.bibliolabs.com
Dist(s): **MyiLibrary.**

Creative Media Publishing, *(978-0-9826435; 978-0-9835393; 978-1-938438; 978-1-950298)* 10606 La Alba Dr, Whittier, CA 90603-2460 USA Tel 714-542-1212
E-mail: info@creativemedia.net
Web site: http://www.CreativeMedia.net
Dist(s): **Lulu Pr., Inc.**

Creative Medicine: Healing Through Words, LLC, *(978-0-9965324; 978-0-9986011; 978-978-099-000-8; 978-978-099-001-5; 978-978-099-002-2; 978-978-099-003-9; 978-978-099-004-6; 978-978-099-005-3; 978-978-099-006-0; 978-978-099-007-7; 978-978-099-008-4; 978-978-099-653-6)* P.O. Box 2749, Tappahannock, VA 22560 USA Tel 804-833-4171
E-mail: Ronnie@creative-medicine.com
Web site: www.creative-medicine.com.

Creative Mind Energy, *(978-1-939424)* 110 E Broadway, Missoula, MT 59802 USA; *Imprints:* Vault Comics (Vault Comics)
E-mail: damian@vaultcomics.com; publisher@vaultcomics.com
Web site: www.vaultcomics.com; www.creativemindenergy.com
Dist(s): **Diamond Comic Distributors, Inc.**
Diamond Bk. Distributors.

Creative Minds Pubns., *(978-0-9769737; 978-0-578-58785-1; 978-0-578-65146-0)* Orders Addr.: 2325 Crowncrest Dr., Richmond, VA 23233 USA Tel 804-740-6010; Fax: 804-798-1531
E-mail: kcstarke@aol.com
Dist(s): **Follett School Solutions.**

Creative Ministry Solutions, *(978-1-58302)* P.O. Box 472258, Aurora, CO 80011 USA
E-mail: kj@creativemin.com
Web site: www.creativemin.com.

Creative Noggin, *(978-0-9899450)* 29610 Double Eagle Cir., Boerne, TX 78015 USA Tel 830-981-8222
E-mail: tracy@creativenoggin.com
Dist(s): **Independent Pubs. Group.**

Creative Nutrition & Wellness, *(978-0-615-12437-7)* P.O. Box 7000-233, Redondo Beach, CA 90277 USA Fax: 310-792-0428
Web site: http://www.creativenutrition.com.

Creative Paperbacks *Imprint of* **Creative Co., The**

Creative Publishing, *(978-0-9744833)* 2221 Justin Rd., No. 119-123, Flower Mound, TX 75028 USA Tel 281-251-1751 (phone/fax) Do not confuse with companies with the same or similar name in Roseboro, NC, Greenville, SC, Lawrenceville, GA, Shrevport, LA, College Station, TX, Tustin, CA
E-mail: support@creativekidsonthemove.com
Web site: http://www.creativekidsonthemove.com.

Creative Publishing Consultants, *(978-0-9824730)* 19 Hilltopper Ct., Blythewood, SC 29016-8745 USA.

Creative Publishing International *Imprint of* **Quarto Publishing Group USA**

Creative Publishing International *Imprint of* **Quarto Publishing Group USA**

Creative Quill Publishing, Inc., *(978-0-9709906)* Orders Addr.: P.O. Box 4028, Salem, OR 97302 USA; Edit Addr.: 460 Myers S., Salem, OR 97302 USA Tel 503-363-2843
E-mail: mavist@aol.com; Creativequill@aol.com
Web site: http://www.creativequill.us.

Creative Sharp Presentations, Incorporated *See* **SHARP Literacy, Inc.**

Creative Sources, *(978-0-9759613)* 105 N. Harvest Crest Ct., Highland, IL 62249 USA
E-mail: lynnette@kidsdoread.com
Web site: http://www.KidsDoRead.com.

Creative Styles *See* **JFW, Ltd.**

Creative Success Works, *(978-0-9759551)* 752 E. Lake Lndg., Marietta, GA 30062-3876 USA
E-mail: creativesuccess@comcast.net
Web site: http://www.creativesuccessworks.com.

Creative Teaching Assocs., *(978-1-878669; 978-1-930818; 978-1-931474; 978-1-932918)* Orders Addr.: P.O. Box 7766, Fresno, CA 93747 USA (SAN 297-6803) Tel 559-294-2141 Toll Free: 800-767-4282 (800-767-4CTA); Edit Addr.: P.O. Box 7766, Fresno, CA 93747-7766 USA
Web site: http://www.mastercta.com
Dist(s): **Follett School Solutions.**

Creative Teaching Pr., Inc., *(978-0-88160; 978-0-916119; 978-1-57471; 978-1-59198; 978-1-60689; 978-1-61601; 978-1-62186; 978-1-63445; 978-1-68310; 978-1-64474)* Orders Addr.: P.O. Box 2723, Huntington Beach, CA 92647-0723 USA Tel 714-895-5047; Fax: 714-895-6547; Toll Free Fax: 800-444-4287; Edit Addr.: 6262 Katella Ave., Cypress, CA 90630 USA (SAN 294-9180) Tel 714-895-5047; Toll Free Fax: 800-229-9929; Toll Free: 800-444-4287; *Imprints:* Learning Works, The (The Lrning Works)
E-mail: toni.gardner@creativeteaching.com; webmaster@creativeteaching.com; we.listen@creativeteaching.com; emond.ling@creativeteaching.com
Web site: http://www.creativeteaching.com; http://www.thelearningworks.com; http://www.learntoreadkidsclub.com
Dist(s): **Follett School Solutions**
Pacific Learning, Inc.

Creative Texts Publishers *See* **Creative Texts Pubs., LLC**

Creative Texts Pubs., LLC, *(978-0-692-32201-7; 978-0-692-32220-8; 978-0-692-42754-5; 978-0-692-42766-8; 978-0-692-42772-9; 978-0-692-42777-4; 978-0-692-42846-7; 978-0-692-42868-9; 978-0-692-42875-7; 978-0-692-42882-5; 978-0-692-42919-8; 978-0-692-42927-3; 978-0-692-42986-0; 978-0-692-43308-9; 978-0-692-43311-9; 978-0-692-43323-2; 978-0-692-43324-9; 978-0-692-43331-7; 978-0-692-43340-9; 978-0-692-43346-1; 978-0-692-43349-2; 978-0-692-43353-9; 978-0-692-43362-1; 978-0-692-43390-4; 978-0-692-43395-9; 978-0-692-43412-3;) P.O. Box 50, Barto, PA 19504 USA Tel 610-945-7586*
E-mail: info@creativetexts.com
Web site: http://www.creativetexts.com
Dist(s): **Ingram Bk. Co.**
Ingram Content Group.

Creative Thinkers, Incorporated *See* **Let's Think-kids Foundation, Inc.**

Creative Unity Productions, *(978-0-9822796; 978-1-949402)* 1550 Harrison Dr., Greenwood, IN 46143 USA (SAN 857-748X)
E-mail: CreativeUnityPublishing@gmail.com; CreationsByDonna@gmail.com
Web site: http://www.creativeunitypublishing.net; http://www.creativeunitypublishing.com.

Creative Well, The, *(978-0-9700108)* P.O. Box 2121, Ashtabula, OH 44005 USA Tel 440-964-0338.

Creative with Words Pubns., *(978-0-936945)* P.O. Box 223226, Carmel, CA 93922 USA (SAN 658-6961) Fax: 408-655-8627
E-mail: cwwpub@usa.net.

Creative Works, *(978-0-9727499)* 3747 Redwood Cir., Palo Alto, CA 94306 USA Tel 650-493-3747.

Creative Writing & Publishing Co., *(978-1-887636)* P.O. Box 511848, Milwaukee, WI 53203-0311 USA
E-mail: Cbritt1@wi.rr.com.

Creative Writing Pr., Inc., *(978-0-9708382)* 1830 Stephenson Hwy., Troy, MI 48083-2173 USA Toll Free: 800-760-6397
E-mail: rodgers@mich.com
Web site: http://thepoetrylady.com.

Creative Year 2014, The *See* **Frog Prince Pr.**

CreativeMedia, Incorporated *See* **Creative Media Publishing**

Publisher Name Index

Creativity Pr., *(978-1-934396; 978-0-9952290-2-0)* P.O. Box 1313, Anacortes, WA 98221 USA Do not confuse with Creativity Press in Cleveland, OH
E-mail: anne@Aanneolwin.com
Web site: http://www.creativitypress.com.

Creatopia Productions - Lamy, New Mexico, *(978-0-9637467; 978-0-9854527)* 719 1/2 No. B, Lamy, NM 87540-9682 USA Tel 505-204-3892
E-mail: wrayl@hotmail.com
Web site: http://www.members.tripod.com/~lyne4lyne/
Dist(s): **Adventures Unlimited Pr.**
Barnes & Noble Bks.-Imports
CreateSpace Independent Publishing Platform.

Credible Math, LLC., *(978-0-9903831)* 20 Baltimore Ave, Piscataway, NJ 08854 USA Tel 732-356-3329
E-mail: deborahharey@aol.com.

Credo Hse. Pubs., *(978-0-9787620; 978-1-935391; 978-1-62586)* 2200 Boyd Ct NE, Grand Rapids, MI 49525-6714 USA
E-mail: connect@credocommunications.net
Web site: http://www.credohousepublishers.com.

Credo Italia, *(978-0-9768375)* Orders Addr.: 350 Bay St., Suite 100-124, San Francisco, CA 94123 USA
E-mail: info@ClintAdams.com
Web site: http://www.ClintAdams.com.

Creed, Julie, *(978-0-9728181)* 17 Los Abitos, Rancho Santa Margarita, CA 92688 USA
E-mail: julie@qabranding.com
Web site: http://www.qabranding.com.

Creek Sound Bks., *(978-0-9743840)* 120 Misty Way, Cosby, TN 37722 USA Tel 606-523-5324
E-mail: rapowell7@msn.com.

Creekside Publishing, *(978-0-9972349)* 14 Mill St., Morris, NY 13808 USA Tel 607-263-5531
E-mail: LesDieh60@aol.com
Web site: www.lesleyadiehl.com.

Creekside Publishing, *(978-0-692-69750-4; 978-1-951763)* 2310 Homestead Rd. Suite C1-155, Los Altos, CA 94024-7302 USA Tel 408-730-1511
E-mail: hansonreading@gmail.com
Web site: www.hansonreading.com.

Creepy Little Productions, *(978-0-9704159)* 3726 W. Augusta Ave., Phoenix, AZ 85051 USA Tel 602-625-6596; Fax: 602-242-3046
E-mail: christy@atgproductions.com; madamem@creepylittlestories.com
Web site: http://www.creepylittlestories.com
Dist(s): **PSI (Publisher Services, Inc.).**

Creevy, Anne *See* **ABC Bks.**

Creflo Dollar Ministries Pubns., *(978-1-931172; 978-1-59089)* Orders Addr.: P.O. Box 490124, College Park, GA 30349 USA Tel 770-210-5700; Fax: 770-210-5701; Edit Addr.: 2500 Burdett Rd., College Park, GA 30349 USA
E-mail: mfleming@worldchangers.org; mocarter@worldchangers.org; dfidler@worldchangers.org; tdavis@worldchangers.org
Web site: http://www.creflodollarministries.org
Dist(s): **Independent Pubs. Group**
Send The Light Distribution LLC.

Creotz Ediciones SL (ESP) *(978-84-941473) Dist. by* **IPG Chicago.**

CreoXimius Publishing Company, *(978-0-9776617)* 970 E. Smith Rd., Medina, OH 44256 USA
Web site: http://www.debrae.com.

Crescent Moon Pr., *(978-0-9816011; 978-0-9818484; 978-0-9823065; 978-0-9841805; 978-0-9828200; 978-0-9846394; 978-1-937254; 978-1-939173; 978-0-9906274; 978-0-9908827; 978-0-9862871)* 1385 Hwy. 35, Box 269, Middletown, NJ 07748 USA
E-mail: publisher@crescentmoonpress.com
Web site: http://www.crescentmoonpress.com.

Crescent Moon Publishing (GBR) *(978-1-86171; 978-1-871846) Dist. by* **IndiCo.**

CREST Pubns., *(978-0-9725546; 978-0-9912995)* P.O. Box 481022, Charlotte, NC 28269 USA Do not confuse with Crest Publications, Richardson, TX
Web site: http://www.crestpub.com.

Crested Tern Publishing, *(978-0-578-19682-4)* 2251 Winged Foot Ct., Oxnard, CA 93036 USA.

Creston Bks., *(978-1-939547)* 965 Creston Rd., Berkeley, CA 94708 USA Tel 510-928-1765
E-mail: solsetimo@yahoo.com
Dist(s): **Lerner Publishing Group**
Publishers Group West (PGW)
Two Rivers Distribution.

Crews Pubns., LLC, *(978-0-9795236)* 7483 Garnet Dr., Jonesboro, GA 30236 USA Tel 770-617-9688
E-mail: crewspublications@yahoo.com
Web site: http://www.gscrews.com.

Cribsheet Publishing *See* **Blue Shoe Publishing**

Cricket Bks., *(978-0-8126)* Div. of Carus Publishing Co., 70 E. Lake St. Ste. 300, Chicago, IL 60601-5945 USA Tel 312-701-1720
Web site: http://www.cricketmag.com/home.asp
Dist(s): **Cobblestone Publishing Co.**
Ebsco Publishing
Follett School Solutions.

Cricket Cottage Publishing, LLC, *(978-0-9991224)* 6799 Calistoga Cir., Port Orange, FL 32128 USA Tel 323-207-6213
E-mail: m.owenmurray@gmail.com
Web site: thecricketpublishing.com.

Cricket Productions, Incorporated *See* **Scrumps Entertainment, Inc.**

Cricket Rohman, *(978-0-9896971; 978-0-9975270; 978-0-9994819; 978-1-7355672)* 7618 E. Callisto Cir. No. 123, Tucson, AZ 85715 USA Tel 520-490-7430
E-mail: cricket@cricketrohman.com
Web site: www.cricketrohman.com.

Cricket XPress of Minnesota, *(978-0-9822534)* 504 Bluebird Ct., Sartell, MN 56377 USA Tel 320-267-8978
E-mail: CricketXPressMN@charter.net.

Crickhollow Bks. *Imprint of* **Great Lakes Literary, LLC**

Cridge Mumbly LLC *See* **Cridge Mumbly Publishing**

Cridge Mumbly Publishing, *(978-1-7326245)* 19172 Laurenrae St., Riverside, CA 92508 USA Tel 909-512-2658
E-mail: peirce@yahoo.com
Web site: peirce-clayton.squarespace.com.

CrimethInc. Workers' Collective, *(978-0-9709101; 978-0-9989822)* P.O. Box 13998, Salem, OR 97309 USA Tel 928-222-9129
E-mail: house@crimethinc.com
Web site: http://www.crimethinc.com
Dist(s): **AK Pr. Distribution.**

Crimson Cloak Publishing, *(978-0-692-30069-5; 978-0-692-31345-9; 978-0-692-32698-5; 978-0-692-33222-1; 978-0-692-36488-8; 978-1-68160)* P.O. Box 36, Pilot Knob, MO 63663 USA Tel 573-639-7591
E-mail: carly@crimsoncloakpublishing; rhianna_al_mere@yahoo.com
Web site: www.crimsoncloakpubliishing.com
Dist(s): **Ingram Publisher Services.**

Crimson Oak Publishing LLC, *(978-0-9822725; 978-0-9829505)* P.O. Box 1389, Pullman, WA 99163 USA
E-mail: info@crimsonoakpublishing.com
Web site: http://www.crimsonoakpublishing.com
Dist(s): **Smashwords.**

Crimson Tree Publishing *Imprint of* **Clean Teen Publishing**

Crippen & Landru Pubs., *(978-1-885941; 978-1-932009; 978-1-936363)* Orders Addr.: P.O. Box 9315, Norfolk, VA 23505-9315 USA Tel 757-622-6656 (phone/fax); Toll Free: 877-622-6656 (phone/fax); Edit Addr.: 627 New Hampshire Ave., Norfolk, VA 23508 USA Tel 757-622-6656 (phone/fax)
E-mail: info@crippenlandru.com
Web site: http://www.crippenlandru.com
Dist(s): **Follett School Solutions.**

Criqueville Pr., *(978-0-9705404)* Orders Addr.: P.O. Box 1227, Princeton, NJ 08542-1227 USA Tel 908-359-7834; Edit Addr.: 2 Dogwood Ln., Princeton, NJ 08542-1227 USA (SAN 255-982X)
E-mail: criquevillepress@hotmail.com.

Crises Research Pr., *(978-0-86627)* 301 W. 45th St., New York, NY 10036 USA (SAN 238-9274).

Crispin Bks. *Imprint of* **Great Lakes Literary, LLC**

Crispus Medical Pr., *(978-0-9640389)* 7923 Leschi Rd., SW, Lakewood, WA 98498 USA Toll Free: 877-464-6469.

Crist, Rachel, *(978-0-578-56390-9)* 2612 W. Laredo St., Broken Arrow, OK 74012 USA Tel 918-944-8333
E-mail: raechull315@gmail.com
Web site: www.rachelcrist.com
Dist(s): **Ingram Content Group.**

Cristal Publishing Co., *(978-0-9779124)* P.O. Box 14-4828, Coral Gables, FL 33114-4828 USA
E-mail: cristal228@bellsouth.net
Dist(s): **Ediciones Universal**
Follett School Solutions.

Critical Path Publishing, *(978-0-9740605)* P.O. Box 1073, Clayton, CA 94517-9073 USA Do not confuse with Critical Path Publishing Company in Denville, NJ
E-mail: cpp@silcon.com
Dist(s): **Book Publishing Co.**

Critical Thinking Books & Software *See* **Critical Thinking Co., The**

Critical Thinking Co., The, *(978-0-89455; 978-0-910974; 978-1-60144; 978-1-64420)* Orders Addr.: 1991 Sherman Ave Ste 200, North Bend, OR 97459 USA (SAN 207-0510) Tel 800-458-4849 Toll Free: 800-458-4849
E-mail: GaleO@criticalthinking.com; AbbeyH@criticalthinking.com; service@criticalthinking.com
Web site: http://www.criticalthinking.com
Dist(s): **Follett School Solutions.**

Critter Camp Inc., *(978-0-9772825)* 1190 Scenic Ave., Lummi Island, WA 98262 USA Tel 360-758-4269 (phone/fax)
E-mail: midiana@clearwire.net.

Critter Pubns., *(978-1-928972)* P.O. Box 413, Leicester, MA 01524-0413 USA
E-mail: del@critterp.com
Web site: http://www.critterp.com.

Critter Publishing, *(978-0-9754615)* Orders Addr.: P.O. Box 585, Readfield, ME 04355 USA Tel 207-685-5527 (phone/fax); Edit Addr.: 70 Walker Rd., Readfield, ME 04355 USA
E-mail: soniccomics@gwi.net
Web site: http://www.sonicpublishing.com.

CritterKin., *(978-0-9960657)* 107 Killam Ct., Cary, NC 27513 USA Tel 919-535-8472
E-mail: JenaBall@CritterKin.com
Web site: www.critterkin.com
Dist(s): **Lulu Pr., Inc.**

Critters Up Close *Imprint of* **National Wildlife Federation**

CrittersInc., *(978-0-9745997)* 19611 Longview Terr., Salinas, CA 93908 USA
Web site: http://www.crittersinc.com.

CRLE Publishing, *(978-0-9972129)* P.O. Box 70437, Odessa, TX 79769 USA Tel 432-553-5867
E-mail: robyn.mitchell1@yahoo.com
Web site: https://www.facebook.com/robynmitchellauthor.

CRM Enterprises, *(978-0-615-13155-9; 978-0-615-13278-5; 978-0-615-33279-6; 978-0-615-96051-7; 978-0-692-80739-2; 978-0-692-19775-2)* 411 Coram Avenue, Shelton, CT 06484 USA.

Croce, Pat & Co., *(978-0-9897533)* P.O. Box 520A, Villanova, PA 19085 USA Tel 610-520-1890; Fax: 610-525-5279
E-mail: sbarbacane@piratesoul.com.

Crocodile Bks. *Imprint of* **Interlink Publishing Group, Inc.**

Crocodiles Not Waterlilies Entertainment, *(978-0-9798297)* 58 Maiden Ln., Fifth Flr., San Francisco, CA 94108 USA (SAN 854-4921) Fax: 801-892-2230
E-mail: jodeen@crocpond.com.

Crofton Creek Pr., *(978-0-9700917; 978-0-9767268)* 2303 Gregg Rd., SW, South Boardman, MI 49680 USA Tel 231-369-2325; Fax: 231-369-4382; Toll Free: 877-255-3117
E-mail: publisher@croftoncreek.com
Web site: http://www.croftoncreek.com
Dist(s): **Partners Bk. Distributing, Inc.**
Wayne State Univ. Pr.

Cromulent Pr., *(978-1-7326840)* 145 Flowering Grove Ln., Mooresville, NC 28115 USA Tel 703-554-7530
E-mail: indiegantz@gmail.com
Dist(s): **CreateSpace Independent Publishing Platform.**

Cronier, Brett, *(978-0-692-15190-7; 978-0-692-15191-4; 978-0-578-42221-3; 978-0-578-42222-0)* 3604 Kelliebrook Ln., Moss Point, MS 39562 USA Tel 228-218-7086
E-mail: brettgcronier@gmail.com
Dist(s): **Ingram Content Group.**

Cronies, *(978-1-929566)* Div. of Reproductive Images, 22738 Roscoe Blvd., No. 225, Canoga Park, CA 91304-3350 USA Tel 818-773-4888; Fax: 818-773-8808; Toll Free: 800-232-8099
E-mail: SethJ@CRONIES.com.

Cronus College, *(978-0-9760045; 978-0-9779897)* Div. of e-Pluribus Unum Publishing Co., P.O. Box 941, Lafayette, CA 94549 USA; *Imprints:* Reluctant Reader Books (ReluctRead)
Web site: http://www.cronuscollege.com.

Crooked Creek Publishing, LLC, *(978-0-9786084)* Orders Addr.: P.O. Box 479, Iola, WI 54945 USA Tel 715-445-5359; Edit Addr.: 460 E State St., Iola, WI 54945 USA
E-mail: crookedcreekpublishing@gmail.com
Dist(s): **Stevens International.**

Crooked River Pr., *(978-0-9778586)* P.O. Box 21, Cuyahoga Falls, OH 44221 USA Tel 330-701-3375; *Imprints:* Blue Jay Books (Blue Jay Bks)
E-mail: Books@CrookedRiverPress.com
Web site: http://www.CrookedRiverPress.com.

Crooked Tail Pr., *(978-1-946380)* 2302 115th AVE SE, Lake Stevens, WA 98258 USA Tel 425-350-2625
E-mail: joy@thecontentvixen.com
Web site: crookedtailpress.com.

Crosam Pr., *(978-0-9774822; 978-0-9790337; 978-0-9798351; 978-0-9818903)* Orders Addr.: 681 Beverly Dr., Lake Wales, FL 33853 USA Tel 863-676-5737; Fax: 863-676-2285; Toll Free: 877-676-2285
E-mail: winksampson22@aol.com
Web site: http://www.feathersandfur.com; http://www.crosampress.com.

Crosby Advanced Medical Systems Inc., *(978-0-9846293)* 13556 Dornoch Dr., Ste. 1, Orlando, FL 32828 USA Tel 407-823-9502.

Cross & Crown Publishing, *(978-0-9785523; 978-0-9817728; 978-0-9886778)* 342 Meadow Green Dr., Ringgold, GA 30736 USA Tel 706-937-3798
E-mail: eddunlop@juno.com
Web site: http://www.dunlopministries.com
Dist(s): **Follett School Solutions.**

Cross Dove Publishing, LLC, *(978-0-9656513; 978-1-7335856)* 1704 Esplanade, Front, Redondo Beach, CA 90277-8710 USA Tel 310-375-8400; Fax: 310-373-5912; 27 West 20Th St., New York, NY 10011
Web site: http://www.marysson.com; http://www.crossdove.com
Dist(s): **Follett School Solutions**
MyiLibrary.

Cross, Michael John, *(978-1-7331414)* 36 Island Pond Rd., Atkinson, NH 03811 USA Tel 603-362-3612
E-mail: lotharcross@hotmail.com.

Cross Pointe Printing, *(978-0-9742154)* 14417 N. 42nd St., Phoenix, AZ 85032-5437 USA
E-mail: dan@crosspointeprinting.com.

Cross Product Pubns., *(978-0-9793087; 978-0-9826837)* 3222 Cascade Hills Dr., NW, Cleveland, TN 37312 USA.

Cross Pubns., *(978-0-9771926; 978-0-9850996; 978-1-7349330)* Orders Addr.: 502 E. Liberty Ave., Stillwater, OK 74075 USA Tel 405-564-5641 Do not confuse with Cross Publications in Safford, AZ, Savannah, GA
Web site: www.lulu.com/greenpheon7
Dist(s): **Lulu Pr., Inc.**

Cross Reference Imprints, *(978-0-9725139)* 3607 Hycliffe Ave., Louisville, KY 40207 USA Tel 502-897-2719
E-mail: Pneuma@eclipsetel.com.

Cross Time *Imprint of* **Crossquarter Publishing Group**

Cross Training Publishing, *(978-1-887002; 978-1-929478; 978-0-9821652; 978-0-9845750; 978-1-938254; 978-0-578-22976-8; 978-1-952222)* P.O. Box 1874, Keary, NE 68848 USA (SAN 298-7406) Tel 308-293-3891; Fax: 308-338-2058; Toll Free: 800-430-8588; 16329 Josphine St., Omaha, NE 68136 Tel 308-293-3891
E-mail: gordon@crosstrainingpublishing.com; gthiessen@mac.com
Web site: http://www.crosstrainingpublishing.com
Dist(s): **Follett School Solutions.**

CrossBearers Publishing, *(978-0-9716365)* Div. of Reconciliation Ministries, Inc., Orders Addr.: 3101 Troost Ave., Kansas City, MO 64109 USA Tel 816-931-4751; Fax: 816-931-0142; P.O. Box 45642, Kansas City, MO 64171 Tel 816-449-2825; Fax: 816-449-5231; *Imprints:* St. Nicholas Press (St Nich Pr)
E-mail: frpaisius@hotmail.com; stnicholaspress@gmail.com
Web site: http://www.stmaryofegypt.net/.

CrossGeneration Comics, Inc., *(978-1-931484; 978-1-59314)* 9030 Lake Chase Island Way, Tampa, FL 33626-1942 USA
E-mail: jbreitbeil@crossgen.com
Web site: http://www.crossgen.com
Dist(s): **Diamond Comic Distributors, Inc.**

Crossing Guard Bks. *Imprint of* **Crossing Guard Bks., LLC**

Crossing Guard Bks., LLC, *(978-0-9770141)* Orders Addr.: P.O. Box 1792, Loveland, CO 80538 USA Tel 970-672-8078; *Imprints:* Crossing Guard Books (CrossGrdBks)
E-mail: Sarah@CrossingGuardBooks.com
Web site: http://www.CrossingGuardBooks.com.

Crossing Trails Pubns., *(978-0-9726095)* 4804 Kentwood Ln., Woodbridge, VA 22193 USA Tel 703-590-4449; Fax: 703-878-2119
E-mail: whnesbitt@compuserve.com
Web site: http://www.crossingtrails.com.

Cross-Lengua Productions *See* **KALEXT Productions, LLC**

Cross-Over, *(978-0-9749455; 978-0-9882835; 978-0-9987894)* 190 Vista Linda Ave., Durango, CO 81303 USA Tel 970-385-1809 (phone/fax); Toll Free: 866-385-1809
E-mail: info@homeschoolhowtos.com
Web site: http://fastphonics.weebly.com/; http://homeschoolhowtos.com/.

Crossover Comics *See* **Gavila Publishing**

Crossquarter Publishing Group, *(978-1-890109)* Div. of Earth Healers Inc., Orders Addr.: P.O. Box 23749, Santa Fe, NM 87502 USA Tel 505-690-3923 (phone); Fax: 214-975-9715 (fax); Edit Addr.: P.O. Box 23749, Santa Fe, NM 87502-3749 USA; *Imprints:* Cross Time (Crosstime)
E-mail: info@crossquarter.com
Web site: http://www.crossquarter.com
Dist(s): **Follett School Solutions**
New Leaf Distributing Co., Inc.

Crossroad Pr., *(978-0-9834348; 978-1-937530; 978-1-941408; 978-1-946025; 978-1-948929; 978-1-949914; 978-1-950565; 978-1-951510; 978-1-952979)* 141 Brayden Dr., HERTFORD, NC 27944 USA Tel 252-340-3952; *Imprints:* Wonderstruck Books (Wonderstruck); Mystique Press (Mystique Pr); Otherside Press (MYID_S_OTHERSI)
E-mail: publisher@crossroadpress.com
Web site: http://store.crossroadpress.com
Dist(s): **Follett School Solutions.**

†**Crossroad Publishing Co., The**, *(978-0-8245)* 831 Chestnut Ridge Rd., Spring Valley, NY 10977-6356 USA (SAN 287-0118)
E-mail: production@crossroadpublishing.com; publisher@crossoradpublishing.com
Web site: http://www.crossroadpublishing.com
Dist(s): **Independent Pubs. Group**; *CIP.*

CrossStaff Publishing, *(978-0-9743876; 978-0-9800755)* P.O. Box 288, Broken Arrow, OK 74013 USA Tel 918-369-9293; Fax: 413-723-4384; Toll Free: 866-862-2278
E-mail: info@crossstaff.com
Web site: http://www.crossstaff.com.

Crosswalk Bks., *(978-0-9746269)* P.O. Box 176, American Fork, UT 84003 USA (SAN 255-7657)
Web site: http://www.crosswalkbooks.com.

†**Crossway**, *(978-0-89107; 978-1-58134; 978-1-4335; 978-1-68216)* Div. of Good News Pubs., 1300 Crescent St., Wheaton, IL 60187 USA (SAN 211-7991) Tel 708-682-4300; Fax: 630-682-4785; Toll Free: 800-323-3890 (sales only); *Imprints:* Crossway Bibles (Crossway Bibles)
E-mail: permissions@gnpcb.org; service@crossway.org; info@crossway.org
Web site: http://www.crossway.org
Dist(s): **Follett School Solutions**
L I M Productions, LLC
Vision Video; *CIP.*

Crossway Bibles *Imprint of* **Crossway**

Crossway Books *See* **Crossway**

Crossways International, *(978-1-891245)* 7930 Computer Ave., S., Minneapolis, MN 55435-5415 USA Tel 952-832-5454; Fax: 952-832-5553; Toll Free: 800-257-7308
E-mail: info@crossways.org
Web site: http://www.crossways.org.

Crosswinds Bks., *(978-0-9726573)* P.O. Box 143, Keller, TX 76244 USA
E-mail: jroach35@earthlink.net.

Crosswinds Pr., Inc., *(978-0-9825559; 978-0-9838155)* 126 Crosswinds Dr., Groton, CT 06340 USA
Web site: http://www.crosswindspress.com.

Crouch, Valeria *See* **Zig the Pig**

Crouse, Donna J., *(978-0-9765339)* P.O. Box 250, Jersey, VA 22481 USA Tel 540-775-7787; Fax: 540-775-1682
E-mail: df_crouse@msn.com.

Crow & Pitcher Pr., *(978-0-9987214)* P.O. Box 1294, Shingle Springs, CA 95682-1294 USA Tel 530-672-0143
E-mail: angelicarjackson@yahoo.com
Web site: https://www.crowandpitcherpress.com/.

Crow Dog Pr., *(978-0-9727656)* 541 Hunter Ave., Modesto, CA 95350 USA
E-mail: jackrandom@earthlink.net
Web site: http://www.jackrandom.com.

Crow, R.L. Pubns., *(978-0-9722958; 978-0-9971780; 978-1-7356296)* P.O. Box 262, Penn Valley, CA 95946 USA
E-mail: wsgainer@comcast.net
Dist(s): **SPD-Small Pr. Distribution.**

Crowder, Jack L., *(978-0-9616589)* Orders Addr.: P.O. Box 250, Bernalillo, NM 87004 USA (SAN 659-8064) Tel 505-867-5812 (phone/fax); Edit Addr.: 500 Beehive Ln., Bernalillo, NM 87004 USA (SAN 659-8072)
E-mail: crowdercon@aol.com.

Crowe, L.J. *See* **ibukku, LLC**

Crowell, Peter T. Pubns., *(978-0-9740290)* 102 Wilson Rd., Phoenixville, PA 19460 USA
E-mail: petertcrowell@gmail.com
Web site: http://www.petertcrowell.com; callmescythe.com
Dist(s): **Partners Bk. Distributing, Inc.**

Crown *Imprint of* **Potter/Ten Speed/Harmony/Rodale**

Crown Atlantic Publishing, *(978-0-9883375; 978-1-7326123)* 2000 Mariposa Vista Ln. No. 104, St. Augustine, FL 32084 USA Tel 407-925-3053
E-mail: philipucf23@yahoo.com.

Crown Books For Young Readers *Imprint of* **Random Hse. Children's Bks.**

Crown Hse. Publishing LLC, *(978-1-899836; 978-1-904424; 978-1-84590; 978-0-9823573; 978-1-935810; 978-1-78135; 978-1-78583)* Orders Addr.: P.O. Box 2223, Williston, VT 05495 USA Fax: 802-864-7626; Toll Free: 877-925-1213; Edit Addr.: Crown Bldg., Bancyfelin, Carmarthen, Dyfed SA33 5ND GBR Tel 01267 211345; 01267 211880; Fax: 01267 211882; 81 Brook Hills Dr., White Plains, NY 10605 Tel 914-946-3517; Toll Free: 866-272-8497; *Imprints:* Independent Thinking Press (IndThinking)
E-mail: books@crownhouse.co.uk; info@CHPUS.com
Web site: http://www.crownhouse.co.uk/; http://www.CHPUS.com; http://www.crownhousepublishing.com
Dist(s): **MyiLibrary.**

Crown Media Publishing *See* **Crown Media Publishing**

Crown Media Publishing, *(978-0-692-60979-8; 978-0-692-61041-1; 978-0-692-61106-7; 978-0-692-61190-6; 978-0-692-63234-5; 978-0-692-63291-8; 978-0-692-63333-5; 978-0-9990279)* P.O. Box 4838, Omaha, NE 68104 USA Tel 4025782578
Dist(s): **CreateSpace Independent Publishing Platform.**

Crown Peak Publishing, *(978-0-9645663)* Orders Addr.: P.O. Box 317, New Castle, CO 81647 USA Tel 970-618-1748
E-mail: ann@annsphotos.com; ann@annramseydesign.com; ann@annlouiseramsey.com
Web site: http://www.annramseydesign.com; http://www.annlouiseramsey.com; http://www.annramseyphotography.com.

†Crown Publishing Group, The, Div. of Random Hse., Inc., Orders Addr.: 400 Hahn Rd., Westminster, MD 21157 USA Tel 410-848-1900; Toll Free Fax: 800-659-2436; Toll Free: 800-733-3000; 800-726-0600; Edit Addr.: 1745 Broadway, New York, NY 10019 USA (SAN 200-2639) Tel 212-751-2600; Toll Free Fax: 800-659-2436; *Imprints:* Clarkson Potter (Clarkson Potter); Potter Style (Potter Style); Convergent Books (Convergent Bk); Multnomah (Multnom Bks); WaterBrook (WaterBrook)
E-mail: customerservice@randomnhouse.com; crownpublicity@randomhouse.com
Web site: http://www.randomhouse.com/
Dist(s): **Follett School Solutions**
MyiLibrary
Penguin Random Hse. Distribution
Penguin Random Hse. LLC
Random Hse., Inc.; *CIP.*

Crown/Archetype, 1745 Broadway, New York, NY 10019 USA; *Imprints:* Broadway Books (BwayBks)
Dist(s): **Penguin Random Hse. Distribution**
Penguin Random Hse. LLC.

Crowne Pointe *See* **White Phoenix**

Crowned Warrior Publishing *Imprint of* **Walters, Steve Ministries**

CrowsNest Publishing, *(978-0-9710225)* 11513 Crows Nest Rd., Clarksville, MD 21029-1601 USA Tel 410-531-3110
E-mail: hannon@erols.com.

Crowther, Debra, *(978-0-9741295)* P.O. Box 1870, Three Rivers, TX 78071 USA Tel 361-786-4703; Fax: 361-786-2579
Web site: http://www.jackthewestie.com.

Cruce de Caminos, *(978-0-9885392)* 10 Akron St., Suite 100, Cambridge, MA 02138-1281 USA Tel 617-384-9499
E-mail: crucedecaminos.org@gmail.com.

Crucifiction Games, *(978-0-9778263)* P.O. Box 654, Selah, WA 98942 USA Tel 509-697-7393; 509-952-6270
E-mail: cweedin@crucifictiongames.com
Web site: http://www.crucifictiongames.com
Dist(s): **Ingram Content Group.**

Crumb Elbow Publishing, *(978-0-89904)* P.O. Box 294, Rhododendron, OR 97049 USA (SAN 679-128X) Tel 503-622-4798.

CrumbGobbler Pr. *Imprint of* **Downtown Wetmore Pr.**

Crumly, Billie, *(978-0-9760577)* P.O. Box 281, Geraldine, AL 35974 USA.

Crumm, David Media, LLC, *(978-1-934879; 978-1-939880; 978-1-942011)* 42015 Ford Rd., Suite 234, Canton, MI 48187 USA (SAN 855-3637) Tel 734-786-3813
E-mail: admin@DavidCrummMedia.com
Web site: http://www.ReadTheSpirit.com.

Crunchpeep Media, *(978-0-9749469)* a/o Steven Merahn, 1700 Market St., 6th Flr., Philadelphia, PA 19103 USA Tel 215-832-0181
E-mail: smerahn@crunchpeep.com.

Crusade for World Revival (GBR) *(978-1-85345) Dist. by* **BTPS.**

Crush Publishing, *(978-0-9798869; 978-0-9853434; 978-0-9910756; 978-0-9995994; 978-1-950935)* P.O. Box 6088, Gardnerville, NV 89460 USA Do not confuse with Crush Publishing in Brooklyn, NY
E-mail: veronica@veronicablade.com
Web site: http://www.crushpublishing.com.

Crushing Hearts and Black Butterfly Publishing, *(978-0-615-60362-9; 978-0-615-60460-2; 978-0-615-60592-0; 978-0-615-60593-7; 978-0-615-60597-5; 978-0-615-61380-2; 978-0-615-61435-9; 978-0-615-62403-7; 978-0-615-63475-3; 978-0-615-66682-2; 978-0-615-66683-9; 978-0-615-66684-6; 978-0-615-66760-7; 978-0-615-67525-1; 978-0-615-68166-5; 978-0-615-68247-1; 978-0-615-69025-4; 978-0-615-70249-0; 978-0-615-70607-8; 978-0-615-70608-5; 978-0-615-70656-6; 978-0-615-71144-7; 978-0-615-72063-0; 978-0-615-72064-7; 978-0-615-72065-4; 978-0-615-72906-0;) 710 Saratoga Cir., Algonquin, IL 60102 USA Tel 224-234-9677*
Web site: www.crushingheartsandblackbutterfly.com
Dist(s): **CreateSpace Independent Publishing Platform.**

Crying Cougar Pr., *(978-0-615-31150-0; 978-0-615-33106-5; 978-0-615-34888-9; 978-0-615-40439-4; 978-0-615-53634-7; 978-0-9859802; 978-1-7339646)* 3559 Ruffin Rd. Suite 155, San Diego, CA 92123 USA
Dist(s): **Smashwords.**

Crypto Editions *Imprint of* **Hancock Hse. Pubs.**

Crysalis Publishing, Inc., *(978-0-9745190)* 10 Main St., Suite 4A, PMB 227, Woodbridge, NJ 07095 USA
Web site: http://www.chrysalispublishinc.com.

crysta luna studios, *(978-0-615-43657-9; 978-0-9887006)* 14995 SW Onyx Ct., Beaverton, OR 97007 USA Tel 503-933-1817
E-mail: smirlsmirl@gmail.com.

Crystal Ball Publishing, LLC., *(978-1-932277)* 107 Skiff Ave., Frankfort, NY 13340 USA
E-mail: Nerbo@msn.com; Sales@CrystalBallPublishing.com; Insight@CrystalBallPublishing.com
Web site: http://www.crystalballpublishing.com; http://www.gypsykids.com.

Crystal Bks. *Imprint of* **Words In The Works, LLC**

Crystal Journeys Publishing, *(978-1-880737)* 130 Cochise Dr., Sedona, AZ 86351-7927 USA Tel 520-284-5730
Dist(s): **Light Technology Publishing, LLC.**

Crystal Mosaic Bks., *(978-0-9836303; 978-0-9911061; 978-0-9981136; 978-1-7322046)* PO Box 1276, Hillsboro, OR 97123 USA
E-mail: raymond@macalino.com.

Crystal Pr., *(978-0-9632123; 978-0-9670886; 978-0-9746109)* 1750 Orr Ave., Simi Valley, CA 93065 USA Tel 805-527-4369; Fax: 805-582-3949 Do not confuse with Crystal Pr. in Houston, TX
E-mail: crystalpress@aol.com
Web site: http://www.Crystalpress.org.

Crystal Productions, *(978-0-924509; 978-1-56290)* Orders Addr.: 1812 Johns Dr., Glenview, IL 60025 USA (SAN 920-8224); Edit Addr.: 1812 Johns Dr., Glenview, IL 60025 USA (SAN 653-2489) Tel 847-657-8144; Fax: 847-657-8149; Toll Free Fax: 800-657-8149; Toll Free: 800-255-8629
E-mail: custserv@crystalproductions.com
Web site: http://www.crystalproductions.com
Dist(s): **Baker & Taylor Fulfillment, Inc.**
Follett School Solutions.

Crystal Springs Bks. *Imprint of* **Staff Development for Educators**

CS Media Resources, *(978-0-9764992)* Orders Addr.: 12 W. Willow Grove Ave. Suite 121, Philadelphia, PA 19118-3952 USA Toll Free: 877-866-8309
E-mail: csmr@csmediaresources.com
Web site: http://www.csmediaresources.com.

CSE Publishing, *(978-0-9743567)* 706 Radcliffe Ave., Lynn Haven, FL 32444-3039 USA (SAN 255-5581) Fax: 850-271-9874; Toll Free: 866-262-8776
E-mail: tchardy@bellsouth.net.

CSI Publishing *See* **Decere Publishing**

CSIRO Publishing (AUS) *(978-1-922173; 978-1-4863) Dist. by* **Stylus Pub VA.**

CSS Backlist *Imprint of* **Chicken Soup for the Soul Publishing, LLC**

CSS Publishing, *(978-0-9721679)* 108A Gallegos Ln., Tularosa, NM 88352 USA (SAN 254-6477) Fax: 505-585-4908 Do not confuse with C S S Publishing Company in Lima, OH
E-mail: rblanks@netmdc.com; csspublishing@hotmail.com.

CT Bookshelf, *(978-0-9837301; 978-0-9972140; 978-0-9974963)* 309 4th St. SE No. 5, Washington, DC 20003 USA Tel 202-546-7126
E-mail: author.travis@gmail.com
Web site: www.travisbooks.com.

CTaylorGo, *(978-0-578-40657-2; 978-0-578-50796-5)* 885 Briarcliff Rd. NE. #29, Atlanta, GA 30306 USA Tel 404-374-8449
E-mail: courtney.cnt@gmail.com.

CTC Publishing, *(978-0-9747789; 978-1-934073)* 10431 Lawyers Rd., Vienna, VA 22181-2822 USA (SAN 851-7908) Toll Free: 800-942-0962
E-mail: pitts@ndmc.com
Web site: http://www.couragetochange.com/
Dist(s): **Follett School Solutions.**

CTO Bks., *(978-0-9724411)* Div. of CTO Publishing LLC, Orders Addr.: P.O. Box 825, Kokomo, IN 46903 USA
E-mail: ctobooks@gmail.com
Web site: http://www.ctobooks.com
Dist(s): **MyiLibrary**
ebrary, Inc.

Ctr. for Curatorial Studies *Imprint of* **Bard College Pubns. Office**

Ctrl+Alt+Del Prodns., *(978-0-9764678)* P.O. Box 206392, New Haven, CT 06520 USA Tel 508-274-5804
E-mail: absath@ctrlaltdel-online.com
Web site: http://www.ctrlaltdel-online.com.

Cub Bks. *Imprint of* **Global Business Information Strategies, Inc.**

Cubbie Blue Publishing, *(978-0-9706341; 978-1-932824)* 546 Flanders Dr., Saint Louis, MO 63122-1618 USA; *Imprints:* Ravencrest (Ravencrest)
E-mail: rahandler@earthlink.net
Web site: ravencrestpublishing.com
Dist(s): **BookBaby.**

Cubby Hole Tales, *(978-0-9754591)* 524 Moores Mill Rd., Pelzer, SC 29669 USA Tel 864-947-6426
E-mail: telvajo@bellsouth.net
Web site: http://www.talesfromtwocousins.com.

Cube Marketing, *(978-0-9893091)* 51 9th Ave., Newark, NJ 07107 USA Tel 973-482-4101
E-mail: deidre.knight@gmail.com.

Cube17, Inc., *(978-0-9821425; 978-1-945196)* 4364 Bonita Rd. - No. 241, Bonita, CA 91902 USA Tel 619-852-6942
E-mail: Jorge@JorgeOlson.com
Web site: http://www.jorgeolson.com.

Cuccia, Louis, *(978-0-9727415)* 603 Winthrop, Smyrna, TN 37167 USA Tel 615-355-6821; Fax: 615-355-0171
E-mail: Lcuccia@aol.com.

Cuddehe Services *See* **Found Link**

Cudworth, Melissa, *(978-0-692-14317-9; 978-0-578-53124-3)* 34529 SE Linden Loop, Snoqualmie, WA 98065 USA Tel 206-300-9957
E-mail: melissa.cudworth@gmail.com
Dist(s): **CreateSpace Independent Publishing Platform.**

Cuento de Luz SL (ESP) *(978-84-937814; 978-84-15241; 978-84-938240; 978-84-15503; 978-84-15619; 978-84-15784; 978-84-16078; 978-84-16147) Dist. by* **PerseuPGW.**

Culican, J.A. *See* **Dragon Realm Pr.**

Cullor Bks. (CAN) *(978-0-9684576) Dist. by* **Lone Pine.**

Cully, Amanda, *(978-0-9971120)* 5303 e village rd, Long beach, CA 90808 USA Tel 562-494-6179
E-mail: Blebow75@aol.com.

Culpepper, Felix International, Inc., *(978-0-9740435)* Orders Addr.: P.O. Box 70, Jefferson City, TN 37760-0070 USA (SAN 255-2752) Tel 865-475-4993; Fax: 914-470-1091; Edit Addr.: 2476 Tarr Rd., Talbott, TN 37877 USA
E-mail: gfac@cshore.com; peteculpepper@helpkidswhohavecancer.org; pete@felixculpepper.com
Web site: http://www.bigboxhead.com; http://www.felixculpepper.com
Dist(s): **American Wholesale Bk. Co.**

Cult Classics Pub., *(978-0-692-54687-1; 978-0-9981068)* 1613 A Black Duck Terr., Carrollton, TX 75010 USA Tel 214-731-8767
Web site: www.Cultclassicspublisher.com
Dist(s): **CreateSpace Independent Publishing Platform.**

Cultural Connections, *(978-0-9636629; 978-1-57371)* 23499 Shakeridge Rd., Volcano, CA 95689 USA Toll Free: 888-234-5412
E-mail: culture123@volcano.net.

Culturatti Ink, *(978-0-9712383; 978-0-692-42185-7; 978-0-692-42186-4; 978-0-692-92033-6; 978-0-692-06343-9; 978-0-692-10351-7; 978-0-578-40944-3)* 9465 Counselors Row Suite 200, Indianapolis, IN, IN 46240 USA
E-mail: erika@culturattikids.net
Web site: http://www.culturattiink.com.

Culture Connection, The *See* **Culturatti Ink**

Culture Hse., *(978-0-9676080; 978-0-9819484)* Orders Addr.: P.O. Box 293, Newton, IA 50208 USA Tel 641-792-0920; Edit Addr.: 3830 Harbor Ave., Newton, IA 50208-9040 USA
E-mail: museum@pcpartner.net
Web site: http://www.mike-chapman.com.

Culture of Life, Inc., *(978-0-9761457)* 1054 Windy Knoll Rd., West Chester, PA 19382-7433 USA.

CultureGrams World Edition *Imprint of* **ProQuest LLC**

Culturelink Pr., *(978-0-9759276)* Orders Addr.: P.O. Box 3538, San Diego, CA 92163 USA (SAN 256-1174); Edit Addr.: 1435 Essex St., No.3, San Diego, CA 92103 USA
Web site: http://www.culturelinkpress.com.

Cumberland Hse. *Imprint of* **Sourcebooks, Inc.**

Cummings Pr., *(978-0-9767063)* 1939 Mt. Vernon Pl., Dunwoody, GA 30338-4417 USA Tel 770-512-8115 (phone/fax).

Cummins Associates International *See* **CAI Publishing**

Cummins, Judi, *(978-0-9760377)* Orders Addr.: P.O. Box 10 Chosen Spot Apartments, Canandaigua, NY 14424 USA
E-mail: jcummins1@rochester.rr.com.

Cumquat Publishing Company *See* **Floppinfish Publishing Co., Ltd.**

Cumuli, *(978-0-9709730)* Div. of Cumuli, Inc., P.O. Box 1174, Port Orchard, WA 98366 USA Tel 360-871-9493 (phone/fax)
E-mail: fletcher@cumuli.com; susan@cumuli.com
Web site: http://www.cumuli.com; http://www.cumulipress.com.

Cune *See* **Cune Pr., LLC**

Cune Pr., LLC, *(978-1-885942; 978-1-61457; 978-1-951082)* Div. of Scott Davis Co., P.O. Box 31024, Seattle, WA 98103 USA (SAN 298-3648) Tel 206-930-1659; Fax: 206-774-0592
E-mail: therese.nasr@cunepress.com; scott.davis@cunepress.com
Web site: http://www.cunepress.com; www.cunepress.info; www.cunepress.org; http://www.cunepress.net
Dist(s): **Publishers Group West (PGW)**
Smashwords.

Cupola Pr., *(978-0-9793345; 978-0-9834046; 978-0-9857932)* 3280 Withers Ave., Lafayette, CA 94549-2128 USA Tel 925-285-7754
E-mail: info@cupolapress.com
Web site: http://www.cupolapress.com
Dist(s): **Independent Pubs. Group**
MyiLibrary.

Cuppa Tea Productions, Inc., *(978-0-9992405)* 1313 Maltman Ave, Los Angeles, CA 90026 USA Tel 310-803-0594
E-mail: 1devonkelly@gmail.com.

†Curbstone Pr., *(978-0-915306; 978-1-880684; 978-1-931896)* P.O. Box 45, Willimantic, CT 06226-0045 USA (SAN 209-4282)
E-mail: info@curbstone.org
Web site: http://www.curbstone.org
Dist(s): **Chicago Distribution Ctr.**
Lectorum Pubns., Inc.
SPD-Small Pr. Distribution; *CIP.*

Curcumin Bks. *Imprint of* **Davlaw Press**

Cure Media Group, *(978-0-9997666)* 2 Clarke Dr, Cranbury, NJ 08512 USA Tel 609-529-9622; Fax: 609-529-9622
E-mail: nglasser@mdmag.com.

Curio Creative *Imprint of* **Wasteland Pr.**

Curiosity Bks. *Imprint of* **Curiosity Ink Media, LLC**

Curiosity Ink Media, LLC, *(978-1-948206)* 4352 FORMAN AVE, TOLUCA LAKE, CA 91602 USA Tel 310-792-0338; *Imprints:* Curiosity Books (MYID_Y_CURIOSI)
E-mail: jon@curiosityinkmedia.com
Web site: curiosityinkmedia.com
Dist(s): **Publishers Group West (PGW).**

Curiosity Quills Pr., *(978-1-62007; 978-1-948099)* Orders Addr.: P.O. Box 2160, Reston, VA 20195 USA (SAN 920-9700) Tel 800-998-2509
E-mail: editor@curiosityquills.com
Web site: http://curiosityquills.com.

Curiosmith, *(978-0-9817505; 978-1-935626; 978-1-941281; 978-1-946145)* P.O. Box 390293, Minneapolis, MN 55439-0293 USA (SAN 856-4450)
E-mail: shopkeeper@curiosmith.com
Web site: http://www.curiosmith.com.

Curious Cat Bks. *Imprint of* **Legacy Bound**

Curious Kids Guides, *(978-0-9789140)* 2561 Bunker Hill, Ann Arbor, MI 48105-3432 USA Tel 734-665-0533
E-mail: eisbruchs@aol.com
Web site: http://www.CuriousKidsGuides.com
Dist(s): **Partners Bk. Distributing, Inc.**

CuriousDots, *(978-0-9893751)* 81 Prospect St., Acton, MA 01720 USA Tel 978-263-1713; Fax: 978-263-1713
E-mail: curiousdots@gmail.com.

Curragh Pr. (IRL) *(978-1-85607) Dist. by* **Casemate Pubs.**

Currach Pr. (IRL) *(978-1-85607) Dist. by* **Dufour.**

Curran, M.J., *(978-0-9768984)* 640 Gooseberry Dr., No. 1207, Longmont, CO 80503 USA Tel 720-206-9099
E-mail: mjcurran@hotmail.com.

Curran Pr. and Editorial Consulting, LLC, *(978-1-970002)* 20 Smith Rd., Rockport, MA 01966 USA
E-mail: damaris@curraneditorial.com
Web site: curranpress.curraneditorial.com.

Currency Pr. (AUS) *(978-0-86819; 978-0-9596937; 978-1-921428; 978-1-921429; 978-1-925004; 978-1-925005; 978-1-925210; 978-1-925359; 978-1-76062) Dist. by* **Antipodes Bks.**

Current Clinical Strategies Publishing, *(978-0-9626030; 978-1-881528; 978-1-929622; 978-1-934323)* P.O. Box 1753, Blue Jay, CA 92317 USA (SAN 298-4490) Tel 949-348-8404; Fax: 949-348-8405; Toll Free Fax: 800-965-9420; Toll Free: 800-331-8227
E-mail: info@ccspublishing.com
Web site: http://www.ccspublishing.com/ccs
Dist(s): **Majors, J. A. Co.**
Matthews Medical Bk. Co.
Rittenhouse Bk. Distributors.

Current Publishing Corp., *(978-1-878663)* 30151 Tomas St., Rancho Santa Margarita, CA 92688 USA Toll Free: 800-729-7234.

Curriculum Associates, Incorporated *See* **Curriculum Assocs., LLC**

Curriculum Assocs., LLC, *(978-0-7609; 978-0-89187; 978-1-55915; 978-1-4957; 978-1-7280; 978-1-6630)* Orders Addr.: P.O. Box 2001, North Billerica, MA 01862-0901 USA (SAN 659-6304) Toll Free: 800-225-0248; Edit Addr.: 153 Rangeway Rd., North Billerica, MA 01862 USA Tel 978-667-8000; Toll Free Fax: 800-366-1158; Toll Free: 800-225-0248
E-mail: info@curriculumassociates.com; info@cainc.com; aclark@cainc.com
Web site: http://www.curriculumassociates.com.

Curriculum Concepts International, *(978-0-9786500; 978-1-60409)* 80 Fifth Ave., Suite 1503, New York, NY 10011 USA Tel 212-242-7827; Fax: 212-242-3523
Web site: www.cciny.net.

Curriculum Publishing, Presbyterian Church (U. S. A.), *(978-1-57153)* 100 Witherspoon St., Louisville, KY 40202-1396 USA Tel 502-569-5090; Fax: 502-569-8329; Toll Free: 800-524-2612; *Imprints:* Witherspoon Press (Witherspoon Pr)
Web site: http://www.pcusa.org/pcusa/currpub; http://www.bridgeresources.org
Dist(s): **Westminster John Knox Pr.**

Currie & Smith Publishing *See* **T.Y.M. Publishing**

Currier Davis Publishing *See* **GRAND Media, LLC**

Currituck Booksmiths, *(978-0-9965845)* 1959 Peace Haven Rd No. 246, Winston Salem, NC 27106 USA Tel 888-833-0360
E-mail: cfh1@prospectivepress.com
Web site: prospectivepress.com.

Curry Brothers Publishing Group, *(978-0-9798364; 978-0-9818956)* 608 Sandy Spring Trail, Madison, TN 37115 USA
E-mail: cbmpg@yahoo.com
Web site: http://currybrotherspublishing.com.

Cursack Bks., *(978-1-933439)* 31 Hubbard Rd., Dover, NH 03820 USA
E-mail: info@cursackbooks.com
Web site: http://www.cursackbooks.com
Dist(s): **Ediciones Universal.**

Curtis Aikens, Inc. *See* **Currituck Booksmiths**

Curtis Elliott Designs, Ltd., *(978-0-9742438)* 5250 Franklin St., Unit C-1, Hilliard, OH 43026 USA Tel 614-771-7978
E-mail: info@creativecoloringbooks.com
Web site: http://www.creativecoloringbooks.com.

Curtis Publishing Company *See* **Cedar Creek Publishing Service**

Custom Museum Publishing LLC, *(978-0-9788008; 978-0-9825684; 978-0-9827021; 978-1-936447; 978-1-938883; 978-1-63381)* 558 Main St., Rockland, ME 04841 USA (SAN 851-660X) Tel 207-594-0090
E-mail: info@custommuseumpublishing.com
Web site: http://www.custommuseumpublishing.com.

Customer Centered Consulting Group, Inc., *(978-0-9762493)* 5729 Lebanon Dr., Suite 144-222, Frisco, TX 75034 USA Tel 469-633-9833; Fax: 469-633-9843
E-mail: dreed@cccginc.com
Web site: http://www.cccginc.com.

Custureri, Mary *See* **Taylor and Seale Publishing**

Cute & Cuddly Productions, Inc., *(978-0-9761318)* 4401 Shallowford Rd., Suite 162-161, Roswell, GA 30075 USA Tel 678-478-6071 (phone/fax)
E-mail: cuteandcuddlyproductions@msn.com
Web site: http://www.bigbillandbuddies.com.

Cutelli, Nick, *(978-0-692-11508-4)* 918 N. Havenhurst Dr. Unit 109, WEST HOLLYWOOD, CA 90046 USA Tel 312-613-4969
E-mail: ncutelli@gmail.com
Dist(s): **Ingram Content Group.**

Cutie Series Co., The, *(978-0-9987568)* 11035 Lavender Hill Dr., Las Vegas, NV 89135 USA Tel 516-459-7966
E-mail: feliciadijohn@gmail.com.

CVD Publishing, *(978-0-9743520)* 1254 Grizzly Flat Ct., Auburn, CA 95603 USA Tel 530-885-4988
E-mail: grizlyflat@jps.net
Web site: http://www.CVDbooks.com.

CVTrahan Publishing, LLC *Imprint of* **Trahan, Virginia A. - Author**

CWG Pr., *(978-0-9788186; 978-0-9906714)* 1517 NE. 5th Ter Apt 1, Fort Lauderdale, FL 33304 USA Tel 954-524-5953
E-mail: editor@cwgpress.com
Web site: http://www.cwgpress.com.

CWLA Pr. *Imprint of* **Child Welfare League of America, Inc.**

CWS Studios, Inc., *(978-0-9785827; 978-0-615-92291-1)* 5414 W. Barry Ave., Chicago, IL 60641 USA
Web site: http://www.cws-studios.com.

Cyber Education, *(978-0-9980728)* 6377 Marquis Ct., Oak Park, CA 91377 USA Tel 818-414-5674
E-mail: lori@lorigetz.com.

Cyber Haus, *(978-1-931373)* 159 Delaware Ave., #145, Delmar, NY 12054 USA Tel 518-478-9798
E-mail: cyhaus@msn.com
Web site: http://www.revolutionaryday.com/; http://www.cyhaus.com/.

Cyber Publishing Co., *(978-0-9637419; 978-0-9747870)* 421 Ave. De Teresa, Grants Pass, OR 97526 USA (SAN 255-691X) Tel 541-474-1077; Fax: 541-474-2829
E-mail: intrchild@aol.com.

Cyber Tiger Pr., *(978-0-615-18259-9)* Planetarium Station, New York, NY 10024 USA
E-mail: bill@billweberstudios.com
Dist(s): **Lulu Pr., Inc.**

Cyberlab Publishing, *(978-0-9746501)* P.O. Box 618, Dimondale, MI 48821-0618 USA Tel 517-974-8068; Fax: 517-887-9029
E-mail: ministerjd@yahoo.com
Web site: http://www.cyberlabpublishing.com.

Cyberosia Publishing, *(978-0-9709474; 978-0-9742713)* 3864 Shelley Dr., Mobile, AL 36693-3933 USA
E-mail: scottobrown@gmail.com
Dist(s): **Diamond Distributors, Inc.**

Cyberwizard Productions, *(978-0-9795788; 978-0-9815669; 978-0-9821352; 978-1-936021)* 1403 iron Springs Rd. No. 36, Prescott, AZ 86305 USA;
Imprints: Banana Oil Books (Banana Oil)
Web site: http://cyberwizardproductions.com; http://www.cyberwizardproductions.com/Chaco_Canyon_Books/; http://wildplainspress.webs.com; http://www.cyberwizardproductions.com/Altered_Dimensions_Press; http://www.cyberwizardproductions.com/Banana_Oil_Books/; http://www.cyberwizardproductions.com/Diminuendo_Poetry/; http://firesidemysteries.webs.com; http://www.cyberwizardproductions.com/Toy_Box_Books/
Dist(s): **Send The Light Distribution LLC**

Cyclops Pr., *(978-0-9740269)* 1342 Van Buren Ave., Saint Paul, MN 55104-1926 USA.

Cyclotour Guide Bks., *(978-1-889602)* Orders Addr.: P.O. Box 10585, Rochester, NY 14610-0585 USA; Edit Addr.: 160 Harvard St., Rochester, NY 14607 USA
E-mail: cyclotour@cyclotour.com; cyclotour@frontiernet.net
Web site: http://www.cyclotour.com.

Cygnet Publishing Group, Inc./Coolreading.com (CAN) *(978-1-55305) Dist. by* **Orca Bk Pub.**

Cymbal Technique 101, *(978-0-9762593)* 440 Ross Rd., Fort Walton Beach, FL 32547 USA
E-mail: edward_capps@cymbaltechnique101.com
Web site: http://www.cymbaltechnique101.com.

Cynthia Eden *See* **Hocus Pocus Publishing, Inc.**

Cynthia Harvest Moon Intuitive Psychic Medium, *(978-0-692-96767-6)* 47732 Cty. 27, Becida, MN 56678 USA Tel 218-854-7265
E-mail: 4darling58@live.com
Web site: www.cynthiaharvestmoon.us.

Cypress Bay Publishing, *(978-0-9746747)* 910 W. Harney Ln., Lodi, CA 95242 USA (SAN 255-6928) Tel 209-365-6114
E-mail: nclaus@clearwire.net.

Cypress Communications, *(978-0-9636412; 978-0-9896043)* 35 E. Rosemont Ave., Alexandria, VA 22301 USA Tel 703-548-0532 (phone/fax) Do not confuse with companies with similar names in Leawood, KS, Saint Paul, MN, Cypress, TX
E-mail: jcclifford@earthlink.net
Web site: http://www.lighthousehistory.info; http://www.CivilWarDrummerBoy.com
Dist(s): **Partners Bk. Distributing, Inc.**

Cypress Knees Publishing, *(978-0-9745863; 978-0-9763757)* Div. of Top Brass Outdoors, Orders Addr.: P.O. Box 209, Starkville, MS 39760 USA Tel 662-323-1559; Fax: 662-323-7466; Edit Addr.: 312 Industrial Pk., Rd., Starkville, MS 39759 USA
E-mail: eric@topbrasstackle.com
Web site: http://www.topbrasstackle.com; http://www.outdooryouthadventures.com.

Cypress Knoll Prs., *(978-0-578-19357-1; 978-0-692-92433-4; 978-0-692-08720-6; 978-0-578-41513-0; 978-1-7335913)* 4070 CR 3070, Cookville, TX 75558 USA.

CyPress Pubns., *(978-0-9672585; 978-0-9776958; 978-1-935083)* P.O. Box 2636, Tallahassee, FL 32316-2636 USA Fax: 850-254-7112
E-mail: lraymond@nettally.com
Web site: http://cypresspublications.com
Dist(s): **Smashwords.**

Cypress Publishing *See* **Cypress Communications**

Cypress River Publishing, *(978-0-692-90901-0; 978-0-692-91278-2; 978-0-692-98702-5)* 1402 Vino Blanc Ct., SOUTHLAKE, TX 76092 USA Tel 817-903-2064
E-mail: agellert@yahoo.com
Dist(s): **Ingram Content Group.**

Cyr Design Publishing, *(978-0-9774543)* P.O. Box 1662, Nashua, NH 03061-1662 USA
Web site: http://cyrdesign.com.

Cyrano Bks., *(978-0-9990993; 978-0-692-08214-0; 978-1-7322739; 978-0-578-61568-4; 978-1-7358942)* 918 12th avenue, 1000, honolulu, HI 96816 USA Tel 808-492-4553; Fax: 808-492-4553
E-mail: cmackey11@icloud.com
Web site: www.cyranobooks.com.

Cyrano Bks., *(978-0-615-55618-5; 978-0-9892699)* 3348 kaunaoa St., Honolulu, HI 96815 USA Tel 808-381-5205
E-mail: cindykm@hawaii.rr.com
Web site: www.cyranobooks.com.

Czarnecki, Janina, *(978-0-9888517)* 426 Clifton Blvd., Clifton, NJ 07013 USA Tel 973-249-1164
E-mail: janina.czarnecki@gmail.com.

Czechoslovak Genealogical Society International, *(978-0-9651932)* Orders Addr.: P.O. Box 16225, Saint Paul, MN 55116-0225 USA Tel 763-595-7799; Edit Addr.: 8582 Timberwood Rd., Woodbury, MN 55125-7620 USA Tel 651-739-7543
E-mail: cgsi@comcast.net
Web site: http://www.cgsi.org.

D. A. W. Enterprise, *(978-0-9628081)* 1314 Bainbridge St., Philadelphia, PA 19147 USA Tel 215-424-2016.

D & S Marketing Systems, Inc., *(978-1-878621; 978-0-9787199; 978-1-934780)* 1205 38th St., Brooklyn, NY 11218-3705 USA Tel 718-633-8383; Fax: 718-633-8385; Toll Free: 800-633-8383
E-mail: dsmarketing@aol.com; info@dsmarketing.com
Web site: http://www.dsmarketing.com.

D B W, Incorporated *See* **Just Like Me, Inc.**

DDDD Pubns., *(978-0-9635341; 978-1-885519)* 3407 Brown Rd., Saint Louis, MO 63114-4329 USA (SAN 631-2675).

D H Publishing LLC, *(978-0-9800263)* 515 E. Carefree Hwy., No. 652, Phoenix, AZ 85085-8839 USA
E-mail: deserthillspublishing@hotmail.com.

D K Publishing, Incorporated *See* **Dorling Kindersley Publishing, Inc.**

D. W. Ink, *(978-1-892313)* P.O. Box 5470, Huntsville, AL 35814 USA Fax: 205-721-1269.

D. W. Publishing, *(978-0-9741774)* 226 McFarland St., Grand Blanc, MI 48439 USA Tel 810-695-8985
E-mail: dan@dwpublishing.com
Web site: http://www.dwpublishing.com.

Da Capo Lifelong *Imprint of* **Hachette Bks.**

Da Capo Pr. Inc. *Imprint of* **Hachette Bks.**

Da Wong Bks., *(978-0-9744360; 978-0-615-73234-3)* 4070 Cactus Rd., Shingle Springs, CA 95682 USA Tel 530-676-6060 (phone/fax)
E-mail: eslhotel@yahoo.com.

DAAB Media Gmbh (DEU) *(978-3-942597) Dist. by* **InnovativeLog.**

Dabel Brothers Production LLC. *See* **Dabel Brothers Publishing LLC**

Dabel Brothers Publishing LLC, *(978-0-9764011; 978-0-9779333; 978-0-9973065; 978-0-692-87763-0; 978-0-9996163)* 6070 Autumn View Trail, Acworth, GA 30101 USA
E-mail: ldabel@dabelbrothers.com
Web site: http://www.dabelbrothers.com/
Dist(s): **Diamond Comic Distributors, Inc. Diamond Bk. Distributors.**

Dabrishus, Mara, *(978-0-9961872)* 16 Pepper Creek Dr., Pepper Pike, OH 44124 USA Tel 412-818-2116
E-mail: mdabris@gmail.com
Web site: www.maradabrishus.com.

DAC Educational Pubns., *(978-1-930731)* 4325 Carlton Pl., Yorba Linda, CA 92886 USA
E-mail: DACpublis@aol.com.

DaChosen Publishing, *(978-0-9762627; 978-1-951047)* 1931 BRIAN WAY, GA 30033, DECATUR, GA 30033 USA Tel 404-926-6563
E-mail: dachosenorg@gmail.com
Web site: http://www.dachosen.org.

Daddy Bean Bks., *(978-0-9842929)* 42 W. 38th St., Suite 1001, New York, NY 10018 USA Tel 212-840-2326
E-mail: Pwalsh@walshfamilymedia.com
Web site: http://www.walshfamilymedia.com.

Daddy's Heroes, Inc., *(978-0-9792111)* 4799 Baxter St., Santa Barbara, CA 93110 USA
E-mail: karun@daddysheroes.com
Web site: http://www.daddysheroes.com.

Dadielte Production, *(978-0-9799273; 978-0-9981419)* Orders Addr.: 12910 Fontainebleau Dr., Moreno Valley, CA 92556-1266 USA (SAN 854-7645)
E-mail: gema118@hotmail.com.

Daedalian Press *See* **Biabe Publishing**

Dafina *Imprint of* **Kensington Publishing Corp.**

Dahle, Mark Portfolios, *(978-0-615-68498-7; 978-0-615-68502-1; 978-0-615-68515-1; 978-0-615-68518-2; 978-0-615-68718-6; 978-0-615-68727-8; 978-0-615-68729-2; 978-0-615-68732-2; 978-0-615-68733-9; 978-0-615-68735-3; 978-0-615-75042-2; 978-0-615-75046-0; 978-0-615-75047-7; 978-0-615-75049-1; 978-0-615-75053-8; 978-0-615-75054-5; 978-0-615-93016-9; 978-0-615-93750-2; 978-0-615-98110-9; 978-0-615-98111-6; 978-0-692-02252-8; 978-0-692-21589-0; 978-0-692-37061-2; 978-0-692-39866-1; 978-0-692-42329-5; 978-0-692-42332-5;) 1645 Emerald St., 2U, San Diego, CA 92109 USA Tel 858-581-1645*
E-mail: MarkDahle@aol.com
Dist(s): **CreateSpace Independent Publishing Platform.**

Dahomey Publishing Co., *(978-0-9723570)* Orders Addr.: 50 Hall Rd., Winchendon, MA 01475 USA (SAN 255-4542) Tel 978-297-1820; Fax: 978-297-2519
Web site: http://www.DahomeyPublishing.com.

Dailey International Pubs., *(978-0-9666251)* 500 Laurel Oaks Ln., Alpharetta, GA 30004-4508 USA
E-mail: franklyn@daileyint.com
Web site: http://www.daileyint.com.

Dailor, Dylan, *(978-0-692-14740-5)* 42 Kittling Ridge Ln., Rochester, NY 14612 USA Tel 585-353-2582
E-mail: DDailor11@gmail.com.

Daimon Verlag (CHE) *(978-3-85630) Dist. by* **BTPS.**

Daisy Mae Bks., *(978-0-692-04361-5; 978-0-692-04423-0; 978-0-578-46281-3)* 8255 N. Denny Rd., Bloomington, IN 47404 USA Tel 812-327-8493
E-mail: sbaker8493@yahoo.com
Dist(s): **Ingram Content Group.**

Daisy Publishing, *(978-0-9740641)* P.O. Box 681171, Franklin, TN 37068 USA Do not confuse with Daisy Publishing in Massapequa Park, NY, Altoona, PA.

Dakitab, Inc., *(978-0-9791059)* Orders Addr.: 2906 W. Grand Blvd., Detroit, MI 48202 USA (SAN 852-4408) Fax: 248-360-6148
E-mail: aid@awaytoread.com
Web site: http://www.awaytoread.com.

Dakota Assocs., Inc., *(978-0-615-14589-1; 978-0-615-18375-6)* P.O. Box 321, W. Bloomfield, NY 14585 USA
Web site: http://www.dakotaassociates.com
Dist(s): **Lulu Pr., Inc.**

Dakota Bks., *(978-0-9632861)* Orders Addr.: 2801 Daubenbiss, No. 1, Soquel, CA 95073 USA (SAN 630-9445) Tel 831-477-7174
E-mail: llogan@cruzio.com.

Dakota Legends, *(978-0-692-65514-6)* 510 S Extension Rd Apt 1044, Mesa, AZ 85210 USA Tel 480-202-7714
Web site: www.timpanogoslegend.com
Dist(s): **CreateSpace Independent Publishing Platform.**

Dakota Rose, *(978-0-9727056)* 23725 260th Ave., Okaton, SD 57562 USA Tel 605-669-2529
E-mail: dakotarose746@goldenwest.net.

Dakota Skies Photography *See* **Johnny Sundby Photography**

Dale Seymour Publications *Imprint of* **Savvas Learning Co.**

Dale, Shelley *See* **Norman Bks.**

Daley, Robert, *(978-0-9800839)* P.O. Box 5518, Keaau, HI 96749-5518 USA Tel 808-982-6688; Fax: 808-982-7824
E-mail: thedaleys@bythebookministries.org.

Dally, James W. Associates *See* **College Hse. Enterprises, LLC**

Dalton Publishing (GBR) *(978-0-9541886) Dist. by* **Midpt Trade.**

Dalton, Steven, *(978-0-692-14600-2; 978-0-692-14601-9)* 12164 S. 3410 W., Riverton, UT 84065 USA Tel 801-403-4144
E-mail: captainteancum@hotmail.com
Dist(s): **Ingram Content Group.**

Dalton, William, *(978-0-9764395)* 1338 N. Laurel Ave., West Hollywood, CA 90046 USA Tel 310-800-0811
E-mail: urban_mystic@yahoo.com.

Damamli Publishing Co., *(978-0-9753584)* 25A Crescent Dr., No.171, Pleasant Hill, CA 94523-3501 USA (SAN 256-100X) Fax: 923-674-9461
E-mail: tookie@tookie.com; president@damamli.com
Web site: http://www.damamli.com.

Damiano Sara, Janeen, *(978-0-9786404)* 108 W. Village Dr., Saint Augustine, FL 32095 USA
Web site: http://www.wheresilly.com.

Damnation Bks., *(978-1-61572; 978-1-62929)* P.O. Box 3931, Santa Rosa, CA 95402-9998 USA
Web site: http://www.damnationbooks.com; http://www.eternalpress.biz.

Dan Dan Fantasy, *(978-0-9834315)* 18483 Five Points, Redford, MI 48240 USA Tel 734-776-5478
E-mail: paintballman@sbcglobal.net.

Dan, Rebekah, *(978-0-692-94753-1)* 1150 Loma Vista Way, Vista, CA 92084 USA Tel 760-298-9404
E-mail: singtonations@gmail.com
Dist(s): **Ingram Content Group.**

Dance & Movement Pr. *Imprint of* **Rosen Publishing Group, Inc., The**

Dance Horizons *Imprint of* **Princeton Bk. Co. Pubs.**

Dancer's Publishing, *(978-0-9749848)* 2103 Harrison NW, Suite 2-336, Olympia, WA 98502 USA.

Dances With Horses, Inc., *(978-0-9763489)* P.O. Box 819, Rexburg, ID 83440 USA Tel 800-871-7635; Fax: 208-356-7817; Toll Free: 800-871-7635
E-mail: frankbell@horsewhisperer.com
Web site: http://www.horsewhisperer.com.

Dancing Dakini Pr., *(978-0-9836333)* 77 Morning Sun Dr., Sedona, AZ 86336 USA Tel 505-466-1887
E-mail: editor@dancingdakinipress.com
Web site: www.dancingdakinipress.com.

Dancing Force, The, *(978-0-9726119)* 2249 Reeves Creek Rd., Suite B, Selma, OR 97538 USA (SAN 255-156X) Tel 541-597-2093 (phone/fax)
E-mail: dancingforce@ureach.com
Dist(s): **DeVorss & Co.**

Dancing Journey Pr., *(978-0-9847662)* 434 Ulman Rd., Thetford Center, VT 05075 USA Tel 802-785-4717
E-mail: Ginger.Wallis@valley.net.

Dancing Magic Heart Bk., *(978-0-9790041)* Div. of Douglas/Steinman Productions, 1841 Broadway, Suite 1103, New York, NY 10023 USA Tel 212-765-9848; Fax: 212-765-9848
E-mail: faithdouglas@earthlink.net
Web site: http://www.douglas-steinman.com
Dist(s): **New Leaf Resources.**

Dancing Mommy Pr., *(978-0-9971084)* 242 St. Paul Dr., Alamo, CA 94507 USA Tel 925-876-4546
E-mail: jeryl@ronjer.com.

Dancing Moon Pr., *(978-1-892076; 978-1-937493; 978-1-945587)* 61535 S Hwy 97 Ste. 5 No. 623, Bend, OR 97702 USA Tel 541-574-7708 (work)
E-mail: kim@dancingmoonpress.com
Web site: http://www.dancingmoonpress.com
Dist(s): **Partners/West Book Distributors.**

Dancing Spirit Publishing, LLC, *(978-0-9997064)* P.O. Box 102, Forked River, NJ 08731 USA Tel 732-403-7146
E-mail: s4mmy415@gmail.com
Web site: DancingSpiritPublishing.com.

Dancing With Bear Publishing, *(978-0-9988339; 978-1-7325905; 978-1-7342841)* P.O. Box 281, San Marcos, TX 78667 USA Tel 512-665-6188 Do not confuse with Dancing With Bear Publishing in Antlers, OK
E-mail: debbieroppolo@gmail.com
Web site: dwbpublishing.com.

Dancing Words Pr., Inc., *(978-0-9716346)* Orders Addr.: P.O. Box 1575, Severna Park, MD 21146 USA; Edit Addr.: 12 Sonneborn Ln., Severna Park, MD 21146 USA Tel 410-647-1441 (phone/fax)
E-mail: dwpinc@aol.com
Web site: http://www.dancingwordspress.com
Dist(s): **Quality Bks., Inc.**

D&C Publishing, *(978-0-692-77041-2; 978-0-692-78854-7; 978-0-692-19084-5)* 2062 S. Taylor, cleveland heights, OH 44118 USA Tel 216-321-1101
E-mail: ladoshaw@yahoo.com
Web site: www.lwrightbooks.com.

Dandelion Publishing, *(978-0-9793930)* 6234 Eliza Ln., North Las Vegas, NV 89031 USA (SAN 853-330X)
E-mail: sand.d@cox.net
Web site: http://DandelionPublishing.com.

Dandy Lion Pubns., *(978-0-931724; 978-1-883055)* P.O. Box 190, Sn Luis Obisp, CA 93406-0190 USA (SAN 211-5565) Toll Free: 800-776-8032
E-mail: dandy@dandylionbooks.com
Web site: http://www.dandylionbooks.com.

Dangberg, Grace Foundation, Incorporated *See* **Sage Hill Pubs., LLC**

Daniel & Daniel, Pubs., Inc., *(978-0-931832; 978-0-936784; 978-1-56474; 978-1-880284)* P.O. Box 2790, McKinleyville, CA 95519 USA (SAN 215-1995) Tel 707-839-3495; Fax: 707-839-3242; Toll Free: 800-662-8351
E-mail: dandd@danielpublishing.com
Web site: http://www.danielpublishing.com
Dist(s): **SCB Distributors.**

Daniel, Onicka J, *(978-0-692-90518-0; 978-0-692-95713-4; 978-0-692-08712-1; 978-0-578-40429-5)* 562 Candle Ln. No. 101, Newport News, VA 23608 USA Tel 757-358-3677
E-mail: theholidayboys@outlook.com
Web site: www.theholidayboy.com.

Daniel's Hse. Publishing, *(978-0-9637200; 978-0-692-01895-8; 978-0-692-9915033; 978-0-692-66397-4; 978-0-692-84229-4; 978-0-9988590)* P.O. Box 623, Huntington, IN 46750 USA Tel 260-356-7569; Fax: 260-356-7594.

Dankworth Publishing, *(978-0-9855676; 978-0-9987888)* 309 Reamer Pl., Oberlin, OH 44074 USA Tel 612-309-5126 E-mail: mindybrueggemann@yahoo.com.

DanMar Publishing, *(978-0-9749407)* 112 E. Pennsylvania Blvd., Feasterville, PA 19053 USA Tel 215-364-1112; Fax: 215-364-3231 E-mail: drlavanga@aol.com Web site: http://www.drlavanga.com.

Danny & Ester's Fortunate Adventures, *(978-0-9833667)* 1979 Willow Ave., Worthington, MN 56187 USA Tel 507-376-5889 E-mail: mccuen@mchsi.com *Dist(s):* **Adventure Pubns.**

Dante's Publishing *See* **Solomon's Bks.**

Dantone, Desni, *(978-0-9895090)* 114 Alderwood Dr., Greensburg, PA 15601 USA Tel 724-261-0096 *Dist(s):* **CreateSpace Independent Publishing Platform.**

Danza Pubns., *(978-0-9774552)* P.O. Box 252053, West Bloomfield, MI 48325 USA Toll Free: 800-457-2157 Web site: http://www.elaineserling.com.

D.A.P./Distributed Art Pubs., *(978-1-881616; 978-1-891024; 978-1-933045; 978-1-935202; 978-1-938922; 978-1-942884; 978-1-63681)* Orders Addr.: 75 Broad St., Suite 630, New York, NY 10004 USA (SAN 630-6446) Tel 212-627-1999; Fax: 212-627-9484; Toll Free Fax: 800-478-3128; Toll Free: 800-338-2665 E-mail: dap@dapinc.com Web site: http://www.artbook.com/.

Dar Asadeeq Publishing & Distribution, Inc., *(978-0-615-52712-3; 978-0-9853772)* 646 Oaklawn Ave., Chula Vista, CA 91910 USA Tel 619-761-5329 E-mail: alsadeeq.usa@gmail.com Web site: www.daralsadeeq.com.

Dara Publishing LLC, *(978-0-9975059; 978-0-692-98947-0; 978-1-7321362)* 1649 Nostrand Ave., Brooklyn, NY 11226 USA Tel 347-962-8363 E-mail: denifa@yahoo.com.

Darby Creek *Imprint of* **Lerner Publishing Group**

Dare to Dream Scholarship, Incorporated *See* **Cole Publishing**

Dargaud Publishing Co. (FRA) *(978-0-917201; 978-2-205) Dist. by* **Distribks Inc.**

Daring, Doe, *(978-0-9853543)* 601 N. Elm St., Comanche, TX 84105 USA Tel 469-688-6888 E-mail: doedaring@gmail.com.

Dark Circle Comics *Imprint of* **Archie Comic Pubns., Inc.**

Dark Cloud Bks., *(978-0-9978296; 978-0-692-91121-1; 978-0-578-49281-0; 978-0-578-49284-1)* 2808 Bent Leaf Dr., Valrico, FL 33594 USA Tel 813-601-2965 E-mail: stevealtier@outlook.com Web site: www.stevealtier.com.

Dark Continents Publishing, *(978-0-9831603; 978-0-9836245; 978-0-9848931; 978-0-615-68082-8; 978-0-615-69182-4; 978-0-615-71013-6; 978-0-615-71015-0; 978-0-615-71017-4; 978-0-615-71018-1; 978-0-615-71019-8; 978-0-615-71840-8; 978-0-615-83145-9; 978-0-615-84491-6; 978-0-615-88140-9; 978-0-615-91582-1; 978-0-615-96489-8; 978-0-615-97495-8; 978-0-692-24951-2) P.O. Box 276, Tiskilwa, IL 61368 USA Tel 815-646-4748* E-mail: DMYoungquist@darkcontinents.com Web site: www.darkcontinents.com *Dist(s):* **CreateSpace Independent Publishing Platform.**

Dark Forest Pr., *(978-0-9764226)* 1310 N. Oak St., Apt. 408, Arlington, VA 22209 USA Tel 202-368-4341; P.O. Box 9133, Arlington, VA 22210 (SAN 256-4475) Tel 202-368-4341 Do not confuse with Dark Forest Press in Denver, CO.

Dark Horse Books *Imprint of* **Dark Horse Comics**

Dark Horse Comics, *(978-1-56971; 978-1-878574; 978-1-59307; 978-1-59582; 978-1-59617; 978-1-61655; 978-1-61659; 978-1-62115; 978-1-63008; 978-1-5067)* 10956 SE Main St., Milwaukie, OR 97222 USA Tel 503-652-8815; Fax: 503-654-9440; *Imprints:* Dark Horse Books (Dark Horse Bks) E-mail: dhcomics@darkhorse.com Web site: http://www.darkhorse.com *Dist(s):* **Children's Plus, Inc.** **Diamond Comic Distributors, Inc.** **Diamond Bk. Distributors** **Penguin Random Hse. Distribution** **Penguin Random Hse. LLC** **Random Hse., Inc.**

Dark Mantle Publishing, *(978-0-692-97450-6)* 1301 n dunbarton oaks ln, Liberty Lake, WA 99019 USA Tel 253-905-9563 E-mail: empirial995@gmail.com.

A Dark Matter Pubn., *(978-0-578-22252-3)* 63 E. 9th St., Apt. 7R, New York, NY 10003-6302 USA Tel 972 0506899049 E-mail: adarkmatterpublication@gmail.com.

Dark Oak Pr., *(978-0-9660744; 978-0-9788777; 978-0-9823745; 978-1-937035; 978-1-941754; 978-1-949817)* Div. of Kerlak Enterprises, Inc., 1779 Kirby Pkwy., Suite 1-373, Memphis, TN 38138 USA (SAN 857-9776) E-mail: agilbreath@kerlakpublishing.com; service@kerlakpublishing.com; agilbreath@darkoakpress.com Web site: http://www.darkoakpress.com; http://www,darkoakpress.com.

Dark Overlord Media *See* **Empty Set Entertainment**

Dark Passages *Imprint of* **Whorl Bks.**

Dark Skull Studios, *(978-0-9797080)* 17711 Barker Bluff Ln., Cypress, TX 77433 USA (SAN 854-1922) Tel 832-220-6734 E-mail: richardleon@darkskullstudios.com Web site: http://www.darkskullstudios.com.

Dark Star Publishing, *(978-0-9897435; 978-0-9984263; 978-0-9986260)* P.O. Box 667, Richmond, MI 48062 USA Tel 810-858-1135 E-mail: dayne87@comcast.net Web site: www.bloodandshadows.net.

Darker Intentions Pr., *(978-0-9769612; 978-0-9827597)* P.O. Box 569, Freehold Twp., NJ 07728-0569 USA Tel 732-299-6212 E-mail: jzdakota@hotmail.com.

Darkerwood Publishing Group, *(978-0-9669788; 978-0-9788975; 978-1-938839)* P.O. Box 2011, Arvada, CO 80001 USA E-mail: swordarkeereon@gmail.com; ofs.admin@gmail.com; darkerwoodpublishing@gmail.com Web site: http://www.demonolatry.org/dbpub.htm.

Darling & Co. *Imprint of* **Laughing Elephant**

Darling Pr. LLC, *(978-0-9765761)* Orders Addr.: 19740 SW 49th Ave., Tualatin, OR 97062 USA Web site: http://www.darlingpress.com *Dist(s):* **Bottman Design, Inc.**

Darlyng & Co. Publisher *See* **Darlyng & Co. Publishing**

Darlyng & Co. Publishing, *(978-1-7337778)* 1585 Yanceyville St., No. 14292, Greensboro, NC 27405 USA Tel 929-376-8584 E-mail: info@darlyngandco.com Web site: www.darlyngandco.com.

Darnell Publishing, *(978-0-9755616)* P.O. Box 341825, Tampa, FL 33694 USA Web site: http://www.abrink.com.

Dar-Salaam.org, *(978-1-948117)* P.O. Box 55573, Houston, TX 77255 USA Tel 713-364-4649 E-mail: hope99@gmail.com.

Dart Publishing, *(978-0-692-80432-2; 978-0-692-84334-5; 978-0-578-54227-0; 978-0-578-56167-7)* 1198 Spruance St., San Jose, CA 95128 USA Tel 408-280-7611 E-mail: juliedart@comcast.ney.

DASANBOOKS, *(978-0-9819542; 978-0-9828016; 978-0-9839594)* 120 Sylvan Ave., Englewood Cliffs, NJ 07632 USA *Dist(s):* **Midpoint Trade Bks., Inc.**

Dash & Doodles Productions, *(978-0-615-22279-0; 978-0-578-08121-2)* 4810 Kellywood Dr., Glen Allen, VA 23060 USA Tel 804-527-1033 E-mail: dashanddoodles@aol.com Web site: http://www.askdash.com *Dist(s):* **Lulu Pr., Inc.**

Data Trace Legal Publishers, Incorporated *See* **Data Trace Publishing, Co.**

Data Trace Publishing, Co., *(978-0-9637468; 978-1-57400)* Orders Addr.: P.O. Box 1239, Brooklandville, MD 21022 USA Tel 410-494-4994; Fax: 410-494-0515; Toll Free: 800-342-0454; Edit Addr.: 110 West Rd., Suite 227, Towson, MD 21204 USA E-mail: info@datatrace.com Web site: http://www.datatrace.com/legal.

Databooks *See* **Chandler Hse. Pr.**

Daughter Culture Pubns., *(978-0-935281)* P.O. Box 127924, San Diego, CA 92112 USA (SAN 695-7447) Tel 619-432-5491.

Daughters Arise, LLC, *(978-0-9744178)* 2648 E. Workman Ave., Suite 314, West Covina, CA 91791 USA Tel 770-808-1199; Fax: 770-216-1626 E-mail: fhenley@daughtersarise.com Web site: http://www.daughtersarise.com.

Daughtrey Publishing Hse., *(978-0-578-46710-8)* 5024 3/4 Hayter Ave., Lakewood, CA 90712 USA Tel 562-333-5353 E-mail: sdaughtrey@icloud.com.

Daven, Christian Publishing, *(978-0-578-00257-6)* 6504 Mendius Ave., NE, Albuquerque, NM 87109 USA Tel 505-315-2984 *Dist(s):* **Lulu Pr., Inc.**

Davenport, May Pubs., *(978-0-943864; 978-0-9603118; 978-0-9794140)* 26313 Purissima Rd., Los Altos Hills, CA 94022-4539 USA (SAN 212-467X) Tel 650-947-1325; Fax: 650-947-1373 E-mail: mdbooks@earthlink.net *Dist(s):* **Todd Communications.**

Davenport, Sheena, *(978-0-9747625)* 3535 Riverview Approach, Ellenwood, GA 30294 USA Tel 404-241-3106 E-mail: szdavenport@yahoo.com.

Davey, Daisy & Pete - The Things We Can Dream, *(978-0-578-40850-7; 978-0-578-46097-0)* 5 Novilla, Laguna, CA 92677 USA Tel 951-907-0762 E-mail: tehunter9@yahoo.com *Dist(s):* **CreateSpace Independent Publishing Platform.**

David & Charles Pubs. (GBR) *(978-0-7153; 978-1-4463) Dist. by* **TwoRivers.**

David, Elizabeth A., *(978-0-9740170)* P.O. Box 766, Fairhaven, MA 02719-0700 USA Tel 508-979-5593 E-mail: yasny@comcast.net Web site: http://www.zorena.com.

David Fickling Bks. *Imprint of* **Random Hse. Children's Bks.**

†David, Jonathan Pubs., Inc., *(978-0-8246)* 68-22 Eliot Ave., Middle Village, NY 11379 USA (SAN 169-5274) Tel 718-456-8611; Fax: 718-894-2818 E-mail: jondavpub@aol.com Web site: http://www.jdbooks.com; *CIP.*

†Davidson, Harlan Inc., *(978-0-88295)* 773 Glenn Ave., Wheeling, IL 60090-6000 USA (SAN 201-2375) Tel 847-541-9720; Fax: 847-541-9830 E-mail: harlandavidson@harlandavidson.com Web site: http://www.harlandavidson.com; *CIP.*

Davies, Sean, *(978-0-692-96866-6)* 514 Americas Way 8806, Box Elder, SD 57719 USA Tel 314-409-0306 E-mail: incrediblemicrobiome@gmail.com.

Davis, A. S. Media Group, *(978-0-9666352; 978-0-9729150; 978-0-9759022; 978-0-9766013; 978-0-9776245; 978-0-9787719; 978-1-934724)* Orders Addr.: P.O. Box 590780, San Francisco, CA 94159 USA E-mail: info@greenlinepub.com Web site: http://www.greenlinepub.com.

Davis Bks. LLC, *(978-0-9770142)* Orders Addr.: P.O. Box 6291, Cincinnati, OH 45206 USA Tel 513-687-1943 E-mail: georgedisselkamp@yahoo.com Web site: http://www.davisbooks.cjb.net *Dist(s):* **Docustar.**

Davis, Brittney, *(978-0-578-47171-6; 978-0-578-47172-3)* 5143 Derby Forest Dr. N., Jacksonville, FL 32258 USA Tel 904-844-3998 E-mail: brittney3583@yahoo.com *Dist(s):* **Ingram Content Group.**

Davis, Gregory B., *(978-0-578-21354-5)* 8 Aintree Walk, Sewell, NJ 08080 USA Tel 856-904-5097 E-mail: gregbdavis@comcast.net.

Davis, James (Jim), *(978-0-9760960)* 1700 W. Washington St. Apt. A507, Springfield, IL 62702-6447 USA.

Davis, Kristalin, *(978-0-578-59675-4)* P.O. Box P.O. Box 84, Howe, OK 74940 USA Tel 760-898-9764 E-mail: kristalin.davis@yahoo.com.

Davis, nathaniel *See* **Davis, Nathaniel**

Davis, Nathaniel, *(978-0-9997822)* 1627 McDonald St., Houston, TX 77007 USA Tel 281-755-7779 E-mail: peanutbutterandjam2017@gmail.com.

Davis, Paul *See* **Royal Hse. Publishing**

Davis Pubns., Inc., *(978-0-87192; 978-1-61528; 978-1-64164)* 50 Portland St., Worcester, MA 01608 USA (SAN 201-3002) Tel 508-754-7201; Fax: 508-791-0779; Toll Free: 800-533-2847 E-mail: rfrederics@davisart.com; mnicholson@davisart.com Web site: http://www.davisart.com *Dist(s):* **Sterling Publishing Co., Inc.**

Davis, Tamela *See* **JacKris Publishing**

Davis, Wayne *See* **LoGiudice Publishing**

Davlaw Press, *(978-0-9776917)* Orders Addr.: P.O. Box 4317, Harrisburg, PA 17111 USA (SAN 257-9863) Tel 717-441-5451; Fax: 717-441-4925; *Imprints:* Curcumin Books (Curcumin Bks) E-mail: larry@davlawpress.com Web site: http://www.davlawpress.com.

†Davus Publishing, *(978-0-915317)* P.O. Box 292, Buffalo, NY 14213-7101 USA (SAN 289-9787) Tel 519-426-2077; 150 Norfolk St., S., Simcoe, ON N3Y 2W2 Tel 519-426-0105; Fax: 519-426-2027 E-mail: davus@kwic.com; davuspub@sympatico.ca Web site: http://www.kwic.com/~davus; http://www3.sympatico.ca/drbeasley; http://www.davuspublishing.com *Dist(s):* **Coutts Information Services;** *CIP.*

DAW *Imprint of* **DAW**

DAW, 375 Hudson St., 3rd Flr., New York, NY 10014 USA; *Imprints:* DAW (DAW) *Dist(s):* **Penguin Random Hse. Distribution** **Penguin Random Hse. LLC.**

Dawasoft, *(978-0-9764218)* 150-35 119th Rd., Jamaica, NY 11434 USA Tel 347-954-6479 E-mail: dawasoft@yahoo.com.

Dawn Chorus Pr. *Imprint of* **Perennis, Sophia**

Dawn of a New Day Pubns., The *Imprint of* **Konkori International**

Dawn of Day Childrens Publishing Co., Inc., *(978-0-9666857)* 73 Ireland Pl., PMB 201, Amityville, NY 11757 USA (SAN 253-0198) Tel 631-225-5513; Fax: 631-225-5431; Toll Free: 800-575-7040 E-mail: information@dawnofday.com Web site: http://www.dawnofday.com.

Dawn Pubns., *(978-0-916124; 978-1-878265; 978-1-883220; 978-1-58469)* 12402 Bitney Springs Rd., Nevada City, CA 95959 USA (SAN 856-8294) Tel 530-478-0111; Fax: 530-274-7778; Toll Free: 800-545-7475 Do not confuse with Dawn Pubns. in Pasadena, TX E-mail: nature@dawnpub.com; info@dawnpub.com Web site: http://www.dawnpub.com *Dist(s):* **Brodart Co.** **Children's Plus, Inc.** **Common Ground Distributors, Inc.** **Follett School Solutions** **Ingram Bk. Co.** **Sourcebooks, Inc.** **Territory Titles.**

Dawn Pubns. *Imprint of* **Sourcebooks, Inc.**

DawQuin LLC, *(978-0-9842787)* P.O. Box 1800, Troy, MI 48099 USA (SAN 858-9461) Tel 248-765-7276 E-mail: publisher@dawquin.com Web site: www.dawquin.com.

Day By Day *See* **Day By Day Recovery Resources, LLC**

Day By Day Recovery Resources, LLC, *(978-0-9674915; 978-1-934569)* 510 Astor Ave, Kingman, AZ 86409 USA Tel 887-447-1683 E-mail: business@pocketsponsor.com Web site: http://www.day-by-day.org; http://www.PocketSponsor.com *Dist(s):* **Mentor Bks.**

Day I Hit a Home Run Enterprise, The, *(978-0-9831950)* 7389 Brookville Rd., Oxford, OH 45056 USA Tel 513-290-2189 E-mail: mullenmike122@yahoo.com Web site: www.thedayihitahomerun.com.

Day to Day Bks. *Imprint of* **Day to Day Enterprises**

Day to Day Enterprises, *(978-1-890905)* Orders Addr.: 8396 Maryland Rd., Lake Shore, MD 21122-4655 USA (SAN 299-7118) Tel 443-817-2129; *Imprints:* Eco Fiction Books (Eco Fiction Bks); Day to Day Books (Day2Day) E-mail: books@daytodayenterprises.com Web site: http://www.daytodayenterprises.com; http://www.totallystories.com *Dist(s):* **Book Clearing Hse.**

Day3 Productions, Inc., *(978-0-9777361)* 215 Tower Rd, McKenzie, TN 38201 USA (SAN 850-0770) Tel 731-352-6081 E-mail: jeff@day3productions.com Web site: http://www.day3productions.com.

Daybreak Pr., *(978-0-578-05238-0; 978-0-578-09509-7)* 314 W. 92nd St., 2F, New York, NY 10025 USA; 2307 Broadway, New York, NY 10024 E-mail: lesliefourton2gmail.com.

Daydreamers Pr. *Imprint of* **Penn, Carlotta**

Daylight Bks., *(978-0-9632177; 978-0-9840220)* 671 W. 193rd St. #4j New York, New York, NY 10040 USA Tel 646-265-3294 E-mail: smartin34@earthlink.net *Dist(s):* **ebrary, Inc.**

Daylight Pubs., *(978-0-9764103; 978-0-9792755)* 8255 S Wright Pl., Broken Arrow, OK 74014 USA Tel 918-357-1266 E-mail: kathy@daylightpublishers.com Web site: http://www.daylightpublishers.com.

DayOne Pubns. (GBR) *(978-0-902548; 978-1-903087; 978-1-84625) Dist. by* **STL Dist.**

Days of Glory Publishing, *(978-0-9770206)* 28 Branden Way, Tolland, CT 06084 USA.

DaySpring Cards, *(978-1-58061; 978-1-884009; 978-1-59449; 978-1-60116; 978-1-60817; 978-1-61494; 978-1-63116; 978-1-68408; 978-1-64454; 978-1-64870)* P.O. Box 1010, Siloam Springs, AR 72761 USA (SAN 298-6302) Tel 479-524-9301; Fax: 479-524-9477; Toll Free: 800-944-8000 E-mail: jkaufman@dayspring.com; laurak@dayspring.com; calis@dayspring.com; dang@dayspring.com Web site: http://www.dayspring.com *Dist(s):* **TNT Media Group, Inc.**

Daystar Press *See* **TopNotch Pr.**

Dayton International Peace Museum *See* **Peace Power Pr.**

Dayton Publishing, *(978-0-9893290; 978-0-9970032; 978-1-7325265; 978-1-7351716)* 608 Barbara Ave., Solana Beach, CA 92075 USA Tel 858-775-3629 E-mail: linneadayt@aol.com.

Dazsling Inc., *(978-0-9749170)* P.O. Box 236, Allston, MA 02134 USA Web site: http://www.rootfriends.com.

DC Comics, *(978-0-930289; 978-1-56389; 978-1-4012; 978-1-7995)* Div. of Warner Bros.- A Time Warner Entertainment Co., 1700 Broadway, New York, NY 10019 USA Tel 212-636-5400; Fax: 212-636-5979; *Imprints:* Vertigo (Vertigo); Paradox (Paradox); A B C (A B C); Wildstorm (Wildstorm); DC Kids (DCKids); MAD (MAD DC); DC Ink (DC Ink); DC Zoom (DC Zoom); Jinxworld (Jinxworld) E-mail: booksales@dccomics.com Web site: http://www.dccomics.com *Dist(s):* **Children's Plus, Inc.** **Eastern News Distributors** **MyiLibrary** **Penguin Random Hse. Distribution** **Penguin Random Hse. LLC** **Random Hse., Inc.**

DC Ink *Imprint of* **DC Comics**

DC Kids *Imprint of* **DC Comics**

DC Zoom *Imprint of* **DC Comics**

DCTS Publishing, *(978-0-9653904)* Div. of Hamilton Ministry, P.O. Box 40216, Santa Barbara, CA 93140 USA Tel 805-570-3168; Toll Free: 800-965-8150 E-mail: dennis@dctspub.com Web site: http://www.dctspub.com.

de Blegny, Nick Publishing, *(978-0-615-82516-8; 978-0-615-92205-8; 978-0-615-95925-2; 978-0-692-32582-7; 978-0-692-32583-4; 978-0-692-61843-1; 978-0-692-67559-5; 978-0-692-14919-5; 978-1-7332647)* 63 Mount Vernon Street, Apt 9, Boston, MA 02108 USA Tel 12019843148 *Dist(s):* **CreateSpace Independent Publishing Platform.**

De Boer, Cynthia L. Author/Speaker, *(978-1-7321384)* P.O. Box 50014, Henderson, NV 89016 USA Tel 702-293-0612 E-mail: c.deboerauthorspeaker@gmail.com Web site: www.CynthiaLDeBoer.com.

de Contreras, Lantz *See* **Angelic Prince Publishing, The**

de Fosseway, Marquis (GBR) *(978-0-9561561) Dist. by* **LuluCom.**

De La Flor (ARG) *(978-950-515) Dist. by* **LD Bks Inc.**

De La Luz Pubns., *(978-0-9748326)* 121 W. Hickory St., Denton, TX 76201 USA Tel 940-367-1651; Fax: 940-323-0488 E-mail: ccarrasco1@chater.net.

DE LA O LLC, *(978-0-578-41239-9)* 85 John St. 5C, New York, NY 10038 USA Tel 773-600-3799 E-mail: SD.DELAO@GMAIL.COM *Dist(s):* **Independent Pub.**

De Loach, George P., *(978-0-9768362)* 475 W. Fallen Leaf Cir., Wasilla, AK 99654 USA Tel 907-376-2680 E-mail: gdeloach@juno.com.

De Portola Pr., *(978-0-692-47363-4; 978-0-692-18673-2)* 33780 Linda Rosea Rd., Temecula, CA 92592 USA Tel 951-551-5338 *Dist(s):* **CreateSpace Independent Publishing Platform.**

Dead Fossil Entertainment, *(978-0-578-56868-3; 978-0-578-59357-9)* 4020 E Altadena Ave, Phoenix, AZ 85028 USA Tel 480-266-3808 E-mail: deadfossil@carldang.com Web site: https://carldang.com.

Deaf Missions, *(978-1-59799)* Orders Addr.: 21199 Greenview Rd., Council Bluffs, IA 51503-4190 USA E-mail: joseph@deafmissions.com Web site: http://www.deafmissions.com.

Deal, Darlene, *(978-0-9747299)* P.O. Box 521, North Hollywood, CA 91603-0521 USA Tel 818-752-7065 (phone/fax).

Deane, Jennifer Inc., *(978-0-9825112)* 1061 5th Ave. N., Naples, FL 34102 USA E-mail: Jenniferdeane@earthlink.net; Jennifer@JenniferDeane.com Web site: http://www.Jenniferdeane.com; http://www.SiennaBooks.com; http://www.musemediapublishing.com.

DeAngelis, Anthony, *(978-0-9754853)* 101 Cypress Ave., San Bruno, CA 94066-5420 USA E-mail: a.deangelis@worldnet.att.net.

Dean's Bks., Inc., *(978-0-9728607)* 1426 S. Kansas Ave., Topeka, KS 66612 USA Tel 785-357-4708 E-mail: contact@oilcanbook.com Web site: http://www.oilcanbook.com.

Dear You, *(978-1-7321177)* 134-27 166th Pl. No. 10c, Jamaica, NY 11434 USA Tel 646-601-3802 E-mail: Nasheemad@gmail.com.

Dearborn Publishing, *(978-1-891685)* Div. of The Mae Group LLC, E-mail: johngraham@att.net.

Dearborn Real Estate Education *Imprint of* **Kaplan Publishing**

Dearborn Trade, A Kaplan Professional Company *See* **Kaplan Publishing**

Deats, Dorie, *(978-1-7326064)* 3617 General Taylor St., New Orleans, LA 70125 USA Tel 607-342-8754 E-mail: dorie.deats@gmail.com.

Deb on Air Bks., *(978-0-9727615)* Orders Addr.: P.O. Box 580055, Elk Grove, CA 95758 USA Tel 916-684-3551.

Debate, Editorial (ESP) *(978-84-7444; 978-84-8306) Dist. by* **AIMS Intl.**

Debi, Kennedy *See* **nJoy Bks.**

Deborah Remington Charitable Trust for the Visual Arts, *(978-0-692-75785-7)* 325 E. 79th St., New York, NY 10075 USA Tel 212-535-7050 E-mail: mmbart1@gmail.com Web site: deborahremington.com *Dist(s):* **D.A.P./Distributed Art Pubs.**

Debra L. Wood, *(978-0-578-43189-5; 978-0-578-64475-2)* 381 Colebrook Rd., Gansevoort, NY 12831 USA Tel 518-695-2055 E-mail: jibbitsohio@aol.com, tsart@live.com *Dist(s):* **Ingram Content Group.**

DeCa Communications, LLC, *(978-0-9762262)* 300 Williamsburg Dr., Mandeville, LA 70471 USA Web site: http://www.decacom.info.

Decent Hill, *(978-1-936085)* Div. of Decent Hill Pubs., LLC, Orders Addr.: 6100 Oak Tree Blvd., Ste 200, Independence, OH 44131 USA (SAN 858-2483) Tel 216-236-3315 Personal Cell Phone; Toll Free: 866-688-5325 (phone/fax) E-mail: Support@DecentHill.com Web site: http://www.DecentHill.com *Dist(s):* **Baker & Taylor Publisher Services (BTPS).**

Decent Hill Publishers *See* **Decent Hill**

Decere Publishing, *(978-0-9717013; 978-0-9816572)* 5590 Bunky Way, Atlanta, GA 30338 USA Tel 404-474-2830; Fax: 770-399-5883 Do not confuse with CSI Publishing in Monterey Park, CA E-mail: mark@decere.com Web site: http://www.decere.com.

Decesare, Jason, *(978-0-578-50578-7; 978-0-578-50579-4)* 174 Water St., Warren, RI 02885 USA Tel 401-473-6231 E-mail: j.dece1010@gmail.com.

Dedalus Bks. Ltd. (GBR) *(978-0-946626; 978-1-873982; 978-1-903517; 978-1-904556; 978-1-907650; 978-1-909232; 978-1-910213; 978-1-912868) Dist. by* **SCB Distributo.**

Dedushkiny Skazki, *(978-0-692-17234-6; 978-0-692-17238-4)* 5677 Nesbitt Ln., JACKSONVILLE, FL 32277 USA Tel 904-434-0062 E-mail: z.arbatskiy@gmail.com *Dist(s):* **Ingram Content Group.**

Deep Dish Design, *(978-0-9755033)* 15012 Cherry Ln., Burnsville, MN 55306 USA E-mail: jb@deepdishdesign.com Web site: http://www.deepdishdesign.com.

Deep River Bks., *(978-0-9712311; 978-0-9747190; 978-1-933204; 978-1-935265; 978-1-937756; 978-1-940269; 978-1-63269)* 1610 W. Williamson Ave., Sisters, OR 97759 USA Tel 541-549-1139 E-mail: bill@deepriverbooks.com Web site: http://www.deepriverbooks.com/ *Dist(s):* **Baker & Taylor Publisher Services (BTPS) Send The Light Distribution LLC.**

Deep Roots Pubns., *(978-0-9671713; 978-0-9819528)* Orders Addr.: P.O. Box 114, Saratoga, NY 12866 USA Tel 518-583-8920; Fax: 518-584-3919; Edit Addr.: 229 Lake Ave., Saratoga, NY 12866 USA E-mail: drpalmer2002@yahoo.com Web site: http://www.deeprootspublications.com *Dist(s):* **North Country Bks., Inc.**

Deep Sea Publishing, *(978-0-9834276; 978-1-939535)* 1109 Devon St., Herndon, VA 2010 USA (SAN 860-164X) Tel 571-455-2027 E-mail: erhughes@deepseapublishing.com Web site: www.deepseapublishing.com *Dist(s):* **Lulu Pr., Inc.**

Deep Waters Pr., *(978-0-9748171)* Suite 100, 77 Court St., Laconia, NH 03246 USA (SAN 255-8777) Tel 603-520-1214; P.O. Box 452, Meredith, NH 03253 Tel 603-524-2585 E-mail: halclyon@yahoo.com; deepwaterspress@yahoo.com Web site: http://www.DeepWaterspress.com.

Deeper Revelation Bks., *(978-0-942507; 978-1-949297)* P.O. Box 4260, Cleveland, TN 37320 USA (SAN 667-3619) Tel 423-478-2843; 423-614-7399; Fax: 423-479-2980 E-mail: pastormikeshreve@gmail.com; vicki@deeperrevelationbooks.org; mikeshreve@shreveministries.org Web site: http://www.deeperrevelationbooks.org; http://www.shreveministries.org *Dist(s):* **Anchor Distributors Whitaker Hse.**

Deeper Roots Pubns. & Media, *(978-1-930547)* Orders Addr.: 13 W. Lakeshore Dr., Cherokee Village, AR 72529 USA E-mail: deeperroots@aol.com Web site: http://www.DeeperRoots.com.

Deeper Waters, *(978-0-615-36602-9; 978-0-615-43255-7; 978-0-615-58840-7)* 11520 Grandview Rd., Kansas City,, MO 64137 USA Tel 816-765-9900 E-mail: blake.cadwell@gmail.com.

Deepercalling Media, Inc., *(978-0-9726135; 978-1-59601)* 1200 Mt. Diablo Blvd., Suite 108, Walnut Creek, CA 94596 USA (SAN 254-9360) Fax: 925-939-4010 E-mail: info@deepercalling.com Web site: http://www.deepercalling.com *Dist(s):* **Whitaker Hse.**

Deer Creek Publishing, *(978-0-9651452)* Orders Addr.: P.O. Box 2594, Nevada City, CA 95959 USA Fax: 530-478-1759 Do not confuse with Deer Creek Publishing, Provo, UT.

Deer Oaks, Inc., *(978-0-9764700)* P.O. Box 429, Barrington, IL 60011-0429 USA.

Deerbrook Editions, *(978-0-9712488; 978-0-9828100; 978-0-9904287; 978-0-9975051; 978-0-9991062; 978-0-9600293; 978-1-7343884)* P.O. Box 542, Cumberland, ME 04021-0542 USA Tel 207-233-0158 E-mail: jewilh@gmail.com Web site: http://www.deerbrookeditions.com; http://deerbrookeditions.wordpress.com *Dist(s):* **SPD-Small Pr. Distribution.**

DefConOne Publishing, *(978-0-615-90595-2; 978-0-692-27021-9; 978-0-692-39732-9; 978-0-692-46014-6; 978-0-692-51470-2; 978-0-692-53013-9; 978-0-692-54329-0; 978-0-692-59172-7; 978-0-692-62764-8; 978-0-692-65123-0; 978-0-692-72847-5; 978-0-9977936; 978-1-948280)* 12550 Greenwood Ave N, No. 202, Seattle, WA 98133 USA Tel 206-902-8249 E-mail: bolthy@bolthy.com Web site: www.defconone.com *Dist(s):* **CreateSpace Independent Publishing Platform.**

Defense Acquisition University *Imprint of* **United States Government Printing Office**

Defense Dept. *Imprint of* **United States Government Printing Office**

Defense Research LLC, *(978-0-9749873)* 211 Kirkland Ave. Apt. 216, Kirkland, WA 98033-6578 USA E-mail: sales@defenseresearch.org Web site: http://www.defenseresearch.org.

Defiance In Print, *(978-0-9771641)* Orders Addr.: 9412 S Belfort Cr, Tamarac, FL 33321 USA (SAN 256-9663) Tel 561-235-1828 E-mail: miller2554@gmail.com.

Defiant Pr. *Imprint of* **Passkey Online Educational Services**

Defined Mind, Inc., *(978-0-9763767)* 580 Broadway, Suite 912, New York, NY 10012 USA Tel 212-925-5138 (Hours: M-F 9:30 am-5:30 pm) E-mail: info@defmind.com Web site: http://www.defmind.com.

DeForest Pr., *(978-0-9649922; 978-1-930374; 978-0-615-99631-8)* Orders Addr.: P.O. Box 383, Rogers, MN 55374 USA Tel 763-428-2997; Fax: 877-747-3123; Toll Free: 877-747-3123; Edit Addr.: P.O. Box 383, Rogers, MN 55374 USA E-mail: shane@deforestpress.com Web site: http://www.deforestpress.com.

DeFranco Entertainment, *(978-1-929845)* P.O. Box 1425, Thousand Oaks, CA 91358-1425 USA Fax: 805-376-2953 E-mail: tdefranco@vcnet.com.

Degenhardt, Scott, *(978-0-9765671)* P.O. Box 11182, Murfreesboro, TN 37129 USA Tel 615-890-9484 E-mail: anything@thedegshop.com Web site: http://www.thedegshop.com.

DeGraaf Publishing, *(978-0-9678385)* 903 W. Morse St., Plant City, FL 33563 USA Tel 813-752-2348; 813-967-7489 (Cell phone) E-mail: robdegraaf@verizon.net Web site: http://www.degraafpublishing.com.

Degree Network, LLC *See* **Marilux Pr.**

Dehghanpisheh, Corine, *(978-0-9851930; 978-0-692-41280-0; 978-0-9978985)* P.O. Box 30302, New York, NY 10011 USA Tel 646-580-8655 E-mail: cmardi2@gmail.com.

DeimosWeb Publishing, *(978-1-950485)* 2727 David Lee Dr., Parkersburg, WV 26101 USA Tel 606-371-7706 E-mail: deimosweb@gmail.com Web site: www.leonarddhilleyii.com.

Deitch, Jeffrey Inc., *(978-0-9633037; 978-0-9648530; 978-0-9753243; 978-0-9778686; 978-0-9815771)* 76 Grand St., New York, NY 10013 USA Tel 212-343-7300 E-mail: info@deitch.com Web site: http://www.deitch.com *Dist(s):* **D.A.P./Distributed Art Pubs.**

Dejohn Enterprises, *(978-0-9754528)* 1121 Elm St., Peekskill, NY 10566 USA E-mail: dejohnenterprise@aol.com Web site: http://www.thereturnofsf.com.

Deka Pr., *(978-0-9645045)* P.O. Box 812, Christmas Valley, OR 97641 USA Tel 541-576-3900; Fax: 541-576-3909 E-mail: katym@teleport.com.

DEKpress *See* **Parent Positive Pr.**

DeKruyff, Ruth, *(978-0-9797549)* Orders Addr.: P.O. Box 380604, San Antonio, TX 78268 USA; Edit Addr.: 5911 Forest Rim, San Antonio, TX 78240 USA.

Del Alma Pubns., LLC, *(978-0-9822422)* 1713 Delmar, Zapata, TX 78076 USA Tel 956-278-0760 E-mail: delalmapublications@gmail.com Web site: www.delalmapublications.com.

Del Gatto, Maria, *(978-0-9747509)* 2227 South 3rd St., Philadelphia, PA 19148 USA Tel 215-271-7165 Web site: http://www.shapettes.com.

Del George, Dana, *(978-0-578-00730-4)* 1025 1/2 Magnolia St., South Pasadena, CA 91030 USA *Dist(s):* **Lulu Pr., Inc.**

Del Rey *Imprint of* **Random House Publishing Group**

Del Sol Pubns., *(978-0-9722936)* P.O. Box 1112, Ventura, CA 93002 USA Do not confuse with Del Sol Publications in Two River, WI E-mail: info@delsolpublications.com Web site: http://www.delsolpublications.com.

Del Sol Publishing, *(978-1-58186)* 29257 Bassett Rd., Westlake, OH 44145 USA (SAN 299-4178) Tel 440-892-5524; Fax: 440-892-5546; Toll Free: 888-335-7651 E-mail: delsolbooks@telocity.com *Dist(s):* **Lectorum Pubns., Inc.**

Delabarre Publishing, *(978-0-9829247; 978-0-9836125; 978-1-61941)* P.O. Box 714, Conway, MA 01341 USA Tel 413-475-0087 E-mail: jeff@jeffrutherford.com.

Delacorte Bks. for Young Readers *Imprint of* **Random Hse. Children's Bks.**

Delacorte Pr *Imprint of* **Random House Publishing Group**

Delacorte Pr. *Imprint of* **Random House Publishing Group**

Delacorte Pr. *Imprint of* **Random Hse. Children's Bks.**

Delaney Green, *(978-0-9982633)* 1928 Ohm Ave., Eau Claire, WI 54701 USA Tel 715-839-7411 E-mail: fitzfool74@gmail.com Web site: http://www.delaneygreenwriter.com/.

Delatorre, Maria *See* **Father's Hse. Publishing**

DeLaVega, T., *(978-0-9754328)* Orders Addr.: P.O. Box 760, Hanapepe, HI 96716 USA Tel 808-335-2704; Fax: 808-335-5469; Edit Addr.: 3691 Uwao St., Hanapepe, HI 96716 USA E-mail: tim.delavega@verizon.net Web site: http://www.napaliphoto.com.

†Delaware &Lehigh National Heritage Corridor, Inc., *(978-0-930973)* Orders Addr.: 2750 Hugh Moore Pk. Rd., Easton, PA 18042 USA; Edit Addr.: 2750 Hugh Moore Pk. Rd., Easton, PA 18042-7743 USA (SAN 678-8831) Tel 610-923-3548; *Imprints:* Canal History & Technology Press (Canal Hist Tech) E-mail: archives@delawareandlehigh.org; finance@delawareandlehigh.org Web site: http://www.canals.org; http://www.delawareandlehigh.org; *CIP.*

Deletrea *See* **Deletrea**

Deletrea, *(978-0-9972904; 978-1-7351219)* 1650 Coral Way Suite 502, Miami, FL 33145 USA Tel 954-562-7784 E-mail: casandra@deletrea.net Web site: www.deletrea.net *Dist(s):* **Legato Pubs. Group Publishers Group West (PGW).**

Delirious Scribbles Ink, *(978-1-944357)* 1645 Sheba Dr., Columbus, GA 31904 USA Tel 706-478-7776 E-mail: author@michaeljallen.net; ink@deliriousscribbles.com Web site: www.deliriousscribbles.com *Dist(s):* **CreateSpace Independent Publishing Platform Ingram Content Group.**

Delittle Storyteller Co., *(978-1-892633)* Orders Addr.: 1562 Pinehurst Dr., Casselberry, FL 32707 USA Tel 407-699-7769 E-mail: delittlestoryteller@yahoo.com Web site: http://www.delittlestoryteller.com.

Dell, Jacob J., *(978-0-9744544)* 6518 Chasethorn Dr., San Antonio, TX 78249-4825 USA E-mail: books@jacobjdell.com Web site: http://www.jacobjdell.com/books.

Dellas, Melanie, *(978-0-9830163)* 4405 Pescadero Ave., San Diego, CA 92107 USA Tel 858-442-7916 E-mail: mdellas@hotmail.com Web site: http://www.Mythological-Creatures.com.

Dellinger, Hampton, *(978-0-615-24971-1)* 4306 Peachway Dr., Durham, NC 27705 USA *Dist(s):* **Lulu Pr., Inc.**

Dellwin Publishing Co., Inc., *(978-0-9765267)* P.O. Box 23391, Brooklyn, NY 11202-3391 USA E-mail: dellwin5@aol.com Web site: http://www.therockmastersystem.com.

†Delmar Cengage Learning, *(978-0-314; 978-0-7668; 978-0-7693; 978-0-8273; 978-0-87350; 978-0-916032; 978-0-944132; 978-0-9653629; 978-1-56253; 978-1-56593; 978-1-56930; 978-1-4018; 978-1-4180; 978-1-4283; 978-1-4354; 978-1-7319)* Div. of Cengage Learning, Orders Addr.: c/o Thomson Learning Order Fulfillment, P.O. Box 6904, Florence, KY 41022 USA Toll Free Fax: 800 487 8488; Toll Free: 800 347 7707; c/o Thomson Delmar Learning Clinical Health Care Series, P.O. Box 3419, Scranton, PA 18505-0419 Fax: 570-347-9072; Toll Free: 888-427-5800; Edit Addr.: P.O. Box 15015, Albany, NY 12212-5015 USA (SAN 206-7544) Tel 518-348-2300; Fax: 518-373-6345; Toll Free: 800-998-7498; 5 Maxwell Dr., Clifton Park, NY 12065- (SAN 658-0440) Tel 518-348-2300; Fax: 518-881-1256; Toll Free: 800-998-7498 E-mail: matthew.grover@thomson.com; clinicalmanuals@thomson.com Web site: http://www.delmarlearning.com; http://www.clinicalmanuals.com/ *Dist(s):* **CENGAGE Learning Follett School Solutions Gryphon Hse., Inc. OptumInsight, Inc. Pearson Education Rittenhouse Bk. Distributors ebrary, Inc.**; *CIP.*

Delor Francis Pr., *(978-0-9838947)* 873 Atwells Ave., Providence, RI 02909 USA Tel 401-421-1222 E-mail: publisher@delorfrancis.com Web site: www.delorfrancis.com.

DeLorme, *(978-0-89933)* P.O. Box 298, Yarmouth, ME 04096 USA (SAN 220-1208) Tel 207-846-7000; Fax: 207-846-7051; Toll Free Fax: 800-575-2244 (orders); Toll Free: 800-335-6763 (orders only) E-mail: reseller@delorme.com Web site: http://www.delorme.com *Dist(s):* **Benchmark LLC Hammond World Atlas Corp. Langenscheidt Publishing Group Many Feathers Bks. & Maps Rand McNally.**

DeLorme Mapping Company *See* **DeLorme**

Delphi Bks., *(978-0-9663397; 978-0-9765185; 978-0-9846015; 978-1-7320512)* Orders Addr.: P.O. Box 6435, Lee's Summit, MO 64064 USA Toll Free: 800-431-1579 (orders) E-mail: DelphiBks@yahoo.com Web site: http://www.DelphiBooks.us; http://www.FranBaker.com *Dist(s):* **Brodart Co. Emery-Pratt Co. Midwest Library Service.**

Delphinium *Imprint of* **HarperCollins Pubs.**

Delta Education, Incorporated *See* **Delta Education, LLC**

Delta Education, LLC, *(978-0-87504; 978-1-58356; 978-1-59242; 978-1-59821; 978-1-60395; 978-1-60902; 978-1-62571; 978-1-64011)* 80 Northwest Blvd., Nashua, NH 03063 USA (SAN 630-1711) Toll Free: 800-442-5444 E-mail: ngosselin@delta-edu.com Web site: http://www.delta-education.com.

Delta Gamma Ctr., *(978-0-9748523)* 1750 S. Big Bend Blvd., Saint Louis, MO 63117-2402 USA Toll Free: 800-341-4310 E-mail: info@dgckids.org Web site: http://www.dgckids.org.

Delta Stream Media, *(978-0-9776939; 978-1-945899)* Div. of Natural Math, 309 Silvercliff, Cary, NC 27513 USA (SAN 257-9987) Tel 919-388-1721 E-mail: maria@naturalmath.com Web site: http://www.naturalmath.com *Dist(s):* **American Mathematical Society Natural Math.**

Delta Systems Company, Inc., *(978-0-937354; 978-1-887744; 978-1-932748; 978-1-934960; 978-1-936299; 978-1-936402; 978-1-62167)* Orders Addr.: 1400 Miller Pkwy., McHenry, IL 60050-7030 USA (SAN 220-0457) Tel 815-363-3582; Fax: 815-363-2948; Toll Free Fax: 800-909-9901; Toll Free: 800-323-8270; *Imprints:* Raven Tree Press (Raven Tree Pr) E-mail: d.patchin@DeltaPublishing.com; L.Bruell@DeltaPublishing.com; j.patchin@deltapublishing.com; Web site: http://www.deltapublishing.com; http://www.raventreepress.com *Dist(s):* **Follett Media Distribution National Bk. Network.**

DeLuca, Robert John, *(978-1-7320596)* 7 Whittier Dr., Friendswood, TX 77546 USA Tel 713-501-1515 E-mail: bobdeluca66@gmail.com.

DeMaio, Carlo A., *(978-1-7322583; 978-1-950219)* 1990 KINGS HWY, FAIRFIELD, CT 06824-6112 USA Tel 203-395-6760 E-mail: Carlo.DeMaio@gmail.com.

DeMara-Kirby & Assocs., LLC., *(978-1-947442)* P.O. Box 720335, Mcallen, TX 78504 USA Tel 956-802-0004 E-mail: christinademara@aol.com.

DEMDACO, *(978-1-932139)* Div. of DD Traders, Inc., 5000 W. 134th St., Leawood, KS 66209-7806 USA Toll Free: 888-336-3226 Web site: http://www.demdaco.com.

Demeter Books *See* **Lake Street Pr.**

DeMosi *See* **DeMosi Publishing**

DeMosi Publishing, *(978-0-9708523)* Orders Addr.: P.O. Box 60606, Chicago, IL 60660 USA E-mail: demosipublishing@email.com.

Den Publishing Co., *(978-0-9742195)* P.O. Box 93336, Albuquerque, NM 87199-3336 USA Fax: 505-822-8035.

DeNicest Concepts, *(978-0-9763973)* P.O. Box 1831, Buffalo, NY 14240 USA.

Denim Design Lab LLC, *(978-0-9773012)* P.O. Box 5853, San Clemente, CA 92674-9998 USA Tel 949-366-3307; Fax: 949-366-3304 E-mail: denimdesignlab@aol.com Web site: http://www.denimdesignlab.com.

Denison, T. S. & Co., Inc., *(978-0-513)* Orders Addr.: P.O. Box 1650, Grand Rapids, MI 49501-5431 USA (SAN 201-3142) Tel 616-802-3000; Fax: 616-802-3009; Toll Free Fax: 800-543-2690; Toll Free: 800-253-5469 *Dist(s):* **Lectorum Pubns., Inc.**

Denlinger, Dennis, *(978-0-9742567)* Orders Addr.: 46 Purdy St., Harrison, NY 10528 USA; Edit Addr.: P.O. Box 60431, Sacramento, CA 95860-0431 USA Tel

916-488-9643 Phone/fax); Toll Free: 800-431-1579 fulfilment
E-mail: dennis@footarch.com
Web site: http://www.footarch.com
Dist(s): **Book Clearing Hse.**

Denney Literary Services, (*978-0-9654698; 978-0-9707469*) 2907 Noah St., Chattanooga, TN 37406-1928 USA Tel 423-622-0419; *Imprints:* DLS Books (DLS Bks)
E-mail: denney2907@earthlink.net.

Dennis West, (*978-0-9978774*) 8212 Sleeping Bear Dr NW, Albuquerque, NM 87120 USA Tel 214-505-0179
E-mail: cwickwire@att.net.

Dennison, Donna, (*978-0-9760484*) 121 Tuxedo, San Antonio, TX 78209-3712 USA.

Densmore-Reid Pubns., (*978-0-9700827*) 67 S. 24th St., Richmond, IN 47374 USA Tel 765-939-2984 (phone/fax)
E-mail: ddgreens@netscape.net
Web site: http://www.densmorereid.com/.

Dental Wellness Institute, (*978-0-9815630*) 321 S. Main St., No. 503, Sebastopol, CA 95472 USA (SAN 855-8795) Tel 707-829-7220; Toll Free: 800-335-7755
E-mail: dentwell@pacbell.net
Web site: http://www.dentalwellness4u.com
Dist(s): **Cardinal Pubs. Group.**

Denver Broncos, (*978-0-9759579*) INVESCO Field at Mile High, 1701 Bryant St., Suite 900, Denver, CO 80204 USA
Web site: http://www.denverbroncos.com.

Denwit Publishing, (*978-0-9960973*) 822 Cotton Grove Rd., Jackson, TN 38305 USA Tel 731-616-5099
E-mail: gcdenwiddie@gmail.com
Web site: gcdenwiddie.com.

DEO Consulting, Inc., (*978-0-9728793*) 16334 Boardwalk Terr., Orland Hills, IL 60477 USA
E-mail: dale@mbd2.com
Web site: http://www.mbd2.com.

DePalma, Vanessa, (*978-0-9728135*) 49 Tropez Point, Rochester, NY 14626 USA Tel 585-723-9699
E-mail: vdepalma@frontiernet.net.

Dept. of Chamorro Affairs, (*978-1-883488*) P.O. Box 2950, Hagatna, GU 96932 USA Tel 671-477-6447
E-mail: lbaguon@yahoo.com
Web site: http://www.dca.guam.gov.

Depot Bks., (*978-0-9717611*) Orders Addr.: 87 Throckmorton Ave., Mill Valley, CA 94941 USA; Edit Addr.: 8 Madrona St., Mill Valley, CA 94941 USA.

Dept. of the Army *Imprint of* **United States Government Printing Office**

Dercum Audio, (*978-1-55656*) 1501 County Hospital Rd., Nashville, TN 37218 USA (SAN 658-7607) Tel 615-254-2408
E-mail: DawsonC@locc.com
Web site: http://www.bookcase.com/Dercum
Dist(s): **APG Sales & Distribution Services.**

Dercum Press/Dercum Audio *See* **Dercum Audio**

Derke, Connie, (*978-0-9747063*) 6418 W. 13100 S., Herriman, UT 84065 USA Tel 801-254-8711
E-mail: derke1904@msn.com.

Derrick, Paul, (*978-0-9744875*) Orders Addr.: 918 N. 30th St., Waco, TX 76707-2502 USA Tel 254-753-6920 (phone/fax)
E-mail: pjderrick@aol.com
Web site: http://stargazerpaul.com.

Derry Lane Publishing, (*978-0-692-82325-5; 978-0-692-83659-0*) 1225 Derry Ln., WEST CHESTER, PA 19380 USA Tel 314-800-7731
E-mail: priyaponnapula@gmail.com; priyaponnapula@gmail.com.

Derrydale Pr., The, (*978-1-56416; 978-1-58667*) Div. of Rowman & Littlefield Publishing Group, Orders Addr.: 15200 NBN Way, Blue Ridge Summit, PA 17214 USA Tel 717-794-3800 (Sales, Customer Service, MIS, Royalties, Inventory Mgmt., Dist., Credit & Collections); Fax: 717-794-3803 (Customer Service &/or orders only); 717-794-3857 (Sales & MIS); 717-794-3856 (Royalties, Inventory Mgmt., & Dist.); Toll Free Fax: 800-338-4550 (Customer Service &/or orders); Toll Free: 800-462-6420 (Customer Service &/or orders); Edit Addr.: 4501 Forbes Blvd., Lanham, MD 20706 USA Tel 301-459-3366; Fax: 301-459-5748
E-mail: sdriver@derrydalepress.com
Web site: http://www.derrydalepress.com
Dist(s): **MyiLibrary**
National Bk. Network
Rowman & Littlefield Publishers, Inc.
ebrary, Inc.

Dershowitz, Adena, (*978-0-692-05378-2*) 2540 Shore Blvd. 1st Flr., ASTORIA, NY 11102 USA Tel 570-575-8433
E-mail: adenardershowitz@gmail.com
Dist(s): **Ingram Content Group.**

Desdemona's Dreams LLC, (*978-0-9968874*) 4229 N. Derbigny, New Orleans, LA 70117 USA Tel 818-645-7390
E-mail: zachmohr77@gmail.com
Web site: https://desdemonasdreams.com/.

†Deseret Bk. Co., (*978-0-87579; 978-0-87747; 978-1-57345; 978-1-59038; 978-1-60641; 978-1-60907; 978-1-60908; 978-1-62972; 978-1-62973; 978-1-64933*) Div. of Deseret Management Corp., P.O. Box 30178, Salt Lake City, UT 84130 USA (SAN 150-763X) Tel 801-517-3165 (Wholesale Dept.); 801-534-1515; Fax: 801-517-3338; Toll Free: 800-453-3876; *Imprints:* Bookcraft, Incorporated (Bkcraft Inc); Shadow Mountain (ShadMtn)
E-mail: wholesale@deseretbook.com; dbwhsale@deseretbook.com
Web site: http://www.deseretbook.com; http://www.shadowmountain.com
Dist(s): **Blackstone Audio, Inc.**
Shadow Mountain Publishing; *CIP.*

Desert Badger Pr., (*978-0-9767555*) 4147 E. Megan Dr., Tucson, AZ 85712 USA
Web site: http://www.elderlawtucson.com.

Desert Bear Publishing, (*978-0-9765389*) P.O. Box 72313, Phoenix, AZ 85050 USA Tel 480-538-0842; Fax: 602-926-2429.

Desert Hills Publishing *See* **D H Publishing LLC**

Desert Palm Pr., (*978-1-942976; 978-1-948327*) 1961 Main St. Suite 220, Watsonville, CA 95076 USA Tel 831-234-9556
E-mail: rleefitz@gmail.com
Web site: www.desertpalmpress.com.

Desert Sage Pr., (*978-0-615-72020-3; 978-0-9897133*) P.O. Box 357, Eagle, ID 83616 USA Tel 208-860-2464; Fax: 208-938-1554
Web site: www.desertsagepress.com
Dist(s): **CreateSpace Independent Publishing Platform.**

Desert Song Productions, (*978-0-9743402*) P.O. Box 35052, Tucson, AZ 85740 USA
E-mail: brian@brianjharris.com
Web site: http://www.brianjharris.com.

Desert Well Network, LLC *See* **Kamal**

Desert West Publishing, (*978-0-578-03542-0*) P.O. Box 35, Fairview, UT 84629 USA
Dist(s): **Lulu Pr., Inc.**

DesertStar Communications, LLC, (*978-0-9769815*) Orders Addr.: P.O. Box 243988, Boynton Beach, FL 33424-3988 USA
Web site: http://www.desertstarcommunications.com.

Desideramus Publishing, (*978-0-9975883*) 802 Peachwood Bend Dr., Houston, TX 77077 USA Tel 281-597-8867
E-mail: Barbarabdenson@gmail.com
Web site: Desideramus.com.

Design Media Publishing Ltd. (HKG) (*978-988-19738-4-9; 978-988-12967*) *Dist. by* **BTPS.**

Design Originals *Imprint of* **Fox Chapel Publishing Co., Inc.**

Design Pr. Bks. *Imprint of* **Savannah College of Art & Design Exhibitions**

Design Studio Pr., (*978-0-9726676; 978-1-933492; 978-1-62465*) Orders Addr.: 5022 Eagle Rock Blvd., Los Angeles, CA 90041 USA
Web site: http://www.designstudiopress.com
Dist(s): **Diamond Bk. Distributors**
Ingram Publisher Services.

Design Vault, LLC *See* **Design Vault Pr., LLC**

Design Vault Pr., LLC, (*978-0-9768974; 978-0-615-93708-3; 978-0-692-68465-8; 978-1-7351818*) 11813 E 105th St N, Owasso, OK 74055 USA Tel 918.625.1483
Web site: www.designvaultpress.com
Dist(s): **CreateSpace Independent Publishing Platform.**

DesignAbility, (*978-0-9786425*) P.O. Box 9988, Salt Lake City, UT 84109 USA
Web site: http://www.design-ability.com.

Designed World Learning, LLC, (*978-0-9763351*) Suite 105-124, 1933 Hwy. 35, Wall, NJ 07719 USA
Web site: http://www.designedworldlearning.com.

Designer Discipline, (*978-0-692-09750-2; 978-0-692-15182-2; 978-0-692-16568-3*) 3521 Marcey Creek Rd., Laurel, MD 20724 USA Tel 646-246-4063
E-mail: shawnadoyle@outlook.com
Dist(s): **Ingram Content Group.**

Designs For Progress, Inc., (*978-0-9793902*) 24601 Milfay Rd., No. 5, Depew, OK 74028 USA
E-mail: dmccalment@aol.com.

Desktop Prepress Services, (*978-0-615-15679-8; 978-0-615-15817-4; 978-0-615-19039-6; 978-0-615-19643-5; 978-0-615-19723-4; 978-0-615-25624-5; 978-0-578-00420-4; 978-0-578-01448-7; 978-0-578-02385-4; 978-0-578-02469-1; 978-0-578-03167-5; 978-0-578-04693-8; 978-0-578-08235-6; 978-0-578-15292-9) 808 S. New Bethel Blvd., Ada, OK 74820 USA*
Web site: http://www.desktopprepress.com
Dist(s): **Lulu Pr., Inc.**

Deste Foundation (GRC) *Dist. by* **Dist Art Pubs.**

Destination Pubs. *Imprint of* **Pulte, Therese Marie**

Destination Wonder Pr., (*978-1-949752*) P.O. Box 505, Laguna Beach, CA 92652 USA Tel 760-989-2226
E-mail: requests@destinationwonderpress.com
Web site: www.destinationwonderpress.com.

Destined For Greatness Publisher *See* **Empowering People Pub.**

Destinee Media, (*978-0-9759082; 978-0-9832768; 978-1-938367; 978-0-578-47597-4*) c/o McCall, 301 Iberian Way, Apt. 253, Sandpoint, ID 83864 USA
Web site: http://www.destineemedia.com.

Destiny Hse. Publishing, (*978-1-936867*) P.O. Box 19774, Detroit, MI 48219 USA Tel 888-890-9455
E-mail: destinyhousepublishing1@yahoo.com.

Destiny Image Europe (ITA) (*978-88-900588; 978-88-89127; 978-88-96727*) *Dist. by* **STL Dist.**

Destiny Image Pubs., (*978-0-7684; 978-0-914903; 978-1-56043; 978-0-9716036*) 167 Walnut Bottom Rd., Shippensburg, PA 17257 USA (SAN 253-4339) Tel 717-532-3040; Fax: 717-532-9291; Toll Free: 800-722-6774
E-mail: dnj@destinyimage.com
Web site: http://www.destinyimage.com
Dist(s): **Anchor Distributors**
Appalachian Bible Co.
Send The Light Distribution LLC
Spring Arbor Distributors, Inc.

Detail Press *See* **Blue Tree LLC**

Determined Productions, Inc., (*978-0-915696*) P.O. Box 2150, San Francisco, CA 94126-2150 USA (SAN 212-7385) Tel 415-433-0660; Fax: 415-421-0929.

Detroit International Pr., (*978-0-9766622*) 900 Wilshire Dr. Ste. 202, Troy, MI 48084-1600 USA
E-mail: vince@detroitip.com.

Dettling Moreno, Elizabeth, (*978-0-692-18190-4*) 1811 FM. 1299 Rd., Wharton, TX 77488 USA Tel 979-282-9626
E-mail: praise77488@sbcglobal.net
Dist(s): **Ingram Content Group.**

Dettman Design Services, (*978-0-615-38527-3*) 718 Logan Ave., Elgin, IL 60120 USA Tel 847-888-2178
E-mail: t.dettman@sbcglobal.net.

Deutscher Taschenbuch Verlag GmbH & Co KG (DEU) (*978-3-423*) *Dist. by* **Distribks Inc.**

Deux *Imprint of* **Aurora Publishing, Inc.**

DeuxRay Productions, (*978-0-615-52915-8*) 2401 Capitan Ave., San Diego, CA 92104 USA Tel 619-987-5505; Fax: 619-291-4404
E-mail: deuxray@cox.net
Web site: www.inmyownbackyard.org.

Devadoss, Donna, (*978-1-7338464*) 3855 Creek Rd., Andover, OH 44003 USA Tel 440-858-2185
E-mail: donnadvds@yahoo.com.

Developmental Studies Center *See* **Center for the Collaborative Classroom**

Developmental Vision Concepts, (*978-0-9635507; 978-0-9747810*) Orders Addr.: P.O. Box 400, Tehachapi, CA 93581 USA Tel 661-822-3106; Edit Addr.: 316 S. Green, Tehachapi, CA 93581 USA
E-mail: stoebner@lightspeed.net.

Devenny, Jenny, (*978-0-692-78650-5*) 257 Gold St. Apt. 1002, Brooklyn, NY 10009 USA Tel 917-232-7377
E-mail: jennydevenny@gmail.com.

Devere Publishng, Inc., (*978-0-9787988*) P.O. Box 970965, Orem, UT 84097-0965 USA (SAN 851-6456) Tel 801-434-7558 (phone/fax)
E-mail: boblamx@gmail.com
Web site: http://winningorlosing.com.

Devil's Due Digital, Inc. - A Checker Digital Co., (*978-0-9710249; 978-0-9741664; 978-0-9753808; 978-1-933160; 978-1-61799*) 217 Byers Rd., Miamisburg, OH 45342 USA
E-mail: info@checkerbpg.com
Web site: http://www.checkerbpg.com
Dist(s): **Brodart Co.**
Haven Distributors
Tales of Wonder.com.

Devil's Due Publishing, Inc., (*978-1-932796; 978-1-934692; 978-1-7332250*) 2217 W. Roscoe St., Chicago, IL 60618-6209 USA
E-mail: swells@devilsdue.net; d.davis@devilsdue.net
Web site: http://www.devilsdue.net
Dist(s): **Diamond Comic Distributors, Inc.**
Diamond Bk. Distributors
Publishers Group West (PGW).

†Devin-Adair Pubs., Inc., (*978-0-8159*) P.O. Box A, Old Greenwich, CT 06870 USA (SAN 112-062X) Tel 203-531-7755; Fax: 718-359-8568; *CIP.*

DeVincentis, Anna, (*978-0-692-86032-8; 978-0-692-87091-4*) 5200 N Ocean Blvd, Lauderdale by the Sea, FL 33308 USA Tel 954-907-3923
E-mail: annadevincentis@gmail.com
Dist(s): **CreateSpace Independent Publishing Platform.**

Devlin, Jacob, (*978-1-7324984; 978-1-7342803*) 2801 N Park Ave., No. 3, Tucson, AZ 85719 USA Tel 520-647-4572
E-mail: authorjakedevlin@gmail.com
Dist(s): **Ingram Content Group.**

Devonfield, (*978-0-692-34077-6; 978-1-7329612*) 16921 Via de Santa Fe P.O. Box 5005 No. 178, Rancho Santa Fe, CA 92067 USA Tel 858-436-5667; *Imprints:* Britfield (MYID_X_BRITFIE)
E-mail: crsdevonfield@gmail.com
Web site: www.Devonfieldllc.com.

Devonshire Bks., (*978-0-615-33660-2*) 918 W. Browning St., Appleton, WI 54914 USA Tel 920-954-5733
E-mail: flwrgirl3@hotmail.com.

Devora Publishing *Imprint of* **Simcha Media Group**

DeVore & Sons, Incorporated *See* **Fireside Catholic Bibles**

DeVorss & Co., (*978-0-87516*) Orders Addr.: P.O. Box 1389, Camarillo, CA 93011-1389 USA (SAN 168-9886) Tel 805-322-9010; Fax: 805-322-9011; Toll Free: 800-843-5743; Edit Addr.: 553 Constitution Ave., Camarillo, CA 93012-8510 USA; *Imprints:* Devorss Publications (Devorss Pubns)
E-mail: service@devorss.com
Web site: http://www.devorss.com
Dist(s): **Health and Growth Assocs.**
New Leaf Distributing Co., Inc.

Devorss Pubns. *Imprint of* **DeVorss & Co.**

Dew Bear Enterprises, Inc., (*978-1-942261*) 1289 N Fordham Blvd PMB 413, Chapel Hill, NC 27514 USA Tel 919-382-0068
E-mail: dewbear@mindspring.com
Web site: dewbear.com.

DeWard Publishing Co., Ltd., (*978-0-9798893; 978-0-9819703; 978-1-936341; 978-1-947929*) P.O. Box 6259, Chillicothe, OH 45601 USA Toll Free: 800-300-9778
E-mail: nathan_ward@hotmail.com
Web site: http://www.dewardpublishing.com.

Dewberry Pr., (*978-0-9854076; 978-0-9910340*) P.O. Box 604, Pflugerville, TX 78660 USA Tel 512-522-0596
E-mail: dewberrypress@yahoo.com
Web site: www.dewberrypress.com
Dist(s): **Ingram Content Group.**

Dewey Does *See* **A B C-123 Publishing**

Dewey Pubns., Inc., (*978-0-9615053; 978-1-878810; 978-1-932612; 978-1-934651; 978-1-941825*) 1840 Wilson Blvd Suite 203, Arlington, VA 22201 USA (SAN 694-1451) Tel 703-524-1355
E-mail: deweypublications@gmail.com
Web site: http://www.deweypub.com.

Dewey's Good News Balloons *See* **Glen Enterprises**

Dey Street Bks. *Imprint of* **HarperCollins Pubs.**

Dezaim Productions and Management, LLC, (*978-0-9770111*) 1385 Chancellor Cir., Bensalem, PA 19020 USA.

Deziner Media International, (*978-0-9743971; 978-0-615-23060-3; 978-0-615-28400-2; 978-0-9819912*) P.O. Box 239, Marrero, LA 70073 USA Tel 504-292-9101; 1472 Ames Blvd., Marrero, LA 70072
E-mail: dezinermedia@aol.com
Web site: http://www.writeabc123.com.

DFC Pubs., (*978-0-9793987*) 31 W. Smith St., Amityville, NY 11701 USA (SAN 853-3695)
E-mail: contactus@urbanclubbooks.com
Web site: http://www.urbanclubbooks.com.

DG Bks. Publishing *Imprint of* **Digital Golden Solutions LLC**

dg ink, (*978-0-9772577*) Orders Addr.: P.O. Box 1182, Daly City, CA 94017-1182 USA Tel 650-994-2662; Fax: 650-991-3050; *Imprints:* Ascribed (Ascribed)
E-mail: dg@dg-ink.net; info@dg-ink.net
Web site: http://www.dg-ink.net
Dist(s): **Follett School Solutions.**

DGriffith Publishing, (*978-1-7337270*) 4217 Braidwood Dr, Fort Collins, CO 80524 USA Tel 970-566-0058
E-mail: djofc51@gmail.com
Web site: Munchkintales.com.

DH Strategies, (*978-0-9864080; 978-1-7347427*) 317 N. Fourth St., Festus, MO 63028 USA Tel 978-989-5433
E-mail: sdewitthall@gmail.com
Web site: www.ipromotebooks.com.

†Dharma Publishing, (*978-0-89800; 978-0-913546*) Orders Addr.: 35788 Hauser Bridge Rd., Cazadero, CA 95421 USA (SAN 201-2723) Tel 707-847-3717; Fax: 707-847-3380; Toll Free: 800-873-4276
E-mail: contact@dharmapublishing.com; hughj@mangalamresearch.org; order@dharmapublishing.com
Web site: http://www.kumnyeyoga.com; http://www.centerforskillfulmeans.com; http://www.enjoysitting.com; http://www.mangalamresearch.org; http://www.dharmapublishing.com/
Dist(s): **National Bk. Network**
Wisdom Pubns.; *CIP.*

DHUNAMI, (*978-0-615-21482-5; 978-0-615-32994-9; 978-1-7356332*)
E-mail: paulji@dhunami.guru
Web site: https://www.dhunami.guru.

Di Angelo Pubns., (*978-0-9850853; 978-1-942549*) 4265 San Felipe No. 1100, Houston, TX 77027 USA Tel 713-960-6636
E-mail: sales@diangelopublications.com; info@diangelopublications.com
Web site: www.diangelopublications.com.

Di Bella, Brenda, (*978-0-615-38253-1*) 6643 Haskell Ave. No. 205, Van Nuys, CA 91406 USA Tel 818-235-3040
E-mail: comiab@yahoo.com
Web site: http://www.imuptobigthings.com.

Di Capua, Michael *Imprint of* **Scholastic, Inc.**

di Capua, Michael Bks. *Imprint of* **Hyperion Bks. for Children**

Di Maggio, Richard *See* **Consumer Pr., The**

Diakonia Publishing, (*978-0-9676528; 978-0-9725609; 978-0-9747278; 978-0-9772483; 978-0-9800877*) P.O. Box 9512, Greensboro, NC 27429-0512 USA Tel 336-707-2610
E-mail: diakoniapublishing@hotmail.com
Web site: http://www.ephesians412.com.

Dial *Imprint of* **Penguin Publishing Group**

Dial Bks *Imprint of* **Penguin Young Readers Group**

Dial Bks *Imprint of* **Penguin Publishing Group**

Dialogue Systems, Incorporated *See* **Metropolitan Teaching & Learning Co.**

Dialogues in Self Discovery LLC, (*978-1-934450*) P.O. Box 43161, Montclair, NJ 07043 USA (SAN 853-2745) Tel 973-714-2800; Fax: 973-746-2853
E-mail: discoveroption@aol.com.

Diamond Bk. Distributors, (*978-1-64031*) Div. of Diamond Comic Distributors, Inc., Orders Addr.: 1966 Greenspring Dr., Suite 300, Timonium, MD 21093 USA (SAN 110-9502) Tel 410-560-7100; Fax: 410-560-2583; Toll Free: 800-452-6642; *Imprints:* William M. Gaines Agent, INC. (WILLIAM M. GAI)
E-mail: books@diamondbookdistributors.com
Web site: http://www.diamondcomics.com; http://www.diamondbookdistributors.com/
Dist(s): **Elsevier**
MyiLibrary
SCB Distributors
SPD-Small Pr. Distribution.

Diamond Book Distributors Inc. *See* **Diamond Comic Distributors, Inc.**

Diamond Clear Vision *Imprint of* **Illumination Arts LLC**

Diamond Comic Distributors, Inc., (*978-1-59396; 978-1-60584*) 1966 Greenspring Dr., Suite 300, Timonium, MD 21093 USA Tel 410-560-7100; Fax: 410-560-2583; Toll Free: 800-452-6642
E-mail: books@diamondbookdistributors.com
Web site: http://www.diamondbookdistributors.com/
Dist(s): **Diamond Bk. Distributors.**

Diamond Creek Publishing, (*978-0-9713811*) P.O. Box 2068, Flagstaff, AZ 86003-2068 USA
Web site: http://www.apathways.com.

Diamond Event Planning, Inc., (*978-0-9766901*) 50-44 193rd St., Fresh Meadows, NY 11365 USA Tel 718-357-6144; Fax: 718-357-6685
E-mail: bridepro@aol.com
Web site: http://www.awedwitharedhead.com.

Diamond Farm Bk. Pubs., Div. of Yesteryear Toys & Books, Inc., Orders Addr.: P.O. Box 537, Alexandria Bay, NY

Publisher Name Index

13607 USA (SAN 674-9054) Tel 613-475-1771; Fax: 613-475-3748; Toll Free Fax: 800-305-5138 (Order Line); Toll Free: 800-481-1353 (Order Line)
E-mail: info@diamondfarm.com
Web site: http://www.diamondfarm.com.

Diamond Fly Publishing, Inc., *(978-0-9817938)* 5224 Kings Mills Rd. Suite 264, Mason, OH 45040-2319 USA (SAN 856-566X)
Web site: http://www.diamondflypublishing.com.

Diamond Media Pr., *(978-1-7333011; 978-1-951302)* 217 Fieldstone Dr., Fraziers Bottom, WV 25082 USA Tel 888-322-7392
E-mail: nicole.regner@diamondmediapress.com
Web site: https://diamondmediapress.com/.

Diamond Select Toys & Collectibles, *(978-1-931724)* Div. of Diamond Comics Distributors, 1966 Greenspring Dr., Suite 300, Timonium, MD 21093 USA Tel 410-560-7100; Fax: 410-560-7589; Toll Free: 800-452-6642
E-mail: wjason@diamondcomics.com
Web site: http://www.diamondselecttoys.com
Dist(s): **Diamond Comic Distributors, Inc.**
Diamond Bk. Distributors
Simon & Schuster, Inc.

Diamond Spine Publishing, *(978-0-9765119; 978-0-9906238)* 42 Lake Ave., Ext., Suite 188, Danbury, CT 06811 USA Fax: 203-775-3311
E-mail: steeling@sinfulnyms.com.

Diamond Springs Pr., *(978-0-9729940)* 8085 Diamond Springs Dr., Helena, MT 59602 USA Tel 406-458-9220
E-mail: sagewood@qwest.net.

Diamond Star Pr., *(978-0-9774335; 978-1-7324591)* P.O. Box 490817, Los Angeles, CA 90049-0817 USA (SAN 257-6457)
E-mail: info@diamondstarpress.com.

Diamond Triple C Ranch, *(978-0-9790652)* 801 Floral Vale Blvd., Yardley, PA 19067 USA (SAN 852-324X) Tel 215-497-3188; Fax: 215-497-3190
Web site: http://www.diamondtriplecranch.com.

DIANE Publishing Co., *(978-0-7881; 978-0-941375; 978-1-56806; 978-0-7567; 978-1-4223; 978-1-4289; 978-1-4379; 978-1-4578)* Orders Addr.: P.O. Box 617, Darby, PA 19023-0617 USA (SAN 667-1217) Tel 610-461-6200; Fax: 610-461-6130; Toll Free: 800-782-3833; Edit Addr.: 330 Pusey Ave., No. 3 rear, Collingdale, PA 19023 USA Tel 610-461-6200; Fax: 610-461-6130; Toll Free: 800-782-3833
E-mail: cfisher@dianepublishing.net
Web site: http://www.dianepublishing.net.

Diarmuid Inc., *(978-1-59347)* Orders Addr.: P.O. Box 357580, Gainesville, FL 32635 USA Toll Free: 877-475-3277; Edit Addr.: 2630 N.W. 41st St., Suite D-1, Gainesville, FL 32606 USA
E-mail: kuc49@aol.com; dalia@greatleaps.com
Web site: http://www.greatleaps.com.

DiaShah Pr., LLC, *(978-0-9761207)* Orders Addr.: P.O. Box 43804, Nottingham, MD 21236 USA
E-mail: diashahpress@yahoo.com
Web site: http://www.debrasawyer.com; http://www.diashahpress.com.

DIASOT Pubns., *(978-0-9844649)* P.O. Box 705, Pittsburg, KS 66762 USA (SAN 859-4759)
E-mail: DIASOTPublications@gmail.com.

Diaspora Vibes Publishing, LLC *See* **Autherine Publishing**

Diaz, Bethany, *(978-0-692-76474-9; 978-0-692-76476-3; 978-0-692-79593-4; 978-0-692-79666-5; 978-0-578-67940-2)* 895 Riverside Dr Apt E157, WENATCHEE, WA 98801 USA Tel 253-820-3953.

Diaz, Olga L, *(978-1-948918)* 2017 Rowe Ave NE, Grand Rapids, MI 40505 USA Tel 616-307-8555; *Imprints*: LectoCultura (MYID_S_LECTOCU)
E-mail: lectocultura2018@gmail.com.

Dibble Institute for Marriage Education, The, *(978-0-9652427; 978-0-9761349; 978-0-9828395; 978-1-940815)* Orders Addr.: P.O. Box 7881, Berkeley, CA 94707-0881 USA Tel 510-528-7975 (Main Office); Fax: 972-226-2824 (Customer Service Fax); Toll Free: 800-695-7975 (Customer Service); Edit Addr.: 728 Coventry Rd., Kensington, CA 94707 USA
E-mail: relationshipskills@DibbleInstitute.org
Web site: http://www.buildingrelationshipskills.org; http://www.DibbleInstitute.org.

Dickens Ghost Publishing, *(978-0-9996219)* 912 Scott St., Beaufort, SC 29902 USA Tel 843-812-3589
E-mail: kimpoovey@gmail.com.

Dickerman, David, *(978-0-692-76993-5; 978-0-692-76994-2)* 317 Hale St., PENNINGTON, NJ 08534 USA Tel 347-834-7819.

Dickow, Gregory Ministries, *(978-1-932833)* Orders Addr.: P.O. Box 7000, Chicago, IL 60680 USA Tel 847-645-9100; Fax: 847-842-9200; Edit Addr.: 2500 Beverly Rd., Hoffman Estates, IL 60192 USA
E-mail: gdmpartnerrelations@changinglives.org
Web site: http://www.changinglives.org.

Dickson Keanaghan, LLC, *(978-0-9749146; 978-1-933230)* 265 Jerusalem Ave., Hicksville, Long Island,, NY 11801-4931 USA Tel 516-578-5874 cell phone; Fax: 516-433-5734 office fax
E-mail: jckunzjr@dicksonkeanaghan.com
Web site: DicksonKeanaghan.com
Dist(s): **Ingram Content Group.**

Dickson-Keanaghan Publishing Group, LLC *See* **Dickson Keanaghan, LLC**

Dictionary Project, Inc., The, *(978-0-9745292; 978-0-9771777; 978-1-934669)* P.O. Box 566, Sullivan's Island, SC 29482 USA (SAN 255-5999)
E-mail: wordpower2@aol.com.

Didax Educational Resources, Inc., *(978-1-58324; 978-1-885111)* 395 Main St., Rowley, MA 01969 USA Tel 978-948-2340 (ext. 350); Fax: 978-948-2813; Toll Free: 800-458-0024
Web site: http://www.didax.com.

Die Gestalten Verlag (DEU) *(978-3-931126; 978-3-89955)* *Dist. by* **IngramPubServ.**

Diettribe Enterprises *See* **Steve Diet Goedde**

Dietz Pr., *(978-0-87517; 978-0-692-55454-8; 978-0-692-55455-5)* Orders Addr.: 930 Winfield Rd., Petersburg, VA 23803-4748 USA Tel 804-733-0123; Fax: 804-733-3514; Toll Free: 800-391-6833
E-mail: wsmith@owenprinting.com; customerservice@dietzpress.com
Web site: http://www.dietzpress.com
Dist(s): **American Wholesale Bk. Co.**
Barnes&Noble.com
Emery-Pratt Co.
Follett School Solutions.

Different Friends, *(978-1-892750)* Orders Addr.: P.O. Box 40208, Cincinnati, OH 45240 USA Tel 513-825-1514; Edit Addr.: 703 Yorkhaven Rd., Cincinnati, OH 45246 USA.

Different Mousetrap Pr. LLC, *(978-0-615-65392-1; 978-0-9890696)* 1100 19th Avenue, No. 108 Unit J, Fargo, ND 58102-2269 USA
E-mail: mrw1980@lycos.com; maxwestart@gmail.com
Web site: http://maxwestart.deviantart.com; http://sunnyvillestories.com.

Different Worlds Pubns., *(978-0-9753999)* 1600 Portola Dr., San Francisco, CA 94127-1402 USA (SAN 256-0577)
E-mail: info@diffworlds.com
Web site: http://www.diffworlds.com.

DiFrancesco, Joe, *(978-0-9712682)* 35 Meadow Creek Ln., Glenmoore, PA 19343-2017 USA
E-mail: josephdifran@comcast.net.

Digging Clams n Oregon, *(978-0-9767508)* P.O. Box 746, Newport, OR 97365 USA (SAN 850-9700) Tel 541-265-5847
E-mail: williamlackner001@msn.com.

Digibots Corp., *(978-0-9755725)* Orders Addr.: P.O. Box 6803, Katy, TX 77491 USA Tel 281-599-1095; Fax: 281-599-0391; Toll Free: 877-375-8794; Edit Addr.: 3710 Havenmoor Pl., Katy, TX 77449 USA
E-mail: drew3710@msn.com
Web site: http://www.digibots.us.

Digireads.com *See* **Digireads.com Publishing**

Digireads.com Publishing, *(978-0-9753222; 978-1-59625; 978-1-59674; 978-1-4209)* 3921 Harvard Rd., Lawrence, KS 66049 USA
E-mail: digireads@yahoo.com
Web site: http://www.digireads.com
Dist(s): **Ingram Publisher Services**
Ingram Content Group
Neeland Media, LLC.

Digital Antiquaria, Inc., *(978-1-58057)* 2 Sand Hill Rd., Morristown, NJ 07960-5928 USA
E-mail: info@DigitalAntiquaria.com
Web site: http://digitalantiquaria.com.

Digital Golden Solutions LLC, *(978-1-948040; 978-1-950280; 978-1-64916)* 11807 Westheimer Rd. Suite 550 PMB 846, HOUSTON, TX 77077 USA Tel 281-305-9245; *Imprints*: DG Books Publishing (MYID_Y_DG BKS)
E-mail: digitalgoldensolutions@gmail.com
Dist(s): **Ingram Content Group.**

Digital Kidz Publishing Hse., *(978-1-7327314)* 5010 Aberdeen Pkwy., Amarillo, TX 79119 USA Tel 806-316-6067
E-mail: kyla@kylahashmi.com.

Digital Manga Distribution *See* **Digital Manga Publishing**

Digital Manga Publishing, *(978-1-56970)* Div. of Digital Manga, Inc., 1487 W. 178th St. Ste. 300, Gardena, CA 90248-3253 USA (SAN 111-817X) Toll Free: 866-897-7300
E-mail: contact@emanga.com
Web site: http://www.dmpbooks.com/
Dist(s): **Diamond Comic Distributors, Inc.**
Diamond Bk. Distributors
Random Hse., Inc.

Digital Quest Inc., *(978-1-934873; 978-1-947262)* 525 Thomastown Ln., Ridgeland, MS 39157 USA Tel 601-856-2237; Fax: 601-856-2576
Web site: http://www.digitalquest.com.

Digital Scanning, Inc., *(978-1-58218)* 344 Gannett Rd., Scituate, MA 02066 USA (SAN 299-8734) Tel 781-545-2100
E-mail: info@digitalscanning.com
Web site: http://www.digitalscanning.com
Dist(s): **Ingram Content Group**
TextStream
ebrary, Inc.

Digital Tech Frontier, LLC., *(978-0-9830127; 978-0-9905354; 978-0-692-51963-9)* Orders Addr.: 2610 E. Mohawk Ln. No. 120, Phoenix, AZ 85050 USA Tel 480-290-2195
E-mail: rsiddell@popartoys.com.

Digital Vista, Inc., *(978-0-9817625; 978-0-9976807; 978-0-9983375; 978-1-950052)* 24 Amity Pl., Massapequa, NY 11758 USA (SAN 856-4825); *Imprints*: DV Books (MYID_W_DV BKS)
E-mail: info@digitalvista.net.

digital@batesjackson llc *See* **Bates Jackson Engraving Co., Inc.**

DigitalKu, *(978-0-9763168)* 7913 N. Highview Dr., Milwaukee, WI 53223 USA
Web site: http://www.digitalku.com/.

Digi-Tall Media, *(978-0-9785728; 978-0-9793944; 978-0-9802093; 978-0-9840655; 978-0-9828950; 978-0-9837334; 978-0-9850007; 978-0-9894024; 978-0-9913654; 978-0-9863958; 978-0-9972356; 978-0-9982406; 978-0-9989286; 978-1-7332411)* 6205 Oregon Ct., Plano, TX 75023 USA Tel 972-352-0324 Digi Tall Media Distributor
E-mail: editorshepherd@gmail.com
Web site: https://www.instagram.com/digi.tall.media.ig/; https://twitter.com/DigiTallMedia1; https://www.facebook.com/groups/207015945987971/; https://www.facebook.com/Digi.Tall.Media.books/; http://www.digi-tall-media.com; http://www.story-e-books.com.

Digitex-U Pubns., *(978-0-615-15579-1)* 6655 Malyern Ave., Philadelphia, PA 19151 USA Tel 215-738-4678
E-mail: raincloud1@gmail.com
Web site: http://www.myspace.com/raincoud1
Dist(s): **Lulu Pr., Inc.**

DiGuiseppi, Joseph, *(978-0-9768348)* Orders Addr.: 4 Richmond Rd., Newtown, CT 06470-1214 USA
E-mail: joedigspi@hotmail.com
Web site: http://www.joedigspi.com.

Dillies, Lyn, *(978-0-615-66530-6; 978-0-615-67484-1)* 15 Laurel Ln., Westport, MA 02790 USA Tel 508-636-2484
E-mail: lyn@magicoflyn.com.

Dilligaf Publishing, *(978-0-9639070; 978-0-9701020; 978-1-931207)* Orders Addr.: 98 Main St., Ellsworth, ME 04605 USA Tel 207-667-5351
E-mail: studio3marty@acadia.net; vze277g4@verizon.net.

Dillon, Elena, *(978-0-9886353; 978-0-9908804)* 15035 Live Oak Springs, Canyon Country, CA 91387 USA Tel 661-406-2369
E-mail: info@elenadillon.com.

Dilly Green Bean Games, *(978-0-9744698; 978-0-9801898)* 33 Hillview Rd., Gorham, ME 04038 USA
E-mail: dillygreenbeangames@dillygreenbeangames.com; jay@indirpg.com; jay@dillygreenbeangames.com
Web site: http://www.dillygreenbeangames.com.

Dimensions, *(978-0-9882694)* 1595 Parliament Ct., Fairfield, OH 45014 USA Tel 513-829-4196; Fax: 513-829-4545
E-mail: hw2000@zoomtown.com
Web site: http://www.henryhwilliamson.com.

Dimensions in Media, Inc., *(978-0-9762273)* 24191 N. Forest Dr., Lake Zurich, IL 60047 USA Tel 847-726-2093
E-mail: debbie@dimensionsinmedia.com
Web site: http://www.be-still.com.

Dingles & Co., *(978-1-891997; 978-1-59646)* P.O. Box 508, Sea Girt, NJ 08750 USA
E-mail: dinglesco@aol.com
Dist(s): **Central Programs**
Gumdrop Bks.

Dingobi Publishing, *(978-0-9772819)* P.O. Box 4533, Rock Island, IL 61204-4533 USA.

Dings Bks., *(978-0-9748890)* 411 Schoolhouse Ln., Shippensburg, PA 17257 USA
E-mail: dingscenter@yahoo.com.

Dino Entertainment AG (DEU) *(978-3-89748; 978-3-932268)* *Dist. by* **Distribks Inc.**

Dinosaur Fund, *(978-0-9748618)* 711 E. St. SE, No. 104, Washington, DC 20003-2879 USA Tel 202-547-3326
E-mail: dinosaurfund@juno.com; shill@laser-image.com
Web site: http://www.dinosaurfund.org.

Dinoship, Inc., *(978-0-9728585; 978-1-933384)* 105 W. 73rd St., No. 1B, New York, NY 10023 USA Tel 212-721-5056; Fax: 212-595-0247; 299 Broadway, No. 1016, New York, NY 10007
E-mail: bob@dinoship.com
Web site: http://www.dinoship.com.

DinRo, *(978-0-9744412)* 7545 Gladstone Dr., No. 205, Naperville, IL 60565 USA Fax: 630-305-3695.

Diogenes Verlag AG (CHE) *(978-3-257)* *Dist. by* **Intl Bk Import.**

Diogenes Verlag AG (CHE) *(978-3-257)* *Dist. by* **Distribks Inc.**

Diomo Square Bks., *(978-0-9765948)* 4911 SW 43rd Ave., Portland, OR 97206-5011 USA
E-mail: diomo@earthlink.net.

Dion's Pubn., *(978-0-9795739; 978-0-9836893)* 3002 Royston Rd., Charlotte, NC 28208 USA Tel 574-307-2496
E-mail: tokereke@gmail.com.

Diplodocus Pr., *(978-0-9771346; 978-0-9800149; 978-0-9860533; 978-1-940999)* 6828 Laurel Canyon Blvd., No. 203, North Hollywood, CA 91605 USA
E-mail: order@diplodocuspress.com
Web site: http://www.diplodocuspress.com.

DIPS publishing Inc, *(978-1-946818)* 4229 e 124, Cleveland, OH 44105 USA Tel 216-801-7886
E-mail: Davidawright73@gmail.com.

Dire Wolf Bks., *(978-1-943934)* 3300 N. Main St. Suite D 153, Anderson, SC 29621 USA Tel 843-269-5167
E-mail: bpatterson@direwolfbooks.com
Web site: www.direwolfbooks.com.

Direct Access Publishing, *(978-0-9796473)* 1402 Auburn Wy No. No. 232, Auburn, WA 98002 USA (SAN 853-9952) Tel 206-725-3001; Toll Free: 877-725-3009
E-mail: directt_access@yahoo.com.

Direct World Publishing, *(978-0-9787591; 978-0-9987832; 978-1-948562)* Orders Addr.: 15507 S. Normandie Ave No. 316, Gardena, CA 90247 USA Tel 949-302-7738; Edit Addr.: 15507 S. Normandie Ave No. 316, Gardena, CA 90247 USA Tel 949-302-7738
E-mail: jennifer@jenniferyu.com; yu@directworldapp.com; yu@directworldpublishing.com
Web site: www.JenniferYu.com; www.directworldpublishing.com.

Directions in Education, Training & Consultation, *(978-0-9664681)* Orders Addr.: P.O. Box 2478, Gig Harbor, WA 98335 USA Tel 253-858-7261; Edit Addr.: 4720 Birchtree Ln., NW, Gig Harbor, WA 98335 USA
E-mail: lbaker@HarborNet.com
Web site: http://www.pebblesinthepond.com.

DirkDesigns, LLC, *(978-0-9790923)* P.O. Box 3754, West Lafayette, IN 47996 USA.

Dirks Publishing *See* **Dirks Publishing, LLC**

Dirks Publishing, LLC, *(978-0-9823145)* P.O. Box 348, Rantoul, IL 61866-0348 USA Fax: 206-339-8510
E-mail: julie@dirkspublishing.com
Web site: http://www.dirkspublishing.com.

Disciple One Publishing, *(978-0-9791883)* Div. of Disciple Group Production, 10153 1/2 Riverside Dr., No. 467, Toluca Lake, CA 91602 USA Tel 323-654-8579
E-mail: baronjay@yourlittleblackbook.net
Web site: http://www.yourlittleblackbook.net
Dist(s): **Lushena Bks.**

Disciple Publishing Co., *(978-0-615-23763-3)* P.O. Box 554, Beaufort, SC 29901 USA Tel 843-379-9955; Fax: 843-379-9956; Toll Free: 866-245-8182
E-mail: dpc@hargray.com
Web site: http://www.dpchope.com.

Discipleship Pubns. International, *(978-1-57782; 978-1-884553)* 300 5th Ave. Ste. 5, Waltham, MA 02451-8749 USA Toll Free: 888-374-2665
E-mail: spjones@icoc.org; dpibooks@icoc.org
Web site: http://www.dpibooks.org
Dist(s): **Baker & Taylor Publisher Services (BTPS)**
ebrary, Inc.

Discipleship Resources *Imprint of* **Upper Room Bks.**

Discover Writing Company *See* **Discover Writing Pr.**

Discover Writing Pr., *(978-0-9656574; 978-1-931492)* Orders Addr.: P.O. Box 264, Shoreham, VT 05770 USA Tel 802-897-7022; Fax: 802-897-2084; Toll Free: 800-613-8055
E-mail: registrar@discoverwriting.com; ann@discoverwriting.com; administrator@discoverwriting.com; barry@discoverwriting.com
Web site: http://www.discoverwriting.com.

Discover Your Northwest, *(978-0-914019)* 164 S. Jackson St., Seattle, WA 98104 USA (SAN 286-8504) Tel 206-220-4140; Fax: 206-479-4170
E-mail: nwia-publications@nwpubliclands.org
Web site: http://www.nwpubliclands.com
Dist(s): **Hopkins Fulfillment Services**
Partners/West Book Distributors
Univ. of Washington Pr.

Discoveries Publishing llc, *(978-0-9998318)* 100 silver beach Ave. No. 124, daytona beach, FL 32115 USA Tel 860-214-8066
E-mail: acernst24@gmail.com.

DiscoverNet, *(978-0-9728053; 978-0-9742787; 978-0-9746943; 978-1-932813)* 1105 Walnut St. #f-160-25, Cary, NC 27511 USA Tel 919-301-0109; Fax: 919-557-2261
E-mail: lharte@discovernet.com
Web site: http://www.althosbooks.com.

DiscoverRoo *Imprint of* **Pop!**

Discovery Communications *See* **Discovery Education**

Discovery Education, *(978-1-56331; 978-1-58738; 978-1-59527; 978-1-60288; 978-1-60711; 978-0-9824299; 978-1-61629; 978-1-61708; 978-1-61828; 978-1-68220)* One Discovery Pl., Silver Spring, MD 20910 USA Tel 240-662-2000; Toll Free: 888-892-3484
E-mail: megan.faller@discovery.com; sara_fisher@discovery.com
Web site: http://www.discoveryeducation.com
Dist(s): **Explorations**
Follett School Solutions
Insight Guides
Langenscheidt Publishing Group.

Discovery Enterprises, Limited *See* **History Compass, LLC**

Discovery Hse. Pubs., *(978-0-929239; 978-1-57293; 978-1-62707; 978-1-64070)* Div. of R B C Ministries, Orders Addr.: P.O. Box 3566, Grand Rapids, MI 49501 USA (SAN 248-8949) Tel 616-942-9218; Fax: 616-957-5741; Toll Free: 800-653-8333; Edit Addr.: 3000 Kraft Ave., SE, Grand Rapids, MI 49512 USA (SAN 248-8957) Tel 616-942-6770; Fax: 616-974-2224
E-mail: melissa.wade@odb.org; lisa.luckenbaugh@odb.org; carol.waltman@odb.org
Web site: http://www.dhp.org
Dist(s): **CLC Pubns.**

Discovery Pr. Pubns., Inc., *(978-0-9645159)* 400 E. 3rd Ave., No. 901, Denver, CO 80203 USA (SAN 298-5691) Tel 303-355-9689; Fax: 303-733-3474
E-mail: discoverypresspub@comcast.net
Web site: http://www.discoverypresspub.com
Dist(s): **Brodart Co.**
Quality Bks., Inc.

Discovery Pubns. (GBR) *(978-0-9538222; 978-0-9550458)* *Dist. by* **Irish Bks Media.**

Disenos del Arte, Inc., *(978-0-9820784)* P.O. Box 11441, San Juan, PR 00910 USA Tel 787-722-1060; Fax: 787-728-3092
E-mail: dasant@delartepr.com
Web site: http://www.delartepr.com.

Disinformation Co. Ltd., The, *(978-0-9713942; 978-0-9729529; 978-1-932857; 978-1-934708; 978-1-939517)* 220 E. 23rd St., Suite 500, New York, NY 10010 USA
E-mail: books@disinfo.com
Dist(s): **Follett School Solutions**
Red Wheel/Weiser
ebrary, Inc.

Dismondy, Maria Inc., *(978-0-615-47393-2; 978-0-615-51620-2; 978-0-9848558; 978-0-9976085; 978-1-7328418; 978-1-7330359; 978-1-7353451)* Orders Addr.: 5449 Sylvia, Dearborn, MI 48124 USA Tel 248-302-1800; *Imprints*: Cardinal Rule Press (CardinalRule)
E-mail: mariadismondy@mac.com
Web site: http://www.cardinalrulepress.com
Dist(s): **Independent Pubs. Group**
Partners Bk. Distributing, Inc.

Disney Editions *Imprint of* **Disney Pr.**

Disney Lucasfilm Press *Imprint of* **Disney Publishing Worldwide**

†**Disney Pr.,** *(978-0-7868; 978-1-56282; 978-1-4231)* Div. of Disney Bk. Publishing, Inc., A Walt Disney Co., 44 S. Broadway. Flr. 16, White Plains, NY 10601-4411 USA Toll Free: 800-759-0190; *Imprints:* Disney Editions (Disney Ed); Riordan, Rick (RRiordan)
Web site: http://www.disney.com/disneybooks/index.html
Dist(s): **Children's Plus, Inc. Hachette Bk. Group Libros Sin Fronteras Little Brown & Co. Perfection Learning Corp.**; *CIP.*

Disney Publishing Worldwide, *(978-1-892309; 978-1-931580; 978-1-4231; 978-1-4847; 978-1-368; 978-1-368-01377-2)* Subs. of Walt Disney Productions, 44 S. Broadway, 10th Flr., White Plains, NY 10601 USA Tel 914-288-4316; 1101 Flower St., Glendale, CA 91201; *Imprints:* Marvel Press (Marvel Pr); Disney Lucasfilm Press (Lucasfilm Pr)
Web site: http://www.disney.go.com; http://www.hyperionbooksforchildren.com; books.disney.com
Dist(s): **Blackstone Audio, Inc. Children's Plus, Inc. Follett School Solutions Hachette Bk. Group.**

Disneyland/Vista Records & Tapes *See* **Walt Disney Records**

Disposition Sketch Bks. *Imprint of* **MacBride, E. J. Pubn., Inc.**

Disruptive Publishing, *(978-1-59654; 978-1-60872; 978-1-62657)* 735 Ivy League Ln., Rockville, MD 20850 USA
E-mail: service.blackmask@gmail.com
Web site: http://www.dispub.com
Dist(s): **Diamond Bk. Distributors.**

Dissected Lives (Auto Biographies) *Imprint of* **Speedy Publishing LLC**

DiStasi Advisors, LLC, *(978-0-692-49826-2; 978-1-7327067)* 5029 Bristol CT, Loveland, OH 45140 USA Tel (513) 477-7624
Dist(s): **CreateSpace Independent Publishing Platform.**

Distinct Pr., *(978-0-9916089; 978-1-943103)* 6822 22nd Ave. N., St. Petersburg, FL 33710-3918 USA Tel 727-238-7884
E-mail: theageofattraction@gmail.com; waldorfinspired@yahoo.com
Web site: www.DistinctPress.com
Dist(s): **Ingram Content Group.**

Distractions Ink, *(978-0-9713389; 978-0-9821921; 978-0-9827826; 978-0-9835250; 978-0-9838074; 978-0-9852740; 978-0-9852807; 978-0-9884276; 978-0-9889582; 978-0-9913878; 978-0-9861307; 978-0-9970959; 978-0-9980595; 978-0-9990831; 978-0-9996274; 978-1-7330336)* Orders Addr.: P.O. Box 15971, Rio Rancho, NM 87144 USA Tel 719-495-1562
E-mail: marcialmcclure@cs.com
Web site: http://www.marcialynnmcclure.com.

Distribooks, Inc., Div. of MED, Inc., 8124 N. Ridgeway, Skokie, IL 60076 USA (SAN 630-9763) Tel 847-676-1596; Fax: 847-676-1195
E-mail: info@distribooks.com.

Distribuidora Norma, Inc., *(978-1-881700; 978-1-935164)* Div. of Carvajal International, Orders Addr.: P.O. Box 195040, San Juan, PR 00919-5040 USA Tel 787-788-5050; Fax: 787-788-7161; Edit Addr.: Carretera 869 Km 1.5 Barrio Palmas Royal Industrial, Catano, PR 00962 USA
Web site: http://www.norma.com.

Distribuidora Plaza Mayor, 1500 Ave. Ponce de Leon Local 2 El Cinco, San Juan, PR 1 USA.

éditeur, Annika Parance (CAN) *(978-2-923830) Dist. by* **Firefly Bks Limited.**

Éditions Chouette (CAN) *(978-2-89450; 978-2-921198; 978-2-9800909; 978-2-89718; 978-2-924734) Dist. by* **Distribks Inc.**

Éditions Tourbillon (FRA) *(978-2-84801; 979-10-276) Dist. by* **HachBkGrp.**

Ditto Enterprises, *(978-0-9967559)* 119 Grove Clover Ln., Montgomery, TX 77316 USA Tel 713-824-3105
E-mail: denfield97@aol.com.

Diverse Medium *See* **Diverse Mediumz**

Diverse Mediumz, *(978-1-7320989)* 15814 Pryor Dr, Missouri city, TX 77489 USA Tel 832-203-9133
E-mail: tiana31510@gmail.com.

Diversified A+ Pubns., *(978-0-9773526)* P.O. Box 13, Winchendon, MA 01475 USA
E-mail: Dpipub@aol.com
Web site: http://www.dpublications.com.

Diversified Publishing, 1745 Broadway, New York, NY 10019 USA; *Imprints:* Living Language (LiviLang); Random House Large Print (RH LargeP)
Dist(s): **Penguin Random Hse. Distribution Penguin Random Hse. LLC Random Hse., Inc.**

Diversion Bks. *Imprint of* **Diversion Publishing Corp.**

Diversion Books *See* **Diversion Publishing Corp.**

Diversion Pr., *(978-1-935290)* P.O. Box 30277, Clarksville, TN 37040 USA (SAN 857-0264)
E-mail: diversionpress@yahoo.com
Web site: http://www.diversionpress.com.

Diversion Publishing Corp., *(978-0-9845151; 978-0-9829050; 978-0-9833371; 978-0-9838395; 978-0-9839885; 978-1-938120; 978-1-62681; 978-1-68230; 978-1-63576)* 443 Park Aveue S., Ste. 1008, New York, NY 10016 USA (SAN 990-6304) Tel 212-675-5556; 212-961-6390; *Imprints:* Diversion Books (DiversionBks); EverAfter Romance (EverAfterRoman)
E-mail: info@diversionbooks.com; charles@efit.com
Web site: http://www.diversionbooks.com
Dist(s): **Children's Plus, Inc. Ingram Publisher Services MyiLibrary Open Road Integrated Media, Inc. Smashwords Two Rivers Distribution.**

Diversity Foundation, The, *(978-0-9797193)* 505 W., 10200 S., South Jordan, UT 84095 USA Tel 801-553-4556; Fax: 801-553-4600; Toll Free: 888-216-2122
Web site: http://www.thediversityfoundation.org
Dist(s): **Partners Pubs. Group, Inc.**

Diversity Ink Publishing, *(978-0-9767258)* P.O. Box 2414, Santa Maria, CA 93457 USA.

Diversity Matters Pr., *(978-0-578-06591-5; 978-0-9839020)* 5555 DTC Pkwy., Suite C3200, Greenwood Village, CO 80111 USA.

Dividion Group, LLC, The, *(978-0-9769366)* Orders Addr.: P.O. Box 2678, North Canton, OH 44720 USA
E-mail: tumekash22@aol.com; bigheds@bigheds.com
Web site: http://www.bigheds.com.

Divine House Ministries *See* **Kingdom Sound Pubs.**

Divine Inspiration Publishing, LLC, *(978-0-9820490)* P.O. Box 210414, Auburn Hills, MI 48326 USA (SAN 857-1090) Fax: 248-927-0357
E-mail: stevecogswell@comcast.net; scogswell@divineinspirationpublishing.com
Web site: http://www.divineinsirationpublishing.com.

Divine Intertwine Publishing, *(978-0-9754489)* P.O. Box 4088, Ocean City, MD 21843 USA.

Divine Mercy Pr., *(978-0-9755471)* 3216 Mission Ave. Apt. 138, Oceanside, CA 92058-1348 USA
E-mail: divinemercy@hypersurf.com.

Divine Ministry of North Florida, Inc., *(978-0-9773356)* P.O. Box 5668, Gainesville, FL 32627-5668 USA (SAN 257-3652)
E-mail: ade0201@yahoo.com
Web site: http://www.divineministry.net.

Divine Physiology International Ministries, *(978-0-9983379)* P.O. Box 159175, Nashville, TN 37215 USA Tel 615-509-5557
E-mail: bnalnc@aol.com.

Dixon, Emma, *(978-0-692-95138-5)* 475 S Perkins Rd No. 708, Memphis, TN 38117 USA Tel 385-209-6542
E-mail: cristina_wilson@yahoo.com.

Dixon, Nell, *(978-0-9864033)* 820 S. MacArthur Blvd., Coppell, TX 75019 USA Tel 972-510-5574
E-mail: nelldixonministries@hotmail.com.

DJ Blues Publishing, *(978-0-9743985)* 403 Dula Cir., Duncanville, TX 75116 USA
E-mail: hipdjblues@earthlink.net
Web site: http://www.djblues.com.

DJ Inkers *Imprint of* **Carson-Dellosa Publishing, LLC**

DK *Imprint of* **Dorling Kindersley Publishing, Inc.**

DK *Imprint of* **DK Games**

DK Children *Imprint of* **Dorling Kindersley Publishing, Inc.**

DK Games, 1745 Broadway, New York, NY 10019 USA; *Imprints:* Prima Games (Prima Games); DK (DK)
Dist(s): **Penguin Random Hse. Distribution Penguin Random Hse. LLC.**

Dksmo-Press, Izdatel'skaja firma (RUS) *(978-5-04) Dist. by* **Distribks Inc.**

DL Grant, LLC, *(978-0-9853713; 978-0-9882084; 978-0-9889947; 978-0-9914542; 978-1-942017)*
E-mail: dgauthor@gmail.com.

DL Publishing, *(978-0-9797699)* 487 Harvard Avenue, North Baldwin, NY 11428 USA Tel 646-240-1633
E-mail: lesleynu@yahoo.com
Web site: www.lesleynurse.com
Dist(s): **Lulu Pr., Inc.**

DLG, LLC *See* **DL Grant, LLC**

dLife - For Your Diabetes Life, *(978-0-9777463)* Div. of LifeMed Media, 101 Franklin St., Westport, CT 06880-0688 USA (SAN 850-1254) Tel 203-454-6985; Fax: 203-454-6986
E-mail: info@dlife.com
Web site: http://www.dlife.com.

DLS Bks. *Imprint of* **Denney Literary Services**

DM Creative, *(978-0-9798445)* 16032 Samoa Ct., Tega Cay, SC 29708-2970 USA
Web site: http://www.hamstersam.com/; http://davemcdonald.com/.

Dm Productions, *(978-0-615-14860-1; 978-0-615-15990-4)* 10596 N. Washington Blvd., Indianapolis, IN 46280 USA
Web site: http://dmprod.blogspot.com/
Dist(s): **Lulu Pr., Inc.**

DMH Pr., Inc., *(978-0-9746153)* 10 Beachside Dr., No. 302, Vero Beach, FL 32963 USA (SAN 256-0127) Fax: 631-325-1340
Web site: http://www.dollyadventures.com.

DMT Publishing, *(978-0-9726189; 978-0-9749144; 978-0-9785553; 978-0-9800813; 978-0-9824259; 978-1-935821)* 900 N. 400 W. , Bldg. 12, North Salt Lake, UT 84054 USA
Web site: http://www.dmtpublishing.com.

DNA Pr., *(978-0-9664027; 978-0-9748765; 978-1-933255)* P.O. Box 572, Eagleville, PA 19408-0572 USA (SAN 256-5005) Fax: 501-694-5495
E-mail: editors@dnapress.com
Web site: http://www.dnapress.com.

DNA2Market, *(978-0-9992689)* 6800 W. McGlochlin St., Boise, ID 83709 USA Tel 208-870-1911
E-mail: beckydembowski@gmail.com.

do be you, *(978-0-9794262)* 229 Vincent Ave. N., Minneapolis, MN 55405 USA
E-mail: info@i-get-around.com
Web site: http://www.i-get-around.com.

Do Good Pr., *(978-0-9974263)* 9950 Scripps Lake Blvd. No. 104, San Diego, CA 92131 USA Tel 858-800-5080
E-mail: info@dogoodpress.com
Web site: www.dogoodpress.com.

Do Life Right, Inc., *(978-0-9824829; 978-1-937848)* P.O. Box 61, Sahuarita, AZ 85629 USA
E-mail: lisa@wrightontimebooks.com
Web site: http://www.doliferight.com
Dist(s): **CreateSpace Independent Publishing Platform.**

Do The Write Thing Foundation of DC, *(978-1-930357; 978-0-692-86055-7; 978-1-7350773)* 56 T. St. , NW, Washington, DC 20001-1009 USA Tel 202-758-0397; Fax: 202-758-0397
E-mail: chillshl@netscape.net; dothewritething1@gmail.com
Web site: www.dothewritethingdc.com.

Do Well Studio, *(978-0-692-86200-1)* 68 Tupper Rd. No. 7, Sandwich, MA 02563 USA Tel 617-966-4636
E-mail: donna@dowellstudio.com
Web site: dowellstudio.com.

DOAN, DEIRDRA *See* **Tapestry Productions**

Dobie Book Publishing *See* **Mowery, Julia**

Dobson, Kathy, *(978-0-9982820)* 7 Chestnut St., Rhinebeck, NY 12572 USA Tel 617-276-7050
E-mail: kldobson@gmail.com.

Doc Publishing, *(978-0-615-46526-5; 978-0-615-58218-4; 978-0-9967370; 978-1-7358559)* 1149 Brookshire Dr., New Castle, PA 16101 USA Tel 724-658-2189
E-mail: juliannmangino@yahoo.com
Web site: www.docpublishing.org
Dist(s): **Lulu Pr., Inc.**

Doc Roe Publishing, *(978-0-692-06979-0; 978-0-692-16579-9; 978-0-578-48545-4; 978-0-578-48546-1; 978-0-578-60412-1)* 1641 Creek Wood Dr., Midlothian, TX 76065 USA Tel 214-450-3939
E-mail: docroegrandson@gmail.com.

Dockery, Robert, *(978-0-692-12903-6; 978-0-692-12907-4; 978-0-578-66709-6; 978-0-578-66712-6)* 64 INNESS Dr., TARPON SPRINGS, FL 34689 USA Tel 727-938-6029
E-mail: rdock@knology.net
Dist(s): **Ingram Content Group.**

Dockter, Toni, *(978-0-9712201)* P.O. Box 1532, Soquel, CA 95073-1532 USA
E-mail: tonette101@aol.com
Web site: http://percyveerance.com.

Doctor Dolittle's Library *Imprint of* **PhotoGraphics Publishing**

DocUmeant Publishing, *(978-0-9788831; 978-0-9825608; 978-0-9826005; 978-0-9832122; 978-1-937801; 978-0-692-30306-1; 978-1-950075)* Orders Addr.: 1730 Rainbow Dr., Clearwater, FL 33755 USA Tel 727-565-2130; Fax: 727-446-2217; Edit Addr.: 244 5th Avenue, Suite G-200, New York, NY 10001 USA; *Imprints:* DP Kids Press (DP Kids Pr)
E-mail: ceo@calomarllc.com; publisher@documeantpublishing.com
Web site: http://www.DocUmeantPublishing.com
Dist(s): **CreateSpace Independent Publishing Platform Ingram Content Group Lulu Pr., Inc.**

Dodi Pr., *(978-0-9767273; 978-0-9851067)* Orders Addr.: 384 Northyard Blvd., NW, Suite 100 #72, Atlanta, GA 30313 USA (SAN 860-3200)
E-mail: cherilnc@cherilnclarke.com; monica.r.bey@gmail.com; cheril@phenomenalwriting.com
Web site: http://www.myfamilyproducts.com; http://www.dodipress.com.

Dog Ear Publishing, LLC, *(978-0-9762173; 978-0-9766603; 978-1-59858; 978-1-60844; 978-1-4575)* 4010 W. 86th St., Suite H, Indianapolis, IN 46268 USA Tel 317-228-3656; Fax: 317-489-3506; Toll Free: 866-823-9613
E-mail: rayr@dogearpublishing.net
Web site: http://www.dogearpublishing.net
Dist(s): **Ingram Publisher Services Ingram Content Group Lulu Pr., Inc. Smashwords.**

Dog Hair Pr., *(978-1-7324914)* 7706 Marine Rd. 129, North Bergen, NJ 07047 USA Tel 201-295-9992
E-mail: cntp@optonline.net.

DOG ON A LOG Bks. *Imprint of* **Jojoba Pr.**

Dog Soldier Pr., *(978-0-9718658)* P.O. Box 1782, Ranchos de Taos, NM 87557-1782 USA (SAN 254-4733) Tel 575-770-1040
E-mail: dogsoldier@newmexico.com
Web site: http://www.dogsoldierpress.com.

Dog-Eared Pubns., *(978-0-941042)* Orders Addr.: P.O. Box 620863, Middleton, WI 53562-0863 USA (SAN 281-6059) Tel 608-831-1410 (phone/fax); Toll Free: 888-364-3277; Edit Addr.: 4642 Toepfer Rd., Middleton, WI 53562 USA
E-mail: field@dog-eared.com
Web site: http://www.dog-eared.com
Dist(s): **Common Ground Distributors, Inc. Paradise Cay Pubns. Partners/West Book Distributors.**

Doggerel Daze, *(978-0-9722820)* 10144 Riedel Pl., Cupertino, CA 95014 USA.

Doggy Diva Show, Inc., The, *(978-0-692-15017-7; 978-0-578-67286-1)* 1800 2nd St. Suite 750, SARASOTA, FL 34236 USA Tel 941-447-4441
E-mail: doggydivashow@aol.com
Dist(s): **Ingram Content Group.**

DogHouse Pr., *(978-0-9761497)* 150 Chestnut St., Park Forest, IL 60466 USA Toll Free: 877-413-8997
E-mail: kimberly@rjsystems.us
Web site: http://www.doghousepress.com.

Doghouse Publishing, Incorporated *See* **Mess Hall Writers**

Dogs Doing Jobs, LLC, *(978-0-9992365)* 224 SHANNON CT, INWOOD, WV 25428 USA Tel 703-980-1442
E-mail: alwssales@gmail.com.

Dogs in Hats Children's Publishing Co., *(978-1-59445)* P.O. Box 182, Grand Haven, MI 49417 USA Tel 616-844-2220; Fax: 616-844-2922
E-mail: customerservice@dogsinhats.com
Web site: http://www.dogsinhats.com
Dist(s): **Follett School Solutions.**

Dogs4dogs, *(978-0-9771265)* P.O. Box 675432, Rancho Santa Fe, CA 92067-5432 USA
Web site: http://www.dogs4dogs.com.

Dogtown Artworks, *(978-0-9777126)* 704 N. Main St. Suite 102, Tuscola, IL 61953 USA Tel 217-689-4575
E-mail: dogtownartworks@mac.com; dogtownartworks@gmail.com; pringle.photography@gmail.com
Web site: http://www.dogtownartworks.com.

Dogwalk Pr., *(978-0-9766846)* Div. of Dan Gersten & Assocs., LLC, 29636 Quail Run Dr., Agoura Hills, CA 91301 USA Tel 818-735-0280; Fax: 818-991-1838
Web site: http://www.askcurtisthedog.com.

Dogwise *See* **Dogwise Publishing**

Dogwise Publishing, *(978-1-929242; 978-1-61781)* Orders Addr.: 403 S. Mission, Wentachee, WA 98801 USA (SAN 631-1415) Tel 509-663-9115; Fax: 509-662-7233; Toll Free: 800-776-2665
E-mail: mail@dogwise.com; charlenew@dogwise.com; nate.woodward@dogwise.com
Web site: http://www.dogwise.com.

Dohate Pr., *(978-0-9767003)* Orders Addr.: 1809 Brookhaven Dr., Austin, TX 78704 USA Tel 512-442-0576
E-mail: donbutlerbooks@earthlink.net.

Doherty, Tom Assocs., LLC, *(978-0-312; 978-0-7653; 978-0-8125)* Div. of Holtzbrinck Publishers, Orders Addr.: 16365 James Madison Hwy., Gordonsville, VA 22942-8501 USA Toll Free Fax: 800-672-2054; Toll Free: 888-330-8477; Edit Addr.: 175 Fifth Ave., New York, NY 10010 USA Tel 212-674-5151; Fax: 540-672-7540 (customer service); *Imprints:* Forge Books (Forge Bks); Orb Books (Orb Bks); Tor Books (Tor Books); Starscape (Starscape); Tor Fantasy (Tor Fan); Tor Science Fiction (TorSciFic); Tor Teen (Tor Teen); Tor Romance (Tor Romance)
E-mail: inquiries@tor.com
Web site: http://www.tor.com/
Dist(s): **Cambridge Univ. Pr. Children's Plus, Inc. CreateSpace Independent Publishing Platform Libros Sin Fronteras Macmillan MyiLibrary Perfection Learning Corp. Westminster John Knox Pr.**

Doing Good Ministries, *(978-0-9667054)* 217 Bayview Way, Chula Vista, CA 91910 USA Tel 619-476-7230
E-mail: moehlenpah@aol.com
Web site: http://www.doinggood.org.

Dokument forlag, Fotograf Malcolm Jacobsson (SWE) *(978-91-973981; 978-91-85639) Dist. by* **SCB Distributo.**

Doley Pubns., *(978-0-9985699)* 4934 Garden Grove Rd., Grand Prairie, TX 75052 USA Tel 972-606-6755
E-mail: stacy.antonino@gmail.com.

Dollison Road Bks., *(978-0-9855540)* 247 E. 4700 N., Provo, UT 84604 USA Tel 417-883-0601
E-mail: JeanStringam@gmail.com
Web site: jeanstringam.com; DollisonRoadBooks.com.

Dollworks, *(978-0-9760064; 978-1-60304)* 6693 Lake Shore Dr., Newport, MI 48166-9716 USA; P.O. Box 66075, Newport, MI 48166
E-mail: nanciejack@aol.com.

Dolly Dimple Ink Children's Bks., *(978-0-9773506)* 5484 Atlantic View, Saint Augustine, FL 32080 USA Tel 904-460-0997
E-mail: effiemaeshearin@aol.com
Web site: http://www.dollydimpleink.com.

Dolphin Media *See* **Blue Brush Media**

Dolphin Publishing, *(978-1-878400)* P.O. Box 16656, West Palm Beach, FL 33416-6656 USA Tel 561-585-8901; Toll Free: 800-547-7867 Do not confuse with companies with the same name in Richardson, TX, Mattawan, MI
E-mail: nicotinefree@bellsouth.net
Web site: http://www.davidcjones.com.

Dolphins Publishing, *(978-0-9892565)* 1931 SW 17th Pl., Cape Coral, FL 33991 USA
E-mail: coach4u13@yahoo.com.

Domestic Policy Association *See* **National Issues Forums Institute**

Dominick Pictures, *(978-0-9726092)* P.O. Box 1925, New York, NY 10013 USA.

Dominie Elementary *Imprint of* **Savvas Learning Co.**

Dominie Pr., Inc., *(978-0-7685; 978-1-56270)* Div. of Pearson Learning, 145 S. Mount Zion Rd., Lebanon, IN 46052-8186 USA (SAN 630-947X) Toll Free: 800-232-4570
E-mail: info@dominie.com
Web site: http://www.dominie.com.

Dominik, Karen, *(978-0-578-70159-2)* 23211 Foxberry Ln., Bonita Springs, FL 34135 USA Tel 239-287-5756
E-mail: dominikkad@aol.com.

Dominion Publishing, *(978-0-692-87247-5; 978-0-578-45589-1; 978-0-578-58139-2;*

978-0-578-71806-4) P.O. Box 130, Sodus, MI 49126 USA Tel 770-862-5890
E-mail: cornellburtonjr@gmail.com; cornellburtonjr@gmail.com; cornellburtonjr@gmail.com
Web site: www.DominionRevival.com
Dist(s): **CreateSpace Independent Publishing Platform.**

DOMINIONHOUSE Publishing & Design, (*978-0-9755234; 978-0-9815463; 978-0-9828366; 978-0-9839869; 978-0-9888718; 978-0-9905031; 978-0-9971980; 978-1-7323126; 978-1-7353091*) Orders Addr.: P.O. Box 681938, Orlando, FL 32868 USA Tel 407-703-4800 (phone/fax)
Web site: http://www.mydominionhouse.com.

Don Cohen-The Mathman, (*978-0-9621674; 978-0-9779493*) Orders Addr.: 809 Stratford Dr., Champaign, IL 61821-4140 USA (SAN 251-866X) Tel 217-356-4555; Fax: 217-356-4593; Toll Free: 800-356-4559
E-mail: mathman@shout.net
Web site: http://www.shout.net/~mathman
Dist(s): **Rainbow Re-Source Ctr.**

Don Paul Publishing, LLC, (*978-0-9655792; 978-0-9816477; 978-1-941818*) P.O. Box 17062, Portland, OR 97217 USA Tel 503-764-9100
E-mail: jenna7jennifer@gmail.com; jennifer@donpaulpublishing.com
Web site: http://www.donpaulpublishing.com.

Don Quixote Publishing Co. Inc., (*978-0-9749196; 978-0-578-06784-1*) 905 Brickell Bay Dr., Unit 230, Miami, FL 33131 USA (SAN 255-884X) Tel 305-379-6151; Fax: 305-379-5156
E-mail: panza1209@aol.com; camote@manuelmartinezdreamer.com
Web site: http://www.manuelmartinezdreamer.com.

Don Rand's Classy Collectibles, (*978-0-9773775*) 26585 Fawn., Lake Forest, CA 92630-6728 USA.

DoNascimento.com/Books *See* **Briggs & Schuster**

Donegal Publishing Co., (*978-0-9788128*) Orders Addr.: 1850 Industrial St., #307, Los Angeles, CA 90021 USA (SAN 851-6782) Tel 310-598-6340; Fax: 310-349-3441; Toll Free: 866-964-4919
E-mail: editor@donegalpublishing.com; richie-d@comcast.net; donegalpublishing@mac.com
Web site: http://www.donegalpublishing.com; http://www.jerryland.net.

Dong, Jianming, (*978-0-692-80729-3*) 3181 Louis Rd., PALO ALTO, CA 94303 USA Tel 408-685-1089
E-mail: dongjianming@gmail.com; dongjianming@gmail.com.

Donkey Duck Enterprises, LLC, (*978-0-578-19757-9; 978-0-578-19906-1*) 1315 Deneb Ct., Walnut Creek, CA 94597 USA.

Donkey Penguin, (*978-1-7329164*) 310 S Delaware Ave. Apt. D, Tampa, FL 33606 USA Tel 813-505-4009
E-mail: denisehaunstetter@yahoo.com
Web site: www.donkeypenguin.com.

Donkey Publishing, (*978-0-9887454*) 16582 Hutchison Rd., Odessa, FL 33556 USA Tel 813-781-7143
E-mail: TOM@BRAYFIELDS.COM.

Donkey Quest Books *See* **Donkey's Quest Pr.**

Donkey's Quest Pr., (*978-0-9961139*) 40 Sherwood Rd., Medford, MA 02155 USA
E-mail: ccbaha1@gmail.com
Web site: http://donkeysquestpress.com.

Donnellan, Martha *See* **Pine Cone Pr.**

Donning Co. Pubs., (*978-0-89865; 978-0-915442; 978-1-57864; 978-1-68184*) Subs. of Walsworth Publishing Co., Inc., 184 Business Park Dr. Suite 206, Virginia Bch, VA 23462 USA (SAN 211-6316) Toll Free: 800-296-8572
E-mail: dcpr3@pilot.infi.net
Web site: http://www.donning.com
Dist(s): **Chicago Distribution Ctr.**
Schiffer Publishing, Ltd.

Donor Sibling Registry, (*978-0-692-10693-8; 978-0-692-12226-6; 978-0-692-14016-1; 978-0-578-63337-4; 978-0-578-63338-1*) P.O. Box 1571, Nederland, CO 80466 USA Tel 303-258-0902
E-mail: wendy@donorsiblingregistry.com
Dist(s): **Ingram Content Group.**

Donovan, Kevin M. *See* **Billy the Bear & His Friends, Inc.**

Dont "Diss" Abilities, (*978-1-7323298*) 726 S Nebraska St., Unit 95, Chandler, AZ 85225 USA Tel 480-688-8346
E-mail: nsharvick@cox.net.

Don't Eat Any Bugs Prodns., (*978-0-9728177; 978-0-9802314; 978-0-9887329; 978-1-7326165*) P.O. Box 291, Tehachapi, CA 93581 USA
E-mail: Ray@rayfriesen.com
Web site: http://www.donteatanybugs.com
Dist(s): **National Bk. Network.**

Don't Look Publishing, (*978-0-9728234*) P.O. Box 486, Moose Lake, MN 55767 USA.

Don't Run With Knives Publications *See* **Academic Solutions, Inc.**

Don't Stop Publishing, (*978-0-9992753; 978-1-947884*) 5940 S Rainbow Blvd Ste 400 No. 55447, Las Vegas, NV 89118 USA Tel 702-329-9980
E-mail: jwagner@qtpublish.com.

Don't Sweat It, Inc., (*978-0-9888712; 978-0-692-63804-0; 978-0-692-63805-7*) 547 N. Las Palmas Ave., Los Angeles, CA 90004 USA Tel 310-435-7713
E-mail: ivana@princessivana.com
Web site: www.dontsweatitmedia.com.

Dontstickdontstuff, (*978-0-9888861*) 5426 E. Via Los Caballos, Paradise Valley, AZ 85253 USA Tel 480-600-4690
E-mail: dontstickdontstuff@gmail.com
Dist(s): **BookBaby**
New Shelves Distribution.

Doodle and Peck Publishing, (*978-0-692-26513-0; 978-0-692-45586-9; 978-0-692-45589-0; 978-0-9966205; 978-0-9972351; 978-0-9983271; 978-0-9989302; 978-0-9992497; 978-1-7323637; 978-1-7327713; 978-1-7337170; 978-1-7333462; 978-1-7346072; 978-1-7358306*) 413 Cedarburg Ct., Yukon, OK 73099 USA Tel 405-354-7422
E-mail: iluvrocksmj@yahoo.com
Web site: www.doodleandpeck.com.

Doodle Publishing, (*978-0-9719518*) 2219 Tam-O-Shanter Ct., Carmel, IN 46032 USA Tel 317-538-6995
E-mail: adam10spro@aol.com.

Doodlebops *Imprint of* **Cookie Jar**

DoodleCake *Imprint of* **Irresistible Pr., LLC**

Dooley Bks., Ltd, (*978-0-9786605*) 53 W. Jackson No. 1240, CHICAGO, IL 60604 USA
Web site: http://www.Dooleybooks.com.

Doolittle Edutainment Corp., (*978-0-9793144*) 2445 Fifth Ave., Suite 440, San Diego, CA 92101 USA (SAN 853-0912)
Web site: http://www.doolittleedutainment.com.

Doorlight Pubns., (*978-0-9778372; 978-0-9838653; 978-0-9982233*) 4 Central Ave., South Hadley, MA 01075 USA.

Doorposts, (*978-1-891206*) 5905 SW Lookingglass Dr., Gaston, OR 97119-9241 USA Tel 503-357-4749; Fax: 503-357-4909 Do not confuse with Doorposts, Lansdale, PA
E-mail: orders@doorposts.com
Web site: http://www.doorposts.com.

Doozybird Publishing, (*978-1-7331853*) P.O. Box 6991, Sherwood, AR 72124 USA Tel 501-448-6613
E-mail: doozybird@icloud.com.

Dora, Liza *See* **Liza Dora Bks.**

Dorcas Pubns., LLC, (*978-0-9769829*) 890 Woodland Ave., Corydon, IN 47112 USA Tel 812-738-4361; Fax: 812-738-2259
E-mail: wfwilson@aol.com
Web site: http://www.dorcaspublications.com.

Dorcas Publishing, (*978-0-9762375*) Div. of Heavenly Patchwork Charity Bks., Orders Addr.: 12101 N. MacArthur, Suite 137, Oklahoma City, OK 73162-1800 USA Tel 405-751-3885 (phone/fax)
E-mail: buckboardquilts@cox.net
Web site: http://www.heavenlypatchwork.com.

Dorchester Publishing Co., Inc., (*978-0-505; 978-0-8439; 978-1-4285*) Orders Addr.: 200 Madison Ave., Suite 2000, New York, NY 10016 USA (SAN 264-0090); P.O. Box 6640, Wayne, PA 19087 Toll Free: 800-481-9191
Dist(s): **MyiLibrary.**

Dorhauer, Amanda, (*978-1-7327442*) 109 Delta Dr., Oakwood, IL 61858 USA Tel 314-337-2599
E-mail: greendayltd@yahoo.com.

Dorianneart, (*978-0-9988128*) 4217 waipua st, Kilauea, HI 96754 USA Tel 808-652-8605
E-mail: dw@dorianneart.com
Web site: PukeyPoetry.com.

Dork Storm Pr., (*978-1-930964; 978-1-933288*) P.O. Box 45063, Madison, WI 53744 USA Fax: 608-225-1352
Web site: http://www.dorkstorm.com
Dist(s): **PSI (Publisher Services, Inc.).**

†Dorling Kindersley Publishing, Inc., (*978-0-7894; 978-1-56458; 978-1-879431; 978-0-7566; 978-1-4654*) Div. of Penguin Publishing Group, 375 Hudson St., 2nd Flr., New York, NY 10014 USA (SAN 253-0791) Tel 212-213-4800; Fax: 212-213-5240; Toll Free: 877-342-5357 (orders only); *Imprints:* Alpha (AlphaUSA); DK (DKUSA); DK Children (DKChildren)
E-mail: Annemarie.Cancienne@dk.com; customer.service@dk.com
Web site: http://www.dk.com
Dist(s): **Children's Plus, Inc.**
Continental Bk. Co., Inc.
Ebsco Publishing
Follett School Solutions
Penguin Random Hse. Distribution
Penguin Random Hse. LLC
Penguin Publishing Group
Hale, Robert & Co., Inc.
Sunburst Communications, Inc.; *CIP.*

Dormouse Productions, Inc., (*978-1-889300*) 25 NE 99th St., Miami, FL 33138-2338 USA Tel 305-379-4990; Fax: 305-379-7990
E-mail: dmouse@juno.com.

Dorn Enterprises *See* **Susy Dorn Productions, LLC**

Dorob International Ltd., (*978-0-9910985*) 1402 Pointe Gate Dr., Livingston, NJ 07039 USA Tel 973-995-9249
E-mail: rdg@genesysassociates.com.

Dorothy, a publishing project, (*978-0-9844693; 978-0-9897607; 978-0-9973666; 978-1-948980*) P.O. Box 300433, Saint Louis, MO 63130 USA
E-mail: editors@dorothyproject.com
Web site: http://www.dorothyproject.com
Dist(s): **SPD-Small Pr. Distribution.**

Dorothy Payne & Virginia Letourneau, (*978-0-9747823*) 300 E. 33rd St., Apt. 7C, New York, NY 10016 USA
Web site: http://www.cityislandclamdigger.com.

Dorothy-Frances Bks., (*978-0-9911099; 978-0-692-27734-8; 978-0-9997911; 978-1-7338878; 978-1-7334865; 978-1-7355366*) 6469 NW 80th Terr, Parkland, FL 33067 USA Tel 954-742-7777
E-mail: drhdel@gmail.com
Dist(s): **CreateSpace Independent Publishing Platform.**

Dorrance Publishing Co., Inc., (*978-0-8059; 978-1-4349; 978-1-4809; 978-1-64426; 978-1-64530; 978-1-64610; 978-1-64702; 978-1-64804; 978-1-64913; 978-1-64957; 978-1-63661*) 701 Smithfield St. Third Flr., Pittsburgh, PA 15222 USA (SAN 201-3363) Tel 412-288-4543; Fax: 412-288-1786; Toll Free: 800-788-7654; 800-695-7599; *Imprints:* RoseDog Books (RoseDog Bks)
E-mail: rpiotrowski@dorrancepublishing.com; dorrordr@dorrancepublishing.com
Web site: http://www.dorrancepublishing.com; www.dorrancebookstore.com.

Dorry Pr., (*978-0-615-67780-4; 978-0-615-75213-6; 978-0-615-76920-2; 978-0-615-76921-9; 978-0-692-20424-5; 978-0-692-22048-1; 978-0-692-45609-5; 978-0-9983796; 978-1-951386*) P.O. Box 16537, Chesapeake, VA 23322 USA Tel 757-277-9739; 1041 Baydon Ln., Chesapeake, VA 23322
E-mail: sherryajones@yahoo.com
Dist(s): **CreateSpace Independent Publishing Platform.**

†Dorset Hse. Publishing, (*978-0-932633*) 3143 Broadway Suite 2b, New York, NY 10027 USA (SAN 687-794X) Tel 212-620-4053; Fax: 212-727-1044; Toll Free: 800-342-6657
E-mail: info@dorsethouse.com; littlewest@dorsethouse.com
Web site: http://www.dorsethouse.com; http://www.littlewestpress.com; *CIP.*

Dory Pr., (*978-0-9633240*) 13396 Wakefield Rd., Sedley, VA 23878 USA Tel 757-220-9206.

Doses of Reality, Inc., (*978-0-9754024*) 634 Ceape Ave, Oshkosh, WI 54901 USA Tel 920-573-9884
E-mail: dosesofreality@yahoo.com.

Dot Dot Bks., (*978-0-9670750*) 420 16th St., Bellingham, WA 98225 USA Tel 360-220-1686
E-mail: dana.rozier@gmail.com
Dist(s): **Small Pr. United.**

Dot EDU (Educational & Textbooks) *Imprint of* **Speedy Publishing LLC**

Dothan Publishing *See* **Moriah Ministries**

Dottir Pr., (*978-1-948340*) 33 Fifth Ave., New York, NY 10003 USA Tel 917-753-8091
E-mail: jb@dottirpress.com
Web site: dottirpress.com
Dist(s): **Consortium Bk. Sales & Distribution.**

Double B Pubns., (*978-0-929526*) 4123 N. Longview, Phoenix, AZ 85014 USA (SAN 249-6615) Tel 602-996-7129; Fax: 602-996-6928
E-mail: bfischerppg@aol.com.

Double Bridge Publishing, 9812 Mahogany Dr., Gaithersburg, MD 20878 USA Tel 240-551-4274
E-mail: editor@doublebridgepublishing.com
Web site: www.doublebridgepublishing.com.

Double Dagger Pr., (*978-0-9729293*) 256 Ridge Ave., Gettysburg, PA 17325-2404 USA (SAN 255-7517) Tel 717-334-5392
E-mail: mplank@doubledaggerpress.com
Web site: http://www.doubledaggerpress.com.

Double Edge Pr., (*978-0-9774452; 978-0-9819514; 978-1-938002*) Orders Addr.: 72 Ellview Rd., Scenery Hill, PA 15360 USA (SAN 257-5019) Tel 724-518-6737; *Imprints:* Hummingbird World Media (HummbirdWrld)
E-mail: cuttingedge@atlanticbb.net
Web site: http://www.doubleedgepress.com
Dist(s): **ebrary, Inc.**

DOUBLE R Bks. *Imprint of* **Rodrigue & Sons Co./Double R Books Publishing**

Double R Publishing, LLC, (*978-0-9713381; 978-0-9718696; 978-0-9770534*) 7301 W. Flagler St., Miami, FL 33144 USA Tel 305-262-4240; Fax: 305-262-4115; Toll Free: 877-262-4240
E-mail: abcsbook@abcsbook.com
Web site: http://www.abcsbook.com
Dist(s): **ABC'S Bk. Supply, Inc.**

Double Roads *See* **Karenzo Media**

Doubleday *Imprint of* **Knopf Doubleday Publishing Group**

Doubleday Bks. for Young Readers *Imprint of* **Random Hse. Children's Bks.**

Doubleday Canada, Ltd. (CAN) (*978-0-385; 978-0-7704*) *Dist. by* **Random.**

Doubleday Publishing *See* **Knopf Doubleday Publishing Group**

Doubleday Religious Publishing Group, The, Div. of Random Hse., Inc., Orders Addr.: 400 Hahn Rd., Westminster, MD 21157 USA Tel 410-848-1900; Toll Free: 800-726-0600 (customer service); 800-733-3000; Edit Addr.: 12265 Oracle Blvd., Suite 200, Colorado Springs, CO 80921 USA (SAN 299-4682) Tel 719-590-4999; Fax: 719-590-8977; Toll Free Fax: 800-294-5686; Toll Free: 800-603-7051; *Imprints:* Multnomah (Mltnmah) Do not confuse with WaterBrook Pr., Great Falls, VA
Web site: http://www.randomhouse.com/waterbrook
Dist(s): **Anchor Distributors**
MyiLibrary
Penguin Random Hse. Distribution
Penguin Random Hse. LLC
Random Hse., Inc.

DOUBLE-R BKS. *Imprint of* **Rodrigue & Sons Co./Double R Books Publishing**

DoubleStar, LLC, (*978-0-9742558*) 9672 Litzsinger Rd., Saint Louis, MO 63124-1494 USA
E-mail: doublestarllc@sbcglobal.net
Web site: http://www.cogno.com.

Dougherty, Elizabeth *See* **School Street Bks.**

Douglas, Bettye Forum, Inc., The, (*978-0-9703183*) 6608 N. Western Ave., No. 327, Oklahoma City, OK 73116 USA Tel 405-528-1773; Fax: 405-842-7541; Toll Free: 800-354-0680
E-mail: bettye_douglas@excite.com
Web site: http://www.bettyedouglas.com.

Dougy Ctr., (*978-1-890534*) Orders Addr.: P.O. Box 86852, Portland, OR 97286 USA Tel 503-542-4833; Fax: 503-777-3097; Edit Addr.: 3909 SE 52nd Ave., Portland, OR 97206 USA
E-mail: kailyn@dougy.org
Web site: http://www.dougy.org.

Doulos Christou Pr., (*978-0-9744796; 978-1-934406*) 57 N. Ruial St. Englewood Christian Church, Indianapolis, IN 46201-3330 USA
E-mail: douloschristoupress@yahoo.com
Web site: http://www.douloschristou.com.

Doumlele, Carol, (*978-0-9992578*) 1500 Jamaica Ct., Marco Island, FL 34145 USA Tel 239-777-0492
E-mail: doumleca@embarqmail.com.

Dove Books and Audio *Imprint of* **Phoenix Bks., Inc.**

Dove Hollow Bks., (*978-0-9969383*) P.O. Box 665, Denton, TX 76202 USA Tel 817-233-8546
E-mail: sarahmactavishtx@gmail.com.

Dove Publishing, Inc., (*978-0-9766578*) P.O. Box 310326, Atlanta, GA 31131 USA Do not confuse with companies with the same or similar name in Houston, TX, Decatur, GA, Forest heights, MD, Lake Konkonkma, NY
Web site: http://www.dovepub.com.

†Dover Pubns., Inc., (*978-0-486; 978-1-60660*) Div. of Courier Corporation, 31 E. Second St., Mineola, NY 11501 USA (SAN 201-338X) Tel 516-294-7000; Fax: 516-873-1401 (orders only); Toll Free: 800-223-3130 (orders only); *Imprints:* Ixia Press (IxiaPr)
E-mail: rights@doverpublications.com
Web site: http://www.doverdirect.com; http://www.doverpublications.com
Dist(s): **Continental Bk. Co., Inc.**
INscribe Digital
Independent Pubs. Group
MyiLibrary
Beeler, Thomas T. Pub.; *CIP.*

DoveTail Hse., Inc., (*978-0-9706244; 978-0-9772935; 978-0-9800099; 978-0-9862832; 978-1-943181*) P.O. Box 501995, San Diego, CA 92150 USA Tel 858-581-5954; Fax: 858-668-1771
E-mail: dovepub@san.rr.com.

Dovetail Publishing, (*978-0-9651284*) P.O. Box 19945, Kalamazoo, MI 49019 USA Tel 616-342-2900; Fax: 616-342-1012; Toll Free: 800-222-0070
E-mail: dovetail@mich.com
Web site: http://www.mich.com/~dovetail
Dist(s): **Quality Bks., Inc.**

Down County Media *See* **Bad Choices Media**

Down East Bks., (*978-0-89272; 978-0-924357*) Div. of Rowman & Littlefield Publishing Group, Inc., P.O. Box 679, Camden, ME 04843 USA (SAN 208-6301) Tel 207-594-9544; Fax: 207-594-0147; Toll Free: 800-766-1670 Wholesale orders; 800-685-7962 Retail orders
E-mail: pblanchard@downeast.com; tbregy@downeast.com
Web site: http://www.countrysportpress.com; http://www.downeastbooks.com
Dist(s): **Follett School Solutions**
MyiLibrary
National Bk. Network
Rowman & Littlefield Publishers, Inc.
TNT Media Group, Inc.
ebrary, Inc.

Down The Road Publishing, (*978-0-9754427*) 172 White Oak Dr., Batesville, IN 47006 USA (SAN 256-2227)
E-mail: timt@downtheroad.org
Web site: http://www.downtheroad.org.

Down The Shore Publishing Corp., (*978-0-945582; 978-0-9615208; 978-1-59322*) Orders Addr.: P.O. Box 100, West Creek, NJ 08092 USA Tel 609-812-5076; Fax: 609-812-5098; Edit Addr.: P.O. Box 100, West Creek, NJ 08092 USA (SAN 661-082X)
E-mail: info@down-the-shore.com; orders@down-the-shore.com; downshore@gmail.com
Web site: http://www.down-the-shore.com
Dist(s): **Partners Bk. Distributing, Inc.**
Sourcebooks, Inc.

Down-To-Earth-Bks., (*978-1-878115*) P.O. Box 488, Ashfield, MA 01330 USA Tel 413-628-0227
E-mail: maryskole@aol.com
Web site: http://www.spinninglobe.net.

Downtown Bookworks, (*978-1-935703; 978-1-941367; 978-1-950587*) 285 W. Broadway, Suite 600, New York, NY 10013 USA Tel 646-613-0707
Dist(s): **Diamond Comic Distributors, Inc.**
Simon & Schuster, Inc.

Downtown Wetmore Pr., (*978-0-9795302*) Orders Addr.: 13451 Wetmore Rd., San Antonio, TX 78247 USA (SAN 853-7070) Tel 210-490-7222; Fax: 210-490-8222; Toll Free Fax: 877-490-8222; Toll Free: 877-490-7222; *Imprints:* CrumbGobbler Press (CrumbGobbler)
E-mail: downtownwetmore@earthlink.net; info@crumbgobbler.com
Web site: http://www.downtownwetmore.com.

DP Group LLC, The *See* **DP Group LLC, The**

DP Group LLC, The, (*978-0-9978230; 978-1-949513*) 150 Wrenn Drive, No. 584, cary, NC 27512 USA Tel 919-452-6966
E-mail: divpriti@gmail.com.

DP Kids Pr. *Imprint of* **DocUmeant Publishing**

Dr. Gazebo Publishing *See* **Snow In Sarasota Publishing**

Dr. Ingrid Wright, (*978-0-9992143*) 5505 W. Buckskin Trail, Phoenix, AZ 85083-4302 USA Tel 951-440-7063
E-mail: ingridwright07@yahoo.com
Web site: IngridWrightFineArt.com.

Dr. Jay, LLC, (*978-0-9860063*) P.O. Box 422, Green Farms, CT 06838 USA
E-mail: yroehler@bookpublishing.com.

Dr. Joyce STARR Publishing, (*978-0-9792333; 978-0-9882394*) Orders Addr.: 20533 Biscayne Blvd., No. 509, Aventura, FL 33180 USA Tel 786-693-4223
E-mail: joyce.starr@gmail.com
Web site: http://drjoycestarr.com; http://starrpublications.com; http://starrpublishing.com.

Dr Ma Publishing, (*978-0-9995813*) 119 N. Fairfax Ave., No. 188, Los Angeles, CA 90036 USA Tel 469-250-0884
E-mail: edna@drednabrands.com
Web site: drEdnabrands.com.

Dr. Mark Stuart Berlin *See* **Berlin, Stuart**

Dr. Mary's Bks., (*978-0-9765453*) 180 90th Ave. SE, Kensal, ND 58455 USA Tel 701-435-2388
E-mail: dwayneerickson@agristar.net
Web site: http://www.shopnd.com.

Dr. Patricia Garfield's Ctr. for Creative Dreami, *(978-0-692-79633-7; 978-0-692-79635-1; 978-0-578-77503-6)* 130 Rancho Dr., TIBURON, CA 94920 USA Tel 415-383-7770.

Dr. Publishing, 2 Kenen Ct., Burlingame, CA 94010 USA Tel 916-548-2113
E-mail: Drbcool29@aol.com.

Draft2Digital, *(978-1-4977; 978-1-4989; 978-1-5014; 978-1-5022; 978-1-5070; 978-1-5130; 978-1-5163; 978-1-5199; 978-1-5242; 978-1-5337; 978-1-5365; 978-1-5401; 978-1-386; 978-1-393; 978-0-578-64452-3)* 5629 SE 67th St., Oklahoma City, OK 73135 USA Fax: 866-358-6413; Toll Free Fax: 866-358-6413; Toll Free: 866-336-5099; 9400 N. Broadway Ext. Ste. 410, Oklahoma City, OK 73114 Tel 866-336-5099
E-mail: support@draft2digital.com
Web site: www.draft2digital.com
Dist(s): **Independent Pubs. Group.**

Dragon Dog Press, Incorporated *See* **Ryu Cope**

Dragon Gate Media, *(978-1-7324359)* 307 Lexington Cir., Newport Beach, CA 92660 USA Tel 949-723-1088
E-mail: carolj10@aol.com.

Dragon Hill Publishing (CAN) *(978-1-896124) Dist. by* **Lone Pine.**

Dragon Hoard Pr. *Imprint of* **IYF Publishing**

Dragon Pup Pr., *(978-0-578-45522-8)* 7360 Stoney Pointe, Liberty Township, OH 45044 USA Tel 513-265-3160
E-mail: kftbooks@outlook.com
Web site: katherinethomasart.com.

Dragon Realm Pr., *(978-0-692-73198-7; 978-0-692-98866-4; 978-0-692-09895-0; 978-0-692-15184-6; 978-1-949621)* 45 Twin Oaks Dr., Bridgeton, NJ 08302 USA Tel 856-332-5306
E-mail: jaculican@gmail.com
Web site: www.dragonrealmpress.com.

Dragon Scale Publishing, *(978-1-943183)* 8466 N Stonebridge LN, Eagle Mountain, UT 84005 USA Tel 801-471-0502
E-mail: Dragonscalebooks@outlook.com
Web site: www.Dragonscalepublishing.com.

Dragon Tree Bks., *(978-0-9884024; 978-0-9916200; 978-0-9862641; 978-0-9963081; 978-0-9974513; 978-0-9977478; 978-0-9995488; 978-1-7326613; 978-1-7337577; 978-1-7343332; 978-1-7348915)* 1620 SW 5th Ave., Pompano Beach, FL 33060 USA Tel 954-788-4775
E-mail: editors@editingforauthors.com
Web site: http://editingforauthors.com.

Dragon Wings Publishing, *(978-0-9748951)* Orders Addr.: Kaybee Images Marketing Order Division PO Box 659, Dallas, OR 97338 USA.

Dragonbrush Arts, *(978-0-9960374)* 34242 Vauxhill Dr. Apt. No. 7, Paw Paw, MI 49079 USA Tel 269-254-0663
E-mail: d.monroe@dragonbrusher.com
Web site: dragonbrusher.com.

Dragoneagle Pr., *(978-0-9787465)* Orders Addr.: P.O. Box Box 30856, Bethesda, MD 20824 USA Tel 732-861-0449; Fax: 301-897-2786
E-mail: info@dragoneagle.com
Web site: http://www.dragoneagle.com.

DragonEye Publishing, *(978-0-9767832; 978-1-61500)* Orders Addr.: c/o ISOTUT Publisher, 753 Linden Place, Apt A, Elmira, NY 14901 USA (SAN 857-7110) Tel 607-333-5256 For questions about ordering
E-mail: Michael.Kiser@DragonEyePublishers.com
Web site: https://www.DragonEyePublishers.com.

Dragonfeather Bks. *Imprint of* **Bedazzled Ink Publishing Co.**

Dragonfly Bks. *Imprint of* **Random Hse. Children's Bks.**

Dragonfly Entertainment, *(978-0-9745213)* 97 Chartwell Ct., Rochester, NY 14618-5376 USA; *Imprints:* Dragonfly Flipz (Dragonfly Flipz)
E-mail: dfly@earthlink.net
Web site: http://www.dragonflyent.net.

Dragonfly Farms: The Great Adventure, *(978-0-578-40926-9)* 1803 E. Hickory Hill Rd., Argyle, TX 76226 USA Tel 817-881-3383
E-mail: jennjennortiz@yahoo.com
Dist(s): **CreateSpace Independent Publishing Platform.**

Dragonfly Flipz *Imprint of* **Dragonfly Entertainment**

Dragonfly Ministries, *(978-0-9788289)* 295 Noble Cir., Vernon Hills, IL 60061-2927 USA
E-mail: info@dragonflyministries.com
Web site: http://www.dragonflyministries.com.

Dragonfly Publishing, Inc., *(978-0-9710473; 978-0-9755888; 978-0-9765786; 978-0-9778651; 978-0-9787421; 978-0-9794660; 978-0-9797574; 978-0-9801376; 978-0-9817049; 978-0-9819080; 978-0-9840980; 978-1-936381; 978-1-941278; 978-1-949187)* 2440 Twin Ridge Dr., Edmond, OK 73034-1943 USA Do not confuse with companies with the same or similar name in Mount Enterprise, TX , Whethersfield, CT , San Antonio, TX ,
Web site: http://www.dragonflypubs.com
Dist(s): **Smashwords.**

Dragonflyer Pr., *(978-0-944933)* Div. of American Water Gardens, Inc., 2460 N. Euclid Ave., Upland, CA 91784-1184 USA (SAN 245-7660) Toll Free: 800-558-0676
E-mail: info@dragonflyerpress.com; cuber@uberadv.com
Web site: http://www.vnwg.com; http://www.dragonflyerpress.com
Dist(s): **Midpoint Trade Bks., Inc.**

Dragongate Publishing, *(978-0-9765178; 978-0-578-67655-5; 978-1-7354042)* 44-119 Bayview Haven Pl., Kaneohe, HI 96744 USA Tel 808-534-0452; 1519 Nuuanu Ave., No.18, Honolulu, HI 96817-3739 (SAN 256-4939) Tel 808-234-5508
E-mail: dragongate@hawaii.rr.com.

Dragonhawk Publishing, *(978-1-888767)* Div. of Life Magic Enterprises, Inc., P.O. Box 1316, Jackson, TN 38302 USA Tel 901-987-3334; Fax: 901-987-2484
Dist(s): **Austin & Company, Inc.**
New Leaf Distributing Co., Inc.

Dragonon, Inc., *(978-0-9763398)* 9378 Mason Montgomery Rd., Suite 108, Mason, OH 45040 USA (SAN 256-3398) Tel 513-227-9224
E-mail: dmeyer@dragonon.com.

Dragon's Roost Pr., *(978-0-615-97909-0; 978-0-9988878; 978-1-7351233)* 207 Gardendale, Ferndale, MI 48220 USA Tel 1 (248) 259-9680
E-mail: editor@thedragonsroost.net
Web site: http://thedragonsroost.net/styled-3/index.html
Dist(s): **CreateSpace Independent Publishing Platform.**

Dragonscale Pr., *(978-0-9994291)* 613 Gray Head Ln., Knightdale, NC 27545 USA Tel 919-266-6292
E-mail: landsman.nic1129@gmail.com.

Dragonseed Pr., *(978-0-9678115)* Orders Addr.: 19020 Brookfield Dr., Chagrin Falls, OH 44023 USA
E-mail: dragonseedpress@aol.com
Web site: http://www.m-c-ryan.com.

Dragonsoul Bks., *(978-0-692-51453-5; 978-0-692-51841-0; 978-0-692-19827-8)* P.O. Box 885, Mechanicsburg, PA 17055 USA Tel 717-648-7012
E-mail: natalie@nataliedamschroder.com
Web site: www.nataliedamschroder.com
Dist(s): **CreateSpace Independent Publishing Platform.**

DragonWing Bks., *(978-0-9761444)* 9107 Brunners Run Ct., Columbia, MD 21045 USA Tel 301-509-5451
E-mail: liz@dragonwingbooks.com
Web site: http://www.dragonwingbooks.com.

Drake, Edwin, *(978-0-9743405)* R.R. 5, Box 5417, Saylorsburg, PA 18353 USA Tel 570-992-2914
E-mail: edrakee@enter.net.

Drake Feltham Publishing, *(978-0-578-10548-2)* 22113 Palos Verdes Blvd., Torrance, CA 90503 USA
Dist(s): **Outskirts Pr., Inc.**

Drake Univ., Anderson Gallery, *(978-0-9749296)* 25th St. & Carpenter Ave., Des Moines, IA 50311 USA Tel 515-271-1994; Fax: 515-271-2558
E-mail: cira.pascual-marquina@drake.edu
Web site: http://www.drake.edu/andersongallery.

Drake Valley Pr., *(978-0-9728186; 978-0-9785632; 978-1-935970)* P.O. Box 979, Clinton, MS 39060 USA Toll Free: 866-442-4990 (fax on demand & phone/fax)
Web site: http://www.drakevalleypress.com
Dist(s): **Palari Publishing LLP.**

Drama Publishers *See* **Quite Specific Media Group, Ltd.**

Drama Tree Pr., *(978-0-9741670; 978-0-9821852; 978-0-9985676)* 150 Iota Ct., Madison, WI 53706 USA
E-mail: dramatree@mail.com
Web site: http://www.dramatree.com.

Dramaline Pubns., *(978-0-940669; 978-0-9611792)* 36851 Palm View Rd., Rancho Mirage, CA 92270-2417 USA (SAN 285-239X) Tel 760-770-6076; Fax: 760-770-4507
E-mail: drama.line@verizon.net
Web site: http://www.dramaline.com
Dist(s): **Distributors, The.**

DramaQueen, L.L.C., *(978-0-9766045; 978-1-933809; 978-1-60331)* Orders Addr.: P.O. Box 2626, Stafford, TX 77497 USA Fax: 281-498-4723; Toll Free: 800-883-1518 (ext. 2)
E-mail: orders@onedramaqueen.com; info@onedramaqueen.com
Web site: http://www.onedramaqueen.com
Dist(s): **AAA Anime Distribution.**

Dramatic Ellipsis, *(978-0-9984397)* P.O. Box 980882, Houston, TX 77098 USA Tel 281-773-2648; *Imprints:* Drivel & Drool (MYID_F_DRIVEL)
E-mail: enparekh@dramaticellipsis.com
Web site: drivelanddrool.com.

Dramatic Improvements Publishing, *(978-0-9768251)* 226 Perrine Ave., Auburn, NY 13021-1715 USA
E-mail: twoods@dramaimp.com
Web site: http://www.dramaimp.com.

Dramatic Pen Press, LLC, The *See* **Dramatic Pen Pr., LLC, The**

Dramatic Publishing Co., *(978-0-87129; 978-1-58342; 978-1-61959)* Orders Addr.: 311 Washington St., Woodstock, IL 60098 USA (SAN 201-5676) Tel 815-338-7170; Fax: 815-338-8981; Toll Free Fax: 800-334-5302; Toll Free: 800-448-7469
E-mail: kjusten@dpcplays.com
Web site: http://www.dramaticpublishing.com.

Dramatists Play Service, Inc., *(978-0-8222)* 440 Park Ave., S., New York, NY 10016 USA (SAN 207-5717) Tel 212-683-8960; Fax: 212-213-1539
E-mail: postmaster@dramatists.com
Web site: http://www.dramatists.com.

Drane, John Wanzer, *(978-0-578-10633-5)* 5 Derry Dr., Horse Shoe, NC 28742 USA.

Draper Publishing, *(978-0-9913342)* 1701 Willow Oak Ln., Dalton, GA 30721 USA Tel 706-260-5496
E-mail: duraniemaria39@yahoo.com
Web site: mariarochelle.com.

Draw Three Lines Publishing, *(978-0-9749418; 978-0-9826202)* P.O. Box 1522, Hillsboro, OR 97123 USA Tel 503-648-9905
E-mail: hastings@draw3lines.com
Web site: http://www.draw3lines.com.

Drawing From History, *(978-0-692-05234-1; 978-0-578-53831-0)* 215 W. Prospect St., Angola, IN 46703 USA Tel 260-665-1988
E-mail: drawingsmiles@yahoo.com
Web site: www.drawingsmiles.com.

Drawn & Quarterly Pubns. (CAN) *(978-0-9696701; 978-1-896597; 978-1-894937; 978-1-897299; 978-1-77046) Dist. by* **Macmillan.**

DrDryland.Com, LLC, *(978-0-9766490)* P.O. Box 1281, Ashland, OR 97520 USA
Web site: http://www.DrDryland.Com.

Dream A World *Imprint of* **BrassHeart Music**

Dream Bee Pubns., *(978-0-9661572)* 3325 C 1/2 Rd., Palisade, CO 81526 USA Tel 970-434-7501
E-mail: bee@dreambee.com
Web site: http://www.dreambee.com
Dist(s): **Bks. West**
Partners/West Book Distributors.

Dream Big Toy Co., *(978-1-940731)* 249 Merton Ave., Alen Ellyn, IL 60137 USA Tel 877-351-1031
E-mail: jnorgaard@dreambigtoycompany.com
Dist(s): **MyiLibrary.**

Dream Creek Pr., *(978-0-9771515)* 401 Taylor St., Ashland, OR 97520 USA
E-mail: bethart@mind.net
Web site: http://www.bbcreativecards.com.

Dream Dance Pubns., *(978-0-9769192; 978-0-692-96655-6)* 375 Kirkland Ave, Kirkland, WA 98033 USA Tel 425-246-7829
E-mail: briggs870@msn.com.

Dream Factory Bks., *(978-0-9701195)* Orders Addr.: P.O. Box 874, Enumclaw, WA 98022 USA (SAN 253-2611) Tel 360-663-0508; Fax: 360-825-7952; Toll Free Fax: 877-377-7030; Edit Addr.: 58402 114th St., E., Enumclaw, WA 98022-7305 USA
E-mail: sensei@earthlink.net
Web site: http://dreamfactorybooks.com.

Dream, Feral LLC, *(978-0-9835970)* 774 Mays Blvd. Ste 10-473, Incline Village, NV 89451 USA Tel 415-555-1212
E-mail: susan@feraldream.com.

Dream Fetchers, *(978-0-578-22846-4)* 8192 Sandcove Cir., Huntington Beach, CA 92646 USA.

Dream House Pr., *(978-0-9671555)* 2714 Ophelia Ct., San Jose, CA 95122 USA Tel 408-274-4574; Fax: 408-274-0786; Toll Free: 877-274-4574
E-mail: mr_art@prodigy.net; dreamhousepress@yahoo.com
Dist(s): **Brodart Co.**
Midwest Library Service
Milligan News Co., Inc.
Partners/West Book Distributors
Yankee Bk. Peddler, Inc.

Dream Image Pr., LLC, *(978-0-9744812)* P.O. Box 454, Northbrook, IL 60065-0454 USA Tel 847-480-8998
E-mail: drashley@dreamimagepress.com
Dist(s): **Follett School Solutions.**

Dream On Pubns., *(978-0-9761151)* Orders Addr.: P.O. Box 190265, Fort Lauderdale, FL 33319 USA (SAN 256-2057)
E-mail: books@dreamonpublications.com.

Dream Publications, I, Incorporated *See* **BOOKGEMSFORKIDS**

Dream Ridge Pr., *(978-0-9792084)* P.O. Box 625, Aurelia, IA 51005 USA Tel 712-660-8409
E-mail: rainbowfarm2006@yahoo.com; tpeiffer67@yahoo.com
Web site: http://www.lulu.com/trishacp; http://www.rainbowfarmbooks.com; http://www.authorsden.com/trishacp
Dist(s): **Lulu Pr., Inc.**

Dream Scape Publishing, LLC, *(978-0-9795519; 978-0-615-13650-9)* 805 Dunwood Ct., Chesapeake, VA 23322 USA Tel 757-717-2734
E-mail: dreamscape2@cox.net.

Dream Secret Inc., The, *(978-0-615-18103-5)* P.O. Box 2012, Sandy, UT 84091 USA Tel 801-518-7770
E-mail: lscread@yahoo.com.

Dream Ship Publishing Co., *(978-0-9729155)* 1512 River Rock Trace, Woodstock, GA 30188 USA
E-mail: info@dreamshipbooks.com.

Dream Star Productions, *(978-0-9772027)* Orbisson Sq. 4306 S. Peoria Ave., Ste 705, Tulsa, OK 74105-3922 USA Tel 918-630-7580; Fax: 918-749-1717
Web site: http://www.kbaustin.com.

Dream Weaver Ministries, Inc., *(978-0-9800259)* Pmb#123 1631 Rock Springs Rd., Apopka, FL 32712-2229 USA (SAN 855-0239) Toll Free: 888-397-7772.

Dream Workshop Publishing Co., LLC, The, *(978-0-9786940)* Orders Addr.: 4421 Bachelor Creek Rd., Asheboro, NC 27205 USA (SAN 851-3635) Tel 336-879-8108
E-mail: info@dreamworkshoppub.com; publisher@dreamworkshoppub.com
Web site: http://www.dreamworkshoppub.com; http://www.spenceraliens.com.

Dream Yard Pr., *(978-0-615-72969-5)* 1085 Washington Ave., Bronx, NY 10456 USA Tel 718-588-8007; Fax: 718-588-8310
E-mail: neilwald@aol.com
Web site: dreamyard.com; neilwaldman.com.

Dream&Achieve Bks., *(978-0-9859298)* 2609 W. 84th Pl., Merrillville, IN 46410 USA Tel 219-218-5145
Web site: www.weenzcat.com.

Dreambridge, *(978-0-692-10136-0; 978-0-692-10397-5)* 927 Bellview Ave. No. 1, Ashland, OR 97520 USA Tel 541-482-8954
E-mail: angel@thedreambridge.com
Dist(s): **Ingram Content Group.**

Dreamcatcher Bks., *(978-0-9848484)* 892 Jensen Ln., Windsor, CA 95492 USA Tel 707-292-0272 Do not confuse with Dreamcatcher Books in Las Vegas, NM
E-mail: alvarezgang@yahoo.com
Web site: http://www.jenniferlynnalvarez.com/.

Dream-Catcher Pubns., *(978-0-9752878)* 22265 Petersburg, Eastpointe, MI 48021 USA.

DreamDog Pr., *(978-0-9666199)* 2308 Mount Vernon Ave., Alexandria, VA 22301-1328 USA
E-mail: rainey@dreamdog.com
Web site: http://www.dreamdog.com.

DreamerLand, *(978-0-9763250)* Orders Addr.: 1018 3rd St., Hermosa Beach, CA 90254 USA Tel 310-406-9371
E-mail: christo@dreamerland.com; info@dreamerland.com
Web site: http://www.Dreamerland.com
Dist(s): **Diamond Bk. Distributors.**

DreamHse. Publishing Inc.,

Dreaming Big Pubns., *(978-0-692-67563-2; 978-0-692-70106-5; 978-0-692-74058-3; 978-1-947381)* 102 First E. St, Sumrall, MS 39482 USA Tel 601-394-8813
Dist(s): **CreateSpace Independent Publishing Platform.**

Dreaming World Bks., *(978-0-615-96020-3; 978-0-615-99045-3; 978-0-692-22696-4; 978-0-692-23006-0; 978-0-692-26821-6; 978-0-692-28839-9; 978-0-692-56077-8; 978-0-692-61841-7; 978-1-948662)* 2409 35th Ave, Rock Island, IL 61201 USA Tel 309-721-2298
Dist(s): **CreateSpace Independent Publishing Platform.**

DreamLand Mediaworks LLC, *(978-0-9884657)* 3712 Lake Catherine Dr., Harvey, LA 70058 USA Tel 504-756-5589; Fax: 504-366-2606
E-mail: Jacqueline_Buffinet@yahoo.com.

Dreams 2 Wings LLC, *(978-0-9797781)* 100 N. 72nd Ave., Wausau, WI 54401 USA Tel 715-842-1133; Fax: 715-842-1155
E-mail: fred@lanepatents.com.

Dreams Due Media Group, Inc., *(978-0-9789202)* P.O. Box 1018, Firestone, CO 80520 USA Tel 303-241-3155 Toll Free: 877-462-1710
Web site: http://www.dreamsdue.com.

Dreams of Dragons, *(978-0-578-12149-9; 978-0-615-97831-4)* P.O. Box 312, Malden, MO 63863 USA Tel 573-576-7435
E-mail: drwilliamembry@yahoo.com
Web site: http://www.drakoandrawr.com.

Dreamscape, LLC *See* **Dreamscape Media, LLC**

Dreamscape Media, LLC, *(978-0-9745563; 978-0-9747118; 978-0-9760996; 978-0-9761981; 978-0-9771510; 978-0-9772338; 978-0-9774680; 978-0-9776262; 978-0-9777098; 978-1-933938; 978-1-61120; 978-1-62406; 978-1-62923; 978-1-63379; 978-1-68141; 978-1-68262; 978-1-5200; 978-1-9749; 978-1-6905; 978-1-6620) Orders Addr.: 1417 Timberwolf Dr., Holland, OH 43538 USA Tel 419-867-6965*
E-mail: kruiz@dreamscapeab.com; molah@dreamscapeab.com
Web site: http://www.dreamscapeab.com
Dist(s): **Findaway World, LLC**
Follett School Solutions
Ingram Publisher Services
Recorded Bks., Inc.

Dreamschooner Pr., *(978-0-9899128)* 15 Beacon St., Natick, MA 01760 USA Tel 773-368-4386
E-mail: rfelty@gmail.com
Web site: dreamschoonerpress.com.

Dreamspinner Pr., *(978-0-9795048; 978-0-9801018; 978-0-9815084; 978-0-9817372; 978-1-935192; 978-1-61581; 978-1-61372; 978-1-62380; 978-1-62798; 978-1-63216; 978-1-63476; 978-1-63477; 978-1-63533; 978-1-64080; 978-1-64108; 978-1-64405)* 5032 Capital Cir. SW Suite 2, PMB #279, Tallahassee, FL 32305-7886 USA (SAN 915-5562); *Imprints:* Harmony Ink Press (HarmonyInk); DSP Publications (DSPPubns)
E-mail: contact@dreamspinnerpress.com
Web site: http://www.dreamspinnerpress.com
Dist(s): **INscribe Digital**
Independent Pubs. Group.

Dreamstreet Studios, Inc. (A Div. of DSMV Industries, Inc.), *(978-0-9892295)* 1800 Grand Ave., Nashville, TN 37212 USA Tel 615-321-9029
E-mail: songmerch@aol.com.

Dreamtime Publishing, *(978-0-9741726)* P.O. Box 834, Tahlequah, OK 74465 USA Tel 918-456-8639.

Dreamwand, *(978-0-615-32313-8; 978-0-9913715)* 715 N. Croft Ave., Los Angeles, CA 90069-5303 USA Tel 323-424-4095
E-mail: dreamwandbooks@yahoo.com; theafflictedgirls@dreamwand.net
Web site: http://www.theafflictedgirls.com.

DreamWorks Animation Pr., *(978-1-941341; 978-1-943452)* 1000 Flower St., Glendale, CA 91201 USA Tel 818-695-3997
E-mail: samantha.suchland@dreamworks.com.

Dreighton Pubns., *(978-0-9981870)* 2645 Kingston rd, Leonard, MI 48367 USA Tel 810-429-0734
E-mail: Jpelkey@residentialhomehealth.com.

Dreistadt, Jessica R., *(978-0-578-02239-0)* 1700 Sullivan Trail, No. 311, Easton, PA 18040 USA
Dist(s): **Lulu Pr., Inc.**

Dressler, Avi, *(978-0-9744309)* 35 Old Brick Rd., East Hills, NY 11577-1816 USA.

Dressler, Craig, *(978-0-9778247)* 5341 NE Webster Ct., Portland, OR 97218 USA Tel 503-281-4214.

Drew Squared Publishing, *(978-0-578-21799-4)* 12232 Oakmont Cir., Knoxville, TN 37934 USA.

Driftwood Pr., *(978-0-9638803)* Orders Addr.: P.O. Box 284, Yachats, OR 97498 USA; Edit Addr.: 62 Gender Dr., Yachats, OR 97498 USA Tel 541-547-3484
E-mail: njguni@clubinernet.fr.

Drinian Pr., LLC, *(978-0-9785165; 978-0-9820609; 978-0-9833069; 978-1-941929)* Orders Addr.: P.O. Box 63, Huron, OH 44839 USA
E-mail: drinianpress@frontier.com
Web site: http://drinianpress.com; http://smithwrite.net.

Drinking Gourd Pr., *(978-0-578-13425-3; 978-0-578-13426-0)* 414 Jefferson Ave., Apt. 1, Brooklyn, NY 11221 USA.

Drivel & Drool *Imprint of* **Dramatic Ellipsis**

Driving Vision, Inc., *(978-0-9766329)* 2117 S. Ventura Dr., Tempe, AZ 85282 USA
Web site: http://www.drivingvision.com.

DrMaster Pubns. Inc., *(978-1-59796)* 48531 Warm Springs Blvd., Suite 408, Fremont, CA 94539 USA Tel 510-687-1388 (phone/fax)
Web site: http://www.drmasterpublications.com
Dist(s): **Diamond Comic Distributors, Inc.**
Diamond Bk. Distributors.

Droemersche Verlagsanstalt Th. Knaur Nachf. - GmbH & Co. (DEU) *(978-3-426) Dist. by* **Distribks Inc.**

Drollery Pr., *(978-0-940920)* 1524 Benton St., Alameda, CA 94501-2420 USA (SAN 223-1808) Tel 510-521-4087.

Dronen, Christina, *(978-0-9997520)* 10705 Northgate St, Culver City, CA 90230 USA Tel 310-710-7614
E-mail: c3stina@gmail.com
Web site: christinadronen.com.

Droogle Inc., *(978-0-578-19933-7; 978-0-692-19024-1; 978-0-578-43477-3; 978-0-578-49174-5; 978-1-7332045)* 3513 Oates Dr., Raleigh, NC 27604 USA
Web site: www.droogledots.com.

DRS Publishing LLC, *(978-0-9852089)* 505 N. Link Rd., Johns Creek, GA 30022 USA Tel 770-475-1772
E-mail: drspubl363@aol.com; drspubl363@aol.com; drspubl@mindspring.com.

DRT Pr., *(978-1-933084)* Orders Addr.: P.O. Box 427, Pittsboro, NC 27312 USA Tel 919-360-7073; Fax: 866-562-5040; Edit Addr.: 395 Bill Thomas Rd., Moncure, NC 27559 USA
E-mail: editorial@drtpress.com
Web site: http://www.drtpress.com
Dist(s): **BWI**
Bk. Hse., The
Brodart Co.
Follett School Solutions
Quality Bks., Inc.

Drucker, Samantha Diener, *(978-0-692-92225-5)* 6070 Oak Bluff Way, Lake Worth, FL 33467 USA Tel 561-568-6430
E-mail: diener.samantha@gmail.com
Dist(s): **CreateSpace Independent Publishing Platform.**

Drummond Publishing Group, The, *(978-0-9755080; 978-1-59763)* 4 Collins Ave., Plymouth, MA 02360-4809 USA Do not confuse with Rec#s 786442, 791375, 1194043
E-mail: f_allen@drummondpub.com
Web site: http://www.drummondpub.com.

Drumstick Media, *(978-0-9764791)* Div. of Old Goats, Inc., 5805 Hwy. 93 S., Whitefish, MT 59937 USA Tel 406-862-8938; Fax: 406-862-8936; Toll Free: 800-404-8279
E-mail: robert@drumstickmedia.com; james@drumstickmedia.com
Web site: http://www.baxterowengraham.com; http://www.drumstickmedia.com.

Drunk Duck Comics, *(978-0-9748960)* P.O. Box 869, Pittston, PA 18640 USA
E-mail: rubbermallet@verizon.net; arrkelaan@hotmail.com
Web site: http://www.drunkduck.com.

Dry Climate Press *See* **Dry Climate Studios**

Dry Climate Studios, *(978-0-9856429; 978-0-9906858; 978-0-9908195; 978-1-942402)* 5119 NE 42nd St., Seattle, WA 98105 USA Tel 206-877-2093
Web site: www.dryclimatestudios.com
Dist(s): **Baker & Taylor Publisher Services (BTPS)**
Publishers Group West (PGW).

Dry, Paul Bks., Inc., *(978-0-9664913; 978-0-9679675; 978-1-58988)* 1616 Walnut St. Ste. 808, Philadelphia, PA 19103-5308 USA
E-mail: pdb@pauldrybooks.com
Web site: http://www.pauldrybooks.com
Dist(s): **Consortium Bk. Sales & Distribution.**

Dryad Pr., *(978-0-931848; 978-1-928755)* P.O. Box 11233, Takoma Park, MD 20913 USA (SAN 206-197X) Tel 301-891-3729
E-mail: dryadpress@yahoo.com
Web site: http://www.dryadpress.com
Dist(s): **SPD-Small Pr. Distribution.**

Dryden Publishing, *(978-0-9644370; 978-1-929204)* P.O. Box 482, Dryden, WA 98821-0482 USA
E-mail: dryden@csiconnect.com.

Dryland, David *See* **DrDryland.Com, LLC**

DSA Publishing & Design, Inc., *(978-0-9774451; 978-0-9818229; 978-0-9848057)* 6900 Edgewater Dr., Mckinney, TX 75070 USA
Web site: http://www.dsapubs.com
Dist(s): **Chicago Distribution Ctr.**

DSP Pubns. *Imprint of* **Dreamspinner Pr.**

DTaylor Bks., *(978-0-615-36081-2)* 415 Armour Dr., Apt. 12204, Atlanta, GA 30324 USA Tel 404-838-9678.

DTC Press *See* **Sweetbeet Bks.**

DTJ, LLC, *(978-0-9765731)* P.O. Box 635, Sequim, WA 98382 USA.

D-Tower Pubns., *(978-0-9770386)* 8028 Pine St., Ethel, LA 70730-3853 USA Tel 225-335-0802
E-mail: swbloopers@yahoo.com.

Dube, Tory, *(978-0-9886193)* 3168 41st St. No. 1f, Astoria, NY 11103 USA Tel 603-781-1440
E-mail: torydube@gmail.com
Web site: www.lovelythankyou.com.

Dubois, Ricardo S., *(978-0-615-15411-4; 978-0-615-15412-1; 978-0-615-15413-8; 978-0-615-16958-3; 978-0-615-17232-3; 978-0-615-18220-9; 978-0-615-19724-1)* 16015 Creekround Dr., Praireville, LA 70769 USA Tel 225-802-6001
E-mail: craftycajun@yahoo.com
Dist(s): **Lulu Pr., Inc.**

Duckett, Brenda, *(978-0-615-17289-7)* 27 Millswood Dr., Clarkville, TN 37042 USA Tel 931-906-8649
E-mail: bduckett1@bellsouth.net
Dist(s): **Lulu Pr., Inc.**

Duckpond Publishing, Inc., *(978-0-9720350)* 130 Hillside Ln., Roswell, GA 30076 USA Tel 770-649-9947; Fax: 770-594-8058
E-mail: theducks@duckpondpublishing.com
Web site: http://www.duckpondpublishing.com.

Dude Publishing *Imprint of* **National Professional Resources, Inc.**

Dudek, Ilene, *(978-0-692-89507-8; 978-0-692-94660-2; 978-0-692-04481-0; 978-0-578-40624-4; 978-0-578-53171-7; 978-0-578-70642-9)* 36 Rhoda Ave., Nutley, NJ 07110 USA Tel 201-390-4381
E-mail: Ilene_Catania@Yahoo.com
Web site: www.littleantstories.com.

Dudek, Mike, *(978-0-9740380; 978-0-9968182)* 505 Duwell St., Johnston, PA 15906 USA Tel 814-536-1500; Fax: 814-536-8952
E-mail: mike@dudekins.com; jetset15906@yahoo.com
Web site: www.rascaljokes.com.

Dudley Court Press, *(978-0-9819291; 978-0-9825396; 978-0-9829054; 978-0-9831383; 978-0-615-65426-3; 978-0-615-65428-7; 978-0-9881897; 978-1-940013; 978-0-9908416; 978-0-9970119; 978-1-945401)* Orders Addr.: PO Box 102 35 Dudley Ct., Sonoita, AZ 85637 USA; *Imprints:* Canterbury House Publishing, Limited (CHPDdlyCrt)
Web site: www.dudleycourtpress.com
Dist(s): **CreateSpace Independent Publishing Platform**
INscribe Digital
Independent Pubs. Group
Smashwords.

Dudley, Joshua Patrick, *(978-0-615-16396-3; 978-0-615-18871-3)* 4 Heritage Village Dr., Unit 102, Nashua, NH 03062 USA Tel 603-459-9687
E-mail: admin@joshuapatrickdudley.com; lostinozbook@yahoo.com
Web site: http://www.ostinozbook.com; http://www.lostinozbook.com
Dist(s): **Lulu Pr., Inc.**

DUENDE Bks., *(978-0-9777973; 978-0-615-14984-4; 978-0-615-15099-4)* Div. of DeCo Communications, 13900 Fiji Way, Apt. 306, Marina del Rey, CA 90292 USA Tel 310-486-0983
E-mail: denizr@verizon.net
Web site: http://www.duendebooks.blogspot.com
Dist(s): **Lulu Pr., Inc.**

Duet *Imprint of* **Novelstream, LLC**

†Dufour Editions, Inc., *(978-0-8023)* Orders Addr.: P.O. Box 7, Chester Springs, PA 19425-0007 USA (SAN 201-341X) Tel 610-458-5005; Fax: 610-458-7103; Toll Free: 800-869-5677
E-mail: info@dufoureditions.com
Web site: http://www.dufoureditions.com
Dist(s): **Casemate Pubs. & Bk. Distributors, LLC**; *CIP.*

Duke & Oscar, *(978-0-692-04831-3)* 1521 Boyd Pointe Way, Vienna, VA 22182 USA Tel 408-223-5177
E-mail: czeffy@gmail.com.

Duke Publishing & Software Corp., *(978-0-9745406)* P.O. Box 3429, Los Altos, CA 94024 USA Tel 408-245-3853; Fax: 408-245-9289
E-mail: info@aboutthekids.org
Web site: http://www.aboutthekids.org.

†Duke Univ. Pr., *(978-0-8223; 978-1-4780)* P.O. Box 90660, Durham, NC 27708-0660 USA (SAN 201-3436) Tel 919-687-3600; Fax: 919-688-4574; 905 W. Main S., Ste.18B, Durham, NC 27701 Tel 919-687-3600; Fax: 919-688-4574; Toll Free: 888-651-0122
E-mail: orders@dukepress.edu; subscriptions@dukepress.edu; hlw@dukeupress.edu
Web site: http://www.dukeupress.edu
Dist(s): **MyiLibrary**
ebrary, Inc.; *CIP.*

Dukes World, Inc., *(978-0-9664506)* P.O. Box 85, Yonkers, NY 10704 USA Tel 917-403-7661
E-mail: dukesworldinc@aol.com
Web site: http://www.chillstreetgang.com.

Dulany, Joseph P., *(978-0-9708830)* 6200 Oregon Ave NW Apt. 236, Washington, DC 20015-1529 USA
E-mail: josephdulany@msn.com
Web site: http://www.onceasoldier.com.

Duling Designs, *(978-0-9743445)* P.O. Box 1996, Marco Island, FL 34146-1996 USA
E-mail: jsduling87@aol.com.

†Dumbarton Oaks, *(978-0-88402)* Orders Addr.: c/o Hopkins Fulfillment Services, P.O. Box 50370, Baltimore, MD 21211-4370 USA (SAN 665-6870) Tel 410-516-6965; Fax: 410-516-6998; Toll Free: 800-537-5487; Edit Addr.: 1703 32nd St., NW, Washington, DC 20007 USA (SAN 293-2547) Tel 202-777-0092; Fax: 202-298-8407
E-mail: doaksbooks@doaks.org
Web site: http://www.doaks.org/publications.html
Dist(s): **Harvard Univ. Pr.**; *CIP.*

Dume Publishing *See* **Corman Productions**

Dumplinz Bk. Publishing, *(978-0-615-80362-3; 978-0-9964684)* 2305 Holland Ave. Apt. 1-G, Bronx, NY 10467 USA Tel 718-944-2414
E-mail: isreba1949@optonline.net.

Dunamis Development, *(978-0-9767066)* 3972-J Barranca Pkwy., Suite 115, Irvine, CA 92606 USA Tel 949-263-0063.

Dundurn (CAN) *(978-0-88762; 978-0-88882; 978-0-88924; 978-0-919028; 978-0-919670; 978-0-9690454; 978-1-55002; 978-1-55488; 978-1-4597; 978-1-77070) Dist. by* **IngramPubServ.**

Dunlop, Edward *See* **Cross & Crown Publishing**

Dunn, Hunter, *(978-0-9761732)* 410 Old Spring Rd., Danville, VA 24540-5206 USA.

Dunn, Michael *See* **Big Secret, The**

Dunne, Thomas Bks. *Imprint of* **St. Martin's Pr.**

Dunnigan, Stefanie and Tina Traina, *(978-0-9962796)* 155 Evergreen Rd., Ramsey, NJ 07446 USA Tel 201-452-4190
E-mail: savvyscribblers@gmail.com
Web site: www.traveltailsbooks.com.

Dunton Publishing, *(978-0-615-55848-6; 978-0-615-56429-6; 978-0-615-76368-2; 978-0-615-76615-7; 978-0-692-48457-9; 978-0-692-48492-0; 978-0-692-54319-1; 978-0-692-73280-9; 978-0-692-06924-0; 978-0-578-40647-3)* P.O. Box 4, New York, NY 10023 USA Tel 212-799-7402
Web site: duntonpublishing.com
Dist(s): **CreateSpace Independent Publishing Platform.**

Duo Pr. Llc (US) *Imprint of* **Duo Pr. LLC**

Duo Pr. LLC, *(978-0-9796213; 978-0-9825295; 978-0-9838121; 978-1-938093; 978-1-946064; 978-1-947458; 978-1-950500)* 265 Stanmore Rd., Baltimore, MD 21212 USA; *Imprints:* Duo Press Llc (US) (DUO PRESS LLC)
E-mail: info@duopressbooks.com
Web site: http://www.duopressbooks.com
Dist(s): **MyiLibrary**
Workman Publishing Co., Inc.
ebrary, Inc.

Duplicates Printing, *(978-0-9749953)* Orders Addr.: P.O. Box 2398, Pawleys Island, SC 29585 USA Tel 843-237-3998; Edit Addr.: 14329 Ocean Hwy. Unit 115, Pawleys Isl, SC 29585-4816 USA
E-mail: slingshot@sc.rr.com.

Dupuis North Publishing, *(978-0-9749199)* 76 N. Church St., Clayton, GA 30525 USA Tel 828-524-9520; Fax: 828-349-1945.

Duracell & the National Ctr. for Missing & Exploited Children (NCMEC), *(978-0-9795307)* 415 Nadison Ave., New York, NY 10018 USA Tel 212-613-4904.

duran, oscar, *(978-0-615-72225-2; 978-0-9886109)* 6204 sw 18th St, Miramar, FL 33023 USA Tel 954-986-4082; Fax: 954-986-4082
Dist(s): **CreateSpace Independent Publishing Platform.**

Durban House Press, Incorporated *See* **Fireside Pr., Inc.**

Durland Alternatives Library, *(978-0-9740184)* 127 Anabel Taylor Hall, Ithaca, NY 14853-1001 USA Tel 607-255-6486; Fax: 607-255-9985
E-mail: alt-lib@cornell.edu
Web site: http://www.alternativeslibrary.org.

Durst, Sanford J., *(978-0-915262; 978-0-942666; 978-1-886720)* 106 Woodcleft Ave., Freeport, NY 11520 USA (SAN 211-6987) Tel 516-867-3333; Fax: 516-867-3397
E-mail: sjdbooks@verizon.net.

Dust Bunny Games LLC, *(978-0-9747833)* Orders Addr.: 3744 Mistflower Ln., Naperville, IL 60564-5921 USA Tel 630-244-0335; Fax: 630-922-6995; Edit Addr.: 3744 Mistflower Ln., Naperville, IL 60564-5921 USA
E-mail: info@dustbunnygames.com
Web site: http://www.dustbunnygames.com.

DuSum Publishing, LLC, *(978-0-9911276; 978-0-9997044; 978-1-7329780)* 549 5th St. NW, Hickory, NC 28601 USA Tel 828-328-5955
E-mail: rdonepudi1969@gmail.com.

Duthaluru, Vidhya, *(978-0-9797657)* 247 Levinberg Ln., Wayne, NJ 07470 USA.

Dutton *Imprint of* **Penguin Publishing Group**

Dutton Books for Young Readers *Imprint of* **Penguin Young Readers Group**

Dutton Caliber *Imprint of* **Penguin Publishing Group**

Dutton Juvenile *Imprint of* **Penguin Publishing Group**

Dutton, Mary, *(978-0-692-90204-2)* 1408 Adams St., PORT TOWNSEND, WA 98368 USA Tel 360-344-2498
E-mail: mhdcashew@juno.com
Dist(s): **Ingram Content Group.**

Duval Publishing, *(978-0-9745637)* Orders Addr.: P.O. Box 4255, Key West, FL 33041 USA Toll Free: 800-355-8562; Edit Addr.: 3717 Eagle Ave., Key West, FL 33040 USA
Web site: http://www.southerncoastaldesigns.com.

DV Bks. *Imprint of* **Digital Vista, Inc.**

DVTVFilm, *(978-0-9678094)* 3 Temi Rd., Framingham, MA 01701 USA
E-mail: todd@dvtvfilm.com; info@themonkeykingsdaughter.com; todd@themonkeykingsdaughter.com
Web site: http://www.dvtvfilm.com; http://www.themonkeykingsdaughter.com.

Dwitt Publishing, *(978-0-9741352)* 9249 17th St SE, Saint Cloud, MN 56304-9709 USA
E-mail: dickawit@aol.com
Web site: http://www.dwittpublishing.com.

DWP, *(978-0-692-17974-1; 978-0-578-40120-1; 978-0-578-48090-9; 978-1-7330092)* 5070 SW 141st Ave., Beaverton, OR 97005 USA Tel 503-807-2012
E-mail: polanddw@comcast.net.

Dyeing Arts, *(978-0-9817244; 978-1-7357139)* 231 Mcallister Ave., Kentfield, CA 94904-1631 USA
E-mail: joytroyer@aol.com
Web site: http://www.DyeingArts.com.

Dyer, Rose *See* **Funnel Time Bks.**

Dykema Engineering, Incorporated *See* **Dykema Publishing Co.**

Dykema, Marjorie *See* **One Coin Publishing, LLC**

Dykema Publishing Co., *(978-0-9660705; 978-0-9701538)* Div. of Dykema Engineering, Inc., 3264 W. Normandy Ave., Roseburg, OR 97470 USA Tel 541-957-0259; Fax: 541-677-7146
E-mail: odykema@mcsi.net
Web site: http://www.oregonwriters.com.

Dykes, William R. III, *(978-0-9740987)* 317 Luchase Rd., Linden, VA 22642 USA.

Dylanna Publishing, Inc., *(978-1-942268; 978-1-947243; 978-1-949651; 978-1-64790)* 423 S CREEK DR, OSPREY, FL 34229 USA
E-mail: juliegrady@comcast.net
Web site: www.creativecoloring.co.

Dynagraphix *Imprint of* **Elliott, Jane**

Dynamic Forces, Incorporated *See* **Dynamic Forces, Inc.**

Dynamic Forces, Inc., *(978-0-9749638; 978-1-933305; 978-1-60690; 978-1-5241)* 113 Gaither Dr., Ste. 205 Suite B, Mt. Laurel, NJ 08054 USA; *Imprints:* Dynamite Entertainment (Dyna Enter)
E-mail: marketing@dynamite.com
Web site: http://www.dynamicforces.com; http://www.dynamite.com
Dist(s): **Diamond Comic Distributors, Inc.**
Diamond Bk. Distributors.

Dynamic Publishing Co., Inc., *(978-0-9656808)* Orders Addr.: P.O. Box 120, Calumet City, IL 60409 USA Tel 708-868-0512; Fax: 708-868-0549; Toll Free: 800-884-1840 Do not confuse with Dynamic Publishing, Sugar Land, TX,
E-mail: dpc123@ymail.com
Web site: http://www.DynamicPublishingCompany.com.

Dynamiq Press LLC *See* **Rustik Haws LLC**

Dynamite Entertainment *Imprint of* **Dynamic Forces, Inc.**

DynaStudy, Inc., *(978-0-9776270; 978-0-9777909; 978-1-933854; 978-1-935005)* 1401 Broadway St. Suite 100, Marble Falls, TX 78654 USA
E-mail: info@dynastudy.com
Web site: http://dynanotes.com.

Dynasty Publishing, Inc., *(978-0-9790444; 978-0-9793490)* P.O. Box 11997, Kansas City, MO 64138-0997 USA Do not confuse with Dynasty Publishing in Honolulu, HI
E-mail: info@dynastypublishinginc.com
Web site: http://www.dynastypublishinginc.com.

DysCovered Publishing *Imprint of* **Lawson, Tracy**

Dyson, Sarah, *(978-1-7334845)* P.O. Box 17253, Jonesboro, AR 72403 USA Tel 870-351-1015
E-mail: Sarah.mdyson@outlook.com.

DZ Publishing, LLC, *(978-0-9753660; 978-0-9889975)* 7360 Lincoln Dr., #2, Scottsdale, AZ 85258 USA Tel 949-922-7042
E-mail: szipp22@gmail.com
Web site: http://www.mycollegesuccess.com.

E & D Bks., Ltd., *(978-0-9794413)* P.O. Box 211, Ruby, NY 12475 USA (SAN 853-4314)
E-mail: info@buddyboobysbirthmark.com
Web site: http://www.buddyboobysbirthmark.com
Dist(s): **Beekman Bks., Inc.**

E & E Publishing, *(978-0-9719898; 978-0-9748933; 978-0-9791606; 978-0-9831499)* P.O. Box 3346, Omaha, NE 68103 USA Tel 402-578-2563 Do not confuse with E & E Publishing, Junction City, OR
E-mail: EveHeidiWrites@gmail.com.

E & H Publishing Co., Inc., *(978-0-9717295)* P.O. Box 4, Burkeville, VA 23922 USA
E-mail: greanes@earthlink.net.

EBP Latin America Group, Inc., *(978-1-56409)* 175 E. Delaware Pl. Apt. 8806, Chicago, IL 60611-7753 USA.

E B S C O Industries, Inc., *(978-0-913956; 978-1-888751)* Orders Addr.: P.O. Box 1943, Birmingham, AL 35201-1943 USA (SAN 201-3584) Tel 205-991-6600; Fax: 205-995-1636; Toll Free: 800-826-3024; Edit Addr.: 5724 Hwy. 280 E., Birmingham, AL 35242 USA
Web site: http://www.ebsco.com.

E C Jackson, *(978-0-9961812; 978-1-7329592)* P.O. Box 701886, Tulsa, OK 74170 USA Tel 918-493-5004
E-mail: christieok8@cox.net.

ECO Herpetological Pub. & Dist., *(978-0-9713197; 978-0-9767334; 978-0-9788979; 978-0-9832789; 978-0-9852936; 978-1-938850)* 4 Rattlesnake Canyon Rd., Rodeo, NM 88056 USA Tel 575-557-5757; Fax: 575-557-7575
E-mail: ecoorders@hotmail.com
Web site: http://www.reptileshirts.com
Dist(s): **BookBaby**
Serpent's Tale Natural History Bk. Distributors, Inc.
T-Rex Products.

EECI, Inc., *(978-0-9649379; 978-0-9722686; 978-1-933193)* 8055 W. Manchester Ave., 1st Flr., Playa Del Rey, CA 90293 USA
E-mail: rwoo@eecinternational.com.

E. F. S. Online Publishing, *(978-0-9701344)* Div. of E. F. S. Enterprises, Inc., 2844 Eighth Ave., Suite 6-E, New York, NY 10039 USA Tel 212-283-8899; Fax: 212-283-6280
E-mail: efsenterprises@hotmail.com
Web site: http://www.efs-enterprises.com.

E Innovative Ideas, *(978-0-9799540)* 800 SE 4th St., Suite 501, Fort Lauderdale, FL 33301 USA Tel 954-527-1070
E-mail: einnovate@aol.com.

E. J. Publishing, *(978-0-9764444; 978-0-9770303)* 4529 Hillcrest Rd., Birmingham, AL 35224-2818 USA Toll Free Fax: 866-864-6087; Toll Free: 866-864-6085
E-mail: elysia@ejpub.com
Web site: http://www.ejpub.com
Dist(s): **Baker & Taylor International**
CreateSpace Independent Publishing Platform.

EKS Publishing Co., *(978-0-939144)* 322 Castro St., Oakland, CA 94607-3028 USA (SAN 216-1281) Tel 510-251-9100; Fax: 510-251-9102; Toll Free: 877-743-2739
E-mail: orders@EKSpublishing.com
Web site: http://www.ekspublishing.com.

E M C Publishing *See* **EMC/Paradigm Publishing**

EMG Networks, *(978-1-56843)* Div. of Educational Management Group, 1 Lake St., No. 3B-47, Upper Saddle River, NJ 07458-1813 USA Tel 602-970-3250; Fax: 602-970-3460; Toll Free: 800-842-6791.

E M McIntyre, (978-0-9988993) 2125 S. 108th St., Omaha, NE 68144 USA Tel 402-393-3971; *Imprints:* Little Hound Publishing (MYD_M_LITTLE)
E-mail: redkingtrilogy@gmail.com.

E M Pubns., (978-0-9749739; 978-0-9794331; 978-0-9893569; 978-0-9905099; 978-0-9997469) Orders Addr.: P.O. Box 780900, Wichita, KS 67278-0900 USA
Web site: http://www.enloeministries.org.

ERIC Clearinghouse on Rural Education & Small Schls., (978-1-880785) Div. of Appalachia Educational Laboratory, Inc., Orders Addr.: P.O. Box 1348, Charleston, WV 25325-1348 USA Tel 304-347-0437; Fax: 304-347-0467; Toll Free: 800-624-9120; Edit Addr.: 1031 Quarrier St., Suite 610, Charleston, WV 25301 USA
E-mail: ericrc@ael.org
Web site: http://www.ael.org/eric.

ESP, Inc., (978-0-8209) Orders Addr.: P.O. Box 839, Tampa, FL 33601-0839 USA; Edit Addr.: 1212 N. 39th St., Suite 444, Tampa, FL 33605-5890 USA (SAN 241-497X) Do not confuse with E S P Inc., Woodlands, TX
E-mail: epublish@tampalay.rr.com
Web site: http://www.espbooks.com.

†ETC Pubns., (978-0-88280) 700 E. Vereda del Sur, Palm Springs, CA 92262 USA (SAN 124-8766) Tel 760-325-5352; Fax: 760-325-8841; Toll Free: 800-382-7869
E-mail: etcbooks@earthlink.net; *CIP.*

E T Nedder *Imprint of* **Paulist Pr.**

E3 Concepts LLC, (978-0-9797375) 3311 Mulberry Dr., Bloomington, IN 47401 USA Tel 812-360-7488; Fax: 888-876-5152
E-mail: chris.berry@linkedblocks.com
Web site: http://www.linkedblocks.com.

E3 Resources, (978-1-933383) 317 Main St., Suite 207, Franklin, TN 37064 USA (SAN 631-9076) Toll Free: 888-354-9411
Web site: http://www.e3resources.org.

Eager Minds Pr. *Imprint of* **Warehousing & Fulfillment Specialists, LLC (WFS, LLC)**

Eagle Bk. Bindery, (978-0-9772304; 978-1-934333) 2704 Camelot Ave., NW, Cedar Rapids, IA 52405 USA Tel 319-265-8210
E-mail: sales@eaglebookbindery.com
Web site: http://www.eaglebookbindery.com.

Eagle Creek Pubns., LLC, (978-0-9769093) P.O. Box 781166, Indianapolis, IN 46278 USA (SAN 257-3490) Tel 317-870-9902; Fax: 317-870-9904; Toll Free: 866-870-9903 Do not Confuse with Eagle Creek Publications in Prior Lake, MN
E-mail: ben@eaglecreekpubs.com
Web site: http://www.eaglecreekpubs.com.

Eagle Editions, Ltd., (978-0-914144; 978-0-9660706; 978-0-9721060; 978-0-9761034; 978-0-9794035) Orders Addr.: P.O. Box 580, Hamilton, MT 59840 USA Tel 406-363-5415; Fax: 406-375-9270; Toll Free: 800-255-1830; Edit Addr.: 752 Bobcat Ln., Hamilton, MT 59840 USA
E-mail: eagle@eagle-editions.com
Web site: http://www.eagle-editions.com
Dist(s): **Hachette Bk. Group**
MBI Distribution Services/Quayside Distribution.

Eagle Eye Consultancy (UK) Ltd, (978-0-9996283) 4 Regency Mews Tadcaster Rd., York, YO241LL GBR Tel 798-180-7467
E-mail: thejontyolivier@gmail.com
Web site: jontyolivier.com.

Eagle Eye Consultancy US, Inc. *See* **Eagle Eye Consultancy (UK) Ltd**

Eagle Publishing *See* **Majestic Eagle Publishing**

Eagle River Type & Graphics *See* **Northbooks**

Eagle Trail Pr., (978-0-9851876; 978-0-9892807; 978-0-9974267) P.O. Box 3671, Parker, CO 80134 USA Tel 720-295-2208
E-mail: info@EagleTrailPress.com.

Eagle Tree Pr., (978-0-9792499) Div. of M. Kay Howell, P.O. Box 1060, Rainier, OR 97048-1060 USA (SAN 852-8950)
Web site: http://fairyempire.biz.

Eaglebrook Press *See* **Oldcastle Publishing**

Eaglehouse, Carolyn, (978-0-9773263) 521 E. Uwchlan Ave., Chester Springs, PA 19425 USA
Web site: http://www.chesterspringscreamery.com.

Eaglemont Pr., (978-0-9662257; 978-0-9748411; 978-1-60040) 13228 NE 20th St. Ste. 300, Bellevue, WA 98005-2049 USA (SAN 254-2102) Toll Free: 877-590-9744
E-mail: info@eaglemontpress.com
Web site: http://www.eaglemontpress.com.

Eaglemoss Publications Ltd (GBR) (978-0-947837; 978-1-85167; 978-1-85629; 978-1-85875) *Dist. by* **Peng Rand Hse.**

Eagle's Wings Educational Materials, (978-1-931292) P.O. Box 502, Duncan, OK 73534 USA Tel 580-252-1555 (phone/fax)
E-mail: info@EaglesWingsEd.com
Web site: http://www.EaglesWingsEd.com.

Eaglesquest Publishing, (978-0-9745860) LTN Enterprises, 11852 Shady Acres Ct., Riverton, UT 84065 USA
E-mail: lestertn@earthlink.net
Web site: http://www.thepaddedgirdle.com; http://www.findingyour new normal.com.

Eakin Pr. *Imprint of* **Eakin Pr.**

†Eakin Pr., (978-0-89015; 978-1-57168; 978-0-9789150; 978-1-934645; 978-1-935632) Div. of Sunbelt Media, P.O. Box 90159, Austin, TX 78709-0159 USA (SAN 207-3633) Tel 254-235-6161; Fax: 254-235-6230; Toll Free: 800-880-8642; *Imprints:* Eakin Press (Eakin Pr); Nortex Press (Nortex Pr)
E-mail: sales@eakinpress.com; kris@eakinpress.com
Web site: http://www.eakinpress.com
Dist(s): **Children's Plus, Inc.**
Follett School Solutions
Hervey's Booklink & Cookbook Warehouse
Twentieth Century Christian Bks.
Wolverine Distributing, Inc.; *CIP.*

Eardley Pubns., (978-0-937630) Div. of Elizabeth Claire, Inc., Orders Addr.: 2100 Mccomas Way Suite 607, Virginia Beach, VA 23456 USA (SAN 215-6377) Tel 757-430-4308; Fax: 757-430-4309; Toll Free: 888-296-1090
E-mail: eceardley@aol.com
Web site: http://www.elizabethclaire.com
Dist(s): **BookLink, Inc.**
Delta Systems Company, Inc.

Early Foundations Pubs., (978-0-9670728; 978-0-9742131; 978-1-936215) P.O. Box 442, Jenison, MI 49429 USA
E-mail: orders@efpublishers.org
Web site: http://www.efpublishers.org.

Early Learning Assessment 2000, (978-0-9667830; 978-0-9746447) P.O. Box 21003, Roanoke, VA 24018 USA
E-mail: eanaatwork@aol.com.

Early Learning Foundation, LLC, (978-0-9755415) 5184 Milroy, Brighton, MI 48116 USA
E-mail: bob@earlylearningfoundation.com
Web site: http://www.earlylearningfoundation.com
Dist(s): **Independent Pubs. Group**
Midpoint Trade Bks., Inc.

Early Light Pr., LLC, (978-0-9799179) P.O. Box 317, Boyds, MD 20841-0317 USA
E-mail: lee@earlylightpress.com
Web site: http://www.earlylightpress.com
Dist(s): **MyiLibrary.**

Early Rise Pubns., (978-0-9741082) Orders Addr.: 350 S. Cty. Rd., Suite 102-134, Palm Beach, FL 33480 USA Tel 877-419-3648 (phone/fax)
E-mail: info@earlyrisepublications.com
Web site: http://www.earlyrisepublications.com
Dist(s): **CreateSpace Independent Publishing Platform.**

EarlyLight Bks., Inc., (978-0-9797455; 978-0-9832014; 978-0-9853037) P.O. Box 984, Clyde, NC 28721 USA
Web site: http://www.earlylightbooks.com
Dist(s): **Charlesbridge Publishing, Inc.**
Penguin Random Hse. Distribution
Penguin Random Hse. LLC
Random Hse., Inc.

Earnshaw Bks. (HKG) (978-988-17149) *Dist. by* **IPG Chicago.**

Earth Arts NW, (978-0-9792207) P.O. Box 25183, Portland, OR 97298-0183 USA
E-mail: tribal@spiritone.com
Web site: http://www.earthandspirit.org.

Earth Aware Editions *Imprint of* **Insight Editions**

Earth Aware Editions *Imprint of* **Mandala Publishing**

Earth Star Pubns., (978-0-944851) P.O. Box 117, Pagosa Springs, CO 81147-1800 USA (SAN 244-9315) Tel 970-731-0694; Fax: 970-731-0694 call first
E-mail: starbeacon@gmail.com
Web site: http://earthstar.tripod.com.

Earthatone Enterprises, (978-0-578-03024-1; 978-0-9914892) 244 5th Ave., No.2643, New York, NY 10016 USA Tel 212-252-6859; Fax: 208-977-3697
E-mail: earthatone@aol.com
Web site: http://www.earthatone.com.

EarthBound Bks., (978-0-9771818) P.O. Box 549, North Egremont, MA 01252 USA (SAN 256-9183) Tel 413-528-9042
E-mail: info@earthboundbooks.com
Web site: www.earthboundbooks.com.

Earthdancer Bks. *Imprint of* **Inner Traditions International, Ltd.**

Earthen Vessel Production, Inc., (978-1-887400) 3620 Greenwood Dr., Kelseyville, CA 95451 USA Tel 707-279-9621; Fax: 707-279-8769
E-mail: books@earthen.com; request@earthen.com
Web site: http://www.earthen.com.

Earthlight *See* **Light24**

Earthling Pr. *Imprint of* **Awe-Struck Publishing**

Earthshaker Bks., (978-0-9790357) 400 Melville Ave., Saint Louis, MO 63130 USA (SAN 852-2545) Tel 314-862-8177
E-mail: albonnie@mindspring.com
Dist(s): **MyiLibrary**
ebrary, Inc.

EarthTime Pubns., (978-0-9663286) Orders Addr.: 5662 Calle Real, #169, Santa Barbara, CA 93117 USA (SAN 299-5727) Tel 805-898-2263; Fax: 805-898-9460
E-mail: donna@seemamoon.com
Web site: http://www.seemamoon.com.

Earthwalk Pr., (978-0-915749) 5432 La Jolla Hermosa Ave., La Jolla, CA 92037-7613 USA (SAN 293-9258)
Dist(s): **Booklines Hawaii, Ltd.**
Langenscheidt Publishing Group.

EarthWardProject, (978-0-9984596) 20 E. Main St., Haverhill, MA 01830 USA Tel 978-807-1805
E-mail: runawaydandelion@gmail.com.

Earthways *See* **Earthways Guided Canoe Trips and School of Wilderness Living**

Earthways Guided Canoe Trips and School of Wilderness Living, (978-0-9761714) 159 Earthways Rd., Canaan, ME 04924 USA Tel 207-426-8138
E-mail: info@earthways.net
Web site: http://www.earthways.net.

Ear Twiggles Productions, Inc., (978-0-9762573) 14610 Luna Media, San Diego, CA 92127 USA Tel 858-756-8644; Fax: 858-756-8235
E-mail: contactus@eartwiggles.com
Web site: http://www.eartwiggles.com.

Eas'l Pubns., (978-1-57377) Div. of The Idea Shop, Inc., Orders Addr.: P.O. Box 22088, Saint Louis, MO 63126 USA Tel 314-892-9222; Fax: 314-892-9607; Edit Addr.: 11150 Lindbergh Business Ct., Suite 107, Saint Louis, MO 63123 USA
E-mail: easlpub@l1.net
Web site: http://www.easlpublications.com.

East End Hospice, Inc., (978-0-9754932) Orders Addr.: P.O. Box 1048, Westhampton Beach, NY 11978 USA Tel 631-288-8400; Fax: 631-288-8492; Edit Addr.: 481 Westhampton River Head Rd., Westhampton Beach, NY 11978 USA
E-mail: info@eeh.org
Web site: http://www.eeh.org.

East River Pr., (978-0-9791283) 455 FDR Dr., No. B1205, New York, NY 10002-5915 USA Do not confuse with companies with the same or similar name in Largo, MD, NEw YOrk, NY, Chester, NY.

East Stream Group, LLC, (978-0-9910342) 46 Bonnie Brae Dr., Weaverville, NC 28787 USA Tel 828-775-4812
E-mail: robin@eaststreamgroup.com; stefan@eaststreamgroup.com.

East West Discovery Pr., (978-0-9669437; 978-0-9701654; 978-0-9799339; 978-0-9821675; 978-0-9832278; 978-0-9856237; 978-0-9913454; 978-0-9973947; 978-1-949567) P.O. Box 3585, Manhattan Beach, CA 90266 USA Tel 310-545-3730; Fax: 310-545-3731
E-mail: info@eastwestdiscovery.com; icy@eastwestdiscovery.com
Web site: http://www.eastwestdiscovery.com
Dist(s): **Follett School Solutions**
Independent Pubs. Group.

East West Hse, (978-0-9778403) 899 S. Plymouth Ct. Apt 2106, Chicago, IL 60605 USA.

Easter Island Foundation, (978-1-880636) Orders Addr.: P.O. Box 6774, Los Osos, CA 93412-6774 USA Tel 805-528-8558; Fax: 805-534-9301
E-mail: eif@att.net
Web site: http://www.islandheritage.org.

Easter, Robert C. Sr., (978-1-885257) 4212 Lost Ridge Dr., Austin, TX 78731 USA Tel 512-346-1692; Fax: 512-349-0802; Toll Free: 800-848-5593
Dist(s): **Quality Bks., Inc.**

Eastern Digital Resources, (978-0-9815953) P.O. Box 1451, Clearwater, SC 29822 USA Tel 803-439-2938
E-mail: jrigdon@researchonline.net; sales@researchonline.net
Web site: http://www.researchonline.net.

†Eastern National, (978-0-915992; 978-1-888213; 978-1-59091) 470 Maryland Dr., Suite 1, Fort Washington, PA 19034 USA (SAN 630-4044)
E-mail: erich@Easternnational.org
Web site: http://www.easternnational.org; *CIP.*

Eastern National Park & Monument Association *See* **Eastern National**

Eastern Slope Publisher, (978-0-9746996; 978-0-9839956) Orders Addr.: P.O. Box 20357, Reno, NV 89515-0357 USA; Edit Addr.: 205 Urban Rd., Reno, NV 89509-3662 USA
E-mail: pdcafferata@sbcglobal.net.

Eastland Studios *See* **Eastwind Studios**

Eastlight Pr., (978-0-9743121) 1976 Savanna, Fairfield, IA 52556 USA
E-mail: gadef@mac.com.

Easton Studio Pr., LLC, (978-0-9743806; 978-0-9798248; 978-1-935212; 978-1-63226) P.O. Box 3131, Westport, CT 06880-3131 USA; *Imprints:* Prospecta Press (ProspectaPr)
Web site: http://www.eastonsp.com/live/
Dist(s): **Ingram Publisher Services**
MyiLibrary
Two Rivers Distribution
ebrary, Inc.

Eastpoint Enterprises, (978-0-9996386) 2228 Nelson Ave Apt. B, Redondo Beach, CA 90278 USA Tel 323-423-8359
E-mail: efadw@msn.com
Web site: glenshoffmanbooks.com.

Eastwaterfront Pr., (978-0-9769771) P.O. Box 220-554, Brooklyn, NY 11222 USA
E-mail: pdolack@gis.net.

Eastwind Studios, (978-0-9755635; 978-0-615-36383-7; 978-0-615-36384-4; 978-0-615-36385-1) P.O. Box 750, San Bernardino, CA 92402 USA Tel 909-725-7337
E-mail: lindaadams35@yahoo.com; philyeh@mac.com
Web site: http://www.ideaship.com; http://www.wingedtiger.com
Dist(s): **Booklines Hawaii, Ltd.**

Eastword Publications Development, Incorporated *See* **Lincoln Library Pr., Inc., The**

Easy Reach Corp., (978-0-615-50973-0; 978-0-615-59362-3; 978-0-9883620) HC 76 Box 121, Daisy, OK 74540 USA Tel 918-569-4803
E-mail: npyle@kiamichiwb.org.

Eat Your Peas Publishing, (978-0-9743210) 330 Conestoga Rd., Wayne, PA 19087 USA Tel 610-995-0495; Fax: 610-995-0496
E-mail: lisa@richeyassociates.com
Web site: http://www.mannerstogo.com.

Eazeland Publishing *See* **McDaniel Publishing Hse.**

EB Benjamin, LLC, (978-0-615-38727-7; 978-0-615-43887-0) 413 Mosby Dr, Leesburg, VA 20175 USA Tel 219-669-8474
E-mail: solalife@gmail.com
Dist(s): **CreateSpace Independent Publishing Platform.**

Ebed Pr., (978-0-9741927; 978-1-933484; 978-0-9774825; 978-1-934050) 3103 Villa Ave., Bronx, NY 11468-1356 USA Tel 718-788-2484; Fax: 718-788-7760; Toll Free: 800-224-7808
E-mail: info@ebedpress.com
Web site: http://www.ebedpress.com.

Ebeling, Vicki, (978-0-9779768; 978-0-9981925) 1250 6th St., Hermosa beach, CA 90254 USA Tel 310-530-0770
E-mail: books@pieravenuepublishing.com
Web site: http://www.educatingamerica.us
Dist(s): **Baker & Taylor Publisher Services (BTPS).**

Ebenezer A.M.E. Church, (978-0-9748834) 7707 Allentown Rd., Fort Washington, MD 20744 USA Tel 301-248-8833; Fax: 301-248-6894
Web site: http://www.ebenezerame.org.

Ebks. On The Net *Imprint of* **Write Words, Inc.**

EBL Coaching, (978-0-9772110; 978-0-9778391) 167 E. 82nd St., Suite 1A, New York, NY 10023 USA Tel 646-342-9380; Fax: 212-937-2305
E-mail: elevy@eblcoaching.com
Web site: http://www.eblcoaching.com.

Ebon Research Systems *See* **Ebon Research Systems Publishing, LLC**

Ebon Research Systems Publishing, LLC, (978-0-915960; 978-0-9648313) 812 Sweetwater Club Blvd., Longwood, FL 32779 USA (SAN 254-6698) Tel 407-786-9200; Fax: 407-682-2384
E-mail: femillionaire@embarqmail.com
Web site: http://www.daretobebooks.com; http://www.ebonresearchsystems.com.

Ebony Pearl's World Bks. & Publishing, (978-0-9988715) 194 Ormond St. SW, Atlanta, GA 30315 USA Tel 404-396-5833; Fax: 404-396-5833
E-mail: alishajohnsonedu@gmail.com.

EbonyEnergy Publishing, Incorporated *See* **GEM Bk. Club**

eBookit.com, (978-1-4566) Div. of Archieboy Holdings, LLC, 365 Boston Post Rd., No. 311, Sudbury, MA 01776 USA
Web site: http://www.ebookit.com.

eBooks2go *See* **eBooks2go Inc**

eBooks2go Inc, (978-1-61813; 978-1-5457) 1111 N. Plaza Dr., Ste. 300, Schaumburg, IL 60173 USA Tel 847-598-1150
E-mail: ram@ebooks2go.net
Web site: www.gantecpublishing.com; http://www.ebooks2go.com/.

E-Booksgen, (978-1-893767) 40 Sandy Pond South, East Wakefield, NH 03830 USA Tel 603-522-9951
E-mail: e-booksgen@e-booksgen.com
Web site: http://www.e-booksgen.com; http://www.e-booksgen.com/E-WW2DOC.html.

eBooksOnDisk.com, (978-0-9719101; 978-1-932157) Orders Addr.: P.O. Box 30432, Gulf Breeze, FL 32503 USA Tel 850-261-1981
E-mail: thomas@ebooksondisk.com
Web site: http://www.ebooksondisk.com; http://www.confederatemilitaryhistory.com
Dist(s): **CreateSpace Independent Publishing Platform**
Ingram Content Group.

ebooksonthe.net *See* **Write Words, Inc.**

ebooksonthe.net *See* **Dilligaf Publishing**

eBookstand Books *See* **Bookstand Publishing**

E-BookTime LLC, (978-0-9717625; 978-1-932701; 978-1-59824; 978-1-60862) 6598 Pumpkin Rd., Montgomery, AL 36108 USA Toll Free: 877-613-2665
E-mail: publishing@e-booktime.com
Web site: http://www.e-booktime.com.

Ebright, David, (978-1-7322277) 152 Moses Creek Blvd, St Augustine, FL 32086 USA Tel 904-466-4173
E-mail: jaxpop8@hotmail.com.

Ebury Publishing (GBR) (978-0-09; 978-0-426; 978-0-7126; 978-0-7535; 978-0-85223; 978-0-86369; 978-1-85227; 978-0-907080; 978-0-903446; 978-1-905042; 978-1-904978; 978-0-427; 978-1-84670; 978-1-905264; 978-1-4735) *Dist. by* **IPG Chicago.**

EC Pr. Bks., (978-0-9983615; 978-1-7330224) 6456 Dwane Ave, San Diego, CA 92120 USA Tel 760-791-3033
E-mail: elizabethchennamchetty@gmail.com
Web site: elizabethchennamchetty.com.

EC Publishing LLC, (978-1-970160; 978-1-953821) 416 Marion Oaks Pass, Ocala, FL 34473 USA Tel 918-938-2068; 352-667-9279
E-mail: ecpublishingllc@outlook.com
Web site: ecpublishing.com
Dist(s): **Ingram Content Group.**

Ecco *Imprint of* **HarperCollins Pubs.**

ecEmedia, a Div. of The EC Corp., (978-0-9822242; 978-1-948623) 10511 Hardin Valley Rd, Knoxville, TN 37932 USA Tel 865-789-8324; Fax: 865-789-8324
E-mail: orlinob@gmail.com
Web site: ecEmedia.net.

Echelon Press Publishing, (978-1-59080) Orders Addr.: 9055 Thamesmeade Rd. Apt. G, Laurel, MD 20723-5807 USA; *Imprints:* Quake (Quake)
E-mail: admin@echelonpress.com; echelonpress@gmail.com
Web site: http://www.echelonpress.com; http://quakeme.com
Dist(s): **Brodart Co.**
Ingram Content Group
Partners Bk. Distributing, Inc.
Smashwords.

Echo Point Bks. and Media, (978-0-9638784; 978-0-615-56118-9; 978-1-62654; 978-1-63561; 978-1-64837) Orders Addr.: 22 Browne Court, No. 100, Brattleboro, VT 05301 USA
E-mail: editorial@echopointbooks.com; fred@epbm.mygbiz.com
Web site: www.echopointbooks.com
Dist(s): **Rodale Institute Bookstore.**

Echo Valley Pr, (978-0-9860734) P.O. Box 449, Glen Arbor, MI 49636 USA.

Echoes Joint Venture, *(978-0-9759995)* Intensive English Program, UD, 1845 E. Northgate Dr., Irving, TX 75062 USA.

ECity Publishing *Imprint of* **ECity Publishing**

E-City Publishing, *(978-0-615-16430-4)* 150 Rustic Ridge Rd., Fredericksburg, VA 22405 USA
Dist(s): **Publishers Services.**

ECity Publishing, *(978-0-9716006; 978-0-9830425; 978-1-7341046)* Orders Addr.: P.O. Box 5033, Everglades City, FL 34139 USA Tel 239-695-2905; 102 E. Broadway, Everglades City, FL 34139; *Imprints:* ECity Publishing (ECity Pubng)
E-mail: ecitypublishing@earthlink.net
Web site: http://www.ecity-publishing.com.

Eckankar, *(978-1-57043)* Orders Addr.: P.O. Box 27300, Minneapolis, MN 55427 USA (SAN 253-7192) Fax: 952-380-2295; Toll Free: 800-568-3463
E-mail: eckbooks@eckankar.org
Web site: http://www.eckankar.org
Dist(s): **BookMobile.**

Eckerd College Leadership Development Institute, *(978-0-9764173)* 4200 54th Ave. S., St. Petersburg, FL 33711 USA Tel 727-864-8213; Fax: 727-864-7575; Toll Free: 800-753-0444
E-mail: ldi@eckerd.edu
Web site: http://www.eckerd.edu/ldi.

Eckl, Joseph J., *(978-0-9746686)* 346 Country Brook Ln., Harvard, IL 60033-7807 USA
E-mail: ecklindpl@aol.com.

Ecky Thump Bks., Inc., *(978-0-9815883)* 1411 N. California St., Burbank, CA 91505-1902 USA
Web site: http://www.achristmasbox.com
Dist(s): **Partners Pubs. Group, Inc.**

Eclectic Dragon Pr., *(978-0-9746016)* P.O. Box 91, Laie, HI 96762-1294 USA.

Eclipse Pr. *Imprint of* **Blood-Horse, Inc., The**

Eclipse Solutions (UK) Ltd. (GBR) *(978-0-9556910) Dist. by* **LuluCom.**

Eco Fiction Bks. *Imprint of* **Day to Day Enterprises**

Eco Images, *(978-0-938423)* Orders Addr.: P.O. Box 61413, Virginia Beach, VA 23466-1413 USA (SAN 661-230X); Edit Addr.: 4132 Blackwater Rd., Virginia Beach, VA 23457 USA (SAN 661-2318) Tel 757-421-3929
E-mail: wildfood@cox.net
Web site: http://www.ecoimages-us.com.

Eco-Busters, *(978-1-885091)* 1198 Old Castleberry Rd, Brewton, AL 36426 USA.

Eco-Justice Pr., LLC, *(978-0-9660370; 978-0-9891296; 978-1-945432)* P.O. Box 5409, Eugene, OR 97405 USA; *Imprints:* Aurora Books (AuroraBks)
E-mail: info@ecojusticepress.com; orders@ecojusticepress.com
Web site: ecojusticepress.com.

Ecology Comics, *(978-0-9643421)* 465 B. Kawailoa Rd., Kailua, HI 96734 USA Tel 808-261-1018; Fax: 808-531-3177.

EcoSeekers, The, *(978-0-9798800)* P.O. Box 637, Nyack, NY 10960 USA (SAN 854-6339)
E-mail: info@theecoseekers.com
Web site: http://www.theecoseekers.com
Dist(s): **Midpoint Trade Bks., Inc.**

Eco-thumb Publishing Co., *(978-0-9778536)* 1212 S. Naper Blvd., Suite 119-337, Naperville, IL 60540 USA (SAN 850-4113) Tel 630-853-9758
Web site: http://www.ecothumb.com; http://www.sendmethesoap.com.

ECS Learning Systems, Inc., *(978-0-944459; 978-1-57022; 978-1-58232; 978-1-60539)* P.O. Box 440, Bulverde, TX 78163 USA (SAN 243-6167) Toll Free Fax: 877-688-3226; Toll Free: 800-688-3224
Web site: http://www.ecslearningsystems.com.

Ecstatic Exchange, The, *(978-0-615-13570-0; 978-0-615-13599-1; 978-0-615-14273-9; 978-0-615-14505-1; 978-0-615-15116-8; 978-0-615-16308-6; 978-0-615-18394-7; 978-0-615-18412-8; 978-0-615-20490-1; 978-0-615-22182-3; 978-0-615-23628-5; 978-0-578-00773-1; 978-0-578-01004-5; 978-0-578-01084-7; 978-0-578-01690-0; 978-0-578-02569-8; 978-0-578-02765-4; 978-0-578-04677-8; 978-0-578-04905-2; 978-0-578-06116-0; 978-0-578-07145-9; 978-0-578-07482-5; 978-0-578-07608-9; 978-0-578-08293-6; 978-0-578-08512-8; 978-0-578-08891-4;) 6470 Morris Pk. Rd., Philadelphia, PA 19151 USA Tel 215-477-8927*
E-mail: abdalhayy@danielmoorepoetry.com
Web site: http://www.danielmoorepoetry.com; www.ecstaticxchange.wordpress.com
Dist(s): **Lulu Pr., Inc.**

Ectopic Publishing, *(978-0-9759695)* 3638 Lovejoy Ct. NE, Olympia, WA 98506 USA
E-mail: bryanrandall@ectopicpublishing.com
Web site: http://www.ectopicpublishing.com.

ECW Pr. (CAN) *(978-0-920763; 978-0-920802; 978-1-55022; 978-1-77041; 978-1-55490; 978-1-77090; 978-1-77305) Dist. by* **BTPS.**

Ed. Acespanish S.A.C.- Lima, Peru, *(978-0-9762361)* 4806 Alta Loma Dr., Austin, TX 78749 USA Tel 512-784-6333
Web site: http://www.acespanish.com.

E.D. Insight Bks., *(978-0-9761552)* P.O. Box 514, Beverly Hills, CA 90213-0514 USA
E-mail: brady@edinsight.com
Web site: http://www.edinsight.com.

Ed Musica, *(978-1-932637)* 1219 La Casa Dr., San Marcos, CA 92078 USA
E-mail: alfredo@edmusica.com
Web site: www.edmusica.com.

Edamex, Editores Asociados Mexicanos, S. A. de C. V. (MEX) *(978-968-409; 978-970-661) Dist. by* **Giron Bks.**

EDC Publishing, *(978-0-7460; 978-0-86020; 978-0-88110; 978-1-58086; 978-0-7945; 978-1-60130)* Orders Addr.: P.O. Box 470663, Tulsa, OK 74147-0663 USA (SAN 658-0505); Edit Addr.: 10302 E. 55th Pl., Tulsa, OK 74146-6515 USA (SAN 107-5322) Tel 918-622-4522; Fax: 918-665-7919; Toll Free Fax: 800-747-4509; Toll Free: 800-475-4522; *Imprints:* Usborne (UsborneU)
E-mail: edc@edcpub.com
Web site: http://www.edcpub.com
Dist(s): **Children's Plus, Inc.**
Continental Bk. Co., Inc.
Lectorum Pubns., Inc.
Libros Sin Fronteras.

EDCO Publishing, Inc., *(978-0-9712692; 978-0-9749412; 978-0-9798088)* 2648 Lapeer Rd., Auburn Hills, MI 48326 USA (SAN 254-4261) Fax: 248-475-9122; Toll Free: 888-510-3326
E-mail: lynette@edcopublishing.com; martha@edcopublishing.com
Web site: http://www.edcopublishing.com
Dist(s): **Partners Bk. Distributing, Inc.**

EDCON Publishing Group, *(978-0-8481; 978-1-56872)* 30 Montauk Blvd., Oakdale, NY 11769 USA Tel 631-567-7227; Fax: 631-567-8745; Toll Free Fax: 888-518-1564; Toll Free: 888-553-3266
E-mail: dale@edconpublishing.com
Web site: http://www.edconpublishing.com
Dist(s): **Findaway World, LLC**
Follett School Solutions.

Eddie Crabtree Ministries, *(978-0-9765830)* Orders Addr.: P.O. Box 846, Salem, VA 24153 USA Tel 540-562-1500; Fax: 540-562-2695; Edit Addr.: 1928 Loch Haven Dr., Roanoke, VA 24019 USA
E-mail: eddiecrabtreeministries@valleywordministries.org.

Eddy, The Writings of Mary Baker, *(978-0-87510; 978-0-87952)* Orders Addr.: 210 Massachusetts Ave P03-25, Boston, MA 02115 USA (SAN 203-6541) Tel 617-450-2517
E-mail: gilibertos@csps.com
Web site: http://www.spirituality.com.

Edebé (ESP) *(978-84-236; 978-84-683; 978-84-300-1909-0) Dist. by* **Ediciones.**

Edebé (ESP) *(978-84-236; 978-84-683; 978-84-300-1909-0) Dist. by* **Lectorum Pubns.**

Edelsa Grupo Didascalia, S.A. (ESP) *(978-84-389; 978-84-7711; 978-84-85786) Dist. by* **Distribks Inc.**

Edelsa Grupo Didascalia, S.A. (ESP) *(978-84-389; 978-84-7711; 978-84-85786) Dist. by* **Continental Bk.**

Edelson, Madelyn, *(978-0-9770131)* 69 Bay Ave., H, Huntington, NY 11743 USA
E-mail: mbedelson@optonline.net
Web site: http://www.beechwindpress.com.

Eden Entertainment Ltd., Inc., *(978-0-9672819; 978-0-9835380)* 1277 1st St. Suite 1, Key West, FL 33040 USA Tel 305-294-7928
E-mail: MarcusVarner@Hotmail.com; DanielJReynen@Hotmail.com
Web site: http://www.truesecretof.com; http://www.dietisdead.com; http://www.webefit.com.

Eden Studios, Inc., *(978-1-891153; 978-1-933105)* 6 Dogwood Ln., Londonville, NY 12211 USA Tel 518-331-2063; Fax: 425-962-2593
E-mail: edenprod@aol.com
Web site: http://www.edenstudios.net
Dist(s): **PSI (Publisher Services, Inc.).**

EdenTree Publishing, *(978-0-692-78131-9; 978-0-9982113)* P.O. Box 1174, PORTSMOUTH, OH 45662 USA Tel 740-285-3954
E-mail: frwamock@yahoo.com.

Edes Publishing Co., *(978-0-9788010; 978-1-943472)* 1224 E. Hadley, Las Cruces, NM 88001 USA (SAN 851-6561)
E-mail: publisher@edes.net
Web site: http://www.edes.net.

Edgar Road Publishing, *(978-0-615-20414-7)* 938 Tuxedo Blvd., Webster Groves, MO 63119 USA Tel 314-541-9235; Fax: 314-961-9044
E-mail: edgarroadpublishing@gmail.com
Dist(s): **R J Communications, LLC.**

Edge, Inc., *(978-0-692-70443-1; 978-0-9996501)* 6141 Arbutus Dr., Pensacola, FL 32504 USA Tel 850-516-7251; Fax: 850-516-7251
E-mail: deborah-edge@cox.net
Web site: www.edgetherapyseminars.

Edgecliff Pr. LLC., *(978-0-9798659; 978-0-9819271; 978-0-9844622; 978-0-9839486)* Mid-century Modern Bldg. 9066 Long Ln., Cincinnati, OH 45231 USA (SAN 854-6150) Tel 513-348-9120 Hours 9 to 5 EST
E-mail: Info@edgecliffpress.com
Web site: http://www.edgecliffpress.com; http://www.edgecliffkids.com.

EDGEucation Publishing, *(978-1-932689)* Orders Addr.: P.O. Box 852013, Yukon, OK 73085-2013 USA; Edit Addr.: 1441 NW 47th St., Oklahoma City, OK 73085-2013 USA
E-mail: edgeucation@sbcglobal.net.

Edgewood Publishing, LLC, *(978-0-9792645)* P.O. Box 153, Adell, WI 53001 USA Tel 920-994-2483.

Ediciones Alas, Inc., *(978-0-9753799)* Orders Addr.: P.O. Box 327495, Fort Lauderdale, FL 33332 USA; Edit Addr.: 6061 SW 195th Ave., Pembroke Pines, FL 33332 USA
E-mail: mm@milymolo.com
Web site: http://www.milymolo.com.

Ediciones Alfaguara (ESP) *(978-84-204) Dist. by* **Santillana.**

Ediciones Alfaguara (ESP) *(978-84-204) Dist. by* **Lectorum Pubns.**

Ediciones B (ESP) *(978-84-406; 978-84-7735; 978-84-666; 978-84-9872; 978-84-15420) Dist. by* **Peng Rand Hse.**

Ediciones B Mexico (MEX) *(978-84-406; 978-84-7735; 978-607-480) Dist. by* **Peng Rand Hse.**

Ediciones Cocoli, *(978-0-9650197; 978-0-9994064)* P.O. Box 9023072, San Juan, PR 00902 USA Tel 787-354-8264
E-mail: sofiasaezmatos@gmail.com.

Ediciones Cátedra (ESP) *(978-84-376) Dist. by* **Continental Bk.**

Ediciones de la Torre (ESP) *(978-84-7960; 978-84-85277; 978-84-85866; 978-84-86587) Dist. by* **Libros Fronteras.**

Ediciones de la Torre (ESP) *(978-84-7960; 978-84-85277; 978-84-85866; 978-84-86587) Dist. by* **AIMS Intl.**

Ediciones del Bronce (ESP) *(978-84-8453; 978-84-89854) Dist. by* **Planeta.**

Ediciones del Laberinto (ESP) *(978-84-8483; 978-84-87482) Dist. by* **Ediciones.**

Ediciones Destino (ESP) *(978-84-233; 978-84-9710) Dist. by* **AIMS Intl.**

Ediciones Destino (ESP) *(978-84-233; 978-84-9710) Dist. by* **Planeta.**

Ediciones Destino (ESP) *(978-84-233; 978-84-9710) Dist. by* **Continental Bk.**

Ediciones Destino (ESP) *(978-84-233; 978-84-9710) Dist. by* **Lectorum Pubns.**

Ediciones DiQueSi (ESP) *Dist. by* **Lectorum Pubns.**

Ediciones El Pozo, *(978-0-9821364; 978-0-9884286; 978-0-9861812; 978-0-9986971)* 37 Fairview St., Apt. 4, Oneonta, NY 13820 USA (SAN 857-3581) Tel 607-353-9277
E-mail: gustavoa1234@hotmail.com
Web site: http://www.employees.oneonta.edu/arangog/.

Ediciones El Salvaje Refinado *See* **Refined Savage Editions / Ediciones El Salvaje Refinado, The**

Ediciones Eleos, *(978-0-9650058; 978-1-881741)* Orders Addr.: Urb. Los Montes 164 Calle Pitirre, Dorado, PR 00646 USA
E-mail: fjortiz@edicioneseleos.com
Web site: http://www.edicioneseleos.com
Dist(s): **Lushena Bks.**

Ediciones Eleos, Incorporated *See* **Ediciones Eleos**

Ediciones La Fragatina (ESP) *(978-84-16226) Dist. by* **IPG Chicago.**

Ediciones la Gota de Agua, *(978-0-9771987; 978-0-9819303; 978-0-9964627; 978-1-7337513)* 1937 Pemberton St., Philadelphia, PA 19146-1825 USA Tel 215-546-9421
E-mail: info@edicioneslagotadeagua.com
Web site: http://edicioneslagotadeagua.com
Dist(s): **Ediciones Universal**
GOBI Library Solutionis from EBSCO.

Ediciones Lea S.A. (ARG) *(978-987-1257; 978-987-21776; 978-987-22032; 978-987-22079; 978-987-634; 978-987-718) Dist. by* **IPG Chicago.**

Ediciones Lerner *Imprint of* **Lerner Publishing Group**

Ediciones Norte, Inc., *(978-1-931928)* P.O. Box 29461, San Juan, PR 00929-0461 USA Tel 787-701-0909; Fax: 787-701-0922
Web site: http://www.edicionesnorte.com
Dist(s): **Independent Pubs. Group.**

Ediciones Nuevo Espacio *See* **Ediciones Nuevo Espacio-AcademicPressENE**

Ediciones Nuevo Espacio-AcademicPressENE, *(978-1-930879)* Orders Addr.: 39 Redfern Rd., Eatontown, NJ 07724 USA
E-mail: AcademicPressENE@gmail.com
Web site: http://www.editorialene.com; http://www.editorial-ene.com
Dist(s): **Book Wholesalers, Inc.**
Brodart Co.

Ediciones Obelisco (ESP) *(978-84-7720; 978-84-86000; 978-84-9777; 978-84-940745; 978-84-941549; 978-84-16117) Dist. by* **Spanish.**

Ediciones Oniro S.A. (ESP) *(978-84-89920; 978-84-922523; 978-84-9754; 978-84-95456) Dist. by* **Bilingual Pubns.**

Ediciones Oniro S.A. (ESP) *(978-84-89920; 978-84-922523; 978-84-9754; 978-84-95456) Dist. by* **Lectorum Pubns.**

Ediciones Rodeno (ESP) *(978-84-938364; 978-84-942689) Dist. by* **IPG Chicago.**

Ediciones Santillana, Inc., *(978-1-57581; 978-1-60484; 978-1-61875)* Div. of Santillana-S. A. (SP), P.O. Box 195462, San Juan, PR 00919-5462 USA Tel 787-781-9800; Fax: 787-782-6149; Toll Free: 800-981-9822
E-mail: molivero@santillanapr.net; areynoso@santillanapr.net; cvazquez@santillanapr.net
Web site: http://www.gruposantillana.com
Dist(s): **Santillana USA Publishing Co., Inc.**

Ediciones Situm, Incorporated *See* **Biblio Services, Inc.**

Ediciones SM, *(978-1-933279; 978-1-934801; 978-1-935556; 978-1-936534; 978-1-939075; 978-1-940343; 978-1-63014; 978-1-64486)* Barrio Palmas, 776 Calle 7 Suite 2, Catano, PR 00962-6335 USA Tel 787-625-9800; Fax: 787-625-9799
Web site: http://www.ediciones-smpr.com.

Ediciones Universal, *(978-0-89729; 978-1-59388)* Orders Addr.: P.O. Box 450353, Miami, FL 33245-0353 USA (SAN 658-0548); Edit Addr.: 3090 SW Eighth St., Miami, FL 33135 USA (SAN 207-2203) Tel 305-642-3355; Fax: 305-642-7978
E-mail: marta@ediciones.com; ediciones@ediciones.com
Web site: http://www.ediciones.com
Dist(s): **Lectorum Pubns., Inc.**

Ediciones Urano de México (MEX) *(978-607-95139; 978-607-7835; 978-607-9344) Dist. by* **Spanish.**

Ediciones Urano S. A. (ESP) *(978-84-7953; 978-84-95618; 978-84-95752; 978-84-86344; 978-84-95787; 978-84-96711; 978-84-96886; 978-84-92916; 978-84-9944) Dist. by* **Spanish.**

Ediciones y Distribuciones Codice, S.A. (ESP) *(978-84-357) Dist. by* **Continental Bk.**

Edifytainment Bks., *(978-0-9753427)* 213 Regent Cir., Inglewood, CA 90301 USA Tel 310-677-9744
E-mail: edifytainmentbooks@prodigy.net
Web site: http://www.bobettejamison-harrison.com/edifytainmentbooks.html.

Edilupa Ediciones, S.L. (ESP) *(978-84-932571; 978-84-932843; 978-84-96252; 978-84-96609) Dist. by* **Lectorum Pubns.**

Edimat Libros, S. A. (ESP) *(978-84-8403; 978-84-923200; 978-84-95002; 978-84-9764; 978-84-9794) Dist. by* **Lectorum Pubns.**

eDimples, Inc., *(978-0-9787759)* 9249 S. Broadway, 200-161, Highlands Ranch, CO 80129 USA Tel 303-284-1331 (phone/fax)
E-mail: greg@edimples.com
Web site: http://www.edimples.com.

Edinboro Bk. Arts Collective, *(978-0-9747001)* Orders Addr.: P.O. Box 77, Edinboro, PA 16412 USA; Edit Addr.: 103 Tarbell Ln., Edinboro, PA 16412 USA
E-mail: winterberger@edinboro.edu.

Edinborough Pr., *(978-1-889020)* P.O. Box 13790, Roseville, MN 55113-2293 USA (SAN 299-2825) Tel 651-415-1034; Toll Free Fax: 800-566-6145; Toll Free: 888-251-6336 (Orders Only)
E-mail: books@edinborough.com
Web site: http://www.edinborough.com
Dist(s): **ebrary, Inc.**

Edinburgh Univ. Pr. (GBR) *(978-0-7486; 978-0-85224; 978-1-4744) Dist. by* **TwoRivers.**

Edinumen, Editorial (ESP) *(978-84-89756; 978-84-85789; 978-84-95986; 978-84-9848) Dist. by* **Cambridge U Pr.**

Edit et Cetera *See* **Edit et Cetera Ltd.**

Edit et Cetera Ltd., *(978-0-9746122; 978-0-9769989; 978-0-9832270)* P.O. Box 551, Canon City, CO 81215 USA
E-mail: familybookhouse@aol.com
Web site: http://www.familybookhouse.com.

EDITER'S Publishing Hse., *(978-0-9706814; 978-0-9743743)* 654 Schafer Pl., Escondido, CA 92025 USA Tel 619-339-7030; Fax: 760-294-2685
E-mail: books@editers.com
Web site: http://www.editers.com.

EDITER'S Publishing Hse. (MEX) *(978-968-6966; 978-968-5432) Dist. by* **EDITERS Pub Hse.**

Editex, Editorial S.A. (ESP) *(978-84-7131) Dist. by* **Lectorum Pubns.**

Editing Mee, *(978-1-7348905; 978-1-953109)* 3985 S 900 E Apt 116 0, Salt Lake City, UT 84124 USA Tel 8016744934
E-mail: esuggs92@gmail.com
Dist(s): **Ingram Content Group.**

Edition Axel Menges GmbH (DEU) *(978-3-930698; 978-3-932565; 978-3-936681) Dist. by* **Natl Bk Netwk.**

Edition Chimaira (DEU) *(978-3-930612; 978-3-89973) Dist. by* **Serpents Tale.**

Edition Q, Inc., *(978-0-86715; 978-1-883695)* 551 N. Kimberly Dr., Carol Stream, IL 60188-1881 USA Tel 630-682-3223; Fax: 630-682-3907; Toll Free: 800-421-0387
E-mail: quintpub@aol.com; service@quintbook.com
Web site: http://www.quintpub.com.

Editions de la Montagne Verte, Inc. (CAN) *(978-0-9737681; 978-1-897277) Dist. by* **Lone Pine.**

Editions de la Paix (CAN) *(978-2-921255; 978-2-922565; 978-2-9800785; 978-2-89599) Dist. by* **World of Reading.**

Editions du Petit Music (FRA) *(978-2-84607) Dist. by* **Distribks Inc.**

Editions du Seuil (FRA) *(978-2-02) Dist. by* **Distribks Inc.**

Editions Fleurus (FRA) *(978-2-215; 978-2-250; 978-2-7289) Dist. by* **Distribks Inc.**

Editions Milan (FRA) *(978-2-7459; 978-2-84113; 978-2-86726; 978-2-408) Dist. by* **Distribks Inc.**

Editora Campamocha, *(978-1-934802)* 1609 Chicago Av., McAllen, TX 78501 USA.

Editores Mexicanos Unidos (MEX) *(978-968-15) Dist. by* **Ediciones.**

Editorial Anagrama S.A. (ESP) *(978-84-339) Dist. by* **Spanish.**

Editorial Betania *See* **Grupo Nelson**

Editorial Brief (ESP) *(978-84-931888) Dist. by* **IPG Chicago.**

Editorial Buenas Letras *Imprint of* **Rosen Publishing Group, Inc., The**

Editorial Busqueda, *(978-0-9744408; 978-0-9760652; 978-0-9798461; 978-0-9843607)* Calle Pinero, No. 113, San Juan, PR 00925-3612 USA.

Editorial Campana, *(978-0-9725611; 978-1-934370)* 19 W. 85th St., New York, NY 10024 USA (SAN 854-2791) Tel 212-721-4062 (phone/fax); *Imprints:* Campanita Books (Campanita Bks)
E-mail: gycultura@aol.com
Web site: http://www.editorialcampana.com
Dist(s): **Downtown Bk. Ctr., Inc.**

Editorial Cultural, Inc., *(978-1-56758; 978-84-399)* Orders Addr.: P.O. Box 21056, San Juan, PR 00928 USA; Edit Addr.: Calle Robles, No. 51, San Juan, PR 00928 USA
E-mail: angiev@editorialculturalpr.com; alamo48@gmail.com
Web site: http://www.editorialculturalpr.com.

Editorial de Nuevo Extremo S.A. (ARG) *(978-950-9681; 978-987-1068; 978-987-1427; 978-987-609) Dist. by* **IPG Chicago.**

Editorial Diana, S.A. (MEX) *(978-968-13) Dist. by* **Giron Bks.**

Editorial Diana, S.A. (MEX) *(978-968-13) Dist. by* **Continental Bk.**

Editorial Diana, S.A. (MEX) *(978-968-13) Dist. by* **Lectorum Pubns.**

Editorial Edaf, S.L. (ESP) *(978-84-7640; 978-84-7166; 978-84-414) Dist. by* **Spanish.**

Editorial El Antillano, Inc., *(978-0-9755661; 978-0-9793026; 978-1-7326361)* 104 Jefferson St., Suite 5-B, Santurce, PR 00911 USA Tel 787-982-4060
E-mail: olga_otero@mspr.net
Web site: http://www.elantillano.com.

Editorial Everest, S.A (ESP) *(978-84-441) Dist. by* **Lectorum Pubns.**

Editorial Flamboyant (ESP) *Dist. by* **Lectorum Pubns.**

Editorial Guipil *Imprint of* **Guipil Pr.**

Editorial Hidra (ESP) *Dist. by* **Lectorum Pubns.**

Editorial Homagno, *(978-0-9727467)* Div. of Homagno Group, Inc., P.O. Box 960227, Miami, FL 33296 USA
Web site: http://www.homagno.com.

Editorial Humanitas, *(978-0-9650104)* Orders Addr.: 2006 23rd Ave., E., Seattle, WA 98112-2936 USA Tel 206-616-9394
E-mail: oberle@mindspring.com
Web site: http://www.mindspring.com/~oberle/PRbirds.htm
Dist(s): **Representaciones Borinquenas, Inc.**

Editorial Imagen, *(978-1-64081; 978-1-64521)* 364 E Main St. Suite 1003, Middletown, DE 19709 USA; *Imprints:* Educando Kids (MYID_M_EDUCAND); Inspira (MYID_Y_INSPIRB).

Editorial John Louis von Neumann, Inc., *(978-0-9748297; 978-0-9779982)* Urb. Villa Fontana, 3NS-15 Via Lourdes, Carolina, PR 00983-4650 USA Tel 787-630-6330; Fax: 787-257-4979
E-mail: josejuandiaz@gmail.com
Web site: http://josejuandiaz.com
Dist(s): **Representaciones Borinquenas, Inc.**

Editorial Leetra (MEX) *Dist. by* **Lectorum Pubns.**

Editorial Libre Albedrio (ESP) *(978-84-947462; 978-84-944172; 978-84-942313) Dist. by* **Lectorum Pubns.**

Editorial Libros en Red, *(978-1-59754; 978-1-62915)* 5018 57th Ave., Apt. B8, Bladensburg, MD 20710 USA
E-mail: administracion@librosenred.com
Web site: http://www.librosenred.com
Dist(s): **Ediciones Universal.**

Editorial Libsa, S.A. (ESP) *(978-84-7630; 978-84-662) Dist. by* **Continental Bk.**

Editorial Libsa, S.A. (ESP) *(978-84-7630; 978-84-662) Dist. by* **Lectorum Pubns.**

Editorial Lumen (ESP) *(978-84-264) Dist. by* **Distribks Inc.**

Editorial Lumen (ESP) *(978-84-264) Dist. by* **Lectorum Pubns.**

Editorial Miglo Inc., *(978-0-9671705)* 1560 Grand Concourse, Apt. 504, Bronx, NY 10457 USA
E-mail: jcmalone01@aol.com
Web site: http://www.edimiglo.com.

Editorial Mundo Hispano *Imprint of* **Casa Bautista de Publicaciones**

Editorial Oceano de Mexico (MEX) *(978-607-400) Dist. by* **IPG Chicago.**

Editorial Panamericana, Inc., *(978-1-881744; 978-1-934139; 978-1-61725)* Orders Addr.: Urb. Puerto Nuevo 1336 F.d. Roosevelt Ave., San Juan, PR 00920 USA Tel 787-277-7988; Fax: 787-277-7240; Edit Addr.: P.O. Box 25189, San Juan, PR 00928-5189 USA Tel 787-277-7988; Fax: 787-277-7240
E-mail: info@editorialpanamericana.com; cbaez@editorialpanamericana.com
Web site: http://www.editorialpanamericana.com.

Editorial Pax (MEX) *(978-968-860; 978-968-461) Dist. by* **IPG Chicago.**

Editorial Planeta, S. A. (ESP) *(978-84-08; 978-84-320; 978-84-395; 978-84-8460; 978-970-37) Dist. by* **Lectorum Pubns.**

Editorial Planeta, S. A. (ESP) *(978-84-08; 978-84-320; 978-84-395; 978-84-8460; 978-970-37) Dist. by* **TwoRivers.**

Editorial Plaza Mayor, Inc., *(978-1-56328)* Avenida Ponce De Leon 1527, Barrio El Cinco, Rio Piedras, PR 00926 USA Tel 787-764-0455; Fax: 787-764-0465
E-mail: patrigut@prtc.net
Dist(s): **Continental Bk. Co., Inc.**
Ediciones Universal
Lectorum Pubns., Inc.
Libros Sin Fronteras.

Editorial Porrua (MEX) *(978-968-432; 978-968-452; 978-970-07) Dist. by* **Continental Bk.**

Editorial Portavoz *Imprint of* **Kregel Pubns.**

Editorial Resources, Inc., *(978-0-9745923)* 4510 Seneca St., Pasadena, TX 77504-3568 USA
E-mail: anng@editorial-resources.com
Web site: http://www.editorial-resources.com.

Editorial Sendas Antiguas, LLC, *(978-1-932789)* 1730 Leffingwell Ave., Grand Rapids, MI 49525-4532 USA Tel 616-365-9073 (phone/fax); 616-365-0699; Fax: 616-365-1990
E-mail: info@sendasantiguas.com; sales@sendasantiguas.com; greendykbill@aol.com
Web site: http://www.sendasantiguas.com
Dist(s): **Send The Light Distribution LLC.**

Editorial Sudamericana S.A. (ARG) *(978-950-07; 978-950-37) Dist. by* **Distribks Inc.**

Editorial Sudamericana S.A. (ARG) *(978-950-07; 978-950-37) Dist. by* **Lectorum Pubns.**

Editorial Unilit, *(978-0-7899; 978-0-945792; 978-1-56063)* Div. of Spanish Hse., Inc., 1360 NW 88th Ave., Miami, FL 33172-3093 USA (SAN 247-5979) Tel 305-592-6136; Fax: 305-592-0087; Toll Free: 800-767-7726
E-mail: sales1@unidial.com
Web site: http://www.editorialunilit.com/
Dist(s): **Bethany Hse. Pubs.**
Lectorum Pubns., Inc.
Pura Vida Bks., Inc.

Editorial Vida Abundante, *(978-0-9765828)* P.O. Box 1073, Fajardo, PR 00738 USA Tel 787-860-3555
Web site: http://www.vidaabundante.org.

Editorial Voluntad S.A. (COL) *(978-958-02) Dist. by* **Distr Norma.**

Editorial Voluntad S.A. (COL) *(978-958-02) Dist. by* **Continental Bk.**

Editorium, The, *(978-1-60096; 978-1-4341)* 3907 Marsha Dr., West Jordan, UT 84081 USA Tel 801-750-2498 Cell; *Imprints:* Boomer Books (BoomerBks); Classic Books Library (ClassicBks); Waking Lion Press (WakingLion)
E-mail: lyon.jack@gmail.com
Web site: http://www.editorium.com; http://www.wakinglionpress.com; http://www.templehillbooks.com.

Edivision Compania Editorial, S.A. de C.V. (MEX) *(978-968-890) Dist. by* **Continental Bk.**

Edizioni PIEMME spa (ITA) *(978-88-384; 978-88-566; 978-88-585) Dist. by* **Distribks Inc.**

Edmondson, Dayne *See* **Dark Star Publishing**

Edmund, Neo, *(978-0-9883808)* 15135 Ryon Ave., Bellflower, CA 90706 USA Tel 562-324-3860
E-mail: neo@neoedmund.com.

EDR, *(978-0-9794615)* P.O. Box 22, Waterport, NY 14571 USA
E-mail: sakina@edrsinc.com
Web site: http://www.edrsinc.com; http://www.omariworld.com.

EdTechLens, *(978-0-9912337)* 1834 Lenox Rd., SCHENECTADY, NY 12308 USA Tel 518-393-9460
E-mail: ellen@ellensenisi.com
Web site: https://www.edtechlens.com
Dist(s): **Follett School Solutions.**

Edu Designs, *(978-0-9795017; 978-1-7348434)* Orders Addr.: PO Box 660518 Apt B, Arcadia, CA 91066 USA Tel 626-940-4768; Edit Addr.: P.O. Box 660518, Arcadia, CA 91066 USA Tel 626-940-4768
E-mail: edudesigns.org@gmail.com
Web site: http://www.edudesigns.org.

Educa Vision Inc., *(978-1-881839; 978-1-58432; 978-1-62632; 978-1-64382)* 7550 NW 47th Ave., Coconut Creek, FL 33073 USA (SAN 760-873X) Tel 954-968-7433; Fax: 954-970-0330
E-mail: educa@aol.com
Web site: http://www.educavision.com; http://www.educabrazil.org; http://www.caribbeanstudiespress.com; www.educalanguage.com
Dist(s): **Follett School Solutions.**

Educando Kids *Imprint of* **Editorial Imagen**

Educare Pr., *(978-0-944638)* P.O. Box 17222, Seattle, WA 98107 USA Tel 206-782-4797; Fax: 206-782-4802 Do not confuse with EduCare, Colorado Springs, CO
E-mail: educarepress@hotmail.com
Web site: http://www.educarepress.com.

Education and More, Inc., *(978-0-9755809)* 1760 Clayton Cir., Cumming, GA 30040-7860 USA Tel 678-455-7667
E-mail: education@educationandmore.com
Web site: http://www.educationandmore.com.

Education Ctr., Inc., *(978-1-56234)* Orders Addr.: P.O. Box 9753, Greensboro, NC 27429 USA Tel 336-854-0309; Fax: 336-547-1590; Toll Free: 800-334-0298; Edit Addr.: 3515 W. Market St., Greensboro, NC 27403 USA (SAN 256-6311) Fax: 336-851-8218; 4224 Tudor Ln. Ste. 101, Greensboro, NC 27410-8145 (SAN 256-632X); *Imprints:* Mailbox Books, The (The Mailbox Bks)
E-mail: jmartin@theeducationcenter.com; mjones@themailbox.com
Web site: http://theeducationcenter.com; http://www.themailbox.com
Dist(s): **Sharpe, M.E. Inc.**

Education Services Australia Ltd. (AUS) *(978-1-86366; 978-0-9758070; 978-1-74200; 978-0-646-19608-4; 978-0-646-21423-8; 978-0-646-24402-0; 978-0-646-24701-4; 978-0-646-25530-9) Dist. by* **Cheng Tsui.**

Education That, LLC, *(978-0-692-73656-2; 978-0-692-77912-5; 978-0-9984254)* 5850 Waterloo Rd. Suite 140, Columbia, MD 21045 USA Tel 443-324-7388; 5850 Waterloo Rd. Suite 140, Columbia, MD 21045
E-mail: mbooker@educationthat.com
Web site: www.educationthat.com.

Educational Activities, Inc., *(978-0-7925; 978-0-89525; 978-0-914296; 978-1-55737)* Orders Addr.: P.O. Box 87, Baldwin, NY 11510 USA; Edit Addr.: 1947 Grand Ave., Baldwin, NY 11510 USA (SAN 207-4400) Tel 516-223-4666; Fax: 516-623-9282; Toll Free: 800-797-3223
E-mail: learn@edact.com
Web site: http://www.edact.com
Dist(s): **Follett School Solutions.**

Educational Adventures *See* **Mighty Kids Media**

Educational Adventures Publishing, *(978-0-9864134)* 12840 Normandy Ln., Los Altos Hills, CA 94022 USA Tel 650-948-5742
E-mail: easyandhealthycooking@yahoo.com.

Educational Consulting by Design, LLC, *(978-0-692-59277-9)* 216 Anderson Rd, Glenoma, WA 98336 USA Tel 360-280-8841
E-mail: jcollierllc@gmail.com.

Educational Development Corporation *See* **EDC Publishing**

Educational Dynamics, LLC, *(978-0-9987753)* 19400 Stubblefield Ln., Edmonad, OK 73012 USA Tel 405-341-4411
E-mail: dcastlerich@gmail.com
Web site: http://wwdonnacastlerichardson.com.

Educational Expertise, LLC, *(978-0-9713450)* 427 E. Belvedere Ave., Baltimore, MD 21212 USA
Web site: http://www.educationalexpertise.com.

Educational Impressions, *(978-0-910857; 978-1-56644)* Orders Addr.: P.O. Box 77, Hawthorne, NJ 07507 USA (SAN 274-4899) Tel 973-423-4666; Fax: 973-423-5569; Toll Free: 800-451-7450; Edit Addr.: 210 Sixth Ave., Hawthorne, NJ 07507 USA
E-mail: awpeller@word.net.att.net
Web site: http://www.awpeller.com
Dist(s): **Continental Bk. Co., Inc.**

Educational Media Corp., *(978-0-932796; 978-1-930572)* Orders Addr.: 1443 Old York Rd., Wartminster, PA 18974 USA Fax: 215-956-9041; Toll Free: 800-448-2197; Edit Addr.: 4256 Central Ave. NE, Minneapolis, MN 55421-2920 USA (SAN 212-4203) Tel 763-781-0088; Fax: 763-781-7753; Toll Free: 800-966-3382
E-mail: emedia@educationalmedia.com
Web site: http://www.educationalmedia.com.

Educational Publishing Concepts, Inc., *(978-1-892354)* P.O. Box 665, Wheaton, IL 60189 USA Tel 630-653-5336; Fax: 630-653-5368 Do not confuse with Educational Publishing Concepts, Inc., Walla Walla, WA
E-mail: Jerryw@newkidsmedia.com
Web site: http://www.newkidsmedia.com.

Educational Publishing LLC, *(978-1-60436)* Orders Addr.: 51 Saw Mill Pond Rd., Edison, NJ 08817-6025 USA Toll Free: 800-554-2296; Edit Addr.: 10 W. 33rd St. Rm. 910, New York, NY 10001-3306 USA (SAN 854-2422)
Web site: http://www.earlystartchild.com.

Educational Research & Applications, LLC, *(978-0-9762724)* P.O. Box 1242, Danville, CA 94526 USA.

Educational Resources, Inc., *(978-1-931574)* 1691 Highland Pkwy., Saint Paul, MN 55116 USA Tel 651-592-3688; Fax: 651-690-2188 Do not confuse with companies with same name in Shawnee Mission, KS, Columbia, SC, Elgin, IL
E-mail: Edres1691@aol.com
Web site: http://www.eduresources.org.

Educational Solutions, Inc., *(978-0-87825)* 99 University Pl., 6th Flr., New York, NY 10003-4555 USA (SAN 205-6186) Tel 212-674-2988 Do not confuse with Educational Solutions, Stafford, TX.

Educational Testing Service, *(978-0-88685)* P.O. Box 6108, Princeton, NJ 08541-6108 USA (SAN 238-034X) Tel 609-771-7243; Fax: 609-771-7385 Do not confuse with Educational Testing Service in Washington, DC
E-mail: lsavadge@ets.org; j.womack@ets.org; cbrodsky@ets.org
Web site: http://www.ets.org.

Educational Tools, Inc., *(978-0-9766802; 978-0-9774310; 978-1-933797)* 3500 Beachwood Ct., Suite 102, Jacksonville, FL 32224 USA Fax: 904-998-1941; Toll Free: 800-586-9940
E-mail: rpettus@educationaltools.org
Web site: http://www.educationaltools.org.

Educational Video Resources *See* **Summit Interactive**

Educators for the Environment *See* **Energy Education Group**

Educators Publishing Service, Inc., *(978-0-8388; 978-1-4293)* P.O. Box 9031, Cambridge, MA 02139-9031 USA (SAN 201-8225) Toll Free: 800-435-7728; 625 Mount Auburn St., Cambridge, MA 02138
E-mail: epsbooks@epsbooks.com
Web site: http://www.epsbooks.com.

Educ-Easy Bks., *(978-0-9664217; 978-0-9912724; 978-0-9864034; 978-0-9963893; 978-0-9968972; 978-1-7324211)* POB 6366, Greenville, SC 29606 USA Tel 910-798-5042
E-mail: gisela.hausmann@yahoo.com.

EDUKIT, L.L.C., *(978-0-9765917)* P.O. Box 821, Suffern, NY 10901 USA
E-mail: edukitco@aol.com
Web site: http://www.edukit.biz.

EduMatch, *(978-0-692-99178-7; 978-0-692-04640-1; 978-0-692-06333-0; 978-1-7322487; 978-1-970133; 978-1-953852)* P.O. Box 150324, Alexandria, VA 22192 USA Tel 703-398-0533; 415-862-8240
E-mail: sarah@edumatch.org; edumatchbooks@edumatchers.org
Web site: www.edumatch.org; www.edumatchpublishing.com
Dist(s): **CreateSpace Independent Publishing Platform.**

Edupress, Inc., *(978-1-56472)* P.O. Box 800, Fort Atkinson, WI 53538-0800 USA Toll Free: 800-835-7978 Do not confuse with EduPress, Pittsburgh, PA
E-mail: info@edupressinc.com
Web site: http://www.edupressinc.com.

Edu-Steps, Inc., *(978-0-9771101; 978-0-9863690)* Orders Addr.: 4644 N. 22nd St. Suite 1161, Phoenix, AZ 85016-4699 USA Tel 480-570-3888; Fax: 602-795-6837
E-mail: patdoran@edu-steps.com
Web site: http://www.edu-steps.com.

Edutech Learning Resource Ctr., *(978-0-9768208)* 1361 NE 158 St., North Miami Beach, FL 33162 USA Tel 305-947-6393
E-mail: edutech_learning@yahoo.com.

Edutunes, *(978-1-930979)* 2067 Rurline Dr., Saint Louis, MO 63146 USA Tel 808-728-8863
E-mail: missjenny@edutunes.com
Web site: http://www.edutunes.com.

Edward, Isaac Adams, *(978-0-692-80001-0)* 2527 S. Meridian St., Puyallup, WA 98373 USA Tel 206-886-5453
E-mail: menatiworld@hotmail.com.

Edwards, Idella, *(978-0-615-56814-0; 978-0-615-65355-6; 978-0-9896802; 978-0-9986662; 978-1-7327963)* 602 Lake Harbor Dr., Marion, IL 62959 USA Tel 618-997-5237
E-mail: idellapearl@frontier.com.

Edwards, Michael, *(978-0-9720952)* 310 N. Front St., Suite No. 4, Box 248, Wilmington, NC 28401 USA
E-mail: neversanever@hotmail.com.

Edwards, R. G. Publishing, *(978-0-615-13336-2; 978-0-615-16739-8; 978-0-615-17785-4)* P.O. Box 978, Goodlettsville, TN 37070 USA
Dist(s): **Lulu Pr., Inc.**

Edwards, R.G. Publlishing *See* **Edwards, R. G. Publishing**

ee publishing & productions, inc., *(978-0-9753843; 978-0-9798466)* P.O. Box 7006, Fairfax Station, VA 22039 USA Tel 703-256-1721 (phone/fax)
E-mail: info@eeppinc.com; lsaker@eepinc.com
Web site: http://www.eeppinc.com.

eeBoo Corp., *(978-1-59461; 978-1-68227)* 170 West 74th St., Ste. 102, New York, NY 10023 USA (SAN 860-4371) Fax: 212-678-1922
E-mail: christine@eeboo.com
Web site: http://www.eeboo.com.

Eelman's Pr., *(978-0-9747053)* Orders Addr.: P.O. Box Box 359, South Orleans, MA 02662 USA Tel 607-277-0612; Edit Addr.: Davis Rd., South Orleans, MA 02662 USA.

Eepie Pr., *(978-0-9755606)* 1412 Greenbrier Pkwy., Suite 145-B, Norfolk, VA 23320 USA Tel 757-424-5868; Fax: 757-424-5845
E-mail: info@eepiepress.com
Web site: http://www.eepiepress.com
Dist(s): **Print & Ship.**

Eerdmans Bks For Young Readers *Imprint of* **Eerdmans, William B. Publishing Co.**

†Eerdmans, William B. Publishing Co., *(978-0-8028; 978-1-4674)* 2140 Oak Industrial Dr NE, Grand Rapids, MI 49505 USA (SAN 220-0058) Tel 616-459-4591; Fax: 616-459-6540; Toll Free: 800-253-7521 (orders); *Imprints:* Eerdmans Books For Young Readers (Eerdmans Bks)
E-mail: info@eerdmans.com; customerservice@eerdmans.com
Web site: http://www.eerdmans.com
Dist(s): **Children's Plus, Inc.**
Faith Alive Christian Resources
Forward Movement Pubns.
INscribe Digital
Ingram Content Group
Send The Light Distribution LLC; *CIP.*

Eernisse, Rachel, *(978-0-692-97874-0)* 2320 W Windmill Ave, NAMPA, ID 83651 USA Tel 408-796-9963
E-mail: racheleernisse@gmail.com
Dist(s): **Ingram Content Group.**

Eeyagi Tales, *(978-1-7327679)* 225 Skyridge Dr, Atlanta, GA 30350 USA Tel 678-320-0386; Toll Free: 678-320-0386
Web site: www.eeyagitales.com
Dist(s): **CreateSpace Independent Publishing Platform.**

EFFE Bks., *(978-0-9773583)* P.O. Box 3448, Winter Park, FL 32790-23448 USA (SAN 257-3784) Tel 407-645-2326
E-mail: tfunaro@summittech.us
Web site: http://www.effebooks.com
Dist(s): **Midpoint Trade Bks., Inc.**

Effective Literacy Methods, *(978-0-9706094)* 57 Knollwood Dr., Rochester, NY 14618-3512 USA
E-mail: info@newphonics.com; rkb@newphonics.com
Web site: http://www.newphonics.com.

Efforts Unified, *(978-0-9763523)* 244 Fifth Ave., No. N259, New York, NY 10001 USA.

EG Bks., *(978-0-615-54589-9; 978-0-615-55920-9)* 360 Oak St., Oakfield, WI 53065 USA Tel 920-583-3329
E-mail: e.garner3@gmail.com.

Egap Gifa Bks. *Imprint of* **Leafcollecting.com Publishing Co.**

Egbert, Bill, *(978-0-9979779)* 3507 N Cole Rd No. 101, Boise, ID 83704-0770 USA
E-mail: begbert2@yahoo.com.

Egg Hill Pubns., *(978-0-9652351; 978-0-692-56474-5; 978-0-692-16533-1; 978-0-692-16534-8)* Orders Addr.: 113 Cottontail Ln., Centre Hall, PA 16828-8508 USA Tel 814-360-4401
E-mail: jandhfra2@yahoo.com
Dist(s): **Partners Bk. Distributing, Inc.**

Egger Publishing, Inc., *(978-1-886050; 978-1-934262)* P.O. Box 12248, Scottsdale, AZ 85267 USA Tel 480-596-5100; Fax: 480-951-2276; Toll Free: 888-937-7355
E-mail: regger@sittonspelling.com
Web site: http://www.sittonspelling.com
Dist(s): **Northwest Textbook Depository.**

EGM Pr., *(978-0-692-13687-4)* 2600 Somerset Dr., Nashville, TN 37217 USA Tel 615-917-4473
E-mail: karuis@comcast.net.

Egmont Bks., Ltd. (GBR) *(978-0-416; 978-0-603; 978-0-7497; 978-0-7498; 978-1-4052; 978-0-7555; 978-1-78031) Dist. by* **HarperCollins Pubs.**

Egmont Bks., Ltd. (GBR) *(978-0-416; 978-0-603; 978-0-7497; 978-0-7498; 978-1-4052; 978-0-7555; 978-1-78031) Dist. by* **Children Plus.**

Egmont Bks., Ltd. (GBR) *(978-0-416; 978-0-603; 978-0-7497; 978-0-7498; 978-1-4052; 978-0-7555; 978-1-78031) Dist. by* **IPG Chicago.**

Egmont Bks., Ltd. (GBR) *(978-0-416; 978-0-603; 978-0-7497; 978-0-7498; 978-1-4052; 978-0-7555; 978-1-78031) Dist. by* **Trafalgar.**

Ehly, Bridgette, *(978-1-7328733)* 3005 Darby Creek Dr., Crestwood, KY 40014 USA Tel 502-905-7376
E-mail: bridgettejacobs@gmail.com
Web site: excellentfiction.com.

Eifrig Publishing, *(978-0-9795518; 978-1-936172; 978-1-63233)* P.O. Box 66, Lemont, PA 16851-0066 USA (SAN 858-6462) Fax: 888-340-6543; Toll Free: 888-340-6543
E-mail: contact@eifrigpublishing.com
Web site: http://www.eifrigpublishing.com
Dist(s): **Baker & Taylor Publisher Services (BTPS)**
BookBaby
Follett School Solutions.

Eileen Reno Maurer, *(978-0-692-16262-0; 978-0-578-40857-6; 978-0-578-42376-0; 978-0-578-42377-7)* 2241 Baxter Canyon Rd., VISTA, CA 92081 USA Tel 760-420-5938
E-mail: eileenmaurer@yahoo.com
Dist(s): **Ingram Content Group.**

Eileen/Morris *See* **Shnoozles, LLC**

EJMP, *(978-0-615-77563-0)* 2421 SW Candletree Dr Apt 6, Topeka, KS 66614 USA Tel 785-338-0625
Dist(s): **CreateSpace Independent Publishing Platform.**

EK Success Ltd., *(978-1-930232)* P.O. Box 1141, Clifton, NJ 07014-1141 USA Tel 973-458-0092; Fax: 973-594-0545; Toll Free: 800-524-1349
E-mail: success@eksuccess.com
Web site: http://www.eksuccess.com.

EKADOO Publishing Group, *(978-0-9747387)* Orders Addr.: P.O. Box 2286, North Redondo Beach, CA 90278 USA Toll Free: 877-252-3404; Edit Addr.: 123 West First St., Suite 675, Casper, WY 82601 USA
E-mail: info@ekadoo.com
Web site: http://www.ekadoo.com.

Ekaré,
Dist(s): **Lectorum Pubns., Inc.**

Ekaré Europa S.L. (ESP) *(978-84-933060; 978-84-934863; 978-84-936504; 978-84-937212; 978-84-937767; 978-84-936843; 978-84-938429; 978-84-939138; 978-84-939912; 978-84-940256; 978-84-941247; 978-84-941716; 978-84-942081; 978-84-943038; 978-84-944050; 978-84-944291; 978-84-946699; 978-84-947431) Dist. by* **Lectorum Pubns.**

Ekare, Ediciones (VEN) *(978-980-257; 978-84-8351; 978-84-937212; 978-84-937767) Dist. by* **Mariuccia Iaconi Bk Imports.**

Ekare, Ediciones (VEN) *(978-980-257; 978-84-8351; 978-84-937212; 978-84-937767) Dist. by* **Lectorum Pubns.**

Eklektika Pr., Inc., *(978-0-9651672; 978-0-9765465; 978-0-9823250)* Orders Addr.: P.O. Box 157, Chelsea, MI 48118 USA Tel 734-730-5161; Edit Addr.: 6401 Conway Rd., Chelsea, MI 48118 USA
Web site: http://www.theseniorsguide.com; http://www.meandmycaregivers.com
Dist(s): **Alliance Bk. Co.**
Distributors, The.

EKR Pubns., *(978-0-9791348)* 257 N. Calderwood St., #356, Alcoa, TN 37701-2111 USA (SAN 852-5293) Tel 727-517-2767 (publisher contact); Toll Free Fax: 866-790-0417 (orders/publisher); Toll Free: 800-266-5564 (orders/AtlasBooks)
Web site: http://www.willigetsahistorylesson.com; http://www.ekrpublications.com.

Ekwike Books & Publishing *See* **Orange County Publishing**

El Aleph Editores, S.A. (ESP) *(978-84-7669; 978-84-85501) Dist. by* **Ediciones.**

El Assali, Amira, *(978-0-9777650)* 23842 Alicia Pkwy Apt. 248, Mission Viejo, CA 92691 USA Tel 714-478-2114
E-mail: amiraalassaly@hotmail.com.

El Brown Training Solutions, *(978-0-9909512)* 2987 District Ave, Fairfax, VA 22031 USA Tel 571-422-3636
E-mail: elbrown@kinderjam.com
Web site: www.elbrowntrainings.com.

El Cid Editor Incorporated, *(978-0-9669968; 978-1-4135; 978-1-4492; 978-1-5129)* Div. of E-Libro Corp., 17555 Atlantic Blvd. # 4, Sunny Isl Bch, FL 33160-2996 USA; 16699 Collins Ave., No. 1003, Miami, FL 33160 Tel 305-466-0155
E-mail: editor@e-libro.com
Web site: http://www.e-libro.net; http://www.e-libro.com
Dist(s): **MyiLibrary**
ProQuest LLC
ebrary, Inc.

El Gato de Hojalata (ARG) *(978-987-668; 978-987-705; 978-987-751) Dist. by* **Peng Rand Hse.**

El Hogar y La Moda, S.A. (ESP) *(978-84-7183) Dist. by* **AIMS Intl.**

El Jefe, *(978-0-9742840)* P.O. Box 7871, Pueblo West, CO 81007 USA
E-mail: rearch145@aol.com.

El Publications *See* **Jesus Estanislado**

El Zarape Pr., *(978-0-9789954; 978-0-692-69574-6; 978-0-692-72032-5; 978-1-7328106)* 1413 Jay Ave., McAllen, TX 78504-3327 USA (SAN 852-1514)
E-mail: elzarapepress@gmail.com
Dist(s): **CreateSpace Independent Publishing Platform.**

Eland' Ra, *(978-0-9862361)* 27 Ellsworth Rd., West Hartford, CT 06107 USA Tel 860-543-3302
E-mail: elandra4444@gmail.com
Web site: www.ElandraArts.com.

Elder Star Pr., *(978-0-578-41282-5; 978-0-578-49060-1; 978-0-578-58687-8)* 3617 Homeway Dr., Los Angeles, CA 90008 USA Tel 614-266-7482
E-mail: johndbuell3@gmail.com
Dist(s): **Independent Pub.**

Elderberry Press, Inc., *(978-0-9658407; 978-1-930859; 978-1-932762; 978-1-934956)* 1393 Old Homestead Rd., Oakland, OR 97462 USA (SAN 254-6604) Tel 541-459-6043 Do not confuse with Elderberry Pr., Encinitas, CA
E-mail: editor@elderberrypress.com
Web site: http://www.elderberrypress.com
Dist(s): **Smashwords.**

Eldergivers, *(978-0-9742262)* 1755 Clay St., San Francisco, CA 94109 USA
E-mail: info@eldergivers.org
Web site: http://www.eldergivers.org.

Eldorado Ink, *(978-1-932904; 978-1-61900)* P.O. Box 100097, Pittsburgh, PA 15233-4842 USA Tel 412-688-0444; Fax: 412-688-8545; Toll Free: 800-783-6767
E-mail: info@eldoradoink.com
Web site: http://www.eldoradoink.com.

Elea Pr., *(978-0-615-34357-0; 978-0-615-67531-2; 978-0-615-75642-4; 978-0-692-21410-7)* 7922 Sequoia Dr., Roanoke, VA 24019 USA
Web site: http://www.nursiesbook.com; http://www.nightweaning.com
Dist(s): **Ingram Content Group.**

eLectio Publishing, *(978-0-615-77551-7; 978-0-615-79001-5; 978-0-615-79469-3; 978-0-615-79864-6; 978-0-615-80543-6; 978-0-615-81846-7; 978-0-615-82555-7; 978-0-615-82645-5; 978-0-615-83096-4; 978-0-615-83772-7; 978-0-615-83878-6; 978-0-615-84548-7; 978-0-615-85867-8; 978-0-615-87769-3; 978-0-615-88179-9; 978-0-615-88473-8; 978-0-615-90365-1; 978-0-615-90866-3; 978-0-615-91122-9; 978-0-615-91680-4; 978-0-615-92441-0; 978-0-615-93116-6; 978-0-615-93337-5; 978-0-615-93550-8; 978-0-615-93822-6; 978-0-615-94869-0;) 1361 Bristol Ln., Aubrey, TX 76227 USA Tel 2149988361*
Web site: http://www.eLectioPublishing.com
Dist(s): **CreateSpace Independent Publishing Platform**
Ingram Publisher Services.

Electret Scientific Co., *(978-0-917406)* P.O. Box 4132, Star City, WV 26504 USA (SAN 206-4715) Tel 304-594-1639 (phone/fax)
E-mail: U1a00439@wvnet.edu.

Electric Moon Publishing, *(978-1-943027)* P.O. Box 466, Stromsburg, NE 68666 USA Tel 402-366-2033
E-mail: laree.lindburg@gmail.com
Web site: www.emoonpublishing.com
Dist(s): **Whitaker Hse.**

Electric Theatre Radio Hour, *(978-0-9848486)* 2200 Market St. Suite 735, Galveston, TX 77550 USA Tel 409-750-8915
E-mail: brendadonaloio@sbcglobal.net.

Eleftheria Publishing, *(978-0-9826040)* 6041 N. Fifth Pl., Phoenix, AZ 85012 USA Tel 602-214-5695
E-mail: michael@michaelenewton.com
Web site: http://www.eleftheriapublishing.com
Dist(s): **Ingram Content Group.**

Elemental Pubs., *(978-0-9765403)* 4404 Whistling Way, Raleigh, NC 27616 USA Tel 919-217-2092.

Elemental Publishing LLC *See* **Elemental Science Inc.**

Elemental Science Inc., *(978-1-935614; 978-1-953490)* 1800 Kraft DR Suite 207, Blacksburg, VA 24060 USA
E-mail: info@elementalscience.com
Web site: http://www.elementalscience.com.

Elena Marcus Negoita, *(978-0-615-57545-2)* 2240 Blake St. No. 315, Berkeley, CA 94704 USA
Web site: www.doghappiness.net
Dist(s): **CreateSpace Independent Publishing Platform.**

Elephant Rock Bks. YA *Imprint of* **Elephant Rock Productions, Inc.**

Elephant Rock Productions, Inc., *(978-0-9753746; 978-0-615-43463-6; 978-0-615-52977-6; 978-0-9846700; 978-0-9895155; 978-0-9968649; 978-1-7324141)* Orders Addr.: P.O. Box 119, Ashford, CT 06278 USA Fax: 860-477-0845; *Imprints:* Elephant Rock Books YA (MYID_X_ELEPHAN)
E-mail: elephantrockorders@gmail.com
Web site: http://www.erpmedia.net/books
Dist(s): **Follett School Solutions**
INscribe Digital
Independent Pubs. Group
MyiLibrary.

ElephantSide Pr., *(978-0-9716873)* 33 Bedford St., Suite 10, Lexington, MA 02420 USA (SAN 255-4062).

Eleuthera Press *See* **Windsong Publishing Co.**

Elevé Arts Publishing *See* **Eleve Publishing**

Elevator Group, The, *(978-0-9786854; 978-0-9820384; 978-0-9819719; 978-0-9824945; 978-0-9825282)* P.O. Box 207, Paoli, PA 19301 USA (SAN 851-3104) Tel 610-296-4966; Fax: 610-644-4436; P.O. Box 207, Paoli, PA 19301 Tel 610-296-4966; Fax: 610-644-4436
E-mail: TheElevatorGroup@comcast.net
Web site: http://www.TheElevatorGroup.com; http://www.TEGFaith.com
Dist(s): **MyiLibrary**
ebrary, Inc.

Eleve Publishing, *(978-0-9827304)* 3001 S. Jay St., Denver, CO 80227 USA Tel 720-560-2448
E-mail: larryelwood@gmail.com.

Eleviv Publishing Group, *(978-0-615-61316-1; 978-0-9886289; 978-0-615-89408-9; 978-0-615-98912-9; 978-0-615-99808-4; 978-0-615-99962-3; 978-0-692-22473-1; 978-0-692-30857-8; 978-0-692-35753-8; 978-0-692-35754-5; 978-0-692-40653-3; 978-0-692-42663-0; 978-0-692-42723-1; 978-0-692-45815-0; 978-0-692-45827-3; 978-0-692-56068-6; 978-0-692-57879-7; 978-0-692-59882-5; 978-0-692-65038-7; 978-0-692-66118-5; 978-0-692-72894-9; 978-0-692-06694-2; 978-0-692-08511-0; 978-0-692-13413-9; 978-0-578-44137-5; 978-0-578-44138-2; 978-)*
Web site: www.elevivpublishing.com
Dist(s): **CreateSpace Independent Publishing Platform.**

Elf Garb, *(978-0-615-64129-4; 978-0-9881822)* 96 Idlewell Bld, Weymouth, MA 02188 USA Tel 781-331-7949
E-mail: kelley@elfgarb.com
Web site: www.elfgarb.com.

Elfa Bks., *(978-0-578-10974-9; 978-0-578-10978-7; 978-0-578-11908-3; 978-0-578-12216-8; 978-0-578-12227-4; 978-0-578-12965-5; 978-0-578-12975-4; 978-0-578-13661-5; 978-0-578-13735-3)* 14967 Merlot Dr., Sterling Heights, MI 48312 USA Tel 586-634-4321
E-mail: elfabooks@yahoo.com
Web site: http://www.elfabooks.com.

Elfen Media, *(978-0-9992311)* P.O. Box 66103, Austin, TX 78766 USA Tel 512-333-4600
E-mail: c.bair@christopherbair.com
Web site: http://www.elfenmedia.com/.

Elgar, Edward Publishing, Inc., *(978-1-84064; 978-1-85278; 978-1-85898; 978-1-84376; 978-1-84542; 978-1-84720)* Orders Addr.: P.O. Box 960, Herndon, VA 20172-0960 USA Tel 800-390-3149; Fax: 802-864-7626; Edit Addr.: 9 Dewey Ct., Northampton, MA 01060-3815 USA (SAN 299-4615)
E-mail: elgarinfo@e-elgar.com; kwight@e-elgar.com; asturmer@e-elgar.com
Web site: http://www.e-elgar.com
Dist(s): **Books International, Inc.**
MyiLibrary.

Elgea Publishing, *(978-0-9972884)* 11960 Tivoli Pk. Row, San Diego, CA 92128 USA Tel 858-649-6311
E-mail: chornermd108@aol.com
Web site: www.drchristinehorner.com.

Elias Pubns., LLC, *(978-0-9726247)* P.O. Box 49704, Sarasota, FL 34230 USA Tel 941-556-5656; Fax: 720-920-7262
E-mail: eliaspublications@hotmail.com
Web site: http://www.eliaspublications.com.

Eliassen Creative, *(978-1-937160; 978-0-9892097)* 10328 Horseback Ridge Ave., las Vegas, NV 89144 USA Tel 702-328-2637
E-mail: sunshinenelson@hotmail.com.

eLiberty Pr., *(978-0-9755608)* 2250 N. University Pkwy. No. 4888, Provo, UT 84604 USA Tel 801-427-6630; Fax: 801-373-5999
E-mail: info@elibertypress.com; sales@elibertypress.com
Web site: http://www.elibertypress.com
Dist(s): **Alibris**
Powells.com.

Elim Publishing, *(978-0-9713711; 978-1-59919)* Div. of Elim Gospel Church, 1679 Dalton Rd., Lima, NY 14485 USA Tel 716-624-5560; Fax: 716-624-9677
E-mail: randy@elimpublishing.com
Web site: http://www.elimpublishing.com
Dist(s): **Ingram Content Group.**

Elissian Publishing Co., *(978-0-615-47664-3)* 9715 FM 620 N No. 11203, Austin, TX 78726 USA Tel 512-913-5553; Fax: 512-436-9796
E-mail: demiolesen@hotmail.com.

Elizabeth Dettling Moreno *See* **Dettling Moreno, Elizabeth**

Elizabooks, *(978-0-9762839)* 5515 Catfish Ct., Waunakee, WI 53597 USA Tel 608-849-1984; Fax: 608-849-1985; Toll Free: 888-603-1984
E-mail: liz@elizabookspublishing.com
Web site: http://www.elizabooks.com.

Elk Lake Publishing, Inc., *(978-0-9793543; 978-0-9913727; 978-0-9903062; 978-0-692-32584-1; 978-1-942513; 978-1-944430; 978-1-946638; 978-1-948888; 978-1-950051; 978-1-951080; 978-1-951970; 978-1-64949)* 35 Dogwood Dr, Plymouth, MA 02360 USA (SAN 853-2001) Tel 508-746-1734
Web site: http://elklakepublishing.com.

Elk River Pr., *(978-0-9710389)* 1125 Central Ave., Charleston, WV 25302 USA Tel 304-342-1848; Fax: 304-343-0594 Do not confuse with companies with the same or similar name in Altamont, KS, Athens, AL.
E-mail: wvbooks@verizon.net
Web site: http://www.wvbookco.com
Dist(s): **West Virginia Book Co., The.**

Elkarez Publishing Co., *(978-0-9819100)* 327 Sheldon Ave., Staten Island, NY 10312 USA Tel 718-966-5205
E-mail: info@elkarezpublishing.com
Web site: http://www.elkarezpublishing.com.

Eller Books *See* **Brethren Pr.**

Ellie Claire *Imprint of* **Worthy Publishing**

Elliott, Ann T, *(978-0-692-18507-0)* 601 E. Micheltorena St. Unit 105, Santa Barbara, CA 93103 USA Tel 707-694-1914
E-mail: annelliottart@gmail.com
Dist(s): **Ingram Content Group.**

Elliott, Jane, *(978-0-9741254)* 707 Country Club Rd., Schofield, WI 54476 USA; *Imprints:* Dynagraphix (Dynagraphix).

Ellipsis Pr., *(978-0-9637536; 978-1-940400)* 3555 78th St., #41, New York, NY 11372 USA Tel 718-840-9373 Do not confuse with Ellipsis Pr. in Campbell, CA
E-mail: info@ellipsispress.com
Web site: http://www.ellipsispress.com
Dist(s): **SPD-Small Pr. Distribution.**

Ellis Pr., The, *(978-0-933180; 978-0-944024)* Div. of Spoon River Poetry Pr., P.O. Box 6, Granite Falls, MN 56241 USA (SAN 214-008X) Tel 507-537-6463 Do not confuse with Ellis Pr., in Charlottesville, VA
E-mail: pichaske@southwest.msus.edu
Web site: http://www.southwest.msus.edu/faculty/pichaske/plains.htm.

Ellison, Penny, *(978-0-9771121)* Orders Addr.: P.O. Box 510082, Miami, FL 33151 USA Tel 786-222-1443; Edit Addr.: 4877 Registry Ln NW, Kennesaw, GA 30152-2891 USA.

Elm Grove Publishing, *(978-1-943492)* 351 Sharon Dr., San Antonio, TX 78216 USA Tel 210-683-9716
E-mail: diane@elmgrovepublishing.com
Web site: www.elmgrovepublishing.com.

Elm Hill, Div. of HarperCollins Christian Publishing, 836 S. Western Dr., Bloomington, IN 47403 USA Tel 317-552-0111; Toll Free: 888-880-4403
Web site: https://elmhillbooks.com
Dist(s): **Nelson, Thomas Inc.**

Elma Colletes & Sons, *(978-0-9719337)* 5895 Gardens Reach Cove, Memphis, TN 38120-2523 USA Fax: 901-747-0040
E-mail: mschnap1@midsouth.rr.com.

Elmdale Park Books, *(978-0-9860593)* PO BOX 26553, OVERLAND PARK, KS 66225 USA Tel 913-908-0129; Fax: 913-945-1426
E-mail: tekobernard@yahoo.com
Web site: www.tekobernard.com.

Elnoir Jane Publishing, *(978-0-578-45111-4)* 6200 E. Sam Houston Pkwy. N. No. 8202, Houston, TX 77049 USA Tel 832-874-8897
E-mail: lashandramhall@gmail.com
Dist(s): **Ingram Content Group.**

Elohim Bks., *(978-0-9768831)* Orders Addr.: P.O. Box 1027, Howell, MI 48844 USA.

Eloquence Pr., *(978-0-9753300; 978-0-9824954; 978-0-9913283; 978-0-692-89832-1)* Orders Addr.: 51689 Via Bendita, La Quinta, CA 92253 USA (SAN 255-9676) Tel 760-698-8482
E-mail: jeadon@cox.net; jeadon2@gmail.com
Web site: http://www.eadonbooks.com; http://www.theamericandramaseries.com; http://.

Eloquent Bks. *Imprint of* **Strategic Book Publishing & Rights Agency (SBPRA)**

Eloquent Rascals, *(978-0-9907094; 978-0-9989949)* 30 Lorden Ln., Weare, NH 03281 USA Tel 845-787-3832
E-mail: eloquentrascals@gmail.com
Web site: www.EloquentRascals.com.

Elora Media, LLC, *(978-0-9786813)* PMB 112, 1201 Yelm Ave., Yelm, WA 98597-9859 USA Tel 360-894-6369
E-mail: betsy@eloramedia.com.

Elora Pr., *(978-0-9786813)* Div. of Elora Media, LLC, PMB 112, 1201 Yelm Ave., Yelm, WA 98597-9859 USA (SAN 851-3228) Toll Free: 888-440-8972
E-mail: betsy@eloramedia.com
Web site: http://www.eloramedia.com.

Elotos Pr., LLC, *(978-0-9821737)* 1220 N. Market St., Suite 808, Wilmington, DE 19808 USA
E-mail: info@elotos.com
Web site: http://www.ELOTOS.com.

ELP Bks., *(978-0-9841650)* P.O. Box 1506, Gardena, CA 90249 USA (SAN 858-6098) Tel 213-928-6724
E-mail: emmja_p@sbcglobal.net
Web site: http://www.elpbooks.net.

Elsevier *Imprint of* **Elsevier - Health Sciences Div.**

Elsevier - Health Sciences Div., *(978-0-323; 978-0-443; 978-0-444; 978-0-7020; 978-0-7216; 978-0-7234; 978-0-7236; 978-0-7506; 978-0-8016; 978-0-8151; 978-0-920513; 978-0-932883; 978-1-55664; 978-1-56053; 978-1-898507; 978-1-932141; 978-1-4160; 978-1-4377; 978-1-4557)* Subs. of Elsevier Science, Orders Addr.: a/o Customer Service, 3251 Riverport Ln., Maryland Heights, MO 63043 USA Tel 314-453-7010; Fax: 314-447-8030; Toll Free Fax: 800-535-9935; Toll Free: 800-545-2522; 800-460-3110 (Customers Outside US); 1799 Highway 50, Linn, MO 65051 (SAN 200-2280); Edit Addr.: 1600 John F. Kennedy Blvd., Suite 1800, Philadelphia, PA 19103-2899 USA Tel 215-239-3900; Fax: 215-239-3990; Toll Free: 800-523-4069; *Imprints:* Mosby (MosElsHlth); Elsevier (ElsevHlth)
E-mail: usbkinfo@elsevier.com
Web site: http://www.elsevier.com; http://www.us.elsevierhealth.com/
Dist(s): **Elsevier**
MyiLibrary
TNT Media Group, Inc.
ebrary, Inc.

Elsevier Science - Health Sciences Division *See* **Elsevier - Health Sciences Div.**

Elsewhere Editions *Imprint of* **Steerforth Pr.**

Elsie Publishing Co., *(978-1-7327573)* 2950 Van Ness St. NW Apt 319, Washington, DC 20008 USA Tel 202-670-3282
E-mail: elsie1guerrero@gmail.com
Web site: www.elsieguerrero.com.

Eltsar Pr., *(978-0-9769275; 978-0-9833990; 978-0-9850892)* 40453 Cherokee Oaks Dr., Three Rivers, CA 93271-9617 USA Tel 559-561-3270
Dist(s): **Lulu Pr., Inc.**

Elucidate Publishing, *(978-0-615-18146-2; 978-0-615-18228-5; 978-0-9825299; 978-0-9887120; 978-1-948370)* P.O. Box 1262, Hermitage, PA 16148 USA Do not confuse with Elucidate Publishing in Salt Lake City, UT
Web site: http://www.ellamkaye.com; http://www.lkhunsaker.com; http://www.elucidations.us
Dist(s): **Lulu Pr., Inc.**
Smashwords.

Elv Enterprises, *(978-0-9829669)* P.O. Box 2225, La Jolla, CA 92038 USA Tel 858-336-6499
E-mail: rainierpage@ymail.com.

Elva Resa Publishing, LLC, *(978-0-9657483; 978-1-934617)* 8362 Tamarack Village, Suite 119-106, Saint Paul, MN 55125 USA Tel 651-357-8770 orders & general info; Fax: 501-641-0777 orders accepted by fax; *Imprints:* Alma Little (Alma Little)
E-mail: orders@elvaresa.com
Web site: http://www.elvaresa.com
Dist(s): **Follett School Solutions**
Independent Pubs. Group.

ELW Pubns., *(978-0-9766233)* 1831 Secretary's Rd., Scottsville, VA 24590 USA Tel 434-295-1678; *Imprints:* His Grace Is Sufficient (HGIS)
E-mail: bridgeministry@aol.com.

Elysian Editions *Imprint of* **Princeton Bk. Co. Pubs.**

Elysian Hills, (*978-0-9635589*) Orders Addr.: P.O. Box 40693, Albuquerque, NM 87196 USA Tel 505-897-2734; Fax: 505-897-4614; Edit Addr.: 919 Western Meadows, Albuquerque, NM 87114 USA E-mail: EdDziczek@aol.com.

Elytra & Antenna, (*978-0-9719129; 978-0-9802401*) 4663 Ruby Ln., Brunswick Hills, OH 44212 USA Tel 330-273-1918 E-mail: elytraandantenna@lycos.com Web site: http://www.elytraandantenna.com.

ELZ Publishing, (*978-0-9772717*) 33 Sheridan Rd., Wellesley, MA 02481 USA Tel 781-237-7417; Fax: 781-237-7429 E-mail: elzahniser@mindspring.com Web site: http://elzpublishing.com.

EM Greenberg Pr., Inc., (*978-0-9634561; 978-0-615-40288-8*) 1245 Sixteenth St., Suite 210, Santa Monica, CA 90402 USA Tel 310-454-0502 (phone/fax) E-mail: elainergordonphd@gmail.com Web site: http://elainegordon.com.

Emaculate Publishing, (*978-1-931855*) P.O. Box 1804, Woodbridge, VA 22195-1074 USA (SAN 254-2005) E-mail: emaculatepublishing@yahoo.com; info@emaculatepublishing.com Web site: http://www.emaculatepublishing.com.

eMaginationFlow, Incorporated *See* **CuriousDots**

Eman Publishing, (*978-0-9841275; 978-1-935948*) P.O. Box 404, Fishers, IN 46038 USA Web site: http://www.EmanPublishing.com.

Emarketing Of Michigan, LLC, (*978-0-615-38985-1; 978-0-615-88247-5*) Orders Addr.: 11127 Kings Ct., Sterling Heights, MI 48312 USA Tel 586-838-0099; Fax: 586-275-2295 Web site: http://www.readwithmax.com; http://www.emarketingofmichigan.com.

Ember *Imprint of* **Random Hse. Children's Bks.**

Ember, (*978-0-692-90256-1; 978-0-578-49336-7*) 15520 Mill Creek Blvd., Mill Creek, WA 98012 USA Tel 858-722-4339 E-mail: annaholmeswritesbooks@gmail.com *Dist(s):* **CreateSpace Independent Publishing Platform.**

Embolden Bks., (*978-1-7322526*) P.O. Box 1228, Cairo, NY 12413 USA Tel 518-819-1662 E-mail: childofmuses@gmail.com.

Embrace Communications, (*978-0-9668878*) 6887 Red Mountain Rd., Livermore, CO 80536 USA Tel 970-416-9076; Fax: 970-407-0083 E-mail: suengayReynolds@aol.com *Dist(s):* **Spring Arbor Distributors, Inc.**

Embracing Life, (*978-0-9985540*) 709 Phar Lap Ln., Bahama, NC 27503 USA Tel 919-308-8889 E-mail: lfovercash@gmail.com.

EMC Publishing, (*978-0-9884707; 978-0-692-36034-7*) 11718 S.E. Federal Hwy. #245, Hobe Sound, FL 33455 USA Tel 504-669-9099.

†EMC/Paradigm Publishing, (*978-0-7638; 978-0-8219; 978-0-88436; 978-0-912022; 978-1-56118; 978-1-5338*) Div. of EMC Corp., 875 Montreal Way, Saint Paul, MN 55102 USA (SAN 201-3800) Toll Free Fax: 800-328-4564; Toll Free: 800-328-1452 E-mail: publish@emcp.com; educate@emcp.com Web site: http://www.emcp.com *Dist(s):* **Continental Bk. Co., Inc.**; *CIP.*

Emecé Editores S.A. (ARG) (*978-950-04; 978-950-519*) *Dist. by* **Planeta.**

Emecé Editores S.A. (ARG) (*978-950-04; 978-950-519*) *Dist. by* **Lectorum Pubns.**

Emece Editores (ESP) (*978-84-95908*) *Dist. by* **Ediciones.**

Emece Editores (ESP) (*978-84-95908*) *Dist. by* **Lectorum Pubns.**

EMedia Corp., (*978-1-891155*) 664 NE Northlake Way, Seattle, WA 98105-6428 USA Toll Free: 888-363-3424 E-mail: custserv@emediamusic.com Web site: http://www.emediamusic.com.

Emerald *Imprint of* **Emerald Bk. Co.**

Emerald Bk. Co., (*978-1-934572; 978-1-937110*) Div. of Greenleaf Bk. Group, 4425 Mo Pac Expy., Suite 600, Austin, TX 78735 USA; *Imprints:* Emerald (Emerald USA) *Dist(s):* **Greenleaf Book Group** **MyiLibrary.**

Emerald Bks., (*978-1-883002; 978-1-932096; 978-1-62486*) Orders Addr.: P.O. Box 635, Lynnwood, WA 98046 USA (SAN 298-7538) Tel 425-771-1153; Fax: 425-775-2383; Toll Free: 800-922-2143; Edit Addr.: 7825 230th St. SW, Edmonds, WA 98026 USA Do not confuse with Emerald Bks. in Westfield, NJ E-mail: wlwalsh@seanet.com Web site: http://www.ywampublishing.com *Dist(s):* **YWAM Publishing.**

Emerald City Publishing, (*978-0-9675082*) Do not confuse with A Class Act, Sierra Madre, CA E-mail: eagle3.fox1@gmail.com.

Emerald Funding Corp, (*978-0-692-52542-5; 978-0-692-80620-3; 978-0-692-12589-2*) 7029 Caviro Ln., BOYNTON BEACH, FL 33437 USA Tel 954-961-3352.

Emerald Hse. Group, Inc., (*978-1-889893; 978-1-932307; 978-1-935507; 978-1-62020; 978-1-64960*) 411 Univ. Ridge, Suite B14, Greenville, SC 29601 USA Tel 864-235-2434; Fax: 864-235-2491; Toll Free: 800-209-8570; *Imprints:* Ambassador-Emerald, International (Ambassador-Emerald); Ambassador International (Ambassador Intl) E-mail: info@emeraldhouse.com Web site: http://www.emeraldhouse.com; www.ambassador-international.com *Dist(s):* **Christian Bk. Distributors** **Follett School Solutions** **Spring Arbor Distributors, Inc.**

Emerald Light Pr., (*978-0-9990977*) 20229 Darlington Dr., Montgomery Village, MD 20886 USA Tel 301-651-9881 E-mail: kate@katekennelly.com Web site: http://www.katekennelly.com.

Emerald Shamrock Pr. LLC, (*978-0-9841880*) 1031 Parkland Rd., Lake Orion, MI 48360 USA (SAN 858-6675) Tel 248-393-6082 E-mail: bridget.mary@comcast.net Web site: http://www.onechildoneplanet.com.

Emerald Star Pr., (*978-0-615-29908-2; 978-0-615-36644-9; 978-0-615-39280-6; 978-0-9831993*) P.O. Box 2621, Atlanta, GA 30331 USA.

Emerson & Tilman, (*978-0-9827835; 978-1-947151*) 129 17th St., Suite 55, Washougal, WA 98671 USA Tel 360-835-3543 E-mail: Blythe@1blythe.com.

EmersonInk, (*978-1-7323603*) 46 Grandview Ave., White Plains, NY 10605 USA Tel 917-273-5353 E-mail: salwaemerson@gmail.com *Dist(s):* **CreateSpace Independent Publishing Platform.**

EMI CMG Distribution, E-mail: distribution@emicmg.com Web site: http://www.emicmgdistribution.com.

Emidra Publishing, (*978-0-9723569*) P.O. Box 770, Fair Oaks, CA 95628 USA (SAN 255-0369) Tel 916-961-2540 (phone/fax); 10416 Fair Oaks Blvd., Fair Oaks, CA 95628 E-mail: emidra@msn.com Web site: http://www.emidrapublishing.com.

Emilia, Cara Pr., (*978-1-7329722*) 414 23rd St., Sacramento, CA 95816 USA Tel 805-503-5716 E-mail: caraemiliadesigns@gmail.com Web site: www.caraemilia.com.

EMK Pr., (*978-0-9726244; 978-1-942571*) Div. of EMK Group, LLC, 16 Mt. Bethel Rd., No. 219, Warren, NJ 07059 USA (SAN 255-0318) Tel 732-469-7544; Fax: 732-469-7861 E-mail: carriekitze@emkpress.com Web site: http://www.emkpress.com *Dist(s):* **Quality Bks., Inc.**

Emma Lindberg, (*978-0-9997307*) 3406 Stagecoach Rd, Durham, NC 27713 USA Tel 919-808-6019 E-mail: Emilyi@eliglobal.com.

EMMA Pubns., (*978-0-9800074*) P.O. Box 654, Northville, MI 48168 USA (SAN 854-977X) E-mail: info@emmapublications.com Web site: http://www.emmapublications.com *Dist(s):* **Partners Bk. Distributing, Inc.**

Emma, Sasha, (*978-1-7335173*) 5208 Drystack Ln., Glen Allen, VA 23059 USA Tel 804-938-5574 E-mail: timo.selvaraj@gmail.com.

Emma's Pantry, (*978-0-9648437*) 0373 Sopris Creek Rd., #7, Basalt, CO 81621 USA Tel 970-927-4661 E-mail: eewalling@yahoo.com Web site: http://www.pages.prodigy.com/legends/.

Emmaus Road, International, (*978-1-880185*) 7150 Tanner Ct., San Diego, CA 92111 USA Tel 619-292-7020 E-mail: emmaus_road@eri.com Web site: http://www.eri.org.

Emmaus Road Publishing, (*978-0-9663223; 978-1-931018; 978-1-937155; 978-1-940329; 978-1-941447; 978-1-63446; 978-1-945125; 978-1-947792; 978-1-949013; 978-1-64585*) 1468 Parkview Cir., Steubenville, OH 43952 USA Tel 740-264-9535; Fax: 740-283-4011; Toll Free: 800-398-5470 E-mail: cerickson@emmausroad.org Web site: http://www.emmausroad.org.

Emnes Systems, (*978-0-9661636*) 7212 Antares Dr., Suite 100, Gaithersburg, MD 20879 USA Tel 240-683-8502 E-mail: ecfchang@msn.com Web site: http://www.emnes.com.

Emotional Content, LLC, (*978-0-9817543*) 1445 S. Carmelina Ave., Los Angeles, CA 90025 USA E-mail: info@biographicnovel.com; eiji@wadirum.com; latinsamurai@gmail.com Web site: http://www.biographicnovel.com; http://www.emotionalcontent.net.

Empak Publishing Co., (*978-0-922162; 978-0-9616156*) Subs. of Empak Enterprises, Inc., P.O. Box 8596, Chicago, IL 60680-8596 USA (SAN 699-9182) Tel 312-642-3434; Fax: 312-642-9657; Toll Free: 800-477-4554 E-mail: empak@email.msn.com Web site: http://www.empakpub.com.

Empire Holdings *Imprint of* **Kodel Group, LLC, The**

Empire Holdins - Literary Division for Young Readers *Imprint of* **Kodel Group, LLC, The**

Empire Publishing, (*978-0-9766246*) 1117 Desert Ln., Suite 1362, Las Vegas, NV 89102 USA Fax: 413-714-5213.

Empire Publishing Service, (*978-1-58690*) P.O. Box 1344, Studio City, CA 91614-0344 USA (SAN 630-5687) Tel 818-784-8918 E-mail: empirepubsvc@att.net.

Empower Pr., (*978-0-9673093; 978-0-9823344*) Div. of Terry Tripp Ministries, Orders Addr.: P.O. Box 899, Gallatin, TN 37066 USA Tel 615-491-3007; Edit Addr.: 2105 Cages Bend Rd., Gallatin, TN 37066 USA E-mail: klimley@aol.com Web site: http://empowerpress.com.

Empowered Entertainment, (*978-0-9767076*) 5853 Liberty Creek Dr. N., Indianapolis, IN 46254 USA E-mail: andrew@chameleonchronicles.com Web site: http://www.chameleonchronicles.com.

Empowered Faith International *See* **Enlightened Living Ministries International**

Empowered Flower Girl, (*978-0-9978800*) 4921 Crooks, M-11, Royal Oak, MI 48073 USA Tel 313-492-3879 E-mail: rkamaria@gmail.com Web site: www.empoweredflowergirl.com.

Empowering People Pub., (*978-0-9762639; 978-0-578-16865-4*) Orders Addr.: P.O. Box 329, Rex, GA 30273 USA Tel 850-328-1698 E-mail: Drtina2@gmail.com; altrellpipkin@yahoo.com Web site: http://www.tinapipkin.com; http://www.empoweringpeopleinc.com; http://www.altrellpipkin.com.

Emprise Publishing *See* **Emprise Publishing & Media**

Emprise Publishing & Media, (*978-0-9717581; 978-0-9725121*) 3643 South Ave., Springfield, MO 65807 USA E-mail: martyb@powermarkcomics.com.

Empty Harbor Productions, LLC, (*978-0-9790699*) 4 Sarah Lynn Ln., Suite 127, Conroe, TX 77303 USA Toll Free: 866-419-2921 E-mail: emptyharbor@msn.com Web site: http://www.sticman.net.

Empty Set Entertainment, (*978-0-615-28744-7; 978-0-615-36542-8; 978-0-9831963; 978-1-939366*) Orders Addr.: PO Box 122710, San Diego, CA 92112-2710 USA (SAN 920-7694) *Dist(s):* **Baker & Taylor Publisher Services (BTPS)** **BookBaby.**

Empty Sky *Imprint of* **Zeromayo Studios, LLP**

Empyrion Publishing, (*978-0-692-21367-4; 978-0-692-22501-1; 978-0-692-23065-7; 978-0-692-25133-1; 978-0-692-26300-6; 978-0-692-29670-7; 978-0-692-32818-7; 978-0-692-34586-3; 978-0-692-35427-8; 978-0-692-35803-0; 978-0-692-37463-4; 978-0-692-39027-6; 978-0-692-39961-3; 978-0-692-50806-0; 978-0-692-53646-9; 978-0-692-56921-4; 978-0-692-57186-6; 978-0-692-57448-5; 978-0-692-58459-0; 978-0-692-59421-6; 978-0-692-60449-6; 978-0-692-61946-9; 978-0-692-62947-5; 978-0-692-71074-6; 978-0-692-71963-3; 978-0-9981013) PO Box 140914, Broken Arrow, OK 74014 USA Tel 9184512676 Do not confuse with Empyrion Publishing in Winter Garden, FL* E-mail: rickmanis@hotmail.com *Dist(s):* **CreateSpace Independent Publishing Platform.**

Emu Editions, (*978-0-692-46644-5*) 543 Virginia Ave, Harrisonburg, VA 22802 USA Tel 5405744414 *Dist(s):* **CreateSpace Independent Publishing Platform.**

En Prose Pubns., (*978-0-9989163; 978-1-948166*) 6564 Loisdale Ct. Suite 600, Springfield, VA 22150 USA Tel 703-992-3600 E-mail: nicolealbertjones@gmail.com Web site: enprose.org.

En Route Bks. & Media, (*978-0-9988940; 978-0-9991143; 978-0-9994704; 978-0-9996670; 978-0-9998814; 978-1-7324148; 978-1-7325949; 978-1-950108; 978-1-952464*) 5705 Rhodes Ave., Saint Louis, MO 63109 USA Tel 314-706-1009; Fax: 314-706-1009 E-mail: smahfood@holyapostles.edu Web site: http://www.enroutebooksandmedia.com.

Enchanted Forest Publishing, (*978-0-9910700*) P.O. Box 453, Volcano, HI 96785-0453 USA Tel 808-333-8052 E-mail: enchantedforestpublishing@gmail.com.

Enchanted Lion Bks., LLC, (*978-1-59270*) 201 Richards St. Ste. 4, Brooklyn, NY 11231-1537 USA E-mail: zoeclaud@earthlink.com; enchantedlionbooks@yahoo.com *Dist(s):* **Consortium Bk. Sales & Distribution** **Farrar, Straus & Giroux** **Two Rivers Distribution.**

Enchanted Pages Publishing LLC, (*978-0-9843361; 978-1-941739*) P.O. Box 88876, Carol Stream, IL 60188 USA Tel 630-432-0915 E-mail: enchantedpagespublishing@gmail.com Web site: ourenchantedpages.com.

Enchanted Self Pr., (*978-0-9798952*) 603 S. Edgemere Dr., West Allenhurst, NJ 07711 USA.

Enchantment Pr., (*978-0-9832074*) 14 Valle Escondido, Placitas, NM 87043 USA Tel 505-350-0227 E-mail: lisa.goldman@comcast.net.

Enclave *Imprint of* **Gilead Publishing, LLC**

Encore Performance Publishing, (*978-1-57514*) Orders Addr.: P.O. Box 692, Orem, UT 84059 USA Tel 801-785-9343; Fax: 801-785-9394 E-mail: encoreplay@aol.com Web site: http://www.encoreplay.com.

Encore Pubns., (*978-0-9798718*) P.O. Box 117, Stoughton, WI 53589 USA Tel 608-877-9692; Fax: 608-877-9693 E-mail: masonfinancial@charter.net; bonita.mason@peachbandana.com Web site: http://PeachBandana.com.

Encounter Bks., (*978-1-893554; 978-1-59403; 978-1-64177*) Div. of Encounter for Culture & Education, Inc., 900 Broadway., Suite 601, New York, NY 10003-1237 USA (SAN 253-1585) Toll Free Fax: 877-811-1461 (orders); Toll Free: 800-786-3839 (inquiries, MS proposals) E-mail: kwong@encounterbooks.com Web site: http://www.encounterbooks.com *Dist(s):* **Ebsco Publishing** **Ingram Publisher Services** **MyiLibrary** **Two Rivers Distribution** **ebrary, Inc.**

Encyclopaedia Britannica, Inc., (*978-0-7826; 978-0-8347; 978-0-85229; 978-0-87827; 978-1-59339; 978-1-60835; 978-1-61535; 978-0-9823819; 978-0-9823820; 978-0-9823821; 978-0-9823822; 978-0-9823823; 978-0-9823824; 978-1-62513; 978-1-68382*) 325 N. La Salle St., Chicago, IL 60654 USA (SAN 204-1464) Toll Free Fax: 800-344-9624 (fax orders); Toll Free: 800-323-1229; 800-621-3900 (orders); 2nd Flr., Unity Wharf Mill St., London, SE1 2BH Tel 020 7500 7800; Fax: 020 7500 7878 E-mail: enquiries@britannica.co.uk; contact@eb.com Web site: http://www.eb.com; http://www.britannica.co.uk *Dist(s):* **Continental Bk. Co., Inc.** **Ebsco Publishing** **Follett School Solutions** **MyiLibrary** **Pearson Education** **Pearson Technology Group** **ebrary, Inc.**

Endeavor Press *See* **Endeavor Publishing**

Endeavor Pr., (*978-0-9728656*) P.O. Box 4307, Chicago, IL 60680 USA Tel 312-420-6675 Do not confuse with Endeavor Press in Gilbert, AZ E-mail: rogerrange@endeavorpress.net Web site: http://www.endeavorpress.com.

Endeavor Publishing, (*978-0-9743843*) 4204 E. Marshall Ave., Gilbert, AZ 85297 USA Tel 480-632-1306 (phone/fax) Do not confuse with Endeavor Press in Annapolis, MD E-mail: endeavorpublishing@yahoo.com Web site: http://www.dowkump.com.

Endicott & Hugh Bks., (*978-0-9823167; 978-0-9837115; 978-0-9894291; 978-0-9993646*) P.O. Box 13305, Burton, WA 98013 USA E-mail: info@endicottandhughbooks.com Web site: http://www.endicottandhughbooks.com *Dist(s):* **Partners/West Book Distributors.**

Endurance Pr., (*978-0-9856746; 978-0-9960146; 978-0-9964975; 978-0-9988756; 978-1-7335503*) 577 N. Cardigan Ave., Star, ID 83669 USA Tel 208-794-5647 E-mail: robert@endurancepress.com Web site: www.endurancepress.com.

Energetic Press, LLC *See* **Four Dolphins Pr., LLC**

Energion Pubns., (*978-1-893729; 978-1-938434; 978-1-63199*) P.O. Box 841, Gonzalez, FL 32560 USA Tel 850-525-3916 E-mail: pubs@energion.com Web site: http://www.energion.com; https://energiondirect.com.

Energy Education Group, (*978-0-9744765*) Div. of The California Study, Inc., Orders Addr.: 664 Hilary Dr., Tiburon, CA 94920 USA Tel 415-435-4574; Fax: 415-435-7737 E-mail: energyforkeeps@aol.com Web site: http://www.energyforkeeps.org *Dist(s):* **PixyJack Pr., Inc.**

Enfini Innovations, (*978-0-692-17507-1; 978-0-692-17598-9; 978-0-578-63638-2; 978-0-578-63639-9; 978-0-578-67559-6*) 1541 Jonathan Ave., Cincinnati, OH 45207 USA Tel 513-238-1484 E-mail: ztm82@yahoo.com *Dist(s):* **Ingram Content Group.**

Engage-N-Learn *See* **Zishka Publishing**

EngGoGIC, LLC, (*978-0-9882142*) P.O. Box 364, PLAINSBORO, NJ 08536 USA Tel 609-716-6165 E-mail: contact@enggogic.com *Dist(s):* **BookBaby.**

Engine Hse. Bks., (*978-0-615-19130-0; 978-0-615-19495-0; 978-0-615-20663-9; 978-0-615-21565-5; 978-0-578-00775-5; 978-0-578-01960-4; 978-1-936211*) 330 WCR 16½, Longmont, CO 80504 USA Web site: http://www.enginehousebooks.com *Dist(s):* **Lulu Pr., Inc.** **Smashwords.**

Engineering is Elementary, (*978-0-918866; 978-0-9774084; 978-1-933758; 978-1-936789; 978-1-940314; 978-1-7348782; 978-1-952749; 978-1-63619*) 1 Science Pk., Boston, MA 02114 USA (SAN 210-4687) Tel 617-589-0230 E-mail: mhiggins@mos.org Web site: www.mos.org/eie.

Enginuity, LLC, (*978-1-929645*) Orders Addr.: P.O. Box 20607, San Jose, CA 95160 USA Tel 408-268-9740; Toll Free Fax: 888-268-9740; Toll Free: 888-618-4263; Edit Addr.: 3629 Bryant St., Palo Alto, CA 94306-4209 USA E-mail: sales@enginuity.com; support@enqinuity.com Web site: http://www.enginuity.com.

Englefield & Arnold, Incorporated *See* **Englefield & Assocs., Inc.**

Englefield & Assocs., Inc., (*978-1-884183; 978-1-59230*) Div. of Show What You Know Publishing, Orders Addr.: P.O. Box 341348, Columbus, OH 43234-1348 USA Tel 614-764-1211; Fax: 614-764-1311; Toll Free: 877-727-7464 (877-PASSING); Edit Addr.: 6344 Nicholas Dr., Columbus, OH 43235 USA E-mail: eapub@eapublishing.com; marketing@eapublishing.com Web site: http://www.showwhatyouknowpublishing.com/.

Engler, Sherry E, (*978-1-7321786*) 195 S Engler Ln., PAYSON, AZ 85541 USA Tel 928-595-4088 E-mail: sherryengler@gmail.com Web site: sherryengler.com.

English Garden Talk Pr., (*978-0-9763572; 978-0-9779257; 978-0-9858431; 978-0-9915290; 978-0-9971342; 978-0-9995535; 978-1-7342095*) 536 W. Hoptree Ct., Louisville, CO 80027 USA E-mail: sanddollar5643@aol.com *Dist(s):* **Lulu Pr., Inc.**

Enhancing Health, Inc., (*978-0-9744479*) P.O. Box 1882, Duluth, GA 30096 USA E-mail: info@thefittgolfer.com.

Publisher Name Index

ENHEART Publishing, *(978-0-9654899; 978-0-9838882)* Orders Addr.: P.O. Box 620086, Charlotte, NC 28262 USA Tel 980-272-1410 (phone/fax)
E-mail: info@enheartpublishing.com
Web site: http://www.enheartpublishing.com
Dist(s): **BookBaby**
Parnassus Bk. Distributors.

Enigma Productions *See* **Enigmaw Studios**

Enigmaw Studios, *(978-0-9794321)* 923 W. Stephen Ave, clawson, MI 48017 USA
Web site: http://www.enigmaw.com.

Enisen Publishing, *(978-0-9702908; 978-0-9763070)* 2118 Wilshire Blvd., # 351, Santa Monica, CA 90403-5784 USA (SAN 253-3308) Tel 310-989-4069; Fax: 310-576-7278 Do not confuse with companies with the same name in Clermont, FL, Hollywood, CA, Otis Orchards, WA
E-mail: publishing@enisen.com
Web site: http://www.enisen.com.

Enlighten Learning, *(978-0-9755865)* 269 S. Beverly Dr., No. 139, Beverly Hills, CA 90212 USA Tel 310-358-2995.

Enlighten Pubns., *(978-0-9706226)* Orders Addr.: P.O. Box 525, Vauxhall, NJ 07088 USA Toll Free: 866-862-8626
E-mail: books@enlightenpublications.com
Web site: http://www.authorsden.com/jackiehardrick; www.enlightenpublications.com.

Enlightened Bks., *(978-0-9769541; 978-0-692-02980-0)* Orders Addr.: P.O. Box 7423, NewPort Beach, CA 92658 USA Tel 949-644-1376; Edit Addr.: 1 Belcourt Dr., Newport Beach, CA 92660 USA
E-mail: enlightenedbooks13@gmail.com
Web site: http://www.enlightenedbooks.com.

Enlightened Learners Publishing, *(978-0-692-86351-0; 978-0-692-86392-3; 978-0-692-87855-2)* 1935 Sabra Dr, Tallahassee, FL 32303 USA Tel 631-949-6886
E-mail: quashierf@yahoo.com.

Enlightened Living Ministries International, *(978-0-9768416)* P.O. Box 156, Marietta, GA 30061 USA Tel 770-218-6215
E-mail: doctorbell@ecclive.org
Web site: http://www.empoweredfaith.org; https://www.enlightenedliving.info.

Ennis, Scott, *(978-0-692-71256-6; 978-0-692-82285-2; 978-1-7343125)* 3751 Sommers St., Jacksonville, FL 32205 USA Tel 904-673-5994
Dist(s): **CreateSpace Independent Publishing Platform.**

Enricharamics, Inc., *(978-1-889654)* 8416-905 O'Connor Ct., Richmond, VA 23228 USA Tel 804-747-5826.

Ensign Benson Bks., LLC, *(978-0-615-62737-3; 978-0-9892846)* Orders Addr.: P.O. Box PO Box 609, Gloucester, VA 23061 USA Tel 315-955-8727
E-mail: info@bookbridgepress.com
Web site: www.adventuresofonyx.com
Dist(s): **Independent Pubs. Group**
Itasca Bks.
Midpoint Trade Bks., Inc.

Ensign Peak *Imprint of* **Shadow Mountain Publishing**

Enslow Elementary *Imprint of* **Enslow Publishing, LLC**

Enslow Publishers, Incorporated *See* **Enslow Publishing, LLC**

Enslow Publishing *Imprint of* **Enslow Publishing, LLC**

†**Enslow Publishing, LLC,** *(978-0-7660; 978-0-89490; 978-1-59845; 978-1-4644; 978-1-4645; 978-1-4646; 978-1-62285; 978-1-62293; 978-1-62324; 978-1-62400; 978-1-9785)* Orders Addr.: P.O. Box 398, Berkeley Heights, NJ 07922-0398 USA (SAN 213-7518) Tel 908-771-9400; Fax: 908-771-0925; Toll Free: 800-398-2504; Edit Addr.: 40 Industrial Rd., Berkeley Heights, NJ 07922-0398 USA; 101 W. 23rd St., Ste, 240, New York, NY 10011 Toll Free Fax: 877-980-4454; Toll Free: 800-398-2504; *Imprints:* MyReportLinks.com Books (MyRptLnks); Enslow Elementary (Enslow Elmntry); Enslow Publishing (EnslowPubng); West 44 Books (MYID_T_WEST 44)
E-mail: ginas@enslow.com; customerservice@enslow.com; hollyc@rosenpub.com
Web site: http://www.enslow.com; http://www.chasingroses.com; http://www.jasminehealth.com; http://www.enslowclassroom.com; http://www.myreportlinks.com; www.speedingstar.com; www.bluewaveclassroom.com; www.scarletvoyage.com
Dist(s): **Follett School Solutions**
MyiLibrary; *CIP.*

Entangled Publishing, LLC, *(978-1-937044; 978-1-62061; 978-1-62266; 978-1-63375; 978-1-943113; 978-1-943114; 978-1-943336; 978-1-943892; 978-1-68281; 978-1-64063; 978-1-64937)* 10940 S Parker Rd Suite 327, Parker, CO 80134 USA Fax: 970-797-9107; *Imprints:* Entangled Teen (EntangledTeen)
E-mail: publisher@entangledpublishing.com
Web site: http://www.entangledpublishing.com
Dist(s): **Ingram Content Group**
Macmillan
MyiLibrary
Two Rivers Distribution
Westminster John Knox Pr.

Entangled Teen *Imprint of* **Entangled Publishing, LLC**

Entegrity Choice Publishing, *(978-0-692-28050-8; 978-0-9909397; 978-0-9974859; 978-0-692-90991-1; 978-0-9991780; 978-1-7325767; 978-1-7330301; 978-1-7351739)* .

Entelechy Education, LLC, *(978-0-9887813)* 10810 Symphony Way, Columbia, MD 21044 USA Tel 410-730-5570
E-mail: Gary@EntelechyEd.com
Web site: www.EntelechyEd.com.

Enterprise Incorporated *See* **TLK Pubns.**

Enterprise Leaf Pr., *(978-0-692-05867-1; 978-0-692-17333-6; 978-0-578-52061-2)* 792 Columbus Ave. APT. 4S, New York, NY 10025 USA Tel 917-623-4686
E-mail: sarayaharon1@gmail.com
Dist(s): **Ingram Content Group.**

Enterprize Publishing Co., Inc., *(978-1-893490)* 1036 Parkway Blvd., Brookings, SD 57006 USA Tel 605-692-7778; Fax: 605-997-3194
E-mail: cfcecil@home.com.

Entertainment Ministry, The, *(978-0-9707798; 978-0-9717316; 978-0-9728003; 978-0-9765142; 978-0-9791259; 978-0-9817549; 978-0-9827891)* 5584 Mountain Rd., Antioch, TN 37013-2311 USA Toll Free: 800-999-0101
Web site: http://www.entmin.com
Dist(s): **Send The Light Distribution LLC.**

Entertainment Pubns., Inc., *(978-1-880248; 978-1-58553; 978-1-59878; 978-1-60967; 978-1-949012; 978-1-950493)* 1401 Crooks Rd. Suite 150, Troy, MI 48084 USA Tel 248-404-1000
E-mail: NationalRetail@entertainment.com
Web site: http://www.entertainment.com
Dist(s): **Waldenbooks, Inc.**

Entertainment Publications Operating Company, Incorporated *See* **Entertainment Pubns., Inc.**

Enthusi Adams, Inc., *(978-0-9670245)* 2792 W. Pekin Rd., Spring Boro, OH 45066 USA Tel 937-743-6381; Fax: 513-743-3292
E-mail: enthusiadams@earthlink.net
Web site: http://www.enthusiadams.com.

Entomological Society of America, *(978-0-938522; 978-0-9776209; 978-0-9966674)* 10001 Derekwood Ln., Suite 100, Lanham, MD 20706-4876 USA (SAN 200-9307) Tel 301-731-4535; Fax: 301-731-4538
E-mail: esa@entsoc.org
Web site: http://www.entsoc.org.

Entropy's Espresso, *(978-0-615-64648-0; 978-0-692-36413-0; 978-0-692-93063-2)*
Dist(s): **CreateSpace Independent Publishing Platform.**

Entry Way Publishing *See* **Digi-Tall Media**

EnviCare Consulting, Inc., *(978-0-9710925)* Orders Addr.: 2809 Blairmont Dr., Midland, MI 48642 USA Tel 989-839-9177
E-mail: bstrawter@chartermi.net
Web site: http://www.envicareinc.com.

Environmental Protection Agency *Imprint of* **United States Government Printing Office**

Environmental Systems Research Institute *See* **ESRI, Inc.**

Environments, Inc., *(978-1-59794)* P.O. Box 1348, Beaufort, SC 29901-1348 USA Tel 843-846-8155; Fax: 843-846-2999; Toll Free Fax: 800-343-2987; Toll Free: 800-342-4453
E-mail: environments@eichild.com
Web site: http://www.eichild.com.

Envisage Publishing, *(978-0-9729042)* Orders Addr.: P.O. Box 557, Queens Village, NY 11428 USA; Edit Addr.: 89-52 208th St., Queens Village, NY 11427 USA
E-mail: dmdavoren@hotmail.com
Web site: http://www.envisagepublishing.com
Dist(s): **Lulu Pr., Inc.**

Envision Editions, Limited *See* **Envision Editions Ltd.**

Envision Editions Ltd., *(978-0-9762814)* Orders Addr.: P.O. Box 442, Gaylord, MI 49734 USA; Edit Addr.: 2020 Brink Trail, Gaylord, MI 49735 USA.

Envision EMI, Inc., *(978-0-9745760)* 1919 Gallows Rd. Ste. 700, Vienna, VA 22182-4007 USA.

EoH Publishing *See* **WE, LLC**

E-O-L Publishing Corp., *(978-0-9753705)* P.O. Box 110 Keely Circle, New Smyrna Beach, FL 32168 USA
E-mail: jvoss2@cfl.rr.com
Web site: http://www.eolpublishing.com.

Eos *Imprint of* **HarperCollins Pubs.**

EPEI Press *See* **EPEI Pr.**

EPEI Pr., *(978-0-9729065)* Orders Addr.: 1450 S. New Wilke Rd., Suite 102, Arlington Heights, IL 60005 USA Tel 847-670-6992; Fax: 847-670-7466; Toll Free: 877-670-7444; Edit Addr.: 1749 Golf Rd., No. 204, Mount Prospect, IL 60056 USA
E-mail: sara@getprepared.org
Web site: http://www.getprepared.org.

Ephemeron Pr., *(978-0-912290)* 1510 Perdidio Ct., Melbourne, FL 32940 USA Tel 321-752-0167
E-mail: johnknapp2@gmail.com
Web site: http://www.ephemeronpress.com.

EPI Bks., *(978-0-9726075; 978-0-9796536; 978-0-9843655; 978-0-9826006)* 2364 Roll Dr., San Diego, CA 92154 USA Fax: 619-869-8501; *Imprints:* EPI Kid Books (EPI Kid Bks)
Web site: http://www.EPIBooks.com
Dist(s): **Anderson Merchandisers.**

EPI Kid Bks. *Imprint of* **EPI Bks.**

Epic Bks. *Imprint of* **Bellwether Media**

Epic Edge *Imprint of* **EPIC Pr.**

Epic Escape *Imprint of* **EPIC Pr.**

Epic Extreme *Imprint of* **EPIC Pr.**

Epic Pr. *Imprint of* **ABDO Publishing Co.**

EPIC Pr., *(978-1-68076)* Div. of ADBO Publishing Group, 8000 W. 78th St., Suite 310, Edna, MN 55439 USA Toll Free Fax: 800-862-3480; Toll Free: 800-800-1312; *Imprints:* Epic Edge (EpicEdge); Epic Escape (EpicEscape); Epic Extreme (EpicExtreme)
Web site: https://abdopublishing.com/
Dist(s): **ABDO Publishing Co.**

Epic Pr., *(978-0-9801061; 978-1-941185)* P.O. Box 141624, Austin, TX 78714-1624 USA
E-mail: sh@epic-press.com
Web site: http://www.epic-press.com.

EPIC Publishing Co., *(978-0-9674025; 978-0-9763870; 978-0-9995925)* 1405 Ten Palms Ct., Las Vegas, NV 89117-1404 USA (SAN 253-2840) Do not confuse with companies with the same or similar name in Erie, PA, Canon City, CO, Greeley, CO
E-mail: rxl@epicpublishing.com
Web site: http://www.epicpublishing.com.

Epicality Bks., LLC, *(978-0-9838594)* 4501 Pk. Glen Rd., No. 216, St. Louis Park, MN 55416 USA Tel 612-751-7947
E-mail: matthewjamesbeier@gmail.com.

Epicenter Literary Software, *(978-0-9760222; 978-1-938609)* 6514 Seventh St., NW, Washington, DC 20012-2622 USA Tel 202-829-2427
E-mail: carolivia@carolivia.org
Web site: http://www.carolivia.org.

Epicenter Pr., Inc., *(978-0-945397; 978-0-9708493; 978-0-9724944; 978-0-9745014; 978-0-9790470; 978-1-60381; 978-0-9800825; 978-1-935347; 978-1-941890)* Orders Addr.: 6524 NE 181st St., No. 2, Kenmore, WA 98028 USA (SAN 246-9405) Do not confuse with companies with similar names in Kanehoe, HI, Long Beach, CA, Oakland, CA
E-mail: info@epicenterpress.com; phil@epicenterpress.com; aubrey@epicenterpress.com
Web site: http://www.epicenterpress.com
Dist(s): **Open Road Integrated Media, Inc.**
Smashwords.

Epigraph Bks., *(978-0-9726357; 978-0-9749359; 978-0-9766843; 978-0-9789427; 978-0-9798828; 978-0-9823246; 978-0-9824530; 978-0-9825255; 978-0-9826441; 978-0-9830517; 978-0-9833589; 978-1-936940; 978-1-939681; 978-1-944037; 978-1-948626; 978-1-948796; 978-1-951937) a/o Monkfish Book Publishing Company, 22 E. Market St., Ste. 304, Rhinebeck, NY 12572 USA*
Web site: http://www.epigrahps.com
Dist(s): **MyiLibrary**
SPD-Small Pr. Distribution.

Episode.Media, *(978-0-9986610)* 5060 S. Hillcrest Ln., Veradale, WA 99037 USA Tel 509-435-7401
E-mail: dandaines.episode@gmail.com
Web site: www.dandaines.com; www.Episode.media.

Epistelogic, *(978-0-9748319)* 47 White Pl., Bloomington, IL 61701-1859 USA Tel 309-826-4808
Web site: http://www.epistelogic.com; http://www.scholarpress.com
Dist(s): **Savant Bk. Distribution Co.**

e-Pluribus Unum Publishing Company *See* **Cronus College**

Epoca, Editorial, S.A. de C.V. (MEX) *(978-968-6769; 978-970-627) Dist. by* **Giron Bks.**

EPOCH Studios, LLC, *(978-0-9970208; 978-0-9975570)* 2645 Rosalyn Ln. SE, Smyrna, GA 30080 USA Tel 773-896-6276
E-mail: dxbrooks@aol.com; jbrooks@worldsofepoch.com
Web site: http://www.worldsofepoch.com.

Eppy's Creations, *(978-0-615-16983-5)* P.O. Box 1103, Swansboro, NC 28584 USA
Dist(s): **Lulu Pr., Inc.**

eProduction Services *See* **Kepler Pr.**

EPS Digital, *(978-0-9772315)* P.O. Box 5185, De Pere, WI 54115-5185 USA.

ePub Bud, *(978-1-61061; 978-1-61979; 978-1-62154; 978-1-62314; 978-1-62590; 978-1-62776; 978-1-62840)* 427 California Ave., Santa Monica, CA 90403 USA Tel 310-980-4668
E-mail: josh@epubbud.com
Web site: http://www.epubbud.com
Dist(s): **BookBaby**
INscribe Digital
Lulu Pr., Inc.

ePublishing Works!, *(978-1-61417; 978-1-947833; 978-1-64457)* 644 Shrewsbury Commons Ave, No. 249, Shrewsbury, PA 17349 USA Tel 866-846-5123; Fax: 866-846-5123
E-mail: epublishingworks@ebookprep.com
Web site: www.epublishingworks.com
Dist(s): **INscribe Digital**
Independent Pubs. Group
Ingram Publisher Services.

EQUALS *Imprint of* **Univ. of California, Berkeley, Lawrence Hall of Science**

Equidata Publishing, *(978-0-9714185)* Orders Addr.: P.O. Box 8116, Surprise, AZ 85374 USA Tel 623-476-7503; Edit Addr.: 13781 W. Crocus Dr. Surprise, Az 85379, Surprise, AZ 85379 USA
E-mail: jobrien6@cox.net
Web site: http://www.equidatapublishing.com.

Equimax USA, Inc., *(978-0-9668082)* HC65 Box 271, Alpine, TX 79830 USA Tel 432-371-2610; Fax: 432-371-2612; Toll Free: 800-759-9494
E-mail: employment@equimax.com
Web site: http://www.equixmax.com.

Equine Graphics Publishing Group, *(978-1-887932; 978-0-9855309; 978-0-9962336)* Orders Addr.: 58 Indian Hill Rd., Uncasville, CT 06382 USA Tel 860-892-8891; *Imprints:* SmallHorse Press (SmallHorse Pr)
E-mail: editor@newconcordpress.com; toniweeone@smallhorse.com; info@equinegraphicspublishing.com; sales@romancingthehorse.com
Web site: http://www.smallhorse.com; http://www.newconcordpress.com; http://www.equinegraphicspublishing.com; http://www.tonileland.com
Dist(s): **Smashwords.**

Equitel Publishing Co., *(978-0-9789131)* 53 Mount Ida Rd., Suite.2, Dorchester, MA 02122-1735 USA
Web site: http://www.equitelpublishing.com.

Erazo, Carlos, *(978-0-9759757; 978-0-9796253)* P.O. Box 2111, Bayamon, PR 00960-2111 USA
E-mail: erazo2001@prtc.net
Web site: http://www.erazolabor.com
Dist(s): **Representaciones Borinquenas, Inc.**

Erewhon Bks., *(978-1-64566)* Erewhon Books, New York, NY 10001 USA Tel 205-626-9663
E-mail: liz@erewhonbooks.com
Web site: www.erewhonbooks.com
Dist(s): **Workman Publishing Co., Inc.**

Erickson Pr., *(978-1-60217)* Orders Addr.: P.O. Box 33, Yankton, SD 57078 USA (SAN 852-0402); Edit Addr.: 329 Broadway, Yankton, SD 57078 USA
Web site: http://www.ericksonpress.com.

Erickson, Rakel L., *(978-0-9744422)* P.O. Box 86, Fertile, MN 56540-0086 USA
E-mail: thomas_robinson@unl.nodak.edu.

Erickson, Tim, *(978-1-59492)* 8801 Fremont Ave S., Minneapolis, MN 55420-2642 USA
E-mail: terickson21@mn.rr.com
Web site: http://www.deathswhisper.com.

Erie Harbor Productions, *(978-0-9717828)* Orders Addr.: 223 W. Cornell Ave., Suite B, Pontiac, MI 48340 USA
E-mail: harbormaster@erieharbor.com
Web site: http://www.erieharbor.com.

ErieKIDS, Inc., *(978-0-9779822)* 4544 W. Ridge Rd., Suite One, Erie, PA 16506 USA (SAN 850-668X) Tel 814-835-3430
Web site: http://www.eriekids.com.

Eriginal Bks. LLC, *(978-0-9829213; 978-1-61370)* 13868 SW 151 Ct., Miami, FL 33196 USA Tel 305-763-2706; 10854 SW 88 St Suite 220, Miami, FL 33176
E-mail: marlene.moleon@gmail.com.

Erin Go Bragh Publishing, *(978-0-9882745; 978-1-941345)* 1885 FM 2673 No. 3, Canyon Lake, TX 78133 USA Tel 830-515-8187; Fax: 866-652-5165
E-mail: kjs@hamiltontroll.com; kjs@kathleensbooks.com; kathleen@eringobraghpublishing.com
Web site: www.HamiltonTroll.com; www.ErinGoBraghPublishing.com; www.KathleensBooks.com.

Erin Kelly Roberts Flores, *(978-0-692-18743-2; 978-0-692-18744-9)* 35280 Prestwick Ct., Round Hill, VA 20141 USA Tel 949-533-3218
E-mail: kellywahine@gmail.com
Dist(s): **Ingram Content Group.**

Eringer Travel Guides *See* **Writer's Cramp, Inc.**

Erinsillart, *(978-0-9779155)* 739 31 ave, san francisco, CA 94121 USA Tel 415-816-0766
E-mail: erin@erinsillart.com
Web site: http://www.erinsillart.com.

Ernest Michael Olivarez Publishing LLC, *(978-1-7328080)* 1011 Wembley Rd., Arlington, TX 76014 USA Tel 817-525-5187
E-mail: emolivarez@yahoo.com
Web site: josethereindeer.com.

ERPublishing, LLC, *(978-0-9766568)* P.O. Box 152, Old Greenwich, CT 06870 USA
Web site: http://www.erpublishing.com.

ERTLL Pubs., *(978-0-9909929; 978-1-7342708)* 7216 Lotus Ave. No. 7, San Gabriel, CA 91775 USA Tel 626-258-9946
E-mail: RANDYERTLL@YAHOO.COM
Web site: www.randyjuradoertl.com.

Ervin, Imogene *See* **Finer Moments**

Ervin, Randy, *(978-0-578-05732-3; 978-0-578-09147-1; 978-0-578-16686-5; 978-0-578-18433-3; 978-0-578-75824-4)* 1113 Stinson Ave., Mattoon, IL 61938 USA
E-mail: randyjervin@icloud.com
Dist(s): **Independent Pub.**

Ervin, Robert E., *(978-0-9746189)* 552 Keystone Station Rd., Jackson, OH 45640 USA Tel 740-286-2693; Fax: 740-286-0756
E-mail: multicominc@adelphia.net
Web site: http://johnhuntmorgan.com.

Erwin, Amy Leaf *See* **Leaf Publishing, LLC**

Eryn Lace, *(978-0-615-38779-6)* 223 Pacific St. Unit B, Santa Monica, CA 90405 USA Tel 323-620-7434
E-mail: jwkobernick@hotmail.com.

Escape Hatch Bks., *(978-0-9976397)* 27 Main St., Jaffrey, NH 03452 USA Tel 603-721-1230
E-mail: ehb@escapehatchbooks.com
Web site: www.escapehatchbooks.com.

Escher, Ursula, *(978-0-9718609)* Bookmasters (high Mountain Pub) 30 Amberwood Pkwy. P.o. Box 388, Ashland, OH 44805 USA Tel 818-645-8621
E-mail: uescher@hotmail.com.

Eschia Bks. (CAN) *(978-0-9810942; 978-1-926696) Dist. by* **Lone Pine.**

Escuela de Musica *See* **Ed Musica**

Eslinger Hse. Publishing, *(978-0-9763033)* 17762 Neff Ranch Rd., Yorba Linda, CA 92886-9013 USA
E-mail: gilberstadt@earthlink.net.

Esmaili, Inc., *(978-0-9656185)* P.O. Box 421382, Dallas, TX 75342 USA Tel 214-521-9600; Fax: 214-526-9617.

ESOL Publishing, *(978-0-9793761)* 10305 Colony View Dr., Fairfax, VA 22032 USA (SAN 853-2796) Tel 703-250-7097
E-mail: ESOLPublishing@aol.com; mcpuginrodas@aol.com
Web site: http://www.Createspace.com/3382900
Dist(s): **CreateSpace Independent Publishing Platform**
Reading Matters, Inc.

Espasa Calpe, S.A. (ESP) *(978-84-239; 978-84-339; 978-84-8326; 978-84-670) Dist. by* **Libros Fronteras.**

Espasa Calpe, S.A. (ESP) *(978-84-239; 978-84-339; 978-84-8326; 978-84-670) Dist. by* **Planeta.**

Espasa Calpe, S.A. (ESP) *(978-84-239; 978-84-339; 978-84-8326; 978-84-670) Dist. by* **Distribks Inc.**

Espasa Calpe, S.A. (ESP) *(978-84-239; 978-84-339; 978-84-8326; 978-84-670) Dist. by* **Continental Bk.**

Espasa Calpe, S.A. (ESP) *(978-84-239; 978-84-339; 978-84-8326; 978-84-670) Dist. by* **Ediciones.**

Espasa Calpe, S.A. (ESP) *(978-84-239; 978-84-339; 978-84-8326; 978-84-670) Dist. by* **Lectorum Pubns.**

Esperanza Pr., *(978-0-692-30570-6)* 12089 N. 75th St., Longmont, CO 80503 USA Tel 303-772-9868
Dist(s): **CreateSpace Independent Publishing Platform.**

Espial Design, *(978-0-692-60881-4; 978-0-692-79727-3; 978-1-7321435)* 16020 SE 42nd Pl., Bellevue, WA 98006 USA Tel 425-615-5609
E-mail: slk_macia@hotmail.com
Web site: www.espialdesign.com
Dist(s): **CreateSpace Independent Publishing Platform.**

Esquire Publishing, Inc., *(978-0-9745045; 978-0-9816554)* 5900 Harper Rd., Suite 107, Solon, OH 44139 USA (SAN 856-146X) Tel 440-528-0156; Fax: 440-528-0157
E-mail: esq@pollock-law.com
Web site: http://www.monsterbooks.net
Dist(s): **Partners Pubs. Group, Inc.**

ESRI, Inc., *(978-1-879102; 978-1-58948)* 380 New York St., Redlands, CA 92373-8100 USA Fax: 909-307-3082; Toll Free: 800-447-9778; *Imprints:* ESRI Press (ESRI Pr)
E-mail: esripress@esri.com
Web site: http://www.esri.com/esripress
Dist(s): **Cengage Gale**
Independent Pubs. Group
Ingram Publisher Services
MyiLibrary
Trans-Atlantic Pubns., Inc.

ESRI Pr. *Imprint of* **ESRI, Inc.**

Essential Library *Imprint of* **ABDO Publishing Co.**

Estreno Plays, *(978-0-9631212; 978-1-888463)* 18 Van Hise Dr., Perrineville, NJ 08535 USA Tel 609-443-4787; Fax: 212-346-1435
E-mail: iridelens@aol.com; sberardini@aol.com
Web site:
http://www.rci.rutgers.edu/~estrplay/webpage.html.

ETA hand2mind *See* **hand2mind**

Etcetera Pr. LLC, *(978-0-9785160; 978-0-9826781; 978-1-936824)* 146 Hills W. Way, Richland, WA 99352 USA (SAN 850-864X)
E-mail: mreilly@etcpress.net
Web site: http://etcpress.net
Dist(s): **CreateSpace Independent Publishing Platform**
Independently Published
Ingram Content Group.

Etch *Imprint of* **Houghton Mifflin Harcourt Publishing Co.**

Eternal Foundations Curriculum, *(978-1-932505)* P.O. Box 1213, Atascadero, CA 93423 USA Tel 805-466-1910
E-mail: tsgaddis@tcsn.net.

Eternal Studios, *(978-1-887814)* 15235 Rainhollow, Houston, TX 77070 USA Tel 713-370-8384
Dist(s): **Diamond Comic Distributors, Inc.**

Eternity Pr., *(978-0-9758989)* 2828 Brannon Ave., Saint Louis, MO 63139-1438 USA Toll Free: 800-886-7587; 1 Brounger Rd., Constantia, 7806 Tel 447521578414
Web site: http://www.cenveo.com
Dist(s): **Smashwords.**

Ethan Ellenberg Literary Agency, *(978-1-68068)* 155 Suffolk St., # 2R, New York, NY 10002 USA Tel 212-431-4554.

Ethics Trading (GBR) *(978-0-9556887) Dist. by* **LuluCom.**

Ethos Of Commerce Pubs., Ltd., *(978-0-9741412)* 3535 E. Coast Hwy. No. 216, Corona del Mar, CA 92625 USA Tel 949-862-5826
E-mail: ethosofcommerce@yahoo.com
Web site: http://www.geocities.com/EthosOfCommerce.

Etiquette, Etc., LLC *See* **CKK Educational, LLC.**

ETN, Inc., *(978-0-9759629; 978-0-9855450)* 3540 W. Sahara Ave., No. 25, Las Vegas, NV 89102 USA
E-mail: eworth@etnbooks.com.

Etopia Pr., *(978-1-936751; 978-1-937976; 978-1-939194; 978-1-940223; 978-1-941692; 978-1-944138; 978-1-947135; 978-1-949719)* 117 Bellevue Ave. Ste. 202B, Newport, RI 02840 USA Tel 401-846-0010
E-mail: apmelton@gmail.com
Web site: www.etopia-press.net.

eTreasures Publishing, *(978-0-9740537)* Orders Addr.: P.O. Box 71813, Newnan, GA 30271 USA Tel 770-683-8032; Edit Addr.: 4442 Lafayette St., Marianna, FL 32446 USA Tel 850-209-0329
E-mail: publisher@etreasurespublishing.com
Web site: http://www.etreasurespublishing.com
Dist(s): **Smashwords.**

Etruscan Pr., *(978-0-9718228; 978-0-9745995; 978-0-9797450; 978-0-9819687; 978-0-9832944; 978-0-9839346; 978-0-9886922; 978-0-9897532; 978-0-9903221; 978-0-9977455; 978-0-9987508; 978-0-9997534; 978-1-7336741)* 84 West South St., Wilkes-Barre, PA 18766 USA Tel 570-408-4546; Fax: 570-408-3333
E-mail: bill@etruscanpress.org
Web site: http://www.etruscanpress.org
Dist(s): **Consortium Bk. Sales & Distribution**
MyiLibrary
SPD-Small Pr. Distribution.

ETS Publishing, *(978-0-9816642)* Orders Addr.: 9341 Clovercroft Rd., Franklin, TN 37067 USA (SAN 856-1583)
E-mail: info@etspublishinghouse.com
Web site: http://www.thisbespromise.com; http://www.etspublishing.com.

Ettelloc Publishing, *(978-0-615-78622-3; 978-0-615-83429-0; 978-0-9898304)* 734 Franklin Avenue, Suite 235, Garden City, NY 11530 USA Tel 5169244411
Dist(s): **CreateSpace Independent Publishing Platform.**

Ettrick Bks., *(978-0-9963451)* P.O. Box 340488, New York, NY 11234 USA Tel 602-743-7426
E-mail: ettrickbooks2015@gmail.com.

Eudon Publishing, *(978-0-9765423)* P.O. Box 9, Goddard, KS 67052 USA Tel 316-210-4649; Fax: 316-233-1075
E-mail: gsmith@EudonPublishing.com
Web site: http://www.EudonPublishing.com
Dist(s): **BWI**
Brodart Co.
Follett School Solutions.

eugenusr STUDIOS *See* **eugenus STUDIOS, LLC**

eugenus STUDIOS, *(978-0-578-09572-1)* 445 Lakeview Rd., Craryville, NY 12521 USA
E-mail: victor@eugenus.com
Web site: http://www.captaincrossbones.com; http://www.eugenus.com.

eugenus STUDIOS, LLC, *(978-0-9885030; 978-0-9989154; 978-0-692-05160-3; 978-1-7330671)* P.O. Box 213, Valatie, NY 12184 USA Tel 518-610-8270; Fax: 518-610-8270.

Eupanapue-Auntella's Rooster Pubns., *(978-0-615-32789-1)* P.O. Box 5803, Denver, CO 80217-5803 USA Tel 720-272-5570; *Imprints:* RoosterBugglePue Books (RoosBugglePue)
E-mail: Eupanapue_AuntellasRoosterPub@q.com
Web site: http://www.roosterbugglepue.com.

Euphema Press, *(978-0-9779600)* P.O. Box 2314, Bowie, MD 20718 USA
Web site: http://www.euphema.com.

Eureka Productions, *(978-0-9712464; 978-0-9746648; 978-0-9787919; 978-0-9825630; 978-0-9963888)* 8778 Oak Grove Rd., Mount Horeb, WI 53572 USA
Web site: http://www.graphicclassics.com
Dist(s): **Diamond Comic Distributors, Inc.**
Diamond Bk. Distributors.

Europa Editions, Inc., *(978-1-933372; 978-1-60945; 978-0-9968778)* Div. of Edizioni E/O (Rome, Italy), 214 W. 29th St Suite 1003, New York, NY 10001 USA; Italian Office, Via Gabriela Camozzi 1, Roma, 00195
E-mail: diego@europaeditions.com; editor@europaeditions.com
Web site: http://www.europaeditions.com/
Dist(s): **MyiLibrary**
Open Road Integrated Media, Inc.
Penguin Publishing Group
Publishers Group West (PGW)
Random Hse., Inc.

European Language Institute (ITA) *(978-88-8148; 978-88-85148; 978-88-536) Dist. by* **Distribks Inc.**

Eusebian Publishing, *(978-1-947805)* 5348 Vegas Drive, Suite 1670, Las Vegas, NV 89108 USA Tel 916-291-9903
E-mail: Eusebianpublishing@gmail.com
Web site: https://www.eusebian.com/.

EV Publishing Corp., *(978-0-9727787)* 1628 E. Southern Ave., Suite 9, PMB 237, Tempe, AZ 85282 USA Fax: 480-966-8627
E-mail: info@evpub.com
Web site: http://www.evpub.com.

Eva Publishing, LLC, *(978-0-9786799)* 345 W. Broadway, Shelbyville, IN 46176 USA (SAN 851-321X) Tel 317-398-0231 (phone/fax)
E-mail: jmesser@lightbound.com.

EvaHarleyChiphe, *(978-0-692-10905-2)* P.O. Box 524, Clio, SC 29525 USA Tel 843-862-8524
E-mail: echiphe@gmail.com
Web site: www.evaharleychiphe.com.

EvangeCube International *See* **E3 Resources**

Evangel Author Services, *(978-1-933858; 978-0-9823957)* Div. of Brethren in Christ Media Ministries, 2000 Evangel Way, P.O. Box 189, Nappanee, IN 46550 USA Tel 574-773-3164; Fax: 574-773-5934; Toll Free: 800-253-9315
E-mail: info@evangelpublishing.com; sales@evangelpublishing.com
Web site: http://www.evangelpress.com; http://www.evangelpublishing.com.

Evangel Press *See* **Evangel Publishing Hse.**

Evangel Publishing Hse., *(978-0-916035; 978-1-928915; 978-1-934233; 978-0-692-00906-2)* Div. of Brethren in Christ Media Ministries, Orders Addr.: P.O. Box 189, Nappanee, IN 46550 USA (SAN 211-7940) Tel 574-773-3164; Fax: 574-773-5934; Toll Free: 800-253-9315 (order); Edit Addr.: 2000 Evangel Way, Nappanee, IN 46550 USA Fax: 574-773-5934; Toll Free: 800-253-9315
E-mail: sales@evangelpublishing.com
Web site: http://www.evangelpublishing.com
Dist(s): **Anchor Distributors**
Partners Bk. Distributing, Inc.
Spring Arbor Distributors, Inc.

evangeline, *(978-0-692-04736-1; 978-1-7320290)* 5437 upland way, Philadelphia, PA 19131 USA Tel 610-803-6539
E-mail: ink4inc@gmail.com.

Evangelista, Susan, *(978-0-9769602)* 1261 W. Fulton Ave., Grand Rapids,, MI 49504 USA
Web site: http://micart.net.

Evan-Moor Educational Pubs., *(978-1-55799; 978-1-59673; 978-1-4409; 978-1-60792; 978-1-60793; 978-1-935353; 978-1-60823; 978-1-60963; 978-1-61365; 978-1-61366; 978-1-61367; 978-1-61368; 978-1-62938; 978-1-64514)* Sub. of Evan-Moor Corporation, 18 Lower Ragsdale Dr., Monterey, CA 93940 USA (SAN 242-5394) Tel 800-976-1915; 831-649-5901; Fax: 831-649-6256; Toll Free Fax: 800-777-4332; Toll Free: 800-777-4362
E-mail: customerservice@evan-moor.com; sterling@evan-moor.com
Web site: http://www.evan-moor.com
Dist(s): **Follett School Solutions**
Spring Arbor Distributors, Inc.

Evans Brothers, Ltd. (GBR) *(978-0-237) Dist. by* **Children Plus.**

†Evans, M. & Co., Inc., *(978-0-87131; 978-1-59077)* 216 E. 49th St., New York, NY 10017 USA (SAN 203-4050) Tel 212-688-2810
E-mail: editorial@mevans.com
Dist(s): **MyiLibrary**
National Bk. Network
Rowman & Littlefield Publishers, Inc.
ebrary, Inc.; *CIP.*

Evans, Robert, *(978-0-9766468; 978-0-9884466)* 1065 Saint Helena Way, Sebastopol, CA 95472 USA
E-mail: rgevans@sonic.net.

Evening Star Enterprise, Inc., *(978-0-9790210; 978-0-9841611)* Orders Addr.: P.O. Box 254, Wilmore, KY 40390-1072 USA (SAN 852-2111) Tel 859-421-0243; Edit Addr.: 408 Kinlaw Dr., Wilmore, KY 40390-1072 USA
E-mail: Rgray@Eveningstarenterprise.com
Web site:
http://www.eveningstarenterprise.com/Home.html.

Evening Sun Pr., *(978-0-9726781)* 8332 Melrose Ave., West Hollywood, CA 90069 USA Tel 310-657-9092
E-mail: lc@pictureentertainment.com.

Evenson, Laurel, *(978-0-9666834)* 675 Moon Lake Dr., Cambridge, MN 55008 USA Tel 612-689-4093.

Event-Based Science Institute, Inc., *(978-0-9747576)* 6609 Paxton Rd., Rockville, MD 20852-3659 USA
Web site: http://www.eventbasedscience.com.

Ever Wonder Bks., *(978-0-692-37551-8; 978-0-9966505)* 1620 Rose Walk Dr, Hoover, AL 35244 USA Tel 205-739-8558
Dist(s): **CreateSpace Independent Publishing Platform.**

EverAfter Romance *Imprint of* **Diversion Publishing Corp.**

EverAfterPr., *(978-0-578-40973-3; 978-0-578-40974-0)* 3085 Blackthorn Rd., Riverwoods, IL 60015 USA Tel 224-500-2752
E-mail: kanemcloughlin@outlook.com
Dist(s): **Ingram Content Group.**

Everbind *Imprint of* **Marco Bk. Co.**

Everbind/Marco Book Company *See* **Marco Bk. Co.**

Eveready Letter & Advertising Inc., *(978-0-9758714; 978-0-9777623; 978-0-9814694; 978-0-9820757; 978-0-9826118; 978-0-9837256; 978-0-9858365; 978-0-9897161; 978-0-9963917; 978-0-9981522)* 7105 Peach Court Suite 110, Brentwood, TN 37027 USA
Web site: http://eveready-usa.com
Dist(s): **Ingram Publisher Services.**

Everest Bks., *(978-0-9754146)* 16026 N. 54th St., Scottsdale, AZ 85254 USA Tel 602-684-5644; Fax: 602-595-7152
E-mail: grahamhfoster@msn.com
Web site: http://www.pacificseminars.com.

Everest Editora (ESP) *(978-84-241; 978-972-750) Dist. by* **Continental Bk.**

Everest Editora (ESP) *(978-84-241; 978-972-750) Dist. by* **Lectorum Pubns.**

Everett Pr. *Imprint of* **State Standards Publishing, LLC**

Everette Publishing (EP), LLC, *(978-0-9672539)* 106 Tillerson Dr., Newport News, VA 23602 USA Tel 757-344-9092; 757-877-6943; Fax: 757-988-0909
E-mail: EverettePublish@cox.net
Web site: http://www.Webunlimted.com.

Everfield Pr., *(978-1-946785)* 19005 SW 13th AVE, NEWBERRY, FL 32669 USA Tel 352-514-8701
E-mail: karenwhiteporter@gmail.com
Web site: karenwporter.

Evergreen Farm *Imprint of* **Gilead Publishing, LLC**

Evergreen Pr. *Imprint of* **Genesis Communications, Inc.**

Evergreen Press *See* **Genesis Communications, Inc.**

Evergreen Pr. LLC, *(978-0-9995825)* P.O. Box 22071, Tampa, FL 33622 USA Tel 813-240-1942
E-mail: evergreenpressllc@gmail.com
Web site: evergreenpressllc.com.

Evergreen Pr. of Brainerd, LLC, *(978-0-9661599; 978-0-9755252; 978-0-9819766)* P.O. Box 465, Brainerd, MN 56401 USA Tel 218-851-4843; 201 W. Laurel St., Brainerd, MN 56401
E-mail: tenlee@evergreenpress.net
Web site: http://www.evergreenpress.net.

Everlasting Publishing, *(978-0-9778083; 978-0-9824844; 978-0-9852739; 978-0-9983858; 978-1-7348047)* P.O. Box 1061, Yakima, WA 98907 USA (SAN 850-2919) Tel 509-225-9829; P.O. Box 1061, Yakima, WA 98907 Tel 509-225-9829
E-mail: dpride42@gmail.com
Web site: http://everlastingpublishing.org.

Everwas Publishing, *(978-0-9777735)* 200 Broken Arrow Way S., Sedona, AZ 86351-8743 USA Tel 928-284-0457; Fax: 928-284-9225
E-mail: kroyce88@esedona.net.

Everybody Run Music, *(978-0-578-04648-8)* 186-A W. Lemon Ave., Monrovia, CA 91016 USA
E-mail: eshouse@hotmail.com.

Everyday Learning Corp., *(978-0-9630009; 978-1-57039; 978-1-877817)* 2 Prudential Plaza, Suite 1200, Chicago, IL 60601 USA Tel 312-233-7820; Fax: 312-540-5848; Toll Free: 800-382-7670
Web site: http://www.everydaylearning.com.

Everyday Mathtools Publishing Company *See* **Everyday Learning Corp.**

Everydaysanctuary Pubns., *(978-0-9761900)* 12514 Maria Cir., Broomfield, CO 80020-5324 USA
Web site: http://www.everydaysanctuary.net.

Everyman Chess (GBR) *(978-1-85744; 978-1-78194) Dist. by* **Natl Bk Netwk.**

Everyman's Library *Imprint of* **Knopf Doubleday Publishing Group**

Everything *Imprint of* **Adams Media Corp.**

Everything Journals, *(978-0-9980714)* 4544 Cielo Ln., Las Vegas, NV 89130 USA Tel 702-458-2201
E-mail: mignard2201@gmail.com.

Evey, *(978-1-7336844)* 62 N. Sabra Ave., Oak Park, CA 91377 USA Tel 310-696-9148
E-mail: evey@eveyclothing.com
Web site: www.EveyClothing.com.

Evil Hat Productions LLC, *(978-0-9771534; 978-1-61317)* Orders Addr.: 1905 Blackbriar St, Silver Spring, MD 20903 USA Tel 240-EHP-BLUE (240-347-2583)
E-mail: feedback@evilhat.com
Web site: http://www.evilhat.com/
Dist(s): **Diamond Comic Distributors, Inc.**
Diamond Bk. Distributors.

Evil Twin Pubns., *(978-0-9712972; 978-0-9763355)* P.O. Box 2, Livingston Manor, NY 12758 USA Tel 917-971-2450
E-mail: info@eviltwinpublications.com
Web site: http://www.eviltwinpublications.com
Dist(s): **AK Pr. Distribution**
D.A.P./Distributed Art Pubs.

eVision, LLC, *(978-0-9768579)* Orders Addr.: 334 Sixth Ave. S., Birmingham, AL 35205 USA Tel 205-283-7690; Fax: 205-252-3090
Web site: http://www.eVisionLLC.net
Dist(s): **Parnassus Bk. Distributors.**

Evolved Publishing, *(978-0-615-60885-3; 978-0-615-61939-2; 978-1-62253)* Orders Addr.: 4985 N 125th St, Butler, WI 53007 USA
E-mail: Admin@EvolvedPub.com
Web site: http://www.evolvedpub.com/press/
Dist(s): **CreateSpace Independent Publishing Platform**
Draft2Digital
Ingram Content Group
Smashwords.

Evolved Self Publishing, *(978-0-9779470)* 723 Springtown Rd., Tillson, NY 12486 USA Tel 845-658-8270; Fax: 845-658-3718
E-mail: publisher@evolvedself.com
Web site: http://www.evolvedself.com
Dist(s): **Smashwords.**

Evolved Teacher Pr. *Imprint of* **499**

EvoraBooks, LLC, *(978-0-9725071)* P.O. Box 397, Canton, CT 06019 USA
E-mail: evorabooks@snet.net
Web site: http://www.booksbyevora.com.

Ewers Family Partnership, *(978-0-9987475)* 404 Ridge Rd., Boulder City, NV 89005 USA Tel 702-294-7718; Fax: 702-294-7718
E-mail: lifelake@embarqmail.com.

Ewuramma, *(978-0-9849805)* 1850 Lafayette Ave. Apt. 3A, Bronx, NY 10473 USA Tel 646-220-6432
E-mail: adomkwa1@gmail.com.

Exact Change, *(978-1-878972)* 5 Brewster St., Cambridge, MA 02138 USA Tel 617-492-5405
E-mail: dk@exactchange.com; ny@exactchange.com
Web site: http://www.exactchange.com
Dist(s): **D.A.P./Distributed Art Pubs.**

Exambusters *Imprint of* **Ace Academics, Inc.**

Examined Solutions PTE. Ltd., *(978-1-68374)* 9450 SW Gemini Dr., No. 21372, Beaverton, OR 97008 USA (SAN 990-1426) Tel 888-248-4521
E-mail: admin@speedypublishing.com; examinedsolutions@gmail.com.

ExamWise *Imprint of* **Total Recall Learning, Inc.**

Excalibur Bks., *(978-1-7330921)* 2635 Second Ave., No. 828, San Diego, CA 92103 USA Tel 619-892-7004
E-mail: simon.grey.yokai@gmail.com.

Exceed, LLC, *(978-0-9771722)* 715 E. 100 N., Lindon, UT 84042 USA (SAN 256-8519) Tel 801-785-7931
E-mail: kcooper@exceed.bz
Web site: http://www.exceed.bz.

Excel Digital Pr., *(978-0-9712249; 978-0-9718254; 978-0-9749202; 978-0-9786376; 978-1-7328955)* Orders Addr.: P.O. Box 703978, Carrollton, TX 75007 USA Tel 214-228-8636; Fax: 214-228-8636; Edit Addr.: 1614 Saxony Pl., Carrollton, TX 75007 USA
E-mail: exceldigitalpress@yahoo.com
Web site: http://www.exceldigitalpress.com.

Excel Heritage Group, Inc., *(978-0-692-88807-0)* 2007 Remington Oaks Cir, CARY, NC 27519 USA Tel 678-549-6517
Dist(s): **Ingram Content Group.**

Excellence Enterprises, *(978-0-9627735)* 3040 Aspen Ln., Palmdale, CA 93550-7985 USA Tel 661-267-2220; Fax: 661-267-2946
E-mail: lavonne.taylor@sbcglobal.net
Web site: http://vonnieshealthspot.com.

Excellence Student Incentives, *(978-0-9789612)* 18942 Muirland, Detroit, MI 48221 USA (SAN 852-1107) Tel 313-646-6079; Fax: 313-449-0396
E-mail: beatthemeap@yahoo.com
Web site: http://www.beatthemeap.com.

Excellent Bks., *(978-0-9628014; 978-1-880780)*
E-mail: books@excellentbooks.com
Web site: http://www.excellentbooks.com.

Excite Kids Pr. *Imprint of* **Publishing Services @ Thomson-Shore**

Executive Books *See* **Tremendous Life Bks.**

Executive Performances, Inc., *(978-0-9748220)* P.O. Box 93, Palos Park, IL 60464 USA; *Imprints:* Executive Performances Publishing (Exec Perform Pubng)
E-mail: magicriz@aol.com.

Executive Performances Publishing *Imprint of* **Executive Performances, Inc.**

Publisher Name Index

Exeter Pr., (978-0-9700612; 978-0-9797407) Orders Addr.: 223 Commonwealth Ave., Boston, MA 02116 USA Tel 617-267-7720; Fax: 617-262-6948; Edit Addr.: 223 Commonwealth Ave., Boston, MA 02116 USA (SAN 854-2554)
E-mail: davidburke@commonwealthfilms.com
Web site: http://www.exeterpress.com.

Exhibit A *Imprint of* **Scholastic, Inc.**

Exhibit A *Imprint of* **TR Bks.**

Exhibit A Pr., (978-0-9633954; 978-0-9815519) 4657 Cajon Way, San Diego, CA 92115 USA Tel 619-286-6350; Fax: 619-286-1591
E-mail: mail@exhibitapress.com
Web site: http://www.exhibitapress.com
Dist(s): **Baker & Taylor Publisher Services (BTPS) Independent Pubs. Group MyiLibrary.**

Exile Editions, Ltd. (CAN) (978-0-920428; 978-1-55096) *Dist. by* **IPG Chicago.**

Exisle Publishing Pty Ltd. (AUS) (978-1-921497; 978-1-921966; 978-1-925335; 978-0-646-95875-0; 978-1-925820) *Dist. by* **HachBkGrp.**

Exit Studio, (978-0-9640868; 978-0-9831891) 1466 N. Quinn St., Arlington, VA 22209 USA Tel 703-312-7121; Fax: 703-894-2741
E-mail: efontanez@exitstudio.com
Web site: http://www.exitstudio.com
Dist(s): **Follett School Solutions.**

Exley, Helen Giftbooks (GBR) (978-0-905521; 978-1-85015; 978-1-86187; 978-1-905130; 978-1-84634; 978-1-78485) *Dist. by* **Natl Bk Netwk.**

Exodus 35:31 Artistry LLC, (978-0-9989256) 49 S. Syracuse St., Denver, CO 80230 USA
E-mail: kimbaltz@hotmail.com; kimbaltz@hotmail.com; kimbaltz@hotmail.com; exoduskb@gmail.com
Dist(s): **CreateSpace Independent Publishing Platform.**

ExpandingBooks.com, (978-0-9721764; 978-1-934443) 200 W. 34th, Suite 953, Anchorage, AK 99503 USA Tel 907-278-9800; Fax: 877-552-7200
E-mail: cherylkirk@gmail.com; expandingbooks@gmail.com
Web site: http://www.expandingpress.com; http://www.expandingbooks
Dist(s): **Taku Graphics.**

Experiment LLC, The, (978-1-61519) 260 Fifth Ave., Suite 3 S., New York, NY 10001-6425 USA (SAN 857-961X)
E-mail: info@theexperimentpublishing.com
Web site: http://www.theexperimentpublishing.com
Dist(s): **Open Road Integrated Media, Inc. Timber Pr., Inc. Workman Publishing Co., Inc.**

Expert Systems for Teachers *Imprint of* **Teaching Point, Inc.**

Explorations Early Learning, (978-0-615-15718-4; 978-0-615-15719-1) 1524 Summit St., Sioux City, IA 51103 USA Tel 712-262-1627
E-mail: jeffajohnson@cableone.net
Web site: http://www.explorationsearlylearning.com
Dist(s): **Lulu Pr., Inc.**

Explorer Media *Imprint of* **Simon & Barklee, Inc./ExplorerMedia**

Explorer's Bible Study, (978-1-889015; 978-0-9787993; 978-1-935424) 2652 Hwy. 46 S., Dickson, TN 37055 USA Tel 615-446-7316; Fax: 615-446-7951; Toll Free: 800-657-2874; P.O. Box 425, Dickson, TN 37056 Toll Free: 800-657-2874
Web site: http://www.explorerbiblestudy.org.

Exploring California Insects *Imprint of* **Insect Sciences Museum of California**

Exploring ExPr.ion LLC, (978-0-692-10412-5; 978-1-7324823) 122 Lakewood Dr, Kingsland, GA 31548 USA Tel 405-795-4824
E-mail: exploringexpression@gmail.com.

Express Bks. *Imprint of* **Bellwether Media**

Expressions Woven, (978-0-9668179) P.O. Box 1004, Waterford, CT 06385 USA Tel 860-442-1332; Fax: 860-447-9916
E-mail: dreaminthelight@alum.rpi.edu
Web site: http://www.poetryin.com
Dist(s): **Ingram Content Group.**

Expressive Design Group, Inc., (978-0-9845278; 978-1-936676) 49 Garfield St., Holyoke, MA 01040 USA (SAN 859-6654) Tel 413-315-6296; Fax: 413-315-6271; Toll Free: 800-848-6685
E-mail: richard.marks@theedg.net
Web site: http://www.theedg.net.

Expressive Ink, (978-0-9759362) Orders Addr.: P.O. Box 74, Foreston, MN 56330 USA; Edit Addr.: 305 Pheasant Ln., Foreston, MN 56330-5540 USA Tel 320-294-4022
E-mail: express@bctelco.net
Web site: http://www.natknows.com.

Exquisite Thoughts, Incorporated *See* **CCP Publishing & Entertainment**

Extejt, Gabriele *See* **McGab Publishing**

Extended Blessings, (978-0-9984267) 3807 Stonecreek Cir SW, Conyers, GA 30094 USA Tel 404-934-8352; Fax: 404-934-8352
E-mail: msdonita76@gmail.com.

Extra Point Pubs., (978-0-9801749; 978-0-9840847; 978-0-9846377; 978-0-9882595; 978-0-9904882; 978-0-9973309) Orders Addr.: P.O. Box 871, Perry, GA 31069 USA; Edit Addr.: 315 Hampton Ct., Perry, GA 31069 USA (SAN 855-4129) Tel 478-224-3267; Fax: 478-218-0306
Web site: http://www.die-hardfans.com.

Extreme Explorers LLC, (978-0-9996666) 14113 Deep Lake Dr, Orlando, FL 32826 USA Tel 859-433-6585
E-mail: MrsHasford@gmail.com.

Eye Bks. (GBR) (978-1-903070; 978-1-908646; 978-1-78563) *Dist. by* **IPG Chicago.**

Eye Contact Media, (978-0-9729187) 1344 Disc Dr., No. 105, Sparks, NV 89436 USA
Web site: http://www.eyecontactmedia.com.

Eye of Newt, The, (978-0-9762565) 5203 Cedar Springs Rd, Dallas, TX 75235-8537 USA Tel 214-520-1739
Web site: http://www.theyeofnewt.com.

Eyres, John, (978-0-9769762) 12713 Willowyck Dr., Saint Louis, MO 63146 USA.

E-z Clothin' *Imprint of* **Prince Zone Publishing**

EZ Comics, (978-0-9795887) 12, Pine Top Rd., Barrington, RI 02806-1706 USA
E-mail: vshah.ezcomics@gmail.com; vshah@ezcomics.com
Web site: http://ezcomics.com.

EZ Muzik Publishing, (978-0-615-24181-4; 978-0-9822805; 978-0-692-01686-2) P.O. Box 50826, Santa barbara, CA 93108 USA Tel 805-886-0799
E-mail: patrikpiano@aol.com.

Ezra's Earth Publishing, (978-0-9727855) P.O. Box 3036, South Pasadena, CA 91031 USA (SAN 255-0555)
E-mail: information@ezrasearth.com
Web site: http://www.ezrasearth.com
Dist(s): **Quality Bks., Inc.**

Ezra's Engine Publishing *See* **Ezra's Earth Publishing**

F & S Music KS Publishing Co., (978-0-9745630; 978-0-9765787) Orders Addr.: P.O. Box 11805, Jackson, MS 39283 USA; Edit Addr.: 1902 Queens Road Ave., Jackson, MS 39213 USA
E-mail: lanniespann@yahoo.com
Web site: lanniespannmcbride.com.

FC&A Publishing, (978-0-915099; 978-1-890957; 978-1-932470; 978-1-935574) 103 Clover Green, Peachtree City, GA 30269-1695 USA (SAN 289-7946) Tel 770-487-6307; Fax: 770-631-4357; Toll Free: 800-537-1275
E-mail: charlotte_carpenter@fca.com; anne_kaufmann@fca.com
Web site: http://www.fca.com.

F E A Publishing *See* **FEA Ministries**

FA LLC, (978-0-692-74187-0; 978-0-692-79747-1) 7582 Cresthill Dr., Longmont, CO 80504 USA Tel 303-859-0121; Toll Free: 303-859-0121
Dist(s): **CreateSpace Independent Publishing Platform.**

Fabbri Editori - RCS Libri (ITA) (978-88-450; 978-88-451; 978-88-452; 978-88-454) *Dist. by* **Distribks Inc.**

Faber & Faber Children's Bks. *Imprint of* **Faber & Faber, Inc.**

†Faber & Faber, Inc., (978-0-571) Affil. of Farrar, Straus & Giroux, LLC, Orders Addr.: c/o Van Holtzbrinck Publishing Services, 16365 James Madison Hwy., Gordonsville, VA 22942 USA Fax: 540-572-7540; Toll Free: 888-330-8477; Edit Addr.: 19 Union Sq., W, New York, NY 10003-3304 USA (SAN 218-7256) Tel 212-741-6900; Fax: 212-633-9385; *Imprints:* Faber & Faber Children's Books (F&FChildrens)
E-mail: sales@fsgbooks.com
Web site: http://www.fsgbooks.com
Dist(s): **Continental Bk. Co., Inc. ISD Macmillan MyiLibrary Penguin Random Hse. Distribution Penguin Random Hse. LLC Publishers Group West (PGW)**; *CIP.*

Faber & Faber, Ltd. (GBR) (978-0-571; 978-1-78335) *Dist. by* **Alfred Pub.**

Faber, David *See* **Faber Pr.**

Faber Music, Ltd. (GBR) (978-0-571) *Dist. by* **Alfred Pub.**

Faber Piano Adventuresr, (978-1-61677) 3042 Creek Dr., Ann Arbor, MI 48108 USA Tel 734-975-1995; Fax: 734-332-7823
Dist(s): **Leonard, Hal Corp.**

Faber Pr., (978-0-9768763) Orders Addr.: 5638 Lake Murray Blvd., No.206, La Mesa, CA 91942 USA (SAN 256-8071) Tel 619-517-2662; Fax: 619-255-2354
E-mail: annavennis@yahoo.com
Web site: http://www.becauseofromek.com.

Fabled Films LLC, (978-1-944020) 200 Park Ave. S., New York, NY 10003 USA Tel 212-220-5804; *Imprints:* Fabled Films Press LLC (Fabled Film)
E-mail: StaceyAshton@fabledfilms.com
Web site: www.fabledfilms.com
Dist(s): **Consortium Bk. Sales & Distribution.**

Fabled Films Pr. LLC *Imprint of* **Fabled Films LLC**

Fablefy LLC, (978-0-578-18496-8) 2515 Plaza Dr., Woodbridge, NJ 07095 USA.

FableVision Pr., (978-1-891405) 308 Congress St. # 6, Boston, MA 02210-1027 USA Toll Free: 888-240-3734
E-mail: info@fablevision.com; shoppe@fablevision.com
Web site: http://www.fablevision.com; http://www.fablevision.com/shoppe.

Fabula, (978-0-9915194; 978-0-9915195) P.O. Box 2709, Redmond, WA 98073 USA Tel 314-495-6939
E-mail: kkennedy0929@gmail.com.

Fabulicity Lifestyle Creations, (978-1-7324186) 429 Main Rd, Maryville, TN 37804 USA Tel 865-679-7948
E-mail: rheimerman@bellsouth.net.

Face 2 Face Games Publishing, (978-0-9728197; 978-0-9761156) 36 The Arcade, 65 Weybosset St., Providence, RI 02903 USA Tel 401-351-0362 (phone/fax)
E-mail: lwhalen@face2facegames.com
Web site: http://www.face2facegames.com
Dist(s): **PSI (Publisher Services, Inc.).**

Factors Pr., (978-0-9700582) Orders Addr.: 14718 Ellison Ave., Omaha, NE 68116-4336 USA
E-mail: Info@FactorsPress.com.

†Facts On File, Inc., (978-0-8160; 978-0-87196; 978-1-60413; 978-1-4381; 978-1-61753) Orders Addr.: 132 W. 31st St., 17th Flr., New York, NY 10001-2006 USA (SAN 201-4696) Tel 212-967-8800; 212-896-4296 (customer service); Fax: 917-339-0325; 917-339-0323; Toll Free Fax: 800-678-3633; Toll Free: 800-322-8755; *Imprints:* Checkmark Books (Checkmark); Ferguson Publishing Company (Ferg Pub Co); Chelsea House (ChelsHse); Chelsea Clubhouse (ChelseaClub); Bloom's Literary Criticism (Bloom's Lit); World Almanac Books (WrldAlmanac)
E-mail: custserv@factsonfile.com; Sales@ChelseaHouse.com
Web site: http://www.factsonfile.com; http://www.fergpubco.com; http://www.chelseahouse.com
Dist(s): **Casemate Academic CreateSpace Independent Publishing Platform Ebsco Publishing Follett School Solutions Infobase Learning MyiLibrary Simon & Schuster, Inc. ebrary, Inc.**; *CIP.*

Faden, Ellen, (978-0-9821231) 145 Plaza Dr., Suite 207-224, Vallejo, CA 94590 USA (SAN 857-3166) Tel 415-342-1552
E-mail: efaden1@gmail.com
Web site: http://www.kabbalah-dating.com.

Fagiolina Pr., (978-0-9986527) 4605 8th Street, NW, Washington, DC 20011 USA Tel 202-819-4646
E-mail: ninahalper@gmail.com
Web site: www.fagiolinapress.com.

Fahnestock Pr., (978-0-9747981) 310 Dennytown Rd., Putman Valley, NY 10579-1423 USA (SAN 255-8564) Tel 212-894-1219
E-mail: weigman676@aol.com.

Fair, Barbara A., (978-0-9621174) Orders Addr.: P.O. Box 241155, Detroit, MI 48224 USA (SAN 250-7447); Edit Addr.: P.O. Box 26101, Fraser, MI 48026-6101 USA (SAN 250-7455).

Fair Havens Pubns., (978-0-9664803) P.O. Box 1238, Gainsville, TX 76241 USA Tel 940-668-6044; Fax: 940-668-6984; Toll Free: 800-771-4861
E-mail: fairhavens@fairhavenspub.com
Web site: http://www.fairhavenspub.com; http://www.ageofgrace.com
Dist(s): **Anchor Distributors Spring Arbor Distributors, Inc.**

Fair Page Media LLC, (978-0-9989098) 626 W. Springfield Rd., Springfield, PA 19064-1626 USA Tel 484-432-1486
E-mail: joelmanon.jm@gmail.com
Dist(s): **Ingram Content Group.**

Fair Winds Pr. *Imprint of* **Quarto Publishing Group USA**

Fairchild Bks. *Imprint of* **Bloomsbury Academic & Professional**

Fairchild Bks., (978-0-87005; 978-1-56367; 978-1-60901) Div. of Bloomsbury Publishing, c/o Sandra Washington, 750 Third Ave., 8th Floor, New York, NY 10017 USA (SAN 201-470X) Tel 212-630-3875; Fax: 212-630-3868; Toll Free: 800-932-4724
Web site: http://www.fairchildbooks.com
Dist(s): **Bloomsbury Publishing USA MyiLibrary.**

Fairfax Lectern, Inc., The, (978-0-9701756) 4280-Redwood Hwy., No. 11, San Rafael, CA 94903 USA Tel 415-479-1128; Fax: 415-479-9024
E-mail: scallsed@aol.com
Web site: http://www.fairfax-lectern.com; http://www.professordave.com
Dist(s): .

Fairfield Language Technologies *See* **Rosetta Stone Ltd.**

Fairhaven Bk. Pubs., (978-1-929649) P.O. Box 105, Lucerne Valley, CA 92356 USA Tel 760-248-1086
E-mail: fairhaven-books@outlook.com
Web site: http://www.worldpeace2.com; http://www.themotivationsolution.net; http://www.forebrain.org;
Dist(s): **Quality Bks., Inc.**

Fairland Bks., (978-0-9818154) P.O. Box 63, West Friendship, MD 21794 USA
Web site: http://fairlandbooks.com
Dist(s): **Emerald Bk. Co.**

†Fairmont Pr., Inc., (978-0-88173; 978-0-915586) 700 Indian Trail, Lilburn, GA 30047 USA (SAN 207-5946) Tel 770-925-9388; Fax: 770-381-9865
Web site: http://www.fairmontpress.com
Dist(s): **Assn. of Energy Engineers CRC Pr. LLC Ebsco Publishing Lulu Pr., Inc. Taylor & Francis Group**; *CIP.*

Fairway Pr. *Imprint of* **CSS Publishing Co.**

Fairwood Pr., (978-0-9668184; 978-0-9746573; 978-1-933846; 978-0-9789078; 978-0-9820730) 21528 104th St. Ct. E., Bonney Lake, WA 98391 USA Tel 253-269-2640; *Imprints:* Media Man! Productions (MeidaMan)
E-mail: patrick@fairwoodpress.com
Web site: http://www.fairwoodpress.com.

Fairy Faye Pubns. (GBR) (978-0-9928269; 978-0-9933842) *Dist. by* **IPG Chicago.**

†Faith Alive Christian Resources, (978-0-930265; 978-0-933140; 978-1-56212; 978-1-59255; 978-1-62025) 2850 Kalamazoo Ave., SE, Grand Rapids, MI 49560 USA (SAN 212-727X) Tel 616-224-0784; Fax: 616-224-0834; Toll Free Fax: 888-642-8606; Toll Free: 800-333-8300; P.O. Box 5070, Burlington, ON L7R 3Y8 Toll Free Fax: 888-642-8606; Toll Free: 800-333-8300
E-mail: sales@faithaliveresources.org
Web site: http://www.faithaliveresources.org
Dist(s): **Lulu Pr., Inc.**; *CIP.*

Faith & Action Team, (978-1-931984; 978-1-60382) 429 Us Hwy. 65, Walnut Shade, MO 65771 USA
E-mail: elizabeth@faithandactionseries.org
Web site: http://www.faithandactionseries.org; http://www.seriefeyaccion.org
Dist(s): **MyiLibrary.**

Faith & Action/RD *See* **Faith & Action Team**

Faith & Life Pr., (978-0-87303) Orders Addr.: P.O. Box 347, Newton, KS 67114-0347 USA (SAN 658-0637) Tel 316-283-5100; Fax: 316-283-0454; Toll Free: 800-245-7894 (orders only); Edit Addr.: 718 Main St., Newton, KS 67114-0347 USA (SAN 201-4726)
E-mail: flp@gcmc.org
Web site: http://www.2southwind.net/~gcmc/flp.html
Dist(s): **Herald Pr. Spring Arbor Distributors, Inc.**

Faith Baptist Church Publications *See* **FBC Pubns. & Printing**

Faith Bks. & MORE, (978-0-9820197; 978-0-9841729; 978-0-9842378; 978-0-9845779; 978-0-9846507; 978-0-9852729; 978-0-9860159; 978-0-9860247; 978-1-939761) 3255 Lawrenceville-Suwanee Rd., Suite P250, Suwanee, GA 30024 USA (SAN 857-0337) Tel 678-232-6156; Fax: 888-479-4540
E-mail: publishing@faithbooksandmore.com
Web site: http://www.faithbooksandmore.com; http://www.facebook.com/corpconnoisseur; http://www.facebook.com/faithbooksandmorepublishing.

Faith Communications *Imprint of* **Health Communications, Inc.**

Faith Pubns., (978-0-9743167) 5301 Edgewood Rd., College Park, MD 20740 USA Tel 301-982-2061 Do not confuse with companies with the same name in Milton, FL, Haviland, KS
E-mail: faith@alhuda.org.

Faith, Substance & Evidence, (978-0-692-99106-0; 978-0-692-18628-2; 978-0-692-18794-4; 978-0-692-18796-8; 978-0-692-18800-2) 24706 Timberlake Dr., Greenwood, MO 64034 USA Tel 816-394-8816
E-mail: eacroteau@gmail.com
Dist(s): **Ingram Content Group.**

Faithful Life Pubs., (978-0-9749836; 978-0-9821408; 978-0-9824931; 978-0-9845208; 978-0-9829105; 978-0-9832039; 978-1-937129; 978-1-63073) Div. of With Integrity Ministries, 3335 Galaxy Way, North Fort Myers, FL 33903-1419 USA Tel 239-652-0135; Toll Free: 800-699-2623
E-mail: editor@FLPublishers.com
Web site: http://www.faithfullife.com; http://www.FLPublishers.com.

Faithful Publishing, (978-0-9759941; 978-0-9779889; 978-1-940911) P.O. Box 345, Buford, GA 30515-0345 USA Tel 770-932-7335; Fax: 678-482-4446; *Imprints:* Pixelated Publishing (Pixel Pubng)
E-mail: faithfulpublishing@yahoo.com; alwzapri@bellsouth.net
Web site: http://www.eighttwelvepublishing.com.

FAITHTOGO, (978-0-9765898) P.O. Box 17273, San Antonio, TX 78217 USA
E-mail: faithtogo@msn.com
Web site: http://www.faithtogo.com.

FaithWalker Publishing *Imprint of* **Markowitz, Darryl**

Faithwords *Imprint of* **FaithWords**

FaithWords, (978-0-446) 10 Cadillac Dr., Suite 220, Brentwood, TN 37027 USA Tel 615-221-0962; Toll Free: 800-423-1247; *Imprints:* Faithwords (Faithwrds); Jelly Telly Press (Jelly Telly Pr)
E-mail: fwpublicity@hbgusa.com
Dist(s): **Blackstone Audio, Inc. Hachette Bk. Group MyiLibrary.**

FAL Enterprises LLC, (978-0-9843047; 978-0-9837515; 978-0-9849400; 978-0-9986231; 978-1-7322584) P.O. Box 140189, Howard Beach, NY 11414 USA (SAN 859-0109)
E-mail: minerva_francesca@yahoo.com
Web site: http://www.falenterprises.com
Dist(s): **BookBaby Independent Pubs. Group Innovative Logistics Midpoint Trade Bks., Inc.**

Falcon Guides *Imprint of* **Globe Pequot Pr., The**

Falcon Pr. International, (978-1-884459) 2150 Almaden Rd., No. 141, San Jose, CA 95125 USA Tel 408-677-4875
E-mail: getty@gettyambau.com.

Falcon Publishing LTD, (978-0-9746959) P.O. Box 6099, Kingwood, TX 77325 USA
E-mail: gwen@falconpublishing.com
Web site: http://www.falconpublishing.com.

Falcor Bks., (978-0-9723530) P.O. Box 1055, Yorktown, VA 23692-1055 USA Tel 757-872-6649; Toll Free: 866-872-6649
E-mail: info@falcorbooks.com
Web site: http://www.falcorbooks.com.

†Falk Art Reference, (978-0-932087) Div. of artprice.com, Orders Addr.: P.O. Box 833, Madison, CT 06443 USA (SAN 686-5240) Tel 203-245-2246; Fax: 203-245-5116; Toll Free: 800-278-4274; Edit Addr.: 61 Beekman Pl., Madison, CT 06443-2400 USA Do not confuse with companies with the same name in Tacoma, WA
E-mail: info@falkart.com
Web site: http://www.falkart.com; http://www.artprice.com; *CIP.*

Fall Rose Bks., (978-0-9742185) 7 Riverwoods Dr. Apt D211, Exeter, NH 03833 USA Tel 207-439-2878
Web site: http://www.fallrosebooks.com.

Fallick, Barbara, (978-0-692-31163-9; 978-0-9997020) 1650 Gold St., Eureka, UT 84628 USA Tel 801-746-9052; 801-746-9064; *Imprints:* Gold Street Publishers (Gold Street Pubs)
E-mail: goldstreetpublishers@gmail.com.

Falls Media *See* **Seven Footer Pr.**

FAM Publications *See* **iFAM Publishing, LLC**

Fame's Eternal Bks., LLC, *(978-0-9753721)* 15740 Rockford Rd. #312, Plymouth, MN 55446 USA Tel 512-468-8873
E-mail: tammymate@aol.com
Web site: http://www.fameseternalbooks.com.

Familius LLC, *(978-1-938301; 978-1-939629; 978-1-942672; 978-1-942934; 978-1-944822; 978-1-945547; 978-1-64170)* 1254 Commerce Way, Sanger, CA 93657 USA (SAN 990-1515) Tel 801-552-7298; 559-876-2170
E-mail: christopher@familius.com
Web site: www.familius.com
Dist(s): **MyiLibrary**
Workman Publishing Co., Inc.

Family Bks., *(978-0-9728460)* Orders Addr.: P.O. Box 730, Petaluma, CA 94953-0730 USA Do not confuse with companies with the same name in Glendale, CA, Dana Point, CA
E-mail: familybooks2003@yahoo.com.

Family Bks. at Home, *(978-0-9753127; 978-1-933200)* 375 Hudson St., 2nd Flr., New York, NY 10014-3657 USA.

Family Enterprises, *(978-0-9773858)* 2678 Challis Creek Rd., Box 981, Challis, ID 83226-0981 USA Do not confuse with Family Enterprises in Milwaukee, WI.

Family Guidance & Outreach Ctr. of Lubbock, *(978-0-9767215)* 5 Briercroft Office Pk., Lubbock, TX 79412-3007 USA Tel 806-747-5577; Fax: 806-747-5119
E-mail: wedwards23@cox.net.

Family Harvest Church, *(978-1-889723)* 18500 92nd Ave., Tinley Park, IL 60477 USA (SAN 801-4817) Tel 708-614-6000; Fax: 708-614-8288; Toll Free: 800-622-0017
E-mail: winner@winninginlife.org
Web site: http://www.winninginlife.org
Dist(s): **Smashwords.**

Family Learning Assn., Inc., *(978-0-9719874)* 3925 Hagan St. Ste. 103, Bloomington, IN 47401-8649 USA
Web site: http://www.kidscanlearn.com.

Family Legacy Ministries, *(978-0-9797879)* Orders Addr.: P.O. Box 811, Rocky Point, NC 28457 USA Tel 910-675-1825
E-mail: publishing@familylegacyministries.org
Web site: http://www.familylegacyministries.org.

Family Life Productions, *(978-1-883761)* 2460 Hobbit Ln., Fallbrook, CA 92028-3679 USA (SAN 239-1090) Tel 760-728-6437; Fax: 760-728-5309; Toll Free: 800-886-2767.

Family Nutrition Ctr. P.C., *(978-0-9770756)* 98 Harding Rd., Glen Rock, NJ 07452-1317 USA
E-mail: everyday7foods@earthlink.net.

Family Of Man Pr., The *Imprint of* **Hutchison, G.F. Pr.**

Family Plays, *(978-0-87602; 978-0-88680)* Div. of Dramatic Publishing, Orders Addr.: 311 Washington St., Woodstock, IL 60098-3308 USA (SAN 282-7433) Tel 815-338-7170
E-mail: msergel@dpcplays.com
Web site: http://www.familyplays.com; http://www.dramaticpublishing.com.

Family Rocks, The, *(978-0-9747466)* 256 S. Robertson Blvd., Beverly Hills, CA 90211-2898 USA Tel 310-358-5106; Fax: 310-734-1594
E-mail: sales@coupon-directory.com
Web site: http://www.coupon-directory.com.

Family Value Publishing, *(978-0-9645180)* R.R. 2, Box 110A, Nevis, MN 56467 USA Tel 218-732-1349.

Family Value Series, *(978-0-9894443)* 257 Blazer Ave, Eugene, OR 97404 USA Tel 541-345-5110
E-mail: rasorprogram@aol.com
Dist(s): **Lulu Pr., Inc.**

FamilyLife, *(978-1-57229; 978-1-60200)* Div. of Campus Crusade for Christ, 5800 Ranch Dr., Little Rock, AR 72223 USA Tel 501-223-8663; Fax: 501-224-2529; Toll Free: 800-404-5052
Web site: http://www.familylife.com.

Familyman Ministries, *(978-0-9821941; 978-1-937639)* 611 S. Main St., Milford, IN 46542 USA Tel 574-658-4376
Web site: http://www.familymanweb.com.

Fan, Mary, *(978-1-7321986)* 20 2nd St., Jersey City, NJ 07302 USA Tel 609-240-9808
E-mail: astralcolt@gmail.com
Dist(s): **Ingram Content Group.**

FancyCrazy Publishing, *(978-0-9745386)* 254 Harrison St., 1st Fl., Nutley, NJ 07110 USA Tel 917-279-5920
E-mail: fch3000@yahoo.com; baltazarray@gmail.com
Web site: http://www.FancyCrazyHydrants.TV.

Fandemonium Bks. *Imprint of* **Fandemonium Ltd.**

Fandemonium Ltd., *(978-0-9547343; 978-1-905586; 978-1-80070)* Orders Addr.: 3 Browns Rd., Surbiton, KT58SP GBR; Edit Addr.: P.O. Box 2178, Decatur, GA 30031 USA; *Imprints:* Fandemonium Books (FndmnmBks)
E-mail: fandemonium@blueyonder.co.uk
Web site: http://www.stargatenovels.com.

Fanning, Neli, *(978-0-692-19555-0)* 5654 W. Cornelia Ave., Chicago, IL 60634 USA Tel 347-307-2326
E-mail: nelilalanne@gmail.com
Dist(s): **Ingram Content Group.**

Fantagraphics Bks., *(978-0-930193; 978-1-56097; 978-1-60699; 978-1-68396)* 7563 Lake City Way, NE, Seattle, WA 98115 USA (SAN 251-5571) Tel 206-524-1967; Fax: 206-524-2104; Toll Free: 800-657-1100
E-mail: zura@fantagraphics.com; diva@eroscomix.com; fbicomix@fantagraphics.com
Web site: http://www.fantagraphics.com; http://eroscomix.com
Dist(s): **Diamond Comic Distributors, Inc.**
Diamond Bk. Distributors
Norton, W. W. & Co., Inc.

Fantasías Puertorriqueñas, *(978-0-9785676)* calle Mendez Vigo No. 275, Dorado, PR 00646 USA Tel 787-796-6154
E-mail: drelfrenrios@prtc.net.

Fantasy Flight Games *See* **Asmodee North America, Inc.**

Fantasy Island Pr., *(978-0-9766628)* 320 W. 7th St., Beach Heaven, NJ 08008 USA Tel 609-492-4000; Fax: 609-492-3512
E-mail: webmaster@fantasyislandpark.com
Web site: http://www.fantasyislandpark.com.

Fantasy Prone Comics, *(978-0-9762842; 978-0-615-32076-2; 978-0-615-36782-8; 978-0-615-39550-0)* 3625 Fredonia Dr., Suite 2, Hollywood, CA 90068 USA (SAN 631-8606) Tel 310-270-6612
E-mail: blakeleibel1@hotmail.com
Web site: http://www.fantasyprone.com
Dist(s): **Diamond Bk. Distributors.**

Far Out Pr., *(978-0-9915285; 978-1-7333589)* 2915 California St., San Francisco, CA 94115 USA Tel 415-746-0430
E-mail: citizenwriter2010@gmail.com
Web site: http://faroutpress.com/.

Farah, Barbara, *(978-0-9769346)* P.O. Box 350, Center Harbor, NH 03226 USA Tel 603-253-7142
E-mail: bbfarah@yahoo.com.

Faraway Publishing, *(978-0-9710130)* Orders Addr.: P.O. Box 765, Highlands, NC 28741-0765 USA Fax: 828-526-5622
E-mail: faraway@nctv.com.

FarBeyond Publishing LLC, *(978-1-936872)* 8185 SW Birchwood Rd., Portland, OR 97225 USA (SAN 920-5276) Tel 503-683-3013
E-mail: publish@farbeyond.com
Web site: http://farbeyond.com
Dist(s): **CreateSpace Independent Publishing Platform**
Quality Bks., Inc.

Farcountry Pr., *(978-0-938314; 978-1-56037; 978-1-59152)* Orders Addr.: P.O. Box 5630, Helena, MT 59604 USA (SAN 220-0732) Tel 406-422-1263; Fax: 406-443-5480; Toll Free: 800-821-3874; 2750 Broadwater, Helena, MT 59602; *Imprints:* Sweetgrass Books (SweetgrassBks)
E-mail: books@farcountrypress.com
Web site: http://www.farcountrypress.com
Dist(s): **INscribe Digital**
Partners Bk. Distributing, Inc.
TNT Media Group, Inc.

Farmer Valley Publishing, *(978-1-7328384)* 779 Cty. Rd., Jackson, MO 63755 USA Tel 573-833-6509
E-mail: rechenberg@yahoo.com
Web site: www.marykoeberlrechenbergwriter.com.

Farmer's Daughter Pr., *(978-0-615-66088-2; 978-0-692-37657-7; 978-0-9979274)* P.O. Box 772, Hebron, CT 06248 USA Tel 860-384-3049
Dist(s): **CreateSpace Independent Publishing Platform.**

Faros Bks. (GBR) *(978-1-913060; 978-1-9164091) Dist. by* **IPG Chicago.**

Farrand Avenue Faith Publishing, *(978-0-9887841)* 301 Lakeside Dr., Walkerton, IN 46574 USA Tel 219-369-9302
E-mail: wordgirl_mary.allen@yahoo.com.

Farrar, Straus & Giroux *Imprint of* **Farrar, Straus & Giroux**

†Farrar, Straus & Giroux, *(978-0-374)* Div. of Holtzbrinck Publishers, Orders Addr.: c/o Holtzbrinck Publishers, 16365 James Madison Hwy., Gordonsville, VA 22942 USA Toll Free Fax: 800-672-2054; Toll Free: 888-330-8477; Edit Addr.: 18 W. 18th St., New York, NY 10011-4607 USA (SAN 206-782X); *Imprints:* Farrar, Straus & Giroux (FarStraGir); Hill & Wang (Hil-Wang); Farrar, Straus & Giroux (BYR) (FSGBYR)
E-mail: sales@fsgee.com; fsg.editorial@fsgee.com
Web site: http://www.fsgbooks.com/
Dist(s): **Children's Plus, Inc.**
Continental Bk. Co., Inc.
Lectorum Pubns., Inc.
Macmillan
MyiLibrary
Perfection Learning Corp.
SPD-Small Pr. Distribution
Westminster John Knox Pr.; *CIP.*

Farrar, Straus & Giroux (BYR) *Imprint of* **Farrar, Straus & Giroux**

Farrell Writes, LLC, *(978-0-692-70163-8; 978-0-9991278)* 5859 Landau Dr., Southaven, MS 38671 USA Tel 901-606-5407
E-mail: farrellwrites@gmail.com
Web site: http://farrellwrites.com
Dist(s): **CreateSpace Independent Publishing Platform.**

F.A.S.T. Learning LLC, *(978-1-59792)* 3447 S Birch St, Denver, CO 80222 USA Tel 720-537-7599
E-mail: becky@crsuccesslearning.com
Web site: http://www.fastlearningllc.com.

FASTLANE LLC, *(978-1-64193; 978-1-0717)* PO Box 85073, Richmond, VA 23285 USA; *Imprints:* Bold Illustrations (BoldIllustration).

Fastlane LLC, *(978-0-9966017)* P.O. Box 85073, Richmond, VA 23285-5073 USA
E-mail: fastlanellcproducts@gmail.com.

FastPrncil, Inc., *(978-1-60746; 978-1-61933; 978-1-63364; 978-1-4999; 978-1-68133)* 1608 W. Campbell Ave. Suite 239, Campbell, CA 95008 USA Tel 408-540-7571; Fax: 408-540-7572; *Imprints:* Premiere (PremierPenc)
E-mail: operations@fastpencil.com; author_services@fastpencil.com
Web site: http://www.fastpencil.com.

FastPublishing.com *See* **ExpandingBooks.com**

Fasttrack Teaching Materials, *(978-1-893742)* 6215 Lavell Court, Springfield, VA 22152 USA Tel 703-644-4612
E-mail: davburns@fasttrackteaching.com.

Fated Hearts Publishing, *(978-0-9997834; 978-0-578-44491-8)* 25 Country Lake Dr., Oak Ridge, NJ 07438 USA Tel 201-693-1580
E-mail: jpg2msmc@gmail.com
Web site: http://www.jpgrider.com/.

Father & Son Publishing, *(978-0-942407; 978-1-935802)* 4909 N. Monroe St., Tallahassee, FL 32303 USA (SAN 667-0229) Tel 850-562-3927; 850-562-0907; Fax: 850-562-0916; Toll Free: 800-741-2712 (orders only)
E-mail: lance@fatherson.com; jean@fatherson.com
Web site: http://www.fatherson.com
Dist(s): **Dot Gibson Distribution.**

Father's Hse. Publishing, *(978-0-9785308)* Orders Addr.: P.O. Box 161597, Miami, FL 33116 USA Fax: 305-235-0352
E-mail: mariadelatorre9@bellsouth.net.

Father's Pr., LLC, *(978-0-9779407; 978-0-9795394; 978-0-9824982; 978-0-9825321; 978-0-9833739)* 2424 SE 6th. St., Lee's Summit, MO 64063 USA Tel 816-600-6288 (phone/fax)
E-mail: fatherspress@yahoo.com
Web site: http://www.fatherspress.com.

Fauna Nirvana LLC, *(978-0-9982242)* 21015 Sylvanwood Ave., Lakewood, CA 90715 USA Tel 626-278-9845
E-mail: steverbarrett7@gmail.com
Web site: www.averyandmasa.com.

Faux Paw Media Group, *(978-0-9777340; 978-0-9779539; 978-0-9825387; 978-1-935824)* 718 Cliff Dr., Laguna Beach, CA 92651 USA (SAN 850-637X)
Web site: http://www.fauxpawproductions.com.

FAVA Pr., *(978-0-9801396)* 1401 Sherman St., Geneva, OH 44041 USA (SAN 855-3173).

Favonian Books *See* **Arts and Minds Studio Inc.**

Favorable Impressions, *(978-0-7808; 978-0-9674698; 978-1-931360)* Div. of Elm Park Pr., Orders Addr.: P.O. Box 69018, Pleasant Ridge, MI 48069 USA Tel 248-544-2421 (phone/fax); Toll Free: 866-246-2341; Edit Addr.: 9 Elm Park Blvd., Pleasant Ridge, MI 48069 USA
E-mail: danoptt@tir.com; danoepp@tir.com.

Favored Publishing, Inc., *(978-0-9791374)* P.O. Box 734, Jackson, MS 39205-0734 USA Tel 601-316-2193
E-mail: jriley_collins@yahoo.com.

Favorite Uncle Bks., LLC, *(978-0-9711665)* 23228 Lawrence, Dearborn, MI 48128 USA Tel 313-406-2040
E-mail: john@johntocco.com.

Favorite World Pr. LLC, *(978-1-948751)* 33 W 84th St., Fourth Flr., New York, NY 10024 USA Tel 646-722-7082
E-mail: lfrench@favoriteworldpress.com.

Favortwou Publishing, *(978-0-9774107; 978-0-9799006; 978-0-615-12362-2; 978-0-9823883)* 6339 Harbin Woods Dr., Morrow, GA 30260-1835 USA
E-mail: favortwou@hotmail.com
Web site: http://www.favortwov.net.

Fawkes Pr., LLC, *(978-1-945419)* 724 Timberoaks Dr., Azle, TX 76020 USA Tel 817-919-0638
E-mail: jodi_thompson@yahoo.com
Web site: www.fawkespress.com.

Faye Bks., *(978-0-615-16371-0; 978-0-615-16610-0; 978-0-615-16737-4; 978-0-578-02146-1)* 305 Halls Ln., Shepherdsville, KY 40165 USA; P.O. Box 387, Shepherdsville, KY 40165
Web site: http://www.fayebooks.zoomshare.com
Dist(s): **Lulu Pr., Inc.**

FayeHouse. Pr. International, *(978-0-9655222)* 1568 St. Margaret's Rd., Annapolis, MD 21401 USA Tel 443-822-9144; Fax: 410-349-9413 (Call before faxing)
E-mail: Charletfaye@aol.com.

Fayette Pr., *(978-0-615-95121-8; 978-0-692-37661-4; 978-0-692-62969-7; 978-0-9982078; 978-1-953419)* 1106 Main St. No. 1471, Bastrop, TX 78602 USA Tel 512-998-9781
E-mail: jamie@jamiesfoley.com
Web site: http://www.jamiesfoley.com; http://www.fayettepress.com
Dist(s): **CreateSpace Independent Publishing Platform.**

FayRe Pr., *(978-0-9771301)* 513 Mount Evans Rd., Golden, CO 80401 USA (SAN 257-9340) Tel 303-526-7726 (phone/fax)
E-mail: theblueumbrella@earthlink.net.

FBC Pubns. & Printing, *(978-1-933594; 978-1-60208)* 3794 Oleander Ave., Fort Pierce, FL 34982 USA Tel 772-461-6460; Fax: 772-461-6474
E-mail: printing@fbcpublications.com
Web site: http://www.fbcpublications.com.

FBS Publishing Co., *(978-0-615-18629-0; 978-0-615-18633-7; 978-0-615-21316-3)* 5520 Grandview Ln., Doylestown, PA 18902 USA Tel 877-853-2267
Dist(s): **Publishers Services.**

F.C.E. Publishing, *(978-0-615-46463-3; 978-0-692-63419-6; 978-0-692-83736-8; 978-0-692-94214-7; 978-0-692-97980-8)* 1020 Amber Falls Ln., North Las Vegas, NV 89081 USA Tel 702-900-8434; Fax: 702-459-7805
E-mail: jazzwlv@gmail.com.

FEA Ministries, *(978-0-9618730; 978-0-9749168; 978-1-933716)* Orders Addr.: P.O. Box 1065, Hobe Sound, FL 33475 USA (SAN 668-6877) Tel 772-546-8426; Fax: 772-546-9379; Edit Addr.: 11305 SE Gomez Ave., Hobe Sound, FL 33455 USA
E-mail: orders@gospelpublishingmission.org
Web site: http://www.gospelpublishingmission.org.

Fear2love Pr., *(978-1-937861)* P.O. Box 1824, Point Roberts, WA 98281 USA Tel 814-409-8083
E-mail: lisa@fear2love.com.

FEARON *Imprint of* **Savvas Learning Co.**

Feather Insight Pr., *(978-0-9982769)* 6710 94th St. Ct NW, Gig Harbor, WA 98332-8455 USA Tel 906-361-1047
E-mail: alexandrafolz@gmail.com.

Feather River Publishing, *(978-0-615-16630-8)* 28 S. Garfield Ave., North Platte, NE 69101 USA Tel 308-532-4025
Dist(s): **Publishers Services.**

Feather Rock Bks., Inc., *(978-1-934066)* Orders Addr.: 4245 Chippewa Ln., Maple Plain, MN 55359 USA; Edit Addr.: P.O. Box 99, Maple Plain, MN 55359 USA (SAN 851-1829) Tel 952-473-9091
E-mail: jadams@featherrockbooks.com
Web site: http://www.featherrockbooks.com.

Feather Star Pr., *(978-1-7327242)* P.O. Box 295, Springfield, NH 03284 USA Tel 603-867-1908
E-mail: featherstarpress@gmail.com.

Featherproof Bks., *(978-0-9771992; 978-0-9825808; 978-0-9831863)* 2108 W. North Ave. No. 2N, Chicago, IL 60647 USA
E-mail: mail@featherproof.com
Web site: http://www.featherproof.com
Dist(s): **MyiLibrary**
Publishers Group West (PGW).

Federal Emergency Management Agency *Imprint of* **United States Government Printing Office**

Federal Street Pr., *(978-1-892859; 978-1-59695)* Div. of Merriam Webster, Inc., P.O. Box 281, Springfield, MA 01102 USA (SAN 859-4678) Fax: 413-731-5979; 47 Federal St., Springfield, MA 01105
E-mail: info@federalstreetpress.com; lbrodeur@m-w.com
Web site: http://www.federalstreetpress.com.

Federation Pr. (AUS) *(978-1-86287; 978-1-876067; 978-0-646-17924-7; 978-1-76002) Dist. by* **Gaunt.**

Feed My Sheep, *(978-0-9768958)* P.O. Box 16438, Rural Hall, NC 27045 USA Do not confuse with Feed My Sheep in Brunswick, GA, Detroit, MI.

Feed My Sheep Bks., *(978-0-9769152)* P.O. Box 05340, Detroit, MI 48205 USA Do not confuse with companies with the same name in Rural Hall, NC, Brunswick, GA.

Feeding Minds Pr., *(978-1-948898)* 600 Maryland Ave SW, Washington, DC 20024 USA Tel 202-406-3737
E-mail: juliad@fb.org
Web site: www.feedingmindspress.com
Dist(s): **Independent Pubs. Group**
Small Pr. United.

Feeley, Lisa & Craig *See* **CMK Pubs. LLC**

Fegley, Elizabeth *See* **Healing Hands Pr.**

Feil, *(978-0-9741588)* 15 Fox Meadow Ln., Merrimack, NH 03054 USA
Web site: http://www.theservingart.com/creativewriting.

Fein, Bruce, *(978-0-9745049)* 5400 Lochmor Ave., Las Vegas, NV 89130 USA
Web site: http://www.oxymoronbooks.com.

Feiner, Bob, *(978-0-9989148)* 6605 Dogwood Creek Dr., Austin, TX 78746 USA Tel 512-289-4737; Fax: 512-289-4737
E-mail: bobfeiner@yahoo.com.

Feiwel & Friends *Imprint of* **Feiwel & Friends**

Feiwel & Friends, *(978-0-312)* 175 Fifth Ave., New York, NY 10010 USA Tel 646-307-5151; *Imprints:* Feiwel & Friends (Feiwel)
Web site: http://www.holtzbrinckus.com
Dist(s): **Children's Plus, Inc.**
Macmillan
Perfection Learning Corp.
Westminster John Knox Pr.

Feldheim, Philipp Incorporated *See* **Feldheim Pubs.**

†Feldheim Pubs., *(978-0-87306; 978-1-58330; 978-1-59826; 978-1-68025)* 208 Airport Executive Park., Nanuet, NY 10954-5262 USA (SAN 106-6307) Toll Free: 800-237-7149
E-mail: sales@feldheim.com; eli@feldheim.com
Web site: http://www.feldheim.com
Dist(s): **David, Jonathan Pubs., Inc.**
Libros Sin Fronteras; *CIP.*

Feldick, Les Ministries, *(978-1-885344)* 30706 W. Lona Valley Rd., Kinta, OK 74552 USA Tel 918-768-3218; Fax: 918-768-3219; Toll Free: 800-369-7856
Web site: http://www.lesfeldick.org.

Feldman, Enrique C, *(978-0-9974877)* 4927 N. Sabino Gulch Ct., Tucson, AZ 85750 USA Tel 520-861-3001
E-mail: enriquehankfeldman@gmail.com
Web site: www.globallearning.foundation.

Felix Comics, Inc., *(978-0-615-12660-9)* 123 Rt. 23 S., Hamburg, NJ 07419 USA Toll Free: 800-343-3549 (800-34-FELIX)
Web site: http://www.felixthecat.com.

Fell Pr., The, *(978-0-9759430)* 8926 N. Greenwood, No. 289, Niles, IL 60714 USA
Web site: http://www.thefellpress.com
Dist(s): **SCB Distributors.**

Fellowship Pr., *(978-0-914390; 978-1-943388)* 5820 Overbrook Ave., Philadelphia, PA 19131 USA (SAN 201-6117) Tel 215-879-8929; Fax: 215-879-6307; Toll Free: 888-786-1786
E-mail: info@bmf.org
Web site: http://www.bmf.org
Dist(s): **Ilmhouse Inc.**
New Leaf Distributing Co., Inc.
Omega Pubns., Inc.

Felony & Mayhem, LLC, *(978-1-933397; 978-1-934609; 978-1-937384; 978-1-63194)* 156 Waverly Pl., New York, NY 10014 USA Tel 212-731-2440; Fax: 212-656-1227
E-mail: jmusha@felonyandmayhem.com
Web site: http://www.felonyandmayhem.com
Dist(s): **MyiLibrary**
National Bk. Network.

Felsen Ink, *(978-1-62272)* 1599 NW 101st St., Clive, IA 50325 USA Tel 515-226-9372
E-mail: holly.welch@gmail.com
Web site: www.felsenink.com.

†Feminist Pr. at The City Univ. of New York, *(978-0-912670; 978-0-935312; 978-1-55861; 978-1-936932; 978-1-952177)* 365 Fifth Ave., New

York, NY 10016 USA (SAN 213-6813) Tel 212-817-7915; Fax: 212-817-2988
E-mail: jisu@feministpress.org; info@feministpress.org
Web site: http://www.feministpress.org
Dist(s): **Consortium Bk. Sales & Distribution**
Continental Bk. Co., Inc.
CreateSpace Independent Publishing Platform
MyiLibrary
Open Road Integrated Media, Inc.
SPD-Small Pr. Distribution
Women Ink; *CIP.*

Fence Bks. *Imprint of* **Fence Magazine, Inc.**

Fence Magazine, Inc., *(978-0-9663324; 978-0-9713189; 978-0-9740909; 978-0-9771064; 978-1-934200; 978-0-9864373; 978-1-944380)* Div. of Fence Bks., New Library 320 Univ. At Albany 1400 Washington Ave., Albany, NY 12222 USA Tel 518-591-8162 (phone/fax); *Imprints:* Fence Books (Fence Bks)
E-mail: fence@albany.edu
Web site: http://www.fencemag.com; http://www.fencebooks.com
Dist(s): **DeBoer, Bernhard Inc.**
Consortium Bk. Sales & Distribution
SPD-Small Pr. Distribution
Univ. Pr. of New England.

Fencepost Communications Inc., *(978-0-9776487)* Orders Addr.: P.O. Box Fencepost Communications, Inc., P O Box 398, Hinsdale, IL 60522-0398 USA Tel 630-850-9755; Toll Free: 888-648-0008; Edit Addr.: 49 1/2 S. Washington St., Hinsdale, IL 60521 USA.

Feng Liu Productions, *(978-0-9727089)* P.O. Box 248, Mill Valley, CA 94942 USA
Dist(s): **Independent Pubs. Group.**

Fennell Adventures, *(978-0-692-94917-7; 978-0-692-95485-0; 978-0-692-04902-0; 978-0-692-08736-7; 978-1-7324796; 978-1-7338306)* 8064 S. fulton Pkwy., fairburn, GA 30213 USA Tel 302-565-9474
E-mail: jennayefennell@yahoo.com.

Fen's Rim, *(978-0-9713603)* Orders Addr.: P.O. Box 885, Elk Rapids, MI 49629 USA Tel 231-264-6800; Edit Addr.: 104 Dexter St., Elk Rapids, MI 49629 USA
E-mail: mail@fensrim.com
Web site: http://www.fensrim.com.

Fenton Publishing Company *See* **Octopus Publishing Co.**

Fenwyn Pr., *(978-0-913062)* Orders Addr.: P.O. Box 245, Rapid City, SD 57709 USA Tel 605-343-6070; Fax: 605-348-2108; Toll Free: 800-821-6343; Edit Addr.: 3635 Homestead St., Rapid City, SD 57703 USA.

Feral Hse., *(978-0-922915; 978-1-932595; 978-1-936239; 978-1-62731)* 1240 W. Sims Way, No. 124, Port Townsend, WA 98368 USA (SAN 251-5423) Tel 323-666-3311; Fax: 323-297-4331
E-mail: info@feralhouse.com
Web site: http://www.feralhouse.com
Dist(s): **Consortium Bk. Sales & Distribution**
MyiLibrary
ebrary, Inc.

Feral Pr., Inc., *(978-0-9649349; 978-1-930094)* 304 Strawberry Field Rd., Flat Rock, NC 28731 USA Tel 828-694-0438; Fax: 828-694-0438; *Imprints:* Rivet Books (Rivet Bks)
E-mail: gchet@feralpressinc.com
Web site: http://www.feralpressinc.com.

Fergus & Lady Publishing, *(978-0-9786975)* 2310 Del Mar Rd., No. 10, Montrose, CA 91020 USA.

Ferguson, Linda, *(978-0-9755288)* 383 Alewine Dr., Boaz, AL 35957-5034 USA
E-mail: lkinspire@yahoo.com
Web site: http://www.l-n-kinspirationalbooks.com/.

Ferguson Publishing Co. *Imprint of* **Facts On File, Inc.**

Ferguson, Suzanie Pamela, *(978-0-9658745)* 4609 Maplewood Dr., Suffolk, VA 23435 USA Tel 757-483-5721
E-mail: lferg72184@aol.com.

Fern Creek Pr., *(978-0-9625737; 978-1-893651)* P.O. Box 1322, Clayton, GA 30525 USA Tel 706-782-5379; Fax: 706-782-5379
E-mail: brian@ferncreekpress.com
Web site: http://rabun.net/boyd.

Fern Creek Publishing *See* **Fern Creek Pr.**

Fern Rock Falls Pr., *(978-0-9762409)* 22105 Fisk Rd., Noti, OR 97461-9718 USA Tel 541-935-3920
E-mail: dandq@rio.com.

Fernandez, Mary Lynne, *(978-0-9840031)* 300 Ctr. Drive, Suite G 181, Superior, CO 80027 USA Tel 303-246-6825
E-mail: marylynne@marylynnefernandez.com.

Fernandez USA Publishing, 203 Argonne Ave., Suite B, PMB 151, Long Beach, CA 90803-1777 USA Tel 562-901-2370; Fax: 562-901-2372; Toll Free: 800-814-8080
Web site: http://www.fernandezusa.com
Dist(s): **Continental Bk. Co., Inc.**

Ferne Pr. *Imprint of* **Nelson Publishing & Marketing**

Fernhouse Pr., *(978-0-9759363)* P.O. Box 73, Woodstock, VT 05067 USA
Web site: http://www.fernhouse.com.

Fernhurst Bks. (GBR) *(978-0-906754; 978-1-898660; 978-1-904475; 978-1-909911) Dist. by* **Casemate Pubs.**

Fernwood & Hedges Bks., *(978-0-615-72092-0; 978-0-9890698; 978-0-615-80386-9; 978-0-615-81583-1)* 7612 Fountain Ave., West Hollywood, CA 90046 USA Tel 213-910-2887
Dist(s): **CreateSpace Independent Publishing Platform.**

Fernwood Publishing Co., Ltd. (CAN) *(978-1-55266; 978-1-895686; 978-1-77363) Dist. by* **Col U Pr.**

Ferree, Rebecca Ann, *(978-0-692-07066-6)* 3207 N. 31st St, TACOMA, WA 98407 USA Tel 253-752-9060
E-mail: ferreet@asme.org
Dist(s): **Ingram Content Group.**

ferrocement.com, *(978-0-9748016)* P.O. Box 31 S. St., Bernardston, MA 01337-0133 USA Fax: 413-648-9098
E-mail: garrett@ferrocement.com.

Fertig, Howard Incorporated *See* **Fertig, Howard Publisher**

†Fertig, Howard Publisher, *(978-0-86527)* Orders Addr.: 80 E. 11th St., New York, NY 10003 USA (SAN 201-4777) Tel 212-982-7922; Fax: 212-982-1099
E-mail: orders@hfertigbooks.com
Web site: http://www.hfertigbooks.com; *CIP.*

Fetch! Publishing, *(978-0-9746324)* 27881 La Paz Rd., Suite G-124, Laguna Niguel, CA 92677 USA Fax: 877-426-3809; Toll Free Fax: 877-426-3809; Toll Free: 877-899-9454
Web site: http://fetchpublishing.com.

Fetiform Teratoma Productions, *(978-0-692-07054-3; 978-0-692-12868-8; 978-0-578-57993-1)* 19053 Nordhoff St. 304, northridge, CA 91324 USA Tel 818-626-0392
E-mail: haitisworst@hotmail.com
Dist(s): **Independent Pub.**

Fey, Sid Designs, Inc., *(978-0-9753530)* Box 184, 335 E. Geneva Rd., Carol Stream, IL 60188 USA Tel 630-668-6607; Fax: 630-668-6282
E-mail: zpdduda@earthlink.net
Web site: http://www.thebeinggame.com.

Fichter, Brittany, *(978-1-949710)* 302 SEARIGHT DR., FORT BRAGG, NC 28307 USA Tel 702-513-2147
E-mail: BRITTANYFICHTERFICTION@GMAIL.COM
Web site: BrittanyFichterFiction.com.

Fickling, David Bks. (GBR) *(978-1-910200; 978-1-910989; 978-1-78845) Dist. by* **Peng Rand Hse.**

Fiction Focus *See* **Story Direction**

Fiction House *See* **Fortuna Pubns.**

Fiction Publishing, Inc., *(978-0-9796752; 978-0-9814956; 978-0-9819727; 978-0-9825086; 978-0-9826168; 978-0-9827442; 978-0-9830007; 978-0-9837803)* 5626 Travelers Way, Fort Pierce, FL 34982 USA Tel 772-489-5811
E-mail: fictionpub@bellsouth.net
Web site: http://www.fictionpublishinginc.com.

Fiction Works, The, *(978-1-58124)* Orders Addr.: 3328 SW Cascade Ave., Corvallis, OR 97333 USA Tel 541-730-2044; Fax: 541-738-2648
E-mail: fictionworks@me.com
Web site: http://www.fictionworks.com
Dist(s): **Brodart Co.**
Untreed Reads Publishing, LLC.

FictionSpin, *(978-0-9724007; 978-0-9817897)* P.O. Box 885, Pacific Palisades, CA 90272 USA (SAN 255-0431) Tel 310-456-0677
E-mail: ASCBooks@aol.com; FictionSpin@aol.com
Web site: http://ASCBooks@aol.com; http://www.fictionspin.com.

Fiddlehead Pr., *(978-0-615-88594-0; 978-0-615-90572-3; 978-0-692-02414-0; 978-1-68013)* 2129 Bethel St. NE, Olympia, WA 98506 USA Tel 360-357-7800
Dist(s): **CreateSpace Independent Publishing Platform.**

Fiddlesticks Press *See* **Periwinkle Pr.**

Fideli Publishing, Inc., *(978-1-60414; 978-1-948638)*
E-mail: info@fidelipublishing.com
Web site: http://www.fidelipublishing.com
Dist(s): **BookBaby**
Greenleaf Book Group
MyiLibrary
Smashwords.

Fidelity Heart Publishing, *(978-0-9748522)* Orders Addr.: P.O. Box 1758, Houston, TX 77251 USA; Edit Addr.: 3923 Teal Run Pl., Ct, Fresno, TX 77545-7049 USA
E-mail: slmccraw@fidelityheart.com
Web site: http://www.fidelityheart.com.

Field Mouse Productions, *(978-0-9647586; 978-0-9888021)* Div. of Associated Design Services, Inc., Orders Addr.: P.O. Box 392, Grand Island, NE 68802 USA Tel 308-380-3315; 308-380-3215; Edit Addr.: 454 8th Ave., Palmer, NE 68864 USA
E-mail: skidi@aol.com; rtstron@aol.com; JeanLukesh@aol.com
Web site: http://www.fieldmousebooks.com; http://www.fieldmouseproductions.com
Dist(s): **Ingram Content Group.**

Field Stone Pubs., *(978-0-9645272)* 331 Fields Hill Rd., Conway, MA 01341 USA Tel 413-369-4091
E-mail: author@johnrdixonbooks.com
Web site: http://www.JohnRDixonBooks.com.

Fielder Group, *(978-0-9639986; 978-0-9789058)* Orders Addr.: P.O. Box 510, Benton, KY 42025 USA Tel 888-255-9248; Fax: 270-362-7130; Toll Free: 888-255-9248
E-mail: barbara@thefieldergroupusa.com
Web site: http://www.thefieldergroupusa.com.

Fielder, John Publishing, *(978-0-9832769; 978-0-9860004; 978-0-9914990; 978-0-9985080; 978-1-7344429)* P.O. Box 26890, Silverthorne, CO 80497 USA Tel 303-907-2179
E-mail: john@johnfielder.com.

Fieldhouse LLC, *(978-0-9768353)* P.O. Box 541, Lawrence, KS 66044 USA
Dist(s): **Independent Pubs. Group**
Midpoint Trade Bks., Inc.

Fields Communications & Publishing *See* **Fields Publishing, Inc.**

Fields of Gold Publishing, Inc., *(978-0-9746296; 978-0-9848034; 978-1-940894)* P.O. Box 128438, Nashville, TN 37212-3304 USA Tel 615-335-2014; 615-567-3371; *Imprints:* Fog Ink (FogInk)
E-mail: tneftzger@comcast.net; amy@fogink.com
Web site: http://www.fogink.com
Dist(s): **Brodart Co.**
Ingram Content Group.

Fields Publishing, Inc., *(978-1-57843)* 8120 Sawyer Brown Rd. Ste. 108, Nashville, TN 37221-1410 USA
E-mail: Fieldsco@mindspring.com
Web site: http://www.fieldspublishing.com.

Fieldstone Hill Pr., *(978-0-9767762)* 321 Old Saluda Dam Rd., Easley, SC 29640 USA
Web site: http://www.fieldstone-hill.net.

Fierce Girl Publishing Hse., *(978-0-9993880)* 4160 gunnison ct, Estero, FL 33928 USA Tel 952-356-9607
E-mail: georginakane@hotmail.com.

Fierce Publishing, *(978-0-9980154)* 501 Fletcher Ave., Indianapolis, IN 46203 USA.

Fiery Studios, *(978-0-9743110)* P.O. Box 51595, Kalamazoo, MI 49005-1595 USA
Web site: http://www.vogelein.com
Dist(s): **Diamond Comic Distributors, Inc.**
Diamond Bk. Distributors.

Fifth Avenue Pr. *Imprint of* **Ann Arbor District Library**

Fifth Ave Pr., *(978-0-9755390)* 413 Salt Pond Rd., Bethany Beach, DE 19930 USA Tel 302-537-9633; Fax: 302-537-0210; Toll Free: 800-862-6443 Do not confuse with Fifth Avenue Press in Fargo, ND and New York, NY.
E-mail: bethanybil@aol.com
Web site: http://www.e-studio8.com/fifthstreetpress.

Fifth Element Publishing, *(978-0-578-41645-8; 978-0-578-50765-1; 978-1-7344152)*
E-mail: dianalundblade@gmail.com
Dist(s): **Ingram Content Group.**

Fifth Hse. Pubs. (CAN) *(978-0-920079; 978-1-895618; 978-1-894004; 978-1-894856; 978-1-897252; 978-1-927083) Dist. by* **Firefly Bks Limited.**

Fifth Paw Press *See* **Jocko Publishing**

Fifth Pillar Bks., *(978-1-950972)* La Jolla, San Diego, CA 92037 USA Tel 858-926-5828
E-mail: info@fifthpillarbooks.com
Web site: www.fifthpillarbooks.com.

Fifth Ribb Publishing, *(978-0-9848104)* 7827 Olive Blvd, UNIVERSITY CITY, MO 63130 USA (SAN 991-0786) Tel 314-349-1122
E-mail: pamela.blair@eyeseeme.com.

Fig & The Vine, LLC, The, *(978-0-9841087; 978-0-615-49661-0; 978-0-615-62717-5; 978-0-9883370; 978-0-692-48233-9; 978-0-578-60456-5)* Orders Addr.: 753 Winthrop St., Mount Pleasant, SC 29464-2946 USA Fax: 843-881-8425; Toll Free Fax: 843-881-8425
E-mail: figandvine@mail.com; wadamacofarms@mail.com
Web site: http://thefigandthevinemedia.com.

Fig Factor Media LLC *Imprint of* **JJR Marketing Consultants LLC**

Fighting Words Publishing, *(978-0-9755279)* P.O. Box 7, Highwood, IL 60040 USA Tel 847-266-1965; Fax: 847-266-0840
E-mail: magmem@aol.com; rmk@robertmkatzmanwriter.com
Web site: http://www.fightingwordsbook.com; http://www.robertmkatzmanwriter.com.

Figueroa Pr., *(978-0-9727625; 978-1-932800)* 840 Childs Way, Suite 401-E, Los Angeles, CA 90089-2540 USA Tel 213-743-4801; Fax: 213-743-4808
Web site: http://www.figueroapress.com.

Figure 8 Pr., *(978-0-9630376)* Orders Addr.: P.O. Box 248, Rolling Ground, WI 54631 USA
E-mail: figure8press@gmail.com
Web site: http://figure8press.com.

Figures In Motion, *(978-0-9818566; 978-1-944481)* 6055 E. Hemmi Ln., Bellingham, WA 98226 USA (SAN 856-7336) Tel 360-966-3500; 510-482-8500
E-mail: cathy@figuresinmotion.com; info@figuresinmotion.com
Web site: http://www.figuresinmotion.com.

Filaretos, William, *(978-0-9724520)* 220 W. Canton St. # 3, Boston, MA 02116-5814 USA
E-mail: william_filaretos@thepotionoftime.com
Web site: http://www.ThePotionofTime.com.

Filion, Rita-Anneliese, *(978-0-9749142)* 26 Elizabeth Ln., Saratoga Springs, NY 12866-2804 USA
E-mail: sirdino@noblebones.com
Web site: http://www.noblebones.com.

Filippucci-Kotz, Renee, *(978-0-578-40718-0)* 6908 Clear Sailing Ln., Raleigh, NC 27615 USA Tel 919-706-5283
E-mail: booksbyrenee@att.net
Dist(s): **Ingram Content Group.**

Filiquarian Publishing, LLC, *(978-0-9770505; 978-1-59986)* Orders Addr.: 110 W. Grant St. Unit 2c, Minneapolis, MN 55403 USA Tel 612-207-2335; *Imprints:* FQ Classics (FQ Classics).

Fillet Of Horn Publishing, *(978-0-9753077)* 35000 Muskrat Rd., Barnesville, OH 43713 USA Tel 740-758-5050; Fax: 740-758-5114
Web site: http://www.filletofhorn.com
Dist(s): **Baker & Taylor Publisher Services (BTPS)**
ebrary, Inc.

Film Black Friday, LLC., The, *(978-0-692-08334-5)* 1450 stokes ave, ATLANTA, GA 30310 USA Tel 404-642-5903
E-mail: thefilmblackfriday@gmail.com
Dist(s): **Ingram Content Group.**

Film Ideas, Inc., *(978-1-57557; 978-1-60572)* 308 N. Wolf Rd., Wheeling, IL 60090 USA Tel 847-419-0255; Fax: 847-419-8933; Toll Free: 800-475-3456
E-mail: info@filmideas.com
Web site: http://www.filmideas.com
Dist(s): **Follett School Solutions.**

Filsinger & Co., Ltd., *(978-0-916754)* 288 W. 12th St., New York, NY 10014 USA (SAN 208-3574) Tel 212-243-7421.

Filter Pr., LLC, *(978-0-86541; 978-0-910584)* P.O. Box 95, Palmer Lake, CO 80133 USA (SAN 201-484X) Tel 719-481-2420 (phone/fax); Toll Free: 888-570-2663
E-mail: info@filterpressbooks.com; doris@filterpressbooks.com
Web site: http://www.filterpressbooks.com.

Financial Safari Pr., *(978-0-9777993)* 1135 Kildaire Farm Rd., Suite 200, Cary, NC 27512 USA Tel 919-657-4201
E-mail: capitaltax@gmail.com.

Finch Bks. Co., *(978-0-9661457)* Orders Addr.: P.O. Box 545, Tularosa, NM 88352 USA; Edit Addr.: 1418 Apple Ave., Tularosa, NM 88352 USA Tel 505-585-8037; Fax: 505-585-8039
Dist(s): **MBI Distribution Services/Quayside Distribution.**

Find Your Way Publishing, Inc., *(978-0-9824692; 978-0-9849322; 978-1-945290)* P.O. Box 667, Norway, ME 04268 USA
E-mail: melissa@findyourwaypublishing.com
Web site: http://www.findyourwaypublishing.com.

Findaway World, LLC, *(978-1-59895; 978-1-60252; 978-1-60514; 978-1-60640; 978-1-60775; 978-1-60812; 978-1-60847; 978-1-61545; 978-1-61574; 978-1-61587; 978-1-61637; 978-1-61657; 978-1-61707; 978-1-4676; 978-1-5094; 978-1-9871; 978-1-0942; 978-1-6622; 978-1-6649)* 31999 Aurora Rd., Solon, OH 44139 USA (SAN 853-8778) Tel 440-893-0808 x108
Web site: http://www.findawayworld.com; http://www.playawaydigital.com
Dist(s): **Follett School Solutions**
MyiLibrary.

Findhorn Press *Imprint of* **Inner Traditions International, Ltd.**

Finding My Way Bks., *(978-0-9903543; 978-0-9863792; 978-0-9964449; 978-0-9968357; 978-1-944764; 978-1-947541)* 3512 SW Huntoon St., Topeka, KS 66604 USA Tel 785-273-6239
E-mail: jo.mach@findingmywaybooks.com; findingmywaybooks@gmail.com
Web site: http://www.findingmywaybooks.com
Dist(s): **Brown Books Publishing Group**
Ingram Publisher Services.

Finding the Cause, LLC, 39738 Calle Azucar, Murrieta, CA 92562 USA Tel 760-724-8104
E-mail: Dr.king@findingthecause.com
Web site: Www.FindingTheCause.com.

Finding the JEMS, *(978-1-7323622)*
E-mail: findingthejems@gmail.com.

Fine Art Editions *Imprint of* **North American International**

Fine Feather Pr. Ltd. (GBR) *(978-1-908489) Dist. by* **IPG Chicago.**

Fine Print Pr., The, *(978-0-9644365; 978-1-888960)* 350 Ward Ave., Suite 106, Honolulu, HI 96814-4091 USA Fax: 425-955-1909
E-mail: info@fineprintpress.com
Web site: http://www.fineprintpress.com
Dist(s): **Independent Pubs. Group**
Midpoint Trade Bks., Inc.
Partners Pubs. Group, Inc.

Fine Print Publishing Company *See* **GO Publishing Co.**

Fineo Editorial, S.L. (ESP) *(978-84-16470) Dist. by* **IPG Chicago.**

Finer Moments, *(978-0-9771549)* P.O. Box 22102, Robbinsdale, MN 55422 USA Tel 612-302-7830
E-mail: finermoments@earthlink.net
Web site: http://www.finermoments.net.

Finest Bks., *(978-1-935679)* 959 W. Jericho Tpke., Smithtown, NY 11787 USA Tel 615-479-0877; Fax: 631-864-1565
E-mail: michaelsheahan@msn.com
Web site: http://www.finestbks.com.

Fingerprint Bks., *(978-0-9709861)* P.O. Box 534, Redlands, CA 92373 USA (SAN 253-7923) Tel 909-307-9993 (phone/fax)
E-mail: mglis2t@earthlink.net.

Finial Publishing, *(978-1-933791)* P.O. Box 346, Mercer Island, WA 98040 USA
Web site: http://www.finialpublishing.com.

Finkelstein, Ruth, *(978-0-9628157)* 27 Saddle River Rd., Airmont, NY 10952-3034 USA.

Finlay Prints, Inc., *(978-0-9766998)* Orders Addr.: 74 Fifth Ave., 6D, New York, NY 10011 USA Tel 212-463-7173
E-mail: finlayprints@earthlink.net.

Finn & Remy, LLC, *(978-1-7322788)* 5834 Richmond Ave, DALLAS, TX 75206 USA Tel 214-538-5342
E-mail: artbyjanedu@gmail.com
Web site: www.finnandremy.com.

Finnegan, Jeanette Gray Jr., *(978-0-578-46566-1)* 46044 Cape Point Way, Buxton, NC 27920 USA Tel 252-305-7077
E-mail: Tedtorok@gmail.com
Web site: Thelighthousekids.com.

Finneran, Lisa, *(978-0-9777744)* 9709 River Rd., Newport News, VA 23601-2360 USA
E-mail: arkangels@cox.net.

Finney Co., Inc., *(978-0-89317; 978-0-912486; 978-0-933855; 978-0-9617767; 978-0-9639705; 978-1-880654; 978-1-893272)* Orders Addr.: 8075 215th St. W., Lakeville, MN 55044 USA (SAN 206-412X) Tel 952-469-6699; Fax: 952-469-1968; Toll Free Fax: 800-330-6232; Toll Free: 800-846-7027; *Imprints:* Windward Publishing (Windward Publng); Lone Oak Press, Limited (LoneOak)
E-mail: feedback@finneyco.com
Web site: http://www.finneyco.com; http://www.ecopress.com; http://www.pogopress.com; http://www.astragalpress.com
Dist(s): **Book Wholesalers, Inc.**
Brodart Co.
Follett School Solutions

National Bk. Network
Rowman & Littlefield Publishers, Inc.
Southern Bk. Service.

Fire Flies Entertainment, LLC, *(978-0-9787302)* 1077 North Ave., Suite 114, Elizabeth, NJ 07208 USA Tel 212-561-1654; Fax: 908-351-1888
Dist(s): **INscribe Digital.**

Fire Mountain Pr., *(978-1-929374)* Orders Addr.: P.O. Box 3851, Hillsboro, OR 97123 USA Tel 503-846-9057 (phone/fax); 503-219-5643 (phone/fax)
Web site: http://www.firemountainpress.com.

Fire Pit Creek Publishing, *(978-0-9845362)* 31208 E. Heidelberger Rd., Buckner, MO 64016 USA.

Fire Quill Publishing, *(978-0-9969748; 978-0-9984714; 978-1-947649)* 2686 Baughman Ave, Columbus, OH 43211 USA Tel 480-819-5205
E-mail: erichbester@hotmail.com.

Firebird *Imprint of* **Penguin Young Readers Group**

Firebird Creative, *(978-1-63023)* 12042 SE Sunnyside Rd No. 385, Clackamas, OR 97015 USA
E-mail: mark@resurrectionhouse.com
Web site: http://firebirdcreative.net; http://www.archepress.com; http://www.underlandpress.com; http://www.resurrectionhouse.com
Dist(s): **MyiLibrary**
Publishers Group West (PGW).

Firebreak Publishing Co., *(978-0-9761448)* Orders Addr.: P.O. Box 995, Pacific Palisades, CA 90272-0995 USA Tel 310-454-3105
E-mail: r.brodie@verizon.net
Web site: http://www.firebreakpublishing.com.

Firebug Fairy Tales, *(978-0-615-58954-1; 978-0-615-58955-8)* P.O. Box 680396, Charlotte, NC 28216 USA Tel 704-398-9923
E-mail: ejkisinger@yahoo.com.

Firefall *See* **Firefall Editions**

Firefall Editions, *(978-0-915090; 978-1-939434)* Div. of Firefallmedia, 4905 Tunlaw St., Alexandria, VA 22312 USA Tel 510-549-2461; *Imprints:* California Street (Calif St)
E-mail: firefallmedia@att.net; literary@att.net
Web site: http://www.firefallmedia.com; http://www.firefallfilms.com; http://www.blotbooks.com; http://www.lostshoerecords.com; http://www.sim-book.com; http://www.lovinglicks.com; http://www.blue-loves.com; http://www.metech.us; http://www.shift-alt-delete.com; http://www.spacespa.net; http://www.1across.com; http://mz.firefallmedia.com; http://www.scifun.us
Dist(s): **Audible.com**
Brodart Co.
Follett School Solutions.

Firefly Bks., Ltd., *(978-0-920668; 978-1-55209; 978-1-895565; 978-1-896284; 978-1-55297; 978-1-55407)* Orders Addr.: c/o Frontier Distributing, 1000 Young St., Suite 160, Tonawanda, NY 14150 USA (SAN 630-611X) Tel 203-222-9700; Toll Free Fax: 800-565-6034; Toll Free: 800-387-5085; Edit Addr.: 8514 Long Canyon Dr., Austin, TX 78730-2813 USA
E-mail: service@fireflybooks.com
Web site: http://www.fireflybooks.com/
Dist(s): **Children's Plus, Inc.**
Lectorum Pubns., Inc.

Firefly Games, *(978-0-9747671)* 7525 Garden Gate Dr., Citrus Hts, CA 95621-1909 USA
E-mail: patrick@firefly-games.com
Web site: http://www.firefly-games.com.

FireFly Lights, *(978-0-9856863)* 1403 Delano St. No. 7, Houston, TX 77003 USA Tel 281-536-3915
E-mail: lacycameywrites@gmail.com.

Firefly Press *See* **Pretty Cool Bks.**

FireFly Publishings & Entertainment *See* **FireFly Publishings & Entertainment LLC**

FireFly Publishings & Entertainment LLC, *(978-0-9774126; 978-0-9846428)* Orders Addr.: P.O. Box 1346, Snellville, GA 30078 USA; Edit Addr.: 845 Common Oak Pl., Lawrenceville, GA 30045 USA (SAN 257-6597)
E-mail: fireflypublishingent@yahoo.com; dorced58@yahoo.com
Web site: http://www.fireflypublishingent.com
Dist(s): **Follett School Solutions.**

Fireglass Publishing, *(978-0-9857523)* 2593 NE Kevos Pond Dr., Poulsbo, WA 98370 USA
E-mail: fiction@slwhyte.com.

FireHydrant Creative Studios, Inc., *(978-0-9826066; 978-1-937176)* 52 Huntleigh Woods, Saint Louis, MO 63132 USA Tel 314-822-0833
E-mail: administrator@FireHydrantCS.com
Web site: http://www.FireHydrantCS.com.

Firelight Press, Inc., *(978-0-9786555; 978-1-934517)* 550 Larchmont Dr., Cincinnati, OH 45215 USA (SAN 851-2353); P.O. Box 15758, Cincinnati, OH 45215 Tel 513-646-6803; Fax: 513-821-2830 Do not confuse with companies with the same name in Independence, MO, Solvang, CA
E-mail: books@firelightpress.com
Web site: http://firelightpress.com.

Firelight Publishing, Inc., *(978-0-9707206)* Orders Addr.: P.O. Box 444, Sublimity, OR 97385-0444 USA Toll Free: 866-347-3544; Edit Addr.: 226 Division St., SW, Sublimity, OR 97385-9637 USA Tel 503-767-0444; Fax: 503-769-8980; Toll Free: 866-347-3544
E-mail: info@firelightpublishing.com; editor@firelightpublishing.com; webmaster@firelightpublishing.com; orders@firelightpublishing.com
Web site: http://www.firelightpublishing.com
Dist(s): **Partners/West Book Distributors.**

Firenze Pr., *(978-0-9711236)* Orders Addr.: P.O. Box 6892, Wyomissing, PA 19610-0892 USA (SAN 254-315X); Edit Addr.: 612 Museum Rd., Reading, PA 19610-0892 USA Tel 610-374-7048 Do not confuse with Leonardo Pr., Camden, ME
E-mail: hailejohnjr@msn.com; HaileJohnJr@msn.com; InkPenCJH@msn.com
Web site: http://caroljhaile.com.

Fireproof Ministries, *(978-0-9741849)* P.O. Box 150169, Grand Rapids, MI 49515 USA
E-mail: info@fireproofministries.com
Web site: http://www.fireproofministries.com.

Fireship Pr., *(978-1-934757; 978-1-935585; 978-1-61179; 978-1-7320305; 978-1-7353545)* P.O. Box 68412, Tucson, AZ 85737 USA Tel 520-360-6228
E-mail: tmg@en.com
Web site: http://www.FireshipPress.com.

Fireside Catholic Bibles, *(978-1-55665)* Div. of Fireside Catholic Bibles, Orders Addr.: P.O. Box 780189, Wichita, KS 67278-0189 USA Tel 316-267-3211; Fax: 316-267-1850; Toll Free: 888-676-2040; Edit Addr.: 9020 E. 35th St., N., Wichita, KS 67226 USA (SAN 854-0780)
E-mail: info@firesidebibles.com; llear@devore.cc
Web site: http://www.firesidebibles.com
Dist(s): **Spring Arbor Distributors, Inc.**

Fireside Critters, *(978-0-9753248)* Orders Addr.: P.O. Box 283, Vermilion, OH 44089 USA; Edit Addr.: P.O. Box 283, Vermillion, OH 44089 USA
E-mail: FiresideCritters@AOL.com.

Fireside Pr., Inc., *(978-1-930754; 978-0-9779863; 978-0-9800067; 978-0-9818486; 978-1-935451; 978-0-9825292; 978-1-935764)* 10000 N. Central Exp, Suite 400, Dallas, TX 75231 USA
E-mail: info@durbanhouse.com; john7@durbanhouse.com
Web site: http://www.durbanhouse.com
Dist(s): **BookMasters**
MyiLibrary
National Bk. Network
ebrary, Inc.

Firesidenook, *(978-0-9887214)* 10072 Forestedge Ln, Miamisburg, OH 45342 USA Tel 937-776-0019
E-mail: strangedad1@yahoo.com.

Firestorm Editions, *(978-0-9855541)* 14314 Rockdale Rd., Clear Spring, MD 21722 USA Tel 815-642-0700
E-mail: cashives@gmail.com.

Firewater Media Group (CAN) *(978-0-9812439) Dist. by* **IPG Chicago.**

Fireweed Pr., *(978-0-9772528)* Orders Addr.: P.O. Box 31037, Seattle, WA 98103 USA; Edit Addr.: 1807 N. 36th St., Seattle, WA 98103 USA Do not confuse with Fireweed Press in Falls Church, VA Fairbanks, AK, Madison, WI, Evergreen, CO AJ
E-mail: fireweedpress@comcast.net.

Fireweed Pr., *(978-1-878660)* Orders Addr.: P.O. Box 482, Madison, WI 53701-0482 USA; Edit Addr.: 638 Gately Terr., Madison, WI 53711 USA Tel 608-233-0300 Do not confuse with companies with same name in Falls Church, VA, Fairbanks, AK, Evergreen, CO Seattle, WA
E-mail: tmccormi@wisc.edu.

First Assist Pubns., *(978-0-9724865)* P.O. Box 608, Woodland Hills, CA 91365 USA Fax: 818-346-8988
E-mail: e21sherr@aol.com.

First Associates Publishing, *(978-0-9618835)* P.O. Box 1281, Richmond, VA 23218-1281 USA (SAN 242-5289) Tel 804-254-0662; Fax: 804-524-5138; Toll Free: 877-247-8343
E-mail: earl@fapbooks.com.

First Avenue Editions *Imprint of* **Lerner Publishing Group**

First Biographies *Imprint of* **Reynolds, Morgan Inc.**

First Bks., *(978-0-912301; 978-0-9823476; 978-1-61007; 978-1-937090)* 6750 SW Franklin St., Suite A, Portland, OR 97223 USA (SAN 297-9063) Tel 503-968-6777; Fax: 503-968-6779
E-mail: customerservice@firstbooks.com
Web site: http://www.firstbooks.com
Dist(s): **Bookazine Co., Inc.**
Partners Bk. Distributing, Inc.

First Century Publishing, *(978-1-885273)* Div. of First Century Church Ministries, P.O. Box 130, Delmar, NY 12054 USA Tel 518-439-3544; Fax: 518-439-0105; Toll Free: 800-570-6060
E-mail: dnbubar1@nycap.rr.com; 1century@nycap.rr.com
Web site: http://www.firstcenturypublishing.com
Dist(s): **Send The Light Distribution LLC.**

First Choice Entertainment *See* **Papilion Pr.**

First Christmas Project, *(978-0-9769828)* 333 Brooks Bend, Brownsburg, IN 46112 USA
Web site: http://www.firstchristmaspresent.com
Dist(s): **Send The Light Distribution LLC.**

First Church Iam, The Schl. of Life Ministry of Solehealism, The (GBR) *(978-1-873478) Dist. by* **Consort Bk Sales.**

First Class Fitness Systems, Inc., *(978-0-9747008)* 23901 Civic Ctr. Way, Suite 342, Malibu, CA 90265 USA Tel 310-456-3043
E-mail: Mario@myfitfamily.com
Web site: http://myfitfamily.com.

First Edition Design eBook Publishing, *(978-0-9837342; 978-1-937520; 978-1-62287; 978-1-5069)* 5202 Old Ashwood Dr., Sarasota, FL 34233 USA (SAN 860-2719) Tel 941-921-2607; Fax: 617-249-1694; P.O. Box 20217, Sarasota, FL 34276 Tel 941-921-2607; Fax: 941-866-7510
E-mail: dgordon@firsteditiondesign.com
Web site: http://www.firsteditiondesignpublishing.com.

First Flight Bks., *(978-0-9763675; 978-0-9836035; 978-0-9860666; 978-0-9974973)* Div. of The Copy Workshop, 2144 N. Hudson, RB, Chicago, IL 60614 USA Tel 773-871-1179; Fax: 773-281-4643
E-mail: firstflightbooks@aol.com
Web site: http://www.firstflightbooks.com.

First Lady Pr., *(978-0-9995630; 978-1-7324308; 978-1-7338897; 978-1-7331134)* 5224 Jackpine Rd., Bemidji, MN 56601 USA Tel 218-766-0753
E-mail: schlichtingbarb@gmail.com.

First Light Publishing, *(978-0-9754411; 978-0-692-51651-5; 978-0-692-51652-2)* 14402 Twickenham Pl., Chesterfield, VA 23832 USA Do not confuse with First Light Publishing in Chagrin Falls, OH
E-mail: briantherock@cs.com
Dist(s): **Parklane Publishing.**

First Mom's Club, The, *(978-0-9704876; 978-0-9728180; 978-0-9764557; 978-1-935822)* 367 Eric Way, Grants Pass, OR 97526-8820 USA
E-mail: dianne@thefirstmomsclub.com
Web site: http://www.thefirstmomsclub.com
Dist(s): **Alliance Bk. Co.**

First Person Publishing *See* **Concinnity Initiatives**

First Second Bks. *Imprint of* **Roaring Brook Pr.**

First Stage Concepts, *(978-0-9667719; 978-1-931430)* Orders Addr.: P.O. Box 3390, Redondo Beach, CA 90277-1390 USA Tel 310-371-6834; Fax: 310-370-3392; Edit Addr.: 5410 W. 190th St., No. 98, Torrance, CA 90503-1045 USA
E-mail: quickstartguitar@msn.com
Web site: http://www.QuickStartGuitar.com.

First Steps Pr., *(978-0-9659944)* Orders Addr.: P.O. Box 380122, Clinton Township, MI 48038-0060 USA Tel 810-463-5670; Edit Addr.: 38453 Gail, Clinton Township, MI 48036 USA.

First Steps Publishing, *(978-0-9833164; 978-1-937333; 978-0-9837225; 978-0-9852431; 978-1-938985; 978-1-944072; 978-1-945146)* 105 Westwind St., Gleneden Beach, OR 97388 USA Tel 541-961-7641; *Imprints:* White Parrot Press (MYID_H_WHITE P)
E-mail: sfparrott@firststepspublishing.com
Web site: https://www.ChristopherMatthewsPub.com/; https://www.FiresidePress.com/; https://www.FirstStepsPublishing.com.

First Word Publishing, The, *(978-0-9708590)* 305 Lind Ave., SW, No. 9, Renton, WA 98055 USA Tel 425-254-8575
E-mail: dejonfw@ayhoo.com.

Firsthand *Imprint of* **Heinemann**

First-Sight Publishing, *(978-0-9770363)* 9636 Nevada Ave., Chatsworth, CA 91311 USA Tel 818-207-6334
E-mail: sabrinawright1961@yahoo.com.

Fiscal Pink, LlC, *(978-0-9974001)* 13502 Arrowwood Ln., Bowie, MD 20715 USA Tel 301-875-9020
E-mail: sharon@fiscalpink.com
Web site: www.fiscalpink.com.

Fischer, Carl LLC, *(978-0-8258)* Orders Addr.: 588 N. Gulph Rd. Ste. B, King Of Prussa, PA 19406-2831 USA Toll Free: 800-762-2328; Edit Addr.: 65 Bleeker St., New York, NY 10012-2420 USA (SAN 107-4245) Tel 212-772-0900; Fax: 212-477-6996; Toll Free: 800-762-2328
E-mail: cf-info@carlfischer.com
Web site: http://www.carlfischer.com
Dist(s): **Follett School Solutions**
Leonard, Hal Corp.

Fish Creek Productions, LLC, *(978-0-9973651)* P.O. Box 131401, Spring, TX 77393 USA Tel 832-341-2372
E-mail: contact@fishcreekproductions.com.

Fish Decoy.com, Ltd., *(978-0-9748721; 978-0-9759386)* Orders Addr.: P.O. Box 321, Cross River, NY 10518 USA (SAN 256-1093) Tel 914-533-5181; Edit Addr.: 71 Conant Valley Rd., Pound Ridge, NY 10576 USA; 218 Honey Hallow Rd., Pound Ridge, NY 10576
Web site: http://www.fishdecoystore.com
Dist(s): **Antique Collectors' Club.**

Fish Head Pubns., LLC, *(978-1-934627)* 5013 W. Buckskin Tr., Glendale, AZ 85310 USA
Web site: http://www.fishheadpublications.com.

Fish Out of Water Bks., *(978-0-9899087; 978-1-947886)* 2747 Parkwood Ave., Ann Arbor, MI 48104 USA Tel 734-975-6896
E-mail: fowbooks@gmail.com
Web site: www.fowbooks.com
Dist(s): **Independent Pubs. Group**
Small Pr. United.

Fish Tales Publishing, *(978-0-9795860)* Orders Addr.: 65 Glen Rd., PMB 128, Garner, NC 27529 USA (SAN 853-8344) Tel 919-320-7428
E-mail: Books@fishtales.org
Web site: http://www.fishtales.org.

Fishbowl International, Inc., *(978-0-9745188; 978-0-9765619)* Orders Addr.: P.O. Box 362, Roxie, MS 39661 USA Tel 601-384-0219; Fax: 601-384-1667
E-mail: fishbowlinternational@yahoo.com
Web site: http://www.fishbowlinternational.com.

Fishcake Publishing, Incorporated *See* **Benicia Literary Arts**

Fisher Amelie, *(978-0-615-48662-8; 978-0-615-58205-4; 978-0-9888125; 978-0-9978976)* 905 Dee Ln., Bedford, TX 76022 USA Tel 817-657-0252
E-mail: mediastem@hotmail.com.

Fisher & Hale Publishing, *(978-0-9742037)* Div. of Horizon Bks., Orders Addr.: 6525 Gunpark Dr. 370, #250, Boulder, CO 80301 USA; Edit Addr.: 18841 E. Cornell Ave., Aurora, CO 80013 USA
E-mail: slmclean@hotmail.com
Web site: http://www.fisherhale.com.

Fisher Enterprises, *(978-0-9767265)* P.O. Box 1342, Eagle, ID 83616 USA Tel 208-939-6650; Fax: 208-939-7480 Do not confuse with Fisher Enterprises, Inc. In Edmonds, WA
E-mail: ggfisher@earthlink.net.

Fisher Hill, *(978-1-878253)* 5267 Warner Ave., No. 166, Huntington Beach, CA 92649 USA (SAN 254-1289) Tel 714-377-9353; Fax: 714-377-9495; Toll Free: 800-214-8110
E-mail: fisher.k@mac.com
Web site: http://www.Fisher-Hill.com
Dist(s): **Delta Systems Company, Inc.**

Fisher, John Wilfred, *(978-0-9771093)* 25216 Arrow Highline Rd., Juliaetta, ID 83535 USA Tel 208-843-7159
E-mail: jwfisher@starband.net.

Fisher King Enterprises, *(978-0-9776076; 978-0-9810344; 978-1-926715; 978-1-77169)* 30 N Gould St Suite 10570, Sheridan, WY 82801 USA (SAN 257-7410) Tel 307-222-9575; 831-238-7799; Fax: 831-621-4667; *Imprints:* il piccolo editions (il piccolo)
E-mail: orders@fisherkingpress.com; fisherkingpress@gmail.com
Web site: http://www.fisherkingpress.com
Dist(s): **Fisher King Bks.**

Fisher King Press *See* **Fisher King Enterprises**

Fisher Wilcoxon *See* **Fisher Hill**

Fisher-Paner Publishing, *(978-0-615-19778-4; 978-0-615-23931-6)* 1919 Sorrento Pl., Richmond, VA 23238 USA
Dist(s): **Lulu Pr., Inc.**

Fishers Media *See* **Hendrickson, Thomas L**

Fishman, Greg *See* **Fishman, Greg Jazz Studios**

Fishman, Greg Jazz Studios, *(978-0-9766153; 978-0-9843492; 978-0-9914078)* 824 Custer Ave., Evanston, IL 60202 USA
E-mail: greg1111@aol.com
Web site: http://www.gregfishmanjazzstudios.com.

Fishnet Pubns./Ministries, *(978-0-9667517)* 8440 Fairwind Ct., Indianapolis, IN 46256 USA
E-mail: canddjohnson@comcast.net.

Fisticuff Publishing, 2529 Whetstone ln, Myrtle Beach, SC 29579 USA Tel 607-759-5075
Dist(s): **CreateSpace Independent Publishing Platform.**

Fit Kids, *(978-0-9709301)* 175 W. 200 S., Suite 2012, Salt Lake City, UT 84101-1459 USA Tel 801-521-0109; Fax: 801-521-8360; Toll Free: 888-234-8543
E-mail: brucebellco@earthlink.net
Web site: http://www.fitkids.org.

Fit Kids Publishing, *(978-0-9895095)* P.O. Box 4149, Auburn, CA 95604 USA Tel 650-339-2727
E-mail: katherine@fitkidspublishing.com
Web site: http://www.fitkidspublishing.com
Dist(s): **Partners Pubs. Group, Inc.**

Fitch, Michele Marko, *(978-0-615-14996-7)* 2103 Wilkerson St., South Boston, MA 24592 USA
E-mail: familyfitch@myembarg.com
Dist(s): **Lulu Pr., Inc.**

Fitness Information Technology, Inc., *(978-0-9627926; 978-1-885693; 978-1-935412; 978-1-940067)* Orders Addr.: P.O. Box 6116, Morgantown, WV 26506 USA; Edit Addr.: 375 Birch St., Morgantown, WV 26506-6116 USA Tel 304-293-6888; Fax: 304-293-6658; Toll Free: 800-477-4348
E-mail: ICPE@mail.wvu.edu; matthew.brann@mail.wvu.edu
Web site: http://www.fitinfotech.com
Dist(s): **Cardinal Pubs. Group**
National Bk. Network
Unifacmanu International Trading Co., Inc.
ebrary, Inc.

Fitzerald, Seeking String, *(978-0-692-09906-3)* 29431 US HWY 160, South Fork, CO 81154 USA Tel 719-480-1858
E-mail: dplucinskihotel@yahoo.com
Dist(s): **CreateSpace Independent Publishing Platform.**

Fitzgerald Bks., *(978-1-887238; 978-1-59054; 978-1-4242)* Div. of Central Programs, Inc., Orders Addr.: P.O. Box 505, Bethany, MO 64424 USA Tel 660-425-7777; Fax: 660-425-3929; Toll Free: 800-821-7199; Edit Addr.: 802 N. 41st St., Bethany, MO 64424 USA
E-mail: wecare@gumdropbooks.com
Web site: http://www.gumdropbooks.com
Dist(s): **Gumdrop Bks.**

Fitzgerald, Caryn, *(978-0-615-17982-7; 978-0-615-21500-6)* P.O. Box 1343, Mansfield, TX 76063 USA
Web site: http://www.samifitzgerald.com
Dist(s): **Lulu Pr., Inc.**

Fitzhenry & Whiteside, Ltd. (CAN) *(978-0-88902; 978-1-55005; 978-1-55041; 978-1-55455) Dist. by* **Firefly Bks Limited.**

Fitzhenry & Whiteside, Ltd. (CAN) *(978-0-88902; 978-1-55005; 978-1-55041; 978-1-55455) Dist. by* **Children Plus.**

Fitzroy Bks. *Imprint of* **Regal Hse. Publishing, LLC**

Five Degrees of Frannie, *(978-0-9679115)* P.O. Box 178, North Greece, NY 14515 USA Tel 716-467-9136
E-mail: ohfrannie@aol.com.

Five Oaks Pr., *(978-0-9779325)* P.O. Box 251, Lake Lure, NC 28746-0251 USA
E-mail: davidklett@bellsouth.net
Web site: http://www.lakelurechronicles.com.

Five O'clock Dog, *(978-0-9767887)* Orchid # 1170, Corona del Mar, CA 92625 USA Tel 949-422-5909
Web site: http://www.fiveodog.com.

Five Ponds Pr., *(978-0-9727156; 978-0-9824133; 978-0-9824583; 978-1-935813)* 30 Hidden Spring Dr., Weston, CT 06883-1144 USA
E-mail: lou@fivepondspress.com
Web site: http://www.fivepondspress.com.

Five Star *Imprint of* **Cengage Gale**

Five Star Christian Pubns., *(978-0-9740142; 978-0-9777291)* 312 SE 24th Ave., Cape Coral, FL 33990 USA Tel 239-574-1000
E-mail: info@5scp.com
Web site: http://www.gulfcoastbaptistchurch.com; www.fivestarchristianministries.com.

Five Star Pr., (978-0-9673102) Orders Addr.: P.O. Box 8454, Richmond, VA 23226 USA Tel 804-282-6069; Edit Addr.: 1910 Byrd Ave., Suite 12, Richmond, VA 23230 USA.

Five Star Publications, Incorporated *See* **Story Monsters LLC**

Five Star Trade *Imprint of* **Cengage Gale**

Five Valleys Publishing (GBR) (978-0-9566042) *Dist. by* **LightSource CS.**

FizzBang Science, (978-0-9718480) 807 Murlay Dr., Plain City, OH 43064 USA Tel 614-873-8860 (phone/fax)
E-mail: blrohrig@worldnet.att.net
Web site: http://www.fizzbangscience.com.

Flaghouse, Inc., (978-0-9713648; 978-1-932032) 601 Rte. 46 W., Hasbrouck Heights, NJ 07604-3116 USA (SAN 631-3086) Tel 201-288-7600; Fax: 201-288-7887; Toll Free Fax: 800-793-7900
Web site: http://www.flaghouse.com.

Flagship Church Resources *Imprint of* **Group Publishing, Inc.**

Flamburis, Georgia, (978-0-615-47908-8) 5 Griggs Pl., Allston, MA 02134 USA Tel 617-783-9425
E-mail: gf_mae@yahoo.com.

Flame Tree Publishing (GBR) (978-1-874634; 978-1-903817; 978-1-904041; 978-1-84451; 978-1-84786; 978-1-78361; 978-1-83964) *Dist. by* **BTPS.**

Flaming Pen Pr., (978-0-615-27115-6; 978-0-615-28423-1; 978-0-615-34476-8; 978-0-615-36650-0; 978-0-615-41089-0; 978-0-615-93500-3; 978-1-950677) 114 Kingsdale Ct, Simpsonville, SC 29680 USA
Web site: www.flamingpenpress.com
Dist(s): **CreateSpace Independent Publishing Platform.**

Flammarion et Cie (FRA) (978-2-08) *Dist. by* **Distribks Inc.**

Flammer, Josephine, (978-0-615-16197-6; 978-0-615-25550-7) P.O. Box 225, Adirondack, NY 128008 USA
E-mail: joannflammer@aol.com
Web site: http://joannflammer.com
Dist(s): **Lulu Pr., Inc.**

Flash & Fancy Bks., (978-0-692-04518-3) 835 Front St. No. C, Georgetown, SC 29440 USA Tel 757-705-6745
E-mail: flashandfancy@gmail.com
Dist(s): **Ingram Content Group.**

Flash Blasters, Incorporated *See* **Ace Academics, Inc.**

Flashlight Pr., (978-0-9729225; 978-0-9799746; 978-1-936261; 978-1-947277) 527 Empire Blvd., Brooklyn, NY 11225-3121 USA
E-mail: ed.assist@flashlightpress.com
Web site: http://www.flashlightpress.com
Dist(s): **Independent Pubs. Group**
MyiLibrary
ebrary, Inc.

FlashPaws Productions, (978-0-9674929) 7714 Rolling Fork Ln., Houston, TX 77040-3432 USA Tel 713-896-8484 (phone/fax)
E-mail: info@flashpaws.com
Web site: http://www.flashpaws.com
Dist(s): **Greenleaf Book Group.**

Flat Hammock Pr., (978-0-9718303; 978-0-9758699; 978-0-9773725; 978-0-9795949; 978-0-9818960) 5 Church St., Mystic, CT 06355 USA Tel 860-572-2722; Fax: 860-572-2755
E-mail: info@flathammockpress.com
Web site: http://www.flathammockpress.com.

Flat Kids *Imprint of* **Smart Smiles Co., The**

Flat Pond Publishing, (978-0-9979179) 32 Flat Pond Cir., Mashpee, MA 02649 USA Tel 860-214-2121
E-mail: foxgroupct@yahoo.com.

Flat Sole Studio *Imprint of* **Skywater Publishing Co.**

Flatiron Bks., (978-1-250-08290-9) Div. of Macmillan, 175 Fifth Ave., New York, NY 10010 USA Tel 646-307-5151
Web site: www.flatironbooks.com
Dist(s): **Macmillan**
Westminster John Knox Pr.

Flaxenfluff Pr., LLC, (978-0-9743890) P.O. Box 2287, Broken Arrow, OK 74013 USA
Web site: http://www.flaxenfluff.com.

Fleischhacker, Daniel, (978-0-578-49196-7; 978-0-578-51290-7) 1911 Grand Ave., Kalamazoo, MI 49006 USA Tel 269-381-4191
E-mail: drdanf@gmail.com
Dist(s): **CreateSpace Independent Publishing Platform.**

Fleming, G. Faye *See* **Faye Bks.**

Fleming, Randall, (978-0-9841616) P.O. Box 252, Point Reyes Station, CA 94956 USA.

Fletcher, C J Publishing LLC, (978-0-9755255) Orders Addr.: P.O. Box 784, Independence, KS 67301 USA (SAN 256-1050) Tel 620-331-5182; Fax: 620-331-5183; Toll Free: 800-814-8513; Edit Addr.: 212- 214 E. Myrtle, Independence, KS 67301 USA
E-mail: cjdcpa@cableone.net.

Fletcher, Kerstin, (978-0-9891660) 3529 San Sonita Pl., Santa Rosa, CA 95403 USA Tel 707-523-2174
E-mail: rb1993@sbcglobal.net.

Fletcher, Robert *See* **Iron Mountain Pr.**

Fleur Art Productions, (978-0-9741277) 32 N. Goodwin Ave., Elmsford, NY 10523 USA Fax: 914-206-3558; Toll Free: 866-353-8727; *Imprints:* Fleur Publishing (Fleur Pubng)
E-mail: agents@fleur.ws
Web site: http://www.fleur.ws
Dist(s): **E-Pros DG.**

Fleur De Lis Publishing, LLC, (978-0-9821956) P.O. Box 2521, South Portland, ME 04116-252121 USA
E-mail: cmunson667@aol.com.

Fleur Publishing *Imprint of* **Fleur Art Productions**

Fleuve Noir (FRA) (978-2-265) *Dist. by* **Distribks Inc.**

Flickerfawn *Imprint of* **Barton Bks.**

Flight Time LLC, (978-0-9858024; 978-0-9943153-4-2) 12182 Deer Chase Dr., Cincinnati, OH 45240 USA Tel 513-702-3126
E-mail: lalakems@aol.com.

FlightBooks, (978-0-9834147) 1800 S. Ocean Blvd. Villa C, Boca Raton, FL 33432 USA Tel 561-750-2057
E-mail: reneblanco@bellsouth.net.

Flinders Pr., (978-0-9843955) P.O. Box 3975, Burbank, CA 91508-3975 USA (SAN 859-2829) Tel 818-714-0455
E-mail: flinderspress@gmail.com
Web site: http://www.flinderspress.com.

Flinn Scientific, Inc., (978-1-877991; 978-1-933709) Orders Addr.: P.O. Box 219, Batavia, IL 60510 USA (SAN 630-1800) Fax: 866-452-1436; Toll Free: 800-452-1261; Edit Addr.: 770 N. Raddant Rd., Batavia, IL 60510 USA
E-mail: flinn@flinnsci.com.

Flip n Flop Learning, LLC, (978-0-9801772; 978-0-9853372; 978-1-7334384; 978-1-7353114) 6752 Castenson Rd., Bryan, TX 77808 USA
E-mail: senoragose@verizon.net
Web site: http://www.flipfloplearning.com.

Flip Publishing, (978-0-9769342) P.O. Box 1072, Hawthorne, CA 90251 USA
E-mail: flippublishing@yahoo.com
Web site: www.flippublishing.net.

Flipp Sports, (978-0-9744443) 960 Turnpike St., Canton, MA 02021 USA Tel 781-821-8788; Fax: 781-821-4088
E-mail: jmarnikovic@flippsports.com
Web site: http://www.flippsports.com.

Flippin' Bks. LLC, (978-0-9742500) 25450 Williams Ridge, Warrenton, MO 63383 USA Tel 636-456-6224
E-mail: thw@flippinbooks.com
Web site: http://www.flippinbooks.com.

Floating Castles Media Inc. (CAN) (978-1-988736) *Dist. by* **IPG Chicago.**

Floating World Editions, (978-1-891640; 978-1-953225) 26 Jack Corner Rd., Warren, CT 06777 USA Tel 860-868-0890
E-mail: rfurse@floatingworldeditions.com
Web site: http://www.floatingworldeditions.com
Dist(s): **Antique Collectors' Club**
National Bk. Network.

FloBound Poems Publications, (978-0-9705819) Orders Addr.: P.O. Box 3101, Fredericksburg, VA 22402-3101 USA
E-mail: floboundpoems@aol.com; morningpoemsflog@aol.com
Web site: http://www.floboundpoems.com.

Flood Crest Pr., (978-1-934130) 604 E. Spring St., New Albany, IN 47150 USA Tel 812-944-5116; Fax: 812-944-5277
E-mail: ops@destinationsbooksellers.com
Web site: http://www.destinationsbooksellers.com.

Flood, Tim, (978-0-9797159) 1349 E. Ellis Dr., Tucson, AZ 85719 USA
Web site: http://www.dreamsofaballinflight.com.

Floodgate Publishing, (978-0-9761355) P.O. Box 1475, Castle Rock, WA 98611 USA.

Floppinfish Publishing Co., Ltd., (978-0-9629124; 978-0-615-70203-2; 978-0-692-34807-9; 978-0-692-87027-3; 978-0-578-52462-7) P.O. Box 4932, Saint Louis, MO 63108 USA Tel 314-567-8697
E-mail: wm4932@yahoo.com
Web site: http://www.JoeKeylon.com; http://www.pixofpeople.com
Dist(s): **Big River Distribution**
Partners Bk. Distributing, Inc.

Floppy Cat Co., (978-0-9823818) 2315 Devon Ave., Tea, SD 57064 USA
E-mail: jenn@greenleafbookgroup.com.

Flora Delaterre Productions, (978-0-9792302) P.O. Box 8474, Missoula, MT 59807 USA Tel 406-728-2977
Web site: http://www.floradelaterre.com.

Florencia Gimenez-Levit, (978-0-692-18100-3) 7227 Desert Jewel, El Paso, TX 79912 USA Tel 915-401-2536
E-mail: ceflovipa@msn.com.

Flores, Angie, (978-0-9979738) 3650 Newton St. No. 31, Torrance, CA 90505 USA Tel 310-408-3764
E-mail: crafty125@hotmail.com.

Flores, Travis *See* **Inclusive Global Inc.**

Floricanto Pr., (978-0-915745; 978-0-9796457; 978-1-951088) Div. of Inter American Development, 7177 Walnut Canyon Rd., Moorpark, CA 93021-1110 USA (SAN 293-9169) Tel 415-793-2662; Fax: 805-517-2991
E-mail: info@floricantopress.com; rcabello@floricantopress.com
Web site: http://www.floricantopress.com.

Florida Div. of Historical Resources, (978-0-9642289; 978-1-889030) Div. of Florida Dept. of State, c/o Bureau of Historic Preservation, 500 S. Bronough St., Tallahassee, FL 32399-0250 USA Tel 850-487-2333; Fax: 850-922-0496; Toll Free: 800-847-7278
Web site: http://www.flheritage.com.

Florida Historical Society, (978-1-886104; 978-0-9771079; 978-0-9817337; 978-1-949810) 435 Brevard Ave., Cocoa, FL 32922 USA Tel 321-690-1971; *Imprints:* Chapin House Books (Chapin Hse)
E-mail: FHSPress@myfloridahistory.org; chris.brotemarkle@myfloridahistory.org
Web site: www.floridabooks.net; www.myfloridahistory.org.

Florida Kids Pr., Inc., (978-0-9792304; 978-0-9863325) 11802 Magnolia Falls Dr., Jacksonville, FL 32258-2587 USA
Web site: http://www.janewoodbooks.com
Dist(s): **Partners Bk. Distributing, Inc.**

Florida Science Source, Inc., (978-0-944961) Orders Addr.: P.O. Box 8217, Longboat Key, FL 34228-8217 USA (SAN 245-6974); Edit Addr.: 28 Eagle Ridge Rd., Sapphire, NC 28774-9681 USA (SAN 245-6982)
E-mail: fssource@aol.com
Web site: http://www.ultimacitrus.com/fssource.

Floris Bks. (GBR) (978-0-86315; 978-0-903540; 978-1-78250) *Dist. by* **Consort Bk Sales.**

Floris Bks. (GBR) (978-0-86315; 978-0-903540; 978-1-78250) *Dist. by* **Gryphon Hse.**

Floris Bks. (GBR) (978-0-86315; 978-0-903540; 978-1-78250) *Dist. by* **SteinerBooks Inc.**

Flourish Publishing Hse., (978-0-9851659) P.O. Box 1661, Frisco, CO 80443 USA Tel 405-760-1118
E-mail: garystallings@yahoo.com.

Flower Press *See* **Flowerfield Enterprises**

Flower Publishing, (978-0-9852608) 1003 Deer Creek Church Rd., Forest Hill, MD 21050 USA Tel 443-528-3033
E-mail: gfdbuilders@yahoo.com.

Flower Sprouts, (978-0-615-21179-4; 978-0-615-21180-0; 978-0-615-21683-6) P.O. Box 1843, Morro Bay, CA 93443 USA Tel 805-772-5808 (phone/fax); 245 Morro Bay Blvd., Morro Bay, CA 1111
Web site: http://www.seawindgallery.com
Dist(s): **Lulu Pr., Inc.**

Flowerfield Enterprises, (978-0-942256) 10332 Shaver Rd., Kalamazoo, MI 49024-6744 USA (SAN 217-7358) Tel 269-327-0108; Fax: 269-327-7009
E-mail: nancy@wormwoman.com
Web site: http://www.wormwoman.com.

Flowerpot Pr., (978-1-68461) Div. of MitSo Media Inc., 142 Second Ave., N., Franklin, TN 37064 USA Tel 615-479-0695
E-mail: infor@flowerpotpress.com; anne@flowerpotpress.com
Web site: http://www.flowerpotpress.com
Dist(s): **Baker & Taylor Publisher Services (BTPS).**

Fluckiger, Jay D. *See* **Harmony Hse. Publishing Co.**

Fluckiger, Kory, (978-0-615-15654-5) 3640 Gramercy Ave., Ogden, UT 84403 USA Tel 801-791-3461
E-mail: kory@koryfluckiger.com
Web site: http://www.koryfluckiger.com
Dist(s): **Lulu Pr., Inc.**

Fluency Fast Language Classes, Inc., (978-0-9824687) Orders Addr.: P.O. Box 165, Manitou Springs, CO 80829 USA Tel 719-633-6000; Toll Free: 866-999-3583; Edit Addr.: 707 Manitou Blvd., Colorado Springs, CO 80904 USA
E-mail: karen@fluencyfast.com
Web site: http://www.fluencyfast.com.

Fluency Matters, (978-0-9777911; 978-1-934958; 978-1-935575; 978-1-940408; 978-1-945956; 978-1-64498) TPRS Publishing, Inc., P.O. Box 13409, Chandler, AZ 85248 USA Tel 480-821-8608; Fax: 480-963-3463; Toll Free: 800-877-4738
E-mail: patgaab@gmail.com
Web site: http://www.tprstorytelling.com.

Flugul Pubng, (978-0-9779390) P.O. Box 6090, Cincinnati, OH 45206 USA
E-mail: VLI@flugulpublishing.com
Web site: http://www.Flugulpublishing.com
Dist(s): **Lulu Pr., Inc.**

Fluharty, Linda Cunningham, (978-0-9759097) 833 Carnforth Dr., Baton Rouge, LA 70810 USA
E-mail: LCFlu@aol.com
Web site: http://www.lindapages.com.

Flutter-By Productions, (978-0-9714734) 1415 Panther Ln. # 214, Naples, FL 34109-7874 USA
Web site: http://www.flutter-byproductions.com
Dist(s): **APG Sales & Distribution Services.**

Flux *Imprint of* **North Star Editions**

Flux *Imprint of* **Llewellyn Pubns.**

Flyaway Bks. *Imprint of* **Westminster John Knox Pr.**

Flying Cloud Bks., (978-0-615-13477-2) 123 Moore Rd., Sudbury, MA 01776 USA
E-mail: mail@paulgreenspan.com
Web site: http://www.paulgreenspan.com
Dist(s): **Lulu Pr., Inc.**

Flying Dolphin Pr. *Imprint of* **Knopf Doubleday Publishing Group**

Flying Eagle Pubns., (978-0-9766268; 978-1-7327688) 139 Brown., Tecumseh, MI 49286 USA
E-mail: dflyingeagle@flyingeaglepublications.com
Web site: http://www.flyingeaglepublications.com/.

Flying Eye Bks. (GBR) (978-1-909263; 978-1-911171; 978-1-912497) *Dist. by* **Peng Rand Hse.**

Flying Frog Pubs.,
Dist(s): **Ideals Pubns.**

Flying Frog Publishing, (978-0-9666647) 567 Westcove Dr., Wasilla, AK 99654-7161 USA Tel 907-373-6994 (phone/fax); Toll Free: 888-673-6994 Do not confuse with Flying Frog Publishing, Reisterstown, MD
E-mail: jobshlh@corecom.net
Web site: http://www.galaxymall.com/children/alaskariddles
Dist(s): **Todd Communications**
Wizard Works.

Flying Frog Publishing, Inc., (978-1-57755; 978-1-884628; 978-1-934967; 978-1-60745; 978-1-63560) 2219 York Rd., Suite 300, Lutherville, MD 21093 USA Tel 443-901-2100; Fax: 443-901-2104
Web site: http://www.flyingfrogpub.com
Dist(s): **Ideals Pubns.**

Flying Owl Pubns, (978-0-9820769) 2268 Brighton, Holland, MI 49424 USA Tel 616-399-3857
E-mail: denuyl@chartermi.net.

Flying Pig Publishing, (978-0-9746110) P.O. Box 304, Harvard, MA 01451 USA
E-mail: douglee41@yahoo.com
Web site: http://deelee.net.

Flying Point Pr., (978-0-9904604) The Pilot House, Boston, MA 02110 USA Tel 617-734-7560
E-mail: peggy@flyingpointpress.com.

Flying Rhino Productions, Incorporated *See* **Flying Rhinoceros, Inc.**

Flying Rhinoceros, Inc., (978-1-883772; 978-1-59168; 978-0-9822773) 1440 NW Overton St., Portland, OR 97209 USA (SAN 857-7501) Tel 503-552-8777; Fax: 503-445-8375; Toll Free: 800-537-4466
E-mail: flyingrhino@flyingrhino.com; melson@flyingrhino.com
Web site: http://www.flyingrhino.com.

Flying Scroll Publishing, LLC, (978-0-9742432; 978-0-9848099) P.O. Box 246, Fort Atkinson, WI 53538 USA Tel 920-723-3454
E-mail: info@flyingscrollpublishing.com
Web site: http://www.flyingscrollpublishing.com.

Flying Solo Pr., LLC, (978-1-940137) 1116 Cherokee St, Denver, CO 80204 USA Tel 303-733-3751
E-mail: paulaertker@gmail.com
Web site: www.crimetravelers.com.

Flying Squirrel Press *See* **Heritage Heart Farm**

Flying Thru Life Pubns., (978-0-692-43750-6; 978-0-692-78797-7; 978-1-7324937) P.O. Box 3351, San Diego, CA 92163 USA Tel 619-368-9410
Web site: www.flyingthrulife.com
Dist(s): **CreateSpace Independent Publishing Platform.**

Flying Turtle Publishing, (978-0-615-31741-0; 978-0-9851492; 978-0-9911378; 978-0-9907104; 978-0-9989979) 7216 Birch Ave., Hammond, IN 46324 USA
Web site: http://flyingturtlepublishing.com
Dist(s): **Smashwords.**

Flying Wren Studio, (978-0-9980141) 508 Liberty St., Petosky, MI 49770 USA.

Flyleaf Publishing, (978-0-9658246; 978-1-929262; 978-1-60541) Orders Addr.: P.O. Box 287, Lyme, NH 03768-0185 USA Tel 800-449-7006; Fax: 888-619-6419; P.O. Box 287, Lyme, NH 03768-0287 Toll Free: 800-449-7006; *Imprints:* Books To Remember (Bks To Remember)
E-mail: laura@flyleafpublishing.com
Web site: http://www.flyleafpublishing.com.

Flywheel Publishing Co., (978-1-930826) Orders Addr.: 1375 Sunnyhills Rd., Oakland, CA 94610 USA (SAN 253-2441) Tel 510-407-7577; Fax: 510-373-6060
E-mail: admin@flywheel.us
Web site: http://www.flywheel.us.

FM Rocks Kids, LLC *See* **Playdate Kids Publishing**

FMA Publishing, (978-0-9774411) 1920 Pacific Ave. No. 16152, Long Beach, CA 90806 USA (SAN 257-4977) Tel 310-438-3483; Fax: 310-438-3486
E-mail: info@fmapublishing.com
Web site: http://www.fmapublishing.com.

Fo Guang Shan International Translation Ctr., (978-1-943211) 3456 Glenmark Dr., Hacienda Heights, CA 91745 USA Tel 626-330-8361
E-mail: fgsitc@gmail.com
Web site: fgsitc.org.

Focus *Imprint of* **Hackett Publishing Co., Inc.**

Focus Group, Inc., (978-0-9766968) 2201 SW 152nd St. Ste. 3, Burien, WA 98166-2080 USA
E-mail: pubs@focusgroupseattle.com.

†Focus on the Family Publishing, (978-0-929608; 978-1-56179; 978-1-58997; 978-1-60482; 978-1-62405; 978-1-62471; 978-1-68332; 978-1-68424; 978-1-68428; 978-1-64607) 8605 Explorer Dr., Colorado Springs, CO 80920 USA (SAN 250-0949) Fax: 719-531-3356; Toll Free: 800-232-6459
E-mail: robert.huntrods@fotf.org; permissions@fotf.org
Web site: http://www.focusonthefamily.com
Dist(s): **Follett School Solutions**
Gospel Light Pubns.
Nelson, Tommy
Tyndale Hse. Pubs.
Zondervan; *CIP.*

Focus Publishing, (978-1-885904; 978-1-936141) Orders Addr.: P.O. Box 665, Bemidji, MN 56619 USA Tel 218-759-9816 Toll Free: 800-913-6287; Edit Addr.: 502 Third St., NW, Bemidji, MN 56601 USA
E-mail: jan@focuspublishing.com
Web site: http://focuspublishing.com
Dist(s): **Spring Arbor Distributors, Inc.**

Focus Readers *Imprint of* **North Star Editions**

Fog City Pr., (978-1-875137; 978-1-887451; 978-1-892374; 978-1-929156; 978-1-74089) Subs. of Weldon Owen, Inc., 2215-R Market St., No. 123, San Francisco, CA 94114 USA Tel 415-626-9636
E-mail: gilblock@sirius.com
Dist(s): **INscribe Digital**
Ingram Publisher Services.

Fog Ink *Imprint of* **Fields of Gold Publishing, Inc.**

Foglight Pr., (978-0-9755848) Orders Addr.: P.O. Box 160322, Sacramento, CA 95816 USA
E-mail: info@foglightpress.com
Web site: http://www.foglightpress.com
Dist(s): **Bookazine Co., Inc.**

folder leaf *Imprint of* **Story Time Stories That Rhyme**

Foley, Mark, (978-0-615-19609-1) 4 3rd Ave., Annville, PA 17003 USA
Dist(s): **Lulu Pr., Inc.**

Folk Prophet Bks., (978-0-578-00160-9) 140 S. 200 E., Lindon, UT 84042 USA
E-mail: books@folkprophet.com
Dist(s): **Lulu Pr., Inc.**

Folklore Publishing (CAN) (978-1-894864; 978-1-897206; 978-1-926677) *Dist. by* **Lone Pine.**

Follett Library Resources *See* **Follett School Solutions**

Follett School Solutions, (978-0-329; 978-0-88153; 978-0-924917; 978-1-4898; 978-1-5160; 978-1-5181; 978-1-5379; 978-1-5444; 978-1-5490; 978-1-7254; 978-1-7137) Div. of the Follett Corp., Orders Addr.: a/o McHenry Warehouse, 1340 Ridgeview Dr., McHenry, IL 60050 USA (SAN 169-1902) Toll Free: 888-511-5114; a/o Patti Hall: R & R Bindery Services, 499 Rachel Rd.,

Girard, IL 62640 (SAN 155-8412) Tel 815-759-1700; *Imprints:* Follettbound (Follettbnd)
Web site: http://www.follett.com
Dist(s): **Baker & Taylor Bks.**

Follettbound *Imprint of* **Follett School Solutions**

Follmer Group, The, *(978-0-925065; 978-1-933478; 978-1-935871; 978-1-943137)* 5758 S. Blackstone Ave., Chicago, IL 60637 USA Tel 773-643-1902; Fax: 773-643-1903
E-mail: david@thedavidfollmergroup.com
Web site: http://www.thedavidfollmergroup.com.

Folsom Fallies Pr., *(978-0-9760790)* Orders Addr.: P.O. Box 348, Folsom, NM 88419 USA Tel 505-278-2520
E-mail: kristene@folsomfallies.com
Web site: http://www.folsomfallies.com.

Fomenky Publishing, *(978-0-615-97545-0; 978-0-9988929)* 3333 164TH ST SW Apt No. 1613, LYNNWOOD, WA 98087 USA Tel 925-367-5478
E-mail: Berthina@CNATOMD.COM; Kellen@Colemanprfirm.com
Web site: www.FOMENKYPUBLISHING.COM; Colemanprfirm.com; WWW.CHRISTIANSTAR.ME.

Fond du Lac Head Start, *(978-0-615-69899-1)* 1720 Big Lake Rd., Cloquet, MN 55720 USA Tel 218-878-8130; Fax: 218-878-8115
E-mail: barbaraforcier@fdlrez.com
Web site: fdlrez.com.

Fondo de Cultura Económcia,
Dist(s): **Fondo de Cultura Economica USA.**

Fondo de Cultura Economica USA, 2293 Verus St., San Diego, CA 92154 USA (SAN 860-1380) Tel 619-429-0455; Fax: 619-651-9684; Toll Free: 800-532-3872
E-mail: orders@fceusa.com; drazo@fceusa.com; fondosales@fceusa.com
Web site: http://www.fceusa.com
Dist(s): **Giron Bks.**
Latin American Book Source, Inc.
Lectorum Pubns., Inc.

Fondo Editorial Grania, Fundacion Hogares Juveniles Campesinos (COL) *(978-958-8233; 978-958-9321)* *Dist. by* **Chelsea Green Pub.**

Fons Vitae *See* **Fons Vitae of Kentucky, Inc.**

Fons Vitae of Kentucky, Inc., *(978-1-887752; 978-1-941610)* 49 Mockingbird Valley Dr., Louisville, KY 40207-1366 USA Tel 502-897-3641
E-mail: fonsvitaeky@aol.com
Web site: http://www.fonsvitae.com
Dist(s): **Independent Pubs. Group.**

Fontanka (GBR) *(978-0-9543095; 978-1-906257)* *Dist. by* **Natl Bk Netwk.**

Food Allergy & Anaphylaxis Network, *(978-1-882541)* 11781 Lee Jackson Hwy. Suite 160, Fairfax, VA 22033 USA Tel 703-691-3179; Fax: 703-691-2713; Toll Free: 800-929-4040
E-mail: faan@foodallergy.org
Web site: http://www.foodallergy.org.

Food Allergy Network *See* **Food Allergy & Anaphylaxis Network**

Food & Agriculture Organization of the United Nations (ITA) *(978-92-5)* *Dist. by* **Rowman.**

Food Enhancement Enterprises, *(978-0-9747247)* Orders Addr.: P.O. Box 60581, Sacramento, CA 95680 USA; Edit Addr.: 2148 Bluebird Ln., Sacramento, CA 95821 USA
E-mail: hsdell@lanset.com
Web site: http://www.pizzareconsidered.com.

Food Marketing Consultants, Inc., *(978-0-9763307; 978-1-59949)* 2805 N. Commerce Pkwy., Miramar, FL 33025 USA Tel 954-322-2668 Toll Free: 877-493-2633
Web site: http://www.colorallabout.com.

Food Network Kitchens *Imprint of* **Meredith Bks.**

Food Safety & Inspection Service *Imprint of* **United States Government Printing Office**

FoodPlay Productions, *(978-0-9642858)* 1 Sunset Ave., Hatfield, MA 01038 USA Tel 413-247-5400; Fax: 413-247-5405; Toll Free: 800-366-3752 (Orders)
E-mail: store@foodplay.com
Web site: http://www.foodplay.com
Dist(s): **Partners Pubs. Group, Inc.**

Foolosophy Media, *(978-0-9779928)* 1528 Primrose Ln., Panama City, FL 32404 USA (SAN 850-8186) Tel 850-871-2304; 850-899-1972; Fax: 850-871-2304
E-mail: wisemullet@gmail.com.

Foothill-Hydroponics, *(978-0-9669557)* 10705 Burbank Blvd., N., North Hollywood, CA 91601 USA Tel 818-760-0688; Fax: 818-760-4025
E-mail: mohsen@foothillhydroponics.com
Web site: http://www.foothill-hydroponic.com.

Footprints Pr., *(978-0-9679813)* 71 Hudson St., New York, NY 10013 USA Tel 212-267-9300; Fax: 212-267-9400.

For Children With Love Pubns., *(978-0-578-00980-3; 978-0-9831221; 978-0-9994002; 978-0-578-74995-2)* 23 Robkins rd, Avon, CT 06001 USA Tel 860-940-9878; 23 Robkins rd, Avon , CT 06001
E-mail: Cathy.forchildren@gmail.com
Web site: http://www.forchildrenwithlove.com.

For Dummies *Imprint of* **Wiley, John & Sons, Inc.**

For Him Pr., *(978-0-9858899)* P.O. Box 2207, Morristown, TN 37816 USA Tel 423-307-8137
E-mail: claudia-scribe@live.com
Web site: claudia-clues.com.

For Little Folks, *(978-0-9771236)* P.O. Box 571, Dresden, OH 43821 USA.

For Such A Time As This Ministries, *(978-0-9725890)* 510 Swank Rd., Hollsopple, PA 15935-8116 USA Tel 814-479-7710; Fax: 814-479-4874; Toll Free: 877-378-4374
E-mail: jpstobaugh@aol.com
Web site: http://www.forsuchatimeasthis.com.

For The Love of Dog Bks., *(978-0-9761124)* 635 NE Buffalo, Portland, OR 97211 USA Tel 503-286-5351
E-mail: stelljes@aol.com
Web site: http://www.silvertonbobbie.com
Dist(s): **Far West Bk. Service**
Partners/West Book Distributors.

Forbes Custom Publishing, *(978-0-8281)* Div. of Forbes, Inc., 60 Fifth Ave., New York, NY 10011 USA (SAN 206-9032) Tel 212-620-2200; Fax: 212-367-4862; Toll Free: 800-242-8786
E-mail: customerservice@forbes.net
Dist(s): **Institute for Healthcare Advancement.**

Forbes Literary Ltd. Inc., *(978-0-9776284)* P.O. Box 494, Grover, MO 63040-1621 USA Tel 314-753-6142; Fax: 636-405-1963
E-mail: forbeslit@sbcgobal.net
Web site: http://www.forbesliterary.com.

Force of Nature LLC, *(978-0-692-87979-5; 978-0-692-94113-3; 978-0-692-04818-4; 978-0-692-08542-4)* 12289 Jamboree Dr, Eastvale, CA 91752 USA
E-mail: info@4orceofnature.com.

Ford, Angela J., *(978-0-692-16876-9)* 2011 Richard Jones Rd L5, Nashville, TN 37215 USA Tel 615-627-6347.

Fore Angels Pr., *(978-0-9658920; 978-0-9799947)* 267 Woodbury Rd., Huntington, NY 11743 USA Tel 631-385-0336
E-mail: annaarts@verizon.net.

Foreign Policy Assn., *(978-0-87124)* 551 Fifth Ave. Suite 3000, New York, NY 10176 USA (SAN 212-9426) Tel 212-481-8100; Fax: 212-481-9275; Toll Free: 800-628-5754; 800-477-5836 (orders)
Web site: http://www.fpa.org.

Forelle Graphics, *(978-0-9770918)* 1015 Atlantic Blvd., Suite 89, Atlantic Beach, FL 32233 USA
E-mail: forelle-graphics@yahoo.com.

Forest Hill Publishing, LLC, *(978-0-9759251; 978-0-9771113)* 13200 Forest Hill Ave., East Cleveland, OH 44112 USA Tel 216-761-8316 (phone/fax); Tel 253-799-8316; *Imprints:* PlayGround (PlayGrnd OH); SpringTree (SpringTree); FortuneChild (FortuneChild) Do not confuse with Forest Hill Publishing in Downers Grove, IL
E-mail: email@foresthillpublishing.com
Web site: http://www.foresthillpublishing.com.

Forest Hse. Publishing Co., Inc., *(978-1-56674; 978-1-878363)* P.O. Box 738, Lake Forest, IL 60045 USA Tel 847-295-8287; Fax: 847-295-8201; Toll Free: 800-394-7323.

Forest Lane Bks., *(978-0-9996735)* P.O. Box 371006, San Diego, CA 92137 USA Tel 619-269-5433
E-mail: ruthmacpete@gmail.com.

Forest Service *Imprint of* **United States Government Printing Office**

Forest Woods Media Productions *Imprint of* **Bunny & The Crocodile Pr., The**

Foresta, David Samuel, *(978-0-578-42370-8)* 3277 Bighorn Cir., Corona, CA 92881 USA Tel 951-549-0789
E-mail: dforesta@arbonne.com.

Forever *Imprint of* **Grand Central Publishing**

Forge Bks. *Imprint of* **Doherty, Tom Assocs., LLC**

Forgotten Bks., *(978-0-60506; 978-1-60620; 978-1-60680; 978-1-4400; 978-1-4510)* 8345 NW 66th St., Miami, FL 33166 USA (SAN 854-9354)
E-mail: director@forgottenbooks.org
Web site: http://www.forgottenbooks.org/
Dist(s): **CreateSpace Independent Publishing Platform.**

Fork in the Road Pubs., *(978-0-9740825)* 1883 145th Pl. SE, Bellevue, WA 98007-6019 USA Tel 425-644-4285
Web site: http://www.raincitycookingschool.com.

Forks Pr., *(978-0-9816641)* 4-02 Summit Ave., Fair Lawn, NJ 07410 USA (SAN 856-1575) Tel 201-310-3297; 646-208-2161
E-mail: info@forkspress.com
Web site: http://www.forkspress.com.

Formac Publishing Co., Ltd. (CAN) *(978-0-88780; 978-0-921921; 978-1-55277; 978-1-4595)* *Dist. by* **Casemate Pubs.**

Formac Publishing Co., Ltd. (CAN) *(978-0-88780; 978-0-921921; 978-1-55277; 978-1-4595)* *Dist. by* **Lerner Pub.**

Forsberg, Michael Photography, *(978-0-9754964)* 100 N. 8th St., Suite 150, Lincoln, NE 68508-1369 USA Toll Free: 888-812-3790 Do not confuse with Platte Publishing Company in Denver, CO
E-mail: patty@michaelforsberg.com
Web site: http://www.michaelforsberg.com
Dist(s): **Univ. of Nebraska Pr.**

Fortitude Graphic Design & Printing, *(978-0-9741611; 978-0-578-06241-9; 978-0-9863173; 978-0-9977136; 978-0-692-88090-6; 978-0-9991334; 978-1-7328399; 978-1-7353600)* 841 Gibson St., Kalamazoo, MI 49001-2540 USA
E-mail: fortitude2@sbcglobal.net
Web site: www.comvoicesonline.com; www.fortitudegdp.com.

Fortner, Ray, *(978-0-9726365)* Orders Addr.: 3501 Baisden Rd., Pensacola, FL 32503-3458 USA.

Fortress Pr. *Imprint of* **Augsburg Fortress, Pubs.**

Fortuna Pubns., *(978-0-692-28905-1; 978-0-692-29870-1; 978-0-692-30039-8; 978-0-692-31178-3; 978-0-692-35913-6; 978-0-692-36240-2; 978-1-947964; 978-1-64720)* 12127 Mall Blvd Ste A507, Victorville, CA 92392 USA Tel 442-247-8962
E-mail: fortunapublications@gmail.com
Web site: www.fortunapublications.com
Dist(s): **CreateSpace Independent Publishing Platform.**

FortuneChild *Imprint of* **Forest Hill Publishing, LLC**

Forward Comix, *(978-0-9886114; 978-0-9904747; 978-1-7344969)* 467 Bay Ridge Pkwy., Brooklyn, NY 11209 USA Tel 718-921-8789
E-mail: jerome@forwardcomix.com
Web site: forwardcomix.com.

Forward Communications *See* **NetNia Publishing Co.**

Forward Movement Pubns., *(978-0-88028)* 300 West Fourth St., Cincinnati, OH 45202 USA (SAN 208-3841) Tel 513-721-6659; Fax: 513-721-0729; Toll Free: 800-543-1813 (orders only)
E-mail: Orders@forwarddaybyday.com
Web site: http://www.forwardmovement.org
Dist(s): **Baker & Taylor Publisher Services (BTPS).**

Forword, *(978-0-9623937)* 16526 W. 78th St., Suite 335, Eden Prairie, MN 55346 USA Tel 612-944-7761; Fax: 612-944-8674.

Foster Branch Publishing, 20 Poplar St., No. 2, Jersey City, NJ 07307 USA
E-mail: dolphinupatree@hotmail.com.

Foster, Dennis, *(978-0-9771956)* P.O. Box 363, Millwood, VA 22646 USA.

Foster, Hicks & Assocs., *(978-0-9790709)* Orders Addr.: 4053 Harlan St., loft 201, Emeryville, CA 94608-9460 USA Tel 510-540-1241
E-mail: info@fosterhicks.com.

Foster, Walter Publishing, Incorporated *See* **Quarto Publishing Group USA**

Foston Adolescent Workshop, Inc., *(978-0-9641709; 978-1-930362)* P.O. Box 726, Clarksville, TN 37041 USA Tel 931-906-4623; Fax: 931-645-3500; Toll Free: 800-418-0374
E-mail: minfoston@aol.com
Web site: http://www.drfoston.com.

Fotopia Pr., *(978-0-9970996)* 9501 S. King Dr., Chicago, IL 60628 USA Tel 773-318-9485
E-mail: adamfotos@rocketmail.com
Web site: adamfotos.com.

Fouch, Robert L., *(978-0-9907913)* 26 Ivy Pl., Valley Stream, NY 11581 USA Tel 516-569-0125
E-mail: robfouch@aol.com
Web site: robertlfouch.com.

Foulsham, W. Co., Ltd. (GBR) *(978-0-572)* *Dist. by* **APG.**

Found Link, *(978-0-615-43601-2; 978-0-9836659)* 13125 Ladybank Ln., Herndon, VA 20171 USA Tel 703-966-2175
E-mail: jlcuddehe@verizon.net
Web site: www.CuddeheServices.com.

Foundation For Cosmetic Surgery, The, *(978-0-9799438)* 400 Newport Center Dr. Ste. 800, Newport Beach, CA 92660-7607 USA
E-mail: bryan@griffinpublishing.com; ffps2007@yahoo.com
Web site: http://www.beautybybrennan.com.

Foundation, Pr. The, *(978-0-9765987)* P.O. Box 182, Westport, CT 06881 USA Do not confuse with companies with the same name in New York, NY, Anaheim, CA
Web site: http://www.thefoundationpress.com.

Foundation Pr., *(978-0-9767272)* 13832 Gimbert Ln., Santa Ana, CA 92705-2849 USA Do not confuse with companies with the same name in New York, NY, Westport, CT.

Foundations for Learning, LLC, *(978-0-9726479; 978-1-933546)* 246 W. Manson Hwy., PMB 144, Chelan, WA 98816 USA Toll Free: 800-553-5950
E-mail: info@gophonics.com
Web site: http://www.gophonics.com.

Foundations in Brass *See* **Cymbal Technique 101**

Foundation, Inc., *(978-0-9797125; 978-0-9859251)* 701 E. Gate Dr. Suite 300, Mt. Laurel, NJ 08054 USA Tel 856-533-1600; Fax: 856-533-1601; Toll Free: 888-977-5437
E-mail: rmclaughlin@foundationsinc.org
Web site: http://www.foundationsinc.org.

Founders Hse. Publishing LLC, *(978-0-9843764; 978-0-692-34395-1; 978-0-692-38422-0; 978-0-692-38427-5; 978-0-692-38945-4; 978-0-692-39110-5; 978-0-692-43655-4; 978-0-692-45654-5; 978-0-692-45897-6; 978-0-692-48863-8; 978-0-692-55429-6; 978-0-692-57197-2; 978-0-692-67911-1; 978-0-692-73490-2; 978-1-945810) 614 Wayne St., Danville, IL 61832 USA*
E-mail: amkilgore@foundershousepublishing.com; sckilgore@foundershousepublishing.com
Web site: http://www.foundershousepublishing.com
Dist(s): **CreateSpace Independent Publishing Platform.**

Fountain Blue Publishing, *(978-0-615-81358-5; 978-1-62868)* P.O. Box 657, Squaw Valley, CA 93675 USA Tel 213-986-6835
E-mail: fountainbluepublishing@gmail.com
Web site: www.fountainbluepublishing.com.

Fountain Publishing, *(978-0-9659164; 978-0-9748423; 978-0-9822172; 978-1-936665)* Orders Addr.: P.O. Box 80011, Rochester, MI 48308 USA (SAN 253-8571) Tel 248-651-2934; Toll Free: 877-736-8598; Edit Addr.: 375 Olivewood Ct., Rochester, MI 48306 USA Tel 810-651-1153 Do not confuse with Fountain Publishing in Pittsburgh, PA
E-mail: ftnpublish@aol.com; jk@fountainpublishing.com
Web site: http://www.fountainpublishing.com.

Fountain Square Publishing, *(978-0-9724421)* 786 Old Ludlow, Cincinnati, OH 45220 USA.

Fountains of Financial Services, LLC, *(978-0-9719706)* 626 S. Ninth St., Las Vegas, NV 89101 USA Tel 702-382-9833; Fax: 702-382-0375
E-mail: pgfox711@aol.com.

Four Blocks, Div. of Carson-Dellosa Publishing Company, Inc., Orders Addr.: P.O. Box 35665, Greensboro, NC 27425 USA Tel 336-632-0084; Fax: 336-808-3249; Toll Free: 800-321-0943
Dist(s): **Carson-Dellosa Publishing, LLC.**

Four Corners Magazine LLC, *(978-0-578-46178-6; 978-0-578-47860-9)* P.O. Box 2252, Flagstaff, AZ 86003 USA Tel 928-300-4452
E-mail: sedonamag@gmail.com.

Four Corners Publishing Co., Inc., *(978-1-893577)* 45 W. Tenth St., New York, NY 10011 USA Tel 212-673-5226; Fax: 516-771-1243
E-mail: RLutnick@aol.com.

Four Dolphins Pr. *Imprint of* **Four Dolphins Pr., LLC**

Four Dolphins Pr., *(978-0-9745746)* Orders Addr.: P.O. Box 93601, Los Angeles, CA 90093 USA (SAN 255-626X) Tel 323-304-2053; Edit Addr.: 2700 N. Cahuenga Blvd., E., Suite 1403, Los Angeles, CA 90068-2139 USA.

Four Dolphins Pr., LLC, *(978-0-9799315)* P.O. Box 833, Scott Depot, WV 25560 USA Tel 304-757-8125; *Imprints:* Four Dolphins Press (Four Dolphin)
Web site: http://www.SadMadGladBooks.com.

Four Dolphins Press/Smart Communications, Incorporated *See* **Four Dolphins Pr.**

Four Elephants Pr., *(978-1-940051; 978-0-9998324)* 11828 La Grange Ave., Los Angeles, CA 90025 USA Tel 310-477-4564
E-mail: annaka.harris@gmail.com
Dist(s): **MyiLibrary**
Publishers Group West (PGW).

Four Foot Pr. LLC, *(978-0-9820817)* 12647 Galveston Ct., Suite 114, Manassas, VA 20112 USA
E-mail: dcgenesis@hotmail.com; fourfootpress@yahoo.com
Web site: http://fourfootpress.com.

Four Menards, The, *(978-0-9887969; 978-0-9891734; 978-0-9903872; 978-0-9904521)* P.O. Box 17265, Asheville, NC 28816 USA Tel 828-335-0284; Fax: 828-484-9873
E-mail: thefourmenards@gmail.com
Web site: N/A.

Four Oaks Publishing *Imprint of* **Santacroce, John**

Four Panel Pr., *(978-0-9674102; 978-0-9971090)* P.O. Box 50032, Eugene, OR 97405 USA Tel 541-343-6436; Fax: 541-684-0787
E-mail: tedlay@comcast.net
Web site: http://www.stonesoupcartoons.com
Dist(s): **Baker & Taylor Publisher Services (BTPS).**

Four Phoenixes Publishing, *(978-0-9976205)* 6407 N. Post Oak Rd., Peoria, IL 61603 USA Tel 309-256-6406
E-mail: joechianakas@gmail.com.

Four Pine Farms *See* **Four Pines Farms**

Four Pines Farms, *(978-0-9860701)* 683 Feldhauser Rd, Frederic, MI 49733 USA
E-mail: yroehler@bookpublishing.com.

Four Seasons Bks., Inc., *(978-0-9666858; 978-1-893595)* P.O. Box 395, Ben Wheeler, TX 75754 USA Tel 903-963-1442; Fax: 903-963-1525; Toll Free: 800-852-7484
E-mail: hcmarlow@yahoo.com; editor@fourseasonsbookstore.com
Web site: http://www.herbmarlow.com; http://www.fourseasonsbookstore.com.

Four Seasons Pubs., *(978-0-9656811; 978-1-891929; 978-1-932497)* Orders Addr.: P.O. Box 51, Titusville, FL 32781 USA Tel 321-632-2932; Fax: 321-632-2935; Edit Addr.: 4350 N. U.S. Hwy. 1, Cocoa, FL 32927 USA
E-mail: fseasons@bellsouth.net
Dist(s): **Follett School Solutions.**

Four Seasons Publishing, *(978-0-578-05005-8)* 105 Ansley Pl., Harlem, GA 30814 USA
E-mail: tedhoodjr@arkansas.net
Web site: http://www.thecardinalnest.com.

Four Sonkist Angels, *(978-0-9753117)* 4985 Wiltshire Ln., Suwanee, GA 30024 USA
E-mail: Michelle@FourSonkistAngels.com
Web site: http://www.FourSonkistAngels.com.

Four Star Publishing, *(978-0-9815894)* P.O. Box 871784, Canton, MI 48187 USA
E-mail: fourstarpublishing@comcast.net.

Four Star Publishing, *(978-0-9851990)* P.O. Box 871784, Canton, MI 48187 USA Tel 734-945-6714
E-mail: larryandmonica@comcast.net
Dist(s): **Greenleaf Book Group.**

FourFront Media & Music, *(978-0-9743420)* Orders Addr.: 1245 S. 128th St., Seattle, WA 98168 USA Tel 206-282-6116
E-mail: chris@chrisknab.net
Web site: http://www.fourfrontmusic.com.

Foursquare Media, ICFG, *(978-0-9635581; 978-0-9802392)* 1910 W. Sunset Blvd., Suite 200, Los Angeles, CA 90026 USA Tel 213-989-4493; Fax: 213-413-3824
E-mail: rwulfestieg@foursquare.org
Web site: http://www.foursquare.org.

Fourth Generation Pubs., *(978-0-9706186)* PMB 146,14625 Baltimore Ave., Laurel, MD 20707-4902 USA (SAN 253-5513) Tel 301-497-9948.

Fox Chapel Publishing Co., Inc., *(978-0-932944; 978-1-56523; 978-1-57421; 978-1-58011; 978-1-880029; 978-1-85974; 978-1-903366; 978-0-9777004; 978-1-905523; 978-1-60765; 978-1-906853; 978-1-4971; 978-1-4972; 978-1-5048; 978-1-908397; 978-1-910456; 978-1-64124; 978-1-64178)* Orders Addr.: 1970 Broad St., East Petersburg, PA 17520 USA (SAN 920-8887) Tel 717-560-4703; Fax: 717-560-4702; Toll Free Fax: 888-369-2885; Toll Free: 800-457-9112 (orders); Edit Addr.: 903 Square St., Mount Joy, PA 17552 USA Fax: 888-369-2885; Toll Free: 1-800-457-9112; *Imprints:* Design Originals (Design Orig); CompanionHouse Books (CompanionBks); Quiet Fox Designs (QuietFox)
E-mail: sales@carvingworld.com; alan@foxchapelpublishing.com; Younger@foxchapelpublishing.com; sales@foxchapelpublishing.com
Web site: http://www.foxchapelpublishing.com/; http://www.scrollsawer.com/; http://www.carvingworld.com;

http://www.foxchapelpublishing.com; www.d-originals.com
Dist(s): **Two Rivers Distribution.**

Fox, Kenneth *See* **Flat Pond Publishing**

Fox Print Bks., (*978-0-9729587*) 200 Seashore Ave., Peaks Island, ME 04108 USA Tel 207-899-0781
E-mail: eleanor.morse@gmail.com.

Fox Ridge Pubns., (*978-0-9856215; 978-0-9904281; 978-0-9967683*) 10490 Fox Ridge Dr., Hillsboro, WI 54634 USA Tel 715-630-2433
E-mail: lisalickel@gmail.com.

Fox Run Pr., LLC, (*978-0-9819607; 978-0-9825930*) 7840 Bullet Rd., Peyton, CO 80831 USA
Web site: http://www.FoxRunPress.com; http://www.ShadowFoxBook.com.

Fox Song Bks., (*978-0-9744989; 978-0-9837310*) Orders Addr.: P.O. Box 548, Ferndale, WA 98248 USA
E-mail: fox@foxsongbooks.com; orders@foxsongbooks.com; amy.foxsongbooks@gmail.com; foxsongbooks@gmail.com
Web site: http://foxsongbooks.com
Dist(s): **Ingram Content Group.**

Fox Valley Habitat for Humanity, (*978-0-9914127*) 1300 S. Broadway, Montgomery, IL 60538 USA Tel 630-859-3333
E-mail: R.Kelso@foxvalleyhabitat.org
Web site: www.foxvalleyhabitat.org.

FoxAcre Pr., (*978-0-9671783; 978-0-9709711; 978-0-9818487; 978-1-936771*) 401 Ethan Allen Ave., Takoma Park, MD 20912 USA Fax: 301-560-2482
E-mail: info@foxacre.com
Web site: http://www.foxacre.com
Dist(s): **Smashwords.**

Foxcroft, Jennifer, (*978-0-9909895*) P.O. Box 2886, Denver, CO 80201 USA
E-mail: jenfoxy@me.com
Web site: jenniferfoxcroft.com.

FoxRock, Inc., (*978-0-9643740; 978-0-9714705*) 61 Fourth Ave., No. 4, New York, NY 10003 USA Tel 212-505-6880; Fax: 212-673-1039
E-mail: evergreen@nyc.rr.com
Web site: http://www.evergreenreview.com.

Fox's Den Publishing, (*978-0-9816107*) P.O. Box 6156, Sevierville, TN 37864-6156 USA
E-mail: foxsdenpublishing@hotmail.com.

FoxTales Pr., (*978-1-942023*) P.O. Box 329, Jefferson, OR 97352 USA Tel 503-689-0100
E-mail: danimariehoots@yahoo.com
Web site: http://foxtalespress.com.

FPI Publishing, (*978-0-9768215*) P.O. Box 247, Havre de Grace, MD 21078 USA Tel 410-459-9087
E-mail: gyleen@colourfulstitches.com
Web site: http://www.colourfulstitches.com.

FQ Classics *Imprint of* **Filiquarian Publishing, LLC**

FR Publishing *Imprint of* **Razavi, Firouzeh Bks.**

Fragile X Assn. of Georgia, (*978-0-9727865*) 3161 W. Somerset Ct., Marietta, GA 30067-5045 USA Tel 770-988-9275; Fax: 770-988-8255; Rood End Hse., 6 Stortford Rd., Great Dunmow, CM6 1DA Tel 01371 875100
E-mail: info@fragilex.k-web.co.uk; frax@bellsouth.net
Web site: www.fragilex.org.uk; http://www.myextraspecialbrother.com.

Fragmenta Editorial (ESP) (*978-84-92416*) *Dist. by* **IPG Chicago.**

Fragrance Ministries, (*978-0-9745260*) 2900 Government Way, No. 161, Coeur d'Alene, ID 83815 USA
E-mail: fragranceministries@yahoo.com
Web site: http://www.fragranceministries.com.

Frances, Celia, (*978-0-692-13655-3*) 424 Parker Ave, DEAL PARK, NJ 07723 USA Tel 732-829-1288
E-mail: celia.ezon@gmail.com
Dist(s): **Ingram Content Group.**

Frances More International Teaching Systems, (*978-0-9768234*) Div. of Gray Squirrel, Inc., P.O. Box 26659, Collegeville, PA 19426 USA Tel 610-724-6331
E-mail: sales@graysquirrel.org; francesmore.hangingrock@xtra.co.nz
Web site: http://www.qwertyqik.com; http://www.fingerithmatic.com.

Francesca Studios, (*978-0-9741060*) 26 Dole Hill Rd., Holden, ME 04429 USA.

Franciscan Media, (*978-0-86716; 978-0-912228; 978-1-61636; 978-1-63253; 978-1-63254*) Subs. of Franciscan Friars (St. John Baptist Province), 28 W. Liberty St., Cincinnati, OH 45202 USA (SAN 204-6237) Tel 513-241-5615; Fax: 513-241-1197; Toll Free: 800-488-0488; *Imprints:* Servant Books (ServBks)
E-mail: caroleD11@AmericanCatholic.org
Web site: http://www.AmericanCatholic.org
Dist(s): **Forward Movement Pubns.**
SPD-Small Pr. Distribution
Spring Arbor Distributors, Inc.
St. Anthony Messenger Press.

Franckowiak, Jon, (*978-0-9715415*) 4981 Shallow Ridge Rd., NE., Kennesaw, GA 30144 USA
E-mail: psukeljon@aol.com
Dist(s): **Partners Bk. Distributing, Inc.**

Franco, Nick Art, (*978-0-615-24474-7; 978-0-578-03402-7*) 5757 W. Euglie Ave., No. 2050, Glendale, AZ 85304 USA
E-mail: nickfrancoart@yahoo.com
Web site: http://www.nickfrancoart.com
Dist(s): **Lulu Pr., Inc.**

Frank Schaffer Pubns. *Imprint of* **Carson-Dellosa Publishing, LLC**

Frankel, David, (*978-0-692-83220-2*) 221 Walton St., WEST HEMPSTEAD, NY 11552 USA Tel 718-404-8914
E-mail: jeffwcrawford5+LVP0003251@gmail.com; jeffwcrawford5+LVP0003251@gmail.com.

Frankie Dove Publishing, (*978-0-9786487; 978-0-9987731*) P.O. Box 3875, Federal Way, WA 98063-3875 USA (SAN 851-2051)
E-mail: georgepettingell@frankiedovepublishing.com.

Franklin Green Publishing, (*978-0-9826387; 978-1-936487*) 500 Wilson Pike Cir. Suite 100, Brentwood, TN 37027 USA Tel 615-277-5553
E-mail: lgessner@coolspringspress.com
Dist(s): **Hachette Bk. Group**
Independent Pubs. Group
MBI Distribution Services/Quayside Distribution
Midpoint Trade Bks., Inc.
MyiLibrary.

Franklin, J.E., (*978-0-9746669*) P.O. Box 517, New York, NY 10031 USA Tel 212-283-8666
E-mail: je413@aol.com
Web site: http://www.geocities.com/haveplaywilltravel/playseries.html.

Franklin, Lauren, (*978-0-9972386*) 24827 whitewater, Murrieta, CA 92563 USA Tel 619-384-3914
E-mail: laurenfranklin23@yahoo.com
Web site: Babblingbeth.com.

Franklin Mason Pr., (*978-0-9679227; 978-0-9760469; 978-0-9857218; 978-0-9977250*) Orders Addr.: P.O. Box 3808, Trenton, NJ 08629 USA (SAN 253-1828) Tel 609-291-5030; Fax: 609-291-7807; 415 Route 68, Columbus, NJ 08022
E-mail: lwill0517@aol.com
Web site: http://www.franklinmasonpress.com; http://www.nickyfifth.com
Dist(s): **BMI Educational Services.**

Franklin Publishing, (*978-0-9708129*) 1917 Warrington Rd., SW, Roanoke, VA 24015-3037 USA Tel 540-982-1654 (phone/fax on demand) Do not confuse with Franklin Publishing, Tempe, AZ, Chandler, AZ
E-mail: ampaw@aol.com.

Franklin Scribes, (*978-0-615-68198-6; 978-0-9886433; 978-1-941516*) 301 Apache Ledge, Cibolo, TX 78108 USA Tel 210-363-3843
E-mail: franklinscribeswrites@gmail.com
Web site: www.franklinscribes.com
Dist(s): **CreateSpace Independent Publishing Platform**
Independently Published
Ingram Bk. Co.

Franklin, Stephanie Michelle *See* **Heavenly Realm Publishing**

Franklin Street Books *See* **Inkwater Pr.**

Fransson, Wade *See* **Something Or Other Publishing**

Frayed Pages Publishing *See* **Frayed Pages Publishing**

Frayed Pages Publishing, (*978-0-9753397*) P.O. Box 705, Pickens, SC 29671 USA
E-mail: cjr@watkinsandwatkins.com
Dist(s): **Continental Enterprises Group, Inc. (CEG).**

Frazier, Jeffrey R. *See* **Egg Hill Pubns.**

Frazier, Jeremy A., (*978-0-692-78756-4*) 208 Mairead Dr., DOTHAN, AL 36301 USA Tel 803-586-5040.

Fred Pinsocket Productions, (*978-0-9907941*) 5070 Betlo Ct., San Jose, CA 95130 USA Tel 408-252-7383
E-mail: musicnews@PeterApel.com.

Frederic, Marc *See* **World of Whimsy Productions, LLC**

Frederic Thomas USA, Inc., (*978-1-945546*) 5621 Strand Blvd, Naples, FL 34110 USA Tel 239-593-8000
E-mail: jbelyea@fredericthomasusa.com
Web site: http://fredericthomasusa.com/.

Fredonia Bks., (*978-1-58963; 978-1-4101*) 4440 NW 73rd Ave., PTY 362, Miami, FL 33166-6437 USA Tel 407-650-2537 (phone/fax)
E-mail: blp@fredoniabooks.com
Web site: http://www.fredoniabooks.com.

Fredrickson, Anne, (*978-0-615-20146-7*) 6905 290th St. W., Northfield, MN 55057 USA
Dist(s): **Aardvark Global Publishing.**

Free Assn. Bks. Ltd. (GBR) (*978-0-946960; 978-1-85343; 978-1-911383*) *Dist. by* **IPG Chicago.**

Free Focus Publishing, (*978-0-9826747*) P.O. Box 716, Blaine, WA 98231 USA Tel 310-562-8165 (phone/fax).

Free People Publishing, (*978-0-9838131; 978-0-9991163*) 10 Parker Cir., Salem, NH 03079 USA Tel 603-898-6124
E-mail: jzygmont@jeffreyzygmont.com
Web site: jeffreyzygmont.com.

Free Pr. *Imprint of* **Free Pr.**

†Free Pr., (*978-0-02; 978-0-669; 978-0-671; 978-0-684; 978-0-7432*) Orders Addr.: 100 Front St., Riverside, NJ 08075 USA; Edit Addr.: 1230 Ave. of the Americas, New York, NY 10020 USA; *Imprints:* Free Press (Free Imp)
Dist(s): **CreateSpace Independent Publishing Platform**
Simon & Schuster
Simon & Schuster, Inc.; *CIP.*

Free Pr. Pubs., (*978-0-943751*) Orders Addr.: P.O. Box 4717, Monroe, LA 71211 USA (SAN 242-6242) Tel 318-388-1310; Fax: 318-388-2911
E-mail: RooseveltWright@prodigy.net
Web site: http://www.sermonideas.com.

F.R.E.E. Publishing House, (*978-0-86639; 978-0-9762472*) Div. of Friends of Refugees of Eastern Europe, 1383 President St., Brooklyn, NY 11213 USA Tel 718-467-0860 ext 118; Fax: 718-467-2146
E-mail: publications@russianjewry.org
Web site: http://www.JRBooks.org.

Free Spirit Artworks, LLC, (*978-0-9996760*) 1125 Lamar Ave, Altamonte Springs, FL 32714 USA Tel 732-778-0351
E-mail: jessica333@yahoo.com.

†Free Spirit Publishing, Inc., (*978-0-915793; 978-1-57542; 978-1-63198*) 6325 Sandburg Rd., Ste. 100, Warehouse Docks 42/43, Golden Valley, MN 55427-3674 USA (SAN 293-9584) Tel 612-338-2068; Fax: 612-337-5050; Toll Free: 800-735-7323
E-mail: help4kids@freespirit.com
Web site: http://www.freespirit.com
Dist(s): **Brodart Co.**
Children's Plus, Inc.
Follett School Solutions
Independent Pubs. Group
MyiLibrary; *CIP.*

Free Your Mind Publishing, (*978-0-9760056*) P.O. Box 70, Boston, MA 02131 USA Fax: 202-889-5056; 2724 Knox Terrace, SE, Washington, DC 20020 (SAN 256-1883) Do nopt confuse with Free Your Mind Publishing in Indianapolis, IN
E-mail: omekongo@omekongo.com
Web site: http://www.freeyourmindpublishing.com
Dist(s): **Smashwords.**

Freedom Archives, The, (*978-0-9727422; 978-0-9790789*) 522 Valencia St., San Francisco, CA 94110 USA Tel 415-863-9977
E-mail: info@freedomarchives.org
Web site: http://www.freedomarchives.org
Dist(s): **AK Pr. Distribution**
Consortium Bk. Sales & Distribution
SPD-Small Pr. Distribution.

Freedom of Speech Publishing, Inc., (*978-1-938634*) 4552 W 138 Terr, Leawood, KS 66224 USA Tel 815-290-9605
E-mail: admin@freedomofspeechpublishing.com
Web site: www.freedomofspeechpublishing.com.

Freedom Pr., (*978-0-9664326*) P.O. Box 2228, Wrightwood, CA 92397-2228 USA Tel 505-573-0737 Do not confuse with companies with the same name in Allentown, PA, Scottsdale, AZ, Pawcatuck, CT, Southaven, MS, Liberty Lake, WA, Saint Louis, MO, Nutley, NJ
E-mail: freedompress@hotmail.com
Web site: http://freedompress.4t.com
Dist(s): **Bristlecone Publishing Co.**
New Leaf Distributing Co., Inc.

Freedom Reading Foundation, Incorporated *See* **Edu-Steps, Inc.**

Freedom Three Publishing, (*978-0-9714254*) 310 N. Indian Hill Blvd., #442, Claremont, CA 91711 USA Tel 909-447-5320
E-mail: info@freedomthree.com
Web site: http://www.freedomthree.com; http://www.joelharper.net; http://www.allthewaytotheocean.com
Dist(s): **Leonard, Hal Corp.**

Freedom Voices Pubns., (*978-0-915117; 978-0-9625153*) Div. of Tenderloin Reflection & Education Ctr., P.O. Box 423115, San Francisco, CA 94142 USA
E-mail: jess@freedomvoices.org; spottywest@freedomvoices.org; art@arthazelwood.com
Web site: http://www.freedomvoices.org
Dist(s): **AK Pr. Distribution**
Ingram Content Group
SPD-Small Pr. Distribution.

Freedom's Hammer, (*978-0-9884780; 978-1-7359236*) 11 Country Squire Ct., Greenville, SC 29615 USA Tel 864-386-1146
E-mail: cfors10917@aol.com.

Freefox Publishing, (*978-0-9801527*) Orders Addr.: 32 Doncaster Cir., Lynnfield, MA 01940 USA
Web site: http://www.freefoxpublishing.com.

Freelance Fridge, LLC, (*978-0-578-42245-9; 978-0-578-60157-1*) 3806 E. Santa Fe Ln., Gilbert, AZ 85297 USA Tel 480-688-5289
E-mail: jameskoenig1@yahoo.com
Dist(s): **Ingram Content Group.**

FreeStar Pr., (*978-0-9661315*) P.O. Box 54552, Cincinnati, OH 45254-0552 USA Tel 513-734-0102
E-mail: Freestarpr@aol.com.

Freestone *Imprint of* **Peachtree Publishing Co. Inc.**

Freet Publishing, (*978-0-9676717*) Orders Addr.: P.O. Box 219, Willow Hill, PA 17271-0219 USA Tel 717-349-7873 (phone/fax); Edit Addr.: 18028 Pigeon Hill Rd., Willow Hill, PA 17271-0219 USA
E-mail: freepbl@pa.net.

Freeverse Enterprises Inc., (*978-0-9743789*) 1200 E. River Rd. C-35, Tucson, AZ 85718 USA.

Freeze Time Media, (*978-0-9858103; 978-0-9913550; 978-0-9966883; 978-1-946702*) 7133 Depew Ct., Arvada, CO 80003 USA Tel 303-885-8736
E-mail: difreeze@gmail.com
Web site: www.difreeze.com.

Fremantle Pr. (AUS) (*978-1-86368; 978-0-909144; 978-0-949206; 978-1-920731; 978-1-921064; 978-1-921361; 978-1-921696; 978-1-921888; 978-0-646-39543-2; 978-0-646-50123-9; 978-1-922089; 978-1-925160; 978-1-925161; 978-1-925162; 978-1-925163; 978-1-925164; 978-1-925591; 978-1-925815; 978-1-925816; 978-1-76099*) *Dist. by* **IPG Chicago.**

French & European Pubns., Inc., (*978-0-320; 978-0-7859; 978-0-8288; 978-1-5479*) 425 E. 58th St., Suite 27D, New York, NY 10022-2379 USA (SAN 206-8109) Fax: 212-265-1094
E-mail: livresny@gmail.com; frenchbookstore@aol.com
Web site: http://www.frencheuropean.com.

French, Samuel , Inc. *Imprint of* **Concord Theatricals**

French, Samuel , Ltd. *Imprint of* **Concord Theatricals**

French Workshop, The *See* **Aaron Levy Pubns., LLC**

FREOMM Publishing, (*978-0-9659891*) 77635 Malone Cir., Palm Desert, CA 92211 USA Tel 760-772-6628; Fax: 760-772-0169
E-mail: odyssey@odysseyofthesoul.org
Web site: http://www.odysseyofthesoul.org
Dist(s): **New Leaf Publishing Group.**

Fresh Ink Group, (*978-1-936442; 978-1-947867; 978-1-947893*) 23 Lake Breeze Dr., Guntersville, AL 35976 USA Tel 256-606-6204
E-mail: info@freshinkgroup.com
Web site: freshinkgroup.com.

Freundship Pr., LLC, (*978-0-9822204; 978-0-9839957*) P.O. Box 9171, Boise, ID 83707 USA Tel 208-407-7457
E-mail: info@freundshippress.com
Web site: http://www.freundshippress.com.

Frias, Marilyn, (*978-0-692-83460-2*) 100 Meadowood Dr, ASPEN, CO 81611 USA Tel 970-618-5050
E-mail: jeffwcrawford5+LVP0003264@gmail.com; jeffwcrawford5+LVP0003264@gmail.com.

Frick Art & Historical Ctr.,The, (*978-0-9703425; 978-0-615-57373-1; 978-0-615-57374-8*) 7227 Reynolds St., Pittsburgh, PA 15208 USA Tel 412-371-0600; Fax: 412-241-5393
E-mail: tsmart@frickart.org; info@frickart.org
Web site: http://www.frickart.org.

Fried, Scott *See* **TALKAIDS, Inc.**

Frieda B., (*978-0-9843862*) 55 Long Hill Dr., Somers, CT 06071 USA (SAN 859-2640)
Web site: http://www.friedab.com.

Friedman, Michael Publishing Group, Inc., (*978-0-9627134; 978-1-56799; 978-1-58663; 978-1-4114*) Div. of Barnes & Noble, Inc., 122 Fifth Ave., Fifth Flr., New York, NY 10011 USA (SAN 248-9732) Tel 212-685-6610; Fax: 212-633-3327
E-mail: rlamarche@bn.com
Web site: http://www.metrobooks.com
Dist(s): **MyiLibrary**
Sterling Publishing Co., Inc.
Texas A&M Univ. Pr.

Friedman, Yuda, (*978-0-9677313*) 11 Quickway Rd. Unit 103, Monroe, NY 10950-8804 USA.

Friedrich, Paul, (*978-0-9793676*) 323 W. Martin St., SPC 70, Raleigh, NC 27601 USA
Web site: http://onionheadmonster.com.

Friend Family Ministries, (*978-0-9767524*) 1601 Hamilton Richmond Rd., Hamilton, OH 45013 USA.

Friendly Isles Pr., (*978-0-9678979*) Orders Addr.: 8503 Sun Harbor Dr., Bakersfield, CA 93312 USA Tel 661-587-0645
E-mail: ofalisiate@yahoo.com.

Friendly Planet, (*978-0-9742469*) 101 Third St., Cambridge, MA 02141 USA; *Imprints:* Big Books for Little People (Big Bks)
E-mail: mike@friendlyplanet.org
Web site: http://www.friendlyplanet.org.

Friendly Planet Club, (*978-0-692-17569-9*) 3301 Michelson Dr., Apt. No. 1521, Irvine, CA 92612 USA Tel 949-573-3517
E-mail: yaya1582@gmail.com
Web site: https://www.friendlyplanet.club/.

Friends of Hildene, Inc., (*978-0-9754917; 978-0-692-31124-0*) 1005 Hildene Rd., PO Box 377, Manchester, VT 05254 USA Tel 802-362-1788; Fax: 802-362-1564
Web site: http://www.hildene.org.

Friends of Lulu, (*978-0-9740960*) P.O. Box 1114, New York, NY 10013-0866 USA
E-mail: info@friends-lulu.org
Web site: http://www.friends-lulu.org/.

Friends Of The Goshen Grange, The, (*978-0-9771473*) P.O. Box 1016, Goshen, NH 03752-1016 USA.

Friends of Vail Foundation *See* **Proverbial Girl Publishing**

†Friends United Pr., (*978-0-913408; 978-0-944350*) 101 Quaker Hill Dr., Richmond, IN 47374 USA (SAN 201-5803) Tel 765-962-7573; Fax: 765-966-1293; Toll Free: 800-537-8839
E-mail: friendspress@fum.org
Web site: http://www.fum.org
Dist(s): **Independent Pubs. Group**; *CIP.*

Friends Without a Border, (*978-0-9653574*) 1123 Broadway Ste. 1210, New York, NY 10010-2007 USA
E-mail: fwab@fwab.org
Web site: http://www.fwab.org
Dist(s): **SCB Distributors.**

Frog Bks. *Imprint of* **North Atlantic Bks.**

Frog Children's Bks. *Imprint of* **North Atlantic Bks.**

Frog Legs Ink *Imprint of* **Gauthier Pubns. Inc.**

Frog Ltd. *Imprint of* **North Atlantic Bks.**

Frog Pond Enterprises, (*978-0-615-12821-4; 978-0-9915037*) 2821 Sheffield Ct., Trophy Club, TX 76262 USA Tel 862-502-4827
E-mail: joyclassalive2@gmail.com
Web site: www.joyclassalive.com; http://www.joyforchurches.com.

Frog Prince Bks., (*978-1-7325410; 978-1-7348242*) 442 E. Shore Trl, Sparta, NJ 07871 USA Tel 973-670-8324
E-mail: frogprincebooks@gmail.com
Web site: www.frogprincebooks.net.

Frog Prince Pr., (*978-0-615-91119-9; 978-0-9908323*) 480 N Walnut St, Boise, ID 83712 USA Tel 5129647997
Web site: elisabethsharpmcketta.com
Dist(s): **CreateSpace Independent Publishing Platform.**

Frog Street Pr., (*978-1-60128; 978-1-63237; 978-1-63636*) 800 Industrial Blvd Suite 100, Grapevine, TX 76051 USA (SAN 851-0806) Tel 800-884-3764; Fax: 800-759-3828; Toll Free Fax: 800-759-3828; Toll Free: 800-884-3764
E-mail: bhunt@frogstreet.com; mtyndall@frogstreet.com
Web site: http://www.frogstreet.com.

F.R.O.G. the Rock Pubns., (*978-0-9727142*) 3524 Parkview Dr., Marietta, GA 30062 USA Tel 770-587-4902; Fax: 770-993-0394
E-mail: frogtherock@aol.com.

Froglogic Concepts LLC *See* **Leadline Publishing**

From Inside the Heart, *(978-0-9729599; 978-0-9833729; 978-0-692-13261-6; 978-0-578-46492-3)* 3244 NW Melville Dr, Bend, OR 97703 USA (SAN 255-4593) Tel 541-410-1478
E-mail: judysbend@gmail.com.

From My Shelf Bks. & Gifts, *(978-0-692-59255-7; 978-0-692-64770-7; 978-0-692-72287-9; 978-0-692-72460-6; 978-0-692-76063-5; 978-0-692-76325-4; 978-0-692-79938-3; 978-0-692-80112-3)* 7 E. Ave, Suite 101, Wellsboro, PA 16901 USA Tel 570-724-5793
E-mail: from_my_shelf@yahoo.com.

From the Asylum Bks. & Pr., *(978-0-9715860)* P.O. Box 1516, Dickinson, TX 77539 USA
Web site: http://www.fromtheasylum.com.

From Your Doctor To You, LLC, *(978-0-692-78615-4; 978-0-9984610)* 8340 Merion Dr., Duluth, GA 30097 USA Tel 404-427-6239
E-mail: fatufoma@hotmail.com.

Front Porch Publishing, *(978-0-9998139)* 1086 Seefried Ln., Blackfoot, ID 83221 USA Tel 208-694-3484
E-mail: coniet7@hotmail.com.

Front Street *Imprint of* **Boyds Mills Pr.**

Front Street/Cricket Books *See* **Cricket Bks.**

Fronte, Kathy, *(978-0-9727725)* 5604 Greenwood Cir., Naples, FL 34112 USA.

Frontier Books *See* **Frontier Pr.**

Frontier Image Pr., *(978-0-9634309; 978-1-888571)* Orders Addr.: P.O. Box 3055, Silver City, NM 88061 USA Tel 505-534-4032; Fax: 505-590-1301
E-mail: frontr@cybermcs.com.

Frontier Pr., *(978-0-9768465)* 180 E. Ocean Blvd., Fl 4, Long Beach, CA 90802-9080 USA Tel 562-491-8331; Fax: 562-491-8791
E-mail: new_frontier@usw.salvationarmy.org.

Frontiera, Deborah *See* **Jade Enterprises**

Frontline *Imprint of* **Charisma Media**

Frontline Communications *See* **YWAM Publishing**

Frontline Pr., *(978-0-930201)* Orders Addr.: P.O. Box 764499, Dallas, TX 75376-4499 USA Tel 972-572-8336; Fax: 972-572-8335 Do not confuse with companies with the same or similar name in Washington, DC, Taylors, SC, Charlston, SC
E-mail: info@youthdirect.org
Web site: http://www.youthdirect.org.

Frost, C. A., *(978-0-9847236)* 8113 Cloverglen Ln., Fort Worth, TX 76123 USA Tel 817-994-2420
E-mail: theewordnerd@yahoo.com.

Frost Hollow Pubs., LLC, *(978-0-9658523; 978-0-9720922; 978-0-9794273; 978-0-9829636; 978-0-9890965; 978-0-9989136)* 411 Barlow Cemetery Rd., Woodstock, CT 06281 USA Tel 860-974-2081; Fax: 860-974-0813; Toll Free: 877-974-2081
E-mail: frosthollow@mindspring.com
Web site: http://www.frosthollowpub.com.

Frugal Bear Communications, *(978-0-9678694)* P.O. Box 5154, Inglewood, CA 90310 USA; *Imprints:* FrugalBear.com (FrugalBear)
E-mail: regresa@hotmail.com; frugalbear@email.com
Web site: http://www.frugalbear.com.

FrugalBear.com *Imprint of* **Frugal Bear Communications**

Fruit Springs, LLC, *(978-1-970016)* 17330 W Ctr. Rd., Omaha, NE 68130 USA Tel 402-884-5995
E-mail: fruitsprings@conciergemarketing.com.

Fruitbearer Publishing, LLC, *(978-1-886068; 978-1-938796)* Orders Addr.: P.O. Box 777, Georgetown, DE 19947 USA (SAN 920-380X) Tel 302-856-6649; Fax: 302-856-7742; Edit Addr.: 107 Elizabeth St., Georgetown, DE 19947 USA
E-mail: cfa@candyabbott.com; info@fruitbearer.com
Web site: http://www.fruitbearer.com
Dist(s): **BookBaby**
Ingram Content Group.

Fruitful Tree Publishing, *(978-0-9986677; 978-1-7341845)* 509 Aspen Glade Ct., Lexington, SC 29072 USA.

Fruition Online Publishing, *(978-0-9712079)* Div. of Cherokee Ventures, 120 St. Albans Dr., #469, Raleigh, NC 27609 USA Tel 919-743-2500; Fax: 919-743-2501
E-mail: customersupport@fruitiononline.com
Web site: http://www.fruitiononline.com.

Fry, Debbie, *(978-0-9759647)* 301 N. Gleason Ave., Fowler, CA 93625-2162 USA.

F/S *Imprint of* **Worthy Publishing**

FT Richards Publishing, *(978-0-9746561)* 41 Tailwinds Ln., North East, MD 21901 USA
Web site: http://www.fairwindsstables.com.

Ft. Valley Geology Study Ctr. *Imprint of* **InterPress**

FTD, *(978-0-9747637)* 3113 Woodcreek Dr., Downers Grove, IL 60515 USA Toll Free: 800-383-6659.

FTL Pubns., *(978-0-9653575; 978-0-9825232; 978-1-936881)* Orders Addr.: P.O. Box 1363, Minnetonka, MN 55345-0363 USA Tel 952-938-4275; Edit Addr.: 5137 Clear Springs Dr., Minnetonka, MN 55345-4312 USA
E-mail: mail@ftlpublications.com
Web site: http://www.FTLPublications.com
Dist(s): **Diamond Comic Distributors, Inc.**
Smashwords.

Fuchs, Monique, *(978-1-7335624)* 118 Franklin St., No. 3, Brookline, MA 02445 USA Tel 617-738-1739
E-mail: monique_fuchs@yahoo.com.

Fuel Media Group, Inc., *(978-0-9772047)* 15305 NW 60th Ave. Suite 100, Miami Lakes, FL 33014 USA Tel 305-822-7000
E-mail: bob@calvarywired.com
Web site: http://www.fuelmg.com.

†Fulcrum Publishing, *(978-0-912347; 978-1-55591; 978-1-56373; 978-1-936218; 978-1-938486; 978-1-68275)* Orders Addr.: 4690 Table Mountain Dr. Suite 100, Golden, CO 80403 USA (SAN 200-2825) Toll Free Fax: 800-726-7112; Toll Free: 800-992-2908
E-mail: info@fulcrumbooks.com
Web site: http://www.fulcrumbooks.com
Dist(s): **Abraham Assocs. Inc.**
Alibris
Copyright Clearance Ctr., Inc.
Independent Pubs. Group
MyiLibrary
ebrary, Inc.; *CIP.*

Fulfill Publishing, *(978-0-9969449)* 3871 S. 850 W., Riverdale, UT 84405 USA Tel 801-695-1673
E-mail: brownjo76@comcast.net.

Full Circle Media, Inc. *Imprint of* **Atma Global Knowledge Media, Inc.**

Full Circle Pr. *Imprint of* **WillowTree Pr., L.L.C.**

Full City Press *See* **Lychgate Pr.**

Full Court Pr., *(978-0-9709477; 978-0-578-01482-1; 978-0-578-02337-3; 978-0-578-02841-5; 978-0-578-03345-7; 978-0-578-05544-2; 978-0-578-05545-9; 978-0-9846113; 978-0-9833711; 978-0-9837411; 978-0-9849536; 978-1-938812; 978-1-946989; 978-1-953728)* 601 Palisade Ave., Englewood Cliffs, NJ 07632 USA Fax: 201-567-7202
Web site: http://writingcenternj.com
Dist(s): **Follett School Solutions.**

Full Cycle Pubns., *(978-0-615-43266-3; 978-0-615-50132-1; 978-0-615-68186-3; 978-0-615-78628-5; 978-0-615-81244-1; 978-0-9905819; 978-0-9966422; 978-1-7325961)* 5837 S. 157 W., Salt Lake City, UT 84107 USA (SAN 860-0953) Tel 213-804-4891
E-mail: nabila@earthlink.net
Dist(s): **BookBaby.**

Full Effect Gospel Ministries, Inc., *(978-0-9679516; 978-0-615-76085-8; 978-0-692-29621-9; 978-1-7338592)* 900 New Lots Ave, Brooklyn, NY 11208 USA Tel 7189270476
Web site: www.effect900.com
Dist(s): **CreateSpace Independent Publishing Platform.**

Full Gospel Family Pubns., *(978-0-9745599)* 419 E. Taft Ave., Appleton, WI 54915-2079 USA Tel 920-734-6693
E-mail: character@characterbuildingforfamilies.com; pilgrims@juno.com
Web site: http://www.characterbuildingforfamilies.com.

Full House Productions, *(978-0-615-27092-0; 978-0-9832564)* 2466 Center Point Rd., Fredericksburg, TX 78624 USA.

Full Moon Creations, Incorporated *See* **LeLeu, Lisa Studios! Inc.**

Full Moon Press *See* **King's Way Pr.**

Full Moon Publishing, LLC, *(978-0-615-81984-6; 978-0-615-84647-7; 978-0-615-89471-3; 978-0-615-89533-8; 978-0-615-99886-2; 978-0-692-20136-7; 978-0-692-02366-2; 978-0-692-02367-9; 978-0-692-20350-7; 978-0-692-22127-3; 978-0-692-40867-4; 978-0-692-43932-6; 978-0-692-47046-6; 978-0-692-53018-4; 978-0-692-58018-9; 978-0-692-58662-4; 978-0-692-58663-1; 978-0-692-60312-3; 978-0-692-63908-5; 978-0-692-65568-9; 978-0-692-66138-3; 978-0-692-68604-1; 978-0-692-68605-8; 978-0-692-74504-5; 978-1-946232)* 110 Evergreen St., Glade Spring, VA 24340 USA Tel 276-451-0331
E-mail: rondacaudill@yahoo.com
Dist(s): **CreateSpace Independent Publishing Platform.**

Full Moon Publishing LLC, *(978-0-9666021; 978-0-9785402; 978-0-9820352; 978-0-9846357; 978-0-9888683; 978-0-9976707)* Orders Addr.: 433 Mystic Point Dr., Bluffton, SC 29909 USA Tel 219-688-3093 Do not confuse with Full Moon Publishing, Norton, MA
E-mail: fullmoonpub@sc.rr.com
Web site: http://www.fullmoonpub.com
Dist(s): **Smashwords.**

Full Quart Pr. *Imprint of* **Holly Hall Pubns., Inc.**

Full Satchel Pr. (CAN) *(978-0-9731960) Dist. by* **MYID_F_GATEWOO.**

Full Tilt Pr. (NZL) *(978-0-473-24742-3) Dist. by* **Lerner Pub.**

Fullerton Bks., Inc., *(978-0-9652918)* Orders Addr.: P.O. Box 1, Waveland, MS 39576 USA Tel 972-412-3131; 228-457-5323; Fax: 509-278-0766
E-mail: info@vincevance.com
Web site: http://www.vincevance.com.

FullofPep Pubns., *(978-0-9760684)* P.O. Box 367, Columbia, SC 29202 USA
E-mail: fullofpeppublications@yahoo.com.

Fulton Bks., *(978-1-63338; 978-1-64654; 978-1-64952)* Orders Addr.: 296 Chestnut St, Meadville, PA 16335 USA; Edit Addr.: 296 Chestnut St., Meadville, PA 16335 USA Tel 877-210-0816
E-mail: dusty@fultonbooks.com
Web site: fultonbooks.com.

Fulton, David Pubs. (GBR) *(978-1-85346; 978-1-84312) Dist. by* **Taylor and Fran.**

Fultus *See* **Fultus Corp.**

Fultus Corp., *(978-0-9744339; 978-1-59682)* P.O. Box 50095, Palo Alto, CA 94303 USA Fax: 650-745-0873; *Imprints:* Fultus Publishing (Ful Pubng)
E-mail: production@fultus.com
Web site: http://www.fultus.com; http://elibrary.fultus.com; http://store.fultus.com; http://writers.fultus.com
Dist(s): **Ingram Content Group.**

Fultus Publishing *Imprint of* **Fultus Corp.**

Fun 4 Kids Publishing *Imprint of* **Stray Dog Pr., LLC**

Fun Family Publishing, *(978-1-7331631)* 9033 SW Burnham St., Portland, OR 97223 USA Tel 503-449-4631
E-mail: kameronkh@yahoo.com
Web site: lamikeandotis.com.

Fun Fitness Publishing, *(978-0-9762483; 978-0-615-35686-0)* 16 Paulsboro Rd., Woolwich, NJ 08055 USA Tel 609-410-3717 (phone/fax); Fax: 609-257-4079
E-mail: jeyre2@comcast.net; funfitness@comcast.net
Web site: http://www.janeeyre-art.com; http://www.funfitnesstraining.weebly.com.

Fun Places Publishing, *(978-0-9646737; 978-0-9833832)* 6124 Capetown St., Lakewood, CA 90713 USA Tel 562-867-5223
E-mail: orders@funplaces.com
Web site: http://www.funplaces.com
Dist(s): **American West Bks.**
Sunbelt Pubns., Inc.

Fun Publishing Co., *(978-0-938293)* 2121 Alpine Pl., No. 402, Cincinnati, OH 45206 USA (SAN 661-1761) Tel 513-533-3636; Fax: 513-421-7269 Do not confuse with companies with the same or similar names in Scottsdale, AZ, Fort Lauderdale, FL, Indianapolis, IN
E-mail: funpublish@aol.com
Web site: http://www.funpublishing.com.

Fun Time Flowers *See* **Flower Sprouts**

Fun to Read Bks. with Royally Good Morals *Imprint of* **MKADesigns**

Funcastle Pubns., *(978-0-9645771)* Orders Addr.: P.O. Box 51217, Riverside, CA 92517 USA Tel 951-653-5200; Fax: 951-653-4300; Edit Addr.: 20833 Millbrook St., Riverside, CA 92508 USA
Dist(s): **Independent Pubs. Group.**

Functional Fitness, LLC, *(978-0-9815551; 978-0-9995034)* 102 Twin Oaks Way, Kemah, TX 77565 USA Tel 281-704-8804
E-mail: functionalfitness@peoplepc.com; patbrill@peoplepc.com
Web site: http://www.functionalfitnessllc.org.

Fundacion Intermon (ESP) *(978-84-604; 978-84-8452; 978-84-89970; 978-84-921977) Dist. by* **Mariuccia Iaconi Bk Imports.**

Fundacion Intermon (ESP) *(978-84-604; 978-84-8452; 978-84-89970; 978-84-921977) Dist. by* **Lectorum Pubns.**

Fundamental Christian Endeavors, *(978-1-931787)* 49191 Cherokee Rd., Newberry Springs, CA 92365 USA Tel 760-257-3503; Fax: 760-652-4808
Web site: http://www.ironwood.org.

Fundamental Wesleyan Pubs., *(978-0-9629383; 978-0-9761003; 978-0-9914251; 978-1-7327926)* 2120 Culverson Ave., Evansville, IN 47714 USA Tel 812-476-2996
E-mail: victorpau@aol.com
Web site: http://www.fwponline.cc.

FUNdamentals/Leap In Faith, *(978-0-9834645)* P.O. Box 491, Abingdon, MD 21009 USA Tel 443-484-2512
E-mail: Fundamentals123@aol.com
Web site: Fundamentals123.com
Dist(s): **Partners Pubs. Group, Inc.**

Fundcraft Publishing, *(978-1-931413; 978-1-935397)* Orders Addr.: P.O. Box 340, Collerville, TN 38027 USA Tel 901-853-7070; Fax: 901-853-6196; Edit Addr.: 410 Hwy. 72 W., Collierville, TN 38017 USA Tel 901-853-7070
E-mail: info@fundcraft.com
Web site: http://www.fundcraft.com.

FungChung, Nikko M, *(978-0-9981497)* 505 Benton Drive, Apt. 4312, Allen, TX 75013 USA Tel 347-724-0000; Fax: 347-724-0000
E-mail: nikko.fungchung@gmail.com
Web site: www.awabookseries.com.

Funk, Sherree *See* **Serving One Lord Resources**

Funnel Cloud 9, Inc., *(978-0-9767297)* 545 Tom Treece Rd., Morristown, TN 37814 USA
Web site: http://www.fc9.net.

Funnel Time Bks., *(978-0-9600123)* 2475 S Huckleberry CT, Heber City, UT 84032 USA.

Funny Bone Bks., *(978-0-9771836; 978-0-9790240; 978-0-9799121; 978-0-9822288; 978-0-9841507)* 3435 Golden Ave., No. 302, Apt. 302, Cincinnati, OH 45226 USA
E-mail: dpendery@newforms.com
Web site: http://www.bookmasters.com/funnybones.

FunnyGuy.Comedy, *(978-0-9747398)* 123 N. Kings Rd., Los Angeles, CA 90048 USA
E-mail: dave@funnyguy.com
Web site: http://www.funnyguy.com.

FunStitch Studio *Imprint of* **C & T Publishing**

Fur, George, *(978-0-9752985)* 165 Laurel Ave., Menlo Park, CA 94025 USA
E-mail: yfur@msn.com.

Furry Purry Pr., *(978-0-692-64005-0; 978-0-692-98224-2; 978-0-578-43122-2)* 514 Duck Puddle Rd., Waldoboro, ME 04572 USA Tel 207-563-7127
E-mail: tx22@tidewater.net.

Fury Publishing & Distributing, *(978-0-9747049)* 325 Washington Ave. No. 214, Kent, WA 98032 USA Tel 253-520-3111
E-mail: furypublishing@msn.com
Web site: http://www.fury2000.com.

Futech Educational Products, Inc., *(978-0-9627001; 978-1-889192)* 2999 N. 44th St., Suite 225, Phoenix, AZ 85018-7248 USA Tel 602-808-8765; Fax: 602-278-5667; Toll Free: 800-597-6278.

Future Bookworms LLC, 30 N. Gould St., Ste 4000, Sheridan, WY 82801 USA Tel 707-702-3069; Fax: 707-312-8175
E-mail: admin@futurebookworms.com
Web site: http://futurebookworms.com.

Future Comics, *(978-0-9744225)* 220 W. Brandon Blvd., Brandon, FL 33511 USA Tel 813-655-1900; Fax: 813-662-3250; Toll Free: 877-226-6427
E-mail: info@futurecomicsonline.com
Web site: http://www.futurecomicsonline.com.

Future Education, Incorporated *See* **Future Horizons, Inc.**

Future Horizons, Inc., *(978-1-885477; 978-1-932565; 978-1-935274; 978-1-935567; 978-0-9860673; 978-1-941765; 978-1-949177)* 721 W. Abram St., Arlington, TX 76013 USA Tel 817-277-0727; Fax: 817-277-2270; Toll Free: 800-489-0727
E-mail: kelly@fhautism.com
Web site: http://www.FHautism.com
Dist(s): **BookBaby**
Follett School Solutions
Ingram Publisher Services
MyiLibrary.

Future Hse. Publishing, *(978-0-615-65449-2; 978-0-9891253; 978-0-9966193; 978-1-944452; 978-1-950020)* 434 N 150 E, Lindon, UT 84042 USA Tel 310-266-7839
E-mail: books@futurehousepublishing.com
Web site: www.futurehousepublishing.com
Dist(s): **CreateSpace Independent Publishing Platform**
Familius LLC
Workman Publishing Co., Inc.

Fuze Publishing, LLC, *(978-0-9841412; 978-0-9849908; 978-0-9897306; 978-0-9965553; 978-0-9974956; 978-0-9998089)* 2305-C Ashland Street, No. 312, Ashland, OR 97520 USA.

FuzionPrint, *(978-0-9844611; 978-0-9909039; 978-0-9974938; 978-1-946195)* Orders Addr.: 1250 E 115th St, Burnsville, MN 55337 USA Tel 612-781-2815; Fax: 612-294-3068; Edit Addr.: c/o Brian C. Aubitz, 9948 Portland Ave. S., Bloomington, MN 55420 USA
E-mail: info@fuzionprint.com
Web site: http://www.fuzionprint.com.

FWB Pubns., *(978-0-9829070; 978-0-9847974; 978-0-9887437; 978-0-615-85868-5; 978-1-940609; 978-0-615-87554-5; 978-0-615-87589-7; 978-0-615-89973-2; 978-0-615-91387-2; 978-0-615-94095-3; 978-0-692-21431-2; 978-0-692-30634-5; 978-0-692-30835-6; 978-0-692-34282-4)* 1006 Rayme Dr., COLUMBUS, OH 43207-8738 USA Tel 573-330-7728
E-mail: alton.loveless@prodigy.net
Dist(s): **CreateSpace Independent Publishing Platform.**

FWOMP Publishing, *(978-0-9760096)* 935 Lighthouse Ave. No. 21, Pacific Grove, CA 93950 USA
Web site: http://www.fwomp.com
Dist(s): **Sunbelt Pubns., Inc.**

FX Digital Photo, *(978-0-9769009)* 9 Maison Way, Toms River, NJ 08757-6413 USA
Web site: http://www.fxdigitalphoto.com.

Fyhrie, Stephanie, *(978-0-9989821; 978-0-9989821-0-6)* 13316 E 7th Ave, Spokane Valley, WA 99216 USA Tel 509-499-1445
E-mail: tc@taylorchristianmarketing.com.

G & K Publishing, *(978-0-615-15770-2)* P.O. Box 445, Johnstown, OH 43031 USA
E-mail: eking@byroncarmichael.com
Web site: http://www.byroncarmichael.com; http://GandKPublishing.com.

G & R Publishing, *(978-1-56383)* 507 Industrial St., Waverly, IA 50677 USA Toll Free Fax: 800-866-7496; Toll Free: 800-383-1679; 800-887-4445
E-mail: gandr@gandrpublishing.com; gifts@cqbookstore.com
Web site: http://www.cookbookprinting.com; http://www.cqbookstore.com
Dist(s): **CQ Products.**

G Arts LLC, *(978-0-9721152; 978-0-9765851; 978-0-9777531; 978-0-9793384; 978-0-9801557; 978-0-9822669; 978-0-9823412; 978-0-9823799; 978-0-9832702; 978-0-9851696; 978-0-9881745; 978-0-9891704; 978-0-9913419; 978-0-9903808; 978-0-9905320; 978-0-9862500; 978-0-9962930; 978-1-943876)* 322 W. 57th St. No. 19T, New York, NY 10019 USA Tel 212-362-9119; Fax: 646-607-4433
E-mail: accounting@glitteratiincorporated.com
Web site: http://www.glitteratiincorporated.com
Dist(s): **National Bk. Network.**

G. B. Enterprises *See* **Kent Communications, Ltd.**

G C B Publishing *See* **Holly Hall Pubns., Inc.**

G F W C of South Dakota/Daughters of Dakota *See* **Sky Carrier Pr.**

G. G. Brown, *(978-0-692-78431-0)* P.O. Box 221161, Hollywood, FL 33004 USA Tel 954-638-2858
E-mail: ggbrown@yahoo.com.

G I A Pubns., Inc., *(978-0-941050; 978-1-57999; 978-1-62277)* 7404 S. Mason Ave., Chicago, IL 60638 USA (SAN 205-3217) Tel 708-496-3800; Fax: 708-496-3828; Toll Free: 800-442-1358
E-mail: custserv@giamusic.com
Web site: http://www.giamusic.com
Dist(s): **Faith Alive Christian Resources**
Independent Pubs. Group
MyiLibrary.

G J & B Publishing, *(978-0-9635006)* 22442 University Ave., N., Cedar, MN 55011 USA Tel 612-434-0786.

G. Lamar Wilkie, *(978-0-9971141)* 784 Toliver Lake Rd., Manchester, TN 37355 USA Tel 931-952-3736
E-mail: wilkie_family@hotmail.com.

G Publishing *See* **G Publishing LLC**

G Publishing LLC, *(978-0-9727582; 978-0-9773267; 978-0-9776780; 978-0-9788536; 978-0-9790691; 978-0-9796978; 978-0-9801297; 978-0-9814650; 978-0-9820002; 978-0-9823533; 978-0-9843426; 978-0-9834307; 978-0-9849360; 978-0-9883374; 978-0-9862379; 978-0-9971579; 978-0-9985990;*

978-0-9998578; 978-1-7340865; 978-1-7355579; 978-1-7357302) P.O. Box 24374, *Detroit, MI 48224-2348 USA Toll Free: 866-882-1159; 4826 Harvard Rd., Detroit, MI 48224 Do not confuse with G Publishing in Sebastopol, CA*
E-mail: jhun@gpublishingsuccess.com; juthegen@sbcglobal.net
Web site: http://www.gpublishingsuccess.com.

G R M Assocs., *(978-0-933813; 978-0-929093)* 290 W. End Ave., 16A, New York, NY 11111 USA Tel 212-874-5964; Fax: 212-874-6425; *Imprints:* Taylor Productions (Taylor Prods)
Dist(s): **Independent Pubs. Group.**

G R Publishing, *(978-0-9668530)* 460 Brookside Way, Felton, CA 95018 USA
E-mail: pub@grandmarose.com
Web site: http://www.grandmarose.com.

G R T Pubns., *(978-0-9678420; 978-0-9716906)* P.O. Box 1845, Provo, UT 84603 USA Tel 801-374-2587 (phone/fax)
E-mail: grtpublications@juno.com
Web site: http://www.rogerpminert.

G Schirmer, Inc. *Imprint of* **Leonard, Hal Corp.**

G T Labs, *(978-0-9660106; 978-0-9788037)* P.O. Box 8145, Ann Arbor, MI 48107 USA Tel 734-994-0474; Fax: 734-764-4487
E-mail: info@gt-labs.com
Web site: http://www.gt-labs.com
Dist(s): **Diamond Comic Distributors, Inc.**
Diamond Bk. Distributors.

G340 Publishing, *(978-0-9843837)* 7115 N. Division St. Suite B #132, Spokane, WA 99207-2242 USA (SAN 859-2462) Tel 509-850-0340
E-mail: service @g340.com; grealy@gmail.com
Web site: http://g340.com.

Gabriel Pr., *(978-0-9721888)* 255 Calle San Sebastian, San Juan, PR 00901 USA Do not confuse with companies with the same name in Phoenix, AZ, Ventura, CA, Fort Lauderdale, FL, Saratoga, CA, Sacramento, CA, San Juan, PR, Littleton, CO
E-mail: paolanogueras@gmail.com
Web site: http://www.paolanogueras.net
Dist(s): **Lectorum Pubns., Inc.**

Gabriel Resources, Orders Addr.: P.O. Box 1047, Waynesboro, GA 30830 USA Tel 706-554-1594; Fax: 706-554-7444; Toll Free: 800-732-6657 (8MORE-BOOKS); Edit Addr.: 129 Mobilization Dr., Waynesboro, GA 30830 USA.

Gabriele Capelli Editore Sagl (CHE) *(978-88-87469) Dist. by* **SPD-Small Pr Dist.**

Gabrielle, Ava, *(978-0-578-42242-8)* P.O. Box 177, Exmore, VA 23350 USA Tel 757-442-4195
E-mail: avagabrielle@esprittv.com.

Gaff Pr., *(978-0-9619629)* Orders Addr.: P.O. Box 1024, Astoria, OR 97103 USA (SAN 245-8403); Edit Addr.: P.O. Box 1024, Astoria, OR 97103-1024 USA (SAN 245-8411)
E-mail: gaffpres@pacifier.com
Web site: http://www.gaffpress.com.

Gaffney, Linda, *(978-0-9787501)* Orders Addr.: PMB 2682 2103 Harrison Ave., NW, Olympia, WA 98502 USA Tel 360-584-8566
Web site: http://www.HomeplacePress.com.

Gagnier Enterprises, *(978-0-9993302; 978-0-9995944)* 1514 Canterbury Ln., Fernandina Beach, FL 32034 USA Tel 904-261-3601
E-mail: frankandsue@gagnierenterprises.com.

Gago, Noel, *(978-0-692-44889-2; 978-0-692-72531-3; 978-0-692-72538-2; 978-0-692-09490-7; 978-0-578-45548-8)* 14261 nw 22nd st, PEMBROKE PINES, FL 33028 USA Tel 7182165431.

Gail's Guides, *(978-1-881005)* Orders Addr.: 134 West Canyonview Dr., Longview, WA 98632 USA
E-mail: guides@oz.net; info@gailsguides.com
Web site: http://www.gailsguides.com
Dist(s): **Anderson News - Tacoma**
Aramark
American News Company
Partners/West Book Distributors.

Gain Literacy Skills / Lynette Gain Williams, *(978-0-9779063)* 10659 Rookwood Dr., San Diego, CA 92131-1619 USA (SAN 850-5608)
E-mail: gainliteracy@sbcglobal.net.

Gaines, Alan, *(978-0-692-06251-7)* 8214 S. 3rd Ave., Inglewood, CA 90305 USA Tel 219-406-8028
E-mail: gainesalan22@gmail.com
Dist(s): **Ingram Content Group.**

Gakken Plus Co., Ltd. (JPN) *(978-4-05) Dist. by* **S and S Inc.**

Galactic Bookforge, *(978-0-9990324)* 11752 leibacher ave, Norwalk, CA 90650 USA Tel 562-760-4392
E-mail: Aceeducator123@gmail.com.

Galactic Bks., *(978-0-9769400)* 9827 Endora Ct., Owings Mills, MD 21117 USA
Web site: http://www.galacticbooks.usafreespace.com.

Galactic Pr., *(978-1-7329452)* 1154 E.223rd St. 2nd Fl., Bronx, NY 10466 USA Tel 646-341-3880
E-mail: bfaust646@aol.com.

Galahad Publishing, *(978-0-918483)* 6035 Vantage Ave., Suite 100, North Hollywood, CA 91606-4637 USA (SAN 657-680X) Tel 818-761-5198; Fax: 818-766-8645; Toll Free: 888-349-4878
Web site: http://www.GalahadPublishing.com.

Galaxia Publishing Group, LLC, *(978-0-9741657)* P.O. Box 61054, Phoenix, AZ 85082-1054 USA Tel 480-279-0836; Fax: 480-279-0863
E-mail: info@galaxiapg.com; LatonyaJordanSmith@yahoo.com
Web site: http://www.galaxiapg.com.

Galaxias Productions, *(978-0-9835631; 978-0-9850529)* 200 W. 90th St. No. 9B, New York, NY 10024 USA Tel 212-712-1540
E-mail: alwooten411@yahoo.com
Web site: www.arthurwooten.com
Dist(s): **Smashwords.**

Galaxy Bks., *(978-0-9671358; 978-0-9935428-2-4)* 244 Madison Ave., PMB 231, New York, NY 10016-2817 USA Fax: 212-428-6747; Toll Free: 877-425-2992
E-mail: Galaxybooks@yahoo.com.

Galaxy Pr., LLC, *(978-1-59212; 978-1-61986)* Orders Addr.: 7051 Hollywood Blvd., Suite 200, Hollywood, CA 90028 USA (SAN 254-6906) Tel 323-466-7815; Fax: 323-466-7817; Edit Addr.: 6121 Malburg Way, vernon, CA 90058 USA
E-mail: jwills@galaxypress.com; kcatalano@galaxypress.com; jgoodwin@galaxypress.com; sarahc@galaxypress.com
Web site: http://www.galaxypress.com/; http://www.battlefieldearth.com; http://www.writersofthefuture.com; http://www.goldenagestories.com
Dist(s): **Follett School Solutions**
Gumdrop Bks.

Galbraith, Sondra R. , *(978-0-578-17085-5)* 10291 Loridan Lane, Sandy, UT 84092 USA.

Gale ECCO, Print Editions *Imprint of* **Creative Media Partners, LLC**

Gale, Study Guides *Imprint of* **Creative Media Partners, LLC**

Galen Pr., Ltd., *(978-1-883620)* Orders Addr.: P.O. Box 64400, Tucson, AZ 85728-4400 USA (SAN 254-1823) Tel 520-577-8363; Fax: 520-529-6459; Toll Free: 800-442-5369 (orders only) Do not confuse with Galen Pr. in Madison, NJ
E-mail: ml@galenpress.com; sales@galenpress.com
Web site: http://www.galenpress.com
Dist(s): **Majors, J. A. Co.**
Matthews Medical Bk. Co.
Rittenhouse Bk. Distributors.

Gali Girls, Inc., *(978-0-9773673)* 48 Cranford Pl., Teaneck, NJ 07666 USA Tel 201-862-1989
Web site: http://www.galigirls.com.

Galileo Pr., *(978-0-913123; 978-0-9817519)* 3222 Rocking Horse, Aiken, SC 29801 USA (SAN 240-6543) Do not confuse with companies with the same or similar name in Edmonds, WA, Brooklyn, NY
E-mail: jawendell@aol.com
Dist(s): **Pathway Bk. Service**
SPD-Small Pr. Distribution.

Galison, *(978-0-7353; 978-0-929648; 978-0-939456; 978-1-56155)* Div. of The McEvoy Group, 28 W. 44th St., Suite 1411-12, New York, NY 10036 USA Tel 212-354-8840; Fax: 212-944-8682; Toll Free: 800-322-6663; *Imprints:* Mudpuppy (Mudpuppy)
E-mail: sales@galison.com
Web site: http://www.galison.com
Dist(s): **Hachette Bk. Group**
McEvoy Group, The.

Gall, Frank, *(978-0-692-18621-3)* 9622 Poynes Dr, Houston, TX 77065 USA Tel 832-567-4892
E-mail: frankcgall@gmail.com.

Gallagher, Carole M., *(978-0-9702197)* 431 S. Main St., Williamstown, NJ 08094 USA Tel 856-875-1575; Fax: 856-875-1998.

Gallant Gold Media *See* **Gallant Gold Media LLC**

Gallant Gold Media LLC, *(978-0-9653035; 978-1-890570; 978-1-58584)* P.O. Box 10404, Burke, VA 22009 USA Tel 310-926-4100 (phone/fax) Do not confuse with Huckleberry Pr., Gig Harbor, WA
E-mail: gallantgoldmedia@gmail.com; noreenwise@gallantgoldmedia.com
Web site: https://www.gallantgold.com.

Gallant Hse. Publishing, *(978-0-9660373)* 1329 Hwy. 395n, Ste 10 Pmb 114, Gardnerville, NV 89410 USA Toll Free: 877-577-2244
E-mail: gallanthouse@hotmail.com.

Gallant Pr., *(978-0-9990879; 978-1-952553)* 18228 Hastings Way, Porter, CA 91326 USA Tel 323-363-2743
E-mail: production@gallantpress.com
Web site: www.gallantpress.com.

†Gallaudet Univ. Pr., *(978-0-913580; 978-0-930323; 978-1-56368; 978-1-944838)* 800 Florida Ave., NE, Washington, DC 20002-3695 USA (SAN 205-261X) Tel 202-651-5488; Fax: 202-651-5489; Toll Free Fax: 800-621-8476; Toll Free: 888-630-9347 (TTY)
E-mail: valencia.simmons@gallaudet.edu
Web site: http://gupress.gallaudet.edu
Dist(s): **Chicago Distribution Ctr.**
Ebsco Publishing
Follett School Solutions; *CIP.*

Gallery Bks. *Imprint of* **Gallery Bks.**

Gallery Bks., 1230 Ave. of the Americas, New York, NY 10020 USA; *Imprints:* Gallery Books (Gallery Imp)
Dist(s): **Simon & Schuster, Inc.**

Galletti, Barbara, *(978-0-9748737)* 2509 Lawnside Rd., Timonium, MD 21093-2605 USA Tel 410-252-6568
E-mail: gallettinotes@hotmail.com.

Gallimard, Editions (FRA) *(978-2-07) Dist. by* **Distribks Inc.**

Gallopade International, *(978-0-635; 978-0-7933; 978-0-935326; 978-1-55609)* Orders Addr.: 6000 Shakerag Hl. # 314, Peachtree Cty, GA 30269-6523 USA (SAN 213-8441) Toll Free Fax: 800-871-2979; Toll Free: 800-536-2438; *Imprints:* Marsh, Carole Family CD-Rom (C Marsh); Marsh, Carole Books (C Mrsh Bks); Marsh, Carole Mysteries (CarolMarshMyst)
E-mail: michael@gallopade.com
Web site: http://www.gallopade.com
Dist(s): **Children's Plus, Inc.**
Follett School Solutions.

Gallopade: Publishing Group *See* **Gallopade International**

Gallup Pr., *(978-1-59562)* 1251 Avenue of the Americas, 23rd Fl., New York, NY 10020 USA Tel 212-899-4709; Fax: 212-899-4899; Toll Free: 877-242-5587
Web site: http://www.gallup.com
Dist(s): **MyiLibrary**
Simon & Schuster
Simon & Schuster, Inc.

GALT, DANIEL Bks., LLC, *(978-0-9992257)* 650 Univ. Cir., Athens, GA 30605 USA Tel 706-351-3180; Fax: 706-351-3180
E-mail: danielgaltbooks@gmail.com
Web site: https://danielgaltbooks.wordpress.com/.

Galway Pr., *(978-0-9963482)* 51999 hwy 19, stratford, OK 74872 USA Tel 580-759-9698
E-mail: kissb4ugo@gmail.com.

Gambit Pubns., Ltd. (GBR) *(978-1-901983; 978-1-904600; 978-1-906454; 978-1-910093) Dist. by* **TwoRivers.**

Game Changer Ga LLC, *(978-0-692-91915-6; 978-0-692-91979-8; 978-0-692-99638-6)* 3708 tamer Ln., LILBURN, GA 30047 USA Tel 678-789-7485
E-mail: renniecurran@me.com
Dist(s): **Ingram Content Group.**

Game Day Press *See* **Timberwood Pr.**

Game Designers' Workshop, *(978-0-943580; 978-1-55878)* 1418 N. Clinton Blvd., Bloomington, IL 61701 USA (SAN 240-656X) Tel 309-531-4076
E-mail: farfuture@gmail.com
Dist(s): **PSI (Publisher Services, Inc.).**

Games Workshop, Ltd. (GBR) *(978-1-84154; 978-1-869893; 978-1-872372; 978-1-907964; 978-1-78253) Dist. by* **S and S Inc.**

Gametasia, *(978-0-692-32164-5; 978-0-9862942; 978-0-692-97852-8; 978-0-578-44579-3)* 14252 Morning Glory Rd., Tustin, CA 92680 USA Tel 714-838-9408
E-mail: pamela@freedomwithinfoundation.org.

Gam-Jam Publishing Company *See* **Pendleton Publishing, Inc.**

Gamlin, Stephen, *(978-0-9767993)* P.O. Box 5, Goffstown, NH 03045 USA Tel 603-560-3360; Fax: 603-774-8698; Toll Free: 877-560-3360
E-mail: Steve@InspiredBySteve.com
Web site: http://www.InspiredBySteve.com.

Gamoke, John, *(978-0-9771290)* 6645 Humboldt Ave. S., Richfield, MN 55423 USA; *Imprints:* JoZanephine Originals (MYID_Z_JOZANEP).

GanDale Associates Houston *See* **Holocaust Museum Houston**

Ganeshan, Rajeshwari Iyer, *(978-0-692-14768-9)* 2289 Pinnacle Ct., Erie, PA 16506 USA Tel 262-309-8749
E-mail: ragasspace@gmail.com
Dist(s): **Ingram Content Group.**

Gannon, Ryan, *(978-0-9991760)* 2626 King ST., Denver, CO 80211 USA Tel 720-475-6738
E-mail: ryanwritergannon@gmail.com
Dist(s): **CreateSpace Independent Publishing Platform.**

Gant, Linda G. Gifted Creations *See* **Readers Are Leaders**

Gantt Smith Publishing Hse., *(978-0-9847885)* 875 Victor Ave. Apt., 235, Inglewood, CA 90302 USA Tel 310-673-5114
E-mail: migs13@sbcglobal.net.

Gaon Bks., *(978-0-9820657; 978-0-9825439; 978-1-935604)* Div. of Gaon Institute for Tolerance Studies, P.O. Box 23924, Santa Fe, NM 87502-3924 USA Tel 505-920-7771
E-mail: gaonbooks@gmail.com
Web site: http://www.gaonbooks.com.

Gap Tooth Publishing *Imprint of* **Charles River Pr.**

Garamella, Priscilla, *(978-0-692-99433-7)* 19 Squire Ct., Brookfield, CT 06804 USA Tel 203-313-0819
E-mail: pgaramella@gmail.com.

Garbage Factory, The, *(978-0-692-58125-4; 978-0-9975227)* 188 Lyndon Ave., Athens, GA 30601 USA Tel 706-248-8626
E-mail: johnnypence@gmail.com
Web site: garbagefactory.com.

Garcia, Cezanne, *(978-0-9728041)* 30405 Cupeno Ln., Temecula, CA 92592-2540 USA Tel 951-506-6407 (phone\fax)
E-mail: stgarcia@fda.net.

Garcia, Jeffrey, *(978-0-9840942)* 3000 Avenida Ciruela, Carlsbad, CA 92009 USA Tel 760-822-0222.

Garden Fleetfoot Pr., *(978-0-9762544)* Orders Addr.: P.O. Box 1188, Okemos, MI 48805 USA
E-mail: info@gardenfleetfoot.com
Web site: http://gardenfleetfoot.com
Dist(s): **Partners Pubs. Group, Inc.**

Garden Gallery, *(978-0-9996323)* 247 Lawrence Rd. 216, Black Rock, AR 72415 USA Tel 870-878-1801
E-mail: jdsclark55@yahoo.com.

Garden, Randa, *(978-0-615-12322-6)* 3503 Portia Pl., Norfolk, NE 68701 USA Tel 402-371-0544
E-mail: jrgarden@cableone.net
Web site: www.pennythepenguin.com.

Gardner, Colin, *(978-0-9720348; 978-0-615-11851-2)* 1677 S. 75 E., Bouniful, UT 84010-5218 USA Tel 801-296-2109 (phone/fax)
E-mail: colingardner@juno.com.

Gardner, Dianne Lynn, *(978-0-692-47613-0; 978-0-692-89976-2; 978-0-692-90949-2; 978-0-692-91279-9; 978-0-692-92044-2; 978-0-692-92048-0; 978-0-692-92874-5; 978-0-692-97612-8; 978-0-692-98797-1; 978-0-692-98798-8; 978-0-692-05912-8; 978-0-692-05913-5; 978-0-692-05979-1; 978-0-692-15188-4; 978-0-578-45959-2)* 9385 *Olalla Valley Rd. SE, Port Orchard, WA 98367 USA Tel 253-851-0339*
Web site: http://gardnersart.com
Dist(s): **CreateSpace Independent Publishing Platform.**

Gardner Pubns., *(978-0-9659163)* 235 E. Main St., No. 119, Hendersonville, TN 37075 USA Tel 615-824-5100; Fax: 615-824-3400; Toll Free: 800-297-8179
E-mail: harveylgardner@bbsco.com
Web site: http://www.bbsco.com.

Gareth Stevens Hi-Lo Must Reads *Imprint of* **Stevens, Gareth Publishing LLLP**

Gareth Stevens Learning Library *Imprint of* **Stevens, Gareth Publishing LLLP**

Gareth Stevens Secondary Library *Imprint of* **Stevens, Gareth Publishing LLLP**

Garfein, Stanley, *(978-0-9787422)* 1110 Lasswade Dr., Tallahassee, FL 32312-2845 USA Tel 850-385-1538; Fax: 850-531-0276
E-mail: StaGarfein@aol.com.

Garfield, M., *(978-0-615-96149-1; 978-0-9964136)* 609 Mills St., Lafayette, CO 80026 USA Tel 303-604-6540; *Imprints:* Pennaeth Publishing (Pennaeth Pub)
E-mail: m.garfield@comcast.net.

Garing, Bernard, *(978-0-9765809)* 6304 Caleigh Dr., Charlestown, IN 47111-7713 USA.

Garland City Bks. of Watertown, *(978-0-9890509)* P.O. Box 604, Black River, NY 13612 USA Tel 315-783-0728
E-mail: rothensu@yahoo.com.

Garland, Daniel, *(978-0-9768414)* 6247 Cascade Hwy., NE, Silverton, OR 97381 USA
E-mail: danielgarland@msn.com.

Garland E. Stafford III, *(978-0-578-41744-8)* 875 Cashen Dr., Fernandina Beach, FL 32034 USA Tel 904-556-3015
E-mail: treystafford51@gmail.com
Dist(s): **Independent Pub.**

Garlic Pr., *(978-0-931993; 978-1-930820)* Orders Addr.: 899 S. College Mall, Suite 381, Bloomington, IN 47401 USA (SAN 686-1105) Tel 800-789-0554; Toll Free Fax: 800-789-5576 Do not confuse with companies with the same name in Kirkwood, MO, New London, NH, Abingdon MD, Lenox MA, Kansas City, MO
E-mail: garlic.press@att.net
Web site: http://www.garlicpress.com.

Garr, Sherry B., *(978-0-9759866)* 3456 S. Mulberry Dr., Saint George, UT 84790 USA
Web site: http://www.gumfounded.com.

Garrelts, Christopher *See* **Squarey Head, Inc.**

Garrett, Debbie Behan, *(978-0-615-24202-6; 978-0-615-42184-1)* P.O. Box 210571, Dallas, TX 75211-0571 USA Tel 214-337-5928; Fax: 214-337-8127
E-mail: blackdolls@sbcglobal.net
Web site: http://blackdollcollecting.com.

Garrigues Hse. Pubs., *(978-0-9620844; 978-1-931014)* 2746 Stein Ln., Lewisburg, PA 17837 USA (SAN 249-969X) Tel 570-204-2906; 2746 Stein Ln., Lewisburg, PA 17837 (SAN 249-9703)
E-mail: jim@garrigueshouse.com
Web site: http://www.garrigueshouse.com.

Garry & Donna, LLC, *(978-0-9815617)* P.O. Box 30021, Las Vegas, NV 89173 USA.

Garteiz, John, *(978-0-578-40228-4; 978-1-7337634)* 7316 Steilacoom Blvd. SW, Lakewood, WA 98499 USA Tel 253-970-7095
E-mail: jgarteizalaska@gmail.com.

Gasior, Julie, *(978-0-615-18824-9; 978-0-615-18884-3)* 6404 Shadow Oaks Ct., Monmouth Jct, NJ 08852-2297 USA
E-mail: juliespotions@gmail.com
Web site: http://juliespotions.com
Dist(s): **Lulu Pr., Inc.**

Gask Castle Pr., *(978-0-9843717)* 1725 Starmont Trail, Knoxville, TN 37909 USA Tel 865-310-8947
E-mail: phillip@gaskcastlepress.com.

Gaslight Pubns., *(978-0-934468)* P.O. Box 1344, Studio City, CA 91614-0344 USA Tel 818-784-8918
Dist(s): **Empire Publishing Service**
Players Pr., Inc.

GASLight Publishing, *(978-0-9754796; 978-1-933869)* P.O. Box 1025, Leander, TX 78646 USA Tel 512-528-1727; Fax: 512-259-8671
E-mail: ken@gaslightpublishing.com; kenschaefer@totalaccess.net
Web site: http://www.gsalightpublishing.com
Dist(s): **Smashwords.**

Gatbonton, Beverly Mabanglo, *(978-1-7322791)* 1083 Independence Blvd, Virginia Beach, VA 23455 USA Tel 757-270-0443
E-mail: bevmmg@gmail.com.

Gatekeeper Pr. *Imprint of* **Gatekeeper Pr.**

Gatekeeper Pr., *(978-0-9724102; 978-1-932549; 978-1-936910; 978-1-61984; 978-1-64237; 978-1-6629)* 2167 Stringtown Rd Suite 109, Columbus, OH 43123 USA Toll Free: 888-234-6896; *Imprints:* Gatekeeper Press (GatekeeperPr); BlogIntoBook.com (BlogIntoBook); Quintessential Press (MYID_L_QUINTES); Breezy Way Publishing (Breezy Way P)
Web site: http://www.priceworldpublishing.com; http://www.GatekeeperPress.com
Dist(s): **Cardinal Pubs. Group**
INscribe Digital
Independent Pubs. Group
MyiLibrary.

GateKeepers International, Incorporated, *(978-0-9745483)* 15245 Jessie Dr., Colorado Springs, CO 80921 USA
E-mail: Femritegki@gmail.com
Web site: http://www.gatekeepersintl.org.

GateKeepers Ministries International, *(978-0-9754535; 978-0-578-21738-3)* 3600 Earl Ave., Pennsauken, NJ 08110 USA Tel 856-406-6101 Toll Free: 866-910-2810
E-mail: gatekeepersmintl@aol.com
Web site: http://www.gkmi.org.

Gateway Hse. Publishing, *(978-0-9995258)* 38 N Gateway, Toms River, NJ 08753 USA Tel 732-239-6752
E-mail: info@gatewayhousepublishing.com
Web site: gatewayhousepublishing.com.

Gateway Learning Corporation *See* **HOP, LLC**

Gateways Bks. & Tapes, *(978-0-89556)* Div. of I.D.H.H.B., Inc., P.O. Box 370, Nevada City, CA 95959 USA (SAN 211-3635) Tel 530-477-8101; Fax: 530-272-0184; Toll Free: 800-869-0658
E-mail: orders@gatewaysbooksandtapes.com; info@gatewaysbooksandtapes.com
Web site: http://www.gatewaysbooksandtapes.com
Dist(s): **Independent Pubs. Group**
MyiLibrary
ebrary, Inc.

Gatewood Pr., *(978-0-9710427)* P.O. Box 356, Johnson City, TX 78636 USA Tel 832-723-7313 Do not confuse with Wilson & Associates, Gig Harbor, WA
E-mail: alvincoog@me.com.

Gathering Place Pubs., Inc., *(978-0-9754622; 978-0-615-38236-4; 978-0-9828311)* P.O. Box 341, Kaysville, UT 84037-8403 USA (SAN 256-0658) Fax: 801-451-6008
E-mail: sales@stonesquest.com
Web site: http://www.rebuildshattereddreams.com; http://www.stonesquest.com.

Gatorbytes *Imprint of* **Univ. Pr. of Florida**

†Gaunt, Inc., *(978-0-912004; 978-1-56169; 978-1-60449)* 3011 Gulf Dr., Holmes Beach, FL 34217-2199 USA (SAN 202-9413) Tel 941-778-5211; Fax: 941-778-5252
E-mail: info@gaunt.com; sales@gaunt.com
Web site: http://www.gaunt.com; *CIP.*

Gaunt, William W. & Sons, Incorporated *See* **Gaunt, Inc.**

Gauntlet, Inc., *(978-0-9629659; 978-1-887368; 978-1-934267)* 5307 Arroyo St., Colorado Springs, CO 80922 USA Tel 719-591-5566; Fax: 719-591-6676
E-mail: gauntlet66@aol.com; info@gauntletpress.com
Web site: http://www.gauntletpress.com
Dist(s): **Independent Pubs. Group.**

Gauthier Pubns. Inc., *(978-0-9820812; 978-0-9833593; 978-0-615-71779-1; 978-1-942314)* P.O. Box 806241, Saint Clair Shores, MI 48080 USA (SAN 857-2119) Tel 313-458-7141; Fax: 586-279-1515; *Imprints:* Frog Legs Ink (Frog Legs Ink); Hungry Goat Press (Hungry Goat)
E-mail: info@gauthierpublications.com
Web site: http://www.FrogLegsInk.com; http://www.EATaBOOK.com
Dist(s): **BWI**
Brodart Co.
CreateSpace Independent Publishing Platform
Diamond Bk. Distributors
Follett School Solutions
OverDrive, Inc.

Gavila Publishing, *(978-0-9748466)* 20-23 43 St., Astoria, NY 11105 USA
Web site: http://www.gavila.com.

Gavin, Fred Enterprises, *(978-0-935668)* 96 Byron St., East Boston, MA 02128 USA (SAN 221-1629).

Gaviota Ediciones (ESP) *(978-84-392) Dist. by* **Lectorum Pubns.**

Gavlak, L.J. Publishing, *(978-0-9740357)* Orders Addr.: P.O. Box 72, Kylertown, PA 16847 USA Tel 814-345-6391; Edit Addr.: Rollingston Rd., Kylertown, PA 16847 USA
E-mail: largav@juno.com.

Gazarik, Rebecca, *(978-0-9802258)* 637 Pine Run Rd., Apollo, PA 15613-9313 USA
Web site: http://www.rebeccagazarik.com/.

Gazelle Pr. *Imprint of* **Genesis Communications, Inc.**

Gazing In Publishing, *(978-0-9839318)* P.O. Box 197, Columbia, SC 29147 USA Tel 803-743-8810
E-mail: winmilawe@gmail.com.

Gazoobi Tales, *(978-0-9679364)* P.O. Box 19614, Seattle, WA 98109-6614 USA
E-mail: info@gazoobitales.com
Web site: http://www.gazoobitales.com.

GB Pr., *(978-0-578-02613-8; 978-0-615-35332-6; 978-0-9828241)* P.O. Box 27224, Boise, ID 83716 USA Tel 208-863-9045
E-mail: ken.mcconnell@gmail.com
Web site: http://gb-press.com
Dist(s): **Lulu Pr., Inc.**

GB4K Inc, *(978-0-9989161)* 250 Ennisbrook Dr SE, Smyrna, GA 30082 USA Tel 404-987-9096
E-mail: tjay3@gb4kinc.com.

GDG Publishing, *(978-0-9787549; 978-0-9796625; 978-0-9797952; 978-0-9855335)* Orders Addr.: 2063 Continental Dr. NE, Atlanta, GA 30345 USA (SAN 851-5182) Tel 404-248-0012; Fax: 404-248-1487 Do not confuse with GDG Publishing in Oxnard, CA
E-mail: glennondesign@comcast.net
Web site: http://www.gdgpublishing.com.

GDL Multimedia, LLC, *(978-1-60245)* 2513 179th Ave E., Lake Tapps, WA 98391-6453 USA
E-mail: greg@gdlmultimedia.com
Web site: http://www.gdlmultimedia.com
Dist(s): **KSG Distributing.**

GDM Consulting Services LLC, *(978-0-9763738)* 5 Alluvium Lakes Dr., Voorhees, NJ 08043 USA
Web site: http://www.gdmcs.com.

G.E. Books *See* **Vision Bks. LLC**

Gecko Pr. (NZL) *(978-0-9582598; 978-0-9582787; 978-0-9582720; 978-1-877467; 978-1-877579; 978-1-927271; 978-1-77657) Dist. by* **Lerner Pub.**

Geckostufs, Incorporated *See* **Words & Pictures Publishing, Inc.**

Geddes, Anne Publishing (AUS) *(978-1-921652; 978-1-922024) Dist. by* **TwoRivers.**

Geekdazzle, *(978-0-692-80608-1)* 9 Ashford Pl., Albertson, NY 11507 USA Tel 516-294-3335
E-mail: dvtuozzo@gmail.com
Web site: geekdazzle.com.

Geez Pr., *(978-0-9816574)* P.O. Box 711, Elmore, OH 43416-0711 USA
Web site: http://home.woh.rr.com/geezpress.

Gefen Bks., *(978-0-86343)* 11 Edison Pl., Springfield, NJ 07081 USA (SAN 856-8065)
E-mail: gefenny@gefenpublishing.com
Web site: http://www.gefenpublishing.com.

Gefen Publishing Hse., Ltd (ISR) *(978-965-229) Dist. by* **Strauss Cnslts.**

Gefen Publishing Hse., Ltd (ISR) *(978-965-229) Dist. by* **Gefen Bks.**

Geist, Sabrina, *(978-0-692-69506-7; 978-0-692-93941-3)* 5628 Cofeen, Sheridan, WY 82801 USA Tel 307-259-6419
E-mail: glannie@msn.com.

Gelos Pubns., *(978-0-9964157; 978-0-9972657; 978-1-7345226)* 332 S. Michigan Ave., Chicago, IL 60604 USA Tel 631-979-5990
E-mail: iansadler64@gmail.com
Dist(s): **Independent Pubs. Group**
Midpoint Trade Bks., Inc.

GEM Bk. Club, *(978-0-9722795; 978-0-9755092; 978-1-59825)* Div. of Highest Good Pubns., Orders Addr.: P.O. Box 43476, Chicago, IL 60643 USA (SAN 255-3953) Tel 773-445-4946; Fax: 773-233-5178; Toll Free: 877-447-1266; *Imprints:* Highest Good Publications (Highest Good Pubns)
E-mail: cherylwash@icloud.com; info@ebonyenergypublishing.com; cherylwash@yahoo.com
Web site: http://www.cherylwash.com; www.globalexecutivemedia.com; www.gembookclub.com; http://www.ebonyenergy.com; http://gemliteraryfoundation.org; http://ebonyenergybooks.com; http://ebonyenergykids.com; http://www.ebonyenergypublishing.com; http://highestgoodpublications.com; http://pocketbooksforyoursoul.com
Dist(s): **Biblio Distribution**
ebrary, Inc.

Gem Bk. Pubs., *(978-0-9633723; 978-1-887651)* Div. of Fred Ward Productions, Inc., Orders Addr.: 2575 Barrymore Dr., Malibu, CA 90265-2955 USA Tel 310-456-9949; Fax: 310-456-9799
E-mail: fred@fredwardgems.com; charlotte@fredwardgems.com
Web site: http://www.fredwardgems.com/.

Gem Printing, *(978-0-9743429)* Orders Addr.: 600 Reisterstown Rd., Suite 200G, Baltimore, MD 21208 USA Tel 410-764-1617; Fax: 410-764-7471; *Imprints:* American Poets Society (Amer Poets)
E-mail: poetryamericaorders@yahoo.com
Web site: http://www.poetryamerica.com.

Gem Pubns., *(978-0-9742354)* 3520 McNally Ave., Altadena, CA 91001 USA
E-mail: gregmiddleton@earthlink.net
Web site: http://www.gempublications.com.

Gemini Bk. Pubns., *(978-0-615-99427-7; 978-0-9978433)* 7137 Promenade Dr. Apt 602, Boca Raton, FL 33433 USA Tel 561-910-1145
Dist(s): **CreateSpace Independent Publishing Platform.**

GemmaMedia, *(978-1-934848; 978-1-936846)* 230 Commercial St., Boston, MA 02109 USA (SAN 855-2037)
E-mail: info@gemmamedia.com; trish@gemmamedia.com
Web site: http://www.gemmamedia.com
Dist(s): **Ingram Publisher Services**
MyiLibrary.

GEMS *Imprint of* **Univ. of California, Berkeley, Lawrence Hall of Science**

Gems International Incorporated *See* **Gems International, LLC**

Gems International, LLC, *(978-0-9728626)* 119 Fern St., Darby, PA 19023 USA
E-mail: polishmeprofessional@gmail.com
Web site: www.rayfieldsrules.com.

Gemstone Literary, *(978-0-9801692)* 27943 Seco Canyon Rd., No. 212, Los Angeles, CA 91350 USA
Web site: http://www.GemTal.com.

Gemstone Publishing, Inc., *(978-0-911903; 978-1-888472; 978-1-60360)* Div. of Diamond Comic Distributors, Inc., 1966 Greenspring Dr., Suite 405, Timonium, MD 21093 USA Tel 410-427-9432; Fax: 410-252-4582 Do not confuse with companies with same or similar names in Thornville, OH, Lebanon, OR, Lauderdale Lakes, FL, Sugarland, TX
Web site: http://www.gemstonepub.com
Dist(s): **Diamond Comic Distributors, Inc.**
Diamond Bk. Distributors
SPD-Small Pr. Distribution.

Gen Manga Entertainment, Inc., *(978-0-9836134; 978-0-9850644; 978-1-939012)* 250 Pk. Ave., Suite 7002, New York, NY 10177 USA Tel 646-535-0090
E-mail: editor@genmanga.com
Web site: http://www.genmanga.com
Dist(s): **Diamond Comic Distributors, Inc.**
Diamond Bk. Distributors.

GenBeam LLC, *(978-1-7325080; 978-1-950491)* 912 Candlewood Dr., El Dorado Hills, CA 95762 USA Tel 916-296-3202; *Imprints:* Tinker Toddlers (MYID_A_TINKER)
E-mail: kaur.handeep@gmail.com.

Gene Caven, *(978-0-578-09100-6; 978-0-9987416)* 61 Hidden Hill Rd, Tryon, NC 28782 USA Tel 828-817-9160.

Genealogical Publishing Company, Incorporated *See* **Genealogical.com**

†Genealogical.com, *(978-0-8063)* 3600 Clipper Mill Rd. Suite 260, Baltimore, MD 21211-1953 USA (SAN 206-8370) Toll Free: 800-296-6687 (orders & customer service); 3600 Clipper Mill Rd. Suite 260, Baltimore, MD 21211 (SAN 920-8755) Tel 410-837-8271; Fax: 410-752-8492
E-mail: hoffman@genealogical.com
Web site: http://www.Genealogical.com; *CIP.*

General Board of Global Ministries, The United Methodist Church, *(978-1-890569; 978-1-933663)* 475 Riverside Dr. Rm. 1473, New York, NY 10115 USA Tel 212-870-3731; Fax: 212-870-3654; *Imprints:* WD/GBGM Books (WD GBGM)
E-mail: cscott@gbgm-umc.org; KDonato@gbgm-umc.org
Web site: http://www.gbgm-umc.org
Dist(s): **Cokesbury**
Mission Resource Ctr.

General Bks. LLC, *(978-1-234; 978-1-77045; 978-1-150; 978-1-151; 978-1-152; 978-1-153; 978-1-154; 978-1-155; 978-1-156; 978-1-157; 978-1-158; 978-1-159; 978-1-230; 978-1-231; 978-1-232; 978-1-233; 978-1-235; 978-1-236; 978-1-238; 978-1-239; 978-1-130)* Orders Addr.: Box 29000, NAS485, Miami, FL 33102 USA
E-mail: support@general-books.net
Web site: www.general-books.net.

Generosity Philosophy, *(978-0-9961703)* 9848 Bobcat St., Aumsville, OR 97325 USA Tel 503-507-7069
E-mail: kim.trumbo@gmail.com.

Genesis Communications, Inc., *(978-0-9637311; 978-1-58169)* P.O. Box 191540, Mobile, AL 36619 USA Tel 251-861-2525; Fax: 251-287-2222; Toll Free: 800-367-8203; *Imprints:* Evergreen Press (Evergrn Pr AL); Gazelle Press (Gazelle Pr); Axiom Press (Axiom Press)
E-mail: Jeff@evergreen777.com
Web site: http://www.evergreenpress.com
Dist(s): **BookBaby**
Spring Arbor Distributors, Inc.

Genet Pr. LLC, *(978-0-9846663)* 9907 Cranapple Ct., Springdale, MD 20774 USA Tel 301-636-6353
E-mail: mayimona_ngwala@hotmail.com
Web site: www.genetpress.com.

Genius In A Bottle Technology Corp, *(978-0-9768429)* Orders Addr.: 910 NW 42nd St., Miami, FL 33127-2755 USA
E-mail: geniusinfo@geniusinabottle.net
Web site: http://www.geniusinabottle.net; http://www.cafepress.com/forevergirl; http://www.cafepress.com/geniusbooks; http://www.cafepress.com/gumo; http://www.cafepress.com/gkid; http://www.cafepress.com/cleversunburst; http://www.cafepress.com/tou; http://www.cafepress.com/foreverman; http://www.cafepress.com/forever4; http://www.cafepress.com/whateverr; http://www.cafepress.com/robospace; http://www.cafepress.com/battlegirlgear; http://www.cafepress.com/geniusinabottle; http://www.ca

Gennesaret Pr., *(978-0-9845541; 978-0-9997343)* 202 Persimmon Pl., Apex, NC 27523 USA (SAN 859-7278) Tel 919-633-0929
E-mail: joel@joelschnoor.com
Web site: http://www.auntruthgrammar.com.

Gentle Giraffe Pr., *(978-0-9747921; 978-0-9777394; 978-0-9801746)* 7405 Barra Dr., Bethesda, MD 20817 USA Tel 202-423-4205; Fax: 334-460-0724; Toll Free: 888-424-4723
E-mail: info@gentlegiraffe.com
Web site: http://www.gentlegiraffe.com.

Gentle Thoughts for Hard Spots, *(978-0-9988274)* 401 RIVER ROCK Rd., CHALLIS, ID 83226 USA Tel 298-833-4681
E-mail: karenw@custertel.net.

Gently Spoken Communications, *(978-0-9711794; 978-0-9746491; 978-0-9776096; 978-0-615-11369-2; 978-0-615-11845-1; 978-0-692-55642-9)* P.O. Box 365, St. Francis, MN 55070 USA Tel 763-506-9933; Fax: 763-506-9934; Toll Free: 877-224-7886
E-mail: info@gentlyspoken.com
Web site: http://www.gentlyspoken.com.

Genuine Prints, LLC, *(978-0-615-23040-5)* P.O. Box 328, Carpentersville, IL 60110 USA Fax: 847-844-9073; Toll Free: 888-853-0001
E-mail: info@nicoandlola.com
Web site: http://www.nicoandlola.com.

Geographic Tongue, LLC, *(978-0-9841685)* P.O. Box 31461, Tucson, AZ 85751-1461 USA
Web site: http://www.GeographicTongueEditions.com.

Geography Matters, Inc., *(978-0-9702403; 978-1-931397; 978-1-62863)* P.O. Box 92, Nancy, KY 42544 USA Tel 606-636-4678; Fax: 606-636-4697; Toll Free: 800-426-4650
E-mail: geomatters@geomatters.com
Web site: http://www.geomatters.com.

George, H. Publishing, *(978-0-9728183)* Orders Addr.: 14513 Bayes Ave., Lakewood, OH 44107 USA Tel 216-319-4575
E-mail: ninthohio@sbcglobal.net.

George, Tricia Artist, *(978-1-7338865)* 122 Paul Dr., San Rafael, CA 94903 USA Tel 415-577-5595
E-mail: info@triciageorge.com
Web site: www.triciageorge.com.

Geoscience Information Services, *(978-0-9777100)* Orders Addr.: P.O. Box 911, West Falmouth, MA 02574-0911 USA Tel 508-540-6490
E-mail: geoinfo@comcast.net.

Gequalsa, *(978-0-9792518)* 2710 Walnut St., Orlando, FL 32806 USA.

Gerardian Inkspot & Paint Society, *(978-0-9786675)* St. Gerard's Church, 240 W. Robb Ave., Lima, OH 45801 USA.

Gerber, Brandy Fine Art, *(978-1-7325942)* 8494 Ida Ctr. Rd, Ida, MI 48140 USA Tel 734-755-4039
E-mail: brandygerber@hotmail.com
Web site: www.brandygerber,com.

Gerber, Judie *See* **Seachild**

Gere Publishing, *(978-0-9743995; 978-0-9981987)* 113 Leonard Rd., Shutesbury, MA 01072-9783 USA (SAN 257-4594) Tel 413-259-1741
E-mail: claudia@claudiagereco.com
Web site: http://www.gerepublishing.com.

Gerhardt, Paul L., *(978-0-615-13556-4; 978-0-615-16208-9; 978-0-615-16270-6; 978-0-615-23707-7; 978-0-615-23721-3)* P.O. Box 111141, Tacoma, WA 98411 USA
Web site: http://www.paulgerhardt.com
Dist(s): **Lulu Pr., Inc.**

Geringer, Laura Book *Imprint of* **HarperCollins Pubs.**

Gernand, Linda, *(978-0-9755025)* 523 Oyster Creek Dr., Richwood, TX 77531 USA.

Gerson Group, The, *(978-0-578-58402-7)* 127 Tullamore Trail, Tyrone, GA 30290 USA Tel 770-827-7977
E-mail: gersongroup45@gmail.com.

Gersten, Dan & Associates LLC *See* **Dogwalk Pr.**

Gerstenblatt, Judith Furedi *See* **Lucky & Me Productions, Inc.**

Gerstorff, Katherine, *(978-0-692-16431-0)* 700 Race St., Jonesboro, IN 46938 USA Tel 765-603-8457
E-mail: gerstorff@gmail.com
Dist(s): **Ingram Content Group.**

gertrude m Bks. *Imprint of* **Circling Rivers**

Gestalt Pubns., *(978-0-9764065)* 3828 Clinton Ave. S., Minneapolis, MN 55409-1314 USA Tel 612-822-4419.

Gestalt Publishing Pty, Ltd. (AUS) *(978-0-9775628; 978-0-9807823; 978-1-922023; 978-1-922335) Dist. by* **D C D.**

Get Happy Tips, LLC, *(978-0-9860272)* 515 SW 18th Ave. No. 19, Fort Lauderdale, FL 33312 USA Tel 786-314-8199
E-mail: gethappytips@gmail.com
Web site: http://www.gethappytips.com.

Get It Factory, The, *(978-0-578-44095-8; 978-0-578-44596-0; 978-1-7337019; 978-1-7333079; 978-1-953011)* 1021 25th Ave SW, Great Falls, MT 59404 USA Tel 406-217-8644
E-mail: ryanacra@sugarbeetfalls.com
Web site: www.thegetitfactory.com.

Get Kids Golfing, *(978-0-692-92660-4)* 3669 Fanwood Ave, LONG BEACH, CA 90808 USA Tel 562-552-4681
E-mail: info@getkidsgolfing.com
Dist(s): **Ingram Content Group.**

Get Life Right Foundation, The *See* **Life Force Bks.**

Get Published, *(978-1-4501; 978-1-4525)* 1663 Liberty Dr., Bloomington, IN 47403 USA Tel 812-650-0913; Fax: 812-339-6554; Toll Free: 877-217-3420 Do not confuse with Get Published in Valparaiso, IN
E-mail: customersupport@dellartepress.com
Dist(s): **Author Solutions, Inc.**
CreateSpace Independent Publishing Platform.

Get the Word Out, Inc, *(978-1-7337970)* 39293 Plymouth Rd., Livonia, MI 48150 USA Tel 734-521-6579
E-mail: letsgwo@gmail.com.

Getchu Bks. *Imprint of* **Lake 7 Creative, LLC**

Gettier Group LLC, *(978-0-9860882; 978-0-9971906; 978-0-9994595; 978-1-7358925)* 43150 Broadlands Ctr. Plaza Box 152-218, Broadlands, VA 20148-3800 USA Tel 703-307-7091
E-mail: denisetimpko@verizon.net
Web site: www.gettiergroup.net.

Getting There, *(978-0-9707274)* P.O. Box 1412, Asheville, NC 28802-1412 USA Tel 828-645-5908
E-mail: bmayers@charter.net
Web site: http://www.paddlingasheville.com
Dist(s): **Common Ground Distributors, Inc.**

Getty, J. Paul Trust Publications *See* **Getty Pubns.**

†Getty Pubns., *(978-0-89236; 978-0-941103; 978-1-60606; 978-1-947440)* Orders Addr.: P.O. Box 49659, Los Angeles, CA 90049-0659 USA Tel 310-440-7333; Fax: 818-779-0051; Edit Addr.: 1200 Getty Ctr. Dr., Suite 500, Los Angeles, CA 90049-1682 USA (SAN 208-2276) Tel 310-440-7365; Fax: 310-440-7758; Toll Free: 800-223-3431; *Imprints:* J. Paul Getty Museum (J P Getty)
E-mail: pubsinfo@getty.edu; pubsinfo@getting.edu; mwinter@getty.edu
Web site: http://www.getty.edu/publications
Dist(s): **Abrams, Inc.**
Casemate Academic
Chicago Distribution Ctr.
Hachette Bk. Group
Lectorum Pubns., Inc.
Libros Sin Fronteras
Oxford Univ. Pr., Inc.; *CIP.*

GFC Pr., *(978-0-9792132; 978-0-9840789; 978-0-9839256)* P.O. Box 294, Inglewood, CA 90306 USA (SAN 858-2297) Do not confuse with companies with the same or similar name in Odenton, MD, Cove, OR, Livingston, TX, Dallas, TX, Dunlap, TN, Hume, CA
E-mail: rjdriver5@gmail.com.

GGMI Incorporated *See* **God's Glory Media**

Ghim, John Yun, *(978-0-9656864)* 1139 Queen Anne Pl. Apt. 106, Los Angeles, CA 90019-7105 USA
E-mail: coolghim@yahoo.com.

Publisher Name Index

GHL Publishing LLC, *(978-0-9726419)* P.O. Box 26462, Collegeville, PA 19426 USA (SAN 254-9875) Tel 610-831-1442; Fax: 610-831-1443
E-mail: c.lagunilla@att.net
Web site: http://www.GHLPublishing.com.

Gholson, C. D., *(978-0-9725974)* 2341 W. Pierce, Harrison, MI 48625 USA Tel 898-539-5312
E-mail: goatlocker@msn.com.

Ghost Hse. Bks. *Imprint of* **Lone Pine Publishing USA**

Ghost Hunter Productions, *(978-0-9717234; 978-1-934307)* P.O. Box 1199, Helena, MT 59624 USA
E-mail: info@ibw-books.com
Web site: http://www.ibw-books.com.

G-Host Publishing, *(978-0-9649088)* Orders Addr.: 8701 Lava Pl., West Hills, CA 91304-2126 USA Tel 818-340-6676 (phone/fax)
E-mail: robanne@ix.netcom.com.

Giant in the Playground, *(978-0-9766580; 978-0-9854139)* 2417 Welsh Rd., Suite 21 No. 328, Philadelphia, PA 19114 USA
E-mail: rich@giantitp.com
Web site: http://www.giantitp.com
Dist(s): **Diamond Comic Distributors, Inc.**
Diamond Bk. Distributors.

Giant in the Playground Games *See* **Giant in the Playground**

Giant Robot Bks., *(978-0-9749492)* P.O. Box 641639, Los Angeles, CA 90064 USA Tel 310-479-7311
E-mail: books@giantrobot.com
Web site: http://www.giantrobot.com
Dist(s): **Trucatriche.**

Gibbons-Fitts Ink, *(978-1-941387)* 14 Hillcrest, Tuscaloosa, AL 35401 USA Tel 205-752-5934
E-mail: billfittsauthor@att.net
Web site: billfittsauthor.com.

Gibbs, Andrea, 615 Kentucky Dr., Rochester Hills, MI 48307 USA Tel 248-495-9881
E-mail: andrealynngibbs@gmail.com.

Gibbs Publishing, *(978-0-9969509)* 8 Evergreen Terr., Ballston Lake, NY 12019 USA Tel 518-877-0759
E-mail: gibbs.pubco@gmail.com.

†Gibbs Smith, Publisher, *(978-0-87905; 978-0-941711; 978-1-58685; 978-1-4236)* Orders Addr.: P.O. Box 667, Layton, UT 84041 USA (SAN 201-9906) Tel 801-544-9800; Fax: 801-544-5582; Toll Free Fax: 800-213-3023 (orders); Toll Free: 800-748-5439 (orders); 800-835-4993 (Customer Service order only); Edit Addr.: 1877 E. Gentile St., Layton, UT 84040 USA Tel 801-544-9800; Fax: 801-546-8853; *Imprints:* Anorak Press (Anorak Pr)
E-mail: info@gibbs-smith.com; tradeorders@gibbs-smith.com
Web site: http://www.gibbs-smith.com
Dist(s): **Open Road Integrated Media, Inc.**
Publishers Group West (PGW)
Publishers Group International, Inc.; *CIP.*

Gibson Bks. *Imprint of* **Glory Days Group Publishing**

Gibson, C. R. Co., *(978-0-7667; 978-0-8378; 978-0-937970)* 401 BNA Dr., Bldg 200, Suite 600, Nashville, TN 37217 USA Toll Free: 800-243-6004 (ext. 2895)
E-mail: customerservice@crgibson.com
Web site: http://www.andersonpress.com.

Gibson, Cita, *(978-0-9727964)* P.O. Box 411236, Melbourne, FL 32941 USA Tel 316-210-6422; Fax: 321-757-7385
E-mail: maloon57@aol.com
Web site: http://www.citagibson.com.

Gibson Hse., *(978-0-9855158; 978-0-9861541; 978-1-948721)* 1348 Heather Hill Crescent, Flossmoor, IL 60422 USA Tel 708-647-0908; *Imprints:* Gibson House Press (MYID_V_GIBSON)
E-mail: deb@gibsonhousepress.com; info@gibsonhousepress.com
Web site: www.gibsonhousepress.com
Dist(s): **Independent Pubs. Group.**

Gibson Hse. Pr. *Imprint of* **Gibson Hse.**

Gibson Tech Ed, Incorporated *See* **GSS Tech Ed**

Gichigami Pr., *(978-0-9906846)* 34145 Pacific Coast Hwy. No. 343, Dana Point, CA 92629 USA Tel 313-310-9115
E-mail: mb@letschatbooks.com
Web site: www.letschatabooutbooks.com.

Giddy Up, LLC, *(978-1-932125; 978-1-59524)* 3630 Plaza Dr., Ann Arbor, MI 48108 USA (SAN 255-6847)
E-mail: stiehl@giddyup.com
Web site: http://www.giddyup.com.

Giesy, Mitchell, *(978-0-9993723)* 242 Vine Cliff Dr., Harvest, AL 35749 USA Tel 256-348-8906
E-mail: mitchgiesy@gmail.com.

Gift Gardens *See* **Gift Gardens Pr.**

Gift Gardens Pr., *(978-0-692-09535-5; 978-1-7329293)* 5133 Waterman Blvd., Saint Louis, MO 63108 USA Tel 314-249-8500
E-mail: arthur.culbert@gmail.com
Web site: giftgardens.org.

Gifted Education Pr., *(978-0-910609)* Orders Addr.: P.O. Box 1586, Manassas, VA 20108 USA; Edit Addr.: 10201 Yuma Ct., Manassas, VA 20109 USA (SAN 694-132X) Tel 703-369-5017; Toll Free: 800-484-1406 (code 6857)
E-mail: mfisher345@home.com
Web site: http://GIFTEDEDPRESS.COM.

Gifted Genie Publishing, *(978-0-9897187)* 149 Forestbrook Dr., Madison, AL 35757 USA Tel 256-527-2692; Fax: 866-819-4954
E-mail: giftedgenie1@hotmail.com.

Gifted Kids Bks., *(978-0-692-08230-0)* 207 Hillside Ave., New Hyde Park, NY 11040 USA Tel 718-673-0310
E-mail: mahvashfm@gmail.com.

Gifted Psychology Press, Incorporated *See* **Great Potential Pr., Inc.**

Gigarjian, Ani & Linda Avedikian, *(978-0-9717799)* 169 S. Main St., Sherborn, MA 01770 USA
E-mail: gigarjian@comcast.net
Web site: http://www.armeniankids.com.

Giggletins *Imprint of* **Le Bk. Moderne, LLC**

Giggling Gorilla Productions, LLC, *(978-0-9770700)* 3444 Laredo Ln., Escondido, CA 92025-7807 USA
E-mail: zoomanmike@earthlink.net
Web site: http://www.gigglinggorillaproductions.com.

GiGi Bks., *(978-0-9740847)* 17480 Old Waterford Rd., Leesburg, VA 20176 USA Tel 703-669-9781; Fax: 703-669-9782
E-mail: ganderson@gigiaudiobooks.com
Web site: http://www.gigiaudiobooks.com.

Gigi Costa, *(978-0-692-11572-5)* 3191 Coral Way, Coral Gables, FL 33145 USA Tel 305-978-3266
E-mail: gc@costalawmiami.com.

Gigi Enterprises, *(978-0-615-12926-6)* P.O. Box 133, Irvington, NY 10533-0133 USA Fax: 914-591-9249
E-mail: sonia0904@aol.com.

Gil Harp Bks., *(978-1-7335441)* 569 Cty. Line Rd., Wayne, PA 19087 USA Tel 917-971-3337
E-mail: javiergaray@gmail.com.

GIL Pubns., *(978-0-9626035; 978-0-9802185; 978-0-615-75814-5)* P.O. Box 80275, Brooklyn, NY 11208 USA Fax: 718-386-6434
E-mail: kumasi@gilpublications.com
Web site: http://www.gilpublications.com
Dist(s): **A & B Distributors & Pubs. Group**
Bk. Hse., Inc., The.

Gilbert, Drexel Enterprises, Inc., *(978-0-9818464)* Orders Addr.: P.O. Box 364, Daphne, AL 36526 USA
E-mail: drexelgilbert@drexelgilbert.com
Web site: http://www.drexelgilbert.com.

Gilbert Square Bks., *(978-0-9745308)* 2115 Plymouth SE, Grand Rapids, MI 49506 USA Tel 616-245-1050
E-mail: kvidro2003@yahoo.com
Web site: http://www.squarepears.com.

Gilboy Publishing, *(978-0-9774696)* 3521 River Narrows Rd., Hilliard, OH 43026-7833 USA.

Gilchrist & Guy Publishing, *(978-0-9747990)* 2112 Colina Vista Way, Costa Mesa, CA 92627 USA
E-mail: rguy2112@comcast.net.

Gilded Dog Enterprises LLC, *(978-0-9793483)* 106 High Point Dr., Churchville, PA 18966 USA (SAN 853-1943) Tel 215-322-5592; Fax: 215-396-6832
Web site: http://gildeddog.com.

Gilder Lehrman Institute of American History, The, *(978-0-9663843; 978-1-932821; 978-0-9970330; 978-1-953611)* Orders Addr.: 49 W. 45th St., 6th Flr., New York, NY 10036 USA Tel 646-366-9666; Fax: 646-366-9669
E-mail: ahlstrom@gilderlehrman.org
Web site: http://www.gilderlehrman.org.

Gile, John Communications *See* **JGC/United Publishing Corps**

Gilead Publishing, LLC, *(978-1-68370)* 304 E. Forest Ave., Wheaton, IL 60187 USA; *Imprints:* Enclave (EnclaveUSA); Evergreen Farm (EvergreenFarm)
Web site: www.gileadpublishing.com
Dist(s): **Kregel Pubns.**

Giles, D. Ltd. (GBR) *(978-1-904832; 978-1-907804; 978-1-911282) Dist. by* **Consort Bk Sales.**

Giles, W. Marie *See* **Giles, Willie M.**

Giles, Willie M., *(978-0-9728944)* Orders Addr.: P.O. Box 3757, Pensacola, FL 32516-3757 USA
Web site: http://www.wix.com/booksbywmariegiles
Dist(s): **CreateSpace Independent Publishing Platform.**

Gilgit Pr., LLC, *(978-0-9746283)* P.O. Box 4881, Richmond, VA 23220 USA
Web site: http://www.gilgitpress.com.

Gill Bks. (IRL) *Dist. by* **Casemate Pubs.**

Gill, Jim Music, *(978-0-9679038; 978-0-9815721)* Subs. of Jim Gill, Inc., Orders Addr.: P.O. Box 2263, Oak Park, IL 60303 USA Tel 708-763-9864; Fax: 708-763-9888; Edit Addr.: 835 N. Kenilworth Ave., Oak Park, IL 60303-9888 USA
E-mail: jimgill@jimgill.com
Web site: http://www.jimgill.com.

Gillespie, Lauren, *(978-0-692-19996-1)* 1311 N Main St, Naperville, IL 60563 USA Tel 480-840-5137
E-mail: orafrying@hotmail.com.

Gillette, Frances A., *(978-0-9636066)* P.O. Box 351, Yacolt, WA 98675 USA
E-mail: copia@copia.com; ward@infinitecolor.com; lithoinusa@centurytel.net
Web site: http://www.copia.com
Dist(s): **Adventure Pubns.**
Publishers Group West (PGW).

Gillgren, John, *(978-0-9798530)* 20716 Rainsboro Dr., Ashburn, VA 20147 USA (SAN 854-5502) Tel 703-724-1150.

Gilliam, T. & Associates, LLC, *(978-0-9762703)* 1696 Georgetown Rd., Unit B, Hudson, OH 44236 USA Tel 330-342-5940; Fax: 330-463-5730; Toll Free: 877-316-5097
E-mail: tgilliam@healthybodyweight.com
Web site: http://www.healthybodyweight.com.

Gilliam-Wilson, Tia, *(978-0-9986073)* P.O. Box 352, Gibsonville, NC 27249 USA Tel 336-267-6998
E-mail: tiagilliamwilson@gmail.com; tiagilliamwilson@gmail.com; tiagilliamwilson@gmail.com
Dist(s): **CreateSpace Independent Publishing Platform.**

Gillis-Smith, *(978-1-7331652)* 12555 Cherry Grove St., Moorpark, CA 93021 USA Tel 805-558-0561
E-mail: greg@gillis-smith.com
Web site: Gillis-SmithAuthor.com.

Gilpatrick, Gil, *(978-0-9650507)* Orders Addr.: P.O. Box 461, Skowhegan, ME 04976 USA Tel 207-453-6959; Edit Addr.: 369 Middle Rd., Fairfield, ME 04937 USA
E-mail: gil@gilgilpatrick.com
Web site: http://www.gilgilpatrick.com.

Gimme Gimme Toys & Games, Inc., *(978-0-9762524)* 1418 N. Clinton Blvd., Bloomington, IL 61701 USA
Web site: http://www.gimmegimme.ca
Dist(s): **PSI (Publisher Services, Inc.).**

Gina Art Books *See* **Pipton Pr.**

Gina's Ink, *(978-0-9740454)* P.O. Box 11650, Denver, CO 80211 USA
Web site: http://www.cassandrasangel.com.

Ginebra, Fidel, *(978-0-615-15410-7)* Urb. La Plata, M-19 Calle Rubi, Cayey, PR 00736 USA
E-mail: fbloodguard@gmail.com
Dist(s): **Lulu Pr., Inc.**

Ginger Nielson - Children's Bk. Illustration, *(978-0-615-92252-2; 978-0-9913093; 978-0-692-78023-7; 978-0-578-41662-5; 978-0-578-44108-5; 978-0-578-50225-0; 978-0-578-51323-2; 978-0-578-53427-5; 978-0-578-74028-7; 978-0-578-77783-2)* 278 Sand Hill Rd., Peterborough, NH 03458 USA Tel 603-924-3775; *Imprints:* HallaVision Publishing (MYID_X_HALLAVI)
E-mail: gingernielson@gmail.com.

Ginger Pr., The, *(978-0-9785151)* P.O. Box 45753, Omaha, NE 68145-0753 USA
Dist(s): **Greenleaf Book Group**
Independent Pubs. Group.

Gingerbread Hse., *(978-0-940112)* 602 Montauk Hwy., Westhampton Beach, NY 11978 USA (SAN 217-0760) Tel 631-288-5119; Fax: 631-288-5179 Do not confuse with Gingerbread House, The, Savannah GA
Web site: http://www.gingerbreadbooks.com
Dist(s): **Independent Pubs. Group.**

Gingko Pr. *Imprint of* **Gingko Pr., Inc.**

Gingko Pr., Inc., *(978-1-58423; 978-1-934471)* Orders Addr.: 1321 Fifth St., Berkeley, CA 94710 USA (SAN 860-4436) Tel 510-898-1195; Fax: 510-898-1196; *Imprints:* Gingko Press (Gingko) Do not confuse with Gingko Pr. in New York, NY
E-mail: account@gingkopress.com
Web site: http://www.gingkopress.com
Dist(s): **Ingram Publisher Services**
MyiLibrary
Publishers Group West (PGW).

Ginter, Judy, *(978-0-692-16194-4)* 11291 E. Wesley Ave., Aurora, CO 80014 USA Tel 303-695-8608
E-mail: jginter@msn.com
Dist(s): **Ingram Content Group.**

GIP House *See* **Summit Hse. Pubs.**

Girasol Collectables Inc., *(978-0-9797639; 978-0-9820890; 978-0-9820891; 978-0-9854755)* P.O. Box 5289, Mansfield, OH 44901-5289 USA
Web site: http://www.girasolcollectables.com.

Girl Named Pants, Inc., A, *(978-0-9755959)* 8954 Stonebriar Dr., Clarence Ctr., NY 14032-9373 USA
Web site: http://www.agirlnamedpants.com.

Girl Pr., Inc., *(978-0-9659754)* P.O. Box 480389, Los Angeles, CA 90048-1389 USA
E-mail: gp@girlpress.com
Web site: http://www.girlpress.com.

Girl Scouts of the USA, *(978-0-88441)* 420 Fifth Ave., New York, NY 10018 USA (SAN 203-4611) Tel 212-852-8000; Fax: 212-852-6511
E-mail: bnelson@girlscouts.org
Web site: http://www.girlscouts.org/.

Girl Twirl Comics, *(978-0-9742450; 978-0-9766707; 978-0-9794207)* Orders Addr.: P.O. Box 88, Sebastopol, CA 95473 USA Tel 707-546-7121 Do not confuse with Jane's World in Seattle, WA
Web site: http://www.janecomics.com
Dist(s): **Diamond Comic Distributors, Inc.**
Diamond Bk. Distributors.

Girls Explore *Imprint of* **Girls Explore LLC**

Girls Explore LLC, *(978-0-9749456)* Orders Addr.: P.O. Box 54, Basking Ridge, NJ 07920 USA (SAN 256-2677) Fax: 908-842-9166; *Imprints:* Girls Explore (GilExplore)
Web site: http://www.girls-explore.com
Dist(s): **Brodart Co.**

Girls In Da Game Publishing, *(978-0-9674454)* Orders Addr.: 5916 Las Virgenes Rd. No. 596, Calabasas, CA 91302 USA
E-mail: corneliagailgroundup@gmail.com
Web site: http://www.facebookthenewlook.com
Dist(s): **Ingram Content Group.**

GIRLS KNOW HOW *Imprint of* **NouSoma Communications, Inc.**

Girls of Faith, *(978-0-9764304)* P.O. Box 535, Rogersville, MO 65742 USA
E-mail: orders@girlsoffaith.com
Web site: http://www.girlsoffaith.com.

Girls-Connect *See* **Bizzy Girls Publishing**

Girn-Dolce, Nora, *(978-0-9974642)* 8502 139th Ave NE, Redmond, WA 98052 USA Tel 425-502-2223
E-mail: gironnora@hotmail.com.

Giro Pr., *(978-1-878857)* Orders Addr.: P.O. Box 203, Croton-on-Hudson, NY 10520 USA Tel 914-271-8924; Fax: 914-271-6552; Edit Addr.: 44 Morningside Dr., Croton-on-Hudson, NY 10520 USA
E-mail: info@giropress.com
Web site: http://www.giropress.com.

Giron Bks., *(978-0-9741393; 978-0-9915442)* 2141 W. 21st St., Chicago, IL 60608-2608 USA Tel 773-847-3000; Fax: 773-847-9197; Toll Free: 800-405-4276
E-mail: juanmanuel@gironbooks.com
Web site: http://www.gironbooks.com.

Gish Creative, *(978-0-9728507; 978-0-615-74202-1)* 1940-A Fountainview, PMB 116, Houston, TX 77057 USA Tel 713-532-1173 (phone/fax)
Web site: http://www.gishcreative.com; http://www.thesummerbook.com.

Giunti Gruppo Editoriale (ITA) *(978-88-09; 978-88-507; 978-88-440) Dist. by* **Distribks Inc.**

Giusti-Gambini, J.M. Publishing, LLC, *(978-0-615-36873-3; 978-0-9896496)* 7259 Creeks Bend Ct., West Bloomfield, MI 48322 USA Tel 248-855-0869
E-mail: jogambini@comcast.net
Web site: http://www.poetino.com; http://www.jmgiusti-gambinipublishing.com.

Gival Pr., LLC, *(978-1-928589; 978-1-940724)* P.O. Box PO Box 3812, Arlington, VA 22203 USA (SAN 852-9787) Tel 703-351-0079 (phone)
E-mail: givalpress@yahoo.com
Web site: http://www.givalpress.com; http://www.givalpressstore.com
Dist(s): **CreateSpace Independent Publishing Platform**
Ediciones Universal
Follett School Solutions.

Givens, Diane C. , *(978-1-7328014)* 8253 Seven Oaks Dr., Jonesboro, GA 30236 USA Tel 678-914-9355
E-mail: dianegivens3@gmail.com.

Givens, Florence Rosie *See* **FloBound Poems Publications**

Givinity Pr., *(978-0-9728654; 978-1-943803)* 3374 Maplewood Ct., Fargo, ND 58104-6224 USA (SAN 255-1527) Tel 701-235-4241; Fax: 701-280-2016; Toll Free: 866-221-5860
E-mail: ellen@givinity.com
Web site: http://www.givinity.com
Dist(s): **Brodart Co.**
Follett School Solutions.

GiWU Publishing, *(978-1-7335752)* 134 S. Mason, Chicago, IL 60644 USA Tel 773-688-5128
E-mail: Info@Giwupublishing.com
Web site: www.Giwupublishing.com.

Gizicki-Lipson, Coryn *See* **In the Sky Publishing**

Gizmo Enterprises, Inc., *(978-0-9759638; 978-1-7322455)* Orders Addr.: 6511 Nova Driver No. 108, Davie, FL 33317 USA
E-mail: Perrytheinventor+bowker@gmail.com; perry@colorcutter.com
Web site: http://www.colorcutter.com; http://www.gizmoLine.com.

Gizmo Pr., *(978-0-9749911)* 6990 Poco Bueno Cir., Sparks, NV 89436 USA Tel 775-626-4533; Fax: 775-425-5290
E-mail: mjarcher@aol.com; greg.nielsen@charter.net.

GL Design, *(978-0-9745882; 978-1-933983)* 3345 Chisholm Trail Apt 206, Boulder, CO 80301 USA
E-mail: distrib@gldesignpub.com
Web site: http://www.gldesignpub.com
Dist(s): **Ingram Content Group.**

Gladstone Publishing, *(978-1-928681)* Orders Addr.: 27 Sunny Bend, Newark, DE 19702 USA (SAN 254-8410) Tel 302-533-6831 Do not confuse with Gladstone Publishing, Prescott, AZ
E-mail: admin@yourinnerconfidence.com
Web site: http://www.yourinnerconfidence.com/smart-sojourner; http://www.yourinnerconfidence.com/smart-sojourner
Dist(s): **BookBaby.**

Glas Daggre Publishing, 61 collins St., ATTLEBORO, MA 02703 USA Tel 585-978-1057
E-mail: srstjean@gmail.com
Dist(s): **Ingram Content Group.**

Glass, Michael B. & Assocs., Inc., *(978-0-940429)* 735 Calebs Path/Glaro Bldg., Hauppauge, NY 11788 USA (SAN 664-3574).

Glass Onion Publishing, *(978-0-9986381; 978-1-947678)* 16685 Lake Circle Dr., No. 1020, Fort Myers, FL 33908 USA Tel 239-910-1355; *Imprints:* Happy Dolphin Press (MYID_U_HAPPY D)
E-mail: editor@happydolphinpress.com
Web site: www.PubSmithPress.com; www.GlassOnionPublishing.com; www.HappyDolphinPress.com.

†Glastonbury Pr., *(978-0-944963)* Orders Addr.: 454 Las Gallinas Ave., No. 108, San Rafael, CA 94903 USA Tel 415-492-2140; 415-686-4150 Do not confuse with Glastonbury Pr., Whittier, CA
E-mail: starstone@comcast.net; misty@glastonburypress.com
Web site: http://www.glastonburypress.com
Dist(s): **CreateSpace Independent Publishing Platform**; *CIP.*

Glavin, Kevin, *(978-0-9825466)* 23 Vassar Aisle, Irvine, CA 92612 USA
E-mail: admin@kevinglavinpublishing.com
Web site: http://www.rockstarsrainbow.com; http://www.kevinglavinpublishing.com.

Gleasner, Bill & Diana Inc., *(978-0-9651185)* 7994 Holly Ct., Denver, NC 28037 USA Tel 704-483-9301; Fax: 704-483-6309
E-mail: dgleasner@aol.com
Dist(s): **Booklines Hawaii, Ltd.**

Glen Enterprises, *(978-1-880215)* 1202 Wildwood Dr., Deer Park, TX 77536 USA Tel 281-479-2759
E-mail: purdys@flash.net.

Glenbridge Publishing, Ltd., *(978-0-944435)* 19923 E. Long Ave., Centennial, CO 80016 USA (SAN 243-5403) Tel 720-870-8381; Fax: 720-230-1209; Toll Free: 800-986-4135 (orders only)
E-mail: glenbridge@qwestoffice.net
Web site: http://www.glenbridgepublishing.com.

Glencannon Pr., *(978-0-9637586; 978-1-889901)* Orders Addr.: P.O. Box 1428, El Cerrito, CA 94530 USA; *Imprints:* Palo Alto Books (Palo Alto)
E-mail: merships@yahoo.com
Web site: http://www.glencannon.com.

†Glencoe/McGraw-Hill, *(978-0-02; 978-0-07)* Div. of The McGraw-Hill Education Group, 8787 Orion Pl.,

Columbus, OH 43240-4027 USA Toll Free: 800-334-7344
E-mail: customer.service@mcgraw-hill.com
Web site: http://www.glencoe.com
Dist(s): **Follett School Solutions**
Libros Sin Fronteras
McGraw-Hill Cos., The; *CIP.*

Glenhaven Pr., *(978-0-9637265; 978-0-9741279)* 24871 Pylos Way, Mission Viejo, CA 92691 USA Tel 949-770-1486
E-mail: glenhavn@thevision.net; jacki@hydrasystems.com
Dist(s): **J & J Bk. Sales.**

Glenmere Pr., *(978-0-9852948; 978-0-9903139)* Orders Addr.: 26 Kings Ridge Rd., Warwick, NY 10990 USA
E-mail: lois@glenmerepress.com; lois@wingedbooks.com
Web site: http://www.glenmerepress.com; http://www.wingedbooks.com
Dist(s): **CreateSpace Independent Publishing Platform**
INscribe Digital
Independent Pubs. Group
Ingram Content Group.

Glenn, Lauren, *(978-0-9772459)* 2436 Oakdale St., Tallahassee, FL 32308 USA.

Glenn, Peter Pubns., *(978-0-87314)* 824 E. Atlantic Ave. Ste. 7, Delray Beach, FL 33483-5300 USA (SAN 201-9930)
E-mail: gjames@pgdirect.com
Web site: http://www.pgdirect.com.

Glenn Young Bks., *(978-1-55783)* 253 W. 72nd St., New York, NY 10023 USA Tel 212-595-2082
Dist(s): **Leonard, Hal Corp.**
National Bk. Network.

Glenneyre Pr. LLC, *(978-0-9768040; 978-1-934602)* 20555 Devonshire St., Box 203, Chatsworth, CA 91311-9133 USA
E-mail: myn@wordsushi.com
Web site: http://www.glenneyrepress.com.

Glens Falls Printing LLC, *(978-1-933575)* 51 Hudson Ave., Glens Falls, NY 12801 USA (SAN 256-7148) Tel 518-793-0555; Fax: 518-793-8624; Toll Free: 866-793-0555
E-mail: bob@gfprinting.com
Web site: http://www.gfprinting.com; http://www.spiritoftheadirondacksbook.com; http://www.commonmanbooks.com.

Glitter Creek, Inc., *(978-0-9744520)* 2919 Westridge Ave., Cincinnati, OH 45238 USA Toll Free: 888-982-7335
Web site: http://www.glittercreek.com.

Glitterati Incorporated *See* **G Arts LLC**

GLM Publishing, *(978-0-578-14076-6; 978-0-9863604; 978-0-9973325)* 2165 NW 30th Rd., Boca Raton, FL 33431 USA.

Global Academic Publishing, *(978-0-9633277; 978-1-883058; 978-1-58684)* Global Academic Publishing, Binghamton Univ., Binghamton, NY 13902-6000 USA Tel 607-777-4495; 607-777-2745 (contact Barnes & Noble for orders); Fax: 607-777-6132
E-mail: gporders@binghamton.edu
Web site: http://www.academicpublishing.binghamton.edu
Dist(s): **Hesteria Records & Publishing Co.**
State Univ. of New York Pr.

Global Age Publishing/Global Academy Pr., *(978-1-887176)* 16057 Tampa Palms Blvd., W., No. 219, Tampa, FL 33647 USA Tel 813-991-4982; Fax: 813-973-8166.

Global Alliances, *(978-0-9759126)* 82-09 166th St., Hillcrest, NY 11432 USA.

Global Authors Pubns., *(978-0-9728513; 978-0-9742161; 978-0-9766449; 978-0-9779680; 978-0-9798087; 978-0-9821223; 978-0-9845926; 978-0-9846536; 978-0-9861109)* P.O. Box 954, Green Cove Springs, FL 32043 USA; 730 Donnelly St., Eustis, FL 32726 Tel 904-425-1608
E-mail: gapbook@yahoo.com
Web site: http://www.globalauthorspublications.com.

Global Awareness Publishing Co., *(978-1-885888)* 1102 Hickory St., Madison, WI 53715-1726 USA.

Global Business Info USA *See* **Global Pro Info USA**

Global Business Information Strategies, Inc., *(978-1-60231)* Orders Addr.: P.O. Box 610135, Newton, MA 02461 USA (SAN 852-1980) Tel 617-795-0519; Fax: 617-795-0211; Edit Addr.: 965 Walnut St., Suite 100, Newton, MA 02461 USA; *Imprints:* Cub Books (Cub Bks)
E-mail: publishing@gbisi.com
Web site: http://gbisi.com.

Global Commitment Publishing, *(978-1-884931)* Div. of Alpert & Assocs., 3544 Winfield Ln., NW, Washington, DC 20007 USA Tel 202-338-4975; Fax: 202-835-0668; 5505 Connecticut Ave., Washington, DC 20015.

Global Communications *See* **Inner Light - Global Communications**

Global Community Communications Publishing, *(978-0-9647357; 978-0-9822423; 978-1-937919)* P.O. Box 1613, Tubac, AZ 85646-1613 USA Tel 520-603-9932
E-mail: info@GlobalCommunityCommunicationsPublishing.org
Web site: http://www.GlobalCommunityCommunicationsPublishing.org.

Global Content Ventures, *(978-0-9799901)* P.O. Box 6370, Lancaster, PA 17607 USA.

Global counseling & coaching services , inc, *(978-0-9905718; 978-1-7328275)* 650 Maitland Ave, Altamonte Springs, FL 32701 USA Tel 781-254-1602
E-mail: Drstem14@gmail.com
Web site: www.drstemspeaks.com; www.amazon.com; Www.drstemmie.com.

Global Education Advance, *(978-0-9796019; 978-0-9801674; 978-1-935434; 978-1-950839)* 345 Barton Rd. at Lone Mountain, Dayton, TN 37321-7635 USA Tel 423-775-2949
E-mail: GlobalEdAdvance@aol.com
Web site: http://www.globaledadvance.org.

Global Education Resources, LLC, *(978-1-934046)* 37 Station Rd., Madison, NJ 07940 USA (SAN 851-1012) Tel 973-410-0840; Fax: 973-410-1603
E-mail: myoshida@globaledresources.com
Web site: http://www.globaledresources.com.

Global Goddess Pr., *(978-0-692-71437-9)* 20212 Village 20, Camarillo, CA 93012 USA Tel 805-504-5050
E-mail: endangeredabcs@yahoo.com.

Global Institute for Maximizing Potential, Incorporated, *(978-0-9772020; 978-0-9825776; 978-0-9830337)* 92 Mt. Zion Way, Ocean Grove, NJ 07756 USA Tel 732-776-7360
E-mail: richert@globalinst.com
Web site: http://www.globalinst.com.

Global Learning, Inc., *(978-1-59867)* 1001 SE Water Ave., Suite 310, Portland, OR 97214 USA Toll Free: 888-548-2787 Do not confuse with Global Learning Inc. in Brielle, NJ
Web site: http://www.litart.com.

Global Partnership, LLC, *(978-0-9644706)* Orders Addr.: P.O. Box 894, Murray, KY 42071 USA (SAN 255-4186) Tel 562-884-0062; Edit Addr.: 100 N. 6th St., Murray, KY 42071 USA
E-mail: steveneschmitt@cs.com; erin@wakeuplive.com
Web site: http://www.businessolympians.com
Dist(s): **Seven Locks Pr.**

Global Pr., *(978-0-9792151)* 2083 Ridge Point Dr., Los Angeles, CA 90049 USA Tel 310-476-8336.

Global Pro Info USA, *(978-0-7397; 978-0-9646241; 978-1-57751; 978-1-4330; 978-1-4387; 978-1-5145)* 6301 Stevenson Ave Suite 1317, Alexandria, VA 22304 USA Tel 703-370-8082; Fax: 703-370-8082; 6301 Stevenson Ave., # 1317, Alexandria, VA 22304 Tel 202-656-2103; Fax: 202-546-3275 Do not confuse with International Business Pubn., Inc. in Cincinnati, OH
E-mail: ibpusa3@gmail.com
Web site: http://www.ibpus.com
Dist(s): **Lulu Pr., Inc.**

Global Publications (S S I P S) *See* **Global Academic Publishing**

Global Publishing, *(978-0-911649)* 51 Bell Rock Plaza, Suite A, PMB 511, Sedona, AZ 86351 USA (SAN 299-3627) Tel 928-284-5544; Fax: 928-284-5545 Do not confuse with companies with the same or similar name in Meimingham, MI, Costa Mesa, CA, Las Angeles, CA, Florence, MA, Memphis, TN, Sauk Rapids, MN, Fort Lauderdale, FL, Fort Worth, TX, Salt Lake City, UT
E-mail: minorwood@earthlink.net
Web site: http://www.wealthysoul.com
Dist(s): **New Leaf Distributing Co., Inc.**

Global Summit Hse., 511 Ave. of the Americas, Unit 949, New York, NY 10011 USA Tel 347-901-4929
E-mail: karensmith@globalsummithouse.com.

Global Truth Publishing, *(978-0-9740465)* Orders Addr.: 1001 Bridgeway, Suite 474, Sausalito, CA 94965 USA Tel 415-331-1102; Fax: 415-331-2265
E-mail: sales@globaltruthpublishing.com
Web site: http://www.globaltruthpublishing.com.

Global Village Kids, LLC, *(978-0-9760472)* 4111 Calavo Dr., La Mesa, CA 91941-7051 USA Tel 619-303-0929; Fax: 925-888-8471
E-mail: seth.burns@globalvillagekids.com
Web site: http://www.globalvillagekids.com
Dist(s): **AV Cafe, Inc., The**
BWI
Iaconi, Mariuccia Bk. Imports
Wayland Audio-Visual.

GlobalVision Travel Resources, Inc., *(978-0-9800147)* 4831 Las Virgenes Rd., No. 115, Calabasas, CA 91302-1911 USA
E-mail: LCohen@getglobalvision.com
Web site: http://getglobalvision.com.

GLOBE *Imprint of* **Savvas Learning Co.**

Globe Fearon Educational Publishing, *(978-0-13; 978-0-8224; 978-0-8359; 978-0-87065; 978-0-88102; 978-0-912925; 978-0-915510; 978-1-55555; 978-1-55675)* Div. of Pearson Education Corporate Communications, Orders Addr.: 4350 Equity Dr., P.O. Box 2649, Columbus, OH 43216-2649 USA Toll Free Fax: 800-393-3156; Toll Free: 800-848-9500; 800-321-3106 (customer service); Edit Addr.: One Lake St., Upper Saddle River, NJ 07458 USA
Web site: http://www.pearsonschool.com
Dist(s): **Cambridge Bk. Co.**
Follett School Solutions
IFSTA.

†Globe Pequot Pr., The, *(978-0-7627; 978-0-87106; 978-0-88742; 978-0-914788; 978-0-933469; 978-0-934802; 978-0-941130; 978-1-56440; 978-1-57034; 978-1-57392; 978-1-58574; 978-1-59228; 978-1-59921; 978-1-4779; 978-1-4930)* Orders Addr.: P.O. Box 480, Guilford, CT 06437-0480 USA (SAN 201-9892) Tel 888-249-7586; Toll Free Fax: 800-820-2329 (in Connecticut); Toll Free: 800-243-0495 (24 hours); 800-336-8334; Edit Addr.: 246 Goose Ln., Guilford, CT 06437 USA Tel 203-458-4500; Fax: 203-458-4600; Toll Free Fax: 800-336-8334; *Imprints:* Lyons Press (Lyons); Falcon Guides (Fal-Guides); TwoDot (Two-D)
E-mail: info@globepequot.com
Web site: http://www.globepequot.com
Dist(s): **Chelsea Green Publishing**
MyiLibrary
National Bk. Network
Rowman & Littlefield Publishers, Inc.; *CIP.*

Globe Pubs., *(978-0-9623663; 978-1-882614)* 724 Fair Meadows Dr., Saginaw, TX 76179-1017 USA.

Globe Publishing, *(978-0-9765168)* Orders Addr.: P.O. Box 3040, Pensacola, FL 32516-3040 USA Tel 850-453-3453; Fax: 850-456-6001; Edit Addr.: 8590 Hwy 98 W., Pensacola, FL 32506 USA Do not confuse with Globe Publishing in Salt Lake City, UT
Web site: http://www.gme.org.

Globetrotta Productions, *(978-0-692-69235-6)* 1706 Fox Hill Rd., Sheboygan, WI 53081 USA Tel 920-334-0937
E-mail: lctrotta53072@yahoo.com.

Globo, Editora SA (BRA) *(978-85-217; 978-85-250) Dist. by* **Distribks Inc.**

Globo Libros, *(978-0-9706953)* Orders Addr.: P.O. Box 4025, Sunnyside, NY 11104 USA; Edit Addr.: 402 E. 64th St. Apt. 6C, New York, NY 10021-7826 USA
E-mail: dstockwell@globolibros.com
Web site: http://www.globolibros.com.

Glolar Multimedia Productions, *(978-0-9707746)* P.O. Box 721452, San Diego, CA 92172-1452 USA
E-mail: info@Glolar.com; info@glolar.com
Web site: http://www.glolar.com.

Glory Be Collectibles, *(978-0-9795127; 978-0-578-06528-1; 978-0-578-07491-7)* 2169 Green Canyon Rd., Fallbrook, CA 92028 USA (SAN 853-6627) Tel 760-723-5222; Fax: 760-723-4433
E-mail: sales@glorybe.com
Web site: http://www.glorybe.com.

Glory Bound Books Las Vegas *See* **Glorybound Publishing**

Glory Days Group Publishing, *(978-0-9755145)* P.O. Box 1869, Glen Burnie, MD 21060-1869 USA Tel 410-766-0005 (phone/fax); *Imprints:* Gibson Books (Gibson Bks)
E-mail: drgibson123@yahoo.com
Web site: http://www.glorydayspublishing2day4u.com.

Glorybound Publishing, *(978-0-9766718; 978-0-9779654; 978-0-9802481; 978-1-60789)* 349 S. 6th St., Camp Verde, AZ 86322 USA (SAN 256-4564) Do not confuse with Glory Bound Books in Marlette, MI
E-mail: sherihauser@yahoo.com; gloryboundpublishing@yahoo.com
Web site: http://www.gloryboundpublishing.com.

Glover Publishing and Community Outsourcing, *(978-0-692-81946-3; 978-0-9986222)* 16306 Thornridge Dr., Grand Blanc, MI 48501 USA Tel 810-423-5118
E-mail: gg.writer.glove@gmail.com; gg.writer.glove@gmail.com; gg.writer.glove@gmail.com
Web site: www.GloverPCO.com
Dist(s): **CreateSpace Independent Publishing Platform.**

Glow Word Bks., *(978-0-9859834; 978-1-942514)* P.O. Box 705, Willernie, MN 55090 USA Tel 720-443-3320
E-mail: glowwordbooks@gmail.com
Web site: http://www.glowwordbooks.com
Dist(s): **CreateSpace Independent Publishing Platform**
Ingram Content Group.

Glowacki, Helen, *(978-0-9847211; 978-0-9890214; 978-0-9893807; 978-0-9913916)* 2319 Saratoga Bay Dr., West Palm Beach, FL 33409 USA Tel 561-845-8493
E-mail: wally_helen@yahoo.com
Web site: www.helenglowacki.com.

Glynworks Publishing, *(978-0-9795912)* 2630 International Dr. #929b, Ypsilanti, MI 48197 USA
Web site: http://www.glynworkspublishing.com
Dist(s): **Ingram Content Group.**

GMC Distribution (GBR) *(978-0-946819; 978-1-86108; 978-1-78494) Dist. by* **IngramPubServ.**

GMEC Publishing, *(978-0-9794302)* P.O. Box 4470, Lake Tahoe, NV 89449-4470 USA Tel 704-992-2272; Fax: 704-992-2271
E-mail: MrsButtar@aol.com; StoriesThatTeach@aol.com
Web site: http://www.DebbieButtar.com; http://www.ChildrensStoriesThatTeach.com.

GMI Bks., *(978-0-9841809)* 7250 Franklin Ave., No.1407, Hollywood, CA 90046 USA
E-mail: richard@thegirlfromatlantis.com; doubleosix@aol.com
Web site: http://www.thegirlfromatlantis.com.

GMKelso, *(978-1-7331092)* 20620 Youpon Ln, PORTER, TX 77365 USA Tel 281-755-7330
E-mail: pegasusfury333@yahoo.com
Dist(s): **Ingram Content Group.**

Gnatcatcher Children'S Bks., *(978-0-9778005)* 1451 E. Armando Dr., Long Beach, CA 90807 USA Tel 562-427-1200
E-mail: maryhoch@excite.com.

GND Publishing *See* **Y-IREAD Publishing**

Gnosophia Pubs., *(978-0-9773391)* 3800 New Hampshire Ave. NW Apt 507, Washington, DC 20011-7932 USA (SAN 257-3210) Tel 202-709-7580; Toll Free Fax: 866-525-0247
E-mail: admin@wisdomforthesoul.org; info@wisdomforthesoul.org; admin@gnosophia.com
Web site: http://www.wisdomforthesoul.org; http://www.gnosophia.com.

Go Ask Anyone, Inc., *(978-0-9742866)* 38 Irwin St., No.3, Winthrop, MA 02152 USA
Web site: http://www.goaskanyone.com.

Go Daddy Productions, Inc., *(978-0-9753938)* 2010 Ripley Point Ct., Odenton, MD 21113 USA Tel 443-226-4747
E-mail: mejagan@yahoo.com
Web site: http://www.go-daddyproductions.com.

Go Flag Football, *(978-0-9772203)* 1978 Shiloh Valley Trail, Kennesaw, GA 30144 USA
Web site: http://www.goflagfootball.com.

Go Jolly Bks., *(978-0-9822824; 978-1-942937)* P.O. Box 2203, Port Angeles, WA 98362 USA
Web site: http://www.gojollybooks.com.

GO Publishing Co., *(978-0-9640713; 978-1-892951; 978-0-9998032; 978-0-578-73897-0)* Orders Addr.: 338 Wekiva Cove Rd., Longwood, FL 32779 USA Tel 407-463-5464
E-mail: wmg@fprint.net.

Go Team, LLC, *(978-0-9797040)* 1427 Heatherwood Rd., Columbia, SC 29205 USA (SAN 854-1566)
E-mail: deliacorrigan@mindspring.com
Web site: http://www.goteambooks.com.

Goal Pubns., *(978-0-9979125; 978-1-949768)* 710 River View Ln., Norwich, CT 06374 USA Tel 860-546-8377
E-mail: professionaljunk@anthroaquatic.com
Web site: www.goalpublications.com.

Goat Song Publishing, *(978-0-692-90923-2; 978-0-692-92333-7; 978-0-692-98176-4; 978-0-692-06808-3)* 7619 Hwy. 70 S PO Box 218482, NASHVILLE, TN 37221 USA Tel 703-407-4654
E-mail: goatsongpub@gmail.com
Dist(s): **CreateSpace Independent Publishing Platform**
Ingram Content Group.

Goatee Graphics, *(978-0-9657257)* P.O. Box 591840, San Francisco, CA 94159-1840 USA (SAN 256-8985) Tel 415-272-6117
E-mail: goatee848@yahoo.com
Web site: http://www.undertherimbook.com.

Goblin Fern Pr. *Imprint of* **HenschelHAUS Publishing, Inc.**

Goddess Enterprises *See* **Goodness Experience, The**

†Godine, David R. Pub., *(978-0-87923; 978-1-56792; 978-1-57423)* Orders Addr.: P.O. Box 450, Jaffrey, NH 03452 USA Tel 603-532-4100; Fax: 603-532-5940; Toll Free Fax: 800-226-0934; Toll Free: 800-344-4771; Edit Addr.: Fifteen Court Sq., Suite 320, Boston, MA 02108 USA (SAN 213-4381) Tel 617-451-9600; Fax: 617-350-0250; *Imprints:* Non Pareil Books (Non Pareil Bk)
E-mail: info@godine.com; order@godine.com
Web site: http://www.godine.com
Dist(s): **Baker & Taylor International**
INscribe Digital
Independent Pubs. Group
Ingram Publisher Services
MyiLibrary
Two Rivers Distribution
eBookit.com; *CIP.*

Godinez-Hammermaster Design, *(978-0-9773205)* Orders Addr.: 411 Garonne St., Oxnard, CA 93036 USA; Edit Addr.: 122 Eugenia Dr., Ventura, CA 93003 USA (SAN 257-7127)
E-mail: artposter3@gmail.com.

Godiva Girl Records & Publishing, Incorporated *See* **Girls In Da Game Publishing**

God's Bible School & College *See* **Revivalist Pr., The**

God's Glory Media, *(978-0-9772647; 978-1-7327861)* Div. of God's Glory Ministries International Inc., P.O. Box 1430, Dacula, GA 30019 USA (SAN 257-1528)
E-mail: office@godsglory.org
Web site: http://www.GodsGlory.org.

God's Greatest Gift, LLC, *(978-0-9796477)* Orders Addr.: P.O. Box 185, Manchester, MI 48158-8513 USA (SAN 853-9855) Tel 734-320-5111; Edit Addr.: 520 City Rd., Manchester, MI 48158-8513 USA Fax: 734-428-0084
E-mail: godsgreatestgift@comcast.net
Web site: http://www.godsgreatestgift.net
Dist(s): **Partners Pubs. Group, Inc.**

God's World Publications *See* **God's World Pubns. Inc.**

God's World Pubns. Inc., *(978-1-882440; 978-0-9844605; 978-0-9855957)* 12 All Souls Crescent, Asheville, NC 28803 USA (SAN 254-1696) Tel 828-253-8063; Fax: 828-253-1556
E-mail: edufeedback@ gwpub.com; pub@gwnews.com
Web site: http://www.learnwithworld.com/writewithworld/.

Godspeed Pr., *(978-0-9798250)* 430 Davis Dr., Suite 270, Morrisville, NC 27560 USA Tel 404-457-4097
E-mail: deanthewriter@gmail.com.

Goff Bks. *Imprint of* **ORO Editions**

GoGo Pr., *(978-0-9769028)* Orders Addr.: 6007 Hickory Valley Rd., Nashville, TN 37205 USA (SAN 257-1412) Tel 615-356-6571; Fax: 615-356-9609
E-mail: info@gogopress.com; paul@pbuff.com
Web site: http://www.gogopress.com.

Goin' Native, Inc., *(978-0-9891323; 978-0-692-83288-2)* P.O. Box 617153, Orlando, FL 32861 USA Tel 407-897-3522; Fax: 407-896-4614
E-mail: info@goinnative.com.

GoKnow, Incorporated *See* **GoKnow Learning**

GoKnow Learning, *(978-0-9762083; 978-0-9767504; 978-0-9786499)* 2084 S. State St., Ann Arbor, MI 48104-4608 USA Toll Free: 877-482-3439
Web site: http://www.goknow.com.

Golaboff, Laura J., *(978-0-9996184)* 4797 Westfield Dr., Hampstead, MD 21074 USA Tel 410-374-3435
E-mail: jlgolab@verizon.net.

Golan, Hanna, *(978-0-9779723)* 17340 Hamlin St., Lake Balboa, CA 91406 USA (SAN 850-7732) Tel 818-342-4969
E-mail: hannagolan2000@yahoo.com
Web site: http://blessthechildren.com.

GO-LA-NV Pr., *(978-0-9741828)* P.O. Box 1897, Huntsville, TX 77342-1897 USA Tel 936-291-2906
E-mail: rhvann@sbcglobal.net.

Gold 5 Publishing, *(978-0-9904017)* 5599 Sherwood Ct., Newburgh, IN 47630 USA Tel 334-614-6103
E-mail: gold5publishing@gmail.com.

Gold Angel Press *See* **ONLY1EARTH, LLC**

Gold Boy Music & Pubn., *(978-0-9761992)* 108 Highland Tr., Chapel Hill, NC 27516 USA (SAN 256-2499) Tel 919-500-3023
E-mail: rob@musicgoldboy.com
Web site: thechristmasauntie.com; http://www.musicgoldboy.com
Dist(s): **BCH Fulfillment & Distribution.**

Publisher Name Index

Gold Boy Music & Publishing *See* **Gold Boy Music & Pubn.**

Gold Charm Publishing, LLC, *(978-0-9744855)* Orders Addr.: P.O. Box 161, Nottingham, NH 03290 USA Tel 603-942-7925 (phone/fax); Edit Addr.: 82 Priest Rd., Nottingham, NH 03290 USA.

Gold Design, LLC *See* **Toy Rocket Studios, LLC**

Gold Leaf Pr., *(978-1-886769)* Orders Addr.: 2229 Alter Rd., Detroit, MI 48215 USA Tel 313-331-3571; 262-342-0018 Oleand Publications; Fax: 313-308-3063; 262-342-0018 Oleand Publications; Toll Free: 800-838-8854 Do not confuse with companies with the same name in Seattle, WA, Starke FL
E-mail: rebecca@goldleafpress.com; wings@oleand.com
Web site: http://www.goldleafpress.com; http://www.oleand.com
Dist(s): **Oleand Pubns.**

Gold Street Pr., *(978-1-934533)* 814 Montgomery St., San Francisco, CA 94133 USA Tel 415-291-0100; Fax: 415-291-8841
E-mail: michelled!@weldonowen.com
Web site: http://www.weldonowen.com; http://www.goldstreetpress.com.

Gold Street Pubs. *Imprint of* **Fallick, Barbara**

Gold Sun Publishing, *(978-0-9886549; 978-0-578-53091-8; 978-0-578-55939-1; 978-0-578-69936-3; 978-1-7354679)* 1325 Wolf St., Philadelphia, PA 19148 USA Tel 610-241-0256
E-mail: Roncostello@mail.com.

Golden Alley Pr., *(978-0-9895265; 978-0-9984429; 978-1-7320276; 978-1-7333055)* 37 S. 6th St., Emmaus, PA 18049 USA Tel 610-966-4440
E-mail: nsayre@goldenalleypress.com
Web site: http://www.goldenalleypress.com.

Golden Anchor Pr., *(978-1-886864)* 625 Elrod Rd., Bowling Green, KY 42104 USA Tel 270-780-9334
E-mail: smithdale2@aol.com; goldnanchr@aol.com
Web site: http://www.Everykidawinner.com
Dist(s): **Partners/West Book Distributors**
Quality Bks., Inc.
Unique Bks., Inc.

Golden Bks. *Imprint of* **Random Hse. Children's Bks.**

Golden Bks. *Imprint of* **Random Hse., Inc.**

Golden Bks. Adult Publishing Group *Imprint of* **St. Martin's Pr.**

Golden, Brian *See* **PastWays Inc.**

Golden Crown Publishing, LLC, *(978-1-7342322)* 445 Pk. St, Deerfield, MI 49238 USA Tel 419-350-1796
E-mail: sarah@sarah-sutton.com
Web site: www.sarah-sutton.com.

Golden Door Pr., *(978-0-692-96859-8)* 82 ellen st, Riverhead, NY 11901 USA Tel 631-727-6728
E-mail: bmasonrast@aol.com.

Golden Eagle Publishing Hse., Inc., *(978-0-9744205; 978-0-9753533; 978-0-9759122; 978-0-9769364)* 9201 Wilshire Blvd., Suite 205, Beverly Hills, CA 90210 USA Tel 310-273-9176; Fax: 310-273-0954
E-mail: info@goldeneaglepublishing.com
Web site: http://www.goldeneaglepublishing.com
Dist(s): **Greenleaf Book Group.**

Golden Gate National Parks Conservancy, *(978-0-9625206; 978-1-883869; 978-1-932519)* 201 Fort Mason, 3rd Flr., San Francisco, CA 94123 USA Tel 415-561-3000; Fax: 415-561-3033
Web site: http://www.parksconservancy.org/
Dist(s): **Yosemite Conservancy.**

Golden Gate Publishing, *(978-0-9856631)* P.O. Box 27478, San Francisco, CA 94127 USA Tel 415-753-2930
E-mail: GoldenGatePublishing@gmail.com
Web site: GoldenGatePublish.com.

Golden Gryphon Pr., *(978-0-9655901; 978-1-930846)* 3002 Perkins Rd., Urbana, IL 61802 USA (SAN 299-1829) Tel 217-384-4205 (phone/fax); Fax: 217-352-9748
E-mail: Gryphon@goldengryphon.com
Web site: http://www.goldengryphon.com
Dist(s): **MyiLibrary**
ebrary, Inc.

Golden Guides from Saint Martin's Pr. *Imprint of* **St. Martin's Pr.**

Golden Harvest Publishing Co., *(978-0-9747904)* 4849 Valley Rd., Rosedale, VA 24280 USA Tel 276-880-9862; Fax: 276-880-1146
E-mail: adda@mounet.com.

Golden Imprint Pubns., *(978-0-9989194)* P.O. Box 20333, Rancho Santa Fe, CA 92067 USA Tel 858-754-7987
E-mail: darcyneils@yahoo.com
Web site: www.goldenimrintpublications.com.

Golden Inspirational *Imprint of* **Random Hse. Children's Bks.**

GOLDEN LIBERTY, *(978-0-578-59944-1)* 7521 Carpenter St., Port Richey, FL 34668 USA Tel 727-831-8301
E-mail: gloriateschofficial@gmail.com.

Golden Light Factory, *(978-1-7327645)* 4006 Darling Hill Rd, East Burke, VT 05832 USA Tel 802-626-5152
E-mail: hope@goldenlightfactory.com
Web site: www.goldenlightfactory.com.

Golden Mastermind Seminars, Inc., *(978-0-9740924; 978-1-934919; 978-0-692-03130-8; 978-0-578-20058-3)* Orders Addr.: 6507 Pacific Ave., Suite 329, Stockton, CA 95207 USA (SAN 255-2639) Fax: 209-467-3260; Toll Free: 800-595-6632
E-mail: Jeff@goldenmastermind.com; Carolyn@goldenmastermind.com
Web site: http://www.goldenmastermind.com.

Golden Monkey Publishing, LLC, *(978-0-9719632)* 24 Meadowood Ln., Old Saybrook, CT 06475 USA (SAN 254-5322)
Web site: http://www.goldenmonkeypublishing.com.

Golden Moon Design, *(978-0-692-93327-5)* 3815 N. Kedzie Ave. Unit 3S, Chicago, IL 60618 USA Tel 773-817-5386
E-mail: hemanshoe@gmail.com
Dist(s): **Ingram Content Group.**

Golden Oak Publishers *See* **Golden Oak Pubs. L.P.**

Golden Oak Pubs. L.P., *(978-1-929248; 978-1-936346)* Orders Addr.: P.O. Box 136967, Fort Worth, TX 76163 USA Tel 800-479-3545; Toll Free Fax: 800-479-3545
E-mail: MattS@goldenoakpublishers.com
Web site: http://www.HaroldBullock.com.

Golden Peach Publishing, *(978-1-930655)* 1223 Wilshire Blvd., #1510, Santa Monica, CA 90403 USA Tel 310-623-0835; 310-272-6809
E-mail: marketing@goldenpeachbooks.com; info@goldenpeachbooks.com; goldenpeachbooks@gmail.com
Web site: http://goldenpeachbooks.com.

Golden Perils Pr., *(978-0-615-15007-9; 978-0-615-19452-3; 978-0-578-00320-7; 978-0-578-00360-3; 978-0-578-00361-0)* 2 McKee Dr., Old Orchard Beach, ME 04064 USA Tel 207-934-3074
E-mail: goldenperils@aol.com
Web site: http://www.howardhopkins.com
Dist(s): **Lulu Pr., Inc.**

Golden Poppy Pubns., *(978-0-9890572; 978-1-945329)* 14313 Valley Vista Blvd., Sherman Oaks, CA 91423 USA Tel 818-501-8423
E-mail: dnehamen@gmail.com.

Golden Rain Tree Pr., *(978-0-9744107)* Div. of Leland Foerster Photography, 307 Fowles St., Oceanside, CA 92054 USA Tel 760-433-2554 (phone/fax)
E-mail: lelandfoerster@sbcglobal.net
Web site: http://www.lelandfoerster.com
Dist(s): **Sunbelt Pubns., Inc.**

Golden Valley Pr., *(978-0-9718053)* 24905 Mica Ridge Rd., Custer, SD 57730 USA
E-mail: horsted@dakotaphoto.com
Web site: http://www.goldenvalleypress.com.

Golden Voice Enterprises, *(978-0-9643301)* 8503 Summerdale Rd., No. 371, San Diego, CA 92126 USA.

Golden West Publishers *Imprint of* **American Traveler Pr.**

Golden Wings Enterprises, *(978-0-9700103; 978-0-9749241; 978-0-9794340)* P.O. Box 468, Orem, UT 84059-0468 USA
E-mail: BJ@bjrowley.com
Web site: http://www.bjrowley.com.

Golden/Disney *Imprint of* **Random Hse. Children's Bks.**

Goldenrod Pr., *(978-0-9748333)* Orders Addr.: P.O. Box 71, Algona, IA 50511 USA Tel 515-295-7090; Edit Addr.: 2509 S. State St., Algona, IA 50511-7296 USA
E-mail: slotjm@yahoo.com.

Goldest Karat Publishing, *(978-1-939509)* 340 S LEMON AVE No. 1077, Walnut, CA 91789 USA Tel 404-409-5252
E-mail: cswainbates@gmail.com.

Goldhirsh, Julia, *(978-0-578-55290-3; 978-0-578-56704-4; 978-1-7351697)* 4739 NW 30th St., Coconut Creek, FL 33063 USA Tel 954-812-9644
E-mail: bluemoonroze@gmail.com.

Goldie McCoppertop Publishing, *(978-0-692-05348-5; 978-0-692-12354-6)* 2082 SE Bristol St No. 215, Newport Beach, CA 92660 USA Tel 949-636-5964
E-mail: goldiemccoppertop@gmail.com
Dist(s): **CreateSpace Independent Publishing Platform.**

Goldleaf Games, LLC, *(978-0-9748757)* P.O. Box 804, Lawrence, KS 66044 USA
E-mail: gary@goldleafgames.com
Web site: http://www.goldleafgames.com.

Goldman Hse. Publishing, *(978-0-9815627; 978-0-9892935; 978-0-9864361; 978-0-9997331)* P.O. Box 6029-117, Artesia, CA 90702 USA
E-mail: goldmanhousepublishing@gmail.com.

Goldmann, Wilhelm Verlag GmbH (DEU) *(978-3-442) Dist. by* **Distribks Inc.**

Goldminds Publishing *Imprint of* **Amphorae Publishing Group**

Goldner, Harriet LLC, *(978-0-9779676)* P.O. Box 480003, Delray Beach, FL 33448 USA
E-mail: hgoldnerbooks@bellsouth.net
Web site: http://www.JewishFamilyFun.com.

Goldsberry, Booty, *(978-0-9792875)* 10 Windsor Pl., Poland, ME 04274 USA Tel 207-998-5710
E-mail: elattanzi@bookmasters.com.

GoldTouch Pr., *(978-1-7337013; 978-1-7337014; 978-1-7332264; 978-1-7332265; 978-1-7333366; 978-1-7333367; 978-1-7334028; 978-1-7334396; 978-1-951461; 978-1-952155; 978-1-953791)* 420 Lexington Ave., Suite 300, New York, NY 10170 USA Tel 917-108-1114
E-mail: arianna.parker@goldtouchpress.com
Web site: goldtouchpress.com.

Goldwrite Publishing, *(978-0-9767933; 978-0-615-13858-9; 978-1-7333188)* 11414 Vinea Ln., Hampton, GA 30228 USA Tel 678 510-6941
E-mail: asheagold@yahoo.com
Dist(s): **BookBaby**
Lulu Pr., Inc.

Golfing Bee, LLC, *(978-0-692-78420-4; 978-0-9983495)* 8815 First Bloom Rd., Charlotte, NC 28277 USA Tel 503-507-2712
E-mail: golfingbee45@gmail.com.

Golightly Publishing, *(978-0-9617721; 978-0-9966544; 978-1-7339277)* P.O. Box 181533, Dallas, TX 75218-1533 USA (SAN 665-1259) Tel 214-415-6156
E-mail: golightlyinfo@aol.com; david@sellbox.com.

Golly Gee-pers, *(978-0-9964175)* 923 Mountain View Dr., Lafayette, CA 94549 USA Tel 925-324-4418
E-mail: gollygee_pers@yahoo.com
Web site: www.gollygee-pers.com.

Golob, Julie, *(978-0-9996456)* 105 S. Jefferson St.,, Kearney, MO 64060 USA Tel 406-230-0824
E-mail: jgoloski@gmail.com
Web site: juliegolob.com.

Gom Foxtail *Imprint of* **Gom Publishing, LLC**

Gom Publishing, LLC, *(978-0-9729197; 978-1-932966)* P.O. Box 211110, Columbus, OH 43221 USA (SAN 255-3988) Tel 614-876-7097; Toll Free Fax: 866-422-8292; Toll Free: 866-466-2608; *Imprints:* Gom Foxtail (Gom Foxtail)
E-mail: sfox@gompublishing.com
Web site: http://www.gompublishing.com.

Gomez Expeditions, *(978-1-7321369; 978-1-7333160)* P.O. Box 246, Nash, TX 75569 USA Tel 910-286-8576
E-mail: sil.gomez@yahoo.com.

Goncalves, John, *(978-0-692-09746-5; 978-0-692-09747-2)* 406 12th Ave. SE, MINNEAPOLIS, MN 55414 USA Tel 401-257-9015
E-mail: john_goncalves@alumni.brown.edu
Dist(s): **Ingram Content Group.**

Gonsalves, Theresa Joyce, *(978-0-9762347; 978-1-62193)* 2725 Grafton Ct., LAS VEGAS, NV 89117 USA
E-mail: tjgmanage@gmail.com
Web site: http://www.theresagonsalves.com
Dist(s): **BCH Fulfillment & Distribution.**

Gonzalez, David J. Ministries, *(978-0-9741561)* P.O. Box 847, Lake Delton, WI 53940 USA Tel 608-254-5150
E-mail: dgm@mountainfaith.org
Web site: http://www.mountainfaith.org.

Good Beginnings Publishing, LLC, *(978-0-692-84463-2)* 5625 Platte Dr., Ellenwood, GA 30294 USA Tel 404-759-9002
E-mail: aleroa12@hotmail.com.

Good Bks. *Imprint of* **Skyhorse Publishing Co., Inc.**

Good Catch Publishing, *(978-0-9772383; 978-0-9785152; 978-0-9792475; 978-1-934635; 978-1-938478; 978-1-68085)* Orders Addr.: P.O. Box 6551, Aloha, OR 97007 USA (SAN 257-0289) Tel 503-475-2005; Fax: 503-356-9685; Toll Free: 877-967-3224; Edit Addr.: 4074 NW 169th Ave., Beaverton, OR 97006 USA Fax: 503-356-9685; Toll Free: 877-967-3224
E-mail: nathanlindley@goodcatchpublishing.com; admingcp@gmail.com
Web site: http://www.goodcatchpublishing.com; http://www.testimonybooks.com.

Good Fun Bks., *(978-0-9995591)* 6716 Gleason Ave. NW, Albuquerque, NM 87120-4409 USA Tel 505-321-8142
E-mail: csteiner5@msn.com
Web site: goodfunbooks.com.

Good Harbor Pr., *(978-0-9799638; 978-0-615-32057-1)* 80 Walsh St., Medford, MA 02155 USA Tel 781-396-1733.

Good Luck Black Cat Bks., *(978-0-692-73385-1; 978-0-9988846)* 3745 Quitman, Denver, CO 80212 USA Tel 303-587-5402
E-mail: nikiknaub@gmail.com
Dist(s): **Independent Pubs. Group.**

Good News Connections, *(978-0-9728900)* Orders Addr.: P.O. Box 66573, Austin, TX 78766 USA Toll Free: 888-899-3207 Do not confuse with The Good News Connections, Inc. in Orlando, FL
E-mail: stayton@xc.org
Web site: http://www.GoodNewsConnections.com.

Good News Fellowship Ministries, *(978-0-9629559; 978-1-888081; 978-1-7344999)* Div. of Funtasy Pubns., 220 Sleepy Creek Rd., Macon, GA 31210-5720 USA Tel 478-757-8071; Fax: 478-757-0136; Toll Free: 800-300-9630
E-mail: goodnews@reynoldscable.net
Web site: http://www.goodnews.netministries.org; http://kathiewaltersministry.com
Dist(s): **Anchor Distributors.**

Good News Productions, International, *(978-1-59305)* Orders Addr.: P.O. Box 222, Joplin, MO 64802-0222 USA Tel 417-782-0060; Fax: 417-782-3999; Edit Addr.: 2111 N. Main, Joplin, MO 64802-0222 USA
E-mail: gnpi@gnpi.org
Web site: http://www.gnpi.org.

Good Newz Dudez, *(978-0-9765568)* 4906 Hopespring Dr., Orlando, FL 32829 USA Tel 407-970-3828.

Good Night Bks., *(978-0-9777979; 978-1-60219)* 36 Route 6A, Sandwich, MA 02563 USA
E-mail: adam@goodnightourworld.com
Web site: http://goodnightbooks.com
Dist(s): **Islander Group**
MyiLibrary
Penguin Random Hse. Distribution
Penguin Random Hse. LLC
Random Hse., Inc.
ebrary, Inc.

Good Reading Bks., *(978-1-888042; 978-0-578-17942-1)* Div. of Southern Printing, Imaging & Typography, Inc., 153 Shady Oaks Dr., Lafayette, LA 70506 USA.

Good Roots Publishing, *(978-0-9745187)* Orders Addr.: P.O. Box 3493, Homer, AK 99603-3493 USA Tel 907-235-5283; Edit Addr.: 62315 Fireweed Ave., Homer, AK 99603-3493 USA
Dist(s): **Wizard Works.**

Good Sound Publishing, *(978-0-9821563; 978-1-935743)* 295 Olive Ave., Palo Alto, CA 94306 USA Fax: 650-227-2320; Toll Free: 888-686-2669
E-mail: info@goodsoundpublishing.com
Web site: http://www.goodsoundpublishing.com.

Good Success Publishing, *(978-0-9837895; 978-0-9978332; 978-1-7355882)* P.O. Box 134, Oxon Hill, MD 20750 USA Tel 301-467-8885
E-mail: info@drcelesteowens.com
Web site: www.drcelesteowens.com
Dist(s): **BookBaby.**

Good Thoughts Publishing *See* **Cardinal Pr.**

Good Times at Home LLC, *(978-0-9840338)* 1933 Hwy. 35 Suite 105-335, Belmar, NJ 07719 USA Tel 732-803-1902
E-mail: vinnie@vinniecurto.com.

Good Turn Publishing, *(978-0-9794393)* 1 Bancroft Rd., Wellesley, MA 02481 USA
Web site: http://www.goodturnpublishing.com.

Good Works Pr., *(978-0-9634472; 978-1-888572)* 4121 Whitfield Ave., Fort Worth, TX 76109 USA Tel 817-927-8808.

Good Works Publishing Hse., *(978-0-9744733)* P.O. Box 52217, Houston, TX 77052-2217 USA Tel 832-267-7366; 346-234-3031
E-mail: wonderlandhudson@yahoo.com.

Good Year Bks. *Imprint of* **Celebration Pr.**

Good Year Bks., *(978-1-59647)* P.O. Box 91858, Tucson, AZ 85752-1858 USA (SAN 854-4050) Toll Free Fax: 888-511-1501; Toll Free: 888-511-1530
E-mail: publisher@goodyearbooks.com; sales@goodyearbooks.com; marketing@goodyearbooks.com; orders@goodyearbooks.com
Web site: http://www.goodyearbooks.com.

Goodall, Barry, *(978-0-9763932)* 218 Tucker Sta. Rd, Louisville, KY 40243 USA Tel 502-817-8530
E-mail: bgoodal1@jefferson.k12.ky.us.

Goode, Ty *See* **Tytam Publishing**

Goodheart-Willcox Pub., *(978-0-87006; 978-1-56637; 978-1-59070; 978-1-60525; 978-1-61960; 978-1-63126; 978-1-68311; 978-1-63563; 978-1-64564; 978-1-64925)* Orders Addr.: 18604 West Creek Dr., Tinley Park, IL 60477-6243 USA (SAN 203-4387) Tel 708-687-5000; Fax: 708-687-5068; Toll Free Fax: 888-409-3900; Toll Free: 800-323-0440
E-mail: custserv@g-w.com; jff@g-w.com
Web site: http://www.g-w.com.

goodluck, marquita Publishing, *(978-0-692-19580-2; 978-0-692-19942-8; 978-0-578-59017-2)* 14111 Arbor Forest Dr., Rockville, MD 20850 USA Tel 240-383-7687
E-mail: marquita.goodluck@gmail.com
Dist(s): **Ingram Content Group.**

Goodman, Kathleen, *(978-1-7336080)* 2328 10th Ave E, Seattle, WA 98102 USA Tel 615-708-4238
E-mail: mkgoodman11@gmail.com.

goodman, peggy, *(978-0-9990606)* 212 windsor ave, glasgow, KY 42141 USA Tel 270-651-6366
E-mail: cag3@glasgow-ky.com.

Goodmedia Communications, LLC, *(978-0-615-60107-6; 978-0-9883237; 978-0-9911148; 978-1-7327046)* 25 Highland Pk. Village, No. 100-810, Dallas, TX 75205 USA Tel 214-240-4503
E-mail: info@GoodMediaCommunications.com
Web site: www.GoodMediaCommunications.com.

Goodness Experience, The, *(978-0-9653077; 978-0-692-27102-5; 978-0-692-03668-6)* 2101 Palm Canyon Ct., Las Vegas, NV 89117-1941 USA.

Goodtimes Software *See* **GT Interactive Software**

Goodwin, Brian, *(978-0-615-16104-4)* 53-823 Kamehameha Hwy., Hauula, HI 96717-9658 USA
Dist(s): **Lulu Pr., Inc.**

Goodwin, Evelyn, *(978-0-615-16145-7; 978-0-615-16344-4)* 2345 Ala Wai Blvd. Apt. 917, Honolulu, HI 96815-5017 USA
Dist(s): **Lulu Pr., Inc.**

goodworksebooks.com, *(978-0-9773192)* 3084 CR 310, Brazoria, TX 77422 USA
Web site: http://goodworksebooks.com.

GoodyGoody Bks., *(978-0-9702546; 978-0-9995920)* P.O. Box 1073, Sun City, AZ 85372-1073 USA
E-mail: charlie-the-cat@cox.net
Web site: http://www.charliethecat.com.

Goodykoontz, Jared, *(978-0-692-04422-3; 978-0-578-45862-5; 978-0-578-54505-9)* 10520 Shields Rd., Ostrander, OH 43061 USA Tel 614-315-5258
E-mail: Jaredgoodykoontz@gmail.com
Dist(s): **Ingram Content Group.**

Goofy Guru Publishing, *(978-0-9726130)* 405 Kiowa Pl., Boulder, CO 80303 USA.

Goon Dog Publishing, *(978-0-9791612)* 309 W. 14th, Suite 32, New York, NY 10014-0014 USA (SAN 852-6206) Tel 212-645-2096
E-mail: monk@ispwest.com
Web site: http://owenopolis.com.

Goops Unlimited, *(978-0-9712368; 978-0-9834865)* P.O. Box 1809, Battle Ground, WA 98604-1809 USA Tel 360-687-1891; Fax: 360-687-2097; Toll Free: 800-861-1891
E-mail: barbara@thegoops.com
Web site: http://www.thegoops.com.

Goose Creek Pubs., Inc., *(978-1-59633)* 4227 Vermont Ave., Louisville, KY 40211 USA Tel 502-714-9985
E-mail: wanda@goosecreekpublishers.com
Web site: http://www.goosecreekpublishers.com.

Goose River Pr., *(978-1-930648; 978-1-59713)* 3400 Friendship Rd., Waldoboro, ME 04572 USA Tel 207-832-6665
E-mail: gooseriverpress@roadrunner.com
Web site: http://www.gooseriverpress.com
Dist(s): **Ingram Content Group.**

Gooseberry Patch *Imprint of* **Rowman & Littlefield Publishers, Inc.**

Goosebottom Bks. LLC, *(978-0-9845098; 978-0-9834256; 978-1-937463)* 543 Trinidad Ln., Foster City, CA 94404-6061 USA (SAN 859-8029) Tel 650-204-4076
E-mail: info@goosebottombooks.com; shirin.bridges@goosebottombooks.com
Web site: http://www.goosebottombooks.com
Dist(s): **Publishers Group West (PGW).**

Gordon Rocket, *(978-1-941037)* P.O. Box 120023, Chula, CA 91912 USA Tel 619-272-8235
E-mail: mxreynoso@gmail.com
Web site: gordonrocket.com.

Gordon, Scott, *(978-0-9963574)* 30 Serenity Ln., Laguna Niguel, CA 92677 USA Tel 949-280-2799
E-mail: repioneer32@gmail.com.

Goretti Publishing, *(978-0-9778451)* Orders Addr.: 1150 N. Loop 1604 W., Ste. 108-410, San Antonio, TX 78248 USA (SAN 850-3176) Tel 210-274-2769; Fax: 210-493-6080 attn: 410
E-mail: publishedworks@aol.com
Web site: http://www.thetexasmermaid.com
Dist(s): **Bk. Marketing Plus.**

Gorgias Pr., LLC, *(978-0-9713097; 978-0-9715986; 978-1-931956; 978-1-59333; 978-1-60724; 978-1-61719; 978-1-61143; 978-1-4632)* 954 River Rd., Piscataway, NJ 08854-5504 USA (SAN 853-0629)
E-mail: info@gorgiaspress.com; sales@gorgiaspress.com
Web site: http://www.gorgiaspress.com
Dist(s): **De Gruyter, Inc.**
ebrary, Inc.

Gormer, Jennifer Hobson, *(978-0-692-96829-1)* P.O. Box 382623, DUNCANVILLE, TX 75138 USA Tel 972-302-0082
E-mail: hobson.jennifer@gmail.com
Dist(s): **Ingram Content Group.**

Gormley Publishing, *(978-0-9794500; 978-0-9827503; 978-0-692-61920-9)* Orders Addr.: 1520 Courtney Dr., Washington Court House, OH 43160-8920 USA
Web site: http://www.gormleypublishing.com

Gorp Group Pr., The, *(978-0-9724249)* 7450 OLIVETAS Ave. No. 386, LA JOLLA, CA 92037 USA Tel 858-412-4424; 208-720-7980; Toll Free: 888-729-4677
E-mail: gorp2@earthlink.net
Web site: http://www.thegorp.com.

†Gospel Advocate Co., Inc., *(978-0-89225)* Orders Addr.: P.O. Box 150, Nashville, TN 37202 USA (SAN 205-2792) Tel 615-254-8781; Fax: 615-254-7411; Toll Free: 800-251-8446; Edit Addr.: 1006 Elm Hill Pike, Nashville, TN 37210 USA (SAN 662-0213)
E-mail: kerry@gospeladvocate.com; keaton@gospeladvocate.com; haimericus@juno.com
Web site: http://www.gospeladvocate.com; *CIP.*

Gospel Grown, *(978-1-7336615)* 974 Breckenridge Ln. No. 295, Louisville, KY 40207-4619 USA Tel 502-514-9513
E-mail: contact@gospelgrown.org
Web site: www.gospelgrown.org.

Gospel Light *Imprint of* **Gospel Light Pubns.**

Gospel Light Pubns., *(978-0-8307)* Orders Addr.: 1957 Eastman Ave., Ventura, CA 93003 USA (SAN 299-0873) Tel 805-644-9721; Fax: 805-289-0200; Toll Free: 800-446-7735 (orders only); *Imprints:* Gospel Light (Gospel Light); Regal Books (Regal Bks) Do not confuse with companies with similar names in Brooklyn, NY, Delight, AR
E-mail: info@gospellight.com; kyleloffelmacher@gospellight.com
Web site: http://www.gospellight.com
Dist(s): **Christian Bk. Distributors**
Cook, David C.
Faith Alive Christian Resources.

Gospel Missionary Union, *(978-0-9617490; 978-1-890940)* 10000 N. Oak Trafficway, Kansas City, MO 64155 USA (SAN 664-1830) Tel 816-734-8500; Fax: 816-734-4601
E-mail: info@gmu.org
Web site: http://www.gmu.org.

†Gospel Publishing Hse., *(978-0-88243; 978-1-60731)* Div. of General Council of the Assemblies of God, 1445 N. Boonville Ave., Springfield, MO 65802-1894 USA (SAN 206-8826) Tel 417-862-2781; Fax: 417-862-5881; Toll Free Fax: 800-328-0294; Toll Free: 800-641-4310 (orders only)
E-mail: webmaster@gph.com
Web site: http://www.gospelpublishing.com
Dist(s): **Appalachian Bible Co.**
Ingram Publisher Services
Lulu Pr., Inc.
MyiLibrary
Spring Arbor Distributors, Inc.; *CIP.*

Gospel Puzzles *See* **Cluster Storm Publishing**

Goss, Nicholas, *(978-1-7321815)* 100 Hiram Ct, Spring Hill, TN 37174 USA Tel 615-596-6923
E-mail: nickthegoss@gmail.com.

Gossamer Bks., *(978-0-9729016)* 444 Eastwood Dr., Petaluma, CA 94954 USA (SAN 255-2671) Tel 707-765-1992; Fax: 707-765-6507 Do not confuse with Gossamer Books LLC in Belmont, CA
E-mail: dcr530@cs.com.

Gossamer Bks., LLC, *(978-0-9742502)* P.O. Box 455, Belmont, CA 94002 USA Fax: 650-257-4058 Do not confuse with Gossamer Books in Petaluma, CA
E-mail: info@gossamerbooks.com
Web site: http://www.gossamerbooks.com.

Gossamer Wings Pr., *(978-1-7321544)* 23 Telfair Dr., Beaufort, SC 29907 USA Tel 859-644-7077
E-mail: rjchamberlain71@gmail.com
Web site: www.rchamberlainart.com.

Gosselin, Matthew S., *(978-0-692-07476-3; 978-0-692-07483-1; 978-0-692-09304-7; 978-0-692-09305-4; 978-0-578-67389-9)* 872 Crooked Branch Dr., CLERMONT, FL 34711 USA Tel 407-504-8253
E-mail: mattgosselin@gmail.com
Web site: http://www.MattGosselin.com
Dist(s): **Ingram Content Group.**

GoTandem *Imprint of* **Barbour Publishing, Inc.**

Gothenburg Bks., *(978-1-7327275; 978-1-7338677; 978-1-7333081)* 1797 Channing Ave, PALO ALTO, CA 94303 USA Tel 650-561-4101
E-mail: jillianbeckerwriter@gmail.com.

Gothic Image Pubns. (GBR) *(978-0-906362) Dist. by* **SCB Distributo.**

Gottabeareason *See* **Rhodes, Candice Sumner**

Gottlieb, Rachel E, *(978-0-692-60407-6)* 62 Old Orchard Ln., Scarsdale, NY 10583 USA Tel 917-494-7236
E-mail: raycraz1@gmail.com.

Goulart-Johnston, Michelle, *(978-0-9980932)* 1375 E Grand Ave. No. 318, Arroyo Grande, CA 93420 USA Tel 805-539-9214
E-mail: michgoulart@gmail.com.

Goulasche Pr., *(978-0-9771466)* 1352 Ithilien, Excelsior, MN 55331 USA.

Gourley, Deb Nelson *See* **Astri My Astri Publishing**

Govinda Yoga Play, *(978-0-692-16098-5; 978-1-7326062)* 10 Faye Cir., Marblehead, MA 01945 USA Tel 781-639-3543
E-mail: ajgiven@comcast.net
Dist(s): **Ingram Content Group.**

Gozo Bks. *Imprint of* **Premio Publishing & Gozo Bks., LLC**

Gozo Books, LLC *See* **Premio Publishing & Gozo Bks., LLC**

G.P. Hoffman Publishing, *(978-0-9798230)* 2224 Heather Ln., Lincoln, NE 68512 USA.

G.P. Putnam's Sons *Imprint of* **Penguin Publishing Group**

G.P. Putnam's Sons Books for Young Readers *Imprint of* **Penguin Young Readers Group**

G.P. Putnam's Sons Books for Young Readers *Imprint of* **Penguin Publishing Group**

Grace Acres Pr., *(978-1-60265)* P.O. Box 22, Larkspur, CO 80118 USA (SAN 852-5978) Tel 303-681-9995; Fax: 303-681-2716
E-mail: Anne@GraceAcresPress.com
Web site: http://www.graceacrespress.com.

Grace & Mercy Publishing, *(978-0-9672049; 978-0-9764763)* Orders Addr.: P.O. Box 11531, Fort Wayne, IN 46857 USA; Edit Addr.: 7408 Mill Run, Suite B, Fort Wayne, IN 46819 USA.

Grace Communications Publishing *See* **Grace Publishing**

Grace Contrino Abrams Peace Education Foundation *See* **Peace Education Foundation**

Grace Hse. Pr., *(978-0-9995368; 978-1-7332888)* 3717 Blackhawk Rd, Eagan, MN 55122 USA Tel 763-438-5289
E-mail: bethanyatazadeh@yahoo.com
Web site: www.bethanyatazadeh.com; www.gracehousepress.com.

Grace Hse. Publishing, *(978-0-9633633)* Div. of R. Allan McCauley Law Office, 6237 N. 15th St., Phoenix, AZ 85014 USA Tel 602-265-9151 Do not confuse with Grace House Publishing in Mahomet, IL.

Grace Publishing, *(978-1-893555)* Div. of Abundant Grace Fellowship, 11118 Robious Rd., Richmond, VA 23235-3724 USA Toll Free: 877-884-7223 Do not confuse with companies with companies with the same name in Seattle, WA, Farmington Hills, MI, Broken Arrow, OK, Waldorf, MD, Elma, NY, Woodinville, WA & New Prague, MN
E-mail: drmhunt@bellsouth.net; carylives@atthi.com; dremlenehunt@earthlink.net
Web site: http://www.abundantgrace.org; http://www.drmarlenehunt.com.

Grace Publishing, *(978-0-9769985)* P.O. Box 17980, Seattle, WA 98123 USA (SAN 256-6257) Tel 206-818-9769 Do not confuse with companies with the same name in Farmington Hills, MI, Broken Arrow, OK, Waldorf, MD, Richmond, VA, Elma, NY, Woodinville, WA & New Prague, MN
E-mail: vonukk@comcast.net
Web site: http://www.rcberg.com.

Grace to Grow Pubns., *(978-0-9709488; 978-0-9745499; 978-0-9764247; 978-0-9778936; 978-0-9800594; 978-0-9819603; 978-1-62289)* Orders Addr.: 507 State St., Hammond, IN 46320 USA Tel 219-932-0711
E-mail: carol.hunter@pulseprint.org; abby.amoros@pulseprint.org
Web site: https://gracetogrowpublications.com; http://www.pulseprint.org.

Grace Walk Ministries *See* **Grace Walk Resources, LLC**

Grace Walk Resources, LLC, *(978-0-9664736)* Orders Addr.: P.O. Box 6537, Douglasville, GA 30135 USA Tel 800-472-2311; Toll Free: 800-472-2311
E-mail: info@gracewalk.org
Web site: http://www.gracewalk.org.

Graceffa, Leilani, *(978-1-7335558; 978-1-7350952; 978-0-578-76251-7)* 167 Brooklyn Way, Pooler, GA 31322 USA Tel 912-508-6700
E-mail: Japanesemagnolia@icloud.com.

GraceNotes Pr. *Imprint of* **New Shelves Bks.**

GraceWorks Interactive, *(978-0-9760548; 978-1-935915)* P.O. Box 2613, Corvallis, OR 97339-2613 USA Toll Free: 877-785-3496 (phone/fax)
E-mail: tim@graceworksinteractive.com
Web site: http://www.graceworksinteractive.com.

Grady Bunch Bks., LLC, *(978-0-9990075)* 7887 N. 16th St. 204, Phoenix, AZ 85020 USA Tel 602-475-1718
E-mail: joannegrady@gmail.com.

Graffeg Limited (GBR) *(978-0-9544334; 978-1-905582; 978-1-909823) Dist. by* **IPG Chicago.**

grafixCORP, *(978-0-9778374)* Orders Addr.: P.O. Box 1441, Mount Vernon, WA 98273-9827 USA
Web site: http://www.grafixCORP.com.

Grafton and Scratch Pubs. (CAN) *(978-0-9879023; 978-0-9881216; 978-1-927979; 978-1-926495) Dist. by* **BTPS.**

Graham Bay, Jeanette, *(978-0-9771210)* 770 Victor Rd., Macedon, NY 14502 USA.

Graham Cracker Kids, *(978-0-9716475; 978-0-615-11409-5)* 1661 Hunt Rd., El Cajon, CA 92019 USA Tel 619-258-7571; Fax: 619-258-5412
E-mail: grmcrkrkds@aol.com
Web site: http://www.grahamcrackerkids.com.

Graham, Inna, 13825 Robinson Ct., Oklahoma City, OK 73170 USA Tel 405-602-4984
E-mail: Inna.shch@gmail.com
Dist(s): **Ingram Content Group.**

Graham, Rita, *(978-0-578-13165-8)*.

Grain Valley Press *See* **Grain Valley Publishing**

Grain Valley Publishing, *(978-1-7323047)* 1818 W. 18th St. No. 291, Wichita, KS 67203 USA Tel 316-734-7196
E-mail: grainvalleypress@gmail.com
Web site: www.GrantOverstake.com.

Grampa Jones's Publishing Co., *(978-0-9748266; 978-0-615-11169-8; 978-0-9893868)* P.O. Box 93, Heron, MT 59844-0093 USA (SAN 214-4700)
Web site: http://www.become-a-millionaire.com.

Gran Gran Series, *(978-0-9840237)* 8549 Hartham Pk. Ave., Raleigh, NC 27616 USA Tel 919-295-4750
E-mail: mhopkins25@nc.rr.com.

Grand Bks., Inc., *(978-0-930809)* P.O. Box 212, Crystal, MI 48818 USA (SAN 677-6361) Tel 517-875-4674; 517-235-4427
E-mail: jwrites@yahoo.com.

Grand Canyon Association *See* **Grand Canyon Conservancy**

Grand Canyon Conservancy, *(978-0-938216; 978-1-934656)* Orders Addr.: P.O. Box 399, Grand Canyon, AZ 86023-0399 USA (SAN 215-7675) Tel 928-638-7141; 928-863-3893; Fax: 928-638-2494; Toll Free: 800-858-2808
E-mail: lsantamaria@grandcanyon.org; acrrison@grandcanyon.org
Web site: http://www.grandcanyon.org.

Grand Canyon Orphan, *(978-0-9764260)* P.O. Box 438, Mina, NV 89422 USA
E-mail: info@grandcanyonorphan.com
Web site: http://www.grandcanyonorphan.com.

Grand Central Art, *(978-0-9771696; 978-0-9817987; 978-1-7331888)* 125 N. Broadway, Santa Ana, CA 92701 USA (SAN 256-8284) Tel 714-567-7238
E-mail: tgayer@fullerton.edu
Web site: http://www.grandcentralartcenter.com
Dist(s): **SCB Distributors.**

Grand Central Press *See* **Grand Central Art**

†Grand Central Publishing, *(978-0-445; 978-0-446; 978-0-7595; 978-1-4555; 978-1-5387; 978-1-5460)* Orders Addr.: c/o Little Brown & Co., 3 Center Plaza, Boston, MA 02108-2084 USA Toll Free Fax: 800-286-9471; Toll Free: 800-759-0190; Edit Addr.: 237 Park Ave., New York, NY 10017 USA (SAN 281-8892) Fax: 800-331-1664; Toll Free Fax: 800-759-0190; 1290 Avenue of the Americas, New York, NY 10104; *Imprints:* Vision (VisionC); Business Plus (Busn Plus); Forever (Forever); Sixth Avenue Books (SixthAveBks); 5 Spot (FiveSpot); Aspect (Aspect); Jimmy Patterson (JimmyPat)
E-mail: renee.supriano@twbg.com; customer.service@hbgusa.com
Web site: http://www.hbgusa.com
Dist(s): **Blackstone Audio, Inc.**
Findaway World, LLC
Follett School Solutions
Hachette Bk. Group
Lectorum Pubns., Inc.
Libros Sin Fronteras
Little Brown & Co.
MyiLibrary
Perelandra, Ltd.
Beeler, Thomas T. Pub.
TextStream
Thorndike Pr.
iPublish.com; *CIP.*

Grand County Historical Assn., *(978-1-7322461)* P.O. Box 165, Hot Sulphur Springs, CO 80451 USA Tel 970-725-3939
E-mail: shanna@grandcountyhistory.org
Web site: grandcountyhistory.org.

Grand Daisy Pr., *(978-0-9848608; 978-0-9962843)* 625 Stetson Rd., Elkins Park, PA 19027-2524 USA Tel 215-380-6710
E-mail: karenptoz@gmail.com
Web site: www.granddaisypress.com; www.karentoz.com.

Grand Hank Productions, Inc., *(978-0-9767236)* P.O. Box 23488, Philadelphia, PA 19143 USA Tel 215-724-5260
Web site: http://www.grandhank.com.

Grand Kidz, The *Imprint of* **Vertical Connect Pr.**

Grand Marais Publishing, *(978-0-615-34796-7)* 1441 Huntington Dr., No. 234, South Pasadena, CA 91030 USA Tel 626-441-1154
E-mail: grandmaraispublishing@gmail.com.

GRAND Media, LLC, *(978-0-930507; 978-0-615-51541-0)* 4791 Baywood Point Dr. S., Gulfport, FL 33711 USA (SAN 670-963X) Tel 727-327-9039; Fax: 727-323-9587
E-mail: jonmicocci@att.net
Web site: http://www.deathfromchildabuse.com.

Grand Productions, *(978-0-9795386)* 1914 Karly Ct., Panama City, FL 32405 USA (SAN 853-7194).

Grand Teton Assn., *(978-0-931895; 978-1-940093)* P.O. Box 170, Moose, WY 83012 USA (SAN 686-0303) Tel 307-739-3606; Fax: 307-739-3423
E-mail: grte_assoc@partner.nps.gov
Web site: http://www.grandtetonpark.org.

Grand Teton Natural History Association *See* **Grand Teton Assn.**

Grand Valley State Univ., *(978-0-9709811)* 1 Campus Dr., 107 Lake Superior Hall, Allendale, MI 49401 USA Tel 616-895-3488
E-mail: royer@river.it.gvsu.edu
Dist(s): **Michigan State Univ. Pr.**

Grandfeather Pr., *(978-0-9832355)* 1221 S. 7th St., Renton, WA 98057 USA Tel 425-902-1852
E-mail: publishing@grandfeather.com
Web site: www.grandfeather.com
Dist(s): **Ingram Content Group.**

Grandin Bk. Co., *(978-0-910523)* P.O. Box 2206, Provo, UT 84603-2206 USA (SAN 260-1931) Tel 801-225-2020; Fax: 801-222-0176; Toll Free: 800-292-2003.

Grandkidsandme, Inc., *(978-0-9741710)* 1764 Hampshire Ave., Saint Paul, MN 55116 USA (SAN 255-3902) Tel 651-695-1988; Fax: 651-699-5966
E-mail: don@grandkidsandme.com
Web site: http://www.grandkidsandme.com.

Grandma Chubby's Bks., *(978-0-9728535)* P.O. Box 902308, Sandy, UT 84090-2308 USA Tel 801-571-6617; Fax: 801-571-2285
E-mail: lsashby@juno.com
Dist(s): **Granite Publishing & Distribution.**

"Grandma's Hope Notes", *(978-0-9677477)* P.O. Box 868, Anchor Point, AK 99556 USA Tel 907-235-0502 (phone/fax).

Grandoc Publishing, *(978-0-9761739)* 3923 Hidden Way NE, Rochester, MN 55906-5590 USA Tel 507-287-9121
E-mail: grandoc@mac.com; drjohngraner@mac.com.

Grandreams Bks., Inc., *(978-1-59340)* Div. of Robert Frederick, 360 Hurst St., Linden, NJ 07036 USA (SAN 254-9832) Fax: 908-523-0373
E-mail: ssullivan@grandreamsbooks.com.

Granite Publishing & Distribution, *(978-1-890558; 978-1-930980; 978-1-932280; 978-1-59936)* 868 N. 1430 W., Orem, UT 84057 USA (SAN 631-0605) Tel 801-229-9023; Fax: 801-229-1924; Toll Free: 800-574-5779 Do not confuse with companies with same or similar names in Madison, WI, Columbus, NC
E-mail: granite@granitepublishing.biz; gregg@granitepublishing.biz
Web site: http://granitepublishing.biz.

Granite Publishing, LLC, *(978-0-926524; 978-0-9632310; 978-1-893183)* P.O. Box 1429, Columbus, NC 28722 USA Tel 828-894-3088; Fax: 828-894-8454; Toll Free: 800-366-0264 Do not confuse with companies with same or similar names in Madison, WI, Orem, UT, Siloam Springs, AR
E-mail: brian@5thworld.com
Web site: http://www.5thworld.com
Dist(s): **New Leaf Distributing Co., Inc.**
Smashwords.

Granity Studios, *(978-1-949520)* 10 Park Terr. E., New York, NY 10034 USA Tel 646-221-2714
Dist(s): **Two Rivers Distribution.**

Grannie Annie Family Story Celebration, The, *(978-0-9677685; 978-0-9793296; 978-0-9969394)* P.O. Box 11343, Saint Louis, MO 63105 USA Tel 314-550-6396; Fax: 636-527-2822
E-mail: familystories@thegrannieannie.org
Web site: http://www.TheGrannieAnnie.org.

Granny's Pub Co., *(978-0-9749950)* P.O. Box 1701, Granbury, TX 76048 USA Tel 817-605-9004; Fax: 817-605-1180
E-mail: granny@loralie.com
Web site: http://www.loralie.com.

Grant, Irma, *(978-0-9996033)* 848 Sylvaner Dr., Pleasanton, CA 94566 USA Tel 919-460-5301
E-mail: irmawgrant@gmail.com
Web site: www.irmagrant.com.

Grant, Melinda Gail *See* **Keebie Pr.**

Grant, Tahlonna *See* **BeanSprout Bks.**

Grape Elephant MarketPr., *(978-0-9760646)* 13025 Ct. Pl., Burnsville, MN 55337 USA Tel 612-281-2566
E-mail: jill@grapeelephant.com
Web site: http://www.grapeelephant.com.

Graphic Arts Bks. *Imprint of* **West Margin Pr.**

Graphic Arts Books *See* **West Margin Pr.**

Graphic Expressions *See* **Graphics North**

Graphic Novels *Imprint of* **Spotlight**

Graphic Planet - Fiction *Imprint of* **Magic Wagon**

Graphic Universe™ *Imprint of* **Lerner Publishing Group**

Graphically Speaking, Inc., *(978-0-9729975)* 15509 Lloyd St., Omaha, NE 68144 USA Tel 402-330-1144; Fax: 402-334-3311
E-mail: fontstudios@cox.net
Web site: http://www.fontstudios.com.

Graphics North, *(978-0-692-79724-2)* 42 Mela Ln., Rancho Palos Verdes, CA 90275 USA Tel 310-780-0643
E-mail: brengreen@gmail.com.

Graphics North, *(978-0-9643452; 978-0-615-29759-0; 978-0-9829503)* P.O. Box 218, Jay, NY 12941 USA Tel 518-946-7741
E-mail: graphicsnorth@yahoo.com
Web site: graphicsnorth.com.

Graphic-Sha (JPN) *(978-4-7661) Dist. by* **Diamond Book Dists.**

Graphic-Sha (JPN) *(978-4-7661) Dist. by* **D C D.**

Graphic International, Inc., *(978-0-916189)* 8780 19th St., No. 199, Alto Loma, CA 91701 USA (SAN 294-9342) Tel 909-987-1921; Fax: 435-514-5975
E-mail: lmartres@phototripusa.com
Web site: http://www.phototripusa.com
Dist(s): **Bks. West**
Canyonlands Pubns.
Mountain n' Air Bks.

Graphis, U.S., Inc., *(978-1-888001; 978-1-931241; 978-1-932026)* Orders Addr.: c/o ABDI, Inc., Buncher Commerce Pk. Ave. A, Bldg. 16, Leetsdale, PA 15056-1304 USA Tel 412-741-3679; Fax: 412-741-0934; Toll Free: 800-209-4234 (for Canada & USA); Edit Addr.: 307 Fifth Ave., 10th Flr., New York, NY 10016 USA Tel 212-532-9387 (ext. 226)
Web site: http://www.graphis.com
Dist(s): **Innovative Logistics**
National Bk. Network
Watson-Guptill Pubns., Inc.

Graphite Pr., *(978-0-9755810; 978-1-938313)* 2025 Lexington Parkway, Niskayuna, NY 12309-4205 USA (SAN 256-0712) Tel 518-303-6006
E-mail: publish@graphitepress.com
Web site: http://graphitepress.com.

Graphix *Imprint of* **Scholastic, Inc.**

Graphix Network, (*978-0-9740673; 978-0-9752832; 978-0-9762301; 978-0-9777043*) Orders Addr.: P.O. Box 2745, Evans, GA 30809 USA Tel 706-210-1000; Fax: 706-210-1111; Edit Addr.: 4104 Colben Blvd., Suite C, Evans, GA 30809 USA Tel 706-210-1000; Fax: 706-210-1111
E-mail: graphixnetwork@hotmail.com; sales@graphixnetwork.com
Web site: http://www.graphixnetwork.com.

Grappling Arts Pubns., LLC, (*978-0-9721097*) 1282 Watson Ave., Costa Mesa, CA 92626 USA
E-mail: info@grapplingarts.net
Web site: http://www.grapplingarts.net
Dist(s): **Baker & Taylor Publisher Services (BTPS)**
Cardinal Pubs. Group.

Grass Root Enterprises, (*978-1-886075*) 16315 Forest Way Dr., Houston, TX 77090-4716 USA Tel 281-444-4103; Fax: 281-444-5804.

Grassdale Publishers, Incorporated *See* **Saxon Pubs., Inc.**

Grasshopper Dream Productions, (*978-0-615-12337-0; 978-0-615-12724-8; 978-0-615-35616-7*) Orders Addr.: P.O. Box 1831, Saint Petersburg, FL 33731-1831 USA Tel 813-382-4230; Edit Addr.: 121 E. Davis Blvd., No. 104, Tampa, FL 33731 USA
E-mail: kokopelli911@hotmail.com
Web site: http://www.kokopelli-butterfly.com.

Grassleaf Publishing, (*978-0-9990716; 978-1-7334913*) 533 Derby Downs, Lebanon, TN 37087-8607 USA Tel 615-477-5743
E-mail: grassleafbooks@gmail.com.

Grassroots Educational Service *See* **Right On Programs, Inc.**

Grassroots Publishing Group, (*978-0-9794805; 978-0-9975677*) 9404 Southwick Dr., Bakersfield, CA 93312 USA (SAN 853-5493) Tel 661-368-2624; Fax: 661-368-2624; 4560 Woodlands Village Dr., Orlando, FL 32835
E-mail: nesta@sbcglobal.net.

Grateful Abundance Publishing, (*978-0-692-06796-3*) 51 Day Ave., Newark, OH 43055 USA Tel 740-334-9438
E-mail: dayleandtom@gmail.com
Dist(s): **Ingram Content Group.**

Grateful Day Pr., (*978-0-9882804*) 24 Dewey Mt Rd., Saranac Lake, NY 12983 USA Tel 518-891-2278; Fax: 518-891-1645
E-mail: gratefuldaypress@gmail.com.

Grateful Steps, (*978-0-9789548; 978-1-935130; 978-0-9962490; 978-1-945714*) 1091 Hendersonville Rd., Asheville, NC 28801 USA (SAN 856-471X) Tel 828-277-0998; Fax: 828-277-8027
Web site: http://www.gratefulsteps.com.

Gratia et Veritas Press *See* **Papillon Publishing**

Gratitude Works, (*978-0-578-13447-5*) 6255 Whitsett Ave, North Hollywood, CA 91606 USA.

Grau, Ryon, (*978-0-9772559*) 6824 Falstone Dr., Frederick, MD 21702 USA
E-mail: ryon@landmarkletters.com
Web site: http://www.spankledelia.com.

Gravino, Nicholas, (*978-0-615-24099-2*) 8935 Oldham Way, West Palm Bch, FL 33412-1110 USA
Web site: http://www.apilotsmemoirsfromthegroundup.com.

Gravitas Pubns., Inc., (*978-0-9749149; 978-0-9765097; 978-0-9799459; 978-0-9817731; 978-0-9823163; 978-1-936114; 978-1-941181; 978-1-950415; 978-1-953542*) PO Box 90338, Albuquerque, NM 97199 USA Tel 505-266-2761; Fax: 505-266-2762; Toll Free: 888-466-2761
E-mail: office@gravitaspublications.com
Web site: http://www.gravitaspublications.com.

Gravley, Debbie Bybee, (*978-0-9771793*) Orders Addr.: P.O. Box 268, Gaston, OR 97119 USA; Edit Addr.: 12320 S.W. Springhill Rd., Gaston, OR 97119 USA.

Graw, Victoria, (*978-0-9787901*) P.O. Box 458, Orange, MA 01364 USA (SAN 851-6138)
E-mail: Vgraw@aol.com.

Gray and Company, Publishers, (*978-0-9631738; 978-1-886228; 978-1-59851; 978-1-938441*) Orders Addr.: 1588 E. 40th St., 3A, Cleveland, OH 44103 USA Tel 216-431-2665; Fax: 216-431-7933; Toll Free: 800-915-3609
E-mail: sales@grayco.com
Web site: http://www.grayco.com.

Gray & Gold Publishing, (*978-1-945888; 978-1-64001; 978-1-64520; 978-1-7008*) 14546 Brook Hollow Blvd Num 349, San Antonio, TX 78232 USA
E-mail: sean@papeteriebleu.com.

Gray Jay Bks., (*978-0-9754539*)
E-mail: Contact@GrayJaybooks.com
Web site: http://www.grayjaybooks.com.

Gray, John, (*978-0-578-43434-6*) 1128 Springfield Valley Rd., Morrisville, NC 27560 USA Tel 318-401-5033; *Imprints:* Misguided Ink (MYID_L_MISGUID)
E-mail: johndonatron@gmail.com.

Gray, Jolie, (*978-1-7340647*) P.O. Box 273, Gonzales, TX 78629 USA Tel 830-857-1731
E-mail: jolie.gray@gmail.com
Dist(s): **Ingram Content Group.**

Gray Publishing, (*978-1-7327006*) 549 Hancock St., Brooklyn, NY 11233 USA Tel 201-320-7396
E-mail: babawesleygray1943@gmail.com.

Gray, Susan *See* **Two's Company**

Graye Castle Pr., (*978-0-692-10934-2; 978-0-692-11865-8*) 202 Brookfield Ave, Chattanooga, TN 37411 USA Tel 423-760-8662
E-mail: kendra@kendrayoung.com.

Grayer Publishing, (*978-0-9785536*) P.O. Box 788, Flossmoor, IL 60422 USA
E-mail: ac@grayerpublishing.com
Web site: http://www.grayerpublishing.com.

Graymalkin Media, (*978-1-935169; 978-1-63168; 978-1-63507*) Orders Addr.: 1413 Greenfield Ave., Suite 103, Los Angeles, CA 90025 USA Tel 310-231-8202 (phone/fax)
Web site: http://www.graymalkin.com
Dist(s): **Follett School Solutions**
Midwest Tape.

Grayson, Kate, (*978-0-9774357*) 2307 58th Ave. E., Bradenton, FL 34203 USA (SAN 257-5000)
E-mail: kgrayson1@aol.com.

Graziano, Claudia *See* **Meerkat's Adventures Bks.**

GRC Bks., (*978-0-578-06866-4; 978-0-578-08611-8; 978-0-578-12011-9*) 704 Robinson Rd., Sebastopol, CA 95472 USA Tel 707-829-9191
E-mail: martyr@sonic.net
Dist(s): **Lulu Pr., Inc.**

Great AD-Ventures, (*978-0-9665053*) P.O. Box 8011, Boise, ID 83707 USA Fax: 208-336-5797; Toll Free: 800-390-5687
E-mail: theplace@lesbois.com; book@freeread.com
Web site: http://www.freeread.com/.

Great Adventures Publishing, (*978-0-9747972*) 465 Hill St., Laguna Beach, CA 92651 USA Tel 949-494-5797
E-mail: paigeturner5@hotmail.com.

Great American Pr., The, (*978-0-9777996; 978-0-9798776; 978-0-9814627*) 551 League City Pkwy., League City, TX 77573 USA (SAN 850-2773) Tel 281-557-4300 (phone/fax)
Web site: http://www.thegreatamericanpress.com.

Great American Pubs., (*978-0-9779053; 978-1-934817*) 171 Lone Pine Church Rd., Lena, MS 39094 USA Tel 601-854-5954; Fax: 601-854-5958
E-mail: info@gapublishers.com; ssimmons@gapublishers.com
Web site: http://www.greatamericanpublishers.com
Dist(s): **Appalachian Bk. Distributors**
Bk. Marketing Plus
Bks. West
Dot Gibson Distribution
Forest Sales & Distributing Co.
Rumpf, Raymond & Son
Southwest Cookbook Distributors.

Great Authors Online, (*978-0-9773869*) 16440 Monterey St., Lake Elsinore, CA 92530 USA Tel 951-674-3246; Fax: 951-245-3608
E-mail: rodgerolsen@yahoo.com
Web site: http://greatauthorsonline.com.

Great Big Comics *See* **Great Big Comics, Big Tex Films**

Great Big Comics, Big Tex Films, (*978-0-9746784; 978-0-9844728; 978-0-615-49875-1*) Div. of The Big Tex Movin' Picture Company, LLC, 31 E. Bonneymead Cir., The Woodlands, TX 77381 USA
E-mail: bh@wondervista.com; avast@shebuccaneer.com
Web site: http://www.wondervista.com; http://www.greatbigcomics.com
Dist(s): **Diamond Distributors, Inc.**

Great Bks. Foundation, (*978-0-945159; 978-1-880323; 978-1-933147; 978-1-939014; 978-1-951782*) 35 E. Wacker Dr. Ste. 400, Chicago, IL 60601-2105 USA (SAN 205-3292) Toll Free: 800-222-5870
E-mail: hurleyp@greatbooks.org
Web site: http://www.greatbooks.org.

Great Character Development Workbook, The, (*978-0-9728417*) P.O. Box 1852, Kingston, WA 98346 USA
Web site: http://www.thegreatcharacterdevelopmentworkbook.com.

Great Dog Literary LLC, (*978-0-692-94683-1; 978-0-9993912; 978-1-7331337; 978-1-951388*) P.O. Box 456, Craryville, NY 12521 USA Tel 917-207-8703
E-mail: liz@greatdogliterary.com
Dist(s): **Ingram Content Group.**

Great Expectations Bk. Co., (*978-1-883934*) P.O. Box 2067, Eugene, OR 07402 USA Tel 541-343-2647; Fax: 541-343-0568
E-mail: fred@pinehillgraphics.com.

Great I-AM Publishing Co., The, (*978-0-9762788*) Orders Addr.: P.O. Box 30412, Wilmington, DE 19805 USA Tel 302-888-2477; Fax: 302-416-5085; Edit Addr.: 25 Roselane Rosegate, New Castle, DE 19720 USA
E-mail: watkinstyree2@aol.com.

Great Ideas for Teaching, Inc., (*978-1-886143*) Orders Addr.: P.O. Box 444, Wrightsville Beach, NC 28480-0444 USA Tel 910-256-4494; Fax: 910-256-4493; Toll Free Fax: 800-839-8498; Toll Free: 800-839-8339; Edit Addr.: 6800 Wrightsville Ave., No. 16, Wilmington, NC 28403 USA
E-mail: gift@wilmington.net
Web site: http://www.gift-inc.com.

Great Ideas Pr., Ltd., (*978-1-884949*) 4130 166th Pl. SW, Lynnwood, WA 98037 USA Tel 425-774-6611
E-mail: JamesRobert@jamesrobertdeal.com
Web site: http://www.whattoserveagoddess.com.

Great Kids Helping Great Kids, Incorporated *See* **America's Great Stories**

Great Lakes Bks. *Imprint of* **Wayne State Univ. Pr.**

Great Lakes Design, (*978-0-9761274*) P.O. Box 511534, Milwaukee, WI 53203 USA
Web site: http://www.vikingadventure.net.

Great Lakes Literary, LLC, (*978-1-883953; 978-1-933987*) 3147 S. Pennsylvania Ave., Milwaukee, WI 53207 USA; *Imprints:* Crickhollow Books (Crickhollow); Crispin Books (CrispinBks); Blue Horse Books (BlueHorse)
E-mail: info@CrickhollowBooks.com
Web site: http://www.CrickhollowBooks.com; http://www.CrispinBooks.com
Dist(s): **BookBaby**
BookMobile
Itasca Bks.

Great Lakes Literary, LLCorp. *See* **Great Lakes Literary, LLC**

Great Lakes Press, Inc., (*978-0-9614760; 978-1-881018; 978-1-939085*) Orders Addr.: P.O. Box 374, Cottleville, MO 63338 USA Fax: 636-273-6086
E-mail: service@glpbooks.com
Web site: http://www.glpbooks.com; http://www.greatlakespress.com.

Great Mastiff Corp., (*978-0-9759166*) 9945 E. Whitebirch Rd., Port wing, WI 54865 USA Tel 715-774-3247
E-mail: greatmastiff@hotmail.com
Web site: http://www.greatmastiff.com.

Great Nation Publishing, (*978-0-578-05549-7; 978-0-578-06529-8; 978-0-615-44374-4; 978-0-615-60214-1; 978-0-9891056*) Orders Addr.: 3828 Salem Rd., No. 56, Covington, GA 30016 USA
E-mail: brian@authorbrianthompson.com
Web site: http://www.authorbrianthompson.com
Dist(s): **Smashwords.**

Great Ocean Publishers *See* **Great River Bks.**

Great Persuader Publishing, The, (*978-0-9712581*)
E-mail: greatpersuader@hotmail.com; Info@Poetryisalive.com.

Great Plains Pr., (*978-0-9632459; 978-0-9861616*) 1103 Canyon Rd., Santa Fe, NM 87501 USA
E-mail: dirk@rainbowplace.com
Web site: http://www.greatplainspress.com/.

Great Plains Pubns. (CAN) (*978-0-9697804; 978-1-894283; 978-1-926531; 978-1-927855; 978-1-77337*) *Dist. by* **IPG Chicago.**

†Great Potential Pr., Inc., (*978-0-910707; 978-1-935067*) 1650 N. Kolb, Suite 200, Tucson, AZ 85715 USA (SAN 260-2385) Tel 520-777-6161; Fax: 520-777-6217
E-mail: info@greatpotentialpress.com
Web site: http://www.facebook.com/GreatPotentialPress; http://www.greatpotentialpress.com
Dist(s): **Bookmen, Inc.**; *CIP.*

Great Reads Bks., (*978-0-9718694*) P.O. Box 2112, Bellaire, TX 77402-2112 USA (SAN 254-5462)
E-mail: greatreadsbooks@earthlink.net; publish@novelpro.com
Web site: http://www.novelpro.com.

†Great River Bks., (*978-0-915556*) 161 M St., Salt Lake City, UT 84103 USA (SAN 207-527X) Tel 801-532-4833
E-mail: info@greatriverbooks.com
Web site: http://www.greatriverbooks.com
Dist(s): **Crown Hse. Publishing LLC**
Independent Pubs. Group
Midpoint Trade Bks., Inc.; *CIP.*

Great Smoky Mountains Assn., (*978-0-937207*) 115 Park Headquarters Rd., Gatlinburg, TN 37738 USA (SAN 658-7267) Tel 865-436-7318; Fax: 865-436-6884
E-mail: aaron@gsmassoc.org
Web site: http://www.smokiesinformation.org
Dist(s): **Publishers Group West (PGW).**

Great Smoky Mountains Natural History Association *See* **Great Smoky Mountains Assn.**

Great Source Education Group, Inc., (*978-0-669; 978-0-9638133; 978-1-57185*) Subs. of Houghton Mifflin Harcourt Supplemental Pubs., 181 Ballardvale St., Wilmington, MA 01887 USA Tel 978-661-1500; Fax: 978-661-1331; Toll Free Fax: 800-289-3994; Toll Free: 800-289-4490
Web site: http://www.greatsource.com
Dist(s): **Houghton Mifflin Harcourt Publishing Co.**

Great Texas Line Pr., (*978-1-892588*) Orders Addr.: P.O. Box 11105, Fort Worth, TX 76110 USA Tel 817-922-8929; Fax: 817-926-0420
E-mail: greattexas@hotmail.com
Web site: http://www.greattexasline.com
Dist(s): **Baker & Taylor Bks.**
Bk. Marketing Plus
Bks. West
Forest Sales & Distributing Co.

Great Valley Bks. *Imprint of* **Heyday**

Great West Publishing, (*978-0-9796199; 978-0-9974553*) Orders Addr.: P.O. Box 31631, Tucson, AZ 85751-1631 USA (SAN 853-9146); *Imprints:* Sentry Books (Sentry Bks)
Web site: http://www.sentrybooks.com.

Great White Bird Publishing, (*978-0-9792474*) Orders Addr.: P.O. Box 667, Hiram, GA 30141-0667 USA Tel 770-947-6817; *Imprints:* GWB (GWB)
E-mail: davidthackston@bellsouth.net
Web site: http://www.myspace.com/thackston.

Greater Cincinnati TV Educational Foundation, (*978-0-9744419*) 1223 Central Pkwy., Cincinnati, OH 45214-2812 USA Tel 513-381-4033; Fax: 513-381-7520; *Imprints:* CET (Cet)
E-mail: edtech@wcet.pbs.org
Web site: http://www.wcet.org.

Greater Truth Pubs., (*978-0-9653078; 978-1-937151*) P.O. Box 4332, Lafayette, IN 47903 USA Do not confuse with Griffin Publishing, Glendale, CA
E-mail: gtp@ao-soft.com
Web site: http://www.ao-soft.com/gtpub/.

Greatest Books Pub., (*978-1-937775; 978-1-62236; 978-81-8423-059-8*) 2764 N. Green Valley Pkwy., Henderson, NV 89014 USA Tel 951-760-8499
E-mail: lbbooks1234@gmail.com.

Greatful Geek Publishing, (*978-0-578-22716-0; 978-0-578-22717-7*) 2301 E. Rock Creek Rd., Norman, OK 73071 USA.

GreatWineFinds.com *See* **GWF Publishing & Henry's Helpers**

GreeHee Publishing, (*978-0-9779590*) Orders Addr.: 125 Susan St., Myrtle Creek, OR 97457-9741 USA Tel 541-863-6631
E-mail: astrologyandmore@gmail.com
Web site: http://www.greehee.com; http://www.talesoftamoor.com
Dist(s): **Quality Bks., Inc.**
Smashwords.

Green & Purple Publishing *See* **Green & Purple Publishing**

Green & Purple Publishing, (*978-1-7321212; 978-1-950190*) 44864 Linalou Ranch Rd, Temecula, CA 92592 USA Tel 909-938-9932
E-mail: pambowen909@gmail.com
Web site: pamellabowen.com; greenandpurplepublishing.com.

Green Apple Lessons, Inc., (*978-0-692-98638-7; 978-0-692-12278-5; 978-0-578-50526-8*) 24110 Venetian Dr., Richmond, TX 77406 USA Tel 832-612-1224
E-mail: julieannesavage@protonmail.com
Dist(s): **Ingram Content Group.**

Green Beanie Bks., (*978-1-937499*) P.O. Box 7405, Bonney Lake, WA 98391 USA Tel 253-862-4711
E-mail: carla@greenbeaniebooks.com
Web site: greenbeaniebooks.com
Dist(s): **American West Bks.**

Green, C. K. *See* **Kingston Publishing Co.**

Green Card Voices, (*978-0-692-51151-0; 978-0-692-57281-8; 978-0-9974960; 978-1-949523; 978-1-7327906*) 2611 1st Ave S, Minneapolis, MN 55408 USA Tel 612-889-7635
E-mail: greencardvoices@gmail.com
Web site: http://www.greencardvoices.com/
Dist(s): **Consortium Bk. Sales & Distribution**
CreateSpace Independent Publishing Platform.

†Green Dragon Bks., (*978-0-89334; 978-1-62386*) 2875 S. Ocean Blvd. Ste 200, Palm Beach, FL 33480 USA (SAN 658-0882) Toll Free Fax: 888-874-8844; Toll Free: 800-874-8844; *Imprints:* Humanics Learning (Humanics Lrng) Do not confuse with Humanics ErgoSystems, Inc., Reseda, CA
E-mail: info@greendragonbooks.com
Web site: http://www.greendragonbooks.com; http://www.humanicslearning.com; http://www.humanicsdealer.com
Dist(s): **Borders, Inc.**
Midpoint Trade Bks., Inc.
New Leaf Distributing Co., Inc.
Two Rivers Distribution; *CIP.*

Green E-Bks., (*978-1-938848; 978-0-9990528; 978-0-9994577; 978-1-7329882*) 6145 N. Tapestry Way, Boise, ID 83714 USA Tel 208-608-8325; Fax: 208-441-6024
E-mail: jason@greene-books.com.

Green Egg Media, Incorporated *See* **Three Sixteen Publishing**

Green Ghost Press *See* **Waide Aaron Riddle**

Green Goat Bks., (*978-0-615-15585-2*) P.O. Box 11256, Bainbridge Island, WA 98110 USA Tel 206-842-3412; Fax: 206-842-0570; Toll Free: 866-776-4543
E-mail: contact@greengoatbooks.com
Web site: http://www.greengoatbooks.com
Dist(s): **Greenleaf Book Group.**

Green Hill Publishers *See* **Jameson Bks., Inc.**

Green Igric Pr., (*978-0-9776170*) P.O. Box 82454, Columbus, OH 43202 USA Tel 614-267-9426.

Green Irene, (*978-0-9742280*) P.O. Box 5, Huron, OH 44839 USA
E-mail: chager@buckeye-express.com
Web site: http://www.redandgreenchoices.com.

Green Key Books *See* **Practical Christianity Foundation**

Green Kids Club, Inc., (*978-0-9836602; 978-1-939871*) 1425 Higham St., Idaho Falls, ID 83402 USA Tel 208-528-8718
E-mail: peggy_hinman@yahoo.com.

Green Kids Pr., LLC, (*978-1-939377*) 23 T St. NW, Washington, DC 20001-1008 USA (SAN 920-458X) Tel 202-518-7070; Fax: 202-588-0931
E-mail: jucles@hotmail.com
Web site: www.Green-KidsPress.com
Dist(s): **Independent Pubs. Group**
Midpoint Trade Bks., Inc.
Partners Pubs. Group, Inc.

Green Lady Pr., The *Imprint of* **RealityIsBooks.com, Inc.**

Green Leaf Publishing *See* **BookWise Publishing**

Green Light Bks. and Publishing, LLC, (*978-0-9755110*) Orders Addr.: 4509 Lake Lawne Ave., Orlando, FL 32808 USA
E-mail: juan_chisholm@yahoo.com
Web site: http://www.greenlightbooks.org.

Green Mansion Pr. LLC, (*978-0-9714612; 978-0-9746457*) 501 E. 79th St., Suite 16A, New York, NY 10021-0773 USA (SAN 254-2684) Tel 212-396-2667; Fax: 212-937-4685
E-mail: info@greenmansionpress.com
Web site: http://www.greenmansionpress.com.

Green, Mary, (*978-0-9764639*) 737 Buffalo Valley Rd., Cookeville, TN 38501-3862 USA
E-mail: greenmajt@frontiernet.net
Web site: http://www.bigfootlady.net.

Green Monkey Bks. *Imprint of* **Purple Sword Pubns., LLC**

Green Nest LLC, (*978-0-9772392*) 18662 Macarthur Blvd. Suite 200, Irvine, CA 92612 USA Fax: 949-387-3806
Web site: http://www.greennest.com
Dist(s): **Pathway Bk. Service.**

Green Owl, Inc., (*978-0-9727273*) 23834 SE 248th St., Maple Valley, WA 98038 USA (SAN 255-0679)
E-mail: owl@greenowl.org
Web site: http://www.greenowl.org.

Green Pastures Pr., (*978-0-9627643; 978-1-884377*) HC 67, Box 91-A, Mifflin, PA 17058 USA Tel 717-436-9115.

Green Pastures Publishing, Inc., (*978-0-9664276; 978-0-9720580*) Orders Addr.: P.O. Box 804, Windsor, CO 80550 USA Tel 970-686-7242
Dist(s): **Independent Pubs. Group.**

Green Ronin Publishing, (*978-0-9701048; 978-0-9714380; 978-0-9723599; 978-0-9726756; 978-1-932442; 978-1-934547; 978-1-949160*) Orders Addr.: P.O. Box

1723, Renton, WA 98057-1723 USA Tel 206-725-2839; Fax: 206-725-2980; Edit Addr.: 6731 29th Ave., S, Seattle, WA 98108 USA
E-mail: pramas@greenronin.com; nicole@greenronin.com
Web site: http://www.greenronin.com
Dist(s): **Diamond Comic Distributors, Inc.**
Diamond Bk. Distributors.

Green Sheet Inc., The, *(978-0-9670947)* P.O. Box 6008, Petaluma, CA 94955-6008 USA Fax: 707-586-1738; Toll Free: 800-757-4441
E-mail: grnsht@aol.com
Web site: http://www.greensheet.com.

Green Tiger Pr. *Imprint of* **Laughing Elephant**

Green, Tim, *(978-0-578-51360-7; 978-0-578-51388-1; 978-0-578-51389-8; 978-0-578-51390-4)* 9127 Cresta Dr., Los Angeles, CA 90035 USA Tel 310-365-4865
E-mail: tmrtim@gmail.com
Dist(s): **Ingram Content Group.**

Green Writers Pr., *(978-0-9893104; 978-0-9899838; 978-0-9960872; 978-0-9909733; 978-0-9961357; 978-0-9962676; 978-0-9968973; 978-0-9974528; 978-0-9982604; 978-0-9987012; 978-0-9990766; 978-0-9994995; 978-1-7320815; 978-1-7322662; 978-1-7327434; 978-1-7328540; 978-1-7336534; 978-1-950584) 34 Miller Rd., Brattleboro, VT 05301 USA Tel 802-380-1121*
E-mail: dcdesignteamvt@gmail.com
Web site: www.greenwriterspress.com
Dist(s): **Independent Pubs. Group**
Midpoint Trade Bks., Inc.

Greenberg, Carmel *See* **Kicks and Giggles Today**

Greenberg, Melanie Hope, *(978-0-692-11664-7; 978-0-578-55212-5; 978-0-578-61903-3)* 168 Hicks St., Brooklyn, NY 11201 USA Tel 718-522-7026
E-mail: melhopegreenberg@aol.com
Web site: http://melaniehopegreenberg.blogspot.com.

Greenberg, Scott *See* **Jump Start Performance Programs**

Greenberry Publishing, LLC *See* **Authors Pr.**

Greenblatt, Kim, *(978-0-9777282; 978-1-60622)* 6600 Melba Ave., West Hills, CA 91307 USA (SAN 850-0649).

Greenbrier/Scentex *See* **Bright of America**

Greenbush Pr., *(978-0-9766720; 978-0-9836460; 978-0-615-95792-0; 978-0-9600297)* Orders Addr.: 21518 Karpathos Ln., Spring, TX 77388-3262 USA (SAN 256-5048) Tel 832-469-1033 Office
E-mail: frank@depressionproofchurch.com; frank@frankbecker.com; frank@greenbushpress.com
Web site: http://www.frankbecker.com.

Greene & Sandell, *(978-0-9834681)* 45 Church St. Apt. 1, Boston, MA 02116 USA Tel 617-426-7278
E-mail: greenesandell@gmail.com.

Greene, A.S. & Co., *(978-0-9761723)* 1828 Kings Hwy., Lincoln Park, MI 48146 USA Fax: 313-388-0447
E-mail: anitazoya@yahoo.com.

Greene Bark Pr., Inc., *(978-1-880851)* P.O. Box 1108, Bridgeport, CT 06601-1108 USA Tel 203-372-4861; Fax: 203-371-5856
E-mail: Greenebark@aol.com
Web site: http://www.greenebarkpress.com.

Greene, Brenda H. *See* **Three Willows Pr.**

Greene, Marjorie A., *(978-0-9741764)* 124 Caughman Park Dr., Columbia, SC 29209 USA Tel 803-783-5430; Fax: 803-783-5430
E-mail: remaininme@msn.com.

Greenfield Enterprises, Ltd. (HKG) *(978-962-563) Dist. by* **Cheng Tsui.**

Greenhaven Pr., Inc. *Imprint of* **Cengage Gale**

Greenhaven Publishing *Imprint of* **Cengage Gale**

Greenhaven Publishing *Imprint of* **Greenhaven Publishing LLC**

Greenhaven Publishing LLC, *(978-1-5345)* 353 3rd Ave., Suite 255, New York, NY 10010 USA (SAN 990-171X) Tel 212-420-1205; Fax: 212-614-7385; Toll Free Fax: 844-317-7405; Toll Free: 844-317-7404; *Imprints*: KidHaven Publishing (KidHaven Publ); Lucent Press (Lucent Pr); Greenhaven Publishing (GreenHav)
E-mail: gh_custserv@greenhaven.com; hollyc@rosenpub.com
Dist(s): **Rosen Publishing Group, Inc., The.**

Greenhill Bks. (GBR) *(978-0-947898; 978-1-85367; 978-1-78438) Dist. by* **HachBkGrp.**

Greenhill Bks. (GBR) *(978-0-947898; 978-1-85367; 978-1-78438) Dist. by* **Casemate Pubs.**

Greenleaf Book Group, *(978-0-9665319; 978-1-929774; 978-0-9790842; 978-1-60832; 978-1-61486; 978-1-62634)* Orders Addr.: 4005-B Banister Ln., Austin, TX 78704 USA Tel 512-891-6100; Fax: 512-891-6150; Toll Free: 800-932-5420; Edit Addr.: P.O. Box 91869, Austin, TX 78709 USA; *Imprints*: Greenleaf Book Group Press (GBGP)
E-mail: tanya@greenleafbookgroup.com
Web site: http://www.greenleafbookgroup.com
Dist(s): **CreateSpace Independent Publishing Platform**
D.A.P./Distributed Art Pubs.

Greenleaf Book Group Pr. *Imprint of* **Greenleaf Book Group**

Greenleaf Pr., *(978-1-882514)* 1570 Old Laguardo Rd E., Lebanon, TN 37087-8958 USA (SAN 297-8555) Toll Free Fax: 866-725-0785 Do not confuse with Greenleaf Pr., Breckenridge, CO
E-mail: info@greenleafpress.com
Web site: http://www.greenleafpress.com.

Greenleaf Publishing, Inc., *(978-0-578-42560-3; 978-0-578-70790-7)* 5531 W. 93rd St., Bloomington, MN 55437-1941 USA Tel 952-856-2505
E-mail: davegreenleaf@comcast.net
Web site: http://www.greenleafpub.com.

Greenlees Publishing, *(978-1-951098)* 7848 Bavaria Rd., Victoria, MN 55386 USA Tel 323-477-5703
E-mail: lisaumhoefer@gmail.com.

Greenline Publications *See* **Davis, A. S. Media Group**

GreenPoint Computer Services *See* **GIL Pubns.**

Greenroom Bks., *(978-0-9712163)* 12 N. Juniper St., Hampton, VA 23669-2416 USA (SAN 254-2501) Tel 757-726-2651 (phone/fax)
E-mail: brad@greenroombooks.com; publisher@greenroombooks.com
Web site: http://www.greenroombooks.com
Dist(s): **Brodart Co.**

Greens' Pubns., *(978-0-9975003)* 409 Misty Ridge Way, Woodstock, GA 30189 USA Tel 678-403-1892
E-mail: darrylgreenpubs@gmail.com
Web site: www.greenspublications.com.

Greensboro Historical Museum, Inc., *(978-0-9747456)* 130 Summit Ave., Greensboro, NC 27401-3016 USA Tel 336-373-2043; Fax: 336-373-2204
Web site: http://www.greensborohistory.org.

Greentown Glass Co., *(978-0-9723958)* Orders Addr.: P.O. Box 771, Westfield, IN 46074-0771 USA Tel 765-455-0595; Edit Addr.: 3703 Robin Dr., Kokomo, IN 46902 USA
Web site: http://www.greentownglasscompany.com.

Greenville Family Partnership, *(978-0-9759699)* P.O. Box 10203, Greenville, SC 29603-0203 USA Tel 864-467-4099; Fax: 864-467-4102
Web site: http://www.redribbonworks.org.

Greenwillow Bks. *Imprint of* **HarperCollins Pubs.**

Greenwoman Publishing, LLC, *(978-0-9897056; 978-0-9905385)*
E-mail: maefayne@msn.com
Web site: http://www.greenwomanmagazine.com.

Greenwood *Imprint of* **ABC-CLIO, LLC**

Greenwood Hill Pr., *(978-0-9797868; 978-0-9836382; 978-0-9846912; 978-0-9881748; 978-0-9915961; 978-0-9989643)* W 7048 Savannah Ln., Delavan, WI 53115 USA; *Imprints*: OddInt Media (OddIntMedia)
E-mail: mjohnson@fullpo.com.

Greenwood, Lisa K., *(978-0-692-08066-5)* 5960 Munger Rd., Dayton, OH 45459 USA Tel 937-609-0891
E-mail: tgreenwood@greentreegroup.com.

Greenwood, Lori Ministries, Inc., *(978-0-9747956)* Orders Addr.: 17622 32nd Pl W., Lynnwood, WA 98037-7714 USA (SAN 255-8297)
E-mail: lgministries@cs.com
Web site: http://www.thevisionlink.com.

Greenwood Street Publishing. GSP, *(978-0-9745553)* 1539 W. Townley Ave., Phoenix, AZ 85021 USA Tel 602-997-4444; Fax: 602-997-5959 Do not confuse with Greenwood Publishing in Wixom, MI
E-mail: julie@gg-az.com; info@greenwoodstreet.com
Web site: http://www.greenwoodstreet.com.

Gregory, Charles, *(978-0-9745432)* 17697 Palmer St., Melvindale, MI 48122 USA (SAN 255-7991) Tel 313-389-2836
E-mail: charles_gregory@ameritech.net
Web site: http://www.charles_gregory/index.html
Dist(s): **Lulu Pr., Inc.**

Gregory, Charles Matthew, *(978-0-9766442)* 5101 Boarshead Rd. No. 102, Minnetonka, MN 55345 USA Tel 612-845-7134
Web site: www.mikascomic.com.

Grendel Roleplaying, *(978-1-929928)* 2341 San Juan Ct., Portales, NM 88130 USA
E-mail: author@paulbspence.com
Web site: http://www.paulbspence.com.

Grenevitch, Betsy Coffman, *(978-0-9747113)* 1450 Hewatt Rd., Lilburn, GA 30047 USA Tel 678-344-6100 (phone/fax)
E-mail: blindangel@joimail.com.

Grenwood Publishing *See* **Greenwood Street Publishing. GSP**

Gresham, Joel, *(978-0-9708446)* 2201 Morgan Pl., Atlanta, GA 30324 USA Tel 404-512-0445
E-mail: undercolorjg@yahoo.com.

Grettler, Kelly, *(978-0-692-80151-2; 978-0-692-07558-6; 978-0-578-57187-4)* .

Grey Gate Media, LLC, *(978-0-9787318; 978-0-9801004; 978-1-61807)* 20 Fisherville Rd., #173, Concord, NH 03303 USA Tel 603-801-2208; Fax: 603-676-7882; *Imprints*: Little Blue Flower Press (Little Blue Flow).

Grey Gecko Pr., *(978-0-9836185; 978-0-9854400; 978-1-938821; 978-1-945760)* 565 S Mason Rd Ste 154, Katy, TX 77450 USA Tel 713-489-5731
E-mail: jason@greygeckopress.com
Web site: http://www.greygeckopress.com
Dist(s): **Ingram Content Group.**

†Grey Hse. Publishing, *(978-0-939300; 978-1-891482; 978-1-930956; 978-1-59237; 978-1-61925; 978-1-68217; 978-1-64265)* 4919 Rte. 22 PO Box 56, Amenia, NY 12501 USA Tel 518-789-8700; Fax: 518-789-0556; Toll Free: 800-562-2139; 4919 Rte. 22 PO Box 56, Amenia, NY 12501 Tel 518-789-8700; Fax: 518-789-0556; Toll Free: 800-562-2139; *Imprints*: Universal Reference Publications (Universal Ref Pubns)
E-mail: books@greyhouse.com
Web site: http://www.greyhouse.com
Dist(s): **Ebsco Publishing**
MyiLibrary
ebrary, Inc.; *CIP.*

Grey Stone Bks. (GBR) *(978-0-9515996; 978-1-902017) Dist. by* **PerseuPGW.**

GreyCore Pr., *(978-0-9671851; 978-0-9742074)* 3833 Hilton Ave NE, Albuquerque, NM 87110-1059 USA
E-mail: joan123@frontiernet.net.

Greyhound Bks., *(978-0-9724136; 978-1-59677)* 2000 Stock Creek Rd., Knoxville, TN 37920 USA Tel 865-405-3002
E-mail: cynmob@aol.com; editor@bushidopress.com
Web site: http://www.dogbooks.org.

Greyson Media Associates, *(978-1-68399)* 122 W Main St No. 49394, Cookeville, TN 38506 USA
Web site: ChristopherGreyson.com; www.greysonmediaassociates.com.

Greystone Books Ltd. (CAN) *(978-1-55365; 978-1-77100; 978-1-77164) Dist. by* **PerseuPGW.**

Grid Pr. *Imprint of* **L & R Publishing, LLC**

Grief Watch, *(978-0-9615197; 978-0-9724241; 978-0-9916312; 978-0-692-37070-4)* Div. of Metanoia Peace Community United Methodist Church, 2116 NE 18th Ave., Portland, OR 97212 USA (SAN 694-2911) Tel 503-284-7426; Fax: 503-282-8985
E-mail: webmaster@griefwatch.com
Web site: http://www.griefwatch.com
Dist(s): **ACTA Pubns.**
CreateSpace Independent Publishing Platform.

GRIFFIN *See* **Griffin**

Griffin, *(978-0-312-60750-0)* 915 Electric Ave., Venice, CA 90291 USA.

Griffin Comics *Imprint of* **Corbett Features**

Griffin, Curtis Monroe, *(978-0-9749583)* 3250 Oneal Cir., Boulder, CO 80301-1424 USA.

Griffin Group Publishing LLC, *(978-0-692-01920-7)* 3419 Westminister Suite 320, Dallas, TX 75205 USA.

Griffin Publishing *See* **Greater Truth Pubs.**

Griffin Publishing Group, *(978-1-58000; 978-1-882180)* P.O. Box 28627, Santa Ana, CA 92799-8627 USA Toll Free: 800-472-9741 Do not confuse with Griffin Publishing, Ogden, UT
E-mail: griffinbooks@earthlink.net; mvonarx@griffinpublishing.com
Web site: http://www.griffinpublishing.com
Dist(s): **BHB Fullfillment**
Sundaykool Bulletins.

Griffin, Sandi Zambarano, *(978-1-883838)* 10840 Kimberfyld Ln., Port Saint Lucie, FL 34986 USA Tel 561-461-6830
Dist(s): **Bookazine Co., Inc.**

Griffis, Teri Errico, *(978-0-692-88542-0)* 1935 Treebark Dr., Charleston, SC 29414 USA Tel 203-450-7051; Fax: 203-450-7051
E-mail: teresaerrico05@yahoo.com.

Griffith, John *See* **Rosetta Stone Communications**

Griffith, Tara, *(978-0-692-83481-7)* 1330 Worley Ave NW, CANTON, OH 44703 USA Tel 330-617-3594
E-mail: jeffwcrawford5+LVP0003269@gmail.com; jeffwcrawford5+LVP0003269@gmail.com.

Griggs Music Co., *(978-0-9753385)* 228 Pope Bend Rd., Cedar Creek, TX 78612 USA Tel 512-303-2744
Web site: http://www.griggsmusic.net.

Grigsby, Cynthia, *(978-0-9786840)* 4304 Hillyer St., Fairfax, VA 22032-1418 USA
E-mail: cgrigsby6@yahoo.com.

Griha, *(978-0-9748503)* 23 Iron Bark Ln., Aliso Viejo, CA 92656 USA
Web site: http://www.griha.com.

Grijalbo, Editorial (MEX) *(978-968-419; 978-970-05) Dist. by* **AIMS Intl.**

Grijalbo, Editorial (MEX) *(978-968-419; 978-970-05) Dist. by* **Continental Bk.**

Grijalbo Mondadori, S.A.-Junior (ESP) *(978-84-253; 978-84-397; 978-84-7419; 978-84-478; 978-84-7423) Dist. by* **Continental Bk.**

Grijalbo Mondadori, S.A.-Montena (ESP) *(978-84-7515; 978-84-85297; 978-84-8441) Dist. by* **Lectorum Pubns.**

Grijalbo-Dargaud, S.A. Editores (ESP) *(978-84-7510) Dist. by* **Distribks Inc.**

Grimes, Richard, *(978-0-9770594)* 111 Lankford Dr., Georgetown, KY 40324 USA.

Gripper Products, *(978-0-916176)* 787 N. 24th St., Philadelphia, PA 19130-2540 USA (SAN 206-3816) Tel 215-765-9362
E-mail: reluctantspy@gmail.com
Web site: http://www.lookunderrocks.com
Dist(s): **CreateSpace Independent Publishing Platform**
Ingram Content Group
Smashwords.

Grivante Pr., *(978-1-62676)* P.O. Box 1392, Sagle, ID 83860 USA Tel 208-660-7294; *Imprints*: Melanin Origins, LLC (MYID_G_MELANIN)
E-mail: grivante@gmail.com
Web site: www.grivantepress.com.

Grizlegirl Productions *See* **Bookateer Publishing**

Grizzly Adams Productions, Inc., *(978-0-9667985; 978-1-929296; 978-1-931602; 978-1-933424; 978-1-934646)* Orders Addr.: P.O. Box 298, Baker City, OR 97814 USA; Edit Addr.: 2850 Myrtle St., Baker City, OR 97814 USA
Dist(s): **Send The Light Distribution LLC.**

Grizzly Bks Publishing, *(978-0-9747951; 978-0-9749634)* Orders Addr.: PMB Box 136, Dahlonega, GA 30533 USA Tel 706-864-2349 (phone/fax); Edit Addr.: 240 Wal-Mart Way, Dahlonega, GA 30533 USA
E-mail: ancient12@linkamerica.net
Web site: http://www.grizzlybookz.com.

Grizzly Ridge Publishing, *(978-0-9793963)* P.O. Box 268, West Glacier, MT 59936 USA
Web site: http://www.grizzlyridgepublishing.com.

Grolier *Imprint of* **Scholastic Library Publishing**

Grolier Online *Imprint of* **Scholastic Library Publishing**

Grolier Publishing *See* **Scholastic Library Publishing**

Grolier Publishing, *(978-0-516; 978-0-531)* 90 Old Sherman Tpke., Danbury, CT 06816E USA Tel 203-797-3500; Fax: 203-797-3657
E-mail: agraham@grolier.com
Web site: www.scholasticlibrary.com.

Grosinger, Crain Publishing, *(978-0-9720054)* Orders Addr.: P.O. Box 55, Mandan, ND 58554 USA Tel 701-202-1293; Edit Addr.: 210 Collins Ave., Mandan, ND 58554 USA
Web site: http://www.johnsbook.net; http://www.crainbooks.com
Dist(s): **Partners Bk. Distributing, Inc.**

Gross, H. H., *(978-0-9754699)* P.O. Box 122606, San Diego, CA 92112 USA
E-mail: hhgross@lycos.com
Web site: http://www.hhgross.net.

Gross, Roxanna, *(978-0-615-16398-7)* 3 S. Cedarwood Ct., Alexandria, KY 41001 USA
E-mail: roxie@zoomtown.com
Dist(s): **Lulu Pr., Inc.**

Grosset & Dunlap *Imprint of* **Penguin Young Readers Group**

Grosset & Dunlap *Imprint of* **Penguin Publishing Group**

Grossman, Dina *See* **Tzipora Pubns., Inc.**

Groundbreaking Pr., *(978-0-9718562; 978-0-9745624; 978-0-9765821; 978-0-9773535; 978-0-9777795; 978-0-9793542; 978-0-9831030; 978-0-9850651; 978-1-7339001)* 2050 Ruby Lane #1, Fairfield, IA 52556 USA Tel 512-339-4000; Fax: 512-458-1648
E-mail: bradfregger@gmail.com
Web site: http://www.groundbreaking.com.

Groundwood Bks. (CAN) *(978-0-88899; 978-1-55498) Dist. by* **PerseuPGW.**

Group Books *See* **Group Publishing, Inc.**

†Group Publishing, Inc., *(978-0-7644; 978-0-931529; 978-0-936664; 978-1-55945; 978-1-4707)* Orders Addr.: 1515 Cascade Ave., Loveland, CO 80538-8681 USA (SAN 214-4689) Tel 970-669-3836; Fax: 970-679-4373; Toll Free: 800-635-0404; 800-447-1070 (consumer orders only); 800-541-5200 (trade orders only); *Imprints*: Flagship Church Resources (Flagship Church)
E-mail: sjohnson@group.com
Web site: http://www.group.com
Dist(s): **Appalachian Bible Co.**
Faith Alive Christian Resources
Spring Arbor Distributors, Inc.
Twentieth Century Christian Bks.; *CIP.*

Grove Creek Publishing, LLC, *(978-1-933963)* 1159 N. 950 E., Pleasant Grove, UT 84062 USA Tel 801-471-5652
E-mail: noonws@yahoo.com
Web site: http://www.grovecreekpublishing.com.

Grove Educational Technologies, *(978-0-936735)* 6435 Yamhill St., SE, Portland, OR 97215-2027 USA (SAN 699-9840); 27 Hy Pl., Lake Grove, NY 11755 (SAN 699-9859)
E-mail: geta@juno.com.

†Grove/Atlantic, Inc., *(978-0-8021; 978-0-87113; 978-1-55584; 978-1-61185)* 841 Broadway, 4th Flr., New York, NY 10003-4793 USA (SAN 201-4890) Tel 212-614-7850; Fax: 212-614-7886; Toll Free: 800-521-0178; *Imprints*: Black Cat (BlackCat)
Web site: http://www.groveatlantic.com/
Dist(s): **MyiLibrary**
Open Road Integrated Media, Inc.
Publishers Group West (PGW)
Two Rivers Distribution; *CIP.*

Growing & Learning Pr., *(978-0-9795773)* 228 Woodward Ave, Buffalo, NY 14214 USA (SAN 853-8093).

Growing Art Pr., *(978-1-934367)* 419 NW 16th St., Corvallis, OR 97330 USA (SAN 852-9612)
E-mail: stickmaker@comcast.net.

Growing Communities for Peace, *(978-0-9646676)* P.O. Box 248, Scandia, MN 55073 USA Tel 651-257-2478; Fax: 651-257-2095
Web site: http://www.peacemaker.org.

Growing Field *Imprint of* **Growing Field Bks.**

Growing Field Bks., *(978-0-9770391; 978-0-9857057; 978-0-9891881)* 2012 Pacific Ct., Fort Collins, CO 80528 USA (SAN 851-7193); *Imprints*: Growing Field (Growing Field) Do not confuse with companies with the same or similar name in Lawrence, KSThomaston, CT, Los Angeles, CA, Huntsville, AL, New YOrk, NY, Glen Head, NY
E-mail: Mhoog@growingfield.com
Web site: http://www.Growingfield.com
Dist(s): **Brodart Co.**
Follett School Solutions
Hertzberg-New Method Inc.

Growing Little Readers, *(978-0-9777150)* 1105 Kyle Ct., Chesapeake, VA 23322 USA
Web site: http://growinglittlereaders.com.

Growing Senses Pubns., *(978-0-9973189)* 5842 Cranbrook Trail, Traverse City, MI 49685 USA Tel 231-881-4138
E-mail: growingsensespublications@gmail.com.

Growing with the Saints, Inc., *(978-0-9798889)* 2812 Longwood Ct., Fort Wayne, IN 46845 USA Tel 260-489-8493
E-mail: melissa@growingwiththesaints.com
Web site: http://www.growingwiththesaints.com.

Growing Years *Imprint of* **Port Town Publishing**

Growsies, *(978-0-9980949)* 10905 Tree Cactus Loop, Land O Lakes, FL 34638 USA Tel 727-641-7944
E-mail: growsiestories@gmail.com
Web site: www.growsiestories.wordpress.com.

Growth Affirming Co., *(978-0-9913804)* 2760 150th Ave., Clear Lake, MN 55319-9561 USA Tel 763-856-8646
E-mail: growthaffirm@izoom.net
Web site: Growthaffirm.com.

Growth Publishing, *(978-1-893505)* Div. of Growth Central LLC, Orders Addr.: 6545 N. Via Divina, Tucson, AZ 85750-0971 USA Tel 520-299-2550; Fax: 520-577-6998
E-mail: growthcentral@gmail.com
Web site: http://www.growthcentral.com/.

Growth-Ink, *(978-0-9799636)* 4025 State St., No. 9, Santa Barbara, CA 93110 USA (SAN 854-9303)
E-mail: Growthink1@aol.com.

Gruber Enterprises, *(978-0-9770413)* 21521 Finlan, Saint Clair Shores, MI 48080 USA
Web site: http://www.thelegendofthebrog.com.

Grubish, Donald, *(978-0-9771179)* 1326 Goodwin Ave N., Saint Paul, MN 55128-6164 USA.

Grubnedor Pr., *(978-0-9795407; 978-0-9989368; 978-0-578-58511-6; 978-0-578-58512-3; 978-0-578-63474-6)* 8121 Allison Pl., Arvada, CO 80005 USA (SAN 853-7186)
E-mail: dmrodenburg@comcast.net
Web site: grubnedorpress.com.

Grupo Anaya, S.A. (ESP) *(978-84-207; 978-84-667; 978-84-678; 978-84-698) Dist. by* **AIMS Intl.**

Grupo Anaya, S.A. (ESP) *(978-84-207; 978-84-667; 978-84-678; 978-84-698) Dist. by* **Distribks Inc.**

Grupo Anaya, S.A. (ESP) *(978-84-207; 978-84-667; 978-84-678; 978-84-698) Dist. by* **Continental Bk.**

Grupo Anaya, S.A. (ESP) *(978-84-207; 978-84-667; 978-84-678; 978-84-698) Dist. by* **Lectorum Pubns.**

Grupo Nelson, *(978-0-8499; 978-0-88113; 978-0-89922; 978-1-60255)* Div. of Thomas Nelson, Inc., 501 Nelson Pl., Nashville, TN 37217 USA (SAN 240-6349) Tel 615-889-9000; Fax: 615-883-9376; Toll Free: 800-251-4000
Web site: http://www.editorialcaribe.com
Dist(s): **Ediciones Universal**
HarperCollins Christian Publishing
Libros Sin Fronteras
Luciano Bks.
Nelson, Thomas Inc.
Pan De Vida Distributors
Peniel Productions
Twentieth Century Christian Bks.
Zondervan.

Gryphon House Inc *Imprint of* **Gryphon Hse., Inc.**

Gryphon Hse., Inc., *(978-0-87659; 978-0-917505; 978-1-58904; 978-1-63650)* Orders Addr.: 6848 Leon's Way, Lewisville, NC 27023 USA (SAN 169-3190) Tel 800-638-0928; Fax: 800-638-7576; Toll Free: 800-638-0928; *Imprints:* Robins Lane Press (Robins Ln Pr); School Age Notes (School-Age); Gryphon House Inc (GHI)
E-mail: info@ghbooks.com
Web site: http://www.gryphonhouse.com
Dist(s): **CENGAGE Learning**
Children's Plus, Inc.
INscribe Digital
MyiLibrary
ebrary, Inc.

Gryphon Pr., The, *(978-0-940719)* 6808 Margarets Ln., Edina, MN 55439 USA Tel 952-941-5993; Fax: 952-941-6593
E-mail: eb6@earthlink.net
Dist(s): **Consortium Bk. Sales & Distribution.**

G.S. Enterprises of America Inc., *(978-0-9763141)* P.O. Box 776, Frankfort, KY 40602-0776 USA Tel 502-227-8226; Fax: 502-227-8223
E-mail: lstafford173@gmail.com
Web site: http://www.bedtimeboomer.com.

GS Publishers *See* **GSVQ Publishing**

GSD Publishing, *(978-0-9724658)* 5589 Nix Rd., Fayetteville, NC 28314 USA Tel 910-864-5033.

GSP Players, LLC, *(978-0-9792640)* 8033 Sunset Blvd., No. 1024, Los Angeles, CA 90046 USA.

G-Square Publishing, *(978-0-692-10481-1)* 888c 8th Ave. suite 424, New York, NY 10019 USA Tel 917-681-2810
E-mail: G-Square-pub@optimum.net
Web site: G-Square.org.

GSR Communications, *(978-0-9717507)* 6090 SW Elm Ave., Beaverton, OR 97005 USA
E-mail: gsr@teleport.com.

GSS Tech Ed, *(978-0-9712340; 978-0-9895576)* 31500 Grape St. Bldg. 3-364, Lake Elsinore, CA 92532 USA Tel 951-471-4932; Fax: 951-471-4981; Toll Free Fax: 866-367-6180; Toll Free: 800-422-1100
Web site: http://www.GSSTechEd.com
Dist(s): **All Electronics Corp.**
Pitsco Education.

GSVQ Publishing, *(978-1-933156)* 1350 E. Flamingo Rd., Suite 50, Las Vegas, NV 89119-5263 USA Tel 866-347-9244; *Imprints:* VisionQuest Kids (VisionQuest Kids); Visikid Books (Visikid Bks)
E-mail: contactus@gsvisionquest.com
Web site: http://www.gsvisionquest.com; http://www.visikidbooks.com.

GT Bks. LLC, *(978-0-9765845)* 19 Housman Ct., Maplewood, NJ 07040-3006 USA
Web site: http://www.gtbooks.net.

GT Interactive Software, *(978-1-56893; 978-1-58869)* 417 Fifth Ave., New York, NY 10016 USA Tel 212-726-4243; Fax: 212-726-4204
E-mail: efierro@gtinteractive.com
Web site: http://gtinteractive.com.

Guadeloupe, Emmanuel & Augustine 'Gus' Logie *See* **Plain Vision Publishing**

Guangdong New Era Publishing Hse. (CHN) *(978-7-5405; 978-7-5583) Dist. by* **Chinasprout.**

Guardian Angel Publishing, *(978-0-9763990)* 415 Meadow View Dr., Lavon, TX 75166-1245 USA Do not confuse with companies with the same or similar name in Carby, OR, Saint Louis, MO
E-mail: admin@tommytellbooks.com
Web site: http://www.tommytellbooks.com.

Guardian Angel Publishing, Inc., *(978-1-933090; 978-1-935137; 978-1-61633; 978-1-951545)* 12430 Tesson Ferry Rd., No. 186, Saint Louis, MO 63128 USA (SAN 858-7833) Do not confuse with companies with same name in Canby, OR and Hubbard, OR., The Colony, TX
E-mail: publisher@guardianangelpublishing.com
Web site: http://www.guardianangelpublishing.com.

Guardian of Truth Foundation *See* **Truth Publications, Inc.**

Guardian Publishing, *(978-0-615-69862-5; 978-0-9892163; 978-0-9912385; 978-0-9909008; 978-0-9965569; 978-1-7340643)* 8044 Montgomery Rd. Suite 440, Cincinnati, OH 45213 USA Tel 800-554-7233; Fax: 866-913-4911
E-mail: jmiller@ojmgroup.com
Web site: www.guardpub.com.

Guardians of Order (CAN) *(978-0-9682431; 978-1-894525) Dist. by* **PSI Ga.**

Guardsman Press *See* **Moondance Publishing**

Guemann, Steven, *(978-0-9909120)* 13870 Idaho Maryland Rd., Nevada City, CA 95959 USA Tel 530-274-9245
E-mail: sguemann@sbcglobal.net.

Guerra, Justin A., *(978-0-692-87963-4; 978-0-692-98756-8)* 14685 Eagle River Rd, EASTVALE, CA 92880 USA Tel 760-912-3560
E-mail: jeffwcrawford5+LVP0003671@gmail.com; jeffwcrawford5+LVP0003671@gmail.com.

Guest Cottage, Incorporated, The, 8821 Hwy 47, Woodruff, WI 54568 USA Tel 715-358-5195; Fax: 715-358-9456
E-mail: amherst@networth.net
Web site: www.amherstpress.com
Dist(s): **Chicago Distribution Ctr.**

Guevara, Alexis S., *(978-0-9765663)* 1625 Palo Alto St., No. 208, Los Angeles, CA 90026 USA
E-mail: sa_guevara@msn.com
Web site: http://www.selectaUSA.com; http://www.alexisguevara.com.

Guia, Elizabeth, *(978-0-9764280)* 15060 SW 104 St. #1613, Miami, FL 33196 USA
E-mail: eguiam@live.com.

Guide to South Florida Off-Road Bicycling *See* **DeGraaf Publishing**

Guideline Pubns. Co., *(978-1-882951)* Div. of Marketing Support Services, Orders Addr.: P.O. Box 801094, Atlanta, GA 30101 USA Fax: 770-424-0778; Toll Free: 800-552-1076
E-mail: sales@guidelinepub.com
Web site: http://www.guidelinepub.com.

Guiding Horizons, *(978-0-9749763)* 2201 Heritage Crest Dr., Valrico, FL 33594-5120 USA
Web site: http://www.guidinghorizons.com.

Guidry Assocs., Inc., *(978-0-9724667)* P.O. Box 2280, Winchester, VA 22604 USA Tel 540-545-8800; *Imprints:* Who's Who In Sports (Who's Who In Sp)
E-mail: info@whoswhoinsports.com
Web site: http://www.whoswhoinsports.com.

Guiffre Bk. Publishing, *(978-0-9830172)* Orders Addr.: P.O. Box 202, Inlet, NY 13360 USA; Edit Addr.: 298 Salt Meadow Cove, Kiawah Island, SC 29455 USA Tel 843-714-7040; 315-357-3422; 843-789-3269
E-mail: misspatrish@gmail.com; wguiffre@frontiernet.net.

Guilford Pubns., *(978-0-89862; 978-1-57230; 978-1-59385; 978-1-60623; 978-1-60918; 978-1-4625)* Orders Addr.: 370 Seventh Avenue, Suite 1200, New York, NY 10001-1020 USA (SAN 212-9442) Tel 212-431-9800; Fax: 212-966-6708; Toll Free: 800-365-7006
E-mail: info@guilford.com
Web site: http://www.guilford.com
Dist(s): **Ebsco Publishing**
MyiLibrary
Rittenhouse Bk. Distributors
Taylor & Francis Group
ebrary, Inc.

Guilin City Publishing, *(978-0-9818622)* P.O. Box 9621, Pittsburgh, PA 15226 USA
E-mail: info@guilincitypublishing.com
Web site: http://www.guilincitypublishing.com.

Guilty Mom Pr., *(978-0-9708415)* 172 Dolphin Cir., Marina, CA 93933 USA Tel 831-384-8459
E-mail: plumtckrd@aol.com
Dist(s): **One Small Voice Foundation.**

Guipil Pr., *(978-0-9992367; 978-1-7335328; 978-1-7332447; 978-1-953689)* 4300 Sheridan St. 246, Hollywood, FL 33021 USA Tel 305-790-6338; *Imprints:* Editorial Guipil (MYID_I_ED.IAL)
E-mail: rebecasegebre@gmail.com
Web site: http://guipilpress.com/; http://editorialguipil.com/.

GuitarVoyager Inc., *(978-0-9785992)* 3616 Calvend Ln., Kensington, MD 20895 USA Tel 240-486-3849; Fax: 301-949-1647
E-mail: guitarvoyager@gmail.com
Web site: http://www.guitarvoyager.com.

Gullah Giri Publishing, *(978-0-9967540)*
E-mail: bftafwife1@yahoo.com.

Gulley Institute of Creative Learning, Inc., *(978-1-928561)* Orders Addr.: P.O. Box 652, Meridian, MS 39302 USA Tel 601-483-0963; Fax: 601-483-0962; Edit Addr.: P.O. Box 1266, Inglewood, CA 90308-1266 USA
E-mail: Gulstem7@aol.com.

Gulley, Wayne, *(978-0-9843505; 978-0-9886117; 978-0-9981252)* P.O. Box 8807, Spring Valley Lake (Victorville), CA 92395 USA
E-mail: wagpublishing@me.com
Web site: www.michelangelotangelo.com.

Gulliver Bks. *Imprint of* **Harcourt Children's Bks.**

GULP Pr., *(978-1-7323810)* W3685 Jostad Rd, Mindoro, WI 54644 USA Tel 608-338-9992
E-mail: beth.mattson@gmail.com
Web site: bethmattson.com.

Gultepe, Evin, *(978-1-7345359)* 2815 Autumn Estates 0, SAN JOSE, CA 95135 USA Tel 8572774901
E-mail: evingultepe@gmail.com
Dist(s): **Ingram Content Group.**

Gumbo Multimedia Entertainment, *(978-0-9762838; 978-0-9832329)* P.O. Box 371641, Miami, FL 32821 USA
E-mail: srodriguez@lushenabks.com; Jeff@JeffRivera.com
Web site: http://www.JeffRivera.com; http://www.GumboWriters.com
Dist(s): **NetSource Distribution**
Smashwords.

Gumdrop Pr., *(978-0-692-50194-8; 978-0-692-54667-3; 978-0-692-54669-7; 978-0-692-54843-1; 978-0-692-56291-8; 978-0-692-56420-2; 978-0-692-56869-9; 978-0-692-57148-4; 978-0-692-57399-0; 978-0-692-57563-5; 978-0-692-57788-2; 978-0-692-57967-1; 978-0-692-57996-1; 978-0-692-58001-1; 978-0-692-58022-6; 978-0-692-58025-7; 978-0-692-58067-7; 978-0-692-58070-7; 978-0-692-58071-4; 978-0-692-58081-3; 978-0-692-58117-9; 978-0-692-58122-3; 978-0-692-58128-5; 978-0-692-58169-8; 978-0-692-58187-2; 978-0-692-58194-0;) 12220 Maycheck Ln, Bowie, MD 20715 USA; Imprints:* Big Blue World Books (Big Blue W)
Web site: http://www.gumdroppress.com
Dist(s): **CreateSpace Independent Publishing Platform.**

GumShoe Press, *(978-0-9777538)* Orders Addr.: 411 Chartley Pk. Rd., Reisterstown, MD 21136 USA (SAN 850-1769) Tel 410-971-8229
E-mail: tjmysteryauthor@aol.com
Web site: http://www.authorsden.com/tjperkins.

Gunderson, Lisa M., *(978-0-692-96692-1; 978-0-692-96768-3; 978-0-692-12699-8)* 6423 W 94th St, Oak Lawn, IL 60453 USA Tel 708-945-7968; *Imprints:* Tea Time Socials, LLC (Tea Time S)
E-mail: lmgmarketingchicago@gmail.com
Web site: www.teatimesocials.com.

Guppy Publishing LLC, *(978-0-9788553)* PMB 221, 6749 S. Westnedge, Suite K, Portage, MI 49002 USA Fax: 269-327-3168
E-mail: dkennis@charter.net
Web site: http://www.guppypublishing.com.

Gupton, Gary Neil, *(978-0-692-95396-9; 978-0-692-97766-8; 978-0-692-14874-7)* 1109 Hampton Pines Ct., LELAND, NC 28451 USA Tel 9103710033
E-mail: g.guppy63@gmail.com
Dist(s): **Ingram Content Group.**

Gurevich, Leonid, *(978-0-9753458)* 4 Remington Ln., Plymouth, MA 02360-1424 USA
E-mail: lgurev3007@aol.com.

Guru Graphics, *(978-0-9729759)* 500 Creekside Ct., Golden, CO 80403-1903 USA Tel 303-278-0177
E-mail: levropes@attbi.com.

Gurze Bks *Imprint of* **Turner Publishing Co.**

Gustav's Library, *(978-0-9758914)* 1011 E. High St., Davenport, IA 52803 USA Tel 563-323-2283
E-mail: gustav@gustavslibrary.com
Web site: http://www.gustavslibrary.com.

Gutenberg Publishers *See* **Albatross Pubs.**

Guzman, Maria del C., *(978-0-9855639)* 39 Arenas St., Aguirre, PR 00794 USA Tel 787-853-2542
E-mail: mguzman_aguirre@yahoo.com.

GW Publishing (GBR) *(978-0-9535397; 978-0-9546701; 978-0-9551564; 978-0-9554145; 978-0-9561211; 978-0-9570844) Dist. by* **MYID_F_GATEWOO.**

Gwarmekia, *(978-0-615-61445-8; 978-0-692-52428-2; 978-0-692-17810-2; 978-0-692-18855-2)* 924 9th Ave., Pleasant Grove, AL 35127 USA Tel 256-682-6834
E-mail: gwarmekia.germany@gmail.com.

Gwasg Prifysgol Cymru / Univ. of Wales Pr. (GBR) *(978-0-7083; 978-0-900768; 978-1-900477; 978-1-78316) Dist. by* **Chicago Distribution Ctr.**

GWB *Imprint of* **Great White Bird Publishing**

Gwenwst Bks., *(978-0-9914423)* P.O. Box 457, Willernie, MN 55090 USA Tel 651-280-7232
E-mail: John.digley@gmail.com
Web site: Pending.

GWF Publishing & Henry's Helpers, *(978-0-9768442)*
E-mail: henryshelpers@yahoo.com
Web site: http://www.henryshelpers.com.

GWOG, *(978-0-692-08311-6; 978-1-7344104)* 318 Plaza Del Sol Pk., Houston, TX 77020 USA Tel 832-233-9494
E-mail: elliotgarcia01@gmail.com.

GWW Publishing Co. *See* **Relentless Publishing Hse.**

GYATRi Media, *(978-0-9988778)* 269 S Western Ave No. 212, Los Angeles, CA 90004 USA Tel 310-426-8899
E-mail: strangeway.ji@gmail.com.

Gye Nyame Hse., *(978-1-886098)* Orders Addr.: P.O. Box 42248, Philadelphia, PA 19101 USA (SAN 299-0415) Tel 215 229 1751; Edit Addr.: 6810 Old York Rd., Philadelphia, PA 19126 USA Tel 215-548-2175
E-mail: gyenyamehouse@aol.com.

Gye Nyame Press *See* **Love II Learn Bks.**

Gypsy Heart Pr., *(978-0-9832514; 978-0-9969984; 978-1-950714)* 127 RAINBOW Dr. No. 2756, Livingston, TX 77399 USA Tel 979-417-2482
E-mail: erin@erin-casey.com
Web site: http://gypsyheartpress.com; http://courageousheartpress.com; http://mywritersconnection.com/
Dist(s): **Ingram Publisher Services.**

Gypsy Hill Publishing,

Gypsy Pubns., *(978-0-9842375; 978-1-938768)* 325 Green Oak Dr., Troy, OH 45373-4396 USA
E-mail: fishermh@juno.com; meg.fisher@yahoo.com
Web site: http://www.gypsypublications.com.

Gypsy Shadow Publishing Co., *(978-0-9844521; 978-0-9834027; 978-1-61950)* 222 Llano St., Lockhart, TX 78644 USA Tel 512-428-8816
E-mail: cholley@gypsyshadow.com
Web site: http://www.gypsyshadow.com
Dist(s): **Smashwords.**

Gyromagnetic Pr., *(978-0-9764790; 978-1-7334070)* 228 Smith Cross Rd., Cooperstown, NY 13326 USA
E-mail: coinmagic1@aol.com
Web site: http://www.geocities.com/larrybarnowsky/.

H & R Magic Bks., *(978-0-9727938)* 3839 Liles Ln., Humble, TX 77396 USA Tel 281-540-7229
Web site: http://www.magicbookshop.com.

H Bar Pr., *(978-0-9794104; 978-0-9893092; 978-1-7324594)* 729 Westview St., Philadelphia, PA 19119-3533 USA (SAN 853-3644) Tel 215-844-8054; Fax: 215-844-1399
E-mail: kwford@verizon.net; hbar.press@verizon.net
Dist(s): **Smashwords.**

H E C Software, Inc., *(978-0-928424; 978-1-62382)* 60 N. Cutler Dr., No. 101, North Salt Lake, UT 84054 USA (SAN 669-6201) Tel 801-295-7054; Fax: 801-295-7088; Toll Free: 800-333-0054
E-mail: info@readinghorizons.com
Web site: http://www.readinghorizons.com.

H H Krsna Balaram Swami, *(978-0-9631403)* Orders Addr.: P.O. Box 27127, Baltimore, MD 21230 USA; Edit Addr.: 1613 Webster St., Baltimore, MD 21230 USA Tel 301-752-7531.

H M Bricker, *(978-0-615-42163-6; 978-0-9838738)* Orders Addr.: 2279 Grass Lake Rd., Lindenhurst, IL 60046 USA
E-mail: santanobeard@comcast.net; birdman1211@comcast.net
Web site: http://www.grandpabrickerbooks.com.

H M S Pubns., Inc., *(978-1-888732)* P.O. Box 524, Niantic, CT 06357 USA Tel 860-739-3187; Toll Free: 888-739-3187
E-mail: hmspublications@earthlink.net
Dist(s): **Follett School Solutions**
Quality Bks., Inc.
ebrary, Inc.

H. O. M. E. (Holding Onto Memorable Experiences) *See* **Do The Write Thing Foundation of DC**

H R M Software *See* **Human Relations Media**

HSA Pubns., *(978-0-910621; 978-1-931166)* 4 W. 43rd St., New York, NY 10036 USA (SAN 270-6490) Tel 212-997-0050; Fax: 212-768-7149.

Haag Environmental Press *See* **Haag Pr.**

Haag Pr., *(978-0-9665497; 978-0-9710260; 978-0-9797511)* Div. of Haag Environmental Co., Inc., Orders Addr.: 315 E. Market St., Sandusky, OH 44870 USA (SAN 852-6583) Tel 419-621-9329; Fax: 419-621-8669
E-mail: haagpress@aol.com; help@haagpress.com
Web site: http://www.haagpress.com.

Haan Graphic Publishing Services, Limited *See* **Southfarm Pr.**

Haas, Melissa, *(978-0-578-06935-7; 978-0-9897689)* 711 Bellaire Ave., Pittsburgh, PA 15226 USA
E-mail: catulathebook@gmail.com
Web site: http://www.catulathebook.com.

Habakkuk Publishing, *(978-0-9798082; 978-0-9827769; 978-0-692-62872-0; 978-0-578-21055-1)* P.O. Box 871601, Canton, MI 48187 USA; 9376 Westwind Dr., Livonia, MI 48150
Web site: http://www.dudleyministries.com.

Haber-Schaim & Associates *See* **Science Curriculum, Inc.**

Hability Solution Services, Inc., *(978-1-932062)* P.O. Box 2595, Kearney, NE 68848 USA Tel 308-338-9238; Fax: 308-338-9208; Toll Free: 888-814-3238
E-mail: info@habsol.com; info@ideamagicbooks.com
Web site: http://www.habsol.com; http://www.ideamagicbooks.com.

Habit House *See* **Roedway Pr.**

Hachai Publications, Incorporated *See* **Hachai Publishing**

Hachai Publishing, *(978-0-922613; 978-1-929628; 978-1-945560)* 527 Empire Blvd., Brooklyn, NY 11225 USA (SAN 251-3749) Tel 718-633-0100; Fax: 718-633-0103
E-mail: info@hachai.com
Web site: http://www.hachai.com
Dist(s): **Kerem Publishing.**

Hachette Antoine, *(978-0-692-94283-3)* 525 W 28th St, New York, NY 10001 USA Tel 917-993-0758
E-mail: chaker@chakerkhazaal.com
Web site: http://www.hachette.com/en/maison/hachette-antoine.

Hachette Audio, *(978-1-57042; 978-1-58621; 978-1-59483; 978-1-60024; 978-1-60788; 978-1-5491)* Div. of Hachette Book Group, 1290 Ave. of the Americas, New York, NY 10104 USA Tel 212-364-1100; Fax: 212-364-1923; Toll Free: 800-759-0190
E-mail: audiobooks.publicity@hbgusa.com
Web site: http://www.hachettebookgroupusa.com/publishing_hachette-audio.aspx
Dist(s): **Blackstone Audio, Inc.**
Findaway World, LLC
Follett School Solutions
Grand Central Publishing
Hachette Bk. Group
Libros Sin Fronteras
Landmark Audiobooks.

Hachette AudioBooks *See* **Hachette Audio**

Hachette Australia (AUS) *(978-0-340; 978-0-450; 978-0-7336; 978-0-7267; 978-0-7316-4988-4; 978-0-646-26970-2; 978-0-646-26972-6; 978-0-646-42250-3) Dist. by* **HachBkGrp.**

Hachette Bks. *Imprint of* **Hachette Bks.**

Hachette Bk. Group, *(978-0-446; 978-1-60286; 978-1-60941; 978-1-61113; 978-1-61969; 978-1-4789; 978-1-64732)* Div. of Hachette Group Livre, Orders Addr.: 3 Center Plaza, Boston, MA 02108 USA (SAN 852-5463) Tel 617-263-1828; Toll Free Fax: 800-286-9471; Toll Free: 800-759-0190; Edit Addr.: P.O. Box 2146, Johannesburg, 2196 ZAF Tel 2711 783-7565; Fax: 2711 883-6866
Web site: http://www.hachettebookgroup.com
Dist(s): **Blackstone Audio, Inc.**
Findaway World, LLC
Follett School Solutions
MyiLibrary
Perfection Learning Corp.
Time Inc. Bks.

Hachette Bks., *(978-0-201; 978-0-306; 978-0-7382; 978-0-938289; 978-0-946771; 978-0-9627613; 978-1-55561; 978-1-58097; 978-1-873376; 978-1-882810; 978-1-885119)* Div. of Hachette Book Group, Orders Addr.: 3 Center Plaza, Boston, MA 02108-2084 USA Tel 617-227-0730; Toll Free Fax: 800-286-9471; Toll Free: 800-759-0730; Edit Addr.: 237 Park Ave., New York, NY 10017 USA Tel 212-364-0600; Fax: 212-364-0952; *Imprints:* Hachette Books (HachetteBks); Black Dog & Leventhal Publishers, Inc. (BlackDog Lev); Da Capo Lifelong (DaCapoLF); Da Capo Press, Incorporated (DaCapoPRI)
Dist(s): **Blackstone Audio, Inc.**
Hachette Bk. Group
MyiLibrary
Open Road Integrated Media, Inc.

Hachette Children's Group (GBR) *(978-0-7502; 978-1-85881; 978-1-84255; 978-1-4440; 978-1-4449)* *Dist. by* **HachBkGrp.**

Hachette Children's Group (GBR) *(978-0-7502; 978-1-85881; 978-1-84255; 978-1-4440; 978-1-4449)* *Dist. by* **IPG Chicago.**

Hachette Groupe Livre (FRA) *(978-2-01)* *Dist. by* **Distribks Inc.**

†Hackett Publishing Co., Inc., *(978-0-87220; 978-0-915144; 978-0-915145; 978-0-941051; 978-1-58510; 978-1-60384; 978-1-62466; 978-1-64792; 978-1-64793)* Orders Addr.: P.O. Box 44937, Indianapolis, IN 46244-0937 USA (SAN 201-6044) Tel 317-635-9250; Fax: 317-635-9292; Toll Free Fax: 800-783-9213; *Imprints:* Focus (FocusUSA)
E-mail: customer@hackettpublishing.com; lizw@hackettpublishing.com
Web site: http://www.hackettpublishing.com
Dist(s): **ebrary, Inc.**; *CIP.*

Hadassah's Crown LLC *See* **Hadassah's Crown Publishing, LLC**

Hadassah's Crown Publishing, LLC, *(978-0-9981230; 978-0-692-98525-0; 978-0-9980269; 978-1-950894)* 634 NE Main St., No. 1263, Simpsonville, SC 29681 USA Tel 864-708-1214
E-mail: soncunnlev@gmail.com
Web site: http://HadassahsCrownPublishing.com.

Hadrosaur Pr., *(978-1-885093)* P.O. Box 2194, Mesilla Park, NM 88047-2194 USA Tel 505-527-4163; *Imprints:* LBF/Hadrosaur (LBF Hadrs)
E-mail: hadrosaur@zianet.com
Web site: http://www.hadrosaur.com.

Hafabanana Press *See* **KB Bks. & More**

Hagan, Theda *See* **Hagan, Theda Bks.**

Hagan, Theda Bks., *(978-0-9678032; 978-0-9827155)* 47 Comer Dr., Madisonville, KY 42431 USA Tel 270-821-6968
E-mail: thedahagan@yahoo.com
Web site: http://www.heavenlyharborbooks.com/default.htm.

Hager, Robert, *(978-0-9727676)* 101 Crawford, Suite 2C, Houston, TX 77002 USA
Web site: http://www.saurcana.com/pages/about_author.html.

Hahn, Beverly, *(978-0-9722494)* Orders Addr.: P.O. Box 66, Hilmak, CA 95324 USA; Edit Addr.: 9613 Ailanthus Ave., Delhi, CA 95315 USA (SAN 254-7376).

Hairball Pr., *(978-0-9646781)* 2318 2nd Ave., Suite 591, Seattle, WA 98121 USA Tel 206-932-8173.

Hairston Enterprises, LLC, *(978-0-9762958)* 582 Bristol Ln., Birmingham, AL 35226 USA Tel 205-369-4022
E-mail: kchairston@yahoo.com
Web site: http://www.forgottenrules.com; http://www.forgottenrules.org; http://www.theforgottenrules.com; http://www.theforgottenrules.org.

Hairston, Rodney, *(978-0-9760689)* 75 Fern Oak Cir. Apt. 201, Stafford, VA 22554-8459 USA
E-mail: rhairston@jbmanagement.com.

Haislip, Allen, *(978-0-9767640)* Orders Addr.: 32 Marquette Dr., Florissant, MO 63031-3839 USA.

Haiti World, *(978-0-9793039)* P.O. Box 5663, Vernon Hills, IL 60061 USA Tel 847-514-9967
E-mail: haitiworld@yahoo.com.

Halbur Publishing, *(978-0-9603520)* 142 Angela Dr., Santa Rosa, CA 95403-1702 USA (SAN 212-9469)
E-mail: dhalbur@sonic.net.

Halcyon Pr., *(978-0-941970)* 18-05 215 St., Flushing, NY 11360 USA (SAN 238-244X) Tel 212-631-9640 Do not confuse with companies with same or similar name in Hendersonville, NC, Dallas, TX, Houston, TX.

Halcyon Pr., Ltd., *(978-0-9706054; 978-1-931823; 978-0-9830676)* P.O. Box 260, Pearland, TX 77588-0260 USA (SAN 253-9934) Toll Free: 866-774-5786 Do not confuse with companies with same or similar name in Hendersonville, NC, Flushing, NY, Dallas, TX
E-mail: david.raley@gmail.com
Web site: http://www.halcyonpress.com
Dist(s): **Bk. Marketing Plus.**

Haldane Mason, Ltd. (GBR) *(978-1-902463; 978-1-905339; 978-1-909720)* *Dist. by* **Trans-Atl Phila.**

Hale Kuamo'o Hawaiian Language Ctr. at UHH, *(978-0-9665331; 978-1-930339; 978-0-9741580)* Div. of Ka Haka 'Ula o Ke'elikolani/College of Hawaiian Language at UH Hilo, 200 W. Kawili St., Hilo, HI 96720-4091 USA Tel 808-974-7339; Fax: 808-974-7686
E-mail: contact@ahapunanaleo.org
Web site: http://www.olelo.hawaii.edu; http://www.ahapunanaleo.org.

Hale Publishing, *(978-0-9636219; 978-0-9729583; 978-0-9772268; 978-0-9815257; 978-0-9823379; 978-0-9845039; 978-0-9833075; 978-0-9847746; 978-0-9858893; 978-1-939847)* 1712 N. Forest St., Amarillo, TX 79106 USA Tel 806-376-9900 Toll Free: 800-378-1317
E-mail: books@ibreastfeeding.com; alicia.ingram@halepublishing.com
Web site: http://www.ibreastfeeding.com.

Haley's, *(978-0-9626308; 978-1-884540; 978-0-9897667; 978-0-9916102; 978-0-9967730; 978-0-9982735; 978-1-948380)* Orders Addr.: 488 S. Main St., Athol, MA 01331 USA Tel 978-249-9400 (phone/fax); Toll Free: 800-215-8805 (phone/fax); Edit Addr.: 488 S. Main St., Athol, MA 01331 USA
E-mail: haley.antique@verizon.net
Dist(s): **Follett School Solutions.**

Half Nelson Enterprises, *(978-1-947934)* 306 Greenup St., Covington, KY 41011 USA Tel 513-607-1206
E-mail: richardhunt07@gmail.com.

Half-Pint Kids, Inc., *(978-1-59256)* Orders Addr.: 646 Crabapple Ln., Ellwood City, PA 16117 USA Tel 724-809-8023
Web site: http://halfpintkids.com.

Hall & Humphries Publishing Hse., *(978-0-9758521)* Orders Addr.: P.O. Box 371021, Decatur, GA 30037-1021 USA; Edit Addr.: 2652 Rainbow Pkwy., Decatur, GA 30034 USA Tel 404-625-4486.

Hall, Annalisa, *(978-0-615-22113-7)* 14271 Anabelle Dr., Poway, CA 92064 USA
Dist(s): **Lulu Pr., Inc.**

Hall, Dana, *(978-0-578-40551-3)* 10 Whaton Oaks Ct., Greensboro, NC 27409 USA Tel 336-501-4334
E-mail: danahallgso@gmail.com
Dist(s): **Ingram Content Group.**

Hall, Joan, *(978-0-692-00148-6)* 1209 Jolliff Rd., Chesapeake, VA 23321 USA Tel 757-620-8871.

Hall, Kenneth, *(978-0-615-19649-7)* 1857 Morris Ave., Lincoln Park, MI 48146-1328 USA
E-mail: kenhall321@yahoo.com
Dist(s): **Lulu Pr., Inc.**

Hall, Monique P. Productions, *(978-0-9772634)* 167 Wyatt Earp Loop, Nolanville, TX 76559 USA (SAN 851-6391) Tel 254-462-2990
E-mail: nickiepop777@gmail.com; moniquephallproductions@gmail.com
Web site: http://nickiepopart.com.

Hall, Nancy Inc., *(978-1-884270)* 7 W. 18th St., 6th Flr., New York, NY 10011 USA Tel 212-674-3408; Fax: 212-353-1521
E-mail: Nhallinc@aol.com.

Hall Press *See* **Hallcienda**

Hall, Stephen & Denise, *(978-0-9753305)* 1237 Prairie Dell Rd., Union, MO 63084-4310 USA
E-mail: wordsofahunter@cs.com.

HallaVision Publishing *Imprint of* **Ginger Nielson - Children's Bk. Illustration**

Hallcienda, *(978-0-932218; 978-0-578-54705-3)* Orders Addr.: P.O. Box 9066, San Bernardino, CA 92427 USA (SAN 211-7061) Tel 909-887-3466; P.O. Box 9066, San Bernardino, CA 92427 (SAN 665-7060) Tel 909-887-3466.

Hallelujah Acres Publishing, *(978-0-929619)* P.O. Box 2388, Shelby, NC 28151 USA (SAN 249-7891) Tel 704-481-1700; Fax: 704-481-0345
E-mail: chet@hacres.com
Web site: http://www.hacres.com
Dist(s): **Send The Light Distribution LLC.**

Haller Company, The, *(978-0-9743961)* Orders Addr.: P.O. Box 207, Burlingame, CA 94010 USA Tel 650-348-3900; Fax: 650-558-9012; Edit Addr.: 1325 Howard Ave., Burlingame, CA 94010 USA
Web site: http://www.hallercompany.com.

Hallmark Card, Inc., *(978-0-87529; 978-1-59530; 978-1-63059)* 2501 McGee, Kansas City, MO 64141-6580 USA (SAN 202-2672) Tel 816-274-5111
Dist(s): **Univ. of New Mexico Pr.**

Hallmark Emporium, *(978-0-9665055)* 9201 Russell Ave., S., Bloomington, MN 55431 USA Tel 612-884-2601; Fax: 612-703-0218
E-mail: dead541@aol.com
Web site: http://members.aol.com/dead 541/index.html.

HallowStyle, LLC, *(978-0-9853082)* 20 Robert Dr., Hyde Park, NY 12538 USA Tel 914-489-9529
E-mail: donnadavies@hallowstyle.com
Web site: www.hallowstyle.com.

Halo Publishing International, *(978-0-9718350; 978-0-9797429; 978-1-935268; 978-1-61244; 978-1-78280)* 5549 Canal Rd., Cleveland, OH 44125 USA
Web site: http://www.halopublishing.com.

Hambrick, Brandy, *(978-0-578-18543-9; 978-0-578-21029-2)* 888 Rockdale Ave, Cincinnati, OH 45229 USA.

Hameray Publishing Group, Inc., *(978-1-60559; 978-1-62817; 978-1-64039; 978-1-64387; 978-1-64941)* 11545 Sorrento Valley Rd., Suite 310, San Diego, CA 92121 USA Tel 858-369-5200; Fax: 858-369-5201; Toll Free Fax: 858-369-5209; Toll Free: 866-918-6173
E-mail: christine@hameraypublishing.com
Web site: http://www.hameraypublishing.com.

Hamilton Bks., *(978-0-7618)* Div. of Rowman & Littlefield Publishing Group, Orders Addr.: 15200 NBN Way, Blue Ridge Summit, PA 17214 USA Tel 717-794-3800 (Sales, Customer Service, MIS, Royalties, Inventory Mgmt., Dist., Credit & Collections); Fax: 717-794-3803 (Customer Service &/or orders only); 717-794-3857 (Sales & MIS); 717-794-3856 Royalties, Inventory Mgmt. & Dist.); Toll Free Fax: 800-338-4550 (Customer Service &/ or orders); Toll Free: 800-462-6420 (Customer Service &/ or orders); Edit Addr.: 4501 Forbes Blvd., Suite 200, Lanham, MD 20706 USA Tel 301-459-3366; Fax: 301-459-5748 Short Discount, please contact rlpgsales@rowman.com
Web site: http://www.rlpgbooks.com
Dist(s): **Follett School Solutions**
MyiLibrary
National Bk. Network
Rowman & Littlefield Publishers, Inc.
ebrary, Inc.

Hamilton Ministries *See* **DCTS Publishing**

Hamilton Stone Editions, *(978-0-9654043; 978-0-9714873; 978-0-9801786; 978-0-9836668; 978-0-9903767)* P.O. Box 43, Maplewood, NJ 07040 USA; *Imprints:* Irene Weinberger Books (IWeinberger)
E-mail: meredithsuewillis@gmail.com; hstone@hamiltonstone.org
Web site: http://www.hamiltonstone.org
Dist(s): **Smashwords.**

Hamline Univ. Pr., *(978-0-9633686; 978-0-9723721; 978-1-934458)* 1536 Hewitt Ave., MS-C1916, Saint Paul, MN 55104-2490 USA
E-mail: bhansonhegg01@hamline.edu
Web site: http://www.hamline.edu.

Hammad, Salma *See* **Lucent Interpretations, LLC**

Hammersmark Books *See* **Kluis Publishing, LLC**

Hammond, Incorporated *See* **Hammond World Atlas Corp.**

Hammond, Roger, *(978-0-9763822)* 4915 Avon Ln., Sarasota, FL 34238 USA
Web site: http://www.pelithepelican.com.

†Hammond World Atlas Corp., *(978-0-7230; 978-0-8437)* Subs. of Langenscheidt Pubs., Inc., 193 Morris Ave., Springfield, NJ 07081-1211 USA (SAN 202-2702)
E-mail: rstrung@americanmap.com
Web site: http://www.Hammondmap.com
Dist(s): **Langenscheidt Publishing Group**; *CIP.*

Hampton Roads Publishing Co., Inc., *(978-0-9624375; 978-1-57174; 978-1-878901)* Orders Addr.: P.O. Box 8107, Charlottesvle, VA 22906-8107 USA (SAN 299-8874) Toll Free Fax: 800-766-9042; Toll Free: 800-766-8009
E-mail: hrpc@hrpub.com
Web site: http://www.hamptonroadspub.com
Dist(s): **Hay Hse., Inc.**
Red Wheel/Weiser.

Hampton-Brown Books *See* **National Geographic School Publishing, Inc.**

Hamster Huey Pr., *(978-0-9749090)* 7627 84th Ave., Ct., NW, Gig Harbor, WA 98335-6237 USA Tel 253-851-7839; Fax: 253-853-3493
E-mail: phs@oz.net
Web site: http://www.hamsterhueypress.com.

Hamster Pr., *(978-0-9645669; 978-0-9724630)* Orders Addr.: P.O. Box 27471, Seattle, WA 98125 USA Fax: 206-363-2878
E-mail: hamstrpres@aol.com
Web site: http://www.billschelly.com
Dist(s): **Diamond Comic Distributors, Inc.**
FM International
Syco Distribution.

Hanako Studio *See* **CKNY Paw Productions**

†Hancock Hse. Pubs., *(978-0-88839; 978-0-919654; 978-1-55205)* No. 104- 4550 Birch Bay-Lynden Rd, Blaine, WA 98230-9436 USA (SAN 665-7079) Tel 604-538-1114; Fax: 604-538-2262; Toll Free Fax: 800-983-2262; Toll Free: 800-938-1114; 19313 Zero Ave., Surrey, BC V3S 9R9 (SAN 115-3730); *Imprints:* Crypto Editions (MYID_W_CRYPTO)
E-mail: sales@hancockhouse.com
Web site: http://www.hancockhouse.com; *CIP.*

Hand Print Pr., *(978-0-9679846; 978-0-615-74893-1; 978-0-9914762)* Orders Addr.: P.O. Box 576, Blodgett, OR 97326 USA Tel 541-438-4300; Edit Addr.: 395 Grant Creek Rd., Eddyville, OR 97343 USA
E-mail: kiko@handprintpress.com; potlatch@cmug.com
Web site: http://www.handprintpress.com
Dist(s): **Chelsea Green Publishing**
CreateSpace Independent Publishing Platform.

†hand2mind, *(978-0-7406; 978-0-914040; 978-0-923832; 978-0-938587; 978-1-57162; 978-1-57452; 978-1-63406)* 500 Greenview Ct., Vernon Hills, IL 60061 USA (SAN 285-7553) Tel 847-816-5050; Fax: 847-816-5066; Toll Free: 800-445-5985; *Imprints:* SunSprouts (SUNSPROUTS); Super Source The (SUPER SOURCE)
E-mail: info@hand2mind.com
Web site: http://www.hand2mind.com; *CIP.*

Handersen Publishing, *(978-1-941429; 978-1-947854; 978-1-64703)* PO Box 21843, Lincoln, NE 68542 USA
E-mail: editors@handersenpublishing.com; stinkwavesmagazine@hotmail.com
Web site: http://handersenpublishing.com/; www.stinkwavesmagazine.com.

Handfinger Pr., *(978-0-9838294)* 833 Eastview Ave., Delray Beach, FL 33483 USA Tel 561-654-8680; Fax: 561-684-1508
E-mail: wendyg52@hotmail.com
Dist(s): **Independent Pubs. Group.**

H&H Publishing, *(978-0-9975411)* 2403 Craig Rd Se, Olympia, WA 98501 USA Tel 360-918-6976
E-mail: puzzlebabe2002@yahoo.com.

Handle Your Business Girl Publishing, *(978-1-886853)* 1006 Deerfield trace, Mebane, NC 27302 USA (SAN 298-5101) Tel 919-244-6321 Do not confuse with Joshua Publishing, Aurora, CO, Lenexa, KS
E-mail: info@handleyourbusinessgirl.com
Web site: www.paiceducationgroup.org; www.handleyourbusinessgirl.com.

H&M Systems Software, Inc., *(978-1-885936)* 600 E. Crescent Ave., Suite 203, U Saddle Riv, NJ 07458-1846 USA Toll Free: 800-327-3713; *Imprints:* StudioLine Photo (StudioLine)
E-mail: Info@HM-Software.com
Web site: http://www.Gameware.com; http://www.HM-Software.com; http://www.StudioLine.biz
Dist(s): **Victory Multimedia.**

Handprint Bks. *Imprint of* **Chronicle Bks. LLC**

Handprint Bks., *(978-1-929766; 978-1-59354)* 413 Sixth Ave., Brooklyn, NY 11215-3310 USA
E-mail: publisher@handprintbooks.com
Web site: http://www.handprintbooks.com
Dist(s): **Chronicle Bks. LLC**
Hachette Bk. Group
Learning Connection, The
Penton Overseas, Inc.
Random Hse., Inc.

Hands to the Plow, Inc., *(978-1-930914)* P.O. Box 567, Webster, WI 54893 USA Tel 715-349-7185
E-mail: tomkelby@handstotheplow.org
Web site: http://www.handstotheplow.org.

Handsome Prince Publishing, *(978-0-9910536; 978-0-9908048; 978-0-9961115)* 2712 Occidental Dr., Sacramento, CA 95826 USA Tel 916-801-5376
E-mail: jam43210@gmail.com
Web site: HandsomePrincePublishing.com.

Handstand Kids, *(978-0-9792107; 978-0-9847476)* 23346 Pk. Colombo, Calabasas, CA 91302 USA (SAN 852-7822) Tel 818-917-7200
E-mail: yvette@handstandkids.com
Web site: http://www.handstandkids.com.

H&W Publishing Inc., *(978-0-9800934)* P.O. Box 53515, Cincinnati, OH 45253 USA Tel 513-687-3968; Fax: 513-761-4221
E-mail: kwatkins1@fuse.net
Web site: http://www.handwpublishing.com.

Handwriting Without Tears, *(978-1-891627; 978-1-934825; 978-1-939814; 978-1-948729; 978-1-950578; 978-1-952970)* Div. of No Tears Learning Inc., 8001 MacArthur Blvd., Cabin John, MD 20818-1607 USA Tel 301-263-2700; Fax: 301-263-2707; Toll Free: 888-983-8409
Web site: http://www.hwtears.com; http://www.getsetforschool.com.

Hanford Mead Pubs., Inc., *(978-0-9643158; 978-1-59275)* P.O. Box 8051, Santa Cruz, CA 95061 USA (SAN 253-9195) Tel 831-459-6855; Fax: 831-426-4474
E-mail: info@hanfordmead.com
Web site: http://www.hanfordmead.com; http://www.soulcollage.com; http://www.ethicsofcaring.com
Dist(s): **New Leaf Distributing Co., Inc.**

†Hanging Loose Pr., *(978-0-914610; 978-1-882413; 978-1-931236; 978-1-934909)* 231 Wyckoff St., Brooklyn, NY 11217 USA (SAN 206-4960) Fax: 212-243-7499
E-mail: print225@aol.com
Web site: http://www.hangingloosepress.com
Dist(s): **Partners/West Book Distributors**
SPD-Small Pr. Distribution; *CIP.*

Hank of America Consulting LLC, *(978-0-692-09239-2; 978-0-692-09241-5; 978-0-692-10267-1; 978-0-692-15867-8; 978-0-692-15869-2; 978-0-578-53482-4)* 11 Riverside DR APT 6kw, NEW YORK, NY 10023 USA Tel 917-686-1979
E-mail: henry.lihn@gmail.com
Dist(s): **Ingram Content Group.**

Hanks, Scott, *(978-0-9794157; 978-0-9799518; 978-0-9815083)* 1781 E. 800th Rd., Lawrence, KS 66049 USA (SAN 853-4098) Tel 785-887-2203; Fax: 785-887-2204
E-mail: mt@heritagebaptistchurch.cc
Web site: http://www.heritagebaptistchurch.cc.

Hanna Concern Publishing *See* **Ariella Publishing**

Hannacroix Creek Bks., Inc., *(978-1-889262; 978-1-938998)* 1127 High Ridge Rd., No. 110, Stamford, CT 06905-1203 USA (SAN 299-9560) Tel 203-968-8098; Fax: 203-968-0193
E-mail: Hannacroix@aol.com
Web site: http://www.hannacroixcreekbooks.com
Dist(s): **Brodart Co.**
CreateSpace Independent Publishing Platform
Emery-Pratt Co.
Follett School Solutions
Midwest Library Service
Quality Bks., Inc.
TextStream
Unique Bks., Inc.

Hannel Educational Consulting, *(978-0-9764776)* 1131 W. Palm Ln., Phoenix, AZ 85007-1536 USA Tel 602-524-7647; Fax: 602-253-2693
Web site: http://www.hannel.com.

Hannibal Bks., *(978-0-929292; 978-1-934749; 978-1-61315)* Div. of KLMK Communications, Inc., Orders Addr.: 313 S. 11th St. Suite A, Garland, TX 75040 USA Tel 800-747-0738; Fax: 888-252-3022; Toll Free Fax: 888-252-3022; Toll Free: 800-747-0738; Edit Addr.: 313 S. 11th St., Garland, TX 75040 USA Fax: 888-252-3022
E-mail: hannibalbooks@earthlink.net; orders@hannibalbooks.com; louismoore@hannibalbooks.com
Web site: http://www.hannibalbooks.com
Dist(s): **Ingram Content Group**
Spring Arbor Distributors, Inc.

Hannover Hse. *Imprint of* **Truman Pr., Inc.**

Hansen, Charles Educational Music & Bks., Inc., *(978-0-8494)* 1820 West Ave., Miami Beach, FL 33139 USA (SAN 205-0609) Tel 305-532-5461; Fax: 305-672-8729
E-mail: khansen507@aol.com
Web site: http://www.hansenpublications.com/
Dist(s): **Hansen Hse.**

Hansen, Diane, *(978-0-9761988)* P.O. Box 1051, Redondo Beach, CA 90278 USA Tel 310-379-8006
Web site: http://thosearemyprivateparts.com.

Hansen, Marc Stuff!, *(978-0-9794643)* P.O. Box 621, Greenville, MI 48838 USA
E-mail: marchansenstuff@gmail.com
Web site: http://www.marchansenstuff.com.

Hanson, Tracie, *(978-0-9799185)* Orders Addr.: 94 Pletcher Dr., Yorkville, IL 60560 USA Tel 815-440-5681
E-mail: tracie777@sbcglobal.net
Web site: http://www.newworldbaby.net.

Happy About, *(978-0-9633302; 978-1-60005; 978-1-60773)* 21265 Stevens Creek Blvd., Suite 205, Cupertino, CA 95014 USA Tel 408-257-3000
E-mail: info@happyabout.info
Web site: http://www.happyabout.info
Dist(s): **Ebsco Publishing**
MyiLibrary
OverDrive, Inc.

Happy Apple Bks., *(978-0-9890903)* 852 Riven Oak Dr., Murrells Inlet, SC 29576 USA Tel 843-458-8740
E-mail: wickedisbetter@yahoo.com; mattellerin@yahoo.com
Web site: http://www.happyapplebooks.com.

Happy Bks. Pr., *(978-0-9787826)* 29877 Westhaven Dr., Agoura, CA 91301 USA Tel 818-879-1268
E-mail: ghuyette@charter.net; happybookspress@vrillustration.com
Web site: http://www.vrillustration.com.

Happy Cat Bks. (GBR) *(978-1-899248; 978-1-903285; 978-1-905117) Dist. by* **Star Brght Bks.**

Happy Day *Imprint of* **Tyndale Hse. Pubs.**

Happy Dolphin Pr. *Imprint of* **Glass Onion Publishing**

Happy Dolphin Press *See* **Glass Onion Publishing**

Happy Hamster Press, The *See* **Imagination Workshop, The**

Happy Heart Kids Publishing, *(978-0-9763143)* Orders Addr.: 2912 Beane Rd., Lenoir, NC 28645-8653 USA (SAN 256-3029) Tel 828-302-9500; 828-754-4126 (phone/fax); Fax: 828-758-8409
E-mail: mshelen@charter.net
Web site: http://www.happyheartkids.com.

Happy Hearts Family, The, *(978-0-615-34485-0; 978-0-9899470)* 2044 Loggia, Newport Beach, CA 92660 USA Tel 949-701-8296
E-mail: marlanal@cox.net
Web site: http://thehappyheartsfamily.com.

Happy Holliday Bks., *(978-0-692-54584-3; 978-0-692-95833-9; 978-0-692-08125-9; 978-0-578-50486-5)* P.O. Box 324, Glendale, CA 91209 USA Tel 818-568-4492
E-mail: thefoodaintttheproblem@gmail.com.

Happy Horse Publishing, Ltd., *(978-0-9727849)* Orders Addr.: P.O. Box 15767, Chevy Chase, MD 20825 USA Tel 301-589-8888; Edit Addr.: 5910 Connecticut Ave., Chevy Chase, MD 70875 USA
E-mail: eashe@happyhorse.us
Web site: http://www.happyhorsekids.com.

HAPPY HOUSE PR., *(978-0-615-87080-9; 978-0-615-88154-6)* 1301 Birdsall St., Old Hickory, TN 37138 USA Tel 6155547064 Do not confuse with Happy House Press in Tillamook, OR
Web site: www.happyhousepress.com
Dist(s): **CreateSpace Independent Publishing Platform.**

Happy Kamperz, *(978-0-578-22287-5; 978-0-578-22288-2)* 13180 Garrett Hwy., Suite F PMB 78, Oakland, MD 21550 USA
Dist(s): **Outskirts Pr., Inc.**

Happy Kappy Karacters, *(978-0-615-45522-8; 978-0-615-65651-9)* 20 Secora Rd., Suite 312, Monsey, NY 10952 USA
E-mail: georgegisser@aol.com; marshall@nydesign.com
Web site: www.nydesign.com; www.kappythekangaroo.com.

Happy Publishing, *(978-0-615-73531-3; 978-0-9895554; 978-0-9896332; 978-0-9961712; 978-0-9983708; 978-0-9996603)* 7052 Santa Teresa Blvd No. 72, San Jose, CA 95139 USA Tel 408-416-7090
E-mail: happypublishing@gmail.com
Web site: http://www.HappyPublishing.net.

Happy Viking Crafts, *(978-0-9740175)* Orders Addr.: P.O. Box 35, Mahomet, IL 61853 USA; Edit Addr.: 1001 Sunrise Cir., Mahomet, IL 61853-3536 USA Tel 217-586-2497.

Happy Women Publishing Co., *(978-0-9745627)* 11487 57th St E., Parrish, FL 34219-5818 USA
E-mail: hwp@toerrific.com
Web site: http://toerrific.com
Dist(s): **Continental Enterprises Group, Inc. (CEG).**

Happy Woods Pr., *(978-0-9894691)* 400 Davey Glen Rd. No. 4323, Belmont, CA 94002 USA Tel 650-802-8369
E-mail: meechie2@sbcglobal.net.

HappyFeet Bks., *(978-0-9992492; 978-1-7329617)* 146 Essex St., Deep River, CT 06417 USA Tel 860-328-1106
E-mail: don@happyfeetbooks.com
Web site: www.happyfeetbooks.com.

Happyland Media, *(978-0-9726418)* Orders Addr.: P.O. Box 20398, Castro Valley, CA 94546 USA; Edit Addr.: 20283 Santa Marie Ave., Castro Valley, CA 94546 USA
E-mail: info@happylandmedia.com
Web site: http://www.happylandmedia.com.

Harambee Pr., *(978-0-9769846)* P.O. Box 353, Macatawa, MI 49434 USA
Web site: http://www.harambeepress.com.

Harbinger Pr., *(978-0-9674736; 978-0-9723998)* 2711 Buford Rd. PMB 383, Richmond, VA 23235-2423 USA (SAN 299-9994) Do not confuse with companies with the same or similar names in Woodland Hills, CA, Corte Madera, CA
E-mail: keith@harbpress.com
Web site: http://www.harbpress.com.

Harbor Hse., *(978-1-891799)* 629 Stevens Xing., Augusta, GA 30907-9566 USA; *Imprints:* Bat Wing Press (Bat Wing Pr)
E-mail: peggycheney@harborhousebooks.com; harborhouse@harborhousebooks.com
Web site: http://www.harborhousebooks.com.

Harbor Hse. Pubs., Inc., *(978-0-937360)* 221 Water St., Boyne City, MI 49712 USA (SAN 200-5751) Tel 616-582-2814; Fax: 616-582-3392; Toll Free: 800-491-1760
E-mail: harbor@harborhouse.com
Web site: http://www.harborhouse.com.

Harbor Island Bks., *(978-0-9741787)* 1214 W. Boston Post Rd., No. 245, Mamaroneck, NY 10543 USA (SAN 255-9137) Tel 914-420-9782; Fax: 914-835-7897
E-mail: publisher@lyingawake.net; hfurbush@earthlink.net
Web site: http://www.lyingawake.net/
Dist(s): **Partners/West Book Distributors.**

Harbor Mountain Pr., *(978-0-9786009; 978-0-9815560; 978-0-9882755)* P.O. Box 519, Brownsville, VT 05037 USA
Web site: http://www.harbormountainpress.org; www.spdbooks.org; petermoney.com
Dist(s): **GenPop Bks.**
SPD-Small Pr. Distribution.

Harbor Pr., Inc., *(978-0-936197)* Orders Addr.: P.O. Box 1656, Gig Harbor, WA 98335 USA (SAN 696-8953) Tel 253-851-5190; Fax: 253-851-5191; Edit Addr.: P.O. Box 1656, Gig Harbor, WA 98335-3656 USA (SAN 696-8961) Do not confuse with companies with the same name in Friday Harbor, WA, Austin, TX, Ardmore, PA
E-mail: young2327@mindspring.com
Web site: http://www.harborpress.com
Dist(s): **National Bk. Network.**

Harborseal Publishing Co., *(978-0-9652963; 978-0-9787308)* Orders Addr.: P.O. Box 126, Seal Cove, ME 04674-0126 USA Tel 207-244-7753; Edit Addr.: Rte. 102, Captain's Quarters Rd., Seal Cove, ME 04674 USA
Dist(s): **Magazines, Inc.**

HarborTown Histories, *(978-0-9710984)* 6 Harbor Way, Santa Barbara, CA 93109 USA
E-mail: baker@sbcc.net.

Harbour Arts, LLC, *(978-0-9778196)* 1790 Philippe Pkwy., Safety Harbor, FL 34695 USA
Web site: http://www.harbourarts.com.

Harbour Bks. *Imprint of* **Mariner Publishing**

Harbour Publishing Co., Ltd. (CAN) *(978-0-920080; 978-1-55017) Dist. by* **PerseuPGW.**

Harbourside Pr., *(978-0-9740552)* 7892 Sailboat Key Blvd., Suite 506, South Pasadena, FL 33707 USA Tel 727-543-5855
E-mail: harbours@harboursidepress.com
Web site: http://www.harboursidepress.com
Dist(s): **Greenleaf Book Group.**

Harcourt Achieve *See* **Houghton Mifflin Harcourt Supplemental Pubs.**

Harcourt Brace & Company *See* **Harcourt Trade Pubs.**

Harcourt Brace School Publishers *See* **Harcourt Schl. Pubs.**

Harcourt Briggs, *(978-0-692-91301-7; 978-0-692-96875-8)* 2020 Penn Ave., NW Suite 343, WASHINGTON, DC 20006 USA Tel 202-841-4682
E-mail: funmi@ffjohn.com
Dist(s): **Ingram Content Group.**

Harcourt Children's Bks *Imprint of* **Harcourt Children's Bks.**

Harcourt Children's Bks., *(978-0-15)* Div. of Houghton Mifflin Harcourt Trade & Reference Pubs., Orders Addr.: 6277 Sea Harbor Dr., Orlando, FL 32887 USA Toll Free Fax: 800-235-0256; Toll Free: 800-543-1918; 465 S. Lincoln Dr., Troy, MO 63379 Toll Free Fax: 800-235-0266; Toll Free: 800-543-1918; Edit Addr.: 15 E. 26th St., 15th Flr., New York, NY 10010 USA Tel 212-592-1000; Fax: 212-592-1011; 525 B St., Suite 1900, San Diego, CA 92101 Tel 619-231-6616; *Imprints:* Gulliver Books (Gulliver Bks); Red Wagon Books (Red Wagon Bks); Harcourt Children's Books (HCB)
E-mail: Andrew.porter@harcourt.com
Web site: http://www.HarcourtBooks.com
Dist(s): **Children's Plus, Inc.**
Houghton Mifflin Harcourt Publishing Co.
Harcourt Trade Pubs.

Harcourt Schl. Pubs., *(978-0-15)* Div. of Houghton Mifflin Harcouty School Publishers, 9205 Southpark Ctr. Loop, Orlando, FL 32819 USA (SAN 299-4585) Tel 407-345-2000; Fax: 407-352-3445; Toll Free Fax: 800-874-6418 (orders); Toll Free: 800-225-5425 (orders)
E-mail: hbspcs@harcourt.com
Web site: http://www.harcourtschool.com/
Dist(s): **Houghton Mifflin Harcourt Trade & Reference Pubs.**
Lectorum Pubns., Inc.

†Harcourt Trade Pubs., *(978-0-15)* Div. of Houghton Mifflin Harcourt Trade & Reference Pubs., Orders Addr.: 6277 Sea Harbor Dr., Orlando, FL 32887 USA (SAN 200-285X) Tel 619-699-6707; Toll Free Fax: 800-235-0256; Toll Free: 800-543-1918 (trade orders, inquiries, claims); Edit Addr.: 15 E. 26th St., New York, NY 10010 USA Tel 212-592-1000; Fax: 212-592-1011; 525 B St., Suite 1900, San Diego, CA 92101-4495 (SAN 200-2736) Tel 619-231-6616; *Imprints:* Silver Whistle (Silver Whistle)
E-mail: andrewporter@harcourt.com
Web site: http://www.HarcourtBooks.com
Dist(s): **MyiLibrary**; *CIP.*

hard girl bk. club, *(978-0-9748712)* 4143 S. Adelle, Mesa, AZ 85212 USA Tel 480-241-1351; Fax: 480-354-4727; Toll Free: 800-307-5261
E-mail: tkempton@cox.net
Web site: http://hardgirlbookclub.com.

Hard Made Books *See* **HM Bks.**

Hard Shell Word Factory, *(978-1-58200; 978-0-7599)* Orders Addr.: 6470a Glenway Ave. #109, Cincinnati, OH 45211 USA (SAN 631-4899) Toll Free Fax: 888-460-4752; Toll Free: 888-232-0808; Edit Addr.: 6470a Glenway Ave. #109, Cincinnati, OH 45211 USA Toll Free: 888-232-0808
E-mail: books@hardshell.com; books@mundania.com
Web site: http://www.hardshell.com
Dist(s): **CreateSpace Independent Publishing Platform**
American News Company.

Hardeman, *(978-0-692-91025-2; 978-0-692-94242-0)* 2662 River Eagle Ct, Sherwood, AR 72120 USA Tel 501-256-6359
E-mail: Royhardeman@delivering2morrowsfuture.com.

Harder, Polly *See* **R. H. Publishing**

Hardie Grant Bks. (AUS) *(978-1-86498; 978-1-876719; 978-1-74066; 978-1-74270; 978-1-74273; 978-0-9807835; 978-0-646-49937-6; 978-1-74358; 978-1-74379) Dist. by* **HachBkGrp.**

Hardie Grant Egmont Pty, Ltd. (AUS) *(978-1-920878; 978-1-921098; 978-1-921288; 978-1-921417; 978-1-921502; 978-1-921564; 978-1-921690; 978-1-921759; 978-1-921848; 978-1-74297; 978-1-76012; 978-1-76050) Dist. by* **IPG Chicago.**

Hardin Publishing, LLC, *(978-0-9742704)* 1380 W. Paces Ferry Rd., Suite 180, Atlanta, GA 30327 USA Tel 404-504-6619; Fax: 404-264-3583 Do not confuse with Hardin Publishing Company in Avera, GA
E-mail: proper@piedmont-atl.com; yntema@hardinpublishing.net
Web site: http://www.hardinpublishing.net.

Harding Hse. Publishing Sebice Inc., *(978-1-933630; 978-1-937211; 978-1-62524)* 220 Front St., Vestal, NY 13850-1514 USA; *Imprints:* Anamchara Books (Anamchara Bks); Village Earth Press (Village Earth); Candlewood Press (Candlewood Pr.)
E-mail: info@anamcharabooks.com
Web site: http://www.hardinghousepages.com; http://www.villageearthpress.com; http://www.anamcharabooks.com
Dist(s): **Follett School Solutions**
Smashwords.

Hardnett Publishing, *(978-0-9789310; 978-0-692-21182-3)* 2114 Keithshire Ct., Conyers, GA 30013 USA
E-mail: info@hardnettpublishing.com
Web site: http://www.hardnettpublishing.com.

Hardtke Publishing Co., *(978-0-9718166)* 2217 Second Ave. E., No. 1, Hibbing, MN 55746-1966 USA (SAN 254-4601) Tel 218-262-6510
Web site: http://www.libertyandlove.com/.

Hardway Pr, *(978-0-9717148; 978-0-9840221; 978-0-9974422; 978-0-692-94359-5; 978-0-578-60308-7)* 2547 La Cara Ave., Las Vegas, NV 89121 USA Tel 702-373-2609
Web site: http://www.brianrouff.com.

Hardy Ink LLC, *(978-1-7329442)* 3605 Woodcliff Dr., Kalamazoo, MI 49008 USA Tel 269-544-2225
E-mail: hardyinkllc@gmail.com
Web site: www.hardyink.com.

Hardy, John M. Publishing Company *See* **Texas Bk. Pubs. Assn.**

Hargrave Pr., *(978-0-9744885; 978-0-9817195)* P.O. Box 524, Nantucket, MA 02554 USA (SAN 856-3519)
E-mail: sales@hargravepress.com
Web site: http://www.hargravepress.com
Dist(s): **BookMasters.**

Hargrove Grey Publishing *Imprint of* **Phebe Phillips, Inc.**

Hargroves, Ann *See* **Hargroves Publishing Co.**

Hargroves Publishing Co., *(978-0-9742277)* P.O. Box 985, Virginia Beach, VA 23451-0985 USA
Web site: http://www.annhhargroves.com.

Harlan Publishing Company *See* **Diakonia Publishing**

Harlan Rose Publishing, *(978-0-9853466)* 920 Fall Creek, Grapevine, TX 76051 USA Tel 469-951-8499
E-mail: Flyingunicorn99@yahoo.com.

Harlem Pr., LLC., *(978-0-692-97471-1; 978-0-578-73961-8)* 7 William St., Montclair, NJ 07042 USA Tel 973-619-3266; Fax: 973-619-3266
E-mail: coryajones@me.com
Web site: HarlemPressLLC.com.

Harlequin Enterprises, Ltd. (CAN) *(978-0-373; 978-1-55166; 978-1-58314; 978-1-55254; 978-0-7783; 978-1-55373; 978-1-4268; 978-1-4592; 978-1-4603; 978-84-687-2370-9; 978-0-919622; 978-1-335; 978-1-4880; 978-1-4882) Dist. by* **HarperCollins Pubs.**

Harlin Jacque Pubns., *(978-0-940938)* Orders Addr.: P.O. Box 336, Garden City, NY 11530 USA (SAN 281-7667) Tel 516-489-0120; Fax: 516-292-9120; Edit Addr.: 89 Surrey Ln., Hempstead, NY 11550-3521 USA (SAN 281-7659) Tel 516-489-8564; *Imprints:* Pen & Rose Press (Pen&Rose Pr)
E-mail: harlinjacquepub@aol.com
Web site: http://www.lindamichellebaron.com.

Harmon Creek Pr., *(978-0-9820852)* 1763 Diamond Head Dr., Tiki Island, TX 77554 USA
E-mail: lnicholson@bookpublishing.com.

Harmony Healing Hse., *(978-0-9787179; 978-0-9854037)* 530 Miramonte Ave., Lakeport, CA 95453 USA (SAN 851-3570).

Harmony Hse. Publishing Co., *(978-0-9725289)* P.O. Box 858, Rexburg, ID 83440 USA Tel 208-359-1595 (phone/fax)
E-mail: jaydef@cableone.net
Web site: http://www.debtfreestepbystep.com.

Harmony Hse. *Imprint of* **Twin Flame Productions**

Harmony Ink Pr. *Imprint of* **Dreamspinner Pr.**

Harmony Pubns., LLC, *(978-0-9787586)* 100 W. Sta. Sq. Dr. Suite 230, Pittsburgh, PA 15219 USA (SAN 851-5468) Tel 412-670-3901; Fax: 724-934-4275
E-mail: harmonypublications@hotmail.com
Web site: http://www.colormyworld.info/.

Harmony Spirit Publishing Co., Inc., *(978-0-9762392)* 148 Westgate Dr., Saint Peters, MO 63376 USA
E-mail: lynowak@mail.win.org.

Harn Museum of Art, *(978-0-9629384; 978-0-9762552; 978-0-9833085; 978-1-7343235)* Div. of University of Florida, Orders Addr.: P.O. Box 112700, Gainesville, FL 32611-2700 USA; Edit Addr.: SW 34th St. & Hull Rd., Gainesville, FL 32611-2700 USA Tel 352-392-9826 (x2116); Fax: 352-392-3892
E-mail: twroath@harn.ufl.edu
Web site: http://www.harn.ufl.edu
Dist(s): **Univ. Pr. of Florida.**

Harold, Elsie L., *(978-0-9764644)* 1701 Eleni Ct., Virginia Bch, VA 23453-2886 USA
E-mail: turtlelsie@aol.com.

Harper Design *Imprint of* **HarperCollins Pubs.**

Harper Entertainment *Imprint of* **HarperCollins Pubs.**

Harper Girl Pr., *(978-0-692-85347-4; 978-0-692-92746-5; 978-0-692-07731-3)* 4210 Willshire Ave., Baltimore, MD 21206 USA
E-mail: michelle@iheartgratitude.com
Web site: www.harpergirlpress.com.

Harper, Janice N, *(978-0-692-88338-9)* 3657 Evans Mill Rd., Lithonia, GA 30038 USA Tel 706-593-4023
E-mail: jnh2005@netzero.net.

Harper, Joel D. *See* **Freedom Three Publishing**

Harper Kids Hse., *(978-0-9747218)* 10061 Riverside Dr., Suite 438, Toluca Lake, CA 91602 USA Tel 818-955-5301; *Imprints:* Young Women Programming (YWProgram)
E-mail: hannah@hannahsway.com
Web site: http://www.hannasway.com
Dist(s): **HarperCollins Pubs.**

Harper Paperbacks *Imprint of* **HarperCollins Pubs.**

Harper Perennial *Imprint of* **HarperCollins Pubs.**

Harper Torch *Imprint of* **HarperCollins Pubs.**

Harper Trophy *Imprint of* **HarperCollins Pubs.**

Harper, Vicky *See* **Little Bookstore Who Could, The**

Harper Voyager *Imprint of* **HarperCollins Pubs.**

Harper-Arrington Publishing, *(978-0-9764161)* 18701 Grand River Ave., 105, Detroit, MI 48223 USA Tel 313-283-4494; Fax: 248-281-0373; Toll Free: 888-435-9234
E-mail: info@harperarringtonmedia.com
Web site: http://www.hapub.com/.

HarperChildren's Audio *Imprint of* **HarperCollins Pubs.**

HarperCollins *Imprint of* **HarperCollins Pubs.**

HarperCollins *Imprint of* **HarperCollins Pubs.**

HarperCollins *Imprint of* **HarperCollins Pubs.**

HarperCollins Canada, Ltd. (CAN) *(978-0-00; 978-0-06; 978-0-690; 978-1-84887; 978-1-4434) Dist. by* **HarperCollins Pubs.**

HarperCollins Christian Publishing, Div. of HarperCollins Publishers, Orders Addr.: P.O. Box 141000, Nashville, TN 37214 USA Toll Free: 800-251-4000; Edit Addr.: 3900 Sparks Dr. SE, Grand Rapids, MI 49546 USA Toll Free: 800-226-1122; *Imprints:* HarperCollins Español (HarpCEspanol)
Web site: http://www.harpercollinschristian.com/
Dist(s): **Brilliance Publishing, Inc.**
Nelson, Thomas Inc.
Zondervan.

HarperCollins Español *Imprint of* **HarperCollins Christian Publishing**

HarperCollins Español, 501 Nelson Pl., Nashville, TN 37214 USA
E-mail: hce@harpercollins.com
Dist(s): **HarperCollins Pubs.**

†HarperCollins Pubs., *(978-0-00; 978-0-06; 978-0-380; 978-0-688; 978-0-690; 978-0-694; 978-0-87795; 978-1-55710)* Div. of News Corp., Orders Addr.: 1000 Keystone Industrial Pk., Scranton, PA 18512-4621 USA (SAN 215-3742) Tel 570-941-1500; Toll Free Fax: 800-822-4090; Toll Free: 800-242-7737 (orders only); Edit Addr.: 10 E. 53rd St., New York, NY 10022-5299 USA (SAN 200-2086) Tel 212-207-7000; *Imprints:* HarperCollins (HarpColl UK); Julie Andrews Collection (Julie Andrews); Harper Trophy (HarperTrophy); HarperFestival (HarperFestival); Cotler, Joanna Books (JoCotler); Geringer, Laura Book (LauraGeringer); Greenwillow Books (GreenwillowBks); HarperCollins (HarperCollCh); HarperChildren's Audio (HarperChildAud); Tegen, Katherine Books (KTegenBooks); Morrow, William & Company (WmMorrow); Avon Books (AvonBooks); Harper Torch (HarperTorch); Eos (Eos Harper); Harper Entertainment (HarperEntert); HarperCollins (HarperCollinsT); Harper Perennial (HarperPerenl); Harper Paperbacks (HarperPaper); Amistad (AmistadHarper); Rayo (Rayo Harper); Ecco (Ecco Harper); ReganBooks (ReganBooks); Collins (Collins); Morrow, William Cookbooks (MorrowCookbks); Harper Design (HDesign); HarperTeen (HarperTeen); HarperLuxe (HarperLuxe); HarperOne (HarperOne); William Morrow Paperbacks (WILLIAM MORROW); Balzer & Bray (Balzer & Bray); Walden Pond Press (Walden Pond); Avon Impulse (AVON IMPULSE); Newmarket for It Books (NewmarkforitBks); Witness Impulse (WitnessImp); Harper Voyager (HarperVoyager); Dey

Street Books (DeyStBks); Delphinium (Delphinium HC); Quill Tree Books (QuillTreeBks)
Web site: http://www.harpercollins.com; http://www.harpercollinschildrens.com
Dist(s): **Blackstone Audio, Inc.**
Casemate Academic
Children's Plus, Inc.
Ebsco Publishing
Findaway World, LLC
Follett School Solutions
F&W Media, Inc.
Lectorum Pubns., Inc.
MyiLibrary
Outskirts Pr., Inc.
Zondervan; *CIP.*

HarperCollins Pubs. Australia (AUS) *(978-0-207; 978-0-7322; 978-0-85835; 978-1-86256; 978-1-86371; 978-1-86378; 978-1-876288; 978-0-7304; 978-1-74050; 978-1-921504; 978-1-4607; 978-1-74309; 978-0-7316-3320-3; 978-0-646-10869-8; 978-0-646-39434-3; 978-1-922033) Dist. by* **HarperCollins Pubs.**

HarperCollins Pubs. Ltd. (GBR) *(978-0-00; 978-0-01; 978-0-06; 978-0-246; 978-0-261; 978-0-586; 978-0-85152; 978-0-411; 978-1-55468) Dist. by* **HarperCollins Pubs.**

HarperCollins Pubs. Ltd. (GBR) *(978-0-00; 978-0-01; 978-0-06; 978-0-246; 978-0-261; 978-0-586; 978-0-85152; 978-0-411; 978-1-55468) Dist. by* **IPG Chicago.**

HarperCollins Pubs. Ltd. (GBR) *(978-0-00; 978-0-01; 978-0-06; 978-0-246; 978-0-261; 978-0-586; 978-0-85152; 978-0-411; 978-1-55468) Dist. by* **Trafalgar.**

HarperFestival *Imprint of* **HarperCollins Pubs.**

HarperLuxe *Imprint of* **HarperCollins Pubs.**

HarperOne *Imprint of* **HarperCollins Pubs.**

HarperTeen *Imprint of* **HarperCollins Pubs.**

Harpeth Ridge Pr., *(978-0-9974449)* 304 Harpeth Ridge Dr., Nashville, TN 37221 USA Tel 615-352-1672
E-mail: judithwolfmandell@gmail.com.

Harptoons Publishing, *(978-0-615-35469-9; 978-0-615-41337-2; 978-0-615-45321-7; 978-0-615-59572-6; 978-0-615-68599-1; 978-0-9960197; 978-0-9995290)* 1081 State Rt. 28 Suite B No. 168, Milford, OH 45150 USA (SAN 859-6921) Tel 614-315-9427
E-mail: steve@studioharpster.com
Web site: www.harptoons.com.

Harrassowitz (DEU) *(978-3-447) Dist. by* **ISD USA.**

Harren Communications, LLC, *(978-0-9667359; 978-0-9831032)* Southern Belle Books, P.O. Box 242, Midway, FL 32343 USA Tel 850-294-8923; Fax: 850-539-9731; *Imprints:* BeanPole Books (BeanPole Bks)
E-mail: publisher@beanpolebooks.com
Web site: http://www.beanpolebooks.net
Dist(s): **Two Rivers Distribution.**

Harren Press/Harren Professional Press *See* **Harren Communications, LLC**

Harrington Artwerkes Booksellers, *(978-0-9778042)* P.O. Box 10648, Burke, VA 22009-0648 USA
E-mail: sjph@cox.net
Web site: http://www.amazingartbros.com.

Harrington Park Pr. *Imprint of* **Haworth Pr., Inc., The**

Harriot Publishing, *(978-0-578-17487-7; 978-0-578-19268-0; 978-0-578-19269-7; 978-0-692-05564-9)* 1504 Filmore Rd, Fort Washington, MD 20744 USA.

Harris, Candice *See* **Harris, K Publishing, Inc.**

Harris Communications, Inc., *(978-0-9727520)* 15155 Technology Dr., Eden Prairie, MN 55344-2277 USA (SAN 255-0512) Tel 952-906-1180; Fax: 952-906-1099; Toll Free: 800-825-6758
E-mail: mail@harriscomm.com
Web site: http://www.harriscomm.com.

Harris, H. E. & Company *See* **Whitman Publishing LLC**

Harris, Jennifer, *(978-0-9989251)* 1821 Barker Rd., Thompsons Station, TN 37179 USA Tel 615-299-6268
E-mail: jeffandjenniferharris@gmail.com.

Harris, Jessica, *(978-0-692-84752-7)* P.O. Box 2044, MONTGOMERY VILLAGE, MD 20886 USA Tel 240-449-4458
E-mail: jeffwcrawford5+LVP0003345@gmail.com; jeffwcrawford5+LVP0003345@gmail.com.

Harris, K Publishing, Inc., *(978-0-9770331)* P.O. Box 3091, Brandon, FL 33509-3091 USA
Web site: http://www.khpinc.com.

Harris, K.L. *See* **Make-believe Pr. LLC**

Harris, Monica *See* **Keep Empowering Yourself Successfully**

Harris, Noah, *(978-0-578-42504-7; 978-0-578-46408-4)* 9 Rosebay Ct., Hattiesburg, MS 39402 USA Tel 601-325-0982
E-mail: noahharris0131@gmail.com
Dist(s): **Independent Pub.**

Harris, Pleshette Communications Inc. Publishing, *(978-0-9754380)* P.O. Box 491282, Lawrenceville, GA 30049 USA Tel 678-910-6128; Fax: 770-237-9358
E-mail: contact@phc1.org
Web site: http://phc1.org.

Harris, Polly, *(978-0-9749375)* 6041 E Akron St., Mesa, AZ 85205 USA Tel 480-654-1213
E-mail: pollyharris@sbcglobal.net.

Harris Publishing, Inc., *(978-1-7340950)* 360 B St., Idaho Falls, ID 83402 USA Tel 208-542-2221
E-mail: janet@harrispublishing.com.

Harris, Samuel, *(978-0-9759253)* 21660 Boschome Dr., Kildeer, IL 60047-8616 USA
E-mail: sf864@aol.com; eharris864@aol.com
Dist(s): **Partners Bk. Distributing, Inc.**

Harrison and James, *(978-0-692-54055-8; 978-0-692-77913-2; 978-0-692-81389-8)* 11300 S Fairfield Ave, Chicago, IL 60655 USA Tel 773-238-9978
Dist(s): **CreateSpace Independent Publishing Platform.**

Harrison, Bobby, *(978-0-9771752)* 444 Shooting Star Tr., Gurley, AL 35748 USA Tel 256-776-2003; Fax: 256-776-2003
E-mail: bnharri@aol.com; ivorybillwp@aol.com
Web site: http://www.bobbyharrison.com
Dist(s): **Impact Photographics.**

Harrison, Gloria M., *(978-1-949185)* P.O. Box PO Box, Dover, DE 19903 USA Tel 302-736-3706
E-mail: hallelu@verizon.net.

Harrison House, Incorporated *See* **Harrison House Pubs.**

†**Harrison House Pubs.**, *(978-0-89274; 978-1-57794; 978-1-60683; 978-1-68031)* Orders Addr.: P.O. Box 35035, Tulsa, OK 74153 USA (SAN 208-676X) Tel 918-523-5700; Toll Free Fax: 800-830-5688; Toll Free: 800-888-4126; Edit Addr.: 7498 E. 46th Pl., Tulsa, OK 74145 USA Tel 918-523-5700; Toll Free Fax: 800-830-5688; Toll Free: 800-888-4126
E-mail: smckee@norimediagroup.com; jinori@norimediagroup.com; lisad@harrisonhouse.com; juliew@harrisonhouse.com
Web site: http://www.harrisonhouse.com
Dist(s): **Anchor Distributors**
Appalachian Bible Co.
Destiny Image Pubs.
Distributors, The
Spring Arbor Distributors, Inc.; *CIP.*

Harry & Stephanie Bks., *(978-0-9760875)* P.O. Box 172, Bronxville, NY 10708 USA Tel 914-961-6601
E-mail: harryandstephanie@yahoo.com
Web site: http://www.harryandstephanie.com.

Harseal Publications *See* **Harborseal Publishing Co.**

Hart, Chris Bks. *Imprint of* **Sixth&Spring Bks.**

hart Hse. publishing's, *(978-0-692-68612-6; 978-0-692-88008-1; 978-0-692-92066-4; 978-0-692-96780-5; 978-0-692-14929-4)* 406 E. Walton, Warrenton, MO 63383 USA Tel 636-359-3073
E-mail: cshart45@gmail.com
Web site: harthousepublishings.com
Dist(s): **CreateSpace Independent Publishing Platform.**

Hart Street Pubs., *(978-0-9793637)* 12157 Antibes St., Jacksonville, FL 32224 USA.

Hart-Burn Pr., *(978-0-9740318)* P.O. Box 99, Newton Junction, NH 03859-0099 USA
E-mail: stevehart7@yahoo.com
Web site: http://www.facebook.com/stevehart7
Dist(s): **Smashwords.**

Hartland Pubns., *(978-0-923309; 978-1-60564)* Div. of Hartland Institute of Health & Education, P.O. Box 1, Rapidan, VA 22733 USA (SAN 252-0834) Tel 540-672-3566; Fax: 540-672-3568; Toll Free: 800-774-3566
E-mail: jcarmouche@hartland.edu
Web site: http://www.hartlandpublications.com; http://www.hartlandbooks.com.

Hartlyn Kids Media, LLC, *(978-0-615-48984-1; 978-0-615-50182-6; 978-0-615-50503-9; 978-0-615-54948-4)* 45 Cowles St., Hartford, CT 06114 USA Tel 866-962-9993
E-mail: info@hartlynkids.com
Web site: http://www.hartlynkids.com.

Hartsuyker, Alice, *(978-0-9770441)* 1258 Fordham Dr. Apt. 204, Glendale Hts, IL 60139-4869 USA
E-mail: info@insidedharma.org; info@alicememoir.com
Web site: http://www.insidedharma.org; http://www.alicememoir.com.

Hart-Whitlow Pubs., *(978-0-9637951)* 1845 Brandywine Dr., Lenoir City, TN 37772 USA Tel 865-986-8553
E-mail: dickins@utk.edu.

Hartwood Publishing Group, LLC, The, *(978-1-62916)* 12372 W Woodland Ave., Avondale, AZ 85323 USA Tel 347-427-8966
E-mail: georgia@hartwoodpublishing.com
Web site: www.hartwoodpublishing.com
Dist(s): **INscribe Digital**
Independent Pubs. Group.

Harvard Business Review Pr., *(978-0-87584; 978-1-57851; 978-1-59139; 978-1-4221; 978-1-62527; 978-1-63369; 978-1-64782)* 60 Harvard Way, Boston, MA 02163 USA (SAN 202-277X) Tel 617-783-7400; 617 495 6181; Fax: 617-783-7492; Toll Free: 888-500-1016 6-19-01 faxed 2nd prefix app, charge, KC
E-mail: corpcustserv@hbsp.harvard.edu
Web site: http://www.hbsp.harvard.edu; http://www.harvardbusinessonline.com
Dist(s): **Ingram Publisher Services**
McGraw-Hill Professional Publishing
MyiLibrary
Two Rivers Distribution.

Harvard Business School Press *See* **Harvard Business Review Pr.**

†**Harvard Common Pr.**, *(978-0-87645; 978-0-916782)* 535 Albany St., Boston, MA 02118 USA (SAN 208-6778) Tel 617-423-5803; Fax: 617-695-9794; Toll Free: 888-657-3755
E-mail: orders@harvardcommonpress.com
Web site: http://www.harvardcommonpress.com
Dist(s): **Houghton Mifflin Harcourt Publishing Co.**
Houghton Mifflin Harcourt Trade & Reference Pubs.
Hachette Bk. Group
Independent Pubs. Group
MyiLibrary
Quarto Publishing Group USA
ebrary, Inc.; *CIP.*

Harvard Education Publishing Group (HEPG), *(978-0-916690; 978-1-891792; 978-1-934742; 978-1-61250; 978-1-68253)* Orders Addr.: c/o Pssc, Harvard Education Press 46 Development Rd., Fitchburg, MA 01420 USA Fax: 978-348-1233 (book order); Toll Free: 888-437-1437 Book Order Line; Edit Addr.: 8 Story St., First Flr., Cambridge, MA 02138 USA (SAN 913-9753) Tel 617-495-3432 editorial office phone; Fax: 617-496-3584 (orders); *Imprints:* Harvard Educational Review Reprint Series (Harv Ed Review)
E-mail: laura_clos@harvard.edu; sumita_mukherji@gse.harvard.edu; christina_deyoung@gse.harvard.edu
Web site: hepg.org.

Harvard Educational Review Reprint Series *Imprint of* **Harvard Education Publishing Group (HEPG)**

Harvard Perspectives in American Sports *Imprint of* **Harvard Perspectives Pr.**

Harvard Perspectives Pr., *(978-0-9715778)* P.O. Box 400827, Cambridge, MA 02140-0009 USA; *Imprints:* Harvard Perspectives in American Sports (Harvard Pers Amer Sp)
E-mail: harvardperspecpr@aol.com; indieKindle@gmail.com
Web site: http://indieKindle.blogspot.com.

†**Harvard Univ. Pr.**, *(978-0-674; 978-0-916724; 978-0-935617)* Orders Addr.: c/o Triliteral LLC, 100 Maple Ridge Dr., Cumberland, RI 02864 USA Tel 401-531-2800; Fax: 401-531-2801; Toll Free Fax: 800-406-9145; Toll Free: 800-405-1619; 800-448-2242; Edit Addr.: 79 Garden St., Cambridge, MA 02138 USA (SAN 200-2043) Tel 617-495-2600; Fax: 617-495-5898; *Imprints:* Belknap Press (Belknap)
E-mail: contact_hup@harvard.edu
Web site: http://www.hup.harvard.edu
Dist(s): **Blackstone Audio, Inc.**
Casemate Academic
De Gruyter, Inc.
Ebsco Publishing
Wiley, John & Sons, Inc.
ebrary, Inc.; *CIP.*

Harvest Hse. Pubs., *(978-0-7369; 978-0-89081; 978-1-56507)* 990 Owen Loop, N., Eugene, OR 97402-9173 USA (SAN 207-4745) Tel 541-302-0729; Fax: 541-302-0731; Toll Free: 888-501-6991
E-mail: pat.mathis@harvesthousepublishers.com; onix@harvesthousepublishers.com
Web site: http://www.harvesthousepublishers.com
Dist(s): **Faith Alive Christian Resources**
INscribe Digital
Independent Pubs. Group
Lulu Pr., Inc.
MyiLibrary
Twentieth Century Christian Bks.

Harvest Moon Bks. *Imprint of* **Tully, Jennifer Cahill**

Harvest Pubns., *(978-0-9654272)* 1928 Oxbow Rd., Minneapolis, KS 67467 USA Tel 913-392-2750 Do not confuse with companies with same name in Berkeley, CA, Arlington Heights, IL, Fort Worth, TX, Jacksonville, TX
E-mail: Adharvest@juno.com
Web site: http://www.pma-online.org/list/7345.html.

Harvest Sun Pr., LLC, *(978-0-9743668)* Orders Addr.: P.O. Box 826, Fairacres, NM 88033 USA Tel 479-283-4000; Fax: 505-526-6930; Edit Addr.: 4109 Broken Arrow Cv., Springdale, AR 72764-7503 USA
E-mail: info@harvestsunpress.com
Web site: http://www.harvestsunpress.com.

Harvey, Alan, *(978-0-9766354)* P.O. Box 235, Chapel Hill, NC 27514 USA; *Imprints:* Big H Books (Big H Bks)
Web site: http://www.lorneharvey.com.

Harwell, William, *(978-0-9728274)* HC 63 Box 1, Hanna, UT 84031 USA.

Hashmi, Kyla *See* **Digital Kidz Publishing Hse.**

Haskell & Judy Rosenthal, *(978-0-9966802)* 2215 Briar Branch Dr., Houston, TX 77042 USA Tel 713-785-4278
E-mail: brosenthal@fb.com.

Haskell, Rachael A., *(978-0-615-21356-9; 978-0-615-25625-2)* 6177 Sun Blvd., No. 404, Staint Petersburg, FL 33715 USA Tel 727-698-2543; Fax: 727-865-6507
E-mail: hangingwithib@yahoo.com
Dist(s): **Lulu Pr., Inc.**

Hassan, Marian, *(978-0-9766616)* 430 Mendota Rd. W., Suite 219, West Saint Paul, MN 55118 USA
E-mail: mhassan1@yahoo.com.

Hasse, Brenda, *(978-0-9906312; 978-1-7347786)* P.O. Box 124, Fenton, MI 48430 USA Tel 810-955-6121
E-mail: bmh730@aol.com.

Hat Trick Publishing, *(978-0-9860405)* 8169 Outer Dr., S., Traverse City, MI 49685 USA.

Hatch Ideas, Inc., *(978-0-9792558)* P.O. Box 14, Pine Plains, NY 12567 USA.

HATCHBACK Publishing, *(978-0-9778155; 978-0-9817338; 978-0-9891934; 978-0-9906859; 978-0-9988295; 978-1-948708)* P.O. Box 494, Genesee, MI 48437 USA Tel 810-394-8612
E-mail: cynthia@hatchbackpublishing.com
Web site: http://www.cynthialhatcher.com.

Hatherleigh Co., Ltd., The, *(978-1-57826; 978-1-886330)* 5-22 46th Ave., Suite 200, Long Island City, NY 11101-5215 USA (SAN 298-878X) Tel 212-832-1584; Fax: 212-832-1502; Toll Free Fax: 800-621-8892; Toll Free: 800-367-2550; *Imprints:* Hatherleigh Press (Hath Pr)
E-mail: info@hatherleigh.com
Web site: http://www.hatherleigh.com; http://www.getfitnow.com
Dist(s): **MyiLibrary**
Penguin Random Hse. Distribution
Penguin Random Hse. LLC
Random Hse., Inc.

Hatherleigh Pr. *Imprint of* **Hatherleigh Co., Ltd., The**

Hathi Chiti Bks. for Kids, *(978-0-615-37071-2; 978-0-615-37072-9; 978-0-9829362)* 203 Rivington St. Suite 2L, New York, NY 10002 USA Tel 212-920-1844
Web site: http://www.hathichiti.com
Dist(s): **National Bk. Network.**

Hatje Cantz Verlag GmbH & Co KG (DEU) *(978-3-7757) Dist. by* **Dist Art Pubs.**

Hatpin Press *See* **MusiKinesis**

Hatton, Robert, *(978-0-692-79740-2)* 12010 Teeside Dr., Fredericksburg, VA 22407 USA Tel 804-310-8246
E-mail: robertlhattonsr@gmail.com.

Hausen, Julie, *(978-0-692-98786-5)* P.O. Box 12153, Beaumont, TX 77726-2153 USA Tel 409-767-0300
E-mail: hausen.julie@gmail.com.

Have Hope Publishing, *(978-0-9762044)* Orders Addr.: P.O. Box 20892, Baltimore, MD 21209 USA Tel 410-367-6179 (phone/fax); Edit Addr.: 5033 Yellowwood Ave., Baltimore, MD 21209 USA
E-mail: teachertalk@jhu.edu.

Haven Bks., *(978-0-9659480; 978-1-58436)* 10153 1/2 Riverside Dr., Suite 629, North Hollywood, CA 91602 USA Tel 818-503-2518; Fax: 818-508-0299
E-mail: Havenbks@aol.com; reya@havenbooks.net; info@havenbooks.net
Web site: http://www.havenbooks.net
Dist(s): **National Bk. Network**
ebrary, Inc.

Haven Harbor, *(978-0-9729863)* P.O. Box 2197, Huntington Beach, CA 92647-0197 USA
Web site: http://www.havenharbor.com.

HavenBound Publishing, *(978-0-9761733)* Orders Addr.: 1076 Pinnacle Dr., Waynesville, NC 28786 USA; Edit Addr.: 1305 Old Balsam Rd., Waynesville, NC 28786 USA; *Imprints:* HBHavenBound Publishing (HBHavenBnd)
E-mail: joseph@introductiontojesus.com; carolyn@havenbound.net; havenbound@havenbound.net.

Haver, Nancy, *(978-0-9795696)* 19 Moorland St., Amherst, MA 01002 USA Tel 413-549-1337
E-mail: nhaver@crocker.com.

Havet Pr., *(978-0-9882798; 978-0-9864148; 978-0-9983132; 978-1-7346789)* 9519 130th Ave. NE, Kirkland, WA 98033 USA Tel 425-736-7303
E-mail: kortemary@comcast.net.

Hawaii Fine Art Studio, *(978-0-615-21549-5)* 1028 Tirol Ln., Lake Arrowhead, CA 92352 USA.

Hawaii Fishing News, *(978-0-944462; 978-0-9884939)* 6650 Hawaii Kai Dr., No. 201, Honolulu, HI 96825 USA (SAN 243-6612) Tel 808-395-4499; Fax: 808-396-3474
E-mail: fishnews@pixi.com
Web site: http://www.hawaiifishingnews.com/hfn
Dist(s): **Booklines Hawaii, Ltd.**

HAWAII Way Publishing *See* **Hawaii Way Publishing**

Hawaii Way Publishing, *(978-1-945384)* 4118 W. Harold Ct., Visalia, CA 93291 USA Tel 559-972-4168
E-mail: hawaiiwaypublishing@gmail.com
Web site: www.hawaiiwaypublishing.com.

Hawaiian Service, Inc., *(978-0-930492)* 94-527 Puahi St., Waipahu, HI 96797-4208 USA (SAN 205-0463) Tel 808-676-5026; Fax: 808-676-5156
Dist(s): **Booklines Hawaii, Ltd.**

Hawaya, Inc., *(978-0-9644149)* Orders Addr.: P.O. Box 300, Kailua, HI 96734 USA Tel 808-261-0589; Fax: 808-531-0957; Edit Addr.: 1564 Ulupii St., Kailua, HI 96734 USA
E-mail: ksullivan@pixi.com
Dist(s): **Booklines Hawaii, Ltd.**

Hawk Mountaintop Publishing, *(978-0-9672162)* P.O. Box 88, Piercy, CA 95587 USA Tel 707-247-3409
E-mail: hawk@saber.net.

Hawk Planners, *(978-0-9759702; 978-0-9776843)* 916 Silver Spur Rd. Suite 203, Rolling Hills Estates, CA 90274 USA Toll Free: 888-442-9575
E-mail: matthawkphd@msn.com
Web site: http://www.hawkplanners.com; http://www.satorsports.com
Dist(s): **Cardinal Pubs. Group.**

HAWK Publishing Group, *(978-0-9673131; 978-1-930709)* 7107 S. Yale, No. 345, Tulsa, OK 74136 USA (SAN 299-9293) Tel 918-492-3677; Fax: 918-492-2120
E-mail: wb@hawkpub.com
Web site: http://www.hawkpub.com
Dist(s): **Baker & Taylor Publisher Services (BTPS).**

Hawkeye Enterprises, *(978-0-9743061)* P.O. Box 252, Seal Rock, OR 97376-0252 USA Tel 541-563-4577
E-mail: hawkeye@oregonfast.net.

Hawks, Lyn, *(978-0-9888837)* 310 Ferguson Rd., Chapel Hill, NC 27516 USA Tel 919-929-5344
E-mail: lynhawks@gmail.com
Web site: www.lynhawks.com.

Haworth, Margaret, *(978-0-9740313)* 1625 W. May St. Apt. 3, Wichita, KS 67213-3578 USA.

†**Haworth Pr., Inc., The**, *(978-0-7890; 978-0-86656; 978-0-917724; 978-1-56022; 978-1-56023; 978-1-56024)* Div. of Taylor & Francis Group, 325 Chestnut St., Philadelphia, PA 19106-2614 USA (SAN 211-0156) Toll Free Fax: 800-895-0582; Toll Free: 800-429-6784; *Imprints:* Harrington Park Press (Harrington Park)
E-mail: orders@haworthpress.com; getinfo@haworthpress.com; barnold@haworthpress.com; docdelivery@haworthpress.com; tbronstein@haworthpress.com
Web site: http://www.haworthpress.com
Dist(s): **Barnes & Noble, Inc.**
Bookazine Co., Inc.
Borders, Inc.
Columbia Univ. Pr.
Distributors, The
Matthews Medical Bk. Co.
New Leaf Distributing Co., Inc.

Quality Bks., Inc.
Rittenhouse Bk. Distributors
SPD-Small Pr. Distribution
Unique Bks., Inc.
Waldenbooks, Inc.; *CIP.*

Hawthorn Pr. (GBR) *(978-0-9507062; 978-1-869890; 978-1-903458; 978-1-907359; 978-1-912480) Dist. by* **IPG Chicago.**

Hawthorne Bks. & Literary Arts, Inc., *(978-0-9716915; 978-0-9766311; 978-0-9790188; 978-0-9833049; 978-0-9834775; 978-0-9838504; 978-0-9860007; 978-0-9893604; 978-0-9904370; 978-0-9970683; 978-0-9988257)* 2201 NE 23rd Ave. 3rd Flr., Portland, OR 97212 USA
E-mail: rhughes@hawthornebooks.com
Web site: Http://hawthornebooks.com
Dist(s): **Publishers Group West (PGW).**

†Hay Hse., Inc., *(978-0-937611; 978-0-945923; 978-1-56170; 978-1-891751; 978-1-58825; 978-1-4019)* Orders Addr.: P.O. Box 5100, Carlsbad, CA 92018-5100 USA (SAN 630-477X) Tel 760-431-7695 ext 112; Fax: 760-431-6948; Toll Free Fax: 800-650-5115 (orders only); Toll Free: 800-654-5126 (orders only); 2776 Loker Ave. W, Carlsbad, CA 92010 (SAN 257-3024) Tel 800-654-5126; Fax: 800-650-5115; *Imprints:* Hay House Lifestyles (Hay Hse Lifestyles)
E-mail: kjohnson@hayhouse.com; pcrowe@hayhouse.com
Web site: http://www.hayhouse.com
Dist(s): **Follett School Solutions**
Lectorum Pubns., Inc.
Penguin Random Hse. Distribution
Penguin Random Hse. LLC; *CIP.*

Hay Hse. Lifestyles *Imprint of* **Hay Hse., Inc.**

Haydenburri Lane, *(978-0-9758785; 978-0-9801849; 978-0-9822149)* 6114 LaSalle Ave., No. 285, Oakland, CA 94611-2802 USA Toll Free: 888-425-2636
Web site: http://www.haydenburrilane.com.

Hayles, Nanette E., *(978-0-9986666)* 6631 NE 159th St., Vancouver, WA 98686 USA Tel 360-977-5597
E-mail: nehayles@gmail.com.

HayMarBks., LLC, *(978-0-9848736)* 1719 Plantation Oaks Dr., Jacksonville, FL 32223 USA Tel 904-655-0801
E-mail: dianeharperbooks@gmail.com
Web site: www.haymarbooks.com.

Haymarket Bks., *(978-1-931859; 978-1-60846; 978-1-64259)* 4015 N. Rockwell, Chicago, IL 60618 USA Tel 773-583-7884
E-mail: orders@haymarketbooks.org
Web site: http://www.haymarketbooks.org
Dist(s): **Consortium Bk. Sales & Distribution**
MyiLibrary
Open Road Integrated Media, Inc.
ebrary, Inc.

Haynes Manuals, Inc., *(978-0-8019; 978-1-56392; 978-1-85010; 978-1-85960; 978-1-62092)* Subdivision of J H Haynes, 861 Lawrence Dr., Newbury Park, CA 91320 USA (SAN 200-9838) Tel 805-498-6703; Fax: 805-498-2867; Toll Free: 800-442-9637; 1299 Bridgestone Pkwy., LaVergne, TN 37086 Fax: 615-793-5325; Toll Free: 800-242-4637
Web site: http://www.haynes.com/
Dist(s): **Delmar Cengage Learning**
Hachette Bk. Group
MBI Distribution Services/Quayside Distribution
Quarto Publishing Group USA.

Haynes Publications, Incorporated *See* **Haynes Manuals, Inc.**

Haynes Publishing Group P.L.C. (GBR) *(978-0-85696; 978-0-900550; 978-1-56392; 978-1-85010; 978-1-85260; 978-1-85960; 978-1-84425; 978-0-85733; 978-1-78521) Dist. by* **HachBkGrp.**

Haynes,Chilton,

Hayse, Emily, *(978-0-692-10514-6; 978-1-7332428)* 1939 Pero Lake Rd., Lapeer, MI 48446 USA Tel 810-510-0122
E-mail: blessedhopeem@aol.com.

HazardousWeather Preparedness Institute, *(978-0-9742794)* 5203 N. Oaks Dr., Greensboro, NC 27455-1229 USA
E-mail: rjackson@weatherpreparedness.com
Web site: http://www.weatherpreparedness.com.

Hazel Street Productions, *(978-0-9786988)* P.O. Box 5936, Sherman Oaks, CA 91413-5936 USA
Web site: http://www.hazelst.com.

†Hazelden, *(978-0-89486; 978-0-89638; 978-0-935908; 978-0-942421; 978-1-56246; 978-1-56838; 978-1-59285; 978-1-61649; 978-1-63634)* 15251 Pleasant Valley Rd., P.o. Box 176, Center City, MN 55012-0176 USA (SAN 209-4010) Fax: 651-213-4044; Toll Free: 800-328-9000; P.O. Box 176, RW4, Center City, MN 55012 Tel 651-213-4000; Toll Free: 800-328-9000
E-mail: bosterbauer@hazelden.org
Web site: http://www.hazelden.org
Dist(s): **BookMobile**
Follett School Solutions
Health Communications, Inc.
MyiLibrary
Simon & Schuster, Inc.
ebrary, Inc.; *CIP.*

Hazelden Publishing & Educational Services *See* **Hazelden**

Hazlett, Sandra , *(978-0-578-18864-5)* 843 North 1500 Rd., Lawrence, KS 66049 USA.

Hazy Dell Pr., *(978-0-9965787; 978-1-948931)* 2925 SE 50th Ave., Portland, OR 97206 USA Tel 206-779-3626
E-mail: hazydellpress@gmail.com
Web site: www.hazydellpress.com
Dist(s): **Consortium Bk. Sales & Distribution.**

HB Publishing *See* **Nadine Lalich**

HBHavenBound Publishing *Imprint of* **HavenBound Publishing**

H.B.P., Inc., *(978-0-9753285; 978-0-9789617; 978-0-9853898; 978-0-9971299; 978-0-692-19636-6)* 952 Frederick St., Hagerstown, MD 21740 USA
E-mail: jdaniels@hbp.com
Web site: http://www.hbp.com.

HCI Teens *Imprint of* **Health Communications, Inc.**

Head of Zeus (GBR) *(978-1-908800; 978-1-78185; 978-1-78408; 978-1-78669; 978-1-78497; 978-1-78854; 978-1-80024; 978-1-83893) Dist. by* **IPG Chicago.**

Head On Dialogue Publishing, *(978-0-9770550)* Orders Addr.: P.O. Box 11400, Oakland, CA 94611 USA; Edit Addr.: 509 El Dorado No. 309, Piedmont, CA 94611 USA Tel 510-677-3267
E-mail: headondialogue@yahoo.com.

Head Pr. Publishing, *(978-0-9758924; 978-0-9832837)* 3804 Pk. Bend Dr., Flower Mound, TX 75022 USA Tel 817-410-9490
E-mail: headpresspublish@aol.com
Web site: http://www.headpress.info
Dist(s): **Send The Light Distribution LLC.**

Headline Bks., Inc., *(978-0-929915; 978-0-938467; 978-1-882658; 978-1-946664; 978-1-951556)* Orders Addr.: P.O. Box 52, Terra Alta, WV 26764 USA (SAN 250-8559) Tel 304-789-3001; Fax: 304-789-6427; Toll Free: 800-570-5951; *Imprints:* Publisher Page (Pub Page); Headline Kids (HeadlineKids)
E-mail: cathy@headlinebooks.com
Web site: http://www.headlinebooks.com
Dist(s): **American Wholesale Bk. Co.**
American West Bks.
Brodart Co.
Coutts Information Services
Follett School Solutions
Midwest Library Service
News Group, The.

Headline Kids *Imprint of* **Headline Bks., Inc.**

Headline Publishing Group (GBR) *(978-0-7472; 978-0-7553; 978-1-4722) Dist. by* **HachBkGrp.**

Headline Publishing Group (GBR) *(978-0-7472; 978-0-7553; 978-1-4722) Dist. by* **Trafalgar.**

Headrick, Gordon, *(978-0-9771385)* M. F. W. High School 1775 W. Lowell Ave., Tracy, CA 95376 USA.

Heads First (1st), *(978-0-9761969)* 4207 Magnolia Ln., Sugar Land, TX 77478 USA Tel 281-844-3719
E-mail: heads1st@aol.com
Web site: http://www.headsfirst.com.

Healing Arts Pr. *Imprint of* **Inner Traditions International, Ltd.**

Healing Flood Bks., Inc., *(978-0-9746497)* Orders Addr.: 3108 N. Longmore St., Chandler, AZ 85224 USA
E-mail: freebook@healingflood.com; prb@healingflood.com; sales@hospitalbooks.net; jerry@hospitalbooks.net; marketing@healingflood.com
Web site: http://www.healingflood.com; http://www.hospitalbooks.net.

Healing Hands Pr., *(978-0-9747686)* Div. of Holistic Home Health Care, 1329 N. Wembley Cir., Port Orange, FL 32128 USA Tel 386-322-4888
Web site: http://www.love-heals.com.

Healing Heart's Publishing Co., *(978-0-692-18461-5)* 10955 Quail Cove Ct., Nampa, ID 83687 USA Tel 208-914-4628
E-mail: heatherorchard88@gmail.com
Dist(s): **CreateSpace Independent Publishing Platform.**

Healing Society, Inc., *(978-0-9720282; 978-1-932843)* Orders Addr.: P.O. Box 4503, Sedona, AZ 86340-9978 USA; Edit Addr.: 6560 Hwy. 179, Suite 114, Sedona, AZ 86351 USA Toll Free: 877-504-1106
E-mail: dcrenshaw@hspub.com; moh@hspub.com
Web site: http://www.healingsociety.com; http://www.bodynbrain.com
Dist(s): **New Leaf Distributing Co., Inc.**

Healing Tree Arts, *(978-0-9779643)* P.O. Box 3398, Laguna Hills, CA 92654 USA (SAN 850-7775)
E-mail: healingtreearts@yahoo.com
Web site: http://www.healingtreearts.com.

healologie, 2467 Adelaide, Abbotsford, CA 11111 USA Tel 778-552-5117
E-mail: jassal.lakhbir@gmail.com.

Health & Beauty Ctr., LLC, *(978-0-9747253)* P.O. Box 363, Oregon City, OR 97045 USA Toll Free: 888-648-7771
E-mail: support@healthnbeauty.com; support@perfect-prescription.com
Web site: http://www.healthnbeauty.com; http://www.perfect-prescription.com.

Health & Human Services Dept. *Imprint of* **United States Government Printing Office**

†Health Communications, Inc., *(978-0-932194; 978-1-55874; 978-0-7573; 978-0-9910732)* Orders Addr.: 3201 SW 15th St., Deerfield Beach, FL 33442-8190 USA (SAN 212-100X) Tel 954-360-0909; Fax: 954-360-0034; Toll Free: 800-441-5569; *Imprints:* HCI Teens (HCi Teens); Faith Communications (Faith Comns) Do not confuse with Health Communications, Inc., Edison, NJ
E-mail: terip@hcibooks.com; lorig@hcibooks.com
Web site: http://www.hcibooks.com
Dist(s): **Bookazine Co., Inc.**
Children's Plus, Inc.
Islander Group
Partners/West Book Distributors
Simon & Schuster, Inc.
Southern Bk. Service
Western Pubns. Service; *CIP.*

Health New England, *(978-0-9777159)* One Monarch Pl., Springfield, MA 01144-1500 USA (SAN 850-0436) Tel 413-787-4000; Toll Free: 800-842-4464
Web site: http://www.hne.com; http://www.hnestore.com; http://www.hnewhizkidz.com.

Health Press *See* **Health Press NA Incorporated**

Health Press NA Incorporated, *(978-0-929173)* P.O. Box 37470, Albuquerque, NM 87176 USA (SAN 248-5036) Tel 505-888-1394; Fax: 505-212-0612
E-mail: goodbooks@healthpress.com
Web site: http://www.healthpress.com.

Health Success Media, LLC, *(978-0-9820121)* P.O. Box 21092, Bradenton, FL 34204 USA (SAN 857-0043)
E-mail: elana.devorah@gmail.com; Elana@ConquerProstateCancer.com
Web site: http://www.ConquerProstateCancer.com.

Healthful Living Bks. *Imprint of* **Unique Executive Pubs.**

HealthMark Multimedia, *(978-0-9717399)* 1828 L St., NW, Suite 250, Washington, DC 20036 USA
E-mail: hm@healthmarkmultimedia.com; amcfarren@healthmarkmultimedia.com
Web site: http://www.HealthMarkMultimedia.com.

Healthnets, *(978-0-615-20972-2)* 2921 Emmorton Rd., Abingdon, MD 21009 USA Tel 410-515-7858
E-mail: milleniumdiet@gmail.com
Web site: http://www.Milleniumdiet.com/.

Healthoot, Inc., *(978-0-9968393)* P.O. Box 2782, Running Springs, CA 92382 USA Tel 909-261-5205
E-mail: jaimestiansen@gmail.com.

HealthSprings, LLC, *(978-0-9718120; 978-0-9740697; 978-0-9748263)* 1759 Grandstand, San Antonio, TX 78238 USA Tel 210-521-7650; Fax: 210-521-7141
E-mail: sabra@zoeyzones.com
Web site: http://www.zoeyzones.com.

HealthTeacher, *(978-0-9785578; 978-0-9817969)* 5200 Maryland Way Ste. 100, Brentwood, TN 37027-5072 USA Toll Free: 800-514-1362
E-mail: tod@relegent.com
Web site: http://www.healthteacher.com.

Healthy Life Press *See* **Healthy Life Pr., LLC**

Healthy Life Pr., Inc., *(978-0-9727328)* Orders Addr.: 1574 Gulf Rd., PMB 72, Point Roberts, WA 98281-9602 USA; Edit Addr.: 2667 Stellar Ct., Coquitlam, BC V3E 1H1 CAN Tel 604-682-5838; Fax: 604-468-1217
E-mail: rszefler@shaw.ca; info@starthealthylife.com
Web site: http://www.starthealthylife.com.

Healthy Life Pr., LLC, *(978-0-9821466; 978-0-9825800; 978-1-939267; 978-0-578-59920-5; 978-1-7342916)* Orders Addr.: 12838 Southampton Cir., Bristol, VA 24202 USA Toll Free: 877-331-2766
Web site: http://www.healthylifepress.com
Dist(s): **CreateSpace Independent Publishing Platform**
Outskirts Pr., Inc.
Send The Light Distribution LLC.

Hear My Heart Publishing, *(978-0-9862331; 978-1-945620)* 313 E. Oak St., Skiatook, OK 74070 USA Tel 918-510-1483
E-mail: hearmyheart02@yahoo.com
Web site: hearmyheart.net.

Heard Word Publishing, LLC, *(978-0-9801060)* 3051 W. 105th Ave. No. 350253, Westminster, CO 80031 USA
E-mail: hispublishingllc@yahoo.com; Beatrice@TheGetOverItGal.com
Web site: www.TheGetOverItGal.com.

Hearst Book Group *See* **Hearst Magazine Media**

Hearst Communications, Inc., *(978-0-87851; 978-1-58816)* 250 W. 55th St., New York, NY 10019-5288 USA
E-mail: jdeval@hearst.com
Web site: http://www.hearst.com
Dist(s): **Hearst Bks.**
Sterling Publishing Co., Inc.

Hearst Magazine Media, *(978-1-950785)* Orders Addr.: 300 W. 57th St., New York, NY 10019 USA Tel 212-649-2000
E-mail: andy.nelson63@gmail.com
Dist(s): **Penguin Random Hse. Distribution**
Penguin Random Hse. LLC.

Heart 4 Clowning Pr., A, *(978-0-9799093)* 905 Hwy 321 NW., No. 215, Hickory, NC 28601 USA Tel 828-326-0662
E-mail: aheart4clowning@gmail.com
Web site: http://www.AHeart4Clowning.com.

Heart & Harp LLC, *(978-0-9742174)* Orders Addr.: P.O. Box 818, Walled Lake, MI 48390-0818 USA Tel 313-938-9847
E-mail: HeartandHarp@comcast.net
Web site: http://www.heartandharp.net.

Heart Arbor Bks., *(978-1-891452)* Orders Addr.: P.O. Box 542, Grand River, OH 44045 USA (SAN 299-6073) Tel 440-257-0722; Toll Free: 877-977-4422.

Heart Bound Pr., *(978-0-615-25721-1; 978-0-578-73329-6)* Orders Addr.: 2141 Via Pacheco, Palos Verdes, CA 90274 USA Tel 310-375-3716; Fax: 310-373-2702
E-mail: heartboundpublishing@yahoo.com.

Heart Communications, *(978-0-9694176; 978-0-9747516)* P.O. Box 710791, Oak Hill, VA 20171 USA (SAN 116-404X) Tel 641-715-3900 (ext. 20889)
E-mail: info@heartcommunications.com
Web site: http://www.HeartCommunications.com.

Heart Flame Publishing, *(978-0-9726618)* P.O. Box 790038, Virgin, UT 84779-0038 USA (SAN 853-2532) Fax: 435-635-2613
Web site: http://www.heartflamepublishing.com.

Heart Of Dixie Publishing *See* **Bluewater Pubns.**

Heart Path Publishing, *(978-0-9712305)* P.O. Box 44, Keene, TX 76059 USA Tel 817-681-3877 Do not confuse with Heart Path Publishing, Atlanta, GA
Web site: http://www.guidemagazine.org.

Heart Seed Pr., *(978-0-615-37628-8; 978-0-9831945; 978-0-578-72051-7; 978-0-578-72052-4)* 3710 Little Walnut Rd. Spc3, Silver City, NM 88061 USA Tel 575-956-5891
E-mail: acircleisdrawn@gmail.com
Web site: http://acircleisdrawn.org.

Heart to Heart Publishing, Inc., *(978-0-9742806; 978-0-9802486; 978-1-937008)* Orders Addr.: P.O. Box PO Box 50644, Bowling Green, KY 42102 USA Tel 270-526-5589; Edit Addr.: P.O. Box PO Box 50644, Bowling Green, KY 42102 USA Tel 270-526-5589
E-mail: linda@hearttoheartpublishinginc.com
Web site: http://www.lindajhawkins.com; http://www.hearttoheartpublishinginc.com
Dist(s): **BookBaby.**

Heart-centered Productions, *(978-0-692-15583-7; 978-0-692-15585-1)* 282 N 300 E Unit D, American Fork, UT 84003 USA Tel 801-602-2699
E-mail: scotty_amour@yahoo.com
Dist(s): **Ingram Content Group.**

Heartfelt Bks., *(978-0-9763933)* 149 Thunderbird Trail, Carol Stream, IL 60188-1982 USA.

HeartFelt Stories LLC, *(978-0-9778113)* 5767 Kempton Run Ct., Columbus, OH 43235 USA (SAN 850-3036)
E-mail: heartfeltstories@hotmail.com
Web site: http://www.heartfeltstoriesllc.com
Dist(s): **Blu Sky Media Group.**

Heartful Loving Pr., *(978-0-9723639)* Div. of Ilui International, 1450 Orange Grove Ave., Santa Barbara, CA 93105 USA Tel 805-687-7442; Fax: 805-687-3042
E-mail: howard@heartfullovingpress.com
Web site: http://www.heartfullovingpress.com; http://www.howtobeafamily.com; http://www.firstloveremembrances.com; http://www.howtobethebestlover.com
Dist(s): **Partners Bk. Distributing, Inc.**

Hearthstone Rose, *(978-0-9836682)* 1156 Valleyview Dr., Lawrence, PA 15055 USA Tel 724-746-0662
E-mail: conniedonaldson@comcast.net.

Heartland Foundation, Inc., *(978-0-943177)* Orders Addr.: P.O. Box 887, Ames, IA 50010 USA Toll Free: 866-385-2027; Edit Addr.: 413 Northwestern Ave., Ames, IA 50010 USA (SAN 668-3010) Tel 515-232-1054
E-mail: issn@att.net
Web site: http://mcmillenbooks.com
Dist(s): **McMillen Bk. Distributors.**

Heartlight Girls, *(978-0-9787689)* P.O. Box 370546, Denver, CO 80237 USA Tel 303-690-5603
E-mail: debra @heartlightgirls.com; debragano@aol.com
Web site: http://www.heartlightgirls.com.

Heartohopia Pr., *(978-0-9725184)* 2007 NE 59 Pl., Suite 105, Fort Lauderdale, FL 33308 USA
Web site: http://www.heartohopia.com.

HeartQuake Publishing *See* **Hunt Thompson Media**

Heartrock Pr., *(978-0-9817668)* P.O. Box 135, Langley, WA 98260 USA Tel 360-321-5603
Web site: http://NWDragons.com.

Heart's Path LLC *See* **Breadcrumbs LLC**

Heartsome Press *See* **Heartsome Publishing**

Heartsome Publishing, *(978-0-9726408)* 220 Norfolk St., Walpole, MA 2081 USA Tel 508-553-3858; Fax: 508-668-1998
Web site: http://www.nolobsterplease.com/.

Heartsome Publishing, *(978-0-9726408)* 220 Norfolk St., Walpole, MA 02081 USA Tel 508-553-3858; Fax: 508-668-1998
E-mail: rrhearts@comcast.net
Web site: http://www.nolobsterplease.com/.

Heartstrings Publishing, *(978-0-9760733)* Orders Addr.: P.O. Box 8255, Fernando Beach, FL 32035 USA; Edit Addr.: Marchette Burette Market, Amelia Island Plantation, Fernandina Beach, FL 32034 USA
E-mail: mledien@aol.com.

Heart-to-Heart Pubns., *(978-0-9744565)* 18237 N. 51st Pl., Scottsdale, AZ 85254 USA Tel 602-485-0793
E-mail: cpruett1@cox.net.

Heath, Jonathan Publishing, *(978-0-9715837)* 10 Willowstream Dr., Vernon, CT 06066 USA Tel 860-875-8373
E-mail: lenpam@snet.net.

Heath Publishing *See* **Lockwood House Publishing**

Heather & Highlands Publishing, *(978-1-58478)* Div. of Heather & Highlands Publishing, Orders Addr.: 2384 Tokay Ct., Paradise, CA 95969 USA (SAN 254-0932) Tel 530-876-8986; Fax: 530-876-8989; Toll Free: 888-999-2358; *Imprints:* Highland Children's Press (Hghlnd Child)
E-mail: pawprintsorders@pawprintspress.com; pawprints@pawprintspress.com; tew@tewatsononline.com; heatherandhighlands@heatherandhighlandspublishing.com
Web site: http://www.pawprintspress.com; http://www.tewatsononline.com; http://heatherandhighlandspublishing.com
Dist(s): **Book Wholesalers, Inc.**
Brodart Co.

Heavenly C. Publishing, *(978-0-9746361)* P.O. Box 335, West Chester, OH 45071 USA
Web site: http://www.heavenlyCPublishing.com.

Heavenly Realm Publishing, *(978-0-9714874; 978-0-9825589; 978-0-9828802; 978-0-9833418; 978-0-9835202; 978-0-9839969; 978-1-937911; 978-1-944383)* Orders Addr.: P.O. Box 682532, Houston, TX 77268 USA Tel 866-216-0696; Toll Free: 877-599-3237
E-mail: heavenlyrealm@heavenlyrealmpublishing.com
Web site: http://www.heavenlyrealmpublishing.com
Dist(s): **Ingram Content Group.**

Heavy Metal Magazine, *(978-1-882931; 978-1-932413; 978-1-935351)* Div. of Metal Mammoth, Inc., 100 H. Village Ave., Suite IV, Rockville Centre, NY 11570-4801 USA Tel 516-594-2130; Fax: 516-594-2133
E-mail: heavymetal1@rcn.com
Web site: http://metaltv.com
Dist(s): **Diamond Comic Distributors, Inc.**
TNT Media Group, Inc.

Hebler, Dave, *(978-0-9765392)* 5891 S. Military Trail, 5A-PMB, Lake Worth, FL 33463-6920 USA Tel 561-642-6696
E-mail: daveahebler@aol.com
Web site: http://www.protectingwomen.com.

Hebler, Michael, *(978-0-615-39525-8; 978-0-9833884; 978-0-692-67408-6; 978-0-692-70134-8)* 1344 Kingswood Ct., Fort Myers, FL 33919 USA Tel 562-857-1524; *Imprints:* Night After Night Publications, Incorporated (NightAfterNight)
E-mail: michaelhebler@gmail.com
Web site: http://www.michaelhebler.com
Dist(s): **CreateSpace Independent Publishing Platform.**

Hecker, Mark Daniel, *(978-0-692-91079-5)* 1606 Isherwood St. NE No. 2, WASHINGTON, DC 20003 USA Tel 215-205-9902
E-mail: mhecker616@gmail.com
Dist(s): **Ingram Content Group.**

Hedgebury (AUS) *(978-0-9873437) Dist. by* **NewShelves.**

Hedgehog Hill Pr., *(978-0-615-90068-1; 978-0-692-53693-3; 978-0-692-53695-7; 978-0-692-53696-4; 978-0-692-53804-3; 978-0-692-56005-1; 978-0-692-68211-1; 978-0-692-68510-5; 978-0-692-69829-7; 978-0-692-72830-7; 978-0-692-72835-2; 978-0-692-78517-1; 978-0-692-79765-5; 978-0-692-91674-2; 978-0-692-91758-9; 978-0-692-06689-8) 7 Urban Dr., Anderson, IN 46011 USA Tel 765-639-5930*
Dist(s): **CreateSpace Independent Publishing Platform.**

Hedger, Ralph, *(978-0-9753880)* 208 Chaucer Rd., Charlottesville, VA 22901-2215 USA
E-mail: rehedger@aol.com.

Heel Verlag GmbH (DEU) *(978-3-89365; 978-3-922858; 978-3-89880; 978-3-95843) Dist. by* **Natl Bk Netwk.**

Heerema, Dina, *(978-0-692-23844-8)* 401 Riverview Dr., Totowa, NJ 07512 USA Tel 973-200-0560
E-mail: dina23n@hotmail.com.

Heersink, Roland, *(978-0-9770473)* 18303 Starboard Dr., Houston, TX 77058-4362 USA
Web site: http://www.fairytunes.com.

Heflin & Thrall Language Pubns., Inc., *(978-0-9723341)* 2109 Stanford, Jacksonville, TX 75766 USA Toll Free: 888-313-3310
E-mail: jheflin@language-publications.com.

Hegemony Pr., *(978-0-9754114)* 5205 Pacific Ave., Tacoma, WA 98405 USA Tel 253-671-2665; Fax: 253-475-2665; Toll Free: 888-671-2665.

Heiderer, Conrad, *(978-0-9746699)* P.O. Box 405, Glen Arbor, MI 49636 USA Tel 231-334-6680 Toll Free: 888-877-0994
E-mail: cehj1200@hotmail.com
Web site: http://www.twigma.com.

Heifer Project International, *(978-0-9755996; 978-0-9798439; 978-0-9819788)* Orders Addr.: 1 World Ave., Little Rock, AR 72203-8058 USA Tel 800-422-1311; Fax: 501-907-2802
E-mail: info@heifer.org
Web site: http://www.heifer.org.

Heights Series, The, *(978-0-692-16632-1)* 511 Andrews Dr., Hampton, GA 30228 USA Tel 305-586-2495
E-mail: denarriuspennell206@outlook.com
Dist(s): **Ingram Content Group.**

Heinemann *Imprint of* **Capstone**

Heinemann *Imprint of* **Heinemann-Raintree**

†Heinemann, *(978-0-325; 978-0-434; 978-0-435; 978-1-59469)* Orders Addr.: P.O. Box 6926, Portsmouth, NH 03802 USA Toll Free: 800-225-5800; Edit Addr.: 361 Hanover St., Portsmouth, NH 03801 USA (SAN 210-5829) Tel 603-431-7894; Fax: 603-431-7840; *Imprints:* Firsthand (Firsthnd)
E-mail: info@heinemann.com
Web site: http://www.heinemann.com
Dist(s): **ABC-CLIO, LLC**
Capstone
Follett School Solutions
Leonard, Hal Corp.
Pearson Education
Trans-Atlantic Pubns., Inc.; *CIP.*

Heinemann Educational Books, Incorporated *See* **Heinemann**

.Heinemann-Raintree *See* **Heinemann-Raintree**

Heinemann-Raintree, *(978-0-431; 978-1-57572; 978-1-58810; 978-1-4034; 978-1-4109; 978-1-4329; 978-1-4846)* Div. of Capstone, Orders Addr.: 1710 Roe Crest Dr., North Mankato, MN 56003 USA; Halley Court Freepost PO Box 1125, Oxford, OX2 8YY; *Imprints:* Heinemann (Heinem); Raintree (RaintreeCap); NA-r (NA-r)
Dist(s): **Capstone**
Follett School Solutions
Lectorum Pubns., Inc.

Heinle & Heinle Publishers, Inc. *See* **Cengage Heinle**

Heinrich Publishing LLC, *(978-0-578-57110-2)* 1140 N. 27th Ave., Bozeman, MT 59718 USA Tel 605-645-8436
E-mail: savinglikeasloth@gmail.com
Dist(s): **Ingram Content Group.**

Heinrich, Tyson Chul, *(978-0-615-23894-4; 978-0-578-00492-1; 978-0-578-01337-4; 978-0-578-01343-5; 978-0-9962209)* 4295 Hitch Blvd., Moorpark, CA 93021 USA
Web site: http://www.tysonheinrich.com.

Heins Pubns., *(978-0-9671762; 978-0-9748680)* 2016 Leonard Ct., Eau Claire, WI 54703 USA Toll Free: 800-554-3467
E-mail: revheins@wwt.net.

Heinz, Derek *See* **Heinz, Derek**

Heinz, Derek, *(978-0-578-19115-7; 978-0-692-98514-4)* 1124 NE Lilac St. 107, Issaquah, WA 98029 USA.

Helen Bolton Ministries *See* **Bolton Publishing LLC**

Helen Darling *See* **My Darling-Tots Pubns.**

Heliand Publishing Corp., *(978-0-9770712)* P.O. Box 477, Pleasant Grove, UT 84062 USA
E-mail: submissions@heliandpublishing.com
Web site: http://www.heliandpublishing.com

Heliograph, Inc., *(978-0-9668926; 978-1-930658)* 26 Porter St., Somerville, MA 02143-2215 USA
E-mail: info@heliograph.com
Web site: http://www.heliograph.com.

Heliotrope Bks., LLC, *(978-0-9816198; 978-0-9832940; 978-0-9904012; 978-1-942762)* 125 E. 4th St., New York, NY 10003 USA Tel 212-477-1783
E-mail: publishers@heliotropebooks.com; nonirose@earthlink.net
Web site: http://www.heliotropebooks.com
Dist(s): **Ingram Publisher Services.**

Helkenn, Brady, *(978-1-7340909)* 815 Tennessee St, San Francisco, CA 94107 USA Tel 415-637-0541
E-mail: bhelkenn@gmail.com.

Hellgate Pr. *Imprint of* **L & R Publishing, LLC**

Helm Literary Publishing *See* **Helm Publishing**

Helm Publishing, *(978-0-9723011; 978-0-9760919; 978-0-9769193; 978-0-9778205; 978-0-9792328; 978-0-9801780; 978-0-9820605; 978-0-9841397; 978-0-9830109; 978-0-9850488)* Orders Addr.: 861 37th Ave. N Apt D, St. Petersburg, FL 33704 USA (SAN 254-7562) Tel 815-621-3336; Edit Addr.: 861 27th Ave. N Apt D, St. Petersburg, FL 33704 USA Tel 727-623-5014
E-mail: dianne@publishersdrive.com
Web site: http://www.publishersdrive.com.

Helms, Jo Publishing, *(978-0-9745319)* 824 S. Schaefer St., Appleton, WI 54915 USA
E-mail: cheesedawg@earthlink.net; ilovegrizz@earthlink.net
Web site: http://www.grizz.20megsfree.com.

Helmshines, *(978-0-9969893)* 11203 Ranch Rd. 2222 Unit 2005, AUSTIN, TX 78730 USA Tel 770-630-3620
E-mail: Melissa.Hines.Helms@gmail.com.

HELORO Publishing Group, *(978-0-9785435; 978-0-615-15932-4; 978-0-615-15933-1; 978-0-615-16034-4)* 860 Appletree Ct., Northbrook, IL 60062-3402 USA (SAN 850-9549) Tel 847-207-1087 mobile phone Do not confuse with companies with the same or similar name in Minneapolis, MN, Great Neck, NY
Web site: http://www.HELORO.com
Dist(s): **Lulu Pr., Inc.**

H.E.L.P. for Self-Education, *(978-0-9766991)* 960 Perth Rd., Troutman, NC 28166 USA Tel 704-528-5866; Fax: 704-585-9397
E-mail: swedship@bellsouth.net
Web site: http://www.home.bellsouth.net/p/pwp-helpeducate.

Helping Hands Children's Bks., *(978-0-9762274)* 421 26th St., Marion, IA 52302 USA Tel 319-373-4169
E-mail: mary@mysak.com.

Helping Hands Therapeutic Services, *(978-0-9855978)* P.O. Box 1452, Columbus, GA 31902 USA Tel 770-310-0510
E-mail: mirrorbuzz99@gmail.com.

Helpingwords, *(978-0-615-16066-5; 978-0-615-23505-9; 978-0-578-03620-5; 978-0-578-05059-1; 978-0-578-06008-8; 978-0-9828529; 978-0-9977922)* 66 Prospect St., Manchester, NH 03104 USA Tel 603-668-1975
E-mail: kathy@kathybrodsky.com
Web site: http://www.kathybrodsky.com
Dist(s): **Enfield Publishing & Distribution Co., Inc.**

Helps4Teachers, *(978-0-9778548)* 145 Gardenside Ct., Fallbrook, CA 92028 USA (SAN 850-4180) Tel 760-723-0504
E-mail: rstur@roadrunner.com
Web site: http://www.helps4teachers.com.

Hemed Books, Incorporated *See* **Lambda Pubs., Inc.**

Henderson Publishing, *(978-1-891029)* Orders Addr.: 811 Eva's Walk, Pounding Mill, VA 24637 USA Tel 276-964-2291.

Hendley, Jeff *See* **L'Edge Pr.**

Hendricks, J. L., *(978-0-9974915; 978-1-952634)* 1649 Ironwood PL Unit B, Corona, CA 92879 USA Tel 951-314-6464
E-mail: jlhendricksauthor@gmail.com.

Hendrickson Publishers, Incorporated *See* **Hendrickson Pubs. Marketing, LLC**

†Hendrickson Pubs. Marketing, LLC, *(978-0-913573; 978-0-917006; 978-0-943575; 978-1-56563; 978-1-59856; 978-1-61970; 978-1-68307)* Orders Addr.: P.O. Box 3473, Peabody, MA 01961-3473 USA (SAN 285-2772) Fax: 978-531-8146; Toll Free: 800-358-3111; Edit Addr.: 140 Summit St., Peabody, MA 01960 USA (SAN 663-6594) Fax: 978-573-8414 Do not confuse with Hendrickson Group, Sandy Hook, CT
E-mail: editorial@hendrickson.com
Web site: http://www.hendrickson.com; *CIP.*

Hendrickson, Thomas L, *(978-0-9817011)* 19910 W. Monroe St., Buckeye, AZ 85326 USA
Web site: http://www.fishersmedia.com.

Henisz, Jerzy E., *(978-0-615-13851-0)* Orders Addr.: P.O. Box 1089, Sharon, CT 06069 USA; Edit Addr.: 33 Hospital Hill Rd., Sharon, CT 06069 USA
Dist(s): **Lulu Pr., Inc.**

Henry, Ian Pubns. (GBR) *(978-0-86025) Dist. by* **Players Pr.**

Henry, Ian Pubns. (GBR) *(978-0-86025) Dist. by* **Empire Pub Srvs.**

Henry, Nelson K. Jr, *(978-0-578-43221-2)* 215 Hidden Springs Dr., Durham, NC 27703 USA Tel 919-824-0370
E-mail: nkhjr05@gmail.com.

Henry, Patti, *(978-0-9817155)* 9114 Tepee Trail, Houston, TX 77064 USA (SAN 856-3268) Tel 281-894-4131
E-mail: patti@patti-henry.com
Web site: http://www.patti-henry.com.

Henry Quill Pr., *(978-1-883960)* 7340 Lake Dr., Fremont, MI 49412-9146 USA Tel 231-924-3026; Fax: 231-928-2802.

HenschelHAUS Publishing, Inc., *(978-0-9647663; 978-0-9722099; 978-1-59598)* 6450 W. Forest Home Ave., Suite 102, Milwaukee, WI 53220 USA Tel 414-486-0653; Fax: 262-565-2058; *Imprints:* Goblin Fern Press (Goblin Fern)
E-mail: kira@henschelHAUSbooks.com
Web site: http://www.goblinfernpress.com; http://www.mavenmarkbooks.com; http://www.henschelHAUSbooks.com; http://www.threetowerspress.com
Dist(s): **Smashwords.**

Hensley, Michael, *(978-0-9747389)* P.O. Box 2952, Ranchos de Taos, NM 87557 USA
Web site: http://www.michaelmhensley.com.

Henzel, Richard, *(978-0-9747237; 978-0-9826688; 978-0-9846715)* 1106 N. Taylor, Oak Park, IL 60302 USA Tel 312-296-8396
E-mail: richard@richardhenzel.com
Web site: http://www.richardhenzel.com; http://www.richardhenzel.com/marktwain
Dist(s): **Audible.com**
Midwest Tape.

†Herald Pr., *(978-0-8361; 978-1-5138)* Div. of MennoMedia, Inc., Orders Addr.: 1251 Virginia Ave., Harrisonburg, VA 22802 USA (SAN 202-2915) Fax: 1-316-283-0454; Toll Free: 1-800-245-7894; 800-631-6535 (Canada only) Do not confuse with Herald Pr., Charlotte, NC
E-mail: info@mennomedia.org
Web site: http://www.mennomedia.org
Dist(s): **Ebsco Publishing**
Faith Alive Christian Resources
Send The Light Distribution LLC
Spring Arbor Distributors, Inc.; *CIP.*

†Herald Publishing Hse., *(978-0-8309)* Orders Addr.: P.O. Box 390, Independence, MO 64051-0390 USA Tel 816-521-3015; Fax: 816-521-3066 (customer services); Toll Free: 800-767-8181; Edit Addr.: 1001W. Walnut St., Independence, MO 64051-0390 USA (SAN 111-7556) Tel 816-257-0200
E-mail: sales@HeraldHouse.org
Web site: http://www.heraldhouse.org; *CIP.*

Heraver, Jamie Renee, *(978-0-692-15830-2; 978-0-578-57078-5)* P.O. Box 16, Huntington Beach, CA 92648 USA Tel 714-916-2422
E-mail: jheraver@yahoo.com
Dist(s): **CreateSpace Independent Publishing Platform.**

Herdman, Susan E., *(978-0-578-01491-3)* 4639 Sunset Ridge, Santa Fe, NM 87507 USA
E-mail: susan@susanheerdman.com
Web site: http://americanadolescents.com
Dist(s): **Lulu Pr., Inc.**

Here with an ear publishing, *(978-0-9995675)* 7629 Lorimar Dr., Reynoldsburg, OH 43068 USA Tel 614-591-2687
E-mail: daviddwriter@gmail.com.

Heredia, Denise, *(978-0-692-10461-3)* 11819 Central Ave. Apt 213, CHINO, CA 91710 USA Tel 626-905-2517
E-mail: niecyntab@yahoo.com
Dist(s): **Ingram Content Group.**

Heritage Bks., *(978-0-7884; 978-0-917890; 978-0-940907; 978-1-55613; 978-1-888265; 978-1-58549; 978-1-68034)* 5810 Ruatan St, Berwyn Heights, MD 20740 USA (SAN 209-3367) Tel 800-876-6103; Fax: 800-876-6103; Toll Free: 800-876-6103
E-mail: Info@HeritageBooks.com
Web site: http://www.HeritageBooks.com; http://www.WillowBendBooks.com
Dist(s): **CreateSpace Independent Publishing Platform.**

Heritage Builders, LLC, *(978-0-615-30423-6; 978-0-615-30734-3; 978-0-615-30735-0; 978-0-615-31024-4; 978-0-692-00827-0; 978-1-939011; 978-1-940242; 978-1-941437; 978-1-942603; 978-1-945549)* 3105 Locan Ave., Clovis, CA 93619 USA
Dist(s): **MyiLibrary**
Publishers Group West (PGW).

Heritage Heart Farm, *(978-0-9706348)* Orders Addr.: 21387 Rd. 128, Oakwood, OH 45873 USA Tel 419-594-2258
E-mail: heritageheartfarm@roadrunner.com; kohart@tds.net
Web site: http://www.heritageheartfarm.com.

Heritage Hse. (CAN) *(978-0-919214; 978-1-895811; 978-1-894384; 978-0-9690546; 978-1-894974; 978-1-926613; 978-1-926936; 978-1-927051; 978-1-927527; 978-1-77203) Dist. by* **Orca Bk Pub.**

Heritage Music Pr., *(978-0-89328)* Div. of The Lorenz Corp., Orders Addr.: 501 E. Third St., Dayton, OH 45401-0802 USA Tel 937-228-6118; Toll Free: 800-444-1144
E-mail: order@lorenz.com
Web site: http://www.lorenz.com.

Heritage National Publishing, *(978-0-9983202)* 412 S. White St. No. 129, Athens, TN 37303 USA Tel 423-920-0776
E-mail: mountmaaziah@aol.com.

Heritage Pr. Pubns., LLC, *(978-1-937660; 978-1-945464)* 10231 Shallow Creek Dr., Collinsville, MS 39325 USA Tel 601-737-2086; Fax: 888-340-3668
E-mail: hannemoon@heritagepresspublications.com
Web site: heritagepresspublications.com.

Heritage Publishing, *(978-0-9672363)* 23507 E. State Rte. P, Pleasant Hill, MO 64080 USA Tel 816-540-4768; 913-338-3893 Do not confuse with companies with the same or similar names in Dallas, TX, Enumclaw, WA, Chicago, IL, Beverly Hills, CA, Loveland, CO, Valley Center, KS, Peabody, MA, Whitesboro, TX, Pleasant Hill, MO, Springdale, AR, Charlotte, NC, Thomasville, GA, North Little Rock, AR, Baton Rouge, LA, Stockton, CA, carthage, MO
E-mail: peggytucker@juno.com.

Heritage Publishing, *(978-0-692-39278-2; 978-0-692-57340-2; 978-0-692-62722-8; 978-0-9974318; 978-0-692-72236-7; 978-0-692-81935-7; 978-0-9987766)* 1261 Andrew Donelson, Hermitage, TN 37076 USA Tel 615-440-6228
E-mail: jsteph1135@gmail.com.

Heritage Publishing Co., *(978-0-9787462)* 4393 Mission Inn Ave., Riverside, CA 92501 USA (SAN 851-5247) Tel 951-788-7878; Fax: 951-788-1206
E-mail: rich1rodriguez@sbcglobal.net; isabel@isabelelias.com
Web site: http://IsabelElias.com.

Heritage Youth, Inc., *(978-0-9740753)* 6245 Esplanade Ave., Baton Rouge, LA 70806-6144 USA.

Hermes Hse. Pr., *(978-0-9912614)* 1197 Village Cove NE, Atlanta, GA 30319 USA Tel 404-844-3049
E-mail: juleshermes@hermeshousepress.com
Web site: www.hermeshousepress.com.

Hermes Pr., *(978-0-9710311; 978-1-932563; 978-1-61345)* 2100 Wilmington Rd., New Castle, PA 16105-1931 USA Tel 724-652-0511; Fax: 724-652-5597 Do not confuse with companies with same or similar names in Brooks, ME, Vista, CA. Ferndale, MI
Web site: http://www.hermespress.com
Dist(s): **Diamond Comic Distributors, Inc.**
Diamond Bk. Distributors.

Hermes Pubs., Inc., *(978-0-9766543)* P.O. Box 186, Roselle Park, NJ 07207 USA (SAN 256-453X) Toll Free: 888-557-5527
E-mail: dollarnet@aol.com.

Hermit Chum Publishing, *(978-0-9760317)* 6901 S. McClinteck, No. 245, Tempe, AZ 89283 USA.

Hermit's Grove, The, *(978-0-9655687; 978-0-9863639)* 16501 County 13, Houston, MN 55943 USA Tel 507-896-3339
E-mail: paul@thehermitsgrove.org
Web site: http://www.thehermitsgrove.org
Dist(s): **New Leaf Distributing Co., Inc.**

Hern, Nick Bks., Ltd. (GBR) *(978-1-85459; 978-1-84842; 978-1-78001; 978-1-78460; 978-1-78850; 978-1-83904) Dist. by* **Consort Bk Sales.**

Hernandez, Theresa, *(978-0-9908688; 978-0-9969393)* 13880 Royal Dornoch Sq., San Diego, CA 92128 USA Tel 858-449-7490
E-mail: theresahernandez1@gmail.com
Web site: http://thhernandez.com.

Hero Builder Comics, *(978-0-615-31157-9)* 1713 Golden Ct., Bellingham, WA 98226 USA.

Hero Dog Pubns., *(978-0-9743659)* 14 Eastview Ave., Pleasantville, NY 10570 USA (SAN 255-545X) Tel 914-525-6483
E-mail: herodogpubl@msn.com
Web site: www.herodogpublications.com
Dist(s): **BCH Fulfillment & Distribution.**

Herobrine Publishing, *(978-0-615-94047-2; 978-0-692-36105-4; 978-0-692-36106-1; 978-0-692-36369-0; 978-0-692-36679-0; 978-0-692-36690-5; 978-0-9864441; 978-1-943330; 978-1-7326265)* 18340 Yorba Linda Blvd Suite 107-119, Yorba Linda, CA 92886 USA Tel 7147439845; *Imprints:* Zack Zombie Publishing (MYID_C_ZACK ZO)
E-mail: info@herobrinepublishing.com; info@zackzombiepublishing.com
Web site: http://sapientbizsolutions.com
Dist(s): **CreateSpace Independent Publishing Platform.**

Heroes & Leaders, *(978-0-9801408)* 616 Kaufman St., Forney, TX 75126 USA (SAN 855-3165)
Web site: http://www.zertelo.com.

Heroic Publishing, Inc., *(978-0-929729)* 6433 California Ave., Long Beach, CA 90805 USA (SAN 250-0582) Tel 562-428-4124 (phone/fax)
E-mail: heroicpub@aol.com
Web site: http://www.heroicpub.com
Dist(s): **Diamond Comic Distributors, Inc.**

Herow Pr. *Imprint of* **Krantz, Heather**

Herrington Teddy Bears, *(978-0-9722343)* 8945 Research Dr., Irvine, CA 92618-4237 USA Toll Free: 866-482-2327
E-mail: chris@herringtonco.com
Web site: http://www.herringtonteddybears.com.

Herrod, Ron L. Evangelism Ministries Association (R.H.E.M.A), *(978-0-9763789)* P.O. Box 6447, Sevierville, TN 37864 USA
E-mail: emily@ronherrod.org; ron@ronherrod.org
Web site: http://ronherrod.org.

hersh, patrice, *(978-0-692-76668-2; 978-0-692-84974-3)* 1865 jacob st, cortlandt manor, NY 10567 USA Tel 914-737-6095
E-mail: pattihersh@aol.com.

Hershberger, Ivan & Fannie, *(978-0-9725806)* 8219 CR 192, Holmesville, OH 44633 USA.

Hershenson, Bruce, *(978-1-887893)* Orders Addr.: P.O. Box 874, West Plains, MO 65775 USA Tel 417-256-9616; Fax: 417-257-6948
E-mail: mail@emovieposter.com
Web site: http://www.emovieposter.com
Dist(s): **Austin & Company, Inc.**
Partners Pubs. Group, Inc.

Heryin Publishing Corp., *(978-0-9762056; 978-0-9787550; 978-0-9845523)* 1033 E. Main St., No. 202, Alhambra, CA 91801 USA Tel 626-289-2238; Fax: 626-289-3865
E-mail: info@heryin.com.

Publisher Name Index

Herzog, Joyce, (978-1-887225) 900 Airport Rd., #21, Chattanooga, TN 37421 USA Tel 423-553-6387
E-mail: joyceoffice@aol.com
Web site: http://JoyceHerzog.com; http://JoyceHerzog.info; http://ScaredyCatReadingSystem.com.

Hesperus Pr. (GBR) (978-1-84391; 978-1-78094) Dist. by **IPG Chicago.**

Hester Publishing, (978-0-9789388) 219 Blackberry Cir., Colchester, VT 05446 USA
E-mail: sales@hesterpublishing.com
Web site: http://hesterpublishing.com.

Hetherington Hall, (978-0-9839963) 888 Logan St. Suite 9A, Denver, CO 80203 USA Tel 720-883-4848
E-mail: lisa@hetheringtonhall.com
Web site: www.hetheringtonhall.com.

Hetman Publishing (GBR) (978-0-9561592) Dist. by **LuluCom.**

Hewell Publishing, (978-1-56870) 2722 N. Josey Ln. Suite 100, Carrollton, TX 75007 USA
E-mail: sally.hewell@alphagraphics.com
Web site: http://www.hewellpublishing.com.

Hewett, Katherine J.E., (978-0-578-03065-4; 978-0-578-09202-7) 625 Gregory Dr. Apt. 85, Crp Christi, TX 78412-3061 USA
E-mail: kathewett@aol.com
Dist(s): **Lulu Pr., Inc.**

Hewitt Research Foundation, Inc., (978-0-913717; 978-1-57896) Orders Addr.: P.O. Box 9, Washougal, WA 98671 USA (SAN 286-1852) Tel 360-835-8708; Fax: 360-835-8697; Toll Free: 800-348-1750; Edit Addr.: 2103 B St., Washougal, WA 98671 USA
E-mail: hewitths@aol.com
Web site: http://www.homeeducation.org.

Hewitt Research, Incorporated See **Hewitt Research Foundation, Inc.**

Hexagon Blue, (978-0-9729958) P.O. Box 1790, Issaquah, WA 98027-0073 USA (SAN 255-3406)
E-mail: maryjesse@gmail.com
Web site: http://www.hexagonblue.com
Dist(s): **Ingram Bk. Co.**
Quality Bks., Inc.

Hey U.G.L.Y., Inc., (978-0-9759004; 978-0-692-15994-1) 8057 N. 300 E., Rolling Prairie, IN 46371 USA
Web site: http://www.heyugly.org.

Heyday, (978-0-930588; 978-0-9666691; 978-1-890771; 978-1-59714) Orders Addr.: P.O. Box 9145, Berkeley, CA 94709 USA (SAN 207-2351) Tel 510-549-3564; Fax: 510-549-1889; 1633 University Ave., Berkeley, CA 94703-1424; Imprints: Great Valley Books (Grt Valley Bks)
E-mail: orders@heydaybooks.com; david@heydaybooks.com; christopher@heydaybooks.com
Web site: http://www.heydaybooks.com
Dist(s): **Open Road Integrated Media, Inc.**
Publishers Group West (PGW).

Heyday Books See **Heyday**

Heyer Publishing, (978-1-7338784) 8505 Oak Way, Arvada, CO 80005 USA Tel 303-808-2230
E-mail: claudiaswest@yahoo.com
Web site: GrammyGiggles.com.

Heyokah Publishing Co., (978-0-9656124; 978-1-930910) 7244 Lattigo Dr., Nampa, ID 83687 USA Tel 208-465-5809
E-mail: hiheyokah@aol.com
Dist(s): **New Leaf Distributing Co., Inc.**

Heywood, Joseph, (978-0-692-82719-2; 978-0-692-82723-9) .

Hez-N-Tales, (978-0-9745349) 11037 Hopewell Rd., Boaz, KY 42027 USA
Web site: http://www.feedinghislambs.org.

HF Group, LLC., The, (978-0-615-33762-3) 1010 N. Sycamore St., North Manchester, IN 46962 USA Tel 260-982-2107
E-mail: sfultz@thehfgroup.com
Dist(s): **Lectorum Pubns., Inc.**

HH Castle-Mac Publishing, (978-0-615-21892-2; 978-0-9826684) 2833 Joppa Ave. S., Suite 2510, St. Louis Park, MN 55416 USA.

Hi Jinx Imprint of **Black Rabbit Bks.**

Hi Jinx Pr., (978-1-57650) P.O. Box 1814, Davis, CA 95617-1814 USA Tel 530-759-8514; Fax: 530-759-8639.

Hi Willow Research & Publishing, (978-0-931510; 978-1-933170) Orders Addr.: P.O. Box 720400, San Jose, CA 95172-0400 USA (SAN 211-3945) Toll Free: 800-873-3043
E-mail: sales@lmcsource.com
Web site: http://www.lmcsource.com
Dist(s): **Follett School Solutions**
L M C Source.

Hibiscus Publishing, (978-0-9792963; 978-0-9842831) 1499 Gormican Ln., Naples, FL 34110 USA Fax: 239-514-0238
E-mail: hibiscus311@comcast.net
Web site: http://www.hibiscuspublishing.com.

Hiccup Cottage Pubns., (978-0-9718724) 316 10th St., NE, Charlottesville, VA 22902 USA Tel 434-980-5347
E-mail: hiccupcottage@yahoo.com.

Hickle Pickle Publishing, (978-1-881958) 4450 Allison Dr., Michigan Center, MI 49254 USA Tel 517-764-1117
E-mail: hicklepickle@modempool.com
Web site: www.hicklepickle.com.

Hickory Bark Productions, (978-0-9748047) 3355 N. Five Mile Rd., Suite 332, Boise, ID 83713 USA Tel 208-322-7239.

Hickory Grove Pr., (978-0-9679915; 978-0-9854725) Orders Addr.: 3151 Treeco Ln., Bellevue, IA 52031 USA Tel 563-583-4767 (phone/fax) Do not confuse with Hickory Grove Pr., Canton, OH
E-mail: challengemath@aol.com
Web site: http://www.challengemath.com.

Hickory Tales Publishing, (978-0-9709104; 978-0-9787555) Orders Addr.: 841 Newberry St., Bowling Green, KY 42103 USA Tel 270-791-3242
E-mail: jadonel@aol.com
Web site: http://www.hickorytales.com.

Hickory Tree Publishing, (978-0-9893157; 978-0-9985754; 978-1-7334091) 123 High St., Ashland, OR 97520 USA Tel 541-864-0541
E-mail: finley.ra@gmail.com
Web site: http://www.hickorytreebooks.blogspot.com
Dist(s): **eBookit.com.**

Hidden Bower Pr., (978-0-578-50818-4) 210 Main St. No. 1021, Farmington, CT 06032 USA Tel 860-897-0828
E-mail: katie@katiejgallagher.com
Dist(s): **Ingram Content Group.**

Hidden Cache Media, (978-0-692-57398-3; 978-0-9981078) 7 Cedar Rd., Wallingford, PA 19086 USA Tel 610-800-9437
Web site: joykieffer.com
Dist(s): **CreateSpace Independent Publishing Platform.**

Hidden Curriculum Education, (978-0-9755103) Orders Addr.: P.O. Box 222041, Hollywood, FL 33022 USA Tel 954-457-8098; Fax: 954-457-3331
Web site: http://www.collegefaqbook.com.

Hidden Forest Pubs., (978-0-9755117) 269 Co. Hwy. 250, Guin, AL 35563-2700 USA.

Hidden Helm Pr., (978-1-949604) 42 Aldwick Rise, Fairport, NY 14450 USA Tel 585-269-8692
E-mail: elicelata@gmail.com.

Hidden Manna Pubns., (978-0-9891683; 978-0-9915261; 978-0-9864066; 978-1-7347503) 53 Solar Rd., Oldtown, ID 83822 USA Tel 208-412-3087
E-mail: artnbooks@gmail.com
Web site: www.gentleshepherd.com.

Hidden Oasis Publishing, (978-0-9884636) P.O. Box 80, Kimberton, PA 19442 USA Tel 610-935-2711
E-mail: pcbaxter@verizon.net.

Hidden Path Pubn., Inc., (978-0-9711534) 304 Briarwood Rd., Statesville, NC 28677 USA Tel 704-878-0716; 704-224-4832
E-mail: dkellysteele@aol.com.

Hidden Pictures, (978-0-9678159; 978-0-9843088) Orders Addr.: P.O. Box 63, Tipp City, OH 45371-9103 USA (SAN 253-6862) Tel 937-667-6288; Fax: 937-669-4178
E-mail: liz@hiddenpictures.com
Web site: http://www.hiddenpicturepuzzle.com.

Hidden Talent Pr., (978-0-9776114) Orders Addr.: P.O. Box 9052, Missoula, MT 59807 USA
Web site: http://www.iysofwar.com.

Hidden Valley Farm Pub., (978-0-615-17173-9) P.O. Box 172, Perry, NY 14530 USA
E-mail: theotherherald@yahoo.com
Web site: http://www.tfrice.etsy.com
Dist(s): **Lulu Pr., Inc.**

Hidden Wolf Bks., (978-0-9911045; 978-0-9968922; 978-0-9994345) 155 W. Genung St., St. Augustine, FL 32086 USA Tel 904-797-5964
E-mail: nsinatsch@hotmail.com.

HiddenSpring Imprint of **Paulist Pr.**

Hide & Seek Ministries, (978-0-9994901) P.O. Box 1835, Springfield, MO 65801 USA Tel 417-522-3597
E-mail: contact@hsm4kids.com
Web site: www.hideandseekministries.com.

Hide-a-Way Publishing, (978-0-9988999) 1405 Westview Ln., Northlake, TX 76226 USA Tel 469-418-3296
E-mail: hideawaypublishingcompany@gmail.com
Web site: www.hideawaypublishing.com.

Hieble, Helen, (978-0-615-77684-2; 978-0-692-79708-2) 685 Knox Rd., Wayne, PA 19087 USA Tel 610-688-4961; Fax: 610-688-0869
Dist(s): **CreateSpace Independent Publishing Platform.**

Hierophant Publishing Services See **Hieropub LLC**

Hierophantasm, (978-0-9837905) 190 W. Fifth Ave. P. O. Box 792, Clifton, IL 60927 USA Tel 815-694-0010
E-mail: Andy@hierophantasm.com
Web site: hierophantasm.com.

Hieropub LLC, (978-0-9727940) P.O. Box 895, Pottstown, PA 19464 USA Tel 610-705-0282
E-mail: patholl@hieropub.com; pholl@comcast.net
Web site: http://www.hieropub.com; http://www.hatheadbooks.com
Dist(s): **Quality Bks., Inc.**

Higgins, Christine, (978-0-9976649) 571 Woodbine Ave., Towson, MD 21204 USA Tel 410-825-6404
E-mail: chriswrite73@comcast.net.

Higgins Publishing, (978-0-9815202; 978-1-941580) P.O. Box 1463, Cedar Hill, TX 75106 USA Tel 510-473-5054
E-mail: contact@higginspublishing.com
Web site: http://www.higginspublishing.com.

Higginson Bk. Co., (978-0-7404; 978-0-8328) 148 Washington St., Salem, MA 01970 USA (SAN 247-9400) Tel 978-745-7170; Fax: 978-745-8025
E-mail: higginsn@cove.com
Web site: http://higginsonbooks.com.

— **High Art Forms, LLC,** (978-0-9962188; 978-0-9992019) P.O. Box 49194, Cookeville, TN 38506 USA Tel 844-370-1730; Fax: 931-537-2218
E-mail: highartforms@frontier.com
Web site: www.highartforms.com.

High Bar Bks., (978-1-950361) 3515 Glover Rd, Easton, PA 18040 USA Tel 307-752-7935
E-mail: highbarbooks@gmx.com.

High Country Conservation Advocates, (978-0-692-90486-2) PO Box 1066 716 Elk Ave., CRESTED BUTTE, CO 81224 USA Tel 970-349-7104
E-mail: office@hccacb.org
Dist(s): **Ingram Content Group.**

High Desert Productions, (978-0-9652920) Orders Addr.: P.O. Box 5506, Bisbee, AZ 85603 USA Tel 520-432-5288; Edit Addr.: 511 Mance St., Bisbee, AZ 85603 USA
Dist(s): **Rio Nuevo Pubs.**

High Ground Productions, Incorporated See **High Ground Pubns.**

High Ground Pubns., (978-0-9720153) 80 Supai Dr., Sedona, AZ 86351 USA (SAN 254-5748) Tel 360-945-2485
E-mail: Karen@amatteroftime.org
Web site: http://www.amatteroftime.org.

High Hill Pr., (978-1-60653) 2731 Cumberland Landing, Saint Charles, MO 63303 USA (SAN 856-2806) Tel 636-928-2212
E-mail: HighHillPress@aol.com
Web site: http://www.highhillpress.com.

High Hopes Publishing, (978-0-9708417; 978-0-9905129) Subs. of Communication Arts Multimedia, Inc., 1618 Williams Dr., Suite No. 5, Georgetown, TX 78628 USA Tel 512-868-0548 (phone/fax); Toll Free: 888-742-0074
E-mail: mail@commartsmultimedia.com
Web site: http://www.highhopespublishing.com.

High Interest Publishing (HIP) (CAN) (978-0-9731237; 978-1-897039; 978-1-926847) Dist. by **Children Plus.**

High Mountain Publishing See **Escher, Ursula**

High Noon Bks., (978-0-87879; 978-1-57128) Div. of Academic Therapy Publications, Inc., 20 Leveroni Ct., Novato, CA 94949-5746 USA Tel 415-883-3314; Toll Free: 800-422-7249
E-mail: customerservice@academictheapy.com
Web site: http://www.highnoonbooks.com.

High Standards Publishing, Incorporated See **True Exposures Publishing, Inc.**

High Star Pr., (978-0-9981808) 217 Teaberry Ln., South Abington Township, PA 18411 USA Tel 570-479-6491
E-mail: cindynoonan49@gmail.com
Web site: cindynoonan.com.

High Tide Pubns., (978-0-9884637; 978-0-615-72863-6; 978-0-692-34939-7; 978-0-692-37913-4; 978-0-692-38423-7; 978-0-692-45585-2; 978-0-692-45595-1; 978-0-692-50369-0; 978-0-692-54851-6; 978-0-692-56405-9; 978-0-692-57700-4; 978-0-692-57708-0; 978-0-692-57961-9; 978-0-692-60854-8; 978-0-692-62932-1; 978-0-692-67079-8; 978-0-692-70597-1; 978-0-692-74482-6; 978-1-945990) Orders Addr.: 1000 Bland Point Rd, Deltaville, VA 23043 USA Tel 804-776-8478
E-mail: hightidepublications@yahoo.com
Web site: redmarblepublishing.com; hightidepublications.com
Dist(s): **CreateSpace Independent Publishing Platform**
Ingram Publisher Services.

Higher Age Pr., (978-0-9979034) 5222 Univ. Ave NE, No. 304A, Seattle, WA 98105 USA Tel 425-891-9129
E-mail: hansenjake@hotmail.com
Web site: jakehansennovels.com.

Higher Balance Institute, (978-0-9759080; 978-1-939410) 515 NW Saltzman Rd., No.726, Portland, OR 97229 USA Tel 503-646-4000; Toll Free: 800-935-4007
E-mail: publishing@higherbalance.com
Web site: http://www.higherbalance.com.

Higher Ground Pr., (978-0-9766062; 978-0-9838321) Orders Addr.: P.O. Box PO 1381, Allen, TX 75013 USA Tel 214-680-9779
E-mail: info@highergroundpress.com
Web site: http://www.highergroundpress.com
Dist(s): **Brigham Distribution.**

Higher Power Publishing, (978-0-9787631) 702 Twilight Dr., Garland, TX 75040 USA Tel 214-298-9563
E-mail: higherpowerpublishing@hotmail.com
Web site: http://www.higherpowerpublishing.biz
Dist(s): **Ingram Content Group.**

Higher Priority Publishing See **Arlington & Ameilia**

Highest Good Pubns. Imprint of **GEM Bk. Club**

Highland Children's Pr. Imprint of **Heather & Highlands Publishing**

Highland Press See **Highland Pr. Publishing**

Highland Pr., (978-0-910722) 10108 Johns Rd., Boerne, TX 78006 USA (SAN 204-0522) Do not confuse with companies of the same name or similar in Birmingham, AL, Wilsonville, OR, Tonasket, WA, Bryson City, NC, San Rafael, CA, High Springs, FL.

Highland Pr., (978-0-9630273) Div. of The Alabama Booksmith, 5512 Crestwood Blvd., Birmingham, AL 35212-4131 USA (SAN 297-8628) Do not confuse with companies with the same name in Boerne, TX, Wilsonville, OR, Tonasket, WA, Bryson City, NC, San Rafael, CA, High Springs, FL
E-mail: booksmith@mindspring.com.

Highland Pr. Publishing, (978-0-9746249; 978-0-9787139; 978-0-9800356; 978-0-9815573; 978-0-9818550; 978-0-9823615; 978-0-9842499; 978-0-9833960; 978-0-9846541; 978-0-9850690; 978-0-9895262; 978-0-9916439; 978-1-942606) Orders Addr.: P.O. Box 2292, High Springs, FL 32655 USA (SAN 851-4275); Imprints: Pandora (Pandora) Do not confuse with companies with the same or similar name in Sacramento, CA, Birmingham, AL, Wilsonville, ORBoerne, TX, San Rafael, CA, Bryson City, NC, Tonasket, WA
E-mail: The.Highland.Press@gmail.com; Mickeytl@aol.com
Web site: http://www.highlandpress.org.

Highlight Publishing, (978-0-9741734) P.O. Box 27, Little Falls, MN 56345 USA Tel 320-630-1463; Toll Free: 866-336-6681
E-mail: books@highlightpublishing.com
Web site: http://www.highlightpublishing.com.

Highlights Imprint of **Boyds Mills Pr.**

Highlights for Children, (978-0-87534) Orders Addr.: P.O. Box 269, Columbus, OH 43216-0269 USA (SAN 281-7810) Tel 614-486-0631; Fax: 614-876-8564; Toll Free: 800-255-9517; Edit Addr.: 803 Church St., Honesdale, PA 18431 USA (SAN 281-7802) Tel 570-253-1080; Fax: 570-253-1179
E-mail: eds@highlights.com
Web site: http://www.highlights.com
Dist(s): **Boyds Mills Pr.**
Hachette Bk. Group
INscribe Digital
Ingram Publisher Services
Penguin Random Hse. Distribution
Penguin Random Hse. LLC.

Highlights of Chicago Pr., (978-0-9710487; 978-0-9907771) 4325 N. Central Park Ave., Chicago, IL 60618 USA Tel 773-509-0008 (phone/fax)
E-mail: bturner@highlightsofchicago.com
Web site: http://www.highlightsofchicago.com.

High-Lonesome Bks., (978-0-944383) Orders Addr.: P.O. Box 878, Silver City, NM 88062 USA (SAN 243-3079) Tel 505-388-3763; Fax: 505-388-5705; Toll Free: 800-380-7323 (orders only)
E-mail: Cherie@High-LonesomeBooks.com
Web site: http://www.high-lonesomebooks.com.

High-Pitched Hum Inc., (978-0-9759818; 978-0-9777290; 978-0-9787995; 978-0-9792780; 978-1-934666; 978-0-9885818; 978-0-9914847) 321 15th St., N., Jacksonville Beach, FL 32250 USA
E-mail: breynolds@jettyman.com
Web site: http://www.highpitchedhum.net.

HighPoint Publishing, Inc., (978-1-933190) Orders Addr.: 3975 E. Highway 290., Dripping Spgs, TX 78620-4287 USA (SAN 256-2952)
E-mail: kenc@highpointpublishing.com; milena@highpointpublishing.com
Web site: http://www.HighPointPublishing.com.

HighReach Learning, Incorporated Imprint of **Carson-Dellosa Publishing, LLC**

†High/Scope Pr., (978-0-929816; 978-0-931114; 978-1-57379) Div. of High/Scope Educational Research Foundation, 600 N. River St., Ypsilanti, MI 48198-2898 USA (SAN 211-9617) Tel 734-485-2000; Fax: 734-485-0704; Toll Free Fax: 800-442-4329 (orders); Toll Free: 800-407-7377 (orders only)
E-mail: info@highscope.org
Web site: http://www.highscope.org
Dist(s): **CENGAGE Learning**
Delmar Cengage Learning
Follett School Solutions; CIP.

Highsmith Inc., (978-0-913853; 978-0-917846; 978-1-57950; 978-1-932146; 978-1-59847; 978-1-60213) P.O. Box 5210, Janesville, WI 53547-5210 USA (SAN 159-8740) Toll Free: 800-448-4887; 401 S. Wright Rd., Janesville, WI 53547 (SAN 858-9674) Toll Free Fax: 800-835-2329; Toll Free: 800-554-4661; Imprints: Upstart Books (Upstart Bks)
Web site: http://www.highsmith.com
Dist(s): **Mackin Bk. Co.**

Highsmith Press, LLC See **Highsmith Inc.**

Highview Creative, (978-0-9978518) 1433 Highview Ave, Eagan, MN 55121 USA Tel 651-303-5202
E-mail: larossin@comcast.net.

Hignites, Tom Miracle Studio, (978-1-934017) Orders Addr.: 1977 Mayfield Rd., Richfield, WI 53076-5307 USA (SAN 850-9611) Tel 262-628-5577; Fax: 262-628-5580; Edit Addr.: 3070 Hwy. 145, Richfield, WI 53076-5307 USA
E-mail: jbrown@miracle-homes.com
Web site: http://tomhignitesmiraclestudios.com.

Hilarity Waters Pr., (978-0-615-49668-9) 1117 SW 126th St., Oklahoma City, OK 73170 USA Tel 405-990-9891
E-mail: andrews.africabound@gmail.com
Web site: www.hilaritywaterspress.com.

Hildebrand, Betty, (978-0-9753729) 116 Rosetta Ct., Springdale, OH 45246 USA
E-mail: deona@bethart.com
Web site: http://www.bethart.com.

Hildebrandt, Sara, (978-0-578-45179-4; 978-0-578-45201-2) 14321 NE30th St. Unit AA, Vancouver, WA 98682-8257 USA Tel 360-975-9173
E-mail: sara.hildebrandt@outlook.com
Dist(s): **Ingram Content Group.**

Hill & Wang Imprint of **Farrar, Straus & Giroux**

Hill, Lawrence Bks. Imprint of **Chicago Review Pr., Inc.**

Hill, Monica See **Penway Publishing LLC**

Hill, Napoleon Foundation, (978-1-880369) Friends of Napoleon Hill, 19458 S. La Grange Rd., Mokena, IL 60448 USA Tel 847-998-0408; Fax: 847-998-6890; Toll Free Fax: 800-957-9124; Toll Free: 800-957-9114
E-mail: 70543.3377@compuserve.com
Web site: http://www.naphill.org.

Hill Publishing See **SunHill Pubs.**

Hill, Shamirrah, (978-0-692-93805-8) 1015 W Grant St, Unit 2016, Phoenix, AZ 85007 USA Tel 623-295-2806
E-mail: info@shymonsterstory.com.

Hill Song Pr., (978-0-9745159; 978-0-692-29132-0; 978-0-692-41911-3; 978-0-692-68393-4; 978-0-692-82104-6; 978-0-692-88303-7; 978-0-692-11598-5; 978-0-578-65257-3) Orders Addr.: P.O. Box 486, Lawrence, KS 66044 USA Tel 785-330-3779; Toll Free: 800-266-5564; Edit Addr.: 3807 Hunters Hill Dr., Lawrence, KS 66049 USA
E-mail: tom.mach@yahoo.com
Web site: http://www.hillsongpress.com
Dist(s): **CreateSpace Independent Publishing Platform.**

Hill, Stephanie & Clarissa, (978-0-9785539) P.O. Box 13212, Baltimore, MD 21203-3212 USA (SAN 850-9816) Tel 443-838-9426
E-mail: sachedesignsinc@yahoo.com
Web site: http://www.sachedesigns.com.

Hill Street Pr., LLC, *(978-1-892514; 978-1-58818)* P.O. Box 49468, Athens, GA 30604-9468 USA Toll Free: 800-295-0365
E-mail: info@hillstreetpress.com
Web site: http://www.hillstreetpress.com
Dist(s): **Gibbs Smith, Publisher**
Beeler, Thomas T. Pub.

Hillegass, Anette, *(978-0-692-80034-8; 978-0-692-81058-3; 978-0-692-07155-7)* .

Hilliard Pr., *(978-0-9912792; 978-0-9966962; 978-0-9990090; 978-1-7342711)* 204 Dandridge Dr., Franklin, TN 37067 USA Tel 931-446-0047
E-mail: jessasexton@gmail.com.

Hillrow Editions, *(978-0-9897958)* 150 Spreading Oak Dr., Scotts Valley, CA 95066 USA Tel 831-439-9888
E-mail: chriz9@yahoo.com.

Hillside Education, *(978-0-9766386; 978-0-9798469; 978-0-9831800; 978-0-9885106; 978-0-9906720; 978-0-9969986; 978-0-9976647; 978-0-9991706; 978-1-7331383)* 475 Bidwell Hill Rd., Lake Ariel, PA 18436 USA (SAN 257-4446)
E-mail: info@hillsideeducation.com; sales@hillsideeducation.com
Web site: http://www.hillsideeducation.com.

Hillside Pr., *(978-0-9815895)* P.O. Box 241, Midway, FL 32343 USA
E-mail: ljhill@hillsidepress.net
Web site: http://www.hillsidepress.net
Dist(s): **Two Rivers Distribution.**

Hillside Pr., *(978-0-9627530)* Affil. of Ridgetop Pr., 280 E. Birch Hill Rd., Fairbanks, AK 99712 USA Tel 907-457-7834; Fax: 907-457-7835; Toll Free: 800-390-8999 Do not confuse with companies with the same name in Los Angeles, CA, Carversville, PA, Vista, CA, Collegeville, PA, Wolcott, CT
E-mail: jhaigh@polarnet.com
Web site: http://www2.polarnet.com/~jhaigh/
Dist(s): **American News Company**
Partners/West Book Distributors
Todd Communications.

Hilton Publishing *See* **Hilton Publishing Co.**

Hilton Publishing Co., *(978-0-9654553; 978-0-9675258; 978-0-9716067; 978-0-9743144; 978-0-9764443; 978-0-9773160; 978-0-9777779; 978-0-9800649; 978-0-9815381; 978-0-9841447; 978-0-9847566; 978-0-9904283; 978-0-9983282)* Orders Addr.: 1630 45th Ave. Ste. 103, Munster, IN 46321-3959 USA Toll Free: 866-455-1070
E-mail: info@hiltonpub.com
Web site: http://www.hiltonpub.com
Dist(s): **SCB Distributors.**

Himari Publishing, *(978-0-9981543)* 335 E. Albertoni St. No. 200-314, Carson, CA 90746 USA Tel 310-766-0487
E-mail: himaripublishing@gmail.com.

Himminbjorg Publishing, Inc., *(978-0-9749416)* P.O. Box 6493, Napa, CA 94581 USA Tel 707-251-9526 (phone/fax)
E-mail: himminbjorg@aol.com
Web site: http://www.wyrdsway.com.

HINDS FEET PUBLISHING, *(978-0-9988206)* 3022 W I-44 Service Rd., No. 57043, Oklahoma City, OK 73112 USA Tel 405-412-6218; Fax: 405-285-5590
E-mail: hindsfeetpublishing@gmail.com
Web site: www.hindsfeetpublishing.com.

Hines, Jerry, *(978-0-615-17723-6)* 2660 Suzanne Cir., White Bear Lake, MN 55110 USA
E-mail: jerryhines@comcast.net
Dist(s): **Lulu Pr., Inc.**

Hinman, Bobbie E. Incorporated *See* **Best Fairy Bks.**

Hinman Publishing, *(978-0-9723525)* 2943 Breakwater Way, Longmont, CO 80503 USA
E-mail: jshinman@earthlink.net.

Hinson, Rebecca Publishing, *(978-1-938360; 978-1-942765; 978-1-947623)* Orders Addr.: 818 N. Palmway, Lake Worth, FL 33460 USA Tel 561-267-5756
E-mail: rebeccahinson@bellsouth.net
Dist(s): **Follett School Solutions.**

Hinterland Sky Pr., *(978-0-9818880)* 37 W. Black Oak Dr., Asheville, NC 28804-1809 USA
E-mail: frances.ruiz@gmail.com
Web site: http://www.hinterlandsky.com.

HinterWelt Enterprises, LLC, *(978-0-9740096)* 7504 W. Hickory Creek Dr., Frankfort, IL 60423-9094 USA
E-mail: winna@hinterwelt.com
Web site: http://www.hinterwelt.com.

Hip Hop Schl. Hse., *(978-0-9768674)* 8618 S. Constance, Chicago, IL 60617 USA Tel 793-218-4204.

Hip Me Publishing, *(978-1-7337395)* 1560 Adams St., Denver, CO 80206 USA Tel 720-232-6514
E-mail: taraemrick@hotmail.com
Web site: www.whyyoubelong.com.

Hippocratic Pr., The, *(978-0-9753516)* 281A Fairhaven Hill Rd., Concord, MA 01742 USA Tel 978-369-0739
E-mail: ccowanmd@hippocraticpress.com
Web site: http://www.hippocraticpress.com.

†Hippocrene Bks., Inc., *(978-0-7818; 978-0-87052; 978-0-88254)* 171 Madison Ave., New York, NY 10016-1002 USA (SAN 213-2060) Tel 718-454-2366 (sales); 212-685-4371 (editorial); Fax: 718-454-1391 (sales/order inquiry); 212-779-9338 (editorial)
E-mail: hippocre@ix.netcom.com
Web site: http://www.hippocrenebooks.com
Dist(s): **Continental Bk. Co., Inc.**
Ingram Publisher Services
Two Rivers Distribution; *CIP.*

Hired Pen, Inc., The *See* **Acacia Publishing, Inc.**

His Feast Publishing, *(978-0-9677722)* Div. of Feast of Tabernacles Ministries, 2720 Mallow Pl., Loveland, CO 80537 USA
E-mail: Hisfeasts@gmail.com; 4Donnamae@gmail.com.

His Grace Is Sufficient *Imprint of* **ELW Pubns.**

His Hands, Inc., *(978-0-9720881)* Orders Addr.: P.O. Box 7063, Oak Ridge, TN 37831 USA Tel 865-482-9562; Edit Addr.: 82 E. Tennesse Ave., Apt. 117, Oak Ridge, TN 37830 USA (SAN 255-2930) Tel 865-482-9562
E-mail: hishandstn@netzero.com
Web site: http://www.hishands.org.

His Kids Publishing, Inc., *(978-0-9720417)* Orders Addr.: P.O. Box 72172, Marietta, GA 30007 USA Tel 770-998-3240; Fax: 770-998-4943; Edit Addr.: 1544 Sandpoint Dr., Roswell, GA 30075 USA
E-mail: management@intrag-publishing.com
Web site: http://www.intrag-publishing.com.

His Pen Publishing, LLC, *(978-0-9798020; 978-1-944643)*
E-mail: authorlacricia@ymail.com; publisher@hispenpublishing.com; author@lacriciaangelle.com
Web site: http://www.lacriciaangelle.com; www.hispenpublishing.com
Dist(s): **Smashwords.**

H.I.S. Publishing LLC *See* **Heard Word Publishing, LLC**

His Sonshine, Inc., *(978-0-9758880)* 13214 Barwick Rd., Del Ray Beach, FL 33445 USA.

His Story, *(978-0-9766951)* 1409 Coolhurst, Sherwood, AR 72120 USA
Web site: http://www.hisstory.org.

His Work Christian Publishing, *(978-0-9778328; 978-0-9798290; 978-0-9799189; 978-0-615-43443-8; 978-0-9854469)* Div. of His Work Christian Ministries, Orders Addr.: P.O. Box 563, Ward Cove, AK 99928 USA Tel 206-274-8474; Fax: 614-388-0664
E-mail: hiswork@hisworkpub.com; editor@hisworkpub.com
Web site: http://www.hisworkpub.com
Dist(s): **Ingram Content Group.**

Hispanic Institute of Social Issues, *(978-0-9771167; 978-0-9797814; 978-1-936885)* P.O. Box 50553, Mesa, AZ 85208-0028 USA
Web site: http://www.hisi.org.

Histart Books *See* **Histart Pr.**

Histart Pr., *(978-0-9915597)* 1300 30th St APT A1-12, BOULDER, CO 80303 USA Tel 786-354-3631
E-mail: maritillo@gmail.com
Web site: https://histartpress.com/.

Historic Mint Co., The, *(978-0-9753767)* 36 Sandwedge Dr., Henderson, NV 89074-1714 USA Toll Free: 877-264-6266
Web site: http://www.historicmint.com.

Historic Philadelphia, Inc., *(978-0-9855319)* 150 S. Independence Mall, W. Suite 550, Philadelphia, PA 19106 USA Tel 215-629-5801
E-mail: debiflora@about-books.com; msdariaf@gmail.com
Web site: http://www.historicphiladelphia.org.

Historic Pr.-South, *(978-0-9645990)* Orders Addr.: P.O. Box 407, Gatlinburg, TN 37738 USA Tel 423-436-4163; Toll Free: 800-279-2603; Edit Addr.: 367 Buckhorn Rd., Gatlinburg, TN 37738 USA.

Historic Tours of America, Inc., *(978-0-9752698)* 201 Front St., Suite 224, Key West, FL 33040 USA Tel 305-292-8920; Fax: 305-295-4999
E-mail: psmith@historictours.com
Web site: http://www.historictours.com.

Historical Pages Company *See* **Birch Island**

Historical Society of Western Pennsylvania, *(978-0-936340)* 1212 Smallman St., Pittsburgh, PA 15222-4208 USA (SAN 214-0276)
E-mail: babutko@heinzhistorycenter.org
Web site: http://www.einzhistorycenter.org.

History Compass, LLC, *(978-1-57960; 978-1-878668; 978-1-932663)* 25 Leslie Rd., Auburndale, MA 02466 USA (SAN 297-2611) Tel 617-332-2202; Fax: 617-332-2210
E-mail: info@historycompass.com; lisa@historycompass.com
Web site: http://www.historycompass.com
Dist(s): **Follett School Solutions**
Ingram Publisher Services
Social Studies Schl. Service.

History Factory, *(978-1-882771)* 14140 Parke Long Ct., Suite G, Chantilly, VA 20151 USA Tel 703-631-0500; Fax: 703-631-1124
E-mail: info@historyfactory.com.

History Gal's Publishing, *(978-0-578-10958-9)* 8344 W. Smith Rd, Medina, OH 44256 USA.

History Hse Pubs., *(978-0-9679158)* 10624 Tuppence Ct., Rockville, MD 20850 USA Do not confuse with History House Press, Rocky Mount, VA.

History Jukebox, LLC, *(978-0-9791118)* P.O. Box 467, Marshall, MI 49068 USA Tel 269-781-8357; Fax: 269-781-8760; Toll Free: 866-977-7664
E-mail: info@historyjukebox.org
Web site: http://www.historyjukebox.org.

History Pr. Ltd.,The (GBR) *(978-0-7509; 978-0-7524; 978-0-86299; 978-0-904387; 978-1-84165; 978-1-84015) Dist. by* **IPG Chicago.**

History Pr., The *Imprint of* **Arcadia Publishing**

Hit Products, *(978-0-9836437)* 6004 Carol St., San Diego, CA 92115 USA Tel 619-286-3661
E-mail: victor2b4@aol.com.

HI-Tech Software, *(978-1-928618; 978-1-936735)* 10 Little Tarn Ct., Hamburg, NJ 07419-1262 USA
E-mail: harry@htsoftware.com
Web site: http://www.htsoftware.com.

Hither Creek Pr., *(978-0-9700555)* 14 Holman St., Laconia, NH 03246-3016 USA Do not confuse with Hither Creek Press in Nantucket, MA
E-mail: hithercreekpress@aol.com.

Hi-Time Pflaum *See* **Pflaum Publishing Group**

HITN, *(978-1-64094)* 63 flushing Ave. bldg. 292 Ste. 211, Brooklyn, NY 11205 USA Tel 646-731-3520; Fax: 212-966-5725
E-mail: mpedroza@hitn.org
Web site: www.hitn.org
Dist(s): **Simon & Schuster, Inc.**

Hive Collective, *(978-0-9884774)* 30 Shelburne Rd., Merrimack, NH 03054 USA Tel 603-423-1071
E-mail: stan@findtheaxis.com
Web site: http://hiveauthors.wordpress.com.

HK Comics Ltd. (HKG) *(978-962-85278; 978-988-98437; 978-988-97972) Dist. by* **Diamond Book Dists.**

HM Bks., *(978-0-9796476; 978-0-9820126)* Div. of HM Entertainment Inc.,
E-mail: meja_mwangi@yahoo.com; mejamwangi@yahoo.com
Web site: http://www.mejamwangi.com; http://www.skylineafrica.com.

HMH Books For Young Readers *Imprint of* **Houghton Mifflin Harcourt Publishing Co.**

HMSI, Inc., *(978-0-615-29442-1; 978-0-9842662; 978-0-9826945; 978-0-9851996)* 50768 Van Buren Dr., Plymouth, MI 48170 USA
Web site: http://www.PublishHMSI.com.

HNB Publishing, *(978-0-9664286; 978-0-9728061; 978-0-9828874)* Orders Addr.: 250 W. 78th St., No. 3FF, New York, NY 10024 USA Tel 212-873-5382; 347-260-1376
E-mail: sales@hnbpub.com
Web site: http://www.hnbpub.com.

Hoaki Bks. SL (ESP) *(978-84-936408; 978-84-92810; 978-84-935438; 978-84-935881; 978-84-936508; 978-84-15967; 978-84-17084; 978-84-17656; 978-84-17412; 978-84-16851; 978-84-16504) Dist. by* **Consort Bk Sales.**

Hoard, W.D. & Sons Co., *(978-0-932147; 978-0-9960753)* P.O. Box 801, Fort Atkinson, WI 53538-0801 USA (SAN 686-4341) Tel 920-563-5551; Fax: 920-563-7298;
Imprints: Hoard's Dairyman (Hoards Dairyman)
Web site: http://www.hoards.com.

Hoard's Dairyman *Imprint of* **Hoard, W.D. & Sons Co.**

Hobar Pubns., *(978-0-89317; 978-0-913163; 978-0-933855; 978-0-9616847; 978-1-55797)* Div. of Finney Co., Orders Addr.: 8075 215th St. W., Lakeville, MN 55044 USA (SAN 283-1120) Tel 952-469-6699; Fax: 952-469-1968; Toll Free Fax: 800-330-6232; Toll Free: 800-846-7027
E-mail: feedback@finneyco.com
Web site: http://www.finney-hobar.com
Dist(s): **Book Wholesalers, Inc.**
Brodart Co.
Follett School Solutions
Midpoint Trade Bks., Inc.
National Bk. Network
Rowman & Littlefield Publishers, Inc.
Southern Bk. Service.

Hobbes End Publishing, LLC, *(978-0-9763510; 978-0-9859110)* Div. of Hobbes End Entertainment, P.O. Box 193, Aubrey, TX 76227 USA
Web site: http://www.hobbesendpublishing.com
Dist(s): **Smashwords.**

Hobblebush Bks., *(978-0-9636413; 978-0-9760896; 978-0-9801672; 978-0-9845921; 978-1-939449)* PO Box 1285, Concord, NH 03302 USA
E-mail: info@hobblebush.com; kirsty@hobblebush.com
Web site: www.hobblebush.com
Dist(s): **Distributors, The**
SPD-Small Pr. Distribution.

Hobbs, Brenda F., *(978-0-9772970)* 14303 Greenview Rd., Detroit, MI 48223 USA
E-mail: bhobbs101@aol.com.

Hobbs, Constance (GBR) *(978-0-9556783) Dist. by* **LuluCom.**

Hobby Horse Publishing, LLC, *(978-0-615-89154-5)* P.O. Box 22, Peterborough, NH 03458 USA Tel 555-555-5555
E-mail: info@hobbyhorsepublishing.com
Web site: www.HobbyHorsePublishing.com.

Hobby Hse. Publishing Group, *(978-0-9727179)* Orders Addr.: 48 Hickory Hill Rd., Box 1527, Jackson, NJ 08527 USA
Web site: http://www.hobbyhousepublishinggroup.com.

Hobnob Pr., *(978-0-9663241)* 2 W. Northfield Rd., Livingston, NJ 07039-3789 USA
Dist(s): **Diamond Comic Distributors, Inc.**

Hochman, Steven, *(978-0-9887975)* 5 Wendover Ct., Mount Laurel, NJ 08054 USA Tel 856-778-1282
E-mail: hoc@me.com.

Hocks Out Press, *(978-0-578-14723-9; 978-0-578-15306-3; 978-0-9964421)* .

Hocus Pocus Publishing, Inc., *(978-0-9855544; 978-0-9910276; 978-1-942840; 978-1-952824)* PO Box 2960, Daphne, AL 36526 USA Tel 251-454-3244
E-mail: nicholasroussos@gmail.com; cynthia@cynthiaeden.com; info@hocuspocuspublishing.com
Web site: https://hocuspocuspublishing.com; https://cynthiaeden.com.

Hodder & Stoughton (GBR) *(978-0-245; 978-0-340; 978-0-550; 978-0-7131; 978-0-7195; 978-1-85998; 978-1-84032; 978-1-84456; 978-1-84854; 978-1-4447; 978-1-4736) Dist. by* **HachBkGrp.**

Hodder & Stoughton (GBR) *(978-0-245; 978-0-340; 978-0-550; 978-0-7131; 978-0-7195; 978-1-85998; 978-1-84032; 978-1-84456; 978-1-84854; 978-1-4447; 978-1-4736) Dist. by* **Trafalgar.**

Hodder Education Group (GBR) *(978-0-340; 978-0-412; 978-0-450; 978-0-7122; 978-0-7131; 978-0-7506; 978-0-85264; 978-0-947054; 978-0-86003; 978-1-874958; 978-1-902984; 978-1-4441; 978-1-905735; 978-1-4718) Dist. by* **IngramPubServ.**

Hodder Education Group (GBR) *(978-0-340; 978-0-412; 978-0-450; 978-0-7122; 978-0-7131; 978-0-7506; 978-0-85264; 978-0-947054; 978-0-86003; 978-1-874958; 978-1-902984; 978-1-4441; 978-1-905735; 978-1-4718) Dist. by* **Trans-Atl Phila.**

Hoffman, Mark *See* **Hramiec Hoffman Publishing**

Hoffmann Partnership, The, *(978-0-9753106)* 349 Martin Ln., Bloomingdale, IL 60108-1326 USA
E-mail: Catherine@WriteHappy.com; info@writehappy.com
Web site: http://www.writehappy.com
Dist(s): **Publishers' Graphics, L.L.C.**

Hoffmaster, Casey Camille, *(978-0-692-13484-9)* 1225 Catherine Ct., CARBONDALE, CO 81623 USA Tel 561-252-1610
E-mail: casey.c.hoffmaster@gmail.com
Dist(s): **Ingram Content Group.**

Hogan Publishing LLC, *(978-0-9779504)* 2708 E. Edison, Tucson, AZ 85716 USA
E-mail: benjamin@madseadog.com
Web site: http://www.madseadog.com.

Hogrefe & Huber Publishers *See* **Hogrefe Publishing**

†Hogrefe Publishing, *(978-0-88937; 978-1-61676; 978-1-61334)* Subs. of Hogrefe Publishing GmbH, Orders Addr.: a/o Customer Service Dept., 30 Amberwood Pkwy., Ashland, OH 44805 USA Fax: 419-281-6883; Toll Free: 800-228-3749; Edit Addr.: 361 Newbury St. 5th Flr., Boston, MA 02115 USA (SAN 293-2792) Tel 857-880-2002
E-mail: customerservice@hogrefe.com; publishing@hogrefe.com
Web site: http://www.hogrefe.com/
Dist(s): **Baker & Taylor Publisher Services (BTPS)**
Coutts Information Services
Majors Scientific Bks., Inc.
Matthews Medical Bk. Co.
Metapress
Rittenhouse Bk. Distributors; *CIP.*

Hogs Back Bks. (GBR) *(978-1-907432) Dist. by* **IPG Chicago.**

Hohm Pr., *(978-0-934252; 978-1-890772; 978-1-935387)* Div. of Hohm, Inc., P.O. Box 2501, Prescott, AZ 86302 USA (SAN 221-0924) Tel 520-778-9189; Fax: 520-717-1779; Toll Free: 800-381-2700 (orders only)
E-mail: staff@hohmpress.com; pinedr@goodnet.com; hpproduction@cableone.net
Web site: http://www.hohmpress.com
Dist(s): **SCB Distributors.**

Holbrook Studios, *(978-0-9762440)* Orders Addr.: P.O. Box 3064, Beverly Hills, CA 90212 USA; Edit Addr.: 754 E. S. Temple, Salt Lake city, UT 84102 USA.

Hole's Greenhouses & Gardens, Ltd. (CAN) *(978-0-9682791; 978-1-894728) Dist. by* **Lone Pine.**

Holes In My Socks Publishing, *(978-0-9771891; 978-0-578-41680-9)* P.O. Box 266, Paola, KS 66071 USA Tel 913-557-4508
E-mail: stephgun2@aol.com; christydreiling@att.net.

†Holiday Hse., Inc., *(978-0-8234)* Orders Addr.: 425 Madison Ave., New York, NY 10017 USA (SAN 202-3008) Tel 212-688-0085; Fax: 212-688-0395;
Imprints: Margaret Ferguson Books (M Ferguson Bks); Neal Porter Books (Neal Porter)
E-mail: holiday@holidayhouse.com
Web site: http://www.holidayhouse.com
Dist(s): **Children's Plus, Inc.**
MyiLibrary
Open Road Integrated Media, Inc.
Penguin Random Hse. Distribution
Penguin Random Hse. LLC
Random Hse., Inc.; *CIP.*

Holiness.com, *(978-0-9743831)* 1271 Washington Ave., PMB 165, San Leandro, CA 94577 USA Tel 510-384-8082
E-mail: suppliers@holiness.com
Web site: http://www.holiness.com.

Holism Publishing, *(978-0-9818297)* Orders Addr.: P.O. Box 3385, Palm Beach, FL 33480-1585 USA Tel 561-533-7704 (phone/fax)
E-mail: curecare@bellsouth.net; info@holismpublishing.com
Web site: http://www.HolismPublishing.com; http://www.HolismMovement.com
Dist(s): **New Leaf Distributing Co., Inc.**

Holland Brown, *(978-0-9797006; 978-0-9897544)* 2509 Portland Ave The Anchor Bldg., Louisville, KY 40202-1008 USA
E-mail: stephanie@thegreenbuilding.com
Web site: http://www.hollandbrownbooks.com.

Holland, Gretchen, *(978-0-9768340)* 4437 Craig Dr., Fort Collins, CO 80526 USA Tel 970-282-1338.

Hollandays Publishing Corp., *(978-0-9708224; 978-0-9728844; 978-0-9753239; 978-0-9769459; 978-0-9799003)* 8459 N. Main St. Ste. 118, Dayton, OH 45415-1324 USA Toll Free: 800-792-3537
E-mail: zhensler@hollandays.net
Web site: http://www.hollandays.net
Dist(s): **Partners Bk. Distributing, Inc.**

Hollar, Cheryl Public Relations, *(978-0-9763826)* Orders Addr.: 218 S. Cheatham St., Franklinton, NC 27525 USA Tel 919-494-2150
E-mail: cherylhollar@yahoo.com; billythebunnybooks@yahoo.com.

Hollenbach, David A, *(978-0-578-41371-6)* 342 Merchant Ave., Marion, OH 43302 USA Tel 740-361-2168
E-mail: daveh8000@gmail.com
Dist(s): **Ingram Content Group.**

Hollingale Bks. LLC, *(978-0-9907895)* 55 N. Merchant St. No. 1481, American Fork, UT 84003 USA Tel 801-855-6448
E-mail: paige@hollingale.com
Web site: www.hollingale.com.

Hollingsworth, Kenneth, *(978-0-9771572)* 2215 Janet Ct., Cedar Hill, TX 75104-1021 USA (SAN 256-8926)
Web site: http://www.hollingsworthtexas.com/plantingtheseeds.

Hollow Mountain Publishing LLC, (*978-0-9981676*) 2266 Possum Hollow Dr, Camdenton, MO 65020 USA Tel 573-207-0699
E-mail: diannakilpack@outlook.com.

Holloway, Greg, (*978-0-9908100*) 107 Ashburne Glen Ln, Ovilla, TX 75154 USA Tel 214-325-8357
E-mail: info@48hrbooks.com
Web site: hollowaygreg.com.

Holly Hall Pubns., Inc., (*978-0-9645396; 978-1-888306*) P.O. Box 254, Elkton, MD 21922-0254 USA Tel 410-392-2300; Fax: 410-620-9877; Toll Free: 800-211-0719; *Imprints:* Full Quart Press (Full Quart Pr)
Dist(s): **Spring Arbor Distributors, Inc.**

Holly Hill Pr., (*978-0-578-01217-9; 978-0-578-03837-7; 978-0-578-03971-8; 978-0-578-08282-0; 978-0-692-03326-5; 978-0-578-40816-3; 978-0-578-41542-0*) 3 Earl Rd., Box 36, East Sandwich, MA 02537 USA; 135 Corn Shop Ln., Farmington, ME 04938
E-mail: jbeanpalmer@yahoo.com
Dist(s): **Independent Pub.**

HollyBear Pr., (*978-0-9651067*) Orders Addr.: P.O. Box 4257, Prescott, AZ 86302-4257 USA Tel 928-776-4689; Edit Addr.: 910 Stevens Dr., Prescott, AZ 86305 USA
E-mail: monamc2@msn.com.

Hollygrove Publishing, Inc., (*978-0-9777939; 978-0-9840904*) 4100 W. Eldorado Pkwy., Suite 100-182, McKinney, TX 75070 USA (SAN 850-170X) Tel 972-837-6191
E-mail: bsmith@hollygrovepublishing.com
Web site: http://www.hollygrovepublishing.com.

Hollym International Corp., (*978-0-930878; 978-1-56591*) Orders Addr.: 2647 Gateway Rd. No. 105-223, Carlsbad, CA 92009 USA Tel 760-814-9880; Fax: 908-353-0255; Edit Addr.: 2647 Gateway Rd. No. 105-223, Carlbad, CA 92009 USA (SAN 211-0172) Tel 760-814-9880; Fax: 908-353-0255 Do not confuse with Hollym Corporation Pubs., New York, NY
E-mail: gracepresa@gmail.com; contact@hollym.com
Web site: http://www.hollym.com.

Hollywood Jesus Bks., (*978-0-9759577; 978-0-9787554*) P.O. Box 48282, Burien, WA 98166 USA Tel 206-241-6149
E-mail: editor@hjbooks.com
Web site: http://www.hjbooks.com.

Hollywood Operating System, (*978-1-893899*) 3108 W. Magnolia Blvd., Burbank, CA 91505-3045 USA
E-mail: hollywoodos@aol.com
Web site: http://www.HollywoodOS.com.

HollywoodComics.com, LLC, (*978-0-9740711; 978-1-932983; 978-1-934543; 978-1-935558; 978-1-61227; 978-1-64932*) 18321 Ventura Blvd. Suite 915 Attn: Greg M. Seigel, Tarzana, CA 91356 USA (SAN 255-366X) Tel 818-385-0284; *Imprints:* Black Coat Press (Black Coat Pr)
E-mail: info@hollywoodcomics.com; info@riviereblanche.com; jean-marc@hollywoodcomics.com; info@blackcoatpress.com
Web site: http://www.hexagoncomics.com; http://www.blackcoatpress.com; http://www.riviereblanche.com.

Holmade Publishing, (*978-0-578-20055-2; 978-0-578-20056-9*) 22431 Philiprimm St., Woodland Hills, CA 91367 USA Tel 818-887-4123
E-mail: michaelrholm@yahoo.com,.

Holman Bible Pubs. *Imprint of* **B&H Publishing Group**

Holman, Doris Anne, (*978-0-9667192; 978-0-9758630*) 5 Oak Ledge Rd., Harpswell, ME 04079 USA.

Holmes Bookshop *Imprint of* **Belle Lumiere True News**

Holmes Investments & Holdings LLC, (*978-0-9962102; 978-0-9992369*) P.O. Box 1021, Lakewood, CA 90714 USA Tel 562-472-8202
E-mail: quentinholmes@hotmail.com
Web site: www.quentinholmes.com
Dist(s): **Ingram Content Group.**

Holocaust Museum Houston, (*978-0-9659781; 978-0-9773988*) 5401 Caroline St., Houston, TX 77004-6804 USA Tel 713-942-8000; Fax: 713-942-7953
E-mail: info@hmh.org
Web site: http://www.hmh.org
Dist(s): **Hervey's Booklink & Cookbook Warehouse.**

Holocaust Survivors' Memoirs Project, (*978-0-9760739; 978-0-9814686*) c/o World Jewish Congress, 633 Third Ave., Flr. 21, New York, NY 10017 USA Fax: 212-318-6176
E-mail: survivorsmemoirs@aol.com.

Holofcener, Mark, (*978-0-9718626*) 7323 Island Cir., Boulder, CO 80301-3905 USA
E-mail: mark@evansadventure.com
Web site: http://www.evansadventure.com.

Holography Sells, (*978-0-9741087*) 1305 Kirks Ln., Dresher, PA 19025 USA (SAN 255-3627)
E-mail: sales@snookybook.com
Web site: http://www.snookybook.com.

Holt Enterprise, LLC, (*978-0-9740016*) Orders Addr.: P.O. Box 414, Riverside, NJ 08075 USA (SAN 255-2760) Tel 856-764-7043; Fax: 856-764-0851; Toll Free: 888-944-4658; Edit Addr.: 147 N. Fairview St., Riverside, NJ 08075 USA
E-mail: HoltEnterprise@comcast.net; holt109@comcast.net
Dist(s): **Quality Bks., Inc.**

Holt, Henry & Co. *Imprint of* **Holt, Henry & Co.**

Holt, Henry & Co. Bks. For Young Readers *Imprint of* **Holt, Henry & Co.**

†Holt, Henry & Co., (*978-0-03; 978-0-8050*) Div. of Holtzbrinck Publishers, Orders Addr.: 16365 James Madison Hwy., Gordonsville, VA 22942-8501 USA Toll Free Fax: 800-672-2054; Toll Free: 888-330-8477; Edit Addr.: 115 W. 18th St., 5th Flr., New York, NY 10011 USA (SAN 200-6472) Tel 212-886-9200; Fax: 540-672-7540 (customer service); *Imprints:* Metropolitan Books (Metropol Bks); Times Books (Times Bks); Holt, Henry & Company (HenHolt); Holt, Henry & Company Books For Young Readers (HH Bks Yng Read); Holt Paperback (Holt Paperbck)
E-mail: info@hholt.com
Web site: http://www.henryholt.com
Dist(s): **Children's Plus, Inc.**
Giron Bks.
Lectorum Pubns., Inc.
Macmillan
Perfection Learning Corp.
Westminster John Knox Pr.
Weston Woods Studios, Inc.; *CIP.*

Holt, Max Media., (*978-0-9966104; 978-1-944537*) 303 Casacabel Pl, Mt Juliet, TN 37122 USA Tel 731-819-4241
E-mail: sandymaxholt@yahoo.com
Web site: www.maxholtmedia.com.

Holt McDougal, (*978-0-395; 978-0-8123; 978-0-86609; 978-0-88343; 978-0-618*) Subs. of Houghton Mifflin Harcourt Publishing Co., Orders Addr.: 1900 S. Batavia Ave., Geneva, IL 60134 USA Toll Free: 888-872-8380; Edit Addr.: P.O. Box 1667, Evanston, IL 60204 USA (SAN 202-2532) Toll Free: 800-323-5435; 800-462-6595 (customer service); 909 Davis St., Evanston, IL 60201 Tel 847-869-2300; Fax: 847-869-0841
Web site: http://www.mcdougallittell.com.

Holt Paperback *Imprint of* **Holt, Henry & Co.**

Holt Smith, Ltd., (*978-0-9886493; 978-0-692-31193-6; 978-0-692-31279-7; 978-0-692-55473-9; 978-0-692-57280-1; 978-0-692-57286-3; 978-0-692-58679-2; 978-0-692-68801-4; 978-0-692-70258-1; 978-0-692-70856-9; 978-0-692-72171-1; 978-0-9977938; 978-1-946777*) 101 W. 23rd Apt. 2Q, New York, NY 10011 USA Tel 917-553-3143
E-mail: support@holtsmith.com
Dist(s): **CreateSpace Independent Publishing Platform.**

Holtz Creative Enterprises, (*978-0-9817247; 978-0-9837617*) 3103 Terry Ln., Eau Claire, WI 54703 USA Tel 715-835-2705
E-mail: holtzenterprises@sbcglobal.net.

Holtzbrinck Publishers *See* **Macmillan**

Holy Child Pubns., (*978-0-615-27752-3; 978-0-615-33948-1; 978-0-615-37502-1; 978-0-615-45181-7; 978-0-615-58648-9; 978-0-615-69219-7; 978-0-615-81249-6; 978-0-692-47633-8; 978-0-692-80495-7; 978-0-692-11629-6; 978-0-578-55615-4; 978-0-578-55616-1*) P.O. Box 954, Fairburn, GA 30213 USA
Web site: http://www.holychildpublications.com.

HOLY COW Bk. Pubs., (*978-0-9773407; 978-0-615-83382-8; 978-1-953232*) 3321 Hugo Ln., Timmonsville, SC 29161 USA Tel 843-229-4641
E-mail: ralphy_jmm@yahoo.com; ollyaga@gmail.com.

Holy Heroes LLC, (*978-0-9801121; 978-1-936330*) 728 Hanna Woods, Cramerton, NC 28032 USA (SAN 855-2401)
E-mail: kandkdavison@bellsouth.net
Web site: http://www.holyheroes.com.

Holy Macro! Bks. *Imprint of* **Tickling Keys, Inc.**

Holy Trinity Monastery, (*978-0-88465; 978-1-942699*) P.O. Box 36, Jordanville, NY 13361-0036 USA (SAN 207-3501) Tel 315-858-0940; Fax: 315-858-0505
Dist(s): **Independent Pubs. Group.**

Holzwarth Pubns. (DEU) (*978-3-935567; 978-3-00*) *Dist. by* **Dist Art Pubs.**

Hom, Jonathan, (*978-0-9974103*) 132 Cityhomes Ln., Foster City, CA 94404 USA Tel 650-477-5315
E-mail: w00tw00tjon@gmail.com.

Homa & Sekey Bks., (*978-0-9665421; 978-1-931907; 978-1-62246*) 3rd Floor, North Tower Mack-Cali Center III 140 East Ridgewood Ave, Paramus, NJ 07652 USA Tel 800-870-HOMA (4662) (Orders only); 201-261-8810; Fax: 201-261-8890
E-mail: info@homabooks.com
Web site: http://www.homabooks.com
Dist(s): **Independent Pubs. Group.**

Homagno Group, Incorporated *See* **Editorial Homagno**

Home Box Office, Inc., (*978-0-910765; 978-0-9828167*) 1100 Sixth Ave., New York, NY 10036 USA (SAN 260-2032) Tel 212-512-1000.

Home Discipleship Pr., (*978-0-9753133; 978-0-9785678*) 6645 W. Steger Rd., Monee, IL 60449 USA Tel 708-235-1901; Fax: 708-235-1904
E-mail: leaders@homediscipleship.orf
Web site: http://www.homediscipleshippress.org.

Home Planet Bks., (*978-0-9743712; 978-0-9887978*) 2300 8th St., Olivenhain, CA 92024-6565 USA Tel 760-634-4947
E-mail: sales@homeplanetbooks.com.

Home Sales Enhancements *See* **Castlebrook Pubns.**

Home Schl. in the Woods, (*978-0-9720265; 978-0-9815523; 978-0-9842041; 978-0-9913678*) 3997 Roosevelt Hwy., Holley, NY 14470 USA Tel 585-964-8188
E-mail: eduardoopak@yahoo.com
Web site: http://www.homeschoolinthewoods.com.

Homecooked Entertainment, (*978-0-9994628*) 4070 Woodman Canyon, Sherman Oaks, CA 91423 USA Tel 310-924-2731
E-mail: al@homecookedentertainment.com.

Homegrown Pubns.,LLC, (*978-0-9799635*) P.O. Box 173, Red Wing, MN 55066 USA
Web site: http://www.homegrownpublications.com.

Homelight Pr., (*978-0-9749936*) P.O. Box 1901, Huntersville, NC 28070-1901 USA Toll Free: 877-438-6657
E-mail: homeligh@bellsouth.net.

Homer Historical Society, (*978-0-9770022*) 107 N. Main St., Homer, IL 61849 USA Tel 217-896-2549.

Homes for the Homeless Institute, Inc., (*978-0-9641784; 978-0-9724425; 978-0-9825533*) 50 Cooper Sq. Flr. 4, New York, NY 10003-7144 USA; *Imprints:* White Tiger Press (Wht Tiger Pr)
E-mail: info@icphusa.org
Web site: www.icphusa.org; www.whitetigerpress.org.

HomeScholar Bks., (*978-0-9754934*) 2311 Harrison Rd., Nashville, NC 27856 USA Tel 252-459-9279; *Imprints:* Literary Lessons (LitLessons)
Web site: http://www.homescholarbooks.com.

Homeschool Journey, (*978-0-9762918; 978-0-9825006*) 4625 Devon, Lisle, IL 60532 USA Tel 630-277-6200
E-mail: homeschooljourney@gmail.com
Web site: http://www.homeschooljourney.com.

Homestead Publishing, (*978-0-943972*) 4388 17th St., San Francisco, CA 94114 USA (SAN 241-029X) Tel 415-621-5039
E-mail: info@homesteadpublishing.net
Web site: http://homesteadpublishing.net; http://www.homesteadpublishing.net.

Honey Girl Bks., (*978-0-9984432*) 1725 41st Ave SW, Seattle, WA 98116 USA Tel 574-400-9362
E-mail: juliawsea@gmail.com
Web site: honeygirlbooks.com/.

Honey Locust Pr. *Imprint of* **Wolfmont, LLC**

Honeybee in the Garden, LLC, (*978-0-9857996; 978-1-7323630*) 11619 Greenlane Dr., Potomac, MD 20854 USA Tel 301-765-6248
E-mail: dband@dbandart.com
Web site: www.dbandart.com.

Honeycomb Adventures Pr., LLC, (*978-0-9820886; 978-0-9836808*) P.O. Box 1215, Hemingway, SC 29554 USA Tel 843-558-0133
E-mail: queenbjan@sc.rr.com
Web site: http://honeycombadventures.com
Dist(s): **Ingram Content Group.**

Honeycomb Inc., (*978-0-9793799*) 1017 Avon, Flint, MI 48503 USA (SAN 853-3024) Tel 810-397-8025; Fax: 810-234-1794
E-mail: tandtvison@aol.com
Web site: http://www.101waysyoucansave.com.

Honeysuckle Acres, (*978-0-9963033*) 146 Rockfish Run Rd., Scottsville, VA 24590 USA Tel 434-566-6675
E-mail: kayepearse@gmail.com.

Honor Bound Bks., (*978-0-615-91638-5; 978-0-692-02434-8; 978-0-692-21785-6; 978-0-692-28323-3; 978-0-692-48896-6; 978-0-692-64187-3; 978-0-692-64346-4; 978-0-9977785; 978-1-951587*) 422 W Meadow Creek Way, Middleton, ID 83644 USA Tel 208-800-1355 Do not confuse with Honor Bound Books in Sacramento, CA
Web site: www.honorboundbooks.com
Dist(s): **CreateSpace Independent Publishing Platform.**

Honorable Pr., (*978-0-9719727*) 2432 Wilshire Ct., Decatur, GA 30035 USA.

HonorNet, (*978-0-9753036; 978-0-9788726; 978-0-9820590; 978-1-938021*) P.O. Box 910, Sapulpa, OK 74067 USA
E-mail: mail@honornet.net
Web site: http://honornet.net
Dist(s): **Destiny Image Pubs.**
Whitaker Hse.

Hood, Alan C. & Co., Inc., (*978-0-911469*) P.O. Box 775, Chambersburg, PA 17201 USA (SAN 270-8221) Tel 717-267-0867; Fax: 717-267-0572; Toll Free Fax: 888-844-9433; 4501 Forbes Blvd., Lanham, MD 20706
E-mail: hoodbooks@pa.net
Web site: http://www.hoodbooks.com
Dist(s): **Follett School Solutions.**

Hood, Ted *See* **Four Seasons Publishing**

Hooker, Lou, (*978-0-9755106*) 6900 Chamberlain, Fremont, MI 49412 USA Tel 231-924-3555
E-mail: lvhook@ncats.net.

Hoopoe Bks. *Imprint of* **I S H K**

Hooser, Jack M Van, (*978-0-692-06208-1; 978-0-692-06224-1*) 2809 Meadow Rose Dr., Nashville, TN 37206 USA Tel 615-308-0822
E-mail: jogarrett35@gmail.com
Dist(s): **Ingram Content Group.**

Hoot N' Cackle Pr., (*978-0-9659381*) 1928 S. Mayfair, Springfield, MO 65804 USA Tel 417-887-0837; Fax: 417-886-3994
E-mail: rlipe@usipp.net
Web site: http://www.mowrites4kids.drury.edu/authors/lipe/.

Hoots, Dani *See* **FoxTales Pr.**

Hoover, Linda, (*978-0-9981806*) 3050 Craig Rd, Springfield, OH 45502 USA Tel 397-631-1566
E-mail: lhoover2@Hotmail.com.

HOP, LLC, (*978-1-887942; 978-1-931020; 978-1-933863; 978-1-60143; 978-1-60242; 978-1-60498; 978-1-60499*) Educate, Inc., 1407 Fleet St. Flr. 1, Baltimore, MD 21231-2859 USA
Web site: http://www.hookedonphonics.com
Dist(s): **Simon & Schuster, Inc.**

Hope Belle LLC, (*978-0-692-16751-9; 978-0-692-16752-6*) 247 W. 145th St. Apt. 1D, NEW YORK, NY 10039 USA Tel 646-489-9409
E-mail: hopebelle1@gmail.com
Dist(s): **Ingram Content Group.**

Hope Chest Legacy, Inc., (*978-1-59565*) P.O. Box 1398, Littlerock, CA 93543 USA Toll Free: 888-554-7292
E-mail: hopechestlegacy@aol.com
Web site: http://hopechestlegacy.com.

Hope Farm Pr. & Bookshop, (*978-0-910746*) 15 Jane St., Saugerties, NY 12477-1511 USA (SAN 204-0697) Toll Free: 800-883-5778 (orders)
E-mail: hopefarm@hopefarm.com
Web site: http://www.hopefarm.com; http://www.hopefarmbooks.com
Dist(s): **North Country Bks., Inc.**

Hope for Families, Inc., (*978-0-9676489*) P.O. Box 238, Hatfield, PA 19440 USA Tel 215-280-5369
E-mail: lbmbam@fast.net.

Hope Harvest Ministries *See* **Hope Harvest Publishing**

Hope Harvest Publishing, (*978-0-9716523; 978-0-9763695; 978-0-9771318; 978-0-9779898*) Div. of H&H Bindery & Distribution Centre, P.O. Box 8353, Kentwood, MI 49518 USA Tel 616-307-3080; Fax: 616-458-8991
E-mail: hopeharvest@comcast.net
Web site: http://www.hopeharvest.com; http://www.blessly.com
Dist(s): **Anchor Distributors**
Anderson Merchandisers
H & H Distribution
Spirit Filled Pr., Inc.
Spring Arbor Distributors, Inc.

Hope International Printshop, (*978-0-9748096*) Orders Addr.: P.O. Box 1182, Hobe Sound, FL 33475 USA; Edit Addr.: 8436 SE Bayberry Terr., Hobe Sound, FL 33475 USA.

Hope of Vision Publishing, (*978-0-9753795; 978-0-9818253; 978-0-9831371; 978-0-9837082; 978-0-9852746; 978-0-9884773; 978-0-9912483; 978-1-942871*) 43 Yale St., Bridgeport, CT 06605 USA (SAN 856-6410) Tel 203-338-1301; Fax: 203-413-1593
Web site: http://www.hopeofvisionpublishing.com.

Hope Pr., (*978-1-878267*) Orders Addr.: P.O. Box 188, Duarte, CA 91009-0188 USA (SAN 200-3244) Tel 626-303-0644; Fax: 626-358-3520; Toll Free: 800-321-4039; Edit Addr.: 1110 Mill Run, Monvaia, CA 91016 USA Tel 626-303-0644 Do not confuse with Hope Pr., Pittsville, WI
E-mail: hoepress@earthink.net; dcomings@earthlink.net
Web site: http://www.hopepress.com; http://www.didmancreatedgod.com.

Hope Publishing Hse., (*978-0-932727; 978-7-5379; 978-1-932717*) Affil. of Southern California Ecumenical Council, P.O. Box 60008, Pasadena, CA 91116 USA (SAN 688-4849) Tel 626-792-6123; Fax: 626-792-2121; Toll Free: 800-326-2671 (orders only)
E-mail: hopepub@sbcglobal.net
Web site: http://hope-pub.com
Dist(s): **Chinasprout, Inc.**
Send The Light Distribution LLC.

Hope Rekindled Pr. *See* **Risen Heart Pr.**

Hope Through Healing Pubns., (*978-0-9743626*) P.O. Box 310, Yelm, WA 98597 USA
E-mail: jennifer@correctthetext.com
Web site: http://www.CorrectTheText.com.

Hopecopious Productions, (*978-0-9982922*) 1720 SW 346th Pl, Federal Way, WA 98023 USA Tel 253-927-9279; Fax: 253-927-9279
E-mail: Connect@Hopecopious.com
Web site: Hopecopious.com.

HopeRoad Publishing Ltd (GBR) (*978-1-908446*) *Dist. by* **IPG Chicago.**

Hopewell Pubns., LLC, (*978-0-9726906; 978-1-933435*) P.O. Box 11, Titusville, NJ 08560-0011 USA Tel 609-818-1049; Fax: 609-964-1718 Do not confuse with companies with the same or similar name in Longmont, CO, Austin, TX, Springdale, AZ
E-mail: publisher@hopepubs.com
Web site: http://www.hopepubs.com
Dist(s): **Univ. Pr. of New England.**

Hopkins, KC, (*978-0-615-23929-3*) 409 Orchid Trail, Franklin, TN 37174 USA Tel 615-618-4997
E-mail: kchopkins1276@yahoo.com
Dist(s): **Lulu Pr., Inc.**

Hopkins Publishing, (*978-0-9839326; 978-1-62080*) 201 Faircrest Dr. No. 3687, Cleburne, TX 76033 USA Tel 210-595-9313; *Imprints:* Azimuth Media (Azimuth Me)
E-mail: leah@hopkinspublishing.com; justin@hopkinspublishing.com
Web site: http://www.facebook.com/churchofchristbooks; http://hopkinspublishing.com/; http://twitter.com/#!/cofcbooks; https://www.smashwords.com/profile/view/hopkinspublishing
Dist(s): **Ingram Content Group**
Send The Light Distribution LLC.

Hoppenbrouwers, Toke *See* **Monte Nido Pr.**

Hopping Mad Pr., (*978-0-692-98113-9; 978-0-692-98114-6*) 219 East N. D St., Gas City, IN 46933 USA Tel 765-667-4822
E-mail: Ardbrowncda@Live.com.

HOPS Pr., LLC, (*978-1-892784*) Orders Addr.: 12 Quartz St., Pony, MT 59747-0697 USA Tel 406-685-3222
E-mail: orders@hollowtop.com
Web site: http://www.hopspress.com
Dist(s): **Chelsea Green Publishing**
Lone Pine Publishing USA
Mountain Pr. Publishing Co., Inc.

Horan Publishing, (*978-0-9769980*) P.O. Box 740485, Orange City, FL 32774-0485 USA
E-mail: horanpublishing@wmconnect.com.

Horizon Bks., (*978-0-9787987*) Orders Addr.: 768 Hardtimes Rd., Farmville, VA 23901 USA (SAN 851-6243) Tel 434-390-7732 (phone/fax)
E-mail: eicherjs@kinex.net
Web site: http://www.readingwithhorizon.com.

Horizon Line Pr., *(978-0-9749426)* 77 N. River Dr., Roseburg, OR 97470 USA
E-mail: dj@knights-of-avalon.com
Web site: http://www.knights-of-avalon.net/.

Horizon Pubs. & Distributors, Inc., *(978-0-88290)* Orders Addr.: P.O. Box 490, Bountiful, UT 84011-0490 USA.

Horizon Pubs. *Imprint of* **Cedar Fort, Inc./CFI Distribution**

Horizons *Imprint of* **Alpha Omega Pubns., Inc.**

Horowitz Creative Media, Incorporated *See* **ArtMar Productions**

Horse & Dragon Publishing, *(978-0-9759488)* 241 Coast Hill Dr., Suite A, Indian Harbour Beach, FL 32937 USA Tel 321-821-2220; Fax: 321-821-2226; Toll Free: 877-374-6815
E-mail: bob@robertclark.us
Web site: http://www.robertclark.us.

Horse Creek Pubns., *(978-0-9722217)* 945 Mockingbird Ln., Norman, OK 73071-4802 USA
E-mail: sue.schrems@horsecreekpublications.com
Web site: http://www.horsecreekpublications.com.

Horseyolo, *(978-0-9966602)* 20 Minuteman Dr., Bluffton, SC 29910 USA Tel 843-368-2115
E-mail: mikoszshowhorses@gmail.com
Web site: horseyolo.com.

Horton, David *See* **Negro Publishing, LLC**

Horvath, Janet, *(978-0-9713735)* 122 Virginia St., Saint Paul, MN 55102 USA (SAN 255-5441) Tel 612-870-4200; Fax: 612-454-2554
E-mail: jhorvathcello@hotmail.com
Web site: http://www.playinglesshurt.com.

Ho's, Jane Children Bks., *(978-0-9619126)* 700 Kipling Ct., El Sobrante, CA 94803 USA (SAN 243-4954) Tel 510-222-2621.

Hosannah Pubns., *(978-0-9786031)* 507 W. Manheim St., Bldg.18 , Apt.D, Philadelphia, PA 19144-4859 USA Tel 215-991-6154; Fax: 215-991-0609
E-mail: fourhosannah@verizon.net.

Hoskins, Jenny, *(978-1-7324318)* 104 E. Fairview Ave. No. 282 Meridian, Meridian, ID 83642 USA Tel 208-996-2692
E-mail: jennyhoskins0213@gmail.com
Web site: jennyhoskins.com.

Hospice & Community Care Pubns., *(978-0-9774691)* Orders Addr.: P.O. Box 993, Rock Hill, SC 29731 USA (SAN 257-6309) Tel 803-329-4663; Fax: 803-329-5935; Toll Free: 800-895-2273; Edit Addr.: P.O. Box 993, Rock Hill, SC 29731-6993 USA
Web site: http://www.hospicecommunitycare.org.

Hospice of Saint John, The, *(978-0-9742849)* 1320 Everett Ct., Lakewood, CO 80215 USA.

Hot Chocolate Pr., *(978-0-9910626; 978-0-9961710; 978-0-692-95409-6; 978-0-692-11452-0; 978-1-7333341)* 338 Zeppelin Way, Fort Collins, CO 80524 USA Tel 970-556-0908
E-mail: kerrie.flanagan@gmail.com
Dist(s): **BookBaby.**

Hot off the Pr., *(978-0-933491; 978-0-9605904; 978-1-56231; 978-1-59776)* 1250 NW 3rd Ave., Canby, OR 97013 USA (SAN 216-3977) Toll Free: 800-227-9595
E-mail: info@hotp.com
Web site: http://www.craftpizazz.com.

Hot Page Pr. *Imprint of* **Potter Assocs.**

HotComb Pr., *(978-0-9787940)* 6230 Wilshire Blvd., Suite 805, Los Angeles, CA 90048-5104 USA
E-mail: info@hotcombpress.com
Web site: http://hotcombpress.com.

HotDiggetyDog Pr., *(978-0-9741417; 978-0-9844645)* P.O. Box 747, Shepherdsville, KY 40165 USA Tel 502-376-5966; Fax: 208-474-1227
E-mail: leighanne@thewoodybooks.com
Web site: http://www.thewoodybooks.com.

Houghton Mifflin Bks. for Children *Imprint of* **Houghton Mifflin Harcourt Trade & Reference Pubs.**

Houghton Mifflin Company *See* **Houghton Mifflin Harcourt Publishing Co.**

Houghton Mifflin Company (School Division) *See* **Houghton Mifflin Harcourt School Pubs.**

Houghton Mifflin Company Trade & Reference Division *See* **Houghton Mifflin Harcourt Trade & Reference Pubs.**

Houghton Mifflin Harcourt Learning Technology, *(978-0-7630; 978-1-930106)* Div. of Houghton Mifflin Harcourt Publishing Co., 100 Pine St. Ste. 1900, San Francisco, CA 94111-5205 USA Toll Free: 800-223-6925; 125 Cambridgepark Dr., Cambridge, MA 02140-2329
E-mail: info@riverdeep.net; international@riverdeep.net
Web site: http://www.riverdeep.com
Dist(s): **Follett School Solutions**
Open Road Integrated Media, Inc.

†Houghton Mifflin Harcourt Publishing Co., *(978-0-395; 978-0-87466; 978-0-9631591; 978-1-57630; 978-1-881527; 978-0-618; 978-0-544; 978-0-547; 978-1-328; 978-0-358)* Orders Addr.: 9205 Southpark Ctr. Loop, Orlando, FL 32819 USA Toll Free: 800-225-3362; Edit Addr.: 222 Berkeley St., Boston, MA 02116 USA (SAN 215-3793) Tel 617-351-5000; 125 High St., Boston, MA 02110; *Imprints:* Clarion Books (Clarion Bk); Betty Crocker (Betty Crocker); HMH Books For Young Readers (HMH Bks FYR); John Joseph Adams (John Joseph); Versify (Versify); Etch (ETCH)
Web site: http://www.hmco.com
Dist(s): **Blackstone Audio, Inc.**
CENGAGE Learning
Cheng & Tsui Co.
Children's Plus, Inc.
Continental Bk. Co., Inc.
hand2mind
Ebsco Publishing
Firebrand Technologies
Follett School Solutions
Houghton Mifflin Harcourt Trade & Reference Pubs.
Houghton Mifflin Harcourt Supplemental Pubs.
Larousse Kingfisher Chambers, Inc.
Lectorum Pubns., Inc.
MyiLibrary
Open Road Integrated Media, Inc.
Perelandra, Ltd.
TextStream
ebrary, Inc.; *CIP.*

Houghton Mifflin Harcourt School Pubs., *(978-0-395; 978-0-669)* Orders Addr.: 1900 Batavia Ave., Geneva, IL 60134-3399 USA Toll Free Fax: 800-733-2098; Toll Free: 800-733-2828; 1175 N. Stemmons Fwy., Lewisville, TX 75067-2516 Toll Free: 800-733-2828; Edit Addr.: 222 Berkeley St., Boston, MA 02116 USA Tel 617-351-5000; Fax: 617-227-5409
E-mail: eduwebmaster@hmco.com
Web site: http://www.eduplace.com
Dist(s): **Follett School Solutions.**

Houghton Mifflin Harcourt Supplemental Pubs., *(978-1-60032; 978-1-60277)* 10801 N. Mopac Expressway, Bldg. 3, Austin, TX 78759 USA
Web site: www.harcourtachieve.com.

Houghton Mifflin Harcourt Trade & Reference Pubs., *(978-0-395; 978-0-89919; 978-0-618)* Orders Addr.: 9205 Southpark Ctr. Loop, Orlando, FL 32819 USA Tel 978-661-1300; Toll Free: 800-225-3362; Edit Addr.: 222 Berkeley St., Boston, MA 02116 USA (SAN 200-2388) Tel 617-351-5000; Fax: 617-227-5409; 215 Park Ave S., 12th Flr., New York, NY 10003-1621; *Imprints:* Clarion Books (Clarion Bk); Sandpiper (Sandpiper); Houghton Mifflin Books for Children (HMBC)
E-mail: trade_sub_rights@hmco.com
Web site: http://www.hmco.com/; http://www.houghtonmifflinbooks.com
Dist(s): **Blackstone Audio, Inc.**
CENGAGE Learning
Children's Plus, Inc.
CreateSpace Independent Publishing Platform
Ebsco Publishing
Follett School Solutions
Houghton Mifflin Harcourt Publishing Co.
Harcourt Trade Pubs.
Lectorum Pubns., Inc.
MyiLibrary
Open Road Integrated Media, Inc.

Ho'ulu Hou Project: Stories Told by Us *Imprint of* **Na Kamalei Koolauloa Early Education Program**

Hound Dog Pr., The, *(978-0-578-42526-9)* 6710 River Springs Ct. NW, Atlanta, GA 30328 USA Tel 404-256-0078
E-mail: jimewing21@hotmail.com.

HourGlass Publishing, *(978-0-9860205; 978-1-946223)* 2095 Hwy. 211 NW Suite 2F-152, Braselton, GA 30517 USA Tel 678-439-9229; Fax: 866-855-1971
E-mail: info@hourglasspublishing.com
Web site: www.HourGlassPublishing.com.

House, David, *(978-0-9777086)* 1488 Madelyn Ave SE, Salem, OR 97306-3552 USA
Web site: http://www.space-worthy.com.

House of Anansi Pr. (CAN) *(978-0-88784; 978-1-77089; 978-1-4870) Dist. by* **PerseuPGW.**

House of David *See* **Key of David Publishing**

Hse. of Mistofer Christopher, *(978-1-7321266)* 114-10 202 St., Saint Albans, NY 11412 USA Tel 347-415-6485
E-mail: mistoferchristopher@gmail.com
Web site: Www.mistoferchristopher@gmail.com.

House of Prayer Ministries, Inc., *(978-1-882825)* 2428 Florian Ct., Decatur, IL 62526 USA Tel 217-428-7077 (phone/fax)
E-mail: vikischerer@comcast.net
Web site: www.houseofprayerministries.com.

House of the Guilded Scribe, *(978-0-615-28905-2; 978-0-615-55608-6; 978-0-9914351)* P.O. Box 432, Mount Pocono, PA 18344 USA
E-mail: sales@prissyandmissy.com; theguildedscribe@gmail.com
Web site: http://www.wonderfulwondersart.com; http://www.prissyandmissy.com; http://www.prissyandmissy.com.

House of The Lord Fellowship, *(978-0-9673530)* Orders Addr.: P.O. Box 235, Lock Haven, PA 17745 USA Tel 570-748-6455; Fax: 570-748-6858; Edit Addr.: 201 W. Main St., Lock Haven, PA 17745 USA
E-mail: ssnyder@houseofthelordfellowship.org
Web site: http://www.houseofthelordfellowship.org.

House of Usher *See* **Abysso Bks.**

House Upon A Hill Bks., *(978-0-9795826)* Orders Addr.: P.O. Box 140322, Broken Arrow, OK 74014 USA; Edit Addr.: 19546 E. 42nd St. S., Broken Arrow, OK 74014 USA.

Houston Enterprises, *(978-0-9712861; 978-0-9907800; 978-0-9862339; 978-0-9862349)* Orders Addr.: 6320 Rucker Rd. Suite E, Indianapolis, IN 46220 USA Tel 317-726-1901; Fax: 317-726-1902; Toll Free: 888-826-8082
E-mail: info@scotthouston.com
Web site: http://www.scotthouston.com.

Houston Zoo, Inc., *(978-0-9762385)* 1513 N. MAcGregor, Houston, TX 77030 USA Tel 713-533-6500; Fax: 713-533-6755
E-mail: gwarfield@houstonzoo.org
Web site: http://www.houstonzoo.org.

Houstons Pr., *(978-0-578-42900-7; 978-0-578-44878-7; 978-1-7334575)* 3035 Stone Mountain St, Lithonia, GA 30058 USA Tel 678-235-4183
E-mail: houstonspressllc@gmail.com.

Houts & Home Pubns. LLC, *(978-0-9855084)* 26162 Ridge Dr., Maryville, MO 64468 USA Tel 660-562-3122
E-mail: sase@cebridge.net
Web site: www.houtsandhome.com.

How 2 Creative Services, *(978-0-9893405)* 3220 18th St. S. Suite 8C, Fargo, ND 58104 USA Tel 701-866-4661
E-mail: mark@how2cs.com
Web site: www.how2cs.com.

"How Do You Know", *(978-0-9675574)* Orders Addr.: P.O. Box 831172, Stone Mountain, GA 30083 USA
E-mail: pjgastonbooks@yahoo.com.

How Great Thou ART Pubns., *(978-0-9700405; 978-0-9717874; 978-0-9859000)* Orders Addr.: P.O. Box 48, Mcfarlan, NC 28102-0048 USA Tel 704-851-3117; Fax: 704-851-3111; Toll Free: 800-982-3729; Edit Addr.: 357 McFarlin Rd, Morven, NC 28119 USA
E-mail: matthew@howgreatthouart.com
Web site: http://www.howgreatthouart.com/.

How to Make & Keep Friends, LLC, *(978-0-692-53121-1; 978-0-9972808)* 1 Industrial Way, Tyngsboro, MA 01879 USA Tel 978-392-9865; *Imprints:* Social Success Central, LLC (MYID_B_SOCIAL)
Web site: www.howtomakeandkeepfriends.com
Dist(s): **CreateSpace Independent Publishing Platform.**

Howard Bks. *Imprint of* **Howard Bks.**

Howard Bks., Div. of SIMON & SCHUSTER, 1230 Ave. of the Americas, New York, NY 10020 USA; *Imprints:* Howard Books (Howard Imp)
Dist(s): **Simon & Schuster, Inc.**

Howard, Emma Bks., *(978-1-886551)* P.O. Box 385, New York, NY 10024-0385 USA Tel 212-996-2590 (phone/fax)
E-mail: emmahowardbooks@verizon.net
Web site: http://www.EellGrassGirls.com.

Howard, Marissa, *(978-0-9985935)* 104 Hampton Loop Unit 1, Minot AFB, ND 58704 USA Tel 719-439-5500
E-mail: marissahowardbooks@gmail.com.

Howard Printing, Inc., *(978-0-9793790)* 14 Noahs Ln., Brattleboro, VT 05301 USA Tel 802-254-3550; Fax: 802-257-1453
E-mail: info@howardprintinginc.com
Web site: http://www.howardprintinginc.com.

Howard-Hirsch *See* **Howard-Hirsch Publishing**

Howard-Hirsch Publishing, *(978-0-9802307)* P.O. Box 786, Green, OH 44720 USA (SAN 855-5524)
Web site: http://www.Howardhirschpublishing.com.

Howe, Tina Field, *(978-0-9768585)* P.O. Box 581, Waverly, NY 14892 USA (SAN 256-8276) Tel 607-329-2458
Web site: http://www.tinafieldhowe.com.

Howell Bk. Hse. *Imprint of* **Wiley, John & Sons, Inc.**

Howell Canyon Pr., *(978-1-931210)* 1475 N Bundy Dr., Los Angeles, CA 90049 USA (SAN 255-3015) Toll Free: 888-252-0411 (Orders)
E-mail: info@HowellCanyonPress.com
Web site: http://www.AddisonTheDog.com; http://www.howellcanyonpress.com/; http://www.drdeanhowell.com/; http://www.TrishaHowell.com
Dist(s): **Ingram Publisher Services.**

Howell, M Kay *See* **Eagle Tree Pr.**

Howell, Mallory, *(978-1-7324216)* 128 Tom Pate Rd., Johnson City, TN 37604 USA Tel 423-647-3259
E-mail: mallii02@yahoo.com.

Howell, Steven, *(978-0-615-15346-9; 978-0-615-19997-9)* 697 Superior Ln., Clarksville, TN 37043 USA Tel 931-358-6022
E-mail: mrmrshowell2@yahoo.com
Dist(s): **Lulu Pr., Inc.**

Howie, C.J. Co., *(978-1-885275)* 1695 Quigley Rd., Columbus, OH 43227-3433 USA Tel 614-237-5474.

HP Bks. *Imprint of* **Penguin Publishing Group**

HPN Publishing, *(978-0-9768451)* 22902 Sonriente Trail, Trabuco Canyon, CA 92679 USA.

HR Dowling, *(978-0-692-83760-3; 978-0-578-40147-8)* 5006 51st Ave SW, Seattle, WA 98136 USA Tel 206-747-2055
E-mail: hrdowling@hotmail.com.

H.R. Wallace Publishing, *(978-0-692-31112-7; 978-0-692-31125-7; 978-0-692-31138-7; 978-0-692-31621-4; 978-0-692-31624-5; 978-0-692-31627-6; 978-0-692-31634-4; 978-0-692-31635-1; 978-0-692-31637-5; 978-0-692-31639-9; 978-0-692-31644-3; 978-0-692-31646-7; 978-0-692-31648-1; 978-0-692-31649-8; 978-0-692-31651-1; 978-0-692-31660-3; 978-0-692-31667-2; 978-0-692-31668-9; 978-0-692-32363-2; 978-0-692-32368-7; 978-0-692-32370-0; 978-0-692-32374-8; 978-0-692-32377-9; 978-0-692-32378-6; 978-0-692-32501-8; 978-0-692-32502-5;) 909 Mayfield Rd., Sharpsville, PA 16150 USA*
Dist(s): **CreateSpace Independent Publishing Platform.**

Hramiec Hoffman Publishing, *(978-0-9746901)* 6911 M-119 Hwy., Harbor Springs, MI 49740 USA Tel 231-526-1011
Dist(s): **Partners Bk. Distributing, Inc.**

Hub City Pr., *(978-0-9638731; 978-1-891885; 978-1-938235)* Orders Addr.: 186 West Main St., Spartanburg, SC 29306 USA Tel 864-577-9349; Fax: 864-577-0188
E-mail: bteter@bellsouth.net
Web site: http://www.hubcity.org
Dist(s): **Blair**
Publishers Group West (PGW).

Hub City Writers Project *See* **Hub City Pr.**

Hubbard Scientific, Inc., *(978-0-8331)* Orders Addr.: P.O. Box 760, Chippewa Falls, WI 54729-1468 USA (SAN 202-3121) Tel 715-723-4427; Fax: 715-723-8021; Toll Free: 800-323-8368; Edit Addr.: P.O. Box 760, Chippewa Fls, WI 54729-0760 USA
Web site: http://www.hubbardscientific.com.

Hubbell, Gerald, *(978-0-9762042)* 4127 Roanoke Rd., Kansas City, MO 64111 USA Tel 816-531-4427
Web site: http://www.malverack.com.

Huckleberry Hill Adventure LLC, *(978-0-692-89191-9; 978-0-578-46430-5)* 4055 El Bosque Dr., Pebble Beach, CA 93953 USA Tel 831-233-0937
E-mail: huckleberryhilladventure@gmail.com
Web site: huckleberryhilladventure.com.

Hudson, Bidenia, *(978-0-692-91356-7; 978-0-578-40023-5)* 701 HARVEST GROVE Ln. SE, CONYERS, GA 30013 USA Tel 678-806-5439
E-mail: BHudsonMinistry@gmail.com
Dist(s): **Ingram Content Group.**

Hudson Bks., *(978-0-9749860; 978-0-9762502; 978-0-9764459; 978-0-9767789; 978-0-9786296; 978-0-9822553)* 244 Madison Ave., No. 254, New York, NY 10016 USA Fax: 718-225-5556; Toll Free: 877-822-2500
Web site: http://www.thefloatinggallery.com.

Hudson Hills Press, Incorporated *See* **Hudson Hills Pr. LLC**

†Hudson Hills Pr. LLC, *(978-0-933920; 978-0-9646042; 978-1-55595)* Orders Addr.: P.O. Box 205, Manchester, VT 05254 USA; Edit Addr.: 74-2 Union St., Manchester, VT 05254 USA (SAN 213-0815) Tel 802-362-6450; Fax: 802-362-6459
E-mail: artbooks@hudsonhills.com
Web site: http://www.hudsonhills.com/
Dist(s): **Art Institute of Chicago**
National Bk. Network; *CIP.*

Hudson House Publishing & Productions *See* **Whorl Bks.**

Hudson, Jessie, *(978-0-9778922)* 14814 Forward Pass, San Antonio, TX 78248 USA
Web site: http://www.OLLIEANDFRIENDS.com.

Hudson, Mary C., *(978-0-9627745; 978-0-9722937)* 1125 Karen Way, Mountainview, CA 94040 USA Tel 650-948-1270.

Hudson Publishing Group, The *See* **Just Us Bks., Inc.**

Hudson, Russ, *(978-0-692-96385-2)* 1080 Pinnacle Rd, LIBERTY, ME 04949 USA Tel 802-738-0775
E-mail: russ@cannabizconsultant.com
Dist(s): **Ingram Content Group.**

Hufnagel Software, *(978-0-9743881)* P.O. Box 747, Clarion, PA 16214-0747 USA Tel 814-226-5600; Fax: 814-226-5551
Web site: http://www.hufsoft.com/books.

Hughes, Betty Barber *See* **Puwaii International, LLC**

Huginn & Muninn, *(978-1-937571)* 1240 W. Sims Way No. 93, Port Townsend, WA 98368 USA Tel 206-202-0998
E-mail: 2ravens@gmx.com; wyrddesign@unseen.is; huginnandmuninn@gmx.com; heathenmama@gmx.com; carrie@carrieoverton.com; carrie@huginnandmuninn.net
Web site: huginnandmuninn.net.

Hugo House Publishers, Ltd., *(978-1-936449; 978-1-948261)* 3361 W. Monmouth Ave., Englewood, CO 80110-6336 USA Tel 303-762-1469; Fax: 303-993-5639
E-mail: Patricia@HugoHousePublishers.com.

Hugs Bks. *Imprint of* **Indie Artist Pr.**

Huia Pubs. (NZL) *(978-0-908975; 978-1-877266; 978-1-877241; 978-1-877283; 978-1-86969; 978-0-9582517; 978-1-77550; 978-1-77550-255-5; 978-1-77550-297-5; 978-1-77550-244-9; 978-1-77550-295-1; 978-1-77550-238-8; 978-1-77550-294-4; 978-1-77550-239-5; 978-1-77550-257-9; 978-1-77550-241-8; 978-1-77550-243-2; 978-1-77550-252-4; 978-1-77550-296-8; 978-1-77550-250-0; 978-1-77550-242-5; 978-1-77550-247-0; 978-1-77550-253-1; 978-1-77550-240-1; 978-1-77550-245-6; 978-1-77550-254-8; 978-1-77550-248-7; 978-1-77550-256-2) Dist. by* **UH Pr.**

Hula Moon Pr., *(978-0-9794649)* P.O. Box 11173, Honolulu, HI 96828 USA Tel 808-947-6470
Dist(s): **BookBaby.**

Hulme Publishing, *(978-0-9991262)* 9 Mountain Laurel Dr., Greenwich, CT 06831 USA Tel 203-622-5131
E-mail: dhulme@optonline.net.

Human Consciousness Consortium, *(978-1-7324336)* 6595 Roswell Rd. G1143, Atlanta, GA 30328 USA Tel 833-300-9990
E-mail: snicholas007@gmail.com
Web site: http://SusanNicholas.org.

Human Factor LLC, *(978-0-9816472)* P.O. Box 3742, Washington, DC 20027 USA (SAN 856-1109)
E-mail: info@humanfactor.net
Web site: http://www.humanfactor.net.

†Human Kinetics, *(978-0-7360; 978-0-87322; 978-0-88011; 978-0-918438; 978-0-931250; 978-1-4504; 978-1-4925; 978-1-7182)* Orders Addr.: P.O. Box 5076, Champaign, IL 61825-5076 USA (SAN 211-7088) Tel 217-351-5076; Toll Free: 800-747-4457; Edit Addr.: 1607 N. Market St., Champaign, IL 61820 USA (SAN 658-0866) Tel 217-351-5076; Fax: 217-351-1549; Toll Free: 800-747-4457
E-mail: humank@hkusa.com; info@hkusa.com
Web site: http://www.humankinetics.com; http://www.hkusa.com
Dist(s): **Follett School Solutions**
MyiLibrary
ebrary, Inc.; *CIP.*

Human Kinetics Publishers *See* **Human Kinetics**

Human Relations Media, *(978-1-55548; 978-1-62706)* 41 Kensico Dr., Mount Kisco, NY 10549 USA (SAN 287-4873) Tel 914-244-0486; Fax: 914-244-0485; Toll Free: 800-431-2050
Web site: http://www.hrmvideo.com.

Human Values 4 Kids Foundation, The, *(978-0-9798986; 978-1-7331428)* Orders Addr.: 11498 Pyrites Way, Gold

River, CA 95670-6226 USA; Edit Addr.: 11498 Pyrites Way, Gold River, CA 95670-6226 USA
E-mail: vvnambiar@sbcglobal.net
Web site: https://www.hv4k.org/; http://www.thehumanvalues4kidsfoundation.org.

†**Humana Pr.**, *(978-0-89603; 978-1-58829; 978-1-59259; 978-1-59745; 978-1-934115; 978-1-60327; 978-1-60761; 978-1-61737; 978-1-61779; 978-1-62703)* 233 Spring St., New York, NY 10013 USA (SAN 212-3606) Fax: 212-460-1575; Toll Free: 800-SPRINGER
E-mail: service-ny@springer.com
Web site: http://humanapress.com; http://www.springer.com
Dist(s): **American Assn. for Clinical Chemistry, Inc.**
CreateSpace Independent Publishing Platform
Ebsco Publishing
Metapress
MyiLibrary
Palgrave Macmillan
Rittenhouse Bk. Distributors
Springer
ebrary, Inc.; *CIP.*

Humane Society Pr. *Imprint of* **National Assn. for Humane & Environmental Education**

Humanics Learning *Imprint of* **Green Dragon Bks.**

Humanics Publishing Group *See* **Green Dragon Bks.**

Humanist Pr. *Imprint of* **American Humanist Assn.**

Humanness Project Pr., The, *(978-0-9891086)* 63 Beacon Cir., Cranston, RI 02910 USA Tel 401-467-9240
E-mail: colbyahopkins@gmail.com.

Humanoids, Inc., *(978-0-9672401; 978-1-930652; 978-1-59465; 978-1-64337)* Orders Addr.: 8033 Sunset Blvd. #628, Los Angeles, CA 90046 USA Tel 323-522-5466; Fax: 323-892-2848
E-mail: alex.donoghue@humanoids.com
Web site: http://www.humanoids.com/
Dist(s): **Diamond Comic Distributors, Inc.**
DKE Toys
Ingram Publisher Services
Simon & Schuster, Inc.

Humble Heart Publishing, *(978-0-9712922)* 267 Crane Orchard Rd., Brewster, WA 98812 USA
Web site: humblehearpublishing.com.

Humming Meadow Ranch, *(978-0-9766431)* 47265 Twin Pines Rd., Banning, CA 92220-9656 USA Tel 951-849-1803; Fax: 951-849-9091
E-mail: elaine@hummingmeadowranch.com
Web site: http://www.hummingmeadowranch.com.

Hummingbird Jewel Pr., *(978-0-9981700)* 137 So. Reeves Dr., No. 405, Beverly Hills, CA 90212 USA Tel 310-278-3189
E-mail: rjslewis@aol.com.

Hummingbird Mountain Pr., *(978-0-9746792)* P.O. Box 127, Midpines, CA 95345-0127 USA
Web site: http://www.sierratel.com/hummingbirdmountain.

Hummingbird World Media *Imprint of* **Double Edge Pr.**

Humor & Communication, *(978-0-9677844; 978-0-9820466)* 709 Doe Trail, Edmond, OK 73012 USA
E-mail: hduncan2@cox.net
Web site: http://www.hallduncan.com.

Humphrey, Daniel, *(978-1-7336598)* 7508 Red Oak Ct., Lincoln, NE 68516 USA Tel 402-489-6705
E-mail: dmhumphrey31@yahoo.com.

Humphreys, Kevin, *(978-0-9745727)* P.O. Box 10731, Spokane, WA 99220 USA; 1312 N. Brook Terrace St., Spokane, WA 99224-5678.

Hundred Ways LLC, A, *(978-0-9789544)* 18034 Ventura Blvd., No. 491, Encino, CA 91316 USA Tel 818-708-0558
E-mail: admin@ahundredways.com
Web site: http://www.whenwordsdream.com.

Hungry Bear Publishing, *(978-0-9754007; 978-0-9857607)* Orders Addr.: 40 McClelland St., Saranac Lake, NY 12983 USA Tel 518-891-5559
Web site: http://www.hungrybearpublishing.com
Dist(s): **North Country Bks., Inc.**

Hungry Goat Pr. *Imprint of* **Gauthier Pubns. Inc.**

Hungry Tiger Pr., *(978-0-9644988; 978-1-929527)* 5995 Dandridge Ln., Suite 121, San Diego, CA 92115-6575 USA
E-mail: books@hungrytigerpress.com
Web site: http://www.hungrytigerpress.com.

Hungry Tomato r *Imprint of* **Lerner Publishing Group**

Hungry Tomato Ltd. (GBR) *(978-1-910684; 978-1-912108)* *Dist. by* **BTPS.**

Hunt, J. L. Publishing, *(978-0-9769401)* Orders Addr.: 27881 La Paz Rd., Suite G-124, Laguna Niguel, CA 92677 USA Tel 949-751-7511; Fax: 949-363-8559
E-mail: james@chewnomore.com.

Hunt, J.L. Publishing *See* **Hunt, J. L. Publishing**

Hunt, John Publishing Ltd. (GBR) *(978-1-85608; 978-1-903019; 978-1-84298; 978-1-903816; 978-1-905047; 978-1-84694; 978-1-78099) Dist. by* **Natl Bk Netwk.**

Hunt, John Publishing Ltd. (GBR) *(978-1-85608; 978-1-903019; 978-1-84298; 978-1-903816; 978-1-905047; 978-1-84694; 978-1-78099) Dist. by* **STL Dist.**

Hunt Thompson Media, *(978-0-9630377)*
E-mail: cjhunt@huntthompsonmedia.com; cjhunt3@gmail.com
Web site: http://www.PerfectHumanDiet.com; http://www.HuntThompsonMedia.com; www.CJHuntReports.com.

Hunter Hse. *Imprint of* **Turner Publishing Co.**

Hunter, J. H. Publishing, *(978-0-9718274)* 8100 Schmuck Rd., Evansville, IN 47712 USA Tel 812-985-5013.

Hunter, Julius K. *See* **J.K.H. Enterprises**

Hunter, Karen Media, *(978-0-9820221; 978-0-9845060)* P.O. Box 632, South Orange, NJ 07079 USA (SAN 857-0167)
Web site: http://www.karenhuntermedia.com; http://www.karenhuntermedia.com; www.readourbooks.com.

Hunter Pubns., *(978-0-9654185)* P.O. Box 433, Vallejo, CA 94589 USA Tel 707-645-8714; Fax: 707-644-7880.

Hunter Publishing, Inc., *(978-1-55650; 978-1-58843)* Orders Addr.: 222 Clematis St., West Palm Beach, FL 33401 USA Do not confuse with Hunter Publishing, Inc., Hobe Sound, FL
E-mail: comments@hunterpublishing.com
Web site: http://www.hunterpublishing.com
Dist(s): **Ebsco Publishing**
MyiLibrary
ebrary, Inc.

Hunter, Torrance, *(978-0-692-94807-1)* 1210 Concord Pl, MISSOURI CITY, TX 77459 USA Tel 713-435-9734
E-mail: torrancehunter1@gmail.com
Dist(s): **Independent Pub.**

HuntForMo Creations, *(978-0-9740182)* 3718 Brentford Rd., Randallstown, MD 21133 USA Toll Free: 800-327-9779
E-mail: monique@huntformo.com
Web site: http://www.huntformo.com.

Huntington Library Pr., *(978-0-87328)* Div. of Huntington Library, Art Collections & Botanical Gardens, 1151 Oxford Rd., San Marino, CA 91108 USA (SAN 202-313X) Tel 626-405-2172; Fax: 626-585-0794
E-mail: booksales@huntington.org
Web site: http://www.Huntington.org/HEHPubs.html
Dist(s): **Angel City Pr.**
California Princeton Fulfillment Services
D.A.P./Distributed Art Pubs.
Gibbs Smith, Publisher.

Huntington Library Publications *See* **Huntington Library Pr.**

Huntington Ludlow Media Group, *(978-0-9789057)* 5320 Maverick Dr., Grand Prairie, TX 75052-2617 USA (SAN 851-9080)
Web site: http://www.huntingtonludlow.com.

Huntley, Shannon, *(978-0-578-55297-2)* 1003 Creech Rd, Garner, NC 27529 USA Tel 919-637-6905
E-mail: brainbunts@gmail.com.

Huntly Hse., *(978-0-9885349; 978-0-615-73405-7)* 1965 Murcer Ln., Elgin, IL 60123 USA Tel 847-312-5904
E-mail: cfurtick@huntlyhouse.com
Web site: www.huntlyhouse.com.

Hunton, Carroll & Wenonah, *(978-0-9758873)* P.O. Box 1048, Albuquerque, NM 87103-1048 USA
E-mail: alan@excelstaff.com.

Huqua Pr., *(978-0-615-43791-0; 978-0-9838120; 978-0-9906966; 978-0-692-41669-3; 978-0-692-17579-8; 978-0-578-41353-2; 978-0-578-52073-5; 978-0-578-55090-9; 978-1-7353844)* 8730 Sunset Blvd., Los Angeles, CA 90069 USA Tel 818-981-5262
E-mail: judy@magpyemedia.com
Dist(s): **MyiLibrary**
Open Road Integrated Media, Inc.

Huron River Pr., *(978-1-932399)*
E-mail: info@huronriverpress.com
Web site: http://www.huronriverpress.com
Dist(s): **Partners Bk. Distributing, Inc.**

Hurst, Carol Consultants, *(978-0-9748509)* 41 Colony Dr., Westfield, MA 01085 USA Tel 413-562-3412
E-mail: carol@carolhurst.com
Web site: http://www.carolhurst.com
Dist(s): **Follett School Solutions.**

Huseby, Kirby, *(978-0-9778494)* P.O. Box 8034, Kentwood, MI 49518 USA
E-mail: staytoond@aol.com.

Husk, Braxton, *(978-0-578-18412-8)* 30 Bitterwoord Circle, The Woodlands, TX 77381 USA.

Huskies Pub *Imprint of* **Lulu Pr., Inc.**

Huskies Pub *Imprint of* **MacLaren-Cochrane Publishing, Inc.**

Husky Trail Pr. LLC, *(978-0-9722918; 978-1-935258)* Orders Addr.: P.O. Box 705, East Lyme, CT 06333-0705 USA Tel 860-739-7644; Fax: 860-739-3702
Web site: http://www.huskytrailpress.com.

Huss Publishing *See* **Huss, Sally Inc.**

Huss, Sally Inc., *(978-0-9822625; 978-0-692-31737-2; 978-0-692-33084-5; 978-0-692-33945-9; 978-0-692-34415-6; 978-0-692-34837-6; 978-0-692-35119-2; 978-0-692-35180-2; 978-0-692-35238-0; 978-0-692-35546-6; 978-0-692-36087-3; 978-0-692-36353-9; 978-0-692-36513-7; 978-0-692-36666-0; 978-0-692-38150-2; 978-0-692-38247-9; 978-0-692-38875-4; 978-0-692-39364-2; 978-0-692-39483-0; 978-0-692-39581-3; 978-0-692-39598-1; 978-0-692-39683-4; 978-0-692-39848-7; 978-0-692-40015-9; 978-0-692-40262-7; 978-0-692-40587-1; 978-) Orders Addr.: 10 El Sereno Dr., Colorado Springs, CO 80906 USA*
Dist(s): **CreateSpace Independent Publishing Platform.**

Hussl, Gloria, *(978-0-9791468)* 5818 Trinity Rd., Needville, TX 77461 USA Tel 832-595-5678
E-mail: gloriasunrisefarms@yahoo.com.

Hutchings, John Pubs., *(978-1-935014)* 621 Dogleg Ln., Bartlett, IL 60103 USA Tel 630-736-6088; *Imprints*: Lessons From The Vine (LFTV)
E-mail: kaththompson@att.net.

Hutchison, G.F. Pr., *(978-1-885631; 978-0-9796279)* 319 S. Block, Suite 17, Fayetteville, AR 72701-6484 USA Tel 479-587-1726; *Imprints*: Family Of Man Press, The (Family Of Man Pr)
E-mail: drwriterguy@netscape.net
Web site: http://www.thehappinessplace.com.

Hutman Productions, *(978-0-9702386; 978-0-9833573; 978-0-9854486; 978-1-7320830; 978-1-7352875)* P.O. Box 268, Linthicum, MD 21090 USA Tel 410-789-0930
E-mail: cbladey@mail.bcpl.net
Web site: http://www./cbladey.com/hutmanA.html.

Hutt, Sarah, *(978-0-9743417)* 1140 Washington St., No. 7, Boston, MA 02118 USA Tel 617-482-4722
Web site: http://www.mymotherslegacy.com.

Hutton Electronic Publishing, *(978-0-9742894; 978-0-9785171; 978-0-9888775)* 160 N. Compo Rd., Westport, CT 06880 USA
E-mail: huttonbooks@hotmail.com
Web site: http://www.huttonelectronicpublishing.com.

Huu, Andre, *(978-0-578-40283-3)* 4911 Harvest Chase Ln., Sugar Land, TX 77479 USA Tel 832-418-8860
E-mail: andrePT228@aol.com
Web site: www.golfroundofyourlife.com.

Huzon Fyrst Pr., *(978-0-9970483)* 19805 Shearwater Point Dr., Cornelius, NC 28031 USA Tel 704-892-8899
E-mail: wolfeskin@hotmail.com
Web site: www.149waystowipeyourass.com.

Hybrid Age Pr., *(978-1-7323192)* 34 Dodd St, Montclair, NJ 07042 USA Tel 862-220-1634
E-mail: tanejaarchitecture@gmail.com; info@hybridagepress.com
Web site: hybridagepress.com.

Hydra Productions Online LLC, *(978-1-951178)* 2500 E Pk. Blvd, Plano, TX 75074 USA Tel 214-298-3132
E-mail: hydraproductions2018@gmail.com.

Hydra Pubns., *(978-0-615-43242-7; 978-0-615-49378-7; 978-0-615-49820-1; 978-0-615-49950-5; 978-0-615-50445-2; 978-0-615-56017-5; 978-0-615-56345-9; 978-0-615-56584-2; 978-0-615-59650-1; 978-0-615-59651-8; 978-0-615-59822-2; 978-0-615-60737-5; 978-0-615-63328-2; 978-0-615-63783-9; 978-0-615-63858-4; 978-0-615-63863-8; 978-0-615-63882-9; 978-0-615-65016-6; 978-0-615-67766-8; 978-0-615-67970-9; 978-0-615-67972-3; 978-0-615-67974-7; 978-0-615-68018-7; 978-0-615-68422-2; 978-0-615-68969-2; 978-0-615-69010-0;) 337 Clifty Dr., Madison, IN 47250 USA Tel 812-574-4113*
Web site: http://www.hydrapublications.com
Dist(s): **CreateSpace Independent Publishing Platform**
Dummy Record Do Not USE!!!!.

Hydra Publishing *See* **Hylas Publishing**

Hydrangea Pr., *(978-0-9768418)* 22 Plumer Rd., Epping, NH 03042 USA Tel 603-679-9544
E-mail: mswegles@comcast.net
Web site: http://www.plumercrest.com.

Hylas Publishing, *(978-1-59258)* 129 Main St., Irvington, NY 10533 USA Fax: 914-591-3220
E-mail: hydrapublishing@mac.com
Dist(s): **St. Martin's Pr.**

Hyles Publications *See* **Grace to Grow Pubns.**

Hylton, Scott, *(978-0-615-97172-8)* 32215 Big Oak LN, Castaic, CA 91384 USA Tel 661-702-9972
E-mail: oneworldpeacenow@yahoo.com.

Hymns Ancient & Modern Ltd (GBR) *(978-0-334; 978-1-85311; 978-0-907547; 978-1-84825) Dist. by* **Westminster John Knox.**

†**Hyperion Bks. for Children**, *(978-0-7868; 978-1-56282)* Div. of Disney Bk. Publishing, Inc., A Walt Disney Co., Orders Addr.: 3 Center Plaza, Boston, MA 02108 USA Toll Free: 800-759-0190; Edit Addr.: 114 Fifth Ave., New York, NY 10011 USA Tel 212-633-4400; Fax: 212-633-4833; *Imprints*: Jump at the Sun (Jump at the Sun); Volo (Volo); di Capua, Michael Books (diCapua Bks)
Web site: http://www.disney.com; http://www.hyperionbooksforchildren.com
Dist(s): **Children's Plus, Inc.**
Disney Publishing Worldwide
Hachette Bk. Group
Little Brown & Co.; *CIP.*

†**Hyperion Paperbacks for Children**, *(978-0-7868; 978-1-56282)* Div. of Disney Bk. Publishing, Inc., A Walt Disney Co., 114 Fifth Ave., New York, NY 10011 USA Tel 212-633-4400; Fax: 212-633-4833
Web site: http://www.disney.com
Dist(s): **Hachette Bk. Group**
Little Brown & Co.; *CIP.*

†**Hyperion Pr.**, *(978-0-7868; 978-1-56282; 978-1-4013)* Div. of Disney Bk. Publishing, Inc., A Walt Disney Co., Orders Addr.: c/o HarperCollins Publishers, 1000 Keystone Industrial Park, Scranton, PA 18512-4621 USA Toll Free: 800-242-7737; Edit Addr.: 114 Fifth Ave., New York, NY 110011 USA Tel 917-661-2000
Web site: http://www.hyperionbooks.com
Dist(s): **Blackstone Audio, Inc.**
Children's Plus, Inc.
Follett School Solutions
Hachette Bk. Group
MyiLibrary; *CIP.*

hyperwerks *See* **Hyperwerks Entertainment**

Hyperwerks Entertainment, *(978-0-9770213)* 1830 Stoner Ave. Apt. 6, Los Angeles, CA 90025-7319 USA
Web site: http://www.hyperwerks.com.

HyphenatedPr., *(978-0-615-75998-2)* 6737 Roosevelt Dr, Sylvania, OH 43560 USA Tel 419-340-4654
E-mail: chadmichaelsimon@gmail.com.

i ZGOOL Media, *(978-0-9885898)* 100 Andover Pk. W Suite 150-237, Tukwila, WA 98188 USA Tel 206-851-1065
E-mail: fredbc11@gmail.com.

I AM Foundation, The, *(978-0-9645224; 978-0-9831780; 978-0-615-70944-4)* 7825 Fay Ave., Suite 200, La Jolla, CA 92037 USA Tel 619-297-7010
E-mail: iam@iamfoundation.org
Web site: http://www.iamfoundation.org
Dist(s): **CreateSpace Independent Publishing Platform**
DeVorss & Co.
New Leaf Distributing Co., Inc.

I Am My Life Publishing, LLC, *(978-0-9973805)* 611 Pennsylvania Ave., SE No. 120, Washington, DC 20003 USA Tel 720-252-9578; *Imprints*: Kaleidoscope Books (KaleidoscopebKS)
E-mail: rachelfosterstuart@gmail.com.

I AM Publishing, *(978-0-9905276)* 2370 Hwy 89A No. 11, Sedona, AZ 86336 USA Tel 805-729-0515
E-mail: danielposney@gmail.com
Web site: www.OneWhiteStone.com.

I Am Your Playground LLC, *(978-0-9769580)* P.O. Box 301, Fanwood, NJ 07023-0301 USA Fax: 908-301-0777; Toll Free: 888-759-4736 (888-PLY-GRND)
E-mail: john@iamyourplayground.com
Web site: http://www.iamyourplayground.com.

I & L Publishing, *(978-0-9661244; 978-1-930002)* 174 Oak Dr. Pkwy., Oroville, CA 95966 USA Tel 530-589-5048; Fax: 530-589-3551; Toll Free: 888-443-4722
E-mail: iolamoore@juno.com
Dist(s): **Morris Publishing.**

i. b. d., Ltd., *(978-0-88431)* 24 Hudson St., Kinderhook, NY 12106 USA (SAN 630-7779) Tel 518-758-1755; Fax: 518-758-6702
E-mail: lankhof@ibdltd.com
Web site: http://www.ibdltd.com.

IBE, Inc., *(978-0-916547; 978-0-9785848)* Div. of Inspiration Bks. East, Inc., Orders Addr.: P.O. Box 352, Jemison, AL 35085 USA (SAN 295-4672) Tel 205-646-2941; Edit Addr.: 170 Cty. Rd. 749, Jemison, AL 35085 USA
E-mail: communications@inbookseast.org
Web site: http://www.inbookseast.org.

I. B. Hoofinit Co., *(978-1-928890)* Orders Addr.: 94 Rte. 130, Forestdale, MA 02644 USA
E-mail: ibhoofinit@yahoo.com
Web site: http://ibhoofinit.com.

I. B. Tauris & Co., Ltd. (GBR) *(978-0-302; 978-0-85667; 978-1-85043; 978-1-86064; 978-1-84511; 978-1-84885; 978-1-78076; 978-0-85773; 978-1-78453; 978-0-85772; 978-0-85771; 978-1-78130; 978-1-78672; 978-1-78673; 978-1-78831) Dist. by* **Macmillan.**

I C A, *(978-0-9747506)* P.O. Box 910, Wayne, MI 48184-9998 USA Fax: 734-595-1869
E-mail: codemanray@aol.com
Web site: http://www.thefemalecode.com.

I C Legacy LLC, *(978-1-7320698)* 18 First Ave, Westbury, NY 11590 USA Tel 646-883-5393
E-mail: creations@iclegacy.com
Web site: www.iclegacy.com.

I Can Do All Things Productions, *(978-0-9745787)* 8 Loveland St., Madison, NJ 07940 USA Tel 973-377-5970; Fax: 973-377-5970
E-mail: seucony@optonline.net
Web site: http://www.perfectpraisebooks.com.

I E E E * Standards *See* **IEEE**

I F V, Inc., *(978-1-931861)* 1045 Coddington Rd., Ithaca, NY 14850 USA
E-mail: ifv@lightlink.com
Web site: http://www.classicalfencing.com.

I Follow the Leader, LLC, *(978-1-7321045)* 2001 Windcliff Dr., Marietta, GA 30067 USA Tel 404-324-6310
E-mail: thegreenfamilybooks@gmail.com
Web site: thegreenfamilybooks.com.

I Global, *(978-0-692-29250-1; 978-0-692-32768-5; 978-0-692-32769-2; 978-0-692-32770-8; 978-0-692-32771-5; 978-0-692-32772-2; 978-0-692-32774-6; 978-0-692-32775-3)* 400 Shelton St., Greensboro, NC 27405 USA Tel 3105703425.

I Have A Voice Enterprises, *(978-0-9746192)* P.O. Box 83, Peshtigo, WI 54157 USA
Web site: http://www.thehidersstory.com.

I Play Math Games *See* **IPMG Publishing**

I S H K, *(978-0-86304; 978-0-900860; 978-1-883536; 978-1-933779; 978-1-942698; 978-1-944493; 978-1-946270; 978-1-949013; 978-1-949358; 978-1-953292)* Div. of Institute for the Study of Human Knowledge, Orders Addr.: P.O. Box 400541, Cambridge, MA 02140 USA (SAN 226-4536) Tel 617-497-4124; Fax: 617-500-0268; Toll Free Fax: 800-223-4200; Toll Free: 800-222-4745; Edit Addr.: Ishk-hoopoe 171 Main St. #140, Los Altos, CA 94022 USA Tel 650-948-9428; *Imprints*: Malor Books (Malor Bks); Hoopoe Books (Hoopoe Books)
E-mail: ishkbooks@aol.com; ishkadm@aol.com
Web site: http://www.ishk.net; http://www.hoopoebooks.com.

I S M Teaching Systems, Inc., *(978-1-56775)* 14132 Desert Willow, El Paso, TX 79938 USA Tel 915-856-6365; Fax: 915-856-6367; Toll Free: 800-453-4476
E-mail: Email4ism@aol.com
Web site: http://www16.inetba.com/ismteachingsystemsinc.

I S R P Press *See* **Sound Reading Solutions**

I Save A Tree, *(978-0-9714299; 978-0-9744670; 978-0-9745659; 978-1-61015)* Orders Addr.: P.O. Box 3006, Arcadia, FL 34265 USA
Web site: http://www.garrettbooks.com; http://www.isaveatree.com.

I See Puppy, LLP, *(978-0-9774277)* Orders Addr.: 107 Richard Mine Rd., Dover, NJ 07801 USA (SAN 257-554X) Tel 973-361-8637; Fax: 973-361-8035
E-mail: info@iseepuppy.com
Web site: http://www.iseepuppy.com.

I WANNA BEE DESIGNS, *(978-0-9986664)* 2117 Markland Dr., Chesapeake, VA 23325 USA Tel 757-424-1357
E-mail: maadukes@yahoo.com.

i wantz Publishing, *(978-0-9727998)* P.O. Box 9305, Grand Rapids, MI 49509-0305 USA
E-mail: elizabeth@iwantz.com
Web site: http://www.iwantz.com.

i-5 Publishing LLC, *(978-0-87714; 978-0-944875; 978-0-9629525; 978-1-882770; 978-1-889540; 978-1-931993; 978-1-59378; 978-0-9745407; 978-1-933342; 978-1-933958; 978-1-935484; 978-1-937049; 978-1-62008; 978-1-62187)* 10 Bridge St., Bldg. C, Metuchen, NJ 08840 USA Tel 949-855-8822 (ext. 1003); Fax: 732-960-3107
Dist(s): **MyiLibrary**
Two Rivers Distribution.

IAC Publishing, *(978-0-9748383)* 3432 Denny St., No. 3, Pittsburgh, PA 15201 USA Toll Free: 877-592-0237
Web site: http://www.irishamericancatholic.com.

Iaconi, Mariuccia Bk. Imports, *(978-0-9628720)* P.O. Box 77023, San Francisco, CA 94107-0023 USA (SAN 161-1364) Toll Free: 800-955-9577
E-mail: mibibook@ixnetcom.com
Web site: http://www.mibibook.com
Dist(s): **Lectorum Pubns., Inc.**

IAHunt, *(978-0-9986851)* 7102 Capitol View Dr., McLean, VA 22101 USA Tel 703-893-0809
E-mail: iah2nd@aol.com.

IamCoach.com Publishing, *(978-0-9754761)* P.O. Box 60088, King of Prussia, PA 19406 USA
E-mail: publishing@iamcoach.com
Web site: http://www.IamCoach.com/chess/publishing/
Dist(s): **SCB Distributors.**

IAMPress, *(978-0-9768782; 978-0-9794839)* 3053 Dumbarton Rd., Memphis, TN 38128 USA Tel 901-358-2226; Fax: 901-358-8102
E-mail: renford@iam-cor.org
Web site: http://www.iam-cor.org
Dist(s): **Lulu Pr., Inc.**

IAMSA Creations, LLC *See* **Unlimited Possibilities Publishing, LLC**

Iberian Press *See* **7 Robots, Inc.**

Ibex Pubs., Inc., *(978-0-936347; 978-1-58814)* Orders Addr.: P.O. Box 30087, Bethesda, MD 20824 USA (SAN 696-866X) Tel 301-718-8188; Fax: 301-907-8707; Toll Free: 888-718-8188
E-mail: info@ibexpub.com
Web site: http://www.ibexpublishers.com.

IBJ Custom Publishing, *(978-0-9745673; 978-0-9776675; 978-0-9798830; 978-1-934922; 978-1-939550; 978-1-950143)* 41 E. Washington St., Suite 200, Indianapolis, IN 46204 USA.

IBJ Media Custom Publishing *See* **IBJ Custom Publishing**

IBks., Inc.,
Dist(s): **National Bk. Network.**

ibooks, Inc., *(978-0-671; 978-0-7434; 978-1-58824; 978-1-59176; 978-1-59687; 978-1-59687-543-2)* 100 Jericho Quadrangle. Ste. 300, Jericho, NY 11753-2702 USA; *Imprints:* Milk & Cookies (Milk-Cookie); ipicturebooks (Ipicbks)
Web site: http://www.ibooksinc.com.

ibooks, Incorporated/ipictures.com *See* **ibooks, Inc.**

ibukku, LLC, *(978-0-9896324; 978-0-9862586; 978-0-9965541; 978-1-944278; 978-1-946035; 978-1-64086)* 3723 Haven Ave. Suite 109, Menlo Park, CA 94025 USA Tel 650-204-1962
E-mail: luiscrowe@gmail.com; ljcrowe@ibukku.com
Web site: https://ibukku.com.

I C Creative, Inc., *(978-0-9742714)* 2300 Michigan Ct., Suite B, Arlington, TX 76016 USA Tel 817-459-8079; Fax: 817-460-0430
E-mail: joi@stayintouchmail.com
Web site: http://www.stayintouchmail.com.

ICAN Press *See* **Black Forest Pr.**

ICanPublish, *(978-0-9711480)* Div. of Heckman Bindery, Inc., P.O. Box 89, North Manchester, IN 46962 USA (SAN 253-9500) Tel 260-982-2107; Fax: 260-982-1130; Toll Free: 800-334-3628
E-mail: dave_mcintyre@heckmanbindery.com.

Ice Age Park and Trail Foundation, Inc., *(978-0-9627079)* 2453 Atwood Ave. STOP 4, Madison, WI 53704-5682 USA
E-mail: iat@iceagetrail.org
Web site: http://www.iceagetrail.org.

Ice Cube Pr., LLC, *(978-1-888160; 978-1-948509)* 205 N. Front St., North Liberty, IA 52317 USA (SAN 298-9085) Tel 319-626-2055; 319-594-6022
E-mail: steve@icecubepress.com
Web site: http://www.icecubepress.com
Dist(s): **Quality Bks., Inc.**

Ice Mountain Publishing, *(978-0-9748814)* P.O. Box 1418, Salida, CO 81201 USA
E-mail: nathanward@amigo.net.

Ice Wine Productions, Inc., *(978-0-9981666)* 4415 N Bayview Rd., Southold, NY 11971 USA Tel 631-765-8287
E-mail: writegw@gmail.com
Web site: www.geoffreywellsfiction.com.

Icecat Bks., *(978-0-9764308; 978-0-9768670)* 1243 Old Canyon Dr., Hacienda Heights, CA 91745 USA Tel 626-333-2430
E-mail: contact@icecatbooks.com
Web site: http://www.icecatbooks.com.

Ichabod Ink, *(978-0-9766641)* 418 Lake George Cir., West Chester, PA 19382 USA.

iCharacter.org, *(978-1-62387; 978-1-63474)* Orders Addr.: 6-9 Trinity St., Dublin, 2 IRL; *Imprints:* Kidible (Kidible)
E-mail: info@icharacter.org
Web site: www.icharacter.org.

Icicle Falls Publishing Co., *(978-0-9749360)* Orders Addr.: HC 31, Box 5118A, Wasilla, AK 99654 USA; Edit Addr.: Hc31 B0x 5118a, Wasilla, AK 99654 USA
Web site: www.alaskanstoires.com
Dist(s): **American News Company.**

Icon Group International, Inc., *(978-0-7576; 978-0-7418; 978-0-597; 978-0-497; 978-0-546; 978-1-114)* Div. of Icon Group, Ltd., P.O. Box 27740, Las Vegas, NV 89126-7440 USA (SAN 299-8122) Tel 858-635-9410; Fax: 858-635-9414
E-mail: ula@icongroupbooks.com; meta@icongroupbooks.com; orders@icongroupbooks.com
Web site: http://www.icongrouponline.com
Dist(s): **CreateSpace Independent Publishing Platform**
Ebsco Publishing
MyiLibrary.

Icon Language Systems, Inc. *See* **Ampersand, Inc.**

Idaho State Journal, *(978-0-9749865; 978-0-615-47497-7)* Orders Addr.: P.O. Box 431, Pocatello, ID 83204 USA; Edit Addr.: P.O. Box 431, Pocatello, ID 83204-0431 USA
Web site: http://www.journalnet.com.

Idea & Design Works, LLC, *(978-0-9712282; 978-0-9719775; 978-1-932382; 978-1-933239; 978-1-60010; 978-1-61377; 978-1-62302; 978-1-63140; 978-1-68405; 978-1-68406; 978-1-64936)* 2765 Truxtun Rd., San Diego, CA 92106 USA (SAN 255-1926) Tel 858-270-1315; Fax: 858-270-1308; 5080 Santa Fe St., San Diego, CA 92109-1609; *Imprints:* Worthwhile Books (Worthwhile Bks)
E-mail: chris@idwpublishing.com
Web site: http://www.idwpublishing.com/
Dist(s): **Chicago Distribution Ctr.**
Children's Plus, Inc.
Diamond Comic Distributors, Inc.
Diamond Bk. Distributors
L P C Group
MyiLibrary
Open Road Integrated Media, Inc.
Penguin Random Hse. Distribution
Penguin Random Hse. LLC
Random Hse., Inc.

Idea, Inc., *(978-0-9701566)* 403 5th Pl NW, Austin, MN 55912-3051 USA Toll Free: 800-828-1231 (phone/fax)
E-mail: Idea_inc@smig.net
Web site: http://www.ccjournal.com.

Idea Network LA Inc., *(978-0-9773301)* 201 S. Santa Fe Ave. No. 105, Los Angeles, CA 90012 USA Tel 213-613-1252; Fax: 213-613-1440.

Ideal Pubns. *Imprint of* **Worthy Publishing**

IdeaList Enterprises, Inc., *(978-0-9758794)* P.O. Box 1967, Evanston, IL 60204 USA.

IdeaStormPress, *(978-0-9820686; 978-1-945313)* 296 Hanbury Dr., Lake Zurich, IL 60047 USA
Web site: http://www.ideastormpress.com.

Ideate Prairie, *(978-0-9762564)* P.O. Box 65, Genoa, IL 60135 USA Tel 815-986-6577; *Imprints:* American Dog (Am Dog)
E-mail: cpierce@ideate-prairie.com
Web site: http://www.americandogtales.com; http://www.ideate-prairie.com.

Identity Pr., *(978-0-9753482)* P.O. Box 46224, Cincinnati, OH 45246-0224 USA Tel 513-313-5907 Do not confuse with companies with the same or similar name in Fountain Valley, CA, Cambridge, MA
E-mail: discovteenesteem@aol.com.

Idle Winter Pr., *(978-0-615-75103-0; 978-0-615-75329-4; 978-0-615-75375-1; 978-0-615-75790-2; 978-0-615-89153-8; 978-0-692-36927-2; 978-0-692-37191-6; 978-0-692-37441-2; 978-0-692-37871-7; 978-0-692-37934-9; 978-0-692-37993-6; 978-0-692-38122-9; 978-0-692-38502-9; 978-0-692-41873-4; 978-0-692-41874-1; 978-0-692-45244-8; 978-0-692-55074-8; 978-0-692-68244-9; 978-1-945687) 4525 SE 61st Ave., Portland, OR 97206 USA Tel 503-772-1214*
Web site: http://IdleWinter.com
Dist(s): **CreateSpace Independent Publishing Platform.**

Idlehour Entertainment, *(978-0-9778063)* P.O. Box 12048, Glendale, AZ 85318 USA (SAN 850-3001) Tel 623-780-1434; Fax: 623-780-1438
Web site: http://www.idlehourentertainment.com.

Idyllworks, LLC, *(978-0-9794647)* 2904 Rippling Brook Ln., Dickinson, TX 77539-6199 USA
Web site: http://www.JamboNation.com.

†IEEE, *(978-0-7803; 978-0-87942; 978-1-55937; 978-0-7381; 978-1-4244; 978-1-61284; 978-1-4577; 978-1-4673; 978-1-62195; 978-1-4799; 978-1-5044; 978-1-5090; 978-1-5386; 978-1-7281; 978-1-6654)* Orders Addr.: P.O. Box 1331, Piscataway, NJ 08855-1331 USA (SAN 250-6130) Tel 732-981-0060; Fax: 732-981-0027; Toll Free: 800-701-4333; Edit Addr.: 445 Hoes Ln., Piscataway, NJ 08855-1331 USA Tel 732-981-0060; 732-981-5300; 732-562-3828; 800-678-4333; 732-562-3966; Fax: 732-981-1769; 732-562-1746; 732-562-1971
E-mail: confpubs@ieee.org; customer-service@ieee.org
Web site: http://www.ieee.org
Dist(s): **Curran Assocs., Inc.**
MyiLibrary
Oxford Univ. Pr., Inc.
Wiley, John & Sons, Inc.; *CIP.*

IEP Resources *Imprint of* **Attainment Co., Inc.**

iFAM Publishing, LLC, *(978-0-9861924)* 3035 SE Maricamp Rd. Ste 104-222, Ocala, FL 34471 USA
E-mail: ifam.publishing@gmail.com.

IFLY Bks., *(978-0-9758888)* P.O. Box 894134, Temecula, CA 92589 USA.

I.Form Ink, Publishing, *(978-0-9763274)* Div. of Insu-Form, Inc., 41921 Beacon Hill, Suite A, Palm Desert, CA 92211 USA Tel 760-779-0657; Fax: 760-779-5143
E-mail: john@hackergroup.org.

IFWG Publishing (AUS) *(978-0-646-56641-2; 978-0-646-59588-7; 978-0-9923020; 978-0-9923654; 978-1-925148; 978-0-9945229; 978-1-925496; 978-1-925759; 978-1-925956) Dist. by* **IPG Chicago.**

IFWG Publishing Inc., *(978-0-9843298; 978-0-615-50936-5; 978-0-615-51846-6; 978-0-615-52105-3; 978-0-615-55249-1; 978-0-615-55424-2; 978-0-615-55642-0; 978-0-615-56093-9; 978-0-615-56121-9)* 302 Horseshoe Ln., Rockaway Beach, MO 65740 USA (SAN 859-0842) Toll Free: 800-337-3038
E-mail: ifwg-publishing@live.com; r.a.knowlton@ifwgpublishing.com
Web site: http://ifwgpublishing.weebly.com/index.html
Dist(s): **CreateSpace Independent Publishing Platform.**

Ig Publishing *See* **Ig Publishing, Inc.**

Ig Publishing, Inc., *(978-0-9703125; 978-0-9752517; 978-0-9771972; 978-0-9788431; 978-0-9815040; 978-1-935439; 978-1-939601; 978-1-63246)* 260 ACADEMY St., South Orange, NJ 07079 USA (SAN 254-0444)
Web site: http://www.igpub.com
Dist(s): **Children's Plus, Inc.**
Consortium Bk. Sales & Distribution
SPD-Small Pr. Distribution
ebrary, Inc.

IGC Japan Ltd., *(978-0-578-42441-5)* 279 E. 52nd St., San Bernardino, CA 92404 USA Tel 909-883-0299
E-mail: lance@igcjapan.com
Dist(s): **Independent Pub.**

IGI Pr., *(978-0-9709443; 978-0-9777121; 978-0-9799963; 978-0-9820870; 978-0-9825503; 978-0-9829273)* 241 First Ave. N., Minneapolis, MN 55401 USA (SAN 854-1876) Tel 612-338-8973 Toll Free: 888-805-8973
E-mail: igi@igipublishing.com
Web site: http://www.igipublishing.com.

IGlobal Educational Services, *(978-0-9882271; 978-1-944346)* 1000 Heritage Ctr. Cir., Round Rock, TX 78664 USA Tel 800-427-8422
E-mail: iglobal.educational@gmail.com.

Igloo Bks. (GBR) *(978-1-84561; 978-1-84817; 978-1-84852; 978-0-85734; 978-0-85780; 978-1-78197; 978-1-78343; 978-1-78440; 978-1-78557; 978-1-78670; 978-1-78810) Dist. by* **S and S Inc.**

IGMI Publishing, *(978-0-9655933)* Div. of PrissyH, P.O. Box 1735, Las Vegas, NM 87745-9602 USA Tel 505-425-9292
E-mail: favplagget@aol.com.

Ignatius Pr., *(978-0-89870; 978-1-58617; 978-1-62164; 978-1-68149; 978-1-64229)* Orders Addr.: P.O. Box 1339, Fort Collins, CO 80522-1339 USA (SAN 855-3556) Tel 970-221-3920; Fax: 970-221-3964; Toll Free Fax: 800-278-3566; Toll Free: 877-320-9276 (bookstore orders); 800-651-1531 (credit card orders, no minimum, individual orders); 1915 Astor Rd. Sycamore, Sycamore, IL 60178 (SAN 991-4595); Edit Addr.: 1348 10th Ave., San Francisco, CA 94122 USA (SAN 214-3887) Toll Free: 800-651-1531
E-mail: info@ignatius.com
Web site: http://www.ignatius.com
Dist(s): **Follett School Solutions**
Independent Pubs. Group
Midpoint Trade Bks., Inc.
Spring Arbor Distributors, Inc.

Ignite! Learning, *(978-0-9791935; 978-0-9798418; 978-1-934763; 978-1-937822)* 2905 San Gabriel Suite 212, Austin, TX 78705 USA Tel 512-697-7000; Fax: 512-697-7001; Toll Free: 866-464-4648
E-mail: support@ignitelearning.com; jbohls@ignitelearning.com
Web site: http://www.ignitelearning.com.

Ignite Reality, *(978-0-9776771; 978-0-9816258)* P.O. Box 1804, Burlingame, CA 94011-1804 USA (SAN 856-0781)
E-mail: drjenniferleigh@gmail.com
Web site: http://www.drjenniferaustinleigh.com.

Ignition Pr. *Imprint of* **Publishing Services @ Thomson-Shore**

igou, asia, *(978-0-692-67491-8; 978-0-692-75292-0)* 317 Riblett Ln., Wilmington, DE 19808 USA Tel 302-332-7564.

IGR Limited *See* **EKADOO Publishing Group**

Iguana Adventures Publishing *See* **Publish To Go Pubns.**

I.H.S. Pubs., *(978-0-9847656)* 3920 S. Old Hwy. 94 Suite 33, St. Charles, MO 63304 USA Tel 636-447-6000.

II, Paul Duane Rhodeman, *(978-0-578-44805-3)* 2445 Wedgwood Dr. W., Florissant, MO 63033 USA Tel 314-225-8922
E-mail: pdrhodemanii@gmail.com
Dist(s): **Ingram Content Group.**

IIEI Pr., *(978-0-9773098; 978-0-9797244; 978-0-615-52608-9)* 11225 N. 28th Dr., Suite B-201, Phoenix, AZ 85029 USA Tel 602-648-5750; Fax: 602-648-5755; Toll Free: 800-474-8013
E-mail: info@expandglobal.com
Web site: http://www.expandglobal.com/iiel-press/.

Ijiwola Pr., Gregory *Imprint of* **Summit Hse. Pubs.**

IJN Publishing, Inc., *(978-1-933894)* 724 NE. 4th St. #9, Hallandale, FL 33009 USA (SAN 850-4474) Fax: 954-457-2277; P.O. Box 630577, Miami, FL 33163
E-mail: gerald@ijnpublishing.com
Web site: http://www.whatliesbeneaththebed.com; http://www.ijnpublishing.com.

IJustWantToSleep, Inc., *(978-0-9744357)* 18 Timothy Ln., Candler, NC 28715 USA
E-mail: store@ijustwanttosleep.com; author@ijustwanttosleep.com
Web site: http://www.ijustwanttosleep.com.

IKIDS *Imprint of* **Innovative Kids**

il piccolo editions *Imprint of* **Fisher King Enterprises**

Ile Orunmila Communications, *(978-0-9644247; 978-0-9714949; 978-0-9825100)* Orders Addr.: P.O. Box 2326, San Bernardino, CA 92405 USA Tel 909-475-5851; Fax: 909-475-5850; Toll Free: 888-678-6645; Edit Addr.: 515 W. 21st St., San Bernardino, CA 92405 USA
E-mail: fsorunmila@aol.com
Web site: http://www.IleOrunmila.com
Dist(s): **Original Pubns.**

Ilui International *See* **Heartful Loving Pr.**

Illumify Media Group, *(978-0-9987896; 978-1-947360; 978-1-949021)* 6561 S. Simms Way, Littleton, CO 80127 USA Tel 303-523-4813
E-mail: mklassen@illumifymedia.com
Web site: www.illumifymedia.com
Dist(s): **Independent Pubs. Group**
Midpoint Trade Bks., Inc.

Illumina Publishing, *(978-0-9718600; 978-0-9818092)* P.O. Box 2643, Friday Harbor, WA 98250-2643 USA Tel 360-378-6047
E-mail: illumina@rockisland.com
Web site: http://www.illuminapublishing.com; http://www.illuminabookdesign.com.

Illuminate YA *Imprint of* **LPC**

Illumination Arts *See* **Inspire Every Child dba Illumination Arts**

Illumination Arts LLC, *(978-0-9829225; 978-0-9846874)* 6788 Lakeview Dr, FRAZIER PARK, CA 93225 USA Tel 617-472-1443; 661-289-5007; *Imprints:* Diamond Clear Vision (DiamondClear)
E-mail: thpjr52@aol.com
Web site: http://www.illuminationarts.us; http://www.diamondclearvision.com.

Illumination Arts Publishing Co., Inc., *(978-0-935699; 978-0-9701907; 978-0-9740190)* Orders Addr.: P.O. Box 1865, Bellevue, WA 98009 USA (SAN 696-2599) Tel 425-644-7185; Fax: 425-644-9274; Toll Free: 888-210-8216; Edit Addr.: 808 6th St S. Ste. 200, Kirkland, WA 98033-6768 USA
E-mail: liteinfo@illumin.com
Web site: http://www.illumin.com
Dist(s): **DeVorss & Co.**
Follett School Solutions
Koen Pacific
New Leaf Distributing Co., Inc.
Partners/West Book Distributors
Quality Bks., Inc.

Illumination Pubns., *(978-0-9789511)* 2802 Floore Ct., Louisville, KY 40299-1610 USA (SAN 852-0313) Tel 502-491-5664 Do not confuse with Illumination Publications in West Toluca lake, CA.

Illumination Studios, *(978-0-9741381)* 5924 Woodoak Dr., Dallas, TX 75249 USA
E-mail: contact@illuminationstudios.com
Web site: http://www.illuminationstudios.com.

Illusion Factory, The, *(978-0-9747331; 978-1-932949)* 21800 Burbank Blvd., Suite 225, Woodland Hills, CA 91367 USA (SAN 255-7096) Tel 818-598-8400; Fax: 818-598-8494
E-mail: ewong@illusionfactory.com
Web site: http://www.illusionfactory.com.

Illusionary Magic LLC, *(978-0-9834201)* 104 Donato Cir., Scotch Plains, NJ 07076 USA Tel 877-322-2723; Fax: 908-322-0421
E-mail: info@bradross.com
Web site: http://www.BradRoss.com.

Illustrate to Educate, *(978-0-9892732)* 2313 Quincy St. Apt. No. 2, Durham, NC 27703 USA Tel 919-908-1254
E-mail: everettar@hotmail.com.

Illustrated Bks. *Imprint of* **Jorge Pinto Bks.**

ILMHOUSE LLC, *(978-0-9726607)* P.O. Box 535, Unionville, PA 19375-0535 USA
Web site: http://www.thetruemarriage.com.

ILT Publishing, *(978-0-9774409)* Div. of Integrated Learning Technology, Inc., 1410 Steeplechase Rd., Downingtown, PA 19335 USA (SAN 257-4950) Tel 484-883-7107 (phone/fax)
E-mail: info@iltpublishing.com; rebejames@smartmail.com; presetco@iltpublishing.com
Web site: http://www.iltpublishing.com; http://www.tommilance.com; http://rebejames.com.

I.M. Enterprises, *(978-0-9777882)* P.O. Box 111, Rochester, MA 02770 USA (SAN 850-1645); *Imprints:* Light Works Publishing (Light Works)
E-mail: imenterprises@hotmail.com
Web site: http://www.imenterprises.org.

IM Pr., *(978-0-9654651; 978-0-9716911; 978-0-615-43634-0; 978-0-9857952)* Orders Addr.: P.O. Box 5346, Takoma Park, MD 20913-5346 USA Tel 301-587-1202; Edit Addr.: 7214 Cedar Ave., Takoma Park, MD 20912 USA Do not confuse with companies with the same name in Cincinnati, OH, Fairfax Station, VA
E-mail: efaine@yahoo.com
Web site: http://www.takoma.com/ned/home.htm
Dist(s): **Book Clearing Hse.**

Imaajinn This, *(978-0-9767342)* P.O. Box 294, West Haven, CT 06516 USA (SAN 256-484X) Tel 203-710-4906
Web site: http://www.robleyblake.com.

Image Cascade Publishing, *(978-0-9639607; 978-1-930009; 978-1-59511)* 420 Lexington Ave., Suite 300, New York, NY 10170 USA (SAN 253-2972) Tel 212-297-6240; Toll Free: 800-691-7779
E-mail: jc@imagecascade.com
Web site: http://www.imagecascade.com
Dist(s): **Baker & Taylor Publisher Services (BTPS).**

Image Comics, *(978-1-58240; 978-1-887279; 978-1-60706; 978-1-63215; 978-1-5343)* 2001 Center St., Berkeley, CA 94704 USA
E-mail: info@imagecomics.com
Web site: http://www.imagecomics.com/
Dist(s): **Diamond Comic Distributors, Inc.**
Diamond Bk. Distributors
L P C Group
Simon & Schuster, Inc.
Trucatriche.

Image Express Inc., *(978-0-9664634; 978-0-615-50572-5)* P.O. Box 66536, Austin, TX 78766 USA Tel 512-401-4900; Toll Free: 888-794-4300
Web site: http://greatday.com
Dist(s): **CreateSpace Independent Publishing Platform.**

Image Formation, *(978-0-9763440)* 23233 N. Pima, No. 113-102, Scottsdale, AZ 85255 USA
E-mail: lance@themummymountainstory.com
Web site: http://www.themummymountainstory.com.

Image Pr., Inc., *(978-1-891548)* Orders Addr.: P.O. Box 2407, Edmond, OK 73083-2407 USA Tel 405-844-6007; Fax: 405-348-5577; Edit Addr.: 247 N. Broadway, Suite 101, Edmond, OK 73034 USA.

Image Publishing, Ltd., *(978-0-911897)* Subs. of Roger Miller Photo, Ltd., 1411 Hollins St., Baltimore, MD 21223 USA (SAN 264-6781) Tel 410-566-1222; 410-233-1234; Fax: 410-233-1241 Do not confuse with companies with the same or similar names in Encino, CA, Wilton, CT
E-mail: rmpl.ipl@verizon.net
Web site: http://www.rogermillerphoto.com.

IMAGECRAFTERS, *(978-0-9773478)* Orders Addr.: 1644 Masters Ct., Naperville, IL 60563 USA (SAN 257-3709) Tel 630-355-1449
E-mail: imgcft@mc.net.

Imagery Pr., *(978-0-9754287)* P.O. Box 337, Carpinteria, CA 93014-0337 USA
E-mail: books@imagerypress.com.

Images & Pages, *(978-0-9788332)* P.O. Box 118120, Carrolton, TX 75007 USA
E-mail: deguzman@imagesandpages.com
Web site: http://imagesandpages.com.

Images Company *See* **Images SI Inc.**

Images For Presentation, *(978-0-9749531)* 176 Second St., Saint James, NY 11780 USA Tel 631-361-7908
E-mail: imagesforpres@aol.com.

Images from the Past, Inc., *(978-1-884592)* 155 W. Main St., P.O. Box 137, Bennington, VT 05201-0137 USA Tel 802-442-3204 (phone/fax); Toll Free: 888-442-3204
E-mail: info@ImagesfromthePast.com
Web site: http://www.ImagesfromthePast.com
Dist(s): **Ingram Publisher Services.**

Images Pr., *(978-1-891577)* 27920 Roble Alto St., Los Altos Hills, CA 94022 USA (SAN 299-4844) Tel 650-948-9251; 650-948-8251; Fax: 650-941-6114 Do not confuse with companies with the same name in San Leandro, CA, New York, NY
E-mail: bugsmom2@aol.com
Web site: http://www.images-press.com
Dist(s): **Quality Bks., Inc.**

Images SI Inc., *(978-0-9677017; 978-1-62385)* 109 Woods of Arden Rd., Staten Island, NY 10312 USA
E-mail: john.iovine@gmail.com; sales@imagesco.com; john.iovine@imagesco.com; melissa@imagesco.com
Web site: http://www.imagesco.com.

Images Unlimited Publishing, *(978-0-930643)* P.O. Box 305, Maryville, MO 64468 USA (SAN 242-0163) Tel 660-582-4279; *Imprints:* Snaptail Press (Snaptail Pr)
E-mail: images@cebridge.net; info@imagesunlimitedpub.com; Lee@imagesunlimitedpub.com
Web site: http://www.imagesunlimitedpub.com; http://www.snaptail.com; http://www.snaptailpress.com; http://www.imagesunlimitedpublishing.com; http://www.cookingandkids.com/blog; http://www.healthykidseatingtips.com; http://www.caringmomshealthykids.com
Dist(s): **Brodart Co.**
Follett School Solutions.

Imaginarium Pr., *(978-0-615-45112-1; 978-0-9978066; 978-1-7334752)* 254 W. 98th St. Apt.1E, New York, NY 10025 USA Tel 410-963-1854
E-mail: josephrbecker@gmail.com.

Imaginary Lines, Incorporated *See* **Sally Ride Science**

Imagination Arts Pubns., *(978-0-9746119)* P.O. Box 103, Mahwah, NJ 07430 USA Tel 201-529-5105; Fax: 201-529-5105
E-mail: imaginationarts@optonline.net
Web site: http://www.iapbooks.com.

Imagination Bk. Works, *(978-0-692-88301-3; 978-0-692-07550-0; 978-0-692-14913-3; 978-0-578-68300-3)* 10N164 Chapman Rd, hampshire, IL 60140 USA Tel 630-337-9019
Dist(s): **CreateSpace Independent Publishing Platform.**

Imagination Publishing-Orlando, *(978-0-9817123; 978-0-615-38566-2)* P.O. Box 802, Loughman, FL 33858 USA (SAN 856-3152)
E-mail: paul@HubbleRevealsCreation.com
Web site: http://www.TheSecretDoorway.com; http://www.HubbleRevealsCreation.com/
Dist(s): **BookBaby.**

Imagination Stage, Inc., *(978-0-9723729)* 4908 Auburn Ave., Bethesda, MD 20814 USA Tel 301-961-6060; Fax: 301-718-9526
E-mail: lagogliati@aol.com
Web site: http://www.imaginationstage.org.

Imagination Station Pr., *(978-0-9742575)* 4560 N. 25th Rd., Arlington, VA 22207-4147 USA Tel 703-528-5828
E-mail: epyatt1@comcast.net.

Imagination Workshop, The, *(978-0-9744437)* 4150 Abbott Ave., N., Minneapolis, MN 55422 USA
E-mail: imaginationworkshop@yahoo.com.

Imaginative Publishing, Ltd., *(978-0-9743335; 978-0-9767948)* P.O. Box 150008, Fort Worth, TX 76108 USA Tel 817-246-6436 (phone/fax); Toll Free: 877-246-6436 (phone/fax)
E-mail: publisher@imaginativepublishing.com
Web site: http://www.imaginativepublishing.com.

Imaginator Pr., *(978-0-9745603; 978-1-936917)* 6400 Baltimore National Pike Suite 170A-194, Baltimore, MD 21228-3915 USA
E-mail: sruth@ImaginatorPress.com
Web site: http://www.ImaginatorPress.com
Dist(s): **Beagle Bay Bks.**
Ingram Content Group.

Imagine Books *See* **Imagine! Studios**

Imagine Creatively *Imprint of* **Roseberg, Anders**

Imagine Publishing *Imprint of* **Charlesbridge Publishing, Inc.**

Imagine Publishing, *(978-0-9758899)* 7620 Dogleg Rd., Dayton, OH 45414 USA Fax: 937-890-7949
E-mail: skyblu40@earthlink.net.

Imagine! Studios, *(978-0-9761317; 978-0-9764353; 978-0-9767913; 978-1-937944)* PO Box 1362, Sarasota, FL 34230 USA Tel 941-999-1278
E-mail: contact@artsimage.com
Web site: http://www.artsimagine.com
Dist(s): **BookBaby.**

Imagine That Enterprises, *(978-0-9723067)* P.O. Box 29315, Saint Louis, MO 63126 USA
E-mail: underthedove@hotmail.com
Web site: http://www.underthedove.com.

Imagine the Possibilities, LLC *See* **Imagining Possibilities**

Imagineland, Ltd., *(978-0-9765038)* P.O. Box 10134, College Station, TX 77842-0134 USA
Web site: http://www.imagineland.com
Dist(s): **Smashwords.**

IMAGINEX, LLC, *(978-0-9753620)* P.O. Box 1375, Frisco, TX 75034 USA; *Imprints:* Bible Game (BibleGame)
Web site: http://www.imnex.net.

Imagining Possibilities, *(978-0-9747426)* P.O. Box 266, Gwynedd Valley, PA 19437-0266 USA.

Imago, *(978-0-9765179)* 14220 Duckett Rd., Brandywine, MD 20613-9343 USA Tel 856-812-0400; Toll Free Fax: 866-268-9003; Toll Free: 866-413-6864.

Imago Pr., *(978-0-9725303; 978-0-9799341; 978-1-935437; 978-0-9981791)* 3710 E. Edison St., Tucson, AZ 85716-2912 USA; *Imprints:* As Sabr Publications (AsSabr)
Web site: http://www.imagobooks.com; http://www.oasisjournal.org.

ImaJinn Bks. *Imprint of* **BelleBks., Inc.**

Imani Productions, *(978-0-615-14325-5)* 2261 Bernwood Dr., Erie, PA 16510 USA Tel 814-897-0502
E-mail: umemesababu@aol.com
Web site: http://www.imaniproductions.org.

Imani-MCHS, *(978-0-9729586)* 3445 W. 66th Pl., Chicago, IL 60629 USA Tel 773-925-6473
E-mail: imanimchs@aol.com.

I-Mar, *(978-0-9741052)* 5150 Rancho Rd., Huntingtn Bch, CA 92647-2074 USA
Web site: http://www.i-mar.net.

ImaRa Publishing, *(978-0-9843111)* Orders Addr.: 3002 230th Ln., SE, Sammamish, WA 98075 USA
E-mail: vrpearce@msn.com
Web site: http://www.imarapublishing.com.

ImBost Inc., *(978-0-9848626)* 158 E. 100 St. Ste 6R, New York, NY 10029 USA Tel 917-482-5178
E-mail: taekwontales@gmail.com.

Imbrifex Bks., *(978-0-9972369; 978-1-945501)* 8275 S. Eastern Ave., Las Vegas, NV 89123 USA Tel 702-320-4866
E-mail: mark@imbrifex.com
Dist(s): **Legato Pubs. Group**
Publishers Group West (PGW).

Imdalind Pr., *(978-0-9884837; 978-0-9914313; 978-0-9964632; 978-1-949725)* 6980 S. Boulder Dr., Cottonwood Heights, UT 84121 USA Tel 385-229-7434
E-mail: me@rebeccaethington.com.

Immediex Publishing, *(978-1-932968)* 540 Evelyn Pl., Beverly Hills, CA 90210 USA Tel 310-273-1585
E-mail: rodney@immediex.com
Web site: www.immediex.com
Dist(s): **Smashwords.**

Immedium, *(978-1-59702)* P.O. Box 31846, San Francisco, CA 94131 USA
Web site: http://www.immedium.com
Dist(s): **Consortium Bk. Sales & Distribution**
MyiLibrary.

Immortal Works LLC, *(978-0-692-78113-5; 978-0-692-83650-7; 978-0-692-88092-0; 978-0-9990205; 978-1-7324674; 978-1-7339085; 978-1-7343866; 978-1-7349046; 978-1-953491)* 1505 Glenrose Dr., SALT LAKE CITY, UT 84104 USA Tel 801-651-4024.

Immortality Pr., *(978-0-9795753)* 1005 Winthrope Chase Dr., Alpharetta, GA 30004 USA
E-mail: publisher@immortalitypress.com; order@immortalitypress.com
Web site: http://www.immortalitypress.com.

IMMPACT Communications *See* **Humble Heart Publishing**

Imogen Rose, *(978-0-615-34507-9; 978-0-615-37681-3; 978-0-9828002; 978-0-9850797; 978-0-9856766; 978-1-940015)* 18 Westwinds Dr., Princeton Junction, NJ 08550 USA
E-mail: portalchronicles@hotmail.com
Dist(s): **Lulu Pr., Inc.**
Smashwords.

IMPACT Books *Imprint of* **Penguin Publishing Group**

Impact Pubns., *(978-0-942710; 978-1-57023)* Div. of Development Concepts, Inc., 7820 Sudley Rd Ste 100, Manassas, VA 20109 USA (SAN 240-1142) Tel 703-361-7300; Fax: 703-335-9486 Do not confuse with companies with the same name in Evanston, IL, Mandeville, LA, Southfield, MI
E-mail: krannich@impactpublications.com
Web site: http://www.impactpublications.com
Dist(s): **Follett School Solutions**
MyiLibrary
National Bk. Network
ebrary, Inc.

Impact Publications, Incorporated *See* **Specialty Pr., Inc.**

Impact Pubs. *Imprint of* **New Harbinger Pubns.**

Impetus Pr., *(978-0-9776693)* P.O. Box 10025, Iowa City, IA 52240-0001 USA Tel 319-321-6282 Do not confuse with Impetus Press in Atlanta, GA
E-mail: jennifer@impetuspress.com
Web site: http://www.impetuspress.com
Dist(s): **SPD-Small Pr. Distribution.**

Important Publishing, 12759 NE Whitaker Way R993, Portland, OR 97230 USA Tel 971-247-4552
E-mail: tommy@sleekpublishers.com
Dist(s): **Ingram Content Group.**

Impossible Dreams Publishing Co., *(978-0-9786422)* 4123 Rancho Grande Pl., NW., Albuquerque, NM 87120 USA (SAN 851-139X)
E-mail: Quixote1818@aol.com
Web site: http://www.impossibledreamspub.com
Dist(s): **Baker & Taylor Publisher Services (BTPS).**

Impresa Bk. Group, *(978-0-9908713; 978-0-692-99307-1; 978-0-578-51460-4)* PO Box 5506, Somerset, NJ 08875 USA Tel 732-649-3604
E-mail: books@kamrynadams.com
Web site: www.kamrynadams.com/books.

Impressions By Veronica, *(978-0-692-80171-0)* .

Impressions Ink, *(978-1-882626)* 3918 Peachtree Ln., Memphis, TN 38135-9115 USA Tel 901-388-5382; Fax: 901-385-0256; Toll Free: 800-388-5382.

Imprexions Publishing Co., *(978-0-9742922)* 4398 Dunkeld Rd., Reno, NV 89519 USA
E-mail: listinsky@hotmail.com.

Imprint (IND) *(978-81-902436) Dist. by* **Macmillan.**

ImPrint, *(978-0-9850454)* 30-84 14th St. Apt. 6, Astoria, NY 11102 USA Tel 347-392-1280
E-mail: charlesm.fraser@hammerandcyclemessengerservice.com.

Imprint.li, *(978-0-9894891; 978-0-9897418)* 11015 122nd Ave. Kp N., Gig Harbor, WA 98329 USA Tel 253-853-4199
E-mail: carolyn@imprint.li
Web site: www.imprint.li.

Imprints, *(978-1-883986)* Div. of Spectrum Bks., Orders Addr.: P.O. Box 4365, Thousand Oaks, CA 91359 USA Tel 808-707-3336; Fax: 808-707-4446; Edit Addr.: 32151 Sailview Ln., Westlake Village, CA 91359 USA
Dist(s): **Continental Bk. Co., Inc.**

Impulse Surf, *(978-0-9744247)* Orders Addr.: 1106 Second St., PMB 823, Encinitas, CA 92024 USA Tel 760-431-6883; Fax: 760-436-7158; Edit Addr.: 7200 Ponto Dr., Carlsbad, CA 92009 USA
E-mail: franklinlives@yahoo.com
Web site: http://www.impulsesurf.com.

In A Bind Bks., *(978-0-9981182)* 1025 W Univ. Ave Apt 5, San Diego, CA 92103 USA Tel 619-665-4085
E-mail: emartin529@live.com
Web site: ErikCMartin.com.

In Ardua Tendit Pr., *(978-0-9749673)* 464 Leton Dr., Columbia, SC 29210 USA Tel 803-608-0804
E-mail: mail@jessmaccallum.com
Web site: http://www.jessmaccallum.com
Dist(s): **BookBaby.**

In Audio *Imprint of* **Sound Room Pubs., Inc.**

In Between Bks., *(978-0-935430; 978-0-9802007)* P.O. Box 790, Sausalito, CA 94966 USA (SAN 213-6236) Tel 415-383-8447; Fax: 415-381-1938; 415-381-3513
E-mail: inbetweenbooks@atthebutterflytree.com; karla@inbetweenbooks.com; juno@inbetweenbooks.com
Web site: http://www.atthebutterflytree.com.

In Cahoots, *(978-0-9745990)* 105 Los Padres Way, Unit 6, Buellton, CA 93427 USA Do not confuse with In Cahoots in Marietta, GA
Dist(s): **SPD-Small Pr. Distribution.**

In Cider Pr., *(978-0-9721716)* P.O. Box 228, Barton, VT 05822 USA Tel 802-754-8889.

In Easy Steps Ltd. (GBR) *(978-1-84078) Dist. by* **PerseuPGW.**

In Heels Publishing, *(978-0-578-15732-0; 978-0-692-80485-8; 978-0-9989264)* 17412 Ventura Blvd, No. 441, Encino, CA 91316 USA.

In Motion Books Incorporated *See* **Dakitab, Inc.**

In Our Words Inc., *(978-1-938040)* 6104 City Pl., Edgewater, NJ 07020 USA Tel 201-280-7399
E-mail: ahn.jaesuk@gmail.com.

In Search Of The Universal Truth (ISOTUT) *See* **DragonEye Publishing**

In the Desert, *(978-0-9744005)* 7990 E. Snyder Rd., No. 5106, Tucson, AZ 85750-9009 USA
Web site: http://www.inthedesert.biz.

In the Hands of a Child, *(978-1-60308)* Eclectically Me Niki, 3271 Kerlikowske Rd., Coloma, MI 49038-8913 USA
E-mail: sales@handsofachild.com
Web site: http://www.Handsofachild.com; http://www.eclecticallymeniki.com.

In The Hse. Publishing Co., *(978-0-9760441)* 1122 N. 84th St., Seattle, WA 98103 USA
E-mail: projectfile@hotmail.com
Web site: http://www.projectgirl.com.

In The Lead Publishing *See* **Lone Cypress Pubs.**

In the Sky Publishing, *(978-0-9740438)* Orders Addr.: 26300 Ford Rd., No. 407, Dearborn Heights, MI 48127 USA Tel 313-792-0694
E-mail: cmlipson@wideopenwest.com
Web site: http://www.intheskypublishing.com.

In the Think of Things *See* **Rainbow Resource Ctr., Inc.**

In the Think of Things *Imprint of* **Rainbow Resource Ctr., Inc.**

In This Together Media, *(978-0-9858956; 978-0-9898166)* 5 Evergreen Ln., Larchmont, NY 10538 USA Tel 914-833-1189
E-mail: calbertine@gmail.com
Web site: www.inthistogethermedia.com
Dist(s): **INscribe Digital.**

In Time Pubns., Inc., *(978-0-9762857)* P.O. Box 190537, Fort Lauderdale, FL 33319 USA
Web site: http://www.intimepublications.com.

In Your Heart Lives a Rainbow, *(978-0-9857824)* 25 Strauss Ave., Selden, NY 11784 USA Tel 516-483-1899
E-mail: kare4you2@yahoo.com.

Inane Blabbering Bks. (GBR) *(978-0-9559798) Dist. by* **LuluCom.**

Inanna Pubns. & Education, Inc. (CAN) *(978-0-9681290; 978-0-9736709; 978-0-9782233; 978-0-9808822; 978-1-926708; 978-1-77133) Dist. by* **SPD-Small Pr Dist.**

Incentive Pubns., Inc., *(978-0-86530; 978-0-913916; 978-1-62950)* 233 N. Michigan Ave., Suite 2000, Chicago, IL 60601 USA (SAN 203-8005) Toll Free: 800-421-2830
E-mail: info@incentivepublications.com
Web site: http://www.incentivepublications.com
Dist(s): **MyiLibrary**
ebrary, Inc.

Inch By Inch Pubns., LLC, *(978-0-9670941)* P.O. Box 15, Okemos, MI 48805 USA Tel 716-688-1515; Fax: 716-636-4058; Toll Free: 877-462-4967
E-mail: chofher@aol.com
Web site: http://www.inchbyinchbooks.com
Dist(s): **Partners Pubs. Group, Inc.**

Inclement Pr., *(978-0-9819736; 978-0-9886669)* P.O. Box 120, Sidney, IA 51652 USA.

INCLUDAS Publishing, *(978-0-9861927; 978-1-949983)* 32315 Corte Zamora, Temecula, CA 92592 USA Tel 951-795-6847
E-mail: luda.gogolushko@includas.com.

Inclusive Books LLC, *(978-0-9778143)* 3027 New Natchez Trace, Nashville, TN 37215 USA Tel 615-383-1065
E-mail: estelle@estellecondra.com
Web site: http://www.inclusivebooks.com.

Inclusive Global Inc., *(978-0-9759077)* P.O. Box 143, Newport, OH 45768 USA Tel 740-516-1143 (phone/fax)
E-mail: sparkeythespider@aol.com
Web site: http://www.inclusive.global; http://www.sparkeythespider.com; http://www.travisflores.org.

Incorgnito Publishing Pr. *Imprint of* **Market Management Group**

Incorporated Trustees of the Gospel Worker Society, The, *(978-0-9617506; 978-1-59843; 978-1-934981; 978-1-935338; 978-1-936272; 978-1-936897; 978-1-936898; 978-1-64495)* Div. of Union Gospel Pr., 1980 Brookpark Rd., Cleveland, OH 44109 USA (SAN 664-2845) Toll Free: 800-638-9988
Web site: http://www.uniongospelpress.com.

Incredible Kid, LLC, *(978-0-9755836)* 7095 Hollywood Blvd., Suite 461, Hollywood, CA 90028 USA.

Independence Books *See* **America Star Bks.**

Independent Media Institute *See* **AlterNet Bks.**

Independent Pub., *(978-1-4243; 978-1-59975; 978-1-60402; 978-1-60461; 978-1-60530; 978-1-60585; 978-1-60643; 978-1-60702; 978-1-60725; 978-1-60743; 978-1-61539; 978-1-61584; 978-1-61623; 978-1-61658; 978-1-4507; 978-1-4675; 978-1-4951; 978-0-9927847; 978-1-5323;-1-5323-0640-2; 978-1-7923) Div. of Bar Code Graphics, 875 N. Michigan Ave., Suite 2650, Chicago, IL 60615 USA Fax: 312-595-0725; Toll Free: 800-662-0701; 65 E. Wacker Pl., 18th Flr., Chicago, IL 60601 Tel 312-595-0600; Toll Free: 800-662-0703 Do not confuse with Independent Publishers in Bountiful, UT*
E-mail: pubserv@barcode-us.com
Web site: http://www.publisherservices-us.com; http://www.isbn-us.com
Dist(s): **Consortium Bk. Sales & Distribution**
D.A.P./Distributed Art Pubs.
Ebsco Publishing
Epicenter Pr., Inc.
Follett School Solutions
Greenleaf Book Group
Leonard, Hal Corp.
Hay Hse., Inc.
Independent Pubs. Group
Ingram Publisher Services
Lulu Pr., Inc.
Midpoint Trade Bks., Inc.
Outskirts Pr., Inc.
SCB Distributors
SPD-Small Pr. Distribution
Smashwords
TNT Media Group, Inc.
Univ. of Arkansas Pr.
eBookit.com
ebrary, Inc.

Independent Pub., *(978-1-62951; 978-1-63041; 978-1-63102; 978-1-63415; 978-1-943438; 978-1-943579; 978-1-943730; 978-1-943932; 978-1-944169; 978-1-944170; 978-1-944171; 978-1-944541; 978-1-944819; 978-1-944820; 978-1-945239; 978-1-945563; 978-1-63535; 978-1-947099) 427 California Ave Unit 1, Santa Monica, CA 90403 USA Tel 310-980-4668 Do not*

confuse with Independent Publisher in Chicago, IL, Pasadena, CA
E-mail: ahoohooahoo@yahoo.com
Dist(s): **Lulu Pr., Inc.**

Independent Publisher Services, *(978-1-4243; 978-0-692-73622-7)* Orders Addr.: 444 N. Michigan Ave., #3500, Chicago, IL 60611 USA Toll Free: 800-662-0701
E-mail: sales@barcode-us.com
Dist(s): **Follett School Solutions**
Islander Group
Miller Trade Bk. Marketing.

Independent Pubs. Group, *(978-1-4956)* Subs. of Chicago Review Pr., 814 N. Franklin, Chicago, IL 60610 USA (SAN 201-2936) Tel 312-337-0747; Fax: 312-337-5985; Toll Free: 800-888-4741
E-mail: frontdesk@ipgbook.com
Web site: http://www.ipgbook.com; http://www.trafalgarsquarepublishing.com.

Independent Spirit Publishing, *(978-0-9666919; 978-0-578-09203-4; 978-0-615-86951-3; 978-0-615-93315-3; 978-0-615-95976-4)* 15994 325th St., Goodhue, MN 55027 USA
Web site: http://www.nataliebuskethomas.com
Dist(s): **Lulu Pr., Inc.**

Independent Thinking Press *Imprint of* **Crown Hse. Publishing LLC**

Independently published *See* **Independently Published**

Independently Published, *(978-1-5190; 978-0-692-55139-4; 978-0-692-55141-7; 978-0-692-55142-4; 978-0-692-55143-1; 978-0-692-55144-8; 978-0-692-55146-2; 978-0-692-55147-9; 978-0-692-55149-3; 978-0-692-55150-9; 978-0-692-55151-6; 978-0-692-55153-0; 978-0-692-55155-4; 978-0-692-55156-1; 978-0-692-55157-8; 978-0-692-55158-5; 978-0-692-55159-2; 978-0-692-55160-8; 978-0-692-55161-5; 978-0-692-55162-2; 978-0-692-55163-9; 978-0-692-55164-6; 978-0-692-55165-3; 978-0-692-55166-0; 978-0-692-55167-7; 978-0-692-55168-4; 978-0-6) 4900 LaCross Rd, North Charleston, SC 29406 USA Tel 206-740-4926 Do not confuse with Independently Published in Maquoketa, IA*
E-mail: abstossn@createspace.com
Dist(s): **Amazon Digital Services Inc.**
Orca Bk. Pubs. USA.

INDI Best *Imprint of* **INDI, LLC**

INDI, LLC, *(978-0-9789247; 978-1-935636)* 15508 W. Bell Rd. Suite 101-315, Surprise, AZ 85374-3436 USA Tel 623-556-2751; Fax: 602-524-7550; *Imprints:* INDI Best (INDIBest)
E-mail: jerry@writersreaders.com
Web site: http://www.writersreaders.com
Dist(s): **BookBaby**
Smashwords.

INDI Publishing Group *See* **INDI, LLC**

Indian Hill Gallery of Fine Photography, *(978-0-9669079)* 671 River Rd., Wells, VT 05774 USA Tel 802-325-2274; Fax: 802-325-2276
E-mail: info@stephenschaub.com
Web site: http://www.indianhillgallery.com
Dist(s): **RAM Pubns. & Distribution.**

Indian Territory Publishing, *(978-0-9727068)* P.O. Box 43, Bennington, OK 74723-0043 USA
E-mail: wes@wesparker-itp.com; wes.parker@us.army.mil
Web site: http://www.wesparker-itp.com.

†Indiana Historical Society, *(978-0-87195)* 450 W. Ohio St., Indianapolis, IN 46202-3269 USA (SAN 201-5234) Tel 317-233-9557; 317-232-1882; Fax: 317-233-0857; Toll Free: 800-447-1830
E-mail: rvaught@indianahistory.org; cbennett@indianahistory.org
Web site: http://www.indianahistory.org
Dist(s): **Distributors, The**
Indiana Univ. Pr.; *CIP.*

†Indiana Univ. Pr., *(978-0-253; 978-0-86196)* 601 N. Morton St., Bloomington, IN 47404-3797 USA (SAN 202-5647) Fax: 812-855-7931; Toll Free: 800-842-6796; *Imprints:* Quarry Books (Quarry Books)
E-mail: iuporder@indiana.edu
Web site: http://www.iupress.indiana.edu
Dist(s): **Blackstone Audio, Inc.**
Ebsco Publishing
Ingram Publisher Services
Ingram Content Group
MyiLibrary
Open Road Integrated Media, Inc.
Transaction Pubs.
Two Rivers Distribution
ebrary, Inc.; *CIP.*

., Orders Addr.: 528 E. Lorain St., Oberlin, OH 44074-1298 USA (SAN 134-2118) Tel 440-775-7777; Toll Free Fax: 800-344-5059; Toll Free: 800-321-3883 (orders only); 800-458-9303 (backorder status only); 800-334-9882 (support programs/technical support); Whitlow Campus Store-indiCo 1 1550 Clarke Dr., DUBUQUE, IA 52001-3198 (SAN 990-560X)
E-mail: service@goindico.com; orders@goindico.com
Web site: http://www.nacscorp.com.

INDICOMM, *(978-0-578-43404-9; 978-1-7358536)* P.O. Box 714, Grayson, GA 30017 USA Tel 216-393-7973
E-mail: info.indicomm@gmail.com
Dist(s): **CreateSpace Independent Publishing Platform.**

Indie Artist Pr., *(978-1-62522)* Orders Addr.: 90 W 100 N No. 6, Price, UT 84501 USA; *Imprints:* Hugs Books (Hugs Bks)
Web site: http://www.indieartistpress.com
Dist(s): **Suite 3 Productions.**

Indie Publishing Group, *(978-0-692-43389-8; 978-1-988656)* 242 W dilcrest, Florence, KY 41042 USA Tel (859)3718242
Web site: JacobCartlidge.com
Dist(s): **CreateSpace Independent Publishing Platform.**

IndieArtz, Inc., *(978-0-9753252)* 1650 Margaret St., Suite 302-131, Jacksonville, FL 32204-3869 USA
Web site: http://www.indieartz.com.

IndieGo Publishing LLC *See* **INDIEGO PUBLISHING LLC**

INDIEGO PUBLISHING LLC, *(978-0-9846685; 978-0-9887048; 978-0-9916307; 978-0-9860953; 978-0-9976021; 978-1-946824)*
E-mail: indiegopublishing@gmail.com
Web site: http://www.indiegopublishing.com/; Http://www.designindiego.com.

Indigo Custom Publishing *See* **Sphinx Publishing**

Indigo Hse. Publishing, LLC, *(978-0-615-17978-0; 978-0-9820687; 978-1-951578)* 22018 N 33rd Pl., Phoenix, AZ 85050 USA
Web site: http://www.leiastone.com.

Indigo Impressions, *(978-0-9788339)* Orders Addr.: P.O. Box 501, Speonk, NY 11972-0501 USA
E-mail: meghanspd@yahoo.com
Dist(s): **BookBaby.**

Indigo, LLC, *(978-0-9758995)* 7486 North Shore Rd., Norfolk, VA 23505 USA Tel 757-622-3319
E-mail: lee@indigoart.net
Web site: http://www.indigoart.net
Dist(s): **Norfolk SPCA.**

Indigo Pubns., *(978-0-9646680)* Orders Addr.: 68-1030 Mauna Lani Point Dr., Kamuela, HI 96743 USA (SAN 298-9921) Tel 808-345-2001; 808-345-0805
E-mail: mel@malinowski.com; judy@malinowski.com
Web site: http://www.snorkelguides.com.

Indigo Sea Pr., LLC, *(978-1-935171; 978-1-938101; 978-1-63066)* 931-B S. Main St., Box 145, Kernersville, NC 27284 USA
E-mail: willhodam@yahoo.com; indigoseapress@gmail.com
Web site: http://secondwindpublishing.com/; http://indigoseapress.com
Dist(s): **Smashwords.**

Indigo Skye, *(978-0-9994924)* 1517 Mackenzie St., WASHINGTON, IL 61571 USA Tel 309-472-0565
E-mail: Indigo.Skye@comcast.net.

Individualized Education Systems/Poppy Lane Publishing, *(978-0-938911)* Orders Addr.: P.O. Box 5136, Fresno, CA 93755 USA (SAN 661-8405) Tel 559-299-4639; Edit Addr.: 134 Poppy Ln., Clovis, CA 93612 USA (SAN 661-8413)
E-mail: Bette1234@aol.com
Web site: http://www.poppylane.com
Dist(s): **American West Bks.**

IndoEuropeanPublishing.com, *(978-1-60444)* 4215 Vineland Ave., No. 17, Studio City, CA 91602 USA
E-mail: Alfredagha@gmail.com
Web site: http://IndoEuropeanPublishing.com.

Indomita Press, *(978-0-578-20983-8)* 17 Colby Ct., Sacramento, CA 95825 USA Tel 646-477-7810
E-mail: pjoshualaskey@hotmail.com
Web site: indomitapress.com.

Indulgence Pr., *(978-0-9742191)* 250 N. 3rd Ave. #224, Minneapolis, MN 55401 USA Tel 612-379-4743
Web site: http://www.indulgencepress.com.

Industrial Gingerbread, *(978-0-9860691)* 61-33 ALDERTON ST, REGO PARK, NY 11374 USA Tel 718-478-8537
E-mail: richard.a.west@jpmchase.com.

Indy Pub, *(978-1-0878; 978-1-0879; 978-1-0880; 978-1-0881; 978-1-0882; 978-0-578-64405-9; 978-0-578-64518-6; 978-0-578-64713-5; 978-0-578-66570-2; 978-0-578-67285-4; 978-0-578-70875-1; 978-0-578-70940-6; 978-0-578-72593-2; 978-0-578-75332-4; 978-0-578-75333-1; 978-0-578-75336-2; 978-0-578-75734-6; 978-0-578-76746-8; 978-0-578-77291-2) Ingram Content Group, One Ingram Blvd., LaVergne, TN 37086 USA.*

IndyPublish.com, *(978-1-58827; 978-1-4043; 978-1-4142; 978-1-4219; 978-1-4280; 978-1-4353; 978-1-4378; 978-1-4491)* 170 Gore St. Suite 405, Cambridge, MA 02141 USA
E-mail: info@indypublish.com
Dist(s): **Ingram Content Group**
TextStream.

InExTra LLC, *(978-1-946972)* 929 Lehigh Cir., Naperville, IL 60565 USA Tel 773-340-9259
E-mail: walz@inextra.biz.

Infant Learning Co., The, *(978-0-9657510; 978-1-931026)* 5009 Isle Royal Ct., Oceanside, CA 92057 USA Tel 760-630-6204; Fax: 760-630-3894; Toll Free: 888-463-2681
E-mail: brendan@infantlearning.com; lisa@infantlearning.com
Web site: http://www.infantlearning.com; http://www.yourbabycanread.com
Dist(s): **Penton Overseas, Inc.**

Infini Pr., LLC, *(978-1-932457)* Orders Addr.: P.O. Box 9096, Cincinnati, OH 45209-9096 USA Toll Free: 800-765-5885; Edit Addr.: 1120 Ave. of the Americas, Fourth Flr., New York, NY 10036 USA; *Imprints:* Asia for Kids (Asia for Kids)
E-mail: info@infinipress.com
Web site: http://www.infinipress.com
Dist(s): **Follett School Solutions**
Master Communications, Inc.

Infinite Adventure, *(978-0-9790720)* 6043 S. Danielson Way, Chandler, AZ 85249 USA
E-mail: amb0457@cox.net
Web site: http://www.members.cox.net/valuevolga.

Infinite Light Publishing, *(978-0-9884537; 978-0-9970467; 978-1-947925)* 5142 Hollister Ave. No. 115, Santa Barbara, CA 93111 USA Tel 805-350-3239
E-mail: ayn@infinitelightpublishing.com; info@infinitelightpublishing.com; aynsgold@yahoo.com
Web site: www.ayncatessullivan.com; www.astoryofbecoming.net; www.infinitelightpublishing.com
Dist(s): **BCH Fulfillment & Distribution**
New Leaf Distributing Co., Inc.

Infinite Love Publishing, *(978-0-9794827)* 15127 NE 24th St., No. 341, Redmond, WA 98052 USA (SAN 853-5264) Toll Free: 888-733-7105
E-mail: sales@jackiechristie.com; dotti@dotdesign.net
Web site: http://www.jackiechristie.com.

Infinite Visions Forum, *(978-0-9770405)* Orders Addr.: P.O. Box 938, La Verne, CA 91750 USA Tel 909-593-7332 (phone/fax); Edit Addr.: 4095 Fruit St., SP 938, La Verne, CA 91750 USA
E-mail: ivforum@aol.com.

Infinity Flower Publishing, LLC *Imprint of* **Barrera, Elizabeth Paige**

Infinity Oak Bks., *(978-0-9885066)* Orders Addr.: P.O. Box 195964, Dallas, TX 75219 USA Tel 972-803-4744
E-mail: jillksayre@me.com.

Infinity One Publishing, *(978-0-9772888)* P.O. Box 725394, Atlanta, GA 31139 USA Tel 678-760-6664; Fax: 617-507-8352
E-mail: thesleepysteve@yahoo.com.

Infinity Publishing *See* **Macro Publishing Group**

Infinity Publishing, *(978-0-9665678; 978-1-892896; 978-0-7414; 978-1-4958)* Div. of Buy Books On The Web.Com, 1094 New Dehaven St., Suite 100, West Conshohocken, PA 19428 USA Tel 610-941-9999; Fax: 610-941-9959; Toll Free: 877-289-2665
E-mail: info@infinitypublishing.com
Web site: http://www.buybooksontheweb.com; http://www.infinitypublishing.com/
Dist(s): **Smashwords.**

Infinity Publishing, *(978-0-9640184)* 8525 Evergreen Ln., Darien, IL 60561 USA Tel 708-985-2300; Fax: 708-985-2339 Do not confuse with companies with same name in Seattle WA, Lansing IL, West Palm Beach, FL.

Infinity Publishing Co., *(978-0-9799487)* 11111 N. Scottsdale Rd., Suite 205, Scottsdale, AZ 85260 USA Tel 480-703-0606
E-mail: pchambers8@cox.net
Web site: http://www.infinitypublishingcompany.com.

Infinity Studios LLC, *(978-1-59697)* 2601 Hilltop Dr. Apt. 815, San Pablo, CA 94806-5797 USA Do not confuse with companies with the same or similar name in Austin, TX
E-mail: info@infinitystudios.com
Web site: http://www.infinitystudios.com
Dist(s): **Diamond Comic Distributors, Inc.**
Diamond Bk. Distributors.

Influence, *(978-1-936699; 978-1-937830; 978-1-938309; 978-1-62912)* 1445 N. Boonville Ave., Springfield, MO 65802 USA Tel 417-831-8000; Fax: 417-862-5881
E-mail: apargo@ag.org; SUPPORT@INFLUENCERESOURCES.COM; tbledsoe@ag.org
Web site: http://store.influenceresources.com/
Dist(s): **Baker & Taylor Publisher Services (BTPS)**
Lulu Pr., Inc.
MyiLibrary
ebrary, Inc.

Infobus, Inc., *(978-0-9771184)* 19 Yellow Brook Rd., Holmdel, NJ 07733-1967 USA Tel 732-332-0232.

InfoHi Publishing, *(978-0-9678605; 978-0-9717849)* P.O. Box 1688, Fremont, CA 94538 USA Tel 831-685-1063
E-mail: linda@infohi.com
Web site: http://www.infohi.com
Dist(s): **Booklines Hawaii, Ltd.**

INFORMA INC, *(978-0-692-90984-3; 978-1-948346; 978-1-948817; 978-1-949338; 978-1-950024; 978-1-950771; 978-1-951306; 978-1-951822; 978-1-952309; 978-1-952852)* 30 Wall St 8th Flr., New York City , NY 10005 USA Tel 866-257-9368; 607 Deemer PL Suite 424, New Castle, DE 19720 Tel 866-256-1278
E-mail: vanessa.jones@bookartpress.us.

Information Age Publishing, Inc., *(978-1-930608; 978-1-931576; 978-1-59311; 978-1-60752; 978-1-61735; 978-1-62396; 978-1-68123; 978-1-64113; 978-1-64802)* P.O. Box 79049, Charlotte, NC 28271 USA (SAN 925-9228) Tel 704-752-9125; Fax: 704-752-9113 Do not confuse with Information Age Publishing in Exeter, NH
E-mail: iap@infoagepub.com; info@infoagepub.com
Web site: http://www.infoagepub.com
Dist(s): **ebrary, Inc.**

Infusionmedia Publishing, *(978-0-9704852; 978-0-9718677; 978-0-9796586; 978-0-9843101)* 140 N. 8th St., Suite 205, Lincoln, NE 68508-1358 USA (SAN 253-9136) Tel 402-477-2065 (phone/fax)
E-mail: info@infusionmediapublishing.com
Web site: http://www.infusionmediapublishing.com
Dist(s): **Smashwords.**

Ingenuity 31 Inc., *(978-0-578-05331-8)* 109 N. Church St., Waynesboro, PA 17268 USA
E-mail: ingenuity31@yahoo.com.

Ingle, Rosalie, *(978-0-578-09876-0)* P.O. Box 8636, St. Joseph, MO 64508 USA.

Ingleside Pr., *(978-1-929883)* P.O. Box 30029, Baltimore, MD 21215 USA
E-mail: inglesidepress@yahoo.com
Web site: http://inkwell62.wixsite.com/inglesidepress.

Ingram Bk. Co., *(978-1-61522; 978-1-60894)* Subs. of Ingram Industries, Inc., Orders Addr.: 1 Ingram Blvd., P.O. Box 3006, La Vergne, TN 37086-1986 USA (SAN 169-7978) Tel 615-213-5000; Fax: 615-213-3976 (Electronic Orders); Toll Free Fax: 800-285-3296 (fax inquiry US & Canada); 800-876-0186 (orders); 877-663-5367 (Canadian orders); Toll Free: 800-937-8000 (orders only); 800-937-8200 (customer service US & Canada); 800-289-0687 (Canadian orders only customer service); 800-234-6737 (electronic orders US & Canada)) Do not confuse with Ingram Pr., Sacramento, CA
E-mail: flashback@ingrambook.com; customerservice@ingrambook.com; ics-sales@ingrambook.com
Web site: http://www.ingrambook.com.

Ingram Content Group, Orders Addr.: 1246 Heil Quaker Blvd., LaVergne, TN 37086 USA (SAN 179-6976) Tel 615-213-4595; Fax: 615-213-4426; 860 Nestle Way - LSI Lightning Source, Breingsville, PA 18031 (SAN 920-4288)
E-mail: terri.jones@lightningsource.com.

Ingram Publisher Services, Orders Addr.: Customer Services, Box 512 1 Ingram Blvd., LaVergne, TN 37086 USA Toll Free Fax: 800-838-1149; Edit Addr.: 1 Ingram Blvd., LaVergne, TN 37086 USA (SAN 631-8630) Tel 615-793-5000; Fax: 615-213-5811
E-mail: customer.service@ingrampublisherservices.com; Publisher@ingrampublisherservices.com; Retailer@ingrampublisherservices.com
Web site: http://www.ingrampublisherservices.com.

Ingram, Sean Inc., *(978-0-9749049; 978-0-615-11910-6)* 176 Lane Rd., Stantonsburg, NC 27883 USA Tel 919-517-7326; Fax: 919-870-7227
E-mail: sean@seaningram.com
Web site: http://www.seaningram.com.

Ingram's Nutrition Consultations, *(978-0-9769379)* 43889 Bayview Ave. Apt. 40107, Clinton Twp, MI 48038-7073 USA; 7701 Corporate Dr., No.212, Houston, TX 77036 (SAN 850-5179) Tel 281-513-4596; Fax: 713-771-2177
E-mail: admin@ingramsnutritionconsultations.com
Web site: http://www.ingram's nutrition.com.

IngramSpark *See* **Indy Pub**

INgrooves *See* **INscribe Digital**

Inhabit Education (CAN) *(978-0-9938975; 978-0-9940216; 978-1-77266; 978-1-987876; 978-1-987958; 978-0-2287) Dist. by* **Consort Bk Sales.**

Inhabit Media Inc. (CAN) *(978-0-9782186; 978-1-926569; 978-1-927095; 978-1-77227) Dist. by* **Consort Bk Sales.**

Inheritance Pr., Inc., *(978-0-9638086; 978-0-9749501)* Orders Addr.: P.O. Box 580, Trenton, NC 28585-0580 USA; Edit Addr.: 388 Henderson Ln., Trenton, NC 28585 USA.

Inherst, Marie, *(978-0-9749785)* 52670 TH 180, Beallsville, OH 43716-9226 USA.

Ink & Feathers Comics, *(978-0-9664974)* Div. of Ink & Feathers Calligraphy, Orders Addr.: 202 E. Grove St., Streator, IL 61364 USA Tel 815-672-1171
E-mail: nerwonduh@hotmail.com
Web site: http://www.ifcomics.com.

Ink & Quill Pubs. *Imprint of* **Mystic Pubs., Inc.**

Ink & Scribe, *(978-0-9679817; 978-1-931947)* Div. of Wise River Companies, Inc., 3101 Kintzley Ct. Unit J, Laporte, CO 80535-9393 USA Toll Free: 888-616-7720
E-mail: books@northfortynews.com
Web site: http://www.inkandscribe.com.

Ink Monster, *(978-0-9894050; 978-0-9960864; 978-0-9906352; 978-1-943858)* 2405 St. George St., Los Angeles, CA 90027 USA Tel 310-721-5400
E-mail: info@inkmonsterbooks.com
Dist(s): **INscribe Digital**
Independent Pubs. Group.

Ink Well, *(978-0-9767578)* P.O. Box 786, Winlock, WA 98596 USA; *Imprints:* Ink Well Publishing (I W P) Do not confuse with Ink Well in Hermosa Beach, CA.

Ink Well Publishing *Imprint of* **Ink Well**

Inkberry Pr., *(978-0-9742148)* 15521 Shell Point Blvd., Fort Myers, FL 33908 USA Tel 239-466-2757
E-mail: wallykain@comcast.net.

Inkberry Pr., *(978-0-9838293)* 4110 S. Highland Dr. Suite 340, Salt Lake City, UT 84124 USA Tel 801-949-1083
E-mail: editorial@leatherwoodpress.com.

Inkblot Bks., *(978-1-932461)* Orders Addr.: 1285 Stratford Ave STE-G No. 115, Dixon, CA 95620 USA; Edit Addr.: 415 Mast Ct, Dixon, CA 95620 USA
E-mail: kathompson@gmail.com
Web site: http://www.inkblotbooks.com
Dist(s): **Smashwords.**

Inkchanted Publishing LLC, *(978-0-578-43819-1)* P.O. Box 572, Princeton, LA 71067 USA Tel 318-518-0800
E-mail: inkchantedpublishing@gmail.com.

InkDrops Publishing, *(978-1-7337947)* 73 N. State Rd., Upper Darby, PA 19082 USA Tel 267-574-1545; *Imprints:* Brown Brainy Brilliant Books (MYID_R_BROWN)
E-mail: inkdropspublications@gmail.com.

Inkling Bks., *(978-1-58742)* 584 Homewood Dr., Auburn, AL 36830 USA Tel 334-369-9613
E-mail: editor@inklingbooks.com
Web site: http://www.inklingbooks.com/
Dist(s): **CreateSpace Independent Publishing Platform**
Smashwords.

Inklings Publishing, *(978-0-9910211; 978-1-944428)* 7222 Granvia Dr., Houston, TX 77083 USA Tel 281-736-7168
E-mail: fbrady.03@comcast.net
Web site: http://inklingspublishing.com.

Inknbeans Pr., *(978-0-615-62429-7; 978-0-615-62896-7; 978-0-615-63408-1; 978-0-615-64400-4; 978-0-615-68085-9; 978-0-615-71952-8; 978-0-615-72837-7; 978-0-615-73222-0; 978-0-9886670; 978-0-615-73861-1; 978-0-615-74204-5; 978-0-615-74488-9; 978-0-615-74719-4; 978-0-615-74944-0; 978-0-615-74958-7; 978-0-615-74961-7;*

978-0-615-75145-0; 978-0-615-75791-9; 978-0-615-75854-1; 978-0-615-76442-9; 978-0-615-76749-9; 978-0-615-77178-6; 978-0-615-77534-0; 978-0-615-78970-5; 978-0-615-80657-0; 978-0-615-81135-2; 978-) 25060 Hancock Ave. Bldg 103 Suite 458, Murrieta, CA 92560 USA Tel 951-471-8184
Web site: inknbeans.com
Dist(s): **CreateSpace Independent Publishing Platform**
Steuben Pr.

Inkshares, *(978-1-941758; 978-1-942645; 978-1-947848; 978-1-950301)* 415 Jackson St Suite B, San Francisco, CA 94111 USA Tel 919-418-0895
E-mail: thad@inkshares.com
Web site: http://www.inkshares.com
Dist(s): **Ingram Publisher Services.**

Inkspil Publishing, *(978-0-9833877; 978-0-615-79874-5)* 1676 W. Bryn Mawr, Chicago, IL 60660 USA Tel 708-824-8465
E-mail: inkspillbooks@gmail.com
Web site: www.inkspillbooks.com
Dist(s): **CreateSpace Independent Publishing Platform.**

Inkspil Publishing House *See* **Inkspil Publishing**

Inkwater Pr., *(978-0-9719414; 978-1-59299; 978-1-62901)* Div. of First Books, 6750 SW Franklin St., Suite A, Portland, OR 97223 USA Tel 503-968-6777; Fax: 503-968-6779
E-mail: orders@inkwaterpress.com
Web site: http://www.inkwaterpress.com; http://www.firstbooks.com.

Inkwell Books LLC, *(978-0-9658158; 978-0-9718155; 978-0-9728118; 978-0-9749701; 978-0-9766340; 978-0-9786202; 978-0-9814648; 978-0-9829589; 978-0-9833247; 978-0-9848019; 978-0-9852501; 978-0-9883568; 978-1-939625; 978-0-9861743; 978-0-578-50033-1; 978-0-578-66486-6; 978-0-578-70836-2) Orders Addr.: 10632 N. Scottsdale Rd. Unit 695, Scottsdale, AZ 85254 USA Tel 480-315-3781*
E-mail: info@inkwellbooksllc.com
Web site: http://inkwellbooksllc.com/.

Inkwell Productions, LLC *See* **Inkwell Books LLC**

InMediaRes Productions, *(978-0-9792047; 978-1-934857; 978-1-936876; 978-1-941582; 978-1-942487; 978-1-947335)* 303 91st Ave., PMB 202 E502, Lake Stevens, WA 98258 USA Fax: 425-948-1301; *Imprints:* Catalyst Game Labs (Catalyst Game)
Web site: http://www.imrpro.com; http://www.catalystgamelabs.com
Dist(s): **PSI (Publisher Services, Inc.).**

Innate Foundation Publishing, *(978-0-9745866)* 9682 Sherwood Dr., Blaine, WA 98230 USA Tel 360-441-9156
E-mail: rca@robertclydeafolter.com
Web site: http://www.innatefoundation.com.

Inner Circle Publishing, *(978-0-9770682)* 1407 Crane St., Schenectady, NY 12303 USA Tel 518-377-0548.

Inner City Publications *See* **Citified Pubns.**

Inner Coaching, *(978-0-9636027)* 1108 Western Ave., Watertown, WI 53094 USA Tel 920-262-0439; Fax: 920-261-8801
E-mail: kids@readysetrelax.com
Web site: http://www.innercoaching.com
Dist(s): **Independent Pubs. Group**
New Leaf Distributing Co., Inc.
Quality Bks., Inc.

Inner Light - Global Communications, *(978-0-938294; 978-1-892062; 978-1-60611)* Orders Addr.: P.O. Box 753, New Brunswick, NJ 08903 USA (SAN 662-0191) Tel 646-331-6777; Edit Addr.: 1231 Hamilton St., Somerset, NJ 08873 USA
E-mail: mrufo@hotmail.com
Dist(s): **Distributors, The**
Distributors International
New Leaf Distributing Co., Inc.
Quality Bks., Inc.
Red Wheel/Weiser
Unique Bks., Inc.

Inner Quality Publishing, *(978-0-9988319)* 13258 Spruce Run Dr., North Royalton, OH 44133 USA Tel 440-877-9390; *Imprints:* Nana Says (NanaSays)
E-mail: lauren@centerforinnerquality.com.

†Inner Traditions International, Ltd., *(978-0-89281; 978-0-905249; 978-1-899171; 978-0-906191; 978-0-9504268; 978-1-84409; 978-1-59477; 978-1-62055; 978-1-64411)* Orders Addr.: P.O. Box 388, Rochester, VT 05767-0388 USA Tel 802-767-3174; Fax: 802-767-3726; Toll Free Fax: 800-246-8648; Edit Addr.: One Park St., Rochester, VT 05767 USA (SAN 208-6948) Tel 802-767-3174; Fax: 802-767-3726; *Imprints:* Healing Arts Press (Heal Arts VT); Bindu Books (Bindu Bks); Findhorn Press (FindhornPr); Earthdancer Books (EarthdancerBks)
E-mail: customerservice@innertraditions.com; info@innertraditions.com
Web site: http://www.innertraditions.com
Dist(s): **Beekman Bks., Inc.**
Book Wholesalers, Inc.
Bookazine Co., Inc.
Brodart Co.
Independent Pub.
Integral Yoga Pubns.
Library Sales of N.J.
Lotus Pr.
MyiLibrary
New Leaf Distributing Co., Inc.
Nutri-Bks. Corp.
Partners/West Book Distributors
Quality Bks., Inc.
Simon & Schuster
Simon & Schuster, Inc.
Unique Bks., Inc.; *CIP.*

Inner Wisdom Pubns., *(978-0-9656741; 978-0-9774921)* 22850 Summit Rd., Los Gatos, CA 95033 USA (SAN 299-2450) Tel 408-353-2050; Fax: 408-353-4663; Toll Free: 888-468-4335
E-mail: 15minutemiracle@verizon.net
Web site: http://www.15MinuteMiracle.com.

InnerChamp Bks., *(978-0-9663949)* P.O. Box 11362, Santa Rosa, CA 95406 USA Tel 707-571-8023; Fax: 707-546-3764
E-mail: inrchamp@aol.com
Web site: http://www.innerchamp.com.

Innerchild Publishing, Inc., *(978-0-9768078)* Orders Addr.: P.O. Box 142317, Fayetteville, GA 30214-2317 USA.

Innerchoice Publishing, *(978-0-9625486; 978-1-56499)* 24426 S. Main, Carson, CA 90745 USA Tel 310-816-3085; Fax: 310-816-3092
Dist(s): **Jalmar Pr.**

InnerCircle Publishing, *(978-1-882918; 978-0-9723191; 978-0-9755214; 978-0-9762924)* 522 Sadie St. Apt. 2, Laurens, IA 50554-1553 USA
Web site: http://www.innercirclepublishing.com; http://www.rev-press.com.

InnerPrize Group, LLC, *(978-1-947485)* 411 SE Delaware Ave. Unit 204, ANKENY, IA 50021 USA Tel 312-399-0886; *Imprints:* Mine Rich In Gems (MYID_B_MINE RI)
E-mail: innerprizeceo@gmail.com; innerprizecfo@gmail.com; innerprizecco@gmail.com; lilishang9@gmail.com
Web site: www.innerprizegroup.com; www.auntielili.com; www.minerichingems.com.

InnerRESOURCES Pubns., *(978-0-9728389)* 109 E. 73rd St., New York, NY 10021 USA
E-mail: jeff@jefflandau.com; jefflandau@innerresources.org
Web site: http://jeffs.smugmug.com/; http://www.jefflandau.com; http://www.innerresources.org; http://www.flickr.com/photos/8ideas/
Dist(s): **Ingram Content Group.**

innertuber, *(978-0-9742742)* 2124 NE 7th St., Gainesville, FL 32609 USA.

Innov8 Studios, *(978-0-9754544)* 16 Cedarwood Dr., Ballston Lake, NY 12019 USA
E-mail: innov8studios@nycap.rr.com.

Innovation Game, The, *(978-0-9643819)* 8509 Irvington Ave., Bethesda, MD 20817 USA Tel 301-530-4299.

Innovation Pr., The, *(978-1-943147)* 391 SE Crystal Creek Cir, Issaquah, WA 98027 USA Tel 360-870-9988
E-mail: acltro@theinnovationpress.com
Web site: http://www.theinnovationpress.com
Dist(s): **Baker & Taylor Publisher Services (BTPS)**
Legato Pubs. Group.

Innovative Christian Pubns. *Imprint of* **Baker Trittin Pr.**

Innovative Eggz LLC, *(978-1-945644; 978-1-64032)* 148 Carson Valley Way, Santa Fe, NM 87508 USA Tel 517-817-8093; *Imprints:* Puppet Theater Books (MYID_H_PUPPET) .

Innovative Kids, *(978-1-58476; 978-1-60169)* Div. of Innovative USA, Inc., 18 Ann St., Norwalk, CT 06854-2258 USA Tel 203-838-6400; Fax: 203-855-5582; *Imprints:* IKIDS (IKIDS)
E-mail: info@innovativekids.com
Web site: http://www.innovativekids.com
Dist(s): **Hachette Bk. Group.**

Innovative Language, LLC, *(978-0-9765236)* P.O. Box 1593, Eugene, OR 97440-1593 USA.

Innovative Logistics, Orders Addr.: 575 Prospect St., Lakewood, NJ 08701 USA (SAN 760-6532) Tel 732-534-7001; 732-363-5679; Fax: 732-363-0338
E-mail: innlogorders@innlog.net
Web site: http://www.innlog.net.

Innovo Pr. *Imprint of* **Innovo Publishing, LLC**

Innovo Publishing, LLC, *(978-0-9815403; 978-1-936076; 978-1-61314)* 159 College St., Collierville, TN 38017 USA Fax: 901-221-4055; Toll Free: 888-546-2111; *Imprints:* Innovo Press (Innovo Pr)
E-mail: info@innovopublishing.com
Web site: http://www.innovopublishing.com.

Inprint Bks., *(978-0-9814510; 978-0-9973316)* 1223 Wilshire Blvd., Suite 1413, Santa Monica, CA 90403 USA (SAN 855-5923).

INscribe Digital, *(978-1-61750; 978-1-62517)* Div. of Independent Publishers Group, 55 Francisco St. Suite 710, San Francsico, CA 94105 USA; *Imprints:* Brown Girls Publishing (BrownGirls)
E-mail: digitalpublishing@ingrooves.com
Web site: http://www.INscribeDigital.com
Dist(s): **Independent Pubs. Group**
Lulu Pr., Inc.

Insect Lore, *(978-1-891541)* Orders Addr.: P.O. Box 1535, Shafter, CA 93263 USA Tel 661-746-6047; Fax: 661-746-0334; Toll Free: 800-548-3284; Edit Addr.: 132 S. Beech St., Shafter, CA 93263 USA
E-mail: john@insectlore.com
Web site: http://www.insectlore.com.

Insect Sciences Museum of California, *(978-0-9764454)* 3644 Calafia Ave., Oakland, CA 94605 USA; *Imprints:* Exploring California Insects (Ex CA In)
E-mail: insectnet@aol.com
Web site: http://www.bugpeople.org.

Insight Editions, *(978-1-933784; 978-1-60887; 978-0-615-39977-5; 978-0-615-50360-8; 978-0-615-50366-0; 978-1-68298; 978-1-68383; 978-1-64722)* 800 A St., San Rafael, CA 94901 USA; P.O. Box 3088, San Rafael, CA 94912 Tel 415-526-1370; Fax: 866-509-0515 eFax; *Imprints:* Earth Aware Editions (EarthAware)
Dist(s): **Hachette Bk. Group**
Simon & Schuster, Inc.

Insight Publishing Group, *(978-1-930027; 978-1-932503)* Div. of Insight International, Inc., 8801 S. Yale, Suite 410, Tulsa, OK 74137 USA Tel 918-493-1718; Fax: 918-493-2219; Toll Free: 800-924-8264 Do not confuse with companies with similar names in Parker, CO, Yreka,CA, Jacksonville, FL, Woodbridge, VA, Salt Lake City, UT
E-mail: info@freshword.com
Web site: http://www.freshword.com
Dist(s): **Smashwords.**

Insight Services, Inc, *(978-0-9786034)* 1020 Hummingbird Ct., Springfield, TN 37172-5563 USA (SAN 851-092X); *Imprints:* Children's Insight (Children's Insight)
E-mail: childrensinsight@learnlivebetter.com
Web site: http://www.learnlivebetter.com.

Insight Studios, LLC *See* **Bugeye Bks.**

Insight Technical Education, *(978-0-9722058; 978-0-9755280)* 13410 NE 92nd St., Vancouver, WA 98682 USA Tel 360-852-6152
E-mail: webinfo@sixbranches.com
Web site: http://www.insightteched.com.

Insights Productions - Innovating Education, *(978-0-9753827)* P.O. Box 1323, Fall City, WA 98024 USA Tel 206-391-5993; Fax: 425-222-7549
E-mail: alandelaossa@centurytel.net.

Inspira *Imprint of* **Editorial Imagen**

Inspirasian Pr. LLC, *(978-0-9743882)* P.O. Box 460256, San Francisco, CA 94146-0256 USA Tel 415-282-7925; Fax: 415-282-6427
Web site: http://www.inspirasian.com.

Inspiration Pr. Inc., *(978-0-9798395)* 8598 N. W. St., Coral Springs, FL 33071 USA
Dist(s): **TNT Media Group, Inc.**

Inspiration Software, Inc., *(978-0-928539; 978-1-932463; 978-1-933238; 978-1-934425)* 9400 SW Beaverton Hillsdale Hwy., No. 300, Beaverton, OR 97005 USA (SAN 670-8234) Toll Free: 800-877-4292
E-mail: jbrooks@inspiration.com
Web site: http://www.inspiration.com
Dist(s): **Follett School Solutions.**

Inspirational Hse. of America, *(978-0-9768598)* 93 Jay Ln., Gasburg, VA 23857 USA.

Inspirations by Grace LaJoy, *(978-0-9747583; 978-0-9814607; 978-0-615-34652-6; 978-0-9829404; 978-0-9987117; 978-0-692-89959-5; 978-0-692-89977-9; 978-1-7341868)* P.O. Box 181, Raymore, MO 64083 USA
Web site: http://www.gracelajoy.com.

Inspire Bks., *(978-1-950685)* 9243 Pipilo St., San Diego, CA 92129 USA Tel 330-416-4916
E-mail: beth@inspire-books.com
Web site: www.inspire-books.com.

Inspire Every Child dba Illumination Arts, *(978-0-615-50779-8; 978-0-9855417)* 808 6th St. S., Ste 200, Kirkland, WA 98033 USA Tel 425-968-5097; Fax: 425-968-5634
E-mail: jthompson@illumin.com
Web site: www.illumin.com.

Inspire Media, LLC *See* **Motivision Media**

Inspire Press, Inc., *(978-0-9741800)* P.O. Box 33241, Los Gatos, CA 95030 USA Tel 408-395-2003; Fax: 408-904-4662
E-mail: sharper@inspirepress.com
Web site: http://www.inspirepress.com.

Inspire Pubns., *(978-0-9725292)* 13229 Middle Canyon Rd., Carmel Valley, CA 93924 USA (SAN 255-1225) Tel 831-917-6059; Fax: 831-659-8460
E-mail: larryhayes@mynamestartswith.com; lhayes@mynamestartswith.com
Web site: http://www.mynamestartswith.com.

Inspire U., LLC, *(978-0-9792361)* 30520 Rancho California Rd., Suite 107-64, Temecula, CA 92591 USA (SAN 852-8535).

Inspired By Family, *(978-0-9787074)* 1332 Westmore Ct., Srevens Point, WI 54481 USA
Web site: http://www.inspiredbyfamily.com.

Inspired by the Beach Co., *(978-0-9790415)* Orders Addr.: P.O. Box 174, Simpsonville, MD 21150-0174 USA
E-mail: mjareaux@ureach.com
Web site: http://www.26thingstoteach.com.

Inspired By the Beach Publishing *See* **Inspired by the Beach Co.**

InspirEd Educators, *(978-1-933558; 978-1-938275)* 350 Waverly Hall Cir., Roswell, GA 30075 USA Tel 770-649-7571; Fax: 770-642-7568; Toll Free: 866-WE-INSPIRE (866-934-6774)
E-mail: sharon@inspirededucators.com; lainey@inspirededucators.com
Web site: http://www.inspirededucators.com.

Inspired Idea, *(978-1-931203)* 4105 Buckthorn Ct., Flower Mound, TX 75028 USA
E-mail: Eve@pharaohsofthebible.com; Eve@Engelbrite.com
Web site: https://inspiredideapress.com; http://www.kneelingmedia.org.

Inspired Imaginations, LLC, *(978-0-9903752; 978-1-945200)* 1405 S. Bascom Ave., San Jose, CA 95128 USA Tel 408-835-5911
E-mail: todd@maxrhymes.com
Dist(s): **Follett School Solutions.**

Inspired Studios Inc., *(978-0-7396; 978-0-88149; 978-1-57713; 978-1-943758; 978-1-64183)* 9920 Royal Cardigan Way, West Palm Beach, FL 33411 USA (SAN 287-7589) Tel 561-333-9142; Fax: 561-333-9143
E-mail: DKasen@Inspired-Studios.com; dkasen@inspired-studios.com
Web site: http://www.peterpan.com; www.inspired-Studios.com
Dist(s): **Follett School Solutions**
INscribe Digital
Independent Pubs. Group
Midwest Tape.

InspireGrowth Enterprises, LLC, *(978-0-578-55405-1; 978-0-578-55407-5; 978-1-7340080)* 108 Jefferson St., Highland Mills, NY 10930 USA Tel 646-246-0911
E-mail: stevepiriano@yahoo.com
Dist(s): **Ingram Content Group.**

Inspiring Voices *Imprint of* **Author Solutions, Inc.**

Inspirio, *(978-0-310)* 5300 Patterson Ave., SE, Grand Rapids, MI 49530 USA Tel 1-800-727-3480
E-mail: zprod@zondervan.com
Web site: http://www.zondervan.com
Dist(s): **Zondervan.**

Instant Help Books *Imprint of* **New Harbinger Pubns.**

Instant Pub., *(978-1-59196; 978-1-59872; 978-1-60458; 978-1-61422)* Orders Addr.: P.O. Box 985, Collierville, TN 38027 USA Tel 901-853-7070; Fax: 901-853-6196; Toll Free: 800-259-2592; Edit Addr.: 410 Hwy, 72 W., Collierville, TN 38017 USA
Web site: http://www.instantpublisher.com
Dist(s): **BookBaby**
Lulu Pr., Inc.
Smashwords.

Instantpublisher.com *See* **Instant Pub.**

Institute For Behavior Change Incorporated The, *(978-0-9770503)* 9900 W. Sample Rd., Suite 300, Coral Springs, FL 33065 USA Tel 954-755-6639; Fax: 954-755-4100
E-mail: rhall3318@acn.net
Web site: http://www.afterthestormchildrensbook.com.

Institute for Conscious Change, The, *(978-0-9743443)* Div. of BioPlan Associates, Inc., Orders Addr.: 8987 E. Tanque Verde Rd. Ste. 309, Tucson, AZ 85749-9399 USA
E-mail: info@ConsciousChange.org
Web site: http://www.ConsciousChange.org.

Institute for Creation Research, *(978-0-932766; 978-1-935587; 978-1-946246)* 1806 Royal Ln., Dallas, TX 75229 USA Tel 214-615-8300.

Institute for Disabilities Research & Training, Inc., *(978-0-9667589; 978-0-9752933; 978-0-9760818; 978-0-9789373)* 11323 Amherst Ave., Wheaton, MD 20902 USA Tel 301-942-4326; Fax: 301-942-4439
E-mail: sales@idrt.com
Web site: http://www.idrt.com.

Institute for Economic Democracy Pr., Inc., *(978-0-9624423; 978-0-9753555; 978-1-933567)* 13851 N. 103rd Ave., Sun City, AZ 85351-4520 USA Tel 623-583-2518; Toll Free: 888-533-1020 (credit card orders)
E-mail: cc@ccus.info; ied@ied.info
Web site: http://www.ied.info.

Institute for Food & Development Policy/Food First Bks., *(978-0-935028; 978-0-9970989)* 398 60th St., Oakland, CA 94618-1212 USA (SAN 213-327X) Tel 510-654-4400; Fax: 510-654-4551
E-mail: marthak@foodfirst.org
Web site: http://www.foodfirst.org
Dist(s): **L P C Group**
Two Rivers Distribution.

Institute For Outdoor Awareness, Inc, *(978-0-9835176; 978-0-9915227)* 41 Linden Ave., Rutledge, PA 19070 USA Tel 610-544-8335
E-mail: phil@bartowassoc.com
Web site: phil@bartowassoc.com.

Institute for Preventative Sports Med., *(978-0-9745655)* P.O. Box 7032, Ann Arbor, MI 48107 USA Tel 734-434-3390; Fax: 734-572-4503
E-mail: admin@ipsm.org
Web site: http://www.ipsm.org.

Institute for Vaishnava Studies, *(978-0-9981871)* 1515 NW 7th Pl., Gainesville, FL 32603-1208 USA Tel 570-814-2150
E-mail: ivspublishing@gmail.com.

Institute of Cybernetics Research, Inc., *(978-1-893375; 978-1-58578)* Orders Addr.: 15 W. 139th St. Apt. 10G, New York, NY 10037-1516 USA
E-mail: icri@usa.net; journal_of_amateur_computing-subscribe@yahoogroups.com
Web site: http://groups.yahoo.com/groups/journal_of_amateur_computing/join
Dist(s): **American Heritage Magazine**
Analos Magazine
Theme Stream, Inc.
Wiley, John & Sons, Inc.

Institute of Early American History & Culture *See* **Omohundro Institute of Early American History & Culture**

Institute of Physics Publishing, *(978-0-7503; 978-0-85274; 978-0-85498)* The Public Ledte Bldg., Suite 1035 150 S. Independence Mall, W., Philadelphia, PA 19106 USA (SAN 298-2315) Tel 215-627-0880; Fax: 215-627-0879; Toll Free: 800-632-0880; Dirac House Temple Back, Bristol, BS1 6BE Tel 44 (0) 117 929 7481; Fax: 44 (0) 117 930 1186
E-mail: book.enquiries@iop.org
Web site: http://bookmark.iop.org
Dist(s): **CRC Pr. LLC**
National Bk. Network.

Instream Flow Council, *(978-0-9716743)* c/o Wyoming Game & Fish, 5400 Bishop Blvd., Cheyenne, WY 82002 USA Tel 307-777-4600; Fax: 307-777-4611
E-mail: tannea@state.wy.us.

Instructional Fair *Imprint of* **Carson-Dellosa Publishing, LLC**

Instructional Resources Co., *(978-1-879478)* P.O. Box 111704, Anchorage, AK 99511-1704 USA Tel 907-345-6689 (phone/fax)
E-mail: susan@susancanthony.com
Web site: http://www.susancanthony.com.

Instrument Society of America *See* **ISA**

Insu-Form, Incorporated *See* **I.Form Ink, Publishing**

Intaglio, Inc., (*978-0-9748034*) P.O. Box 211296, Montgomery, AL 36109 USA Tel 706-593-2749; Fax: 334-260-9373
E-mail: sperez@intaglioinc.com
Web site: http://www.intaglioinc.com.

Intaglio Pr., (*978-0-944091*) Orders Addr.: P.O. Box 9952, College Station, TX 77842 USA (SAN 242-7133) Tel 409-696-7800; Toll Free: 800-768-5565; Edit Addr.: 8709 Bent Tree, College Station, TX 77845 USA (SAN 242-7141)
E-mail: HDETHL9414@aol.com.

†Integral Yoga Pubns., (*978-0-932040; 978-1-938477*) Satchidananda Ashram-Yogaville, 108 Yogaville Way, Buckingham, VA 23921 USA (SAN 285-0338) Tel 434-969-3121 ex 102; Fax: 434-969-1303; Toll Free: 800-262-1008 (orders)
Web site: http://www.yogaville.org
Dist(s): **Baker & Taylor Publisher Services (BTPS)**
MyiLibrary
New Leaf Distributing Co., Inc.
ebrary, Inc.; *CIP.*

integrated health publishing, (*978-0-615-72324-2; 978-0-9981472; 978-0-578-46893-8*) 9305 fraser Ln., Chesterland, OH 44026 USA Tel 2164692160
Web site: doctorlori.net
Dist(s): **CreateSpace Independent Publishing Platform.**

Integrity Consulting Enterprise, LLC, (*978-0-9964038*) P.O. Box 651, Menomonee Falls, WI 53052 USA Tel 262-292-9533; 875 N. Michigan Avenue, Suite 3100 John Hancock Ctr., Chicago, IL 60611; *Imprints:* Riley Press (Riley P)
E-mail: candegail@gmail.com; carolyn@lifetc.org
Web site: www.megalife.life; www.rileypress.com; www.integrityce.com; www.carolynganderson.com.

Intelligent Concepts, Inc., (*978-0-9740612*) 1889 N. Airport Dr., Lehi, UT 84043 USA Tel 801-766-0262
E-mail: joe@intelcon.biz
Web site: http://www.intelcon.biz.

Intelligent Design Pr., Ltd., (*978-0-9993322*) 1150 First Ave., STE 511, King of Prussia, PA 19406 USA Tel 732-757-7989
E-mail: steph.krell@gmail.com.

Intellipop, LLC, (*978-0-9743805*) 2701 Troy Center Dr., Suite 275, Troy, MI 48084 USA Tel 248-269-6091; Fax: 248-269-6092
E-mail: info@intellipop.com
Web site: http://www.intellipop.com.

Intense Media, LLC, (*978-0-615-31401-3; 978-0-9854709*) 3324 E. Carla Vista Dr., Gilbert, AZ 85295 USA
Dist(s): **CreateSpace Independent Publishing Platform**
Ingram Content Group.

Interaction Point Games, LLC, (*978-1-936326*) 4544 Chowen Ave. N., Robbinsdale, MN 55422 USA
E-mail: brent@interactionpoint.com; info@interactionpoint.com
Web site: http://www.interactionpoint.com.

Interaction Pubs., Inc., (*978-1-57336*) Orders Addr.: P.O. Box 900, Fort Atkinson, WI 53538 USA; Edit Addr.: W5527 State Rd. 106, Fort Atkinson, WI 53538-0800 USA (SAN 631-2950) Tel 920-563-9571; Fax: 920-563-7395; Toll Free: 800-359-0961
E-mail: sales@interact-simulations.com; interact@highsmith.com
Web site: http://www.interact-simulations.com/; http://www.teachinteract.com.

Interactive Eye, L.L.C. *Imprint of* **Interactive Knowledge, Inc.**

Interactive Knowledge, Inc., (*978-0-9759464*) 142 High St., No. 618, Portland, ME 04101 USA Tel 207-775-2278; Fax: 413-778-6861; *Imprints:* Interactive Eye, L.L.C. (InterEye) Do not confuse with Interactive Knowledge, Inc., Charlotte, NC
E-mail: support@iknow.net
Web site: http://www.iknow.net.

Interactive Media Publishing, (*978-0-9744391; 978-1-934332*) Orders Addr.: P.O. Box 1407, Phoenix, OR 97535-1407 USA (SAN 256-095X) Tel 541-535-5552; Fax: 888-900-1598; *Imprints:* Once Upon A Time in a Classroom (OnceUponTime)
E-mail: orders@i-mediapub.com; linda@i-mediapub.com
Web site: http://www.interactivemediapub.com; http://www.edfortech.com; http://www.exploringrobotics.com
Dist(s): **New Leaf Distributing Co., Inc.**

Interactive Publishing Corporation (CAN) (*978-0-9918589*) *Dist. by* **IPG Chicago.**

Interactive Pubns. Pty, Ltd. (AUS) (*978-1-876819; 978-1-921479; 978-1-921869; 978-0-646-32685-6; 978-0-646-32746-4; 978-1-922120; 978-1-925231; 978-1-922332*) *Dist. by* **LightSource CS.**

Interactive Pubns. Pty, Ltd. (AUS) (*978-1-876819; 978-1-921479; 978-1-921869; 978-0-646-32685-6; 978-0-646-32746-4; 978-1-922120; 978-1-925231; 978-1-922332*) *Dist. by* **CreateSpace.**

Interactive Stories, (*978-0-692-23199-9; 978-0-692-36847-3; 978-0-692-37008-7; 978-1-945906*) 2001 Kingston Rd, Farmington, UT 84025 USA Tel 801-867-7493
Web site: http://minecraft-interactive.com
Dist(s): **CreateSpace Independent Publishing Platform.**

Intercollegiate Studies Institute, Incorporated *See* **ISI Bks.**

Intercultural Communication Services, Inc., (*978-0-9741881; 978-0-9773359*) 2580 SW 76th Ave., Portland, OR 97225-3305 USA Fax: 503-292-6817
E-mail: jolinda@jolindaosborne.com
Web site: http://www.jolindaosborne.com.

Interdimensional Pr., (*978-0-9827753; 978-0-9911970*) 480 Lakeview Dr. Suite 107, Brentwood, CA 94513 USA Tel 925-513-1596 (phone/fax)
E-mail: pmcculley@comcast.net
Dist(s): **Ingram Content Group.**

Interface Publishing *See* **IGI Pr.**

Interior Dept. *Imprint of* **United States Government Printing Office**

Interlink Bks. *Imprint of* **Interlink Publishing Group, Inc.**

Interlink Publishing Group, Inc., (*978-0-940793; 978-1-56656; 978-1-62371*) 46 Crosby St., Northampton, MA 01060-1804 USA (SAN 664-8908) Tel 413-582-7054; Fax: 413-582-6731; Toll Free: 800-238-5465; *Imprints:* Crocodile Books (Crocodile Bks); Interlink Books (Interlink Bks); Clockroot Books (Clockroot)
E-mail: info@interlinkbooks.com; editor@interlinkbooks.com
Web site: http://www.interlinkbooks.com
Dist(s): **MyiLibrary**
Publishers Group West (PGW).

Interlink Resources International *See* **CJR**

Interlude Pr. *Imprint of* **Novelstream, LLC**

Intermedia Publishing Group, (*978-0-9820458; 978-0-9819682; 978-1-935529; 978-1-935906; 978-1-937654; 978-0-615-56309-1*) Orders Addr.: P.O. Box 2825, Peoria, AZ 85380 USA Tel 623-337-8710; Fax: 623-867-9469
E-mail: halton@intermediapr.com; ldavis@intermediapr.com
Web site: http://www.intermediapub.com.

Intermedio Editores S.A. (COL) (*978-958-637*) *Dist. by* **Random.**

International Alliance Pro-Publishing, LLC, (*978-1-60942*) 7260 W. Azure Dr. 140-744, Las Vegas, NV 89130 USA Tel 206-339-9080
E-mail: therebox@yahoo.com
Web site: http://www.iappublishing.net.

International Arts & Artists, (*978-0-9662859; 978-0-9767102; 978-0-9883497; 978-0-9973099*) 9 Hillyer Ct., NW, Washington, DC 20008 USA Fax: 202-333-0758
E-mail: design@artsandartists.org; designstudio@artsandartists.org
Web site: http://www.artsandartists.org
Dist(s): **Tuttle Publishing**
Univ. of Washington Pr.

†International Bk. Ctr., Inc., (*978-0-86685; 978-0-917062*) 2007 Laurel Dr., P.O. Box 295, Troy, MI 48099 USA (SAN 169-4014) Tel 248-879-7920; 586-254-7230; Fax: 586-254-7230
E-mail: ibc@ibcbooks.com
Web site: http://www.ibcbooks.com; *CIP.*

International Bk. Import Service, Inc., Orders Addr.: 161 Main St., P.O. Box 8188, Lynchburg, TN 37352-8188 USA (SAN 630-5679) Tel 931-759-7400; Fax: 931-759-7555; Toll Free: 800-277-4247
E-mail: IBIS@IBIService.com
Web site: http://www.IBIService.com.

International Children's Books *See* **Calabrese, Christine**

International Church of the Foursquare Gospel *See* **Foursquare Media, ICFG**

International Comics & Entertainment L.L.C., (*978-1-929090; 978-1-932575*) 1005 Mahone St., Fredericksburg, VA 22401 USA Tel 540-899-9186; Fax: 540-899-9196
E-mail: kblue@ic-ent.com
Web site: http://www.ic-ent.com
Dist(s): **Diamond Comic Distributors, Inc.**

International Council for Computers in Education *See* **International Society for Technology in Education**

International Council for Gender Studies, (*978-1-929656*) Orders Addr.: P.O. Box 702, Waxahachie, TX 75168 USA Fax: 972-937-9930; Toll Free: 800-317-6958
E-mail: rivilian@yahoo.com; icgsinfo@yahoo.com
Web site: http://www.fiveaspects.com; www.5aspects.org.

International Debate Education Assn., (*978-0-9702130; 978-0-9720541; 978-1-932716; 978-1-61770*) 224 W. 57th St., New York, NY 10019 USA Tel 212-547-6932; Fax: 646-557-2416; 105 E. 22nd St. Suite 915, New York, NY 10010 Tel 212-300-6076 x9
E-mail: martin.greenwald@opensocietyfoundations.org
Web site: http://www.idebate.org
Dist(s): **Books International, Inc.**

International Development Ctr., (*978-0-9774483; 978-0-9799873*) P.O. Box 25163, Arlington, VA 22202 USA Tel 703-766-0643
E-mail: mi.productions@yahoo.com; ouatiss@yahoo.com.

International Educational Improvement Ctr. Pr., (*978-1-884169*) Orders Addr.: c/o Dr. Archie W. Earl, Sr., Mathematics Dept. School of Science & Technology Norfork State University, Norfolk, VA 23504 USA Tel 757-823-9564
E-mail: awearl@nsu.edu
Web site: http://www.webspawner.com/users/ieicpress/index.html.

International Graphic Group, (*978-0-9821692*) 838 Reedy St., Cincinnati, OH 45202 USA Tel 513-321-7884; Fax: 513-621-1619
E-mail: sales@iggbooks.com.

International Institute for Ecological Agriculture, (*978-0-9790437*) 309 Cedar St. No.127, Santa Cruz, CA 95060 USA (SAN 852-2847) Tel 831-471-9164; Toll Free: 888-737-6228
E-mail: ourstore@permaculture.com
Web site: http://www.permaculture.com.

International Language Centre, 1753 Connecticut Ave., NW, Washington, DC 20009 USA (SAN 209-1615) Tel 202-332-2894; Fax: 202-462-6657
E-mail: richard@newsinform.com; zisa@newsinform.com
Web site: http://www.newsinform.com.

International Learning Systems, Incorporated *See* **International Language Centre**

International Linguistics Corp., (*978-0-939990; 978-1-887371; 978-0-9814540*) 12220 Blue Ridge Blvd., Suite G, Grandview, MO 64030 USA (SAN 220-2573)
E-mail: jennifer@learnables.com
Web site: http://www.learnables.com.

International Localization Network, (*978-1-935018; 978-1-945423*) 109 Sunset Ct. No. 2., Hamburg, NY 14075 USA Tel 913-773-8323
E-mail: randy2905@gmail.com
Web site: www.ilncenter.com.

International Marine/Ragged Mountain Pr. *Imprint of* **McGraw-Hill Professional Publishing**

†International Monetary Fund, (*978-0-939934; 978-1-55775; 978-1-58906; 978-1-61635; 978-1-4518; 978-1-4519; 978-1-4527; 978-1-4552; 978-1-4623; 978-1-4639; 978-1-4755; 978-1-4843; 978-1-4983; 978-1-5135*) c/o Publications Department, 700 19th St., NW, Washington, DC 20431 USA (SAN 203-8188) Tel 202-623-7899
E-mail: tdelrosario@imf.org; salavi@imf.org; jbeardow@imf.org
Web site: http://www.imf.org; http://.www.cibrary.imf.org
Dist(s): **Bernan Assocs.**
MyiLibrary
Rowman & Littlefield Publishers, Inc.
ebrary, Inc.; *CIP.*

International Pacific Halibut Commission, (*978-0-9776931*) P.O. Box 95009, Seattle, WA 98145-2009 USA Tel 206-634-1838
E-mail: lauri@iphc.washington.edu
Web site: http://www.iphc.washington.edu.

International Scientific Ctr., (*978-0-9630594*) 2655 E. 21st St., Brooklyn, NY 11235 USA Tel 718-368-2918.

International Society for Technology in Education, (*978-0-924667; 978-1-56484*) 175 W. Broadway., Suite 300, Eugene, OR 97401-3003 USA (SAN 296-7693) Toll Free: 800-336-5191
E-mail: iste@iste.org
Web site: http://www.iste.org
Dist(s): **Follett School Solutions**
Ingram Publisher Services.

International Society of Sephardic Leadership Council *See* **ISLC**

International Specialized Book Services *See* **ISBS Publisher Services**

International Step by Step Assn., (*978-1-931854; 978-1-60195*) 400 W. 59th St., New York, NY 10019 USA
E-mail: info@issa.nl
Web site: http://www.issa.nl.

International Training, Incorporated *See* **ITI Holdings, Inc.**

International Univ. Line, (*978-0-9636817; 978-0-9720774*) P.O. Box 2525, La Jolla, CA 92038 USA Tel 858-457-0595; Fax: 858-581-9073
E-mail: info@iul-press.com.

International Vaquero Productions, (*978-0-9761103*) 730 W. 8th St., Claremont, CA 91711 USA
E-mail: ivp1@me.com
Web site: http://www.kurtbeardsley.com.

International Wizard of Oz Club, The, (*978-1-930764*) P.O. Box 26249, San Francisco, CA 94126-6249 USA Fax: 510-642-7589 Do not confuse with International Wizard of OZ Club, Appleton, WI
E-mail: phanff@library.berkeley.edu
Web site: http://ozclub.org.

Interpact Press *See* **Schwartau, Winn LLC**

Interplay Productions, (*978-1-57629*) 16815 Von Karman Ave., Irvine, CA 92606-4920 USA Tel 714-553-6655; Fax: 714-252-2820.

InterPress, (*978-0-9744173*) 14056 Fort Valley Rd., Fort Valley, VA 22652 USA; *Imprints:* Fort Valley Geology Study Center (Ft Valley)
E-mail: wjmelson@shentel.net
Web site: http://interpressusa.com.

Interpreting Time's Past, LLC, (*978-0-692-31046-5; 978-0-9964304; 978-1-7328333*) 450 Old Richmond Rd. S, Crab Orchard, KY 40419 USA Tel 770-364-6512
E-mail: connie@cmhuddleston.com
Web site: www.cmhuddleston.com.

InterRelations Collaborative, Inc., (*978-0-9761753*) P.O. Box 6280, Hamden, CT 06517-3503 USA.

Interset Pr., (*978-1-57433*) Orders Addr.: 35 Burns Hill Rd., Wilton, NH 03086 USA Tel 603-654-2949
E-mail: artistafloat@earthlink.net; woad@earthlink.net
Dist(s): **Lulu Pr., Inc.**

Interstellar Publishing Co., (*978-0-9645957; 978-1-889599*) Orders Addr.: P.O. Box 7306, Beverly Hills, CA 90212 USA (SAN 298-5829) Tel 310-247-8154 (orders); Fax: 310-247-0622
E-mail: Interstlr@aol.com
Web site: http://www.interstellarpublishing.com.

Interstellar Trading & Publishing Company *See* **Interstellar Publishing Co.**

†InterVarsity Pr., (*978-0-8308; 978-0-87784; 978-1-5140*) Div. of InterVarsity Christian Fellowship of the USA, Orders Addr.: P.O. Box 1400, Downers Grove, IL 60515 USA (SAN 202-7089) Tel 630-734-4000; Fax: 630-734-4200; Toll Free: 800-843-7225 (other depts.); 800-843-9487 (orders); 800-843-1019 (customer service); 800-873-0143 (electronic ordering); *Imprints:* IVP Books (IVP Bks)
E-mail: email@ivpress.com
Web site: http://www.ivpress.com
Dist(s): **INscribe Digital**
Midpoint Trade Bks., Inc.
christianaudio
ebrary, Inc.; *CIP.*

Intervisual/Piggy Toes *Imprint of* **Bendon, Inc.**

InterWeave Corp., (*978-0-9771936; 978-0-9841041*) Orders Addr.: 5364 Ehrlich Rd. No. 248, Tampa, FL 33624 USA Tel 813-933-4431; Fax: 813-933-4311
E-mail: kimberly@wheredoyoufindgod.com; kking@wheredoyoufindgod.com
Web site: http://www.wheredoyoufindgod.com.

IntoPrint Publishing LLC, (*978-1-62352; 978-0-578-44926-5*) 4322 Harding Pike, SUite 417, Nashville, TN 37205 USA Tel 615-210-8593
E-mail: jpcampbell3@mac.com; jonathanperry@comcast.net.

Intralife Systems Publishing, (*978-0-9703102*) P.O. Box 1555, Layton, UT 84041 USA Tel 801-544-2470; Fax: 801-544-2518
E-mail: admin@frogbuster.com
Web site: http://www.frogbuster.com.

Intrepid Films, LLC, (*978-1-929931*) Orders Addr.: P.O. Box 566, Boulder, CO 80306-0566 USA Tel 303-443-2426; Fax: 303-541-9737; Toll Free: 800-279-0802
E-mail: sportinc@msn.com; marya@intrepidfilms.com
Web site: http://www.intrepidfilms.com.

Intrepid Ink, LLC, (*978-0-9843857; 978-1-935774; 978-1-937022; 978-1-943403*) Orders Addr.: P.O. Box 302, McFarland, WI 53558 USA Tel 608-318-3636; *Imprints:* Resurrected Press (ResurrectedPr)
E-mail: publisher@intrepidink.com; irene@intrepidink.com
Web site: http://www.intrepidink.com.

Intrigue Publishing, (*978-0-9762181; 978-0-9794788; 978-0-9893696; 978-1-940758; 978-1-7337793*) 10200 Twisted Stalk Ct., Upper Marlboro, MD 20772 USA
E-mail: dbcamacho@hotmail.com
Web site: http://www.intriguepublishing.com
Dist(s): **Independent Pubs. Group.**

Intuitive Arts Pr., (*978-0-9741334*) 15 E. Northwest Hwy., Suite 15 B, Palatine, IL 60067 USA
E-mail: katychance@juno.com
Web site: http://www.peakperformanceliving.info.

invenTEAM, LLC *See* **From Inside the Heart**

Investigaciones LLEJ *See* **KCL Publishing & Tutoring**

Investing for Kids *Imprint of* **LINX Corp.**

Invisible College Pr., LLC, The, (*978-1-931468*) Orders Addr.: P.O. Box 209, Woodbridge, VA 22194 USA Tel 703-590-4005; Edit Addr.: 1206 N. Danville St., Arlington, VA 22201 USA; 3703 Del Mar Dr., Woodbridge, VA 22193
E-mail: manager@invispress.com
Web site: http://www.invispress.com/.

Invision Pubns., (*978-0-9767337*) 1136 Sherman Ave., Suite C4, Bronx, NY 10456 USA Tel 718-538-6102
E-mail: puzzles@puzzlesforus.com
Web site: http://www.puzzlesforus.com.

Invoke A Blessing Inc., (*978-0-9831902*) P.O. Box 163772, Fort Worth, TX 76161-3772 USA
E-mail: yuritereshchenko@hotmail.com; Yuritereshchenko@hotmail.com.

Invoke A Blessing Ministry *See* **Invoke A Blessing Inc.**

Inward Core, Inc., (*978-0-9796546*) Orders Addr.: P.O. Box 792, Roswell, GA 30077 USA (SAN 854-0284)
E-mail: nancialeath@inwardcore.com; passionnancia@gmail.com
Web site: http://www.inwardcorebooks.com.

Inward Reflections, Inc., (*978-0-9746783*) P.O. Box 1747, Brockton, MA 02303-1747 USA
E-mail: inwardreflections@homestead.com.

Inyati Press, (*978-0-9777440*) P.O. Box 453, fulton, CA 95439 USA
E-mail: milton@webbellis.org
Web site: http://www.webbellis.org.

I.Om.Be Pr., (*978-1-882161*) Orders Addr.: P.O. Box 1387, New York, NY 10159 USA
Web site: http://about.me/josefinaBaezAyombeT.

IONA Pubs., (*978-1-948056*) 413 Mosby Dr, Leesburg, VA 20175 USA Tel 219-669-8474
E-mail: ben@ionapublishers.com.

IOS Pr., Inc., (*978-90-407; 978-90-5199; 978-90-6275; 978-0-9673355; 978-1-58603; 978-90-298; 978-1-60750; 978-1-61499; 978-1-64368*) 4502 Rachael Manor Dr., Fairfax, VA 22032 USA Tel 703-323-5600; Fax: 703-323-3668; Nieuwe Hemweg 6B, Amsterdam, 1013 BG (SAN 858-995X) Tel 31 (0)20 688 33 55; Fax: 31 (0)20 687 00 19
E-mail: iosbooks@iospress.com; orders@iospress.com
Web site: http://www.iospress.com
Dist(s): **Ebsco Publishing**
Metapress
MyiLibrary
ebrary, Inc.

Iowa Greyhound Association *See* **McKinnon, Robert Scott**

Ipaatti, (*978-0-9984282*) 12500 Flatwood circel, Fairfax, VA 22033 USA Tel 703-901-7904
E-mail: kumar.sivalingam@ipaatti.com
Web site: www.ipaatti.com.

ipicturebooks *Imprint of* **ibooks, Inc.**

iPlayMusic, Inc., (*978-0-9760487; 978-0-9797683*) P.O. Box 391775, Mountain View, CA 94039 USA Tel 650-969-3387; Fax: 650-969-3680; Toll Free: 866-594-3344
E-mail: quincy@iplaymusic.com
Web site: http://www.iplaymusic.com
Dist(s): **Leonard, Hal Corp.**
Music Sales Corp.

IPMG Publishing, (*978-1-934218*) 18362 Erin Bay, Eden Prairie, MN 55347 USA (SAN 852-2057)
E-mail: webmaster@iplaymathgames.com
Web site: http://www.iplaymathgames.com.

Ippolito, Eva Marie, (*978-0-9705350; 978-0-615-11326-5*) 10316 W. Oakmont Dr., Sun City, AZ 85351-3528 USA.

iPulpFiction.com, (*978-0-9828090; 978-0-692-37516-7; 978-0-692-37518-1; 978-0-692-37526-6; 978-0-692-38410-7; 978-0-692-38411-4; 978-0-692-38412-1; 978-0-692-38413-8; 978-0-692-38414-5; 978-0-692-38428-2; 978-0-692-38690-3; 978-0-692-41603-7; 978-0-692-45613-2; 978-0-692-45695-8; 978-0-692-46161-7; 978-0-692-46508-0; 978-0-692-48539-2; 978-0-692-66826-9; 978-0-692-95944-2; 978-0-692-96162-9; 978-0-692-96166-7; 978-0-692-97715-6) 1630 W. Gail Dr., Chandler, AZ 85224 USA Tel 480-773-8958*
E-mail: publisher@ipulpfiction.com
Web site: http://www.iPulpFiction.com
Dist(s): **CreateSpace Independent Publishing Platform.**

Iran Books *See* **Ibex Pubs., Inc.**

Irene, Jan Pubns., (*978-0-9653428*) Orders Addr.: P.O. Box 934, Sonora, CA 95370 USA Tel 209-532-2470; Fax: 209-532-0277; Edit Addr.: 19575 Roselyn Ln., Sonora, CA 95370 USA
E-mail: janirene@mlode.com.

Irene Press *See* **Quindaro Pr.**

Irene Weinberger Bks. *Imprint of* **Hamilton Stone Editions**

Iris Pallas-Luke E-Writings/E-Literature, (*978-0-9765637*) 12472 Lake Underhill Rd., Suite 267, Orlando, FL 32828 USA
E-mail: irispallasluke@msn.com; noir@noirpallasluke.com
Web site: http://www.irispallas-luke.com; http://www.barbarapallas-luke.com; http://www.vemninapallas-luke.com; http://www.noirpallas-luke.com.

Iris Pr. *Imprint of* **Iris Publishing Group, Inc., The**

Iris Publishing Group, Inc., The, (*978-0-916078; 978-1-60454*) 969 Oak Ridge Turnpike, No. 328, Oak Ridge, TN 37830-8832 USA Tel 865-483-0837; Fax: 865-481-3793; Toll Free: 800-881-2119; *Imprints:* Iris Press (Iris)
E-mail: rcumming@irisbooks.com
Web site: htt://irisbooks.com.

Irish American Bk. Co., Subs. of Roberts Rinehart Pubs., Inc., P.O. Box 666, Niwot, CO 80544-0666 USA Tel 303-652-2710; Fax: 303-652-2689; Toll Free: 800-452-7115
E-mail: irishbooks@aol.com
Web site: http://www.irishvillage.com.

Irish Bks. & Media, Inc., (*978-0-937702*) Orders Addr.: 2904 41st Ave S., Minneapolis, MN 55406-1814 USA (SAN 111-8870) Toll Free: 800-229-3505 Do not confuse with Irish Bks. in New York, NY
E-mail: Irishbook@aol.com
Web site: http://www.irishbook.com.

Irish Genealogical Foundation, (*978-0-940134*) Div. of O'Laughlin Pr., P.O. Box 7575, Kansas City, MO 64116 USA (SAN 218-4834) Tel 816-454-2410
E-mail: mike@Irishroots.com
Web site: http://www.IrishRoots.com
Dist(s): **Irish Bks. & Media, Inc.**

Iron Arm International, (*978-0-9746989*) 1 Reid St., Amsterdam, NY 12010-3424 USA Tel 518-842-9299
E-mail: Ironarm1@aol.com
Web site: http://www.uechiryu-karate.com
Dist(s): **Tuttle Publishing.**

Iron Circus Comics, (*978-0-9708731; 978-0-9794080; 978-0-9890207; 978-1-945820*) Orders Addr.: 329 W 18th St Suite 604, Chicago, IL 60616 USA
Web site: http://www.ironcircus.com
Dist(s): **Consortium Bk. Sales & Distribution**
Diamond Comic Distributors, Inc.

Iron Fire Publishng Co., (*978-0-9817791*) 3702 Manhattan Ave., Suite 101, Fort Collins, CO 80526 USA (SAN 856-5465)
E-mail: mike@iron-fire.com
Web site: http://www.destinationstationseries.com.

Iron Mountain Pr., (*978-0-9722961*) Orders Addr.: P.O. Box 7, New Milford, NY 10959 USA (SAN 256-0097)
E-mail: info@ironmountainpress.com
Web site: http://www.ironmountainpress.com.

Iron Stream Media, (*978-1-56309; 978-1-59669*) 100 Missionary Ridge, Birmingham, AL 35242 USA Toll Free Fax: 888-811-9934; *Imprints:* New Hope Publishers (NewHopePub)
Dist(s): **Baker & Taylor Publisher Services (BTPS).**

Ironbound Pr., (*978-0-9763857*) P.O. Box 250, Winter Harbor, ME 04693-0250 USA Tel 207-963-2355; Fax: 320-323-2434 Do not confuse with Ironbound Pr. in Scotch Plains, NJ
E-mail: sales@ironboundpress.com
Web site: http://www.ironboundpress.com.

Ironcreek Pr., (*978-0-9766017*) 147 S. Randolph Ave., Asheboro, NC 27203 USA Tel 336-521-9105
E-mail: crottymartha@yahoo.com.

Ironcroft Publishing, (*978-0-9771688*) 11093 Alberta Dr., Brighton, MI 48114 USA
Web site: http://www.ironcroft.com
Dist(s): **BookBaby**
Partners Bk. Distributing, Inc.

Irongate Pr., (*978-0-9754746*) Orders Addr.: 1237 W. Seascape Dr., Gilbert, AZ 85233 USA Tel 480-813-2056
E-mail: jpascoe@irongatepress.com; j3pascoe@gmail.com
Web site: http://www.irongatepress.com
Dist(s): **Canyonlands Pubns.**
Forest Sales & Distributing Co.
Rio Nuevo Pubs.

Ironhorse Publishing Co., (*978-0-9747039*) 308 B W. Market St., Gratz, PA 17030 USA Fax: 717-365-7399 do not confuse with Ironhorse Publishing in Hayden Lake, ID
E-mail: pennvalleyprint@epix.net.

Irresistible Pr., LLC, (*978-1-946047*) 150 Ogilvie Dr., John Day, OR 97845 USA Tel 541-575-4387; *Imprints:* DoodleCake (DoodleCake)
E-mail: ccnrs@craigemcmillan.com
Web site: www.irresistiblepress.com
Dist(s): **Ingram Publisher Services**
Ingram Content Group.

†Irvington Pubs., (*978-0-512; 978-0-8290; 978-0-8422; 978-0-89197*) Orders Addr.: P.O. Box 286, New York, NY 10276-0286 USA Fax: 212-861-0998; Toll Free Fax: 800-455-5520; Toll Free: 800-472-6037
Dist(s): **Addicus Bks.**
MyiLibrary; *CIP.*

Irwin, Christine, (*978-0-615-15008-6; 978-0-578-00787-8*) 4N 265 Avard Rd., West Chicago, IL 60185 USA
Dist(s): **Lulu Pr., Inc.**

Irwin, Esther L., (*978-0-9778462*) 3531 Grove Dr., Cheyenne, WY 82001 USA Tel 307-632-2060
E-mail: Elivroman@bresnan.net.

†ISA, (*978-0-87664; 978-1-55617; 978-0-9791330; 978-0-9792343; 978-1-934394; 978-1-936007; 978-1-937560; 978-1-939660; 978-1-941546; 978-1-945541; 978-1-64331*) 67 Alexander Dr., Research Triangle Park, NC 27709 USA (SAN 202-7054) Tel 919-549-8411; Fax: 919-549-8288
E-mail: info@isa.org; ebell@isa.org; lelrod@isa.org
Web site: http://www.isa.org
Dist(s): **INscribe Digital**; *CIP.*

Isaac Publishing *See* **Ajoyin Publishing, Inc.**

Isaac Publishing, (*978-0-9787141; 978-0-9825218; 978-0-9853109; 978-0-9885930; 978-0-9892905; 978-0-9916145; 978-0-9967245; 978-0-9977033; 978-1-7321952; 978-1-952450*) 80 Abbeyville Rd., Lancaster, PA 17603 USA Tel 703-288-1681
E-mail: usa@barnabasaid.org
Web site: https://isaac-publishing.com/
Dist(s): **BookBaby**
Independent Pubs. Group
Midpoint Trade Bks., Inc.
Send The Light Distribution LLC.

Isaacs, John, (*978-0-9779606*) 643 N. Main St., Lawrenceburg, KY 40342 USA (SAN 850-6191) Tel 502-418-1521
E-mail: jisaacs@kheaa.com.

Isabella Media Inc, (*978-0-9994459; 978-1-7330416; 978-1-7357256*) 270 Bellevue Ave, Newport, RI 02840 USA Tel 401-354-2445
E-mail: steveg@isabellamedia.com
Web site: www.isabellabooks.com; www.isabellamedia.com.

Isabella Products, Inc., (*978-1-936503; 978-1-62334; 978-1-63083; 978-1-68186*) 23 Bradford St. 2nd Flr., Concord, MA 01742 USA Tel 978-287-0007; Fax: 309-405-1865; *Imprints:* StarWalk Kids Media (StarWalkKids)
E-mail: liz.nealon@isabellaproducts.com; support@fablelearning.com; gabrielle.howard@fablelearning.com
Web site: http://www.fablelearning.com; http://www.isabellaproducts.com
Dist(s): **INscribe Digital**
Independent Pubs. Group
StarWalk Kids.

ISBS Publisher Services, 920 NE 58th Ave., Suite 300, Portland, OR 97213-3786 USA (SAN 169-7129) Tel 503-287-3093; Fax: 503-280-8832; Toll Free: 800-944-6190
E-mail: info@isbs.com
Web site: http://www.isbs.com
Dist(s): **ebrary, Inc.**

iScribe Pubns. LLC, (*978-0-9883126*) 1006 Westbriar Dr., Henrico, VA 23238 USA Tel 804-441-3400; Fax: 804-741-7741
E-mail: info@iscribepublications.com.

ISD, 70 Enterprise Dr., Suite 2, Bristol, CT 06010 USA Tel 860-584-6546; Fax: 860-540-1001
E-mail: orders@isdistribution.com
Web site: https://www.isdistribution.com/.

Isha Enterprises, Inc., (*978-0-936981*) P.O. Box 25970, Scottsdale, AZ 85255 USA (SAN 658-7895) Tel 480-502-9454; Fax: 480-991-5635; Toll Free: 800-641-6015
E-mail: info@easygrammar.com
Web site: http://www.easygrammar.com.

Ishi Pr. International, (*978-0-923891*) Div. of The Ishi Pr. (Japan), 461 Peachstone Terr., San Rafael, CA 94903-1327 USA (SAN 249-0749) Tel 917-507-7226
E-mail: samhsloan@gmail.com
Web site: http://www.anusha.com/ordering.html.

ISI Bks., (*978-1-882926; 978-1-932236; 978-1-933859; 978-1-935191; 978-1-61017*) 3901 Centerville Rd., Wilmington, DE 19807-1938 USA Toll Free Fax: 800-621-8476 (orders in the US & CAN); Toll Free: 800-526-7022; 800-621-2736 (orders M-F in the US & CAN)
E-mail: bookpub@isi.org
Web site: http://www.isibooks.org
Dist(s): **Chicago Distribution Ctr.**
MyiLibrary
Open Road Integrated Media, Inc.
Open Road Distribution
Univ. of Chicago Pr.

ISIS Large Print Bks. (GBR) (*978-0-7531; 978-1-85089; 978-1-85695*) *Dist. by* **Transaction Pubs.**

Isis Publishing Hse., Inc., (*978-0-9662281*) 4620 Kings Hwy., Brooklyn, NY 11234 USA
E-mail: isispublishingco@aol.com.

Iskierka, Kristine, (*978-0-692-13533-4; 978-0-692-13534-1; 978-0-692-15852-4; 978-0-692-17114-1*) 16515 Yakima St. N.W., Andover, MN 55304 USA Tel 763-355-7680
E-mail: krisiskierka@gmail.com
Dist(s): **Ingram Content Group.**

Islamic Bk. Service, 1209 Cleburne, Hoston, TX 77004 USA (SAN 169-2453) Tel 713-528-1440; Fax: 713-528-1085.

Islamic Ctr. of Sacramento, The, (*978-0-9769245*) Div. of Sacramento Computers, c/o Sacramento Computers, 2022 4th St. #2, Sacramento, CA 95818 USA
E-mail: shamdani@mindspring.com
Web site: http://www.hineaf.net.

Islamic Foundation, Ltd. (GBR) (*978-0-9503954; 978-0-86037*) *Dist. by* **Consort Bk Sales.**

Islamic Supreme Council of America, (*978-1-930409; 978-1-938058*) Orders Addr.: 17195 Silver Pkwy. #401 Fenton, MI 48430, Fenton, MI 48430 USA Tel 810-593-1222; Fax: 810-815-0518; Toll Free: 800-278-6624; Edit Addr.: 17195 Silver Pkwy. #401 Fenton Michigan 48430, Fenton, MI 48430 USA
E-mail: staff@islamicsupremecouncil.org; aliyah@sunnah.org
Web site: http://www.islamicsupremecouncil.org; http://www.worde.org.

Island Friends LLC, (*978-0-9729987*) 11 Promontory Ct., Hilton Head Island, SC 29928 USA
E-mail: benjo@adelphia.net
Web site: http://www.islandfriends.net
Dist(s): **Sandlapper Publishing Co., Inc.**

Island Heritage Publishing, (*978-0-89610; 978-0-931548; 978-1-59700*) Div. of The Madden Corp., 94-411 Koaki St., Waipahu, HI 96797 USA (SAN 211-1403) Tel 808-564-8800; Fax: 808-564-8888; Toll Free: 800-468-2800
E-mail: ihorders@welcometotheislands.com
Web site: http://www.welcometotheislands.com
Dist(s): **Independent Pubs. Group**
Madden Corp., The
Midpoint Trade Bks., Inc.

Island In The Sky Publishing Co., (*978-0-9760328*) 60 Meadow Lakes, East Windsor, NJ 08520 USA
Web site: http://www.MemoriesOfWWII.com.

Island Ink, (*978-0-9657849*) Orders Addr.: P.O. Box 1818, Indiantown, FL 34956 USA Tel 561-597-3778; Fax: 561-597-4691.

Island Institute, (*978-0-942719; 978-0-9835613*) 386 Main St., Box 648, Rockland, ME 04841-3345 USA (SAN 667-7274) Tel 207-594-9209; Fax: 207-594-9314
E-mail: inquiry@islandinstitute.org; publications@islandinstitute.org
Web site: http://www.islandinstitute.org
Dist(s): **Magazines, Inc.**

Island Media Publishing, LLC, (*978-0-9829908*) 120 N. 15th St., Fernandina Beach, FL 32034 USA Tel 904-556-3002
E-mail: islandmediapublishing@gmail.com.

Island Moon Pr., (*978-0-9755605*) P.O. Box 956, Oaks, PA 19456-0956 USA Tel 610-935-2378; Toll Free: 877-252-8262
E-mail: islandquest@msn.com
Web site: http://www.IslandMoonPress.com.

Island Nation Pr., LLC, (*978-0-9657437; 978-1-892738*) Orders Addr.: 144 Rowayton Woods Dr., Norwalk, CT 06854 USA Tel 203-852-0028; Fax: 203-852-0528; Toll Free: 888-356-1450 [Direct Order Line]
E-mail: cvaleallen@earthlink.net
Web site: http://www.charlottevaleallen.com.

Island Paradise Publishing, (*978-0-9705889; 978-0-9855153*) Orders Addr.: P.O. Box 163, Haleiwa, HI 96712 USA Tel 808-638-9640; Edit Addr.: 59-465 KeWaena Rd., Haleiwa, HI 96712 USA
E-mail: CooperKool@Hawaii.rr.com
Dist(s): **Booklines Hawaii, Ltd.**

Islandport Pr., Inc., (*978-0-9671662; 978-0-9763231; 978-1-934031; 978-1-939017; 978-1-944762; 978-1-952143*) Orders Addr.: P.O. Box 10, Yarmouth, ME 04096 USA Tel 207-846-3344; Fax: 207-846-3955; Edit Addr.: 267 US Rte. 1, Suite B, Yarmouth, ME 04096 USA
E-mail: deanlunt@islandportpress.com
Web site: http://www.islandportpress.com
Dist(s): **Baker & Taylor Publisher Services (BTPS)**
Follett School Solutions
INscribe Digital
Independent Pubs. Group
MyiLibrary
ebrary, Inc.

IslandWood, (*978-0-9821633*) Orders Addr.: 4450 Blakely Ave. NE, Bainbridge Island, WA 98110 USA Tel 206-855-4300; Fax: 206-855-4301
Web site: http://www.IslandWood.org.

ISLC, (*978-0-9763226*) c/o Alfassa, 15 W. 16th St., 6th Flr., New York, NY 10011 USA Tel 917-207-4344
E-mail: shelomo@alfassa.com.

Isle of Dogs Publishing, Co., (*978-0-9741321*) 4008 - 83rd Ave. SE, Snohomish, WA 98290 USA
E-mail: connieraestrain@msn.com; ConnieRaeStrain@IsleofDogsPublishing.com
Web site: http://www.isleofdogspublishing.com.

Isles of the Sea Pubs., (*978-0-9728126*) Orders Addr.: P.O. Box 51352, Provo, UT 84605-1352 USA Tel 801-427-5209; Edit Addr.: 2052 S. California Ave., No. 12, Provo, UT 84044 USA
E-mail: drrlesa@hotmail.com.

Islewest Publishing, (*978-0-9641919; 978-1-888461*) Div. of Carlisle Communications, Ltd., 4242 Chavenelle Dr., Dubuque, IA 52002-2650 USA (SAN 299-5018)
E-mail: mjgraham@carcomm.com
Web site: http://www.islewest.com
Dist(s): **Independent Pubs. Group.**

Israel Book Shop *See* **Israel Bookshop Pubns.**

Israel Bookshop Pubns., (*978-0-9670705; 978-1-931681; 978-1-60091*) 501 Prospect St., No. 97, Lakewood, NJ 08701 USA Tel 732-901-3009; Fax: 732-901-4012; Toll Free: 888-536-7427
E-mail: sales@israelbookshoppublications.com
Web site: http://www.israelbookshoppublications.com.

ISS, (*978-1-934942*) 2 Shaker Rd. Ste. D103, Shirley, MA 01464-2535 USA (SAN 855-6164)
E-mail: print@issexpress.com
Web site: http://www.imagesoftware.com.

Istoria Hse., (*978-0-9816538*) Orders Addr.: P.O. Box 6342, Vernon Hills, IL 60061 USA (SAN 856-1370)
E-mail: info@istoriahouse.com
Web site: http://www.istoriahouse.com.

Italica Pr., (*978-0-934977; 978-1-59910*) 595 Main St., Suite 605, New York, NY 10044 USA (SAN 695-1805) Tel 917-371-0563
E-mail: inquiries@italicapress.com
Web site: http://www.italicapress.com.

Itasca Bks., (*978-0-9767054*) Orders Addr.: 5120 Cedar Lake Rd. S., Minneapolis, MN 55416 USA (SAN 855-3823) Tel 952-345-4488; Fax: 952-920-0541; Toll Free: 800-901-3480
E-mail: mjung@itascabooks.com
Web site: http://www.itascabooks.com
Dist(s): **BookMobile.**

iTeenBooks Inc., (*978-0-9798997; 978-0-9852925*) P.O. Box 171, Middletown, NJ 07748-0171 USA.

Ithaca Pr. *Imprint of* **Authors & Artists Publishers of New York, Inc.**

Ithuriel's Spear, (*978-0-9749502; 978-0-9793390; 978-0-9835791; 978-1-943209*) 939 Eddy St., Apt. 102, San Francisco, CA 94109 USA Tel 415-440-3204 plainfeather@gmail.com
E-mail: plainfeather@gmail.com
Web site: http://www.ithuriel.com
Dist(s): **BookMobile**
SPD-Small Pr. Distribution.

ITI Holdings, Inc., (*978-1-931451; 978-1-61011*) 1321 SE Decker Ave, Stuart, FL 34994 USA Tel 207-729-4201; Fax: 207-729-4453; Toll Free: 888-778-9073
E-mail: flemming.elleboe@tdisdi.com; brian.carney@tdisdi.com; worldhq@tdisdi.com
Web site: http://www.tdisdi.com.

Itiya Publishing, Inc., (*978-0-9770312*) 217 Ave. Unvi. Interanericana PMB 161, San German, PR 00683 USA
E-mail: gpita@itiyainc.com
Web site: http://www.itiyainc.com.

ITRON Publishing, (*978-0-9786863*) 6510 LBJ Freeway, Suite 200, Dallas, TX 75240 USA (SAN 851-2817) Tel 972-934-2811; Fax: 972-934-1705.

It's A Habit! Co., The, (*978-0-9713664*) 2238 Harwood St., Los Angeles, CA 90031-1238 USA Tel 323-254-7772
Web site: http://www.itsahabit.com.

It's a Lifestyle Fitness, (*978-0-9890227*) 1 Evergreen Pl., Morristown, NJ 07960 USA (SAN 920-783X) Tel 973-267-2121
E-mail: gregorycrawford@ymail.com.

It's About Time, Herff Jones Education Division *See* **It's About Time, Herff Jones Education Div.**

It's About Time, Herff Jones Education Div., (*978-1-891629; 978-1-58591; 978-1-60720; 978-1-68231*) Orders Addr.: 333 N. Bedford Rd. # 110, Mt. Kisco, NY 10549 USA Tel 914-273-2233; Fax: 914-273-2227; Toll Free: 888-698-8463 Do not confuse with companies with the same name in Los Gatos, CA, Santa Monica, CA
E-mail: gerneralinfo@herffjones.com
Web site: http://www.its-about-time.com.

It's Good 2B Good LLC,
Dist(s): **Baker & Taylor Publisher Services (BTPS).**

It's Me Briana, LLC, (*978-0-9793904; 978-0-9838492*) P.O. Box 12386, Atlanta, GA 30355 USA
Web site: http://www.brianasneighborhood.com.

It's My Hair! Magazine, (*978-0-692-74966-1; 978-0-692-77197-6; 978-0-692-83141-0; 978-0-692-88297-9; 978-0-692-93394-7*) P.O. Box 18593, ATLANTA, GA 31126 USA Tel 470-755-2061.

ITSMEEE Industries, (*978-0-9677231*) 13918 E. Mississippi Ave., No 213, Aurora, CO 80012 USA Tel 303-229-7584
E-mail: itsmeeeindustries@outlook.com.

Itsy Bitsy Muslims *See* **Itsy Bitsy Muslims**

Itsy Bitsy Muslims, (*978-1-7321600*)
E-mail: alielsayed.92@gmail.com; Elsayed.neda@gmail.com
Web site: https://www.itsybitsymuslims.com/.

Itty Bitty Bks., (*978-0-9760691*) 1682 NW 785 Rd., Bates City, MO 64011 USA Tel 816-697-3617 (phone/fax)
E-mail: waynedyer@gmail.com.

Itty Bitty Kitty *Imprint of* **Singing Moon Pr.**

Itty Bitty Witch Works, (*978-0-9768573*) P.O. Box 532, Kernville, CA 93238 USA Tel 760-376-3973 (phone/fax)
E-mail: ittybittywitch@sierranet.us
Web site: http://ittybittywitch.com.

iUniverse, Inc. *Imprint of* **iUniverse, Inc.**

iUniverse, Inc., (*978-0-9665514; 978-1-58348; 978-0-9668591; 978-1-893652; 978-0-595; 978-0-9795279; 978-1-60528; 978-1-4401; 978-1-936236; 978-1-4502; 978-1-4620; 978-1-4697; 978-1-4759; 978-1-4917; 978-1-5320; 978-1-6632*) Orders Addr.: 1663 Liberty Dr., Suite 300, Bloomington, IN 47403 USA (SAN 254-9425) Toll Free: 800-288-4677; *Imprints:* Writers Club Press (Writers Club Pr); Writer's Showcase Press (Writers Showcase); Backinprint.com (Backinprint); ASJA Press (ASJA Pr); Authors Choice Press (Authors Choice Pr); Mystery Writers of America Presents (Myst Write Amer); Mystery & Suspense Press (Mystery & Suspense); Weekly Reader Teacher's Press (Weekly Rd Tch); Writers

Advantage Press (Writers Adv Pr); iUniverse, Inc. (iUni Inc); iUniverse Star (iUniverse Star)
Web site: http://www.iUniverse.com; http://iuniverse.com; www.balboapress.com
Dist(s): **Author Solutions, Inc.**
Baker & Taylor Publisher Services (BTPS)
CreateSpace Independent Publishing Platform
Smashwords
Zondervan.

iUniverse Star *Imprint of* **iUniverse, Inc.**

iUniverse.com, Incorporated *See* **iUniverse, Inc.**

Iverson, Theodore, *(978-0-9747378)* P.O. Box 3671, Grand Canyon, AZ 86023-3671 USA.

Ivey Leaf Publishing, *(978-0-9981801)* 8508 Jean Parrish Ct. NE, Albuquerque, NM 87122 USA Tel 505-400-1785
Dist(s): **CreateSpace Independent Publishing Platform.**

Ivoryton Pr., *(978-0-9814663)* P.O. Box 485, Ivoryton, CT 06442 USA Tel 860-581-8133
E-mail: Ivoryton.Press@gmail.com.

IVP Bks. *Imprint of* **InterVarsity Pr.**

Ivy Advising LLC, *(978-0-9771568)* 50 Livingston St., Brooklyn, NY 11201 USA (SAN 256-8934).

Ivy Fund, The, *(978-0-9754003)* 33 Irving St., Waltham, MA 02451-0758 USA
E-mail: courtney@ivysplace.org
Web site: http://ivysplace.org.

Ivy Group, The (GBR) *Dist. by* **HachBkGrp.**

Ivy Hill Bunch, LLC, *(978-0-9743619)* P.O. Box 1053, La Quinta, CA 92253 USA Tel 760-771-0834; Fax: 760-771-1910; Toll Free: 866-892-5795
E-mail: lynn@ivyhillbunch.com
Web site: http://www.saddyandgladdy.com.

Ivy House Publishing Group *Imprint of* **Pentland Pr., Inc.**

Ivy Pr., The (GBR) *(978-1-905695; 978-1-908005; 978-1-907332; 978-1-78240) Dist. by* **HachBkGrp.**

IvyStone Pr., *(978-0-9755771)* P.O. Box 50, Emmalena, KY 41740 USA
E-mail: hodson@tgtel.com
Web site: http://www.mountainrainbow.com.

iwishyouicecreamandcake, *(978-0-9792019)* 3871 W. Millers Bridge Rd., Tallahassee, FL 32312 USA Fax: 850-893-9616
E-mail: carolhmoore@yahoo.com
Web site: http://iwishyouicecreamandcake.com.

Ixia Pr. *Imprint of* **Dover Pubns., Inc.**

Iyengar, Malathi, *(978-0-9753912)* 14748 Morrison St., Sherman Oaks, CA 91403 USA
E-mail: msiyengar@yahoo.com
Web site: http://www.rangoli.org.

IYF Publishing, *(978-0-692-69861-7; 978-0-9998780; 978-1-7345152)* 501 S Jackson St, Beverly Hills, FL 34465 USA Tel 239-272-8613; *Imprints:* Dragon Hoard Press (MYID_Y_DRAGON)
Web site: www.SandyLenderInk.com
Dist(s): **CreateSpace Independent Publishing Platform.**

iynx publishing (GBR) *(978-0-9535413; 978-0-9540583) Dist. by* **Dufour.**

IZA Publishing Co., *(978-0-9674241)* 253 Pvt. Rd. 2410, Uvalde County, TX 78801 USA Tel 361-946-3132; Fax: 361-946-2000
E-mail: smith-ma@swbell.net.

IZS, Inc., *(978-0-9764684)* 34 E. Franklin St., Bellbrook, OH 45305-1746 USA Tel 937-848-8896
E-mail: pantherbay@aol.com
Web site: http://www.pantherbay.com.

IzzyBella Bks., *(978-0-578-49304-6; 978-0-578-56938-3; 978-0-578-63492-0)* 8828 Meridian Pl. NE B 102, Lake Stevens, WA 98258 USA Tel 360-784-9390
E-mail: abbi.mckee@yahoo.com.

J A G Pubns., *(978-0-943327)* 11288 Ventura Blvd., No. 301, Studio City, CA 91604 USA (SAN 668-4157) Tel 818-505-9002 (phone/fax) Do not confuse with Jag Publications in Los Angeles, CA
E-mail: info@jagpublications-esl.com
Web site: http://www.jagpublications-esl.com.

J A Interests, Inc., *(978-0-9769648)* P.O. Box 1472, Versailles, KY 40383 USA.

J A S Pr., Inc., *(978-0-9666920; 978-0-9773316)* Orders Addr.: P.O. Box 1925, Bolingbrook, IL 60440 USA Tel 630-226-1635; Edit Addr.: 155 Ashcroft Dr., Bolingbrook, IL 60490 USA Tel 630-226-1635
E-mail: jaspress@mindspring.com.

J & J Publishing Co., *(978-0-9759831)* Box 305, 9728 US Hwy. 277, Elgin, OK 73538 USA Do not confuse with companies with same or similar name in Los Angeles, CA, Buffalo, NY, Englewood, CO, Darien, IL, Frankfurt, IL MD
E-mail: djw73@aol.com.

J & J Publishing Co., *(978-0-9705008; 978-0-615-73754-6; 978-0-9961018)* P.O. Box 291205, Columbia, SC 29229 USA Tel 803-968-5196
E-mail: jjpublisher@yahoo.com
Web site: http://www.jandjpublishingonline.com.

J & K Publishing, *(978-0-9790487)* 5221 Collins St., Suite 101, Panama City, FL 32404 USA
E-mail: jnbowen@netscape.com.

J&M Publishing, *(978-0-9646590)* 2417 Valley View Rd., Narvon, PA 17555 USA Tel 610-286-5489 Do not confuse with companies with the same name in Lebanon, TN, Fayetteville, NC, Phoenix, AZ.

J B Communications, Inc., *(978-1-55987)* 101 W. 55th St., No. 2D, New York, NY 10019-5346 USA Tel 212-246-0900; *Imprints:* Sunny Books (Sunny Bks).

J. B. J. Enterprises *See* **Morgan, E. A.**

J. Caro & Associates *See* **Cowboy Collector Pubns.**

J J Publishing, *(978-0-9604610)* 1312 Arthur St., Hollywood, FL 33019 USA (SAN 220-0090) Tel 954-929-3559 (phone/fax).

J. K. Eckert & Co., Inc., *(978-0-9835675; 978-0-9913571; 978-0-9915252; 978-0-692-27860-4)* 513 Dona Dr., Nokomis, FL 34275 USA Tel 941-882-8760; *Imprints:* Susanna Lagoon Books (SusLagoonBks)
E-mail: tech@jkeckert.com.

J L Publishing Co., *(978-0-9740774)* 2901 Ranch Rd, Apt. 511, Paragould, AR 72450 USA.

J M D's Business Services, *(978-0-9712641)* 67 Darling St., Southington, CT 06489 USA
E-mail: jmdsbussrv@liquidchariot.com
Web site: http://www.jmdsbusinessservices.com; http://www.liquidchariot.com.

J. M. Jensen, *(978-0-578-42147-6; 978-0-578-42167-4)* 9606 Fox Den Dr., Littleton, CO 80125 USA Tel 970-372-6263
E-mail: jmjensenart@yahoo.com
Dist(s): **Ingram Content Group.**

J M Pubns., *(978-0-9638007)* Orders Addr.: P.O. Box 753427, Memphis, TN 38115 USA; Edit Addr.: 3830 Scottsdale Ave., Memphis, TN 38115 USA (SAN 255-0598) Tel 901-368-3414; Fax: 901-566-1978; Toll Free: 888-321-4747
E-mail: jmpub1@midsouth.rr.com
Web site: http://www.jmpublications.com.

J. Paul Getty Museum *Imprint of* **Getty Pubns.**

J. Taylor Publishing, *(978-0-9834058; 978-1-937744)* 5448 Apex Peakway No. 198, Apex, NC 27502 USA Tel 919-249-7318
E-mail: production@jtaylorpublishing.com
Web site: http://www.jtaylorpublishing.com.

J2B Publishing LLC, *(978-0-9911994; 978-1-941927; 978-1-948747)* 4251 Columbia Pk. Rd., Pomfret, MD 20675 USA Tel 202-557-8097
E-mail: GladToDoIt@gmail.com
Web site: www.GladToDoIt.net; www.J2BLLC.com.

J3Russell, LLC., *(978-1-7350437)* 575 NE 162nd St., Miami, FL 33162 USA Tel 786-838-7403
E-mail: j3russell@yahoo.com
Web site: http://www.j3russellbooks.wordpress.com
Dist(s): **Ingram Content Group.**

JA Pubns., Ltd., *(978-0-9746093; 978-0-9794124)* Orders Addr.: P.O. Box 7275, Loveland, CO 80537 USA Tel 970-776-8395; Fax: 970-692-2492
E-mail: julieaydlott@gmail.com; info@japbulicationsltd.com
Web site: http://www.startabookkeepingbusiness.com/; http://www.thevitalicsystem.com
Dist(s): **Emery-Pratt Co.**
Midwest Library Service.

Jabberwocky Literary Agency, Inc., *(978-1-936535; 978-1-62567)* Orders Addr.: P.O. Box 4558, Sunnyside, NY 11104 USA Tel 718-392-5985; Edit Addr.: 41-16 47th Ave., No. 2D, Sunnyside, NY 11104 USA Tel 718-392-5985
E-mail: jessie@awfulagent.com
Web site: www.awfulagent.com
Dist(s): **INscribe Digital**
Independent Pubs. Group
Open Road Integrated Media, Inc.

Jacana Media (ZAF) *(978-1-874955; 978-1-919931; 978-1-919777; 978-1-4314; 978-1-928420) Dist. by* **IPG Chicago.**

Jacera Publishing, *(978-1-943992)* 14918 EL TESORO DR, HOUSTON, TX 77083 USA Tel 281-772-2549
E-mail: jen.m.gabler@gmail.com.

Jack Hook Publishing, *(978-0-9837863)* 1288 Columbus Ave., No. 279, San Francisco, CA 94133 USA Tel 310-889-4728
E-mail: susan.saville@jackhook.com
Web site: www.jackhook.com.

Jack Walker Pr., *(978-1-945378)* 945 Bay View Cir., Mukwonago, WI 53149 USA Tel 262-955-6675
E-mail: amyloujenkins@gmail.com
Web site: www.JackWalkerPress.com.

Jackal Moon Pr. *Imprint of* **P. Anastasia**

JacKris Publishing, *(978-0-9772923; 978-0-9821196; 978-0-9826608; 978-0-9836089)*
E-mail: sales@growingwithgrammar.com; tonydee64@sbcglobal.net
Web site: http://www.jackrispublishing.com; http://www.growingwithgrammar.com.

Jack's Bookshelf, Inc., *(978-1-928907)* 224 Woodland Dr., Vista, CA 92083 USA.

Jackson, Amber, *(978-0-692-84096-2; 978-0-578-60073-4)* 5390 Amber Cove Way, FLOWERY BRANCH, GA 30542 USA Tel 404-694-4387
E-mail: jeffwcrawford5+LVP0003324@gmail.com; jeffwcrawford5+LVP0003324@gmail.com.

Jackson Joy LLC, *(978-0-692-84728-2; 978-0-692-84760-2; 978-0-692-07028-4)* P.O. Box 922, GRAYSON, GA 30017 USA Tel 770-375-0635
E-mail: jeffwcrawford5+LVP0003332@gmail.com; jeffwcrawford5+LVP0003332@gmail.com.

Jackson, Linda *See* **Jackson Publishing**

Jackson, Lucas L. *See* **RBHC LLC.**

Jackson Publishing, *(978-0-9716442)* 7661 Forstoria Cove, Southaven, MS 38672 USA Tel 901-413-5748 Do not confuse with companies with the same name in Jackson, MS; Clarkston, MI
E-mail: jackson35015@bellsouth.net.

Jackson, Robert, *(978-0-9761420)* 12807 Prospect Knolls Dr., Bowie, MD 20720 USA
E-mail: trebor_jackson@yahoo.com
Web site: http://www.amazinglibertеens.com.

Jacobob Pr., LLC, *(978-0-9705827; 978-0-9772817; 978-0-9820960; 978-0-9838072; 978-0-9852887; 978-0-9857477; 978-0-9860361; 978-0-9911151; 978-0-9914066; 978-0-9916416; 978-0-692-53701-5; 978-0-692-55660-3)* 11035 Ridge Forest Ct., Saint Louis, MO 63126-3429 USA (SAN 257-1862) Tel 314-843-4829
E-mail: jacobobsw@sbcglobal.net
Web site: http://jacobobpress.com
Dist(s): **Follett School Solutions**
Jacobob Pr. Distributing
Unique Bks., Inc.

Jacobs, Karen, *(978-0-9850440; 978-0-9982119)* 40 Indian Carry Rd., Moultonbourgh, NH 03254 USA Tel 617-838-1872
E-mail: kjacobs@bu.edu.

Jacqueline Bell *See* **Body by Bella, LLC**

Jacqueline Beverly Hills, *(978-0-9664783)* 650 The Village, Unit 215, Redondo Beach, CA 90277-2734 USA
E-mail: jacquih3@yahoo.com
Web site: http://jbhbooks.com.

Jacquet-Acea, Russell, *(978-0-9771919)* 3645 Whitman Ave. N., Seattle, WA 98103 USA Tel 206-547-7026; Fax: 810-454-1721
E-mail: rjacquet2@msn.com
Web site: http://rjacquet.tripod.com.

JADA Pr., *(978-0-9747501; 978-0-9761110; 978-0-9764115; 978-0-9771343; 978-0-9788724; 978-0-9800629; 978-0-9843558; 978-0-9848365; 978-0-9907961)* 4375 Confederate Point Rd. #6-H, Jacksonville, FL 32210 USA Tel 904-226-8876 (leave a message)
Web site: http://www.jadapress.com.

JadaStar *See* **Star Publish LLC**

Jade Enterprises, *(978-0-9753410)* 11807 S. Fair Hollow Ln., Suite 106, Houston, TX 77043-1033 USA Tel 713-416-0109
Web site: http://www.authorsden.com/deborahkfrontiera.

Jade Publishing, *(978-0-9985390; 978-1-949299)* 700 Ciro St., Donna, TX 78537 USA Tel 956-570-1023
E-mail: rossylima@jadepublishing.org
Web site: www.jadepublishing.org.

Jade Ram Publishing, *(978-1-877721)* 3003 Wendy's Way, No. 9, Anchorage, AK 99517-1466 USA Tel 907-248-0979; Fax: 907-272-8432
E-mail: jaderam@alaska.net
Dist(s): **Publication Consultants**
Todd Communications
Wizard Works.

Jade Tree Bks., *(978-0-9888610)* P.O. Box 2132, Cherry Hill, NJ 08034 USA Tel 215-913-3456
E-mail: pangj@comcast.net.

Jadenaila Publishing, *(978-0-615-12544-2)* 7340 S. Union Creek Way 5G, Salt Lake City, UT 84047 USA Tel 801-916-1037
E-mail: kidsbooksbynaila@hotmail.com
Web site: http://www.kidsbooksbynaila.com.

Jades Publishing, *(978-0-9743352)* Orders Addr.: P.O. Box 485, Fayette, OH 43521 USA Tel 419-237-3128; Edit Addr.: 24022-T, Fayette, OH 43521 USA
E-mail: amadsj@bright.net; amadsj@bright.nett.

Jaffe Book Solutions, Div. of Booksource, 1230 Macklind Ave, Saint Louis, MO 63110-1432 USA
Dist(s): **Booksource, The.**

Jaffee, Diane, *(978-0-692-19766-0; 978-1-7350254)* 7799 Wills Run Ln, Blacklick, OH 43004 USA Tel 614-933-0608
E-mail: Jaffwoman@gmail.com.

Jaffrey, Kamal, *(978-0-9753673)* 400 Technology Sq., Cambridge, MA 02139 USA.

Jahs Publishing Group, *(978-0-9701144; 978-0-9747550; 978-0-615-49893-5; 978-0-615-50005-8)* 6304 Somerset Rd., Riverdale, MD 20737 USA Tel 301-326-6468
Web site: http://www.jahspublishing.com
Dist(s): **CreateSpace Independent Publishing Platform.**

Jajou, Rafee, *(978-0-692-19219-1)* 7341 Cornell Ave., La Mesa, CA 91942 USA Tel 619-204-6291
E-mail: rjajou@gmail.com
Dist(s): **Ingram Content Group.**

Jakkar Enterprises, *(978-0-692-15099-3; 978-0-692-15949-1; 978-0-692-17649-8; 978-0-578-43447-6; 978-0-578-51473-4; 978-0-578-54902-6; 978-0-578-55096-1; 978-0-578-69512-9; 978-0-578-69513-6)* 777 W. Germantown Pike Apt. 926, Plymouth Meeting, PA 19462 USA Tel 215-300-2904
E-mail: lenny1908@yahoo.com
Web site: www.leonardandersonjr.com.

Jakki Joy Publishing, *(978-0-692-69630-9; 978-1-7339436)* 7010 Alpine Way, Yakima, WA 98908 USA Tel 509-930-4611
Dist(s): **CreateSpace Independent Publishing Platform.**

Jakobi Publishing, LLC, *(978-0-9972358)* 5820 Perry Rd., Elkton, FL 32033 USA Tel 904-377-3915
E-mail: heather.hamel@hotmail. om
Web site: heatherhamel.com.

Jalali, Yassaman *See* **Saman Publishing**

Jalmar Pr., *(978-0-915190; 978-0-935266; 978-1-880396; 978-1-931061)* Subs. of B. L. Winch & Assocs., P.O. Box 370, Fawnskin, CA 92333-0370 USA (SAN 113-3640) Toll Free: 800-662-9662 (orders)
E-mail: jalmarpress@att.net
Web site: http://jalmarpress.com
Dist(s): **Winch, B. L. & Assocs.**
Brodart Co.

JA-M Pubs., LLC, *(978-0-9728975)* 2358 Pinewood Blvd., Bitely, MI 49309 USA Tel 231-745-8641; 269-363-2955 Do not confuse with companies with the same or similar name in Mount Pleasant, SC, Comstock Park, MI
E-mail: joycex4@msn.com; jandmck@gmail.com
Web site: http://ja-mpublishers.weebly.com.

Jama Kids, *(978-0-9772711)* 612 N. St., Beaufort, SC 29902 USA Tel 843-522-1577
E-mail: janspringle@earthlink.net.

Jamaldinian, Yousef, *(978-0-9766657)* 5207 Olley Ln., Burke, VA 22015 USA Tel 571-212-9471
E-mail: joedinian@yahoo.com.

JaMarque Publishing *See* **JK Pr.**

James, JoAnn, *(978-0-9764406)* P.O. Box 11459, Eugene, OR 97440 USA
E-mail: joann_james@comcast.net.

James Lorimer & Co. Ltd., Pubs. (CAN) *(978-0-88862; 978-1-55028; 978-1-55277; 978-1-4594) Dist. by* **Casemate Pubs.**

James Lorimer & Co. Ltd., Pubs. (CAN) *(978-0-88862; 978-1-55028; 978-1-55277; 978-1-4594) Dist. by* **Children Plus.**

James Lorimer & Co. Ltd., Pubs. (CAN) *(978-0-88862; 978-1-55028; 978-1-55277; 978-1-4594) Dist. by* **Lerner Pub.**

James Matthew Thompson, *(978-0-692-17501-9)* 762 Coriander Rd., Blythewood, SC 29016 USA Tel 803-466-4006
E-mail: jamathompson@gmail.com
Dist(s): **Ingram Content Group.**

James Stevenson Pub., *(978-1-885852)* 1500 Oliver Rd., Suite K-109, Fairfield, CA 94533 USA Tel 707-469-0237; Fax: 206-350-2954
E-mail: ceo@jspub.com
Web site: http://www.jspub.com
Dist(s): **Marangio, Charles F. Distribution.**

†**Jameson Bks., Inc.,** *(978-0-89803; 978-0-915463; 978-0-916054)* 722 Columbus St., P.O. Box 738, Ottawa, IL 61350 USA (SAN 281-7578) Tel 815-434-7905; Fax: 815-434-7907; Toll Free: 800-426-1357
E-mail: jamesonbooks@yahoo.com
Dist(s): **Midpoint Trade Bks., Inc.;** *CIP.*

Jamestown, *(978-0-07; 978-0-8092; 978-0-8442; 978-0-89061; 978-0-913327; 978-0-941263; 978-1-56943)* Div. of Glencoe/McGraw-Hill, Orders Addr.: P.O. Box 543, Blacklick, OH 43004-0543 USA Fax: 614-860-1877; Toll Free: 800-334-7344; Edit Addr.: P.O. Box 508, Columbus, OH 43216 USA Toll Free: 800-872-7323
Web site: http://www.jamestowneducation.com
Dist(s): **Libros Sin Fronteras**
McGraw-Hill Cos., The.

Jamie Jai, 687 Valley View Way, Travis AFB, CA 94535 USA Tel 214-498-0406
E-mail: Jamiejaifitness@gmail.com
Dist(s): **Ingram Content Group.**

Jamiram Publishing, *(978-0-9790434)* 1760 Harbeck Rd., Grants Pass, OR 97527 USA
Web site: http://jamiram.com.

Jamisonk.com, *(978-0-692-08517-2; 978-0-692-08518-9; 978-0-692-08985-9; 978-0-578-55500-3; 978-0-578-62136-4)* Tiny Ranch 5 Paso Mediano, Carmel Valley, CA 93924 USA Tel 831-236-2036
E-mail: jamisonk@mac.com
Dist(s): **Ingram Content Group.**

JamSum Limited, *(978-0-9770754)* 621 S. Main St., Bellefontaine, OH 43311-1725 USA Toll Free: 866-857-2061
E-mail: publish@jamsum.com
Web site: http://www.jamsum.com.

Jan & San *See* **Jerome, Janice**

Jan-Carol Publishing, INC., *(978-0-9767793; 978-0-9801504; 978-0-9822337; 978-0-9841870; 978-0-9843192; 978-0-9845470; 978-0-9846398; 978-0-9834885; 978-0-9848050; 978-0-9850272; 978-1-939289; 978-1-945619; 978-1-950895)* Orders Addr.: PO Box 701, Johnson City, TN 37605 USA Tel 423-926-9983; *Imprints:* Little Creek Books (LittleCreek)
Web site: www.voicemagazineforwomen.com; www.jancarolpublishing.com.

Jandie Jams Music LLC, *(978-0-9796150)* 1036 Katy Ln., Longmont, CO 80504 USA (SAN 853-8999)
E-mail: jandiejams@comcast.net
Web site: http://www.kidcleveronline.com.

J&M Pubs, *(978-0-9726492)* Orders Addr.: P.O. Box 648, Florence, SC 29501 USA Fax: 410-981-5456; Toll Free: 800-989-1170
E-mail: jmpublishers@comcast.net
Web site: http://www.jmpublishers.net.

Jane & Street Pubs. Ltd., *(978-0-9745077)* 302-A W. 12th St., No. 197, New York, NY 10014 USA
Web site: http://www.janeandstreet.com.

Janelle Pubns., Inc., *(978-0-9626739; 978-1-890265)* Orders Addr.: P.O. Box 811, De Kalb, IL 60115-0811 USA Tel 815-756-2300; Fax: 815-756-4799; Toll Free: 800-888-8834; Edit Addr.: 1189 Twombley Rd., De Kalb, IL 60115 USA
E-mail: info@janellepublications.com
Web site: http://www.janellepublications.com.

Jane's World *See* **Girl Twirl Comics**

Janik Pr., *(978-0-9883938)* P.O. Box 12034, Fort Wayne, IN 46862 USA Tel 260-804-8044
E-mail: nikbenedict@yahoo.com.

Janis, Tim Ensemble, Inc., *(978-0-9773335)* P.O. Box 315, Kennebunk, ME 04043 USA (SAN 257-280X) Tel 207-985-3463.

Jank Publishing LLC, *(978-0-9845572)* Orders Addr.: 3081 Farmstead Ct., Grayson, GA 30017 USA Tel 718-415-3401
E-mail: kevinwrites4u@gmail.com.

Janneck Bks., *(978-1-7322236; 978-1-7329687; 978-1-950434)* 100 N. Prospect St, Crescent City, FL 32112 USA Tel 904-874-2608
E-mail: turtlemay@gmail.com.

Janosky, Brandon, *(978-0-692-83634-7)* 905 Evans Ave, Kirkwood, MO 63122 USA Tel 314-315-7006
E-mail: brandon@daddytries.com
Web site: www.daddytries.com.

Jan's Bks., *(978-0-9797139)* Orders Addr.: 1780 Phillips, Berkley, MI 48072 USA Tel 248-545-5160.

Jan's Looks & Books *See* **Jan's Bks.**
Jansen, Marilyn, *(978-0-9761070)* P.O. Box 278, Makawao, HI 96768 USA Tel 808-572-0699 phone/fax
E-mail: jamarilyn2008@aol.com
Web site: http://amaryllisofhawaii.com
Dist(s): **Booklines Hawaii, Ltd.**
Jansen, Michael, *(978-0-578-41166-8; 978-0-578-41168-2; 978-0-578-49333-6; 978-0-578-49334-3)* 5942 N. Michigan St., Portland, OR 97217 USA Tel 503-826-3547
E-mail: mikedjansen@gmail.com
Dist(s): **Ingram Content Group.**
Janze Pubns., *(978-0-9629142; 978-0-9794955)* 930 Bargo St, London, KY 40741-2713 USA
E-mail: janzepub@windstream.net.
Japan Pubns. (U.S.A.), Inc., *(978-0-87040; 978-1-57883)* Subs. of Japan Pubns., Inc. (Tokyo, Japan), 160 Spruce Knob Rd., Middletown Springs, VT 05757-4432 USA (SAN 680-0513) Tel 802-235-2814
Dist(s): **Diamond Comic Distributors, Inc.**
Diamond Bk. Distributors
Oxford Univ. Pr., Inc.
Japanime Co., Ltd. (JPN) *(978-4-921205) Dist. by* **Diamond Book Dists.**
Japanime Co., Ltd. (JPN) *(978-4-921205) Dist. by* **D C D.**
Jappa Pubns., *(978-0-9720694)* 1808 N. 79th St., Kansas City, KS 66112 USA Tel 913-205-2361
E-mail: Ongi.entertainment@gmx.com
Web site: http://www.pandaoki.com.
Jappamation Studios *See* **Jappa Pubns.**
Jarndyce & Jarndyce Pr., *(978-0-9721916; 978-0-9772720; 978-0-9817269; 978-0-9836173; 978-0-9894271; 978-0-9910077; 978-0-9864238; 978-0-9995747; 978-1-7327493; 978-1-7349967; 978-1-7355873)* Div. of PSA Consulting, Inc., 305 Snow Shoe Dr., Southgate, KY 41071 USA (SAN 860-2433) Tel 513-382-4315; 513-304-3633; Fax: 855-361-8591
Web site: http://www.cincybooks.com
Dist(s): **BookBaby.**
Jarrel, Ashley Creations Inc, *(978-0-578-56421-0)* 6831 Hwy. 53 W., Dawsonville, GA 30534 USA Tel 678-776-2620
E-mail: Ashleybrandtjarrel@gmail.com.
Jarrett Publishing Co., *(978-0-9624723; 978-1-882422; 978-0-9795493; 978-1-935022)* P.O. Box 1460, Ronkonkoma, NY 11779-0426 USA Toll Free: 800-859-7679
E-mail: info@jarrettpub.com
Web site: http://www.jarrettpub.com.
Jarvis Printing *See* **Mitchell, Damien Pardow**
Jasmine Pr., *(978-0-930069)* 2224 Ogden Ave., Bensalem, PA 19020 USA (SAN 669-9650) Tel 215-244-0525.
Jasnans Publishing Co., *(978-0-9761759)* P.O. Box 873633, Wasilla, AK 99687-3633 USA
E-mail: hallalfa@mtaonline.net
Web site: http://www.jasnanspublishing.com.
Jason & Nordic Pubs., *(978-0-944727)* P.O. Box 441, Hollidaysburg, PA 16648 USA (SAN 244-9374) Tel 814-696-2920; Fax: 814-696-4250; *Imprints:* Turtle Books (Turtle Books)
E-mail: turtlbks@jasonandnordic.com
Web site: http://www.jasonandnordic.com.
Jason Foundation for Education *See* **JASON Project, The**
Jason Jacques Gallery Pr. The, *(978-0-9788371; 978-0-615-55775-5; 978-0-578-41302-0)* 29 E. 73rd St., No. 1, New York, NY 10021-3501 USA (SAN 851-7568) Tel 212-535-7500; Fax: 212-535-5757
E-mail: jason@jasonjacques.com
Web site: http://www.jasonjacques.com.
JASON Project, The, *(978-0-9763809; 978-0-9787574; 978-1-935211; 978-1-945126)* Orders Addr.: 44983 Knoll Sq. Suite 150, Ashburn, VA 20147 USA Tel 703-822-7238; Fax: 703-673-1060; Toll Free: 888-527-6600
E-mail: info@jason.org
Web site: http://www.jason.org.
Jasper State Brand, Inc., *(978-0-9820228; 978-0-9833366)* 311 N. Robertson Blvd., Suite 363, Beverly Hills, CA 90211 USA (SAN 857-0213) Tel 310-801-7737
E-mail: judith@jasperstate.com.
Jatkar, Deven *See* **MonkeyMantra**
Jauregui, Julian, *(978-0-578-43568-8)* 4214 Lotus Ave., Sacramento, CA 95823 USA Tel 661-563-4453
E-mail: Julianjauregui77@yahoo.com
Dist(s): **Ingram Content Group.**
javariBook, *(978-0-9679161)* P.O. Box 230551, New York, NY 10023 USA
E-mail: javaribook@javari.com
Web site: http://www.javaribook.com; http://www.globalwidetrade.com.
Jawbone Publishing Corp., *(978-0-9702959; 978-1-59094)* 1540 Happy Valley Cir., Newnan, GA 30263-4035 USA (SAN 253-5335); *Imprints:* Top Shelf (Top); Jawbreakers for Kids (Jawbreakers)
E-mail: marketing@jawbonepublishing.com
Web site: http://www.jawbonepublishing.com.
Jawbreakers for Kids *Imprint of* **Jawbone Publishing Corp.**
JaxPublishing.net, *(978-0-9798316)* 11727 Invierno Dr., San Diego, CA 92124-2883 USA Tel 619-757-7016; Fax: 858-277-6418
E-mail: atom@atomart.net
Web site: http://www.atomart.net.
Jay, Ronald Publishing, *(978-0-9744383)* 301 33rd St., Fort Madison, IA 52627 USA (SAN 255-769X) Tel 319-372-4781
E-mail: racrooks@lisco.com.
Jay Street Pubs., *(978-0-9639999; 978-1-889534)* Div. of G-Communications, P.O. Box 230944, New York, NY 10023-0016 USA
E-mail: jaystpub@i-2000.com.
JayJo Bks., LLC, *(978-0-9639449; 978-1-891383)* Orders Addr.: P.O. Box 760, Plainview, NY 11803-0760 USA (SAN 178-5435) Tel 516-349-5520; Fax: 800-262-1886; Toll Free: 800-999-6884; Edit Addr.: 45 Executive Dr. Ste. 201, Plainview, NY 11803-1738 USA
E-mail: jayjobook@guidancechannel.com
Web site: http://www.jayjo.com
Dist(s): **Follett School Solutions**
Quality Bks., Inc.
Unique Bks., Inc.
Jaylil Publishing Co., *(978-0-9748165)* Orders Addr.: P.O. Box 656551, Flushing, NY 11365 USA
E-mail: jaylilpublishing@aol.com
Web site: http://www.jaylilpublishing.com
Dist(s): **Culture Plus Bk. Distributors**
Seaburn Bks.
JayZ Pubns., *(978-0-578-18666-5; 978-0-578-21162-6)* 48 S. New York Rd., B-7, Smithville, NJ 08205 USA.
Jazwares Distribution, Inc., *(978-0-9724983; 978-0-9765714; 978-1-933752)* 555 Sawgrass Corporate Pkwy., Sunrise, FL 33325-6211 USA
E-mail: julio@jazwares.com
Web site: http://www.projectkitsforkids.com.
Jazz Path Publishing, *(978-0-9760977)* P.O. Box 381810, Cambridge, MA 02238 USA
Web site: http://www.jazzpath.com.
Jazzy Kitty Greetings Marketing & Publishing Company *See* **Jazzy Kitty Pubns.**
Jazzy Kitty Pubns., *(978-0-9768540; 978-0-9843255; 978-0-9830548; 978-0-9851453; 978-0-9892656; 978-0-9916648; 978-0-9970848; 978-0-9988433; 978-0-692-10602-0; 978-1-7324523; 978-1-7349014; 978-1-7357874)*
E-mail: anelda@jazzykittypublications.com; jazzykittygreetingpublishing@gmail.com
Web site: http://www.jazzykittypublications.com.
JB Information Station, *(978-0-934334)* P.O. Box 19333, Saint Louis, MO 63125 USA (SAN 213-4128) Tel 314-638-3404; 3888 Via Miralesta Dr., Saint Louis, MO 63125
E-mail: empoweredparenting@earthlink.net
Web site: http://www.JoanBramsch.com.
JBall Publishing, *(978-0-9764179)* 393 W. 300 N., Smithfield, UT 84335 USA Tel 435-563-9437
Web site: http://pumpkinglow.com.
JBiRD iNK, Ltd., *(978-0-9715253; 978-0-9850732)* 109 Knutson Dr., Madison, WI 53704 USA Tel 608-554-0803
E-mail: info@jbirdink.com
Web site: http://www.jbirdink.com.
JBT Publishing, *(978-0-9792059)* Orders Addr.: 1485 Christina Ln., Lake Forest, IL 60045 USA (SAN 852-7644) Tel 781-760-2357; Fax: 419-735-0603
E-mail: jtedesco@gis.net.
JC Burdine, P.O. Box 3017, SOUTHAMPTON, NY 11968 USA Tel 646-352-1413
E-mail: jcburdine1@aol.com
Dist(s): **Ingram Content Group.**
JCCJ Pr., *(978-0-9770207)* 81 River Rd., Norfolk, MA 02056 USA Tel 508-528-4767.
JCTT, LLC, *(978-0-9766926; 978-1-7338960)* 412 Capote Peak Dr., Georgetown, TX 78633 USA
E-mail: linleyw@msn.com
Web site: http://www.mathemagicians.info.
JD Entertainment, *(978-0-9772240)* 1731 Cherry Rd., Memphis, TN 38117 USA
E-mail: directorrsp@yahoo.com
Web site: http://www.jkdenny.com
Dist(s): **Partners Bk. Distributing, Inc.**
J.D. Hines, *(978-0-578-42047-9; 978-0-578-47336-9; 978-0-578-47341-3; 978-0-578-49357-2; 978-0-578-57818-7; 978-0-578-58350-1; 978-0-578-58532-1; 978-0-578-58824-7; 978-0-578-60020-8; 978-0-578-60124-3; 978-0-578-72920-6; 978-0-578-72922-0; 978-1-7357396)* 2380 Central Ave., Riverside, CA 92506 USA Tel 951-784-7024
E-mail: jdwriter@rocketmail.com
Dist(s): **Ingram Content Group.**
JD Publishing, *(978-0-9793972)* Div. of Redpsych Production, P.O. Box 696, Fairfax, CA 94978 USA (SAN 853-3431) Tel 773-793-7622
E-mail: redpsychproductions@yahoo.com
Web site: http://www.redpsych.com; http://www.monkeyandtheengineer.com.
JE Solinski, *(978-0-9989096)* 80 Danbury Dr., Redding, CA 96003 USA Tel 530-339-6268
E-mail: jody@jesolinski.com
Web site: jesolinski.com.
Jeb Cool Kids Entertainment, Inc, *(978-0-9744123; 978-0-9859430)* 8208 Norton Ave., Unit 2, Los Angeles, CA 90046 USA
E-mail: jebcoolkids@gmail.com
Web site: http://www.jebcoolkids.com
Dist(s): **BookBaby.**
JEC Publishing Company *See* **Recipe Pubs.**
Jeffers Pr., *(978-0-9745776; 978-0-9777618)* 2700 Neilson Way, Suite 1428, Santa Monica, CA 90405 USA Tel 310-450-4008; Toll Free: 877-450-4008
E-mail: mark@jefferspress.com
Web site: http://www.jefferspress.com
Dist(s): **National Bk. Network.**
Jefferson Pr., *(978-0-9718974; 978-0-9778086; 978-0-9800164; 978-0-615-27680-9)* P.O. Box 115, Lookout Mountain, TN 37350 USA
E-mail: dmagee@jeffersonpress.com; info@jeffersonpress.com
Web site: http://www.jeffersonpress.com.
Jefferson, Thomas University Press *See* **Truman State Univ. Pr.**
Jeffrey Sterling, *(978-0-692-17587-3)* 5808 Woodrow Wilson Blvd. NE, St. Petersburg, FL 33703 USA Tel 727-798-5850
E-mail: Scottsterling81@gmail.com
Dist(s): **Ingram Content Group.**
Jelly Telly Pr. *Imprint of* **FaithWords**
Jellyroll Productions *See* **Osborne Enterprises Publishing**
JEM Bks., Inc., *(978-0-9754317)* 10466 E. Sheena Dr., Scottsdale, AZ 85255-1742 USA
E-mail: rmahoney@jem-books.com
Web site: http://www.jem-books.com.
Jen Jen W. Cherieperrault, *(978-0-9984684)* 40 Musket Dr., shirley, NY 11967 USA Tel 347-319-2747; Fax: 631-399-2919
E-mail: netnich@gmail.com.
Jenis Group, LLC, *(978-1-942674)* 975 Alvin St., San Diego, CA 92114-1838 USA Tel 619-955-9284
E-mail: aynixon@yahoo.com.
Jenkins-Simmons, Glenda, *(978-0-9758586)* 692 Mulberry Dr., Biloxi, MS 39532 USA Tel 228-388-7540
E-mail: res55472@cs.com.
Jennie's Music Room Bks., *(978-0-9842392)* 4241 Filmore St., Chincoteague Island, VA 23336 USA (SAN 858-8236)
Web site: http://www.ginasfamilystore.com; http://www.jmrbooks.com
Dist(s): **Smashwords.**
Jennifer Lynne Kennard, *(978-0-692-34412-5; 978-0-692-56862-0; 978-0-578-43066-9; 978-0-578-48077-0)* 1135 Belvidere Dr., Nashville, TN 37204-3915 USA Tel 615-424-4529
E-mail: jenniferlynnkennard@gmail.com.
Jennings, J. Publishing Company *See* **Jennings Publishing**
Jennings Publishing, *(978-0-9700038)* 5012 Kahn St., Carmichael, CA 95608 USA Tel 916-863-1638; Fax: 916-863-5807
E-mail: jane@jenningspub.com
Web site: http://www.jenningspub.com
Dist(s): **Omnibus Pr.**
Jenpet Publishing, *(978-0-9726794)* P.O. Box 2542, Alameda, CA 94501 USA Tel 510-521-3582
E-mail: jj@jenpet.com
Web site: http://www.jenpet.com.
JenPrint Pubns., LLC, *(978-0-9653791)* 12195 Hwy. 92 Suite 114-162, Woodstock, GA 30188 USA
E-mail: margarette@jenprint.com
Web site: http://www.jenprint.com
Dist(s): **Book Clearing Hse.**
Follett School Solutions
Quality Bks., Inc.
Jensen, Lissa, *(978-0-9666973)* 958 Summer Holly Ln., Encinitas, CA 92024 USA Tel 760-944-6345.
JENSEN, TRAVIS, *(978-0-9754439)* 600 N. Central Ave. #533, Glendale, CA 91203 USA
E-mail: TRAVIS@TRAVISJENSENPHOTO.COM
Web site: http://WWW.TRAVISJENSENPHOTO.COM.
Jensonbooks, *(978-0-9794414)* P.O. Box 416, Greenfield, MA 01302-0416 USA (SAN 853-4322).
Jentmedia, *(978-0-578-03676-2)* P.O. Box 1304, Lonbard, IL 60148 USA
Dist(s): **Lulu Pr., Inc.**
Jeremy's Things, *(978-0-9747878)* 410 Fifth Ave., 2nd Flr., Brooklyn, NY 11215 USA Tel 718-788-3987
E-mail: jeremy@jeremybullis.com
Web site: http://www.jeremybullis.com.
Jeriel Works, *(978-0-9994364)* 2855 Poirier Rd., Blanchard, ID 83804 USA Tel 208-437-0719
E-mail: jessicapaintsjesus@hotmail.com.
Jeriger Pr., *(978-1-59810)* P.O. Box 1249, Stafford, TX 77477-1249 USA Tel 888-447-5495 (phone/fax)
E-mail: info@jeriger.com
Web site: http://www.jeriger.com.
Jerome, Janice, *(978-0-9729741)* 273 Roy Huie Rd., Riverdale, GA 30274 USA
E-mail: feedback@providerhouse.com
Web site: http://www.providerhouse.com.
Jersey Classic Publishing, *(978-0-9765261)* 75 Locust Ave., Wallington, NJ 07057 USA.
Jerusalem Pubns., *(978-0-9707572; 978-0-9743911; 978-0-9761862; 978-0-9773885; 978-0-9792230; 978-0-9815567; 978-0-9844921; 978-0-9888958; 978-0-9863253; 978-0-9987055)* 4917 Ravenswood Dr., Apt. 513, San Antonio, TX 78232 USA Tel 732-901-3009; Fax: 732-901-4012
E-mail: rapaport@netvision.net.il
Web site: http://www.israelbookshop.com/; http://www.feldheim.com/
Dist(s): **Feldheim Pubs.**
Israel Bookshop Pubns.
Jessa Lynn Pease Garrett, *(978-0-578-43550-3; 978-0-578-43888-7; 978-0-578-70803-4; 978-0-578-70804-1)* 1432 Shades Crest Rd., Hoover, AL 35226 USA Tel 678-794-6356
E-mail: Jessalynnpease@gmail.com
Dist(s): **Ingram Content Group.**
Jessian Pr., *(978-0-692-70523-0)* 21 Saddlerock Dr., Poughkeepsie, NY 12603 USA Tel 917-833-4580
Dist(s): **CreateSpace Independent Publishing Platform.**
Jessica Nelson, *(978-0-692-95114-9; 978-0-692-95115-6; 978-0-692-95394-5; 978-0-692-95397-6; 978-0-692-95403-4)* 2318 n 450 w, Harrisville, UT 84414 USA Tel 801-505-1323
E-mail: jeffwcrawford5+LVP0003523@gmail.com; jeffwcrawford5+LVP0003523@gmail.com.
Jessie Street Pr., *(978-0-9888080)* P.O. Box 3013, Sausalito, CA 94966 USA Tel 415-806-4083
E-mail: btcolor@yahoo.com
Web site: www.jessiestreetpress.com.
JESSPress *See* **JESSPress/Susie Yakowicz**
JESSPress/Susie Yakowicz, *(978-0-9652546)* 4231 Wexford Way, Eagan, MN 55122 USA Tel 651-681-9537
E-mail: syakowicz@comcast.net
Web site: http://www.jesspress.com; susieyakowicz.com/blog.
Jester Bks., *(978-0-9723382)* 39 E. 12th St., 506, New York, NY 10003 USA Tel 212-529-9209 Do not confuse with companies with the same or similar names in Woodland Hills, CA, Orinda, CA
E-mail: davidmkorn@earthlink.net.
Jesus Estanislado, *(978-0-9776291)* P.O. Box 6373, Lakewood, CA 90714 USA
E-mail: jesscortez01@gmail.com.
Jet City Comics *Imprint of* **Amazon Publishing**
JETM Publishing & Distribution *See* **I Am Your Playground LLC**
Jetpack Publishing, *(978-0-9898533)* 3 Maybrook Dr., Glenville, NY 12302 USA Tel 518-929-1895
E-mail: ethancrownberry@nycap.rr.com.
Jetty Hse. *Imprint of* **Randall, Peter E. Pub.**
Jetway Geographer, LLC, *(978-0-9711640)* Orders Addr.: 431 S. Cooke, Helena, MT 59601 USA Tel 406-586-6879
E-mail: jgeographer@bresnan.net
Web site: www.jetwaygeographer.com.
Jew-El Pr. Co., *(978-0-9767618)* 40022 Milkmaid Ln., Murrieta, CA 92562 USA Tel 951-600-7054 (phone/fax)
E-mail: jew-el-press@verizon.net
Web site: http://www.jew-el-press.com.
Jewel Publishing, *(978-0-9744944)* P.O. Box 38, Chino Hills, CA 91709 USA Fax: 909-606-1092 Do not confuse with companies with the same or similar name in Baltimore, MD, Denver, CO, Detroit, MI, Cincinnati, OH
E-mail: cmckee7721@aol.com.
Jewel Publishing LLC, *(978-0-9629715; 978-1-936499)* Orders Addr.: 6815 W. Floyd Ave., Denver, CO 80227 USA Tel 303-980-1957 Do not confuse with companies with similar names in Cincinnati, OH, New York, NY, Baltimore, MD, Detroit, MI, Chino Hills, CA
E-mail: sandy7lardinois@gmail.com; sandy@jewelpublishing.com
Web site: http://jewelpublishing.com.
Jewell Histories, *(978-0-9678413)* 143 Breckenridge St., Gettysburg, PA 17325 USA Tel 717-420-5344
E-mail: jewellhistories@superpa.net.
Jewell, Vickie, *(978-0-692-99078-0)* 1702 S. 7th ave. No. 17, Marshalltown, IA 50158 USA Tel 641-750-8041
E-mail: vtjewell@outlook.com.
Jewish Community Federation of Rochester, NY, Inc., *(978-0-9710686)* 441 East Ave., Rochester, NY 14607 USA Tel 585-461-0490; Fax: 585-461-0912
E-mail: bappelbaum@jewishrochester.org
Web site: http://www.jewishrochester.org
Dist(s): **Wayne State Univ. Pr.**
Jewish Educational Media, *(978-1-931607; 978-1-932349; 978-0-9890522)* 784 Eastern Pkwy., Suite 403, Brooklyn, NY 11213 USA Tel 718-774-6000; Fax: 718-774-3402
E-mail: eli@jemedia.org
Web site: http://www.jemedia.org
Dist(s): **Kehot Pubn. Society.**
Jewish Girls Unite, *(978-0-9841624; 978-0-578-40595-7; 978-0-578-44571-7; 978-0-578-53297-4; 978-0-578-55652-9; 978-0-578-68652-3; 978-0-578-70328-2)* P.O. Box 215, Sharon, MA 02067-0215 USA (SAN 858-5938) Toll Free: 888-492-5324
E-mail: leahmcaras@gmail.com
Web site: http://www.yaldah.com.
Jewish Learning Group, The, *(978-1-891293)* 6 Tokay Ln., Monsey, NY 10952-1701 USA Toll Free: 888-565-3276
E-mail: info@jewishlearninggroup.com
Web site: http://www.jewishlearninggroup.com
Dist(s): **Independent Pubs. Group.**
Jewish Lights Publishing *Imprint of* **LongHill Partners, Inc.**
†Jewish Pubn. Society, *(978-0-8276)* Orders Addr.: 22883 Quicksilver Dr., Dulles, VA 20166 USA (SAN 253-9446) Tel 703-661-1165; 703-661-1529; Fax: 703-661-1501; Toll Free: 800-355-1165; Edit Addr.: 2100 Arch St., 2nd Flr., Philadelphia, PA 19103-1399 USA Tel 215-832-0600
E-mail: marketing@jewishpub.org
Web site: http://www.jewishpub.org
Dist(s): **Ebsco Publishing**
MyiLibrary
Univ. of Nebraska Pr.; *CIP.*
JFA Productions, *(978-0-9723024)* 806 Homestead Ave., Maybrook, NY 12543 USA Tel 845-427-5008
E-mail: carrdero@warwick.net.
Jfalcock, *(978-0-9890111)* 4262 Althea Way, Palm Beach Gardens, FL 33410 USA Tel 561-252-3350
E-mail: jfalcock@gmail.com.
JFAR Bks., *(978-0-615-45886-1)* Orders Addr.: P.O. Box 331621, West Hartford, CT 06133 USA Tel 617-388-2489
E-mail: J_Farquharson@yahoo.com
Web site: www.PlaytimetoBedtime.com.
JFK Online Studios, LLC, *(978-0-9742249)* 293 2nd Ave., West Haven, CT 06516-5127 USA
Web site: http://www.jfkonlinestudios.com.
JFW, Ltd., *(978-0-9710071)* 400 N. Church St., Unit 602, Charlotte, NC 28202 USA Tel 704-277-8378 (phone/fax)
E-mail: create2000@earthlink.net; jfwbird@earthlink.com.
JG Pr. *Imprint of* **World Pubns. Group, Inc.**

JGC/United Publishing Corps., *(978-0-910941)* 1717 Harlem Blvd., Rockford, IL 61103 USA (SAN 270-5109) Tel 815-968-6601
E-mail: mailbox@jgcunited.com
Web site: http://www.jgcunited.com.

J.G.R. Enterprises, *(978-0-9758746)* 100 Oak St., Patchogue, NY 11772 USA Tel 631-790-0932
E-mail: joannros12@aol.com.

JGracia Publishing, *(978-0-9837403)* 2998 Valley View Cir., Powder Springs, GA 30127 USA Tel 678-668-6286
E-mail: jgraciaenterprises@gmail.com
Dist(s): **Lulu Pr., Inc.**

Jib & Jigger, Inc., *(978-0-692-17283-4)* 826 E. Pk. Ave., Port Townsend, WA 98368 USA Tel 800-979-1930
E-mail: josh@smallcraftadvisor.com
Dist(s): **Ingram Content Group.**

Jill Knapp-Zitron *See* **Sunflower Pr.**

JIMAPCO, Inc., *(978-1-56914)* Orders Addr.: P.O. Box 1137, Clifton Park, NY 12065 USA Fax: 518-899-5093; Toll Free: 800-627-7123; Edit Addr.: 2095 Rte. 9, Round Lake, NY 12151 USA Tel 518-899-5091
E-mail: cfisk@jimapco.com
Dist(s): **Benchmark LLC**
Langenscheidt Publishing Group
Rand McNally.

Jimmy Patterson *Imprint of* **Grand Central Publishing**

Jimmy Patterson *Imprint of* **Little Brown & Co.**

Jimmyland Corp., *(978-0-9760140; 978-0-9792672; 978-0-9820618; 978-0-9837021)* Jimmyland Corp., Orders Addr.: 2804 E. Crosley Dr., Suite H, West Palm Beach, FL 33415 USA Tel 561-602-1400
E-mail: jimmydrobinson@comcast.net
Web site: http://www.jimmydrobinson.com
Dist(s): **BookBaby.**

Jimsam Incorporated *See* **Jimsam Inc. Publishing**

Jimsam Inc. Publishing, *(978-0-9790768; 978-0-9816914; 978-0-9820587; 978-0-9841074; 978-0-615-57183-6; 978-0-615-66583-2; 978-0-615-67879-5)* P.O. Box 3363, Riverview, FL 33569 USA Tel 813-748-9523
E-mail: contact@jimsaminc.com; ms1free@aol.com
Web site: http://www.jimsam-inc.com.

Jinks, Elizabeth Schneider, *(978-0-9666312)* 7624 W. Mauna Loa Ln., Peoria, AZ 85381-4388 USA Tel 602-486-5362
E-mail: ee_jinks@qwest.net.

JINKS Studio Art & Publishing, *(978-0-9749672)* Orders Addr.: 9421 Woodlief Rd., Wake Forest, NC 27587-8993 USA
E-mail: jinksstudio@comcast.net
Web site: http://www.jinksstudio.com.

Jinxworld *Imprint of* **DC Comics**

Jiovanie, *(978-0-578-10152-1)* 503 La Costa, Leander, TX 78641 USA.

JIST Life *Imprint of* **JIST Publishing**

†JIST Publishing, *(978-0-942784; 978-1-56370; 978-1-57112; 978-1-59357; 978-1-63332)* Div. of EMC Publishing, 875 Montreal Way, Saint Paul, MN 55102 USA (SAN 240-2351) Tel 651-290-2800 Toll Free Fax: 800-547-8329; *Imprints:* KIDSRIGHTS (Kidsrts); JIST Works (JIST Works); JIST Life (JIST Lfe)
E-mail: info@jist.com
Web site: http://www.jist.com
Dist(s): **Cardinal Pubs. Group**
Ebsco Publishing
Follett School Solutions
Linx Educational Publishing, Inc.
MyiLibrary
O'Reilly Media, Inc.; *CIP.*

JIST Works *Imprint of* **JIST Publishing**

JIST Works, Incorporated *See* **JIST Publishing**

Jitterbug Bks., *(978-0-9763031; 978-0-615-49452-4)* 25 Whale Rock Rd., Jamestown, RI 02835 USA Tel 401-423-2823
E-mail: jitterbugbooks@cox.net.

J.J. Pips Publishing, *(978-0-9982343)* 2461 Santa Monica Blvd., Suite 519, Santa Monica, CA 90404 USA Tel 310-710-5345
E-mail: jj@jjpips.com
Web site: http://www.jjpips.com.

JJR Marketing Consultants LLC, *(978-0-615-36808-5; 978-0-9971605; 978-0-9990012; 978-1-7324916; 978-1-7330635; 978-1-7342369; 978-1-7345680; 978-1-952779)* 843 Hathaway Ct., North Aurora, IL 60542 USA Tel 630-441-6057; Fax: 630-786-6116; *Imprints:* Fig Factor Media LLC (Fig Factor)
E-mail: jackie@jjrmarketing.com.

JK Pr., *(978-0-9667853; 978-0-9667853-1-9; 978-1-7329347; 978-1-7359233)* 2054 SW 25th ST, Redmond, OR 97756 USA
E-mail: james5of7@yahoo.com.

J.K.H. Enterprises, *(978-0-9761422)* MSC 5033, Busch Student Center 20 N. Grand Blvd., Saint Louis, MO 63103 USA
E-mail: juliushunter@slu.edu
Web site: http://juliushunter.tripod.com.

JL De Castro, *(978-1-7324219)* P.O. Box 25, Hummels Wharf, PA 17831-0025 USA Tel 570-374-8294
E-mail: jldecastrolivros@yahoo.com
Web site: janetldecastro.com.

JL Thomas Pub., *(978-0-9786537)* 1287 Hadaway Trl., Lawrenceville, GA 30043-4670 USA
E-mail: jlthomas@jlthomas-author.com
Web site: http://jlthomas-author.com.

JLM CD-ROM Publishing Co., *(978-0-9749905)* 150 Idora Ave., San Francisco, CA 94127-1016 USA (SAN 255-9552)
Web site: http://www.jlmcd-rompublishing.com.

JM Publishing, *(978-0-578-14249-4; 978-0-9907424)*.

J.M. Roman *See* **Jose M. Roman**

JM Studio, *(978-1-7321442)* 48 E. 1050 N., Chesterton, IN 46304 USA Tel 219-926-8937
E-mail: mullindesign@gmail.com.

JM2 Publishing Co., *(978-0-9767210)* 6316 Monte Cresta, Richmond, CA 94806 USA Fax: 510-237-4305
E-mail: jeanmock@comcast.net.

JMC Printing, *(978-0-9638586)* Div. of JMC Marketing, Orders Addr.: 6730 W. 84th Cir. Suite 88, Arvada, CO 80003 USA Tel 303-564-1606 mobile
E-mail: jmcpublishing@aol.com.

JMG Studio, *(978-0-9771117)* Div. of John-Marc Grob Studios, 6 Southwind Dr., Flanders, NJ 07836 USA (SAN 256-8691) Tel 973-347-5399
E-mail: johnmarc@jmgstudio.net
Web site: http://www.jmgstudio.net.

JMK Music Publishing, *(978-0-9743218)* 22 Maple Ln., Northborough, MA 01532 USA
Web site: http://www.jmkmusicpub.com.

J.N. Courtney Pubns., *(978-0-9967059)* 51 Hilltop Dr., Penfield, NY 14526 USA Tel 585-313-1995
E-mail: jeancourt59@gmail.com.

JNB Pr., *(978-0-615-38122-0; 978-0-692-79347-3; 978-0-9993017)* 40 Glen St., Melrose, MA 02176 USA Tel 617-957-2076; Fax: 617-957-2076
E-mail: janice@janicecooks.com
Web site: https://janicecooks.com/.

J-Novel Club, *(978-1-7183)* 4411 Yorkshire Ct., Shavano Pk., TX 78249 USA Tel 201-775-2414
E-mail: contact@j-novel.club
Web site: http://www.j-novel.club
Dist(s): **Ingram Publisher Services.**

JoAnn Vergona Krapp & Gene Zaner, *(978-0-9722576)* 94 Sunset Ave., Farmingdale, NY 11735 USA
E-mail: jkrapp1940@aol.com.

Joanne Faye Pr., *(978-0-9747375)* c/o Goblin Fern Pr., Inc., 852 Hemlock Dr., Verona, WI 53593 USA Tel 608-835-5523; Fax: 608-442-0212
E-mail: jritland@mac.com
Web site: http://www.loveybooks.com.

Joanne Frances Pr., *(978-0-9777640)* Orders Addr.: 210 Piney Hill Rd., Oakland, MI 48363-1449 USA Toll Free: 800-960-2347
Web site: http://www.JoanneFrancesPress.com.

JoAnne/Horatio Books *See* **Gumbo Multimedia Entertainment**

JoBen Books, LLC *See* **Unveiled Media, LLC**

Jocko Publishing, *(978-0-9816188)* 4247 Eagle Rock Blvd Unit 502, Los Angeles, CA 90065 USA Tel 718-288-6141
E-mail: jbozak@jockopublishing.com; jonbozak@gmail.com
Web site: http://www.jockopublishing.com; www.warriorkid.com
Dist(s): **Ebsco Publishing.**

Jodan Collections, *(978-0-9747181)* Orders Addr.: 2716 N. Univ. Rd., Spokane, WA 99206 USA Tel 509-927-1882; Edit Addr.: 6405 S. Dishman Mica Rd., Spokane, WA 99206 USA
E-mail: joanne@inlandbindery.com
Web site: http://www.inlandbindery.com.

Jodaviste Publishing, *(978-0-9789016)* P.O. Box 473444, Charlotte, NC 28247 USA (SAN 851-920X)
E-mail: jodavistepublishing@earthlink.net
Web site: www.margosmagictrunk.com.

Joe Girl Ink, *(978-0-9766080)* 111S. Morgan, No. 502, Chicago, IL 60607 USA.

Joe Joe Dawson, *(978-0-692-70463-9; 978-0-692-87713-5; 978-0-692-97245-8; 978-0-692-05949-4; 978-0-692-18205-5; 978-0-692-18206-2; 978-0-692-19908-4; 978-0-578-40269-7; 978-0-578-42130-8; 978-0-578-42415-6; 978-0-578-43891-7; 978-0-578-44456-7; 978-0-578-51625-7; 978-0-578-52644-7; 978-0-578-62380-1; 978-0-578-69190-9; 978-0-578-69191-6; 978-0-578-69193-0)*.

Joel-Taiwo, Olubusola, *(978-0-578-41500-0)* 5415 N. Sheridan Rd. Apt. 2807, Chicago, IL 60640 USA Tel 312-890-5198
E-mail: author4kidss@gmail.com
Dist(s): **Ingram Content Group.**

Joewolf Pubs., *(978-0-9671344)* Orders Addr.: P.O. Box 80127, Conyer, GA 30013 USA Tel 770-922-6655; Fax: 770-388-0521
E-mail: joewolf@bellsouth.net.

Joey Bks. *Imprint of* **Acclaim Pr., Inc.**

Joey Publishing, *(978-0-9799444)* 300 Atlantic St., Suite 500, Stamford, CT 06902 USA Fax: 203-363-7825
E-mail: jeanne@joeypublishing.com.

Johannesen Printing & Publishing, *(978-1-881084)* Orders Addr.: P.O. Box 24, Whitethorn, CA 95589 USA Tel 707-986-7465; Fax: 707-986-1656
E-mail: books@johannesen.com
Web site: http://www.johannesen.com.

John, *(978-0-9886232)* 4303 Inlet Rd, Marietta, GA 30066 USA Tel 404-457-9981
E-mail: altj1a@gmail.com.

John Joseph Adams *Imprint of* **Houghton Mifflin Harcourt Publishing Co.**

John M. Jimerson, *(978-0-578-44197-9)* 5900 Timber Creek Ln. No. 1315, Raleigh, NC 27612 USA Tel 919-561-1950
E-mail: john@johnjimerson.com
Dist(s): **Ingram Content Group.**

Johnny Sundby Photography, *(978-0-9747152)* 4780 Easy St., Rapid City, SD 57702 USA Tel 605-343-5646; Fax: 605-342-0139
E-mail: dsp@rap.midco.net
Web site: http://www.johnnysundby.com.

Johnnycopywriter, *(978-0-692-93913-0)* 825 Bayshore Dr Apt 505, Pensacola, FL 32507 USA Tel 850-723-6923; Fax: 850-723-6923
E-mail: johnglgskns@gmail.com
Web site: johncwaite.com.

Johnson, Anthony, *(978-0-9773760)* P.O. Box 731, Burbank, CA 91503-0731 USA (SAN 257-4187) Fax: 818-558-6771
E-mail: leedobug@hotmail.com.

Johnson Bks. *Imprint of* **Bower Hse.**

Johnson, Bonnie, *(978-0-9769756)* Orders Addr.: 6 Son Ct., Valley Center, KS 67147-2659 USA.

Johnson, Colleen, *(978-0-9785002)* 2500 63rd St NW, Minot, ND 58703 USA Tel 701-839-5768
E-mail: gchristi@minot.com
Web site: http://icecreamforbreakfastbook.com.

Dr. Dionna Hancock Johnson International Corp., *(978-0-9913988)* 2328 Spice Pecan Way, Palmdale, CA 93551 USA Tel 858-869-7368
E-mail: energeticlifecoaching@gmail.com.

Johnson, Earl Photography, *(978-0-9649645; 978-0-9779024)* Orders Addr.: P.O. Box 870165, Stone Mountain, GA 30087 USA Tel 678-476-3950; Fax: 678-476-3951
E-mail: books@earljohnsontruckbooks.com
Web site: http://earljohnsontruckbooks.com.

Johnson, Gary, *(978-0-9791794)* 938 E. Lois Ln., Phoenix, AZ 85020-1189 USA (SAN 852-6931) Tel 602-944-7517 (phone/fax); Toll Free: 888-665-2762
E-mail: gjohnson@molarman.com
Web site: http://www.molarman.com.

Johnson, James *See* **Strategies Publishing Co.**

Johnson, Jenna Elizabeth, *(978-0-9976442)* 729 Calle Bendita, Arroyo Grande, CA 93420 USA Tel 805-478-0244
E-mail: authorjejohnson@gmail.com
Web site: www.jennaelizabethjohnson.com.

Johnson, Renee B., *(978-0-578-46891-4; 978-1-7340409)* 2900 Gilbert Ln, Alton, IL 62002-5504 USA Tel 618-465-0764
E-mail: Rbj2040@aol.com.

Johnson, Suzanne, *(978-0-9968220; 978-1-7325921)* 814 Chickasaw Ave., Auburn, AL 36830 USA Tel 504-301-6414
E-mail: suzannej3523@gmail.com
Web site: http://www.suzannejohnsonauthor.com.

Johnson Tribe Publishing, *(978-0-9896733; 978-0-692-30715-1; 978-0-9977522; 978-0-692-14788-7; 978-0-578-43285-4; 978-1-7337844; 978-1-7352637)* 1484 Uncle Ben Dr., Powder Springs, GA 30127 USA Tel 770-815-6477
E-mail: johnsontribepublishing@gmail.com
Web site: dradairspeaks.net; johnsontribepublishing.com.

Johnson-Young,, Jill LCSW, *(978-0-692-97586-2; 978-0-9997886)* 6840 Indiana Ave., Riverside, CA 92506 USA Tel 951-778-0230
E-mail: jilljohnsonyoung@gmail.com
Dist(s): **CreateSpace Independent Publishing Platform.**

Johnston, Ann, *(978-0-9656776)* Orders Addr.: P.O. Box 388, Ashland, OH 44805 USA Toll Free: 800-247-6553 (ordering & shipping information); Edit Addr.: P.O. Box 944, Lake Oswego, OR 97034 USA (SAN 852-9043) Tel 503-635-6791; Fax: 503-675-0366
E-mail: order@bookmaster.com
Web site: http://www.annjohnston.net
Dist(s): **CreateSpace Independent Publishing Platform.**

Johnston, Ann, *(978-0-9796010)* 2409 Crest St., Alexandria, VA 22302 USA Tel 703-629-2175
E-mail: growhealthy@gmail.com.

Johnston, Don Inc., *(978-1-893376; 978-1-58702; 978-1-4105)* Orders Addr.: 26799 W. Commerce Dr., Volo, IL 60073 USA Tel 847-740-0749; Fax: 847-740-7326; Toll Free: 800-999-4660
Web site: http://www.donjohnston.com.

Johnston, Lissa, *(978-0-9973068)* 721 Wildwood Rd., Leesville, SC 29070 USA Tel 803-487-9385
E-mail: lissajohnston@gmail.com.

Johnston-Brown, Anne Publishing Co. *See* **Retriever Pr.**

Joint Committee on Printing *Imprint of* **United States Government Printing Office**

Joint Committee on Taxation *Imprint of* **United States Government Printing Office**

Joint Heir Multimedia, *(978-0-9796148)* P.O. Box 108, Edgewater, NJ 07020 USA
Web site: http://www.jointheirmultimedia.net.

Joint Publishing Co. (HKG) *(978-962-04) Dist. by* **Chinasprout.**

Joint Publishing Co. (HKG) *(978-962-04) Dist. by* **China Bks.**

Jojoba Pr., *(978-1-949471; 978-1-64831)* P.O. Box 1281, Tucson, AZ 85702 USA; *Imprints:* DOG ON A LOG Books (MYID_T_DOG ON)
E-mail: jojobapress@gmail.com
Web site: www.dogonalogbooks.com.

Jokar Productions, LLC *See* **Save Our Seas, Ltd.**

Jolley Chronicles, *(978-1-7331821)* 606 20 Rd, Grand Junction, CO 81507 USA Tel 970-361-1520
E-mail: tylerhjolley@gmail.com
Web site: http://www.jolleychronicles.com.

Jolly Fish Pr. *Imprint of* **North Star Editions**

Jolly Geranium, Inc., *(978-0-9644524)* 2953 E. Pawnee Dr., Sierra Vista, AZ 85635-8511 USA Tel 520-321-4747.

Jolly Learning, Ltd. (GBR) *(978-1-870946; 978-1-903619; 978-1-84414) Dist. by* **Am Intl Dist.**

Jollyrhymes, *(978-1-7336364; 978-1-952717)* 1586 Johnson St., North Bend, OR 97459 USA Tel 541-252-1397
E-mail: jollyllama23@gmail.com
Web site: www.jollyrhymes.com.

Jolt, *(978-0-9831498)* Orders Addr.: P.O. Box 201013, Montgomery, AL 36120 USA Tel 256-390-3722
E-mail: information@jolt-books.com
Web site: http://www.jolt-books.com.

Jonathan, *(978-0-9910704)* P.O. Box 113, Bayville, NJ 08721 USA Tel 609-290-3728
E-mail: jonathan@jonathan-mcelroy.com.

†Jones & Bartlett Learning, LLC, *(978-0-7637; 978-0-86720; 978-1-4496; 978-1-284)* 5 Wall St., Burlington, MA 01803 USA (SAN 285-0893) Toll Free: 800-832-0034
Web site: http://www.jblearning.com
Dist(s): **Ebsco Publishing**
Rittenhouse Bk. Distributors
ebrary, Inc.; *CIP.*

Jones & Bartlett Publishers, Incorporated *See* **Jones & Bartlett Learning, LLC**

Jones, Augustine R., *(978-0-9743223)* 4213 N. Knoll Ridge Rd. Apt. B2, Peoria, IL 61614-7439 USA.

Jones, Bob University Press *See* **BJU Pr.**

Jones Bks., *(978-0-9721217; 978-0-9763539; 978-0-9790475)* 3 Loon Ln., Madison, WI 53717-1854 USA
E-mail: info@jonesbooks.com
Web site: http://www.jonesbooks.com.

Jones, Kaylie Books *Imprint of* **Akashic Bks.**

Jones, Kirk, *(978-0-9759688)* P.O. Box 74702, Richmond, VA 23236 USA
E-mail: kirkjonesillustrations@juno.com.

Jones, Linda, *(978-0-9776450)* 2700 Woodland Park Dr. Apt. 705, Houston, TX 77082-6605 USA
E-mail: amiasthefirst@aol.com.

Jones, Marla F. *See* **Doodle and Peck Publishing**

Jones, Vivian Ann, *(978-0-692-91819-7)* 574 Dandelion Loop, Kyle, TX 78640 USA Tel 512-743-8174
E-mail: padellatemp4@yahoo.com.

JonesHarvest Publishing, *(978-0-9794455; 978-1-60388)* 5400 E. State Rd. 45, Bloomington, IN 47408 USA Tel 812-323-2330; Fax: 812-323-2339; Toll Free: 877-400-0075
E-mail: jonesharvest@sbcglobal.net
Web site: http://www.jonesharvest.com.

Jonquil Books *See* **Miglior Pr.**

Jon'taar Graphxs, *(978-0-9764385)* 75 Lantern Chase Dr., Delaware, OH 43015 USA Tel 740-972-6321
E-mail: msuplicki@jontaar.com; information@mirthburdz.com
Web site: http://www.jontaar.com; http://www.mirthburdz.com.

Jordan Music Productions, Inc., *(978-1-895523; 978-1-894262; 978-1-55386)* M.P.O. Box 490, Niagara Falls, NY 14302-0490 USA
E-mail: sjordan@sara-jordan.com
Web site: http://www.sara-jordan.com; http://www.SongsThatTeach.com; http://www.edu-mart.com
Dist(s): **Follett Media Distribution**
iLeon.

Jordan Publishing Hse., *(978-1-890875)* Orders Addr.: P.O. Box 671, Columbia, CA 95310 USA Fax: 209-532-5503; Edit Addr.: 22620 Parrotts Ferry Rd., Columbia, CA 95310 USA Do not confuse with companies with the same name in Las Vegas, NV, Nappanee, IN, Reston, VA, Phoenix, AZ, Prescott, AZ
E-mail: gpview@erli.net.

Jordan, Sara Publishing, *(978-1-895523; 978-1-894262; 978-1-55386)* Div. of Jordan Music Productions, Inc., Orders Addr.: M.P.O. Box 490, Niagara Falls, NY 14302-0490 USA (SAN 118-959X) Tel 416-760-7664; Fax: 416-762-2770; Toll Free Fax: 800-229-3855; Toll Free: 800-567-7733
E-mail: sjordan@sara-jordan.com
Web site: http://www.edu-mart.com; http://www.sara-jordan.com; http://www.songsthatteach.com
Dist(s): **Follett School Solutions.**

Jordan Valley Heritage Hse., *(978-0-939810)* P.O. Box 99, Stayton, OR 97383-0099 USA (SAN 216-7425) Tel 503-769-4236
E-mail: jvhh5@wvi.com.

Jorge Pinto Bks., *(978-0-9742615; 978-0-9774724; 978-0-9790766; 978-0-9795576; 978-0-9801147; 978-1-934978)* 6216 Vorlich Ln., Bethesda, MD 20816 USA (SAN 853-7526); *Imprints:* Illustrated Books (Illus Bks)
Web site: http://www.pintobooks.com; jpintobooks.com
Dist(s): **D.A.P./Distributed Art Pubs.**

Jorlan Publishing *See* **Jorlan Publishing, Inc.**

Jorlan Publishing, Inc., *(978-0-9710696; 978-1-933830)* P.O. Box 2882, Cedar City, UT 84721-2882 USA
Web site: http://www.jorlanpublishing.com.

Jose M. Roman, *(978-0-692-60566-0; 978-1-7324943)* 200 Thunderbird Hill Rd., Sebring, FL 33872 USA Tel 863-414-1621
E-mail: jmr508@yahoo.com
Dist(s): **CreateSpace Independent Publishing Platform.**

Joseph, Dr. Angela Banner, *(978-1-943945)* 37-29 104th Street, Apt. 3D, Corona, NY 11368 USA Tel 347-669-0151
Dist(s): **CreateSpace Independent Publishing Platform.**

Joseph Henry Pr. *Imprint of* **National Academies Pr.**

Joseph Pubns., *(978-0-9773243)* P.O. Box 401, Killington, VT 05751 USA Tel 917-502-7328
Web site: http://www.josephpublications.com.

Joseph's Coat Publishing *See* **Breezy Reads**

Joseph's Heartprint, *(978-0-9787035)* 728 Creek Rd., Carlisle, PA 17013 USA Tel 717-258-8796; Fax: 717-243-4254
E-mail: george@catholicartworks.com
Web site: http://www.catholicartworks.com.

Joseph's Labor, *(978-0-9729800)* P.O. Box 176265, Covington, KY 41017-6265 USA Tel 859-578-8112
E-mail: JosephsLabor@aol.com.

Publisher Name Index

Joshua Pr., Inc. (CAN) *(978-1-894400) Dist. by* **Gabriel Res.**

Joshua Publishing *See* **Handle Your Business Girl Publishing**

Joshua Tree Publishing, *(978-0-9710954; 978-0-9768677; 978-0-9778311; 978-0-9823703; 978-0-9845904; 978-0-9829803; 978-0-9886577; 978-1-941049)* 3 Golf Ctr. No. 201, Hoffman Estates, IL 60169 USA Tel 312-893-7525; 3 Golf Ctr. No. 201, Hoffman Estates, IL 60169 Tel 312-893-7525 Do not confuse with companies with the same or similar names in Mentor, OH, Lake San Marcos, CA
E-mail: info@joshuatreepublishing.com
Web site: http://joshuatreepublishing.com; http://centaurbooks.com; http://chiralhouse.com.

Jossey-Bass *Imprint of* **Wiley, John & Sons, Inc.**

Jostens Bks., *(978-0-9759530; 978-0-9788398)* 116 Independence Dr., Indian Trail, NC 28079-9452 USA Toll Free: 800-458-0319
E-mail: sherry.clontz@jostens.com
Web site: http://www.jostens.com.

Jots & Tittles Publishing, *(978-0-9894379)* 310 W. 39th St., Vancouver, WA 98660 USA Tel 360-566-2781
E-mail: ghost@writingasaghost.com.

Joubert, Christopher, *(978-0-692-19093-7; 978-0-692-19094-4)* 5420 Downs Rd., Beaumont, TX 77705-6900 USA Tel 409-673-9073
E-mail: cjoubert11@aol.com
Dist(s): **Ingram Content Group.**

Journals Unlimited, Inc., *(978-1-892033; 978-0-9818414; 978-0-9842578; 978-0-9832414; 978-0-9859025; 978-0-9907307; 978-0-9973031; 978-0-9995079; 978-1-7345331)* P.O. Box 1882, Bay City, MI 48706 USA Tel 989-686-3377; Fax: 989-686-3380; Toll Free Fax: 800-897-8529; Toll Free: 800-897-8528
E-mail: orders@journalsunlimited.com
Web site: http://www.journalsunlimited.com.

Journalstone, *(978-0-9828119; 978-1-936564; 978-1-940161; 978-1-942712; 978-1-945373; 978-1-947654; 978-1-950305)* 3205 Sassafras Trl, Carbondale, IL 62901 USA Tel 415-235-6734
E-mail: christophercpayne@journalstone.com
Web site: http://journalstone.com.

Journey of a Dream Pr., *(978-0-9749876; 978-0-9818251; 978-0-9839777; 978-0-9897142)* 2888 Winchester Ct., Duluth, GA 30096 USA Tel 770-789-9796
E-mail: journeyofadream@comcast.net
Web site: www.journeyofadream.com.

Journey Pubns., LLC, *(978-0-9728716; 978-0-9748087; 978-0-9772078; 978-0-9798171)* Orders Addr.: P.O. Box 2442, Warminster, PA 18974-2442 USA (SAN 255-1675) Do not confuse with companies with the same or similar names in Woodstock, NY, Savannah, GA, Avon Park, FL, Metairie, LA, Lacey, WA
E-mail: journeypubs@aol.com
Web site: http://www.journeypublications.com.

Journey Stone Creations, LLC, *(978-0-9758709; 978-1-59958)* 3533 Danbury Rd., Fairfield, OH 45014 USA Fax: 513-860-0176; *Imprints:* A.W.A. Gang (AWA Gang)
E-mail: pat@journeystonecreations.com
Web site: http://www.journeystonecreations.com; http://www.myezbookclub.com; http://www.jscbooks.com.

JourneyForth *Imprint of* **BJU Pr.**

Journeys Press *See* **Whirlwind Publishing Group**

JourneytimeBks., *(978-0-615-43624-1; 978-0-692-43867-1)* 407 8TH Ave,, TROY, NY 12182 USA Tel 518-237-8622
E-mail: mgraber@journeytimebooks.com.

Journique Publishing Group, Inc., *(978-0-9795586)* P.O. Box 524, Knightdale, NC 27545 USA Fax: 407-796-6394
E-mail: pjordan@journique.com
Web site: http://www.journique.com
Dist(s): **Ingram Content Group.**

Joy of my Youth Pubns., The, *(978-0-9774345)* P.O. Box 128702, Cincinnati, OH 45212 USA Tel 513-531-2709
E-mail: thejoyofmyyouth@netzero.net
Web site: http://www.thejoyofmyyouth.com.

Joy on Your Shoulders TM, *(978-0-9840353)* P.O. Box 951, Pisgah Forest, NC 28768 USA Tel 440-476-0960
E-mail: createjoyfulness@yahoo.com.

J.O.Y. Pubns., *(978-0-9762975)* 186 Gatewood Ave., Rochester, NY 14624-1737 USA Do not confuse with companies with the same or similar name in Santa Maria, CA Gardena, CA, Pittsboro, NC, Woburn, MA
E-mail: rainbowvillagecc@yahoo.com; rainbowvillage@homewithGod.net
Web site: www.our.homewithGod.com/rainbowvillage/.

J.O.Y. Publishing, *(978-0-9755454)* Orders Addr.: P.O. Box 540912, Merritt Island, FL 32594-0912 USA; *Imprints:* Laughing Zebra - Books for Children (Laugh Zebra)
E-mail: jdelgado@laughing-zebra-children-books.com
Web site: http://zooprisepartyfiestazoorpresa.blogspot.com; http://www.laughing-zebra-children-books.com.

Joya Cultural Enterprises Inc., *(978-0-9904135)* 4644 W. Gandy Blvd. 4 - 102, Tampa, FL 33611 USA Tel 813-388-8385
E-mail: info@joya-inc.com.

Joyce Miriam Friedman, *(978-0-578-41520-8; 978-0-578-48355-9)* 50 Dorset Rd., Waban, MA 02468-1406 USA Tel 617-645-3186
E-mail: joycefriedman625@gmail.com
Dist(s): **Ingram Content Group.**

JoyceHerzog.com, Incorporated *See* **Herzog, Joyce**

Joyful by Design, *(978-0-9976590; 978-1-7340288)* 4025 Forsythe Way, Tallahassee, FL 32309 USA Tel 850-570-0415
E-mail: sarajoym@yahoo.com
Web site: www.saramarchessault.com.

Joyful Learning Publications, LLC, *(978-0-9836580)* 3148 Plainfield Ave NE suite 153, Grand Rapids, MI 49525-3285 USA Tel 207-693-5257
E-mail: sandyjane05@yahoo.com.

Joyful Learning Publishing *See* **Joyful Learning Publications, LLC**

Joyful Noise, *(978-0-9772109)* 312 Stonewall Rd., Concord, VA 24538 USA (SAN 257-0149)
E-mail: j.b.designs@att.net.

Joyful Pubs., *(978-0-9992868)* 941 Fry Rd, Greenwood, IN 46142 USA Tel 317-888-3333
E-mail: kiwidenis@gmail.com.

Joyride Bks., *(978-1-937791)* 9200 Alpine Rd., La Honda, CA 94020 USA Tel 650-747-0796 (phone/fax); *Imprints:* Kid Fuse (Kid Fuse)
E-mail: laurie@fuseliterary.com; joyridebooks@gmail.com; gordon@fuseliterary.com
Web site: http://fuseliterary.com/shortfuse; http://joyridebooks.com.

JoyRox, LLC, *(978-0-9754972)* 11585 Hooker St., Westminster, CO 80031-7121 USA
E-mail: info@joy-rox.com
Web site: http://www.joy-rox.com.

JoySoul Corp., *(978-0-9727786)* Orders Addr.: 1214 Rose St., Lisbon, ND 58054-0071 USA
E-mail: jscontact@joysoul.com
Web site: http://www.joysoul.com.

JoyWrites, *(978-1-7322831)* 10430 Morado Cir. No. 1820, Austin, TX 78759 USA Tel 512-796-6974
E-mail: joy@joywrites.com.

JoZanephine Originals *Imprint of* **Gamoke, John**

JPA Assocs., *(978-0-9727125)* 11026 Maple Rd., Lafayette, CO 80026 USA Tel 303-665-6764.

JR Comics (KOR) *(978-89-94208; 978-89-92836; 978-89-98341) Dist. by* **Lerner Pub.**

Jr Imagination, *(978-0-9837404; 978-0-9893189)* 17310 Trosa St., Granada Hills, CA 91344 USA Tel 818-366-4194; Fax: 818-366-2134
E-mail: marty@jrimagination.com
Web site: http://www.jrimagination.com; http://www.samatart.com; http://www.doublemgraphics.com.

JRP Ringier Kunstverlag AG (CHE) *(978-2-940271; 978-3-905701; 978-3-905770; 978-3-03764; 978-3-905829) Dist. by* **Dist Art Pubs.**

JRSK Bks., *(978-0-9837709; 978-0-9850733)* 1120 Ellison Pk. Cir., Denton, TX 76205 USA Tel 940-383-0426
E-mail: jrskipling@yahoo.com
Web site: www.jrodneyshort.com.

JRV Publishing, *(978-0-9771250)* P.O. Box 82, West Simsbury, CT 06092 USA
E-mail: jverney1@jrvpublishing.com.

JSP Bks., *(978-0-9728519)* 6886 Hickory Lake Cove, Memphis, TN 38119 USA Tel 901-757-0694
E-mail: contact@jspbooks.com
Web site: http://www.jspbooks.com.

JU Pr., *(978-0-578-52674-4)* 1709 S. State Rte. 560, Urbana, OH 43078 USA Tel 937-869-3882
E-mail: Jessie.k.uthoff@gmail.com.

Juba Bks. *Imprint of* **NetNia Publishing Co.**

Judah Bks., Inc., *(978-0-9767469)* 3535 W. Tierra Buena Ln., Apt. No. A273, Phoenix, AZ 85053 USA.

Judaica Pr., Inc., The, *(978-0-910818; 978-1-880582; 978-1-932443; 978-1-60763)* 123 Ditmas Ave., Brooklyn, NY 11218 USA (SAN 204-9856) Tel 718-972-6200; Fax: 718-972-6204; Toll Free: 800-972-6201; *Imprints:* Shayach Comics (Shayach Comics)
E-mail: info@judaicapress.com
Web site: http://www.judaicapress.com.

Judd, Robert, *(978-0-692-05202-0)* P.O. Box 186, Forest City, NC 28043 USA Tel 828-245-3950; Fax: 828-245-3950
E-mail: robertjudd7067@att.net.

JuDe Publishing, *(978-0-9712585)* Orders Addr.: P.O. Box 264 s lacienega blvd #1283, beverly hills, CA 90211 USA Tel 310-600-9729
E-mail: judepublishing@yahoo.com
Dist(s): **Bookazine Co., Inc.**

Judie, Sharon Y., *(978-0-692-93298-8)* 19281 Rocky Summit Dr., Perris, CA 92570 USA Tel 310-818-3662
E-mail: sharon.judie@gmail.com.

Judith VT Wilson, *(978-0-692-07753-5; 978-0-692-14615-6)* 191 Delhi Ct, Smyrna, DE 19977 USA Tel 302-653-6862
E-mail: jwilson191@comcast.net
Web site: www.growingsmartercenter.com.

†Judson Pr., *(978-0-8170)* Div. of American Baptist Churches, U.S.A., Orders Addr.: 1075 First Ave., King of Prussia, PA 19406 USA (SAN 201-0348) Fax: 610-768-2107; Toll Free: 800-458-3766
E-mail: gale.tull@abhms.org
Web site: http://www.judsonpress.com
Dist(s): **Anchor Distributors**
Spring Arbor Distributors, Inc.; *CIP.*

Juice & Berriesr, The *Imprint of* **Asiana Media**

Jujapa Pr., *(978-0-9650233; 978-1-7321976; 978-1-952493)* PO Box 269, Hansville, WA 98340 USA.

Julenda Enterprises, *(978-0-9747994)* 219 E. El Valle, Green Valley, AZ 85614-2903 USA Tel 520-393-0071
E-mail: judylgarcia@aol.com
Web site: http://www.judylenore.com.

Julian's Legacy, *(978-0-615-22488-6; 978-0-578-48848-6)* 65 Futch Rd., Allenhurst, 31313 SUN
Web site: http://www.inhisowntime.com.

Julie Andrews Collection *Imprint of* **HarperCollins Pubs.**

Julie Causton, phD, *(978-0-578-44374-4)* 7704 Berkshire Pkwy., Manlius, NY 13104 USA Tel 315-692-2026
E-mail: julie@inclusiveschooling.com
Dist(s): **Ingram Content Group.**

Juliette's Adventures, 85 Sturbridge Ln., Grand Island, NY 14072 USA Tel 716-773-3694
E-mail: dawn_cardin@yahoo.com
Dist(s): **Ingram Content Group.**

Julio C. Malone *See* **Editorial Miglo Inc.**

Julson, D. K., *(978-0-9746564; 978-0-615-11699-0)* 28704 County Hwy B., Richland Ctr, WI 53581-6721 USA.

July Publishing Inc. *See* **Social Motion Publishing**

July-Eight Publishing *See* **Three Socks Publishing**

Jumbo Minds, Inc., *(978-1-944049)* P.O. Box 1153, Fairport, NY 14450 USA Tel 585-747-4242
E-mail: admin@JumboMinds.com
Web site: JumboMinds.com.

Jump at the Sun *Imprint of* **Hyperion Bks. for Children**

Jump! Inc. *See* **Jump! Inc.**

Jump! Inc., *(978-1-62031; 978-1-62496; 978-1-64128; 978-1-64527)* 5357 Penn Ave. S., Minneapolis, MN 55419 USA (SAN 920-8143) Tel 888-960-1346; *Imprints:* Bullfrog Books (BullfrogBks); Pogo (Pogo)
E-mail: casie@jumplibrary.com
Web site: http://www.jumplibrary.com
Dist(s): **Follett School Solutions**
Independent Pubs. Group.

Jump Pr., *(978-0-9754902; 978-0-9980733)* P.O. Box 600743, Newtonville, MA 02460-2210 USA
E-mail: emily@emilysper.com
Web site: http://blueirisdesign.com.

Jump Start Performance Programs, *(978-1-893962)* P.O. Box 3448, Van Nuys, CA 91407 USA Toll Free Fax: 800-990-9667; Toll Free: 800-450-0432
E-mail: scott@scottgreenberg.com
Web site: http://www.scottgreenberg.com.

Jumping Cow Pr., *(978-0-9801433; 978-0-9980010; 978-1-7356962)* P.O. Box 2732, Briarcliff Manor, NY 10510 USA (SAN 855-305X) Tel 914-373-9816
E-mail: jumpingcowpress@gmail.com
Web site: http://www.JumpingCowPress.com
Dist(s): **Brown Books Publishing Group.**

Jumping Jack Pr., *(978-0-9795441; 978-1-60580; 978-1-62348)* Div. of Up With Paper, LLC, 6049 Hi-Tek Ct., Mason, OH 45040 USA Tel 513-759-7473; Fax: 513-336-3119
E-mail: info@upwithpaper.com; georgew@upwithpaper.com
Web site: http://www.jumpingjackpress.com
Dist(s): **Ingram Publisher Services.**

June & Lucy, *(978-1-64608)* 627 Stoneway Dr, San Antonio, TX 78258 USA Tel 210-569-9083
E-mail: bowker@junelucy.com.

June & The Wolves Publishing, *(978-0-615-74511-4; 978-0-615-89550-5; 978-0-692-36512-0)* 148 E St. RD 177, FEASTERVILLE, PA 19053 USA Tel 480-999-1877
Dist(s): **CreateSpace Independent Publishing Platform.**

June Bks., LLC, *(978-0-9835558)* 408 W. Lotta St. Suite No. 1, Sioux Falls, SD 57105 USA Tel 512-630-3380
E-mail: trevor@junebooks.com; hello@junebooks.com
Web site: http://www.junebooks.com.

Junebug Bks. *Imprint of* **NewSouth, Inc.**

JuneOne Publishing Hub, *(978-0-9763082)* 27762 Antonio Pkwy., L1-404, Ladera Ranch, CA 92694 USA Tel 949-364-6179; Fax: 757-299-4407; *Imprints:* A JuneOne Production (A JuneOne Prod)
E-mail: info@juneonehub.com
Web site: http://www.juneonehub.com.

Junge, Michael, *(978-0-692-75722-2; 978-0-692-75723-9; 978-0-692-77029-0)* 10 Algerwood, Ladera Ranch, CA 92694 USA Tel 949-887-6085.

Jungle Communications, Incorporation *See* **Allergic Child Publishing Group**

JUNGLE Gym, The, *(978-0-578-42236-7)* 8566 N. Oswego Ave., Portland, OR 97203 USA Tel 312-802-2323
E-mail: antonfrederickcobb@gmail.com
Dist(s): **Ingram Content Group.**

Jungle Hse. Pubns., *(978-0-9769332)* Orders Addr.: 736 Cardium St., Sanibel, FL 33957-6704 USA Tel 239-395-4518
E-mail: junglehousepub@yahoo.com
Web site: http://junglehousepublications.com.

Jungle Jeep Press *See* **Jungle Wagon Pr.**

Jungle Tales, *(978-0-615-70807-2)* 229 edgecomb Ave Apt No. 3, New York, NY 10030 USA Tel 714-856-1768
E-mail: Jeff.Zorrilla@gmail.com.

Jungle Wagon Pr., *(978-0-9834092; 978-0-9904271)* 5116 Didier Ave., Rockford, IL 61101 USA (SAN 920-6426) Tel 815-988-9048
E-mail: junglewagonpress@gmail.com
Web site: http://www.junglewagonpress.com.

Jungler *See* **Yunka Publishing**

Junior History Pr., *(978-0-9744556)* Orders Addr.: P.O. Box 157, Summerville, SC 29484-0157 USA Tel 843-873-8117; Edit Addr.: 1311 Jahnz Ave., Summerville, SC 29485 USA
E-mail: gteaster@juniorhistory.com
Web site: http://www.juniorhistory.com.

Junior League of Central Westchester, *(978-0-615-16563-9)* 1039 Post Rd., Scarsdale, NY 10583 USA Tel 914-723-6139; Fax: 914-723-6016
E-mail: jlcw@verizon.net
Web site: http://www.jlcentralwestchester.org.

Junior League of Grand Rapids Michigan, Inc., *(978-0-9611316; 978-0-9634927)* 25 Sheldon Blvd., Suite 124, Grand Rapids, MI 49503 USA (SAN 282-9452) Tel 616-451-0452; Fax: 616-451-1936
E-mail: juniorleague@iserv.net
Web site: http://www.juniorleaguegr.com.

Junior League of Omaha, *(978-0-9609146)* 608 N. 108th Ct., Omaha, NE 68154-1762 USA (SAN 241-5348) Tel 402-330-0197.

Junior League of Tyler, Inc., The, *(978-0-9607122)* 1919 S. Donnybrook, Tyler, TX 75701 USA (SAN 238-9975) Tel 903-593-8141; Fax: 903-595-1362.

Juniper Berry Pr., *(978-0-9760076)* 6609 Cornelia Dr., Edina, MN 55435 USA Tel 952-285-4447
E-mail: gjudso@aol.com
Web site: http://www.juniperberrypress.com.

Juniper Grove, *(978-1-60355)* 2129 E. Stearns, Fayetteville, AR 72703 USA (SAN 853-5078)
E-mail: JuniperGrove@gmail.com
Web site: http://www.junipergrove.com
Dist(s): **CreateSpace Independent Publishing Platform.**

Juniper Publishing (CAN) *(978-1-988002) Dist. by* **S and S Inc.**

Juping Horse Pr., *(978-0-615-55671-0; 978-0-615-75585-4)* 845 N. 27th St., Philadelphia, PA 19130 USA Tel 215-978-0844
E-mail: karin@jumpinghorsepress.com
Web site: http://www.jumpinghorsepress.com.

Jupiter Coins *See* **Adventure in Discovery**

Jupiter Kids (Childrens & Kids Fiction) *Imprint of* **Speedy Publishing LLC**

juputer2 bks., *(978-0-9779404)* 309 Claymille Pl., Nashville, TN 37207 USA
Web site: http://www.juputer2books.com.

Juris Prudence LLC, *(978-1-946456)* 5115 8th St. NW, Washington, DC 20011 USA Tel 804-937-4598
Dist(s): **CreateSpace Independent Publishing Platform.**

Just Be Publishing, Inc., *(978-0-9668219)* 746 E. Rosemore Ct., Salt Lake City, UT 84107 USA (SAN 299-7479) Tel 801-265-3435 (phone/fax)
E-mail: bl_ehrler@att.net
Web site: http://www.justbepublishing.com.

Just Chill Pubns., *(978-0-9726548)* P.O. Box 5990, Chicago, IL 60680 USA
E-mail: chill1960@comcast.net; contact@justchill.org; contact@communityaccesstoresources.org
Web site: http://www.justchill.org; http://www.communityaccesstoresources.org.

Just Enjoyable Memorable Story Bks., *(978-0-9724472)* 8258 Balsam Way, Arvada, CO 80005 USA
E-mail: jemsbooks@hotmail.com.

Just For Kids Pr., LLC, *(978-1-934650; 978-1-935498; 978-1-935747; 978-1-936918; 978-1-937962)* 360 Hurst St., Linden, NJ 07036 USA
E-mail: ssullivan@justforkidspress.com.

Just Fun Bks. & Things, *(978-0-692-87442-4; 978-0-9990471)* 4991 Manor Ridge Ln., San Diego, CA 92130 USA Tel 858-461-1935
E-mail: barbgay95@gmail.com.

Just Jessica, L.L.C., *(978-0-692-92654-3; 978-0-578-63561-3; 978-0-578-63563-7)* 529 Brooklyn Tpke., Hampton, CT 06247 USA Tel 203-218-7864
E-mail: Fred.wills@att.net
Web site: Just Jessica.org.

Just Like Me, Inc., *(978-1-928889)* 525 Tailgate Terr., Landover, MD 20785 USA
E-mail: jlm1922@gmail.com
Web site: http://www.justlikemeworld.com
Dist(s): **Ingram Bk. Co.**

Just Me Productions, *(978-0-9821118)* 4255 Us 1 S., Suite 18-212, Saint Augustine, FL 32086 USA Tel 904-797-7242
Web site: http://www.justmeproductions.com.

Just Think Bks. *Imprint of* **Canary Connect Pubns.**

Just Us Bks., Inc., *(978-0-940975; 978-1-933491)* 395 Pleasant Valley Way Suite B, West Orange, NJ 07052 USA (SAN 664-7413) Tel 973-672-7701; *Imprints:* Sankofa Books (Sankofa Bks)
E-mail: justusbook@aol.com
Web site: http://www.justusbooks.com.

Just Us Bks., Inc., *(978-1-60349)* 395 Pleasant Valley Way Suite B, West Orange, NJ 07052 USA Tel 973-672-7701; Fax: 973-677-7570; *Imprints:* Marimba Books (MarimbaBks)
E-mail: justusbook@aol.com
Dist(s): **Just Us Bks., Inc.**

Just Write Bks., *(978-0-9722839; 978-0-9766533; 978-0-9777614; 978-0-9788628; 978-1-934949; 978-1-944386)* Just Write Communications, 14 MUNROE LN, TOPSHAM, ME 04086 USA (SAN 855-5109) Tel 207-837-0558; 207-729-3600
E-mail: jstwrite@jstwrite.com
Web site: http://www.jstwrite.com.

Justice Brothers Publishing *See* **Justice, Israel**

Justice, Israel, *(978-0-9997969)* 2429 Arborwood Dr, Valrico, FL 33596 USA Tel 813-956-7605
E-mail: israeljustice04@gmail.com.

Justice Link Publishing, *(978-0-692-00612-2)* P.O. Box 3144, Glendale, CA 91221 USA.

Justkym, *(978-0-692-90715-3)* 1907 Rambling Ln., Brandon, FL 33510 USA Tel 813-317-1004
E-mail: justkym@gmail.com.

JustTheBox, LLC, *(978-0-692-92371-9)* 600 Excel Cir, SE, Brownsboro, AL 35741 USA Tel 256-457-5355
E-mail: rdunford21@gmail.com
Dist(s): **Independent Pub.**

Juvenescent Research Corp., *(978-0-9600148; 978-1-884996)* 807 Riverside Dr., Apt. 1F, New York, NY 10032 USA (SAN 206-7250) Tel 212-795-3749
Dist(s): **Barnes & Noble, Inc.**

Juventud, Editorial (ESP) *(978-84-261) Dist. by* **AIMS Intl.**

Juventud, Editorial (ESP) *(978-84-261) Dist. by* **Distribks Inc.**

Juventud, Editorial (ESP) *(978-84-261) Dist. by* **Continental Bk.**

Juventud, Editorial (ESP) *(978-84-261) Dist. by* **Lectorum Pubns.**

JVED Publishing, *(978-0-9768833)* 13570 Grove Dr. No. 361, Maple Grove, MN 55311 USA
Web site: http://www.jvedpublishing.org.

JVGray, *(978-0-9982387)* 71 Snowden Ave, Ossining, NY 10562 USA Tel 914-713-4104
E-mail: jvgray01@gmail.com
Web site: jvgray.com.

JWall Publishing, *(978-0-9760518)* 287 Jones Rd., Statham, GA 30666 USA Tel 770-725-7465.

JWD Publishing, *(978-0-9816437; 978-0-9843365; 978-0-9846315; 978-1-941574)* P.O. Box 1481, Hiram, GA 30141 USA Tel 912-687-5546
E-mail: jwpublishing@gmail.com
Web site: http://www.revolutionarydisciples.com; www.jaribooks.com.

JYZ Books, LLC *See* **JYZ Bks., LLC**

K and K Publishing, *(978-0-9828886)* P.O. Box 20517, Carson City, NV 89721 USA Tel 775-885-7986
E-mail: okmarge@charter.net; marge@kankpublishing.com
Web site: http://kankpublishing.com.

K. F. Enterprises *See* **Production Assocs., Inc.**

K Jacks Publishing, *(978-0-9978108)* 20 Deerfield Dr., Franklin, NJ 07416 USA Tel 973-827-0684
E-mail: kristenjaccodine@hotmail.com.

K T Graphics, *(978-0-9755259)* 5300 Standing Rock Pl., Las Vegas, NV 89130 USA Tel 702-808-3773
Web site: http://www.ktgraphicsolutions.com.

K Yee, *(978-0-9992730)* 3126 Allen Way, Santa Clara, CA 95051 USA Tel 650-714-1005
E-mail: greencows2@gmail.com.

K12, *(978-1-931728; 978-1-60153)* 2300 Corporate Park Dr., Herndon, VA 20171 USA Tel 703-483-7000; Fax: 703-483-7330
Web site: http://www.k12.com.

K-Twelve MicroMedia Publishing, Inc., *(978-0-943646; 978-1-56419)* 16 McKee Dr., Mahwah, NJ 07430 USA (SAN 286-990X) Tel 201-529-4500; Fax: 201-529-5282; Toll Free: 800-292-1997
E-mail: sales@k12mmp.com
Web site: http://www.k12mmp.com.

K4K Bks. LLC, *(978-1-935368)* 21 N 13th St, Niles, MI 49120 USA
E-mail: editorial_staff@K4KBooks.com
Web site: http://www.K4KBooks.com.

KA Productions, LLC, *(978-1-888018)* Orders Addr.: P.O. Box 21, Alexandria, VA 22313-0021 USA Tel 703-371-4325 (phone/fax); *Imprints:* Word of Mouth Books (Word of Mouth Bks)
E-mail: stephanie@bookinaday.com
Web site: http://www.kwamealexander.com
Dist(s): **SPD-Small Pr. Distribution.**

Kabet Pr. (GBR) *(978-0-948662) Dist. by* **Empire Pub Srvs.**

Kadima Pr., *(978-0-9723229)* 410 Pine St. No., 802 C, Abilene, TX 79601-5163 USA Fax: 501-636-7425
E-mail: KadimaPress@juno.com
Web site: http://www.kadimapress.com; http://www.AuntLaya.com
Dist(s): **Bks. West.**

Kaeden Bks. *Imprint of* **Kaeden Corp.**

Kaeden Corp., *(978-1-57874; 978-1-879835; 978-1-61181; 978-1-63584; 978-1-64132)* Orders Addr.: P.O. Box 16190, Rocky River, OH 44116 USA Tel 440-617-1400; Fax: 440-617-1403; Toll Free: 800-890-7323; *Imprints:* Kaeden Books (Kaeden)
E-mail: info@kaeden.com; gurmston@kaeden.com; customerservice@kaeden.com
Web site: http://www.kaeden.com
Dist(s): **Follett School Solutions.**

Kagan Cooperative Learning *See* **Kagan Publishing**

Kagan Publishing, *(978-1-879097; 978-1-933445)* Div. of Resources for Teachers, Orders Addr.: P.O. Box 72008, San Clemente, CA 92673 USA Tel 949-545-6300; Fax: 949-545-6301; Toll Free: 800-933-2667
E-mail: carol@kaganonline.com; parker@kaganonline.com; Hannah@KaganOnline.com
Web site: http://www.kaganonline.com.

Kagelmacher, Leonard W. *See* **Buffalo Arts Publishing**

Kahl, Helen Barry, *(978-0-692-13055-1; 978-0-692-19734-9)* 907 Governor Bridge Rd., Davidsonville, MD 21035 USA Tel 202-528-7569
E-mail: helenbarry@msn.com
Dist(s): **CreateSpace Independent Publishing Platform.**

kahla, bob, *(978-1-882820; 978-0-692-75067-4)* P.O. Box 134, Stowell, TX 77661 USA Tel 409-201-4614
E-mail: poss1108@msn.com.

Kahley, Glenn, *(978-0-9788914)* 1575 England Dr., Columbus, OH 43240 USA
E-mail: kahley.1@osu.edu.

Kai Adventures, *(978-0-692-63587-2)* 10700 Brunswick Rd., Apt. 107, Bloomington, MN 55438 USA Tel 612-987-5945
E-mail: juneoliver2@aol.com; joliver@isd271.org.

Kaimanu Prodns., Ltd., *(978-0-9764474)* 135-A Kaimanu Pl., Kihei, HI 96753 USA Tel 808-268-9092; Fax: 808-442-0013
E-mail: customerservice@kaimanu.net
Web site: http://www.kaimanu.net
Dist(s): **Booklines Hawaii, Ltd.**

Kaio Publications, Inc. *See* **Kaio Pubns., Inc.**

Kaio Pubns., Inc., *(978-0-9960430; 978-1-7326661; 978-1-952955)* 2119 Autumn Cove Cir., Fleming Island, FL 32003 USA Tel 615-828-4363
E-mail: joe@kaiopublications.org
Web site: www.kaiopublications.org.

Kairos Publishing, *(978-0-9665831; 978-0-9818864; 978-0-615-92130-3; 978-0-692-65816-1; 978-0-692-67177-1)* Orders Addr.: P.O. Box 450, Clarence, NY 14031 USA Tel 716-759-1058; Edit Addr.: 10501 Main St., Clarence, NY 14031 USA Do not confuse with Kairos Publishing in Llano de San Juan, NM
E-mail: office@eagleswings.to
Web site: http://www.eagleswings.to
Dist(s): **Destiny Image Pubs.**
Send The Light Distribution LLC.

KAK, *(978-0-615-40229-1)* 776 Highland Hills Dr., Howard, OH 43028 USA Tel 740-294-3202
E-mail: saucie776@yahoo.com.

Kalandraka Ediciones Andalucía, S.L. (ESP) *(978-84-96388; 978-84-933755; 978-84-933759; 978-84-933780) Dist. by* **Lectorum Pubns.**

Kalandraka Editora, S.L. (ESP) *(978-84-8464; 978-84-923553; 978-84-95123) Dist. by* **Mariuccia Iaconi Bk Imports.**

Kalandraka Editora, S.L. (ESP) *(978-84-8464; 978-84-923553; 978-84-95123) Dist. by* **Lectorum Pubns.**

Kalawantis Computer Services, Incorporated *See* **Kalawantis Publishing Services, Inc**

Kalawantis Publishing Services, Inc, *(978-0-9665909)* Orders Addr.: P.O. Box 25004, Charlotte, NC 28227 USA Tel 704-754-1108
E-mail: publisher@kalawantis.com
Web site: http://www.kalawantis.com.

Kalcom Publishing, *(978-0-9797530)* 84-01 Lefferts Blvd., Kew Gardens, NY 11415 USA Tel 718-805-5555
E-mail: yek@kalcom.com.

Kaleidoscope Bks. *Imprint of* **I Am My Life Publishing, LLC**

Kaleta Publishing, LLC, *(978-0-615-39881-5; 978-0-9830222)* 161 Trail E., Pataskala, OH 43062 USA Tel 614-352-3583
E-mail: mindyjkaleta@gmail.com
Dist(s): **MyiLibrary.**

KALEXT Productions, LLC, *(978-0-9617451; 978-0-9748792)* 12795 75th Lane N., West Palm Beach, FL 33412 USA (SAN 664-0613) Tel 561-310-4338; Fax: 561-790-6294 Call 561-310-4338 first
E-mail: xela319@comcast.net
Web site: http://www.bilingualgames.com; http://www.biznizgames.com.

Kalindi Pr., *(978-1-935826; 978-0-9838455)* 2508 Shadow Valley Ranch Rd., Prescott, AZ 86305 USA Tel 928-636-3759
E-mail: balazuccarello@gmail.com
Web site: http://www.kalindipress.com
Dist(s): **SCB Distributors.**

Kaliyan Publishing, *(978-0-9762065)* P.O. Box 473, Stephens City, VA 22655-9998 USA.

†Kalmbach Publishing Co., Bks. Div., *(978-0-8238; 978-0-87116; 978-0-89024; 978-0-89778; 978-0-913135; 978-0-933168; 978-1-62700)* Orders Addr.: P.O. Box 1612, Waukesha, WI 53186 USA (SAN 201-0399) Tel 262-796-8776 Toll Free: 800-533-6644 (customer sales); 800-446-5489 (customer service); 800-558-1544 (trade sales); Edit Addr.: 21027 Crossroads Cir., Waukesha, WI 53186 USA Tel 262-796-8776
E-mail: customerservice@kalmbach.com
Web site: http://corporate.kalmbach.com/; http://kalmbach.com
Dist(s): **Publishers Group West (PGW)**
Watson-Guptill Pubns., Inc.; *CIP.*

Kalmia Publishing, *(978-0-9676620)* Orders Addr.: 826 Amiford Dr., San Diego, CA 92107 USA Tel 619-222-7074 (phone/fax)
E-mail: pixieh@mymailstation.com; folsom@islc.net
Web site: http://www.islc.net/~folsom/language.

Kaloustian, Varak, *(978-0-9987773; 978-1-7338185)* 13903 Otsego St., Sherman Oaks, CA 91423 USA Tel 818-383-0621; *Imprints:* TLOV Publishing (MYID_H_TLOV PU)
E-mail: info@thelegendofv.com
Web site: thelegendofv.com.

KAM Publishing, *(978-0-9795474)* Orders Addr.: 1716 Worley St., Durant, OK 74701-2468 USA
E-mail: sharonm@llibs.com
Web site: http://www.llibs.com
Dist(s): **Library Integrated Solutions & Assocs.**

Kamahoi Pr. *Imprint of* **Bishop Museum Pr.**

Kamal, *(978-1-59236)* P.O. Box 1026 Florin Rd, #303, Sacramento, CA 95831 USA
E-mail: admin04@desertwellnetwork.com
Web site: http://www.DesertWellNetwork.com
Dist(s): **Ingram Content Group.**

KAMAL Pubns., *(978-0-9651552; 978-1-59236-028-4)* 445C E. Cheyenne Mountain Blvd., No. 243, Colorado Springs, CO 80906 USA Tel 719-579-9777; Fax: 719-579-8221; Toll Free: 800-231-9341
E-mail: creative.organizing@worldnet.att.net; kitaos@aol.com.

Kamara, Feremusu, *(978-0-692-19390-7)* 1224 Waugh Chapel Rd, Gambrills, MD 21054 USA Tel 202-378-8185
E-mail: musukamara@hotmail.com.

Kamaron Institute Pr., Div. of Kamaron Institute for Rapid Business Results, 104 Strawflower Path, Peachtree City, GA 30269 USA
E-mail: info@kamaron.org; kamaroninstitute@earthlink.net
Web site: http://www.kamaron.org.

†Kamehameha Publishing, *(978-0-87336)* 567 S. King St., Suite 118, Honolulu, HI 96813 USA Tel 808-534-8205; Fax: 808-541-5305
E-mail: publishing@ksbe.edu
Web site: http://www.kamehamehapublishing.org
Dist(s): **Bess Pr., Inc.**
Booklines Hawaii, Ltd.
Follett School Solutions
Native Bks.; *CIP.*

Kamehameha Schools Press *See* **Kamehameha Publishing**

Kana'i Records, *(978-0-9754567)* 95-1168 Makaikai St. Apt. 113, Mililani, HI 96789-4392 USA
E-mail: bhelemano@aol.com
Dist(s): **Booklines Hawaii, Ltd.**

K&B Products, *(978-0-9646181; 978-0-9740841; 978-0-9772372; 978-1-935122)* P.O. Box 548, Yellville, AR 72687 USA Toll Free Fax: 888-871-5856; Toll Free: 800-700-5096
E-mail: brmp@aol.com
Web site: http://www.thecompletepet.com; http://www.whitehallpublishing.com
Dist(s): **Western International, Inc.**

Kandon Publishing *See* **Kandon UnLtd., Inc.**

Kandon UnLtd., Inc., *(978-0-9829277; 978-0-9912905; 978-1-970163)* 6977 Navajo Rd. No. 105, San Diego, CA 92119 USA
Web site: http://kandonunlimited.com/.

Kane, Gillian, *(978-0-692-14579-1)* 3305 Gina Lynne Ct., Murrysville, PA 15668 USA Tel 724-325-9047
E-mail: 15kaneg@comcast.net
Dist(s): **Ingram Content Group.**

Kane, Kimberly Brougham, *(978-0-615-17610-9; 978-0-578-04556-6)* 1406 Campfire Rd., Lake Charles, LA 70611 USA
Web site: http://www.mommysheart.com
Dist(s): **Lulu Pr., Inc.**

†Kane Miller, *(978-0-916291; 978-1-929132; 978-1-933605; 978-1-935279; 978-1-61067; 978-1-68464)* Div. of EDC Publishing, Orders Addr.: P.O. Box 470663, Tulsa, OK 74146 USA (SAN 295-8945) Tel 800-475-4522; 918-622-4522; Fax: 800-743-5660; Edit Addr.: P.O. Box 8515, La Jolla, CA 92038 USA Tel 858-456-0540
E-mail: info@kanemiller.com
Web site: http://www.kanemiller.com; http://www.edcpub.com
Dist(s): **Children's Plus, Inc.**
EDC Publishing; *CIP.*

Kane/Miller#Book Publishers, Incorporated *See* **Kane Miller**

Kanlearn, Inc., *(978-0-9772077)* 8950 W. Olympic Blvd., No. 128, Beverly Hills, CA 90211 USA Tel 310-430-6806
E-mail: mattie3rd@yahoo.com
Web site: www.thekanlearnfoundation.com.

Kansas Alumni Assoc., *(978-0-9742918)* 1266 Oread Ave., Lawrence, KS 66044 USA
Web site: http://www.kualumni.org.

Kansas City Guidebooks, *(978-0-9763873)* P.O. Box 14082, Parkville, MO 64152 USA
Web site: http://www.kckidsguide.com.

Kanto Productions, LLC, *(978-1-929956)* P.O. Box 630435, Simi Valley, CA 93063 USA Tel 805-584-9639; Fax: 310-507-0142; Toll Free: 800-335-2686
E-mail: info@atophill.com
Web site: http://www.atophill.com.

Kaplan, Hadas, *(978-0-578-21404-7; 978-0-578-46844-0; 978-0-578-47442-7; 978-0-578-74858-0)* 8131 Havitshire Way Apt. 101, Centerville, OH 45458 USA.

†Kaplan Publishing, *(978-0-7931; 978-0-88462; 978-0-913864; 978-0-936894; 978-0-942103; 978-1-57410; 978-1-60714; 978-1-60978; 978-1-61865; 978-1-62523; 978-1-5062)* 395 Hudson St., New York, NY 10014 USA (SAN 211-2280); 395 Hudson St., New City, NY 10014; *Imprints:* Dearborn Real Estate Education (Dearbrn Real Est Ed); Barron's Educational Series, Incorporated (BarronsEd)
E-mail: deb.darrock@kaplan.com; shayna.webb@kaplan.com; alexander.noya@kaplan.com
Web site: http://www.kaplanpublishing.com; http://www.kaplanprofessional.com
Dist(s): **BookBaby**
Cranbury International
Dearborn Financial Publishing, Inc.
JAGCO & Associates Inc.
LibreDigital
MBI Distribution Services/Quayside Distribution
Simon & Schuster
Simon & Schuster, Inc.; *CIP.*

Kapp Bks. LLC, *(978-1-60346; 978-1-64035)* Orders Addr.: 204-Mohan Complex , H block Market Phase 1, New Delhi, 110052 IND; Edit Addr.: 3602 Rocky Meadow Ct., Fairfax, VA 22033 USA Fax: 703-621-7162
E-mail: pravin@kappbooks.com; sundeep@macawbooks.com
Web site: http://www.kappbooks.com; http://www.macawbooks.com/.

Karadi Tales Co. Pvt, Ltd. (IND) *(978-81-8190) Dist. by* **Consort Bk Sales.**

Karadjian, Kayl, *(978-0-692-79862-1; 978-0-9989635)* 14324 Lake Price Dr., ORLANDO, FL 32826 USA Tel 954-551-8169.

Kar-Ben Publishing *Imprint of* **Lerner Publishing Group**

Kardec, Allan Educational Society, *(978-0-9649907)* 5020 N. Eighth St., Philadelphia, PA 19120 USA Tel 215-329-4010 (phone/fax)
E-mail: akesbooks@cox.net
Web site: http://www.allan-kardec.org.

Karen Pokras Toz *See* **Grand Daisy Pr.**

Karenzo Media, *(978-0-9798164; 978-0-9899318)* 451 Tequesta Dr, Tequesta, FL 33469 USA Tel 772-882-8582
E-mail: karenzomedia@gmail.com; khsilvestri@live.com
Web site: http://www.karenyvonnehamilton.com; http://www.publishersmarketplace.com/members/kazsilvestri/; http://www.writingyourlifetales.com.

karilogue, *(978-0-9994504)* 2211 urbana pike, ijamsville, MD 21754 USA Tel 301-401-9951
E-mail: kariann.marti@gmail.com
Web site: www.karilogue.com.

Karina Library Pr., *(978-0-9824491; 978-1-937902)* P.O. Box 35, Ojai, CA 93024-9302 USA Tel 805-500-4535
E-mail: michael@karinalibrary.com; sails@karinalibrary.com
Web site: http://www.karinalibrary.com.

Karleen Tauszik *See* **Tip Top Bks.**

Karlin, Malcolm, *(978-0-692-16851-6; 978-0-692-16854-7; 978-0-692-17566-8; 978-0-692-19405-8; 978-0-692-19413-3)* 1065 Pk. Ave., New York, NY 10128 USA Tel 212-779-3375
E-mail: mkarlin@karlinpimsler.com
Dist(s): **Ingram Content Group.**

Karma Kollection LLC, *(978-0-9896966; 978-0-692-33207-8; 978-0-692-33208-5)* 549 W. Eugenie St., Chicago, IL 60614 USA Tel 312-952-0776
E-mail: roopaweber@gmail.com
Web site: www.messypenny.com.

Karma Valley Music, *(978-0-9746011)* 505 Lovins Ln., Somerset, KY 42503 USA Tel 606-274-5194
E-mail: flo@floydlovins.com.

Karnak Co., *(978-0-9630951)* Orders Addr.: P.O. Box 497-158, Chicago, IL 60649-7158 USA Tel 773-684-5298; Edit Addr.: 1616 E. 50th Pl., No. 5-C, Chicago, IL 60615 USA
E-mail: t.greer57@yahoo.com.

Karosa Publishing, *(978-0-9706312)* 4636 Almond Ln., Boulder, CO 80301 USA Tel 303-484-8856 Do not confuse with companies with same or similar name in Lower Burnell, PA, Paradise Valley, AZ, Sheffield, PA, hailey, ID
E-mail: karpub@comcast.net
Web site: http://www.spadesbook.com.

Karsonkina, Tatiana, *(978-0-9779672)* P.O. Box 191, Brooklyn, NY 11223 USA.

Karten, Ryan, *(978-0-9987424)* 1020 N Vista St., West Hollywood, CA 90046 USA Tel 323-810-5841; Fax: 323-810-5841
E-mail: ryankarten@gmail.com
Web site: ryankarten.com.

Karuna Press *See* **Utopia Pr.**

Karyn Henley Resources *Imprint of* **Child Sensitive Communication, LLC**

Kaseberg, W. G. Publishing, *(978-0-9761138)* 49 Red Bud Ln., Glen Carbon, IL 62034 USA Tel 618-288-5269; Fax: 618-288-0712
E-mail: wgkasebergpub@empowering.com.

Kashvi'sArtwork, *(978-0-692-04749-1; 978-0-692-05070-5)* 6605 W. 126th Terr., Overland Park, KS 66209 USA Tel 913-660-0945
E-mail: kashvi.silswal@gmail.com
Dist(s): **Ingram Content Group.**

Kasian Publishing, *(978-1-943207; 978-1-951871)* 15582 Eastbrook Ln., Apple Valley, MN 55124 USA Tel 612-414-9173
E-mail: kristin@kristinvanrisseghem.com
Web site: www.kristinvanrisseghem.com.

Kasson Publishing, *(978-0-9729435)* 201 E. St., Elmo Rd., Austin, TX 78745-1217 USA Tel 512-447-1988 (phone/fax)
E-mail: publishing@kassonscastings.com
Web site: http://www.kassonscastings.com.

Kasten, Victoria *See* **Victoria Tecken**

Kat Tales Publishing *See* **EMC Publishing**

Kat Tales Publishing, *(978-0-9744330)* 2515 Clarkson St., Denver, CO 80205 USA Tel 303-394-6380
E-mail: alluptojah@aol.com.

KAtastroPHE, *(978-0-9769698)* 6389 Florio St., Oakland, CA 94618 USA Tel 510-601-9631
E-mail: info@katastrophemusic.com
Web site: http://www.katastrophemusic.com.

Katheryn Maddox Haddad *Imprint of* **Northern Lights Publishing Hse.**

Kathryn Sommer, *(978-0-9719665)* 205 N. Cleveland Ave., Garnett, KS 66032 USA (SAN 254-5527)
Web site: http://www.msmediaproduction.com.

Kathy Dawson Books *Imprint of* **Penguin Young Readers Group**

Kathy Wall, *(978-0-9971001)* 101 Sierra Point Rd., Brisbane, CA 94005 USA Tel 415-608-4168
E-mail: kwallprudential@aol.com.

Kathy's Pen, *(978-0-9777034)* 24 Ridgewood Pkwy, Newport News, VA 23608 USA Tel 757-872-6258
E-mail: regmcc@cox.net
Web site: http://www.kathyspen.com.

Kati Bee & Friends Publishing, *(978-0-9793760)* 8304 Limonite Ave. Suite D-3, Riverside, CA 92509 USA (SAN 853-2818) Tel 951-685-7256; Fax: 951-332-0436
E-mail: ContactKati@katibeeandfriends.com
Web site: http://www.katibeeandfriends.com.

Katie Cook, *(978-0-9883554)* 1201 Kenwood Dr., Nashville, TN 37216 USA Tel 615-430-8128
E-mail: cookontv@comcast.net.

Katrina Denise, *(978-0-692-77541-7; 978-0-692-84082-5; 978-1-7343535)* 26 Pickersgill Sq., Owings Mills, MD 21117 USA Tel 443-416-5177
Dist(s): **CreateSpace Independent Publishing Platform.**

Kat's Kids Kreation, A, *(978-0-9749516)* 413 Fairlawn Ave., Saint Louis, MO 63119-2614 USA Fax: 314-963-0494
E-mail: katbuck123@aol.com.

Katsoris, Nicholas C. *See* **NK Pubns.**

Kattan, Peter I., *(978-0-615-15334-6; 978-0-615-18718-1; 978-0-578-03642-7)* 147-29 182nd St. Box AMM 2232, Springfield Gardens, NY 11413 USA Tel 718-553-8740
E-mail: info@kindergardensudoku.com; info@petrabooks.com
Web site: http://www.kindergardensudoku.com
Dist(s): **Lulu Pr., Inc.**

Katy Warren, *(978-0-9995221)* 8747 Phinney Ave N, No. 6, Seattle, WA 98103 USA Tel 206-291-2021
E-mail: kathlyn_warren@yahoo.com; tulipandpiggy@gmail.com.

Katydid Pubns., *(978-1-879945)* Orders Addr.: P.O. Box 526, Point Lookout, MO 65726 USA; Edit Addr.: Acacia Club Rd., Hollister, MO 65672 USA Tel 417-335-8134
E-mail: mgcameron@aol.com; kay@camerons-crag.com
Web site: http://www.katydid-publications.com.

Katydid Publishing LLC, *(978-0-9724272)* 5845 Eldorado, San Joaquin, CA 93660 USA Tel 559-693-4565 Do not confuse with Latydid Publishing in Mincie, IN.

Katzman, Lori, *(978-1-7335992)* 24 Claremont Dr., Short Hills, NJ 07078 USA Tel 732-809-7499
E-mail: lakatzman@me.com.

Kaukini Ranch Pr., *(978-0-9643674)* P.O. Box 2462, Wailuku, HI 96793 USA Tel 808-244-3371; Fax: 808-395-0738.

Kav Books, Incorporated *See* **Royal Fireworks Publishing Co.**

Kawainui Pr., *(978-0-943357)* P.O. Box 163, Captain Cook, HI 96704 USA (SAN 668-6427) Tel 808-328-9126 (phone/fax)
E-mail: herbkane@kona.net
Web site: http://www.hitrade.com
Dist(s): **Booklines Hawaii, Ltd.**

Kay, James Publishing, *(978-0-9728288; 978-0-9850113; 978-1-943245)* Orders Addr.: P.O. Box 470733, Tulsa, OK 74147-0733 USA
E-mail: alongtheway89@sbcglobal.net
Web site: www.jameskaypublishing.com.

Kay, Janet Consulting, *(978-0-9768786)* 115 Brighton Pk., Battle Creek, MI 49015 USA.

Kay Kay Publishing, LLC, *(978-0-9987769)* 19 Clyde Road, Suite 202, Somerset, NJ 08873 USA Tel 732-873-6464; Fax: 732-873-6480
E-mail: khebbon@yahoo.com
Web site: www.kaykaypublishing.com.

Kay Productions LLC, *(978-0-9707201)* Orders Addr.: 1115 W. Lincoln Ave., Suite 107, Yakima, WA 98902 USA Tel 509-853-0860; Fax: 509-853-0861; Toll Free: 800-619-4345; Edit Addr.: 732 Summitview Ave., Suite 628, Yakima, WA 98902 USA Do not confuse with Kay Productions, San Rafael, CA
E-mail: marketing@kayproductions.com
Web site: http://www.kayproductions.com.

Kay, Sjoukje, *(978-0-9789698)* 4500 Broadway Suite 6i, New York, NY 10040 USA
E-mail: pdolan@fairpoint.net
Web site: http://www.thedonutyogi.com.

Kaya 20 LLC, *(978-1-948633)* 1039 Constitution Way, Cumming, GA 30040-1295 USA Tel 404-618-8988; *Imprints:* Kitab Press (Kitab Pr)
E-mail: kaya20llc@gmail.com.

Kaya Production *See* **Muae Publishing, Inc.**

KayStar Publishing, *(978-0-9749886)* P.O. Box 571, Saddle River, NJ 07458 USA Fax: 201-825-3912.

Kazi Pubns., Inc., *(978-0-933511; 978-0-935782; 978-1-56744; 978-1-871031; 978-1-930637)* 3023 W. Belmont Ave., Chicago, IL 60618 USA (SAN 162-3397) Tel 773-267-7001; Fax: 773-267-7002
E-mail: info@kazi.org
Web site: http://www.kazi.org.

KB Bks. & More, *(978-0-9761128; 978-1-934486)* Orders Addr.: P.O. Box 56, Channing, TX 79018 USA Tel 806-235-2665; Fax: 866-282-1658; 715 Sante Fe, Channing, TX 79018 Fax: 866-282-1658
E-mail: kbbooks@windstream.net
Dist(s): **Follett School Solutions.**

KB Publishing, *(978-0-9768129)* 11 Running Fox Rd., Columbia, SC 29223 USA.

KBA, LLC, *(978-1-880931)* P.O. Box 3673, Carbondale, IL 62902 USA Tel 618-549-2893
E-mail: thriving@colorado.net
Web site: http://www.benziger.org.

KBR Mutti's Pubns., *(978-0-9762664)* P.O. Box 907431, Santa Barbara, CA 93190 USA
E-mail: kbrmuttis@cox.net
Web site: http://www.matthewsbox.com.

K.C. Fox Publishing, *(978-0-9767078)* Div. of The Kerr Co., P.O. Box 5446, Takoma Park, MD 20913 USA Tel 301-434-9191
E-mail: publisher@kcfoxpublishing.com
Web site: http://www.poutorpurpose.com; http://www.kcfoxpublishing.com.

KC13 Corp., *(978-1-945918)* 5440 Strand No. 203, Hawthorne, CA 90250 USA Tel 909-576-7002
E-mail: kccorp13@gmail.com.

KCI Sports *See* **KCI Sports Publishing**

KCI Sports Publishing, *(978-0-9758769; 978-0-9798729; 978-0-9843882; 978-0-9831985; 978-0-9837337; 978-0-9885458; 978-1-940056)* 3340 Whiting Ave., Suite 5, Stevens Point, WI 54481 USA Fax: 715-344-2668; Toll Free: 800-697-3756
Web site: http://www.kcisports.com
Dist(s): **Partners Bk. Distributing, Inc.**

KCL Publishing & Tutoring, *(978-0-692-05332-4; 978-0-692-18636-7; 978-0-578-46591-3; 978-0-578-50656-2; 978-1-7334681)* 683 SE Juniper Ave., Dallas, OR 97338 USA Tel 503-910-4445
E-mail: kathy.martin123@gmail.com
Dist(s): **CreateSpace Independent Publishing Platform.**

K.Co.Kids, LLC, *(978-0-9801423)* 6804 Peter's Path, Colleyville, TX 76034 USA (SAN 855-3092) Tel 817-886-8402
E-mail: kristine@kcokids.com
Web site: http://www.kcokids.com; http://www.katieandthemagicumbrella.com
Dist(s): **Midpoint Trade Bks., Inc.**

KDC Enterprises, *(978-0-692-13866-3)* 12523 S Union Ave., Chicago, IL 60628 USA Tel 773-671-2463
E-mail: kdcvictory@yahoo.com
Web site: kdc.enterprises.com.

Keaster, Diane W. *See* **ZC Horses Series of Children's Bks.**

Keebie Pr. *Imprint of* **Keebie Pr.**

Keebie Pr., *(978-0-692-91210-2; 978-0-692-91211-9; 978-0-692-92913-1; 978-0-692-98591-5; 978-0-692-98592-2; 978-0-692-98832-9; 978-0-578-42135-3; 978-0-578-42137-7; 978-0-578-42333-3; 978-0-578-54500-4; 978-1-7358875)* 327 N. Brooke Dr., CANTON, GA 30115 USA Tel 925-768-2102; *Imprints:* Keebie Press (Keebie Press)
E-mail: melindagailauthor@gmail.com
Web site: www.MelindaGailBooks.com
Dist(s): **Ingram Content Group.**

Keen Communications *See* **AdventureKEEN**

Keenan Tyler Paine, *(978-0-9740907)* 1715 Brae Burn Rd., Altadena, CA 91001 USA (SAN 255-3414)
E-mail: pmgoddard@earthlink.net.

Keene Publishing, *(978-0-9724853; 978-0-9766805; 978-0-9792371; 978-0-9815972)* P.O. Box 54, Warwick, NY 10990-0054 USA (SAN 254-8631) Tel 845-987-7750; Fax: 845-987-7845; *Imprints:* Moo Press (Moo)
E-mail: dtinney@KeeneBooks.com; info@KeeneBooks.com; mbrowne@KeeneBoooks.com
Web site: http://www.KeeneBooks.com.

Keen's Martial Arts Academy, *(978-0-9702958; 978-1-60243)* Orders Addr.: P.O. Box 144, Tannersville, PA 18372-0144 USA (SAN 852-3002)
E-mail: LOHON6@msn.com
Web site: http://www.kmaa.info.

Keenspot Entertainment, *(978-0-9722350; 978-1-932775)* Orders Addr.: P.O. Box 110, Cresbard, SD 57435 USA Tel 605-324-3332; Toll Free: 888- 533-6776
E-mail: TeriCrosby@gmail.com
Web site: http://www.keenspot.com
Dist(s): **Simon & Schuster, Inc.**

Keep Bks., *(978-1-893986)* Div. of The Ohio State Univ., 1100 Kinnear Rd., Columbus, OH 43212 USA Tel 800-678-6484; Fax: 614-688-3452; Toll Free: 800-678-6484
E-mail: keepbooks@osu.edu
Web site: http://www.keepbooks.org.

Keep Coming Back *See* **Puddledancer Pr.**

Keep Empowering Yourself Successfully, *(978-0-9762009)* 5630 S. Division, Grand Rapids, MI 49548 USA Tel 616-261-3000; Fax: 616-261-3355
E-mail: monicaharris@grar.com
Web site: http://www.successfulkeys.com.

Keep Hope Alive, *(978-1-887831)* P.O. Box 270041, West Allis, WI 53227 USA Tel 414-545-6539; Fax: 414-329-0653
E-mail: khope@access4less.net
Web site: http://www.keephopealive.org
Dist(s): **New Leaf Distributing Co., Inc.**

Keep Me Company Publishing Co., *(978-0-9718632)* 214 Blue Ridge Rd., Plymouth Meeting, PA 19462 USA Tel 610-828-2641.

Keepers of Wisdom and Peace Bks., *(978-0-9844079)* P.O. Box 1314, Woodstock, NY 12498 USA (SAN 859-3159) Tel 845-679-9258
E-mail: KeepersofWisdomandPeace@gmail.com
Web site: http://KeepersofWisdomandPeace.com
Dist(s): **Ingram Publisher Services.**

Keepsake Productions *Imprint of* **Keepsake Productions**

Keepsake Productions, *(978-0-615-63929-1; 978-0-9882979)* 2485 W. Mericrest Way, Queen Creek, AZ 85142-6066 USA Tel 480-659-9682; *Imprints:* Keepsake Productions (KeepsakeProdns)
Dist(s): **CreateSpace Independent Publishing Platform.**

Keepworthy Creations LLC, *(978-0-9833155)* P.O. Box 3529, Peoria, IL 61612 USA
E-mail: bob@keepworthy.com
Web site: www.keepworthy.com.

Kehas, Alethea, *(978-0-692-92157-9; 978-0-692-12357-7; 978-0-578-40031-0)* 26 Jonathan Ln, Bow, NH 03304 USA Tel 603-233-1846
E-mail: aekehas@gmail.com
Dist(s): **Independent Pub.**

Kehot Pubn. Society, *(978-0-8266)* Div. of Merkos L'Inyonei Chinuch, Orders Addr.: 291 Kingston Ave., Brooklyn, NY 11213 USA Tel 718-778-0226; Fax: 718-778-4148; Toll Free: 877-463-7567 (877-4MERKOS); Edit Addr.: 770 Eastern Pkwy., Brooklyn, NY 11213 USA (SAN 220-7060) Tel 718-604-2785
E-mail: orders@kehotonline.com; info@kehot.com
Web site: http://www.kehotonline.com
Dist(s): **Follet Higher Education Grp Follett School Solutions.**

Keira Pr., *(978-0-9824506)* P.O. Box 815, Joliet, IL 60434 USA Tel 815-726-4200
Web site: http://www.keirapress.com.

Keith Pubns., LLC, *(978-1-936372; 978-1-62882)* Orders Addr.: 1526 W. Sea Haze Dr., Gilbert, AZ 85233 USA
E-mail: KeithPublications@cox.net; mary@keithpublications.com
Web site: http://www.keithpublications.com.

Keiva DA, *(978-1-7335596)* 131 E. Central Ave., Maywood, NJ 07607 USA Tel 201-888-6060
E-mail: keivada@gmail.com.

Kelley, James *See* **Lypton Publishing**

Kelley, L. A., *(978-1-7321537)* 513 Pheasant Ct., Pensacola, FL 32514 USA Tel 850-477-0067
E-mail: l.a.kelley.author@gmail.com.

Kelley, Mark, *(978-1-880865; 978-0-9744053)* Orders Addr.: P.O. Box 32077, Juneau, AK 99803 USA Tel 907-586-1993; Fax: 907-586-1201; Edit Addr.: PO Box 32077, Juneau, AK 99803 USA
E-mail: photos@markkelley.com
Web site: http://www.markkelley.com.

KelleyGreenworks Publishing, *(978-0-9791029)* Orders Addr.: 607 Woodsman Way, Crownsville, MD 21032 USA
Web site: http://www.readysetgo-organic.com.

Kellie Ann Briseno, *(978-0-578-57205-5; 978-0-578-60915-7; 978-0-578-77522-7)* 807 Rockcress Dr., Mansfield, TX 76063 USA Tel 817-807-3870
E-mail: kellie.briseno@gmail.com.

Kelly Bear Pr., Inc., *(978-0-9621054)* 20493 Pine Vista, Bend, OR 97702 USA (SAN 250-5746) Fax: 541-330-6846; Toll Free: 800-431-1934 (orders only)
E-mail: kellybear@bendcable.com
Web site: http://www.kellybear.com
Dist(s): **Sunburst Visual Media.**

Kelly Cochran Publishing, *(978-0-578-42665-5)* 2261 N Beachwood Dr. K-114, Los Angeles, CA 90068 USA Tel 205-265-0102
E-mail: caremoresharemore@gmail.com
Dist(s): **Independent Pub.**

Kelly, D Scott, *(978-0-9755482)* 208 W. Lincoln, Charlevoix, MI 49720 USA Tel 231-547-1144; Fax: 231-547-4970
E-mail: info@basesteencenter.org
Web site: http://www.basesteencenter.org.

Kelly, Elaine A., *(978-0-578-06873-2)* 5 Appletree Ln., Newtown Square, PA 19073 USA
E-mail: eakgck@hotmail.com.

Kelly, Jason Pr., *(978-0-9664387)* 15 Ken Pratt Blvd. Suite 200, Longmont, CO 80501 USA Tel 303-772-7209
E-mail: jason@jasonkelly.com
Web site: http://www.JasonKelly.com
Dist(s): **BookBaby.**

Kelly, Katherine, *(978-0-9773481)* 4203 Cty. Rd., 3100, Lubbock, TX 79403-7869 USA
E-mail: kellytomkat@sptc.net
Web site: www.informationsleuth.wordpress.com.

Kelly, Kimberly, *(978-0-9747363)* 9801 E. Homestead Rd., Poplar, WI 54864 USA
E-mail: kimkellykimkelly@yahoo.com
Dist(s): **Partners Bk. Distributing, Inc.**

Kelly Lee Culbreth, *(978-0-578-43267-0; 978-0-578-49777-8; 978-0-578-56447-0)* 641 Creek Oak Dr., Murfreesboro, TN 37128 USA Tel 615-480-7747
E-mail: studio627@gmail.com
Dist(s): **Ingram Content Group.**

Kelly, Tiffany, *(978-0-692-83022-2; 978-0-578-71835-4)* 9001 Bramblewood Way, Elk Grove, CA 95758 USA Tel 916-877-0378; Fax: 916-877-0378
E-mail: TiffanyKelly616@yahoo.com.

Kelsey Enterprises Publishing *See* **Cheval International**

†Kelsey Street Pr., *(978-0-932716)* 2824 Kelsey St., Berkeley, CA 94705-2302 USA (SAN 212-6729)
E-mail: kelseyst@sirius.com
Web site: http://www.kelseyst.com
Dist(s): **BookMobile SPD-Small Pr. Distribution**; *CIP.*

Kelton, Inc., *(978-0-692-86206-3)* 200 2nd Ave SE, Sleepy Eye, MN 56085 USA Tel 715-533-5880
E-mail: jediblender1986@gmail.com.

Kempston, Megan, *(978-0-9975660)* 19275 Hidden Springs Ln., Boulder Creek, CA 95006 USA Tel 520-904-0546
E-mail: megankempston@gmail.com.

Kemtec Educational Corp., *(978-1-877960)* 4780 Interstate Dr., Cincinnati, OH 45246-1112 USA Toll Free: 877-536-8321
E-mail: prekem@kemtecscience.com
Web site: http://www.kemtecscience.com.

Ken Pr., *(978-1-928771)* 4001 N. Paseo de los Rancheros, Tucson, AZ 85745 USA (SAN 299-9714) Tel 520-743-3200; Fax: 520-743-3210
E-mail: office@kenpress.com
Web site: http://www.kenpress.com
Dist(s): **Distributors, The.**

Kenamar, Inc., *(978-0-9753207)* P.O. Box 689, West Dundee, IL 60110-0689 USA
E-mail: kenamarpublish@aol.com.

Kendahl Hse. Pr. *Imprint of* **Youngs, Bettie Bks.**

Kendall Hunt Publishing Co., *(978-0-7872; 978-0-8403; 978-0-7575; 978-1-4652; 978-1-5249; 978-1-7924)* Orders Addr.: P.O. Box 1840, Dubuque, IA 52004-1840 USA; Edit Addr.: 4050 Westmark Dr., Dubuque, IA 52002 USA (SAN 203-9184) Tel 563-589-1000; Fax: 563-589-1046; Toll Free Fax: 800-772-9165; Toll Free: 800-228-0810
E-mail: orders@kendallhunt.com; kkelly@kendallhunt.com
Web site: http://www.kendallhunt.com
Dist(s): **Smashwords.**

Kendar Publishing Company *See* **Kendar Publishing, Inc.**

Kendar Publishing, Inc., *(978-1-889506)* 310 5th St., Suite 101, Racine, WI 53403 USA Tel 262-632-4070; Fax: 262-632-7089; Toll Free: 866-632-7040.

Kendu Films, *(978-0-615-19233-8; 978-0-9825050; 978-0-9977328)* Orders Addr.: 27068 la paz rd, No. 543, Aliso Viejo, CA 92656 USA
Web site: http://www.kendufilms.com
Dist(s): **Publishers Services.**

Kenealy, Kevin Patrick, *(978-0-692-15485-4; 978-0-692-15487-8; 978-0-692-15576-9; 978-0-692-15577-6)* 14307 Wooded Path Ln., Orland Park, IL 60462 USA Tel 708-299-2486
E-mail: kevin.kenealy@gmail.com
Dist(s): **Ingram Content Group.**

Kennebec Large Print *Imprint of* **Cengage Gale**

Kennedy Christian Publishing, *(978-0-9743136)* P.O. Box 5385, Texarkana, TX 75505-5385 USA
E-mail: knndytgr@aol.com.

Kennedy Enterprises, LLC, *(978-0-9836230)* 600 Baver St., Clarksburg, WV 26301 USA Tel 304-685-1239
E-mail: kennedykonnection@yahoo.com
Dist(s): **Lulu Pr., Inc.**

Kenneth B. White, *(978-0-9979291; 978-0-692-04983-9; 978-1-7340222; 978-1-7354384)* 1108 Wellesley Ave., Modesto, CA 95350 USA Tel 209-567-0600.

Kensington Bks. *Imprint of* **Kensington Publishing Corp.**

Kensington Publishing Corp., *(978-0-7860; 978-0-8065; 978-0-8184; 978-0-8217; 978-1-55817; 978-1-57566; 978-0-7582; 978-1-4201; 978-1-59983; 978-1-60183; 978-0-9817144; 978-0-9818905; 978-0-9824170; 978-0-9841132; 978-1-61650; 978-1-61773; 978-1-4967; 978-1-5161; 978-1-63573) 119 W. 40th St., New York, NY 10018 USA Tel 212-407-1500; Fax: 212-935-0699; Toll Free: 800-221-2647; 499 North Canon Dr., Beverly Hills, CA 90210 Tel 310-887-7082;* *Imprints:* Kensington Books (Knsington); Dafina (Dafina); K-Teen (K-TEEN); K-Teen/Dafina (K-TEEN/DAFINA); Urban Renaissance (Urban Renais)
E-mail: jmclean@kensingtonbooks.com; melley@kensingtonbooks.com
Web site: http://www.kensingtonbooks.com
Dist(s): **Children's Plus, Inc. Ebsco Publishing Independent Pubs. Group MyiLibrary Open Road Integrated Media, Inc. Penguin Random Hse. Distribution Penguin Random Hse. LLC Penguin Publishing Group Random Hse., Inc. Worldwide Media Service, Inc.**

Kent Communications, Ltd., *(978-0-9627106; 978-1-888206; 978-0-9830963)* Orders Addr.: 25 Poplar Plain Rd., Westport, CT 06880 USA Tel 203-454-9646; *Imprints:* Kent Press (Kent Pr)
E-mail: mhoule@gbiplaw.com
Dist(s): **Independent Pubs. Group MyiLibrary National Bk. Network Small Pr. United.**

Kent Fine Art *See* **Kent Gallery**

Kent Gallery, *(978-1-878607)* P.O. Box 684, New York, NY 10012-0013 USA
E-mail: info@kentfineart.net
Web site: http://www.kentfineart.net.

Kent Pr. *Imprint of* **Kent Communications, Ltd.**

†Kent State Univ. Pr., *(978-0-87338; 978-1-60635; 978-1-61277; 978-1-63101)* Orders Addr.: c/o BookMasters, Inc., 30 Amberwood Pkwy., Ashland, OH 44805 USA Tel 419-281-1802; Fax: 419-281-6883; Toll Free: 800-247-6553; Edit Addr.: 1118 Univ. Library Bldg. 1125 Risman Dr., Kent, OH 44242-0001 USA (SAN 201-0437) Tel 330-672-7913; Fax: 330-672-3104; *Imprints:* Black Squirrel Books (Blck Squir)
E-mail: scash@kent.edu
Web site: http://www.kentstateuniversitypress.com
Dist(s): **Baker & Taylor Publisher Services (BTPS) Follett School Solutions MyiLibrary Partners Bk. Distributing, Inc. ebrary, Inc.**; *CIP.*

Keogh, Anne, *(978-1-938993)* 132 S. Battery St., Charleston, SC 29401 USA Tel 843-722-7350
E-mail: akeogh98@hotmail.com
Web site: www.annetoddbooks.com.

Kepler Pr., *(978-0-9713770)* Orders Addr.: P.O. Box 400326, Cambridge, MA 02140 USA (SAN 255-6014) Tel 617-413-7204
E-mail: ealex@keplerpress.com
Web site: http://www.keplerpress.com
Dist(s): **Ingram Content Group.**

Keriouspyeseries LLC, *(978-0-615-45033-9; 978-0-615-55447-1; 978-0-9899654; 978-0-692-88383-9; 978-1-7324965)* 12437 N. Portland Ave., Mequon, WI 53092 USA Tel 262-243-1299
E-mail: keriouspyeseries@att.net.

Kerlak Enterprises, Inc. *See* **Dark Oak Pr.**

Kerpluggo Bks. LLC, *(978-0-9762429)* 1015 W. Webster Ave., Suite 3, Chicago, IL 60614 USA Tel 773-665-8075
E-mail: mbwillian2@yahoo.com.

Kerr, Alex, *(978-0-9753076)* 145 Lincoln Rd. Apt. 2L, Brooklyn, NY 11225-4017 USA
E-mail: alexkerr@earthlink.net.

Kerr, Charles H. Publishing Co., *(978-0-88286; 978-1-7326067)* Orders Addr.: 8901 S. Exchange Ave., Chicago, IL 60617 USA (SAN 207-7043) Tel 773-465-7774 (orders); 847-328-2132 (orders); Fax: 773-472-7857 (orders)
E-mail: charles.h.kerr.pub@gmail.com; arcane@ripco.com
Web site: http://www.charleshkerr.net
Dist(s): **SPD-Small Pr. Distribution.**

Kerr Company, The *See* **K.C. Fox Publishing**

Kerr, Justin & Shelley, *(978-0-9766408)* 10735 Atascadero Ave., Atascadero, CA 93422-5723 USA
Web site: http://www.kirra-rincon.com.

Kessinger Publishing Company *See* **Kessinger Publishing, LLC**

Kessinger Publishing, LLC, *(978-0-7661; 978-0-922802; 978-1-56459; 978-1-4179; 978-1-4191; 978-1-4192; 978-1-4253; 978-1-4254; 978-1-4286; 978-1-4304; 978-1-4325; 978-1-4326; 978-0-548; 978-1-4365; 978-1-4366; 978-1-4367; 978-1-4368; 978-1-4369; 978-1-4370; 978-1-4371; 978-1-4372; 978-1-4373; 978-1-4374; 978-1-104; 978-1-120; 978-1-160; 978-1-161; 978-1-162; 978-1-163; 978-1-164; 978-1-165; 978-1-166; 978-1-167; 978-1-168; 978-1-169) Orders Addr.: P.O. Box 1404, Whitefish, MT 59937 USA (SAN 251-4621) Fax: 406-897-7825*
E-mail: kpreply55@runbox.com
Web site: http://www.kessinger.net
Dist(s): **Ingram Content Group.**

Kesterson & Associates *See* **Big Valley Publishing**

Kestrel Pubns., *(978-0-9628472; 978-0-9881925)* 1811 Stonewood Dr., Dayton, OH 45432-4002 USA Tel 937-426-5110; Fax: 937-320-1832; Toll Free: 800-314-4678 (orders only)
E-mail: invisiblel@aol.com.

Keszler, E., *(978-0-615-19548-3; 978-0-615-36360-8)* 6779 Sienna Club Pl., Lauderhill, FL 33319 USA E-mail: uniqueart613@gmail.com.

Ketabe Gooya Publishing LLC, *(978-1-933429)* Orders Addr.: 6400 Canoga Ave., Suite 355, Woodland Hills, CA 91367 USA Tel 818-346-8338; Toll Free: 800-515-0069 E-mail: nasser@farrokh.us Web site: http://www.ketabegooya.com.

Ketman Publishing *See* **Wooster Bk. Co., The**

Kevin W W Blackley Bks., LLC, *(978-0-9960839; 978-1-950039)* 280 E. Treehaven Rd, BUFFALO, NY 14215 USA Tel 716-316-6336 E-mail: kevin.blackley@gmail.com.

kevindkone, *(978-0-9997562)* 10116 lonesome pine Dr., knoxville, TN 37932 USA Tel 801-380-1142 E-mail: kevindkone@gmail.com.

Kew Publishing (GBR) *(978-0-947643; 978-1-900347; 978-0-85521; 978-1-84246) Dist. by* **Chicago Distribution Ctr.**

Key Answer Products, Inc., *(978-0-9642823)* 108 S. Third St., Suite 4, Bloomingdale, IL 60108 USA (SAN 255-805X) Tel 630-893-4007; Fax: 630-893-4030; Toll Free: 800-539-1233 E-mail: dcowhey@ci-inc.com Web site: http://www.ci-inc/what/what.htm.

Key of David Publishing, *(978-1-886987)* Subs. of House of David, Orders Addr.: PO Box 947, Palatka, FL 32178 USA Tel 800-829-8777 (phone/fax); Toll Free: 800-829-8777 Do not confuse with Key of David Publishing, Poughquag, NY E-mail: info@redeemedisrael.com Web site: http://www.keyofdavidpublishing.com.

Key Publishers, Incorporated *See* **City Creek Pr., Inc.**

Keyboarding First, LLC, *(978-0-9768426)* 6919 Prairie Dr., Middleton, WI 53562-5356 USA Tel 608-836-4404 (phone/fax); Fax: 608-836-4405 E-mail: psm.janet@tds.net.

KEYGARD, *(978-0-9767086)* Orders Addr.: 7887 Broadway, Suite 506, San Antonio, TX 78209 USA Tel 210-829-5074; Fax: 210-829-5132 E-mail: bhkeyser@aol.com.

Keyhole Pr., *(978-0-9821512; 978-0-615-59031-8; 978-0-615-61927-9; 978-0-692-83815-0)* Div. of Dzanc Bks., E-mail: info@keyholepress.com Web site: http://www.keyholepress.com *Dist(s):* **Consortium Bk. Sales & Distribution CreateSpace Independent Publishing Platform MyiLibrary Smashwords.**

Keys For Kids Publishing Company *See* **Amazing Drama Anointed Voices Original Music**

Keysquake Music, *(978-0-9760837)* 42 Blackfoot Ct., Guilford, CT 06437 USA E-mail: bgillie48@yahoo.com Web site: http://www.briangillie.com.

Keystone College Pr., *(978-0-9623862; 978-1-879205; 978-1-64042)* One College Green, La Plume, PA 18440-0200 USA Tel 570-945-5141 x 3007; *Imprints:* Swingin' Bridge Books (SwinginBridge) E-mail: raymond.hammond@keystone.edu; nightshadepress@keystone.edu; kcpress@keystone.edu Web site: http://www.keystone.edu.

Keytochange Publishing, Inc., *(978-0-9729798)* 7484 University Ave. Ste. T, La Mesa, CA 91941-6030 USA E-mail: sjones@keytochange.com Web site: http://www.keytochange.com.

Keywords Press *Imprint of* **Atria Bks.**

Khalexandra Bks., *(978-1-949558)* 500 Westover Dr. No. 13880, Sanford, NC 27330 USA Tel 937-421-6511 E-mail: khalexandra80@gmail.com Web site: www.khalexandra.com.

Khalfani, Natasha, *(978-0-692-38558-6)* 4500 Governor Pratt Ct., Upper Marlboro, MD 20772 USA Tel 301-580-3786 E-mail: khalfani.law@gmail.com.

KHallBks., *(978-0-692-78291-0; 978-0-692-79187-5; 978-0-692-04582-4; 978-1-7337717)* P.O. Box 623, Austin, MN 55912 USA Tel 507-993-8929; Fax: 800-903-8160 E-mail: khallbooks@gmail.com Web site: idovideostories.com; khallbooks.com; cornerconfessions.com.

Khanna, Rachel, *(978-0-9779568)* 163 John St., Greenwich, CT 06831 USA (SAN 850-7260) Web site: http://www.liveeatcookhealthy.com.

Khesed Foundation, *(978-0-9785077)* Orders Addr.: 633 S. Plymouth Ct, Chicago, IL 60605-6060 USA Tel 615-792-1449; Edit Addr.: 1030 Trouble Ct., No. 1005, Ashland City, TN 37015-6060 USA (SAN 850-7236) E-mail: hankbo@juno.com.

Khunum Productions, Inc., *(978-0-9797010)* Khunum Productions, Inc. 149 Bainbridge St., Suite 3, Brooklyn, NY 11233 USA Tel 718-924-8779 E-mail: Khunumproductions@gmail.com; Nehprii@msn.com Web site: http://www.NehpriiAmenii.com.

Kiazpora LLC, *(978-0-9966362; 978-1-946057)* P.O. Box 2184, Union City, CA 94587 USA Tel 408-230-0340 E-mail: info@kiazpora.com.

Kick The Ball, *(978-0-9790396; 978-1-934372; 978-1-61320)* Orders Addr.: 8595 Columbus Pike Suite 197, Lewis Center, OH 43035 USA E-mail: pfwilson@triviagamebooks.com; tprippey@triviagamebooks.com Web site: http://www.triviagamebooks.com; http://www.bythenumberbook.com *Dist(s):* **Partners Bk. Distributing, Inc.**

Kickapoo Farms *See* **Genuine Prints, LLC**

Kicks and Giggles Today, *(978-0-615-20924-1; 978-0-615-54874-6)* P.O. Box 1023, Ross, CA 94957 USA Web site: http://www.kicksandgigglestoday.com.

Kicky Cane Pr., *(978-1-7342789)* 221 W. Illinois St., Bellingham, WA 98225 USA Tel 206-992-9259 E-mail: courtneyshannonstrand@gmail.com Web site: courtneyshannonstrand.com.

Kid by Kid, Incorporated, *(978-0-9745496)* 54249 Myrica Dr., Macomb, MI 48042 USA Tel 586-781-2345 (phone/fax) E-mail: kidbykid@comcast.net Web site: http://www.crystalkids.net.

Kid Fuse *Imprint of* **Joyride Bks.**

Kid Niche Christian Bks., *(978-0-9852712; 978-0-9904626; 978-0-9994837)* 9958 Edgewood Ave, Traverse City, MI 49686-5845 USA.

Kid Niche Publishing *See* **Kid Niche Christian Bks.**

Kid Prep, Inc., *(978-1-58312)* 6942 FM 1960 E-132, Humble, TX 77346 USA Tel 281-852-5261; Fax: 281-852-4901; *Imprints:* Little Chameleon Books (Little Chameleon) E-mail: customerservice@kidprep.com Web site: http://www.kidprep.com.

KiD Sounds, *(978-0-9767650)* P.O. Box 13888, Las Vegas, NV 89112-1888 USA Web site: http://www.kid-sounds.com.

kid2kid publishing, *(978-0-615-48783-0; 978-0-692-58147-6)* 2577 Cove Point Pl., Virginia Beach, VA 23455 USA Tel 757-375-5020 E-mail: kfk1313@yahoo.com *Dist(s):* **CreateSpace Independent Publishing Platform.**

KidBiz 3000 *See* **Achieve3000**

KidBookInk Publishing, LLC, *(978-0-9776772)* Orders Addr.: 25809 Nichols Rd., Columbia Station, OH 44028 USA (SAN 257-9103) Tel 440-725-7587; Fax: 440-236-5356; Toll Free: 888-978-1669 E-mail: dbvanhorn@yahoo.com Web site: http://www.kidbookink.com; http://www.storyboard4kidz. com.

Kidder, Clark, *(978-0-615-15313-1; 978-0-692-58895-6; 978-0-692-82942-4)* 1620 Sienna Crossing, Janesville, WI 53546 USA Web site: http://www.clarkkidder.com.

Kidderature Publishing, *(978-0-9729703)* P.O. Box 612, Hammondsport, NY 14840 USA Tel 607-292-3026 E-mail: bobhicks@citlink.net Web site: http://www.kidderature.com.

Kiddy Chronicles Publishing (CAN) *(978-0-9699203; 978-0-9733994) Dist. by* **Firefly Bks Limited.**

Kid-E Bks. *Imprint of* **Word Productions LLC**

Kidhaven *Imprint of* **Cengage Gale**

KidHaven Publishing *Imprint of* **Cengage Gale**

KidHaven Publishing *Imprint of* **Greenhaven Publishing LLC**

Kidible *Imprint of* **iCharacter.org**

Kidpub Pr., *(978-0-9840807; 978-1-936184; 978-1-61018)* P.O. Box 724, North Attleboro, MA 02761 USA (SAN 858-365X) Tel 401-466-4176; Toll Free: 800-252-5224 (orders/editorial) E-mail: pd@kidpub.com; orders@kidpub.com Web site: http://bookstore.kidpub.com; http://www.kidpub.com.

Kidrich Corp., *(978-0-9761051)* 347 5th Ave., Suite 610, New York, NY 10016 USA Tel 718-767-5135; Toll Free: 800-231-7385 Web site: http://www.kidrich.com.

Kids 4 Ever, *(978-0-9764433)* P.O. Box 1784, Holland, MI 49422 USA Tel 616-566-1231 E-mail: kids4ever@charter.net Web site: http://www.kids4everbooks.com.

Kids Activity Publishing, *(978-1-946525)* E-mail: activitypublishingkids@gmail.com.

Kids Ahead Bks. *Imprint of* **WND Bks, Inc.**

Kids At Heart Publishing & Books *See* **Kids At Heart Publishing, LLC**

Kids At Heart Publishing, LLC, *(978-0-615-36340-0; 978-0-9828109; 978-0-9836641; 978-0-9855202; 978-0-9886360; 978-0-9899472; 978-0-9905734; 978-0-9964962; 978-0-9969574; 978-1-946171)* P.O. Box 492, Milton, IN 47357 USA Tel 765-478-5873 *Dist(s):* **Davis/Books Distribution.**

Kids At Our House, Inc., The, *(978-0-9705773; 978-1-942390)* Orders Addr.: 47 Stoneham Pl., Metuchen, NJ 08840 USA Tel 732-548-1779 E-mail: info@dannyandkim.com Web site: www.dannyandkim.com *Dist(s):* **Follett School Solutions Indig, Stanley M. Specialty Pubn.**

Kids Bk. Pr., *(978-0-692-23217-0; 978-0-692-37117-6; 978-0-692-37484-9; 978-0-692-46037-5; 978-0-692-51635-5; 978-0-692-51675-1; 978-0-692-54962-9; 978-0-692-56562-9; 978-0-692-58944-1; 978-0-692-59953-2; 978-0-692-61637-6; 978-0-692-62920-8; 978-0-692-71803-2; 978-0-692-73023-2) 1352 E. Sunshine, Springfield, MO 65804 USA Tel 417-881-6537* E-mail: skizholmes@sbcglobal.net *Dist(s):* **CreateSpace Independent Publishing Platform.**

Kids Camping Bks., *(978-1-951633)* 6960 Kirkridge Ct., Shelby Township, MI 48316 USA Tel 703-597-1511 E-mail: teamsponsler@gmail.com Web site: www.kidscampingbooks.com.

Kids Can *Imprint of* **Proactive Publishing**

Kids Can Pr., Ltd. (CAN) *(978-0-919964; 978-0-921103; 978-1-55074; 978-1-55337; 978-1-894786; 978-1-55453; 978-1-77138) Dist. by* **HachBkGrp.**

Kids Can Pr., Ltd. (CAN) *(978-0-919964; 978-0-921103; 978-1-55074; 978-1-55337; 978-1-894786; 978-1-55453; 978-1-77138) Dist. by* **Children Plus.**

Kids Can Pr., Ltd. (CAN) *(978-0-919964; 978-0-921103; 978-1-55074; 978-1-55337; 978-1-894786; 978-1-55453; 978-1-77138) Dist. by* **Perfect Learn.**

Kids Children & Teens World 2000 & Beyond, *(978-0-9747543)* Orders Addr.: P.O. Box 385, Brandywine, MD 20613 USA Fax: 301-372-9979; Edit Addr.: 8300 Belding Ct., Brandywine, MD 20613 USA E-mail: djospeh301@aol.com.

Kid's Creative Classics *Imprint of* **BrassHeart Music**

Kids, Critters & Country Publishing, *(978-0-9755200)* P.O. Box 866874, Plano, TX 75086-6874 USA E-mail: jlarsen@chasewest.com Web site: http://www.kidscrittersandcountry.com.

Kids Donate, Inc., *(978-0-9754131)* 221 Chesley Ln., Chapel Hill, NC 27514 USA Tel 919-967-0882.

Kids For Health, Inc., *(978-0-9759517; 978-1-933847)* P.O. Box 326, Springdale, AR 72763 USA Tel 479-756-9551; Fax: 479-756-0949.

Kids Go Europe, Inc., *(978-0-9772699)* P.O. Box 4014, Menlo Park, CA 94026 USA Tel 650-743-7404 E-mail: info@kidsgoeurope.com Web site: http://www.kidsgoeurope.com.

Kids in Ministry International, *(978-0-9767647; 978-0-9815940)* P.O. Box 549, Mandan, ND 58554-0549 USA Web site: http://www.kidsinministry.com.

Kids' Library *Imprint of* **Aurora Pubs., Inc.**

Kids Life Pr., *(978-0-9755348; 978-0-9903172)* P.O. Box 3484, Pismo Beach, CA 93448-3484 USA Fax: 805-888-2838; Toll Free: 800-262-8973 E-mail: tuzee@charter.net.

Kids Rehab Spa, *(978-0-692-92453-2)* 1220 Heritage Lakes Dr., Mableton, GA 30126 USA Tel 404-317-4894 E-mail: Kimgreene563@gmail.com.

Kid's Shelf, *(978-0-9729339)* 19600 Baker Rd., Gambier, OH 43022 USA Tel 740-247-2427.

Kids Think Big LLC, *(978-0-9797362)* P.O. Box 11013, Greenwich, CT 06831 USA (SAN 854-2597) E-mail: info@kidsthinkbig.com Web site: http://www.kidsthinkbig.com *Dist(s):* **Distributors, The Follett School Solutions.**

Kids Write On, LLC, *(978-0-615-23574-5)* Orders Addr.: P.O. Box 700924, Dallas, TX 75370 USA Tel 972-862-7257; Fax: 972-862-0194; Toll Free: 877-596-7257 Web site: http://www.thestaplercaper.com.

Kids1st Bks. *Imprint of* **BC Publishing**

Kidsafety of America, *(978-1-884413)* 6288 Susana St., Chino, CA 91710 USA E-mail: peter@kidsafetystore.com Web site: http://www.kidsafetystore.com *Dist(s):* **Follett School Solutions.**

Kidsbooks, Incorporated *See* **Kidsbooks, LLC**

Kidsbooks, LLC, *(978-0-942025; 978-1-56156; 978-1-58865; 978-1-62885)* 3535 W. Peterson Ave., Chicago, IL 60659 USA (SAN 666-3729) E-mail: sales@kidsbooks.com Web site: http://www.kidsbooks.com *Dist(s):* **Independent Pubs. Group.**

KidsCanPublish.Org, *(978-0-692-76150-2; 978-0-692-77349-9; 978-0-692-78442-6; 978-0-692-84092-4; 978-0-692-07621-7)* 1020 Brookview Ct., Morgan Hill, CA 95037 USA Tel 408-607-0986 E-mail: kidscanpublish@gmail.com Web site: www.KidsCanPublish.Org.

Kidscope, Inc., *(978-0-9647798)* 2045 Peachtree Rd NE Ste. 150, Atlanta, GA 30309-1405 USA.

KidsDiscuss.com, *(978-0-9749244)* PCS, Orders Addr.: P.O. Box 6102, Edmonds, WA 98026 USA E-mail: JeanTracy@KidsDiscuss.com Web site: http://www.KidsDiscuss.com.

KidsGive, LLC, *(978-0-9792912; 978-0-9845910)* 5757 W. Century Blvd., Suite 800, Box 8, Los Angeles, CA 90045 USA (SAN 853-0297) Tel 310-665-9777; Fax: 310-665-9494 E-mail: lmuniz@kidsgive.com Web site: http://www.kidsgive.com.

Kidskills America *Imprint of* **Kidskills International**

Kidskills International, *(978-0-9710641)* Div. of Creekside Creations, 1031 Cahoon Rd., Westlake, OH 44145-1232 USA Tel 440-835-5071 (phone/fax); *Imprints:* Kidskills America (Kidskills Amer) E-mail: kidskills@wowway.com; diane@kidskills.com Web site: http://www.kidskills.com.

KIDSRIGHTS *Imprint of* **JIST Publishing**

Kidsrights, 10100 Park Cedar Dr., Charlotte, NC 28210 USA (SAN 299-2809) Tel 704-541-0100; Fax: 704-541-0113; Toll Free: 888-970-5437 Do not confuse with Kidsrights, Mount Dora, FL.

Kidstalk, LLC, *(978-0-9776144)* P.O. Box 520, Sherman, TX 75091 USA (SAN 257-7992) Tel 903-436-0858; Fax: 903-893-1614 E-mail: kidstalk@cableone.net Web site: http://www.kidstalkmag.com.

Kidstory Pr., *(978-0-9772231)* P.O. Box 75, Brighton, MI 48116-0075 USA Tel 517-204-9030 E-mail: kidstorypress@comcast.net Web site: http://www.kidstorypress.home.comcast.net.

KidsWorld Bks. (CAN) *(978-0-9938401; 978-1-988183; 978-0-9940069) Dist. by* **Lone Pine.**

Kidware Software, LLC, *(978-1-937161; 978-1-937161-25-5; 978-1-951077)* P.O. Box 701, Maple Valley, WA 98038 USA Tel 425-413-1185 E-mail: phil@kidwaresoftware.com; phil@biblebytebooks.com Web site: http://www.kidwaresoftware.com; http://www.biblebytebooks.com; http://www.computerscienceforkids.com.

Kidwick Bks., *(978-0-9703809)* 363 S. Saltair Ave., First Fl., Los Angelas, CA 90049 USA Tel 310-471-2472; Fax: 310-861-8111 E-mail: mail@kidwick.com Web site: http://www.kidwick.com *Dist(s):* **National Bk. Network.**

Kidz & Katz Publishing Co., *(978-1-883371)* 752 Brandon Pl., Wheeling, IL 60090 USA Fax: 708-860-0513.

Kidz By Dezign Pr., Inc., *(978-0-9771030)* 1881 Kingston Way, Lawrenceville, GA 30044 USA (SAN 256-7121) Tel 770-962-2181; Fax: 678-615-2247; Toll Free: 800-719-5439 E-mail: info@slumbergirls.com Web site: http://www.slumbergirls.com.

Kidz Entertainment, Inc., *(978-0-9795049; 978-0-9891954)* P.O. Box 0301, Baldwin, NY 11510 USA Fax: 516-223-6546 E-mail: dcorrado@optonline.net Web site: http://www.chanteusemusic.com.

Kidz Krave Inc., *(978-0-9764144)* P.O. Box 88350, Houston, TX 77288 USA Web site: http://www.prettypainful.com.

Kidzpoetz Publishing, *(978-0-9760220)* P.O. Box 621, New City, NY 10956 USA Tel 845-536-5505; Fax: 845-323-4272 E-mail: robertkurkela@kidzpoetz.com Web site: http://www.kidzpoetz.com *Dist(s):* **Quality Bks., Inc.**

Kidzup Productions, *(978-1-894281; 978-1-894677)* 555 VT Rte. 78, Suite 146, Box 717, Swanton, VT 05488 USA Toll Free: 888-321-5437 (888-321-KIDS) E-mail: info@kidzup.com Web site: http://www.kidzup.com *Dist(s):* **Penton Overseas, Inc.**

Kieliszewski, Shelia, *(978-0-615-25575-0; 978-0-578-00002-2)* 2192 Willow Springs Dr., Stevens Point, WI 54481 USA E-mail: shellabrt@yahoo.com *Dist(s):* **Lulu Pr., Inc.**

Kies Publishing Co., *(978-0-9767437)* Orders Addr.: P.O. Box 923572, Sylmar, CA 91392-3572 USA Tel 818-367-8416 E-mail: kies@kies.org Web site: http://www.kies.org.

Kila Springs Pr., *(978-0-9716481; 978-1-7338479)* Div. of Kila Springs Group, 4231 Oak Meadow Rd., Placerville, CA 95667 USA Tel 530-621-2297; Fax: 206-202-1309 E-mail: press@kilasprings.net Web site: http://kilasprings.net/KSPress.html.

Kilbride, Harry, *(978-0-578-14015-5; 978-0-578-14016-2)*.

Killer Sports Publishing, *(978-1-933135)* Orders Addr.: P.O. Box 862, Berea, OH 44017 USA Tel 440-239-1854; Edit Addr.: 201 S. Rocky River Rd., Berea, OH 44017 USA Web site: http://www.killersports.com.

Killingbeck, Dale, *(978-0-9762758)* 18300 Tustin Rd., Tustin, MI 49677 USA Tel 231-829-3084.

Kilsby, Raymond *See* **RK Enterprises, Inc.**

Kimber Stories, *(978-0-9767773)* Orders Addr.: P.O. Box 143, Woodlake, CA 93286 USA; Edit Addr.: 37811 Millwood Dr., Woodlake, CA 93286 USA E-mail: kimberstories@yahoo.com.

Kimberlite Publishing Co., *(978-0-9632675)* 44091 Olive Ave., Hemet, CA 92544-2609 USA Tel 951-927-7726 Do not confuse with Kimberlite Publishing, Ventura, CA E-mail: frumpypapa@yahoo.com.

Kimberly M. Nesmith, *(978-1-7333696)* 33 Cogdill Pl., Pawleys Island, SC 29585 USA Tel 843-833-4323 E-mail: kimberlymeans@gmail.com *Dist(s):* **Ingram Content Group.**

Kimberly Pr., LLC, *(978-0-9668611)* 100 Westport Ave., Norwalk, CT 06851 USA (SAN 251-2483) Tel 203-750-6101; Fax: 203-846-3472.

Kimble, George J., *(978-0-9767024)* 4941 Hickory Woods E., Antioch, TN 37013 USA Web site: http://www.theroadpoet.com.

Kin Pr., *(978-0-9989293)* P.O. Box 682, Higganum, CT 06441 USA Tel 860-301-9064 E-mail: affinitystudio@yahoo.com Web site: www.kinpress.org.

Kind Critter Junction, *(978-0-9752842)* P.O. Box 30249, Indianapolis, IN 46220 USA Toll Free: 888-366-3525 E-mail: info@kindcritterjunction.com Web site: http://www.kindcritterjunction.com.

Kind Eye Publishing, *(978-0-9992262)* P.O. Box 511, MASON, OH 45040 USA Tel 202-270-8470 E-mail: avanti@kindeyepublishing.com Web site: www.kindeyepublishing.com.

Kinder Shpiel USA, Inc., *(978-1-937637; 978-1-68091)* 199 Lee Ave. PMB 148, Brooklyn, NY 11211 USA Tel 718-305-7540 Web site: WWW.Kindershpiel.com.

KinderBach L.L.C., *(978-0-9773005)* P.O. Box 336, Hudson, IA 50643 USA (SAN 257-2397) Toll Free: 866-988-9814 E-mail: info@kinderbach.com Web site: http://www.kinderbach.com.

Kinderhaus Publishing Co., *(978-0-578-05104-8)* 2970 Edgewick Dr., Glendale, CA 91206 USA E-mail: bettyfritz@kinderhauspublishing.com.

Kindermusik International, *(978-0-945613; 978-1-931127; 978-1-58987; 978-1-948952)* Orders Addr.: 2606 Phoenix Dr., Greensboro, NC 27406 USA (SAN 247-3747) Tel 336-273-3363; Fax: 336-273-2023; Toll

Free: 800-628-5687; Edit Addr.: 6204 Corporate Park Dr., Browns Summit, NC 27214 USA (SAN 247-3755)
E-mail: info@kindermusik.com; dkells@kindermusik.com
Web site: http://www.kindermusik.com.

Kindness Learning Co. LLC, The, *(978-0-9967943)* 300 E 54th St Apt 34BC, New York, NY 10022 USA Tel 914-752-8378
E-mail: carazelas@gmail.com.

Kindness Queen's Empire, The, *(978-0-9889060)* 7850 Wildwood Rd., Jacksonville, FL 32211-6046 USA Tel 904-723-0116
E-mail: dbsmith10@comcast.net.

Kindred Press *See* **Kindred Productions**

Kindred Productions, *(978-0-921788; 978-0-919797)* Orders Addr.: 315 S. Lincoln St., Hillsboro, KS 67063 USA Tel 316-947-3151; Fax: 316-947-3266; Toll Free: 800-545-7322
E-mail: kindred@mbconf.ca
Web site: http://www.mbconf.org/kindred.htm
Dist(s): **Spring Arbor Distributors, Inc.**

Kindred Trade LLC, *(978-0-692-08598-1)* 2809 W Bluefield Ave., Phoenix, AZ 85053 USA Tel 602-315-0259
E-mail: sales@kindredtrade.com
Web site: www.thedesertmermaid.com.

Kinfolk Research Pr., *(978-0-9712564)* P.O. Box 6303, Plymouth, MI 48170 USA Tel 734-454-1883
E-mail: KinfolkPress@aol.com
Web site: http://cheekfamilychronicles.homestead.com/CheekFamilyChronicles.html.

King & Castle Publishing LLC *See* **King & Castle Publishing LLC**

King & Castle Publishing LLC, *(978-1-949778)* 2134 W Ditch Creek Dr, Meridian, ID 83646 USA Tel 623-455-6426
E-mail: kelvan@yahoo.com.

King Joe Educational Enterprises, Inc., *(978-0-9728596; 978-0-9773902)* Orders Addr.: P.O. Box 86, Los Alamitos, CA 90720 USA Tel 562-430-8600; Fax: 562-598-5940; Toll Free: 866-818-5464 (866-818-KING); Edit Addr.: 3112 Inverness Dr., Los Almitos, CA 90720 USA
E-mail: lindarodgers@kingjoe.com
Web site: http://www.kingjoe.com.

King, Joel, *(978-0-9787820)* 547 McLean Ave., Hopkinsville, KY 42240 USA
E-mail: joelk3@bellsouth.net.

King, Julia, *(978-0-615-34585-7; 978-0-615-37032-3; 978-0-9839827)* 13565 Watsonville Rd., Morgan Hill, CA 95037 USA Tel 408-591-6465
E-mail: wyethia3@yahoo.com.

King, Marcy, *(978-0-9850752)* 4107 Sunset Ave., Chester, VA 23831 USA Tel 804-683-0517
E-mail: marcy.king@yahoo.com.

King Production, A, *(978-0-9755811; 978-0-9843325; 978-0-9860045; 978-0-9913890; 978-1-942217)* P.O. Box 912, Collierville, TN 38017 USA Tel 917-279-1363; Fax: 201-624-7225
E-mail: joyking1993@yahoo.com
Web site: www.joydejaking.com
Dist(s): **Children's Plus, Inc.**

King St Bks./Stabler-Leadbeater Apothecary Museum, *(978-0-9763945)* 410 S Fairfax St., Alexandria, VA 22314 USA Fax: 703-456-7890
Web site: http://apothecarymuseum.org.

King, Terri Ann *See* **Paulus Publishing**

Kingdom Builders Pubn., *(978-0-578-12048-5; 978-0-578-13238-9; 978-0-578-13304-1; 978-0-578-13488-8; 978-0-578-13932-6; 978-0-578-13991-3; 978-0-578-14385-9; 978-0-578-14627-0; 978-0-578-14843-4; 978-0-578-14903-5; 978-0-578-14909-7; 978-0-578-15487-9; 978-0-692-38109-0; 978-0-692-38120-5; 978-0-692-38123-6; 978-0-692-39146-4; 978-0-692-40038-8; 978-0-578-15969-0; 978-0-692-41566-5; 978-0-692-45673-6; 978-0-692-45674-3; 978-0-692-45975-1; 978-0-692-50699-8; 978-0-692-52648-4; 978-0-692-53342-0; 978-0-692-53343-7;) 1641 Omarest Dr., Columbia, SC 29210 USA*
Web site: www.kingdombuilderspublications.com
Dist(s): **CreateSpace Independent Publishing Platform.**

Kingdom Door Publishing LLC, *(978-0-9974913)* P.O. Box 2144, Amarillo, TX 79105 USA Tel 806-676-5087
E-mail: wholehearted8@yahoo.com
Web site: kingdomdoor.org.

Kingdom Kaught Publishing LLC, *(978-0-9824550; 978-0-9964040; 978-0-9982100; 978-1-947741)* 1350 Blair Dr., Odenton, MD 21113 USA (SAN 858-2033)
E-mail: kingdompublishingllc@gmail.com
Web site: http://www.kingdompublishingllc.com.

Kingdom Publishers *See* **Cathedral of the Holy Spirit**

Kingdom Publishing Co., *(978-0-9765636)* 17100 Halsted St., Harvey, IL 60426-6131 USA.

Kingdom Publishing Group, Inc., *(978-0-9745324; 978-0-9772964; 978-0-9792074; 978-0-9796130; 978-0-9801564; 978-0-9817706; 978-0-9821411; 978-0-9824084; 978-0-9825104; 978-0-9825849; 978-0-9826370; 978-0-9827484; 978-0-9829775; 978-0-9831452; 978-0-9833651; 978-0-9835721; 978-0-9839090; 978-0-9848940; 978-0-9852679; 978-0-9854693; 978-0-9896581; 978-0-9862492; 978-0-9962629; 978-0-9971518) P.O. Box 3273, Henrico, VA 23228-9705 USA*
Web site: http://www.kingdompublishing.org.

Kingdom Sound Pubs., *(978-0-9662666; 978-0-9856206)* Orders Addr.: P.O. Box 371917, Decatur, GA 30037 USA Tel 404-384-3795; Edit Addr.: 3622 Summit Trace, Suite 400, Decatur, GA 30034 USA
E-mail: kvjackson@yahoo.com.

Kingdom Talk Publishing, Incorporated *See* **Rapha Publishing**

Kingfisher *Imprint of* **Roaring Brook Pr.**

Kingfisher Bks., *(978-0-9662218)* Orders Addr.: P.O. Box 4628, Helena, MT 59604 USA Tel 406-442-2168; Toll Free: 800-879-4576; Edit Addr.: 2480 Broadway, No. 18D, Helena, MT 59601 USA
Dist(s): **Houghton Mifflin Harcourt Trade & Reference Pubs.**
Partners/West Book Distributors.

Kingfisher Publications, plc (GBR) *(978-0-7523; 978-0-7534; 978-1-85697; 978-0-86272) Dist. by* **Children Plus.**

KingMaker Bks. LLC, *(978-0-9744870)* 13315 E. Cindy St., Chandler, AZ 85225 USA
E-mail: mbogumill@juno.com.

King's Kids Trading Cards, Inc., *(978-0-9703880)* P.O. Box 923271, Sylmar, CA 91392-3271 USA Fax: 818-364-2443; Toll Free: 800-910-2690
E-mail: visioninprint@brandx.net
Web site: http://www.kingskidscards.com.

King'S Land Pr. Inc,

King's Treasure Box Ministries, The, *(978-0-9910841)* 7735 Castle Combe Ct., Cumming, GA 30040 USA Tel 678-455-3710
E-mail: roy.nancyj@gmail.com
Web site: www.kingstreasurebox.org.

King's Way Pr., *(978-0-9814748; 978-0-615-22720-7; 978-0-615-29920-4; 978-0-692-67787-2; 978-0-692-70065-5; 978-0-692-70141-6; 978-0-692-70487-5; 978-0-692-71717-2; 978-0-9988367)* 3721 New Macland Rd. Suite 200-141, Powder Springs, GA 30127 USA (SAN 855-6539) Tel 404-642-5113
E-mail: publisher@kings-way-press.com
Web site: https://stolenjesus.com/; http://www.kwp-books.com
Dist(s): **CreateSpace Independent Publishing Platform.**

Kingston Pr. (CAN) *(978-1-894997) Dist. by* **SCB Distributo.**

Kingston Publishing Co., *(978-0-9969540; 978-1-949050; 978-1-970068; 978-1-64533)* 1521 NW 31st St., Lawton, OK 73505 USA
E-mail: crystal@kingstonpublishing.com
Web site: http://www.kingstonpublishing.com.

Kingsway Pubns. (GBR) *(978-0-85476; 978-0-86065; 978-0-902088; 978-1-84291) Dist. by* **STL Dist.**

KiniArt Publishing, *(978-0-578-06335-5)* 658 SE Jerome St., Oak Harbor, WA 98277 USA
E-mail: publishing@kiniart.com
Dist(s): **Lulu Pr., Inc.**

KINJIN Global, *(978-0-9759152)* 4960 SW 32nd Ave., Dania Beach, FL 33312 USA Tel 347-826-6272
E-mail: i@dangoldman.net
Web site: http://dangoldman.net; http://redlightproperties.com.

Kinkachoo Pr., The, *(978-0-9729285)*
Web site: http://www.zhibit.org/bolan.

Kinkajou Pr. *Imprint of* **Artemesia Publishing, LLC**

Kinsey, Michael, *(978-0-578-67223-6; 978-0-578-67227-4)* 53 W. 8th St. 4RE, New York, NY 10011 USA Tel 6504715670
E-mail: michael.charles.kinsey@gmail.com
Dist(s): **Ingram Content Group.**

Kip Kids of New York, *(978-0-9789384)* 85 Christopher St., Suite No. 5B, New York, NY 10014 USA
E-mail: KipKids@aol.com
Web site: http://www.KipKids.com.

Kirin Rise Studios, LLC, *(978-1-946003)* 120 e. anita ave, mount prospect, IL 60056 USA Tel 847-800-9679
E-mail: info@kirinrise.com
Web site: kirinrise.com.

Kirkham, Sharon Birlson, *(978-0-9767100)* 1530 Michigan Ave., La Porte, IN 46350 USA
Dist(s): **INscribe Digital.**

KIRKLAND, JUSTIN B., *(978-0-615-81456-8)* 906 BENDLETON TRACE, ALPHARETTA, GA 30004 USA Tel 404-434-8035
E-mail: KIRKLANDJUSTIN@YMAIL.COM.

Kiss A Me Productions, Inc., *(978-1-890343)* 90 Garfield Ave., Sayville, NY 11782 USA Tel 516-589-4886; Fax: 516-218-8927; Toll Free: 888-547-7263.

KISSFAQ.COM Publishing, *(978-0-9722253; 978-0-9822537; 978-0-9977658; 978-0-9997765; 978-1-7344412)* P.O. Box 210686, San Francisco, CA 94121-0686 USA
E-mail: kissfaq@outlook.com
Web site: http://www.kissfaq.com/
Dist(s): **CreateSpace Independent Publishing Platform.**

KitaabWorld.Com, LLC, *(978-0-9995476)* P.O. Box 268, MENLO PARK, CA 94025 USA Tel 650-421-3409
E-mail: gauri@kitaabworld.com
Dist(s): **Ingram Content Group.**

Kitab Pr. *Imprint of* **Kaya 20 LLC**

Kitanie Bks., *(978-0-9821262; 978-0-9841195; 978-1-935734)* P.O. Box 97, Saratoga Springs, NY 12866 USA (SAN 857-3263)
Web site: http://www.kitanie.com.

Kitanie Coloring Books *See* **Kitanie Bks.**

Kitchen Table Pubs., *(978-0-9707685)* Orders Addr.: 136 Cook-McDonald Rd., Collins, MS 39428 USA Tel 601-765-8329; Edit Addr.: 802 S. Cherry St., Collins, MS 39428 USA Tel 601-765-8329
E-mail: knight3230@bellsouth.net.

Kite Tales Publishing, *(978-1-935332)* 9122 N Tennyson Dr, Milwaukee, WI 53217 USA Tel 414-803-9259
E-mail: cbohlen@wi.rr.com
Web site: http://kitetalespublishing.com.

Kitson Bks., LLC, *(978-1-7333001)* 2707 Lisbon St., East Liverpool, OH 43920 USA Tel 330-708-3975
E-mail: jws1701@comcast.net
Web site: www.jwkitson.com.

Kitsune Bks., *(978-0-9792700; 978-0-9819495; 978-0-9827409; 978-0-9840058; 978-0-9840059)* P.O. Box 1154, Crawfordville, FL 32326-1154 USA (SAN 852-9760) Tel 850-926-3464
E-mail: anne@kitsunebooks.com; contact@kitsunebooks.com
Web site: http://www.kitsunebooks.com
Dist(s): **Bella Distribution**
Smashwords.

Kitsune Inc., *(978-0-692-53331-4; 978-0-9978028; 978-0-9989942; 978-1-951904)* 10610 S. 48th St. 2090, Phoenix, AZ 85044 USA Tel 480-235-8151
Web site: http://varnellbrandon.wix.com/brandon-author
Dist(s): **CreateSpace Independent Publishing Platform.**

Kittyco Pr., *(978-1-937922)* 6D Auburn Ct., Alexandria, VA 22305 USA Tel 703-684-3699
E-mail: kittyerussell@comcast.net.

Kiva Publishing, Inc., *(978-1-885772)* 21731 E. Buckskin Dr., Walnut, CA 91789 USA Tel 909-595-6833; Fax: 909-860-5424; Toll Free: 800-634-5482
E-mail: kivapub@aol.com
Web site: http://www.kivapub.com
Dist(s): **Canyonlands Pubns.**
New Leaf Distributing Co., Inc.
Quality Bks., Inc.
Rio Nuevo Pubs.

Kivel, Lee, *(978-0-9774999)* 6010 E. Paseo Santa Teresa, Tucson, AZ 85750 USA Tel 520-529-2802
E-mail: ghostriver@gainusa.com.

KiwE Publishing, Ltd., *(978-1-931195; 978-1-933973)* 2980 Glacier St., Anchorage, AK 99508 USA Tel 907-333-5493
E-mail: kiwe@kiwepublishing.com
Web site: http://www.kiwepublishing.com.

Kiwi Media Group, Inc., *(978-0-9743319)* P.O. Box 493, Hopkinton, MA 01748 USA Tel 508-435-4986; Fax: 508-435-0378.

Kiwi Publishing *See* **Kiwi Media Group, Inc.**

Kiykioglu, Tamer, *(978-0-578-49227-8)* 13350 SW Lancewood St, Beaverton, OR 97008 USA Tel 503-330-0196
E-mail: Tamerk007@gmail.com.

KJ Pubns., *(978-0-9792383)* 7069 Middlebury Dr., Boynton Beach, FL 33436 USA
E-mail: contactus@kidshyperspace.com
Web site: http://www.thenutrigang.com.

Kjasen, *(978-0-692-68195-4; 978-0-692-69120-5; 978-0-692-70341-0; 978-0-692-71040-1; 978-0-692-71147-7; 978-0-692-71188-0; 978-0-692-71192-7; 978-0-692-71675-5; 978-0-692-72916-8; 978-0-9977821; 978-1-7328521)* 2215 Rippling Rill St, San Antonio, TX 78232 USA Tel 210-788-0452; Toll Free: 210-788-0452
Dist(s): **CreateSpace Independent Publishing Platform.**

Kjelberg & Sons, Incorporated *See* **Kjellberg, Inc.**

Kjellberg, Inc., *(978-0-912868)* 805 W. Liberty Dr., Wheaton, IL 60187-4844 USA (SAN 201-5102) Tel 630-653-2244; Fax: 630-653-6233; *Imprints:* Kjellberg Publishers (Kjellberg Pubs)
E-mail: wsc@kjellbergprinting.com
Web site: http://kjellbergprinting.com.

Kjellberg Pubs. *Imprint of* **Kjellberg, Inc.**

KK, *(978-1-940689)* 149 Amapola Ave, Pacifica, CA 94044 USA Tel 650-284-3303
E-mail: kk@kk.org
Web site: http://www.kk.org.

Klapheke, Alisha, *(978-0-9987379; 978-0-9998314)* 3975 New Hwy. 96 W, Franklin, TN 37064 USA Tel 615-440-3717
E-mail: alisha@alishaklapheke.com.

Klare & Taylor Publishing Company *See* **Klare Taylor Pubs.**

Klare Taylor Pubs., *(978-0-9764403)* P.O. Box 637, Ashland, OR 97520 USA
Web site: http://www.klaretaylorpublishers.com; http://www.pacificwestcom.com/klare; http://www.pacificwestcom.com/amazon; http://www.pacificwestcom.com/shipsofchildren; http://www.pacificwestcom.com/richardpoem.

KLC Publishing, *(978-0-9995734)* P.O. Box 10162, Dothan, AL 36303 USA Tel 334-405-4519
E-mail: info@tianapatrice.com
Dist(s): **CreateSpace Independent Publishing Platform.**

K,L.Corgliano, *(978-0-615-56735-8)* 926 Holly hills Ct., Keller, TX 76248 USA Tel 817-914-2344
E-mail: corgliano@verizon.net.

Klemm, Rebecca Charitable Foundation *See* **NumbersAlive! Pr.**

Klett, Ernst, Verlag GmbH (DEU) *(978-3-12) Dist. by* **Intl Bk Import.**

Klett, Ernst, Verlag GmbH (DEU) *(978-3-12) Dist. by* **Continental Bk.**

Kline, Tom *See* **Reality Check Pubns.**

Kloria Publishing LLC, *(978-1-933737)* Orders Addr.: 401 E. 8th St. Suite 214-568, Sioux Falls, SD 57103 USA
E-mail: orders@kloria.com
Web site: http://www.kloria.com/
Dist(s): **Concordia Publishing Hse.**

KLS LifeChange Ministries *Imprint of* **Skinner, Kerry L.**

KLT & Assocs., *(978-0-9799119)* 11829 E. Parkview Ln., Scottsdale, AZ 85255 USA Tel 480-342-9638.

Kluis Publishing, LLC, *(978-0-9776878; 978-0-9830382)* Orders Addr.: 901 Twelve Oaks Ctr. Dr. Suite 907, Wayzata, MN 55391 USA Tel 952-767-5504; Toll Free: 888-345-2855
E-mail: info@kluispublishing.com; kt@alkluis.com
Web site: http://www.alkluis.com.

Klutz, *(978-0-932592; 978-1-57054; 978-1-878257; 978-1-59174)* Div. of Scholastic, Inc., 450 Lambert St., Palo Alto, CA 94306 USA (SAN 212-7539) Tel 650-857-0888; Fax: 650-857-9110; Toll Free: 800-737-4123; *Imprints:* Chicken Socks (Chick Socks); Klutz Certified (Klutz Cert)
E-mail: thefolks@klutz.com
Web site: http://www.klutz.com
Dist(s): **Scholastic, Inc.**

Klutz Certified *Imprint of* **Klutz**

Klutz Latino (MEX) *Dist. by* **IPG Chicago.**

KMB Creative, *(978-0-692-19239-9; 978-0-578-40991-7)* 1409 Tuscany Way, Boyton Beach, FL 33435 USA Tel 561-449-7071
E-mail: too2koi@gmail.com
Web site: www.kellymbcreative.com.

KMR Scripts, *(978-1-932240)* P.O. Box 189, Webster City, IA 50595 USA
Web site: http://www.kmrscripts.com.

KnackPacks, Inc., *(978-0-9726619)* P.O. Box 3716, Oak Park, IL 60303-3716 USA Tel 708-358-1760
E-mail: comments@knackpacks.com
Web site: http://www.knackpacks.com.

KnausWorks, *(978-0-9758742)* 4160-87 Jade St., Capitola, CA 95010 USA
E-mail: ltrsfmspace@aol.com.

Knee Patch Publishing, *(978-1-7323319)* 1643 Coastal Rd, Brooksville, ME 04617 USA Tel 808-866-8046
E-mail: abrambarrett@gmail.com.

Knee-High Adventures, *(978-0-615-16825-8)* 13450 Oak Hollow, Cypress, TX 77429 USA
Web site: http://www.davidsdonkeytales.com
Dist(s): **Lulu Pr., Inc.**

Knight Publishing, *(978-0-9740535)* P.O. Box 7452, Fremont, CA 94537-7452 USA Tel 209-743-7390; Fax: 510-818-1166
E-mail: knightpublishing@sbcglobal.net; childrenbooks@sbcglobal.net.

Knight Watch Publishing, *(978-0-9974351)* 8663 Oak Dr, Rancho Cucamonga, CA 91730 USA Tel 626-824-1099
E-mail: contact@knightwatchpublishing.com
Web site: www.knightwatchpublishing.com.

Knights of Soul Publishing *See* **DHUNAMI**

KNK Books *See* **California is Me**

KnockKnock LLC, *(978-1-60106; 978-1-68349)* 11111 Jefferson Blvd No. 5167, Culver City, CA 90231 USA Tel 310-396-4132; Fax: 310-396-4385; Toll Free: 800-656-5662
E-mail: kk1@knockknockstuff.com; gil.vizconde@whosthere.com; ops@whosthere.com
Web site: http://www.knockknockstuff.com.

†Knoll, Allen A. Pubs., *(978-0-9627297; 978-1-888310)* 200 W. Victoria St., Santa Barbara, CA 93101 USA (SAN 299-0539) Tel 805-564-3377 (orders); Fax: 805-966-6657 (orders); Toll Free: 800-777-7623 (orders)
E-mail: accounts@knollpublishers.com
Web site: http://www.knollpublishers.com
Dist(s): **Brodart Co.**
Follett School Solutions; *CIP.*

†Knopf, Alfred A. Inc., *(978-0-394)* Div. of The Knopf Publishing Group, Orders Addr.: 400 Hahn Rd., Westminster, MD 21157 USA Tel 410-848-1900; Toll Free: 800-726-0600 (orders); Edit Addr.: 1745 Broadway, New York, NY 10019 USA (SAN 202-5825) Tel 212-782-9000; Toll Free: 800-726-0600
E-mail: customerservice@randomhouse.com
Web site: http://www.randomhouse.com/knopf
Dist(s): **Libros Sin Fronteras**
MyiLibrary
Penguin Random Hse. Distribution
Penguin Random Hse. LLC
Random Hse., Inc.; *CIP.*

Knopf Bks. for Young Readers *Imprint of* **Random Hse. Children's Bks.**

†Knopf Doubleday Publishing Group, *(978-0-307)* Div. of Doubleday Broadway Publishing Group, Orders Addr.: 400 Hahn Rd., Westminster, MD 21157 USA (SAN 281-6083) Tel 410-848-1900; Toll Free: 800-726-0600; Edit Addr.: 1745 Broadway, New York, NY 10019 USA (SAN 201-0089) Tel 212-782-9000; 212-572-4961 Bulk orders; Toll Free Fax: 800-659-2436 Orders only; Toll Free: 800-669-1536 Electronic orders; 800-726-0600 Customer service; *Imprints:* Doubleday (Double); Flying Dolphin Press (FDP); Everyman's Library (Everymns Lib); Pantheon (Pantheon); Schocken (Schocken); Vintage (Vin Bks); Anchor (AncKPG); Vintage Espanol (VintageEsp)
E-mail: ddaypub@randomhouse.com
Web site: http://www.doubleday.com
Dist(s): **Children's Plus, Inc.**
Follett School Solutions
MyiLibrary
Penguin Random Hse. Distribution
Penguin Random Hse. LLC
Random Hse., Inc.; *CIP.*

Knosis, LLC *See* **SkyMark Corp.**

Knot Garden Pr., *(978-0-9655018)* 7712 Eagle Creek Dr., Dayton, OH 45459 USA Tel 937-433-2592 (phone/fax)
E-mail: marthaboice@aol.com.

Knott, Joan, *(978-0-9779895)* 132 W. High St., Jackson, MI 49203 USA.

Know Me Pubn. LLC, *(978-0-9790934)* Orders Addr.: 1679 Valdosta Cir., Pontiac, MI 48340 USA Tel 248-212-0204
E-mail: knowmepub@yahoo.com
Web site: http://www.cwren.bravehost.com.

Know Wonder Publishing, LLC, *(978-0-615-18112-7)* 12832 71st Ave., Kirkland, WA 98034 USA
Dist(s): **Publishers Services.**

Knowing Pr., The, *(978-0-936927)* Orders Addr.: 400 Sycamore, McAllen, TX 78501 USA (SAN 658-361X) Tel 956-686-4033
E-mail: janseale@rgv.rr.com.

Knowledge Box Central, *(978-1-61625; 978-1-62472)* 403 N. Jodie St., Shreveport, LA 71007 USA Tel 318-207-2454
Web site: http://www.knowledgeboxcentral.com.

Knowledge College Planning, *(978-0-9761218)* P.O. Box 321, Stockbridge, GA 30281 USA Tel 770-331-0739
Web site: http://www.kcplan.com.

Knowledge Kids Enterprises, Incorporated *See* **LeapFrog Enterprises, Inc.**

Knowledge Power Communications, *(978-0-9818790; 978-0-9854107; 978-0-9888644; 978-0-9907199; 978-0-9967162; 978-0-9976622; 978-0-9981701; 978-0-9993455; 978-1-7322665; 978-1-950936)* 24307 Magic Mountain Pkwy, No. 386, Valencia, CA 91355 USA (SAN 856-8189) Tel 661-513-0308
Web site: http://www.knowledgepowerinc.com.

Knowledge Quest, *(978-1-932786)* P.O. Box 474, Boring, OR 97009-0474 USA Tel 503-663-1210; Fax: 503-663-0670 Do not confuse with Knowledge Quest, Dieterich, IL
E-mail: orders@knowledgequestmaps.com; terri@knowledgequestmaps.com
Web site: http://www.knowledgequestmaps.com.

Knowledge Wand, LLC, *(978-0-9766680)* 100 Kennewyck Cir., Slingerlands, NY 12159 USA Tel 518-456-3110; Fax: 518-456-6990; Toll Free: 800-376-5669
E-mail: djahnel@gmail.com
Web site: http://www.knowledgewand.com.

KnowledgeGain Inc., *(978-0-9779844)* 3936 Hwy 52 N, Suite 121, Rochester, MN 55901 USA (SAN 850-802X) Tel 507-398-2384; Fax: 928-832-6568
E-mail: Publisher@KnowledgeGain.com
Web site: http://www.KnowledgeGain.com.

Knowtivate, LLC, *(978-0-9787021)* Orders Addr.: 116 Milton St., Lake Mills, WI 53551-5355 USA Tel 920-478-3936; Edit Addr.: N7894 Cty. Rd., O, Waterloo, WI 53594-5355 USA
Web site: http://www.knowtivate.com.

Knox, John Press *See* **Westminster John Knox Pr.**

KO Kids Bks., *(978-0-9723946)* 16 Baytree Rd., San Rafael, CA 94903-3801 USA
Web site: http://www.kokidsbooks.com
Dist(s): **Publishers Group West (PGW).**

Koala Jo Publishing, *(978-0-9764698)* Orders Addr.: 352 N. El Camino Real, San Mateo, CA 94401 USA
Web site: http://www.koalajo.com.

KOBZ, *(978-0-9772222)* 2230 Rockingham Dr., Maryville, TN 37803 USA Tel 865-980-7755.

Koch, Chris, *(978-0-9764338)* 3344 Louisville Rd., Harrodsburg, KY 40330-9190 USA.

Kochevar, Steven, *(978-0-9763546)* 7 Beth Lee Dr., Grafton, MA 01519-1139 USA.

†Kodansha America, Inc., *(978-0-87011; 978-1-56836; 978-1-935429; 978-1-61262; 978-1-63236; 978-1-64651)* 451 Park Ave S. Flr. 7, New York, NY 10016-7390 USA (SAN 201-0526) Toll Free: 800-451-7556; *Imprints:* Vertical (Vertical)
E-mail: t-sumi@kodansha-usa.com; ka-koide@kodansha.co.jp
Web site: http://kodanshacomics.com/; www.kodanshausa.com
Dist(s): **Oxford Univ. Pr., Inc.**
Penguin Random Hse. Distribution
Penguin Random Hse. LLC
Random Hse., Inc.; *CIP.*

Kodansha International (JPN) *(978-4-7700) Dist. by* **Cheng Tsui.**

Kodansha International (JPN) *(978-4-7700) Dist. by* **Peng Rand Hse.**

Kodansha International (JPN) *(978-4-7700) Dist. by* **Kodansha.**

Kodansha USA Publishing *See* **Kodansha America, Inc.**

Kodel Group, LLC, The, *(978-0-9844784; 978-0-9850142; 978-1-62485)* Orders Addr.: P.O. Box 38, Grants Pass, OR 97528-0003 USA (SAN 859-4961) Tel 541-471-1234; Edit Addr.: 132 NW 6th St., Grants Pass, OR 97528 USA; *Imprints:* Empire Holdings (Empire Holds); Empire Holdins - Literary Division for Young Readers (EH LDYR)
E-mail: info@kodelgroup.com
Web site: stevietenderheart.com; kodelempire.com.

Kodzo Bks., *(978-1-943960)* 1125 Hilltop Dr., Rock Springs, WY 82901 USA Tel 801-414-2550
E-mail: lkodzo@live.com.

Koehntopp, James, *(978-0-578-61820-3)* 715 Harrison Ct., West Bend, WI 53090 USA Tel 715-379-5013
E-mail: shazam791@yahoo.com.

Koenisha Pubns., *(978-0-9700458; 978-0-9718758; 978-0-9741685; 978-0-9759621; 978-0-9800098; 978-1-7351485)* 3196-53rd St., Hamilton, MI 49419 USA
E-mail: shar@sewingmachinemuseum.com
Web site: http://www.koenisha.com; www.sewingmachinemuseum.com.

Kofford, Greg Books, Inc., *(978-1-58958)* P.O. Box 1362, Draper, UT 84020 USA (SAN 253-5882) Tel 801-572-7417; Fax: 801-576-0583
E-mail: gregk@koffordbooks.com
Web site: http://www.gregkofford.com.

Kogan Page, Ltd. (GBR) *(978-0-7494; 978-0-85038; 978-1-85091; 978-1-78966; 978-1-78757; 978-1-78967) Dist. by* **IngramPubServ.**

Kogan, Sheila, 8 Highland Blvd., Kensington, CA 94707 USA Tel 510-527-9741
E-mail: sheilakogan@hotmail.com
Dist(s): **Ingram Content Group.**

Koho Pono, LLC, *(978-0-9845424; 978-1-938282; 978-1-941379)* 15024 SE Pinegrove Loop, Clackamas, OR 97015-7629 USA (SAN 859-6956) Tel 503-723-7392
E-mail: burrs@kohopono.com
Web site: http://kohopono.com.

Kokila *Imprint of* **Penguin Young Readers Group**

Kokopelli Pr., *(978-0-9759270)* 9611 Paseo del Rey NE, Albuquerque, NM 87111-1649 USA Do not confuse with companies with the same name in Las Cruces, NM, Sedona, AZ.

Kolaj, Paul, *(978-0-578-42916-8)* 245 Main St., White Plains, NY 10601 USA Tel 914-413-6100
E-mail: pk@famousfamiglia.com
Dist(s): **Ingram Content Group.**

Koldarana Pubns., *(978-1-884993)* Orders Addr.: P.O. Box 973, Dover, AR 72837 USA; Edit Addr.: 958 SR 164 E., Dover, AR 72837 USA
E-mail: ctn47496@yahoo.com.

Kollath-Stensaas Pubs., *(978-0-9673793; 978-0-9792006; 978-1-936571)* 394 Lake Ave., S., Suite 406, Duluth, MN 55802 USA Tel 218-341-3350
E-mail: sparkystensaas@hotmail.com
Web site: http://www.kollathstensaas.com
Dist(s): **Adventure Pubns.**
Publishers Group West (PGW).

Kolluri, Alina M., *(978-0-9787319)* 10124 Queens Park Dr., Tampa, FL 33647-3179 USA
E-mail: alinakolluri@yahoo.com.

Komikwerks, LLC, *(978-0-9742803; 978-0-9778809; 978-1-933925)* 1 Ruth St., Worcester, MA 01602 USA; *Imprints:* Actionopolis (Actionopolis); Agent of Danger (AgentofDanger)
E-mail: patrick@komikwerks.com; shannon@komikwerks.com; kristendenton@gmail.com
Web site: http://www.komikwerks.com; http://www.actionopolis.com.

Kommon Cents, Inc., *(978-0-9745982)* Orders Addr.: P.O. Box 313274, Jamaica, NY 11431-3274 USA Tel 917-541-8568; Toll Free: 877-566-2368
E-mail: info@kommoncents.com
Web site: http://www.kommoncents.com.

Kommon Cents Publishing Company *See* **Kommon Cents, Inc.**

Konaa Publishing *See* **Smallbag Bks.**

Konecky & Konecky *Imprint of* **Konecky, William S. Assocs., Inc.**

Konecky, William S. Assocs., Inc., *(978-0-914427; 978-1-56852)* 72 Ayers Point Rd., Old Saybrook, CT 06475-4301 USA (SAN 663-2432) Tel 860-388-0878; Fax: 860-388-0273; *Imprints:* Konecky & Konecky (Konecky & Konecky)
E-mail: seankon@comcast.net.

Konkori International, *(978-0-9647012)* P.O. Box 102441, Denver, CO 80250 USA Tel 303-744-6318; Fax: 303-296-9113; *Imprints:* Dawn of a New Day Publications, The (Dawn of a New Day)
E-mail: dabdulai@yahoo.com
Dist(s): **Emery-Pratt Co.**

Konopka, Ann Marie, *(978-0-615-18598-9)* 20 Palmer Rd., Kendall Pk., NJ 08824 USA Tel 732-821-5415
E-mail: annmkonopka@yahoo.com
Dist(s): **Lulu Pr., Inc.**

Konstellation Pr., *(978-0-9987482; 978-0-9991989; 978-1-7346421)* 4367 Narragansett Ave., San Diego, CA 92107 USA Tel 619-517-5017
E-mail: corneliafeye@gmail.com.

Kontis, Alethea, *(978-1-942541)* PO Box 512, Mims, FL 32754 USA
E-mail: akontis@gmail.com
Web site: http://www.aletheakontis.com.

Kookalook Publishing, *(978-0-9706323)* 53 Garden Pl., Brooklyn, NY 11201-4501 USA
E-mail: kookypubs@hotmail.com.

Korab, Kat *See* **Purple Unicorn Pr.**

Korean Culture Research, Inc., *(978-0-9762990)* 38 W. 32nd St., Suite 1112, New York, NY 10001 USA Tel 212-563-5763; Fax: 212-563-6707
E-mail: leekle@sprynet.com
Web site: http://www.learnkoreannow.com.

Kores, Michelle, *(978-0-692-78763-2; 978-0-692-78765-6)* 633 Montrose Ave., Delano, MN 55328 USA Tel 701-446-7048.

Koroknay, Thomas, *(978-0-9749705)* 3718 Lindsey Rd., Lexington, KY 44904 USA Tel 419-884-0222.

Kory Industries, *(978-0-578-40186-7; 978-0-578-42596-2; 978-0-578-50961-7; 978-0-578-68647-9; 978-0-578-68648-6)* 17617 SE 293rd PL, KENT, WA 98042 USA Tel 425-941-9352
E-mail: flyacecat@hotmail.com
Dist(s): **Ingram Content Group.**

Kotowicz, Anetta *See* **ArtsKindred**

Kotzig Publishing, Inc., *(978-0-9715411; 978-0-9767163)* 1109 NW 16th St., Delray Beach, FL 33444 USA
E-mail: susan@kotzigpublishing.com
Web site: http://www.kotzigpublishing.com
Dist(s): **Independent Pubs. Group.**

Kountz Marketing Group *See* **Texas Pride Publishing**

Kovels Antiques, Inc., *(978-0-9646683; 978-0-9970825)* 22000 Shaker Blvd., Shaker Heights, OH 44122 USA Tel 216-752-2252; Fax: 216-752-3115; Toll Free: 800-303-1996
E-mail: kkovel@kovels.com
Web site: www.kovels.com.

Kowalewski, Billie, *(978-0-692-04643-2; 978-0-578-48323-8)* P.O. Box 106, MOODUS, CT 06469 USA Tel 860-861-5115
E-mail: billie@enlightenedbook.net
Dist(s): **Ingram Content Group.**

Koyama Pr. (CAN) *(978-0-9784810; 978-0-9879630; 978-0-9868739; 978-1-927668) Dist. by* **Consort Bk Sales.**

KP Bks., *(978-0-9748549)* 354 Sequoia Ct., Antioch, IL 60002-2600 USA
E-mail: pudaitem@sbcglobal.net; bluehorizon1@sbcglobal.net; marylpk625@me.com.

KPT Publishing, LLC, *(978-1-944833)* 2600 E. 26th St., Minneapolis, MN 55406 USA Tel 612-721-5017; Fax: 612-721-7968
E-mail: david.koechel@kpadesign.com
Web site: KPTpublishing.com
Dist(s): **Penguin Random Hse. Distribution**
Penguin Random Hse. LLC.

Kraemer, Jean, *(978-0-9897694)* 28627 Essex St., Roseville, MI 48066 USA Tel 586-777-0113
E-mail: jeangirlk60@att.net.

Kramer, H.J. Inc., *(978-0-915811; 978-1-932073)* P.O. Box 1082, Tiburon, CA 94920 USA (SAN 294-0833) Fax: 415-435-5364; Toll Free: 800-972-6657
E-mail: hjkramer@jps.net
Web site: http://www.newworldlibrary.com
Dist(s): **New Leaf Distributing Co., Inc.**
New World Library
Publishers Group West (PGW).

Kramer, Sarah, *(978-0-692-99173-2)* 3909 W 124th St., Leawood, KS 66209 USA Tel 417-214-6721
E-mail: sarahfarrellkramer@gmail.com
Dist(s): **Ingram Content Group.**

Kranichfeld, Andrew, *(978-0-692-51647-8; 978-0-692-51648-5; 978-0-692-51649-2; 978-0-692-52541-8; 978-0-692-61529-4; 978-0-692-84206-5)* 3425 Kingsbridge Ave. Apt. 606, BRONX, NY 10463 USA Tel 914-227-0645.

Krantz, Heather, *(978-0-9987037; 978-1-952881)* 2967 NW Starview Dr, Bend, OR 97703 USA Tel 541-948-5641; *Imprints:* Herow Press (HerowPr)
E-mail: zwillinga@bendbroadband.com.

Krash Publishing *See* **Place Mark Bks.**

Krassa, Arlene, *(978-0-578-45100-8; 978-0-578-45105-3)* 14520 Fincher Rd., Ball Ground, GA 30107 USA Tel 678-848-8041
E-mail: arlenekrassa@gmail.com
Dist(s): **Ingram Content Group.**

Kraszewski, Terry, *(978-0-9821989)* 2162 Avenida De La Playa, La Jolla, CA 92037 USA (SAN 857-5223) Tel 858-456-9283; Fax: 858-456-9551
E-mail: ricswave@cox.net
Web site: http://www.surfangelbook.com.

Krause, Claudia, *(978-0-9655689)* P.O. Box 7083, Capistrano Beach, CA 92624 USA Tel 714-492-7778.

Kravec & Kravec & Associates *See* **Bellaboozle Books, Inc.**

Krazy Duck Productions, *(978-0-9776739; 978-0-9961622)* Orders Addr.: P.O. Box 105, Danville, KY 40423 USA Tel 606-787-2571; Fax: 606-787-8207; Edit Addr.: 2227 Wood Creek Rd., Liberty, KY 42539 USA
E-mail: KrazyduckProductions@msn.com
Web site: http://www.krazyduck.com.

KRBY Creations, LLC, *(978-0-9745715)* 2 Leeds Ct., Brick, NJ 08724-4011 USA
E-mail: krbyenterprises@comcast.net
Web site: http://www.krbycreations.com.

Kreations, *(978-0-9766621)* 19842 Needles St., Chatsworth, CA 91311 USA
E-mail: kreations@socal.rr.com
Web site: http://www.skelanimals.com.

Kreativ Kaos, *(978-0-9790572)* P.O. Box 27955, Anaheim Hills, CA 92809 USA (SAN 852-310X)
E-mail: admin@kreativkaos.com
Web site: http://www.kreativkaos.com.

Kreative Character Kreations, Inc., *(978-0-9641381)* 9 Endicott Dr., Huntington, NY 11743 USA Tel 516-673-8230; Fax: 516-346-6620.

Kreative X-Pressions Pubns., *(978-0-9798536; 978-0-9800552)* Orders Addr.: 87 Kennedy Dr., Colchester, CT 06415-1315 USA (SAN 854-5561) Tel 860-537-2673
E-mail: novelwriter@comcast.net
Web site: http://www.kreativexpressionsonline.com.

KreativeMindz Prodns. LLC, P.O. Box 2413, New York, NY 10108 USA Tel 212-222-3069
E-mail: KLB@kreativemindzproductions.com
Web site: http://www.kreativemindzproductions.

Kreder, Mary Ellen DeLuca, *(978-0-615-92430-4; 978-0-9913232)* 364 Quaker St., Wallkill, NY 12589 USA Tel 845-853-2803
E-mail: MaryEd4466@verizon.net.

†Kregel Pubns., *(978-0-8254)* Div. of Kregel, Inc., Orders Addr.: P.O. Box 2607, Grand Rapids, MI 49501-2607 USA (SAN 206-9792) Tel 616-451-4775; Fax: 616-451-9330; Toll Free: 800-733-2607; Edit Addr.: 733 Wealthy St., SE., Grand Rapids, MI 49503-5553 USA (SAN 298-9115); *Imprints:* Editorial Portavoz (Edit Portavoz)
E-mail: kregelbooks@kregel.com; acquisitions@kregel.com
Web site: http://www.kregel.com
Dist(s): **Faith Alive Christian Resources**
INscribe Digital
Send The Light Distribution LLC
Spring Arbor Distributors, Inc.; *CIP.*

Kreizel Enterprises, Inc., *(978-0-9729232)* P.O. Box 224, Monsey, NY 10952 USA; 26 Charles Ln., Spring Valley, NY 10977-3330
E-mail: info@kreizelplating.com; books@kreizelplating.com.

Kremer Pubns, Inc., *(978-0-9707591; 978-0-9745631; 978-0-9817272)* 12615 W. Custer Ave., Butler, WI 53007 USA Toll Free: 800-669-0887
E-mail: info@kremerpublications.com
Web site: http://www.kremerpublications.com.

Krickett Enterprises, *(978-1-7333567)* 18013 Duncan St., Encino, CA 91316 USA Tel 818-384-1697
E-mail: krickett@drumtolearn.com
Dist(s): **Ingram Content Group.**

Krickle Forest Adventures, *(978-0-9855997)* 4081 Jeri Rd., Interlochen, MI 49643 USA Tel 231-753-6025
E-mail: customerservice@krickleforest.com
Web site: http://www.krickleforest.com.

Kringle Enterprises Company *See* **North Pole Pr.**

Kris, *(978-0-9984291)* 660 King Street, Apt 302, San Francisco, CA 94107 USA Tel 617-763-6129
E-mail: krishanthirondonfuentes@gmail.com.

Krisaran Publishing Co., *(978-0-9773146)* 850 NC 55 E., Mount Olive, NC 28365 USA (SAN 257-3903)
E-mail: bjackson@esn.net; brenda@krisaran.com
Web site: http://www.krisaran.com.

Krishnamurti Pubns., *(978-1-888004; 978-1-934989)* Orders Addr.: Krishnamurti Foundation Of America 134 Besant Rd., Ojai, CA 93024-1560 USA Toll Free: 866-552-6651; Krishnamurti Foundation Trust Brockwood Pk., Bramdean, SO24 0LQ
E-mail: info@kpublications.com; publications@brockwood.org.uk
Web site: http://www.jkrishnamurti.org/info
Dist(s): **CreateSpace Independent Publishing Platform**
MyiLibrary
SCB Distributors.

Krishnan, Laura, *(978-0-692-78397-9)* 13560 NE 54th PL, BELLEVUE, WA 98005 USA Tel 832-687-3560.

KRO Publishing *See* **Preschool Prep Co.**

Kronos Publishing, *(978-0-615-44390-4; 978-0-9833951)* 297 Billerica Rd., Chelmsford, MA 01730 USA Tel 978-947-3042
E-mail: Indrani.Ghosal@kronos.com
Web site: kronos.com
Dist(s): **INscribe Digital.**

Kruger, Wolfgang Verlag, GmbH (DEU) *(978-3-8105) Dist. by* **Intl Bk Import.**

Kruger, Wolfgang Verlag, GmbH (DEU) *(978-3-8105) Dist. by* **Distribks Inc.**

Krullstone Publishing, LLC, *(978-0-9833237; 978-0-9882170; 978-0-9889578; 978-1-941851)* 114 Oakwood Ave., FAIRHOPE, AL 36532 USA (SAN 860-1240) Tel 251-270-7173
E-mail: charlotte@krullstone.com
Web site: www.krullstone.com
Dist(s): **Krullstone Distributing, LLC**
Smashwords.

Krystal Lee Enterprises (KLE Publishing), *(978-0-9971378; 978-1-945066)* 1264 Mill Crest Walk NW, Conyers, GA 30012 USA Tel 404-667-2051
E-mail: krystalleeenterprises@gmail.com
Web site: www.klepub.com.

K's Kids Publishing, *(978-0-9797208)* 12706 SW 94 Ct., Miami, FL 33176 USA (SAN 854-1892) Tel 305-969-5570
E-mail: ks_kids@bellsouth.net.

†Ktav Publishing Hse., Inc., *(978-0-87068; 978-0-88125; 978-1-60280; 978-965-524)* Orders Addr.: 930 Newark Ave. 4th Flr., Jersey City, NJ 07306 USA (SAN 201-0038) Tel 201-963-9524; Fax: 201-963-0102; Toll Free Fax: 800-626-7517 (orders)
E-mail: orders@ktav.com; editor@ktav.com; questions@ktav.com
Web site: http://www.ktav.com
Dist(s): **Academic Studies Pr.**
ISD
eBookit.com; *CIP.*

K-Teen *Imprint of* **Kensington Publishing Corp.**

K-Teen/Dafina *Imprint of* **Kensington Publishing Corp.**

ktf-writers-studio, *(978-0-615-41134-7; 978-0-615-44161-0; 978-3-9523908; 978-0-578-10595-6; 978-0-9913395; 978-0-9969890; 978-0-9986927)* 5712 Ashley Sq. S., Memphis, TN 38120 USA Tel 901-683-4210; 478 W. Racquet Club Pl., Memphis, TN 38117
E-mail: frigonomfr@aol.com; ktf-writers-studio@hotmail.com
Web site: www.ktf-writers-studio.ch.

KTH Investment Group, *(978-0-692-85894-3; 978-0-692-08213-3; 978-0-692-09811-0; 978-0-692-09812-7; 978-0-578-42213-8; 978-0-578-42215-2)* 592 N Peppercorn Ln., Rossville, GA 30741 USA Tel 423-463-2720
E-mail: jeffwcrawford5+LVP0003448@gmail.com; jeffwcrawford5+LVP0003448@gmail.com.

Kube Publishing Ltd. (GBR) *(978-1-84774) Dist. by* **Consort Bk Sales.**

Kudu, *(978-0-9849294; 978-1-938624; 978-1-943294; 978-1-950718)* 390 Baymoor Way, Lake Mary, FL 32746 USA Tel 407-900-5838
E-mail: matt@kudupub.com
Dist(s): **Send The Light Distribution LLC**
Whitaker Hse.

Kudzu King Productions, *(978-0-9961370)* 864 Heiferhorn Trace, Columbus, GA 31904 USA Tel 706-315-9117
E-mail: stephen.scott@mchsi.com
Web site: www.thekudzuking.com.

Kulupi Pr., *(978-0-9661867; 978-0-9817653)* 5082 Warm Springs Rd., Glen Ellen, CA 95442 USA Tel 707-996-1149
E-mail: kulupi@vom.com
Web site: http://www.kulupi.com
Dist(s): **Partners Bk. Distributing, Inc.**

Kumon Publishing North America, Inc., *(978-1-933241; 978-4-7743; 978-1-934968; 978-1-935800; 978-1-941082; 978-0-692-47466-2; 978-0-692-57875-9; 978-0-692-59884-9; 978-0-692-67737-7; 978-0-692-69890-7; 978-0-692-74109-2; 978-0-692-76435-0; 978-0-692-76436-7; 978-0-692-76437-4; 978-0-692-76438-1; 978-0-692-76658-3; 978-0-692-76659-0; 978-0-692-76660-6; 978-0-692-76661-3; 978-0-692-76662-0; 978-0-692-86678-8; 978-0-692-86679-5; 978-0-9859219; 978-0-9998787; 978-1-7331689; 978-1-953845)* 55 Challenger Rd. Suite 300, Ridgefield

Park, NJ 07666 USA Tel 201-836-2105; Fax: 201-836-1559; Toll Free: 800-657-7970; 4-10-18 Takanawa Minato-Ku, 13th Flr. Chiyoda-ku, Tokyo, 108-8617 Tel 0081 0332343485; Fax: 0081 0332344018
E-mail: books@kumon.com
Web site: http://www.kumonbooks.com
Dist(s): **Bookazine Co., Inc.**
Independent Pubs. Group
Ingram Publisher Services
Sterling Publishing Co., Inc.

Kumon U.S.A., Inc., *(978-0-9702092)* 300 Frank W. Burr Blvd., Teaneck, NJ 07666 USA
E-mail: falcbooks@home.com

Kunce, Craig LLC *See* **Windhill Bks. LLC**

Kung, Jeannie M., *(978-0-578-18737-2)* 815 S. Songbird Cir., Anaheim Hills, CA 92808 USA Tel 714-809-5634
E-mail: jeanniekung@sbcglobal.net.

Kunz, Matt, *(978-0-9976298)* 730 Sable Pointe Rd, Milton, GA 30004 USA Tel 404-386-0354
E-mail: mkunz59@hotmail.com.

Kuperman, Marina, *(978-0-9801109)* 8 Forge Rd., Hewitt, NJ 07421 USA Tel 973-728-0835
E-mail: marinakuperman@yahoo.com
Web site: http://turtlefeetsurfersbeat.com.

Kupu Kupu Pr., *(978-0-9883448)* 1710 Franklin No. 300, Oakland, CA 94612 USA Tel 510-452-1912
E-mail: inno@designaction.org
Web site: http://aisforactivist.com.

Kurban, Mary, *(978-0-692-67003-3; 978-0-692-67648-6; 978-0-692-70535-3; 978-0-692-71575-8; 978-0-692-77582-0; 978-0-692-77604-9; 978-1-7332598; 978-1-7332599; 978-1-7355591)* 1310 N. Avon St., BURBANK, CA 91505 USA Tel 818-848-3108
E-mail: makurban@hotmail.com.

Kurdyla, E L Publishing LLC, *(978-1-61751)* Orders Addr.: P.O. Box 958, Bowie, MD 20718-0958 USA Tel 301-805-2191; Fax: 301-805-2192; Edit Addr.: P.O. Box 958, Bowie, MD 20718-0958 USA Tel 301-805-2191; Fax: 301-805-2192; *Imprints:* 4th Division Press (FourthDiv)
E-mail: publisher@kurdylapublishing.com
Web site: http://www.kurdylapublishing.com.

Kurjan, Sally, *(978-0-692-13852-6; 978-0-692-19276-4; 978-0-578-44656-1; 978-0-578-52747-5; 978-0-578-70592-7)* 1703 Warner Ct., Mineral Ridge, OH 44440 USA Tel 330-519-5319
E-mail: sally3510@hotmail.com
Web site: www.bernietheoneeyedpuppy.com.

Kurtz Art Studio Inc, *(978-0-9982674)* 64 Austin Storey Cir., Newnan, GA 30263 USA Tel 404-435-3647
E-mail: kurtzartwork@gmail.com
Web site: johnkurtzart.com.

Kurz, Ron, *(978-0-939829)* P.O. Box 95551, Las Vegas, NV 89193 USA (SAN 663-8333) Tel 702-837-6395 (phone/fax); 3060 Sunrise Heights Dr., Henderson, NV 89052 (SAN 663-8341) Tel 702-870-5968
E-mail: ronkurz@earthlink.net
Web site: http://www.ronkurz.com.

Kush Univ. Pr., *(978-1-893731)* Orders Addr.: 8247 S. Oglesby Ave., Chicago, IL 60617 USA Tel 773-598-5707; *Imprints:* Mandolin House (MandolinHse)
E-mail: esmith334@kushuniversitypress.net
Web site: http://kushuniversitypress.net/opencart/; http://kushuniversitypress.net/KU_press.html.

Kutie Kari Bks., Inc., *(978-1-884149)* 4189 Ethan Dr., Eagan, MN 55123 USA Tel 651-450-7427
E-mail: gharbo@garyharbo.com
Web site: http://www.garyharbo.com.

Kvale Good Natured Games LLC, *(978-0-9793583)* 771 Parkview Ave., Saint Paul, MN 55117-4045 USA Tel 651-204-6781; Fax: 651-204-6966
E-mail: admin@kvalegames.com
Web site: http://www.kvalegames.com.

Kvalvasser, Leonid, *(978-0-9753110)* 1124 Blake Ct. # 1A, Brooklyn, NY 11235-5219 USA.

Kwazy Kitty Publishing Co., *(978-0-9770012)* Orders Addr.: P.O. Box 178, Monkton, MD 21111-0178 USA.

KWIP, Inc., *(978-0-9790267; 978-0-692-25867-5)* 1400 Broadway Blvd., Polk City, FL 33868 USA
E-mail: stevec@fantasyofflight.com.

Kwist, Karla, *(978-0-9795046)* 2420 Golden Arrow, Las Vegas, NV 89120 USA Tel 702-768-8406
E-mail: karlakk@aol.com
Web site: http://www.karlakwist.com.

Kyburg Publishing, *(978-1-7337650)* 1307 W. Hawk Ct., Nampa, ID 83651 USA Tel 208-697-3478
E-mail: authorbenjaminvogt@gmail.com.

Kymberli Mulford, Inc., *(978-1-7323504; 978-1-7329444)* 869 E Schaumburg Rd., PMB 218, Schaumburg, IL 60169 USA Tel 847-627-0984
E-mail: onionskin1@gmail.com
Web site: www.kymberlimulford.com.

Kyoodoz, *(978-0-9771172)* Orders Addr.: P.O. Box 5431, Beaverton, OR 97006-0431 USA
E-mail: customerservice@kyoodoz.com; sales@kyoodoz.com
Web site: http://www.kyoodoz.com.

L A 411 Publishing Company *See* **Reed Business Information**

L. A. Eng Bks., *(978-0-9748598)* 231 W. Hillcrest Blvd., Inglewood, CA 90301 USA
E-mail: luis_arevalo@lennox.k12.ca.us.

L. A. Media, LLC *See* **Mardi Gras Publishing, LLC**

L & L Enterprises, *(978-0-9760046)* 6960 W. Peoria Ave. LOT 132, Peoria, AZ 85345-6038 USA
Web site: https://www.latinandlanguage.com.

L & R Publishing, LLC, *(978-1-55571)* Subs. of Publishing Services, Inc., P.O. Box 3531, Ashland, OR 97520 USA (SAN 218-9240) Tel 541-973-5154; *Imprints:* Hellgate Press (Hellgate Pr); Grid Press (Grid Pr); Paloma Books (PalomaBks)
E-mail: harley@hellgatepress.com
Web site: http://www.hellgatepress.com
Dist(s): **Independent Pubs. Group**
Midpoint Trade Bks., Inc.
MyiLibrary
ebrary, Inc.

L. C. D., *(978-0-941414)* 663 Calle Miramar, Redondo Beach, CA 90277 USA (SAN 239-0035) Tel 310-375-6336
E-mail: lenduncan@earthlink.net
Web site: http://www.phonicsplus.com.

LED Publishing, *(978-1-885674)* Div. of Logical Expression In Design, 1730 M St. NW, Suite 407, Washington, DC 20036 USA Tel 703-558-0100; Fax: 703-558-4970.

L G Productions *See* **L G Publishing**

L G Publishing, *(978-0-9768486)* Orders Addr.: 281 Fielding, Ferndale, MI 48220 USA
E-mail: admin@lgproductions.info
Web site: http://www.lgproductions.info.

L L Teach, *(978-0-9676545; 978-1-931104)* 709 Country Club Rd., Bridgewater, NJ 08807-1601 USA Tel 908-575-8830; Fax: 908-704-1730; Toll Free: 800-575-7670
E-mail: ann4480@aol.com; llteach5757670@aol.com
Web site: http://www.LLteach.com.

LMA Publishing, *(978-1-892426)* Div. of Lifestyle Management Assocs., 111 Grove St., Apt. 1, West Roxbury, MA 02132 USA Tel 617-325-6752 (phone/fax)
E-mail: pentzj@ix.netcom.com
Web site: http://www.lifestylemanagement.com.

L P D Enterprises *See* **LPD Pr.**

L W S Bks., *(978-0-9704361)* 227 Bayshore Dr., Hendersonville, TN 37075 USA Tel 615-826-3871; Fax: 615-826-3883; Toll Free: 800-643-4718
E-mail: clazzy@mindspring.com
Web site: http://www.janethan.com; http://www.imsonofman.com.

L W S Publishers *See* **L W S Bks.**

La Caille Nous Publishing Co., *(978-0-9647635; 978-0-9718191)* 328 Flatbush Ave, Suite 240, Brooklyn, NY 11238 USA Tel 212-726-1293; Fax: 212-591-6465
E-mail: gcadet@lcnpub.com.

La Di La Dah, *(978-0-9816629)* 5508 Vantage Point Rd., Columbia, MD 21044-2631 USA
E-mail: r.higgins@xs4all.net
Dist(s): **Lulu Pr., Inc.**

La Frontera Publishing, *(978-0-9785634; 978-0-9857551; 978-0-9974757)* 1712 Pioneer Ave., Suite 181, Cheyenne, WY 82001 USA (SAN 851-0180) Tel 307-778-4752 general office number
E-mail: company@lafronterapublishing.com
Web site: http://www.lafronterapublishing.com
Dist(s): **Univ. of New Mexico Pr.**

La Galera, S.A. Editorial (ESP) *(978-84-246; 978-84-7515; 978-84-85297) Dist. by* **AIMS Intl.**

La Galera, S.A. Editorial (ESP) *(978-84-246; 978-84-7515; 978-84-85297) Dist. by* **Lectorum Pubns.**

La Librairie Parisienne, *(978-0-615-54542-4; 978-0-9886058)* 17844 Porto Marina Way, Pacific Palisades, CA 90272 USA Tel 424-268-4898; 310-343-1941
E-mail: JACKIEMANCUSO@GMAIL.COM; steve@lalibrairieparisienne.com
Web site: http://www.jackiemancuso.com/la-librairie-parisienne
Dist(s): **Independent Pubs. Group.**

La Luz Comics, *(978-0-9755193)* 1516 10th Ave. S., No. 6, Minneapolis, MN 55404-1795 USA
E-mail: sam@samhiti.com
Web site: http://www.samhiti.com.

La Mancha Publishing Group, *(978-1-890701)* 14534 Victory Blvd., Van Nuys, CA 91411 USA Tel 818-994-8195.

La Montagne Secrete (CAN) *(978-2-923163) Dist. by* **IPG Chicago.**

La Oferta Publishing Co., *(978-0-9665876; 978-0-9791624)* 1376 N. Fourth St., San Jose, CA 95112 USA Tel 408-436-7850; Fax: 408-436-7861; Toll Free: 800-336-7850
E-mail: sales@laoferta.com; mary@laoferta.com
Web site: http://www.laoferta.com
Dist(s): **Bilingual Pubns. Co., The**
Lectorum Pubns., Inc.
Libros Sin Fronteras
SPD-Small Pr. Distribution.

la Orilla Farm, *(978-0-9986447; 978-0-9986447-0-7)* 2401 Black Mesa Loop SW, Albuquerque, NM 87105 USA Tel 505-877-2877
E-mail: skreed47@gmail.com.

La Puerta Pubns., *(978-0-692-99026-1; 978-0-692-99855-7; 978-1-948563)* 4510 Catalina Pkwy., McFarland, WI 53558 USA Tel 608-772-3894
E-mail: lapuertapublications@gmail.com
Dist(s): **CreateSpace Independent Publishing Platform.**

LA Ruocco, *(978-0-9743454; 978-1-941593)* Orders Addr.: 31 Lake St., Brooklyn, NY 11223 USA
E-mail: laruocco@cs.com.

Laasya Design, *(978-0-9774147)* 400 N. Catalina St., Burbank, CA 91505 USA
E-mail: info@laasyadesign.com
Web site: http://www.laasyadesign.com.

Lab-Aids, Inc., *(978-1-887725; 978-1-933298; 978-1-60301; 978-1-63093)* 17 Colt Ct., Ronkonkoma, NY 11779 USA Tel 631-737-1133; Fax: 631-737-1286; Toll Free Fax: 800-381-8003
E-mail: lab-aids@lab.aids.com.

Labarco, *(978-0-9762439)* P.O. Box 1734, Alief, TX 77411 USA
Web site: http://www.cushcity.com; http://www.Amazon.com.

L'Abeille Publishing Incorporated *See* **Orndee Omnimedia, Inc.**

Labor, Editorial S. A. (ESP) *(978-84-335) Dist. by* **Continental Bk.**

Labosh Publishing, *(978-0-9744341)* P.O. Box 588, East Petersburg, PA 17520-0588 USA Tel 717-898-3813 (phone/fax)
E-mail: laboshpublishing@msn.com
Web site: http://laboshpublishing.com.

Lab-Volt Systems, Inc., *(978-0-86657; 978-1-60533)* Orders Addr.: P.O. Box 686, Farmingdale, NJ 07727 USA (SAN 238-7050) Tel 732-938-2000 Toll Free: 800-522-8658
E-mail: us@labvolt.com; Ivanbrug@labvolt.com
Web site: http://www.labvolt.com.

Lacey Productions, *(978-0-9771076)* 611 Druid Rd., Suite 705, Clearwater, FL 33767 USA
E-mail: sherry@laceyproductions.com
Web site: http://www.laceyproductions.com.

Lacey Publishing Co., *(978-0-9709249)* 29 Bounty Rd W., Benbrook, TX 76132-1003 USA Tel 817-738-3185 (phone/fax)
E-mail: jamesb50@charter.net
Web site: http://www.marfalightsresearch.com
Dist(s): **MyiLibrary**
ebrary, Inc.

LaChrisAnd Productions, *(978-0-9765063)* P.O. Box 969, Desert Hot Springs, CA 92240 USA Tel 760-309-2263
Web site: http://www.lachrisandproductions.com.

Lackner, William *See* **Digging Clams n Oregon**

Ladd, David Pr., *(978-0-9774563)* 56 Coolidge Ave., South Portland, ME 04106 USA Tel 207-767-2836
E-mail: davidladdpress@yahoo.com.

Ladd-Reese Group, LLC, The, *(978-0-9980271)* 5069 Parkside Cir., Hoover, AL 35244 USA Tel 205-533-5392
E-mail: theladdreesegroup@gmail.com.

LaDow Publishing, *(978-0-9723623)* 308 Reynolds Ln., West Chester, PA 19380-3300 USA Tel 219-689-4565; Fax: 610-918-9571
E-mail: wmladow@aol.com
Web site: http://www.wmladow.com.

Lady Hawk Pr., *(978-0-9829082)* 3831 Abbey Ct., Newbury Park, CA 91320 USA Tel 310-460-8744
Web site: ladyhawkpress.com
Dist(s): **ebrary, Inc.**

Lady Illyria Pr., *(978-0-9765572)* 30 Lamprey Ln., Lee, NH 03824 USA Tel 603-659-3826
E-mail: patricia.emison@unh.edu.

Lady Knight Enterprises Publishing, *(978-0-615-44985-2; 978-0-615-67175-8; 978-0-615-79318-4; 978-0-692-16488-4; 978-0-692-17728-0; 978-0-9980263; 978-1-7358663)* 3628 Satellite Blvd. #956265, Duluth, GA 30095 USA Tel 678 667-2311; 3628 Satellite Blvd., Duluth, GA 30095 Tel 678-667-2311
E-mail: ladyrhondaknight@gmail.com
Web site: http://rhondaknight.com
Dist(s): **CreateSpace Independent Publishing Platform**
Dummy Record Do Not USE!!!!.

Ladybug Writings, *(978-1-7322968)* P.O. Box 310786, New Braunfels, TX 78131 USA Tel 432-853-6409
E-mail: authorkwendt@gmail.com
Web site: www.kwendt.online.

Laffin Minor Pr., *(978-0-9770516)* P.O. Box 273, Alma, CO 80420 USA Tel 970-409-8857; Fax: 207-967-5492
E-mail: lydia@laffinminorpress.com
Web site: http://www.laffinminorpress.com.

Lagesse Stevens *Imprint of* **Martell Publishing Co**

Laguna Press/BTI *See* **Cerebral Press International**

Lainez, Stephanie, *(978-0-9820358)* P.O. Box 1471, La Mirada, CA 90637-1471 USA (SAN 857-068X)
E-mail: storyhousebooks@yahoo.com.

Lake 7 Creative, LLC, *(978-0-9774122; 978-0-9821187; 978-0-9883662; 978-1-940647)* 3419 Vincent Ave. N., Minneapolis, MN 55412 USA (SAN 257-5167) Tel 612-412-5493; *Imprints:* Getchu Books (Getchu Bks)
E-mail: ryan@lake7creative.com
Web site: http://www.lake7creative.com
Dist(s): **Adventure Pubns.**
Publishers Group West (PGW).

Lake Isle Pr., Inc., *(978-0-9627403; 978-1-891105)* 16 W. 32nd St., Suite 10B, New York, NY 10001 USA Tel 212-273-0796; Fax: 212-273-0198; Toll Free: 800-462-6420 (Orders only)
E-mail: lakeisle@earthlink.net; hiroko@lakeislepress.com
Web site: http://www.lakeislepress.com
Dist(s): **National Bk. Network.**

Lake Limericks, *(978-0-9761711)* P.O. Box 478, Lake Waccamaw, NC 28450 USA Tel 910-646-4998; Fax: 910-371-1133
E-mail: aldrich@weblnk.net.

Lake 'n Moor, Ltd., *(978-1-936748)* Orders Addr.: 5448 Apex Peakway No. 315, Apex, NC 27502 USA Tel 919-815-9769; Edit Addr.: 5448 Apex Peakway No. 315, Apex, NC 27502 USA Tel 919-815-9769
E-mail: info@lakenmoor.com.

Lake Street Pr., *(978-1-936181)* 4918 N Oakley Ave., Chicago, IL 60625 USA
Web site: http://www.lakestreetpress.com
Dist(s): **Ingram Content Group**
Partners Pubs. Group, Inc.
Quality Bks., Inc.

Lake Street Pubs., *(978-1-58417)* Orders Addr.: 4537 Chowen Ave S., Minneapolis, MN 55410-1364 USA
E-mail: compass@sd.cybernex.net.

Lake Superior Port Cities, Incorporated *See* **Lake Superior Publishing LLC**

Lake Superior Publishing LLC, *(978-0-942235; 978-1-938229)* Orders Addr.: P.O. Box 16417, Duluth, MN 55816-0417 USA Tel 218-722-5002; Fax: 218-722-4096; Toll Free: 888-244-5253; Edit Addr.: 310 E. Superior St. #125, Duluth, MN 55802-3134 USA (SAN 666-9980)
E-mail: edit@lakesuperior.com
Web site: http://www.lakesuperior.com.

Lakefront Research LLC, *(978-0-9764665)* P.O. Box 667, East Hampstead, NH 03826-0667 USA.

Lakeshore Curriculum Materials Company *See* **Lakeshore Learning Materials**

Lakeshore Learning Materials, *(978-1-929255; 978-1-58970; 978-1-59746; 978-1-60666)* Orders Addr.: 2695 E. Dominguez St., Carson, CA 90895 USA (SAN 630-0251) Toll Free: 800-421-5354; Edit Addr.: 2695 E. Dominguez St., Carson, CA 90895 USA Tel 310-537-8600; Fax: 310-632-8314
E-mail: ubeckham@lakeshorelearning.com
Web site: http://www.lakeshorelearning.com.

Lakeside Pr., *(978-1-879653; 978-0-9978959)* Do not confuse with companies with the same name in Anacortes, WA, Tamarac, FL
E-mail: larry.martin@roadrunner.com.

Lakeside Publishing MI, *(978-0-9907446)* 6175 Kinyon Dr., Brighton, MI 48116 USA Tel 810-599-0481
E-mail: carol.trembath3@gmail.com.

Lakeview Pr., *(978-0-9749677)* c/o Jan Devereux, 255 Lakeview Ave., Cambridge, MA 02138 USA Do not confuse with Lake View Press in New Orleans, LA, Mooresville, NC, Lake Oswego, OR.

Lakin, Laqwacia, *(978-0-9891103)* 3290 Osterley Way, Cumming, GA 30041 USA Tel 678-237-8495
E-mail: llakin.consulting@gmail.com.

Lakota Language Consortium, Inc., *(978-0-9761082; 978-0-9821107; 978-0-9834363; 978-1-941461)* 2620 N Walnut St. Suite 1280, Bloomington, IN 47404 USA Tel 812-961-0140; Fax: 812-961-0141; Toll Free: 888-525-6828
E-mail: orders@lakhota.org; sales@lakhota.org
Web site: http://www.lakhota.org; http://www.languagepress.com; http://www.llcbookstore.com.

Lamar, Mel Ministries *See* **Lamar, Melvin Productions**

Lamar, Melvin Productions, *(978-0-9716068)* 900 Downtowner Blvd., Apt. 89, Mobile, AL 36609-5409 USA
E-mail: melvinelamar@att.net; melvinlamar31@gmail.com.

Lamb, Wendy Bks. *Imprint of* **Random Hse. Children's Bks.**

Lambda Pubs., Inc., *(978-0-915361; 978-1-55774)* 3709 13th Ave., Brooklyn, NY 11218-3622 USA (SAN 291-0640) Tel 718-972-5449; Fax: 718-972-6307
E-mail: judaica@email.msn.com.

Lambert Bk. Hse., Inc., *(978-0-89315)* 4139 Parkway Dr., Florence, AL 35630-6347 USA (SAN 180-5169) Tel 256-764-4098; 256-764-4090; Fax: 256-766-9200; Toll Free: 800-551-8511
E-mail: info@lambertbookhouse.com
Web site: http://www.lambertbookhouse.com.

LaMothe, Karin, *(978-0-9728763)* P.O. Box 672, Belleville, MI 48112-0672 USA
Web site: http://www.angelslullaby.com.

Lamp Post Inc., *(978-0-9708587; 978-1-933428; 978-1-60039)* 29348 Ariel St., Murrieta, CA 92563 USA
E-mail: burner@lamppostpubs.com
Web site: http://www.lamppostpubs.com
Dist(s): **Diamond Comic Distributors, Inc.**
Diamond Bk. Distributors.

Lamp Post Publishing, Inc., *(978-1-892135)* 1741 Tallman Hollow Rd., Montoursville, PA 17754 USA (SAN 253-4681) Tel 570-435-2804; Fax: 570-435-2803; Toll Free: 800-326-9273
E-mail: lamppostp@aol.com
Web site: http://www.lamppostpublishing.com; http://www.beyondthegloesmur.com; http://www.heartstringsbio.com.

Lamplight Pubns., *(978-0-615-23329-1; 978-0-9819815)* 11123W US Hwy 60, Olive Hill, KY 41164 USA
E-mail: joan2728@windstream.net.

Lampo Licensing, LLC *See* **Ramsey Pr.**

Lampstand Pr., Ltd., *(978-1-935301)* Orders Addr.: P.O. Box 5798, Derwood, MD 20855 USA Tel 301-963-0808; Fax: 301-963-1868; Toll Free: 800-705-7487; Edit Addr.: 8073 Snouffer School Rd., Derwood, MD 20855 USA
Web site: http://www.lampstandpress.com.

Amur Bks., *(978-0-9776563; 978-0-9847118; 978-0-9855601; 978-0-9894940; 978-0-9914901; 978-0-9908299; 978-0-9963966)* P.O. Box 102697, Denver, CO 80250 USA Tel 303-777-4155
E-mail: amurbooks@msn.com
Web site: http://www.childrenare.com.

LaMuth Publishing Company *See* **Fairhaven Bk. Pubs.**

Lamweg Publishing, *(978-0-9801146)* 176 W. 100 S., Kouts, IN 46347 USA Tel 219-766-2174.

Lancaster, Paula, *(978-1-7322513)* 4809 Briercrest Ct., Bowie, MD 20720 USA Tel 301-262-2366
E-mail: paula@paulalancaster.com.

Landauer Corporation *See* **Landauer Publishing, LLC**

Landauer Publishing, LLC, *(978-0-9646870; 978-1-890621; 978-0-9770166; 978-0-9793711; 978-0-9800688; 978-0-9818040; 978-0-9825586; 978-1-935726; 978-1-947163)* 3100 100th St., Urbandale, IA 50322 USA (SAN 915-2334) Tel 515-287-2144; Fax: 515 276 5102; Toll Free: 800-557-2144; 3100 100th St., Urbandale, IA 50322 (SAN 915-2334) Tel 515-287-2144; Fax: 515 276 5102; Toll Free: 800-557-2144
E-mail: info@landauercorp.com; jeramy@landauercorp.com; acounting@landauercorp.com
Web site: http://www.landauerpub.com
Dist(s): **American Wholesale Bk. Co.**
Baker & Taylor Bks.
Bookazine Co., Inc.

Brodart Co.
Fox Chapel Publishing Co., Inc.

Landfall Co., The, *(978-0-9747445)* 18640 Mack Ave., P.O. Box 36551, Grosse Pointe Farms, MI 48236 USA Fax: 313-886-6250
E-mail: mhslandfall@landfallcompany.com.

Landmark Editions, Incorporated *See* **landmark Hse., Ltd.**

landmark Hse., Ltd., *(978-0-933849; 978-0-9822874)* 1949 Foxridge Dr., Kansas City, KS 66106 USA
Web site: http://www.landmarkhouse.com.

Landmark Publishing Inc., *(978-0-9726738)* P.O. Box 46403, Minneapolis, MN 55446 USA (SAN 254-9689) Tel 763-694-8907; Fax: 763-694-8909
E-mail: info@brainerdbound.com
Web site: http://www.brainerdbound.com.

Landrum, Warren, *(978-0-9787355; 978-1-7333195)* 1334 E. Chandler Blvd., Suite 5-D67, Phoenix, AZ 85048 USA
E-mail: warrenglandrum@hotmail.com.

Landstrider Pr., *(978-0-9969936)* 2944 NE Sawdust Hill Rd, Poulsbo, WA 98370 USA Tel 206-498-7944
E-mail: bors.vesterby@gmail.com.

Lane, Sondra Corp., *(978-0-9743874)* 2436 N. Federal Hwy., No. 300, Lighthouse Point, FL 33064 USA
Web site: http://www.hallelujahkids.com.

Lane, Veronica Bks., *(978-0-9637597; 978-0-9762743; 978-0-9826513; 978-0-9910083; 978-0-9992573; 978-1-7341800; 978-1-7351910)* Orders Addr.: 2554 Lincoln Blvd., Suite 142, Venice, CA 90291 USA (SAN 298-1157) Toll Free: 800-651-1001 (phone/fax)
E-mail: etan@veronicalanebooks.com
Web site: http://www.veronicalanebooks.com
Dist(s): **Bored Feet Pr.**
DeVorss & Co.
Follett School Solutions
INscribe Digital
Independent Pubs. Group
Integral Yoga Pubns.
New Leaf Distributing Co., Inc.

Lang Graphics, Ltd., *(978-0-933617; 978-1-55962; 978-1-57832; 978-0-7412)* Div. of Perfect Timing, Inc., Orders Addr.: P.O. Box 1605, Waukesha, WI 53188 USA; Edit Addr.: 514 Wells St., Delafield, WI 53018 USA (SAN 692-4689) Tel 414-646-3399; Fax: 414-646-2224; Toll Free: 800-262-2611
E-mail: support@shop.lang.com
Web site: http://www.lang.com
Dist(s): **TNT Media Group, Inc.**

Lang Verhaal Co., *(978-0-578-41140-8; 978-0-578-41707-3; 978-1-7339503)* 3902 N Kenneth Ave Flr. 2, Chicago, IL 60641 USA Tel 630-777-1056
E-mail: jaynesnoelle@gmail.com
Dist(s): **Ingram Content Group.**

Langenscheidt Publishing Group, *(978-0-88729; 978-1-58573)* Subs. of Langenscheidt KG, Orders Addr.: 15 Tyger River Dr., Duncan, SC 29334 USA Fax: 888-773-7979; Toll Free: 800-432-6277; Edit Addr.: 36-36 33rd St., Long Island City, NY 11106 USA
Web site: http://www.americanmap.com; http://www.langenscheidt.com
Dist(s): **Bilingual Pubns. Co., The**
Ingram Publisher Services.

Lange-Patton, Lorraine, *(978-0-9752874)* P.O. Box 96811, Las Vegas, NV 89193-6811 USA.

Langille, Cody, *(978-0-692-87818-7; 978-0-692-87819-4)* 1808 S 2095 W, Woods Cross, UT 84087 USA Tel 801-358-8934
E-mail: jeffwcrawford5+LVP0003669@gmail.com; jeffwcrawford5+LVP0003669@gmail.com.

Langley, Jan *See* **Captain & Harry LLC, The**

Langley, Rachel, *(978-0-578-43763-7; 978-0-578-44664-6; 978-0-578-66803-1; 978-0-578-66804-8)* 1557 Inland Ave., Charleston, SC 29412 USA Tel 706-399-7896
E-mail: rlangley13@gmail.com
Dist(s): **Ingram Content Group.**

LangMarc Publishing, *(978-1-880292)* Orders Addr.: P.O. Box 90488, Austin, TX 78709 USA (SAN 297-519X) Tel 512-394-0989; Fax: 512-394-0829; Toll Free: 800-864-1648 (orders only); Edit Addr.: 7500 Shadowridge Run, No. 28, Austin, TX 78749 USA
E-mail: langmarc@booksails.com
Web site: http://www.langmarc.com.

Langson, Bridgett Bell, *(978-0-9994376)* 2330 Thornridge Rd, Charlotte, NC 28226 USA Tel 704-582-0982; *Imprints:* Tale Wag Press (Tale Wag Pr)
E-mail: bblangson@aol.com.

Language 911, Inc., *(978-1-933451)* 12924 Calais Cir., Palm Beach Gardens, FL 33410 USA.

Language Adventure Pubns., *(978-0-9671053; 978-0-9976698)* 2311 E. Stadium Blvd., Suite 105 N, Ann Arbor, MI 48104 USA Tel 734-763-8378; Fax: 734-769-8409
E-mail: andrearojo@aol.com.

Language Quest Corp., *(978-0-9744691)* 1 Tartan Lakes, Westmont, IL 60559 USA.

Language Research Educational Series, *(978-0-9609446)* 4309 20th St., NE, Washington, DC 20018 USA (SAN 260-0927) Tel 202-636-9306
E-mail: lresduke@gmail.com.

Language Resource Manual for Schools *Imprint of* **Language Treasures**

Language Transformer Bks. *Imprint of* **Velichko, Vera**

Language Treasures, *(978-0-9765293)* 2141 SE 113th Ave., Portland, OR 97216 USA; *Imprints:* Language Resource Manual for Schools (L R M S)
E-mail: vrisk@comcast.net
Web site: http://www.languagetreasures.com.

Language Workshop for Children, The, *(978-0-9754205; 978-0-9755659; 978-0-9759664; 978-0-9819458)* 888 Lexington Ave., 2nd Flr., New York, NY 10065 USA (SAN 256-0704)
E-mail: info@professortoto.com
Web site: http://www.professortoto.com
Dist(s): **China Books & Periodicals, Inc.**

Lanico Media Hse., *(978-0-9886772; 978-0-9862057; 978-0-9967799; 978-0-9986520)* 206 Curve Dr. No. 13, Monroe, LA 71203 USA Tel 318-805-6589
E-mail: lacresha.hayes@gmail.com
Web site: www.lanicomediahouse.com.

LANIUS Software *See* **PassionQuest Technologies, LLC**

Lanoue, Michelle, *(978-0-692-10170-4; 978-0-692-11265-6)* 81 Cummings Rd., Athol, MA 01331 USA Tel 978-868-5825
E-mail: lanoue72@yahoo.com
Dist(s): **Ingram Content Group.**

Lanphier Pr., *(978-0-9762151; 978-0-9786039; 978-1-934570)* Div. of Corporate Chaplains of America, 1300 Corporate Chaplain Dr., Wake Forest, NC 27587-6596 USA
E-mail: dwhite@chaplain.org
Dist(s): **Send The Light Distribution LLC.**

Lantana Publishing (GBR) *(978-0-9932253; 978-1-911373)* *Dist. by* **Lerner Pub.**

Lantern Books *See* **Lantern Publishing & Media**

Lantern Publishing & Media, *(978-1-930051; 978-1-59056)* Div. of Booklight, Inc., 128 2nd Pl., Brooklyn, NY 11231-4102 USA
E-mail: martin@booklightinc.com
Web site: http://www.booklightinc.com
Dist(s): **Red Wheel/Weiser**
Smashwords
SteinerBooks, Inc.

Lapid, Yosef, *(978-0-9973899; 978-0-9993361; 978-1-949091)* 928 Raleigh Rd., Las Cruces, NM 88005 USA Tel 575-524-3201
E-mail: ioji158@gmail.com.

LAPOP (Latin American Public Opinion Project), *(978-0-9777042; 978-0-9792178; 978-0-9817299; 978-0-9821456; 978-0-9846260; 978-0-9846303; 978-1-939186)* 230 Appleton Pl, PMB 505 PSCI Dept at Vanderbily Univ., Nashville, TN 37203 USA
E-mail: liz.zechmeister@vanderbilt.edu
Web site: http://vanderbilt.edu/lapop.

Laramie, Charles, *(978-0-9769536)* 11 W. St., Fair Haven, VT 05743 USA Tel 802-265-3538
E-mail: chucklaramie@adelphia.net.

†Laredo Publishing Co., Inc., *(978-1-56492)* 465 Westview Ave., Englewood, NJ 07631 USA Tel 201-408-4048; Fax: 201-408-5011
E-mail: info@laredopublishing.com
Web site: http://www.laredopublishing.com; *CIP.*

Large Print Bk. Co., The, *(978-1-59688)* P.O. Box 970, Sanbornville, NH 03872-0970 USA Tel 603-569-4215
Web site: largeprintbookco.com.

Large Print Pr. *Imprint of* **Thorndike Pr.**

Lark Bks., *(978-0-937274; 978-1-57990; 978-1-887374; 978-1-60059; 978-1-4547)* Div. of Sterling Publishing Co., Inc., 67 Broadway St., Asheville, NC 28801-2919 USA (SAN 219-9947)
E-mail: info@larkbooks.com
Web site: http://www.larkbooks.com
Dist(s): **Hearst Bks.**
Sterling Publishing Co., Inc.

†Larksdale, *(978-0-89896)* P.O. Box 801222, Houston, TX 77280 USA (SAN 220-0643) Tel 713-461-7200; Fax: 713-467-4770 (purchase orders); Toll Free: 877-461-7200; *CIP.*

Larksong Productions *See* **Larksong Productions, Earthsong, Inc.**

Larksong Productions, Earthsong, Inc., *(978-0-9744878)* Div. of Earthsong, Inc., 1663 N. Circle Dr., Tempe, AZ 85281 USA Tel 480-599-4830
E-mail: mail@meadowlarkmusic.com; lynn@lynntrombetta.com; trombetta.wordsmith@gmail.com
Web site: http://www.meadowlarkmusic.com; http://choosinggreatness.com/; http://www.lynntrombetta.com.

Larousse, Ediciones, S. A. de C. V. (MEX) *(978-968-6042; 978-968-6147; 978-968-6347; 978-970-607; 978-970-22)* *Dist. by* **HM.**

Larousse, Ediciones, S. A. de C. V. (MEX) *(978-968-6042; 978-968-6147; 978-968-6347; 978-970-607; 978-970-22)* *Dist. by* **Giron Bks.**

Larousse, Ediciones, S. A. de C. V. (MEX) *(978-968-6042; 978-968-6147; 978-968-6347; 978-970-607; 978-970-22)* *Dist. by* **Continental Bk.**

Larousse, Editions (FRA) *(978-2-03)* *Dist. by* **HM.**

Larousse, Editions (FRA) *(978-2-03)* *Dist. by* **IPG Chicago.**

Larousse Kingfisher Chambers, Inc., *(978-0-7534; 978-1-85697)* 215 Park Ave., S., New York, NY 10003 USA (SAN 297-7540); 181 Ballardvale St., Wilmington, MA 01887
Dist(s): **Macmillan.**

Larry Huch Ministries, *(978-0-9745301)* Orders Addr.: P.O. Box 2197, Mansfield, TX 76063-0039 USA
E-mail: cory@larryhuchministries.com
Web site: http://www.larryhuchministries.com
Dist(s): **Anchor Distributors.**

Lars Muller Pubs. (CHE) *(978-3-907044; 978-3-906700; 978-3-907078; 978-3-03778)* *Dist. by* **Dist Art Pubs.**

Larson Learning, Inc., *(978-0-9639121; 978-1-58123; 978-1-887050)* Div. of Larson Texts, Inc., 1762 Norcross Rd., Erie, PA 16510-3838 USA Tel 814-824-6365; Fax: 814-824-6377; Toll Free: 800-530-2355
Web site: http://www.larsonlearning.com.

Larson Pubns., *(978-0-943914; 978-1-936012)* 4936 Rte. 414, Burdett, NY 14818 USA (SAN 241-130X) Tel 607-546-9342; Fax: 607-546-9344; Toll Free: 800-828-2197 Do not confuse with Larson Pubns., Joliet, IL
E-mail: larson@lightlink.com
Web site: http://www.larsonpublications.org
Dist(s): **National Bk. Network**
New Leaf Distributing Co., Inc.
Red Wheel/Weiser
ebrary, Inc.

Larstan Publishing, Inc., *(978-0-9764266; 978-0-9776895; 978-0-9789182)* 209 Canterbury Ct., Blue Bell, PA 19422 USA (SAN 256-3460) Fax: 707-922-7280
E-mail: sgenkin@larstan.net
Web site: http://www.theblackbooks.com.

LaRyssa K. Hodges, *(978-0-578-42133-9; 978-0-578-49315-2)* 5139 W. Headstall Trail, Phoenix, AZ 85083 USA Tel 770-312-2193
E-mail: laryssa68@icloud.com
Dist(s): **Ingram Content Group.**

Laser Productions *See* **Global Publishing**

Lash & Assocs. Publishing/Training, Inc., *(978-1-931117)* Orders Addr.: 100 Boardwalk Dr. Suite 150, Youngsville, NC 27596 USA Tel 919-556-0300 phone; Fax: 919-556-0900 fax
E-mail: keith@lapublishing.com
Web site: http://www.lapublishing.com.

Last Gasp Eco-Funnies, Incorporated *See* **Last Gasp of San Francisco**

Last Gasp of San Francisco, *(978-0-86719)* Orders Addr.: 777 Florida St., San Francisco, CA 94110 USA (SAN 216-8308); Edit Addr.: 777 Florida St., San Francisco, CA 94110-2025 USA (SAN 170-3242) Tel 415-824-6636; Fax: 415-824-1836; Toll Free: 800-366-5121
E-mail: colin@lastgasp.com
Web site: http://www.lastgasp.com
Dist(s): **SCB Distributors.**

Last Knight Publishing *See* **Last Knight Publishing Co.**

Last Knight Publishing Co., *(978-0-9720442)* P.O. Box 270006, Fort Collins, CO 80527 USA Tel 970-391-6857
Web site: http://www.lastknightpublishing.com
Dist(s): **Bks. West.**

Last Play Publishing, *(978-0-9760181)* 17931 Inverness Ave., Baton Rouge, LA 70810 USA Tel 225-751-6419
E-mail: djones@dow.com.

Lasting Bks. Publishing Co., *(978-0-9767511)* 8433 Briggs Dr., Roseville, CA 95747-5951 USA
E-mail: director@lastingbooks.com
Web site: http://www.lastingbooks.com.

Lata de Sal Editorial S.L. (ESP) *(978-84-940584; 978-84-941136; 978-84-941784; 978-84-942451; 978-84-942867)* *Dist. by* **Lectorum Pubns.**

Latham, Jon Bks., *(978-1-7322763)* 455 Bliss Ave., Clovis, CA 93611 USA Tel 559-900-7158
E-mail: mnjonman@gmail.com
Web site: www.jonlathambooks.com.

Latinarte *See* **I.Om.Be Pr.**

Latino, Frank Publishing Co., *(978-0-9640474)* 6806 Newport Lake Cir., Boca Raton, FL 33496 USA Tel 561-241-3880; Fax: 561-995-6975; Toll Free: 800-922-8565
E-mail: frank@hollyboy.com
Web site: http://www.hollyboy.com.

Latino Literacy Press *See* **Lectura Bks.**

Latitude 20 *Imprint of* **Univ. of Hawaii Pr.**

Lato, Greg, *(978-0-692-91633-9)* 16 Marian Ave, Narragansett, RI 02882 USA Tel 401-952-1581
E-mail: greglato@gmail.com.

Lauco Pr., *(978-0-692-32492-9; 978-0-692-48432-6; 978-0-9976422)* 8206 Kittama Dr., Clinton, MD 20735 USA Tel 3018683221; Toll Free: 3018683221
Dist(s): **CreateSpace Independent Publishing Platform.**

Laudati, Joe, *(978-0-615-20324-9; 978-0-578-06902-9)* 425 E. 76th St., No. 9B, New York, NY 10021-2516 USA Tel 212-737-3515
E-mail: joelaudati33@earthlink.net
Web site: http://www.joelaudati.com
Dist(s): **Lulu Pr., Inc.**

Lauerman, Rosalie, *(978-0-692-50783-4; 978-0-692-08224-9)* 1201 Redtail Cir., Woodstock, IL 60098 USA Tel 815-337-3501
E-mail: rosalielauerman@msn.com.

Laugh-A-Lot Bks., *(978-0-615-28469-9)* 25 W. Broadway, Apt. 310, Long Beach, NY 11561 USA
Web site: http://www.laughalotpoetry.com; http://www.laughalotbooks.com.

Laughing Baby Pubns., *(978-0-615-18948-2)* 3662 Big Spring Rd., Lake Almanor, CA 96137 USA Tel 530-596-4397
E-mail: jennifer@babyinspirations.net
Web site: http://www.laughingbabypublications.com.

Laughing Elephant, *(978-0-9621131; 978-1-883211; 978-1-59583; 978-1-5149)* Orders Addr.: 3645 Interlake Ave., N., Seattle, WA 98103 USA Tel 206-447-9229; Fax: 206-447-9189; Toll Free: 800-354-0400 (orders only); Edit Addr.: 4649 Sunnyside Ave., N., Seattle, WA 98103 USA (SAN 250-7722) Tel 206-632-7075; Fax: 206-632-0466; *Imprints:* Darling & Company (Darling & Comp); Green Tiger Press (Grn Tiger Pr)
E-mail: laughingelephant@laughingelephant.com
Web site: http://www.laughingelephant.com
Dist(s): **Ingram Publisher Services.**

Laughing Gull Pr., *(978-0-9726699)* P.O. Box 23272, Brooklyn, NY 11202-3272 USA
E-mail: laughinggullpress@earthlink.net.

Laughing Rhino Bks., *(978-0-9859603)* 23830 25th Dr. SE, Bothell, WA 98021 USA Tel 425-420-8144
E-mail: gordon.glessner@gmail.com
Web site: www.laughinrhinobooks.com.

Laughing Zebra - Bks. for Children *Imprint of* **J.O.Y. Publishing**

Laurel *Imprint of* **Random House Publishing Group**

Laurel & Herbert, Inc., *(978-0-9619155)* P.O. Box 440266, Sugarloaf Shores, FL 33044 USA (SAN 243-4687) Tel 305-745-3506; Fax: 305-745-9070.

Laurel Leaf *Imprint of* **Random Hse. Children's Bks.**

Laurel Press *See* **Laurel & Herbert, Inc.**

Laurel Rose Publishing, *(978-0-692-41643-3; 978-0-692-42391-2; 978-0-692-56797-5; 978-1-944583)* 1930 Holston Rd, Senatobia, MS 38619 USA Tel 6625196505; Toll Free: 6626120703
Web site: www.laurelrosepublishing.com
Dist(s): **CreateSpace Independent Publishing Platform.**

Laurel Valley Graphics, Inc., *(978-0-9717475; 978-0-9853454)* 1511 Monastery Dr., Latrobe, PA 15650 USA Fax: 724-532-1957
Web site: http://www.lvgraphics.net.

Lauren Elizabeth Design, *(978-0-9779594)* 2002 Duboin Rd, New Iberia, LA 70560 USA
E-mail: chad@turnkeybid.com.

Lauren Simone Publishing Company *See* **Lauren Simone Publishing Hse.**

Lauren Simone Publishing Hse., *(978-0-9979520; 978-1-948071)* 41 Henderson Dr., East Hartford, CT 06108 USA Tel 860-478-3897
E-mail: laurensimonepubs@gmail.com
Web site: http://laurensimonepubs.weebly.com/.

Laurob Pr., *(978-0-9787376)* 4204 Anjou Ct., Chico, CA 95973 USA.

Laurus Books *See* **Laurus Co., Inc., The**

Laurus Co., The, Orders Addr.: 524 Guinevere Court, McDonough, GA 30252 USA (SAN 858-608X) Tel 678-814-4047; Fax: 678-272-7255; Toll Free: 800-596-7370
E-mail: thelaurusco@charter.net
Web site: http://www.thelauruscompany.com.

LaVa Pubns., *(978-0-9638838; 978-0-9714261; 978-0-9761449; 978-0-9792400)* Div. of Field O Dreams Farm, Orders Addr.: P.O. Box 9372, Dothan, AL 36303 USA (SAN 255-2027)
E-mail: spharr@centurytel.net.

Lavabrook Publishing Group, *(978-0-9892064; 978-1-942662)* 234 Castillo St., Unit A, Santa Barbara, CA 93101 USA Tel 805-637-4813
E-mail: dricchiazzi@gmail.com.

Lavender Books *See* **Lavender Bks.**

Lavender Bks., *(978-0-9742739)* Orders Addr.: P.O. Box 3555, Culver City, CA 90231-3555 USA; Edit Addr.: 11111 Jefferson Blvd., Culver City, CA 90230 USA
E-mail: lavenderbooks333@sbcglobal.net.

Lavergne, Teresa *See* **Teresa E Lavergne**

Lavoie, Louis, *(978-0-9791018)* 1300 W. Medicine Lake Dr., No. 211, Plymouth, MN 55441 USA
E-mail: lavoielouis6@hotmail.com.

Law Offices of Harry Glick, *(978-0-9717419)* 100 Quentin Rossevelt Blvd. No. 511, Garden City, NY 11530 USA Tel 516-456-1088; Fax: 805-473-9025
Web site: http://www.harryglick.com.

Lawe Street Bks., *(978-0-9713179)* 1818 S. Lawe St., Appleton, WI 54915 USA Tel 920-739-4577
E-mail: stedjee@aol.com.

Lawells Publishing, *(978-0-934981)* P.O. Box 1338, Royal Oak, MI 48068-1338 USA (SAN 694-602X) Tel 248-543-5297
E-mail: lawells@tm.net
Web site: http://www.lawells.net.

LawMux Pr. *Imprint of* **Skelley, James**

Lawrence Educational Services, Inc., *(978-1-932959; 978-1-59699)* Orders Addr.: P.O. Box 6256, Bridgewater, NJ 08807 USA Tel 908-575-8830; Fax: 908-704-1730; Toll Free: 800-575-7670; Edit Addr.: 674 Rte. 202-206 N, Suite 4, Bridgewater, NJ 08807 USA
E-mail: llteach5757670@aol.com
Web site: http://www.llteach.com.

Lawrence Publishing, *(978-0-9716039)* Div. of Educational Services & Publications, 2935 E. Rose Ln., Phoenix, AZ 85016 USA Tel 602-912-9553 Do not confuse with companies with the same or similar names in Flower Mound, TX, Van Nuys, CA, Los Angeles, CA, Wichita, KS, Baton Rouge, LA
E-mail: llawre2222@aol.com; walton90@alltel.net.

Lawson, Archie B., *(978-0-9762660)* 1168 Shashas Way, Riverton, UT 84065-4111 USA Tel 801-302-0440
E-mail: archiebl@msn.com.

Lawson, Tracy, *(978-0-9966108)* 702 Lipscomb Ave., Dallas, TX 75214 USA Tel 614-439-6291; *Imprints:* DysCovered Publishing (DysCovered)
E-mail: tracy.s.lawson@gmail.com
Web site: http://counteractbook.com.

Layla the Ladybug Bk. Publishing, *(978-0-692-59563-3; 978-0-9988693)* P.O. Box 3246, McKinney, TX 75070 USA Tel 817-504-9094
E-mail: lemonscd7@yahoo.com.

Layman Theologian Ministries, *(978-0-692-13099-5; 978-0-692-13100-8; 978-0-692-14894-5; 978-0-692-16646-8; 978-0-692-17632-0; 978-0-578-44392-8; 978-0-578-50562-6)* 597 W. Burrough Rd., BOWDOIN, ME 04287 USA Tel 207-248-1007
E-mail: davidthms600@gmail.com
Dist(s): **Ingram Content Group.**

Layne Morgan Media, Inc., *(978-0-9762904; 978-0-9772007; 978-0-9774803; 978-1-4265)* 2101 W. Chesterfield Blvd. Ste. A102, Springfield, MO 65807-8672 USA
E-mail: kimberlym@laynemorgan.com
Web site: http://www.laynemorgan.com.

LB Kids *Imprint of* **Little, Brown Bks. for Young Readers**

LBF Bks., LLC, *(978-0-9754533; 978-0-9773082)* Orders Addr.: P.O. Box 7989, Pittsburgh, PA 15216 USA; Edit Addr.: 1537 Dormont Ave., Pittsburgh, PA 15216 USA
E-mail: lbf@lbfbooks.com.

LBF/Hadrosaur *Imprint of* **Hadrosaur Pr.**

Publisher Name Index

L'Chaim Pubns., *(978-0-9766946)* 521 Fifth Ave., Suite 1740, New York, NY 10175 USA
E-mail: lchaim@att.biz
Web site: http://lchaimpublications.com/.

LD Bks., Inc., *(978-0-9772669; 978-0-9785897; 978-1-939048; 978-1-940281; 978-1-943387)* 8313 NW 68th St., Miami, FL 33166 USA (SAN 631-8088) Tel 305-406-2292; Fax: 305-406-2293
E-mail: vilmac@ldbooks.com; sales@ldbooks.com
Web site: http://www.sinlimites.net; http://www.ldbooks.com.

LD Coach, LLC, *(978-0-9745938; 978-0-9764112)* 1401 Johnson Ferry Rd., Suite 328-C13, Marietta, GA 30062-5241 USA Toll Free: 888-848-6224
E-mail: bill.allen@ldcoach.com
Web site: http://www.ldcoach.com.

LDS & Assocs., *(978-1-883574)* Orders Addr.: 13681 Newport Ave., Suite 8 #831, Tustin, CA 92780 USA Toll Free: 800-331-3610
E-mail: trainers@ldsassoc.com
Web site: http://www.ldsassoc.com.

Le Bk. Moderne, LLC, *(978-0-9768450)* 2849 W. 23rd Ave., Denver, CO 80211 USA Tel 303-523-6401; *Imprints:* Giggletins (Gigglet)
E-mail: michael@lebookmoderne.com
Web site: http://www.lebookmoderne.com.

Le Gendre, Kimaada, *(978-1-7326320)* 115-44 217th St., Queens, NY 11411 USA Tel 917-795-5344
E-mail: naturebellainc@gmail.com.

Le Petit Chien, *(978-0-9717019)* 2415 Daybreaker Dr., Park City, UT 84098 USA.

Le Reve Enterprises, LLC *See* **13th & Joan**

Le Robert (FRA) *(978-2-85036; 978-2-84902) Dist. by* **Distribks Inc.**

Le Robert (FRA) *(978-2-85036; 978-2-84902) Dist. by* **Continental Bk.**

Le Rue Publishing, *(978-0-9985437; 978-1-7335960; 978-1-951714)* 320 S. Boston Ave., Ste. 1030, Tulsa, OK 74103 USA Tel 918-216-0180
E-mail: robertsdenton@gmail.com
Web site: www.leruepublishing.com.

Lead Life Pr., LLC, *(978-0-9762408)* The Lead Life Institute, 2111 Deerfield Dr., New Hope, PA 18938 USA Tel 215 794 8516; Fax: 215 794 8532
E-mail: mdec@leadlifeinstitute.com.

Lead U, *(978-0-578-55634-5)* 511 3rd Ave., Asbury Park, NJ 07712 USA Tel 732-998-4027
E-mail: jd.wilson@leaduthere.com
Web site: www.leaduthere.com.

Leaderbrook, *(978-0-9719079)* P.O. Box 864, Amherst, OH 44001-0864 USA Tel 440-985-5844
E-mail: timothy@clevelandceo.com
Web site: http://www.leaderbrook.com.

LeaderMetrix Inc., *(978-1-7325236)* 3321 Caldeira Dr., Livermore, CA 94550 USA Tel 408-832-8111
E-mail: gary@leadermetrix.com
Web site: www.leadermetrix.com.

Leaders Pr., *(978-0-9831547; 978-1-943386)* ul Okolna 83 F Poland, Czestochowa, NY 42-200 USA Tel 060-477-2048
E-mail: alina.rutkowska@gmail.com
Dist(s): **Blackstone Audio, Inc.**
Ingram Publisher Services.

Leadership Development Group, The, *(978-0-692-21198-4; 978-0-578-44950-0; 978-0-578-76418-4)* 1043 Grand Ave., St Paul, MN 55105 USA Tel 651-399-3556
E-mail: dd@theLDG.org
Web site: www.theLDG.org.

Leadership Horizons, LLC, *(978-0-9668868)* 959 Keystone Way, Carmel, IN 46032-2823 USA Tel 317-844-5587; Fax: 317-581-9226; Toll Free: 888-262-2477
E-mail: ron@leadershiphorizons.com.

Leadership Loft, The *See* **Green Owl, Inc.**

LeaderTreks NFP, *(978-1-934577; 978-1-939031)* 25w560 Geneva Rd. #30, Carol Stream, IL 60188 USA Tel 630-668-0936; Fax: 630-668-0980; Toll Free: 800-502-0699
E-mail: danc@leadertreks.com; angie@leadertreks.com
Web site: http://www.leadertreks.com; http://www.leadertreks.org.

Leading Lady Pubns., *(978-0-9776746; 978-0-9798084; 978-0-9802468; 978-0-9818753)* Orders Addr.: P.O. Box 35, Worton, MD 21678 USA Toll Free: 800-597-9428; Edit Addr.: 306 Sunrise Ave., Ridgely, MD 21660 USA
Web site: http://www.publishyourchristianbook.com
Dist(s): **CreateSpace Independent Publishing Platform**
Lushena Bks.

Leadline Publishing, *(978-0-9801464)* Orders Addr.: 2101 NW Corporate Blvd Ste 206, Boca Raton, FL 33431 USA
Web site: http://www.teamfroglogic.com.

Leaf & Vine Bks, *(978-0-9786087; 978-0-615-18762-4)* 387 Ivy St., San Francisco, CA 94102 USA
E-mail: editor@leafvinebooks.com
Dist(s): **Lulu Pr., Inc.**

Leaf Publishing, LLC, *(978-0-692-19308-2; 978-0-578-44020-0; 978-0-578-49097-7; 978-0-578-51021-7)* 1470 Baracoa Ave., Coral Gables, FL 33146 USA Tel 305-725-8821
E-mail: amy.l.erwin@comcast.net.

Leaf Storm Pr., *(978-0-9914105; 978-0-9970207; 978-1-945652)* P.O. Box 4670, Santa Fe, NM 87502 USA (SAN 920-7406)
E-mail: LeafStormPress@gmail.com
Web site: http://leafstormpress.com
Dist(s): **Legato Pubs. Group**
Publishers Group West (PGW).

Leafcollecting.com Publishing Co., *(978-0-9747654)* 189 N. Jefferson Ave., Bradley, IL 60915-1829 USA Tel 815-932-0850; *Imprints:* Egap Gifa Books (Egap Gifa Bks)
E-mail: Darlene@leafcollecting.com; Thegreatlakes189@yahoo.com
Web site: http://www.leafcollecting.com.

Leafcutter Pr., LLC, *(978-0-9818734; 978-0-9997992)* P.O. Box 102, Southworth, WA 98386 USA (SAN 856-7999) Tel 360-990-5422
E-mail: kevinhwirth@gmail.com.

Leafwood Pubs. *Imprint of* **Abilene Christian Univ. Pr.**

Leah Venegas, *(978-0-578-40046-4; 978-0-578-41972-5)* 1017 Klondyke Loop, Somers, MT 59932 USA Tel 406-858-0496
E-mail: leah@leahvenegas.com
Dist(s): **Ingram Content Group.**

Lean Pr., *(978-1-932475)* Div. of Hopefuls, Inc., Orders Addr.: P.O. Box 80334, Portland, OR 97280-1334 USA (SAN 255-6286) Tel 503-708-4415; Fax: 503-626-9098
E-mail: sean@leanpress.com; mike@leanpress.com
Web site: http://www.leanpress.com.

Leaning Rock Pr., *(978-0-9994985; 978-0-9998744; 978-1-7328519; 978-1-950323)* P.O. Box 44, Gales Ferry, CT 06335 USA Tel 860-464-6454; 860-235-2552
E-mail: leaningrockpress.gmail.com; bobrobinnelson@hotmail.com
Web site: www.colibrichildrensadventures.com; www.colibrichildrenspress.com; www.leaningrockpress.com.

Leap Bks., *(978-1-61603)* P.O. Box 112, Reidsville, NC 27320-0112 USA (SAN 858-5431)
E-mail: leapbks@gmail.com
Web site: http://www.leapbks.com.

Leap Forward Pubns., *(978-0-9743664)* 12108 Scribe Dr., Austin, TX 78759-3133 USA
E-mail: mjanthony@sbcglobal.net.

L.E.A.P. (Learning through an Expanded Arts Program, Inc), *(978-0-9713649)* 441 W. End Ave., Suite 2G, New York, NY 10024 USA Tel 212-769-4160; Fax: 212-724-4479
E-mail: leap@leapnyc.org
Web site: http://www.leapnyc.org.

Leap Year Marketing, *(978-0-692-08633-9; 978-0-692-17389-3)* 18 Towle Pasture Dr., EPSOM, NH 03234 USA Tel 603-344-8843
E-mail: jmrwtpl@gmail.com
Dist(s): **Ingram Content Group.**

LeapFrog Enterprises, Inc., *(978-1-58605; 978-1-932256; 978-1-59319; 978-1-60685)* 6401 Hollis St., Suite 125, Emeryville, CA 94608 USA Tel 510-420-5000; Fax: 510-596-6821; *Imprints:* LeapFrog School House (LeapSchHse)
E-mail: crymer@leapfrog.com; leo_lui@vtech.com; mtellegen@leapfrog.com
Web site: http://www.leapfrog.com.

Leapfrog Pr., *(978-0-9654578; 978-0-9679520; 978-0-9728984; 978-0-9796415; 978-0-9815148; 978-1-935248; 978-1-948585)* Orders Addr.: P.O. Box 2110, Teaticket, MA 02536 USA; Edit Addr.: 59 Tanglewood Dr., Teaticket, MA 02536 USA Do not confuse with Leapfrog Pr., Wyandotte, MI
E-mail: books@leapfrogpress.com; lisa@leapfrogpress.com
Web site: http://www.leapfrogpress.com
Dist(s): **Consortium Bk. Sales & Distribution**
MyiLibrary
SPD-Small Pr. Distribution.

Leapfrog Press, Incorporated, The *See* **Leapfrog Pr.**

LeapFrog Schl. Hse. *Imprint of* **LeapFrog Enterprises, Inc.**

Leaping Antelope Productions, *(978-0-9659222; 978-0-9762059)* Div. of Armadillo Pr., Orders Addr.: 101 Industrial Way Ste. 10, Belmont, CA 94002-8207 USA (SAN 253-7974) Toll Free: 888-909-5327
E-mail: print123@leapingantelope.com
Web site: http://www.leapingantelope.com
Dist(s): **Distributors, The**
Quality Bks., Inc.

Learn & Sign Funtime *See* **Learn & Sign Funtime Bks.**

Learn & Sign Funtime Bks., *(978-0-9753717)* Orders Addr.: 0255 E. Yellowstone Trail, Hamlet, IN 46532 USA Tel 219-775-7080; Fax: 888-308-2606; 0255 E. Yellowstone Trail Hamlet, In 46532, Hamlet, IN 46532
E-mail: learnandsign@aol.com; jujub121@aol.com.

Learn As You Grow, L.L.C., *(978-0-9824652)* P.O. Box 103, Mount Horeb, WI 53572 USA
E-mail: chad.lindley@learnasyougrow.com.

Learn2study, *(978-0-9729557)* 1935 Columbia Pike No. 24, Arlington, VA 22204 USA
Web site: http://www.learn2study.org.

Learning Abilities Bks., *(978-0-9658853; 978-0-9720267)* 166 Glyndale Cir., Brunswick, GA 31520 USA (SAN 850-3087) Tel 912-264-5308; Fax: 775-305-0063; Toll Free: 800-779-5088
E-mail: contactlab@gate.net
Web site: http://www.gate.net/~labooks.

Learning All About Me, LLC, *(978-0-9763961)* Orders Addr.: P.O. Box 161923, Boiling Springs, SC 29316 USA; Edit Addr.: 8 Montford Ave., Boiling Springs, SC 29316 USA.

Learning Challenge, Inc., *(978-1-59203)* 36 Washington St., Wellesley, MA 02481 USA Tel 781-239-9900; Fax: 781-239-3273
Web site: http://www.learningchallenge.com.

Learning Connection, The, *(978-1-56831)* Orders Addr.: 4100 Silver Star Rd. Ste. D, Orlando, FL 32808-4618 USA Toll Free: 800-218-8489
Web site: http://www.tlconnection.com.

Learning Curve Brands, Incorporated *See* **TOMY International, Inc.**

Learning Fasten-Ations, Inc., *(978-0-9673268; 978-0-9729476)* 5014-16th Ave., Suite 195, Brooklyn, NY 11204 USA Tel 718-854-3808; Fax: 718-854-9436; Toll Free: 800-252-8152
Web site: http://www.velcroboards.com.

Learning in Motion, *(978-1-889775)* 113 Cooper St., Santa Cruz, CA 95060-4526 USA Toll Free: 800-560-5670 Do not confuse with Learning in Motion, Mount Laurel, NJ
Web site: http://www.learn.motion.com.

Learning Line Media, The, *(978-0-9831191; 978-0-9971257)* 451 A E. Ojai Ave., Ojai, CA 93023 USA Tel 805-218-2443
E-mail: dave@ojaidigital.com; dreeser@davidreeser.com; dvw@thelearninglinemedia.com
Web site: bluejayink.com.

Learning Links Inc., *(978-0-7675; 978-0-88122; 978-0-934048; 978-1-56982)* Orders Addr.: 26 Haypress Road, Cranbury, NJ 08512 USA (SAN 241-3302) Tel 516-437-9071; Fax: 516-437-5392; Toll Free: 800-724-2616
E-mail: info@learninglinks.com
Web site: http://www.learninglinks.com; http://www.novel-ties.com/estore/search/.

Learning Management Systems *See* **Active Learning Corp.**

Learning Net, The, *(978-1-887946)* 567 Catnip Rd., Cullowhee, NC 28723 USA Tel 828-293-2542.

Learning Parent, The, *(978-0-9708770; 978-0-9777685; 978-0-9785859; 978-0-9860433)* 2430 Sunnymeade Rd., Rustburg, VA 24588 USA Tel 434-845-8345; Fax: 434-845-3020
E-mail: learningparent@aol.com
Web site: http://www.thelearningparent.com.

Learning Props, *(978-0-9741549; 978-0-9768706; 978-1-935292)* P.O. Box 774, Racine, WI 53401 USA Toll Free: 877-776-7750
E-mail: bev@learningprops.com
Web site: http://www.learningprops.com
Dist(s): **Follett School Solutions.**

Learning Research Associates, Incorporated *See* **National Reading Styles Institute, Inc.**

Learning Resources, Inc., *(978-1-56911)* 380 N. Fairway Dr., Vernon Hills, IL 60061 USA (SAN 630-057X) Tel 847-573-8400; Fax: 847-573-8425
E-mail: info@learningresources.com
Web site: http://www.learningresources.com.

Learning Series Pr., *(978-0-9769701)* P.O. Box 590812, Fort Lauderdale, FL 33359 USA (SAN 256-6060) Tel 954-552-4855
E-mail: mdgeddes@comcast.net
Web site: http://www.learningtodream.com.

Learning to Give, *(978-0-9774155)* 16924 Buchanan St., Grand Haven, MI 49417-8625 USA
Web site: http://www.learningtogive.org.

Learning Together, *(978-1-931840)* 5509b W. Friendly Ave. Ste. 201, Greensboro, NC 27410-4279 USA
E-mail: wtlecl@aol.com.

Learning Tools Co., *(978-0-938017)* Orders Addr.: P.O. Box 657, Berkeley Springs, WV 25411 USA (SAN 692-7297) Tel 304-258-1304; Edit Addr.: 714 Rockwell St., Berkeley Springs, WV 25422 USA.

Learning Wood, LLC, *(978-1-933577)* 3535 W. Peterson Ave., Chicago, IL 60659 USA Tel 773-509-0707; Fax: 773-509-0404.

Learning Works, The *Imprint of* **Creative Teaching Pr., Inc.**

Learning Wrap-Ups, Inc., *(978-0-943343; 978-1-59204)* 1660 West Gordon Ave., No. 4, Layton, UT 84041 USA (SAN 668-3975) Tel 801-497-0050; Fax: 801-497-0063; Toll Free: 800-992-4966
E-mail: info@learningwrapups.com
Web site: http://www.learningwrapups.com.

Learning ZoneXpress, *(978-1-57175)* Orders Addr.: P.O. Box 1022, Owatonna, MN 55060 USA Tel 507-455-9076; Fax: 507-455-3380; Toll Free: 888-455-7003
E-mail: customerservice@learningzonexpress.com
Web site: http://www.learningzonexpress.com
Dist(s): **Follett School Solutions.**

LearningExpress, LLC, *(978-1-57685; 978-1-61103)* 2 Rector St., Flr. 26, New York, NY 10006-3754 USA Tel 646-274-6453; 800-295-9556
E-mail: info@learnatest.com; customerservice@learnatest.com
Web site: http://www.learnatest.com
Dist(s): **MyiLibrary**
National Bk. Network
ebrary, Inc.

LearningSuccess Pr., *(978-0-9772350)* 1147 E. Main St., Ventura, CA 93001 USA (SAN 257-0726) Tel 805-648-1739
Web site: http://www.learningsuccessinstitute.com.

Learnovation, LLC, *(978-0-9705790; 978-0-9796434; 978-0-9969528)* Orders Addr.: P.O. Box 502150, Indianapolis, IN 46250 USA (SAN 255-4577); Edit Addr.: 10831 Thistle Ridge, Fishers, IN 46038 USA Tel 317-577-1190; Fax: 317-598-0816; Toll Free: 888-577-1190
E-mail: anna@learnovation.com; karen@learnovation.com
Web site: http://learnovation.com.

Leatherbound Bestsellers, *(978-1-62715)* Orders Addr.: 20325 N. 51st. Ave. Suite 134, Glendale, AZ 85308 USA Tel 602-616-4334
E-mail: leatherboundbestsellers@gmail.com
Web site: www.leatherboundbestsellers.com.

Leatherbound Booksellers *See* **Leatherbound Bestsellers**

Leatherman, Diane *See* **Bounty Project, The**

Leathers Publishing, *(978-0-9646898; 978-1-890622; 978-1-58597)* Div. of Ad Ctr., 4500 College Blvd., Overland Park, KS 66211-1760 USA Tel 913-498-2625; Fax: 913-498-1561; Toll Free: 888-888-7696
E-mail: barbara@leatherspublishing.com
Web site: http://www.leatherspublishing.com.

Leatherwood Press *See* **Walnut Springs Bks.**

Leatherwood Publishing, *(978-0-9741725)* 20395 Cty. 86, Long Prairie, MN 56347 USA Tel 320-732-2879
E-mail: tann0042@umn.edu
Web site: http://www.alexweb.net/whimsy/index.htm.

Leave No Sister Behind Pubns., *(978-0-9787004)* Orders Addr.: 13 Pecan Ln., Long Beach, MS 39560 USA (SAN 851-3759)
E-mail: info@leavenosisterbehind.net
Web site: http://www.leavenosisterbehind.net
Dist(s): **Ingram Content Group.**

LeBlanc, Terry Leonard, *(978-0-9755913)* Orders Addr.: P.O. Box 387, Loyalton, CA 96118 USA; Edit Addr.: 805 Mill St., Loyalton, CA 96118 USA
E-mail: terrythetrashman@cwo.com.

Lectio Ediciones (ESP) *(978-84-96754; 978-84-15088) Dist. by* **IPG Chicago.**

LectoCultura *Imprint of* **Diaz, Olga L**

Lectorum Pubns., Inc., *(978-0-9625162; 978-1-880507; 978-1-930332; 978-1-933032; 978-1-941802; 978-1-63245; 978-1-64684)* Orders Addr.: 205 Chubb Ave, Lyndhurst, NJ 07071 USA (SAN 990-0802) Tel 201-559-2232; Edit Addr.: 205 Chubb Ave., Lyndhurst, NJ 07071 USA (SAN 860-0597) Tel 201-559-2200; Fax: 201-559-2201; Toll Free Fax: 877-532-8676; Toll Free: 800-345-5946
E-mail: acorrea@lectorum.com
Web site: http://www.lectorum.com; http://www.librerialectorum.com
Dist(s): **Children's Plus, Inc.**
Libros Sin Fronteras
MyiLibrary
Perfection Learning Corp.

Lectorum, S.A. de C.V. (MEX) *(978-968-7748; 978-968-5270; 978-970-732) Dist. by* **LD Bks Inc.**

Lectura Bks., *(978-0-9716580; 978-0-9772852; 978-1-60448)* 1107 Fair Oaks Ave., Suite 225, South Pasadena, CA 91030 USA
E-mail: ktdelmonte@lecturabooks.com; info@lecturabooks.com
Web site: http://www.lecturabooks.com.

Lectura Colaborativa (ARG) *(978-987-45) Dist. by* **IPG Chicago.**

Lederer/Messianic Jewish Publishers & Distributors *See* **Messianic Jewish Pubs.**

Ledford Publishing, *(978-0-9840777; 978-1-951466)* 16117 Hwy 101 S No. 64, BROOKINGS, OR 97415 USA (SAN 858-3587) Tel 541-661-8170
E-mail: dledford11@gmail.com
Web site: http://www.fructosemalabsorptionhelp.com; http://www.brewtourbooks.com/; https://rardledford.homesteadcloud.com/.

L'Edge Pr., *(978-0-9762014; 978-1-935256)* P.O. Box 1653, Boone, NC 28607 USA
E-mail: jeffhendley@charter.net
Web site: http://www.upsidedownministries.com.

LeDor Publishing, *(978-0-9747382)* 4885 McKnight Rd., No. 350, Pittsburgh, PA 15237 USA Tel 888-624-9094; Fax: 412-421-1628; Toll Free: 888-624-9094
E-mail: drichman@ledorgroup.com
Web site: http://www.ledorgroup.com.

Lee & Low Bks., Inc., *(978-0-89239; 978-1-880000; 978-1-885008; 978-1-58430; 978-1-60060; 978-1-62014; 978-1-64379)* 95 Madison Ave., New York, NY 10016 USA (SAN 920-7546) Tel 212-779-4400 (General info./Editorial); Fax: 212-683-1894 (orders); Toll Free: 888-320-3190 (ext. 28, orders); *Imprints:* Tu Books (Tu Books); Children's Book Press (ChilBkPr); Shen's Books (ShensBks)
E-mail: clow@leeandlow.com
Web site: http://www.leeandlow.com
Dist(s): **Children's Plus, Inc.**
Follett School Solutions
Lectorum Pubns., Inc.
Perfection Learning Corp.

Lee Bks., *(978-0-9660653)* Orders Addr.: 514 Jamacha Rd., No. 16J, El Cajon, CA 92019 USA Tel 619-447-8789 Do not confuse with other companies with the same or similar names in San Anselmo, CA, Columbia, SC
E-mail: leebooks@juno.com
Web site: http://www.readatleebooks.com.

Lee, Collin, *(978-0-692-82896-0; 978-0-692-82897-7)*
E-mail: jeffwcrawford5+LVP0003213@gmail.com; jeffwcrawford5+LVP0003213@gmail.com.

Lee, Deborah I, *(978-0-9858839)* 3800 Bexley Sq., Reno, NV 89503 USA Tel 775-848-7797
E-mail: debbaleereno@yahoo.com.

Lee Enterprise Group *See* **Lee's Pr. and Publishing Co.**

Lee, Howard, *(978-0-9766137)* 191 Lorraine Dr., Berkeley Heights, NJ 07922 USA.

Lee Instruments, *(978-0-9704913)* Orders Addr.: P.O. Box 460-999, Leeds, UT 84746 USA; Edit Addr.: 555 E. 900 N., Leeds, UT 84746 USA; 1050 N. Main, Leeds, UT 84746 USA Tel 435-879-6907
E-mail: leeinst@infowest.com; violguy@infowest.com
Web site: http://kevinleeluthier.com.

Lee, J. & L. Co., *(978-0-934904)* P.O. Box 5575, Lincoln, NE 68505 USA (SAN 213-8557) Tel 402-488-4416; Fax: 402-489-2770; Toll Free: 888-665-0999
E-mail: leebooks@radiks.net
Web site: http://www.leebooksellers.com
Dist(s): **Big River Distribution.**

Lee, James V. *See* **Salado Pr., LLC**

Lee, Keith Russel Publishing *See* **Lee, Keith Russel Publishing Hse.**

Lee, Keith Russel Publishing Hse., *(978-0-9768684)* 6223 Spruce St., Philadelphia, PA 19139 USA
E-mail: krlteaches@gmail.com
Web site: http://www.keithrlee.com.

Lee, Michael, *(978-0-9766830)* 5503 Harvard, Detroit, MI 48224 USA.

Lee, Quentin Daschel, *(978-0-9789007)* 4949 Harris Ave., Las Vegas, NV 89110 USA (SAN 851-867X) Tel 702-463-9692.

Lee, Shelley, *(978-0-9786757)* Orders Addr.: 441 Frazee Ave., Suite A, Bowling Green, OH 43402-1834 USA Tel 419-354-4673
E-mail: bgpc@wcnet.org
Web site: http://BeforeIKnewYou.com.

LeeBurton Publishing, *(978-0-9768307; 978-0-692-36454-3; 978-0-9963863)* 1112 S. Holly Dr., Sioux Falls, SD 57105 USA Tel 605-334-8149; Fax: 605-334-2479
E-mail: compasscse@sio.midco.net.

Leedan Publishing, *(978-1-893802; 978-0-9991828)* 65 S. Orchard Dr., Park Forest, IL 60466 USA Tel 858-999-4329
E-mail: antigone.blackwell@hotmail.com
Web site: www.adsloane.com.

Leelanau Pr., *(978-0-9742068; 978-0-9785465)* 6898 MacFarlane Rd., Glen Arbor, MI 49636 USA
Web site: leelanaupress.com
Dist(s): **Partners Bk. Distributing, Inc.**

Lee's Pr. and Publishing Co., *(978-0-615-78939-2; 978-0-692-62219-3; 978-0-692-63484-4; 978-0-692-69067-3; 978-0-692-69812-9; 978-0-692-72335-7; 978-0-692-74689-9; 978-0-9978623; 978-0-9993103; 978-1-7329441)* 3310 Rehobeth Church Rd Apt S, Greensboro, NC 27406 USA Tel 3362809845
Dist(s): **CreateSpace Independent Publishing Platform.**

Leeth, Dawna, *(978-0-9799184)* Orders Addr.: 400 W. Bay Dr., Largo, FL 33770 USA Fax: 727-536-6863.

Leeway Pubs., *(978-0-9744929)* Div. of Leeway Artisans, Orders Addr.: P.O. Box 1577, Laurel, MD 20707 USA Tel 301-404-3355
E-mail: info@LeewayArtisans.com
Web site: http://www.LeewayArtisans.com.

Lefall & Co., Inc., *(978-0-9761778)* 2020 Edmondson Ave., Baltimore, MD 21223 USA (SAN 256-2596)
E-mail: lefallandco@aol.com
Web site: http://www.jockobook.com.

Leffler, Susan, *(978-0-9906244)* P.O. Box 4352, Tumwater, WA 98501 USA Tel 360-866-1841
E-mail: whitestarloghome@hotmail.com.

Left - Write Ink, *(978-0-9761301)* 8407 Shadow Oaks, College Station, TX 77845 USA (SAN 256-2383) Tel 979-693-0224
E-mail: lwink2@aol.com.

Left Brain Craft Brain, *(978-0-692-78236-1)* 516 Balra Dr., EL CERRITO, CA 94530 USA Tel 510-909-4971.

Left Field,Angel Gate,

Left Hand Pubs., LLC, *(978-0-9996839; 978-1-949241)* 1417 Sadler Rd. No. 245, Fernandina Beach, FL 32034 USA Tel 980-505-7677
E-mail: editor@lefthandpublishers.com
Web site: http://LeftHandPublishers.com.

Left Hand Publishing Co., *(978-0-9744799)* P.O. Box 253, Moose Lake, MN 55767 USA
E-mail: nemadji@computerpro.com
Web site: http://computerpro.com/~nemadji.

Left Paw Pr., *(978-0-9818360; 978-0-615-17884-4; 978-0-9829132; 978-0-9838044; 978-1-943356)* Orders Addr.: P.O. Box 133, Greens Fork, IN 47345 USA; Edit Addr.: 17 Washington Blvd., Greens Fork, IN 47345 USA
E-mail: lauren@laurenoriginals.com
Web site: http://www.leftpawpress.com
Dist(s): **Lulu Pr., Inc.**

Left Shoe Lost, *(978-0-9986932)* 66 Maple Ave, Maplewood, NJ 07040 USA Tel 310-614-0693
E-mail: daelo@me.com.

Legacies & Memories, *(978-0-9759533; 978-0-9972523; 978-1-7322135; 978-1-7347007)* 5 Willard Dr., No. 644, Saint Augustine, FL 32086 USA
E-mail: info@legaciesandmemories.com
Web site: http://www.legaciesandmemories.com.

Legacy *Imprint of* **WordWright.biz, Inc.**

Legacy Book Publishing, Incorporated *See* **Legacy Family History, Inc.**

Legacy Bound, *(978-0-9677057; 978-0-9766264; 978-0-9794202; 978-0-9801045; 978-0-9819307; 978-0-9835189; 978-0-9883508; 978-0-9904014)* 5 N. Central Ave., Ely, MN 55731 USA Tel 800-909-9698; *Imprints:* Curious Cat Books (Curious Cat Bks)
E-mail: laura@legacybound.net; brad@legacybound.net
Web site: http://www.legacybound.net
Dist(s): **Baker & Taylor Publisher Services (BTPS)**
Brodart Co.
Eastern National
Follet Higher Education Grp.

Legacy Bound, Inc *See* **Legacy Bound**

Legacy Family History, Inc., *(978-0-9655835; 978-0-9716705; 978-0-9998770)* 5902 Woodshire Ln., Highland, UT 84003 USA Tel 801-763-1686 (phone/fax)
E-mail: tristantolman@comcast.net
Dist(s): **Send The Light Distribution LLC.**

Legacy Group Productions, LLC, *(978-0-9740585)* 3980 Greenmount Rd., Harrisonburg, VA 22802-0504 USA Toll Free: 877-227-6027
E-mail: cheryl@legacymatters.org
Web site: http://www.legacymatters.org.

Legacy Planning Partners, LLC, *(978-0-9719177; 978-0-9823220)* 254 Plaza Dr., Suite B, Oviedo, FL 32765 USA Tel 407-977-8080; Fax: 407-977-8078
E-mail: peggy@hoytbryan.com.

Legacy Pr. *Imprint of* **Rainbow Pubs. & Legacy Pr.**

Legacy Pr., *(978-0-9653198; 978-0-9777897)* 11381 Mallard Dr., Rochester, IL 62563 USA Tel 217-498-8159; Fax: 217-498-7178 Do not confuse with companies with the same or similar name in Pensacola, FL, Fort Lauderdale, FL, Columbus, GA, Thinelander, WI, Sacremento, CA, Hollywood, FL, Fairfax, VA, Argle, TX
E-mail: legacypressbooks@aol.com
Web site: http://legacypress.homestead.com.

Legacy Pr. of Florida, inc, *(978-0-9980128; 978-1-947718)* 1883 Lee Rd., Winter Park, FL 32789 USA Tel 407-647-3787; Fax: 321-594-7637
E-mail: gabrielvaughn@earthlink.net
Web site: LegacyBookPublishing.com.

Legacy Pubns., *(978-0-933101)* Subs. of Pace Communications, Inc., Orders Addr.: 1301 Carolina St., Greensboro, NC 27401 USA (SAN 860-4495) Tel 800-248-3204; Fax: 336-378-8271 Do not confuse with companies with the same or similar name in Tumon GU, Overland KS, Brentwood TN, Canyon TX, Irving TX, Lilburn GA, Midlothian, VA
E-mail: legacy.publications@paceco.com
Web site: http://www.legacypublications.com.

Legacy Pubs., *(978-1-932957)* 1866 Oak Harbor Dr., Ocean Isle Beach, NC 28469 USA Tel 910-755-6873 Do not confuse with Legacy Publishers in Natural Bridge, VA, Austin, TX
E-mail: mtdixon@atmc.net.

Legacy Pubs., *(978-0-9754685)* 12126 Trotwood Dr., Austin, TX 78753 USA Tel 512-837-5366 Do not confuse with Legacy Publishers in Snellville GA, Natural Bridge VA
E-mail: legacypublishers@austin.rr.com.

Legacy Pubs. International, *(978-1-880809)* P.O. Box 9690, Rcho Santa Fe, CA 92067-4690 USA (SAN 257-0718)
E-mail: Michele@LegacyPublishersInternational.com; dmiller@hccweb.org
Web site: http://www.LegacyPublishersInternational.com
Dist(s): **Destiny Image Pubs.**

Legacy Publishing Services, Inc., *(978-0-9628733; 978-0-9708395; 978-0-9764982; 978-0-9776777; 978-1-934449; 978-1-937952)* 1883 Lee Rd. Ste. B, Winter Park, FL 32789-2108 USA Tel 407-647-3787 Do not confuse with companies with the same or similar name in Ojai, CA, Berkeley, CA, Atlanta, GA, West Chester, OH, Birmingham, AL, Daty, TX, Fort Meyers, Fl, Baton Rouge, LA
E-mail: legacybookpublishing@yahoo.com; legacypublishing@earthlink.net
Web site: http://www.legacybookpublishing.com
Dist(s): **BookBaby.**

Legacy Tree, LLC, *(978-0-9974834)* 19537 Lake Rd., Rocky River, OH 44116 USA Tel 216-509-2828
E-mail: ckozak@scratchoffworks.com
Web site: www.thejesusfamilytree.com
Dist(s): **Ingram Publisher Services**
Spring Arbor Distributors, Inc.

Legaia Bks. USA, *(978-1-946946; 978-1-948738; 978-1-950543; 978-1-951932)* 555 Fayetteville St. Suite 201, Raleigh, NC 27601 USA Tel 704-216-4194
E-mail: michael.luke@legaiabooks.com.

Legend eXpress Publishing, *(978-0-9773648; 978-0-9846324; 978-0-9982261)* 3831 E. Clovis Ave., Mesa, AZ 85206-8520 USA Tel 480-664-1047; Fax: 800-528-0295
E-mail: jc@lxpaz.com
Web site: http://www.lxpaz.com.

Legend Publishing Co., *(978-0-615-22552-4; 978-0-615-22553-1; 978-0-615-22554-8; 978-0-9821687; 978-0-9909373; 978-0-9991813)* Orders Addr.: P.O. Box 429, Garden City, MI 48136 USA Tel 734-595-0663; Edit Addr.: 33807 Calumet Ct., Westland, MI 48186 USA
E-mail: bobwilly81897@Yahoo.com.

Legendary Comics, *(978-1-937278; 978-1-68116)* 2900 W Alameda Ave. 15th Flr., Suite 1500, Burbank, CA 91522 USA
E-mail: bschreck@legendary.com
Web site: www.legendary.com
Dist(s): **Penguin Random Hse. Distribution**
Penguin Random Hse. LLC
Random Hse., Inc.
Simon & Schuster, Inc.

Legenderry.com, *(978-0-9776967)* 6154 Meadowbrook Dr., Morrison, CO 80465 USA Fax: 720-222-0490
Web site: http://www.legenderry.com.

LegendMaker Scriptoria, *(978-0-9759355)* 9400 Wade Blvd. #817, Frisco, TX 75035 USA Tel 413-313-9127
E-mail: scriptoria@legendmaker.com
Web site: http://legendmaker.com.

Legends of Erin, *(978-0-9996189)* 19342 Saylor Terr., Santa Ana, CA 92705 USA Tel 714-333-7225
E-mail: meadowgriffin@yahoo.com
Web site: www.legendsoferin.com.

Legends of the West Publishing Co., *(978-0-9786904)* 174 Santa Rosa Ave., Sausalito, CA 94965-2060 USA (SAN 851-2825) Do not Copnfuse with Know DeFeet Publishing Company 2 Different companies. LD
E-mail: knowdefeet@aol.com.

Legler, Caroline, *(978-0-9771233)* Orders Addr.: 1930 Bonanza Ct., Winter Park, FL 32792 USA
E-mail: glegler@cfl.rr.com.

Legwork Team Publishing, *(978-0-578-00665-9; 978-0-578-00666-6; 978-0-578-01705-1; 978-0-578-01865-2; 978-0-578-01866-9; 978-0-578-01999-4; 978-0-578-02016-7; 978-0-578-02310-6; 978-0-578-02407-3; 978-0-578-02845-3; 978-0-9841535; 978-0-9843539; 978-0-9827337; 978-1-935905) 4 Peacock Ln., Commack, NY 11725 USA*
Web site: http://www.legworkteam.com
Dist(s): **Follett School Solutions.**

leharperwilliamsdesign group, *(978-0-615-37424-6)* 3819 Wake Forest Rd., Decatur, GA 30034 USA Tel 770-593-4687; Fax: 770-593-5466
E-mail: lhwdesign@me.com
Web site: http://leharperwilliamsdesign.com.

Lehman Publishing, *(978-0-9792686)* 15997 Hough, Allenton, MI 48002 USA
E-mail: dlehman@iwarp.net; dana@lehmanpublishing.com
Web site: http://www.lehmanpublishing.com
Dist(s): **Partners Bk. Distributing, Inc.**

Lehmann, Peter Publishing, *(978-0-9788399)* P.O. Box 11284, Eugene, OR 97440-3484 USA Tel 541-345-9106; Fax: 541-345-3737; Toll Free: 877-623-7743
E-mail: info@peter-lehmann-publishing.com
Web site: http://www.peter-lehmann-publishing.com.

Lehua, Inc., *(978-0-9647491)* P.o. Box 25548, Honolulu, HI 96825-0548 USA
E-mail: lehua@ohia.com
Web site: http://www.lehuainc.com
Dist(s): **Booklines Hawaii, Ltd.**

Leicester Bay Bks., *(978-0-615-68523-6; 978-0-615-69470-2; 978-0-615-90725-3; 978-0-692-23263-7; 978-0-692-34862-8; 978-0-692-36091-0; 978-0-692-46080-1; 978-0-692-63220-8; 978-0-692-73508-4; 978-0-692-93091-5; 978-0-692-95237-5)* 3877 Leicester Bay, South Jordan, UT 84095 USA Tel 801-282-8159
Web site: www.leicesterbaybooks.com
Dist(s): **CreateSpace Independent Publishing Platform.**

Leigh, Kimbra, *(978-0-9718851)* P.O. Box 20255, Rochester, NY 14602 USA
Web site: http://www.kimbraleigh.com.

Leiser, Savannah, *(978-0-9991614)* 4654 N Kenmore Ave, Chicago, IL 60640 USA Tel 302-593-9779
E-mail: savyleiser@gmail.com
Web site: savyleiser.com.

Leisure Arts, Inc., *(978-0-942237; 978-1-57486; 978-1-60140; 978-1-60900; 978-1-4647)* Orders Addr.: 5701 Ranch Dr., Little Rock, AR 72223 USA (SAN 666-9565) Tel 501-868-8800; Fax: 501-868-1001; Toll Free Fax: 877-710-5603; Toll Free: 800-643-8030 (customer service); 800-526-5111
E-mail: hermine_linz@leisurearts.com
Web site: http://www.leisurearts.com
Dist(s): **Checker Distributors**
Midpoint Trade Bks., Inc.
Notions Marketing.

Leisure Time Pr., *(978-0-9890270)* 27259 Prescott Way, Temecula, CA 92591 USA Tel 951-219-3168
E-mail: j13m@aol.com
Web site: www.leisuretimepress.com.

Lekha Murali *Imprint of* **Lekha Vippu**

Lekha Pubs., LLC, *(978-0-9725901; 978-1-937675; 978-1-951569)* 263 Ridgeview Dr., Tracy, CA 95377 USA Tel 209-666-2068
Web site: http://www.lekhaink.com.

Lekha Vippu, *(978-0-692-13010-0; 978-1-7327053)* 12807 Duck Pond Dr, GERMANTOWN, MD 20874 USA Tel 301-250-5745; *Imprints:* Lekha Murali (Lekha Murali)
E-mail: lekhavippu@gmail.com
Web site: lmexpressions.com
Dist(s): **Ingram Content Group.**

LeLeu, Lisa Puppet Show Bks. *Imprint of* **LeLeu, Lisa Studios! Inc.**

LeLeu, Lisa Studios! Inc., *(978-0-9710537; 978-0-9770299)* 100 Mechanics St., Doylestown, PA 18901 USA Tel 215-345-1233; Fax: 215-348-5378; *Imprints:* LeLeu, Lisa Puppet Show Books (L LeLeu Puppet)
E-mail: lisa.leleu@lisaleleustudios.com; Frederic.Leleu@LisaLeLeuStudios.com
Web site: http://www.LisaLeLeuStudios.com.

Lemniscaat *Imprint of* **Boyds Mills Pr.**

Lemniscaat USA, *(978-1-935954)* 413 Sixth Ave., New York, NY 11215 USA Tel 718-768-3696; Fax: 718-369-0844
E-mail: janetta@lemniscaat.nl
Web site: http://www.lemniscaatusa.com/
Dist(s): **Ingram Publisher Services.**

Lemon Grove Pr., *(978-0-9815240)* 1158 26th St. #502, Santa Monica,, CA 90403 USA Tel 310-471-1740; Fax: 310-476-7627
E-mail: info@lemongrovepress.com
Web site: http://www.lemongrovepress.com
Dist(s): **Brodart Co.**
MyiLibrary
ebrary, Inc.

Lemon Pr. LLC, *(978-0-9844183; 978-1-936617)* Orders Addr.: P.O. Box 459, Emerson, GA 30137 USA (SAN 859-3477) Tel 404-791-7742
E-mail: lemonpresspublishing@gmail.com
Web site: http://www.lemonpresspublishing.com
Dist(s): **Smashwords.**

Lemon Shark Pr., *(978-0-9741067)* 1604 Marbella Dr., Vista, CA 92081-5463 USA Tel 760-727-2850 [phone after 9AM PCT]
E-mail: lemonsharkpress@yahoo.com
Web site: http://www.lemonsharkpress.com
Dist(s): **Coutts Information Services**
Eastern Bk. Co.
Yankee Bk. Peddler, Inc.

Lemon Sherbet Pr., *(978-0-9897411)* 87 Guernsey St., Roslindale, MA 02131 USA Tel 781-799-5412
E-mail: lemonsherbetpress@gmail.com.

Lemon Vision Productions, *(978-1-934789)* 27475 Ynez Rd., No. 642, Temecula, CA 92591 USA (SAN 854-9346) Tel 951-526-2942 Toll Free: 866-580-1675
E-mail: info@lemonvision.com
Web site: http://www.lemonvision.com.

Lemonade Bks., *(978-0-9994330)* 7701 Covered Bridge Dr, Austin, TX 78736 USA Tel 949-302-1760; Fax: 949-302-1760
E-mail: ann.orsinger@gmail.com
Web site: www.lemonade-books.com.

Lemondrop Pr., *(978-0-9704718)* 2121 Loudenslager Dr., Thompson's Station, TN 37179 USA.

Lemonflavor Productions, *(978-0-9740169)* 100 Pk. Ave., 18th Flr. (Dept. MSM), New York, NY 10017 USA Tel 212-316-4278; Fax: 212-937-2211
E-mail: info@lemonflavor.com
Web site: http://www.lemonflavor.com.

Lemur Conservation Foundation, *(978-0-9766009; 978-0-9856728; 978-0-615-97588-7)* P.O. Box 249, Myakka City, FL 34251 USA Tel 941-322-8494; Fax: 941-322-9264
Web site: http://www.lemurreserve.org.

Leni Bks., *(978-0-9828173)* 11036 S. Tripp, Oak Lawn, IL 60453 USA Tel 708-712-4021; Fax: 708-398-1546
E-mail: ntalty@me.com
Web site: http://cilie-yack-is-under-attack.com.

LENKK Pr., *(978-0-9988004)* 9612 Albert Dr, Dublin, CA 94568 USA Tel 925-289-0120
E-mail: julie@jkroyce.com
Web site: www.jkroyce.com.

Leo Publishing, *(978-0-9834735; 978-1-941157)* 303 Augusta Cir., Saint Augustine, FL 32086 USA Tel 310-598-8943
E-mail: lp10leo@gmail.com.

Leo Publishing Works, Inc., *(978-0-615-35488-0)* 3 Monroe Pkwy., Suite P455, Lake Oswego, OR 97035 USA Tel 800-675-7564; Fax: 888-362-5891
E-mail: bethany@leopublishingworks.com
Web site: http://www.LeoPublishingWorks.com.

Leonard, Dennis Publications *See* **Legacy Pubs. International**

†Leonard, Hal Corp., *(978-0-634; 978-0-7935; 978-0-87910; 978-0-87930; 978-0-88188; 978-0-931340; 978-0-9607350; 978-1-56516; 978-1-57467; 978-1-4234; 978-1-936098; 978-1-61713; 978-1-61774; 978-1-61780; 978-1-4584; 978-1-4768; 978-1-4803; 978-1-62906; 978-1-4950; 978-1-5400; 978-1-7051) Orders Addr.: P.O. Box 13819, Milwaukee, WI 53213-0819 USA Tel 414-774-3630; Fax: 414-774-3259; Toll Free: 800-524-4425; Edit Addr.: 7777 W. Bluemound Rd., Milwaukee, WI 53213 USA (SAN 239-250X) Tel 414-777-3630; Fax: 414-774-4176; Imprints:* G Schirmer, Incorporated (G Schirmer); Limelight Editions (LimelightEd); Amadeus Press (AmadeusPress); Applause Theatre & Cinema (ApplauseTheatr)
E-mail: halinfo@halleonard.com
Web site: http://www.halleonard.com
Dist(s): **Follett School Solutions**
Giron Bks.
Hachette Bk. Group
MyiLibrary
National Bk. Network
Penguin Random Hse. Distribution
Penguin Random Hse. LLC
Penguin Publishing Group
Rowman & Littlefield Publishers, Inc.; *CIP.*

Leonard Pr., *(978-0-9769114; 978-1-934223)* P.O. Box 752, Bolivar, MO 65613-0752 USA Tel 417-326-5001
Web site: http://www.leonardpress.com.

Leonardo Press *See* **Firenze Pr.**

Leonardoverse Books, *(978-0-615-63333-6; 978-0-615-73882-6; 978-0-615-76677-5; 978-0-615-87076-2; 978-0-615-95841-5; 978-0-692-65694-5; 978-0-692-07536-4; 978-0-692-07573-9; 978-0-692-14044-4; 978-0-692-14045-1; 978-0-692-14046-8; 978-0-692-14060-4; 978-0-692-14090-1) 4998 Maxwell Landing Dr., Nolensville, TN 37135 USA*
E-mail: leo.ramirez7@icloud.com
Web site: http://Leonardoverse.com
Dist(s): **CreateSpace Independent Publishing Platform.**

Leonard's, Stew Holdings, LLC *See* **Kimberly Pr., LLC**

Leonine Pubs. LLC, *(978-0-9843001; 978-0-9836740; 978-0-9859483; 978-0-9887729; 978-0-9860552; 978-1-942190)* P.O. Box 1040, Laveen, AZ 85339 USA Tel 602-237-7487
E-mail: laura@leoninepublishers.com; info@leoninepublishers.com
Web site: http://www.leoninepublishers.com.

Leopard Books LLC *See* **Kids Activity Publishing**

Lerner Digital *Imprint of* **Lerner Publishing Group**

†Lerner Publishing Group, *(978-0-7613; 978-0-8225; 978-0-87406; 978-0-87614; 978-0-929371; 978-0-930494; 978-1-57505; 978-1-58013; 978-1-58196; 978-1-4677; 978-1-5124; 978-1-5415; 978-1-7284)* Orders Addr.: 1251 Washington Ave. N., Minneapolis, MN 55401 USA (SAN 256-0283) Tel 612-332-3344; Fax: 612-204-9208; Edit Addr.: 241 First Ave., N., Minneapolis, MN 55401 USA (SAN 201-0828) Tel 612-332-3344; Fax: 612-215-6230; Toll Free Fax: 800-332-1132; Toll Free: 800-328-4929; *Imprints:* First Avenue Editions (First Ave Edns); Lerner Publications (Lerner Publctns); Carolrhoda Books (Carolrho Bks); Ediciones Lerner (EdiciLerner); Millbrook Press (Millbrok Pr); Twenty-First Century Books (TwentFrstCent); Graphic Universe™ (Graphic Univ); Kar-Ben Publishing (Kar-Ben); Carolrhoda Lab™ (CarolrhodaLAB); Darby Creek (DarbyCreek); Lerner Digital (LernerDigital); Hungry Tomato r (Hungry Tomato); Zest Books (ZstBk)
E-mail: info@lernerbooks.com; custserve@lernerbooks.com
Web site: http://www.lernerbooks.com; http://www.karben.com
Dist(s): **Children's Plus, Inc.**
Ebsco Publishing
Follett School Solutions
Hachette Bk. Group
Ingram Publisher Services
MyiLibrary

Open Road Integrated Media, Inc.
Perfection Learning Corp.; *CIP.*

Lerner Pubns. *Imprint of* **Lerner Publishing Group**

LERN-LEARN, *(978-0-9763195)* 340 Vallejo Dr., Suite 82, Millbrae, CA 94030 USA.

Lerue Pr., LLC, *(978-0-9797460; 978-1-938814)* Orders Addr.: 280 Greg St., #10, Reno, NV 89502 USA Tel 775-849-3814
E-mail: janiceh@lerurpress.com; custserv@leruepress.com; lrp@lrpnv.com
Web site: http://www.leruepress.com; http://www.lrpnv.com
Dist(s): **Ingram Bk. Co.**

Les Lurn Pubs., *(978-0-9792000)* 5451 Bancroft Ave., Oakland, CA 94601 USA (SAN 852-7512).

Les Penseurs, *(978-0-9764999; 978-0-9820676)* 309 Weatherstone Ln., Marietta, GA 30068 USA Tel 678-575-7052; Fax: 678-560-1580
E-mail: jsands@lespenseurs.com
Web site: http://www.lespenseurs.com.

Lesen Pub., *(978-0-9767200)* 2207 Shermont Pl., Brandon, FL 33511 USA Tel 813-857-6629; Fax: 813-684-7876
E-mail: jem2207@aol.com.

Leslie, Beverly J., *(978-0-9769722)* 1911 Patton Pl., Lithonia, GA 30058 USA Tel 770-987-8769; Fax: 770-987-8018
E-mail: bjleslie1@comcast.net; Beverly@lesliegraphicdesigns.com
Web site: http://LeslieGraphicDesigns.com.

Less is More Publishing, LLC, *(978-0-9769618)* 405 N. Woodlawn Ave., Kirkwood, MO 63122 USA
Web site: http://www.aboutheaven.net
Dist(s): **Big River Distribution.**

Less Pr., *(978-0-9657367)* 100 Hannah Niles Way, Braintree, MA 02184-7261 USA Tel 781-848-0555.

Lesson Ladder, *(978-0-9848657; 978-0-9884499; 978-0-9964067)* 21 Orient Ave, Melrose, MA 02176 USA Tel 800-301-4647
E-mail: accounting@xamonline.com
Dist(s): **Ingram Publisher Services.**

Lessons From The Vine *Imprint of* **Hutchings, John Pubs.**

LeTay Publishing, *(978-0-9753434; 978-0-9830731)* Div. of LeTay Corp., Orders Addr.: P.O. Box 170233, Atlanta, GA 30317 USA Tel 404-667-2810
E-mail: booksales@letaypublishing.com; publisher@letaypublishing.com
Web site: http://www.letaypublishing.com
Dist(s): **Ingram Content Group.**

Lethe Pr., *(978-1-59021)* 118 Heritage Ave., Maple Shade, NJ 08052 USA Tel 609-410-7391
E-mail: lethepress@aol.com; editor@lethepressbooks.com
Web site: http://www.lethepressbooks.com
Dist(s): **Bookazine Co., Inc.**
Smashwords.

Letona, Oscar, *(978-0-615-24938-4)* 51 Cedar Pl., Yonkers, NY 10705 USA
E-mail: mrletona@thetrojancurse.com; mrletona@hotmail.com
Web site: http://www.thetrojancurse.com.

Letourneau, *(978-0-692-07912-6)* 49 W. Gill Rd., Gill, MA 01354 USA Tel 413-863-8291
E-mail: dolly.letourneau@yahoo.com.

Lets Go Publish, *(978-0-9899957; 978-0-9962454; 978-0-9977667; 978-0-9980848; 978-0-9982683; 978-0-9986282; 978-0-9988111; 978-1-947402; 978-1-951562)* 11 Marjorie Ave., Wilkes Barre, PA 18702 USA Tel 570-829-5926
E-mail: jmac@kellyconsulting.com; bkelly@kellyconsulting.com
Web site: http://letsgopublish.com; http://www.bookhawkers.com
Dist(s): **BookHawkers Internet BookSeller.**

Let's Grow Leaders, *(978-1-7322647)* 8505 Young Rivers Ct., Laurel, MD 20723 USA Tel 303-898-7018
E-mail: david.dye@letsgrowleaders.com
Web site: https://letsgrowleaders.com.

Let's Learn Library of Knowledge Series, *(978-0-9771015)* P.O. Box 9910, Canoga Park, CA 91309-9910 USA (SAN 256-7849)
E-mail: letslearn@letslearnlibrary.net
Web site: http://www.letslearnlibrary.net.

Let's Pretend Childrens Bks., *(978-0-9986480; 978-1-7324256)* 126 Fitchburg Dr, Woodstock, GA 30189 USA Tel 404-644-6888; Fax: 404-644-6888
E-mail: pcsclean@bellsouth.net.

Let's Think-kids Foundation, Inc., *(978-1-58237)* 3925 Blackburn Ln., Burtonsville, MD 20866 USA Toll Free: 800-841-2883
E-mail: thinkkids@aol.com; sftierno@aol.com
Web site: http://www.LTKF.org.

Lettra *See* **Lettra Pr. LLC**

Lettra Pr. LLC, *(978-1-949746; 978-1-64552; 978-1-951559; 978-1-951913; 978-1-953150)* 30 N. Gould St. Ste. 4753, Sheridan, WY 82801 USA
E-mail: chrisclay@lettrapress.com
Web site: www.lettrapress.com.

Levanter Publishing, *(978-0-9847237; 978-1-940576)* 910 S. Skylake Dr., Woodland Hills, UT 84653 USA Tel 801-423-8409
E-mail: loislane@digis.net
Dist(s): **Smashwords.**

Level 4 Press, Inc., *(978-0-9768001; 978-1-933769; 978-1-64630)* 13518 Jamul Dr., Jamul, CA 91935 USA Tel 619-669-3100; Fax: 619-374-7311
E-mail: william@level4press.com
Web site: http://www.level4press.com
Dist(s): **Follett School Solutions**
Independent Pubs. Group
Midpoint Trade Bks., Inc.
MyiLibrary.

Level 603 LLC, *(978-0-9747615)* 133 Washington St. No. 1203, Dover, NH 03821 USA
Dist(s): **Unique Bks., Inc.**

Level Green Bks., *(978-0-9788771)* 11 Level Green Rd., Brooktondale, NY 14817 USA (SAN 851-8319).

Level Ground Pr., *(978-0-9773461)* 2810 San Paula Ave., Dallas, TX 75228 USA Tel 214-796-2135
Web site: http://www.levelgroundfilms.com.

Levenger Pr., *(978-1-929154)* 420 S. Congress Ave., Delray Beach, FL 33445 USA Tel 561-276-2436; Fax: 561-276-3584
E-mail: mvogel@levenger.com
Web site: http://www.levenger.com.

Leverage Factory, *(978-0-9773000)* 38 Rogerson Dr., Chapel Hill, NC 27517-4037 USA (SAN 257-2710)
E-mail: info@leveragefactory.com
Web site: http://www.beawriter.us; http://www.leveragefactory.com
Dist(s): **Independent Pubs. Group.**

Levi Bass Publishing, *(978-0-9835651)* PO Box 608355, Orlando, FL 32860 USA Tel 407-709-0578; Fax: 407-271-8552
E-mail: carolyndenise@ymail.com
Web site: www.carolyndenise.com.

Levine, Arthur A. Bks. *Imprint of* **Scholastic, Inc.**

Levine, Bette M., *(978-0-9721094)* 4605 Regiment Way, Manlius, NY 13104 USA
E-mail: rampa505@aol.com.

Levine Querido, *(978-1-64614)* 220 E 74th St, New York, NY 10021 USA Tel 201-983-9470
E-mail: nick@levinequerido.com
Web site: www.levinequerido.com
Dist(s): **Chronicle Bks. LLC**
Hachette Bk. Group.

Levinson, Ralph D, *(978-1-7327889)* 10563 Troon Ave., Los Angeles, CA 90064 USA Tel 310-839-1075; Fax: 310-839-1075
E-mail: ralphdlevinson@gmail.com
Web site: ralphlevinson.com.

levitin, sarah, *(978-0-578-43972-3)* 891 33rd Ave., San Francisco, CA 94121 USA Tel 415-305-7808
E-mail: sarah_ll@sbcglobal.net
Dist(s): **Ingram Content Group.**

Levity Pr., *(978-0-615-64986-3; 978-0-615-68151-1; 978-0-615-70890-4; 978-0-615-70893-5; 978-1-939896)* 10170 Palm Glen Dr. No. 46, Santee, CA 92071 USA
Web site: www.englishcorner.me
Dist(s): **CreateSpace Independent Publishing Platform.**

Lewis & Clark Bicentennial Corps of Discovery Arch, *(978-0-9763970)* 1907 NE 75th Ave., Portland, OR 97213 USA Tel 503-201-2494
E-mail: faith.ruffing@bicencorpsarchive.com
Web site: http://www.bicencorpsarchive.com.

Lewis International, Inc., *(978-0-9666771; 978-1-930983)* 2201 NW 102nd Pl., No. 1, Miami, FL 33172 USA Tel 305-436-7984; Fax: 305-436-7985; Toll Free: 800-259-5962.

Lewis Lynn Bks., *(978-0-9745544)* 1143 N. Carey Ave., Clovis, CA 93611-7371 USA Fax: 559-322-9038
E-mail: cconn@cwnet.com
Web site: http://www.borainiansector.com.

Lewis-Thornton, Rae, *(978-0-9747983)* 1507 E. 53rd St., Suite 315, Chicago, IL 60615 USA Tel 773-643-4316; Fax: 773-643-4356
E-mail: rae_lewis_thornton@hotmail.com
Web site: http://www.raelewisthornton.org.

Lexicon Marketing Corporation *See* **Lexicon Marketing, LLC**

Lexicon Marketing, LLC, *(978-1-59172)* 6380 Wilshire Blvd. Ste. 1400, Los Angeles, CA 90048-5018 USA
E-mail: Jbelletti@lexiconmarketing.com; icruz@lexiconmarketing.com.

Lexingford Publishing, *(978-0-9844938; 978-0-9859480; 978-0-9863343; 978-0-9963948; 978-0-9981665; 978-0-9986060; 978-1-947373; 978-1-7329576)* 255 redlands st., Playa del Rey, CA 90293 USA (SAN 859-5674) Tel 415-328-5465
E-mail: abell@clarkson.edu.

Lexington Books *See* **Lexington Bks.**

Lexington Bks., *(978-0-7391; 978-1-4985; 978-1-9787; 978-1-7936)* Div. of Rowman & Littlefield Publishing Group, Inc., Orders Addr.: 15200 NBN Way, Blue Ridge Summit, PA 17214 USA Tel 717-794-3800 (Sales, Customer Service, MIS, Royalties, Inventory Mgmt., Dist., Credit & Collections); Fax: 717-794-3803 (Customer Service &/or orders only); 717-794-3857 (Sales & MIS); 717-794-3856 (Royalties, Inventory Mgmt., & Dist.); Toll Free Fax: 800-338-4550 (Customer Service &/or orders); Toll Free: 800-462-6420 (Customer Service &/or orders); 67 Mowat Ave., Suite 241, Toronto, ON M6K 3E3 Tel 416-534-1660; Fax: 416-534-3699; Edit Addr.: 4501 Forbes Blvd., Blvd., Ste. 200, Lanham, MD 20706 USA Tel 301-459-3366; Fax: 301-429-5749; Toll Free: 1-800-462-6420 Short Discount, contact rlpgsales@rowman.com
E-mail: custserv@rowman.com; edebusk@rowman.com; lexingtonbooks@rowman.com
Web site: http://www.lexingtonbooks.com; http://www.rlpgbooks.com; http://www.rowman.com
Dist(s): **CreateSpace Independent Publishing Platform**
Ebsco Publishing
Follett School Solutions
MyiLibrary
National Bk. Network
Rowman & Littlefield Publishers, Inc.
Send The Light Distribution LLC
Transaction Pubs.
ebrary, Inc.

Lexington Pubs., *(978-1-933361)* P.O. Box 750018, Arlington Heights, MA 02475 USA
E-mail: lexingtonpublishers@gmail.com.

Leyva, Barbara, *(978-0-9729056)* P.O. Box 3295, Clewiston, FL 33440-3295 USA; *Imprints:* Balticbard Publishing (Balticbard Pub)
E-mail: balticbard@yahoo.com
Web site: http://www.geocities.com/balticbard/index.html.

LFF Consultant, *(978-0-9843472)* 127 Peck Hill 1200 Harford Ave, N.Scituate, RI 02857 USA (SAN 859-1326) Tel 401-688-0217
E-mail: admin@lifestyleinstitute.org
Web site: Lifestyleinstitute.org.

L.G. Publishing, *(978-0-615-16242-3)* P.O. Box 5098, Sarasota, FL 34277 USA Tel 941-312-4725
E-mail: glickmanfamily@aol.com.

LGE Performance Systems, Inc., *(978-0-9778776)* 9757 Lake Nona Rd., Orlando, FL 32827 USA (SAN 850-5055) Tel 407-438-9911; Fax: 407-438-6667.

LGR Productions *See* **LGR Publishing, Inc.**

LGR Publishing, Inc., *(978-0-9657610)* 3219 NW C St., Richmond, IN 47374 USA Tel 765-939-8924 (phone/fax)
E-mail: jwilde@indiana.edu; mcphd@infocom.com
Web site: http://www.angerchillout.com.

Lóguez Ediciones (ESP) *(978-84-85334; 978-84-89804; 978-84-96646) Dist. by* **Lectorum Pubns.**

LH Pubns. & Productions, *(978-0-9749013)* Orders Addr.: P.O. Box 914, Center Harbor, NH 03226 USA
E-mail: mcat_lh@yahoo.com
Web site: http://www.laurahickey.com.

LHC Publishing, *(978-0-615-71668-8; 978-0-615-86013-8; 978-0-615-93103-6; 978-0-692-02397-6; 978-0-692-47441-9; 978-0-692-47443-3; 978-0-9970254; 978-1-7323733; 978-1-952517)*
E-mail: yvijones@hotmail.com
Web site: www.LHCpublishing.com
Dist(s): **CreateSpace Independent Publishing Platform.**

Li, Richard T., *(978-0-9675988)* 4554 Rose Tree Ct., Fort Worth, TX 76137 USA Tel 817-656-5178; Fax: 817-656-4138.

LiArt-Literature & Art, *(978-1-931481)* P.O. Box 245686, Pembroke Pines, FL 33024-5686 USA Tel 954-986-6886 (phone/fax)
E-mail: liartpe@aol.com.

Liber Publishing Hse., *(978-1-950425)* Orders Addr.: Tres de Abril St., Punta Princessa, Labangon, Cebu City, 6000 PHL Tel 315-820-1714; Edit Addr.: Tres de Abril St., Punta Princessa, Labangon, Cebu City, 6000 PHL Tel 315-820-1714
E-mail: bookprojects18@gmail.com
Web site: www.liberpublishing.com; www.royalehousepub.com.

Liberation's Publishing, *(978-0-9843827; 978-0-615-76642-3; 978-0-9891348; 978-0-692-02160-6; 978-0-692-02161-3; 978-0-692-02162-0; 978-0-692-02163-7; 978-0-692-02164-4; 978-0-692-27755-3; 978-0-692-36183-2; 978-0-692-37137-4; 978-0-692-37138-1; 978-0-692-39174-7; 978-0-692-39217-1; 978-0-692-42144-4; 978-0-692-42913-6; 978-0-692-53789-3; 978-1-7320846; 978-1-7326934; 978-1-7336754; 978-1-951300) 29680 Hwy 50 E, West Point, MS 39773 USA (SAN 859-242X) Tel 662-605-0382*
E-mail: nicole@liberationspublishing.com
Web site: http://www.liberationspublishing.com
Dist(s): **CreateSpace Independent Publishing Platform**
Ingram Content Group
Lulu Pr., Inc.

Libertary Company *See* **Booktrope**

Liberty Artists Management, *(978-0-9785427)* Orders Addr.: 31 Liberty St., Catskill, NY 12414-1442 USA
E-mail: admin@libertyartists.com
Web site: http://www.beckyblume.com; http://www.libertyartists.com.

Liberty Communications House *See* **JB Information Station**

Liberty Fund, Inc., *(978-0-86597; 978-0-913966; 978-1-61487)* Orders Addr.: c/o Total Response, Inc., 5804 Churchman By-Pass, Indianapolis, IN 46203 USA; Edit Addr.: 8335 Allison Pointe Trail, No. 300, Indianapolis, IN 46250-1684 USA (SAN 202-6740) Tel 317-842-0880; Fax: 317-579-6060; Toll Free: 800-866-3520; 800-955-8335 (customer service); *Imprints:* Amagi Books (Amagi Bks)
E-mail: webmaster@libertyfund.org
Web site: http://www.libertyfund.org
Dist(s): **Chicago Distribution Ctr.**
Ingram Publisher Services
MyiLibrary
ebrary, Inc.

Liberty Hill Publishing *Imprint of* **Salem Author Services**

Liberty Manuals Co., *(978-0-9710748; 978-0-9820955; 978-1-940069)* Orders Addr.: P.O. Box 453, Rumson, NJ 07760 USA Tel 732-842-3000; Fax: 732-741-5820.

Liberty Publishing Group, *(978-1-893095; 978-1-946291)* Div. of The Holton Consulting Group, Inc., Orders Addr.: 1405 Autumn Ridge Dr., Durham, NC 27712-2680 USA Tel 919-767-9620; Toll Free Fax: 866-500-7697; Toll Free: 877-819-7489
E-mail: bil@holtonconsulting.com; cher@holtonconsulting.com
Web site: http://www.holtonconsulting.com; http://www.prosperityPublishing.com; http://www.themetaphysicalwebsite.com
Dist(s): **Prosperity Publishing Hse.**
Smashwords.

Liberty Publishing Hse., Inc., *(978-0-914481; 978-1-932686; 978-1-62804)* P.O. Box 1058, New York, NY 10024-0547 USA (SAN 289-6869)
E-mail: info@libertypublishinghouse.com
Web site: https://www.libertypublishinghouse.com.

Liberty St. *Imprint of* **Time Inc. Bks.**

Liberty University Press, *(978-0-9819357; 978-1-935986; 978-0-9976828; 978-1-7326376)* 1971 University Blvd., Lynchburg, VA 24502 USA Tel 434-592-3100
E-mail: libertyuniversitypress@liberty.edu.

Librado Pr., *(978-1-879571)* 11223 Leatherwood Dr., Reston, VA 22091 USA Tel 703-476-0516 Do not confuse with Librad Press in San Francisco, CA.

Librairie du Liban Pubns. (FRA) *Dist. by* **Intl Bk Ctr.**

Librairie Larousse (FRA) *(978-2-03) Dist. by* **Distribks Inc.**

Libraries Unlimited *Imprint of* **ABC-CLIO, LLC**

Library Assn. of La Jolla, *(978-0-9744804; 978-0-9828289)* 1008 Wall St., La Jolla, CA 92037-4418 USA Tel 858-454-5872; Fax: 858-454-5835; *Imprints:* Athenaeum Music & Arts Library (Athenaeum Music)
E-mail: Athlibrary@pacbell.net; kpeterson@ljathenaeum.org.

Library of America, The, *(978-0-940450; 978-1-883011; 978-1-931082; 978-1-59853)* Div. of Literary Classics of the U. S., Inc., 14 E. 60th St., New York, NY 10022 USA (SAN 286-9918) Tel 212-308-3360; Fax: 212-750-8352
E-mail: info@loa.org
Web site: http://www.loa.org
Dist(s): **MyiLibrary**
Penguin Random Hse. Distribution
Penguin Random Hse. LLC
Penguin Publishing Group
Random Hse., Inc.

Library Reprints, Inc., *(978-0-7222)* Orders Addr.: P.O. Box 890820, Temecula, CA 92589-0820 USA (SAN 254-0258) Fax: 951-767-1803; 951-767-0133
E-mail: newbookorders@gmail.com
Dist(s): **Amazon Digital Services Inc.**

Library Sales of N.J., *(978-1-888032)* Orders Addr.: P.O. Box 335, Garwood, NJ 07027-0335 USA Tel 908-232-1446; Edit Addr.: 607 S. Chestnut St., Westfield, NJ 07090-1369 USA
E-mail: Librarysalesofnj@aol.com.

Library Tales Publishing, Inc., *(978-0-615-39884-6; 978-0-578-07458-0; 978-0-578-07790-1; 978-0-615-47817-3; 978-0-615-48528-7; 978-0-615-50393-6; 978-0-615-51583-0; 978-0-615-52116-9; 978-0-615-56273-5; 978-0-615-56822-5; 978-0-615-56823-2; 978-0-615-65368-6; 978-0-615-66879-6; 978-0-615-69556-3; 978-0-615-74800-9; 978-0-615-75793-3; 978-0-615-76875-5; 978-0-615-77415-2; 978-0-615-83527-3; 978-0-615-83638-6; 978-0-615-86816-5; 978-0-615-91241-7; 978-0-615-91251-6; 978-0-615-91956-0; 978-0-615-94763-1; 978-0-615-94799-0;) Div. of Library Tales Entertainment Group, 180 Riverside Blvd 40C, New York, NY 10069 USA*
E-mail: Office@Librarytales.com
Web site: http://www.librarytalespublishing.com
Dist(s): **CreateSpace Independent Publishing Platform**
Ingram Content Group.

LIBRI Bks., Division of Seasons & A Muse, Incorporated *See* **LIBRI Pubs.**

LIBRI Pubs., *(978-0-9763952)* P.O. Box 5849, Playa Del Rey, CA 90296-5849 USA Tel 310-827-6495; Fax: 310-827-8166
E-mail: libri@seasonsandamuse.com
Web site: http://www.seasonsandamuse.com.

Libris Draconis Pr., *(978-0-9728124)* PMB 279 1296 E. Gibson Rd., Suite A, Woodland, CA 95776 USA (SAN 255-1179)
Dist(s): **Baker & Taylor Publisher Services (BTPS).**

Libro Studio LLC, *(978-1-63578)* 1012 Pk. Ave. NW., Willmar, MN 56201 USA Tel 320-293-7702; Fax: 320-293-7702
E-mail: LibroStudioLLC@gmail.com.

Libros del Asteroide (ESP) *(978-84-934315; 978-84-935018; 978-84-92663; 978-84-935448; 978-84-935914; 978-84-936597) Dist. by* **IPG Chicago.**

Libros del Zorro Rojo (ESP) *(978-84-933361; 978-84-933976; 978-84-934032; 978-84-96509; 978-84-92412; 978-84-940336; 978-84-941041; 978-84-941619; 978-84-941645; 978-84-942473; 978-84-942918) Dist. by* **Lectorum Pubns.**

Libros Desafio, *(978-0-939125; 978-1-55883; 978-1-55955)* Subs. of CRC Pubns., 2850 Kalamazoo Ave., SE, Grand Rapids, MI 49560 USA (SAN 248-9775) Tel 616-224-0785; Fax: 616-224-0834; Toll Free: 800-333-8300
E-mail: info@librosdesafio.org
Web site: http://www.librosdesafio.org.

Libros, Encouraging Cultural Literacy, *(978-0-9675413; 978-0-9710860)* Orders Addr.: P.O. Box 453, Long Beach, NY 11561 USA Tel 516-889-6077; Fax: 516-889-6365; Toll Free: 800-260-9915; Edit Addr.: 160 LaFayette Blvd., Long Beach, NY 11561 USA (SAN 253-374X)
E-mail: librospress@msn.com
Web site: http://www.librospress.com.

Libros in Spanish, LLC, 1941 NE 147th Terr., North Miami, FL 33181 USA Tel 786-274-1556; Fax: 305-948-0333
E-mail: admin@librosinspanish.com.

Libros Liguori *Imprint of* **Liguori Pubns.**

Libros Para Ninos *Imprint of* **Libros Para Ninos**

Libros Para Ninos, Div. of Simon & Schuster Children's Publishing, 1230 Ave. of the Americas, New York, NY 10020 USA; *Imprints:* Libros Para Ninos (LibPara)
Dist(s): **Simon & Schuster**
Simon & Schuster, Inc.

Libros Publishing, *(978-0-9837458; 978-0-9851769; 978-0-9906713; 978-0-9987031)* 24040 Camino Del Avion No. A225, Monarch Beach, CA 92629 USA Tel 949-201-9477; Fax: 949-661-9098
E-mail: librospublishing@cox.net
Dist(s): **Baker & Taylor Publisher Services (BTPS)**
Follett School Solutions
ebrary, Inc.

Libros Sin Fronteras, P.O. Box 2085, Olympia, WA 98507 USA Tel 360-357-4332; Fax: 360-357-4964
E-mail: info@librossinfronteras.com
Web site: http://www.librossinfronteras.com.

Libros-Latin American Treasures For Kids *See* **Libros, Encouraging Cultural Literacy**

Librujas, *(978-0-9771566)* 4335 Van Nuys Blvd., Suite 117, Sherman Oaks, CA 91403 USA (SAN 256-887X) Tel 818-905-7221
E-mail: jamie@librujas.com; patricia@librujas.com
Web site: http://www.librujas.com
Dist(s): **Quality Bks., Inc.**

Liburdi, Mariana *See* **Happy Hearts Family, The**

Lickel, Lisa Publishing, also operating as Five Loaves *See* **Fox Ridge Pubns.**

Lieberherr, Ruth, *(978-1-7328877)* 8 Red Coach Ln., Winchester, MA 01890 USA Tel 781-721-2663
E-mail: ruth.lieberherr@gmail.com
Dist(s): **Ingram Content Group.**

Life Action Inc., *(978-0-940110; 978-0-9667124; 978-1-934718)* Orders Addr.: P.O. Box 31, Buchanan, MI 49107 USA Tel 269-697-8600; Fax: 269-695-2974; Toll Free: 800-321-1538; Edit Addr.: 2727 Niles Buchanan Rd., Buchanan, MI 49107 USA (SAN 220-2859)
Web site: http://www.lifeaction.org; http://www.ReviveOurHearts.com.

Life Action Publishing *See* **Life Action Inc.**

Life by Design Youth Leadership Resources *See* **Youthleadership.com**

Life Changers International Church *See* **Dickow, Gregory Ministries**

Life Chronicles Publishing, *(978-0-692-64191-0; 978-0-692-77302-4; 978-0-692-84946-0; 978-0-9989114; 978-0-692-98651-6; 978-1-7328944; 978-1-950649)* 4414 S 318th St, FEDERAL WAY, WA 98023 USA Tel 253-508-8876
E-mail: sharon.blake@outlook.com
Web site: www.lifechroniclespublishing.com
Dist(s): **CreateSpace Independent Publishing Platform.**

Life force, *(978-0-9985790)* 7007 W. indian school Rd., Phoenix, AZ 85033 USA Tel 845-200-4962
E-mail: maryamnisajudan@gmail.com.

Life Force Bks., *(978-0-9795331; 978-0-9896540; 978-0-9962386; 978-1-7324453)* P.O. Box 302, Bayside, CA 95524 USA; *Imprints:* Zardoz Press (ZardozPr)
E-mail: jjsemple@suddenlink.net; jjsemple@lifeforcebooks.com
Web site: http://www.lifeforcebooks.com; http://www.goldenflowermeditation.com; http://www.commonsensekundalini.com; http://www.kundaliniconsortium.org/
Dist(s): **Smashwords.**

Life is a Story Problem LLC, *(978-1-63270)* 2910 N. Powers No. 326, Colorado Springs, CO 80922 USA Tel 720-940-8153
E-mail: demcadams@demcadams.com
Web site: www.demcadams.com.

Life Letters Publishing, *(978-0-9746022)* P.O. Box 360111, Strongsville, OH 44136 USA
E-mail: lifeletter@aol.com
Web site: http://www.lifeletter.net.

Life Line, Inc., *(978-0-9647089)* P.O. Box 7990, New York, NY 10116-8715 USA Tel 212-947-0661; Fax: 212-947-0681 Do not confuse with Life Lines, Rimrock, AZ
E-mail: lifel@aol.com.

Life Line Publishing, *(978-0-9761604)* P.O. Box 1482, Bridgeport, CT 06601-1482 USA Do not confuse with Life Line Publishing in Franklin, VA.

Life Link Worldwide Pubs., *(978-1-880608)* 175 Raymond Ct., Fayetteville, GA 30214 USA Tel 770-994-1683.

Life of Asil, The, *(978-0-615-31907-0)* 8302 turnberry St., Rowlett , TX 75089 USA.

Life Pubs. International, *(978-0-7361; 978-0-943258; 978-1-890219)* 1625 N. Robberson Ave., Springfield, MO 65803 USA (SAN 213-5817) Tel 417-831-7766; Fax: 417-831-6445; Toll Free: 888-776-2425
E-mail: info@lifepublishers.org
Dist(s): **Charisma Media.**

Life Rich Publishing *Imprint of* **AuthorHouse**

Life Sentence Publishing, Inc., *(978-0-9832016; 978-1-62245)* P.O. Box 652, Abbotsford, WI 54405 USA Tel 715-223-3013; *Imprints:* ANEKO Press (ANEKOPr)
E-mail: jeremiah@lspbooks.com
Web site: zeiset.org; http://www.anekopress.com
Dist(s): **Ingram Publisher Services**
Ingram Content Group
North Star Editions
Send The Light Distribution LLC
Spring Arbor Distributors, Inc.

Life Story Publishing, LLC *See* **Wizard Academies, LLC**

Life Works Pr., *(978-0-9755938)* P.O. Box 2174, Clinton, MD 20735 USA Tel 602-561-1354; Toll Free: 888-786-7526
Web site: http://www.byrongarrett.com.

Lifeforce Enterprises, Inc., *(978-0-9709796)* 250 Pacific Ave., Suite 326, Long Beach, CA 90802 USA Tel 562-366-2617; Toll Free: 866-543-3367
E-mail: ajyager@entertheforce.com
Web site: http://www.entertheforce.com
Dist(s): **Midpoint Trade Bks., Inc.**

Lifelight Bks., *(978-0-9743801)* 2629 262nd Pl SE, Sammamish, WA 98075-7900 USA (SAN 850-8070)
E-mail: lynne@lifelightbooks.com
Web site: http://www.lifelightbooks.com.

LifeLine Studios, Inc., *(978-0-9714753)* 1390 W. Main St., Lancaster, TX 75146 USA Tel 972-275-0468; Fax: 972-275-0469
E-mail: afoutsjr@lifelinestudios.com
Web site: http://www.lifelinestudio.com.

Lifelong Friends Pub., *(978-0-9971221)* po box 483, Mansfield Center, CT 06250 USA Tel 860-428-7691
E-mail: ssptbp@charter.net
Web site: www.lifelongfriends.com.

Lifepac *Imprint of* **Alpha Omega Pubns., Inc.**

Liferays Publishing, *(978-0-9795397)* 5390 Elliott Rd., Powder Springs, GA 30127-3803 USA Tel 770-943-6123
E-mail: liferays@bellsouth.net
Web site: http://liferays02.googlepages.com/home.

LifeReloaded *See* **LifeReloaded Specialty Publishing LLC**

LifeReloaded Specialty Publishing LLC, *(978-0-9776414; 978-1-60800)* 2256 Huber Dr., Manheim, PA 17545 USA; *Imprints:* American Literary Publishing (Amer Literary)
E-mail: admin@lifereloaded.com; Editor@LifeReloaded.com; Sales@LifeReloaded.com; Publisher@LifeReloaded.com
Web site: http://www.LifeReloaded.com; http://www.GhostTrainToFreedom.com; http://www.MooKittyFindsAHome.Com; http://www.JMPMysterySeries.com.

Life's Journey of Hope Pubns., *(978-0-9747815)* Orders Addr.: P.O. Box 1277, Groton, MA 01450 USA (SAN 255-7789) Tel 978-448-1252; Edit Addr.: 90 Martins Pond Rd., Groton, MA 01450 USA
E-mail: LLeonard@lifesjourneyofhope.com; lifesjourneyofhope@hotmail.com
Web site: http://www.lifesjourneyofhope.com.

Lifeskills Press *See* **Uplift Pr.**

LifeSong Pubs., *(978-0-9718306; 978-0-9799116)* Orders Addr.: P.O. Box 183, Somis, CA 93066-0183 USA Tel 805-504-3916; Toll Free: 866-266-6917
Web site: http://www.lifesongpublishers.com
Dist(s): **Send The Light Distribution LLC.**

Lifestage, Inc., *(978-0-9799905)* 496 Smithtown ByPass, Suite 202, Smithtown, NY 11787 USA (SAN 854-9192) Tel 631-366-4265
E-mail: lifestage_2000@yahoo.com
Web site: http://www.lifestage.org.

LifeStory Publishing, *(978-0-9758988; 978-0-578-41243-6; 978-0-578-58575-8)* 5328 Runnymede Rd., Jackson, MS 39211 USA Tel 601-978-3478
E-mail: maxwell@thewellpublishing.org.

LifeTime Media, Inc., *(978-0-9675967; 978-0-9816368; 978-0-9822171; 978-0-9823975)* 352 Seventh Ave., 7th Flr., New York, NY 10001 USA (SAN 856-0978) Tel 212-631-7524; Fax: 212-631-7529
E-mail: sales@lifetimemedia.com; jgrace@lifetimemedia.com
Web site: http://www.lifetimemedia.com
Dist(s): **Two Rivers Distribution.**

Lifetime Relationship Center *See* **Intralife Systems Publishing**

Lifetrack Resources, *(978-0-9743826)* 709 Univ. Ave. W., Saint Paul, MN 55104-4804 USA Tel 651-227-8471; Fax: 651-227-0621
E-mail: familiestogether@lifetrackresources.org
Web site: http://www.lifetrackresources.org.

Lifevest *Imprint of* **Lifevest Publishing, Inc.**

Lifevest Publishing, Inc., *(978-0-9724680; 978-1-932338; 978-1-59879)* 4910 E. Dry Creek Rd., Suite 170, Centennial, CO 80122 USA Tel 303-221-1007; Fax: 303-771-1166; Toll Free Fax: 877-843-1007; *Imprints:* Lifevest (Livevst)
E-mail: ric.simmons@lifevestpublishing.com; publisher@lifevestpublishing.com
Web site: http://www.lifevestpublishing.com.

LifeWay Christian Resources, *(978-0-7673; 978-0-633; 978-1-4158; 978-1-4300; 978-1-5359; 978-1-0877)* Div. of The Southern Baptist Convention, One Lifeway Plaza, Nashville, TN 37234 USA Tel 615-251-2000; Fax: 615-277-8221 (product info., ordering, order tracking); 615-251-2626 (shipping/transportation); Toll Free Fax: 800-296-4036; Toll Free: 800-458-2772 (product info., ordering); 800-251-3225; *Imprints:* Serendipity House (Serendip Hse)
E-mail: customerservice@lifeway.com; support.lifeway.com
Web site: http://www.lifewaystores.com; http://www.lifeway.com; http://www.bhpublishinggroup.com
Dist(s): **Spring Arbor Distributors, Inc.**

Liffey Pr., The (IRL) *(978-1-904148; 978-1-905785; 978-1-908308) Dist. by* **Dufour.**

Light & Life Publishing Co., *(978-0-937032; 978-1-880971; 978-1-933654)* Orders Addr.: 4808 Park Glen Rd., Minneapolis, MN 55416 USA (SAN 213-8565) Tel 952-925-3888; Fax: 888-925-3918; Toll Free Fax: 888-925-3918
E-mail: ivy@light-n-life.com
Web site: http://www.light-n-life.com.

Light Bugs Publishing, *(978-0-9765514)* 1400 Champions Green Dr., Gulf Breeze, FL 32563 USA Tel 850-932-9325
E-mail: allen911@bellsouth.net; russ@lightbugspublishing.com; jan@lightbugspublishing.com
Web site: http://www.lightbugspublishing.com.

Light Energy Bks., *(978-0-9740480)* 731 Mandana Blvd., Oakland, CA 94610 USA Tel 510-268-9999.

Light Horse Publishing, *(978-0-9966754)* 2500 Sawmill Rd., Santa Fe, NM 87505 USA Tel 505-660-4456
E-mail: camkattell@yahoo.com.

Light Internal Publishing, *(978-0-9823732)* Orders Addr.: 6130 E. Fair Ave., Centennial, CO 80111 USA (SAN 857-9822)
E-mail: marnie@lightinternal.com
Web site: http://www.lightinternal.com.

Light Line, *(978-0-9773244)* 353 E. Pittsfield St., Pennsville, NJ 08070 USA (SAN 257-2540) Toll Free: 877-427-8271
E-mail: jildadf@comcast.net.

Light Messages Publishing, *(978-0-9679937; 978-0-9800756; 978-1-61153)* 5216 Tahoe Dr., Durham, NC 27713 USA (SAN 920-9298) Tel 919-361-5041; Toll Free Fax: 866-585-4635; *Imprints:* Torchflame Books (TorchflameBks)
E-mail: books@lightmessages.com
Web site: http://www.lightmessages.com
Dist(s): **INscribe Digital**
Independent Pubs. Group
New Leaf Distributing Co., Inc.

Light Network, The, *(978-0-9966403; 978-0-9975727; 978-0-9987043; 978-1-7320268; 978-1-7335939; 978-1-7330436; 978-1-7341814; 978-1-7356648)* 151 4th St. W., Ketchum, ID 83340 USA Tel 208-721-3324
E-mail: keidikeating@yahoo.co.uk
Web site: www.thelightnetwork.com.

Light of Logos Pr., *(978-0-615-82703-2; 978-0-9896356)* 15 Fairfield Rd, Wayland, MA 01778 USA
E-mail: yuegang_zhang@yahoo.com.

Light Pubns., *(978-0-9702642; 978-0-9824707; 978-1-940060)* Orders Addr.: P.O. Box 2462, Providence, RI 02906 USA Tel 401-272-8707; Edit Addr.: 393 Morris Ave., Providence, RI 02906 USA (SAN 852-7407) Tel 401-272-8707
E-mail: info@lightpublications.com
Web site: http://www.lightpublications.com.

Light Sword Publishing, LLC *See* **LSP Digital, LLC**

Light Works Publishing *Imprint of* **I.M. Enterprises**

Light24, *(978-0-9700002)* Orders Addr.: 85-42 160th St., Jamaica Queens, NY 11432 USA Tel 718-526-7021 Do not confuse with companies with the same name in Worthington, OH, Kirkland, WA.

LightBurst Media, *(978-0-692-59600-5; 978-0-692-63807-1; 978-0-692-63810-1; 978-0-692-63813-2; 978-0-692-64039-5; 978-0-692-64283-2; 978-0-692-65893-2; 978-0-692-66096-6; 978-0-692-67320-1; 978-0-692-70346-5; 978-0-692-70858-3; 978-0-692-70961-0; 978-0-692-71084-5; 978-0-692-73769-9; 978-0-9979389) 3226 se gladstone st, portland, OR 97202 USA Tel 347-551-3121*
Web site: www.lightburstmedia.com
Dist(s): **CreateSpace Independent Publishing Platform.**

Lighted Hill, *(978-0-9966539; 978-0-692-50004-0)* 189 Corinth Church Rd, Alma, GA 31510 USA Tel 912-310-1184
E-mail: joshua.horton@sfwbcmail.com
Dist(s): **CreateSpace Independent Publishing Platform.**

Lighted Lamp Pr., *(978-1-888350)* Orders Addr.: P.O. Box 1234, Wheat Ridge, CO 80034 USA; Edit Addr.: 4945 Gray St., Denver, CO 80212 USA (SAN 298-8348)
E-mail: robertjinye@msn.com.

Lighten Pr., *(978-0-9980410)* 2633 N. 22nd St., Mesa, AZ 85213 USA
E-mail: authororasmith@gmail.com
Web site: www.lightenpress.com.

Lighthearted Pr., Inc., *(978-0-9659225)* Orders Addr.: P.O. Box 90125, Portland, OR 97290 USA Tel 503-786-3085; Fax: 503-786-0315; Edit Addr.: 10585 SE Fairway Dr., Portland, OR 97266 USA
E-mail: davis@lightheartedpress.com
Web site: http://www.lightheartedpress.com.

Lighthouse Bk. Publishing, *(978-0-9791168)* Orders Addr.: P.O. Box 310534, Houston, TX 77231 USA Toll Free: 800-247-9100
E-mail: book@journeytoseetheking.com
Web site: http://www.journeytoseetheking.com.

Lighthouse Christian Products Co., *(978-0-9712894)* 1050 Remington Rd., Schaumburg, IL 60173-4518 USA
Web site: http://lcpgifts.com.

Lighthouse eBooks *See* **Lighthouse Publishing**

Lighthouse for Leaders, *(978-0-9820576)* P.O. Box 1990, San Benito, TX 78586 USA; *Imprints:* Lighthouse for Leaders, A (LighthseforLea)
Web site: http://www.LighthouseforLeaders.com.

Lighthouse for Leaders, A *Imprint of* **Lighthouse for Leaders**

Lighthouse Point Pr., *(978-0-9637966; 978-0-9792998)* Div. of Yearick-Millea, Inc., 7412 Lighthouse Point, Pittsburgh, PA 15221 USA Tel 412-242-9382; Fax: 412-242-9382
Web site: http://lighthousepointpress.com.

LightHouse Pr., *(978-0-9703823; 978-0-9724442; 978-0-9747189; 978-0-9762898; 978-0-9791372; 978-0-9823218)* 2053 Williams Valley Dr., Madison, TN 37115-7610 USA Do not confuse with companies with the same or similar names in Culver City, CA, Millersburg, OH, York, ME, Marblehead, MA, Deerfield Beach, FL, La Junta, CO, Rochester, NY, San Mateo, CA.

Lighthouse Pr., Inc., *(978-0-9677347; 978-0-9795392)* 5448 Apex Peakway #230, Apex, NC 27502-3924 USA (SAN 253-0961) Do not confuse with companies with the same or similar names in York, ME, Marblehead, MA, La Junta, CO, Deerfield Beach, FL, San Mateo, CA, Sanford, MI, Minneapolis, MN, Millersburg, OH
E-mail: swagner@lighthouse-press.com
Web site: http://www.lighthouse-press.com
Dist(s): **Independent Pubs. Group**
Midpoint Trade Bks., Inc.

Lighthouse Publication *See* **MainSpringBks.**

Lighthouse Publications *See* **I AM Foundation, The**

Lighthouse Publishing *See* **LightHse. Publishing**

LightHse. Publishing, *(978-0-9755438)* 6761 W. Sonnet Dr., Glendale, AZ 85308 USA Tel 602-535-9379; Fax: 858-720-8733; Toll Free: 888-357-7313
E-mail: julieginn@gmail.com.

Lighthouse Publishing, *(978-0-9773766; 978-0-9797863; 978-1-935079; 978-0-9981577; 978-1-64373)* 754 Roxholly Walk, Buford, GA 30518 USA (SAN 257-4330)
E-mail: andyoverett@lighthousechristianpublishing.com
Web site: http://www.lighthouseebooks.com; http://www.lighthousechristianpublishing.com; http://www.loneoakpublishing.com
Dist(s): **CreateSpace Independent Publishing Platform.**

Lighthouse Publishing of the Carolinas *See* **LPC**

LightHse. Pr. *Imprint of* **Agape Inc**

Lightly Pr., *(978-0-9794452)* 26 Quay Ct., No. 65, sacramento, CA 95831-1540 USA Tel 916-427-7840
E-mail: regdown@hotmail.com.

Lightnin Bug Pr., *(978-0-9824289)* 422 S. Maple, Harrison, AR 72690-5832 USA (SAN 858-1428).

Lightning Bug Flix *See* **Santa Fe Communications, Inc.**

Lightning Bug Learning Corporation *See* **Lightning Bug Learning Pr.**

Lightning Bug Learning Pr., *(978-0-9817826; 978-0-9832098)* Reviewer Relations Dept. 316 Mid Valley Ctr., #130, Carmel, CA 93923 USA (SAN 856-5449) Tel 831-250-1866; Fax: 971-250-2582; Toll Free: 877-695-7312
E-mail: mail@lightningbuglearning.com
Web site: http://www.lightningbuglearning.com; http://www.lightningbuglearningpress.com
Dist(s): **Book Clearing Hse.**

Lightning Creek *See* **Perceval Pr.**

Lightning Fast Bk. Publishing, *(978-0-9916682; 978-0-9965411; 978-0-9974925; 978-0-9994653; 978-1-7348113)* 1812 Hollydale Rd., Fort Washington, MD 20744 USA Tel 240-605-1106
E-mail: matt@matthewchorne.com
Web site: www.lfbookpublishing.com.

Lightning Source, LLC *See* **Ingram Content Group**

LightningBolt Pr., *(978-0-9746398)* 1481 Applegate Dr. Suite 101, Naperville, IL 60565-1225 USA Tel 630-778-7310; Fax: 630-778-7890
E-mail: info@mygreatdebate.net
Web site: http://www.greatdebate.net.

Lightport Bks., *(978-0-9712425)* P.O. Box 7112, Berkeley, CA 94707 USA
E-mail: haconrad@earthlink.net
Web site: http://www.lightportbooks.com.

Lightwatcher Publishing *See* **Illumina Publishing**

Ligonier Ministries, *(978-1-56769; 978-1-64289)* Orders Addr.: P.O. Box 547500, Orlando, FL 32854-7500 USA Tel 407-333-4244; Fax: 407-333-4233; Edit Addr.: 400 Technology Park Dr., Lake Mary, FL 32746 USA; *Imprints:* Reformation Trust Publishing (ReformTrust)
Web site: http://www.ligonier.org
Dist(s): **christianaudio.**

Liguori Pubns., *(978-0-7648; 978-0-89243)* One Liguori Dr., Liguori, MO 63057-9999 USA (SAN 202-6783) Tel 636-464-2500; Fax: 636-464-8449; Toll Free Fax: 800-325-9526; Toll Free: 800-325-9521 (orders); *Imprints:* Libros Liguori (Libros Liguori)
E-mail: liguori@liguori.org
Web site: http://www.liguori.org
Dist(s): **ACTA Pubns.**
Follett School Solutions
MyiLibrary.

LikeMinds Pr., *(978-0-9764724; 978-0-9915853)* Orders Addr.: 3151 Airway Ave. Suite K-205 Suite K-205, Costa Mesa, CA 92626 USA Fax: 714-556-2354
E-mail: shendl@cox.net
Web site: http://www.likemindspress.com.

Lil' Libros *Imprint of* **Little Libros, LLC**

Lilac Pr., *(978-0-9662568)* Orders Addr.: P.O. Box 1356, Scottsdale, AZ 85252-1356 USA Fax: 480-368-5551; Edit Addr.: 6268 N. 85th St., Scottsdale, AZ 85250 USA
E-mail: lilacp@cholesterolnodiet.com; lilacp@frontiernet.net
Web site: http://www.cholesterolnodiet.com.

Lilacs in Litearture, *(978-0-692-74509-0; 978-0-692-74510-6; 978-0-9981958; 978-1-7340099)* 3014 Coventry Ct., Cocoa, FL 32926 USA Tel 321-525-9612
E-mail: wandalu64@gmail.com
Web site: www.wandaluthman.wordpress.com.

LiliArte, *(978-0-692-88040-1; 978-0-692-92873-8)* 21 SHENEMAN DR, BELLA VISTA, AR 72715 USA Tel 501-588-1365
E-mail: christyhn@yahoo.com.

Lillenas Publishing Co., *(978-0-8341)* Div. of Nazarene Publishing Hse., P.O. Box 419527, Kansas City, MO 64141 USA (SAN 298-7619) Tel 816-931-1900; Fax: 816-753-4071; Toll Free Fax: 800-849-9827; Toll Free: 800-877-0700 (Orders Only)
E-mail: music@lillenas.com
Web site: http://www.lillenas.com
Dist(s): **The Foundry Publishing**
Leonard, Hal Corp.
Spring Arbor Distributors, Inc.

Lillian Press *See* **Smith & Assocs.**

Lillis, Holly, *(978-0-9762733)* P.O. Box 1082, Aptos, CA 95001-0000 USA.

Lill-Till Pr., *(978-0-9742808)* 15305 Walvern Blvd., Maple Heights, OH 44137 USA.

Lily & Co. Publishing, *(978-1-929265)* Orders Addr.: 15 Willow Rd., Greenville, RI 02828 USA
E-mail: erinesquedesign@mac.com
Web site: http://www.lilycopublishing.com.

Lily The Reindeer, *(978-0-692-87764-7; 978-0-692-15777-0)* 55 Myrtle Pk. Point, Ponte Vedra, FL 32081 USA Tel 516-819-1234; Toll Free: 516-819-1234
E-mail: jackbunkerdavid@aol.com; jackbunkerdavid@aol.com; jackbunkerdavid@aol.com
Web site: https://lilythereindeer.com/
Dist(s): **CreateSpace Independent Publishing Platform.**

Lily Wish Factory, *(978-0-9792472)* 44 W. Main St., Mystic, CT 06355 USA (SAN 852-8861) Tel 860-245-0629
E-mail: shipandshimmer@aol.com
Web site: http://shipandshimmer.com.

Lima Bear Pr LLC, The, *(978-1-933872)* 2305 MacDonough Rd., Wilmington, DE 19805 USA
E-mail: lbp.books@yahoo.com
Web site: http://www.limabearpress.com.

Limelight Editions *Imprint of* **Leonard, Hal Corp.**

Limerock Bks., *(978-0-9746589)* 15 Mechanic St., Thomaston, ME 04861 USA Tel 207-354-8191 Do not confuse with Limerock Books, Inc., New Canaan, CT
E-mail: limebks@midcoast.com
Web site: http://www.ChristopherFahy.com
Dist(s): **Brodart Co.**

Limitless Bks., *(978-0-9998865)* 101 Parkhurst Rd, Gansevoot, NY 12831 USA Tel 518-396-8376
E-mail: ian@bicyclebenefits.org
Web site: www.limitlessbooks.us.

Limitless Ink Press, LLC, *(978-1-939672; 978-0-615-93665-9; 978-1-947218)* P.O. Box 8802, Erie, PA 16505 USA Tel 913-271-7804
E-mail: patricemichelle@gmail.com.

Limitless Publishing, LLC, *(978-0-615-68509-0; 978-0-615-76957-8; 978-0-615-78296-6; 978-0-615-78347-5; 978-0-615-68058; 978-1-64034)* 701 N. Kalaheo, Kailua, HI 96734 USA
E-mail: jennifer@limitlesspublishing.com; dixie@limitlesspublishing.com
Web site: http://www.limitlesspublishing.com
Dist(s): **CreateSpace Independent Publishing Platform.**

Lincoln Bks., *(978-0-9910560)* 406 Diana Ct., Highland Heights, OH 44124 USA Tel 440-813-0274
E-mail: robthomas@hotmail.com
Web site: Rob Thomas.

Lincoln, Emma *See* **Awesome Bk. Publishing**

Lincoln Learning Solutions, *(978-0-9816745; 978-1-935193; 978-1-936318; 978-1-938165; 978-1-943303; 978-1-944075; 978-1-68379)* 294 Massachusetts Ave., Rochester, PA 15074 USA Toll Free: 866-990-6637
Web site: http://www.nndsonline.org; linconlearningsolutions.org.

Lincoln Library Pr., Inc., The, *(978-0-912168)* Orders Addr.: 812 Huron Rd., SE, Suite 401, Cleveland, OH 44115-1126 USA (SAN 205-5953) Fax: 216-781-9559 (phone/fax); Toll Free: 800-516-2656
E-mail: tgall@thelincolnlibrary.com
Web site: http://www.thelincolnlibrary.com
Dist(s): **Follett School Solutions**
INscribe Digital.

Lincoln Public Schls., *(978-0-9671920)* P.O. Box 82889, Lincoln, NE 68501 USA (SAN 508-9964) Tel 401-436-1628; Fax: 401-436-1638
E-mail: dpeters@lps.org
Web site: http://www.lps.org.

Lincross Publishing, *(978-0-9987566; 978-0-9991896; 978-1-948581)* 4480 - H South Cobb Drive, Suite 391, Smyrna, GA 30080 USA Tel 678-308-9971
E-mail: lincrosspublishing@gmail.com
Web site: www.lincrosspublishing.com.

Linda Cardillo, Author *See* **Bellastoria Pr.**

Linda Hall Library, *(978-0-9763590)* 5109 Cherry St., Kansas City, MO 64110-2498 USA Tel 816-363-4600; Fax: 816-926-8790
E-mail: bradleyb@lindahall.org
Web site: http://www.lindahall.org.

Linda Kaye's Birthdaybakers, Partymakers, *(978-0-9759161)* 195 East 76th St., New York, NY 10021 USA Tel 212-288-7112; Fax: 212-879-6785
E-mail: lindak@partymakers.com
Web site: http://www.partymakers.com.

Linda M. Penn Author, *(978-0-9852488; 978-0-9908807; 978-1-7321454)* 2023 Eagles Landing Dr., Lagrange, KY 40031 USA Tel 502-262-7870
E-mail: lindampenn@gmail.com.

Lindaloo Enterprises, *(978-0-9800923; 978-1-937564)* P.O. Box 90135, Santa Barbara, CA 93190 USA; *Imprints:* Classic Bookwrights (ClassicBook)
E-mail: sales@lindaloo.com
Web site: http://www.lindaloo.com; http://www.tporigami.com
Dist(s): **Ingram Content Group.**

Linden Hill Publishing, *(978-0-9704754; 978-0-9820153)* Subs. of Arcadia Productions, 11923 Somerset Ave., Princess Anne, MD 21853 USA Tel 410-651-0757 (phone/fax)
E-mail: lindenhill2@comcast.net
Web site: http://www.lindenhill.net.

Linden Publishing Co., Inc., *(978-0-941936; 978-1-933502; 978-1-61035)* 2006 S. Mary, Fresno, CA 93721 USA (SAN 238-6089) Tel 559-233-6633 (phone/fax); Toll Free: 800-345-4447 (orders only); *Imprints:* Craven Street Books (Craven St Bks) Do not confuse with LInden Publishing in Avon, NY
E-mail: richard@lindenpub.com
Web site: http://www.lindenpub.com
Dist(s): **CreateSpace Independent Publishing Platform**
Ingram Publisher Services
Quality Bks., Inc.
Smashwords.

Lindisfarne Bks. *Imprint of* **SteinerBooks, Inc.**

Lindsay Pubns., Inc., *(978-0-917914; 978-1-55918)* Orders Addr.: P.O. Box 12, Bradley, IL 60915 USA (SAN 209-9462) Tel 815-935-5353; Fax: 815-935-5477.

Lindsley, David Studio, *(978-0-9796008)* P.O. Box 431, Springville, UT 84663 USA.

Line By Lion Pubns. *Imprint of* **3 Fates Pr.**

Linear Wave Publishing, *(978-0-9767196)* P.O. Box 177, Liberty, KY 42539-0177 USA Tel 606-787-8189
E-mail: blaine.staat@linearwavepublishing.com
Web site: http://www.linearwavepublishing.com.

Linehan Authors, *(978-1-7336855)* 807 Callant Dr., Little River, SC 29566 USA Tel 860-942-1623
E-mail: judithlinehan@gmail.com; thomas.linehan@yahoo.com
Web site: www.linehanauthors.com.

Lingenfelser, Lynda L., *(978-0-615-13290-7; 978-0-615-14072-8)* 3284 Spruce Creek Glen, Daytona Beach, FL 32198 USA; P.O. Box 290714, Port Orange, FL 32129
Dist(s): **Lulu Pr., Inc.**

Linger Longer Books *See* **Artists' Orchard, LLC, The**

Lingo Pr. LLC, *(978-0-9777419)* 1020 Janet Dr., Lakeland, FL 33805 USA (SAN 850-119X) Tel 863-868-5996 (phone/fax)
E-mail: customerservice@lingopress.com
Web site: http://www.lingopress.com.

Linguatechnics Publishing, *(978-0-9767837)* 2114 Pauline Blvd., Ann Arbor, MI 48103 USA Tel 734-662-0434; Fax: 734-662-0248
E-mail: info@linguatechnics.com
Web site: http://www.linguatechnics.com.

LinguaText, Limited *See* **LinguaText, LLC**

LinguaText, LLC, *(978-0-936388; 978-0-942566; 978-1-58871; 978-1-58977)* Orders Addr.: 103 Walker Way, Newark, DE 19711-6119 USA (SAN 238-0307) Tel 302-453-8695
E-mail: text@linguatextbooks.com; libros@juandelacuesta.com
Web site: http://www.LinguatextLtd.com; http://www.MoliereandCo.com; http://www.LinguaTextBooks.com; http://www.CervantesandCo.com; http://www.EuropeanMasterpieces.com; http://www.JuandelaCuesta.com
Dist(s): **Baker & Taylor Publisher Services (BTPS)**
Follett School Solutions
Yankee Bk. Peddler, Inc.

LinguiSystems, Inc., *(978-0-7606; 978-1-55999)* 3100 Fourth Ave., East Moline, IL 61244-9700 USA Tel 309-755-2300; Fax: 309-755-2377; Toll Free: 800-776-4332; 800-577-4555
E-mail: kmicka@linguisystems.com
Web site: http://www.linguisystems.com.

Linhardt, Mitch, *(978-0-578-13379-9; 978-0-578-17373-3; 978-0-578-18616-0; 978-0-578-18748-8)* 921 Union Pl., Herculaneum, MO 63048 USA Tel 314-229-8689
E-mail: mclinhardt@yahoo.com.

Linive Kreyol Publishing, *(978-0-9720954)* 339 Howell Dr. SE, Suite 3-F, Atlanta, GA 30316 USA.

Link & Rosie Pr., *(978-0-9762434)* Orders Addr.: c/o Goblin Fern Press, Inc., 1118 Sequoia Trail, Madison, WI 53713 USA Tel 608-335-0542; Fax: 608-210-7235
E-mail: ssharron@sbcglobal.net
Web site: http://www.linkandrosie.com.

Linky & Dinky Enterprises, *(978-0-9768588)* P.O. Box 418, Oldsmar, FL 34677 USA
E-mail: uncle-url@linkydinky.com
Web site: http://www.linkydinky.com.

Linmore Publishing, Inc., *(978-0-916591; 978-1-934472)* Orders Addr.: P.O. Box 1545, Palatine, IL 60078 USA (SAN 662-2291) Fax: 612-729-9125; Toll Free: 800-336-3656
E-mail: linmore@linmore.com
Web site: http://www.linmore.com.

LinWood Hse. Publishing, *(978-0-9753098; 978-0-692-98408-6; 978-1-7321891)* 3652 Kissimmee Pk. Rd., Saint Cloud, FL 34772 USA Tel 407-595-6220
E-mail: zippityzem@comcast.net
Dist(s): **CreateSpace Independent Publishing Platform**
Smashwords.

Linworth Publishing, Inc. *Imprint of* **ABC-CLIO, LLC**

LINX Corp., *(978-0-9642386; 978-0-9802118; 978-1-936961)* P.O. Box 613, Great Falls, VA 22066 USA Tel 703-216-9314; *Imprints:* Investing for Kids (Investing); VRguy publishing (VRguy)
E-mail: orders@linxcorp.com; steve@linxcorp.com
Web site: http://www.linxcorp.com
Dist(s): **Bookazine Co., Inc.**

Linx Educational Publishing, Inc., *(978-1-891818; 978-0-9797510)* P.O. Box 50009, Jacksonville Beach, FL 32240 USA Tel 904-241-1861; Fax: 904-241-3279; Toll Free Fax: 888-546-9338; Toll Free: 800-717-5469
E-mail: mimi@lixedu.com; info@linxedu.com
Web site: http://www.linxedu.com
Dist(s): **American Assn. for Vocational Instructional Materials**
Films Media Group
Follett School Solutions
JIST Publishing
S V E & Churchill Media.

†Lion Bks., *(978-0-87460)* 235 Garth Rd. Apt. D5A, Scarsdale, NY 10583-3994 USA (SAN 241-7529)
Dist(s): **Baker & Taylor Publisher Services (BTPS)**; *CIP.*

Lion Forge *Imprint of* **Oni Pr., Inc.**

Lion Hudson PLC (GBR) *(978-0-7459; 978-0-85648; 978-0-85721) Dist. by* **IPG Chicago.**

Lion Hudson PLC (GBR) *(978-0-7459; 978-0-85648; 978-0-85721) Dist. by* **Trafalgar.**

Lion Hudson PLC (GBR) *(978-0-7459; 978-0-85648; 978-0-85721) Dist. by* **Kregel.**

Lion Prints Publishing *See* **DL Publishing**

Lion Stone Bks., *(978-0-9658486; 978-0-9859618)* Orders Addr.: 4921 Aurora Dr., Kensington, MD 20895 USA Tel 301-949-3204; Fax: 301-949-3860
E-mail: lionstone@juno.com
Dist(s): **Book Wholesalers, Inc.**
Brodart Co.
Follett School Solutions.

Lionel A. Blanchard, Pub., *(978-0-9972984; 978-1-7335858)* 2580 Dixon Dr., Santa Clara, CA 95051 USA Tel 408-406-8470
E-mail: l.a.blanchard@comcast.net.

Lioness Publishing, *(978-0-9961606)* 2120 W.96th St., Los Angeles, CA 90047 USA Tel 323-477-3530
E-mail: livia.latrice@gmail.com.

Lionheart Foundation, The, *(978-0-9644933; 978-0-9799338; 978-0-578-59124-7; 978-0-578-62058-9; 978-0-578-68961-6; 978-0-578-74284-7; 978-0-578-76336-1)* P.O. Box 194, Boston, MA 02117 USA Tel 781-444-6667; Fax: 781-444-6855
E-mail: judith@lionheart.org
Web site: http://www.lionheart.org.

Lionheart Group Publishing, *(978-0-9845127; 978-1-938505)* Div. of Lionheart Group, LLC, 1501 Main St No. 1023, Canon City, CO 81215 USA
E-mail: admin@lionheartgrouppublishing.com
Web site: www.redenginepress.com; www.lionheartgrouppublishing.com.

Lionheart Pr., *(978-0-9964246)* 3711 Fews Ford Ln., Durham, NC 27712 USA Tel 919-812-6204
E-mail: hejafred@gmail.com
Web site: www.timberhowligan.com.

Lion's Crest Pr., *(978-0-9763798)* 1900 S. Rock Rd., Suite 5205, Wichita, KS 67207 USA Tel 316-305-5813.

Lions Den Publishing, LLC, *(978-0-9786786)* P.O. Box 91254, Washington, DC 20090-1254 USA (SAN 851-2477) Tel 202-256-0508.

Lion's Tale Pr., LLC, *(978-0-9748478)* 4895 Kings Valley Dr., Suite 200, Roswell, GA 30075 USA Tel 770-998-3302; Fax: 770-998-3874
E-mail: ebbenator@mindspring.com.

LionX Publishing, *(978-0-9716085)* 24988 Blue Ravine Rd., #108-113, Folsom, CA 95630 USA (SAN 254-2021) Tel 916-939-9422; Fax: 916-939-9424
E-mail: info@lionxpublishing.com
Web site: http://www.lionxpublishing.com.

LIP Publishing LLC, *(978-0-9771114)* 903 Oakridge Dr, Suite 100, Round Rock, TX 78681 USA
E-mail: thelifeip@yahoo.com
Web site: http://www.thelifeip.com.

†Lippincott Williams & Wilkins, *(978-0-316; 978-0-397; 978-0-683; 978-0-7817; 978-0-8067; 978-0-8121; 978-0-88167; 978-0-89004; 978-0-89313; 978-0-89640; 978-0-911216; 978-1-881063; 978-1-60547; 978-1-60831; 978-1-60929; 978-1-4698)* Orders Addr.: P.O. Box 1620, Hagerstown, MD 21741 USA Fax: 301-223-2400; Toll Free: 800-638-3030; Edit Addr.: 530 Walnut St., Philadelphia, PA 19106-3621 USA (SAN 201-0933) Tel 215-521-8300; Fax: 215-521-8902; Toll Free: 800-638-3030; 351 W. Camden St., Baltimore, MD 21201 Tel 410-528-4000; 410-528-4209
E-mail: custserv@lww.com; orders@lww.com
Web site: http://www.lww.com
Dist(s): **Igaku-Shoin Medical Pubs.**
MyiLibrary; *CIP.*

Lippincott-Raven Publishers *See* **Lippincott Williams & Wilkins**

Liquid Space Publishing, *(978-0-9710366)* 37 Endicott St., Salem, MA 01970 USA Tel 978-745-5529
E-mail: donniedives@earthlink.net
Web site: http://www.home.earthlink.net/~donniedives.

Lire Bks., *(978-0-9849323; 978-1-939652)* 7 Debaun Pl., Spring Valley, NY 10977 USA Tel 845-659-2018
E-mail: raedanbocs@gmail.com
Web site: lirebooks.com; http://simplylire.com/.

Lisa Bushong-Holgate, *(978-0-692-94611-4)* 5216 Univ. Dr., Santa Barbara, CA 93111 USA Tel 510-265-4714
E-mail: lmbushong@yahoo.com.

Lisa The Weather Wonder Inc., *(978-0-9740997)* 187 Summer Lake Dr., Marietta, GA 30060 USA
Web site: http://www.lisamozer.com.

Lisboa, David, *(978-0-9752740)* 9060 Palisade Ave., Apt. 307, North Bergan, NJ 07047 USA Tel 201-869-3494.

Listen & Live Audio, Inc., *(978-1-885408; 978-1-931953; 978-1-59316)* Orders Addr.: P.O. Box 817, Roseland, NJ 07068 USA Tel 201-558-9000; Fax: 201-558-9800; Toll Free: 800-653-9400; Edit Addr.: 1700 Manhattan Ave., Union City, NJ 07087-5473 USA
E-mail: Alfred@Listenandlive.com
Web site: http://www.listenandlive.com
Dist(s): **Audible.com**
Ebsco Publishing
Findaway World, LLC
Follett School Solutions
OverDrive, Inc.
Smashwords.

Listening Library *Imprint of* **Random Hse. Audio Publishing Group**

Lister, Tresina, *(978-0-9791171)* 541 S. Staunton Dr., Tucson, AZ 85710 USA Tel 520-751-8630.

Lit Noire Publishing, *(978-0-9719052; 978-0-578-50965-5)* P.O. Box 26183, Brooklyn, NY 11201 USA Tel 212-656-1762
E-mail: duewa@duewaworld.com
Web site: http://www.duewaworld.com
Dist(s): **CreateSpace Independent Publishing Platform**
Lulu Pr., Inc.

Lit Torch Publishing, *(978-1-887357)* 4204 Danmire Dr., Richardson, TX 75082 USA Tel 312-239-8633 (phone/fax)
E-mail: littorch@gmail.com
Web site: http://www.littorch.com.

Lit Verlag (DEU) *(978-3-8258; 978-3-89473; 978-3-88660; 978-3-643) Dist. by* **IPG Chicago.**

Literacy Resources, Inc., *(978-0-9759575; 978-1-947260)* 143 Franklin Ave., River Forest, IL 60305-2113 USA Tel 708-366-5947; Fax: 708-366-9149
E-mail: tcorless@literacyresourcesinc.com
Web site: http://www.literacyresourcesinc.com.

Literal Publishing Inc., *(978-0-9770287; 978-0-9897957; 978-1-942307)* 5425 Renwick Dr., Houston, TX 77081 USA Tel 713-626-1433.

Literally Speaking Publishing Hse., *(978-1-929642)* 2020 Pennsylvania Ave., NW, No. 406, Washington, DC 20006 USA (SAN 852-8896) Tel 202-491-5774; Fax: 202-403-3535
E-mail: Distribution@LiterallySpeaking.com; bookinfo@literallyspeaking.com
Web site: http://www.literallyspeaking.com.

Literary Architects, LLC, *(978-1-933669)* 1427 W. 86th St., Suite 324, Indianapolis, IN 46260 USA Tel 317-462-6329
E-mail: info@literaryarchitects.com
Web site: http://www.literaryarchitects.com.

Literary Legacies Publishing, *(978-0-692-95440-9; 978-0-692-15422-9; 978-0-692-15965-1; 978-0-578-49765-5; 978-0-578-49766-2; 978-0-578-49767-9)* 1355 James Ct., Morgan Hill, CA 95037 USA Tel 4084107886
E-mail: info@literarylegacies.org
Dist(s): **CreateSpace Independent Publishing Platform.**

Literary Lessons *Imprint of* **HomeScholar Bks.**

Literary Licensing, LLC, *(978-1-258; 978-1-4940; 978-1-4941; 978-1-4978; 978-1-4979; 978-1-4980; 978-1-4981)* P.O. Box 1404, Whitefish, MT 59937 USA Fax: 406-897-7825
E-mail: literarylicensing@runbox.com
Web site: http://www.literarylicensing.com
Dist(s): **ISD.**

Literary Works Specialist, *(978-0-9746687)* P.O. Box 58908, New Orleans, LA 70158-8908 USA
E-mail: rdomio@aol.com
Web site: http://www.lwspublishing.net.

Literate Chigger Pr., Ink, Inc., The, *(978-0-9759042; 978-0-615-56517-0)* 1175 Queen Anne Rd., Teaneck, NJ 07666 USA Tel 201-741-6529
E-mail: emily@hipbo.org.

Literature Dramatization Pr., *(978-0-9644186)* 1089 Sunset Cliffs Blvd., San Diego, CA 92107-4037 USA Tel 619-222-2462
Dist(s): **Educational Bk. Distributors**
Empire Publishing Service
Lectorum Pubns., Inc.

LITHBTH Educational Services, *(978-0-9744920)* P.O. Box 55495, Hayward, CA 94545-5495 USA
E-mail: teachingkids@mindspring.com
Web site: http://www.home.mindspring.com/~teachingkids.

Litho Tech, LLC, *(978-0-9742791)* 3045 Highland Ave., Grants Pass, OR 97526 USA Tel 541-479-8905; Fax: 541-474-6937
E-mail: gpprint@charterinternet.com; lithotech541@charter.net.

Litkus Pr., *(978-1-932629)* P.O. Box 34785, Los Angeles, CA 90034 USA Tel 310-391-5629
E-mail: litkuspress@earthlink.net.

Litmocracy Pubns., *(978-0-9798861)* 9175 Middlefield Dr., Riverside, CA 92508 USA (SAN 854-6606)
E-mail: dscotese@litmocracy.com
Web site: http://www.litmocracy.com.

Little A *Imprint of* **Amazon Publishing**

Little Acorn Assocs., Inc., *(978-0-9741579; 978-0-9844010; 978-1-937257; 978-1-946557)*
E-mail: liiacorn53@gmail.com.

Little Acorn Associates, Incorporated *See* **Little Acorn Assocs., Inc.**

Little Acorn LLC, *(978-0-9766703; 978-0-9964448)* Orders Addr.: 112 W. Calista Dr., Tahlequah, OK 74464-7446 USA
E-mail: info@littleacornkids.net
Web site: http://www.littleacornkids.net.

Little Adventures *Imprint of* **Amberjack Publishing Co.**

Little Balloon Pr., *(978-0-9843922)* 988 Belmont Terr., No. 2, Sunnyvale, CA 94086 USA (SAN 859-2721)
Web site: http://www.littleballoonpress.com.

Little Band Man Co., LLC, The, *(978-0-615-12596-1)* 1415 Easy St., New Iberia, LA 70560 USA Tel 337-365-4136; Fax: 337-365-4137
E-mail: jady@littlebandman.com
Web site: http://www.littlebandman.com.

Little Bay Pr., *(978-0-9745192)* 40 Salmon Beach, Tacoma, WA 98407 USA Tel 253-756-0987
E-mail: kcampbell@littlebaypress.com
Web site: http://www.littlebaypress.com.

Little Bear Pr., *(978-0-615-57443-1; 978-0-615-90320-0)* 448 Pear Tree Point Rd., Chestertown, MD 21620 USA Tel 301-775-0164; 410-778-6270
Dist(s): **CreateSpace Independent Publishing Platform.**

Little Bee Books Inc., *(978-1-4998)* Div. of Bonnier Publishing USA, 251 Park Ave. S., 12th Flr., New York,

NY 10016 USA Tel 917-280-6600; Toll Free: 844-321-0237; *Imprints:* Sizzle Press (SizzlePr); BuzzPop (BuzzPop)
E-mail: info@littlebeebooks.com
Web site: http://www.littlebeebooks.com
Dist(s): **Children's Plus, Inc.**
Simon & Schuster, Inc.

Little Big Bay LLC, *(978-0-9834330; 978-0-9892822; 978-0-9968071)* 124 E. Bennett St., Mellen, WI 54546 USA Tel 715-919-0179
E-mail: ros@winternet.com
Web site: www.littlebigbay.com
Dist(s): **Ingram Publisher Services**
Ingram Content Group.

Little Big Tomes, 1275 Trail Ridge Dr., Canyon Lake, TX 78133 USA Tel 830-899-6888
E-mail: cottage@gvtc.com.

Little Bigfoot *Imprint of* **Sasquatch Bks.**

Little Bird Bks., *(978-0-615-66291-6; 978-0-9913003)* 585 Mountain View Rd., Santa Cruz, CA 95065 USA
E-mail: masperling@gmail.com.

Little Bird Publishing, *(978-0-9728838)* 285 W. 8th St., Ship Bottom, NJ 08008 USA Tel 609-494-7485; Fax: 609-494-9569
E-mail: gwennhotaling@aol.com
Web site: http://www.gwennhotaling.com.

Little Black Paws Publishing, *(978-0-9992704)* 2803 Sarento Pl. No. 107, Palm Beach Gardens, FL 33410 USA Tel 203-249-9838
E-mail: sandramendelson@yahoo.com.

Little Blue Flower Pr. *Imprint of* **Grey Gate Media, LLC**

Little Blue Hse., 1600 Cliff Rd. E, Burnsville, MN 55337 USA; *Imprints:* Little Blue Readers (LBlueRead)
Dist(s): **North Star Editions.**

Little Blue Pr., *(978-0-9725584)* 14403 Little Blue Rd., Kansan City, MO 64136 USA Tel 816-455-1110
E-mail: littlebluepress@softhome.net.

Little Blue Readers *Imprint of* **Little Blue Hse.**

Little Bookroom *Imprint of* **New York Review of Bks., Inc., The**

Little Bookstore Who Could, The, *(978-0-9746997)* 1303 Windsong Way, Augusta, GA 30907 USA Tel 706-868-0075
E-mail: vickyharperselah@yahoo.com; vicky@thelittlebookstorethatcould.com
Web site: http://www.thelittlebookstorethatcould.coom.

Little Boots Publishing, *(978-0-9767230)* P.O. Box 3110, Pawtucket, RI 02861 USA Tel 401-475-5852 (phone/fax)
E-mail: Info@littlebootspublishing.com
Web site: http://www.littlebootspublishing.com.

Little Britches Childrens Bks., *(978-0-9798189)* P.O. Box 1188, Willow, AK 99688-1188 USA.

†Little Brown & Co., *(978-0-316; 978-0-8212; 978-0-7595)* Div. of Hachette Bk. Group, Orders Addr.: 3 Center Plaza, Boston, MA 02108-2084 USA (SAN 630-7248) Tel 617-227-0730; Toll Free Fax: 800-286-9471; Toll Free: 800-759-0190; Edit Addr.: 237 Park Ave., New York, NY 10017 USA (SAN 200-2205) Tel 212-364-0600; Fax: 212-364-0952; *Imprints:* Back Bay Books (Back Bay); Reagan Arthur Books (ReagArthur); Jimmy Patterson (JimmyPat); Bulfinch (Bulfinch)
E-mail: customer.service@hbgusa.com
Web site: http://www.hachettebookgroup.com
Dist(s): **Blackstone Audio, Inc.**
Children's Plus, Inc.
Continental Bk. Co., Inc.
Follett School Solutions
Grand Central Publishing
Hachette Bk. Group
Hastings Bks.
Lectorum Pubns., Inc.
MyiLibrary
Rounder Kids Music Distribution
Beeler, Thomas T. Pub.
TextStream
Thorndike Pr.; *CIP.*

Little, Brown Book Group Ltd. (GBR) *(978-0-09; 978-0-316; 978-0-349; 978-0-351; 978-0-7088; 978-0-7474; 978-0-7499; 978-0-7515; 978-0-8212; 978-0-86188; 978-0-948164; 978-1-85004; 978-1-85487; 978-1-85703; 978-1-85018; 978-1-84119; 978-0-7221; 978-0-86007; 978-0-9536151; 978-1-903608; 978-1-84529; 978-1-84528; 978-1-84901; 978-1-4087; 978-1-908974) Dist. by* **HachBkGrp.**

Little, Brown Bks. for Young Readers, *(978-0-316; 978-0-8212; 978-0-7595; 978-0-7596)* Div. of Hachette Bk. Group, 1271 Ave. of the Americas, New York, NY 10020 USA Tel 212-522-8700; Fax: 212-522-2067; Toll Free: 800-343-9204; 3 Center Plaza, Boston, MA 02108-2084 USA Tel 617-227-0730; Toll Free Fax: 800-286-9471; Toll Free: 800-759-0190; *Imprints:* Tingley, Megan Books (Megan Tingley Bks); Poppy (Poppy); LB Kids (LBKids)
Dist(s): **Blackstone Audio, Inc.**
Children's Plus, Inc.
Follett School Solutions
Grand Central Publishing
Hachette Bk. Group
Lectorum Pubns., Inc.
Little Brown & Co.
MyiLibrary.

Little Brown Children's Books *See* **Little, Brown Bks. for Young Readers**

Little Bunny Bks., *(978-0-615-46734-4; 978-0-615-58595-6; 978-0-615-66757-7; 978-0-692-48194-3)* P.O. Box 151, Cabin John, MD 20818 USA Tel 978-712-8669
E-mail: littlebunnybooks@gmail.com
Dist(s): **CreateSpace Independent Publishing Platform.**

Little Buzz Bk. Club, *(978-0-9975981; 978-1-947099-46-3)* 2146 Roswell Rd., Marietta, GA 30062 USA Tel 770-744-9390; Fax: 770-744-9390
E-mail: membership@littlebuzzbookclub.com
Web site: www.littlebuzzbookclub.com.

Little CAB Pr., *(978-0-692-76264-6)* 17220 E Desert Ln., GILBERT, AZ 85234 USA Tel 602-791-8410
Dist(s): **Independent Pub.**

Little Cabbagehead Books *See* **Luthie M West**

Little Chameleon Bks. *Imprint of* **Kid Prep, Inc.**

Little Clive Pr., *(978-0-615-58866-7; 978-0-615-69435-1; 978-0-615-79920-9; 978-0-9911479)* 306 N. 19th Ave., Kelso, WA 98626 USA Tel 503-381-3923
E-mail: bendertzu@yahoo.com; joey.wardell@gmail.com
Web site: www.littleclivepress.com.

Little Cottonwood River Bks., *(978-0-9884268)* 2918 71st St., Dundee, MN 56131 USA Tel 507-274-5316
E-mail: paplowp@gmail.com.

Little Creek Bks. *Imprint of* **Jan-Carol Publishing, INC.**

Little Creek Press, *(978-0-9828023; 978-0-9849245; 978-0-9896431; 978-0-9899780; 978-0-9899784; 978-1-942586)* Div. of Kristin Mitchell Design, LLC, 5341 Sunny Ridge Rd., Mineral Point, WI 53565 USA (SAN 920-2862) Tel 608-987-3370
E-mail: info@littlecreekpress.com
Web site: www.littlecreekpress.com
Dist(s): **Independent Pubs. Group.**

Little Cubans, LLC, *(978-1-934113)* P.O. Box 260944, Pembroke Pines, FL 33026-7944 USA
E-mail: littlecubans@bellsouth.net
Web site: http://www.littlecubans.com.

Little, Cynthia M. *See* **Sleepless Warrior Publishing**

Little Danny's Bks. Inc., *(978-1-7328515; 978-1-7339326)* 16900 Heller Ln., Saint Robert, MO 65584 USA Tel 805-320-8058
E-mail: littledannysbooks@gmail.com.

Little Deer Pr., *(978-1-891360)* P.O. Box 1220, Rainier, WA 98576 USA Tel 360-894-3459
E-mail: mollypiper@hotmail.com
Web site: http://www.focusbloom.com.

Little Devil Bks., *(978-0-9858280; 978-0-9911534)* 5139 Maxon Terr., Sanford, FL 32771 USA Tel 407-443-6494
E-mail: dave@littledevilbooks.com
Web site: www.littledevilbooks.com
Dist(s): **Ingram Content Group**
Smashwords.

Little Dixie Publishing Co., *(978-0-9628099)* Orders Addr.: P.O. Box 215, Wynnewood, OK 73098 USA Tel 405-665-4811 Do not confuse with Rebel Pr., Chino, CA
E-mail: LittleDixie@itinet.net
Web site: www.michaelandrewgrissom.com.

Little Dog Pubns., *(978-0-9774143)* P.O. Box 8680, Kansas City Missouri, MO 64114-0680 USA (SAN 257-5051)
E-mail: jeffr@littledogpress.net
Web site: http://littledogpress.net.

Little Feet Pr., *(978-0-9990120)* 13913 Boquita Dr., Del Mar, CA 92014 USA Tel 650-714-8004
E-mail: dani.chammas@gmail.com.

Little Fiddle Co., Inc., The, *(978-0-9700489; 978-0-9798643)* 700 Kinderkamack Rd., Oradell, NJ 07649 USA Fax: 201-265-6499; Toll Free: 888-678-5636
E-mail: info@minimaestro.com; jeofficemgr@osen.us
Web site: http://www.minimaestro.com
Dist(s): **Penton Overseas, Inc.**

Little Germ That Could..Creations, Inc., The, *(978-0-9763233; 978-0-9960186)* 6815 Edgewater Dr., No.108, Coral Gables, FL 33133 USA Tel 305-775-0281
Web site: www.littlegerm.com.

Little Grandma Bks., *(978-0-692-55126-4; 978-0-692-60419-9; 978-0-9997637)* 813 Los Arboles NW, Albuquerque, NM 87107 USA
Dist(s): **CreateSpace Independent Publishing Platform.**

Little Grasshopper Bks. *Imprint of* **Publications International, Ltd.**

Little Guardians, Inc., *(978-0-9660879)* 111 Melody Dr., Metairie, LA 70001 USA Tel 504-837-3328; Fax: 504-835-9993; Toll Free: 800-582-4923.

Little Hands Bk. Co., LLC, *(978-0-9814878)* 32094 Vintage Way, Afton, OK 74331-5600 USA
Web site: http://www.littlehandsbook.com.

Little Hare Bks. (AUS) *(978-1-877003; 978-1-921049; 978-1-921272; 978-1-921541; 978-1-921714; 978-1-921894) Dist. by* **IPG Chicago.**

Little Hat Bks., *(978-0-9980763)* 13216 Mira Mar Dr, Sylmar, CA 91342 USA Tel 818-632-2909
E-mail: cloudgirlbook@gmail.com.

Little Hero, *(978-0-9769057)* P.O. Box 771371, Orlando, FL 32877 USA
E-mail: whitlockmatt@hotmail.com
Web site: http://www.littlehero.net.

Little Hill Pubs., *(978-0-9835048)* Orders Addr.: P.O. Box 282, Ashland, MA 01721 USA; Edit Addr.: 18 Pennock Rd., Ashland, MA 01721 USA Tel 508-881-0011
E-mail: contact@littlehillpublishers.com.

Little Hippo Bks., *(978-1-949679; 978-1-950416; 978-1-950951; 978-1-951356; 978-1-952137; 978-1-952592; 978-1-953756)* 145 Pinelawn Rd., Melville, NY 11747 USA Tel 631-390-8822
E-mail: cleone@usmediapartners.net; kdoherty@usmediapartners.net
Web site: www.littlehippobooks.com.

Little Hound Publishing *Imprint of* **E M McIntyre**

Little Hse. Pr., *(978-0-9773812)* 3618 Bayshore Rd., Sarasota, FL 34234 USA
Dist(s): **Independent Pubs. Group**
MyiLibrary.

Little Hse. Site Tours LLC, *(978-0-9765951)* 2430 Marlette Rd., Applegate, MI 48401 USA Tel 810-633-9973; Fax: 810-633-9027
E-mail: lhsitetours@email.com
Web site: http://www.lhsitetours.homestead.com.

Little Island (IRL) *(978-1-84840; 978-1-908195; 978-1-910411; 978-1-910031) Dist. by* **IPG Chicago.**

Little Island Press (NZL) *(978-1-877484) Dist. by* **UH Pr.**

Little Johnny Bks., *(978-0-692-09259-0; 978-0-692-09706-9; 978-0-578-44093-4; 978-0-578-44118-4)* 720 Williams White Rd, Zebulon, NC 27597 USA Tel 919-426-5527
E-mail: alfordjp88@gmail.com
Dist(s): **CreateSpace Independent Publishing Platform.**

Little Labradoodle Publishing, LLC, *(978-1-7324566; 978-1-7339605)* 245 Manton St., Pawtucket, RI 02861 USA Tel 401-288-9957
E-mail: info@thelittlelabradoodle.com
Web site: www.thelittlelabradoodle.com.

Little Lamb Bks., *(978-0-9986243; 978-1-7323158; 978-1-7332828; 978-1-953456)* P.O. Box 211724, Bedford, TX 76021 USA
E-mail: rachel@littlelambbooks.com
Web site: www.littlelambbooks.com
Dist(s): **Independent Pubs. Group**
Ingram Content Group
Small Pr. United.

Little League Pr., *(978-0-9747883)* P.O. Box 249, Stanleytown, VA 24168 USA
E-mail: hooneybgood@adelphia.net
Dist(s): **Bassett Printing Corp.**

Little Libros, LLC, *(978-0-9861099; 978-1-947971; 978-1-948066)* Orders Addr.: 1960 Hawkins Cir., Los Angeles, CA 90001 USA (SAN 990-6312) Tel 323-484-9758; *Imprints:* Lil' Libros (LIL LIBROS)
E-mail: hola@littlelibros.com; info@littlelibros.com
Web site: www.LilLibros.com; www.LittleLibros.com
Dist(s): **Gibbs Smith, Publisher.**

Little Light Pr., *(978-0-9755374)* Orders Addr.: 549 Broadway, Bethpage, NY 11714 USA Tel 516-938-3343 Do not confuse with Little Light Press in Oklahoma City, OK
E-mail: littlelightpress@yahoo.com
Web site: http://www.littlelightpress.biz.

Little Linguists Press, *(978-0-9777085)* P.O. Box 169, Owings Mills, MD 21117 USA.

Little Lion Pr., *(978-0-9796393)* 4911 Cumberland Ave., Chevy Chase, MD 20815 USA Tel 301-980-4344; Fax: 301-656-0086.

Little Lollipop Pr., *(978-0-9996151)* 4125 Glenshire St., Houston, TX 77025 USA Tel 615-779-6594
E-mail: lkjaxn@gmail.com
Web site: www.littlelollipoppress.com.

Little Lost Creations, *(978-0-9965766; 978-1-7352850)* 3650 N. 3650 W, Darlington, ID 83255 USA Tel 208-406-4777
E-mail: brendaskidsbooks@gmail.com
Web site: https://brendaskidsbooks.com.

Little Lyrics Pubns., *(978-1-893429)* 12310 Old Barn Rd., Elbert, CO 80106 USA Tel 719-495-4941
E-mail: littlelyrics@prodigy.com
Web site: http://www.littlelyrics.com.

little m Bks., *(978-0-9830487)* 756 Pompton Ave., Cedar Grove, NJ 07009 USA Tel 201-704-7886
E-mail: wmadsen@me.com.

Little Mai Pr., *(978-1-893237)* 102 River Dr., Lake Hiawatha, NJ 07034 USA Tel 973-331-9648; Fax: 973-331-1856; Toll Free: 800-438-2719
E-mail: lmaipress@aol.com; f1promo@aol.com
Web site: http://www.littlemaipress.com.

Little Melody Pr. *Imprint of* **Brighter Minds Children's Publishing**

Little Moose Pr., *(978-0-9720227; 978-0-9786049; 978-0-9841021; 978-0-9841441; 978-0-9831161; 978-0-9838386; 978-0-9893988)* Orders Addr.: 269 S. Beverly Dr. #1065, Beverly Hills, CA 90212 USA (SAN 254-9778) Tel 310-862-2574; 310-862-2575; Toll Free: 866-234-0626
E-mail: ellen@littlemoosepresspub.com; bookshep@mac.com
Web site: http://www.littlemoosepresspub.com; www.louisegaylordauthor.com; www.pippinpb.com
Dist(s): **Book Clearing Hse.**
Pathway Bks.
Smashwords.

Little Munchkin Bks., *(978-0-9773936)* 2893 Rockefeller Rd., Willoughby Hills, OH 44092-1423 USA (SAN 257-411X) Tel 440-585-4950
E-mail: tara_tabernik@yahoo.com
Web site: http://www.littlemunchkinbooks.com.

Little Noggin LLC, *(978-0-9743760)* 1350 Grand Summit Dr., Suite 288, Reno, NV 89523 USA Tel 916-435-9737; Fax: 530-673-9680
E-mail: info@akidatart.com
Web site: http://www.akidatart.com.

Little Ones *Imprint of* **Port Town Publishing**

Little Owl Publishing, *(978-0-9894685)* 377 Oliver Smith Rd, Flintville, TN 37335 USA Tel 931-492-3042
E-mail: kellyrmichaels@gmail.com
Web site: www.kellyrmichaels.com.

Little P Pr. Co., *(978-0-9853430)* 6387 Camp Bowie Blvd Ste B PMB No. 292, Fort Worth, TX 76116 USA Tel 817-501-8229
E-mail: pitch129@aol.com
Web site: ChazzKids.com.

Little Patriot Pr. *Imprint of* **Regnery Publishing, Inc., An Eagle Publishing Co.**

Little Paws Pr. *Imprint of* **Veillette, Roseanne**

Little Pear Pr., *(978-0-9746911)* P.O. Box 343, Seekonk, MA 02771-1409 USA
Web site: http://www.littlepearpress.com.

Little Pemberley Pr., *(978-0-9763359)* Orders Addr.: 1528 Tulane St., Suite F, Houston, TX 77008-4146 USA Tel 713-862-8542; Fax: 713-862-6399
E-mail: littlepemberleypress@hotmail.com
Web site: http://www.giraffeofmontana.com; http://www.littlepemberleypress.com.

Little People Bks., *(978-0-9764114)* 2 Victor Ave., Worcester, MA 01603 USA Tel 508-963-2004.

Little Petals *Imprint of* **Roses Are READ Productions**

Little Pickle Pr. *Imprint of* **Sourcebooks, Inc.**

Little Pickle Press LLC *See* **March 4th, Inc.**

Little Pigeon Bks., *(978-0-9818976)* 5354 Washington St., Downers Grove, IL 60515 USA Tel 630-541-3700
Dist(s): **ebrary, Inc.**

Little Pink Dog Bks. (AUS) *(978-0-9946269; 978-0-6482563; 978-0-6486528; 978-0-6489640; 978-0-6489641) Dist. by* **HachBkGrp.**

Little Prince Publishing, *(978-0-615-46053-6; 978-0-615-46977-5; 978-0-615-47049-8; 978-0-9835220; 978-0-615-58516-1; 978-0-615-59301-2; 978-0-615-59908-3; 978-0-615-59909-0; 978-1-939947; 978-0-692-56834-7)* 7942 Indica Ct., North Charleston, SC 29418 USA
E-mail: sybilnelson@hotmail.com
Web site: www.sybilnelson.com; www.littleprincepublishing.com
Dist(s): **CreateSpace Independent Publishing Platform**
Dummy Record Do Not USE!!!!
Smashwords.

Little Red Acorns *Imprint of* **Little Red Tree Publishing LLC**

Little Red Cat Publishing, *(978-0-9726375)* 939A Terra Bella Ave., Mountainview, CA 94043 USA (SAN 254-9549) Tel 650-960-4040; Fax: 650-960-1040
E-mail: email@comprintingco.com; e-mail@comprintingco.com.

Little Red Tree Publishing LLC, *(978-0-9789446; 978-1-935656)* 635 Ocean Ave., New London, 06320 SUN (SAN 852-0143) Tel 860-287-1660; *Imprints:* Little Red Acorns (LR Acorns)
E-mail: mikelinnard@yahoo.co.uk
Web site: http://www.littleredtree.com.

Little Redhaired Girl Publishing, Inc., *(978-0-9729264)* 120 Riverside Blvd., #2e, New York, NY 10069 USA (SAN 857-6041) Fax: 225-410-6739; *Imprints:* Books for Brats (Books for Brats)
E-mail: booksforbrats@aol.com
Web site: http://www.booksforbrats.com.

Little River Bookshelf, *(978-0-9769856)* 2707 Silver Leaf Ct., Grapevine, TX 76051 USA Tel 817-308-2510
E-mail: mark.storer@usa.net.

Little Santa Bks., Inc., *(978-0-615-17411-2)* P.O. Box 806, Buffalo, NY 14220 USA Tel 716-316-1545
E-mail: sergioroguez@gmail.com
Web site: http://www.littlesantaclaus.com.

Little Scary Mouse, *(978-1-7326042)*
E-mail: littlescarymouse@gmail.com.

Little Scribblers Bks., LLC, *(978-0-9747689)* 2545 NW 55th Pl., Oklahoma City, OK 73112-7101 USA Tel 405-615-8662
E-mail: littlescribblers@cox.net
Web site: http://www.littlescribblers.com.

Little Shepherd *Imprint of* **Scholastic, Inc.**

Little Simon *Imprint of* **Little Simon**

Little Simon, *(978-0-671; 978-0-689; 978-1-4169)* Div. of Simon & Schuster Children's Publishing, 1230 Ave. of the Americas, New York, NY 10020 USA; *Imprints:* Little Simon (LSimon)
Dist(s): **Children's Plus, Inc.**
Simon & Schuster
Simon & Schuster, Inc.

Little Simon Inspirations *Imprint of* **Little Simon Inspirations**

Little Simon Inspirations, Div. of Simon & Schuster Children's Publishing, 1230 Ave. of the Americas, New York, NY 10020 USA; *Imprints:* Little Simon Inspirations (LSimonInsp)
Dist(s): **Simon & Schuster, Inc.**

Little Soundprints *Imprint of* **Soundprints**

Little Sparrow *Imprint of* **Blue Sparrow Bks.**

Little Sprout Publishing Hse., *(978-0-9779194)* Orders Addr.: 520 Berry Way, La Habra, CA 90631 USA; *Imprints:* Psalms for Kidz (Psalms for Kidz)
Web site: http://psalmsforkidz.com.

Little Steps Bks (AUS) *(978-0-9805750; 978-0-9807237; 978-1-921928-59-8; 978-1-921928-62-8; 978-1-921928-63-5; 978-1-921928-64-2; 978-1-921928-74-1; 978-1-925117; 978-1-925545; 978-0-6482673; 978-0-6482674; 978-1-925839; 978-1-922358) Dist. by* **IPG Chicago.**

Little Steps Bks (AUS) *(978-0-9805750; 978-0-9807237; 978-1-921928-59-8; 978-1-921928-62-8; 978-1-921928-63-5; 978-1-921928-64-2; 978-1-921928-74-1; 978-1-925117; 978-1-925545; 978-0-6482673; 978-0-6482674; 978-1-925839; 978-1-922358) Dist. by* **Lerner Pub.**

Little Thoughts For Little Ones Publishing, Inc., *(978-0-9748884; 978-0-9861870)* Orders Addr.: P.O. Box 665, Tavernier, FL 33070 USA Fax: 305-852-4274
E-mail: vhandelsman@att.net
Web site: http://www.littlethoughtspublishing.net.

Little Tiger Pr., *(978-1-888444; 978-1-58431)* Div. of Futech Interactive Products, 39 S. La Salle St. Ste. 1410, Chicago, IL 60603-1706 USA Toll Free: 800-541-2205 Do not confuse Little Tiger Press in San Francisco, CA
E-mail: jody@futechsales.com
Dist(s): **Futech Educational Products, Inc.**
Lectorum Pubns., Inc.
MyiLibrary.

Publisher Name Index

Little Treasure Bks., *(978-0-9639838; 978-0-9814571)* P.O. Box 362, Bensalem, PA 19020-0362 USA
Web site: http://www.littletreasurebooks.com.

Little Treasure Publications, Incorporated *See* **Little Treasure Bks.**

Little T's Corner *See* **Zadunajsky, Donna M.**

Little Tule Bks., *(978-0-9773133)* P.O. Box 549, Carmel Valley, CA 93924-0549 USA (SAN 257-2311) Tel 831-659-0107; Fax: 831-659-0106
E-mail: bill@littletulebooks.com
Web site: http://www.littletulebooks.com.

Little Vegan Monsters Publishing, *(978-0-9787590)* P.O. Box 9258, New Haven, CT 06533 USA
E-mail: Lourdes@littleveganmonsters.com
Web site: http://www.littleveganmonsters.com.

Little Way Pr., *(978-0-9764691)* 18252 Little Fuller Rd., Twain Harte, CA 95383 USA
Web site: http://www.littlewaypress.com
Dist(s): **Catholic Heritage Curricula.**

Little Willow Tree Bks., *(978-0-9743795)* 4900 Dodd St., Lynchburg, VA 24502 USA Do not confuse with Willow Tree Press in Monsey, NY
E-mail: willowtreebooks@yahoo.com.

Little Wooden Bks., *(978-0-929949)* 11001 S. Degray Ln., Spokane, WA 99224 USA (SAN 250-7943) Tel 509-932-4729.

Little Worm Publishing, *(978-0-9911382)* 920 Litchfield Pl., Roswell, GA 30076 USA Tel 706-258-8925
E-mail: hetheringtonlin@gmail.com
Web site: www.littlewormpub.com.

Littletonhouse Publishing, *(978-0-9746849)* Orders Addr.: P.O. Box 2954, Littleton, CO 80161-2954 USA (SAN 256-3371) Tel 303-740-2003; Fax: 303-771-0305
E-mail: info@thesecretcovebook.com; treis@littletonhousepublishing.com
Web site: http://www.thesecretcovebook.com; http://www.virobacter.com.

Liturgical Pr. Bks. *Imprint of* **Liturgical Pr.**

†Liturgical Pr., *(978-0-8146; 978-0-916134)* Div. of Order of St. Benedict, Inc., Orders Addr.: a/o St. Johns Abbey, P.O. Box 7500, Collegeville, MN 56321-7500 USA (SAN 202-2494) Tel 320-363-2213; 612 363 2326; Fax: 320-363-3299; Toll Free Fax: 800-445-5899; Toll Free: 800-858-5450; *Imprints:* Liturgical Press Books (Liturg Pr Bks)
E-mail: sales@litpress.org; bwoods@csbsju.edu
Web site: http://www.litpress.org; http://sjbible.org; http://cistercianpublications.com
Dist(s): **BookMobile**
Metapress
MyiLibrary; *CIP.*

Liturgies, PC, *(978-0-578-40675-6; 978-0-578-42606-8; 978-0-578-50885-6; 978-0-578-56276-6; 978-0-578-60052-9)* 3426 Admiralty Ln., Indianapolis, IN 46240 USA Tel 317-402-2139
E-mail: drtim@liturgies.org
Dist(s): **Ingram Content Group.**

Liturgy Training Pubns., *(978-0-929650; 978-0-930467; 978-1-56854; 978-1-61671; 978-1-61833)* Div. of Archdiocese of Chicago, 3949 S. Racine Ave., Chicago, IL 60609-2523 USA (SAN 670-9052) Toll Free Fax: 800-933-7094 (orders); Toll Free: 800-933-1800 (orders); *Imprints:* Catechesis of the Good Shepherd (Catechesis Good Shepherd)
E-mail: lguzman@ltp.org
Web site: http://www.ltp.org
Dist(s): **Faith Alive Christian Resources.**

Litwin, April Lynn, *(978-0-692-18539-1; 978-0-692-18540-7)* 273 Lyceum Ave., Philadelphia, PA 19128 USA Tel 732-616-7576
E-mail: alitwin273@gmail.com
Dist(s): **Ingram Content Group.**

Liu, Katrina, *(978-1-7339671; 978-1-953281)* 57 Arbor St., San Francisco, CA 94131 USA Tel 415-265-8888
E-mail: katrinaliu@gmail.com.

Live Like Noah Foundation, *(978-1-7325254)* 7033 Quartz Ave, Winnetka, CA 91306 USA Tel 818-339-1216
E-mail: keith.michaelis@hotmail.com
Web site: www.livelikenoah.org.

Live Oak Games, *(978-0-9764394)* P.O. Box 780932, Orlando, FL 32878 USA Toll Free Fax: 800-214-4632 (phone/fax)
E-mail: sales@liveoakgames.com
Web site: http://www.liveoakgames.com.

Live Oak Media, *(978-0-87499; 978-0-941078; 978-1-59112; 978-1-59519; 978-1-4301)* Orders Addr.: P.O. Box 652, Pine Plains, NY 12567-0652 USA (SAN 217-3921) Tel 518-398-1010; Fax: 518-398-1070; Toll Free: 800-788-1121
E-mail: info@liveoakmedia.com
Web site: http://www.liveoakmedia.com
Dist(s): **AudioGO**
Ebsco Publishing
Findaway World, LLC
Follett School Solutions
Greathall Productions, Inc.
Lectorum Pubns., Inc.
Lerner Publishing Group.

†Liveright Publishing Corp., *(978-0-87140; 978-1-63149)* Subs. of W. W. Norton Co., Inc., 500 Fifth Ave., New York, NY 10110 USA (SAN 201-0976) Tel 212-354-5500; Fax: 212-869-0856; Toll Free Fax: 800-458-6515; Toll Free: 800-233-4830
Web site: http://www.wwnorton.com
Dist(s): **Penguin Random Hse. Distribution**
Penguin Random Hse. LLC; *CIP.*

Liverpool Univ. Pr. (GBR) *(978-0-7463; 978-0-85323; 978-1-84631; 978-1-78138; 978-1-78694; 978-1-78962; 978-1-80034)* *Dist. by* **OUP.**

Living Bks. Pr., *(978-0-9790876; 978-0-9818093; 978-1-938192)* 5497 S. Gilmore Rd., Mount Pleasant, MI 48858 USA (SAN 852-4114) Toll Free: 888-331-3481
E-mail: lbcinfo@livingbookscurriculum.com
Web site: http://www.livingbookscurriculum.com.

Living Breathing Story Pubns., *(978-0-578-41938-1)* 8039 Genesta Ave., Van Nuys, CA 91406 USA Tel 805-217-9199
E-mail: kellyanott@gmail.com
Dist(s): **Independent Pub.**

Living Dead Pr., *(978-1-935458; 978-1-61199)* 58 Dedham St., Revere, MA 02151 USA
Dist(s): **Smashwords.**

Living History Pr., *(978-0-9664925)* 7426 Elmwood Ave., Middleton, WI 53562 USA Tel 608-836-7426; Fax: 608-836-0176 Do not confuse with Living History Pr., Bellevue, WA
E-mail: pferd@itis.com
Web site: http://www.inwave.com/Milton/MiltonHouse/.

Living in Grace, *(978-0-9659319)* 10051 Siegen Ln., Baton Rouge, LA 70810 USA Tel 504-769-8844; Fax: 504-767-5655; Toll Free: 800-484-2046 ext. 9506
E-mail: QRBC@aol.com.

Living Ink Bks. *Imprint of* **AMG Pubs.**

Living Language *Imprint of* **Diversified Publishing**

Living Library Pr., *(978-0-692-74615-8; 978-0-692-81047-7; 978-0-692-83664-4; 978-0-692-87488-2; 978-0-692-97395-0; 978-0-692-07532-6; 978-0-692-09071-8; 978-0-578-42451-4; 978-0-578-48822-6; 978-0-578-50090-4; 978-0-578-58239-9)* 318 Meadow Dr., BRISTOL, VA 24201 USA Tel 276-644-9169.

Living Life Publishing Co., *(978-0-9768773; 978-0-9769166; 978-0-9774499; 978-1-934796)* Div. of Bianca Productions, LLC, 24165 IH-10, W., Suite 217-474, San Antonio, TX 78257 USA (SAN 256-5684) Tel 210-698-6392; Fax: 210-698-1754
E-mail: livinglifepublishing@msn.com
Web site: http://www.livinglifepublishing.com; http://www.biancaproductions.com.

Living Ministry, Inc., *(978-0-9763167)* 800 Prospect Blvd., Pasadena, CA 91103 USA Tel 626-356-9491; Fax: 626-584-0290
Web site: http://www.livingministry.com.

Living Room Adventures, *(978-0-578-16641-4; 978-0-692-79945-1; 978-0-692-99751-2)* 9545 S 2500 W, South Jordan, UT 84095 USA Tel 801-414-5790; Fax: 866-226-0309
E-mail: mattsprunt@gmail.co
Dist(s): **CreateSpace Independent Publishing Platform.**

Living Stone Arts, *(978-0-9763901)* 3806 Owl Dr., Rolling Meadows, IL 60008 USA
Web site: http://www.livingstonearts.com.

Living Stream Ministry, *(978-0-7363; 978-0-87083; 978-1-57593; 978-1-5360)* 2431 W. La Palma Ave., Anaheim, CA 92801 USA (SAN 253-4266) Tel 714-236-6001; 714-991-4681; Fax: 714-991-4685; Toll Free: 800-549-5164
E-mail: books@lsm.org
Web site: http://www.lsm.org
Dist(s): **Anchor Distributors**
Spring Arbor Distributors, Inc.

Living the Good News *Imprint of* **Church Publishing, Inc.**

Living Tree Pr., *(978-1-7320355; 978-1-7330477)* 1325 W Sunshine, Springfield, MO 65807 USA Tel 317-507-3239
E-mail: editor@livingtreepress.com
Web site: livingtreepress.com.

Living Water Pubns., *(978-1-59521)* P.O. Box 4653, Rockford, IL 61110-4653 USA Fax: 815-394-0140 Do not confuse with Living Water Publications in Edwardsville, KS
E-mail: lwministry@aol.com
Web site: http://www.livingwaterpublications.org.

Living Waters Publishing Co., *(978-0-9798154; 978-0-9814532; 978-0-9821153)* P.O. Box 1361, Marion, AR 72364-1361 USA
E-mail: administration@livingwaterspc.com
Web site: http://www.livingwaterspc.com
Dist(s): **Ingram Content Group.**

Livingston Pr., *(978-0-930501; 978-0-942979; 978-1-931982; 978-1-60489)* Div. of Univ. Of West Alabama, Orders Addr.: Sta. 22, One College Dr. Univ. of W. Alabama, Livingston, AL 35470 USA (SAN 851-917X) Tel 205-652-3470 Do not confuse with Livingston Pr., Anaheim, CA
E-mail: jwt@uwa.edu
Web site: https://livingstonpress.uwa.edu
Dist(s): **SPD-Small Pr. Distribution.**

Livingstone Corporation *See* **Barton-Veerman Co.**

Livity Books LLc *See* **Livity Bks. LLC**

Livity Bks. LLC, *(978-1-941632)* 1110 C Parkside Green Dr., Greenacres, FL 33415 USA Tel 561-373-4439
E-mail: lifegatepublishing@yahoo.com.

Livraria Martins Editora (BRA) *(978-85-336)* *Dist. by* **Distribks Inc.**

Liza Dora Bks., *(978-0-692-43392-8; 978-0-692-43393-5; 978-0-692-53087-0; 978-0-692-59885-6; 978-0-692-88259-7; 978-0-578-47420-5; 978-1-7340576)* 2205 Charlestown, Clarksville, TN 37043 USA Tel 713-534-7538
E-mail: lizabrightdora@gmail.com.

LizStar Bks, *(978-0-9779753)* 2648 Jolly Acres Rd., White Hall, MD 21161 USA Tel 410-557-9388
E-mail: tracy@lizstarbooks.com
Web site: http://www.lizstarbooks.com.

Lizzie Joy Lukens, *(978-0-692-97943-3)* 924 Bedford Ave SW, Canton, OH 44710 USA Tel 330-754-8984; Fax: 330-754-8984
E-mail: creativelizzie@gmail.com.

Lizzy Anne's Adventures, *(978-0-9845887; 978-0-9835168)* P.O. Box 97, Monrovia, MD 21770-0097 USA (SAN 859-8320)
Web site: http://www.lizzyannesadventures.com.

LJK Publishing LLC, *(978-0-9771476)* P.O. Box 993, Springer, NM 87747 USA Tel 505-483-2451 (fax as well - phone to turn on)
E-mail: chieftalkjaw@aol.com.

LJM Publishing, *(978-0-615-46906-5; 978-0-615-48518-8; 978-0-9897175; 978-0-615-92333-8; 978-0-9861946)* 2597 CR 2101, Palestine, TX 75801 USA Tel 214-956-5656; 817-703-1844
Web site: www.RachelsLittleQuoteBook.org
Dist(s): **CreateSpace Independent Publishing Platform.**

Llama Press *See* **Birchall Publishing**

†Llewellyn Pubns., *(978-0-7387; 978-0-87542; 978-1-56718)* Div. of Llewellyn Worldwide, Ltd., Orders Addr.: 2143 Wooddale Dr., Woodbury, MN 55125-2989 USA Tel 651-291-1970; Fax: 651-291-1908; Toll Free: 800-843-6666; *Imprints:* Flux (FluxUSA)
E-mail: sales@llewellyn.com
Web site: http://www.llewellyn.com; http://www.midnightinkbooks.com
Dist(s): **Children's Plus, Inc.**
Follett School Solutions
Lectorum Pubns., Inc.
Libros Sin Fronteras
Llewellyn Worldwide Ltd.
New Leaf Distributing Co., Inc.
Partners/West Book Distributors
Perrone; *CIP.*

Llumina Christian Bks. *Imprint of* **Aeon Publishing Inc.**

Llumina Kids *Imprint of* **Aeon Publishing Inc.**

Llumina Pr. *Imprint of* **Aeon Publishing Inc.**

LM Azpiazu, *(978-0-692-58185-8; 978-0-692-59170-3)* 3519 Woodlawn Dr., HONOLULU, HI 96822 USA Tel 808-988-6158.

LM Digital, *(978-0-9760770)* 4501 Mirador Dr., Pleasanton, CA 94566-7435 USA
E-mail: luke@lm-digital.com
Web site: http://www.lm-digital.com.

LMA Publishing, *(978-0-692-63132-4)* 8635 W Sahara Ave, Las Vegas, NV 89117 USA Tel 310-402-8677
E-mail: mzabner08@gmail.com.

LMBPN Publishing, *(978-1-64202; 978-1-64971)* PMB 196 2540 S. Maryland Pkwy, Las Vegas, NV 89109 USA Tel 239-821-7655
E-mail: steve@lmbpn.com
Web site: www.lmbpn.com.

LMS Bks., *(978-0-9764185)* 1007 Manor Dr., Ripon, CA 95366 USA Tel 209-599-4685.

LMW Works, *(978-1-889584)* 85 St. Michael Way NE., Hanceville, AL 35077 USA Tel 716-946-1060
E-mail: lynne@lmwworks.com; pviverito@yahoo.com
Web site: http://www.lmwworks.com.

LOA Quantum Growth LLC, *(978-0-9786158)* 7805 Tylerton Dr., Raleigh, NC 27613-1554 USA Tel 919-368-8041; Fax: 919-571-8769
E-mail: publisher@loaquantumgrowth.com
Web site: http://www.loaquantumgrowth.com.

Lobster Pr. (CAN) *(978-1-894222; 978-1-897073)* *Dist. by* **Orca Bk Pub.**

Local Color Pr., *(978-0-9716607; 978-0-578-18575-0; 978-0-578-18576-7)* 526 W. 26th St., Studio No. 506, New York, NY 10001 USA Tel 212-242-2660; Fax: 212-242-2661
E-mail: localcolorpress@aol.com
Web site: http://www.localcolorpress.com.

Local History Co., The, *(978-0-9711835; 978-0-9744715; 978-0-9770429)* Orders Addr.: 112 N. Woodland Rd., Pittsburgh, PA 15232 USA (SAN 257-5264); *Imprints:* Towers Maguire Publishing (Towers Mag)
E-mail: Sales@TheLocalHistoryCompany.com; Sales@TowersMaguire.com
Web site: http://www.TheLocalHistoryCompany.com; http://www.TowersMaguire.com.

Lock & Mane, *(978-0-615-20562-5; 978-0-615-30969-9; 978-0-615-62282-8)* 2012 Spring Garden St., No. 3, Philadelphia, PA 19130 USA.

Lockman, James Consulting, *(978-0-9759988)* P.O. Box 278, Gorham, ME 04038-0278 USA
E-mail: james@jameslockman.com
Web site: http://www.jameslockman.com.

Lockman, Vic, *(978-0-936175)* 233 Rogue River Hwy No. 360, Grants Pass, OR 97527 USA (SAN 697-2063) Fax: 541-472-1083
E-mail: vlockman@budget.net.

Lockwood House Publishing, *(978-0-578-07258-6; 978-0-578-15354-4; 978-0-578-15986-7; 978-0-578-16662-9; 978-0-578-18530-9; 978-0-578-18592-7; 978-0-578-20154-2; 978-1-7321478)* 103 Seaview Ave., Monmouth Beach, NJ 07750 USA.

Lodestone Pr., *(978-0-9678922)* 17 Appleby Rd., Suite B-2, Wellesley, MA 02482 USA
E-mail: books@lodestone.nu
Web site: http://www.lodestone.nu.

Loew-Cornell, Inc., *(978-0-9776925; 978-0-9794445)* Div. of Jarden Corporation, 2834 Schoeneck Rd., Macungie, PA 18062-9679 USA
E-mail: joleary@loew-cornell.com
Web site: http://www.loew-cornell.com
Dist(s): **Watson-Guptill Pubns., Inc.**

Loewe Verlag GmbH (DEU) *(978-3-7855; 978-3-8390; 978-3-7320; 978-3-7432)* *Dist. by* **Distribks Inc.**

LoewenHerz-Creative *See* **LHC Publishing**

LOF Publishing, *(978-0-9764441)* Orders Addr.: 7500 Bellerive, Suite 412, Houston, TX 77036 USA Tel 832-251-6867
E-mail: pslam144ym@aol.com; info@lofpublishing.com
Web site: http://www.lofpublishing.com; http://www.mbridges05.com.

Log Cabin Bks., *(978-0-9755548; 978-0-9848911; 978-0-9973251; 978-0-692-07651-4; 978-1-7330891)* 6607 Craine Lake Rd., Hamilton, NY 13346 USA Tel 315-750-9157
Web site: http://www.logcabinbooks.us/; http://www.logcabinbooks.com/.

Logan Bks., *(978-0-9728691)* P.O. Box 21451, Columbia Heights, MN 55421 USA
Web site: http://www.loganbooks.com.

Logan Hse., *(978-0-9674123; 978-0-9769935)* Orders Addr.: Rte. 1, Box 154, Winside, NE 68790 USA Tel 402-286-4891; Edit Addr.: Rte. 1 Box 154, Winside, NE 68790 USA
E-mail: jim@loganhousepress.com
Web site: http://www.loganhousepress.com.

Logic of English, Inc, *(978-1-936706; 978-1-942154; 978-1-950632)* 4865 19th St. NW Suite 130, Rochester, MN 55901 USA (SAN 860-0694)
E-mail: jenny@logicofenglish.com
Web site: http://www.logicofenglish.com/.

LoGiudice Publishing, *(978-1-940803)* 749 Silver Bluff Rd. E62, Aiken, SC 29803 USA Tel 260-499-0777
E-mail: odavis909@yahoo.com.

Logos Productions, Inc., *(978-0-9618891; 978-1-885361)* 6160 Carmen Ave., E., Inver Grove Heights, MN 55076-4422 USA Tel 612-451-9945; Fax: 612-457-4617; Toll Free: 800-328-0200 Do not confuse with Logos Productions, Carmel, CA
E-mail: lpstaff@mn.uswest.net
Web site: http://www.1logos.com.

LOGOS System Assocs., *(978-0-9727146; 978-0-9752605; 978-0-9768168)* 1405 Frey Rd., Pittsburgh, PA 15235 USA Tel 412-372-1341; Fax: 412-372-8447; Toll Free: 877-937-2572
E-mail: patjanssen@logos-system.org
Web site: http://www.logos-system.org.

Logos-Rhema Publishing *See* **Triumph Publishing**

Lollipop Media Productions, LP, *(978-0-9815111; 978-0-9824926; 978-0-9909073)* 3600 S. Harbor Blvd. Apt No. 81 Apt. No. 81, Channel Islands Harbor, CA 93035 USA
E-mail: Suzy@keopu.com.

Lollipop Publishing, LLC, *(978-0-615-30165-5)* 10710 Moore Cir., Westminster, CO 80021 USA.

Lollipop Publishing, LLC, *(978-0-9709793; 978-1-931737)* P.O. Box 6354, Chesterfield, MO 63006-6354 USA Tel 314-434-6011; Fax: 314-434-6040; Toll Free: 800-383-7767
E-mail: jbenigas@aol.com
Web site: http://www.lollippoppublishing.com.

LolliWolliWorld Infant Products!, *(978-0-692-85138-8; 978-0-692-99931-8; 978-0-692-09392-4; 978-0-692-17814-0)* 330 S.W. 43rd St Suite K 532, RENTON, WA 98057 USA Tel 206-484-8907
E-mail: jeffwcrawford5+LVP0003382@gmail.com; jeffwcrawford5+LVP0003382@gmail.com.

Lollypop Bks., *(978-1-7323550)* 25 Burriana, SAN CLEMENTE, CA 92672 USA Tel 949-361-9316
E-mail: ashley@lollypopbooks.com; steve@lollypopbooks.com
Web site: www.lollypopbooks.com
Dist(s): **Ingram Content Group.**

Loma, LLC, *(978-0-9769460)* 6 Bryan Valley Ct., O'Fallon, MO 63366-3465 USA
E-mail: dudleytg@aol.com.

London Publishing, *(978-0-578-15413-8; 978-0-578-16496-0; 978-0-578-16507-3)* 84 Red Alder Court, Danville, CA 94506 USA
E-mail: jrespanosa@yahoo.com
Web site: http://www.myspiffykids.com
Dist(s): **Outskirts Pr., Inc.**

London Town Pr., *(978-0-9666490; 978-0-9766134; 978-0-9799759)* 2026 Hilldale Dr., La Canada, CA 91011 USA
E-mail: martin@londontownpress.com
Web site: http://www.londontownpress.com
Dist(s): **Publishers Group West (PGW).**

Lone Butte Pr., *(978-0-9666860; 978-0-9893518)* 32 S. Fork Extended, Santa Fe, NM 87508 USA Tel 505-424-3574; Fax: 505-473-1227
E-mail: wilddogbooks@cnsp.com
Dist(s): **Wild Dog Bks.**

Lone Cypress Pubs., *(978-0-9741413)* 3588 Hwy. 138 S.E., No. 193, Stockbridge, GA 30281 USA Tel 404-421-7445
E-mail: graysenwalles@yahoo.com
Web site: http://www.lonecypresspublishers.com.

Lone Dragonfly Bks., *(978-0-9967350)* 5565 Seminary Rd. Apt. 105, Falls Church, MD 22041 USA Tel 443-824-6854
E-mail: geoff@lonedragonflybooks.com
Web site: http://lonedragonflybooks.com.

Lone Oak Pr., Ltd. *Imprint of* **Finney Co., Inc.**

Lone Pine Publishing USA, Orders Addr.: 1808 B St., NW Suite 140, Auburn, WA 98001 USA (SAN 859-0427) Tel 253-394-0400; Fax: 253-394-0405; Toll Free Fax: 800-548-1169; Toll Free: 800-518-3541; *Imprints:* Ghost House Books (Ghost Hse Bks)
E-mail: mikec@lonepinepublishing.com
Web site: http://www.lonepinepublishing.com; http://www.companyscoming.com/; http://overtimebooks.com; http://www.folklorepublishing.com/.

Lone Star Bks., *(978-1-58907)* Orders Addr.: 15200 NBN Way, Blue Ridge Summit, PA 17214 USA Tel 717-794-3800 ((Sales, Customer Service, MIS, Royalties, Inventory Mgmt., Dist., Credit & Collections); Fax: 717-794-3803 (Customer Service &/or orders only); 717-794-3857 (Sales & MIS); 717-794-3856 (Royalties, Inventory Mgmt., & Dist.); Toll Free Fax: 800-338-4550 (Customer Service &/or orders); Toll Free: 800-462-6420 (Customer Service &/or orders); Edit Addr.: 4501 Forbes Blvd., Suite 200, Lanham, MD

20706 USA Toll Free Fax: 301-459-5748; Toll Free: 301-459-3366
Dist(s): **National Bk. Network.**

Lone Star Pubns., *(978-0-9766157)* P.O. Box 810872, Dallas, TX 75381 USA Do not confuse with Lone Star Publication in Dallas, TX
E-mail: info@lonestarpublications.com
Web site: http://www.lonestarpublications.com.

Lone Star Publishing Co., *(978-0-9777274)* 906 SW St., Lucie W. Blvd., Port Saint Lucie, FL 34986 USA Tel 772-486-3214; Fax: 772-785-8496 do not confuse with companies with the same name in Paradise, TX, Amarillo, TX, Bryan, TX.

Lone Wolf Productions *See* **Canis Lupus Productions**

Lonejack Mountain Pr., *(978-0-9729101)* P.O. Box 28424, Bellingham, WA 98228-0424 USA.

Lonely Child Pr., *(978-0-9969401)* 16200 Mitchell Creek Dr., Fort Bragg, CA 95437 USA Tel 707-964-6810
E-mail: grorby@mcn.org
Web site: www.ginnyrorby.org.

Lonely Planet Global Ltd. (IRL) *(978-1-78657; 978-1-78701; 978-1-78868)* *Dist. by* **HachBkGrp.**

Lonely Planet Pubns., *(978-1-55992)* Orders Addr.: 124 Linden St., Oakland, CA 94607 USA (SAN 659-6541) Tel 510-893-8555; Fax: 510-893-8572; Toll Free: 800-275-8555 (orders, 9am - 5pm Pacific Time); 230 Franklin Rd., Bldg. 2B, Franklin, TN 37064; Edit Addr.: 315 W 36th St., 10th Flr., New York, NY 10018 USA
E-mail: orders@lonelyplanet.com; lonelyplanet.kids@lonelyplanet.com; customerservice@lonelyplanet.com
Web site: http://www.lonelyplanet.com.

Lonely Swan Bks. *Imprint of* **Cosmic Gargoyle Creative Solutions**

Lonestar Abilene Publishing *Imprint of* **LoneStar Abilene Publishing, LLC**

LoneStar Abilene Publishing, LLC, *(978-0-9749725)* 402 Cedar St., Suite 208, Abilene, TX 79601 USA Tel 325-676-9800; Fax: 325-676-2790; *Imprints:* Lonestar Abilene Publishing (LoneStarAbil)
E-mail: michael@yrbks.com
Web site: http://www.yrbks.com/LoneStar.html.

Long Beach City Schl. District, *(978-0-9677925)* 235 Lido Blvd., Lido Beach, NY 11561 USA Tel 516-897-2104; Fax: 516-897-2107
E-mail: RLF@li.net.

Long Bridge Publishing, *(978-0-9842723; 978-1-938712)* 2875 Benjamin Ave., San Jose, CA 95124 USA
E-mail: info@longbridgepublishing.com; orders@longbridgepublishing.com
Web site: http://www.longbridgepublishing.com
Dist(s): **Ingram Content Group.**

Long Dash Publishing, *(978-1-59899)* 49 Orchard St., Hackensack, NJ 07601-4806 USA
E-mail: longdash@gmail.com
Web site: http://www.longdash.com.

Long, George Children's Books, *(978-0-9844946)* P.O. Box 3672, Irmo, SC 29063 USA Tel 803-781-5528
E-mail: GL@GeorgeLongChildrensBooks.com
Web site: www.GeorgeLongChildrensBooks.com.

Long Life Publishing Co., *(978-0-9725836)* P.O. Box 1564, Escondido, CA 92033 USA.

Long Riders' Guild Pr., The, *(978-1-59048)* 2201 Coyle Ln., Walla Walla, WA 99362-8873 USA
E-mail: longriders@thelongridersguild.com
Web site: http://www.thelongridersguild.com.

Long Stories LLC, *(978-0-615-15295-0; 978-0-615-18961-1)* N3865 County Rd. H, Lake Geneva, WI 53147 USA
E-mail: chad@lycanjournal.com
Web site: http://www.lycanjournal.com.

Longevity Publishing, LLC, *(978-0-9777323)* Orders Addr.: 10179 E. Pinewood Ave., Englewood, CO 80111 USA Tel 720-489-7243
E-mail: info@longevitypublishing.com
Web site: http://www.longevitypublishing.com
Dist(s): **Partners Bk. Distributing, Inc.**

LongHill Partners, Inc., *(978-0-943763; 978-1-58023; 978-1-879045; 978-1-893361; 978-1-59473; 978-0-9904152)* P.O. Box 237, Woodstock, VT 05091 USA; *Imprints:* Jewish Lights Publishing (JewishLights); Skylight Paths Publishing (SkylightPaths)
E-mail: production@longhillpartners.com
Dist(s): **Ingram Publisher Services.**

Longhorn Creek Pr., *(978-0-9714358; 978-0-9764026; 978-0-615-99574-8)* 3780 County Road 4317., De Kalb, TX 75559-5681 USA
E-mail: editor@longhorncreekpress.com; Ron@longhorncreekpress.com
Web site: http://www.longhorncreekpress.com
Dist(s): **CreateSpace Independent Publishing Platform**
Gatewood Pr.

Longleaf Services, Orders Addr.: P.O. Box 8895, Chapel Hill, NC 27515-8895 USA Tel 800-848-6224; Fax: 800-272-6817; 919-962-2704 (24 hours)
E-mail: customerservice@longleafservices.org; orders@longleafservices.org
Web site: http://www.longleafservices.org/.

Longline Imprints Ltd, *(978-1-7326530)* 11956 KIOWA AVE APT 9, Los Angeles, CA 90049-5908 USA Tel 753-509-3876
E-mail: peterwibaux@theindiaroad.com.

Longman Publishing, *(978-0-02; 978-0-06; 978-0-13; 978-0-201; 978-0-205; 978-0-321; 978-0-582; 978-0-673; 978-0-7248; 978-0-8013; 978-1-57322; 978-0-7339)* 75 Arlington St., Boston, MA 02116 USA Tel 617-848-7500
Web site: http://www.aw-bc.com
Dist(s): **Giron Bks.**
Libros Sin Fronteras
Pearson Education.

†**Longman Publishing Group**, *(978-0-13; 978-0-201; 978-0-321; 978-0-582; 978-0-8013)* Div. of Addison Wesley Longman, Inc., The Longman Bldg., 10 Bank St., White Plains, NY 10606-1951 USA (SAN 202-6856) Tel 914-993-5000; Fax: 914-997-8115 800-922-0579 (college, bkstores, customer service only)
Web site: http://www.pearsonlongman.com
Dist(s): **Coronet Bks.**
Giron Bks.
MyiLibrary
Pearson Education
Pearson Technology Group
Sourcebooks, Inc.
Trans-Atlantic Pubns., Inc.; *CIP.*

Longoria, Eugene R., *(978-0-9796818)* 2222 W. Central Ave., Coolidge, AZ 85228 USA (SAN 854-1116)
E-mail: ElJunior@ElJunior.com
Web site: http://eljunior.com; http://eugenelongoria.com.

Longs Peak Publishing, Incorporated *See* **Crossing Guard Bks., LLC**

Longseller S.A. (ARG) *(978-987-550; 978-987-9481; 978-987-98516)* *Dist. by* **Libros Fronteras.**

Longseller S.A. (ARG) *(978-987-550; 978-987-9481; 978-987-98516)* *Dist. by* **Bilingual Pubns.**

LongTale Publishing, LLC, *(978-0-9818054; 978-0-9854705; 978-1-941515)* P.O. Box 266597, Houston, TX 77207-6597 USA Fax: 713-896-9701
Web site: http://www.iggytheiguana.com.

Longwood Publishing, *(978-0-692-51554-9; 978-0-692-73478-0; 978-1-7324181)* 14 Longwood Dr., Kennebunk, ME 04043 USA Tel 207-468-7100
Dist(s): **CreateSpace Independent Publishing Platform.**

LonnaDee Pr., *(978-0-9898594)* 24171 Frontage Rd, Bozeman, MT 59718 USA Tel 972-800-2153
E-mail: chounzet@gmail.com
Web site: www.diamondwilson.com.

Look Again Pr., LLC, *(978-0-9801113)* 2461 Mountain Vista Dr., Birmingham, AL 35243 USA (SAN 855-2266) Tel 205-823-8556
Web site: www.lookagainpress.com
Dist(s): **CreateSpace Independent Publishing Platform.**

Look, Learn & Do Pubns., *(978-1-893327)* 24 Highland Blvd., Kensington, CA 94707 USA Fax: 510-524-7577
E-mail: professor@lldkids.com
Web site: http://www.looklearnanddo.com
Dist(s): **Ten Speed Pr.**

Look-About Bks., *(978-0-9800208)* P.O. Box 1907, Nampa, ID 83653 USA (SAN 854-9869) Tel 208-466-6260
E-mail: lpowersraptor@msn.com
Web site: http://www.look-aboutbooks.com.

Looking Glass Library *Imprint of* **Magic Wagon**

Loon Song Publishing, *(978-0-9965070)* P.O. Box 14663, Portland, OR 97293 USA Tel 503-267-6339
E-mail: nick@nvasilieff.com
Web site: www.nvasilieff.com.

Loonfeather Pr., *(978-0-926147)* Orders Addr.: P.O. Box 1212, Bemidji, MN 56619 USA
E-mail: books@loonfeatherpress.com
Web site: http://www.loonfeatherpress.com.

Loose Cannon, *(978-0-9851292; 978-1-939812; 978-1-944476)* 444 Sutter St., Petaluma, CA 94954 USA Tel 530-762-7002
E-mail: stevhutch@loose-cannon.com.

Loose Change, *(978-0-944707)* 936 Sixth St., Los Banos, CA 93635 USA (SAN 244-9692) Tel 209-826-3797; Fax: 209-826-1514
E-mail: nco4242@sbcglobal.net.

Loose In The Lab, *(978-0-9660965; 978-1-931801)* 9462 S. 560 W., Sandy, UT 84070 USA Tel 801-568-9596; Fax: 801-568-9586; Toll Free: 888-403-1189
E-mail: mail@looseinthelab.com
Web site: http://www.looseinthelab.com.

Loose Leaves Publishing, *(978-1-62432)* 4218 E. Allison Rd, Tucson, AZ 85712 USA Tel 520-310-7528
E-mail: Talminia@gmail.com.

Loosey Goosey Pr., *(978-0-9820991)* 1111 Shive Ln. No. 200, Bowling Green, KY 42103 USA (SAN 857-2623)
Web site: http://www.ganderpress.com.

Lopata, Melanie ~ Author, *(978-0-578-45341-5)* 208 Stimson St, Herkimer, NY 13350 USA Tel 315-940-1555
E-mail: melanie.author@yahoo.com
Web site: http://melanielopata.weebly.com/.

Lopez, Daniela J., *(978-0-692-96618-1; 978-0-692-12471-0; 978-0-578-59508-5)* 826 E. 16th Street, Apt 4B, Brooklyn, NY 11230 USA Tel 718-781-6246
E-mail: tallgirldani@gmail.com
Dist(s): **CreateSpace Independent Publishing Platform.**

Lopez, David, *(978-0-9744097)* 3441 Twinberry Ct., Bonita Springs, FL 34134 USA Tel 239-947-2532 (phone/fax)
E-mail: jazzpop@aol.com
Web site: http://www.maddiesmagicmarkers.com.

Loquacious Publishing Co., *(978-0-9763811)* 2115 Wintermere Pointe Dr., Winter Garden, FL 34787-5439 USA.

Loqueleo *Imprint of* **Santillana USA Publishing Co., Inc.**

Lord & Dooney Pr., *(978-1-7328166)* 145 Town Ctr., Corte Madera, CA 94925 USA Tel 415-235-8557
E-mail: wcafdn@yahoo.com
Web site: margotelainejones.com.

Lore, Czidor LLC, *(978-0-9903799; 978-0-9971227; 978-0-9993829)* 421 San Eduardo Ter., Sunnyvale, CA 94085 USA Tel 408-746-5779
E-mail: czidorlorellc@outlook.com
Dist(s): **Lulu Pr., Inc.**

LORE Mountain Productions, *(978-0-9970294; 978-1-946807)* 20875 Jerusalem Grade, Lower Lake, CA 95457 USA Tel 707-987-8577; *Imprints:* MonkeyBear Publishing (MonkeyBear Pub)
E-mail: info@loremountain.com
Web site: www.gracieandmonkeybear.com; www.loremountain.com.

Lorenc, Micah, *(978-0-692-50795-7)* 9604 Dawn Trl, San Antonio, TX 78254 USA Tel 210-417-8178
E-mail: micahlorenc@gmail.com.

Lorenz Corp., The, *(978-0-7877; 978-0-88335; 978-0-89328; 978-1-55863; 978-1-57310; 978-1-885564; 978-1-4291)* 501 E. Third St., Dayton, OH 45401-0802 USA (SAN 208-7413) Tel 937-228-6118; Fax: 937-223-2042; Toll Free: 800-444-1144
E-mail: service@lorenz.com
Web site: http://www.lorenz.com.

Lorenz Educational Pubs., *(978-1-885564)* Div. of The Lorenz Corp., 501 E. Third St., Dayton, OH 45401-0802 USA Tel 937-228-6118 (phone/fax); Fax: 937-223-2042; Toll Free: 800-444-1144
Web site: http://www.lorenzeducationalpress.com
Dist(s): **Rainbow Horizons Publishing, Inc.**

Lorenz, Theo, *(978-0-9975738)* 1773 Lafond Ave, Saint Paul, MN 55104-1716 USA Tel 651-278-7865
E-mail: tiernsshadow@gmail.com.

Lorian Assn., The, *(978-0-936878)* P.O. Box 1368, Issaquah, WA 98027 USA (SAN 666-6663) Tel 425-427-9071
E-mail: info@lorian.org
Web site: http://www.lorian.org.

Lorian Press *See* **Lorian Assn., The**

Lorimer & Pine Press *See* **Lorimer Pr.**

Lorimer Pr., *(978-0-9704651; 978-0-9789342; 978-0-9826171; 978-0-9838936; 978-0-9897885; 978-0-9961884)* Div. of LBR Holdings, Orders Addr.: 619 Lorimer Rd., Davidson, NC 28036 USA; Edit Addr.: P.O. Box 1013, Davidson, NC 28036 USA Tel 704-896-8998
E-mail: leslie.b@att.net
Dist(s): **Independent Pubs. Group**
Midpoint Trade Bks., Inc.
Partners Pubs. Group, Inc.

Lorito Bks., Inc., *(978-0-9815686; 978-0-9842981; 978-0-9835197; 978-0-9883561; 978-0-9904930; 978-0-9998903)* 10395 W. 74th Pl., Arvada, CO 80005 USA (SAN 855-8876) Fax: 303-425-3277; Toll Free: 800-420-6936
Web site: http://www.loritobooks.com
Dist(s): **Follett School Solutions.**

Lormax Communications, *(978-0-9641239)* P.O. Box 40304, Raleigh, NC 27629 USA Tel 919-878-9108.

Los Alamos Historical Society Publications *See* **Bathtub Row Pr.**

Los Andes Publishing Co., *(978-0-9637065; 978-1-57159)* P.O. Box 190, Chino Hills, CA 91709 USA Tel 562-789-1540; Toll Free: 800-532-8872
E-mail: losandes@losandes.com
Web site: http://www.losandes.com
Dist(s): **Lectorum Pubns., Inc.**

Los Espada, *(978-0-692-75653-9; 978-0-692-93404-3; 978-0-692-99059-9; 978-0-692-10489-7; 978-0-578-65894-0)* 111-03 76 Dr., Forest Hills, NY 11375 USA Tel 917-406-4498
E-mail: losespada@yahoo.com
Web site: losepada.com
Dist(s): **CreateSpace Independent Publishing Platform.**

Los Perros Publishing Co., *(978-0-9764685)* 3565 Parches Cove, Union Grove, AL 35175-8422 USA
E-mail: jr@losperros.com; mrgsd@hiwaay.net
Web site: http://www.mrgsd.com.

Losantiville Pr., Inc., *(978-0-9794946; 978-1-7326293)* Orders Addr.: P.O. Box 42604, Cincinnati, OH 45242-6040 USA; Edit Addr.: 7012 Beech Hollow Dr., Cincinnati, OH 45236 USA
E-mail: losantivillepress@fuse.net.

Lost Art Pr. LLC, *(978-0-9850777; 978-0-9906230; 978-0-9978702; 978-1-7322100; 978-1-7333916)* 26 Greenbriar Ave., Fort Mitchell, KY 41017 USA Tel 859-445-6075
E-mail: cms@lostartpress.com
Web site: http://www.lostartpress.com.

Lost Candy Bar Pr., LLC, *(978-0-9786794)* P.O. Box 5193, Madison, WI 53705-0193 USA Tel 608-233-5690; Fax: 608-231-2312
Web site: http://www.lostcandybarpress.com.

Lost Classic Bks.,
Dist(s): **National Bk. Network.**

Lost Classics Bk. Co., *(978-0-9652735; 978-1-890623)* Orders Addr.: P.O. Box 1756, Fort Collins, CO 80522 USA Tel 970-493-3793 (Distribution Center); Toll Free Fax: 888-211-2665 (Libraries & Schools); Toll Free: 888-611-2665 (credit card orders only); Edit Addr.: P.O. Box 3429, Lake Wales, FL 33859-3429 USA Tel 863-678-3149; Fax: 863-678-0802
E-mail: mgeditor@lostclassicsbooks.com
Web site: http://lcbcbooks.com; http://www.lcbcbooks.com/homeright.htm
Dist(s): **National Bk. Network.**

Lost Coast Pr., *(978-1-882897; 978-1-935448)* 155 Cypress St., Fort Bragg, CA 95437 USA Tel 707-964-9520; Fax: 707-964-7531; Toll Free: 800-773-7782
E-mail: forms@cypresshouse.com
Web site: http://www.cypresshouse.com
Dist(s): **Continental Bk. Co., Inc.**
Cypress Hse.
New Leaf Distributing Co., Inc.
Partners/West Book Distributors.

Lost Hills Bks., *(978-0-9798535)* P.O. Box 3054, Duluth, MN 55803 USA (SAN 854-5553)
Web site: http://www.losthillsbks.com.

Lost Lake Pr., *(978-0-9906450; 978-0-9981736)* N7130 N. Lost Lake Rd., Randolph, WI 53956 USA Tel 920-326-5554
E-mail: LostLakePress@gmail.com
Web site: http://www.LostLakePress.com.

Lost Language Pr. LLC, *(978-0-9975009)* 1128 Chesterton Dr., Richardson, TX 75080 USA Tel 214-340-9837
E-mail: fbuchly@sbcglobal.net
Web site: buchly.wordpress.com.

Lost Scout Pr., *(978-0-9741310)* P.O. Box 86, Loveland, OH 45140-0086 USA (SAN 255-7193) Fax: 719-457-5952; 1283 Sand Trap Ct., Loveland, OH 45140-6060
E-mail: hq@lostscout.com
Web site: http://www.lostscout.com.

Lotti, Marc, *(978-1-932341)* P.O. Box 5841, Carefree, AZ 85377-5841 USA
E-mail: mlotti@mandragore.com.

Lotus Art Works Inc., *(978-0-9800637)* 11833 Mississippi Ave., Suite 200, Los Angeles, CA 90025 USA Tel 310-442-3335.

Lotus Blossom Bks., *(978-0-9801414)* 1220 Rosecrans St., No. 325, San Diego, CA 92106 USA (SAN 855-3181) Tel 619-224-7771
E-mail: publisher@lotusblossombooks.com
Web site: http://www.lotusblossombooks.com
Dist(s): **BookBaby.**

Lotus Lights Publications *See* **Lotus Pr.**

Lotus Petal Publishing, *(978-0-9787672; 978-0-9820949)* Div. of Lotus Petal, P.O. Box 1394, Nashville, IN 47448-1394 USA Tel 812-988-1250; Toll Free Fax: 800-867-4851
E-mail: info@lotuspetalpublishing.com
Web site: http://www.lotuspetalpublishing.com.

Lotus Pond Media, *(978-0-9791021)* 176 Broadway, Suite 9C, New York, NY 10038 USA Tel 212-608-3329
E-mail: scgrant@goatkids.net; scgrant@customerresearchcenter.com
Web site: http://www.goatkids.net; http://www.highimpactquality.com.

Lotus Pr., *(978-0-910261; 978-0-914955; 978-0-940676; 978-0-940985; 978-0-941524; 978-1-60869)* Div. of Lotus Brands, Inc., P.O. Box 325, Twin Lakes, WI 53181 USA (SAN 239-1120) Tel 262-889-2461; Fax: 262-889-8591; Toll Free: 800-824-6396 Do not confuse with companies with the same or similar name in Lotus, CA, Westerville, OH, Bokeelia, FL, Brattleboro, VT, Detroit, MI, Tobyhanna, PA
E-mail: lotuspress@lotuspress.com
Web site: http://www.lotuspress.com
Dist(s): **National Bk. Network.**

Lotus Publications *See* **Johnson, Earl Photography**

Louck, Cheryl, *(978-0-9744230)* 2708 Avalon Ln., Montgomery, IL 60538 USA Tel 630-853-0653
Web site: http://www.cheryllouck.com.

Loughton Bks., *(978-0-9704974)* 101 W. 23rd St., New York, KS 37215 USA Do not confuse with companies with similar names in Newport, RI, San Diego, CA, Mary Esther, FL,
E-mail: mbraden@loghtonbooks.com
Web site: http://www.loughtonbooks.com.

Louisana Museum of Modern Art (DNK) *(978-87-90029; 978-87-91607; 978-87-92877)* *Dist. by* **Dist Art Pubs.**

Louisiana Ladybug Pr., *(978-0-9753435)* 210 Pinecrest Rd., Arcadia, LA 71001 USA
Web site: http://www.LouisianaPotpourriFromAtoZ.com.

†**Louisiana State Univ. Pr.**, *(978-0-8071)* 3990 W. Lakeshore Dr., Baton Rouge, LA 70808 USA Tel 225-578-6294; Fax: 225-578-6461; Toll Free Fax: 800-272-6817; Toll Free: 800-848-6224
E-mail: lsupress@lsu.edu
Web site: http://lsupress.org/
Dist(s): **Ebsco Publishing**
Longleaf Services
ebrary, Inc.; *CIP.*

Love + Lifestyle Media Group (CAN) *(978-0-9920874; 978-1-77210)* *Dist. by* **BTPS.**

Love & Blessings *See* **Self-Mastery Pr.**

Love Bug Bks., *(978-0-9787174)* 1117 Ariana Rd., Suite 102, San Marcos, CA 92069-8122 USA Tel 760-798-9415; Fax: 760-798-9415
E-mail: rolwink@cox.net
Web site: http://www.lovebugbooks.com.

Love Cultivating Editions, *(978-0-9744999)* 2665 Reed Rd., Hood River, OR 97031-9609 USA
Web site: http://www.lovecultivatingeditions.com.

Love II Learn Bks., *(978-0-9796679)* 860 Johnson Ferry Rd., Suite 140-345, Atlanta, GA 30342 USA (SAN 854-0535) Tel 404-808-0458
Web site: http://www.booksbykobie.com; http://www.loveiilearbooks.com
Dist(s): **Baker & Taylor Publisher Services (BTPS).**

Love Ink LLC, *(978-1-940426)* 65257 Solar Rd, Montrose, CO 81403 USA
E-mail: Love_Ink_LLC@outlook.com
Web site: www.love-ink-llc.com.

Love Language Pubns., *(978-0-9749924)* 2111 E. Santa Fe, No. 268, Olathe, KS 66062 USA
E-mail: anne@lovelanguageforbabies.com
Web site: http://www.lovelanguageforbabies.com.

Love of Kids Bks. Publishing, *(978-0-692-91699-5)* 164 Rendition Dr., None, Mcdonough, GA 30253 USA Tel 770-912-1124
E-mail: loveofkidsbookspublishing@gmail.com.

Love Truth, *(978-0-9977016)* 353 SW Wakonda Beach Rd., Waldport, OR 97394 USA Tel 541-832-1300
E-mail: jeanann_w@yahoo.com
Web site: http://joshua-mom.blogspot.com/.

Love Your Life, *(978-0-9664806; 978-0-9798554; 978-0-9820477)* Orders Addr.: P.O. Box 2, Red Lion, PA 17356 USA (SAN 256-1387) Tel 717-200-2852; Fax:

Publisher Name Index

310-496-0716; Edit Addr.: 755 Conndly Dr., Red Lion, PA 17356 USA Tel 717-200-2852; Fax: 310-496-0716
E-mail: publish@loveyourlife.com
Web site: http://www.loveyourlife.com
Dist(s): **Ingram Publisher Services.**

Loveland Pr., LLC, *(978-0-9662696; 978-0-9744851)* P.O. Box 7001, Loveland, CO 80537-0001 USA Tel 970-593-9557 Toll Free: 800-593-9557
E-mail: info@lovelandpress.com
Web site: http://www.lovelandpress.com.

LoveLight Media, *(978-0-9893181)* 216 Regina Dr., Fort Collins, CO 80525 USA Tel 970-218-2592
E-mail: Deidre@lovelightmedia.com
Web site: None yet.

Love-LovePublishing, *(978-0-9852015; 978-0-9973200; 978-1-7334454)* P.O. Box 258136, Madison, WI 53725 USA Tel 608-576-2064
E-mail: contact@screenwritersdaily.com
Web site: http://love-lovepublishing.com.

Love's Creative Resources, *(978-1-929548)* Orders Addr.: P.O. Box 44306, Charlotte, NC 28215 USA Tel 704-563-7469
E-mail: ml9734@yahoo.com.

Lovestruck Literary, *(978-0-9833980; 978-0-9856574; 978-0-9960356)* 1643 Rodney Dr. APT 1, Los Angeles, CA 90027 USA
E-mail: afletcher@lovestruckliterary.com
Web site: lovestruckliterary.com
Dist(s): **Smashwords.**

LoveWorld Publishing, *(978-978-51521-6-6)* ., ., CA 1 USA
Web site: http://www.rhapsodyofrealities.org
Dist(s): **Smashwords**
Whitaker Hse.

Lovin Ovens, Inc., *(978-0-9617468)* 57 Chof Trail, Flagstaff, AZ 86001 USA (SAN 664-1180) Tel 928-525-1527
E-mail: GandCFox@msn.com.

Loving Guidance, Inc., *(978-1-889609; 978-1-7350640)* P.O. Box 622407, Oviedo, FL 32762 USA Tel 407-366-0233; 407-977-8862; Fax: 407-366-4293; Toll Free: 800-842-2846; 50 Smith St., Oviedo, FL 32765-9608
E-mail: bryan@lovingguidance.com; kate@lovingguidance.com; becky.bailey@consciousdiscipline.com
Web site: http://www.beckybailey.com; http://www.consciousdiscipline.com
Dist(s): **Gryphon Hse., Inc.**

Loving Healing Pr., Inc., *(978-1-932690; 978-1-61599)* 5145 Pontiac Trail, Ann Arbor, MI 48105-9279 USA (SAN 255-7770) Tel 734-662-6864; Fax: 734-663-6861; Toll Free: 888-761-6268; *Imprints:* Marvelous Spirit Press (MarvelousSpir)
E-mail: info@lovinghealing.com
Web site: http://www.beyondtrauma.com/; http://www.TurtleDolphinDreams.com; http://www.TIRbook.com; http://www.LifeSkillsBook.com; http://www.VictorianHeritage.com; http://www.PhysicalLoss.com; http://www.gotparts.org; http://www.lovinghealing.com/
Dist(s): **New Leaf Distributing Co., Inc.**
Quality Bks., Inc.
ebrary, Inc.

Lovstad, Joel Publishing, *(978-0-9749058)* 701 Henry St., No. 203, Waunakee, WI 53597 USA
E-mail: jlfred@chorus.net
Web site: http://www.joellovstad-books.com.

Low Fat Express, Incorporated *See* **Learning ZoneXpress**

†Lowell Hse., *(978-0-7373; 978-0-8092; 978-0-929923; 978-1-56565)* 2020 Avenue of the Stars, Suite 300, Los Angeles, CA 90067-4704 USA (SAN 250-863X) Tel 310-552-7555; Fax: 310-552-7573
Dist(s): **Independent Pubs. Group**
McGraw-Hill Trade; *CIP.*

Lowell Hse. Juvenile, *(978-0-7373; 978-0-929923; 978-1-56565)* 2020 Avenue of the Stars, No. 300, Los Angeles, CA 90067 USA Tel 310-552-7555; Fax: 310-552-7573; *Imprints:* Roxbury Park Juvenile (Roxbury Pk Juvenile)
Dist(s): **McGraw-Hill Trade.**

Lowell, Meryl, *(978-0-578-21442-9; 978-1-7342037)* 1221 Ottawa Dr., South Lake Tahoe, CA 96150 USA Tel 352-427-8525
E-mail: meryllowell@yahoo.com
Web site: www.merylbestlowell.com.

Lowell Milken Ctr. for Unsung Heroes, *(978-0-9988266)* 1 S. Main, Fort Scott, KS 66701 USA Tel 620-223-1312
E-mail: lmcwerling@gmail.com
Web site: lowellmilkencenter.org.

†Lowell Pr., The, Gallion Communications, *(978-0-913504; 978-0-932845)* Orders Addr.: P.O. Box 411877, Kansas City, MO 64141-1877 USA (SAN 207-0774) Tel 816-753-4545; Fax: 816-753-4057; Toll Free: 800-736-7660 Do not confuse with Lowell Pr. in Eugene, OR
E-mail: plowell@accessus.net; sales@thelowellpress.com
Web site: http://www.thelowellpress.com; *CIP.*

Lowell, Shelley, *(978-0-9765344)* Orders Addr.: c/o Montage Gallery, 925 South Charles St., Baltimore, MD 21230 USA.

Lower Kuskokwim Schl. District, *(978-1-58084)* Orders Addr.: P.O. Box 305, Bethel, AK 99559 USA Tel 907-543-4928; Fax: 907-543-4935
E-mail: catalog@fc.lksd-do.org
Web site: http://www.lksd.org/catalog.

Lower Lane Publishing LLC, *(978-0-9797790)* 2105 Carehill Rd., Vienna, VA 22181 USA.

Lowney, Amanda *See* **Amanda Lowney Bks. LLC**

Lowrance, Carrie, *(978-0-9995069)* 1900 Highview Rd. Apt. C8, East Peoria, IL 61611 USA Tel 309-444-0209
E-mail: Carrie.Lowrance@yahoo.com
Web site: www.carrielowrance.com.

Loyola Grupo de Comunicacion (ESP) *Dist. by* **Lectorum Pubns.**

†Loyola Pr., *(978-0-8294)* 3441 N. Ashland Ave., Chicago, IL 60657 USA (SAN 211-6537) Tel 773-281-1818; Fax: 773-281-0555; Toll Free: 800-621-1008
E-mail: customerservice@loyolapress.com
Web site: http://www.loyolabooks.org
Dist(s): **ISD**
Spring Arbor Distributors, Inc.; *CIP.*

LP Publishing, *(978-0-578-00530-0; 978-0-578-01791-4; 978-0-615-56110-3; 978-0-9859790)* 2941 S. Cornett Dr., Ridgefield, WA 98642 USA
Dist(s): **Lulu Pr., Inc.**

L.Patrick Publishing, *(978-0-9774418)* 2710 W. 76th St., Inglewood, CA 90305 USA.

LPC, *(978-0-9822065; 978-0-9833196; 978-0-9847655; 978-1-938499; 978-0-615-89890-2; 978-1-941103; 978-1-946016; 978-1-64526)* Div. of Christian Devotions Ministries, Orders Addr.: 2333 Barton Oaks Dr., Raleigh, NC 27614 USA; *Imprints:* Brimstone Fiction (BrimstoneFict); Illuminate YA (Illuminate YA)
E-mail: lighthousepublishingcarolinas@gmail.com
Web site: http://LPCBooks.com
Dist(s): **CreateSpace Independent Publishing Platform**
Spring Arbor Distributors, Inc.

LPD Pr., *(978-0-9641542; 978-1-890689; 978-1-936744; 978-1-943681)* 925 Salamanca, NW, Los Ranchos, NM 87107-5647 USA Tel 505-344-9382; Fax: 505-345-5129; *Imprints:* Rio Grande Books (Rio Grande Bks)
E-mail: LPDPress@q.com
Web site: http://www.nmsantos.com
Dist(s): **Smashwords.**

LRS, *(978-1-58118)* 14214 S. Figueroa St., Los Angeles, CA 90061-1034 USA Tel 310-354-2610; Fax: 310-354-2601; Toll Free: 800-255-5002
E-mail: lrsprint@aol.com
Web site: http://www.lrs-largeprint.com
Dist(s): **Beeler, Thomas T. Pub.**

LSG Pubns., *(978-1-933532)* 29165 Clover Ln., Big Pine Key, FL 33043-6046 USA
E-mail: lisagaljanic@optonline.net
Web site: http://www.lsgpublications.com.

LSP *Imprint of* **LSP Digital, LLC**

LSP Digital, LLC, *(978-0-9792030; 978-0-9800733; 978-0-9817654)* P.O. Box 851556, Westland, MI 48185 USA Tel 734-355-3733; Fax: 734-261-0155; *Imprints:* LSP (LSP USA)
E-mail: admin@lspdigital.com
Web site: http://www.lspdigital.com.

LTI Publishing, *(978-0-9743048)* Div. of Let's Talk Interactive, Inc., P.O. Box 371, Huntersville, NC 28070 USA
E-mail: art@LTIPublishing.net
Web site: http://www.letstalkinterctive.com; http://www.FathersTouch.com; http://www.SexualAbuse.ws; http://www.ChildHoodItShouldNotHurt.com; http://www.ChildHoodShouldNotHurt.com; http://www.AgainstSexualAbuse.org; http://www.LetsTalkCounseling.com.

LTL Media LLC, *(978-0-9785744)* P.O. Box 12766, Tempe, AZ 85284 USA
Web site: http://www.mylittlethinkers.com.

Lu, Melissa Productions, *(978-0-9726832)* 5356 Rose Ridge Ln., Colorado Springs, CO 80917 USA Fax: 719-594-6993
E-mail: patsy@melissalu.com
Web site: http://www.melissalu.com.

Lua Publishing, *(978-0-9746304)* P.O. Box 3250, Fairfield, CA 94533 USA Tel 707-426-9480
E-mail: info@luapublishing.com
Web site: http://www.luapublishing.com
Dist(s): **New Leaf Distributing Co., Inc.**

Luath Pr. Ltd. (GBR) *(978-0-946487; 978-1-84282; 978-1-905222; 978-1-906307; 978-1-906817; 978-1-908373; 978-1-910021) Dist. by* **IngramPubServ.**

Luath Pr. Ltd. (GBR) *(978-0-946487; 978-1-84282; 978-1-905222; 978-1-906307; 978-1-906817; 978-1-908373; 978-1-910021) Dist. by* **Midpt Trade.**

Luath Pr. Ltd. (GBR) *(978-0-946487; 978-1-84282; 978-1-905222; 978-1-906307; 978-1-906817; 978-1-908373; 978-1-910021) Dist. by* **IPG Chicago.**

Lubbers, Theresa *See* **Mr. Emmett Publishing**

Lucas Co., *(978-0-9715916)* P.O. Box 9245, Moscow, ID 83843 USA
Web site: http://www.lucasco.com.

Lucas Enterprises, *(978-0-9770611)* P.O. Box 9201, Chico, CA 95927 USA
E-mail: lucasent1@earthlink.net.

Lucas, Mattie, *(978-0-9762456)* P.O. Box 47070, Windsor Mills, MD 21244 USA Fax: 410-944-2597
E-mail: bishop@digc.org.

Lucas Violet *Imprint of* **Clocktower Hill Research & Publishing Group, LLC**

†Luce, Robert B. Pubs., *(978-0-88331)* Owned by Renaissance Book Services Corp., 2490 Black Rock Tpke., Fairfield, CT 06432 USA Tel 203-372-0300; Fax: 203-374-4766; Toll Free: 800-786-5427
E-mail: info@aslanpublishing.com
Web site: http://www.aslanpublishing.com
Dist(s): **APG Sales & Distribution Services**; *CIP.*

Lucent Bks. *Imprint of* **Cengage Gale**

Lucent Interpretations, LLC, *(978-0-9787849; 978-1-935146)* P.O. Box 3931, Lisle, IL 60532-8831 USA (SAN 856-6364)
E-mail: salmahammad@hotmail.com.

Lucent Pr. *Imprint of* **Greenhaven Publishing LLC**

Lucia Pubs., *(978-0-9762297)* Orders Addr.: P.O. Box 3, Churubusco, IN 46723-0003 USA Tel 260-693-0852; Fax: 260-693-0082; Edit Addr.: 209C S. Main St., Churubusco, IN 46723 USA
E-mail: diannegg@peoplepc.com; giannakeff@iquest.net
Web site: http://www.luciapublishers.com.

Lucky & Me Productions, Inc., *(978-0-9721256; 978-0-615-71754-8)* Orders Addr.: 410 East 74th St., 6H, New York, NY 10021-3918 USA (SAN 255-0873) Tel 212-288-7203; Fax: 401-783-7815 call before faxing/not always on
E-mail: writermyst@aol.com
Web site: http://www.dearjohnlennon.com
Dist(s): **CreateSpace Independent Publishing Platform.**

Lucky Bamboo Crafts, *(978-0-9884648)* P.O. Box 1022, Yarmouth, ME 04096 USA Tel 207-310-8101
E-mail: info@luckybamboocrafts.com
Web site: http://www.luckybamboocrafts.com
Dist(s): **Independent Pubs. Group.**

Lucky Bear Pubns., *(978-0-9729938)* 1144 Langwood Dr., Gallatin, TN 37066 USA Tel 615-452-3242 (phone/fax)
E-mail: perryluckybear@comcast.net
Web site: http://www.myluckybear.com.

Lucky Duck Designs, *(978-0-9790632)* P.O. Box 2192, Petaluma, CA 94953-2192 USA
E-mail: stuart@lucky-duck.com
Web site: http://www.lucky-duck.com.

Lucky Jenny Publishing, *(978-0-9847982; 978-0-615-69429-0; 978-0-615-87941-3; 978-0-615-88036-5; 978-0-615-88053-2; 978-0-615-92528-8; 978-0-615-93423-5; 978-0-615-97849-9; 978-0-692-26564-2; 978-0-692-33703-5; 978-0-692-34748-5; 978-0-692-35226-7; 978-0-692-35675-3; 978-0-692-44777-2; 978-0-692-46799-2; 978-0-692-48929-1; 978-0-692-61369-6; 978-0-692-66141-3; 978-1-7323301) P.O. Box 331, Plymouth, CA 95669 USA Tel 209-256-2465*
E-mail: publisher@luckyjenny.com
Web site: www.luckyjenny.com
Dist(s): **CreateSpace Independent Publishing Platform**
Ingram Content Group.

Lucky Publications *See* **Covered Wagon Publishing LLC**

Lucky Red Pr., LLC, *(978-0-9790690)* 10061 Riverside Dr., Suite 812, Toluca Lake, CA 91602 USA Tel 818-795-2388; Fax: 818-566-4995
E-mail: Susan@frankiespals.com
Web site: http://www.frankiespals.com.

Lucky 3 Ranch, Inc., *(978-1-928624)* 2457 S. County Rd. 19, Loveland, CO 80537-9044 USA Tel 970-663-0066; Fax: 970-663-0676; Toll Free: 800-816-7566
E-mail: meredith@luckythreeranch.com
Web site: http://www.luckythreeranch.com/
Dist(s): **MediaTech Productions.**

LuckySports, *(978-0-935938)* 39844 Somerset Ave., Palm Desert, CA 92211 USA (SAN 213-7453) Tel 760-861-2174 (cell)
E-mail: chuck@LuckySports.net
Web site: http://www.bogiegolf.com; http://www.sportcartoonbooks.com; http://www.LuckySports.net.

Lucy Rose Publishing LLC, *(978-0-9789386; 978-0-9821936)* P.O. Box 3034, Fort Polk, LA 71459 USA
E-mail: admin@lucyrosepublishing.com
Web site: http://www.lucyrosepublishing.com.

Ludwig Creative, Inc., *(978-0-578-55326-9; 978-0-578-63568-2)* P.O. Box 25505, Portland, OR 97298-0505 USA Tel 503-329-9873; Fax: 503-297-7773
E-mail: trudy@trudyludwig.com
Web site: trudyludwig.com.

Ludwig, Michael, *(978-0-692-14696-5; 978-0-692-14699-6)* 20 W. St., West Hatfield, MA 01088 USA Tel 774-200-7707
E-mail: mike.luddy@yahoo.com
Dist(s): **Ingram Content Group.**

Lueck Studios, *(978-0-9774547)* 8353 11th Ave. NW, Seattle, WA 98117 USA (SAN 257-6023)
E-mail: jenny@lueckstudios.com
Web site: http://www.chicabee.com
Dist(s): **Baker & Taylor Publisher Services (BTPS).**

Luisalchemy *See* **Alchemy Hero Publishing**

Luke & Lori Bks., *(978-0-9747792)* Orders Addr.: 5908 90th St., Lubbock, TX 79424 USA Tel 806-783-9941; Fax: 806-783-3099
E-mail: Melissa@lukeandlori.com
Web site: http://www.LukeAndLori.com.

Lukeman Literary Management, Ltd., *(978-0-9829537; 978-0-9839778; 978-0-9849753; 978-1-939416; 978-1-63291; 978-1-64029; 978-1-0943)* 157 Bedford Ave., Brooklyn, NY 11211 USA Tel 718-599-8988; Fax: 775-264-2189
E-mail: noah@lukeman.com.

Lulilite Productions, *(978-0-9759631)* P.O. Box 20847, Sedona, AZ 86341-0847 USA Tel 928-284-5442 (phone/fax)
E-mail: ariamagi@npgcable.com
Web site: http://www.lulilites.com.

Lulu Enterprises Inc. *See* **Lulu Pr., Inc.**

Lulu Pr., Inc., *(978-1-4116; 978-1-84728; 978-1-4303; 978-1-4357; 978-0-60552; 978-0-557; 978-1-4583; 978-1-257; 978-1-105; 978-1-300; 978-1-4834; 978-1-304; 978-1-312; 978-1-326; 978-1-329; 978-1-365; 978-1-5342; 978-0-6927338-7; 978-0-359; 978-0-578-42336-4; 978-1-68470; 978-1-68471; 978-1-68474; 978-1-716; 978-0-578-73052-3) 627 Davis Dr. Suite 300, Morrisville, NC 27560 USA Tel 919-459-5858 919-447-3198; 26-28 Hammersmith Grove, London, W6 7BA; Imprints:* Huskies Pub (MYID_X_HUSKIES)
E-mail: rbraynin@lulu.com; dllamas@lulu.com
Dist(s): **Amazon Digital Services Inc.**
Booklines Hawaii, Ltd.
Copyright Clearance Ctr., Inc.
CreateSpace Independent Publishing Platform
Ingram Content Group
Smashwords
Valjean Pr.

Lulu.com (GBR) *(978-1-84753; 978-1-4092; 978-1-4461; 978-1-4457; 978-1-4452; 978-1-84799; 978-1-4476; 978-1-4466; 978-1-4467; 978-1-4475; 978-1-4477; 978-1-4478; 978-1-4709; 978-1-4710; 978-1-291; 978-1-4717; 978-1-4716; 978-1-326; 978-1-387; 978-1-7947; 978-1-7948; 978-0-244; 978-1-6780; 978-1-6781) Dist. by* **LuluCom.**

Lumadix Pr., *(978-0-9981647)* 1615 Buck St, West Linn, OR 97068 USA Tel 503-707-1438
E-mail: rio4koviak@gmail.com
Web site: www.riokoviak.com.

Lumen (ARG) *(978-950-724; 978-950-9017; 978-987-00) Dist. by* **Lectorum Pubns.**

LUMEN-US Pubns., *(978-0-9703611; 978-0-9787788; 978-0-9794862; 978-0-9815359; 978-0-9819935; 978-1-936405)* 234 Main St., Park Forest, IL 60466-2098 USA Toll Free: 866-219-9637
E-mail: Lumenuspubl@aol.com
Web site: http://www.lumen-us.com
Dist(s): **BookBaby.**

Lumina Pr. LLC, *(978-0-9708442)* P.O. Box 1106, Wrightsville Beach, NC 28480-1106 USA Do not confuse with Lumina Press in Springfield, MO
E-mail: david@luminapress.com
Dist(s): **Two Rivers Distribution.**

Luminare Pr., LLC, *(978-1-937303; 978-1-944733; 978-1-64388)* 467 W. 17th Ave., Eugene, OR 97401 USA Tel 541-554-7574
E-mail: pmarshall17@comcast.net.

Luminary Media Group *Imprint of* **Pine Orchard, Inc.**

Luminate 7 Publishing, *(978-0-9765496)* 676 A 9th Ave., No. 142, New York, NY 10036 USA Tel 917-647-6740; Fax: 212-957-9191
E-mail: luminate7@aol.com.

Luminations Media Group, Inc., *(978-0-9821199; 978-1-61222)* P.O. Box 538, Monterey Park, CA 91754 USA Tel 626-571-0115
E-mail: office@luminationsmedia.com
Web site: http://www.LuminationsMedia.com.

Luminis Bks., Inc., *(978-1-935462; 978-1-941311)* 13245 Blacktern Way, Carmel, IN 46033 USA (SAN 857-8125) Tel 317-250-9539
E-mail: publisher@luminisbooks.com
Web site: http://www.luminisbooks.com
Dist(s): **MyiLibrary**
ebrary, Inc.

Lumpkin, Carol *See* **Peace Rug Company, Inc., The**

Luna Publishing, *(978-0-9791785)* Orders Addr.: 5815 82nd St., No. 145, PMB 137, Lubbock, TX 79424 USA Tel 806-687-3479; Fax: 806-687-3401 Do not confuse with Luna PUblishing Company in Los Angeles, CA
E-mail: ccrmgr2@nts-online.net
Web site: http://www.lunapublish.com.

Luna, Rachel Nickerson *See* **Howard, Emma Bks.**

Luna Rising *Imprint of* **Northland Publishing**

Lunada Pr., LLC, *(978-0-937176)* 2510 W. 237th, Suite 100, Torrence, CA 90505 USA Tel 435-632-8349
E-mail: jeannemaree@charter.net
Dist(s): **Ingram Content Group.**

Lunar Donut Pr., *(978-0-9725638)* P.O. Box 692625, Orlando, FL 32869 USA Tel 407-298-7779; Fax: 407-298-7779
E-mail: caricatureconnection@cfl.rr.com
Web site: http://www.caricatureconnection.com.

Lunasea Studios, *(978-0-9799290)* 9450 Mira Mesa Blvd., Suite B-107, San Diego, CA 92126 USA
Web site: http://www.lunasea-studios.com/.

Lunatic Pr., *(978-0-9772590)* P.O. Box 4571, West Hills, CA 91308 USA
Web site: http://www.lunaticpress.com.

Lunchbox Lessons, *(978-1-60507)* 970 E. Broadway, Suite 406, Jackson, WY 83001 USA (SAN 854-9540) Tel 307-462-4173
E-mail: info@lunchboxlessons.com
Web site: http://www.lunchboxlessons.com.

Lunchbox Stories Inc., *(978-0-9798059)* 20425 NW Quail Hollow Dr., Portland, OR 97229 USA
Web site: http://www.lunchboxstories.com.

Lundblade, Diana *See* **Fifth Element Publishing**

Lundy, Dylan, *(978-0-578-19800-2)* 2955 Talon Court, Virginia Beach, VA 23453 USA.

Luse, Sandra I., *(978-0-615-22394-0)* P.O. Box 431, Wilber, NE 68465 USA Tel 402-821-2641.

Lushena Bks., *(978-1-930097; 978-1-63182)* 607 Country Club Dr., Unit E, Bensenville, IL 60106 USA (SAN 630-5105) Tel 630-238-8708; Fax: 630-238-8824
E-mail: Lushenabks@yahoo.com
Web site: http://www.lushenabks.com/.

Lutherworth Pr., The (GBR) *(978-0-7188) Dist. by* **ISD USA.**

Luthie M West, *(978-0-9986548; 978-1-7322514)* 3979 N. Clarey St., Eugene, OR 97402 USA Tel 541-915-1664
E-mail: Arpeer@gmail.com.

Lutz, William G., *(978-0-615-15622-4; 978-0-615-18287-2; 978-0-615-21273-9)* 10248 Ramm Rd., Whitehouse, OH 43571 USA
Dist(s): **Lulu Pr., Inc.**

Luv U Bks., *(978-0-9715322)* P.O. Box 42037, Cincinnati, OH 45242-0037 USA
E-mail: luvubooks@fuse.net
Web site: http://www.luvubooks.com.

Luvlife Publishing, *(978-0-9764316)* Orders Addr.: 69 Shore Dr., Old Lyme, CT 06371 USA Tel 860-434-0723
E-mail: mistilove@earthlink.net
Web site: http://www.snakesofnewengland.com.

LuvLuv *Imprint of* **Aurora Publishing, Inc.**

L.W. Communications, *(978-0-9723378)* 16815 Victory Blvd. #226, Van Nuys, CA 91406-5550 USA Tel 818-787-9550 (phone, fax - call first)
E-mail: lancecoach@aol.com
Web site: http://www.lancecoach.com.

Lycan Valley Press *See* **Lycan Valley Press Pubns.**

Lycan Valley Press Pubns., *(978-0-9987489; 978-1-64562)* 1625 E. 72nd St, STE 700 PMB 132, Tacoma, WA 98404 USA Tel 425-270-7097
E-mail: writer.mj.sydney@gmail.com
Web site: www.TheCrowsInMyAttic.com; www.LycanValley.com.

Lyceum Books, Incorporated *See* **Follmer Group, The**

Lychgate Pr., *(978-0-615-65502-4; 978-0-9882887; 978-0-9976116)* 529 N.W. 31st St., Corvallis, OR 97330 USA Tel 541-752-5211
Web site: editor@fullcitypress.com
Dist(s): **CreateSpace Independent Publishing Platform.**

Lynch, Marietta & Patricia Perry, *(978-0-9610962)* 240 Atlantic Rd., Gloucester, MA 01930 USA (SAN 265-2722) Tel 508-283-6322.

Lynda Fern Bks., *(978-0-9961982)* 12918 Oakland Hills Ct., Jacksonville, FL 32225 USA Tel 904-565-8495
E-mail: lyndafernbooks@gmail.com.

Lynn Tyner Mitchum & James Rogers, *(978-0-9745191)* P.O. Box 5799, Sevierville, TN 37864 USA
Web site: http://jamesrogersonline.com.

Lynne Ellen, Inc., *(978-0-9748889)* 670 N. Stiles Dr., Charleston, SC 29412 USA Tel 843-817-2530
E-mail: lynne@metoomommy.com.

Lynn's Bookshelf, *(978-0-9618608)* Orders Addr.: P.O. Box 2224, Boise, ID 83701 USA (SAN 667-1314) Tel 208-331-1987 (phone/fax); Edit Addr.: 3423 Scenic Dr., Boise, ID 83703 USA
E-mail: decker.barbara@ymail.com; lynnsbooks@cableone.net.

†Lynx Hse. Pr., *(978-0-89924)* 420 W. 24th Ave., Spokane, WA 99203-1922 USA (SAN 250-3344) Tel 309-624-4594; Fax: 309-623-4238
E-mail: cnhowell@mail.ewu.edu
Dist(s): **SPD-Small Pr. Distribution**
Univ. of Washington Pr.; *CIP.*

Lyon, Ernest Media Productions, *(978-0-9741328; 978-0-9991661)* P.O. Box 26101, San Francisco, CA 94126-6101 USA (SAN 255-7460) Tel 415-387-5569 (phone/fax)
E-mail: davidlyon@mindspring.com.

Lyons Pr. *Imprint of* **Globe Pequot Pr., The**

Lypton Publishing, *(978-0-9752780)* 35409 S. Fairbank Point, Drummond Island, MI 49726 USA (SAN 256-0143).

Lyrical Learning, *(978-0-9646367; 978-0-9741635; 978-0-692-37347-7; 978-0-692-38790-0; 978-0-9964731)* 8008 Cardwell Hill, Corvallis, OR 97330 USA Tel 541-754-3579 (phone/fax); Toll Free: 800-761-0906
Web site: http://www.lyricallearning.com.

Lyrically Korrect Publishing, *(978-0-9727776)* 5402 Belle Vista Ave., Baltimore, MD 21206 USA; *Imprints:* Book Her Publications (Bk Hr Pubns)
Web site: http://www.sheribooker.com.

M & B Publishing, *(978-0-9758580)* 930 Edgecliffs Dr., Langley, WA 98260 USA
E-mail: wistful@whidbey.com.

M & D Publishing, Inc., *(978-0-9768667)* '2980 SE Fairway W., Stuart, FL 34997 USA Tel 772-286-9781; Fax: 772-286-5169 Do not confuse with M & D Publishing in Phoenix, AZ
E-mail: manddpublishing@bellsouth.net.

M D C T Publishing, *(978-0-9674491; 978-0-692-06540-2; 978-0-692-06544-0; 978-0-578-42274-9; 978-0-578-43146-8; 978-0-578-54083-2; 978-0-578-54088-7; 978-0-578-59982-3)* 31990 SW Village Crest Ln., Wilsonville, OR 97070-8427 USA
E-mail: mdundy@teleport.com
Dist(s): **Partners/West Book Distributors.**

M G L S, Inc., *(978-0-9601682; 978-1-888833)* 700 S. First St., Marshall, MN 56258 USA (SAN 212-2170) Tel 507-532-4311; Fax: 507-532-4313
E-mail: carberry@mgls.com.

M K L Publishing, *(978-0-9746204)* Orders Addr.: P.O. Box 407, Ballston Spa, NY 12020 USA; Edit Addr.: 5019 Fairground Ave., Ballston Spa, NY 12020 USA
E-mail: mklpublishing@aol.com.

M L E S *See* **Pathway Bk. Service**

MM Co., *(978-1-883473)* 15007 Avon St., Independence, MO 64055 USA Tel 816-246-6365.

M Q Pubns., *(978-1-84072; 978-1-897954; 978-1-84601; 978-0-9797400)* 12 The Ivories 6-8 Northampton St., London, N1 2HY GBR Tel 020 7359 2244; Fax: 020 7359 1616; 49 W. 24th St., 8th Flr., New York, NY 10010 Tel 212-223-2320; Fax: 212-675-8026; Toll Free: 800-398-2848
E-mail: mail@mqpublications.com
Web site: http://www.mqpublications.com
Dist(s): **Advanced Global Distribution Services**
Hachette Bk. Group
Ingram Publisher Services
Mercedes Distribution Ctr., Inc.
Sterling Publishing Co., Inc.
Wybel Marketing Group.

M R L, Inc., *(978-1-892860)* 1445 Cannon St., Louisville, CO 80027-1453 USA Tel 303-666-8164
E-mail: moyazena@aol.com.

M T E, Ltd., *(978-1-888679)* 3095 S. Trenton St., Denver, CO 80231-4164 USA Tel 303-696-0839.

M2M Partners, *(978-0-9768884)* P.O. Box 60923, Phoenix, AZ 85082-0923 USA Toll Free: 800-658-8790
Web site: http://www.mamaroses.com; http://www.printserve.net; http://www.nonnieskitchen.com
Dist(s): **Partners/West Book Distributors.**

MAA Pr. *Imprint of* **American Mathematical Society**

MAAT Resources, Inc., *(978-0-9624096; 978-1-893447)* 130 East Grand Ave., South San Francisco, CA 94080 USA Tel 650-871-4449; 650-871-4111; Fax: 650-871-4551; *Imprints:* Bilingual Language Materials (Biling Lang)
E-mail: info@blmteachaids.com
Web site: http://www.blmteachaids.com/; http://www.transparentpower.com/.

Mabbul Publishing Co., *(978-0-9762860)* 915 Hunting Horn Way, Evans, GA 30809 USA
Web site: http://www.mabbul.com.

Mabela Publishing, *(978-0-9981307; 978-0-9995544)* 602 1st Ave E, Oskaloosa, IA 52577 USA Tel 641-295-1871; Fax: 641-295-1871
E-mail: karikaydb@gmail.com.

Mabrey, Chris, *(978-0-9979042)* 5410 Nighthawk Dr, Indianapolis, IN 46254 USA Tel 317-513-6413
E-mail: cmabrey@comcast.net.

MAC Productions, *(978-1-878591)* P.O. Box 84, Duvall, WA 98019 USA Tel 425-256-2652; Fax: 425-749-7065
E-mail: macproductions1@verizon.net
Web site: http://www.macsgolfguides.com
Dist(s): **Partners/West Book Distributors.**

MacAdam/Cage Publishing, Inc., *(978-1-878448; 978-0-9673701; 978-1-931561; 978-1-59692)* 155 Sansome St., Suite 550, San Francisco, CA 94104 USA (SAN 299-9730) Tel 415-986-7503; Fax: 415-986-7414
E-mail: david@macadamcage.com
Web site: http://www.macadamcage.com.

Macalester Park Publishing Co., Inc., *(978-0-910924; 978-0-930286; 978-1-886158)* 24558 546th Ave., Austin, MN 55912 USA (SAN 110-8077) Tel 507-396-0135; Toll Free: 800-407-9078
E-mail: macalesterpark@macalesterpark.com
Web site: http://www.macalesterpark.com
Dist(s): **Bookmen, Inc.**
Spring Arbor Distributors, Inc.

Macaronic Pr., *(978-0-9766859; 978-1-59864)* P.O. Box 1542, Sebastopol, CA 95473-1542 USA Tel 707-813-7047; Toll Free: 888-364-8253
E-mail: vivienka@msn.com
Web site: http://www.macaronicpress.com.

Macaulay, David Studio *Imprint of* **Roaring Brook Pr.**

Macauley, Myron Christian, *(978-0-578-05300-4)* 106 Monroe St., No. 2, Brooklyn, NY 11216 USA
E-mail: danae@kgn6.com.

Macaw Books LLC *See* **Kapp Bks. LLC**

MacBeath, Emmaline, *(978-1-7324073)* P.O. Box 55014, Shoreline, WA 98155 USA Tel 541-653-6904
E-mail: emmalinerosebooks@gmail.com
Web site: https://emmalinerosebooks.com.

MacBride, E. J. Pubn., Inc., *(978-1-892511)* 129 W. 147th St., No. 20B, New York, NY 10039 USA; *Imprints:* Disposition Sketch Books (Disposition Sketch).

MacGill, William V. & Company, *(978-0-9744720)* 1000 N. Lombard Rd., Lombard, IL 60148-1232 USA Tel 800-323-2841; Toll Free Fax: 800-727-3433
E-mail: macgill@macgill.com; nickh@macgill.com
Web site: http://www.macgill.com.

MacGregor, Doug, *(978-0-9654843; 978-0-9995030)* 1578 Rosada Way, Fort Myers, FL 33901 USA Tel 941-337-3980
E-mail: mactoons@comcast.net.

MacHillock Publishing, *(978-0-9744996; 978-1-7334439)* 9158 Selborne Ln. 30268, Palmetto , GA 30268 USA
E-mail: sdh@mindspring.com
Dist(s): **Independent Pubs. Group**
MyiLibrary.

MacIntyre Purcell Publishing Inc. (CAN) *(978-0-9738063; 978-0-9784784; 978-0-9810941; 978-1-926916; 978-1-927097; 978-1-77276) Dist. by* **BTPS.**

Mackenzie Smiles, LLC, *(978-0-9790347; 978-0-9815761)* P.O. Box 1373, Sausalito, CA 94965 USA Toll Free: 888-800-5978; P.O. Box 1373, Sausalito, CA 94965
Web site: http://www.mackenziesmiles.com.

Mackie, Valencia *See* **CRE Lease Talk, Incorporated**

Mackin, Dan, *(978-0-615-12303-5)* 8395 SE Palm St., Hobe Sound, FL 33455 USA Tel 772-546-3008; Fax: 772-546-5374
E-mail: danmackinartist@aol.com
Web site: http://www.danmackin.com.

Mackinac Island Press, Inc. *Imprint of* **Charlesbridge Publishing, Inc.**

Mackinac Island State Park Commission *See* **Mackinac State Historic Parks**

Mackinac State Historic Parks, *(978-0-911872)* Orders Addr.: P.O. Box 873, Mackinaw City, MI 49701 USA; Edit Addr.: 207 W. Sinclair, Mackinaw City, MI 49701 USA (SAN 202-5981) Tel 231-436-5564; Fax: 231-436-4210.

MackStorm Productions, Inc., *(978-0-9753078)* 1410 Prairie Crossing Dr., West Chicago, IL 60185 USA Tel 630-231-3998
E-mail: marilee@americanslidechart.com.

MacLaren-Cochrane Publishing *See* **MacLaren-Cochrane Publishing, Inc.**

MacLaren-Cochrane Publishing, Inc., *(978-1-64372)* 4325 Lafayette Dr, El Dorado Hills, CA 95762 USA; *Imprints:* Huskies Pub (MYID_X_HUSKIES)
E-mail: Tannya@maclaren-cochranepublishing.com
Web site: www.maclaren-cochranepublishing.com
Dist(s): **Follett School Solutions.**

MacMenamin Pr., *(978-0-9761414)* P.O. Box 133, Zionsville, PA 18092 USA Tel 610-739-9527
E-mail: sales@macmenaminpress.com
Web site: http://www.macmenaminpress.com.

Macmillan, *(978-0-374; 978-1-4668; 978-1-68274)* Div. of Holtzbrinck Publishing, Orders Addr.: 16365 James Madison Hwy., Gordonsville, VA 22942 USA (SAN 631-5011) Tel 540-672-7600; Fax: 540-672-7664; 540-672-7540 (Customer Service); Toll Free Fax: 800-672-2054 (Order Dept.); Toll Free: 888-330-8477; Edit Addr.: 175 Fifth Ave., 20th Flr., New York, NY 10010 USA Tel 212-674-5151; Fax: 212-677-6487; Toll Free Fax: 800-258-2769; Toll Free: 800-488-5233
E-mail: customerservice@mpsvirginia.com
Web site: http://www.macmillan.com
Dist(s): **Children's Plus, Inc.**
Child's World, Inc., The
Follett School Solutions
National Bk. Network
ebrary, Inc.

Macmillan Audio, *(978-0-940687; 978-1-55927; 978-1-893564; 978-1-59397; 978-1-59768; 978-1-4272)* Div. of Macmillan, Orders Addr.: 16365 James Madison Hwy., Gordonsville, VA 22942-8501 USA Toll Free Fax: 800-672-2054; Toll Free: 888-330-8477; Edit Addr.: 175 Fifth Ave., Suite 315, New York, NY 10010 USA (SAN 665-1275) Tel 646-307-5000; Fax: 917-534-0980; Toll Free: 800-221-7945
E-mail: audio@hbpub.com
Web site: http://www.macmillanaudio.com
Dist(s): **AudioGO**
Findaway World, LLC
Follett School Solutions
Landmark Audiobooks
MPS
Macmillan.

Macmillan Caribbean (GBR) *(978-0-333; 978-1-4050) Dist. by* **Interlink Pub.**

Macmillan Education, Ltd. (GBR) *(978-0-333; 978-1-4050; 978-0-230; 978-1-4472; 978-1-349; 978-1-78632; 978-1-380) Dist. by* **Players Pr.**

†Macmillan Publishing Co., Inc., *(978-0-02; 978-0-87605; 978-0-89256)* Orders Addr.: 200 Old Tappan Rd., Old Tappan, NJ 07675 USA (SAN 202-5574)
Dist(s): **MyiLibrary**; *CIP.*

Macmillan Pubs., Ltd. (GBR) *(978-0-330; 978-0-333; 978-1-4050) Dist. by* **IPG Chicago.**

Macmillan Pubs., Ltd. (GBR) *(978-0-330; 978-0-333; 978-1-4050) Dist. by* **Trafalgar.**

Macmillan Reference USA *Imprint of* **Cengage Gale**

Macmillan/McGraw-Hill Schl. Div., *(978-0-02)* Div. of The McGraw-Hill Education Group, Orders Addr.: 220 E. Daniel Dale Rd., DeSoto, TX 75115 USA Fax: 972-228-1982; Toll Free: 800-442-9685
Dist(s): **McGraw-Hill Cos., The.**

Macro Publishing Group, *(978-0-9702699; 978-0-9754130; 978-0-9826829; 978-1-7326225; 978-1-7331782; 978-1-952871)* 1507 E. 53rd Street, No. 858, Chicago, IL 60615 USA Tel 773-263-6512; Toll Free: 888-854-8823 (phone/fax)
E-mail: lissawoodson@aol.com
Dist(s): **INscribe Digital**
Independent Pubs. Group.

Macromedia Education *Imprint of* **Macromedia, Inc.**

Macromedia, Inc., *(978-0-9742273; 978-1-932719)* 600 Townsend St., San Francisco, CA 94103 USA Tel 415-252-2000; Fax: 415-832-5555; Toll Free: 800-457-1774; *Imprints:* Macromedia Education (Macromedia Educ) Do not confuse with Macromedia, Inc. in Lake Placid, NY
Web site: http://www.macromedia.com/education.

Macy, Carolyn, *(978-0-9988838; 978-0-9989127; 978-1-7328604)* 6227 81st Ave. N.E., Norman, OK 73026 USA Tel 405-401-2012
E-mail: cmacy2@aol.com.

MAD *Imprint of* **DC Comics**

Mad Creek Bks. *Imprint of* **Ohio State Univ. Pr.**

Mad Dash Co., The, *(978-0-9975965)* 111 Windermere Way, Warwick, RI 02886 USA Tel 401-527-5700
E-mail: lumpybones@gmail.com.

Mad Hatter Publishing, Inc., *(978-0-9994692)* P.O. Box 20973, Ferndale, MI 48220-0973 USA Tel 248-560-7372
E-mail: info@madhatterpublishinginc.com.

Mad Libs *Imprint of* **Penguin Young Readers Group**

Mad Yak Pr., *(978-0-9717995)* 8232 Styers Ct., Laurel, MD 20723-2100 USA Tel 301-317-8817
Dist(s): **Diamond Comic Distributors, Inc.**
Diamond Bk. Distributors.

Madame Cat Publishing, *(978-0-9983859)* 6491 Smooth Thorn Ct, Jacksonville, FL 32258 USA Tel 904-955-9967
E-mail: meldow14@gmail.com.

Madame Fifi Pubns., *(978-0-9667418; 978-0-9762900; 978-0-9821707)* P.O. Box 310967, Newington, CT 06131-0967 USA
Web site: http://www.madamefifi3.com.

Madd Mindz Publishing, Inc., *(978-0-9802262)* P.O. Box 20437, Brooklyn, NY 11202-0437 USA Tel 347-661-4030; Fax: 718-425-9919
E-mail: C.Brandon@MaddMindzPublishing.com
Web site: http://www.maddmindzpublishing.com.

Maddness, Inc., *(978-0-9761619)* P.O. Box 76551, Oklahoma City, OK 73147-2551 USA
E-mail: osheashamir@aol.com
Web site: http://www.osheashamir.com.

Mader, Lothar, *(978-0-615-24577-5; 978-0-578-05621-0)* 2130 Professional Dr., Suite 240, Roseville, CA 95661 USA
Dist(s): **Lulu Pr., Inc.**

Madison, Dr. Ron *See* **Ned's Head Productions**

Maerkle Pr., *(978-0-9721966; 978-0-9819479)* 66 E. Shore Blvd., Timberlake, OH 44095 USA Tel 440-269-8653; Fax: 440-269-8035
Web site: http://www.maerklepress.com.

Maerov, Jeffrey, *(978-0-578-11402-6; 978-0-578-11504-7)* 24 Fecamp, Newport Coast, CA 92657 USA.

Maestro Classics, *(978-1-932684)* Div. of Simon & Simon, LLC, Orders Addr.: 1745 Broadway 17th Fl, New York, NY 10019 USA Tel 212-519-9847
E-mail: bsimon@maestroclassics.com
Web site: http://www.MaestroClassics.com
Dist(s): **CD Baby**
Follett School Solutions.

Maestro Learning, *(978-0-9740533)* 24 Chilton St., Cambridge, MA 02138-6802 USA
E-mail: peter@maestrolearning.com
Web site: http://www.maestrolearning.com.

MaestroMedia Pr., *(978-0-9773731)* 408 Pearl St., Richmond, IN 47374 USA Tel 765-962-8380
E-mail: rosecitysp@msn.com.

Maeva, Ediciones, S.A. (ESP) *(978-84-86478; 978-84-95354; 978-84-92695; 978-84-96231; 978-84-96748; 978-84-15120; 978-84-15532; 978-84-15893; 978-84-17108) Dist. by* **Lectorum Pubns.**

Magabala Bks. (AUS) *(978-0-9588101; 978-1-875641; 978-1-921248; 978-0-7316-0335-0; 978-0-7316-1622-0; 978-0-7316-1623-7; 978-0-7316-1736-4; 978-0-7316-3328-9; 978-0-646-22120-5; 978-0-646-26784-5; 978-1-922142; 978-1-925360; 978-1-925768; 978-1-925936) Dist. by* **IPG Chicago.**

Mage Pubs., Inc., *(978-0-934211; 978-1-933823; 978-1-949445)* 1408 35th St., NW, Washington, DC 20007 USA (SAN 693-0476) Tel 202-342-1642; Fax: 202-342-9269; Toll Free: 800-962-0922 (orders only)
E-mail: as@mage.com
Web site: http://www.mage.com.

Magee, Burke & Glenna, *(978-0-9748424)* Orders Addr.: P.O. Box 581, Carnation, WA 98014 USA; Edit Addr.: 2015 290th Ave., NE, Carnation, WA 98014 USA
E-mail: rtg@returntogod.com
Web site: http://www.returntogod.com.

Maggid *Imprint of* **Toby Pr. LLC, The**

MaggieMooseTracks, *(978-0-9895205)* 1766 Sand Hill Rd., No. 102, Palo Alto, CA 94304 USA Tel 650-322-8860
E-mail: girlfins@aol.com.

Magic Cat (GBR) *Dist. by* **HachBkGrp.**

Magic Crystal Pr., *(978-0-9986487)* 727 W. 7th St. Suite 503, Los Angeles, CA 90017 USA Tel 949-278-8005
E-mail: jrc@magiccrystalpress.com
Web site: www.magiccrystalpress.com.

Magic Factory, LLC, The, *(978-1-938155)* Orders Addr.: 3818 Somerset Dr., Durham, NC 27707 USA Tel 310-943-6972; Edit Addr.: 3818 Somerset Dr., Durham, NC 27707 USA Tel 310-943-6972 (Tel/Fax)
E-mail: orders@magicfactory.com; orders@magicfactory.com; info@magicfactory.com; books@magicfactory.com
Web site: http://magicfactory.com; http://signofthesandman.com; http://rangerbaldy.com.

Magic Lamp Pr., *(978-1-56891; 978-1-882629)* Div. of Magic Lamp Productions, 1838 Washington Way, Venice, CA 90291-4704 USA (SAN 256-1670) Tel 310-822-2985; Fax: 310-827-9123; Toll Free: 800-367-9661
E-mail: videopage@earthlink.net
Web site: http://www.magiclamppress.com
Dist(s): **Smashwords.**

Magic Lamp Productions *See* **Magic Lamp Pr.**

Magic Moon Bks., LLC, *(978-0-615-77740-9; 978-0-9983137)* 8663 Equinox Cir, Bingham Canyon, UT 84037-2039 USA Tel 385-495-6393
Dist(s): **CreateSpace Independent Publishing Platform.**

Magic Mountain Pr., *(978-0-9715946; 978-1-7338765)* P.O. Box 1933, Asheville, NC 28802 USA Tel 828-231-0041 Do not confuse with Magic Mountain Press, The in Lafayette, IN
E-mail: karon@ashevillerealtygroup.com
Web site: http://www.the12keys.com.

Magic of African Rhythm (TMOAR), The, *(978-0-9820926)* Orders Addr.: P.O. Box 14724, Raleigh, NC 27620-4724 USA Tel 919-828-1906; Fax: 419-781-8209
E-mail: shabutaso@gmail.com.

Magic Penny Pr., *(978-0-9982777)* 3336 Lone Hill Ln, Encinitas, CA 92024 USA Tel 858-367-8541
E-mail: massiveart@gmail.com.

Magic Penny Reading, *(978-0-9761987; 978-0-9899114)* 61 Wehrle Dr., Amherst, NY 14225 USA Tel 800-873-0396; Fax: 888-728-0754
E-mail: sandyschneider@magicpennyreading.org
Web site: http://magicpennyreading.org.

Magic Picture Frame Studio, LLC, *(978-0-9749269)* Orders Addr.: P.O. Box 2603, Issaquah, WA 98027 USA Tel 425-222-7562
E-mail: publisher@magicpictureframe.com; mvm@magicpictureframe.com; class@magicpictureframe.com
Web site: http://www.magicpictureframe.com
Dist(s): **Baker & Taylor Publisher Services (BTPS).**

Magic Propaganda Mill, *(978-0-9760117)* Please Send All Correspondence To: Info@mpmill.com, Brooklyn, NY 11238 USA
E-mail: info@mpmill.com
Web site: http://www.magicpropagandamill.com.

Magic Space, *(978-0-615-32034-2; 978-0-9983113)* 14749 Croft St., Dade City, FL 33525 USA Tel 352-521-5653.

Magic Valley Pubs., *(978-0-9716681; 978-0-9774833; 978-0-9785509; 978-0-9800879; 978-0-9821496; 978-0-9845275)* 6390 E. Willow St., Long Beach, CA

90815 USA Tel 562-795-0289; Fax: 562-795-0490 Do not confuse with Magic Valley Publishers in Burly, ID
Web site: http://www.magicvalleypub.com.

Magic Wagon, (978-1-60270; 978-1-61641) Div. of ADBO Publishing Group, Orders Addr.: P.O. Box 398166, Minneapolis, MN 55439-8166 USA Fax: 952-831-1632; Toll Free: 800-458-8399; Edit Addr.: 8000 W. 78th St., Suite 310, Edina, MN 55439 USA Toll Free: 800-458-8399; *Imprints:* Looking Glass Library (LookngGlassLib); Graphic Planet - Fiction (Graphic Planet); Short Tales (Short Tales); Calico Chapter Books (CalicoChap Bks); Spellbound (SpellboundUSA)
E-mail: info@abdopublishing.com
Web site: http://www.abdopublishing.com
Dist(s): **ABDO Publishing Co.**
Follett School Solutions
MyiLibrary.

Magic Woman Pubns., (978-0-9760062) 1527 Veteran Ave., Suite 7, Los Angeles, CA 90024-5566 USA Tel 310-478-7743; Fax: 310-478-9892
E-mail: artdivin@yahoo.com
Web site: http://www.magicwomanpublications.com.

Magic Wordweaver Pr., (978-0-9754116; 978-0-615-12456-8) Orders Addr.: P.O. Box 1315, Conifer, CO 80433 USA (SAN 255-8459) Tel 303-838-7515 (phone/fax); Edit Addr.: 29580 S. Sunset Trail, Conifer, CO 80433 USA
E-mail: premalee108@yahoo.com.

Magic Works Publishing & Production, (978-0-9799545) 27 Greenmoor, Irvine, CA 92614 USA Tel 714-309-4824; Fax: 949-651-8895
E-mail: selina@superachievement.net
Web site: http://SuperAchievement.net.

Magical Beginnings, (978-0-692-54966-7; 978-0-692-59310-3; 978-0-692-61084-8; 978-0-692-61356-6; 978-0-692-62334-3; 978-0-9973594; 978-0-692-65326-5; 978-0-692-71224-5) 10940 S. Parker Rd. No. 791, Parker, CO 80134-7440 USA
Web site: www.FairyVillageBooks.com
Dist(s): **CreateSpace Independent Publishing Platform.**

Magical Bk. Works, (978-1-943196; 978-0-692-42748-4; 978-0-692-44762-8; 978-0-692-57982-4; 978-0-692-61750-2; 978-0-692-66030-0; 978-0-692-68311-8; 978-0-692-71417-1; 978-0-692-71697-7) 2597 Amethyst Dr., Suite 10, Santa Clara, CA 95051-1154 USA Tel 408-480-0505; Fax: 512-727-0580
E-mail: pennyannecole@gmail.com
Web site: www.magicalbookworks.com
Dist(s): **CreateSpace Independent Publishing Platform.**

Magical Child Bks. *Imprint of* **Shades of White**

Magical Creations, (978-0-9744879) P.O. Box 324, Chicago Park, CA 95712 USA Tel 530-477-7429
E-mail: doris_rainville@hotmail.com.

Magical Mischief Maker, (978-0-9754004) P.O. Box 1075, Douglasville, GA 30133 USA
Web site: http://www.magicalmischiefmaker.com.

MagicStar Inc., (978-0-9821387) 2021 Midwest Rd., Suite 200, Oak Brook, IL 60523 USA (SAN 857-3336) Tel 510-740-4045
E-mail: publisher@magicstarpub.com
Web site: http://www.magicstarpub.com.

Magination, (978-1-881597) 3579 E. Foothill Blvd., No. 330, Pasadena, CA 91107 USA Tel 626-306-1190; Fax: 626-306-1193.

Magination Pr. *Imprint of* **American Psychological Assn.**

Magiscule Publishing Group, L.L.C., (978-0-9772232) 12 Armstrong Ave., Suite 3 W., Providence, RI 02903 USA Fax: 401-861-7030
E-mail: Krystalstream@excite.com.

Magna Large Print Bks. (GBR) (978-0-7505; 978-0-86009; 978-1-84137; 978-1-85057; 978-1-78502) *Dist. by* **Ulverscroft US.**

Magnatic Music, (978-0-9719897) 13806 Delaney Rd., Dale City, VA 22193 USA
E-mail: alstonsongs@aol.com.

Magner Publishing *See* **Magner Publishing & American Binding & Publishing**

Magner Publishing & American Binding & Publishing, (978-1-929416; 978-1-60080) P.O. Box 60049, Corpus Christi, TX 78466 USA Tel 361-658-4221; Toll Free: 800-863-3708
E-mail: rmmagner@pyramid3.net
Web site: http://www.americanbindingpublishing.com.

Magness, Robert Pubns., LLC, (978-0-9774577) 1412 Kent St., Sturgis, MI 49091-2334 USA Tel 269-651-7473
E-mail: sengam@netzero.com.

Magnetar Venture Group, LLC, (978-0-692-37543-3; 978-0-9861212) P.O. Box 540324, Houston, TX 77254 USA Tel 5127632652
Dist(s): **CreateSpace Independent Publishing Platform.**

Magnetic Image, Inc., (978-0-9678542) 900 SW 13th St., Boca Raton, FL 33486 USA
E-mail: info@magneticimageinc.com
Web site: http://www.magneticimageinc.com.

Magnetic Pr., (978-1-942367; 978-1-951719) 5415 N Sheridan Rd Apt 5101, CHICAGO, IL 60640 USA Tel 312-259-7356
E-mail: mike@magnetic-press.com
Web site: www.magnetic-press.com
Dist(s): **Diamond Comic Distributors, Inc.**

Magni Co., The, (978-1-882330; 978-1-937026) Orders Addr.: 1402 S. Custer Rd. Suite 201, McKinney, TX 75072 USA Tel 972-540-2050; Fax: 972-540-1057; Edit Addr.: 7106 Wellington Point Rd., McKinney, TX 75072 USA Tel 972-540-2050; Fax: 972-540-1057
E-mail: sales@magnico.com; info@magnico.com
Web site: http://www.magnico.com
Dist(s): **Book Publishing Co.**

Magnolia Nook Pubns., (978-0-692-80164-2; 978-0-692-06306-4) 145 Delatte Ln., Gheens, LA 70355 USA Tel 985-258-6351
E-mail: magnolianook@yahoo.com
Web site: https://magnolianookpublications.com.

Magpie Children's Bks., (978-1-7321012) 158 N 300 E, Provo, UT 84606 USA Tel 623-742-5820
E-mail: morty.joshua@gmail.com
Web site: www.joshualeemortensen.com.

Magpie Press *See* **Magpie Pr., Pine Mountain Club, CA**

Magpie Pr., Pine Mountain Club, CA, Orders Addr.: P.O. Box 6434, Pine Mountain Club, CA 93222-6434 USA Tel 661-242-1265 (phone/fax) Do not confuse with Magpie Pr. in Wallington, NJ
E-mail: MagSmith1265@msn.com
Web site: www.magpiepress.com.

Magrane, Etna International, (978-0-9741167) 8 Hill Point Ave., San Francisco, CA 94117 USA Tel 415-681-5157; Fax: 415-681-5820
E-mail: emagrane@aol.com.

Magsimba Pr., (978-1-932956) 1821 Bruce Rd., NE, Atlanta, GA 30329-2508 USA Tel 404-633-9153
E-mail: info@magsimba.org
Web site: http://www.magsimba.org; http://www.tagalog1.com/Ordinary/Learn_Filipino.jsp
Dist(s): **Quality Bks., Inc.**

Mahle,, Robin D. Author, (978-1-7325592) 6905 Ashley Dr., Colorado Springs, CO 80922 USA Tel 979-595-7183
E-mail: author@robindmahle.com
Web site: robindmahle.com.

MAHVL Publishing, (978-0-9790072) P.O. Box 134, Deerfield, IL 60015-0134 USA
Web site: http://michaelslewismd.com
Dist(s): **Chicago Distribution Ctr.**
Ingram Publisher Services.

Maia Ocean Printing, (978-0-692-08522-6) 2101 E Trant Rd., Kingsville, TX 78363 USA Tel 305-780-9062
E-mail: simplebychoice@gmail.com
Dist(s): **Ingram Content Group.**

Mailbox Bks., The *Imprint of* **Education Ctr., Inc.**

Main Asset Pubns., (978-0-9667617) P.O. Box 1153, Teaneck, NJ 07666 USA Tel 201-837-6400; Fax: 201-837-8842
E-mail: mathispublishing@aol.com
Web site: http://www.whyarentumarried.com.

Main Coon Publishing, (978-0-9983035) 58 St. George Rd., Wingdale, NY 12594 USA Tel 845-832-6076
E-mail: osusanna@outlook.com.

Main Event Pr., (978-0-9774129) 1714 Boxwood Cir., Saint Cloud, MN 56303-0148 USA.

Main Frame Pr., (978-0-615-49914-7; 978-0-9856790) 858 Third Ave. No. 320, Chula Vista, CA 91911 USA Tel 619-253-4312
E-mail: gilbert@gilbertklein.com
Web site: www.football101.net.

Main Street Pubns., (978-0-9745033) 11810 Dice Rd., Freeland, MI 48623 USA.

Main Street Publishing, Inc. *See* **Main St Publishing, Inc.**

Main St Publishing, Inc., (978-0-9666676; 978-0-9710470; 978-0-9741294; 978-0-9748591; 978-0-9760414; 978-0-9765369; 978-0-9776480; 978-0-9785934; 978-0-9791154; 978-1-934615; 978-1-939999) 206 E. Main, Suite 207, Jackson, TN 38301 USA Fax: 731-427-7380; Toll Free: 866-457-7379; *Imprints:* MSP (MSP) Do not confuse with companies with same or similar names in Kingston, NJ, Shorewood, WI, Osage Beach MO,
E-mail: editor@mainstreetpublishing.com
Web site: http://www.mainstreetpublishing.com.

Maine Mediator, The, (978-0-9991718) 25 Stony Brook Way, Bar Harbor, ME 04609 USA Tel 601-618-6447
E-mail: trishmadell@gmail.com.

MainSpringBks., (978-1-946854; 978-1-947352; 978-1-64133) 5901 W Century Blvd. Suite 750, Los Angeles, CA 90045 USA
E-mail: production@mainspringbooks.com
Web site: https://mainspringbooks.com/.

Mainstay, LLC, (978-0-9798854) 4134 W. View Pointe Dr., Highland, UT 84003 USA
Web site: http://www.MainstayEducation.com.

Mainstay Publishing, (978-0-9832901; 978-0-9899479) Mainstay Publishing P.O. Box 293, Middletown, DE 19709 USA Tel 302-223-6636
E-mail: denise@mainstaypublishing.com.

Mainstream Ctr., Schl. for the Deaf, The, (978-0-9797287) 48 Round Hill Rd., Northampton, MA 01060-2124 USA Tel 413-582-1121; Fax: 413-586-6654
E-mail: akot@clarkeschool.org
Web site: http://www.clarkeschool.org.

Mainstream Connections Publishing, (978-1-60336) 10103 Queens Cir., Ocean City, MD 21842 USA Tel 410-213-7861 fax or email requests; *Imprints:* Adventures of Everyday Geniuses, The (Adv Evryday)
E-mail: barb.esham@mainstreamconnections.org; lisa.spielman@mainstreamconnections.org
Web site: http://www.mainstreamconnections.org
Dist(s): **Brodart Co.**
Emery-Pratt Co.
Follett School Solutions
Quality Bks., Inc.
Yankee Bk. Peddler, Inc.

Mainstreet Systems & Software Inc., (978-0-9726871) P.O. Box 577, Harleysville, PA 19438-0577 USA (SAN 255-335X) Toll Free: 800-257-4535
E-mail: epwhelan@netcarrier.com
Web site: http://www.promotecopyrights.com.

Maire, Lucy Bedoya, (978-0-9768436) Orders Addr.: P.O. Box 2632, Westport, CT 06880 USA Tel 203-454-5204; Fax: 203-454-5204; Edit Addr.: 19 River Oak Rd., Westport, CT 06880 USA
E-mail: twelvetreasures@yahoo.com
Dist(s): **Raimond Graphics Inc.**

Majestic Eagle Publishing, (978-0-9797495) Div. of James J. Brown & Assoc., Inc., 6649 Navajo, Lincolnwood, IL 60712 USA Tel 847-679-3447; Fax: 847-679-6191
E-mail: jola1@aol.com.

Majestic Kids *Imprint of* **MP Pubns., Inc.**

Majestic Publishing, LLC, (978-0-9755314; 978-1-942156) Orders Addr.: P.O. Box 1560, Lithonia, GA 30058 USA Tel 770-482-9129 Do not confuse with Majestic Publishing, LLC in Santa Barbara, CA
E-mail: majpublish@gmail.com
Web site: http://www.majesticpublishing.net.

Majesty Publishing, (978-0-9754839) 12 Paddock Ln., Hampton, VA 23669 USA
E-mail: customerservice@faithfrontier.com
Web site: http://www.faithfrontier.com.

Major, Christina, (978-0-692-02524-6; 978-0-692-46530-1) 1910 Yosemite Ave. No. 205, Simi Valley, CA 93063 USA Tel 818-517-1076
E-mail: delphina2k@gmail.com
Web site: http://www.horizonscape.com.

Major Masterpieces *See* **Major Masterpieces Ltd.**

Major Masterpieces Ltd., (978-0-692-52666-8; 978-1-7336564) 1842 First Ave., Pottsville, PA 17901 USA Tel 570-622-9364
E-mail: nannettebrophymajor@gmail.com
Web site: www.majormasterpieces.com.

Majority Press, Incorporated, The *See* **Majority Pr., The**

Majority Pr., The, (978-0-912469) Orders Addr.: 46 Development Rd., Fitchburg, MA 01420 USA (SAN 249-3012) Tel 978-342-9676; Fax: 978-348-1233; Edit Addr.: P.O. Box 538, Dover, MA 02030 USA (SAN 265-2757) Tel 508-744-6097 (phone/fax)
E-mail: tmpress@earthlink.net
Web site: http://www.themajoritypress.com
Dist(s): **A & B Distributors & Pubs. Group**
Lexicon Pubns., Inc.

Majzik, Bill *See* **Mill Creek Metro Publishing**

Makai Concepts, LLC, (978-0-9744035) Orders Addr.: 3 King William Ct., Hilton Head Island, SC 29926 USA (SAN 255-6219)
E-mail: betsys@hargray.com.

Makdan Publishing, (978-0-9819283) P.O. Box 7560, Bonney Lake, WA 98391 USA Tel 253-720-1059
E-mail: jimlandgraf@hotmail.com.

Make Believe Ideas (GBR) (978-1-905051; 978-1-84610; 978-1-84879; 978-1-78065; 978-1-78235; 978-1-78393; 978-1-78598) *Dist. by* **Nelson.**

MAKE BELIEVE PUBLISHING, (978-0-692-90006-2; 978-0-9998833) P.O. Box 1009, BLANCHARD, OK 73010 USA Tel 661-549-2498
E-mail: MakeBelieve63@hotmail.com
Web site: makebelievepublishing.com; www.authordebbiefogle.com
Dist(s): **CreateSpace Independent Publishing Platform.**

Make Me A Story Pr., (978-1-878847) 1737 N. 2580 E. Rd., Sheldon, IL 60966 USA Tel 815-429-3501 (phone/fax)
E-mail: info@earthesquirrel.com
Web site: http://www.earthesquirrel.com.

Make-A-Wish Middle Tennessee, (978-0-578-54356-7; 978-0-578-54892-0; 978-0-578-61226-3; 978-0-578-63451-7) 600 Hill Ave. Suite 201, Nashville, TN 37210 USA Tel 615-221-2200
E-mail: Ltemple@middletennessee.wish.org
Dist(s): **Ingram Content Group.**

Make-believe Pr. LLC, (978-1-7323686) 3106 Blackberry Lane., Columbia, MO 65201 USA Tel 310-906-7730
E-mail: masterofmakebelieve@gmail.com
Web site: www.make-believepress.com.

Maker, Azmaira H. *See* **Aspiring Families Press**

Malachite Quills Publishing *See* **MQuills Publishing**

Malamih Publishing Hse., (978-0-9820804) 4311 Jamboree Rd., No. 170, Newport Beach, CA 92660 USA.

Malamute Pr., (978-0-9722180) Orders Addr.: P.O. Box W, Aspen, CO 81612 USA; Edit Addr.: P.O. Box W, Aspen, CO 81612-7424 USA
E-mail: info@dodogsvote.com; sales@malamutepress.com
Web site: http://www.malamutepress.com.

Malbrough, Michael, (978-0-9758893) 163-167 N. Pk. St., Apt. 5, East Orange, NJ 07019 USA.

Malcolm Down Publishing Ltd. (GBR) (978-1-910786; 978-1-912863) *Dist. by* **BTPS.**

Malenga, Mubita, (978-0-9991946; 978-0-578-40787-6; 978-1-7345744) 8641 N. Servite Dr. Unit 205, Milwaukee, WI 53223 USA Tel 414-688-5333
E-mail: mubitam@yahoo.com.

Malibu Bks. for Children, (978-1-929084) Div. of Malibu Films, Inc., 48 Broad St., No. 134, Red Bank, NJ 07701 USA Tel 732-933-0446 (phone/fax); Toll Free: 888-629-9947 (phone/fax)
E-mail: malibuinc@aol.com
Web site: http://www.malibubooks.com.

Malik, Sakinah A. *See* **EDR**

Mallon Publishing (AUS) (978-1-875696) *Dist. by* **D C D.**

Malone-Ballard Book Publishers, (978-0-9729484) 160 S. Third St., Lansing, IA 52151 USA Tel 319-389-7174 (phone/fax)
Web site: http://www.malone-ballard.com
Dist(s): **Partners Bk. Distributing, Inc.**

Malor Bks. *Imprint of* **I S H K**

Malpaso Ediciones SL (ESP) (978-84-15996; 978-84-16420; 978-84-17081) *Dist. by* **IPG Chicago.**

Mama Incense Publishing, (978-0-9761523) P.O. Box 4635, Long Beach, CA 90804-9998 USA Tel 310-490-9097
E-mail: mama@mamaincense.com
Web site: http://www.mamaincense.com.

Mama Specific Productions, (978-0-9749480) P.O. Box 110393, Cleveland, OH 44111-0393 USA Tel 440-396-1963; Fax: 801-640-2494; *Imprints:* MSPpress (MSPpr)
E-mail: info@msppress.com; trula@MSPpress.com
Web site: http://www.msppress.com.

Mama's Boyz, Inc., (978-0-9796132; 978-1-7323184) 304 Main Ave. #114, Norwalk, CT 06851 USA (SAN 854-1914)
E-mail: jerrycraft@aol.com
Web site: http://www.jerrycraft.net
Dist(s): **Follett School Solutions.**

MaMbabooks.com, (978-0-9817448; 978-0-9887867; 978-1-948407) Div. of Mamba Books & Publishing, 355 Liberty St., Dendron, VA 23839 USA
E-mail: mambabooks@gmail.com
Web site: http://www.mambabooks.com; http://www.mambabooks.biz.

Mammoth, Math, (978-1-942715) 915 Lounds St., Inverness, FL 34450 USA Tel 813-728-9831
E-mail: maria_miller@mathmammoth.com
Web site: www.mathmammoth.com.

Mamoo Hse., (978-1-933014) 17 W. Browning Rd., Collingswood, NJ 08108 USA Tel 856-858-6616
E-mail: melisma@earthlink.net
Web site: http://www.mamoohouse.com.

MAMP Creations, (978-0-9772210) P.O. Box 1316 Landmark Trail South, Hopkins, MN 55343 USA Tel 952-938-9320 (phone/fax); *Imprints:* Phil the Pill & Friends (Phil PillFrnds)
E-mail: APritcha6@gmail.com; mampcreations@gmail.com
Web site: http://https://www.amazon.com/M.-Ann-Machen-Pritchard/e/B002BM9DLM/; http://www.cafepress.com/mampcreations.

Management Services, (978-0-9747418) 302 S. 2nd St. Apt. 711, Champaign, IL 61820-4141 USA Do not confuse with Managment Services Incorporated in Atlanta, GA
E-mail: aepelbaum@yahoo.com
Web site: http://moscowtechchicago.com.

Manassas Museum, The, (978-1-886826) Orders Addr.: P.O. Box 560, Manassas, VA 20108 USA Tel 703-368-1873; Edit Addr.: 9101 Prince William St., Manassas, VA 201110-5615 USA
Web site: http://www.manassasmuseum.org.

Mance Ian Wright, (978-0-578-42961-8) 600 Benton St., Mountain Home, AR 72653 USA Tel 870-580-0166
E-mail: adaniels.wright@gmail.com
Dist(s): **Ingram Content Group.**

Mandala Publishing, (978-0-945475; 978-1-886069; 978-1-932771; 978-1-60109) 3160 Kerner Blvd. Ste. 108, San Rafael, CA 94901-5454 USA Toll Free: 800-688-2218 (orders only); *Imprints:* Earth Aware Editions (Earth Aware)
E-mail: info@mandala.org
Web site: http://www.mandala.org; http://earthawareeditions.com/catalog/
Dist(s): **MyiLibrary**
Simon & Schuster, Inc.

Mandala Publishing Group *See* **Mandala Publishing**

Mandel Vilar Pr., (978-1-942134) 19 Oxford Ct., Simsbury, CT 06070 USA Tel 860-431-5269; *Imprints:* Moment Books (MYID_G_MOMENT)
E-mail: Robert@americasforconservation.org
Web site: www.mvpress.org
Dist(s): **Consortium Bk. Sales & Distribution.**

Mandell, Ted, (978-0-9749156) 2232 Pine Creek Ct., South Bend, IN 46628 USA Tel 574-631-6953
E-mail: tmandell@nd.edu.

Mandeville, Terry M., (978-0-9762475) 7933 NE 124th St., Kirkland, WA 98034 USA
E-mail: terrymand@aol.com.

M&J Southwest, Inc., (978-0-9744534) 4402 E. Desert Willow Rd., Phoenix, AZ 85044 USA Tel 480-940-4046
E-mail: michaelc@gotwords.com
Web site: http://www.gotwords.com.

Mandolin House *See* **Kush Univ. Pr.**

Mandolin Hse. *Imprint of* **Kush Univ. Pr.**

Mandracchia Bks. *Imprint of* **Mandracchia, Charles**

Mandracchia, Charles, (978-0-9721957) 7914 Rockaway Beach Blvd. Apt. 6L, Rockaway Beac, NY 11693-2081 USA; *Imprints:* Mandracchia Books (Mandracchia Bks)
E-mail: charlesmandracchia@yahoo.com
Web site: http://www.kungfoogrannys.com; http://www.showtoonz.com.

Mandragora (ITA) (978-88-7461; 978-88-85957) *Dist. by* **Natl Bk Netwk.**

Mandy & Andy Bks., Inc., (978-0-9772757) 124 Meridian Ave., Poinciana, FL 34759-3241 USA (SAN 257-1765) Tel 407-319-3880; 863-427-4643
E-mail: wadams23@cfl.rr.com
Web site: http://mandyandandybooks.com.

Mandy & Pandy Bks., LLC, (978-0-9800156; 978-0-9834411) 2590 Cook Creek Ct., Ann Arbor, MI 48103 USA Tel 734-904-1916
E-mail: tsinkule@heulegordon.com
Dist(s): **China Books & Periodicals, Inc.**

Manga 18 *Imprint of* **Central Park Media Corp.**

Manga Classics Inc., (978-1-947808) 2194 Esperanca Ave., Santa Clara, CA 95054 USA Tel 647-400-8366; Fax: 647-400-8366
E-mail: erikko@gmail.com
Web site: www.mangaclassics.com
Dist(s): **Diamond Comic Distributors, Inc.**
Diamond Bk. Distributors.

Manga Punk, (978-0-9748966) P.O. Box 966, Meadows of Dan, VA 24120 USA
Web site: http://www.mangapunk.com.

MANGACANDY, LLC, (*978-0-9785891*) 13937 W. 73rd St., Shawnee, KS 66216 USA Tel 913-638-9940
E-mail: nami.bunny@gmail.com
Web site: http://www.mangacandy.com.

Mango (FRA) (*978-2-7404; 978-2-84270; 978-2-910635*) *Dist. by* **Distribks Inc.**

Mango Media, (*978-1-63353; 978-1-64250*) 2850 Douglas Rd. Suite 301, Coral Gables, FL 33134 USA (SAN 920-8275) Tel 305-428-2299; *Imprints:* Conari Press (ConariMango)
E-mail: info@mangomedia.us
Web site: www.mangomedia.us
Dist(s): **Ingram Publisher Services**
MyiLibrary
Open Road Integrated Media, Inc.
Red Wheel/Weiser.

Mango Tree Pr., (*978-0-9708571*) Orders Addr.: P.O. Box 853, Mackinaw City, MI 49701 USA Tel 231-627-7322 (phone/fax); Edit Addr.: 2562 Pinewood Cir., Cheboygan, MI 49721 USA
E-mail: ids@mangotreepress.com; lds@mangotreepress.com
Web site: http://www.mangotreepress.com
Dist(s): **Partners Bk. Distributing, Inc.**

Mangrove Seed Expressions *Imprint of* **Mangrove Seed, Inc.**

Mangrove Seed, Inc., (*978-0-9797158*) Orders Addr.: P.O. Box 2, Sarasota, FL 34230-0002 USA Toll Free: 866-549-1549 to contact publisher; P.O. Box 02, Sarasota, FL 34230; *Imprints:* Mangrove Seed Expressions (Mangve Seed)
E-mail: dan@mangroveseed.org
Web site: http://www.mangroveseed.org; http://www.mangroveseedchronicles.com.

Mangrum, Kaylea J., (*978-0-9883009*) 1521 Carrick Dr., Murfreesboro, TN 37128 USA Tel 615-579-3663
E-mail: donmangrum@yahoo.com; phillipmangrum@mac.com.

Mangrum-Strichart Learning Resources, (*978-0-9745999; 978-0-9797723; 978-0-9978079; 978-1-7336069*) 2634 Glendale Dr., Loveland, CO 80538 USA Tel 970-593-1586; Fax: 970-962-0057; Toll Free: 866-409-0585
E-mail: study@mangrum-strichart.com
Web site: http://www.mangrum-strichart.com.

Manhattan Academia, (*978-0-615-16120-4; 978-0-615-18454-8; 978-0-615-18503-3; 978-1-936581*) 26 Norwood Terr., Millburn, NJ 07041 USA
Web site: http://www.manhattanacademia.com
Dist(s): **Lulu Pr., Inc.**

Manic D Pr., (*978-0-916397; 978-1-933149; 978-1-945665*) Orders Addr.: P.O. Box 410804, San Francisco, CA 94141 USA (SAN 670-6932) Tel 415-648-8288 (phone/fax); Edit Addr.: 250 Banks St., San Francisco, CA 94110 USA
E-mail: info@manicdpress.com
Web site: http://www.manicdpress.com
Dist(s): **Consortium Bk. Sales & Distribution**
Last Gasp of San Francisco
MyiLibrary
SPD-Small Pr. Distribution.

Manifest Pubns., (*978-0-9627896; 978-1-929354*) Orders Addr.: P.O. Box 429, Carpinteria, CA 93014 USA Tel 805-684-4905; Fax: 805-684-3100; Edit Addr.: P.O. Box 429, Carpinteria, CA 93014-0429 USA
E-mail: editor@manifestpub.com; publisher@manifestpub.com
Web site: http://www.manifestpub.com
Dist(s): **Sunbelt Pubns., Inc.**

Manifesting Pages Publishing *See* **MITWA**

Manifold Grace Publishing Hse., (*978-1-937400; 978-1-952926*) 25163 Greenbrooke Dr., Southfield, MI 48033 USA Tel 248-910-5616
E-mail: darlene@mgph.org
Web site: manifoldgracepublishinghouse.com
Dist(s): **BookBaby.**

Maninge Mali, (*978-0-9729698*) 204 Garden Pl., Radnor, PA 19087 USA (SAN 255-4623) Tel 610-254-0846
E-mail: maningemali@aol.com.

Manis, Shirley, (*978-0-9839286*) 2205 Francesco Cr., Capitola, CA 95010 USA Tel 831-462-4126
E-mail: smanis@cruzio.com.

Manitowish River Pr., (*978-0-9656763; 978-0-9998157*) 4245N State Hwy. 47, Mercer, WI 54547 USA (SAN 990-8900) Tel 715-476-2828
E-mail: manitowish@centurytel.net
Web site: www.manitowishriverpress.com
Dist(s): **Adventure Pubns.**

Mankamyer, Laura, (*978-0-9728431*) 343 Stonebrook Dr., Canonsburg, PA 15317-3409 USA.

Mann Publishing Group, (*978-0-9726888; 978-1-932577; 978-1-933673*) 710 Main St., 6th Flr., Rollinsford, NH 03869 USA (SAN 255-5409) Tel 603-601-0325; Fax: 603-601-0334; Toll Free: 877-877-6266; *Imprints:* BookMann Press (BkMann Pr)
E-mail: tmann@mannpublishing.com
Web site: http://www.askopus.com; http://www.rationalpress.com; http://www.agilitypress.com; http://www.incpress.com; http://www.mannpublishing.com.

Mann Publishing Inc. *See* **Mann Publishing Group**

Manners Toy Co., LLC, (*978-0-615-17967-4*) Orders Addr.: 2546 Lochness Rd, Richmond, VA 23235 USA Tel 804-307-5154
E-mail: mmadore@mannerstoycompany.com.

Mannheim Steamroller L.L.C., (*978-0-9656909; 978-0-9754149*) 9130 Mormon Bridge Rd., Omaha, NE 68152 USA Tel 402-457-4341; Fax: 402-457-4332
Web site: http://www.amgram.com; www.mannheimsteamroller.com.

Manning Pubns. Co., (*978-1-884777; 978-1-930110; 978-1-932394; 978-1-933988; 978-1-935182; 978-1-61729; 978-1-63343*) 180 Broad St. Apt. #1323, Saintmpford, CT 06901 USA; 178 S. Hill Dr., Westamptomn, NJ 08060 Tel 609-835-2793
E-mail: kidi@manning.com
Web site: http://www.manning.com
Dist(s): **Ebsco Publishing**
O'Reilly Media, Inc.
Simon & Schuster, Inc.

Manns, Marlo, (*978-0-9976399*) 7631 S. Perry Ave., Chicago, IL 60620 USA Tel 773-690-0175
E-mail: myheartknewlove@yahoo.com.

Manoa Pr., (*978-1-891839*) 2702 Menoa Rd., Honolulu, HI 96822 USA Tel 808-988-4904
Dist(s): **Native Bks.**

Manor Hse. Publishing Co., Inc., (*978-0-9645844; 978-0-9796239; 978-0-9836634; 978-0-9858774*) 880 Louis Dr., Warminster, PA 18974-2819 USA Tel 215-259-1700 Toll Free: 800-768-3222
E-mail: rdean@mgadvertising.com
Web site: http://www.poolspaliving.com.

Mansfield, J. Hse. Publishing Co., (*978-0-9707428*) P.O. Box 191575, Los Angeles, CA 90019 USA Fax: 323-935-6169
E-mail: jlmansfield@usa.net.

Mansion Publishing, Ltd., (*978-0-9675941*) c/o The Maggiore Companies, 60 Myopia Rd., Winchester, MA 01890 USA Tel 781-729-7210; 781-718-2003; Fax: 781-729-6444
E-mail: mansionpub@aol.com
Web site: http://wdressingthewholeperson.com.

Mantra Lingua (GBR) (*978-1-85269; 978-1-947679; 978-1-84444; 978-1-84611*) *Dist. by* **Chinasprout.**

Manual In Truth, A, (*978-0-9763252*) P.O. Box 541486, Miami, FL 33054 USA
E-mail: customersupport@amanualintruth.com
Web site: http://www.amanualintruth.com.

Manufacturing Application Konsulting Engineering (MAKE)in, (*978-1-62495*) 705 W. Azure Ln., Litchfield PArk, AZ 85340 USA Tel 469-265-8212
E-mail: trythaiketco@gmail.com
Web site: www.trythaiketco.com
Dist(s): **Lulu Pr., Inc.**

Many Kites Pr., (*978-0-9618469; 978-0-9729002*) Orders Addr.: P.O. Box 711, Cass Lake, MN 56633 USA Tel 605-341-4232 (phone/fax); Toll Free: 800-486-8940; Edit Addr.: 6511 160th St. NW, Cass Lake, MN 56633 USA
E-mail: info@manykites.com; jamie@manykites.com
Web site: http://www.manykites.com; http://www.manykites.org
Dist(s): **Smashwords.**

Many Voice Pr., (*978-0-9795185; 978-0-9833679; 978-1-7336918*) Flathead Valley Community College 777 Grandview Dr., Kalispell, MT 59901 USA (SAN 853-6686) Tel 406-756-3907; Fax: 406-756-3815 Do not confuse with companies with the same name in Long Islanf City, NY, Cincinnati, OH
E-mail: ljaegermontana@hotmail.com
Dist(s): **SPD-Small Pr. Distribution.**

Manzanita Falls Pubs., (*978-0-9763916*) P.O. Box 991920, Redding, CA 96099-1920 USA (SAN 256-3347)
Web site: http://www.manzanitafallspublishers.com.

MAP Creative LLC, (*978-0-9856967*) Orders Addr.: 128 Hamilton Rd, Bloomfield Hills, MI 48301 USA Tel 248-731-7065
E-mail: mattdamman@gmail.com
Web site: www.thesmallsports.com.

Mapin Publishing Pvt. Ltd (IND) (*978-81-85822; 978-81-88204*) *Dist. by* **Natl Bk Netwk.**

Maple Bend Farms Pr., (*978-0-9740799*) 4804 Laurel Canyon Blvd., Suite 224, Valley Village, CA 91607 USA
E-mail: ocsage@aol.com
Web site: http://www.maplebend.com.

Maple Canyon Co., (*978-0-9669760; 978-0-9787164*) P.O. Box 565, Mapleton, UT 84663 USA Tel 801-489-8948
E-mail: chuckclifton@maplecanyon.com; customerservice@maplecanyon.com
Web site: http://www.maplecanyon.com.

Maple Corners Press *Imprint of* **Attic Studio Publishing Hse.**

Maple Creek Media, (*978-0-9837967; 978-0-9859678; 978-0-9895471; 978-0-9912442; 978-0-9907392; 978-1-942914*) 1194 N. Carroll St., Hampstead, MD 21074 USA Tel 410-259-8295
E-mail: craig.schenning@maplecreekmedia.com
Web site: http://www.maplecreekmedia.com.

maple, Jessie, (*978-0-94817-0*) 658 HANSELL ST SE, Atlanta, GA 30312 USA Tel 347-551-0250
E-mail: jessielmaple@aol.com.

Maple Lane Writing & Desktop Publishing, (*978-0-9667527*) 16821 W. County Hill Rd., Hayward, WI 54843 USA Tel 715-634-9600; Fax: 715-634-1871
E-mail: mapleln@win.bright.net.

Maple Leaf Ctr., (*978-0-9759850; 978-0-9827210*) 167 N. Main St., Wallingford, VT 05773 USA Tel 802-446-3601; Fax: 802-446-3801
E-mail: mapleleaf@vermontel.net
Web site: http://www.mapleleafcenter.com.

Maple Leaf Publishing *See* **Spreeda Publishing**

Maple Pr., (*978-1-882029; 978-1-938232*) 481 E. San Carlos St, San Jose, CA 95112 USA (SAN 248-1375) Tel 408-297-1000; Fax: 408-297-1057
E-mail: copy@maplepress.net.

Maple Road Publishing, Inc., (*978-0-9844453*) Orders Addr.: P.O. Box 10143, McLean, VA 22102 USA
Web site: http://www.mapleroadpublishing.com.

Maps For Kids Inc., (*978-0-9759433*) 1550 Poly Dr., Billings, MT 59102 USA Tel 406-238-7131; Fax: 406-259-4021; Toll Free: 877-897-7131
E-mail: banjo@floberg.com
Web site: http://www.mapsforkids.com.

Maps.com, (*978-1-930194*) 120 Cremona Dr. Ste. 260, Goleta, CA 93117-5564 USA (SAN 254-4180) Toll Free: 800-929-4627
E-mail: info@maps.com
Web site: http://www.maps.com
Dist(s): **Cram, George F. Co., Inc.**

Marable, Justin, (*978-0-9831104*) 136 SW Kendall Ave., Topeka, KS 66606 USA Tel 785-286-7944
E-mail: justinmarableks@gmail.com.

Maracle, Derek, (*978-0-9991138; 978-1-7321056; 978-1-950594*) 13 Wesley St, Camden, DE 19934 USA Tel 302-697-1243; *Imprints:* Bickering Owls Publishing (BickeringOwls)
E-mail: dcm1977@comcast.net.

Marak, Michael, (*978-0-9795866*) 6205 Daffan Ln., Austin, TX 78724-1501 USA
E-mail: sue@rezulting.com.

Marandu, Thobias L., (*978-0-9767605*) 2913 Columbiana Rd. Apt. B, Birmingham, AL 35216-3537 USA
E-mail: tlekundayo@yahoo.com.

Marble Hse. Editions, (*978-0-9677047; 978-0-9786745; 978-0-9815345; 978-0-9834030; 978-0-9966224; 978-1-7332299*) 67-66 108th Street, Suite D27, Forest Hills, NY 11375 USA (SAN 253-6536); 67-66 108th Street, Suite D27, Forest Hills, NY 11375 (SAN 253-6536)
E-mail: elizabethuhlig7@gmail.com
Web site: http://www.marble-house-editions.com/.

Marble Mountain Pr., (*978-0-9748552*) PMB 214, 2019 Aero Way, Suite 103, Medford, OR 97504 USA Tel 530-926-2473
E-mail: marblemountain@snowcrest.net
Web site: http://www.rvinnz.com.

Marcabru Publishing, (*978-0-615-61495-3*) 108 E. 38th St., New York, NY 10016 USA Tel 917-596-0650
Web site: www.glennberger.net
Dist(s): **CreateSpace Independent Publishing Platform.**

Marcasa Bks., (*978-0-9763015*) Paloma del Lago No. 67, Campolago, Cidra, PR 00739-9361 USA Tel 787-960-3517 (phone/fax)
E-mail: mmartinezpr@gmail.com.

March 4th, Inc., (*978-0-9840806; 978-0-9829938; 978-1-939775*) 3701 Sacramento St. #494, San Francisco, CA 94118 USA (SAN 858-3641) Fax: 415-366-1520; Toll Free: 877-415-4488
E-mail: info@littlepicklepress.com
Web site: http://www.littlepicklepress.com
Dist(s): **Ingram Publisher Services**
MyiLibrary
Publishers Group West (PGW)
Sourcebooks, Inc.

March Media, Inc., (*978-0-9634824*) 1114 Oman Dr., Brentwood, TN 37027 USA Tel 615-377-1146; Fax: 615-373-1705
E-mail: etta.wilson@comcast.net.

March Street Pr., (*978-0-9624453; 978-1-882983; 978-0-9745909; 978-1-59661*) 3413 Wilshire Dr., Greensboro, NC 27408-2923 USA Fax: 336-282-9754 prefer orders by email (rbixby@earthlink.net)
E-mail: rbixby@earthlink.net
Web site: http://www.marchstreetpress.com
Dist(s): **Bottom Dog Pr.**

Marcia's Menagerie, (*978-0-9777359*) 2960 W. Stuart St., A-203, Fort Collins, CO 80526 USA Tel 970-493-6373
E-mail: tangome27@hotmail.com.

Marcinson Pr., (*978-0-9893732; 978-0-9967207; 978-1-946932*) 11111-70 San Jose Blvd. Suite 136, Jacksonville, FL 32223 USA Tel 352-263-0910
E-mail: editor@marcinsonpress.com.

Marco Bk. Co., (*978-0-9710756; 978-0-9729765*) 60 Industrail Rd., Lodi, NJ 07644 USA Tel 973-458-0485; Fax: 973-458-5289; Toll Free: 800-842-4234; *Imprints:* Everbind (Everbind)
E-mail: everbind5@aol.com
Dist(s): **Bks. & Media, Inc.**

MAR*CO Products, Inc., (*978-1-57543; 978-1-884063*) Orders Addr.: 1443 Old York Rd., Warminster, PA 18974 USA Tel 215-956-0313; Fax: 215-956-9041; Toll Free: 800-448-2197
E-mail: csfunk@marcoproducts.com; marcoproducts@comcast.net
Web site: http://www.store.yahoo.com/marcoproducts; http://www.marcoproducts.com.

Marcoux, Tom Media, LLC, (*978-0-9624660; 978-0-9800511; 978-0-615-78342-0; 978-0-615-78657-5; 978-0-615-80157-5; 978-0-615-80934-2; 978-0-615-81302-8; 978-0-615-83582-2; 978-0-615-91576-0; 978-0-615-92869-2; 978-0-615-97539-9; 978-0-615-99188-7; 978-0-692-21096-3; 978-0-692-22704-6; 978-0-692-22972-9; 978-0-692-23525-6; 978-0-692-33069-2; 978-0-692-35850-4; 978-0-692-38436-7; 978-0-692-45951-5; 978-0-692-52718-4; 978-0-692-56195-9; 978-0-692-60115-0; 978-0-692-60208-9; 978-0-692-63808-8; 978-0-692-64737-0; 978-0-69) 674 Morse Ave. Unit F, Sunnyvale, CA 94085 USA Tel 415-572-6609*
Dist(s): **CreateSpace Independent Publishing Platform.**

Marczak Innovations, (*978-0-692-85726-7; 978-0-692-19627-4; 978-0-578-74872-6*) 38 Oxford Rd, Newport News, VA 23606 USA Tel 757-207-0231
E-mail: chris.marczak.1@gmail.com; info@chrismarczak.com
Dist(s): **CreateSpace Independent Publishing Platform.**

Mardi Gras Publishing, LLC, (*978-0-9787262; 978-0-9789024; 978-0-9789986; 978-0-9790649; 978-0-9791570; 978-1-934329*) 6845 Hwy. 90 E. Suite 255, Daphne, AL 36526 USA
E-mail: contactlamedia@gmail.com
Web site: http://lamediaonline.com.

Mardick Pr., (*978-1-940413*) P.O. Box 10701, Houston, TX 77206 USA Tel 713-254-7285; *Imprints:* Blackbirch Press, Incorporated (Blackbirch Pr)
E-mail: publisher@mardickpress.com.

Marduk Publishing Inc., (*978-1-893138*) Orders Addr.: a/o Marduk Publishing Inc., P.O. Box 480608, Delray Beach, FL 33448 USA (SAN 256-3053) Tel 561-638-6070; 516 695-8077; Toll Free: 888-462-7385 (phone/fax)
E-mail: docbloc@marduk1.com; docbloc@marpub.com; docbloc@hotmail.com
Web site: http://www.marpub.com; http://www.marduk1.com; http://www.all-a.us; http://www.all-ace.com.

Marn Green Publishing, Inc., (*978-1-934277*) 5630 Memorial Ave N. # 3, Stillwater, MN 55082-1087 USA (SAN 852-4920) Toll Free: 800-287-1512
E-mail: toddsnow@marengreen.com
Web site: http://www.marengreen.com.

Maresca, Wendi, (*978-0-9772897*) 6130 Murifield Dr., Gurnee, IL 60031-5357 USA.

Margaret Ferguson Books *Imprint of* **Holiday Hse., Inc.**

Margaret Weis Productions, Ltd., (*978-1-931567; 978-1-936685*) P.O. Box 1131, Williams Bay, WI 53191 USA Fax: 866-668-5730 Do not confuse with Sovereign Pr. in Rochester, WA
E-mail: margaret@margaretweis.com; christi@margaretweis.com
Web site: http://www.margaretweis.com
Dist(s): **Diamond Comic Distributors, Inc.**
Diamond Bk. Distributors
PSI (Publisher Services, Inc.).

Margolis, Amy Publishing, (*978-0-9776692*) Orders Addr.: 31 Saddle Ln., Old Brookville, NY 11545 USA (SAN 257-9294)
E-mail: Amy@ButterfliesandMagicalWings.com
Web site: http://www.ButterfliesandMagicalWings.com.

Margolis, Marion, (*978-0-9753184*) 1 W. 72nd St., Apt. No. 95, New York, NY 10023 USA Tel 212-595-7555
E-mail: chasmargolis@aol.com
Dist(s): **Xlibris Corp.**

Marhouse, Inc., (*978-0-9752703*) Orders Addr.: a/o Marhouse Inc., P.O. Box 150605, Altamonte Springs, FL 32715 USA Tel 407-499-5307 (phone/fax)
E-mail: marhouse12@yahoo.com
Web site: http://www.adventurefox.com.

Marian Pr., (*978-0-944203; 978-1-932773; 978-1-59614*) Marian Helpers Ctr., Eden Hill, Stockbridge, MA 01263-0004 USA (SAN 243-1548) Tel 413-298-3691; Fax: 413-298-1356; Toll Free: 800-462-7426
E-mail: marianpress@marian.org
Web site: http://www.marian.org
Dist(s): **Send The Light Distribution LLC.**

Marianist Pr., (*978-0-9628309*) Orders Addr.: 1116 Imperial Blvd., Kettering, OH 45419-2434 USA Tel 937-298-8509; Edit Addr.: 233 E. Helena St., Dayton, OH 45404-1003 USA.

Marianne Richmond Studios, Inc. *Imprint of* **Sourcebooks, Inc.**

Marilux Pr., (*978-0-9710281*) 4100 Corporate Sq., Suite 161, Naples, FL 34104 USA Tel 239-398-7018; Fax: 917-591-0387
E-mail: sales@mariluxpress.com
Web site: http://www.MariluxPress.com.

Marimba Bks. *Imprint of* **Just Us Bks., Inc.**

Marinaro, Stacy, (*978-0-615-20684-4; 978-0-615-20807-7; 978-0-615-20883-1; 978-0-615-21988-2; 978-0-578-02365-6*) 420 Matthews St., Bristol, CT 06010 USA
E-mail: stacymarinaro@yahoo.com
Dist(s): **Lulu Pr., Inc.**

Mariner Publishing, (*978-0-9768238; 978-0-9776841; 978-0-9800077; 978-0-9820172; 978-0-9841128; 978-0-9833478; 978-0-9835565; 978-0-9849214; 978-0-9909653; 978-0-9975226; 978-0-9992885; 978-0-9997629; 978-1-7339720; 978-1-7341842; 978-1-7349136*) Div. of Mariner Media, Inc., 131 W. 21st St., Buena Vista, VA 24416 USA Tel 540-264-0021; Fax: 540-261-1881; *Imprints:* Harbour Books (HarbourBks) Do not confuse with Mariner Publishing in Tampa, FL Oklahoma City, OK
E-mail: andy@marinermedia.com
Web site: http://www.marinermedia.com
Dist(s): **Virginia Pubns.**

Marion Street Pr., LLC, (*978-0-9665176; 978-0-9710050; 978-0-9729937; 978-1-933338; 978-1-936863*) 4207 SE. Woodstock Blvd. #168, Portland, OR 97206 USA Toll Free Fax: 866-571-8359
E-mail: marionstreetpress@gmail.com
Web site: http://www.acornguild.com; http://www.marionstreetpress.com
Dist(s): **Independent Pubs. Group.**

Maritime Kids Quest Pr., (*978-0-9761178*) P.O. Box 700, Manteo, NC 27954 USA Tel 252-473-6933
E-mail: maritimekidsquest@earthlink.net.

Maritime Museum Assn. of San Diego, (*978-0-944580*) 1492 N. Harbor Dr., San Diego, CA 92101 USA (SAN 279-5027) Tel 619-234-9153; Fax: 619-234-8345
E-mail: museumstore@sdmaritime.com
Web site: http://www.sdmaritime.com/mains'lhaul
Dist(s): **Sunbelt Pubns., Inc.**

MARK & Assocs. LLC, (*978-0-692-13906-6*) 1622 Country Club Dr., Pittsburgh, PA 15237 USA Tel 412-369-8231
E-mail: reginakmunsch@gmail.com.

Marked Writers Publishing, (*978-0-692-36079-8; 978-0-692-36179-5; 978-0-692-38117-5; 978-0-692-41586-3; 978-0-692-41587-0; 978-0-692-41588-7; 978-0-692-45389-6; 978-0-692-53897-5; 978-0-692-59419-3;*

978-0-692-60911-8; 978-0-692-60912-5; 978-0-692-84543-1; 978-0-692-88868-1; 978-0-692-88869-8; 978-0-692-90722-1; 978-0-692-04653-1; 978-0-692-14283-7; 978-0-578-21503-7; 978-0-578-45854-0; 978-1-7334333) 5809 LAGO VISTA DR, CORPUS CHRISTI, TX 78418 USA Tel 3617286518; 5809 Lago Vista Dr., Corpus Christi, TX 78414
Dist(s): **CreateSpace Independent Publishing Platform.**

Marker, Margaret Penfield, (*978-0-9716721*) 64 Colonial Dr., Rancho Mirage, CA 92270-1600 USA
E-mail: tmlrmarker@aol.com.

Market 1 Group Inc., (*978-0-9748109*) 118 Worthington Business Ctr. 1550 Douglas Ave., Charleston, IL 61920 USA Tel 217-345-8281
E-mail: bmcelwee@consolidated.net
Web site: http://www.familyjourneys.net.

Market Management Group, (*978-0-9861953; 978-0-9969111; 978-1-944589*) 300 E Bellevue Dr. Unit 208, Pasadena, CA 91101 USA Tel 888-859-0792; *Imprints:* Incorgnito Publishing Press (MYID_H_INCORGN)
E-mail: mconant@incorgnitobooks.com
Dist(s): **Independent Pubs. Group**
Midpoint Trade Bks., Inc.

Market Place Publisher *See* **Market Place Publishing**

Market Place Publishing, (*978-1-7326799*) 11442 CALIFORNIA, BRIDGMAN, MI 49106-9362 USA Tel 269-449-1100
E-mail: cherissehavlicek@gmail.com
Web site: http://AuthorCherisse.com/.

Markins Enterprises, (*978-0-937729*) 2039 SE 45th Ave., Portland, OR 97215 USA (SAN 659-3224) Tel 503-235-1036.

Markowitz, Darryl, (*978-0-9818469*) 354 Park Blvd., Worthington, OH 43085 USA Tel 412-613-1733; *Imprints:* FaithWalker Publishing (FaithWalker)
Web site: http://www.thefaithwalkerseries.com.

Marks, Ginger *See* **DocUmeant Publishing**

Marks, William *See* **MPC Pr. International**

Markwin Pr., (*978-0-9740793*) Orders Addr.: P.O. Box 1143, Silver Springs, NV 89429 USA Tel 775-577-0676; Edit Addr.: 3220 E. 9th St., Silver Springs, NV 89429 USA
E-mail: softgaits@wildblue.com
Web site: www.TheFabulousFloatingHorses.com.

Marlena Brown-Holcomb, (*978-0-578-41006-7*) 905 W. Idylwild Dr., Midwest City, OK 73110 USA Tel 405-414-3711
E-mail: lenabrow38@yahoo.com
Dist(s): **Independent Pub.**

Marley-Goeste, (*978-1-7320306*) 9 Old Timber Ln., Palos Park, IL 60464 USA Tel 708-846-9630
E-mail: marc.mattson@gmail.com.

Marlor Pr., Inc., (*978-0-943400; 978-1-892147*) 4304 Brigadoon Dr., Saint Paul, MN 55126 USA (SAN 240-7140) Tel 651-484-4600; Fax: 651-490-1182; Toll Free: 800-669-4908
E-mail: marlor@minn.net
Dist(s): **Independent Pubs. Group**
MyiLibrary.

MarMooWorks,LLC, (*978-0-9853579; 978-0-9853580*) 318 Beverly Dr., Erie, PA 16505 USA Tel 814-454-1888
E-mail: mamoodey@gmail.com
Web site: jason@conveyorarts.org.

Maroma Bks., (*978-0-9796465*) 5615 Kirby Dr., Suite 820, Houston, TX 77005 USA Toll Free Fax: 800-525-0910; Toll Free: 888-627-6628
E-mail: molly@maromabooks.com
Web site: http://www.maromabooks.com
Dist(s): **Ingram Content Group.**

Marquand Bks., Inc., (*978-0-9706394; 978-0-9744202; 978-0-9778028; 978-0-9815762; 978-0-615-22812-9; 978-0-615-27788-2; 978-0-615-31547-8; 978-0-615-31690-1; 978-0-615-33169-0; 978-0-615-35171-1; 978-0-615-35172-8; 978-0-615-36404-9; 978-0-615-39016-1; 978-0-615-39126-7; 978-0-615-39579-1; 978-0-615-41782-0; 978-0-615-45883-0; 978-0-615-47180-8; 978-0-615-55154-8; 978-0-615-56154-7; 978-0-615-56155-4; 978-0-615-56156-1; 978-0-615-56210-0; 978-0-615-56585-9; 978-0-9849864; 978-0-615-59005-9; 978-0-615-59427-9; 9) 1400 2nd Ave, Seattle, WA 98101 USA Tel 206-624-2030; Fax: 206-624-1821*
E-mail: Adrian@luciamarquand.com
Web site: http://www.luciamarquand.com
Dist(s): **Antique Collectors' Club**
D.A.P./Distributed Art Pubs.
National Bk. Network
Two Rivers Distribution
Univ. of Oklahoma Pr.
Univ. of Washington Pr.

Marquette Bks., (*978-0-922993; 978-0-9816018; 978-0-9826597; 978-0-9833476; 978-1-7327197*) 16421 N. 31st Ave., Phoenix, AZ 85053 USA (SAN 251-5261) Tel 509-290-9240
E-mail: books@marquettebooks.com
Web site: http://www.marquettebooks.com
Dist(s): **Ambassador Bks. & Media**
Bk. Hse., The
Brodart Co.
Coutts Information Services
Eastern Bk. Co.
Emery-Pratt Co.
Levant USA, Inc.
Midwest Library Service
Blackwell.

Marquette Books, LLC *See* **Marquette Bks.**

Marquise Publishing, (*978-0-9745264*) 11459 Mayfield Rd Suite 338, Cleveland, OH 44106 USA
E-mail: marquisepublishing@gmail.com
Web site: http://www.marquisepublishing.com.

Marrero, Rafael, (*978-0-9747569*) 2121 Red Rd., Ave., Coral Gables, FL 33155-2232 USA Tel 305-267-0163
E-mail: rafelitomarrero@hotmail.com.

Marriwell Publishing, (*978-0-9742891*) P.O. Box 116, Center Valley, PA 18034 USA Tel 610-282-6807; Fax: 610-282-0909
Web site: http://www.marriwell.com.

Mars Media Publishers *See* **Audio Holdings, LLC**

Marsh, Carole Bks. *Imprint of* **Gallopade International**

Marsh, Carole Family CD-Rom *Imprint of* **Gallopade International**

Marsh, Carole Mysteries *Imprint of* **Gallopade International**

Marsh Creek Pr., (*978-0-937750*) Div. of Don Aslett, Inc., Orders Addr.: P.O. Box 700, Pocatello, ID 83204 USA (SAN 216-1028) Tel 208-232-3535; Fax: 208-235-5481; Edit Addr.: 311 S. Fifth Ave., Pocatello, ID 83201 USA
E-mail: Tobih@aol.com
Web site: http://www.aslett.com.

Marsh Media *See* **Witcher Productions**

Marsh, Thomas E. Inc., (*978-0-9633682*) 914 Franklin Ave., Youngstown, OH 44502 USA Tel 216-743-8600; Toll Free: 800-845-7930.

Marshall, Angela, (*978-0-692-98157-3*) 10221 MAIN ST, HANOVERTON, OH 44423 USA Tel 330-853-0889
E-mail: redcow06@gmail.com.

Marshall Cavendish (GBR) (*978-0-7614; 978-0-86307; 978-1-85435; 978-0-9533784; 978-1-902741; 978-0-462; 978-0-85080; 978-1-905992*) *Dist. by* **Marshall C.**

†Marshall Cavendish Corp., (*978-0-7614; 978-0-85685; 978-0-86307; 978-1-85435; 978-1-60870*) Member of Times Publishing Group, 99 White Plains Rd., Tarrytown, NY 10591-9001 USA (SAN 238-437X) Tel 914-332-8888; Fax: 914-332-8882; Toll Free: 800-821-9881; *Imprints:* Cavendish Children's Books (Cav Child Bks)
E-mail: mce@marshallcavendish.com
Web site: www.MCEducation.us
Dist(s): **BookBaby**
Brilliance Publishing, Inc.
Children's Plus, Inc.
Ebsco Publishing
Follett School Solutions
Fujii Assocs.
Lectorum Pubns., Inc.
MyiLibrary
National Bk. Network; *CIP.*

Marshall Cavendish International (Asia) Private Ltd. (SGP) (*978-981-204; 978-981-232; 978-2-85700; 978-981-261; 978-981-4302; 978-981-4312; 978-981-4328; 978-981-4346; 978-981-4351; 978-981-4361; 978-981-4382; 978-981-4398; 978-981-4408; 978-981-4426; 978-981-4430; 978-981-4433; 978-981-4435; 978-981-4484; 978-981-4516; 978-981-4561; 978-981-4771; 978-981-4828; 978-981-4794*) *Dist. by* **Natl Bk Netwk.**

Marshall, George Publishing, (*978-0-9729403*) P.O. Box 375, Bedford, VA 24523 USA.

Marshall, John High Schl. Alumni Assn., (*978-0-9759618*) 347 Pineview Cir., Berea, OH 44017 USA
E-mail: jmhalumni@ameritech.com
Web site: http://www.jmhalumni.com.

Marshlands Group LLC, (*978-0-692-98575-5; 978-0-692-98760-5; 978-0-9600605*) 13728 Poppleton Ct., Charlotte, NC 28273 USA
E-mail: marshlandsgroup@gmail.com
Dist(s): **CreateSpace Independent Publishing Platform**
Ingram Content Group.

Martell Publishing Co, (*978-1-893181; 978-1-930200*) P.O. Box 83554, San Diego, CA 92138-3554 USA Toll Free Fax: 800-805-3329; *Imprints:* Lagesse Stevens (LagesseS)
E-mail: martell@martellpublishing.com.

Martella, Liz, (*978-0-615-14941-7; 978-0-615-25506-4*) 393 Lathrop Rd., Lathrop, CA 95330 USA
E-mail: lizmartella@yahoo.com
Web site: http://www.lulu.com/lizmartella
Dist(s): **Lulu Pr., Inc.**

Marten Pr., (*978-1-7324588*) 3646 W Keyworth Dr., South Jordan, UT 84095 USA Tel 801-319-6982
E-mail: kaylmoody@gmail.com
Dist(s): **Ingram Content Group.**

Marti Bks., (*978-0-9766006*) Orders Addr.: P.O. Box 603, West Tisbury, MA 02575 USA Tel 508-696-7496 (phone/fax); Edit Addr.: 635 State Rd., West Tisbury, MA 02575 USA
E-mail: fferr2@aol.com
Web site: http://www.martibooks.com.

Martin, Amy, (*978-0-9882051*) 2733 Braden Way, Lexington, KY 40509 USA Tel 859-797-0156
E-mail: amart71@rocketmail.com.

Martin & Brothers, (*978-0-9719842; 978-0-9767500*) Orders Addr.: P.O. Box 122, Abbott, TX 76621 USA Tel 254-235-8588; Edit Addr.: 101 Bordon, Abbott, TX 76621 USA
E-mail: martinbrothers@aol.com.

Martin, Carolyn, (*978-0-9746808*) 1890 N. 36th St., Galesburg, MI 49053-9528 USA Tel 269-665-9953 Do not confuse with Carolyn Martin in Philadelphia, PA
E-mail: carmartin@earthlink.net
Web site: http://www.finefrets.com/metalhorses.

Martin, Danielle, (*978-0-578-41023-4*) 192 S 6th St, Jefferson, OR 97352 USA Tel 541-788-7875
E-mail: daniellemccallister@hotmail.com
Dist(s): **Ingram Content Group.**

Martin, Elizabeth B., (*978-0-578-12912-9; 978-0-578-12913-6; 978-0-9910543; 978-0-9904213*)
E-mail: elizabeth@elizabethbmartin.com
Dist(s): **Lulu Pr., Inc.**

Martin, Jack & Assocs., (*978-0-9649530*) Orders Addr.: 9422 S. Saginaw, Grand Blanc, MI 48439 USA Tel 810-694-5698; Fax: 810-694-7851
E-mail: jdmart@tir.com
Web site: http://www.Pre-Apprenticetraining.com.

Martin, James Jr., (*978-0-9799465*) P.O. Box 4207, Greenwitch, CT 06831 USA Fax: 516-060-1177
E-mail: JMJ723@optonline.com
Web site: http://williamthegarbagetruck.com.

Martin, Kevin, (*978-0-578-10705-9*) 7450 Globe Rd., Lenoir, NC 28645 USA.

Martin Publishing, (*978-0-9753992*) 1600 S. 30th, Lot 36, Escanaba, MI 49829 USA Do not confuse with companies with the same or similar name in Fort Morgan, CO; Tampico, IL; La Mesa, CA; Perry, OK; Cowpens, SC; Lincoln, ME.

Martina Franklin Poole, (*978-0-578-42884-0*) P.O. Box 21122, Keizer, OR 97303 USA Tel 541-505-0386
E-mail: martina.f.poole@gmail.com
Dist(s): **Ingram Content Group.**

Martinez, Leroy F., (*978-0-9748002*) 4045 E. 3rd St. Unit 111, Long Beach, CA 90814-2883 USA Tel 562-443-7727
Web site: http://leroymartinez.com.

Martinez, Patty & Logan, (*978-1-7332949*) 176 Broadway, New York, NY 10038 USA Tel 212-665-0252
E-mail: patty@pattyadams.net.

Martinez, Richard A., (*978-1-7329511*) 8961 Jackson St., Weedsport, NY 13166 USA Tel 315-237-8959
E-mail: capt.jack1064@gmail.com.

†Martingale & Co., (*978-0-943574; 978-1-56477; 978-1-60468; 978-1-68356*) Orders Addr.: 19021 120th Ave. NE. Suite 102, Bothell, WA 98011 USA (SAN 665-7923) Tel 425-483-3313; Fax: 425-486-7596; Toll Free: 800-426-3126; *Imprints:* That Patchwork Place (That Patchwrk Pl)
E-mail: ssanta@martingale-pub.com; mburns@martingale-pub.com; info@martingale-pub.com
Web site: http://www.martingale-pub.com
Dist(s): **Bookazine Co., Inc.**; *CIP.*

Martino,, Carmela Arquilla freelance writing *See* **Arquilla Pr.**

Martino Fine Bks., (*978-1-57898; 978-1-888262; 978-1-61427; 978-1-68422*) P.O. Box 913, Eastford, CT 06242 USA Tel 860-974-2277; 118 Westford Rd., Eastford, CT 06242
E-mail: martinofinebooks@hotmail.com
Web site: http://www.martinofinebooks.com.

Martino Publishing *See* **Martino Fine Bks.**

Martin's *See* **Green Pastures Pr.**

Marvel Age *Imprint of* **Spotlight**

Marvel Enterprises, Incorporated *See* **Marvel Worldwide, Inc.**

Marvel Pr. *Imprint of* **Disney Publishing Worldwide**

Marvel Worldwide, Inc., (*978-0-7851; 978-0-87135; 978-0-939766; 978-0-9604146; 978-1-4695; 978-1-302*) Subs. of The Walt Disney Co, 135 W. 50th St., New York, NY 10020 USA (SAN 216-9088); c/o Marvel Enterprises Japan, Inc., Hill House B, 9-10 Hachiyama-cho Sibuya, Tokyo, 150-0034
E-mail: mail@marvel.com; amorales@marvel.com
Web site: http://www.marvel.com
Dist(s): **Children's Plus, Inc.**
Hachette Bk. Group.

Marvelous Dream, (*978-0-9771016*) Div. of Marvelous World LLC, P.O. Box 252, Bloomfield, NJ 07003-9998 USA (SAN 256-7857).

Marvelous Spirit Pr. *Imprint of* **Loving Healing Pr., Inc.**

MarWel Enterprises, Inc., (*978-0-9759582*) P.O. Box 31227, Washington, DC 20030 USA
E-mail: marwel@earthlink.net.

Marx Group, The, (*978-0-9773962; 978-1-935309*) 2111 Jefferson Davis Hwy. 303N., Arlington, VA 22202 USA Tel 703-418-1956; Fax: 703-418-0224
E-mail: don@themarxgroup.com
Web site: http://www.the marxgroup.com.

Marx, Jeff, (*978-0-9667824; 978-0-9793134*) 3160 N. 35th St., Hollywood, FL 33021-2630 USA (SAN 853-1021)
E-mail: JeffMarx@schoolelection.com
Web site: http://www.schoolelection.com.

Mary B./French, (*978-0-9852821*) 1355 Pine St. # 5, San Francisco, CA 94109 USA Tel 415-931-8691.

Mary Ryan, (*978-0-578-40941-2; 978-0-578-40963-4; 978-1-7338945*) 135 Bear Wallow Ln. Site 47, Sedona, AZ 86336 USA Tel 443-909-6297
E-mail: MaryTruly92@icloud.com
Dist(s): **Ingram Content Group.**

Mary Sunshine Bks., (*978-0-9652337*) 1710 Sunnymede Ave., South Bend, IN 46615 USA Tel 219-233-6064; Fax: 219-631-6767; Toll Free: 800-231-6580.

Maryann, (*978-1-7320725*) P.O. Box 770624, Woodside, NY 11377-0624 USA Tel 646-620-8402
E-mail: SantaMaria1345@yahoo.com.

Maryknoll Fathers & Brothers *See* **Maryknoll Missioners**

Maryknoll Missioners, (*978-0-941395*) P.O. Box 308, Maryknoll, NY 15054-0308 USA (SAN 219-3752) Tel 914-941-7590; Toll Free: 800-227-8523
E-mail: jgoldbeck@maryknoll.org.

†Maryland Ctr. for History & Culture, (*978-0-938420; 978-0-9842135; 978-0-9965944*) 610 Pk. Ave., Baltimore, MD 21201 USA (SAN 203-9788) Tel 410-685-3750; Fax: 410-385-2105
E-mail: mkado@mdhs.org
Web site: http://www.mdhs.org
Dist(s): **Hood, Alan C. & Co., Inc.**
Johns Hopkins Univ. Pr.; *CIP.*

Maryland Historical Society *See* **Maryland Ctr. for History & Culture**

Maryland Secretarial Services, Inc., (*978-0-692-31692-4; 978-0-692-31693-1; 978-0-692-31694-8; 978-0-692-56468-4*) 12105 Whiston Ct, Bowie, MD 20715 USA Tel 3013527927.

Maryleigh Bucher *See* **Bucher, Maryleigh**

Maryruth Bks., Inc., (*978-0-9713518; 978-0-9720295; 978-0-9746475; 978-1-933624; 978-1-62544*) 18660 Ravenna Rd. Bldg. 2, Chagrin Falls, OH 44023 USA Tel 440-834-1105; Toll Free Fax: 800-951-4077
E-mail: admin@maryruthbooks.com
Web site: http://www.maryruthbooks.com.

Marzetta Bks., (*978-0-9657033*) P.O. Box 274, Lombard, IL 60148 USA Tel 630-424-1403
E-mail: marzetta@concentric.net.

Masalai Pr., (*978-0-9714127*) 368 Capricorn Ave., Oakland, CA 94611-2058 USA
E-mail: THSlone@yahoo.com
Web site: http://THSlone.tripod.com/masalaipress.html.

Mascot Bks., Inc., (*978-0-9743442; 978-1-932888; 978-1-934878; 978-1-936319; 978-1-937406; 978-1-62086; 978-1-63177; 978-1-68401; 978-1-64307; 978-1-64543*) 620 Herndon Pkwy. Suite 320, Herndon, VA 20170 USA Tel 703-437-3584; Fax: 703-437-3554; Toll Free: 877-862-7568
E-mail: debbie@mascotbooks.com; naren@mascotbooks.com; kristin@mascotbooks.com
Web site: http://www.mascotbooks.com
Dist(s): **Partners Bk. Distributing, Inc.**

Mascots for Kids, (*978-0-9762636*) Div. of Wells Yeager Best Co., Inc., 400 S. 7th St., Lafayette, IN 47901 USA Tel 765-742-7648; Fax: 765-742-1049
E-mail: aklink@nlci.com
Web site: http://www.mascotsforkids.com
Dist(s): **Indiana Univ. Pr.**
Ingram Publisher Services
Two Rivers Distribution.

Masha, Segun Inc., (*978-0-9755927; 978-1-7336338*) Div. of SEGUN MASHA, INC., 57 WADDELL STREET, SW, MARIETTA, GA 30060 USA
E-mail: segunmashainc@gmail.com
Web site: http://www.segunmasha.com; www.marketplacemissions.com.

Mashack Productions *See* **HOLY COW Bk. Pubs.**

MASK, ACE, (*978-0-692-81950-0; 978-0-692-13064-3; 978-0-692-13736-9; 978-0-578-75934-0*) 1988 HEATHER CIRCLE, BREA, CA 92821 USA Tel 714-529-0850
E-mail: acemask@yahoo.com; acemask@yahoo.com.

mason, cathy, (*978-0-692-18311-3; 978-0-692-18340-3*) 7516 Georgia Ridge Rd., Alma, AR 72921 USA Tel 479-997-2774
E-mail: cathy@cathymasonfineart.com
Dist(s): **Ingram Content Group.**

Mason Crest, (*978-1-59084; 978-1-59482; 978-1-4222*) Div. of Highlights Inc., Orders Addr.: 450 Parkway Dr., Suite D, Broomall, PA 19008-0914 USA Tel 610-543-6200; Fax: 610-543-3878; Toll Free: 866-627-2665 (866-MCP-Book)
E-mail: gbaffa@masoncrest.com
Web site: http://www.masoncrest.com
Dist(s): **Follett School Solutions**
Simon & Schuster, Inc.
Smashwords.

Mason Crest Publishers *See* **Mason Crest**

Mason Mill Publishing Hse., (*978-0-9986455*) 4371 Allen Dr, Brownsburg, IN 46112 USA Tel 317-225-3412
E-mail: authorsavannahgoins@gmail.com.

Massachusetts Continuing Legal Education, Inc., (*978-0-944490; 978-1-57589; 978-1-68345*) 10 Winter Pl., Boston, MA 02108 USA (SAN 226-3033) Tel 617-482-2205; Fax: 617-482-9498; Toll Free: 800-966-6253
Web site: http://www.mcle.org.

Massey Publishing, (*978-0-9640883*) P.O. Box 8945, Atlanta, GA 31106-0945 USA Tel 404-406-5034 (phone/fax)
E-mail: galemassey7@aol.com
Dist(s): **New Leaf Distributing Co., Inc.**

Massey University Press (NZL) (*978-0-9941300; 978-0-9941325; 978-0-9941363; 978-0-9941407; 978-0-9941415; 978-0-9941473; 978-0-9951001; 978-0-9951029; 978-0-9951095; 978-0-9951135; 978-0-9951230; 978-0-9951229; 978-0-9951318; 978-0-9951354; 978-0-9951378*) *Dist. by* **IPG Chicago.**

Master Books *Imprint of* **New Leaf Publishing Group**

Master Communications, Inc., (*978-1-888194; 978-1-60480*) 2692 Madison Rd., Suite N1-307 N1-307, Cincinnati, OH 45208 USA (SAN 299-2140) Tel 513-563-3100; Fax: 513-563-3105; Toll Free: 800-765-5885
E-mail: sales@master-comm.com
Web site: http://www.worldculturemedia.com; http://www.master-comm.com
Dist(s): **Follett School Solutions.**

Master Pr., (*978-0-9646543; 978-0-9759049; 978-0-9790296; 978-0-9834326; 978-0-9885057; 978-0-9913121; 978-0-9993750*) 318 SE. 4th Terrace, Cape Coral, FL 33990 USA Tel 239-772-0634 (phone/fax); Fax: 239-772-0634; Toll Free: 800-325-9136
E-mail: neil@ezraproject.org.

Master Publishing, Inc., (*978-0-945053*) 6019 W. Howard St., Niles, IL 60714-4801 USA (SAN 245-8829)
E-mail: pete@w5yi.com
Web site: http://www.MasterPublishing.com; http://www.ForrestMims.com; http://www.w5yi.org
Dist(s): **WFiveYI Group, Inc., The.**

Master Strategies Publishing, (*978-0-9766485*) 5806 Chatsworth Ct., Arlington, TX 76018 USA Toll Free: 888-792-5105.

Mastermind Resource Group, *(978-1-7333883)* 1248 Lacey Oak Loop, Round Rock, TX 78681 USA Tel 512-964-1631
E-mail: maverickmoses@gmail.com.

Masterpiece Creations Graphics & Publishing, *(978-0-615-23057-3; 978-0-9842171)* 305 Friendship Ln., Suite 100, Gettysburg, PA 17325 USA (SAN 858-7507) Tel 717-337-1829
E-mail: dj@masterpiececreations.biz
Web site: http://www.masterpiececreations.biz.

MasterVision, *(978-1-55919)* 969 Park Ave., New York, NY 10028 USA Tel 212-879-0448
E-mail: stadin1@aol.com
Web site: http://www.mastervision.com/.

Mastery Education Corporation *See* **Charlesbridge Publishing, Inc.**

Mastery For Strings Pubns., *(978-0-9753919)* 1005 Meriden Ln., Austin, TX 78703 USA Tel 512-474-8196
E-mail: musipro@aol.com.

Mastery Learning Systems, *(978-1-888976)* 532 N. School St., Ukiah, CA 95482 USA Fax: 707-462-9307; Toll Free: 800-433-4181 (phone/fax)
E-mail: mastery@pacific.net
Web site: http://www.masterylearningsystems.com.

Masthof Pr., *(978-1-883294; 978-1-930353; 978-1-932864; 978-1-60126)* 219 Mill Rd., Morgantown, PA 19543-9701 USA Tel 610-286-0258; Fax: 610-286-6860
E-mail: mast@masthof.com
Web site: http://www.masthof.com.

Matchstick Literary, 3000 Atrium Way, Mt. Laurel, NJ 08054 USA Tel 888-306-8885
E-mail: mgomez@matchliterary.com
Web site: www.matchliterary.com.

Matchu Pichu Press *See* **Matchu Pichu Pr.**

Matchu Pichu Pr., *(978-1-7328684)* 1740 Tristen Dr., Newtown, PA 18940 USA Tel 610-574-4746
E-mail: matthew.elliot.sherman@gmail.com
Web site: http://www.matthew-sherman.com.

Mateboer, Johannes Aart, *(978-0-9759487)* Div. of Captain's Publishing, 6514 Wakehurst Rd., Charlotte, NC 28226 USA Tel 704-540-7617 (phone/fax)
E-mail: hlmateboer@hotmail.com
Web site: http://www.captainspublishing.com
Dist(s): **eBookit.com.**

Math Essentials, *(978-0-9666211; 978-0-9821901; 978-0-9843629; 978-0-9994433; 978-1-7335018; 978-1-7345880)* P.O. Box 1723, Los Gatos, CA 95031 USA (SAN 991-0069) Fax: 408-358-3738; Toll Free: 866-444-6284; 265 Carlton Ct., Los Gatos, CA 95032
E-mail: math.essentials@verizon.net
Web site: http://www.mathessentials.com.

Math in Motion *See* **Crane Bks.**

Math Solutions, *(978-0-941355; 978-1-935099)* Div. of Marilyn Burns Education Assocs., Orders Addr.: 150 Gate 5 Rd., Sausalito, CA 94965 USA (SAN 665-5424) Tel 415-332-4181; Fax: 415-331-1931; Toll Free Fax: 877-942-8837; Toll Free: 800-868-9092
E-mail: info@mathsolutions.com; jcross@mathsolutions.com; jwayland@mathsolutions.com
Web site: http://www.mathsolutions.com
Dist(s): **MyiLibrary**
Scholastic, Inc.

Math Solutions Publications *See* **Math Solutions**

Math Studio, The, *(978-1-929362)* 271 Lafayette St., Salem, MA 01970-5404 USA
E-mail: cdraper@mathstudio.com
Web site: http://www.mathstudio.com.

Math4Minors LLC, *(978-1-7328503)* 321 Rt 59 No. 444, Tallman, NY 10982 USA Tel 845-369-7723
E-mail: info@mathmilemarkers.com
Web site: www.mathmilemarkers.com.

Mathematical Sciences Research Institute, *(978-0-9639903; 978-0-9824800)* 17 Gauss Way, Berkeley, CA 94720-5070 USA Tel 510-642-0143; Fax: 510-642-8609
E-mail: librarian@msri.org
Web site: http://www.msri.org/.

Mathematical Solutions Publishing Company *See* **Twianie Roberts Consulting**

Mathieson Creative Media, *(978-1-940350)* 9140 SW Chelan Pl, Beaverton, OR 97008 USA
E-mail: MathiesonCreativeMedia@outlook.com.

Mathis, Stefan, *(978-0-692-89659-4)* 420 Somerset Dr, AUBURNDALE, FL 33823 USA Tel 863-585-9621
Dist(s): **Ingram Content Group.**

MathisJones Communications, LLC, *(978-0-9799482; 978-0-9840117; 978-0-9850542; 978-0-9853093; 978-0-9889643; 978-0-9964948; 978-1-7321345)* Orders Addr.: P.O. Box 569, Chesterfield, MO 63006-0569 USA (SAN 854-8102) Tel 636-938-1100; Fax: 636-349-1100; Edit Addr.: 1 Putt Ln., Eureka, MO 63025-2828 USA
E-mail: info@mathisjones.com
Web site: monographpublishing.com
Dist(s): **eBookit.com.**

Mathis-Njie, Joan J. *See* **Anointed Pubs.**

MATHSTORY.COM, *(978-0-9702641)* Div. of Rak Productions, P.O. Box 20226, New York, NY 10025-1511 USA Tel 212-864-5462
E-mail: mathstory2000@aol.com
Web site: http://mathstory.com.

MathWord Pr., LLC, *(978-0-9840425; 978-1-939431)* 97 Fennbrook Dr., Hamden, CT 06517 USA Tel 203-288-8114
E-mail: mathwordpress@aol.com
Web site: mwpenn.com.

Matinicus Pr., *(978-0-9765689)* 734 Cleveland Ave., Brackenridge, PA 15014-1501 USA.

Matisse Studios, *(978-0-9630069)* 4572 Via Marina 207, Marina Del Rey, CA 90292 USA
E-mail: LauriAnneMatisse@gmail.com
Web site: www.laurimatisse.com; http://www.matissestudios.com; www.evesmemoirs.com.

Matter of Africa America Time, *(978-0-9760523)* 2114 Vincent Ave. N., Minneapolis, MN 55411 USA.

Matthew E Nordin, *(978-0-578-47509-7; 978-0-578-61523-3; 978-1-7355573)* 105 Broad St., Grinnell, IA 50112 USA Tel 402-670-3664
E-mail: matthewenordin@gmail.com
Dist(s): **Ingram Content Group.**

Matthew Upholz, *(978-0-578-42185-8)* 13 Scofield Ct., Bloomington, IL 61704 USA Tel 440-829-1628
E-mail: scottbowlshiner@gmail.com
Dist(s): **Ingram Content Group.**

Matting Leah Publishing Co., *(978-0-9761528; 978-0-9905764)* P.O. Box 265, Warwick, NY 10990-0265 USA
Web site: http://www.mattingleahpublishing.com.

Matzah Ball Bks., *(978-0-9753629)* 3469 Redwood Ave., Los Angeles, CA 90066 USA
E-mail: info@matzahballbooks.com
Web site: http://www.matzahballbooks.com.

Mau, C. Publishing Co., *(978-0-9778843)* Orders Addr.: P.O. Box 30084, Edmond, OK 73003-0002 USA
E-mail: cmaupublishing@cox.net.

Maui Arthoughts Co., *(978-0-945045)* P.O. Box 967, Wailuku, HI 96793-0967 USA (SAN 245-8799) Tel 808-244-0156; Toll Free: 800-403-3472
E-mail: books@maui.net
Web site: http://www.booksmaui.com
Dist(s): **Quality Bks., Inc.**

Mauldin Publishing & Literacy House, *(978-0-9786565)*
E-mail: mauldinpublishingliteracyhouse@gmail.com
Web site: http://www.naypree-enterprises.com.

Maupin House Publishing *Imprint of* **Capstone**

Maval Medical Education *See* **Maval Publishing, Inc.**

Maval Publishing, Inc., *(978-1-884083; 978-1-59134)* Div. of Maval Printing Co., 5335 Victoria Cir., Firestone, CO 80504 USA Tel 303-682-9424
E-mail: info@jejerre.com
Web site: http://www.jejerre.com
Dist(s): **Majors Scientific Bks., Inc.**
Matthews Medical Bk. Co.

Maven Of Memory Publishing, *(978-0-9768042; 978-0-9833277; 978-0-9864412)* P.O. Box 398, Hurst, TX 76053-0398 USA Fax: 817-282-0000
Web site: http://www.mavenofmemory.com.

MavenMark Books, LLC *See* **HenschelHAUS Publishing, Inc.**

Maverick Arts Publishing (GBR) *(978-1-84886) Dist. by* **Lerner Pub.**

Maverick Bks. *Imprint of* **Trinity Univ. Pr.**

Maverick Bks., *(978-0-9672355)* P.O. Box 897, Woodstock, NY 12498 USA (SAN 253-9284) Toll Free: 866-478-9266 (phone/fax) Do not confuse with Maverick Books, Perryton, TX
E-mail: maverickbooks@aol.com; hank1@ptsi.net.

Maverick Bks., Inc., *(978-0-916941; 978-0-9608612; 978-1-59188)* Orders Addr.: P.O. Box 549, Perryton, TX 79070 USA (SAN 240-7183) Tel 806-435-7611; Fax: 806-435-2410; Edit Addr.: 14492 N.W. Loop 143, Perryton, TX 78070 USA Do not confuse with Maverick Books, Woodstock, NY
E-mail: hank1@ptsi.net
Web site: http://www.hankthecowdog.com
Dist(s): **Follett School Solutions**
Ingram Publisher Services.

Maverick Press *See* **Maverick Bks.**

Mawco, Inc., *(978-0-9853523)* 22172 Bakers Mill Rd., Dacula, GA 30019 USA Tel 404-202-7615
E-mail: a1missy@aol.com.

Mawi, Inc., *(978-0-9743901)* P.O. Box 471666, Chicago, IL 60647-6525 USA
E-mail: info@mawibooks.com
Web site: http://www.mawibooks.com.

Max Publication, Inc., *(978-0-9633577; 978-0-9799882; 978-0-692-76992-8; 978-0-9995882)* Div. of DL Services, Inc., Orders Addr.: 825 Malvern Hill, Alpharetta, GA 30022 USA Tel 770-851-0935; Fax: 770-740-0188
E-mail: Info@mrandmrsitaly.com
Web site: www.mrandmrsitaly.com; www.mrandmrsitaly.com.

MAX Publishing, LLC, *(978-1-970097)* 5252 Olde Towne Rd Suite A, Williamsburg, VA 23188 USA
E-mail: tagconsulting123@gmail.com
Web site: www.tijuanagholson.com.

Max West *See* **Different Mousetrap Pr. LLC**

Maxim Pr., *(978-0-9767096)* 6947 Coal Creek Pkwy. SE, No. 137, Newcastle, WA 98059-3159 USA
E-mail: lg@maximpress.com
Web site: http://www.maximpress.com/.

Maximilian Pr. Pubs., *(978-0-9668650; 978-1-930211; 978-0-9827717)* Orders Addr.: P.O. Box 64841, Virginia Beach, VA 23467-4841 USA Tel 757-482-2273; Fax: 757-482-0325; Edit Addr.: 920 S. Battlefield Blvd., No. 100, Chesapeake, VA 23322 USA
E-mail: mp-publishing@inter-source.org
Web site: http://www.maximilianpressbookpublishers.com/.

Maximus Publishing, *(978-0-9792439)* P.O. Box 4455, Whitefish, MT 59937-4455 USA (SAN 852-8829)
E-mail: MaximusPublishing@bresnan.net
Web site: http://www.maximuspublishing.com.

Maxwell, Andre, *(978-0-578-10115-6; 978-0-578-10116-3; 978-0-9881811)* 722 Sawyer St. SE, Olympia, WA 98501 USA Tel 253-509-4022
E-mail: aleighmaxwell@gmail.com
Dist(s): **Follett School Solutions.**

Maxwell, Joseph *See* **LifeStory Publishing**

Maxwell, Mackenzie, *(978-0-692-05134-4; 978-0-692-05135-1)* 7209 Deerfield Dr., Rowlett, TX 75089 USA Tel 2145044598
E-mail: freelance.mackenzie@gmail.com
Dist(s): **Ingram Content Group.**

May 3rd Bks., Inc., *(978-0-692-72921-2; 978-1-945891)* 201 E. Patrick St. No. 3212, Frederick, MD 21701 USA Tel 202-740-5137
E-mail: info@may3rdbooks.com
Web site: www.may3rdbooks.com.

May, Cynthia D., *(978-0-615-12578-7)* 7720 W. 14 Rd., Mesick, MI 49668-9792 USA.

May December Pubns. LLC, *(978-0-9845372; 978-1-936730; 978-1-940734)* P.O. Box 5132, Beaverton, OR 97006 USA
E-mail: twbrown@maydecemberpublications.com
Web site: http://www.maydecemberpublications.com.

May, L. B. & Assocs., 3517 Neal Dr., Knoxville, TN 37918 USA Tel 865-922-7490; Fax: 865-922-7492
E-mail: lbmay@aol.com.

MAY Publishing, *(978-0-9881804)* P.O. Box 1212, Midlothian, VA 23113 USA Tel 804-423-1452
E-mail: maypublishing@yourish.com
Web site: http://merylyourish.com/.

Maya & Me Pubns., *(978-0-692-47111-1; 978-0-9972566)* 12060 Cty. Line Rd Suite J No. 197, Madison, AL 35756 USA Tel 520-241-6559
E-mail: efalva@yahoo.com
Web site: www.maya-and-me.com.

Mayhaven Publishing, Inc., *(978-1-878044; 978-1-932278; 978-1-939695)* P.O. Box PO Box 557, Mahomet, IL 618530557 USA Tel 217-586-4493; *Imprints:* Wild Rose (Wld Rose)
E-mail: mayhavenpublishing@mchsi.com
Web site: http://www.mayhavenpublishing.com
Dist(s): **Brodart Co.**
Deseret Bk. Co.
Distributors, The
Follett School Solutions
Mumford Library Bks., Inc.
Quality Bks., Inc.

Mayhem Bks., *(978-0-9770055)* P.O. Box 313, Bon Secour, AL 36511 USA
E-mail: sweetzer@gulftel.com.

Maylin, Grace, *(978-0-9792384)* 204 S. Roycroft Blvd., Cheektowaga, NY 14225 USA
E-mail: gmds@adelphia.net.

Maynard, Vernal *See* **Maynard, Vernal Hugo**

Maynard, Vernal Hugo, *(978-0-692-91009-2; 978-0-692-05785-8; 978-0-692-05786-5; 978-0-692-05787-2; 978-0-692-07746-7; 978-0-692-17816-4; 978-0-692-17817-1; 978-0-578-48739-7; 978-0-578-48741-0)* 306 Mt. Bethel Rd., Harmony, NC 28634 USA Tel 816-922-9357
E-mail: junecaniel@gmail.com; info@jcaniel.com
Dist(s): **CreateSpace Independent Publishing Platform.**

Maynestream Pr., *(978-0-9715183)* 3189 Cocoplum Cir., Coconut Creek, FL 33063 USA
E-mail: contact@maynestream.com
Web site: http://www.weirdthings.com.

Mayo, Jerry, *(978-0-9985792)* 7524 Via Desierto NE, Albuquerque, NM 87113 USA Tel 505-344-1857
E-mail: Mayo505@gmail.com.

Mayo, Johnny, *(978-0-9765918)* P.O. Box 5484, Columbia, SC 29250 USA Tel 803-767-6756
E-mail: k9heroes@att.net
Web site: http://www.bucksheroes.com.

Mayor of Venice, *(978-0-9998956; 978-1-950698)* 2302 Pacific Ave., Venice, CA 90291 USA Tel 650-740-5018
E-mail: felivesey@gmail.com
Web site: www.ignisla.com
Dist(s): **Ingram Content Group.**

Mayreni *Imprint of* **Mayreni Publishing**

Mayreni Publishing, *(978-0-9653718; 978-1-931834)* P.O. Box 5881, Monterey, CA 93944-5881 USA Tel 831-655-4377 (phone/fax); *Imprints:* Mayreni (Mayreni)
E-mail: mayrenipublishing@comcast.net; vatcheg@gmail.com
Web site: http://www.mayreni.com.

Maytag Messerschmitt Media Concern, *(978-0-9768470)* 931 W. 19th St., Santa Ana, CA 92706 USA.

Mazaa, LLC, *(978-0-9849624)* 1555 Botelho Dr., No. 433, Walnut Creek, CA 94596 USA Tel 925-954-7182
E-mail: jofarrell@mazaallc.com.

Maze Creek Studio, *(978-0-9742285)* Orders Addr.: 1495 E. Thirteenth St., Carthage, MO 64836-9507 USA Tel 417-359-8787
E-mail: studio@andythomas.com
Web site: http://www.andythomas.com.

Mazeology, *(978-0-9793043)* 284 W. 12th St., No. 2, New York, NY 10014-6000 USA Tel 212-929-0734
E-mail: mazeology@yahoo.com
Web site: http://www.mazeology.net.

Mazie, Bernard *See* **Pangus Publishing**

Mazo Pubs., *(978-965-90462; 978-965-7344; 978-1-936778; 978-1-946124)* P.O. Box 10474, Jacksonville, FL 32247 USA Tel 815-301-3559 (phone/fax)
E-mail: mazopublishers@gmail.com; cm@mazopublishers.com
Web site: http://www.mazopublishers.com
Dist(s): **Smashwords.**

Mazur, Kathy *See* **Spring Ducks Bks., LLC**

MB Publishing, LLC, *(978-0-9624166; 978-0-9850814; 978-0-9913646; 978-0-9908430; 978-0-9994463)* 7831 Woodmont Ave., Pmb 312, Bethesda, MD 20814 USA Toll Free: 866-530-4732
Web site: http://www.mbpublishing.com
Dist(s): **BWI**
BookBaby
Quality Bks., Inc.

MBG Creations, *(978-0-578-41008-1)* 9214 Sydney Ln., Brentwood, TN 37027 USA Tel 336-209-1180
E-mail: Katgulliano@gmail.com
Dist(s): **Ingram Content Group.**

Mbonglou, Franziska, *(978-0-578-58549-9)* 2609 Amy Dr., Jeffersonville, PA 19403 USA Tel 610-805-5277
E-mail: gmbonglou@yahoo.com.

MBS Onsite llc *See* **This Little Light Productions**

MBT, *(978-0-9768419)* P.O. Box 215, Guilford, CT 06437 USA.

MC Basset, LLC, *(978-0-9774800)* P.O. Box 241, Asbury, NJ 08802 USA Tel 908-537-6410 (phone/fax)
E-mail: mkuderka@mcbasset.com.

M.C. Beynon, *(978-0-578-49900-0; 978-0-578-49907-9; 978-1-7349499)* 4955 Bode Ln., McHenry, IL 60050 USA Tel 773-619-9264
E-mail: merwojo73@yahoo.com
Dist(s): **Ingram Content Group.**

MC Math Comics, *(978-0-9728453)* 720 Sutton Dr., Carlisle, PA 17013 USA Tel 717-243-4470
E-mail: clarkcherry@aol.com
Web site: http://plusman.org.

MC Publishing & Design Group, *(978-0-578-00109-8; 978-0-9966696)* 4207 Forest Ln., Nacogdoches, TX 75965 USA Toll Free: 800-781-4890.

MC Wheeler Enterprises, *(978-0-692-68048-3; 978-0-692-80814-6)* 657 Highland Ave., FALL RIVER, MA 02720 USA Tel 401-835-2718.

MC123 *See* **Taven Hill Studio**

MCA Denver, *(978-0-692-76221-9; 978-0-692-76318-6; 978-0-692-78930-8; 978-0-692-87222-2; 978-0-578-43484-1; 978-0-578-72961-9)* 1485 Delgany St., Denver, CO 80202 USA Tel 720-236-1813
E-mail: zoel@mcadenver.org
Web site: www.mcadenver.org
Dist(s): **D.A.P./Distributed Art Pubs.**

McArdle, Donald, *(978-0-615-14212-8)* 11556 110th Ter., Largo, FL 33778-3716 USA
Web site: http://www.santaandbugsy.com
Dist(s): **Lulu Pr., Inc.**

McBeth, Mary, *(978-0-692-06303-3; 978-0-692-06328-6)* 710 S. Loop St., San Marco, TX 78666 USA Tel 210-393-6883
E-mail: megmcbeth@yahoo.com
Dist(s): **Ingram Content Group.**

McBook Pubs., LLC, *(978-0-9705777)* Orders Addr.: P.O. Box 35513, Tulsa, OK 74005 USA Tel 918-671-6656
E-mail: jdokla@cableone.net.

McBride Collection of Stories LLC, *(978-0-692-81414-7; 978-0-692-82418-4; 978-0-692-84474-8; 978-0-692-85606-2; 978-0-692-03985-4; 978-0-692-03986-1)* 70-02 Parsons Blvd, No. 7c, Fresh Meadows, NY 11365 USA Tel 917-771-4463
E-mail: mcbridestories@gmail.com
Dist(s): **CreateSpace Independent Publishing Platform.**

McBride, Danielle, *(978-0-578-44099-6; 978-0-578-44101-6)* 147-24 230th St., Jamaica, NY 11413 USA Tel 917-771-4463
E-mail: amaritasway@gmail.com
Dist(s): **Ingram Content Group.**

McBride, Heddrick, *(978-0-615-70075-5; 978-0-615-70923-9; 978-0-615-71693-0; 978-0-615-72059-3; 978-0-615-72339-6; 978-0-615-78846-3; 978-0-615-86353-5; 978-0-615-91076-5; 978-0-615-95937-5; 978-0-692-68651-5)* 70-02 parsons blvd. apt 7c, Flushing, NY 11365 USA Tel 917-771-4463
Web site: www.mcbride-collection-of-stories.com
Dist(s): **CreateSpace Independent Publishing Platform.**

McCaid Paul Books, *(978-0-9996145; 978-1-7357299)* P.O. Box 909, DeFuniak Springs, FL 32435 USA Tel 850-305-6343
E-mail: cmccaidpaul@gmail.com.

McCall, Philip Lee II *See* **Cathal Entertainment**

McCaney Publishing, Inc., *(978-0-692-09204-0)* 12400 Hwy. 157, Florence, AL 35633 USA Tel 256-483-6080
E-mail: maurice_mccaney@yahoo.com.

McCarthy, Maria Skantzaris, *(978-0-9755844)* P.O. Box 1308, Westford, MA 01886 USA
E-mail: msmccarthy@mindspring.com.

McCarthy, Sally Studios, *(978-0-9898968)* 7 Patriot Ln., Whitman, MA 02382 USA Tel 781-771-3394
E-mail: sallyjm@comcast.net.

McCarthy-Contreras, Shannon, *(978-0-692-99294-4)* 2872 W Ribera Pl, Tucson, AZ 85742 USA Tel 520-981-6620
E-mail: smccarthc@gmail.com
Dist(s): **Ingram Content Group.**

McCaw, Pat, *(978-1-7328606)* 27335 205th Ave, Eldridge, IA 52748 USA Tel 563-285-9163
E-mail: patmccawauthor@gmail.com.

McClain Printing Co., *(978-0-87012)* Orders Addr.: P.O. Box 403, Parsons, WV 26287-0403 USA (SAN 203-9478) Tel 304-478-2881; Fax: 304-478-4658; Toll Free: 800-654-7179
E-mail: mcclain@mcclainprinting.com; mmckinnie@mcclainprinting.com
Web site: http://www.McClainPrinting.com.

McClanahan Publishing Hse., Inc., *(978-0-913383; 978-1-934898; 978-0-9829785; 978-0-615-40157-7; 978-0-9836687; 978-0-9847933; 978-0-9895424; 978-0-9897078)* P.O. Box 100, Kuttawa, KY 42055 USA (SAN 285-8371) Tel 270-388-9388; Fax: 270-388-6186; Toll Free: 800-544-6959
E-mail: books@kybooks.com
Web site: http://www.kybooks.com
Dist(s): **Partners Bk. Distributing, Inc.**

McClelland & Stewart (CAN) *(978-0-396; 978-0-7710) Dist. by* **Peng Rand Hse.**

McClelland & Stewart (CAN) *(978-0-396; 978-0-7710) Dist. by* **Random.**

McClenney Publishing *See* **First Associates Publishing**

McConnell, Eric, *(978-0-578-48113-5; 978-0-578-62782-3; 978-0-578-76813-7)* 4023 Cody Rd., Sherman Oaks, CA 91403 USA Tel 818-789-3571
E-mail: ericsurf8@sbcglobal.net
Dist(s): **Ingram Content Group.**

McCormick, Susan *See* **Carroll Pr.**

McCourtie, Anne, *(978-0-9744448)* 15700 154th Rd., Mayetta, KS 66509 USA.

McCowan, Linda, *(978-0-9814596)* 1739 S. Hwy., 89 A, Kanab, UT 84741 USA.

McCoy, Amy, *(978-0-692-65141-4; 978-1-7330362)* 142 Fairview Terr., South Glastonbury, CT 06073 USA Tel 516-551-9390
Dist(s): **CreateSpace Independent Publishing Platform.**

McCracken, Amie, *(978-0-9981052)* 716 Frederick St, Royal Oak, MI 48067 USA Tel 313-539-9087
E-mail: amie.mccracken@gmail.com.

McCray, Kathy *See* **Kathy's Pen**

McCray-Garrison, Rispba, *(978-0-692-15397-0; 978-0-692-16987-2; 978-0-692-16989-6)* 5009 Isla Canela Ln., League City, TX 77573 USA Tel 409-599-9934
E-mail: rispba.garrison@gmail.com
Dist(s): **CreateSpace Independent Publishing Platform.**

McDaniel, Megan Faux *See* **25 Dreams Educational Media**

McDaniel Publishing Hse., *(978-1-7332194)* 670 Watson Cove, Stone Mountain, GA 30087 USA Tel 678-978-4409
E-mail: mcdanielsyl@gmail.com.

McDonald & Woodward Publishing Co., The, *(978-0-939923; 978-1-935778)* Orders Addr.: 431-B E. College St., Granville, OH 43023-1319 USA (SAN 663-6977) Tel 740-321-1140; Fax: 740-321-1141; Toll Free: 800-233-8787
E-mail: mwpubco@mwpubco.com
Web site: http://www.mwpubco.com.

McDonald Publishing Co., *(978-1-55708; 978-1-934256; 978-1-937664; 978-1-943600)* 567 Hanley Industrial Ct., Saint Louis, MO 63144 USA (SAN 249-5813) Tel 314-781-7400; Toll Free: 800-722-8080
E-mail: janet@mcdonaldpublishing.com.

McDonald, Wendy Goodall MD, *(978-0-9993341)* 4241 S. Martin Luther King, Dr., CHICAGO, IL 60653 USA Tel 312-320-6862; Fax: 312-320-6862
E-mail: wendygmcdonald16@gmail.com
Web site: dreverywoman.com.

McDougal Littell Incorporated *See* **Holt McDougal**

McDougal Publishing Co., *(978-1-58158; 978-1-884369)* Orders Addr.: P.O. Box 3595, Hagerstown, MD 21742-3595 USA (SAN 856-8286) Tel 301-797-6637; Fax: 301-733-2767; Toll Free: 800-962-3684
E-mail: publishing@mcdougal.org
Web site: http://www.mcdougalpublishing.com.

McDowell Health-Science Bks., LLC, *(978-0-9741238)* P.O. Box 81, Lafayette, CO 80026 USA Tel 303-570-7231; Fax: 303-604-0773
E-mail: McDPubCo@mcdowellpublishing.com; McDPubCo@aol.com; healthscience@mcdowellpublishing.com
Web site: http://www.mcdowellpublishing.com.

McElderry, Margaret K. Bks. *Imprint of* **McElderry, Margaret K. Bks.**

McElderry, Margaret K. Bks., Div. of Simon & Schuster Children's Publishing, 1230 Ave. of the Americas, New York, NY 10020 USA; *Imprints:* McElderry, Margaret K. Books (MMcElderry)
Dist(s): **Children's Plus, Inc.**
Simon & Schuster, Inc.

McElreath, K.M., *(978-0-9769271)* 10420 Rivertown Rd., Fairburn, GA 30213 USA Tel 770-969-1718; Fax: 770-969-0183
E-mail: tmcelreath@bellsouth.net.

McElroy & Assocs., *(978-0-9673917)* 6651 Avignon Blvd., Falls Church, VA 22043-1724 USA Tel 703-237-5993; Fax: 703-237-5994
E-mail: roland@mcelroyassoc.com
Web site: http://www.mcelroyassoc.com.

McEvoy, N. L., *(978-0-615-95144-7; 978-0-9908933)* 3767 Winding Lake Cir., Orlando, FL 32835 USA Tel 8477369375
Dist(s): **CreateSpace Independent Publishing Platform.**

McEwen, Judith A., *(978-0-9780693)* 22342 Chimayo Bend, San Antonio, TX 78258 USA Tel 210-630-9226; Fax: 210-595-7490
E-mail: chickensonthego@hotmail.com
Web site: http://www.chickensonthego.com.

McFadden, Linnea, *(978-0-9984681)* 1740 Alden Ln., Wyomissing, PA 19610 USA Tel 610-656-9173
E-mail: lbqtmm@gmail.com.

†McFarland & Co., Inc. Pubs., *(978-0-7864; 978-0-89950; 978-1-4766)* Orders Addr.: P.O. Box 611, Jefferson, NC 28640 USA (SAN 215-093X) Tel 336-246-4460; Fax: 336-246-5018; 336-246-4403; Toll Free: 800-253-2187 (orders only); Edit Addr.: 960 Hwy., 88 W., Jefferson, NC 28640 USA
E-mail: info@mcfarlandpub.com; vtomlinson@mcfarlandpub.com
Web site: http://www.mcfarlandbooks.com
Dist(s): **Ebsco Publishing**
Follett School Solutions
Metapress
MyiLibrary
ebrary, Inc.; *CIP.*

McFinn Press *See* **Captain McFinn and Friends LLC, McFinn Pr.**

McGab Publishing, *(978-0-9788092)* 12438 Prather Ave., Pt Charlotte, FL 33981-1352 USA
Web site: http://weirdobook.com.

McGarry, Donna *See* **Pollux Ink**

McGee, Tori *See* **Rowboat Pr.**

McGinley, Aaron, *(978-1-7330859)* 27 Willowick Dr., Asheville, NC 28803 USA Tel 828-808-8425
E-mail: aaronmcginley001@gmail.com
Dist(s): **Ingram Content Group.**

McGovern, Matthew /700acres Communications, *(978-0-9749445)* 27 McGovern Dr., Buxton, ME 04093 USA
E-mail: matt@mattmcgovern.com
Web site: http://www.mattmcgovern.com.

McGowan, Linda G. LLC dba LM, *(978-1-7336947)* 27200 Cty. Rd. 313, Lot 19, Buena Vista, CO 81211 USA Tel 719-238-2590
E-mail: ragingravin@gmail.com
Web site: www.unicornandthemaster.com.

McGraw, Jason A., *(978-0-615-13681-3)* 254 Westminster Rd., Rochester, NY 14607 USA Tel 585-771-7777
E-mail: jaymcgraw18@aol.com
Dist(s): **Lulu Pr., Inc.**

†McGraw-Hill Cos., The, *(978-0-07)* 6480 Jimmy Carter Blvd., Norcross, GA 30071-1701 USA (SAN 254-881X) Tel 614-755-5637; Fax: 614-755-5611; Orders Addr.: 860 Taylor Station Rd., Blacklick, OH 43004-0545 USA (SAN 200-254X) Fax: 614-755-5645; Toll Free: 800-722-4726 (orders & customer service); 800-338-3987 (college); 800-525-5003 (subscriptions); 800-352-3566 (books - US/Canada orders); P.O. Box 545, Blacklick, OH 43004-0545 Fax: 614-759-3759; Toll Free: 877-833-5524
E-mail: customer.service@mcgraw-hill.com
Web site: http://www.mcgraw-hill.com; http://www.ebooks.mcgraw-hill.com/
Dist(s): **Cambridge Univ. Pr.**
Children's Plus, Inc.
Ebsco Publishing
Libros Sin Fronteras
McGraw-Hill Osborne
McGraw-Hill Create (TM)
MyiLibrary
Sams Technical Publishing, LLC
ebrary, Inc.; *CIP.*

McGraw-Hill Education (GBR) *(978-0-07) Dist. by* **McGraw.**

McGraw-Hill Education, *(978-1-259; 978-1-260; 978-1-264; 978-1-265; 978-1-266)* Two Penn Plaza, New York, NY 10121-2298 USA Tel 212-904-2000; a/o The Mcgraw-Hill Companies, 8787 Orion Pl., Columbus, OH 43240 (SAN 256-3908) Tel 614-755-5637; Fax: 614-755-5611
E-mail: customer.service@mcgraw-hill.com
Web site: http://www.mheducation.com/custserv.html; http://www.mcgraw-hill.com
Dist(s): **Brilliance Publishing, Inc.**
McGraw-Hill Cos., The
McGraw-Hill Professional Publishing
McGraw-Hill Higher Education
MyiLibrary
ebrary, Inc.

McGraw-Hill Higher Education, *(978-0-07; 978-1-121)* Orders Addr.: P.O. Box 545, Blacklick, OH 43004-0545 USA Toll Free: 800-338-3987; Edit Addr.: 1333 Burr Ridge Pkwy., 3rd Flr., Burr Ridge, IL 60527 USA; *Imprints:* McGraw-Hill/Dushkin (Dshkn McG-Hill); McGraw-Hill Science, Engineering & Mathematics (McG-H Sci Eng)
E-mail: customer.service@mcgraw-hill.com
Web site: http://www.mhhe.com
Dist(s): **Follett School Solutions**
McGraw-Hill US Higher Ed USE Legacy
McGraw-Hill US Higher Ed USE
McGraw-Hill Cos., The
McGraw-Hill Education
McGraw-Hill Professional Publishing
MyiLibrary
Oxford Univ. Pr., Inc.
ebrary, Inc.

McGraw-Hill Osborne, *(978-0-07; 978-0-88134; 978-0-931988)* Div. of The McGraw-Hill Professional, 160 Spear St. Flr. 7, San Francisco, CA 94105-1544 USA (SAN 274-3450) Toll Free: 800-227-0900
E-mail: customer.service@mcgraw-hill.com
Web site: http://www.osborne.com
Dist(s): **Ebsco Publishing**
McGraw-Hill Cos., The
MyiLibrary
ebrary, Inc.

McGraw-Hill Professional Book Group *See* **McGraw-Hill Schl. Education Group**

McGraw-Hill Professional Publishing, *(978-0-07)* Div. of McGraw-Hill Higher Education, Orders Addr.: P.O. Box 545, Blacklick, OH 43004-0545 USA Fax: 614-755-5645; Toll Free: 800-722-4726; Edit Addr.: 2 Penn Plaza, New York, NY 10121-2298 USA Tel 212-904-2000; *Imprints:* International Marine/Ragged Mountain Press (Inter Mar/Rag)
Dist(s): **AMACOM**
American Pharmacists Assn.
Berrett-Koehler Pubs., Inc.
Ebsco Publishing
Entrepreneur Media Inc/Entrepreneur Pr.
Harvard Business Review Pr.
McGraw-Hill Cos., The
McGraw-Hill Medical Publishing Div.
McGraw-Hill Trade
MyiLibrary
ebrary, Inc.

McGraw-Hill Schl. Education Group, *(978-0-07; 978-0-7602; 978-0-8306; 978-0-911314; 978-0-917253; 978-1-55738; 978-1-307)* Div. of The McGraw-Hill Companies, Orders Addr.: P.O. Box 545, Blacklick, OH 43004-0545 USA Fax: 614-755-5645; Toll Free: 800-442-9685 (customer service); 800-722-4726; Edit Addr.: 8787 Orion Pl., Columbus, OH 43240 USA Tel 614-430-4000; Toll Free: 800-344-7344; c/o Grand Rapids Distribution Center, 3195 Wilson NW, Grand Rapids, MI 49544 (SAN 253-6420) Fax: 614-755-5611
E-mail: customer.service@mcgraw-hill.com
Web site: http://www.accessmedbooks.com; http://www.MHEducation.com
Dist(s): **Ebsco Publishing**
McGraw-Hill Cos., The
Urban Land Institute
ebrary, Inc.

McGraw-Hill Science, Engineering & Mathematics *Imprint of* **McGraw-Hill Higher Education**

McGraw-Hill Trade, *(978-0-07; 978-0-658; 978-0-8442)* Div. of McGraw-Hill Professional, Orders Addr.: P.O. Box 545, Blacklick, OH 43004-0545 USA Tel 800-722-4726; Fax: 614-755-5645; Edit Addr.: 2 Penn Plaza, New York, NY 10121 USA Tel 212-904-2000; *Imprints:* Passport Books (Passport Bks)
E-mail: Jeffrey_Krames@mcgraw-hill.com
Web site: http://www.books.mcgraw-hill.com
Dist(s): **Ebsco Publishing**
McGraw-Hill Cos., The
MyiLibrary
ebrary, Inc.

McGraw-Hill/Contemporary, *(978-0-658; 978-0-8092; 978-0-8325; 978-0-8442; 978-0-88499; 978-0-89061; 978-0-913327; 978-0-940279; 978-0-941263; 978-0-9630646; 978-1-56626; 978-1-56943; 978-1-57028)* Div. of McGraw-Hill Higher Education, Orders Addr.: P.O. Box 545, Blacklick, OH 43004-0545 USA Toll Free Fax: 800-998-3103; Toll Free: 800-621-1918; Edit Addr.: 4255 W. Touhy Ave., Lincolnwood, IL 60712 USA (SAN 169-2208) Tel 847-679-5500; Fax: 847-679-2494; Toll Free Fax: 800-998-3103; Toll Free: 800-323-4900; *Imprints:* National Textbook Company (Natl Textbk Co)
E-mail: ntcpub@tribune.com
Web site: http://www.ntc-cb.com
Dist(s): **Continental Bk. Co., Inc.**
Ebsco Publishing
Giron Bks.
Libros Sin Fronteras
McGraw-Hill Cos., The
ebrary, Inc.

McGraw-Hill/Dushkin *Imprint of* **McGraw-Hill Higher Education**

McHay, Micki, *(978-0-9786826)* 8212 Dolphin Bay Ct., Las Vegas, NV 89128 USA (SAN 854-655X).

McIntyre, Connie *See* **Grannie Annie Family Story Celebration, The**

McJimpsey, Erica *See* **RUACH PUBLISHING Co.**

McKatlib Pr., *(978-0-9745440)* P.O. Box 76693, Atlanta, GA 30358-1693 USA
Web site: http://www.bethanyadventures.com.

†McKay, David Co., Inc., *(978-0-679; 978-0-88326; 978-0-89440)* Subs. of Random Hse., Inc., Orders Addr.: 400 Hahn Rd., Westminster, MD 21157 USA Tel 410-848-1900; Toll Free: 800-733-3000 (orders only); Edit Addr.: 201 E. 50th St., MD 4-6, New York, NY 10022 USA (SAN 200-240X) Tel 212-751-2600; Fax: 212-872-8026
Dist(s): **Libros Sin Fronteras**; *CIP.*

McKellen-Caffey, *(978-0-9794191)* 15543 Sprig St., Chino Hills, CA 91709-2853 USA (SAN 853-4144) Tel 909-393-0894
E-mail: mckellencaffey@yahoo.com
Web site: http://chiselhedgehog.com.

McKenna, Mark, *(978-0-9727681)* P.O. Box 633, Florida, NY 10921 USA.

McKenna Publishing Group, *(978-0-9713659; 978-1-932172)* 425 Poa Pl., San Luis Obispo, CA 93405 USA Tel 805-550-1667; Fax: 805-783-2317
E-mail: ric@mckennapubgrp.com
Web site: http://www.mckennapubgrp.com
Dist(s): **Booklines Hawaii, Ltd.**

McKenny, Stephanie L. *See* **J & J Publishing Co.**

McKenzie, Cheryl, *(978-1-7320103)* 21436 Roaring Water Way, Los Gatos, CA 95033 USA Tel 408-335-3442; *Imprints:* C. Lee McKenzie (C Lee Mc)
E-mail: clee38@gmail.com
Dist(s): **Ingram Content Group.**

McKinney, David, *(978-0-692-42801-6; 978-0-692-60111-2; 978-0-692-86325-1; 978-0-692-98324-9)* 7311 E 64 St, Tulsa, OK 74133 USA Tel 918-252-2360 Do not confuse with David McKinney in Phoenix, AZ
E-mail: sardsfamily@cox.net.

McKinnon, Robert Scott, *(978-0-9651943)* 1608 Seventh St., S., Great Falls, MT 59405 USA Tel 406-452-3500
E-mail: maddog526@bresnan.net
Web site: http://home.bresnan.net/~maddog526/.

McKiver, Debbie dba Strong & Healthy Temple, *(978-0-692-18080-8)* 2650 Foxglove Dr SW, MARIETTA, GA 30064 USA Tel 770-850-0603
E-mail: debmac@bellsouth.net
Dist(s): **Ingram Content Group.**

McLellan Bks., *(978-0-9747536)* Orders Addr.: P.O. Box 341, Claymont, DE 19703-0341 USA Tel 302-798-4006; Fax: 302-798-2567
E-mail: richardmclellan@dca.net; richard@mclellanbooks.com
Web site: http://www.mclellanbooks.com.

MCM Prime, Inc., *(978-0-9742351)* 6355 E. Duke Ranch Rd., Pearce, AZ 85625-6113 USA Tel 520-824-4051; Fax: 775-249-9133
E-mail: paulmc@vtc.net
Web site: http://www.mcmprime.pair.com/mcmpindx.htm.

MCM Publishing *Imprint of* **Thompson, Jeniffer**

McManus, Steve, *(978-0-9964485; 978-1-7349083)* 5807 Radford Ave, Valley Village, CA 91607 USA Tel 323-573-0986
E-mail: steve@stevemcmanus.com.

McMillan, Carol, *(978-0-9907106)* 12 Marigold Dr, Bellingham, WA 98229 USA Tel 509-429-0293
E-mail: sylvanease@msn.com.

McMillen Publishing, *(978-0-9635812; 978-1-888223)* Orders Addr.: 304 Main St., Ames, IA 50010 USA (SAN 254-9085) Tel 515-232-0208; Fax: 515-232-0402 (orders); Toll Free: 800-750-6997 (In Iowa); 800-453-3960 (Outside Iowa)
E-mail: denise.sunvold@sigler.com
Web site: http://www.mcmillenbooks.com.

McMurtrey, Martin A., *(978-0-9623961)* 808 Camden, San Antonio, TX 78215 USA Tel 210-223-9680.

McNair Publishing, *(978-0-9976408)* 1751 Mizell Ave., Winter Park, FL 32789 USA Tel 407-644-5662
E-mail: TrudyMcNair@outlook.com
Web site: www.mcnairpublishing.com.

McNatmar Ventures LLC, *(978-0-9787540)* P.O. Box 1324, Clover, SC 29710-7533 USA Tel 803-222-4043
E-mail: rhcisjdm@comporium.net
Web site: http://www.mcnatmar.com.

McNaughton Publishing, *(978-1-64640)* 1776 White Oak Dr., Eugene, OR 97405 USA Tel 800-313-0999
E-mail: info@mcnaughtonpublishing.com.

McNeil & Richards, *(978-0-9825602)* 2715 N. Wisconsin Ave., Peoria, IL 61603 USA.

McNeil Publishing, *(978-1-7340908)* 130 Veracruz Dr., Ponte Vedra Beach, FL 32082 USA Tel 904-742-8487
E-mail: vivianpinner@gmail.com
Web site: vivianpinnertherapy.com.

McNeill, Lance, *(978-0-692-75992-9; 978-0-692-75994-3; 978-0-692-97350-9; 978-0-692-16251-4; 978-0-578-53977-5)* 6200 Honey Dew Ct., AUSTIN, TX 78749 USA Tel 512-964-6040.

McPeake Design, *(978-0-578-14032-2; 978-0-692-92511-9)*

McPhaul Publisher *See* **CJ Publishing Co.**

McPugh, Kathleen, *(978-0-9742062)* Orders Addr.: P.O. Box 8372, Fresno, CA 93747 USA; Edit Addr.: P.O. Box 2552, Fallbrook, CA 92088-2552 USA
Web site: http://home.att.net/~kathfreeman/book.html; http://home.att.net/~kathfreeman
Dist(s): **Ingram Content Group.**

McQueen Publishing Co., *(978-0-917186)* 1211 S. Osceola Ave., Orlando, FL 32806-2223 USA (SAN 203-9516).

MCrc Industries, LLC, *(978-0-692-10760-7; 978-0-692-13581-5; 978-0-692-13718-5; 978-0-692-14425-1; 978-0-692-14426-8; 978-0-692-14442-8; 978-1-7325521)* 603 E Oakland Ave., OAKLAND, FL 34787 USA Tel 407-245-1254; *Imprints:* ANGI PERRETTI (MYID_G_ANGI PE)
E-mail: angi@angiarts.com; angiperretti@outlook.com; mc@mrcannabisrc.com; angiperretti@gmail.com
Web site: http://www.angiarts.com; http://www.mrcannabisrc.com; http://www.angiperretti.com; https://www.MCrcShop.com
Dist(s): **Ingram Content Group.**

McRitchie, Mike, *(978-0-578-03644-1)* 109 Falcon Creek Dr., McKinney, TX 75070 USA Tel 972-540-6800
E-mail: mmcritchie@tx.rr.com
Dist(s): **Lulu Pr., Inc.**

Mcruffy Pr., *(978-1-59269)* P.O. Box 212, Raymore, MO 64083 USA Tel 816-331-2500; Fax: 816-331-3868; Toll Free Fax: 888-967-1300; Toll Free: 888-967-1200
E-mail: brian@mcruffy.com
Web site: http://www.mcruffy.

McSellin Ray II, *(978-0-692-17897-3; 978-0-692-17898-0)* 157 Forest Pl., Stockbridge, GA 30281 USA Tel 404-664-4036
E-mail: mcsellinr@gmail.com
Dist(s): **Ingram Content Group.**

McSweeney's Books *See* **McSweeney's Publishing**

McSweeney's Publishing, *(978-0-9703355; 978-0-9719047; 978-1-932416; 978-1-934781; 978-1-936365; 978-1-938073; 978-1-940450; 978-1-944211)* Orders Addr.: 849 Valencia St., San Francisco, CA 94110-1736 USA (SAN 254-3184)
E-mail: custservice@mcsweeneys.net
Web site: http://www.mcsweeneys.net
Dist(s): **Baker & Taylor Publisher Services (BTPS)**
MyiLibrary
Publishers Group West (PGW).

MCW Publishing, *(978-0-9753773)* 50 Brookdale Ave., Rochester, NY 14621 USA Tel 585-317-5780
E-mail: itm2000@hotmail.com.

McWilliams Mediation Group Ltd., *(978-0-9768663; 978-1-7350243)* P.O. Box 6216, Denver, CO 80206 USA (SAN 257-5442) Tel 303-830-0171
E-mail: joan@peacefinder.com
Web site: http://www.peacefinder.com
Dist(s): **ebrary, Inc.**

McWitty Pr., Inc., *(978-0-9755618; 978-0-9852227; 978-0-9977554)* 1835 NE Miami Gardens Dr. 150, MIAMI, FL 33179 USA Tel 305-466-0652
E-mail: jo@momentumtours.com
Web site: http://www.mcwittypress.com
Dist(s): **MyiLibrary**
Publishers Group West (PGW).

McWong Ink, *(978-0-9820881)* 440 Kent Ave., Apt. PH1B, Brooklyn, NY 11211 USA
Web site: http://www.gordonandlili.com
Dist(s): **Emerald Bk. Co.**
Greenleaf Book Group.

m.d. hughes, *(978-0-9788541)* 9 Pasadena Rd., Branford, CT 06405 USA
Web site: http://www.cryofthefalcon.com.

Avitable Pub., *(978-0-9769794; 978-0-578-09899-9)* P.O. Box 38, East Meadow, NY 11554 USA Fax: 516-826-6843
E-mail: milliemsrd@aol.com
Web site: http://www.CaloriestheBottomLine.com.

ME Media LLC *See* **Tiger Tales**

Me On the Page, *(978-0-578-42980-9; 978-1-7338064)* 2895 Dandelion Cir., Antioch, CA 94531 USA Tel 925-382-8986
E-mail: Pelang@comcast.net
Dist(s): **Ingram Content Group.**

Mead, Brian Publishing, *(978-0-9717509)* 203 E. Grove Rd., Long Grove, IA 52756 USA (SAN 255-2329)
E-mail: meadpub@juno.com; mattedeye@aol.com.

Mead Lommen Publishing *See* **Calaroga Publishing**

Meadow Road Publishing, *(978-1-7334393)* 360 Bayhead Dr, Melbourne, FL 32940-7705 USA Tel 321-543-7054
E-mail: SillyYaya@SillyYaya.com
Web site: SillyYaya.com.

†Meadowbrook Pr., *(978-0-88166; 978-0-915658)* 5451 Smetana Dr., Minnetonka, MN 55343 USA (SAN 207-3404) Tel 612-930-1100; Fax: 612-930-1940; Toll Free: 800-338-2232
E-mail: mballard@meadowbrookpress.com
Web site: http://www.meadowbrookpress.com
Dist(s): **Hachette Bk. Group**
Simon & Schuster
Simon & Schuster Children's Publishing; *CIP.*

Meadowlark, *(978-0-692-26616-8; 978-0-692-43466-6; 978-0-9966801; 978-0-692-56779-1; 978-1-7322410; 978-1-7342477)* Orders Addr.: P.O. Box 333, Emporia, KS 66801 USA; Edit Addr.: 206 Rural St., Emporia, KS 66801 USA Tel 620-794-9320
Web site: www.meadowlark-books.com
Dist(s): **CreateSpace Independent Publishing Platform.**

Meadowview Pubs., *(978-0-9741218)* Orders Addr.: P.O. Box 444, Portlant, CT 06480 USA Tel 860-342-2646; Edit Addr.: 221 E. Cotton Hill Rd., Portland, CT 06480 USA
E-mail: marketbase@peoplepc.com.

MeAgain Publishing, *(978-0-9993012)* 3180 Fox Squirrel Dr., Orange Park, FL 32073 USA Tel 904-338-3008
E-mail: beth@meagainpublishing.com
Web site: www.meagainpublishing.com.

Means To An End, *(978-0-9995852)* 7250 Old Redmond Rd. Apt M147, Redmond, WA 98052-6817 USA Tel 425-861-8042
E-mail: vsches@frontier.com.

MEAR LLC, *(978-0-9787628)* 636 Twp. Rd., 2724, Loudonville, OH 44842 USA Tel 419-994-3462 (phone/fax)
E-mail: mearllc@gmail.com
Web site: www.twralphabetbook.com.

MEC Publishing, *(978-0-9746865)* 1923 W. 17th St., Santa Ana, CA 92706 USA (SAN 256-405X)
E-mail: mecpublishing@aol.com
Web site: http://www.mecpublishing.com.

Mechanech Pubns., *(978-0-9702861; 978-0-9856497)* 4 Kaser Terr., Monsey, NY 10952 USA Tel 914-352-1926.

Mechling Bookbindery, *(978-0-9703825; 978-0-9744657; 978-0-9760563; 978-0-9793772; 978-0-9841400; 978-1-938184)* Div. of Mechling Associates, Inc., Orders Addr.: 1124 Oneida Valley Rd., Route 38, Chicora, PA 16025-3820 USA Tel 724-287-2120; Fax: 724-285-9231; Toll Free: 800-941-3735
E-mail: sales@mechlingbooks.com
Web site: http://www.mechlingbooks.com.

Medal Bks., *(978-0-9764300; 978-0-9785667)* P.O. Box 7231, Clearwater, FL 33758-7231 USA
E-mail: ronan@ronanblaze.com
Web site: http://www.ronanblaze.com.

Medallion Pr., Inc., *(978-0-9743639; 978-1-932815; 978-1-933836; 978-1-934755; 978-1-60542; 978-1-942546)* Orders Addr.: 4222 Meridian Pkwy. Ste 110, Aurora, IL 60504 USA (SAN 255-5360) Tel 630-513-8316; Fax: 630-513-8362
E-mail: jeanne@medallinmediagroup.com
Web site: http://www.medallionmediagroup.com
Dist(s): **Legato Pubs. Group**
MyiLibrary
Publishers Group West (PGW).

Meder, Julia, *(978-0-9967304; 978-1-944260)* Kurpfalzstr. 156, Neustadt, 67435 DEU Tel 984-255-5049
E-mail: info@dreamfinder-coaching.com.

Medernach, T.K. *See* **ThunderBolt Pubns.**

Media Alert!, *(978-0-9676616)* P.O. Box 735, Littleton, CO 80160-0735 USA Toll Free: 800-986-5560 (code 02)
E-mail: CNFsueLS@aol.com.

Media Angels, Inc. *See* **Knowledge Box Central**

Media Angels, Inc., *(978-0-9700385; 978-1-931941)* Orders Addr.: 15720 S. Pebble Ln., Fort Myers, FL 33912-2341 USA
E-mail: felice@mediaangels.com
Web site: http://www.mediaangels.com
Dist(s): **Send The Light Distribution LLC.**

Media Assocs., *(978-0-918501)* Orders Addr.: P.O. Box 1221, Galt, CA 95632 USA (SAN 657-3207) Tel 209-280-8609; Toll Free: 800-373-1897; *Imprints:* Archives Pr. (Archives Pr) Do not confuse with Media Assocs., Marina Del Rey, CA
E-mail: lovekillsbook@gmail.com; moyturra@gmail.com
Web site: www.hankharrison.com.

Media Blasters, Inc., *(978-1-890228; 978-1-58655; 978-1-59883)* 132 W. 36th St. Rm. 401, New York, NY 10018-8837 USA (SAN 859-5712)
E-mail: info@media-blasters.com
Web site: http://www.media-blasters.com; http://www.kittymedia.com
Dist(s): **Diamond Comic Distributors, Inc.**
Diamond Bk. Distributors
Follett School Solutions.

Media Creations, Incorporated *See* **Aeon Publishing Inc.**

Media For Life, *(978-0-9675068)* 300 Main St. No. 540, Madison, NJ 07940 USA Fax: 201-490-1801
E-mail: EduFun@aol.com.

Media Hatchery, *(978-0-9971276)* 42 Green Lake Dr., Orchard Park, NY 14127 USA Tel 716-245-1634
E-mail: bill@mediahatchery.com
Web site: MediaHatchery.com.

Media Magic New York, *(978-0-9744211)* 15 W. 39th St., 13th Flr., New York, NY 10018 USA Tel 212-926-5575
E-mail: mediamagicny@aol.com; info@mediamagic-ny.com.

Media Man! Productions *Imprint of* **Fairwood Pr.**

Media Publishing Group, The, *(978-0-692-82027-8)* 11 Penn plaza 5th Flr., NEW YORK, NY 10001 USA Tel 718-473-9819
E-mail: Sylfronia.king@mail.com; Sylfronia.king@mail.com.

Media Rodzina (POL) *(978-83-7278; 978-83-85594) Dist. by* **Distribks Inc.**

Medical Alternative Pr., *(978-0-9660882)* 4173 Fieldbrook Rd., West Bloomfield, MI 48323 USA Tel 248-851-3372; Fax: 248-851-0421; Toll Free: 888-647-5616 Do not confuse with Medical Alternative Pr., Colleyville, TX
E-mail: alselko@hotmail.com
Web site: http://www.drbrownstein.com.

Medical Manor Bks., *(978-0-934232)* Subs. of Manor Hse. Pubns., Inc., 3501 Newberry Rd., Philadelphia, PA 19154 USA (SAN 217-2526) Tel 800-343-8464; Fax: 215-440-9255; Toll Free: 800-343-8464
E-mail: info@diet-step.com; sales@diet-step.com; sales@medicalmanorbooks.com; marketing@diet-step.com; DrWalk@diet-step.com; info@medicalmanorbooks.com
Web site: http://www.medicalmanorbooks.com/; http://www.peace-healingbooks.com; http://www.manorhousepublications.com
Dist(s): **Baker & Taylor Publisher Services (BTPS)**
Distributors, The
Follett School Solutions
Quality Bks., Inc.
Unique Bks., Inc.
ebrary, Inc.

Medici Publishing, Inc., *(978-0-9743791; 978-0-9823853)* P.O. Box 282, Beulah, CO 81023 USA Tel 719-485-1167
E-mail: marcprat@juno.com
Web site: http://www.medicibooks.org.

Medicine Wheel Education (CAN) *(978-0-9938694; 978-1-989122) Dist. by* **Orca Bk Pub.**

Medicine Woman Inc., The, *(978-0-9771906)* Orders Addr.: P.O. Box 613, Cascade, ID 83611 USA Tel 208-382-6653; Edit Addr.: 843 S. Main Hwy. 55, Cascade, ID 83611 USA
E-mail: tmw@ctcweb.net
Web site: http://www.themedicinewoman.com.

Medicus Pr., Inc., *(978-0-9787727)* P.O. Box 284, Leonia, NJ 07605-0284 USA (SAN 851-5905) Tel 201-816-7363; Fax: 201-266-0537
E-mail: medicuspress@yahoo.com.

Medina Publishing, Ltd. (GBR) *(978-0-9570233; 978-1-909339; 978-0-9564170; 978-0-9567081) Dist. by* **Casemate Pubs.**

Medio Media *See* **Medio Media Publishing**

Medio Media Publishing, *(978-0-9666941; 978-0-9725627; 978-1-933182)* 627 N. 6th Ave., Tucson, AZ 85705-8330 USA Toll Free: 800-324-8305
E-mail: JoeD846136@aol.com; meditate@mediomedia.org
Web site: http://www.mediomedia.org
Dist(s): **Continuum International Publishing Group, Inc.**
Macmillan
National Bk. Network.

Medley, *(978-1-890034)* 1620 Los Alamos, SW, Albuquerque, NM 87104 USA Tel 505-247-3921; *Imprints:* Medley Publications (Medley Pubns)
E-mail: litchman@unm.edu.

Medley, Cynthia, *(978-0-9861178; 978-0-9974021; 978-0-9989748; 978-1-7342690)* 805 Brunson St., Prairie du Chien, WI 53821 USA Tel 608-379-1691
E-mail: cmedley49@yahoo.com.

Medley Pubns. *Imprint of* **Medley**

MedPress & Quality Publishers *See* **Quality Pubs.**

Medusa Road Pr., *(978-0-9779295)* 6 Rte. 75, Norton Hill, NY 12083 USA Tel 518-966-5281
E-mail: MedusaRoadStudio@aol.com
Web site: http://CarolynsWebsite.net.

Medwag Publishing, *(978-0-9654963)* P.O. Box 36037, Richmond, VA 23235 USA Tel 804-794-8186
E-mail: alrx1@juno.com.

Meehl Foundation Pr., *(978-0-9767049)* P.O. Box 2089, Brazoria, TX 77422-2089 USA Tel 979-798-7972
E-mail: meehlfou@meehlfoundation.org
Web site: http://www.meehlfoundation.org.

MeeraMasi, Inc., *(978-0-9773645; 978-0-9797191)* 449 London Pk. Ct., San Jose, CA 95136 USA Tel 408-365-8044; Fax: 408-225-8586
E-mail: info@meeramasi.com; sonali@meeramasi.com
Web site: http://www.meeramasi.com.

Meerkat Pr., *(978-0-692-37854-0; 978-0-9966262; 978-1-946154)* 200 River Vista Dr. Suite 522, Atlanta, GA 30339 USA Tel 678-439-7675
Web site: www.meerkatpress.com
Dist(s): **CreateSpace Independent Publishing Platform**
Independent Pubs. Group
Midpoint Trade Bks., Inc.

Meerkat's Adventures Bks., *(978-0-9778072)* 510 Diamond St, Suite A, San Francisco, CA 94114 USA (SAN 850-2862)
Web site: http://www.meerkatsadventures.com.

Meet Bks., LLC, *(978-0-615-31579-9; 978-0-615-38973-8)* 806 Seale Ave., Palo Alto, CA 94303 USA.

Meet the Author *Imprint of* **Owen, Richard C. Pubs., Inc.**

MeetMinnie, *(978-0-9997646)* P.O. Box 1628, Columbia, MD 21044 USA Tel 443-808-3201
E-mail: books@meetminnie.com
Web site: www.meetminnie.com.

Mefford, David, *(978-0-9762143)* 274 W. 700 N., American Fork, UT 84003 USA
E-mail: david@mefford.org.

Meg and Lucy Bks. (GBR) *Dist. by* **IPG Chicago.**

Megami Pr. LLC, *(978-0-615-39156-4; 978-0-615-40446-2; 978-0-9853471)* P.O. Box 128557, Nashville, TN 37212 USA
E-mail: Megamipress@gmail.com
Web site: http://www.megamipress.com.

Megtree Organics, *(978-1-948347)* 3914 Clear Creek Ct, Richardson, TX 75082 USA Tel 214-242-9141
E-mail: bijoy@megtree.com.

Megyeri, Graham Bks., *(978-0-9711971; 978-0-9791994)* 439 Lakeview Blvd., Albert Lea, MN 56007 USA Tel 507-377-1255; Toll Free: 866-755-5942
E-mail: minnmemory@aol.com
Web site: http://www.minnesotamemories.com
Dist(s): **Partners Bk. Distributing, Inc.**

Mehr Iran Publishing Co. *See* **Mehriran Publishing Co.**

Mehriran Publishing Co., *(978-0-9633129)* 14900 Talking Rock Ct., Suite B, N. Potomac, MD 20878 USA Tel 301-279-6778; Fax: 301-738-2174
E-mail: pirnia@pirnia.com
Web site: http://www.pirnia.com.

Mehta Publishers (IND) *(978-93-83222) Dist. by* **IPG Chicago.**

MEIER Enterprises Inc., *(978-0-9726808)* 8697 Gage Blvd., Kennewick, WA 99336 USA Tel 509-735-1589; Fax: 509-783-5075; Toll Free: 800-239-7589
E-mail: sranderson@meierinc.com; info@learningtowrite.com
Web site: http://www.meierinc.com; http://www.learningtowrite.comw.

Meirovich, Igal, *(978-0-9820556; 978-1-60796)* 6408 Elray Dr., Apt. E, Baltimore, MD 21209 USA Tel 410-764-6423
E-mail: lightoncds@gmail.com
Dist(s): **BookBaby**
Lulu Pr., Inc.

Meister-Home, Inc., *(978-0-9702497)* P.O. Box 471250, Charlotte, NC 28247-1250 USA (SAN 256-1794) Tel 704-968-6741; Fax: 704-544-2034; *Imprints:* Meister-Home Press (Meister-Home Pr)
E-mail: ragilmartin@hotmail.com; rgilmartin@meister-home.com
Web site: http://www.meister-home.com.

Meister-Home Pr. *Imprint of* **Meister-Home, Inc.**

Mel Bay Pubns., Inc., *(978-0-7866; 978-0-87166; 978-1-56222; 978-1-60974; 978-1-61065; 978-1-61911; 978-1-5134)* 1734 Gilsinn Ln., Fenton, MO 63026 USA (SAN 657-3630) Tel 636-257-3970; Fax: 636-257-5062; Toll Free: 800-863-5229
E-mail: email@melbay.com; sharon@melbay.com
Web site: http://www.melbay.com; www.melbaydealers.com
Dist(s): **Alfred Publishing Co., Inc.**

Mel Ona, *(978-0-9716585)* Div. of ONA New Body - New Life, Inc., 1203 Kamehame Dr., Honolulu, HI 96825 USA
E-mail: doctormelona@gmail.com
Web site: http://www.doctormelona.com
Dist(s): **Baker & Taylor Publisher Services (BTPS).**

Melanie, *(978-0-692-64200-9)* 208 Stimson St, Herkimer, NY 13350 USA Tel 315-219-1316
E-mail: melanie.lopata@yahoo.com.

Melanie Hooyenga, *(978-0-692-72747-8; 978-0-692-72753-9; 978-0-692-72755-3; 978-0-692-04449-0)* 15008 Lakeshore Dr., GRAND HAVEN, MI 49417 USA Tel 616-502-6410.

Melanin Grace Publishing, LLC, *(978-0-692-87205-5; 978-0-692-87206-2; 978-0-692-97827-6; 978-0-692-97828-3)* 7440 Maple Spice Ave, CANAL WINCHESTER, OH 43110 USA Tel 614-946-6475
E-mail: jeffwcrawford5+LVP0003584@gmail.com; jeffwcrawford5+LVP0003584@gmail.com.

Melanin Origins, LLC *Imprint of* **Grivante Pr.**

Melbourne Univ. Publishing (AUS) *(978-0-522; 978-0-646-05507-7) Dist. by* **IPG Chicago.**

Melbournestyle Bks. (AUS) *(978-0-9757047; 978-0-9924917; 978-0-6485684) Dist. by* **IPG Chicago.**

Melissa & Doug, LLC, *(978-1-950013; 978-1-951733)* P.O. Box 590, Westport, CT 06881 USA Tel 203-762-4500
E-mail: NRitchey@melissaanddoug.com.

Melissa Productions, Inc., *(978-0-9842394; 978-0-9834751; 978-0-9898293)* 2003 Arundale Ln., Matthews, NC 28104 USA (SAN 858-8252) Tel 704-246-7304
E-mail: melissa@melissaproductions.com
Web site: http://www.melissaproductions.com.

MelissaCrickard, *(978-0-692-22392-5; 978-0-692-25853-8; 978-0-692-91565-3; 978-0-9992059; 978-1-7325856; 978-1-7326808; 978-1-951482)* 483 Park Pl., Grand Island, NY 14072 USA Tel 7168648978
Dist(s): **CreateSpace Independent Publishing Platform.**

MELJAMES, Inc., *(978-0-9755195; 978-1-933419)* 107 Suncreek Dr., Suite 300, Allen, TX 75013 USA
Web site: http://www.meljamesinc.com.

Melland Publishing, LLC, *(978-0-9966876; 978-0-9971885; 978-0-9998957)* 5515 Hargrove Ave., Caldwell, ID 83607 USA Tel 208-546-1306
E-mail: v19501971@msn.com
Web site: www.maryvine.com.

mellano, jean, *(978-0-692-53981-1; 978-0-692-06685-0)* 3620 demott ave, wantagh, NY 11793 USA Tel 516-221-5951
E-mail: spinjunkie53@hotmail.com
Web site: www.slippedaway.org.

†Mellen, Edwin Pr., The, *(978-0-7734; 978-0-88946; 978-0-935106; 978-0-7799; 978-1-4955)* Orders Addr.: P.O. Box 67, Queenston, ON L0S 1L0 CAN; Edit Addr.: P.O. Box 450, Lewiston, NY 14092-0450 USA (SAN 207-110X) Tel 716-754-2266; 716-754-2788; Fax: 716-754-1860
E-mail: sales@mellenpress.com
Web site: http://www.mellenpress.com; *CIP.*

Melquist, Justin, *(978-0-578-45882-3)* 2504 Fircrest Blvd., Anacortes, WA 98221 USA Tel 360-320-3895
E-mail: justin.melquist@gmail.com
Dist(s): **Ingram Content Group.**

Melton Hill Media, *(978-0-9816793; 978-0-9990919)* 9119 Solway Ferry Rd., Oak Ridge, TN 37830 USA (SAN 856-2288)
E-mail: wendy@meltonhillmedia.com
Web site: http://www.familyroadmap.org; http://www.meltonhillmedia.com.

Melzee's Production, *(978-0-9722738)* P.O. Box 394, Hawthorne, CA 90251-0394 USA Tel 310-263-7804
E-mail: melzee3@juno.com.

Me+Mi Publishing, *(978-0-9679748; 978-1-931398)* 400 Knoll St. Ste. B, Wheaton, IL 60187-4557 USA Toll Free: 888-251-1444
E-mail: m3@memima.com
Web site: http://www.memima.com
Dist(s): **Lectorum Pubns., Inc.**
Quality Bks., Inc.

Memoir Bks., *(978-0-9793387; 978-1-937748)* Div. of Heidelberg Graphics, Orders Addr.: 2 Stansbury Ct., Chico, CA 95928 USA Tel 530-342-6582
Web site: http://www.heidelberggraphics.com.

Memoria Pr., *(978-1-930953; 978-1-61538; 978-1-5477)* Orders Addr.: 4603 Poplar Level Rd., Louisville, KY 40213-2337 USA Toll Free: 877-862-1097
E-mail: magister@memoriapress.com
Web site: http://www.memoriapress.com
Dist(s): **Chicago Distribution Ctr.**

Memories Publishing, *(978-0-9748984)* P.O. Box 82516, Austin, TX 78708 USA Tel 512-907-1821
E-mail: mindyred@aol.com.

MENDIAS, LJ, *(978-0-692-94394-6)* 23765 Jayhawk Ave, COLORADO SPRINGS, CO 80928 USA Tel 719-683-7424
E-mail: createillustratedesign@gmail.com
Dist(s): **Ingram Content Group.**

Mennonite Board of Missions *See* **Mennonite Mission Network**

Mennonite Mission Network, *(978-1-877736; 978-1-933845)* 500 S. Main St., P.O. Box 370, Elkhart, IN 46515-0370 USA Tel 219-294-7523; Fax: 574-294-8669; Toll Free: 866-866-2872
E-mail: Beyond@MennoniteMission.net
Web site: http://www.mennonitemission.net
Dist(s): **Follett School Solutions**
Herald Pr.

Mennonite Pr. Inc., *(978-0-9772745; 978-0-692-03234-3)* Orders Addr.: P.O. Box 867, Newton, KS 67114 USA Tel 316-283-4680; Fax: 316-283-2068; Toll Free: 800-536-4686; Edit Addr.: 532 N. Oliver Rd., Newton, KS 67114 USA
E-mail: reliability@mennonitepress.com
Web site: http://www.mennonitepress.com.

Mental Health Historic Preservation Society Of Central Illinois, *(978-0-9748742)* 209 Arnold Ave., East Peoria, IL 61611 USA Tel 309-699-3051
E-mail: aparr12345@aol.com
Dist(s): **Partners Bk. Distributing, Inc.**

Mental Wellness Publishing House *See* **Wellness pH**

Mentoring Minds, LP, *(978-0-9763559; 978-0-9767940; 978-1-935123; 978-1-938935; 978-1-62763)* P.O. Box 8843, Tyler, TX 75711 USA Fax: 800-838-8186; Toll Free: 800-585-5258
E-mail: gavin@mentoringminds.com
Web site: http://www.mentoring-minds.com.

MentorSource, LLC, *(978-0-9773324)* P.O. Box 24436, Minneapolis, MN 55424 USA Tel 612-269-8242
E-mail: gianna_bl@msn.com
Web site: http://www.rosyproses.com.

Mentzer Printing Ink, *(978-0-9746705; 978-0-9786276; 978-0-9797502; 978-0-9894927)* 1054 Virginia Ave., Indianapolis, IN 46203-1754 USA Toll Free: 800-514-6017
E-mail: info@m2print.com
Web site: http://www.m2print.com.

Menucha Pubs. Inc., *(978-1-61465)* 1235 38th St., BROOKLYN, NY 11218 USA (SAN 860-2115) Tel 718-232-0856; Fax: 718-232-0856
E-mail: hirsch@menuchapublishers.com.

Meraki Co. *See* **Meraki Co.**

Meraki Co., *(978-0-578-21845-8)* 7386 Long Lake Rd. SE, Port Orchard, WA 98367 USA Tel 210-910-7428
E-mail: juliannefritz14@gmail.com.

†Mercer Univ. Pr., *(978-0-86554; 978-0-88146)* 1501 Mercer Univ. Dr., Macon, GA 31207 USA (SAN 220-0716) Tel 478-301-2880; Fax: 478-301-2585; Toll Free: 866-895-1472
E-mail: mupressorders@mercer.edu
Web site: http://www.mupress.org; *CIP.*

Mercesart, *(978-0-9907894)* 65 Dean St., Hicksville, NY 11801 USA Tel 646-269-2080
E-mail: Mercesart@hotmail.com
Web site:
Dist(s): **Lulu Pr., Inc.**

Merchant Bks. *Imprint of* **Rough Draft Printing**

Mercier Pr., Ltd., The (IRL) *(978-0-85342; 978-1-85635; 978-1-86023; 978-1-78117) Dist. by* **Casemate Pubs.**

Mercury Publishing, Inc., *(978-0-9778793)* Orders Addr.: 35 Fieldstone Way, Alpharetta, GA 30005 USA (SAN 850-5020)
E-mail: goga7n@gmail.com
Dist(s): **BCH Fulfillment & Distribution.**

Publisher Name Index

Mercury West Publishing, *(978-1-948577)* 4748 Shands Dr, Mesquite, TX 75150 USA Tel 404-580-2958
E-mail: authorcmhealy@gmail.com.

Mercy Grace Publishing, *(978-0-615-70230-8; 978-0-692-93247-6; 978-0-692-96818-5; 978-0-578-49654-2)* 20 Morses Pond RD, Wellesley, MA 02482 USA Tel 7812352048
E-mail: belogour@aol.com.

Mercy Place, Inc., *(978-0-9677402; 978-0-9707919)* P.O. Box 134, Shippensburg, PA 17257 USA Tel 717-532-6899; Fax: 717-532-8646; Toll Free: 800-722-6774
E-mail: mpm@reapernet.com
Web site: http://mercyplace.com
Dist(s): **Destiny Image Pubs.**

†Meredith Bks., *(978-0-696; 978-0-89721; 978-0-917102)* Div. of Meredith Corp., Orders Addr.: 1716 Locust St., LN-110, Des Moines, IA 50309-3023 USA (SAN 202-4055) Tel 515-284-2363; 515-284-2126 (sales); Fax: 515-284-3371; Toll Free: 800-678-8091; *Imprints:* Food Network Kitchens (Food Net) Do not confuse with Meredith Pr. in Skaneateles, NY
E-mail: John.OBannon@meredith.com
Web site: http://www.bhgstore.com
Dist(s): **Children's Plus, Inc.**
Follett School Solutions
MyiLibrary
Sterling Publishing Co., Inc.; *CIP.*

Meredith Etc, *(978-0-692-46265-2; 978-0-692-46804-3; 978-0-692-60643-8; 978-0-692-62432-6; 978-0-692-69480-0; 978-0-692-71820-9; 978-0-9993226; 978-1-7341578)*
Dist(s): **CreateSpace Independent Publishing Platform.**

Meredith Group Ltd., The, *(978-0-9765341)* Orders Addr.: 24 N. Bryn Mawr Ave., Box117, Bryn Mawr, PA 19010 USA (SAN 256-4920) Tel 610-642-0199; Edit Addr.: 71 Eden View Rd. # 6, Elizabethtown, PA 17022-3124 USA
E-mail: mmbellamy1@verizon.net
Web site: http://www.goldiesbook.com.

Meridia Pubs. LLC, *(978-0-615-40498-1; 978-0-9832330; 978-0-9904031)* 29439 Sayle Dr., Willoughby Hills, OH 44092 USA Tel 440-944-8047
E-mail: al.ruksenas@gmail.com
Dist(s): **BookBaby**
Smashwords.

Meridian Creative Group *See* **Larson Learning, Inc.**

Meritage Publishing, *(978-0-9769866)* Orders Addr.: 12339 Meritage Ct., Rancho Cucamonga, CA 91739 USA
E-mail: meritagepub@charter.net
Dist(s): **Quality Bks., Inc.**

Meriwether Publishing *Imprint of* **Meriwether Publishing, Ltd.**

Meriwether Publishing, Ltd., *(978-0-916260; 978-1-56608)* Div. of Pioneer Drama Service, Inc., Orders Addr.: P.O. Box 4267, Englewood, CO 80155-4267 USA (SAN 208-4716) Tel 303-779-4035; Fax: 303-779-4315; P.O. Box 4267, Englewood, CO 80155 (SAN 990-2856) Tel 303-779-4035; Fax: 303-779-4315; Edit Addr.: 9707 E. Easter Ln. Suite A, Englewood, CO 80112 USA Tel 303-779-4035; *Imprints:* Meriwether Publishing (MeriwetherPub)
E-mail: lori@pioneerdrama.com; books@pioneerdrama.com; wholesale@pioneerdrama.com
Web site: http://https://www.christianpub.com/; http://www.pioneerdrama.com
Dist(s): **Follett School Solutions**
Ingram Publisher Services.

Merkos L'Inyonei Chinuch, *(978-0-8266)* 291 Kingston Ave., Brooklyn, NY 11213 USA Tel 718-778-0226; Fax: 718-778-4148
E-mail: yonason@kehot.net
Web site: http://www.kehotonline.com.

Merlin, Debbi, *(978-0-9793568)* 12339 Scarcella Ln., Stafford, TX 77477-1609 USA (SAN 853-232X)
E-mail: merlin@merlinmagic.cc
Web site: http://www.merlinmagic.cc.

Merlin Enterprises, *(978-0-9761017)* Orders Addr.: 11881 S. Fortuna Rd., No. 451, Yuma, AZ 85367 USA
E-mail: napuff@gmail.com
Web site: http://cafepress.com/npuff.

Merlot Group, LLC, The, *(978-0-9816123; 978-0-9887117)* P.O. Box 302, Covington, KY 41012-0302 USA Tel 859-743-1003
Web site: http://www.merlotgroup.com
Dist(s): **Lulu Pr., Inc.**

Meroe Publishing, *(978-0-9768306)* P.O. Box 664, Cusseta, GA 31805 USA
E-mail: tonieshort@meroepublishing.com
Web site: http://www.meroepublishing.com.

Merriam-Webster *Imprint of* **Merriam-Webster, Inc.**

Merriam-Webster, Inc., *(978-0-87779; 978-1-68150)* Subs. of Encyclopaedia Britannica, Inc., Orders Addr.: 47 Federal St., Springfield, MA 01102 USA (SAN 202-6244) Tel 413-734-3134; Fax: 413-731-5979; 413-734-2014; Toll Free: 800-828-1880; *Imprints:* Merriam-Webster (Merriam-Webstr)
E-mail: sales@Merriam-Webster.com; orders@Merriam-Webster.com; jsantoro@Merriam-Webster.com
Web site: http://www.WordCentral.com; http://www.Merriam-Webster.com
Dist(s): **CENGAGE Learning**
Delmar Cengage Learning
Perfection Learning Corp.

Merril Pr., *(978-0-936783)* 12500 NE Tenth Pl., Bellevue, WA 98005 USA (SAN 699-9387) Tel 425-454-7009; Fax: 425-451-3959
E-mail: editor@merrilpress.com
Web site: http://www.merrilpress.com
Dist(s): **Independent Pubs. Group**
Midpoint Trade Bks., Inc.

Merrimack Bk. Works, *(978-0-9799090)* 23 Pleasant St., No. 508, Newburyport, MA 01950-2632 USA (SAN 854-7424) Tel 978-417-9277
E-mail: mary@maryleemattison.com
Web site: http://www.maryleemattison.com.

Merrimack Media, *(978-1-939166; 978-1-945756)* 665 Washington St. No. 2507, Boston, MA 02111 USA Tel 508-932-0865
E-mail: jenny@merrimackmedia.com
Web site: http://merrimackmedia.com.

Merritt Publishing *See* **Silver Lake Publishing**

Merriwell, Frank Inc., *(978-0-8373)* Subs. of National Learning Corp., 212 Michael Dr., Syosset, NY 11791 USA (SAN 209-259X) Tel 516-921-8888; Toll Free: 800-645-6337.

Merry Dissonance Pr., *(978-1-939919)* 3113 Soaring Eagle Ln., Castle Rock, CO 80109 USA Tel 213-448-7701
E-mail: donnamazzitelli@gmail.com
Web site: merrydissonancepress.com.

Merry Lane Pr., *(978-0-9744307)* 18 E. 16th St., 7th Flr., New York, NY 10003 USA Tel 212-633-6505; Fax: 212-242-6077
E-mail: alan@merrylanepress.com
Web site: http://www.merrylanepress.com.

Merry Tales Publishing, *(978-0-9845471)* 209 Bobbitt Rd., Clayton, NC 27520-6557 USA (SAN 859-709X) Tel 919-550-0107.

Merryant Pubs., *(978-1-877599)* P.O. Box 1921, Vashon, WA 98070-1921 USA Toll Free: 800-228-8958
E-mail: jmboule@aol.com.

Merrybooks & More, *(978-0-9615407; 978-1-882607)* 1214 Rugby Rd., Charlottesville, VA 22903 USA (SAN 695-5053) Tel 804-979-3658; Fax: 804-296-8446; Toll Free: 800-959-2665.

Mesmer, Sandy Bergstrom Designs, *(978-1-7336945)* 1509 Bonair St., Clearwater, FL 33755 USA Tel 727-452-5745
E-mail: sandy@smesmer.com
Web site: https://www.etsy.com/shop/SandyMesmerDesigns.

Mesorah Pubns., Ltd., *(978-0-89906; 978-1-57819; 978-1-4226)* 4401 Second Ave., Brooklyn, NY 11232 USA (SAN 213-1269) Tel 718-921-9000 Toll Free: 800-637-6724; *Imprints:* ArtScroll Series (ArtScroll Series); Shaar Press (Shaar Pr)
E-mail: info@ArtScroll.com
Web site: http://www.artscroll.com.

Mesquite Tress Pr., LLC, *(978-0-9729835)* Orders Addr.: P.O. Box 17513, Louisville, KY 40217 USA; Edit Addr.: 212 W. Ormsby Ave, Louisville, KY 40203 USA
Web site: http://www.onetinytwig.com; http://www.mesquitetreepress.com; http://bluegrassbreeze.com.

Mess Hall Writers, *(978-1-885531)* P.O. Box 1551, Jeffersonville, IN 47130 USA Tel 812-288-9888; Fax: 812-288-9695
E-mail: fooddudes2@aol.com.

Message In a Bottle Translators *See* **Pangloss Publishing**

Messiah Publishing - Pearables, *(978-0-9792446)* P.O. Box 272000, Fort Collins, CO 80527 USA (SAN 852-8837) Tel 719-549-0662
Web site: http://www.pearables.com.

Messianic Jewish Pubs., *(978-1-880226; 978-1-936716; 978-1-7339354; 978-1-951833)* Div. of The Lewis & Harriet Lederer Foundation, Inc., 6120 Day Long Ln., Clarksville, MD 21029 USA Tel 410-531-6644; Fax: 410-531-9440; Toll Free: 800-410-7367 (individual orders only)
Web site: http://www.MessianicJewish.net
Dist(s): **Anchor Distributors**
Baker & Taylor Publisher Services (BTPS)
Christian Bk. Distributors
INscribe Digital
Ingram Content Group
Messianic Jewish Resources International
Spring Arbor Distributors, Inc.

Messianic Perspectives, *(978-0-9674319; 978-0-9882120; 978-0-9898240)* Orders Addr.: P.O. Box 345, San Antonio, TX 78292-0345 USA Tel 210-226-0421; Fax: 210-226-2140; Toll Free: 800-926-5397; Edit Addr.: 611 Broadway St., San Antonio, TX 78215 USA
E-mail: info@cjfm.org
Web site: http://www.cjfm.org.

Messimer, Maria S, *(978-0-578-43171-0; 978-0-578-44132-0; 978-0-578-50848-1; 978-0-578-51225-9; 978-0-578-54301-7; 978-0-578-54307-9; 978-0-578-56645-0; 978-0-578-56820-1)* 5375 Main St., Kelseyville, CA 95451 USA Tel 707 245-5445
E-mail: msmessimer@msn.com
Dist(s): **Ingram Content Group.**

Messineo, Joe *See* **Socrates Solutions Incorporated**

Meta Adventures *See* **Meta Adventures Publishing & DIA Publishing**

Meta Adventures Publishing & DIA Publishing, *(978-0-9721202)* Orders Addr.: P.O. Box 1894, Sedona, AZ 86339 USA (SAN 254-6183) Tel 928-204-1560
E-mail: info@dreamsinaction.us; publishing@dreamsinaction.us; orderinfo@dreamsinaction.us
Web site: http://www.dreamsinaction.us; http://www.MrSedona.com
Dist(s): **Dreams in Action Distribution.**

Metacognition Pr., *(978-0-9859707)* 48 Michael Ln., Orinda, CA 94563 USA Tel 925-360-9159
E-mail: Metacognitionblog@yahoo.com.

Metal Lunchbox Publishing, *(978-0-9843437; 978-1-7335118)* 5257 Buckeystown Pike #508, Frederick, MD 21704 USA (SAN 859-1202) Tel 412-916-0211
E-mail: info@metallunchboxpublishing.com
Web site: http://www.metallunchboxpublishing.com.

Metalmark Pr., *(978-0-9767239)* 7116 New Sharon Church Rd., Rougemont, NC 27572 USA
E-mail: birdcr@concentric.net
Web site: http://www.rlephoto.com.

Metamedix, Incorporated *See* **Science2Discover, Inc.**

Metamorphosis, *(978-0-9774589)* 100 State St S., Kirkland, WA 98033-6667 USA
E-mail: christinemerritt@earthlink.net
Web site: http://www.iahp.com/metamorphosis.

Metaphrog (GBR) *(978-0-9534932; 978-0-9545984) Dist. by* **D C D.**

Metapublishing, *(978-0-9654522)* 500 Center Ave. Apt. 211, Westwood, NJ 07675-1677 USA Do not confuse with Metapublishing, North Miami Beach, FL
Dist(s): **New Leaf Distributing Co., Inc.**

Metchnikoff, Elie Memorial Library, *(978-0-9634067)* 230 Orange St., No. 6, Oakland, CA 94610-4139 USA Tel 510-444-3435; Fax: 510-642-7175
E-mail: bibel@lonemountain-art.com.

Metonymy Pr. (CAN) *(978-0-9940471; 978-1-9990588) Dist. by* **SPD-Small Pr Dist.**

Metric Moon Press *See* **Graphite Pr.**

Metrix, *(978-0-692-19417-1)* 13250 W. Lincoln Hwy A502, Dekalb, IL 60115 USA Tel 815-995-7207
E-mail: Cassiemdodd1@gmail.com
Dist(s): **CreateSpace Independent Publishing Platform.**

Metro Bks., *(978-0-9752732)* 1706 W. Jarvis, 1W, Chicago, IL 60626 USA.

Metropolitan Bks. *Imprint of* **Holt, Henry & Co.**

Metropolitan Museum of Art, The, *(978-0-87099; 978-1-58839)* 1000 Fifth Ave., New York, NY 10028 USA (SAN 202-6279) Tel 212-879-5500; Fax: 212-396-5062
Web site: http://www.metmuseum.org
Dist(s): **California Princeton Fulfillment Services**
Casemate Academic
Chicago Distribution Ctr.
Continental Bk. Co., Inc.
Princeton Univ. Pr.
Yale Univ. Pr.

Metropolitan Teaching & Learning Co., *(978-0-928415; 978-1-58120; 978-1-58830)* 317 Madison Ave., New York, NY 10017 USA Tel 212-475-8826; Fax: 212-475-8311; Toll Free: 800-235-6931
Web site: http://metrotlc.com.

Meyer & Meyer Sport, Ltd. (GBR) *(978-1-84126; 978-1-78255) Dist. by* **Cardinal.**

Meyer & Meyer Sport, Ltd. (GBR) *(978-1-84126; 978-1-78255) Dist. by* **Lewis Intl Inc.**

Meyer Enterprises *See* **Western New York Wares, Inc.**

Meyer, Tjaden, *(978-0-9744536)* Orders Addr.: P.O. Box 230015, Saint Louis, MO 63123 USA Tel 314-352-2253; Edit Addr.: 7045 Parkwood St., Saint Louis, MO 63116 USA
E-mail: klmeyer@worldnet.att.net.

Meza, Marti, *(978-0-615-16571-4)* 1515 W. 7th St., Apt. 4-D, Brooklyn, NY 11204 USA
Dist(s): **Lulu Pr., Inc.**

MF Unlimited, *(978-0-9712278)* P.O. Box 55346, Atlanta, GA 30308 USA
Web site: http://www.mfunews.com
Dist(s): **Ingram Content Group.**

Mfg Application Konsulting Engineering, *(978-0-9762208)* 1071 E. 425 N., Ogden, UT 84404 USA.

M-Graphics *Imprint of* **M-Graphics Publishing**

M-Graphics Publishing, *(978-0-9753075; 978-0-9777003; 978-0-9792808; 978-1-934881; 978-1-940220; 978-1-950319)* One Dead Eye Run, Swampscott, MA 01907 USA Tel 781-990-8778 Weekdays 9AM - 4 PM; *Imprints:* M-Graphics (M-Grap)
E-mail: mgraphics.books@gmail.com
Web site: http://www.mgraphics-publishing.com.

M.H. Gill & Co. U. C. (IRL) *(978-0-7171) Dist. by* **Dufour.**

MHC Ministries, *(978-0-9895422)* 1170 NE 133rd St., North Miami, FL 33161 USA Tel 786-286-5210
E-mail: mmuc31@gmail.com
Web site: www.mhcministries.com.

Mia Sharon, Inc., *(978-0-9759098)* 600 Academy Dr., No. 130, Northbrook, IL 60062 USA Tel 847-826-8196
Web site: http://www.miasharon.com.

†Micah Pubns., *(978-0-916288)* 255 Humphrey St., Marblehead, MA 01945 USA (SAN 209-1577) Tel 781-631-7601; Fax: 781-639-0772; Toll Free: 877-268-9963
E-mail: micah@micahbooks.com
Web site: http://www.micahbooks.com
Dist(s): **Book Publishing Co.**
David, Jonathan Pubs., Inc.; *CIP.*

Miceli, *(978-0-9888654)* P.O. Box 2027, Danvers, MA 01923 USA Tel 978-626-1429
E-mail: mary_miceli@comcast.net.

Miceli, Mary Anne, *(978-0-578-08747-4; 978-0-578-10145-3; 978-0-578-10979-4)* 10 Daniels Rd., Wenham, MA 01984 USA; P.O. Box 2027, Danvers, MA 01923
E-mail: mary_miceli@comcast.net
Web site: bostonnorthshorestoriesandpoems.com.

Micelle Pr., Inc., *(978-0-9608752; 978-1-870228)* Orders Addr.: P.O. Box 1519, Port Washington, NY 11050-0306 USA Tel 516-767-7171; Fax: 516-944-9824
E-mail: micellepress@googlemail.com
Web site: http://www.scholium.com
Dist(s): **Scholium International, Inc.**

MiceWorks, *(978-0-9764719)* 544 13th Ave., W., Kirkland, WA 98033 USA.

Michael Neugebauer Bks. *Imprint of* **North-South Bks., Inc.**

Michael-Christopher Bks., *(978-0-9710398)* Orders Addr.: P.O. Box 75313, Washington, DC 20013-0313 USA Tel 301-927-3179
E-mail: mc@michael-christopher.com
Web site: http://www.michael-christopher.com
Dist(s): **BookBaby.**

MichaelsMind LLC *See* **Right Stuff Kids Bks.**

Michaelson Entertainment, *(978-0-9727702; 978-1-932530; 978-1-60730)* 36 Cabrillo Terr., Aliso Viejo, CA 92656 USA Tel 949-916-0575 phone; Fax: 949-916-0574 fax; *Imprints:* 101 Book (101 Bk); ABC Book (ABCBk)
E-mail: brad@michaelsonentertainment.com
Web site: http://www.michaelsonentertainment.com
Dist(s): **Partners Bk. Distributing, Inc.**

Michalek, Curtis, *(978-0-9786177)* P.O. Box 403, Montezuma, IA 50171 USA Tel 641-623-3368
E-mail: c.a.michalek@hotmail.com
Web site: www.aluris.com.

Michele, Mary, *(978-0-615-25486-9)* 27638 N. 45th Way, Cave Creek, AZ 85331 USA Tel 602-952-8604
E-mail: scriptsrelief@cox.net
Dist(s): **Lulu Pr., Inc.**

Michelle, Patrice *See* **Limitless Ink Press, LLC**

michelle s lazurek-author, *(978-0-692-89435-4; 978-0-692-18987-0)* 3 alliance ave, coudersport, PA 16915 USA Tel 814-274-9298
E-mail: michellelazurek@yahoo.com
Web site: www.michellelazurek.com.

Michelle's A & E (KOR) *(978-89-954869) Dist. by* **APG.**

Michelle's Bks. & More, Ltd. Co., *(978-0-9763080)* 800 Fabric X-Press Way, Dallas, TX 75234 USA Tel 972-625-1444; Fax: 972-406-1321
E-mail: michelle@michellesbooks.com
Web site: http://www.michellesbooks.com.

Michelle's Designs, *(978-0-9789694; 978-0-9817663; 978-0-9842520)* 3702 Sandpoint Ct, Carlsbad, CA 92010 USA Tel 760-720-4335; Fax: 802-609-2629
E-mail: patterns@michelles-designs.com; jen@condormedia.com
Web site: http://www.michelles-designs.com.

Michigan Publishing, *(978-0-9745109; 978-1-4181; 978-1-4255; 978-1-60785; 978-1-64315)* Div. of University of Michigan Library, 1210 Buhr Bldg. 839 Greene St., Ann Arbor, MI 48109 USA (SAN 255-9889)
E-mail: spo.pod@umich.edu; lib.pod@umich.edu
Web site: http://www.lib.umich.edu/michigan-publishing
Dist(s): **Chicago Distribution Ctr.**

Michigan State Univ., Julian Samora Research Institute, *(978-0-9650557)* 301 Nisbet Bldg., 1407 S. Harrison, East Lansing, MI 48823-586 USA Tel 517-432-1317; Fax: 517-432-2221
E-mail: info@jsri.msu.edu
Web site: http://jsri.msu.edu.

†Michigan State Univ. Pr., *(978-0-87013; 978-0-937191; 978-1-60917; 978-1-61186; 978-1-938065; 978-1-62895; 978-1-62896; 978-1-941258; 978-0-9967252; 978-1-68430; 978-1-947134; 978-1-948314)* Orders Addr.: 1405 S. Harrison Rd. Suite 25, East Lansing, MI 48823-5245 USA (SAN 202-6295) Tel 517-884-6901; Fax: 517-432-2611; Toll Free: 800-621-2736; 800-621-8476
E-mail: msupress@msupress.org
Web site: http://www.msupress.org
Dist(s): **Chicago Distribution Ctr.**; *CIP.*

mickego art, *(978-0-692-89076-9; 978-0-692-16315-3)* 12257 Hill Rd., Swartz Creek, MI 48473 USA Tel 989-277-1585
Dist(s): **Ingram Content Group.**

Micro Publishing Media, Inc., *(978-0-9827716; 978-1-936517; 978-1-944068; 978-1-953321)* 29 Pk. St., Stockbridge, MA 01262 USA; *Imprints:* Pop Pop Press (Pop Pop Pr)
E-mail: Deborah@micropublishingmedia.com
Web site: http://www.micropublishingmedia.com
Dist(s): **Cardinal Pubs. Group.**

Microcosm Publishing, *(978-0-9726967; 978-0-9770557; 978-0-9788665; 978-1-934620; 978-1-62106; 978-1-64841)* Orders Addr.: 2752 N. Williams Ave., Portland, OR 97227 USA Toll Free Fax: 888-503-0599; *Imprints:* Microcosmos (Microcosmos)
E-mail: joe@microcosmpublishing.com
Web site: http://www.microcosmpublishing.com
Dist(s): **Baker & Taylor Publisher Services (BTPS)**
Publishers Group West (PGW).

Microcosmos *Imprint of* **Microcosm Publishing**

Microsoft Pr. *Imprint of* **Pearson Education**

†Microsoft Pr., *(978-0-7356; 978-0-914845; 978-0-925550; 978-1-55615; 978-1-57231; 978-1-879021)* Orders Addr.: 3 Center Plaza, Boston, MA 02108-2084 USA Toll Free: 800-677-7377; Edit Addr.: One Microsoft Way, Redmond, WA 98052-6399 USA (SAN 264-9969) Tel 425-882-8080; 206-882-8080; 425-703-0942; Fax: 425-936-7329 Do not confuse with Microsoft Pr., Dunmore, PA
E-mail: msporder@msn.com; duanedr@microsoft.com; chriscai@microsoft.com
Web site: http://www.microsoft.com/mspress/
Dist(s): **Follett School Solutions**
Pearson Education; *CIP.*

Mid Ohio Chiropractic, *(978-0-9989090; 978-1-7346488)* 714 N. Sandusky Aveunue, Upper SAndusky, OH 43351 USA Tel 419-294-0832
E-mail: BettyLok@live.com.

Mid-Atlantic Highlands Publishing *Imprint of* **Publishers Place, Inc.**

Middelhauve Verlags GmbH (DEU) *(978-3-7876) Dist. by* **Distribks Inc.**

†Middle Atlantic Pr., *(978-0-912608; 978-0-9705804; 978-0-9754419)* 400 Pond View Dr., Moorestown, NJ 08057 USA Tel 856-273-9062; Fax: 856-273-7526
E-mail: blake@middleatlanticpress.com; info@middleatlanticpress.com
Web site: http://www.middleatlanticpress.com
Dist(s): **Partners Bk. Distributing, Inc.**; *CIP.*

Middle River Pr., *(978-0-9785656; 978-0-9817036; 978-0-9846071; 978-0-9838203; 978-0-9857295; 978-0-9896724; 978-0-9964086; 978-1-946886)* 1498 NE 30th Ct., Oakland Park, FL 33334-4414 USA Tel 954-630-8192
E-mail: info@middleriverpress.com
Web site: http://www.middleriverpress.com.

Middleburry Hse. Publishing, *(978-0-9792067)* 3225 Middleburry Ln., Charleston, SC 29414 USA
Web site: http://www.rwridley.com; http://www.choytcaldwell.com.

Middleton Classics *See* **Middleton Publishing**

Middleton Publishing, *(978-0-9787871; 978-1-935702; 978-1-63104)* P.O. Box 226, Williamstown, NY 13493 USA (SAN 851-6308)
Web site: http://www.uniquecoloring.com.

Midnight Hologram, LLC, *(978-1-938516)* 1180 Beacon Hill Crossing, Alpharetta, GA 30005 USA Tel 678-393-0420
E-mail: yvet77@comcast.net
Web site: www.midnighthologram.com.

Midpoint Trade Bks., Inc., *(978-1-940416)* Orders Addr.: 1263 Southwest Blvd., Kansas City, KS 66103 USA (SAN 631-3736) Tel 913-831-2233; Fax: 913-362-7401; Toll Free: 800-742-6139 (consumer orders); Edit Addr.: 27 W. 20th St., No. 1102, New York, NY 10011 USA (SAN 631-1075) Tel 212-727-0190; Fax: 212-727-0195
E-mail: info@midpointtrade.com
Web site: http://www.midpointtrade.com; http://www.midpointtradebooks.com/
Dist(s): **Ingram Bk. Co.**
ebrary, Inc.

MidRun Pr., *(978-0-9664095; 978-0-9824397)* 90 Larch Row, Wenham, MA 01984-1624 USA Tel 978-468-9953 (phone/fax)
E-mail: midrunpress@aol.com
Web site: http://www.midrunpress.com.

Midwest Christian Center *See* **Family Harvest Church**

Midwest Cylinder Management, Inc., *(978-0-9729026)* 1203 Paramount Pkwy., Batavia, IL 60510-1458 USA Tel 630-673-9770; Fax: 630-406-9922
E-mail: prminalt@yahoo.com
Web site: http://www.kidsmenus.com.

Midwest Graphics, Inc., *(978-0-9776893)* 180 N. Wacker Dr., Suite 104, Chicago, IL 60606 USA Tel 312-641-2236; Fax: 312-641-2256
E-mail: mark@mwgchicago.com
Web site: http://www.mwgchicago.com.

Midwest Screen and Media Production *See* **Kathryn Sommer**

Midwest Writng, *(978-0-9778290; 978-0-9818089; 978-0-9834116; 978-0-9906190; 978-1-7334802)* c/o RIPL 401 19th St., Rock Island, IL 61201 USA Tel 309-732-7330
Web site: http://www.mwcqc.org.

Mielcarek, David, *(978-0-9785480)* 3387 Ocean Beach Hwy, Longview, WA 98632 USA
E-mail: thebook@timeforyourmind.com
Web site: http://timeforyourmind.com.

Mighty Kids Media, *(978-0-9765953; 978-0-9770455; 978-1-933934; 978-0-9884241)* 4201 Congress St, Suite 451, Charlotte, NC 28209 USA Toll Free Fax: 877-723-3388 Do not confuse with companies with the same name in Dobbs Ferry, NY, Medofrd, OR, Lanett, AL
Web site: http://www.dangerrangers.com.

Mighty Lion Ventures, *(978-0-615-30860-9; 978-0-9831449)* P.O. Box 2950, Cypress, TX 77410 USA.

Mighty Media Junior Readers *Imprint of* **Mighty Media Pr.**

Mighty Media Kids *Imprint of* **Mighty Media Pr.**

Mighty Media Pr., *(978-0-9765201; 978-0-9798249; 978-0-9824584; 978-0-9830219; 978-1-938063)* Div. of Mighty Media, 1201 Currie Ave., Minneapolis, MN 55403 USA Tel 612-455-0252; Fax: 612-338-4817; *Imprints:* Mighty Media Junior Readers (MMJrRead); Mighty Media Kids (MMKids)
E-mail: info@scarlettapress.com; josh@scarlettapress.com
Web site: http://www.mightymediapress.com
Dist(s): **Continental Enterprises Group, Inc. (CEG)**
MyiLibrary
Publishers Group West (PGW).

Mighty Publishing, LLC, *(978-0-9966739)* 701 Niagara St, Denver, CO 80220 USA Tel 303-355-3120
E-mail: kbcinspires@gmail.com.

Miglior Pr., *(978-0-9827614; 978-0-9836484)* P.O. Box 7487, Athens, GA 30604 USA Tel 706-338-0017
E-mail: info@migliorpress.com
Web site: http://migliorpress.com.

Mijade Editions (BEL) *(978-2-87142) Dist. by* **Distribks Inc.**

Mikaya Pr., *(978-0-9650493; 978-1-931414)* 12 Bedford St., New York, NY 10014 USA Tel 212-647-1831; Fax: 212-727-0236
E-mail: Waldman@Mikaya.com
Web site: http://www.mikaya.com
Dist(s): **Firefly Bks., Ltd.**

Mikazuki Jujitsu *See* **Mikazuki Publishing Hse.**

Mikazuki Publishing Hse., *(978-0-615-47311-6; 978-0-615-48054-1; 978-0-9835946; 978-1-937981; 978-0-9910285; 978-1-942825)* 530 E. 8th St. Suite 400, Los Angeles, CA 90014 USA Tel 010-982-2379
E-mail: kambizmostofizadeh1@gmail.com
Web site: http://www.MikazukiPublishing.com
Dist(s): **BookBaby**
Ingram Content Group.

Mike-Auri Bks., *(978-0-9747587)* P.O. Box 420966, Del Rio, TX 78842 USA Tel 830-774-2789
E-mail: dfitzgibbon@stx.rr.com
Web site: http://www.texasredhen.com; http://www.mikeauri.com.

Mike-Mike Distribution, *(978-0-9741043)* 1003 N., Fifth St., Champaign, IL 61820 USA Tel 217-352-4215.

Mikenzi's Kardz & Bks. Llc., *(978-0-9792647)* 1115 S. Alhambra Cir., Coral Gables, FL 33146-3711 USA
E-mail: sgbarrow@hotmail.com.

Milano, Jacque & Assocs., *(978-0-9728432)* 700 N. Dobson Rd., No. 15, Chandler, AZ 85224 USA; *Imprints:* Carefree Publishing (Carefree Pubng)
Web site: http://www.carefreepublishing.com.

Mile High Pr., Ltd., *(978-1-885331)* Div. of Briles Group, Inc., Orders Addr.: P.O. Box 460880, Aurora, CO 80046 USA Tel 303-627-9179; Fax: 303-627-9184; Toll Free: 800-594-0800; Edit Addr.: 14160 E. Bellewood Dr., Aurora, CO 80015 USA Tel 303-745-4590
E-mail: info@milehighpress.com; milehighpress@aol.com.

Mile Oak Publishing, Inc. (CAN) *(978-1-896819) Dist. by* **Austin and Co.**

Miles & Assocs., *(978-0-9778623)* P.O. Box 15566, Phoenix, AZ 85060 USA Tel 386-446-9291
E-mail: drlinda03@aol.com
Web site: http://www.thenewmarriage.com.

Miles Kelly Publishing, Ltd. (GBR) *(978-1-902947; 978-1-84236; 978-1-84810; 978-1-78209; 978-1-78617) Dist. by* **Parkwest Pubns.**

Miles, Linda *See* **Miles & Assocs.**

Miles Music, *(978-0-9710446)* Div. of Miles Enterprises, 3060 Larson Rd., Weippe, ID 83553 USA Tel 208-435-4600; Fax: 208-435-1116
E-mail: milesmusic@idamail.com
Web site: http://www.idamall.com.

Milestone Pr., Inc., *(978-0-9631861; 978-1-889596)* Orders Addr.: P.O. Box 158, Almond, NC 28702 USA Tel 828-488-6601 (phone/fax)
E-mail: maryellenhammond@milestonepress.com
Web site: http://www.milestonepress.com
Dist(s): **America's Cycling Pubns.**
Common Ground Distributors, Inc.

Milestones Publishing, *(978-0-9786154)* P.O. Box 1556, Wylie, TX 75098 USA Tel 214-403-9852; Fax: 972-442-1613
E-mail: kaylasadams@hotmail.com
Web site: http://www.kaylaadams.net.

Milet Publishing, *(978-1-84059)* P.O. Box 2459, Chicago, IL 60690-2459 USA
E-mail: info@milet.com
Web site: http://www.milet.com
Dist(s): **Chinasprout, Inc.**
Independent Pubs. Group
Tuttle Publishing.

Milk & Cookies *Imprint of* **ibooks, Inc.**

Milk Mug Publishing, *(978-0-9721882)* 9190 W. Olympic Blvd., Suite 253, Beverly Hills, CA 90212 USA Tel 310-278-1153 (phone/fax)
E-mail: orders@thehoopsterbook.com
Web site: http://www.thehoopsterbook.com
Dist(s): **SCB Distributors.**

Milken Family Foundation, *(978-0-9646425)* 1250 Fourth St., 4th Flr., Santa Monica, CA 90404-1353 USA Tel 310-998-2825; Fax: 310-998-2899
E-mail: jboone@mff.org
Web site: http://www.milkenexchange.org.

Milkweed Editions, *(978-0-915943; 978-1-57131)* 1011 Washington Ave. S., Suite 300, Minneapolis, MN 55415-1246 USA (SAN 294-0671) Tel 612-332-3192; Fax: 612-215-2550; Toll Free: 800-520-6455
E-mail: market@milkweed.org
Web site: http://www.milkweed.org; http://www.worldashome.org
Dist(s): **MyiLibrary**
Publishers Group West (PGW).

Mill City Press, Inc *Imprint of* **Salem Author Services**

Mill Creek Metro Publishing, *(978-0-9741989)* P.O. Box 90134, Youngstown, OH 44509 USA Tel 330-797-0024
E-mail: ianjcue@ianjcue.com
Web site: http://www.ianjcue.com
Dist(s): **Book Clearing Hse.**

Mill Creek Pr., *(978-0-9897760; 978-0-9916474; 978-1-942236; 978-1-951085)* 2308 Mt Vernon Ave Suite 408, Alexandria, VA 22301 USA Tel 703-638-8395; *Imprints:* At Home With Cristin (MYID_U_AT HOME)
E-mail: cristin@cristinharber.com.

Mill Park Publishing, *(978-0-9728225; 978-0-9883980; 978-0-9975871)* E & M Group, LLC, 6676 N Double Eagle Ln, Meridian, ID 83616 USA Tel 208-890-8122
E-mail: elaine@elaineambrose.com; elaine@millparkpublishing.com
Web site: http://www.Elaineambrose.com; www.millparkpublishing.com
Dist(s): **Lulu Pr., Inc.**

Mill Street Forward, The, *(978-0-9654628)* 15 1/2 Van Houten St., Apt. 117, Paterson, NJ 07505 USA Tel 973-345-9539.

Millbrook Pr. *Imprint of* **Lerner Publishing Group**

Millennial Mind Publishing *Imprint of* **American Bk. Publishing Group**

Millennium Marketing & Publishing, *(978-1-886161)* 2455 Glen Hill Dr., Indianapolis, IN 46240-3460 USA Tel 317-815-9828; Fax: 317-815-9829
E-mail: MMPbooks@comcast.net
Web site: http://www.chicksguidetofootball.com
Dist(s): **Cardinal Pubs. Group**
Journey Pubns., LLC
Quality Bks., Inc.

Millennium Workshop Production, *(978-0-9725344)* 11501 Maple Ridge Rd., Reston, VA 20190-3604 USA (SAN 255-1624) Tel 703-925-0610 (phone/fax)
E-mail: victor@millenniumworkshop.com
Web site: http://www.millenniumworkshop.com.

Miller, Ann *See* **Jaylil Publishing Co.**

Miller, Bruce, *(978-0-9765598)* 10011 Bridgeport Way SW., Suite 1500 PMB128, Lakewood, WA 98499 USA Tel 253-227-2292
E-mail: warofpowers@comcast.net.

Miller, Deanna, *(978-0-9725424)* 12215 Fuller St., Silver Spring, MD 20902 USA
E-mail: info@deannamiller.com
Web site: http://www.deannamiller.com.

Miller, Debra Juanita, *(978-0-9706782; 978-0-9776014)* P.O. Box 20593, Chicago, IL 60620 USA
E-mail: monogrambooklets@yahoo.com; djpmspinsstories@yahoo.com.

Miller, Don G., *(978-0-615-12836-8)* 5051 S. 172nd. St., Omaha, NE 68135 USA.

Miller, Elizabeth, *(978-0-692-10115-5; 978-0-692-10126-1)* 6641 Golf Club Dr., Longmont, CO 80503 USA Tel 303-949-1932
E-mail: liz.w.miller@icloud.com
Dist(s): **Ingram Content Group.**

Miller, J. Cris & Assocs., *(978-0-9725308)* 10555 W. 74th St., Countryside, IL 60525 USA Tel 708-579-1707 (phone/fax)
E-mail: jcmtales@hotmail.com.

Miller, J. Garnet Ltd. (GBR) *(978-0-85343) Dist. by* **Empire Pub Srvs.**

Miller, Michael, *(978-0-9723474; 978-0-9743522; 978-0-9825155; 978-0-9839356)* 2418 Hagerman St., Colorado Springs, CO 80904 USA Tel 719-600-9315; Fax: 501-421-1495
E-mail: michael@mail.sabineundmichael.com
Web site: http://www.sabineundmichael.com.

Miller, Peter Mitchell *See* **Silver Print Pr., Inc.**

Miller, Randy, *(978-0-9770530)* 17 N. Rd., Alstead, NH 03602 USA Tel 603-835-7889
E-mail: jrmiller@sover.net
Web site: http://www.randymillerprints.com.

Miller, Sharon, *(978-0-9774756)* 4544 Foco Rd., Standish, MI 48658 USA
E-mail: sjmlady@gmail.com.

Miller, Smit Enterprises, *(978-0-9769433)* 112 Misty Creek Dr., Colorado Springs, CO 80132-6032 USA
E-mail: dawn@dawnsmit.com.

MillerWords, *(978-0-615-94052-6; 978-0-692-41237-4; 978-0-692-48617-7; 978-0-692-56102-7; 978-0-692-61478-5; 978-0-692-63441-7; 978-0-692-65983-0; 978-0-692-66359-2; 978-0-692-74074-3; 978-0-692-74075-0; 978-0-692-74141-2; 978-0-9982986; 978-0-9996195; 978-1-7342676) P.O. Box 322, Lansing, KS 66043 USA Tel 352-385-4499*
E-mail: mark@millerwords.com
Web site: www.millerwords.com
Dist(s): **CreateSpace Independent Publishing Platform.**

MillerWrite, Inc., *(978-0-9723948)* 2875-F Northtowne Ln., No. 302, Reno, NV 89512-2062 USA Tel 775-673-2152
E-mail: chrisshelton78@msn.com; jmiller@millerwrite.com
Web site: http://www.millerwrite.com.

Millfree Mursaps Media, *(978-0-9904093; 978-1-7327873)* Orders Addr.: P.O. Box 52772, New Orleans, LA 70152 USA Tel 504-233-3369
E-mail: ryan@millfreemursaps.com
Web site: millfreemursaps.com
Dist(s): **Independent Pubs. Group.**

Milligan Books *See* **Professional Publishing Hse. LLC**

Million Words Publishing, LLC, *(978-1-891282; 978-0-578-47415-1)* 1946 Mora Ln., Jennings, MO 63136 USA.

Millman, Selena, *(978-0-9793058; 978-0-9794584; 978-0-9795756; 978-0-9798417; 978-0-9798603; 978-0-9802400; 978-0-615-15137-3; 978-0-615-23804-3; 978-0-578-00466-2; 978-0-578-00564-5)* 4984 Ridgebury, Lyndhurst, OH 44124 USA
Web site: http://www.freewebs.com/heal4michael
Dist(s): **Lulu Pr., Inc.**

Millmark Education, *(978-1-4334; 978-1-61618)* Orders Addr.: 7272 Wisconsin Ave, Suite 300, Bethesda, MD 20814-2081 USA (SAN 852-4912) Tel 301-941-1974; Fax: 301-656-0183; Edit Addr.: 7272 Wisconsin Ave. Suite 300, Suite 300, Bethesda, MD 20814-2081 USA
E-mail: rachel.moir@millmarkeducation.com; info@millmarkeducation.com
Web site: http://www.millmarkeducation.com/.

Mills & Morris Publishing Corporation *See* **Bluebonnets, Boots & Bks. Pr.**

Milner Crest Publishing, LLC, *(978-0-9820651)* P.O. Box 10754, Portland, OR 97296-0754 USA (SAN 857-1376)
E-mail: danielbruton@gmail.com
Web site: http://www.milnercrestpublishing.com
Dist(s): **BookBaby.**

Milner, Ommi, *(978-0-692-16998-8)* 8180 Vincetta Dr, LA MESA, CA 91942 USA Tel 619-254-0696
E-mail: ommi.milner@hotmail.com.

Milo Educational Bks. & Resources, *(978-1-933668; 978-1-60698)* P.O. Box 41353, Houston, TX 77241-1353 USA Tel 713-466-6456; Fax: 713-896-6456
E-mail: milo_books@yahoo.com
Web site: http://www.miloeducationalbooks.com.

MiLo Ink Bks., *(978-0-615-70687-0; 978-0-9910909)* 10353 Sophia Ave., Granada Hills, CA 91344 USA
Dist(s): **CreateSpace Independent Publishing Platform.**

Milstein & Hauptman Publishing *See* **Wonderful Publishing**

Miltenberg, Robert Allen, *(978-0-615-63925-3; 978-0-615-66467-5; 978-0-615-77522-7; 978-0-9893031)* 210 LIME KEY Ln., NAPLES, FL 34114 USA Tel 310-994-2407
E-mail: Rmiltenberg@yahoo.com
Web site: www.blurb.com; www.artworq.com.

MiMar Publishing, *(978-0-9754241; 978-0-615-16688-9; 978-0-615-16689-6)* 714 Enchanted Rock Trail, Georgetown, TX 78633 USA
Web site: http://www.bakerstreetbunch.com
Dist(s): **Lulu Pr., Inc.**

Mimaxion, *(978-1-68321)* 40 E. Main St., Newark, DE 19711 USA (SAN 990-0896)
E-mail: cedric.dufay@gmail.com; admin@speedypublishing.com
Web site: http://www.mimaxion.com/.

Mimi Bee Pubns., *(978-0-9745944)* Orders Addr.: P.O. Box 188, Accord, NY 12404 USA
E-mail: mimibee@att.com
Web site: http://mrallergyhead.com.

Mimi's Funhouse, LLC, *(978-0-9841589)* 10611A Crystal Cove Dr., Magnolia, TX 77354 USA
Web site: http://www.mimisfunhouse.com.

Mims Hse., *(978-0-9798621; 978-0-9852134; 978-1-62944)* 1309 S. Broadway, Little Rock, AR 72209 USA
Web site: mimshouse.com.

Minardi Photography, *(978-1-878444)* 5501 Harvest Scene Ct., Columbia, MD 21044 USA Tel 410-964-5403; Fax: 410-964-5643.

Minch, John Publishing, *(978-0-9631090; 978-0-9990251)* 27441 Betanzos, Mission Viejo, CA 92692 USA Tel 714-501-4162
E-mail: jmainc@earthlink.net.

Mind - Stretch, *(978-0-9676409)* 3124 Landrum Rd., Columbus, NC 28722 USA Tel 828-863-4235; Fax: 828-863-2584; Toll Free: 888-538-8911
E-mail: marklevin@alltel.net
Web site: http://www.mindstretch.com.

Mind Candy, LLC, *(978-0-9786929)* P.O. Box 2185, Garden City, NY 11531-2185 USA (SAN 851-3392) Tel 516-318-4433
Web site: http://mindcandymedia.com.

Mind Trip Press *See* **Big Ransom Studio**

Mindanao Publishing Co., *(978-0-9710841)* 1222 Hazel St., N., Saint. Paul, MN 55119-4500 USA Tel 651-274-6602; Fax: 651-771-9772
E-mail: jararick@worldnet.att.net
Web site: http://www.sanpedrocollege.org; http://www.eslseminarschina.org; http://www.eslseminars.org; http://www.ielts4nurses.org.

Mind/Body Workshops, *(978-0-9748548)* 131 S. Euclid, Westfield, NJ 07090 USA Tel 718-273-3682
Web site: http://www.kickoutstress.com.

Mindcastle Bks., Inc., *(978-0-9677204)* Orders Addr.: P.O. Box 3005, Woodinville, WA 98072 USA Tel 425-424-8860; Fax: 425-398-1354
E-mail: vanessa@mindcastle.com
Web site: http://www.mindcastle.com.

MindCatcher Pr., *(978-0-9724113)* 284 Mattison Dr., Concord, MA 01742 USA Tel 978-369-7868
E-mail: marian@mindcatcherpress.com
Web site: http://www.mindcatcherpress.com; http://www.readylady.com.

Mindful Matters LLC, *(978-0-692-05033-0)* P.O. Box 3, Hazlet, NJ 07730 USA Tel 908-358-5249
E-mail: nikki@mindfulmattersliving.com
Web site: www.mindfulmattersliving.com.

Mindful Wonders, LLC, *(978-0-578-67378-3; 978-0-578-68214-3)* 1187 40th Ave NE 0, ST PETERSBURG, FL 33703 USA Tel 4402125110
E-mail: mindfulwonders@gmail.com
Web site: www.mindfulwonders.com
Dist(s): **Ingram Content Group.**

Mindfull Publishing, *(978-0-9669551)* 177 W. Norwalk Rd., Norwalk, CT 06850 USA Tel 203-831-0855
E-mail: mindfullpub@hotmail.com
Web site: http://www.homestead.com/mindfullpublishing/.

Mindfull Publishing Co., *(978-0-9720308)* Orders Addr.: P.O. Box 34, Clairton, PA 15025 USA Toll Free: 888-946-0816; Edit Addr.: 329 Mitchell Ave., Clairton, PA 15025 USA
E-mail: gbberryauthor@yahoo.com.

MindMaze Publishing Co., *(978-0-9747668)* P.O. Box 251278, Woodbury, MN 55125 USA
E-mail: mindmaze@comcast.net.

Mindo Pr., *(978-0-9747971)* P.O. Box 34, Danielsville, PA 18038-9754 USA
E-mail: rshade@fast.net.

MindOH! Foundation, The, *(978-0-9773689)* 2525 Robinhood St., Houston, TX 77005 USA (SAN 257-3741) Tel 713-533-1138 Toll Free: 866-646-3641
Web site: http://www.mindohfoundation.org.

Mindset CS, *(978-0-9989794)* 123 2nd St. Apt 1, Laurel, MD 20707 USA Tel 202-696-0487
E-mail: sudanrr@yahoo.com
Web site: createmindset.com.

Mindsong Math, *(978-0-9758592)* 7757 N. Basin Way, Boise, ID 83714 USA Tel 208-371-7668
E-mail: karlalaland@gmail.com
Web site: http://www.thewhaleslibrary.com.

Publisher Name Index

MindsOrb, Inc., *(978-0-9741877)* P.O. Box 162706, Austin, TX 78716 USA
Web site: http://www.mindsorb.com.

Mindstir Media, *(978-0-9819648; 978-0-9836771; 978-0-9853650; 978-0-9858398; 978-0-9883162; 978-0-9885180; 978-0-9886409; 978-0-9889595; 978-0-9890288; 978-0-9892711; 978-0-9894748; 978-0-9897168; 978-0-9898820; 978-0-9910324; 978-0-9911512; 978-0-9913190; 978-0-9914884; 978-0-9916230; 978-0-9903626; 978-0-9906106; 978-0-9908137; 978-0-9862149; 978-0-9863057; 978-0-9961434; 978-0-9962872; 978-0-9964615; 978-0-9967294; 978-0-9969689; 978-0-9970334; 978-0-9972233; 978-0-9973575; 978-0-9975435; 978-0-9977466;) 1931 Woodbury Ave. No. 182, Portsmouth, NH 03801 USA Toll Free: 800-767-0531*
Web site: www.mindstirmedia.com
Dist(s): **Smashwords.**

MindWare Holdings, Inc., *(978-0-9648481; 978-1-892069; 978-1-933054; 978-1-936300)* 2100 County Rd. C W., Roseville, MN 55113 USA (SAN 859-9157) Fax: 651-582-0556; Toll Free: 800-999-0398
Web site: http://mindware.com.

Mindwing Concepts, Inc., *(978-0-9761393; 978-0-9769527; 978-0-9791307; 978-0-9792917; 978-0-9793185; 978-0-9816818; 978-0-9996043)* 1 Federal St. Bldg. 103-1, Springfield, MA 01105 USA Toll Free: 888-228-9746
Web site: http://www.mindwingconcepts.com.

MindWorks Pr., *(978-1-886554)* 4019 Westerly Pl., Suite 108, Newport Beach, CA 92660 USA (SAN 850-4873) Tel 949.266.3714; Fax: 949.266.3770; Toll Free: 800-626-2720
E-mail: mindworkspress@aol.com; sposs@amenclinic.com
Web site: http://www.mindworkspress.com
Dist(s): **Lulu Pr., Inc.**

Mine Rich In Gems *Imprint of* **InnerPrize Group, LLC**

Minecraft Interactive *See* **Interactive Stories**

Minerva Bks., *(978-0-9620125)* Div. of Hulbert Performance Rating, Inc., 316 Commerce St., Alexandria, VA 22314 USA (SAN 247-493X) Tel 703-683-5905 Do not confuse with companies with the same or similar name in Palo Alto, CA, New York, NY, Louisville, KY.

Minerva Bks., Ltd., *(978-0-8056)* 30 W. 26th St., New York, NY 10010 USA (SAN 205-8367) Tel 212-675-0465; Fax: 212-675-0573 Do not confuse with companies with the same or similar name in Alexandria, VA, Palo Alto, CA, Louisville, KY
Dist(s): **Continental Bk. Co., Inc.**
Lectorum Pubns., Inc.

Mini Enterprises - M.E. *See* **AGB Publishing**

Minikin Pr., *(978-0-9772320)* P.O. Box 528, Barrington, RI 02806-0280 USA (SAN 257-0076) Tel 401-245-7960
E-mail: jill@minikinpress.com
Web site: http://www.minikinpress.com.

Minimal Pr., The, *(978-0-9742516; 978-0-615-25627-6; 978-0-615-25629-0; 978-0-9824665)* 406 Colchester Ave., Burlington, VT 05401 USA
Dist(s): **Lulu Pr., Inc.**

Mink, Connie J *See* **Saturn Music & Entertainment**

Minko, Alyssa, *(978-0-692-09217-0)* 131 Oak Mills Crossing, WEST HENRIETTA, NY 14586 USA Tel 724-575-2210
E-mail: btswu.art@gmail.com
Dist(s): **Ingram Content Group.**

Minna Pr., *(978-0-9829630; 978-1-7324034; 978-1-7353069)* 108 Hamilton Ave., Lehigh Acres, FL 33936 USA Tel 239-308-6139
E-mail: lj1838@gmail.com
Dist(s): **BookBaby.**

Minna Press & Inspire Publications *See* **Minna Pr.**

Minnesota Assn. for Children's Mental Health, *(978-0-9820482)* 165 Western Ave., N., Suite 2, Saint Paul, MN 55102 USA Tel 651-644-7333; Fax: 651-644-7391; Toll Free: 800-528-4511
E-mail: info@macmh.org
Web site: http://www.macmh.org.

Minnesota Department of Economic Security *See* **Minnesota Dept. Employment & Economic Development**

Minnesota Dept. Employment & Economic Development, *(978-0-9670505; 978-0-9845780; 978-0-615-50484-1)* 332 Minnesota St. Ste. E200, Saint Paul, MN 55101-1349 USA Toll Free: 888-234-1114
E-mail: Amy.yerkes@state.mn.us
Web site: http://www.positivelyminnesota.com.

†Minnesota Historical Society Pr., *(978-0-87351; 978-1-68134)* Orders Addr.: 11030 S. Langley Ave., Chicago, IL 60628 USA Toll Free Fax: 800-621-8476; Toll Free: 800-621-2736; Edit Addr.: 345 Kellogg Blvd., W., Saint Paul, MN 55102-1906 USA (SAN 202-6384) Tel 651-297-2221; 651-259-3202; Fax: 651-297-1345; Toll Free: 800-647-7827; *Imprints:* Borealis Book (Borealis Book)
E-mail: greg.britton@mnhs.org
Web site: http://www.mnhs.org/mhspress; mnhspress.org
Dist(s): **BookMobile**
Chicago Distribution Ctr.
Ingram Publisher Services; *CIP.*

Minnesota Humanities Ctr., *(978-0-9629298; 978-1-931016; 978-0-578-03464-5; 978-0-9884539)* 987 E. Ivy Ave., Saint Paul, MN 55106-2046 USA Tel 651-774-0105 Toll Free: 866-268-7293
E-mail: info@minnesotahumanities.org
Web site: http://www.minnesotahumanities.org.

Minnesota Humanities Commission *See* **Minnesota Humanities Ctr.**

Minnesota's Bookstore, *(978-0-9647451; 978-0-9754338)* 660 Olive St., Saint Paul, MN 55155 USA Tel 651-297-3000; Fax: 651-215-5733; Toll Free: 800-657-3757
E-mail: mnbookstore@state.mn.us
Web site: http://www.minnesotasbookstore.com
Dist(s): **Univ. of Texas Pr.**

Minnewaska Pr., *(978-0-9799410)* 1406 S Darling Dr. NW, Alexandria, MN 56308 USA
E-mail: minnewaskapress@yahoo.com
Web site: http://www.debmercier.com.

Minnie Troy Pubs., *(978-0-9727480; 978-0-9997346)* Div. of Historically Speaking, 309 Union St., Murfreesboro, NC 27855 USA Tel 252-398-5098
E-mail: lion5098@aol.com.

Minon, S.A. (ESP) *(978-84-355) Dist. by* **Lectorum Pubns.**

Minotaur Bks. *Imprint of* **St. Martin's Pr.**

Minotauro Ediciones (ESP) *(978-84-450) Dist. by* **Planeta.**

Minotauro Ediciones (ESP) *(978-84-450) Dist. by* **Distribks Inc.**

Minotauro Ediciones (ESP) *(978-84-450) Dist. by* **Lectorum Pubns.**

Minted Prose, LLC, *(978-0-9744287; 978-0-9905721; 978-0-9965454)* 176 Broadway, Suite 11A, New York, NY 10038 USA (SAN 255-6138) Tel 646-789-7368; Fax: 347-493-3545
E-mail: linda@mintedprose.com
Web site: http://www.mintedprose.com; http://www.traitordachshund.com
Dist(s): **CreateSpace Independent Publishing Platform**
Independent Pubs. Group
MyiLibrary.

Minton, Art, *(978-0-615-15948-5)* Orders Addr.: P.O. Box 16294, Jackson, MS 39236-6294 USA Tel 601-966-6699; Fax: 206-202-3329; Edit Addr.: 1939 Cherokee Dr., jackson, MS 39211 USA
E-mail: rentjackson@gmail.com
Web site: http://birdingforchildren.com.

Minuteman Press of Green Bay *See* **EPS Digital**

Mira Pr., The, *(978-0-9762947)* P.O. Box 590207, Newton Centre, MA 02459 USA.

Miracle Pr., *(978-0-929889)* 2808 W. Lexington Way, Edmond, OK 73003-4224 USA (SAN 250-975X) Tel 405-359-0369; Fax: 703-883-1861
E-mail: miraclepress@cox.net.

Miraculous Fingerprints Pubs., *(978-1-886134)* 74565 Dillon Rd., MH 15, Desert Hot Springs, CA 92241 USA Tel 760-251-3037.

Miramax Bks., *(978-0-7868; 978-1-4013; 978-1-4464)* Div. of Walt Disney Productions, 11 Beach St., 5th Flr., New York, NY 10013 USA Fax: 212-625-5075
Web site: http://www.miramax.com
Dist(s): **Children's Plus, Inc.**
Disney Publishing Worldwide
Hachette Bk. Group
Hyperion Pr.

MiraQuest, *(978-0-9748329; 978-0-615-26973-3; 978-0-9819958)* Orders Addr.: P.O. Box 29722, Los Angeles, CA 90029-0722 USA
Web site: http://www.islandlili.com
Dist(s): **Ingram Content Group.**

Mirasee, *(978-0-692-97782-8; 978-0-9996500)* 4200 Cabarrus Ct. E., Greensboro, NC 27407 USA Tel 336-404-7165
E-mail: ashlee@mirasee.com
Web site: www.mirasee.com.

Miraux Publishing *See* **Publify Consulting**

Mireya *See* **WAO Publishing**

Mirhady, Farhad, *(978-0-9760323)* 2055 Beverly Beach Dr NW, Olympia, WA 98502-3427 USA
E-mail: fmirhady@comcast.net
Web site: http://www.poeticliterature.com.

MIROGLYPHICS, *(978-0-9773064; 978-0-9801073)* Orders Addr.: 5734 N. 4th St., Philadelphia, PA 19120 USA (SAN 257-2451) Tel 215-224-2486; *Imprints:* Romoulous (Romoulous)
E-mail: germic2008@gmail.com; mnik1972@aol.com
Web site: http://www.miroglyphics.biz
Dist(s): **Ingram Content Group.**

Mirror Pond Publishing, *(978-0-9777683)* 63090 Casey Pl., Bend, OR 97701 USA Tel 541-385-6927
E-mail: speedyread@hotmail.com.

Mirror Publishing, *(978-0-9796519; 978-0-9800675; 978-0-9815904; 978-0-9817521; 978-0-9821171; 978-0-9822560; 978-1-936046; 978-1-936352; 978-1-61225)* 6434 W. Dixon St., Milwaukee, WI 53214-1750 USA Tel 414-763-1034
E-mail: info@pagesofwonder.com
Web site: http://www.pagesofwonder.com
Dist(s): **Ingram Content Group.**

Mirrorstone *Imprint of* **Wizards of the Coast**

MirthMarks Publishing, *(978-0-9789591)* 675 Deis Dr., STE 123, Fairfield, OH 45014 USA
E-mail: flymaster@coppershoo.com.

Misch Masch *See* **Prime Bks.**

Mischief Productions, *(978-0-9998328)* 15 Vine Ave, Quincy, MA 02169 USA Tel 720-503-6697
E-mail: Cujo2828@gmail.com.

Misfit Mous *See* **Misfit Mouse**

Misfit Mouse, *(978-0-578-11067-7; 978-0-578-12084-3; 978-0-578-15002-4; 978-0-692-42251-9; 978-0-692-48383-1; 978-0-9972406)* 3382 Habersham Rd. NW, Atlanta, GA 30305 USA
Web site: www.misfitmouse.com.

Misguided Ink *Imprint of* **Gray, John**

MissFoxCreations, *(978-0-692-18325-0; 978-0-578-51496-3; 978-1-7346681)* 323 W4 St., New York, NY 10014 USA Tel 917-586-1850
E-mail: lightfox82@gmail.com
Dist(s): **CreateSpace Independent Publishing Platform.**

Missing Lid Bk.Hse., *(978-0-9838068)* 13526 Omega Cir., Littleton, CO 80124 USA Tel 303-799-8982
E-mail: tjterbush@yahoo.com.

Missing Piece Pr., *(978-0-9703729; 978-0-9977959; 978-1-7340123; 978-1-7350312)* 37042 S. Hollygreen Dr., Tucson, AZ 857398 USA Tel 520-338-2582
E-mail: Questions@MissingPiecePress.com
Web site: http://www.missingpiecepress.com
Dist(s): **Reveal Entertainment, Inc.**

Mission City Pr., Inc., *(978-1-928749; 978-1-934306)* 8122 Datapoint Dr. Ste. 1000, San Antonio, TX 78229-3273 USA Toll Free: 800-840-2641
E-mail: busaffair@missioncitypress.com
Web site: http://www.alifeoffaith.com
Dist(s): **Zondervan.**

Mission Creek Studios, *(978-0-929702)* 1040 Mission Canyon Rd., Santa Barbara, CA 93105-2122 USA (SAN 249-9630) Tel 805-682-6724; Fax: 805-682-6761
E-mail: dave@missioncreek.com
Web site: http://www.missioncreek.com.

Mission Manuscripts, Inc., *(978-0-9768880)* 1000 Jorie Blvd., Suite 206, Oak Brook, IL 60523 USA Tel 630-990-0220; Fax: 630-990-2556
E-mail: kathy.hill@arends-inc.com.

Mission Mill Museum, *(978-0-9753484)* 1313 Mill St., SE, Salem, OR 97301 USA Tel 503-585-7012; Fax: 503-588-9902
E-mail: info@missionmill.org
Web site: http://www.missionmill.org.

Mission Partners, *(978-1-7346186)* 7201 Wisconsin Ave, BETHESDA, MD 20814 USA Tel 301-585-5034
E-mail: carrie@mission.partners
Web site: mission.partners.

Mision Ridge Pr., *(978-0-9763956)* 4660 Eastus Dr., San Jose, CA 95129 USA.

†Mississippi Museum of Art, *(978-1-887422)* 380 S. Lamar St., Jackson, MS 39201-4007 USA (SAN 279-6198)
E-mail: rpb@netdoor.com
Web site: http://www.msmuseumart.org
Dist(s): **Pennsylvania State Univ. Pr.**
Univ. Pr. of Mississippi
Univ. of Washington Pr.; *CIP.*

Missouri Botanical Garden Pr., *(978-0-915279; 978-1-930723; 978-1-935641)* Orders Addr.: P.O. Box 299, Saint Louis, MO 63166-0299 USA (SAN 290-0157) Tel 314-577-9547 marketing and publishing questions; Toll Free: 888-271-1930 orders department; Edit Addr.: 4500 Shaw Blvd., Saint Louis, MO 63110 USA
E-mail: mbgpress@mobot.org; press.coordinator@mobot.org; allison.brock@mobot.org
Web site: http://www.mbgpress.org
Dist(s): **Chicago Distribution Ctr.**

Missouri Historical Society Pr., *(978-1-883982)* Orders Addr.: P.O. Box 11940, Saint Louis, MO 63112-0040 USA Fax: 314-746-4548
E-mail: jstevens@mohistory.org
Web site: http://www.mohistory.org
Dist(s): **Chicago Distribution Ctr.**
SPD-Small Pr. Distribution
Univ. of Missouri Pr.
Univ. of New Mexico Pr.
Wayne State Univ. Pr.

Missy Sheldrake, *(978-1-7345896)* 6818 Chasewood Cir., Centreville, VA 20121 USA Tel 703-203-2420
E-mail: Missy@variable.org
Dist(s): **Ingram Content Group.**

Mister C Music, *(978-0-9755333)* P.O. Box 28, Rochester, PA 15074 USA Toll Free: 877-687-4258
E-mail: misterc437@aol.com
Web site: http://www.mistercmusic.com.

Mistofer Christopher *See* **Hse. of Mistofer Christopher**

†MIT Pr., *(978-0-262; 978-0-89706)* Orders Addr.: c/o Triliteral LLC, 100 Maple Ridge Dr., Cumberland, RI 02864 USA Tel 401-531-2800; Fax: 401-531-2801; Toll Free Fax: 800-406-9145; Toll Free: 800-405-1619; Edit Addr.: One Rogers St., Cambridge, MA 02142-1209 USA (SAN 202-6414) Tel 617-253-5646; Fax: 617-253-6779
E-mail: orders@triliteral.org
Web site: http://mitpress.mit.edu
Dist(s): **Ebsco Publishing**
MyiLibrary
Penguin Random Hse. Distribution
Penguin Random Hse. LLC
TriLiteral, LLC
Wiley, John & Sons, Inc.
ebrary, Inc.; *CIP.*

Mitchell, Carol *See* **CaribbeanReads**

Mitchell, Damien Pardow, *(978-0-615-18469-2)* 13834 Doolittle Dr., San Leandro, CA 94577 USA
Web site: http://jarvisprinting.com
Dist(s): **Publishers Services.**

Mitchell, Karan, *(978-0-9763793)* 79 Baruch Dr., Apt.5E, New York, NY 10002-3659 USA Tel 212-982-7977
E-mail: mtchllkm@aol.com.

Mitchell Lane Pubs., *(978-1-883845; 978-1-58415; 978-1-61228; 978-1-68020)* 2001 SW 31st Ave, Hallandale, FL 33009 USA (SAN 858-3749) Tel 954-985-9400; Fax: 954-987-2200; Toll Free: 800-814-5484
E-mail: Phil@mitchellane.com
Web site: http://www.mitchelllane.com.

Mitchell Lane Publishers, Incorporated *See* **Mitchell Lane Pubs.**

Mitchell, P. S., *(978-0-615-80354-8)* 3682 King St. Unit 16831, Alexandria, VA 22302 USA Tel 571-214-4805
E-mail: psmitchellbook@gmail.com.

Mitchell Publishing, *(978-1-7322689)* 212 Peach Grove Pl., Mauldin, SC 29662 USA Tel 843-860-6742
E-mail: katisha.mitchell@gmail.com.

Mitchell Publishing, Incorporated *See* **Teaching & Learning Co.**

Mitchell Publishing, Inc., *(978-0-938188)* 160 Spear St. Ste. 700, San Francisco, CA 94105-1562 USA (SAN 215-7896) Toll Free: 800-435-2665 Do not confuse with companies with the same or similar names in Spokane, WA, Medina, NY, Medicine Lodge, KS.

Mitre's Touch Gallery, The, *(978-0-9764384)* 1414 Adams Ave., La Grande, OR 97850 USA Tel 541-963-3477
E-mail: weframe@eoni.com.

Mitten Pr. *Imprint of* **Ann Arbor Editions LLC**

MITWA, *(978-0-692-90196-0; 978-0-692-96959-5; 978-0-692-97666-1; 978-0-692-08942-2; 978-0-578-61119-8)* 949 OAK CREEK CIR, APT C, DOUGLASVILLE, GA 30134 USA Tel 404-374-5196; Fax: 404-374-5196
E-mail: info@manifestinginc.com.

Mixta Publishing Co., *(978-0-9675951)* 3179 San Francisco Ave., Long Beach, CA 90806 USA Tel 562-427-4270
E-mail: michael.archuleta@gte.net; michael@mixtapublishing.com
Web site: http://www.mixtapublishing.com; http://www.mixtapublishing.net
Dist(s): **Leonard, Hal Corp.**

Mizzou Media - University BookStores *See* **Mizzou Publishing - The Mizzou Store**

Mizzou Publishing - The Mizzou Store, *(978-1-61600)* Div. of University of Missouri, Mu Student Ctr. 911 E. Rollins St., Columbia, MO 65211 USA Tel 573-882-8567; Fax: 573-884-8050
E-mail: mizzoupublishing@missouri.edu.

MJ Brooks Co., *(978-0-9787864)* 767 N. Pine St., Colville, WA 99114 USA Tel 808-347-1311
E-mail: amakihi@startmail.com.

MJA Creative, LLC, *(978-0-9910894; 978-1-7324180)* P.O. Box 3997, Covington, LA 70434 USA Tel 985-789-3423
E-mail: mike@mikeartell.com
Web site: www.mikeartell.com.

MJS Music & Entertainment, LLC, *(978-0-9762917; 978-0-9817451)* 9699 W. Fort Island Trail, Crystal River, FL 34429 USA Tel 352-257-3261; Fax: 352-795-1658 Do not confuse with comapnies with the same or similar name in Boyertown, PA, Searsport, ME
E-mail: msternal@mjspublications.com; wriverroad@aol.com
Web site: http://www.mjspublications.com
Dist(s): **Dumont, Charles Son, Inc.**
Omnibus Pr.
TNT Media Group, Inc.

MJS Music Publications *See* **MJS Music & Entertainment, LLC**

MJS Publishing Group LLC, *(978-0-9764336)* P.O. Box 6582, Evanston, IL 60204-6582 USA Tel 847-869-5901; Fax: 847-745-0219
E-mail: mjspg@ameritech.net
Web site: http://www.mjspub.com.

MK Pubs., *(978-0-9993790; 978-1-7320448; 978-1-7346643)* 3901 Bixler Church RD, Westminster, MD 21158 USA Tel 410-857-6373
E-mail: monakerby@gmail.com.

MK Publishing, *(978-0-9720484; 978-0-9747147; 978-0-9760534; 978-0-9763271; 978-0-9770933; 978-0-9785081)* 25123 22nd Ave. S., Saint Cloud, MN 56301 USA; P.O. Box 945, St Cloud, MN 56302 (SAN 256-4092) Tel 320-252-1023; Fax: 320-252-4574
Web site: http://www.yourbookpublisher.net
Dist(s): **Closet Case Bks.**
J & N Creations, LLC
JMS Distribution
Main Trail Productions
Ozark Bk. Distributors
Perfume River Pubns.
Puzzle Piece Pubns.

MKADesigns, *(978-0-9745839; 978-0-578-74636-4)* 5 American Ave., Huntsville, AL 35824 USA Tel 256-721-0200; *Imprints:* Fun to Read Books with Royally Good Morals (Fun to Read Bk)
E-mail: mike.dozier@mkadesigns.com
Web site: http://www.mkadesigns.com.

ML Networks *Imprint of* **Sonis, Gabriela**

ML Publishing, *(978-0-9768347)* Div. of MIHP, 31500 Dequindre Rd., Warren, MI 48092-1057 USA Tel 586-268-6942
E-mail: smclaughlin@mihp.net
Web site: http://mlpublishing.com.

MLM Ranch Publishing, *(978-0-9743098)* P.O. Box 910251, St. George, UT 84791 USA.

MLR Pr., LLC, *(978-0-9793110; 978-1-934531; 978-0-615-13459-8; 978-1-60820; 978-1-944770; 978-1-64122)* 3052 Gaines Waterport Rd., Albion, NY 14411 USA (SAN 853-1013) Tel 585-589-7831
E-mail: mlrpress@gmail.com
Web site: http://www.mlrpress.com
Dist(s): **Lulu Pr., Inc.**

MMB Enterprises, LLC, *(978-0-9747443; 978-0-615-57676-3)* Orders Addr.: P.O. Box 5887, Santa Barbara, CA 93150 USA
E-mail: pabujack@me.com
Web site: http://www.michellemadridbranch.com.

MMG Technology Corp., *(978-0-9754886)* 379 Amherst St., Suite 204, Nashua, NH 03063 USA
Web site: http://www.the-common.com.

MMJ Foundation, *(978-0-9827972)* 4350 Von Karman, 4th Flr., Newport Beach, CA 92660 USA Tel 949-244-5544
E-mail: mjanavs@hotmail.com.

M-m-mauleg Publishing, *(978-0-9790111)* Orders Addr.: P.O. Box 5258, Mangilao, GU 96923 USA; Edit Addr.: 303 University Dr., Mangila, GU 96923-5258 USA
E-mail: millhoff@uog.edu.

MMP *See* **Millennium Marketing & Publishing**

MNMC, (*978-0-9728518; 978-0-9763532*) 17 Old Shelter Rock Rd., Danbury, CT 06810 USA Tel 203-798-6936; Toll Free: 866-210-0004
E-mail: order@muslimplanet.com
Web site: http://www.muslimpublisher.com.

Mo MacPhail, (*978-1-7320581*) 95 Hillside Dr., East Longmeadow, MA 01028 USA Tel 413-250-9753
E-mail: momacphail@aol.com.

Mo Peanuts Publishing, (*978-0-9971513*) 1019 Ft. Salonga Rd., Northport, NY 11768 USA Tel 631-682-1768
E-mail: trelfp@gmail.com
Web site: www.TheAlienClub.com.

Mobius Communications, Ltd., (*978-1-891304; 978-1-928583*) Div. of Publication Services, Inc., 1802 S. Duncan Rd., Champaign, IL 61822-5222 USA Fax: 217-398-3923; Toll Free: 800-662-4875
Web site: http://www.8-mobius.com.

Mocha Enterprises, (*978-0-9707163*) 6322 Chesapeake Cir., Stockton, CA 95219 USA (SAN 253-620X) Tel 209-478-0635 (phone/fax); 209-946-3064
E-mail: mochaenterprises@aol.com
Web site: http://www.welcometotheprofessionalwork.com.

Mockingbird Cottage Pr., (*978-0-692-68327-9; 978-0-9983519*) 1014 Richland Ct, Ashland City, TN Bell USA Tel 615-473-2757
Dist(s): **CreateSpace Independent Publishing Platform.**

Mockingbird Lane Pr., (*978-0-9856906; 978-0-9889542; 978-0-9893105*) 2441 Washington Rd., Maynard, AR 72444 USA Tel 870-647-2137
E-mail: mockingbirdlanepress@gmail.com.

Mockingbird Publishing, (*978-0-9828528*) Orders Addr.: P.O. Box 442, Fairhope, AL 36533 USA Tel 334-546-0710
E-mail: ashley@mockingbirdpublishing.com
Web site: http://www.mockingbirdpublishing.com.

Modern Curriculum Pr. *Imprint of* **Savvas Learning Co.**

†Modern Curriculum Pr., (*978-0-7652; 978-0-8136; 978-0-87895*) Div. of Pearson Education, Orders Addr.: P.O. Box 2500, Lebanon, IN 46052-3009 USA (SAN 206-6572) Toll Free: 800-526-9907 (Customer Service)
Web site: http://www.pearsonlearning.com
Dist(s): **Follett School Solutions**
Lectorum Pubns., Inc.
Pearson Learning; *CIP.*

Modern Evil Pr., (*978-1-934516*) 913 S 2nd Ave, Phoenix, AZ 85003-2511 USA Tel 602-999-6449
E-mail: teel@modernevil.com
Web site: http://modernevil.com/
Dist(s): **Smashwords.**

Modern Learning Pr., (*978-0-935493; 978-1-56762*) P.O. Box 167, Rosemont, NJ 08556 USA Tel 609-397-2214; Fax: 845-277-3548; Toll Free Fax: 888-558-7350; Toll Free: 800-627-5867
E-mail: Rlow@tasa.com.

Modern Library *Imprint of* **Random House Publishing Group**

Modern Living Media *See* **Pirouz, Raymond**

Modern Publishing, (*978-0-7666; 978-0-87449; 978-1-56144*) Div. of Unisystems, Inc., 155 E. 55th St., New York, NY 10022 USA (SAN 253-2921) Tel 212-826-0850; Fax: 212-759-9096
E-mail: info@modernpublishing.com
Web site: http://www.modernpublishing.com.

MoGho Bks., LLC, (*978-0-9712559; 978-0-615-11888-8*) Box 200, 9801 Hartley Rd., Hallsville, MO 65255 USA Tel 573-696-3537 (phone/fax)
E-mail: moghobks@tranquility.net
Dist(s): **Cowley Distributing, Inc.**
Univ. of Missouri Pr.

Mogul Comics, (*978-0-9657723*) 102 6th Ave. 2nd Flr., WaterVliet, NY 12189 USA.

Moheke Pr., (*978-0-692-77907-1; 978-0-692-19036-4; 978-0-578-60751-1*) 34 Walnut Pl., Huntington, NY 11743 USA Tel 631-385-8708
Dist(s): **CreateSpace Independent Publishing Platform.**

Mohsena Memorial Foundation, Inc., (*978-0-9617273*) P.O. Box 2309, Princeton, NJ 08543 USA (SAN 663-5075) Tel 609-799-6545; Fax: 609-799-7311.

Mohsena Memorial Trust *See* **Mohsena Memorial Foundation, Inc.**

MoJo InkWorks, (*978-0-9820381*) 16 Foxglove Row, Riverhead, NY 11901 USA Tel 516-695-6690
E-mail: maureensullivan@gmail.com
Web site: http://www.maureensullivancommunications.com.

Mokum Media (NLD) (*978-90-828756*) *Dist. by* **IPG Chicago.**

Molino, Editorial (ESP) (*978-84-272*) *Dist. by* **AIMS Intl.**

Molino, Editorial (ESP) (*978-84-272*) *Dist. by* **Santillana.**

Molino, Editorial (ESP) (*978-84-272*) *Dist. by* **Distribks Inc.**

Molino, Editorial (ESP) (*978-84-272*) *Dist. by* **Continental Bk.**

Molino, Editorial (ESP) (*978-84-272*) *Dist. by* **Lectorum Pubns.**

Molino RBA,
Dist(s): **Lectorum Pubns., Inc.**

Molly Brave, (*978-1-61245*) 3682 Quiet Pond Ln., Sarasota, FL 34235 USA Tel 941-955-0091
E-mail: mollybrave@gmail.com
Web site: http://www.mollybrave.com.

Molly The Owl Bks., (*978-0-9828638*) 2033 San Elijo Ave. No. 482, Cardiff by the Sea, CA 92007 USA Tel 760-716-6535
E-mail: eric@ericblehm.com
Web site: http://www.mollytheowlbooks.com.

Moltiverse, (*978-0-9761844*) Orders Addr.: 76 northampton ave, springfield, MA 01109 USA Tel 413-433-6456; Edit Addr.: 76 northampton ave, springfield, MA 01109 USA
E-mail: pricevanray@gmail.com
Web site: http://pricevanray.com.

Mom of 4, The *See* **Anna Stilianessis**

Moment Bks. *Imprint of* **Mandel Vilar Pr.**

Momentpoint Media, (*978-0-9710448*) 2385 Friesian Rd., York, PA 17406 USA Tel 717-848-4528 (phone/fax) Do not confuse with Moment Point Press Inc. of NH/ME.
E-mail: momentpoint@suscom.net
Web site: http://www.momentpointmedia.com.

MOMENTUM *Imprint of* **Child's World, Inc., The**

Momentum Books, Limited *See* **Momentum Bks., LLC**

Momentum Bks., LLC, (*978-0-9618726; 978-1-879094; 978-1-938018*) Div. of Hour Media, LLC, 117 W. Third St., Royal Oak, MI 48067 USA (SAN 668-7067) Tel 248-691-1800; Fax: 248-691-4531
E-mail: info@momentumbooks.com
Web site: http://www.momentumbooks.com
Dist(s): **Baker & Taylor Publisher Services (BTPS)**
SCB Distributors
TNT Media Group, Inc.

Mometrix Media LLC, (*978-1-60971; 978-1-61072; 978-1-61073; 978-1-61402; 978-1-61403; 978-1-62120; 978-1-62733; 978-1-63094; 978-1-5167*) 3827 Phelan No. 179, Beaumont, TX 77707 USA (SAN 860-0430) Tel 800-673-8175.

MomGeek.com *Imprint of* **Wood Designs, Inc.**

Momma Dot Publishing LLC, (*978-0-9967667*) 11632 18th St SE, Lake Stevens, WA 98258 USA Tel 425-314-9746
E-mail: thenuetzs@gmail.com.

Mommy Has Tattoos, (*978-0-9770232*) P.O. Box 231059, New York, NY 10023-0023 USA
E-mail: info@mommyhastattoos.com
Web site: http://www.mommyhastattoos.com.

Mommy Workshop Bks., (*978-0-9817565*) P.O. Box 265, Doylestown, PA 18901 USA (SAN 856-4655) Tel 215-489-8649; Fax: 480-393-5692
E-mail: kristie@mommyworkshop.com
Web site: http://www.mommyworkshop.com/.

Momosa Publishing LLC, (*978-0-9844804; 978-0-9970808; 978-0-9986531; 978-0-9994151; 978-1-7323016; 978-1-950459*) Orders Addr.: 765 Front St., Hellertown, PA 18055 USA (SAN 859-5224)
E-mail: jennifer@momosapublishing.com
Dist(s): **National Bk. Network.**

Momotombo Pr., (*978-0-9710465; 978-0-9797446*) Institute for Latino/University of Notre Dame, Notre Dame, IN 46556 USA; Inst. for Latino Studies Univ. of Notre Dame 230 McKenna Hall, Notre Dame, IN 46556
E-mail: faragon@nd.edu
Web site: http://www.momotombopress.com
Dist(s): **SPD-Small Pr. Distribution.**

Mom's Pride Enterprises, (*978-0-9720549*) 16521 N. 69th Dr., Peoria, AZ 85382 USA Tel 623-487-7589; Fax: 623-487-1504
E-mail: mrsb4kids@yahoo.com
Web site: http://www.mrsbstorytime.com.

Monacelli Pr., Inc., (*978-1-58093; 978-1-885254*) 1745 Broadway, New York, NY 10019-4305 USA Tel 212-782-9000
E-mail: info@monaddcellipress.com
Web site: http://www.monacellipress.com
Dist(s): **Hachette Bk. Group**
MyiLibrary
Penguin Random Hse. Distribution
Penguin Random Hse. LLC
Penguin Publishing Group
Random Hse., Inc.

Monarch Baby Publishing, (*978-0-9749499*) Orders Addr.: P.O. Box 22, Salem, VA 24153 USA Tel 504-669-1044
E-mail: monarchbaby@blackbutterflyrecords.com
Web site: http://blackbutterflyrecords.com\monarch_baby_publishing.thml.

Monarch Pubs., (*978-0-9774038; 978-0-615-12659-3*) Orders Addr.: 305 Holly Tree Ln., Simpsonville, SC 29681 USA
E-mail: joconnor@uscupstate.edu
Web site: http://www.monarchpublishers.com
Dist(s): **Follett School Solutions**
Parnassus Bk. Distributors
Bryan, R. L.

Monarch Publishing Hse., (*978-0-9797861*) 2573 Lake Cir., Jackson, MS 39211-6630 USA (SAN 859-4627) Tel 601-982-1233.

Monarchs in the Classroom, (*978-0-9800653*) 1980 Folwell Ave., 200 Hodson Hall, Saint Paul, MN 55108 USA Tel 612-624-8706; Fax: 612-625-5299
E-mail: oberh001@umn.edu
Web site: http://www.monarchlab.org.

Mondadori (ITA) (*978-88-04; 978-88-356; 978-88-86372; 978-88-520; 978-88-521*) *Dist. by* **Distribks Inc.**

Monday Creek Publishing, (*978-0-692-83683-5; 978-0-692-85102-9; 978-0-692-86331-2; 978-0-692-86452-4; 978-0-692-87827-9; 978-0-692-87898-9; 978-0-692-88706-6; 978-0-692-88741-7; 978-0-692-89299-2; 978-0-692-89826-0; 978-0-692-91214-0; 978-0-692-91631-5; 978-0-692-92731-1; 978-0-692-93730-3; 978-0-692-96396-8; 978-0-692-96419-4; 978-0-692-96759-1; 978-0-692-96947-2; 978-0-692-98321-8; 978-0-692-04512-1; 978-0-692-06638-6; 978-0-692-06990-5; 978-0-692-07295-0; 978-0-692-09300-9; 978-0-692-10561-0; 978-0-692-10676-1;) P.O. Box 399, Buchtel, OH 45716 USA Tel 740-590-3987*
E-mail: gmcknight11@gmail.com
Web site: http://gmcknight.com
Dist(s): **CreateSpace Independent Publishing Platform.**

Mondial, (*978-1-59569*) 203 W 107th St., No. 6C, New York, NY 10025 USA
E-mail: contact@mondialbooks.com
Web site: http://www.mondialbooks.com
Dist(s): **Smashwords.**

Mondo Fax Publishing, (*978-0-9710095*) 26235 Ravenhill Rd., Suite M, Santa Clarita, CA 91350-4754 USA Tel 661-250-0990; Fax: 661-251-4452
E-mail: argapc@socal.rr.com
Web site: http://mondofax.com.

Mondo Publishing, (*978-1-57255; 978-1-879531; 978-1-58653; 978-1-59034; 978-1-59336; 978-1-60201; 978-1-60715; 978-1-61736; 978-1-62889; 978-1-63060; 978-1-63061; 978-1-68156; 978-1-64064*) Div. of Music Plus, Inc., 980 6th Ave., New York, NY 10018 USA Toll Free: 888-268-3560
E-mail: ckracuna@mondopub.com
Web site: http://www.mondopub.com.

Money Management Books *See* **Prism Hse. Media**

Mongoose Pr., (*978-0-9791482; 978-1-936277*) 1005 Boylston St., Suite 324, Newton Highlands, MA 02461 USA Tel 617-875-6298
E-mail: info@mongoosepress.com
Web site: http://www.MongoosePress.com
Dist(s): **MyiLibrary**
National Bk. Network
ebrary, Inc.

Mongoose Publishing (GBR) (*978-1-903980; 978-1-904577; 978-1-904854; 978-1-905176; 978-1-905476; 978-1-905471; 978-1-905850; 978-1-906103; 978-1-906508; 978-1-907218*) *Dist. by* **Diamond Book Dists.**

Monique Patrice Hall *See* **Hall, Monique P. Productions**

Monkey Barrel Pr., (*978-0-9802000*) 4738 Andrea Way, Union City, CA 94587 USA
Web site: http://www.monkeybarrelpress.com.

Monkey Brain Factory, (*978-0-692-93725-9*) 245 N Alvarado St No. 305, Los Angeles, CA 90026 USA Tel 213-291-5633
E-mail: brandonifd@gmail.com
Dist(s): **CreateSpace Independent Publishing Platform.**

Monkey Business *See* **Monkeying Around**

MonkeyBear Publishing *Imprint of* **LORE Mountain Productions**

MonkeyGod Enterprises, (*978-0-9708094; 978-0-9717729; 978-0-9728197*) Div. of Face 2 Face Games Publishing, 36 The Arcade, 65 Weybosset St., Providence, RI 02903 USA Tel 401-351-0362 (phone/fax)
E-mail: fmf@pipeline.com
Web site: http://www.monkeygodenterprses.com.

Monkeying Around, (*978-0-9700437; 978-0-9799753; 978-0-9975907*) P.O. Box 10131, Rochester, NY 14610 USA Tel 585-256-2660; Fax: 585-442-2965
E-mail: info@monkeyingaround.com
Web site: http://www.monkeyingaround.com.

MonkeyMantra, (*978-0-692-59340-0; 978-0-9977181*) 2050 Jamison Pl., Santa Clara, CA 95051 USA Tel 408-506-0156
E-mail: jatkar.deven@gmail.com.

Monkeyshines Publishers *See* **Allosaurus Pubs.**

Monkeytoes Pr., (*978-0-615-12555-8*) 125 Sycamore Rd., Braintree, MA 02184-7318 USA
E-mail: jvgandkdlarson@comcast.net
Web site: http://www.monkeytoespress.com.

Monnin, Philip, (*978-0-9969639; 978-0-9982907*) 5220 Creekmonte Dr, Oakland Township, MI 48306 USA Tel 248-701-1995
E-mail: pmonnin@yahoo.com.

Monocle Pr., (*978-1-7321189; 978-1-952938*) 11600 Broadway Ext, Oklahoma City, OK 73114 USA Tel 405-507-6447
E-mail: christina@monoclepress.com
Web site: www.monoclepress.com.

Monogram Booklets *See* **Miller, Debra Juanita**

Monolith Graphics, (*978-0-9675756; 978-0-9788857; 978-0-9824899*) Orders Addr.: P.O. Box 360801, Strongsville, OH 44136 USA
E-mail: goth@monolithgraphics.com; nox@noxarcana.com
Web site: http://www.monolithgraphics.com; http://www.noxarcana.com.

Monroe Educational Media, (*978-0-9721146*) 2965 Taylor Rd., Reynoldsburg, OH 43068 USA Tel 614-866-4289; Fax: 740-927-9131
E-mail: jon@gooddebt.com
Web site: http://www.monroemedia.com.

Monroe, Guy, (*978-0-9742443*) P.O. Box 2325, Newport, OR 97365-0171 USA Toll Free: 877-562-3866
Web site: http://www.pinerystreet.com.

Monroe Media *See* **Monroe Educational Media**

Monsoon Bks. Pte. Ltd. (SGP) (*978-981-05; 978-981-4358; 978-981-4423; 978-981-4625*) *Dist. by* **Natl Bk Netwk.**

Monsoon Bks. Pte. Ltd. (SGP) (*978-981-05; 978-981-4358; 978-981-4423; 978-981-4625*) *Dist. by* **Tuttle Pubng.**

Monster Ivy Publishing, (*978-0-9987426; 978-1-948095*) 104 Candis CT, Springtown, TX 76082 USA Tel 817-805-4418
E-mail: marycgray@icloud.com.

MonsterHaven, (*978-0-615-38690-4*) 385 Camino dos Palos, Thousand Oaks, CA 91360 USA Tel 805-208-8383
E-mail: marmaxdesigns@hotmail.com
Web site: http://www.monsterhaven.com.

Monsters in My Head, LLC, The, (*978-0-9792860; 978-0-9914952*) 344 Grove St. #119, Jersey City, NJ 07302 USA (SAN 853-0254) Tel 917-881-8326
E-mail: info@worrywoos.com
Web site: http://www.worrywoos.com.

Montag Pr., (*978-0-9822809; 978-1-940233*) 1066 47th Ave., Unit #9, Oakland, CA 94601 USA Tel 916-806-8341
E-mail: c.lanfranco@gmail.com
Dist(s): **SPD-Small Pr. Distribution.**

Montana Publishing Group *See* **Loughton Bks.**

Montanha Pr., (*978-0-9743380*) 1547 Palos Verdes Mall , Suite 139, Walnut Creek, CA 94597 USA.

Monte Nido Pr., (*978-0-9742663*) Rm 9L19, 1240 Mission Rd., Los Angeles,, CA 90033 USA Tel 323-226-3406; Fax: 323-226-3440
E-mail: hoppenbrou@earthlink.net
Web site: http://www.toke.hoppenbrouwers.net.

Montemayor Pr., (*978-0-9674477; 978-1-932727*) P.O. Box 526, Millburn, NJ 07041 USA Tel 973-761-1341
E-mail: mail@montemayorpress.com
Web site: http://www.montemayorpress.com.

†Monterey Bay Aquarium, (*978-1-878244*) 886 Cannery Row, Monterey, CA 93940 USA Tel 831-648-4942; 408-648-4800; 831-648-4847; Fax: 831-644-7568; Toll Free: 877-665-2665
E-mail: mmckenzie@mbayaq.org
Web site: http://www.montereybayaquarium.org; *CIP.*

Monterey Bay Sancturary Foundation, (*978-0-9742810*) 299 Foam St., Monterey, CA 93940 USA
E-mail: info@mbnmsf.org
Web site: http://www.mbnmsf.org
Dist(s): **Sunbelt Pubns., Inc.**

Montessori Advantage, (*978-0-9766453*) Orders Addr.: P.O. Box 272, Wickatunk, NJ 07765 USA Toll Free: 888-946-2114; Edit Addr.: 257 Rt. 79N, Wickatunk, NJ 07765 USA.

Montevallo Historical Pr., (*978-0-9658624*) 9052 Old Hickory Ct., Manassas, VA 20110 USA Tel 703-789-2407
E-mail: dean@mhpress.com
Web site: https://www.mhpress.com.

Montevallo Historical Press, Incorporated *See* **Montevallo Historical Pr.**

Montgomery County Historical Society, (*978-0-9720965*) 1000 Carillon Blvd., Dayton, OH 45409-2023 USA Do not confuse with Montgomery County Historical Society in Rockville MD, Fort Johnson NY
Web site: http://www.daytonhistory.org.

Montlake Romance *Imprint of* **Amazon Publishing**

Montoya, Amanda, (*978-0-578-45106-0; 978-0-578-45594-5*) 202 Woodway Dr., Laredo, TX 78041 USA Tel 956-286-8848
E-mail: amandamontoya4@icloud.com
Dist(s): **Ingram Content Group.**

Montville Pr., (*978-0-9706527*) P.O. Box 4304, Greensboro, NC 27410-4304 USA Tel 336-292-8268; Fax: 336-218-0410
E-mail: bas236@aol.com.

Moo Pr. *Imprint of* **Keene Publishing**

Moo Press, Incorporated *See* **Keene Publishing**

†Moody Pubs., (*978-0-8024; 978-1-881273; 978-1-60066*) Div. of Moody Bible Institute, Orders Addr.: 210 W. Chestnut, Chicago, IL 60610 USA; Edit Addr.: 820 N. LaSalle, Chicago, IL 60610 USA (SAN 202-5604) Tel 312-329-2101; Fax: 312-329-2144; Toll Free: 800-678-8812; 215 W. Locust, Chicago, IL 60610 (SAN 297-6404) Tel 312-329-2110; Fax: 312-329-8062; Toll Free: 800-678-8001; *Imprints:* Northfield Publishing (Northfield); WingSpread Publishers (WingSpre Pub)
E-mail: mpcustomerservice@moody.edu
Web site: http://www.moodypublishers.com
Dist(s): **Anchor Distributors**
BJU Pr.
Children's Plus, Inc.
Follett School Solutions
Send The Light Distribution LLC; *CIP.*

Moody Valley, (*978-1-59513*) 475 Church Hollow Rd., Boone, NC 28607 USA Tel 828-963-5331; Fax: 828-963-4101
E-mail: moodyvalley@skybest.com
Web site: http://www.moodyvalley.com
Dist(s): **Partners Bk. Distributing, Inc.**

Moody, William, (*978-0-9762556*) 301 Willard Hall, Univ. of Delaware, Newark, DE 19711 USA Tel 302-831-1658; Fax: 302-831-0591
E-mail: wmoody@udel.edu
Web site: http://www.udel.edu/educ/solveit.htm.

Mookind Pr., (*978-0-9792761*) 1600 S. Eads St., Suite 822N, Arlington, VA 22202 USA Tel 703-920-1884
E-mail: cnadel999@yahoo.com.

Moombaya Bks., (*978-0-9766799*) 2118 Wilshire Blvd., Suite 528, Santa Monica, CA 90403-9040 USA
E-mail: diponzagroup@aol.com.

Moon, Alice *See* **PeachMoon Publishing**

Moon Bear Pr., (*978-0-944164*) P.O. Box 468, Velarde, NM 87582 USA (SAN 242-9144) Tel 505-852-4897
E-mail: orders@moonbearpress.com
Web site: http://www.moonbearpress.com
Dist(s): **New Leaf Distributing Co., Inc.**

Moon Bound Pr. LLC, (*978-0-9967401*) 208 Seamoor Dr, Fredericksburg, TX 78624 USA Tel 830-613-0100
E-mail: stephanie_kay88@yahoo.com
Web site: www.stephaniekneese.com.

Moon Chaser Publishing, (*978-0-9987338*) 220 Mare Pond Pl., Hampstead, NC 28443 USA Tel 714-713-2831
E-mail: ask1rd@aol.com.

Moon Lantern Studios, (*978-1-7337601*) 234 N Kenwood St, Glendale, CA 91206 USA Tel 805-698-9311
E-mail: tim@teruo.com
Web site: moonlanternstudios.com.

Moon Leaf Publishing LLC, (*978-0-9997612*) 876 N. Water St, Henderson, NV 89011 USA Tel 702-743-5289
E-mail: moontime@prodigy.net
Dist(s): **Ingram Content Group.**

Moon Mountain Publishing, Inc., (*978-0-9677929; 978-1-931659*) P.O. Box 188, West Rockport, ME

04865 USA Tel 207-236-0958; Fax: 978-719-6290; Toll Free: 800-353-5877
E-mail: hello@moonmountainpub.com
Web site: http://www.moonmountainpub.com.

Moon Over Mountains Publishing (M.O.M.), (*978-1-891665*) Div. of Gallery of Diamonds Jewelers, 1528 Brookhollow Dr. Suite 200, Santa Ana, CA 92705 USA (SAN 299-5492) Tel 714-549-2000; Fax: 714-545-8000; Toll Free: 800-667-4440
E-mail: info@galleryofdiamonds.com
Web site: http://www.whymomdeservesadiamond.com.

Moon Pie Pr., (*978-0-9761744*) 53 Faye Dr., Smithfield, VA 23430 USA Tel 757-356-1690
E-mail: cathyk@visi.net
Web site: http://www.moonpiepress.net.

Moon Trail Bks., (*978-0-9773140*) 24 W. 4th St., Bethlehem, PA 18015-1604 USA (SAN 850-6922) Tel 610-866-6482
E-mail: pnmca21@aol.com.

Moon Travel Handbooks *See* **Avalon Publishing**

Moon Valley Productions, (*978-0-934290*) P.O. Box 1342, Healdsburg, CA 95448 USA (SAN 221-2900) Tel 707-823-9340; 707-523-8525
E-mail: zaksartandsoul@yahoo.com
Web site: http://www.zakzalkine.com.

Moonbow Pr., LLc, (*978-0-9789092*) P.O. Box 95, Bethel, OH 45106 USA (SAN 851-9110).

Moondance *Imprint of* **Quarto Publishing Group USA**

Moondance Publishing, (*978-0-9671865; 978-1-931524*) Orders Addr.: P.O. Box 16, Upper Black Eddy, PA 18972 USA Tel 610-442-1951; Fax: 610-982-5331; Edit Addr.: 1525 Oak Ln., Upper Black Eddy, PA 18972 USA (SAN 254-5101) Tel 610-442-1951
E-mail: caravan@moondancepublishing.com
Web site: http://www.moondancepublishing.com.

Moonjar, LLC, (*978-0-9724282; 978-0-9764231*) 612 19th Ave., E., Seattle, WA 98112 USA Fax: 206-726-0769; Toll Free: 888-323-0001
E-mail: contact@moonjar.com
Web site: http://www.moonjar.com
Dist(s): **Ten Speed Pr.**

Moonlight Bks., (*978-0-9971833; 978-1-945360; 978-1-7327603; 978-1-950244*) 160 W 77th St, New York, NY 10024 USA Tel 212-799-6416
E-mail: sunnydaysbook@gmail.com
Web site: www.jeanjoachimbooks.com.

Moonlight Publishing, Ltd. (GBR) (*978-0-907144; 978-1-85103*) *Dist. by* **IPG Chicago.**

MoonRattles, (*978-0-9790920*) P.O. Box 939, Carmel, CA 93921 USA; 70 Dapplegray Rd., Bell Canyon, CA 91307 (SAN 854-2201) Fax: 818-932-9631; Toll Free: 800-961-6073
E-mail: info@moonrattles.com
Web site: http://www.moonrattles.com.

Moons & Stars Publishing For Children, (*978-1-929063*) Div. of Moon Star Unlimited, Inc., P.O. Box 1763, Pasadena, TX 77505 USA Tel 713-473-7120; Fax: 713-473-1105
E-mail: services@dorpexpress.com
Web site: http://www.dorpexpress.com.

Moonshell Bks., Inc. *Imprint of* **Shelley Adina**

Moonshine Cove Publishing LLC, (*978-1-937327; 978-1-945181; 978-1-952439*) 150 Willow Pt., Abbeville, SC 29620 USA Tel 864-446-7570
E-mail: publisher@moonshinecovepublishing.com
Web site: http://moonshinecovepublishing.com
Dist(s): **Ingram Content Group.**

Moonspinners Enterprise, 2787 N. Cambridge Rd., JEFFERSONVILLE, VT 05464 USA Tel 888-785-4888
E-mail: lesleynase@moonspinnersenterprise.com
Dist(s): **Ingram Content Group.**

MoonStar Pr., (*978-0-9672107*) 4360 E. Main St., Suite 408, Ventura, CA 93003 USA Tel 805-648-7753
E-mail: toutzhag@earthlink.net
Dist(s): **New Leaf Distributing Co., Inc.**

Moonstone, (*978-0-9710129; 978-0-9712937; 978-0-9721668; 978-0-9726443; 978-0-9748501; 978-1-933076; 978-1-936814; 978-1-944017*) Div. of Amazing Fantasy Comic Shop Ltd., 582 Torrence Ave., Calumet City, IL 60409 USA Fax: 708-891-0644
E-mail: afbooks_frankfort@sbcglobal.net
Web site: http://www.moonstonebooks.com
Dist(s): **Diamond Comic Distributors, Inc.**
Diamond Bk. Distributors.

Moonstone Lily Publishing, (*978-0-9992724*) P.O. Box PO Box 90367, San Diego, CA 92169 USA Tel 858-361-5239; Fax: 858-361-5239
E-mail: publisher@moonstonelily.com
Web site: http://moonstonelily.com/.

Moonstone Pr., LLC, (*978-0-9707768; 978-0-9727697; 978-0-9769542; 978-0-9834983*) 4816 Carrington Cir., Sarasota, FL 34243 USA (SAN 852-5625) Tel 301-765-1081; Fax: 301-765-0510
E-mail: mazeprod@erols.com
Web site: http://www.moonstonepress.net
Dist(s): **Independent Pubs. Group**
Lectorum Pubns., Inc.
PSI (Publisher Services, Inc.).

Moonswept Pr., (*978-0-9718629; 978-1-60087*) 20203 Goshen Rd. No. 374, Gaithersburg, MD 20879 USA Tel 240-389-3459
Web site: http://www.moonsweptpress.com.

Moonview Pr., (*978-0-9828987*) 5460 Linda Ln., Santa Rosa, CA 95404 USA Tel 707-578-2269
E-mail: ctmarkee@gmail.com
Web site: http://www.charlesmarkee.comzbandit
Dist(s): **Smashwords.**

Moonwater Products, (*978-0-9769033*) 63 Roycroft Dr., Rochester, NY 14621 USA
E-mail: djed_ra_maat@yahoo.com.

Moore, Ammanuel, (*978-0-9744060*) P.O. Box 3295, Baltimore, MD 21228 USA Tel 410-788-7271
E-mail: info@acmoorebooks.com
Web site: http://www.acmoorebooks.com.

Moore, Evans, (*978-0-9709762*) P.O. Box 30311, Washington, DC 20030 USA Tel 202-889-3648
E-mail: evansmoore@hotmail.com.

Moore, Greg Publishing, (*978-0-9639495*) Orders Addr.: 6202 Wallina Ct., SE, Salem, OR 97309 USA Tel 503-749-1393; Fax: 503-588-7707
E-mail: yoyo@tdn.com.

Moore, Hugh Historical Park & Museums, Incorporated *See* **Delaware &Lehigh National Heritage Corridor, Inc.**

Moore, Hullihen, (*978-0-9785775*) P.O. Box 116, Oldhams, VA 22529 USA (SAN 850-9468).

Moore, Lonnie W. *See* **I & L Publishing**

Moore Publishing, (*978-0-9800791*) 646 Beautiful Run Rd., Madison, VA 22727 USA.

Moore, Sharon, (*978-0-578-03132-3; 978-1-946195; 978-1-946195-12-8*) 1009 Bay Ridge Ave., No.138, Annapolis, MD 21403 USA Tel 410-757-1474; Toll Free: 877-786-6564
E-mail: sharon@sharon-moore.com.

Moose Egg Productions, (*978-0-578-48781-6*) 1139 Trinity Trl, Saginaw, TX 76131 USA Tel 817-739-1006
E-mail: mooseegg1982@yahoo.com
Web site: www.mooseeggproductions.com.

Moose Hill Bks., Inc., (*978-0-9728627*) P.O. Box 222271, Anchorage, AK 99522 USA (SAN 255-1616)
E-mail: publisher@moosehillbooks.com
Web site: http://www.moosehillbooks.com.

Moose Run Productions, (*978-0-9766315*) 22010 Highview, Clinton Township, MI 48036 USA Tel 586-718-7700
Web site: http://www.moose-run.com.

Moosehead Publishing, (*978-0-615-43399-8; 978-0-692-49597-1; 978-0-692-51854-0; 978-0-692-54977-3*) 3 Marsh Rd., Tiburon, CA 94920 USA Tel 415-990-5019
Dist(s): **CreateSpace Independent Publishing Platform**
Dummy Record Do Not USE!!!!.

Moppet Bks., (*978-0-9977145; 978-0-9988205; 978-1-7337921*) 15608 S. New Century Dr., Gardena, CA 90248 USA Tel 323-717-3976
E-mail: fredrik@kinderguides.com
Web site: www.kinderguides.com
Dist(s): **SCB Distributors.**

Morals & Values Pr., (*978-0-9754191; 978-0-9842140; 978-0-9898501; 978-1-7355487*) P. O. Box 4785, Los Angeles, CA 90231 USA
E-mail: mischa@mischainspires.com
Web site: http://www.moralsandvaluespress.com; http://www.greatnessnow.org.

Moran, Kristyna, (*978-0-692-79225-4*) 5016 Thorne Dr. #14, LA MESA, CA 91942 USA Tel 619-787-3785.

Morari Specialties Inc., (*978-0-9770618*) 13901 SW 22nd St., Miami, FL 33175-7006 USA
Web site: http://www.morarispecialties.com.

Morcan, Dorina, (*978-0-9763663*) P.O. Box 1564, Malvern, AR 72104 USA Fax: 501-262-4127
E-mail: dmorcan@ix.netcom.com.

More Books Press *See* **SCOJO ENTERTAINMENT**

More, Frances International Teaching Systems *See* **Frances More International Teaching Systems**

More, Francisco J., (*978-0-9747851*) 221 Majorca Ave., No. 207, Coral Gables, FL 33134-4429 USA Tel 305-448-5081.

More Heart Than Talent Publishing, Incorporated *See* **Golden Mastermind Seminars, Inc.**

More Pr., (*978-0-9743394*) Div. of More Consulting Co., 1634 E. 53rd St., Chicago, IL 60615-4389 USA
E-mail: shaharimoore@aol.com.

M.O.R.E. Pubs., (*978-0-9719984; 978-0-9758549; 978-0-9801647; 978-0-9820354; 978-0-9830325; 978-0-692-27449-1; 978-1-945344*) Orders Addr.: P.O. Box 621, Collierville, TN 38027-0621 USA; Edit Addr.: 4466 Elvis Presley Blvd. 1st Memphis Plaza - Suite 103, Memphis, TN 38116 USA (SAN 255-1055)
E-mail: stlouiswpguild@aol.com; MOREPublishersCO@AOL.com
Web site: http://www.MOREPublishers.biz; http://www.TheScaleMagazine.MagCloud.com.

More to Life Publishing, (*978-0-9632564; 978-0-9766971; 978-0-9825746; 978-0-9949-9251*) 1549 22nd St N, Arlington, VA 22209 USA; Aarekoidu tee 10 Alliku Kula, Saue vald, Harjumaa, 76403 Tel 372 50 81 944
E-mail: kimismore@gmail.com; morepublish@gmail.com
Web site: http://www.askrealjesus.com; http://www.morepublish.com
Dist(s): **SCB Distributors.**

Morehouse Education Resources, (*978-1-60674*) 1313 Steele St., Suite 400, Denver, CO 80203 USA Tel 303-832-4427; Fax: 202-832-4971; Toll Free: 800-242-1918
Web site: http://www.morehouseeducation.org
Dist(s): **Abingdon Pr.**
Church Publishing, Inc.
Open Road Integrated Media, Inc.

Morehouse Publishing *Imprint of* **Church Publishing, Inc.**

Morelmasters LLC, (*978-0-615-12829-0*) Orders Addr.: 6294 Reynolds Ridge Rd., Potosi, WI 53820 USA Tel 608-732-2175; Fax: 608-763-2799
E-mail: morelmasters@tds.net
Web site: http://www.morelmasters.com.

Morewellson, Ltd *See* **Morewellson, Ltd.**

Morewellson, Ltd., (*978-0-9994402; 978-1-950452*) P.O. Box 49726, Colorado Springs, CO 80949-9726 USA Tel 719-460-5425
E-mail: vikki@vikkiwalton.com.

Morgan & Claypool Pubs., (*978-1-59829; 978-1-60845; 978-1-62705; 978-1-970001; 978-1-68173; 978-1-68174; 978-1-947487; 978-1-64327; 978-1-63639*) Orders Addr.: a/o c/o. bLogistics, 82 Winter Sport Ln., Williston, VT 05495 USA (SAN 256-5153) Tel 888-822-9942; Edit Addr.: 1210 5th Ave. Suite 250, San Rafael, CA 94901 USA Tel 415-785-8003; Fax: 415-785-2507
E-mail: info@morganclaypool.com
Web site: http://www.morganclaypool.com
Dist(s): **American International Distribution Corp. ebrary, Inc.**

Morgan, E. A., (*978-0-9631975*) Orders Addr.: P.O. Box 7452, Naples, FL 34101 USA Fax: 941-598-9809
E-mail: rhymetime@mailstation.com.

Morgan, Elizabeth Jane, (*978-0-692-92320-7; 978-0-692-04614-2; 978-0-692-07610-1*) 2245 E. Racquet Club Rd., PALM SPRINGS, CA 92262 USA Tel 760-413-1458
E-mail: ejm92262@gmail.com
Dist(s): **Ingram Content Group.**

Morgan Foundation Pubs.: International Published Innovations, (*978-1-885679*) Orders Addr.: 182 Fourth St., Ashland, OR 97520 USA Fax: 815-550-4456
E-mail: morganfoundation@earthlink.net
Web site: http://www.morganfoundationpublishers.com.

Morgan James Publishing, (*978-0-9746133; 978-0-9758570; 978-0-9760901; 978-0-9768491; 978-1-933596; 978-1-60037; 978-0-9815058; 978-0-9817906; 978-0-9820750; 978-0-9823793; 978-0-9846170; 978-0-9828590; 978-0-9833715; 978-0-9835013; 978-1-61448; 978-0-9837125; 978-0-9840316; 978-1-938467; 978-1-63047; 978-1-63195; 978-1-68350; 978-0-9985823; 978-1-64279*) *Div. of Morgan James, LLC, 23rd Flr. 5 Penn Plaza, New York, NY 10001 USA*
Web site: http://www.morganjamespublishing.com
Dist(s): **Ingram Publisher Services**
Ingram Content Group
Lulu Pr., Inc.
MyiLibrary
Open Road Integrated Media, Inc.

Morgan Publishing Co., (*978-0-9639940*) Orders Addr.: P.O. Box 28718, San Jose, CA 95159 USA (SAN 298-1432) Fax: 408-637-1674; Edit Addr.: 338 Fifth St., Hollister, CA 95023 USA Tel 408-637-7031.

Morgan Publishing, Incorporated *See* **Augustine Pr.**

Morgan Rice *Imprint of* **Morgan Rice Bks.**

Morgan Rice Bks., Div. of Lukeman Literary Management Ltd., 157 Bedford Ave., Brooklyn, NY 11211 USA Tel 718-599-8988; Fax: 718-264-2189; *Imprints:* Morgan Rice (MYID_X_MORGAN) ; Noah Lukeman (MYID_P_NOAH LU)
Dist(s): **Lukeman Literary Management, Ltd. MyiLibrary.**

Morgan's Magical Media, (*978-0-692-65214-5; 978-0-578-17921-6; 978-0-692-69248-6; 978-0-692-76332-2*) 2 Foxhall Ct., Silver Spring, MD 20906 USA Tel 301-525-5699
Dist(s): **CreateSpace Independent Publishing Platform.**

Moriah Ministries, (*978-0-9728454; 978-0-9774836*) P.O. Box 23823, Chagrin Falls, OH 44023 USA Tel 440-543-9304 (phone/fax)
E-mail: info@davidicdance.com; info@moriahministries.org
Web site: http://www.davidicdance.com; http://www.moriahministries.org.

Morin, Frank *See* **Whipsaw Pr.**

Mormon Comics, (*978-0-9764965*) 435 N. 150 W., Blackfoot, ID 83221 USA Tel 208-785-4558 (phone/fax)
E-mail: info@mormoncomics.com
Web site: http://www.mormoncomics.com.

Mornin' Light Media, (*978-0-9763534*) Orders Addr.: 31203 N. Course View, Franklin, TN 37067 USA; *Imprints:* Mornin'Light Media (MorninLight)
E-mail: shawnsurber@comcast.net; hopebook@bellsouth.net
Web site: http://www.thehopebook.com.

morning circle media, (*978-0-9834702; 978-0-578-65314-3; 978-0-578-71951-1*) 519 Toll Rd., Oreland, PA 19075 USA Tel 215-572-9375
E-mail: cynthiakreilick@aol.com.

†Morning Glory Pr., Inc., (*978-0-930934; 978-1-885356; 978-1-932538; 978-0-9844283*) 6595 San Haroldo Way, Buena Park, CA 90620 USA (SAN 211-2558) 888-327-4362; Toll Free: 888-612-8254 Do not confuse with Morning Glory Press in Nashua, NH
E-mail: jwl@morningglorypress.com; info@morningglorypress.com
Web site: http://www.morningglorypress.com
Dist(s): **MyiLibrary**; *CIP.*

Morning Glory Pubns., (*978-0-9762929*) Orders Addr.: 1104 Blue ridge Dr., Clarkston, MI 48348 USA
E-mail: klinejane@hotmail.com.

Morning Joy Media, (*978-0-9826102; 978-1-937107*) 359 Bridge St., Spring City, PA 19475 USA Tel 610-256-2906
E-mail: debbie@morningjoymedia.com
Web site: http://www.morningjoymedia.com
Dist(s): **BookBaby.**

Morning Star Music Pubs., (*978-0-944529*) 1727 Larkin Williams Rd., Fenton, MO 63026 USA (SAN 243-8496)
E-mail: morningstar@morningstarmusic.com
Web site: http://www.morningstarmusic.com
Dist(s): **BookBaby.**

Morning Sun Bks., Inc., (*978-0-9619058; 978-1-58248; 978-1-878887*) 9 Pheasant Ln., Scotch Plains, NJ 07076 USA (SAN 243-1157) Tel 908-755-5454; Fax: 908-755-5455
E-mail: morningsunbooks@comcast.net
Web site: http://www.morningsunbooks.com
Dist(s): **Walthers, William K. Inc.**

MorningGlory Publishing, (*978-0-9705090*) Orders Addr.: P.O. Box 15523, Plantation, FL 33318-5523 USA Tel 954-370-7205; Fax: 954-370-6817; Edit Addr.: 9951 NW Sixth Ct., Plantation, FL 33324 USA
E-mail: tandtsm@aol.com.

Morningside Publishing, LLC, (*978-1-936210*) 1705 W Riley Rd, Payson, AZ 85541 USA (SAN 858-835X)
Web site: http://www.morningsidepublishing.com
Dist(s): **Smashwords.**

Morningstar Christian Chapel, (*978-0-9715733; 978-0-9729477; 978-0-9842943; 978-1-940198; 978-0-9964131*) 16241 Leffingwell Rd., Whittier, CA 90603 USA Tel 562-943-0297; Fax: 562-943-3608
E-mail: jacobeelen@morningstarcc.org
Web site: http://www.morningstarcc.org.

MorningStar Pubns., Inc., (*978-1-878327; 978-1-929371; 978-1-59933; 978-1-60708*) Div. of MorningStar Fellowship Church, 375 Star Light Dr., Fort Mill, SC 29715 USA Tel 803-802-5544 (phone/fax); Toll Free: 800-542-0278 (orders only) Do not confuse with Morningstar Pubns., Boulder, CO
E-mail: info@morningstarministries.org
Web site: http://www.morningstarministries.org
Dist(s): **Anchor Distributors**
Destiny Image Pubs.
Whitaker Hse.

Morningtide Pr., (*978-0-9790395*) P.O. Box 312, St. Augustine, FL 32085-0312 USA
Web site: http://www.morningtidepress.com
Dist(s): **Quality Bks., Inc.**

Mornin'Light Media *Imprint of* **Mornin' Light Media**

Morris, Nicole, (*978-0-692-89340-1*) 5 Washington Ave, PRINCETON, NJ 08540 USA Tel 908-256-4205
E-mail: lilniki45@gmail.com
Dist(s): **Ingram Content Group.**

Morris Publishing, (*978-0-7392; 978-0-9631249; 978-1-57502; 978-1-885591; 978-0-9863567*) Orders Addr.: P.O. Box 2110, Kearney, NE 68847 USA Fax: 308-237-0263; Toll Free: 800-650-7888 Do not confuse with companies with the same Wesley Chapel, FL, Elkhart, IN
Web site: http://www.morrispublishing.com.

Morris, Shanon, (*978-1-7325821*) 272 W. 117th st Apt 2E, NEW YORK, NY 10026 USA Tel 516-972-4513
E-mail: shanonmorris@gmail.com
Web site: www.shanonmorris.com.

Morris, Tami *See* **2B Pr.**

Morrison Meyer Pr., (*978-1-7323292*) 31 Le Conte, Laguna Niguel, CA 92677 USA Tel 949-395-8364
E-mail: Paulecke@gmail.com.

Morrison-Andrews, Sharalyn, (*978-0-9962889; 978-0-9974305; 978-0-9975343; 978-1-7335614*) P.O. Box 2829, South Portland, ME 04116 USA Tel 207-799-3664
E-mail: sharalynlovesanimals@gmail.com
Web site: sharalynlovesanimals.com.

Morrow Circle Publishing, LLC, (*978-0-9989801*) 7333 Woodward Claypool Rd., Morrow, OH 45152 USA Tel 513-310-0280
E-mail: Janet@JanetKassalenAuthor.com
Web site: www.JanetKassalenAuthor.com.

Morrow, William Cookbooks *Imprint of* **HarperCollins Pubs.**

Morrow, William & Co. *Imprint of* **HarperCollins Pubs.**

Morten Moore Publishing, (*978-0-9672576; 978-0-9991108*) Div. of K & M Marketing, 415 E. Mohawk, Flagstaff, AZ 86001 USA Tel 928-380-4982; Fax: 000-000-0000
Dist(s): **Canyonlands Pubns.**

Mortensen, Joshua *See* **Magpie Children's Bks.**

Morton Arts Media, (*978-0-9796868*) P.O. Box 233, Cornelius, NC 28031 USA.

Morton Bks., (*978-1-929188*) 47 Stewart Ave., Irvington, NJ 07111 USA Tel 973-374-8327; Fax: 973-374-1125
E-mail: rmo1033555@aol.com
Web site: http://www.mortonbooks.com.

MOS, Inc., (*978-0-9778570*) 5271 E MANN RD, Pekin, IN 47165-8807 USA Tel 812-967-2531; Fax: 812-967-2980; Toll Free: 800-451-3993
E-mail: info@joyfulcatholic.com
Web site: http://www.traditionalcatholicpublishing.com/.

Mo's Nose, LLC, (*978-0-9816255*) 222 Palisades Ave., Santa Monica, CA 90402-2734 USA (SAN 856-0811) Tel 310-451-8125
Web site: http://www.mosnose.com
Dist(s): **Independent Pubs. Group**
Midpoint Trade Bks., Inc.

Mosaic Paradigm Group, LLC, (*978-0-578-07392-7; 978-0-9852542*) 3 Pasco Ct., Pikesville, MD 21208 USA (SAN 920-2889) Tel 877-733-7308
E-mail: info@mpg-publishing.com
Web site: http://www.mpg-publishing.com.

Mosaic Pr. (CAN) (*978-0-88962; 978-1-77161*) *Dist. by* **IPG Chicago.**

Mosaic Publishing *See* **Branded Black Publishing**

Mosby *Imprint of* **Elsevier - Health Sciences Div.**

Moscow Ballet *Imprint of* **Sports Marketing International, Inc.**

Mosdos Pr., (*978-0-9671009; 978-0-9742160; 978-0-9801670; 978-0-9858078; 978-0-9888286*) Div. of Mosdos Ohr Hatorah, 1508 Warrensville Ctr. Rd., Cleveland, OH 44121 USA Tel 216-291-4158; Fax: 216-291-4169
E-mail: mosdospress@moh1.org; jfactor@moh1.org
Web site: http://www.mosdospress.com.

Moselle Productions, Inc., (*978-0-9701289*) P.O. Box 1304, League City, TX 77574 USA Tel 732-623-9908; Toll Free: 800-598-2519
Web site: http://www.mangoeandmarlie.com.

Mosely, Winifred, (*978-0-9769610*) 6600 E. River Rd., Tucson, AZ 85750 USA Tel 520-327-3681
E-mail: njmosely@comcast.net.

For full information on wholesalers and distributors, refer to the Wholesaler and Distributor Name Index

Moshire Pr., *(978-0-615-39082-6)* 2355 Carlysle Cove, Lawrenceville, GA 30044 USA Tel 404-784-5987
Web site: http://www.moshirepress.com.

Mosley, Kim, *(978-0-9663215)* 1312 W. 40th St., Austin, TX 78756-3615 USA Tel 512-762-6790
E-mail: mrkimmosley@gmail.com
Web site: http://kimmosley.com/workbook.

Moss, Francis C., *(978-1-7327910)* 7709 Vista Rd., Joshua Tree, CA 92252 USA Tel 818-692-1575
E-mail: fcmoss@gmail.com.

Moss, Michael, *(978-0-9763003)* 610 Prestwick Dr., Frankfort, IL 60423 USA Tel 312-437-7827 (312-437-STAR)
Web site: http://www.5starpc.com.

Moss Press Publishing, *(978-0-578-12603-6)* 616 Corporate Way Suite 2-4348, Valley Cottage, NY 10989 USA.

Mosscovered Gumbo Barn, *(978-0-9725853)* 15960 Highland Rd., Baton Rouge, LA 70810 USA
Dist(s): **Greenleaf Book Group.**

Mossy Moot, *(978-0-9977134)* 127 KINGS HWY, HACKETTSTOWN, NJ 07840 USA Tel 908-852-7050
E-mail: Susimage66@gmail.com.

Mostats, Marie C., *(978-0-9742848)* Orders Addr.: P.O. Box 230053, Las Vegas, NV 89123-0001 USA; Edit Addr.: 608 NW 29th St., Wilton Manors, FL 33311-2443 USA.

Mot de Mere Publishing, *(978-0-692-15641-4; 978-0-578-45015-5; 978-0-578-45658-4; 978-0-578-48293-4; 978-0-578-51508-3)* 27506 N. 3979 Dr., Ochelata, OK 74051 USA Tel 918-277-7691
E-mail: scon555@gmail.com.

Mother Bear Pr., *(978-0-692-19773-8; 978-0-692-04346-2)* 1590 Amsterdam Ave. Apt. 22, New York, NY 10031 USA Tel 225-505-2203
E-mail: dcassidy1228@gmail.com
Dist(s): **Ingram Content Group.**

Mother Goose Programs, *(978-0-9753985; 978-0-9841366; 978-1-935784)* P.O. Box 423, Chester, VT 05143-0423 USA
E-mail: debbi@mothergooseprograms.org
Web site: http://www.mothergooseprograms.org
Dist(s): **National Bk. Network.**

Mother Hubbard & Co. LLC *Imprint of* **Mother Hubbard & Co. LLC**

Mother Hubbard & Co. LLC, *(978-0-692-18722-7; 978-0-578-41143-9; 978-1-7330681)* 3375 Centerville Hwy. No. 391385, Snellville, GA 30039 USA Tel 404-740-7835; *Imprints:* Mother Hubbard & Co. LLC (MYID_Z_MOTHER)
E-mail: MotherHubbardCo@gmail.com
Web site: MotherHubbard.us.

Mother Lode Pr. LLC, *(978-0-615-34241-2; 978-0-692-78184-5)* P.O. Box 2526, Bay Saint Louis, MS 39521 USA Tel 571-926-3443
E-mail: jonfaust@helicopterharry.com.

Mother Moose Pr., *(978-0-9724570)* Orders Addr.: 21010 Southbank St., PMB No. 435, Potomac Falls, VA 20165 USA Tel 571-223-6472
E-mail: books@mothermoosepress.com
Web site: http://www.mothermoosepress.com.

Mother Necessity Inc., *(978-0-9796579)* P.O. Box 2135, Bonita Springs, FL 34133 USA
E-mail: cfergus@mothernecessity.com
Web site: http://www.mothernecessity.com.

M.O.T.H.E.R. Publishing Co., Inc., The, *(978-0-9718431)* Orders Addr.: P.O. Box 477, Rock Springs, WY 82902 USA Tel 307-382-5027; Fax: 307-382-6492; Edit Addr.: 616 Elias Ave., Rock Springs, WY 82901 USA
E-mail: motherpublishing@wyoming.com
Web site: http://www.motherpublishing.com.

Motherboard Bks., *(978-0-9749653; 978-0-692-42438-4; 978-0-692-42562-6; 978-0-692-43162-7)* P.O. Box 430041, Saint Louis, MO 63143 USA
E-mail: info@motherboardbooks.com
Web site: http://motherboardbooks.com
Dist(s): **CreateSpace Independent Publishing Platform.**

Motherhood Printing & Etc., *(978-1-60225)* Orders Addr.: 45973 Rd. 795, Ansley, NE 68814-5126 USA (SAN 852-1212) Tel 308-880-1021; Fax: 308-732-3280
E-mail: mary@motherhoodprinting.com
Web site: http://motherhoodprinting.com.

Motherly Way Enterprises, *(978-0-9671428)* P.O. Box 11, Marylhurst, OR 97036-0011 USA Tel 503-723-2879; Toll Free: 877-666-7929
E-mail: julie@motherlyway.com
Web site: http://www.motherlyway.com.

Mother's Love Publishing, A, *(978-0-9777022)* 4962 Bristol Rock Rd, Florissant, MO 63033 USA (SAN 257-9707)
Dist(s): **Lushena Bks.**

Mothwing Pr. *Imprint of* **Mothwing.com**

Mothwing.com, *(978-0-9724528)* 80 Sheffield Rd., Waltham, MA 02451-2374 USA Tel 781-899-8153; *Imprints:* Mothwing Press (Mothwng Pr)
E-mail: mothwingpress@mothwing.com; andylevesque@rcn.com
Web site: http://www.mothwing.com/mothwingpress.

Motina Bks., *(978-1-945060)* 811 Rockefeller Ln., Allen, TX 75002 USA Tel 303-668-0440
E-mail: diane@warthog.com.

Motion Fitness LLC, *(978-0-9744568)* P.O. Box 2179, Palatine, IL 60078-2179 USA
E-mail: sales@motionfitness.com
Web site: http://www.motionfitness.com.

Motivision Media, *(978-0-9722332)* 9528 Blossom Valley Rd., El Cajon, CA 92021 USA
E-mail: dehaven@motivisionmedia.com; dehaven1@cox.net
Web site: http://www.motivisionmedia.com; http://www.MyFootballMentor.com.

Motorbooks *Imprint of* **Quarto Publishing Group USA**

†**Mott Media**, *(978-0-88062; 978-0-915134; 978-0-940319)* 1130 Fenway Cir., Fenton, MI 48430 USA (SAN 207-1460) Tel 810-714-4280; Fax: 810-714-2077 Do not confuse with Mott Media in Stamford, CT
E-mail: sales@mottmedia.com; bill@mottmedia.com
Web site: http://www.mottmedia.com
Dist(s): **Spring Arbor Distributors, Inc.**; *CIP.*

Mottley, William, *(978-0-9769216)* 428 N. Genito Rd., Burkeville, VA 23922 USA Tel 434-767-5594
E-mail: emottley@ceva.net
Web site: http://www.narrowstrip.com.

Motto, Amy, *(978-0-692-14862-4; 978-0-692-14935-5; 978-0-692-14939-3)* 1915 Myrtle Ave, Las Cruces, NM 88001 USA Tel 575-541-8070
E-mail: ray.karen7@gmail.com
Dist(s): **Ingram Content Group.**

Moulton, Shirley *See* **Magic Moon Bks., LLC**

Mount Baldy Pr., Inc., *(978-0-9715863)* P.O. Box 469, Boulder, CO 80306-0469 USA (SAN 254-2625) Tel 415-413-8052; Fax: 303-532-1007
E-mail: simeon@mountbaldy.com
Web site: http://www.mountbaldy.com
Dist(s): **New Leaf Distributing Co., Inc.**
Quality Bks., Inc.

Mount Helicon Pr. *Imprint of* **Rock, James A. & Co. Pubs.**

Mount Olive College Pr., *(978-0-9627087; 978-1-880994; 978-1-59761)* Mount Olive College, Administration Bldg. 634 Henderson St., Mount Olive, NC 28365 USA (SAN 297-7729) Tel 919-658-2502; Toll Free Fax: 800-653-0854.

Mount Rushmore Bookstores, *(978-0-9646798; 978-0-9752617; 978-0-9798823; 978-0-692-63993-1)* Div. of Mount Rushmore National Memorial Society, 13030 Hwy. 244, Keystone, SD 57751 USA Tel 605-341-8883; Fax: 605-341-0433; Toll Free: 800-699-3142
E-mail: debbie_ketel@mtrushmore.org
Web site: http://www.mountrushmoresociety.com
Dist(s): **Partners Distributing.**

Mount Rushmore History Association *See* **Mount Rushmore Bookstores**

†**Mount Vernon Ladies' Assn. of the Union**, *(978-0-931917)* Orders Addr.: P.O. Box 110, Mount Vernon, VA 22121 USA (SAN 225-3976); Edit Addr.: 3200 Mount Vernon Memorial Hwy., Mount Vernon, VA 22121 USA
E-mail: ajohnson@mountvernon.org
Web site: http://www.mountvernon.org
Dist(s): **University of Virginia Pr.**
Wimmer Cookbooks; *CIP.*

Mountain Air Bks., *(978-0-615-24940-7; 978-0-615-24941-4; 978-0-615-26703-6; 978-0-615-29319-6; 978-0-615-29829-0; 978-0-615-41620-5; 978-0-615-56237-7; 978-0-615-64830-9)* 1045 University Ave. Apt. 2, Rochester, NY 14607-1624 USA
E-mail: scottkny@yahoo.com; mairbooks123@yahoo.com.

Mountain Bk. Co., P.O. Box 778, Broomfield, CO 80038-0778 USA Tel 303-436-1982; Fax: 917-386-2769
E-mail: wordguise@aol.com
Web site: http://www.mountainbook.org.

Mountain Brook Ink, *(978-0-9960068; 978-1-943959)* 26 Moore Rd., White Salmon, WA 98672 USA Tel 509-493-3953
E-mail: miraleef@gmail.com
Web site: www.miraleeferrell.com.

Mountain Gap Bks., *(978-0-692-98919-7; 978-1-7323277; 978-1-7329720)* 221 Forestview Dr., Jonesborough, TN 37659-5622 USA Tel 423-773-7225
E-mail: bjmg1049@gmail.com; publisher@mountaingapbooks.com
Web site: mountaingapbooks.com.

Mountain Girl Press *See* **Jan-Carol Publishing, INC.**

Mountain Horse Pr., *(978-0-9995431)* 1859 Tower Rd., St. Johnsbury, VT 05819 USA Tel 802-748-5455
E-mail: robin.kristoff@gmail.com
Web site: mountainhorsepress.com.

Mountain Maid *See* **Light Messages Publishing**

Mountain Memories Bks. *Imprint of* **Quarrier Pr.**

Mountain Ministries, *(978-0-9787761)* 18055 100th St., Lindsay, OK 73052-3308 USA Do not confuse with Mountain Ministries Sitka, Alaska.

Mountain n' Air Bks., *(978-1-879415)* Div. of Mountain n' Air Sports, Inc., Orders Addr.: P.O. Box 12540, La Crescenta, CA 91224 USA (SAN 630-5598) Tel 818-248-9345; Toll Free Fax: 800-303-5578; Toll Free: 800-446-9696; Edit Addr.: 2947-A Hololulu Ave., La Crescenta, CA 91214 USA (SAN 631-4198); *Imprints:* Bearly Cooking (Bearly Cooking)
E-mail: books@mountain-n-air.com
Web site: http://mountain-n-air.com
Dist(s): **CreateSpace Independent Publishing Platform.**

Mountain Path Pr., *(978-0-9653149)* 111 Bank St., Ste 152, Grass Valley, CA 95945 USA Toll Free: 888-224-9997
E-mail: Info@MountainPathPress.com
Web site: http://www.mountainpathpress.com
Dist(s): **Bks. West**
Integral Yoga Pubns.
New Leaf Distributing Co., Inc.
Partners Bk. Distributing, Inc.

Mountain Path Publications *See* **Mountain Path Pr.**

†**Mountain Pr. Publishing Co., Inc.**, *(978-0-87842)* Orders Addr.: P.O. Box 2399, Missoula, MT 59806-2399 USA (SAN 202-8832) Tel 406-728-1900; Fax: 406-728-1635; Toll Free: 800-234-5308; Edit Addr.: 1301 S. Third West, Missoula, MT 59801 USA (SAN 662-0868)
E-mail: jrimel@mtnpress.com; info@mtnpress.com; anne@mtnpress.com
Web site: http://www.mountain-press.com
Dist(s): **Bks. West**
Partners Bk. Distributing, Inc.; *CIP.*

Mountain States Specialties, *(978-0-9726022)* 1671 Valtec Ln., Boulder, CO 80301 USA Tel 303-444-6186 Toll Free: 800-353-2147.

Mountain Stream Publishing, *(978-0-615-89002-9; 978-0-692-22188-4; 978-0-692-26072-2; 978-0-692-28524-4; 978-0-692-33655-7; 978-0-692-33933-6; 978-0-692-35039-3; 978-0-692-37723-9; 978-0-692-52377-3; 978-0-692-76014-7)* 5327 W. HILL Rd., BOISE, ID 83703 USA Tel 2088639839
Dist(s): **CreateSpace Independent Publishing Platform.**

Mountain Thunder Publishing, *(978-0-615-69738-3; 978-0-9887625)* P.O. Box 6264, Snowmass Village, CO 81615 USA Tel 6462836884
Dist(s): **CreateSpace Independent Publishing Platform.**

Mountain Valley Publishing, LLC, *(978-1-59453; 978-1-60002; 978-1-934940)* Orders Addr.: 1420 Maple Ct., Martinsville, IN 46151 USA Tel 765-349-8908; Fax: 765-349-8908
E-mail: bdenton308@comcast.net
Web site: http://www.mountainvalleypublishing.com.

Mountain Voices Pubs., *(978-0-9671908)* Orders Addr.: 2 Junaluska Rd., Andrews, NC 28901 USA Tel 828-321-5553; Fax: 828-321-2446
E-mail: MountainTeller@mountainvoice.com
Web site: http://www.mountainvoice.com.

Mountain World Media LLC, *(978-0-9763309)* Orders Addr.: P.O. Box 687, Telluride, CO 81435 USA Tel 970-729-0289; Edit Addr.: 135 Hillside Ln., Telluride, CO 81435 USA
E-mail: damon@mountainworldmedia.com
Web site: http://www.mountainworldmedia.com
Dist(s): **Alpenbooks Pr. LLC**
Bks. West.

Mountaintop Pr., *(978-0-9711106)* Orders Addr.: P.O. Box 550, Cary, NC 27512-0550 USA Tel 919-567-9550; Fax: 919-567-9694; Edit Addr.: 201-D Foliage Cir., Cary, NC 27511 USA
Dist(s): **Send The Light Distribution LLC.**

MountainView *Imprint of* **Treble Heart Bks.**

Mountan Creek Pubns., *(978-0-615-52752-9; 978-0-615-55170-8; 978-0-9853574)* 80 Post Ave., Rochester, NY 14619 USA Tel 585-966-9669
E-mail: nailahbaniti@gmail.com
Web site: Mountaincreekpublications.com.

Mountcastle, Deirdre D. PA, *(978-0-9992073)* 16 Marshview Dr., St Augustine, FL 32080-9182 USA Tel 904-687-5667
E-mail: Dee.Mountcastle.Books@gmail.com.

Mountz Media & Publishing, *(978-0-9840673; 978-0-9891429; 978-1-7347117)* Orders Addr.: P.O. Box 702398, Tulsa, OK 74170 USA; Edit Addr.: 5721 E. 101st Pl., Tulsa, OK 74137 USA
E-mail: mamountz@cox.net.

Mouse Prints Pr. (NLD) *(978-90-818368; 978-94-91613)* *Dist. by* **IngramPubServ.**

Mouse! Publishing, *(978-0-9643512)* Orders Addr.: P.O. Box 1674, Honolulu, HI 96806 USA Tel 808-625-7522; Fax: 808-284-5516; Edit Addr.: 419 South St., Suite 133, Honolulu, HI 96813 USA
Dist(s): **Booklines Hawaii, Ltd.**

Mouse Works, *(978-0-7364; 978-1-57082)* Div. of Disney Bk. Publishing, Inc., A Walt Disney Co., 114 Fifth Ave., New York, NY 10011 USA (SAN 298-0797) Tel 212-633-4400; Fax: 212-633-4811
Web site: http://www.disneybooks.com
Dist(s): **Random Hse., Inc.**

Mousetime Bks. *Imprint of* **Mousetime Media LLC**

Mousetime Media LLC, *(978-0-9723213)* 7960-B Soquel Dr., No. 297, Aptos, CA 95003 USA; *Imprints:* Mousetime Books (Msetime Bks)
E-mail: books@mousetime.com
Web site: http://www.mousetime.com.

Move Bks., LLC, *(978-0-9854810; 978-0-9970513; 978-0-692-73732-3; 978-0-692-97736-1; 978-1-7322137)* 10 N. Main St., Beacon Falls, CT 06403 USA Tel 203-709-0490
Web site: http://www.move-books.com
Dist(s): **Independent Pubs. Group**
MyiLibrary
Small Pr. United.

Move Mountains Publishing, *(978-0-9991698)* 2925 Gulf Fwy S Ste. B-248, League City, TX 77573 USA Tel 281-671-7689
E-mail: gobedolive@gmail.com.

Movement Makers International, *(978-0-9766930)* P.O. Box 3940, Broken Arrow, OK 74013-3940 USA
Web site: http://www.j12.com.

Movies for the Ear, LLC, *(978-1-935793)* 8362 Tamarack Village No. 119-327, St. Paul, MN 55125 USA Tel 612-209-3884
E-mail: moviesfortheear@comcast.net
Web site: www.CreepersMysteries.com
Dist(s): **Ingram Content Group.**

Moving Finger Pr., *(978-0-9774214)* 369 Jersey St., San Francisco, CA 94114-3709 USA Tel 415-285-0926; Fax: 415-840-0038
E-mail: editor@movingfingerpress.com
Web site: http://movingfingerpress.com.

Moving Stories, *(978-0-9986877)* P.O. Box 371505, Las Vegas, NV 89137 USA Tel 702-793-8376
E-mail: arlenacohen@gmail.com
Web site: acohenauthor.wordpress.com.

Mowery, Julia, *(978-0-9710529)* 6308 Starfish Ave, North Port, FL 34291 USA
E-mail: storyteller2000@msn.com; storytellerjm@aol.com
Web site: http://dobiebookpublishing.com.

Moznaim Publishing Corp., *(978-0-940118; 978-1-885220)* 4304 12th Ave., Brooklyn, NY 11219 USA (SAN 214-4123) Tel 718-438-7680; Fax: 718-438-1305; Toll Free: 800-364-5118.

MP Pubns., Inc., *(978-0-9823601)* Orders Addr.: P.O. Box 2061, Clifton, NJ 07015-9831 USA Tel 973-471-1787; Toll Free: 877-673-8346; *Imprints:* Majestic Kids (MajesticKids)
E-mail: info@mpministries.org
Web site: http://www.mpministries.org.

MP Publishing Ltd. (GBR) *(978-0-9555792; 978-1-84982)* *Dist. by* **IPG Chicago.**

MP2ME Enterprise, *(978-0-9717947; 978-0-9776679; 978-0-9841360)* 2125 NE. Newton Ln., Issaquah, WA 98029 USA Tel 425-326-0335
E-mail: mpighin1@comcast.net
Dist(s): **Ingram Content Group.**

MPC Pr. International, *(978-0-9628453; 978-0-9715541)* P.O. Box 26142, San Fransisco, CA 94126-6142 USA
E-mail: info@laughingcookiejar.com
Web site: http://www.laughingcookiejar.com.

MPI Publishing, *(978-0-9960179)* 173 Torringford St, Winsted, CT 06098 USA Tel 860-909-1011
E-mail: jldost@aol.com.

MPR Publishing, *(978-0-9831857)* 3550 N. Daisy Dr., Rialto, CA 92377 USA Tel 323-259-2884
E-mail: sales@mprpublishing.com.

MPublishing *See* **Michigan Publishing**

MQuills Publishing, *(978-0-615-55835-6; 978-0-615-56307-7; 978-0-615-63989-5; 978-1-62375)* 4179 Choteau Cir., Rancho Cordova, CA 95742 USA Tel 916-205-6999; *Imprints:* Caliburn Books (Caliburn Bks); Paramance (Paramance)
E-mail: mquills@mquills.com
Web site: www.mquills.com
Dist(s): **CreateSpace Independent Publishing Platform**
Ingram Content Group.

Mr. Cal Cumin, *(978-0-9987788)* 9433 Hwy 87, shepherd, MT 59079 USA Tel 406-690-1763; Fax: 406-690-1763
E-mail: cuminster@gmail.com.

Mr Do It All, Inc., *(978-0-9722038)* 2212 S. Chickasaw Trail, No. 220, Orlando, FL 32825 USA Toll Free: 800-425-9206
E-mail: info@planet-heller.com
Web site: http://www.planet-heller.com.

Mr. Emmett Publishing, *(978-0-9759346)* 37 Harleston Pl., Charleston, SC 29401 USA Tel 843-853-5728
E-mail: talubbers@comcast.net.

Mr. Fuzzy Ears LLC, *(978-0-692-14309-4; 978-0-692-18421-9; 978-0-692-18424-0)* 4970 N. Grandview Dr., Peoria Heights, IL 61616 USA Tel 317-753-1028
E-mail: Donna@CarrRoberts.com
Dist(s): **Ingram Content Group.**

Mr Nick Productions, *(978-0-692-35762-0; 978-0-692-60806-7; 978-0-692-65952-6; 978-0-692-85504-1; 978-0-692-85547-8; 978-0-692-10167-4; 978-0-692-10169-8; 978-0-578-47954-5; 978-0-578-47955-2; 978-0-578-50645-6; 978-0-578-54782-4; 978-0-578-58877-3; 978-0-578-63692-4; 978-0-578-68046-0; 978-0-578-68307-2; 978-0-578-69452-8; 978-0-578-69453-5; 978-0-578-69456-6; 978-0-578-69484-9; 978-0-578-69514-3; 978-0-578-69558-7; 978-0-578-69559-4; 978-0-578-70320-6; 978-0-578-74253-3) 16 Wayto Ln., Ballston Lake, NY 12019 USA Tel 518-598-4194.*

Mr. Theodore Bear, *(978-0-9862968)* 5720 Belaire cir, Granbury, TX 76048 USA Tel 8174080634; Toll Free: 8174080634
Web site: http://mrtheobear.blogspot.com/
Dist(s): **CreateSpace Independent Publishing Platform.**

Mr. V. Consulting Services, *(978-0-692-75108-4; 978-0-692-94960-3; 978-1-7323085)* 938 Buck Way, Sevierville, TN 37876 USA Tel 210-365-1843
E-mail: villareal.mark@yahoo.com
Web site: www.markvillareal.com.

Mracek, Ann, *(978-0-9766488)* 22 Morwood Ln., Creve Coeur, MO 63141 USA (SAN 257-0009) Tel 314-432-5713; Fax: 314-569-2202
E-mail: anmracek@springmail.com.

MrDuz.com, *(978-0-9796226)* 1325 W. Sunshine No. 515, Springfield, MO 65807 USA (SAN 853-9332) Tel 417-831-9898; Fax: 417-863-6655 (please include To: MrDuz.com on cover pg.); Toll Free: 866-966-7389
E-mail: patrick@patrickwellman.com; patrick@mrduz.com
Web site: http://www.mrduz.com; http://www.patrickwellman.com.

MrExcel.com Publishing *See* **Tickling Keys, Inc.**

MRG Professional Services, *(978-0-9760310)* 6255 Cherry Ln. Farm Dr., West Chester, OH 45069 USA
E-mail: kgillis85@gmail.com.

MRN Pubns., *(978-0-9630495)* 1417 Noble St., Longwood, FL 32750 USA Tel 407-831-2947 (phone/fax)
E-mail: marjorie@partnersinlearning.com
Web site: http://www.partnersinglelearning.com.

Mroczka Media, *(978-0-9846800; 978-1-938397; 978-0-692-54800-4; 978-0-692-55469-2; 978-0-692-56464-6)* 7202 Barker Cypress Rd. Suite

Publisher Name Index

10302, Cypress, TX 77433 USA; *Imprints:* Pagan Writers Press (PaganWriters)
E-mail: angie@mroczkamedia.com
Web site: http://www.lostenchantressbooks.com
Dist(s): **CreateSpace Independent Publishing Platform.**

Mrs, (978-1-7329078) 702 Commercial Ste. 1C, Emporia, KS 66801 USA Tel 620-340-1001
E-mail: debirsik@gmail.com
Web site: dairsik.wordpress.com.

Mrs. L's Reading Room, (978-0-9767278) Orders Addr.: 110 Wedgefield Dr., Hilton Head Island, SC 29926 USA Tel 843-682-2820 (telephone/fax)
Web site: http://www.readroom.com.

Mrs. Raven's World, (978-0-578-42837-6; 978-0-578-42839-0) 2524 Cty. Rt. 60, Elmira, NY 14901 USA Tel 607-873-8011
E-mail: mrsravensworld@gmail.com
Dist(s): **Ingram Content Group.**

Mrs. Weisz Books *See* **Mrs. Weisz Bks.**

Mrs Wordsmith Ltd. (GBR) (978-1-9996107) *Dist. by* **S and S Inc.**

M.S.C. Bks. *Imprint of* **Mustard Seed Comics**

MSJ Music Publighing, (978-0-9764521) P.O. Box 3185, Rancho Santa Fe, CA 92067-3185 USA.

MSP *Imprint of* **Main St Publishing, Inc.**

MSPpress *Imprint of* **Mama Specific Productions**

MsRevenda.com, (978-0-9768538) P.O. Box 370109, Decatur, GA 30037 USA
Web site: http://www.msrevenda.com.

M.T. Publishing Co., Inc., (978-1-932439; 978-1-934729; 978-1-938730; 978-1-945306; 978-1-949478) Orders Addr.: P.O. Box 6802, Evansville, IN 47719-6802 USA Toll Free: 888-263-4702; Edit Addr.: 209 NW 8th St., Evansville, IN 47708 USA
Web site: http://www.mtpublishing.com.

mTrellis Publishing, Inc., (978-0-9663281; 978-1-930650) Orders Addr.: P.O. Box 280, New York Mills, MN 56567 USA (SAN 299-6669) Fax: 218-385-3708; Toll Free: 800-513-0115
E-mail: trellis2@aol.com; mary@trellispublishing.com
Web site: http://www.trellispublishing.com
Dist(s): **Independent Pubs. Group**
MyiLibrary
Small Pr. United.

MTV Bks. *Imprint of* **MTV Books**

MTV Books, 1230 Ave. of the Americas, New York, NY 10020 USA; *Imprints:* MTV Books (MTV Imp)
Dist(s): **Simon & Schuster, Inc.**

Mu Alpha Theta, National High Schl. Mathematics Club, (978-0-940790) 601 Elm Ave., Rm. 423, Norman, OK 73019 USA (SAN 204-0077) Tel 405-325-4489; Fax: 405-325-7184
E-mail: matheta@ou.edu
Web site: http://www.mualphatheta.org.

Muae Publishing, Inc., (978-1-885030; 978-1-935717) c/o 3620 S Vermont Ave KAP 462, Los Angeles, CA 90089 USA
E-mail: sunyoung@panix.com; kaya@kaya.com
Web site: http://www.kaya.com
Dist(s): **D.A.P./Distributed Art Pubs.**
SPD-Small Pr. Distribution
Two Rivers Distribution.

Mud Pie Pr., (978-0-9714941) 4201 Morrow Ave., Waco, TX 76710 USA Tel 254-716-3193
E-mail: bjelmore@msn.com; belmore1@hot.rr.com
Web site: http://www.mudpiepress.com
Dist(s): **Quality Bks., Inc.**

Mud Puddle, Inc., (978-1-59412; 978-1-60311) 54 W. 21st St., Suite 601, New York, NY 10010 USA Tel 212-647-9168.

Muddle Puddle Bks. (CAN) (978-0-9686586) *Dist. by* **BTPS.**

Muddy Boots Pr., (978-1-63076; 978-0-692-44652-2) 421 Ponderosa Dr, Harker Heights, TX 76548 USA Tel 240-515-1042
Web site: www.muddybootspress.com
Dist(s): **CreateSpace Independent Publishing Platform**
National Bk. Network
Rowman & Littlefield Publishers, Inc.

Mudpuppy *Imprint of* **Galison**

Mudpuppy Pr., (978-0-7353; 978-0-929648; 978-0-939456; 978-1-56155) Div. of Galison Bks., 28 W. 44th St., Suite 1411, New York, NY 10036 USA (SAN 216-3888) Tel 212-354-8840
Dist(s): **Hachette Bk. Group.**

Mueller, Mary L. Bks. LLC, (978-0-692-90164-9; 978-0-692-90545-6) 1352 Holmes Landing Dr, FLEMING ISLE, FL 32003 USA Tel 239-823-5240
E-mail: talktomarymueller@gmail.com
Dist(s): **Ingram Content Group.**

Mugen Pr., (978-1-942920) 110 Isolda Dr., Pittsburgh, PA 15209 USA Tel 412-401-3264
E-mail: mugenpress@gmail.com
Web site: www.mugenpress.com.

Mugsy and Sugar Pressed, (978-0-9798886) 1117 Nobb Hill Dr., West Chester, PA 19380 USA
E-mail: tlaurento@comcast.net.

Mukund Pubns., (978-0-9663831) 3033 Arbor Bnd., Birmingham, AL 35244-1573 USA
E-mail: pratibhakhare@hotmail.com
Web site: http://www.learnhindi.com.

Mulholland Teacher Resources *See* **Sonic Sword Productions**

Mullen, Peter, (978-0-692-77226-3; 978-0-692-77229-4) 440 Dixon Landing Rd. Apt# I-306, MILPITAS, CA 95035 USA Tel 408-691-6581.

Mullen Pr., (978-1-7323458) 4600 POWDER MILL RD STE 450, Beltsville, MD 20705 USA Tel 240-351-7269
E-mail: contact.us@mullenpress.com
Web site: www.MullenPress.com.

Mulley, Bradley, (978-0-9996420) 133 Steep Mountain Ct., Livermore, CO 80546 USA Tel 970-407-7271
E-mail: bradmulley@gmail.com.

Mullings Media, (978-0-9767657) P.O. Box 934, Woodbridge, NJ 07095 USA.

Mullins Pubns. & Apparel, LLC, (978-0-9760160) 6600 Plaza Dr., No.2000, New Orleans, LA 70127 USA.

Mulry, Peter J., (978-0-692-78821-9) 2401 Bayshore Blvd .No. 1002, Tampa, FL 33629 USA Tel 850-221-1045
E-mail: pete@petemulry.com
Web site: www.peterjmulryfoundation.org.

Multables, Inc., (978-0-9645004) 6398 S. Louthan St., Littleton, CO 80120 USA Tel 303-794-0786; Toll Free: 800-320-6857.

Multicultural Pubns., (978-0-9634932; 978-1-884242) 936 Slosson St., Akron, OH 44320 USA Tel 330-865-9578; Fax: 330-734-0737; Toll Free: 800-238-0297
E-mail: multiculturalpub@prodigy.net
Web site: http://www.multiculturalpub.net
Dist(s): **Brodart Co.**
Follett School Solutions.

Multi-Language Pubns., (978-0-9703210; 978-1-931891) 2500 George Dieter, El Paso, TX 79936 USA Tel 915-857-5852; Fax: 915-857-7644; Toll Free: 800-876-1388
E-mail: paul.hartman@wels.net; jan.gamble@wels.net.

Multi-Language Publications Program *See* **Multi-Language Pubns.**

Multnomah *Imprint of* **Doubleday Religious Publishing Group, The**

Multnomah Bks. *Imprint of* **Crown Publishing Group, The**

Mumblefish Bks., (978-0-9759649) Orders Addr.: P.O. Box 139, Point Pleasant, PA 18950-0139 USA Tel 215-297-5002; Fax: 215-297-5299
E-mail: info@mumblefishbooks.com
Web site: http://mumblefishboooks.com.

Mumford Institute, (978-0-615-25457-9; 978-0-692-00349-7) 330 Shore Dr., Unit C5, Highlands, NJ 07732 USA Tel 732-291-8243.

Munagala, Krithi, (978-0-692-12315-7; 978-1-7332943) PO Box 1324, Folsom, CA 95763 USA Tel 916-753-5085
E-mail: kreativekrithi@gmail.com
Web site: www.kreativekrithi.com.

Mundania Pr. *Imprint of* **Mundania Pr.**

Mundania Pr., (978-0-9723670; 978-1-59426; 978-1-60659) 6470A Glenway Ave., No. 109, Cincinnati, OH 45211 USA (SAN 255-013X) Tel 513-490-2822; Fax: 513-598-9220; *Imprints:* Mundania Press (MundPr)
E-mail: bob@mundania.com; books@mundania.com
Web site: http://www.mundania.com; http://www.phaze.com
Dist(s): **Ingram Content Group.**

Munson, Craig *See* **Fleur De Lis Publishing, LLC**

Murasaki Pr., (978-1-7328995) 4902 W. Wind Trail No. 103, Austin, TX 78745 USA Tel 512-790-3526
E-mail: brittajensen@me.com
Web site: www.britta-jensen.com.

Murdoch Bks. Pty Ltd. (AUS) (978-0-86411; 978-1-74045; 978-1-921259; 978-1-921208; 978-1-74196; 978-1-74266; 978-0-7316-4258-8; 978-0-646-32800-3; 978-1-74325; 978-1-74336) *Dist. by* **HachBkGrp.**

Murdock, Bob E., (978-0-9754363) 352 Carly Ln., Rock Hill, SC 29732-7750 USA Tel 803-366-2666 (phone/fax)
E-mail: pbmurdock@comporium.net
Web site: http://www.sermonsforchildren.com.

Murdock Publishing Co., (978-0-9743359; 978-1-934102) Orders Addr.: 127 Belk Ct., Clayton, NC 27520 USA Tel 919-934-2393; Fax: 919-938-2394
Web site: http://www.murdockmedia.com.

Murine Pubns. LLC, (978-0-9753093; 978-0-9792665; 978-0-9815971; 978-0-692-00084-7; 978-0-9824994; 978-1-936690; 978-0-615-58775-2; 978-1-940849; 978-1-950330) Div. of Murine Communications, 1804 Miekle Ave, Woodland, CA 95776 USA
Web site: https://www.bigfontbooks.com
Dist(s): **CreateSpace Independent Publishing Platform**
Ingram Content Group
Lulu Pr., Inc.

Murphey, Hiromi, (978-0-9761350) 4049 Madison Ave. Apt. 102, Culver City, CA 90232-3246 USA
Web site: http://www.nabiland.com.

Murphy, D. L., (978-1-7329658) 4470 Long Ln., Franklin, TN 37064 USA Tel 615-714-0030
E-mail: dlrestivo@aol.com
Web site: Kingslandtales.com.

Murphy, Indera *See* **Tolana Publishing**

Murphy, Michael, (978-0-692-17801-0) 13436 N. Locust St., Dexter, MO 63841 USA Tel 573-624-7144
E-mail: dunning53@hotmail.com
Dist(s): **CreateSpace Independent Publishing Platform.**

Murphy's Bone Publishing, (978-0-9748226) P.O. Box 56835, Sherman Oaks, CA 91413-6835 USA Toll Free: 877-811-2663
E-mail: murphysbone@aol.com
Web site: http://www.murphysbone.com.

Murrah, Emma-Grace, (978-1-7321239) 3002 W. Georgia Rd, Piedmont, SC 29673 USA Tel 864-407-8797
E-mail: bemurrah@gmail.com
Web site: sharpenedarrows4christ@gmail.com.

Murray, Aryn D, (978-0-578-46906-5) 1840 W. Thomas Rd., Apt. 3, Phoenix, AZ 85015 USA Tel 602-810-0668
E-mail: whatawhoot@gmail.com.

Murray, Cynthia, (978-0-578-05770-5; 978-0-578-14613-3) P.O. Box 7564, Charlottesville, VA 22906 USA
E-mail: crm702004@yahoo.com
Web site: http://www.divinewomenofdestiny.com.

Murray, David M., (978-0-9729807) Orders Addr.: ., Seekonk, MA 02916 USA; Edit Addr.: 30 Wnterberry Ln., Seekink, MA 02771-4816 USA.

Murray, Dax, (978-0-692-14243-1) 1705 E. W. Hwy. 117, Silver Spring, MD 20910 USA Tel 202-642-4764
E-mail: dax@dax.codes
Dist(s): **Ingram Content Group.**

Murray, Eleanor, (978-0-692-93265-0) 4701 Port Charlotte, Las Vegas, NV 89131 USA Tel 702-982-8946
E-mail: cassie.salde@aol.com
Dist(s): **Ingram Content Group.**

Murray Hill Bks., LLC, (978-0-9719697; 978-1-935139) 7 Evergreen Ln., Woodstock, NY 12498 USA (SAN 256-3622) Tel 845-679-6749
E-mail: robinsegal@earthlink.net; info@murrayhillbooks.com
Web site: http://www.murrayhillbooks.com
Dist(s): **Learning Connection, The.**

Murray, Regina Waldron, (978-0-9636918; 978-0-9664042) 300 Hollinshead Spring Rd. Apt. AL137, Skillman, NJ 08558-2049 USA
E-mail: reginawmurray@yahoo.com.

Musa Publishing, (978-1-61937; 978-1-68009) 4815 Iron Horse Trail, Colorado Springs, CO 80917 USA Tel 719-393-2398
E-mail: kerry@musapublishing.com
Web site: www.musapublishing.com.

Muscatello Publishing, (978-0-9722774) P.O. Box 620011, Orlando, FL 32862-0011 USA Tel 407-888-3060; Fax: 407-650-3222; Toll Free: 877-888-3060
E-mail: info@muscatellopublishing.com
Web site: http://www.muscatellopublishing.com.

Muscle Bks. *Imprint of* **AGM Communications**

Muse Media LLC *See* **Deane, Jennifer Inc.**

Museum of Fine Arts, Houston, (978-0-89090) P.O. Box 6826, Houston, TX 77265-6826 USA (SAN 202-2559) Tel 713-639-7300
Dist(s): **D.A.P./Distributed Art Pubs.**
Texas A&M Univ. Pr.
Two Rivers Distribution
Univ. of Texas Pr.
Yale Univ. Pr.

Museum of Glass, (978-0-9726649; 978-0-692-46250-8; 978-0-692-78193-7) 1801 Dock St., Tacoma, WA 98402 USA Toll Free: 866-468-7386 (866-4-MUSEUM)
Web site: http://www.museumofglass.org
Dist(s): **Univ. of Washington Pr.**

Museum of Glass: International Center for Contemporary Art *See* **Museum of Glass**

Museum of Modern Art, (978-0-87070; 978-1-63345) 11 W. 53 St., New York, NY 10019-5497 USA (SAN 202-5809) Tel 212-708-9700; Fax: 212-333-1127; Toll Free: 800-447-6662 (orders)
E-mail: MoMA_Publications@moma.org
Web site: http://www.moma.org/publications
Dist(s): **Abrams, Inc.**
D.A.P./Distributed Art Pubs.
Hachette Bk. Group.

Museum of New Mexico Pr., (978-0-89013) Div. of New Mexico Department of Cultural Affairs, Orders Addr.: 11030 S. Langley Ave., Chicago, IL 60628 USA (SAN 202-2575) Tel 773-702-7000; 800-621-2736; Fax: 773-702-7212; Toll Free: 800-249-7737; Edit Addr.: P.O. Box 2087, Santa Fe, NM 87504-2087 USA Tel 505-476-1160
E-mail: orders@press.uchicago.edu
Web site: http://www.mnmpress.org
Dist(s): **Chicago Distribution Ctr.**

Museum of Science *See* **Engineering is Elementary**

Museum of Texas Tech Univ., (978-0-9640188; 978-1-929330) Div. of Texas Tech Univ., 3301 4th St., Box 43191, Lubbock, TX 79409-3191 USA Tel 806-742-2442; Fax: 806-742-1136
E-mail: museum.texastech@ttu.edu
Web site: http://www.museum.ttu.edu.

Museum of the Bible *Imprint of* **Worthy Publishing**

Museum of the Bible Bks. *Imprint of* **Worthy Publishing**

Museyon, (978-0-9822320; 978-0-9846334; 978-1-938450; 978-1-940842) Orders Addr.: 1177 Ave. Of The Americas, 5th Flr., New York, NY 10036 USA (SAN 857-6033)
E-mail: chiba@museyon.com
Web site: http://www.museyon.com
Dist(s): **Independent Pubs. Group**
MyiLibrary.

Museyon Guides *See* **Museyon**

Mushgush Pr., (978-0-9795818) 335 Cantlegate Close, Johns Creek, GA 30022 USA
Web site: http://tidalpress.com.

Mushkins, (978-0-9987478) 14 Waldron Pl., Palm Coast, FL 32164 USA Tel 386-569-5684
E-mail: mushmom@bellsouth.net
Web site: www.mushkins.com.

Mushroom Cloud Pr. of Orlando, (978-0-9679552) 278 Leslie Ln., Lake Mary, FL 32746 USA Tel 407-328-7311
E-mail: mushroomcloudpress@hotmail.com.

Music Awareness, (978-0-9753599) P.O. Box 188, Amherst, MA 01004 USA Tel 413-253-4216; Fax: 413-253-1397
E-mail: pwb@valinet.com
Web site: http://www.musicawareness.com.

Music Bks. & Games, (978-0-9744427) P.O. Box 97, McNeil, TX 78651 USA
E-mail: info@musicbooksandgames.com
Web site: http://www.musicbooksandgames.com/.

Music City Publishing, (978-1-933215) P.O. Box 41696, Nashville, TN 37204-1696 USA (SAN 256-288X)
E-mail: manager@musiccitypublishing.com
Web site: http://www.musiccitypublishing.com.

Music for Little People, Inc., (978-1-56628; 978-1-877737) 390 Lake Benbow Dr., No. C, Garberville, CA 95542 USA Tel 707-923-3991; Fax: 707-923-3241; Toll Free: 800-346-4445
Web site: http://www.musicforlittlepeople.com
Dist(s): **Educational Record Ctr., Inc.**
Follett School Solutions
Goldenrod Music, Inc.
Linden Tree Children's Records & Bks.
Music Design, Inc.
New Leaf Distributing Co., Inc.
Rounder Kids Music Distribution
Western Record Sales.

Music Institute of California, (978-0-9624062; 978-1-883993) Orders Addr.: P.O. Box 3535, Vista, CA 92085-3535 USA (SAN 297-5955) Tel 760-891-0226
Dist(s): **BookBaby**
Brodart Co.

Music, Movement & Magination Bks., (978-0-9818635; 978-1-935572) 3165 S. Alma School Rd., Suite 29-195, Chandler, AZ 85248 USA (SAN 856-7662) Tel 480-247-3129; Fax: 480-634-7148; Toll Free: 888-637-1313
E-mail: info@MMMKids.com
Web site: http://www.MMMKids.com.

Music Resources International *See* **Kindermusik International**

Music Sales Corp., (978-0-7119; 978-0-8256; 978-1-84609) Orders Addr.: 445 Bellvale Rd., P.O. Box 572, Chester, NY 10918 USA (SAN 662-0876) Tel 845-469-2271; Fax: 845-469-7544; Toll Free Fax: 800-345-6842; Toll Free: 800-431-7187; Edit Addr.: 257 Park Ave., S., 20th Flr., New York, NY 10010 USA (SAN 282-0277) Tel 212-254-2100; Fax: 212-254-2103; *Imprints:* Amsco Music (Amsco Music); Chester Music (Chester Music)
E-mail: info@musicsales.com
Web site: http://www.musicroom.com; http://www.musicsales.com
Dist(s): **Beekman Bks., Inc.**
Dumont, Charles Son, Inc.
Chesbro Music Co.
Leonard, Hal Corp.
Ingram Publisher Services
Quality Bks., Inc.

Music Together, LLC, (978-0-615-32865-2; 978-0-9855719; 978-0-9897814) 66 Witherspoon St., Princeton, NJ 08542 USA Tel 609-945-0354
Web site: http://www.musictogether.com.

Musical Linguist, The, (978-0-9706829) Orders Addr.: 14419 Greenwood Ave. N., Suite A, No. 354, Seattle, WA 98133 USA Fax: 509-693-4160; Toll Free: 866-297-2128
E-mail: mlinguist@aol.com
Web site: http://www.musicalspanish.com.

Musical Novels Press *See* **Golden Poppy Pubns.**

Musictech College Pr., (978-0-9729879) 19 Exchange St., E., Saint Paul, MN 55101 USA Tel 651-291-0177; Fax: 651-291-0366; Toll Free: 800-594-9500
E-mail: dsmith@musictech.com
Web site: http://www.musictech.com.

MusicWorks, (978-0-9763194; 978-0-9820900) Orders Addr.: P.O. Box 1971, Maryland Heights, MO 63043 USA; Edit Addr.: 13233 Amiot Dr., Saint Louis, MO 63146 USA; P.O. Box 1971, Saint Louis, MO 63043 (SAN 857-2291) Tel 314-439-5334 Do not confuse with MusicWorks in Marietta, GA
Web site: http://www.the-music-works.com; http://www.the-music-works.net.

MusiKinesis, (978-0-9701416) 3734 Cross Bow Ct., Ellicott City, MD 21042 USA Fax: 410-465-8472
E-mail: monicadale@musikinesis.com
Web site: http://www.musikinesis.com.

Muslim Writers Publishing, (978-0-9767861; 978-0-9793577; 978-0-9819770; 978-0-9854638) 1029-B5 Avent Hill., Raleigh, NC 27606 USA Tel 919-817-8656
E-mail: debmcnichol@gmail.com
Web site: http://www.muslimwriterspublishing.com
Dist(s): **Smashwords.**

Mustang BKS, (978-0-9766270) P.O. Box 1193, Crooked River Ranch, OR 97760 USA Tel 541-504-9620.

Mustard Hill Pr., (978-0-9977897) 492 Pala Way, Sacramento, CA 95819 USA Tel 916-455-2797
E-mail: caron@caronvikre.com.

Mustard Seed Comics, (978-0-9769819; 978-0-9826975; 978-0-9964631) 1609 Stoney Grove Church Rd., Warrenton, GA 30828 USA Tel 706-466-1633; *Imprints:* M.S.C. Books (MSCBks)
E-mail: mail@mustardseedcomics.com; benitomsc@yahoo.com
Web site: http://www.mustardseedcomics.com.

Mustard Seed Pr., (978-0-9797703) 263 Northampton Rd., Amherst, MA 01002 USA
Web site: http://www.bagelsbuddyandme.com.

Muszynski, James A., (978-0-9766461) 1446 Yoder Rd., Manister, MI 49660 USA Tel 231-723-6500 (phone/fax)
E-mail: lsmuszyk@hotmail.com
Web site: http://www.jaminjimbooks.com.

Mutaneers, (978-1-892619) 1011 Univ. Village, Salt Lake City, UT 84108 USA Tel 707-616-6893
E-mail: mutaneers@gmail.com
Web site: http://www.mutaneers.com; http://www.crazyuseful.com.

Mutant Prophet Publishing, (978-0-9864420; 978-0-692-13289-0) 4933 Rock Haven Dr. SW, Lilburn, GA 30047 USA Tel 678-266-0262
E-mail: violethaze999@yahoo.com.

Mutasian Entertainment, LLC, (978-0-578-07221-0; 978-0-578-07222-7; 978-0-578-07236-4; 978-0-692-01674-9; 978-0-9856002; 978-0-692-10632-7; 978-0-692-13535-8) 4440 PGA Blvd. Suite 600, Palm Beach Gardens, FL 31410 USA Tel 912-665-1048; Fax: 912-354-3220
E-mail: brigitte@mutasia.com
Web site: www.mutasia.com
Dist(s): **Independent Pubs. Group**
Midpoint Trade Bks., Inc.

Mutual Publishing LLC, (978-0-935180; 978-1-56647; 978-1-939487; 978-0-9971305; 978-1-949307; 978-1-7325030; 978-1-7347824) 1215 Center St., Suite

210, Honolulu, HI 96816 USA (SAN 222-6359) Tel 808-732-1709; Fax: 808-734-4094
E-mail: info@mutualpublishing.com
Web site: http://www.mutualpublishing.com
Dist(s): **Booklines Hawaii, Ltd.**
Islander Group
Mel Bay Pubns., Inc.

MVCD, Inc., *(978-0-9753617)* 4711 E. Falcon Dr., Suite 251, Mesa, AZ 85215 USA.

MVmedia, *(978-0-9800842; 978-0-9960167; 978-0-9992789; 978-1-7346279)* 145 Ridgewood Dr., Fayetteville, GA 30215 USA.

MVP Kids Media, 7205 E. Southern Ave., #105, Mesa, AZ 85209 USA Tel 480-495-7694
E-mail: info@realMVPkids.com
Web site: http://www.realMVPkids.com
Dist(s): **Baker & Taylor Publisher Services (BTPS).**

MX No Fear, *(978-0-9766918)* 2251 Faraday Ave., Suite A, Carlsbad, CA 92008 USA Toll Free: 866-787-3691
Web site: http://www.mxnofear.com.

My Ancestors, My Heroes *Imprint of* **Parker-Wallace Publishing Co., LLC**

My Bench Productions, *(978-0-9977858; 978-0-9977858-0-7)* 5479 Wellesley Dr., Calabasas, CA 91302 USA Tel 818-880-6811
E-mail: lauren@mybenchproductions.com
Dist(s): **Greenleaf Book Group.**

My Campus Adventure, Inc., *(978-1-935159)* Orders Addr.: 7705 Orly Ct., Plano, TX 75025 USA (SAN 856-6690)
E-mail: kim@mycampusadventure.com
Web site: http://www.mycampusadventure.com.

My Children Publishing Inc., *(978-0-9799376)* 17410 Vinwood Ln., Yorba Linda, CA 92886 USA (SAN 854-7890)
Web site: http://www.mychildrenpublishing.com.

My Darling-Tots Pubns., *(978-0-9797674)* 8593 Pantherburn Trace, Cordova, TN 38018 USA
E-mail: hdarling30@yahoo.com
Web site: http://www.helendarling.com.

My Grandma & Me Pubs., *(978-0-9742732)* 1275 E. Parks Rd., Saint Johns, MI 48879 USA
E-mail: info@mygrandmaandme.com; janemarysinke@gmail.com
Web site: http://www.mygrandmaandme.com
Dist(s): **Partners Pubs. Group, Inc.**

My Heart Yours Publishing, *(978-1-932721)* P.O. Box 4975, Wheaton, IL 60187 USA (SAN 255-6774)
E-mail: tanya@myheartyours.com; jeannine@myheartyours.com
Web site: http://www.myheartyours.com.

My Journey Bks., *(978-0-9766295)* P.O. Box 1169, Olney, MD 20830-1169 USA Toll Free: 877-965-2665
E-mail: KGF@billiesworld.com; KGF@myjourneybooks.com
Web site: http://www.billiesworld.com; http://www.myjourneybooks.com.

My Kinda Bks., *(978-0-9830781)* P.O. Box 1035, Lake Oswego, OR 97034 USA Tel 512-923-4501
E-mail: mykindabooks@gmail.com
Web site: www.mykindabooks.com.

My Little Jessie Pr., *(978-0-9740743)* Orders Addr.: P.O. Box 529, Bethel, VT 05032 USA (SAN 255-321X) Tel 802-234-9725; Edit Addr.: One Cushing Ave., Bethel, VT 05032 USA
E-mail: jhaywardburnham@aol.com.

My Little One, Incorporated *See* **Mylo Publishing**

My Lyric's Hse., *(978-0-9761446)* 593 Vanderbilt Ave., No. 135, Brooklyn, NY 11238 USA Tel 347-408-7786
E-mail: itsmeisha@yahoo.com.

My Pal Mark, *(978-0-9823750)* 9-15 Essex Pl., Fair Lawn, NJ 07410 USA
E-mail: mypalmark@aol.com
Web site: http://www.mypalmark.com.

My Purple Toes, LLC, *(978-0-9844556; 978-0-9834778)* P.O. Box 826, Mt. Pleasant, SC 29465 USA
E-mail: blair@blairhahnbooks.com
Web site: http://www.blairhahnbooks.com; http://www.mypurpletoes.com
Dist(s): **Emerald Bk. Co.**

My Second Language Publishing, USA, *(978-0-615-23709-1; 978-0-615-24460-0; 978-0-615-26150-8; 978-0-615-26238-3; 978-0-615-26239-0; 978-0-615-26240-6; 978-0-578-00208-8; 978-0-578-00209-5; 978-0-578-02214-7)* 165 River Hills Dr., Clayton, NC 27527 USA
E-mail: publisher@mysecondlanguagepublishingusa.com
Web site: http://www.mysecondlanguagepublishingusa.com
Dist(s): **Lulu Pr., Inc.**

My Special Thoughts, *(978-0-9743019)* P.O. Box 150747, Nashville, TN 37215 USA Fax: 615-297-3138
Web site: http://www.myspecialthoughts.com.

My Student-Athlete, Inc., *(978-0-9767250)* P.O. Box 15, Redan, GA 30074 USA Tel 770-981-3000
Web site: http://www.morethanvictories.com.

My Sunshine Bks., *(978-0-9749561)* 1370 Little Brier Creek Rd., Warrenton, GA 30828 USA Toll Free: 800-765-4663.

My Three Sisters Publishing, *(978-0-615-73283-1; 978-0-615-73697-6; 978-0-615-73769-0; 978-0-615-74341-7; 978-0-615-74542-8; 978-0-615-74664-7; 978-0-615-74890-0; 978-0-615-74922-8; 978-0-615-75048-4; 978-0-615-75245-7; 978-0-615-75261-7; 978-0-615-75276-1; 978-0-615-75367-6; 978-0-615-75421-5; 978-0-615-75460-4; 978-0-615-75518-2; 978-0-615-75534-2; 978-0-615-75556-4; 978-0-615-75716-2; 978-0-615-75752-0; 978-0-615-75770-4; 978-0-615-75825-1; 978-0-615-75897-8; 978-0-615-75904-3; 978-0-615-75910-4; 978-0-615-75938-8;)* 13817 W. Rovey Ave., Litchfield Park, AZ 85340 USA Tel 847-769-9824
E-mail: Jenniseco@aol.com
Dist(s): **CreateSpace Independent Publishing Platform.**

My Three Sons *See* **Life of Asil, The**

My Time Pubns., *(978-0-9820530; 978-0-9843257; 978-0-9830518)* 2984 Spring Falls Dr., West Carrollton, OH 45449 USA Tel 937-344-4805
E-mail: leila@mytimepublications.com; ljeff25@yahoo.com
Web site: http://www.mytimepublications.com.

MyBoys3 Pr., *(978-0-9893414; 978-0-9861473; 978-1-947881)* P.O. Box 2555, Midlothian, VA 23113 USA
E-mail: steve@myboys3.com
Web site: www.stevensawyerbooks.com; www.myboys3.com.

Myers, Connie Ellis *See* **Say Out Loud, LLC**

Myers, Jack Ministries, Inc., *(978-0-9720928)* P.O. Box 158, Orland Park, IL 60462-0158 USA
E-mail: jmm.revival@juno.com
Web site: http://www.jackmyersministries.com.

Myers Publishing Co., *(978-0-9745210; 978-0-9745929)* Orders Addr.: 207 Shelley Ct., Roseville, CA 95747 USA Tel 916-987-7668 (phone/fax) Do not confuse with Myers Publishing Company in Tarpon Springs, FL
E-mail: myerspubco@myerspublishing.com
Web site: http://www.myerspublishing.com.

Myers Publishing Co., *(978-0-9729381)* 1426 Vermont Ave., Tarpon Springs, FL 34689-3871 USA Tel 727-938-6855; Fax: 727-934-4562 Do not confuse with Myers Publishing Company in Sacramento, CA
E-mail: kmyers2@tampabay.rr.com.

MyHandiwork, *(978-0-9742555)* 7520 Walker St., Saint Louis Park, MN 55426-4042 USA Fax: 952-935-2840
E-mail: myhandiwork@earthlink.net
Web site: http://www.myhandiwork.com.

MYHRECO, *(978-0-9753704)* 9033 1/2 Hubbard St., Culver City, CA 90232-2508 USA.

Mylemarks LLC, *(978-0-9964154)* P.O. Box 1252, Chesapeake, VA 23327 USA Tel 757-620-8539
E-mail: andrew.jatau@mylemarks.com.

Mylo Publishing, *(978-0-9910341)* 10052 E. Gelding Dr., Scottsdale, AZ 85260 USA Tel 682-465-6845
E-mail: znscurry@hotmail.com
Web site: www.mylopublishing.com.

Mymilou Pr., *(978-0-615-93163-0; 978-0-692-79069-4)* 2923 Bighorn Dr., Corona, CA 92881 USA Tel 714-390-6139
E-mail: amarestaing@hotmail.com.

Myrddin Publishing Group, *(978-0-9883828; 978-1-939296; 978-1-68063)* 54 Mill Pond Rd., Jackson, NJ 08527 USA Tel 732-822-8920
E-mail: alisondeluca@hotmail.com; cjjasp@gmail.com
Dist(s): **Lulu Pr., Inc.**

MyReportLinks.com Bks. *Imprint of* **Enslow Publishing, LLC**

Myrin Institute, Incorporated *See* **Orion Society, The**

Myrtle Learns, *(978-1-930694)* Orders Addr.: P.O. Box 3645, Rancho Cucamonga, CA 91729 USA Fax: 909-428-2401 (phone/fax); Edit Addr.: 14034 Fort Ross Ct., Fontana, CA 92336 USA Tel 909-428-2401
E-mail: jaajdeem@aol.com
Web site: http://myrtlelearns.com.

MySheri Enterprises, LLC, *(978-0-9766782)* P.O. Box 141111, Detroit, MI 48214 USA.

Myst of the Oracle Corp., *(978-0-9786812)* P.O. Box 133, Piney Creek, NC 28663 USA
E-mail: administrator@mystoftheoracle.com
Web site: http://www.mystoftheoracle.com.

Mysteries by Vincent, LLC, *(978-1-932169)* Orders Addr.: 2707 Mountain Green Trail, Kingwood, TX 77345 USA Tel 281-312-0120; Toll Free: 866-946-3864 1-866-WHODUNIT
E-mail: robert@mysteriesbyvincent.com; cindy@mysteriesbyvincent.com
Web site: http://www.mysteriesbyvincent.com; http://www.buckleyandbogey.com; http://www.whodunitpress.com.

Mystery & Suspense Pr. *Imprint of* **iUniverse, Inc.**

Mystery Writers of America Presents *Imprint of* **iUniverse, Inc.**

mysterygirl publishing *See* **Mysterygirl Publishing**

Mysterygirl Publishing, *(978-0-692-28118-5; 978-0-692-30501-0; 978-0-692-40686-1; 978-0-692-40740-0; 978-0-692-90018-5)* 15 Fairview Ln., Springfield, IL 62711 USA Tel 217-836-0229
E-mail: mlibrisigle@yahoo.com
Web site: www.marleyparker.com
Dist(s): **CreateSpace Independent Publishing Platform.**

Mystic Arts, LLC, *(978-0-9771700)* P.O. Box 1110, Riverton, UT 84065 USA (SAN 256-8217)
Web site: http://www.reading-with-kids.com.

Mystic Harbor Pr., LLC, *(978-1-933660; 978-0-578-01793-8; 978-1-61899)* Orders Addr.: P.O. Box 1707, Conroe, TX 77305 USA (SAN 257-2680) Tel 281-826-4026 (phone/fax); *Imprints*: Tadpole Press 4 Kids (Tadpole Pr)
E-mail: cmcginnis@smoothsailingpress.com
Web site: http://www.smoothsailingpress.com
Dist(s): **Follet Higher Education Grp**
Ingram Content Group.

Mystic Hippo Media Publishing, *(978-0-9848694)* 5 Bald Hill Ct., Saint Peters, MO 63376 USA Tel 636-922-3593
E-mail: 88fingerslouie@att.net.

Mystic Jaguar Publishing, *(978-0-9792294)* 10821 Margate Rd., Suite A, Silver Spring, MD 20901-1615 USA (SAN 852-8365)
E-mail: Mysticjaguar@verizon.net.

Mystic Night Bks. *Imprint of* **Pink Stucco Pr.**

Mystic Pubs., Inc., *(978-0-9727840; 978-1-934051; 978-1-941271; 978-1-948266)* 614 Mosswood Dr., Henderson, NV 89002 USA; *Imprints*: Ink & Quill Publishers (Ink&Quill)
E-mail: richard@themackennasaga.com
Web site: http://www.mysticpublishers.com; www.iqpublishing.com; www.newlinkpublishing.com
Dist(s): **ebrary, Inc.**

Mystic Publishing, *(978-0-9747454)* 16613 195th Ave., Mystic, IA 52574-8678 USA Do not confuse with Mystic Publishing in North, VA
E-mail: sharon@freddiethefrog.com; sharon@freddiethefrogbooks.com
Dist(s): **Leonard, Hal Corp.**

Mystic Ridge Bks., *(978-0-9672182; 978-0-9742845)* Div. of Mystic Ridge Productions, Inc., 222 Main St., Sutie 142, Farmington, CT 06032 USA (SAN 853-9898)
E-mail: mysticridge@att.net
Web site: http://www.mysticridgebooks.com; http://www.blackjacktoday.com; http://www.helixeye.com.

Mystic River Ink, *(978-0-9724752)* P.O. Box 441357, Somerville, MA 02144 USA
Web site: http://www.mysticriverink.com.

Mystic Seaport Museum, Inc., *(978-0-913372; 978-0-939510)* 75 Greenmanville Ave., Mystic, CT 06355-0990 USA (SAN 213-7550) Tel 860-572-5347; Fax: 860-572-5348; Toll Free: 800-248-1066
E-mail: publications@mysticseaport.org; wholesale@mysticseaport.org
Web site: http://www.mysticseaport.org
Dist(s): **Peabody Essex Museum**
Univ. Pr. of New England.

Mystic Waters Publishing *See* **Winkelstein Studios**

Mystic World Pr., *(978-0-9854289)* 115 San Jose Ave. No. 2, San Francisco, CA 94110 USA Tel 415-373-8533
E-mail: william@mysticworldpress.com.

Mystical Publishing, *(978-0-578-19966-5)* 4200 Maple Leaf Dr., New Orleans, LA 70131 USA Tel 504-579-6534
E-mail: keiffertj@gmail.com.

Mystical Willow Productions, *(978-0-9763205)* P.O. Box 95, Wheaton, IL 60189 USA
E-mail: mysticalwillow@comcast.net.

MysticMountain Pr., *(978-0-9905938)* 483 Apache Rd., Arrey, NM 87930 USA Tel 505-550-5530
E-mail: sheilaofthejungle@yahoo.com.

Mystique International, Ltd., *(978-0-9745333)* 2533 N. Carson St., Suite 593, Carson City, NV 89706-0147 USA
E-mail: metamind@eznet.net.

Mystique Pr. *Imprint of* **Crossroad Pr.**

Myth Breakers *See* **Happy About**

MYTHIKAS, *(978-0-9983011)* 8215 Lake Dr., Doral, FL 33166 USA Tel 786-487-8049; Fax: 786-545-7636
E-mail: infomythikas@gmail.com.

MythSeries, *(978-0-9776472)* P.O. Box 211, Millville, MN 55957 USA (SAN 257-8743) Tel 507-798-2450
E-mail: lisa@mythseries.com
Web site: http://mythseries.com.

Mz. Rosa Notions, *(978-0-9740267)* P.O. Box 114, Turlock, CA 95380 USA
E-mail: ninarule62@aol.com.

NAPSAC Reproductions, *(978-0-934426; 978-1-932747; 978-0-615-45573-0)* Rte. 4, Box 646, Marble Hill, MO 63764 USA (SAN 222-4607) Tel 573-238-4846; Fax: 573-238-2010
E-mail: napsac@clas.net
Dist(s): **Send The Light Distribution LLC.**

N&N Publishing Co., Inc., *(978-0-9606036; 978-0-935487)* 18 Montgomery St., Middletown, NY 10940 USA (SAN 216-4221) Tel 845-342-1677; Fax: 845-342-6910; Toll Free: 800-664-8398; *Imprints*: STAReviews (STAReviews); X-treme Reviews (X-treme Reviews)
E-mail: info@nandnpublishing.com; sales@nandnpublishing.com
Web site: http://www.nandnpublishing.com; http://www.nn4text.com; http://www.starreview.com; http://www.big8review.com.

N Gallerie Pr. LLC, *(978-0-9818347; 978-0-9962748)* Div. of N Gallerie Studios, LLC, Orders Addr.: 1213 Culbreth Dr. Suite 233, Wilmington, NC 28405 USA Tel 910-398-6411
E-mail: sales@ngallerie.com
Web site: http://www.ngallerie.com.

N2Print *Imprint of* **New Age World Publishing**

N8TIVE, *(978-0-9769575)* 620 S. 19th St., Philadelphia, PA 19146 USA
Web site: http://www.n8tve.com.

Na Kamalei Koolauloa Early Education Program, *(978-0-9773495; 978-0-9760892; 978-1-935111)* P.O. Box 900, Hauula, HI 96717 USA Tel 808-237-8500; Fax: 808-237-8501; *Imprints*: Ho'ulu Hou Project: Stories Told by Us (Houlu Hou)
E-mail: nkpublishing@nakamalei.org
Web site: http://www.nakamalei.org.

Nabors, Murray W., *(978-0-615-38301-9; 978-0-615-40572-8; 978-0-615-49157-8; 978-0-615-85999-6)* 3051 NE State Rte. W., Saint Joseph, MO 64507 USA Tel 816-244-0354
E-mail: mnabors@missouriwestern.edu.

Nabu Pr. *Imprint of* **Creative Media Partners, LLC**

NACSCORP, Incorporated *See* .

NADER, LILLIAN, *(978-1-7323175)* 18421 Lemon Drive, Apt 507, YORBA LINDA, CA 92886 USA Tel 714-693-0951
E-mail: LNADER1910@SBCGLOBAL.NET
Web site: https://lilliannader.com.

Naderi, Fariedeh, *(978-1-7322683)* 4656 Lawson Dr., Decatur,, IL 62526 USA Tel 217-358-6100
E-mail: naderi.farideh@gmail.com.

Nadine Lalich, *(978-0-9711776; 978-0-615-19967-2)*
E-mail: nadinelalich@yahoo.com
Web site: http://hbpublishing.net.

Nadores Publishing & Research, *(978-0-9797847)* Orders Addr.: P.O. Box 1202, Gilroy, CA 95021-1202 USA
E-mail: regulo-zapata@Verizon.net
Web site: http://www.nadorespublishing.com.

Nags Head Art, Inc., *(978-0-9616344; 978-1-878405)* Orders Addr.: P.O. Box 2149, Manteo, NC 27954 USA (SAN 200-9145) Tel 252-441-7480; Fax: 252-475-9893; Toll Free Fax: 800-246-7014; Toll Free: 800-541-2722; Edit Addr.: 7728 Virginia Dare Trail, Manteo, NC 27954 USA (SAN 658-8107)
E-mail: suzannetate@yahoo.com
Web site: http://www.suzannetate.com
Dist(s): **Florida Classics Library**
Mistco, Inc.

NA-h *Imprint of* **Capstone**

NAHSH M'ISTAH Pub., *(978-0-9665427)* 8614 E. Dahlia Dr., Scottsdale, AZ 85260 USA Tel 480-998-8189
E-mail: nashmista@aol.com.

Naim, Deborah, *(978-0-9762828)* 20801 Biscayne Blvd., Suite 403, Aventura, FL 33180 USA
E-mail: dnaim@mercadeoecologico.com.

Nakota Publishing, *(978-0-9882442)* 7240 W Shaw Butte, Peoria, AZ 85345 USA Tel 602-750-3662
E-mail: vltreude@cox.net.

NAL *Imprint of* **Penguin Publishing Group**

Nambennett Publishing, *(978-0-9742208)* 11748 Fremont Ave. N., Seattle, WA 98133 USA
E-mail: kelly@nambennett.com
Web site: http://www.nambennett.com.

namelos llc, *(978-1-60898)* 133 Main Ave., South Hampton, NH 03827 USA Tel 828-221-
E-mail: roxburgh@namelos.com
Web site: http://www.namelos.com.

Nana Says *Imprint of* **Inner Quality Publishing**

Nana's Stories, *(978-0-9857362)* 22 St. Nicholas Ave., Worcester, MA 01606 USA Tel 508-560-5888
E-mail: kfinneron@yahoo.com.

Nancy Becklean Tobin *See* **Thalian Bks.**

Nancy Paulsen Bks. *Imprint of* **Penguin Publishing Group**

Nancy Paulsen Books *Imprint of* **Penguin Young Readers Group**

Nancy's Artworks, *(978-0-9748074)* Orders Addr.: 6185 Faxon Ct., Colorado Spgs, CO 80922-1839 USA
E-mail: sales@nancyweb.com
Web site: http://www.multcamp.com; http://www.nancyweb.com; http://www.seanotes.net.

Nanie C. Memeh, *(978-1-7327876)* 17433 52nd Ave W, Lynnwood, WA 98037 USA Tel 253-202-1225
E-mail: n.m.divis@gmail.com.

NANUQ Publishing, *(978-0-9795400; 978-0-692-97169-7)* 111 Linwood Ave., Williamsville, NY 14221 USA Tel 716-634-4379
E-mail: cralt37@yahoo.com.

NAO Pubns., *(978-0-9760838)* 35895 Conroy Rd., Suite 1015, Orlando, FL 32839 USA
E-mail: bbgwyn12@netzero.net; briangwyn@bellsouth.net
Web site: http://www.notanotheroverdraft.com; http://notanotheroverdraft.blogspot.com.

Naphtali Publishing, *(978-0-692-90267-7)* 2221 80th Ave, Unit B, OAKLAND, CA 94605 USA Tel 510-332-2782
E-mail: janrenee418@gmail.com.

NAPNAP, *(978-0-9749769)* 20 Brace Rd., Suite 200, Cherry Hill, NJ 08034-2634 USA Tel 856-857-9700; Fax: 856-857-1600
E-mail: info@napnap.org
Web site: http://www.napnap.org.

Napue & Tucker Publishing, L.L.C. *See* **NT Publishing, L.L.C.**

NA-r *Imprint of* **Capstone**

NA-r *Imprint of* **Heinemann-Raintree**

Narragansett Graphics, *(978-0-615-12390-5)* P.O. Box 1492, Coventry, RI 02816-0029 USA
E-mail: lsousa@narragansettgraphics.com
Web site: http://www.narragansettgraphics.com.

NarraGarden LLC, *(978-0-9907434)*
E-mail: info@narragarden.com; bradley.blankenship@gmail.com
Web site: www.papadadandme.com; www.narragarden.com.

Nash, Patrick, *(978-1-7342771)* 46 Hancock St., Wrentham, MA 02093 USA Tel 508-282-9202
E-mail: pnash5@comcast.net.

Nassau-Street.com, *(978-1-60290)* Nassau Street Media LLC, 1130 W. Washington St., #94 W. Chicago, Il 60186-3025, West Chicago, IL 60185 USA
E-mail: talk-to-us@nassaustreetmedia.com
Web site: http://nassau-street.com.

Nastari, Nadine, *(978-0-9798387)* 8408 Salerno Rd., Fort Pierce, FL 34951-4506 USA
Web site: http://www.three-leggedcat.com.

NASW Pr. *Imprint of* **National Assn. of Social Workers/NASW Pr.**

Natavi Guides, *(978-0-9719392; 978-1-932204)* 44 Pine St., West Newton, MA 02465-1425 USA
E-mail: info@nataviguides.com
Web site: http://www.nataviguides.com.

Nathan, Fernand (FRA) *(978-2-09) Dist. by* **Distribks Inc.**

Nathaniel Max Rock, *(978-0-9749392; 978-1-59980)* 1418 S. Orange Ave., Monterey Park, CA 91755 USA
Web site: http://rockmath.com.

†National Academies Pr., *(978-0-309)* Orders Addr.: 8700 Spectrum Dr., Landover, MD 20785 USA; Edit Addr.: 500 Fifth St., NW Lockbox 285, Washington, DC 20001 USA (SAN 202-8891) Tel 202-334-3313; Fax:

Publisher Name Index

202-334-2451; Toll Free: 888-624-7654; *Imprints:* Joseph Henry Press (Joseph Henry Pr)
E-mail: zjones@nas.edu
Web site: http://www.nap.edu
Dist(s): **Ebsco Publishing**
MyiLibrary
ebrary, Inc.; *CIP.*

National Academy Press *See* **National Academies Pr.**

†National Archives & Records Administration, (*978-0-911333; 978-1-880875*) Orders Addr.: 700 Pennsylvania Ave., NW, Washington, DC 20408 USA (SAN 210-363X) Tel 301-713-6800; Fax: 310-713-6169; Toll Free: 800-234-8861
E-mail: katherine.coram@nara.gov
Web site: http://www.nara.gov
Dist(s): **United States Government Printing Office**; *CIP.*

National Assn. for Humane & Environmental Education, (*978-0-941246*) Div. of Humane Society of the U.S., P.O. Box 362, East Haddam, CT 06423 USA (SAN 285-0680) Tel 860-434-8666; Fax: 860-434-9579; *Imprints:* Humane Society Press (Humane Soc Pr)
E-mail: nahee@nahee.org
Web site: http://www.nahee.org.

National Assn. for Visually Handicapped, (*978-0-89064*) 3201 Balboa St., San Francisco, CA 94121 USA (SAN 202-0971) Tel 415-221-3201; Fax: 415-221-8754; 111 E. 59th St. # 6, New York, NY 10022-1202 (SAN 669-1870)
E-mail: staff@navh.org
Web site: http://www.navh.org.

†National Assn. of Social Workers/NASW Pr., (*978-0-87101*) Orders Addr.: P.O. Box 431, Annapolis Junction, MD 20701 USA Fax: 301-206-7989; Toll Free: 800-227-3590; Edit Addr.: 750 First St., NE, Suite 700, Washington, DC 20002-4241 USA (SAN 202-893X) Tel 202-408-8600; Fax: 202-336-8312; Toll Free: 800-638-8799; *Imprints:* N A S W Press (NASW Pr)
E-mail: press@naswdc.org
Web site: http://www.naswpress.org; *CIP.*

National Assn. of Speed & Explosion, (*978-0-938074*) P.O. Box 1784, Kill Devil Hills, NC 27948 USA (SAN 215-6148) Tel 252-441-1185; Fax: 252-449-4125
E-mail: naseinc@aol.com.

National Bk. Network, Div. of Rowman & Littlefield Pubs., Inc., Orders Addr.: 15200 NBN Way, Blue Ridge Summit, PA 17214 USA (SAN 630-0065) Tel 717-794-3800; Fax: 717-794-3828; Toll Free Fax: 800-338-4550 (Customer Service); Toll Free: 800-462-6420 (Customer Service); a/o Les Petriw, 67 Mowat Ave., Suite 241, Toronto, ON M6P 3K3 Tel 416-534-1660; Fax: 416-534-3699
E-mail: custserv@nbnbooks.com
Web site: http://www.nbnbooks.com.

National Braille Pr., (*978-0-939173*) Orders Addr.: 88 St. Stephen St., Boston, MA 02115 USA (SAN 273-0952) Tel 617-266-6160; Fax: 617-437-0456; Toll Free: 800-548-7323
E-mail: orders@nbp.org
Web site: http://www.nbp.org.

National Ctr. For Youth Issues, (*978-1-931636; 978-1-937870*) Orders Addr.: P.O. Box 22185, Chattanooga, TN 37422-2185 USA Tel 423-899-5714; Fax: 423-899-4547; Toll Free: 800-477-8277; Edit Addr.: 6101 Preservation Dr., Chattanooga, TN 37416 USA (SAN 990-1590)
E-mail: info@ncyi.org
Web site: http://www.ncyi.org
Dist(s): **Follett School Solutions**
MAR*CO Products, Inc.
Youthlight, Inc.

National Children's Book Project *See* **Public Square Bks.**

National Conference of State Legislatures, (*978-0-941336; 978-1-55516; 978-1-58024*) 7700 E. First Pl., Denver, CO 80230-7143 USA (SAN 225-1000) Tel 303-364-7700; Fax: 303-364-7800
E-mail: rita.morris@ncsl.org
Web site: http://www.ncsl.org.

†National Council of Teachers of English, (*978-0-8141*) Orders Addr.: 1111 W. Kenyon Rd., Urbana, IL 61801-1096 USA (SAN 202-9049) Tel 217-328-3870 Main Switchboard; Fax: 217-328-0977 Editorial Fax; 217-328-9645 Customer Service Fax; Toll Free: 800-369-6283 Main Switchboard Toll Free Tel; 877-369-6283 Customer Service Toll Free Tel
E-mail: kaustin@ncte.org; orders@ncte.org
Web site: http://www.ncte.org
Dist(s): **APG Sales & Distribution Services**; *CIP.*

†National Council of Teachers of Mathematics, (*978-0-87353; 978-1-68054*) 1906 Association Dr., Reston, VA 20191-1502 USA (SAN 202-9057) Tel 703-620-9840; Fax: 703-476-2970; 703-715-9536; Toll Free Fax: 800-220-8483; Toll Free: 800-235-7566 (orders only)
E-mail: info@nctm.org; cnoddin@nctm.org
Web site: http://www.nctm.org; *CIP.*

National Crime Prevention Council, (*978-0-934513; 978-1-929888; 978-1-59686*) 2345 Crystal Dr. Suite 500, Arlington, VA 22202 USA (SAN 693-8574) Tel 202-466-6272; Fax: 202-296-1356; Toll Free: 800-627-2911 (orders only) Do not confuse with The National Crime Prevention Assn., also in Washington, D.C.
E-mail: kirby@ncpc.org; demenno@ncpc.org
Web site: http://www.ncpc.org; http://www.mcgruff.org.

National Dance Education Organization, (*978-1-930798*) 8609 2nd Ave. Ste. 203B, Silver Spring, MD 20910-6359 USA
E-mail: ndeo@erols.com
Web site: http://www.ndeo.org
Dist(s): **Chicago Distribution Ctr.**

National Deacons Association *See* **Tommy Bks. Pubng.**

National Defense University *Imprint of* **United States Government Printing Office**

†National Education Assn., (*978-0-8106*) Orders Addr.: P.O. Box 404846, Atlanta, GA 30384-4846 USA (SAN 203-7262) Tel 202-822-7208; Fax: 202-822-7377; Toll Free: 800-229-4200; Edit Addr.: 1201 16th St., NW. Suite 514, Washington, DC 20036 USA Tel 770-280-4080; Fax: 770-280-4134
E-mail: nea-orders@pbd.com
Web site: http://www.nea.org/books; *CIP.*

National Educational Systems, Inc., (*978-1-893493*) P.O. Box 691450, San Antonio, TX 78269-1450 USA Toll Free: 800-442-2604.

National Film Network LLC, (*978-0-8026*) Orders Addr.: 4501 Forbes Blvd., Lanham, MD 20706 USA (SAN 630-1878) Tel 301-459-8020 ext 2066
E-mail: info@nationalfilmnetwork.com
Web site: http://www.nationalfilmnetwork.com.

National Foundation for Teaching Entrepreneurship, The, (*978-1-890859*) Orders Addr.: 120 Wall St., 29th Flr., New York, NY 10005 USA Tel 212-232-3333; Fax: 212-232-2244; Toll Free: 800-367-6383
E-mail: nfte@nfte.com
Web site: http://www.nfte.com.

National Gallery of Australia (AUS) (*978-0-646-30472-4*) *Dist. by* **U of Wash Pr.**

National Gallery of Victoria (AUS) (*978-1-925432*) *Dist. by* **Natl Bk Netwk.**

National Gallery of Victoria (AUS) (*978-1-925432*) *Dist. by* **Antique Collect.**

National Gallery Singapore (SGP) (*978-981-09-1091-4; 978-981-09-7349-0; 978-981-09-7352-0; 978-981-09-7353-7; 978-981-09-7384-1; 978-981-09-7385-8; 978-981-09-7498-5; 978-981-09-8433-5; 978-981-09-9561-4; 978-981-11-0189-2; 978-981-11-0190-8; 978-981-11-0608-8; 978-981-11-2236-1; 978-981-11-2373-3; 978-981-11-2374-0; 978-981-11-2375-7*) *Dist. by* **Pa St U Pr.**

National Geographic Children's Bks. *Imprint of* **National Geographic Society**

National Geographic Learning *Imprint of* **CENGAGE Learning**

National Geographic School Publishing, Inc., (*978-0-7362; 978-0-917837; 978-1-56334*) Div. of CENGAGE Learning, Orders Addr.: 10650 Toebben Dr., Independence, KY 41051 USA Tel 859-282-5700; Toll Free Fax: 800-487-8488; Toll Free: 800-354-9706; 888-915-3276; Edit Addr.: 1 Lower Ragsdale Dr., Bldg. 1, Suite 200, Monterey, CA 93940 USA
Web site: http://www.hampton-brown.com
Dist(s): **CENGAGE Learning.**

†National Geographic Society, (*978-0-7922; 978-0-87044; 978-1-4262; 978-1-4263*) 1145 17th St., NW, Washington, DC 20036 USA (SAN 202-8956) Tel 202-857-7000; Fax: 301-921-1575; Toll Free: 800-647-5463; 800-548-9797 (TTD users only); *Imprints:* National Geographic Children's Books (NGCB)
E-mail: askngs@nationalgeographic.com
Web site: http://nationalgeographic.com
Dist(s): **Benchmark LLC**
Children's Plus, Inc.
Follett Media Distribution
Follett School Solutions
Hachette Bk. Group
Lectorum Pubns., Inc.
MyiLibrary
Penguin Random Hse. Distribution
Penguin Random Hse. LLC
Rand McNally
Random Hse., Inc.
Simon & Schuster, Inc.; *CIP.*

National Honor Roll, LLC, (*978-0-9714201; 978-0-9721652; 978-0-9729406; 978-1-932654*) 777 Sunrise Hwy. Ste. 300, Lynbrook, NY 11563-2950 USA Toll Free: 800-416-2185
Web site: http://www.nationalhonorroll.org.

National Horseman Publishing Inc., The, (*978-0-9762854*) 16101 N. 82nd St., Suite 10, Scottsdale, AZ 85260-1830 USA Tel 480-922-5202
Web site: http://www.tnh1865.com.

National Institute on Alcohol Abuse & Alcoholism *Imprint of* **United States Government Printing Office**

National Issues Forums Institute, (*978-0-945639; 978-1-943028; 978-1-946206*) 100 Commons Rd., Dayton, OH 45459 USA (SAN 247-2163) Tel 937-434-7300; Fax: 937-439-9804; Toll Free: 800-221-3657
E-mail: dsacksteder@kettering.org
Web site: http://www.nifi.org
Dist(s): **Atlas Bks.**
Baker & Taylor Publisher Services (BTPS).

National Learning Corp., (*978-0-8293; 978-0-8373; 978-1-7318; 978-1-7993*) 212 Michael Dr., Syosset, NY 11791 USA (SAN 206-8869) Tel 516-921-8888; Fax: 516-921-8743; Toll Free: 800-645-6337; *Imprints:* Passbooks (Passbooks)
E-mail: sales@passbooks.com
Web site: nlcpassbooks@aim.com
Dist(s): **Independent Pubs. Group.**

National Marfan Foundation, The, (*978-0-918335*) 22 Manhasset Ave., Prt Washingtn, NY 11050-2023 USA (SAN 657-2855) Toll Free: 800-862-7326
E-mail: staff@marfan.org
Web site: http://www.marfan.org.

National Marine Fisheries Service *Imprint of* **United States Government Printing Office**

National Maritime Museum (GBR) (*978-0-905555; 978-0-948065; 978-0-9501764; 978-1-906367*) *Dist. by* **Casemate Pubs.**

National Network of Digital Schools *See* **Lincoln Learning Solutions**

†National Park Service Div. of Pubns., (*978-0-912627*) Harpers Ferry Ctr., Harpers Ferry, WV 25425 USA (SAN 282-7980) Tel 304-535-6018; Fax: 304-535-6144
Dist(s): **United States Government Printing Office**; *CIP.*

National Professional Resources, Inc., (*978-1-887943; 978-1-934032; 978-0-9819919; 978-1-935609; 978-1-938539; 978-1-949961*) BarCharts Publishing c/o Jason Scerbo 6000 Pk. of Commerce Blvd., Suite D, Boca Raton, FL 33487 USA Tel 800-453-7461; Toll Free: 800-453-7461; *Imprints:* Dude Publishing (Dude Pubng)
E-mail: lhanson@NPRinc.com; lkehoe@nprinc.com
Web site: http://www.NPRinc.com
Dist(s): **Baum & Beaulieu Assocs.**
CEC: Council for Exceptional Children
Complete Book & Media Supply
Follett School Solutions
Master Teacher
National School Products
Park Pl.
QEP, Inc. Professional Bks.

National Reading Styles Institute, Inc., (*978-0-929192; 978-1-883186; 978-1-933533*) Orders Addr.: P.O. Box 737, Syosset, NY 11791 USA (SAN 248-8191) Tel 516-921-5500; Fax: 516-921-5591; Toll Free: 800-331-3117; Edit Addr.: 179 Lafayette Dr., Syosset, NY 11791 USA (SAN 248-8205)
E-mail: readingstyle@nrsi.com
Web site: http://www.literacy.org; http://www.nrsi.com.

National Rehabilitation Services *See* **Northern Speech Services**

National Review, Inc., (*978-0-9627841; 978-0-9758998; 978-0-9847650*) 215 Lexington Ave., 4th Flr., New York, NY 10016 USA (SAN 226-1685) Tel 212-679-7330; Fax: 212-696-0340
E-mail: jfowler@nationalreview.com
Web site: http://www.nationalreview.com
Dist(s): **Chicago Distribution Ctr.**

National Science Resources Center (NSRC) *See* **Smithsonian Science Education Ctr. (SSEC)**

†National Science Teachers Assn., (*978-0-87355; 978-1-933531; 978-1-935155; 978-1-936137; 978-1-936959; 978-1-938946; 978-1-941316; 978-1-68140; 978-1-952109*) 1840 Wilson Blvd., Arlington, VA 22201 USA (SAN 203-7173) 703-243-7177; Toll Free Fax: 888-433-0526 (orders); Toll Free: 800-277-5300 (orders); 800-722-6782
E-mail: pubsales@nsta.org; dyudkin@nsta.org
Web site: http://www.nsta.org/store
Dist(s): **Ebsco Publishing**
Independent Pubs. Group
MyiLibrary
ebrary, Inc.; *CIP.*

National Self-Esteem Resources & Development Ctr., (*978-0-9632276*) 851 Irwin St., Suite 205, San Rafael, CA 94901-3343 USA Tel 415-457-4411; Fax: 415-457-0356.

National Society of Professional Engineers, (*978-0-915409*) 1420 King St., Alexandria, VA 22314-2715 USA (SAN 225-168X) Tel 703-684-2800; Fax: 703-836-4875; Toll Free: 888-285-6773
E-mail: customer.service@nspe.org
Web site: http://www.nspe.org.

National Textbook Co. *Imprint of* **McGraw-Hill/Contemporary**

National Training Network, Inc., (*978-1-57290*) Orders Addr.: P.O. Box 36, Summerfield, NC 27358 USA
E-mail: l.schueren@ntnmath.com
Web site: http://www.ntnmath.com.

National Wildlife Federation, (*978-0-937934; 978-1-888153; 978-1-932396; 978-1-938811; 978-1-946318*) 1260 Audubon Rd., Park Hills, KY 41011-1904 USA (SAN 215-8299) Toll Free: 800-477-5034; *Imprints:* Zoo Books (Zoo Bks); Critters Up Close (Critters Up Close)
E-mail: sales@zoobooks.com
Web site: http://www.zoobooks.com.

National Writers Pr., The, (*978-0-88100*) Div. of National Writers Assn., 17011 Lincoln Ave., No. 421, Parker, CO 80134 USA (SAN 240-320X) Tel 720-851-1944; Fax: 303-841-2607
E-mail: natlwritersassn@hotmail.com
Web site: http://www.nationalwriters.com.

National Writing Institute, (*978-1-888344*) PMB 248, 624 W. University Dr., Denton, TX 76201-1889 USA Tel 940-382-0044; Fax: 940-383-4414; Toll Free Fax: 888-663-7855; Toll Free: 800-688-5375
E-mail: info@writingstrands.com
Web site: http://www.writingstrands.com.

Nations Hope, Inc., The, (*978-0-9761415*) P.O. Box 691446, Orlando, FL 32869-1446 USA
Web site: http://www.nationshope.org.

Native American Pubns., (*978-0-9745867*) Orders Addr.: P.O. Box 9, Dulac, LA 70353-0009 USA Tel 985-223-3857; Edit Addr.: 443 Ashland Dr., Houma, LA 70363-7283 USA
E-mail: ccbilliot@aol.com.

Native Nature *See* **Niche Publishing & Marketing**

Native Sun Pr., (*978-0-9746848*) Orders Addr.: P.O. Box 1139, Summerland, CA 93067 USA (SAN 255-6839) Tel 805-969-2234 (phone/fax); Edit Addr.: 2240 Banner Ave., Summerland, CA 93067 USA.

Native Voices *Imprint of* **Book Publishing Co.**

Natl Bk. Network,
Dist(s): **Perfection Learning Corp.**

NaTroy Publishing Co., (*978-0-9755246*) Orders Addr.: P.O. Box 93442, Cleveland, OH 44101 USA Tel 216-376-4810.

Natural Genius Bks., (*978-0-9765070*) P.O. Box 191088, Sacramento, CA 95819 USA Toll Free: 800-917-9321
E-mail: mjsee3@earthlink.net
Web site: http://www.naturalgeniusbooks.com.

Natural Heritage/Natural History, Inc. (CAN) (*978-0-920474; 978-1-896219; 978-1-897045*) *Dist. by* **IngramPubServ.**

Natural History Museum Pubns. (GBR) (*978-0-565*) *Dist. by* **IPG Chicago.**

Natural Learning Concepts, Inc., (*978-0-9778866; 978-0-9800300*) 21 Gallatin Dr., Suite B, Dix Hills, NY 11746 USA Tel 631-858-0188 (phone/fax); Toll Free: 800-823-3430
E-mail: sales@nlconcepts.com
Web site: http://www.nlconcepts.com.

Natural Life Energy LLC, (*978-1-7320958*) 13130 SW 16th St., Davie, FL 33325 USA Tel 917-450-4717
E-mail: aqiyl.henry@gmail.com
Web site: http://www.naturallifeenergy.com.

Natural Math *See* **Delta Stream Media**

Naturally You Can Sing, (*978-0-9708397*) 3026 South St., East Troy, WI 53120 USA (SAN 255-4712)
E-mail: mary@flowformsamerica.com
Web site: http://www.maturallyyoucansing.com
Dist(s): **SteinerBooks, Inc.**

Nature Connection, (*978-0-9996944*) 31745 410th St., St. Peter, MN 56082 USA Tel 507-931-4399
E-mail: jbieder@wildblue.net.

Nature, Inc., (*978-0-692-97495-7*) 4195 Cedarcrest Ln., Anacortes, WA 98221 USA Tel 360-969-6170
E-mail: info@natureday.com
Dist(s): **Ingram Content Group.**

Nature Works Press, (*978-0-915965*) Orders Addr.: P.O. Box 469, Talent, OR 97540 USA (SAN 293-9738) Tel 541-535-3189; Toll Free Fax: 866-749-3077
E-mail: irene@natureworkspress.com; natureworks1@gmail.com
Web site: http://www.natureworkspress.com
Dist(s): **Bks. West**
Partners/West Book Distributors.

Naturegraph Pubs., Inc., (*978-0-87961; 978-0-911010*) Box 1047, 3543 Indian Creek Rd., Happy Camp, CA 96039 USA (SAN 202-8999) Tel 530-493-5353; Fax: 530-493-5240; Toll Free: 800-390-5353
E-mail: nature@sisqtel.net
Web site: http://www.naturegraph.com
Dist(s): **American West Bks.**
Gem Guides Bk. Co.
New Leaf Distributing Co., Inc.
Sunbelt Pubns., Inc.

NaturEncyclopedia *Imprint of* **Stemmer Hse. Pubs.**

Natures Beauty Publishing, (*978-0-9754701*) P.O. Box 107, Oxford, MI 48371-0107 USA Tel 248-236-9314; Fax: 248-236-9315
E-mail: Ron@Naturesbeautyphotography.com
Web site: http://www.naturesbeautyphotography.com.

Nature's Hopes & Heroes, (*978-0-9822942*) 265 Kings Hwy., Boulder Creek, CA 95006 USA Tel 831-423-8973
E-mail: jimcruz@cruzers.com.

Nature's Pr., (*978-0-9741883*) Orders Addr.: P.O. Box 371, Mercer, WI 54547 USA
Web site: http://www.naturespressbooks.com.

Naumann, Jennifer, (*978-0-9883902*) 2777 420th Ave, Elmore, MN 56027 USA Tel 507-943-3673
E-mail: jen.naumann@yahoo.com.

†Naval Institute Pr., (*978-0-87021; 978-1-55750; 978-1-59114; 978-1-61251; 978-1-68247; 978-1-68269*) Orders Addr.: 291 Wood Rd, Annapolis, MD 21402-5034 USA (SAN 662-0930) Tel 410-268-6110; Fax: 410-295-1084; Toll Free: 800-233-8764; Edit Addr.: 291 Wood Rd., Beach Hall, Annapolis, MD 21402-5034 USA (SAN 202-9006)
E-mail: tskord@usni.org; books@usni.org
Web site: http://www.usni.org
Dist(s): **Fujii Assocs.**
MyiLibrary
Publishers Group West (PGW); *CIP.*

Navarro, Sandra *See* **Cornsilk Pr.**

NavPress Publishing Group, (*978-0-89109; 978-1-57683; 978-1-60006; 978-1-61521; 978-1-61747; 978-1-61291; 978-1-63146; 978-1-64158*) 3820 N. 30th St., Colorado Springs, CO 80904 USA Fax: 719-260-7223; Toll Free Fax: 800-343-3902; Toll Free: 800-366-7788; *Imprints:* Th1nk Books (Th1nk Bks)
Web site: http://www.navpress.com
Dist(s): **Follett School Solutions**
Tyndale Hse. Pubs.

Nay Seyers *See* **WARTS etc.**

Nay Vogel Photography & Design, (*978-0-692-80195-6; 978-0-692-81723-0*) .

Naylor, Christopher, (*978-0-692-12074-3; 978-0-578-40320-5*) 2804 E 9th Ave Apt 23, WINFIELD, KS 67156 USA Tel 316-648-9013
E-mail: cjmnaylor@yahoo.com
Dist(s): **Ingram Content Group.**

Naynay Bks *See* **Naynay Bks.**

Naynay Bks., (*978-0-9769589*) 122 Arbor Rd., NW, Minerva, OH 44657 USA
E-mail: naynaybooks@aol.com
Web site: http://www.naynaybooks.com.

Naypree Enterprises, LLC *See* **Mauldin Publishing & Literacy House**

Nazarene Publishing House *See* **The Foundry Publishing**

NBM Publishing Co., (*978-0-918348; 978-1-56163; 978-1-68112*) Orders Addr.: 40 Exchange Pl., Suite 1308, New York, NY 10005 USA (SAN 210-0835) Tel 212-643-5407; Fax: 212-643-1545; Toll Free: 800-886-1223; Edit Addr.: 160 Broadway, Suite. 700, E. Wing, New York, NY 10038 USA Tel 646-559-4681; Fax: 212-643-1545; Toll Free: 800-886-1223; *Imprints:* Comics Lit (Comics Lit); Amerotica (Amerotica)
E-mail: catalog@nbmpublishing.com
Web site: http://www.nbmpub.com
Dist(s): **Independent Pubs. Group**
MyiLibrary.

N'Deeo Beauty *See* **N'Deeo, LLC**

N'Deeo, LLC, *(978-0-9724203; 978-0-9753811)* Orders Addr.: P.O. Box 460574, Aurora, CO 80046 USA Tel 770-896-6606; P.O. Box 1425, Mableton, GA 30126; Edit Addr.: 20511 E. Union Ave., Aurora, CO 80015 USA
E-mail: cservice@ndeeo.com
Web site: http://www.ndeeo.com.

Ndegwa, Catherine W., *(978-0-9742688)* Orders Addr.: P.O. Box 220411, Saint Louis, MO 63122-0411 USA; Edit Addr.: 119 Oakside Ln., Saint Louis, MO 63122-0411 USA
E-mail: catherine@varietystl.com.

NdueCzon Publishing Group, *(978-0-9755679)* P.O. Box 341825, Tampa, FL 33694 USA Tel 813-269-9351; Fax: 813-968-1941
E-mail: ndueczon@aol.com
Dist(s): **Culture Plus Bk. Distributors.**

Neal, Ann-Marie F, *(978-0-9747734; 978-0-9862096)* 903 Dale St., Edgewater, MD 21037 USA Tel 401-662-2411
E-mail: sunflower683@reagan.com
Web site: http://www.clarencethefrog.com.

Neal Morgan Publishing, *(978-0-9786117)* 51 Arrowgate Dr., Randolph, NJ 07869 USA Tel 973-598-9601; Fax: 973-927-8722
E-mail: Daleb6@aol.com.

Neal Porter Bks *Imprint of* **Holiday Hse., Inc.**

†Neal-Schuman Pubs., Inc., *(978-0-918212; 978-1-55570)* Div. of American Library Assn., 100 William St., Suite 2004, New York, NY 10038 USA (SAN 210-2455) Tel 212-925-8650; Fax: 212-219-8916; Toll Free Fax: 800-584-2414
E-mail: info@neal-schuman.com
Web site: http://www.neal-schuman.com
Dist(s): **ebrary, Inc.**; *CIP.*

Nearaway Far Pubns., *(978-0-9969878)* 22330 Victory Blvd., Woodland Hills, CA 91367 USA Tel 805-300-0738
E-mail: thehopefulprince@gmail.com
Web site: thehopefulprince.com.

Nebador Archives, *(978-1-936253)* P.O. Box 592, Kelso, WA 98626 USA
E-mail: jzc23@nebador.com
Web site: http://www.nebador.com.

Nebbadoon Pr., *(978-1-891331)* Div. of Nebbadoon, Inc., Orders Addr.: 371 Hubbard St., Glastonbury, CT 06033 USA Toll Free: 800-500-9086
E-mail: george@4554.com
Web site: http://www.nebbadoonpress.com.

Nebe, Charles, *(978-0-9773091)* Orders Addr.: P.O. Box 631143, Irving, TX 75063-1143 USA
Web site: http://www.boonefiles.com.

Nebraska Wealth.com, *(978-0-9746206)* 1803 Stagecoach Rd., Grand Island, NE 68801 USA
Web site: http://www.nebraskawealth.com.

Necessary Evil Pr., *(978-0-9753635)* P.O. Box 178, Escanaba, MI 49829 USA
E-mail: info@necessaryevilpress.com
Web site: http://www.necessaryevilpress.com.

Nechalec Pr., *(978-0-692-06188-6; 978-0-692-06506-8; 978-0-578-48645-1)* 448 E. Due W. Ave., Madison, TN 37115 USA Tel 615-496-8953
E-mail: jondbwriter@gmail.com
Dist(s): **Ingram Content Group.**

Nectar Pubns., *(978-0-9859986)* P.O. Box 6552, Savannah, GA 31404 USA Tel 912-631-9214
E-mail: contact@nectarpublications.com
Web site: www.nectarpublications.com.

Ned's Head Productions, *(978-1-887206)* 307 State St., Apt. B3, Johnstown, PA 15905 USA (SAN 253-8059) Tel 814-255-6646 (phone/fax)
E-mail: drron@charter.net
Web site: http://nedsheadbooks.com
Dist(s): **APG Sales & Distribution Services.**

Need To Know Publishing, *(978-1-940705)* 11019 N. 73rd St., Scottsdale, AZ 85260 USA Tel 888-377-3158; Fax: 888-377-3158
E-mail: brad@needtoknowpublishing.com
Dist(s): **MyiLibrary**
Publishers Group West (PGW).

Neely, Judy, *(978-1-893968)* 54505 NW Scofield Rd., Buxton, OR 97109 USA Tel 503-324-8222; Fax: 503-324-8252
E-mail: jneely@neelyranch.com
Web site: http://www.neelyranch.com.

Neema's Children Literature Assn., Inc., *(978-0-9740653)* Orders Addr.: P.O. Box 440073, Chicago, IL 60644-1937 USA Tel 773-378-0607; Fax: 773-378-0042; Edit Addr.: 5345 W. Ferdinand St., Chicago, IL 60644-1937 USA Tel 773-575-4639
E-mail: nclapub@gmail.com.

Nefu Bks. *Imprint of* **Africana Homestead Legacy Pubs., Inc.**

Negro Publishing LLC *Imprint of* **Negro Publishing, LLC**

Negro Publishing, LLC, *(978-0-9763583)* Orders Addr.: P.O. Box 78, Mableton, GA 30126 USA Tel 770-265-0822; Fax: 770-948-2460; *Imprints:* Negro Publishing LLC (Negro Pub)
E-mail: supadave@negropublishing.com; dhhorton_2000@yahoo.com
Web site: http://www.negropublishing.com
Dist(s): **Culture Plus Bk. Distributors.**

NEHA Training LLC, *(978-0-944111)* 720 S. Colorado Blvd. Ste. 1000N, Denver, CO 80246-1926 USA
E-mail: support@nehatraining.com
Web site: http://www.nehatraining.com.

Neighborhood Pubs., *(978-0-615-75249-5)* 3317 Manor Rd., Austin, TX 78723 USA Tel 512-291-2314
E-mail: johnatpbp@yahoo.com.

Nelsbok Publishing, *(978-0-9763072)* 3312 Cedar Ave S., Minneapolis, MN 55407-2335 USA
Web site: http://www.nelsbok.com.

Nelsen, Margie, *(978-0-615-22008-6; 978-0-615-25480-7)* 804 Spruce Pl., Saint Peter, MN 56082 USA
E-mail: margienelsen@mchsi.com
Web site: http://www.snugglebooks.com.

Nelson, Linda J., *(978-0-692-18458-5; 978-0-578-50119-2)* 47 N. Rd., NEW IPSWICH, NH 03071 USA Tel 603-878-2121
E-mail: linda_nel@msn.com
Dist(s): **Ingram Content Group.**

Nelson Publishing & Marketing, *(978-1-933916; 978-0-9785075; 978-1-938326)* 366 Welch Rd., Northville, MI 48167-1160 USA Tel 248-735-0418; *Imprints:* Ferne Press (Ferne Press)
E-mail: marian@nelsonpublishingandmarketing.com; kris@nelsonpublishingandmarketing.com
Web site: http://nelsonpublishingandmarketing.com
Dist(s): **Partners Pubs. Group, Inc.**

Nelson Publishing, LLC, *(978-0-9794171)* 15480 Annapolis Road, Suite No. 202-216, Bowie, MD 20715 USA; *Imprints:* Adventures of Hillary, The (AdventuresHillary)
E-mail: info@nelson-publishing.com
Web site: http://www.nelson-publishing.com.

Nelson, R. E. & Assoc., *(978-0-9749636)* 1535 SW Plass Ave., Topeka, KS 66604 USA Tel 785-235-3041
Web site: http://www.renelson.com.

Nelson, Roy *See* **Nelson, R. E. & Assoc.**

†Nelson, Thomas Inc., *(978-0-529; 978-0-7852; 978-0-8407; 978-0-8499; 978-0-86605; 978-0-88113; 978-0-89840; 978-0-89922; 978-0-918956; 978-0-7180; 978-1-4002; 978-1-4003; 978-1-4016; 978-1-59145; 978-1-4041; 978-1-59554; 978-1-59555; 978-1-4185; 978-1-59951; 978-1-4261; 978-1-60255; 978-1-4845; 978-1-5000; 978-1-5314; 978-1-6623) Div. of HarperCollins Christian Publishing, Orders Addr.: P.O. Box 141000, Nashville, TN 37214-1000 USA (SAN 209-3820) Fax: 615-902-1866; Toll Free: 800-251-4000; Edit Addr.: 501 Nelson Pl., Nashville, TN 37214 USA*
Web site: http://www.harpercollinschristian.com
Dist(s): **Brilliance Publishing, Inc.**
Christian Bk. Distributors
CreateSpace Independent Publishing Platform
Follett School Solutions
Twentieth Century Christian Bks.; *CIP.*

Nelson Thornes Ltd. (GBR) *(978-0-17; 978-0-7487; 978-0-85950; 978-1-871402; 978-1-873732; 978-1-4085) Dist. by* **Trans-Atl Phila.**

Nelson Thornes Ltd. (GBR) *(978-0-17; 978-0-7487; 978-0-85950; 978-1-871402; 978-1-873732; 978-1-4085) Dist. by* **OUP.**

Nelson, Tracy C., *(978-0-9990974)* 4011 Overcup Oak Ln., Cary, NC 27519 USA Tel 919-408-9911; Fax: 919-408-9911
E-mail: stephy.costarica@gmail.com.

Nemec LLC, *(978-1-947608)* 3812 Elbert Ave, Alexandria, VA 22305 USA Tel 571-214-4222
E-mail: GaleNemecBooks@gmail.com
Web site: www.GaleNemecBooks.com.

NEMESIS Enterprises, L.P., *(978-0-9713230)* Orders Addr.: 1048 S. Wardsboro Rd., Wardsboro, VT 05355 USA
E-mail: nemesis@myfairpoint.net
Web site: http://www.gophergo.com.

Nemo Publishing, LLC, *(978-0-9817132)* 86 Newbury St., Portland, ME 04101 USA (SAN 856-3381) Tel 207-761-0807; Fax: 207-775-5567
E-mail: tami@maine.rr.com
Web site: http://www.captneli.com
Dist(s): **Diamond Comic Distributors, Inc.**
Diamond Bk. Distributors.

Nemsi Bks., *(978-0-9718164; 978-0-9766400; 978-0-9794855; 978-0-9815313; 978-0-9821427; 978-0-9825011)* Div. of Morphtek.com, Inc., P.O. Box 191, Pierpont, SD 57468-0191 USA Fax: 605-325-3393
E-mail: psiccusa@dailypost.com
Web site: http://www.nemsi-books.net.

Neo-Tech Publishing Co., *(978-0-911752)* P.O. Box PO Box 531330, Henderson, NV 89053-1330 USA (SAN 202-3156)
E-mail: rapper@neo-tech.com
Web site: http://www.neo-tech.com; http://www.neo-tech.com/front/cservice.html.

Nerdel Co., The, *(978-0-9823357)* 1000 West McNab Road, Pompano Beach, FL 33069 USA (SAN 858-7205)
Web site: http://www.nerdel.com.

NERO International Holding Co., Inc. *See* **Valenti, Joseph**

NESFA Pr. *Imprint of* **New England Science Fiction Assn., Inc.**

Neshee Pubn., *(978-0-9747017; 978-0-9770907; 978-0-9785794; 978-0-9823053)* P.O. Box 48028, Philadelphia, PA 19144 USA
E-mail: info@nesheepublicaiton.com
Web site: http://www.nesheepublication.com.

Neshui Publishing, Inc., *(978-0-9652528; 978-1-931190)* 6310 Rosebury Ave. #2, Saint Louis, MO 63105 USA
E-mail: info@neshuipress.com
Web site: http://www.neshuipress.com
Dist(s): **Raven West Coast Distribution.**

Nesting Tree Bks. *Imprint of* **Raven Publishing Inc. of Montana**

NetClinger, *(978-0-9760308)* P.O. Box 38144, Houston, TX 77238-8144 USA
Web site: http://www.netclinger.com.

Netcomics, *(978-1-60009)* P.O. Box 16484, Jersey City, NJ 07306 USA
Dist(s): **Diamond Comic Distributors, Inc.**
Diamond Bk. Distributors.

NetNia Publishing Co., *(978-1-884163)* 9218 Rockbrook Dr., Dallas, TX 75220 USA; *Imprints:* Juba Books (Juba Bks)
E-mail: jeffery.bradley@outlook.com
Web site: http://www.howtogrowdreadlocks.com; http://www.netnia.com; http://www.africanamericanchildrenplays.com
Dist(s): **Ingram Content Group.**

NETroplex Books *See* **Yankee Cowboy**

Network CPU Learning Technologies, *(978-1-932257)* 172 Fifth Ave., Suite 37, Brooklyn, NY 11217-3504 USA (SAN 254-9298)
E-mail: roxceyluv@yahoo.com.

NETWORK Inc., The, *(978-1-878234)* Div. of NETWORK, Inc., 136 Fenno Dr., Rowley, MA 01969-1004 USA Tel 978-948-7764; Fax: 978-948-7836; Toll Free: 800-877-5400
E-mail: info@thenetworkinc.org
Web site: http://www.thenetworkinc.org.

Networking Univ., *(978-0-9885108)* 4900 Brook Ln., Anna, TX 75409 USA Tel 214-592-5196
E-mail: DebraPope@Networking-University.com.

Networlding, *(978-0-9883471; 978-1-944027)* 910 W Madison, No. 905E, IL, IL 60607 USA Tel 312-560-0982; Fax: 312-560-0982
E-mail: melissa@networlding.com
Web site: www.networlding.com.

Neuburger Publishing, *(978-0-9762419)* Orders Addr.: P.O. Box 3928, Taulatin, OR 97062-3928 USA Tel 503-925-0400; Edit Addr.: 24386 SW Baker Rd., Sherwood, OR 97140 USA
Web site: http://www.takethefearoutofmath.com.

Neugebauer, Michael (Publishing) Limited (HKG) *(978-988-15126; 978-988-15127; 978-988-15128; 978-988-15953; 978-988-15854; 978-988-15955; 978-988-18485; 978-988-19152; 978-988-19153; 978-988-19154; 978-988-97794; 978-988-8240; 978-988-15954; 978-988-8341; 978-988-8342) Dist. by* **Peng Rand Hse.**

Neumann Pr. *Imprint of* **TAN Bks.**

Neurosculpting Institute, *(978-0-692-80006-5)*
Dist(s): **CreateSpace Independent Publishing Platform.**

Nevaeh Publishing, LLC, *(978-0-9787899; 978-0-9839187)* 3523 Morton's Landing Dr., Ellenwood, GA 30294 USA (SAN 851-6111) Tel 404-216-6111
E-mail: dwanabrams@gmail.com
Web site: http://www.dwanabrams.com
Dist(s): **Smashwords.**

Never Not Knitting, *(978-0-9883249)* P.O. Box 1635, Atascadero, CA 93423 USA Tel 805-270-5648
E-mail: nevernotknitting@gmail.com
Web site: www.nevernotknitting.com
Dist(s): **Independent Pubs. Group.**

Never Quit Productions, Inc., *(978-0-615-26231-4)* 4832 Wind Hill Ct. W., Fort Worth, TX 76179 USA
Dist(s): **Lulu Pr., Inc.**

Never Stop Reading Never Stop Learning, *(978-0-9741750)* 3221 S. Indiana St., Lakewood, CO 80228 USA Tel 303-829-8699
E-mail: neverstopreading@aol.com
Web site: http://www.jdmcdoil.com.

Neverland Publishing Co., LLC, *(978-0-9826971; 978-0-9888290; 978-0-9903148; 978-0-9965595)* 24 NW 102 St., Miami Shores, FL 33150 USA (SAN 990-0187) Tel 786-521-0731
E-mail: editor@neverlandpublishing.com
Web site: http://www.neverlandpublishing.com.

Nevruz, Cori, *(978-0-692-89979-3; 978-0-692-92312-2; 978-0-692-12243-3; 978-0-692-15523-3; 978-0-692-16469-3; 978-0-578-41158-3; 978-0-578-44673-8; 978-0-578-50825-2; 978-0-578-57209-3; 978-0-578-67292-2; 978-0-578-67296-0)* 1121 Military Cutoff, Wilmington, NC 28405 USA Tel 919-610-8532
E-mail: corinevruz@gmail.com.

New Academia Publishing, LLC, *(978-0-9744934; 978-0-9767042; 978-0-9777908; 978-0-9787713; 978-0-9794488; 978-0-9800814; 978-0-9818654; 978-0-9823867; 978-0-9844062; 978-0-9828061; 978-0-615-43269-4; 978-0-9832451; 978-0-9836899; 978-0-9845832; 978-0-9855698; 978-0-9860216;-0-9886376; 978-0-9899169; 978-0-9915047; 978-0-9904471; 978-0-9906939; 978-0-9864353; 978-0-9966484; 978-0-9974962; 978-0-9981477; 978-0-9986433; 978-0-9995572; 978-1-7326988; 978-0-578-50586-2; 978-1-7330408; 978-1-7333980; 978-1-7348659; 978-1-) 4401-A Connecticut Ave. NW No. 236, Washington, DC 20008 USA; Imprints:* Vellum Books (Vellum)
Web site: http://www.newacademia.com
Dist(s): **Ingram Content Group**
eBookit.com.

New Age Beauty Corp, *(978-0-578-50265-6; 978-1-7346298)* 6296 SW 165 Pl., Miami, FL 33193 USA Tel 720-202-1360
E-mail: looleebook@gmail.com
Dist(s): **Ingram Content Group.**

New Age Dimensions, Incorporated *See* **Adrema Pr.**

New Age World Publishing, *(978-1-59405)* 27 Dove Ln., El Sobrante, CA 94803-2827 USA; *Imprints:* N2Print (N2Print)
E-mail: nawpublishing@hotmail.com
Web site: http://www.nawpublishing.com.

New & Living Way Publishing Co., *(978-0-910003)* P.O. Box 830384, Tuskegee, AL 36083-0384 USA (SAN 241-2314) Tel 334-727-5372
E-mail: nlwpc@bellsouth.net; clgpgt@bellsouth.net
Web site: http://www.clgpgt.org/NLW/nlw1.html.

New & Living Way Publishing House *See* **New & Living Way Publishing Co.**

New Art & Vision, LLC, *(978-0-9742322)* 1360 E. 300 N., Layton, UT 84040 USA Tel 801-543-3383
E-mail: bnybo@elmojackson.com
Web site: http://www.elmojackson.com.

New Awareness Network, Inc., *(978-0-9652855; 978-0-9711198; 978-0-9768978; 978-0-9849285; 978-0-9894058; 978-0-9960986; 978-0-9975404; 978-1-7325883)* 86 Dennis St., Manhasset, NY 11030 USA Tel 516-869-9108; 516-365-1547; Fax: 516-365-1624
E-mail: sumari@sethcenter.com
Web site: http://www.sethcenter.com.

New Baby Productions, *(978-0-9818530)* Orders Addr.: 4143 Tanglewood Ct., Bloomfield Township, MI 48301 USA (SAN 856-7298)
E-mail: eric@elementalfources.com
Web site: http://www.ElementalFources.com
Dist(s): **Haven Distributors**
Ingram Content Group.

New Birth Publishing, *(978-0-9755489)* 1900 Preston Rd., No. 267, PMB 264, Plano, TX 75093 USA
Web site: http://www.newbirthpublishing.com.

New Buds Publishing Hse. (CHN) *(978-7-5307) Dist. by* **Chinasprout.**

New Canaan Publishing Co. LLC, *(978-1-889658)* 2384 N. Hwy. 341, Rossville, GA 30741 USA Tel 423-285-8672
E-mail: djm@newcanaanpublishing.com
Web site: http://www.newcanaanpublishing.com
Dist(s): **Send The Light Distribution LLC.**

New Castle Publishing Co., *(978-0-9740195)* 512 Wadsworth Dr., Richmond, VA 23236 USA
E-mail: newcastlepubl@aol.com.

New Century Pr., *(978-0-9748013)* P.O. Box 73381, Richmond, VA 23235-8040 USA Tel 804-897-2824 Do not confuse with companies with the same or similar name in Bermuda Dunes CA, Chula Vista CA, New York NY
E-mail: newcenturypress@aol.com.

New Century Pr., *(978-1-890035)* Orders Addr.: 1055 Bay Blvd., Suite C, Chula Vista, CA 91911-1628 USA (SAN 859-3760) Tel 619-476-7400; Fax: 619-476-7474; Toll Free: 800-519-2465 (orders) Do not confuse with companies with the same or similar name in Bermuda Dunes CA, New York NY
E-mail: sales@newcenturypress.com
Web site: http://www.newcenturypress.com.

New Century Publishing, LLC, *(978-0-9768052; 978-0-9820729; 978-0-9822344; 978-0-9824711; 978-0-9841819; 978-0-9843666; 978-0-9844661)* 1040 E. 86th St., Suite 42A, Indianapolis, IN 46240 USA Tel 317-663-8741; Fax: 317-663-8745
E-mail: dwcaswell@newcentrypublishing.orrg
Web site: http://www.newcenturypublishing.org.

New City Community Pr., *(978-0-9712996; 978-0-9819560; 978-0-9840429; 978-0-9887635; 978-0-692-83625-5)* 7715 Crittenden St., #222, Philadelphia, PA 191182 USA Tel 315-443-1912 Do not confuse with New City Press in Hyde Park, NY
E-mail: sjparks@syr.edu
Web site: http://www.newcitypress.org
Dist(s): **Chicago Distribution Ctr.**
Longleaf Services
SPD-Small Pr. Distribution.

New City Press *See* **New City Community Pr.**

New City Press *See* **New City Press of the Focolare**

†New City Press of the Focolare, *(978-0-911782; 978-1-56548)* 202 Comforter Blvd., Hyde Park, NY 12538 USA (SAN 203-7335) Tel 845-229-0335; Fax: 845-229-0351; Toll Free: 800-462-5980 (orders only)
E-mail: info@newcitypress.com
Web site: http://www.newcitypress.com; *CIP.*

New Classics Pr., *(978-0-9755704)* 2400 Ridgecroft SE, Grand Rapids, MI 49546 USA.

New Concepts Publishing, *(978-1-891020; 978-1-58608; 978-1-60394)* 5202 Humphreys Rd., Lake Park, GA 31636 USA Tel 229-257-0367; Fax: 229-219-1097
E-mail: newconcepts@newconceptspublishing.com; service@newconceptspublishing.com
Web site: http://www.newconceptspublishing.com
Dist(s): **Smashwords.**

New Dawn Pr., Inc., *(978-0-9729607; 978-1-932705)* 244 S. Randall Rd., No. 90, Elgin, IL 60123 USA
E-mail: maildrop@newdawnpress.com
Web site: http://www.newdawnpress.com.

New Dawn Publishing, *(978-0-9721948)* P.O. Box 11151, Portland, ME 04104 USA Tel 207-839-8809 Do not confuse with companies with the same or similar name in Elk Mills, MD, Dexter, NY
Web site: http://www.mynewdawn.com.

New Day Pr., *(978-0-913678)* c/o Karamu Hse., 2355 E. 89th St., Cleveland, OH 44106 USA (SAN 279-2664) Tel 216-795-7070 ext 228; Fax: 216-795-7073 Do not confuse wtih New Day Press in Las Vegas, NV
E-mail: editor@newdaypress.com.

New Day Publishing, Inc., *(978-0-9789056; 978-0-9798247)* 26 Bluff Ridge Ct., Greensboro, NC 27455 USA Tel 336-545-1545; Fax: 336-545-1640; Toll Free: 866-763-2977 Do not confuse with companies with the same or similar name in Winston-Salem, NC, Phoenix, AZ, North Miami, FL
E-mail: ateich@newdaypublishing.net
Web site: http://www.newdaypublishing.net.

†New Directions Publishing Corp., *(978-0-8112)* 80 Eighth Ave., New York, NY 10011 USA (SAN 202-9081) Tel 212-255-0230; Fax: 212-255-0231; Toll Free: 800-233-4830
E-mail: nd@ndbooks.com
Web site: http://www.ndpublishing.com
Dist(s): **Continental Bk. Co., Inc.**
Norton, W. W. & Co., Inc.
Penguin Random Hse. Distribution
Penguin Random Hse. LLC
SPD-Small Pr. Distribution; *CIP.*

New Eden Publishing, *(978-0-9882368; 978-0-692-32667-1; 978-0-9980950)* 50513 W Esch Trail, Maricopa, AZ 85139 USA Tel 480-217-0776
E-mail: anitasmail3@gmail.com
Dist(s): **Lulu Pr., Inc.**

New England Bible Sales, *(978-0-9839522; 978-1-941776)* 262 Quaker Rd., Sidney, ME 04330 USA Tel 207-512-2636
E-mail: jptbooks@gmail.com
Web site: www.NewEnglandBibleSales.com.

New England Science Fiction Assn., Inc., *(978-0-915368; 978-1-886778; 978-1-61037)* P.O. Box 809, Framingham, MA 01701-0809 USA (SAN 223-8187) Tel 508-653-7397; Fax: 617-776-3243; *Imprints:* N E S F A Press (NESFA Pr)
E-mail: press@nesfa.org
Web site: http://www.nesfa.org/press/.

New Europe Bks., *(978-0-9825781; 978-0-9850623; 978-0-9900043; 978-0-9973169; 978-0-9995416; 978-1-7345379)* 54 Hall Street, Suite 2, Williamstown, MA 01267 USA Tel 413-458-8763; *Imprints:* Young Europe Books (YngEUBks)
E-mail: paul@neweuropebooks.com; info@neweuropebooks.com
Web site: http://www.NewEuropeBooks.com; http://www.NewEuropeBooks.com
Dist(s): **Consortium Bk. Sales & Distribution**
MyiLibrary.

New Family Pr., *(978-0-9742008)* 389 Belmont St., Suite 105, Oakland, CA 94610 USA Tel 510-866-3984
E-mail: newfamilypress@yahoo.com
Dist(s): **Book Wholesalers, Inc.**

New Forums Pr., *(978-0-913507; 978-1-58107)* Orders Addr.: P.O. Box 876, Stillwater, OK 74076 USA (SAN 285-8673) Tel 405-372-6158; Fax: 405-377-2237; Toll Free: 800-606-3766; Edit Addr.: 1018 S. Lewis, Stillwater, OK 74074 USA
E-mail: dougdollar@provalue.net; design@newforums.com
Web site: http://www.newforums.com
Dist(s): **BookBaby.**

New Generation Publishing (GBR) *Dist. by* **IPG Chicago.**

New Global Publishing, *(978-0-9762292; 978-0-9770043; 978-0-9785609; 978-0-9791748; 978-0-9830940; 978-0-9896334)* Orders Addr.: 2310 SE. Bordeaux Ct., Port Saint Lucie, FL 34952 USA
Web site: http://www.newglobalpublishing.com.

New Growth Pr., *(978-0-9762308; 978-0-9770807; 978-0-9785567; 978-1-934885; 978-1-935273; 978-1-936768; 978-1-938267; 978-1-939946; 978-1-942572; 978-1-945270; 978-1-948130; 978-1-64507)* Orders Addr.: P.O. Box 4485, Greensboro, NC 27404 USA; Edit Addr.: 1301 Carolina St. Suite 124, Greensboro, NC 27401 USA Tel 336-378-7775; Fax: 336-464-2722
E-mail: aprentzas@newgrowthpress.com
Web site: https://newgrowthpress.com
Dist(s): **Cook, David C.**

New Harbinger Pubns., *(978-0-934986; 978-1-57224; 978-1-879237; 978-1-60882; 978-1-62625; 978-1-68403; 978-1-64848)* Orders Addr.: 5674 Shattuck Ave., Oakland, CA 94609 USA (SAN 205-0587) Tel 510-652-2002; 510-652-0215; Fax: 510-652-5472; Toll Free: 800-652-1613; *Imprints:* Impact Publishers (ImpactPubs); Instant Help Books (Instant Help Bks)
E-mail: customerservice@newharbinger.com
Web site: http://www.newharbinger.com
Dist(s): **MyiLibrary**
ebrary, Inc.

New Holland Pubs., Ltd. (GBR) *(978-1-85368; 978-1-85974; 978-1-84330; 978-1-84636; 978-1-84537; 978-1-84773; 978-1-78009)* *Dist. by* **Sterling.**

New Holland Pubs. Pty, Ltd. (AUS) *(978-1-86436; 978-1-875580; 978-1-876334; 978-1-877069; 978-1-74110; 978-1-921024; 978-1-921073; 978-1-921072; 978-1-921517; 978-1-921580; 978-1-921655; 978-1-74257; 978-1-74268; 978-1-921740; 978-1-921836; 978-0-7316-1991-7; 978-0-646-15496-1;-1-74337; 978-1-925546; 978-1-76079)* *Dist. by* **IPG Chicago.**

New Holland Pubs. Pty, Ltd. (AUS) *(978-1-86436; 978-1-875580; 978-1-876334; 978-1-877069; 978-1-74110; 978-1-921024; 978-1-921073; 978-1-921072; 978-1-921517; 978-1-921580; 978-1-921655; 978-1-74257; 978-1-74268; 978-1-921740; 978-1-921836; 978-0-7316-1991-7; 978-0-646-15496-1;-1-74337; 978-1-925546; 978-1-76079)* *Dist. by* **Tuttle Pubng.**

New Hope *See* **Woman's Missionary Union**

New Hope Pubs., *(978-0-9651950)* 3501 Yukon Ave., N, New Hope, MN 55427 USA Do not confuse with New Hope Publishers in Birmingham, AL
Dist(s): **B&H Publishing Group**
Baker & Taylor Publisher Services (BTPS).

New Hope Pubs. *Imprint of* **Iron Stream Media**

New Horizon Pr. Pubs., Inc., *(978-0-88282)* Orders Addr.: P.O. Box 669, Far Hills, NJ 07931 USA (SAN 677-119X) Tel 908-604-6311; Fax: 908-604-6330; Toll Free: 800-533-7978 (orders only)
E-mail: nhp@newhorizonpressbooks.com
Web site: http://www.newhorizonpressbooks.com
Dist(s): **Kensington Publishing Corp.**
MyiLibrary
Penguin Publishing Group
Publishers Group West (PGW).

New Horizons Christian Ctr., *(978-0-9728532)* 16 Foxbriar Rd., Hilton Head, SC 29926 USA.

New Horizons Pr., *(978-0-9647933)* Orders Addr.: 26 Nottingham Dr., Cartersville, GA 30121 USA; Edit Addr.: 2815 New South Dr., Marietta, GA 30066 USA Do not confuse with companies with the same name in, Lake Mary, FL, Ferrisburgh, VT, Leesburg, VA, Orlando, FL.

New in Chess *Imprint of* **Continental Sales, Inc.**

New In Chess,Csi *Imprint of* **Continental Sales, Inc.**

New Internationalist Pubns., Ltd. (GBR) *(978-1-869847; 978-0-9540499; 978-1-904456; 978-1-906523; 978-1-78026; 978-1-912408; 978-0-9955900)* *Dist. by* **Consort Bk Sales.**

New Island Books (IRL) *(978-1-85186; 978-1-874597; 978-1-902602; 978-1-904301; 978-1-905494)* *Dist. by* **IPG Chicago.**

New Issues Poetry & Prose, Western Michigan Univ., *(978-0-932826; 978-1-930974; 978-1-936970)* 1903 West Michigan Ave. Western Michigan University, Kalamazoo, MI 49008 USA (SAN 276-6299) Tel 269-387-8185; Fax: 269-387-2562
E-mail: new-issues@wmich.edu
Web site: http://www.wmich.edu/newissues
Dist(s): **Chicago Distribution Ctr.**
SPD-Small Pr. Distribution.

New Kid Safety, *(978-0-9829371)* 4824 Smallwood Rd. Suite 214, Columbia, SC 29223 USA Tel 803-740-0861; Fax: 803-736-0223
E-mail: info@newkidsafety.com
Web site: http://www.newkidsafety.com.

New Leaf Bks. *Imprint of* **WigWam Publishing Co.**

New Leaf Education, Inc. *See* **New Leaf Educ., Inc.**

New Leaf Educ., Inc., *(978-0-9722452; 978-0-9764217; 978-1-933655)* Orders Addr.: P.O. Box 16230, Baltimore, MD 21210 USA Tel 410-467-7835; Fax: 410-951-0419; Edit Addr.: 2050 Rockrose Ave., Baltimore, MD 21211 USA
E-mail: contactus@newleafeducation.com
Web site: http://www.newleafeducation.com.

New Leaf Media, LLC, *(978-1-970072; 978-1-952027)* 410 E. Royal Forrest Blvd., Columbus, OH 43214 USA Tel 951-465-4621
E-mail: info@thenewleafmedia.com; simon.lee@thenewleafmedia.com
Web site: www.thenewleafmedia.com.

New Leaf Pr. *Imprint of* **New Leaf Publishing Group**

New Leaf Press, Incorporated *See* **New Leaf Publishing Group**

New Leaf Publishing Group, *(978-0-89051; 978-0-89221; 978-1-61458; 978-1-68344)* P.O. Box 726, Green Forest, AR 72638 USA (SAN 207-9518) Tel 870-438-5288; Fax: 870-438-5120 Toll Free: 800-643-9535; 800-999-3777; *Imprints:* New Leaf Press (NLP); Master Books (MasterBks) Do not confuse with companies with the same or similar name in Los Angeles, CAStone Mountain, GA
E-mail: nlp@nlpg.com
Web site: http://www.nlpg.com; http://www.masterbooks.com
Dist(s): **MyiLibrary**
Spring Arbor Distributors, Inc.
ebrary, Inc.

New Learning Publishing, *(978-0-9793576)* 123 Wolcott Ave., Rochester, NY 14606 USA (SAN 853-2273) Tel 585-426-9454
E-mail: callen10@rochester.rr.com.

New Library Press LLC, *(978-0-7950)* Orders Addr.: 3419 Chapman Ave. #133, Orange, CA 92869 USA; Edit Addr.: P.O. Box 130, Murrieta, CA 92564 USA
E-mail: newbookorders@gmail.com.

New Life Clarity Publishing, *(978-0-578-43624-1; 978-0-578-44336-2; 978-0-578-46230-1; 978-0-578-46231-8; 978-0-578-51069-9; 978-0-578-51070-5; 978-0-578-54962-0; 978-0-578-54976-7; 978-0-578-55470-9; 978-0-578-55471-6; 978-0-578-57850-7; 978-0-578-57851-4; 978-0-578-59038-7; 978-0-578-59039-4; 978-0-578-59798-0; 978-0-578-59799-7; 978-0-578-77614-9; 978-0-578-77615-6; 978-0-578-77720-7; 978-0-578-77722-1) 205 W. 300 S., Brigham City, UT 84302 USA Tel 435-695-4456*
E-mail: newlifeclaritypublishing@gmail.com
Dist(s): **Ingram Content Group.**

New Life Publishing Hse., *(978-0-9785573)* Orders Addr.: 2835 Cedar Ln., Vienna, VA 22180 USA (SAN 850-8844) Tel 703-942-8440 (phone/fax)
E-mail: garrygenser@me.com.

New Line Bks., *(978-1-57717; 978-1-880908; 978-1-59764)* 245 Eighth Ave., No. 180, New York, NY 10011-1607 USA Toll Free Fax: 888-719-7723; Toll Free: 888-719-7722
E-mail: info@newlinebooks.com
Web site: http://www.newlinebooks.com.

New Millenium Pr., The, *(978-0-9706728)* 311 E. Seventh St., Tama, IA 52339 USA Tel 515-484-2313 Do not confuse with New Millennium Press in Augusta, GA.

New Millennium Bks., *(978-0-9672333)* c/o Gail Mathabane, 901 SW King St. Suite 1006, Portland, OR 97205 USA Tel 503-758-2628 Do not confuse with New Millennium Bks., Petersburg, VA
E-mail: gem@mathabane.com
Web site: http://www.mathabane.com.

New Monic Bks., *(978-0-9652422; 978-0-9840966)* P.O. Box 511314, Punta Gorda, FL 33951-1314 USA Toll Free: 800-741-1295
E-mail: bburchers@earthlink.net
Web site: www.vocabularycartoons.com.

New Montgomery Pr., *(978-0-692-77662-9; 978-0-578-59072-1; 978-0-578-64136-2; 978-1-7347046)* 2422 Dundee Rd, Louisville, KY 40205 USA Tel 502-767-9312
Web site: http://louisrats.wixsite.com/witchrabbit
Dist(s): **CreateSpace Independent Publishing Platform.**

New Native Pr., *(978-1-883197)* P.O. Box 661, Cullowhee, NC 28723 USA Tel 828-293-9237
E-mail: newnativepress@hotmail.com
Dist(s): **SPD-Small Pr. Distribution.**

New Orleans Stories, *(978-0-9758996)* 7401 Slaughter Ln., PMB 5015, Austin, TX 78739 USA Tel 512-923-5015
E-mail: sean@neworleansstories.com
Web site: http://neworleansstories.com
Dist(s): **Forest Sales & Distributing Co.**

New Page Bks. *Imprint of* **Red Wheel/Weiser**

New Paige Pr., LLC, *(978-0-578-19803-3; 978-0-692-09269-9; 978-0-692-15613-1; 978-0-578-48389-4; 978-0-578-49638-2; 978-0-578-52178-7; 978-0-578-53533-3; 978-0-578-53808-2; 978-0-578-55758-8; 978-0-578-59464-4; 978-1-7345980)* 414 Hackensack Ave suite 1126, Hackensack, NJ 07601 USA Tel 917-887-1993
E-mail: jmiletsky@newpaigepress.com
Dist(s): **Independent Pub.**

New Paradigm Bks., *(978-1-892138)* 22491 Vistawood Way, Boca Raton, FL 33428 USA Tel 561-482-5971; Fax: 561-852-8322; Toll Free: 800-808-5179
E-mail: darbyc@earthlink.net
Web site: http://www.newpara.com
Dist(s): **New Leaf Distributing Co., Inc.**

New Paradigm Pubns., *(978-0-615-35944-1; 978-0-9827673; 978-1-7326610)* 12 Cherokee St., Dover, NH 03820 USA (SAN 860-2255) Tel 603-742-4162
E-mail: jim@mastromedia.com; info@newparadigmpublications.com
Web site: http://www.newparadigmpublications.com.

New Poets Series, Incorporated/Chestnut Hills Press/Stonewall *See* **BrickHouse Bks., Inc.**

New Pr., The, *(978-1-56584; 978-1-59558; 978-1-62097)* 38 Greene St., 4th Flr., New York, NY 10013 USA Tel 212 629 8802; Fax: 212 629 8617; Toll Free Fax: 800 458 6515; Toll Free: 800 233 4830
E-mail: newpress@thenewpress.com
Web site: http://www.thenewpress.com
Dist(s): **China Books & Periodicals, Inc.**
MyiLibrary
Open Road Integrated Media, Inc.
Two Rivers Distribution
ebrary, Inc.

New Publications, *(978-0-692-52964-5; 978-1-944156; 978-0-9933594-1-5)* 5 Bradley Rd., Enfield, NH 03585 USA Tel 603-838-6444
E-mail: darin@theinspiragroup.com
Dist(s): **CreateSpace Independent Publishing Platform.**

New Reformation Publications *See* **1517 Publishing**

New Seasons *Imprint of* **Publications International, Ltd.**

New Shelves Bks., *(978-1-935355; 978-0-692-73191-8)* Orders Addr.: 20 Office Pkwy. No. 126, Pittsford, NY 13534 USA (SAN 857-3700) Tel 518-261-1300; Fax: 518-633-1211; *Imprints:* GraceNotes Press (GraceNotes Pr)
Web site: http://www.newshelves.com.

New Shelves Distribution, 103 Remsen St., Cohoes, NY 12047 USA Tel 518-391-2300; Fax: 518-391-2365
Web site: http://www.newshelvesdistribution.com.

New Song Publishing Co., *(978-0-942925)* Div. of Al Menconi Ministries, Orders Addr.: P.O. Box 131147, Carlsbad, CA 92013 USA (SAN 667-8475) Tel 760-591-4696; Toll Free: 800-786-8742; Edit Addr.: 1635 S. Rancho Santa Fe Rd., Suite 105, San Marcos, CA 92069 USA (SAN 667-8483)
E-mail: patty@almenconi.com; al@almenconi.com
Web site: http://www.AlMenconi.com.

New Star Bks., Ltd. (CAN) *(978-0-919573; 978-0-919888; 978-0-921586; 978-1-55420)* *Dist. by* **SPD-Small Pr Dist.**

New Strategist Pr., LLC, *(978-0-9628092; 978-1-885070; 978-1-933588; 978-1-935114; 978-1-935775; 978-1-937737; 978-1-940308)* Orders Addr.: P.O. Box 635, Amityville, NY 11701 USA Tel 631-608-8795; Edit Addr.: 26 Austin Ave., Amityville, NY 11701 USA (SAN 860-4002) Tel 800-848-0842; 631-608-8795; Fax: 631-691-1770
E-mail: accounting@newstrategist.com
Web site: http://www.newstrategist.com
Dist(s): **MyiLibrary.**

New Sweden Pr., *(978-0-9702646)* 10509 Schmidt Ln., Manor, TX 78653 USA Fax: 512-278-1251 Do not confuse with New Sweden Pr., South Saint Paul, MN
E-mail: shrout@mail.utexas.edu.

New Tribes Mission, Inc., *(978-1-890040; 978-1-61565; 978-0-9968348)* 1000 E. First St., Sanford, FL 32771-1487 USA Tel 407-323-3430; Fax: 407-330-0376; 407-547-2450; Toll Free: 800-321-5375
E-mail: ntm@ntm.org; doug_lotz@ntm.org
Web site: http://www.ntm.org.

New Village Pr., *(978-0-9766054; 978-0-9815593; 978-1-61332)* Div. of Architects/Designers/Planners for Social Responsibility, 400 Central Pk. W, 12B, New York, NY 10025 USA Tel 510-717-3101
E-mail: hello@newvillagepress.net
Web site: http://www.newvillagepress.net
Dist(s): **Consortium Bk. Sales & Distribution**
Ingram Publisher Services
MyiLibrary
New York Univ. Pr.
Two Rivers Distribution.

New Virginia Pubns., *(978-0-9755030)* 9185 Matthew Dr., Manassas Park, VA 20111 USA (SAN 256-0453) Tel 703-928-8316; Fax: 703-331-0577
E-mail: lab49@att.net.

New Vision Entertainment, LLC, *(978-0-9778310)* Orders Addr.: 30 Estuary Trail, Clearwater, FL 33759 USA
E-mail: jim@newvisionentertainment.us.

New Voices Publishing Co., *(978-1-931642)* Div. of KidsTerrain, Inc., P.O. Box 560, Wilmington, MA 01887 USA (SAN 253-9047) Tel 978-658-2131; Fax: 978-988-8833 Do not confuse with companies with the same or similar names in Sarasota, FL, Flushing, NY
E-mail: egilmartin@kidsterrain.com
Web site: http://www.newvoicespublishing.com; http://www.kidsterrain.com.

New Wave Bks. & CD, *(978-0-9727753; 978-0-9741493)* Orders Addr.: 7850 S. Normandie Ave., Apt. 69, Los Angeles, CA 90044 USA; Edit Addr.: 11050 Bryant St., No. 292, Yucaipa, CA 92399 USA.

New Wave Internet Services Incorporated *See* **Healthy Life Pr., Inc.**

New Wave Pubns., *(978-0-9749674; 978-0-9786660; 978-0-9800452)* 1419 New York Ave., Rm 3A, New York, NY 11210-1221 USA Do not confuse with New Wave Publications in Lincoln, NE.

†**New Win Publishing,** *(978-0-8329; 978-0-87691)* 9682 Telstar Ave., Suite 110, El Monte, CA 91731 USA (SAN 217-1201) Tel 626-448-4422; *Imprints:* Z Health Books (Z Hlth Bks)
E-mail: info@AcademicLearningCompany.com
Web site: http://www.newwinpublishing.com; *CIP.*

†**New World Library,** *(978-0-931432; 978-0-945934; 978-1-57731; 978-1-880032; 978-1-60868)* 14 Pamaron Way, Novato, CA 94949 USA (SAN 211-8777) Tel 415-884-2100; Fax: 415-884-2199; Toll Free: 800-972-6657 (retail orders only) Do not confuse with New World Library Publishing Co., Los Altos, CA
E-mail: escort@nwlib.com
Web site: http://www.newworldlibrary.com
Dist(s): **Brilliance Publishing, Inc.**
Ebsco Publishing
Islander Group
Landmark Audiobooks
New Leaf Distributing Co., Inc.
Publishers Group West (PGW); *CIP.*

New World Publishing, *(978-0-9771939; 978-0-9776818; 978-0-9787112; 978-0-9796815; 978-0-9821528)* 4540 State Rd., Cleveland, OH 44109 USA Tel 216-635-1671 Do not confuse with New World Publishing in Riverdale, GA, Scottsdale, AZ and Auburn, CA
E-mail: rkisner5@sbcglobal.net
Web site: http://www.silverquillpoetry.net.

New World Revelation Pr., *(978-0-9762105)* Orders Addr.: P.O. Box 839, Ellijay, GA 30540 USA Tel 706-635-7720; Fax: 706-635-8170
E-mail: fess1944@etcmail.com; office@awakeandlive.org
Web site: http://www.awakeandlive.org
Dist(s): **Ingram Content Group.**

New Worlds Press *See* **Institute for Economic Democracy Pr., Inc.**

New Year Publishing, *(978-0-9671565; 978-0-9760095; 978-0-9799885; 978-1-935547; 978-1-61431)* 144 Diablo Ranch Ct., Danville, CA 94506 USA Tel 925-348-0481; Fax: 425-984-7256 Do not confuse with New Year Publishing in Oceanside, CA
E-mail: dmorris@newyearpublishing.com
Web site: http://www.newyearpublishing.com
Dist(s): **Distributors, The**
Innovative Logistics.

New York Review of Bks., Inc., The, *(978-0-940322; 978-1-59017; 978-1-68137)* 435 Hudson St., 3rd Flr. Suite 300, New York, NY 10014 USA (SAN 220-3448) Tel 212-757-8070; Fax: 212-333-5374; *Imprints:* NYR Children's Collection (NY Rev Child); NYRB Classics (NYRB Class); NYRB Kids (NYRB Kids); Little Bookroom (LittleBkrm)
E-mail: mail@nybooks.com; nyrb@nybooks.com
Web site: http://www.nyrb.com
Dist(s): **MyiLibrary**
Penguin Random Hse. Distribution
Penguin Random Hse. LLC
Random Hse., Inc.

New York Times Educational Publishing *Imprint of* **Rosen Publishing Group, Inc., The**

†**New York Univ. Pr.,** *(978-0-8147; 978-1-4798)* Div. of New York Univ., Orders Addr.: 838 Broadway, 3rd Flr., New York, NY 10003-4812 USA (SAN 658-1293) Tel 212-998-2575; Fax: 212-995-3833; Toll Free: 800-996-6987 (ordering); *Imprints:* NYU Press (NYUPr)
E-mail: orders@nyupress.org
Web site: http://www.nyupress.org
Dist(s): **CreateSpace Independent Publishing Platform**
Ebsco Publishing
ISD
Ingram Publisher Services
Two Rivers Distribution
ebrary, Inc.; *CIP.*

Newburyport Pr., *(978-1-882266)* Orders Addr.: P.O. Box 389, Newburyport, MA 01950 USA Tel 978-465-5751; Fax: 978-462-2043; Toll Free: 800-491-4700 (in Massachusetts only); Edit Addr.: 477 Commerce Blvd., Oldsmar, FL 34677-2809 USA
E-mail: mail@newburyportpress.com
Dist(s): **D.A.P./Distributed Art Pubs.**

Newburyport Press, Incorporated *See* **Newburyport Pr.**

Newcastle Bks., 11923 NE Sumner St. Ste. 808916, Portland, OR 97220 USA Tel 503-568-1586
E-mail: newcastlebooksofficial@gmail.com.

NeWest Pubs., Ltd. (CAN) *(978-0-920316; 978-0-920897; 978-1-896300; 978-1-897126; 978-1-927063; 978-1-988732; 978-1-926455)* *Dist. by* **Strauss Cnslts.**

NewLife Publications *See* **Campus Crusade for Christ**

Newman Educational Publishers *See* **Newman Educational Publishing Co.**

Newman Educational Publishing Co., *(978-0-938990)* P.O. Box 461, Glen Ellyn, IL 60138 USA (SAN 239-8273) Tel 630-668-7027
E-mail: blzfootstep@aol.com
Web site: http://www.ugrr.illinois.com.

Newman Springs Publishing, Inc., *(978-1-64096; 978-1-64531; 978-1-64801)* 320 Broad St., Red Bank, NJ 07701 USA Tel 800-305-0243
E-mail: info@newmanspprings.com.

Newmark Learning LLC, *(978-1-60719; 978-1-61269; 978-1-4788)* 629 Fifth Ave., Pelham, NY 10803 USA Tel 1-877-279-8388; 1-877-280-0375
E-mail: bhaggerty@benchmarkeducation.com
Dist(s): **Follett School Solutions.**

Newmarket for It Bks. *Imprint of* **HarperCollins Pubs.**

†Newmarket Pr., *(978-0-937858; 978-1-55704)* Div. of Newmarket Publishing & Communications Corp., 18 E. 48th St., New York, NY 10017 USA (SAN 217-2585) Tel 212-832-3575; Fax: 212-832-3629; Toll Free Fax: 800-458-6515 (trade orders); Toll Free: 800-233-4830 (trade orders)
E-mail: mailbox@newmarketpress.com
Web site: http://www.newmarketpress.com
Dist(s): **MyiLibrary**
Two Rivers Distribution
Worldwide Media Service, Inc.
ebrary, Inc.; *CIP.*

Newport Pr., *(978-0-692-08971-2; 978-0-692-09139-5; 978-0-692-09364-1)* 303 Euer Ct, Folsom, CA 95630 USA Tel 916-890-7083
E-mail: wallace95630@yahoo.com
Dist(s): **CreateSpace Independent Publishing Platform.**

Newport Valley Pr, *(978-0-9778602)* P.O. Box 32, Solon, IA 52333-0032 USA Tel 319-351-8854.

NewSage Pr., LLC, *(978-0-939165)* Orders Addr.: P.O. Box 607, Troutdale, OR 97060-0607 USA (SAN 662-8370) Tel 503-695-2211
E-mail: info@newsagepress.com
Web site: http://www.newsagepress.com
Dist(s): **MyiLibrary**
Publishers Group West (PGW).

NewsChannelChurch *See* **Asiana Media**

NewSound, LLC, 81 Demeritt Pl., Waterbury, VT 05676 USA Tel 802-244-7858; Fax: 802-244-1808; Toll Free: 800-342-0295 (wholesale orders)
E-mail: sales@newsoundmusic.com.

NewSouth Bks. *Imprint of* **NewSouth, Inc.**

NewSouth, Inc., *(978-1-58838; 978-1-60306)* P.O. Box 1588, Montgomery, AL 36102-1588 USA Tel 334-834-3556; Fax: 334-834-3557; Toll Free: 866-639-7688; *Imprints:* NewSouth Books (NewSouth AL); Junebug Books (Junebug Bks)
E-mail: info@newsouthbooks.com
Web site: http://www.newsouthbooks.com
Dist(s): **Blair**
Ingram Publisher Services
ebrary, Inc.

NewSouth Publishing (AUS) *(978-0-86840; 978-0-909465; 978-0-908237; 978-1-921410; 978-1-74223; 978-1-74224; 978-0-646-09872-2; 978-0-646-27463-8)* *Dist. by* **IPG Chicago.**

Newton, J. Britt *See* **Twelve Stones Publishing LLC**

Newtonian Golf & Particle Physics, Inc., *(978-0-9725355)* 107 Bordeaux Ln., Cary, NC 27511 USA Tel 919-469-0180
E-mail: sales@saintmulligan.com
Web site: http://www.stmulligan.com.

New-Wolf Moon Publishing, *(978-0-615-34422-5; 978-0-578-44976-0; 978-0-578-44977-7; 978-0-578-63028-1; 978-0-578-63677-1; 978-0-578-65072-2; 978-0-578-67219-9; 978-0-578-73131-5)* 3035 Washington Blvd., Cleveland Heights, OH 44118 USA Tel 216-371-1668
E-mail: clemys@sbcglobal.net.

New-York Historical Society, *(978-0-916141; 978-1-85759)* Two W. 77th St., New York, NY 10024 USA (SAN 294-975X) Tel 212-873-3400
Dist(s): **Ingram Publisher Services.**

Next Century Foundation *See* **Next Century Publishing Co.**

Next Century Publishing *See* **Pilot Communications Group, Inc.**

Next Century Publishing Co., *(978-0-9632937)* Orders Addr.: P.O. Box 3020, Carefree, AZ 85377 USA; Edit Addr.: 8548 Silver Saddle Dr., Carefree, AZ 85377 USA Tel 602-488-9600
Dist(s): **Indiana Univ. Pr.**
Ingram Publisher Services
Midpoint Trade Bks., Inc.
Two Rivers Distribution.

Next Chapter Pr., *(978-0-9816265)* P.O. Box 1937, Boca Grande, FL 33921 USA.

Next Chapter Pr., *(978-0-692-92978-0)* 590 Hallmark Dr., Martinsburg, WV 25403 USA Tel 304-261-3876
E-mail: nextchapterpress@gmail.com
Dist(s): **Ingram Content Group.**

Next Generation Pr., *(978-0-9762706; 978-0-9815595)* P.O. Box 603252, Providence, RI 02906 USA Tel 401-247-7665; Fax: 401-245-6428
E-mail: info@nextgenerationpress.org
Web site: http://www.nextgenerationpress.org.

Next Step Magazine, Inc., The, *(978-0-9752926)* 86 W. Main St., Victor, NY 14564 USA Tel 585-742-1260; Fax: 585-742-1263; Toll Free: 800-771-3117
Web site: http://www.nextstepmagazine.com.

Next Step Pr., *(978-1-892876)* Sub. of New Wisdom, Inc., 1201 Delta Glen Ct., Vienna, VA 22182-1320 USA Tel 703-757-7945; Fax: 703-757-7946
E-mail: Wyattwooodsmall@compuserve.com
Web site: http://www.peoplepatterns.com; http://www.mindcoach.org
Dist(s): **Two Rivers Distribution.**

Next Stop Publishing, *(978-1-942144)* 3225 McLeod Dr. Suite 100, Las Vegas, NV 89121 USA Tel 702-998-2837; Fax: 702-989-4627
E-mail: info@nextstopinc.com
Web site: www.nextstopinc.com.

Nextone Inc., *(978-1-64112; 978-1-952019)* 2681 Spruill Ave., North Charleston, SC 29405 USA; *Imprints:* Vertel Publishing (VertelPub)
Dist(s): **Independent Pubs. Group.**

Nextpos Corporation *See* **Aldelo Systems Inc.**

Neyborhood Enterprises, *(978-0-578-19088-4; 978-0-578-19089-1; 978-0-9989848)* 178 Maya Ct., St. Augustine, FL 32086 USA.

NF Publishing *See* **SouthWest Pubns.**

Ni, Kaiyao, *(978-0-692-89319-7)* 713 churchill rd, chester springs, PA 19425 USA Tel 517-420-7984
E-mail: nikaiyao@gmail.com.

Nia Publishing Company, Incorporated *See* **Urban Spirit!**

Nicco Boss, LLC, *(978-0-9891635)* 524 Cala Morlanda St., Las Vegas, NV 89138 USA Tel 702-595-4884
E-mail: niccoboss@yahoo.com.

Nicewood Imagined, *(978-0-9720334)* 6823 NW 52nd Ln., Gainesville, FL 32653 USA Tel 352-271-3306 (phone/fax)
E-mail: nicewoodimagined@yahoo.com
Web site: http://www.macecora.com.

Niche Content Pr., *(978-0-9989987)* 671 Eastern Ct., Ridgewood, NJ 07450 USA Tel 732-687-4725; Fax: 732-687-4725
E-mail: anthony@engineeredcontent.com.

Niche Publishing & Marketing, *(978-0-9726628; 978-1-7347388)* 3310 Bexley Pk. Rd., Columbus, OH 43213 USA Tel 614-390-5748
E-mail: sairapriest@me.com
Web site: http://www.nichepublishing.us; http://www.zenofhoarding.com.

NicheMarket.com *See* **Passion Profit Co., The/NicheMarket**

Nicho The Tiger LLC, *(978-0-9820801)* 43-31 223 St., Bayside, NY 11361 USA Tel 347-853-2694.

Nichols, Brady, *(978-0-692-78919-3)* 605 Capricorn Ln., Madison, WI 53718 USA Tel 608-335-3775
E-mail: bnichols07@hotmail.com.

nichols, frank, *(978-0-692-47926-1; 978-0-692-48464-7)* 27110 ben howard rd, MONROE, WA 98272 USA Tel 727-320-3158.

Nick Of Time Media, Inc., *(978-1-940775)* 8661 NW 16th St., Pembroke Pines, FL 33024 USA Tel 888-540-7593
E-mail: Bsamarel33414@yahoo.com
Web site: http://www.nickoftime.us.

Nick The Cat, LLC, *(978-1-936193)* 26541 Dundee Rd., Huntington Woods, MI 48070 USA Tel 313-570-7996
Dist(s): **Baker & Taylor Publisher Services (BTPS).**

Nickel Pr., *(978-1-57122; 978-1-879424)* Div. of S.R. Jacobs & Assocs., 107 Knob Hill Pk. Dr., Reisterstown, MD 21136 USA Do not confuse with Nickel Press, Inc., Enterprise, AL.

Nicksich, Karen M., *(978-0-692-68768-0; 978-0-578-49282-7; 978-0-578-49577-4; 978-0-578-66845-1; 978-0-578-72532-1)* 1641 Brantingham Rd., Richland, WA 99352 USA Tel 509-737-7637
E-mail: emeraldhalo@earthlink.net.

Nicole Publishing, *(978-0-9648278)* Orders Addr.: P.O. Box 557, South Holland, IL 60473-2129 USA Tel 847-339-2739; Fax: 708-339-7357; Edit Addr.: 16416 S. Prairie Ave., South Holland, IL 60473-2129 USA.

Nicolin Fields Publishing, Inc., *(978-0-9637077; 978-1-892066)* 861 Lafayette Rd., Unit 2A, Hampton, NH 03842-1232 USA Toll Free: 800-431-1579 (orders only)
E-mail: nfp@nh.ultranet.com
Web site: http://www.nicolinfields.com
Dist(s): **Alpenbooks Pr. LLC**
Peregrine Outfitters
Quality Bks., Inc.
Univ. Pr. of New England.

Nicoll Creations, *(978-0-9747527)* 5608 Evergreen, Midland, MI 48642 USA Tel 989-839-8293
E-mail: hgnicoll@sbcglobal.net.

Nicolo Whimsey Pr., *(978-1-935550)* 14411 Baden Westwood Rd., Brandywine, MD 20613 USA
Dist(s): **Consortium Bk. Sales & Distribution**
MyiLibrary.

Nicolosi, Gaetano, *(978-0-9763828)* 74 W. Fountain Ave., Delaware, OH 43015-1629 USA
E-mail: ciaogaetano@yahoo.com.

NIEJE Production LLC, *(978-0-692-72812-3; 978-0-692-77187-7; 978-0-578-19895-8; 978-0-578-19899-6; 978-0-692-99480-1)* 1002 Attilio Ct, Harrison City, PA 15636 USA Tel 724-640-8877.

Nielsen, Lester *See* **Eaglesquest Publishing**

Nielsen-Bks., *(978-0-9701670)* 11 Greenway Plaza, No. 2700, Houston, TX 77046 USA Tel 713-963-8740; Fax: 713-572-7728
Web site: http://nielsen-books.com.

Night After Night Pubns., Inc. *Imprint of* **Hebler, Michael**

Night Heron Media, *(978-0-9704729; 978-0-9709987; 978-1-931721; 978-1-933979; 978-1-936474; 978-1-939055; 978-1-942945)* Orders Addr.: 2365 Rice Blvd., Suite 202, Houston, TX 77005 USA Tel 713-533-9300; Fax: 713-528-2432 Do not confuse with Breakaway Bks., Halcottsville, NY
E-mail: info@nightheronmedia.org
Web site: www.nightheronmedia.org
Dist(s): **Baker & Taylor Publisher Services (BTPS)**
Follett School Solutions
Independent Pubs. Group
MyiLibrary
Sterling Publishing Co., Inc.
ebrary, Inc.

Night Howl Productions, *(978-0-9702176)* P.O. Box 1, Clay Center, NE 68933 USA Tel 402-984-2566
E-mail: dirtytricksforchicks@yahoo.com
Dist(s): **AK Pr. Distribution.**

Night Light Pubns., LLC, *(978-0-9740418; 978-0-9743785)* 6101 E. Wethersfield Rd., Scottsdale, AZ 85254 USA Tel 480-948-2607; Fax: 480-948-9921
E-mail: reg@nightlightpublications.com
Web site: http://www.nightlightpublications.com.

Night Sky Bks., *(978-1-59014)* Div. of North-South Books, Inc., 11 E. 26th St., 17th Flr., New York, NY 10010 USA Tel 212-706-4545; Fax: 212-706-4546; Toll Free: 800-282-8257 Do not confuse with companies with the same name in Santa Fe, NM
E-mail: nightsky@northsouth.com
Web site: http://www.northsouth.com
Dist(s): **Ingram Publisher Services**
Lectorum Pubns., Inc.

Night Sky, LLC, *(978-0-9888901)* 4 Buckskin Heights Dr., Danbury, CT 06811 USA Tel 203-826-9690
E-mail: jrivot@yahoo.com.

Nightengale Pr., *(978-0-9743348; 978-0-9761289; 978-1-933449; 978-1-935993; 978-1-945257)* Div. of Nightengale Media LLC, 370 S. Lowe Ave. Suite A-122, Cookeville, TN 38501 USA Tel 931-854-1390; Fax: 866-830-2624
E-mail: publisher@nightengalepress.com
Web site: http://www.nightengalemedia.com.

Nightlight Pr., *(978-0-9982992; 978-1-947607)* Orders Addr.: P.O. Box 8345, Miami, FL 33166 USA
E-mail: hpancakeslab@gmail.com.

Nightwood Editions (CAN) *(978-0-88971)* *Dist. by* **PerseuPGW.**

NIIS Publishing, *(978-0-9745013; 978-0-615-11294-7)* 7349 Milliken, No. 140164, Rancho Cucamonga, CA 91730 USA.

Nile Publishing, *(978-0-9768485)* 213 Hancock St., Brooklyn, NY 11216 USA Tel 718-810-1148 Do not confuse with Nile PUblishing in Cincinnati, OH
E-mail: wale1@hotmail.com.

Nilsson Media, *(978-0-9724771)* Box 1371, Brentwood, TN 37024-1371 USA Tel 615-776-2593; Fax: 615-776-3193; Toll Free: 888-801-5190; *Imprints:* Nilsson, Troy (Troy Nilsson)
E-mail: books@nilssonmedia.org
Web site: http://www.nilssonmedia.com.

Nilsson, Troy *Imprint of* **Nilsson Media**

Nimble Bks. LLC, *(978-0-9754479; 978-0-9765406; 978-0-9777424; 978-0-9788138; 978-0-9799205; 978-1-934840; 978-1-60888)* 1521 Martha Ave., Ann Arbor, MI 48103 USA
E-mail: wfz@nimblebooks.com
Web site: http://www.nimblebooks.com
Dist(s): **Smashwords.**

Nimbus Publishing, Ltd. (CAN) *(978-0-919380; 978-0-920852; 978-0-921054; 978-1-55109; 978-1-77108)* *Dist. by* **BTPS.**

Nimbus Publishing, Ltd. (CAN) *(978-0-919380; 978-0-920852; 978-0-921054; 978-1-55109; 978-1-77108)* *Dist. by* **Orca Bk Pub.**

Nine Petal Pr., *(978-0-9984256)* 702 Keywe Pl., Duncanville, TX 75116 USA Tel 214-226-9352
E-mail: unity9@sbcglobal.net
Web site: www.NinePetalPress.com.

NineStar Pr., *(978-1-945952; 978-1-947139; 978-1-947904; 978-1-948608; 978-1-949340; 978-1-949909; 978-1-950412; 978-1-951057; 978-1-951880; 978-1-64890)* P.O. Box 91792, Albuquerque, NM 87199 USA Tel 505-217-4491
E-mail: kat@ninestarpress.com
Web site: www.ninestarpress.com.

Ninety & Nine Records *See* **Blooming Twig Books LLC**

Ninos Aprenden Ingles Corp., *(978-1-934665)* 15476 NW 77 Ct., No. 360, Miami Lakes, FL 33016 USA (SAN 854-249X)
E-mail: ar@childrenlearninglanguages.com
Web site: http://www.ChildrenLearningLanguages.com.

Ninth Planet Pr., *(978-0-615-41386-0; 978-0-615-54486-1; 978-0-615-60901-0; 978-0-692-26010-4; 978-0-692-41572-6; 978-0-9983351)* 402 Buckeye Trail, Austin, TX 78746 USA Tel 512-330-1726; Fax: 512-289-0595; 909 Live Oak Ridge Rd., Austin, TX 78746
E-mail: bmccandless@austin.rr.com.

Nissi Publications *See* **Nissi Publishing, Inc.**

Nissi Publishing, Inc., *(978-0-944372)* 1404 Summer Ridge Ct., Roanoke, TX 76262 USA (SAN 243-4148) Tel 817-337-8681
E-mail: dfreeman@nissipub.com
Web site: http://www.nissipub.com.

Nistraman Consulting, *(978-0-9706387)* P.O. Box 1314, Brookline, MA 02446 USA
E-mail: alex_belenky@lycos.com.

Nithyananda Univ., *(978-0-9790806; 978-1-934364; 978-1-60607)* 9720 Central Ave., Montclair, CA 91763 USA Tel 909-625-1400
E-mail: galleriaorders@yahoo.com
Web site: http://www.lifeblissfoundation.org.

Nithyananda Yoga & Meditation University *See* **Nithyananda Univ.**

NJL College Preparation, *(978-0-9753913)* 880 Willis Ave., Albertson, NY 11507 USA Tel 516-741-3550
E-mail: njlcp@aol.com
Dist(s): **Topical Review Bk Co., Inc.**

NJM *See* **Allen-Ayers Bks.**

nJoy Bks., *(978-0-9769959)* Orders Addr.: 18 S. 2nd St., Madison, WI 53704 USA
E-mail: office@njoybooks.com
Web site: http://www.njoybooks.com.

NK nPrint *See* **nVision Publishing**

NK Pubns., *(978-0-9705100; 978-0-9841610)* P.O. Box 1735, New York, NY 10101-1735 USA
E-mail: nkatsoris@aol.com
Dist(s): **Michigan State Univ. Pr.**

NKB Bks. LLC, *(978-0-9988101; 978-1-7331064)* 1415 23rd St., Canyon, TX 79015 USA Tel 806-655-4046; Fax: 806-655-5558
E-mail: nkbbooksllc@gmail.com; natalie@nataliebright.com
Web site: nataliebright.com.

NLAlex Publishing *See* **Joe Girl Ink**

No Agenda Publishing, LLC, *(978-1-7320058)* 7594 Wolftever TRL, Ooltewah, TN 37363 USA Tel 423-619-0917
E-mail: april.royer@icloud.com.

No Doubt Imagination, *(978-0-692-11422-3)* 2055 N. Redding Way, Upland, CA 91784 USA Tel 909-200-8034
E-mail: sargent25@roadrunner.com.

No Dream Too Big LLC, *(978-0-9745717; 978-0-9838415)* Div. of AsAMan Thinketh.net LLC, P.O. Box 1220, Melrose, FL 32666 USA
E-mail: ebooks@asamanthinketh.net
Web site: http://www.asamanthinketh.net
Dist(s): **CreateSpace Independent Publishing Platform.**

No Frills Buffalo, *(978-0-578-04711-9; 978-0-578-08224-0; 978-0-615-48945-2; 978-0-615-51315-7; 978-0-615-54031-3; 978-0-615-56207-0; 978-0-615-58847-6; 978-0-615-59426-2; 978-0-615-61034-4; 978-0-615-62237-8; 978-0-615-62696-3; 978-0-615-66171-1; 978-0-615-66520-7; 978-0-615-66821-5; 978-0-615-70800-3; 978-0-615-70801-0; 978-0-615-72411-9; 978-0-615-72567-3; 978-0-615-75542-7; 978-0-615-75973-9; 978-0-615-78493-9; 978-0-615-78813-5; 978-0-615-81005-8; 978-0-615-81239-7; 978-0-615-82396-6; 978-0-615-83012-4;) 119 Dorchester, Buffalo, NY 14213 USA*
E-mail: contact@nofrillsbuffalo.com
Web site: http://nofrillsbuffalo.com
Dist(s): **CreateSpace Independent Publishing Platform**
Ingram Content Group.

No Frills Press Buffalo *See* **No Frills Buffalo**

No Greater Joy Ministries, Inc., *(978-1-892112; 978-0-9786372; 978-1-934794; 978-1-935370; 978-1-61644)* 1000 Pearl Rd., Pleasantville, TN 37033 USA (SAN 914-5958) Toll Free: 866-292-9936
E-mail: ngj@nogreaterjoy.org; cjoyner@nogreaterjoy.org
Web site: http://www.nogreaterjoy.org
Dist(s): **Baker & Taylor Publisher Services (BTPS)**
Follett School Solutions
MyiLibrary
Send The Light Distribution LLC
ebrary, Inc.

No Limits Communications, *(978-0-9712842)* P.O. Box 220, Horsham, PA 19044 USA Tel 215-675-9133; Fax: 215-675-9376.

No Limitz Productions, Inc., *(978-0-9766942)* 3257 Primera Ave., Los Angeles, CA 90068 USA Tel 323-876-7149
E-mail: nolimitz@aol.com
Web site: http://www.suzannelopez.com.

No Name, *(978-1-7323493)* 5926 Cove Point Ct, Columbus, OH 43228 USA Tel 614-572-7409
E-mail: salley.ayad@gmail.com.

No Starch Pr., Inc., *(978-1-886411; 978-1-59327; 978-1-7185)* 555 De Haro St., Suite 250, San Francisco, CA 94107 USA Tel 415-863-9900; Fax: 415-863-9950; Toll Free: 800-420-7240; 245 8th St., San Francisco, CA 94103 Tel 415-863-9900; Fax: 415-863-9950; Toll Free Fax: 800-420-7240 Do not confuse with No Starch Pr., in Berkeley, CA
E-mail: info@nostarch.com
Web site: https://nostarch.com
Dist(s): **Wiley & Sons, Inc., John**
Ebsco Publishing
Follett School Solutions
O'Reilly Media, Inc.
Penguin Random Hse. Distribution
Penguin Random Hse. LLC.

No Voice Left Behind Publishing, *(978-0-9773513)* P.O. Box 1109, Ceres, CA 95307 USA Tel 209-968-3425
E-mail: fernando_pena@sbcglobal.net
Web site: http://www.nvlb.net.

N.O.A.H Bks., *(978-0-615-59068-4; 978-0-9859770)* 1915 Quarterpath Dr., Richmond, TX 77406 USA Tel 832-769-1166; Fax: 713-458-4473; 1915 Quarterpath Dr., Richmond, TX 77406
E-mail: jaiden01@windstream.net; cheryl.hill1914@gmail.com
Web site: http://www.empoweringchildrentoread.blogspot.com/.

Noah Educational Projects *See* **N.O.A.H Bks.**

Noah Lukeman *Imprint of* **Morgan Rice Bks.**

Noble Hero Pr., *(978-0-9768410)* 3754 Salem Walk, No. A1, Northbrook, IL 60062 USA
E-mail: mike@nobleheropress.com
Web site: http://www.nobleheropress.com.

Noble, John A. Collection *See* **Noble Maritime Collection, The**

†Noble Maritime Collection, The, *(978-0-9623017)* 1000 Richmond Terr., Staten Island, NY 10301-1114 USA Tel 718-447-6490
E-mail: erinurban@earthlink.net; *CIP.*

Noble Publishing *See* **20/20 Publishing**

Noble Publishing Assocs., *(978-0-923463; 978-1-56857)* 1300 NE 131st Cir., Vancouver, WA 98685 USA (SAN 251-656X) Tel 360-258-3119; Fax: 360-258-3122; Toll Free: 800-225-5259; 1300 NE 131st St., Vancouver, WA 98685-3164
E-mail: noblebooks@noblepublishing.com
Web site: http://www.noblepublishing.com.

Noble Success Publishing, *(978-0-578-21278-4; 978-0-578-44910-4)* 2048 Igou Crossing Dr., Chattanooga, TN 37421 USA Tel 423-508-9642
E-mail: drdb@noblesuccessllc.com
Web site: johncmaxwellgroup.com/davidbanks.

Noble Washitaw Mothers Olmec Muur Nation *See* **Noble Washitaw Mothers Olmec Muur Trust**

Noble Washitaw Mothers Olmec Muur Trust, *(978-1-931671)* Orders Addr.: P.O. Box 10618, casa grande, AZ 85130 USA; P.O. Box 10618, Casa Grande, AZ 85130
E-mail: fmpublishing2011@gmail.com; free2behealthyandwealthy@gmail.com; mayloemrojo@gmail.com
Web site: http://www.free2behealthyandwealthy.com.

Nobrow Ltd. (GBR) *(978-1-907704; 978-0-9562135; 978-1-910620) Dist. by* **Peng Rand Hse.**

Nodin Pr., *(978-0-931714; 978-1-932472; 978-1-935666; 978-1-947237)* c/o The Bookmen, Inc., 530 N. Third St., Suite 120, Minneapolis, MN 55401 USA (SAN 204-398X) Tel 612-333-6300; Fax: 612-333-6303
Dist(s): **Adventure Pubns.**
Itasca Bks.
Publishers Group West (PGW).

Noel, Jaren, *(978-0-9993015)* 8941 Miami St, Unit 2, Omaha, NE 68134 USA Tel 308-870-1157; Fax: 308-870-1157; *Imprints:* Contemporary Fiction (MYD_FICTION)
E-mail: jaren.zimmerman@gmail.com.

Noesis, Inc., *(978-0-9742091)* 10530 Linden Lake Plaza, Manassas, VA 20109 USA Tel 703-369-2924; Fax: 703-392-7978
E-mail: fstilley@noesis-inc.com
Web site: http://www.noesis-inc.com/drydockhistory.

Noesis Publishing, *(978-0-9794328)* Div. of Noesis Communications International, Orders Addr.: 4425 S., Mo Pac Expway Suite 600, Austin, TX 78735 USA Tel 512-891-6100 Greenleaf Book Group; Edit Addr.: 5777 W. Century Blvd., Suite 200, Los Angeles, CA 90045 USA Tel 310-645-5604 Noesis Publishing; 512-891-6100 Greenleaf Book Group; Fax: 310-215-3018 Noesis Publishing
E-mail: diana@cmsbiz.com; candice@greenleafbookgroup.com
Web site: http://noesispublishing.com; http://www.greenleafbookgroup.com; http://www.kandide.com
Dist(s): **Greenleaf Book Group.**

Noguer y Caralt Editores, S. A. (ESP) *(978-84-217; 978-84-279) Dist. by* **Lectorum Pubns.**

Noixia's Reading Circle, *(978-0-9749122)* 8002 Avenida Navidad, San Diego, CA 92122 USA Tel 858-550-9519
E-mail: contact@noixia.com
Web site: http://www.noixia.com.

Nolia Crown Prods., *(978-0-9767047)* P.O. Box 150682, Arlington, TX 76015 USA
E-mail: noliacrown@gmail.com
Web site: http://www.noliacrown.com.

Noller, Gail, *(978-0-9744877)* 1416 Oakwood Dr., Anoka, MN 55303 USA Tel 763-427-6897
E-mail: nolle005@tc.umn.edu.

NOLO, *(978-0-87337; 978-0-917316; 978-1-4133)* Orders Addr.: 950 Parker St., Berkeley, CA 94710 USA (SAN 206-7935) Tel 510-549-1976; Fax: 510-548-5902; Toll Free Fax: 800-645-0895; Toll Free: 800-728-3555 (customer service); 800-955-4775 (trade orders only)
E-mail: tradecs@nolo.com
Web site: http://www.nolo.com
Dist(s): **Ebsco Publishing**
Ingram Publisher Services
MyiLibrary.

Nolo.com *See* **NOLO**

Nomad Pr., *(978-0-9659258; 978-0-9722026; 978-0-9749344; 978-0-9771294; 978-0-9785037; 978-0-9792268; 978-1-934670; 978-1-936313; 978-1-936749; 978-1-61930; 978-1-64741)* Div. of Nomad Communications, Inc., 2456 Christian St., White River Junction, VT 05001 USA Tel 802-649-1995; Fax: 802-649-2667 Do not confuse with Nomad Pr., Clewiston, FL, Fort Collins, CO
E-mail: rachel@nomadcom.com; rachel@nomadpress.net
Web site: http://www.nomadpress.net
Dist(s): **Baker & Taylor Publisher Services (BTPS)**
Children's Plus, Inc.
Ebsco Publishing
Follett School Solutions
Legato Pubs. Group
MyiLibrary
Publishers Group West (PGW)
Perseus Bks. Group.

Non Pareil Bks. *Imprint of* **Godine, David R. Pub.**

none, *(978-1-949684)* 1213 Wea Ave., Lafayette, IN 47905-1880 USA Tel 765-532-3535
E-mail: gunzai57@gmail.com
Web site: mellygreywriter/weebly.

Nonetheless Pr., *(978-1-932053)* 20332 W. 98th St., Lenexa, KS 66220-2650 USA Tel 913-254-7266; Fax: 913-393-3245
E-mail: mschutte@nonethelesspress.com
Web site: http://www.nonethelesspress.com; http://www.lookingglasspress.com
Dist(s): **Bookazine Co., Inc.**
Brodart Co.
Greenleaf Book Group
Midwest Library Service.

Non-ISBN Publisher, 630 Central Ave., New Providence, NJ 07974 USA.

Noodle Holdings LLC, *(978-0-615-41968-8)* Rood Hill Farm 53 Rood Hill Rd., Sandisfield, MA 01255 USA
E-mail: hoover205@gmail.com
Web site: http://www.stevehooverauthor.com.

Noodle Pr., *(978-0-9601022)* Orders Addr.: P.O. Box 42542, Washington, DC 20015 USA; Edit Addr.: P.O. Box 42542, Washington, DC 20015 USA (SAN 208-7871) Tel 202-363-5078; Fax: 202-364-0090
E-mail: Noodleprss@aol.com.

NOOK Press *See* **Barnes & Noble Pr.**

Noonan, Stefanie, *(978-0-9997378)* 25093 Grange Hall Rd., Philomath, OR 97370 USA Tel 541-760-6703
E-mail: stefnoonan@msn.com.

Nooni Publishing, *(978-0-9796832)* 1211 Garden Lake Dr., Riverdale, GA 30296 USA
E-mail: Nooni-pub@hotmail.com.

Noor Foundation-International, *(978-0-9632067; 978-0-9766972; 978-1-942043)* P.O. Box 758, Hockessin, DE 19707 USA (SAN 854-3712) Tel 302-234-8860; Fax: 208-279-5341; Toll Free: 888-937-2665; 249 Peoples Way, Hockessin, DE 19707
E-mail: cyrusomar@hotmail.com; alnoorfoundation@hotmail.com
Web site: http://www.islamusa.org.

Noorart, Inc., *(978-1-933269)* 1356 Exchange Dr., Richardson, TX 75081 USA; 6126 Clear Creek Dr., Garland, TX 75044
E-mail: ammar@noorart.com
Web site: http://www.noorart.com.

Noorart, Incorporated *See* **Noorart, Inc.**

NooVoo Publishing LLC, *(978-0-9767513)* 28257 Thornybrae, Farmington Hills, MI 48331 USA Tel 248-762-4858
E-mail: glennrader@noovoo.com.

Nop, Mony Publishing, *(978-0-9997918)* 1926 Railroad Ave. No. 102, Livermore, CA 94550 USA Tel 925-575-1602
E-mail: mony@monynop.com.

Nora Hse., *(978-0-9752958)* 9122 White Eagle Ct., Raleigh, NC 27617 USA
E-mail: oren2a@yahoo.com.

Norcor Enterprises, *(978-0-9622469)* 6147 N. Sheridan Rd., Chicago, IL 60660 USA Tel 773-743-6792
E-mail: norcorent@juno.com.

Nordic Studies Pr., *(978-0-9772714)* 5226 N. Sawyer, Chicago, IL 60625-4716 USA (SAN 257-1498) Tel 773-610-4283
E-mail: cpeterson@igc.org
Web site: http://www.nordicstudiespress.com.

Nordikgirl, *(978-0-9997737)* 14192 209th St. N., Scandia, MN 55073 USA Tel 651-491-5151; Fax: 651-491-5151
E-mail: ccolonna15@gmail.com
Web site: www.nordikgirl.com.

Nordskog Publishing, Inc., *(978-0-9796736; 978-0-9824929; 978-0-9827074; 978-0-9831957; 978-0-9882976; 978-0-9903774; 978-0-9974221; 978-1-946497)* Orders Addr.: 4562 Westinghouse St. Suite E., Ventura, CA 93003 USA; Edit Addr.: 2716 Sailor Ave., Ventura, CA 93001 USA
E-mail: Jerry@NordskogPublishing.com; staff@nordskogpublication.com
Web site: http://www.NordskogPublishing.com.

Norfleet Pr., Inc., *(978-0-9649934)* 1 Gracie Ter. Apt. 4C, New York, NY 10028-7956 USA
Dist(s): **Continental Enterprises Group, Inc. (CEG)**
North Country Bks., Inc.

Norgannan Publishing LLC, *(978-0-692-63209-3; 978-0-692-65539-9; 978-0-692-08818-0; 978-1-7323676)* 3630 Terrapin Ln Apt 711, Coral Springs, FL 33067 USA Tel 518-248-0911
Web site: http://www.norgannanpublishing.com
Dist(s): **CreateSpace Independent Publishing Platform.**

Norilana Bks., *(978-1-934169; 978-1-934648; 978-1-60762)* Orders Addr.: P.O. Box 224, Highgate Center, VT 05459-0224 USA (SAN 851-8556); Edit Addr.: 145 Dubois Dr., Highgate Center, VT 05459-0224 USA; *Imprints:* YA Angst (YA Angst)
E-mail: service@norilana.com; vnazarian@gmail.com
Web site: http://www.norilana.com/
Dist(s): **Smashwords.**

NORKY AMERICA, *(978-0-9769209)* Orders Addr.: 4712 Admiralty Way, No. 614, Marina Del Rey, CA 90292 USA Tel 310-985-3039
Web site: http://www.norky.com.

Norma Editorial, S.A. (ESP) *(978-84-7904; 978-84-8431; 978-84-85475; 978-84-86595; 978-84-679) Dist. by* **IPG Chicago.**

Norma Editorial, S.A. (ESP) *(978-84-7904; 978-84-8431; 978-84-85475; 978-84-86595; 978-84-679) Dist. by* **D C D.**

Norma S.A. (COL) *(978-958-04; 978-958-45) Dist. by* **AIMS Intl.**

Norma S.A. (COL) *(978-958-04; 978-958-45) Dist. by* **Distr Norma.**

Norma S.A. (COL) *(978-958-04; 978-958-45) Dist. by* **Continental Bk.**

Norma S.A. (COL) *(978-958-04; 978-958-45) Dist. by* **Lectorum Pubns.**

Norman & Globus, Inc., *(978-1-886978)* Orders Addr.: P.O. Box 20533, El Sobrante, CA 94803 USA; Edit Addr.: 4130 Lakeside Dr., San Pablo, CA 94806-1941 USA
E-mail: info@electrowiz.com; drpenny@sciencewiz.com
Web site: http://www.electrowiz.com; http://www.sciencewiz.com.

Norman Bks., *(978-0-9708617)* 900 Euclid St., Suite 302, Santa Monica, CA 90403 USA Tel 310-899-9310; Fax: 503-961-9523
E-mail: normanbooks411@gmail.com
Web site: http://www.normanbooks.com
Dist(s): **Book Wholesalers, Inc.**
Follett School Solutions
Quality Bks., Inc.
Sunbelt Pubns., Inc.

Norman, Tyrone A., *(978-0-692-09248-4)* 4828 Skyway, Fair Oaks, CA 95628 USA Tel 916-257-3461
E-mail: mrsteppingstone@yahoo.com
Dist(s): **CreateSpace Independent Publishing Platform.**

Nortex Pr. *Imprint of* **Eakin Pr.**

North American International, *(978-0-88265)* P.O. Box 251, Penn Laird, VA 22846 USA (SAN 202-9200) Tel 540-435-6454; *Imprints:* Fine Art Editions (Fine Art Edtns)
E-mail: naibooks@yahoo.com; naibooks@gmail.com
Web site: http://erniehippo.ecrater.com; http://finekidsbooks.webs.com; http://kidsbook.zoomshare.com.

North American Mission Board, SBC, *(978-1-59312)* 4200 North Point Pkwy, Alpharetta, GA 30022-4176 USA Tel 770-410-6100; Fax: 770-410-6051; Toll Free: 866-407-6262
E-mail: marketing@namb.net
Web site: http://www.namb.net.

North American Vexillological Assoc. (NAVA), *(978-0-9747728)* 101 Belair Dr., New Milford, CT 06776 USA
E-mail: tmealf@aol.com
Web site: http://www.nava.org.

†North Atlantic Bks., *(978-0-913028; 978-0-938190; 978-0-942941; 978-1-55643; 978-1-883319; 978-1-58394; 978-1-62317)* Div. of The Society of the Study of Native Art & Science, Orders Addr.: P.O. Box 12327, Berkeley, CA 94712 USA (SAN 203-1655) Fax: 510-559-8277; Toll Free: 800-337-2665 (orders only); Edit Addr.: 1435 4th St. # A, Berkeley, CA 94710-1335 USA; 2526 Martin Luther King Jr. Way, Berkeley, CA 94704 Tel 510-549-4270; Fax: 510-549-4276; *Imprints:* Frog Limited (Frog Ltd); Frog Books (FrogBks); Frog Children's Books (FrogChld)
E-mail: orders@northatlanticbooks.com
Web site: http://www.northatlanticbooks.com
Dist(s): **China Books & Periodicals, Inc.**
MyiLibrary
Nutri-Bks. Corp.
Penguin Random Hse. Distribution
Penguin Random Hse. LLC
Random Hse., Inc.
SPD-Small Pr. Distribution; *CIP.*

North Bay Bks., *(978-0-9725200; 978-0-9749098)* Orders Addr.: P.O. Box 21234, El Sobrante, CA 94820-1234 USA Tel 510-758-4276; Fax: 510-758-4659; Toll Free: 800-870-3194; Edit Addr.: 3110 Whitecliff Ct., Richmond, CA 94803 USA Do not confuse with companies with the same name in El Sobrante, CA, Richmond, CA
Web site: www.northbaybooks.com.

North Bks., *(978-0-939495; 978-1-58287)* P.O. Box 1277, Wickford, RI 02852 USA (SAN 663-4052) Tel 401-294-3682; Fax: 401-294-9491
E-mail: north@ids.net.

North Bound Bks., *(978-0-9759089)* P.O. Box 63, Norwich, VT 05055 USA.

North Cape Pubns., Inc., *(978-1-882391)* P.O. Box 1027, Tustin, CA 92781 USA Tel 714-832-3621; Fax: 714-832-5302; Toll Free: 800-745-9714
E-mail: ncape@ix.netcom.com
Web site: http://www.northcapepubs.com.

North Carolina Division of Archives & History *See* **North Carolina Office of Archives & History**

North Carolina Office of Archives & History, *(978-0-86526)* Orders Addr.: Historical Publications Section 4622 Mail Service Ctr., Raleigh, NC 27699-4622 USA (SAN 203-7246) Tel 919-733-7442 ext. 0; Fax: 919-733-1439
Web site: http://www.ncpublications.com
Dist(s): **Univ. of North Carolina Pr.**

North Carolina State Univ. Humanities Extension Pubns./Program, *(978-1-881507; 978-1-885647)* North Carolina State Univ., Box 8101 026 Winston Hall, Raleigh, NC 27695 USA Tel 919-515-1334; Fax: 919-515-8738
Web site: http://www.ncsu.edu/chass/extension.

North Carolina Symphony Society, Inc., The, *(978-0-9618952)* 4361 Lassiter At North Hills A. Ste. 105, Raleigh, NC 27609-5781 USA (SAN 242-5378).

†North Country Bks., Inc., *(978-0-925168; 978-0-932052; 978-0-9601158; 978-1-59531)* 220 Lafayette Street, Utica, NY 13502 USA (SAN 110-828X) Tel 315-735-4877; Fax: (315) 738-4342
E-mail: ncbooks@verizon.net
Web site: http://www.northcountrybooks.com; *CIP.*

North Country Pr., *(978-0-945980; 978-1-943424)* P.O. Box 501, Unity, ME 04988 USA (SAN 247-9680) Tel 207-948-2208; Fax: 207-948-9000 Do not confuse with North Country Pr., White Cloud, MI
E-mail: info@northcountrypress.com
Web site: http://www.northcountrypress.com.

North Cover Prs, *(978-0-578-18862-1)* 7 North Cover Rd, Old Saybrook, CT 06475 USA.

North Cover Press *See* **North Cover Prs**

North Dakota Center for Distance Education *See* **State Historical Society of North Dakota**

North Dakota State University, Institute for Regional Studies *See* **North Dakota State Uiv. Pr.**

North Dakota State Univ. Libraries, *(978-0-9629777; 978-1-891193)* Orders Addr.: NDSU Dept 2080, Fargo, ND 58105-6050 USA Tel 701-231-8416; Fax: 701-231-7138; Edit Addr.: 1201 Albrecht Blvd., Fargo, ND 58105 USA
E-mail: michael.miller@ndsu.edu; jeremy.kopp@ndsu.edu
Web site: http://library.ndsu.edu/grhc/.

North Dakota State Uiv. Pr., *(978-0-911042; 978-1-946163)* Div. of North Dakota Institute for Regional Studies, Orders Addr.: 1210 Albrecht Blvd., Fargo, ND 58108-6050 USA (SAN 203-1574) Tel 701-231-6848; Fax: 701-231-1047
E-mail: suzzanne.kelley@ndsu.edu; kelley@kindredhouse.net; zachary.vietz@ndsu.edu
Web site: www.ndsupress.org; https://www.facebook.com/NDSUPress/.

North Gap Publishing, *(978-0-9677379)* 636 Golden Hill St., Cheyenne, WY 82009 USA Tel 307-778-8761
E-mail: twalkwyo@hotmail.com.

North Loop Pr. *Imprint of* **Salem Author Services**

North Node LLC, *(978-1-7340857)* 2121 Newcastle Ave., Cardiff by the Sea, CA 92007 USA Tel 760-330-0947
E-mail: cee@ceehunt.com
Web site: www.northnodellc.com.

North Pole Chronicles, *(978-0-9636442)* 7306 Park Ln., Dallas, TX 75225-2462 USA Tel 214-696-1717; Fax: 214-696-5288.

North Pole Pr., *(978-0-9787129; 978-0-9992977; 978-1-7323782; 978-1-7324958; 978-1-7336761)* 432 Ruth Riggs Way, Maryville, TN 37801 USA Tel 865-207-2703
E-mail: tennesseesanta@gmail.com; mary@thenorthpolepress.com; joe@thenorthpolepress.com
Web site: http://thenorthpolepress.com; http://northpolepress.com.

North River Press, Incorporated *See* **North River Pr. Publishing Corp., The**

†North River Pr. Publishing Corp., The, *(978-0-88427)* P.O. Box 567, Great Barrington, MA 01230 USA (SAN 202-1048) Tel 413-528-0034 (phone/fax); Toll Free Fax: 800-266-5329; Toll Free: 800-486-2665
E-mail: agallagher@northriverpress.com
Web site: http://www.northriverpress.com; *CIP.*

North Shore Records, Inc., *(978-0-9746229)* Orders Addr.: P.O. Box 1035, Los Alamos, CA 93440 USA (SAN 257-3733) Tel 800-771-7531
E-mail: info@jacirae.com
Web site: http://www.winningromance.com; http://www.christmaswithlove.com; http://www.theindieguide.com; http://www.winningpoints.net; http://www.jacirae.com; http://www.thequeenofgreen.com; http://www.pennymeals.com.

North Star Editions, *(978-0-9848801; 978-0-9886491; 978-1-939967; 978-1-63163; 978-1-63517; 978-1-63583; 978-1-64185; 978-1-64493; 978-1-64494; 978-1-64619; 978-1-952455)* Subs. of Big Timber Media, 1600 Cliff Rd. E, Burnsville, MN 55337 USA (SAN 990-2325) Tel 952-446-7222; *Imprints:* Flux (FluxUSA); Focus Readers (FocusRead); Jolly Fish Press (JollyFishPr)
E-mail: info@northstareditions.com
Web site: www.fluxnow.com; www.northstareditions.com; www.focusreaders.com
Dist(s): **Children's Plus, Inc.**
Independent Pub.
Llewellyn Pubns.

North Star Press of Saint Cloud *See* **North Star Pr. of St. Cloud**

†North Star Pr. of St. Cloud, *(978-0-87839; 978-1-68201)* P.O. Box 451, Saint Cloud, MN 56302-0451 USA (SAN 203-7491) Tel 320-558-9062; Toll Free: 888-820-1636
E-mail: info@northstarpress.com
Web site: http://www.northstarpress.com
Dist(s): **Independent Pubs. Group**
Midpoint Trade Bks., Inc.
Partners Bk. Distributing, Inc.; *CIP.*

North Star Way *Imprint of* **Simon & Schuster**

North Street Publishing, *(978-0-9883860)* 40 N. St., Grafton, MA 01519 USA Tel 508-839-5298
E-mail: fwvincent@verizon.net.

Northampton Hse., *(978-1-937997; 978-1-950668)* 7018 Wildflower Ln., Franktown, VA 23354 USA Tel 757-442-3013
E-mail: nhp@poyer.com
Web site: www.northampton-house.com.

Northbooks, *(978-0-9653074; 978-0-9720604; 978-0-9789766; 978-0-9815193; 978-0-9830764; 978-0-9888954)* Orders Addr.: P.O. Box 671832, Chugiak, AK 99567 USA Tel 907-696-8973
E-mail: tg@northbooks.com
Web site: http://www.northbooks.com.

Northern Illinois Univ. Pr. *Imprint of* **Cornell Univ. Pr.**

Northern Lights Pr., *(978-0-692-69115-1; 978-0-692-77087-0; 978-0-692-05523-6; 978-0-692-14419-0; 978-1-7337534)* 2403 Dilloway Dr., Midland, MI 48640 USA Tel 989-839-4820
E-mail: jodyhedlund@hotmail.com
Web site: jodyhedlund.com.

Northern Lights Publishing House *See* **Northern Lights Publishing Hse.**

Northern Lights Publishing Hse., *(978-1-948462; 978-1-952261)* 668 W. Jardin Dr., Casa Grande, AZ 85122 USA Tel 520-510-3835; *Imprints:* Katheryn Maddox Haddad (MYID_D_KATHERY)
E-mail: katheryn@inspirationsbykatheryn.com
Web site: https://inspirationsbykatheryn.com.

Northern Publications, Incorporated *See* **Northern Publishing**

Northern Publishing, *(978-0-9639869; 978-0-9741684)* P.O. Box 871803, Wasilla, AK 99687 USA Tel 907-376-6474
E-mail: tony@tonyruss.com
Web site: http://www.tonyruss.com
Dist(s): **American News Company**
Partners Bk. Distributing, Inc.
Partners/West Book Distributors.

Northern Speech Services, *(978-0-9708947; 978-0-9761967; 978-0-9765497; 978-0-9785581; 978-0-9799245; 978-0-9823449; 978-1-935578)* 325 Meecher Rd., Gaylord, MI 49735 USA Toll Free Fax:

888-696-9655; Toll Free: 888-337-3866; P.O. Box 1247, Gaylord, MI 49734
E-mail: tslominski@nss-nrs.com
Web site: http://www.nss-nrs.com
Dist(s): **BookBaby.**

Northern State Univ. Pr., *(978-1-883120)* Div. of NSU Foundation, Orders Addr.: Northern State Univ. 1200 S Jay St, Aberdeen, SD 57401 USA.

Northern Virginia Writing Project, *(978-0-9759524)* GMU, MSN3E4, 4400 University Dr., Fairfax, VA 22030 USA Tel 703-993-1168; Fax: 703-993-1184
E-mail: sbaker@gmu.edu; contact@nvwp.org
Web site: http://www.nvwp.org.

Northfield Publishing *Imprint of* **Moody Pubs.**

Northland Press *See* **Northland Publishing**

†Northland Publishing, *(978-0-87358)* Div. of Rowman & Littlefield Publishing Group, Orders Addr.: P.O. Box 15200 NBN Way, Blue Ridge Summit, PA 17214 USA Tel 301-459-3366; Fax: 301-429-5745; Toll Free Fax: 800-338-4550; Toll Free: 800-462-6420; *Imprints*: Rising Moon Books for Young Readers (Rising Moon Bks); Luna Rising (Luna Rising) Do not confuse with companies with the same or similar name in Memomonie, WI, Cleveland, OH
E-mail: dbreier@nbnbooks.com
Dist(s): **Children's Plus, Inc.**
Fujii Assocs.
Lectorum Pubns., Inc.
Libros Sin Fronteras
Learning Connection, The
National Bk. Network; *CIP.*

Northlight Communications, Inc. *See* **Sign2Me Early Learning / Northlight Communications, Inc.**

Northopolis, *(978-0-615-69125-1; 978-0-9898090)* 1105 Jasmine, Weslaco, TX 78596 USA Tel 956-373-1134
E-mail: rbanda@gmail.com
Web site: www.northopolis.com.

Northshire Pr., *(978-1-60571)* Orders Addr.: P.O. Box 2200, Manchester Center, VT 05255 USA; Edit Addr.: 4869 Main St., Manchester Center, VT 05255 USA Tel 802-362-3565; Fax: 802-362-1233; *Imprints*: Shires Press (Shires Pr)
Web site: http://www.northshire.com/printondemand.

†North-South Bks., Inc., *(978-0-7358; 978-1-55858; 978-1-58717)* 350 7th Ave. Rm. 1400, New York, NY 10001-5013 USA; *Imprints*: Michael Neugebauer Books (M Neugebauer Bks)
E-mail: mnavarro@northsouth.com
Web site: http://www.northsouth.com
Dist(s): **Children's Plus, Inc.**
Continental Bk. Co., Inc.
Ingram Publisher Services
Lectorum Pubns., Inc.
Libros Sin Fronteras
Simon & Schuster, Inc.; *CIP.*

Northstar Entertainment Group, LLC, *(978-0-9741544)* 9009 Danwood Manor Ter., Richmond, VA 23227-1269 USA; *Imprints*: Baby Faye Books (Baby Faye)
E-mail: northstarent2003@yahoo.com
Web site: http://www.northstarent.net.

Northstone Publishing, Inc. (CAN) *(978-1-55145; 978-1-896836; 978-1-77064) Dist. by* **Westminster John Knox.**

Northwest Interpretive Association *See* **Discover Your Northwest**

Northwestern Publishing Hse., *(978-0-8100)* 2949 N. Mayfair Rd., Suite 200, Milwaukee, WI 53222 USA (SAN 206-7943) Tel 414-454-2100; Fax: 414-454-2170
E-mail: kuehlt@nph.wels.net; johnsonr@nph.wels.net
Web site: http://www.nph.net.

Northwestern Univ. Pr., *(978-0-8101)* Orders Addr.: c/o Univ. of Chicago Pr. Distribution Ctr., 11030 S. Langley Ave., Chicago, IL 60628 USA Tel 773-568-1550; Fax: 773-660-2235; Toll Free Fax: 800-621-8476; Toll Free: 800-621-2736; Edit Addr.: 629 Noyes St., Evanston, IL 60208-4210 USA (SAN 202-5787) Tel 847-491-5313; 847-491.2046; Fax: 847-491-8150
E-mail: nupress@northwestern.edu
Web site: http://www.nupress.northwestern.edu
Dist(s): **Chicago Distribution Ctr.**
MyiLibrary
Random Hse., Inc.
Univ. of Chicago Pr.
ebrary, Inc.

Northwind Sailing, Inc., *(978-0-9752700)* P.O. Box 973, Grand Marais, MN 55604-0973 USA.

NorthWord Bks. for Young Readers *Imprint of* **T&N Children's Publishing**

Norton, Frances M., *(978-0-9632938)* 1012 N. Wheaton Ave., Wheaton, IL 60187 USA Tel 630-665-0249.

Norton Simon Museum, *(978-0-9726681; 978-0-9891956)* 411 W. Colorado Blvd., Pasadena, CA 91105 USA (SAN 122-4700) Tel 818-449-6840
E-mail: info@nortonsimon.org
Web site: http://www.nortonsimon.org.

†Norton, W. W. & Co., Inc., *(978-0-393; 978-0-88150; 978-0-914378; 978-0-936399; 978-0-942440; 978-1-58157; 978-1-324; 978-1-68268)* Orders Addr.: c/o National Book Company, 800 Keystone Industrial Pk., Scranton, PA 18512 USA (SAN 157-1869) Tel 570-346-2029; Fax: 570-346-1442; Toll Free Fax: 800-458-6515; Toll Free: 800-233-4830; Edit Addr.: 500 Fifth Ave., New York, NY 10110-0017 USA (SAN 202-5795) Tel 212-354-5500; Fax: 212-869-0856; Toll Free: 800-223-2584; *Imprints*: Norton Young Readers (Norton Young)
Web site: http://www.wwnorton.com
Dist(s): **Penguin Random Hse. Distribution**
Simon & Schuster
Taylor & Francis Group
Wiley, John & Sons, Inc.; *CIP.*

Norton Young Readers *Imprint of* **Norton, W. W. & Co., Inc.**

Norvik Pr. (GBR) *(978-1-870041) Dist. by* **Dufour.**

Norwen Pubns., *(978-0-9852869)* 820 West Shore Dr., Culver, IN 46511 USA.

Norwood Hse. Pr., *(978-1-59953; 978-1-60357; 978-1-68404; 978-1-68450)* Orders Addr.: P.O. Box 316598, Chicago, IL 60631 USA (SAN 257-1552) Tel 773-467-0837; Fax: 773-467-9686; Toll Free Fax: 866-565-2901; Toll Free: 866-565-2900
E-mail: lisa@norwoodhousepress.com
Web site: http://www.norwoodhousepress.com
Dist(s): **Follett School Solutions.**

Nosey Trunk, *(978-0-9911454)* Orders Addr.: 240 Dolores St., No. 216, San Francisco, CA 94103 USA Tel 650-218-2986
E-mail: ranjani_krishnaswamy@hotmail.com.

Nostra Ediciones (MEX) *(978-607-7603) Dist. by* **IPG Chicago.**

Nosy Crow *Imprint of* **Candlewick Pr.**

Not Available Books *Imprint of* **Not Available Comics**

Not Available Comics, *(978-0-9744767)* Orders Addr.: 2627 Pulaski St., Hamtramck, MI 48212 USA; *Imprints*: Not Available Books (NotAvailBks)
E-mail: feazell038@comcast.net
Web site: http://www.cynicalman.com.

Not Home Yet Publishing, *(978-0-615-20928-9; 978-0-615-21258-6)* 8 Catamount Ln., Littleton, CO 80127 USA Tel 303-972-0895
E-mail: nothomeyetmin@msn.com.

Notable Kids Publishing, *(978-0-9970851; 978-1-7333548)* 10267 Celestine Pl., Parker, CO 80134 USA Tel 303-910-1884
E-mail: info@notablekidspublishing.com
Web site: notablekidspublishing.com
Dist(s): **Independent Pubs. Group**
Midpoint Trade Bks., Inc.

Notgrass Co., *(978-1-933410; 978-1-60999)* 975 Roaring River Rd, Gainesboro, TN 38562 USA Tel 800-211-8793; Fax: 800-891-8335; Toll Free: 800-211-8793
E-mail: books@notgrass.com
Web site: http://www.notgrass.com
Dist(s): **BookBaby.**

Nothing But The Truth, LLC, *(978-0-9883754; 978-0-615-73258-9; 978-0-9904652; 978-0-9963074; 978-0-9968999; 978-0-9972962; 978-1-946706)* 1010 Sir Francis Drake Blvd Suite 102, Kentfield, CA 94904 USA Tel 4157067067
Dist(s): **CreateSpace Independent Publishing Platform**
Publishers Group West (PGW).

Notion Pr., Inc., *(978-0-9975577; 978-1-945400; 978-1-945497; 978-1-945579; 978-1-945621; 978-1-945688; 978-1-945825; 978-1-945926; 978-1-946048; 978-1-946129; 978-1-946204; 978-1-946280; 978-1-946390; 978-1-946436; 978-1-946515; 978-1-946556; 978-1-946641; 978-1-946714; 978-1-946822; 978-1-946869; 978-1-946983; 978-1-947027; 978-1-947137; 978-1-947202; 978-1-947283; 978-1-947349; 978-1-947429; 978-1-947498; 978-1-947586; 978-1-947634; 978-1-947697; 978-1-947752; 978-1-947851; 978-1-947949; 978-1-947988; 978) 800 W. El Camino Real, Suite 180,, Mountain View, CA 94040 USA Tel 984-041-8723*
E-mail: editor@notionpress.com
Web site: www.notonpress.com.

NouSoma Communications, Inc., *(978-0-9743604)* 500 Waldron Pk. Dr., Haverford, PA 19041-1932 USA Tel 610-658-5889; *Imprints*: GIRLS KNOW HOW (Girls Know How)
Web site: http://www.nousoma.com; http://girlsknowhow.com/
Dist(s): **Book Wholesalers, Inc.**
Brodart Co.

Nova Blue, Inc., *(978-0-9725584)* 14403 Little Blue Rd., Kansas City, MO 64136 USA Tel 816-737-8895
E-mail: novablueco@aol.com.

Nova Media, Inc., *(978-0-9618567; 978-1-884239)* 1724 N. State St., Big Rapids, MI 49307-9073 USA (SAN 668-0372) Tel 231-796-4637 (phone/fax)
E-mail: trund@netonecom.net
Web site: http://www.novamediainc.com.

Nova Pr., *(978-0-9637371; 978-1-889057; 978-0-692-38359-9; 978-1-944595)* Orders Addr.: 9058 Lloyd Pl., West Hollywood, CA 90069 USA (SAN 858-8317) Tel 310-275-3513; Fax: 310-281-5629; Toll Free: 800-949-6175
E-mail: novapress@aol.com
Web site: http://www.novapress.net
Dist(s): **CreateSpace Independent Publishing Platform**
Ebsco Publishing
Ingram Content Group
ebrary, Inc.

†Nova Science Pubs., Inc., *(978-0-941743; 978-1-56072; 978-1-59033; 978-1-59454; 978-1-60021; 978-1-60456; 978-1-60692; 978-1-60741; 978-1-60876; 978-1-61668; 978-1-61728; 978-1-61761; 978-1-61122; 978-1-61209; 978-1-61324; 978-1-61470; 978-1-62100; 978-1-61942; 978-1-62081; 978-1-62257; 978-1-62417; 978-1-62618; 978-1-62808; 978-1-62948; 978-1-63117; 978-1-63321; 978-1-63463; 978-1-63482; 978-1-63483; 978-1-63484; 978-1-63485; 978-1-5361) 400 Oser Ave., Suite 1600, Hauppauge, NY 11788 USA (SAN 666-0266)*
E-mail: novascience@earthlink.net; novapublishers@earthlink.net; suzy@novapublishers.com; nova.main@novapublishers.com; cathy@novapublishers.com
Web site: http://www.novapublishers.com
Dist(s): **Ebsco Publishing**
ebrary, Inc.; *CIP.*

Novak, Lindy, *(978-0-692-16739-7; 978-1-7331556)* 701 Miner Rd., Orinda, CA 94563 USA Tel 925-258-9432
E-mail: lindy@spottwoode.com.

Novalis, Brigitte *See* **Novalis Pr.**

Novalis Pr., *(978-0-9835035; 978-0-9886559; 978-1-944870)* 46 Lincoln St., Weymouth, MA 02191 USA Tel 781-340-0322
E-mail: brigitte@brigittenovalis.com
Web site: www.brigittenovalisbooks.com
Dist(s): **Smashwords.**

Novanglus Publishing, LLC, *(978-0-9837186)* Orders Addr.: 15 E. Putnam Avenue, No. 232, Greenwich, CT 06830 USA (SAN 920-4504) Tel 203-885-7476; 15 E. Putnam Ave., #232, Greenwich, CT 06830 Tel 203-885-7476; Fax: 203-724-1867
E-mail: mpeacockphd@gmail.com; michelle@novanglus publishing.com
Web site: http://www.novanguspublishing.com; http://fairandsquarebook.com.

Novarena, *(978-1-7328925)* 18 Central St., Woburn, MA 01801 USA Tel 832-381-4233
E-mail: Info@novarena.com
Web site: Www.novarena.com.

Novel Companion LLC, A, *(978-1-948148)* 7500 Nottingham Ave, Shrewsbury, MO 63119 USA Tel 970-231-3999
E-mail: anovelcompanion@gmail.com
Web site: anovelcompanion.com.

Novel Security, *(978-0-578-42305-0; 978-0-578-42309-8)* 3341 Regent Blvd. Ste. 130-363, Irving, TX 75063 USA Tel 214-536-2422
E-mail: lee@leeparrish.com
Dist(s): **Ingram Content Group.**

Novel Units, Inc. *Imprint of* **Classroom Library Co.**

Novello & Co., Ltd. (GBR) *(978-0-85360) Dist. by* **H Leonard.**

Novello Festival Pr., *(978-0-9708972; 978-0-9760963; 978-0-9815192; 978-0-615-15969-0; 978-0-615-16624-7)* Div. of Public Library of Charlotte & Mecklenburg County, 310 N. Tryon St., Charlotte, NC 28202 USA (SAN 254-3206) Tel 704-416-0706
Dist(s): **Blair.**

Novelstream, LLC, *(978-1-941530; 978-1-945053; 978-1-951954)* 4 S. Mill St., Nyack, NY 10960 USA Tel 917-279-2726; *Imprints*: Interlude Press (InterludePr); Duet (Duet)
E-mail: lex@interludepress.com; annie@interludepress.com
Web site: http://interludepress.com; http://duetbooks.com
Dist(s): **Independent Pubs. Group.**

November Media Publishing and Consulting Firm, *(978-0-692-76179-3; 978-0-9981622; 978-0-9990431; 978-0-9998274; 978-1-7326897; 978-1-7337724; 978-0-578-70900-0; 978-1-7354542)* 2212 123rd St., Unit 1, Blue Island, IL 60406 USA Tel 708-515-7114
E-mail: novmedia10@gmail.com
Web site: http://www.novembermediapublishing.com/
Dist(s): **CreateSpace Independent Publishing Platform.**

Novus Via Music Group Inc. (CAN) *(978-1-897379) Dist. by* **H Leonard.**

Now Age Knowledge, *(978-0-9729259)* Orders Addr.: 8315 Lake City Way, NE, Seattle, WA 98115 USA; Edit Addr.: 16626 6th Ave. W. #m301, Lynnwood, WA 98037 USA (SAN 255-2876) Do not confuse with Awaken Publishing in Houston, TX
E-mail: nowageknowledge@gmail.com
Web site: http://nowageknowledge.com.

Now I'm Reading! *Imprint of* **Random Hse. Children's Bks.**

NOW SC Pr., *(978-0-9987391; 978-0-9995845; 978-1-7326611; 978-1-7341809)* 4219 Hartwood Ln., Tampa, FL 33618 USA Tel 253-468-8801
E-mail: liza@nowscpress.com
Web site: www.nowscpress.com.

Nowata Press Publishing Consultants, *(978-0-615-21595-2; 978-0-692-00130-1; 978-0-692-01778-4; 978-0-615-81419-3; 978-0-9907950)* 1338 Old Coach Road, SW, Marietta, GA 30008 USA
E-mail: dmyles3784@yahoo.com
Web site: http://nowatapress.wordpress.com/.

Nowlin, Roberta J, *(978-0-9862905)* 103 Columbia Way, Montrose, CO 81401 USA Tel 818-792-6189
E-mail: robertajeanmurphy@gmail.com.

NPG Newspapers, Inc., *(978-0-9724933)* Orders Addr.: P.O. Box 29, St Joseph, MO 64502-0029 USA Tel 816-271-8500; Fax: 816-271-8631; Toll Free: 800-779-6397; Edit Addr.: 825 Edmond St., St Joseph, MO 64502-0029 USA
E-mail: brucek@npgco.com.

Npustin Pr., *(978-0-9816834; 978-0-9963704)* P.O. Box 683, Arlee, MT 59821-0452 USA
E-mail: npustin@gmail.com
Web site: http://www.npustin.org.

NQSBks., *(978-0-9793168)* 477 Brentview Hills Dr., Nashville, TN 37220 USA Tel 615-832-1125
E-mail: nqsbooks@comcast.net
Web site: http://www.nqsbooks.com.

NRG Pubns., *(978-0-9741647)* 3510 Plum Brook, Missouri City, TX 77459 USA
E-mail: info@nrgpublications.com
Web site: http://www.nrgpublications.com.

NRS Enterprises, *(978-0-615-27983-1)* 2237 NW. Terr. Pines Dr., Bend, OR 97701 USA.

N-Spired Productions, *(978-0-9814774)* P.O. Box 2033, Westfield, NJ 07090 USA Tel 9083720203
Web site: www.NspiredProductions.com
Dist(s): **CreateSpace Independent Publishing Platform**
Lulu Pr., Inc.

NSR Pubns., *(978-0-9761724)* 1482 51st Rd., Douglass, KS 67039 USA Tel 620-986-5472; Toll Free: 866-677-2624
E-mail: gumm@wheatstate.com
Web site: http://www.nsrpublications.com.

NT Publishing, L.L.C., *(978-0-9741864; 978-0-9787123)* P.O. Box 461540, Aurora, CO 80047 USA Tel 303-484-1071; Fax: 303-484-1072
E-mail: questions@ntpublishing.net
Web site: http://www.ntpublishing.net.

NTC/Contemporary Publishing Company *See* **McGraw-Hill/Contemporary**

NUA Multimedia, *(978-0-9777573)* Orders Addr.: 15480 Annapolis Rd., Suite 202, No. 422, Bowie, MD 20715 USA Tel 410-710-2700
E-mail: pr@nuamultimedia.com; orders@nuamultimedia.com
Web site: http://www.soniahayes.com
Dist(s): **Brodart Co.**
Follett School Solutions.

NuAngel, Inc., *(978-0-9626614)* 14717 Friend Rd., Athens, AL 35611 USA Tel 256-729-5000; Fax: 256-729-5111
E-mail: sales@nuangel.com
Web site: www.nuangel.com.

NuBaby, Incorporated *See* **NuAngel, Inc.**

NubeOcho Ediciones (ESP) *(978-84-942360; 978-84-942929; 978-84-17123-11-6) Dist. by* **Consort Bk Sales.**

Nubiangodess Publishing, *(978-0-9744291)* P.O. Box 12224, Columbus, GA 31917-2224 USA
E-mail: ngpublishing@cs.com; admin@nubiangodesspublishing.com
Web site: http://www.nubiangodesspublishing.com.

Nubiano Project, Inc., The, *(978-0-9762837)* P.O. Box 371, Chapel Hill, NC 27514 USA
E-mail: info@thenubianoproject.com.

Nude Son Publishing *See* **Canoed Sun Publishing, LLC**

Nuevo Bks., *(978-1-936745)* 925 Salamanca NW, Los Ranchos, NM 87107 USA Tel 505-344-9382; Fax: 505-345-5129
E-mail: paul@nmsantos.com
Web site: www.NuevoBooks.com.

Nuf-Love Publishing, *(978-0-9636109)* P.O. Box 120976, Clermont, FL 34712 USA
E-mail: ashersbooks@earthlink.net
Web site: http://www.ashersbooks.com.

Nugent, Kristen Independent Publishing, *(978-0-9995768)* 1509 Main Street, Apt 505, Dallas, TX 75201 USA Tel 203-606-1287
E-mail: kristennugent20@gmail.com.

Nui Media & Entertainment, LLC, *(978-0-9817388)* P.O. Box 364, Santa Monica, CA 90406 USA
E-mail: publishing@nui.com.

NUMA LLC, *(978-0-9977196)* P.O. Box 52, Mystic, CT 06355 USA Tel 860-501-3316
E-mail: msoni.author@gmail.com.

Number 6 Publishing LLC, *(978-1-7321116)* 1799 Rampart Dr., Alexandria, VA 22308 USA Tel 703-360-6054
E-mail: sdressing@number6publishing.com.

Number One Fan Pr., *(978-0-615-16416-8; 978-0-615-17221-7; 978-0-615-38550-1; 978-0-615-85320-8)* 34 Robert St., Braintree, MA 02184 USA
Dist(s): **Lulu Pr., Inc.**
Publishers Services.

NumbersAlive! Pr., *(978-0-9853667)* 975 F St., NW., Washington, DC 20004-1454 USA Tel 202-652-1820; Fax: 202-667-5793
E-mail: rebecca@numbersalive.org
Web site: http://www.numbersalive.org.

Nu-Nature, *(978-0-9759008)* 858 Heritage Valley Rd., Norcross, GA 30093 USA Tel 404-376-8917
E-mail: nunatureinfo@aol.com
Web site: http://www.nu-nature.com.

Nunes, H. William, *(978-0-9646934; 978-0-9787994)* 3029 Mark Trail, Glen Carbon, IL 62034 USA Tel 618-288-5185; Fax: 618-205-3053
E-mail: bnunesbook@aol.com
Dist(s): **Big River Distribution**
Partners Bk. Distributing, Inc.

Nur Pubns., *(978-0-9764947)* Orders Addr.: 562 Sawmill River Rd., Millwood, NY 10546 USA
E-mail: s_nadimi@yahoo.com
Web site: http://www.nurpublications.com.

Nuriel, Tal, *(978-0-692-96604-4; 978-0-9997262)* 493 Amsterdam Ave, Apt 2C, New York, NY 10024 USA Tel 646-369-8445
E-mail: tnuriel@gmail.com.

Nursery Bks., *(978-0-9894505)* 30 jannas Ln., Madison, CT 06443 USA Tel 860-308-4303
E-mail: sophie.helenek@gmail.com
Web site: www.nurserybooks.net.

Nurture Wellness now, *(978-0-9998845)* 786 burden lake Rd., Aiken, SC 29803 USA Tel 803-646-1067; Fax: 803-646-1067
E-mail: tania@nurturewellnessnow.com
Web site: nurturewellnessnow.com.

Nurturing Potential, *(978-0-692-96815-4)* 6709 Ave. A, New Orleans, LA 70124 USA Tel 706-201-3927
E-mail: zibbie39@gmail.com.

Nurturing Your Children Pr., *(978-0-9767198)* P.O. Box 5066, Larkspur, CA 94977-5066 USA Tel 415-927-4839 (phone/fax)
E-mail: nurturingpress@aol.com
Web site: http://nurturingyourchildren.com.

Nutrishare Publishing, *(978-0-9764116)* 10519 E. Stockton Blvd., Suite 110, Elk Grove, CA 95624 USA.

Nutrition Network Pubs., Inc., *(978-0-9898633)* 5 Arleigh Rd., Great Neck, NY 11021 USA Tel 516-773-4754
E-mail: daunlester@gmail.com.

Nutshell Publishing *See* **Enisen Publishing**

NuVision Designs, *(978-0-578-19006-8; 978-0-578-19207-9; 978-0-578-19422-6;*

Publisher Name Index

978-0-578-19430-1; 978-0-578-19652-7; 978-0-578-19832-3; 978-0-578-20333-1; 978-0-578-20531-1; 978-0-578-21836-6; 978-0-578-21966-0; 978-0-578-22265-3) P.O. Box 4455, Wilmington, NC 28406 USA; 5027 Lamppost Cir., Wilmington, NC 28403 Tel 240.439.5294
Web site: www.nuvisiondesigns.biz.

NuVision Pubns., LLC, *(978-1-932681; 978-1-59547; 978-1-61536)* 1504 E. 70th St N., Sioux Falls, SD 57104-9429 USA
E-mail: nuvisionpub@gmail.com
Web site: http://www.nuvisionpublications.com
Dist(s): **CreateSpace Independent Publishing Platform**
Ingram Content Group.

Nvision Publishing *Imprint of* **Power Play Media**

nVision Publishing, *(978-0-9766086)* Div. of Written by Nicole Kearney Enterprises, P.O. Box 88731, Indianapolis, IN 46208 USA Tel 317-724-8926
E-mail: nicoleckearney@yahoo.com
Web site: http://www.nicolekearney.com.

N'Writing, *(978-0-9990976)* 14869 Arlington Ave., Allen Park, MI 48101 USA Tel 734-634-1817
E-mail: overstart2002@yahoo.com.

NY Media Works, LLC, *(978-0-9890914)* 112 Franklin St. First Flr., New York, NY 10013 USA (SAN 920-5187) Tel 646-369-5681
E-mail: jgribble@nymediaworks.com
Web site: http://www.nymediaworks.com
Dist(s): **Brodart Co.**
Quality Bks., Inc.

NY Studio Gallery LLC, *(978-0-692-49726-5; 978-0-692-62127-1; 978-0-692-62269-8; 978-0-692-65367-8; 978-0-692-67000-2; 978-0-692-67277-8; 978-0-692-67300-3; 978-0-692-72251-0; 978-0-692-78710-6; 978-0-692-80005-8; 978-0-692-80410-0; 978-0-692-80916-7; 978-0-692-80920-4) 420 N. Ohioville Rd, NEW PALTZ, NY 12561 USA Tel 612-987-1473.*

Nye Products, *(978-0-9746665)* P.O. Box 177, Wexford, PA 15090-0177 USA Tel 724-935-8710
E-mail: nyeproducts@stargate.net
Web site: http://nyeproducts.com; http://www.beverlynye.com/.

Nypa Distributing, LLC, *(978-0-578-08858-7; 978-0-578-08859-4; 978-0-9997400)* 1733 N. 40 E., Tooele, UT 84074 USA Tel 435-224-4286
E-mail: NypaDistributing@gmail.com.

NYR Children's Collection *Imprint of* **New York Review of Bks., Inc., The**

NYRB Classics *Imprint of* **New York Review of Bks., Inc., The**

NYRB Kids *Imprint of* **New York Review of Bks., Inc., The**

NyreePress Literary Group *See* **Create & Blossom, LLC**

NYU Pr. *Imprint of* **New York Univ. Pr.**

O & H Bks., *(978-0-9960057)* 528 Spence Ln Apt 105, Martins Ferry, OH 43935 USA
E-mail: smithgift264@gmail.com
Web site: http://www.oandhbooks.com.

OSS Publishing Co., *(978-0-9660286)* Orders Addr.: P.O. Box 610, White Plains, NY 10603 USA Tel 914-946-6521; Fax: 914-949-5380; Toll Free: 888-677-6521
E-mail: OSSpublishing@att.net
Web site: http://www.osspublishing.com.

Oak Court Pr., *(978-0-9767696)* 34612 Oak Ct., Elizabeth, CO 80107 USA Tel 303-703-6633
E-mail: oakcourtpress@msn.com.

Oak Grove Pr., LLC, *(978-0-615-42153-7)* 61 Thompson Inn Rd., South Bristol,, ME 04568 USA Tel 207-644-8448
E-mail: cgbeau@gwi.net
Dist(s): **Independent Pubs. Group.**

Oak Hill Studios, *(978-0-9848818)* 2150 Farnsworth Dr., O'Fallon, MO 63368 USA Tel 314-560-0041; Fax: 636-978-1135
E-mail: nealwriter1@charter.net
Web site: letterstomillie.com
Dist(s): **BookBaby.**

†Oak Knoll Pr., *(978-0-938768; 978-1-884718; 978-1-58456; 978-1-872116)* 310 Delaware St., New Castle, DE 19720 USA (SAN 216-2776) Tel 302-328-7232; Fax: 302-328-7274; Toll Free: 800-996-2556 Do not confuse with Oak Knoll Press in Hardy, VA
E-mail: oakknoll@oakknoll.com
Web site: http://www.oakknoll.com; *CIP.*

Oak Lake Pr., *(978-0-9744115)* Orders Addr.: 1432 Higuera, San Luis Obispo, CA 93406 USA Tel 916-791-2309; Edit Addr.: P.O. Box 529, Loomis, CA 95650 USA
E-mail: abowler@surewest.net
Web site: http://www.annmartinbowler.net.

Oak Leaf Systems, *(978-0-9659546; 978-0-9848809)* 2710 John Tyler Hwy., Williamsburg, VA 23185 USA Tel 757-208-0200 Landline; 757-634-1441 Mobile
E-mail: carolfeltman@gmail.com
Web site: ATruckNamedTravis.com.

Oak Manor Publishing, Inc., *(978-0-9747361; 978-0-9791757)* 161 Boutwell St., Manchester, NH 03102-2933 USA Tel 603-860-5551
E-mail: customerservice@aokmanorpublishing.com
Web site: http://www.oakmanorpublishing.com.

Oak Ridge Publishing, *(978-0-9814735; 978-0-9843270; 978-0-9851416)* P.O. Box 682, Lady Lake, FL 32158 USA Tel 352-259-7450
E-mail: ldridgley@comcast.net.

Oak Tree Publishing, *(978-1-892343; 978-1-61009)* Orders Addr.: 1820 W. Lacey Blvd. #220, Hanford, CA 93230 USA; *Imprints:* Acorn (AcornIL) Do not confuse with companies with the same or similar name in Virginia Beach, VA, Seminole, FL
E-mail: oaktreepub@aol.com; Publisher@oaktreebooks.com; info@oaktreebooks.com
Web site: http://www.oaktreebooks.com; http://www.otpblog.blogspot.com.

Oak Valley Publishing, *(978-0-9962753)* 14152 S. Senior Band, Draper, UT 84020 USA Tel 951-249-4577
E-mail: arsenalman@me.com.

Oakana Hse., *(978-0-9762197)* Orders Addr.: P.O. Box 1680, Ramona, CA 92065 USA (SAN 257-5418)
Web site: http://OakanaHouse.com.

Oakdale Pr., *(978-0-9656364)* Orders Addr.: P.O. Box 555, Caulfield, MO 65626 USA Tel 417-284-3512; Fax: 417-284-3623 Do not confuse with companies with the same name in Lincoln., MA, Tallahassee, FL
E-mail: oakdale@webound.com
Web site: http://www.oakdalepress.com.

Oaklawn Marketing, Inc., *(978-0-9764628)* P.O. Box 190615, Dallas, TX 75219 USA Tel 713-542-7642; Fax: 832-550-2079
E-mail: admin@bookofcontext.com.

OakTara Publishing Group LLC *See* **Nassau-Street.com**

Oakwood Solutions, LLC, *(978-1-893806; 978-1-933093)* 4 Brookwood Ct., Appleton, WI 54914-8618 USA
E-mail: bschmitz@conovercompany.com; sales@conovercompany.com
Web site: http://www.conovercompany.com.

Oasis, Producciones Generales de Comunicacion, S.L. (ESP) *(978-84-7871; 978-84-7901; 978-84-85351) Dist. by* **Lectorum Pubns.**

Oasis Pubns., *(978-0-9652736; 978-0-9837859)* 2344 Cambridge Dr., Sarasota, FL 34232 USA Tel 941-371-2223; Fax: 941-342-1228
E-mail: oasis.dianne@juno.com
Web site: http://www.nutrikid2.com
Dist(s): **Nelson's Bks.**
New Leaf Distributing Co., Inc.
Teva Nature.

Oasis Studios Inc, *(978-0-9785605)* Orders Addr.: 7701 Witherspoon Dr., Baltimore, OH 43105 USA Tel 740-862-8620
E-mail: ekayzer@hotmail.com
Web site: http://www.championoasisstudios.com
Dist(s): **Send The Light Distribution LLC.**

OASYS Pr., *(978-0-9863965)* 5916 E. Lake Pkwy. Suite 195, McDonough, GA 30253 USA Tel 678-561-5655; Fax: 877-720-8705
E-mail: alonzo@theoasysgroup.com
Web site: www.HiringMadeEasyasPIE.com; www.TheOASYSGroup.com.

†Oberlin College Pr., *(978-0-932440; 978-0-9973355)* 50 N. Professor St., Oberlin, OH 44074 USA (SAN 212-1883) Tel 440-775-8408; Fax: 440-775-8124
E-mail: oc.press@oberlin.edu
Web site: http://www.oberlin.edu/ocpress
Dist(s): **CUP Services**
Chicago Distribution Ctr.; *CIP.*

Oberon Bks., Ltd. (GBR) *(978-0-948230; 978-1-84002; 978-1-870259; 978-1-84943; 978-1-78319; 978-1-78682) Dist. by* **Consort Bk Sales.**

O'Brien, Gerard, *(978-0-9743850)* 115 Essex St., Indian Orchard, MA 01151-1409 USA Tel 413-543-5939
E-mail: gob@ifriendly.com.

OBrien, Kathryn, *(978-0-692-15101-3)* 12740 N.W. 78th Manor, Parkland, FL 33076 USA Tel 312-285-6189
E-mail: kobauthor@yahoo.com
Dist(s): **Ingram Content Group.**

O'Brien, Lara Publishing, *(978-0-9896752)* 47 Davis st, Vineyard Haven, MA 02568 USA Tel 774-563-0292
E-mail: laraeobrien@yahoo.com.

O'Brien Pr., Ltd., The (IRL) *(978-0-86278; 978-0-86322; 978-0-905140; 978-0-9502046; 978-1-902011; 978-1-84717; 978-1-78849) Dist. by* **Casemate Pubs.**

O'Brien Pr., Ltd., The (IRL) *(978-0-86278; 978-0-86322; 978-0-905140; 978-0-9502046; 978-1-902011; 978-1-84717; 978-1-78849) Dist. by* **Dufour.**

OBrien, Wiley Workspace, *(978-0-615-29492-6; 978-0-615-97038-7)* 125 Washington St., Canandaigua, NY 14424 USA
Web site: http://www.WonderlandBook.com.

Ocean Crest Publishing, LLC, *(978-0-9981322)* P.O. Box 842, Palm Beach, FL 33480 USA Tel 561-629-2528
E-mail: chelow@comcast.net
Web site: www.oceancrestpublishing.com.

Ocean Front Bk. Publishing, Inc., *(978-1-934190)* Orders Addr.: 9101 W. Sahara Ave. Suite 105-130, Las Vegas,, NV 89117 USA (SAN 852-0046) Tel 702-499-0608; 9101 W. Sahara Ave. Suite 105-130, Las Vegas,, NV 89117 (SAN 852-0046) Tel 702-499-0608
E-mail: jhorowitz@oceanfrontbooks.com
Web site: http://www.oceanfrontbooks.com.

Ocean World Photography, *(978-0-9766749)* 6461 Running Brook Rd., Manassas, VA 20112 USA
E-mail: wgregorybrown@comcast.net
Web site: http://www.wgregorybrown.com.

OceanAir Publishing *See* **Mayreni Publishing**

Oceano Grupo Editoria, S.A. (ESP) *(978-84-494; 978-84-7069; 978-84-7505; 978-84-7555; 978-84-7764; 978-84-85317; 978-84-9719) Dist. by* **Gale.**

OceanPubns., *(978-1-7321546)* 12827 SW 133rd ST, MIAMI, FL 33186 USA Tel 727-247-6078
E-mail: oceanpublications@gmail.com
Web site: oceanpublications.us.

Oceanus Bks. *Imprint of* **Warrington Pubns.**

Ocher Moon Pr., *(978-0-9765303)* 391 Joppa Mountain Rd., Rutledge, TN 37861 USA Tel 865-828-8280
E-mail: jeri@hopalonggreetings.com
Web site: http://www.hopalonggreetings.com.

O'Connor, Cassidy K. *See* **Celtic Hearts Pr.**

OCRS, Incorporated *See* **River Pr.**

Octagon Pr., Ltd., *(978-0-86304; 978-0-900860)* Orders Addr.: P.O. Box 400541, Cambridge, MA 02140 USA; Edit Addr.: 171 Main St. No. 140, Los Altos , CA 94022 USA
Web site: http://www.octagonpress.com
Dist(s): **I S H K.**

Octagon Pr./ISHK Bk. Service *See* **I S H K**

Octane Pr., *(978-0-9821733; 978-0-9829131; 978-1-937747; 978-1-64234)* Orders Addr.: 815A Brazos St No. 658, Austin, TX 78701 USA Tel 512-430-1943; Edit Addr.: 815a Brazos St. No. 658, Austin, TX 78701 USA (SAN 920-9395) Tel 512-334-9441
E-mail: lee@octanepress.com; sales@octanepress.com
Web site: http://octanepress.com
Dist(s): **Bookazine Co., Inc.**
Ingram Content Group.

OctiRam Publishing Co., *(978-0-9830423)* Orders Addr.: P.O. Box 5859, Vancouver, WA 98668 USA Tel 360-464-7670
E-mail: raski@comcast.net.

Octobooks, *(978-0-9843297)* P.O. Box 1554, La Jolla, CA 92038-1554 USA (SAN 859-0834)
E-mail: jack@octoboks.com; millie@millietheoctopus.com
Web site: http://www.millietheoctopus.com.

Octobre Pr., *(978-0-615-69253-1; 978-0-615-84019-2; 978-0-692-34554-2; 978-0-692-61301-6; 978-0-692-82604-1; 978-0-692-98457-4; 978-1-7329768)* 3310 Oak Brook Ln., Vero Beach, FL 32963 USA Tel 772-538-4805
E-mail: virginiabest@me.com
Web site: http://www.pansythepoodle.com
Dist(s): **National Bk. Network.**

Octopoda Pr., *(978-0-9858506; 978-0-9908818)* P.O. Box 8943, Ketchikan, AK 99901 USA Tel 907-225-8212
E-mail: evon@evonzerbetz.com
Web site: octopodapress.com.

Octopus Publishing Co., *(978-0-9824433)* Div. of Octopus Enterprises LLC, 100 S. River Bend, Jackson, GA 30233-3204 USA
E-mail: rogerfen@bellsouth.net; geletaf@bellsouth.net.

Octopus Publishing Group (GBR) *(978-0-600; 978-0-905879; 978-1-84091; 978-1-86007; 978-1-84202; 978-1-84430; 978-1-904705; 978-1-84403; 978-1-84696; 978-1-905814; 978-1-84898; 978-1-908150; 978-1-907579; 978-1-78157; 978-1-78325) Dist. by* **HachBkGrp.**

Octopus Publishing Group (GBR) *(978-0-600; 978-0-905879; 978-1-84091; 978-1-86007; 978-1-84202; 978-1-84430; 978-1-904705; 978-1-84403; 978-1-84696; 978-1-905814; 978-1-84898; 978-1-908150; 978-1-907579; 978-1-78157; 978-1-78325) Dist. by* **Children Plus.**

Odd Dot *Imprint of* **St. Martin's Pr.**

Odd Duck Ink, Inc., *(978-1-933069)* P.O. Box 533, Norwell, MA 02061-0533 USA
E-mail: jennifer@oddduckink.com
Web site: http://www.oddduckink.com.

OddInt Media *Imprint of* **Greenwood Hill Pr.**

Oddo Publishing, Inc., *(978-0-87783)* Storybook Acres, Box 68, Fayetteville, GA 30214 USA (SAN 282-0757) Tel 770-461-7627.

Odds Bodkin Storytelling Library, The *Imprint of* **Rivertree Productions, Inc.**

ODE, *(978-0-692-87176-8; 978-0-578-41922-0; 978-0-578-46012-3; 978-0-578-46197-7; 978-0-578-70537-8)* 1708C 4th Ave N, Nashville, TN 37208 USA Tel 818-427-1901
E-mail: cdaymusic@gmail.com
Dist(s): **Independent Pub.**

Oden, Rachel, *(978-0-9729914)* 133 E. Graham Ave., Council Bluffs, IA 51503 USA Tel 712-323-7222 (phone/fax)
E-mail: cbmarketadmin@juno.com.

Odenwald Pr., *(978-0-9623216; 978-1-884363)* 6609 Brooks Dr., Temple, TX 76502 USA Tel 254-773-4884; Fax: 254-773-4884
E-mail: CSho777@aol.com
Dist(s): **SMMA Distributors.**

Odeon Livre, *(978-1-947961; 978-1-64574)* 1111 Old Barn Rd., Buffalo Grove, IL 60089 USA Tel 847-917-9575; Fax: 847-917-9575; *Imprints:* Oui Love Books (MYID_Y_OUI LOV)
E-mail: ethan@odeonlivre.com
Web site: https://odeonlivre.com.

odod bks. *Imprint of* **Uncivilized Bks.**

Odon Livre *See* **Odeon Livre**

Odysia Pr., *(978-0-692-98154-2; 978-0-692-99104-6; 978-0-692-99115-2; 978-0-692-99123-7; 978-0-692-99124-4; 978-0-692-04566-4; 978-0-692-19708-0; 978-0-578-42424-8; 978-0-578-42428-6; 978-0-578-42431-6; 978-0-578-44094-1; 978-0-578-44816-9)* 705 B SE Melody Ln. No. 320, LEES SUMMIT, MO 64063 USA Tel 816-607-1801
E-mail: djpedersen@gmail.com
Dist(s): **Ingram Content Group.**

Odyssey Bks. (AUS) *(978-0-9806909; 978-0-9872325; 978-1-922200; 978-1-925652; 978-1-922311) Dist. by* **LightSource CS.**

Oelrich, Josh, *(978-0-692-11120-8)* 300 Koch Dr., Hollister, CA 95023 USA Tel 408-710-0650
E-mail: josh.oelrich@gmail.com
Dist(s): **Ingram Content Group.**

OES, *(978-0-692-07456-5)* W6350 Old Lake Ln., Shawano, WI 54166 USA Tel 715-508-0250
E-mail: doug.pebs@gmail.com.

Off The Record *Imprint of* **College Prowler, Inc.**

Officer Byrd Publishing Co., *(978-0-9787322)* 15730 Williams Cir., Lake Mathews, CA 92570 USA (SAN 851-4712) Tel 951-334-6111
E-mail: officerbyrd@aol.com.

OffTheBookshelf.com *See* **Micro Publishing Media, Inc.**

Oglethorpe Pr., Inc., *(978-1-891495)* 326 Bull St., Savannah, GA 31401 USA Tel 912-231-9900; Fax: 912-234-7258
E-mail: sjackel@comcast.net
Dist(s): **Parnassus Bk. Distributors.**

Ogma Pr., *(978-0-9785853)* 4717 Broad Rd., Syracuse, NY 13215 USA Tel 315-491-9339
E-mail: bernie@ogmapress.com
Web site: http://www.ogmapress.com.

Ogonor, Fyne, *(978-1-7321995; 978-1-951460)* 2579 Jenna Ln., Lithia Springs, GA 30122 USA Tel 404-402-7986
E-mail: fcogonor@gmail.com.

Ogorek, Elchanan, *(978-0-692-76640-8)* .

Oh My Stars Publishing, *(978-0-615-20153-5)* 222 3rd St., Suite 4, Lemoyne, PA 17043 USA
Dist(s): **APG Sales & Distribution Services**
Lulu Pr., Inc.

OHC Group LLC, *(978-0-9763213)* P.O. Box 7839, Westlake Village, CA 91359 USA Tel 805-384-4800
Web site: http://www.onlyheartsclub.com.

Ohio Distinctive Publishing, Inc., *(978-0-9647934; 978-1-936772)* 6500 Fiesta Dr., Columbus, OH 43235 USA Tel 614-459-0453; Fax: 614-457-2488
E-mail: tim@ohio-distinctive.com
Web site: http://www.ohio-distinctive.com.

†Ohio State Univ. Pr., *(978-0-8142)* 1070 Carmack Rd., Columbus, OH 43210 USA (SAN 202-8158) Tel 614-292-6930; 773-568-1550 (orders); Fax: 614-292-2065; Toll Free Fax: 800-621-8476 (orders); Toll Free: 800-621-2736 (orders); *Imprints:* Mad Creek Books (MadCreekBks)
E-mail: ohiostatepress@osu.edu
Web site: http://www.ohiostatepress.org
Dist(s): **Chicago Distribution Ctr.**
Partners Bk. Distributing, Inc.
Univ. of Chicago Pr.; *CIP.*

†Ohio Univ. Pr., *(978-0-8214)* Orders Addr.: 11030 S. Langley Ave., Chicago, IL 60628 USA Tel 773-702-7000; Fax: 773-702-7212; Toll Free Fax: 800-621-8476; Toll Free: 800-621-2736; Edit Addr.: 19 Circle Dr. The Ridges, Athens, OH 45701 USA (SAN 282-0773) Tel 740-593-1154; Fax: 740-593-4536
Web site: https://www.ohioswallow.com/
Dist(s): **Chicago Distribution Ctr.**
Ebsco Publishing
Trajectory, Inc.
Univ. of Chicago Pr.
ebrary, Inc.; *CIP.*

Ohnick Enterprises, *(978-0-9746222)* Orders Addr.: P.O. Box 969, Meade, KS 67864-0969 USA Tel 620-873-2900; Fax: 620-873-2603; Toll Free: 800-794-2356; Edit Addr.: 102 N. Fowler, Meade, KS 67864-0969 USA
E-mail: nancy@prairiebooks.com
Web site: http://backroomprinting.com.

Oka, Joseph *See* **Joseph's Labor**

Okasan & Me, *(978-0-9743613)* 829 N. Sixth St., San Jose, CA 95112 USA
Web site: http://www.okasanandme.com.

O'Keefe, Cameron, 3 N. Covington Meadows, OLIVETTE, MO 63132 USA Tel 314-406-0069
E-mail: iamcameronkillian@gmail.com
Dist(s): **Ingram Content Group.**

Oki, Blessed, *(978-0-9721336)* 2465 Heaton Dri., Suite A, East Point, GA 30344 USA
E-mail: blessiebeke@yahoo.com.

Oklahoma Energy Resources Board, *(978-0-615-19844-6; 978-0-615-39316-2; 978-0-692-63684-8)* 3555 NW 58th St., Suite 430, Oklahoma City, OK 73112 USA Tel 405-942-5323; Fax: 405-942-3435; Toll Free: 800-664-1301
Web site: http://www.oerb.com.

Oklahoma Heritage Assn., *(978-1-885596; 978-1-938923)* Orders Addr.: 1400 Classen Dr., Oklahoma City, OK 73106 USA Tel 405-235-4458; 405-523-3202; Fax: 405-235-2714; Toll Free: 888-501-2059
E-mail: gmc@oklahomaheritage.com
Web site: http://www.oklahomaheritage.com
Dist(s): **Partners Bk. Distributing, Inc.**

Olandar Pr. Ltd., *(978-0-9729502)* Orders Addr.: 2222 Parview Rd., Middleton, WI 53562 USA Tel 608-831-1222; Fax: 608-831-1647
Web site: http://www.leighmccloskey.com.

Ola's Hanalei LTD, *(978-0-9763907)* P.O. Box 488, Hanalei, HI 96714 USA
E-mail: olashanalei@hawaiiantel.net.

Old Bay Publishing, *(978-0-9745854)* 19 Meeting St., Huntsville, AL 35806-5230 USA
E-mail: msikes@hiwaay.net
Dist(s): **Partners Bk. Distributing, Inc.**

Old Bess Publishing Co., *(978-0-9631912; 978-0-9762132)* Orders Addr.: P.O. Box 277, Brunswick, ME 04011 USA Tel 207-725-8575; P.O. Box P.O. Box 277, Brunswick, ME 04011
E-mail: sbutcherr@mcn.net.

Old Coal Publishing, *(978-0-578-54166-2; 978-0-578-65387-7)* 28509 North Pk. Dr., North Olmsted, OH 44070 USA Tel 440-429-6161
E-mail: modernvictorian@yahoo.com.

Old Farm Pr., *(978-0-9788227)* P.O. Box 20894, Oklahoma City, OK 73156-0894 USA (SAN 851-6995) Tel 405-748-7072; Fax: 405-748-7073
E-mail: spi@mbo.net
Web site: http://www.BobbyBrightBooks.com.

Old Farmer's Almanac *Imprint of* **Yankee Publishing, Inc.**

Old Hogan Publishing Co., *(978-0-9638851)* Orders Addr.: P.O. Box 91978, Tucson, AZ 85752 USA Tel 520-579-9321; Fax: 520-579-0502; Toll Free:

800-867-1506; Edit Addr.: 3600 W. Mesa Ridge Trail, Tucson, AZ 85742 USA
E-mail: mgaraway@juno.com
Web site: http://www.oldhogan.com
Dist(s): **Hispanic Bks. Distributors & Pubs., Inc.**
Rio Nuevo Pubs.

Old Hundredth Pr., (*978-0-9793911*) 2885 Gordon Rd., NW, Dover, OH 44622 USA.

O.L.D. Inc., (*978-0-9830470*) 118 N Ross St No. 6, Auburn, AL 36830 USA Tel 334-787-1713
E-mail: cwjones@oldinc.net.

Old Maps, (*978-0-911653; 978-0-9747639*) P.O. Box 54, West Chesterfield, NH 03466 USA (SAN 264-2689)
E-mail: daven@sover.net
Web site: http://www.old-maps.com.

Old Scout Pr., (*978-0-692-85277-4; 978-0-692-11902-0; 978-0-578-54238-6*) 4033 Kingsgate Pl., Charlotte, NC 28211 USA Tel 434-996-7318
E-mail: KDSherry@gmail.com; oldscoutpresscharlotte@gmail.com
Web site: katesliteracycorner.weebly.com; oldscoutpresscharlotte.com.

Old Silver Pr., (*978-0-9800975*) 224 Coonamessett Cir., East Falmouth, MA 02536 USA
E-mail: OldSilverPress@yahoo.com.

Old Soldier Publishing, (*978-0-9764167*) Orders Addr.: P.O. Box 1113, Richmond, TX 77469 USA Tel 281-341-0781 (phone/fax); Edit Addr.: 1110 Pioneer Dr., Richmond, TX 77469 USA
Dist(s): **ebrary, Inc.**

Old St. Augustine Pubns., (*978-0-9833684; 978-0-692-38918-8*) P.O. Box 162056, Altamonte Springs, FL 32716 USA Fax: 407-774-8799
E-mail: doug@oldstaugustinepublications.com
Web site: http://www.oldstaugustinepublications.com
Dist(s): **Ingram Content Group.**

Old Stone Pr., (*978-1-938462*) 520 Old Stone Ln., Louisville, KY 40207 USA Tel 502-693-1506
E-mail: john@oldstonepress.com; john@jhclarkandassociates.com
Web site: http://OldStonePress.com
Dist(s): **Baker & Taylor Publisher Services (BTPS).**

Old Time Stories, (*978-0-9792770*) 116 Beasley Rd., Cusseta, GA 31805-3206 USA.

Old Town Publishing, (*978-1-7329703; 978-1-7338129; 978-1-7332138*) 5014 College View Ave, Los Angeles, CA 90041 USA Tel 818-415-4616
E-mail: uspnow@aol.com
Web site: www.oldtownpublishing.com.

Old Vine Oublishing Co., (*978-0-9794291*) P.O. Box 6774, Pine Mountain Club, CA 93222-6774 USA.

Old West Company, The *See* **Old West Co., The**

Oldcastle Bks., Ltd. (GBR) (*978-0-948353; 978-1-874061; 978-1-84243; 978-1-84344; 978-1-904915*) *Dist. by* **IPG Chicago.**

Oldcastle Publishing, (*978-0-932529*) Orders Addr.: P.O. Box 1193, Escondido, CA 92033 USA (SAN 297-9039) Tel 760-489-0336; Fax: 760-747-1198; Edit Addr.: 3415 Laredo Ln., Escondido, CA 92025 USA (SAN 297-9047)
E-mail: abcurtiss@cox.net
Web site: http://www.abcurtiss.com; http://www.depressionisachoice.com
Dist(s): **National Bk. Network.**

Olde Milford Pr., The, (*978-0-9662019; 978-1-7331780; 978-1-7342334*) Orders Addr.: P.O. Box 5342, Milford, CT 06460 USA; Edit Addr.: 108 Clark Hill Rd., Milford, CT 06460 USA
E-mail: oldemilfordpress@msn.com
Web site: http://www.oldemilfordpress.com.

Olde Springfield Shoppe *See* **Masthof Pr.**

Olde Town Publishing, (*978-0-9755906*) 703 W. Main, Jonesborough, TN 37659 USA
Web site: http://www.drisbell.com.

Olde Towne Publishing, (*978-0-9794935*) P.O. Box 98, Old Mission, MI 49673 USA Do noty confuse with Olde Towne Publishing Company in Fredericksburg, VA
Web site: http://www.strolltraversecity.com
Dist(s): **Partners Bk. Distributing, Inc.**

Oldenworld Bks., (*978-0-578-41700-4; 978-0-578-41703-5; 978-1-7339429*) 9207 NE 104th St., Vancouver, WA 98662 USA Tel 360-771-3367
E-mail: jd@jackdublin.net
Web site: https://JackDublin.net
Dist(s): **Independent Pub.**

O'Leary, Stephanie, (*978-0-692-16597-3; 978-0-692-17154-7; 978-0-692-04451-3*) 1313 N Lucy Montgomery Way, Olathe, KS 66061 USA Tel 316-841-1322
E-mail: caoghlan@yahoo.com
Dist(s): **Ingram Content Group.**

Oleson, Susan, (*978-0-9779251*) 511 E Iowa St, Monona, IA 52159 USA
E-mail: sammytails@netins.net.

Olive & Ink, (*978-0-578-16978-1; 978-0-692-76874-7; 978-0-692-76882-2*) 21 South Main St., Perry, NY 14530 USA.

Olive Branch Publishing, LLC *See* **OlivesAngels Publishing, LLC**

Olive Grove Pubs., (*978-0-9752508*) 1420 King Rd., Hinckley, OH 44233 USA Tel 330-278-4028
E-mail: RSpirko@Roadrunner.com
Web site: http://www.atlasbooks.com
Dist(s): **American Wholesale Booksellers Assn.**
Baker & Taylor Publisher Services (BTPS)
Book$mart, Inc.
New Leaf Distributing Co., Inc.
ebrary, Inc.

Olive Leaf Pubns., (*978-0-9761583*) 782 San Gabriel Loop, New Braunfels, TX 78132 USA (SAN 256-6206) Tel 830-626-7671
E-mail: sharon3572@att.net; sharon3572@icloud.com
Web site: http://www.oliveleafpublications.com
Dist(s): **Ingram Content Group.**

Olive Pr. Pub., (*978-0-9790873; 978-0-9847111; 978-0-9855241; 978-1-941173*) P.O. Box 163, Copenhagen, NY 13626 USA Tel 315-941-6710.

Olive Pr., The, (*978-0-9769298*) Orders Addr.: P.O. Box 2056, Saintllwater, MN 55082 USA Tel 651-251-3063 Do not confuse with Olive Press i Ann Arbor, MI West Orange, NJ Estes Park, CO
E-mail: olivepressinc@yahoo.com
Web site: http://jumpstartfuture.com.

Olive Tree of Life, (*978-0-9768182*) P.O. Box 344, Tijeras, NM 87059 USA
Web site: http://www.olivetreeoflife.com.

Oliver Pr., Inc., (*978-1-881508; 978-1-934545*) Orders Addr.: 5707 W. 36th St., Minneapolis, MN 55416-2510 USA Tel 952-926-8981; Fax: 952-926-8965; Toll Free: 800-865-4837
E-mail: orders@oliverpress.com
Web site: http://www.oliverpress.com.

Oliver Pr. LLC, (*978-0-692-42047-8; 978-0-692-42048-5; 978-0-692-78667-3; 978-0-692-87956-6*) 1935 Chene Ct. Apt. 1505, Detroit, MI 48207 USA Tel 313-744-8543
E-mail: grimlyjane@yahoo.com
Dist(s): **CreateSpace Independent Publishing Platform**
Ingram Content Group.

Oliver, Sarah (GBR) (*978-0-9559820*) *Dist. by* **LuluCom.**

Oliver, Wade, (*978-0-9768030*) P.O. Box 1605, Logan, UT 84322-1605 USA
E-mail: wademan@cache.net
Web site: http://www.dovepage.com.

OlivesAngels Publishing, LLC, (*978-0-9793147*) P.O. Box 940725, Plano, TX 75094-0725 USA (SAN 853-0955) Tel 972-977-4881
E-mail: olivesangels@tx.rr.com.

Olivo, Andy, (*978-0-9743376*) 1807 Glengarry St., Carrollton, TX 75006 USA Tel 972-242-0924; Fax: 972-242-1754; *Imprints*: Brown Books (Brown BksTX).

OLLY Publishing Co., (*978-0-9720427*) 4335 Lake Michigan Dr., NW Suite H, Grand Rapids, MI 49544 USA (SAN 254-587X) Tel 616-735-0553
E-mail: diane@ollypublishing.com
Web site: http://www.ollypublishing.com.

Olms, Georg Verlag AG (DEU) (*978-3-487*) *Dist. by* **IPG Chicago.**

Olmstead LLC *See* **Olmstead Publishing LLC**

Olmstead Publishing LLC, (*978-0-9667696; 978-1-934194*) Orders Addr.: 2629 Grassmoor Lp, Apopka, FL 32712-5005 USA Tel 954-559-0192 (phone); Fax: 650-479-8273
E-mail: olmsteadpublishing@usa.com
Web site: http://www.olmsteadpublishing.com; http://https://squareup.com/market/olmstead-publishing-llc; http://www.facebook.com/olmsteadpublishing.

Olsen, Mary Bks., (*978-0-9715374*) P.O. Box 882, Eastsound, WA 98245-0882 USA
E-mail: mary@maryolsenbooks.com.

Olson, Robin, (*978-0-9818695*) P.O. Box 5294, Laytonsville, MD 20882 USA (SAN 856-7719)
E-mail: robin@robinsweb.com
Web site: http://www.robinsweb.com.

Oma Publishing Co., (*978-0-9747175*) 2217 Eden Rd., Seguin, TX 78155-0179 USA Tel 210-684-3200.

Omaha Bks., (*978-0-9745410; 978-0-9788429; 978-0-9908000*) Div. of Eventive Marketing, 5037 Parker St., Omaha, NE 68104 USA (SAN 857-1295) Tel 402-679-5854
E-mail: kristine.gerber@cox.net; jkgerber@cox.net
Dist(s): **Partners Bk. Distributing, Inc.**

Omaha World-Hearld *See* **Omaha World-Herald**

Omaha World-Herald, (*978-0-615-37076-7; 978-0-615-41175-0; 978-0-615-42369-2; 978-0-615-51155-9; 978-0-615-55822-6; 978-0-615-70853-9; 978-0-615-71539-1; 978-0-615-71549-0; 978-0-615-79394-8; 978-0-615-87516-3; 978-0-615-89513-0; 978-0-615-90983-7; 978-0-692-26499-7; 978-0-692-31051-9; 978-0-692-31055-7; 978-0-692-31859-1; 978-0-692-55512-5; 978-0-692-55518-7; 978-0-692-62399-2; 978-0-692-74658-5; 978-0-692-79875-1; 978-0-692-79878-2; 978-0-692-88708-0; 978-0-692-94259-8; 978-0-692-96277-0; 978-1-7322317; 978-) 1314 Douglas St., Omaha, NE 68102 USA Tel 402-444-1204; Fax: 402-346-7158*
E-mail: rich.warren@owh.com
Web site: http://www.omaha.com.

O'Mara, Michael Bks., Ltd. (GBR) (*978-1-85479; 978-0-946429; 978-0-948397; 978-1-84317; 978-1-903840; 978-1-904613; 978-1-907151; 978-1-78243; 978-1-910552*) *Dist. by* **IngramPubServ.**

O'Mara, Michael Bks., Ltd. (GBR) (*978-1-85479; 978-0-946429; 978-0-948397; 978-1-84317; 978-1-903840; 978-1-904613; 978-1-907151; 978-1-78243; 978-1-910552*) *Dist. by* **Trans-Atl Phila.**

O'Mara, Michael Bks., Ltd. (GBR) (*978-1-85479; 978-0-946429; 978-0-948397; 978-1-84317; 978-1-903840; 978-1-904613; 978-1-907151; 978-1-78243; 978-1-910552*) *Dist. by* **IPG Chicago.**

Omega Hse. Publishing, (*978-0-9672519*) Div. of Spectrum Group, Inc., Orders Addr.: P.O. Box 68, Three Rivers, MI 49093 USA Tel 269-273-7070; Fax: 269-273-7026; Edit Addr.: 58690 US 131, Three Rivers, MI 49093 USA
E-mail: zendra@omega777.com.

Omega Pr., (*978-0-9626087; 978-0-9754923; 978-1-933951*) 5823 N. Mesa, No. 839, El Paso, TX 79912-3340 USA Tel 915-478-1114; 915-219-4210; Toll Free: 888-560-1243 Do not confuse with companies with the same name in Tustin, CA
E-mail: ken@kenhudnall.com
Web site: http://www.omegapress.us; http://www.kenhudnall.com; http://shop.kenhudnall.com.

Omega Prime, LLC, (*978-0-9897588*) 3521 Hartzdale Dr., Camp Hill, PA 17011-7231 USA Tel 717-579-0038
E-mail: SusanRShutt@OmegaPrime.net
Web site: http://www.loveoffizz.com; http://www.fortheloveoffizz.com; http://www.omegaprime.net.

Omega Publishing, (*978-0-9748494*) P.O. Box 53626, Lubbock, TX 79453 USA (SAN 255-8815) Tel 806-748-9880; Fax: 806-748-9870; Toll Free: 877-842-9880 do not confuse with companies iwth the same or similar name in Madisonville, KY, Stockton, GA, Snohomish, WA, Norcross, GA
E-mail: jpartin@omega-pub.com
Web site: http://www.omega-pub.com.

Omega Publishing Hse., (*978-1-886297*) Subs. of B. C. & G. Graphics, Orders Addr.: 2935 Glenwood Ave., Youngstown, OH 44511 USA Tel 330-881-1344; Fax: 330-782-7599
E-mail: omegapublishing@ymail.com; craiga2356@msn.com
Web site: http://omegapublishinghouse.com.

Omen Sky Pubns., (*978-0-9744192*) 3600 Brookewind Way, No. 1201, Lexington, KY 40515 USA Tel 859-543-2026 (phone/fax)
E-mail: omensky@qx.net.

Omni Arts Publishing *Imprint of* **Read Street Publishing, Inc.**

Omni Arts Publishing, Incorporated *See* **Read Street Publishing, Inc.**

Omnibook Co., 1171 Decorah Rd., West Bend, WI 53095-9509 USA (SAN 282-6941) Tel 414-675-2760; Fax: 414-675-2340.

Omnibus Publishing, (*978-0-9740599*) 3402 Beresford Ave., Belmont, CA 94002 USA Tel 650-622-9702; Fax: 650-240-3586
E-mail: yuhogan@omnibuspublishing.com
Web site: http://www.omnibuspublishing.com.

Omnific Publishing, (*978-1-936305; 978-1-62342*) P.O. Box 793871, Dallas, TX 75379 USA Fax: 214-975-4889
E-mail: publisher@omnificpublishing.com
Web site: http://www.omnificpublishing.com
Dist(s): **Ingram Publisher Services**
Simon & Schuster, Inc.

†Omnigraphics, Inc., (*978-0-7808; 978-1-55888*) Orders Addr.: P.O. Box 8002, Aston, PA 19014-8002 USA Tel 800-234-1340; Fax: 800-875-1340; Toll Free Fax: 800-875-1340 (orders & customer service); Toll Free: 800-234-1340 (orders & customer service); Edit Addr.: 615 Griswold, Suite 520, Detroit, MI 48226 USA (SAN 249-2520)
E-mail: info@omnigraphics.com; customerservice@omnigraphics.com
Web site: http://www.omnigraphics.com
Dist(s): **Ebsco Publishing**
Gale Virtual Reference Library
Independent Pubs. Group
Mackin Educational Resources
MyiLibrary
Rittenhouse Bk. Distributors
Visible Ink Pr.
ebrary, Inc.; *CIP.*

Omohundro Institute of Early American History & Culture, (*978-0-910776*) P.O. Box 8781, Williamsburg, VA 23187 USA (SAN 201-5161) Tel 757-221-1116; Fax: 757-221-1047
Dist(s): **Univ. of North Carolina Pr.**

O'More Publishing, (*978-0-9717444; 978-0-9800285; 978-0-9822618; 978-0-9846244; 978-0-9860150; 978-0-9860244*) 423 S. Margin St., Franklin, TN 37064 USA Fax: 615-790-1662; 615-790-1666
E-mail: mhilliard@omorecollege.edu; jsexton@omorecollege.edu
Web site: http://www.omorepublishing.com.

On Cape Pubns., (*978-0-9653283; 978-0-9719547; 978-0-9758502; 978-0-9785766; 978-0-9913401; 978-1-64907*) Orders Addr.: 87 Barley Neck Rd., Orleans, MA 02638 USA Tel 508-385-2108 Toll Free: 877-662-5839
E-mail: chopi@goodnightbooks.com
Web site: http://www.oncapepublications.com.

On The Ball Publishing, (*978-0-615-21079-7; 978-0-615-25047-2; 978-0-615-45284-5; 978-0-615-45296-8; 978-0-9834341*) 12821 Stratford Dr. Suite 114, Oklahoma City, OK 73120 USA Tel 405-549-1174
E-mail: admin@ontheballpublishing.com
Web site: http://www.ontheballpublishing.com
Dist(s): **Lulu Pr., Inc.**

On The Edge Pubns., (*978-0-9762360*) P.O. Box 690007, Stockton, CA 95269 USA Tel 209-473-8553
E-mail: ontheedgepublications@msn.com
Web site: http://www.ontheedgepublications.com.

On The Fly Pubns., (*978-1-61463*) 1359 Vista Ridge Dr., Santaquin, UT 84655 USA Tel 801-208-5637
E-mail: jaimebuckley@wantedhero.com
Web site: http://www.ontheflypublications.com
Dist(s): **Lulu Pr., Inc.**

On the Reelz Pr., (*978-0-9778048*) 13813 Congress Dr., Suite 610, Rockville, MD 20853 USA Tel 202-288-5562
E-mail: ibefg@hotmail.com
Web site: http://www.onthereelz.com.

On the Spot! Bks., (*978-0-9652998*) 1492 Tipperary St., Boulder, CO 80303 USA Tel 303-666-0550
E-mail: onthespotbooks@msn.com
Web site: www.kerryleemaclean.com
Dist(s): **Bks. West**
New Leaf Distributing Co., Inc.

On Tour Publishing, (*978-0-9767234*) Orders Addr.: 512 Northampton St., 151, 303, Edwardsville, PA 18704 USA
E-mail: otp@ontourpublishing.com.

ON Words Publishing, LLC, (*978-0-9787589*) 8720 Ferguson Ave., Savannah, GA 31406 USA.

ONA Healthy Life, L.L.C. *See* **Mel Ona**

Once Upon A Time in a Classroom *Imprint of* **Interactive Media Publishing**

Oncekids, (*978-0-9844207; 978-1-938806*) 119 Maono Pl., Honolulu, HI 96821 USA (SAN 859-3574)
E-mail: oncekids@gmail.com
Dist(s): **Baker & Taylor Publisher Services (BTPS).**

Oncology Nursing Press, Incorporated *See* **Oncology Nursing Society**

Oncology Nursing Society, (*978-1-890504; 978-1-935864; 978-1-63593*) Subs. of Oncology Nursing Society, 125 Enterprise Dr., Pittsburgh, PA 15275-1214 USA (SAN 689-8041) Tel 412-859-6100
E-mail: jholmes@ons.org
Web site: http://www.ons.org.

One Arm Publishing, (*978-0-9746024*) 3344 Via La Selva, Palos Verdes Estates, CA 90274 USA
E-mail: mariana1969@hotmail.com
Web site: http://www.onearmpublishing.com.

One Armed Operation *See* **One Arm Publishing**

One Coin Publishing, LLC, (*978-0-615-31066-4*) 6876 Towhee, Portage, MI 49024 USA.

One Elm Books *Imprint of* **Red Chair Pr.**

One Eyed Pr., (*978-0-9665430; 978-0-615-26684-8*) 272 Rd. 6RT, Cody, WY 82414 USA Tel 307-272-9628; 307-587-6136
E-mail: one_eyed_press@yahoo.com
Web site: http://www.one-eyed-press.com
Dist(s): **Bks. West**
CreateSpace Independent Publishing Platform
Todd Communications.

One Eyed Tiger Publishing, (*978-0-9971588*) 1420 NE Brockman Pl, Seattle, WA 98125 USA Tel 206-228-5954
E-mail: hindmank@gmail.com.

One Faithful Harp Publishing Co., (*978-0-9666701*) 138 N. 2nd St., Catawissa, PA 17820-1210 USA
E-mail: info@onefaithfulharp.com
Web site: http://www.onefaithfulharp.com.

One Horse Pr., (*978-0-9725650*) 963 Maple Hill Dr., Erie, PA 16509 USA Tel 814-923-4086
E-mail: stephanie@stephaniewincik.com
Web site: http://www.stephaniewincik.com.

One in Me, The, (*978-0-9898437*) 503 Wicklow Pl., Acworth, GA 30102 USA Tel 678-324-8750; Fax: 678-324-8750
E-mail: tgodoy@comcast.net.

One In The Son Publishing, (*978-0-9973723*) 16745 SE Division St. No. 127, Portland, OR 97236 USA Tel 503-730-4688
E-mail: littleredappletree@hotmail.com
Web site: oneintheson.com.

One Little Miracle, (*978-0-9743948*) 1449 Highland Ct., Stillwater, MN 55082 USA Tel 651-439-3250
E-mail: allieschield@hotmail.com
Web site: http://www.onelittlemiracle.com.

One Little Spark, (*978-0-615-53981-2; 978-0-578-12711-8*) 239 W. Lime Ave., Monrovia, CA 91016 USA Tel 818-621-3466; Fax: 626-486-9456
E-mail: vicki@onelilspark.com
Web site: onelilspark.com.

One Love Assn. Bks., (*978-0-9776603*) 306 Trillick Ct., Rolesville, NC 27571 USA (SAN 257-8654)
E-mail: ras@newkemet.com; gerald@newkemet.com
Web site: http://www.newkemet.com/gerald.

One Monkey Bks., (*978-0-9777082; 978-1-940722*) 156 Diamond St., San Francisco, CA 94114-2414 USA (SAN 850-0320).

One Moore Bk., (*978-0-615-66119-3; 978-0-615-66120-9; 978-0-615-66121-6; 978-0-615-66122-3; 978-0-615-66123-0; 978-0-615-66124-7; 978-0-615-66125-4; 978-0-615-70631-3; 978-0-615-72179-8; 978-0-615-73636-5; 978-0-615-73900-7; 978-0-615-73998-4; 978-0-615-73999-1; 978-0-615-74001-0; 978-0-615-74002-7; 978-0-615-74004-1; 978-0-615-74005-8; 978-0-615-80172-8; 978-0-615-97703-4; 978-0-692-49285-7; 978-0-692-77875-3; 978-1-7335161) 80 Broad St. 5th Flr. Suite 503, New York, NY 10004 USA Tel 212-837-7818*
Dist(s): **CreateSpace Independent Publishing Platform.**

One Night Bks. *Imprint of* **WordWright.biz, Inc.**

One Odd Duck Bks., (*978-0-578-40036-5*) 122 Alden Ave., Chattanooga, TN 37405 USA Tel 325-668-7808
E-mail: jessalynclairem@gmail.com
Dist(s): **Ingram Content Group.**

One of a Kind Books, Incorporated *See* **Webster Henrietta Publishing**

One Part Rain, (*978-0-692-79233-9*) 340 E. 4380 N., PROVO, UT 84604 USA Tel 801-420-8087.

One Peace Bks., Inc., (*978-0-9785084; 978-1-935548; 978-1-944937; 978-1-64273*) 43-32 22nd St. #204, Long Island City, NY 11101 USA (SAN 850-7430) Tel 718-482-9100; Fax: 718-482-9101
E-mail: mcguire@onepeacebooks.com
Web site: http://www.onepeacebooks.com
Dist(s): **SCB Distributors.**

One Pink Rose, (*978-0-9722991*) 111921 Rawson Rd., Red Bluff, CA 96080 USA
E-mail: pinkwhirlwind@cablespeed.com; squallsknight@yahoo.com
Web site: http://www.darkfedora.com.

One Rib Pubns., (*978-0-9722625; 978-0-9746191; 978-1-944414*) Orders Addr.: 1811 NW 51st St., Fort

Lauderdale, FL 33309 USA Tel 954-489-0141; Edit Addr.: PMB 826, 2001 NW 51st St., Ft. Lauderdale, FL 33309 USA.

1 Sleeve Publishing, (*978-0-9729153*) Orders Addr.: P.O. Box 1865, North Mankato, MN 56002-1865 USA; Edit Addr.: 442 Belgrade Ave., No. 13, North Mankato, MN 56003 USA
E-mail: onesleeve@hotmail.com.

One Source Publishing, LLC, (*978-0-9779374*) 63 Gates St, White River Junction, VT 05001 USA Fax: 802-295-5338
E-mail: hphipps@onesourcefg.com.

One Too Tree Publishing, (*978-0-9820781*) 106 Calendar Ct., No. 108, La Grange, IL 60525-2325 USA (SAN 857-1732)
E-mail: publisher@onetootree.com
Web site: http://www.OneTooTree.com.

One True Faith (Religion & Spirituality) *Imprint of* **Speedy Publishing LLC**

One Voice Recordings, (*978-0-9708022*) 16835 Halper St., Encino, CA 91436 USA Tel 818-501-8145 (phone/fax)
E-mail: ddavies858@aol.com.

One Way Bks., (*978-0-9800451; 978-1-936459*) Div. of Waht About You?, Inc., 2269 S. Univ. Dr. #330, Fort Lauderdale, FL 33324 USA Tel 954-680-9095
Web site: http://www.OneWayBooks.org
Dist(s): **MyiLibrary**
Send The Light Distribution LLC
ebrary, Inc.

One Way Street, Incorporated *See* **Creative Ministry Solutions**

O'Neal, Carolyn, (*978-0-9966878*) 708 Acorn Ln., Charlottesville, VA 22903 USA Tel 434-882-0362
E-mail: carolynoneal@comcast.net
Web site: http://authorcarolynoneal.com/.

O'neal Publishing, (*978-0-615-49338-1; 978-0-9851318; 978-0-9972555; 978-0-9984748*) 2594 Pinewood Ln., Layton, UT 84040 USA Tel 8015445045
E-mail: cindymhogan@yahoo.com
Dist(s): **Brigham Distribution**
CreateSpace Independent Publishing Platform.

OneHope, (*978-1-890525; 978-1-931940; 978-1-59480; 978-1-63049; 978-1-64653*) 600 SW 3rd St., Pompano Beach, FL 33060-6936 USA Toll Free: 800-448-2425
E-mail: andreadragotas@onehope.net
Dist(s): **Whitaker Hse.**

ONeill, Gene & Assoc., (*978-0-9747797*) 10163 Potter Rd., Des Plaines, IL 60016 USA.

O'Neill, Hugh & Assocs., (*978-0-9675919; 978-0-615-76348-4*) Orders Addr.: P.O. Box 1297, Nevada City, CA 95959 USA Tel 530-265-4196; Edit Addr.: 227 Prospect St., Nevada City, CA 95959 USA
E-mail: info@bydb.com
Web site: http://www.bydb.com
Dist(s): **CreateSpace Independent Publishing Platform.**

O'Neill, Jan, (*978-0-9746409*) 5681 Rives Junction Rd., Jackson, MI 49201-9413 USA.

ONeill, Robert L. , (*978-1-7327613*) 437 W. 46th St. No. 4fw, New York, NY 10036 USA Tel 646-431-0956
E-mail: robloneill@aol.com.

O'Neill-Sheehan, Elizabeth, (*978-0-692-69931-7; 978-0-692-76666-8; 978-0-692-76678-1*) 30 Vreeland Ave, East Longmeadow, MA 01028 USA Tel 413-519-5393.

OneLight Publishing, (*978-0-9909270*)
E-mail: JOSHGOTTSEGEN@ME.COM
Web site: http://www.onelightstudios.com.

OneLight Studios *See* **OneLight Publishing**

OneMoreWord Bks., (*978-1-937533; 978-1-62456*) P.O. Box 165, New Philadelphia, OH 44663 USA
Web site: http://HollyLisle.com.

OneShare Educational Pr., (*978-0-9788438*) 3450 Third St. Bldg. 1-D, San Francisco, CA 94124 USA (SAN 851-7487) Tel 415-777-1777; Fax: 415-777-1677; Toll Free: 888-777-6919
Web site: http://www.oneshare.com.

Oneworld Pubns. (GBR) (*978-1-85168; 978-1-78074; 978-1-78607*) *Dist. by* **S and S Inc.**

Oni Pr., Inc., (*978-0-9667127; 978-1-929998; 978-1-932664; 978-1-934964; 978-1-62010*) 1305 SE Martin Luther King Jr. Blvd., Suite A, Portland, OR 97214 USA Tel 503-233-1377; Fax: 503-233-1477; *Imprints:* Lion Forge (LionFrgl)
E-mail: joe@onipress.com
Web site: http://www.onipress.com
Dist(s): **Diamond Comic Distributors, Inc.**
Simon & Schuster, Inc.

Onion River Pr., (*978-0-9657144; 978-0-9976458; 978-1-949066*) 21 Essex Way No. 407, Essex Junction, VT 05452 USA (SAN 990-1736) Tel 802-872-7111 (phone/fax)
E-mail: michael@phoenixbooks.biz; rachelf@phoenixbooks.biz
Web site: http://www.onionriverpress.com; www.phoenixbooks.biz.

ONLY1EARTH, LLC, (*978-0-9763354*) 3146 The Alameda Suite 7, San Jose, CA 95126 USA
E-mail: only1earthinc@gmail.com
Web site: http://www.theturtlekey.com.

Onondaga Hill Publishing, (*978-0-9794908*) 4586 Bloomsbury Dr., Syracuse, NY 13215 USA Tel 315-420-3025
E-mail: mdunn@imsolv.com; matthew@matthewdunn.net
Web site: http://www.matthewdunn.net
Dist(s): **BookBaby.**

Onstage Publishing, LLC, (*978-0-9700752; 978-0-9753367; 978-0-9790857*) Orders Addr.: 190 Lime Quarry Rd., Suite 106 J, Madison, AL 35758 USA Tel 256-461-0661; Fax: 256-461-0661
E-mail: onstage123@knology.net
Web site: http://www.onstagepublishing.com.

ONTRAK, (*978-0-9765502*) P.O. Box 205, Bethel, CT 06801-0153 USA Do not confuse with Ontrak in Yorba Linda, CA
E-mail: plumtrees@snet.net.

Onwuemene Publishing Group, (*978-1-948960*) 8311 Brier Creek Pkwy, Raleigh, NC 27617 USA Tel 919-695-3847
E-mail: opubgroup@gmail.com
Web site: opubgroup.com.

Onyx Pubns., (*978-0-9702628*) 2002 Tioga Pass Way, Antioch, CA 94531 USA Do not confuse with Onyx Publications, Inglewood, CA
E-mail: onyxpub04@aol.com.

ooli & tooli llc, (*978-0-9987126*) 65 crest Dr. N., cresskill, NJ 07626 USA Tel 551-206-5577; Fax: 551-206-5577
E-mail: pollak.ora@gmail.com
Web site: ooliandtooli.com.

Ooligan Pr., (*978-1-932010; 978-1-947845*) Div. of Portland State Univ., Dept. of English, Orders Addr.: Dept. of English Portland State Univ. P.O. Box 751, Portland, OR 97207 USA Tel 503-725-9410; Fax: 503-725-3561; Edit Addr.: 630 SW Mill St., 97201, Rm. Nh405, Portland, OR 97201 USA
E-mail: ooligan@ooliganpress.pdx.edu; agaterud@pdx.edu
Web site: http://www.ooliganpress.pdx.edu; http://www.publishing.pdx.edu
Dist(s): **Ingram Publisher Services.**

OPA Author Services, (*978-0-911041*) Div. of Optimum Performance Associates, 777 W. Chandler Blvd., No. 1322, Chandler, AZ 85225-2511 USA (SAN 254-9255) Tel 480-275-5270; 480-393-1646 (phone/fax)
Web site: http://www.opaauthorservices.com; http://www.opapublishing.com
Dist(s): **OPA Publishing & Distributing.**

OPA Publishing *See* **OPA Author Services**

Opacity, Inc., (*978-0-615-14266-1*) 7086 SW Iron Horse St., Wilsonville, OR 97070 USA
Dist(s): **Lulu Pr., Inc.**

Open Arms Publishing, (*978-0-9770841*) 607 Knob Ct., Fayetteville, NC 28303 USA Tel 910-258-3941
E-mail: sallymander66@earthlink.net; thoglenm@yahoo.com
Web site: http://www.oaim.net.

Open Bk. Publishing, (*978-0-9719167; 978-0-9740321; 978-1-932621*) Rte. 2, Box 2607, Birch Tree, MO 65438 USA Tel 573-292-3368; Fax: 573-292-8115 Do not confuse with Open Book Publising Company in Huntington beach, CA
E-mail: lfann@socket.net; ifann@socket.net
Web site: http://www.openbookpublishing.com.

Open Bk. Publishing Co., (*978-0-9753349*) P.O. Box 3602, Huntington Beach, CA 92649 USA Tel 714-264-7284; Fax: 714-846-6782 Do not confuse with Open Book Publishing in Birch Tree, MO
E-mail: k.cutt@verizon.net
Web site: http://www.openbookpublishingcompany.com.

†Open Court, (*978-0-8126; 978-0-87548; 978-0-89688; 978-0-912050; 978-0-8126-9956-2*) Div. of S R A/McGraw-Hill, 220 E. Daniel Dale Rd., DeSoto, TX 75115 USA Fax: 972-228-1982; Toll Free: 888-772-4543; 800-442-9685 (orders)
Web site: https://www.sraonline.com
Dist(s): **Libros Sin Fronteras**
Publishers Group West (PGW)
SRA/McGraw-Hill; *CIP.*

Open Court Publishing Co., (*978-0-8126; 978-0-87548; 978-0-89688; 978-0-912050*) Div. of Carus Publishing Co., Orders Addr.: c/o Publishers Group West, 1700 Fourth St., Berkeley, CA 94710 USA Fax: 510-528-3444; Toll Free: 800-788-3123; Edit Addr.: 70 E. Lake St. Ste. 300, Chicago, IL 60601-5945 USA Toll Free: 800-815-2280
E-mail: opencourt@caruspub.com
Web site: http://www.opencourtbooks.com
Dist(s): **Follett School Solutions**
MyiLibrary
Publishers Group West (PGW).

Open Door Pr., (*978-1-942264*) 42299 Chisolm Trail, Murrieta, CA 92562 USA Tel 951-461-9072
E-mail: khales@me.com
Web site: www.opendoor-press.com
Dist(s): **Greenleaf Book Group.**

Open Door Publishers, Inc., (*978-0-9841721; 978-1-937138*) 2373 Rte. 9, Mechanicville, NY 12118 USA (SAN 858-625X) Tel 518-899-2097
E-mail: adamiszyn@hotmail.com; ladean@opendoorpublishers.com
Web site: http://www.ladeanwarner.com; http://opendoorpublishers.com/.

Open Gate Publishing, (*978-0-9717036; 978-1-937195; 978-1-950641*) Div. of Open Gate Sangha, Inc., Orders Addr.: P.O. Box 112107, Campbell, CA 95011-2107 USA; Edit Addr.: 1299 Del Mar Ave., Suite 200, San Jose, CA 95128-3548 USA
E-mail: jerilyn@adyashanti.org
Web site: http://www.adyashanti.org
Dist(s): **New Leaf Distributing Co., Inc.**

Open Gate Sangha *See* **Open Gate Publishing**

Open Hand Publishing, LLC, (*978-0-940880*) P.O. Box 20207, Greensboro, NC 27420 USA (SAN 219-6174) Tel 336-292-8585; Fax: 336-292-8588
E-mail: info@openhand.com
Web site: http://www.openhand.com.

Open Heaven Pubns., (*978-0-9752622*) P.O. Box 457, Moravian Falls, NC 28654 USA
Web site: http://www.garyoates.com.

Open Mind Pr., (*978-0-9755157*) P.O. Box 1338, Garden Grove, CA 92844 USA Tel 714-322-3049 Do not confuse with Open Mind Press in Garner, NC
E-mail: openmindpress@albalagh.net
Web site: http://www.openmindpress.com.

Open Pages Publishing, (*978-0-9785937*) Orders Addr.: P.O. Box 420788, Houston, TX 77242 USA (SAN 851-0822); Edit Addr.: 3130 Walnut Bend Ln., Unit No. 317, Houston, TX 77042-4778 USA
E-mail: goodstory@openpagespublishing.com.

Open Range Publishing, (*978-0-615-70962-8; 978-0-9956877-6-9*) 9415 Wolfe Pl., Highlands Ranch, CO 80129 USA Tel 303-346-8483
Dist(s): **CreateSpace Independent Publishing Platform.**

Open Road Integrated Media, Inc., (*978-1-58586; 978-0-7592; 978-1-936317; 978-1-4532; 978-1-61756; 978-0-9832929; 978-1-937624; 978-1-937957; 978-1-938582; 978-0-615-65097-5; 978-1-62467; 978-1-4804; 978-1-4976; 978-1-5040*) 180 Varick St. Suite 816, New York, NY 10014 USA Tel 212-691-0900; Fax: 212-691-0901; 345 Hudson St., Suite 6C, New York, NY 10014 Tel 212-691-0900; Fax: 212-691-0901; *Imprints:* Open Road Young Readers (OPEN ROAD YOUN); Open Road Media E-riginal (OpenRdMedE-rig)
E-mail: acolvin@openroadmedia.com
Web site: http://www.openroadmedia.com
Dist(s): **Children's Plus, Inc.**
Follett School Solutions
Independent Pubs. Group
Ingram Publisher Services
MyiLibrary.

Open Road Media E-riginal *Imprint of* **Open Road Integrated Media, Inc.**

Open Road Young Readers *Imprint of* **Open Road Integrated Media, Inc.**

Open Spaces Publishing (Rupen), LLC, (*978-0-9768752; 978-0-9846494*) 1411 Timberlake Circle, Richardson, TX 75080 USA
E-mail: chistinerhoden@att.net.

Open Suitcase, (*978-0-9985496*) 461 Wildwood Dr., St. Augustine, FL 32086-2903 USA Tel 352-316-2355
E-mail: Myopensuitcase@gmail.com
Web site: Myopensuitcase.com.

Open Texture, (*978-0-9742391; 978-1-933900*) 9457 S. Univ. Blvd. #409, Highlands Ranch, CO 80126 USA Toll Free: 866-546-6459 (phone/fax)
E-mail: sales@opentexture.com
Web site: http://www.opentexture.com.

Open Vision Entertainment Corp., (*978-0-9721825*) 48 Summer St., Stoneham, MA 02180 USA Tel 781-438-7939; Fax: 781-438-8115
Web site: http://www.open-visions.com
Dist(s): **Fell, Frederick Pubs., Inc.**

Open Water Pr., (*978-1-7324597*) 31 Greenlawn Dr, Fairfield, CT 06825 USA Tel 860-917-7424
E-mail: thectwebbers@optonline.net.

Open Window Publishing, (*978-0-9798505*) P.O. Box 1436, Clarkston, MI 48347-1436 USA (SAN 854-5642).

Openvein, (*978-0-9764033*) 3760 SE Morrison St., Portland, OR 97214-3210 USA
Web site: http://www.openvein.com/.

Oppenheim Toy Portfolio, Inc., (*978-0-9664823; 978-0-9721050*) 40 E. Ninth St., Suite 14M, New York, NY 10003 USA (SAN 255-2175) Tel 212-598-0502; Fax: 212-598-9709
E-mail: stephanie@toyportfolio.com
Web site: http://www.toyportfolio.com
Dist(s): **Brodart Co.**

Oppenlander Enterprises LLC, (*978-0-9977800*) 4110 E Morningside Dr., Bloomington, IN 47408 USA Tel 812-391-6310
E-mail: annette.oppenlander@yahoo.com
Web site: annetteoppenlander.com.

Opportune Independent Publishing Co., (*978-0-9965694; 978-1-945532; 978-1-970079; 978-1-63616*) 113 Live Oak St, Houston, TX 77003 USA Tel 832-263-1700; 832-792-8269
E-mail: info@opportunepublishing.com
Web site: www.opportunepublishing.com.

Opposable Thumb Pr., (*978-0-9786570*) P.O. Box 409107, Chicago, IL 60640 USA
E-mail: Dawn@opposablethumbpress.com
Web site: http://opposablethumbpress.com.

Options Galore, (*978-0-9801426*) 22890 S. Woodland Rd., Suite 100, Shaker Heights, OH 44122 USA Tel 216-965-8599.

Optiview Publishing, (*978-0-9723066*) 7725 Martin Mill Pike, Knoxville, TN 37920 USA
E-mail: mmediajohn@ao.com
Web site: http://www.optiviewpubs.com.

OPUS II Bks., (*978-0-9796210*) Orders Addr.: 1216 Purple Sage Loop, Castle Rock, CO 80104 USA (SAN 853-9367) Tel 720-371-1872
E-mail: egualberto@opusiibooks.com
Web site: http://www.opusiibooks.com.

Oracle Institute Pr., LLC, The, (*978-0-9773929; 978-1-937465*) Div. of The Oracle Institute, Orders Addr.: 88 Oracle Way, Independence, VA 24348 USA (SAN 257-4780) Tel 276-773-3308
E-mail: Laura@TheOracleInstitute.org; Eric@TheOracleInstitute.org
Web site: http://www.TheOracleInstitute.org
Dist(s): **Ingram Content Group**
New Leaf Distributing Co., Inc.

Orage Publishing, (*978-0-9740901*) 1460 Wren Ct., Punta Gorda, FL 33950 USA Tel 941-639-6144
E-mail: ntoupsschmitt@comcast.net.

Orange County Historical Society, Inc., (*978-1-932547*) 130 Caroline St., Orange, VA 22960 USA Tel 540-672-5366 (Wednesday afternoon)
E-mail: info@orangecohist.org
Web site: http://www.orangecohist.org.

Orange County Publishing, (*978-0-9661598; 978-0-9789972; 978-1-7326619*) Orders Addr.: P.O. Box 487, Middletown, NY 10940 USA; Edit Addr.: 4417 Edson Ave., Bronx, NY 10466 USA Tel 917-306-7244 (cell)
E-mail: ikebezi@juno.com.

Orange Day Media, (*978-0-615-98797-2; 978-0-9905750*) 4319 S. Ridgewood Ave., Port Orange, FL 32127 USA Tel 386-235-9056
Dist(s): **CreateSpace Independent Publishing Platform.**

Orange Frazer Pr., (*978-0-9619637; 978-1-882203; 978-1-933197; 978-1-939710; 978-1-949248*) Orders Addr.: P.O. Box 214, Wilmington, OH 45177 USA (SAN 245-9299)
E-mail: ofrazer@erinet.com
Web site: http://www.orangefrazer.com
Dist(s): **Partners Bk. Distributing, Inc.**

Orange Hat Publishing, (*978-1-937165; 978-1-943331; 978-1-948365; 978-1-64538*) 259 S. St. Suite B, Waukesha, WI 53186 USA Tel 414-212-5477; *Imprints:* TEN16 Press (MYID_F_TEN16 P)
E-mail: Shannon@orangehatpublishing.com
Web site: www.orangehatpublishing.com; www.tinyspoonpress.com; www.ten16press.com.

Orange, Michael Nicholas, (*978-0-9758877*) Orders Addr.: P.O. Box 236, Half Moon Bay, CA 94019 USA; Edit Addr.: 646 Filbert St., Half Moon Bay, CA 94019-2112 USA.

Orange Ocean Pr., (*978-1-885021*) 127 Bennett Ave., Long Beach, CA 90803-2935 USA; *Imprints:* Tangerine Tide (Tang Tide)
E-mail: nextmag@aol.com.

Orange Spot Publishing, (*978-0-9785191*) P.O. Box 224, Freeland, WA 98249 USA
Web site: http://www.pugetsoundbackyardbirds.com.

OrangeFoot Publishing Co., (*978-0-9760651*) P.O. Box 3694, Pittsburgh, PA 15230-3694 USA
E-mail: orangefootpublishing@zoominternet.net; info@orangefootpublishing.com.

Oratia Media (NZL) (*978-1-877514; 978-0-473-17634-1; 978-0-947506*) *Dist. by* **UH Pr.**

Orb Bks. *Imprint of* **Doherty, Tom Assocs., LLC**

Orbis Publications, Incorporated *See* **Bilingual Dictionaries, Inc.**

Orbit, Div. of Hachette Book Group, 237 Park Ave., New York, NY 10017 USA; *Imprints:* Yen Press (YenOr)
Dist(s): **Blackstone Audio, Inc.**
Hachette Bk. Group
MyiLibrary.

Orca Bk. Pubs. (CAN) (*978-0-920501; 978-1-55143; 978-1-55469; 978-1-4598*) *Dist. by* **Orca Bk Pub.**

Orca Bk. Pubs. USA, (*978-0-920501; 978-1-55143; 978-1-55469*) Orders Addr.: P.O. Box 468, Custer, WA 98240-0468 USA (SAN 630-9674) Tel 250-380-1229; Fax: 250-380-1892; Toll Free: 800-210-5277
E-mail: orca@orcabook.com
Web site: http://www.orcabook.com
Dist(s): **Children's Plus, Inc.**

Orchard Bks. *Imprint of* **Scholastic Library Publishing**

Orchard Bks. *Imprint of* **Scholastic, Inc.**

Orchard Books *See* **Healing Heart's Publishing Co.**

Orchard House Press *See* **Blue Forge Pr.**

Orchard Pr. *Imprint of* **Point Publishing**

Orchid Isle Publishing Co., (*978-1-887916*) 131 Halai St., Hilo, HI 96720 USA.

Orchid Pr. (THA) (*978-974-8299; 978-974-8304; 978-974-86220; 978-974-87426; 978-974-89229; 978-974-87356; 978-974-89212; 978-974-89218; 978-974-89219; 978-974-89271; 978-974-89272; 978-974-524*) *Dist. by* **Natl Bk Netwk.**

Orchid Publishing Co., (*978-0-9740898*) 14906 SW 104 St., Miami, FL 33196 USA.

Orchid Publishing, Inc., (*978-0-9831641; 978-0-9838325*) 333 N. Michigan Ave. Suite 222, Chicago, IL 60601 USA Tel 312-332-7200
E-mail: efimova@russianpointe.com.

Oregon Ctr. for Applied Science, Inc., (*978-1-933898*) 260 E. 11th Ave., Eugene, OR 97401-3291 USA (SAN 850-5284) Toll Free: 888-349-5472
E-mail: orcas@orcasinc.com
Web site: http://www.orcasinc.com.

Oregon State Univ. Extension Service, (*978-1-931979*) Extension & Station Communications 422 Kerr Administration, Corvallis, OR 97331 USA Tel 541-737-0807; Fax: 541-737-0817
Web site: http://extension.oregonstate.edu/eesc/.

†Oregon State Univ. Pr., (*978-0-87071*) 121 The Valley Library, Corvallis, OR 97331 USA (SAN 202-8328) Tel 541-737-3166; 541-737-4620; Fax: 541-737-3170
E-mail: osu.press@oregonstate.edu
Web site: http://osupress.oregonstate.edu/
Dist(s): **American Society of Civil Engineers**
Chicago Distribution Ctr.
Partners Bk. Distributing, Inc.
University of Arizona Pr.
Univ. of Oklahoma Pr.; *CIP.*

O'Reilly & Associates, Incorporated *See* **O'Reilly Media, Inc.**

O'Reilly Media, Inc., (*978-0-937175; 978-1-56592; 978-3-89721; 978-3-930673; 978-4-900900; 978-0-596; 978-4-87311; 978-1-60033; 978-1-4493; 978-1-4919; 978-1-4920; 978-1-4571; 978-1-0981*) Orders Addr.: 1005 Gravenstein Hwy. N., Sebastopol, CA 95472 USA (SAN 658-5973) Fax: 707-829-0104; Toll Free: 800-998-9938; Edit Addr.: 10 Fawcett St. Ste. 4, Cambridge, MA 02138-1175 USA Toll Free:

800-775-7731; 4 Castle St, Farnham, GU9 7HR Tel 01252 71 17 76; Fax: 01252 73 42 11
E-mail: order@oreilly.com; information@oreilly.co.uk; nuts@ora.com; isbn-info@oreilly.com
Web site: http://www.oreilly.com; http://www.editions-oreilly.fr; http://oreilly.co.uk; http://oreilly.com.tw; http://www.ora.com; http://www.oreilly.fr/; http://www.oreilly.com.cn/
Dist(s): **CreateSpace Independent Publishing Platform**
Ebsco Publishing
Follett School Solutions
Ingram Publisher Services
MyiLibrary
Wiley, John & Sons, Inc.

Oren Village, LLC, *(978-0-9777272)* P.O. Box 1111, Worthington, OH 43085 USA Tel 614-937-8513
E-mail: author@alanstjean.com
Web site: http://www.alanstjean.com.

Orenda Pr., LLC, *(978-0-9907453; 978-0-9967920)* P.O. Box 1445, Cedar Park, TX 78630 USA Tel 512-961-0531
E-mail: kristen@orendapress.com
Web site: Orendapress.com.

Oresjozef Pubns., *(978-1-885566)* 167 Canton St., Randolph, MA 02368 USA Tel 781-961-5855; Toll Free: 617-851-0100
E-mail: ojozef@massed.net
Dist(s): **Educa Vision Inc.**
Haitiana Pubns., Inc.

Organ Buddies Inc., *(978-0-615-32940-6)* 110 Blue Ribbon Dr, North Wales, PA 19454 USA Tel 267-253-8462; Fax: 215-393-8464
E-mail: leedowning8@msn.com
Web site: www.organbuddies.com.

OrganWise Guys Inc., The, *(978-0-9648438; 978-1-931212; 978-0-9858048)* 450 Satellite Blvd. NE Suite M, Suwanee, GA 30024 USA Tel 770-844-8686; Fax: 770-844-6580; Toll Free: 800-786-1730 Do not confuse with Wellness, Inc., Boston, MA
E-mail: karen@organwiseguys.com
Web site: http://www.organwiseguys.com.

Orion Publishing Group, Ltd. (GBR) *(978-0-304; 978-0-460; 978-0-575; 978-0-7528; 978-1-85797; 978-1-85798; 978-1-85881; 978-1-86047; 978-1-84188; 978-1-84255; 978-1-905619; 978-1-4091; 978-1-78062; 978-0-85782; 978-1-4072; 978-1-4719; 978-1-78771-955-2) Dist. by* **HachBkGrp.**

Orion Publishing Group, Ltd. (GBR) *(978-0-304; 978-0-460; 978-0-575; 978-0-7528; 978-1-85797; 978-1-85798; 978-1-85881; 978-1-86047; 978-1-84188; 978-1-84255; 978-1-905619; 978-1-4091; 978-1-78062; 978-0-85782; 978-1-4072; 978-1-4719; 978-1-78771-955-2) Dist. by* **Trafalgar.**

Orion Society, The, *(978-0-913098; 978-0-578-62162-3)* Orders Addr.: 187 Main St., Great Barrington, MA 01230-1601 USA (SAN 204-0182) Tel 413-528-4422; Fax: 413-528-0676; Toll Free: 888-909-6568
E-mail: gagne@orionmagazine.org
Web site: http://www.orionmagazine.org.

Orion Wellspring, Inc., *(978-0-9794614)* 20 Blaine St., Seattle, WA 98109 USA Tel 206-931-4656; Fax: 206-374-2149
E-mail: tom.masters@orionwellspring.com; info@orionwellspring.com
Web site: http://www.orionwellspring.com.

Orion-Cosmos, *(978-0-9752725)* 3609 Candleknoll Cir., San Antonio, TX 78244 USA
E-mail: customerservice@orion-cosmos.com
Web site: http://www.orion-cosmos.com.

Orison Pubs., *(978-0-9763800; 978-0-9827944; 978-1-945169)* P.O. Box 188, Grantham, PA 17027 USA
E-mail: marsha@orisonpublishers.com
Web site: http://www.discovertheauthor.com; http://www.orisonpublishers.com
Dist(s): **Independently Published**
Ingram Publisher Services
Pennsylvania State Univ. Pr.

Ormond, Jennifer, *(978-0-9792010)* 77 Pkwy., Quincy, MA 02169 USA
E-mail: jennormond@gmail.com
Web site: http://www.jenniferormond.com.

Orndee Omnimedia, Inc., *(978-0-9774260; 978-0-9822229)* 36 West 37th St. Penthouse, New York, NY 10018 USA Tel 212-203-0363
E-mail: Publishing@Orndee.com
Web site: http://www.Orndee.com.

ORO Editions, *(978-0-9746800; 978-0-9774672; 978-0-9793801; 978-0-9795395; 978-0-9814628; 978-0-9820607; 978-0-9819857; 978-0-9826226; 978-1-935935; 978-1-941806; 978-1-939621; 978-1-940743; 978-1-943532; 978-1-951541)* Orders Addr.: P.O. Box 150338, San Rafael, CA 94915 USA Tel 415-663-0678; Fax: 415-457-3650; Edit Addr.: 31 Commercial Blvd., Suite F, Novato, CA 94945 USA Tel 415-883-3300; Fax: 415-883-3309; *Imprints*: Goff Books (GoffBks)
E-mail: gordon@oroeditions.com; christy@oroeditions.com; info@oroeditions.com
Web site: http://www.oroeditions.com
Dist(s): **D.A.P./Distributed Art Pubs.**
Ingram Publisher Services
Publishers Group West (PGW).

Oron's, *(978-1-947095)* 30 Chapin Rd, Unit 1201, Pine Brook, NJ 07058-9392 USA Tel 973-740-0095
E-mail: ohagit@gmail.com.

Orpen Pr. (IRL) *(978-1-871305; 978-1-84218; 978-1-909895; 978-1-78605; 978-1-909518) Dist. by* **Dufour.**

Orr Bks., *(978-0-9800611; 978-0-9827764; 978-0-9851760)* 608 Seitz St., Easton, PA 18042-6544 USA Tel 610-258-5479
E-mail: derek@beachfrontpress.com; peter@beachfrontpress.com
Web site: http://www.orrbooks.net; http://www.beachfrontpress.com.

Ortells, Alfredo Editorial S.L. (ESP) *(978-84-7189) Dist. by* **Continental Bk.**

Ortiz, Enrique Publishing, *(978-0-615-25622-1; 978-0-615-25637-5; 978-0-615-26124-9; 978-0-578-00134-0; 978-0-578-00135-7)* 1538 Bullbush Way, Oviedo, FL 32765 USA
Dist(s): **Lulu Pr., Inc.**

Osage Bend Publishing Co., *(978-0-9626245; 978-1-58389)* 213 Belair Dr., Jefferson City, MO 65109 USA Tel 573-635-5580; Toll Free: 888-243-9772
E-mail: OBPC@Socket.net
Dist(s): **Follett School Solutions.**

Osanto Univ. Pr. *Imprint of* **Benjamin Franklin Pr.**

Osborne Enterprises Publishing, *(978-0-932117)* P.O. Box 255, Port Townsend, WA 98368 USA (SAN 242-7567) Tel 360-385-1200; Toll Free: 800-246-3255 (orders only)
E-mail: jpo@olympus.net
Web site: http://www.jerryosborne.com.

Osborne Pr., *(978-1-928856)* Div. of David M. Osborne, Inc., 16726 Comstock, Livonia, MI 48154 USA Tel 734-464-7002; Fax: 734-464-6837
E-mail: osborne@mich.com
Web site: http://www.mich.com/~osborne.

Osborne/McGraw-Hill *See* **McGraw-Hill Osborne**

Oscar, Erica, *(978-0-9747262)* 20424 Packard, Detroit, MI 48234 USA.

O'Shea, Ellen Storyteller, *(978-1-7321023)* 751 Old Eaglemount Rd., Port Townsend, WA 98368 USA Tel 360-301-1662
E-mail: elleno@peak.org
Web site: Ellenosheastoryteller.com.

Osherbert Bks., LLC, *(978-0-9885461)* P.O. Box 1591, Gig Harbor, WA 98335 USA Tel 253-651-8997
E-mail: seshell@gmail.com.

Osmosis, LLC, *(978-0-9727886; 978-0-9816281)* 8 Findlay Ave., Hartsdale, NY 10530-2613 USA Tel 914-328-8898; Fax: 914-328-1124; Toll Free: 866-676-6747
E-mail: osmosis@earthlink.net
Web site: http://www.learningbyosmosis.com; http://www.osmosis.tv.

Osprey *Imprint of* **Bloomsbury Publishing USA**

Osprey Pr., *(978-0-9673711)* 2107 Ibis Dr., Buffalo, MN 55313 USA Tel 763-682-4558 Do not confuse with companies with the same or similar names in St. Johnsbury, VT, Wiscasset, ME
E-mail: ospreypress@charter.net
Web site: http://www.planetearthhome.com
Dist(s): **Random Hse., Inc.**

Osteogenesis Imperfecta Foundation, *(978-0-9642189)* 804 W. Diamond Ave., Suite 210, Gaithersburg, MD 20878 USA Tel 301-947-0083; Fax: 301-947-0456; Toll Free: 800-981-2663
E-mail: bonelink@oif.org
Web site: http://www.oif.org.

Ostermeyer Photography, *(978-0-9794228; 978-0-615-74538-1; 978-0-692-02001-2)* 1813 Country Brook Ln., Allen, TX 75002 USA Tel 972-542-7065
E-mail: tim@ostermeyer-photography.com
Web site: http://www.ostermeyer-photography.com.

Ostrageous Publishing, *(978-0-9785144)* P.O. Box 2867, Hot Springs, AK 71914 USA Tel 501-525-4245.

Otago University Pr. (NZL) *(978-0-908569; 978-1-877133; 978-1-877276; 978-1-877372; 978-1-877578; 978-1-988531; 978-1-927322) Dist. by* **IPG Chicago.**

Otherside Pr. *Imprint of* **Crossroad Pr.**

Otis & Randolph Pr., *(978-0-9752516)* 1229 Bishop's Lodge Rd., Santa Fe, NM 87501 USA.

Otis, Beverly J., *(978-0-615-27994-7; 978-0-615-72483-6)* 1138 Oakhill St., Seffner, FL 33584 USA
Web site: http://www.beverlyotis.web.officelive.com.

Otis, Dorcas Marie *See* **Zion Publishing**

Otter Falls Publishing, *(978-0-692-84835-7; 978-0-692-95401-0; 978-0-692-04557-2; 978-0-578-21284-5; 978-0-578-57496-7; 978-0-578-67954-9)* 2085 Bridgewater Blvd S, Cambridge, MN 55008 USA Tel 612-741-9185
E-mail: bbfellerer@yahoo.com.

Otter Run Bks. LLC, *(978-0-9760796)* 16965 Nicolet Rd., Townsend, WI 54175 USA Tel 715-276-6515 (phone/fax)
E-mail: kathiemarsh@yahoo.com
Web site: http://www.otterrunbooks.com.

Otter Track Pr., *(978-0-9848229; 978-0-9998070)* Div. of MRose Group, LLC, 103 Turtle Bend, Georgetown, TX 78628 USA Tel 251-752-2416.

Otter-Barry Bks. (GBR) *(978-1-910959; 978-1-913074) Dist. by* **IPG Chicago.**

OTTN Publishing, *(978-1-59556)* 16 Risler Street, Stockton, NJ 08559 USA Tel 609-397-4005; Fax: 609-397-4007
E-mail: jgallagher@ottnpublishing.com
Web site: http://www.ottnpublishing.com.

Otto PD, *(978-0-692-70958-0; 978-0-9981412)* 4801 Laguna Blvd #105-310, Elk Grove, CA 95758 USA Tel 408-836-8918; Toll Free: 408-836-8918
Dist(s): **CreateSpace Independent Publishing Platform.**

Ouattara, Issoufou *See* **International Development Ctr.**

Oui Love Bks. *Imprint of* **Odeon Livre**

Our Blueprint-A Recipe for Wellness, *(978-0-692-05847-3; 978-0-692-08757-2; 978-0-692-04442-1; 978-0-578-42078-3; 978-0-578-42357-9; 978-0-578-49451-7)* 1442 E. Lincoln Ave No. 310, Orange, CA 92865 USA Tel 714-910-5141
E-mail: TONY@ob4w.com; tonyisactive@gmail.com
Web site: www.ob4w.com
Dist(s): **CreateSpace Independent Publishing Platform.**

†Our Child Pr., *(978-0-9611872; 978-1-893516)* P.O. Box 4379, Philadelphia, PA 19118 USA (SAN 682-272X) Tel 610-308-8988
E-mail: ourchildpress@aol.com
Web site: http://www.ourchildpress.com; *CIP.*

Our Companions, Inc., *(978-0-9753257)* 84 N. Acoma Blvd., No. 100-33, Lake Havasu City, AZ 86403 USA Tel 928-486-4508.

Our Inspiring Stories Publishing Co., *(978-0-9995246)* 6983 Seabreeze Dr., Suite 100, Grand Prairie, TX 75054 USA Tel 682-554-1743
E-mail: sandraannwalters@gmail.com
Web site: www.ourispiringstories.com.

Our Kids Pr., *(978-0-9660884; 978-0-9860290)* Orders Addr.: P.O. Box 486, Bellingham, WA 98227 USA Tel 360-734-2335; Edit Addr.: 3804 Ridgemont Way, Bellingham, WA 98227 USA
Web site: ourkidspress.com.

Our Lady of Victory Schl., *(978-1-931555)* 103 E. Tenth Ave., Post Falls, ID 83854 USA Tel 208-773-7265; Fax: 208-773-1951
E-mail: lepanto@olvs.org
Web site: http://www.olvs.org.

Our Little Secret Pr., *(978-0-9720978)* 140 Timberlink Dr., Grand Island, NY 14072 USA.

Our Story Pubns., *(978-0-9765554)* P.O. Box 7514, Round Rock, TX 78683 USA Tel 512-663-1471
E-mail: nicoleeutsey@ourstorypublications.com
Web site: http://www.ourstorypublications.com.

Our Sunday Visitor, Publishing Div., *(978-0-87973; 978-0-9707756; 978-1-931709; 978-1-59276; 978-1-61278; 978-1-68192)* 200 Noll Plaza, Huntington, IN 46750 USA (SAN 202-8344) Tel 260-356-8400; Fax: 260-359-9117; 260-356-8472; Toll Free: 800-348-2440
E-mail: osvbooks@osv.com; ntopp@osv.com
Web site: http://www.osv.com
Dist(s): **Baker & Taylor International**
MyiLibrary
Spring Arbor Distributors, Inc.

Our World of Books *See* **Good Night Bks.**

OurRainbow Pr., LLC, *(978-0-9752860; 978-1-934214)* Orders Addr.: 2600 Penrick Dr., Marietta, GA 30064-1809 USA Tel 770-514-8794; Toll Free: 877-600-7323
E-mail: publisher@ourrainbow.com; ameadows@ourrainbow.com; anthony.meadows@gmail.com; sheila.meadows@gmail.com
Web site: http://www.ourrainbowpress.com; http://orpbooks.com.

Out of the Box, *(978-0-9726849)* P.O. Box 24234, Minneapolis, MN 55424 USA Tel 612-822-5151; Fax: 612-823-4164
E-mail: info@ootbooks.com
Web site: http://www.ootbooks.com
Dist(s): **Brodart Co.**
Follett School Solutions
Quality Bks., Inc.

Out of the Box Publishing, Inc., *(978-0-9664517; 978-0-9708554; 978-0-9716729; 978-1-932359)* 609 Bennett Rd., Dodgeville, WI 53533 USA (SAN 760-5269) Toll Free: 800-540-4201 Do not confuse with Out of the Box Publishing, Cincinnati, OH
E-mail: sales@otb-games.com; brad@otb-games.com
Web site: http://www.otb-games.com.

Out There Bks., *(978-0-9827906; 978-1-7353204)* 1324 Alta Vista Ave., Austin, TX 78704 USA Tel 512-577-7808.

Outcomes Unlimited Pr., Inc., *(978-0-925640)* P.O. Box 8013, Asheville, NC 28814-8497 USA
E-mail: drdossey@drdossey.com
Web site: http://www.drdossey.com.

Outdoor Originals LLC, *(978-0-9762971)* 1052 California Ave. W., Saint Paul, MN 55117 USA.

Outdoor Writing & Photography, Limited *See* **Visions Of Nature**

Outer Banks Pr., *(978-0-9713890; 978-0-9778924; 978-1-7326805)* Div. of OBBC, Inc., P.O. Box 2829, Kitty Hawk, NC 27949 USA (SAN 254-3958) Tel 252-261-0612; Toll Free Fax: 800-215-9648
E-mail: linda@outerbankspress.com
Web site: http://www.outerbankspress.com.

outerBks., *(978-0-692-37891-5; 978-0-692-43092-7; 978-0-692-70647-3; 978-0-692-92649-9)* 32 jazz way, mt laurel, NJ 08054 USA Tel 856-914-0850
E-mail: rkingsbury32@comcast.net
Web site: http://www.outerbooks.com.

OutFlow Publishing, *(978-1-7329995)* 929 Main St W., Valdese, NC 28690 USA Tel 828-874-4457
E-mail: allenking@outflowpublishing.com
Web site: www.outflowpublishing.com.

Outland Communications, LLC, *(978-0-9714102; 978-1-932820)* Orders Addr.: P.O. Box 534, Skaneateles, NY 13152 USA; Edit Addr.: 4022 Mill Rd., Skaneateles, NY 13152-9319 USA
Web site: http://www.outlandbooks.com.

Outlaw Bks., *(978-0-9656946)* 419 Centre St., Hereford, TX 79045 USA Tel 806-364-2838; Fax: 806-364-5522; Toll Free: 888-583-9408 Do not confuse with Outlaw Books, Bozeman, MT
Dist(s): **Hervey's Booklink & Cookbook Warehouse.**

Outlaw Pubns., *(978-1-886709)* Orders Addr.: P.O. Box 1424, Red Oak, TX 75154 USA Tel 972-504-6608; Edit Addr.: P.O. Box 3043, Desoto, TX 75115 USA.

Outlet Book Company, Incorporated *See* **Random Hse. Value Publishing**

Outlook Publishing, Inc., *(978-0-9711667; 978-0-9817755)* Orders Addr.: P.O. Box 278, Laurel, MT 59044 USA Tel 406-628-4412; Fax: 406-628-8260; Edit Addr.: 415 E. Main St., Laurel, MT 59044 USA
E-mail: publisher@laureloutlook.com
Web site: http://www.laureloutlook.com.

Outlook Words & Art, *(978-0-692-83201-1; 978-0-692-83667-5; 978-0-9986426; 978-0-9986593; 978-1-7320896)* 12057 Open Run Rd., Ellicott City, MD 21042 USA Tel 310-990-5529
E-mail: t.pryce@outlookco.com
Dist(s): **Diamond Comic Distributors, Inc.**
Independent Pubs. Group.

Outreach Publications *See* **DaySpring Cards**

Outrival Publishing, *(978-0-9885603)* P.O. Box 130345, Houston, TX 77219 USA Tel 832-878-6162; Fax: 713-861-1501
E-mail: kimpedigo@gmail.com.

Outside the Box Publishing, LLC, *(978-0-9817398)* 326 2nd St. No. 3, Brooklyn, NY 11215 USA Tel 202-905-3442
E-mail: info@otbpublishing.com; dax@daxdevlonross.com; daxdevlonross@gmail.com
Web site: http://www.otbpublishing.com
Dist(s): **Ingram Content Group.**

Outskirts Pr., Inc., *(978-0-9725874; 978-1-932672; 978-1-59800; 978-1-4327; 978-0-615-20388-1; 978-1-4787; 978-1-9772)* 10940 S. Parker Rd. - 515, Parker, CO 80134 USA (SAN 256-5420)
Web site: http://www.OutskirtsPress.com
Dist(s): **Aardvark Global Publishing**
Smashwords.

Outskirts Press, Incorporation *See* **Outskirts Pr., Inc.**

Ovation Bks., *(978-1-933538; 978-0-9790275; 978-0-9814534)* 2100 Kramer Ln., Suite 300, Austin, TX 78758 USA Tel 512-478-2028; Fax: 512-478-2117
E-mail: awillis@bookpros.com; sboulden@ovationbooks.net
Web site: http://www.bookpros.com; http://www.ovationbooks.net.

Over the Rainbow *Imprint of* **Pearn & Assocs. Inc.**

Over The Rainbow Bks. Publishing, *(978-0-9793882)* 1810 New Palm Way, No. 410, Boynton Beach, FL 33435 USA Tel 561-704-6581
E-mail: famuffy@aol.com.

Over the Rainbow Productions, *(978-0-9661330)* 1715 Rosedale, Suite B, Houston, TX 77004 USA Tel 713-523-1276; Fax: 713-526-0571
E-mail: apb3@prodigy.net
Web site: http://www.imneecie.com.

Overcup Pr., *(978-0-9834917; 978-1-7326103)* 4760 SE 58th Ave., Portland, OR 97206 USA Tel 503-453-0091
E-mail: pat@overcupbooks.com
Web site: www.overcupbooks.com
Dist(s): **SCB Distributors.**

Overdue Bks., *(978-0-9786850)* P.O. Box 259462, Madison, WI 53725 USA Do not confuse with Overdue Books in West Linn, OR
E-mail: theoverduebooks@yahoo.com.

Overhead Pr., LLC, *(978-0-9985067)* 18 Whitetail Crossing, Lunenburg, MA 01462 USA
E-mail: jaredperrine@hotmail.com.

Overlook Connection Pr., The, *(978-0-9633397; 978-1-892950; 978-1-62330)* Orders Addr.: P.O. Box 1934, Hiram, GA 30141 USA Tel 678-567-9777; Edit Addr.: 364 Valerie Cir., Hiram, GA 30141 USA
E-mail: overlookcn@aol.com
Web site: http://www.overlookconnection.com; http://www.overlookconnection.com
Dist(s): **Diamond Comic Distributors, Inc.**

Overlook Pr., The *Imprint of* **Abrams, Inc.**

Overmountain Pr., *(978-0-932807; 978-0-9644613; 978-1-57072; 978-1-935692)* P.O. Box 1261, Johnson City, TN 37605 USA (SAN 687-6641) Tel 423-926-2691; Fax: 423-232-1252; Toll Free: 800-992-2691 (orders only); *Imprints*: Silver Dagger Mysteries (Silver Dagger)
E-mail: beth@overmtn.com
Web site: http://www.silverdaggermysteries.com; http://www.overmountainpress.com
Dist(s): **Partners Pubs. Group, Inc.**

Overstreet, Mae *See* **Overstreet Pub. & Mktg.**

Overstreet Pub. & Mktg., *(978-0-9746253)* P.O. Box 3808, Yountville, CA 94599 USA
Web site: http://www.bettyoverstreet.com.

Overview Publishing, *(978-0-9760685)* 1081 Crown River Pkwy., McDonough, GA 30252 USA Tel 678-583-0898
E-mail: cindy@overviewpublishing.com
Web site: http://www.overviewpublishing.com
Dist(s): **Quality Bks., Inc.**

Owen, Jessica, 16 Via Tranquila, Rancho Santa Margarita, CA 92688 USA Tel 949-300-6702
E-mail: carolowen@coastalexec.com
Dist(s): **Ingram Content Group.**

Owen, Richard C. Pubs., Inc., *(978-0-913461; 978-1-57274; 978-1-878450)* P.O. Box 585, Katonah, NY 10536 USA (SAN 285-1814) Tel 914-232-3903; Fax: 914-232-3977; Toll Free: 800-336-5588 (orders); *Imprints*: Meet the Author (Meet Author); Books for Young Learners (Bks Yng Learn); Author at Work (Author at Work)
Web site: http://www.RCOwen.com.

Owens, David A., *(978-0-578-05417-9)* 4253 October Woods Dr., Antioch, TN 37013 USA.

Owens, Ralinda, *(978-0-9993228)* 5633 Tiger Trail, Fort Worth, TX 76126 USA Tel 817-800-5853
E-mail: ralindaowens@att.net.

Owensby, Legertha, *(978-0-9742789)* 6820 Chiffview Dr., No. E, Indianapolis, IN 46214 USA
E-mail: legethao@yahoo.com
Web site: http://earvino.tripod.com.

Owl About Books Publisher, Incorporated *See* **Owl About Bks. Pubs.**

Publisher Name Index

Owl About Bks. Pubs., *(978-1-937752)* 1632 Royalwood Cir., Joshua, TX 76058 USA Tel 682-553-9078; Fax: 817-558-8983
E-mail: owlaboutbooks@gmail.com
Web site: http://www.owlaboutbooks.com
Dist(s): **Ingram Content Group.**

Owl Creek Farm Bks. *Imprint of* **Owl Tree Pr.**

Owl Creek Media Ltd., *(978-1-60404)* 490 Trego Rd., Waverly, OH 45690 USA Tel 740-493-1939; Toll Free: 800-305-0339 Please leave a message
E-mail: james@owlcreekmedia.com
Web site: http://www.owlcreekmedia.com; http://www.localbookproject.com.

Owl Hollow Pr., *(978-1-945654; 978-1-945654-04-6)* 224 S. Main St. No. 452, Springville, UT 84663 USA Tel 703-597-4720
E-mail: exec.editor@owlhollowpress.com
Web site: https://owlhollowpress.com/.

Owl Hollow Publishing, *(978-0-9726826)* 13704 Lawrence 2187, Verona, MO 65769 USA Tel 417-498-6964
E-mail: zona@mo-net.com.

Owl of Minerva Press *See* **Minerva Bks.**

Owl Pals, *(978-0-9799196)* 10210 NE. 12th St. Unit C301, Bellevue, WA 98004 USA Tel 206-948-2629
Web site: http://www.owlpals.com.

Owl Room Pr., *(978-0-692-95930-5; 978-0-692-08784-8; 978-0-578-46643-9; 978-0-578-58923-7; 978-0-578-61915-6; 978-1-7351366)* 1630 15th Ave SW, Albany, OR 97321 USA Tel 541-223-3894
E-mail: RocketshipGD@yahoo.com
Dist(s): **CreateSpace Independent Publishing Platform.**

Owl Tree Pr., *(978-1-929424)* P.O. Box 292, Saint Helens, OR 97051 USA Tel 503-397-3667; Fax: 503-397-3684; *Imprints:* Owl Creek Farm Books (Owl Creek Farm Bks)
E-mail: jdnyberg@ados.com
Web site: http://www.owltreepress.com.

Owlkids Bks. Inc. (CAN) *(978-0-919872; 978-0-920775; 978-1-895688; 978-2-920660; 978-1-894379; 978-2-89579; 978-1-77147) Dist. by* **PerseuPGW.**

Oxbow Bks., Ltd. (GBR) *(978-0-946897; 978-1-900188; 978-1-84217; 978-1-78297; 978-1-78570) Dist. by* **CasemateAcad.**

Oxbow Bks., *(978-0-9771129)* 76 Presidio Dr., Novato, CA 94949 USA
E-mail: dchaller@horizoncable.com.

Oxfam Publishing (GBR) *(978-0-85598) Dist. by* **Stylus Pub VA.**

Oxford Museum Pr., *(978-1-930127)* 5790 Stillwell-Beckett Rd., Oxford, OH 45056 USA Tel 513-756-9386; Fax: 513-756-9123; Toll Free: 877-127-1941
E-mail: omp@oxfordmuseumpress.com
Web site: http://www.oxfordmuseumpress.com.

Oxford Univ. Pr. (GBR) *(978-0-19) Dist. by* **OUP.**

Oxford Univ. Pr., Inc., *(978-0-19; 978-0-87893; 978-1-60535)* Orders Addr.: 2001 Evans Rd., Cary, NC 27513 USA (SAN 202-5892) Tel 919-677-0977 (general voice); Fax: 919-677-1303 (customer service); Toll Free: 800-445-9714 (customer service - inquiry); 800-451-7556 (customer service - orders); Edit Addr.: 198 Madison Ave., New York, NY 10016-4314 USA (SAN 202-5884) Tel 212-726-6000 (general voice); Fax: 212-726-6440 (general fax)
E-mail: custserv@oup-usa.org; orders@oup-usa.org
Web site: http://www.oup.com/us
Dist(s): **Chicago Distribution Ctr.**
Children's Plus, Inc.
CreateSpace Independent Publishing Platform
Ebsco Publishing
Follett School Solutions
Hancock Hse. Pubs.
ISD
MyiLibrary
Oxford University Press USA - OSO
World Bank Pubns.
ebrary, Inc.

Oxfordshire Publishing Co., *(978-0-9745895)* 900 Lincoln Hwy., Box 180, East Mckeesport, PA 15035 USA Tel 412-823-1700
E-mail: blissman@pghmail.com.

Oyebanji, Adam, *(978-0-692-09941-4; 978-0-692-19443-0; 978-0-692-19444-7)* 4769 Wallingford St. 0, Pittsburgh, PA 15213 USA Tel 7736360268; *Imprints:* Andromeda Press (MYID_Q_ANDROME)
E-mail: adam@adam-alexander.net
Web site: adam-alexander.net
Dist(s): **Ingram Content Group.**

OZA.Inc.Co, *(978-1-7330602)* 2980 Brogans Bluff Dr., Colorado Springs, CO 80919 USA Tel 530-314-1766
E-mail: OZA_1@MSN.COM.

Ozark Mountain Publishing, Inc., *(978-0-9632776; 978-1-886940; 978-1-940265; 978-1-950608; 978-1-950639)* Orders Addr.: P.O. Box 754, Huntsville, AR 72740 USA Tel 479-738-2348; Fax: 479-738-2448; Toll Free: 800-935-0045 Do not confuse with Ozark Mountain Pubs., Springfield, MO
E-mail: nancy@ozarkmt.com
Web site: http://www.ozarkmt.com
Dist(s): **D.A.P./Distributed Art Pubs.**
Red Wheel/Weiser.

Ozark Publishing, *(978-1-56763; 978-1-59381)* P.O. Box 228, Prairie Grove, AR 72753 USA (SAN 298-4318) Tel 214-649-0188; Fax: 501-846-2853; Toll Free: 800-321-5671
E-mail: srg304@aol.com
Web site: http://www.ozarkpublishing.com
Dist(s): **Central Programs**
Gumdrop Bks.

Ozo Pr., *(978-1-946618)* 8098 Hollygrape Ln., Colorado Springs, CO 80927 USA Tel 719-323-1576
E-mail: stacysjensen@gmail.com
Web site: ozopress.com.

Ozone Publishing, Corp., *(978-0-9773285)* PMB 500, RR-8 Box 1995, Bayamon, PR 00956-9676 USA Tel 787-562-5200; Fax: 787-730-0987
E-mail: info@ozonepublishing.net
Web site: http://www.ozonepublishing.net.

Ozten, *(978-0-9752966)* 347 NW 87th St., Seattle, WA 98117 USA
E-mail: shout@ozten.com
Web site: http://www.ozten.com.

P. Anastasia, *(978-0-9862567; 978-0-9974485; 978-1-952425)* P.O. Box 12431, LEXINGTON, KY 40583 USA; *Imprints:* Jackal Moon Press (Jackal Moon)
E-mail: wolferene@gmail.com
Web site: www.fatesaflame.com; www.panastasia.com; www.FluorescenceBooks.com; www.DarkDiaryNovel.com.

P & P Publishing LLC, *(978-0-9797020)* 4957 Lakemont Blvd., SE, Suite C-4, No. 316, Bellevue, WA 98006 USA Tel 425-557-0257 Do not confuse with companies with the same or similar name in Frankermuth, MI, Warren, MI, Temple, TX, Wauwatosa, WI.

P & R Publishing, *(978-0-87552; 978-1-59638; 978-1-62995)* Orders Addr.: 1102 Marble Hill Rd., Harmony, Phillipsburg, NJ 08865 USA (SAN 658-1463) Tel 908-454-0505; Fax: 908-859-2390; Toll Free: 800-631-0094 Do not confuse with P & R Publishing Co. in Sioux Center, IA
E-mail: tara@prpbooks.com; jesse@prpbooks.com
Web site: http://www.prpbooks.com
Dist(s): **CLC Pubns.**
Faith Alive Christian Resources.

P C I Education, *(978-1-884074; 978-1-58804; 978-1-61975)* 4560 Lockhill-Selma, Suite 100, San Antonio, TX 78265-4270 USA Tel 210-377-1999; Fax: 210-377-1121; Toll Free Fax: 888-259-8284; Toll Free: 800-594-4263
E-mail: lboulet@pcieducation.com
Web site: http://www.pcieducation.com
Dist(s): **Attainment Co., Inc.**

P C I Educational Publishing *See* **P C I Education**

P.C. Pubns., *(978-0-9709123; 978-0-578-18965-9)* 22 Williams St., Batavia, NY 14020 USA Tel 716-343-2810 (phone/fax); 444 Ellicott St., Batavia, NY 14020
E-mail: patti.chadwick@juno.com
Web site: http://www.historyswomen.com.

p i kids *Imprint of* **Phoenix International Publications, Inc.**

P K I Ds, *(978-1-929524)* P.O. Box 5666, Vancouver, WA 98668 USA Tel 360-695-0293; Fax: 360-695-6941; Toll Free: 877-557-5437
E-mail: pkids@pkids.org
Web site: http://www.pkids.org.

P.O.W. (Pubns. of Worth), *(978-1-877898)* 2561 E. 1980 N., Layton, UT 84040-7928 USA.

PSI & Assocs., *(978-0-938261; 978-1-55993)* 9745 SW 125th Terr., Miami, FL 33176-4941 USA (SAN 659-834X).

P2 Publishing, *(978-0-9856336)* 10455 N. Central Expwy Suite 109-115, Dallas, TX 75231 USA Tel 214-223-0366
E-mail: pickleproductionspc@gmail.com
Web site: www.PiperandPickle.com.

P4K Publishing, *(978-0-9744570)* 5699 Kanan Rd., Suite 373, Agoura Hills, CA 91301 USA Tel 818-991-5764; Fax: 818-879-9646
E-mail: lori@prosperity4kids.com
Web site: http://www.prosperity4kids.com.

Paarmann, Al International, *(978-0-9715963)* 368 El Gaucho Rd., Santa Barbara, CA 93111 USA Tel 805-964-2830 (phone/fax)
E-mail: alpaarmann@aol.com.

Pace Products, Inc., *(978-1-58295; 978-1-880592)* P.O. Box 470970, Lake Monroe, FL 32747-0970 USA Toll Free: 800-541-7670
E-mail: PaceProd@aol.com
Web site: http://www.paceplace.com.

Pacesetters Bible School *See* **Energion Pubns.**

Pacific Bks., *(978-1-885375)* Orders Addr.: P.O. Box 3562, Santa Barbara, CA 93130 USA (SAN 630-2548) Tel 805-687-8340; Fax: 805-687-2514; Edit Addr.: 2573 Treasure Dr., Santa Barbara, CA 93105 USA; *Imprints:* Shore Line Press (Shore Line Pr).

Pacific Dogwood Pr., *(978-0-9896145)* 6400 Claremont Ave., Richmond, CA 94805 USA Tel 510-255-5067
E-mail: karin@manycycles.com
Web site: www.pacificdogwoodpress.com.

Pacific Heritage Bks., *(978-0-9635906; 978-1-928753)* Orders Addr.: P.O. Box 998, Palos Verdes, CA 90274 USA Tel 310-541-8818; Fax: 310-791-9069; Toll Free: 888-810-9891; Edit Addr.: 532 Via del Monte, Palos Verdes Estates, CA 90274 USA
E-mail: amawong@worldnet.att.net
Web site: http://www.pacificheritagebooks.com
Dist(s): **Distributors, The**
Quality Bks., Inc.

Pacific Learning, Inc., *(978-1-59055; 978-1-60457; 978-1-61391; 978-1-59055-000-7)* Orders Addr.: P.O. Box 2723, Huntington Beach, CA 92647-0723 USA; Edit Addr.: 6262 Katella Ave., Cypress, CA 90630 USA Tel 800-279-0737; Toll Free: 800-279-0737
E-mail: customer.service@pacificlearning.com
Web site: http://www.pacificlearning.com
Dist(s): **Brightpoint Literacy.**

Pacific Moon Pubns., *(978-0-9729524)* Orders Addr.: 2334 Monroe Blvd. Suite 703, Ogden, UT 84401-1727 USA
Dist(s): **Ingram Content Group.**

Pacific Northwest Ballet, *(978-0-9745415)* 301 Mercer St., Seattle, WA 98109 USA Tel 206-441-9411; Fax: 206-441-2440
E-mail: kaolivier@mac.com
Web site: http://www.pnb.org.

Pacific Pr. Pubns., *(978-0-9678122)* 3260 Monument, Ann Arbor, MI 48108 USA Tel 734-975-1877 (phone/fax)
E-mail: hailstormx@aol.com.

†Pacific Pr. Publishing Assn., *(978-0-8163; 978-1-5180)* P.O. Box 5353, Nampa, ID 83653-5353 USA (SAN 202-8409) Tel 208-465-2500; Fax: 208-465-2531; Toll Free: 800-447-7377
E-mail: donlay@pacificpress.com
Web site: http://www.AdventistBookCenter.com; http://www.pacificpress.com; *CIP.*

Pacific Pubs., *(978-0-936521; 978-1-933120)* P.O. Box 480, Bolinas, CA 94924 USA (SAN 697-9335) Tel 415-868-2909; Fax: 415-868-9040
E-mail: tideguy@fastmail.fm
Web site: http://www.tidelog.com.

Pacific Publishing Studio, *(978-0-9823756; 978-0-9824454; 978-1-936136)* 1425 Broadway, No. 435, Seattle, WA 98122 USA.

Pacific Raven Press *See* **Pacific Raven Pr.**

Pacific Raven Pr., *(978-0-9841228; 978-0-9840204; 978-0-9860755)* P.O. Box 195, Wailuku, HI 96793 USA (SAN 931-4946)
E-mail: pacificravenpress@gmail.com
Web site: http://www.pacificravenpress.com.

Pacific Ridge Press, LLC *See* **Parra Grande Pr.**

Pacific View Pr., *(978-1-881896)* 2864 Harrison St., San Francisco, CA 94110 USA Tel 415-285-8538; 510-849-4216; Fax: 415-285-2620; 510-843-5835
E-mail: pvp2@mindspring.com
Web site: http://www.pacificviewpress.com
Dist(s): **Cheng & Tsui Co.**
China Books & Periodicals, Inc.
Chinasprout, Inc.
Publishers Group West (PGW).

Pacifica Island Art, Inc., *(978-0-9727594; 978-0-9758721; 978-1-933735)* Orders Addr.: P.O. Box 120, Haiku, HI 96708 USA Fax: 808-575-2072; Edit Addr.: 810 Haiku Rd., No. 331, Haiku, HI 96708 USA
E-mail: joseph@islandartcards.com
Web site: http://www.islandartcards.com.

Pack, Kristin, *(978-0-9993624)* 938 N Elston Ave, No. 2, Chicago, IL 60642 USA Tel 989-400-8819; Fax: 989-400-8819
E-mail: kristinlynnpack@gmail.com
Web site: www.emmagoestoschool.com.

Packard, Boyle & Jackson *See* **Apollo Pubs.**

Padah Pr., *(978-0-9721269)* Orders Addr.: P.O. Box 231285, Gresham, OR 97281 USA Tel 971-219-1861
E-mail: eileen@padah.net; eileen@eileenscott.com
Web site: http://www.eileenscott.com.

Paddle Wheel Publishing, *(978-0-9657612)* Div. of Arabia Steamboat Museum, 400 Grand Blvd., Kansas City, MO 64106 USA Tel 816-471-1856; Fax: 816-471-1616; Toll Free: 800-471-1856
E-mail: greghawley@comcast.net
Web site: http://www.1856.com.

Paddywhack Lane LLC., *(978-0-9794286; 978-1-936169)* 9849 Bluestar Dr., Parker, CO 80138 USA (SAN 858-6497) Tel 303-841-1163; Fax: 888-840-0169; Toll Free: 800-796-1163
E-mail: bob@paddywhacklane.com
Web site: http://www.paddywhacklane.com.

Padula, Stacy A. *See* **Briley & Baxter Publications**

Padwolf Publishing, Inc., *(978-1-890096)* P.O. Box 117, Yulan, NY 12792-0117 USA Toll Free: 800-484-7284 ext. 7239
E-mail: padwolf@padwolf.com
Web site: http://www.padwolf.com.

Pagan Writers Pr. *Imprint of* **Mroczka Media**

Pagan Writers Press *See* **Mroczka Media**

Page A Day Math, *(978-1-947286; 978-1-948949)* 7661 E. Camino Amistoso, Tucson, AZ 85750 USA Tel 520-780-1079
E-mail: janice@pageadaymath.com
Web site: www.pageadaymath.com.

Page Pond Pr., *(978-0-9913977; 978-0-9907600)* 1512 Hilltop Dr., Tallahassee, FL 32303 USA Tel 850-385-7472
E-mail: susan.womble@gmail.com.

Page Publishing *See* **Page Publishing Inc.**

Page Publishing Inc., *(978-0-9854504; 978-1-62838; 978-1-63417; 978-1-68139; 978-1-68213; 978-1-68289; 978-1-68348; 978-1-68409; 978-1-63568; 978-1-64027; 978-1-64082; 978-1-64138; 978-1-64214; 978-1-64298; 978-1-64334; 978-1-64350; 978-1-64424; 978-1-64462; 978-1-68456; 978-1-64544; 978-1-64584; 978-1-64628; 978-1-64701; 978-1-6624) 101 Tyrellan Ave., Suite 100, New York, NY 10309 USA Toll Free: 866-315-2708; 320 Water St., Conneaut Lake, PA 16316 Toll Free: 866-315-2708*
E-mail: accounts@pagepublishing.com
Web site: http://www.pagepublishing.com.

Page Street Publishing Co., *(978-1-62414; 978-1-64567)* 31 Forest Ave., Essex, MA 01929 USA Tel 978-768-0168
E-mail: williamkiester@gmail.com
Dist(s): **Macmillan**
Westminster John Knox Pr.

Page Two Strategies Inc. (CAN) *Dist. by* **PerseuPGW.**

PageFree Publishing, Inc., *(978-1-929077; 978-1-930252; 978-1-58961)* P.O. Box 60, Otsego, MI 49078-0060 USA Toll Free: 1-866-GO BOOKS
E-mail: pagefreepublish@aol.com; publisher@pagefreepublishing.com
Web site: http://www.pagefreepublishing.com
Dist(s): **BookBaby**
Ingram Content Group
Midpoint Trade Bks., Inc.
Univ. of Hawaii Pr.

PageMaster Publishing, *(978-0-9797759)* 2884 Britton Rd., B34, Perry, MI 48872 USA (SAN 854-3453)
E-mail: Gwen@pagemasterpublishing.com
Web site: http://www.pagemasterpublishing.com.

Pages of Life, *(978-0-615-24716-8; 978-0-615-48466-2; 978-0-615-48467-9)* Div. of Lavender Belle Enterprises, 6328 Joe Klustch Dr., Fort Washington, MD 20744 USA Tel 202-251-2210
E-mail: LavenderBelle@verizon.net
Web site: http://pagesoflife.wordpress.com.

PageSpring Publishing, *(978-1-939403)* 2671 Bristol Rd., Columbus, OH 43221 USA Tel 614-204-2548
E-mail: rseum@pagespringpublishing.com
Web site: www.pagespringpublishing.com; www.luckymarblebooks.com; www.cupofteabooks.com.

PageTurner: Pr. & Media, *(978-1-948304; 978-1-64376; 978-1-64908)* 601 E. Palomar St., Suite C-478, Chula Vista, CA 91911 USA Tel 888-447-9651
E-mail: info@pageturner.us
Web site: www.pageturner.us.

Pageturners Publishing Co., *(978-0-9755102)* Orders Addr.: P.O. Box 6, Jacksonville, FL 32234-0006 USA (SAN 256-1719) Tel 904-266-3393; Fax: 904-266-3394
E-mail: publisher@pageturnerspublishing.com
Web site: http://www.pageturnerspublishing.com.

Paginas de Espuma (ESP) *(978-84-95642; 978-84-931243; 978-84-8393) Dist. by* **Lectorum Pubns.**

Pagkaihang, Katesalin, 55/1 Moo.10, Chang Keng, 50270 THA
E-mail: Katesalin.pagkaihang@icloud.com.

Paidea Classics, *(978-0-9749900; 978-1-947816)* 304 Robinhood Dr., Irving, TX 75061 USA
Web site: http://paideaclassics.org.

Paige Martin Bks., *(978-0-578-06864-0; 978-0-578-08272-1)* 11101 Silver Aspen Ct., Hampton, GA 30228 USA
Dist(s): **Smashwords.**

Paige Publishing, *(978-0-9769375)* 5708 Washington St., Downers Grove, IL 60516 USA Do not confuse with companies with the same or similar name in Lexington, OK, Mesa, AZ La Harba, CA San Antonio, TX.

Paige, Sharyn, *(978-0-692-40687-8)* 250 E. 105th St, New York, NY 10029 USA Tel 917-822-7539
E-mail: shaysensuals@gmail.com.

Paigerac, Patricia & Allan Choi *See* **Paigerac, Patricia M.**

Paigerac, Patricia M., *(978-0-9801137)* 30110 Crown Valley Pkwy., Suite 103, Laguna Niguel, CA 92677 USA.

Paino, Francine, *(978-0-692-59550-3; 978-0-692-96128-5; 978-1-7326489)* 8020 Journeyville Dr., Austin, TX 78735 USA Tel 512-551-2824
E-mail: franpaino@gmail.com
Web site: francinepaino.com
Dist(s): **CreateSpace Independent Publishing Platform.**

Paint Creek Press, Limited *See* **Archus Pr., LLC**

Paintbox Pr., *(978-0-9669433; 978-0-9777905; 978-1-951574)* 3 Malaga Cove Plaza Suite 206, Palos Verdes, CA 90274 USA Tel 800-920-5075; 800-920-5075; Fax: 800-920-5075
E-mail: ppease@paintboxpress.com
Web site: http://www.paintboxpress.com
Dist(s): **Follett School Solutions.**

Paintbrush Tales Publishing, LLC, *(978-0-9846151)* 20 Webber Ave., Beverly, MA 01915 USA Tel 978-239-9895
E-mail: caustin36@yahoo.com.

Painted Daisies Inc., *(978-0-615-34491-1)* 3433 Hwy. 190 PMB 377, Mandeville, LA 70471 USA Tel 985-674-0398; Fax: 985-674-2965; 978 Bald Cypress Dr., Mandeville, LA 70448
E-mail: kborg95@gmail.com.

Painted Gate Publishing, *(978-0-692-41111-7; 978-0-692-41563-4; 978-0-692-42495-7; 978-0-692-42641-8; 978-0-9963480; 978-0-692-44686-7; 978-0-692-45093-2; 978-0-692-45163-2; 978-1-943871; 978-0-578-41474-4; 978-1-952465)* P.O. Box 681, Spearfish, SD 57783 USA Tel (605) 645-1725
Dist(s): **CreateSpace Independent Publishing Platform.**

Painted Horse Pubns., Inc., *(978-0-9708066; 978-0-9729482)* 45 Wingate St., Haverhill, MA 01835 USA Tel 978-521-1740
E-mail: sully@stopforastory.com.

Painted Leaf Publishing, *(978-0-692-49942-9; 978-0-692-49945-0; 978-0-692-16754-0; 978-0-578-52703-1)* 18870 Painted Leaf Ct., JUPITER, FL 33458 USA Tel 561-972-8690.

Painted Pony, Inc., *(978-0-9759806)* Orders Addr.: P.O. Box 661, Fort Washakie, WY 82514 USA Tel 307-335-7330; Fax: 307-335-7332; Edit Addr.: 47 N. Fork Rd., Fort Washakie, WY 82514 USA Do not confuse with companies with similar name in Atlanta, GA and La Conner, WA.
E-mail: ppi@wrdf.org.

Painted Quill Publishing, *(978-0-9909471)* 230 Parker Oaks Ln., Hudson Oaks, TX 76087 USA
E-mail: paintedquill@gmail.com.

Painted Sky Productions *See* **Emerald City Publishing**

Painted WORD Studios, *(978-0-9721845; 978-0-9771809; 978-0-9845644)* P.O. Box 1606, Crosby, TX 77532-1606 USA Tel 281-456-8810 Toll Free: 866-241-7510
E-mail: paintedwordstudios@gmail.com
Web site: http://www.paintedwordstudios.com.

Painter, Annie & Assocs., *(978-1-928875)* P.O. Box 2135, Sisters, OR 97759 USA Tel 541-549-9539 (phone/fax)
E-mail: monamouse@cox.net.

Painting the Pages Publishing, *(978-0-9843487)* 673 Potomac Station Dr., No. 628, Leesburg, VA 20176 USA (SAN 859-1393)
Web site: http://www.paintingthepages.com.

Painting With Words, *(978-0-9743080)* 10 B State St., Windsor, VT 05089 USA Tel 802-674-5514; Fax: 802-674-9810.

Pair'a Spurs Pr., *(978-0-9749518)* Rt. 2 Box 20, Hollis, OK 73550 USA.

Paisley Publishing, *(978-0-9761710)* 7240 Sagebrush Dr., Parker, CO 80138 USA Fax: 303-841-5229 Do not confuse with Paisley Publishing in Anchorage, AK
E-mail: mlheinze11@aol.com.

Paizo Inc., *(978-0-9770071; 978-0-9776778; 978-1-60125; 978-1-64078)* 7120 185th Ave. NE. Ste 120, Redmond, WA 98052-0577 USA
Web site: http://www.paizo.com
Dist(s): **Diamond Comic Distributors, Inc.**
Diamond Bk. Distributors.

Paizo Publishing, LLC *See* **Paizo Inc.**

Pajama Pr. (CAN) *(978-0-9869495; 978-1-927485; 978-1-77278) Dist. by* **IngramPubServ.**

Pajarito, Conejo y Oso *Imprint of* **American Reading Co.**

Paje Publishing, *(978-0-9857768)* 267 Henley Rd., Wynnewood, PA 19096 USA Tel 484-437-3876
E-mail: pajepub@yahoo.com
Dist(s): **Baker & Taylor Publisher Services (BTPS).**

PAJE Publishing Co., *(978-0-9753200)* 267 Henley Rd., Wynnewood, PA 19096 USA Tel 610-642-1729; Fax: 610-642-9891; Toll Free: 877-561-1377
E-mail: jay.scott@verizon.net
Dist(s): **Baker & Taylor Publisher Services (BTPS)**
Quality Bks., Inc.

Pakkins Presents, *(978-0-9700241)* Orders Addr.: P.O. Box 10503, Salinas, CA 93912 USA Tel 831-422-3442; Edit Addr.: 637 Carmelita Dr., No. 23, Salinas, CA 93901 USA
E-mail: Pakkins-Land@worldnet.att.net
Web site: http://www.pakkinsland.com.

Pal Toys, LLC, *(978-0-9726170; 978-0-9763648; 978-0-9841459)* P.O. Box 2531, Palos Verdes Peninsula, CA 90274 USA Tel 310-938-6125 Toll Free: 877-725-8880; 26 Santa Bella Rd., Rolling Hills Estates, CA 90274
E-mail: info@paltoys.com; marymoepal@cox.net
Web site: http://www.paltoys.com.

Palabra, Ediciones S.A. (ESP) *(978-84-7118; 978-84-8239) Dist. by* **Lectorum Pubns.**

Palace Press International *See* **Insight Editions**

Palace Press International *See* **ORO Editions**

Paladin Timeless *Imprint of* **Twilight Times Bks.**

Palari Publishing LLP, *(978-1-928662)* Orders Addr.: P.O. Box 9288, Richmond, VA 23227-0288 USA Tel 804-355-1035; Toll Free Fax: 866-570-6724 (on demand); Toll Free: 866-570-6724; *Imprints:* Richmondmom.com Publishing (Richmondmom)
E-mail: dave@palaribooks.com
Web site: http://www.palaribooks.com
Dist(s): **Bookazine Co., Inc.**
Smashwords.

Palazzo Editions, Ltd. (GBR) *(978-0-9545103; 978-0-9553046; 978-0-9564448; 978-0-9564942; 978-0-9571483; 978-1-78675) Dist. by* **IPG Chicago.**

Pale Horse Bks., *(978-1-939917)* 108 Maid Marion Pl., Williamsburg, VA 23185 USA Tel 757-220-0146
E-mail: jwconl@wm.edu
Web site: palehorsebooks.com.

Pale Silver Rainplop Pr., *(978-0-9794396; 978-0-615-14670-6)* P.O. Box 1285, Sioux City, IA 51102 USA
Web site: http://www.katieandkimbleblog.com
Dist(s): **Lulu Pr., Inc.**

Palgrave *See* **Palgrave Macmillan**

Palgrave Macmillan, *(978-0-312; 978-0-333; 978-1-4039; 978-0-230; 978-1-4472; 978-1-137; 978-1-349; 978-1-78632)* Orders Addr.: 16365 James Madison Hwy., Gordonsville, VA 22942-8501 USA Toll Free Fax: 800-672-2054; Toll Free: 888-330-8477; Edit Addr.: 175 Fifth Ave., New York, NY 10010 USA Tel 212-982-9300; Fax: 212-777-6359; Toll Free Fax: 800 672-2054 (Customer Service); Toll Free: 800-221-7945; 888-330-8477 (Customer Service)
E-mail: customerservice@vhpsva.com
Web site: http://www.palgrave.com
Dist(s): **China Books & Periodicals, Inc.**
Ebsco Publishing
Independent Pubs. Group
Libros Sin Fronteras
Macmillan
MyiLibrary
Springer
Trans-Atlantic Pubns., Inc.
ebrary, Inc.

Palgrave Macmillan Ltd. (GBR) *(978-0-312; 978-0-333; 978-1-4039; 978-0-230; 978-1-137) Dist. by* **Spri.**

PALH, *(978-0-9719458; 978-1-953716)* P.O. Box 5099, Santa Monica, CA 90409 USA
E-mail: palh@aol.com
Web site: http://www.palhbooks.com.

Palibrio, *(978-1-61764; 978-1-5065)* Div. of Author Solutions, Inc., 1663 Liberty Dr., Bloomington, IN 47403 USA Tel 812-674-9757; Fax: 812-355-1576; Toll Free: 877-407-5847
Web site: http://www.palibrio.com
Dist(s): **Author Solutions, Inc.**

Palladium Bks., Inc., *(978-0-916211; 978-1-57457)* 39074 Webb Ct., Westland, MI 48185-7606 USA (SAN 294-9504)
E-mail: palladiumbooks@palladiumbooks.com
Web site: http://www.PalladiumBooks.com.

Palm, *(978-1-7329843)* 6120 Torrington Dr., Reno, NV 89511 USA Tel 775-848-6096
E-mail: dkinsley0321@hotmail.com.

Palm Canyon Pr., *(978-0-9960794)* 24 Crockett St., Rowayton, CT 06853 USA Tel 203-853-1512
E-mail: pmorrison101@gmail.com; pagemcbrier@gmail.com
Web site: www.abracadabratut.com; www.palmcanyonpress.com; www.pagemcbrier.com.

Palm Pen Press, *(978-0-9666942; 978-1-933678)* Orders Addr.: 7881 Barrancas Ave., Bokeelia, FL 33922 USA (SAN 299-7835) Tel 239-283-3975 Toll Free: 877-725-6782
Web site: http://www.dlhavlin.com.

Palm Publishing LLC, *(978-0-9753548)* 1016 N. Dixie Hwy., West Palm Beach, FL 33401 USA Tel 561-833-6333; Fax: 561-833-0070
Web site: http://www.phfpbc.org.

Palm Tree Pubns., *(978-0-9787128; 978-0-9795480; 978-0-9799879; 978-0-9817054; 978-0-9822237; 978-0-9826954; 978-0-9846311; 978-0-9847653; 978-0-9857942; 978-0-9862033)* Div. of Palm Tree Productions, P.O. Box 122, Keller, TX 76244 USA; 4508 Willow Rock ln., Keller, TX 76244 Tel 817-431-8574 Do not confuse with Palm Tree Publications in Baton Rouge, LA
Web site: http://www.palmtreeproductions.net
Dist(s): **BookBaby.**

Palmer, Barbara A., *(978-0-9728228)* 486 Manitou Beach Rd., Hilton, NY 14468 USA Tel 585-392-3391; Fax: 585-392-1322
E-mail: bpforkart@aol.com.

Palmer Enterprises *See* **Palmer Pr., The**

Palmer Lake Historical Society, *(978-0-9755989)* 66 Lower Glenway St., Palmer Lake, CO 80133 USA Tel 719-559-0837
E-mail: plhs@palmerdividehistory.org
Web site: www.PalmerDivideHistory.org.

Palmer Pr., The, *(978-0-912479)* P.O. Box 1347, Loomis, CA 95650 USA (SAN 215-1650) Tel 916-652-3225; Fax: 916-652-8665.

Palmer Publications, Incorporated/Amherst Press *See* **Amherst Pr.**

Palmer Publishing, *(978-0-9744410)* 604 4th N.W., Ardmore, OK 73401 USA Tel 580-504-2609 Do not confuse with companies with the same or similar name in Palmer, AK, Ocala, FL
E-mail: charlsie@duracom.net.

Palmer-Pletsch Assocs., *(978-0-935278; 978-1-61847)* 18200 NW Sauvie Island Rd., Portland, OR 97231 USA
E-mail: info@palmerpletsch.com; wisner.palmerpletsch@gmail.com
Web site: http://www.palmerpletsch.com
Dist(s): **Independent Pubs. Group**
MyiLibrary.

Palmetto Publishing, *(978-1-944313; 978-1-64111; 978-0-578-68178-8; 978-1-64990)* 2681 Spruill Ave, N. Charleston, SC 29405 USA.

Palmetto Publishing Group *See* **Palmetto Publishing**

Palmetto Street Publishing, *(978-0-615-49043-4; 978-0-9848782)* 106 W. Augusta Pl., Greenville, SC 29605 USA Tel 864-242-3906
E-mail: gabbehoward@gmail.com
Web site: n/a.

Palmetto Tree Pr., *(978-0-9742532)* 821 Calhoun St., Columbia, SC 29201 USA (SAN 255-5832) Tel 803-771-9300; Fax: 803-407-0766
E-mail: follybeech@aol.com.

Palmland Publishing *See* **Palm Pen Press**

Palmore, Julie, *(978-0-9722653)* 3203 Harwood, Tyler, TX 75701-7642 USA.

Palo Alto Bks. *Imprint of* **Glencannon Pr.**

Paloma Bks. *Imprint of* **L & R Publishing, LLC**

Palomina Publishing, *(978-0-9763393)* 338 Napa Rd., Sonoma, CA 95476 USA.

Palomino Publishing, *(978-1-892344)* Div. of Programs for the Arts, Inc., 1535 E. Broadway, Tucson, AZ 85719 USA Tel 520-623-4000; Fax: 520-623-9102
E-mail: madaras@worldnet.att.net
Dist(s): **TNT Media Group, Inc.**

Palski, Leona, *(978-0-615-91591-3; 978-0-692-20236-4; 978-0-692-52664-4; 978-0-692-78301-6; 978-0-692-91612-4)* P.O. Box 47, Antes Fort, PA 17720 USA Tel 570-398-2726
E-mail: leonapalski@yahoo.com.

Pamir LLC, *(978-0-9888649)* 460 Jameson Hill Rd., Clinton Corners, NY 12514 USA Tel 845-266-0064
E-mail: natasha_rafi@hotmail.com.

Pampa Publishing, *(978-0-9744675; 978-0-615-11346-3)* Orders Addr.: P.O. Box 3481, Olympia, WA 98509-3481 USA; Edit Addr.: 4613 Shincke Rd. NE, Olympia, WA 98506 USA
E-mail: pampapublishing@comcast.net; ma2ka@home.com.

Pan Asian Pubns. (U S A), Inc., *(978-1-57227)* 29564 Union City Blvd., Union City, CA 94587 USA Tel 510-475-1185; Fax: 510-475-1489
E-mail: schiu@panap.com.

Pan Asia Pubns. (USA), Inc., *(978-1-57227)* 29564 Union City Blvd., Union City, CA 94587 USA (SAN 173-685X) Tel 510-475-1185; Fax: 510-475-1489; Toll Free: 800-909-8088
E-mail: sales@panap.com; hchan@panap.com; info@panap.com
Web site: http://www.panap.com; http://www.cjkv.com
Dist(s): **China Books & Periodicals, Inc.**
Chinasprout, Inc.
Follett School Solutions
Lectorum Pubns., Inc.

Pan Macmillan (GBR) *(978-0-283; 978-0-312; 978-0-330; 978-0-333; 978-0-7522; 978-1-85283; 978-1-4050; 978-1-904633; 978-1-904919; 978-1-905716; 978-1-907360; 978-1-4472; 978-1-909621; 978-1-5098; 978-1-5290) Dist. by* **Macmillan.**

Pan Macmillan (GBR) *(978-0-283; 978-0-312; 978-0-330; 978-0-333; 978-0-7522; 978-1-85283; 978-1-4050; 978-1-904633; 978-1-904919; 978-1-905716; 978-1-907360; 978-1-4472; 978-1-909621; 978-1-5098; 978-1-5290) Dist. by* **Trans-Atl Phila.**

Pan Macmillan (GBR) *(978-0-283; 978-0-312; 978-0-330; 978-0-333; 978-0-7522; 978-1-85283; 978-1-4050; 978-1-904633; 978-1-904919; 978-1-905716; 978-1-907360; 978-1-4472; 978-1-909621; 978-1-5098; 978-1-5290) Dist. by* **Children Plus.**

Pan Macmillan (GBR) *(978-0-283; 978-0-312; 978-0-330; 978-0-333; 978-0-7522; 978-1-85283; 978-1-4050; 978-1-904633; 978-1-904919; 978-1-905716; 978-1-907360; 978-1-4472; 978-1-909621; 978-1-5098; 978-1-5290) Dist. by* **IPG Chicago.**

Pan Macmillan (GBR) *(978-0-283; 978-0-312; 978-0-330; 978-0-333; 978-0-7522; 978-1-85283; 978-1-4050; 978-1-904633; 978-1-904919; 978-1-905716; 978-1-907360; 978-1-4472; 978-1-909621; 978-1-5098; 978-1-5290) Dist. by* **Trafalgar.**

Pan Macmillan Australia Pty, Ltd. (AUS) *(978-0-330; 978-0-7251; 978-0-7329; 978-1-4050; 978-1-74198; 978-1-74197; 978-1-74261; 978-1-74262; 978-1-74303; 978-1-74328; 978-1-74329; 978-1-74334; 978-1-74351; 978-1-74353; 978-1-74354; 978-1-76008; 978-1-76009; 978-1-76030; 978-1-925479; 978-1-925480; 978-1-925481; 978-1-925482; 978-1-925483; 978-1-76055; 978-1-76078; 978-1-76098) Dist. by* **IPG Chicago.**

Panacea Pr., *(978-0-9791309; 978-0-9842147; 978-0-9893645; 978-0-9861012)* P.O. Box 292005, Nashville, TN 37229-2005 USA Tel 615-406-822
E-mail: king2dw@aol.com.

Panacea Publishing, *(978-0-9743432)* Orders Addr.: 5002 Barlow Dr., Round Rock, TX 78681 USA Tel 512-228-1388; Fax: 512-906-1579; Toll Free: 877-723-6110 Do not confuse with Panacea Publishing in North Attleboro MA, South Yarmouth MA
E-mail: sales@panaceabooks.com
Web site: http://www.panaceabooks.com
Dist(s): **Brodart Co.**
Midwest Library Service
Quality Bks., Inc.

Panama Hat Publishing, Ltd., *(978-0-9852202; 978-1-943317)* P.O. Box 343, Green Mountain Falls, CO 80819-0343 USA Tel 970-368-2665
E-mail: admin@panamahatpublishing.com
Web site: http://www.panamahatpublishing.com/.

Pan-American Publishing Co., *(978-0-932906)* P.O. Box 1505, Las Vegas, NM 87701 USA (SAN 212-5366).

Panamericana Editorial (COL) *(978-958-30) Dist. by* **Lectorum Pubns.**

Panda Bear Pr., *(978-0-9724699)* Orders Addr.: 612 Museum Rd., Reading, PA 19611-1427 USA (SAN 255-5328) Tel 610-374-7048; Fax: 610-478-7992
E-mail: HaileJohnJr@msn.com
Web site: http://www.caroljhaile.com
Dist(s): **Firenze Pr.**

PANDA BKS. PR., *(978-0-692-78668-0; 978-0-692-80099-7)* 47 bristol St., thomaston, CT 32968 USA Tel 772-766-6549
E-mail: kramer535@bellsouth.net
Web site: www.musicboxstory.com.

Panda Pubns., *(978-0-9818392)* P.O. Box 595, Wilkes Barre, PA 18703 USA
E-mail: pandapublications@verizon.net; antobianco@msn.com.

Panda Publishing, L.L.C., *(978-0-9740180; 978-1-932724)* Orders Addr.: P.O. Box 670608, Dallas, TX 75367 USA (SAN 255-8165) Toll Free: 800-807-1776; Edit Addr.: 6215 Rex Dr., Dallas, TX 75230 USA; *Imprints:* Bios for Kids (Bios for Kids)
E-mail: info@biosforkids.com.

Pandalily Bks., *(978-0-692-92150-0; 978-0-9995804)* 8505 Laberta Blvd., Savannah, GA 31406 USA Tel 912-704-2301
E-mail: jamie@youhaveawildimagination.com; reservedsav@gmail.com
Web site: youhaveawildimagination.com.

Pandasaurus, LLC, *(978-0-615-63750-1; 978-0-9858227)* 4501 Rosedale Ave, Austin, TX 78756 USA Tel 512-731-6812
E-mail: nmcnair@pandasaurusgames.com
Dist(s): **Independent Pubs. Group.**

Pandia Pr., *(978-0-9766057; 978-0-9798496; 978-0-9977963; 978-1-7334441)* 18400 SE Hwy.42, Weirsdale, FL 32195 USA
Web site: http://www.PandiaPress.com.

Pandora *Imprint of* **Highland Pr. Publishing**

Pandora Press U. S. *See* **Cascadia Publishing Hse., LLC**

PANGAEA, *(978-0-9630180; 978-1-929165)* Orders Addr.: 226 Wheeler St., S., Saint Paul, MN 55105-1927 USA Tel 651-226-2032
E-mail: info@pangaea.org
Web site: http://www.pangaea.org
Dist(s): **Follett School Solutions.**

Pangaea Publishing *See* **PANGAEA**

Pangea Software, Inc., *(978-0-9761505)* 12405 John Simpson Ct., Austin, TX 78732-2112 USA Tel 512-266-9991
Web site: http://www.pangeasoft.net.

Pangloss Pr., *(978-0-9668784; 978-0-692-51345-3)* Orders Addr.: P.O. Box 2225, Ballston Spa, NY 12020 USA Tel 518-584-4034 phone/fax; Edit Addr.: 63 Franklin St., Saratoga, NY 12866 USA Do not confuse with Pangloss Pr., Malibu, CA
E-mail: tuckerb@global2000.net.

Pangloss Publishing, *(978-0-9768586; 978-0-615-12424-7)* 3904 Becker Ave., Austin, TX 78751-5209 USA Fax: 512-453-1486
E-mail: candide@grandecom.net.

Pangus Publishing, *(978-0-9769715)* Orders Addr.: 1637 S. Iseminger St., Philadelphia, PA 19148 USA; Edit Addr.: P.O. Box 15763, Philadelphia, PA 19148 USA.

Panigrahy, Sonia, *(978-0-9975956)* 129 W. 89th St., New York, NY 10024 USA Tel 646-648-1898
E-mail: sonia1211@gmail.com.

†Panjandrum Bks., *(978-0-915572)* 6156 Wilkinson Ave., North Hollywood, CA 91606-4518 USA (SAN 282-1257) Tel 818-985-7259
Dist(s): **Coutts Information Services**
New Leaf Distributing Co., Inc.; *CIP.*

Pankratz Creations, *(978-0-9742637)* 355 S. Fairlane Dr., Tooele, UT 84074-2623 USA
E-mail: customerservice@pankratzcreations.com; pankratz@mstar2.net
Web site: http://www.pankratzcreations.com.

Panline U.S.A., Inc., *(978-0-9713507; 978-0-615-23938-5; 978-0-9822010; 978-0-9847127)* 251 Union St., Northvale, NJ 07647 USA (SAN 920-5772) Tel 201-750-8010; Fax: 201-750-8030
E-mail: info@alextoys.com
Web site: http://www.alextoys.com.

Pannonia Pr., *(978-0-9657793)* P.O. Box 1062, Palatine, IL 60078-1062 USA Tel 847-277-0806; Fax: 847-228-6847
E-mail: pannoniapress2000@sbcglobal.net
Web site: http://www.pannoniapress.com.

Pannycake Pubn., *(978-0-9769538)* 1710 Vallejo St., Unit B, Seaside, CA 93955 USA Tel 831-393-1358; Fax: 831-753-6085
E-mail: carmelalayne@yahoo.com.

Panoply Pubns., *(978-0-9818391)* P.O. Box 2329, North Hollywood, CA 91610-0329 USA Tel 818-761-8757
E-mail: panoplypub@aol.com
Web site: http://www.panoplypublications.com.

Panorama Pr., Inc., *(978-0-9768642)* P.O. Box 183, Boulder, CO 80306-0183 USA.

Pantera Pr. (AUS) *(978-0-9807418; 978-0-9870685; 978-1-921997; 978-1-925399; 978-1-925700; 978-0-6485084; 978-0-6485715; 978-0-6486769; 978-0-6486770; 978-0-6487488; 978-0-6487489; 978-0-6487951; 978-0-6487952; 978-0-6487953; 978-0-6489874; 978-0-6489875; 978-0-6489876) Dist. by* **IPG Chicago.**

Pantheon *Imprint of* **Knopf Doubleday Publishing Group**

Panther Creek Pr., *(978-0-9678343; 978-0-9718361; 978-0-9747839; 978-0-9771797)* Orders Addr.: P.O. Box 130233, Spring, TX 77393-0233 USA (SAN 253-8520); Edit Addr.: 104 Plum Tree Ter. Apt. 115, Houston, TX 77077-5375 USA
E-mail: panthercreek3@hotmail.com; guidamj@juno.com
Web site: http://www.panthercreekpress.com.

Pants On Fire Pr., *(978-0-9827271; 978-0-9860373; 978-0-615-88989-4; 978-0-615-89685-4; 978-0-615-89931-2; 978-0-615-91719-1; 978-0-615-96453-9; 978-0-615-98402-5; 978-0-692-02170-5; 978-0-692-02171-2; 978-0-692-20585-3; 978-0-692-20941-7; 978-0-692-21000-0; 978-0-692-21001-7; 978-0-692-21003-1; 978-0-692-30738-0; 978-0-692-35957-0; 978-0-692-44415-3; 978-0-692-44416-0; 978-0-692-57238-2; 978-0-692-69868-6) 2062 Harbor Cove Way, Winter Garden, FL 34787 USA*
E-mail: david@pantsonfirepress.com; editor@pantsonfirepress.com
Web site: http://www.pantsonfirepress.com
Dist(s): **CreateSpace Independent Publishing Platform**
INscribe Digital
Independent Pubs. Group
Ingram Publisher Services.

Paon Pubns., *(978-0-9711721)* 608 S. Webik Ave, Clawson, MI 48017 USA Tel 248-288-5621.

Papa Koj Bks., *(978-0-9981152)* 21 Washburn Pk., Rochester, NY 14620 USA Tel 330-256-3224
E-mail: cbrownlie@frontiernet.net
Web site: craigbrownlie.com.

Papaloizos Pubns., Inc., *(978-0-932416)* 11720 Auth Ln., Silver Spring, MD 20902-1645 USA (SAN 220-9853) Tel 301-593-0652
E-mail: info@greek123.com
Web site: http://www.greek123.com.

Papas & Nellie Pr., *(978-0-9719925)* 2110 Lakeland Ave., Madison, WI 53704 USA Tel 608-661-0508
E-mail: papasandnellie@tds.net.

Papell, David, *(978-0-615-17531-7; 978-0-615-17931-5; 978-0-615-17932-2)* 5601 Riverdale Ave., Bronx, NY 10471 USA Tel 718-601-3771
E-mail: dpapell@earthlink.net
Web site: http://www.davidpapell.net
Dist(s): **Lulu Pr., Inc.**

Paper Airplane Publishing, LLC, *(978-1-947677)* 2205 Willow, Liberty, TX 77575 USA Tel 281-734-0330
E-mail: lindastreetely@gmail.com
Web site: http://paperairplanepublishing.com/.

Paper Crane Pr., *(978-0-9650833)* P.O. Box 29292, Bellingham, WA 98228-1292 USA Tel 360-676-0266; Toll Free: 800-356-9315
E-mail: carolrj@nas.com
Dist(s): **Brodart Co.**
New Leaf Distributing Co., Inc.
Unique Bks., Inc.
Upper Access, Inc.

Paper Doll Publishing, *(978-0-9748252)* Orders Addr.: a/o Orders, P.O. Box 72028, Phoenix, AZ 85050 USA (SAN 255-8084)
E-mail: michael@paperdollpublishing.com; books@paperdollpublishing.com
Web site: http://www.paperdollpublishing.com.

Paper Jam Publishing, *(978-1-888345)* Orders Addr.: P.O. Box 435, Eastsound, WA 98245 USA Tel 360-376-3200 (phone/fax); Toll Free: 877-757-2665; Edit Addr.: 531 Fern St., Eastsound, WA 98245 USA
E-mail: paperjam@rockisland.com
Web site: http://www.rockisland.com/~paperjam.

Paper Mermaid, The, *(978-1-7322085)* 57 Main St., ROCKPORT, MA 01966 USA Tel 978-546-3553
E-mail: info@papermermaid.com
Web site: www.papermermaid.com; www.romeaday.com
Dist(s): **Ingram Content Group.**

Paper Posie, *(978-0-9707944; 978-0-9774763)* Orders Addr.: 315a Meigs Rd., #167, Santa Barbara, CA 93109 USA Tel 805-569-2398; Fax: 805-563-0166; Toll Free: 800-360-1761
Web site: http://www.paperposie.com; http://www.kidsatweddings.com
Dist(s): **Greenleaf Book Group.**

Paper Studio Pr., *(978-0-9790668; 978-0-9795053; 978-1-935223; 978-1-942490)* Orders Addr.: P.O. Box 14, Kingfield, ME 04947 USA Tel 207-265-2500
Web site: http://paperstudiopress.com.

Paper Tiger, Incorporated, The *See* **Paper Tiger, The**

Paper Tiger, The, *(978-1-889439)* Orders Addr.: 722 Upper Cherrytown Rd., Kerhonkson, NY 12446 USA Tel 845-626-5354
E-mail: fredweiss@papertig.com
Web site: http://www.papertig.com.

Paperbacks for Educators, *(978-0-9702376; 978-1-59721)* 426 W. Front St., Washington, MO 63090 USA (SAN 103-3379) Tel 636-239-1999; Fax: 636-239-4515; Toll Free Fax: 800-514-7323; Toll Free: 800-227-2591
E-mail: paperbacks@usmo.com
Web site: http://www.any-book-in-print.com.

Papercutz, *(978-1-59707; 978-1-62991; 978-1-5458)* 160 Broadway, E. Wing Suite 700, New York, NY 10038 USA (SAN 850-9670) Tel 646-559-4681
E-mail: nantier@papercutz.com
Web site: http://www.papercutz.com
Dist(s): **Children's Plus, Inc.**
Diamond Comic Distributors, Inc.
Macmillan
Westminster John Knox Pr.

Papergraphics Printing, *(978-0-9773322)* 4 John Tyler St., Suite 1, Merrimack, NH 03054-3054 USA Tel 603-880-1835; Fax: 603-880-1751; Toll Free: 800-499-1835
E-mail: prepress@papergraphics.biz
Web site: http://www.papergraphics.biz.

PaperMaze Media, *(978-0-692-08981-1)* 5418 Gosforth Dr., Katy, TX 77449 USA Tel 8329740639
E-mail: iclark@papermaze.media
Dist(s): **Ingram Content Group.**

Papilion Pr., *(978-1-884429)* Orders Addr.: P.O. Box 54502, Phoenix, AZ 85078-4502 USA Tel 602-931-0556
E-mail: firstchoiceent05@msn.com.

Papillon Pr., Inc., *(978-0-9667476)* 23 Seagull Pl., Vero Beach, FL 32960-5212 USA
Dist(s): **New Leaf Distributing Co., Inc.**

Papillon Publishing *Imprint of* **Blue Dolphin Publishing, Inc.**

Papillon Publishing, *(978-0-9651048)* P.O. Box 12044, Dallas, TX 75225 USA Tel 214-722-1297 (phone/fax) Do not confuse with Papillon Publishing in Rochester, MN
E-mail: ford.lawrence@sbcglobal.net.

PAPO Brand *Imprint of* **Planet Bronx Productions**

Papyrus & Pen, *(978-0-9770687)* 2923 Cecil B. Moore Ave., Suite 3, Philadelphia, PA 19121 USA Tel 267-539-7540
E-mail: dmccrary@papyrusandpen.com
Web site: http://www.papyrusandpen.com
Dist(s): **Ingram Publisher Services**
Ingram Content Group.

Papyrus Publishing, Inc., *(978-0-9675581; 978-0-9882883)* Orders Addr.: 7409 Edgewood Ave. N., Brooklyn Park, MN 55428 USA Tel 763-717-8854; Fax: 763-374-7737 Do not confuse with Papyrus Publishing in Missouri City, TX
E-mail: PapyrusPublishing@msn.com
Web site: http://www.mahmoudelkati.com; http://www.papyruspublishinginc.com.

Para-Anchors International, *(978-1-878832)* Orders Addr.: P.O. Box 19, Summerland, CA 93067 USA Tel 805-966-4837; Fax: 805-966-0782; Toll Free: 800-350-7070; Edit Addr.: 21 E. Canon Perdido, Suite 303, Santa Barbara, CA 93101 USA
E-mail: victor1pai@netscape.com; victor1cnp@netscape.com
Web site: http://www.jerustar.com
Dist(s): **Quality Bks., Inc.**

†**Parable Pr.,** *(978-0-917250)* P.O. Box 51, Vinalhaven, ME 04863-0051 USA (SAN 208-4449); *CIP.*

Parable Venture Partners, LLC, *(978-0-9728501)* 12946 SW 133 Ct., Suite B, Miami, FL 33186 USA Tel 305-252-0905; Fax: 305-245-9974
E-mail: info@ethansparables.com
Web site: http://www.ethansparables.com.

Parables & Bks., *(978-0-9833188; 978-1-939682)* 24 S. Front St., Bergenfield, NJ 07621 USA Tel 201-338-4953
E-mail: sandy@parablesandbooks.com
Web site: www.parablesandbooks.com.

Parabola Bks., *(978-0-930407)* 656 Broadway, Suite 615, New York, NY 10012-2317 USA (SAN 219-5763) Tel 212-505-6200; Fax: 212-979-7325; Toll Free: 800-560-6984
E-mail: ads-promo@parabola.org; orders@parabola.org; JoeKulin@aol.com; editors@parabola.org
Web site: http://www.parabola.org/; http://www.cinemaofthespirit.org
Dist(s): **New Leaf Distributing Co., Inc.**

Parabola Magazine/Society for Study of Myth & Tradition *See* **Parabola Bks.**

Parachute Jump Publishing, *(978-0-9852469; 978-0-9888905; 978-0-9915405; 978-0-9903660)* 50 Brighton 1st Rd. Apt. 16D, Brooklyn, NY 11235 USA Tel 718-593-7717
E-mail: kpaulet@verizon.net
Dist(s): **BookBaby**
Ingram Content Group.

Parachute Press, Incorporated *See* **Parachute Publishing, LLC**

Parachute Publishing, LLC, *(978-0-938753; 978-1-57351)* 156 Fifth Ave., New York, NY 10010 USA (SAN 661-5554) Tel 212-691-1421; Fax: 212-645-8769
E-mail: ppibooks@aol.com.

Paraclete Pr., Inc., *(978-0-941478; 978-1-55725; 978-1-61261; 978-1-64060)* Orders Addr.: P.O. Box 1568, Orleans, MA 02653 USA (SAN 282-1508) Fax: 508-255-5705; Toll Free: 800-451-5006; Edit Addr.: 36 Southern Eagle Cartway, Brewster, MA 02631 USA (SAN 664-6239) Do not confuse with companies with the same or similar names in Indianapolis, IN, Pentwater, MI
E-mail: srmercy@paracletepress.com; miao@paracletepress.com
Web site: http://www.paracletepress.com
Dist(s): **BookMasters**
Follett School Solutions
Forward Movement Pubns.
MyiLibrary.

Paradigm Accelerated Curriculum, *(978-1-928629; 978-1-59476)* Div. of Paradigm Alternatives Centers, Inc., Orders Addr.: P.O. Box 200, Dublin, TX 76446-0200 USA Tel 254-445-4272; Fax: 254-445-3947; Edit Addr.: 112 S. Grafton, Dublin, TX 76446-0200 USA
E-mail: learn@pacworks.com
Web site: http://www.pacworks.com.

Paradigm Alternatives Centers, Incorporated *See* **Paradigm Accelerated Curriculum**

Paradigm Publishing, *(978-0-9746013)* Orders Addr.: P.O. Box 872, LaPorte, CO 80535 USA; Edit Addr.: 3106 Kintzley Ct., D, LaPorte, CO 80535 USA Do not confuse with companies with the same or similar name in Oklahoma City OK, San Dimas CA, Chicago IL, McFarland WI, Saint Paul MN, Midvale UT, Pembroke Pines FL, Pocatello ID, Brookline MA, Boulder CO, Laguna Park, TX , Washington, DC
E-mail: sales@paradigmpublish.com
Web site: http://www.paradigmpublish.com.

Paradise Cay Pubns., *(978-0-939837; 978-1-937196)* P.O. Box 29, Arcata, CA 95518-0029 USA (SAN 663-690X) Tel 707-822-9063; Fax: 707-822-9163; Toll Free: 800-736-4509 (orders only)
E-mail: jim@paracay.com
Web site: http://www.paracay.com
Dist(s): **Independent Pubs. Group**
Hale, Robert & Co., Inc.
Univ. of Hawaii Pr.

Paradise Copies, Inc., *(978-0-9836716)* 21 Conz St., Northampton, MA 01060 USA Tel 413-585-0414; Fax: 413-585-0417
E-mail: Carol@paradisecopies.com
Web site: http://paradisecopies.com.

Paradise Pr. & Assocs., LLC, *(978-0-9755970)* P.O. Box 783573, Winter Garden, FL 34778-3573 USA Tel 321-354-5881 (phone/fax)
E-mail: bbeehy@gmail.com
Web site: none.

Paradise Pr., Inc., *(978-1-57657; 978-1-884907; 978-1-4194)* 1776 N. Pine Island Rd. Ste. 218, Plantation, FL 33322-5223 USA Do not confuse with companies with the same or similar names in Crested Butte, CO Corte Madera, CA, Santa Monica, CA, Ridgefield, CA, Chicago, IL, Herdon, VA, Temple Terrace, FL
E-mail: buybooks@paradisepress.us.

Paradise Research Pubns., Inc., *(978-1-885803)* Orders Addr.: P.O. Box 837, Kihei, HI 96753-0837 USA Tel 808-874-4876 (phone/fax)
E-mail: dickb@dickb.com
Web site: http://www.dickb.com/index.html
Dist(s): **Globe Pequot Pr., The**
Good Bk. Publishing Co.

Paradox *Imprint of* **DC Comics**

Paradoxal Pr., *(978-0-9766132)* 28916 NE 34th Ct., Redmond, WA 98053-9114 USA
Web site: http://www.paradoxalpress.com.

Paradoxical Pr., The, *(978-0-9786663)* 48 Cranford Pl., Teaneck, NJ 07666 USA Tel 201-281-8112
E-mail: info@theparadoxicalpress.com
Web site: http://www.theparadoxicalpress.com.

Paraglyph, Inc., *(978-1-932111; 978-1-933097)* 3533 E. Friess Dr., Phoenix, AZ 85032-5318 USA; 3533 E. Friess Dr., Phoenix, AZ 85032-5318; *Imprints:* Paraglyph Press (Paraglyph Pr)
E-mail: ccaldwell@paraglyphpress.com; stevesayre@paraglyphpress.com
Web site: http://www.paraglyphpress.com
Dist(s): **Ingram Publisher Services**
O'Reilly Media, Inc.

Paraglyph Pr. *Imprint of* **Paraglyph, Inc.**

Paragon Agency, Pubs., The *Imprint of* **Paragon Agency, The**

Paragon Agency, The, *(978-1-891030; 978-0-9710012; 978-1-942329)* Orders Addr.: P.O. Box 1281, Orange, CA 92856 USA Tel 714-771-0652; *Imprints:* Paragon Agency, Publishers, The (PAP)
E-mail: Paragon@SpecialBooks.com
Web site: http://www.SpecialBooks.com.

†**Paragon Hse. Pubs.,** *(978-0-88702; 978-0-89226; 978-0-913729; 978-0-943852; 978-1-55778; 978-1-885118; 978-1-61083)* Orders Addr.: 3600 Labore Rd., Suite 1, Saint Paul, MN 55110-4144 USA (SAN 286-1704) Tel 651-644-3087; Fax: 651-644-0997; Toll Free Fax: 800-494-0997; Toll Free: 800-447-3709
E-mail: paragon@paragonhouse.com
Web site: http://www.paragonhouse.com
Dist(s): **Baker & Taylor Publisher Services (BTPS);** *CIP.*

Paraklesis Pr., *(978-1-947446)* 113 Winn Ct, Waleska, GA 30183 USA Tel 404-695-5517
E-mail: sally@sally-apokedak.com.

Parallax, Inc., *(978-1-928982)* 599 Menlo Dr., No. 100, Rocklin, CA 95765-3708 USA Tel 916-624-8333; Fax: 916-624-8003; Toll Free: 888-512-1024
E-mail: info@parallaxinc.com
Web site: http://www.parallaxinc.com.

Parallax Pr., *(978-0-938077; 978-1-888375; 978-1-935209; 978-0-9846271; 978-1-937006; 978-1-941529; 978-1-946764; 978-1-952692)* Orders Addr.: P.O. Box 7355, Berkeley, CA 94707 USA (SAN 663-4494) Tel 510-525-0101; Fax: 510-525-7129; Toll Free: 800-863-5290; Edit Addr.: 2236 6th St., Berkeley, CA 94710-2219 USA; *Imprints:* Plum Blossom Books (Plum Blossom)
E-mail: orders@parallax.org
Web site: http://www.parallax.org
Dist(s): **MyiLibrary**
Penguin Random Hse. Distribution
Penguin Random Hse. LLC
Random Hse., Inc.
SPD-Small Pr. Distribution.

Parallel Vortex, *(978-0-578-20654-7; 978-1-7335610)* 11264 E. Bath Rd, Byron, MI 48418 USA Tel 517-294-5420
E-mail: thechaderway@gmail.com.

Paramance *Imprint of* **MQuills Publishing**

Paraphrase, LLC, *(978-0-9815879; 978-1-953566)* Orders Addr.: P.O. Box 56508, Sherman Oaks, CA 91413 USA (SAN 855-9643) Tel 818-219-4377; Toll Free Fax: 888-863-4377
Web site: http://www.paraphrasellc.com; http://www.espete.com.

Parascension, Inc., *(978-0-9729380; 978-0-615-18212-4)* 222 Oak Grove Rd., Suite 201, Bradfordwoods, PA 15015-1338 USA; *Imprints:* Parascension Press (Parascen)
E-mail: jameshayhurst@zoominternet.net
Web site: http://www.parascension.com; http://www.badcommandments.com; http://www.adventuresofmercurylane.com.

Parascension Pr. *Imprint of* **Parascension, Inc.**

ParaTomb Studios, *(978-0-578-44423-9; 978-1-7336825)* 23441 Via Burriana, Mission Viejo, CA 92691 USA Tel 530-867-7875
E-mail: drew@paratombstudios.com
Web site: paratombstudios.com.

Parent Brigade Company, The, *(978-0-9774998)* 530 New Los Angeles Ave., Suite 115-332, Moorpark, CA 93021 USA Fax: 805-523-0119.

Parent Child Pr., Inc., *(978-0-939195; 978-0-9601016)* Orders Addr.: 11 W 9th St, Santa Rosa, CA 95401 USA (SAN 208-4333) Tel 707-579-3003; Fax: 707-579-1604; Toll Free: 866-727-3682; Edit Addr.: 11 W 9th St, Santa Rosa, CA 95401 USA (SAN 662-7331)
E-mail: smcmath@montessoriservices.com
Web site: http://http://www.montessoriservices.com/parent-child-press.

Parent Perks, Inc., *(978-0-9822150)* 217 Bellevue St., Newton, MA 02458 USA (SAN 857-569X)
E-mail: parentperks@yahoo.com.

Parent Positive Pr., *(978-0-9721502)* 446 Willis Ave., No. 118, Williston Park, NY 11596-0118 USA (SAN 257-4438) Tel 516-997-0051
E-mail: Info@parentpositive.com
Web site: http://www.girlsonlyweightloss.com.

Parental Interventional Tools, Inc, *(978-0-9778274)* P.O. Box 547, Southbury, CT 06488 USA Tel 203-264-1054
E-mail: pittools@aol.com
Web site: http://www.drketch.com; www.pit-inc.com.

†**Parenting Pr., Inc.,** *(978-0-943990; 978-0-9602862; 978-1-884734; 978-1-936903)* Orders Addr.: P.O. Box 75267, Seattle, WA 98175 USA (SAN 215-6938) Tel 206-364-2900; Fax: 206-364-0702; Toll Free: 800-992-6657; Edit Addr.: P.O. Box 75267, Seattle, WA 98175 USA (SAN 699-5500)
E-mail: cthreadgill@ParentingPress.com
Web site: http://www.parentingpress.com
Dist(s): **Brodart Co.**
Follett School Solutions
Independent Pubs. Group
Midwest Library Service
MyiLibrary; *CIP.*

Parents Publishing Group *Imprint of* **Big Tent Bks.**

Pares Forma Press *See* **Pares Forma Pr. Will Way Bks., Inc.**

Pares Forma Pr. Will Way Bks., Inc., *(978-1-7327837; 978-1-7332880)* 212 Will Way, Byron, GA 31008 USA Tel 478-972-3448
E-mail: miepmary@gmail.com; MargaretRodeheaverAuthor@gmail.com
Web site: www.margaretrodeheaver.com.

Paris Pr., *(978-1-880203)* R.R. 2, Box 218, Paris, MO 65275 USA Tel 816-327-5576 Do not confuse with Paris Pr. in Northampton, MA.

Parish, Alex (GBR) *(978-0-9561613) Dist. by* **LuluCom.**

Parity Pr., *(978-0-9762015)* 1450 W. Horizon Ridge Pkwy, B-304-226, Henderson, NV 89012-4480 USA Tel 702-260-8989; Fax: 702-364-8988; Toll Free: 877-260-8989
E-mail: info@paritypress.biz
Web site: http://www.ShiftingRings.com.

Park Ave Pr., *(978-0-9995526)* 110 Park Ave., Yakima, WA 98902 USA Tel 509-339-5464
E-mail: larsen.ideas@gmail.com.

Park Hse. Bks., *(978-0-9755097)* 838 N. 6th St., Saint Clair, MI 48079 USA
E-mail: parkhousebooks@yahoo.com; mmerkau@yahoo.com
Web site: http://www.familyunity.us.

Park Tutor Schl., *(978-0-9612740)* 7200 N. College Ave., Indianapolis, IN 46240 USA (SAN 289-7903) Tel 317-415-2700; Fax: 317-254-2714; Toll Free: 888-782-5861
E-mail: info@parktudor.org
Web site: http://www.parktudor.org.

Parker Girl Publishing, *(978-0-9855074)* 227 Shoreline Dr., Honey Brook, PA 19344 USA Tel 610-496-5070
E-mail: Huganursem@gmail.com.

Parker Hse. Publishing, *(978-0-9895474; 978-0-692-46594-3; 978-0-692-47078-7; 978-0-692-47152-4; 978-0-692-51134-3; 978-0-692-52702-3; 978-0-692-55109-7; 978-0-692-56447-9; 978-0-692-58121-6; 978-0-692-60015-3; 978-0-692-63049-5; 978-0-692-64457-7; 978-0-692-65297-8; 978-0-692-73196-3; 978-0-692-73527-5; 978-0-692-78063-3; 978-0-692-79499-9; 978-0-692-82457-3; 978-0-692-83776-4; 978-0-692-90853-2; 978-0-692-93111-0; 978-0-692-93808-9; 978-0-692-94055-6; 978-0-692-95112-5; 978-0-692-98617-2; 978-1-7328427) 474 Great Oaks Blvd, Monticello, FL 32344 USA Tel 850-997-4595*
E-mail: docneedles@aol.com
Dist(s): **CreateSpace Independent Publishing Platform.**

Parker, Laurie, *(978-0-9729615; 978-0-9980060)* 111 Dunbrook Dr., Starkville, MS 39759 USA.

Parker Publishing Company *See* **Parker-Wallace Publishing Co., LLC**

Parker Publishing Inc., *(978-1-60043)* 12523 Limonite Ave. #440-438, Mira Loma, CA 91752 USA Fax: 681-685-8036
E-mail: miriam@parker-publishing.com
Web site: http://www.parker-publishing.com
Dist(s): **CreateSpace Independent Publishing Platform.**

Parker-Wallace Publishing Co., LLC, *(978-0-9654700; 978-1-893091)* Orders Addr.: P.O. Box 1111, Stroudsburg, PA 18360 USA; *Imprints:* My Ancestors, My Heroes (My Ancestors)
E-mail: thebusiness2@yahoo.com.

Parkhurst Brook Pubs., *(978-0-9615664)* 303 Perrin Rd., Potsdam, NY 13676 USA (SAN 695-9121) Tel 315-265-9037
E-mail: mhcharle@northnet.org.

Parkhurst Brothers, Inc., Pubs., *(978-1-935166; 978-1-62491)* Orders Addr.: 110 West Main, Marion, MI 49665 USA (SAN 856-7107) Tel 5015153224
E-mail: ted@parkhurstbrothers.com
Web site: www.parkhurstbrothers.com; http://www.parkhurstbrothers.com
Dist(s): **Chicago Distribution Ctr.**

Parkhurst, R.M., *(978-0-9770323)* Orders Addr.: P.O. Box 1033, Redwood City, CA 94064 USA; Edit Addr.: P.O. Box 1013, Atascadero, CA 93423-1013 USA
E-mail: parkhurst@bigfoot.com.

Parklane Publishing, *(978-1-59384)* Div. of Book Club of America, 100 Marcus Blvd. Ste. 8, Hauppauge, NY 11788-3749 USA
E-mail: lbaumert@bookclubusa.com
Web site: http://www.parklanepublishing.com.

Parks Publishing *Imprint of* **RBC Publishing Co., Inc.**

Parkside Pubns., Inc., *(978-0-9617266; 978-0-9820774)* 601 Union St. Ste. 2600, Seattle, WA 98101 USA (SAN 663-4907) Do not confuse with Parkside Pubns., Inc., Davis, SD
E-mail: info@parksidepublications.com
Web site: http://www.parksidepublications.com
Dist(s): **Partners Bk. Distributing, Inc.**

Parkway Pr., Ltd., *(978-0-9826641; 978-0-9828089)* 330 Smith St., Niles, OH 44446-1735 USA Tel 330-505-8113
E-mail: dlbrown88@yahoo.com
Web site: www.parkwaypress.com.

Parkway Pubs., Inc., *(978-0-9635752; 978-1-887905; 978-1-933251)*
E-mail: parkwaypub@hotmail.com
Web site: http://www.parkwaypublishers.com
Dist(s): **Blair**
Julia Taylor Ebel.

Parkwest Pubns., Inc., *(978-0-88186)* P.O. Box 310251, Miami, FL 33231 USA (SAN 264-6846) Tel 305-256-7880; Fax: 305-256-7816
E-mail: parkwest@parkwestpubs.com; info@parkwestpubs.com
Web site: http://www.parkwestpubs.com
Dist(s): **Independent Pubs. Group.**

Parlance Publishing, *(978-0-9721032)* Orders Addr.: P.O. Box 841, Columbus, MS 39703-0841 USA (SAN 255-0806) Tel 662-327-4064; Fax: 662-327-4504; Edit Addr.: 1099 Southdown Pkwy., Columbus, MS 39701 USA
E-mail: parlancepub@aol.com; mail@abookery.com
Web site: http://www.parlancepublishing.com; http://www.abookery.com.

Parlor Pr., *(978-0-9724772; 978-1-932559; 978-1-60235; 978-1-64317)* Orders Addr.: 3015 Brackenberry Dr., Anderson, SC 29621 USA (SAN 254-8879) Tel 765-409-2649; Fax: 206-600-5076
E-mail: editor@parlorpress.com; sales@parlorpress.com
Web site: http://www.parlorpress.com
Dist(s): **Ebsco Publishing**
MBS Textbook Exchange, Inc.
SPD-Small Pr. Distribution
ebrary, Inc.

Parra Grande Pr., *(978-0-9815541; 978-0-615-19049-5)* 211 E. Carrillo St., No. 301, Santa Barbara, CA 93101 USA (SAN 855-8671) Tel 805-899-3210; Fax: 805-899-3211 E-mail: jb657@verizon.net.

Parragon Books *Imprint of* **Cottage Door Pr.**

Parragon, Inc., *(978-0-7525; 978-1-85813; 978-1-4054)* Div. of Parragon Publishing, 440 Park Ave. S, 13th Flr., New York, NY 10016 USA (SAN 256-7385) Tel 212-629-9773; Fax: 212-629-9756 *Dist(s):* **Central Programs.**

Parramon Ediciones S.A. (ESP) *(978-84-342) Dist. by* **Distr Norma.**

Parramon Ediciones S.A. (ESP) *(978-84-342) Dist. by* **Continental Bk.**

Parramon Ediciones S.A. (ESP) *(978-84-342) Dist. by* **Lectorum Pubns.**

Parrish, Fayrene, *(978-0-9826717)* 264 Country Club Dr., Avila Beach, CA 93424 USA Tel 805-500-5481 *Dist(s):* **CreateSpace Independent Publishing Platform.**

Parrot Pr., *(978-0-615-17122-7)* 6200 Vista Del Mar, Suite 313, Playa del Rey, CA 90293 USA Tel 310-574-0911 E-mail: mira@miramarmango.com Web site: http://www.parrotstory.com *Dist(s):* **Partners Pubs. Group, Inc.**

PARSEC Ink, *(978-0-9743231; 978-0-615-15280-6; 978-0-615-23540-0; 978-0-578-03103-3)* P.O. Box 3681, Pittsburgh, PA 15230-3681 USA E-mail: dianetumshek@gmail.com; renaissancewomn04@gmail.com Web site: http://parsecink.com/ *Dist(s):* **Lulu Pr., Inc.**

PARSEC Publishing *See* **PARSEC Ink**

Parson Place Pr., LLC, *(978-0-9786567; 978-0-9842163; 978-0-9888528)* 10701 Tanner Williams Rd., Mobile, AL 36608-8846 USA (SAN 851-254X); P.O. Box 8277, Mobile, AL 36689-0277 Tel 251-645-9803 E-mail: info@parsonplacepress.com; mlwhite@parsonplacepress.com Web site: http://www.parsonplacepress.com *Dist(s):* **Ingram Content Group Spring Arbor Distributors, Inc.**

Parsons Porch Bks., *(978-0-9826337; 978-0-9829413; 978-1-936912; 978-0-692-25814-9; 978-0-692-30031-2; 978-0-692-30040-4; 978-0-692-30872-1; 978-0-692-32034-1; 978-0-692-32056-3; 978-0-692-32058-7; 978-0-692-32063-1; 978-0-692-32066-2; 978-0-692-32067-9; 978-0-692-32776-0; 978-0-692-33452-2; 978-0-692-33526-0; 978-0-692-33625-0; 978-0-692-33626-7; 978-0-692-35217-5; 978-0-692-35889-4; 978-0-692-35891-7; 978-0-692-35894-8; 978-0-692-36083-5; 978-0-692-36086-6; 978-0-692-38065-9; 978-0-692-38067-3; 978-0-692-380) 121 Holly Trail NW, Cleveland, TN 37311 USA Tel 423-476-4122* E-mail: dtullock@parsonsporch.com Web site: http://www.parsonsporch.com *Dist(s):* **CreateSpace Independent Publishing Platform.**

Parsons Technology, *(978-1-57264)* Subs. of The Learning Co., Orders Addr.: P.O. Box 100, Hiawatha, IA 52233-0100 USA (SAN 665-6161) Tel 319-395-9626; Fax: 319-378-0335; Toll Free: 800-833-3241 *Dist(s):* **Spring Arbor Distributors, Inc.**

Partae Pr., *(978-0-9662608)* 703 Ivinson Ave., Laramie, WY 82070 USA (SAN 254-1688) Tel 307-745-6893 E-mail: press@partae.com Web site: http://www.partae.com.

Parthenon Pr., *(978-0-9718398)* 4839 Fullmoon Dr., El Sobrante, CA 94803-2139 USA Tel 510-223-6850 Do not confuse with Parthenon Pr., in New York, NY E-mail: wakingthetiger@yahoo.com Web site: http://expage.com/tigerspirit *Dist(s):* **CreateSpace Independent Publishing Platform.**

Parthian Bks. (GBR) *(978-0-9521558; 978-1-902638; 978-1-905762; 978-1-906998; 978-1-907476; 978-1-912681; 978-1-910409) Dist. by* **IPG Chicago.**

PartnerPress.org, *(978-1-944098)* 7668 El Camino Real Ste 104-333, Carlsbad, CA 92009 USA Tel 760-814-1416 E-mail: publish@partnerpress.org.

Partners in Development *See* **Partners in Development Foundation**

Partners in Development Foundation, *(978-1-933835)* 2040 Bachelot St., Honolulu, HI 96817 USA Tel 808-595-2752; Fax: 808-595-4932 E-mail: pid@pidfoundation.org Web site: http://www.pidfoundation.org *Dist(s):* **Islander Group.**

Partners in Learning, Incorporated *See* **MRN Pubns.**

Partridge Pub., *(978-1-4828; 978-1-5437)* 1663 Liberty Dr., Bloomington, IN 47403 USA Tel 812-334-5223; Fax: 812-334-5223; Toll Free: 877-655-1722 E-mail: sfurr@authorsoultions.com; jburns@authorsolutions.com Web site: http://www.partridgepublishing.com.

PartridgeIndia *Imprint of* **Author Solutions, Inc.**

Pascha Pr., *(978-0-9964045)* P.O. Box 944, Schererville, IN 46375 USA Tel 844-472-7242 E-mail: mkunch@paschapress.com Web site: www.paschapress.com.

Pasco Scientific, *(978-1-886998; 978-1-937492)* 10101 Foothills Blvd., Roseville, CA 95678-8905 USA Tel 916-786-3800; Fax: 916-786-8905.

Pascualina Producciones S.A., 150 42nd Ave. E., Seattle, WA 98112 USA Tel 206-940-5412; Fax: 206-621-7956 E-mail: magdelenarossa@aol.com *Dist(s):* **Independent Pubs. Group.**

Pasiteles Publishing Co., *(978-0-9785270)* 743 Belmont St., Belmont, MA 02478 USA Web site: http://www.pasiteles.com.

Passage Publishing, *(978-0-9715926; 978-0-9724619; 978-0-9814833)* Div. of Art by Marianne, P.O. Box 148304, Nashville, TN 37214 USA Tel 615-828-3657 Do not confuse with Passage Publishing in Seattle, WA E-mail: upcountrygirl@comcast.net; marsydotes1@live.com; upcountrygirl7@msn,com Web site: http://www.upcountrycreations.com; http://www.artbymarianne.com.

Passbooks *Imprint of* **National Learning Corp.**

Passion Profit Co., The/NicheMarket, *(978-0-9629202; 978-0-9745313; 978-0-9835808)* Div. of A Company Called W, P.O. Box 503991, SAIPAN, NP 96950 USA Tel 646-481-4238 E-mail: waltonsaipan@gmail.com Web site: http://www.passionprofit.com; http://www.fastandgrowyoung.com; http://www.agelessadept.com; http://www.hiphopbiz.com.

Passionate Purpose, *(978-0-9898579)* 377 Carodon Dr., Ruckersville, VA 22968 USA Tel 850-890-2768 E-mail: wildcatdtt@yahoo.com.

PassionQuest Technologies, LLC, *(978-0-9679338; 978-0-9912611)* P.O. Box 912, Marysville, OH 43040 USA (SAN 254-4326) Tel 707-688-2848; 5055 Business Ctr. Dr. Suite 108, Pmb 110, Fairfield, CA 94534 Tel 707-688-2848; *Imprints:* Wings-on-Disk (Wings Disk) E-mail: john@earnprofitsfromyourpassion.com Web site: http://www.OnMyMountain.com.

Passkey Learning Systems Nevada *See* **Passkey Online Educational Services**

Passkey Online Educational Services, *(978-0-9818971; 978-0-9822660; 978-1-935664; 978-1-937361)* 5348 Vegas Dr. 1670, Las Vegas, NV 89108 USA (SAN 856-8782); *Imprints:* Defiant Press (DefiantPr) E-mail: admin@passkeyonline.com; admin@passkeypublications.com Web site: http://www.passkeypublications.com *Dist(s):* **CreateSpace Independent Publishing Platform Ingram Content Group Lulu Pr., Inc.**

Passport Bks. *Imprint of* **McGraw-Hill Trade**

Pastime Pr., *(978-0-9711632; 978-1-932046)* Div. of CICA Industries, Inc., P.O. Box 741084, Boynton Beach, FL 33474 USA Tel 561-731-3400; Toll Free: 800-370-1174 Do not confuse with Pastime Press in Seattle, WA E-mail: cicausadotcom@aol.com Web site: http://www.pastimepress.com.

Pastime Pubns., *(978-0-9760276)* 1370 Trancas St., No. 372, Napa, CA 94558 USA Do not confuse with Pastime Publications in Walnut Creek, CA; Oakhill, VA; Herndon, VA Web site: http://napavalleypastime.com.

Pastime Pubns., LLC, *(978-0-692-77305-5)* 1303 Waterfront Dr., Virginia Beach, VA 23451 USA Tel 724-961-2922 E-mail: scott@pastimepublicationsllc.com.

Pastorpreneur Ministries, *(978-0-9716489; 978-0-9831958)* Orders Addr.: 6243 Camellia Ct., Rocklin, CA 95765 USA Tel 916-872-5435 E-mail: john@pastorpreneur.com Web site: http://www.pastorpreneur.com.

PastWays Inc., *(978-0-9671075)* Orders Addr.: P.O. Box 551, Farmington, MI 48332-0551 USA Tel 248-701-8112; Edit Addr.: 33414 Oakland, Suite 2, Farmington Hills, MI 48335-3571 USA E-mail: bgolden@pastways.info Web site: http://www.pastways.info.

Patagonia, *(978-0-9790659; 978-0-9801227; 978-1-938340; 978-1-952338)* 259 W. Santa Clara St., Ventura, CA 93001-2717 USA Tel 805-643-8616; Fax: 805-643-2367; Toll Free: 800-638-6464 E-mail: karla_olson@patagonia.com Web site: http://www.Patagonia.com *Dist(s):* **D.A.P./Distributed Art Pubs. MyiLibrary Publishers Group West (PGW).**

Patagonia Books *See* **Patagonia**

Patagonia Pr., *(978-1-882695)* P.O. Box 284, Bagdad, FL 32530 USA Tel 904-623-5790 Do not confuse with Patagonia Pr., Inc., Patagonia AZ E-mail: Patagoniapress@aol.com.

Patchwork Pr., *(978-0-615-88322-9; 978-0-615-91877-8; 978-0-615-93512-6; 978-0-615-98429-2; 978-0-692-20253-1)* 7707 Red Maple Dr., Plainfield, IL 60586 USA Tel 815-416-8236 *Dist(s):* **CreateSpace Independent Publishing Platform.**

Paterson Museum for Italian Girls Press *See* **Mill Street Forward, The**

Path of Peace Inc., The, *(978-0-9766702)* 6610 Dorel St., Suite B, Philadelphia, PA 19142 USA Tel 215-681-6592 E-mail: blessbango@yahoo.com Web site: http://www.thepathofpeace.net.

PathLight Bks. *Imprint of* **Sunesis Publishing Co.**

Pathway Bk. Service, Div. of MLES, Inc., Orders Addr.: 4 White Brook Rd., Gilsum, NH 03448 USA (SAN 170-0545) Tel 603-357-0236; Fax: 603-357-2073; Toll Free: 800-345-6665; P.O. Box 89, Gilsum, NH 03448; Edit Addr.: 34 Production Ave., Keene, NH 03431 USA (SAN 991-2657) Tel 603-357-0236 E-mail: pbs@pathwaybook.com Web site: http://www.pathwaybook.com.

Pathway Pr., *(978-0-87148; 978-1-59684; 978-1-64288)* Div. of Church of God Publishing Hse., Orders Addr.: P.O. Box 2250, Cleveland, TN 37320-2250 USA (SAN 665-7567); Edit Addr.: 1080 Montgomery Ave., Cleveland, TN 37311 USA (SAN 202-8727) Tel 423-476-4512; Fax: 423-478-7616; Toll Free: 800-553-8506 (trade only) Do not confuse with Pathway Press, San Rafael, CA E-mail: stephanie@pathwaypress.org; elaine_mcdavid@pathwaypress.org Web site: http://www.pathwaypress.org.

Pathways into Science, *(978-0-9779427)* 7417 River Falls Dr., Potomac, MD 20854 USA (SAN 850-5683) Tel 301-365-7593 Web site: http://pathwaysintoscience.com.

Patmos, Inc., *(978-0-9741748)* P.O. Box 124, Maple Hill, KS 66507-0124 USA Web site: http://www.patmos.us.

Patmos Publishing, *(978-0-9768545)* 4591 Jernigan Rd., Milton, FL 32571-1921 USA Tel 850-994-0908 (phone/fax) Do not confuse with Patmos Publications in Bristol GBR E-mail: patmosprinting@gmail.com Web site: http://www.patmospublishing.com.

Patou Bks., LLC, *(978-0-9767756)* 1550 Larimer St., Suite 459, Denver, CO 80202-1602 USA.

Patrenialla Turner, Queen , *(978-0-578-14812-0)* .

Patrick Henry College Pr., *(978-0-9714458)* 1 Patrick Henry Cir., Purcellville, VA 20132 USA Tel 540-338-1776; Fax: 540-338-8707 E-mail: info@phc.edu Web site: http://www.phc.edu.

PatrickGeorge (GBR) *(978-0-9562558; 978-1-908473) Dist. by* **IPG Chicago.**

†Patrick's Pr., *(978-0-944322; 978-0-9609412)* Orders Addr.: P.O. Box 5189, Columbus, GA 31906 USA (SAN 274-466X) Tel 706-322-1584; Fax: 706-322-5806; Toll Free: 800-654-1052; Edit Addr.: 2218 Wynnton Rd., Columbus, GA 31906 USA (SAN 243-2773) E-mail: quizbowl@aol.com Web site: http://www.patrickspress.com *Dist(s):* **Peller, A. W. & Assocs.**; *CIP.*

Patriot Media, Inc., *(978-0-9791642; 978-0-9845777; 978-0-9846638; 978-0-9888930; 978-0-9905724; 978-1-7323764)* Orders Addr.: P.O. Box 5414, Niceville, FL 32578 USA Tel 850-897-4204 (phone/fax) E-mail: dari.bradleyceo@patriotmediainc.com; dari@patriotmediainc.com Web site: http://www.patriotmediapublishing.com; http://www.patriotmediainc.com; http://www.patriotmediainternational.com; http://www.silentbattleground.com; http://www.dmulmer.com; http://www.staffmonkeys.com; http://www.paulsherbo.com; http://www.booksbynelson.com; http://www.those67blues.com *Dist(s):* **CreateSpace Independent Publishing Platform.**

Patriot Media Publishing *See* **Patriot Media, Inc.**

Patriot Pr., *(978-0-9796000; 978-1-941020)* 1505 Knoxlyn Rd., Gettysburg, PA 17325 USA (SAN 853-8735) E-mail: patriotpress@live.com Web site: http://www.patriotpressbooks.com; http://www.jessicajamesbooks.com.

Patriot Publishing, *(978-0-9789936)* Ernest Beath, III, 2216 Horn Point Rd., Cambridge, MD 21613-3379 USA Tel 410-228-5771 E-mail: docprb@bluecrab.org.

Patten Point Marketing Services, Incorporated *See* **Liberty Manuals Co.**

Pattern Pr., *(978-0-9729248; 978-1-935559; 978-1-941961)* Orders Addr.: P.O. Box 2737, Fallbrook, CA 92088 USA; Edit Addr.: 40521 De Luz Rd., Fallbrook, CA 92028 USA E-mail: patternpress1@gmail.com Web site: http://www.patternpress.com.

Patterson, Stacey Lynn, *(978-0-578-21593-8)* 1030 Strahley Pl., Pittsburgh, PA 15220 USA Web site: http://shermangc2014.wixsite.com/slpatterson.

Patton, Lashunda, *(978-0-692-27864-2; 978-0-692-09452-5)* 2500 Thomason Cr No. 100, Arlington, TX 76006 USA Tel 817-680-5492 E-mail: lashunda.patton@yahoo.com.

Patty Huston-Holm, *(978-0-692-92156-2; 978-0-692-04996-9; 978-0-692-14271-4; 978-0-578-72034-0)* 9685 Slough Rd., CANAL WINCHESTER, OH 43110 USA Tel 614-837-0164 E-mail: hustonpat@gmail.com *Dist(s):* **Ingram Content Group.**

Patty's Blooming Words, *(978-0-615-78050-4; 978-0-9893303)* 693 Springlake Dr., Franklin, TN 37064 USA Tel 615-790-0109 E-mail: pattysbloomers@me.com.

†Pauline Bks. & Media, *(978-0-8198)* 50 St. Paul's Ave., Boston, MA 02130-3491 USA (SAN 203-8900) Tel 617-522-8911; Fax: 617-524-8035; Toll Free: 800-876-4463 (orders only) E-mail: editorial@pauline.org; kcorina@paulinemedia.com Web site: http://www.PAULINE.org *Dist(s):* **MyiLibrary O'Reilly Media, Inc. St Pauls/Alba Hse. Pubs.**; *CIP.*

†Paulist Pr., *(978-0-8091; 978-1-893757; 978-1-58768; 978-1-61643)* 997 MacArthur Blvd., Mahwah, NJ 07430-2096 USA (SAN 202-5159) Tel 201-825-7300 (ext. 232); Fax: 201-825-8345; Toll Free Fax: 800-836-3161; Toll Free: 800-218-1903; *Imprints:* HiddenSpring (HidSpring); E T Nedder (ETNedder); Ambassador Books (Ambass Bks) E-mail: info@paulistpress.com Web site: http://www.paulistpress.com *Dist(s):* **Bookazine Co., Inc. Spring Arbor Distributors, Inc.**; *CIP.*

Paulsen, Marc Productions, Incorporated *See* **Stance Pubns.**

Paulus Publishing, *(978-0-9744863)* 6115 E. Hillview St., Mesa, AZ 85205 USA.

Paved Roads Productions, *(978-0-9795862)* Orders Addr.: P.O. Box 640173, Pike Road, AL 36064 USA.

Pavilion Bks. (GBR) *(978-0-85177; 978-0-86101; 978-0-86283; 978-1-85470; 978-1-85585; 978-1-85753; 978-1-85833; 978-0-947553; 978-1-84138; 978-1-85561; 978-0-904609; 978-1-85028; 978-1-84065; 978-1-85600; 978-1-902616; 978-1-85993; 978-0-86288; 978-1-84333; 978-1-903954; 978-1-84411; 978-1-86222; 978-1-84340; 978-1-84458; 978-0-86124; 978-1-85841; 978-1-906388; 978-1-908449; 978-1-909397) Dist. by* **Peng Rand Hse.**

Pavilion Bks. (GBR) *(978-0-85177; 978-0-86101; 978-0-86283; 978-1-85470; 978-1-85585; 978-1-85753; 978-1-85833; 978-0-947553; 978-1-84138; 978-1-85561; 978-0-904609; 978-1-85028; 978-1-84065; 978-1-85600; 978-1-902616; 978-1-85993; 978-0-86288; 978-1-84333; 978-1-903954; 978-1-84411; 978-1-86222; 978-1-84340; 978-1-84458; 978-0-86124; 978-1-85841; 978-1-906388; 978-1-908449; 978-1-909397) Dist. by* **Sterling.**

Pavilion Bks. (GBR) *(978-0-85177; 978-0-86101; 978-0-86283; 978-1-85470; 978-1-85585; 978-1-85753; 978-1-85833; 978-0-947553; 978-1-84138; 978-1-85561; 978-0-904609; 978-1-85028; 978-1-84065; 978-1-85600; 978-1-902616; 978-1-85993; 978-0-86288; 978-1-84333; 978-1-903954; 978-1-84411; 978-1-86222; 978-1-84340; 978-1-84458; 978-0-86124; 978-1-85841; 978-1-906388; 978-1-908449; 978-1-909397) Dist. by* **Trafalgar.**

Pavilion Pr., Inc., *(978-1-4145)* 1213 Vine St., Philadelphia, PA 19107 USA Tel 215-569-9779; Fax: 215-569-8814 Web site: http://www.pavilionpress.com.

Pavilion Pubs., *(978-0-88432; 978-1-57970)* Div. of Pavilion Publishers, LLC, P.O. Box 1460, Guilford, CT 06437 USA (SAN 213-957X) Tel 518-605-5179; Toll Free: 800-243-1234 E-mail: Antonydaou@gmail.com; Mcgradylaura@gmail.com Web site: http://www.audioforum.com *Dist(s):* **Bolchazy-Carducci Pubs.**

Paw Print Pubns., *(978-0-9785473)* Orders Addr.: 4206 NE Newbury Ct., Lees Summit, MO 64064-1617 USA (SAN 850-9573) Toll Free: 877-267-9482; *Imprints:* Austin & Charlie Adventures (Austin & Charlie Adventures) E-mail: lparker154@aol.com; pawfacts@aol.com; linda8000@sbcglobal.net Web site: http://www.austincharlieadventures.com *Dist(s):* **Book Clearing Hse.**

Paw Print Publishing, *(978-0-9770898)* Orders Addr.: P.O. Box 48309, Cumberland, NC 28331-8309 USA Web site: www.k9fluffy.com.

Paw Prints *Imprint of* **Baker & Taylor, CATS**

Paw Prints Press *See* **Heather & Highlands Publishing**

Pawl, Jacqueline, *(978-0-578-44031-6)* 676 Cambridge Way, Bolingbrook, IL 60440 USA Tel 630-345-0370 E-mail: jackiepawl21@aol.com *Dist(s):* **Ingram Content Group.**

PawlingPr., *(978-0-692-95226-9)* 24809 Magic Mtn Pkwy, Apt 1733, Valencia, CA 91355 USA Tel 310-730-9060 E-mail: jdmcmah@gmail.com Web site: www.pawlingpress.com.

Paws and Claws Publishing, LLC, *(978-0-9846724; 978-0-9906067; 978-1-946198)* 1586 Skeet Club Rd. Ste 102-175, High Point, NC 27265 USA Tel 336-297-9783 E-mail: jcappoen@pawsandclawspublishing.com Web site: http://www.pawsandclawspublishing.com.

Paws In the Sand Publishing, *(978-0-9790057)* Orders Addr.: 4644 Pepper Mill St., Moorpark, CA 93021-9302 USA (SAN 852-193X) Fax: 805-553-9253 Web site: http://pawsinthesand.com.

Paxen Publishing LLC *See* **Paxen Publishing LLC**

Paxen Publishing LLC, *(978-1-934350; 978-1-7326905; 978-1-7337320; 978-1-7345284; 978-1-7345285; 978-1-7345289; 978-1-7346206; 978-1-7351585; 978-1-7351586; 978-1-7356953)* 2194 Hwy. A1A Suite 208, Indian Harbour Beach, FL 32937 USA Tel 321-425-3030; 866-547-1895 Web site: http://www.paxenpublishing.com.

Paycock Pr., *(978-0-931181; 978-0-9602424)* 3819 N. 13th St., Arlington, VA 22201 USA (SAN 212-5420) Tel 703-525-9296 phone/fax E-mail: gargoyle@gargoylemagazine.com Web site: http://www.gargoylemagazine.com.

Payne, Christine, *(978-0-9740643)* P.O. Box 951, Mountain Home, AR 72654-0951 USA.

Payne, Yadira V. Publishing, *(978-0-9747350)* 341 Lamplighter Ln., Martinez, GA 30907 USA Tel 706-414-9566 E-mail: yvppublishing@knology.net.

PAZ Publishing, *(978-0-942253)* Div. of PAZ Percussion, Orders Addr.: 2415 Bevington St. NW, North Canton, OH 44709-2221 USA (SAN 666-8100) Tel 330-493-6661 (phone/fax) E-mail: PAZPublishing@aol.com Web site: http://www.PAZPublishing.com.

PB&J OmniMedia *Imprint of* **Takahashi & Black**

PBD, Inc., *(978-0-9846038; 978-0-9837260; 978-1-62219)* 1650 Bluegrass Lakes Pkwy., Alpharetta, GA 30004 USA (SAN 126-6039) Tel 770-442-8633; Fax: 770-442-9742 Web site: http://www.pbd.com.

PBL Stories LLC, *(978-0-9792379)* Orders Addr.: P.O. Box 393, Lynn Haven, FL 32444-4272 USA Tel 850-348-0718; Fax: 850-265-9815; Edit Addr.: 1812 S. Hwy. 77, Suite. 115, Lynn Haven, FL 32444-4272 USA E-mail: booksales@pblstories.com Web site: http://www.pblstories.com.

PC Treasures, Inc., *(978-1-933796; 978-1-60072)* 1795 N. Lapeer Rd., Oxford, MI 48371-2415 USA (SAN 857-0930)
E-mail: lthomas@pctreasures.com; jbrandt@pctreasures.com; jadams@pctreasures.com
Web site: http://www.pctreasures.com.

PCS Edventures, Inc., *(978-0-9753193; 978-0-9827203)* 345 Bobwhite Ct., Suite 200, Boise, ID 83706 USA Tel 208-343-3110; Fax: 208-343-1321; Toll Free: 800-429-3110
E-mail: rmwright@pcsedu.com; rgrover@pcsedu.com; agranger@pcsedu.com
Web site: http://www.edventures.com.

PD Hse. Holdings, LLC, *(978-0-9815333; 978-0-9984644)* 910 S. Meadow Dr., Sandusky, OH 44870 USA (SAN 855-806X)
E-mail: pjgron@pjgrondin.com
Web site: http://www.pjgrondin.com.

PDG *Imprint of* **Publishers Design Group, Inc.**

†Peabody Essex Museum, *(978-0-87577; 978-0-88389)* Orders Addr.: East India Sq., Salem, MA 01970 USA Tel 978-745-9500 ext 3047; Fax: 978-740-3622; Toll Free: 800-745-4054 ext 3047
E-mail: wholesale@pem.org
Web site: http://www.pem.org
Dist(s): **Antique Collectors' Club**
Ingram Publisher Services
Univ. Pr. of New England
Univ. of Washington Pr.; *CIP.*

†Peabody Museum of Archaeology & Ethnology, Harvard Univ., Pubns. Dept., *(978-0-87365)* Orders Addr.: 11 Divinity Ave., Cambridge, MA 02138 USA (SAN 203-1426) Tel 617-496-9922; 617-495-3938; Fax: 617-495-7535
E-mail: ddickers@fas.harvard.edu
Web site: http://www.peabody.harvard.edu/publications
Dist(s): **Harvard Univ. Pr.**
Univ. Pr. of New England
Univ. of New Mexico Pr.; *CIP.*

Peabody Publishing Co., *(978-0-9963323)* 325 Thames Dr., Colorado Springs, CO 80906 USA Tel 719-237-8014
E-mail: drphineaspeabody@gmail.com.

Peace B Still Ministries Pr., *(978-0-9752665)* 205 Joel Blvd., Suite 107, Lehigh Acres, FL 33972-0202 USA
E-mail: gduncan316@aol.com.

Peace Education Foundation, *(978-1-878227; 978-1-934760)* 1900 Biscayne Blvd., Miami, FL 33132-1025 USA Tel 305-576-5075; Fax: 305-576-3106; Toll Free: 800-749-8838
Web site: http://www.peaceeducation.com.

Peace Evolutions, LLC, *(978-0-9753837; 978-0-9912489)* P.O. Box 458, Glen Echo, MD 20812-0458 USA (SAN 256-2146) Fax: 301-263-9280
E-mail: info@peace-evolutions.com; julie@peace-evolutions.com
Web site: http://www.peace-evolutions.com.

Peace Hill Press *See* **Well-Trained Mind Pr.**

Peace Love Karma Publishing, *(978-0-9743540)* 2584 Rim Rock Way, Santa Rosa, CA 95404 USA
E-mail: Carol@peacelovekarma.com; 11lovepoet@gmail.com
Web site: http://www.peacelovekarma.com
Dist(s): **New Leaf Distributing Co., Inc.**

Peace of Mind Inc, *(978-0-692-53539-4; 978-0-9976954)* 5540 Nevada Ave. NW, Washington, DC 20015 USA Tel 202-494-2624; *Imprints:* Peace of Mind Press (P M P)
E-mail: teachpeacedc@gmail.com
Web site: www.teachpeaceofmind.com.

Peace of Mind LLC *See* **Peace of Mind Inc**

Peace of Mind Pr. *Imprint of* **Peace of Mind Inc**

Peace Power Pr., *(978-0-9824601)* 6044 Waterloo Rd., Dayton, OH 45402-3015 USA (SAN 858-2254) Tel 937-227-3223
Web site: http://daytonpeacemuseum.org.

Peace Rug Company, Inc., The, *(978-0-9763949)* 407 W. Emery St., Dalton, GA 30720 USA Tel 706-272-0200; Fax: 706-226-2296; Toll Free: 888-732-2378
E-mail: info@peacerug.com
Web site: http://www.peacerug.com.

Peaceable Kingdom Pr., *(978-1-56890; 978-1-59395)* 950 Gilmain, Suite 200, Berkeley, CA 94710 USA Tel 510-558-2051; Fax: 510-558-2052; Toll Free: 800-444-7778 Do not confuse with Peaceable Kingdom Press in Greenville, VA
E-mail: djaffe@pkpress.com
Web site: http://www.pkpress.com.

Peaceable Productions, *(978-0-9709187)* Orders Addr.: P.O. Box 708, Center Hill, FL 33514 USA (SAN 254-4946) Tel 352-793-7516; Edit Addr.: 6698 SE 57th Rd., Center Hill, FL 33514 USA Tel 352-793-7516; Fax: 775-514-8681
E-mail: yvonne@atlantic.net.

Peaceful Daily, Inc., *(978-0-9884926; 978-0-9970143; 978-0-9982579)* 800 Village Walk Suite 103, Guilford, CT 06437 USA Tel 203-298-8077
E-mail: sandy@peacefuldaily.com
Web site: www.peacefuldaily.com.

Peaceful Thoughts Pr., *(978-0-9725118)* 598 Straton Chase SE, Marietta, GA 30067 USA
Web site: http://www.peacefulthoughts.net.

PeaceLight Pr., *(978-0-9971661)* 1206 Lineberry St., Ramseur, NC 27316 USA Tel 336-633-9938
E-mail: chip.womick@twc.com.

Peacemakers Press *See* **Positive Spin Pr.**

Peach Blossom Pubns., *(978-0-941367)* 120 E. Beaver Ave. Apt. 212, State College, PA 16801-4991 USA (SAN 665-4800)
E-mail: inezwaterson@prodigy.net
Dist(s): **Quality Bks., Inc.**

Peach Plum Pr., *(978-0-578-04395-1)* 123 Picnic Ave., San Rafael, CA 94901 USA
E-mail: marymitchelldesign@comcast.net.

Peach Tree Pr., *(978-0-9893120; 978-1-62910)* 1321 Upland Dr., Houston, TX 77043 USA Tel 919-502-0151
E-mail: arpl.dropbox@gmail.com.

PeachMoon Publishing, *(978-0-9795831)* 3915 Bonnett Creek Ln., Hoschton, GA 30548-6204 USA (SAN 853-814X)
E-mail: Alice@peachmoonpublishing.com
Web site: http://luckythelizard.com; http://peachmoonpublishing.com.

Peachtree Junior *Imprint of* **Peachtree Publishing Co. Inc.**

Peachtree Publishers *See* **Peachtree Publishing Co. Inc.**

†Peachtree Publishing Co. Inc., *(978-0-931948; 978-0-934601; 978-1-56145; 978-1-68263)* 1700 Chattahoochee Ave., NW, Atlanta, GA 30318-2112 USA (SAN 212-1999) Tel 404-876-8761; Fax: 404-875-2578; Toll Free Fax: 800-875-8909; Toll Free: 800-241-0113; *Imprints:* Peachtree Junior (Peachtree); Freestone (Freestone)
E-mail: sales@peachtree-online.com; palermo@peachtree-online.com; McManus@peachtree-online.com
Web site: http://www.peachtree-online.com; www.cheshirecheesecat.com; www.christmasinthetrenches.info; www.14cowsforamerica.com
Dist(s): **Children's Plus, Inc.**
Heinecken & Assoc., Ltd.
Lectorum Pubns., Inc.
MyiLibrary
Open Road Integrated Media, Inc.; *CIP.*

Peacock Tree Publishing, *(978-1-9160491)* 52 Parkgrove Dr., Edinburgh, EH4 7QG GBR Tel 07476 303909 Admin
E-mail: madly.chatterjee@gmail.com
Web site: http://www.madlychatterjee.com.

Peak City Publishing, LLC, *(978-1-935711)* 104B N. Salem St., Apex, NC 27502 USA Tel 919-758-9516
Web site: http://www.peakcitypublishing.com.

Peak Writing, LLC, *(978-0-9717330; 978-0-9767961)* Orders Addr.: P.O. Box 14196, Savannah, GA 31416 USA Tel 912-398-2987; Toll Free Fax: 888-226-4811; Edit Addr.: 12 Mercer Rd., Savannah, GA 31411 USA Do not confuse with Peak Writing in Frisco, CO
E-mail: info@peakwriting.com
Dist(s): **Quality Bks., Inc.**
Send The Light Distribution LLC
Spring Arbor Distributors, Inc.

Peaks Pr. LLC, *(978-1-938032)* 630 Race St., Denver, CO 80206 USA Tel 720-560-3779
E-mail: info@peakspress.com
Dist(s): **BookBaby.**

Peanut Butter Publishing, *(978-0-89716; 978-1-59849)* 2207 Fairview Ave. E., Houseboat No. 4, Seattle, WA 98102 USA (SAN 212-7881) Tel 206-860-4900 Toll Free: 877-728-8837
E-mail: ewolfpub@aol.com
Web site: http://www.peanutbutterpublishing.com.

Peapod Pr. *Imprint of* **PublishingWorks**

Peapod Publishing, Inc., *(978-0-9729507; 978-0-9894591)* P.O. Box 951599, Lake Mary, FL 32795-1599 USA Tel 407-333-3030
E-mail: info@peapodpublishing.com
Web site: http://www.adventureswithpawpaw.com; http://www.pawpawspals.org; http://www.peapodpublishing.com; http://www.borntoflybook.com; http://www.born2fly.org
Dist(s): **BookBaby.**

Pearl & Dotty, *(978-0-9772441)* Orders Addr.: P.O. Box 2162, Seattle, WA 98111-2162 USA
E-mail: pearlanddotty@gmail.com; holler@pearlanddotty.com
Web site: http://www.pearlanddotty.com.

Pearl Pr., *(978-0-9741332)* 3104 O St., No. 175, Sacramento, CA 95816 USA Do not confuse with Pearl Press in Nazareth PA, Eastport MI
E-mail: info@pearlpress.net
Web site: http://www.pearlpress.net
Dist(s): **Quality Bks., Inc.**

Pearl Pr., *(978-0-9674525)* Orders Addr.: P.O. Box 266, Eastport, MI 49627 USA (SAN 299-9870) Tel 231-599-2372 (phone/fax); Edit Addr.: 6027 M-88 Hwy., Eastport, MI 49627 USA Do not confuse with Pearl Pr., Nazareth, PA, Sacramento CA
E-mail: Beebystudio@mailbug.com.

Pearl Publishing, LLC, *(978-0-9785264; 978-0-9826175; 978-1-937390)* 2587c Southside Blvd., Melba, ID 83641 USA Tel 888-499-9666
E-mail: info@pearlpublishing.net
Web site: http://wupublishing.com; http://666america.com; http://pearlpublishing.net.

Pearlman, Beth, *(978-0-9767522)* 1773 Diane Rd., Mendota Heights, MN 55118 USA.

Pearls & Ivy Publishing *See* **Monster Ivy Publishing**

Pearlsong Pr., *(978-0-9713247; 978-1-59719)* P.O. Box 58065, Nashville, TN 37205 USA (SAN 255-9188) Tel 615-356-5188
E-mail: contact@pearlsong.com
Web site: http://www.pearlsong.com.

PearlStone Publishing, Inc., *(978-0-9724586; 978-0-9816883; 978-0-9841899; 978-1-936513; 978-1-944348; 978-1-944348-20-5)* 514-201 Daniels St., Raleigh, NC 27603 USA
E-mail: publish@pendiumpublishing.com
Web site: http://www.pendiumpublishing.com.

Pearn & Assocs. Inc., *(978-0-9777318; 978-0-9841683; 978-0-9846523; 978-0-9897242; 978-1-7357731)* 1428 S. California Ave., Suite 4, Loveland, CO 80537-7177 USA Tel 970-599-8924; *Imprints:* Over the Rainbow (Over the Rain)
E-mail: victorpearn@ymail.com.

Pearson Education, *(978-0-13; 978-0-582; 978-0-7686; 978-1-5093)* Orders Addr.: 200 Old Tappan Rd., Old Tappan, NJ 07675 USA (SAN 200-2175) Tel 201-767-5000 (Receptionist); Toll Free Fax: 800-445-6991; Toll Free: 800-428-5331; 800-922-0579; Edit Addr.: One Lake St., Upper Saddle River, NJ 07458 USA Tel 201-236-7000; 201-236-5321; Fax: 201-236-6549; 800 E. 96th St., Suite 300, Indianapolis, IN 46240 Toll Free: 800-571-4580; *Imprints:* Microsoft Press (MicrosoftPress)
E-mail: communications@pearsoned.com
Web site: http://www.pearsoned.com; www.pearson.com
Dist(s): **Gaunt, Inc.**
MyiLibrary
Trans-Atlantic Pubns., Inc.

Pearson Education Australia (AUS) *(978-0-7248; 978-0-7342; 978-0-7312; 978-1-86391; 978-0-7339; 978-0-85859; 978-0-86462; 978-1-74009; 978-1-74140; 978-1-876209; 978-1-74085; 978-1-74103; 978-1-74091; 978-1-74081; 978-1-74206; 978-1-4425; 978-0-86911; 978-0-7316-1261-1; 978-0-646-24199-9; 978-0-646-29552-7; 978-0-646-30941-5; 978-0-646-31855-4; 978-0-646-32904-8; 978-0-646-32905-5; 978-1-4860) Dist. by* **Cheng Tsui.**

Pearson Education, Ltd. (GBR) *(978-0-201; 978-0-273; 978-0-321; 978-0-582; 978-0-673; 978-1-4058; 978-1-84479; 978-1-84658; 978-1-84959; 978-1-84878; 978-1-84776; 978-1-4479; 978-1-292; 978-1-78726) Dist. by* **Trans-Atl Phila.**

Pearson Education, Ltd. (GBR) *(978-0-201; 978-0-273; 978-0-321; 978-0-582; 978-0-673; 978-1-4058; 978-1-84479; 978-1-84658; 978-1-84959; 978-1-84878; 978-1-84776; 978-1-4479; 978-1-292; 978-1-78726) Dist. by* **Pearson Educ.**

Pearson ESL, *(978-0-582)* Div. of Pearson International, 75 Arlington St., Boston, MA 02116 USA
Dist(s): **Pearson Education.**

Pearson Learning, *(978-0-7652; 978-1-4284)* Div of Pearson Education, Orders Addr.: P.O. Box 2500, Lebanon, IN 46052 USA Toll Free Fax: 800-393-3156; Toll Free: 800-321-3106; Edit Addr.: 1 Lake St., U Saddle Riv, NJ 07458-1813 USA Toll Free: 800-526-9907 (Customer Service)
E-mail: jeff.hoitsma@pearsonlearning.com
Web site: http://www.pearsonlearning.com
Dist(s): **Follett School Solutions.**

Pearson School *See* **Savvas Learning Co.**

Pearson, Shelley, *(978-1-7324082)* 16437 SE Stephens St, Portland, OR 97233 USA Tel 503-734-6202
E-mail: shelleypearsonwrites@gmail.com
Web site: shelleypearsonwrites.com.

Peartree r, *(978-0-935343)* Orders Addr.: P.O. Box 14533, Clearwater, FL 33766 USA Tel 727-531-4973 (phone/fax)7275314973
E-mail: peartreebooks@yahoo.com
Web site: http://www.peartree-books.com
Dist(s): **Brodart Co.**
Follett School Solutions.

Pebble *Imprint of* **Capstone**

Pebble Beach Pr., Ltd., *(978-1-883740)* P.O. Box 1171, Pebble Beach, CA 93953-1171 USA Tel 408-372-5559; Fax: 408-375-4525.

Pebbles Pr., *(978-1-7337582)* 130 Malcolm X Blvd, Apt 328, New York, NY 10026 USA Tel 646-541-7127
E-mail: cenydgaleria@mac.com
Web site: www.pebblespress.com.

Pebbleton Pr., *(978-0-9760011)* P.O. Box 1894, Duxbury, MA 02331 USA
E-mail: pebbletonpress@comcast.net
Web site: http://www.pebbletonpress.com.

Pecan Tree Publishing, *(978-0-9821114; 978-0-9832078; 978-0-615-67485-8; 978-0-9888969; 978-1-7328311; 978-1-7341058; 978-1-7347430; 978-1-7358295)* Orders Addr.: 2238 Greene St., Hollywood, FL 33020 USA Tel 786-763-1295
E-mail: adminservices@pecantreebooks.com; info@pecantreebooks.com
Web site: http://www.pecantreebooks.com/shop-ptp.html; http://www.pecantreebooks.com
Dist(s): **Ingram Bk. Co.**

Pecci Educational Pubs., *(978-0-943220)* 440 Davis Ct., No. 405, San Francisco, CA 94111 USA (SAN 240-558X) Tel 415-391-8579; Fax: 970-493-8781
E-mail: pecci@sirius.com
Web site: http://www.onlinereadingteacher.com.

PeDante Pr., *(978-0-9790199; 978-1-940844)* 4 White Oak, Danbury, CT 06410 USA Tel 203-350-9288
E-mail: erikagrey@rocketmail.com
Web site: www.erikagrey.com.

Peddlers Group, *(978-0-9802257; 978-0-9829177)* 1127 Parrish Rd., Leesville, SC 29070 USA Tel 803-657-5324; Fax: 803-753-9824
E-mail: peddlersgroup@gmail.com
Web site: http://www.peddlersgroup.com.

Pedia Learning, Inc. *See* **Logic of English, Inc**

Pedigree Bks., Ltd. (GBR) *(978-1-874507; 978-1-904329; 978-1-906450; 978-1-907602; 978-1-908152) Dist. by* **Diamond Book Dists.**

†Pedipress, Inc., *(978-0-914625)* Orders Addr.: 125 Red Gate Ln., Amherst, MA 01002 USA (SAN 287-7570) Tel 413-549-7798 M - Thurs. 8:30 to 4:30 EST; Fax: 413-549-4095; Toll Free: 800-611-6081 M - Thurs. 8:30 to 4:30 EST
E-mail: tplautassistant@gmail.com
Web site: http://www.pedipress.com
Dist(s): **INscribe Digital**; *CIP.*

Peebco Publishing Hse., The, *(978-0-9644758; 978-0-578-55731-1; 978-0-578-55739-7)* P.O. Box 45333, Saint Louis, MO 63145 USA (SAN 298-6760) Tel 636-346-7179
E-mail: Info@PeebcoPublishing.com
Web site: http://www.PeebcoPublishing.com.

Peek-A-Boo Publishing, *(978-1-943154)* 500 Montgomery St., Alexandria, VA 22314 USA Tel 703-348-9898; *Imprints:* See-Saw Publishing (See-SawPub)
E-mail: info@peekaboopublishing.com
Web site: peekaboopublishing.com.

Peel Productions, Inc., *(978-0-939217; 978-1-943158)* 9415 NE Woodridge, Vancouver, WA 98664 USA; *Imprints:* Blackbirch Press, Incorporated (Blackbirch Pr)
E-mail: ddub@drawbooks.com
Web site: http://www.drawbooks.com; http://www.peelbooks.com; http://www.123draw.com; http://www.1-2-3.draw.com
Dist(s): **F&W Media, Inc.**
Pathway Bk. Service
Two Rivers Distribution.

Peeler, Casey, *(978-0-9906984; 978-0-9961521)* 2424 Olan Dr., Shelby, NC 28152 USA Tel 704-472-9384
E-mail: caseypeelerauthor@gmail.com.

Peepal Tree Pr., Ltd. (GBR) *(978-0-948833; 978-1-900715; 978-1-84523) Dist. by* **IPG Chicago.**

Peeper & Friends *Imprint of* **Tree Of Life Publishing**

Peerless Publishing, L.L.C., *(978-0-9666076)* Orders Addr.: P.O. Box 20466, Ferndale, MI 48220 USA Tel 248-542-1930; Fax: 248-542-3895; Edit Addr.: 414 W. Lewiston, Ferndale, MI 48220 USA
E-mail: peerlesspublishing@ameritech.net
Web site: http://www.spannet.org/peerless/index.html.

Pegasus Bks. for Children, *(978-0-9824095; 978-0-615-82835-0)* P.O. Box 681, Flossmoor, IL 60422 USA Tel 708-990-8111; Fax: 708-747-4659
E-mail: stallionbooks@gmail.com
Web site: http://www.stallionbooks.com
Dist(s): **CreateSpace Independent Publishing Platform.**

Pegasus Pubns., *(978-0-9747023)* 1055 E., 16th St., Brooklyn, NY 11230 USA Do not confuse with companies with the same name in Point Reyes Statio, CA, San Antonio, TX.

Pegatha Press *See* **Rosasharn Pr.**

Peggy's Trunk, *(978-0-9706967)* 3809 Juniper Rd., Baltimore, MD 21218-1828 USA Tel 410-366-1785; Fax: 410-467-0641 (to call first)
E-mail: mdpagan@erols.com.

Peiffer, Trisha Cousineau *See* **Dream Ridge Pr.**

Peine, Jan *See* **Ashway Pr.**

Pelagia Pr. *Imprint of* **Calm Unity Pr.**

Pelican Book Group *See* **Pelican Ventures, LLC**

Pelican Lake Pr., *(978-0-9649139)* Div. of Healthy Lifestyle, Inc., Box 250, Ketchum, ID 83340 USA Tel 858-888-2278
E-mail: tomiselin@gmail.com
Web site: http://www.tomiselin.com.

Pelican Press *See* **Pelican Pr. Pensacola**

Pelican Press *See* **booksonnet.com**

Pelican Pr. Pensacola, *(978-0-9771102; 978-0-9911640; 978-1-7342203)* Div. of The Pelican Enterprise, LLC, Orders Addr.: 9121 Carabella St., Pensacola, FL 32514 USA Tel 850-475-8179; 850-206-4608 preferred Do not confuse with companies with the same name in Prather, CA, Santa Barbara, CA, Aptos, CA, Saint Augustine, FL, Belvedere, CA
E-mail: linda.wasserman@att.net
Dist(s): **BookBaby**
CreateSpace Independent Publishing Platform
Lulu Pr., Inc.

Pelican Publishing *Imprint of* **Arcadia Publishing**

Pelican Ventures, LLC, *(978-0-9712522; 978-0-9842968; 978-1-61116; 978-1-5223)* Div.of Pelican Ventures LLC, Orders Addr.: P.O. Box 1738, Aztec, NM 87410 USA; Edit Addr.: 2307 E. Main St., Farmington, NM 87401 USA; *Imprints:* Watershed Books (WatershedBks)
Web site: http://www.harbourlightbooks.com; http://www.whiterosepublishing.com; http://www.pelicanbookgroup.com
Dist(s): **Independent Pubs. Group.**

Peller, A. W. & Associates, Incorporated *See* **Educational Impressions**

Pemberley Publishing, *(978-1-947032)* 621 Hudson St., Eau Claire, WI 54703 USA Tel 715-456-0880
E-mail: pemberleypublishing@aol.com.

Pemblewick Pr., *(978-0-9656557; 978-0-9718507)* Orders Addr.: P.O. Box 321, Lincoln, MA 01773 USA (SAN 254-0886); Edit Addr.: 155 S. Great Rd., Lincoln, MA 01773 USA Tel 781-259-8832 (phone/fax); 617-259-8389; 617 259 8389
E-mail: pemblewick@aol.com
Web site: http://www.pemblewickpress.com.

Pembroke Pubs., Ltd. (CAN) *(978-0-921217; 978-1-55138) Dist. by* **Stenhsa Pubs.**

Pemmican Pubns., Inc. (CAN) *(978-0-919143; 978-0-921827; 978-1-894717) Dist. by* **Firefly Bks Limited.**

Pen + Ink (GBR) *(978-1-911475) Dist. by* **SCB Distributo.**

Pen & Pad Publishing, *(978-0-9769050)* P.o. Box 2995, Orcutt, CA 93457-2995 USA Tel 805-938-1307
E-mail: JBest@BestFamilyAdventures.com
Web site: http://BestFamilyAdventures.com
Dist(s): **Central Coast Bks.**

Pen & Paper Publishing, *(978-0-9703876)* 5450 Saluson Ave., PMB 15, Culver City, CA 90230 USA Fax: 323-933-3851; Toll Free: 800-662-9066 Do not confuse with Pen & Paper Publishing in Horn Lake, MS
E-mail: sixrags@earthlink.net
Web site: http://www.penandpaper.net.

Pen & Publish Incorporated *See* **Pen & Publish, LLC**

Pen & Publish, LLC, *(978-0-9768391; 978-0-9779530; 978-0-9790446; 978-0-9800429; 978-0-9817264;*

978-0-9823850; 978-0-9842258; 978-0-9844600; 978-0-9845751; 978-0-9846359; 978-0-9852737; 978-0-9859367; 978-1-941799) Orders Addr.: 4719 Holly Hills Ave, Saint Louis, MO 63116 USA; Edit Addr.: 4719 Holly Hills Ave, Saint Louis, MO 63116 USA Tel 314-827-6567; Toll Free: 866-326-7768
E-mail: info@penandpublish.com; paul@penandpublish.com; info@brickmantelbooks.com
Web site: http://www.penandpublish.com; http://transformationmediabooks.com; http://openbookspress.com; http://brickmantelbooks.com
Dist(s): **Smashwords.**

Pen & Rose Pr. *Imprint of* **Harlin Jacque Pubns.**

Pen & Sword Bks. Ltd. (GBR) *(978-0-7232; 978-0-85052; 978-1-84415; 978-1-84468; 978-1-84832; 978-1-84884; 978-1-78159; 978-1-78303; 978-1-78346; 978-1-78383; 978-1-4738; 978-1-78337; 978-1-5267; 978-1-78340)* *Dist. by* **Casemate Pubs.**

Pen & Sword Publishing Co., The, *(978-0-9745798)* 522 N. Holly St., Philadelphia, PA 19104 USA
E-mail: nancy@theaalamgroup.com; nk81dove@yahoo.com; melodicg2003@hotmail.com.

Pen It! Pubns., LLC, *(978-0-692-96536-8; 978-1-948390; 978-1-949609; 978-1-950454; 978-1-951263; 978-1-952011; 978-1-952894)* 5110 W Cty. Rd. 400 N, SCIPIO, IN 47273 USA Tel 812-371-4128
E-mail: penitpublications@yahoo.com
Web site: www.penitpublications.com
Dist(s): **Ingram Content Group.**

Pen Name Publishing, *(978-1-941541)* 54 N. St., Bargersville, IN 46106 USA Tel 317-422-5682
E-mail: dionne@pennamepublishing.com
Web site: www.pennamepublishing.com.

Pen of the Writer, LLC, *(978-0-9786066)* 893 S. Main St. PMB 175, Englewood, OH 45322 USA (SAN 851-1047) Tel 937-307-0760
E-mail: colemanbfp@aol.com; info@penofthewriter.com
Web site: http://www.penofthewriter.com
Dist(s): **Send The Light Distribution LLC**
Smashwords.

Pen Pearls, *(978-0-9989905; 978-1-7355145)* 13653 Thunderhawk Pl., Victorville, CA 92392 USA Tel 760-617-6039; Fax: 888-464-3229
E-mail: suzanneholbrook@yahoo.com
Web site: www.penpearls.com.

Pen Row Productions, *(978-0-9766695)* 9461 Charleville Blvd., No. 506, Beverly Hills, CA 90212 USA Tel 310-924-9167
E-mail: bwasz1@verizon.net
Web site: http://www.penrowproductions.com.

Pencil Point Pr., Inc., *(978-1-58108; 978-1-881641)* P.O. Box 634, New Hope, PA 18938-0634 USA Toll Free: 800-356-1299
E-mail: penpoint@ix.netcom.com
Web site: http://www.pencilpointpress.com.

Pendant Pr., LLC, *(978-0-9906617)* 130 N. Garland Court, No. 1703, Chicago, IL 60602 USA Tel 615-579-4422
E-mail: carolinelee99@yahoo.com
Web site: http://www.maxzyne.com/.

Pendentive Pubns., *(978-0-9853817)* 405 Serrano Dr., Apt. 9-K, San Francisco, CA 94132 USA Tel 415-586-1806
E-mail: mpowers2004@yahoo.com
Dist(s): **Lulu Pr., Inc.**

Pendleton Publishing, *(978-0-578-47649-0; 978-0-578-52782-6)* 106 N. Pendleton Ave., Pendleton, IN 46064 USA Tel 317-430-9677
E-mail: pendletonpublishing@yahoo.com
Dist(s): **Ingram Content Group.**

Pendleton Publishing, Inc., *(978-0-9654480; 978-0-9711564)* Orders Addr.: P.O. Box 5004, Laurel, MD 20726 USA Tel 301-604-4076; Fax: 301-317-5746; Edit Addr.: 3113 Burning Springs Rd., No.1A, Laurel, MD 20724 USA
E-mail: newauthorsandartists@msn.com; gamjampublishing@yahoo.com.

Pendulum Pr., Inc., *(978-0-87232; 978-0-88301)* Academic Bldg., Saw Mill Rd., West Haven, CT 06516 USA (SAN 202-8808) Tel 203-933-2551 Do not confuse with companies with same or similar names in Jacksonville, FL, Palm Coast, FL, Minneapolis, MN.

Penelope Pipp Publishing, *(978-0-9882369)* 38 McCreedy Dr., McHenry, MS 39561 USA Tel 228-254-6711
E-mail: admin@penelopepipp.com
Web site: http://www.penelopepipp.com.

Penfield Bks., *(978-0-941016; 978-0-9603858; 978-1-57216; 978-0-9717025; 978-1-932043)* 215 Brown St., Iowa City, IA 52245 USA Tel 319-337-9998; Fax: 319-351-6846
E-mail: penfield@penfieldbooks.com
Web site: http://www.penfieldpress.com; http://www.penfieldbooks.com
Dist(s): **Partners Bk. Distributing, Inc.**
Penfield Pr.

PenGame Publishing LLC, *(978-0-9771444)* Orders Addr.: P.O. Box 341361, Jamaica, NY 11434 USA (SAN 256-8802)
E-mail: PenGameLLC@aol.com
Web site: http://www.PenGamePublishing.com.

Penguin AudioBooks *Imprint of* **Penguin Publishing Group**

Penguin Bks. *Imprint of* **Penguin Publishing Group**

Penguin Bks. India PVT, Ltd (IND) *(978-0-14; 978-0-670)* *Dist. by* **IPG Chicago.**

Penguin Bks., Ltd. (GBR) *(978-0-14; 978-0-241; 978-0-670; 978-0-7232; 978-1-4059; 978-1-4093)* *Dist. by* **Diamond Book Dists.**

Penguin Bks., Ltd. (GBR) *(978-0-14; 978-0-241; 978-0-670; 978-0-7232; 978-1-4059; 978-1-4093)* *Dist. by* **Penguin Grp USA.**

Penguin Bks., Ltd. (GBR) *(978-0-14; 978-0-241; 978-0-670; 978-0-7232; 978-1-4059; 978-1-4093)* *Dist. by* **IPG Chicago.**

Penguin Bks., Ltd. (GBR) *(978-0-14; 978-0-241; 978-0-670; 978-0-7232; 978-1-4059; 978-1-4093)* *Dist. by* **D C D.**

Penguin Books *Imprint of* **Penguin Young Readers Group**

Penguin Books *Imprint of* **Penguin Publishing Group**

Penguin Canada (CAN) *(978-0-14; 978-0-216; 978-0-451; 978-0-452; 978-0-453; 978-0-670; 978-1-55305; 978-0-7723)* *Dist. by* **Peng Rand Hse.**

Penguin Classics *Imprint of* **Penguin Publishing Group**

Penguin Family Publishing, *(978-0-9637985)* P.O. Box 471, Orland, CA 95963 USA.

Penguin Global *Imprint of* **Penguin Publishing Group**

Penguin Group India (IND) *(978-0-14; 978-0-670)* *Dist. by* **Penguin Grp USA.**

Penguin Group New Zealand, Ltd. (NZL) *(978-0-14; 978-0-670)* *Dist. by* **IPG Chicago.**

Penguin Group (USA) Incorporated *See* **Penguin Publishing Group**

Penguin Ireland (IRL) *(978-1-84488)* *Dist. by* **IPG Chicago.**

Penguin Publishing Group, *(978-0-14; 978-0-399; 978-0-425; 978-0-452; 978-0-525; 978-0-698; 978-0-87477; 978-1-58542; 978-1-933438; 978-1-4295; 978-1-934511; 978-1-4362; 978-1-4406; 978-1-101; 978-1-937007)* Orders Addr.: 405 Murray Hill Pkwy., East Rutherford, NJ 07073-2136 USA (SAN 282-5074) Fax: 201-933-2903 (customer service); Toll Free Fax: 800-227-9604; Toll Free: 800-526-0275 (reseller sales); 800-631-8571 (reseller customer service); 800-788-6262 (individual consumer sales); Edit Addr.: 375 Hudson St., New York, NY 10014 USA Tel 212-366-2000; Fax: 212-366-2666; 405 Murray Hill Pkwy., East Rutherford, NJ 07073 (SAN 852-5455) Tel 201-933-9292; *Imprints:* Ace (Ace Bks); Avery (Avr); Berkley (BerkBks); Dial (Dial); Dutton (Dut); Dutton Juvenile (DuttJuv); Warne (Warne); Putnam Juvenile (PutnaJuv); Grosset & Dunlap (Gross-Dun); HP Books (HPTrade); NAL (NewAmLib); Penguin AudioBooks (PengAudBks); Penguin Classics (PenClassics); Philomel (PhilPG); Planet Dexter (PlanDext); Plume (PlumPG); Portfolio (PortfolTrade); Price Stern Sloan (PSS); Puffin (PufBks); Penguin Global (PenGlobal); Roc (Roc); Razorbill (Razrbl); Riverhead Books (RivhdHC); Sentinel (Senti); Signet (SigBks); Viking Adult (VikiPG); Prentice Hall Press (PHPP); Nancy Paulsen Books (Nancy Paulsen); Warne (WarneUSA); Dial Books (DialYoung); Viking Books for Young Readers (VikingBksforYR); G.P. Putnam's Sons Books for Young Readers (GPPutnam); Philomel Books (PhilomelBks); G.P. Putnam's Sons (GPPutnams); Penguin Books (Penguin Bks); TarcherPerigee (TarcherPerigee); Viking (MYID_L_VIKING); Penguin Books (PenguinYR); Dutton Caliber (DuttonCaliber); IMPACT Books (IMPACTBks)
E-mail: customer.service@us.penguingroup.com
Web site: http://penguingroup.custhelp.com; http://booksellers.penguingroup.com; http://www.penguinputnam.com
Dist(s): **Casemate Pubs. & Bk. Distributors, LLC**
Casemate Academic
Children's Plus, Inc.
Ebsco Publishing
Follett School Solutions
Independent Pubs. Group
Lectorum Pubns., Inc.
MyiLibrary
Penguin Random Hse. Distribution
Pearson Education
Penguin Random Hse. LLC
Perfection Learning Corp.
Viking Penguin
ebrary, Inc.

Penguin Random House Audio Publishing Group, *(978-1-61176)* 375 Hudson St., New York, NY 10014 USA Tel 212-366-2000; Fax: 212-366-2873; *Imprints:* Random House Audio (RHAudio)
Web site: www.penguin.com
Dist(s): **Blackstone Audio, Inc.**
Follett School Solutions
Penguin Random Hse. Distribution
Penguin Random Hse. LLC
Penguin Publishing Group.

Penguin Random House Grupo Editorial (ESP) *(978-84-7888; 978-84-86033; 978-84-8365)* *Dist. by* **Casemate Pubs.**

Penguin Random House Grupo Editorial (ESP) *(978-84-7888; 978-84-86033; 978-84-8365)* *Dist. by* **Peng Rand Hse.**

Penguin Random Hse. Grupo Editorial (USA) LLC, *(978-1-941999; 978-1-945540; 978-1-947783; 978-1-949061; 978-1-64473)* 2711 Centerville Rd., Wilmington, DE 19808 USA Tel 305-527-8286; *Imprints:* Aguilar (Aguilar RH)
E-mail: monica.delgado@penguinrandomhouse.com
Web site: http://www.penguinrandomhousegrupoeditorial.com/en/
Dist(s): **Ingram Publisher Services**
Penguin Random Hse. Distribution
Penguin Random Hse. LLC
Two Rivers Distribution.

Penguin Random Hse. LLC, *(978-0-593; 978-1-101; 978-1-9848)* Orders Addr.: 400 Hahn Rd., Westminster, MD 21157 USA Toll Free Fax: 800-659-2436; Toll Free: 800-733-3000; Edit Addr.: 375 Hudson St. 3rd Flr., New York, NY 10014 USA Tel 212-366-2424
E-mail: brittany.wienke@us.penguingroup.com
Web site: http://www.PenguinRandomHouse.com.

Penguin Random House SEA Pte. Ltd. (SGP) *(978-981-4867; 978-981-4882; 978-981-4914)* *Dist. by* **IPG Chicago.**

Penguin Random House South Africa (ZAF) *(978-0-86977; 978-0-86978; 978-0-86966; 978-1-86825; 978-1-86872; 978-1-875015; 978-1-86870; 978-1-86809; 978-1-86823; 978-0-947024; 978-0-9584195; 978-0-9584468; 978-1-77007; 978-1-4859)* *Dist. by* **Casemate Pubs.**

Penguin Random Hse. (AUS) *(978-0-14; 978-0-670; 978-0-86914; 978-0-7343; 978-1-920989; 978-1-921382; 978-1-921383; 978-1-921384; 978-1-921518; 978-1-74228; 978-1-74253; 978-1-74348; 978-0-85796; 978-0-85797; 978-1-74377; 978-1-76014; 978-1-76089; 978-1-76104)* *Dist. by* **IPG Chicago.**

Penguin Random Hse. (GBR) *(978-0-09; 978-0-224; 978-0-7126; 978-1-86046; 978-1-870516; 978-0-85265; 978-1-84413; 978-1-84657; 978-1-84655; 978-1-84853; 978-1-4881; 978-1-911215; 978-1-78089)* *Dist. by* **IPG Chicago.**

Penguin Random Hse. (GBR) *(978-0-09; 978-0-224; 978-0-7126; 978-1-86046; 978-1-870516; 978-0-85265; 978-1-84413; 978-1-84657; 978-1-84655; 978-1-84853; 978-1-4881; 978-1-911215; 978-1-78089)* *Dist. by* **Trafalgar.**

Penguin Workshop *Imprint of* **Penguin Young Readers Group**

Penguin Young Readers *Imprint of* **Penguin Young Readers Group**

Penguin Young Readers Group, 375 Hudson St., New York, NY 10014 USA; *Imprints:* Speak (SpeakPeng); Puffin Books (PuffPeng); Warne (WarneUSA); Dial Books (DialYoung); Viking Books for Young Readers (VikingBksforYR); Dutton Books for Young Readers (Dutt BksYR); Firebird (Firebird); Razorbill (RazorbillUSA); G.P. Putnam's Sons Books for Young Readers (GPPutnam); Grosset & Dunlap (GrosDunl); Kathy Dawson Books (Kathy Daws); Price Stern Sloan (PriceSternSloan); Philomel Books (PhilomelBks); Nancy Paulsen Books (NancyPaul); Penguin Young Readers (Penguin YR); Penguin Books (PenguinYR); Mad Libs (MadLibs); Penguin Young Readers Licenses (PenYngRead); Penguin Workshop (PenguinWrkshop); Kokila (Kokila)
Dist(s): **Children's Plus, Inc.**
Independent Pubs. Group
Penguin Random Hse. Distribution
Penguin Random Hse. LLC
Penguin Publishing Group.

Penguin Young Readers Licenses *Imprint of* **Penguin Young Readers Group**

Penknife Pr., *(978-0-9741949; 978-1-59997)* 1837 N. Oak Pk. Ave., Chicago, IL 60707 USA Tel 773-733-0830
E-mail: publisher@penknifepress.com
Web site: http://www.penknifepress.com
Dist(s): **Ingram Content Group.**

Pen-L Publishing, *(978-0-9851274; 978-1-940222; 978-1-942428; 978-1-68313)* 12 W. Dickson St., No. 4455, Fayetteville, AR 72702 USA
E-mail: duke@pen-l.com
Web site: Pen-L.com.

Penland, Alexandra Brooke, *(978-0-692-95173-6; 978-0-692-08775-6; 978-0-692-14955-3; 978-0-692-14956-0)* 1513 Olde Hickory Rd. Apt. 3, Coralville, IA 52241 USA Tel 7035097972
E-mail: penlandab@gmail.com
Dist(s): **Ingram Content Group.**

Penlight Pubns., *(978-0-9838685; 978-1-7324955)* 572 Empire Blvd., Brooklyn, NY 11225 USA Tel 718-972-5449
E-mail: urim_pub@netvision.net.il
Web site: www.penlightpublications.com
Dist(s): **Independent Pubs. Group.**

PenLit Publishing, *(978-1-7321263; 978-1-7354329)* 1212 NE 192nd Ave, Portland, OR 97230 USA Tel 503-348-2106
E-mail: nick.buckingham@penlit.com
Web site: www.penlit.com.

Penman Productions, *(978-0-9767978; 978-0-9914804; 978-0-9988968)* P.O. Box 400, Gleneden Beach, OR 97388-0400 USA; *Imprints:* Shalu Children's Series, The (MYID_O_SHALU C)
E-mail: therealnicksharma@gmail.com; penmanproductions@gmail.com; ronsterbooks@gmail.com
Web site: http://www.penmanproductions.com
Dist(s): **Epicenter Pr., Inc.**
Partners Bk. Distributing, Inc.
Partners/West Book Distributors.

Penman Publications *See* **Voice & Vision Pubns.**

Penman Publishing, Inc., *(978-0-9700486; 978-0-9707646; 978-0-9712808; 978-0-9720775; 978-1-932496; 978-1-7322390)* Div. of Pathway Pr., Orders Addr.: P.O. Box 3933, Cleveland, TN 37320-2250 USA; Edit Addr.: 1705 Overhead Bridge Rd., Cleveland, TN 37312 USA Tel 423-478-7613
Web site: http://www.penmanpublishing.com.

Pen-Mar News Distributors *See* **Americana Souvenirs & Gifts**

Penn, Carlotta, *(978-0-692-96718-8; 978-0-9996613)* 272 N 17th St., COLUMBUS, OH 43203 USA Tel 614-599-1170; *Imprints:* Daydreamers Press (DaydreamPr)
E-mail: carlottamichelle@gmail.com
Dist(s): **Ingram Content Group.**

Pennaeth Publishing *Imprint of* **Garfield, M.**

Penned By Fafa, LLC, *(978-0-692-92795-3)* 1709 Walker Ave., Apt. C, Union, NJ 07083 USA Tel 973-651-7838
E-mail: pennedbyfafa@gmail.com
Dist(s): **Ingram Content Group.**

Penner/Lynn Publishing, *(978-0-9763025)* P.O. Box 7393, Naples, FL 34104 USA
E-mail: pennerlynn@msn.com
Web site: http://www.pennerlynn.com.

Pennie Rich Publishing, *(978-0-9820328; 978-0-9824960)* 4755 Cty. Rd. 27, Monte Vista, CO 81144-9314 USA (SAN 857-0884)
E-mail: pennierich@pennierich.com
Web site: http://www.pennierich.com.

†Pennsylvania State Univ. Pr., *(978-0-271; 978-1-64602)* Orders Addr.: 820 N. University Dr., USB-1 Suite C, University Park, PA 16802 USA (SAN 213-5760) Tel 814-865-1327; Fax: 814-863-1408; Toll Free Fax: 877-778-2665 (orders only); Toll Free: 800-326-9180 (orders only)
E-mail: http://www.eisenbrauns.org; info@psupress.org; log-ins@press.psu.edu
Web site: http://www.psupress.org
Dist(s): **Ebsco Publishing**
ISD
MyiLibrary
ebrary, Inc.; *CIP.*

Penny Candy Bks., LLC, *(978-0-9972219; 978-0-9987999; 978-0-9996584; 978-1-7342259)* PO Box 3205, Oklahoma City, OK 73101 USA Tel 405-626-7175
E-mail: alexis@pennycandybooks.com; chad@pennycandybooks.com
Web site: www.pennycandybooks.com
Dist(s): **BookMobile**
Itasca Bks.
Publishers Group West (PGW).

Penny Candy Pr. *Imprint of* **Brighter Minds Children's Publishing**

Penny Laine Papers, Inc., *(978-1-890703)* 2211 Century Center Blvd. Ste. 110, Irving, TX 75062-4960 USA Toll Free: 800-456-6484; *Imprints:* Bookmates (Bkmates)
E-mail: cardwhiz1@mindspring.com.

Penny Lane Pubns., Inc., *(978-0-911211)* P.O. Box 3005, New York, NY 10012-0009 USA (SAN 274-4961) Tel 212-570-9666.

Penny Pr. *Imprint of* **Penny Pubns., LLC**

Penny Pubns., LLC, *(978-0-944422; 978-1-55956; 978-1-59238)* 6 Prowitt St., Norwalk, CT 06855 USA (SAN 243-6485); *Imprints:* Penny Press (Penny Pr)
E-mail: ltrutnau@pennypublications.net
Web site: http://www.pennydellpuzzles.com; http://www.analogsf.com; http://www.asimovs.com; http://www.themysteryplace.com; http://www.dellhoroscope.com; http://www.thecrosswordsclub.com.

Pennydragon Pr., *(978-0-9988614)* 645 Sumner Way No. 5, Oceanside, CA 92058 USA Tel 310-435-2022
E-mail: zoedragon@yahoo.com
Web site: pennydragon.com.

Penny-Farthing Press, Incorporated *See* **Penny-Farthing Productions, Inc.**

Penny-Farthing Productions, Inc., *(978-0-9673683; 978-0-9719012; 978-0-9842143; 978-0-9991709)* One Sugar Creek Ctr. Blvd., Suite 820, Sugar Land, TX 77478 USA Tel 713-780-0300; Fax: 713-780-4004; Toll Free: 800-926-2669
E-mail: corp@pfproductions.com; edit@pfproductions.com; design@pfproductions.com
Web site: http://www.pfpress.com; http://www.pfproductions.com
Dist(s): **Diamond Comic Distributors, Inc.**

Pennypack Productions, Inc., *(978-0-9704184)* 21 Tree Farm Ct., Glen Arm, MD 21057 USA Tel 410-420-3828; Fax: 410-420-2243
E-mail: ppennypack@comcast.net
Web site: http://www.kinderfun.net.

Penny's Publishing *Imprint of* **Balloon Magic**

Pennywhistler's Pr., *(978-0-9623456; 978-0-9727516)* Orders Addr.: P.O. Box 2473, New York, NY 10108 USA Tel 212-247-3231 (phone/fax); Edit Addr.: 467 W. 46th St., New York, NY 10036 USA
E-mail: info@pennywhistle.com
Web site: http://www.pennywhistle.com
Dist(s): **Book Clearing Hse.**
Mel Bay Pubns., Inc.

Pennywise Pubns., Inc., *(978-0-9702944)* 10550 St. Rd. 84, L98, Davie, FL 33324 USA Tel 954-472-8776 (phone/fax)
E-mail: filmpeny@bellsouth.net.

Penrod/Hiawatha Co., *(978-0-942618; 978-1-893624; 978-1-940691)* 10116 M140, Berrien Center, MI 49102 USA (SAN 238-5546) Tel 269-461-6993; Fax: 269-461-4170; Toll Free: 800-632-2823
Web site: http://www.penrodhiawatha.com
Dist(s): **Partners Bk. Distributing, Inc.**

Pentacle Pr., *(978-0-9604760; 978-0-9763500; 978-0-9825047; 978-1-937313)* Orders Addr.: P.O. Box 9400, Scottsdale, AZ 85252 USA (SAN 255-4860) Tel 480-922-2759; Fax: 480-443-8333; Edit Addr.: 5432 E. Desert Jewel Dr., Paradise Valley, AZ 85253 USA
E-mail: djm543@cox.net
Web site: http://www.missionscalifornia.com; http://www.pentacle-press.com
Dist(s): **Sunbelt Pubns., Inc.**

Pentatonic Pr., *(978-0-9773712)* 1232 Second Ave., San Francisco, CA 94122 USA Tel 415-564-1597; Fax: 415-566-6828
E-mail: Goodkindg@aol.com
Web site: http://www.douggoodkin.com
Dist(s): **Independent Pubs. Group**
Midpoint Trade Bks., Inc.

Pen-Tech Professional, *(978-0-9820962)* P.O. Box 67, Greenville, WI 54942 USA Tel 920-203-0563
Web site: http://www.pentechprofessional.com.

Pentland Pr., Inc., *(978-1-57197)* 5122 Bur Oak Cir., Raleigh, NC 27612 USA (SAN 298-5063) Tel 919-782-0281; Fax: 919-781-9042; Toll Free: 800-948-2786; *Imprints:* Ivy House Publishing Group (Ivy Hse Pubng Grp)
E-mail: janetevans@ivyhousebooks.com
Web site: http://www.ivyhousebooks.com
Dist(s): **Independent Pubs. Group.**

Publisher Name Index

Penton Kids *Imprint of* **Penton Overseas, Inc.**
Penton Overseas, Inc., *(978-0-939001; 978-1-56015; 978-1-59125; 978-1-60379)* 1958 Kellogg Ave., Carlsbad, CA 92008 USA (SAN 631-0826) Tel 760-431-0060; Fax: 760-431-8110; Toll Free: 800-748-5804; *Imprints:* Penton Kids (Penton Kids); Smart Kids (Smrt Kds)
E-mail: kellie@pentonoverseas.com; susan@pentonoverseas.com
Web site: http://www.pentonoverseas.com
Dist(s): **Ideals Pubns.**
Pentucket Publishing, *(978-0-615-78644-5; 978-0-615-96648-9; 978-0-692-35910-5; 978-0-692-39153-2; 978-0-692-39154-9; 978-0-692-59416-2; 978-1-948134)* P.O. Box 482, Andover, MA 01810-0009 USA Tel 978-659-2107
Web site: http://www.pentucketpublishing.com/
Dist(s): **CreateSpace Independent Publishing Platform.**
Penury Pr., *(978-0-9676344)* 8701 Utah Ave S., Bloomington, MN 55438 USA Tel 952-829-1811
E-mail: penurypress@hotmail.com
Web site: http://www.penurypress.com
Dist(s): **Adventure Pubns.**
Adventures Unlimited Pr.
Partners Bk. Distributing, Inc.
Penway Publishing LLC, *(978-0-578-49149-3)* P.O. Box 21117, Louisville, KY 40221 USA Tel 502-450-1203
E-mail: penwaypublishing@gmail.com.
Penworthy Co., LLC, The, *(978-0-87617; 978-1-64310; 978-1-64697)* 219 N. Milwaukee St., Milwaukee, WI 53202 USA (SAN 630-2300) Fax: 414-287-4602; Toll Free: 800-262-2665
E-mail: info@penworthy.com
Web site: http://www.penworthy.com.
Penzart, *(978-0-9966940)* 9206 White Chimney Ln., Great Falls, VA 22066 USA Tel 571-989-2432.
People, Incorporated *See* **People Ink Pr.**
People Ink Pr., *(978-0-9858052; 978-0-9893267; 978-0-9862182; 978-0-9977740)* 1219 N. Forest, Williamsville, NY 14223 USA Tel 716-629-3602
E-mail: scrocker@people-inc.org; npalumbo@people-inc.org.
People Ink Pr., *(978-0-9789476; 978-0-9845983)* 1219 N. Forest Rd., Williamsville, NY 14231 USA Tel 716-634-8132; Fax: 716-817-7558
Web site: http://www.people-inc.org.
People Skills International, *(978-1-881165)* Orders Addr.: 2910 Baily Ave., San Diego, CA 92105 USA Tel 619-262-9951; Fax: 619-262-0505
E-mail: idagreene@earthlink.net
Web site: http://www.idagreene.com.
People's Literature Publishing Hse. (CHN) *(978-7-02) Dist. by* **Chinasprout.**
People's Literature Publishing Hse. (CHN) *(978-7-02) Dist. by* **China Bks.**
Pep & Olie Publishing, *(978-0-9912023)* 1355 Hilda Ave. No. 6, Glendale, CA 91205 USA Tel 818-552-2642
E-mail: sahin@ersoz.com
Web site: www.pepandolie.com.
Peppermint Bks., *(978-0-9828852)* P.O. Box 16512, Edina, MN 55416 USA (SAN 859-9424) Tel 651-815-8137
E-mail: orders@peppermintbooks.com
Web site: http://www.peppermintbooks.com.
Peppernut Publishing, *(978-0-9796500)* P.O. Box 31126, Omaha, NE 68131-1126 USA Tel 402-556-5591
E-mail: evyboonyawiroj@yahoo.com.
Peppertree Pr., The, *(978-0-9778525; 978-0-9787740; 978-1-934246; 978-0-9814894; 978-0-9817572; 978-0-9818683; 978-0-9820479; 978-0-9821654; 978-0-9822540; 978-0-9823002; 978-1-936051; 978-1-936343; 978-1-61493)* 1269 First St., Suite 7, Sarasota, FL 34236-5518 USA
Web site: http://www.peppertreepublishing.com.
Peppery Pr., *(978-0-9764813)* 504 Springcreek Dr., Longwood, FL 32779 USA Tel 407-786-6113
E-mail: pruben@cfl.rr.com
Web site: http://www.pepperypress.com.
Per Aspera Pr., *(978-0-9745734; 978-1-941662)* Div. of Viridian City Media, Orders Addr.: 205 Grandview Dr., San Marcos, TX 78666 USA
E-mail: adastra@perasperapress.com
Web site: http://www.perasperapress.com/
Dist(s): **Brodart Co.**
Partners/West Book Distributors.
Peralta Publishing, LLC, *(978-0-9798620)* 9908 E. Desert Trail Ln., Gold Canyon, AZ 85218 USA Tel 480-288-4306
E-mail: thomaspreiss@msn.com.
Perceval Pr., *(978-0-9721436; 978-0-9747078; 978-0-9763009; 978-0-9774869; 978-0-9819747; 978-0-9895616; 978-0-9969227)* 1223 Wishire Blvd. No. F, Santa Monica, CA 90403 USA
E-mail: info@percevelpress.com; michele@percevalpress.com
Web site: http://www.percevalpress.com
Dist(s): **D.A.P./Distributed Art Pubs.**
SPD-Small Pr. Distribution.
Peregrine Communications *Imprint of* **Collins, Robert**
Perelandra Publishing Co., *(978-0-9640858)* Orders Addr.: P.O. Box 697, Cardiff, CA 92007 USA; Edit Addr.: 2387 Montgomery, Cardiff, CA 92007 USA Tel 760-753-4469.
Perennial Dreams Pubns., *(978-0-9764779)* P.O. Box 671, Lehi, UT 84043-0671 USA.
Perennis, Sophia, *(978-0-900588; 978-1-59731)* P.O. Box PO Box 253, El Prado, NM 87529 USA Tel 415-509-6969; *Imprints:* Dawn Chorus Press (DawnChrous)
E-mail: jameswetmore@mac.com
Web site: http://www.sophiaperennis.com
Dist(s): **Ingram Content Group**
SPD-Small Pr. Distribution.
Perennis, Sophia Et Universalis *See* **Perennis, Sophia**
Perfect 4 Preschool, *(978-0-9769239)* 428 N. Nelson St., Arlington, VA 22203 USA (SAN 850-0614) Tel 703-351-5843
E-mail: bjmischel@aol.com
Web site: http://www.perfect4preschool.
Perfect Bound Marketing, *(978-0-9769923; 978-0-9795588; 978-0-9887022; 978-1-939614; 978-1-7339087)* 12558 W. Maya Way, Peoria, AZ 85383 USA Tel 602-996-1766
E-mail: vickie@perfectboundmarketing.press
Web site: www.PerfectBoundMarketing.press
Dist(s): **eBookit.com.**
Perfect Page, The, *(978-0-692-54554-6)* 939 Palm Ave., No. 306, West Hollywood, CA 90069 USA Tel 310-652-8438
E-mail: jamesradford@hotmail.com.
Perfect Praise Publishing, *(978-0-9679240; 978-0-9915735; 978-1-7359061)* 1228 Fourth Ave., E., Williston, ND 58801 USA
E-mail: perfectpraise@dia.net
Web site: http://www.perfect-praise.com.
Perfect Publishing, *(978-0-9895012; 978-0-9915608; 978-1-942688; 978-1-949907; 978-1-64810)* 6030 Marshallee Dr. Suite 711, Elkridge, MD 21075 USA Tel 443-904-4545
E-mail: Natalie@theumbrellasyndicate.com
Web site: https://www.facebook.com/PerfectPublishing.
Perfecting Parenting Pr., *(978-0-9790420)* 3943 Jefferson Ave, Emerald Hills, CA 94062-3437 USA Tel 650-364-4466; Fax: 650-364-2299
Web site: http://www.perfectingparentingpress.com.
Perfection Form Company, The *See* **Perfection Learning Corp.**
Perfection Learning Corp., *(978-0-7807; 978-0-7891; 978-0-8124; 978-0-89598; 978-1-56312; 978-0-7569; 978-1-60686; 978-1-61563; 978-1-61383; 978-1-61384; 978-1-62299; 978-1-62359; 978-1-62765; 978-1-62766; 978-1-62974; 978-1-63419; 978-1-68064; 978-1-68065; 978-1-68240; 978-1-5311; 978-1-6903; 978-1-6636) 1000 N. 2nd Ave., Logan, IA 51546 USA (SAN 221-0010) Tel 712-644-2831; Fax: 712-644-2392; Toll Free Fax: 800-543-2745; Toll Free: 800-831-4190; Imprints:* Covercraft (Covercraft)
E-mail: orders@perfectionlearning.com
Web site: http://www.perfectionlearning.com.
Performance Publishing Group, *(978-0-615-26354-0; 978-0-578-03804-9; 978-0-615-42489-7; 978-0-615-47898-2; 978-0-578-08878-5; 978-0-9839570; 978-0-9847547; 978-0-9915724; 978-0-9906553; 978-0-9861254; 978-0-9965021; 978-0-9975762; 978-1-946629)* 6841 Virginia Pkwy., Suite 103-124, McKinney, TX 75071 USA.
Performance Strategies, *(978-1-942333)* 209 Main Ave., Hayti, SD 57241 USA Tel 605-691-2007
E-mail: coleenliebsch@hotmail.com
Web site: www.PublishPS.com.
Pergot Pr., *(978-0-936865)* 19 Prospect Ave., Sausalito, CA 94965 USA (SAN 699-9441) Tel 415-332-0279; Fax: 415-332-5588.
Perigree *Imprint of* **PRI Publishing/Perigree Publishing**
Perinatal Loss *See* **Grief Watch**
Perio Reports, *(978-0-9659236)* Orders Addr.: P.O. Box 30367, Flagstaff, AZ 86003-0367 USA Tel 520-526-2523; Fax: 520-526-0852; Edit Addr.: 1640 N. Spyglass Way, Flagstaff, AZ 86004 USA
Dist(s): **Jenkins Group, Inc.**
Peripatetic Productions, LLC, *(978-0-578-02360-1; 978-0-9842385)* 4145 Joan Ave., Concord, CA 94521-2737 USA Tel 925-798-1311 (phone/fax)
Web site: http://www.peripateticproductions.com
Dist(s): **Lulu Pr., Inc.**
PeriplusEdition *Imprint of* **Tuttle Publishing**
Periscope Film, LLC, *(978-0-9786388; 978-0-9816526; 978-1-935327; 978-1-935700; 978-1-937684; 978-1-940453)* P.O. Box 341474, Los Angeles, CA 90034 USA
E-mail: contact@periscopefilm.com
Web site: http://www.periscopefilm.com.
Periscope Pr., *(978-0-9718546)* 15736 Horton Ln., Overland Park, KS 66223-3491 USA (SAN 254-9700)
Web site: http://www.hearthisorg.com
Dist(s): **Midwest Library Service**
Quality Bks., Inc.
Periscopefilm.com *See* **Periscope Film, LLC**
Periwinkle Pr., *(978-1-7323592)* 706 McGraw Dr., Fort Collins, CO 80526 USA Tel 970-219-9079
E-mail: maripat.borowski@yahoo.com
Dist(s): **Ingram Content Group.**
Periwinkle Studios, *(978-0-9759385)* P.O. Box 5134, Roselle, IL 60172 USA
E-mail: periwinklestudios@comcast.net.
Perkins Crawford, *(978-0-9762935)* 2605 Treyburne Ln., Owens Crossroads, AL 35763 USA Tel 256-536-5391
E-mail: e_vroom@bellsouth.net
Web site: http://www.perkinscrawford.com.
Perkins Miniatures, *(978-0-9759198)* 1708-59th St., Des Moines, IA 50322 USA Tel 515-279-6639
E-mail: gladon@earthlink.net.
Perkins Schl. for the Blind, *(978-0-9657170; 978-0-9743510; 978-0-615-26039-6; 978-0-9822721; 978-0-9881713; 978-0-692-69882-2; 978-0-9991766; 978-0-9992637; 978-1-947954)* a/o Publications Dept., 175 N. Beacon St., Watertown, MA 02472 USA
Web site: http://www.Perkins.org
Dist(s): **eBookit.com.**
Perkins-Stell, Crystal, *(978-0-9740705)* P.O. Box 8044, Edmond, OK 73013-8044 USA Tel 405-216-0224; Fax: 405-216-0224
E-mail: cleva@crystalstell.com
Web site: http://www.crystalstell.com.
Perks, Brad Lightscapes Photo Gallery, *(978-0-9788442)* 4055 Kimberly Pl., Concord, CA 94521-3359 USA
E-mail: bradperks@yahoo.com; bradperks@pcimagenetwork.com
Web site: http://pcimagenetwork.com; http://bradperks.com.
Perky Penguin Prs, *(978-0-578-18046-5; 978-0-578-18047-2)* 1808 E. Oxford Dr., Tempe, AZ 85283 USA.
Perkyideas Publishing, *(978-0-578-47574-5)* 29266 Pilgrim Ct., Valencia, CA 91354 USA Tel 818-967-3402
E-mail: perkinstmb@yahoo.com.
Perlina Pr., *(978-0-9971333)* 20 Udine St., Arlington, MA 02476 USA Tel 781-643-3162
E-mail: irerasin@yahoo.com.
Perlycross Pubs., *(978-0-9741743)* Orders Addr.: a/o Bryce D. Gibby, P.O. Box 9725, Ogden, UT 84409 USA Tel 801-732-8600; Fax: 801-732-8602; Edit Addr.: 2711 Centerville Rd., Suite 120, PMB 5544, Wilmington, DE 19808 USA.
Perman, LeAnn, *(978-0-615-79750-2; 978-0-9892677)* 2295 S. Hiawassee Rd. Suite 208, Orlando, FL 32835 USA Tel 801-243-8463
Dist(s): **BookBaby**
CreateSpace Independent Publishing Platform.
Permanent Productions, Incorporated *See* **Permanent Productions Publishing**
Permanent Productions Publishing, *(978-0-9818204)* Orders Addr.: 904 Silver Spur Rd., No. 510, Rolling Hills Estates, CA 90274 USA (SAN 856-6348) Tel 310-366-4996; Fax: 310-521-9329; Toll Free: 866-698-7376
E-mail: c.jackson@permproductions.com
Web site: http://www.permproductions.com.
Permiso Por Favor Publishing Co., *(978-0-9747272)* 8568 Riverwood Farms, Cordova, TN 38016 USA Tel 901-756-0663
E-mail: permisoporfavor@hotmail.com.
Permuted Press, 1230 Avenue of the Americas, New York, NY 10020 USA
Dist(s): **Simon & Schuster, Inc.**
Perpendicular Pr., *(978-0-9740234)* 64 Estabrook Rd., Carlisle, MA 01741-1724 USA
E-mail: info@perpendicularpress.com
Web site: http://www.perpendicularpress.com.
Perpetual Motion Machine Publishing, *(978-0-9887488; 978-0-9860594; 978-1-943720)* 152 Dew Fall Trail, Cibolo, TX 78108 USA Tel 210-573-7796
E-mail: pmmpublishing@gmail.com
Web site: www.perpetualpublishing.com.
Perretti, Angi *See* **MCrc Industries, LLC**
Perri, Jessica, *(978-0-692-91830-2)* 600 S Ridgeley, Los Angeles, CA 90036 USA Tel 847-828-4343; *Imprints:* Wild Meadow (WildMeadow)
E-mail: jperri43@gmail.com.
Perri Tales Pubns., *(978-0-9763442)* Orders Addr.: 45 W. 132nd St., Suite 12K, New York City, NY 10037-3123 USA; Edit Addr.: 19601 Kings Hwy., Warrensville Heights, OH 44122 USA
E-mail: perrigaffney@aol.com
Web site: http://www.perritales.com.
Perrin & Kabel Publishing, *(978-0-9725364)* 145 Waverly Dr., Pasadena, CA 91105 USA Tel 626-577-1023; Fax: 626-577-1024
E-mail: perrinkabel@earthlink.net.
Perrin, Leslie, *(978-0-692-11002-7)* 11817 Timbermill Ln, Fredericksburg, VA 22407 USA Tel 540-845-6161
E-mail: lesliekperrin@gmail.com.
Perrine, Jared *See* **Overhead Pr., LLC**
Perronet Pr. (GBR) *(978-0-9543733; 978-0-9547046) Dist. by* **IPG Chicago.**
Perry, Brenda, *(978-0-692-18619-0)* 290 Pk. Ave. W. 122, Denver, CO 80205 USA Tel 720-883-6784
E-mail: bjp830@gmail.com
Dist(s): **Ingram Content Group.**
Perry, Brien, *(978-0-9980260)* 13718 Chandler Blvd., Sherman Oaks, CA 91401 USA Tel 310-977-0129
E-mail: brienjtperry@yahoo.com
Web site: brienperry.com.
Perry Enterprises, *(978-0-941518)* 3907 N. Foothill Dr., Provo, UT 84604 USA (SAN 171-0281) Tel 801-226-1002.
Perry Heights Pr., *(978-0-9630181)* P.O. Box 102, Georgetown, CT 06829 USA Tel 203-767-6509; *Imprints:* A Road to Discovery Series Guide (Rd Discovery)
E-mail: contact@perryheightspress.com; contact@cttrips.com
Web site: http://www.cttrips.com.
Perry, Molly A., *(978-0-692-83558-6)* 3689 Silsby Rd., University Heights, OH 44118 USA Tel 216-990-9519
E-mail: mperry4077@gmail.com
Dist(s): **Independent Pub.**
Perry Pubns./Performance Pr., *(978-0-942442)* P.O. Box 5894, Oak Ridge, TN 37830 USA (SAN 238-1877) Tel 865-927-4912; Fax: 423-927-4912 Do not confuse Perry Publications, Silver Spring, Fl., Boerne, TX
E-mail: larryperry@worldnet.att.net.
Perryman Hse. of Design, *(978-1-7320969)* 260 Waterview Terr., Vallejo, CA 94591 USA Tel 707-319-5903
E-mail: gpman@mail.com.
Pers Publishing, *(978-1-932179)* Div. of Pers Corp., 5255 Stevens Creek Blvd., No. 232-5, Santa Clara, CA 95051-6664 USA (SAN 254-7716) Toll Free Fax: 800-505-7377
E-mail: info@pers.com
Web site: http://www.pers.com; http://www.pers.com/wholesale
Dist(s): **APG Sales & Distribution Services**
Brodart Co.
Emery-Pratt Co.
Quality Bks., Inc.
†Persea Bks., Inc., *(978-0-89255)* 853 Broadway, Suite 604, New York, NY 10003 USA (SAN 212-8233) Tel 212-260-9256; Fax: 212-260-1902
E-mail: info@perseabooks.com
Web site: http://www.perseabooks.com
Dist(s): **Norton, W. W. & Co., Inc.**
Penguin Random Hse. Distribution
Penguin Random Hse. LLC; *CIP.*
Perseus Bks. Group, *(978-0-7382; 978-0-938289; 978-1-58097; 978-1-882810; 978-1-903985; 978-1-78239)* Div. of Hachette Book Group, Orders Addr.: 2465 Central Ave., Suite 200, Boulder, CO 80301-5728 USA Toll Free: 800-343-4499 (customer service); Edit Addr.: 387 Park Ave., S., 12th Flr., New York, NY 10016-8810 USA Tel 212-340-8100; Fax: 212-340-8105
Web site: http://www.perseusbooksgroup.com.
Perseus Distribution *See* **Two Rivers Distribution**
Perseus-PGW *See* **Publishers Group West (PGW)**
Persnickety Pr. *Imprint of* **WunderMill, Inc.**
Personal, *(978-0-9856724)* P.O. Box 661, Monticello, IL 61856 USA Tel 217-649-1589
E-mail: flygri78@gmail.com.
Personal Best Motivional Sciences, Inc., *(978-0-9769988)* P.O. Box 562, Social Circle, GA 30025-0562 USA
Web site: http://www.babysimplerecipe.com/.
Personal Freedom Publishing, *(978-0-615-29044-7; 978-0-615-91370-4; 978-0-9973994)* 410 V Pl. SE, Auburn, WA 98002 USA
Web site: viviangale.com; http://www.thepersonalfreedomcenter.com/.
Personal Genesis Publishing, *(978-0-9747395)* 110 Pacific Ave., No. 204, San Francisco, CA 9411 USA Toll Free: 888-337-7776
Web site: http://www.ForgottenFaces.org.
Personal Power Press *See* **Personal Power Pr.**
Personal Power Pr., *(978-0-9616046; 978-0-9772321; 978-0-9821568)* Div. of Institute for Personal Power, 5225 3 Mile Rd, Bay City, MI 48706 USA (SAN 698-0155) Tel 989-239-8628
E-mail: Personalpowerpress@gmail.com
Web site: www.personalpowerpress.com
Dist(s): **Austin & Company, Inc.**
Independent Pubs. Group
Midpoint Trade Bks., Inc.
Partners Pubs. Group, Inc.
Personal Promise Bible, *(978-0-9759578)* 470 Heritage Hills Dr., Richland, WA 99352 USA Tel 509-627-2607; Fax: 775-402-2106; Toll Free: 866-968-7242
Web site: http://www.personalpromisebible.com.
Personal Security, *(978-0-9675357)* 24366 Falcon, Lake Forest, CA 92630 USA Tel 949-461-9552; Fax: 949-472-8018
E-mail: xwordshicklers@hotmail.com.
Personality Wise *See* **Uniquely You Resources**
Personify Creative, LLC, *(978-1-7329172)* 15429 Schuyler Dr., Omaha, NE 68154 USA Tel 402-493-4727
E-mail: gkerrmc@cox.net.
Personify Pr., *(978-0-9797491)* 1959 Camino a los Cerros, Menlo Park, CA 94025 USA.
Perspective Publishing, Inc., *(978-0-9622036; 978-1-930085)* 2528 Sleepy Hollow Dr., No. A, Glendale, CA 91206 USA Tel 818-502-1270; Fax: 818-502-1272; Toll Free: 800-330-5851 Do not confuse with Perspective Publishing, Memphis, TN
E-mail: books@familyhelp.com
Web site: http://www.familyhelp.com
Dist(s): **Quality Bks., Inc.**
Perspectives Pr., Inc., *(978-0-944934; 978-0-9609504)* P.O. Box 90318, Indianapolis, IN 46290-0318 USA (SAN 262-5059) Tel 317-872-3055
E-mail: patjohnston@perspectivespress.com
Web site: http://www.perspectivespress.com
Dist(s): **Smashwords.**
PES, Inc., *(978-0-9766962)* P.O. Box 5501, Virginia Bch, VA 23471-0501 USA
E-mail: sailingthroughbusiness@cox.net
Web site: http://www.sailingthroughbusiness.com.
PESI, *(978-0-941161; 978-1-55957; 978-0-9722147; 978-0-9749711; 978-0-9790218; 978-0-9820398; 978-1-936128; 978-0-9845254; 978-1-937661; 978-1-68373)* P.O. Box 1000, Eau Claire, WI 54702 USA; 3839 White Ave., Eau Claire, WI 54702; *Imprints:* PESI Publishing & Media (PESIPub)
E-mail: dkirby@pesi.com
Web site: http://www.pesi.com
Dist(s): **Baker & Taylor Publisher Services (BTPS)**
BookBaby.
PESI Publishing & Media *Imprint of* **PESI**
Pesout, Christine, *(978-0-615-47220-1)* 14 Dinan Ct., Lake St. Louis, MO 63367 USA Tel 314-443-6319
E-mail: cpesout@hotmail.com.
Pet Pundit Publishing, *(978-0-9853752; 978-1-948444)* P.O. Box 91733, Austin, TX 78209-1733 USA Tel 512-358-4515
E-mail: cathy@petpundit.com
Web site: www.petpunditpublishing.com.
Petalous Publishing, LLC, *(978-0-9777811)* Orders Addr.: PO Box 285, Farmingdale, NJ 07727 USA.
Peter Pan Industries, Incorporated *See* **Inspired Studios Inc.**
Peter Pauper Pr. Inc., *(978-0-88088; 978-1-59359; 978-1-4413)* Orders Addr.: 202 Mamaroneck Ave., Suite 400, White Plains, NY 10601 USA (SAN 204-9449) Tel 914-681-0144; Fax: 914-681-0389
E-mail: orders@peterpauper.com; customerservice@peterpauper.com
Web site: http://www.peterpauper.com.
PeterCottonBks., *(978-0-692-57072-2)* 2736 Magnolia Woods Dr., Mount Pleasant, SC 29464 USA Tel 843-814-1872
E-mail: petercotto@gmail.com
Web site: www.petercottontales.com.

Peterman, Melvin G. *See* **Insight Technical Education**
Peters & Pardee Pubs., *(978-0-9626279)* Orders Addr.: 1039 NW Hwy. 101, Lincoln City, OR 97367 USA.
Peters, Chelsea, *(978-0-9992786)* 908 Dove Ridge Cir, Nashville, TN 37221 USA Tel 662-816-2554
E-mail: chelspeters7@gmail.com.
Peters, Michelle Lee, *(978-0-692-14933-1; 978-0-692-14936-2)* 2304 S Lakeline Blvd., No. 582, Cedar Park, TX 78613 USA Tel 210-860-8943
E-mail: uxbymichelle@gmail.com
Dist(s): **Ingram Content Group.**
Petersburg Museums, The, *(978-0-9744824)* 15 W. Bank St., Petersburg, VA 23803 USA Tel 804-733-2402 Toll Free: 800-368-3595.
Peterson, Kristi, 127 W. Second St 1E, Monroe, MI 48161 USA Tel 734-731-0482
E-mail: margiekpfudge@gmail.com
Dist(s): **Ingram Content Group.**
Peterson, Mark, *(978-0-692-76713-9; 978-0-692-96981-6; 978-0-692-13912-7; 978-0-692-13913-4; 978-0-692-15178-5)* .
Peterson-Boyce, Linda, *(978-0-9766034)* P.O. Box 2942, North Babylon, NY 11703 USA.
†Peterson's, *(978-0-7689; 978-0-87866; 978-1-56079)* Div. of Nelnet, Orders Addr.: P.O. Box 67005, Lawrenceville, NJ 08648-6105 USA (SAN 200-2167); Edit Addr.: 2000 Lenox Dr., 3rd Flr., Lawrenceville, NJ 08648 USA (SAN 297-5661) Tel 609-896-1800; Fax: 609-896-1811; Toll Free: 800-338-3282 X5660;Customer Service; *Imprints:* Arco (Arco); B.E.S. Publishing (BESPubPete)
E-mail: custsvc@petersons.com
Web site: http://www.petersons.com
Dist(s): **Children's Plus, Inc.**
Hachette Bk. Group
Ingram Publisher Services
MyiLibrary
Simon & Schuster
Two Rivers Distribution; *CIP.*
Petey, Rock & Roo Children's Pubns., *(978-0-9789642)* Orders Addr.: 1657 Broadway, New York, NY 10019 USA (SAN 852-0585)
E-mail: tash@timessquarechurch.org
Web site: http://www.timessquarechurch.org.
Petit Chou Chou, LLC, *(978-0-615-54492-2; 978-0-9882306)* P.O. Box 470875, Fort Worth, TX 76147 USA Tel 817-793-2594
E-mail: jdrez@att.net
Web site: http://goodnightcowtown.com.
Petra Publishing *See* **Petra Publishing Co.**
Petra Publishing Co., *(978-0-9712429)* 385 S. Lemon Ave., Suite E314, Walnut, CA 91789 USA Tel 404-452-3374
E-mail: admin@petrapublishingcompany.com
Web site: http://www.petrapublishingcompany.com; http://www.positivemag.com.
Petrine Day Mitchum, *(978-0-692-93173-8; 978-0-692-94429-5)* P.O. Box 1703, SANTA YNEZ, CA 93460 USA Tel 805-698-3488
E-mail: Trineday@comcast.net
Dist(s): **Ingram Content Group.**
Pet's Playground *See* **Singing Moon Pr.**
Pex Publishing Co., *(978-0-933767)* 8625 Boysenberry Dr., Tampa, FL 33635 USA (SAN 692-7645).
P.F.B. Publishing, *(978-0-9741273)* P.O. Box 149, Warren, OH 44482-0149 USA Fax: 330-373-0211
E-mail: pat@southparktitle.com.
Pflaum Publishing Group, *(978-0-89837; 978-0-937997; 978-1-933178; 978-1-935042; 978-1-939105; 978-1-947358)* Div. of Bayard, Inc., 3055 Kettering Blvd., Suite 100, Dayton, OH 45439 USA (SAN 661-2539) Fax: 937-293-1310; Toll Free Fax: 800-370-4450; Toll Free: 800-543-4383; 3055 Kettering Blvd., Suite 100, Dayton, OH 45439 (SAN 661-2539) Fax: 937-293-1310; Toll Free Fax: 800-370-4450; Toll Free: 800-543-4383
E-mail: service@pflaum.com; lcavender@pflaum.com
Web site: http://www.pflaum.com
Dist(s): **ACTA Pubns.**
P.F.P. Pubs., *(978-0-615-18028-1; 978-0-615-18027-4; 978-0-615-18157-8; 978-0-615-18343-5; 978-0-615-18415-9; 978-0-615-18648-1; 978-0-615-18873-7; 978-0-615-19123-2; 978-0-615-19266-6; 978-0-615-19773-9; 978-0-615-22198-4)* 35 Stone Ridge Blvd., Hermitage, PA 16148 USA
E-mail: p.f.p.publishers@gmail.com
Web site: http://www.pfppublishers.com
Dist(s): **Lulu Pr., Inc.**
PGC Publishing *See* **Hope of Vision Publishing**
PH Publishing, *(978-0-9835863; 978-0-9835863-7-1; 978-1-7320421)* 3446 13th Ave. SW, Naples, FL 34117 USA Tel 239-352-1889
E-mail: pphayton@yahoo.com.
Phaidon Pr. Ltd. (GBR) *(978-0-7148) Dist. by* **HachBkGrp.**
Phaidon Pr., Inc., *(978-0-7148)* 180 Varick St., 14th Flr., New York, NY 10014-4606 USA (SAN 253-3367) Tel 212-652-5400; Fax: 212-652-5410; Toll Free Fax: 800-286-9471 (Orders only); Toll Free: 800-759-0190 (Orders only); 877-742-4366 (Editorial)
E-mail: ussales@phaidon.com
Web site: http://www.phaidon.com
Dist(s): **Children's Plus, Inc.**
Hachette Bk. Group.
Phantom Hill Pr., *(978-1-7328813)* 114 Chocolate Gulch, Ketchum, ID 83340 USA Tel 208-726-4052
E-mail: pattyketchum@gmail.com.
Phantom Pubns., Inc., *(978-0-9625372)* 9451 Page Rd., Wattsburg, PA 16442-2005 USA
Dist(s): **Empire Publishing Service.**
Pharmasoft Publishing *See* **Hale Publishing**
phazelFOZ Co., LLC., The, *(978-0-9819645; 978-0-9834876; 978-0-9859333; 978-0-9960781; 978-0-692-61390-0; 978-0-9974257; 978-0-9988803; 978-1-7328646)* 858 W. Armitage Ave., No. 365, Chicago, IL 60614 USA.
PHD Ink, *(978-0-9897278; 978-1-941104)* P.O. Box 4295, Sarasota, FL 34230 USA Tel 347-661-2073
E-mail: rkclark@aol.com.
Pheasant Tale Productions, *(978-0-9817001)* P.O. Box 73, Skamokawa, WA 98647-0073 USA (SAN 856-2814)
E-mail: rajj@iinet.com; adventureinborneo@gmail.com
Web site: http://https://sites.google.com/site/adventureinborneo/.
Phebe Phillips, Inc., *(978-0-9846454; 978-0-9837820)* P.O. Box 190748, Dallas, TX 75219 USA Tel 214-762-5727; *Imprints:* Hargrove Grey Publishing (Hargrove GP)
E-mail: phebe@phebephillips.com
Web site: http://www.phebephillips.com.
Phelps, Diane *See* **Red Rock Mountain Pr. LLC**
Phelps Publishing, *(978-1-887627)* P.O. Box 22401, Cleveland, OH 44122 USA Tel 216-752-4938; Fax: 216-752-4941
E-mail: earl@phelpspublishing.com; earl@edna-reco.com
Web site: https://www.phelpspublishing.com; https://drawsupercharacters.com/
Dist(s): **Brodart Co.**
Follett School Solutions
Ingram Bk. Co.
Phelps Publishing Company *See* **Phelps Publishing**
Phenomenal One Pr., *(978-0-9841989; 978-0-9850251; 978-0-9969195; 978-1-7329247)* 1463 Akeke Pl., Kailua, HI 96734 USA
E-mail: lprstn@hotmail.com
Web site: http://www.phenomenalonepress.com
Dist(s): **Ingram Content Group**
MyiLibrary.
Phi Sigma Omega, Alpha Kappa Alpha Sorority, Inc., *(978-0-9785269)* P.O. Box 1784, Gonzales, LA 70707-1784 USA Tel 225-936-1665
Web site: http://phisigmaomega2000.org.
Phidal Publishing, Inc./Editions Phidal, Inc. (CAN) *(978-2-89393; 978-2-920129; 978-2-7643) Dist. by* **AIMS Intl.**
Phil the Pill & Friends *Imprint of* **MAMP Creations**
Philadelphia Folklore Project, *(978-0-9644937)* 735 S. 50th St., Philadelphia, PA 19147 USA Tel 215-726-1106; Fax: 215-726-6250
E-mail: pfp@folkloreproject.org
Web site: http://www.folkloreproject.org.
Philadelphia Inquirer, The, *(978-1-58822)* Div. of Philadelphia Newspapers, Inc., 400 N. Broad St., Philadelphia, PA 19101 USA Tel 215-854-2000
Web site: http://www.philly.com.
†Philadelphia Museum of Art, *(978-0-87633)* 2525 Pennsylvania Ave., Philadelphia, PA 19130 USA (SAN 203-0969)
Web site: http://www.philamuseum.org
Dist(s): **Antique Collectors' Club**
Art Media Resources, Inc.
D.A.P./Distributed Art Pubs.
ISD
National Bk. Network
Pennsylvania State Univ. Pr.
Yale Univ. Pr.; *CIP.*
Philio International *See* **Philio Publishing**
Philio Publishing, *(978-0-9622996; 978-0-9964356)* 1138 N. Germantown Pkwy. Suite 101-294, Cordova, TN 38018 USA Tel 901-201-4058
Dist(s): **Lulu Pr., Inc.**
Philip J. Damiani, *(978-0-9980258)* 129 Southridge Dr., Cranberry Twp., PA 16066 USA Tel 412-979-4444
E-mail: pdamiani05@aol.com.
Philipp, Cathy Publishing, *(978-0-9655848)* P.O. Box 1954, Thousand Oaks, CA 91358-1954 USA Tel 805-498-0611; Fax: 805-498-7331
E-mail: phillfam@adelphia.net.
Philippine American Literary House *See* **PALH**
Philippine American Writers & Artists, Inc., *(978-0-9763316; 978-0-9968032; 978-0-9981792)* P.O. Box 31928, San Francisco, CA 94131-0928 USA
E-mail: pawa@pawainc.com
Web site: http://www.pawainc.com.
Philips, Fleur, *(978-0-9889299)* 250 N. College Pk. Dr. No. U33, Upland, CA 91786 USA Tel 909-908-3788
E-mail: fleurphilips@gmail.com
Dist(s): **BookBaby.**
PHILLIPS, JACQUELINE J. LLC., *(978-0-9994550)* 250 Goge Rd., Cliffside Park, NJ 07010 USA Tel 646-526-4781
E-mail: imagecosmetics@yahoo.com
Web site: www.starsbehindthestars.com.
Philograph *Imprint of* **Cascade, Inc.**
Philokalos Pr., *(978-0-9912472)* P.O. Box 3811, McLean, VA 22103 USA Tel 703-586-1353
E-mail: philokalospress@gmail.com
Web site: www.philokalospress.org.
Philomel *Imprint of* **Penguin Publishing Group**
Philomel Bks. *Imprint of* **Penguin Young Readers Group**
Philomel Bks. *Imprint of* **Penguin Publishing Group**
Philos Pr., *(978-0-9831075)* 22545 SW Miami Dr., Tualatin, OR 97062 USA Tel 503-885-8877; Fax: 503-885-1847
E-mail: maryandonian@yahoo.com.
†Philosophical Library, Inc., *(978-0-8022)* P.O. Box 1789, New York, NY 10010 USA (SAN 201-999X) Tel 212-886-1873; Fax: 212-873-6070
Dist(s): **Kensington Publishing Corp.**
MyiLibrary
Open Road Integrated Media, Inc.
Open Road Distribution
Rowman & Littlefield Publishers, Inc.; *CIP.*
Philothea Pr., *(978-0-9826867)* P.O. Box 1262, West Chester, OH 45071 USA Tel 513-805-6766.
Phlare, Inc., *(978-0-9741147)* 9565 W. 52nd Ave., Arvada, CO 80002 USA Tel 303-513-1565; Toll Free: 888-731-2398
Web site: http://www.phlare.com.
Phoenix Bks., Inc., *(978-1-59777; 978-1-60747; 978-1-61467; 978-1-7345201; 978-1-7357227)* 9465 Wilshire Blvd., Suite 840, Beverly Hills, CA 90212-2609 USA; *Imprints:* Pickwick Press (PickwickPr); Dove Books and Audio (Dove Bks).
Phoenix Books, Incorporated *See* **Phoenix Bks., Inc.**
Phoenix Cry Publishing, *(978-0-9995191)* PSC 37 Box 162, APO, AE 09459 USA Tel 405-225-8606
E-mail: jennie.gillham@gmail.com
Web site: www.courageouschiropractor.com.
Phoenix Films & Video, *(978-0-7919)* 2349 Chaffee Dr., Saint Louis, MO 63146 USA (SAN 653-5224) Tel 314-569-0211; Fax: 314-569-2834; Toll Free: 800-221-1274
E-mail: phoenixfilm@worldnet.att.net
Web site: http://www.phoenix-bfa-coronet.com
Dist(s): **Follett School Solutions**
Weston Woods Studios, Inc.
Phoenix Flair Pr., *(978-0-9846124)* 2704 W. Royerton Rd., Muncie, IN 47303 USA (SAN 859-8967).
Phoenix International, Inc., *(978-0-9650485; 978-0-9713470; 978-0-9768007; 978-0-9824295; 978-0-9835615; 978-0-9899356)* 17762 Summer Rain Rd., Fayetteville, AR 72701 USA Tel 479-521-2204 Do not confuse with companies with the same or similar names in Oxon Hill, MD, Nampa, ID
E-mail: john@phoenixupub.com
Web site: http://www.phoenixbase.com
Dist(s): **Chicago Distribution Ctr.**
Univ. of Arkansas Pr.
Phoenix International Publications, Inc., *(978-0-7853; 978-1-4127; 978-1-60553; 978-1-4508; 978-1-5037; 978-1-64269; 978-1-64996)* 8501 West Higgins Rd., Suite 300, Chicago, IL 60631 USA (SAN 860-424X) Tel 312-739-4400; *Imprints:* p i kids (p i kids); Sequoia Publishing & Media LLC (SequoiaPub); Sunbird Books (SunbirdBKS)
E-mail: b2b.customerservice@pikidsmedia.com
Dist(s): **Hachette Bk. Group.**
Phoenix Learning Resources, LLC, *(978-0-7915)* Orders Addr.: P.O. Box 510, Honesdale, PA 18431 USA (SAN 246-148X) Tel 570-251-6871; Fax: 570-253-3227; Toll Free: 800-228-9345
E-mail: rich@phoenixlr.com
Web site: http://www.phoenixlr.com.
Phoenix Publishing, *(978-1-928812)* Orders Addr.: P.O. Box 8231, Missoula, MT 59807 USA Fax: 406-721-6195; Toll Free: 800-549-8371; Edit Addr.: 309 SW Higgins, Missoula, MT 59803 USA Do not confuse with companies with the same or similar names in Redmond, WA, W. Kennebunk, ME, Rocklin, CA, Bloomington, IN, Miami, FL, Fairfield, FL, Tolono, IL, Newark, NJ, Lansing, MI, Alpharetta, GA, Custer, WA, Marina del Ray, CA, Half Moon Bay, CA, New York, NY
E-mail: phoenixl@phoenixpub.com
Web site: http://www.phoenixpub.com.
Phoenix Publishing, *(978-0-615-20417-8)* 308 W. Burnside Ave., Fairland, IN 46126 USA
E-mail: kphoenix_3@sbcglobal.net
Dist(s): **Lulu Pr., Inc.**
Phoenix Rising LLC, *(978-0-9800807)* 11684 Ventura Blvd., Suite 886, Studio City, CA 91604 USA (SAN 855-1464)
E-mail: phoenixrising@earthlink.net.
Phoenix Yard Bks. (GBR) *(978-1-907912) Dist. by* **IPG Chicago.**
Phonic Monic, *(978-1-943241)* 472 Trident Maple Terr., Fremont, CA 94539 USA Tel 510-573-1646
E-mail: cammieho123@gmail.com
Web site: www.phonicmonic.com.
Phosphene Publishing Co., *(978-0-9796968; 978-0-9851477; 978-0-9986316)* 4019 River Dr., Houston, TX 77017 USA.
PhotoGraphics Publishing, *(978-0-9643844; 978-0-9793813; 978-0-9829730)* 23 Cool Water Ct., Palm Coast, FL 32137 USA Tel 386-246-3672; Fax: 386-445-7365; *Imprints:* Doctor Dolittle's Library (Doctor Dolittle)
E-mail: joycehuber47@hotmail.com
Web site: http://www.photographicspublishing.com.
Photographs Naturally, Inc., *(978-0-9710343)* 57 Laurel Oak, Amelia Island, FL 32034 USA Tel 904-277-4403; Fax: 904-277-0749.
Photographs Naturally, Incorporated *See* **Photographs Naturally, Inc.**
Photography in Pearls LLC, *(978-1-7334206)* 1097 Hawthorn Dr, Pawleys Island, SC 29585 USA Tel 843-543-0054
E-mail: photographyinpearls@gmal.com.
PhotoHutch, *(978-0-9824925)* P.O. Box 482, Alamo, CA 94507 USA
Web site: http://www.bisforbufflehead.com; http://www.photohutch.com.
Photon Pubns., *(978-0-9744128; 978-0-615-11954-0)* 7532 Mason Dells Dr., Dallas, TX 75230-3246 USA
E-mail: j1jagger@aol.com
Dist(s): **Baker & Taylor Publisher Services (BTPS).**
Piano Pr, *(978-0-9673325; 978-1-931844)* Orders Addr.: P.O. Box 85, Del Mar, CA 92014-0085 USA Tel 619-884-1401; Fax: 858-755-1104; Edit Addr.: 1425 Ocean Ave., No. 17, Del Mar, CA 92014 USA Tel 619-884-1401
E-mail: eaxford@aol.com; pianopress@pianopress.com; lizaxford@pianopress.com
Web site: http://www.pianopress.com
Dist(s): **Book Wholesalers, Inc.**
Coutts Information Services
Blackwell
Wayland Audio-Visual.
Pianomouse Productions, *(978-0-9889068)* Orders Addr.: 8789 Auburn Folsom Rd. Ste. C416, Granite Bay, CA 95746 USA Tel 916-204-8110
E-mail: kathleen@pianomouse.com
Web site: www.pianomouse.com.
Piñata Books *Imprint of* **Arte Publico Pr.**
Picador, *(978-0-312)* Div. of Holtzbrinck Publishers, Orders Addr.: 16365 James Madison Hwy., Gordonsville, VA 22942-8501 USA Fax: 800-672-2054; Toll Free: 888-330-8477; Edit Addr.: 175 Fifth Ave., New York, NY 10010 USA Tel 212-674-5151; Fax: 540-672-7540 (customer service)
Web site: http://www.picadorusa.com
Dist(s): **Libros Sin Fronteras**
Macmillan
Westminster John Knox Pr.
Picaro Press *See* **One Eyed Pr.**
Piccadilly Bks., Ltd., *(978-0-941599; 978-1-936709)* P.O. Box 25203, Colorado Springs, CO 80936 USA (SAN 665-9969) Tel 719-550-9887
E-mail: info@piccadillybooks.com
Web site: http://www.piccadillybooks.com
Dist(s): **MyiLibrary**
New Leaf Distributing Co., Inc.
Nutri-Bks. Corp.
Piccolo Tales, *(978-0-9881889)* 10640 Riverlake Dr., Knoxville, TN 37922 USA Tel 865-966-0274; Fax: 865-966-0274
E-mail: bc2bls@yahoo.com.
Pick It Publishing, *(978-0-615-26122-5)* P.O. Box 284, Danville, IA 52623 USA
Dist(s): **Lulu Pr., Inc.**
Pick Me Up N Go Publishing Co., *(978-0-615-15832-7)* 10312 S. Prospect Ave., Chicago, IL 60643 USA
E-mail: felice@pickmeupngo.com
Dist(s): **Lulu Pr., Inc.**
Pickett Fennell Group, The, *(978-0-615-31289-7; 978-0-9833864)* 619 Castlewood Dr., Upper Marlboro, MD 20774 USA
E-mail: pfgpublishing@gmail.com.
Pickett Publishing *See* **Pickett Fennell Group, The**
Pickled Eggs Press (TM) *Imprint of* **Bk. Entree(TM)**
Pickled Herring Pr., *(978-0-9778276)* 2380 W. Hill Dr., Madison, WI 53711 USA.
Picklesisters, *(978-0-9767542)* 224 Red Oak Dr E. Apt. F, Sunnyvale, CA 94086-6612 USA
E-mail: editor@picklesisters.com
Web site: http://www.picklesisters.com.
Pickrell, Karen, *(978-0-9993482)* 5717 Balfor Rd., Rocklin, CA 95765 USA Tel 916-435-0256
E-mail: karen_pick@sbcglobal.net
Web site: kareninreallife.com.
Pickup, Terry Lowey *See* **Terry Lowey's Children's Stories, LLC**
Pickwick Pr. *Imprint of* **Phoenix Bks., Inc.**
Picnic Publishing Ltd. (GBR) *(978-0-9556105) Dist. by* **Trans-Atl Phila.**
Pictorial Legends, *(978-0-939031)* Subs. of Event Co., 435 Holland Ave., Los Angeles, CA 90042 USA (SAN 662-8486) Tel 213-254-4416
Dist(s): **Igram Pr.**
Picture Bk. *Imprint of* **Spotlight**
Picture Bk. Learning, Inc., *(978-0-9760725)* P.O. Box 270075, Louisville, CO 80027 USA
E-mail: todd@picturebooklearning.com
Web site: http://www.picturebooklearning.com
Picture Entertainment *See* **Evening Sun Pr.**
Picture Me Books, Incorporated *See* **Playhouse Publishing**
Picture Window Bks. *Imprint of* **Capstone**
Pie in the Sky Publishing, LLC, *(978-1-893815)* 8031 E. Phillips Cir., Centennial, CO 80112 USA
E-mail: PieintheSkyPublishing@msn.com
Web site: http://www.pieintheskypublishing.com
Dist(s): **Bks. West.**
Pie Plate Publishing Co., *(978-0-9855906; 978-1-941175)* P.O. Box 760151, Lathrup Village, MI 48076 USA Tel 248-508-7749
E-mail: joddo@pieplatepublishing.com
Web site: www.pieplatepub.com.
Pieces of Learning, *(978-0-9623835; 978-1-880505; 978-1-931334; 978-1-934358; 978-1-937113)* Div. of Creative Learning Consultants, Inc., 1990 Market Rd., Marion, IL 62959 USA (SAN 298-461X) Tel 618-964-9426; Fax: 618-964-1897; Toll Free Fax: 800-844-0455; Toll Free: 800-729-5137
E-mail: piecesoflearning@frontier.com; stan@piecesoflearning.com
Web site: http://www.piecesoflearning.com.
Piedra Santa, Editorial (GTM) *(978-84-8377; 978-99922-1; 978-99922-58) Dist. by* **Libros Fronteras.**
PIEEYE Publishing, Inc., *(978-0-9759435)* 116 Consumer Sq., Suite 333, Plattsburgh, NY 12901 USA Tel 514-684-0434; Toll Free: 888-474-3393
E-mail: jocelyne@pieeyepublishing.com; info@pieeyepublishing.com
Web site: http://www.pieeyepublishing.com/.
Pier Media, *(978-0-9715980)* Div. of Pier Video, Inc., P.O. Box 190, Gardiner, NY 12525 USA Tel 212-481-0031; Fax: 212-481-0892
E-mail: joe514@aol.com
Web site: http://www.marcusantebi.com.
Pieras Inc. Editorial, *(978-0-9729719)* Div. of Pieras Inc., Y-9 México Ave. and Colorado St. Parkville Extension, Guaynabo, PR 00962-3923 USA (SAN 255-3112) Tel 787-299-4486
E-mail: jorge@elbien.org
Web site: http://www.wakebooks.com
Dist(s): **Ingram Content Group.**
Pieras Incorporated *See* **Pieras Inc. Editorial**

Pierce, Paul, *(978-0-9741819)* 1400 15th St., Columbus, GA 31901 USA
E-mail: prpierce@mindspring.com
Dist(s): **Parnassus Bk. Distributors.**

Pierce Pr., *(978-0-9776396; 978-0-9960975; 978-0-9970681; 978-0-9996592)* P.O. Box 206, Arlington, MA 02746 USA Tel 339-368-5656; Fax: 339-368-5656
E-mail: charlotte@piercepress.com
Web site: http://www.piercepress.com; https://www.facebook.com/daytripperbooks; https://plus.google.com/+CharlottePierce; http://peeragogy.org
Dist(s): **Ingram Publisher Services.**

Pierre Publishing *Imprint of* **Carol J. Pierre, LLC**

Pig Iron Pr., *(978-0-917530)* Orders Addr.: P.O. Box 237, Youngstown, OH 44501 USA (SAN 209-0937) Tel 330-747-6932; Fax: 330-747-0599; Edit Addr.: 26 N. Phelps, Youngstown, OH 44503 USA (SAN 241-8193)
E-mail: pigironpress@cboss.com.

Pikes Peak Library District, *(978-1-56735)* 5550 N. Union, Colorado Springs, CO 80918 USA Tel 719-531-6333; Fax: 719-389-8161
E-mail: tblevins@ppld.org.

Pikku Publishing (GBR) *(978-0-9928050) Dist. by* **IPG Chicago.**

Pik-Ware Publishing, *(978-0-9744190)* P.O. Box 110, Crisfield, MD 21817 USA Tel 410-968-3873 (phone/fax)
E-mail: pat@funkyseagull.com
Web site: http://www.pik-ware.com.

PIL Kids *Imprint of* **Publications International, Ltd.**

Pilate, Victoria, *(978-0-9759665)* P.O. Box 75433, Washington, DC 20013 USA.

Pilgrim Press *See* **Kinfolk Research Pr.**

Pilgrim Pr., The/United Church Pr., *(978-0-8298)* Div. of United Church Board for Homeland Ministries, 700 Prospect Ave. E., Cleveland, OH 44115-1100 USA Tel 216-736-3848; Fax: 216-736-2207
E-mail: ucpress@ucc.org; pilgrim@ucc.org
Web site: http://www.ucpress.com; http://www.pilgrimpress.com
Dist(s): **BookBaby**
Faith Alive Christian Resources
Women Ink.

Pilgrim Voyage Pr., *(978-0-9891166)* 989 Scarlett Pl., Tracy, CA 95376 USA Tel 209-229-1375
E-mail: chase@pilgrimvoyage.com
Web site: www.pilgrimvoyage.com.

Pilinut Pr., Inc., *(978-0-9779576; 978-1-944390)* 41 W. Lee Hwy., Suite 59, #808, Warrenton, VA 20186 USA.

Pill Bug Pr., *(978-0-9761623)* 1868 Bridgeport Ave., Claremont, CA 91711 USA Tel 909-624-9985 (phone/fax).

Pill Hill Pr., *(978-0-9842610; 978-1-61706)* 343 W. 4th St., Chadron, NE 69337 USA
E-mail: pillhillpress@gmail.com
Web site: http://www.pillhillpress.com
Dist(s): **BookBaby.**

Pillar of Enoch Ministry Bks., *(978-0-9759131)* The Pillar of Enoch Ministry, 1708 N. 77th Ave., Elmwood Park, IL 60707-4107 USA
E-mail: helena@pillar-of-enoch.com
Web site: http://www.pillar-of-enoch.com
Dist(s): **Ingram Content Group.**

Pillar Rock Publishing, *(978-0-9764109)* P.O. Box 86571, Portland, OR 97286 USA
Web site: http://www.zoppa.com.

Pillowtalks Publishing, *(978-0-692-82809-0)* 105 Beverly Blvd., Hobart, IN 46342 USA Tel 219-942-1821; Fax: 219-942-1821
E-mail: sherryfinnerty@gmail.com.

Pilot Bks. *Imprint of* **Bellwether Media**

Pilot Communications Group, Inc., *(978-0-9791957; 978-0-9824967; 978-0-9826665; 978-1-936417; 978-1-939268; 978-1-62903)* 317 Appaloosa Trl., Woodway, TX 76712-8816 USA
Dist(s): **Independent Pubs. Group**
Midpoint Trade Bks., Inc.

Pilumeli, Tanya *See* **FAVA Pr.**

Pinata Pubns., *(978-0-934925)* P.O. Box 13252, Oakland, CA 94611 USA (SAN 694-6062) Tel 510-336-0819 (phone/fax)
E-mail: bsalinas@ousd.k12.ca.us
Dist(s): **Lectorum Pubns., Inc.**
Libros Sin Fronteras
Teacher's Discovery.

Pinata Publishing (CAN) *(978-0-9685097; 978-0-9809163) Dist. by* **IPG Chicago.**

Pinchey Hse. Pr., *(978-0-9820342)* 1805 Mummasburg Rd., Gettysburg, PA 17325 USA (SAN 857-0655)
Web site: http://www.ofthewing.com
Dist(s): **Follett School Solutions.**

Pine Cone Pr., *(978-0-9791982; 978-0-692-20517-4)* 2870 Callie Still Rd., Lawrenceville, GA 30045 USA
E-mail: marty@donnellan.com
Web site: http://www.frendibles.com
Dist(s): **CreateSpace Independent Publishing Platform.**

Pine Hill Graphics, *(978-0-9714103; 978-0-9727279; 978-1-933150; 978-0-615-29527-5)* 85334 Lorane Hwy., Eugene, OR 97405 USA Tel 541-343-1364; Fax: 541-343-0568
E-mail: fred@pinehillgraphics.com
Dist(s): **Leonard, Hal Corp.**

Pine Hill Pr., *(978-1-57579)* Div. of Print Right Printing, 1808 N. K Ave., Sioux Falls, SD 57104 USA Tel 605-362-9200; Fax: 605-362-9222 Do not confuse with Pine Hill Pr., Lafayette, CA8
E-mail: print@pinehillpress.com
Web site: http://www.printrightprinting.com.

Pine Orchard, Inc., *(978-0-9645727; 978-1-930580)* Orders Addr.: 2850 Hwy 95 South. P.O. box 9184, Moscow, ID 83843 USA (SAN 253-4258) Tel 208-882-4838; Fax: 208-882-4845; Toll Free: 877-354-7433; *Imprints:* Ulyssian Publications (Ulyssian Pubns); Luminary Media Group (Luminary Media)
E-mail: orders@pineorchard.com; pineorch@pineorchard.com
Web site: http://www.pineorchard.com
Dist(s): **Brodart Co.**

Pine Orchard Press *See* **Pine Orchard, Inc.**

Pine View Pr., *(978-0-9740151)* Orders Addr.: 42 Central St., Southbridge, MA 01550 USA (SAN 255-3309) Tel 508-764-7415; Fax: 508-765-1963
E-mail: shawnpcormier@aol.com
Web site: http://www.pineviewpress.com
Dist(s): **Partners Bk. Distributing, Inc.**

Pineapple Pr., Inc., *(978-0-910923; 978-1-56164; 978-1-68334)* Div. of The Globe Pequot Press, 4501 Forbes Blvd., Suite 200, Lanham, MD 20706 USA (SAN 285-0850) Tel 301-459-3366; Fax: 301-429-5748 Do not confuse with companies with same or similar names in Saint Johns, MI, Middletown, RI, Northampton, MA, Wimberley, TX
Dist(s): **American Wholesale Bk. Co.**
Ingram Publisher Services
MyiLibrary
National Bk. Network
Rowman & Littlefield Publishers, Inc.

Pineapple Publishing and Consulting LLC, *(978-0-9794608; 978-1-938188)* 1046 W. 42nd St., Houston, TX 77018-4314 USA
Web site: http://www.pineapplepublishing.com.

Pinecone Bk. Co., *(978-1-949053)* P.O. Box 65, Evergreen, CO 80437 USA Tel 303-670-3628
E-mail: bethfostered@gmail.com
Web site: BethFosterED.com.

Pinefield Publishing, *(978-0-9746397)* 9801 Fall Creek Rd., Suite 318, Indianpolis, IN 46256 USA Tel 317-258-6211; Fax: 317-576-9154
E-mail: Pinefieldpublishing@comcast.net
Web site: http://www.Pinefieldpublishing.com.

Pines Publishing, *(978-0-9766820)* 9896 Lincoln Rd., Morrison, KY 61270-9498 USA
E-mail: info@pinespublishing.com
Web site: http://www.pinespublishing.com.

Pinetree Pubns., *(978-0-9709408)* 6523 Oregon Chickadee Rd., Weeki Wachee, FL 34613-8353 USA Tel 352-592-5292 (phone/fax)
E-mail: lwnorris@hitter.net; lwnorris@bellsouth.net.

Pink Elephant Pr. The, *(978-0-9772975)* P.O. Box 1153, Jonesboro, GA 30236-1153 USA (SAN 257-2532) Toll Free: 800-583-1439 (phone/fax)
E-mail: info@thepinkelephantpress.com
Web site: http://www.thepinkelephantpress.com.

Pink Granite Pr., *(978-0-9766737)* P.O. Box 231, Thousand Island Park, NY 13692-0231 USA Tel 613-549-6575.

Pink Hyacinth Press *See* **Kelly, Katherine**

Pink Kiss Publishing Co., *(978-0-615-29068-3; 978-0-9828795; 978-0-9835756; 978-0-9847455; 978-0-9851909; 978-0-9858299; 978-0-9885632; 978-0-9895580; 978-0-9904442; 978-0-9962965)* 2316 Greenway Dr., Gautier, MS 39553 USA
E-mail: pinkkisspublishing@pinkkisspublishing.com; glenda099@cableone.net
Web site: http://www.pinkkisspublishing.com.

Pink Lemonade, LLC, *(978-0-9799159)* 297 Sunset Pk. Dr., Prescott, AZ 86303 USA
E-mail: zuzu@cableone.net
Web site: http://www.thecupcakesclub.com.

Pink Pig Pr., *(978-0-9816360)* 980 Broadway, Suite 248, Thornwood, NY 10594 USA Tel 914-747-8188.

Pink Stucco Pr., *(978-0-9717796)* 36 Dexter St., Waltham, MA 02453-5017 USA; *Imprints:* Mystic Night Books (Mystic Night Bks)
E-mail: publishing@pinkstucco.net
Web site: http://www.pinkstucco.net/psp/.

Pink&Brown Publishing, LLP, *(978-0-615-36448-3)* 35 E. Main St. Suite 373, Avon, CT 06001 USA Tel 860-674-0292
E-mail: marycashman@comcast.net
Dist(s): **West.**

Pinkney, Gail, *(978-0-9799320)* 1185 Collier Rd NW Apt. 10E, Atlanta, GA 30318-8218 USA
E-mail: pinkneycorey@yahoo.com
Web site: http://www.dreamteambook.com.

Pinkney Wilcox, JoAnn, *(978-0-9764191)* Orders Addr.: 4044 George Busbee Pkwy. #8304, Kennesaw, GA 30144 USA Tel 678-768-5644
E-mail: joannpwilcox@yahoo.com
Web site: http://www.booksbyjpw.com.

PinkPowerful Bks. *Imprint of* **PinkPowerful LLC**

PinkPowerful LLC, *(978-0-9859171)* 699 W. Magee, No. 6203, Tucson, AZ 85704 USA Tel 650-996-4878; *Imprints:* PinkPowerful Books (PinkPowerfulBks)
Web site: Pinkpowerful.com.

Pinkston, Anastasia, *(978-0-9790515)* 500 Moonraker Dr. Apt. 107, Chesapeake, VA 23320-4051 USA
E-mail: anapinkston@yahoo.com
Web site: http://www.cafepress.com/pinkston.

Pinnacle Press *See* **Mountaintop Pr.**

Pinnacle Press *See* **Capital Communications, Inc.**

Pinnacle Pr., *(978-0-9745542)* 25 Country Estates W., East Durham, NY 12423 USA Tel 518-239-8003 Do not confuse with companies with the same name in Little Rock, AR, Cary, NC, Spokane, WA, Nashville, TN, Franklin, TN, Saint Louis, MO
E-mail: foxykate2001@yahoo.com.

Pinninti Pubs., *(978-0-9703474)* 120 Carter Rd., Princeton, NJ 08540-2111 USA
E-mail: pkrao@dr.com
Web site: http://www.pinnintipublishers.com.

Pinpoint Color *See* **Pinpoint Printing**

Pinpoint Printing, *(978-0-9702324)* 5115 E. Highland Dr., Jonesboro, AR 72401 USA Tel 870-931-6200; Fax: 870-931-5800
E-mail: dkelley@mkbmarketing.com
Web site: http://www.pinpointprinting.com.

Pinter & Martin Ltd. (GBR) *(978-0-9530964; 978-1-905177; 978-1-78066) Dist. by* **Natl Bk. Netwk.**

Pintos, Yoselem G., *(978-0-9800127; 978-1-61196)* 17906 E Mission Ave, Spokane Valley, WA 11423 USA Tel 646-634-9490
E-mail: yoselem@hotmail.com.

Pinup Vintage *See* **Pinup Vintage**

Pinup Vintage, *(978-0-692-76674-3; 978-0-692-76689-7)* .

Pinwheel Bks., *(978-0-9832577; 978-0-9854248; 978-1-940741)* Orders Addr.: PO BOX 491470, Key Biscayne, FL 33149 USA Tel 617-794-7976
E-mail: publisher@pinwheelbooks.com
Web site: www.pinwheelbooks.com.

Pinyon Publishing, *(978-0-9821561; 978-1-936671)* 23847 V66 Trail, Montrose, CO 81403 USA Tel 970-596-8676
E-mail: susanelliott@pinyon-publishing.com
Web site: http://www.pinyon-publishing.com.

Pinz, Shelley Music, *(978-0-9700251)* Orders Addr.: P.O. Box 275, Atlantic Beach, NY 11509 USA Tel 516-371-4437; Fax: 516-371-4437 (*51); Edit Addr.: 2100 Atlantic Blvd., Atlantic Beach, NY 11509 USA.

Pioneer Clubs, *(978-0-9743503; 978-1-934725; 978-0-9853008; 978-0-9885794)* Orders Addr.: P.O. Box 788, Wheaton, IL 60187-0788 USA (SAN 225-4891) Tel 630-293-1600; Fax: 630-293-3053; Toll Free: 800-694-2582; Edit Addr.: 27 W. 130 St. Charles Rd., Carol Stream, IL 60188-1999 USA (SAN 669-2419)
E-mail: info@pioneerclubs.org
Web site: http://www.pioneerclubs.org.

Pioneer Poet Publishing, *(978-0-615-55095-4; 978-0-615-65742-4)* 10651 MacGregor Dr., Pensacola, FL 32514 USA Tel 850-748-8895
E-mail: gincru@gmail.com
Dist(s): **CreateSpace Independent Publishing Platform**
Lulu Pr., Inc.

Pioneer Valley Bks. *Imprint of* **Pioneer Valley Bks.**

Pioneer Valley Bks., *(978-1-58453; 978-1-932570; 978-1-60343)* 155A Industrial Drive, Northhampton, MA 01060 USA Fax: 4137278211; *Imprints:* Pioneer Valley Books (PioValley Bks)
E-mail: lauri@pvep.com; gina@pvep.com; nick@pvep.com
Web site: http://www.pioneervalleybooks.com.

Pioneer Valley Educational Press, Incorporated *See* **Pioneer Valley Bks.**

Piper, Aaron, *(978-0-578-21215-9)* 62 Salzburg Blvd., Columbus, IN 47201 USA Tel 567-204-2841
E-mail: aaronjpiper@hotmail.com.

Piper, J.G., *(978-0-9916561)* P.O. Box 14018, Columbus, OH 43214 USA Tel 614-262-7896
E-mail: books@jgpiper.com
Web site: http://jgpiper.com.

Piper Punches, *(978-0-9910936; 978-1-7353895)* 30 Citori Ct., Troy, MO 63379 USA Tel 636-346-7028
E-mail: denise_mcgrail@yahoo.com
Web site: www.piperpunches.com.

Piper Verlag GmbH (DEU) *(978-3-492; 978-3-89029; 978-3-8225; 978-3-89521; 978-3-921909) Dist. by* **Distribks Inc.**

Pippa's Passion, *(978-0-9988337)* 308 S. Bozeman Ave, Bozeman, MT 59715 USA Tel 406-581-6383
E-mail: edmonia308@yahoo.com.

Pippin & Maxx Arts & Entertain, LLC, *(978-0-9818747)* 533 Choctaw Rd., Jackson, MS 39206-3920 USA (SAN 856-7794) Tel 601-982-9394 (phone/fax)
E-mail: amile@pippinandmaxx.com
Web site: http://www.pippinandmaxx.com.

Pippin Pr., *(978-0-945912)* Orders Addr.: P.O. Box 1347, New York, NY 10028 USA (SAN 247-8366) Tel 212-288-4920; Fax: 732-225-1562; Edit Addr.: 229 E. 85th St., New York, NY 10028 USA.

Pipton Pr., *(978-0-9828203)* Orders Addr.: 1457 Capri Ave., Petaluma, CA 94954 USA; Edit Addr.: 2506 Castello St., Oakland, CA 94602 USA
E-mail: ginaartbooks@gmail.com.

Pirate Island Pr., *(978-0-9799326)* 3750-A Airport Blvd., No. 224, Mobile, AL 36608 USA (SAN 855-0026) Tel 251-650-4147; Fax: 251-928-9841; Toll Free: 877-689-6660
E-mail: pirateisland@bellsouth.net
Web site: http://www.tnrivers.com; http://www.jihadgerm.com.

Pirate Publishing International, *(978-0-9674081)* 6323 St. Andrews Cir., No. 5, Fort Myers, FL 33919-1719 USA Tel 941-939-4845
E-mail: SuperK@juno.com
Dist(s): **ebrary, Inc.**

Pirouz, Raymond, *(978-0-9729815)* Orders Addr.: 2014 Holland Ave. #719, Port Huron, MI 48060 USA (SAN 255-3899)
Web site: http://www.raymondpirouz.com.

Pisteuo Pubns., *(978-0-578-40998-6; 978-0-578-40999-3; 978-0-578-42903-8)* 649 Pecan Ln., Cottonwood Shores, TX 78657 USA Tel 830-220-3408
E-mail: julien@julienjamar.com
Dist(s): **Ingram Content Group.**

P.I.T. Pubns., *(978-0-9760608)* 120 Deweese Dr., Waggaman, LA 70094-2480 USA Tel 504-436-7012.

Pitcher, Jan, *(978-0-9795877)* 208 Tait Ave., Los Gatos, CA 95030 USA
E-mail: janpitcher@verizon.net.

Pitchford, D. L., *(978-0-9987945)* 628 E Morningside, Springfield, MO 65807 USA Tel 417-298-1916; *Imprints:* Straight on till Morningside Prints (Straightontil)
E-mail: dlpitchfordauthor@gmail.com; admin@dlpitchford.com
Web site: dlpitchford.com.

Pitchstone LLC, *(978-0-9728875; 978-0-9844932; 978-0-9852815; 978-1-939578; 978-1-63431)* 848 Sedgefield St., Durham, NC 27705-4251 USA
Web site: http://www.pitchstonepublishing.com
Dist(s): **BookBaby**
Follett School Solutions
Independent Pubs. Group
MyiLibrary
ebrary, Inc.

Pitspopany Pr. *Imprint of* **Simcha Media Group**

Pittsburgh Literary Arts Network LLC, *(978-0-9727319)* P.O. Box 226, Oakmont, PA 15139 USA Tel 412-820-2507; *Imprints:* Blacktypewriter Press (Blacktypewriter Pr)
E-mail: info@blacktypewriter.com
Web site: http://www.blacktypewriter.com.

PitziGil Pr. *Imprint of* **PitziGil Pubns.**

PitziGil Pubns., *(978-0-9846397; 978-0-9914760; 978-0-9970488; 978-0-9985426)* Orders Addr.: P.O. Box 1315, Gaffney, SC 29342-1315 USA (SAN 860-1550) Tel 864-488-7320; *Imprints:* PitziGil Press (PitziGil Pr)
E-mail: pitzigil@yahoo.com; dl@pitzigilpublications.com
Web site: www.pitzigilpublications.com.

Pivot Point Pubns., *(978-1-7335230)* 3 Jersey St., Londonderry, NH 03053 USA Tel 603-770-9288
E-mail: kmcintire5@comcast.net.

Pivotal Force, *(978-0-9740473)* 632 Skyview Rd., Bellville, TX 77418 USA (SAN 256-4319) Tel 979-865-9213
E-mail: pivotalforce@evl.net
Web site: http://www.pivotalforce.com.

Pivotal Publishing, *(978-0-9990332)* 246 Churchill St., Northfield, IL 60093 USA
E-mail: chliu0219@gmail.com.

Pivotal Publishing Inc. *See* **Pivotal Publishing**

Pixel Coast Publishing, *(978-0-9985159)* P.O. Box 17877, Reno, NV 89511 USA Tel 310-339-1019
E-mail: klasekan@gmail.com.

Pixel Kid Publishing, *(978-0-9990681; 978-1-949216)* 690 S US Hwy. 89, Suite 200, Jackson, WY 83001 USA Tel 307-222-9093; Fax: 307-222-9093
E-mail: info@pixelkidpublishing.com.

Pixel Mouse Hse., *(978-1-939322)* P.O. Box 20241, Huntington Station, NY 11746 USA Tel 631-850-3497
E-mail: info@pixelmousehouse.com
Web site: www.pixelmousehouse.com.

Pixelated Publishing *Imprint of* **Faithful Publishing**

Pixel+Ink, *(978-1-64595)* 85 Broad St., New York, NY 10004 USA Tel 917-301-5632
E-mail: bbuck@tbridgemedia.com
Dist(s): **Penguin Random Hse. Distribution**
Penguin Random Hse. LLC.

Pixelpics Publishing, *(978-0-9747826)* 4801 Secret Harbor Dr., Jacksonville, FL 32257 USA
Web site: http://www.pixelpics.net.

Pixels Publishing, *(978-0-9728743)* P.O. Box 10, La Fox, IL 60147 USA
E-mail: customerservice@pixelspublishing.com
Web site: http://www.pixelspublishing.com.

Pixie Ears Pr., *(978-1-939157)* 97 Mountain View Rd., Santa Cruz, CA 95065 USA
E-mail: lisa@pixieearspress.com.

Pixie Stuff LLC, *(978-0-9761421; 978-0-9795832; 978-0-9826081; 978-0-9833364; 978-0-9850897; 978-0-9850898; 978-0-9854666; 978-0-9890806; 978-0-9916167; 978-0-9862115; 978-0-9966836; 978-0-9974255; 978-0-9978570; 978-1-7336728)* Orders Addr.: 18 Brighton Way, Saint Louis, MO 63105 USA Tel 314-721-4107; Fax: 314-721-4107
E-mail: jennifer@thumbsupjohnnie.com; jennifer@hiredink.com
Web site: http://www.thumbsupjohnnie.com; www.hiredink.com.

PixyJack Pr., Inc., *(978-0-9658098; 978-0-9773724; 978-1-936555)* Orders Addr.: P.O. Box 149, Masonville, CO 80541 USA Tel 303-810-2850; Toll Free Fax: 888-273-7499
E-mail: info@pixyjackpress.com
Web site: http://www.pixyjackpress.com.

Pizzazz Publishing, *(978-0-9744936)* Orders Addr.: P.O. Box 415, Victoria, MN 55386 USA Tel 952-368-1903; Fax: 952-944-0399
E-mail: psimenson@aol.com
Web site: http://www.pizzazzpublishing.com
Dist(s): **Quality Bks., Inc.**

PJR Assocs., Ltd., *(978-0-9790796)* Orders Addr.: P.O. Box 2482, Alexandria, VA 22301 USA Fax: 703-683-4348; Edit Addr.: 910 Junior St., Alexandria, VA 22301 USA
E-mail: patrichards@pjrassociates.com
Web site: http://www.pjrassociates.com.

PJs Corner, *(978-0-9745615; 978-1-933158)* P.O. Box 39, Taft, CA 93268 USA Tel 661-765-7216; Fax: 661-770-8608; *Imprints:* Twiglet The Little Christmas Tree (Twiglet)
E-mail: memories@pjscorner.net
Web site: http://www.pjscorner.net.

PJS Publishing, *(978-0-9743177; 978-0-615-40511-7)* 40344 Redbud Dr., Oakhurst, CA 93644 USA Tel 559-641-5994
E-mail: steve@tycooney.com.

PK Bks. Inc., *(978-0-9827347; 978-0-9846799; 978-0-9891177)* 512 Terrace Rd., Bayport, NY 11705-1528 USA
E-mail: jnewbauer6@hotmail.com
Dist(s): **Ingram Content Group.**

pk potts publishing, *(978-0-615-65613-7; 978-0-578-48767-0)* 2058 Pine Field Ct #622, N. Charleston, SC 29405 USA Tel 843-729-0787
Dist(s): **CreateSpace Independent Publishing Platform.**

Place 33 Presses, *(978-0-9915700; 978-0-9915700-2-7)* 10275 Fairfield Ave, Las Vegas, NV 89183 USA Tel 702-717-2137
E-mail: Graphicartist@aol.com
Web site: http://www.place33.org
Dist(s): **Ingram Publisher Services.**

†Place In The Woods, The, *(978-0-932991)* 3900 Glenwood Ave., Golden Valley, MN 55422-5302 USA (SAN 689-058X) Tel 763-374-2120; Fax: 952-593-5593
E-mail: placewoods@aol.com; differentbooks@aol.com
Dist(s): **Social Studies Schl. Service**; *CIP.*

Place Mark Bks., *(978-0-9815991; 978-1-941032)* P.o. Box 602, Conneaut, OH 44030 USA (SAN 855-9929).

Placenames Press *See* **Back Channel Pr.**

Plaidswede Publishing, *(978-0-9626832; 978-0-9755216; 978-0-9790784; 978-0-9840650; 978-0-9837400; 978-0-9889176; 978-0-9962182; 978-1-7323648; 978-1-7333556)* P.O. Box 269, Concord, NH 03302-0269 USA Tel 603-226-1020; Toll Free: 800-267-9044
E-mail: gnews@empire.net
Web site: http://www.plaidswede.com.

Plain View Pr., *(978-0-911051; 978-1-891386; 978-0-9819731; 978-1-935514; 978-1-63210)* Orders Addr.: 1101 W 34th Street, STE 404, Austin, TX 78705 USA (SAN 264-3073)
E-mail: pk@plainviewpress.net; support@plainviewpress.net
Web site: http://www.plainviewpress.net; http://www.plainviewpress.com
Dist(s): .

Plain Vision Publishing, *(978-0-9761628; 978-0-9848234; 978-0-9910594; 978-0-9971664; 978-1-947820)* Eb#141 Paria Dr. Aripero Village Rousillac, La Brea, TTO Tel 868-704-6397; 984 Ashford St., Brooklyn, NY 11207 Tel 347-652-0883 Do not confuse with Plain Vision Publishing in Kihei, HI
E-mail: info@pvppress.com; eguadeloupe@pvppressl.com
Web site: http://www.pvppress.com
Dist(s): **Ingram Content Group.**

Plain White Pr., LLC, *(978-0-9760250; 978-0-9777383; 978-0-9815004; 978-0-9815964; 978-1-936005)* Orders Addr.: 17 Chadwick Rd., West Harrison, NY 10604-1802 USA (SAN 850-0886)
E-mail: julie@plainwhitepress.com
Web site: http://www.plainwhitepress.com.

Plan B Bks, *(978-0-9785798)* P.O. Box 300307, University City, MO 63130 USA
E-mail: abby@planbbooks.com
Web site: http://www.planbbooks.com.

Planet Bronx Productions, *(978-0-9765566)* P.O. Box 672146, Bronx, NY 10467-0803 USA; *Imprints:* PAPO Brand (PAPO)
E-mail: ivanvelezjr@planetbronx.com; admin@planetbronx.com
Web site: http://www.planetbronx.com.

Planet Dexter *Imprint of* **Penguin Publishing Group**

Planet Gina Media, *(978-0-9991410; 978-0-9991410-0-7)* 813 Hayfield Ct., Doylestown, PA 18901 USA Tel 609-678-6494; Fax: 609-678-6494
E-mail: Jenniep.hamel@gmail.com.

Planeta Mexicana Editorial S. A. de C. V. (MEX) *(978-968-406; 978-970-690) Dist. by* **Lectorum Pubns.**

Planeta Publishing *Imprint of* **Planeta Publishing Corp.**

Planeta Publishing Corp., *(978-0-9715256; 978-0-9719950; 978-0-9748724; 978-1-933169; 978-0-9795042)* 999 Ponce De Leon Blvd. Ste. 1045, Coral Gables, FL 33134-3047 USA; *Imprints:* Planeta Publishing (PlanPubng)
E-mail: mnorman@planetapublishing.com
Web site: http://www.planeta.es
Dist(s): **Ediciones Universal**
Ingram Publisher Services
Two Rivers Distribution.

PLANit Brands, LLC, *(978-0-578-49755-6; 978-1-7331188)* P.O. Box 21484, Beaumont, TX 77720 USA
E-mail: donna4430@att.net.

PLANit Lifestyle *See* **PLANit Brands, LLC**

Plankton Pr., *(978-0-9774074)* 5692 Kalanianaole Hwy., Honolulu, HI 96821 USA Tel 808-373-1016; Fax: 808-373-5381
Web site: www.planktonpress.com.

†Planned Parenthood Federation of America, Inc., *(978-0-934586; 978-1-930996; 978-1-935100)* 123 William St. 10th Flr., New York, NY 10038 USA (SAN 205-1281) Tel 212-261-4602
E-mail: julia.scheinbeim@ppfa.org
Web site: https://marketplace.plannedparenthood.org/brochures; *CIP.*

Planning/Communications, *(978-0-9622019; 978-1-884587)* 7215 Oak Ave., River Forest, IL 60305-1935 USA (SAN 253-8717) Tel 708-366-5200; Fax: 708-366-5280; Toll Free: 888-366-5200 (orders only)
E-mail: info@planningcommunications.com; dl@planningcommunications.com
Web site: http://www.jobfindersonline.com; http://www.planningcommunications.com; http://www.dreamitdoit.net.

Plant Kingdom Communications, *(978-0-9834114)* 1503 Gates Ct., Morris Plains, NJ 07950 USA Tel 201-745-5494
E-mail: basia@plantkingdomcommunications.com
Web site: www.PlantKingdomCommunications.com.

Plant the Seed Publishing, *(978-0-9759790)* 4361 Fiesta Ln., Houston, TX 77004 USA Tel 713-747-0026
E-mail: rr4361@aol.com
Web site: http://hometown.aol.com/rr4361/myhomepage/business

Plantain Pr., Inc., *(978-0-9816262)* P.O. Box 37, Cruz Bay, VI 00831-0037 USA (SAN 856-0838) Tel 340-344-6123
E-mail: info@vitaxhelp.com.

Plata Publishing, *(978-1-61268; 978-1-950138)* 4330 N. Civic Ctr. Plaza Suite 100, Scottsdale, AZ 85251 USA Tel 480-998-6971
E-mail: d.leong@richdad.com
Dist(s): **Ingram Publisher Services**
Smashwords
Two Rivers Distribution.

Plataforma Editorial SL (ESP) *(978-84-15115; 978-84-15577; 978-84-15750; 978-84-15880; 978-84-16096; 978-84-16256; 978-84-935962; 978-84-96981) Dist. by* **Lectorum Pubns.**

Platinum Bks., *(978-0-9746503)* P.O. Box 660876, Arcadia, CA 91066-0876 USA (SAN 255-7525) Do not confuse with companies with the same name in Alpharetta, GA, Washington, DC
E-mail: hongdenise@yahoo.com
Web site: http://www.happierkids.com.

Platinum Medallion Children's Bks., *(978-1-929489)* Div. of EDS Design & Animation, 2705 Ridge Rd., Huntingtown, MD 20639 USA Tel 410-535-6992; Fax: 410-535-7643
E-mail: doug@dougweb.com; edsdesign@dsmith.com
Web site: http://www.platinum-medallion.com.

Platinum Paw Pr., *(978-0-9817067; 978-0-692-78049-7; 978-0-9984121; 978-1-7331972)* 1316 Grande Blvd. SE., Rio Rancho, NM 87124 USA (SAN 856-3047)
E-mail: info@platinumpawpress.com
Web site: http://www.platinumpawpress.com.

Platinum Rose Publishing, *(978-0-9742948)* 16619 W. Sierra Hwy., Canyon Country, CA 91351 USA
Web site: http://www.platinumrose.com.

Platte Publishing *See* **Forsberg, Michael Photography**

Platypus Media, L.L.C., *(978-1-930775; 978-1-951995)* Orders Addr.: 725 Eighth St., SE, Washington, DC 20003 USA Tel 202-546-1674; Fax: 202-546-2356; Toll Free: 877-752-8977
E-mail: info@platypusmedia.com
Web site: http://www.platypusmedia.com
Dist(s): **MyiLibrary**
National Bk. Network.

Play Ball Publishing, *(978-0-615-17947-6)* 891 Juliana Cove, Collierville, TN 38017 USA Tel 901-240-1353
E-mail: tmanso9@aol.com.

Play Odyssey Inc., *(978-0-9799441; 978-0-9825931)* 3 Alan Rd., Spring Valley, NY 10977 USA (SAN 854-8463) Tel 520-400-5188; Fax: 310-575-8873
E-mail: mgill@playoi.com
Web site: http://playoi.com; http://worksheetlab.com.

Play Snippets Pr., Inc., *(978-1-7335901)* 5581 Gallery Pk. Dr., Ann Arbor, MI 48103 USA Tel 734-929-5881
E-mail: acusleah@gmail.com.

Playdate Kids Publishing, *(978-1-933721)* 1901 Main St., Santa Monica, CA 90405 USA (SAN 257-571X) Toll Free: 800-587-1501
E-mail: info@fmrockskids.com
Web site: http://www.theplaydatekids.com/.

Player Piano Mouse Productions (PPMP), *(978-0-9797794)* 883 S. Iowa St., Suite 105, Dodgeville, WI 53533 USA.

Player Pr., *(978-0-9623966)* 139-22 Caney Ln., Rosedale, NY 11422 USA Tel 718-528-3285 Do not confuse with Player Press LLC in New York, NY.

Players Pr., Inc., *(978-0-88734)* P.O. Box 1132, Studio City, CA 91614-0132 USA (SAN 239-0213) Tel 818-789-4980
E-mail: Playerspress@att.net
Dist(s): **Empire Publishing Service.**

PlayGround *Imprint of* **Forest Hill Publishing, LLC**

Playground Pr., *(978-0-9790033)* 1951 W. Rochelle Ave., Glendale, WI 53209 USA (SAN 852-1832) Tel 414-352-1590
E-mail: trishwilliams@trishwilliams.net
Web site: http://www.trishwilliams.net.

Playhouse Publishing, *(978-1-57151; 978-1-878338)* 1566 Akron Peninsula Rd., Akron, OH 44313 USA Tel 330-762-6800; Fax: 330-762-2230; Toll Free: 800-762-6775
E-mail: info@playhousepublishing.com
Web site: http://www.nibble-me-books.com; http://www.playhousepublishing.com; http://www.littlelucyandfriends.com.

Playing Pig Pr., *(978-0-9788324)* 922 S. 87th Ave., Omaha, NE 68114 USA (SAN 851-7452) Tel 402-399-0516
E-mail: bettyhan@cox.net
Web site: http://FrecklesandMaya.com.

PlayinTime Productions, Inc., *(978-1-932895; 978-1-59860)* 19525 Valdez Dr., Tarzana, CA 91356-4946 USA Toll Free: 800-310-0087
E-mail: playintime@aol.com
Web site: http://www.playintime.com.

Playmore, Incorporated, Publishers *See* **Waldman Publishing Corp.**

Playor, Editorial, S.A. (ESP) *(978-84-359) Dist. by* **Continental Bk.**

PlayPen Publishing, *(978-0-9855865; 978-0-692-42878-8; 978-0-692-42879-5; 978-0-692-42880-1; 978-0-692-42881-8; 978-0-692-42936-5; 978-0-9994380; 978-1-7343610)* 1469 Panola Rd., Ellenwood, GA 30294 USA Tel 678-708-5398
E-mail: mzrocdyp@aol.com
Web site: http://playpenpublishing.com.

Playroom Pr., *(978-0-9660958)* 1163 Hopper Ave., No. 26, Santa Rosa, CA 95403 USA Tel 707-522-0150
E-mail: rfd5b4@aol.com
Web site: http://www.mansonfamilypicnic.com
Dist(s): **Casemate Pubs. & Bk. Distributors, LLC.**

Playscripts, Inc., *(978-0-9709046; 978-0-9819099; 978-1-62384; 978-1-68069)* 450 Fashion Ave. Ste. 809, New York, NY 10123-0805 USA Toll Free Fax: 866-203-4519
E-mail: info@playscripts.com
Web site: http://www.playscripts.com
Dist(s): **Consortium Bk. Sales & Distribution.**

Playscripts.com *See* **Playscripts, Inc.**

Playwrights Canada Pr. (CAN) *(978-0-88754; 978-0-919834; 978-1-55155) Dist. by* **Consort Bk Sales.**

Plaza & Janes Editories, S.A. (ESP) *(978-84-01) Dist. by* **Distribks Inc.**

Plaza Joven, S.A. (ESP) *(978-84-7655) Dist. by* **Lectorum Pubns.**

Pleasant Company Publications *See* **American Girl Publishing, Inc.**

Pleasant Plains Pr., *(978-0-9790906)* 366 Kingsberry Dr, Suite 100, Annapolis, MD 21409 USA Tel 410-757-1318
E-mail: boaterbrenda@comcast.net
Web site: http://www.pleasantplainspress.com.

Pleasant St. Pr., *(978-0-9792035; 978-1-935025)* P.O. Box 520, Raynham Center, MA 02768 USA (SAN 852-7598) Tel 508-822-3075; Fax: 508-977-2498
E-mail: orders@pleasantstpress.com; info@pleasantstpress.com
Web site: http://www.pleasantstpress.com.

Pleasure Boat Studio *See* **Pleasure Boat Studio: A Literary Pr.**

Pleasure Boat Studio: A Literary Pr., *(978-0-912887; 978-0-9651413; 978-1-929355)* 3710 SW Barton St., Seattle, WA 98126 USA (SAN 299-0075)
E-mail: pleasboat@nyc.rr.com; pleasboatpublishing@gmail.com; irslate88@gmail.com; michaelfdaley@gmail.com
Web site: http://www.pleasureboatstudio.com
Dist(s): **Brodart Co.**
Partners/West Book Distributors
SPD-Small Pr. Distribution
Smashwords.

Plebeian Media, *(978-0-692-82854-0; 978-0-9992658)*
E-mail: juliannorthauthor@gmail.com; juliannorthauthor@gmail.com; juliannorthauthor@gmail.com
Web site: www.juliannorth.com
Dist(s): **CreateSpace Independent Publishing Platform.**

Pleiness Publishing, *(978-0-9742472)* 45937 Duke Dr., Chesterfield Township, MI 48051 USA
E-mail: cpbusy@comcast.net.

PLEO, *(978-0-9660617)* 302 Park Tree Terr Bldg. 1311, Orlando, FL 32825-3474 USA Tel 407-277-3776; 321-297-5531.

pleo leonard productions *See* **PLEO**

Plexus Publishing, Ltd. (GBR) *(978-0-85965) Dist. by* **PerseuPGW.**

Plicata Pr. LLC, *(978-0-9828205; 978-0-9848400; 978-0-9903102; 978-1-7322963)* P.O. Box 32, Gig Harbor, WA 98335 USA Tel 253-851-2444
E-mail: janwalker@centurytel.net; info@plicatapress.com
Web site: http://www.plicatapress.com.

PloohFX Investments, *(978-0-692-15499-1; 978-0-692-15510-3; 978-0-692-19825-4; 978-0-578-40010-5; 978-0-578-40940-5; 978-0-578-75928-9; 978-0-578-75929-6)* 3127 Watsons Bend, Alpharetta, GA 30004 USA Tel 678-749-4063
E-mail: info@zardangs.com
Dist(s): **Ingram Content Group.**

Plouffe, Delci, *(978-0-692-84708-4; 978-0-578-54018-4)* 1102 Clark Ave, Lewistown, MT 59457 USA Tel 406-366-4174
E-mail: jeffwcrawford5+LVP0003374@gmail.com; jeffwcrawford5+LVP0003374@gmail.com.

†Plough Publishing Hse., *(978-0-87486; 978-1-63608)* 151 Bowne Dr., Walden, NY 12586 USA (SAN 202-0092) Tel 845-572-3455; Fax: 845-572-3472; Toll Free: 800-521-8011
E-mail: info@plough.com
Web site: http://www.plough.com
Dist(s): **Ingram Publisher Services**
MyiLibrary
Spring Arbor Distributors, Inc.; *CIP.*

Plowshare Media, *(978-0-9821145; 978-0-9860428; 978-1-7341443)* P.O. Box 278, La Jolla, CA 92038 USA (SAN 857-2933) Tel 858-454-5446
E-mail: tt@plowsharemedia.com
Web site: http://www.plowsharemedia.com.

Pluegl Bks., *(978-0-9760868)* Orders Addr.: P.O. Box 16622, Chapel Hill, NC 27516-6622 USA; Edit Addr.: 114 Waverly Forest Ln., Chapel Hill, NC 27516 USA.

Plum Blossom Bks. *Imprint of* **Parallax Pr.**

Plum Street Pr., *(978-0-692-35865-8)* 550 W. 54th St., New York, NY 10019 USA Tel 310-592-9053
E-mail: laurawilde100@gmail.com
Dist(s): **CreateSpace Independent Publishing Platform.**

Plum Street Press, *(978-1-943169)* Div. of Yes, MAM Creations, P.O. Box 13899, New Orleans, LA 70185-3899 USA Tel 904-307-6411
E-mail: YesMAMCreations@outlook.com.

Plum Tree Pr., *(978-0-9653535; 978-1-892476)* Orders Addr.: 531 Silcott Rd., Clarkston, WA 99403 USA Tel 509-758-2820; 509-332-1520 (Pine Orchard Distributors)
E-mail: bookinfo@pineorchard.com; gpducky@aol.com
Web site: http://www.pineorchard.com/plumtree; http://www.chinchinian.com
Dist(s): **Partners/West Book Distributors**
Pine Orchard, Inc.

Pluma Productions, *(978-1-889848)* Div. of Southern Dominican Province, USA, Orders Addr.: P.O. Box 1138, Los Angeles, CA 90078-1138 USA Tel 213-463-6488; Fax: 213-466-6645; Edit Addr.: 1977 Carmen Ave., Los Angles, CA 90068 USA
E-mail: pluma@eatrhlink.net.

Plume *Imprint of* **Penguin Publishing Group**

Plumlette Publishing, *(978-0-692-15944-6; 978-0-692-15946-0; 978-0-578-60024-6; 978-0-578-60026-0; 978-0-578-60028-4; 978-0-578-75305-8)* 5501 Abercorn St. Suite D, No. 134, Savannah, GA 31405 USA Tel 206-694-9315
E-mail: natalie.broulette@gmail.com
Dist(s): **Ingram Content Group.**

Pluriverse Publishing, *(978-0-9846119)* P.O. Box 3305, Ponte Vedra Beach, FL 32004-3305 USA
E-mail: isbn-registration@epluriverse.com; information@ePluriverse.com
Web site: http://www.ePluriverse.com
Dist(s): **Smashwords.**

Plushy Feely Corp, *(978-0-9837668)* 11 San Rafael Ave., San Anselmo, CA 94960 USA Tel 415-454-4600 (Tel/Fax)
E-mail: kerri@kimochis.com
Web site: www.kimochis.com.

Pluteo Pleno, *(978-1-937847)* 803 S. Durbin St., Casper, WY 82601 USA Tel 307-277-9010
E-mail: pete@pluteopleno.com
Web site: http://www.pluteopleno.com.

Pluto Project, *(978-0-9662982)* 601 Van Ness, No. E3801, San Francisco, CA 94102-3200 USA Tel 415-647-5501; Fax: 415-840-0060; Toll Free: 888-227-5886
E-mail: walter@plutoproject.com
Web site: http://www.plutoproject.com
Dist(s): **New Leaf Distributing Co., Inc.**
Quality Bks., Inc.

Pluton Ediciones (ESP) *Dist. by* **Lectorum Pubns.**

Plyler, Clint, *(978-0-692-18569-8; 978-1-7356561)* 4289 Winchester Rd., Dover, PA 17315 USA Tel 570-604-2014
E-mail: plylermo@gmail.com.

PM, INK, *(978-0-9753852)* 522 aNDERSON aVE., Rockville, MD 20850 USA (SAN 256-0275) Tel 301-424-0638 (phone/fax)
E-mail: pm.ink@verizon.net
Web site: http://www.pmink.net.

PM Moon Pub., LLC, *(978-0-9817777; 978-0-615-15573-9; 978-0-615-15734-4)* 3308 W. 111th St., Cleveland, OH 44111-3642 USA
Dist(s): **Lulu Pr., Inc.**

PM Pr., *(978-1-60486; 978-1-62963)* P.O. Box 23912, Oakland, CA 94623 USA
Web site: http://www.pmpress.org
Dist(s): **AK Pr. Distribution**
Ebsco Publishing
Follett School Solutions
Independent Pubs. Group
ebrary, Inc.

P.M. Publishing, *(978-0-9798346)* Orders Addr.: P.O. Box 185, Lottsburg, VA 22511 USA (SAN 854-5200); Edit Addr.: 353 Walmsley Rd., Callao, VA 22435 USA
E-mail: pinkie_thecat@yahoo.com.

PMK Press *See* **Dancer's Publishing**

Pneuma Life Publishing, Inc., *(978-1-56229)* Orders Addr.: 12138 Central Ave. #251, Mitchellville, MD 20721 USA (SAN 297-3057); *Imprints:* Christian Living Books, Inc. (Christian Livng)
E-mail: info@pneumalife.com; Info@christianlivingbooks.com
Web site: http://www.pneumalife.com; http://christianlivingbooks.com
Dist(s): **Anchor Distributors**
Ingram Content Group
Smashwords
Spring Arbor Distributors, Inc.

Pocamug Pr., *(978-0-9908877; 978-0-9984790; 978-1-7333656)* 5037 Alhambra Rd., Mayslick, KY 41055-9786 USA Tel 702-425-6189
E-mail: michaeld42@aol.com.

POCEE Publishing, *(978-0-9824812)* 1260 Wesley Ave., Pasadena, CA 91104 USA Tel 626-794-8524.

Pocket Books, *(978-1-4165)* 1230 Avenue of the Americas, New York, NY 10020 USA
Dist(s): **Diamond Comic Distributors, Inc.**
Simon & Schuster, Inc.

Pocket Books/Star Trek *Imprint of* **Pocket Bks./Star Trek**

Pocket Bks./Star Trek, 1230 Avenue of the Americas, New York, NY 10020 USA; *Imprints:* Pocket Books/Star Trek (PockBksStar)
Dist(s): **Simon & Schuster, Inc.**

Pocket Pr., Inc., *(978-1-884493; 978-1-61371)* P.O. Box 25124, Portland, OR 97298 USA Toll Free Fax: 877-643-3732; Toll Free: 888-237-2110
E-mail: sales@pocketpressinc.com
Web site: http://www.pocketpressinc.com.

Pocket Pubn., A, *(978-0-9721333)* 6701 Democracy Blvd., Suite 300, Bethesda, MD 20817 USA Tel 301-468-4905 Do not confuse with Pocket Publications in York, PA
E-mail: david_new@msn.com
Web site: http://www.home.talkcity.com/LibertySt/davidwnew.

PockitBook Publishing, Inc., *(978-0-9761716)* P.O. Box 6753, Athens, GA 30604-4120 USA Tel 706-354-8380
E-mail: pockitbook@bellsouth.net
Web site: http://www.pockitbook.com.

Pocol Pr., *(978-1-929763)* Orders Addr.: 6023 Pocol Dr., Clifton, VA 20124-1333 USA (SAN 253-6021) Tel 703-830-5862; Fax: 703-830-5862
E-mail: chrisandtom@erols.com
Web site: http://www.pocolpress.com.

Podengo Publishing, *(978-1-941876)* 123 Mohawk Rd., Lyons, CO 80540 USA Tel 970-324-0861
E-mail: marianwynkoop@hotmail.com.

POE Holistic Health, *(978-0-692-19206-1; 978-0-692-19207-8)* 8 Cottonwood Cir., Shrewsbury, MA 01545 USA Tel 508-769-5884
E-mail: kristenleepoe@yahoo.com
Web site: www.poeholistichealth.com.

Poet Tree Pubns., *(978-0-9658926)* P.O. Box 571444, Salt Lake City, UT 84157-1444 USA Tel 801-685-9398; Fax: 801-262-2324
Dist(s): **Tree Hse. Distribution.**

Poetic Matrix Pr., *(978-0-9714003; 978-0-9789597; 978-0-9824276; 978-0-9827343; 978-0-9852883; 978-0-9860600; 978-0-9981469; 978-1-7337025)* Orders Addr.: P.O. Box 1051, Lake Isabella, CA 93240 USA Tel 559-673-9402
E-mail: poeticmatrix@icloud.com
Web site: http://www.poeticmatrix.com
Dist(s): **Bored Feet Pr.**
SPD-Small Pr. Distribution.

Poetose Pr., *(978-1-945366; 978-1-64672)* 7 Farrington Ave, Allston, MA 02134 USA Tel 401-935-0696
E-mail: meia_geddes@alumni.brown.edu
Dist(s): **Ingram Bk. Co.**

Poet's Passage Pr., The, *(978-0-9841252)* Calle Cruz 203, Old San Juan, PR 00901 USA (SAN 858-4826) Tel 787-567-9235
E-mail: ducart@yahoo.com
Web site: Poetspassage.com.

Poets Wear Prada, *(978-0-9817678; 978-0-9841844; 978-0-615-60020-8; 978-0-615-60651-4; 978-0-615-65019-7; 978-0-615-76123-7; 978-0-615-81963-1; 978-0-615-83322-4; 978-0-615-84885-3; 978-0-615-86358-0; 978-0-615-87926-0; 978-0-615-88477-6; 978-0-615-91007-9; 978-0-615-97110-0; 978-0-615-98830-6; 978-0-692-22769-5; 978-0-692-28457-5; 978-0-692-30379-5; 978-0-692-45069-7; 978-0-692-67933-3; 978-0-9979811; 978-1-946116) 533 Bloomfield St., 2nd Flr., Hoboken, NJ 07030 USA (SAN 856-5031) Tel 201-253-0561 office*
E-mail: poetswearpradanj@att.net; roxy533@yahoo.com
Web site: http://thesmokingbook.blogspot.com; http://poetsweaprada.blogspot.com; http://twitter.com/pradapoet; http://pwpbooks.blogspot.com; http://issuu.com/pradapoet/; http://www.facebook.com/pages/Poets-Wear-Prada/41483895438
Dist(s): **CreateSpace Independent Publishing Platform.**

Pogo *Imprint of* **Jump! Inc.**

Pohl, Brittiany Publishing, *(978-0-692-10794-2)* P.O. Box 2574, ELIZABETH, CO 80107 USA Tel 303-898-0848
E-mail: brittianylpohl@gmail.com.

Pohl, J. Assocs., *(978-0-939332)* 307 N. Shady Ave., Houston, PA 15342 USA (SAN 220-181X) Tel 724-746-1178
E-mail: judepohl@comcast.net.

Pohrte, Dorey Publishing, Inc., *(978-0-9722296)* 917 Maple Rd., Buffalo, NY 14221 USA Tel 716-631-1256
E-mail: kathysue1@adelphia.net.

Point of Grace Entertainment Group, *(978-0-9706112; 978-0-9727644)* 3575 N. Beltline Rd., Suite 345, Irving, TX 75062 USA Tel 972-331-2538; Fax: 972-331-2569; Toll Free: 877-447-2233
E-mail: pgedist@yahoo.com.

Point of Life, Inc., *(978-0-9668069; 978-0-9819367)* 3032 E. Commercial Blvd., Ft. Lauderdale, FL 33308 USA
E-mail: mikmikl@aol.com
Web site: http://www.pointoflife.com.

Point Publishing, *(978-0-9663560)* Orders Addr.: 960 Sage Crest Dr., Wenatchee, WA 98801 USA Tel 509-670-6250; *Imprints:* Orchard Press (Orchard Press) Do not confuse with Point Publishing, Madison, WI
E-mail: thacken@genext.net
Dist(s): **Lulu Pr., Inc.**

Point To Point Publishing, *(978-0-9714147)* 5108 Brittany Dr., Old Hickory, TN 37138 USA Fax: 615-758-8495.

Poisoned Pen Pr., *(978-1-890208; 978-1-929345; 978-1-59058; 978-1-61595; 978-1-4642; 978-1-62886)* Orders Addr.: 6962 E. First Ave., Suite 103, Scottsdale, AZ 85251 USA (SAN 299-6898) Tel 480-945-3375; Fax: 480-949-1707; Toll Free: 800-421-3976; *Imprints:* Poisoned Pencil, The (Poisond Pencil)
E-mail: info@poisonedpenpress.com; sales@poisonedpenpress.com
Web site: http://www.poisonedpenpress.com; www.thepoisonedpencil.com
Dist(s): **INscribe Digital**
Ingram Publisher Services
MyiLibrary
Sourcebooks, Inc.

Poisoned Pencil, The *Imprint of* **Poisoned Pen Pr.**

Pokemon, USA, Inc., *(978-1-933743; 978-1-60438)* 777 108th Ave. NE, Suite 2000, Bellevue, WA 98004 USA
Web site: http://www.pokemon-tcg.com
Dist(s): **Diamond Bk. Distributors**
Simon & Schuster, Inc.

Pokeweed Pr. (CAN) *(978-1-894323) Dist. by* **IngramPubServ.**

Polaire Pubns., *(978-0-9708500; 978-0-9795218; 978-1-936315)* Div. of Polaire Entertainment Group, Inc., 422 Wolf Run Rd., Bartonville, TX 76226 USA (SAN 254-8291)
E-mail: chmeezepal@earthlink.net
Web site: http://www.animalcompanionsandtheirpeople.com
Dist(s): **DeVorss & Co.**

Polar Bear & Co., *(978-1-882190)* Solon Center for Research and Publishing, Orders Addr.: P.O. Box 311, Solon, ME 04979 USA (SAN 858-8902); Edit Addr.: 8 Brook St., Solon, ME 04979 USA
E-mail: paul@polarbearandco.com
Web site: http://www.polarbearandco.com; http://www.polarbearandco.org
Dist(s): **Ingram Content Group**
Magazines, Inc.

Polar Club Publishing, *(978-0-615-22038-3)* 635 Sandy Ridge Dr., Glen Burnie, MD 21061 USA
Dist(s): **Lulu Pr., Inc.**

Polar Surf Enterprises *See* **NORKY AMERICA**

Polaris Bks., *(978-0-9741443)* 11111 W. 8th Ave., Unit A, Lakewood, CO 80215-5516 USA Tel 303-980-0890; Fax: 303-980-0753
E-mail: zubrin@aol.com
Web site: http://www.polarisbooks.net.

Polark, Kelly *See* **Big Smile Pr., LLC**

Polebridge Pr., *(978-0-944344; 978-1-59815)* Orders Addr.: P.O. Box 7268, Santa Rosa, CA 95407 USA Tel 707-523-1323; Fax: 707-523-1350; Toll Free: 877-523-3545
E-mail: accounts@polebridgepress.com
Web site: http://www.polebridgepress.com
Dist(s): **Spring Arbor Distributors, Inc.**

Policy Studies Organization *See* **Westphalia Press**

Polis Bks., *(978-1-940610; 978-1-943818; 978-1-947993; 978-1-951709)* 1201 Hudson St. No. 211S, Hoboken, NJ 07030 USA; *Imprints:* Armina Press (ArminaPr)
E-mail: jpinter@polisbooks.com
Web site: www.polisbooks.com
Dist(s): **MyiLibrary**
Publishers Group West (PGW).

Polistampa (ITA) *(978-88-8304; 978-88-85977) Dist. by* **CasemateAcad.**

Political Status Education Coordinating Commission *See* **Dept. of Chamorro Affairs**

Polity Pr. (GBR) *(978-0-7456; 978-1-5095) Dist. by* **Wiley US.**

Poliva, Oren, *(978-0-692-93318-3; 978-0-9993687; 978-0-9993688)* 8940 Sage Rd., Oakland, CA 94605 USA Tel 510-292-1790
E-mail: polivaoren@hotmail.com.

Polka Dot Publishing, *(978-0-9709995; 978-0-9791072; 978-1-937032)* Orders Addr.: 3312 Woodview Dr., Lafayette, CA 94549 USA Tel 916-570-3839 our Distributor; Edit Addr.: 9034 Western Skies Dr., Reno, NV 89521 USA Tel 775-852-2690
E-mail: lifeoffred@yahoo.com
Web site: http://www.polkadotpublishing.com
Dist(s): **Z-Twist Bks.**

Poll, Michael Publishing *See* **Cornerstone Bk. Pubs.**

Polley Publishing, *(978-1-7320580)* 29 Pond St., Essex, MA 01929 USA Tel 508-641-5535
E-mail: buyersbrokerdiane@gmail.com
Web site: dianepolley.com.

PollieMarieSolutions, *(978-0-578-18749-5)* 2111 E. Blue Lake Dr., Magnolia, TX 77354 USA.

Pollux Ink, *(978-0-9820827; 978-0-615-26320-5; 978-0-9982201)* Div. of Zodiacts, 418 Centre Ave. Nyack, Nyack, NY 10960 USA (SAN 857-2186)
E-mail: mcgarryd6@gmail.com
Web site: http://zodiacts.com
Dist(s): **CreateSpace Independent Publishing Platform**
Lulu Pr., Inc.

PollyRhythm Productions, *(978-0-9701249)* Orders Addr.: P.O. Box 7707, New York, NY 10150 USA Tel 212 688 3900; Toll Free: 800 701 7981
E-mail: prprd@attglobal.net
Web site: http://www.pollyrhythm.com.

Pollywog Bog Bks. (CAN) *(978-0-9810575) Dist. by* **IngramPubServ.**

Polychrome Publishing Corp., *(978-1-879965)* 4509 N. Francisco, Chicago, IL 60625-3808 USA Tel 773-478-4455; Fax: 773-478-0786
E-mail: polypub@earthlink.net
Web site: http://www.home.earthlink.net/~polypub.

Polyface, Inc., *(978-0-9638109)* 363 Shuey Rd., Swoope, VA 24479 USA Tel 540-885-3590; Fax: 540-885-5888
Dist(s): **Chelsea Green Publishing.**

Polyglot Pr., Inc., *(978-1-931927; 978-1-4115)* 111 Caenarvon Ln., Haverford, PA 19041-1049 USA Do not confuse with Polyglot Press in Fairfax, VA
E-mail: david@polyglotpress.com
Web site: http://www.polyglotpress.com.

Polygon Publishing, *(978-0-9764768)* 73 Sutton Pl. W., Palm Desert, CA 92211 USA (SAN 256-4521) Tel 760-346-0544; Fax: 760-406-9333
E-mail: polygnpublishing@aol.com
Web site: http://www.polygonpublishing.com/.

Polytope Pr., *(978-0-9670526)* Div. of Tarescent Synductions, Orders Addr.: P.O. Box 1349, Phoenix, AZ 85001 USA Tel 602-271-9922; Fax: 602-230-1991; Edit Addr.: 321 E. Portland, No. 6, Phoenix, AZ 85004 USA
E-mail: polytope@hotmail.com.

Pomegranate Communications, Inc., *(978-0-7649; 978-0-87654; 978-0-917556; 978-1-56640; 978-1-0875)* Orders Addr.: 19018 NE. Portal Way, Portland, OR 97230 USA (SAN 860-2077) Toll Free: 800-227-1428; Edit Addr.: 19018 NE. Portal Way, Portland, OR 97230 USA Tel 503-328-6500; 503-328-6525; Fax: 503-328-9330; Toll Free: 800-227-1428; *Imprints:* POMEGRANATE KIDS (POMEGRANATEKID)
E-mail: info@pomegranate.com
Web site: http://www.pomegranate.com.

POMEGRANATE KIDS *Imprint of* **Pomegranate Communications, Inc.**

Pomegranate Publishing, *(978-0-9767377)* P.O. Box 43, Carpinteria, CA 93014 USA Do not confuse with Pomegranate Publishing in Loma Linda, CA
Web site: http://www.pomegranatepublishing.com.

Ponder Rose-A, The, *(978-0-692-88996-1)* 110 Keel Ct., Grover, NC 28073 USA Tel 704-487-7224
E-mail: roseoday2@yahoo.com.

Pontrelli, Jeany, *(978-0-9778456)* 6156 Solstice Dr., Sparks, NV 89436 USA.

PONY *Imprint of* **Stabenfeldt Inc.**

Pony Rock Pr., *(978-0-9759598)* 23484 150th Ave. NE, Thief River Falls, MN 56701 USA.

Poodle Suit Publishing, *(978-0-9728429)* P.O. Box 9844, Phoenix, AZ 85068 USA (SAN 255-1608) Tel 602-943-6766 Toll Free: 800-547-8247
E-mail: lougold@cox.net
Web site: http://www.poodlesuit.com.

Poor Magazine, *(978-0-9742007)* 255 9th St., 3, San Francisco, CA 94103 USA Tel 415-863-6306; Fax: 415-865-1932
E-mail: alex@poormagazine.org
Web site: http://www.poormagazine.org.

PoorHse. Publishing LLC, *(978-0-9896335; 978-1-943468)* 905 Myrtle Ave., Big Bear City, CA 92314 USA (SAN 920-6027) Tel 909-272-0059
E-mail: info@poorhousepublishingllc.com
Web site: poorhousepublishingllc.com
Dist(s): **BookBaby**
Small Pr. United.

Pop!, 8000 W. 78th St., Ste. 310, Edina, MN 55439 USA; *Imprints:* Pop! Cody Koala (Pop Cody K); DiscoverRoo (DiscoverRoo)
Web site: https://abdobooks.com/pop-books
Dist(s): **North Star Editions.**

Pop Academy of Music, *(978-0-9887710; 978-0-692-39597-4; 978-0-9961631; 978-1-947029)* 4912 Bendahl valley Terr., Richmond, VA 23237 USA Tel 7576131097
Dist(s): **CreateSpace Independent Publishing Platform.**

Pop! Cody Koala *Imprint of* **Pop!**

Pop Pop Pr. *Imprint of* **Micro Publishing Media, Inc.**

Pop Sandbox, Inc. (CAN) *(978-0-9864884) Dist. by* **Diamond Book Dists.**

Pop the Cork Publishing, *(978-0-9741854)* 1629 McGilvra Blvd., E., Seattle, WA 98112 USA Tel 206-720-9779; Fax: 206-720-9771
E-mail: sallyv@isomedia.com
Dist(s): **Hara Publishing Group.**

Pop The World, *(978-0-9846257)* 462 N. Linden Dr. Ste 430, Beverly Hills, CA 90212 USA Tel 310-274-1462
E-mail: poptheworld@att.net
Web site: www.privilegeofparenting.com.

Pope, Bryson, *(978-0-692-10683-9)* 710 N. 970 E., Springville, UT 84663 USA Tel 801-854-8260
E-mail: brysonrpope@gmail.com
Dist(s): **Ingram Content Group.**

Popol Vuh Press *See* **Talisman Pr.**

Poppy *Imprint of* **Little, Brown Bks. for Young Readers**

Poppy Blossom Pr., *(978-0-615-24059-6)* 8713 Glenbury Ct., S. Suite 102, Jacksonville, FL 32256 USA
E-mail: hello@poppyblossom.com.

Popstheclub.com, Inc., *(978-0-692-29061-3; 978-0-692-43666-0; 978-0-692-43667-7; 978-0-9988382; 978-0-578-47758-9; 978-0-578-47759-6)* 4160 Lyceum Ave., Los Angeles, CA 90066 USA Tel 3107092484.

Popular Truth, Inc., *(978-0-9631547)* P.O. Box 40656, Indianapolis, IN 76260 USA Toll Free: 888-342-8156
E-mail: anyike@netscape.net.

Porpoise Publishing, *(978-1-930328)* Div. of Life On Purpose, Orders Addr.: P.O. Box 834, Flat Rock, NC 28731 USA Tel 828-697-9239; Fax: 828-697-6038; Toll Free: 800-668-0183; Edit Addr.: 1160 W. Blue Ridge Rd., Flat Rock, NC 28731 USA
E-mail: publishing@lifeonpurpose.com
Web site: http://www.lifeonpurpose.com
Dist(s): **BookBaby.**

Porro, Guillermo Fermin III, *(978-0-692-99603-4; 978-0-692-11503-9; 978-0-692-17179-0)* 3307 SE Cty. Rd. 760, Aracdia, FL 34266 USA Tel 786-413-5689
E-mail: dadeshark19@yahoo.com
Dist(s): **Ingram Content Group.**

Port, Cynthia L., *(978-0-9912278)* 2513 E. Poplar Ct., Bloomington, IN 47401 USA Tel 812-322-7897
E-mail: cynthia.l.port@gmail.com.

Port Hole Pubns., *(978-0-9700274; 978-0-9768107; 978-0-9827627; 978-0-9882659; 978-0-9892608; 978-1-943119)* P.O. Box 205, Westlake, OR 97493-0205 USA
E-mail: porthole@digisys.net
Web site: http://www.ellentraylor.com.

Port Ludlow Bks., *(978-0-9729884)* 20 Keefe Ln., Port Ludlow, WA 98365 USA
E-mail: gldyerjr@waypt.com.

Port Town Publishing, *(978-0-9700544; 978-0-9716239; 978-0-9725990; 978-0-9740833; 978-1-59466)* 5832 Lamborn Ave., Superior, WI 54880-6231 USA; *Imprints:* Little Ones (Little Ones); Growing Years (Growing Years)
E-mail: porttownpublish@aol.com
Web site: http://www.porttownpublishing.bigstep.com.

Port Washington Public Library, *(978-0-9615059)* 1 Library Dr., Port Washington, NY 11050 USA (SAN 694-163X) Tel 516-883-4400.

Portable COO, The *See* **Mathieson Creative Media**

Portable Pr. *Imprint of* **Printers Row Publishing Group**

Portable Press *See* **Akashic Bks.**

Portage & Main Pr. (CAN) *(978-0-919566; 978-0-920541; 978-0-9694264; 978-1-894110; 978-1-895411; 978-1-55379) Dist. by* **Orca Bk Pub.**

Portal Ctr. Pr., *(978-1-936902; 978-0-9834956)* 215 Hwy 101 No. 2 P O Box 2024, Waldport, OR 97394 USA; *Imprints:* SpiritBooks (SpiritBooks)
E-mail: editor@portalcenterpress.com; sales@portalcenterpress.com
Web site: portalcenterpress.com.

Portals Publishing, *(978-0-692-51890-8; 978-0-692-52862-4; 978-0-9970512; 978-1-946469)* Denouement Literary Agency PO Box 973, Eagle Lake, FL 33839 USA Tel 863-640-6709
Web site: http://BLISSBooksOnline.com; http://DenouementLit.com; http://portalspublishing.com
Dist(s): **CreateSpace Independent Publishing Platform.**

Porter, Inman, *(978-0-9979766)* 32 Leroy St., Apt. 10, New York, NY 10014 USA Tel 478-290-2815
E-mail: inmanporter@gmail.com
Web site: www.inmanporter.com.

Porter, Rosanna *See* **Raisykinder Publishing**

Portfolio *Imprint of* **Penguin Publishing Group**

Portfolio Press *See* **Portfolio Pr. Corp.**

Portfolio Pr. Corp., *(978-0-942620)* Orders Addr.: 130 Wineow St., Suite 3, Cumberland, MD 21502 USA Tel 301-724-2795; Fax: 301-724-2796; Toll Free: 877-737-1200; Edit Addr.: 1107 Broadway, 12th Flr., New York, NY 10010 USA (SAN 238-5554) Tel 212-989-8700; Fax: 212-691-3073
E-mail: portfolio@hereintown.net
Web site: http://www.portfoliopress.com.

Portico Bks., *(978-0-9664867)* Orders Addr.: P.O. Box 6094, Chesterfield, MO 63006 USA Tel 636-527-2822 (phone/fax); Toll Free: 888-641-5353 (phone/fax); Edit Addr.: 1316 Rusticview Dr., Ballwin, MO 63011 USA
E-mail: info@grammarandmore.com
Web site: http://www.grammarandmore.com.

Portland Press, Incorporated *See* **Chihuly Workshop, Inc.**

Portland State University, Ooligan Press *See* **Ooligan Pr.**

Portland Studios, Inc., *(978-0-9797183)* The Point At Pk. Pl. 112 Poinsett Hwy., Greenville, SC 29609 USA (SAN 854-1744) Tel 864-241-0810; Fax: 864-241-0811
E-mail: jpeterson@portlandstudios.com
Web site: http://www.beowulfthebook.com; http://www.portlandstudios.com
Dist(s): **Pioneer Enterprises.**

Portrait Health Publishing, *(978-0-9853555)* Orders Addr.: 175 E Hawthorn Pkwy. Suite 235, Vernon Hills, IL 60061 USA Tel 847-236-0943
E-mail: info@portraithealthpublishing.com
Web site: http://www.portraithealthpublishing.com.

Portunus Publishing Co., *(978-0-9641330; 978-1-886440)* 27875 Berwick Dr., Carmel, CA 93923 USA Tel 831-622-0604; Fax: 310-399-5644
E-mail: service@portunus.net
Dist(s): **Lectorum Pubns., Inc.**

Positive Action For Christ, *(978-1-929784; 978-0-9719491; 978-1-59557)* 502 W. Pippen St., Whitakers, NC 27891 USA Tel 252-437-7771; Fax: 252-437-3297; Toll Free: 800-688-3008; *Imprints:* ProTeens (ProTeens)
Web site: http://www.positiveaction.org.

Positive Imaging, LLC, *(978-0-615-16787-9; 978-0-615-18693-1; 978-0-9842480; 978-0-9856876; 978-1-944071; 978-1-951776)* 9016 Palace Pwky., Austin, TX 78748 USA (SAN 858-8430) Tel 512-217-4803; 512-282-5717; Fax: 877-288-5496
E-mail: bill@positive-imaging.com; awbenitez@hotmail.com
Web site: http://www.positive-imaging.com; http://www.handyman-business-guide.com/; http://www.woodworking-business.com; http://www.selfpublishingworkbook.com; http://woodworking-biz-solutions.com; http://billbenitez.com; http://self-publish-your-writing.com; http://woodworkingbusinessbook.com; http://selfpublishingworkbook.com; http://woodworking-business-guide.com; http://notesonrelationship.com; http://awilliambenitez.com; http://goodrelationships101.com; http://self-publishing-suppo
Dist(s): **CreateSpace Independent Publishing Platform**
Ingram Bk. Co.
Lulu Pr., Inc.
Smashwords.

Positive Pasta Publishing, LLC, *(978-1-947645)* 8526 Eversham Rd, Henrico, VA 23294 USA Tel 804-385-4150
E-mail: getinspired@positivepasta.com.

Positive Productions, *(978-1-928726)* 934 E. 84th Pl., Suite A, Chicago, IL 60619 USA Tel 773-846-6131; Fax: 773-846-6555; Toll Free: 800-306-3064.

Positive Spin Pr., *(978-0-9773096)* P.O. Box 653, Warren, MI 02885-9998 USA
E-mail: info@positivespinpress.com; lisa@studiocvr.com
Web site: http://www.thehalloweenfairy.com.

Positive Strokes, *(978-0-9673490)* Orders Addr.: P.O. Box 97271, Raleigh, NC 27624 USA
E-mail: pstrokes@aol.com; healheartsbooks@aol.com.

Positively for Kids, Inc., *(978-0-9634650; 978-0-9765722; 978-0-9778237; 978-0-9786838)* P.O. Box 3283, Kirkland, WA 98083-3283 USA Toll Free: 800-600-5437
E-mail: customerservice@positivelyforkids.com
Web site: http://www.positivelyforkids.com
Dist(s): **American West Bks.**
Brodart Co.
Mackin Bk. Co.

Positively Rich, *(978-1-7328391)* 245 Maple St, Moscow, PA 18444 USA Tel 570-977-5434
E-mail: rludka7@hotmail.com.

Possum Products, *(978-0-615-12548-0)* 712 Warren Dr., Annapolis, MD 21403 USA Fax: 410-510-1003; 410-263-4473 (call 410-263-1847 first)
E-mail: possumpalette@aol.com.

Possum Trot Productions LLC, *(978-0-9962289)* Orders Addr.: P.O. Box 15341, Kansas City, MO 64106 USA Tel 816-895-2924
E-mail: info@possumtrotproductions.com
Web site: http://possumtrotkc.com.

Post Hill Pr., *(978-1-64293)* 8115 Isabella Lane., Suite 4, Brentwood, TN 37027 USA Tel 615-261-4646
E-mail: contact@posthillpress.com
Web site: http://www.posthillpress.com
Dist(s): **MyiLibrary**
Simon & Schuster
Simon & Schuster, Inc.

Post Mortem Publications, Inc., *(978-0-615-30090-0; 978-0-9839074; 978-1-941880)* 146 E. Broad St., Groveland, FL 34736 USA.

Post Oak Hill, *(978-0-9636122)* 235 Shady Hill Ln., Double Oak, TX 75067-8270 USA Tel 817-430-1182.

Potenial Psychotherapy Counseling & Remedial Service, *(978-0-9759889)* 1525 E. 53rd St., Suite 516, 11-2, Chicago, IL 60615 USA.

Potential Developing Ministries, Inc., *(978-0-9745554)* 455 Grason Hwy., Suite 111 Box 153, Lawrenceville, GA 30045 USA
E-mail: pdm@winning.com.

Potential Unlimited Publishing *See* **Red Letter Publishing & Media Group**

Potocar, Lisa Y., *(978-0-9990488)* 19 Outlet Rd., Ballston Lake, NY 12019 USA Tel 518-225-9695
E-mail: lisapotocar@gmail.com
Web site: lisapotocarauthor.com.

Potoma, Alison Elise, *(978-1-940602)* 6234 Avalon Dr., Wilmington, MA 01887 USA Tel 845-461-1065
E-mail: alisonpotoma@gmail.com
Web site: www.alisonpotoma.com.

Potter Assocs., *(978-0-9758672)* 2305 Jacob Dr., Santa Clara, UT 84765 USA Tel 435-986-3886; Fax: 435-986-3887; *Imprints:* Hot Page Press (HotPP)
E-mail: stanpot@sisna.com.

Potter Craft *Imprint of* **Potter/Ten Speed/Harmony/Rodale**

Potter Publishing, *(978-0-9856350)* 100 Cherry Tree Hill Ln., Barton, VT 05822 USA Tel 802-525-3311 Do not confuse with Potter Publishing in Elmsford, NY
E-mail: info@cherryyarn.com.

Potter Style *Imprint of* **Crown Publishing Group, The**

Potters Publishing LLC, *(978-0-9745810)* Orders Addr.: 2204 Blackjack Oak St., Ocoee, FL 34761 USA Tel 407-877-7444
Web site: http://www.potterspublishing.com.

Potter/Ten Speed/Harmony/Rodale, 1745 Broadway, New York, NY 10019 USA; *Imprints:* Crown (Crow); Potter Craft (PotterCraft); Ten Speed Press (TenSpeedPr); Watson-Guptill (WatsonG); Rodale Books (Rodale Books)
Dist(s): **MyiLibrary**
Penguin Random Hse. Distribution
Penguin Random Hse. LLC
Random Hse., Inc.

Potter/TenSpeed/Harmony/Rodale *See* **Potter/Ten Speed/Harmony/Rodale**

PottyMD LLC, *(978-0-9762877)* 2216 White Ave., Knoxville, TN 37916 USA Tel 865-525-0000; Fax: 865-525-0262; Toll Free: 877-769-8963
E-mail: support@pottymd.com
Web site: http://www.pottymd.com
Dist(s): **SCB Distributors.**

Poudre Landmarks Foundation, *(978-0-9753849)* 108 N. Meldrum St., Fort Collins, CO 80521 USA Tel 970-221-4220; 970-221-0553
Web site: http://www.poudrelandmarks.com.

Pounce To Success International, Inc., *(978-0-9776074)* 608 1/2 W. Park St., Lamar, CO 81052 USA (SAN 257-7364) Tel 719-201-7470; Toll Free: 800-768-6238.

Pounders Publishing, *(978-0-692-33113-2)* 4545 Barfield Rd, Memphis, TN 38117 USA Tel 901-278-6868
E-mail: pounders@anfa.com.

Pouring the Oil: Poetic Praise Pubns., *(978-0-9760734; 978-0-9841968)* Orders Addr.: P.O. Box 944, Brewster, NY 10509 USA; Edit Addr.: P.O. Box 253, Danbury, CT 06813-0253 USA
E-mail: pouringtheoil@yahoo.com; info@pouringtheoilpublications.com; spoken_word03@yahoo.com
Web site: http://www.pouringtheoilpublications.com.

Powell Hill Pr., *(978-0-9760648)* 8 Packett's Glen, Fairport, NY 14450 USA Tel 585-388-8622
E-mail: scoopwrite@aol.com
Web site: http://www.spiritwolf.info; http://www.powellhillpress.com
Dist(s): **North Country Bks., Inc.**

Power of One , LLC, *(978-0-692-81445-1; 978-0-692-96952-6; 978-0-692-18208-6; 978-0-578-57561-2; 978-1-7351969)* 48641 Denton Rd apt 209, Belleville, MI 48111 USA Tel 734-699-6483
E-mail: lajuana_jackson@att.net.

Power Play Media, *(978-0-9724003; 978-0-9741394; 978-1-934230)* P.O. Box 423, Brandywine, MD 20613 USA Tel 240-375-6908; Fax: 301-579-9913; *Imprints:* Nvision Publishing (NvisPub)
E-mail: tressa428@cs.com
Web site: http://www.nvisionpublishing.com/
Dist(s): **INscribe Digital.**

Power Pr., *(978-0-9748508; 978-0-9825568)* P.O. Box 622, Tyrone, GA 30290 USA Tel 770-486-0758; Fax: 770-486-6687 Do not confuse with Power Press in Torrance CA, Chico CA, Sonoma CA
E-mail: ratto@mindspring.com.

Power Pubns., Inc., *(978-0-9629858; 978-0-9724194; 978-0-615-40283-3; 978-0-615-41417-1)* 185 Randon Terr., Lake Mary, FL 32746 USA (SAN 254-6817) Tel 407-732-4322 (phone/fax) Do not confuse with Power Publications, Inc. in Phoenix, AZ, Mountain City, GA
E-mail: igilbert@cfl.rr.com.

Power Through Faith, *(978-0-9707320)* 1702 Capps St., Durham, NC 27707 USA Tel 919-596-7753.

Power Writings, *(978-0-9641640)* 9019 Wall St., 6F, North Bergen, NJ 07047 USA Fax: 201-869-9179
E-mail: fmelfa02@yahoo.com
Web site: http://www.pharmalanding.com.

Powerband, LLC, *(978-0-9746445)* 16199 Kennedy Rd., Los Gatos, CA 95032-9503 USA Fax: 408-402-0617; 16199 Kennedy Rd., Los Gatos, CA 95032-9503
E-mail: clelliott@mac.com
Web site: http://www.powerbandllc.com.

Power-Glide Foreign Language Courses, *(978-1-58204)* 1682 W. 820 N., Provo, UT 84601 USA Tel 801-373-3973; Fax: 801-343-3912; Toll Free: 800-596-0910
E-mail: deloyh@power-glide.com
Web site: http://www.power-glide.com.

powerHouse Bks. *Imprint of* **powerHse. Bks.**

powerHse. Bks., *(978-1-57687; 978-1-64823)* 32 Adams St, Brooklyn, NY 11201 USA (SAN 850-5845); *Imprints:* powerHouse Books (pwerHse Bks); PowerHouse Kids (PowerKids)
E-mail: info@powerhousebooks.com
Web site: http://www.powerhousebooks.com
Dist(s): **MyiLibrary**
Simon & Schuster, Inc.

powerHouse Cultural Entertainment, Incorporated *See* **powerHse. Bks.**

PowerHouse Kids *Imprint of* **powerHse. Bks.**

PowerKids Pr. *Imprint of* **Rosen Publishing Group, Inc., The**

PowerMark Productions, *(978-0-9705669; 978-0-9713412; 978-0-9717876; 978-0-9729135; 978-0-9747026; 978-0-9749339; 978-0-9795833; 978-0-9827990; 978-1-935980)* Div. of Quest Ministries International, 380 E. Hwy. Cc Suite E104, Nixa, MO 65714 USA Tel 417-724-1222; Fax: 417-724-0119; Toll Free: 877-769-2669
E-mail: linda@qminternational.com
Web site: http://www.powermarkcomics.com
Dist(s): **New Day Christian Distributors Gifts, Inc.**

PowerMoves, *(978-0-9748298)* P.O. Box 92907, Washington, DC 20090 USA Tel 301-568-9111
Web site: http://www.powermoves.org.

Powers, Elaine A., *(978-0-9991669)* 8540 N Yellowstone Ave, ORO VALLEY, AZ 85704 USA Tel 520-297-3402
E-mail: lizlady@comcast.net
Dist(s): **Ingram Content Group.**

Powerstart Pr. *Imprint of* **Rosen Publishing Group, Inc., The**

PowWow Publishing, *(978-0-9819789; 978-0-9859577)* P.O. Box 31855, Tucson, AZ 85751 USA
E-mail: brent@powwowinc.com
Web site: http://www.powwowpublishing.com; http://www.katemathis.net.

P.R.A. Enterprises Incorporated *See* **P.R.A. Publishing**

P.R.A. Publishing, *(978-0-9727703; 978-0-9821407; 978-0-9840142; 978-1-941416)* Orders Addr.: P.O. Box 211701, Martinez, GA 30917 USA (SAN 991-5419) Tel 706-855-6173
E-mail: lucindaclark@phoenixrisingarts.com; info@prapublishing.com; ljclark08@gmail.com
Web site: http://www.prapublishing.com; http://www.phoenixrisingarts.com; http://www.phoenixrisingart.wordpress.com
Dist(s): **BookBaby**
Ingram Content Group.

Practical Christianity Foundation, *(978-0-9705996; 978-1-932587; 978-1-60098)* 2514 Aloha Pl., Holiday, FL 34691 USA (SAN 254-4377) Tel 727-934-0927; Fax: 727-934-4241; Toll Free: 888-278-3300
E-mail: cseitz@greenkeybooks.com
Web site: http://www.greenkeybooks.com
Dist(s): **Send The Light Distribution LLC.**

Practical Green Pr., *(978-0-9834112)* 407 Del Rio Ct., Allen, TX 75013 USA Tel 214-785-8680
E-mail: office@practicalgreenpress.com
Web site: www.practicalgreenpress.com.

PRACTICAL SOLUTIONS Writing, Editing, Consulting, *(978-0-615-19350-2; 978-0-615-19351-9; 978-0-615-32636-8)* P.O. Box 1484, Wake Forest, NC 27588 USA Tel 919-604-4585; Fax: 901-273-1852
E-mail: Jfaulk28@nc.rr.com
Web site: http://stores.lulu.com/store.php?fAcctID=1906985; http://www.jefferyafaulkerson.com
Dist(s): **Lulu Pr., Inc.**

Praeger *Imprint of* **ABC-CLIO, LLC**

Pragma Design, Inc., *(978-1-7322836)* P.O. Box 413, Bertram, TX 78605 USA (SAN 991-1200) Tel 512-277-5424
E-mail: jeffhoo.bowker@pragma-design.com
Web site: www.pragma-design.com; http://pragma.media.

Pragmatic Bookshelf, The *Imprint of* **Pragmatic Programmers, LLC, The**

Pragmatic Programmers, LLC, The, *(978-0-9745140; 978-0-9766940; 978-0-9776166; 978-0-9787392; 978-1-934356; 978-1-937785; 978-1-941222; 978-1-68050)* 9650 Strickland Rd., Suite 103, No. 255, Raleigh, NC 27615 USA; 2831 El Dorado Pkwy., No. 103-381, Frisco, TX 75033 Toll Free Fax: 800-699-7764; *Imprints:* Pragmatic Bookshelf, The (Pragmatic Bkshelf)
E-mail: andy@pragprog.com
Web site: http://www.pragmaticprogrammer.com
Dist(s): **Ingram Publisher Services**
O'Reilly Media, Inc.

Prairie Arts, Inc., *(978-0-9725382)* 3100 Birch Bark Ln., Oklahoma City, OK 73120 USA Tel 405-755-5432; 405-728-1350; Fax: 405-728-9813
E-mail: dgordonart@aol.com.

Prairie Heart Publishing, *(978-0-9793668)* 8967 W. Driftwood Dr., Coeur d'Alene, ID 83814 USA Tel 208-777-8079 (phone/fax)
E-mail: aprairieheart@earthlink.net; sdianewood@earthlink.net
Web site: http://www.prairievirtuedolls.com.

Prairie Hills Publishing, *(978-0-9821084)* 1101 4th St. NW, Watertown, SD 57201 USA
Web site: http://www.prairiehillspublishing.com.

Prairie Moon Pubs., *(978-0-9994765)* P.O. Box 779, Nevada, MO 64772 USA Tel 678-777-2584
E-mail: marilyn.kmay@yahoo.com
Web site: www.PrairieMoonPublishers.com.

Prairie Shore Creative, Inc., *(978-0-9740542)* 2500 S. Corbett, Chicago, IL 60608 USA
E-mail: PSCreative@AOL.come
Web site: http://www.Prairieshorecreative.com.

Prairie Winds Publishing, *(978-0-9778240)* 15154 W. 231st St., Spring Hill, KS 66083 USA Tel 913-592-5002
E-mail: cyndi@gertrudemccluck.com
Web site: http://www.gertrudemccluck.com.

Prairieland Pr., *(978-0-9759829; 978-1-944132)* P.O. Box 2404, Fremont, NE 68026-2404 USA Tel 402-721-0241
E-mail: nlsharpwriter@gmail.com
Web site: http://www.prairielandpress.com; http://writesharp.com.

Pranayama Institute, Inc., The, *(978-0-9724450)* Orders Addr.: P.O. Box 40731, Albuquerque, NM 87196 USA Tel 706-889-5035 (phone/fax); Fax: 505-212-0097
E-mail: ssaranam@pranayama.org; publicity@pranayama.org
Web site: http://www.pranayama.org; http://www.godwithoutreligion.com.

Prancing Pony, The, *(978-0-9763555)* Orders Addr.: 104802 W. Foisy Rd., Prosser, WA 99350 USA
Web site: http://www.herbleonhard.com.

Prather, Anastasia, *(978-0-692-09851-6)* 1916 S 2nd St., SPRINGFIELD, IL 62704 USA Tel 217-720-6974
E-mail: dalek0802@gmail.com
Dist(s): **Ingram Content Group.**

Pratt Ctr. The, *(978-0-9772835)* Orders Addr.: Four Main St., Suite 210, Los Altos, CA 94022 USA Tel 650-949-2997; Fax: 650-949-2442
E-mail: prattcenter@covad.net.

Praxis Pr., Inc., *(978-0-9754305; 978-1-934278)* 1515 Skelton Rd.5-100, Gainesville, GA 30504 USA Tel 770-846-5978
Web site: http://www.praxispress.com.

Prayer Bk. Pr., Inc., *(978-0-87677)* Subs. of Media Judaica, Inc., Orders Addr.: 1363 Fairfield Ave., Bridgeport, CT 06605 USA (SAN 207-0022) Tel 203-384-2284; Edit Addr.: 304 E. 49th St., New York, NY 10017 USA (SAN 282-1788) Tel 212-319-6666.

PRAZZ Pubns., *(978-0-9776356)* Orders Addr.: P.O. Box 636, Upper Marlboro, MD 20773-0636 USA (SAN 257-8212); Edit Addr.: 8419 Thornberry Dr., West Upper Marlboro, MD 20772 USA
E-mail: ycsmallwood@yahoo.com.

Preadtend Publishing, *(978-0-9890174)* 219 Bulifants Blvd., Williamsburg, VA 23188 USA Tel 757-293-8408
E-mail: kendra@pREADtend.com.

Precept Ministries, *(978-1-888655; 978-1-934884; 978-1-62119)* Orders Addr.: P.O. Box 182218, Chattanooga, TN 37422 USA Tel 423-892-6814; Fax: 423-894-2449; Toll Free: 800-763-8280; Edit Addr.: 7324 Noah Reid Rd., Chattanooga, TN 37421 USA
E-mail: info@precept.org; jbundy@precept.org
Web site: http://www.precept.org.

Precious Little Bks., *(978-0-9787235)* 9353 SE. Yardarm Terr., Hobe Sound, FL 33455-3214 USA (SAN 851-3813) Tel 561-307-2367; Fax: 772-545-4944
E-mail: clarke@preciouslittlebooks.com
Web site: http://www.preciouslittlebooks.com.

Precious Moments, Inc., *(978-0-9817159; 978-0-9819885; 978-0-9825809)* 2850 W. Golf Rd., Suite 250, Rolling Meadows, IL 60008 USA (SAN 856-3403)
Web site: http://www.preciousmoments.com
Dist(s): **Midpoint Trade Bks., Inc.**

Precioustymes Entertainment, LLC, *(978-0-9729325; 978-0-9776507)* 229 Governors Pl., No. 138, Bear, DE 19701 USA Tel 302-294-6980 (office line); Fax: 302-294-6980
E-mail: PrecioustymesEnt@aol.com
Web site: http://www.precioustymes.com; http://www.platinumteen.org
Dist(s): **A & B Distributors & Pubs. Group**
Afrikan World Bk. Distributor.

Precision Cad/Cam Systems, Inc., *(978-0-9707464)* 9564 Deereco Rd., Luthvle Timon, MD 21093-2119 USA
E-mail: info@cadcam4u.com
Web site: http://www.cadcam4u.com.

Preferred Enterprises, *(978-1-885143)* P.O. Box 848, Lakewood, NJ 08701-0848 USA.

Preferred Marketing *See* **American Historical Pr.**

PremaNations Publishing, *(978-1-892176)* Div. of PremaNations, Inc., P.O. Box 321447, Cocoa Beach, FL 32932-1447 USA (SAN 299-5808) Tel 310-417-9195; Fax: 407-784-5372; Toll Free Fax: 877-372-4660; Toll Free: 877-372-4664
E-mail: Paradigm@PremaNations.com
Web site: http://www.PremaNations.com
Dist(s): **New Leaf Distributing Co., Inc.**
Quality Bks., Inc.

Prematurely Yours, *(978-0-9614786)* Orders Addr.: P.O. Box 9141, Chesapeake, VA 23321 USA (SAN 692-9907) Tel 757-483-9879; Fax: 757-484-8267; Toll Free: 800-767-0023
E-mail: kbryant@prematurelyyours.com
Web site: http://www.prematurelyyours.com.

Premier Schl. Agendas, *(978-1-884272; 978-1-59923; 978-1-63080)* 400 Sequoia Dr., Ste. 200, Bellingham, WA 98226 USA Tel 360-734-1153; Fax: 360-734-3014; Toll Free Fax: 800-880-3287; Toll Free: 800-447-2034
E-mail: ruth.richardson@schoolspecialty.com; nancy.fosberg@schoolspecialty.com; arielle.bons@schoolspecialty.com; whitney.ochs@schoolspecialty.com
Web site: http://www.premier.us.

Premiere *Imprint of* **FastPrncil, Inc.**

Preminger, Tanya, *(978-0-692-13441-2; 978-0-578-46358-2; 978-0-578-48039-8)* 8391 Beverly Blvd No. 419 C/O Tomer Grassiany, Los Angeles, CA 90048 USA Tel 054-630-9273
E-mail: tanyapr@gmail.com
Web site: sean-wants-to-be-messi.com.

Premio Publishing & Gozo Bks., LLC, *(978-0-9776065; 978-0-615-43691-3; 978-0-615-44230-3; 978-0-615-44305-8; 978-0-615-49278-0; 978-0-9853988; 978-0-615-68823-7; 978-0-615-68824-4; 978-0-615-69229-6; 978-0-615-85615-5; 978-0-615-85616-2; 978-0-615-85617-9; 978-0-615-87686-3; 978-0-692-22096-2; 978-0-692-22097-9; 978-0-692-22098-6; 978-0-692-22099-3; 978-0-692-40797-4; 978-0-692-42677-7; 978-0-692-43639-4; 978-0-692-64859-9; 978-1-7320696; 978-1-951599) Div. of Premio Publishing, 648 W. Wasatch St., Midvale, UT 84047 USA Tel 801-953-3793; Imprints:* Gozo Books (Gozo Bks)
E-mail: karl@premiobooks.com; karlbx@gmail.com
Web site: https://Premiobooks.com; https://gozobooks.com; https://twitter.com/PremioBooks; https://premiopublishing.com; https://twitter.com/karlbeckstrand; https://karlbeckstrand.com
Dist(s): **Baker & Taylor Publisher Services (BTPS)**
Brodart Co.
CreateSpace Independent Publishing Platform
Follett School Solutions
Ingram Bk. Co.
Smashwords.

Premium Pr. America, *(978-0-9637733; 978-1-887654; 978-1-933725)* Div. of Schnitzer Communications, Inc., Orders Addr.: P.O. Box 159015, Nashville, TN 37215-9015 USA Tel 615-256-8484; Fax: 615-256-8524; Toll Free: 800-891-7323; Edit Addr.: 2606 Eugenia Ave., Suite C, Nashville, TN 37211-2177 USA
E-mail: bbsgcs@aol.com
Web site: http://www.premiumpress.com
Dist(s): **Send The Light Distribution LLC.**

Prentice Hall *Imprint of* **Prentice Hall PTR**

Prentice Hall *Imprint of* **Savvas Learning Co.**

Prentice Hall Bks., *(978-0-13)* Orders Addr.: 200 Old Tappan Rd., Old Tappan, NJ 07675 USA Toll Free Fax: 800-445-6991; 800-835-5327; Toll Free: 800-223-1360; 800-282-0693 (Single-Copy Phone Orders)
Web site: http://www.prenhall.com
Dist(s): **Langenscheidt Publishing Group.**

Prentice Hall General Reference & Travel *See* **Prentice Hall Bks.**

Prentice Hall Pr. *Imprint of* **Penguin Publishing Group**

Prentice Hall Pr., *(978-0-13; 978-0-7352)* Orders Addr.: 200 Old Tappan Rd., Old Tappan, NJ 07675 USA; Edit Addr.: 240 Frisch Ct., Paramus, NJ 07652 USA Tel 201-909-6200; Fax: 201-909-6360; Toll Free: 800-288-4745; 800-223-2336 (customer service); a/o Prentice Hall Direct, P.O. Box 11075, Des Moines, IA 50336 Tel 515-284-6719; Toll Free: 800-947-7700
E-mail: pearsoned@eds.com
Web site: http://www.phdirect.com
Dist(s): **Penguin Random Hse. Distribution**
Pearson Education
Penguin Random Hse. LLC
Penguin Publishing Group
ebrary, Inc.

†Prentice Hall PTR, *(978-0-13; 978-0-201; 978-0-672)* Div. of Pearson Technology Group, Orders Addr.: 200 Old Tappan Rd., Old Tappan, NJ 07675 USA Fax: 416-447-2819 (orders - Canada); Toll Free Fax: 800-835-5327 (individual single copy orders - US); 800-445-6991 (government orders); Toll Free: 800-282-0693 (individual single copy orders - US); 800-922-0579 (government orders); 800-567-3800 (orders - Canada); Edit Addr.: 405 Murray Hill Pkwy., E Rutherford, NJ 07073-2136 USA; *Imprints:* Prentice Hall (Prentice Hall)
Web site: http://www.phptr.com/
Dist(s): **Cambridge Bk. Co.**
Continental Bk. Co., Inc.
Ebsco Publishing
IFSTA
MyiLibrary
Pearson Education
Pearson Technology Group
Rittenhouse Bk. Distributors
Trans-Atlantic Pubns., Inc.; *CIP.*

Prentice Hall (Schl. Div.), *(978-0-13)* Div. of Pearson Education, Orders Addr.: P.O. Box 2500, Lebanon, IN 46052-3009 USA Toll Free: 800-848-9500; P.O. Box 2649, Columbus, OH 43216-2649; Edit Addr.: 160 Gould St. (Northeast Region), Needham Heights, MA 02194-2310 USA Tel 617-455-1300; 8445 Freeport Pkwy., Suite 400 (South Central Region), Irving, TX 75063 Tel 214-915-4255
Web site: http://www.phschool.com/
Dist(s): **Pearson Education.**

Prentice-Hall *See* **Prentice Hall PTR**

Prepare For Rain Pr., *(978-0-9889537)*
E-mail: Joel@PrepareForRain.com.

Presbeau Publishing, Inc., *(978-0-9831380; 978-1-7357496)* 6533 S. Ouray St., Aurora, CO 80016 USA Tel 303-690-1177
E-mail: carmens222@comcast.net
Web site: www.presbeaupublishing.com.

Presbyterian & Reformed Publishing Company *See* **P & R Publishing**

Presbyterian Publishing Corporation *See* **Curriculum Publishing, Presbyterian Church (U. S. A.)**

Preschool Prep Co., *(978-0-9767008; 978-0-9770215; 978-0-9801717; 978-0-9820331; 978-1-935610)* P.O. Box 1159, Danville, CA 94526 USA Tel 925-743-1400; Fax: 925-886-4843; Toll Free: 866-451-5600
Web site: http://www.preschoolprepco.com
Dist(s): **Follett School Solutions.**

Presence Publishing, *(978-0-9729676)* Orders Addr.: 25909 Plantation Ave., Denham Springs, LA 70726 USA
E-mail: presencepub@bellsouth.net; sharonelliott@bellsouth.net
Dist(s): **Baker & Taylor Publisher Services (BTPS).**

Preserving Memories, *(978-0-9742576; 978-0-9817835)* 5809 Stonebridge Ln., Waxhaw, NC 28173 USA
Web site: http://www.preservememories.net.

Presidential Publishing, *(978-0-9729095)* Orders Addr.: P.O. Box 221834, Sacramento, CA 95822 USA (SAN 255-1977) Tel 916-447-2460
E-mail: contactus@presidentialcookies.com; contactus@presidentialpublishing.com
Web site: http://www.presidentialcookies.com; http://www.presidentialpublishing.com
Dist(s): **Baker & Taylor Publisher Services (BTPS).**

Press Americana, *(978-0-9789041; 978-0-9829558; 978-0-9967779; 978-1-7353601)* 7095 Hollywood Blvd, 1240, Hollywood, CA 90028-8903 USA (SAN 851-9013) Tel 818-370-1143; Fax: 818-760-1828
E-mail: editor@americanpopularculture.com
Web site: http://www.americanpopularculture.com.

Pr. & Brand Productions, *(978-0-615-25883-6)* 2515 34th St., No. 6, New York, NY 11103 USA Tel 718-267-8771
Dist(s): **Lulu Pr., Inc.**

Press Box Bks. *Imprint of* **Wheatmark, Inc.**

Press North America, *(978-0-938271)* P.O. Box 105, Gustavus, AK 99826 USA (SAN 659-8285) Tel 907-697-2303 (phone/fax, press start); Fax: 907-697-2760.

Press of the Camp Pope Bookshop *See* **Camp Pope Publishing**

Press Release Group Corp., *(978-0-9764633)* Orders Addr.: P.O. Box 651, New York, NY 10276 USA
E-mail: info@prgroup.info
Web site: http://www.prgroup.info.

Pr. Room Editions LLC, *(978-1-62143; 978-1-63494)* 1686 Cliff Rd. E., Burnsville, MN 55337-1300 USA Tel 952-746-7867; Fax: 952-746-4287
E-mail: btemple@reditorial.com
Dist(s): **Amicus Publishing**
North Star Editions
RiverStream Publishing.

Presses Pocket (FRA) *(978-2-266) Dist. by* **Distribks Inc.**

Prestel Publishing, *(978-3-7913)* Orders Addr.: c/o VNU, 575 Prospect St., Lakewood, NJ 08701 USA Tel 732-363-5679; Fax: 732-363-0338; Toll Free Fax: 877-227-6564; Toll Free: 888-463-6110; Edit Addr.: 900 Broadway, Suite 603, New York, NY 10003 USA Tel 212-995-2720; Fax: 212-995-2733
E-mail: sales@prestel-usa.com
Web site: http://www.prestel.com; http://www.die-gestalten.de; http://www.scalo.com
Dist(s): **VNU.**

Prestel Verlag GmbH & Co KG. (DEU) *(978-3-7913) Dist. by* **Peng Rand Hse.**

Preston Publishing, *(978-0-9964464; 978-1-7345879; 978-1-7353855)* 4822 S. 133rd St., Omaha, NE 68137 USA Tel 402-884-5995
E-mail: preston@conciergemarketing.com.

Preston-Speed Pubns., *(978-1-887159; 978-1-931587)* 51 Ridge Rd., Mill Hall, PA 17751 USA Tel 570-726-7844; Fax: 570-726-3547
E-mail: doug@prestonspeed.com
Web site: http://www.prestonspeed.com.

Prestwick Hse., Inc., *(978-1-58049; 978-1-60389; 978-1-60843; 978-1-935464; 978-1-935465; 978-1-935466; 978-1-935467; 978-1-935468; 978-0-9823095; 978-0-9823096; 978-0-9823097; 978-0-692-00136-3; 978-0-692-00137-0; 978-1-62019)* Orders Addr.: P.O. Box 658, Clayton, DE 19938 USA Fax: 302-734-0549; Toll Free: 800-932-4593; Edit Addr.: 58 Artisan Dr., Smyrna, DE 19977 USA (SAN 154-5523) Tel 800-983-4593; Fax: 302-659-2792
E-mail: info@prestwickhouse.com; keith@prestwickhouse.com
Web site: http://www.prestwickhouse.com.

Pretty Cool Bks., *(978-1-7328341)* 3725 Courtois St., Saint Louis, MO 63123-7712 USA Tel 314-631-0320
E-mail: paulkell4842@att.net
Web site: prettycoolbooks.com.

Pretty Paper Pr., *(978-0-9746315; 978-0-9858814)* 14 Everett St., East Orange, NJ 07017 USA
E-mail: moody4u@verizon.net
Web site: http://www.moodyholiday.com.

Pretty Please Pr., Inc., *(978-0-9759378)* 105 E. 29th St., 6th Flr., New York, NY 10016 USA.

Prevention Through Puppetry, Inc., *(978-0-9768827)* 468 Boyle Rd., Port Jefferson Station, NY 11776 USA Tel 631-476-3099; Fax: 631-476-7680
Web site: http://www.sunshinepreventionctr.org.

PrevinPublications *See* **TortoiseBrand Bks.**

PRF Pubs., *(978-0-578-03405-8; 978-0-578-04719-5)* 221 Hopewell Amwell Rd., Hopewell, NJ 08525 USA
E-mail: s.schwinn1@verizon.net
Web site: http://www.henrythelamb.com.

PRH Canada Young Readers (CAN) *Dist. by* **Peng Rand Hse.**

PRI Publishing *See* **PRI Publishing/Perigree Publishing**

PRI Publishing/Perigree Publishing, *(978-0-9703269; 978-0-9835636; 978-0-578-19593-3)* Orders Addr.: 1646 Seascape Cir., Tarpon Springs, FL 34689 USA (SAN 253-3693) Tel 419-869-7901; *Imprints:* Perigree (Perigre) Do not confuse with PRI Publishing, Tampa, FL
E-mail: proreach@aol.com
Web site: http://LowcountryRising.com.

Price, Diane Joan, *(978-0-9789637)* 10508 Courtney Cove, Las Vegas, NV 89144 USA
E-mail: dpcontact@netzero.net.

Price, Mathew Ltd., *(978-1-935021; 978-0-9844366)* 12300 Ford Rd. Ste. 455, Dallas, TX 75234-8136 USA (SAN 856-0471)
Web site: http://www.mathewprice.com.

Price Stern Sloan *Imprint of* **Penguin Young Readers Group**

Price Stern Sloan *Imprint of* **Penguin Publishing Group**

Price World Publishing *See* **Gatekeeper Pr.**

Priceless Ink Publishing Co., Inc., *(978-0-9778937)* Orders Addr.: P.O. Box 218538, Nashville, TN 37221 USA
E-mail: apricelessgiftcom@yahoo.com; audreylprice@yahoo.com
Web site: http://apricelessgift.com.

PricePoint+Publications, *(978-0-9661661; 978-0-9741627; 978-0-9772614; 978-0-9826838; 978-0-9838033)* P.O. Box 26, Alto, NM 88312 USA (SAN 257-067X) Tel 575-973-3277
E-mail: laura@pricepointcreative.com; laurareynoldsdesigner@gmail.com
Web site: http://www.ppcbookpublishing.com; http://www.pricepointcreative.com.

Prickly Pair Bks., *(978-0-578-14536-5; 978-0-578-21252-4; 978-0-578-22392-6; 978-0-578-23157-0)* .

Prickly Pear Pr., *(978-0-9764323)* P.O. Box 69, Sahuarita, AZ 85629-0069 USA Tel 520-625-1587; Fax: 520-625-3655 Do not confuse with Pricly Pear Press in San Francisco CA, Cedar Park TX, Scottsdale AZ, Tucson AZ.
E-mail: pricklypearpress@msn.com
Web site: http://pricklypearpress.info.

Prickly Pr., *(978-1-893463)* 11695 Rosehill Rd, Overland Park, KS 66210 USA Tel 913-648-2034 (phone/fax)
E-mail: ikesmith@kc.rr.com
Web site: http://www.readwest.com/flouncesmith.thm.

Priddy Bks. *Imprint of* **St. Martin's Pr.**

Priest, Gerald L., *(978-0-9743871)* 4801 Allen Rd., Allen Park, MI 48101 USA Toll Free: 800-866-0111.

Priest Rapids Pr., *(978-0-615-85681-0; 978-0-615-92080-1; 978-0-9994629)* 16006 Rd. 28 SW, Mattawa, WA 99349 USA Tel 509-840-9846; 2059 Hudson Ave., Richland, WA 99354 Tel 509-840-9846
E-mail: michelle.priestrapidspress@gmail.com
Web site: www.michelleahansen.com
Dist(s): **CreateSpace Independent Publishing Platform.**

Priester, Jennifer, *(978-1-7320765)* 250 Middleton Ct., ORTONVILLE, MI 48462 USA Tel 810-841-0213
E-mail: Jesusjen@hotmail.com
Dist(s): **Ingram Content Group.**

Prima Games *Imprint of* **Random Hse. Information Group**

Prima Games *Imprint of* **DK Games**

Primary Concepts, Inc., *(978-1-893791; 978-1-60184)* 1338 Seventh St., Berkeley, CA 94710 USA
E-mail: info@primaryconcepts.com
Web site: http://www.primaryconcepts.com.

Primary Concepts/Concepts to Go *See* **Primary Concepts, Inc.**

Primary Sources, *(978-1-881849)* 16442 SE 42nd Pl., Issaquah, WA 98027 USA Tel 425-865-0409 (phone/fax)
E-mail: info@primary-sources.com
Web site: http://www.primary-sources.com/
Dist(s): **Smashwords.**

Prime, *(978-0-8095; 978-0-9668968; 978-1-930997; 978-1-894815)* Div. of Wildside Press, P.O. Box 301, Holicong, PA 18928 USA
E-mail: sean@wildsidepress.com
Web site: http://www.primebooks.net
Dist(s): **Diamond Comic Distributors, Inc.**
Diamond Bk. Distributors.

Prime Bks. *Imprint of* **Prime Bks.**

Prime Bks., *(978-1-60701)* 13862 Crosstie Dr., Germantown, MD 20874 USA; *Imprints:* Prime Books (Prime Bks)
Web site: http://www.prime-books.com/
Dist(s): **Diamond Comic Distributors, Inc.**
Diamond Bk. Distributors.

Primedia eLaunch LLC, *(978-1-62209; 978-1-62890; 978-0-615-88236-9; 978-0-615-88337-3; 978-0-615-88403-5; 978-1-63173; 978-1-63315; 978-1-63443; 978-1-942526; 978-1-942573; 978-1-942574; 978-1-942748; 978-1-942749; 978-0-692-36411-6; 978-1-942844; 978-1-942845; 978-1-942846; 978-1-943090; 978-1-943091; 978-1-943092; 978-1-943093; 978-1-943274; 978-1-943275; 978-1-943276; 978-1-943277; 978-1-943278; 978-1-943279; 978-1-943280; 978-1-943281; 978-0-692-42561-9; 978-1-943842; 978-1-943843; 978-1-943844; 978-1-943845) 5518 Flint St., Shawnee, KS 66203 USA (SAN 935-4808) Tel 214-870-5515*
E-mail: josh@primediaelaunch.com
Web site: http://www.primediaelaunch.com
Dist(s): **Amazon Digital Services Inc.**
BookBaby
Chelsea Green Publishing
CreateSpace Independent Publishing Platform
Lulu Pr., Inc.
eBookit.com.

Primordia, *(978-0-9759007)* P.O. Box 2455, Santa Barbara, CA 93120 USA (SAN 256-1018).

Primrose Hse. Publishing, *(978-0-9988440)* P.O. Box 724723, Atlanta, GA 31139 USA Tel 678-409-0320; Fax: 678-409-0320
E-mail: thevestigemovie@gmail.com
Web site: www.PrimroseHousePublishing.com.

Primrose Layne Pr., *(978-0-692-85825-7)* 494 Landsdown Cir., ROHNERT PARK, CA 94928 USA Tel 707-664-8110
E-mail: jeffwcrawford5+LVP0003479@gmail.com; jeffwcrawford5+LVP0003479@gmail.com.

Primrose Pr., *(978-0-9673171)* Orders Addr.: P.O. Box 2577, Prescott, AZ 86302 USA (SAN 299-9331) Tel 520-445-4567; Fax: 520-445-0517; Edit Addr.: 815 Bertrand Ave., Prescott, AZ 86303 USA Do not confuse with companies with the same name in Antelope, CA, Alhambra, CA, San Francisco, CA.

Primrose Presses *See* **Scarlet Primrose Pr.**

Prince Motivation, *(978-0-692-88507-9)* 1033 SW 167th ave, Pembroke Pines, FL 33027 USA Tel 954-868-8102
E-mail: 954prince@gmail.com
Web site: http://www.instagram.com/IamPaulMompremier.

Prince Zone Publishing, *(978-0-9785256; 978-1-7353648)* Div. of prince george/warzone comics, records, art etc., 2230 E. 113th St. Apt No. 236, los angeles, CA 90059 USA Tel 424-732-9673 cell phone; Fax: 323-484-0158 fax; *Imprints:* E-z Clothin' (EzCloth)
E-mail: warzonecomicswzc@hotmail.com
Web site: http://www.warzonecomicswzc.com.

Princess Khrystle & Prince Michael, Inc., *(978-0-9772565)* Orders Addr.: P.O. Box 960176, Miami, FL 33296 USA; Edit Addr.: 14631 SW 104 Ct., Miami, FL 33176 USA
E-mail: khrystle19@aol.com
Web site: http://www.princesskhrystle.org.

Princeton Architectural Pr., *(978-0-910413; 978-0-9636372; 978-1-56898; 978-1-878271; 978-1-885232; 978-1-61689; 978-1-64896)* Div. of The McEvoy Group, 202 Warren St., Hudson, NY 12534 USA (SAN 260-1176) Tel 518-671-6100
E-mail: sales@papress.com
Web site: http://www.papress.com
Dist(s): **Chronicle Bks. LLC**
Hachette Bk. Group
McEvoy Group, The
Metapress
ebrary, Inc.

Princeton Bk. Co. Pubs., *(978-0-87127; 978-0-916622)* Orders Addr.: P.O. Box 831, Hightstown, NJ 08520-0831 USA (SAN 630-1568) Tel 609-426-0602; Fax: 609-426-1344; Toll Free: 800-220-7149; 614 Rte. 130, Hightstown, NJ 08520 (SAN 244-8076); *Imprints:* Dance Horizons (Dance Horizons); Elysian Editions (Elysian Editions)
E-mail: pbc@dancehorizons.com; elysian@aosi.com
Web site: http://www.dancehorizons.com
Dist(s): **Ebsco Publishing**
Follett School Solutions
Independent Pubs. Group
MyiLibrary.

Princeton Health Pr., *(978-0-933665; 978-0-9835782; 978-1-940175)* 711 Westchester Ave., West Harrison, NY 10604-3504 USA (SAN 692-5391) Toll Free: 800-293-4969
E-mail: ksilloway@nhpamail.com
Web site: http://www.lifeskillstraining.com.

Princeton Review *Imprint of* **Random Hse. Children's Bks.**

†Princeton Univ. Pr., *(978-0-691)* Orders Addr.: California-Princeton Fulfillment Services, 1445 Lower Ferry Rd., Ewing, NJ 08618 USA Tel 800-777-4726; Fax: 800-999-1958; Edit Addr.: 41 William St., Princeton, NJ 08540 USA (SAN 202-0254) Tel 609-258-4900; Fax: 609-258-6305; 3 Market Place, Woodstock, OX20 1SY Tel (0) 1993 814501; Fax: (0) 1993 814504
E-mail: webmaster@pupress.princeton.edu
Web site: http://www.press.princeton.edu
Dist(s): **Casemate Academic**
De Gruyter, Inc.
Ebsco Publishing
ISD
MyiLibrary
Ingram Academic
Princeton University Press_mupo
Two Rivers Distribution
Wiley, John & Sons, Inc.
ebrary, Inc.; *CIP.*

Principle Bks. Pubs., *(978-0-9848410; 978-0-9961897; 978-0-9970069; 978-0-9970070; 978-1-7331855)* 14165 Mt. Pleasant Rd., Jacksonville, FL 32225 USA Tel 904-220-2247 (Tel/Fax)
E-mail: Logosman@aol.com
Web site: http://www.HelenJordanDavis.com.

Prindle House *See* **Prindle Hse. Publishing Co.**

Prindle House Publishing Co. *Imprint of* **Prindle Hse. Publishing Co.**

Prindle Hse. Publishing Co., *(978-0-9759527; 978-0-9819372; 978-0-9826846; 978-0-9835320; 978-0-9889080; 978-1-7333874)* Orders Addr.: P.O. Box 18761, Jacksonville, FL 32229 USA Tel 904-710-6529; Fax: 904-751-9338; Toll Free: 866-877-4635; Edit Addr.: 62 W. 27th St., Jacksonville, FL 32206 USA; *Imprints:* Prindle House Publishing Company (PrinHsePubCo)
E-mail: twylaprindle@yahoo.com
Web site: http://www.prindlehouse.com; http://www.twylaprindle.com; www.kashkids.com.

Prinit Pr., *(978-0-932970)* 211 NW Seventh St., Richmond, IN 47374-4051 USA (SAN 212-680X) Tel 765-966-7130; Fax: 765-966-7131; Toll Free: 800-478-4885
Web site: http://www.printpress.com.

Printers Row Publishing Group, *(978-1-57145; 978-1-59223; 978-1-60710; 978-1-62686; 978-1-68412)* 10350 Barnes Canyon Rd. Suite 100, San Diego, CA 92121 USA; *Imprints:* Thunder Bay Press (Thunder Bay); Silver Dolphin Books (Silver Dolph); Portable Press (Portable Pr); Canterbury Classics (Canterbury Class); Studio Fun International (StudioFun Intl)
Web site: http://www.printersrowpublishinggroup.com/to-order/
Dist(s): **Publishers Group West (PGW)**
Readerlink Distribution Services, LLC
Simon & Schuster, Inc.

Printing Systems, *(978-0-9767595; 978-1-59916)* Orders Addr.: 2249 14th St SW, Akron, OH 44314-2007 USA Toll Free: 800-231-0521
E-mail: info@48HrBooks.com
Web site: http://www.48HrBooks.com.

Printmedia Bks., *(978-0-9778591; 978-0-9788447; 978-0-9790999; 978-1-934379)* Div. of The Printmedia Cos. of Southern California, 3355 E. Miraloma Ave., Bldg. 165, Anaheim, CA 92806 USA Tel 714-729-0789; Fax: 714-729-0790
E-mail: peter@printmediabooks.com; books@printmediabooks.com
Web site: http://www.printmediabooks.com.

printONDEMANDpublisher.com, *(978-0-9765725)* 325 W. Belden Ave., Chicago, IL 60614-3817 USA Tel 773-988-8619; Fax: 773-935-9967
E-mail: george@georgevalko.com
Web site: http://www.printondemandpublisher.com.

Prints By Mail, *(978-0-9740173)* 33 Jose I Garica Rd., Belen, NM 87002 USA; 33 Jose I Garcia Rd., Belen, NM 87002
E-mail: books@printsbymail.com
Web site: http://www.printsbymail.com.

Prioleau, Jivonne, *(978-0-615-25200-1; 978-0-578-00427-3; 978-0-578-08744-3)* 5701 Rafferty Ave., McClellan, CA 95652 USA
Dist(s): **Lulu Pr., Inc.**

Prioritybooks Pubns., *(978-0-9753634; 978-0-9792823; 978-0-9816483; 978-0-9819913; 978-0-9834860; 978-0-9896502)* P.O. Box 2535, Florissant, MO 63033 USA (SAN 853-0130) Tel 314-741-6789 (phone/fax); 314-306-2972; Fax: 314-475-5613
E-mail: rosbeav03@yahoo.com
Web site: http://www.prioritybooks.com
Dist(s): **Brodart Co.**
Follet Higher Education Grp
Ingram Content Group
Lushena Bks.

Prism Comics, *(978-0-9759164)* 2621 E. Madison, Seattle, WA 98122-4711 USA Fax: 206-770-6137
Web site: http://www.prismcomics.org.

Prism Hse. Media, *(978-0-9748088)* Orders Addr.: 126 Quail Hollow Dr., San Jose, CA 95128 USA Tel 407-461-4999
E-mail: paulpelley@gmail.com
Dist(s): **Review & Herald Publishing Assn.**

Pristine Pubs., Inc., *(978-0-9716633)* 18 Buckthorn Cove, Jackson, TN 38305 USA (SAN 254-2420) Tel 731-660-3333 Toll Free: 866-565-3311
E-mail: Kathy@pristinepublishers.com
Web site: http://www.readysetgofitness.com; http://www.questforasdin.com; http://www.pristinepublishers.com; http://www.gabrielsmagicornament.com.

†Pritchett & Hull Assocs., Inc., *(978-0-939838; 978-1-933638; 978-1-934234)* 3440 Oakcliff Rd., NE, Suite 110, Atlanta, GA 30340 USA (SAN 216-9258) Tel 770-451-0602; Fax: 770-454-7130; Toll Free: 800-241-4925
E-mail: phsales@p-h.com
Web site: http://www.p-h.com/; *CIP.*

Privacy Trust Group, The, *(978-0-9777457)* Div. of JR The Trust Group Inc., Orders Addr.: 240 S. Elizabeth #h1-116, ELizabeth, CO 80107 USA (SAN 850-122X) Tel 303-648-3496; Fax: 303-648-3205; Toll Free: 877-648-0119; 240 S. Elizabeth #h1-116, Elizabeth, CO 80107 Tel 303-648-3496; Fax: 303-648-3205
Web site: http://www.privacytrustgroup.com.

Privateer Pr., Inc., *(978-0-9706970; 978-1-933362; 978-1-939480; 978-1-943693)* 13434 NE 16th St. Ste. 120, Bellevue, WA 98005-2335 USA Do not confuse with Privateer Pr. in New Orleans, LA
E-mail: mw@privateerpress.com
Web site: http://www.privateerpress.com
Dist(s): **Diamond Bk. Distributors**
PSI (Publisher Services, Inc.).

Privatgaeste Verlag, *(978-0-9712545)* c/o Ute Kruedewagen, 3168 Harrison St., No. 106, Oakland, CA 94611 USA
Web site: http://www.privatgaeste.com.

Privileged Communications, LLC, *(978-0-9802302)* 844 25th St., Santa Monica, CA 90403 USA Fax: 310-828-9590
E-mail: lester310@earthlink.net
Web site: http://www.theboywhowouldntsitstill.com.

PRL Publishing, *(978-0-9743957)* 2245 E. Colorado Blvd., No. 104 PMB 243, Pasadena, CA 91107 USA Tel 626-255-1743
E-mail: info@prldesigns.com
Web site: http://www.prlpub.com.

†Pro Lingua Assocs., Inc., *(978-0-86647)* Orders Addr.: 74 Cotton Mill Hill, Suite A315, Brattleboro, VT 05301 USA (SAN 216-0579) Tel 802-257-7779; Fax: 802-257-5117; Toll Free: 800-366-4775
E-mail: info@prolinguaassociates.com; orders@prolinguaassociates.com
Web site: http://www.prolinguaassociates.com; http://www.lexicarry.com; *CIP.*

Pro-Actif Communications (GBR) *(978-0-9559121; 978-1-908211)* *Dist. by* **IngramPubServ.**

Proactive Publishing, *(978-0-9767324)* 260 Gateway Dr., Suite 21-C, Bel Air, MD 21014 USA Tel 410-893-9016; Fax: 410-893-9380; *Imprints:* Kids Can (Kids Can)
Web site: http://www.proactive-solutions.net.

Process Inc U. S. *See* **Process Transition International, Inc.**

Process Transition International, Inc., *(978-0-9646008)* P.O. Box 1988, Annapolis, MD 21404 USA Tel 301-261-9921; Fax: 410-295-5037
E-mail: spi@processtransition.com
Web site: http://www.processtransition.com.

Proclaim Publishing, *(978-1-885831)* P.O. Box 415, Palmer, TX 75152-0415 USA
E-mail: jo@awake-ministries.org; mreaves872@earthlink.net.

Production 101, Inc., *(978-0-9729706; 978-0-9767765)*
E-mail: julie@smartkids101.com
Web site: http://www.smartkids101.com
Dist(s): **Big Kids Productions, Inc.**

Production Assocs., Inc., *(978-1-887120)* 1206 W. Collins Ave., Orange, CA 92867 USA Tel 714-771-6519; Fax: 714-771-2456; Toll Free: 800-535-8368
E-mail: mikec@production-associates.com
Web site: http://www.production-associates.com; http://signtospeak.com; http://www.wesign.com
Dist(s): **Brodart Co.**
Follett School Solutions
Independent Pubs. Group.

Productivity, Incorporated *See* **Productivity Pr.**

†Productivity Pr., *(978-0-527; 978-0-915299; 978-1-56327)* Orders Addr.: 7625 Empire Dr., Florence, KY 41042-2919 USA (SAN 290-036X) Toll Free Fax: 800-248-4724; Toll Free: 800-634-7064 (orders)
Dist(s): **CRC Pr. LLC**
MyiLibrary
Taylor & Francis Group; *CIP.*

Products & Activities for Christian Education (PACE) LTD, *(978-0-9964043; 978-1-946904)* P.O. Box 1923, Youngstown, OH 44506 USA Tel 919-215-4456
E-mail: linda@abc-jesus.com
Web site: www.abc-jesus.com.

Products With A Purpose, *(978-0-9641134)* 16430 N. 34th Pl., Phoenix, AZ 85032 USA Tel 602-595-1188
E-mail: maryalice@ev1.net.

Profane Existence, *(978-0-9662035)* P.O. Box 8722, Minneapolis, MN 55408-0722 USA
E-mail: blackened@visi.com
Web site: http://www.propaneexistence.com
Dist(s): **AK Pr. Distribution.**

Professional Book Distributors, Incorporated *See* **PBD, Inc.**

Professional Education Systems, Incorporated *See* **PESI**

Professional Publishing Hse. LLC, *(978-1-881524; 978-0-9719749; 978-0-9725941; 978-0-9742811; 978-0-9753504; 978-0-9759654; 978-0-9764690; 978-0-9767678; 978-0-9771082; 978-0-9786032; 978-0-9792016; 978-0-9799308; 978-0-9815783; 978-0-9824292; 978-0-9826704; 978-0-9834444; 978-0-9853259; 978-0-9891960; 978-0-9861557; 978-0-692-79600-9; 978-0-9983089; 978-1-7328982) 1425 W. Manchester Ave., Suite B, Los Angeles, CA 90047 USA (SAN 852-7563) Tel 323-750-3592; Fax: 323-750-2886*
Web site: http://www.professionalpublishinghouse.com.

Professional Publishing Services *See* **WayaMedia**

Professor Beaver *Imprint of* **Speedy Publishing LLC**

Proficient Support, *(978-0-692-42712-5; 978-0-692-52047-5; 978-0-692-64309-9; 978-0-692-78052-7; 978-0-692-86622-1; 978-0-692-17245-2; 978-0-692-19292-4; 978-0-578-41773-8; 978-0-578-47505-9; 978-0-578-58713-4)* 5467 Benttree Way, Antioch, CA 94531 USA Tel 9257279027.

Profile Bks. Ltd. (GBR) *(978-1-86197; 978-0-9536969; 978-0-9535895; 978-0-9541303; 978-1-903942; 978-0-9547913; 978-1-84668; 978-0-9551384; 978-0-9551904; 978-1-84765; 978-0-9556476; 978-1-906994; 978-1-906507; 978-0-9873178; 978-1-78125; 978-1-908990; 978-1-78816)* *Dist. by* **Consort Bk Sales.**

Profile Entertainment, Inc., *(978-0-88013; 978-0-931064; 978-0-934551)* 475 Park Ave., S., 8th Flr., New York, NY 10016 USA (SAN 212-1247) Tel 212-689-2830; Fax: 212-889-7933
E-mail: dee.erwine@starloggroup.com
Dist(s): **Kable Media Services.**

Profit Publishing, *(978-0-9773757)* 39 W. Trace Creek Dr., Spring, TX 77381 USA.

Profitable Publishing *Imprint of* **Thornton Publishing, Inc.**

Profits Publishing, *(978-1-933817)* Orders Addr.: 1300 Boblett St., Unit A-218, Blaine, WA 98230 USA Fax: 604-944-7993; Toll Free: 866-492-6623
E-mail: bwburnham@gmail.com
Web site: http://www.profitspublishing.com
Dist(s): **Ingram Content Group**
Whitewing Pr.

Profound Impact Group, Inc., *(978-0-9760564; 978-0-9887900; 978-1-942151)* Orders Addr.: P.O. Box 506, Alpharetta, GA 30009 USA Tel 303-437-7827
Web site: http://www.profoundgroup.com; http://www.BusterBlank.com; http://www.DomTesta.com; http://www.EricSwan.com
Dist(s): **Bks. West.**

Progeny Pr., *(978-1-58609)* Div of MG Publishers Group LLC, Orders Addr.: P.O. Box 223, Eau Claire, WI 54702-0223 USA Tel 715-838-0171; Fax: 715-836-0176; Toll Free: 877-776-4369; Edit Addr.: 133 S. State St., Box 100, Fall Creek, WI 54742 USA
E-mail: progeny@progenypress.com
Web site: http://www.progenypress.com.

Progreso, Editorial, S. A. (MEX) *(978-970-641; 978-968-436)* *Dist. by* **Lectorum Pubns.**

Progreso Publishing Group , LLC, *(978-1-930584)* 2733 East Battlefield #283, Springfield, MO 65804 USA Tel 417-234-0084
E-mail: sanderson@progresopublishing.com
Web site: www.progresopublishing.com.

Progressive Language, Inc., *(978-0-9758759; 978-0-9899749)* 5804 Lost Dutchman Ave NE, Albuquerque, NM 87111-5901 USA
Web site: http://www.progresssivelangauge.com.

Progressive Rising Phoenix Pr., LLC, *(978-0-615-68352-2; 978-0-615-68666-0; 978-0-615-68667-7; 978-0-615-69091-9; 978-0-615-70515-6; 978-0-615-74990-7; 978-0-9888568; 978-0-615-76159-6; 978-0-615-77265-3; 978-0-615-78287-4; 978-0-615-80027-1; 978-0-615-86717-5; 978-0-615-87169-1; 978-0-615-89836-0; 978-1-940834; 978-1-944277; 978-1-946329; 978-1-950560) 100 Goldmine Ct., Aledo, IL 76008 USA Tel 817-757-7143*
E-mail: contact@progressiverisingphoenix.com
Web site: www.progressiverisingphoenix.com
Dist(s): **Ingram Publisher Services.**

Project Management Excellence Ctr., Inc., The, *(978-0-9726656; 978-0-9787468)* Div. of Sturgeon Publishing, P.O. Box 30291, Phoenix, AZ 85046-0291 USA Tel 623-321-8068
E-mail: info@perfectscoresoftware.com
Web site: http://www.perfectscoresoftware.com.

Project WET Foundation, *(978-1-888631; 978-0-9857384; 978-0-9903620; 978-0-9907148; 978-1-942416; 978-1-950726)* 1001 W. Oak St. Suite 210, Bozeman, MT 59715 USA Tel 406-585-2236; Fax: 406-522-0394
E-mail: kristen.read@projectwet.org; linda.hveem@projectwet.org; sandra.deyonge@projectwet.org; stephanie.kaleva@projectwet.org
Web site: http://www.projectwet.org.

Projects For Asia, *(978-0-98633-2; 978-0-98634-9)* 1009 cuervo Ct., Chesapeake, VA 23322 USA Tel 916-554-8570
E-mail: pfasia98@aol.com
Dist(s): **Ingram Content Group.**

Prologo Pubns., *(978-0-9764264)* 4109 N. O Connor Rd., Irving, TX 75062-3748 USA
E-mail: layne@msu.edu; prologo@comcast.net
Web site: http://www.prologopublications.com.

Prom Girl Publishing. Inc., *(978-0-9726917)* 808 Broadway, Penthouse C, New York, NY 10003 USA
Web site: http://www.promgirl.com.

†Prometheus Bks., Pubs., *(978-0-87975; 978-1-57392; 978-1-59102; 978-1-61592; 978-1-61614; 978-1-63388)* Orders Addr.: 59 John Glenn Dr., Amherst, NY 14228-2197 USA (SAN 202-0289) Tel 716-691-0133; Fax: 716-691-0137; Toll Free: 800-421-0351
Web site: http://www.prometheusbooks.com
Dist(s): **Casemate Academic**
MyiLibrary
National Bk. Network
Random Hse., Inc.
Rowman & Littlefield Publishers, Inc.
Simon & Schuster, Inc.; *CIP.*

Promocion Editorial Inca S.A., PEISA (PER) *(978-9972-40; 978-9972-721)* *Dist. by* **Mariuccia Iaconi Bk Imports.**

Promontory Pr. (CAN) *(978-0-9866722; 978-1-927559; 978-1-987857)* *Dist. by* **IPG Chicago.**

Promotora de prensa internacional S.A (ESP) *(978-84-936408; 978-84-92810; 978-84-935438; 978-84-935881; 978-84-936508; 978-84-15967)* *Dist. by* **Consort Bk Sales.**

ProNailTech.com, *(978-0-9748796)* P.O. Box 260515, Lakewood, CO 80226 USA Tel 720-935-1761
Web site: http://www.pronailtech.com.

Pronghorn Pr., *(978-0-9714725; 978-1-932636; 978-0-9885533; 978-1-941052)* Orders Addr.: P.O. Box 707, Greybull, WY 82426 USA; Edit Addr.: 335 2nd Ave., N., Greybull, WY 82426 USA
Web site: http://www.pronghornpress.org
Dist(s): **INscribe Digital.**

Pronoun, Inc., *(978-0-9842977; 978-1-936321; 978-0-9846202; 978-1-936792; 978-1-61430; 978-1-62539; 978-1-62921; 978-1-63295; 978-1-63461; 978-1-68105; 978-1-5080; 978-1-5183; 978-1-5312; 978-1-5378; 978-1-64186; 978-1-64203)* Orders Addr.: 229 W. 43rd St. Flr. 8, New York, NY 10036 USA
E-mail: distribution@pronoun.com; alex@pronoun.com
Web site: http://www.pronoun.com.

Prop-Abilities Inc., *(978-0-9827461)* 1502 Fairway Grn, Mamaroneck, NY 10543 USA Tel 914-309-4383.

Propeller Pr., *(978-0-9678577)* P.O. Box 729, Fort Collins, CO 80522 USA (SAN 253-1704) Tel 970-482-8807; Fax: 970-493-1240
E-mail: propress@frii.com
Web site: http://www.propellerpress.com.

Prophecy Pubns., *(978-0-941241)* P.O. Box 7000, Oklahoma City, OK 73153 USA (SAN 665-5319) Tel 405-634-1234; Fax: 405-636-1054; Toll Free: 800-245-5577.

Prophecy, The *Imprint of* **Simon & Son Publishing**

ProPress Bks., Inc., *(978-0-9845197; 978-0-9915627; 978-0-9908641; 978-0-9969945; 978-0-9969946)* 645 Franklin Ave., Massapequa, NY 11758 USA
E-mail: gmpro07@optonline.net
Web site: http://www.ProPressBooks.net.

ProQuest Information and Learning *See* **ProQuest LLC**

ProQuest LLC, *(978-0-14; 978-0-608; 978-0-7837; 978-0-8357; 978-0-88692; 978-0-89093; 978-0-912380; 978-1-55655; 978-0-591; 978-0-9702937; 978-0-599; 978-1-931694; 978-1-59399; 978-0-496; 978-0-542; 978-1-4247; 978-0-9778091; 978-1-60205; 978-1-4345; 978-0-549; 978-1-109; 978-1-124; 978-1-267; 978-1-303; 978-1-321; 978-1-339; 978-1-369; 978-0-355; 978-0-438; 978-1-392; 978-0-578-52671-3; 978-0-578-52672-0; 978-0-578-52673-7; 978-1-7331884; 978-1-7331885; 978-0-578-52675-1; 978-1-0732; 978-1-0739; 978-1-0) 5252 N. Edgewood Dr., Suite 125, Provo, UT 84604 USA Tel 801-765-1737; 789 Eisenhower Pkwy., Ann Arbor, MI 48108 Tel 734-761-4700; Toll Free: 800-521-0600; Imprints:* CultureGrams World Edition (CultureGram Wrld)
E-mail: sales@csa.com
Web site: http://www.culturegrams.com; http://www.proquest.com/
Dist(s): **Cengage Gale.**

Prose & Concepts, *(978-1-7323275; 978-1-952820)* 5 Jeremiahs Ln., Worcester, MA 01602 USA Tel 508-756-5744
E-mail: linhnguyenng@gmail.com
Web site: www.proseandconcepts.com.

ProsePress, *(978-0-9833073; 978-0-9851889; 978-0-9886194; 978-0-9893063; 978-1-941069; 978-1-950768)* 75 Red Maple Dr., Pawleys Island, SC 29585 USA Tel 843-237-9929
E-mail: prose-cons@outlook.com
Web site: prosepress.biz.

Prospect Palo Alto Publishing, *(978-0-9891043)* 435 Tasso Street, Suite 200, Palo Alto, CA 94301 USA Tel 650-327-8800
E-mail: dschnell@prospectventures.com.

Prospect Park Bks., LLC, *(978-0-9753939; 978-0-9844102; 978-0-9834594; 978-1-938849; 978-1-945551; 978-1-7353038)* Orders Addr.: 2359 Lincoln Ave., Altadena, CA 91001 USA
E-mail: colleen@prospectparkbooks.com
Web site: http://www.prospectparkbooks.com
Dist(s): **Consortium Bk. Sales & Distribution**
MyiLibrary
Open Road Integrated Media, Inc.
SCB Distributors.

Prospect Park Publishing *See* **Prospect Park Bks., LLC**

Prospecta Pr. *Imprint of* **Easton Studio Pr., LLC**

Prospective Pr., *(978-1-943419; 978-1-63516)* 1959 Peace Haven Rd No. 246, Winston Salem, NC 27106-4850 USA Tel 888-833-0360
E-mail: contact@prospectivepress.com
Web site: prospectivepress.com.

Prosperity & Profits Unlimited, Distribution Services, P.O. Box 416, Denver, CO 80201-0416 USA (SAN 200-4682) Tel 303-575-5676; Fax: 303-575-1187
E-mail: nonstopsuccess@gmail.com
Web site: http://www.breadpudding.net; http://www.contentprovidermedia.com; http://www.gumbomedia.com.

Prospero's Pr., *(978-0-9727315)* P.O. Box 4616, Boulder, CO 80306-4616 USA (SAN 255-0121) Tel 303-817-5622
Web site: http://www.ahouseforamouse.com.

Protar Hse., LLC, *(978-0-9720910)* 829 Ann St., East Lansing, MI 48823 USA Tel 517-974-7993
E-mail: info@protarhouse.com
Dist(s): **Partners Bk. Distributing, Inc.**

Protea Boekhuis (ZAF) *(978-1-86919; 978-1-919825)* *Dist. by* **Casemate Pubs.**

Protecting Our Diversity (POD), *(978-0-9727714)* P.O. Box 231598, Encinitas, CA 92023-1598 USA Tel 760-944-0852
E-mail: email@kidspod.com
Web site: http://www.kidspod.com.

Protective Hands Communications, *(978-0-9787394; 978-0-9818990; 978-0-9845161; 978-0-615-57240-6; 978-0-615-60403-9; 978-0-615-63600-9; 978-0-9857105; 978-0-9892028; 978-0-692-32229-1; 978-0-692-40426-3; 978-0-692-46613-1; 978-0-9975272; 978-1-7337496; 978-1-7349267)* Orders Addr.: 1668 Essex Ln., Riviera Beach, FL 33404 USA Toll Free: 866-457-1203
E-mail: info@protectivehands.com; steve@protectivehands.com
Web site: http://protectivehands.com.

Protectors of The Wood, *(978-0-692-85933-9; 978-0-692-90065-9; 978-0-692-91472-4; 978-0-692-91475-5; 978-0-578-45016-2; 978-0-578-46955-3)* 1678 8th Ave., BROOKLYN, NY 11215 USA Tel 917-531-3724
E-mail: jeffwcrawford5+LVP0003485@gmail.com; jeffwcrawford5+LVP0003485@gmail.com.

ProTeens *Imprint of* **Positive Action For Christ**

ProTips(TM) Media, *(978-0-9740600)* 810 Adair Pl., Del Rey Oaks, CA 93940 USA
E-mail: tom@rivelli.com
Web site: http://www.protipsmedia.com.

Proton Arts, *(978-0-9752647; 978-0-9905028; 978-1-945857)* 5051 Grand Beech Ct., Haymarket, VA 20169-2586 USA
E-mail: info@protonarts.com
Web site: http://www.protonarts.com.

Proud Peacock Publishing, *(978-0-9859437)* 930 Palm Ave. Apt. 136, West Hollywood, CA 90069 USA Tel 925-520-5528
E-mail: marcelino.rosas@ymail.com.

Proud 2-B Me Publishing!, *(978-0-9655726)* 3653-F Flakes Mill Rd., PMB-F188, Decatur, GA 30034 USA Tel 770-808-2301.

Prous, J. R. S.A. (ESP) *(978-84-499; 978-84-300; 978-84-401; 978-84-86973)* *Dist. by* **Continental Bk.**

Proverbial Girl Publishing, *(978-0-578-54481-6)* 1720 Venture Farms Rd., Pilot Point, TX 76258 USA Tel 940-367-2567
E-mail: cscranch@gmail.com.

Providence Hse Pubs., *(978-1-57736; 978-1-881576)* 238 Seaboard Ln., Franklin, TN 37067 USA Tel 615-771-2020; Fax: 615-771-2002; Toll Free: 800-321-5692
E-mail: books@providencehouse.com
Web site: http://www.providencehouse.com.

Providence Publishing, *(978-0-9651661; 978-0-9753004; 978-0-9819222; 978-1-60934)* 9500 Tomahawk Trail, Fort Worth, TX 76244 USA; 1317 Ben Hur, Houston, TX 77055 Tel 713-480-7069 Do not confuse with companies with the same or similar name in Salt Lake City, UT, Martinez, CA
E-mail: info@providencepublishing.com; woodtee@aol.com
Web site: http://www.providencepublishing.com
Dist(s): **Gatewood Pr.**

Providence Publishing Corporation *See* **Providence Hse Pubs.**

Provine Pr., *(978-1-889883)* 832 Cerrito St., Albany, CA 94706 USA Tel 510-528-7055
E-mail: jmbartlett@sbcglobal.net.

PRPublishing, *(978-0-9712258)* 2830 N. Fifth St., Kalamazoo, MI 49009 USA Tel 616-375-5909; Fax: 616-375-7649
E-mail: freelanceediting@ameritech.net.

PRS Inc., *(978-0-9768441)* PRS Ctr. Suite 200, PO Box 852, Latrobe, PA 15650 USA Tel 724-539-7820; Fax: 724-539-1388; Toll Free: 800-338-3688
E-mail: prsinfo@prsrx.com; alexr@prsrx.com
Web site: http://www.prsrx.com.

Prufrock Pr., *(978-1-882664; 978-1-59363; 978-1-61821; 978-1-64632)* Orders Addr.: P.O. Box 8813, Waco, TX 76714-8813 USA Tel 254-756-3337; Fax: 254-756-3339; Toll Free Fax: 800-240-0333; Toll Free: 800-998-2208; Edit Addr.: 6898 Woodway Dr., Woodway, TX 76712-6158 USA (SAN 851-9188); 1935 Brookdale Rd, Ste 139, Naperville, IL 60563
E-mail: info@prufrock.com
Web site: http://www.prufrock.com
Dist(s): **Follett School Solutions**
MyiLibrary
Sourcebooks, Inc.

Pruggus Publishing, *(978-0-9844037; 978-0-9900225; 978-1-7325779)* P.O. Box 1655, Taos, NM 87571 USA.

Prytania Pr., *(978-0-9742602)* Orders Addr.: P.O. Box 1892, Gray, LA 70359 USA Tel 225-346-8811
E-mail: ameliastreet@go.com.

Psalms for Kidz *Imprint of* **Little Sprout Publishing Hse.**

Pseudepigrapha Publishing, *(978-1-931608)* Div. of Chi Xi Stigma Publishing Co., LLC, 2113 Elmwood Ln., Pueblo, CO 81005-2724 USA Tel 719-564-3025 Do not confuse with Penny Dreadful Publishers in Jackson, MI
E-mail: hrothbeorht@hotmail.com.

PSI (Publisher Services, Inc.), 3095 Kingston Ct., Norcross, GA 30071-1231 USA Toll Free: 800-755-9653; 877-578-4774.

PSI Research *See* **L & R Publishing, LLC**

Psychedelic Otter Publishiing, *(978-1-7321763)* 400 E. 10th St., Leadville, CO 80461 USA Tel 719-293-0148
E-mail: psychedelicotterpublishing@gmail.com
Web site: www.energysmagic.com.

PT Publishing, *(978-0-615-21675-1; 978-0-615-27677-9; 978-0-9839147)* P.O. Box 2668, Oak Bluffs, MA 02557 USA
Dist(s): **Lulu Pr., Inc.**

PTO Pr., *(978-0-9760187)* P.O. Box 5394, Snowmass Village, CO 81615 USA.

P2 Educational Services, Inc., *(978-1-885964)* 4915 S. 146th Cir., Omaha, NE 68137-1402 USA Tel 712-727-3772.

Puarose Publishing, *(978-1-933593)* P.O. Box 1597, Gilroy, CA 95021 USA Tel 408-846-0116
E-mail: admin@puarosepublishing.com
Web site: http://www.puarosepublishing.com.

Public Education Foundation, The, *(978-0-9788980; 978-0-9988332)* 3360 W. Sahara Ave., Suite 160, Las Vegas, NV 89102 USA Tel 702-799-1042; Fax: 702-799-5247
E-mail: dkchristensen@interact.ccsd.net
Web site: http://www.thepef.org.

Public Ink, *(978-0-9772371)* 314 Sandpiper Ct., Novato, CA 94949 USA Fax: 415-883-7669
E-mail: sdunwell@earthlink.net.

Public Square Bks., *(978-1-59497)* 307 Seventh Ave., Suite 1601, New York, NY 10001 USA (SAN 255-8149) Tel 212-604-0415; Fax: 212-604-0390; Toll Free: 800-732-3321
Web site: http://www.publicsquarebooks.com
Dist(s): **Diamond Comic Distributors, Inc.**
Diamond Bk. Distributors.

Public8tion Nation, *(978-0-692-95216-0)* 16331 Willow Bend Ave., Oklahoma City, OK 73165 USA Tel 405-922-6300
E-mail: velazquez0312@yahoo.com.

Publicaciones Citem, S.A. de C.V. (MEX) *(978-970-656; 978-968-6792; 978-968-7668) Dist. by* **Lectorum Pubns.**

Publicaciones Educativas, Inc., *(978-0-9767623; 978-0-9767624; 978-0-9779806)* Orders Addr.: P.O. Box 192337, San Juan, PR 00919-2337 USA Tel 787-250-8252; Fax: 787-274-1671; Edit Addr.: 1117 Ave. Munoz Rivera, San Juan, PR 00925 USA Do not confuse with Publicaciones Educativas, Inc. in Hato Rey, PR, Rio Piedras, PR
E-mail: peduc@coqui.net
Web site: http://www.libreriaeducativapr.com.

Publicaciones Fher, S.A. (ESP) *(978-84-243) Dist. by* **AIMS Intl.**

Publicaciones Papelandia, *(978-0-9759194; 978-0-9765805)* 843 Waukee Pass, San Antonio, TX 78260-1919 USA
E-mail: wjconaway@yahoo.com
Web site: http://www.mexicowalkingtours.com.

Publicaciones Puertorriquenas, Inc., *(978-0-929441; 978-1-881713; 978-1-881720; 978-1-932243; 978-1-933485; 978-1-934630; 978-1-935145; 978-1-935606; 978-1-62537)* Orders Addr.: P.O. Box 195064, San Juan, PR 00919-5064 USA; Edit Addr.: 46 Mayaguez St., San Juan, PR 00917-4915 USA (SAN 249-4272) Tel 787-759-9673; Fax: 787-250-6498
Web site: http://www.publicacionespr.com.

Publicaciones Urbanas, *(978-0-615-41660-1)* Garden HIlls PLaza PMB 359, Carr. 19, Guaynabo, PR 00966 USA Tel 787-793-1164 (phone/fax).

Publicaciones y Ediciones Salamandra, S.A. (ESP) *(978-84-9838) Dist. by* **Peng Rand Hse.**

Publicaciones y Ediciones Salamandra, S.A. (ESP) *(978-84-9838) Dist. by* **Spanish.**

PublicAffairs, *(978-1-891620; 978-1-58648; 978-1-61039; 978-1-5417; 978-1-4789-2184-4)* A Member of Perseus Books Group, 1290 Avenue of the Americas, New York, NY 10104 USA Toll Free: 800-759-0190 (and fax)
E-mail: customer.service@hbgusa.com
Web site: http://www.hbgusa.com
Dist(s): **Blackstone Audio, Inc.**
Ebsco Publishing
Follett School Solutions
Hachette Bk. Group
MyiLibrary
ebrary, Inc.

Publication Consultants, *(978-0-9644809; 978-1-888125; 978-1-59433)* 8370 Eleusis Dr., Anchorage, AK 99502 USA Tel 907-349-2424; Fax: 907-349-2426; *Imprints:* Publishing Consultants (Pubng Consultants)
E-mail: evan@publicationconsultants.com
Web site: http://www.publicationconsultants.com
Dist(s): **INscribe Digital**
American News Company
Todd Communications
Wizard Works.

Publications International, Ltd., *(978-0-7853; 978-0-88176; 978-1-56173; 978-1-4127; 978-1-60553; 978-1-4508; 978-1-68022; 978-1-64030; 978-1-64558)* 8140 Lehigh Ave., Morton Grove, IL 60053-2627 USA (SAN 263-9823) Tel 847-676-3470; Fax: 847-676-3671; Toll Free: 800-745-9299; *Imprints:* New Seasons (New Seasons); PIL Kids (PIL Kids); Little Grasshopper Books (MYID_T_LITTLE GRASSHOPPER BKA)
E-mail: customer_service@pubint.com
Web site: http://www.pilbooks.com
Dist(s): **Penguin Publishing Group**
Send The Light Distribution LLC.

Publications Unltd, *(978-0-9767450)* Orders Addr.: P.O. Box 30752, Raleigh, NC 27622 USA Do not confuse with Publications Unlimited in Lake Worth, FL
E-mail: cfmajors@gmail.com
Web site: http://www.publicationsunltd.com.

PublicSpeakKing, *(978-1-7322127)* 5218 Brookside dr, Madison, WI 53718 USA Tel 848-213-7871
E-mail: vnramakrishna@gmail.com
Web site: www.PublicSpeakKing.com.

Publify Consulting, *(978-0-692-56490-5; 978-0-692-88671-7; 978-0-692-92100-5; 978-0-692-06589-1; 978-1-7338857; 978-1-7343346; 978-1-7347356)* 608 Bohannon Blvd, Orlando , FL 32824 USA Tel 407-308-5948
Dist(s): **CreateSpace Independent Publishing Platform.**

Publish For Christ, Incorporated *See* **Nathaniel Max Rock**

Publish To Go Pubns., *(978-0-9669289; 978-0-9728923; 978-0-9745110)* Orders Addr.: 8812 SW Fishermans Wharf Dr., STUART, FL 34997 USA; Edit Addr.: 8812 SW Fishermans Wharf Dr., STUART, FL 34997 USA Tel 561-350-4770 (phone/fax)
E-mail: marknemcek@comcast.net.

Publish Wholesale, *(978-1-943767; 978-1-970024)* 836 S. Western Dr., Bloomington, IN 47403 USA Tel 812-323-1334
E-mail: isbn@accurance.com
Dist(s): **INscribe Digital.**

PublishAmerica, Inc., *(978-1-893162; 978-1-58851; 978-1-59129; 978-1-59286; 978-1-4137; 978-1-4241; 978-1-60441; 978-1-60474; 978-1-60563; 978-1-60610; 978-1-60672; 978-1-60703; 978-1-60813; 978-1-60836; 978-1-60749; 978-1-61546; 978-1-61582; 978-1-4489; 978-1-4512;-1-4560; 978-1-4626; 978-1-62709; 978-1-63000; 978-1-63004; 978-1-62772; 978-1-62907; 978-1-63084) Div. of America Hse. Bk. Pubs., Orders Addr.: P.O. Box 151, Frederick, MD 21705 USA Fax: 301-631-9073; Edit Addr.: 230 E Patrick St, Frederick, MD 21701 USA; 230 E. Patrick St., Frederick, MD 21701*
E-mail: pratherm@publishamerica.com; support@publishamerica.com; tina@publishamerica.com; retta@publishamerica.com; alice@publishamerica.com
Web site: http://www.publishamerica.com
Dist(s): **America Hse. Bk. Pubs.**

Published by Westview, Inc., *(978-0-9819172; 978-0-9819325; 978-1-935271; 978-1-937763; 978-1-62880; 978-0-692-95380-8; 978-0-692-10895-6)* P.O. Box 210183, Nashville, TN 37082 USA Tel 615-646-6134; Fax: 615-662-0946.

Publisher Media Services *See* **Independent Publisher Services**

Publisher Page *Imprint of* **Headline Bks., Inc.**

Publisher Plus, *(978-1-888537)* Div. of Montana Ole Store, Orders Addr.: 200 Choteau St., Sun River, MT 59483 USA Tel 406-264-5953; Fax: 406-264-5672
E-mail: rebeccahel2000@yahoo.com
Web site: http://www.montanaolestore.com.

Publishers Design Group, Inc., *(978-1-929170)* Orders Addr.: P.O. Box 37, Roseville, CA 95678 USA Tel 916-784-0500; Fax: 916-773-7421; Toll Free: 800-587-6666; Edit Addr.: 1655 Booth Rd., Roseville, CA 95747 USA; *Imprints:* PDG (PDG)
E-mail: books@publishersdesign.com; orders@publishersdesign.com; admin@publishersdesign.com; marketing@publishersdesign.com
Web site: http://www.publishersdesign.com; http://www.tearoomguide.com
Dist(s): **Quality Bks., Inc.**
Send The Light Distribution LLC.

Publishers' Graphics, L.L.C., *(978-0-9663402; 978-1-930847; 978-1-933556; 978-1-934703; 978-1-935590)* 140 Della Ct., Carol Stream, IL 60188 USA (SAN 990-0241) Toll Free: 888-404-3769
Web site: http://www.pubgraphics.com.

Publishers Group West (PGW), Div. of Ingram Content Group, Orders Addr.: 1094 Flex Dr., Jackson, TN 38301-5070 USA (SAN 631-7715) Tel 731-423-1973; Toll Free Fax: 800-351-5073; Toll Free: 800-343-4499; Edit Addr.: 387 Park Avenue South, New York, NY 10016 USA (SAN 631-760X) Tel 212-340-8100; Fax: 212-340-8195
E-mail: info@pgw.com
Web site: http://www.pgw.com/home.

Publishers Place, Inc., *(978-0-9676051; 978-0-9744785; 978-0-9771978; 978-0-9840757; 978-0-9864267; 978-0-9994072)* Div. of Grace Associates, 821 4th Ave., Suite 201, Huntington, WV 25701 USA Tel 304-697-3236; Fax: 304-697-3399; *Imprints:* Mid-Atlantic Highlands Publishing (Mid Atlantic WV)
E-mail: publishersplace@gmail.com
Web site: http://www.publishersplace.org.

Publishers' Pr., *(978-0-943592)* Orders Addr.: P.O. Box 86421, Portland, OR 97286 USA (SAN 240-7558) Do not confuse with Publishers Pr., Salt Lake City, UT.

Publishers Quality Library Service, *(978-1-4844; 978-1-5364)* P.O. Box 159, Crete, IL 60417 USA Tel 708-946-4100; Fax: 708-946-4199; Toll Free Fax: 800-896-7213; Toll Free: 800-230-1279.

Publishers@TreeHouse, The, *(978-0-9708816)* 2658 Patapsco Rd., Finksburg, MD 21048 USA Tel 410-848-9306
E-mail: pix4u@qis.net.

Publishing Assocs., Inc., *(978-0-942683)* Subs. of Financial & Commercial Printing Services, 5020 Montcalm Dr., Atlanta, GA 30331 USA (SAN 667-2183) Tel 404-349-4678; Fax: 404-629-5533
E-mail: fcpublish@aol.com.

Publishing by the Seas *See* **Seven Seas Pr.**

Publishing Consortium, LLC, The, *(978-1-62225)* 435 State Rd. U, Urbana, MO 65767 USA Tel 308-249-4643
E-mail: guy@ny0k.com; guy@guyanthonydemarco.com
Web site: http://www.ThePublishingConsortium.com; http://www.VillainousPress.com.

Publishing Consultants *Imprint of* **Publication Consultants**

Publishing Cooperative, The *Imprint of* **Publishing Factory, The**

Publishing Designs, Inc., *(978-0-929540; 978-1-945127)* Orders Addr.: P.O. Box 3241, Huntsville, AL 35810 USA (SAN 249-6372) Tel 256-533-4301; Fax: 256-533-4302; Edit Addr.: 517 Killingsworth Cove Rd., Gurley, AL 35748 USA (SAN 249-6380) Tel 205-859-9372
E-mail: info@publishingdesigns.com
Dist(s): **Send The Light Distribution LLC**
Twentieth Century Christian Bks.

Publishing Factory, The, *(978-0-9722741)* 1836 Blake St., Suite 200, Denver, CO 80202 USA Tel 303-297-1233; Fax: 303-297-3997; *Imprints:* Publishing Cooperative, The (Publishing Coop)
E-mail: editorinchief@penclay.com.

Publishing Hse. Gelany, *(978-0-9712665; 978-0-9728301; 978-0-9747248; 978-0-9777566; 978-0-9817529; 978-0-9827833)* Orders Addr.: P.O. Box 61472, Staten Island, NY 10306 USA Tel 718-668-1375
E-mail: gelany@juno.com
Web site: http://www.zagorizontom20megsfree.com.

Publishing in Motion, *(978-1-61279)* 2502 Canada bld. No. 1, Glendale, CA 91208 USA Tel 818-547-1554
E-mail: publishinginmotion@yahoo.com
Web site: www.publishinginmotion.com.

Publishing Services @ Thomson-Shore, *(978-0-9841658; 978-1-936672; 978-1-943290; 978-1-7337427; 978-0-578-46731-3; 978-0-578-46732-0)* 7300 W. Joy Rd., Dexter, MI 48130 USA (SAN 991-028X) Tel 734-426-6248; *Imprints:* Excite Kids Press (ExciteKids); Ignition Press (IgnitionPr)
E-mail: jerryf@tshore.com
Web site: http://thomsonshore.com/publishing/
Dist(s): **Seattle Bk. Co.**

Publishing Syndicate LLC,
Dist(s): **MyiLibrary.**

PublishingWorks, *(978-0-9744803; 978-1-933002; 978-1-935557)* 151 Epping Rd., Exeter, NH 03833-4522 USA Toll Free: 800-333-9883; 151 Epping Rd., Exeter, NH 03833-4522 (SAN 850-4806) Toll Free: 800-333-9883; *Imprints:* Townsend, J. N. Publishing (JNTown); Peapod Press (PeapodPr) Do not confuse with The Publishing Works in Waldport, OR
E-mail: bookpub@worldpath.net; jeremy@publishingworks.com
Web site: http://www.publishingworks.com
Dist(s): **MyiLibrary.**

PublishNext *See* **Publishing Services @ Thomson-Shore**

Pucker Art Pubns. *Imprint of* **Pucker Gallery**

Pucker Gallery, *(978-0-9635318; 978-1-879985)* 240 Newbury St. 3rd Flr., Boston, MA 02116-2897 USA Tel 617-267-9473; Fax: 617-424-9759; *Imprints:* Pucker Art Publications (Pucker Art)
E-mail: contactus@puckergallery.com; jeanne@puckergallery.com
Web site: http://www.puckergallery.com
Dist(s): **Longleaf Services**
Syracuse Univ. Pr.
Univ. Pr. of New England
Univ. of Washington Pr.

Pucker Safrai Gallery *See* **Pucker Gallery**

Puckett Publishing, Inc., *(978-0-9764938)* P.O. Box 528, Columbia, IL 62236 USA.

Puddinhead LLC, *(978-0-615-24552-2)* 6470 Fogle Ct., Westerville, OH 43082 USA Tel 614-899-6112.

Puddle Jump Pr., Ltd., *(978-0-9726487)* 763 Rte. 9W, Nyack, NY 10960 USA Tel 914-645-6551 (phone/fax)
E-mail: puddlejumppress@gmail.com
Web site: http://www.puddlejumppress.com
Dist(s): **Follett School Solutions.**

Puddledancer Pr., *(978-0-9647349; 978-1-892005; 978-1-934336)* Orders Addr.: 2240 Encinitas Blvd, Encinitas, CA 92024 USA Toll Free: 877-367-2849; Edit Addr.: 3245 Rim Rock Cir., Encinitas, CA 92024 USA
E-mail: email@puddledancer.com; neill@puddledancer.com; meiji@puddledancer.com
Web site: http://www.puddledancer.com; http://www.nonviolentcommunication.com
Dist(s): **Ebsco Publishing**
Independent Pubs. Group
MyiLibrary
ebrary, Inc.

Puddletown Publishing Group, Inc., *(978-1-61413)* 4125 SE 63rd, Portland, OR 97206 USA Tel 503-320-1242
E-mail: lachance@puddletowngroup.com
Web site: puddletowngroup.com
Dist(s): **BookBaby.**

Pueblo Magico Pr., *(978-1-7323960)* 5849 Castana Ave, Lakewood, CA 90712 USA Tel 562-673-2683
E-mail: kgpenaflorLMFT@gmail.com.

Pueblo Mgico Press *See* **Pueblo Magico Pr.**

Puentes, *(978-0-9993479; 978-1-7322780; 978-1-7333464)* 4 Ingleside Ave., Norwalk, CT 06850 USA Tel 203-671-3165
E-mail: jadegen9@gmail.com.

Puffin *Imprint of* **Penguin Publishing Group**

Puffin Books *Imprint of* **Penguin Young Readers Group**

Puget Sound Bks., *(978-0-9715019)* Div. of Angel Fire Pr., Orders Addr.: 14403 N. Silverado Dr., Fountain Hls, AZ 85268-3048 USA Tel 480-304-2948
E-mail: almoeblog@yahoo.com.

Pugh, Val, *(978-0-692-54429-7; 978-0-692-68624-9; 978-0-9982706)* 3536 Del Rio St., Shreveport, LA 71109 USA Tel 318-550-1272
E-mail: valerie@valpughlove.com
Web site: www.valpughlove.com.

Pulp Collector Press *See* **Adventure Hse.**

Pulte, Therese Marie, *(978-0-9746557)* 1278 Glenneyre St., Suite 39, Laguna Beach, CA 92651 USA; *Imprints:* Destination Publishers (Destin Pubs)
Web site: http://www.destinationpublishers.com.

Pumpkin Hill Productions, *(978-0-9793602)* P.O. Box 165, Hawleyville, CT 06440 USA
E-mail: nmroddas@aol.com.

Pumpkin Patch Publishing, *(978-0-9754823)* 10911 E. Skinner Dr., Scottsdale, AZ 85262 USA.

Pumpkin Ridge Publishing, *(978-0-9754459)* P.O. Box 1668, North Plains, OR 97113-6157 USA (SAN 256-1379) Tel 503-647-5970
E-mail: prpublish@msn.com
Web site: http://www.factoryride.com.

Pumpkin Seed Pr., *(978-0-9700273)* 68335 355th Ave., Humphrey, NE 68642 USA Tel 402-923-1682; Fax: 402-923-9110; Toll Free Fax: 877-923-1682
E-mail: rjnoona@megavision.com; rjnoona@magavision.com
Web site: http://www.usedhomeschoolbooks.com/bgh.htm.

Pumpkin Seeds Pr., *(978-0-615-17159-3)* 24 Uranus Rd., Sewell, NJ 08080 USA
Dist(s): **Lulu Pr., Inc.**

Pumpkins Pansies Bunnies & Bears, *(978-0-9747367)* Orders Addr.: 19 Treevine Ct., The Woodlands, TX 77381 USA Tel 281-785-0755
E-mail: paklppbb@aol.com; tricialowenfield@gmail.com
Web site: http://www.tricialowenfielddesign.com.

Punch Press Publications *See* **New Growth Pr.**

Punching Pandas, *(978-0-9998235; 978-0-578-53038-3; 978-0-578-53039-0; 978-0-578-53576-0)* 11008 NE 68th St, Kirkland, WA 98033 USA Tel 503-475-9824
E-mail: nolen@nolenlee.com.

Punkin Pr., *(978-1-60149)* 1221 S. Sherbourne Dr., Apt. No. 5, Los Angeles, CA 90035 USA
E-mail: punkinpress@hotmail.com
Web site: http://www.punkinpress.net.

Punta Gorda Pr., *(978-1-929528)* 2760 W. Marion Ave., Punta Gorda, FL 33950 USA
E-mail: joeinnovations@gmail.com
Web site: http://www.puntagordapress.com.

Punto de Lectura *Imprint of* **Santillana USA Publishing Co., Inc.**

Puppet Rescue, *(978-0-9799958)* 711 9th St., No. 2, Santa Monica, CA 90402 USA (SAN 854-9516) Tel 310-656-7738
E-mail: darinvents@adelphia.net
Web site: http://www.puppetrescue.com.

Puppet Theater Bks. *Imprint of* **Innovative Eggz LLC**

Puppetry in Practice, *(978-0-9720183)* 1923 Haring St., Brooklyn, NY 11229-3713 USA
E-mail: tovaa@aol.com
Web site: http://www.puppetryinpractice.com.

Puppy Tale, LLC, *(978-0-9903030)* 555 S. Main St., Providence, RI 02903 USA Tel 508-789-2641
E-mail: lkelley9@msn.com
Web site: livefreelovetuggie.com.

Pups & Purrs Pr., *(978-0-9966612)* 4288 S. Alton St., Greenwood Village, CO 80111 USA Tel 303-547-8138
E-mail: sunny@sunnyweber.com
Web site: www.SunnyWeber.com.

Puptattle Pr., Inc., *(978-0-9786947)* 21813 S. Embassy Ave., Carson, CA 90810 USA
Web site: http://www.puptattle.com.

†Purdue Univ. Pr., *(978-0-911198; 978-1-55753; 978-1-61249; 978-1-62260; 978-1-62261; 978-1-62671)* Orders Addr.: P.O. Box 388, Ashland, OH 44805 USA Toll Free: 800-247-6553; Edit Addr.: 504 W. State St. Stewart Ctr. 190, West Lafayette, IN 47907-2058 USA (SAN 203-4026) Tel 765-494-2038; Fax: 765-496-2442 Do not confuse with Purdue Univ. Pubns., same address
E-mail: pupress@purdue.edu
Web site: http://www.thepress.purdue.edu/
Dist(s): **Baker & Taylor Publisher Services (BTPS)**
Ebsco Publishing
Follett School Solutions
Longleaf Services
MyiLibrary
Trajectory, Inc.; *CIP.*

Pure Faith Ministry, 3211 W. Lexington Apt. 1C, Chicago, IL 60624 USA Tel 312-414-5868
E-mail: williamsdarlene70@gmail.com
Dist(s): **Ingram Content Group.**

Pure Joy Pubns., *(978-0-9749578)* P.O. Box 482, Wheat Ridge, CO 80034-0482 USA
E-mail: purejoypublicatrions@comcast.net.

Pureheart UnLtd. media, *(978-1-7327547)* 875 Boynton ave, Bronx, NY 10473 USA Tel 646-260-9987
E-mail: Jphunny3@gmail.com.

PureLight Pubns., *(978-0-9787597; 978-0-615-23432-8; 978-0-9825988)* Orders Addr.: P.O. Box 720193, Dallas, TX 75372 USA Tel 214-770-0206 weekdays 9am to 5 pm
E-mail: pl.publications@yahoo.com; seaonducote@aol.com
Web site: http://www.seaonducoteproductions.com; http://www.purelightpublications.org
Dist(s): **Lulu Pr., Inc.**

Pureplay Pr., *(978-0-9714366; 978-0-9765096; 978-1-7352908)* 11353 Missouri Ave., Los Angeles, CA 90025-5553 USA (SAN 852-5404) Tel 310-479-8773; Fax: 310-473-9384
E-mail: editor@pureplaypress.com
Web site: http://www.pureplaypress.com
Dist(s): **Baker & Taylor Publisher Services (BTPS).**

pureplaypress.com *See* **Pureplay Pr.**

Purfect Promises, *(978-0-9759343)* 149 Summerhill Dr., Rockwall, TX 75032 USA Tel 972-771-9528; Fax: 972-772-5403
E-mail: purfectpromises@aol.com.

Purgatory Publishing, Inc., *(978-1-932867)* 904 Colonial Ct., Coatesville, PA 19320 USA; *Imprints:* West End Games (W End Games)
Web site: http://www.westendgames.com
Dist(s): **Century Pr.**
Diamond Distributors, Inc.

Purity Pr. Pubs., *(978-0-9728797)* P.O. Box 2896, Decatur, GA 30031 USA.

Purple Bear Bks., Inc., *(978-1-933327)* 300 Park Ave., Suite 1700, New York, NY 10022 USA.

Purple Butterfly Pr. *Imprint of* **Kat Biggie Pr.**

Purple Cow Pr., *(978-0-9820983)* 14688 Denmark Ct., Apple Valley, MN 55124 USA Tel 952-322-1419
E-mail: wdwaibel@aol.com
Web site: http://www.rudyslittleworld.com.

Purple Crayon Studios, *(978-0-9706491)* 0-115 Luce, SW, Grand Rapids, MI 49055 USA Tel 616-822-3186; Toll Free Fax: 877-710-2368
E-mail: beryl@pca3d.com
Web site: http://www.mushtons.com.

Purple Finch Pr., *(978-0-9633740)* P.O. Box 758, Dewitt, NY 13214 USA Tel 315-445-8087 (phone/fax)
E-mail: Nbenson@twcny.rr.com.

Purple Haze Pr., *(978-0-9773200; 978-1-935183)* Orders Addr.: 2195 Malibu lake Cir., No. 1134, Naples, FL 34119 USA; Edit Addr.: 2430 Vanderbilt Beach Rd., No. 108, PMB 167, Naples, FL 34109 USA
E-mail: v@purpleV.com; p_tomasello@yahoo.com
Web site: http://www.purplehazepress.com
Dist(s): **Baker & Taylor Publisher Services (BTPS)**
ebrary, Inc.

Purple Hse. Pr., *(978-1-930900; 978-1-948959)* Orders Addr.: P.O. Box 787, Cynthiana, KY 41031 USA; Edit Addr.: 8100 US Hwy. 62 E., Cynthiana, KY 41031-6796 USA
E-mail: ray@purplehousepress.com
Web site: http://www.purplehousepress.com.

For full information on wholesalers and distributors, refer to the Wholesaler and Distributor Name Index

Purple Ink, Inc., *(978-0-9801002; 978-1-939119)* Orders Addr.: P.O. Box 41232, Houston, TX 77241 USA (SAN 855-1987) Tel 713-705-5530; Fax: 713-474-5529
E-mail: onediagage@purpleink.net
Web site: http://www.purpleink.net.

Purple Ink Publishing *See* **Purple Owl Publishing**

Purple Lady Productions, *(978-0-9714506)* P.O. Box 1277, Tiburon, CA 94920-4277 USA Tel 415-435-0720
E-mail: purpleladybythebay@earthlink.net.

Purple Lizard Pr. LLC, *(978-0-9762902)* Orders Addr.: P.O. Box 68883, Tucson, AZ 85737-7076 USA Tel 520-575-6660
E-mail: Julie@PurpleLizardPress.com
Web site: http://www.purplelizardpress.com.

Purple Mountain Pr., Ltd., *(978-0-916346; 978-0-935796; 978-1-930098; 978-0-578-22378-0)* Orders Addr.: P.O. Box 309, Fleischmanns, NY 12430-0309 USA (SAN 222-3716) Tel 845-254-4062; Fax: 845-254-4476; Toll Free: 800-325-2665; Edit Addr.: 1060 Main St., Fleischmanns, NY 12430 USA; 1064 Main St., Fleischmanns, NY 12430 Tel 845-254-4062; Toll Free Fax: 800-325-2665 Do not confuse with Purple Mountain Pr., Carson City, NV
E-mail: purple@catskill.net
Web site: http://www.catskill.net/purple.

Purple Owl Publishing, *(978-1-7326371; 978-1-952800)* 7 Kingman Rd, Newton, MA 02461 USA Tel 617-630-1141
E-mail: dharkins1@verizon.net.

Purple Peaks Pr., *(978-0-9971266)* Orders Addr.: 145 Univ. Dr. No. 3048, Amherst, MA 01004 USA Tel 908-763-6397; Edit Addr.: 145 Univ. Dr. No. 3048, Amherst , MA 01004 USA Tel 908-763-6397
E-mail: mepsteinagain@comcast.net.

Purple Penguin Publishing, *(978-0-9765473)* 3929 Hummingbird Ln., Roanoke, VA 24018 USA Tel 540-400-7220; Toll Free: 800-788-3196
E-mail: tanyapenguin@aol.com
Web site:
http://www.underragingskies.tanyaadams.com.

Purple People, Inc., *(978-0-9707793)* P.O. Box 3194, Sedona, AZ 86340-3194 USA Tel 928-204-6400
E-mail: info@purplepeople.com
Web site: http://www.purplepeople.com.

Purple Pig Publishing, *(978-0-9700380; 978-1-8380523)* Orders Addr.: P.O. Box 1083, Bethel, CT 06801 USA Tel 203-797-1857; Edit Addr.: 7 Wixon Rd., Danbury, CT 06811 USA
E-mail: jshaboo@att.net.

Purple Plume Pr., *(978-0-9744923)* 5980 Peach Ave., Manteca, CA 95337 USA Tel 209-825-7602
E-mail: purpleplumepress@cs.com; purpleplumeprss@cs.com.

Purple Sage Publishing, *(978-0-9674639; 978-0-9836690)* P.O. Box 1431, Goldthwaite, TX 76844 USA Tel 830-563-5223
E-mail: karencrumley@hotmail.com
Dist(s): **BookBaby.**

Purple Sword Pubns., LLC, *(978-1-936165; 978-1-61292)* 6901 E. Calle Bellatrix, Tucson, AZ 85710 USA; *Imprints:* Green Monkey Books (Green Monkey)
E-mail: purpleswordpublications@yahoo.com
Web site: http://www.purplesword.com
Dist(s): **Smashwords.**

Purple Toad Publishing, Inc., *(978-1-62469)* 204 S. Union St., Kennett Square, PA 19348 USA Tel 610-444-8259
E-mail: cynthia@purpletoadpublishing.com.

Purple Unicorn Pr., *(978-0-692-36341-6; 978-0-692-64540-6)* 1635 35th Ave., Seattle, WA 98122 USA Tel 206-909-8562
E-mail: kat@hopmann.org.

Purposeful Pen Publishing, *(978-0-692-04181-9; 978-1-7335789)* 1114 GA Hwy. 96 Suite C-1, No. 353 0, Kathleen, GA 31047 USA Tel 478 213-7892
E-mail: P3@awsindustries-inc.com
Dist(s): **CreateSpace Independent Publishing Platform.**

Purposely Created Publishing Group, *(978-0-615-91309-4; 978-0-615-99099-6; 978-0-692-20774-1; 978-0-692-23081-7; 978-0-692-29474-1; 978-0-692-29487-1; 978-0-692-29749-0; 978-0-692-32010-5; 978-0-692-34783-6; 978-0-692-35442-1; 978-1-942838; 978-1-945558; 978-1-947054; 978-0-692-92776-2; 978-0-692-92779-3; 978-0-692-92780-9; 978-1-948400; 978-1-949134; 978-0-692-19826-1; 978-1-64484) P.O. Box PO BOX 66546, Baltimore, MD 21239 USA Toll Free: 866-674-3340*
E-mail: tie@publishyourgift.com
Web site: www.publishyourgift.com
Dist(s): **CreateSpace Independent Publishing Platform.**

Purpus Publishing, *(978-0-615-65777-6; 978-0-615-75871-8; 978-0-615-76330-9; 978-0-615-93055-8; 978-0-692-22125-9; 978-0-692-26721-9; 978-0-692-35472-8; 978-0-692-78583-6; 978-0-692-94556-8; 978-1-7326402)* 19824 87th Ave. SW, Vashon, WA 98070 USA Tel 206-463-2754
Dist(s): **CreateSpace Independent Publishing Platform.**

PUSH *Imprint of* **Scholastic, Inc.**

Pushkin Children's Bks. *Imprint of* **Steerforth Pr.**

Pushkin Collection *Imprint of* **Steerforth Pr.**

Pushkin Press *Imprint of* **Steerforth Pr.**

Putnam Juvenile *Imprint of* **Penguin Publishing Group**

Putnam Productions, *(978-0-9762728)* P.O. Box 525, Buckner, MO 64016 USA Tel 816-305-6916
E-mail: toby@sagebrushexchange.com
Web site: http://www.prairielabyrinth.com; http://www.chakralabyrinth.com.

Putschakap?n Pr., *(978-0-9978943)* 1720 Spruce St., Philadelphia, PA 19103 USA Tel 267-318-7297
E-mail: edmundweisberg@yahoo.com.

Putumayo World Music & Crafts, *(978-1-885265; 978-1-58759)* Div. of Putumayo, Inc., 324 Lafayette St., 7th Flr., New York, NY 10012 USA Tel 212-625-1400; Fax: 212-460-0095; Toll Free: 800-995-9588
E-mail: info@putumayo.com
Web site: http://www.putumayo.com
Dist(s): **Follett School Solutions**
Recorded Bks., Inc.
Rhino Entertainment Co, A Warner Music Group Co.
Rounder Kids Music Distribution.

Puumakaa Pr., *(978-0-9762387)* Orders Addr.: P.O. Box 500, Na'Alehu, HI 96772 USA; Edit Addr.: 94-6448 Mamalahoa Hwy., Na'Alehu, HI 96772 USA
E-mail: elizabeth@fastnethi.com
Web site: http://www.inka-online.com.

Puwaii International, LLC, *(978-0-9787949)* 7326 N. 61 St., Paradise Valley, AZ 85253 USA
E-mail: jerrelvanier@yahoo.com
Web site: http://www.puwaiiadventures.com.

Puzzlewright *Imprint of* **Sterling Publishing Co., Inc.**

PW.Co., *(978-0-9745102)* 774 Henry St., Apt. 1E, Brooklyn, NY 11231-3153 USA
E-mail: tregeryefim@aol.com.

PXL Media, LLC, *(978-0-9749322)* P.O. Box 99, LeClaire, IA 52753-0099 USA
E-mail: pxlmedia@aol.com.

Pyle, Robert Associates *See* **Avocus Publishing, Inc.**

Pyr Bks. *Imprint of* **Start Publishing LLC**

Pyramid Dancer Pubns., *(978-0-9659913)* P.O. Box 5263, Colorado Spgs, CO 80931-5263 USA
E-mail: rjb@phoenixbonsai.com
Web site: http://www.phoenixbonsai.com.

Pyramid Educational Products, Inc., *(978-1-928598)* Div of Pyramid Educational Consultants, Incorporated, 13 Garfield Way, Newark, DE 19713-3450 USA
E-mail: dbittner@pyramidproducts.com
Web site: http://www.pyramidproducts.com.

Pyramid Pubs., *(978-0-9851514; 978-0-9982014; 978-1-7351068)* 1314 Grandview Cir., Buffalo, MN 55313 USA Tel 763-390-4853
E-mail: patrickday@pyramidpublishers.com.

Pyramid Publishing, Inc., *(978-1-885920; 978-1-934008)* Orders Addr.: P.O. Box 129, Zenda, WI 53195-0129 USA Tel 414-275-3384; Fax: 414-275-3584; P.O. Box 129, Zenda, WI 53195 Do not confuse with companies with the same name in Utica, NY, Montgomery, AL
E-mail: pyramid2mail@gmail.com.

Pyrola Publishing, *(978-0-9618348)* P.O. Box 80961, Fairbanks, AK 99708 USA (SAN 667-3503) Tel 907-455-6469 (phone/fax)
E-mail: mshields@mosquitonet.com
Web site: http://www.maryshields.com.

Pysher, Brock, *(978-0-692-98452-9; 978-0-692-98453-6)* 138 Harvester Ave., Batavia, NY 14020 USA Tel 585-201-8778
E-mail: TheBrassBadger@gmail.com
Dist(s): **Ingram Content Group.**

Pyxie Moss Press *See* **Fun Fitness Publishing**

Q & A Books *See* **Paradoxical Pr., The**

Q & J Bird Pr., LLC, *(978-0-615-16566-0)* 141 Morey Pl., Greensburg, PA 15601 USA
E-mail: icanbe@qandjbirdpress.com
Web site: http://www.qandjbirdpress.com.

QEB Publishing Inc., *(978-1-59566; 978-1-60992; 978-1-68297)* Div. of QED Publishing, 6 Orchard, Ste. 100, Lake Forest, CA 92630 USA Tel 949-380-7510
Web site: http://www.qed-publishing.co.uk; http://www.quarto.com
Dist(s): **Hachette Bk. Group**
Lerner Publishing Group
Quarto Publishing Group USA
Scholastic Bk. Fairs.

QED Publishing *See* **QEB Publishing Inc.**

Quackenbush, Robert Studios, *(978-0-9612518; 978-0-9712757)* Orders Addr.: 460 E. 79th St., Suite 14E, New York, NY 10021 USA (SAN 656-0458) Tel 212-744-3822; Fax: 212-861-2761
E-mail: rqstudios@aol.com
Web site: http://www.rquackenbush.com.

Quackenworth Publishing, *(978-1-933211)* P.O. Box 4747, Culver City, CA 90230-4747 USA Tel 310-945-5634; Fax: 310-945-5709
E-mail: info@quackenworth.com
Web site: http://www.quackenworth.com.

Quad Cities' Learning, Incorporated *See* **Quad City Pr.**

Quad City Pr., *(978-0-9824448; 978-0-9863898; 978-0-692-52738-2)* 2127 3rd St., Suite B, East Moline, IL 61244-2409 USA (SAN 858-1819)
Web site: http://www.weeklywilson.com
Dist(s): **CreateSpace Independent Publishing Platform.**

QuadMama Pr., *(978-1-944701)* 538 Sinton Ave, Colorado Springs, CO 80906 USA Tel 719-391-8980
E-mail: MyBusinessTweets@outlook.com.

Quadradrillion, LLC - Publishing Division *See* **Transaltar Publishing**

Quagan, Brittany, *(978-0-578-20155-9)* P.O. Box 582, East Granby, CT 06026 USA.

Quail High Bks., *(978-0-9825443)* 7120 Patriots Colony Dr., Williamsburg, VA 23188 USA.

Quail Ridge Pr., Inc., *(978-0-937552; 978-1-893062; 978-1-934193; 978-1-938879)* Orders Addr.: P.O. Box 123, Brandon, MS 39043 USA (SAN 257-8794) Tel 601-825-2063; Fax: 601-825-3091; Toll Free Fax: 800-864-1082; Toll Free: 800-343-1583
E-mail: lward@quailridge.com
Web site: http://www.quailridge.com
Dist(s): **Booklines Hawaii, Ltd.**
Gibson, Dot Pubns.
Forest Sales & Distributing Co.
Islander Group
Southwest Cookbook Distributors.

Quake *Imprint of* **Echelon Press Publishing**

Quaker Press of Friends General Conference *See* **QuakerPress**

QuakerPress, *(978-0-9620912; 978-1-888305; 978-1-937768)* Div. of Friends General Conference, 1216 Arch St., 2B, Philadelphia, PA 19107 USA (SAN 225-4484) Tel 215-561-1700; Fax: 215-561-0759; Toll Free: 800-966-4556
E-mail: publications@fgcquaker.org; bookstore@fgcquaker.org
Web site:
http://www.fgcquaker.org/services/fgc-publications.

Quale Pr. LLC, *(978-0-9656161; 978-0-9700663; 978-0-9744503; 978-0-9792999; 978-1-935835; 978-1-939606)* 2 Hillcrest Rd., Niantic, CT 06357 USA Tel 860-739-9153 (phone/fax); P.O. Box 642, Niantic, CT 06357 Tel 860-739-9153
E-mail: central@quale.com
Web site: http://www.quale.com
Dist(s): **ConsuLogic Consulting Services**
SPD-Small Pr. Distribution.

Quality Nature Displays by Eddie Dunbar *See* **Insect Sciences Museum of California**

Quality of Life Publishing Co., *(978-0-9675532; 978-0-9816219; 978-0-9972612)* 6210 Shirley St., Suite 112, Naples, FL 34109-6258 USA Toll Free: 877-513-0099
Web site: http://www.qolpublishing.com
Dist(s): **Baker & Taylor Publisher Services (BTPS).**

Quality Pr., *(978-0-87389; 978-1-951058; 978-1-953079)* Div. of American Society for Quality, 600 N. Plankinton Ave., P.O. Box 3005, Milwaukee, WI 53203 USA (SAN 683-5244) Tel 414-272-8575; Fax: 414-270-8810; Toll Free: 800-248-1946
E-mail: swoodhouse@asq.org
Web site: https://asq.org/quality-press
Dist(s): **American Technical Pubs., Inc.**
Follett School Solutions.

Quality Pubs., *(978-0-9671107)* Orders Addr.: P.O. Box 691546, San Antonio, TX 78269 USA Tel 210-699-9007; Fax: 210-641-6334; Edit Addr.: 11238 Jade Green, San Antonio, TX 78249 USA Toll Free: 888-633-9898
E-mail: aroman@qualitypublishers.com
Web site: http://www.medpress.com.

Quality Publishing Inc., *(978-0-9745741; 978-0-9759309)* 1005 E. Highland Ave., Rome, GA 30161 USA Fax: 706-290-1223; Toll Free: 800-262-4404
E-mail: bbmonday@comcast.net.

Quality Time Publishing *See* **Don't Stop Publishing**

Quantalore *Imprint of* **Spatterlight Pr.**

Quantum Manifestations Publishing, *(978-0-9718099; 978-1-933505)* 1360 University Ave., W. Suite #104-192, Saint Paul, MN 55104 USA Tel 678-227-3162
E-mail: pm@quantumdatingclub.com
Web site:
http://www.quantummanfestationspublishing.com.

Quantum One Publishing, *(978-0-9755681)* 1728 Spruce Ln., Linton, IN 47441 USA Tel 812-847-8708; Fax: 812-847-8712
E-mail: jdsapara@iglide.net.

Quarrier Pr., *(978-0-938985; 978-0-9646197; 978-1-891852; 978-1-942294)* 1125 Central Ave., Charleston, WV 25302 USA Tel 304-342-1848; Fax: 304-343-0594; Toll Free: 888-982-7472; *Imprints:* Mountain Memories Books (Mtn Memories Bks)
E-mail: clemmtstate@gmail.com
Web site: http://www.wvbookco.com
Dist(s): **West Virginia Book Co., The.**

Quarry Bks. *Imprint of* **Quarto Publishing Group USA**

Quarry Bks. *Imprint of* **Indiana Univ. Pr.**

Quarry Books *Imprint of* **Quarto Publishing Group USA**

Quarrystone Bond *See* **Club4Girls Publishing Co.**

Quarter Milestones Publishing, *(978-0-9748216)* Orders Addr.: P.O. Box 441, Milligan College, TN 37682-0441 USA Tel 423-542-0159; Fax: 423-542-9532; Edit Addr.: 1682 Powder Branch Rd., Johnson City, TN 37601-6220 USA
E-mail: qmp@preferred.com
Web site: http://www.quartermilestones.com
Dist(s): **Overmountain Pr.**

Quarterback Press *See* **Why Not Bks.**

Quarto Publishing Group UK (GBR) *(978-0-7112; 978-1-85410; 978-0-948149; 978-0-906053; 978-0-946544; 978-0-906459; 978-1-84092; 978-1-85076; 978-1-84543; 978-1-84507; 978-1-84538; 978-1-84513; 978-1-84780; 978-1-84835; 978-1-78131; 978-1-78171; 978-1-910277; 978-1-78493) Dist. by* **HachBkGrp.**

Quarto Publishing Group USA, *(978-0-7603; 978-0-86573; 978-0-89738; 978-0-912612; 978-0-929261; 978-0-9640392; 978-1-55832; 978-1-56010; 978-1-888608; 978-1-930604; 978-1-58923; 978-1-59186; 978-1-59233; 978-1-59253; 978-1-60058; 978-1-61673; 978-1-936309; 978-1-61058; 978-1-61059; 978-1-61060; 978-1-937994; 978-1-939581; 978-1-62788; 978-1-63106; 978-1-63159; 978-1-63322; 978-1-942875) Orders Addr.: Retail Order Dept., Quayside Publishing Group 18705 Lake Dr. E., Chanhassen, MN 55317 USA Tel 1-952-936-4700; Fax: 1-952-099-9101; Toll Free: 1-800-328-0590; Edit Addr.: 3 Wrigley Suite A, Irvine, CA 92618-2748 USA (SAN 249-051X) Toll Free: 800-426-0099; Imprints:* Creative Publishing International (Creativ Pub); Rockport Publishers (Rockport Pub); Quarry Books (QuarryBks); Walter Foster (WalterFoster); Walter Foster Jr (WalterFostJr); Cool Springs Press (CoolSpringsPr); Race Point Publishing (RacePtPub); Fair Winds Press (FairWindsPr); Motorbooks (Motorbooks); Zenith Press (ZenithPr); Quarry Books (QuarryBksUSA); Rock Point Gift & Stationery (RockPtGift); Voyageur Press (VoyageurUSA); Creative Publishing International (CreatPubIntl); Rockport Publishers (Rockport); Moondance Press (Moondance); Seagrass Press (Seagrass)
E-mail: rebecca.razo@quartous.com
Web site:
https://www.quartoknows.com/division/Quarto-Publishing-Group-USA/
Dist(s): **Arcadia Publishing**
Hachette Bk. Group
Lerner Publishing Group
MyiLibrary.

Quatemion Pr., *(978-0-9672535)* P.O. Box 700564, San Antonio, TX 78270 USA Tel 210-497-1096.

Que, *(978-0-7897; 978-0-88022; 978-1-56529)* Div. of Pearson Technology Group, 201 W. 103rd St., Indianapolis, IN 46290-1094 USA Tel 317-581-3500; Toll Free: 800-428-5331 (orders); 800-858-7674 (customer service) Do not confuse with Que Software, also a division of Macmillan Computer Publishing, same address
E-mail: customerservice@macmillanUSA.com
Web site: http://www.quepublishing.com
Dist(s): **Alpha Bks.**
Ebsco Publishing
MyiLibrary
Pearson Education
Pearson Technology Group
Sams Technical Publishing, LLC.

Quebla, *(978-0-9772738)* P.O. Box 958073, Duluth, GA 30095 USA Tel 404-906-3993
E-mail: support@quebla.com
Web site: http://www.quebla.com.

Queen Adisa, *(978-0-9979672)* 443 Riverbend Apt, Riverside, AL 35135 USA Tel 205-362-5000
E-mail: adisasalim@gmail.com
Web site: www.queenadisa.com.

Queen Alexandra Foundation for Children (CAN) *(978-0-9880536) Dist. by* **Orca Bk Pub.**

Queen Pubns, *(978-0-9778377)* Orders Addr.: P.O. Box 496, Antioch, IL 60002 USA
E-mail: apascascio@comcast.net
Web site: http://www.queenpublications.com.

Queen's Knight, *(978-0-9752810)* 8741 Saline Waterworks Rd., Saline, MI 48176 USA.

Queens Museum of Art, *(978-0-9604514; 978-1-929641)* New York City Bldg., Flushing Meadows Park, Queens, NY 11368-3398 USA (SAN 280-2147) Tel 718-592-9700; Fax: 718-592-5778
Web site: http://www.queensmuseum.org
Dist(s): **D.A.P./Distributed Art Pubs.**
Univ. Pr. of New England.

Quentin Road Ministries *See* **Victory In Grace Ministries**

Quercus Pr., *(978-0-9793444)* P.O. Box 46163, Plymouth, MN 55446-0163 USA (SAN 853-1773)
Web site: http://www.windingoak.com.

Questmarc Publishing, *(978-0-9634251; 978-0-9755801; 978-0-9819946; 978-1-939532)* Orders Addr.: P.O. Box 340, Yankton, SD 57078 USA Tel 605-660-0335; Fax: 605-260-6873; Edit Addr.: 811 W. 8th, Yankton, SD 57078 USA Tel 605-660-0335
E-mail: questmarc@mail.com
Web site: http://www.questmarc.com.

Quick Book Publishing *See* **FREOMM Publishing**

Quick Quest Pubns. LLC, *(978-0-9760372)* Orders Addr.: P.O. Box 9934, Alexandria, VA 22306 USA Toll Free Fax: 800-682-6576; Edit Addr.: P.O. Box 9934, Alexandria, VA 22304 USA Tel 978-726-5713
E-mail: nathanialportis@yahoo.com; mnportis@yahoo.com
Web site: http://www.quickquestpub.com.

Quick Wisdom Publishers *See* **Aylen Publishing**

Quickpresspublishing Incorporated *See* **Quick Quest Pubns. LLC**

Quiet Fox Designs *Imprint of* **Fox Chapel Publishing Co., Inc.**

Quiet Impact, Inc., *(978-0-9713749; 978-0-9754629)* 140 Cherry St., No. 388, Hamilton, MT 59840 USA Tel 406-375-9378; Fax: 406-363-5234; *Imprints:* Character-in-Action (Character-in-Action)
E-mail: elhamilton@quietimpact.com; elhamilton@character-in-action.com
Web site: http://www.character-in-action.com; http://www.quietimpact.com.

Quiet Man, *(978-0-9744251)* 28 W. 44th St., Suite 2105, New York, NY 10036-6600 USA (SAN 255-7150) Tel 212-921-4444; Fax: 212-921-4504
E-mail: dawn@quietman.net
Web site: http://www.quietman.net.

Quiet Man Publishing, *(978-0-9742829)* 27542 Berkshire Hills Pl., Valencia, CA 91354 USA
E-mail: jh1429@yahoo.com
Web site: http://www.Quietmanpublishing.com.

Quiet Owl Bks., *(978-0-615-54891-3; 978-0-615-59366-1; 978-0-615-64284-0; 978-0-615-64677-0; 978-0-615-65835-3; 978-0-9859443; 978-0-615-67800-9; 978-0-9898331)* 85 E. Point Rd., Montrose, PA 18801 USA Tel 323-253-1411; 570-278-6332
E-mail: books@quietowl.com
Web site: http://quietowl.com/
Dist(s): **CreateSpace Independent Publishing Platform**
Dummy Record Do Not USE!!!!.

Publisher Name Index

Quiet Storm Publishing Group, (*978-0-9714296; 978-0-9728819; 978-0-9744084; 978-0-9749608; 978-0-9758571; 978-0-9770070; 978-0-9787528*) Orders Addr.: P.O. Box 1666, Martinsburg, WV 25401 USA; Edit Addr.: 1045 Needmore Rd., Martinsburg, WV 25401 USA
E-mail: quietstormbooks@yahoo.com
Web site: http://www.quietstormpublishing.com.

Quiet Time Pr. *Imprint of* **Quiet Time Publishing**

Quiet Time Press *See* **Quiet Time Publishing**

Quiet Time Publishing, (*978-1-884743; 978-0-9755812; 978-0-9825090*) 14 Westminster Ave. #31 Venice, Ca, Los Angeles, CA 90291 USA Tel 310-452-2922; Fax: 310-399-9206; *Imprints:* Quiet Time Press (QuietTimePr)
E-mail: Quiettimepress@gmail.com; cgreco@earthlink.net
Web site: http://www.quiettimepress.com.

Quiet Vision Publishing, (*978-1-57646; 978-1-891595; 978-1-60545*) Orders Addr.: 12155 Mountain Shadow Rd., Sandy, UT 84092-5812 USA Tel 801-572-4018; Fax: 801-571-8625; Toll Free: 800-442-4018
E-mail: john@quietvision.com; info@quietvision.com
Web site: http://www.quietvision.com.

Quiet Waters Pubns., (*978-0-9663966; 978-1-931475*) 1318 N. Nias Ave., Springfield, MO 65802 USA
E-mail: david.trobisch@gmail.com
Web site: http://www.quietwaterspub.com.

Quigley, Karen, (*978-0-9800449*) P.O. Box 535, Blackwood, NJ 08012 USA (SAN 855-076X)
E-mail: loveelwood @comcast.net
Web site: http://www.EveryoneLovesElwood.com.

Quill & Hearth Publishing Hse., (*978-0-9984597*) 8 Hammer Ln., Rustburg, VA 24588 USA Tel 540-535-8952
E-mail: jessiebiggs@ymail.com.

Quill Driver Bks., (*978-1-884956*) 2006 S. Mary St., Fresno, CA 93721-3311 USA (SAN 298-2196) Toll Free: 800-497-4909
E-mail: info@QuillDriverBooks.com
Web site: http://www.quilldriverbooks.com
Dist(s): **American West Bks.**
Bookazine Co., Inc.
Bookpeople
Heinecken & Assoc., Ltd.
Independent Pubs. Group
Ingram Publisher Services
Libros Sin Fronteras
MyiLibrary
Partners/West Book Distributors
Quality Bks., Inc.
Unique Bks., Inc.

Quill Tree Books *Imprint of* **HarperCollins Pubs.**

Quiller Publishing, Ltd. (GBR) (*978-1-904057; 978-1-84689*) *Dist. by* **IPG Chicago.**

Quillpen, (*978-0-9673504*) 1520 Waverly Dr., Trenton, MI 48183 USA Tel 734-676-1285; Fax: 734-676-9822
E-mail: bfquillpen@msn.com.

Quillquest Books, (*978-0-940075; 978-0-9769272*) Div. of Quillquest Publishing Co., Orders Addr.: 388 Knights Run Dr., Heathsville, VA 22473 USA Tel 804-580-8815; 805-724-3869
E-mail: quillquestbooks@msn.com
Web site: http://www.frankmosco.com; http://www.lulu.com/quillquestbooks
Dist(s): **CreateSpace Independent Publishing Platform**
Ingram Content Group
Lulu Pr., Inc.

Quillrunner Publishing LLC, (*978-0-9796330; 978-0-9851157*) 8423 Los Reyes Ct., NW, Albuquerque, NM 87120 USA (SAN 853-9669) Tel 505-890-0723
E-mail: khickman@comcast.net
Web site: http://www.quillrunner.com.

Quilt in a Day, (*978-0-922705; 978-1-891776*) 1955 Diamond St., Unit A, San Marcos, CA 92069 USA (SAN 251-5644) Tel 760-591-0081; Fax: 760-591-4424; Toll Free: 800-777-4852
E-mail: qiad@quilt-in-a-day.com
Web site: http://www.quilt-in-a-day.com
Dist(s): **MyiLibrary**
ebrary, Inc.

Quimby & Sneet Publications *See* **405 Pubns.**

Quindaro Pr., (*978-0-9669258; 978-0-9764434; 978-1-946248*) 3808 Genessee St., Kansas City, MO 64111 USA Tel 816-200-2276
E-mail: quindaropress@gmail.com
Web site: http://www.quindaropress.com
Dist(s): **Itasca Bks.**

Quindim *See* **KINJIN Global**

Quinlan Pr., (*978-0-933341; 978-0-9611268; 978-1-55770*) 1 Devonshire Pl., No. 3108, Boston, MA 02109-3515 USA (SAN 226-4641).

Quinn Entertainment, (*978-0-9773099*) 7535 Austin Harbour Dr., Cumming, GA 30041 USA (SAN 257-2575) Tel 770-356-3847; Fax: 770-886-1475
E-mail: stephaniequinn@bellsouth.net
Web site: http://www.startabusinessteachingkids.com.

Quinn Micheal Publishing, Incorporated *See* **Rhapsody Branding, Inc.**

†Quintessence Publishing Co., Inc., (*978-0-86715; 978-0-931386; 978-1-85097; 978-1-883695; 978-1-64724*) 4350 Chandler Dr., Hanover Park, IL 60133-6763 USA (SAN 215-9783)
E-mail: service@quintbook.com
Web site: http://www.quintpub.com
Dist(s): **Publishers Group West (PGW)**; *CIP.*

Quintessential Corp., (*978-0-9715298*) P.O. Box 9224, Mclean, VA 22102 USA Tel 703-734-4900
E-mail: info@qproductsarchery.com
Web site: http://qproductsarchery.com.

Quintessential Pr. *Imprint of* **Gatekeeper Pr.**

Quintessential Productions, (*978-1-7337067*) 808 Concord Rd., Marlborough, MA 01752 USA Tel 774-249-4976
E-mail: kathleenquinton@yahoo.com.

Quirk Bks., (*978-1-931686; 978-1-59474; 978-1-68369*) 215 Church St., Philadelphia, PA 19106 USA Tel 215-627-3581; Fax: 215-627-5220
E-mail: jane@quirkbooks.com
Web site: http://www.quirkbooks.com
Dist(s): **Hachette Bk. Group**
MyiLibrary
Penguin Random Hse. Distribution
Penguin Random Hse. LLC
Random Hse., Inc.

Quirkles, The *Imprint of* **Creative 3, LLC**

Quisqueyana Pr., (*978-0-578-62770-0; 978-1-7354562*) 13625 Antelope Sta., Poway, CA 92064-1355 USA Tel 760-532-8442
E-mail: malabi77@hotmail.com
Web site: www.quisqueyanapress.com.

†Quite Specific Media Group, Ltd., (*978-0-89676*) Orders Addr.: 7373 Pyramid Pl., Hollywood, CA 90046-1312 USA (SAN 213-5752) Tel 323-851-5797; Fax: 323-851-5798; *Imprints:* Costume & Fashion Press (Costume & Fashion Pr)
E-mail: info@quitespecificmedia.com
Web site: http://www.quitespecificmedia.com; *CIP.*

Quitt & Quinn, Pubs., (*978-1-7328489*) 4811 Tullamore Dr., Bloomfoeld Hills, MI 48304 USA Tel 248-594-6376
E-mail: wsthomson@mac.com.

Quixote Press *See* **Padwolf Publishing, Inc.**

Quixote Pr., (*978-1-57166; 978-1-878488*) 1854 345th Ave., Wever, IA 52658-9597 USA Tel 319-372-7480; Fax: 319-372-7485; Toll Free: 800-571-2665 Do not confuse with Quixote Pr., Houston, TX, Los Angeles, CA
E-mail: heartsntummies@hotmail.com
Dist(s): **Bookmen, Inc.**

Qum, (*978-1-7320292*) 2000 Ascot Pkwy, Vallejo, CA 94591 USA Tel 510-325-7548; Fax: 707-731-0493
E-mail: hfeltuscurry@gmail.com.

Quoi Happens LLC, (*978-1-7338375*) 6247 S. Locust St., Centennial, CO 80111 USA Tel 508-733-0542
E-mail: jlowryauthor@gmail.com
Web site: janelowry.com.

Quoir, (*978-0-9765222; 978-0-9827446; 978-1-938480; 978-0-9913345*) 11520 Green Ln., Oak Glen, CA 92399 USA Tel 714-403-1922
E-mail: rafael@quoir.com
Web site: www.quoir.com.

QuotationWorld Pubns., (*978-0-9741868*) 3035 Shannon Lakes Dr., N., Tallahassee, FL 32309 USA Tel 850-894-1903 (phone/fax)
E-mail: admin@quotationworld.com
Web site: http://www.quotationworld.com.

Quotidian, Incorporated *See* **Quotidian Pubs.**

Quotidian Pubs., (*978-0-934391*) Orders Addr.: 377 River Rd., Cushing, ME 04563-9502 USA (SAN 693-8094) Tel 207-354-7091
E-mail: judydownmaine@roadrunner.com.

Quranic Educational Society, (*978-0-9760681*) Orders Addr.: P.O. Box 597969, Chicago, IL 60659 USA; Edit Addr.: 6355 N Claremont Ave., Chicago, IL 60659 USA Tel 773-743-9345
E-mail: qeschicago@sbcglobal.net
Web site: http://www.qesonline.org.

R & D Educational Center *See* **Boarding House Publishing**

R & D Publishing of Lakeland, Florida, (*978-0-9797566*) 5709 LaSerena Ave., Lakeland, FL 33809-4262 USA Tel 863-859-2984.

R & J Publishing, (*978-0-615-15136-6*) 1136 5th Ave. S., Anoka, MN 55303-2726 USA
E-mail: bobhelf.1@juno.com.

R & R Advertising, (*978-0-9765225*) 3409 Executive Ctr. Dr., No. 202, Austin, TX 78731 USA Tel 512-342-0110; Fax: 512-342-0142
E-mail: info@rradinc.com
Web site: http://www.rradinc.com.

R & R Publishing, LLC, (*978-0-9764845; 978-0-615-34449-2; 978-0-9829599; 978-0-9830577*) Div. of GlutenFree Passport, Orders Addr.: 80 Burr Ridge Pkwy. Suite 141, Burr Rudge, IL 60527 USA Tel 312-244-3702; Fax: 312-276-8001 Do not confuse with companies with the same or similar name in Torrance, CA, Brimingham, AL, Shelton, WA, San Antonio, TX, Washington, DC, Baldwin City, KS
E-mail: info@rrpublishing.com; kkoeller@glutenfreepassport.com
Web site: http://www.glutenfreepassport.com.

R & S Bks. (SWE) (*978-91-29*) *Dist. by* **Macmillan.**

R & S Pubns., (*978-0-615-18520-0; 978-0-615-18814-0*) 6799 Durham Rd., Whitehall, MI 49461 USA
E-mail: beckywit@charterinternet.com
Web site: http://www.rspublications.com
Dist(s): **Lulu Pr., Inc.**

RBC Publishing Co., Inc., (*978-0-9703178; 978-0-9721547*) Orders Addr.: P.O. Box 1330, Elk Grove, CA 95759 USA Tel 916-685-5578; Fax: 916-685-5958; Edit Addr.: 9107 Voos Ct., Elk Grove, CA 95624 USA; *Imprints:* Parks Publishing (Parks Publ)
E-mail: scituate@citlink.net
Web site: http://www.rbcpublishingco.com.

R.B. Media, Inc., (*978-0-9700021; 978-0-9797932*) 14064 Monterey Estates Dr., Delray Beach, FL 33446-2217 USA Tel 561-498-5922; Fax: 561-498-2369
E-mail: mabudnik@comcast.net
Web site: http://www.rbmediainc.com.

R. E. Farrellbooks, LLC, (*978-0-9759116; 978-0-9963587*) Orders Addr.: 18212 N. 130th Ave, Sun City West, AZ 85375-5015 USA
E-mail: ref40@msn.com
Web site: http://www.refarrellbooks.com.

REP Pubs., (*978-0-9604876*) Orders Addr.: 733 Turrentine Trail, St. Louis, MO 63141 USA (SAN 239-3786) Tel 314-434-1833
E-mail: Richard@reppublishers.com
Web site: www.reppublishers.com
Dist(s): **Unique Bks., Inc.**

R F T Publishing Company *See* **aha! Process, Inc.**

R.H. Boyd Publishing Corp., (*978-1-58942; 978-1-68167*) 6717 Centennial Blvd., Nashville, TN 37209-1049 USA Tel 615-350-8000; Fax: 615-350-9018
E-mail: dgroves@rhboyd.com; lboyd@rhboyd.com
Web site: http://www.rhboydpublishing.com.

R. H. Publishing, (*978-0-9772460; 978-0-9976907; 978-1-945693*) 5021 S. 30th St., Lincoln, NE 68516 USA Tel 214-605-0162
Dist(s): **Ingram Content Group.**

R J Communications, LLC, (*978-0-9700741; 978-1-59664*) 51 E. 42nd St., Suite 1202, New York, NY 10017-5404 USA Tel 212-867-1331; Fax: 212-681-8002; Toll Free: 800-621-2556 (New York)
E-mail: ron@rjcom.com
Web site: http://www.selfpublishing.com; http://www.booksjustbooks.com.

R. N. M., Incorporated *See* **Onion River Pr.**

RSVP Pr., (*978-0-930865; 978-1-60209*) 619 Gay Rd., Monroe, NC 28112-8214 USA (SAN 657-6346)
E-mail: writernet@aol.com
Web site: http://www.rsvpbooks.com; http://www.members.aol.com/writernet/rsvp.htm.

R T A Pr., (*978-1-929768*) Div. of Rochester Teachers Assn., 30 N. Union St., Suite 301, Rochester, NY 14607 USA Tel 716-546-2681; Fax: 716-546-4123
E-mail: ddsigns@servtech.com.

RVS Bks., Inc., (*978-0-9634257*) P.O. Box 683, Lebanon, TN 37088-0683 USA (SAN 298-7325) Tel 615-449-6725; Fax: 615-449-6910.

Rabbit Ears Pr. & Co., (*978-0-9748922*) Orders Addr.: P.O. Box 1952, Davis, CA 95617 USA Tel 530-220-3289
Web site: http://www.rockythemudhen.com
Dist(s): **Partners Bk. Distributing, Inc.**

Rabbit Pubs., (*978-1-943785*) a/o Mr. Mark A. Poe, 1624 W. Northwest Hwy., Arlington Heights, IL 60004 USA Tel 858-513-7150
E-mail: plewis@smartfamilies.com
Web site: www.smartfamilies.com
Dist(s): **Diamond Comic Distributors, Inc.**
Whitaker Hse.

Rabbit Room Pr., (*978-0-615-32542-2; 978-0-9826214; 978-0-9889632; 978-0-9863818; 978-0-9983112; 978-1-7326910; 978-1-951872*) 940 Davidson Dr., Nashville, TN 37205 USA
Web site: http://www.rabbitroom.com.

Rabbit's Foot Pr. *Imprint of* **Blue Mountain Arts Inc.**

Race Point Publishing *Imprint of* **Quarto Publishing Group USA**

Racehorse Publishing *Imprint of* **Skyhorse Publishing Co., Inc.**

Racemaker Pr. LLC, (*978-0-9766683; 978-1-935240; 978-0-9998754*) 39 Church St., Boston, MA 02116 USA (SAN 256-4513) Tel 617-723-6533
E-mail: admin@racemaker.com
Web site: www.racemaker.com.

Rach, W. Dennis, (*978-0-9792579*) 9965 Portofino Dr., Orlando, FL 32832 USA (SAN 852-9299) Tel 407-625-8528
E-mail: dennis@rachfamily.com.

Racing to Joy Press LLC *See* **Linda M. Penn Author**

Racom Communications, (*978-0-9704515; 978-1-933199*) 150 N. Michigan Ave. Ste. 2800, Chicago, IL 60601 USA (SAN 852-7210)
E-mail: rahagle@aol.com
Dist(s): **Baker & Taylor Publisher Services (BTPS).**

Raconteurs, Inc., (*978-0-9621758*) 1305 W. Wisconsin Ave., No. 114, Oconomowoc, WI 53066-2646 USA (SAN 252-080X) Tel 414-567-4009.

Rada Press, Inc., (*978-0-9604212; 978-1-933011*) Orders Addr.: 1277 Fairmount Ave., Saint Paul, MN 55105-2701 USA Fax: 888-288-6401
E-mail: rm@radapress.com
Web site: http://www.radapress.com.

Radford, Marsha, (*978-0-9785872; 978-0-9903726; 978-1-952205*) 1020 W. Angeleno Ave. No. 1, Burbank, CA 91506 USA Tel 818-940-5704
E-mail: writetomarsha@gmail.com
Web site: http://www.arcanaland.com.

Radiance Pubs., (*978-0-918224*) Div. of S. K. Publications, Orders Addr.: 1042 Maple Ave., Lisle, IL 60532 USA Tel 630-577-7624
E-mail: 'nlarson@radiancepublishers.com
Web site: http://www.radiancepublishers.com.

Radical Reformation Bks., (*978-0-9818973*) 34 Cindia Ln, Ephrata, PA 17522 USA (SAN 856-8790) Tel 717-738-9099
E-mail: deantaylorfamily@gmail.com; dean@radicalreformation.net
Web site: http://www.radicalreformation.com.

Radical Women, (*978-0-615-62458-7; 978-0-615-73142-1; 978-0-692-58373-9; 978-0-9983308; 978-1-7325363; 978-1-7340398*) P.O. Box 782, Granbury, TX 76048 USA Tel 817-269-9066
E-mail: lisabell@bylisabell.com
Web site: www.bylisabell.com
Dist(s): **CreateSpace Independent Publishing Platform.**

RADIOIONICS RESEARCH, (*978-1-930216*)
E-mail: bruceperreault@roadrunner.com
Web site: http://www.radioionics.com.

Rae, Karyn Publishing, (*978-0-9960922; 978-1-946847*) 13 Colonel Hazzard Rd., Okatie, SC 29909 USA Tel 573-424-0155
E-mail: krp@karynraepublishing.com
Web site: www.karynraepublishing.com.

Raedan Bocs *See* **Lire Bks.**

Raemark Pr., (*978-1-7325090*) 346 Rd. 21, Sedan, KS 67361 USA Tel 620-216-0332
E-mail: hjspire@yahoo.com
Web site: www.hazelspire.com.

Rafka Pr. LLC, (*978-0-9779628; 978-0-9911958*) P.O. Box 8099, Phoenix, AZ 85066 USA
Web site: http://www.rafkapress.com.

Rag Mag *See* **Black Hat Pr.**

Ragan, Jewel, (*978-0-9853809*) 24206 SE 248th St., Maple Valley, WA 98038 USA Tel 425-413-6032
E-mail: jewelragan@gmail.com.

Rageldar Pr., (*978-0-9993390*) 80 Westminster rd, 2, Rochester, NY 14607 USA Tel 585-727-0207; Fax: 585-727-0207
E-mail: Leah.fricano@yahoo.com.

Ragged Sky Pr., (*978-0-9633092; 978-1-933974*) 270 Griggs Dr., Princeton, NJ 08540 USA
E-mail: ellen_foos@pupress.princeton.edu
Web site: http://Raggedsky.com.

Raging Bull Publishing, LLC *See* **Command Publishing, LLC**

Ragtown Pr., (*978-1-7320968*) 21145 Bank Mill Rd., Saratoga, CA 95070-5706 USA Tel 408-823-2476
E-mail: andrew.john.grose@gmail.com.

Rai Publishing, (*978-0-9765641*) P.O. Box 918, Grover Beach, CA 93483 USA Tel 805-473-9025
E-mail: donrai@ix.netcom.com.

Raider Publishing International, (*978-0-9772054; 978-0-9790799; 978-1-934360; 978-1-935383; 978-1-61667*) 350 5th Ave., 59th Flr., New York, NY 10118 USA Tel 917-267-7912; Toll Free: 800-293-1653
E-mail: johnraider@hotmail.com; jraider@raiderpublishing.com
Web site: http://www.raiderpublishing.com.

Rain Tree Bks., (*978-0-9764129*) Orders Addr.: P.O. Box 1290, DeQueen, AR 71832 USA; Edit Addr.: 146 Treating Plant Rd., DeQueen, AR 71832 USA Tel 870-582-3565.

Rainbow Bks., Inc., (*978-0-935834; 978-1-56825*) P.O. Box 430, Highland City, FL 33846-0430 USA (SAN 213-5515) Tel 863-648-4420; Fax: 863-647-5951 Do not confuse with companies with the same or similar name in Middleburg, VT, Amstgerdam, NY, New York, NY, Sparks, NV
E-mail: RBIbooks@aol.com
Web site: http://www.RainbowBooksInc.com
Dist(s): **BCH Fulfillment & Distribution**
Book Clearing Hse.
Smashwords.

Rainbow Bridge Publishing, (*978-1-887923; 978-1-932210*) Div. of Carson-Dellosa Publishing Co., Inc., Orders Addr.: P.O. Box 571470, Salt Lake City, UT 84157-1470 USA Tel 801-268-8887; Fax: 801-268-2770; Toll Free: 800-598-1441; Edit Addr.: P.O. Box 571470, Salt Lake Cty, UT 84157-1470 USA
E-mail: danell@rbpbooks.com
Web site: http://www.rbpbooks.com
Dist(s): **Carson-Dellosa Publishing, LLC**
Midpoint Trade Bks., Inc.

Rainbow Communications, (*978-0-9725479; 978-0-9728737; 978-0-9888554*) 471 NW Hemlock Ave, Corvallis, OR 97330 USA Tel 541-753-3335
E-mail: varsell4@comcast.net.

†Rainbow Horizons Publishing, Inc., (*978-1-55319*) Orders Addr.: P.O. Box 19729, San Diego, CA 92159 USA Toll Free Fax: 800-663-3608; Toll Free: 800-663-3609; *Imprints:* Classroom Complete Press (Classrm Comp)
E-mail: paul@classroomcompletepress.com
Web site: http://www.ccpinteractive.com; http://www.rainbowhorizons.com; http://www.classroomcompletepress.com
Dist(s): **Follett School Solutions**
OverDrive, Inc.
ebrary, Inc.; *CIP.*

Rainbow Morning Music Alternatives, (*978-0-938663; 978-0-9615696*) 2121 Fairland Rd., Silver Spring, MD 20904 USA (SAN 218-2963) Tel 301-384-9207; Fax: 312-337-5985; Toll Free: 800-881-4741
E-mail: barrylou@ziplink.net
Web site: http://www.barrylou.com
Dist(s): **Independent Pubs. Group**
MyiLibrary.

Rainbow Pony Publishing, (*978-0-9728871*) 368 S. McCaslin Blvd., PMB No. 226, Louisville, CO 80027 USA.

Rainbow Pony Publising *See* **Rainbow Pony Publishing**

Rainbow Publishers *See* **Rainbow Pubs. & Legacy Pr.**

Rainbow Pubs. & Legacy Pr., (*978-0-937282; 978-1-885358; 978-1-58411*) Orders Addr.: P.O. Box 261129, San Diego, CA 92196 USA (SAN 256-4718) Tel 858-668-3260; Fax: 858-668-3328; Toll Free Fax: 800-331-0297; Toll Free: 800-323-7337; Edit Addr.: P.O. Box 70130, Richmond, VA 23255-0130 USA; *Imprints:* Legacy Press (Lgacy Pr)
E-mail: rainbowed@earthlink.net; drmiley@juno.com
Web site: http://www.rainbowpublishers.com
Dist(s): **Appalachian Bible Co.**
Spring Arbor Distributors, Inc.

Rainbow Reach, (*978-0-9829490*) 2340 Bedfordshire Cir., Reston, VA 20191 USA
E-mail: susan@rainbowreach.com
Web site: www.rainbowreach.com
Dist(s): **Ingram Content Group.**

Rainbow Resource Ctr., Inc., (*978-1-933407; 978-1-942446*) P.O. Box 391, Williamsfield, IL 61489 USA; *Imprints:* In the Think of Things (IntheThink).

Rainbow Star Bks., (*978-0-9802363*) P.O. Box 422, Centereach, NY 11720 USA (SAN 855-5680)
Web site: http://www.rainbowstarbooks.com.

Rainbow Star, Incorporated *See* **Rainbow Star Bks.**

Rainbow Valley Publishing Co., *(978-0-9748558)* 2189 Hwy. 90 W., Sulphur, LA 70663 USA Tel 337-528-1157.

Rainbows Within Reach, *(978-0-9705987; 978-0-578-03944-2; 978-0-578-06631-8)* 5765 Westbourne Ave., Columbus, OH 43213 USA
E-mail: debbie@rainbowswithinreach.com
Web site: http://www.rainbowswithinreach.com
Dist(s): **Follett School Solutions**
TNT Media Group, Inc.

Raincoast Bk. Distribution (CAN) *(978-0-920417; 978-1-55192; 978-1-895714; 978-1-894542) Dist. by* **PerseuPGW.**

Raindrop Bks., *(978-0-9766129)* 423 Hicks St., No. 6-H, Brooklyn, NY 11201 USA Tel 718-855-2918
E-mail: lgliessner@aol.com.

Raindrop Bks., *(978-0-9799677)* 10 Sunderland St., Melville, NY 11747 USA
Web site: http://www.learnalongwithlily.com; http://www.raindropbooks.com
Dist(s): **Big Tent Bks.**

Raining Popcorn Media, *(978-0-9797304)* P.O. Box 91244, San Antonio, TX 78209 USA Tel 210-320-0548; Toll Free: 866-503-3088
E-mail: info@rainingpopcorn.com; lisa@rainingpopcorn.com
Web site: http://www.RainingPopcorn.com.

Rains, Charlotte, *(978-0-692-90412-1; 978-0-692-97125-3; 978-0-578-48057-2)* 405 W. Taylor Ave., COOLIDGE, AZ 85128 USA Tel 520-518-5114
E-mail: bokz4kidz@hotmail.com
Dist(s): **Ingram Content Group.**

Rainstorm Pr., *(978-0-615-47986-6; 978-0-615-49269-8; 978-0-615-53082-6; 978-1-937758; 978-1-4748-9005-2)* P.O. Box 391038, Anza, CA 92539 USA Tel 760-270-8641
E-mail: Lyle@rainstormpress.com
Web site: http://www.RainstormPress.com
Dist(s): **CreateSpace Independent Publishing Platform.**

Raintree *Imprint of* **Capstone**

Raintree *Imprint of* **Heinemann-Raintree**

Raintree Steck-Vaughn Publishers *See* **Steck-Vaughn**

Rainy Day Entertainment, LLC *See* **Apologue Entertainment, LLC**

Rairarubia Bks., *(978-0-9712206)* 1000 San Diego Rd., Santa Barbara, CA 93103 USA Fax: 805-966-4697
E-mail: raira@silcom.com
Web site: http://www.rairarubia.com.

Raising World Children LLC, *(978-1-7335649)* 11604 Kenilworth Pl., Glen Allen, VA 23059 USA Tel 908-338-4650
E-mail: aditi.ws@gmail.com
Web site: https://raisingworldchildren.com/.

Raisykinder Publishing, *(978-0-615-21798-7; 978-0-615-27779-0; 978-0-9825530; 978-0-9907348; 978-0-9978111; 978-0-9992760)* 1713 Golden Ct., Bellingham, WA 98226 USA
E-mail: raisykinderpub@aol.com
Web site: http://www.raisykinderpublishing.com.

Rakha, Marwa *See* **Malamih Publishing Hse.**

Rakowski, Diane, *(978-0-9760194)* 11402 W. Parkhill Dr., Littleton, CO 80127-4716 USA
E-mail: dsjsit@juno.com.

Raku Bks., *(978-0-615-12445-2; 978-0-615-12561-9)* Orders Addr.: P.O. Box 51954, Palo Alto, CA 94303 USA
E-mail: rapimus@yahoo.com.

Raku Publishing, *(978-0-9770662)* 30799 Pinetree Rd., No. 411, Pepper Pike, OH 44124 USA Tel 216-299-0613
Dist(s): **BookBaby.**

Ralston Store Publishing, *(978-0-9822585; 978-1-938322)* P.O. Box 4513, Durango, CO 81302-4513 USA
Web site: http://www.ralstonstorepublishing.com
Dist(s): **Smashwords.**

Ramahi, Yasmin, *(978-1-7323382)* 930 NW 35th St., Corvallis, OR 97330 USA Tel 831-224-6449
E-mail: ThePurplePrincessSeries@gmail.com.

Ramos, Raymond G., *(978-0-9855114)* 11600 Mendel Dr. Apt. 3, Orlando, FL 32826 USA Tel 407-756-5730
E-mail: congabuena@yahoo.com.

Ramsey Dean, Inc., *(978-0-9893372)* 1555 N. Dearborn Pkwy. No. 14A, Chicago, IL 60610 USA Tel 312-860-2021
E-mail: ramseydeaninc@gmail.com
Web site: www.ridingonabeamoflight.com.

Ramsey Pr., *(978-0-9635712; 978-0-9718554; 978-0-9720044; 978-0-9726323; 978-0-9753033; 978-0-9769630; 978-0-9774895; 978-0-9777767; 978-0-9785620; 978-0-9786577; 978-1-934629; 978-0-9800873; 978-0-9816839; 978-0-9829862; 978-1-936948; 978-1-937077; 978-1-938400; 978-1-942121) 1749 Mallory Ln., Brentwood, TN 37027 USA Tel 615-515-3223; 888-227-3223; Fax: 615-371-5007; Toll Free: 888-227-3223*
E-mail: ken.murray@daveramsey.com; preston.cannon@daveramsey.com; lauren.kallemeyn@daveramsey.com
Web site: http://www.daveramsey.com
Dist(s): **Ingram Publisher Services**
Nelson, Thomas Inc.

Ranch Gate Bks., *(978-0-9618660)* 2409 Dormarion, Austin, TX 78703 USA (SAN 668-4033) Tel 512-476-2185.

†**RAND Corp., The,** *(978-0-8330; 978-1-9774)* Orders Addr.: P.O. Box 2138, Santa Monica, CA 90407-2138 USA (SAN 218-9291) Tel 310-393-0411; Fax: 310-393-4818; Toll Free: 877-584-8642; Edit Addr.: 1776 Main St., Santa Monica, CA 90401-3208 USA (SAN 665-763X) Tel 310-393-0411; Fax: 412-802-4981
E-mail: jwarren@rand.org; correspondence@rand.org; randell@rand.org; cs@rand.org
Web site: http://www.rand.org
Dist(s): **CreateSpace Independent Publishing Platform**
Ebsco Publishing
MyiLibrary
National Bk. Network
ebrary, Inc.; *CIP.*

†**Rand McNally,** *(978-0-528)* Orders Addr.: 9855 Woods Dr., Skokie, IL 60077-1074 USA Toll Free Fax: 800-934-3479 (Orders); Toll Free: 800-333-0136 (ext. 4771); 800-678-7263 (Orders); 8770 W Bryn Mawr Ave., Chicago, IL 60631 Tel 800-333-0136; Fax: 847-329-6139
E-mail: Education@randmcnally.com
Web site: http://www.randmcnally.com
Dist(s): **Benchmark LLC**
Bryant Altman Map, Inc.; *CIP.*

Rand Media Co, *(978-0-9818935; 978-0-9824390; 978-0-9841393; 978-0-9844418; 978-0-692-01528-5; 978-0-9852818; 978-0-9988392)* Orders Addr.: 265 Post Rd. W., Westport, CT 06880 USA (SAN 925-4919) Tel 203-226-8727; Fax: 203-221-7677; *Imprints:* Skinny On (tm), The (Skinny on)
E-mail: cmonroy@randmediaco.com
Web site: http://www.theskinnyon.com; http://randmediaco.com/money/money-book-1/; http://randmediaco.com/
Dist(s): **Lulu Pr., Inc.**

RAND Publishing *See* **Rand Media Co**

Randall, Charles Inc., *(978-0-9624736; 978-1-890379)* Orders Addr.: 30 Amberwood Pkwy., Ashland, OH 44805 USA Fax: 419-281-6883; Toll Free: 800-247-6553; Edit Addr.: P.O. Box 1656, Orange, CA 92856 USA (SAN 253-7737)
E-mail: peter@randallonline.com
Web site: http://www.randallonline.com; http://www.charlesrandall.com
Dist(s): **Follett School Solutions**
MyiLibrary
ebrary, Inc.

Randall, Cheri, *(978-0-9767213)* P.O. Box 2176, Belton, TX 76513 USA Tel 254-939-8776 (phone/fax)
E-mail: hrandallmail@aol.com
Web site: http://www.harveyrandall.org.

Randall Fraser Publishing *See* **RandallFraser Publishing**

Randall Hse. Pubns., *(978-0-89265; 978-1-61484)* 114 Bush Rd., Nashville, TN 37217 USA (SAN 207-5040) Tel 615-361-1221; Fax: 615-367-0535; Toll Free: 800-877-7030
E-mail: michelle.orr@randallhouse.com
Web site: http://www.randallhouse.com.

Randall International *See* **Randall, Charles Inc.**

†**Randall, Peter E. Pub.,** *(978-0-914339; 978-1-931807; 978-0-9817898; 978-0-9828236; 978-1-937721; 978-0-692-22144-0; 978-1-942155; 978-0-692-51521-1; 978-0-9971567; 978-0-9600735; 978-1-7331500)* 5 Greenleaf Woods Dr., Unit 102, Portsmouth, NH 03801 USA (SAN 223-0496) Tel 603-431-5667; Fax: 603-431-3566; 60 Main St., Nashua, NH 03060 Toll Free: 844-777-7812; *Imprints:* Jetty House (Jetty Hse)
E-mail: deidre.randall@me.com; lois@loishermann.com; media@perpublisher.com
Web site: http://www.perpublisher.com; www.loishermann.com
Dist(s): **Bondcliff Bks.**
BookBaby
Enfield Publishing & Distribution Co., Inc.
MyiLibrary
Pathway Bk. Service; *CIP.*

Randall, Robert E. *See* **Zander Pubns.**

RandallFraser Publishing, *(978-0-9745143)* 2082 Business Ctr. Dr., Suite 163, Irvine, CA 92612 USA Fax: 949-250-9020; Toll Free: 866-339-3999
E-mail: algreen51@comcast.net
Web site: http://www.Deweydooit.com
Dist(s): **National Bk. Network.**

R&B Trading Co., *(978-0-9718784)* 7619 Belmont Stakes Dr., Midlothian, VA 23112 USA (SAN 254-4741) Tel 804-739-8073; Fax: 775-243-6578
E-mail: dwindsofdestiny@aol.com
Web site: http://www.RnBtradingco.net/home.html.

Randle, Ian Pubs., Inc., *(978-0-9729358; 978-0-9742155; 978-0-9753529)* 25 SE Second Ave., Suite 1105, Miami, FL 33131 USA Tel 305-358-1588; Fax: 305-358-1589
E-mail: info@ianrandlepublishers.com
Web site: http://www.ianrandlepublishers.com
Dist(s): **Indiana Univ. Pr.**

R&N Productions, *(978-0-615-14376-7)* 698 Talbert Ave., Simi Valley, CA 93065 USA
E-mail: norm@kuvina.com
Web site: http://www.troublestreet.com
Dist(s): **Lulu Pr., Inc.**

Randolph, Connie, *(978-0-9994285)* 1153 Strada Cristallo, Henderson, NV 89011 USA Tel 330-610-6023
E-mail: casp2800@gmail.com
Web site: casperjoe.com.

Randolph Publishing, *(978-1-932258)* 4125 Braswell Church Rd., Good Hope, GA 30641-160 USA Do not confuse with companies with the same or similar names in Dunnellon, FL, Dallas, TX, Indianapolis, IN, Princeton, TX
E-mail: randolphpublishing@EarthLink.net
Web site: http://www.RandolphPublishing.com.

Random Ace Ink, *(978-0-9978475)* 18950 N Hills Dr., Brookfield, WI 53045 USA Tel 262-527-9963
E-mail: randomaceink@gmail.com.

Random House *Imprint of* **Random House Publishing Group**

Random House Adult Trade Publishing Group *See* **Random House Publishing Group**

Random House Audio *Imprint of* **Penguin Random House Audio Publishing Group**

Random Hse. Audio Publishing Group, Div. of Random House, Inc., Orders Addr.: 400 Hahn Rd., Westminster, MD 21157 USA (SAN 201-3975) Tel 410-848-1900; Toll Free: 800-726-0600; Edit Addr.: 1745 Broadway, New York, NY 10036 USA Tel 212-782-9000; *Imprints:* Listening Library (Listening Lib)
Web site: http://www.randomhouse.com/audio
Dist(s): **Ebsco Publishing**
Follett School Solutions
Penguin Random Hse. Distribution
Penguin Random Hse. LLC
Random Hse., Inc.

Random Hse. Bks. for Young Readers, *(978-0-375; 978-0-394; 978-0-517; 978-0-679; 978-1-4000)* Orders Addr.: 400 Hahn Rd., Westminster, MD 21157 USA; Edit Addr.: 1540 Broadway, New York, NY 10036 USA
Dist(s): **Children's Plus, Inc.**
MyiLibrary.

Random House Children's Books (GBR) *(978-1-4090; 978-1-4464) Dist. by* **IPG Chicago.**

Random House Children's Books (GBR) *(978-1-4090; 978-1-4464) Dist. by* **Perfect Learn.**

Random House Children's Books (GBR) *(978-1-4090; 978-1-4464) Dist. by* **Trafalgar.**

Random Hse. Children's Bks., Div. of Random Hse., Inc., Orders Addr.: 400 Hahn Rd., Westminster, MD 21157 USA Tel 410-848-1900; Toll Free: 800-726-0600; Edit Addr.: 1745 Broadway, 10th Flr., New York, NY 10019 USA Tel 212-782-8491; 212-782-9000; Fax: 212-782-9577; Toll Free: 800-200-3552; *Imprints:* Delacorte Books for Young Readers (Delacorte Bks); Lamb, Wendy Books (Wendy Lamb); Random House Para Ninos (ParaNinos); Crown Books For Young Readers (CBYR); Knopf Books for Young Readers (Knop); RH/Disney (RH Disney); Golden Books (Gold Bks); Random House Books for Young Readers (RHBYR); Bantam Books for Young Readers (BBYngRead); Doubleday Books for Young Readers (Doubleday Bk Yng); Yearling (Year); Dragonfly Books (Dragonfly Bks); Laurel Leaf (LaurelLeaf); Schwartz & Wade (Schwartz & Wade); Golden/Disney (Gold Disney); Robin Corey Books (Robin Corey); Golden Inspirational (Gold Inspir); Ember (Ember); Delacorte Press (DelacortePr); Bluefire (BluefireR); Princeton Review (PrinceReview); Sylvan Learning Publishing (Sylvan Lea); Tricycle Press (Tricycle); Now I'm Reading! (Now Im); David Fickling Books (DavidFickling); Rodale Kids (Rodale Kid); Underlined (Underlined)
E-mail: pmuller@randomhouse.com; kids@random.com
Web site: http://www.randomhouse.com/kids/
Dist(s): **Children's Plus, Inc.**
Follett School Solutions
Libros Sin Fronteras
MyiLibrary
Penguin Random Hse. Distribution
Penguin Random Hse. LLC
Random Hse., Inc.

Random House, Incorporated *See* **Random Hse., Inc.**

†**Random Hse., Inc.,** *(978-0-307; 978-0-345; 978-0-375; 978-0-385; 978-0-394; 978-0-440; 978-0-449; 978-0-517; 978-0-553; 978-0-593; 978-0-609; 978-0-676; 978-0-679; 978-0-7364; 978-0-7366; 978-0-7615; 978-0-7679; 978-0-7704; 978-0-8041; 978-0-8052; 978-0-8129; 978-0-8230; 978-0-87637; 978-0-87665; 978-0-87788; 978-0-88070; 978-0-913369; 978-0-914629; 978-0-930014; 978-0-945564; 978-1-57082; 978-1-57673; 978-1-57856; 978-1-878867; 978-1-884536; 978-1-885305; 978-1-58836; 978-1-4000; 978-1-59052; 978-1-4159; 978-) Div. of Penguin Random House LLC, Orders Addr.: 400 Hahn Rd., Westminster, MD 21157 USA (SAN 202-5515) Tel 410 848 1900; Toll Free Fax: 800 659 2436; Toll Free: 800 726 0600 (customer service/orders); Edit Addr.: 1745 Broadway, New York, NY 10019 USA (SAN 202-5507) Tel 212 782 9000; Fax: 212 302 7985; Imprints:* Golden Books (Golden Books)
E-mail: customerservice@randomhouse.com
Web site: http://www.randomhouse.com
Dist(s): **Ebsco Publishing**
Follett School Solutions
Giron Bks.
Libros Sin Fronteras
MyiLibrary
Penguin Random Hse. Distribution
Penguin Random Hse. LLC
Perfection Learning Corp.; *CIP.*

Random Hse. Information Group, Div. of Random Hse., Inc., Orders Addr.: 400 Hahn Rd., Westminster, MD 21157 USA Tel 410-848-1900; Toll Free: 800-726-0600; Edit Addr.: 1745 Broadway, New York, NY 10019 USA Tel 212-751-2600; Toll Free: 800-726-0600; *Imprints:* Random House Puzzles & Games (RHPG); Prima Games (PrimGames)
E-mail: customerservice@randomhouse.com
Web site: http://www.randomhouse.com/
Dist(s): **Bilingual Pubns. Co., The**
Ediciones Universal
Libros Sin Fronteras
MyiLibrary
Penguin Random Hse. Distribution
Penguin Random Hse. LLC
Random Hse., Inc.
Simon & Schuster, Inc.

Random House Large Print *Imprint of* **Diversified Publishing**

Random Hse. Large Print, Div. of Random House, Inc., Orders Addr.: 400 Hahn Rd., Westminster, MD 21157 USA Tel 410-848-1900 Toll Free: 800-726-0600 (customer service); Edit Addr.: 1745 Broadway, New York, NY 10019 USA Tel 212-782-9000
E-mail: editor@randomhouse.com; customerservice@randomhouse.com
Web site: http://www.randomhouse.com
Dist(s): **Libros Sin Fronteras**
MyiLibrary
Penguin Random Hse. Distribution
Penguin Random Hse. LLC
Random Hse., Inc.
Thorndike Pr.

Random House Para Ninos *Imprint of* **Random Hse. Children's Bks.**

Random House Publishing Group, *(978-1-4070)* Orders Addr.: 400 Hahn Rd., Westminster, MD 21157 USA (SAN 852-5579) Tel 410-848-1900; 410-386-7560; Toll Free: 800-726-0600; Edit Addr.: 1745 Broadway, New York, NY 10019 USA Tel 212-751-2600; Fax: 212-572-4949; Toll Free: 800-726-0600; *Imprints:* Random House Trade Paperbacks (RH Trade Bks); Modern Library (Mod Lib); Villard (Villard Bks); Random House (Random House); Del Rey (Del Rey); Ballantine Books (Ballantine Bks); Bantam (Bant); Delacorte Press (DelacorRHP); Laurel (LaureRH); Delacorte Press (DelacortePr)
E-mail: lstark@randomhouse.com
Dist(s): **Children's Plus, Inc.**
Follett School Solutions
Independent Pubs. Group
Libros Sin Fronteras
MyiLibrary
Penguin Random Hse. Distribution
Penguin Random Hse. LLC
Perfection Learning Corp.
Random Hse., Inc.

Random House Reference & Information Publishing *See* **Random Hse. Information Group**

†**Random Hse. Value Publishing,** Div. of Random House, Inc., Orders Addr.: 400 Hahn Rd., Westminster, MD 21157 USA Tel 410-848-1900 Toll Free: 800-726-0600 (Customer Service); Edit Addr.: 280 Park Ave., 11th Flr., New York, NY 10017 USA Tel 212 572 2400
Web site: http://www.randomhouse.com
Dist(s): **Penguin Random Hse. Distribution**
Penguin Random Hse. LLC
Random Hse., Inc.; *CIP.*

Random Hse. Australia (AUS) *(978-1-86359; 978-0-86824; 978-0-947189; 978-1-86325; 978-0-7338; 978-1-74051; 978-0-900882; 978-1-74166; 978-1-86471; 978-1-4230; 978-1-74274; 978-1-74275; 978-0-646-08769-6; 978-0-646-19362-5; 978-0-646-23850-0; 978-0-646-29047-8; 978-0-646-31636-9; 978-0-646-32934-5; 978-0-85798; 978-1-925324) Dist. by* **IPG Chicago.**

Random Hse. Bks. for Young Readers *Imprint of* **Random Hse. Children's Bks.**

Random Hse. of Canada (CAN) *(978-0-09; 978-0-307; 978-0-375; 978-0-394; 978-0-676; 978-0-679; 978-0-7704; 978-1-4000) Dist. by* **Random.**

Random Hse. Puzzles & Games *Imprint of* **Random Hse. Information Group**

Random Hse. Trade Paperbacks *Imprint of* **Random House Publishing Group**

R&R Blackburn Enterprises, *(978-0-9907603)* P.O. Box 27577, Fresno, CA 93729 USA Tel 559-287-4149
E-mail: rlb737@gmail.com
Web site: www.TwasWithATwist.com.

R&R Endeavors, Inc., *(978-0-9740444)* Orders Addr.: P.O. Box 301, Indianapolis, IN 46217 USA; Edit Addr.: 1350C W. Southport Rd., Indianapolis, IN 46217 USA
E-mail: editor@writerpublishing.com
Web site: http://www.writerpublishing.com.

Randy Jay Richards, *(978-0-578-45210-4)* 1918 S. 19th St., Grand Forks, ND 58201 USA Tel 701-213-2150
E-mail: randyrichards.gop@gmail.com
Dist(s): **Ingram Content Group.**

Rang Jung Yshe Pubns. (HKG) *(978-962-7341) Dist. by* **PerseuPGW.**

Ransom, L. M., *(978-1-7320588)* 1414 S. 102nd Ave., Shelby, MI 49455 USA Tel 231-301-0066
E-mail: linransom75@gmail.com
Web site: lmransom.com.

RAPC - Sparkle & Shine Project, *(978-0-9760282)* 116 Jackson St., Sylva, NC 28779 USA Tel 828-586-0661; Fax: 828-586-0663
Web site: http://www.sparkle-shine.com.

RAPHA, Inc., *(978-0-9740081)* Orders Addr.: P.O. Box 1184, Groton, CT 06340 USA Tel 860-938-2599; Edit Addr.: 45 South Rd., Apt. 9A, Groton, CT 06340 USA Tel 860-514-7266
E-mail: joyindamornin@earthlink.net.

Rapha Publishing, *(978-0-9763686)* 431 Beechwood Ave., Carnegie, PA 15106 USA Tel 412-249-0669
E-mail: raphapublishing@yahoo.com
Web site: http://www.raphapublishing.com/.

Raphel Marketing, Inc., *(978-0-9624808; 978-0-9711542; 978-0-9826644; 978-1-938406)* Orders Addr.: 211 North Ave., St Johnsbury, VT 05819-1626 USA Tel 802-751-8802; *Imprints:* Compass (CompassUSA)
E-mail: neil@raphel.com
Web site: http://www.raphel.com; http://www.brigantinemedia.com; http://compasspublishing.org.

Rapids Christian Pr., Inc., *(978-0-915374)* P.O. Box 717, Ferndale, WA 98248-0717 USA (SAN 205-0986) Tel 360-384-1747
E-mail: gundersonwv@aol.com.

Rapier Publishing Co., LLC, *(978-0-9839483; 978-0-9966083; 978-0-9970307; 978-0-9977029; 978-1-946683)* 135 Lakeside Dr., Dothan, AL 36301 USA Tel 256-553-9410; Fax: 334-699-5550
E-mail: petefannie@aol.com.

Publisher Name Index

Rare Bird Bks., *(978-0-9839255; 978-0-9854902; 978-0-9887456; 978-0-9889312; 978-1-940207; 978-1-942600; 978-0-9971486; 978-0-9974407; 978-1-945572; 978-0-9983147; 978-1-947856; 978-1-64428)* 453 S. Spring St., Suite 302, Los Angeles, CA 90013 USA Tel 213-623-1773; *Imprints:* Vireo Book, A (VireoBk); Secular Media Group (MYID_B_SECULAR)
E-mail: tyson@rarebirdlit.com
Dist(s): **MyiLibrary**
Publishers Group West (PGW)
SPD-Small Pr. Distribution.

R.A.R.E. TALES, *(978-0-9760303)* 14120 River Rd., Fort Myers, FL 33905-7436 USA
E-mail: kphchance@comcast.net
Web site: http://www.raretales.net.

Rarecity Pr., *(978-0-9760959)* 17 Yardley Dr., Medford, NJ 08055 USA Tel 201-788-9746
E-mail: jason@rarecity.com.

Rasa Music Co., *(978-0-9766219)* 409 Glenview Rd., Glenview, IL 60025-3262 USA Tel 847-486-0416; Fax: 847-657-9459
E-mail: lleifer@northpark.edu
Web site: http://www.admin.northpark.edu/lleifer/.

Rascal Treehouse Publishing, *(978-0-9759321)* 1523 Morris St. - Suite 330, Lincoln Park, MI 48146 USA
E-mail: lscoffman@lscoffman.com
Web site: http://www.lscoffman.com.

Raspberry Bks., *(978-0-9848749)* 4346 Mammoth Ave. No. 4, Sherman Oaks, CA 91423 USA Tel 818-633-9190
E-mail: tammy@tammylaframboise.com.

Ratatat Graphics LLC *See* **Studio Moonfall**

Rattle OK Pubns., *(978-0-9626210; 978-1-883965)* Orders Addr.: P.O. Box 5614, Napa, CA 94581 USA (SAN 297-5475) Tel 707-253-9641; Edit Addr.: 296 Homewood Ave., Napa, CA 94558-5617 USA
Dist(s): **Gryphon Hse., Inc.**

Ratway, Michael, *(978-0-9724698)* 216 Midshipman Cir., Stafford, VA 22554-2421 USA
E-mail: yawtar@earthlink.net
Web site: http://www.earthlink.net/~yawtar.

Rauch, Linda Gallery, *(978-0-692-04341-7; 978-0-578-74232-8)* 246 A Ledoux St., Taos, NM 87571 USA Tel 512-417-0116
E-mail: lrauchartist@yahoo.com
Dist(s): **Ingram Content Group.**

Raven Bks. *Imprint of* **Raven Productions**

Raven House Media, *(978-0-9983624)* 1625 SW 173rd Ter, Beaverton, OR 97003 USA Tel 503-459-8547
E-mail: rmseidler@gmail.com
Web site: rmseidler.com.

Raven Mad Studios, *(978-0-9896269)* 16327 197th Ave. NE, Woodinville, WA 98077 USA Tel 206-310-7246
E-mail: randybriley@comcast.net.

Raven Press *See* **Raven House Media**

Raven Productions, *(978-0-9764091)* 325 E. 2550 N, Suite 117, North Ogden, UT 84414 USA Tel 801-782-0872; *Imprints:* Raven Books (RavenBks) Do not confuse with companies with the same or similar name in Delta Junction, AKEly, MN
E-mail: gshaw@post.harvard.edu
Dist(s): **MyiLibrary.**

Raven Productions, Inc., *(978-0-9914157)* Orders Addr.: P.O. Box 188, Ely, MN 55731 USA Do not confuse with companies with the same or similar name in Delta Junction, AK, North Ogden, UT
E-mail: raven@ravenwords.com.

Raven Publishing *See* **Raven Publishing Inc. of Montana**

Raven Publishing Inc. of Montana, *(978-0-9714161; 978-0-9772525; 978-0-9820893; 978-0-9827377; 978-1-937849)* P.O. Box 2866, Norris, MT 59745 USA (SAN 254-5861) Tel 406-685-3545; Fax: 406-685-3599; Toll Free: 866-685-3545; *Imprints:* Nesting Tree Books (NestingTree) Do not confuse with companies with the same or similar name in Bronx, NY, Pittsfield, MA
E-mail: janet@ravenpublishng.net
Web site: http://www.ravenpublishing.net
Dist(s): **Bks. West**
Distributors, The
Follett School Solutions
Partners/West Book Distributors
Quality Bks., Inc.
Smashwords
Wolverine Distributing, Inc.
Western International, Inc.

Raven Rocks Pr., *(978-0-9615961)* 53650 Belmont Ridge, Beallsville, OH 43716 USA (SAN 696-5679) Tel 740-926-1481 (phone/fax)
E-mail: jmrpress@1st.net.

Raven Tree Pr. *Imprint of* **Delta Systems Company, Inc.**

Raven Tree Pr.,Csi *Imprint of* **Continental Sales, Inc.**

Raven Wing, *(978-0-9887762; 978-0-9969351; 978-0-9989157; 978-1-7329767; 978-1-7342468)* 1837 Talon Rd, Rocklin, CA 95765 USA Tel 916-742-0671
E-mail: susan144@me.com
Web site: www.sbalexander.com.

Ravencrest *Imprint of* **Cubbie Blue Publishing**

Ravenhart Pr., *(978-0-9996106)* 8635 W Sahara Avenue, No. 677, Las Vegas, NV 89117 USA Tel 702-219-5698; Fax: 702-219-5698
E-mail: ravenhartpress@gmail.com
Web site: http://ravenhartpress.com.

Ravenhawk Bks., *(978-1-893660)* Div. of The 6DOF Group, 7739 E. Broadway Blvd. Suite 95, Tucson, AZ 85710 USA Tel 520-886-9885 (phone/fax); Toll Free: 800-520-9885
E-mail: 76673.3165@compuserve.com
Web site: http://www.ravenhawk.org.

RavenMark, *(978-0-9713998; 978-0-615-55902-5)* 27 E. State St., Montpelier, VT 05602-3011 USA Tel 802-223-5507
E-mail: rebecca@ravenmark.com
Dist(s): **R. C. Brayshaw.**

Ravensburger Buchverlag Otto Maier GmbH (DEU) *(978-3-473) Dist. by* **Distribks Inc.**

Ravenstone Pr., *(978-0-9659712)* Orders Addr.: Ravenstone Press 2056 Berry Roberts Dr., Sun City Center, FL 33573-6130 USA Tel 813-633-5759; Fax: 813-633-5759; Edit Addr.: 2056 Berry Roberts Dr., Sun City Ctr, FL 33573-6130 USA
E-mail: writerjerri@gmail.com
Web site: http://www.ravenstonepress.com.

Ravenwood Publishing, *(978-0-9899275)* 133 Rob Rd., Brooklin, ME 04616 USA Tel 207-359-2451
E-mail: ruthjohnhowell@gmail.com.

Ravenwood Studios, *(978-0-9718604; 978-1-933420)* P.O. Box 197, Diamond Springs, CA 95619 USA
E-mail: ravenwoodstudios@me.com; maureenedgecomb@me.com; todd.ryan@comcast.net
Web site: http://www.maureenedgecomb.com; http://www.ravenwoodstudios.net; http://www.marcyinmanhattan.com.

Ravette Publishing, Ltd. (GBR) *(978-0-948456; 978-1-85304; 978-0-906710; 978-1-84161) Dist. by* **Parkwest Pubns.**

Ravishing Gecko Publishing, *(978-0-9989938)* 2127 Hopkins Pl. Ct, Duluth, GA 30096 USA Tel 470-564-0914
E-mail: naynuk@ravishinggecko.com.

Raw Dog Screaming Pr., *(978-0-9745031; 978-1-933293; 978-1-935738; 978-1-947879)* 2802 Farris Ln., Bowie, MD 20715 USA (SAN 255-7673)
E-mail: books@rawdogscreaming.com
Web site: http://www.rawdogscreaming.com.

Raw Junior, LLC *See* **TOON Books / RAW Junior, LLC**

Ray, *(978-0-9856890)* 551 Atlanta Ave., San Jose, CA 95125 USA Tel 917-647-4899
E-mail: rnfvento@gmail.com.

Ray Greer, Mary Lou, *(978-0-9749161)* P.O. Box 1740, Eagar, AZ 85925 USA Tel 520-850-6209.

Rayenear Publishing, *(978-0-692-97667-8)* 633 F St., Martinez, CA 94553 USA Tel 925-332-9892
E-mail: rayenearpublishing@gmail.com.

Raynear Publishing *See* **Rayenear Publishing**

Raynestorm Bks. *Imprint of* **Silver Rose Publishing**

Rayo *Imprint of* **HarperCollins Pubs.**

Rayve Productions, Inc., *(978-1-877810)* Orders Addr.: P.O. Box 726, Windsor, CA 95492 USA (SAN 248-4250) Tel 707-838-6200; Fax: 707-838-2220; Toll Free: 800-852-4890
E-mail: rayvepro@aol.com
Web site: http://www.rayveproductions.com; http://www.rayvepro.com
Dist(s): **Brodart Co.**
Follett School Solutions
Lippincott Williams & Wilkins
Quality Bks., Inc.
Unique Bks., Inc.

Razavi, Firouzeh Bks., *(978-0-692-08968-2; 978-0-692-11249-6; 978-0-692-15929-3; 978-0-578-42265-7; 978-0-578-42329-6)* 497 S. El Molino No. 211, Pasadena, CA 91101 USA Tel 626-379-7608; *Imprints:* FR Publishing (FR Publish)
E-mail: thefirouzehrazavi@gmail.com
Dist(s): **CreateSpace Independent Publishing Platform.**

Razorbill *Imprint of* **Penguin Young Readers Group**

Razorbill *Imprint of* **Penguin Publishing Group**

RBA Libros, S.A. (ESP) *(978-84-89662; 978-84-7871; 978-84-7901; 978-84-85351; 978-84-9867; 978-84-9006) Dist. by* **Santillana.**

RBA Libros, S.A. (ESP) *(978-84-89662; 978-84-7871; 978-84-7901; 978-84-85351; 978-84-9867; 978-84-9006) Dist. by* **Lectorum Pubns.**

RBHC LLC., *(978-0-692-99523-5; 978-0-578-45901-1)* 111 E. 26th St. Apt. B9, New York, NY 10010 USA Tel 917-209-0960
E-mail: rugbytrader@gmail.com
Dist(s): **CreateSpace Independent Publishing Platform.**

RBTB Publishing, *(978-0-9977530)* 590 Bloomfield Ave, No. 207, Bloomfield, NJ 07003 USA Tel 973-303-9412
E-mail: kelly@kidpressroom.com
Web site: www.kidpressroom.com.

RCL Benziger Publishing, *(978-0-89505; 978-0-913592; 978-1-55924)* A Kendall Hunt Company, Orders Addr.: 8805 Governor's Hill, Suite 400, Cincinnati, OH 45249 USA (SAN 299-0628) Toll Free Fax: 800-688-8356; Toll Free: 877-275-4725
E-mail: customerservice@rclbenziger.com
Web site: http://www.rclweb.com/
Dist(s): **Spring Arbor Distributors, Inc.**

RD Vincent, *(978-0-692-56221-5)* 4000 Essex Ln. Apt 1301, Houston, TX 77027 USA Tel 845-699-6664
E-mail: rayd792002@yahoo.com.

RDM Publishing, *(978-0-9766038)* 605 CR 1040E, Norris City, IL 62869 USA Tel 618-265-3225
E-mail: earthart@midwest.net.

RDR Bks., *(978-0-9636161; 978-1-57143)* 1487 Glen Ave., Muskegon, MI 49441-3101 USA; 960 S. Sherman, Muskegon, MI 49441
E-mail: books@rdrbooks.com
Web site: http://www.rdrbooks.com
Dist(s): **Alpen Bks**
American West Bks.
Book Wholesalers, Inc.
Bookazine Co., Inc.
Brodart Co.
Follett School Solutions
New Leaf Distributing Co., Inc.
Quality Bks., Inc.
Sunbelt Pubns., Inc.
Unique Bks., Inc.
Yankee Bk. Peddler, Inc.

Re, Joseph Del, *(978-0-692-99876-2)* 777 N. Orange Ave., Orlando, FL 32801 USA Tel 407-595-7336
E-mail: babaoriley74@gmail.com
Dist(s): **Ingram Content Group.**

Reaching Beyond, Inc., *(978-0-9741893)* Orders Addr.: P.O. Box 12364, Columbus, GA 31917-2364 USA Tel 706-573-5942; Edit Addr.: P.O. Box 12364, Columbus, GA 31917-2364 USA
E-mail: nccjohnson@hotmail.com
Web site: http://Www.charlotterjohnson.com
Dist(s): **Book Clearing Hse.**

Reachment Publications *See* **Southeast Media**

Read 2 Children, *(978-0-9755839)* P.O. Box 4113, Warren, NJ 07059 USA Tel 732-805-9073
Web site: http://www.read2children.com.

Read All Over Publishing, *(978-0-9728779)* 17705 Ingleside Rd., Cleveland, OH 44119 USA Tel 216-486-8615 ext. 3
E-mail: readallover@sbcglobal.net.

Read More! Run More!, *(978-0-692-82924-0; 978-0-692-92465-5)* 3900 Woodchase Dr Apt152, HOUSTON, TX 77042 USA Tel 443-739-4339
E-mail: jeffwcrawford5+LVP0003230@gmail.com; jeffwcrawford5+LVP0003230@gmail.com.

Read Publishing, *(978-0-9762868)* Orders Addr.: 3918 Dorcas Dr., Nashville, TN 37215 USA Tel 615-279-9988; Fax: 615-385-2651
E-mail: snea5001@bellsouth.net; jennie0120@aol.com.

Read Street Publishing, Inc., *(978-0-942929)* 133 W. Read St., Baltimore, MD 21201 USA (SAN 667-8505) Tel 410-837-1116; Fax: 410-727-3174; *Imprints:* Omni Arts Publishing (Omni Arts Pubng)
E-mail: editor@omnititles.com; editor@tablespr.com; editor@readstreetpublishing.com
Web site: http://www.omnititles.com; http://www.tablespr.com; http://www.readstreetpublishing.com.

Read Together Bks., *(978-0-9822615)* 8045 230th St, Bellerose Manor, NY 11427-2105 USA Tel 917-757-5868
E-mail: mike@readtogetherbooks.com
Web site: http://www.readtogetherbooks.com.

Read Us For Fun Publishing, *(978-0-9820363)* P.O. Box 623, Dover, MA 02030 USA Tel 508-523-9414
E-mail: mking426@msn.com
Web site: http://readusforfun.com.

Read Well Publishing Inc., *(978-0-9630539; 978-0-9703400; 978-1-933873)* Div. of Apodixis, Inc., Orders Addr.: P.O. Box 671053, Dallas, TX 75367 USA Tel 972-241-1366; Fax: 972-241-5345 (call first); Toll Free: 800-522-3341; Edit Addr.: 3975 High Summit Dr., Dallas, TX 75244 USA
E-mail: jillsmithusa@att.net
Web site: http://www.learning-apodixis.com.

ReadaClassic.com, *(978-1-61104)* Orders Addr.: P.O. Box 7, Cedar Lake, MI 48812 USA Tel 989-244-0030; Edit Addr.: 4769 Feather Trail, Cedar Lake, MI 48812 USA Tel 989-244-0030
E-mail: carijhaus@gmail.com
Web site: http://www.readaclassic.com.

Reader Publishing Group, *(978-0-9837873; 978-1-7323345)* 1900 E. Ocean Blvd. No. 1001, Long Beach, CA 90802 USA Tel 562-900-0953
E-mail: cunham@aol.com.

Readerlink Distribution Services, LLC, *(978-0-934429; 978-1-57145; 978-1-59223; 978-1-60710; 978-1-62686; 978-1-68412; 978-1-64517)* 10350 Barnes Canyon Rd. Suite 100, San Diego, CA 92121 USA (SAN 630-8090) Toll Free: 800-284-3580; *Imprints:* Thunder Bay Press (Thunder Bay); Silver Dolphin Books (Silver Dolph)
E-mail: lnordland@readerlink.com
Web site: http://www.silverdolphinbooks.com; http://www.printersrowpublishinggroup.com; http://www.thunderbaybooks.com/; http://www.bathroomreader.com; http://www.readerlink.com
Dist(s): **Publishers Group West (PGW)**
Simon & Schuster, Inc.

Readers Are Leaders, *(978-0-9673625)* 908 Ashland Dr., Mesquite, TX 75149 USA Tel 972-288-5806 (phone/fax)
E-mail: rlgant@airmail.net.

Readers Are Leaders U.S.A., Inc., *(978-0-9768035; 978-0-9800397)* 2315 SW 5th Ave., Miami, FL 33129-1939 USA (SAN 855-0557)
Web site: http://www.readersareleadersusa.net.

†Reader's Digest Assn., Inc., The, *(978-0-7621; 978-0-89577; 978-0-86438; 978-1-60652)* One Bedford Rd., Pleasantville, NY 10570 USA (SAN 282-2091) Toll Free: 800-463-8820; 800-334-9599; 800-635-5006
Web site: http://www.readersdigest.com; http://www.rd.com
Dist(s): **Children's Plus, Inc.**
Leonard, Hal Corp.
Penguin Publishing Group
Simon & Schuster, Inc.
Tuttle Publishing; *CIP.*

Reader's Digest Children's Bks. *Imprint of* **Studio Fun International**

Reader's Digest Children's Publishing, Incorporated *See* **Studio Fun International**

Reader's Digest Young Families, Inc. *Imprint of* **Studio Fun International**

READERS to EATERS, *(978-0-9836615; 978-0-9984366; 978-0-9980477; 978-1-7351522)* 12437 SE 26th Pl., Bellevue, WA 98005 USA Tel 206-849-1962
E-mail: philip@readerstoeaters.com
Web site: www.ReadersToEaters.com
Dist(s): **Publishers Group West (PGW).**

Reading Co., The *Imprint of* **Rhoades & Assocs.**

Reading Power *Imprint of* **Rosen Publishing Group, Inc., The**

Reading Reading Bks., LLC, *(978-1-933727; 978-1-60892)* P.O. Box 6654, Reading, PA 19610 USA
E-mail: service@rrbooks.com; orangetabbycat2000@yahoo.com
Web site: http://www.rrbooks.com.

Reading Resc., *(978-0-9755561; 978-0-9795648)* 314 Knowles Hill Rd., Alexandria, NH 03222 USA (SAN 853-7771) Tel 603-744-5803 Do not confuse with Reading Resources, Inc. in Worthington, OH
E-mail: laberge001@gmail.com; readingrescources@metrocast.net.

Reading Rock Books *See* **Reading Rock, Inc.**

Reading Rock, Inc., *(978-1-929591)* P.O. Box 67, Athens, MI 49011 USA Tel 616-729-9440
Web site: http://www.Readingrockbook.com.

Reading Studio Pr., *(978-0-9767506)* 250 W. 90th St., Suite 12F, New York, NY 10024 USA Tel 212-724-6232
E-mail: readingstudio@aol.com
Web site: http://www.alphieandthealphabets.com.

Reading Tree Pr., *(978-0-615-92763-3; 978-0-692-38179-3)*
Dist(s): **CreateSpace Independent Publishing Platform.**

Reading with Rose, *(978-0-9891006)* 317 S. Elm St. Loft 313, Owosso, MI 48867 USA Tel 989-274-1053
E-mail: rtithof@gmail.com.

Reading's Fun/Books are Fun, Limited *See* **Bks. Are Fun, Ltd.**

Ready Blade *Imprint of* **Blooming Tree Pr.**

Ready Writer Publishing, LLC, *(978-0-9748748)* P.O. Box 18197, Shreveport, LA 71138 USA Tel 318-470-0538
E-mail: satbeau1@bellsouth.net.

ReadZone Bks. (GBR) *(978-1-78322) Dist. by* **IPG Chicago.**

Reagan Arthur Bks. *Imprint of* **Little Brown & Co.**

Reagent Pr. Bks. for Young Readers *Imprint of* **RP Media**

Reagent Pr. Echo *Imprint of* **RP Media**

Reagent Pr. Signature Editions *Imprint of* **RP Media**

Reagent Press *See* **RP Media**

Reaktion Bks., Ltd. (GBR) *(978-0-948462; 978-1-86189; 978-1-78023; 978-1-78914) Dist. by* **Chicago Distribution Ctr.**

Real Bks. 360, *(978-0-692-97002-7; 978-0-692-14235-6)* 4510 Charlotte Ave., Apt. 301, Nashville, TN 37209 USA Tel 615-829-3600
E-mail: freddy.sturman@gmail.com
Dist(s): **CreateSpace Independent Publishing Platform.**

R.E.A.L. Pubns., *(978-0-9724503; 978-0-9748003)* 109 La Costa Dr., Georgetown, KY 40324 USA (SAN 255-867X) Tel 859-539-2463
E-mail: austinandbelinda@gmail.com
Web site: http://www.arealeducation.com.

R.E.A.L. Publishing *See* **R.E.A.L. Pubns.**

Real Reads Ltd. (GBR) *(978-1-906230; 978-1-911091) Dist. by* **Casemate Pubs.**

Real Simple Bks. *Imprint of* **Time Inc. Bks.**

Real World Productions, *(978-1-60855; 978-1-60856)* 131 Ave. B, No. 1B, New York, NY 10009 USA.

Realistically Speaking Publishing Co., *(978-0-9727874)* 10808 Foothill Blvd. No. 160-260, Rancho Cucamonga , CA 91730 USA
E-mail: sherea@vejauan.com
Web site: http://www.vejauan.com.

Reality Check Pubns., *(978-0-9863364)* 2966 S. Church St. Suite 235, Burlington, NC 27215 USA
E-mail: feedback@realitycheck.org.

Reality Living Publishing, Inc., *(978-0-9643021; 978-1-888220)* 8720 E. 55th St., Kansas City, MO 64129 USA Tel 816-358-1515 ext 2062; Fax: 816-358-3439 ext 2062
E-mail: sehle@kcbt.org
Web site: http://www.realityliving.org.

Realityls Bks. *Imprint of* **RealitylsBooks.com, Inc.**

RealitylsBooks.com, Inc., *(978-0-9791317; 978-0-9817137; 978-0-9843883; 978-0-9847390; 978-0-578-41238-2; 978-1-7334578)* 1327 Winslowe Dr., Unit 304, Palatine, IL 60074 USA Tel 847-305-4657; Toll Free: 866-534-3366; *Imprints:* Realityls Books (Realityls Bks); Green Lady Press, The (GreenLady)
E-mail: publish@realityisbooks.com
Web site: http://www.realityisbooks.com.

Really Big Coloring Bks., Inc., *(978-0-9727833; 978-0-9729753; 978-0-9763186; 978-1-935266; 978-1-61953)* 224 N. Meramec, Saint Louis, MO 63105 USA Tel 314-725-1452; Fax: 314-725-3553; Toll Free: 800-244-2665 (1-800-Big-Book)
E-mail: wayne@bigcoloringbooks.com; ken@bigcoloringbooks.com; derek@bigcoloringbooks.com
Web site: http://www.bigcoloringbook.com; http://www.spanishcoloringbooks.com; http://www.wholesalecoloringbooks.com; http://www.coloringbook.com; http://www.coloringbookpublishers.com
Dist(s): **MeadWestvaco.**

Realms *Imprint of* **Charisma Media**

RealWord Pubns., *(978-0-9743088)* Orders Addr.: P.O. Box 931461, Norcross, GA 30093-1461 USA Fax: 678-406-9178; Edit Addr.: 6450 Indian Acres Trail, Norcross, GA 30093 USA
E-mail: wrcomm@comcast.net
Web site: http://www.climbeveryobstacle.com.

Reardon, Anne E., *(978-1-7320197; 978-1-7344770)* 10725 S. Ocean Dr. -31, Jensen Beach, FL 34957 USA Tel 772-342-4300
E-mail: Annie2yk@aol.com.

Reasor, Teresa J., *(978-0-615-50243-4; 978-0-9850069; 978-0-9886627; 978-1-940047)* P.O. Box 124, Corbin, KY 40702 USA Tel 606-528-0819
Web site: http://www.teresareasor.com
Dist(s): **CreateSpace Independent Publishing Platform**
Smashwords.

Rebecca E Blair *See* **Blair, Rebecca E**

Rebecca Hse., *(978-0-945522)* 1550 California St., Suite 330, San Francisco, CA 94109 USA (SAN 247-1361) Tel 415-752-1453; Toll Free: 800-321-1912 (orders only)
E-mail: Rebeccahse@aol.com
Dist(s): **New Leaf Distributing Co., Inc.**

Rebecca's Bks., *(978-0-9744346)* P.O. Box 644, Watertown, WI 53094 USA.

Rebel Girls *Imprint of* **Timbuktu Labs, inc.**

Rebel Press *See* **Little Dixie Publishing Co.**

Rebel Redd Bks., *(978-0-9984228)* 2807 Doralane, Dodge City, KS 67801 USA Tel 620-682-5070
E-mail: rebelreddbooks@outlook.com

Rebel Satori Pr., *(978-0-9790838; 978-1-60864)* P.O. Box 363, Hulls Cover, ME 04644 USA Fax: 207-669-4200
E-mail: publisher@rebelsatoripress.com
Web site: http://www.rebelsatori.com; http://www.queermojo.net
Dist(s): **Smashwords.**

Rebellion (GBR) *(978-1-904265; 978-1-906735; 978-1-907519; 978-1-84997; 978-1-907992; 978-1-78108; 978-1-78618) Dist. by* **S and S Inc.**

Recipe Pubs., *(978-0-9778057; 978-0-9816282; 978-0-9824801; 978-0-9826424; 978-0-9828531; 978-0-9898137)* Orders Addr.: 610 N. Elmwood Ave, Springfield, MO 65802 USA (SAN 930-8873) Tel 417-619-4939; Toll Free: 800-313-5121
E-mail: jec1963@sbcglobal.net; jec@recipepubs.com
Web site: http://www.recipepubs.com.

Recirculation Art, *(978-0-692-11283-0)* 28 K St. SE, Washington, DC 20003 USA Tel 631-664-2277
E-mail: Recirculationart@gmail.com
Web site: www.recirculationart.com.

Reclam, Philip jun., Verlag GmbH (DEU) *(978-3-15) Dist. by* **Intl Bk Import.**

Record Stockman & Coyote Cowboy *See* **Coyote Cowboy Co.**

Recorded Bks., Inc., *(978-0-7887; 978-1-55690; 978-1-84197; 978-1-4025; 978-1-4193; 978-1-84505; 978-1-4281; 978-1-4361; 978-1-4407; 978-1-4498; 978-1-4561; 978-1-4618; 978-1-4640; 978-1-4703; 978-1-4906; 978-1-5019; 978-1-9800; 978-1-7050)* Subs. of W. F. Howes Limited, Orders Addr.: 270 Skipjack Rd., Prince Frederick, MD 20678 USA (SAN 111-3984) Fax: 410-535-5499; Toll Free: 800-638-1304; 7257 Pkwy. Dr., Hanover, MD 21076 (SAN 920-7414)
E-mail: thelvey@recordedbooks.com
Web site: http://www.rbdigital.com
Dist(s): **Brilliance Publishing, Inc.**
Ebsco Publishing
Follett School Solutions
Ingram Publisher Services.

Recorded Books, LLC *See* **Recorded Bks., Inc.**

Rector Pr., Ltd., *(978-0-7605; 978-0-934393; 978-1-57205)* Orders Addr.: The Ledge House 130 Rattlesnake Gutter Rd. Suite 1000, Leverett, MA 01054-9726 USA (SAN 693-8108) Tel 413-367-0303 (International Book Sales); Fax: 413-367-2853
E-mail: info@rectorpress.com; info@runanywhere.com
Web site: http://www.rectorpress.com; http://twitter.com/Lewisxxxusa; http://twitter.com/Rectorpress.

Rector Tales, *(978-0-9969085)* 22154 Barrington Way, Santa Clarita, CA 91350 USA Tel 661-449-9103
E-mail: cuffsbyrector@gmail.com
Web site: RectorTales.com.

Red 5 Comics (CAN) *(978-0-9809302) Dist. by* **D C D.**

Red & Black Pubs., *(978-0-9791813; 978-1-934941; 978-1-61001)* P.O. Box 7542, Saint Petersburg, FL 33734 USA
E-mail: info@redandblackpublishers.com
Web site: http://www.redandblackpublishers.com.

Red Barn Reading Inc., *(978-0-9753059)* P.O. Box 540, Alanson, MI 49706 USA
E-mail: thecathy@tm.net.

Red Brick Learning *Imprint of* **Capstone**

Red Bud Publishing, *(978-0-9759421)* 2425 Lakeshore Ct., Lebanon, IN 46052 USA.

Red CalacArts Publications *Imprint of* **Calaca Pr.**

Red Carpet Publishing, *(978-0-9719657; 978-0-9722829)* P.O. Box 309, Noblesville, IN 46061-0309 USA (SAN 255-755X) Tel 317-847-9553; Fax: 317-773-5375
Web site: http://www.redcarpetpublishing.com.

Red Chair Pr., *(978-1-936163; 978-1-937529; 978-1-939656; 978-1-63440; 978-1-947159; 978-1-64371)* P.O. Box 333, South Egremont, MA 01258 USA (SAN 858-6209); *Imprints:* Rocking Chair Kids (Rocking Chair Kids); One Elm Books (One Elm Bks)
E-mail: redchairpress@gmail.com; info@redchairpress.com
Web site: http://www.redchairpress.com; http://www.lernerbooks.com
Dist(s): **Follett School Solutions**
Lerner Publishing Group
MyiLibrary.

RED CLAY / Young Pubs. Global Network, *(978-0-9795370)* P.O. Box 4221, Greenville, MS 38704 USA Tel 662-773-2048
E-mail: YPGNtwk@peoplepc.com
Web site: http://www.ypgn.net.

†Red Crane Bks., Inc., *(978-1-878610)* Orders Addr.: P.O. Box 33590, Santa Fe, NM 87954 USA; Edit Addr.: 2008 Rosina St., Suite C, Santa Fe, NM 87505 USA Tel 505-988-7070; Fax: 505-989-7476; Toll Free: 800-922-3392
E-mail: publish@redcrane.com
Web site: http://www.redcrane.com
Dist(s): **Chicago Distribution Ctr.**
Continental Bk. Co., Inc.
Libros Sin Fronteras; *CIP.*

Red Cygnet Pr., *(978-1-60108)* 2245 Enterprise St. Ste. 110, Escondido, CA 92029-2060 USA; *Imprints:* Bearing Books (Bearing Bks)
E-mail: info@redcygnet.com
Web site: http://www.redcygnet.com
Dist(s): **Rosen Publishing Group, Inc., The**
Soundprints.

Red Deer Pr. (CAN) *(978-0-88995) Dist. by* **IngramPubServ.**

Red Deer Pr. (CAN) *(978-0-88995) Dist. by* **Firefly Bks Limited.**

Red Door Pr., *(978-0-9763770)* 1704 Black Oak Ln., Silver Spring, MD 20910 USA Tel 301-588-7599; Fax: 301-838-9771 Do not confuse with Red Door Press in San Francisco, CA
E-mail: trishbaur@comcast.net.

Red Earth Publishing, *(978-0-9767748)* Orders Addr.: 104 Candace Dr., Ponca City, OK 74604 USA Tel 580-763-7003
E-mail: deborahjuckes@gmail.com
Web site: http://www.redearthpub.com.

Red Earth Publishing, *(978-0-9779993)* 2041 NW 20th St., Oklahoma City, OK 73106-1609 USA.

Red Engine Pr., *(978-0-9663276; 978-0-9743758; 978-0-9745652; 978-0-9785158; 978-0-9800064; 978-0-9800332; 978-0-9827923; 978-0-9834930; 978-1-937958; 978-1-943267)* 18942 State Hwy. 13, Suite F107, Branson West, MO 65737 USA Tel 417-230-5555
E-mail: riverroadpress@yahoo.com
Web site: http://www.redenginepress.com.

Red Feather *Imprint of* **Schiffer Publishing, Ltd.**

Red Fox Publishing, *(978-0-692-78504-1; 978-0-692-78506-5)* 19706 N Ramsey Rd, Rathdrum, ID 83858 USA Tel 208-709-7762.

Red Giant Entertainment *Imprint of* **Active Media Publishing, LLC**

Red Giant Publishing, *(978-0-9767661)* P.O. Box 5, San Mateo, CA 94401 USA
E-mail: questions@redgiantpublishing.com
Web site: http://www.redgiantpublishing.com.

Red Hawk Bks., *(978-0-9892851)* 12903 Pt. Richmond Dr., Gig Harbor, WA 98332 USA Tel 253-858-8794; Fax: 253-858-8795
E-mail: torreylystra@gmail.com.

Red Hawk Pr., *(978-0-9971488)* P.O. Box 1083, Bartlesville, OK 74005 USA Tel 918-440-2832
E-mail: marykincaid2001@yahoo.com
Web site: http://marytkincaidauthor.com/.

†Red Hen Pr., *(978-0-931093)* P.O. Box 454, Big Sur, CA 93920 USA (SAN 678-9420) Tel 831-667-2726 (phone/fax) Do not confuse with Red Hen Pr. in Casa Grande, AZ, Granada Hills, CA
E-mail: HopeHen@aol.com
Dist(s): **Book Wholesalers, Inc.**
Brodart Co.
Follett School Solutions; *CIP.*

Red Hen Pr., *(978-1-888996; 978-1-59709; 978-0-9890361; 978-1-63628)* P.O. Box 3537, Granada Hills, CA 91394 USA Tel 818-831-0649; Fax: 818-831-6659
E-mail: editors@redhen.org
Web site: http://www.redhen.org
Dist(s): **Chicago Distribution Ctr.**
Ingram Publisher Services
Mintright, Inc.
SPD-Small Pr. Distribution
Valentine Publishing Group.

Red Hills Writers Project, *(978-0-9759339)* 1509 Hasosaw Nene, Tallahassee, FL 32301 USA Tel 850-216-2016; Fax: 831-308-3285
E-mail: info@redhillswritersproject.org
Web site: http://www.redhillswritersproject.org.

Red Ink Pr., *(978-0-9788401)* 1914 N. Roan St., Suite 106-223, Johnson City, TN 37601 USA (SAN 851-724X) Tel 423-741-2835
Web site: http://www.redinkpress.com
Dist(s): **Book Hub, Inc.**

Red Jacket Pr., *(978-0-9748895)* 3099 Maqua Pl., Mohegan Lake, NY 10547-1054 USA
E-mail: info@redjacketpress.com
Web site: http://www.redjacketpress.com
Dist(s): **Pathway Bk. Service.**

Red Letter Pr., *(978-0-9661199; 978-0-9794420; 978-0-692-43517-5)* Orders Addr.: 6148 Rutledge Hill, Columbia, SC 29209-1315 USA Tel 843-344-2221 Do not confuse with Red Letter Pr., Seattle, WA
E-mail: redletterpress@gmail.com
Web site: http://redletterpress.googlepages.com
Dist(s): **CreateSpace Independent Publishing Platform.**

Red Letter Publishing & Media Group, *(978-0-9740003)* 1015 Newport Harbor, Schaumburg, IL 60193 USA Tel 630-728-6046
E-mail: screenwriter1914@gmail.com.

Red Men Interprises, *(978-0-9744682)* 8 Boton Rd., Lloyd Harbor, NY 11743 USA Tel 516-769-9720
E-mail: jason@drugfreeteen.com
Web site: http://www.drugfreeteen.com.

Red Mitten Bks., LLC, *(978-1-7333034)* 4222 W Bay View Ave, Tampa, FL 33611 USA Tel 813-758-2298
E-mail: barbara.escher@gmail.com
Web site: http://redmittenbooks.com.

Red Mountain Creations, *(978-0-9759858; 978-0-9910804; 978-1-7345037)* P.O. Box 172, High Ridge, MO 63049 USA Tel 636-677-3088; Toll Free: 866-732-4857
E-mail: redmountain@swbell.net
Web site: http://www.byronvonrosenberg.com.

Red Mud Pr., *(978-0-9672996)* Orders Addr.: P.O. Box 1257, Sedona, AZ 86336-4357 USA Tel 520-282-5285; Edit Addr.: 51 Remuda Rd., Sedona, AZ 86336 USA
E-mail: Crawford@sedona.net.

Red Owl Pubns., *(978-0-9754279)* 7857 Sedgewick Dr., Freeland, MI 48623 USA Tel 989-737-4486
E-mail: ckblack@redowlpublications.com
Dist(s): **MyiLibrary.**

Red Penguin Bks., *(978-0-9997460; 978-1-949864; 978-1-952859)* 27 Ontario Rd., Bellerose Village, NY 11001 USA Tel 516-448-4993; Fax: 516-740-5899
E-mail: stephanie@redpenguinbooks.com
Web site: http://redpenguinbooks.com.

Blue Phoenix Bks., *(978-0-9726290; 978-1-937781; 978-1-938969)* 809 W. Dike St., Glendora, CA 91740 USA
E-mail: Service@redphoenixbooks.com; cja@redphoenixbooks.com; claudia.alexander@gmail.com
Web site: http://www.redphoenixbooks.com
Dist(s): **Partners Pubs. Group, Inc.**

Red Planet Pictures, *(978-0-9719031)* 1800 S. Robertson Blvd., No. 153, Los Angeles, CA 90035 USA Tel 310-659-8386 (phone/fax)
E-mail: markm@laube.com
Dist(s): **Consortium Bk. Sales & Distribution.**

Red Poppy Pr., *(978-0-9778249)* 30524 Sparrow Hawk Dr., Canyon Lake, CA 92587 USA
E-mail: dharlenemarie@redpoppypress.co
Web site: http://https://www.dharlenemariefahl.com; http://https://www.redpoppypress.com.

Red Pumpkin Pr., *(978-0-9711572; 978-0-9849284)* P.O. Box 40, Rutledge, TN 37861 USA Tel 865-828-3362; Fax: 865-828-4578
E-mail: centar123@aol.com.

Red River Pr. *Imprint of* **Red River Pr.**

Red River Pr., *(978-0-910653)* 3900 Roy Rd., Suite 37, Shreveport, LA 71107 USA (SAN 270-1774) Fax: 318-309-1653; *Imprints:* Red River Press (Red River Pr)
E-mail: rrp_asi@Bellsouth.net
Web site: http://www.ArchivalServicesInc.com.

Red Rock Mountain Pr. LLC, *(978-0-615-30253-9; 978-0-615-40473-8; 978-0-615-73121-6; 978-0-578-55760-1; 978-0-578-55761-8)* 560 Schnebly Rd., Sedona, AZ 86336 USA.

Red Rock Pr., Inc., *(978-0-9669573; 978-0-9714372; 978-1-933176)* 331 W. 57th. Street, suite 175, New York, NY 10019 USA Tel 212-362-8304; Fax: 212-362-6216; Toll Free: 800-488-8040
E-mail: richard@redrockpress.com
Web site: http://www.redrockpress.com
Dist(s): **MyiLibrary.**

Red Sage Publishing, *(978-0-9648942; 978-0-9754516; 978-1-60310)* Div. of Red Sage Publishing, Inc., P.O. Box 4844, Seminole, FL 33775 USA (SAN 859-0249) Tel 727-391-3847 (phone/fax)
E-mail: alekendall@aol.com
Web site: http://www.eRedSage.com
Dist(s): **Brodart Co.**
Cowley Distributing, Inc.
OverDrive, Inc.

Red Sky Presents, *(978-1-941015)*
E-mail: redskypresents@gmail.com
Web site: www.redskypresents.com.

Red Summit Pubs., *(978-0-615-76924-0; 978-1-944650)* 40538 Calla Lilly St., Murrieta, CA 92629 USA Tel 949-246-0980
E-mail: swoffingtonliterary@gmail.com
Web site: swoffington.com
Dist(s): **CreateSpace Independent Publishing Platform.**

Red Tail Publishing, *(978-0-9635757; 978-0-9847756; 978-1-941950)* Orders Addr.: P.O. Box 1477, Anderson, CA 96007 USA Tel 530-365-5863
E-mail: livingston@redtail.com; info@redtail.com
Web site: http://www.redtail.com.

Red Team Ink, *(978-0-9982349; 978-0-9984881; 978-1-7322129)* 9480 W. River Beach Ln., Boise, ID 83714 USA Tel 208-870-8359; Fax: 208-870-8359
E-mail: Redteamink@gmail.com
Web site: www.redteamink.com.

Red Truck LLC, *(978-0-615-73703-4; 978-0-578-51086-6)* 6568 Finch Ct., Fort Collins, CO 80525 USA Tel 970-215-4191
E-mail: jimcampain@comcast.net.

Red Wagon *See* **Magic Wagon**

Red Wagon Bks. *Imprint of* **Harcourt Children's Bks.**

†Red Wheel/Weiser, *(978-0-87728; 978-0-943233; 978-1-56414; 978-1-57324; 978-1-57863; 978-1-59003; 978-1-60163; 978-1-60925; 978-1-61283; 978-1-61852; 978-1-61940; 978-1-938875; 978-1-63265; 978-1-63341; 978-1-942785; 978-1-64297; 978-0-692-19811-7; 978-1-953650* Div. of Weiser Bks., Orders Addr.: 65 Parker St., Suite 7, Newburyport, MA 01950 USA (SAN 255-8610) Tel 978-465-0504; Fax: 978-465-0243; Toll Free Fax: 877-337-3309; Toll Free: 800-423-7087 (orders only); *Imprints:* New Page Books (New Page Bks); Career Press (CareerPr)
E-mail: customerservice@redwheelweiser.com
Web site: http://www.redwheelweiser.com
Dist(s): **Abyss Distribution**
D.A.P./Distributed Art Pubs.
Ebsco Publishing
Ingram Publisher Services
New Leaf Distributing Co., Inc.
Open Road Integrated Media, Inc.; *CIP.*

Redback Publishing (AUS) *(978-0-9946247; 978-1-925630; 978-1-925860; 978-1-922322) Dist. by* **IPG Chicago.**

Redcay Publishing, *(978-0-615-17346-7)* 2953 Grandview Blvd ., West LAwn, PA 19609 USA Tel 610-678-5636
E-mail: mwkreitz@msn.com
Web site: http://www.divcothelittlemilktruck.com.

Redding, Marion T., *(978-0-9671701)* Orders Addr.: 684 Chaloupe St. SE., Palm Bay, FL 32909-4433 USA (SAN 254-4024) Tel 740-369-4952
E-mail: starbourne53@mac.com; marionredding@icloud.com
Web site: http://www.davidredding.net.

Redding Pr., *(978-0-9658879)* Orders Addr.: c/o Mary Mahony, P.O. Box 366, Belmont, MA 02178 USA Fax: 617-489-9476; Toll Free: 800-267-6012; Edit Addr.: P.O. Box 366, Belmont, MA 02178 USA
E-mail: mary@reddingpress.com
Web site: http://www.channel.com/users/msmahony; http://www.reddingpress.com
Dist(s): **Quality Bks., Inc.**

Redel, Nicole, *(978-0-9769738)* 2125 David Dr., Florissant, MO 63031-4321 USA Tel 314-839-3242
E-mail: gospelpitbull@sbcglobal.net
Web site: http://www.gospelpitbull.com.

Redemption Pr., *(978-1-63232; 978-1-68314; 978-1-7329625; 978-1-64645; 978-1-951310; 978-1-951350)* 1730 Railroad St., Enumclaw, WA 98022 USA Tel 360-226-3488; Toll Free Fax: 855-498-6595; Toll Free: 888-305-2967; P.O. Box 427, Enumclaw, WA 98022 Tel 360-226-3488; Toll Free: 844-273-3336; *Imprints:* Reliant Publishing (MYID_A_RELIANT)
E-mail: accounting@redemption-press.com
Web site: www.redemption-press.com
Dist(s): **Spring Arbor Distributors, Inc.**

Redhawk Publishing, *(978-0-9641861; 978-0-9769267)* Orders Addr.: 602 Pompa St., Carlsbad, NM 88220 USA Tel 505-885-1748; *Imprints:* RWP Books (RWP Bks)
E-mail: randy@rwpbooks.com
Web site: http://www.rwpbooks.com
Dist(s): **CreateSpace Independent Publishing Platform.**

RedJack *See* **Mutaneers**

Redleaf Pr., *(978-0-934140; 978-1-884834; 978-1-929610; 978-1-933653; 978-1-60554)* Div. of Resources for Child Caring, Inc., 10 Yorkton Ct., Saint Paul, MN 55117-1065 USA (SAN 212-8691) Toll Free Fax: 800-641-0115; Toll Free: 800-423-8309
E-mail: sales@redleafpress.org
Web site: http://www.redleafpress.org
Dist(s): **Capstone**
Consortium Bk. Sales & Distribution
Gryphon Hse., Inc.
Lectorum Pubns., Inc.
MyiLibrary.

Redline Bks., *(978-0-9727440)* 2280 Jones Creek Rd., White Bluff, TN 37187 USA Tel 615-797-3043 (phone/fax)
E-mail: redlinebooks@bardyoung.com; bardyoung@bardyoung.com.

RedMEDIA, *(978-0-9721708)* 41 Schermerhorn St., No. 147, Brooklyn, NY 11201 USA Tel 718-857-6638; Fax: 718-857-6427
E-mail: rmedia3@aol.com
Web site: http://www.tgoodlife.com; http://www.ibrooklyn.com/redmedia.

Redmond, Pamela, *(978-0-9760767)* P.O. Box 169, Topping, VA 23169-0169 USA.

Reece, Kim Taylor Prodns. LLC, *(978-0-9660395; 978-1-59779)* 53-866 Kamehameha Hwy., Hauula, HI 96717 USA Tel 808-293-2000; Fax: 808-293-2136; Toll Free: 800-657-7966
E-mail: info@kimtaylorreece.com
Web site: http://www.kimtaylorreece.com
Dist(s): **Booklines Hawaii, Ltd.**
Islander Group.

Reed Business Information, *(978-0-9614276; 978-1-879930; 978-1-931625; 978-0-9764027; 978-0-9851869)* 5900 Wilshire Blvd. Ste. 3100, Los Angeles, CA 90036-5030 USA (SAN 687-3944) Toll Free: 800-545-2411
E-mail: nlongman@reedbusiness.com; steve.atinsky@reedbusiness.com
Web site: http://www.la411.com
Dist(s): **SCB Distributors.**

Reed, Robert D. Pubs., *(978-1-885003; 978-1-931741; 978-1-934759; 978-1-944297)* P.O. Box 1992, Bandon, OR 97411 USA Tel 541-347-9882; Fax: 541-347-9883
E-mail: 4bobreed@msn.com
Web site: http://www.rdrpublishers.com
Dist(s): **Independent Pubs. Group**
Midpoint Trade Bks., Inc.
Todd Communications.

Reedale Karma Pr., *(978-0-615-67492-6; 978-0-615-90362-0; 978-0-692-88606-9; 978-0-692-09330-6; 978-0-692-13563-1)* 52 Timarron Trail, Rochester, NY 14612 USA Tel 585-368-0383
Dist(s): **CreateSpace Independent Publishing Platform.**

Reedswain, Inc., *(978-0-9651020; 978-1-890946; 978-1-59164)* Orders Addr.: 88 Wells Rd., Spring City, PA 19475-8628 USA Toll Free: 800-331-5191
E-mail: bryan@reedswain.com
Web site: http://www.reedswain.com
Dist(s): **Cardinal Pubs. Group.**

Publisher Name Index

Reedy Pr., (*978-0-9753180; 978-1-933370; 978-1-935806; 978-1-68106*) Orders Addr.: P.O. Box 5131, Saint Louis, MO 63139 USA Toll Free Fax: 866-999-6916 fax
E-mail: jstevens@reedypress.com; dkorte@reedypress.com
Web site: http://www.reedypress.com
Dist(s): **Partners Bk. Distributing, Inc.**

Reel Productions, LLC, (*978-0-9675010; 978-0-9707422*) P.O. Box 1069, Monument, CO 80132 USA Toll Free: 800-964-0439
E-mail: support@reelproductions.net; jolene@explorationfilms.com
Web site: http://www.explorationfilms.com; http://www.reelproductions.net
Dist(s): **Exploration Films**
Send The Light Distribution LLC.

Reeves Bay Press, (*978-0-9860833*) 17 Huntington Lane, Flanders, NY 11901 USA.

Reeves, Emily, (*978-0-9821506*) P.O. Box 15861, Savannah, GA 31416 USA.

Reference Service Pr., (*978-0-918276; 978-1-58841*) 5000 Windplay Dr., Suite 4, El Dorado Hills, CA 95762 USA (SAN 210-2633) Tel 916-939-9620; Fax: 916-939-9626
E-mail: findaid@aol.com; info@rspfunding.com
Web site: http://www.rspfunding.com.

ReferencePoint Pr., Inc., (*978-1-60152; 978-1-68282; 978-1-6782*) P.O. Box 27779, San Diego, CA 92198 USA (SAN 858-6845) Tel 858-618-1314; Fax: 858-618-1730; Toll Free: 888-479-6436; 17150 Via Del Campo. Ste. 205, San Diego, CA 92127-2138; *Imprints*: BrightPoint Press (MYID_J_BRIGHTP)
E-mail: dan@referencepointpress.com; orders@referencepointpress.com; info@referencepointpress.com
Web site: http://www.referencepointdigital.com; http://www.brightpointpress.com; http://www.referencepointpress.com.

Refined Savage Editions / Ediciones El Salvaje Refinado, The, (*978-0-9713175; 978-0-9746855; 978-0-9761940; 978-0-9768868; 978-0-9791011; 978-0-9802008; 978-0-9816968*) 10 Delaware Ave., Charleston, WV 25302-1950 USA
E-mail: esrefinado@aol.com
Web site: http://www.esrefinado.net.

Reflection Pr., (*978-0-9843799; 978-1-945289*) 3543 18th St., Ste 17, San Francisco, CA 94110 USA
E-mail: info@reflectionpress.com; manager@reflectionpress.com
Web site: http://www.reflectionpress.com.

Reflection Pr., (*978-0-9671543*) 3430 W. 98th Pl. Unit A, Westminster, CO 80031 USA Tel 303-862-4868 Do not confuse with companies with the same name in Huntsville, AL, Berkeley, CA
E-mail: mbsmith48@gmail.com.

Reflection Publishing, (*978-0-9797618; 978-1-936629*) P.O. Box 2182, Citrus Heights, CA 95621-2182 USA Fax: 916-726-2768
E-mail: contact@reflectpublishing.com
Web site: http://www.reflectpublishing.com.

Reflection Publishing Company *See* **Imprints**

Reflection Publishing Co., (*978-0-9657561; 978-0-9712142*) 1813 4th St W., Palmetto, FL 34221-4303 USA (SAN 299-2787) Toll Free: 888-677-0101
E-mail: lakepm@msn.com
Web site: http://www.reflectionpublishing.com
Dist(s): **Brodart Co.**
Spring Arbor Distributors, Inc.

Reflections Publishing Hse., (*978-0-9837231; 978-0-9965296*) 925 N. Inglewood Ave No. 10, Inglewood, CA 90302 USA Tel 310-695-9800
E-mail: dabellis@sbcglobal.net
Web site: www.reflectionspublishings.net.

Reflections Publishing, Incorporated *See* **GFC Pr.**

Reformation Herald Publishing Assn., (*978-0-9745295; 978-1-934308*) P.O. Box 7240, Roanoke, VA 24019-0240 USA
Web site: http://www.sdarm.org.

Reformation Heritage Bks., (*978-1-892777; 978-1-60178*) 2965 Leonard St., NE, Grand Rapids, MI 49525-5828 USA
E-mail: jay.collier@heritagebooks.org
Web site: http://www.heritagebooks.org
Dist(s): **Send The Light Distribution LLC**
christianaudio.

Reformation Trust Publishing *Imprint of* **Ligonier Ministries**

Reformed Church Pr., Reformed Church in America, (*978-0-916466*) 4500 60th St., SE, Grand Rapids, MI 49512-9670 USA Tel 616-698-7071; Fax: 616-698-6606; Toll Free: 800-968-7221 (orders); 475 Riverside Dr., 18th Flr., New York, NY 10115 (SAN 207-4508)
Dist(s): **Faith Alive Christian Resources.**

Reformed Free Publishing Assn., (*978-0-916206; 978-1-936054; 978-1-944555*) Orders Addr.: 1894 Georgetown Ctr. Dr., Jenison, MI 49428-7137 USA Tel 616-457-5970
E-mail: mail@rfpa.org
Web site: http://www.rfpa.org.

Refugee Pr., (*978-0-692-43628-8; 978-0-692-88712-7; 978-0-692-95136-1; 978-0-578-48744-1; 978-0-578-48745-8; 978-0-578-60339-1*) 2511 Buck Quarter Farm Rd., Hillsborough, NC 27278 USA Tel 919 625-4502
Dist(s): **CreateSpace Independent Publishing Platform.**

Regal Bks. *Imprint of* **Gospel Light Pubns.**

Regal Enterprises, (*978-0-9727771; 978-0-9729960*) 16310 Garfield Ave., Paramount, CA 90723-4806 USA (SAN 255-2477)
Dist(s): **Timberwolf Pr., Inc.**

Regal Hse. Publishing, LLC, (*978-0-9912612; 978-0-9988398; 978-1-947548; 978-1-64603*) 4718 Longhill Ln., Raleigh, NC 27612 USA Tel 919-931-7044; *Imprints*: Fitzroy Books (MYID_F_FITZROY)
E-mail: info@regalhousepublishing.com; editor@regalhousepublishing.com
Web site: www.pactpress.com; www.fitzroybooks.com; https://regalhousepublishing.com
Dist(s): **Independent Pubs. Group.**

ReganBooks *Imprint of* **HarperCollins Pubs.**

Regency Hse., Ltd., (*978-0-9716923*) 6538 Pardee, Taylor, MI 48180-1771 USA Tel 313-291-9242
Dist(s): **Baker & Taylor Publisher Services (BTPS).**

Regenold Publishing, (*978-0-9773085*) P.O. Box 621967, Littleton, CO 80162-1967 USA (SAN 257-2583) Tel 303-797-8881
Web site: http://www.regenoldpublishing.com.

Regent Pr., (*978-0-916147; 978-1-889059; 978-1-58790*) 2747 Regent St., Berkeley, CA 94705-1212 USA (SAN 294-9717) Tel 510-845-1196 Do not confuse with Regent Pr., Oxnard, CA
E-mail: regentpress@mindspring.com
Web site: http://www.regentpress.net
Dist(s): **Ingram Content Group.**

Regina Orthodox Pr., (*978-0-9649141; 978-1-928653*) Orders Addr.: P.O. Box 5288, Salisbury, MA 01952 USA Fax: 978-462-5079; Toll Free: 800-636-2470; Edit Addr.: 6 Second St., Salisbury, MA 01952 USA
E-mail: reginaorthodoxpress@comcast.net
Web site: http://www.reginaorthodoxpress.com
Dist(s): **National Bk. Network.**

Regina Pr., Malhame & Co., (*978-0-88271*) Orders Addr.: P.O. Box 608, Melville, NY 11747-0608 USA (SAN 203-0853) Tel 631-694-8600; Edit Addr.: 10 Hub Dr., Melville, NY 11747 USA
E-mail: customerservice@malhame.com
Web site: http://www.malhame.com/
Dist(s): **Catholic Bk. Publishing Corp.**

Reginetta Pr., LLC, (*978-0-9823714*) P.O. Box 7042, Aurora, IL 60507 USA
Web site: http://www.HookandJill.com; http://www.ReginettaPress.com
Dist(s): **New Leaf Distributing Co., Inc.**

Region 4 Education Service Ctr., (*978-1-932524; 978-1-932797; 978-1-933049; 978-1-933521; 978-1-934950; 978-1-937403; 978-1-945615; 978-1-950577*) 7145 W. Tidwell, Houston, TX 77092-2096 USA Tel 713-462-7708; Fax: 713-744-6514
E-mail: daniesha.debose@esc4.net
Web site: http://www.esc4.net
Dist(s): **Consortium Bk. Sales & Distribution.**

Region IV Education Service Center *See* **Region 4 Education Service Ctr.**

Regional Laboratory for Educational Improvement of the Northeast & Islands *See* **NETWORK Inc., The**

Regnery Gateway, Incorporated *See* **Regnery Publishing, Inc., An Eagle Publishing Co.**

Regnery Kids *Imprint of* **Regnery Publishing, Inc., An Eagle Publishing Co.**

†**Regnery Publishing, Inc., An Eagle Publishing Co.**, (*978-0-89526; 978-1-59698; 978-1-62157; 978-1-68451*) Div. of Caron Broadcasting, Inc., One Massachusetts Ave., NW, Suite 600, Washington, DC 20001 USA (SAN 210-5578) Tel 202-216-0600; *Imprints*: Little Patriot Press (LittlePatriot); Regnery Kids (REGNERY KIDS)
E-mail: sales@regnery.com; matthew.maschino@refnery.com
Web site: http://www.regnery.com
Dist(s): **Continental Bk. Co., Inc.**
Ingram Publisher Services
MyiLibrary
Simon & Schuster, Inc.
Send The Light Distribution LLC
Two Rivers Distribution
ebrary, Inc.; *CIP.*

†**Regular Baptist Pr.**, (*978-0-87227; 978-1-59402; 978-1-60776; 978-1-62940; 978-1-64213*) Div. of General Assn. of Regular Baptist Churches, 1300 N. Meacham Rd., Schaumburg, IL 60173-4806 USA (SAN 205-2229) Tel 847-843-1600 (foreign orders); 708-843-1600; Fax: 847-843-3757; Toll Free: 800-727-4440 (orders only)
E-mail: rbporders@garbc.org
Web site: http://www.regularbaptistpress.org; *CIP.*

Reich, Tina, (*978-1-7343186*) 40 Oleander Ln, Turlock, CA 95380 USA Tel 209-648-2119
E-mail: reichtina320@gmail.com.

Reiki Blessings, (*978-0-9743679*) P.O. Box 2000, Byron, GA 31008-2000 USA (SAN 255-7045) Fax: 801-705-1802
E-mail: reikiblessings@earthlink.net
Web site: http://www.rbpress.com.

Reily Garrett, (*978-0-9989265; 978-1-7339585*) 11400 urieville Ln., Worton, MD 21678 USA Tel 443-480-0639
E-mail: rylankillian@gmail.com
Web site: reilygarrett.com.

Reimann Bks., (*978-0-9820941; 978-0-9838148; 978-0-9852254; 978-1-938743*) Orders Addr.: 305 Parkton Dr, Richlands, NC 28574 USA
E-mail: reimannbooks@gmail.com
Web site: http://www.reimannbooks.com.

Reinoso, Marta, (*978-0-9676203*) World Educational Guild, Inc. 1330 E. 223rd., Suite 501, Carson, CA 90745 USA Tel 310-816-1100; Fax: 310-816-1103
E-mail: wegi@earthnet.com.

Reisman, Dave *See* **Jumping Cow Pr.**

Rejoyce Pubns., (*978-0-9661564*) 5205 Aryshire Dr., Dublin, OH 43017 USA Tel 614-766-2771; Fax: 614-766-1731.

Relationship Resources, Inc., (*978-0-9721728*) P.O. Box 63383, Colorado Springs, CO 80962 USA
E-mail: gaylyn@relationshipresources.org
Web site: http://www.relationshipresources.org
Dist(s): **Send The Light Distribution LLC.**

Relde Publishing, (*978-0-9701863*) Subs. of Solutions Training & Development LLC, P.O. Box 21304, Jackson, MS 39289 USA Tel 601-926-4375; Fax: 601-926-4374; Toll Free: 800-489-3439
E-mail: solut2000@aol.com.

Relentless Publishing Hse., (*978-0-9991975; 978-1-948829*) 136-4 Forum Dr. No. B8, Columbia, SC 29229 USA Tel 803-200-1094
E-mail: info@relentlesspublishing.com
Web site: https://www.relentlesspublishing.com.

Relevant Graces Productions, (*978-0-9822375*) 1044 Cresswood Dr., Richlands, VA 24641 USA.

Relevant Media Group, Inc., (*978-0-9714576; 978-0-9729276; 978-0-9746942; 978-0-9760357; 978-0-9763642; 978-0-9768175; 978-0-9776167; 978-0-9777480*) 1220 Alden Rd., Orlando, FL 32803-2546 USA; 600 Rinehart Rd., Lake Mary, FL 32746
E-mail: nick@relevantmediagroup.com
Web site: http://www.relevantbooks.com/
Dist(s): **Charisma Media.**

Relevant Pages Pr., (*978-0-615-82759-9; 978-0-615-87121-9; 978-0-692-31475-3; 978-0-692-50308-9; 978-0-692-56515-5; 978-0-692-58351-7; 978-0-692-58360-9; 978-0-692-58792-8; 978-0-692-64319-8; 978-0-9982211; 978-1-947303*) 3301 Heathland Way, Mt. Pleasant, SC 29466 USA Tel 843-813-0172
Web site: www.narthexacademyseries.com
Dist(s): **CreateSpace Independent Publishing Platform.**

Relevant Ventures, LLC, (*978-0-9760259*) 4279 Roswell Rd., Suite 102-273, Atlanta, GA 30342-4145 USA (SAN 256-4483) Tel 404-842-1930; Fax: 404-842-1021
E-mail: td3@mac.com; tom@relevantventures.com
Web site: http://www.relevantventures.com.

Reliant Energy, (*978-0-9791383*) 1000 Main St., Houston, TX 77002 USA
E-mail: jmolholt@reliant.com.

Reliant Publishing *Imprint of* **Redemption Pr.**

Religion Res. Institute, (*978-0-9765024; 978-0-578-41422-5; 978-0-578-67382-0*) P.O. Box 7505, Prospect Heights, IL 60070 USA Tel 773-396-0147
E-mail: info@religionresearchinstitute.org
Web site: http://www.religionresearchinstitute.org.

Reluctant Reader Bks. *Imprint of* **Cronus College**

Remarco Publishing, (*978-0-9770762*) P.O. Box 644, Ames, IA 50010 USA (SAN 256-6958) Tel 515-203-0358
Web site: http://www.remarcopublishing.com.

RemarkableMe, (*978-0-9776642*) 3905 W 10260 N, CEDAR HILLS, UT 84062 USA Tel 801-796-6486; Fax: 801-796-6486
E-mail: charless@utahweb.com
Web site: http://www.remarkableme.com.

Remedia Pubns., (*978-1-56175; 978-1-59639; 978-1-61394; 978-1-949581; 978-1-64807*) 15887 N. 76th St., Suite 120, Scottsdale, AZ 85260-1696 USA Tel 602-661-9900; Fax: 602-661-9901; Toll Free: 800-826-4740
E-mail: christina@rempub.com; Becky@rempub.com
Web site: http://www.rempub.com.

Remey, Lisa, (*978-0-9855445*) PSC 2 Box 6496, APO, AE 85718 USA
E-mail: rlremey@aol.com.

Reminders Of Faith, Inc., (*978-0-9748160; 978-0-9763691*) 518 Overhead Dr., Moon Township, PA 15108 USA Fax: 412-264-7857
E-mail: kathyb@remindersoffaith.com
Dist(s): **Send The Light Distribution LLC.**

Remnant Pubns., Inc., (*978-1-883012; 978-1-933291; 978-0-9777445; 978-1-937718; 978-1-62913*) Orders Addr.: 649 E. Chicago Rd., Coldwater, MI 49036-9497 USA Tel 517-279-1304 (ext. 23); Fax: 517-279-1804; Toll Free: 800-423-1319
Web site: http://www.remnantpublications.com.

RemStar Ink, (*978-0-9988791*) 5209 Melvin Ave., Tarzana, CA 91356 USA Tel 818-977-3023
E-mail: remace@yahoo.com.

Renaissance Books *See* **New Millennium Bks.**

Renaissance Learning, Inc., (*978-0-9646404; 978-1-893751; 978-0-9708138; 978-1-931731; 978-1-931819; 978-1-932299; 978-1-59455*) 2911 Peach St., Wisconsin Rapids, WI 54494 USA Tel 715-424-3636; Toll Free: 800-338-4204; P.O. Box 8036, Wisconsin Rapids, WI 54495-8036
E-mail: answers@renlearn.com
Web site: http://www.renlearn.com.

Renaissance Printing *See* **Bookends Pr.**

Renaissance Pubns., (*978-1-929473*) Div. of Mission Renaissance, 5744 San Fernando Rd., Glendale, CA 91202-2104 USA Toll Free: 800-430-4278 Do not confuse with Renaissance Publications, Worthington, OH .

Renegado Pr., The, (*978-0-9754616*) Orders Addr.: 29 Lynn Way, Indiana, PA 15701 USA Tel 724-388-3958
E-mail: mackelly@renegadopress.com
Web site: http://www.theavatarthenovel.com.

Reney Editions, Inc., (*978-0-9752688*) 35 Sands Brook Dr., New Hemstead, NY 10977 USA Tel 845-548-4029
E-mail: ethan@reney.com
Web site: http://www.reney.com.

Renner Writes, (*978-0-9990586; 978-1-7357351*) 1111 E Le Marche Ave, Phoenix, AZ 85022 USA Tel 602-228-7451
E-mail: barb.renner@gmail.com
Web site: www.rennerwrites.com.

Rennie Road Books *See* **Tuxbury Publishing LLC**

Renovo Partners LLC, (*978-1-935310*) 8220 Jones Rd., Suite 100, Houston, TX 77065-5375 USA (SAN 857-1163) Tel 281-677-9568; Fax: 281-677-9480; Toll Free: 877-773-6686
E-mail: customers@renovopartners.com; barhorw@nationwide.com
Web site: http://www.renovopartners.com.

Repko, Marya *See* **ECity Publishing**

Repressed Publishing LLC, (*978-1-4622; 978-1-5042; 978-1-5222*) P.O. Box 1242, Provo, UT 84603 USA; 223 W. Bulldog Blvd., Number 420, Provo, UT 84604 Tel 385-204-4408
E-mail: orders@repressedpublishing; customerservice@repressedpublishing.com
Web site: http://www.repressedpublishing.com/.

†**Reprint Services Corp.**, (*978-0-7812; 978-0-932051; 978-1-4227*) P.O. Box 130, Murrieta, CA 92564-0130 USA (SAN 686-2640) Fax: 951-699-5065
E-mail: Reprintservices@gmail.com; *CIP.*

Requiem Pr., (*978-0-9758542; 978-0-9788687*) Orders Addr.: 3271 Timrod Rd., Bethune, SC 29009 USA Toll Free: 888-708-7675; P.O. Box 7, Bethune, SC 29009 Tel 843-334-6222; Toll Free: 888-708-7675
E-mail: info@requiempress.com
Web site: http://www.requiempress.com.

Research & Education Assn., (*978-0-7386; 978-0-87891*) Div. of Courier Corporation, Orders Addr.: 61 Ethel Rd., W., Piscataway, NJ 08854 USA (SAN 204-6814) Tel 732-819-8880; Fax: 732-819-8808; Toll Free: 800-822-0830
E-mail: jcording@rea.com; info@rea.com
Web site: http://www.rea.com
Dist(s): **Dover Pubns., Inc.**
INscribe Digital
Independent Pubs. Group
MyiLibrary.

†**Research Centre of Kabbalah**, (*978-0-924457; 978-0-943688; 978-1-57189; 978-1-7334303; 978-1-952895*) 83-84 115th St., Richmond Hill, NY 11418 USA (SAN 210-9484) Tel 718-805-9122; Fax: 718-805-5899; Toll Free: 888-522-2252
Web site: http://www.kabbalah.com/kabbalah/
Dist(s): **MyiLibrary**; *CIP.*

Research Evaluation & Statistics *See* **Image Cascade Publishing**

Research In Time Publications, (*978-0-9764341*) 101 Hotchkiss Grove Rd., No. 4, Branford, CT 06405 USA
E-mail: raradune@comcast.net.

Research In Time Publishers *See* **Research In Time Publications**

Research Institute Pr., The, (*978-0-9752986*) 5000 Enighed Pmb 356, Saint John, VI 00830 USA Tel 340-998-9597
E-mail: asewer@triinformation.com; info@triinformation.com
Web site: www.triinformation.com.

Research Pr., (*978-0-87822*) Orders Addr.: P.O. Box 7886, Champaign, IL 61826-9177 USA (SAN 282-2490) Toll Free: 800-519-2707; Edit Addr.: 2612 N. Mattis Ave., Champaign, IL 61822 USA (SAN 282-2482) Tel 217-352-3273; Fax: 217-352-1221 Do not confuse with Research Pr., Prairie Village, KS
E-mail: products@researchpress.com; permissions@researchpress.com
Web site: http://www.researchpress.com.

Resolution Pr., (*978-0-9838886; 978-0-9982423-0-9*) 8301 SW 6th Ave., Portland, OR 97219 USA Tel 503-957-5219
E-mail: betsyshand@hotmail.com
Web site: www.survivingnaturaldisastersbook.com
Dist(s): **Baker & Taylor Publisher Services (BTPS).**

Resort Gifts Unlimited, Incorporated *See* **RGU Group, The**

ReSource Guides, Inc., (*978-0-9755370*) 13110 Vista del Mundo, San Antonio, TX 78216-2200 USA Tel 210-493-3974
E-mail: resource@resourceguides.com
Web site: http://www.resourceguides.com.

Resource Pubns., (*978-0-9626281*) Orders Addr.: P.O. Box 42046, Portland, OR 97242 USA; Edit Addr.: 730 SW 16th, Portland, OR 97205 USA Tel 503-228-4844 Do not confuse with Resource Pubns., Searcy, AR.

†**Resource Pubns., Inc.**, (*978-0-89390*) 160 E. Virginia St., No. 290, San Jose, CA 95112-5876 USA (SAN 209-3081) Tel 408-286-8505; Fax: 408-287-8748; Toll Free: 888-273-7782 Do not confuse with Resource Pubns. in Los Angeles, CA
E-mail: info@rpinet.com
Web site: http://www.rpinet.com
Dist(s): **Empire Publishing Service**
Feldheim Pubs.; *CIP.*

Resource Publishing, (*978-0-9706429; 978-0-615-22022-2; 978-0-692-49159-1*) 3736 Brookwood Rd., Birmingham, AL 35223 USA Tel 205-967-3446 Do not confuse company with same or similar name in Greensboro, NC, Baton Rouge, LA, San Francisco, CA
E-mail: hoytwilson1@charter.net.

Resource Pubns.(OR) *Imprint of* **Wipf & Stock Pubs.**

Resources for Children with Special Needs, Inc., (*978-0-9678365; 978-0-9755116*) 116 E. 16th St., 5th Flr., New York, NY 10003 USA
E-mail: dlittwin@resourcesnyc.org
Web site: http://www.resourcesnyc.org.

Resources for Christian Living *See* **RCL Benziger Publishing**

Resources on the Net Publishing, (*978-0-9722803*) 250 32 St., No. 307, Bellingham, WA 98225-0943 USA.

RESPONDER911, Inc., (*978-0-9746186*) 17011 Beach Blvd., Suite No. 900, Huntington Beach, CA 92647 USA Tel 714-375-6693; Fax: 714-375-6694
Web site: http://www.responder911.com.

Responsible Netizen Institute *See* **Ctr. for Safe & Responsible Internet Use**

Restart Enterprises *See* **DGriffith Publishing**

Restless Bks., *(978-0-9899832; 978-1-63206)* 232 3rd St. No. A111, Brooklyn, NY 11215 USA Tel 646-202-9498
E-mail: joshua@restlessbooks.com
Dist(s): **INscribe Digital**
Publishers Group West (PGW)
Simon & Schuster, Inc.

Restore Order Professional Organizeg *See* **Restore Order Professional Organizing**

Restore Order Professional Organizing, *(978-0-692-18566-7)* 6110 Farmwood Way, Mableton, GA 30126 USA Tel 770-744-5970
E-mail: naeemah.fordgoldson@gmail.com
Web site: www.restoreordernow.com.

Resurrected Pr. *Imprint of* **Intrepid Ink, LLC**

Resurrecting Faith, *(978-0-9729876)* P.O. Box 43217, Minneapolis, MN 55443-0217 USA
E-mail: admin@churchofminneapolis.org; cerise.lewis@comcast.net
Web site: http://www.resurrectingfaith.org; http://www.churchofminneapolis.org.

Resurrection House *See* **Firebird Creative**

Resurrection Pr. *Imprint of* **Catholic Bk. Publishing Corp.**

Resurrection Resources LLC, *(978-0-9653723; 978-0-9710950; 978-0-9792338)* 8362 Tamarack Village, Ste. 119, Woodbury, MN 55125 USA
E-mail: editor@thefathersbooks.com; sales@thefathersbooks.com
Web site: http://www.thefathersbooks.com
Dist(s): **Send The Light Distribution LLC.**

Rethinking Resiliency, LLC, *(978-0-578-53381-0; 978-0-578-62750-2; 978-1-7345026)* 14072 Gordons Ln, Glen Allen, VA 23059 USA Tel 804-709-2777
E-mail: davisal5484@marybaldwin.edu
Web site: www.rethinkingresiliency.com.

Retriever Pr., *(978-0-9760718; 978-0-615-55790-8)* 3689 Ridge Line Dr., San Bernardino, CA 92407 USA.

Retro Recess, *(978-0-9785425)* 3939 Lavista Rd., Suite E, PMB 327, Tucker, GA 30084 USA
E-mail: retrorecess@comcast.net
Web site: http://www.retrorecess.net.

Return To The Word, *(978-0-9709763)* Div of LIFE Fellowship Family Bible Church, 11500 Sheridan Blvd., Westminster, CO 80020 USA Tel 303-451-5433; Fax: 303-469-1787
E-mail: truthquester@aol.com
Web site: http://www.returntotheworld.org.

Retzlaff Publishing Co., *(978-0-9752525)* 1516 Piedmont Pl., Savannah, TX 76227 USA Tel 817-975-1115
E-mail: DonRetzlaff@gmail.com
Web site: http://RPC.macroenterprisesinc.com.

Retzler, Laura, *(978-0-692-98820-6)* 5302 MacArthur Blvd., Washington, DC 20016 USA Tel 202-286-2179
E-mail: lretzler@yahoo.com
Dist(s): **Ingram Content Group.**

REUTS Pubns., *(978-0-9896499; 978-1-942111)* 2369 S 64 St., West Allis, WI 53219 USA Tel 734-658-9818
E-mail: ashley@reuts.com
Web site: http://www.reuts.com.

Revelation Products LLC, *(978-0-9792510)* 11746 Manhattan Ave., Saint Louis, MO 63131-4625 USA Tel 314-984-8180; Fax: 314-984-8194; Toll Free: 888-344-0606
E-mail: info@rpideas.com.

†Revell, *(978-0-8007)* Div. of Baker Publishing Group, Orders Addr.: P.O. Box 6287, Grand Rapids, MI 49516-6287 USA Toll Free Fax: 800-398-3111; Toll Free: 800-877-2665; Edit Addr.: 6030 E. Fulton, Ada, MI 49301 USA Tel 616-676-9185; Fax: 616-676-9573
E-mail: sharlow@bakerbooks.com
Web site: http://www.bakerbooks.com
Dist(s): **Baker Publishing Group**; *CIP.*

Revell, Fleming H. Company *See* **Revell**

Reveno, Katherine, *(978-0-692-94881-1)* 1001 mclynn ave ne, Atlanta, GA 30306 USA Tel 503-716-6500
E-mail: kreveno20@groton.org.

Reverence Design Team Hair Salon, The *See* **D&C Publishing**

Reverence for Life, *(978-1-880757)* P.O. Box 222, Rectortown, VA 20140 USA Tel 540-364-1282; Fax: 540-364-7636
E-mail: sananda@erols.com
Web site: http://www.1spirit.com/sananda.

Reverie Publishing Co., *(978-1-932485)* Orders Addr.: 130 South Wineow St., Suite 3, Cumberland, MD 21502 USA Tel 301-722-2373; Fax: 301-722-2374; Toll Free: 888-721-4999; Edit Addr.: 127 West 96th St., 6-D, New York, NY 10025 USA Tel 212-662-7627
E-mail: info@reveriepublishing.com
Web site: http://www.reveriepublishing.com.

†Review & Herald Publishing Assn., *(978-0-8127; 978-0-8280)* 55 W. Oak Ridge Dr., Hagerstown, MD 21740 USA (SAN 203-3798) Tel 301-393-3000
E-mail: smulkern@rhpa.org
Web site: http://www.reviewandherald.com/
Dist(s): **Spring Arbor Distributors, Inc.**; *CIP.*

Revival Pubns. (GBR) *(978-0-9536768) Dist. by* **Consort Bk Sales.**

Revival Waves of Glory, *(978-0-615-94231-5; 978-0-615-94271-1; 978-0-615-94272-8; 978-0-615-94273-5; 978-0-615-94286-5; 978-0-615-94292-6; 978-0-615-94831-7; 978-0-615-95143-0; 978-0-615-95145-4; 978-0-615-96815-5; 978-0-615-96817-9; 978-0-692-20785-7; 978-0-692-21429-9; 978-0-692-21499-2; 978-0-692-21554-8; 978-0-692-21663-7; 978-0-692-22184-6; 978-0-692-22285-0; 978-0-692-22331-4; 978-0-692-22921-7; 978-0-692-23397-9; 978-0-692-24064-9; 978-0-692-26625-0; 978-0-692-27285-5; 978-0-692-27996-0; 978-0-692-32262-8;)* P.O. Box 596, Litchfield, IL 62056 USA Tel 217-851-0361
E-mail: bill.vincent@yahoo.com
Web site: http://www.revivalwavesofgloryministries.com
Dist(s): **BookBaby**
CreateSpace Independent Publishing Platform
Send The Light Distribution LLC.

Revivalist Pr., The, *(978-0-9749186; 978-0-9891979)* Div. of God's Bible School & College, 1810 Young St., Cincinnati, OH 45202 USA
E-mail: president@gbs.edu
Web site: http://www.gbs.edu.

Revolutionary Strategies, *(978-0-9769354; 978-0-9825493; 978-0-9883527; 978-0-9981269; 978-1-949775)* P.O. Box 900, Dripping Springs, TX 78620 USA Tel 512-858-0974
Web site: http://www.rickgreen.com.

Rexroad International, *(978-0-9817742; 978-1-946650)* Div. of Rexroad International, 616 Upham Pl. NW, Vienna, VA 22180 USA; *Imprints:* Rexroad Kids (MYID_G_REXROAD)
E-mail: fred@rexroad.us; fred.rexroad@yahoo.com
Web site: TannerDent.com; www.fredrexroad.com; WhizTanner.com; http://Rexroad.International
Dist(s): **CreateSpace Independent Publishing Platform**
Ingram Content Group.

Rexroad Kids *Imprint of* **Rexroad International**

Reyes, Jose, *(978-0-9794731)* 422 Sabal Palm Ln., Pearland, TX 77584-7770 USA
E-mail: thelordsfield@sbcglobal.net; riff28@sbcglobal.net.

REYES, MARIA DE LA LUZ, *(978-0-9972790)* 985 SAN PABLO Dr., SAN MARCOS, CA 92078 USA Tel 760-685-3101
E-mail: mdlaluz@icloud.com.

Reynolds & Hearn (GBR) *(978-1-903111; 978-1-905287) Dist. by* **Trafalgar.**

Reynolds, Morgan Inc., *(978-1-883846; 978-1-931798; 978-1-59935)* 620 S. Elm St., Suite 223, Greensboro, NC 27406 USA (SAN 858-4680) Tel 336-275-1311; Fax: 336-275-1152; Toll Free Fax: 800-535-5725; Toll Free: 800-535-1504; *Imprints:* First Biographies (First Biographies)
E-mail: sales@morganreynolds.com; editorial@morganreynolds.com
Web site: http://www.morganreynolds.com
Dist(s): **Follett School Solutions.**

Reynoso, Michelle, *(978-0-9997189)* 11 Henry St., Bergenfield, NJ 07621 USA Tel 973-306-8964; *Imprints:* Caterpillar & Gypsy Moth Press (MYID_F_CATERPI)
E-mail: mtr@MichelleReynoso.com
Web site: http://www.michellereynoso.com.

RFPublishing, *(978-0-9969173)* 244 5th Ave., New York, NY 10001 USA Tel 212-726-1453
E-mail: 007sdropybur007@gmail.com.

RG Mincey Group, LLC, The, *(978-0-9882039; 978-1-63498-451-5)* P.O. Box 1245, Bluffton, SC 29910 USA Tel 678-472-4740
E-mail: rgmincey@gmail.com.

RGC Pr., LLC, *(978-0-9728876; 978-0-9779886)* P.O. Box 2921, Indianapolis, IN 46206-2921 USA (SAN 255-4747) Tel 317-926-0541
E-mail: info@RGCPress.com
Web site: http://www.RGCPress.com.

RGU Group, The, *(978-1-891795)* 560 W. Southern Ave., Tempe, AZ 85282 USA (SAN 299-9366) Tel 480-736-9862; Fax: 480-736-9863; Toll Free: 800-266-5265
E-mail: mpagnozzi@theRGUgroup.com
Web site: http://www.thergugroup.com
Dist(s): **Send The Light Distribution LLC.**

RGZ Consulting, *(978-0-615-80196-4)* P.O. Box 153, South Woodstock, VT 05071 USA Tel 802-457-5861
E-mail: zamenhof@alum.mit.edu.

Rhapado Quick Reference, *(978-0-9719588; 978-0-9814940)* 702 S. Fairview St., Riverside, NJ 08075-3950 USA (SAN 855-7020) Tel 856-255-5492
E-mail: dvillari@rhapado.com
Web site: http://www.rhapadopublishing.com.

Rhapsody Branding, Inc., *(978-0-9667232)* Orders Addr.: 14027 N. Miami Ave., Miami, FL 33168 USA Tel 305-681-0489
E-mail: pumba66@yahoo.com; Don@notw8.com; Don@nightofthewitches.com
Web site: http://www.nightofthewitches.com
Dist(s): **Bk. Warehouse**
Distributors, The
Southern Bk. Service.

Rhapsody Productions *See* **Rhapado Quick Reference**

RH/Disney *Imprint of* **Random Hse. Children's Bks.**

Rhea Leto Media Group, *(978-0-9904727; 978-1-947185)* 6854 Orcutt Ave., Long Beach, CA 90805 USA Tel 424-757-8134
E-mail: Rhea@rhealeto.com; cj@phabb5.org
Web site: www.RheaLeto.Com.

Rheiss, *(978-0-692-91113-6)* 141 Hunter Rd., Simpsonville, SC 29681 USA Tel 607-342-4433
E-mail: rsh023@gmail.com
Dist(s): **CreateSpace Independent Publishing Platform.**

Rhemalda Publishing, *(978-0-615-32885-0; 978-0-9827437; 978-1-936850)* P.O. Box 1790, Moses Lake, WA 98837 USA
E-mail: emmaline@rhemalda.com
Web site: http://www.rhemalda.com; http://shop.rhemalda.com/
Dist(s): **MyiLibrary**
Smashwords.

Rhette Enterprises, Inc., *(978-0-9702319)* 3316 Shorewood Ave., Fort Gratiot, MI 48059 USA Tel 810-385-9416; Fax: 810-385-2304
E-mail: bobjan@futureone.com.

Rhino Entertainment Co, A Warner Music Group Co., *(978-0-7379; 978-0-930589; 978-1-56826; 978-0-9797278)* 3400 W. Olive Ave., Burbank, CA 91505 USA (SAN 677-5454) Tel 818-238-6110; Fax: 818-562-9239
E-mail: gladys.sanchez@wmg.com; tracie.bowers@wmg.com
Web site: http://www.rhino.com.

Rhizoo Publishing, *(978-0-9762723)* P.O. Box 1249, Stephenville, TX 76401 USA.

Rhoades & Assocs., *(978-1-930006; 978-0-9841378)* 8070 19th St., No. 326, Alta Loma, CA 91701 USA (SAN 858-5369) Tel 909-297-3436; Fax: 909-657-5446; Toll Free: 888-699-0685; *Imprints:* Reading Company, The (Reading Co)
E-mail: jacquie@readingcompany.us
Web site: http://www.readingcompany.us.

Rhode Island State Council, International Reading Assn., *(978-0-9664455)* 4 Gardner Ave., North Providence, RI 02911 USA.

Rhode, Steve Inc., *(978-0-9742781; 978-1-59840)* 310 Watkins Pond Blvd., Rockville, MD 20850 USA
E-mail: steve@steverhode.com
Web site: http://www.steverhode.com.

Rhodes, Candice Sumner, *(978-0-9895439)* 268 loch stone st, Fort Mill, SC 29715 USA Tel 323-474-9293
E-mail: candicerhodes@yahoo.com.

Rhodes Educational Pubns., *(978-0-9743214)* P.O. Box 501155, Dallas, TX 75250 USA
Web site: http://www.nativeamericanrhymes.com.

Rhodes, Edwin Books LLC *See* **Rhodes, EL. Bks., LLC**

Rhodes, EL. Bks., LLC, *(978-0-615-24550-8; 978-0-578-01988-8; 978-0-578-03719-6; 978-0-692-82552-5)* 7710 Tinkers Creek Dr., Clinton, MD 20735 USA.

RHS Consulting, *(978-0-9990937)* 104 Pine Lake Dr., Whispering Pines, NC 28327 USA Tel 910-633-1169
E-mail: rhsconsulting@outlook.com.

Rhymeglow LLC, *(978-0-9786912; 978-0-578-15239-4)* Orders Addr.: 14625 Baltimore Ave., #869, Laurel, MD 20707 USA; Edit Addr.: P.O. Box 869, Laurel, MD 20707 USA.

Rhythm & Reasoning Pubns., *(978-1-949301)* 6250 Lyons Rd No. 11, Garland, TX 75043 USA Tel 972-203-1990
E-mail: AlyssaLynnDonovan@tx.rr.com.

Rialp, Ediciones, S.A. (ESP) *(978-84-320; 978-84-321) Dist. by* **Lectorum Pubns.**

Ribbing, John, *(978-0-9987219)* 4866 Charles, Shelby Township, MI 48316 USA Tel 248-310-7551
E-mail: jribbing@yahoo.com.

Ribbonwood Pr., *(978-0-9800291; 978-0-473-38865-2)* P.O. Box 390375, Anza, CA 92539 USA Tel 951-763-2060
E-mail: nancylee202004@yahoo.com.

Ric Design LLC, *(978-0-9758704; 978-0-9859684)* 2245 Stony Hill Rd., Boulder, CO 80305 USA Toll Free: 800-432-7346 (phone/fax)
E-mail: ricdilz13@gmail.com
Dist(s): **Bookazine Co., Inc.**

R.I.C. Publications Asia Co, Inc. (JPN) *(978-4-902216) Dist. by* **CEG.**

R.I.C. Pubns. (AUS) *(978-1-86311; 978-1-74126; 978-1-921750; 978-1-922116; 978-1-925201; 978-1-925431; 978-1-925660; 978-1-925686; 978-1-925698; 978-1-925812; 978-1-925837; 978-1-925926; 978-1-922313; 978-1-922426) Dist. by* **SCB Distributo.**

Ricciardi, Charles, *(978-0-9996986)* 155 Henry Street, No. 404, New York, NY 10002 USA Tel 646-334-0330
E-mail: charlesricciardi@gmail.com
Web site: torinopictures.com.

Rich Gamble Assocs., *(978-0-692-16775-5; 978-1-7338052)* P.O. Box 163, Los Alamos, CA 93440 USA Tel 805-344-3259
E-mail: rlawsongamble@gmail.com
Web site: rlawsongamble.com.

Rich List *See* **Rich Register, The**

Rich Pr., *(978-1-933914)* 4330 N. Civic Center Plaza, #100, Scottsdale, AZ 85251 USA (SAN 850-5209)
E-mail: kathy@richdad.com
Dist(s): **Ingram Publisher Services**
Two Rivers Distribution.

Rich Publishing, *(978-0-9726670)* 4175 W. 5345 S., Salt Lake City, UT 84118 USA Tel 801-965-6200; Fax: 801-965-6199; Toll Free: 800-224-3221 Do not confuse with companies with the same or similar name in Houston, TX, Temecula, CA
E-mail: milton@zeestlouis.com
Web site: http://www.miltonrich.com.

Rich Register, The, *(978-0-9633933; 978-0-9831368)* P.O. Box 29955, Austin, TX 78755 USA Tel 512-477-8871
E-mail: jda@richregister.com
Web site: www.richregister.com.

Richard Hall II, *(978-0-692-07897-6)* 130 Berwick Lakes Blvd., POOLER, GA 31322 USA Tel 912-484-9669
E-mail: lavontrichie@aol.com
Dist(s): **Ingram Content Group.**

Richards, Erin, *(978-0-9911264; 978-1-943800)* 1720 Tahoe Cir., Tracy, CA 95376 USA Tel 209-832-3249
E-mail: erinrichards@att.net
Web site: www.erinrichards.com.

Richards, Markita, *(978-0-578-45805-2; 978-0-578-71391-5; 978-0-578-77757-3)* 12085 Jojo Ct., Hampton, GA 30228 USA Tel 678-668-1454
E-mail: lynn0786@gmail.com.

Richards, Michael, *(978-0-692-16268-2; 978-0-692-16269-9; 978-0-578-61478-6)* 3935 Jasmine St., Paris, TX 75462 USA Tel 972-795-5656
E-mail: Mrichards@reagan.com
Dist(s): **Ingram Content Group.**

Richardson, Lilith, *(978-0-578-00920-9; 978-0-578-04792-8; 978-0-578-07481-8)* 360 Dusty Rd., St. Augustine, FL 32095 USA
Dist(s): **Lulu Pr., Inc.**

Richardson Production, Inc., *(978-0-9761222)* Orders Addr.: P.O. Box 543, Marietta, OH 45750 USA Tel 740-373-0861; Edit Addr.: 177 Acme St., Marietta, OH 45750 USA
Web site: http://www.richardsonproductions.tv.

Richardson Publishing, Inc., *(978-0-9637991; 978-1-935683)* 321 Montgomery Rd. No. 162115, Altamonte Springs, FL 32716-2115 USA Tel 407-529-8539
E-mail: usabookcoach@gmail.com; coachrik@aol.com
Web site: http://www.RickFeeney.com; http://www.PublishingSuccessOnline.com.

Richardson, Whitni, *(978-0-9903665)* 61 Harry S Truman Dr. Apt 23, Largo, MD 20774 USA Tel 443-535-2880
E-mail: richardson.whitni@gmail.com.

Richer Life, LLC, *(978-0-9744617; 978-0-9855699; 978-0-9892884; 978-0-9899001; 978-0-9903291; 978-0-9863544; 978-0-9970831; 978-0-9988773; 978-1-7335693)* 5725 S. 21st Pl., Phoenix, AZ 85040 USA Tel 602-708-4268; Fax: 602-772-4910
E-mail: earlcobb@earthlink.net; earlcobb1@gmail.com; earl@richerlifellc.com; charlotte@richerlifellc.com; cobbcare@yahoo.com
Web site: http://www.richerlifellc.com.

Richer Life, LLC (dba RICHER Publications) *See* **Richer Life, LLC**

Richer Resources Pubns., *(978-0-9776269; 978-0-9797571; 978-0-9818162; 978-1-935238; 978-1-63464)* 1926 N. Woodrow St., Arlington, VA 22207-2410 USA (SAN 853-2931) Tel 800-856-3060; Fax: 703-276-0193
E-mail: info@richerresourcespublications.com; publisher@richerresourcespublications.com
Web site: http://www.richerresourcespublications.com.

Riches Publishing Co., *(978-0-9728219)* P.O. Box 02232, Detroit, MI 48202 USA
E-mail: klrich@sbcglobal.net
Web site: http://www.klrich.com.

Richeson, John W., *(978-0-9675315)* P.O. Box 710371, San Diego, CA 92171 USA
E-mail: john@VBAtech.com
Web site: http://vbatech.com.

Richie, Morgan W., *(978-0-692-06695-9)* 6370 Hawaii Kai Dr. No. 39, Honolulu, HI 96825 USA Tel 808-321-7757
E-mail: morganwrichie@gmail.com
Dist(s): **Ingram Content Group.**

Richlee Publishing, *(978-0-9796265)* 2898 Morning Creek Rd., Chula Vista, CA 91914-4311 USA
E-mail: jmacgregor@cadencemarketinggroup.com.

Richlyn Publishing, *(978-0-9722264)* 12045 W Brandt Pl, Littleton, CO 80127-4572 USA Tel 303-979-8609
E-mail: richlyn2@msn.com
Web site: http://www.richlynpublishing.com.

Richmond *Imprint of* **Santillana USA Publishing Co., Inc.**

Richmondmom.com Publishing *Imprint of* **Palari Publishing LLP**

Rickshaw Press *See* **Ragged Sky Pr.**

Riddering, Maggie, *(978-0-9765977)* P.O. Box 770, Hormigueros, PR 00660 USA Fax: 787-833-2260.

Riddle Creek Publishing, *(978-0-9725894; 978-0-9835009)* 232 Cty. Rd. 19, Haleyville, AL 35565-7416 USA
E-mail: riddlecreek@centurytel.net
Web site: http://www.riddlecreekpublishing.com.

Rider Franklin Reynolds Publishing *See* **Belisarian Bks.**

Riders Elite Academy, Inc., *(978-0-9741628)* 23120 Garrison Rd., Corcoran, MN 55340-9103 USA Tel 763-498-6565 (phone/fax)
E-mail: books@riderselite.com
Web site: http://www.riderselite.com.

Ridge, Jacqueline, *(978-1-7321403)* 130 Shorewood Dr, Valparaiso, IN 46385 USA Tel 219-213-5432
E-mail: jacquelinemridge@gmail.com.

Ridge Rock Pr., *(978-0-9670177)* Div. of Ridge Rock, Inc., Orders Addr.: P.O. Box 255, Healy, AK 99743 USA (SAN 253-6595) Tel 907-322-8185 (cell); 907-683-7737 (phone/fax); Edit Addr.: Mile 261 Parks Hwy., Box 255, Healy, AK 99743 USA
E-mail: ridgerock@gtemail.net
Dist(s): **Todd Communications.**

Ridge Row Press *See* **Univ. of Scranton Pr.**

Ridgewood Group, The, *(978-0-9716907)* P.O. Box 8011, Manchester, CT 06040 USA (SAN 254-3419) Tel 860-432-4537 (phone/fax); *Imprints:* Ridgewood Publishing (Ridgewd Pub)
E-mail: info@theridgewoodgroup.com
Web site: http://www.hermanthecrab.com.

Ridgewood Pr., *(978-0-9650434)* 2160 Aztec Dr., dyersburg, TN 38024 USA Do not confuse with Ridgewood Pr., Jefferson City, MO
E-mail: bartonsn@mac.com.

Ridgewood Publishing *Imprint of* **Ridgewood Group, The**

Ridgway Park Publishing, *(978-0-9706219; 978-0-692-19391-4)* P.O. Box 2591, La Mesa, CA 91943-2591 USA Tel 619-698-3414; Fax: 619-698-2061
E-mail: pamela@crooks.com; editor@ridgwaypark.com
Web site: http://www.ridgwaypark.com
Dist(s): **Sunbelt Pubns., Inc.**

†Rienner, Lynne Pubs., *(978-0-89410; 978-0-931477; 978-0-931816; 978-1-55587; 978-1-56549; 978-1-58826; 978-1-935049; 978-1-62637)* 1800 30th

Publisher Name Index

St., Suite 314, Boulder, CO 80301-1026 USA (SAN 683-1869) Tel 303-444-6684; Fax: 303-444-0824
E-mail: cservice@rienner.com; sglover@rienner.com; questions@rienner.com
Web site: http://www.rienner.com; *CIP.*

Rigby Education, *(978-0-7635; 978-0-7578; 978-1-4189)* Div. of Houghton Mifflin Harcourt Supplemental Pubs., Orders Addr.: 6277 Sea Harbor Dr., 5th Flr., Orlando, FL 32887 USA Toll Free Fax: 877-578-2638; Toll Free: 888-363-4266; Edit Addr.: 10801 N. Mopac Expressway, Bldg. 3, Austin, TX 78759 USA Toll Free Fax: 800-699-9459; Toll Free: 800-531-5015
Web site: http://www.harcourtachieve.com
Dist(s): **Follett School Solutions**
Houghton Mifflin Harcourt Supplemental Pubs.

Riggott, Dean Photography, *(978-0-9659875)* 831 10 1/2 St., SW, Rochester, MN 55902 USA Tel 507-285-5076; Fax: 253-540-6093
Web site: http://www.riggottphoto.com
Dist(s): **Partners Bk. Distributing, Inc.**

Riggs, Jon, *(978-0-692-06813-7)* 912 SE Combs Flat Rd., Prineville, OR 97754 USA Tel 360-597-6110
E-mail: j.riggs4@students.clark.edu.

Riggs, Theresia, *(978-0-9746132)* 8910 Dogwood Dr., Tomball, TX 77375 USA Tel 281-351-2329 (phone/fax)
E-mail: Ohringen@aol.com
Web site: http://www.CosmicSisters.com.

Right On Programs, Inc., *(978-0-933426)* 522 E. Broadway, Suite 101, Glendale, CA 91205 USA (SAN 212-5099) Tel 818-240-1683; Fax: 818-240-2858.

Right Stuff Kids Bks., *(978-0-9704597; 978-1-932317)* 5600 Claire Rose Ln., Atlanta, GA 30327 USA
E-mail: satiller@bellsouth.net
Web site: http://www.michaelsmind.com.

Right Track Reading LLC, *(978-0-9763290)* P.O. Box 1952, Livingston, MT 59047 USA
E-mail: mmgagen@earthlink.net.

Right-Away, Inc., *(978-0-9709095)* P.O. Box 741993, Riverdale, GA 30274 USA Tel 404-798-7508
E-mail: jakiharris2004@yahoo.com; rightaway1@hotmail.com.

Righteous Bks., *(978-0-9883634)* 2801 W. 83rd St., Chicago, IL 60652 USA Tel 773-744-8162
E-mail: righteousrayray@gmail.com.

Righter Publishing Co., Inc., *(978-0-9706823; 978-0-9747735; 978-0-9766032; 978-0-9778948; 978-0-9796209; 978-1-934936; 978-1-938527)* Orders Addr.: 410 River Oaks Pkwy., Timberlake, NC 27583 USA Fax: 336-597-8881
E-mail: righterpub@esinc.net
Web site: http://www.righterbooks.com
Dist(s): **CreateSpace Independent Publishing Platform.**

RiJan Publishing, *(978-0-615-79949-0; 978-0-692-20342-2; 978-0-9906179; 978-1-7329739)* 7100 Chase Oaks Blvd Apt 4411, Plano, TX 75025-5938 USA Tel 4694500784
Web site: www.jansikes.com
Dist(s): **CreateSpace Independent Publishing Platform.**

Riker, Dale, *(978-0-9771621)* 6937 W. Country Club Dr. N, Unit 152, Sarasota, FL 34243-3507 USA.

Riley Pr. *Imprint of* **Integrity Consulting Enterprise, LLC**

Riley Pr., *(978-0-9728958)* P.O. Box 202, Eagle, MI 48822 USA Tel 517-626-7027
E-mail: rileypress@yahoo.com
Web site: http://rileypress.hypermart.net.

Rilly Silly Bk. Co., The, *(978-0-9747054)* 11130 W. Heatherbrae Dr., Phoenix, AZ 85037 USA Tel 623-877-6020
Web site: http://www.rillysilly.com.

Rime Quill Publishing Co., *(978-0-9988709; 978-1-7330283)* 150 Central Ave S No. 320, Wayzata, MN 55391 USA Tel 864-504-9293
E-mail: janetascher@gmail.com
Web site: janholmesfrost.com.

Rincon Point, LLC, *(978-0-692-97467-4; 978-0-578-48064-0)* 140 Riverside Blvd, New York City, NY 10069 USA Tel 559-553-5506
E-mail: kkloss12@gmail.com.

Rincon Publishing Co., *(978-0-9660858)* Orders Addr.: 1913 Skyline Dr., Orem, UT 84097 USA Tel 801-377-7657; Fax: 801-356-2733
E-mail: RinconPub@Utahtrails.com
Web site: http://www.utahtrails.com
Dist(s): **Partners/West Book Distributors.**

Rind, Sherry, *(978-0-9674729)* Orders Addr.: 959 Evonshire Ln., Great Falls, VA 22066 USA; Edit Addr.: 8419 NE 144th St., Bothell, WA 98011-5055 USA
E-mail: AIREBIRD@hotmail.com; KCBROOM@erols.com
Web site: http://www.airedaleterriers.org.

Rindle Books Inc *See* **Rindle Bks. Inc.**

Rindle Bks. Inc., *(978-1-942214)* 1200 Westlake Ave. N, Seattle, WA 98109 USA Tel 206-430-6021
E-mail: mark@rindlebooks.com
Web site: www.rindlebooks.com
Dist(s): **Baker & Taylor Publisher Services (BTPS).**

Rinehart, Roberts Pubs., *(978-0-911797; 978-0-943173; 978-1-57098; 978-1-57140; 978-1-879373; 978-1-58979)* Div. of Rowman & Littlefield Pubs., Inc., Orders Addr.: 15200 NBN Way, Blue Ridge Summit, PA 17214 USA Tel 717-794-3800 (Customer Service &/or orders); Fax: 717-794-3803 (Customer Service &/or orders only); 717-794-3857 (Sales & MIS); 717-794-3856 (Royalties, Inventory Mgmt., & Dist.); Toll Free Fax: 800-338-4550 (Customer Service &/or orders); Toll Free: 800-462-6420 (Customer Service &/or orders); Edit Addr.: 4501 Forbes Blvd., Suite 200, Lanham, MD 20706 USA Tel 301-459-3366; Toll Free: 800-462-6420
E-mail: nrothschild@rowman.com
Web site: http://www.robertsrinehart.com
Dist(s): **Ebsco Publishing**
Follett School Solutions
National Bk. Network
Rowman & Littlefield Publishers, Inc.
ebrary, Inc.

Rio Grande Bks. *Imprint of* **LPD Pr.**

Rio Nuevo Pubs., *(978-0-918080; 978-1-887896; 978-0-9700750; 978-1-933855; 978-1-940322)* Orders Addr.: P.O. Box 5250, Tucson, AZ 85703-0250 USA (SAN 209-3251) Tel 520-623-9558; Fax: 520-624-5888; Toll Free Fax: 800-715-5888; Toll Free: 800-969-9558; Edit Addr.: 451 N. Bonita Ave., Tucson, AZ 85745 USA Tel 602-623-9558; *Imprints:* Rio Nuevo Publishers (Rio Nuevo)
E-mail: info@rionuevo.com; info@treasurechestbooks.com; suzang@rionuevo.com
Web site: http://www.treasurechestbooks.com; http://www.rionuevo.com/
Dist(s): **Treasure Chest Bks.**

Rio Nuevo Pubs. *Imprint of* **Rio Nuevo Pubs.**

Rio Wildflower Pubns., *(978-0-9786168)* P.O. Box 246, Almont, CO 81210 USA Tel 970-642-0272
E-mail: wildflowercd@peoplepc.com.

Riordan, Rick *Imprint of* **Disney Pr.**

Rip Squeak, Inc., *(978-0-9672422; 978-0-9747825)* Orders Addr.: c/o Raven Tree Press, 1400 Miller Pkwy., McHenry, IL 60050 USA Tel 815-363-3582; Fax: 815-363-2948; Edit Addr.: 840 Capitolio Way, Suite B, San Luis Obispo, CA 93401-7130 USA Tel 805-594-0184; Fax: 805-543-5782; Toll Free: 800-251-0654; *Imprints:* Rip Squeak Press (Rip Squeak Pr)
E-mail: Beda@RipSqueak.com; dawnj@delta-systems.com
Web site: http://www.RipSqueak.com; http://www.raventreepress.com
Dist(s): **Delta Systems Company, Inc.**

Rip Squeak Pr. *Imprint of* **Rip Squeak, Inc.**

Ripley Entertainment, Inc., *(978-1-893951; 978-1-60991)* Div. of The Jim Pattison Group, 7576 Kingspointe Pkwy., Suite. 188, Orlando, FL 32819-6510 USA (SAN 299-9498)
E-mail: meyer@ripleys.com; dula@ripleys.com
Web site: http://www.ripleys.com
Dist(s): **Children's Plus, Inc.**
Mint Pubs. Group
Simon & Schuster, Inc.

Rippee, Zachariah J., 308 Pershing St, WILLARD, MO 65781 USA Tel 417-207-0948
E-mail: jeffwcrawford5+LVP0003495@gmail.com; jeffwcrawford5+LVP0003495@gmail.com.

Ripple Grove Pr., *(978-0-9913866; 978-0-9990249)* P.O. Box 86740, Portland, OR 97286 USA Tel 774-230-3556
E-mail: amanda@ripplegrovepress.com
Web site: www.ripplegrovepress.com
Dist(s): **Independent Pubs. Group**
Midpoint Trade Bks., Inc.
Small Pr. United.

Riptide Pr., Inc., *(978-0-9723456)* 233 Walnut Creek Dr., Clayton, NC 27520 USA Tel 919-359-2852; Fax: 919-882-9924 Do not confuse with companies with the same or similar name in New York, NY, Fredericksburg, VA
E-mail: info@riptidebooks.com; info@riptidepress.com
Web site: http://www.riptidebooks.com; http://www.riptidepress.com.

Risa Publications, *(978-0-9771404)* 8424-A Santa Monica Blvd., Suite 175, West Hollywood, CA 90069 USA
Web site: http://www.lisahaisha.com.

Risen Heart Pr., *(978-0-9764497)* 554 Bruns Dr., Rossford, OH 43460 USA Tel 419-666-6269
E-mail: rjbaden@wcnet.org.

Rising Bks., *(978-0-9644456)* P.O. Box 1408, Conyers, GA 30012 USA (SAN 298-5438) Tel 404-378-7464; Fax: 770-761-9865
E-mail: chadfoster@mindspring.com
Web site: www.chadfoster.com.

Rising Moon Bks. for Young Readers *Imprint of* **Northland Publishing**

Rising Son International, Ltd., *(978-0-9915370; 978-0-9961358)* 218 Beach Rd., Washington, MA 01223 USA Tel 413-623-6112
E-mail: annieguthrie@risingsonrecords.com
Web site: www.risingsonrecords.com.

Rising Star Publishers *See* **WeWrite LLC**

Rising Star Studios, LLC., *(978-1-936086; 978-1-936770)* 5251 W. 73rd St. Suite C, Edina, MN 55439 USA Tel 952-831-8532; Fax: 952-831-5809
E-mail: mark@risingstarstudios.com; info@risingstarstudios.com; sales@risingstarstudios.com
Web site: http://www.risingstarstudios.com
Dist(s): **Follett School Solutions.**

Rising Sun Publishing, Inc., *(978-1-880463)* P.O. Box 70906, Marietta, GA 30007-0906 USA Tel 770-518-0369; Fax: 770-587-0862; Toll Free: 800-524-2813 Do not confuse with Rising Sun Pubng in Fairfield, OH
E-mail: info@rspublishing.com; sholland@rspublishing.com
Web site: http://www.rspublishing.com.

Rising Tide Pr., *(978-0-913844)* Div. of American-Canadian Pubs., Inc., P.O. Box 6136, Santa Fe, NM 87502-4595 USA (SAN 298-217X) Do not confuse with Rising Tide Pubs., Tucson, AZ.

Rissarae Designs, *(978-0-692-45001-7; 978-0-692-53652-0; 978-1-7322949)* 621 88th Ave. N. Apt. 3, St. Petersburg, FL 33702 USA Tel 6263241249; Toll Free: 6263241249
Web site: www.thefairybabybooks.com
Dist(s): **CreateSpace Independent Publishing Platform**
Ingram Bk. Co.

Rissylyn, *(978-0-9894933)* 2 12th St. Apt. 1012, Hoboken, NJ 07030 USA Tel 917-859-4751
E-mail: info@dreambigacademy.com.

Ritchie, John Ltd. (GBR) *(978-0-946351; 978-1-904064; 978-1-907731; 978-1-909803; 978-1-910513) Dist. by* **BTPS.**

Ritchie Unlimited Pubns., *(978-0-939656)* 1427 Anderson Rd. Suite B, Springfield, OR 97477 USA (SAN 216-6461) Tel 541-741-0794 (phone/fax)
E-mail: ralph-ritchie@comcast.net
Web site: http://www.ritchieunlimitedpublications.com.

Rite Lite Limited, *(978-0-9772560)* 333 Stanley Ave., Brooklyn, NY 11207 USA Tel 718-498-1700; Fax: 718-498-1251; Toll Free: 800-942-0707
E-mail: mail@riteliteltd.com
Web site: http://www.riteliteltd.com.

Rite Quest, *(978-0-9801484)* 1308 Turnberry Ct., Chesapeake, VA 23320-9445 USA.

Ritz, Lee Pubns., *(978-1-940840)* 2934 Ames St., Wheat Ridge, CO 80214 USA Tel 303-330-2477
E-mail: leeritz@leeritzpublications.com
Web site: www.leeritzpublications.com.

Rivendell Bk. Factory, *(978-0-944353)* 217 Country Club Park Crestline Village, PMB321, Mountain Brook, AL 35213 USA Tel (205) 871-5915; Fax: (205) 871-5945
Dist(s): **Cardinal Pubs. Group.**

River Canyon Pr., *(978-0-9815914; 978-0-9827531)* Orders Addr.: P.O. Box 191, Oakland, OR 97462 USA (SAN 855-9651) Tel 541-530-2061
Web site: http://www.rivercanyonpress.com
Dist(s): **CreateSpace Independent Publishing Platform**
River Canyon Distributing.

River City Kids *Imprint of* **River City Publishing**

River City Pr., *(978-0-9706962; 978-0-9764232; 978-0-9776713)* 4301 Emerson Ave. N., Minneapolis, MN 55412 USA Tel 612-521-9633 (phone/fax); Toll Free: 888-234-3559 Do not confuse with River City Pr. in New Orleans, LA
E-mail: bwolf@rivercitypress.net
Web site: http://www.rivercitypress.net.

River City Publishing, *(978-0-913515; 978-0-9622815; 978-1-57966; 978-1-880216; 978-1-881320)* 1719 Mulberry St., Montgomery, AL 36106 USA (SAN 631-4910) Tel 334-265-6753; Fax: 334-265-8880; Toll Free: 877-408-7078; *Imprints:* River City Kids (River City Kids) Do not confuse with companies with the same or similar names in Richland, WA, South Bend, IN
E-mail: sales@rivercitypublishing.com
Web site: http://www.rivercitypublishing.com.

River Grove Bks., *(978-1-938416; 978-1-63299)* 4005 B Banister Ln. Three Pk. Pl., Austin, TX 78704 USA Tel 512-891-6100
E-mail: jgoff@greenleafbookgroup.com
Dist(s): **Greenleaf Book Group.**

River Lake Pr., *(978-0-615-36951-8)* 1799 Ashland Ave., Saint Paul, MN 55104 USA Tel 651-646-2915
E-mail: bethanymasters@riverlakepress.com
Web site: http://www.bethanymasters.com.

River of Life Publishing, *(978-0-9746345)* 3700 Chestnut Lake Ct., Jonesboro, GA 30236-5502 USA Do not confuse with River of Life Publishing in Kremmling, CO.

River Pointe Pubns., *(978-0-9758805; 978-0-9817258; 978-0-9848103)* 612 River Pointe Ct., Milan, MI 48160 USA Tel 734-439-8031
E-mail: riverptpub@sbcglobal.net.

River Pr., *(978-0-9725796; 978-0-9849909)* Div. of OCRS, Inc., Orders Addr.: 52 Tuscan Way Ste 202 # 404, Saint Augustine, FL 32092 USA (SAN 850-5098) Tel 904-563-6277; Fax: 904-940-5178; Edit Addr.: P.O. Box 551627, Jacksonville, FL 32255 USA
E-mail: wrcsacriver@comcast.net
Web site: http://randycribbsauthor.com.

River Rain Ministries, *(978-0-9792713)* 1302 E. 30th St., Suite A, Texarkana, AR 71854 USA Tel 870-216-2243 (phone/fax)
E-mail: teaching2win@gmail.com.

River Road Pubns., Inc., *(978-0-938682)* 1433 Fulton St., Grand Haven, MI 49417-1572 USA (SAN 253-8172) Toll Free: 800-373-8762
E-mail: Pandex@prodigy.net
Web site: http://www.riverroadpublications.com.

River Sanctuary Publishing, *(978-0-9841140; 978-1-935914; 978-1-952194)* P.O. Box 1561, Felton, CA 95018 USA (SAN 858-4532) Tel 831-335-7283
Web site: http://www.riversanctuarypublishing.com.

River Styx Publishing Co., *(978-0-9788997; 978-1-61704)* 1400 Ash St., Terre Haute, IN 47804 USA; P.O. Box 3246, Terre Haute, IN 47803
E-mail: pessy74@aol.com
Web site: http://fixitprogram.zoomshare.com.

Rivera Engineering, *(978-0-9801695)* 227 Brahan Blvd., San Antonio, TX 78215 USA (SAN 855-3874) Tel 210-771-2662; Fax: 210-226-9027
E-mail: alanegarivera@yahoo.com
Web site: http://www.rivera-engineering.com.

Riverbank Publishing, *(978-0-9753320)* 1917 Winterport Cluster, Reston, VA 20191 USA
Web site: http://www.riverbankpublishing.com.

Riverbend Publishing, *(978-1-931832; 978-1-60639)* Orders Addr.: P.O. Box 5833, Helena, MT 59604 USA Tel 406-449-0200; Fax: 406-449-0330; Toll Free: 866-787-2363; Edit Addr.: 1660 B St., Helena, MT 59601 USA (SAN 254-5020) Do not confuse with companies with the same or similar names in Elizabeth, CO, Marion, KY, Knoxville, TN
Web site: http://www.riverbendpublishing.com
Dist(s): **Bks. West**
High Peak Bks.
National Bk. Network
Partners Bk. Distributing, Inc.
Smashwords
TNT Media Group, Inc.
Wolverine Distributing, Inc.

Rivercity Pr. *Imprint of* **Amereon Ltd.**

RiverCreek Bks., Inc., *(978-0-9745171)* Orders Addr.: P.O. Box 1146, Buies Creek, NC 27506 USA Tel 910-893-8853.

RiverCrest Publishing, *(978-0-9667421; 978-1-930004; 978-1-942091)* Div. of Power of Prophecy, 1708 Patterson Rd., Austin, TX 78733-6507 USA (SAN 920-9972) Tel 512-263-9780; Fax: 512-263-9793; Toll Free: 800-234-9673
E-mail: Prophecy@texemarrs.com
Web site: http://www.texemarrs.com.

Riverdale Bks. *Imprint of* **Riverdale Electronic Bks.**

Riverdale Electronic Books *See* **Riverdale Electronic Bks.**

Riverdale Electronic Bks., *(978-0-9712207; 978-1-932606)* 4420 Bonneville Dr., Cumming, GA 30041 USA Tel 770-891-2710; *Imprints:* Riverdale Books (RiverdBks)
E-mail: jtm@riverdalebooks.com
Web site: http://www.riverdaleebooks.com.

Riverdeep, Incorporated *See* **Houghton Mifflin Harcourt Learning Technology**

RiverEarth, *(978-0-9787722)* Orders Addr.: P.O. Box 245, Southern Pines, NC 28388 USA (SAN 851-5824) Tel 910-795-2285; Edit Addr.: P.O. Box 684, Lenoir, NC 28645 USA
E-mail: info@riverearth.com
Web site: lostseaexpedition.com; http://riverearth.com.

Riverhead Bks. *Imprint of* **Penguin Publishing Group**

RiverPlace Development Corp., *(978-0-9785538)* Orders Addr.: P.O. Box 6218, Reading, PA 19610-0218 USA
E-mail: info@RiverPlacePA.com
Web site: http://www.RiverPlacePA.com.

RIVERRUN BOOKSTORE INC, *(978-0-9856073; 978-0-9885370; 978-1-939739; 978-1-944393; 978-1-950381)* 86 Morning St, Portsmouth, NH 3801 USA Tel 603-431-2100
E-mail: riverrunbookstore@gmail.com.

Rivers, Swannee, *(978-0-9749216; 978-0-578-04160-5)* 1629 Index Ave. Se, Suite No. 400, Renton, WA 98058 USA Fax: 425-277-2950
E-mail: swanneerivers@mindspring.com
Web site: http://www.swanneerivers.com.

Rivershore Bks., *(978-0-615-79091-6; 978-0-615-80212-1; 978-0-615-82977-7; 978-0-615-84337-7; 978-0-615-89413-3; 978-0-615-90629-4; 978-0-615-93301-6; 978-0-615-94046-5; 978-0-615-94307-7; 978-0-615-95626-8; 978-0-615-96614-4; 978-0-615-97239-8; 978-0-615-97851-2; 978-0-615-97975-5; 978-0-692-02353-2; 978-0-692-22526-4; 978-0-692-22528-8; 978-0-692-22625-4; 978-0-692-25882-8; 978-0-692-26386-0; 978-0-692-27118-6; 978-0-692-31180-6; 978-0-692-32102-7; 978-0-692-33564-2; 978-0-692-34741-6; 978-0-692-39052-8;) 9011 Pierce St. NE, Blaine, MN 55434 USA Tel 7636708677*
Web site: www.rivershorebooks.com
Dist(s): **CreateSpace Independent Publishing Platform.**

Riverside Art Museum, *(978-0-9802207; 978-0-692-41917-5)* 3425 Mission Inn Ave., Riverside, CA 92501-3304 USA
E-mail: mcarlson@riversideartmuseum.org
Dist(s): **D.A.P./Distributed Art Pubs.**

Riverside Park Pr., *(978-0-9864246)* 8811 E Florian Ave, Mesa, AZ 85208 USA Tel 480-201-6048
E-mail: valerieipson@ymail.com
Web site: riversideparkpress.com.

Riverstone Group Publishing, *(978-0-9706117; 978-0-9763092; 978-0-9906166; 978-1-7346235)* 331 Laiken Dr., Jasper, GA 30143 USA; 331 Laiken Dr., Jasper, GA 30143 Tel 404-219-1008
E-mail: ep@rsgroup.us
Web site: http://www.riverstonegroup.com.

RiverStream Publishing, *(978-0-9834972; 978-1-62243)* 123 S. Broad St., Mankato, MN 56001 USA Tel 414-378-2480
Web site: https://riverstreampublishing.net.

Rivertide Publishing, *(978-0-9826252)* 890 Kensington Ave., Astoria, OR 97103 USA Tel 503-440-1002
E-mail: leedomkaren@gmail.com.

Rivertree Productions, Inc., *(978-1-882412)* P.O. Box 410, Bradford, NH 03221 USA Tel 603-938-5120; Fax: 603-938-5616; Toll Free: 800-554-1333; *Imprints:* Odds Bodkin Storytelling Library, The (Odds Bodkin)
E-mail: rivertree@conknet.com
Web site: http://www.oddsbodkin.com
Dist(s): **Penton Overseas, Inc.**

Riverview Foundation, *(978-0-9771639)* Orders Addr.: P.O. Box 310, Topsham, ME 04086 USA (SAN 256-8357) Tel 207-729-7399; Fax: 207-797-5676; Edit Addr.: 610 Augusta Rd., Tomsham, ME 04086 USA
E-mail: office@riverviewfoundation.com
Web site: http://www.riverviewfoundation.com.

Rivet Bks. *Imprint of* **Feral Pr., Inc.**

RIXKIN, *(978-0-9842069)* P.O. Box 11922, Atlanta, GA 30355 USA Tel 888-674-1679; Fax: 888-674-2577
E-mail: info@rixkin.com; pr@rixkin.com; orders@rixkin.com
Web site: http://www.rixkin.com
Dist(s): **Quality Bks., Inc.**

†**Rizzoli International Pubns., Inc.,** *(978-0-8478; 978-0-88363; 978-0-941807; 978-1-932183;*

978-1-59962) Subs. of RCS Rizzoli Editore Corp., 300 Park Ave., S., 3rd Flr., New York, NY 10010 USA (SAN 111-9192) Tel 212-387-3400; Fax: 212-387-3535; *Imprints:* White Star (White Star NY); Rizzoli Universe Promotional Books (RUPB); Skira (Skira); Welcome Books (Welcome)
Web site: http://www.rizzoliusa.com/
Dist(s): **Casemate Academic**
D.A.P./Distributed Art Pubs.
Ingram Publisher Services
MyiLibrary
Penguin Random Hse. Distribution
Penguin Random Hse. LLC
Random Hse., Inc.; *CIP.*

Rizzoli Universe Promotional Bks. *Imprint of* **Rizzoli International Pubns., Inc.**

RJ Blackstone Ltd, (*978-0-9769949*) Div. of Stuart and Weitz Publishing,
E-mail: rjblackstone2@aol.com; billing@SEASCAPECENTER.COM
Web site: http://www.stuartweitzpublishing.com
Dist(s): **BookBaby.**

R.J. Bob Chavez Images, (*978-0-9778110*) 5537 Lewis Ct. Unit 201, Arvada, CO 80002 USA Tel 303-423-6982
E-mail: rjbcimages@aol.com.

RJ Pubns., (*978-0-9769277; 978-0-9786373; 978-0-9817773; 978-0-9819998; 978-1-939284*) 290 Dune St., Far Rockaway, NY 11691-2714 USA (SAN 256-5919); P.O. Box 300771, Jamaica, NY 11430
Web site: http://www.rjpublications.com.

RJA Enterprises, (*978-0-615-76035-3; 978-0-692-31377-0; 978-0-692-35527-5; 978-0-692-55194-3; 978-0-692-58517-7; 978-0-692-68642-3; 978-0-692-75532-7; 978-0-692-79835-5; 978-0-692-12173-3; 978-0-578-40450-9; 978-1-7334754*) 2924 Oakton Ridge Cir., Oakton, VA 22124 USA Tel 703-242-1798
Dist(s): **CreateSpace Independent Publishing Platform.**

RJI Publishing, (*978-1-885184*) Orders Addr.: 2800 N. Roadrunner Pkwy. # 701, Las Cruces, NM 88011 USA Tel 575-521-1336
E-mail: rjipublishing@aol.com
Web site: http://www.rjipublishing.com.

RK Enterprises, Inc., (*978-0-9743775*) 22581 NE State Route 3., Belfair, WA 98528-9303 USA
E-mail: rkilsby@wavecable.com
Web site: http://www.gooshu.com.

RMA Publicity LLC dba Sigma's Bookshelf, (*978-0-9987157; 978-0-9996577*) 13540 Knollway Dr. N, MINNETONKA, MN 55305 USA Tel 952-240-2513.

RMB Rocky Mountain Bks. (CAN) (*978-0-921102; 978-0-9690038; 978-1-894765; 978-1-897522; 978-1-926855; 978-1-927330; 978-1-77160*) *Dist. by* **PerseuPGW.**

RMB Rocky Mountain Bks. (CAN) (*978-0-921102; 978-0-9690038; 978-1-894765; 978-1-897522; 978-1-926855; 978-1-927330; 978-1-77160*) *Dist. by* **Orca Bk Pub.**

RNWC Media, LLC, (*978-1-937975*) P.O. Box 559, Pinehurst, TX 77362 USA Tel 281-506-2601; *Imprints:* Young Reader's Library (Young ReadL)
E-mail: gary@rnwcmedia.com
Web site: www.rnwcmedia.com.

Roach, Patricia, (*978-0-9817680*) 17 Hillside Ave., Winsted, CT 06098 USA.

Road Tunes Media, (*978-0-9721725*) Orders Addr.: 534 Hidden Way, Homer, AK 99603 USA (SAN 852-5188)
E-mail: roadtunes@gci.net
Web site: http://www.berniejones.com
Dist(s): **Follett School Solutions.**

Roadracing World Publishing, Inc., (*978-0-9749615*) P.O. Box 1428, Lake Elsinore, CA 92531 USA Tel 951-245-6411 Toll Free: 800-464-8336
E-mail: custsvc@roadracingworld.com
Web site: http://www.roadracingworld.com.

RoadRunner Pr., (*978-1-937054; 978-1-950871*) P.O. Box 2564, Oklahoma City, OK 73101 USA Tel 405-524-6205
E-mail: jeanne@theroadrunnerpress.com
Web site: www.TheRoadRunnerPress.com.

Roadrunner Pr., (*978-0-9636346*) Orders Addr.: 2815 Lake Shore Dr., Michigan City, IN 46360-1619 USA Tel 219-879-0133; 2815 Lake Shore Dr., Michigan City, IN 46360-1619
E-mail: roadrunnerpress@comcast.net
Web site: http://www.halhigdon.com.

Roald Publishing, (*978-0-578-12595-4; 978-0-578-12602-9*) 1139 West Ave., J-9, Lancaster, CA 93534 USA.

Roane Ink LLC, (*978-0-9969750; 978-0-9976869*) 121 Arlette Dr, lafayette, LA 70503 USA Tel 337-278-0169
E-mail: GeorgeR728@aol.com.

Roane, Janice J. *See* **Roane Ink LLC**

Roaring Brook Pr., (*978-0-7613; 978-1-59643*) 115 West 18th Street, New York, NY 10011 USA Tel 212-886-1030; *Imprints:* First Second Books (First Second); Kingfisher (Kingfsh); Macaulay, David Studio (D Macaulay)
Web site: http://www.henryholt.com; http://us.macmillan.com/splash/publishers/roaring-brook-press.html
Dist(s): **Children's Plus, Inc.**
Follett School Solutions
Macmillan
MyiLibrary
Westminster John Knox Pr.

Roban, Whitney *See* **Chandler Publishing**

Robbie Dean Pr., (*978-0-9630608; 978-1-889743; 978-0-9892303; 978-0-9916017; 978-0-9982493; 978-0-9995842; 978-1-7327384; 978-1-7357470*) 2910 E. Eisenhower Pkwy., Ann Arbor, MI 48108 USA Tel 734-973-9511; Fax: 734-973-9475
E-mail: fairyha@aol.com.

Robe Communications, Inc., (*978-0-9817403; 978-1-935831*) 5138 S. Clifton Ave., Springfield, MO 65810 USA Tel 417-887-8793
E-mail: krobe@mchsi.com
Web site: http://www.robbietherabbit.com.

Roberson, Karen, (*978-0-578-42605-1*) 616 7th St., Peru, IL 61354 USA Tel 815-326-1369
E-mail: sweetpea-emt13@hotmail.com.

Robert L. Fouch *See* **Fouch, Robert L.**

Roberts & Ross Publishing *See* **Hugo House Publishers, Ltd.**

Roberts, Hebard D. Bks., (*978-0-692-05085-9*) 6769 Landover Cir., Tallahassee, FL 32317 USA Tel 850-878-1612
E-mail: gailroberts983@gmail.com.

Roberts, Laura, (*978-0-578-43509-1; 978-0-578-45472-6*) 4677 E. Donna Dr., Prescott, AZ 86301 USA Tel 916-202-0380
E-mail: LaRoberts163@gmail.com
Dist(s): **Independent Pub.**

Roberts, Michele, (*978-0-9760188*) P.O. Box 271611, Houston, TX 77277-1611 USA.

Roberts Publishing Co., (*978-0-931764*) 738 32nd St., S. E., Grand Rapids, MI 49548 USA Tel 616-245-1560; Fax: 616-245-1561 (orders can be sent by fax) Do not confuse with companies with the same or similar names in Sacramento, CA, San Marcos, CA, Great Lake, WI, Blaine, WA
E-mail: robertspublishingco@juno.com
Web site: http://www.scoliosishelp.com; http://www.scoliosishelp.org; http://www.robertsbookshelf.comw.

Robertson, Deirdre, (*978-0-692-46152-5*) RT 5 Box 157, KEYSER, WV 26726 USA Tel 3048130345.

Robertson Publishing, (*978-0-9727721; 978-0-9796251; 978-0-9798633; 978-0-9801675; 978-1-935125; 978-1-61170*) 59 N. Santa Cruz Ave., Suite B, Los Gatos, CA 95030 USA Tel 408-354-5957 Toll Free: 888-354-5957
E-mail: alicia.r@robertsonpubblishing.com
Web site: http://www.RobertsonPublishing.com.

Robillard, Kristy, (*978-0-9800870*) 15110 S Oakleigh Ln., Prairieville, LA 70769 USA Fax: 225-744-3276
E-mail: robillard1@eatel.net.

Robin Corey Bks. *Imprint of* **Random Hse. Children's Bks.**

Robinbook, Ediciones S.L. (ESP) (*978-84-7927; 978-84-9917*) *Dist. by* **Lectorum Pubns.**

Robins Lane Pr. *Imprint of* **Gryphon Hse., Inc.**

Robinson, Beth, (*978-0-9799092*) P.O. Box 100, New Deal, TX 79350 USA (SAN 854-7378)
Web site: http://www.drbethrobinson.com.

Robinson, Consuelo, (*978-0-9786767*) P.O. Box 8662, Delray Beach, FL 33482 USA (SAN 851-2868)
E-mail: math1on1@math1on1.com
Web site: www.math1on1.com.

Robinson, Francesca *See* **Francesca Studios**

Robinson, Julia, (*978-0-692-71414-0*) 28885 Fairway Dr, Buena Vista, CO 81211 USA Tel 717-395-2320
E-mail: georgejuliedt@hotmail.com.

Robison Gamble Creative, (*978-1-933497*) 402B W Mt Vernon 272, Nixa, MO 65714 USA Tel 417-581-6008; Fax: 417-581-4542; Toll Free: 877-335-2735
E-mail: carrie@robisoncreative.com
Web site: http://www.robisoncreative.com.

Robot Playground, Inc., (*978-0-615-51355-3; 978-0-615-57232-1; 978-0-615-67487-2; 978-0-9862926*) 5110 LONG MEADOW DR, FRANKLIN, OH 45005 USA Tel 937-371-1240
E-mail: rita@ritajwebb.com
Dist(s): **CreateSpace Independent Publishing Platform.**

Robus, Debbie, (*978-0-9762034*) 31 Timberline Dr., Heber Springs, AR 72543-9417 USA
E-mail: firecrackerbaby57@yahoo.com
Web site: http://firecrackerbaby57.blogspot.com; http://www.workamper.com
Dist(s): **Workamper Bookstore.**

Robyn Z Moon Publishing, (*978-0-615-15292-9; 978-0-615-20370-6*) 3021 Eads Ave., Saint Lois, MO 63104 USA Toll Free: 877-544-0102
E-mail: robynzmoon@gmail.com
Dist(s): **Lulu Pr., Inc.**

Roc *Imprint of* **Penguin Publishing Group**

Roca Bolsillo (ESP) (*978-84-96940; 978-84-92833; 978-84-15729; 978-84-16240*) *Dist. by* **Spanish.**

Roca Editorial (ESP) (*978-84-96284; 978-84-96544; 978-84-96791; 978-84-9918; 978-84-92429; 978-84-16700; 978-84-16867; 978-84-17092*) *Dist. by* **Spanish.**

Roca Editorial (ESP) (*978-84-96284; 978-84-96544; 978-84-96791; 978-84-9918; 978-84-92429; 978-84-16700; 978-84-16867; 978-84-17092*) *Dist. by* **Ediciones.**

Rocco, Editora, Ltda (BRA) (*978-85-325; 978-85-62500*) *Dist. by* **Distribks Inc.**

Rock & Learn Educational Products *See* **Rock 'N Learn, Inc.**

Rock Cliff Media, (*978-0-9791384*) 553 Staci Ct., Ogden, UT 84404 USA
E-mail: info@rockcliffmedia.com
Web site: http://www.rockcliffmedia.com.

Rock Hse. Method, The *Imprint of* **Russell, Fred Publishing**

Rock Ink, (*978-0-9726979*) 2826 Cory Creek Rd., Oroville, CA 95965 USA Tel 530-894-7743; Fax: 530-892-8293
E-mail: mlrock@mariarock.com
Web site: http://www.mariarock.com.

Rock, James A. & Co. Pubs., (*978-0-918736; 978-1-59663*) 900 S. Irby St., #508, Florence, SC 29505-6357 USA (SAN 211-4690) Toll Free: 800-411-2230; 9710 Traville Gateway Dr., No. 305, Rockville, MD 20850; *Imprints:* Castle Keep Press (Castle Keep Pr); Sense of Wonder Press (Sense of Wonder); Mount Helicon Press (Mt Helicon MD)
E-mail: jarrock@sprintmail.com
Web site: http://www.rockpublishing.com; http://www.senseofwonderpress.com.

Rock 'N Learn, Inc., (*978-1-878489; 978-1-934312; 978-1-941722*) Orders Addr.: P.O. Box 3595, Conroe, TX 77305-3595 USA Tel 936-539-2731; Fax: 936-539-2659; Toll Free Fax: 800-801-5481; Toll Free: 800-348-8445; Edit Addr.: 105 Commercial Cir., Conroe, TX 77304 USA
E-mail: info@rocknlearn.com
Web site: http://www.rocknlearn.com
Dist(s): **Big Kids Productions, Inc.**
Follett School Solutions
Rounder Kids Music Distribution.

Rock Paper Pen Pr., (*978-0-578-55349-8*) 1405 River Aspen Rd., Yankton, SD 57078 USA Tel 402-860-1718
E-mail: mzandrews@mzandrews.com.

Rock Point Gift & Stationery *Imprint of* **Quarto Publishing Group USA**

Rock Point Pr., (*978-0-9912516*) 7 Avenida Vista Grande Suite B7-403, Santa Fe, NM 87508 USA Tel 267-304-8521
E-mail: joannavhill@gmail.com
Dist(s): **SCB Distributors.**

Rock Village Publishing, (*978-0-9674204; 978-0-9721389; 978-0-9766356; 978-1-934400*) 41 Walnut St., Middleborough, MA 02346 USA Tel 508-946-4738
E-mail: rockvillage@verizon.net.

Rock Wren Pr., (*978-0-692-96831-4*) 30 Lewis Mountain Ln., Durango, CO 81301 USA Tel 970-259-9179
E-mail: tiffmapel@yahoo.com.

Rockbott'm *See* **Spring Hollow Bks., LLC**

Rocket City Publishing, (*978-1-7325071; 978-1-7352475*) 990 Explorer Blvd. NW, HUNTSVILLE, AL 35811 USA Tel 256-453-4975
E-mail: rocketcitypublishing@gmail.com
Web site: www.rocketcitypublishing.com.

Rocket Press Books Inc. *See* **Rocket Press Publishing, LLC**

Rocket Press Publishing, LLC, (*978-0-9891732; 978-1-5375-9865-9*) 139-B James Comeaux Rd. PMB No. 571, Lafayette, LA 70508 USA Tel 337-591-9845
E-mail: rocketpressbooks@gmail.com
Web site: www.rocketpressbooks.com.

Rocket Ride Bks., (*978-0-9823322*) P.O. Box 1223, Somerset, PA 15501 USA
E-mail: anthonyrotoolo@yahoo.com.

Rocket Science Productions, LLC, (*978-0-9821823; 978-0-9830725; 978-1-937121; 978-1-939954; 978-1-945355*) 5765-F Burke Centre Pkwy., No. 222, Burke, VA 22015 USA (SAN 857-4863) Tel 703-764-8000
E-mail: fmonahan@rsp-llc.com
Dist(s): **Smashwords.**

RockhopperBooks, (*978-0-615-72947-3; 978-0-615-87745-7; 978-0-692-27399-9; 978-0-692-45625-5; 978-0-9965424; 978-0-9986234*) 1944 Gibson Ave, Clovis, CA 93611 USA Tel 559-908-1654
Dist(s): **CreateSpace Independent Publishing Platform.**

Rocking Chair Kids *Imprint of* **Red Chair Pr.**

Rockit Pr., (*978-0-9908011; 978-0-9962160; 978-0-9981719*) 695 Nashville Pike, No. 200, Gallatin, TN 37066 USA Tel 818-850-3020
E-mail: shauna@rockitpress.com; david@rockitpress.com
Web site: http://www.rockitpress.com.

Rockland Press *See* **Peach Tree Pr.**

Rockmill Publishing Co., (*978-0-9764012*) Rockmill Management, Inc., 17360 Hunter Ct., Lake Oswego, OR 97035 USA (SAN 256-5722) Tel 503-989-2590 (phone/fax); 503-806-3970
E-mail: energiesinc@msn.com; tammystarnermotsch@msn.com.

Rockon Publishing, (*978-0-9726255*) 210 Hy Rd., Buda, TX 78610 USA Tel 512-295-4889
E-mail: wermundj@mail.utexas.edu.

Rockport Publishers *Imprint of* **Quarto Publishing Group USA**

Rockport Publishers *Imprint of* **Quarto Publishing Group USA**

Rockridge University Press *See* **Callisto Media Inc.**

Rocksand, LLC, (*978-1-931552*) 238 Greenbrier Dr., Cape Girardeau, MO 63701 USA Tel 877-625-7263
E-mail: bethprints@ymail.com
Web site: http://www.rainbowindow.com.

Rockshow Comedy, Inc., (*978-0-9854699*) 130 Old Town Blvd. N., Argyle, TX 76226 USA Tel 817-915-4296
E-mail: todd@rockshowcomedy.com
Web site: www.rockshowcomedy.com.

RockTuff, (*978-0-9800754*) Orders Addr.: P.O. Box 133, Roscoe, SD 57471 USA (SAN 855-1308) Tel 605-287-4133; Fax: 605-287-4188; Edit Addr.: 34240 Hwy. 12, Roscoe, SD 57471 USA
E-mail: rocktuff@venturecomm.net
Web site: http://www.andreabeyers.com.

Rocky Mountain Bks., (*978-0-9605648; 978-0-692-12711-7*) P.O. Box 100663, Denver, CO 80210 USA (SAN 215-7047) Tel 303-850-9403; Fax: 303-771-6654 (call first)
E-mail: rockymountainbooks@yahoo.com
Web site: www.normasands.com
Dist(s): **Publishers Group West (PGW).**

Rocky Nook, (*978-1-933952; 978-1-937538; 978-1-68198*) Orders Addr.: 802 E. Cota St., 3rd Flr., Santa Barbara, CA 93103 USA (SAN 850-6906) Tel 805-687-8727; Toll Free: 866-687-1118
E-mail: matthias@rockynook.com; info@rockynook.com
Web site: http://www.rockynook.com
Dist(s): **Ingram Publisher Services**
MyiLibrary
O'Reilly Media, Inc.
ebrary, Inc.

Rod & Staff Pubs., Inc., (*978-0-7399*) P.O. Box 3, 14193 Hwy. 172, Crockett, KY 41413 USA (SAN 206-7633) Tel 606-522-4348; Fax: 606-522-4896; Toll Free Fax: 800-643-1244
Web site: http://www.rodstaff.com/.

Rodaian Pr., (*978-1-935436; 978-0-9847167; 978-0-9847986; 978-0-9893251*) P.O. Box 3128, Palm Springs, CA 92263 USA
Web site: http://www.rodaian.com.

Rodale Books *Imprint of* **Potter/Ten Speed/Harmony/Rodale**

Rodale Kids *Imprint of* **Random Hse. Children's Bks.**

†**Rodale Pr., Inc.,** (*978-0-87596; 978-0-87857; 978-1-57954; 978-1-4050; 978-1-59486; 978-1-60529; 978-1-60961; 978-1-62336; 978-1-63565*) Orders Addr.: 16365 James Madison Hwy., Gordonsville, VA 22942-8501 USA Toll Free Fax: 800-672-2054; Toll Free: 888-330-8477; Edit Addr.: 400 S. Tentth St., Emmaus, PA 18098-0099 USA (SAN 200-2477) Tel 610-967-5171; Fax: 215-967-8961; Toll Free: 800-222-4997
E-mail: sara.cox@rodale.com
Web site: rodale.com
Dist(s): **Bilingual Pubns. Co., The**
Children's Plus, Inc.
Lectorum Pubns., Inc.
MBI Distribution Services/Quayside Distribution
Penguin Random Hse. Distribution
Penguin Random Hse. LLC
Send The Light Distribution LLC
St. Martin's Pr.
TNT Media Group, Inc.; *CIP.*

Rodgers, Alan Bks., (*978-1-59818; 978-1-60312; 978-1-60664; 978-1-4638*) 23511 Aliso Creek Rd., No. 120, Alsio Viejo, CA 92656-1341 USA
E-mail: AlanRodg@aol.com; amysterlingcasil@gmail.com; lmdegange@yahoo.com
Web site: http://www.aegypan.com; www.chameleonpublishers.com; http://www.chameleonmedia.co.

Rodgers & Nelsen Publishing Company *See* **Loveland Pr., LLC**

Rodrigue & Sons Company *See* **Rodrigue & Sons Co./Double R Books Publishing**

Rodrigue & Sons Co./Double R Books Publishing, (*978-0-9749026; 978-0-9833975; 978-1-938319*) Orders Addr.: 740 N. H St., Suite 170, Lompoc, CA 93436 USA Tel 805-735-7103 10am - 5pm PST; Fax: 805-737-9846; 740 N. H St., Suite 170, Lompoc, CA 93436 Tel 805-735-7103 10am - 5pm PST; Fax: 805-737-9846; *Imprints:* DOUBLE-R BOOKS (DOUBLE-R); DOUBLE R BOOKS (MYID_E_DOUBLE)
E-mail: publisher@doubleRbooks.com
Web site: http://DoubleRbooks.com
Dist(s): **INscribe Digital**
Independent Pubs. Group
Ingram Bk. Co.

Rodriguez, Estela, (*978-0-9772631*) Orders Addr.: 2050 NW 16th Terr., Apt. E111, Miami, FL 33125 USA Tel 305-549-3039; Edit Addr.: Jose Marti Stat. 27 & 4th St., Miami, FL 33135 USA
E-mail: colorama@bellsouth.net.

Rodriguez, Josue D., 34 Norwood Rd, NEW HAVEN, CT 06513 USA Tel 203-214-3981.

Rodriguez, Michelle, (*978-0-9900061*) 38-33 147th St., Flushing, NY 11354 USA Tel 646-217-9177
E-mail: maliperto1@gmail.com.

Rodriguez, Raul, (*978-0-9912750*) 9619 Judalon Ln, Houston, TX 77063 USA Tel 281-467-6992
E-mail: raul6992@yahoo.com.

Rodro, (*978-0-9744770; 978-1-7328579; 978-1-970056*) 52 Richmond Blvd., No. 3B, Ronkonkoma, NY 11779-3629 USA
Web site: http://www.rodro.com.

Roe, Gary, (*978-1-950382*) 4203 Cripple Creek Ct., College Station, TX 77845 USA Tel 425-422-2222
E-mail: garynroe@gmail.com.

Roedway Pr., (*978-0-9659650*) P.O. Box 903, La Quinta, CA 92253 USA Tel 760-771-9818; Fax: 760-771-9618; Toll Free: 888-694-2248.

Roehm, Nancy Jean, (*978-0-9745591*) 210 Stoney Ridge Dr., Alpharetta, GA 30022-7668 USA
E-mail: njroehm4116@aol.com.

Roger Dean Publishing Co., (*978-0-89328*) Div. of The Lorenz Corp., 501 E. Third St., Dayton, OH 45402-2118 USA Tel 937-228-6118; Toll Free: 800-444-1144
E-mail: order@lorenz.com
Web site: http://www.lorenz.com.

Rogers, Al M. Jr., (*978-0-9760159*) 48151 N. Laura Rogers Rd., Tickfaw, LA 70466 USA
Web site: http://www.lasttrumpgathering.com.

Rogers, Siobain K., (*978-0-615-13289-1*) 103 Harris Cir., Carthage, TX 75633 USA
Web site: http://www.lulu.com/siobainrogers
Dist(s): **Lulu Pr., Inc.**

Rogue Wave Publishing *See* **Tonepoet Publishing**

Rohrer Design, (*978-0-9721138*) 725-17th St., Kenosha, WI 53140-1329 USA
Web site: http://www.rohrer-design.com.

Publisher Name Index

Roisin Dubh Pubns., *(978-0-692-93065-6)* P.O. Box 237, Gardena, CA 90248 USA Tel 310-632-7826 (phone/fax)
E-mail: legacyofpacific@aol.com
Web site: www.alegacyofthepacific.com.

Roland & Eleanor Bergthold, *(978-0-9741193)* 9133 N. Stoneridge Ln., Fresno, CA 93720 USA Tel 559-434-4137
E-mail: rolbergthold@prodigy.net; embergthold@prodigy.net.

Roland Golf Services, *(978-0-9911293)* 8911 Shrockton St., Powell, OH 43065 USA Tel 614-264-0545
E-mail: Rolandgolfservices@gmail.com
Web site: Tonylema.com.

Rolemommy, *(978-0-9822974)* 36 Rutledge Rd., Scarsdale, NY 10583 USA
E-mail: beth@rolemommy.com; mail@plainwhitepress.com.

Rolest P. Inc., *(978-0-9786281; 978-0-9984275; 978-0-692-83116-8; 978-0-9986232)* 1503 Elberta Rd., No. 115, Warner Robins, GA 31093 USA Tel 478-442-6936
E-mail: rolest@juno.com.

Rolling Hills Pr., *(978-0-943978)* 17 Olive Ave., Novato, CA 94945-3428 USA (SAN 282-2601) Do not confuse with Rolling Hills Pr., in Alexandria, VA
E-mail: rhpressllc@aol.com.

Rolling Through Life With TaLisha, *(978-0-578-55018-3; 978-0-578-61823-4; 978-0-9999013)* 9 Highland Blvd., New Castle, DE 19720 USA Tel 302-983-4038
E-mail: talishagrzyb@gmail.com.

Romain, Trevor Co., The, *(978-0-9762843; 978-0-9787783; 978-1-934365; 978-0-9819804; 978-1-936407)* 4412 Spicewood Springs Rd. Suite 705, Austin, TX 78759-8567 USA Toll Free: 877-876-6246
E-mail: sabrina@trevorromain.com
Web site: http://www.TrevorRomain.com; http://www.comicalsense.com.

Roman Candle Publishing, *(978-0-692-12039-2)* 1002 Faculty Dr., Columbus, OH 43221 USA Tel 415-816-5326
E-mail: dustinoverholser@gmail.com
Web site: www.imaginaryninjas.com.

Roman Catholic Bks., *(978-0-912141; 978-1-929291; 978-0-9793540; 978-1-934888)* Div. of Catholic Media Apostolate, Orders Addr.: P.O. Box 2286, Fort Collins, CO 80522 USA Fax: 970-493-8781; Edit Addr.: 1331 Red Cedar Cir., Fort Collins, CO 80524 USA
Web site: http://www.booksforcatholics.com.

Roman, Teresa, *(978-0-9961545)* 5207 Arden Way, Carmichael, CA 95608 USA Tel 904-625-4310
E-mail: gayoba@gmail.com
Web site: teresaromanwrites.com.

Romancing Cathay, *(978-1-932592)* 10050 Montgomery Rd., No. 315, Cincinnati, OH 45242 USA Tel 513-290-7419; Fax: 949-266-8395
E-mail: business@romancingcathay.com
Web site: http://www.romancingcathay.com.

Romani, Gabriella *See* **BBM Bks.**

Romero Empire, *(978-0-578-19278-9)* 16 Blossom St., Leominster, MA 01453 USA.

Romita, Tom, *(978-0-9995928)* 29 Amherst Dr, Hastings on Hudson, NY 10706 USA Tel 914-693-4210
E-mail: tom@tomromita.com
Web site: www.tomromita.com.

Romoulous *Imprint of* **MIROGLYPHICS**

Romoulous Enterprises *See* **MIROGLYPHICS**

Ronald, George Pub., Ltd., *(978-0-85398)* 8325 17th St., N., Saint Petersburg, FL 33702-2843 USA (SAN 679-1859); 3 Rosecroft Ln. Oaklands, Welwyn, AL6 0UB
E-mail: sales@grbooks.com
Web site: www.grbooks.com
Dist(s): **Cambridge Univ. Pr.**

Ronan Enterprises, Inc., *(978-0-9821110)* P.O. Box 574, Richmond, MI 48062 USA.

Rondo Books *See* **Parrish, Fayrene**

Ronin Publishing, *(978-0-914171; 978-1-57951)* P.O. Box 22900, Oakland, CA 94609 USA (SAN 287-5365) Tel 510-420-3669; Fax: 510-420-3672; Toll Free: 800-858-2665 (orders) Do not confuse with Ronin Publishing in Cambridge, MA
E-mail: orders@roninpub.com
Web site: http://www.roninpub.com
Dist(s): **MyiLibrary**
New Leaf Distributing Co., Inc.
Publishers Group West (PGW)
ebrary, Inc.

RonJon Publishing, Incorporated *See* **Hewell Publishing**

Ronsdale Pr. (CAN) *(978-0-921870; 978-1-55380) Dist. by* **SPD-Small Pr Dist.**

Roost Books *Imprint of* **Shambhala Pubns., Inc.**

Rooster Pubns., *(978-0-9792135)* Orders Addr.: 101 S. Page St., Morrisonville, IL 62546-6746 USA; Edit Addr.: 101 S. Page St., Morrisonville, IL 62546-6746 USA
E-mail: grandmotherstewart@msn.com.

RoosterBugglePue Bks. *Imprint of* **Eupanapue-Auntella's Rooster Pubns.**

Roots & Wings, *(978-0-9703319)* 20114 Illinois Rte. 16, Nokomis, IL 62075 USA Tel 217-594-7300; Fax: 217-563-2111 Do not confuse with companies with the same name in Lake Forest, IL, New Paltz, NY, Boulder, CO
E-mail: beltpulley@ccipost.net.

Roots in Myth, *(978-1-949717)* 9223 Spicebrush Dr., Austin, TX 78759 USA Tel 512-797-6974
E-mail: triciajh@yahoo.com.

Roots, Robert, *(978-0-9715336)* 11820 Miramar Pkwy. No. 212, Miramar, FL 33025 USA
E-mail: rbroots22@yahoo.com; rr@robertroots.com
Web site: http://www.robertroots.com.

Rope Ferry Press *See* **Anemone Publishing**

Roque-Velasco, Dr. Ismael, *(978-0-9706319)* P.O. Box 432804, Miami, FL 3243 USA Tel 305-667-6230; 305-740-6724
E-mail: northernismael@aol.com
Web site: http://www.cubaforkids.com
Dist(s): **Lectorum Pubns., Inc.**

Rori Shay Author, *(978-1-7320479)* 3314 264th Ave. NE, REDMOND, WA 98053 USA Tel 571-213-6485
E-mail: ramkraut@gmail.com
Dist(s): **Ingram Content Group.**

Rorschach Entertainment, *(978-0-9748654)* 15806 18th Ave W. Apt. F203, Lynnwood, WA 98087-8755 USA
E-mail: info@rorschachentertainment.com
Web site: http://www.rorschachentertainment.com.

Rosales, Irene, *(978-0-9824348)* PMB 154, 3118 FM 528, Webster, TX 77598 USA.

Rosasharn Pr., *(978-0-615-96746-2; 978-0-9916496; 978-0-692-50595-3)* 1011 Serenity Cir., Auburn, AL 36830 USA Tel 334-750-6280
E-mail: info@pegathapress.com.

Rose, A., *(978-0-692-04963-1; 978-0-692-04964-8; 978-0-578-42827-7; 978-0-578-42828-4)* 1022 20th Ave. NE, Minneapolis, MN 55418 USA Tel 612 701 6262
E-mail: sadee.thompson@gmail.com
Dist(s): **Ingram Content Group.**

Rose Art Industries, Inc., *(978-1-57041)* 6 Regent St., Livingston, NJ 07039 USA Toll Free: 800-272-9667.

Rose Bud Publishing Co. LLC, *(978-0-9836913)* 8245 N. 27th Ave., Apt. 1048, Phoenix, AZ 85051 USA Tel 602-501-4533.

Rose Consultant, *(978-0-578-40200-0; 978-0-578-48402-0; 978-0-578-62948-3)* 8948 SW 211th Ln., Cutler Bay, FL 33189 USA Tel 786-209-4795
E-mail: drpattirose@gmail.com
Web site: https://drpattirose.wixsite.com/website.

Rose, Gary Publishing, *(978-0-9988777; 978-1-7348524)* 4065 River Woods, Auburn, CA 95602 USA Tel 530-885-3067
E-mail: grose1@pacbell.net.

Rose, Lisa Writes, *(978-0-692-06053-7)* 28860 Nottway, Farmington Hills, MI 48331 USA Tel 248-943-0742; Fax: 248-943-0742
E-mail: lchottiner@sbcglobal.net
Web site: www.LisaRoseWrites.com.

Rose Publishing, *(978-0-9655082; 978-1-890947; 978-1-59636; 978-1-62862; 978-1-64938)* Orders Addr.: 140 Summit St., Peabody, MA 01961 USA; Edit Addr.: 140 Summit St., Peabody, MA 01961-3473 USA (SAN 253-0120) Tel 800-358-3111; 978-573-3111; Fax: 978-573-8111 Do not confuse with companies with same or similar names in Flagtown, NJ, Arcadia, CA, Keystone Heights, FL, Salem, OR, Santa Cruz, CA, Tucson, AZ, Alameda, CA, Grand Rapids, MI, Little Rock, AR, Boulder, CO
Web site: http://www.rose-publishing.com; hendricksonrose.com
Dist(s): **Firebrand Technologies**
INscribe Digital
Spring Arbor Distributors, Inc.

Rose River Publishing Co., *(978-0-9707976)* P.O. Box 19864, Alexandria, VA 22320 USA Tel 703-768-2380 (phone/fax)
E-mail: herbpuscheck@cs.com.

Rose Valley Publishing, *(978-0-9765905)* 53762 Kristin Ct., Shelby Township, MI 48316 USA
E-mail: manitoumagic@aol.com
Web site: http://www.rosevalleypublishing.com.

Rose Water Cottage Pr., *(978-0-9853223; 978-0-9961393; 978-1-7352333)* 308 Stewart St., Franklin, TN 37064 USA Tel 615-476-6717
E-mail: tray296@att.net.

Rose Wind Pr., *(978-0-9631232)* Div. of Compass Rose Corp., 1701 Broadway, No. 345, Vancouver, WA 98663 USA Tel 360-693-7742; Fax: 360-693-0950
E-mail: galenahk@aol.com
Web site: http://www.compassart.

Roseberg, Anders, *(978-0-9982323; 978-1-952199)* 14595 S. 1515 W., Bluffdale, UT 84065 USA Tel 801-898-2263; *Imprints:* Imagine Creatively (ImagineCreat)
E-mail: andersrosebergbooks@gmail.com
Web site: www.andersrosebergbooks.wordpress.com; www.andersroseberg.com; https://www.facebook.com/AndersRoseberg/.

RoseDog Bks. *Imprint of* **Dorrance Publishing Co., Inc.**

RoseFountain Pr., LLC, *(978-0-9768051)* 65 High Ridge Rd., No. 163, Stamford, CT 06905-3814 USA (SAN 858-4664)
Dist(s): **BookBaby**
Enfield Publishing & Distribution Co., Inc.

RoseKnows, Inc., *(978-0-9755889)* P.O. Box 5448, McLean, VA 22103-5448 USA
Web site: http://www.playgeist.com.

Rosemaling & Crafts, *(978-0-9674583)* Orders Addr.: 3208 Snowbrush Pl., Fort Collings, CO 80521 USA Tel 970-229-9846; Fax: 970-229-5683
E-mail: diaedwards@cs.com
Web site: http://www.nordic-arts.com.

Rosemary Publishing, *(978-0-692-19340-2; 978-0-692-04304-2; 978-0-578-53544-9)* 1201 Dulles Ave. Apt. 2106, Stafford, TX 77477 USA Tel 832-763-0952
E-mail: theedonnamarie@gmail.com
Dist(s): **Ingram Content Group.**

Rosemont, Ltd., *(978-0-9635811)* 1620 Belmont St., Jackson, MS 39202-1203 USA Tel 601-355-1233.

Rosen & Assocs., Inc., *(978-0-9746811; 978-0-9778973)* P.O. Box 17173, Chapel Hill, NC 27516 USA Tel 919-264-5976; Fax: 919-929-7119
E-mail: info@cashworkbooks.com
Web site: http://www.cashworkbooks.com.

Rosen Central *Imprint of* **Rosen Publishing Group, Inc., The**

Rosen Classroom *Imprint of* **Rosen Publishing Group, Inc., The**

†Rosen Publishing Group, Inc., The, *(978-0-8239; 978-1-56696; 978-1-4042; 978-1-59791; 978-1-4358; 978-1-60851; 978-1-60852; 978-1-60853; 978-1-60854; 978-1-61511; 978-1-61512; 978-1-61513; 978-1-61514; 978-1-61530; 978-1-61531; 978-1-61532; 978-1-61533; 978-1-4488; 978-1-4777; 978-1-4824; 978-1-4994; 978-1-68048; 978-1-5081; 978-1-68416; 978-1-5382; 978-1-5383; 978-1-64282; 978-1-64374; 978-1-7253) a/o Dept. C234561, 29 E. 21st St., New York, NY 10010 USA (SAN 203-3720) Tel 212-777-3017; Fax: 212-358-9588; Toll Free Fax: 888-436-4643; Toll Free: 800-237-9932; Imprints:* PowerKids Press (PowerKids Pr); Rosen Reference (RosenRef); Editorial Buenas Letras (EditBuenas); Powerstart Press (Powerstart Pr); Reading Power (Reading Power); Dance & Movement Press (Dance); Rosen Classroom (RosenClassrm); Britannica Educational Publishing (BritEducPub); Rosen Young Adult (RosenYA); Windmill Books (WindmillBks); Rosen Central (RosenCent); New York Times Educational Publishing (NewYork TEP)
E-mail: hollyc@rosenpub.com; info@rosenpub.com; customerservice@rosenpub.com; hollyc@rosen.pub
Web site: http://www.rosenpublishing.com; http://www.rosendigital.com; http://www.rosenclassroom.com
Dist(s): **Ebsco Publishing**
Encyclopaedia Britannica, Inc.
Follett School Solutions
Stevens, Gareth Publishing LLLP
Lectorum Pubns., Inc.
ebrary, Inc.; *CIP.*

Rosen Publishing Group, Incorporated, The *See* **Rosen Publishing Group, Inc., The**

Rosen Publishing, Inc., *(978-1-881930)* 3000 Chestnut Ave., Suite 300, Baltimore, MD 21211 USA Tel 800-237-9932; Fax: 410-889-1320.

Rosen Reference *Imprint of* **Rosen Publishing Group, Inc., The**

Rosen Young Adult *Imprint of* **Rosen Publishing Group, Inc., The**

Rosenberg, Harvey *See* **Go Jolly Bks.**

Rosenberger, Matthew, *(978-0-9760047; 978-0-9909415)* Div. of ABC Publishing for Kids, One Summit St., Philadelphia, PA 19118 USA (SAN 858-9887) Tel 215-242-4011; Fax: 215-242-9421
E-mail: mgr@kidstravelguides.com
Web site: http://www.kidstravelguides.com.

Roses Are READ Productions, *(978-0-9703489; 978-0-9755093)* P.O. Box 7844, Saint Paul, MN 55107 USA Tel 651-686-8418; Fax: 651-340-5333; *Imprints:* Little Petals (Little Petals)
E-mail: admin@rosesareread.cc.

Rosetta Stone Communications, *(978-0-9759331)* 1971 N. Nowak Ave., Thousand Oaks, CA 91360 USA (SAN 256-1549) Tel 805-370-0010; Fax: 805-435-1541
E-mail: johngriffith@maggio-associates.com
Web site: http://www.scientificgolfer.com.

Rosetta Stone Ltd., *(978-1-58022; 978-1-883972; 978-1-60391; 978-1-60717; 978-1-60829; 978-1-61716; 978-1-62821)* 135 W. Market St., Harrisonburg, VA 22801 USA Toll Free: 800-788-0822
E-mail: info@trstone.com; help@RosettaStone.com
Web site: http://www.rosettastone.com.

Roslin Pr., *(978-1-946290)* 36-03 Stelton Terr., Fair Lawn, NJ 07410 USA Tel 484-557-1269
E-mail: haig@roslin.press.

Rosmen-Izdat (RUS) *(978-5-8451) Dist. by* **Distribks Inc.**

Ross, Alan Publications *See* **Ross Pubns.**

Ross & Perry, Inc., *(978-1-931641; 978-1-931839; 978-1-932080; 978-1-932109; 978-0-9849531)* 3 S. Haddon Ave., Suite 4, Haddonfield, NJ 08003 USA (SAN 253-8555) Tel 856 427-6135; Fax: 856-427-6136
E-mail: grfisheriii@gmail.com
Web site: http://www.rossperry.com; http://www.gporeprints.com
Dist(s): **TextStream.**

Ross, Cathy, *(978-0-9797832)* 1509 Cypress Rd., Olney, IL 62450 USA Tel 618-393-7732; Fax: 618-395-0123
E-mail: devspecinc@yahoo.com.

Ross, Jeanne, *(978-0-9850216)* PO Box 9011 PMB 308, Calexico, CA 92232 USA Tel 720-480-0121
E-mail: Raydiant1s@yahoo.com.

Ross, Liesl, *(978-0-578-42456-9)* 3438 Nicklaus Dr., Rapid City, SD 57702 USA Tel 980-560-4743
E-mail: lieslross1985@yahoo.com
Dist(s): **Ingram Content Group.**

Ross Pubns., *(978-0-9617038)* 1438 W. Lantana Rd., No. 401, Lantana, FL 33462 USA (SAN 662-8230)
E-mail: alanross@aol.com
Web site: http://www.thegenuinejesus.com.

Ross, Warren K Jr, *(978-0-9903086)* 85 Brook St, Wellesley, MA 02482 USA Tel 781-235-5560
E-mail: w@wross.com
Dist(s): **Independent Pubs. Group**
Midpoint Trade Bks., Inc.

Rossi, Debra, *(978-0-9758982)* 813 Wentwood, Southlake, TX 76092 USA.

Rotaplast Pr., *(978-0-9706901)* Orders Addr.: P.O. Box 1100, Kennebunkport, ME 04046 USA Tel 207-967-0118; Edit Addr.: 4 East Ave., Kennebunkport, ME 04046 USA.

Roth Pubns., *(978-0-9832102; 978-1-938428)* P.O. Box 1058, Monsey, NY 10952 USA Tel 845-474-0022; Fax: 845-770-3382
E-mail: solomon@rothpublishers.com
Web site: www.rothpublishers.com.

Roth Publishing *See* **HELORO Publishing Group**

Rothman Editions, *(978-0-692-50288-4; 978-0-692-53384-0; 978-0-692-58566-5; 978-0-692-64413-3; 978-0-692-71266-5; 978-0-692-75332-3; 978-0-692-76020-8; 978-0-692-76489-3; 978-0-692-91369-7; 978-0-692-15187-7)* P.O. Box 53, Cypress, TX 77410 USA Tel 281-382-1655
E-mail: ryvrsann@comcast.net
Web site: https://www.instagram.com/rothmaneditions/
Dist(s): **CreateSpace Independent Publishing Platform.**

Rothwell Digital Imagery, *(978-0-615-18912-3)* Orders Addr.: P.O. Box 383, Westfield, NY 14787 USA Tel 716-326-4319; 716-969-4088 (cell)
E-mail: tlroth@fairpoint.net; tlrothwell@gmail.com; lewisthedragon@live.com
Web site: http://lewisthedragon.com
Dist(s): **R J Communications, LLC.**

Rough Draft Printing, *(978-0-933998; 978-1-60386)* 1280 Queen St., Seaside, OR 97138 USA; *Imprints:* Merchant Books (Merchant Bks).

Round Cow Media Group, *(978-0-9745218)* Orders Addr.: P.O. Box 87, Alpharetta, GA 30009-0087 USA Tel 678-762-9053; Edit Addr.: 2822 Ashleigh Ln., Alpharetta, GA 30004 USA; *Imprints:* Biz4Kids (Biz4Kids)
E-mail: christian@biz4kids.com
Web site: http://www.biz4kids.com.

Round Tower Pr., *(978-0-9765964)* P.O. Box 2942, Paradise, CA 95969-2942 USA Tel 530-872-9705; Fax: 530-872-7732; Toll Free: 888-737-9705
E-mail: thor@roundtowerpress.com
Web site: http://www.roundtowerpress.com.

Rounder Bks., *(978-1-57940)* 29 Lancaster St., Cambridge, MA 02140 USA Tel 617-492-3799
Dist(s): **Leonard, Hal Corp.**

Roundsquare Pr., *(978-0-9717280)* 295 Marble St., Suite 303, Broomfield, CO 80020-2171 USA
E-mail: rs_press@msn.com.

Roundtree Pr. *Imprint of* **Cameron + Co.**

Rourke Educational Media, *(978-0-86592; 978-0-86593; 978-0-86625; 978-1-55916; 978-1-57103; 978-1-58952; 978-1-59515; 978-1-60044; 978-1-60472; 978-1-60694; 978-1-61590; 978-1-61741; 978-1-61236; 978-1-61810; 978-1-62169; 978-1-62717; 978-1-63155; 978-1-63430; 978-1-68191; 978-1-68342; 978-1-64156; 978-1-64369; 978-1-7316) Div. of Carson-Dellosa Publishing, LLC, Orders Addr.: P.O. Box 643328, Vero Beach, FL 32964 USA (SAN 857-0825) Fax: 772-234-6622; Toll Free: 800-394-7055; Edit Addr.: 1701 Hwy. A1A S., Ste 300, Vero Beach, FL 32963 USA Toll Free Fax: 1-888-355-6270; Toll Free: 800-394-7055*
E-mail: rourke@rourkepublishing.com; rbrady@rourkepublishing.com; renee@roukeeducationalmedia.com
Web site: http://www.rourkeeducationalmedia.com
Dist(s): **Carson-Dellosa Publishing, LLC**
Findaway World, LLC
Follett School Solutions
Ideals Pubns.
MyiLibrary.

Rourke Enterprises, Inc., *(978-0-86592)* Div. of Rourke Publishing Group, P.O. Box 3328, Vero Beach, FL 32964-3328 USA Tel 561-234-6001; Fax: 561-234-6622
E-mail: rourke@sunet.net
Web site: http://www.rourkepublishing.com.

Rourke Publishing, LLC *See* **Rourke Educational Media**

Rourke, Ray Publishing Company, Incorporated *See* **Rourke Enterprises, Inc.**

Routledge *Imprint of* **Taylor & Francis Group**

†Routledge, *(978-0-04; 978-0-413; 978-0-415; 978-0-7100; 978-0-87830; 978-1-317)* Member of Taylor & Frances Group, Orders Addr.: 7625 Empire Dr., Florence, KY 41042 USA Toll Free Fax: 800-248-4724 (orders, customer serv.); Toll Free: 800-634-7064 (orders, customer serv.); Edit Addr.: 270 Madison Ave. # 3, New York, NY 10016-0601 USA (SAN 213-196X)
E-mail: cserve@routledge-ny.com; info@routledge-ny.com
Web site: http://www.routledge-ny.com
Dist(s): **CRC Pr. LLC**
Chicago Distribution Ctr.
Ebsco Publishing
MyiLibrary
National Bk. Network
Oxford Univ. Pr., Inc.
Pearson Education
Rowman & Littlefield Publishers, Inc.
Taylor & Francis Group
Women Ink; *CIP.*

Roux Publishing, *(978-0-9976979)* 17518 Amelia Dr, Baton rouge, LA 70810 USA Tel 225-281-3686
E-mail: Jbmoniotte@yahoo.com.

Rovakada, LLC, *(978-0-9845867)* P.O. Box 210324, San Francisco, CA 94121 USA Tel 415-290-6454
E-mail: order@rovakada.com
Dist(s): **National Bk. Network.**

Rowan Mountain Pr., *(978-0-926487)* Orders Addr.: P.O. Box 10111, Blacksburg, VA 24062-0111 USA Tel 540-449-6178; Fax: 540-951-5214; Toll Free: 888-961-3315; Edit Addr.: 2010 Broken Oak Dr., Blacksburg, VA 24060-1448 USA Tel 540-449-6178
E-mail: faulkner@bev.net
Web site: http://www.rowanmountain.com.

Rowboat Pr., *(978-0-578-42401-9; 978-0-578-42676-1; 978-1-7339196)* 138 17th Ave. N., St. Petersburg, FL 33704 USA Tel 727-612-3444
E-mail: toriashleymcgee@gmail.com
Dist(s): **Independent Pub.**

Rowe, Kysha, *(978-0-9769339)* 605 Crested View Ct., Loganville, GA 30052-8926 USA
E-mail: kysha_r@yahoo.com
Web site: http://www.whatcreaturesteachus.com; http://www.focusontheyouth.com.

Rowe Publishing, *(978-0-9833971; 978-0-9851196; 978-1-939054; 978-1-64446)* 655 Old Lifsey Springs Rd, Molena, GA 30258 USA Tel 785-302-0451
E-mail: info@rowepublishingdesign.com
Web site: www.rowepub.com
Dist(s): **Smashwords.**

Rowe Publishing and Design *See* **Rowe Publishing**

Rowfant Pr., *(978-1-929731)* 845 N. Gow, Wichita, KS 67203 USA Tel 316-371-7254
E-mail: b_myers123@live.com
Web site: http://rowfantpress.org.

Rowles, Louis, *(978-0-9708748)* 204 12th Ave., N., Amory, MS 38821-1206 USA Tel 662-256-3865
E-mail: glrowles@network-one.com.

Rowman & Littlefield Education, *(978-0-8108; 978-1-56676; 978-1-57886; 978-1-60709; 978-1-61048; 978-1-4758)* Orders Addr.: 15200 NBN Way, Blue Ridge Summit, PA 17214 USA Tel 717-794-3800 (Sales, Customer Service, MIS, Royalties Inventory); Fax: 717-794-3803 (Customer Service & orders only); 717-794-3857 (Sales & MIS); 717-794-3856 (Royalties, Inventory Mgmt. & Distribution); Toll Free Fax: 800-338-4550 (Customer Service & orders); Toll Free: 800-462-6420 (Customer Service & orders); Edit Addr.: 4501 Forbes Blvd., Suite 200, Lanham, MD 20706 USA Tel 301-459-3366; Fax: 301-459-5748; Toll Free Fax: 800-338-4550; Toll Free: 800-462-6420; 4501 Forbes Blvd Suite 200, Lanham, MD 20706 Short Discount, contact rlpgsales@rowman.com
E-mail: mmcmenamin@rowman.com; tkoerner@rowman.com
Web site: http://www.rlpgbooks.com; http://www.scarecroweducation.com; http://www.rowman.com
Dist(s): **CreateSpace Independent Publishing Platform**
Ebsco Publishing
Follett School Solutions
MyiLibrary
National Bk. Network
Rowman & Littlefield Publishers, Inc.
ebrary, Inc.

†Rowman & Littlefield Publishers, Inc., *(978-0-8476; 978-0-87471; 978-0-9632978; 978-1-56699; 978-1-888052; 978-0-7425; 978-1-931890; 978-1-933494; 978-1-4422; 978-1-936283; 978-1-61281; 978-1-4616; 978-1-4617; 978-1-62093; 978-1-5381; 978-1-68475)* Mem. of Rowman & Littlefield Publishing Group, Inc., Orders Addr.: 15200 NBN Way, Blue Ridge Summit, PA 17214 USA Tel 717-794-3800 (Sales, Customer Service, MIS, Royalties, Inventory; Fax: 717-794-3803 (Customer Service & orders only); 717-794-3857 (Sales & MIS); 717-794-3856 (Royalties, Inventory Mgmt. & Distribution); Toll Free Fax: 800-338-4550 (Customer Service & orders); Toll Free: 800-462-6420 (Customer Service & orders); Edit Addr.: 4501 Forbes Blvd., Suite 200, Lanham, MD 20706 USA Tel 301-459-3366; Fax: 301-459-5748; Toll Free: 800-462-6420; *Imprints:* Gooseberry Patch (GooseberP) Short Discount, please contact rlpgsales@rowman.com
E-mail: rlpgsales@rowman.com; lweston@rowman.com
Web site: http://www.rowmanlittlefield.com; http://www.rlpgbooks.com/bookseller/index.shtml
Dist(s): **CreateSpace Independent Publishing Platform**
Ebsco Publishing
Follett School Solutions
MyiLibrary
National Bk. Network
National Film Network LLC
Send The Light Distribution LLC
Two Rivers Distribution
ebrary, Inc.; *CIP.*

Rowohlt Taschenbuch Verlag GmbH (DEU) *(978-3-499)* *Dist. by* **Distribks Inc.**

Rowohlt Taschenbuch Verlag GmbH (DEU) *(978-3-499)* *Dist. by* **Continental Bk.**

Roxbury Park Juvenile *Imprint of* **Lowell Hse. Juvenile**

Roxby Media Ltd. (GBR) *(978-1-900521; 978-0-9848539)* *Dist. by* **LaurusCo.**

Roy, Wendy, *(978-0-615-59502-3)* 18 Haviland St. No. 15, Boston, MA 02115 USA Tel 617-645-9018
E-mail: contactwendynow@yahoo.com
Web site: http://www.glamgranola.com.

Royal British Columbia Museum (CAN) *(978-0-7718; 978-0-7726)* *Dist. by* **IPG Chicago.**

Royal Brown Publishing, *(978-0-9978541; 978-0-9979611)* 12138 Central Ave., Bowie, MD 20721 USA Tel 301-262-3472
E-mail: tdroyal@gmail.com
Web site: www.royalbrownpublishing.com.

Royal Caliber Pubns., *(978-0-9860785; 978-0-9860824)* 4043 Cypress Landing E., Winter Haven, FL 33884 USA
Dist(s): **Baker & Taylor Publisher Services (BTPS).**

Royal Collins Publishing Group Inc. (CAN) *(978-0-9918338; 978-1-4878; 978-1-927670; 978-1-987821)* *Dist. by* **IPG Chicago.**

Royal Council of the Real Fairyland, LLC, *(978-0-9841188)* 1332 Landfall Dr., Wilmington, NC 28405-2840 USA (SAN 858-4621)
Web site: http://www.therealtoothfairies.com.

Royal Financial Investment Group, *(978-0-578-16296-6; 978-0-578-16297-3; 978-0-578-16298-0; 978-0-9983860)* 1102-A Hwy 56 North, Waynesboro, GA 30830 USA
E-mail: info@royalfinancials.com
Web site: www.royalfinancials.com.

Royal Fireworks Publishing Co., *(978-0-88092; 978-0-89824)* Orders Addr.: P.O. Box 399, Unionville, NY 10988 USA (SAN 240-2394) Tel 845-726-4444; Fax: 845-726-3824; Edit Addr.: 1 First Ave., Unionville, NY 10988 USA
E-mail: rfpress@frontiernet.net
Web site: http://www.rfwp.com/
Dist(s): **Bridge Pubns., Inc.**

Royal Guard Dragon Society, The, *(978-0-9791733)* 706 Hall Ave., White Bear Lake, MN 55110 USA
E-mail: trgdspublications@trgds.com
Web site: http://trgds.com.

Royal Hse. Publishing, *(978-0-9772671)* 2315 Market Pl., Suite E, Huntsville, AL 35801 USA Tel 256-519-2291; Fax: 256-519-2292.

Royal Hues Designs, *(978-0-578-41614-4)* 1204 Village Market Pl. Suite 252, Morrisville, NC 27560 USA Tel 919-665-7691
E-mail: rhdrumgo@royalhuesdesigns.com
Dist(s): **Ingram Content Group.**

Royal Imprint Pr., Inc., *(978-0-9798624)* P.O. Box 342403, Austin, TX 78734 USA
Web site: http://http:www.TheRoyalYacht.net.

Royal Knight Inc., *(978-0-9777110)* 1204 Harbor Dr SE # 100, Rochester, MN 55904-5923 USA
Web site: http://www.royalknightresearch.com.

Royal Limited Partnership, *(978-0-9714798)* P.O. Box 448, Eugene, OR 97440-0448 USA
E-mail: fun@funnix.com
Web site: http://www.funnix.com.

Royal Peacock Publications *See* **Satin Finish Publishing**

Royal Penny Pr., The, *(978-0-9912370)* 9300 Colesville Rd., Silver Spring, MD 20901 USA Tel 240-372-1670
E-mail: sales@royalpennypress.com.

Royal Swan Enterprises, Inc., *(978-0-9793000; 978-0-9977720; 978-1-7336865)* 201 Orchard Ln., Carrboro, NC 27510-2530 USA (SAN 853-0521); *Imprints:* Alazar Press (Alazar Pr)
E-mail: rse@nc.rr.com; alazar.press@gmail.com
Web site: http://www.royal-swan-enterprises.com; http://www.alazar-press.com
Dist(s): **Independent Pubs. Group**
MyiLibrary.

Royall World Productions, *(978-0-9768115)* 1608 N. 13th St., Kansas City, KS 66102 USA Toll Free: 800-331-7668
E-mail: royallworldproductions@unoi.org.

Royalti Virtue, *(978-0-692-18780-7; 978-0-578-48470-9)* 2444 Cole Branch Ct, 1, Indianapolis, IN 46239-7975 USA Tel 317-489-2496
E-mail: royaltivirtue@gmail.com
Web site: royaltivirtue.net.

Royalty Bks. International, Inc., *(978-0-9705458)* Orders Addr.: 2047 Gees Mill Rd. Suite 210, Conyers, GA 30013 USA
E-mail: royaltybooks@gmail.com
Web site: http://www.royaltybooksonline.com.

Royalty Company Two-Thousand, The *See* **Royalty Bks. International, Inc.**

Royalty Patrenia Turner Publications, *(978-0-578-15322-3; 978-0-578-18000-7; 978-0-578-18261-2; 978-0-578-19928-3)* 1532 N. Sedgewick Ave., Chicago, IL 60610 USA.

Royalty Publishing Co., *(978-0-910487)* P.O. Box 2125, Bedford, IN 47421 USA (SAN 260-1265) Fax: 812-278-8785
E-mail: nitaspeaks@nitascoggan.com
Web site: http://www.the-maximum-zone.com.

Rozanski, Johnathan, *(978-0-9983327)* 471 E. Main St., Chicopee, MA 01020 USA Tel 413-594-3155
E-mail: mysteriousmisterenter@gmail.com.

RP Media, *(978-1-57545; 978-1-62716; 978-0-692-62456-2)* Div. of RP Bks., Orders Addr.: P.O. Box 362, East Olympia, WA 98540 USA; *Imprints:* Ruin Mist Publications (Ruin Mist Pubns); Reagent Press Signature Editions (Reagent Pr Sig Edns); Reagent Press Echo (Reagent Pr Echo); Reagent Press Books for Young Readers (RPBTR)
E-mail: sales@reagentpress.com; service@reagentpress.com; rights@reagentpress.com; emma.spring@reagentpress.com
Web site: http://www.reagentpress.com/; http://www.ruinmist.com/; http://books.reagentpress.com/; http://audio.reagentpress.com/; http://video.reagentpress.com/; http://graphics.reagentpress.com/; http://www.wizardsofskyhall.com/; http://www.ruinmistmovie.com/; http://www.themagiclands.com/; http://www.tvpress.com; http://www.bugvillecritters.com/
Dist(s): **CreateSpace Independent Publishing Platform**
EBSCO Media
Ingram Content Group
MyiLibrary
OverDrive, Inc.
ebrary, Inc.

RPG Objects, *(978-0-9724826; 978-0-9743067; 978-1-935432)* 9275 Cedar Forest Rd., Eden Prairie, MN 55347 USA
E-mail: chris@rpgobjects.com
Web site: http://www.rpgobjects.com.

RPJ & Co., Inc., *(978-0-9761122; 978-0-615-27121-7; 978-0-9819980; 978-0-9828277; 978-1-937770)* 1080 Princewood Dr., Orlando, FL 32810-4542 USA; *Imprints:* SPC Books (SPCBks)
E-mail: kathy@rpjandco.com
Web site: http://www.rpjandco1417.com; http://www.rpjandco.com
Dist(s): **Advocate Distribution Solutions**
Ingram Content Group Inc.
Send The Light Distribution LLC
Smashwords.

RPM Publishing *See* **RPM Publishing**

RPM Publishing, *(978-0-9764085; 978-0-9795126; 978-0-692-58325-8; 978-0-692-59412-4; 978-0-9992743; 978-1-7329503; 978-1-7342633; 978-1-7344407)* P.O. Box 841, Coeur d'Alene, ID 83814 USA Tel 425-890-3113
E-mail: sarahgerdesauthor@gmail.com
Web site: http://www.sarahgerdes.com
Dist(s): **CreateSpace Independent Publishing Platform**
Draft2Digital
Smashwords.

R.R Publishing Company *See* **Dara Publishing LLC**

RRJ Publishing, Inc., *(978-0-9857095)* 2073 SilverCrest Dr. unit C, Myrtle Beach, SC 29579 USA Tel 864-497-8392
E-mail: Mstnwright@yahoo.com.

RS Art Studio, *(978-0-9787729)* PO Box 64, Big Bear City, CA 92314 USA Tel 714-724-1480
E-mail: rsart@aol.com
Web site: http://www.rsartstudio.com.

RS Publishing *See* **JD Entertainment**

RTC Publishing, *(978-1-939418; 978-1-947564)* P.O. Box 1603, Deerfield, IL 60015 USA Tel 833-750-5683; Fax: 833-750-5683.

RTE Media, LLC, *(978-0-692-80787-3)* 6 Westhill Rd., Saddle River, NJ 07458 USA Tel 201-934-9675
E-mail: aforment@optonline.net
Web site: www.alisonashleyformento.com.

RTI Publishing, LLC, *(978-0-9769086)* 5685 S. Topaz Pl., Chandler, AZ 85249-5804 USA (SAN 256-6338)
E-mail: rtipublishing@cox.net.

RTMC Organization, LLC, *(978-1-934316)* P.O. Box 15105, Baltimore, MD 21282 USA (SAN 852-6923) Tel 410-900-7834
E-mail: Sales@RTMC.org
Web site: http://www.rtmc.org.

RUACH PUBLISHING Co., *(978-0-692-11085-0; 978-0-692-14575-3; 978-0-578-71284-0; 978-0-578-72487-4; 978-1-7355819)* 1680 E. WHEELER Cir., Macomb, IL 61455 USA Tel 312-401-8777
Web site: www.beginningoftimeplan.com.

Ruano, José A., *(978-0-9792972)* 8909 NW 189 TE, Miami, FL 33018 USA (SAN 853-0610) Tel 305-829-2683; Fax: 305-829-2094
E-mail: jaruano@bellsouth.net.

Rubicon Bks., *(978-0-9771676)* P.O. Box 1167, Silver City, NM 88062-1167 USA Tel 505-388-4585 Do not confuse with companies with the same name in Montrose, CA, Glendale, AZ
E-mail: badarmstrong@signalpeak.net.

Ruby Flower Publishing, *(978-0-615-79530-0; 978-0-615-83334-7; 978-0-615-83335-4; 978-0-615-84482-4; 978-0-615-85898-2; 978-0-615-87136-3; 978-0-9997172)* 527 E. Third Ave. No. 125, New York, NY 10016 USA Tel 2127261453
E-mail: belleusine@gmail.com
Dist(s): **CreateSpace Independent Publishing Platform.**

RUBY GULCH ENTERPRISES LLC, *(978-1-7325793)* P.O. Box 64, Craig, CO 81626 USA Tel 970-824-1908
E-mail: rubygulchenterprises@gmail.com
Dist(s): **Ingram Content Group.**

Ruby Tuesday Books Limited (GBR) *(978-1-909673; 978-1-910549; 978-1-911341)* *Dist. by* **Lerner Pub.**

Ruddick, Jessica Bks. LLC, *(978-1-946164)* 515 Miami Dr., Chesapeake, VA 23323 USA Tel 757-548-0468; Fax: 757-548-0468
E-mail: jmruddick@gmail.com.

Rugg's Recommendations, *(978-0-9608934; 978-1-883062)* P.O. Box 417, Fallbrook, CA 92088-0417 USA (SAN 237-9694) Tel 760-728-4558; Fax: 760-728-4467
E-mail: frugg@thegrid.net
Web site: http://www.ruggsrecommendations.com.

Ruin Mist Pubns. *Imprint of* **RP Media**

Rule 2 Bks., *(978-0-9915511)* 2365 Rice Blvd, Houston, TX 77005 USA Tel 713-533-9300
E-mail: lchambers@brightskypress.com
Web site: www.rule2books.com
Dist(s): **Night Heron Media.**

Rummana Publishing Inc., *(978-0-9990610)* P.O. Box 354, Riverview, FL 33568 USA Tel 412-403-2577
E-mail: rummanapublishing@gmail.com.

Run to Win, LLC, *(978-1-943795)* 135 Maine St. Suite A No. 176, Brunswick, ME 04011 USA Tel 207-615-4819; *Imprints:* Trail Trotter Press (Trail Trotter Pr)
E-mail: blaine@trailtrotterpress.com.

Run With Me Publishing, *(978-0-9776835)* 15447 W. Monterey Ln., Kerman, CA 93630 USA Tel 559-846-6432
E-mail: runwithmepublishing@yahoo.com.

Runamuck Publishing, *(978-0-615-16220-1)* 221 Academy St., Mexico, NY 13114 USA
Dist(s): **Lulu Pr., Inc.**

Runestone Publishing *See* **Walking Elk Pubns.**

Running Girl Productions *See* **Wheelhouse Publishing**

Running Horse Pr., *(978-0-9908979; 978-1-945087)* 700 Lavaca #1400 Pmb 90503, Austin, TX 78701 USA Tel 575-650-2246
E-mail: ecellenb@gmail.com
Web site: http://www.ellenbulkema.com.

Running Moose Publications, *(978-0-9777210)* 42400 Garfield Road, Clinton Township, MI 48038 USA
Dist(s): **Adventure Pubns.**

Running Pr. *Imprint of* **Running Pr.**

Running Pr. Kids *Imprint of* **Running Pr.**

Running Pr. Minature Editions *Imprint of* **Running Pr.**

†Running Pr., *(978-0-7624; 978-0-89471; 978-0-914294; 978-1-56138)* Div. of Perseus Books Group, 125 S. 22nd St., Philadelphia, PA 19103-4399 USA (SAN 204-5702) Tel 215-567-5080; Fax: 215-568-2919; Toll Free Fax: 800-453-2884; Toll Free: 800-345-5359 customer service; *Imprints:* Running Press (RunPr); Running Press Kids (RunningKids); Running Press Miniature Editions (RunMinEdns); Black Dog & Leventhal Publishers, Inc. (BlackDog Lev)
E-mail: support@runningpress.com
Web site: http://www.runningpress.com
Dist(s): **Blackstone Audio, Inc.**
Hachette Bk. Group
MyiLibrary
Open Road Integrated Media, Inc.
Zondervan
ebrary, Inc.; *CIP.*

Running Press Book Publishers *See* **Running Pr.**

Running the Goat, Bks. & Broadsides (CAN) *(978-0-9688712; 978-0-9737578; 978-0-9866113; 978-1-927917)* *Dist. by* **Orca Bk Pub.**

Runny Nose Press L.L.C., *(978-0-9788542)* 24111 Beierman, Warren, MI 48091-1714 USA
Web site: http://www.runnynosepress.com.

Rupa & Co. (IND) *(978-81-7167; 978-81-291)* *Dist. by* **S Asia.**

Rupanuga Vedic College, *(978-0-9650899; 978-0-9728372; 978-1-934405)* Div. of Iskcon Krishnafest, Inc., Orders Addr.: 5201 Paseo Blvd, Kansas City, MO 64110 USA Tel 224-558-8868; Edit Addr.: 5201 Paseo, Kansas City, MO 64110 USA Tel 816-924-5619; Fax: 816-924-5640
E-mail: eternityknowledgebliss@gmail.com; danavir.goswami@pamho.net
Web site: RVC.edu; DanavirGoswami.com; RVC.edu/RVC_BOOKS.html.

Rural Farm Productions, *(978-0-9753542)* 6538 Germanton Rd., Rural Hall, NC 27045 USA Tel 336-969-2202.

Rush, Hailey, *(978-0-692-99626-3)* 2704 Winslow Ridge Dr., Buford, GA 30519 USA Tel 662-871-7497
E-mail: hahumphr@gmail.com
Dist(s): **Ingram Content Group.**

RUSH Pubns. & Educational Consultancy, LLC, *(978-0-9748222; 978-0-9748868; 978-0-9814958)* 1901 60th Pl. E., Suite L7432, Bradenton, FL 34203-5076 USA Tel 941-227-4444
E-mail: meylani@superonline.com
Web site: http://www.rushsociety.com
Dist(s): **Cardinal Pubs. Group.**

Rush, Ricki, *(978-0-9674292)* 123 Gregory Dr., Fairfax, CA 94930 USA Tel 415-457-6422; Fax: 415-456-4459
E-mail: rickicoach@aol.com
Web site: http://lifeworks-coaching.com.

Rushmore Pr. LLC, *(978-1-950818; 978-1-953223)* 7662 Balmoral Mills Ct, Las Vegas, NV 89113 USA Tel 888-733-9607
E-mail: dary@rushmorepress.com; noah@rushmorepress.com
Web site: www.rushmorepress.com.

Russ Invision, *(978-0-9660122; 978-0-9720234; 978-0-9747064; 978-0-9799612; 978-0-9987090; 978-0-9987589)* 3219 Conquista Ave., Long Beach, CA 90808 USA (SAN 854-8315)
E-mail: rivision@aol.com
Web site: http://www.abridgeclub.com.

Russell, Fred Publishing, *(978-0-9764347; 978-0-9789832; 978-0-9796229)* 52 Collis St., West Haven, CT 06516 USA Tel 203-934-2501; Fax: 203-934-8723; Toll Free: 866-968-7685; *Imprints:* Rock House Method, The (The Rock)
E-mail: jp@rockhousemethod.com
Web site: http://www.rockhousemethod.com
Dist(s): **Leonard, Hal Corp.**
Music Sales Corp.

Russell, Hilary, *(978-0-578-50353-0; 978-0-578-51195-5)* 6600 Vanderbilt Ave., Dallas, TX 75214 USA Tel 817-937-4711
E-mail: hilaryrtx@yahoo.com.

Russet & Kensington Pr., *(978-1-940114)* 2066 Russet Dr. Suite 200, Troy, MI 48098 USA Tel 248-515-4247
E-mail: time4equilibrium@hotmail.com.

Rustik Haws LLC, *(978-0-578-51889-3; 978-0-578-51890-9; 978-0-578-53323-0; 978-0-578-53324-7; 978-1-951147; 978-1-952244; 978-1-952617; 978-1-64934)* 5221 Bon Vivant Dr. Apt. 208, TAMPA, FL 33603 USA Tel 813-467-7812
E-mail: services@rustikhaws.com
Dist(s): **Ingram Content Group.**

†Rutgers Univ. Pr., *(978-0-8135; 978-1-9788)* 106 Somerset St., Third Flr., New Brunswick, NJ 08901 USA (SAN 253-2115) Tel 848-445-7786
Web site: http://www.rutgersuniversitypress.org
Dist(s): **Chicago Distribution Ctr.**
De Gruyter, Inc.
Ebsco Publishing
Longleaf Services
MyiLibrary
Univ. of Chicago Pr.
ebrary, Inc.; *CIP.*

Ruth, A. Creations, *(978-0-9656306; 978-0-9907390)* 1860 Wynnewood Ln., Cincinnati, OH 45237 USA Tel 513-821-9027; Fax: 513-821-7762
E-mail: annieruth@fuse.net
Web site: http://www.annieruth.com.

Rutigliano, Joe, *(978-0-9767769)* 178 Ramona Ave., Staten Island, NY 10312-2717 USA.

Rutledge Development, *(978-0-692-99491-7)* 815 Mission Trail, New Braunfels, TX 78130 USA Tel 830-660-1052
E-mail: Clint@clintrutledge.com
Dist(s): **Ingram Content Group.**

Rutledge, Susan *See* **Willow Bend Pr.**

Ruwanga Trading, *(978-0-9615102; 978-0-9701528)* P.O. Box 1027, Puunene, HI 96784 USA (SAN 694-2776)
Dist(s): **Booklines Hawaii, Ltd.**

Ruybal, Michael, *(978-0-9963959)* 4537 Azure Hills, Las Cruces, NM 88011 USA Tel 575-312-2581
E-mail: micru20@gmail.com.

RWP Bks. *Imprint of* **Redhawk Publishing**

Rx Humor, *(978-0-9639002; 978-1-892157)* 2272 Vistamont Dr., Decatur, GA 30033 USA Tel 404-321-0126; Fax: 404-633-9198
E-mail: nshulma@emory.edu.

Ryan Ave Publishing, *(978-0-9760759)* Div. of J. C. Melvin Seminars, Inc., 5738 Hedgeford Ct., Las Vegas, NV 89120 USA Tel 702-454-9822; Fax: 702-454-9821.

Ryan, Karlene Kay Author, *(978-0-9888843)* 5154 N. Woodson, Fresno, CA 93711 USA Tel 559-304-9737; Fax: 559-446-0565
E-mail: karleneryan@comcast.net
Web site: karleneryan.com.

Ryan, Shirley, *(978-0-9754196)* 6480 Havenside Dr., Sacramento, CA 95831-1504 USA
E-mail: shirleyryanphd@gmail.com
Web site: http://www.shirleyryan.net.

Ryan's World, *(978-0-615-49711-2)* 4620 N. Braeswood Blvd. - No 138, Houston, TX 77096 USA Tel 832-754-6700; Fax: 281-915-4505
E-mail: judy@judysworld.info.

Rye Grass Roots Publishing, *(978-0-9788713)* Orders Addr.: P.O. Box 291382, Port Orange, FL 32129-1382 USA (SAN 851-8289) Tel 386-212-1800
E-mail: jamesmhunt@ryegrassroots.com.

Ryherd, Tim Publishing, *(978-0-9749974)* 21479 FM 365, Beaumont, TX 77705 USA.

Ryland, John B. Publishing *See* **DJ Blues Publishing**

Ryland Peters & Small (GBR) *(978-1-84172; 978-1-900518; 978-1-872536; 978-1-903116; 978-1-904991; 978-1-84597; 978-1-906094; 978-1-906525; 978-1-907030; 978-1-84975; 978-1-907563; 978-0-9571409; 978-1-909313; 978-1-78879; 978-1-912983; 978-1-913533)* *Dist. by* **S and S Inc.**

Ryland Peters & Small (GBR) *(978-1-84172; 978-1-900518; 978-1-872536; 978-1-903116; 978-1-904991; 978-1-84597; 978-1-906094; 978-1-906525; 978-1-907030; 978-1-84975; 978-1-907563; 978-0-9571409; 978-1-909313; 978-1-78879; 978-1-912983; 978-1-913533)* *Dist. by* **WIPRO.**

Rymer Bks., *(978-0-934723; 978-0-9600792)* P.O. Box 153, Tollhouse, CA 93667-0153 USA (SAN 207-1010) Tel 209-298-8845.

Ryu Cope, *(978-0-9770121)* P.O. Box 5399, Philadelphia, PA 19135 USA Tel 215-303-5435
E-mail: wakageryucope@gmail.com
Web site: http://www.ryucope.com.

Ryzewski, Deborah, *(978-0-9765302)* 240 Crabapple Ln., Valparaiso, IN 46383 USA.

R.Z. Enterprises of Florida, *(978-0-9792031)* 7640 Prospect Hill Cir., New Port Richey, FL 34654-6376 USA
Web site: http://www.RobertzHicks.com.

S & S Pr., *(978-0-615-14271-5; 978-0-615-14642-3; 978-0-615-14930-1; 978-0-615-14931-8; 978-0-615-14954-7)* 35221 SE Kinsey, Suite 101, Snoqualmie, WA 98065 USA
Web site: http://www.gloriabond.com
Dist(s): **Lulu Pr., Inc.**

SMS Cos., Inc., *(978-0-9669595)* P.O. Box 1184, Smyrna, GA 30081 USA Tel 678-339-0626; Fax: 678-339-0726
E-mail: JMBryant@bellsouth.net
Web site: http://www.smsbooks.com
Dist(s): **Follett School Solutions.**

S.O.C.O. Pubns., *(978-0-910119)* 276 Ward Rd., Mohawk, NY 13407 USA (SAN 241-5720) Tel 315-866-7445
E-mail: copress@borg.com.

S P I E-International Society for Optical Engineering *See* **SPIE**

S. Swan, *(978-1-7342991)* 1143 Becky ln, Lancaster, TX 75134 USA Tel 405-905-0537
E-mail: i.nubes@me.com.

S V E & Churchill Media, *(978-0-7932; 978-0-89290; 978-1-56357)* 6465 N. Avondale Ave., Chicago, IL 60631-1909 USA (SAN 208-3930) Toll Free Fax: 800-624-1678; Toll Free: 800-829-1900
E-mail: custserv@svemedia.com
Web site: http://www.svemedia.com
Dist(s): **Video Project, The**
Weston Woods Studios, Inc.

†SYDA Foundation, *(978-0-911307; 978-0-914602; 978-1-930939)* 371 Brickman Rd., South Fallsburg, NY 12779 USA (SAN 206-5649) Tel 845-434-2000 Toll Free Fax: 888-422-2339 (ordering); Toll Free: 888-422-3334 (ordering); P.O. Box 600, South Fallsburg, NY 12779
Web site: http://www.siddhayoga.org
Dist(s): **Bookpeople**
Independent Pubs. Group
New Leaf Distributing Co., Inc.; *CIP.*

S2 Services, *(978-0-9770928; 978-1-953765)* Orders Addr.: 384 Russell Ave., Gaithersburg, MD 20877 USA; Edit Addr.: 384 Russell Ave., Gaithersburg, MD 20877 USA (SAN 257-3377) Tel 301-493-4982; 301-500-6973
E-mail: socrtwo@s2services.com
Web site: http://www.socrtwo.info/portfolio.htm; http://people.lulu.com/users/index.php?fHomepage=179563
Dist(s): **CafePress.com**
Lulu Pr., Inc.

S.A. Kokinos (ESP) *(978-84-88342; 978-84-96629)* *Dist. by* **Lectorum Pubns.**

Sabeels Publishing, *(978-1-68376)* 40 E. Main St., Newark, DE 19711 USA Tel 902-457-9356
E-mail: isbn@speedy.partners.

Saberlee Bks., *(978-0-9815836; 978-0-9909606; 978-1-7340894)* 168 N. Catalina Ave. Apt. 103, Pasadena CA, CA 91106 USA
E-mail: saberleebooks@yahoo.com
Web site: http://www.lisettebrodey.com; http://facebook.com/BrodeyAuthor.

Sable Creek Pr. LLC, *(978-0-9766823; 978-0-9828875; 978-0-9890667; 978-0-9974953; 978-0-9991157; 978-0-578-61507-3)*
E-mail: sablecreekpress@cox.net
Web site: http://www.sablecreekpress.com; http://janetclarkshay.com.

Sabledrake Enterprises, *(978-0-9702189; 978-0-9771005; 978-0-9844032)* P.O. Box 30751, Seattle, WA 98113 USA Tel 425-317-9241; Fax: 772-673-2381
E-mail: tim@sabledrake.com
Web site: http://www.sabledrake.com.

Sabre Publishing Hse., Inc., *(978-0-9746213)* 201 Huff Lake Ct., Ortonville, MI 48462 USA Tel 248-627-1112; Fax: 248-627-1113
E-mail: mikeatsabre@aol.com.

Sabreen Ali, *(978-0-692-98448-2)* 625 Herb White Way, Pittsburg, CA 94565 USA Tel 510-926-8123
E-mail: fsali324@gmail.com.

Sabyr Pr., *(978-0-9746463)* 2999 Allmon Ln., Missouri Vly, IA 51555-5057 USA
E-mail: info@sabyr.com
Web site: http://www.sabyr.com.

Sachedina, Dr. Shenin Medical Education Products, *(978-0-9778648)* 2200 Glenwood Dr., Winter Park, FL 32792 USA (SAN 850-4377) Tel 407-740-5127
E-mail: Metuandlee@aol.com
Web site: http://www.metuandlee.com.

Sacred Garden Fellowship, *(978-1-932746)* 293 Totem Lodge Rd., Averill Park, NY 12208 USA Tel 802-363-5579
E-mail: sacredgf@gmail.com
Web site: www.sacredgardenfellowship.org.

Sacred Structure Pr., *(978-0-692-07421-3)* 10129 E Elk Lake Dr., Rapid City, MI 49676 USA Tel 231-322-2159
E-mail: shawn@pollackfamily.org
Dist(s): **Ingram Content Group.**

Sacred Truth Publishing, *(978-1-58840)* Div. of Sacred Truth Ministries, Orders Addr.: P.O. Box 18, Mountain City, TN 37683 USA
E-mail: sacredtruthministries@mounet.com.

Saddle & Bridle, Inc., *(978-0-9655501)* 375 Jackson Ave., Saint Louis, MO 63130-4243 USA Tel 314-725-9115; Fax: 314-725-6440
E-mail: saddlebr@saddleandbridle.com
Web site: http://www.saddleandbridle.com.

Saddle Pal Creations, Inc., *(978-0-9663495; 978-1-931353)* Orders Addr.: P.O. Box 872127, Wasilla, AK 99687-2127 USA Tel 907-357-3235; Fax: 907-357-3446
Web site: http://www.alaskachildrensbooks.com
Dist(s): **Partners Bk. Distributing, Inc.**
Partners/West Book Distributors
Wizard Works.

Saddleback Educational Publishing *See* **Saddleback Educational Publishing, Inc.**

Saddleback Educational Publishing, Inc., *(978-1-56254; 978-1-59905; 978-1-60291; 978-1-61651; 978-1-61247; 978-1-62250; 978-1-62670; 978-1-63078; 978-1-68021; 978-1-64598)* 151 Kalmus Dr., J-1, Costa Mesa, CA 92626-4564 USA (SAN 860-0902) Toll Free Fax: 888-734-4010; Toll Free: 800-637-8715
E-mail: contact@saddleback.com; amchugh@sdlback.com; adormanesh@sdlback.com
Web site: http://www.sdlback.com
Dist(s): **Children's Plus, Inc.**
Findaway World, LLC
Follett School Solutions
ebrary, Inc.

Sadie Bks., *(978-0-9816047; 978-0-615-55525-6; 978-0-615-74503-9)* 215 E. Camden Ave., H11, Moorestown, NJ 08057 USA (SAN 856-017X) Tel 856-234-2676; 856-313-0548
E-mail: info@sadie-books.com
Web site: http://www.sadie-books.com
Dist(s): **CreateSpace Independent Publishing Platform**
Dummy Record Do Not USE!!!!
Smashwords.

Sadlier *Imprint of* **Sadlier, William H. Inc.**

Sadlier, William H. Inc., *(978-0-8215; 978-0-87105; 978-1-4217)* 9 Pine St., New York, NY 10005-1002 USA (SAN 204-0948) Tel 212-227-2120; Fax: 212-267-8696; Toll Free: 800-221-5175; *Imprints:* Sadlier (Sadlier)
Web site: http://www.sadlier.com.

†SAE Intl., *(978-0-7680; 978-0-89883; 978-1-56091; 978-1-4686)* 400 Commonwealth Dr., Warrendale, PA 15096 USA (SAN 232-5721) Tel 724-776-4970; Fax: 724-776-0790
E-mail: customerservice@sae.org
Web site: http://www.sae.org; http://books.sae.org/; *CIP.*

Saeligstone, *(978-0-615-15984-3; 978-0-615-15985-0)* 13110 Moselle Forest, helotes, TX 78023 USA
E-mail: peirce1@saeligstone.com
Dist(s): **Lulu Pr., Inc.**

Safari, Ltd., *(978-1-881469)* Orders Addr.: P.O. Box 630685, Miami, FL 33163 USA Tel 305-621-1000; Fax: 305-621-6894; Toll Free: 800-554-5414; Edit Addr.: 1400 NW 159th St., Miami, FL 33169 USA
Web site: http://www.toydirectory.com.

Safari Pr., Inc., *(978-0-940143; 978-1-57157)* 15621 Chemical Ln., Suite B, Huntington Beach, CA 92649 USA (SAN 663-0723) Tel 714-894-9080; Fax: 714-894-4949; Toll Free: 800-451-4788 (orders only)
E-mail: info@safaripress.com
Web site: http://www.safaripress.com
Dist(s): **National Bk. Network.**

Safe Harbor Pubns., *(978-0-9760416)* P.O. Box 396, Titusville, FL 32781 USA
E-mail: admin@rikerbooks.com
Web site: http://www.rikerbooks.com.

Safeblade, Evelyn Colllins, *(978-0-9700655)* W8504 Jellen Rd., Spooner, WI 54801 USA Tel 715-635-7536.

SafePlans, *(978-0-9975811)* 3519 US Alt 19, Palm Harbor, FL 34683 USA Tel 573-636-5377
E-mail: heidi@safeplans.com; brad@safeplans.com
Web site: www.safeplans.com.

Safer Society Pr., *(978-1-884444; 978-1-940234)* Div. of Safer Society Foundation, Inc., Orders Addr.: P.O. Box 340, Brandon, VT 05733-0340 USA Tel 802-247-3132; Fax: 802-247-4233; Edit Addr.: 8-10 Conant Sq., Brandon, VT 05733-1121 USA
E-mail: Theream@saver.net
Web site: http://www.safersociety.org.

Safety Always Matters, Inc., *(978-0-9620584; 978-1-883994)* 222 Wildwood Ct., Bloomingdale, IL 60108 USA (SAN 248-9759) Tel 630-894-1229
Dist(s): **Syndistar, Inc.**

Safeworld Publishing Co., *(978-0-9655604; 978-0-578-15130-4; 978-0-692-31823-2; 978-0-692-31827-0; 978-0-692-31835-5)* 3 Greenshire Ln., Owings Mills, MD 21117-4813 USA Tel 410-356-7233
E-mail: janisraf4@aol.com
Web site: www.declineandfallofallevil.org.

SAGA Pr. *Imprint of* **Smocking Arts Guild of America**

SAGA Press *Imprint of* **Simon & Schuster Bks. For Young Readers**

Sagaponack Bks., *(978-0-9668845; 978-0-9801336; 978-0-9983526; 978-0-9985673; 978-0-9997045; 978-1-7339651; 978-1-7347374)* Orders Addr.: 101 South Walk Pl., Saint Augustine, FL 32086 USA Tel 904-429-7209
E-mail: fran@sagbooks.com
Web site: http://www.SagaponackBooks.com
Dist(s): **Follett Higher Education Grp**
Partners Bk. Distributing, Inc.

Sage, David, *(978-0-9894210; 978-1-7336402)* 67 N. Piney PO Box 208, Story, WY 82842 USA Tel 303-883-4148
E-mail: davesageinstory@gmail.com.

Sage Hill Pubs., LLC, *(978-0-913205)* Orders Addr.: P.O. Box 866, Yerington, NV 89447 USA (SAN 283-0493) Tel 775-463-4188 (phone/fax)
E-mail: booksbysagehill@aol.com.

Sage Pr., *(978-0-9799972)* P.O. Box 981432, Park City, UT 84098 USA (SAN 854-9494) Tel 435-658-1238 Do not confuse with companies with similar name in Evergreen, CO, Phonenix, AZ, Murrieta, CA, Glenwood Springs, CO, San Diego, CA
E-mail: rudyandcoco@hotmail.com
Web site: http://www.rudyandcoco.com
Dist(s): **Itasca Bks.**

†SAGE Pubns., Inc., *(978-0-7619; 978-0-8039; 978-1-4129; 978-1-4522; 978-1-4462; 978-1-4833; 978-1-5063; 978-1-5443; 978-1-0718; 978-1-0719)* 2455 Teller Rd., Thousand Oaks, CA 91360 USA (SAN 204-7217) Tel 800-818-7243; Fax: 800-583-2665; 805-499-0871
E-mail: info@sagepub.com; deborah.vaughn@sagepub.com
Web site: http://www.sagepub.com; http://www.sagepub.co.uk; http://www.pineforge.com; http://sagepub.com
Dist(s): **Ambassador Bks. & Media**
Coutts Information Services
Cranbury International
Ebsco Publishing
Emery-Pratt Co.
MBS Textbook Exchange, Inc.
Midwest Library Service
MyiLibrary
Blackwell
Yankee Bk. Peddler, Inc.
ebrary, Inc.
; *CIP.*

SAGE Pubns., Ltd. (GBR) *(978-0-7619; 978-0-8039; 978-1-903300; 978-1-4129; 978-1-84445; 978-1-84641; 978-1-84860; 978-1-4462; 978-0-85725; 978-0-85702; 978-1-84787; 978-1-4739; 978-1-84920; 978-93-85985)* *Dist. by* **SAGE.**

Sagebrush Entertainment, Inc., *(978-0-9766557)* P.O. Box 261187, Encino, CA 91426-1187 USA Toll Free Fax: 800-881-4577; Toll Free: 800-711-4677
E-mail: info@hopalong.com
Web site: http://www.hopalong.com.

Sagebrush Writings, *(978-1-7322202)* 2900 Bosham Ln., Midlothian, VA 23113 USA Tel 804-937-7007
E-mail: libbymcnamee@yahoo.com
Web site: www.LibbyMcNamee.com.

Sager Group, The, *(978-0-9881785; 978-0-9895241; 978-0-9916629; 978-0-9862679; 978-0-9964901; 978-0-9980793; 978-0-9996338; 978-1-950154)* 5996 La Jolla Corona Dr, La Jolla, CA 92037 USA Tel 619-218-2109
E-mail: info@mikesager.com
Web site: www.TheSagerGroup.net.

Saguaro Bks., LLC, *(978-0-615-98268-7; 978-0-615-98274-8; 978-0-615-99062-0; 978-0-692-20351-4; 978-0-692-24769-3; 978-0-692-27779-9; 978-0-692-83044-4; 978-0-692-06465-8; 978-0-578-43121-5; 978-0-578-45371-2; 978-0-578-67648-7; 978-0-578-69249-4)* 16201 E. Keymar Dr., Fountain Hills, AZ 85268 USA Tel 602-309-7670; Fax: 480-285-4955; Toll Free: 888-229-4159
Web site: www.saguarobooks.com
Dist(s): **CreateSpace Independent Publishing Platform.**

Sahaja Publishing, *(978-0-578-44421-5)* 12117 180th Ave. Ct. NW, Gig Harbor, WA 98329 USA Tel 253-884-2036
E-mail: sahaja@centurytel.net.

Sahtva, *(978-1-7327620)* 2 Northwood Dr, Downingtown, PA 19335-1757 USA Tel 484-784-7190
E-mail: H_mottaleb@yahoo.com
Web site: Www.bigworldlittleom.com.

Saint Andrew Pr., Ltd. (GBR) *(978-0-7152; 978-0-86153)* *Dist. by* **Westminster John Knox.**

Saint Anthony Messenger Press & Franciscan Communications *See* **Franciscan Media**

St. Augustine Pr., *(978-0-9819634; 978-0-578-45139-8)* 809 Copperhead Cir., St. Augustine, FL 32092 USA
Dist(s): **Chicago Distribution Ctr.**

St. Augustine's Pr., Inc., *(978-1-890318; 978-1-58731)* P.O. Box 2285, South Bend, IN 46680 USA Tel 574-291-3500; Fax: 574-291-3700; Toll Free: 888-997-4994
E-mail: bruce@staugustine.net
Web site: http://www.staugustine.net
Dist(s): **Chicago Distribution Ctr.**
Univ. of Chicago Pr.

St. Benedict Pr., LLC, *(978-0-89555; 978-0-9675978; 978-0-9770091; 978-1-935302; 978-1-61890; 978-1-5051)* 13315 Carowinds Blvd Suite Q, Charlotte, NC 28273 USA (SAN 760-789X) Tel 704-731-0651; Fax: 704-884-3262; Toll Free: 800-437-5876
Web site: http://www.saintbenedictpress.com; http://www.tanbooks.com; https://catholiccourses.benedictpress.com/index.php; https://neumann.benedictpress.com/
Dist(s): **Baker & Taylor Publisher Services (BTPS)**
Saint Benedict Pr.

St. Bob Pr., *(978-0-9796988)* 2095 Poplar Ave., Suite 54, Memphis, TN 38104 USA (SAN 854-1523) Tel 901-412-7362
E-mail: murff@saintbobpress.com
Web site: http://www.saintbobpress.com.

St. Clair Pubns., *(978-0-9801704; 978-0-9826302; 978-1-935786; 978-1-947514)* P.O. Box 727, Mc Minnville, TN 37111-0726 USA Tel 931-668-2860; Fax: 931-668-2861; Toll Free: 888-248-0192
E-mail: stan@stclair.net
Web site: http://stan.stclair.net/StClairPublications.html#books.

St. Clair Publishing, *(978-0-615-17629-1)* 3103 Fleece Flower, Austin, TX 78735 USA
Web site: http://www.richardshenderson.com.

Saint Mary's Press of Minnesota *See* **Saint Mary's Press of Minnesota**

Saint Mary's Press of Minnesota, *(978-0-88489; 978-1-59982; 978-1-64121)* 702 Terrace Heights, Winona, MN 55987-1320 USA (SAN 203-073X) Tel 507-457-7900; Fax: 507-457-7990; Toll Free Fax: 800-344-9225; Toll Free: 800-533-8095
E-mail: smpress@smp.org; hwilliams@smp.org
Web site: http://www.smp.org.

St. Nectarios Pr., *(978-0-913026)* 10300 Ashworth Ave., N., Seattle, WA 98133-9410 USA (SAN 203-3542) Tel 206-522-4471; Fax: 206-523-0550; Toll Free: 800-643-4233
E-mail: orders@stnectariospress.com; anneborozan@live.com
Web site: http://www.stnectariospress.com.

St. Nicholas Monastery, *(978-0-9773579)* 1340 Piney Rd., North Fort Myers, FL 33903-3822 USA.

St. Pancratius Pr., *(978-1-943835)* 4001 Pelham Rd. No. 82, Greer, SC 29650 USA Tel 864-320-8085
E-mail: saintpancratiuspress@gmail.com.

Saint Paul Books & Media *See* **Pauline Bks. & Media**

Saint Paul Brotherhood *See* **ACTS Pr.**

St. Vincent Archabbey Pubns., *(978-0-9708216; 978-0-9773909; 978-0-9906855)* 300 Fraser Purchase Rd., Latrobe, PA 15650-2690 USA Tel 724-805-2601; Fax: 724-805-2775
E-mail: kim.metzgar@email.stvincent.edu
Web site: http://www.stvincentstore.com
Dist(s): **Distributors, The.**

St. Vincent College Ctr. for Northern Appalachian Studies, *(978-1-885851)* 300 Fraser Purchase Rd., Latrobe, PA 15650 USA Tel 724-805-2316; Fax: 724-537-4554
E-mail: rwissolik@stvincent.edu
Web site: http://www.stvincent.edu/napp.

†St. Vladimir's Seminary Pr., *(978-0-88141; 978-0-913836; 978-0-9618545; 978-0-9622536; 978-1-879038; 978-1-891295)* 575 Scarsdale Rd., Yonkers, NY 10707 USA (SAN 204-6296) Tel 914-961-8313 x 348; Fax: 914-961-5456 Bookstore fax; 914-961-4507 Press fax; Toll Free: 800-204-2665 Bookstore
E-mail: benedict@svots.edu; ghatrak@svots.edu
Web site: http://www.svspress.com; *CIP.*

Saintly Lisle, *(978-1-7321396)* 5750 Buffington Rd, apt 2208, College Park, GA 30349 USA Tel 708-712-3594
E-mail: jonathan1989@sbcglobal.net.

Saints Of Glory Church, *(978-0-9673342)* Orders Addr.: P.O. Box 8957, Anaheim, CA 92812-0957 USA Tel 714-846-0401; Fax: 714-846-3395; Edit Addr.: 16102 Warmington Ln., Huntington Beach, CA 92649 USA
E-mail: sgcgow@aol.com.

Sakthi Bks., Inc., *(978-0-9752586)* Orders Addr.: 1507 Lone Oak Cir., Fairfield, IA 52556 USA
E-mail: pradheepkumar@hotmail.com
Web site: http://www.matrixjourney.com; http://www.rightawareness.com.

Sakura Pr., *(978-0-9660583)* Hesta Roach 227 Croatan Dr., Oriental, NC 28571 USA Tel 252-249-1929 (phone/fax) Do not confuse with Sakura Pr., Pleasant Hill, OR
E-mail: roachdj@hotmail.com.

Salaam Reads *Imprint of* **Simon & Schuster Bks. For Young Readers**

Salado Pr., LLC, *(978-0-9663870; 978-0-9835342; 978-0-9913118)* Orders Addr.: P.O. Box 470171, Fort Worth, TX 76147 USA Tel 972-215-6116
E-mail: lee@saladopress.com
Web site: http://www.salaodpress.com.

Salani (ITA) *(978-88-7782; 978-88-8451)* *Dist. by* **Distribks Inc.**

Salariya Bk. Co. Ltd. (GBR) *(978-1-904194; 978-1-904642; 978-1-905087; 978-1-905638; 978-1-906370; 978-1-906714; 978-1-907184; 978-1-908759;*

978-1-909645; 978-1-908177; 978-1-908973; 978-1-912006) Dist. by **Sterling.**
Salaud Publishing, *(978-0-9713167)* P.O. Box 11681, Portland, OR 97211 USA Tel 919-963-9135
E-mail: jesse@hastardrecords.com; jesse@bastardrecords.com; jordan_lari@highcountrystudentpublishers.org
Web site: http://www.highcountrystudentpubishers.org; http://www.bastardrecords.com/salaud.htm.
Salazar, JC, *(978-0-9991496)* 805 Bomar No. 2, Houston, TX 77006 USA Tel 832-788-7858
E-mail: csal55@aol.com.
Salch, Megan F., *(978-0-9776154)* 3106 Lawrence St., Houston, TX 77018 USA Tel 713-864-1344.
Salem Academy & College, *(978-0-9789608)* P.O. Box 10548, Winston-Salem, NC 27108 USA
Web site: http://www.salem.edu.
Salem Author Services, *(978-1-931232; 978-1-59160; 978-0-9723806; 978-0-9740030; 978-1-59467; 978-0-9744668; 978-0-9754803; 978-1-59781; 978-0-9764981; 978-0-9769668; 978-1-60034; 978-1-934248; 978-1-60266; 978-0-9798246; 978-0-9798467; 978-1-60477; 978-0-9799120; 978-1-934937; 978-1-934938; 978-0-9802455; 978-0-9802456; 978-1-60647; 978-1-935097; 978-1-935098; 978-1-935204; 978-0-9820938; 978-1-60791; 978-1-935456; 978-1-61579; 978-1-936107; 978-1-936183; 978-0-9841965; 978-1-936198; 978-1-60957; 978-1-936400; 9) Div. of Salem Media Group, 2301 Lucien Way, Suite 415, Maitland, FL 32751 USA Tel 407-339-4217; Fax: 407-339-9898; Toll Free: 866-381-2665; Imprints:* Mill City Press, Inc (Mill City); Two Harbors Press (TwoHarbors); Liberty Hill Publishing (Liberty Hill); North Loop Press (MYID_T_NORTH L)
E-mail: cbenzine@salemauthorservices.com
Web site: http://www.salemauthorservices.com/; www.XulonPress.com; www.MyBookOrders.com; www.millcitypress.net
Dist(s): **INscribe Digital**
Ingram Bk. Co.
Itasca Bks.
eBookit.com.
†Salem Pr., Inc., *(978-0-89356; 978-1-58765)* Div. of EBSCO Publishing, Orders Addr.: 10 Estes St, IPSWICH, MA 01938 USA (SAN 241-8XX) Tel 800-758-5995; Fax: 201-968-1411; Toll Free: 800-221-1592
E-mail: csr@salempress.com
Web site: http://www.salempress.com; http://salempress.com/Store/pages/hwwilson.htm
Dist(s): **Ebsco Publishing**
Grey Hse. Publishing
MyiLibrary
ebrary, Inc.; *CIP.*
Salem Publishing Solutions, Incorporated *See* **Salem Author Services**
Salem Ridge Press LLC, *(978-0-9776786; 978-1-934671)* 4263 Salem Dr., Emmaus, PA 18049 USA
E-mail: customerservice@slaemridgepress.com.
Sales Effectiveness, Inc., *(978-0-9676255)* 221 Riverstone Way, GREER, SC 29651 USA Tel 770-842-8744; 770-552-6612
E-mail: carlos.quintero@gmail.com
Web site: http://www.saleseffectiveness.com.
Salih, Sara *See* **Harlan Rose Publishing**
Salina Bookshelf *See* **Salina Bookshelf Inc**
Salina Bookshelf Inc, *(978-0-9644189; 978-1-893354)* 1120 W. University Ave, Ste. 102, Flagstaff, AZ 86001 USA (SAN 253-0503) Tel 928-527-0070; Fax: 928-526-0386; Toll Free: 877-527-0070
E-mail: elockard@salinabookshelf.com
Web site: http://www.salinabookshelf.com.
Salish Kootenia College Pr., *(978-1-934594)* Orders Addr.: P.O. Box 70, Pablo, MT 59855 USA Tel 406-275-4882; Fax: 406-275-4801; Edit Addr.: 52000 Hwy.93, Pablo, MT 59855 USA
E-mail: bob-bigant@skc.edu
Dist(s): **Stoneydale Pr. Publishing Co.**
Univ. of Nebraska Pr.
Sally Ride Science, *(978-0-9753920; 978-1-933798; 978-1-940073; 978-1-941094)* 9191 Towne Centre Dr. Ste. L101, San Diego, CA 92122-6204 USA Tel 858-638-1432; Fax: 858-638-1419; Toll Free: 800-561-5161
E-mail: tam@sallyridescience.com; bleck@sallyridescience.com
Web site: http://www.sallyridescience.com.
Salmon Hole Poetry Press *See* **Minimal Pr., The**
Salmon Publishing (IRL) *(978-0-948339; 978-1-897648; 978-1-903392; 978-1-910669) Dist. by* **Casemate Pubs.**
Salmon Run Pr., *(978-0-9634000; 978-1-887573)* Orders Addr.: P.O. Box 672130, Chugiak, AK 99567-2130 USA Tel 907-688-4268
E-mail: salmonrp@aol.com
Dist(s): **Partners/West Book Distributors**
SPD-Small Pr. Distribution
Todd Communications
Wizard Works.
Salmon Run Publishing Company *See* **Salmon Run Pr.**
Salt and Light Bks., *(978-0-692-67312-6; 978-0-692-67627-1; 978-0-692-67628-8; 978-1-946417)* P.O. Box 5, Hugoton, KS 67951 USA Tel 620-544-9042
Web site: www.saltandlightbooks.com
Dist(s): **CreateSpace Independent Publishing Platform.**
Salt City Books, *(978-0-9776332)* P.O. Box 6, Farmington, UT 84025-0006 USA (SAN 257-8522) Tel 801-309-7820; Fax: 801-485-2654
E-mail: saltcitybooks@msn.com.
Salt City Systems *See* **Salt Pubs.**
Salt of the Earth Pr., *(978-0-9816949; 978-0-9849183)* W. 4456 Hwy. 63, Springbrook, WI 54875 USA (SAN 856-2555) Fax: 715-318-6417
Web site: http://www.saltpress.com.
Salt Pubs., *(978-0-9709940; 978-0-9725804)* 6163 E. Molloy Rd., East Syracuse, NY 13057 USA Tel 315-437-1139; Fax: 315-463-2055; Toll Free: 800-324-2607
E-mail: salt@twcny.rr.com.
Salt Publishing (GBR) *(978-1-876857; 978-1-901994; 978-1-84471; 978-1-907773; 978-1-78463) Dist. by* **SPD-Small Pr Dist.**
Salty Dog, Inc., The, *(978-0-9793560)* Orders Addr.: a/o Mark Yarbrough, The Salty Dog Inc., 69 Arrow Rd., Hilton Head Island, SC 29928-2992 USA (SAN 853-2338)
Web site: http://www.saltydog.com.
Salty Doll Studios, *(978-0-692-12453-6; 978-0-578-41460-7; 978-0-578-67093-5; 978-0-578-67203-8)* P.O. Box 1392, Farmington, AR 72730 USA Tel 479-530-1586
E-mail: saltydollstudios@yahoo.com
Dist(s): **CreateSpace Independent Publishing Platform.**
Salty Paws Publishing, *(978-0-9986680)* 208 Mariela Ct., Ponte Vedra Beach, FL 32082 USA Tel 904-254-5763
E-mail: rigbym@bellsouth.net
Web site: saltypawspublishing.com.
Salty Pond Pubs., *(978-0-615-45705-5; 978-0-615-56089-2)* 10 Edward Kelly Rd., East Sandwich, MA 02537 USA Tel 781-715-5014; Fax: 508-833-8923
E-mail: jglinehan@comcast.net.
Salty Sea Publishing, *(978-0-692-78475-4)* 2400 NE 99th St., Vancouver, WA 98665 USA Tel 503-929-6941
E-mail: katebeeman@gmail.com
Web site: http://katebeeman.website.
Salvation Army, *(978-0-89216)* 440 W. Nyack Rd., West Nyack, NY 10994 USA (SAN 237-2649) Tel 845-620-7200 Do not confuse with Salvation Army Supplies, Southern, Des Plaines, IL (Southern Territory) or Salvation Army Supplies & Purchasing Dept., Des Plaines, IL or Salvation Army, Des Plaines, IL
Dist(s): **Baker & Taylor Publisher Services (BTPS).**
Salvatorelli, A. Michael, *(978-0-9992734)* 1002 Balcom Ave., Bronx, NY 10465 USA Tel 917-400-9729
E-mail: deaconsalvatorelli@gmail.com.
Salvo Pr. *Imprint of* **Start Publishing LLC**
Salzman Bks. LLC, *(978-0-9842632)* Orders Addr.: P.O. Box 189, Winfield, KS 67156 USA (SAN 858-8910) Tel 620-262-7280; Edit Addr.: 2106 Kickapoo, Winfield, KS 67156 USA
E-mail: jsalzman@salzmanbooks.com
Web site: http://www.salzmanbooks.com.
Saman Publishing, *(978-0-9728020)* 751 Lemonwood Ct., San Jose, CA 95120 USA.
Samantha's Stories Inc. *See* **Samantha's Stories Inc.**
Samantha's Stories Inc., 115 G st spc 14, arcata, CA 95521 USA Tel 707-999-7334
Web site: http://samanthastories.us; http://wellandenglishtutor.com.
Samara Pr., *(978-0-9577556)* c/o Trillium Hse., 241 Bonita, Los Trancos Woods, Portola Valley, CA 94028-8103 USA Tel 650-851-1847.
Sambodh Society, Inc., The, *(978-0-9785969)* 6363 N 24th St., Kalamazoo, MI 49004 USA (SAN 851-0849)
Web site: http://www.sambodh.us.
Same Old Story Productions, *(978-0-9845571; 978-1-945450)* 3993 Ivy Wood Dr., Amelia, OH 45102 USA.
Samhain Publishing, LTD, *(978-1-59998; 978-1-60504; 978-1-60928; 978-1-61921; 978-1-61922; 978-1-61923; 978-1-5139; 978-1-61923-400-0; 978-1-61923-300-3)* Orders Addr.: 11821 Mason Montgomery Rd. 4B, Cincinnati, OH 45249 USA; Edit Addr.: 11821 Mason Montgomery Rd. Suite 4b, Cincinnati, OH 45249 USA (SAN 257-7488) Tel 513-453-4688; Fax: 513-583-0191
E-mail: contracts@samhainpublishing.com
Web site: http://www.samhainpublishing.com.
Samizdat Express *See* **Seltzer Bks.**
Sammi Leigh Melville, *(978-0-578-40600-8)* 248 Maclay St., Harrisburg, PA 17110 USA Tel 508-243-2154
E-mail: Sammileighm@gmail.com
Dist(s): **Ingram Content Group.**
Sammy Bks., *(978-0-9984241)* 1845 Stinnett Rd., Huntingtown, MD 20639 USA Tel 410-535-2188
E-mail: bawilburn@comcast.net
Web site: www.sammybooks.com.
Sams, II, Carl R. Photography, Inc., *(978-0-9671748; 978-0-9770108; 978-0-9827625; 978-0-9989836)* 361 Whispering Pines, Milford, MI 48380-3807 USA (SAN 859-435X) Tel 248-685-2422; Fax: 248-685-1643; Toll Free: 800-552-1867
E-mail: carlsams@carlsams.com
Web site: http://www.carlsams.com; http://www.strangerinthewoods.com
Dist(s): **Follett School Solutions**
Partners Bk. Distributing, Inc.
Samuelson, Norma, *(978-1-7329192)* 26862 Via Corta, San Juan Capistrano, CA 92675 USA Tel 949-291-7465
E-mail: normaillu@cox.net.
San Diego Business Accounting Solutions a Non CPA Firm *See* **JA Pubns., Ltd.**
San Diego County Regional Airport Authority, *(978-0-9745294)* P.O. Box 82776, San Diego, CA 92138-2776 USA Tel 619-400-2400; Fax: 619-400-2866
Web site: http://www.san.org.
San Diego Museum of Man, *(978-0-937808)* 1350 El Prado, Balboa Pk., San Diego, CA 92101-1616 USA Tel 619- 239-2001; Fax: 619- 239-2749
E-mail: khedges@museumofman.org
Web site: http://www.museumofman.org.
San Francisco Art Commission, The, *(978-1-888048)* 800 Chestnut St., San Francisco, CA 94133 USA Tel 415-771-7020; Fax: 415-252-2595; *Imprints:* WritersCorps Books (WrtrsCorps Bks)
Dist(s): **SPD-Small Pr. Distribution.**
San Francisco Story Works, *(978-0-9774227)* 386 Union St., San Francisco, CA 94133-3516 USA (SAN 257-5248)
Web site: http://www.pengey.com; http://www.sanfranciscostoryworks.com.
San Francisco Study Ctr., *(978-0-936434; 978-1-888956)* 1663 Mission St. Suite310, San Francisco, CA 94103 USA (SAN 214-4654) Tel 415-626-1650; Fax: 415-626-7276; Toll Free: 888-281-3757; *Imprints:* Study Center Press (Study Ctr Pr)
E-mail: marjorie@studycenter.org
Web site: http://www.studycenter.org
Dist(s): **Parent Services Project.**
San Juan Publishing, *(978-0-9707399; 978-0-9858897)* Orders Addr.: P.O. Box 923, Woodinville, WA 98072 USA
E-mail: sanjuanbooks@yahoo.com
Dist(s): **Partners Bk. Distributing, Inc.**
Sananda Publications *See* **Reverence for Life**
SanaOhio, *(978-0-692-91401-4)* 2323 Meadowpoint Dr, Troy, OH 45373 USA Tel 859-533-4905
E-mail: phash@sanaohio.com.
Sanchez, Shayla, *(978-0-9993636)* 38553 Blacow Rd., Fremont, CA 94536 USA Tel 510-797-4013
E-mail: shaylasanchez@att.net.
Sancho Storybooks *See* **Joseph Pubns.**
Sanctity Pubns., *(978-0-9983129)* 2732 Webber Ct., Steilacoom, WA 98388 USA Tel 253-292-1317
E-mail: Graciesmail@comcast.net.
Sanctuary Bks., *(978-0-9753334)* P.O. Box 1623, New York, NY 10028 USA Do not confuse with companies with the same or similar name in Mount Juliet, TN, Tampa, FL
E-mail: sanctuarybooks@earthlink.net
Web site: http://www.sanctuarybks.com.
Sanctuary Publishing, Inc., *(978-0-9746995; 978-0-9785334; 978-0-9843754; 978-0-9830018; 978-0-9840392)* 40 Red Butte Rd., Sedona, AZ 86351-7765 USA (SAN 920-1122) Tel 928-284-2269; 928-284-1154; Fax: 928-284-4782
Web site: http://www.SanctuaryPublications.com
Dist(s): **MyiLibrary.**
Sanctuary Publishing, Ltd. (GBR) *(978-1-86074; 978-1-898141) Dist. by* **H Leonard.**
Sand Dreams Pr., LLC, *(978-0-9798656)* P.O. Box 24, Whitehouse Station, NJ 08889-0024 USA (SAN 854-6134) Tel 908-256-4834
E-mail: imre@sanddreamspress.com
Web site: http://www.sanddreamspress.com.
Sand Sage Pr., *(978-0-9793474)* Orders Addr.: P.O. Box 60812, Canyon, TX 79016 USA (SAN 853-1935) Toll Free: 888-655-0875 (phone/fax)
E-mail: psallison@earthlink.net
Web site: http://www.SandSagePress.com.
Sandbox Bks., *(978-0-9755184)* 6561 Portage Rd., DeForest, WI 53532-0000 USA
Web site: http://www.sandboxbooks.com.
Sandbox Publishing, *(978-0-692-59788-0)* 4818 Jumano Ave., San Diego, CA 92117 USA Tel 858-437-1416
Dist(s): **CreateSpace Independent Publishing Platform**
Independent Pubs. Group
Midpoint Trade Bks., Inc.
Sandbridge Sons Publishing, *(978-0-9796039)* 2577 Sandpiper Rd., Virginia Beach, VA 23456 USA.
SandCastle *Imprint of* **ABDO Publishing Co.**
Sandcastle Publishing, *(978-0-9627756; 978-1-883995)* Orders Addr.: P.O. Box 3070, South Pasadena, CA 91031-6070 USA Fax: 323-255-3616; Edit Addr.: 1723 Hill Dr., South Pasadena, CA 91030 USA Tel 213-255-3616 Do not confuse with Sandcastle Publishing, Orleans, MA
E-mail: info@sandcastle-online.com; rwhatley@sandcastle-online.com
Web site: http://www.sandcastle-online.com
Dist(s): **Quality Bks., Inc.**
Unique Bks., Inc.
†Sandlapper Publishing Co., Inc., *(978-0-87844)* Orders Addr.: P.O. Box 730, Orangeburg, SC 29115 USA (SAN 203-2678) Toll Free Fax: 800-337-9420 (orders); Toll Free: 800-849-7263 (orders); Edit Addr.: 1281 Amelia St., NE., Orangeburg, SC 29116 USA Tel 803-533-1658; Fax: 803-534-5223
E-mail: agallman1@bellsouth.net
Web site: http://www.sandlapperpublishing.com
Dist(s): **Follet Higher Education Grp;** *CIP.*
Sandner-Petersen International Bks., *(978-0-9744852)* 5112 Coronado Pkwy., No.11, Cape Coral, FL 33904 USA Tel 739-549-3028; Fax: 239-549-5547.
Sandpiper *Imprint of* **Houghton Mifflin Harcourt Trade & Reference Pubs.**
Sandra Kitabjian, *(978-0-578-59816-1; 978-0-578-60451-0; 978-0-578-73626-6; 978-0-578-74338-7)* 254 S. New Ardmore Ave., Broomall, PA 19008 USA Tel 610-325-3239
E-mail: bellask1@comcast.net.
Sandramantos Publishing, *(978-0-9887848)* 1550 Alpine Trail, San Marcos, TX 78666 USA Tel 512-462-9670
E-mail: manager@Sandramantos.com
Web site: http://princessapril.com.
Sands, Monty, *(978-0-9788038; 978-0-615-25788-4; 978-0-578-15474-9)* P.O. Box 6463, Visalia, CA 93291 USA
E-mail: monger15@juno.com; montysands@yahoo.com.
Sands Pr. (CAN) *(978-0-9936753; 978-1-988281) Dist. by* **IPG Chicago.**
S&S Publishing LLC, *(978-0-9794710)* 1609 Dublin Dr., Silver Spring, MD 20902 USA Tel 301-681-8729
E-mail: xsalinas21@gmail.com.
Sandstein Kommunikation GmbH (DEU) *(978-3-95498) Dist. by* **ISD USA.**
Sandstone Pr. Ltd. (GBR) *(978-0-9546333; 978-1-905207; 978-1-908737; 978-1-910124; 978-1-912240; 978-1-910985; 978-1-913207) Dist. by* **Dufour.**
Sandvik Innovations, LLC, *(978-1-932915; 978-1-935868)* 460 E. Swedesford Rd., Suite 2030, Wayne, PA 19087 USA Tel 610-975-3585; Fax: 610-975-3587
Web site: http://www.sandvikinnovations.com.
Sandvik Publishing, *(978-1-58048; 978-1-881445)* Div. of Sandviks Bokforlag, Norway, 3729 Knights Rd., Bensalem, PA 19020-2908 USA Toll Free: 800-843-2445
E-mail: Nicole@sandvikpublishing.com; cust-serv@sandvikpublishing.com
Web site: http://www.sandviks.com.
Sandy Bay Publishing, *(978-0-9701285)* Orders Addr.: P.O. Box 580, Hatteras, NC 27943-0580 USA Tel 252-986-2195; Fax: 252-986-2372; Edit Addr.: 56187 Pamlico Dr., Hatteras, NC 27973-0580 USA Tel 252-986-2195
E-mail: joannewhale@earthlink.net.
Sandy Putter Pr., *(978-0-578-05153-6)* 9 Meadowview Rd., Asheville, NC 28804 USA.
SANE *See* **Sane**
Sane, *(978-0-692-15473-1; 978-0-578-44232-7; 978-0-578-44234-1; 978-0-578-45069-8; 978-0-578-45117-6; 978-0-578-55264-4)* 640 Eastern Pkwy. Unit 4c, Brooklyn, NY 11213 USA Tel 646-243-0842
E-mail: miriamyerushalmi18@gmail.com
Dist(s): **Ingram Content Group.**
SangFroid Pr., *(978-0-917939)* 34 Water St., Excelsior, MN 55331 USA (SAN 657-0178) Tel 952-474-6220; Fax: 952-474-6221 Do not confuse with Sang Froid in New York, NY.
Sanitaryum, *(978-0-9983352)* 414 Terr. Cir., Lamesa, TX 79331 USA Tel 505-362-6990; *Imprints:* Bookify by Sanitaryum (MYID_R_BKIFY B)
E-mail: nathantafoya@gmail.com
Web site: http://sanitaryum.com/bookify-publishing/; www.sanitaryum.com.
Sankofa Bks. *Imprint of* **Just Us Bks., Inc.**
Sankofa Pr., *(978-0-9654009)* Orders Addr.: P.O. Box 3144, Jacksonville, FL 32206 USA Tel 904-355-0126 (phone/fax); Edit Addr.: 239 W. 40th St., Jacksonville, FL 32206 USA
E-mail: sankofa@leading.net
Web site: http://www.users.southeast.net/~sankofa.
Sankofa Productions *See* **Sankofa Pr.**
Sankofa Project Productions, *(978-0-692-92878-3)* 1601 N Bryant No. 56, Little Rock, AR 72207 USA Tel 501-553-4460; Fax: 501-553-4460
E-mail: cindy@cindy-hurst.com.
SanPaul Group, LLC, The, *(978-0-9670875)* 209 Josephine St., Detroit, MI 48202-1811 USA (SAN 253-6013)
E-mail: gtpspg@cs.com
Web site: http://www.qtpleworld.com.
Sanpitch Pr., *(978-0-9760607)* 141 S. Main, Manti, UT 84642 USA Tel 435-835-6271; Fax: 435-835-8431; Toll Free: 800-748-4660
E-mail: sanman@horseshoetrader.com.
Sans Soucie Studio, *(978-0-692-59323-3; 978-0-692-59522-0; 978-0-692-59523-7; 978-0-9977253)* 8014 Nimrod Trail, Dallas, TX 75238 USA Tel 214-803-0169.
Santa Ana River Pr., *(978-0-9747638)* P.O. Box 5473, Norco, CA 92860 USA (SAN 255-7568)
E-mail: admin@santaanariverpress.com
Web site: http://www.santaanariverpress.com
Dist(s): **Sunbelt Pubns., Inc.**
Santa Fe Communications, Inc., *(978-1-933262)* 1126 S. 70th St. Suite N601, MILWAUKEE, WI 53214 USA
E-mail: bruno@heartofthenation.org; brunojohn2468@gmail.com
Web site: http://www.lightningbugflix.com.
Santa Fe Writers Project, *(978-0-9776799; 978-0-9819661; 978-0-9882252; 978-1-939650; 978-1-7337777; 978-1-951631)* No. 350, 369 Montezuma Ave., Santa Fe, NM 87501 USA (SAN 257-9588)
E-mail: agifford@sfwp.com
Web site: http://www.sfwp.com
Dist(s): **Ebsco Publishing**
Independent Pubs. Group
MyiLibrary
ebrary, Inc.
Santa Monica Pr., *(978-0-9639946; 978-1-891661; 978-1-59580)* Orders Addr.: P.O. Box 1076, Santa Monica, CA 90406 USA (SAN 298-1459) Tel 310-230-7759; Fax: 310-230-7761; Toll Free: 800-784-9553; Edit Addr.: 513 Wilshire Blvd., No. 321, Santa Monica, CA 90401 USA
E-mail: books@santamonicapress.com
Web site: http://www.santamonicapress.com
Dist(s): **Ebsco Publishing**
Legato Pubs. Group
MyiLibrary
Publishers Group West (PGW)
Perseus Bks. Group
ebrary, Inc.
Santacroce, John, *(978-0-615-76887-8; 978-0-9899916)* 2066 Rivers Edge Dr., Rio Rancho, NM 87144 USA Tel 505-450-7096; *Imprints:* Four Oaks Publishing (Four Oaks Pub)
E-mail: johnpsantacroce@gmail.com.
Santiago, Claribel, *(978-0-9744726)* P.O. Box 25345, Tamarac, FL 33320 USA
E-mail: claribel_santiago@hotmail.com
Web site: http://www.claribelsantiago.com.
Santillana *Imprint of* **Santillana USA Publishing Co., Inc.**

Publisher Name Index

Santillana (COL) *(978-958-24) Dist. by* **Santillana.**

Santillana Ecuador (ECU) *(978-9978-07; 978-9942-05; 978-9942-19; 978-9978-29) Dist. by* **Santillana.**

Santillana Ediciones Generales, S.A. de C.V. (MEX) *(978-607-11; 978-607-01) Dist. by* **Santillana.**

Santillana, Editorial, S.A. de C.V. (MEX) *(978-970-29; 978-968-430; 978-970-642) Dist. by* **Santillana.**

Santillana S. A. (URY) *(978-9974-590; 978-9974-671) Dist. by* **Santillana.**

Santillana Texto *Imprint of* **Santillana USA Publishing Co., Inc.**

Santillana USA Publishing Co., Inc., *(978-0-88272; 978-1-56014; 978-1-58105; 978-1-58986; 978-1-59437; 978-1-59820; 978-1-60396; 978-1-61605; 978-1-61435; 978-1-62263; 978-1-63113; 978-1-68292; 978-1-64101)* Div. of Grupo Santillana, 8333 NW 53rd St. Suite 402, Doral, FL 33166 USA (SAN 205-1133) Tel 617-351-4867; Av. Rio Mixcoac No. 274 Col. Acacias, C.P. 0324 Benito Juarez, Ciudad de Mexico, DF,; *Imprints:* Santillana (Santillana Imprint); Richmond (Richmond); Alfaguara (Alfaguara); Punto de Lectura (Punto de Lectura); Santillana Texto (SanTexto); Loqueleo (Loqueleo)
E-mail: dminella@vistahigherlearning.com; esanta@santillanausa.com; customerservice@santillanausa.com
Web site: http://www.loqueleo.com/us
Dist(s): **Barnes & Noble, Inc.**
Bilingual Pubns. Co., The
Children's Plus, Inc.
Continental Bk. Co., Inc.
CreateSpace Independent Publishing Platform
EMC/Paradigm Publishing
Follett School Solutions
Lectorum Pubns., Inc.
Libros Sin Fronteras
Two Rivers Distribution.

Santoon Bks., *(978-0-9744905)* 13533 1/2 Village Dr., Cerritos, CA 90703 USA Tel 562-926-3361; Fax: 562-802-7680
E-mail: santoon@santoon.com.

Santoon Productions, Incorporated *See* **Santoon Bks.**

Santore, Marcia, *(978-0-692-05482-6; 978-0-692-06703-1; 978-0-692-03567-2)* 6 Texas Hill Rd, Plymouth, NH 03264-4226 USA; *Imprints:* Amalgamated Story (MYID_Y_AMALGAM)
E-mail: marcia@amalgamatedstory.com; mlsantore@gmail.com; info@amalgamatedstory.com
Web site: https://www.amalgamatedstory.com/; www.marciasantore.com
Dist(s): **CreateSpace Independent Publishing Platform.**

Sapient Business Solutions *See* **Herobrine Publishing**

Sapling Bks., *(978-0-9650871)* 234 W. Concord Ln., Chicago, IL 60614 USA Tel 312-280-1058; Fax: 312-280-1013.

Sapphire Bks. Publishing, *(978-0-9828608; 978-1-939062; 978-1-943353; 978-1-948232; 978-1-952270)* P.O. Box 8142, Salinas, CA 93912 USA Tel 831-998-7145
E-mail: publisher@sapphirebooks.com; info@sapphirebooks.com
Web site: http://www.sapphirebooks.com.

Saqi Bks. (GBR) *(978-0-86356; 978-1-908906) Dist. by* **Consort Bk Sales.**

Sara Anderson Children's Bks., *(978-0-9702784; 978-0-9911933; 978-1-943459)* 1522 Post Alley No. 206, Seattle, WA 98101 USA Tel 206-285-1520
E-mail: sara@saranderson.com
Web site: http://www.saranderson.com/
Dist(s): **BWI.**

Saraband (Scotland) Ltd. (GBR) *(978-1-887354; 978-1-908643; 978-1-910192) Dist. by* **IPG Chicago.**

Sarah & David LLC, *(978-0-9761648; 978-0-9796785)* P.O. Box 5894, Englewood, NJ 07631-5894 USA Fax: 201-221-7879
Web site: http://www.sarahdavid.com.

SarahRose Children's Bks. *Imprint of* **SarahRose Publishing**

SarahRose Publishing, *(978-0-9745865)* Orders Addr.: 12853 Dusty Willow RD, Manassas, VA 20112 USA Tel 253-232-9561; Edit Addr.: 14101 Parke Long Ct, Suite T, Chantilly, VA 20151 USA Tel 703-457-0429; *Imprints:* SarahRose Children's Books (SarahRose Child Bks)
E-mail: melodycurtiss@gmail.com
Web site: http://www.melodycurtiss.com; http://sarahrosepublishing.tumblr.com.

Sarah's Daughters Publishing *See* **Fidelity Heart Publishing**

Sarajames Poetry, Inc., *(978-0-9767395)* 88 Lawrence Ave., Brooklyn, NY 11230 USA Tel 718-972-2944
E-mail: jamestronan@yahoo.com.

Saranghay Studios, *(978-0-9887068)* 9 Brookside Dr., Foxboro, MA 02035 USA Tel 617-475-0563
E-mail: ray@saranghaystudios.com
Web site: www.saranghaystudios.com.

Saranjon Publishing, *(978-0-9665282)* Orders Addr.: P.O. Box 980, Homer, AK 99603-0980 USA Tel 907-235-8200; Fax: 907-235-8699; Edit Addr.: 385 E. Fairview St., Homer, AK 99603-0980 USA
E-mail: saranjon@alaska.net
Dist(s): **Wizard Works.**

Sarkisyan, Mary, *(978-0-692-15938-5; 978-0-692-15941-5)* 361 E 224th St., Carson, CA 90745 USA Tel 818-261-5956
E-mail: marysarkisyan@gmail.com
Dist(s): **Ingram Content Group.**

Sarvis, Barbara, *(978-0-9831346)* 10 Northgate Dr., Ponte Vedra Beach, FL 32082 USA Tel 904-285-2196
E-mail: barbarasarvis@aol.com.

Saseen, Sharon, *(978-0-9748425)* 403 E. 46th St., Savannah, GA 31405 USA Tel 912-233-1341
E-mail: saseenart@aol.com
Web site: http://www.saseen.com.

Sasquatch Bks., *(978-0-912365; 978-1-57061; 978-0-9821188; 978-1-63217)* 1904 Third Avenue, Suite 710, Seattle, WA 98101 USA (SAN 289-0208) Toll Free: 800-775-0817; *Imprints:* Little Bigfoot (Little Bigfoot)
E-mail: custserv@SasquatchBooks.com
Web site: http://www.sasquatchbooks.com
Dist(s): **MyiLibrary**
Penguin Random Hse. Distribution
Penguin Random Hse. LLC
Random Hse., Inc.

Sasscer, Abby, *(978-0-9854729)* 158 Nazareth Dr., Fort Valley, VA 22652 USA Tel 540-933-6496
E-mail: projectnazareth@yahoo.com.

Sassy Sister Publishing, *(978-0-9975859)*
E-mail: info@sydneyfaith.com
Web site: sydneyfaith.com.

Sastrugi Press *See* **Sastrugi Pr.**

Sastrugi Pr., *(978-0-9960206; 978-1-944986; 978-1-64922)* 335 W. Deloney St. No. E10, Jackson, WY 83001 USA Tel 619-363-5359
E-mail: aaron@sastrugipress.com; alinsdau@yahoo.com
Web site: www.sastrugipress.com.

Satellite Studio, *(978-0-9743968)* P.O. Box 32457, Knoxville, TN 37930-2457 USA Tel 865-691-1450; Fax: 865-691-2464
E-mail: dwilson@dannywilson.com.

Satin Finish Publishing, *(978-0-9764930; 978-0-9800209)* P.O. Box 481351, Kansas City, MO 64131 USA
E-mail: slfoster0826@kc.rr.com.

Satin Sheet Memoirs Publishing *See* **Nowata Press Publishing Consultants**

Saturn International, *(978-0-9764957)* 126 Herricks Rd., Mineola, NY 11501 USA Fax: 516-214-0154.

Saturn Music & Entertainment, *(978-0-692-82106-0; 978-0-692-83847-1; 978-0-692-84418-2; 978-0-692-88897-1; 978-0-692-93821-8; 978-0-692-15655-1; 978-0-578-40456-1)* 120 Madeira Dr. NE No. 220, Albuquerque, NM 91789 USA Tel 360-232-3022
E-mail: saturnmusicandentertainment@gmail.com
Dist(s): **CreateSpace Independent Publishing Platform.**

Satya Hse. Pubns., *(978-0-9729191; 978-0-9818720; 978-1-935874)* Orders Addr.: 22 Turkey St., Hardwick, MA 01037 USA; Edit Addr.: P.O. Box 122, Hardwick, MA 01037 USA Tel 413-477-8743
E-mail: julie@satyahouse.com
Web site: http://https://www.satyahouse.com; http://www.iseethesunbooks.com
Dist(s): **Independent Pubs. Group**
Midpoint Trade Bks., Inc.
OverDrive, Inc.
Smashwords.

Sauerlander AG (CHE) *(978-3-7941) Dist. by* **Distribks Inc.**

Saul, Robert, *(978-0-692-15368-0; 978-0-692-15369-7; 978-0-578-44407-9)* 108 Wimbledon Ct., GREENWOOD, SC 29646 USA Tel 864-980-8372
E-mail: robertsaul@me.com
Dist(s): **Ingram Content Group.**

Sauls, Lynn, *(978-0-615-74910-5; 978-0-615-78903-3; 978-0-9893216)* 14 Alexander St., Alexandria, VA 22314 USA Tel 703-549-5799
E-mail: lynnbsauls@aol.com.

Saunders Bk. Co. (CAN) *(978-1-895058; 978-1-897563; 978-1-926660; 978-1-926722; 978-1-926853; 978-1-77092; 978-1-77308) Dist. by* **RiverStream.**

Saunders Bk. Co. (CAN) *(978-1-895058; 978-1-897563; 978-1-926660; 978-1-926722; 978-1-926853; 978-1-77092; 978-1-77308) Dist. by* **Creative Co.**

Saur, Gregory, *(978-0-9964245; 978-0-692-80648-7; 978-1-949317)* 711 Old Wormley Creek Rd., Yorktown, VA 23692 USA Tel 757-898-1524
E-mail: imalepton@hotmail.com.

Sautrelle Publishing Co., *(978-1-947927)* 4100 W. 12th St., Lawrence, KS 66049 USA Tel 785-218-4046; Fax: 785-865-2966
E-mail: papahooge@gmail.com.

Sauvignon Pr., *(978-0-9889618)* 1459 Brookcliff Dr., Marietta, GA 30062 USA Tel 404-435-6507
E-mail: rewrites1@gmail.com.

Savage Books *See* **Blue Thunder Bks.**

Savage Pr., *(978-1-886028; 978-1-937706)* 14172 E Carlson Rd, Brule, WI 54820 USA Tel 218-391-3070 (phone/fax); 14172 E Carlson Rd., Brule, WI 54820 Tel 218-391-3070
E-mail: mail@savpress.com
Web site: http://www.savpress.com
Dist(s): **Baker & Taylor Bks.**
Partners Bk. Distributing, Inc.

Savanna Pr., *(978-0-9759440)* Orders Addr.: P.O. Box 777, Monte Vista, CO 81144 USA Tel 719-850-2255; Fax: 719-852-2211; Edit Addr.: 67 Gold Cir., Pagosa Springs, CO 81147 USA; P.O. Box 1806, Vryburg, 8600
E-mail: riovista@rmi.net.

Savannah College of Art & Design Exhibitions, *(978-0-9654682; 978-1-893974; 978-0-9797440; 978-0-615-22202-8)* Orders Addr.: P.O. Box 3146, Savannah, GA 31401-3146 USA Tel 912-525-5287; Fax: 912-525-4952; Edit Addr.: 212 W. Hall St., Garden Apt., Savannah, GA 31401 USA; *Imprints:* Design Press Books (Design Press Bks)
E-mail: asalgado@scad.edu
Web site: http://www.scadexhibitions.com
Dist(s): **D.A.P./Distributed Art Pubs.**

Savannah's Safe Publishing Co., *(978-0-692-73903-7; 978-1-7338884)* P.O. Box 972, Vallejo, CA 94590 USA Tel 415-574-1627
E-mail: optimalbf@gmail.com.

Savas, Bachtsoglou, *(978-0-9771020)* 139-02 97th Ave., Jamaica, NY 11435 USA Tel 718-793-0107
E-mail: avipremlall@gmail.com.

Savas Beatie, *(978-1-932714; 978-1-61121)* 989 Governor Dr., Suite 102, El Dorado Hills, CA 95762 USA Tel 916-941-6896; Fax: 916-941-6895
E-mail: sarahs@savasbeatie.com; editorial@savasbeatie.com
Web site: http://www.savasbeatie.com
Dist(s): **Casemate Pubs. & Bk. Distributors, LLC**
MBI Distribution Services/Quayside Distribution
MyiLibrary
Open Road Integrated Media, Inc.
ebrary, Inc.

Save Our Seas, Ltd., *(978-0-9800444)* 626 Elvira Ave., Redondo Beach, CA 90277-9027 USA Tel 310-792-0338; Fax: 310-792-9273
E-mail: jonr@jokarproductions.com
Web site: http://www.saveourseas.com
Dist(s): **National Bk. Network.**

Savor Publishing Hse., Inc., *(978-0-9708296)* 6020 Broken Bow Dr., Citrus Heights, CA 95621 USA Tel 718-846-7277
E-mail: Smarties@SavorPublishing.com; SavorPubHouse@aol.com
Web site: http://www.savorpublishing.com
Dist(s): **Book Clearing Hse.**
Book Wholesalers, Inc.
Follett School Solutions.

Savory Palate, Inc., *(978-1-889374)* 8174 S. Holly, No. 404, Centennial, CO 80122-4004 USA Tel 303-741-5408; Fax: 303-741-0339; Toll Free: 800-741-5418
E-mail: info@savorypalate.com
Web site: http://www.savorypalate.com
Dist(s): **Brodart Co.**
New Leaf Distributing Co., Inc.
Quality Bks., Inc.
Royal Pubns., Inc.

Savory Words, *(978-0-9863552)* P.O. Box 3941, Frederick, MD 21705 USA Tel 240-422-8540
E-mail: info@savorywords.com
Web site: http://www.savorywords.com/.

Savvas Learning Co., *(978-1-59896; 978-1-60637)* 75 Arlington St., Boston, MA 02116 USA; *Imprints:* AGS Secondary (AGS Second); Dominie Elementary (Dominie Elem); FEARON (FEARON); GLOBE (GLOBPS); Celebration Press (Celebration); Dale Seymour Publications (Dale Seymo); Modern Curriculum Press (Mod Curriculu); Scott Foresman (Scott Fores); SILVER BURDETT (SilvBurd); Prentice Hall (PHall)
Dist(s): **Pearson Education.**

Savvy Cyber Kids, Inc., *(978-0-9827968)* 4780 Ashford Dunwoody Rd. Suite A 312, Atlanta, GA 30338 USA Tel 404-955-7233
E-mail: info@savvycyberkids.org
Web site: http://www.savvycyberkids.org.

Savvy Pr., *(978-0-9669877; 978-0-9826069; 978-0-9852115; 978-1-939113)* Orders Addr.: P.O. Box 63, Salem, NY 12865 USA Tel 518-633-4778; Fax: 815 346-2659
E-mail: info@savvypress.com; info@gowanusbooks.com
Web site: http://www.savvypress.com; http://www.sagasf.com; http://www.gowanusbooks.com
Dist(s): **Quality Bks., Inc.**

Sawatch Publishing, *(978-0-9989473)* 116 Wren Ct., Eagle, CO 81631 USA Tel 970-343-0470
E-mail: Jenniferalsever@gmail.com
Web site: www.trinityforestseries.com.

Sawmill Pr., 3326 Hollyberry Dr., VISTA, CA 92084 USA Tel 530-613-2817.

Sawmill Publishing, *(978-0-9749915)* 6444 E. Spring St., No. 215, Long Beach, CA 90815 USA
Web site: www.sawmillpublishing.com.

Sawmill Ridge Publishing, *(978-0-9761924)* 183 Post Oak Dr., Roanoke, VA 24019 USA Tel 540-966-5706.

Saxon Pubs., Inc., *(978-0-939798; 978-1-56577; 978-1-59141)* Div. of Houghton Mifflin Harcourt Supplemental Pubs., Orders Addr.: 6277 Sea Harbor Dr., 5th Flr., Orlando, FL 32887 USA Toll Free Fax: 877-578-2638; Toll Free: 888-363-4266; Edit Addr.: 10801 N. Mopac Expressway, Bldg. 3, Austin, TX 78759 USA (SAN 216-8960) Toll Free: 800-531-5015
Web site: http://www.saxonpublishers.com
Dist(s): **Follett School Solutions**
Houghton Mifflin Harcourt Publishing Co.

Say It Loud! Readers & Writers Series, *(978-0-9779499)* 1507 E. 53rd St., No. 841, Chicago, IL 60615 USA.

Say It Right, *(978-0-9723457; 978-0-9760490; 978-0-9770418; 978-1-934701)* Orders Addr.: P.O. Box 651, Tybee Island, GA 31328 USA Tel 912-228-4556; Fax: 912-480-4214; Toll Free: 888-811-0759
E-mail: jim@sayitright.org
Web site: http://www.sayitright.org.

Say Out Loud, LLC, *(978-0-9799127)* Orders Addr.: 885 Woodstock Rd. Suite 430-373, Roswell, GA 30075 USA (SAN 854-7483) Tel 404-428-7935; Fax: 404-506-9823
E-mail: author@wordstosayoutloud.com
Web site: http://www.wordstosayoutloud.com.

SC & FC Publications, *(978-0-9860794)* P.O. Box 124, Interlochen, MI 49643 USA.

S.C. TreeHouse LLC, *(978-0-692-87157-7; 978-0-578-46600-2; 978-0-578-47363-5; 978-0-578-50969-3; 978-0-578-56517-0; 978-0-578-56680-1)* 183 Parker RD, BENTON, TN 37307 USA Tel 423-715-4694
E-mail: jeffwcrawford5+LVP0003605@gmail.com; jeffwcrawford5+LVP0003605@gmail.com.

Scafe, Claire, *(978-0-9787695)* 7918 John Dr., Cheyenne, WY 82009 USA Tel 307-632-1702
E-mail: skir2@aol.com.

Scandinavia Publishing Hse. (DNK) *(978-87-7247; 978-87-87732; 978-87-7132; 978-87-7203) Dist. by* **Destiny Image Pubs.**

Scandora,

Scanlan, John M., *(978-0-9755405)* 5 Gumtree Rd., No. F-20, Hilton Head, SC 29926 USA (SAN 256-0771) Tel 843-342-2793; Fax: 419-281-6883 (orders); Toll Free: 800-247-6553 (orders)
E-mail: ping1@hargray.com; order@bookmasters.com
Web site: http://www.speedislife.us; http://www.atlasbooks.com.

Scanlan, John M. Literary Services *See* **Scanlan, John M.**

†Scarecrow Pr., Inc., *(978-0-8108; 978-1-57886)* Div. of Rowman & Littlefield Publishing Group, Orders Addr.: 15200 NBN Way, Blue Ridge Summit, PA 17214 USA Tel 717-794-3800 (Sales, Customer Service, MIS, Royalties, Inventory Mgmt., Dist., Credit & Collection); Fax: 717-794-3803 (Customer Service &/or orders); 717-794-3857 (Sales & MIS); 717-794-3856 (Royalties, Inventory Mgmt. & Dist.); Toll Free Fax: 800-338-4550 (Customer Service &/or orders); Toll Free: 800-462-6420 (Customer Service &/or orders); Edit Addr.: 4501 Forbes Blvd., Suite 200, Lanham, MD 20706-4310 USA Tel 301-459-3366; Fax: 301-429-5747 Short Discount, please contact rlpgsales@rowman.com
E-mail: custserv@rowman.com
Web site: http://www.scarecrowpress.com; http://www.rlpgbooks.com
Dist(s): **CreateSpace Independent Publishing Platform**
Ebsco Publishing
Follett School Solutions
MyiLibrary
National Bk. Network
Rowman & Littlefield Publishers, Inc.
ebrary, Inc.; *CIP.*

ScarecrowEducation *See* **Rowman & Littlefield Education**

Scarlet Primrose Pr., *(978-0-9851678)* 308 Blue Heron Cir., Simpsonville, SC 29680 USA Tel 585-545-0032
E-mail: andreacefalo4@gmail.com; scarletprimrosepress@gmail.com
Web site: http://www.andreacefalo.com
Dist(s): **CreateSpace Independent Publishing Platform**
Ingram Content Group
Smashwords.

Scarlett L Pr., *(978-0-615-60059-8; 978-0-9982452)* 7800 E Freeport Pl., Broken Arrow, OK 74014 USA Tel 918-520-5718
Dist(s): **CreateSpace Independent Publishing Platform.**

Scarletta *See* **Mighty Media Pr.**

Scars Pubns. & Design, *(978-1-891470)* 829 Brian Ct., Gurnee, IL 60031 USA
E-mail: Editor@scars.tv
Web site: http://scars.tv.

Scavenger's Pubns., *(978-0-9798792)* 3443 Remington Ct., Eau Claire, WI 54703 USA Tel 715-456-3909
E-mail: ggparadox@hotmail.com.

SCB Distributors, Orders Addr.: 15608 S. New Century Dr., Gardena, CA 90248-2129 USA (SAN 630-4818) Tel 310-532-9400; Fax: 310-532-7001; Toll Free: 800-729-6423 (orders only)
E-mail: info@scbdistributors.com
Web site: http://www.scbdistributors.com.

SCF Pr., *(978-0-9990337)* P.O. Box 329, Merrimac, MA 01860 USA Tel 617-852-2599
E-mail: schoolcounselingfiles@gmail.com.

Schadt, Susan Pr., LLC, *(978-0-9973559; 978-1-7336341)* 4728 Spottswood, Memphis, TN 38117 USA Tel 901-412-2334
E-mail: susan.schadt@sschadtpress.com
Web site: sschadtpress.com
Dist(s): **Ingram Publisher Services.**

Schafer-Post Entomology Pubns., *(978-0-9766855)* Entomology Dept. Hultz Hall, North Dakota State Univ., Fargo, ND 58105 USA Tel 701-231-7582; Fax: 701-231-8557
E-mail: david.rider@ndsu.edu.

Schallert, Ann, *(978-0-578-03425-6)* 10047 Hwy. 104, Tucumcari, NM 88401 USA
E-mail: crossann@shipleysystems.com.

Schaub, Stephen M. Photography *See* **Indian Hill Gallery of Fine Photography**

Scheer Delight Publishing, *(978-0-9671761)* 4030 E. Christy, Wichita, KS 67220-2540 USA (SAN 253-908X) Tel 316-683-2001; Fax: 316-636-1268
E-mail: schdelight@cox.net
Web site: http://scheerdelightpub.com.

Scheller, Debbie, *(978-0-9991885)* 13510 Smith Lake ln, houston, TX 77044 USA Tel 810-877-2852; Fax: 810-877-2852
E-mail: schellerdebbie@gmail.com.

Schermerhorn, Walters Co., *(978-0-9741746; 978-0-9824987)* 740 Purdue Dr., Claremont, CA 91711-3418 USA Tel 909-398-1228
E-mail: lilly.walters@verizon.net
Web site: http://www.motivational-keynote-speakers.com.

Scheuerman, Susan, *(978-0-692-12327-0; 978-0-692-12328-7)* 166 E. Genesee St., SKANEATELES, NY 13152 USA Tel 315-247-6096
E-mail: ryan@ryanzbartlett.com
Dist(s): **Ingram Content Group.**

Schiavi, Sherry *See* **Celltrition**

Schiffer Publishing, Ltd., *(978-0-7643; 978-0-87033; 978-0-88740; 978-0-89538; 978-0-916838; 978-0-9787278; 978-1-5073)* Orders Addr.: 4880 Lower Valley Rd., Atglen, PA 19310 USA (SAN 208-8428) Tel 610-593-1777; Fax: 610-593-2002; *Imprints:* Cornell Maritime Press/Tidewater Publishers (CornellTide); Schiffer Publishing Ltd (SCHIFFER PUBLI); Red Feather (RedFeather)
E-mail: info@schifferbooks.com; karen@schifferbooks.com
Web site: http://www.schifferbooks.com.

Schiffer Publishing Ltd *Imprint of* **Schiffer Publishing, Ltd.**

Schiffner, Frederick A., *(978-0-9765782)* P.O. Box 1047, Spring Mt., PA 19478 USA Tel 610-287-5827
E-mail: fschiffner@fast.net.

Schiller Institute, Inc., *(978-0-9621095; 978-1-882985; 978-0-9997818)* Orders Addr.: P.O. Box 20244, Washington, DC 20041-0244 USA (SAN 250-4944) Tel 703-777-9451 ext 541; Fax: 703-771-3099
E-mail: SchillerInstitutePrinting@gmail.com; swelsh@schillerinstitute.org
Web site: http://www.schillerinstitute.org.

Schisler, Amy MacWilliams, *(978-0-615-93539-3; 978-0-692-40924-4; 978-0-692-49786-9; 978-0-692-77575-2; 978-0-692-83640-8; 978-0-692-94617-6; 978-0-692-94619-0; 978-0-692-94625-1; 978-0-692-98294-5; 978-1-7322242; 978-1-7346907)* 7604 Cooper Point Rd., Bozman, MD 21612 USA Tel 410-725-1693
E-mail: amyschisler@me.com
Web site: amyschislerauthor.com
Dist(s): **CreateSpace Independent Publishing Platform.**

Schleich, James, *(978-0-615-12142-0)* 105 Woodland Dr., Zelienople, PA 16063-9316 USA
E-mail: james@the-soundman.org
Web site: http://www.the-soundman.org.

Schlessinger Media, *(978-1-57225; 978-1-879151)* Div. of Library Video Co., Orders Addr.: P.O. Box 580, Wynnewood, PA 19096 USA Tel 610-645-4000; Fax: 610-645-4050; Toll Free: 800-843-3620; Edit Addr.: 7 Wynnewood Rd., Wynnewood, PA 19096 USA
E-mail: sales@libraryvideo.com
Web site: http://www.libraryvideo.com
Dist(s): **Follett School Solutions**
Library Video Co.
Video Project, The.

Schlessinger Video Productions *See* **Schlessinger Media**

Schley, Michael, *(978-0-9759645)* 2 Oak Pk. Ave., Darien, CT 06820 USA
E-mail: mike_schley@yahoo.com.

Schmaus, Marcia L., *(978-0-692-94546-9; 978-0-692-97555-8)* 5401 34th St. S., Fargo, ND 58104 USA Tel 605-268-3303
E-mail: marsayam67@msn.com
Dist(s): **CreateSpace Independent Publishing Platform.**

Schmidt, Kimberly K, *(978-0-9864009)* 6507 Scottsville Rd., Scottsville, VA 24590 USA Tel 434-286-7226
E-mail: kkjschmidt@gmail.com.

Schmidt, M. Productions, *(978-0-692-09042-8; 978-0-692-09046-6; 978-0-692-09960-5; 978-0-692-09965-0; 978-0-692-11104-8; 978-0-692-12253-2; 978-0-692-15194-5; 978-0-692-15681-0; 978-0-692-15917-0; 978-0-692-15920-0; 978-0-692-17191-2; 978-0-692-17193-6; 978-0-692-17620-7; 978-0-692-17621-4; 978-0-578-44876-3; 978-0-578-44879-4; 978-0-578-45411-5; 978-0-578-45413-9; 978-0-578-51576-2; 978-0-578-51578-6; 978-0-578-59358-6; 978-0-578-64096-9; 978-0-578-64097-6; 978-0-578-73224-4; 978-0-578-73226-8; 978-0-578-77702-3;) P.O. Box 371, Ellsworth, KS 67439 USA Tel 785-472-8665*
E-mail: dcountess.mary@gmail.com
Dist(s): **Ingram Content Group.**

Schmitt, Steven E. *See* **Global Partnership, LLC**

Schmul Publishing Co., Inc., *(978-0-88019)* Orders Addr.: P.O. Box 716, Salem, OH 44460-0716 USA (SAN 180-2771) Tel 330-222-2249; Fax: 330-222-0001; Toll Free: 800-772-6657; Edit Addr.: 3583 Newgarden Rd., Salem, OH 44460 USA
E-mail: spchale@valunet.com
Web site: http://www.wesleyanbooks.com.

Schnitzelbank Press *See* **BeerBooks.com**

Schocken *Imprint of* **Knopf Doubleday Publishing Group**

Schoenberg & Assocs., *(978-0-9748208)* 8033 W. Sunset Blvd., No. 944, Los Angeles, CA 90046 USA
Web site: http://www.rdsphotos.com.

Schoenhof's Foreign Bks., Inc., *(978-0-87774)* 76a Mount Auburn St., Cambridge, MA 02138-5051 USA (SAN 212-0062)
E-mail: info@schoenhofs.com
Web site: http://www.schoenhofs.com.

Scholargy Custom Publishing, Incorporated *See* **Scholargy Publishing, Inc.**

Scholargy Publishing, Inc., *(978-1-58666; 978-1-59247)* 17855 N. Black Cnyon Hwy., Phoenix, AZ 85023 USA (SAN 254-7295) Tel 602-548-5833 (phone/fax); Fax: 602-353-0680
E-mail: stephanie@scholargy.com
Web site: http://www.scholargy.com.

Scholarly Hour, *(978-0-692-92871-4; 978-1-7325487)* 11260 Williams Ct., Carmel, IN 46033 USA Tel 317-440-7088
E-mail: jenny.bryant7@gmail.com.

Scholastic *Imprint of* **Scholastic, Inc.**

Scholastic Canada, Ltd. (CAN) *(978-0-439; 978-0-590; 978-0-7791; 978-1-4431) Dist. by* **PerseuPGW.**

Scholastic en Espanol *Imprint of* **Scholastic, Inc.**

Scholastic, Inc. *Imprint of* **Scholastic, Inc.**

†Scholastic, Inc., *(978-0-439; 978-0-590; 978-0-545; 978-1-338)* 557 Broadway, New York, NY 10012-3999 USA (SAN 202-5442) Fax: 212-343-6802; Toll Free: 800-325-6149 (customer service); *Imprints:* Cartwheel Books (Cartwheel); Scholastic Reference (Scholastic Ref); Blue Sky Press, The (Blue Sky Press); Scholastic (Scholastic); Levine, Arthur A. Books (A A Levine); Orchard Books (Orchard Bks); Scholastic Press (Scholastic Pr); Chicken House, The (Chick Hse); PUSH (PUSH); Scholastic en Espanol (Scholastic en Espanol); Scholastic Nonfiction (Schol Nonfic); Scholastic Paperbacks (Schol Pbk); Sidekicks TM (Sidekicks); Tangerine Press (Tang Pr Sch); Teaching Resources (Teach Res Sch); Graphix (Graphx); Scholastic, Incorporated (SchInc); Teaching Strategies (TeachStrategi); Theory & Practice (Theory & Prac); Little Shepherd (Little Shepard); Di Capua, Michael (Michael DiCapua); WestBow Press (WestBowPr); Exhibit A (Exhibit A); Scholastic Professional (ScholProf)
E-mail: info@scholastic.com
Web site: http://www.scholastic.com
Dist(s): **Blackstone Audio, Inc.**
Brilliance Publishing, Inc.
Children's Plus, Inc.
Ebsco Publishing
Follett School Solutions
Hachette Bk. Group
HarperCollins Pubs.
INscribe Digital
Lectorum Pubns., Inc.
MyiLibrary
Open Road Integrated Media, Inc.
Perfection Learning Corp.; *CIP.*

Scholastic Institute Chokyi Gyaltsen Univ., *(978-0-9973275; 978-0-9990141)* 3433 N Druid Hills Rd. Apt M, Decatur, GA 30033 USA Tel 404-825-8898
E-mail: office@sicgu.org
Web site: www.sicgu.org.

Scholastic Library Publishing, *(978-0-516; 978-0-531; 978-0-7172; 978-1-60631; 978-1-5461)* 90 Old Sherman Tpke., Danbury, CT 06816 USA (SAN 253-8865); *Imprints:* Orchard Books (Orchard Bks); Grolier Online (Grolier Online); Children's Press (Childrens Pr); Grolier (Grolier Schol); Watts, Franklin (Frank Watts)
E-mail: agraham@grolier.com; kbreen@scholastic.com
Web site: http://librarypublishing.scholastic.com
Dist(s): **Booksource, The**
Children's Plus, Inc.
Hachette Bk. Group
Lectorum Pubns., Inc.

Scholastic Nonfiction *Imprint of* **Scholastic, Inc.**

Scholastic Paperbacks *Imprint of* **Scholastic, Inc.**

Scholastic Pr. *Imprint of* **Scholastic, Inc.**

Scholastic Professional *Imprint of* **Scholastic, Inc.**

Scholastic Reference *Imprint of* **Scholastic, Inc.**

Scholte, Sandra, *(978-0-692-16642-0; 978-0-692-18610-7)* 31960 Deerberry Ln., Murrieta, CA 92563 USA Tel 951-397-5144
E-mail: lostinnl@yahoo.com
Dist(s): **CreateSpace Independent Publishing Platform.**

Schonwalder, Helmut, *(978-0-9763287)* P.O. Box 1390, Monterey, CA 93940 USA Tel 831-375-7737
E-mail: helmut@schonwalder.org; helmut@schonwalder.com
Web site: http://www.schonwalder.com; http://www.gastronomical.net; http://www.kaufhouse.info.

School Age Notes *Imprint of* **Gryphon Hse., Inc.**

School Days, *(978-0-9744302)* Orders Addr.: P.O. Box 454, North Carrollton, MS 38947 USA
E-mail: schooldaysmemorybook@yahoo.com
Web site: http://www.schooldaysmemorybook.com
Dist(s): **Wimmer Cookbooks.**

†School for Advanced Research Pr./SAR Pr., *(978-0-933452; 978-1-930618; 978-1-934691; 978-1-938645)* P.O. Box 2188, Santa Fe, NM 87504-2188 USA (SAN 212-6222) Tel 505-954-7206; Fax: 505-954-7241; Toll Free: 888-390-6070
E-mail: press@sarsf.org
Web site: http://www.sarpress.sarweb.org
Dist(s): **Univ. of New Mexico Pr.;** *CIP.*

School Forest Publishing LLC, *(978-0-9996862)* 8906 W. RS Ave., Schoolcraft, MI 49087 USA Tel 269-217-6135
E-mail: davedevisser2@gmail.com.

School of American Research Press *See* **School for Advanced Research Pr./SAR Pr.**

School of Color Publishing, *(978-0-9679628; 978-1-931780)* Div. of The Michael Wilcox School of Color, Inc., P.O. Box 4793, Pinehurst, NC 28374 USA Toll Free: 888-794-5269
E-mail: wilcoxschool@earthlink.net; anne.m.gardner@worldnet.att.net
Web site: http://www.schoolofcolor.com
Dist(s): **F&W Media, Inc.**
Two Rivers Distribution.

Schl. of Government, *(978-1-56011; 978-1-64238)* CB 3330 UNC Chapel Hill, Chapel Hill, NC 27599-3330 USA (SAN 204-8752) Tel 919-966-4119; Fax: 919-962-2707
E-mail: justice@sog.unc.edu; Twomey@sog.unc.edu; horton@sog.unc.edu
Web site: http://www.sog.unc.edu
Dist(s): **Univ. of North Carolina Pr.**
Univ. of Nebraska Pr.

School of Music Publishing Hse. (RUS) *(978-5-9500) Dist. by* **Coronet Bks.**

Schl. Services of California, Inc., *(978-0-9708628; 978-0-9748487; 978-0-9848031)* 1121 L St., No. 1060, Sacramento, CA 95814 USA Tel 916-446-7517; Fax: 916-446-2011
E-mail: susanm@sscal.com
Web site: http://www.sscal.com.

School Specialty, Incorporated, P.O. Box 6031, Cambridge, MA 02139-9031 USA
Dist(s): **Children's Plus, Inc.**

School Street Bks., *(978-0-9845513)* 284 School St., Northboro, MA 01532 USA
Web site: http://www.writtenbyelizabethdougherty.com
Dist(s): **Smashwords.**

Schl. Tools, *(978-0-9754578)* 23418 28th Ave. W, Brier, WA 98036 USA.

School Zone Publishing Co., *(978-0-88743; 978-0-938256; 978-1-58947; 978-1-60041; 978-1-60159; 978-1-68147)* 1819 Industrial Dr., Grand Haven, MI 49417 USA (SAN 289-8314) Tel 616-846-5030; Fax: 616-846-6181; Toll Free: 800-253-0564
E-mail: christyf@schoolzone.com; sharonw@schoolzone.com
Web site: http://www.schoolzone.com.

Schoolhouse Publishing, *(978-0-9758543; 978-0-9845335; 978-0-9834657)* Orders Addr.: 659 Schoolhouse Rd., Telford, PA 18969-2449 USA Toll Free: 877-747-4711
Web site: http://www.shpublishing.com.

Schoolside Pr, *(978-0-9785100)* 7039 Sacred Cir., Sparks, NV 89437 USA Tel 818-884-7349
E-mail: eamartonyi@schoolsidepress.com
Web site: http://Schoolsidpress.com
Dist(s): **Independent Pubs. Group**
Midpoint Trade Bks., Inc.

Schoolwide, Inc., *(978-0-9760421; 978-1-933552; 978-1-937694; 978-1-938508; 978-1-62621; 978-1-68341)* 4250 Veterans Memorial Hwy., Ste. 2000 W, Holbrook, NY 11741 USA Toll Free Fax: 866-333-1130; Toll Free: 800-261-9964
Web site: http://www.schoolwide.com.

Schooner Pubns., *(978-1-929234)* 1610-D Church St. Coastal Ctr., PMB 360, Conway, SC 29526 USA Tel 843-347-9792.

Schott Music Corp., *(978-0-930448)* 35 E 21st ST., 8th Flr., New York, NY 10010 USA
E-mail: scott.wollschleger@eamdllc.com
Dist(s): **Leonard, Hal Corp.**

Schott Musik International GmbH & Co. KG (DEU) *(978-3-7957; 978-3-95983) Dist. by* **H Leonard.**

Schrader, Racheal, *(978-0-9815274)* P.O. Box 15603, Colorado Springs, CO 80935-5603 USA
E-mail: inspired-ink@hotmail.com
Web site: http://inspired-ink.net.

Schroeder, Patrick A. Publications: Civil War Books *See* **Schroeder Pubns.: Civil War Bks.**

Schroeder Pubns.: Civil War Bks., *(978-1-889246)* Orders Addr.: 131 Tanglewood Dr., Lynchburg, VA 24502 USA Tel 434-525-4431; Fax: 434-525-7293
E-mail: civilwarbooks@yahoo.com
Web site: http://www.civilwar-books.com.

Schue, Lori, *(978-0-692-11524-4; 978-0-692-11528-2; 978-0-692-12833-6; 978-0-692-15799-2; 978-0-578-40063-1)* 40377 Stonebrook Hamlet Pl., Waterford, VA 20197 USA Tel 540-882-3743
E-mail: lschue@comcast.net
Dist(s): **Ingram Content Group.**

Schultz, Ryan, *(978-0-9988918)* 19007 111 Pl SE, Snohomish, WA 98290 USA Tel 425-583-9523
E-mail: schultzry@hotmail.com.

Schumar Publishing, *(978-0-692-98181-8)* 1009 N Elbow Ln., Yardley, PA 19067 USA Tel 215-738-1670
E-mail: Sneakersgm@yahoo.com.

Schwarcz, Editora Ltda, Companhia das Letrinhas (BRA) *(978-85-7406) Dist. by* **Distribks Inc.**

Schwartau, Winn LLC, *(978-0-9628700; 978-0-9964019)* Orders Addr.: 545 Westport Dr., Old Hickory, TN 37138-1115 USA
E-mail: sherra@alwayschaos.com; winn@securityexperts.com
Web site: http://www.winnschwartau.com.

Schwartz & Wade Bks. *Imprint of* **Random Hse. Children's Bks.**

Schwartz, Arthur & Company, Incorporated/Woodstocker Books *See* **Woodstocker Books/Arthur Schwartz & Company**

Schwartz, Gary, *(978-0-9975860)* P.O. Box 1123, North Bend, WA 98045 USA Tel 425-831-5667
E-mail: gary@gary-schwartz.com
Web site: http://gary-schwartz.com.

Schwartz, Joel, *(978-0-9785885)* 1315 Cinnamon Dr., Fort Washington, PA 19034-2818 USA
E-mail: jshrink@comcast.net
Web site: http://www.stresslessshrink.com.

Schwartz Marketing, *(978-0-9893046)* 1234 Bloomfield St., Hoboken, NJ 07030 USA Tel 201-656-2223; Fax: 201-656-2223
E-mail: tomschwartz@earthlink.net.

Schwarz Pauper Pr., *(978-0-9621505)* 88 Winwood Dr., Barnstead, NH 03225 USA (SAN 251-4540) Tel 603-776-5680
E-mail: Granitesunset@aol.com.

Sci Fi-Arizona, Inc., *(978-1-929381)* 1931 E. Libra Dr., Tempe, AZ 85283 USA Tel 480-838-6558; *Imprints:* Third Millennium Publishing (Third Millen Pubng)
E-mail: mccollum@scifi-az.com
Web site: http://www.scifi-az.com; http://www.3mpub.com.

Science Academy Software, *(978-0-9623926)* 600 Baychester Ave., Apt 5B, Bronx, NY 10475-4457 USA Tel 718-561-4048.

Science & God, Inc., *(978-0-9745861)* P.O. Box 2036, Labelle, FL 33975-2036 USA Tel 239-218-4543.

Science & Humanities Pr., *(978-1-888725; 978-1-59630)* Subs. of Banis & Assocs., Orders Addr.: P.O. Box 7151, Chesterfield, MO 63006-7151 USA (SAN 299-8459) Tel 636-394-4950; Fax: 800-706-0585; P.O. Box 7151, Chesterfield, MO 63006-7151; Edit Addr.: 1023 Stuyvesant Ln., Manchester, MO 63011-3601 USA Tel 636-394-4950; Toll Free Fax: 800-706-0585; 1023 Stuyvesant Ln., Manchester, MO 63011-3601 Tel 636-394-4950; Toll Free Fax: 800-706-0585; *Imprints:* BeachHouse Books (BeachHouse Bks)
E-mail: banis@sciencehumanitiespress.com; banis@banis-associates.com
Web site: http://www.banis-associates.com; http://www.sciencehumanitiespress.com; http://www.macroprintbooks.com; http://www.stressmyth.com; http://www.normajeanebook.com; http://www.route66book.com; http://www.accessible-travel.com.

Science and Technology Concepts (STC) *Imprint of* **Smithsonian Science Education Ctr. (SSEC)**

Science Curriculum, Inc., *(978-1-882057)* Orders Addr.: 200 Union Blvd. Ste. G18, Lakewood, CO 80228-1845 USA (SAN 248-3637) Toll Free: 888-501-0957; 24 Stone Rd., Belmont, MA 04278
E-mail: marketing@sci-ips.com
Web site: http://www.sci-ips.com.

Science Enterprises, Inc., *(978-0-930116)* 402 N. Blackford St., Indianapolis, IN 46202-3272 USA (SAN 210-6639).

Science, Naturally!, *(978-0-9678020; 978-0-9700106; 978-1-938492)* 725 Eighth St., SE., Washington, DC 20003 USA Tel 202-465-4798; Fax: 202-558-2132; Toll Free: 866-724-9876
E-mail: dia@sciencenaturally.com
Web site: http://www.sciencenaturally.com
Dist(s): **Children's Plus, Inc.**
MyiLibrary
National Bk. Network
ebrary, Inc.

Science of Knowledge Pr., *(978-1-59620)* P.O. Box 324, Little Falls, NJ 07424 USA Fax: 973-272-1102
Web site: http://www.scienceok.com
Dist(s): **Majors, J. A. Co.**

Science of Mind Publishing, *(978-0-911336; 978-0-917849; 978-0-9727184)* Div. of United Church of Religious Science, Orders Addr.: 573 Park Point Dr., Golden, CO 80401-7042 USA (SAN 203-2570) Tel 720-279-1643; 720-496-1370; Fax: 303-526-0913
E-mail: kjohnson@csl.org
Web site: http://www.scienceofmind.com; http://www.spirituallivingpress.com
Dist(s): **DeVorss & Co.**
Red Wheel/Weiser.

Science Pubs., *(978-0-9700733; 978-0-9716445; 978-0-9749755; 978-1-938024)* Div. of BrainMind.com, 677 Elm St., San Jose, CA 95126 USA Do not confuse with companies with the same name in Hudson, WI, Flushing, NY, San Francisco, CA, Missoula, MT, Wolf City, TX
E-mail: RJoseph@BrainMind.com
Web site: http://BrainMind.com; http://Cosmology.com
Dist(s): **MyiLibrary.**

Science Square Publishing, *(978-0-9740861)* 2845 Bowen St., Graton, CA 95444-9347 USA
E-mail: info@sciencesquare.com
Web site: http://www.sciencesquare.com.

Science2Discover, Inc., *(978-0-9673811)* P.O. Box 2435, Del Mar, CA 92014-1735 USA Fax: 858-793-0410; Toll Free: 888-359-6075; 2015 Seaview Ave., Del Mar, CA 92014 Do not confuse with MetaMetrix, Inc., Norcross, GA
E-mail: info@science2discover.com
Web site: http://www.science2discover.com.

Sciencenter, *(978-0-578-00196-8; 978-0-578-00197-5)* 601 First St., Ithaca, NY 14850 USA Tel 607-272-0600
Dist(s): **Lulu Pr., Inc.**

Scientia Est Vox Pr., *(978-0-578-02353-3; 978-0-578-05385-1; 978-0-578-07089-6; 978-0-578-12511-4; 978-0-578-16302-4; 978-0-578-18130-1; 978-0-578-19361-8)* 2338 8th Ave., Terre Haute, IN 47804 USA Tel 812-917-4182; 812-917-4384
E-mail: magicianofoz@hotmail.com
Web site: http://www.magicianofoz.blogspot.com
Dist(s): **Lulu Pr., Inc.**

Scobre Pr. Corp., *(978-0-9708992; 978-0-9741695; 978-0-9741997; 978-0-9766240; 978-1-933423; 978-1-934713; 978-1-61570; 978-1-62920)* 2255 Calle Clara, La Jolla, CA 92037 USA Toll Free: 877-726-2734
E-mail: Scott@bookbuddyaudio.com
Web site: http://www.scobre.com
Dist(s): **Children's Plus, Inc.**
MyiLibrary.

SCOJO ENTERTAINMENT, *(978-0-9651306; 978-0-9786488)* Orders Addr.: P.O. Box 1225, New York, NY 10008 USA
Web site: theportalinthepark.com.

SCOPE Pubns., *(978-0-9759955)* Orders Addr.: 100 Lawrence Ave., Smithtown, NY 11787 USA Tel

Publisher Name Index

631-360-0800; Fax: 631-360-8489 Do not confuse with Scope Publications, Fairfax, OK
E-mail: bkauffman@scopeonline.us
Web site: http://www.scopeonline.us.

Scotland Gate, Inc., *(978-0-9830084; 978-0-9837523; 978-0-9839550; 978-0-9888972; 978-0-9888973)* 176 Edgecliff Dr., Highland Park, IL 60035 USA Tel 847-432-1947
E-mail: mskemp@sbcglobal.net.

Scott, Cassandra Dr Ministries, *(978-0-9882936)* 3802 Hanberry, Pearland, TX 77584 USA Tel 713-550-3370
E-mail: cescott1@aol.com.

Scott, D.& F. Publishing, Inc., *(978-0-941037; 978-1-930566)* Orders Addr.: P.O. Box 821653, North Richland Hills, TX 76182-1653 USA (SAN 665-2875) Tel 817-788-2280; Fax: 817-788-9232; Toll Free: 888-788-2280; Edit Addr.: P.O. Box 821653, N Richlnd Hls, TX 76182-1653 USA; *Imprints:* WestWind Press (WstWind)
E-mail: info@dfscott.com
Web site: http://www.dfscott.com.

Scott Foresman *Imprint of* **Addison-Wesley Educational Pubs., Inc.**

Scott Foresman *Imprint of* **Addison-Wesley Educational Pubs., Inc.**

Scott Foresman *Imprint of* **Savvas Learning Co.**

Scott Foresman *Imprint of* **Addison Wesley Schl.**

Scott, J & N Pubs., *(978-0-9719868)* 10461 NW 20 St., Pembroke Pines, FL 33026 USA Tel 954-432-6578
E-mail: nscott2000@aol.com.

Scott, James *See* **Scott, J & N Pubs.**

Scott, Josephine, *(978-0-9718582; 978-0-9746600)* P.O. Box 55127, Bridgeport, CT 06610 USA
E-mail: jartist@optonline.net
Web site: http://www.ethnicitycards.com
Dist(s): **MyiLibrary**
ebrary, Inc.

Scott, Kirsti, *(978-0-9984995)* 500 Brooktree Ranch Rd, Aptos, CA 95003 USA Tel 831-688-8246
E-mail: kirstiscott@me.com
Web site: http://www.etchedbythesea.com.

†Scott Pubns., Inc., *(978-0-916809; 978-1-893625; 978-0-9787419)* 2145 W. Sherman Blvd., Muskegon, MI 49441-3434 USA Toll Free: 866-733-9382 Do not confuse with Scott Pubns. in Indianapolis, IN
E-mail: contactus@scottpublications.com
Web site: http://www.scottpublications.com; *CIP.*

Scott Publishing Co., *(978-0-9617626; 978-1-930043; 978-0-9908913; 978-0-9982386; 978-0-9991508; 978-0-9998884; 978-1-7328939; 978-1-7345637)* Orders Addr.: P.O. Box 9707, Kalispell, MT 59901 USA (SAN 664-6948) Tel 406-755-0099; Fax: 406-756-0098; Edit Addr.: 1845 Helena Flats Rd., Kalispell, MT 59901-6525 USA (SAN 664-6956) Do not confuse with companies with the same or similar name in Sidney, OH, Houston, TX, Edmonds, WA
E-mail: scott@scottcompnay.net.

Scott, Sue Ann, *(978-1-7329953)* 2010 Richard Garrett, Christiana, TN 37037 USA Tel 615-274-6264
E-mail: testimoniesbysue@comcast.net.

Scottish Children's Pr. (GBR) *(978-1-898218; 978-1-899827) Dist. by* **MYID_F_GATEWOO.**

Scottish Christmas, *(978-0-9726114)* 2369 Joslyn Ct., Lake Orion, MI 48360 USA.

Scottwall Assocs., *(978-0-942087; 978-0-9612790; 978-0-578-01245-2)* 95 Scott St., San Francisco, CA 94117 USA (SAN 289-8322) Tel 415-861-1956; Fax: 415-863-7273
E-mail: scotwall@pacbell.net
Web site: http://www.scottwallpub.com
Dist(s): **Sunbelt Pubns., Inc.**
Todd Communications.

Scott-Waters, Marilyn, *(978-0-9759884)* 1589 Baker St., Costa Mesa, CA 92626 USA
E-mail: msw@scottwatersdesign.com
Web site: http://www.thetoymaker.com.

SCR, Inc., *(978-0-9747582; 978-1-63227)* Orders Addr.: a/o Maximum Logistics, 93 S. JACKSON ST. -46673, SEATTLE, WA 98104 USA (SAN 256-6192)
E-mail: isbn@spamex.com
Web site: http://www.scrbooks.ocom
Dist(s): **Lulu Pr., Inc.**

SCR Publications *See* **SCR, Inc.**

S.C.R.A.P. Gallery, *(978-0-9708135)* 46-350 Arabia St., Indio, CA 92201 USA Tel 760-863-7777; Fax: 760-863-8973; Toll Free: 866-717-2727 (866-71-SCRAP)
E-mail: scrapgallery@earthlink.net
Web site:
http://www.infoteam.com/nonprofit/scrapgallery.

Scrap Paper Pr., *(978-0-9745493)* 6 Manor Dr., Goldens Bridge, NY 10526 USA Tel 914-997-1692; Fax: 914-997-2253.

Scribble & Sons, *(978-0-615-93279-8; 978-0-615-93286-6; 978-0-615-93328-3; 978-0-615-93335-1; 978-0-615-93344-3; 978-0-9916352)* 720 W Idaho #28, Boise, ID 83702 USA Tel 970-556-3740
Web site: www.goodbookco.com
Dist(s): **CreateSpace Independent Publishing Platform**
Independent Pubs. Group.

Scribble Scholars, *(978-1-7348462)* 10756 Glacier Rapids Ct. 0, HENDERSON, NV 89052 USA Tel 7025210497
E-mail: sugarflare@gmail.com.

Scribbler's Sword, *(978-0-9761186)* 1640 Halfacre Rd., Newberry, SC 29108 USA.

Scribbles, *(978-0-615-18473-9)* 3852 Albright Ln., Orlando, FL 32828 USA Tel 321-287-7243; 407-312-3591
Web site: http://www.sunscribbles.com.

Scribbles 'n Lit, *(978-0-692-18937-5; 978-0-578-63459-3)* 102 Wye Way, Chocowinity, NC 27817 USA Tel 252-623-1975
E-mail: eileenlettick@gmail.com
Web site: www.eileenlettick.com.

Scribbulations LLC, *(978-0-9629311; 978-1-935751)* Orders Addr.: P.O. Box 3027TCB, W. Orange, NJ 07052 USA Tel 973-325-1648 Do not confuse with Bookcraft, Inc. in West Valley, UT
E-mail: info@scribbulations.com
Web site: http://www.scribbulations.com.

Scribe Publishing, *(978-0-9727077)* 842 S 2ND ST, Philadelphia, PA 19147 USA Do not confuse with companies with the same or similar name in King City, CA, Murray, UT, Welsh, LA, Seattle, WA, Redan, GA
E-mail: contact@scribenet.com
Web site: http://www.scribenet.com.

Scribe Publishing & Consulting Services, The, *(978-0-9793516)* Div. of TrueLight Ministries, P.O. Box 11013, Tacoma, WA 98411 USA Tel 253-312-9377; Fax: 253-238-6041; *Imprints:* Writing The Vision (Writing The Vision)
E-mail: missmillie59@yahoo.com
Web site: http://www.truelightmin.org.

Scribe Publishing Co., *(978-0-9859562; 978-1-940368; 978-0-9916021; 978-1-7353051)* 29488 Woodward Suite 426, Royal Oak, MI 48073 USA Tel 248-259-0090
E-mail: jennifer@scribe-publishing.com
Web site: http://scribe-publishing.com
Dist(s): **Independent Pubs. Group**
Midpoint Trade Bks., Inc.

Scribe Pubns. (AUS) *(978-0-908011; 978-1-920769; 978-1-921215; 978-1-921372; 978-1-921640; 978-1-921753; 978-1-921844; 978-1-921863; 978-1-921864; 978-1-921942; 978-1-922070; 978-1-922072; 978-1-922247; 978-1-925106; 978-1-925113; 978-1-925228; 978-1-925292; 978-1-925293; 978-1-925307; 978-1-925321; 978-1-925322; 978-1-925500; 978-1-925548; 978-1-947534; 978-1-925693; 978-1-911344; 978-1-925713; 978-1-925849; 978-1-950354; 978-1-925938; 978-1-922310) Dist. by* **Consort Bk Sales.**

Scribe Tribe, Inc., *(978-0-9986339)* 9594 Arbor View Dr N, Boynton Beach, FL 33437 USA Tel 305-206-4488
E-mail: arlene.hauben@gmail.com
Web site: http://scribetribe.com.

Scribe's Closet Pubns., The, *(978-0-9801269; 978-0-9832570; 978-0-9884125; 978-0-9912487; 978-1-943058)* 56 S. Rutherford, Macon, MO 63552 USA
E-mail: scribescloset@gmail.com
Web site: http://www.thescribesclosetpublications.com.

Scribez, Scarebz & Vibez, *(978-0-9853406)* 689 Macon St., Brooklyn, NY 11233 USA Tel 646-267-1459
E-mail: bedstuybelle1@gmail.com.

Scribner *Imprint of* **Scribner**

Scribner, *(978-0-684; 978-0-7432)* Orders Addr.: 100 Front St., Riverside, NJ 08075 USA; Edit Addr.: 1230 Ave. of the Americas, New York, NY 10020 USA; *Imprints:* Scribner (ScribImp)
Dist(s): **Children's Plus, Inc.**
Simon & Schuster
Simon & Schuster, Inc.

Scribolin, *(978-0-9746226)* 10107 Copeland Dr., Manassas, VA 20109 USA Tel 703-257-7683
E-mail: books@scribolin.com
Web site: http://www.scribolin.com.

Scripts Publishing, *(978-1-889826)* Orders Addr.: 638 Hennepin Ter., Mcdonough, GA 30253-5965 USA
E-mail: AtaxiaBooks@aol.com
Web site:
http://www.hometown.aol.com/pathamilto/myhomepage/profile.html.

Scripture Mastery Resources!, *(978-1-933589)* 1814 Cranberry Way, Springville, UT 84663-3930 USA
E-mail: scripturemastery@kenalford.com
Web site: http://www.kenalford.com.

Scripture Memory Fellowship International, *(978-1-880960)* Orders Addr.: P.O. Box 411551, Saint Louis, MO 63141 USA Tel 314-569-0244; Fax: 314-569-0025; Toll Free: 888-569-2560; Edit Addr.: P.O. Box 568, Hannibal, MO 63401-0568 USA
E-mail: memorize@stlnet.com
Web site: http://www.scripturememory.com.

Scripture Union (GBR) *(978-0-85421; 978-0-86201; 978-1-85999; 978-1-873824; 978-1-84427; 978-1-78506) Dist. by* **Gabriel Res.**

Scripture Union (GBR) *(978-0-85421; 978-0-86201; 978-1-85999; 978-1-873824; 978-1-84427; 978-1-78506) Dist. by* **STL Dist.**

Scrivener Bks., *(978-0-9895523; 978-0-9986254; 978-1-949165)* 869 E. 2680 N., Provo, UT 84604 USA Tel 801-368-7374
E-mail: chris@scrivenerbooks.com.

Scroll Group, The, *(978-0-692-76814-3; 978-0-692-04601-2)* 3 Bethesda Metro Ctr. Suite 700, Bethesda, MD 20814 USA Tel 202-748-6093.

†Scroll Pr., Inc., *(978-0-87592)* 2858 Valerie Ct., Merrick, NY 11566 USA (SAN 206-796X) Tel 516-379-4283; *CIP.*

Scroll Publishing Co., *(978-0-924722)* Orders Addr.: P.O. Box 4714, Tyler, TX 75712 USA; Edit Addr.: 22012 Indian Spring Tr., Amberson, PA 17210 USA Tel 717-349-7033; Fax: 717-349-7558
E-mail: customerservice@scrollpublishing.com
Web site: http://www.scrollpublishing.com.

Scrub Jay Journeys, *(978-0-9898122; 978-1-946253)* 205 Wiley Ln., Middleton, TN 38052 USA Tel 407-227-0540
E-mail: author@daviscrossing.com
Dist(s): **Whitaker Hse.**

Scrumps Entertainment, Inc., *(978-0-9672279)* 19320 NW. 47th Ave., Miami, FL 33055 USA Tel 305-624-7231
E-mail: climbcrick@aol.com.

Scuby's DogHse., *(978-0-578-45598-3)* 4013 Rubicon Peak Ct., Las Vegas, NV 89129 USA Tel 702-496-8511
E-mail: lovescuby2@gmail.com
Dist(s): **Ingram Content Group.**

SD Mayer & Assocs. LLP, *(978-0-578-41354-9; 978-0-578-41355-6; 978-0-578-53696-5; 978-0-578-57070-9)* 235 Montgomery St. 30th Flr., San Francisco, CA 94104 USA Tel 415-691-4040
E-mail: info@sdmayer.com
Dist(s): **Independent Pub.**

SDC Publishing, LLC, 221 Berry Ridge Rd., BUCHANAN, VA 24066 USA Tel 540-676-3279
E-mail: allenfmahon@gmail.com
Dist(s): **Ingram Content Group.**

SDH Publishing, *(978-0-9912363)* 134 N. Roosevelt Ave., Fort Collins, CO 80521 USA Tel 970-214-4079
E-mail: shealahenke@yahoo.com
Web site: IDEA33regeneration.com
Dist(s): **BookBaby.**

SDH Studio, LLC, *(978-0-578-46950-8)* 18200 NE 19th Ave., Suite 100, North Miami Beach, FL 33162 USA Tel 305-519-5731
E-mail: stephanie@sdhstudio.com.

SDP Publishing, *(978-0-9824461; 978-0-9829256; 978-0-9885157; 978-0-9889381; 978-0-9899723; 978-0-9911597; 978-0-9913167; 978-0-9905596; 978-0-9862896; 978-0-9964345; 978-0-9968426; 978-0-9972853; 978-0-9977224; 978-0-9981277; 978-0-9984240; 978-0-9986730; 978-0-9992839; 978-1-7321115; 978-1-7327933; 978-1-7338214; 978-1-7342402; 978-1-7343317; 978-1-7356973) Div. of SDP Publishing Solutions, LLC, Orders Addr.: P.O. Box 26, East Bridgewater, MA 02333 USA (SAN 858-1762)*
E-mail: lross@SDPPublishing.com
Web site: http://www.sdppublishingsolutions.com; http://www.PublishAtSweetDreams.com; http://www.sdppublishing.com
Dist(s): **Ingram Content Group.**

SDP Publishing Solutions *See* **SDP Publishing**

SE PrinTech, *(978-0-615-33647-3; 978-0-615-48019-0; 978-0-9847344)* 315 E. Banks St., Glennville, GA 30427 USA Tel 912-654-3610
E-mail: bill@welovetoprint.com.

Se7enth Swan Publishing Group, LLC, *(978-0-615-14849-6)* P.O. Box 16874, Chapel Hill, NC 27516 USA
Web site: http://www.se7enthswan.com
Dist(s): **Lulu Pr., Inc.**

Sea Blue Publishing, *(978-1-948458)* 220 Water St., Brooklyn, NY 11201 USA Tel 310-809-9633
E-mail: 1diannedain@gmail.com.

Sea Chest Bks., *(978-0-9742909)* 11573 Viking Ave., Northridge, CA 91326 USA
E-mail: info@beverlyhillsvideographer.com
Web site: http://www.seachestbooks.com.

Sea Keepers Publishing, *(978-0-9846251)* 936 N. Main St., Akron, OH 44310 USA.

Sea Lion Bks., *(978-0-578-06080-4; 978-0-9828186; 978-0-9836131; 978-0-9857691)* 6070 Autumn View Trail, Acworth, GA 30101 USA
E-mail: david@sealionbooks.com
Dist(s): **BookBaby**
Diamond Bk. Distributors.

Sea Oats Publishing, *(978-0-9798143)* 699-A Sterling Dr., James Island, SC 29412-9135 USA Tel 843-762-2606
E-mail: seaoatspublishing@yahoo.com.

Sea Raven Enterprises *See* **Sea Raven Pr.**

Sea Raven Pr., *(978-0-9768707; 978-0-9821899; 978-0-9827700; 978-0-9838185; 978-0-9858632; 978-0-9913779; 978-1-943737)* Orders Addr.: 223 Town Ctr. Pkwy No. 1484, Sprig Hill , TN 37174 USA Tel 615-241-1277; 223 Town Ctr. Pkwy. No. 1484, Spring Hill, TN 37174
E-mail: searavenpress@nii.net
Web site: https://www.searavenpress.com
Dist(s): **Ingram Content Group.**

Sea Turtle Press *See* **Sierra Muses Pr.**

Sea Wright Publishing, *(978-1-947702)* 1456 Operetta Ave. SE, Palm Bay, FL 32909 USA Tel 321-872-9190
E-mail: info@seawrightpublishing.com
Web site: seawrightpublishing.com.

Seabury Bks. *Imprint of* **Church Publishing, Inc.**

Seachild, *(978-0-9787881)* P.O. Box 2600, Petaluma, CA 94952 USA (SAN 851-6499) Tel 707-762-7316
E-mail: jag@seachild.net
Web site: http://www.seachild.net.

Seacoast Publishing, Inc., *(978-1-878561; 978-1-59421)* P.O. Box 1504, Hartselle, AL 35640 USA Tel 256-367-4195; 256-318-6635; *Imprints:* Blackbirch Press, Incorporated (Blackbirch Pr) Do not confuse with companies with the same name in Monterey, CA, East Hampton, NY
E-mail: Seacoastpub@yahoo.com; Martinebates@charter.net
Web site: http://www.seacoastpublishing.org.

Seaforth Publishing, *(978-0-9725706)* 5818 Three Ponds Ct., West Bloomfield, MI 48324-3124 USA
Dist(s): **MyiLibrary.**

Seagrass *Imprint of* **Quarto Publishing Group USA**

Seagull Bks. (IND) *(978-81-7046) Dist. by* **Chicago Distribution Ctr.**

Seagull Books (GBR) *(978-1-905422; 978-1-906497; 978-0-85742) Dist. by* **Chicago Distribution Ctr.**

Seagull Pr., *(978-0-9753709)* 375-A Maxham Rd., No. 414, Austell, GA 30168 USA Fax: 770-944-3799 Do not confuse with companies with the same name in Oakland, CA, Owings, MD.

Seagull Pr., *(978-0-578-00924-7; 978-0-692-94200-0; 978-0-578-55479-2; 978-0-578-74729-3)* 2 Oakwood Rd., Springfiled, IL 62711 USA
E-mail: ken220@aol.com.

Seal Pr. *Imprint of* **Basic Bks.**

Seal Publishing, LLC, *(978-0-9774062)* P.O. Box 435, Odessa, FL 33556 USA
Web site: http://www.sealswimschool.com.

Seal Rock Publishing, LLC, *(978-0-9763778)* 834 Marshall Rd., Boulder, CO 80305-7337 USA
E-mail: sealrockpub@yahoo.com.

Sealaska Heritage Institute, *(978-0-9825786; 978-0-9853129; 978-0-9963698; 978-1-946019)* 105 S. Seward St. Suite 201, Juneau, AK 99801 USA
E-mail: nobu.koch@sealaska.com.

Sealofters Pr., Inc., *(978-0-9821323; 978-0-9909113; 978-0-9968782; 978-0-9994562)* 32532 Hawks Lake Ln, Sorrento, FL 32776-7737 USA (SAN 857-345X)
E-mail: lori.chappel@hotmail.com.

Seaman, P. David, *(978-0-9755066)* 2645 E. Southern Ave. Apt. A679, Tempe, AZ 85282-7532 USA.

Sean Tigh Pr., *(978-0-9851200)* 1799 Ivy Oak Sq., Reston, VA 20190 USA Tel 321-446-1483
E-mail: kristen@kristenandjoe.com.

Search Pr., Ltd. (GBR) *(978-0-85532; 978-1-903975; 978-1-84448; 978-1-78126; 978-1-78221) Dist. by* **Peng Rand Hse.**

Searchlight Pr., *(978-0-9644609; 978-0-9824802; 978-1-936497)* Orders Addr.: 5634 Ledgestone Dr., Dallas, TX 75214-2026 USA Tel 214-662-5494
E-mail: searchlight@johncunyus.com; info@searchlight-press.com
Web site: http://www.johncunyus.com; http://www.searchlight-press.com.

SearlStudio Publishing, *(978-0-9883670; 978-0-9895062)* 18331 Pines Blvd., No. 322, Pembroke Pines, FL 33029 USA Tel 305-517-7261
E-mail: searlstudio@me.com
Web site: http://www.searlstudio.com.

Sears, Brenda L., *(978-0-692-13305-7)* 5010 SW 19th St., West Park, FL 33023 USA Tel 305-308-8524
E-mail: truelcm@gmail.com.

Sears, M.A., *(978-0-9639785)* 16809 Superior, North Hills, CA 91343 USA; 555 W. Sierra Hwy., Acton, CA 93510 Tel 818-891-8632.

Sears, Stanley, *(978-0-9770067)* Rte. 1 Box 215, Hickman, NE 68372-9686 USA.

Seascape Pr., *(978-0-9769510)* P.O. Box 13132, Jekyll Island, GA 31527 USA Tel 912-635-3263; Fax: 912-635-3264 Do not confuse with Seascape Press, LLC in Santa Barbara, CA.

SeaScape Pr., Ltd., *(978-0-9669741; 978-0-9852381)* 5717 Tanner Ridge Ave., Westlake Vlg, CA 91362-5238 USA (SAN 299-8386) Tel 818-707-3080 Toll Free: 800-929-2906 do not confuse with Seascape Press in Jekyll Island, GA
E-mail: seapress@aol.com; llamensdor@aol.com
Web site: http://www.lenlamensdorf.com.

Seascay Productions, *(978-0-9764152)* 11 Ventnor Dr. Suite 906, Edison, NJ 08820 USA Tel 732-242-3902
E-mail: corporate@seascay.com
Web site: http://www.seascay.com.

Seashell Pr., The, *(978-0-9768866)* 28 Skytop Rd, Ipswich, MA 01938 USA
E-mail: mailbag@theseashellpress.com
Web site: http://www.theseashellpress.com.

Seaside Books *See* **Ladd, David Pr.**

Seasoning Quilting (Arts & Crafts), *(978-1-888413)* 806 Elvie St., Wilson, NC 27893-6116 USA Tel 919-291-7705.

Seasons of Preparation Publishing *See* **Tamara Taylor Edu Publishing LLC**

SeaSquirt Pubns. (GBR) *(978-1-905470) Dist. by* **Basic Dist.**

SeaStar Bks. *Imprint of* **Chronicle Bks. LLC**

Seastory Pr., *(978-0-9673704; 978-0-9768370; 978-0-9799474; 978-0-9821151; 978-1-936818)* 1508 Seminary St. #2, Key West, FL 33040 USA Tel 305-304-6090 mobile
E-mail: sheri@seastorypress.com; seastorypress@gmail.com
Web site: http://www.seastorypress.com
Dist(s): **MyiLibrary**
ebrary, Inc.

Sea-To-Sea Pubns., *(978-1-932889; 978-1-59771)* Div. of Creative Co., 2140 Howard Dr., W., North Mankato, MN 56003 USA
Dist(s): **Creative Co., The**
RiverStream Publishing.

Seattle Review Pr., *(978-0-692-34720-1)* 14232 221st Ave. NE, Woodinville, WA 98077 USA Tel 206-851-2286
Dist(s): **CreateSpace Independent Publishing Platform.**

Seawall Bks., Inc., *(978-0-615-34226-9; 978-0-615-34240-5; 978-0-615-37353-9; 978-0-615-75068-2; 978-0-9893324)* 7 Summit Dr., Hingham, MA 02043 USA Tel 781-749-4284; Fax: 781-749-0977
E-mail: donhussey@aol.com
Web site: http://donhussey.com.

SeaWorld Education Dept. *Imprint of* **SeaWorld, Inc.**

SeaWorld, Inc., *(978-1-893698)* Div. of Anheuser-Busch Adventure Parks, 500 SeaWorld Dr., San Diego, CA 92109 USA (SAN 255-576X) Tel 619-225-4275; Fax: 619-226-3634; Toll Free: 800-237-4268; *Imprints:* SeaWorld Education Department (SeaWorld Educ)
E-mail: swc.education@seaworld.com; debbie.nuzzolo@seaworld.com
Web site: http://www.seaworld.org
Dist(s): **Book Wholesalers, Inc.**
Brodart Co.
Carolina Biological Supply Co.

Second Ark Pubns., *(978-1-889667)* 2907 Kevin Ln., Houston, TX 77043 USA.

Second Base Publishing, *(978-0-9793562; 978-0-9981709)* 6197 Hinterlong Ct, Lisle, IL 60532 USA (SAN 853-2206)
Dist(s): **Ebsco Publishing**
Independent Pubs. Group
MyiLibrary
ebrary, Inc.

Second Sight Enterprises, Inc., *(978-0-9785222)* P.O. Box 251248, Plano, TX 75025 USA (SAN 850-7996)
Web site: http://www.asktheinventors.com.

Second Star Creations, *(978-0-9725977)* 12120 State Line Rd., No. 190, Leawood, KS 66209 USA Tel 913-681-2252
E-mail: jan@secondstar.us
Web site: http://www.secondstar.us.

Second Story Pr. (CAN) *(978-0-921299; 978-0-929005; 978-1-896764; 978-1-897187; 978-1-77260; 978-1-926739; 978-1-926920; 978-1-927583) Dist. by* **Orca Bk Pub.**

Second Time Media & Communications, *(978-0-9727498; 978-0-9815162; 978-0-9840660; 978-0-9831743)* P.O. Box 401367, Redford, MI 48240 USA Tel 800-377-7497
E-mail: secondtimemedia@yahoo.com
Web site: http://www.secondtimemedia.com.

Second Wind Publishing, LLC *See* **Indigo Sea Pr., LLC**

Secret Corners Publishing, *(978-0-615-24083-1; 978-0-615-24084-8)* 3613 ORANGEPOINTE RD, VALRICO, FL 33596 USA
E-mail: mhamlet@secret-corners.com
Web site: http://www.secret-corners.com.

Secret Garden Bookworks, *(978-0-9766283)* Orders Addr.: P.O. Box 1506, Oak Bluffs, MA 02557-1506 USA Tel 508-693-4759; Fax: 508-693-4867; Edit Addr.: 41 Circuit Ave., Oak Bluffs, MA 02557-1506 USA
E-mail: secretgardenmv@peoplepc.com
Web site: http://www.secretgardenbookworks.com.

Secret Hat, L.L.C., The, *(978-0-578-49629-0)* 2007 Columbia Rd., Berkley, MI 48072 USA Tel 248-632-3265
E-mail: peggylosey@gmail.com
Web site: www.thesecrethat.com.

Secret Mountain (CAN) *(978-2-923163; 978-2-924774; 978-2-924217) Dist. by* **IPG Chicago.**

Secret Passage Pr., *(978-1-888695)* 26 Tucker Hollow Rd., North Scituate, RI 02857 USA Tel 401-647-0440; Toll Free: 877-863-4622 (Orders Only)
E-mail: lucindalandon@verizon.net
Web site: http://www.megmackintosh.com
Dist(s): **Ebsco Publishing**
Enfield Publishing & Distribution Co., Inc.
Independent Pubs. Group
MyiLibrary.

Secret Staircase Bks., an imprint of Columbine Publishing Group, LLC *Imprint of* **Columbine Publishing Group, LLC**

Secret Staircase Books, an imprint of Columbine Publishing Group *See* **Columbine Publishing Group, LLC**

Secular Media Group *Imprint of* **Rare Bird Bks.**

Security Studies Pr., *(978-0-9797539)* 650 J St., Suite 405, Lincoln, NE 68508 USA
E-mail: rlund@securitystudies.us
Web site: http://www.securitystudies.us.

Sedell, Kirsten, *(978-0-9800838)* 3 John R's Bend, Berkley, MA 02779 USA
E-mail: ksedell@norton.k12.ma.us.

sedgewick eye Assocs., P.C., *(978-0-9968178)* 44121 harry byrd hwy, No. 175, ashburn, VA 20147 USA Tel 703-725-1698
E-mail: jrsedgewick@verizon.net
Web site: www.sedgewickeye.com.

Sedwick, Daniel Frank LLC, *(978-0-9820818)* P.O. Box 1964, Winter Park, FL 32790-1964 USA Tel 407-975-3325; Fax: 407-975-3327
E-mail: info@sedwickcoins.com
Web site: http://www.sedwickcoins.com.

See abc's LC, *(978-1-890566)* Orders Addr.: P.O. Box 276, Smithfield, UT 84335 USA; Edit Addr.: 9 S. 490 E., Smithfield, UT 84335 USA.

See Movement, *(978-0-9965398)* 415 W. Foothill Blvd. PH 1, Claremont, CA 91711 USA Tel 626-795-4500; Fax: 626-795-4545
E-mail: leatricel@earthlink.net
Web site: www.SeeMovement.com.

See Sharp Pr., *(978-0-9613289; 978-1-884365; 978-1-937276; 978-1-947071)* P.O. Box 1731, Tucson, AZ 85702-1731 USA (SAN 653-8134) Tel 520-628-8720 (phone/fax)
E-mail: info@seesharppress.com
Web site: http://www.seesharppress.com
Dist(s): **Ebsco Publishing**
Independent Pubs. Group
MyiLibrary
ebrary, Inc.

See The Wish, *(978-0-9822134; 978-0-9857676; 978-0-9886716)* 246 Main St., Cold Spring, NY 10516 USA Tel 845-797-9183
Web site: http://www.seethewish.com
Dist(s): **Follett School Solutions.**

Seed Faith Bks, *(978-1-60101)* P.O. Box 12227, Portland, OR 97212-0227 USA (SAN 850-6795)
Web site: http://seedfaithbooks.com.

SeeDEGA, *(978-0-9746586)* Orders Addr.: 46 Violet Pl., Rhinebeck, NY 12572 USA
E-mail: seedega@gmail.com
Web site: http://seedega.com.

Seeding Hearts, *(978-0-9998675)* 10441 Spring Green Blvd No. 805, KATY, TX 77494 USA Tel 713-545-9640
E-mail: divanwinkle@seedinghearts.com
Dist(s): **Ingram Content Group.**

Seedling Pubns. *Imprint of* **Continental Pr., Inc.**

Seeds of Imagination, *(978-0-9600253)* 2241 Hutchison St., Vista, CA 92084 USA
E-mail: lindaappo@sbcglobal.net
Dist(s): **Ingram Content Group.**

SeeHearDo Co., LLC, The, *(978-0-9788089)* 3011 E. 7145 S., Salt Lake City, UT 84121 USA.

Seelcraft Publishing, *(978-0-9728380)* 63 Church St., Suite 201, High Bridge, NJ 08829-1516 USA
Web site: http://www.seelcraft.com.

See-More's Workshop, *(978-1-882601)* Div. of Shadow Box Theatre, 325 West End Ave., New York, NY 10023 USA Tel 212-724-0677; Fax: 212-724-0767
E-mail: sbt@shadowboxtheatre.org
Web site: http://www.shadowboxtheatre.org
Dist(s): **Follett School Solutions**
Professional Media Service Corp.

See-Saw Publishing *Imprint of* **Peek-A-Boo Publishing**

Segal, Berty Inc., *(978-0-938395)* 1749 E. Eucalyptus St., Brea, CA 92821 USA (SAN 630-0553) Tel 714-529-5359; Fax: 714-529-3882
E-mail: bertytprsource@earthlink.net
Web site: http://www.tprsource.com
Dist(s): **Continental Bk. Co., Inc.**

Segal, Robin *See* **Murray Hill Bks., LLC**

Segarra, Angelo, *(978-0-9752664)* 422 Gregg Ave., Santa Fe, NM 87501-1600 USA
Dist(s): **Greenleaf Book Group.**

Seglie, Susan M., *(978-0-9747243)* 1 Deer Run Ln., Pittsburg, KS 66762 USA Fax: 620-232-5819.

Segue Pubs., *(978-0-9671796)* 527 arbor Rd., Cheltenham, PA 19012 USA Tel 215-277-5525 phone
E-mail: seguepublishing@aol.com; kbradford@seguepublishing.com
Web site: seguepublishing.com.

Seif, Daniel J., *(978-0-9983807)* 106 Kingfisher Ln., New Hartford, NY 13413 USA Tel 315-796-2751
E-mail: danseif@roadrunner.com.

Seigle Bks., *(978-0-9852819)* 235 County Rte. 627, Phillipsburg, NJ 08865 USA Tel 908-319-0384
E-mail: prepub@bookmasters.com.

Selah Publishing Group, LLC, *(978-0-9679371; 978-1-58930)* 162 Crescent Dr., Bristol, TN 37620 USA Toll Free Fax: 866-777-8909; Toll Free: 877-616-6451 Do not confuse with the same name in Kingston, NY, Berkley, MI
E-mail: garlen@selahbooks.com
Web site: http://www.selahbooks.com.

Selah Publishing, Incorporated *See* **Selah Publishing Group, LLC**

Selby Dean Ventures, Inc., *(978-0-9716479)* P.O. Box 246, Kure Beach, NC 28449 USA (SAN 852-7539) Tel 910-279-2486
E-mail: fishinstructor@aol.com
Web site: http://www.gullswatch.com; http://www.SelbyDeanVentures.com.

Selective Mutism Anxiety Research & Treatment Ctr., *(978-0-9714800)* 1130 Herkness Dr., Meadowbrook, PA 19046 USA Tel 215 -887-5748; Fax: 215-827-5722
E-mail: dreshiponblum@aol.com
Web site: http://www.selectivemutismcenter.org.

Selector, S.A. de C.V. (MEX) *(978-968-403; 978-970-643; 978-607-453) Dist. by* **Spanish.**

Self Discovery, Inc., *(978-0-692-92892-9; 978-0-9992696)* 5211 NE 27 Ave., Lighthouse Point, FL 33064 USA Tel 954-610-4816
E-mail: shivaliviviani@gmail.com
Dist(s): **Ingram Content Group.**

Self-Discovery LLC, *(978-0-9974831)* 22200 W. Eleven Mile Rd. Unit No. 4232, Southfiled, MI 48037 USA Tel 248-705-9074
E-mail: Info@SelfDiscoverySolutions.com
Web site: http://www.selfdiscoverysolutions.com/.

Self-Esteem Adventures Pr., *(978-0-9747597)* P.O. Box 2145, Universal City, TX 78148 USA Tel 210-595-6952
E-mail: daddybooks@grandecom.net
Web site: http://www.daddybooks.com.

Self-Mastery Pr., *(978-0-9644765; 978-1-7357645)* W. Main St., Carrboro, NC 27510 USA Tel 855-706-4663; 661-904-2416
E-mail: Victoria@ManifestYourGood.com; lovelandcoen@gmail.com
Web site: http://www.ManifestYourGood.com; http://www.Breakthrough2.com
Dist(s): **New Leaf Distributing Co., Inc.**

Self-Realization Fellowship Pubs., *(978-0-87612)* Orders Addr.: 3208 Humboldt St., Los Angeles, CA 90031 USA (SAN 204-5788) Tel 323-276-6002; Fax: 323-276-6003; Toll Free: 888-773-8680; Edit Addr.: 3880 San Rafael Ave., Los Angeles, CA 90065 USA Tel 323-276 6000; 215 K. St., Encinitas, CA 92024 Tel 760-753-2888 ext 471; Fax: 323-276-6003
E-mail: sales@srfpublishers.org
Web site: http://www.srfpublishers.org
Dist(s): **Distributors, The**
TNT Media Group, Inc.

Sellers, Amy, *(978-0-9787632)* 5151 Round Lake Rd., Apopka, FL 32712 USA (SAN 851-5425)
E-mail: amycsellers@yahoo.com
Web site: http://www.amysellers.com.

Sellers Publishing, Inc., *(978-1-56906; 978-1-4162; 978-1-5319)* Orders Addr.: 161 John Roberts Rd, South Portland, ME 04106 USA (SAN 858-1258) Tel 207-772-6833; Fax: 207-772-6814; Toll Free: 800-625-3386 (800-MAKE-FUN); Edit Addr.: 161 John Roberts Rd., South Portland, ME 04106 USA
E-mail: rsp@rsvp.com
Web site: http://www.rsvp.com
Dist(s): **Bookazine Co., Inc.**
MBI Distribution Services/Quayside Distribution
New Leaf Distributing Co., Inc.
Partners Bk. Distributing, Inc.

Sellers, Ronnie Productions, Incorporated *See* **Sellers Publishing, Inc.**

Seltzer Bks., *(978-0-915232; 978-0-931968; 978-1-4553; 978-1-4554)* 33 Gould St., West Roxbury, MA 02132 USA (SAN 207-1037) Tel 617-469-2269
E-mail: seltzer@samizdat.com
Web site: http://www.samizdat.com/; http://store.yahoo.com/samizdat
Dist(s): **Smashwords.**

Sem Fronteiras Pr., Ltd., *(978-0-9642333)* 1530 Palisade Ave., Suite 2F, Fort Lee, NJ 07024 USA (SAN 253-4959) Toll Free Fax: 800-433-5193
E-mail: semfront@superlink.net.

Sem, Gilmore, *(978-0-9742299)* 1822 Carl St., Lauderdale, MN 55113-5203 USA.

Semele Bks., *(978-0-9764937)* 40 Cedar Ln., Princeton, NJ 08540 USA Tel 609-924-6481; Fax: 609-924-0549; Toll Free: 866-967-3835
E-mail: eva@evasiroka.com
Web site: http://www.evasiroka.com.

Semper Studio, *(978-0-9778420)* 4416 Rte. 47, Delmont, NJ 08314 USA (SAN 850-3885) Tel 609-501-3341
E-mail: Catherine@semperstudiosus.com
Web site: http://www.semperstudiosus.com.

Send The Light Distribution LLC, *(978-0-9835608; 978-1-939900)* Orders Addr.: 129 Mobilization Dr., Waynesboro, GA 30830 USA (SAN 631-8894) Tel 706-554-5827; Toll Free Fax: 877-323-4551; Toll Free: 877-323-4550; 100 Biblica Way, Elizabethton, TN 37643-6070 (SAN 630-7388) Tel 423-547-5131 editorial Toll Free Fax: 800-759-2779
E-mail: Customerservice@stl.org
Web site: http://www.stl-publisherservices.com.

Seneca Lake Pr., *(978-1-7321614)* P.O. Box 513, Ithaca, NY 14851 USA Tel 607-387-8425
E-mail: aileeneaster@yahoo.com.

Seneca Mill Pr. LLC, *(978-0-9768986; 978-0-9899595)* P.O. Box 1423, Great Falls, VA 22066 USA
E-mail: senecamillpress@aol.com.

Sensational Bks., *(978-0-9770054)* P.O. Box 261085, Lakewood, CO 80226 USA (SAN 256-6265) Tel 303-238-4760; Fax: 303-205-0614
Web site: http://www.sensationalbooks.com.

Sensational Pubns., *(978-0-9888003; 978-0-9912808; 978-1-944948)* 1756 Cumberland Green Dr Unit 126, saint Charles, IL 60174 USA Tel 630-549-7226
E-mail: cindyjusino@ymail.com
Web site: www.cindyjusino.com; http://www.sensationalpublications.com.

Sensational Publishing *See* **Sensational Pubns.**

Sense of Wonder Pr. *Imprint of* **Rock, James A. & Co. Pubs.**

Senshu, Noriko *See* **Studio Cherry Publishing**

Sensory Resources, *(978-1-893601; 978-1-931615)* Div. of Future Horizons, Inc., P.O. Box 530790, Henderson, NV 89053-0790 USA (SAN 253-8288) Toll Free: 888-357-5867
E-mail: orders@sensoryresources.com
Web site: http://www.sensoryresources.com
Dist(s): **Ingram Publisher Services**
MyiLibrary.

Sentient Pubns., *(978-0-9710786; 978-1-59181)* 1113 Spruce St., Boulder, CO 80302 USA Tel 303-443-2188; Fax: 303-447-1511; Toll Free: 866-588-9846
E-mail: cshaw@sentientpublications.com; dialagzone@aol.com
Web site: http://www.sentientpublications.com/
Dist(s): **National Bk. Network.**

Sentimental Bloke Holdings International, *(978-1-7328957)* 16373 SE 66th St., Bellevue, WA 98006 USA Tel 425-499-0735
E-mail: carol.eckersley@bigpond.com; publisher@sentimentalbloke.com
Web site: www.sentimentalbloke.com.

Sentinel *Imprint of* **Penguin Publishing Group**

Sentinel Publishing, *(978-0-9728291)* 1131 Rossiter Ln., Wayne, PA 19087-2812 USA Tel 610-687-5908; Fax: 610-687-5909 Do not confuse with Sentinel Publishing in Ogden, UT
E-mail: orchidman@snip.net
Web site: http://www.linenpostcards.com.

Sentry Bks. *Imprint of* **Great West Publishing**

Sentry Pr., Inc., *(978-1-889574)* 424 E. Call St., Tallahassee, FL 32301-7693 USA
E-mail: wwrogers@peoplepc.com
Web site: http://sentry-press.com/
Dist(s): **Polk County Historical Assn.**

Seoul Selection (KOR) *(978-89-91913; 978-89-953760; 978-89-97639) Dist. by* **UH Pr.**

Sephyrus *See* **Sephyrus Pr.**

Sephyrus Pr., *(978-0-615-23982-8; 978-0-9830137; 978-1-948728)* 192 Flicker Dr., Sandy, UT 84070 USA Tel 203-414-5694
E-mail: care@sephyrus.com; rachel@sephyrus.com
Web site: http://sephyruspress.com.

SepSha Publishing, *(978-0-9727885)* P.O. Box 462075, Aurora, CO 80046 USA (SAN 255-3007)
Web site: http://www.endtimebooks.com.

Sequent Media, Inc., *(978-0-9746531)* P.O. Box 126325, San Diego, CA 92112 USA
Web site: http://www.sequentmedia.com.

Sequoia Publishing & Media LLC *Imprint of* **Phoenix International Publications, Inc.**

Seraph Publishing, *(978-1-934948)* 7660 Fay Ave., La Jolla, CA 92037-4843 USA
E-mail: info@markmlittle.com.

Seraphemera Bks *See* **Seraphemera Bks.**

Seraphemera Bks., *(978-0-9778989; 978-0-9815516; 978-0-9844441; 978-0-9846464; 978-0-9971384; 978-0-9978698; 978-1-947406)* 211 Greenwood Ave Suite 224, Bethel, CT 06801 USA Tel 832-515-9539
E-mail: three@seraphemera.org
Web site: http://www.seraphemera.org.

Seraphic Pr., *(978-0-9754382)* 1531 Cardiff Ave., Los Angeles, CA 90035 USA (SAN 256-0496) Tel 310-557-0132; Fax: 310-286-9534
E-mail: robert@seraphicpress.com; rjaprod@aol.com
Web site: http://www.seraphicpress.com
Dist(s): **David, Jonathan Pubs., Inc.**

Seraphim Pubns., *(978-0-615-21071-1)* 17641 Gilmore St., Van Nuys, CA 91406 USA
E-mail: toni@seraphimpublications.com
Web site: http://www.seraphimpublications.com.

Seraphina *Imprint of* **Bonita and Hodge Publishing Group**

Seren Bks. (GBR) *(978-0-907476; 978-1-85411; 978-1-78172) Dist. by* **IPG Chicago.**

Serena Bocchino/In His Perfect Time Collection, *(978-0-9767674; 978-0-9838660; 978-0-9961443)* 82 Haas Rd., Basking Ridge, NJ 07920 USA
E-mail: serena@serenabocchino.com
Web site: http://www.serenabocchino.com.

Serendib Pr., *(978-0-615-18889-8)* 1611 N. Bell, No. 3N, Chicago, IL 60647 USA
Dist(s): **Lulu Pr., Inc.**

Serendipity Art & Publishing *See* **Serendipity Art & Publishing**

Serendipity Art & Publishing, *(978-0-692-05369-0; 978-0-692-13288-3)* 2109 Pine Lake Dr., West Columbia, SC 29169 USA Tel 803-760-8445
E-mail: dkerlin50@yahoo.com
Dist(s): **CreateSpace Independent Publishing Platform.**

Serendipity Hse. *Imprint of* **LifeWay Christian Resources**

Serenity Pr., *(978-0-9787981)* 500 SW. 21st Terr., Fort Lauderdale, FL 33312 USA (SAN 851-6251)
E-mail: marty@mwpr.com
Web site: http://www.mwpr.com/Splash.html.

Serenity Pubs. *Imprint of* **Arc Manor**

Serey/Jones Pubs., *(978-1-881276)* 7413 W. Oraibi Dr., Glendale, AZ 85308 USA Tel 623-561-0240; Fax: 623-561-8441
E-mail: info@sereyjones.com.

Serpent's Tale Natural History Bk. Distributors, Inc., *(978-1-885209)* Orders Addr.: P.O. Box 405, Lanesboro, MN 55949-0405 USA (SAN 630-6101) Tel 507-467-8734; Fax: 507-467-8735
E-mail: zoobooks@acegroup.cc
Web site: http://www.zoobooksales.com.

Serprentress Publishing, *(978-0-578-15083-3; 978-0-9862022)* 14816 NE 23rd Ave, Vancouver, WA 98686 USA Tel 360-909-6168
E-mail: yauna.smith@icloud.com.

Serres, Ediciones, S. L. (ESP) *(978-84-88061; 978-84-95040; 978-84-8488) Dist. by* **Lectorum Pubns.**

Servant Bks. *Imprint of* **Franciscan Media**

Serve Man Pr., *(978-0-9768517)* P.O. Box 1445, Easthampton, MA 01027 USA Tel 413-209-1029
E-mail: rokaril@hotmail.com
Web site: http://www.seanwang.com; www.runnersuniverse.com.

Servilibro Ediciones, S.A. (ESP) *(978-84-7971) Dist. by* **Giron Bks.**

Serving Jesus Christ with Joy Ministries, *(978-0-9770078; 978-0-9774428)* Div. of Serving Jesus Christ with Joy, Orders Addr.: 316 E. Ajo, Tucson, AZ 85713 USA Tel 520-406-1674 (Publishing Phone) 520-889-0215 (Publishing Fax)
E-mail: pastorrandy@sjcwj.org; info@sjcwj.org
Web site: http://christianbooks1.com.

Serving One Lord Resources, *(978-0-9823137)* P.O. Box 98, Sewickley, PA 15143 USA
Web site: www.servingonelord.com.

Session Family, *(978-0-9658006)* Orders Addr.: P.O. Box 841, Florissaint, MO 63032 USA Tel 314-972-7705 (phone/fax); Edit Addr.: 16856 Heather Moor Dr., Florissant, MO 63034 USA
E-mail: denise.session@att.net
Web site: http://www.sessionfamily.com.

Set in Stone Pr., *(978-1-7343336)* 5845 Pollard Dr, Westworth Village, TX 76114 USA Tel 817-655-2314
E-mail: skendall@setinstonepress.com
Web site: www.thebackyardtrio.com.

Set on a Hill, *(978-0-9971485)* 11152 Westheimer Rd No. 1115, Houston, TX 77042 USA Tel 832-900-9802
E-mail: info@setonahill.com
Web site: www.setonahill.com.

Seton Pr., *(978-1-60704)* 1350 Progress Dr., Front Royal, VA 22630 USA Tel 540-636-9990; Fax: 540-636-1602
Web site: http://setonhome.org.

Setubandh Pubns., *(978-0-9623674)* 1 Lawson Ln., Great Neck, NY 11023 USA Tel 516-482-6938
Web site: http://www.setubandh.com.

Seven C's Productions, Inc., *(978-0-9910345; 978-1-7338010)* Orders Addr.: 22050 Costanso St., Woodland Hills, CA 91364 USA; Edit Addr.: 22050 Costanso St., Woodland Hills, CA 91364 USA Tel 845-216-9884
E-mail: AuthorMarcClark@gmail.com
Web site: www.TheFablesKingdom.com.

Seven Footer Pr., *(978-0-9740439; 978-0-9788178; 978-1-934734)* 184 Kendrick Pl., Apt. 28, Gaithersburg, MD 20878-5662 USA; 247 W. 30th St., New York, NY 10001-2824
E-mail: david@wouldyourather.com; jnheimberg@aol.com
Web site: http://www.wouldyourather.com; http://www.movieplotgenerator.com
Dist(s): **Publishers Group West (PGW).**

Seven Guns Pr., *(978-0-615-70006-9; 978-0-9884259; 978-0-615-82838-1; 978-0-9899461; 978-0-9974474;*

Publisher Name Index

978-0-9982177) 2405 Jennieville Dr., Davidsonville, MD 21035 USA Tel 4433066691
Dist(s): **CreateSpace Independent Publishing Platform.**

Seven Lions Publishing, *(978-0-615-82629-5; 978-0-615-91348-3; 978-0-615-99504-5; 978-0-692-29016-3; 978-0-692-42608-1; 978-0-692-71739-4; 978-0-9996879)* 8224 Babbler Ln., North Chesterfield, VA 23235 USA Tel 8046775718
Dist(s): **CreateSpace Independent Publishing Platform.**

†Seven Locks Pr., *(978-0-929765; 978-0-932020; 978-0-9615964; 978-1-931643; 978-0-9790950; 978-0-9795852; 978-0-9801270; 978-0-9822293; 978-0-9824957)* P.O. Box 25689, Santa Ana, CA 92799-5689 USA (SAN 211-9781) Toll Free: 800-354-5348
E-mail: sevenlocks@aol.com
Web site: http://www.sevenlockspublishing.com; *CIP.*

Seven Rivers Publishing, *(978-0-9728768; 978-0-615-63339-8)* P.O. Box 682, Crowley, TX 76036-0682 USA Toll Free: 800-544-3770 (Order line: Hendrick-Long)
E-mail: hendrick-long@att.net; djls@sevenriverspublishing.com; sales@sevenriverspublishing.com; seven-rivers@earthlink.net
Web site: http://www.hendricklongpublishing.com; http://www.sevenriverspublishing.com; http://www.smashwords.com/books/view/93148
Dist(s): **CreateSpace Independent Publishing Platform**
Hendrick-Long Publishing Co.
Ingram Content Group
Smashwords.

Seven Seas Entertainment, LLC, *(978-1-933164; 978-1-934876; 978-1-935934; 978-1-937867; 978-1-62692; 978-1-64275; 978-1-64505; 978-1-64827)* 3463 State St., Suite 545, Santa Barbara, CA 93105 USA
Web site: http://www.gomanga.com
Dist(s): **Diamond Comic Distributors, Inc.**
Diamond Bk. Distributors
Macmillan.

Seven Seas Pr., *(978-0-578-06316-4; 978-0-578-06317-1; 978-0-578-06318-8; 978-0-578-06319-5; 978-0-578-06440-6; 978-0-578-06441-3; 978-0-578-06442-0; 978-0-578-06443-7; 978-0-9833381; 978-1-940654)* 2030 Castillo St, Santa Barbara, CA 93105 USA Tel 805-886-6548
E-mail: erikaromer@gmail.com
Web site: sevenseaspress.org.

Seven Stars Trading Co., *(978-0-9743999; 978-0-9863464)* 3543 Marvin St., Annandale, VA 22003 USA Tel 703-573-2939.

Seven Stories Pr., *(978-1-58322; 978-1-888363; 978-1-60980; 978-1-64421)* 140 Watts St., New York, NY 10013 USA Tel 212-226-8760; Fax: 212-226-1411; Toll Free: 800-596-7437; *Imprints:* Siete Cuentos Editorial (Siete Cuentos); Triangle Square (Triangle Sq)
E-mail: info@sevenstories.com
Web site: http://www.sevenstories.com
Dist(s): **Independent Pubs. Group**
MyiLibrary
Penguin Random Hse. Distribution
Penguin Random Hse. LLC
Random Hse., Inc.

SevenHorns Publishing *See* **Sevenhorns Publishing**

Sevenhorns Publishing, *(978-0-9838427; 978-0-9976846; 978-1-7323870; 978-0-9600817; 978-1-7349527)* Orders Addr.: 276 5th Avenue, Suite 704, New York, NY 10001 USA Tel 917-677-4540; Edit Addr.: 276 5th Ave Suite 704, New York, NY 10001 USA Tel 917-677-4540
E-mail: tasha.grant@sevenhornspublishing.com; admin@sevenhornspublishing.com
Web site: http://www.sonsofcaasi.com; http://www.sevenhornspublishing.com
Dist(s): **Ingram Content Group.**

Seventh Mind Publishing, *(978-0-9973547; 978-1-7330158)* 1096 Via Regina, Santa Barbara, CA 93111 USA Tel 805-964-6164
E-mail: britt.andreatta@gmail.com
Web site: www.SeventhMindPublishing.com.

Seventh Sense Publishing, *(978-1-7320813)* 8502 16th st APT 409, Rockville, MD 20850 USA Tel 803-840-6838
E-mail: iamjdixon@gmail.com.

Seventh Street Pr., Div. of Malone-Ballard Book Pubs., 2215 6th Ave. Apt D, Moline, IL 61265 USA
E-mail: bookwoman1110@hotmail.com.

Severn Hse. Pubs., Ltd. (GBR) *(978-0-7278; 978-1-78029; 978-0-9560566; 978-1-78010; 978-1-4483) Dist. by* **IngramPubServ.**

Seward, Bernice, *(978-0-615-98377-6; 978-0-692-33409-6; 978-0-9862879; 978-0-692-71852-0; 978-0-9995378)* P.O. Box 2231, Lewiston, ID 83501 USA
Web site: www.berniceseward.com
Dist(s): **CreateSpace Independent Publishing Platform.**

Seymour, Dale Pubns., *(978-0-201; 978-0-7690; 978-0-86651; 978-1-57232)* Div. of Pearson Learning, Orders Addr.: P.O. Box 2500, Lebanon, OH 43216 USA Toll Free Fax: 800-393-3156; Toll Free: 800-321-3106 (Customer Service); Edit Addr.: 10 Bank St., White Plains, NY 10602-5026 USA (SAN 200-9781) Toll Free Fax: 800-393-3156; Toll Free: 800-237-3142
E-mail: pearson_learning2@prenhall.com
Web site: http://www.pearsonlearning.com; http://www.pearsonlearning.com/rightsPerm.rtf
Dist(s): **Addison-Wesley Educational Pubs., Inc.**

Seymour Institute for Advanced Christian Studies, *(978-0-9765717)* 411 Washington St., Dorchester, MA 02124 USA Tel 617-373-7273; Fax: 617-373-7575
E-mail: erivers@ntlf.org.

Seymour Institute for the Advancement of Christian *See* **Seymour Institute for Advanced Christian Studies**

Seymour Science LLC *See* **Isabella Products, Inc.**

SF Publishing, *(978-0-578-40868-2; 978-0-578-43722-4; 978-0-578-44310-2)* 1405 Dundalk Ave, Baltimore, MD 21222 USA Tel 443-537-0750
E-mail: victoriajhayes@gmail.com.

SFT Pubns., *(978-0-9724384)* Orders Addr.: 3915 S. Cramer Cir., Bloomington, IN 47403 USA (SAN 254-8283) Tel 812-333-8902
E-mail: leilarandle@sbcglobal.net.

Sgian Enterprises, *(978-0-9771197; 978-0-615-12814-6)* 4349 W. Tomahawk Dr., Beverly Hills, FL 34465-4871 USA.

Shaar Pr. *Imprint of* **Mesorah Pubns., Ltd.**

Shades of Me Publishing, *(978-0-9718307)* 3969 Strandhill Rd., Cleveland, OH 44128 USA
E-mail: marybury1927@msn.com.

Shades of White, *(978-0-9796834)* 301 Tenth Ave., Crystal City, MO 63019 USA Tel 314-740-0361; *Imprints:* Magical Child Books (Magical Child)
Web site: http://www.magicalchildbooks.com
Dist(s): **New Leaf Distributing Co., Inc.**

ShadeTree Publishing, LLC, *(978-0-9822632; 978-1-937331)* 1038 N. Eisenhower Dr., No. 274, Beckley, WV 25801 USA (SAN 857-6971)
E-mail: jennifer.minigh@shadetreepublishing.com
Web site: http://www.shadetreepublishing.com.

Shadow Canyon Graphics, *(978-0-9857420)* 454 Somerset Dr., Golden, CO 80401 USA Tel 303 278 0949; Fax: 303-279-5831
E-mail: dnshadow@earthlink.net.

Shadow Mountain *Imprint of* **Shadow Mountain Publishing**

Shadow Mountain *Imprint of* **Shadow Mountain Publishing**

Shadow Mountain *Imprint of* **Deseret Bk. Co.**

Shadow Mountain Publishing, *(978-0-87579; 978-1-57345; 978-1-59038; 978-1-60907)* Div. of Deseret Book Company, P.O. Box 30178, Salt Lake City, UT 84130 USA Tel 801-517-3223; *Imprints:* Shadow Mountain (ShadowMountain); Ensign Peak (EnsPeak); Shadow Mountain (ShadMtn)
E-mail: info@shadowmountain.com
Web site: http://www.shadowmountain.com
Dist(s): **Blackstone Audio, Inc.**
Deseret Bk. Co.

Shadow Pubns., *(978-0-9771424)* P.O. Box 1151, Valley Forge, PA 19482-1151 USA
Web site: http://www.olliedude.com.

ShadowPlay Pr., *(978-0-9638819)* P.O. Box 647, Forreston, IL 61030 USA Tel 815-938-3151; Fax: 815-371-1440
E-mail: sheilawelch@juno.com; ericwelch2@juno.com
Web site: http://www.shadowplay.userworld.com.

Shadowridge Pr., *(978-0-615-71838-5; 978-0-615-78251-5; 978-0-615-79586-7; 978-0-615-79587-4; 978-0-9897796; 978-0-615-94710-5; 978-0-692-37333-0; 978-0-692-37334-7; 978-1-946808)* 1447 Sycamore Dr, Simi Valley, CA 93065 USA Tel 8055017274
Web site: www.shadowridgepress.com
Dist(s): **CreateSpace Independent Publishing Platform.**

Shady Tree Productions, *(978-0-9747352)* 5383 Iron Pen Pl., Columbia, MD 21044 USA Tel 410-997-6337 (phone/fax)
E-mail: shadytreepro@hotmail.com; bigtree_75@msn.com; ronfullwood@returningsoldiers.us.

Shaffer, Dale E., *(978-0-915060)* 478 Jennings Ave., Salem, OH 44460-2732 USA (SAN 206-9067).

Shaffer, Earl Foundation, Inc., *(978-0-9795659)* 1635 Haft Dr., Reynoldsburg, OH 43068-3059 USA Tel 614-751-0029
E-mail: spur@mac.com
Web site: http://www.earlshaffer.org.

Shaffner, Randolph P. *See* **Faraway Publishing**

Shaggy Dog Pr., *(978-0-9722007)* P.O. Box 4436 Reeves Road, Ojai, CA 93023 USA Tel 805-646-1849
E-mail: shaggydogpress@gmail.com.

Shah, Meera, *(978-0-9774219)* 7003 Westminster Ln., Germantown, TN 38138 USA Tel 901-754-7197
E-mail: meeds_46@yahoo.com; merra.meeds46@gmail.com.

Shahine, Lora, *(978-0-9987146)* 1101 Madison St., Seattle, WA 98104 USA Tel 206-515-0000
E-mail: lshahine@pnwfertility.com.

Shahnawaz Khan *See* **Terra Blue Enterprises**

Shahriary, Cathlin, *(978-1-7328453)* 4301 Essex Ct., Flower Mound, TX 75028 USA
E-mail: cshahriary@gmail.com
Dist(s): **Ingram Content Group.**

Shakalot High Entertainment, *(978-0-9721067; 978-0-9796219; 978-1-7358905)* 20687 White Dove Ln., Bend, OR 97702 USA Tel 541-788-4011; 13019 SW 154th Ave., Tigard, OR 97223 Tel 503-548-3336; *Imprints:* Writing Wild & Crazy (Writing Wild)
E-mail: shakalothighentertainment@yahoo.com
Web site: http://www.shakalothigh.com
Dist(s): **Lulu Pr., Inc.**

Shake the Moon Bks., *(978-0-615-25125-7; 978-0-615-53638-5; 978-0-692-14333-9; 978-0-578-55965-0)* 431 N. Hidalgo Ave., ALHAMBRA, CA 91801 USA Tel 818-903-4112
E-mail: info@shakethemoonbooks.com; slangteau@gmail.com
Web site: http://www.shakethemoonbooks.com
Dist(s): **Baker & Taylor Publisher Services (BTPS).**

ShakeB Co., *(978-0-615-24232-3; 978-0-615-41353-2)* 1189 Masselin Ave., Los Angeles, CA 90019 USA.

Shalako Pr., *(978-0-9798898; 978-0-9830608; 978-0-9846811; 978-0-9892917; 978-0-9908878; 978-0-9964235; 978-0-9970679; 978-0-9990070; 978-1-7340795; 978-1-7351297)* P.O. Box 371, Oakdale, CA 95361-0371 USA (SAN 854-6622)
E-mail: major@majormitchell.net
Web site: http://www.shalakopress.com
Dist(s): **Smashwords.**

Shalhout, Ahlam LLC *See* **Expressions Woven**

Shalom Secrets *See* **Socially Smarter**

Shalu Children's Series, The *Imprint of* **Penman Productions**

Shamber Pubns., *(978-0-9771326)* P.O. Box 470321, Lake Monroe, FL 32747-0321 USA
E-mail: unbrokencirclebymcghee@gmail.com.

Shambhala Publications, Incorporated *See* **Shambhala Pubns., Inc.**

†Shambhala Pubns., Inc., *(978-0-8348; 978-0-87773; 978-0-937938; 978-0-9627138; 978-1-55939; 978-1-56957; 978-1-57062; 978-1-930485; 978-1-59030; 978-1-61180; 978-1-64547)* 4720 Walnut St., Boulder, CO 80301 USA (SAN 203-2481) Tel 303-222-9598; 978-829-2599 (international); Toll Free: 888-424-2329 (orders); *Imprints:* Weatherhill, Incorporated (Weathill); Trumpeter (Trumpeter); Roost Books (Roost Bks); Snow Lion Publications, Incorporated (SnowLion); Bala Kids (Bala Kids)
E-mail: editors@shambhala.com; support@shambhala.com; customercare@shambhala.com
Web site: http://www.shambhala.com
Dist(s): **MyiLibrary**
Penguin Random Hse. Distribution
Penguin Random Hse. LLC
Random Hse., Inc.; *CIP.*

Shammah Ministries, *(978-0-9725944)* Orders Addr.: 1346 Oak Pk. Dr., Aransas Pass, TX 78336 USA Tel 361-226-4918
E-mail: tonia@shammah.org; twoolever@gmail.com
Web site: https://toniawoolever.com; http://www.shammah.org.

Shamrock Pr., *(978-0-9675410)* Orders Addr.: P.O. Box 58186, Charleston, WV 25358 USA Tel 304-744-4259 (phone/fax) Do not confuse with Shamrock Pr. in Chattanooga, TN
E-mail: shamrockpress@frontier.com
Web site: www.shamrockpress.com.

Shamrock Publishing, Inc., *(978-0-9743244; 978-0-9759703)* 400 Corey Ave., Wachovia Bldg., 2nd Flr., Saint Pete Beach, FL 33706 USA Tel 727-363-4747; Fax: 727-363-4848; 1220 S. State St., Chicago, IL 60605 Tel 312-212-1143; Fax: 708-371-9576 Do not confuse with Shamrock Publishing, Incorporated in New Orleans, LA
E-mail: tpmac@sprynet.com; bksemmer@blueshamrockpublishing.com.

Shamus B. Publishing, *(978-0-9753671)* 18533 Pond Dr., Abingdon, VA 24211 USA.

Shan Jen Publishing Co., Ltd. (TWN) *(978-986-7517; 978-957-2041; 978-957-8298; 978-957-9658; 978-957-99079) Dist. by* **Chinasprout.**

Shanahan, John Francis Publishing, *(978-0-9618275)* 6727 N. Lightfoot Ave., Chicago, IL 60646 USA (SAN 667-0490) Tel 773-631-6344; Fax: 773-631-6372
E-mail: REPSbooks@aol.com.

Shanbhag, Arun, *(978-0-9790081)* 32 Chatham St., Arlington, MA 02474-2008 USA
E-mail: arun@shanbhag.org.

Shanghai Translation Publishing Hse. (CHN) *(978-7-5327; 978-7-900325; 978-7-88841) Dist. by* **PerseuPGW.**

Shangri-La Pubns., *(978-0-9677201; 978-0-9714683; 978-0-9719496)* Orders Addr.: P.O. Box 65, Warren Center, PA 18851-0065 USA Toll Free: 866-966-6288; Edit Addr.: 3 Coburn Hill Rd., PMB 65, Warren Center, PA 18851 USA Tel 570-395-3423; Fax: 570-395-0146
E-mail: gosline@egypt.net; shangrila@egypt.net; shangri_la_book@hotmail.com
Web site: http://www.shangri-la.0catch.com/.

Shannon Road Pr., *(978-0-9788785; 978-0-9846101)* 16330 Shannon Rd., Los Gatos, CA 95032 USA
E-mail: info@shannonroadpress.com
Web site: http://www.shannonroadpress.com.

Shanti Arts Publishing, *(978-0-9885897; 978-1-941830; 978-1-947067; 978-1-951651)* 193 Hillside Rd., Brunswick, ME 04011 USA Tel 207-837-5760; Fax: 207-725-4909
E-mail: publisher@shantiarts.com
Web site: http://www.shantiarts.com.

Shanti Publishing, *(978-0-615-86491-4; 978-0-615-88564-3; 978-0-615-93871-4; 978-0-692-32474-5; 978-0-692-35882-5; 978-0-692-36270-9; 978-0-692-38178-6; 978-0-692-38320-9; 978-0-692-44042-1; 978-0-692-47800-4; 978-0-9973754; 978-0-692-13178-7)* P.O. Box 6252, Pine Mountain Club, CA 93222 USA Tel 6613199977
Web site: www.ShantiPublishing.com
Dist(s): **CreateSpace Independent Publishing Platform.**

Shapato Publishing, LLC, *(978-0-9821058; 978-0-9826992; 978-0-9833526; 978-0-615-50457-5; 978-0-615-50918-1; 978-0-615-50920-4; 978-0-615-50921-1; 978-0-615-51306-5; 978-0-615-53431-2; 978-0-615-53435-0; 978-0-615-56643-6; 978-0-615-59791-1; 978-0-615-60650-7; 978-0-615-72638-0; 978-0-615-83271-5; 978-0-615-91943-0; 978-0-692-25479-0; 978-0-692-30027-5; 978-0-692-58092-9) Orders Addr.: P.O. Box 476, Everly, IA 51338 USA Tel 712-490-5165; Edit Addr.: 503 E 2nd St., Everly, IA 51338 USA*
E-mail: Jean@midwestwriter.com
Web site: http://www.shapatopublishing.com
Dist(s): **CreateSpace Independent Publishing Platform**
Smashwords.

Shar-Don & Associates, Incorporated *See* **Lovin Ovens, Inc.**

Share & Care Society Inc., *(978-0-9722025)* 3737 El Portal, C/o 57552 29 Palms Hwy. #52, 29 Palms, CA 92284 USA; *Imprints:* True Lightening (True Lght)
E-mail: london_pain@hotmail.com; elizabethbergman@shareandcaresociety.us
Web site: http://shareandcaresociety.us.

Share Publishing, *(978-0-9633705)* Orders Addr.: 313 Laurel Ave., Menlo Park, CA 94025 USA Tel 650-321-5947 (phone/fax)
E-mail: pamelalaw@sbcglobal.net
Web site: http://sharepublishing.com.

ShareInPrint, *(978-1-7330291; 978-1-7355501)* 520 Mapleview Dr., University City, MO 63130 USA Tel 314-863-2476
E-mail: johnmramsay@mac.com
Web site: shareinprint.com; johnmramsay.com.

Sharif, Mboya *See* **Doses of Reality, Inc.**

Shark & Siren Pr., *(978-1-7328605)* 2317 Ebony St, Port Townsend, WA 98368 USA Tel 415-269-2587
E-mail: TRENOR@GMAIL.COM
Web site: www.umijoo.com.

Shark Press *See* **Lemon Shark Pr.**

†Sharp & Dunnigan, *(978-0-918495)* 2700 Richards Rd., Suite 110, Bellevue, WA 98005 USA (SAN 657-3029) Tel 425-467-6565; Fax: 425-467-6564
E-mail: ecovepress@aol.com
Web site: http://elfincovepress.com
Dist(s): **Elfin Cove Pr.**; *CIP.*

Sharp & Dunnigan, Publications, Incorporated *See* **Sharp & Dunnigan**

Sharp, Diana Consulting, *(978-0-9762626)* 5954 Fishhawk Crossing Blvd., Lithia, FL 33547-5878 USA.

SHARP Literacy, Inc., *(978-0-9770816; 978-0-9836222; 978-0-9986683)* 750 N. Lincoln Memorial Dr. Suite 311, Milwaukee, WI 53202 USA Tel 414-270-3388
Web site: http://www.sharpliteracy.org.

Sharpe, Jeannie W., *(978-0-9763117)* 373 Langford Rd., Blythewood, SC 29016 USA Fax: 803-786-4557
E-mail: jws415@aol.com.

Sharpe Writings, *(978-0-9997926)* P.O. Box 194, Norwalk, IA 50211 USA Tel 515-802-7753
E-mail: jakesharpe@mchsi.com.

Shauger, Daniel, *(978-0-9746114)* 12438 Moorpark St., No. 241, Studio City, CA 91605 USA Tel 818-693-6231
E-mail: dan@aperfectswing.com
Web site: http://www.aperfectswing.com.

Shaw, Dana, *(978-0-9791091)* Orders Addr.: P.O. Box 91, Franklin, ME 04634 USA (SAN 852-4815) Tel 207-565-4445; Edit Addr.: 206 Georges Pond Rd., Franklin, ME 04634 USA
E-mail: myfriendzundel@yahoo.com
Web site: http://myfriendzundel.com.

Shawnee Pr., Inc., *(978-0-8256; 978-0-9603394; 978-1-59235)* Subs. of Music Sales Corp., Orders Addr.: P.O. Box 1250, Marshalls Creek, PA 18335 USA Toll Free Fax: 800-345-6842; Toll Free: 800-962-8584; Edit Addr.: 9 Dartmouth Dr., Bldg. 4, Marshalls Creek, PA 18335 USA (SAN 202-084X) Tel 212-254-2100 (copyright & licensing information); 570-476-0550; Fax: 570-476-5247
E-mail: shawnee-info@shawneepress.com
Web site: http://www.shawneepress.com
Dist(s): **Leonard, Hal Corp.**
Music Sales Corp.

Shay, Marissa, *(978-0-9899604)* 575 Watchogue Rd., Staten Island, NY 10314 USA Tel 718-477-0026
E-mail: m.pessolano@yahoo.com.

Shayach Comics *Imprint of* **Judaica Pr., Inc., The**

Shaymaa Publishing Corp., *(978-0-9719581)* P.O. Box 501, Lodi, NJ 07644-0501 USA (SAN 255-738X) Fax: 973-237-0537
E-mail: elhewiemf@juno.com; todaysgy@todaysgym.com; elhewie@lift-4-life.com
Web site: http://www.lift-4-life.com; http://www.todaysgym.com; http://www.shaymaa-publishing.com.

Shayne Publishing, *(978-0-9771192)* 4895 SE 40th St., Des Moines, IA 50320 USA (SAN 256-7997) Tel 515-263-2784
E-mail: dlhuston01@aol.com.

Shazak Productions *Imprint of* **Torah Excel**

She Soars LLC, *(978-0-578-41577-2)* 4407 Sweet Williams Ln., Wilson, NC 27896 USA Tel 252-991-7296
E-mail: hannahsheart7@gmail.com
Dist(s): **Independent Pub.**

She Writes Pr., *(978-1-938314; 978-1-63152; 978-1-64742)* 1563 Solano Ave. No. 546, Berkeley, CA 94707 USA Tel 510-967-9333
E-mail: brooke@warnercoaching.com
Dist(s): **Ingram Publisher Services**
Seattle Bk. Co.

†Shearer Publishing, *(978-0-940672)* 406 Post Oak Rd., Fredericksburg, TX 78624 USA Tel 830-997-6529; Fax: 830-997-9752; Toll Free: 800-458-3808
E-mail: shearer@shearerpub.com
Web site: http://www.shearerpub.com
Dist(s): **Bk. Marketing Plus**
Texas A&M Univ. Pr.; *CIP.*

Shechinah Third Temple, Inc., *(978-0-9723866; 978-0-9817212; 978-0-9895128)* 11583 Pamplona

Blvd., Boynton Beach, FL 33437 USA Tel 561-735-7958; Fax: 561-738-1535
E-mail: thirdtemple@bellsouth.net; jerrypollock@bellsouth.net
Web site: http://www.shechinahthirdtemple.org.

Sheepdog Pr., *(978-0-9742205)* P.O. Box 60, Onancock, VA 23417 USA Tel 888-787-1951; Fax: 888-787-2675
E-mail: publisher@sheepdogpress.com
Web site: http://www.sheepdogpress.com.

Sheepgate Pr., *(978-1-7333733)* 4590 Woodland Brook Dr. SE, Atlanta, GA 30339 USA Tel 770-639-1671
E-mail: emilyhjeffries@gmail.com
Web site: www.emilyhjeffries.com.

Sheepscrot River Pr., *(978-0-9964084)* 147 Eddy Rd., Edgecomb, ME 04556 USA Tel 207-882-5569
E-mail: leawait@roadrunner.com
Web site: www.leawait.com.

Sheets, Judy, *(978-0-9726451)* 2526 Brune Rd., Farmington, MO 63640 USA Tel 573-756-6254
E-mail: judys@i1.net.

Shekinah Productions, *(978-0-9802250; 978-0-578-04316-6; 978-0-578-05243-4; 978-0-578-05610-4; 978-0-578-05834-4; 978-0-578-07417-7; 978-0-578-08092-5; 978-0-578-08093-2; 978-0-578-08094-9; 978-0-578-08182-3; 978-0-578-08415-2; 978-0-578-08869-3; 978-0-578-10324-2; 978-0-578-11645-7; 978-0-578-12000-3; 978-0-578-13210-5; 978-0-578-13328-7; 978-0-578-13499-4; 978-0-578-13962-3; 978-0-578-14057-5; 978-0-578-14114-5; 978-0-578-18040-3; 978-0-578-19525-4; 978-0-578-19715-9; 978-0-578-19716-6; 978-0-578-19838-5; 978-) 8111 Windersgate Drive, Olive Branch, MS 38654 USA Fax: 662-504-4234; P.O. Box 209, Olive Branch, MS 38654*
E-mail: shekinah.productions@yahoo.com
Web site: http://www.skpseminars.com.

Shekinah Publishing Hse., *(978-0-9700976; 978-1-940153)* Orders Addr.: P.O. Box 118811, Carrollton, TX 75011 USA Tel 877-538-1363; Edit Addr.: P.O. Box 118811, Carrollton, TX 75011 USA Fax: 877-538-1363; *Imprints:* Shekinah Publishing House (Shek Pub Hse) Do not confuse with companies with the same or similar names in Cameron, NC, Cameron, NC
E-mail: lpbowk@thebwfg.com; author@shekinahpublishinghouse.com.

Shekinah Publishing Hse. *Imprint of* **Shekinah Publishing Hse.**

Shelby, Lloyd *See* **Painted WORD Studios**

Shelbykay Publishing Co., *(978-0-9744407)* 525 Greenhill Ln., Philadelphia, PA 19128 USA Tel 215-483-6688
E-mail: cdkae@aol.com.

Shelf-Life Bks., *(978-1-880042)* Div. of M.A.P.S., Inc., 2132 Fordem, Madison, WI 53704-0599 USA Tel 608-244-7767; Fax: 608-244-8394.

Shell Beach Publishing, LLC, *(978-0-9706732)* 677 Shell Beach Dr., Lake Charles, LA 70601-5732 USA Tel 433-439-2110
E-mail: kkblake@compuserve.com.

Shell Educational Publishing, *(978-1-4258)* 5301 Oceanus Dr., Huntington Beach, CA 92649 USA Tel 714-489-2080; Fax: 714-230-7070; Toll Free: 888-877-7606; 877-777-3450
E-mail: rkarnik@tcmpub.com; LShill@seppub.com
Web site: http://www.seppub.com; http://www.tcmpub.com
Dist(s): **Follett School Solutions**
Lectorum Pubns., Inc.
Teacher Created Materials, Inc.

Shella, Aaron, *(978-0-578-44271-6; 978-0-578-48198-2)* 1157 Waukegan Rd., Deerfield, IL 60015 USA Tel 847-945-6884; 847 309 2493
E-mail: aaron.shella@gmail.com
Dist(s): **Ingram Content Group.**

Shelle, Carole Creative Arts, *(978-0-9792641)* P.O. Box 52972, Irvine, CA 92619 USA (SAN 852-9493) Toll Free: 800-929-1634.

Shelley Adina, *(978-0-615-52095-7; 978-0-615-62675-8; 978-1-939087; 978-1-950854)* P.O. Box 752, Redwood Estates, CA 95044 USA Tel 408-761-1195; *Imprints:* Moonshell Books, Inc. (MoonshellBks)
Web site: http://www.shelleyadina.com
Dist(s): **Blackstone Audio, Inc.**
CreateSpace Independent Publishing Platform.

Shelly's Adventures LLC, *(978-0-9851845; 978-1-953768)* P.O. Box 2632, Land O Lakes, FL 34639 USA Tel 352-219-7199
E-mail: kentrell@shellysadventuresllc.com; kentrell.martin15@gmail.com; kentrell@shellysadventures.com
Web site: www.shellysadventuresllc.com; www.shellysadventures.com
Dist(s): **Partners Pubs. Group, Inc.**

ShellyShines Bks., *(978-0-9993131)* 9134 Forest Willow Dr., Indianapolis, IN 46234 USA Tel 317-694-1409
E-mail: ShellyShines22@gmail.com
Web site: www.ShellyShines.com.

ShellyShines22@gmail.com *See* **ShellyShines Bks.**

Shelter Harbor Pr., *(978-0-9853230; 978-1-62795)* 605 W. 115th St. Suite 163, New York, NY 10025 USA Tel 212-864-0427; Fax: 212-316-6496
E-mail: Jeanette.Limondjian@gmail.com; info@shelterharborpress.com; jeanette@shelterharborpress.com.

Shelter of Flint, Inc., *(978-0-9740929)* 902 E. 6th St., Flint, MI 48503-2787 USA
E-mail: sof@shelterofflint.com
Web site: http://www.shelterofflint.com.

†Shelter Pubns., Inc., *(978-0-936070)* Orders Addr.: P.O. Box 279, Bolinas, CA 94924 USA (SAN 122-8463) Tel 415-868-0280; Fax: 415-868-9053; Toll Free: 800-307-0131; Edit Addr.: 285 Dogwood Rd, Bolinas, CA 94924 USA
E-mail: shelter@shelterpub.com
Web site: http://www.shelterpub.com
Dist(s): **Bk. Express**
Bookmen, Inc.
Distributors, The
Koen Pacific
Partners/West Book Distributors
Publishers Group West (PGW); *CIP.*

shelterpetsink, *(978-0-9740980)* 16457 Gledhill St., North Hills, CA 91343 USA Fax: 818-892-2112
E-mail: shelterpetsink@shelterpetsink.com; remilove2002@yahoo.com
Web site: http://www.shelterpetsink.com.

Shenandoah County Historical Society, Inc., *(978-0-9795924)* P.O. Box 506, Edinburg, VA 22824 USA Tel 540-465-5570
E-mail: adamsons@shentel.net.

Shenango River Bks., *(978-1-888836)* P.O. Box 631, Sharon, PA 16146 USA Tel 412-342-3811; Fax: 412-342-1583.

Shenanigan Bks., *(978-0-9726614; 978-1-934860)* 84 River Rd., Summit, NJ 07901-1443 USA (SAN 915-7085)
Web site: http://www.shenaniganbooks.com
Dist(s): **Jobson, Oliver H.**

Shenanigans Series,

Shenek, *(978-0-692-08159-4; 978-1-7321464)* 425 Zachary Way, Garner, NC 27529 USA Tel 919-834-3658
E-mail: shenek.alston@gmail.com.

Shen's Bks. *Imprint of* **Lee & Low Bks., Inc.**

Shepard Pubns., *(978-0-938497; 978-1-62035; 978-0-9849616; 978-0-9898649)* P.O. Box 280, Friday Harbor, WA 98250 USA (SAN 661-0536); *Imprints:* Skyhook Press (Skyhook Pr)
Web site: http://www.shepardpub.com
Dist(s): **Ingram Content Group.**

Shepherd Mountain Pr., *(978-0-9749282)* 21 Cargill Rd., Liberty, ME 04949 USA Tel 207-589-4772.

Shepherd Pr. Inc., *(978-0-9663786; 978-0-9723046; 978-0-9767582; 978-0-9815400; 978-0-9824387; 978-0-9830990; 978-1-936908; 978-1-63342)* Orders Addr.: P.O. Box 24, Wapwallopen, PA 18660 USA Tel 570-379-2101; Fax: 570-379-2071; Toll Free: 800-338-1445; Edit Addr.: 437 S. River St., Wapwallopen, PA 18660 USA Do not confuse with companies with the same or similar names in Tappan, NJ, S. Hackensack, NJ, Birmingham, AL, Amityville, NY
E-mail: info@shepherdpress.com
Web site: http://www.shepherdpress.com.

Shepherd's Workshop, LLC, The, *(978-0-9752895)* 8213 Otis Ct., Arvada, CO 80003 USA Toll Free: 888-257-4673
E-mail: info@tsworkshop.com
Web site: http://www.tsworkshop.com.

Sheppard Publishing, *(978-0-9725286)* 3371 Old Forge Rd., Kent, OH 44240 USA Tel 330-325-9658
E-mail: sheppardpublishing@neo.rr.com.

Sheptoski-Forbush, Faith, *(978-0-9985228; 978-1-7340186)* P.O. Box 74688, Romulus, MI 48174-0688 USA Tel 989-255-1326
E-mail: faithsf@yahoo.com.

Sher-A-Craft, *(978-0-9670612)* Div. of Bell Blueprint Co., Inc., 7888 Othello Ave., San Diego, CA 92111 USA Tel 619-278-4830; Fax: 619-278-6830; Toll Free: 877-235-5877.

Sheri McCulley Studio, *(978-0-9981591)* 5928 Hemlock St., Merriam, KS 66202 USA Tel 913-362-0560
E-mail: tseib@aol.com.

Sherian Publishing, *(978-0-9795676)* 2700 Braselton Hwy., Suite 10-390, Dacula, GA 30019-3207 USA Tel 888-276-6730; Fax: 888-209-8212; Toll Free: 888-276-6730
E-mail: sherri.sheusi@sherianinc.com
Web site: http://www.sherianinc.com.

Sheridan Books *See* **KEYGARD**

Sherian County Historical Society Pr., *(978-0-9792871)* Orders Addr.: 850 Sibley Cir., Sheridan, WY 82801-9626 USA
Web site: http://www.sheridancountyhistory.org
Dist(s): **Greenleaf Book Group.**

Sherman Asher Publishing, *(978-0-9644196; 978-1-890932)* P.O. Box 31725, Santa Fe, NM 87594-1725 USA
E-mail: westernedge@santa-fe.net
Web site: http://www.shermanasher.com
Dist(s): **Partners/West Book Distributors**
SCB Distributors.

Sherman, Linda, *(978-0-615-16017-7)* 31557 W. 10 Mile Rd., Farmington, MI 48336 USA Tel 248-476-3433; Fax: 248-476-4307
E-mail: grandmalouie@hotmail.com
Web site: http://grandmalouie.com.

Sheron Enterprises, Inc., *(978-1-891877)* 1035 S. Carley Ct., N Bellmore, NY 11710-2051 USA
E-mail: sheron@concentric.net.

Sherrifmatt9 Publishing Company *See* **Second Time Media & Communications**

Sherry Gansle *See* **Little Big Tomes**

Sherwood, Jae Anne, *(978-0-692-04564-0; 978-0-692-04621-0)* 1002 Moss Haven Ct., Annapolis, MD 21403 USA Tel 703-581-4711
E-mail: toadsville@mac.com
Dist(s): **Ingram Content Group.**

Sherwood Publishing LLC, *(978-0-9987872)* 16480 White Haven DR, Northville, MI 48168 USA Tel 734-420-6932
E-mail: jam@mipalmers.us.

Sheva, Marie, *(978-0-9741736)* 301 Main St., Apt. 8, East Greenwich, RI 02818 USA
E-mail: mariesheva@yearofthedogs.com
Web site: http://www.yearofthedogs.com.

ShiaGnosis, *(978-0-9975945; 978-1-946737; 978-1-946737-00-7)* 1115 Virginia Ave., Hagerstown, MD 21740 USA Tel 301-582-8743
E-mail: ddsodagar@gmail.com
Web site: www.shiagnosis.com; https://heavenlywise.com.

Shields, Kathleen J. *See* **Erin Go Bragh Publishing**

Shiloh Children's Bks., *(978-0-9777923; 978-0-615-81504-6)* P.O. Box 954, Polson, MT 59860 USA Tel 406-531-2281
E-mail: oxman@blackfoot.net.

Shiloh Group *See* **Shiloh Children's Bks.**

Shiloh Kidz *Imprint of* **Barbour Publishing, Inc.**

'Shiloh Run Studios *Imprint of* **Barbour Publishing, Inc.**

Shine On Pubns., *(978-0-9749806)* 12325 Kosich Pl., Saratoga, CA 95070 USA; 12325 Kosich Pl., Saratoga, CA 95070-3575
Web site: http://www.shineonpublications.com.

Shine Publishing Hse., *(978-0-9749467)* 1811 Abbey Oak Dr., Suite 12879, Vienna, VA 22182 USA (SAN 255-9269) Tel 571-432-8922; Fax: 703-448-8443
E-mail: sales@shinepublishing.com
Web site: http://www.shinepublishing.com
Dist(s): **CreateSpace Independent Publishing Platform**
Global Bk. Distributors.

Shine Time Records & Bks., *(978-0-9712398)* Orders Addr.: P.O. Box 331941, Nashville, TN 37203 USA Tel 615-242-9857 (phone/fax); Toll Free: 888-807-4463 (888-80-SHINE)
E-mail: chucwhit@usit.net; info@shinetime.com; info@littleststar.com
Web site: http://www.littleststar.com; http://www.shinetime.com.

Shining Hall *Imprint of* **Twelve Winters Pr.**

Shining Tramp Pr., *(978-0-9749352; 978-0-615-46043-7)* 2114 Harbor View Dr., Rocky Hill, CT 06067 USA Tel 860-563-1899
E-mail: kjmurphy@sbcglobal.net
Dist(s): **CreateSpace Independent Publishing Platform.**

Shinnery Publishing Co., *(978-0-692-80660-9; 978-0-9990572)* 102 W. 2nd St., Colorado City, TX 79512 USA Tel 325-436-1724
E-mail: sharongbarber@sbcglobal.net; sharongbarber@sbcglobal.net; sharongbarber@sbcglobal.net
Dist(s): **CreateSpace Independent Publishing Platform.**

Shinobi Ent., Inc., 14622 Cypress Cottage Ct., Cypress, TX 77429 USA Tel 713-443-5774
E-mail: davewhitfield@comcast.net
Web site: The NewRuleofThree.com
Dist(s): **Diamond Comic Distributors, Inc.**

Shiny Red Ball Publishing, *(978-0-9773608)* 105 Lakeover Dr., Athens, GA 30607 USA
Web site: http://www.shinyredball.com.

Shiptree Pubn., *(978-0-615-77925-6; 978-0-692-20740-6; 978-0-9966682)* 1040 Lunalilo St. Penthouse 2, Honolulu, HI 96822 USA Tel 808 599-3728
Web site: gardnermckay.net
Dist(s): **CreateSpace Independent Publishing Platform.**

Shire *Imprint of* **Bloomsbury Publishing USA**

Shires Press *Imprint of* **Northshire Pr.**

Shirley's Girl Pubns., *(978-0-578-06605-9)* 2165 Silverado St., San Marcos, CA 92078 USA Tel 619-723-8492
E-mail: LVa2thpro@gmail.com.

Shirt Tales *Imprint of* **Brookteam Corp.**

Shively, Lisa Cookbooks, *(978-0-9766756)* P.O. Box 2123, Eden, NC 27289 USA
E-mail: loopi3@earthlink.net; kitchenhelpers@earthlink.net
Web site: http://www.fromourhometoyours.net; http://www.cookingwithlisa.com.

Shiver Hill Bks., *(978-0-9747417)* 1220 Tico Rd., Ojai, CA 93023 USA; 79 S Canyon Diablo Rd. Unit 11, Sedona, AZ 86351 Tel 805-908-1651
E-mail: geraldstanek@yahoo.com
Dist(s): **Lulu Pr., Inc.**

Shivers, Frank Evangelistic Assn., *(978-1-878127)* Orders Addr.: P.O. Box 9991, Columbia, SC 29290 USA
E-mail: fsea@juno.com
Web site: http://FrankShivers.com.

Shnoozles, LLC, *(978-0-9768852; 978-0-9770292)* 8 Canyon Ridge, Irvine, CA 92603 USA
Web site: http://www.shnoozles.com.

Shoetree Publishers, Inc., *(978-0-9785521)* P.O. Box 2122, Chandler, AZ 85244 USA (SAN 850-9859) Fax: 480-812-0182
Web site: http://www.shoetreepublishers.com.

Shooting Star Edition *Imprint of* **American Literary Pr.**

Shooting Star Publishing, *(978-0-9762835)* 1305 E. Fort King St. # 100, Ocala, FL 34471-2443 USA Do not confuse with companies with the same name in Dearborn, MI, Moses Lake, WA
Web site: http://www.shottingstarpublishing.com.

Shope, Diann, *(978-0-9968988)* 1222 20th Ave E., Seattle, WA 98112 USA Tel 206-329-1178
E-mail: eshope12@msn.com
Web site: diannshope.com.

Shope, E. Raymond *See* **Flutter-By Productions**

Shophar So Good, *(978-0-9970778)* 6904 Vantage Avenue, No. 115, North Hollywood, CA 91605 USA Tel 818-765-2600
E-mail: Humbleentertainment@yahoo.com
Web site: shopharsogood.com.

Shore Line Pr. *Imprint of* **Pacific Bks.**

Shorebird Media, *(978-0-9745737)* Orders Addr.: P.O. Box 372, Mukilteo, WA 98275-0372 USA (SAN 255-6359)
E-mail: jeanie.james@verizon.net.

Shorefront N.F.P., *(978-0-9765232; 978-1-946717)* Orders Addr.: P.O. Box 1894, Evanston, IL 60204 USA Tel 847-864-7467; Edit Addr.: P.O. Box 1894, Evanston, IL 60204 USA
Web site: http://shorefrontlegacy.org
Dist(s): **Lulu Pr., Inc.**

Shoreline Pr., *(978-1-887671)* P.O. Box 555, Jamestown, RI 02835 USA Do not confuse with Shoreline Press in Soquel, CA
E-mail: kennethproudfoot@hotmail.com.

Shore Publishing Co., *(978-0-9746846)* PMB 123, 7485 Rush River Dr., Suite 710, Sacramento, CA 95831-5260 USA Tel 916-442-4883; Fax: 916-428-9542.

Shorey Publications *See* **Shorey's Bookstore**

Shorey's Bookstore, *(978-0-8466)* P.O. Box 77316, Seattle, WA 98177-0316 USA (SAN 204-5958) Tel 206-633-2990
E-mail: shorey@serv.net
Web site: http://www.serv.net/shorey.

Short Books *See* **Half-Pint Kids, Inc.**

Short Tales *Imprint of* **Magic Wagon**

Short Term Mission Language Program, *(978-0-9746182)* 3612 Mary Elizabeth Church Rd., Waxhaw, NC 28173-9273 USA
E-mail: info@missionlanguage.com
Web site: http://www.missionlanguage.com.

Shortbread Hill Bk. Co., *(978-0-9799162)* P.O. Box 1565, Veradale, WA 99037 USA (SAN 854-7599)
E-mail: shortbreadhill@hotmail.com.

Shortland Pubns. (U. S. A.) Inc., *(978-0-7699; 978-1-57257)* 19201 120th Ave NE Ste. 100, Bothell, WA 98011-9507 USA
Dist(s): **Heinemann-Raintree**
Wright Group/McGraw-Hill.

Shotwell, Sheila, *(978-0-9994225)* 54 Fitch Pl SE, Grand Rapids, MI 49503 USA Tel 616-451-4401
E-mail: sheilashotwell@aol.com.

Show N' Tell Publishing, *(978-0-615-19210-9; 978-0-9825700; 978-0-9968332; 978-0-9986498)* 56 Drakes Bay Dr., Corona Del Mar, CA 92625 USA Tel 946-644-2293
E-mail: dick@rate.com
Dist(s): **Publishers Services.**

Show What You KnowR Publishing, *(978-1-884183)* 6344 Nicholas Dr, Columbus, OH, OH 43235 USA.

Showcase Writers, *(978-0-9753340)* P.O. Box 13757, Richmond, VA 23225 USA Tel 804-398-1138
E-mail: editor@showcasewriters.com
Web site: http://www.showcasewriters.com.

Showdown Mesa, *(978-0-578-56096-0)* 829 E. Cedar Ct., Fruita, CO 81521 USA Tel 417-379-4685
E-mail: easy112233@gmail.com.

Showtime Bks., *(978-0-9911860)* 140 Sheldon Ave., Staten Island, NY 10312 USA Tel 718-356-2275
E-mail: bwshowtime@aol.com.

Shrewsbury Publishing, *(978-0-9678182)* 3624 Livingston, New Orleans, LA 70118 USA Tel 504-488-5249.

Shrimlife Pr., *(978-0-9997310)* 1 Ronwood Rd., Chestnut Ridge, NY 10977 USA Tel 845-371-2751
E-mail: susan@unlockyourchild.com
Web site: http://www.unlockyourchild.com.

Shulemite Christian Crusade, *(978-0-9714361)* 1420 Armstrong Valley Rd., Halifax, PA 17032-8383 USA (SAN 254-3931) Tel 717-896-8383; Fax: 717-896-8386
E-mail: sherrerd@epix.net
Web site: http://www.chrissherrerd.com.

Shulenberger Publishing, *(978-0-9767355)* 3912 NE 127th St., Seattle, WA 98125 USA (SAN 256-5935) Tel 206-367-5886
E-mail: ericshul@hotmail.com.

Shumpert, Sharon *See* **SYS Publishing**

ShuNu Publishing, *(978-0-9742329)* P.O. Box 2031, Stafford, TX 77497 USA Tel 713-401-8479
E-mail: kmitchellthomas@aol.com.

Shurley Instructional Materials, Inc., *(978-1-881940; 978-1-58561)* 366 Sim Dr., Cabot, AR 72023 USA Tel 501-843-3869; Fax: 501-843-0583; Toll Free: 800-566-2966; Ballad Rd., Cabot, AR 72023
E-mail: shurley@shurley.com
Web site: http://www.shurley.com.

shuster books *See* **Roberts, Hebard D. Bks.**

Shy Cat Pubns., *(978-0-578-40488-2; 978-0-578-40882-8)* 2314 Roosevelt Ave., Redwood City, CA 94061 USA Tel 408-821-5635
E-mail: ashwinsunder@gmail.com
Dist(s): **Ingram Content Group.**

SIA Publishing, LLC, *(978-0-9787344; 978-1-936820)* 204 Wyndom Ct., Goodlettsville, TN 37072-2176 USA
E-mail: donbloomquist@siapublishing.com
Web site: http://www.siapublishing.com
Dist(s): **Smashwords.**

SIA Software, LLC *See* **SIA Publishing, LLC**

Sibyl Merritt, *(978-0-9824565)* 25 Western Ledge Rd., Corea, ME 04624 USA (SAN 858-2157)
E-mail: bparks@maine.edu
Web site: http://sibylmerritt.com
Dist(s): **Ingram Content Group.**

Side FX Partners, LLC, *(978-0-692-82883-0; 978-0-692-83666-8; 978-0-692-83799-3)* 5875 Collins Ave No. 1801, MIAMI BEACH, FL 33140 USA Tel 443-570-4942
E-mail: jeffwcrawford5+LVP0003227@gmail.com; jeffwcrawford5+LVP0003227@gmail.com.

Sidedoor Publishing LLC, *(978-0-9770248)* P.O. Box 18271, San Jose, CA 95158-8271 USA
E-mail: isbn@sidedoorpublishing.com
Web site: http://www.sidedoorpublishing.com.

Sidekicks TM *Imprint of* **Scholastic, Inc.**

Publisher Name Index

Sideline Ink Publishing, *(978-0-9992905; 978-1-7343909)* 2225 W. Berwyn Ave., Chicago, IL 60625 USA Tel 312-343-6273
E-mail: sidelineinkpublishing@gmail.com
Web site: www.creativeclassroomconsulting.com.

Sidewalk Publishing, *(978-0-9766418)* Inform Design, 2809 Forest Hill Cir., SE, Olympia, WA 98501 USA Tel 360-570-9398
E-mail: informbarb@qwest.net
Web site: http://www.sidewalkpublishing.net.

Sidewalk Univ. Pr., *(978-0-9759962)* 1739 Springfield Ave., Maplewood, NJ 07040 USA Tel 973-885-0860
E-mail: sidewalku@msn.com
Web site: http://www.sidewalkuniversity.org.

Sidewinder Publishing LLC, *(978-0-914001)* 4609 Kinney St. SE, Albuquerque, NM 87105 USA Tel 505-998-8000
Web site: http://www.sidewinderpublishing.com/.

Sidran Institute Pr., *(978-0-9629164; 978-1-886968)* Div. of Sidran Institute, P.O. Box 436, Brooklandville, MD 21022 USA Tel 410-825-8888; Fax: 410-560-0134
E-mail: esther.giller@sidran.org
Web site: http://www.sidran.org
Dist(s): **New Leaf Distributing Co., Inc.**
Quality Bks., Inc.

Siebenaler, Sarina, *(978-0-578-60610-1; 978-1-7351996)* 6632 E. Calle De Las Estrellas, Cave Creek, AZ 85331 USA Tel 623-565-0199
E-mail: Sa30siebenaler@gmail.com
Dist(s): **Ingram Content Group.**

Siegrist, Vicky, *(978-0-615-21676-8; 978-0-9820977; 978-0-9824444)* 1478 E. Buder Ave., Millington, MI 48529 USA
Web site: http://www.vickisiegrist.com
Dist(s): **Lulu Pr., Inc.**

Siemers, Robert, *(978-0-9744723)* P.O. Box 549, Koloa, HI 96756-0549 USA Tel 808-635-2905; Toll Free: 888-233-8365
Web site: http://www.teok.com.

Siems, D.R., *(978-0-9794483)* Orders Addr.: P.O. Box 83, Daniel, WY 83115 USA; Edit Addr.: 19 School House Ln., Daniel, WY 83115 USA.

Sienna Bay Pr., *(978-0-9898438; 978-1-945527)* 1409 Timber Ridge Cir., Nashville, TN 37211 USA Tel 615-693-1568
E-mail: shannonlbrown@yahoo.com.

Sierra Club Bks. for Children, *(978-0-87156; 978-1-57805)* Div. of Sierra Club Bks., 85 Second Street, San Francisco, CA 94105 USA Tel 415-977-5500; Fax: 415-977-5792
E-mail: Books.Publishing@sierraclub.org
Web site: http://www.sierraclub.org/books
Dist(s): **Gibbs Smith, Publisher.**

Sierra Muses Pr., *(978-0-9912102)* P.O. Box 942, North San Juan, CA 95960 USA Tel 530-292-3610
E-mail: blisssearcher8@gmail.com.

Sierra Nevada Publishing Hse., *(978-0-9765697)* P.O. Box 50366, Henderson, NV 89016 USA Tel 702-991-1383; Fax: 702-953-8973; Toll Free: 800-254-6266
Web site: http://www.climbonsuccess.com.

Sierra Pr., *(978-0-939365; 978-0-9617651; 978-1-58071)* Div. of Panorama International Productions, Inc., Orders Addr.: 4988 Gold Leaf Dr., Mariposa, CA 95338 USA (SAN 662-6955) Tel 209-966-5071; Fax: 209-966-5073; Toll Free: 800-745-2631; *Imprints:* Wish You Were Here (Wish You Were Here)
E-mail: siepress@sti.net
Web site: http://www.nationalparksusa.com
Dist(s): **Smashwords.**

Sierra Raconteur Publishing, *(978-1-58365; 978-1-58582)* Orders Addr.: P.O. Box 97, Memphis, IN 47143 USA Tel 812-294-4693
E-mail: Lori_soard@yahoo.com.

Sierra Vista Junior High *See* **Sierra Vista Pubns.**

Sierra Vista Pubns., *(978-0-9711314; 978-0-615-11784-3)* Alpine Sports, Orders Addr.: P.O. Box 55391, Valencia, CA 91385 USA Fax: 661-259-8941; Toll Free: 800-330-7734; Edit Addr.: P.O. Box 186, Crystal Bay, NV 89402 USA (SAN 411-5961)
E-mail: alpinesport@earthlink.net
Web site: http://www.alpinebasketball.com
Dist(s): **American West Bks.**
Brigham Distribution.

Siete Cuentos Editorial *Imprint of* **Seven Stories Pr.**

Sigel Pr., *(978-1-905941)* Orders Addr.: 4403 Belmont Ct., Medina, OH 44256 USA (SAN 853-960X) Tel 330-722-2541 (phone/fax); 51a Victoria Rd., Cambridge, CB4 3BW Tel 01223 30 33 03
E-mail: tsigel@sigelpress.com
Web site: http://www.sigelpress.com
Dist(s): **MyiLibrary.**

Sights Productions, *(978-0-9629978; 978-1-886366)* Orders Addr.: 15130 Black Ankle Rd., Mount Airy, MD 21771 USA Tel 410-795-4582; Fax: 410-795-5054
E-mail: eric@sights-productions.com
Web site: http://sights-productions.com
Dist(s): **Brodart Co.**
Follett School Solutions
Kamkyi Bks.
New Leaf Distributing Co., Inc.
Quality Bks., Inc.

Sigi & LuLu Productions, *(978-0-9829864; 978-1-937339)* 3733 Regina Royale Blvd, Sarasota, FL 34238 USA
Web site: www.theadventuresofsigi.com
Dist(s): **Ingram Content Group.**

Sigil Publishing, *(978-0-9728461; 978-0-9785642; 978-0-9846528; 978-0-9860323)* P.O. Box 824, Leland, MI 49654- USA (SAN 255-1667)
Web site: http://www.knightscares.com; www.realheroesread.com
Dist(s): **Partners Bk. Distributing, Inc.**
Quality Bks., Inc.

Sigler Printing & Publishing, Incorporated *See* **McMillen Publishing**

Sigmar (ARG) *(978-950-11) Dist. by* **Mariuccia Iaconi Bk Imports.**

Sigmar (ARG) *(978-950-11) Dist. by* **AIMS Intl.**

Sigmar (ARG) *(978-950-11) Dist. by* **Continental Bk.**

Sigmar (ARG) *(978-950-11) Dist. by* **Lectorum Pubns.**

Sign Up Learning, Incorporated *See* **Language Quest Corp.**

Sign2Me *Imprint of* **Sign2Me Early Learning / Northlight Communications, Inc.**

Sign2Me Early Learning / Northlight Communications, Inc., *(978-0-9668367; 978-1-932354)* Orders Addr.: 11112 47th Ave. W., Mukilteo, WA 98275 USA (SAN 850-7902) Tel 425-493-1903; Fax: 425-493-1904; Edit Addr.: 11112 4th Ave. W., Mukilteo, WA 98275 USA Tel 425-493-1903; Fax: 425-493-1904; Toll Free: 877-744-6263; *Imprints:* Sign2Me (Sign Two Me)
E-mail: btarcea@sign2me.com; acrain@sign2me.com
Web site: http://sign2me.com
Dist(s): **American Wholesale Bk. Co.**

Signal Fire Pr., *(978-0-9764128)* 25260 Terr. Grove Rd., Los Gatos, CA 95033 USA (SAN 256-4351)
Web site: http://www.signalfirepress.com.

Signator Publishing Group Inc., *(978-0-9728472)* 1725 I St. NW., Suite 300, Washington, DC 20006 USA Tel 202-349-3896; Fax: 202-349-3915
E-mail: info@signatorpublishing.com
Web site: http://www.signatorpublishing.com.

Signet *Imprint of* **Penguin Publishing Group**

SignificantFaith.com *See* **Sincerity Publishing**

Sigueme, Ediciones, S.A. (ESP) *(978-84-301) Dist. by* **Augsburg Fortress.**

Sikes Sports Concepts *See* **Old Bay Publishing**

Sikh Research Institute, *(978-1-60411)* P.O. Box 690504, San Antonio, TX 78269 USA (SAN 854-0403)
E-mail: info@sikhri.org
Web site: http://www.sikhri.org.

Sikorski, Lorna D. & Associates *See* **LDS & Assocs.**

Silence Dogood Pr., *(978-0-9861967)* 4141 11th Ave SW, Naples, FL 34116 USA Tel 239-963-5063
E-mail: ronkezeske@gmail.com.

Silent Devil Productions, *(978-0-9752582; 978-0-9786451; 978-0-9789281; 978-0-9791192; 978-0-9796902)* 3777 Center Way, Fairfax, VA 22033 USA
E-mail: silentdevilproductions@hotmail.com
Web site: http://www.silentdevil.com.

Silent Moon Bks., *(978-0-9721457)* P.O. Box 1280, Seeley Lake, MT 59868 USA
E-mail: bschieber@yahoo.com.

Silent Thunder Publishing, *(978-1-938680)* 5663 Balboa Ave. No. 401, San Diego, CA 92111 USA Tel 619-925-0547
E-mail: teresa@teresaburrell.com.

Silhouette Pond Productions, *(978-0-9761169)* P.O. Box 778, Palm Harbor, FL 34682-0778 USA (SAN 256-3886) Tel 727-771-1691
E-mail: ceceenter@tampabay.rr.com
Web site: http://www.silhouettepond.com.

Silk Waters Mooney, *(978-0-9776608)* 316 E. El Paso St., Brackettville, TX 78832 USA Tel 830-563-3443; P.O. Box 393, Brackettville, TX 78832
E-mail: swmooney@pukathemoose.com.

Silly Goose Productions, LLC, *(978-0-9711500)* 525 Cutty Trl. Apt. A, Lakeway, TX 78734-4836 USA
E-mail: sallysue678@yahoo.com; sally@onmyown.com
Web site: http://www.starfishpublishing.com; http://www.onmyown.com
Dist(s): **Follett School Solutions.**

Silly String Media, *(978-0-615-25193-6)* P.O. Box 884, Ross, CA 94957 USA
Web site: http://www.sillystringmedia.com
Dist(s): **Lulu Pr., Inc.**

Sillygeese Publishing, LLC, *(978-0-9987112; 978-1-951521)* P.O. Box 1434, Elgin, TX 78621 USA Tel 512-695-4048
E-mail: mydragonbubbles@gmail.com.

Siloam Pr. *Imprint of* **Charisma Media**

SILSNORRA LLC, *(978-1-951792)* 23 DANE CT, HAMPTON, VA 23666 USA Tel 757-969-9088
E-mail: ivryok@icloud.com.

Silver Bells Publishing Hse., *(978-0-9793517)* 19415 150th Ave., Tustin, MI 49688 USA Tel 231-829-3898
E-mail: dgbelleville@yahoo.com.

Silver Birch Ranch Pr., *(978-0-910421; 978-1-7328241)* Silver Birch Ranch, Star Rte., White Lake, WI 54491 USA (SAN 260-1354) Tel 715-484-8114.

SILVER BURDETT *Imprint of* **Savvas Learning Co.**

†Silver, Burdett & Ginn, Inc., *(978-0-382; 978-0-663; 978-1-4182)* Orders Addr.: P.O. Box 2500, Lebanon, IN 46052 USA Toll Free Fax: 800-841-8939; Toll Free: 800-552-2259; Edit Addr.: P.O. Box 480, Parsippany, NJ 07054 USA (SAN 204-5982); 108 Wilmot Rd., Suite 380, Midwest Div., Deerfield, IL 60015 (SAN 111-6517) Tel 708-945-1240
E-mail: customerservice@scottforesman.com
Web site: http://www.scottforesman.com/; *CIP.*

Silver Cloak Pubns., *(978-0-9777677)* P.O. Box 1027, Carpinteria, CA 93014-1027 USA
E-mail: SilverCloak@aol.com.

Silver Dagger Mysteries *Imprint of* **Overmountain Pr.**

Silver Dolphin Bks. *Imprint of* **Readerlink Distribution Services, LLC**

Silver Dolphin Bks. *Imprint of* **Printers Row Publishing Group**

Silver Dragon Bks. *Imprint of* **Zenescope Entertainment**

Silver Empire, *(978-1-949891)* 102 Wandering Ln, Harvest, AL 35749 USA Tel 256-503-0024
E-mail: russell@silverempire.org
Web site: https://silverempire.org/.

Silver Fire Publishing, *(978-0-9968168; 978-0-9976747; 978-1-7349929)* 701 Georgetown Ave, ELYRIA, OH 44035 USA Tel 440-366-6745
E-mail: theresalinden@oh.rr.com.

Silver Knight Publishing, LLC *See* **Black Forge**

Silver Lake Publishing, *(978-0-930868; 978-1-56343)* 1119 N. Broadway St., Aberdeen, WA 98520-2433 USA (SAN 203-8110) Toll Free: 800-663-3091 Do not confuse with Silver Lake Publishing, Morton, PA
E-mail: publisher@silverlakepublishing.com; SCRIBERE@aol.com; mthorpe@silverlakepub.com
Web site: http://www.silverlakepub.com
Dist(s): **SCB Distributors.**

Silver Leaf Bks., LLC, *(978-0-9744354; 978-0-9787782; 978-1-60975)* Orders Addr.: P.O. Box 6460, Holliston, MA 01746 USA Tel 508-740-6270; Toll Free: 888-823-6450; Edit Addr.: 13 Temi Rd., Holliston, MA 01746 USA
E-mail: Sales@SilverLeafBooks.com
Web site: http://www.silverleafbooks.com.

Silver Linden Pr., *(978-0-9981354)* 1094 37th Pl. NE No. 112, Salem, OR 97301 USA Tel 503-586-8696
E-mail: patti.bowman@msn.com.

Silver Moon Pr., *(978-1-881889; 978-1-893110)* 400 E. 85th St. Apt. 15K, New York, NY 10028-6324 USA Toll Free: 800-874-3320
E-mail: mail@silvermoonpress.com
Web site: http://www.silvermoonpress.com.

Silver Print Pr., Inc., *(978-0-9628064; 978-0-9749890)* Div. of Peter Miller LLC, 20 Crossroad, Suite No. 1, Colbyville, VT 05676 USA (SAN 299-0350) Tel 802-272-8851
E-mail: peter@petermillerphotography.com
Web site: http://www.petermillerphotography.com.

Silver Rim Pr., *(978-1-878611)* 2759 Park Lake Dr., Boulder, CO 80301 USA Tel 303-666-4290 (phone/fax)
E-mail: Sybilset@aol.com.

Silver Rose Publishing, *(978-0-9778211)* P.O. Box 462174, Aurora, CO 80046 USA Tel 303-946-2183; Toll Free: 800-431-1579; *Imprints:* Raynestorm Books (Raynestorm Bks)
E-mail: contact@silverrosepublishing.com
Web site: http://www.silverrosepublishing.com; http://www.bookch.com
Dist(s): **BCH Fulfillment & Distribution.**

Silver Snowflake Publishing, *(978-0-9778476)* P.O. Box 1256, East Greenwich, RI 02818 USA (SAN 850-394X)
E-mail: exteriordesigner@cox.net
Web site: http://www.themagicsceptre.com; http://www.silversnowflakepublishing.com.

Silver Thread Publishing, *(978-0-9844129; 978-0-9858326; 978-0-9861864; 978-0-9991794; 978-1-7353845)* 730 Vista Pacifica Cir., Pismo Beach, CA 93449 USA (SAN 859-3248)
E-mail: jeannie@asilverthread.com
Web site: http://www.asilverthread.com.

Silver Whistle *Imprint of* **Harcourt Trade Pubs.**

Silver Wings Publishing *See* **Snowy Wings Publishing**

SilverBrown Bks., *(978-0-9840922)* 9355 54th Ave., S., Seattle, WA 98118 USA Tel 206-721-3794.

SilverhawkCorp., *(978-0-9772933)* 618 Draper Heights Way, Draper, UT 84020 USA.

Silverman, Toby, *(978-0-9793475)* 1611 Hemlock Farms, Lords Valley, PA 18428 USA
E-mail: tsilverman@noln.com.

Silvey Bk. Publishing, *(978-0-9762446)* P.O. Box 5171, Goodyear, AZ 85338-5171 USA Fax: 623-853-9172
E-mail: silveybooks@earthlink.net.

Simakan Group, The, *(978-0-9767812)* P.O. Box 492496, Atlanta, GA 30349 USA Fax: 770-981-1046
E-mail: info@playingyouragame.com
Web site: http://www.playingyouragame.com.

Simba Publishing Co., *(978-0-9765982)* 5413 Whistler Dr., Tallahassee, FL 32317 USA (SAN 256-4270) Tel 850-878-7741
E-mail: gladys_gikiri@simbapublishingcompany.com
Web site: http://www.simbapublishingcompany.com.

Simba's Publishing, *(978-0-9765475)* P.O. Box 27634, Fresno, CA 93729-7634 USA.

Simbosa Publishing, *(978-0-9996717)* 314 Vineyard Ln, Carlsbad, NM 88220 USA Tel 575-887-5858
E-mail: drlisas@hotmail.com.

Simcha Media Group, *(978-0-943706; 978-965-465; 978-1-930143; 978-1-932687; 978-1-934440; 978-1-936068)* 94 Dwight Pl., Englewood, NJ 07631 USA Tel 201-503-1151; Fax: 201-503-9761; *Imprints:* Devora Publishing (DevorPubng); Pitspopany Press (Pitspopany Pr)
Web site: http://www.pitspopany.com
Dist(s): **Coronet Bks.**
Lulu Pr., Inc.

Simmons, Kristina, *(978-0-9769843)* 40 Christopher Cir., Middletown, CT 06457 USA.

Simmons, Laura, *(978-0-692-16869-1)* P.O. Box 14, Richton Park, IL 60471 USA Tel 708-269-6928
E-mail: tgirl06@att.net
Dist(s): **CreateSpace Independent Publishing Platform.**

Simmons, Sukether Williams *See* **Shrewsbury Publishing**

Simms, Laura Storyteller, *(978-0-9911692)* 814 Broadway, New York, NY 10003 USA Tel 212-674-3479
E-mail: storymentor2010@gmail.com
Web site: http://www.laurasimms.com.

Simon & Barklee, Inc./ExplorerMedia, *(978-0-9704661; 978-0-9714502; 978-0-578-47400-7)* 2280 E. Whidbey Shores Rd., Langley, WA 98260 USA Tel 360-730-2360; Fax: 360-730-2355; *Imprints:* Explorer Media (Explorer Media)
E-mail: cwsch@whidbey.com
Web site: http://simonandbarklee.com
Dist(s): **Quality Bks., Inc.**

Simon & Brown, *(978-0-9814843; 978-1-936041; 978-1-61382; 978-1-7317)* 3140 N 52nd Ave, Hollywood, FL 33021 USA Tel 305-610-7128
E-mail: info@simonandbrown.com
Web site: http://www.simonandbrown.com.

Simon & Northrop of Cal, Incorporated *See* **Martell Publishing Co**

Simon & Schuster, *(978-0-671; 978-0-684; 978-0-689; 978-0-914676; 978-0-7432; 978-1-4165; 978-1-4391; 978-1-4516; 978-1-4767; 978-1-5011; 978-1-9821; 978-1-7214)* Div. of Simon & Schuster, Inc., Orders Addr.: 100 Front St., Riverside, NJ 08075 USA (SAN 200-2442) Toll Free Fax: 800-943-9831; Toll Free: 800-223-2336 (ordering); 800-223-2348 (customer service); Edit Addr.: a/o Subsidiary Rights, 11th Flr., 1230 Avenue of the Americas, New York, NY 10020 USA (SAN 200-2450) Tel 212-698-7000; Fax: 212-698-7007; 212-632-8099 (Rights & Permissions); 212-698-1269 (Pocket Bks. Rights & Permissions); Toll Free: 800-897-7650 (customer financial services); 100 Front St., Riverside, NJ 08075 (SAN 852-5471) Tel 856-824-2175; *Imprints:* Atria Books (Atria); Beyond Words (BWords); North Star Way (NorthStarWay)
E-mail: ssonline_feedback@simonsays.com; consumer.customerservice@simonandschuster.com
Web site: http://www.simonsays.com; http://www.oasis.simonandschuster.com; http://www.simonandschuster.com/
Dist(s): **Cengage Gale**
Giron Bks.
Hachette Bk. Group
Libros Sin Fronteras
Simon & Schuster, Inc.
Studio Fun International
TextStream
Thorndike Pr.
Ulverscroft Large Print Bks., Ltd.

Simon & Schuster Audio, *(978-0-671; 978-0-7435; 978-1-4423)* Orders Addr.: 100 Front St., Riverside, NJ 08075 USA Toll Free Fax: 800-943-9831 (orders); Toll Free: 800-223-2336 (customer service); Edit Addr.: a/o Sub Rights Manager, 11th fl., 1230 Avenue of the Americas, New York, NY 10020 USA Tel 212-698-7000; Fax: 212-698-2370; 212-632-8091 (Rights & Permissions)
Web site: http://www.simonsays.com/subs/index.cfm?areaid=45
Dist(s): **Blackstone Audio, Inc.**
Follett School Solutions
Simon & Schuster
Simon & Schuster, Inc.

Simon & Schuster Bks. For Young Readers *Imprint of* **Simon & Schuster Bks. For Young Readers**

Simon & Schuster Bks. For Young Readers *Imprint of* **Simon & Schuster/Paula Wiseman Bks.**

Simon & Schuster Bks. For Young Readers, Div. of Simon & Schuster Children's Publishing, 1230 Ave. of the Americas, New York, NY 10020 USA; *Imprints:* Simon & Schuster Books For Young Readers (S&SBFYng); Simon & Schuster/Paula Wiseman Books (S&SPaulaW); SAGA Press (SAGA Press); Salaam Reads (SalaamReads)
Dist(s): **Simon & Schuster, Inc.**

Simon & Schuster Canada (CAN) *Dist. by* **S and S Inc.**

Simon & Schuster Children's Publishing, *(978-0-02; 978-0-671; 978-0-684; 978-0-689; 978-0-7434; 978-1-4169; 978-1-4424; 978-0-85707)* Orders Addr.: 100 Front St., Riverside, NJ 08075 USA Toll Free Fax: 800-943-9831; Toll Free: 800-223-2336; Edit Addr.: a/o Subsidiary Rights, 4th floor, 1230 Avenue of the Americas, New York, NY 10020 USA Tel 212-698-7200; Fax: 212-698-2797 (Rights & Permissions); *Imprints:* Aladdin Library (AlaLib); Atheneum Books for Young Readers (AthenSS); Atheneum/Anne Schwartz Books (Anne Schwart); Atheneum/Richard Jackson Books (Rich Jack); Simon Spotlight (SSpot); Simon & Schuster/Paula Wiseman Books (S&SPaulaW); Aladdin Paperbacks (AladdinPaperbcks); Atheneum/Caitlyn Dlouhy Books (Caitlyn Dlou); Aladdin (Aladdin)
Web site: http://www.simonsays.com
Dist(s): **Children's Plus, Inc.**
Follett School Solutions
Lectorum Pubns., Inc.
Simon & Schuster
Simon & Schuster, Inc.

†Simon & Schuster, Inc., *(978-0-02; 978-0-671; 978-0-684; 978-0-689; 978-0-88138; 978-0-914676; 978-0-937860; 978-1-55850; 978-1-58062; 978-0-7432; 978-0-7434; 978-0-7435; 978-1-59337; 978-1-4165; 978-1-4169; 978-1-59869; 978-1-60550; 978-1-4391; 978-1-4405; 978-1-4423; 978-1-4424; 978-1-4516; 978-0-85707; 978-1-4814; 978-1-5072; 978-1-5082; 978-1-5344; 978-1-7971) Div. of Viacom Co., Orders Addr.: 100 Front St., Riverside, NJ 08075 USA Toll Free Fax: 800-943-9831; Toll Free: 800-223-2336 (orders); 800-223-2348 (customer service); Edit Addr.: 1230 Ave. of the Americas, New York, NY 10020 USA Tel 212-698-7000*
E-mail: Consumer.CustomerService@simonandschuster.com
Web site: http://www.simonsays.com; http://www.simonandschuster.com
Dist(s): **Children's Plus, Inc.**
Follett School Solutions; *CIP.*

Simon & Schuster, Ltd. (GBR) *(978-0-671; 978-0-684; 978-0-689; 978-0-7432; 978-0-7434; 978-1-84738; 978-1-84737; 978-0-85720; 978-0-85707; 978-1-84983; 978-1-4711) Dist. by* **S and S Inc.**

Simon & Schuster Trade *See* **Simon & Schuster**

Simon & Schuster/Paula Wiseman Bks. *Imprint of* **Simon & Schuster Children's Publishing**

Simon & Schuster/Paula Wiseman Bks. *Imprint of* **Simon & Schuster Bks. For Young Readers**

Simon & Schuster/Paula Wiseman Bks. *Imprint of* **Simon & Schuster/Paula Wiseman Bks.**

Simon & Schuster/Paula Wiseman Bks., Div. of Simon & Schuster Children's Publishing, 1230 Ave. of the Americas, New York, NY 10020 USA; *Imprints:* Simon & Schuster Books For Young Readers (S&SBFYng);

Simon & Schuster/Paula Wiseman Books (S&SPaulaW)
Dist(s): **Simon & Schuster, Inc.**

Simon & Simon, LLC *See* **Maestro Classics**

Simon & Son Publishing, *(978-0-9773665)* 4995 Paist Rd., Doylestown, PA 18901 USA; *Imprints:* Prophecy, The (Prophecy)
E-mail: frankfsp1@comcast.net
Web site: http://www.simonsonpublishing.com.

Simon, Les, *(978-0-9761914)* Orders Addr.: P.O. Box 57274, Washington, DC 20037-0274 USA Tel 202-659-3639; Fax: 202-457-1155; Edit Addr.: 1400 20th St., NW, No. 805, Washington, DC 20036 USA
E-mail: lessim2003@yahoo.com.

Simon Peter Pr., Inc., *(978-0-9761533; 978-0-9777430; 978-1-936159)* P.O. Box 2187, Oldsmar, FL 34677 USA Fax: 727-772-0368
E-mail: theaben@aol.com
Web site: http://www.simonpeterpress.com
Dist(s): **eBookit.com.**

Simon Pulse *Imprint of* **Simon Pulse**

Simon Pulse, Div.of Simon & Schuster Children's Publishing, 1230 Ave. of the Americas, New York, NY 10020 USA; *Imprints:* Simon Pulse (SimonPulse)
Dist(s): **Children's Plus, Inc.**
Simon & Schuster, Inc.

Simon Pulse/Beyond Words, 1230 Avenue of the Americas, New York, NY 10020 USA
Dist(s): **Simon & Schuster, Inc.**

Simon Pulse/Mercury Ink *Imprint of* **Simon Pulse/Mercury Ink**

Simon Pulse/Mercury Ink, 1230 Avenue of the Americas, New York, NY 10020 USA; *Imprints:* Simon Pulse/Mercury Ink (SimoPulseMer)
Dist(s): **Simon & Schuster, Inc.**

Simon Scribbles *Imprint of* **Simon Scribbles**

Simon Scribbles, Div. of Simon & Schuster Children's Publishing, 1230 Ave. of the Americas, New York, NY 10020 USA; *Imprints:* Simon Scribbles (SScribbles)
Dist(s): **Simon & Schuster, Inc.**

Simon Spotlight *Imprint of* **Simon & Schuster Children's Publishing**

Simon Spotlight *Imprint of* **Simon Spotlight**

Simon Spotlight, Div. of Simon & Schuster Children's Publishing, 1230 Ave. of the Americas, New York, NY 10020 USA; *Imprints:* Simon Spotlight (SimonSpotlight)
Dist(s): **Simon & Schuster, Inc.**

Simon Spotlight/Nickelodeon *Imprint of* **Simon Spotlight/Nickelodeon**

Simon Spotlight/Nickelodeon, Div.of Simon & Schuster Children's Publishing, 1230 Ave. of the Americas, New York, NY 10020 USA; *Imprints:* Simon Spotlight/Nickelodeon (SSpotNick)
Dist(s): **Simon & Schuster, Inc.**

Simone, Julia, *(978-0-692-82697-3; 978-0-692-82698-0)*
E-mail: jeffwcrawford5+LVP0003217@gmail.com; jeffwcrawford5+LVP0003217@gmail.com.

simoneink, llc, *(978-0-692-98877-0)* P.O. Box 25723, Washington, DC 20007 USA Tel 703-534-8100
E-mail: simone@simoneink.com.

Simone's Bks., *(978-0-615-18719-8; 978-0-615-20614-1)* 65 Winding Wood Dr., Apt. 4A, Sayreville, NJ 08872 USA
Dist(s): **Lulu Pr., Inc.**

Simpatico Bks., *(978-0-9771322)* P.O. Box 201, Heber Springs, AR 72543 USA Tel 501-362-2858
Web site: http://www.simpaticobooks.com.

Simple Faith Bks. *Imprint of* **Sunrise Mountain Bks.**

Simple Fish Bk. Co., LLC, *(978-0-9817596; 978-0-9837932)* 5500 Abercorn St., Suite 32, Savannah, GA 31405 USA
E-mail: bbrooks@simplefishbookco.com
Web site: http://www.simplefishbookco.com.

Simple Ink, LLC, *(978-0-9794167)* P.O. Box 1825, Hays, KS 67601 USA
E-mail: gmarconette@simpleink.net; gameck@gmail.com
Web site: http://www.simpleink.net.

Simple Productions *See* **Shepard Pubns.**

Simple Thoughts Pr., LLC, *(978-0-9768557)* Orders Addr.: P.O. Box 759, Northfield, MN 55057 USA; Edit Addr.: 14345 Falk Ave., Northfield, NJ 55057 USA
Web site: http://www.backandforthjournal.com.

Simplemente Maria Pr., *(978-0-9766811; 978-1-7346768)* 2611 Samarkand Dr., Santa Barbara, CA 93105 USA Tel 805-962-2497
E-mail: mary@maryheebner.com
Web site: http://www.simplementemariapress.com; http://www.maryheebner.com.

Simpler Life Pr., *(978-0-9619806)* 1599 S. Uinta Way, Denver, CO 80231 USA (SAN 246-5809) Tel 303-751-2454; Fax: 303-671-5200
E-mail: avs@vansteenhouse.com
Web site: http://www.vansteenhouse.com.

Simplex Pubns., *(978-0-9623113; 978-1-929304)* Orders Addr.: 575 Larkspur Plaza Dr., Unit 4, Larkspur, CA 94939-1476 USA
E-mail: gosmith@pacbell.net
Web site: http://www.simplexpublications.com
Dist(s): **Bookpeople.**

SimpliFun Studios, *(978-1-932839)* 2070 Stratford Dr., Milpitas, CA 95035 USA Tel 408-946-8632; Toll Free: 800-850-4-FUN
E-mail: mail@simplifun.com
Web site: http://www.childrenspartygames.com.

Simply Hooked, *(978-0-692-77545-5)* 12308 Marblehead Dr., Tampa, FL 33626 USA Tel 843-812-7686
E-mail: mwynnsc@hotmail.com
Web site: www.simplyhooked.co.

Simply Read Bks. (CAN) *(978-0-9688768; 978-1-894965; 978-1-897476; 978-1-927018) Dist. by* **IngramPubServ.**

Simply Silly Stories, *(978-0-9838964)* 3603 Forsythia Dr., Wylie, TX 75098 USA Tel 214-597-8999
E-mail: bewilson@simplysillystories.com.

SimplyCMB,LLC, *(978-0-9980042)* 1958 S. Cherry Blossom Ln., Suttons Bay, MI 49682 USA
E-mail: yroehler@bookpublishing.com.

Simpson, Charles B., *(978-0-9703818)* 234 Faulkner Ave., Hazard, KY 41701 USA Tel 606-436-4652
E-mail: cngsimpson@earthlink.net
Web site: http://www.appalachianwriter.com.

Sims, Brianna V. *See* **Growsies**

Simsand Publishing, *(978-0-9765580)* 8 Huntington Pl. Dr., Atlanta, GA 30350 USA Tel 678-458-0759
E-mail: timsanders01@aol.com.

Sinanan, Cindy, *(978-0-9769004)* 10169 New Hampshire Ave., No. 155, Silver Spring, MD 20903 USA
E-mail: mybook@mris.com.

Sincerity Publishing, *(978-0-9848314; 978-1-945915)* 450 Pine Flower Ct., Highlands Ranch, CO 80126 USA
E-mail: hwhitmore12@icloud.com
Web site: http://www.HughWhitmore.com.

Sinclair, A. E., *(978-0-692-78356-6)* 8518 OAK VIEW DR, Chattanooga, TN 37421 USA Tel 423-693-3597
E-mail: aprilsinclair355@gmail.com.

Sinclair, Loretta, *(978-0-615-24452-5; 978-0-615-40432-5; 978-0-9916159; 978-0-9992025)* P.O. Box 2052, Rancho Cordova, CA 95741 USA
E-mail: lori@sinclairinkspot.com
Web site: http://www.sinclairinkspot.com.

Sinclair/Polk, *(978-0-615-20281-5)* 1717 W. Green Tree Rd., No. 204, Glendale, WI 53209 USA Tel 414-704-3207
E-mail: janpolk@janpolk.com; margerysinclair@juno.com
Web site: http://www.janpolk.com; http://www.margerysinclair.com; http://www.ayearofgoodmanners.com
Dist(s): **Signature Bks., LLC.**

SingaporeMath.com, Inc., *(978-0-9741573; 978-1-932906; 978-1-947226)* 19535 SW 129th Ave., Tualatin, OR 97062 USA (SAN 255-6510) Tel 503-557-8100; Fax: 503-557-8103
E-mail: accounting@singaporemath.com; dthomas@singaporemath.com; nicholle@singaporemath.com
Web site: http://www.singaporemath.com.

SingaporeMath.com, Incorporated *See* **SingaporeMath.com, Inc.**

singer, david, *(978-0-692-05439-0; 978-0-692-05478-9; 978-0-9998224; 978-0-692-15279-9; 978-0-692-16541-6; 978-0-692-17280-3; 978-1-7326875)* 19195 Mystic Pointe Dr. Apt. 2606, Aventura, FL 33180 USA Tel 786-525-1815
E-mail: drdsinger@gmail.com; drdsinger@hotmail.com
Web site: www.davidsingerauthor.com
Dist(s): **Ingram Content Group.**

Singing Magpies, *(978-0-692-16621-5)* 12500 Spring Creek Rd., Parker, CO 80138 USA Tel 720-270-3508
E-mail: jenmtaos@gmail.com.

Singing Moon Pr., *(978-0-9770497)* Singing Moon Press #239 2601 S. Minnesota Ave., Ste 105, Sioux Falls, SD 57105-4750 USA; *Imprints:* Itty Bitty Kitty (Itty Bitty Kitty)
E-mail: editor@singingmoonpress.com
Web site: http://www.singingmoonpress.com.

Singing River Pubns., *(978-0-9709575; 978-0-9759953; 978-0-9774831; 978-0-9789870; 978-0-9822596)* Orders Addr.: P.O. Box 72, Ely, MN 55731 USA (SAN 254-136X) Tel 218-365-3498; Fax: 218-365-5792; Edit Addr.: 3365 Wolf Lake Rd., Ely, MN 55731 USA
E-mail: cmoroni@singingriverpublications.com; info@singingriverpublications.com
Web site: http://www.singingriverpublications.com
Dist(s): **Adventure Pubns.**
Partners Bk. Distributing, Inc.

Singing Tree Pr., *(978-0-9708005)* P.O. Box 722, Auburn, CA 95604 USA (SAN 255-4011) Tel 530-823-9284
E-mail: editor@mail.singingtreepress.com; orders@singingtreepress.com
Web site: http://www.singingtreepress.com.

Singing Winds Pr., *(978-1-61955)* 1331 SE Ellis, Dallas, OR 97338 USA Tel 503-551-7241 (phone/fax)
E-mail: singingwindspress@gmail.com
Web site: www.singingwindspress.com.

Siniff Publishing *See* **Country Messenger Pr. Publishing Group, LLC**

Sinolingua (CHN) *(978-7-80052) Dist. by* **China Bks.**

Sinonexus Publishing Co., *(978-0-9787664)* 65 Wethersfield Rd., Bellingham, MA 02019-1045 USA Tel 508-966-4423
E-mail: sinonexus@yahoo.com
Web site: http://www.sinonexus.org.

Sinsinawa Dominicans, Inc., *(978-0-9774934)* 585 Cty. Rd., Z, Sinsinawa, WI 53824-9701 USA Tel 608-748-4411; Fax: 608-748-4491
E-mail: communication@sinsinawa.org
Web site: http://www.sinsinawa.org.

Sioux City Lewis & Clark Interpretive Ctr., The, *(978-0-9753860; 978-0-9785063)* 900 Larsen Pk. Rd., Sioux city, IA 51103 USA Tel 712-224-5242; Fax: 712-224-5244
E-mail: mpoole@siouxcitylcic.com
Web site: http://www.siouxcitylcic.com.

Sippel, Robert, *(978-0-692-84050-4)* 8745 Mcdowell Rd, Scottsdale, AZ 85257 USA Tel 928-254-0081
E-mail: rsippel@mail.com.

Sir Brody Bks., *(978-0-692-39979-8; 978-0-9978611; 978-1-951551)* 605 Sycamore Dr. NE, CLEVELAND, TN 37312 USA Tel 423-595-7005
Web site: sirbrody.com.

Sir Pigglesworth Publishing, Inc., *(978-1-68055)* 1515 N. Town East Blvd., Suite. 138-118, Mesquite, TX 75150 USA Tel 469-416-25
E-mail: bill.wagner@whereintheworldi ssitpi geleswofih.com
Web site: www. whereintheworldissirpigglesworth. com.

Sir Wrinkles Pr., *(978-0-9766639)* 30692 Fox Run Ln., San Juan Capistrano, CA 92675 USA
Web site: http://www.sirwrinklesthebulldog.com.

Siren-BookStrand, Inc., *(978-1-933563; 978-1-60601; 978-1-61034; 978-1-61926; 978-1-62241; 978-1-62242; 978-1-62740; 978-1-62741; 978-1-63258; 978-1-63259; 978-1-68295; 978-1-64010; 978-1-64243; 978-1-64637)* 2500 S. Lamar Blvd., Austin, TX 78704 USA (SAN 256-6869) Toll Free: 866-887-4736
E-mail: diana.debalko@sirenpublishing.com
Web site: http://www.sirenpublishing.com; http://www.sirenbookstrand.com.

Sirius Entertainment, Inc., *(978-1-57989)* Orders Addr.: P.O. Box X, Unadilla, NY 13849 USA Tel 607-369-2620; Fax: 607-369-2623; Edit Addr.: P.O. Box X, Unadilla, NY 13849-0723 USA
E-mail: sirent@aol.com
Dist(s): **Diamond Comic Distributors, Inc.**
Diamond Bk. Distributors.

SIRS Mandarin *See* **SIRS Publishing, Inc.**

†SIRS Publishing, Inc., *(978-0-89777; 978-0-9678914)* Div. of ProQuest Information and Learning, 5201 Congress Ave., Suite 250, Boca Raton, FL 33487 USA (SAN 222-8920) Tel 561-994-0079; Fax: 561-995-4074; Toll Free: 800-521-0600
Web site: http://www.proquestK12.com; *CIP.*

Siruela, Ediciones S.A. (ESP) *(978-84-7844; 978-84-85876; 978-84-15937) Dist. by* **Lectorum Pubns.**

Sistemas Tecnicos de Edicion, S.A. de C.V. (MEX) *(978-968-6579; 978-970-629; 978-968-6048; 978-968-6135; 978-968-6394) Dist. by* **AIMS Intl.**

Sisterhaus Publishing, *(978-0-578-05291-5)* 40555 La Colima Rd., Suite 100, Temecula, CA 92591 USA
E-mail: lisaharding4@yahoo.com.

Sisters of Providence, *(978-1-893789; 978-0-9897397)* a/o Ann Casper, SP, Sisters of Providence Owens Hall, Saint Mary-of-the-Woods, IN 47876 USA Tel 812-535-2800; Fax: 812-535-1009 Do not confuse with Sisters of Providence in Holyoke, MA
E-mail: acasper@spsmw.org
Web site: http://www.sistersofprovidence.org.

Sisters Three Publishing Inc., *(978-0-9787375)* 5026 SW. 94th Ave., Cooper City, FL 33328 USA Fax: 954-885-8007
Web site: http://www.sistersthreeseries.com.

Sisu Home Entertainment, Inc., *(978-1-56086; 978-1-884857)* 340 W. 39th St., 6th Flr., New York, NY 10018 USA Tel 212-779-1559; Fax: 212-779-7115; Toll Free Fax: 888-221-7478; Toll Free: 800-223-7478
E-mail: sisu@sisuent.com
Web site: http://www.sisuent.com
Dist(s): **Follett School Solutions.**

Sitare, Ltd., *(978-0-940178)* Orders Addr.: 1101 N. Rainbow Blvd., No. 52, Las Vegas, NV 89108 USA (SAN 217-0833) Tel 702-990-0688
E-mail: editor@dlvmagazine.com
Web site: http://www.dlvmagazine.com.

SitStayRead, *(978-0-9970312)* 2849 N. Clark St., Chicago, IL 60657 USA Tel 773-661-9251
E-mail: info@sitstayread.org
Web site: http://sitstayread.org.

SivART Gallery, The, *(978-0-692-94926-9; 978-0-578-50746-0)* 9934 Gray Dove Ct., Charlotte, NC 28216 USA Tel 704-607-9728
E-mail: tathompson1987@yahoo.com
Dist(s): **Ingram Content Group.**

Six Foot Press *See* **Six Foot Pr., LLC**

Six Foot Pr., LLC, *(978-1-64442)* 4200 Montrose Blvd., Houston, TX 77006 USA Tel 323-612-8855
E-mail: coertv@6ft.com; charlesk@6ft.com
Dist(s): **Ingram Publisher Services.**

Six Seconds, *(978-0-9629123; 978-0-9716772; 978-0-9797343; 978-1-935667)* Orders Addr.: P.O. Box 1985, Freedom, CA 95019 USA Tel 831-763-1800
E-mail: staff@6seconds.org; jenny@6seconds.org
Web site: http://www.6seconds.org.

Six Suns Publishing, *(978-0-9654200)* P.O. Box 112852, Anchorage, AK 99511 USA Tel 907-344-2905
Dist(s): **Todd Communications**
Wizard Works.

Sixth Avenue Bks. *Imprint of* **Grand Central Publishing**

Sixth&Spring Bks., *(978-1-931543; 978-1-933027; 978-1-936096)* 233 Spring St., 3rd Flr., New York, NY 10013 USA; *Imprints:* Hart, Chris Books (Chris Hart)
E-mail: wendy@sohopublishing.com
Web site: http://sixthandspringbooks.com
Dist(s): **Sterling Publishing Co., Inc.**

Sizzle Pr. *Imprint of* **Little Bee Books Inc.**

SKALIUM Pr., *(978-0-9996836; 978-1-7355001)* 131 Overbrook, Irvine, CA 92620 USA Tel 949-903-9635
E-mail: bvukov71@gmail.com.

Skandisk, Inc., *(978-0-9615394; 978-1-57534)* 6667 W. Old Shakopee Rd., Suite 109, Bloomington, MN 55438-2622 USA (SAN 695-4405) Tel 952-829-8998; Fax: 952-829-8992; Toll Free: 800-468-2424 (orders)
E-mail: lhamnes@skandisk.com; tomten@skandisk.com
Web site: http://www.skandisk.com.

SkateRight Publishing, *(978-0-9798876)* 2913 Cummings, Berkley, MI 48072-4807 USA.

Skazka Publishing, *(978-0-9994522)* P.O. Box 661, Gaston, OR 97119 USA Tel 503-896-6680
E-mail: connect@ekaterinawalter.com.

Skeete, D., *(978-0-9769012)* P.O. Box 737, New York, NY 10030 USA
E-mail: msdss@aol.com
Web site: http://www.hiphopwordsearch.com.

Skelley, James, *(978-1-947847)* 2005 California St. No. 6, Mountain View, CA 94040 USA Tel 417-291-9069; *Imprints:* LawMux Press (Lawmux Pr)
E-mail: jpskelley04@gmail.com.

Skeptical Guitarist Pubns., *(978-0-9665029; 978-0-9788609; 978-1-944210)* Orders Addr.: P.O. Box 5824, Raleigh, NC 27650-5824 USA Tel 919-834-2031; Edit Addr.: 714 Faircloth St., Raleigh, NC 27607-4013 USA
E-mail: bruceemery@mindspring.com
Web site: http://www.skepticalguitarist.com/.

Sketch Publishing, *(978-0-9726764)* 414 S. 43rd St, Philadelphia, PA 19104 USA Tel 215-243-0644
E-mail: msand227@aol.com.

Sketches From The Heart Publishing, *(978-0-9759300)* P.O. Box 3431, Boulder, CO 80307 USA
Web site: www.sketchesfromtheheart.com
Dist(s): **Bks. West**
Common Ground Distributors, Inc.
Partners/West Book Distributors
Quality Bks., Inc.

Skillful & Soulful Pr., *(978-0-9989520)* 3615 Elford Dr., Whittier, CA 90601 USA Tel 626-664-6471
E-mail: skillfulandsoulfulmovement@gmail.com
Web site: www.skillfulandsoulful.com.

Skillin Marketing/Advertising, Inc., *(978-0-578-40414-1; 978-0-578-40415-8)* 7560 St. Marlo CC Pkwy, Duluth, GA 30097 USA Tel 404-663-8837
E-mail: joe@skillinmarketing.com
Dist(s): **Ingram Content Group.**

Skinder-Strauss Assocs., *(978-1-57741)* Orders Addr.: P.O. Box 50, Newark, NJ 07101 USA Tel 973-642-1440; Fax: 973-242-1905; Toll Free: 800-444-4041; Edit Addr.: 240 Mulberry St., Newark, NJ 07101 USA
E-mail: ed@elaw.com
Web site: http://lawdiary.com; http://elaw.com.

Skinned Knee Publishing, *(978-0-9989580; 978-1-949633)* 902 Gardner Rd., Austin, TX 78721 USA Tel 512-203-7939
E-mail: gabgar30@yahoo.com.

Skinner, Emily, *(978-0-9994196)* P.O. Box 8590, Seminole, FL 33775 USA Tel 727-409-6790
E-mail: eskinner@knology.net
Web site: www.emilyskinnerbooks.com.

Skinner Hse. Bks. *Imprint of* **Unitarian Universalist Assn.**

Skinner, Kerry L., *(978-0-9648743; 978-1-931080)* Div. of Think Life/Change, Orders Addr.: 67 N. Marshside Pl., The Woodlands, TX 77389 USA; *Imprints:* KLS LifeChange Ministries (KLS LifeChge)
E-mail: kerry@kerryskinner.com
Web site: http://www.kerryskinner.com.

Skinner, Lynn C., *(978-0-9991679; 978-1-7336531)* 402 W. College St., Ailey, GA 30410 USA Tel 912-583-4741
E-mail: skipandlynn@windstream.net.

Skinny On (tm), The *Imprint of* **Rand Media Co**

Skira *Imprint of* **Rizzoli International Pubns., Inc.**

Skirvan, Pamela, *(978-0-9742943)* P.O. Box 484, New Harbor, ME 04554-0484 USA.

Skookum Bks., *(978-0-692-79518-7; 978-0-9983078; 978-0-9985225)* 1 Manatee Ct, Simpsonville, SC 29681 USA Tel 864-552-1055; Toll Free: 864-552-1055
Dist(s): **CreateSpace Independent Publishing Platform.**

Skromovas, Andrea, *(978-1-7322796)* 5481 Grand Pk. Pl, Boca Raton, FL 33486 USA Tel 954-562-6702
E-mail: andrea.skromovas@hotmail.com.

Sky Blue Pr., *(978-0-9652364; 978-0-9774851; 978-0-9889170; 978-0-9987246; 978-1-7357459)* 20561 Anndyke Way, Germantown, MD 20874 USA Tel 505-603-5738
E-mail: orders@skybluepress.com; skybluepress@skybluepress.com
Web site: http://www.skybluepress.com
Dist(s): **Smashwords.**

Sky Carrier Pr., *(978-1-880589)* P.O. Box 442, Fayetteville, NY 13066 USA Tel 605-486-4310; 315-637-9511
E-mail: swagner711@aol.com.

Sky Pony Pr. *Imprint of* **Skyhorse Publishing Co., Inc.**

†Sky Publishing, *(978-0-933346; 978-1-931559; 978-0-615-38976-9)* Div. of New Track Media, 90 Sherman St. Ste. D, Cambridge, MA 02140-3264 USA (SAN 212-4556) Toll Free: 800-253-0245
E-mail: orders@SkyandTelescope.com
Web site: http://www.skyandtelescope.com
Dist(s): **F&W Media, Inc.**
Sterling Publishing Co., Inc.
Two Rivers Distribution; *CIP.*

Sky Publishing Corporation *See* **Sky Publishing**

Sky Rocket Pr., *(978-0-9724637)* Orders Addr.: 2104 Old York Dr., Keller, TX 76248-5497 USA Tel 817-498-4300; Fax: 757-299-3608
E-mail: robert@rocketvilletexas.com
Web site: http://www.rocketvilletexas.com.

Sky Sun Publishing, *(978-0-578-20088-0; 978-0-578-20247-1)* 12128 Lakeshore Drive, Clermont, FL 34711 USA.

Skybox Event Productions, *(978-0-692-02935-0; 978-0-692-03261-9)* 506 S. Meadows Rd., Covina, CA 91791 USA (SAN 860-4177).

Skybox Publishing *See* **Skybox Event Productions**

Skyd LLC, *(978-0-9963107)* 1543 NW 64th St., Seattle, WA 98107 USA Tel 412-414-6820
E-mail: dan@hellervogel.com
Web site: http://skydmagazine.com.

Skyhook Pr. *Imprint of* **Shepard Pubns.**

Skyhorse Publishing Co., Inc., *(978-0-934672; 978-0-941873; 978-1-56148; 978-1-892389; 978-1-59780; 978-1-60239; 978-1-61608; 978-1-61145;*

978-1-936697; 978-1-61321; 978-1-62087; 978-1-62153; 978-1-62636; 978-1-62872; 978-1-62873; 978-1-62914; 978-1-940456; 978-1-63144; 978-1-63158; 978-1-63220; 978-1-63450; 978-1-68099; 978-1-5107; 978-1-68358) 307 W. 36th Street, Flr. 11, New York, NY 10018 USA Tel 212-643-6816; 212-643-6819; Imprints: Arcade Publishing (ARCADE PUBLISH); Sky Pony Press (SKY PONY PRESS); Allworth Press (Allwrth Pr); Yucca Publishing (Yucca Pub); Good Books (GoodBksUSA); Racehorse Publishing (Racehorse Pub)
E-mail: skyhorsepublishing@gmail.com
Web site: http://www.skyhorsepublishing.com
Dist(s): **Children's Plus, Inc.**
Follett School Solutions
INscribe Digital
MBI Distribution Services/Quayside Distribution
MyiLibrary
National Bk. Network
Open Road Integrated Media, Inc.
Publishers Group West (PGW)
Random Hse., Inc.
Simon & Schuster, Inc.
Sterling Publishing Co., Inc.
Two Rivers Distribution.

Skylar Doreal, (978-0-9667747; 978-0-578-49302-2; 978-0-578-49303-9) 1304 N. Van Buren St., Allentown, PA 18109 USA.

Skylight Paths Publishing Imprint of **LongHill Partners, Inc.**

Skylight Publishing, (978-0-9654853; 978-0-9727055; 978-0-9824775; 978-0-9972528) Orders Addr.: 9 Bartlet St., Suite 70, Andover, MA 01810-3655 USA Tel 978-475-1431 (phone/fax); Toll Free: 888-476-1940
E-mail: support@skylit.com
Web site: http://www.skylit.com.

Skyline Pubn., (978-0-9723493; 978-0-9815846; 978-0-9843602; 978-0-615-66773-7) P.O. Box 295, Stormville, NY 12582-0295 USA; Imprints: Water Forest Press (Wtr Forest) Do not confuse with companies with the same or similar name in Lancaster, OH, Oakland Park, FL
E-mail: skylineeditor@aol.com
Web site: http://www.skylinemagazines.com
Dist(s): **CreateSpace Independent Publishing Platform.**

Skyline Publishing, (978-0-918981) Orders Addr.: P.O. Box 1118, Columbia Falls, MT 59912 USA (SAN 669-8662) Tel 406-892-5560; Fax: 406-892-1922; Edit Addr.: a/o Skyline Publishing, 3101 Hwy. 206, Columbia Falls, MT 59912 USA Do not confuse with companies with similar names in Londonderry, NH, Saint George, UT
E-mail: carolynj@rolandcheek.com
Web site: http://www.rolandcheek.com
Dist(s): **Partners/West Book Distributors.**

SkyMacSyd Publishing, (978-0-9767244) P.O. Box 56363, Little Rock, AR 72215 USA.

SkyMark Corp., (978-0-9769873) 7300 Penn Ave., Pittsburgh, PA 15208 USA Tel 412-371-0680; Fax: 412-371-0681
E-mail: marie.routledge@skymark.com
Web site: http://www.theseus.biz.

Skyrai Publishing, (978-0-692-68252-4; 978-0-9978555) 935 Carla Dr., Troy, IL 62294 USA Tel 309-338-7589
Dist(s): **CreateSpace Independent Publishing Platform.**

Skyscape Imprint of **Amazon Publishing**

Skyscraper Pr. (children's) Imprint of **Windy City Pubs.**

Skyward Bks., (978-0-9777902) Orders Addr.: P.O. Box 56734, Riverside, CA 92517 USA Tel 951-782-0711
E-mail: skywardbooks@msn.com.

Skyward Press See **Skyward Bks.**

Skyward Publishing Co., (978-1-881554) Div. of Paragon Media Corp., 813 Michael St., Kennett, MO 63857 USA (SAN 297-9705) Tel 573-888-5589
E-mail: nfo@skywardpublishing.com
Web site: http://www.skywardpublishing.com; http://www.bransonozarks.com; http://www.brandywineswar.com.

Skywater Publishing Co., (978-0-9793081; 978-0-9818279; 978-1-938237) Orders Addr.: 260 Goodrich Ave., Saint Paul, MN 55102 USA Tel 952-818-2178; Imprints: Flat Sole Studio (FlatSole)
E-mail: info@skywaterpublishing.com
Web site: http://www.solbooks.com
Dist(s): **Follett School Solutions**
Smashwords.

Skyway Pictures LLC., (978-0-692-84306-2) 1700 ROBINSON DR N, SAINT PETERSBURG, FL 33710 USA Tel 321-578-0022; Fax: 727-201-2407
E-mail: tate_mcghee@yahoo.com.

Skyword Pr., (978-0-9740202) Orders Addr.: P.O. Box 1714, Hood River, OR 97031 USA; Edit Addr.: 555 Highline Rd., Hood River, OR 97031 USA.

SL Conradt, LLC, (978-0-615-37381-2) N1685 Amies Ln., Greenville, WI 54942 USA Tel 920-427-0512
E-mail: shanaleeconradt@gmail.com
Web site: http://www.getfitwithfood.com.

SL Resources, (978-1-935040; 978-1-935808) Orders Addr.: P.O. Box 36040, Birmingham, AL 35236 USA Tel 205-985-0760; Fax: 205-403-3969; Toll Free: 800-718-2267; Edit Addr.: 2183 Pkwy. Lake Dr., Hoover, AL 35242 USA
E-mail: products@studentlife.net; bradford@studentlife.net
Web site: http://www.studentlifestore.com.

SLABYPRESS, (978-0-9774118; 978-0-9792622) W25952 State Rd., 95, Arcadia, WI 54612 USA Tel 608-323-7335
E-mail: slabypress@yahoo.com
Web site: http://www.jsiwicki.com.

SLACK, Inc., (978-0-913590; 978-0-943432; 978-1-55642; 978-1-61711; 978-1-63091) 6900 Grove Rd., Thorofare, NJ 08086-9447 USA (SAN 201-8632) Tel 856-848-1000; Fax: 856-853-5991; Toll Free: 800-257-8290
E-mail: orders@slackinc.com; lplummer@slackinc.com
Web site: http://www.slackbooks.com
Dist(s): **Barnes & Noble Bks.-Imports**
Coutts Information Services
Ebsco Publishing
Emery-Pratt Co.
Holt, Henry & Co.
Majors, J. A. Co.
Macmillan
Matthews Medical Bk. Co.
Rittenhouse Bk. Distributors.

Slack Water Pr., (978-0-9797613)
E-mail: jon.adams@slackwaterpress.com
Web site: http://slackwaterpress.com
Dist(s): **Ingram Content Group**
Smashwords.

Slangman Publishing, (978-1-891888; 978-1-947601) Orders Addr.: 12206 Hillslope St., Studio City, CA 91604 USA Tel 818-752-6462; Fax: 413-647-1589
E-mail: info@slangman.com
Web site: http://www.slangman.com
Dist(s): **Delta Systems Company, Inc.**

Slant Imprint of **Wipf & Stock Pubs.**

Slate Falls Pr., LLC, (978-0-578-04697-6; 978-0-578-07199-2; 978-0-578-10560-4; 978-0-578-12468-1; 978-0-578-17224-8; 978-0-578-18544-6; 978-0-578-23865-4) P.O. Box 7062, Loveland, CO 80537 USA; 1124 Harrison Ave., Loveland, CO 80537
Web site: http://www.slatefallspress.com.

Slater Software. Inc., (978-0-9743149) 351 Badger Ln., Guffey, CO 80820-9106 USA Tel 719-479-2255 Toll Free: 877-306-6968
E-mail: jim@slatersoftware.com
Web site: http://www.slatersoftware.com.

Slater-Milligan, Joey, (978-0-9979619) 184 Franklin Street, D17, Brooklyn, NY 11222 USA Tel 631-339-4411
E-mail: joeyslatermilligan@gmail.com.

Slave Labor Bks., (978-0-943151; 978-1-59362) 577 S. Market St., San Jose, CA 95113 USA (SAN 668-1204) Tel 408-971-8929; Fax: 408-279-0451; Toll Free: 800-866-8929; Imprints: Slave Labor Graphics (Slave Labor Graph)
E-mail: dan@slavelabor.com
Web site: http://www.slavelabor.com
Dist(s): **Diamond Comic Distributors, Inc.**
Diamond Bk. Distributors.

Slave Labor Graphics Imprint of **Slave Labor Bks.**

Slavens Enterprises & Marketing Services, LLP See **Slavens Enterprises, LLC.**

Slavens Enterprises, LLC., (978-0-9740348) 13335 SW Violet Ct., Beaverton, OR 97008-5015 USA Toll Free: 877-526-0904; Imprints: Special Editions — Customized Biographies (Special Edns)
E-mail: ricks@slavensmarketing.com.

Slavit, Norma, (978-0-578-22043-7; 978-0-578-22494-7) 1483 Fields Dr., San Jose, CA 95129 USA Tel 408-253-7200
E-mail: normaslavit86@gmail.com.

Sleek Publishing, (978-0-9990479) 5910 W Sumac Ave, Denver, CO 80123 USA Tel 303-562-6695
E-mail: Laura@sleekpublishing.com.

Sleep Garden, Inc., (978-0-9752988) P.O. Box 2365, Menlo Park, CA 94025-2365 USA Toll Free: 877-475-3376
E-mail: marykelley@amsiventures.com
Web site: http://www.zzonesleep.com.

Sleeping Bear Pr., (978-1-57504; 978-1-886947; 978-1-58536) Orders Addr.: P.O. Box 20, Chelsea, MI 48118 USA (SAN 253-8466) Tel 734-475-4411; Fax: 734-475-0787; Toll Free: 800-487-2323; Edit Addr.: 27500 Drake Rd., Farmington Hills, MI 48331 USA
E-mail: customerservice@sleepingbearpress.com
Web site: http://www.sleepingbearpress.com
Dist(s): **Booklines Hawaii, Ltd.**
Cherry Lake Publishing
Children's Plus, Inc.
Follett School Solutions
Keith Distributors
MyiLibrary
Partners Bk. Distributing, Inc.
Southern Bk. Service
Urban Land Institute.

The Sleeping Bear Pr., (978-0-578-19814-9; 978-0-578-19815-6) 2395 S. Huron Pkwy. Suite 200, Ann Arbor, MI 48104 USA Toll Free: 800-487-2323.

Sleepless Warrior Publishing, (978-0-9747707) 14989 Grassy Knoll Ct., Woodbridge, VA 22193 USA (SAN 256-1069) Tel 703-897-9394; Fax: 703-897-0695
E-mail: cynthia.little@comcast.net
Web site: http://www.sleeplesswarrior.com.

Sleepy Creek Music, (978-0-9754633) P.O. Box 2652, Bloomington, IN 47402-2652 USA Tel 812-334-9901
E-mail: grey@greylarsen.com
Web site: http://www.greylarsen.com.

Sleepy Dog Publishing, (978-0-9842560) P.O. Box 2033, Turlock, CA 95381 USA
E-mail: swolsen@sbcglobal.net
Web site: http://sleepydogpublishing.com.

Sleepytown Pr., (978-0-9826344; 978-0-9831738; 978-1-937260) 1709 Valley Creek Rd., Anniston, AL 36207 USA Tel 256-365-1416
E-mail: artnbooks73@yahoo.com
Web site: http://www.sleepytownpress.com.

SLG, (978-0-615-12907-5) 128 C Main St., Agawam, MA 01001 USA
E-mail: slg_gallery@yahoo.com
Web site: http://geocities.com/slg_gallery/about.

Slhoetree Publishers, Incorporated See **Shoetree Publishers, Inc.**

S.L.Hollister, (978-1-7328445) 655 Talcottville Rd. 18, Vernon, CT 06066 USA Tel 860-454-4333
E-mail: s.hollister1@comcast.net
Dist(s): **Ingram Content Group.**

Slice of Lime Publishing, (978-0-9789475) 1415 Easy St., New Iberia, LA 70560 USA Tel 337-365-4136; Fax: 337-365-4137
E-mail: jady@sliceoflime.net
Web site: http://www.sliceoflime.net
Dist(s): **Partners Bk. Distributing, Inc.**

Slim Goodbody Corp., (978-1-887028; 978-0-9708230) Orders Addr.: P.O. Box 242, Lincolnville, ME 04850 USA Tel 207-230-0399; Fax: 207-230-0795; Toll Free: 888-484-1100
E-mail: john@slimgoodbody.com
Web site: http://www.slimgoodbody.com
Dist(s): **INscribe Digital**
Independent Pubs. Group.

Slippers for Hannah (hardcover), (978-0-692-31284-1; 978-0-692-34255-8) 3650 N 3650 W, Moore, ID 83255 USA Tel 2084064777
E-mail: Littlelostcreations@gmail.com.

Slippery Slope Press See **Ideate Prairie**

SLM Bk. Publishing, (978-0-9830039) Orders Addr.: 21204 Pontiac Trail, No. 16, South Lyon, MI 48178 USA
E-mail: joanna@slmbookpublishing.com
Web site: http://www.slmbookpublishing.com.

Slow on the Draw Productions, (978-0-615-48469-3; 978-0-615-74591-6) 12826 Ironstone Way No. 304, Parker, CO 80134 USA Tel 720-838-5176
E-mail: swpaulding@msn.com
Web site: lifelessonsfromandywink.com.

Sluser Publishing, (978-0-578-03599-4; 978-0-578-03634-2; 978-0-578-04034-9; 978-0-578-06031-6; 978-0-578-08065-9; 978-0-578-10299-3; 978-0-578-10318-1; 978-0-578-12746-0; 978-0-578-12986-0) 324 Stonegate Cir. N., Chambersburg, PA 17201 USA.

Slusser, Jan See **RiverCreek Bks., Inc.**

SM Ediciones (ESP) (978-84-348; 978-84-404; 978-84-398; 978-84-675; 978-84-9107; 978-84-9182; 978-84-398-2663-7; 978-84-398-3219-5; 978-84-398-3531-8; 978-84-398-4146-3; 978-84-398-5547-7; 978-84-398-6213-0; 978-84-404-0085-7; 978-84-404-1546-2) Dist. by **Mariuccia Iaconi Bk Imports.**

SM Ediciones (ESP) (978-84-348; 978-84-404; 978-84-398; 978-84-675; 978-84-9107; 978-84-9182; 978-84-398-2663-7; 978-84-398-3219-5; 978-84-398-3531-8; 978-84-398-4146-3; 978-84-398-5547-7; 978-84-398-6213-0; 978-84-404-0085-7; 978-84-404-1546-2) Dist. by **AIMS Intl.**

SM Ediciones (ESP) (978-84-348; 978-84-404; 978-84-398; 978-84-675; 978-84-9107; 978-84-9182; 978-84-398-2663-7; 978-84-398-3219-5; 978-84-398-3531-8; 978-84-398-4146-3; 978-84-398-5547-7; 978-84-398-6213-0; 978-84-404-0085-7; 978-84-404-1546-2) Dist. by **IBD Ltd.**

SM Ediciones (ESP) (978-84-348; 978-84-404; 978-84-398; 978-84-675; 978-84-9107; 978-84-9182; 978-84-398-2663-7; 978-84-398-3219-5; 978-84-398-3531-8; 978-84-398-4146-3; 978-84-398-5547-7; 978-84-398-6213-0; 978-84-404-0085-7; 978-84-404-1546-2) Dist. by **Continental Bk.**

SM Ediciones (ESP) (978-84-348; 978-84-404; 978-84-398; 978-84-675; 978-84-9107; 978-84-9182; 978-84-398-2663-7; 978-84-398-3219-5; 978-84-398-3531-8; 978-84-398-4146-3; 978-84-398-5547-7; 978-84-398-6213-0; 978-84-404-0085-7; 978-84-404-1546-2) Dist. by **Lectorum Pubns.**

Small Batch Bks., (978-0-9829758; 978-1-937650; 978-1-951568) 493 S. Pleasant St., Amherst, MA 01002 USA Tel 413-230-3943
E-mail: fred@smallbatchbooks.com
Web site: www.smallbatchbooks.com
Dist(s): **BookBaby**
Ingram Content Group.

Small Bear Publishing, (978-0-9801662) P.O. Box 842, Livingston, MT 59047 USA
E-mail: BarringtonBear@q.com
Web site: http://www.travelswithbarrington.com.

Small Beer Pr., (978-1-931520; 978-1-61873) 150 Pleasant St. #306, Easthampton, MA 01027 USA Fax: 413-203-1636; Imprints: Big Mouth House (BigMouthHse)
E-mail: info@smallbeerpress.com
Web site: http://www.smallbeerpress.com; http://www.weightlessbooks.com
Dist(s): **Consortium Bk. Sales & Distribution**
MyiLibrary
ebrary, Inc.

Small Fry Beginnings, (978-0-9651690; 978-1-892703) Affil. of LightVision Films, Inc., 6625 Hwy. 53 E. Suite No. 410-212, Dawsonville, GA 30534 USA Tel 770-451-7000
E-mail: dennis@smallfrybeginnings.com
Web site: http://www.smallfrybeginnings.com
Dist(s): **Follett School Solutions**
Ingram Entertainment, Inc.
VPD, Inc.
Valley Media, Inc.

Small Fry Productions See **Small Fry Beginnings**

Small Group, LLC, The, (978-0-578-45676-8) 108 King Sago Ct., Ponte Vedra Beach, FL 32082 USA Tel 843-384-9333
E-mail: briancsmall@gmail.com
Dist(s): **Ingram Content Group.**

Small New York LLC, (978-0-578-16183-9; 978-0-9963985) 676 Third Ave., New York, NY 10017 USA.

Small Press Distribution See **SPD-Small Pr. Distribution**

Small Pr., The, (978-1-933651) Div. of Brown Bks. Publishing Group, 16200 N. Dallay Pkwy., No. 170, Dallas, TX 75248 USA Tel 972-381-0009; Fax: 972-248-4336
Dist(s): **BookBaby**
Open Road Integrated Media, Inc.

Small Publishing, (978-0-692-22459-5; 978-0-692-30147-0; 978-0-692-33282-5; 978-0-692-35425-4; 978-0-692-40481-2; 978-0-692-48561-3; 978-0-692-59717-0; 978-0-692-70869-9; 978-0-692-72714-0; 978-1-946257) P.O. Box 800, Belleview, FL 34421 USA Do not confuse with Small Publishing in Monterey, CA
E-mail: smallpublishing1@gmail.com
Web site: http://smallpublishing.wordpress.com; facebook.com/SmallPublishing
Dist(s): **CreateSpace Independent Publishing Platform.**

Small Waters Publishing, (978-0-9765621) 14251 75th Ave. SE, Atwater, MN 56209 USA Tel 320-894-7904; Fax: 320-235-6418
E-mail: markp@lakesideprintingandadvertising.com.

Small Wonder Publishing, (978-0-9899964) 130 Boniface Dr., Rochester, NY 14620 USA Tel 585-271-3492
E-mail: hdm@smallwonderpublishing.com.

Small Wonders Enterprises, (978-0-9741888) 12210 Fairfax Towne Ctr., PMB No. 901, Fairfax, VA 22033 USA Tel 703-352-0226 Do not confuse with Small Wonders Enterprises in Farmingron, NM
E-mail: snickerdoodle@erols.com
Web site: http://www.snickerdoodleforkids.com.

Small World Toys, (978-0-9774677; 978-0-9776034; 978-0-9795081) P.O. Box 3620, Culver City, CA 90231-3620 USA
Web site: http://www.smallworldtoys.com.

Smallbag Bks., (978-0-9761631) Orders Addr.: 2000 Del Sol, Bowie, MD 20721 USA
E-mail: konaapub@yahoo.com
Web site: http://www.younganddebtfree.com.

SmallHorse Pr. Imprint of **Equine Graphics Publishing Group**

Smallwood, Edward, (978-0-9741282) 1609 Mountain Ashe Ct., Matthews, NC 28105 USA
Web site: http://www.jfrankles.com.

Smart & Smarter Publishing, (978-0-9713530) P.O. Box 1815, Zillah, WA 98953 USA (SAN 255-3104) Tel 877-807-3703 (phone/fax)
E-mail: daviddunham@smartandsmarter.com; services@smartandsmarter.com
Web site: http://www.smartandsmarter.com.

Smart Apple Media Imprint of **Black Rabbit Bks.**

Smart Data Processing, Inc., (978-0-9718439) 14 Molly Pitcher Dr., Manalapan, NJ 07726 USA Tel 732-598-4027; Fax: 732-409-1364
E-mail: info@smartdataprocessing.com
Web site: http://www.smartdataprocessing.com.

Smart Kids Imprint of **Penton Overseas, Inc.**

Smart Kids Publishing See **Smart Kidz Media, Inc.**

Smart Kidz Media, Inc., (978-1-891100; 978-1-939658) 2460 Hobbit Ln., Fallbrook, CA 92028 USA Tel 760-468-1891
Dist(s): **APG Sales & Distribution Services**
Whitaker Hse.

smart Life Ministries, Inc., The, (978-0-9741091) 1649 Springhill St., Chillicothe, MO 64601 USA.

Smart Love Pr., LLC, (978-0-9838664; 978-1-7330897) 400 E. Randolph St. Suite 1905, Chicago, IL 60601 USA Tel 312-970-9846; Fax: 312-278-0441
E-mail: smartlovepress@gmail.com; marthahpieper@smartlovepress.com
Web site: http://www.smartlovepress.com; http://www.jillysterribletempertantrums.com; http://www.mommydaddyihadabaddream.com
Dist(s): **Brigham Distributing.**

Smart Picks, Inc., (978-0-9764785) P.O. Box 771440, Lakewood, OH 44107 USA Tel 216-226-6173; Fax: 216-226-5413
E-mail: games@smartpicks.com.

Smart Poodle Publishing, (978-0-9800307) 3436 Pierce St., Hollywood, FL 33021 USA
E-mail: debbie.glade@comcast.net
Web site: http://www.smartpoodlepublishing.com.

Smart Publishing, (978-0-9761819) P.O. Box 410894, Chicago, IL 60641 USA Tel 773-616-0267
E-mail: halfbakedsistas@aol.com
Web site: http://www.halfbakedsistas.com.

Smart Smiles Co., The, (978-0-9722792; 978-0-9723727; 978-0-9762740; 978-0-9763328) 380 S. Mizner Blvd., No. 1709, Boca Raton, FL 33432 USA Tel 561-347-3075; Imprints: Flat Kids (Flat Kids)
Web site: http://www.smartsmilescompany.com.

SmartBook Media, Inc., (978-1-5105) 350 5th Ave, 59th Floor, New York, NY 10118 USA Toll Free Fax: 866-449-3445; Toll Free: 866-649-3445
E-mail: linda@weigl.com; samantha.nugent@weigl.com
Web site: http://www.asmartbook.com.

SmartBooks Publishing, (978-0-578-20283-9) 29 Banbury Ln, Bloomfield, CT 06002 USA.

Smartinbooks, Inc., (978-0-9761765) Orders Addr.: P.O. Box 729, Paducah, KY 42002-0729 USA; Edit Addr.: 1441 HC Mathis Dr., Paducah, KY 42001 USA
E-mail: hmartin@paducah.com
Web site: http://www.smartinbooks.com.

SmartInk Bks., LLC, *(978-1-932403)* 413 6th Ave., Brooklyn, NY 11215 USA Tel 718-768-3696; Fax: 718-369-0844
E-mail: publisher@smartinkbooks.com
Web site: http://ww.smartinkbooks.com
Dist(s): **Hachette Bk. Group**
Ideals Pubns.
Penton Overseas, Inc.

SmartiPantz Publishing, *(978-0-9747563)* P.O. Box 24014, Minneapolis, MN 55424 USA (SAN 256-0720).

SmartLab *Imprint of* **becker&mayer! books**

SmartPop *Imprint of* **BenBella Bks.**

SMARTseeds Co., LLC, The, *(978-0-9790931)* P.O. Box 100028, Cudahy, WI 53110 USA (SAN 852-4068) Tel 414-433-0500
E-mail: carlos@thesmartseedscompany.com; info@thesmartseedscompany.com
Web site: http://www.thesmartseedscompany.com.

Smartypants Bks., *(978-0-9773550)* P.O. Box 1014, Logandale, NV 89021-1014 USA (SAN 257-3423)
Web site: http://www.smartypants-books.com.

Smartypants Publishing, *(978-0-9792897)* Orders Addr.: P.O. Box 1548, Buckley, WA 98321 USA Tel 253-278-6612
E-mail: christa@smartypantspublishing.com
Web site: http://smartypantspublishing.com.

Smashwords, *(978-1-4523; 978-1-4524; 978-1-4580; 978-1-4581; 978-1-4657; 978-1-4658; 978-1-4659; 978-1-4660; 978-1-4661; 978-1-4760; 978-1-4761; 978-1-4762; 978-1-4763; 978-1-4764; 978-1-301; 978-1-310; 978-1-311; 978-1-370; 978-0-463; 978-0-692-04063-8; 978-0-578-41339-6; 978-1-005) 15951 Gatos Blvd., Suite 16, Los Gatos, CA 95032 USA Tel 408-358-1824; ziya gokalp mah. cimen sk. no:1/1 ikitelli koyu, basaksehir-istanbul, 34306 Tel 90 0538 8939727*
E-mail: bill@smashwords.com
Web site: http://www.smashwords.com
Dist(s): **Lulu Pr., Inc.**

SmatteringsBks., *(978-0-9800130)* P.O. Box 556, Clarence, NY 14031 USA (SAN 854-9931) Tel 716-818-0324
Web site: http://smatteringsbooks.com/books.html.

SMC Pubns., LLC, *(978-0-9729546)* P.O. Box 2684, Branchville, NJ 07826 USA Tel 973-948-7441 (phone/fax) Do not confuse with companies with the same name in Houston, TX, Garden Grove, CA, Corona, CA, West Long Branch, NJ
E-mail: smcpublications@embarqmail.com
Web site: http://www.magi-call.com.

SMC Publishing *See* **SMC Pubns., LLC**

Smethwick Publishing LLC *See* **Oliver Pr. LLC**

Smile Time Publishing, *(978-0-9785961)* P.O. Box B, Del Mar, CA 92014 USA
E-mail: ps@peterstrunk.com
Web site: http://www.smile-time.com.

Smile-a-Lot, LLP, *(978-0-9785132)* 1050 Walnut St. #201, Boulder, CO 80302 USA Tel 303-443-2006; Fax: 303-443-9475; *Imprints:* Smiletown Books (Smiletown Bks)
E-mail: chris@smiletownbooks.com
Web site: http://smiletownbooks.com.

SMiles Productions (SMP), LLC, *(978-0-9768456)* 14241 NE Woodinville-Duvall Rd., Woodinville, WA 98072 USA Tel 425-481-8817; Fax: 425-481-8179
E-mail: language@smilesprod.com
Web site: http://www.smilesprod.com.

Smiletown Bks. *Imprint of* **Smile-a-Lot, LLP**

Smiley Co., *(978-0-9629001)* 401 Anglin St., Smiley, TX 78159-0099 USA (SAN 297-4045) Tel 830-587-6623; Fax: 830-587-6113; Toll Free: 800-584-3655
E-mail: npattesonsmiley@the-cia.net.

Smiley Originals *See* **Smiley Co.**

Smiley, Rhonda, *(978-0-9984492)* 1632 Royal Blvd, Glendale, CA 91207 USA Tel 818-545-8113
E-mail: rjsmiley@aol.com.

Smith & Assocs., *(978-0-9790817)* 70 Goodwin Cir., Hartford, CT 06105 USA (SAN 852-3886) Tel 860-543-0279; Fax: 860-586-8718
Web site: http://www.morningdovepress.com
Dist(s): **Connecticut River Pr.**

Smith & Daniel, *(978-0-9630463; 978-1-889668)* P.O. Box 8097, Jacksonville, FL 32239-0097 USA Toll Free: 800-330-1325.

Smith & Kraus Pubs., Inc., *(978-0-9622722; 978-1-57525; 978-1-880399; 978-1-936232; 978-1-937738; 978-1-943511; 978-1-970012; 978-1-68476)* Orders Addr.: P.O. Box 127, Lyme, NH 03768 USA (SAN 255-1454) Tel 603-643-6431; Toll Free: 877-866-8680; Edit Addr.: P.O. Box 564, Hanover, NH 03755 USA
E-mail: marisasmithkraus@gmail.com; boda@sover.net
Web site: http://www.smithandkraus.com.

Smith, Andrea Joy, *(978-0-9764396)* 2447 Mission Ave, Suite B, Carmichael, CA 95608 USA
E-mail: smithfamdent@aol.com
Web site: http://smileagainnow.com; http://inthechairwithdrsmith.com.

Smith, Barbara Maxine, *(978-0-578-11939-7; 978-0-615-85722-0)* 21103 Gary Dr., Apt 114, Castro Valley, CA 94546 USA.

Smith, Bill O., *(978-0-615-56972-7; 978-0-9895238)* 8489 Timbers Trail, Traverse City, MI 49685 USA Tel 313-515-4328
E-mail: bill@billosmith.com.

Smith, Brenda J. Few *See* **Tall Through Bks.**

Smith, C. Brandt, *(978-0-9768020)* 1910 Scenic Rd., Jonesboro, AR 72401-0220 USA Tel 870-933-1908
E-mail: brandt@walnutstreetbaptist.org.

Smith, David, *(978-0-692-97007-2; 978-0-692-15759-6)* 1025 Oakwood St. SE, North Canton, OH 44720 USA Tel 330-966-9734
E-mail: davidsmith0303@yahoo.com
Dist(s): **CreateSpace Independent Publishing Platform.**

Smith, Deanna *See* **Annade Publishing**

Smith, Debra, *(978-0-9747754)* 1934 Donna Dr., Coupeville, WA 98239 USA.

Smith, Ernest, *(978-0-9729154)* Orders Addr.: 3155 Sharpe Ave. Apt. 304, Memphis, TN 38111-3784 USA
E-mail: ernest725@Hotmail.com.

Smith, Florence B. *See* **Prickly Pr.**

Smith, George Publishing, *(978-0-9740434)* Orders Addr.: 11 Amberwinds Ct., Lakewood, NJ 08701 USA (SAN 255-3716)
E-mail: customer_support@georgesmithpublishing.com
Web site: http://www.georgesmithpublishing.com
Dist(s): **Mountain Bk. Co.**

Smith, Gibbs Publisher *See* **Gibbs Smith, Publisher**

Smith Island Foundation, *(978-0-9754170)* 44108 Bristow Cir., Ashburn, VA 20147 USA Tel 703-729-4462 Phone/Fax
E-mail: books@smithislandfoundation.org; heather@pneumabooks.com
Web site: http://www.smithislandfoundation.org.

Smith, Jennifer W. *See* **Apple House Publishing**

Smith, Joseph L., *(978-0-9754985)* 38118 Village 38, Camarillo, CA 93012 USA
E-mail: cayusekid@earthlink.net.

Smith, Kasper, *(978-0-9744519)* 4251 Fischer, Detroit, MI 48214 USA Tel 313-922-1728
E-mail: pastorsmith@dominionintl.org
Web site: http://www.dominionintl.org.

Smith, Keith Bks., *(978-0-9637682; 978-0-9740764)* 1115 E. Main St., Suite 219, Box 8, Rochester, NY 14609 USA Tel 585-473-6776; Fax: 585-482-2496
E-mail: keith@keithsmithbooks.com
Web site: http://www.keithsmithbooks.com.

Smith Kerr Assocs., *(978-0-9786899; 978-0-9830622; 978-0-692-33644-1)* 1 Government St No. 1, Kittery , ME 03904 USA Tel 207-703-2314; Fax: 207-703-2313; *Imprints:* Seapoint Books ()
E-mail: bizbks@aol.com
Dist(s): **National Bk. Network.**

Smith Knutson Publishing, *(978-0-692-11869-6; 978-0-692-11877-1; 978-0-578-23099-3)* 15414 McClarnden Dr., Fishers, IN 46040 USA
Dist(s): **Ingram Content Group.**

Smith, Lindsay, *(978-0-692-05746-9; 978-0-692-05747-6)* 1143 3rd St NE, Washington, DC 20002 USA Tel 202-286-4999
E-mail: bohemienne@mac.com
Dist(s): **Ingram Content Group.**

Smith, Mason, *(978-0-692-02010-4)* 107 Southland Dr., Richmond, KY 40475-2413 USA Tel 859-582-5960
E-mail: mason.smith@eku.edu.

Smith, Michael *See* **East West Discovery Pr.**

Smith, Mildred C., *(978-0-9778641; 978-0-692-60783-1)* 4200 Cathedral Ave, NW, Apt. 610, Washington, DC 20016 USA Tel 202-363-5352
E-mail: mcs29@georgetown.edu.

Smith Novelty Co., Inc., *(978-0-938765; 978-1-59099; 978-1-934954)* Div. of Smith News Co., Inc., 460 Ninth St., San Francisco, CA 94103-4478 USA (SAN 216-2326) Tel 415-861-4900; Fax: 415-861-5683
E-mail: ken@smithnovelty.com; matt@smithnovelty.com
Web site: http://www.smithnovelty.com.

Smith, Peter Pub., Inc., *(978-0-8446)* Five Lexington Ave., Magnolia, MA 01930 USA (SAN 206-8885) Tel 978-525-3562; Fax: 978-525-3674.

Smith, Ronald J. Sr., *(978-0-9749390)* 1118 S. Thomas St., Apt. 2, Arlington, VA 22204-3640 USA Tel 571-212-1734
E-mail: Breakerdelawa@gmail.com
Dist(s): **Morris Publishing.**

Smith, S. Pubns., *(978-0-9769320)* P.O. Box 122, Severna Park, MD 21146 USA Tel 410-271-0837; Fax: 410-544-0059
E-mail: stew@stewsmith.com
Web site: http://www.stewsmith.com.

Smith, Sharon, *(978-0-9817615)* 13611 SW 285th Terr., Homestead, FL 33033 USA Tel 786-317-0267
E-mail: dexavior1@msn.com.

Smith, Tyjauna, *(978-0-9760112)* P.O. Box 2230 Misty Woods Rd., Lake Cormorant, MS 38641 USA
E-mail: tyjauna@bellsouth.net
Web site: http://www.authorsden.com/tyjaunalsmith.

Smith, Viveca Publishing, *(978-0-9740551; 978-1-7327568)* PMB No. 131, 3001 S. Hardin Blvd., Suite 110, McKinney, TX 75070-9028 USA Tel 214-793-0089; Fax: 972-562-7559
E-mail: vsmithpublishing@aol.com
Web site: http://www.vivecasmithpublishing.com
Dist(s): **BookBaby**
ebrary, Inc.

Smithcraft Pr., *(978-0-9793935; 978-1-62927)* 1718 Ashcroft St., NW, Palm Bay, FL 32907-9474 USA
E-mail: smithcraftpress@gmail.com; questions@smithcraftpress.info; craig@smithcraft.org.

Smithfield Capital Corp., *(978-0-9764670)* 219 S. D. St., Hamilton, OH 45013 USA
E-mail: smithfieldcap@msn.com.

Smithfield Press *See* **Princeton Health Pr.**

Smithsonian Bks. *Imprint of* **Smithsonian Institution Scholarly Pr.**

†Smithsonian Bks., *(978-0-87474; 978-1-56098; 978-1-58834)* Div. of Smithsonian Institution, Orders Addr.: 22883 Quicksilver Dr., Dulles, VA 20166 USA (SAN 253-3383); Edit Addr.: 600 Maryland Ave. SW, Suite 6001, Washington, DC 20024 USA (SAN 206-8044)
Web site: http://www.smithsonianbooks.com
Dist(s): **CreateSpace Independent Publishing Platform**
Ebsco Publishing
MyiLibrary
Penguin Random Hse. Distribution
Penguin Random Hse. LLC
Random Hse., Inc.
Rowman & Littlefield Publishers, Inc.
Wittenborn Art Bks.; *CIP.*

Smithsonian Institution Press *See* **Smithsonian Bks.**

Smithsonian Institution Scholarly Pr., *(978-0-9788460; 978-1-935623; 978-1-944466; 978-0-9992662; 978-0-9992663)* Orders Addr.: P.O. Box 37012, MRC 957, Washington, DC 20013 USA Tel 202-633-3017; Fax: 202-633-3017; *Imprints:* Smithsonian Books (SmithsonBks)
E-mail: schol.press@si.edu
Web site: http://www.scholarlypress.si.edu/
Dist(s): **MyiLibrary**
National Bk. Network
Penguin Random Hse. Distribution
Penguin Random Hse. LLC
Random Hse., Inc.
Rowman & Littlefield Publishers, Inc.

Smithsonian National Museum of the American Indian, *(978-0-9719163; 978-1-933565)* MRC 590 PO Box 37012, Washington, DC 20013-7012 USA; 4th St. & Independence Ave., SW, Washington, DC 20024
E-mail: nmai-pubs@si.edu
Web site: http://www.americanindian.si.edu
Dist(s): **Consortium Bk. Sales & Distribution**
D.A.P./Distributed Art Pubs.
Fulcrum Publishing.

Smithsonian Science Education Ctr. (SSEC), *(978-1-933008; 978-0-9985286; 978-0-9985287; 978-1-7324198; 978-1-7324199; 978-1-7324437; 978-1-7324438; 978-1-7357196; 978-1-7357197)* 901 D St. SW, Suite 704B, Washington, DC 20024 USA Tel 202-633-2992; *Imprints:* Science and Technology Concepts (STC) (Sci & Tech)
E-mail: marohnp@si.edu
Web site: http://www.nsrconline.org; http://carolinacurriculum.com
Dist(s): **Carolina Biological Supply Co.**

Smocking Arts Guild of America, *(978-0-9743959)* P.O. Box 214, Hathorne, MA 01937-0214 USA Tel 800-520-3101; Fax: 978-777-4329; *Imprints:* SAGA Press (SAGA Pr)
E-mail: sagahq@smocking.org
Web site: http://www.smocing.org.

Smokestack Bks. (GBR) *(978-0-9548691; 978-0-9551061; 978-0-9554028; 978-0-9575747; 978-0-9571722; 978-0-9927409; 978-0-9560341; 978-0-9564175; 978-0-9568144; 978-0-9929581) Dist. by* **Dufour.**

Smooth Sailing Press, LLC *See* **Mystic Harbor Pr., LLC**

Smore Bks., *(978-1-7329969)* 2880 Olympic View dr, Chino hills, CA 91709 USA Tel 626-264-2410; Fax: 626-264-2410
E-mail: hyerin.kang@gmail.com.

SMPR, *(978-0-9767898)* 4800 S. Westshore Blvd., Suite 411, Tampa, FL 33611 USA Tel 813-831-8206 (phone/fax); Toll Free Fax: 866-958-1323 (phone/fax)
E-mail: sonja.moffett@smpr.info
Web site: http://www.smpr.info.

†Smyth & Helwys Publishing, Inc., *(978-0-9628455; 978-1-57312; 978-1-880837; 978-1-64173)* 6316 Peake Rd., Macon, GA 31210-3960 USA (SAN 298-7732) Tel 478-757-0564; Fax: 478-757-1305; Toll Free: 800-747-3016
E-mail: bowker@helwys.com
Web site: http://www.helwys.com
Dist(s): **CreateSpace Independent Publishing Platform**; *CIP.*

Snader Publishing Co., *(978-1-945871)* 218 CHESTNUT, HALSTEAD, KS 67056 USA Tel 316-217-4223
E-mail: billbush@usa.com
Web site: snaderpublishing.com.

Snake Country Publishing, *(978-0-9635828)* 16748 W. Linden St., Caldwell, ID 83607-9270 USA Tel 208-459-9233
E-mail: snakecountry@mindspring.com
Dist(s): **Caxton Pr.**

Snake Goddess Bks., *(978-0-9744910)* 11431/2 Gladsy Ave., Long Beach, CA 90804 USA.

Snaptail Pr. *Imprint of* **Images Unlimited Publishing**

Snelsonbks.com, *(978-0-9723935)* 355 N. Diamond Ave., Canon City, CO 81212 USA
E-mail: bs@ris.net
Web site: http://www.snelsonbooks.com.

SNL Publishing, *(978-0-615-48221-7; 978-0-9848368)* 9 Spring Hill Ave., Norwalk, CT 06850 USA Tel 914-671-2252
E-mail: davidalara@aol.com; snlpublishing@aol.com.

Snodgrass, Ruth M., *(978-0-9754867)* 160 Polaris Dr., Dover, OH 44622 USA.

Snojoy Publishing, *(978-0-9743913)* 4509 14th St., Greeley, CO 80634 USA
E-mail: snojoy1@hotmail.com; gnojoy1@hotmail.com.

Snow In Sarasota Publishing, *(978-0-9663335; 978-0-9824611; 978-0-9830362; 978-0-9837685; 978-0-9893840; 978-0-9862979; 978-0-9977126; 978-0-9997415; 978-1-7333492)* 5170 Central Sarasota Pkwy., No.309, Sarasota, FL 34238 USA Tel 941-923-9201; Fax: 941-926-8739
E-mail: sarasota58@aol.com
Web site: http://www.snowinsarasota.com
Dist(s): **Follett School Solutions**
MyiLibrary
ebrary, Inc.

Snow Leopard Publishing, *(978-1-944361)* 171 Durham Rd., Dover, NH 03820 USA (SAN 990-1183) Tel 603-343-8107
E-mail: info@snowleopardpublishing.com
Web site: SnowLeopardPublishing.com.

Snow Lion Publications, Inc, *Imprint of* **Shambhala Pubns., Inc.**

Snow Publishing, *(978-0-692-83769-6; 978-0-692-08848-7)* 5641 High Tor Hill, Columbia, MD 21045 USA Tel 443-812-4240
E-mail: abby.snow@comcast.net; abby.snow@comcast.net; abby.snow@comcast.net
Web site: www.abbysnow.org
Dist(s): **CreateSpace Independent Publishing Platform.**

Snow Tree Bks., *(978-0-9749006)* Orders Addr.: P.O. Box 546, Peabody, MA 01960-7564 USA (SAN 255-965X) Tel 781-592-9866
E-mail: info@snowtreebooks.com
Web site: http://snowtreebooks.com.

Snow Waters Publishing *See* **River Rain Ministries**

Snowbound Bks., *(978-0-9722570)* Orders Addr.: P.O. Box 281327, Lamoille, NV 89828 USA; Edit Addr.: 1291 Country Ln., Lamoille, NV 89828 USA.

Snowbound Pr., Inc., *(978-1-932362)* P.O. Box 698, Littleton, CO 80160-0698 USA Tel 303-347-2869; Fax: 303-386-3232
E-mail: info@snowboundpress.com
Web site: http://www.snowboundpress.com
Dist(s): **Quality Bks., Inc.**

Snowman Learning Center, The, *(978-0-9674666)* 6 Carver St., Plymouth, MA 02360-3301 USA Tel 508-746-5993; Fax: 508-746-8097
E-mail: S.Snowmanph.d@worldnet.att.net.

Snowpuppy, *(978-0-692-02600-7; 978-0-692-30007-7; 978-0-9963244)* 494 riverside Dr., Burley, ID 83318 USA Tel 208 219 9056
Dist(s): **CreateSpace Independent Publishing Platform.**

Snowy Day Distribution & Publishing, A, *(978-0-9844681; 978-1-936615)* P.O. Box 2014, Merrimack, NH 03054 USA Tel 603-493-2276
E-mail: salspiritosr@asnowyday.com
Web site: http://www.asnowyday.com.

Snowy Night Pub., *(978-0-9860324)* 44240 Riverview Ridge Dr., Clinton Township, MI 48038 USA
E-mail: yroehler@bookpublishing.com.

Snowy Plains, *(978-0-9791367)* 270 Flodin Rd., Gwinn, MI 49841 USA
E-mail: jwsnowyplains@yahoo.com.

Snowy Wings Publishing, *(978-1-946202; 978-1-948661; 978-1-952667)* P.O. Box 1035, Turner, OR 97392 USA Tel 209-471-1735
E-mail: lyssa.chiavari@gmail.com.

Snuggle Up Bks., *(978-0-9655530)* 3145 Claremore Ave., Long Beach, CA 90808-4421 USA
E-mail: judybelshe@aol.com.

SnuggleBugzzz Pr., *(978-0-615-38169-5)* 21328 Independence Ave., Lakeville, MN 55044 USA Tel 612-910-0190; Fax: 952-985-4151
E-mail: kathylucilejohnson@att.net
Web site: http://www.snugglebugzzz.com
Dist(s): **West.**

Snyder Enterprises LLC, *(978-0-692-99640-9; 978-0-692-99661-4; 978-0-692-99918-9)* 468 N. Loafer Dr., Elk Ridge, UT 84651 USA Tel 801-687-0563
E-mail: amberley.snyder@hotmail.com
Dist(s): **Ingram Content Group.**

Snyder, Maria V., *(978-1-946381)* 200 Foreman Rd., Elizabethtown, PA 17022 USA Tel 717-475-8036
E-mail: mariavsnyder@gmail.com.

Snyder, Stacy, *(978-0-9600041)* P.O. Box 1411, Rancho Santa Fe, CA 92067 USA
E-mail: stacysnyder@mac.com; anne@wagdesign.be.

Snyder, Ted, *(978-0-9965019)* 8100 Valley Creek Dr., Choctaw, OK 73020 USA Tel 405-590-0794
E-mail: tedsnyder@reagan.com.

Snyder, Vicki, *(978-0-9773187)* 4349 Cimarron Ct., NW, Rochester, MN 55901 USA
E-mail: cctraining@prodigy.net.

Snyder-Winston Pr., *(978-0-9752749)* 23679 Calabasas Rd., No. 186, Calabasas, CA 91302 USA Tel 818-876-0188; Fax: 818-876-0133
E-mail: tedafed@earthlink.net
Web site: http://www.midaskids.com.

SNZ Publishing, *(978-0-9758815)* P.O. Box 32190, Cincinnati, OH 45232 USA (SAN 256-1255)
E-mail: doug@snzpublishing.com
Web site: http://www.snzpublishing.com.

So Pretty In Pink LLC *See* **King Production, A**

So Simple Learning, *(978-0-9772158)* 12463 Rancho Bernardo Rd., PMB 253, San Diego, CA 92128 USA Tel 858-530-5055
E-mail: info@sosimplelearning.com
Web site: http://www.sosimplelearning.com.

So So Little Reads, Inc., *(978-1-947302)* P.O. Box 136, New York, NY 10272 USA Tel 917-512-1706
E-mail: sosolittlereads@gmail.com
Web site: www.sosolittlereads.com.

Soar Publishing, LLC, *(978-0-9721142; 978-0-9825450; 978-0-9838220; 978-0-9888650; 978-0-9962052; 978-0-9992960; 978-1-7321782; 978-1-950269)* 16 Austree Ct., Columbia, SC 29229-7581 USA (SAN 255-4437) Tel 803-699-0633 phone; Fax: 803-699-0634 (phone/fax)
E-mail: smithser@bellsouth.net; smithser1@bellsouth.net
Web site: http://www.soarpublishing.com; http://www.titlewave.com; http://titletales.com
Dist(s): **Follett School Solutions.**

Soaring Sparrow Pr., *(978-1-891262)* 11795 SW Crater Loop, Beaverton, OR 97008 USA Tel 503-644-5960
E-mail: sparrowman@earthlink.net
Web site: www.marvinmallard.com.

Soccer Poet LLC, *(978-0-9896977)* 245 Falling Shoals Dr., Athens, GA 30605 USA Tel 706-201-3858
E-mail: soccerpoet@gmail.com
Web site: www.soccerpoet.com.

Soccertowns LLC, *(978-0-692-27681-5; 978-0-692-29319-5; 978-0-692-29448-2; 978-0-9908808; 978-0-9863584; 978-1-943255)* 4504 W. Memphis St, Broken Arrow, OK 74012 USA Tel 918-893-3121
E-mail: andresvarela@hotmail.com
Web site: www.roundyandfriends.com.

Social Motion Publishing *Imprint of* **Social Motion Publishing**

Social Motion Publishing, *(978-0-9704379; 978-0-9968906; 978-0-578-41752-3)* Orders Addr.: P.O. Box 5301, Herndon, VA 20172-5301 USA; Edit Addr.: P.O. Box 5301, Herndon, VA 20172-5301 USA; *Imprints:* Social Motion Publishing (SocialMotion)
E-mail: andrew@socialmotionpublishing.com
Web site: http://www.JulyPublishing.com; http://www.SocialMotionPublishing.com.

Social Skill Builder, Inc., *(978-0-9819585)* P.O. Box 2430, Leesburg, VA 20177 USA.

Social Studies Schl. Service, *(978-1-56004; 978-1-57596)* Orders Addr.: 10200 Jefferson Blvd., P.O. Box 802, Culver City, CA 90232-0802 USA (SAN 168-9592) Tel 310-839-2436; Fax: 310-839-2249; Toll Free: 800-421-4246
E-mail: access@socialstudies.com
Web site: http://socialstudies.com
Dist(s): **Follett School Solutions.**

Social Success Central, LLC *Imprint of* **How to Make & Keep Friends, LLC**

Socially Smarter, *(978-1-930640)* 349 N. Detroit St., Los Angeles, CA 90036 USA Tel 323-549-0279
E-mail: info@sociallysmarter.com
Web site: sociallysmarter.com
Dist(s): **Feldheim Pubs.**

Sociedad de San Pablo (COL) *(978-958-607) Dist. by* **St Pauls Alba.**

Sociedad de San Pablo (ESP) *Dist. by* **St Pauls Alba.**

Sociedad General Espanola de Libreria (ESP) *(978-84-7143; 978-84-9778) Dist. by* **Distribks Inc.**

Sociedad General Espanola de Libreria (ESP) *(978-84-7143; 978-84-9778) Dist. by* **Continental Bk.**

Society for Developmental Education *See* **Staff Development for Educators**

Society For The Understanding Of Early Child Development, *(978-0-9762509)* 39741 Lynn St., Canton, MI 48187 USA (SAN 256-260X) Tel 734-416-0480; Fax: 734-459-5280
E-mail: rsawhney@infotreeservice.com.

Society for Visual Education, Incorporated *See* **S V E & Churchill Media**

Society of Automotive Engineers, Incorporated *See* **SAE Intl.**

Society of Young Inklings, *(978-0-615-42953-3; 978-0-9839568; 978-0-9910031; 978-0-9981849)* 16 Muller Pl., San Jose, CA 95126 USA Tel 650-861-0508
E-mail: naomi@younginklings.org; info@younginklings.org
Web site: www.younginklings.org
Dist(s): **Lulu Pr., Inc.**

Socrates Solutions Incorporated, *(978-0-692-00121-9; 978-0-615-52175-6; 978-0-9905501)* P.O. Box 18457, San Jose, CA 95158 USA Tel 408-448-4018
E-mail: joemessineo@yahoo.com.

Sofija Zlatanova, *(978-1-7338618)* 6 Clinton St., Cambridge, MA 02139 USA Tel 857-504-5591
E-mail: sofija.zlatanov@gmail.com.

Soft Saints, Inc., *(978-0-9769519)* 5753-G Santa Ana Canyon Rd., No. 378, Anaheim Hills, CA 92807 USA Tel 714-505-3127; Fax: 714-838-5857
E-mail: teri@softsaints.com
Web site: http://www.softsaints.com.

Soft Skull Pr. *Imprint of* **Counterpoint Pr.**

Softlight Pr. LLC, *(978-0-9983623)* P.O. Box 242, Wilton, CT 06897 USA Tel 203-554-8509
E-mail: abbymsmith@icloud.com.

SoftPlay, Inc., *(978-1-931312; 978-1-59292)* 3535 W. Peterson Ave., Chicago, IL 60659 USA (SAN 858-4982) Tel 773-509-0707; Fax: 773-509-0404
E-mail: sales@softplayforkids.com
Web site: http://www.softplayforkids.com.

SoGo Creation, *(978-0-9852052; 978-1-941006; 978-1-944425)* 6830 Via Marinero, Carlsbad, CA 92009 USA Tel 760-710-7144
E-mail: sogocreation@yahoo.com.

Soho Crime *Imprint of* **Soho Pr., Inc.**

Soho Pr., Inc., *(978-0-939149; 978-1-56947; 978-1-61695; 978-1-64129)* 853 Broadway Ste. 1402, New York, NY 10003 USA (SAN 662-5088) Tel 212-260-1900; Fax: 212-260-1902; *Imprints:* Soho Crime (Soho Crime); Soho Teen (Soho Teen)
E-mail: soho@sohopress.com
Web site: http://www.sohopress.com
Dist(s): **MyiLibrary**
Open Road Integrated Media, Inc.
Penguin Random Hse. Distribution
Penguin Random Hse. LLC
Random Hse., Inc.

Soho Publishing Company *See* **Sixth&Spring Bks.**

Soho Teen *Imprint of* **Soho Pr., Inc.**

Soil Science Society of America *See* **ASA-CSSA-SSSA**

SoJam Pr., *(978-0-9761477)* P.O. Box 25163, Woodbury, MN 55125-9998 USA (SAN 256-2359)
E-mail: sojam@comcast.net
Web site: http://www.sojampress.com.

Sojourner Publishing, Inc., *(978-0-9701726; 978-0-9773156; 978-0-9824741)* Orders Addr.: 1208 Chilmark Av, Wake Forest, NC 27587 USA; Edit Addr.: 1208 Chilmark Ave., Wake Forest, NC 27587 USA Do not confuse with companies with the same name in Arlington, WA, Clarkston, MI
E-mail: wandam123@yahoo.com
Web site: http://www.thepaperjourney.com.

Sojourner Stories, *(978-0-9896660)* 4225 Piedmont Mesa Rd., Claremont, CA 91711 USA Tel 562-305-9119
E-mail: sojournerstories@gmail.com.

Sol de Oro Pubns., *(978-0-9754261)* 1004 S. Quinn Ct., Gilbert, AZ 85296-8818 USA Tel 480-892-0582
E-mail: SoldeOroPublications@yahoo.com
Web site: http://www.SoldeOroPublications.50megs.com.

Solar Publishing LLC, *(978-0-9785326)* P.O. Box 2116, Ellicott City, MD 21041 USA (SAN 850-8089) Tel 410-493-1872
E-mail: robyn@solarpub.com
Web site: http://www.solarpub.com
Dist(s): **BookBaby.**

Sole Bks., *(978-0-9844257; 978-1-938591)* P.O. Box 10445, Beverly Hills, CA 90213 USA Tel 424-283-4299
E-mail: yitzhak@wildsoccer.com; info@wildsoccer.com; sales@solebooks.com; taly@wildsoccer.com
Web site: http://www.wildsoccerbunch.com; http://www.solebooks.com.

Solebury Press *See* **Thompson Mill Pr.**

Solel Pubns., *(978-0-9748332)* 309 Concord Ave., Oceanside, NY 11572 USA Tel 516-678-9778.

Solemn Word Publishing, *(978-0-9759717)* P.O. Box 301, Grant City, MO 64456 USA
E-mail: cjblanchard@solemnword.com
Web site: http://www.solemnword.com.

Soler, Michael, *(978-0-9795469)* 74 Sashington Heights Rd., Washington, NH 03280 USA (SAN 853-6996).

Solibros, *(978-0-9755945)* 2215 Peachtree N. Ct., Atlanta, GA 30338 USA
Web site: http://www.solibros.com.

Solid Ground Christian Bks., *(978-0-9710169; 978-1-932474; 978-1-59925)* Orders Addr.: P.O. Box 660132, Vestavia Hills, AL 35266 USA Tel 205-443-0311; Fax: 775-822-5917; Toll Free: 877-666-9469; Edit Addr.: 715 Oak Grove Rd., Birmingham, AL 35209-6503 USA
E-mail: solid-ground-books@juno.com; solid_ground_books@yahoo.com; scgbclassics@juno.com; sgcb@charter.net
Web site: http://www.solid-ground-books.com.

Solid Rock Bks. *Imprint of* **Trumpet In Zion Publishing**

Solid Rock Publishing *See* **Trumpet In Zion Publishing**

SolidA, Inc., *(978-0-9677328)* 9339 Paradise Rd., Kewaskum, WI 53040 USA Tel 262-692-9609
E-mail: deanne@solida.net
Web site: http://www.solida.net.

Solitude Pr., *(978-1-928874)* 212 Brooks St., Williamsburg, VA 23185 USA Tel 757-564-1365
E-mail: zander67@cox.net.

Soloman, Debra, *(978-0-578-20706-3)* 3814 N. 54th Ave., Omaha, NE 68104 USA.

Solomon & Makeda Publishing, *(978-0-9973104; 978-0-9987233; 978-1-947318)* 914 Poplar Ln., Williamstown, NJ 08094 USA Tel 609-334-0643
E-mail: purityinstrength@gmail.com.

Solomon Schechter Day Schl. of Greater Boston, *(978-0-9836623)* 60 Stein Cir., Newton, MA 02459 USA Tel 617-964-7765
E-mail: amy.bardack@ssdsboston.org
Web site: www.ssdsboston.org.

Solomon Waterwine, LLC *See* **Tinsley Phelps, LLC**

Solomon's Bks., *(978-0-9763871; 978-0-9827949; 978-0-9838687; 978-0-615-67340-0)* 1100 Misty Meadows Way, Hampton, GA 30228 USA Tel 470-246-8075
E-mail: mrjquillings@gmail.com
Web site: solomonsbooks.org.

Solovisions *Imprint of* **Comic Library International**

Solsidan Hse., *(978-0-9741620)* Orders Addr.: 104 7th St., Colorado Springs, CO 80906 USA; Edit Addr.: 475 Sunnyside Ave., Eugene, OR 97404 USA
E-mail: solsidanhouse@yahoo.com
Web site: http://www.solsidanhouse.com.

Solutionary Stories Pr., *(978-0-692-79987-1)* 3761 Portland Ct., Carlsbad, CA 92010 USA Tel 760-729-7383
E-mail: writermeeg@gmail.com.

Solutions for Human Services, LLC, *(978-0-9764802)* 25 Vernon Dr., Warren, PA 16365 USA Tel 814-726-1228
E-mail: lindab@westpa.net.

Solving Light Bks., *(978-0-9705438; 978-0-692-26013-5)* 727 Mountalban Dr., Annapolis, MD 21409-4646 USA Tel 410-757-4630
E-mail: rbowlej@comcast.net; nancygjohnson@comcast.net
Web site: http://www.solvinglight.com; http://www.theparthenoncode.com
Dist(s): **BookBaby**
CreateSpace Independent Publishing Platform
Send The Light Distribution LLC.

Some Kids I Know, *(978-0-9768230)* Div. of Some Kids I Know, LLC, W323 N8164 Northcrest Dr., Hartland, WI 53029 USA Tel 262-966-2582
E-mail: thorst@wi.rr.com.

Some Kids I Know, LLC, *(978-0-9768230)* W323 N8164 Northcrest Dr., Hartland, WI 53029 USA.

Someday Ranch, *(978-0-9910180)* P.O. Box 414, Wauna, WA 98395 USA Tel 253-380-0663
E-mail: zookeeper99@comcast.net.

†Somerset Pubs., Inc., *(978-0-403)* 1532 State St., Santa Barbara, CA 93101 USA (SAN 204-6105) Toll Free: 800-937-7947
Dist(s): **North American Bk. Distributors**; *CIP.*

Somerspoint Pr., *(978-0-692-18941-2)* 9633 1/2 Red Pony Ln., El Cajon, CA 92021 USA Tel 619-204-7126
E-mail: arabiandaz@gmail.com
Dist(s): **Ingram Content Group.**

Somerville Hse. Bks., Ltd. (CAN) *(978-0-921051; 978-1-58184; 978-1-895897; 978-1-55286; 978-1-894042) Dist. by* **Penguin Grp USA.**

Something Or Other Publishing, *(978-0-9846938; 978-1-7324511)* 3537 Mammoth Trail, Madison, WI 53719 USA Tel 213-952-9557
E-mail: wfransson@gmail.com
Web site: soopllc.com.

Son of Thunder Pubns., *(978-1-7321638)* 155 Highland Way, Taylors, SC 29687 USA Tel 864-436-5898
E-mail: doberman9@juno.com
Web site: http://www.sonofthunderpublications.org.

Sonfire Media, LLC, *(978-0-9825773; 978-0-9891064)* 974 E. Stuart Dr. Suite D, PMB 232, Galax, VA 24333 USA; *Imprints:* Taberah Press (Taberah Pr)
Web site: http://www.sonfiremedia.com.

Song Revival Fellowship & Ministries *See* **Empower Pr.**

Songadh, Jain Swadhyay Mandir, *(978-0-9748681)* 304 Tall Oak Trail, Tarpon Springs, FL 34688 USA Tel 602-863-1073; 727-376-7290; Fax: 602-863-3557; 727-843-8157
E-mail: kahanguru@hotmail.com.

Songbird Pr., *(978-0-9720913)* Orders Addr.: P.O. Box 99, Freeport, ME 04032 USA Fax: 207-373-1128
Web site: http://www.songbirdpress.biz.

Songpaint, *(978-1-7333488)* 201 Commons Pk. S., Stamford, CT 06902 USA Tel 718-413-8177
E-mail: byron.mccray@gmail.com.

Sonic Sword Productions, *(978-0-9797715)* 1089-A Alice Dr., Suite 327, Sumter, SC 29150 USA Tel 803-983-5084
E-mail: john@jhollandbooks.com
Web site: http://jhollandbooks.com; http://rjwargames.com.

Sonis, Gabriela, *(978-0-692-99275-3)* 2950 NE 188th St, Aventura, FL 33180 USA Tel 571-723-8817; *Imprints:* ML Networks (ML Networks)
E-mail: fs2005@gmail.com.

Sonnenschein Bks. *Imprint of* **Black Forest Pr.**

Sonny Evans, *(978-0-578-19464-6)* 969 Sheridan Rd., Glencoe, IL 60022 USA.

Sonny's Legacy Publishing, *(978-0-9990745; 978-1-7325686)* 3131 Harbinger Ln, Dallas, TX 75287 USA Tel 214-662-2782
E-mail: pcfoland4/pamela@folandtech.com; pamela@pamelafoland.com
Web site: www.meganswor ldbookseries.com.

Sono Nis Pr. (CAN) *(978-0-919203; 978-0-919462; 978-0-9690282; 978-1-55039) Dist. by* **Orca Bk Pub.**

SonoMagnetics *See* **RADIOIONICS RESEARCH**

Son-Rise Pubns. & Distribution Co., *(978-0-936369)* 51 Greenfield Rd., New Wilmington, PA 16142 USA (SAN 698-0031) Tel 724-946-9057; Fax: 724-946-8700; Toll Free: 800-358-0777
Web site: http://www.softspace.com/steelvalley; http://www.sonrisepublications.com.

Sonrise Publishing, *(978-0-9724458; 978-0-9845663; 978-0-9914347)* 131 Galleon St. # 2B, Marina Dl Rey, CA 90292-5973 USA (SAN 254-8348) Do not confuse with companies with the same or similar names in Corte Madera, CA, Ashland, OH
E-mail: annsonrise@aol.com
Web site: http://www.sonrisepublishing.com; http://www.annhamiltonwallace.com
Dist(s): **Baker & Taylor Publisher Services (BTPS).**

Sonrise Stable Bks., *(978-0-9847242; 978-1-7333912)* 20938 Coleman Brake Rd, Milford Center, OH 43045 USA Tel 937-644-1967
E-mail: vicki@vickiwatson.com
Web site: http://www.sonrisestable.com
Dist(s): **Follett School Solutions.**

Sonship Pr. *Imprint of* **21st Century Pr.**

Soothing Waterfalls Bks., *(978-0-692-06438-2; 978-0-692-13368-2; 978-0-692-14711-5)* 155 N Pearl Lake Causeway Unit 212, Altamonte Springs, FL 32714 USA Tel 786-267-4079
E-mail: info@soothingwaterfalls.com
Dist(s): **CreateSpace Independent Publishing Platform.**

†Sophia Institute Pr., *(978-0-918477; 978-1-928832; 978-1-933184; 978-1-62282; 978-1-64413)* Orders Addr.: P.O. Box 5284, Manchester, NH 03108 USA (SAN 657-7172) Tel 603-641-9344; Fax: 603-641-8108; Toll Free: 800-888-9344 Do not confuse with Sophia Pr., Durham, NH
E-mail: production@sophiainstitute.com
Web site: http://www.sophiainstitute.com
Dist(s): **eBookit.com**; *CIP.*

Sophie's Tales, LLC, *(978-0-578-03818-6; 978-0-9851575; 978-0-578-49615-3)* 665 S Skinker Blvd, Saint Louis, MO 63105 USA Tel 516-242-1466
E-mail: mpaticoff@sophiestales.com
Web site: www.sophiestales.com.

Sophrose Entertainment Inc., *(978-0-9800736)* P.O. Box 1989, Cape Canaveral, FL 32920-1989 USA (SAN 855-1286) Tel 321-459-3442 Toll Free: 888-599-7483
E-mail: mail@sophrose.com
Web site: http://www.sophrose.com.

Sopris West Educational Services *See* **Cambium Education, Inc.**

Sora Publishing, *(978-0-9765756)* 1800 Atlantic Blvd., A-405, Key West, FL 33040-5708 USA (SAN 256-4157) Tel 305-296-6699
E-mail: sorapublishing@comcast.net
Web site: http://www.sorapublishing.com.

Sorella Bks., *(978-0-9767351)* P.O. Box 454, Plantsville, CT 06479 USA
E-mail: sorellabooks@yahoo.com
Web site: http://www.sorellabooks.com.

Sorenson, E. Randy, *(978-0-615-16939-2)* 3053 Frederick Pl., West Valley City, UT 84119 USA
Web site: http://www.firstreindeer.com.

Sortis Publishing, *(978-0-9772025; 978-0-9827986)* 2193 E. Claxton Ave., Gilbert, AZ 85297 USA (SAN 256-923X) Tel 480-310-8316; Fax: 480-279-5851
E-mail: tradewebb@wydebeam.com
Web site: http://www.sortispublishing.com.

Soul Attitude Press, *(978-0-578-06870-1; 978-1-939181; 978-1-946338)* P.O. Box 1656, Pinellas Park, FL 33782 USA
Web site: http://www.johnrehg.com.

Soul Family Travels *See* **SFT Pubns.**

Soul Mate Publishing, *(978-1-61935; 978-1-68291; 978-1-64716)* P.O. Box 24, Macedon, NY 14502 USA Tel 315-986-4571
Web site: http://www.soulmatepublishing.com.

Soul Pubns., *(978-0-937327)* 232 Rockford St., Mt. Airy, NC 27030 USA (SAN 658-8050) Tel 336-786-4118 (phone/fax); 3220 Lazelle St. #114, STURGIS, SD 57785 Tel 605-720-0986
Dist(s): **Lulu Pr., Inc.**

Soul Vision Works Publishing, *(978-0-9659538; 978-0-9816254)* P.O. Box 360063, Brooklyn, NY 11236 USA Tel 718-493-7981; Toll Free: 888-789-6757; *Imprints:* Vision Works Publishing (Vis Wrks)
E-mail: info@visionworksonline.net
Web site: http://www.visionworksonline.net.

Soulful Storytellers, Inc., *(978-0-9851628)* 3263 Ave. H, Brooklyn, NY 11210 USA Tel 718-781-7560
E-mail: soulmuze@gmail.com.

Soulo Communications, *(978-0-9778209; 978-0-9825607)* Div. of Soulo Communications, Orders Addr.: 2112 Broadway St., NE Suite 100, Minneapolis, MN 55413-3036 USA Tel 612-788-4341; Fax: 612-788-4347
E-mail: tomh@soulocommunications.com
Web site: http://www.soulocommunications.com
Dist(s): **Partners Pubs. Group, Inc.**

Soulshine Pr., LLC, *(978-0-578-40317-5; 978-1-7336496)* 1650 Red Sky Rd., Wimberley, TX 78676 USA Tel 832-964-4830
E-mail: mollybowen13@gmail.com
Web site: soulshinepress.com.

SoulSong Publishing, *(978-0-9793113)* Div. of SoulSong Enterprises, Orders Addr.: P.O. Box 715, Crestone, CO 81131 USA
E-mail: soulsongpublishing@yahoo.com
Web site: http://www.soulsong.org.

Sound Concepts, Incorporated *See* **Verb Technology, Inc.**

Sound Craft Designs, *(978-0-9771357)* P.O. Box 1563, Poway, CA 92074-1563 USA Tel 858-842-1985
E-mail: info@exploreguitar.com
Web site: http://www.exploreguitar.com.

Sound Library *Imprint of* **AudioGO**

Sound Reading *Imprint of* **Sound Reading Solutions**

Sound Reading Solutions, *(978-0-9704183; 978-0-9742485; 978-0-9743384)* 379 Turkey Hill Rd., Ithaca, NY 14850 USA Tel 607-273-1370 (phone/fax); Toll Free: 800-801-1954; *Imprints:* Sound Reading (Sound Read)
E-mail: info@soundreading.com
Web site: http://www.soundreading.com.

Sound Room Pubs., Inc., *(978-1-883049; 978-1-58472)* Orders Addr.: P.O. Box 3168, Falls Church, VA 22043 USA Tel 540-722-2535; Fax: 540-722-0903; Toll Free: 800-643-0295; Edit Addr.: 100 Weems Ln., Winchester, VA 22601 USA; *Imprints:* In Audio (In Aud)
E-mail: commuterslib@worldnet.att.net
Web site: http://www.inaudio.biz/
Dist(s): **Distributors, The**
Findaway World, LLC
Follett Media Distribution
Follett School Solutions.

Sound View Press *See* **Falk Art Reference**

Soundprints, *(978-0-924483; 978-1-56899; 978-1-931465; 978-1-59249; 978-1-60727)* Div. of Trudy Corp., 353 Main Ave., Norwalk, CT 06851 USA Fax: 203-846-1776; Toll Free: 800-228-7839; *Imprints:* Blackbirch Press, Incorporated (Blackbirch Pr); Little Soundprints (Little Sound)
Web site: http://www.soundprints.com
Dist(s): **Follett School Solutions**
Cengage Gale
Learning Connection, The.

Sounds Devine, *(978-0-9745249)* P.O. Box 251, Arabi, LA 70032 USA Do not confuse with Calliope Publishing in Steamboat Springs, CO
Web site: http://www.soundsdevine.com.

Sounds True, Inc., *(978-1-56455; 978-1-59179; 978-1-60407; 978-1-62203; 978-1-68364; 978-1-64963)* Orders Addr.: P.O. Box 8010, Boulder, CO 80306-8010 USA; Edit Addr.: 413 S. Arthur Ave., Louisville, CO 80027 USA (SAN 850-3532) Tel 303-665-3151; Fax: 303-665-5292; Toll Free: 800-333-9185
Web site: http://www.soundstrue.com
Dist(s): **Macmillan.**

Sounds Write Productions, Inc., *(978-0-9626286; 978-1-890161)* 6685 Norman Ln., San Diego, CA 92120 USA Tel 619-697-6120; Fax: 619-697-6124; Toll Free: 800-976-8639
E-mail: soundswrite@aol.com; info@soundswrite.com
Web site: http://www.soundswrite.com.

Sourcebook Project, The, *(978-0-915554; 978-0-9600712)* P.O. Box 107, Glen Arm, MD 21057 USA (SAN 201-7652) Tel 410-668-6047
Web site: http://www.science-frontiers.com.

Sourcebooks Casablanca *Imprint of* **Sourcebooks, Inc.**

†**Sourcebooks, Inc.,** *(978-0-942061; 978-0-9629162; 978-0-9629803; 978-1-57071; 978-1-57248; 978-1-58182; 978-1-883518; 978-1-887166; 978-1-888952; 978-1-4022; 978-1-932783; 978-1-62047; 978-1-4926; 978-1-7282)* 1935 Brookdale Rd., Suite 139, Naperville, IL 60563 USA (SAN 666-7864) Tel 630-961-3900; Fax: 630-961-2168; Toll Free: 800-727-8866; *Imprints:* Sourcebooks Casablanca (Casablanca); Sourcebooks Landmark (Sourcebks Land); Sourcebooks MediaFusion (MediaFusion); Sourcebooks Jabberwocky (Srcbks Jabber); Marianne Richmond Studios, Incorporated (MarianneRich); Cumberland House (Cumberland); Little Pickle Press (LittlePickle); Dawn Publications (DawnPubnsl)
E-mail: info@sourcebooks.com
Web site: http://www.sourcebooks.com/
Dist(s): **Children's Plus, Inc.**
Ebsco Publishing
Follett School Solutions
Ingram Publisher Services
MyiLibrary
New Leaf Publishing Group
Source Bk. Pubns.; *CIP.*

Sourcebooks Jabberwocky *Imprint of* **Sourcebooks, Inc.**

Sourcebooks Landmark *Imprint of* **Sourcebooks, Inc.**

Sourcebooks MediaFusion *Imprint of* **Sourcebooks, Inc.**

Sourland Mountain Bks., *(978-1-7332865)* 2800 N Bismark Ln, Jupiter, FL 33458 USA Tel 561-762-8242
E-mail: klmgorey12@att.net
Web site: sourlandmountainbooks.com.

South Asia Bks., *(978-0-8364; 978-0-88386)* P.O. Box 502, Columbia, MO 65205 USA (SAN 207-4044) Tel 573-474-0116; Fax: 573-474-8124
E-mail: sabooks@juno.com
Web site: http://www.southasiabooks.com.

South Carolina Geographic Alliance, *(978-0-9768247)* Ctr. of Excellence for Geographic Education, Orders Addr.: Department of Geography, Univ. of S. C., Columbia, SC 29208 USA Toll Free: 888-895-2023
Web site: http://www.cas.sc.edu/cege/.

South Dakota Historical Society Pr., *(978-0-9622621; 978-0-9715171; 978-0-9749195; 978-0-9777955; 978-0-9798940; 978-0-9822749; 978-0-9845041; 978-0-9846505; 978-0-9852817; 978-0-9852905; 978-0-9860355; 978-1-941813)* 900 Governors Dr., Pierre, SD 57501 USA; *Imprints:* South Dakota State Historical Society Press (S Dak St Hist Soc Pr)
E-mail: jennifer.mcintyre@state.sd.us; orders@sdhspress.com; info@sdhspress.com; judy.uecker@state.sd.us
Web site: www.sdhspress.com
Dist(s): **BookBaby.**

South Dakota State Historical Society Pr. *Imprint of* **South Dakota Historical Society Pr.**

South Dakota State Historical Society Press *See* **South Dakota Historical Society Pr.**

South Florida Art Ctr., Inc., *(978-0-9719492)* 924 Lincoln Rd., Suite 205, Miami Beach, FL 33139-2609 USA
Web site: http://www.artcentersf.org.

South Hadley Publishing *See* **Moltiverse**

South Main Media by Mindwatering, *(978-0-9909737)* 520 S. Main St., Wake Forest, NC 27587 USA Tel 919-556-3691
E-mail: nicki@southmainmedia.com
Web site: www.southmainmedia.com.

South River Pr., *(978-0-9770764)* P.O. Box 392, Indianola, IA 50125-5012 USA (SAN 256-6982) Tel 515-962-9375.

Southall, Twyla, *(978-0-9765501)* 5837 Karric Sq. Dr., Dublin, OH 43016 USA
E-mail: twyla@tsouthall.com
Web site: http://www.tsouthall.com.

Southeast Media, *(978-1-888141)* 87 Piedmont Dr., Palm Coast, FL 32164-7085 USA
E-mail: Reachment@msn.com
Web site: http://www-gout-haters.com.

Southern Acres Academy, *(978-0-615-17522-5)* 4955 Hwy. 4, Davenport, NE 68335ed USA
Dist(s): **Lulu Pr., Inc.**

Southern Girl Media, *(978-0-9744423)* Orders Addr.: P.O. Box 373, Festus, MO 63028 USA Tel 760-535-2640
Web site: http://www.masonweaver.com
Dist(s): **Tremendous Life Bks.**

Southern Lion Bks., *(978-0-9662454; 978-0-9794203; 978-1-935272)* 1070 Jordan Rd., Madison, GA 30650 USA Tel 706-474-1667 (Tel. & Fax)
E-mail: taniamcclain@yahoo.com; mcclain2@bellsouth.net
Web site: http://www.southernlionbooks.com.

Southern Living *Imprint of* **Time Inc. Bks.**

Southern Yellow Pine (SYP) Publishing LLC, *(978-1-59616; 978-0-9857062; 978-1-940869)* 4351 Natural Bridge Rd., Tallahassee, FL 32305 USA Tel 850-933-0389; *Imprints:* SYP Kids (SYP Kids)
E-mail: tgerrell@syppublishing.com
Web site: www.syppublishing.com.

Southfarm Pr., *(978-0-913337)* Div. of Haan Graphic Publishing Services, Ltd., P.O. Box 1296, Middletown, CT 06457 USA (SAN 283-4146) Tel 860-346-8798
E-mail: southfar@ix.netcom.com
Web site: http://www.war-books.com; http://www.wandahaan.com.

Southgate Pubs. (GBR) *(978-1-85741) Dist. by* **Parkwest Pubns.**

Southpaw Books LLC, *(978-0-9777720)* Southpaw Books LLC, Maplewood, NJ 07040 USA (SAN 850-1017) Tel 973-313-0843; Fax: 973-313-0843
E-mail: info@southpawbooks.com
Web site: http://southpawbooks.com.

Southport Historical Society, Inc., *(978-1-892444)* P.O. Box 10014, Southport, NC 28461-0014 USA Tel 910-457-6940
E-mail: Furstenau@earthlink.net.

Southwest guns & stuff, *(978-0-9747407)* 4212 Lanshire Ct., Grand Prairie, TX 75052-3164 USA.

Southwest Legal Services, *(978-0-9644908; 978-0-9843383; 978-0-9980306)* Div. of Charlynn Publishing Co., Inc., Orders Addr.: P.O. Box 57091, Tucson, AZ 85732 USA Tel 520-795-1414; Edit Addr.: 4152 E. Fifth St., Tucson, AZ 85711 USA
E-mail: swlsorders@yahoo.com
Web site: http://www.southwestlegalservices.com; http://www.bustedbythefeds.com
Dist(s): **Charlynn Publishing Co., Inc.**

Southwest Parks & Monuments Association *See* **Western National Parks Assn.**

SouthWest Pubns., *(978-1-934345)* Div. of NF Publishing, P.O. Box 782, Kingsport, TN 37662 USA Tel 423-765-1416; Fax: 800-807-9203; Toll Free Fax: 800-807-9203; Toll Free: 800-807-9203
Web site: http://www.southwestpublications.net.

Southwestern Pr., Inc, *(978-0-923176)* Orders Addr.: P.O. Box 4297, Carlsbad, CA 92018-4297 USA (SAN 251-5601) Tel 760-434-8858; Fax: 760-434-8888
E-mail: sharon@southwesternpress.com
Web site: http://www.southwesternpress.com/.

Southwestern Publishing House *See* **Southwestern Publishing Hse., Inc.**

†**Southwestern Publishing Hse., Inc.,** *(978-0-87197; 978-1-935442; 978-1-941800; 978-1-943198)* A member of the Southwestern Family of Companies, Orders Addr.: P.O. Box 305142, Nashville, TN 37230 USA (SAN 204-1197) Tel 615-391-2944; Fax: 615-391-2656; Toll Free: 800-798-1780; Edit Addr.: 2451 Atrium Way, Nashville, TN 37214 USA Fax: 615-391-2815; Toll Free: 800-269-6839; *Imprints:* Beckon Books (BeckonBks) Do not confuse with Favorite Recipes in Vernal, UT
E-mail: info@frpbooks.com; kconnelly@swpublishinghouse.com
Web site: http://www.frpbooks.com; http://www.beckonbooks.com; http://www.swpublishinggroup.com; http://www.greenwichpublishing.com; http://quailridgepress.com; swphbooks.com; https://swphmarketplace.com/; http://southwesternbooks.com; http://frpbooks.com; HistoricHospitalityBooks.com; https://www.swphbooks.com/; bluesneakerpress.com; cookbookmarketplace.com; swpublishinghouse.com
Dist(s): **Cookbook Marketplace, The;** *CIP.*

Souvenir Pr. Ltd. (GBR) *(978-0-285) Dist. by* **Consort Bk Sales.**

Souvenir Pr. Ltd. (GBR) *(978-0-285) Dist. by* **IPG Chicago.**

Sovereign Grace Pubs., Inc., *(978-1-878442; 978-1-58960)* P.O. Box 4998, Lafayette, IN 47903-4998 USA (SAN 299-6847) Toll Free: 800-447-9142 Do not confuse with Sovereign Grace Pubns., Lexington, KY
E-mail: jaygreenxx@iquest.net
Web site: http://www.sovgracepub.com.

Sovereign Press *See* **Margaret Weis Productions, Ltd.**

Sow Forth Publishing LLC, *(978-0-9822262)* P.O. Box 303, Lewis Center, OH 43035-9462 USA (SAN 857-7358)
E-mail: sowforth@insight.rr.com.

Sowash, Rick Publishing Co., *(978-0-9762412)* 338 Milton St. # 1, Cincinnati, OH 45202-0971 USA Toll Free: 888-255-2764
E-mail: rick@sowash.com
Web site: http://www.sowash.com.

Soxwings Publishing, *(978-0-615-20974-6)* 414 Executive Ctr. Blvd., Suite 105, El Paso, TX 79902 USA Tel 915-533-3827; Fax: 915-533-3745; Toll Free: 866-416-3827
E-mail: bobtjr@yahoo.com.

SP Family Productions, LLC, *(978-0-9773134)* 5 Knute Drive, Andover, NJ 07821-3912 USA Tel 973-479-6111
E-mail: seancanning@hotmail.com
Web site: http://www.seancanning.com.

Spalding, Brenda, *(978-0-692-25731-9; 978-0-692-92737-3; 978-0-692-97652-4)* 6109 55th Terr. E., Bradenton, FL 34203 USA Tel 941-739-0496
E-mail: bpspalding@msn.com.

Spalding Education International, *(978-1-935289; 978-1-952494)* 23335 N. 18th Dr., Suite 102, Phoenix, AZ 85027-6301 USA (SAN 857-0310) Tel 623-434-1204; Fax: 623-434-1208
E-mail: jsexton@spalding.org; kporter@spalding.org
Web site: http://www.spalding.org.

Spanish Language Texts, Inc., *(978-0-9710710)* Orders Addr.: P.O. Box 1088, New York, NY 10040 USA; Edit Addr.: 19 Seaman Ave. 2M, New York, NY 10034 USA
Web site: http://www.spanishlanguagetexts.com
Dist(s): **Lectorum Pubns., Inc.**

Spanish Pubs., LLC, 8871 SW 129 Terr., Miami, FL 33176 USA Tel 305-233-3365; Fax: 305-251-1310
E-mail: mariela@spanishpublishers.net
Web site: www.spanishpublishers.net.

Spanish-Live, *(978-0-9816973)* 1033 Imperial Dr., Morgantown, WV 26508 USA
E-mail: lorena@spanish-live.com
Web site: http://www.spanish-live.com.

Spann Productions, *(978-0-9772209)* P.O. Box 10412, Bakersfield, CA 93389 USA Tel 661-832-2135 (phone/fax)
E-mail: spannlake@aol.com.

SpanPress, Inc., *(978-1-58045; 978-1-887578)* 5722 S. Flamingo Rd., Suite 277, Cooper City, FL 33330 USA Tel 305-592-7913; Fax: 305-477-5632; Toll Free: 800-585-8384
Dist(s): **Continental Bk. Co., Inc.**
Lectorum Pubns., Inc.

Spark Hse., *(978-1-936174)* Div. of Augsburg Fortress, Pubs., 100 S. 5th St., Suite 600, Minneapolis, MN 55402 USA Tel 612-330-3305; Fax: 612-330-3514; Toll Free: 800-426-0115; *Imprints:* Sparkhouse Press (Sparkhouse)
E-mail: irene.crooks@augsburgfortress.org
Dist(s): **Augsburg Fortress, Pubs.**

Spark Notes *Imprint of* **Sterling Publishing Co., Inc.**

Spark Publishing Group *Imprint of* **Sterling Publishing Co., Inc.**

Sparkhouse Family *Imprint of* **Augsburg Fortress, Pubs.**

Sparkhouse Pr. *Imprint of* **Spark Hse.**

Sparkledoll Productions, *(978-0-9747832)* P.O. Box 56173, Virginia Beach, VA 23456 USA Tel 757-718-3095
E-mail: books@sparkledoll.com
Web site: http://www.sparkledoll.com/publishing.

Sparklesoup LLC, *(978-0-9714776; 978-1-932379; 978-1-59748; 978-1-61814)* 11700 W. Charleston Blvd., Ste. 170-95, Las Vegas, NV 89135 USA; *Imprints:* The Edge (TheEdge)
E-mail: sparklesoup@aol.com
Web site: http://www.sparklesoup.com; http://www.theedgebooks.com; http://www.kailingowbooks.com
Dist(s): **CreateSpace Independent Publishing Platform**
Ingram Content Group.

Sparklesoup Studios, Incorporated *See* **Sparklesoup LLC**

Sparkling Bks. (GBR) *(978-1-907230) Dist. by* **Pathway Bk Serv.**

Sparkling Pr., *(978-0-9774855)* 137 E. Curtice St., St. Paul, MN 55107 USA Tel 651-227-5248.

SparkNotes *Imprint of* **Barnes & Noble, Inc.**

SparkPr. (a Bks.parks Imprint), *(978-1-940716; 978-1-943006; 978-1-68463)* 80 E. Rio Salado Pkwy., TEMPE, AZ 85281 USA Tel 480-275-4280; 480-650-1688
E-mail: Publishing@sparkpointstudio.com
Web site: gosparkpress.com; http://booksparkspr.com/
Dist(s): **Ingram Publisher Services.**

Sparks Fly, *(978-0-9789445)* 609 Myrtle Ave., Apt 3A, Brooklyn, NY 11205-1470 USA Toll Free: 866-556-2432
E-mail: info@sparksfly.org
Web site: http://www.sparksfly.org.

Sparrow Media Group, Inc., *(978-0-9719304; 978-0-9786018; 978-0-9829526)* P.O. Box 44272, Eden Prairie, MN 55344-4272 USA Tel 952-953-9166
Web site: http://www.sparrowmediagroup.com.

Sparrow's Nest Enterprises, LLC, The, *(978-0-578-41346-4; 978-0-578-60460-2)* 7535 Sparrow Rd., Hopedale, IL 61747 USA Tel 309-210-4758
E-mail: tomlbye@yahoo.com
Dist(s): **Independent Pub.**

Spatterdash Pr., *(978-0-9987565)* 1701 S Splitrock Blvd, Brandon, SD 57005 USA Tel 605-582-2266
E-mail: Tammy.osheim4@gmail.com.

Spatterlight Pr., *(978-1-61947)* 6383 Valley View Rd., Oakland, CA 94611-1226 USA Tel 510-502-1506; *Imprints:* Quantalore (MYID_R_QUANTAL)
E-mail: jhvance2@gmail.com
Web site: jackvance.com.

SPC Bks. *Imprint of* **RPJ & Co., Inc.**

SPCK Publishing (GBR) *(978-0-281; 978-0-7459; 978-0-85969; 978-1-902694) Dist. by* **Pilgrim OH.**

SPCK Publishing (GBR) *(978-0-281; 978-0-7459; 978-0-85969; 978-1-902694) Dist. by* **InterVarsity.**

SPD-Small Pr. Distribution, *(978-0-914068)* 1341 Seventh St., Berkeley, CA 94710-1409 USA (SAN 204-5826) Tel 510-524-1668; Fax: 510-524-0852; Toll Free: 800-869-7553 (orders)
E-mail: orders@spdbooks.org
Web site: http://www.spdbooks.org.

Speak *Imprint of* **Penguin Young Readers Group**

Speak Out Ministry, *(978-0-578-02848-4; 978-0-692-86807-2; 978-0-9993791)* 13844 Carter House Way, Silver Spring, MD 20904 USA Tel 202-412-7957
E-mail: aileencunningham15@gmail.com
Web site: http://www.alphathetaomega.com.

Speakeasy Comics (CAN) *(978-0-9737039; 978-0-9738388) Dist. by* **Diamond Book Dists.**

Speak-Easy Publishing, LLC, *(978-0-9714433; 978-0-9754977)* Orders Addr.: P.O. Box 11377, Takoma Park, MD 20913 USA Tel 202-723-1317
E-mail: jgduarte@speakeasypublishing.com; info@speakeasypublishing.com
Web site: http://www.speakeasypublishing.com
Dist(s): **Lyrical Liquor Productions.**

Speaking Volumes, LLC, *(978-1-935138; 978-1-61232; 978-1-62815; 978-1-64540)* 21 Sleeping Dog Rd., Santa Fe, NM 87508 USA (SAN 856-5880) Tel 505-466-4318; 888-777-8204
E-mail: kurt@speaking-volumes.com
Web site: http://www.speaking-volumes.com/indexflsh.asp; http://.www.speakingvolumes.us
Dist(s): **Follett School Solutions.**

SpeakToChange Enterprise, *(978-0-578-52851-9; 978-1-7353908)* 169 CR 381, Water Valley, MS 38965 USA Tel 662-801-6337
E-mail: speaktochange@yahoo.com.

Special Edition Studios, Inc., *(978-0-9759013)* P.O. Box 7216, Sebring, FL 33872-0104 USA
Web site: http://www.sestudios.com.

Special Editions — Customized Biographies *Imprint of* **Slavens Enterprises, LLC.**

Special Ideas, *(978-1-888547)* P.O. Box 9, Heltonville, IN 47436 USA Tel 812-834-5691 (phone/fax); Toll Free: 800-326-1197
E-mail: karen@special-ideas.com; justice@special-ideas.com
Web site: http://www.bahairesources.com; http://www.interfaithresources.com.

Special Kids Company, Incorporated *See* **Anythings Possible, Inc.**

Special Reads for Special Needs, *(978-0-9702698; 978-0-9795922)* 12025 Merganser Dr., Cincinnati, OH 45246-1542 USA Tel 513-541-7617; Fax: 513-541-2543; Toll Free: 866-553-2042
E-mail: specialreads@aol.com
Web site: http://www.specialreads.com.

Specialized Printing, LLC, *(978-0-615-38944-8)* 2430 NW Broadway St., Albany, OR 97321 USA Tel 800-282-6621
E-mail: ericbrunsvold@gmail.com.

Specialized Quality Pubns., *(978-0-9634906; 978-0-9789582)* 921 11th St., S., Wisconsin Rapids, WI 54494 USA (SAN 299-299X) Tel 715-423-7476; *Imprints:* SQP (SQP)
Web site: http://www.specializedqualitypublications.com/index.htm.

Specialty Educational Pubs., *(978-0-9718488)* P.O. Box 161, New Oxford, PA 17350 USA
E-mail: specialtypublishers@hotmail.com.

Specialty Greetings, *(978-0-9860024)* 2225 Grant St., Eugene, OR 97405 USA Tel 541-344-6400
E-mail: orders@specialtygreetings.com
Web site: http://www.SpecialtyGreetings.com.

Specialty Pr., Inc., *(978-0-9621629; 978-1-886941; 978-1-937761)* 300 NW 70th Ave., Suite 102, Plantation, FL 33317 USA (SAN 251-6977) Tel 954-792-8100; Fax: 954-792-8545; Toll Free: 800-233-9273 Do not confuse with Specialty Pr., Inc., in Ocean, NJ
E-mail: sales@addwarehouse.com
Web site: http://www.addwarehouse.com
Dist(s): **Ebsco Publishing**
Independent Pubs. Group
MyiLibrary.

Specialty Publishing Co., *(978-0-9755199)* 135 E. Saint Charles Rd., Caol Stream, IL 60188 USA (SAN 256-0569) Tel 630-933-0844; Fax: 630-933-0845
Web site: http://www.specialtypub.com.

Species Spectrum LLC, *(978-1-7339209)* P.O. Box 32664, Santa Fe, NM 87594 USA Tel 505-231-2329
E-mail: contact@speciesspectrum.com
Web site: speciesspectrum.com.

Spectacle Films, Inc., *(978-0-9767771)* 2021 Commonwealth Ave. #2, Boston, MA 02135 USA Tel 212-807-0290
E-mail: spectaclefilms@gmail.com; csoling@gmail.com
Web site: http://www.Rumpleville.com; http://www.SpectacleFilms.com.

Spectre Publishing, *(978-0-9709191)* 22316 Haig St., Taylor, MI 48180 USA
E-mail: publisher@spectrepublishing.com
Web site: http://www.spectrepublishing.com
Dist(s): **CreateSpace Independent Publishing Platform.**

Spectrum *Imprint of* **Carson-Dellosa Publishing, LLC**

Spectrum Films Inc., *(978-0-9760906)* 4319 Salisbury Rd., Suite 4, Jacksonville, FL 32216 USA
Web site: http://www.spectrumfilms.tv.

SpeculativeFictionReview.com, *(978-0-9785232)* 22281 Letur, Mission Viejo, CA 92691-1406 USA
Web site: http://www.speculativefictionreview.com.

Speech Bin, Inc., The, *(978-0-937857)* 1965 25th Ave., Vero Beach, FL 32960 USA (SAN 630-1657) Tel 772-770-0007; Fax: 772-770-0006
E-mail: info@speechbin.com
Web site: http://www.speechbin.com.

Speech Kids Texas Pr., *(978-1-933319)* 3802 Beaconsdale Dr., Austin, TX 78727-2951 USA (SAN 256-4122)
E-mail: info@speechkidstexaspress.com
Web site: http://www.speechkidstexaspress.com.

Speech Place Publishing, The, *(978-0-9794102)* 1810-A York Rd., No. 432, Lutherville, MD 21093 USA (SAN 853-3679) Tel 410-517-9026
E-mail: cs@thespeechplace.com
Web site: http://www.thespeechplace.com.

Speech Publishing Hse., *(978-0-9770483)* 1115 Cordova St., Suite 318, Pasadena, CA 91106-3013 USA Tel 626-372-1195
E-mail: jonandspeech@prodigy.net.

Speedwitch Media, *(978-0-9749508; 978-0-9987341)* 645 Tanner Marsh Rd., Guilford, CT 06437-2106 USA
Web site: http://www.speedwitchmedia.com.

Speedy Kids (Children's Fiction) *Imprint of* **Speedy Publishing LLC**

Speedy Publishing Books (General) *Imprint of* **Speedy Publishing LLC**

Speedy Publishing LLC, *(978-1-939643; 978-1-62884; 978-1-63022; 978-1-63187; 978-1-63287; 978-1-63383; 978-1-63428; 978-1-68032; 978-1-63501; 978-1-68127; 978-1-68145; 978-1-68185; 978-1-68212; 978-1-68260; 978-1-68280; 978-1-68305; 978-1-68326; 978-1-68368; 978-1-5419; 978-0-578-40177-5; 978-0-578-40278-9) 7914 Raven Creek Ln., Cypress, TX 77433 USA (SAN 920-6620) Tel 954-379-7796; Fax: 954-379-7796; 40 E. Main St., Newark, DE 19733; Imprints:* Dissected Lives (Auto Biographies) (Dissected Live); Speedy Kids (Children's Fiction) (Speedy Kids); Baby Professor (Education Kids) (Baby Profes); Jupiter Kids (Childrens & Kids Fiction) (Jupiter Kids); One True Faith (Religion & Spirituality) (One True Faith); Dot EDU (Educational & Textbooks) (Dot EDU); Biz Hub (Business & Investing) (Biz Hub); Universal Politics (Politics & Social Sciences) (Univ Politics); Speedy Publishing Books (General)

(SpeedyPub); @ Journals & Notebooks (JournalsN); Professor Beaver (PrBeaver) Web site: http://www.speedypublishing.co.

Speight, Theresa , L.L.C. *See* **Complete in Christ Ministries, Inc.**

Spellbound *Imprint of* **Magic Wagon**

Spellbound River Pr., *(978-0-9911914; 978-1-945017)* P.O. Box 161081, Austin, TX 78716 USA Tel 617 233 6143 E-mail: bondsam@hotmail.com.

†Speller, Robert & Sons, Pubs., Inc., *(978-0-8315)* Orders Addr.: P.O. Box 411, New York, NY 10159 USA (SAN 203-2295) Tel 646-334-8008; P.O. Box 461, New York, NY 10108 (SAN 203-2309); *CIP.*

Spence City *Imprint of* **Spencer Hill Pr.**

Spence Publishing Co., *(978-0-9653208; 978-1-890626)* 5646 Milton St. Ste. 314, Dallas, TX 75206-3923 USA (SAN 257-9383) Toll Free: 888-773-6782 E-mail: tspence@spencepublishing.com Web site: http://www.spencepublishing.com *Dist(s):* **Chicago Distribution Ctr. Vigilante, Richard Bks.**

Spence, Stephen Mark, *(978-0-9705324)* 211 Moore Ave., Buffalo, NY 14223 USA Tel 716-836-5178 E-mail: spence@buffalo.edu Web site: http://www.acsu.buffalo.edu/~spence/.

Spencer Hill Contemporary *Imprint of* **Spencer Hill Pr.**

Spencer Hill Middle Grade *Imprint of* **Spencer Hill Pr.**

Spencer Hill Pr., *(978-0-9845311; 978-0-9831572; 978-1-937053; 978-1-939392; 978-1-63392)* 27 W. 20th St., New York, NY 10011 USA (SAN 859-6573); *Imprints:* Spence City (Spence City); Spencer Hill Contemporary (SpencerHill); Spencer Hill Middle Grade (SpencHill Middl) E-mail: karen@beaufortbooks.com Web site: http://www.spencerhillpress.com; http://www.spencecity.com/ *Dist(s):* **INscribe Digital Independent Pubs. Group Midpoint Trade Bks., Inc.**

Spencer Pr., The, *(978-0-932270)* Div. of The Spencer Group, Nine Tudor Terr., Newton, MA 02466-1509 USA (SAN 205-5651) Tel 617-965-8388; Fax: 617-964-3971 Do not confuse with companies with similar names in Wells, ME, Portland, OR E-mail: jacknusan@aol.com.

Spencer, Russell & Kathlynn, *(978-0-9664055)* Orders Addr.: 2484 Dewberry Ln., Oxnard, CA 93030 USA Tel 805-981-2820 E-mail: RSpencer@windshieldadventures.com Web site: http://www.windshieldadventures.com *Dist(s):* **Gem Guides Bk. Co.**

Spencer's Mill Pr., *(978-0-9771666)* 555 Church St. No. 1501, Nashville, TN 37219 USA (SAN 256-8225) Tel 615 477-2044 E-mail: trudychoices@aol.com Web site: http://www.spencersmillpress.com *Dist(s):* **BookBaby.**

Spending Solutions Pr., *(978-0-9729732)* 4347 W. NW Hwy., Suite 120, PMB 283, Dallas, TX 75220-3864 USA Web site: http://www.spendingsolutions.com.

Sper, Emily *See* **Jump Pr.**

Speranza's Pr., *(978-0-9800327)* P.O. Box 2404, Glenview, IL 60025 USA.

Sphaira Publishing, *(978-0-692-60640-7; 978-1-7323585)* 1855 Tyler Trce, Lawrenceville, GA 30043 USA Tel 470-447-7251 *Dist(s):* **CreateSpace Independent Publishing Platform.**

Sphinx Publishing, *(978-0-9725951; 978-0-9762875; 978-0-9770912; 978-0-9776711; 978-1-934144; 978-1-935921)* 7400 Airport Dr., Macon, GA 31216 USA Toll Free: 866-311-9578; *Imprints:* Blue Marble Books (Blu Marble Bks) E-mail: gpulliam@indigopublishing.us Web site: http://www.indigopublishing.us *Dist(s):* **American Wholesale Bk. Co. Parnassus Bk. Distributors.**

SPI Bks., *(978-0-944007; 978-1-56171)* 99 Spring St., 3rd Flr., New York, NY 10012 USA Tel 212-431-5011; Fax: 212-431-8646 E-mail: ian@spibooks.com Web site: http://www.spibooks.com *Dist(s):* **APG Sales & Distribution Services Two Rivers Distribution.**

Spica Bks., *(978-0-9728531)* 9742 N. 105th Dr., Sun City, AZ 85351 USA Tel 623-583-6764 (phone/fax) E-mail: marilyn@dreamlady.com Web site: http://www.dreamlady.com.

Spicka, Jana Incorporated *See* **Tree of Life Pr.**

Spider Comics, *(978-0-9859884)* 1489 Wallace Dr., Springville, UT 84663 USA Tel 678-386-5550 E-mail: michael@spidercomics.com Web site: www.spidercomics.com.

SPIE, *(978-0-8194; 978-0-89252; 978-1-62841; 978-1-5106)* Orders Addr.: P.O. Box 10, Bellingham, WA 98227-0010 USA (SAN 224-1706) Tel 360-676-3290; Fax: 360-647-1445; Edit Addr.: 1000 20th St., Bellingham, WA 98225 USA (SAN 669-1323) Tel 360-676-3290; Fax: 360-647-1445; Toll Free: 888-504-8171 E-mail: spie@spie.org; kerryg@spie.org; marysu@spie.org Web site: http://www.spie.org/bookstore *Dist(s):* **Wiley, John & Sons, Inc. ebrary, Inc.**

Spineless Bks., *(978-0-9724244; 978-0-9801392; 978-0-9853578; 978-0-9998086)* P.O. Box 91, Urbana, IL 61803 USA Tel 217-722-1033 E-mail: william@spinelessbooks.com Web site: http://www.spinelessbooks.com.

Spinelli, Patti, *(978-0-9742328)* 87 Portland Ave., Dover, NH 03820-3525 USA E-mail: pasbug1010@aol.com.

Spinifex Pr. (AUS) *(978-1-875559; 978-0-908205; 978-1-876756; 978-1-74219; 978-0-646-04196-4; 978-1-925581; 978-1-925950) Dist. by* **IPG Chicago.**

Spinner Bks., *(978-1-59653)* 2030 Harrison St., San Francisco, CA 94110-1310 USA Tel 415-503-1600; Fax: 415-503-0085.

Spinner Pubns., Inc., *(978-0-932027)* 164 William St., New Bedford, MA 02740-6022 USA (SAN 686-0826) Tel 508-994-4564; Fax: 508-994-6925; Toll Free: 800-292-6062 E-mail: spinner@spinnerpub.com Web site: http://www.spinnerpub.com.

Spinning Broom Bks. Publishing, LLC, *(978-0-692-61294-1; 978-0-9983244)* 1997 S. Meadows Dr., Kalispell, MT 59901 USA Tel 406-871-4292 E-mail: spinningbroombooks@gmail.com Web site: http://www.spinningbroombookspublishing.com/ *Dist(s):* **CreateSpace Independent Publishing Platform.**

Spinning Horse Publishing, *(978-0-9842832)* 6320 Cty. Rd. K, Omro, WI 54963 USA Tel 920-685-2094.

SpinSmart Software, *(978-0-9743434)* Orders Addr.: 4717 S. Hydraulic, Wichita, KS 67216 USA E-mail: support@spinsmart.com Web site: http://www.spinsmart.com.

Spinsters Ink *See* **Spinsters Ink Bks.**

†Spinsters Ink Bks., *(978-1-883523; 978-1-935226)* Div. of Southern Belle Bks., P.O. Box 242, Midway, FL 32343 USA (SAN 212-6923) Tel 850-576-2370; Fax: 850-576-3498; Toll Free: 800-301-6860 E-mail: Linda@SpinstersInk.com Web site: http://www.spinstersink.com *Dist(s):* **Bella Distribution SPD-Small Pr. Distribution Two Rivers Distribution**; *CIP.*

Spirit & Life Productions, *(978-0-9788928)* Orders Addr.: 2260 Grand Ave., Baldwin, NY 11510 USA Tel 866-430-3801.

Spirit Arm Publishing *See* **Solemn Word Publishing**

Spirit of Americar *Imprint of* **Child's World, Inc., The**

Spirit Pr. *Imprint of* **Bendon, Inc.**

Spirit Pr., LLC, *(978-1-893075)* Orders Addr.: 1520 NE 21st Ave. #101, Portland, OR 97232 USA Tel 503-954-0012 Do not confuse with companies with the same name in Santa Cruz, CA, Raleigh, NC E-mail: suzannedeak@gmail.com; onespiritpress@gmail.com; spiritpresspublishing@gmail.com Web site: http://www.onespiritpress.com *Dist(s):* **CreateSpace Independent Publishing Platform Ingram Content Group.**

Spirit Productions *See* **Personal Freedom Publishing**

Spirit Publishing LLC, *(978-0-9770967)* 819 Marcy Ave., Brooklyn, NY 11216 USA (SAN 256-7636) Tel 718-230-5605.

SpiritBooks *Imprint of* **Portal Ctr. Pr.**

Spiritbuilding *See* **Spiritbuilding Pubs.**

Spiritbuilding Pubs., *(978-0-9774754; 978-0-9821376; 978-0-9829811; 978-0-9990684)* 9700 Ferry Rd., Waynesville, OH 45068 USA E-mail: mhallen@spiritbuilding.com Web site: http://www.spiritbuilding.com.

Spirited Presentations, *(978-0-9790017)* 4249 Peak Ln., Grand Rapids, MI 49525 USA E-mail: Kathey@spiritedpresentations.com Web site: http://Spiritedpresentations.com.

Spirited Publishing, LLC, *(978-0-9768513)* Orders Addr.: P.O. Box 1796, Appleton, WI 54912-1796 USA Tel 920-419-3340 E-mail: kris@spiritedpublishing.com Web site: http://www.spiritedpublishing.com.

Spiritpoint Press *See* **Bitty Book Pr.**

Spiritual Hse. Pr., The, *(978-0-9656847)* 24 Old Milford Rd., Brookline, NH 03033 USA Tel 603-672-8550 E-mail: blueskies@myfairpoint.net Web site: http://www.TheSpiritualHouse.com.

Spitzer, Lance, *(978-0-615-72525-3)* 226 Crestmoor Cir., Pacifica, CA 94044 USA Tel 650-922-8554 E-mail: lancesherwood@comcast.net.

Spizzirri Pr., Inc., *(978-0-86545)* P.O. Box 9397, Rapid City, SD 57709 USA (SAN 215-2851) Tel 605-348-2749; Fax: 605-348-6251 (orders); Toll Free: 800-325-9819; 800-322-9819 E-mail: spizzpub@aol.com Web site: http://www.spizzirri.com.

Splash Designworks, *(978-0-692-87695-4; 978-0-578-42380-7; 978-0-578-42381-4)* 68 Shore Ln., Milford, DE 19963 USA Tel 302-399-7851 E-mail: info@splashdw.com Web site: www.splashdw.com.

Splendid Benedict, *(978-0-615-90023-0; 978-0-9910809)* 5094 N Agave Trl, Flagstaff, AZ 86001 USA Tel 303-455-1835 *Dist(s):* **CreateSpace Independent Publishing Platform.**

Splendid Torch, *(978-0-9788027; 978-0-615-16717-6; 978-0-615-16784-8)* 2000 St. Regis Dr. #6d, Lombard, IL 60148 USA (SAN 851-6588) Web site: http://www.puglish.com *Dist(s):* **Lulu Pr., Inc.**

Splendors Publishing, *(978-0-9717228)* P.O. Box 1155, Soquel, CA 95073 USA Fax: 831-464-1854 E-mail: lalo@laloflorelli.com Web site: http://www.laloflorelli.com.

Split Level of the Blessed Suburbs Publishing, *(978-0-9761515)* 56 Arbor St., Hartford, CT 06106-1201 USA Tel 860-586-8448 (phone/fax) Web site: http://www.tedpaulsen.com.

Spoken Arts, Inc., *(978-0-8045)* Orders Addr.: 3901 Union Blvd Suite 160, St Louis, MO 63115 USA (SAN 990-7734); Edit Addr.: 1517 Highland valley cir, wildwood, MO 63005 USA (SAN 205-079X) Fax: 845-878-9009; Toll Free: 800-326-4090 E-mail: sales@spokenartsinc.com Web site: http://www.spokenartsinc.com *Dist(s):* **AudioGO Follett Media Distribution Follett School Solutions Lectorum Pubns., Inc. Weston Woods Studios, Inc.**

Spoken Word, The, *(978-0-9637644)* 1031 Michigan Ave. NE, No. 205, Washington, DC 20017 USA Tel 202-832-2368 Do not confuse with Spoken Word, The, Arlington , TX.

SpokenVizions Entertainment Group, LLC, *(978-0-9773834)* P.O. Box 373, Florissant, MO 63032 USA Tel 314-517-8764 E-mail: info@spokenvizions.com Web site: http://www.spokenvizions.com.

Spookatorium, The, *(978-0-9966984)* 1762 Silver Leaf Dr., Loveland, CO 80538 USA E-mail: Spookatorium.info@gmail.com Web site: Spookatorium.com.

Spoon Publishing Hse., *(978-0-615-11213-8)* Div. of A Corpus Polymedia Monolith, 440 E. Broadway, Executive Suite 51, Salt Lake City, UT 84111-2651 USA E-mail: spoonpublishing@corpuspolymedia.com Web site: http://www.corpuspolymedia.com/spoonpublishing/; http://www.spoonpublishing.com.

Spooners Publishing, *(978-0-9766179)* 98 Onteora Ct., Shokan, NY 12481-5610 USA Tel 845-657-8737 E-mail: ecurtis@hvc.rr.com.

Spork *Imprint of* **Clear Fork Publishing**

Sport Story Publishing, *(978-0-9702216)* 740 Lakeview Dr., Palm Harbor, FL 34683 USA Fax: 727-447-3587 E-mail: thoover@tampabay.rr.com.

Sport Workbooks, *(978-0-9787458)* P.O. Box 1623, Pacifica, CA 94044 USA (SAN 851-5093) Tel 650-270-3200 E-mail: baseballmath@hotmail.com.

Sport Your Stuff Corp., *(978-1-931746)* 5025 Longbrook Rd., Winston Salem, NC 27105 USA.

SportAmerica, *(978-1-879498)* P.O. Box 95030, South Jordan, UT 84095 USA Tel 801-253-3360; Fax: 801-253-3361; Toll Free: 800-467-7885 Web site: http://www.sportamerica.com.

Sportime International, *(978-0-9793506)* 3175 Northwoods Pkwy. # A, Norcross, GA 30071-1539 USA E-mail: dkissel@sportime.com Web site: http://www.sportime.com.

Sportiva Bks., *(978-0-692-11783-5; 978-0-692-13805-2; 978-0-9980307; 978-1-7342758)* 11435 Avondale Rd. NE, Redmond, WA 98052 USA Tel 425-405-8010 E-mail: info@acurcio.com; anthony@acurcio.com Web site: www.sportivabooks.com *Dist(s):* **CreateSpace Independent Publishing Platform.**

Sports Challenge Network *See* **Toy Vey Toys**

Sports Illustrated For Kids, *(978-0-316; 978-0-553; 978-1-886749; 978-1-930623)* Div. of Time, Inc., 135 W. 50th St. ., New York, NY 10020-1393 USA Tel 212-522-1212; Fax: 212-522-0926 E-mail: joe_nunziata@sikids.com Web site: http://www.sikids.com *Dist(s):* **Hachette Bk. Group Independent Pubs. Group.**

Sports In Mind, *(978-0-9745066; 978-0-9765074)* 3603 Palm Harbor Blvd., Unit C, Palm Harbor, FL 34683 USA Fax: 727-942-3339 Web site: http://www.ravesystems.com.

Sports Marketing International, Inc., *(978-0-9743082)* 27 E. Housatonic St., Pittsfield, MA 01201-4121 USA Tel 413-499-1733; Fax: 413-499-3820; Toll Free: 800-320-1733; *Imprints:* Moscow Ballet (Moscow Ballet) E-mail: smi@nutcracker.com Web site: http://www.nutcracker.com.

Sports Masters, *(978-1-58382)* Div. of Sports Publishing, Inc., 804 N. Neil St., Champaign, IL 61820 USA Tel 217-363-2072; Fax: 217-363-2073; Toll Free: 877-424-2665 E-mail: choffman@sagamorepub.com *Dist(s):* **Ingram Publisher Services.**

Sports Publishing, LLC, *(978-1-57167; 978-1-58261; 978-1-58382; 978-1-59670)* 804 N. Neil St., Champaign, IL 61820 USA Tel 217-363-2072; Fax: 217-353-2073; Toll Free: 877-424-2665 Do not confuse with Sports Publishing, Champaign, IL E-mail: info@sportspublishingllc.com Web site: http://www.sportspublishingllc.com *Dist(s):* **Hachette Bk. Group Ingram Publisher Services MyiLibrary.**

Sports Touch *See* **Sports Touch/Kate Montgomery**

Sports Touch/Kate Montgomery, *(978-1-878069)* 1625 E. Jackson Blvd., Elkhart, IN 46516 USA E-mail: kate@sportstouch.com; katemontgomery@mac.com Web site: http://www.lulu.com; http://www.sportstouch.com; http://www.createspace.com *Dist(s):* **Lulu Pr., Inc.**

Sportsman's Connection, *(978-1-885010)* Div. of Sportsman's Marketing, Inc., Orders Addr.: P.O. Box 852, Lake Elmo, MN 55042 USA Tel 800-264-0474; Fax: 651-773-3320; Toll Free: 800-777-7461; Edit Addr.: 1810 N. 16th St. Ste. 1, Superior, WI 54880-2597 USA E-mail: info@sportsmansconnection.com Web site: http://www.sportsmansconnection.com *Dist(s):* **Partners Bk. Distributing, Inc.**

SportsZone *Imprint of* **ABDO Publishing Co.**

Spotlight, *(978-1-59961)* Div. of ABDO Publishing Group, Orders Addr.: P.O. Box 398166, Edina, MN 55439-8166 USA Fax: 952-831-1632; Toll Free: 877-877-5939; Edit Addr.: 8000 W. 78th St., Suite 310, Edina, MN 55439 USA; *Imprints:* Chapter Books (ChapBooks); Graphic Novels (GraphicNovel); Picture Book (PicBook); Marvel Age (Marvel Age) E-mail: info@abdopublishing.com Web site: http://www.abdopublishing.com *Dist(s):* **ABDO Publishing Co.**

Spotlight Books *See* **Hannacroix Creek Bks., Inc.**

Spotlight News Publications *See* **Autumn Hse. Publishing**

Spotted Dog Pr., Inc., *(978-0-9647530; 978-1-893343)* Orders Addr.: P.O. Box 1721, Bishop, CA 93515 USA (SAN 257-9936) Tel 760-872-1524; Fax: 800-872-0681; Toll Free: 800-417-2790 Do not confuse with Spotted Dog Pr., Ashland, OR E-mail: wbenti@spotteddogpress.com; store@spotteddogpress.com Web site: http://www.spotteddogpress.com *Dist(s):* **Gem Guides Bk. Co. Partners/West Book Distributors Treasure Chest Bks.**

Spreeda Publishing, *(978-0-9748979)* Div. of SPREEDA, 14204 W. 72nd St., Shawnee, KS 66216 USA Do not confuse with Maple Leaf Publishing in Minneapolis, MN E-mail: karen@spreeda.com Web site: http://www.spreeda.com.

Spriitelee Enterprises, *(978-0-9773460)* P.O. Box 207, Westwood, MA 02090 USA.

Spring Arbor Distributors, Inc., Subs. of Ingram Industries Inc., 4271 Edison Ave., Chino, CA 91710 USA; 7315 Innovation Blvd., Fort Wayne, IN 46818-1371; Edit Addr.: 1 Ingram Blvd., La Vergne, TN 37086-1976 USA Fax: 615-213-5192; Toll Free: 800-395-4340; 800-395-7234 (customer service) E-mail: orders@springarbor.com.

Spring Creek Bk. Co., *(978-1-932898; 978-0-9960974; 978-1-944657)* P.O. Box 1013, Rexburg, ID 83440 USA Tel 801-669-4368 Web site: http://www.springcreekbooks.com *Dist(s):* **Brigham Distribution.**

Spring Ducks Bks., LLC, *(978-0-9761076)* Orders Addr.: P.O. Box 44847, Madison, WI 53744-4847 USA Toll Free: 800-342-4404; Edit Addr.: 222 Carillon Dr., Madison, WI 53705 USA E-mail: kathy@springducks.com Web site: http://www.springducks.com.

Spring Harbor Pr., *(978-0-935891)* Div. of Spring Harbor, Ltd., Orders Addr.: P.O. Box 346, Delmar, NY 12054 USA (SAN 695-9768) Tel 518-478-7817 (phone/fax) E-mail: springharbor@springharborpress.com; info@springharborpress.com Web site: http://www.springharborpress.com.

Spring Hollow Bks., LLC, *(978-0-9665389)* P.O. Box 115, Cave Spring, GA 30124-0115 USA Tel 706-235-5113; Fax: 706-235-0742 Do not confuse with Spring Hollow Bks., Richfield, MN E-mail: jbcjmc@aol.com.

Spring Tide Publishing, *(978-0-9765578)* 1281 N. Ocean Dr. Suite 151, Singer Island, FL 33404 USA Tel 561-632-2278 E-mail: delores@springtidepublishing.com Web site: www.springtidepublishing.com.

Spring Tree Pr., *(978-0-9785007)* P.O. Box 461, Atlantic Highlands, NJ 07716 USA (SAN 850-8429) Tel 732-872-8002; Fax: 732-872-6967 Web site: http://www.springtreepress.com *Dist(s):* **New Leaf Distributing Co., Inc.**

†Springer, *(978-0-387; 978-0-8176; 978-3-211; 978-3-540; 978-3-7908; 978-4-431; 978-1-85233; 978-1-84628; 978-1-4419; 978-1-4612; 978-1-4613; 978-1-4614; 978-1-4615; 978-1-4684; 978-1-4757; 978-1-4899; 978-1-4939; 978-1-5041; 978-1-0716)* Subs. of Springer Science+Business Media, Orders Addr.: P.O. Box 2485, Secaucus, NJ 07096-2485 USA Tel 201-348-4033; Fax: 201-348-4505; Toll Free: 800-777-4643; Edit Addr.: a/o Springer Nature, 233 Spring St., New York, NY 10013-1578 USA (SAN 203-2228) Tel 212-815-0249; 212-460-1500; Fax: 212-460-1575; Toll Free: 800-777-4643 Thomson Delmar Learning Distributes Blanchard & Loeb Nursing Videos Only E-mail: Slu@Springer-ny.com; service-ny@springer.com; customerservice@springernature.com.com Web site: http://www.springeronline.com; http://www.springer.com *Dist(s):* **Ebsco Publishing Metapress MyiLibrary Palgrave Macmillan Rittenhouse Bk. Distributors ebrary, Inc.**; *CIP.*

Springer, Mary Jane, *(978-0-578-22443-5; 978-0-578-67932-7)* 26029 S. Saddletree Dr., Sun Lakes, AZ 85248 USA Tel 815-985-4258 E-mail: maryspringer1109@gmail.com.

†Springer Publishing Co., Inc., *(978-0-8261; 978-0-939957; 978-1-888799; 978-1-932603; 978-0-9771597; 978-1-933864; 978-1-935281; 978-1-936287; 978-1-936303; 978-1-61705; 978-1-62070)* 11 W. 42nd St., 15th Fl., New York, NY 10036 USA (SAN 203-2236) Tel 212-431-4370; Fax: 212-941-7842; Toll Free: 877-687-7476 E-mail: Springer@springerpub.com; journals@springerpub.com; Editorial@springerpub.com; cs@springerpub.com Web site: http://www.springerpub.com *Dist(s):* **CreateSpace Independent Publishing Platform**

Ebsco Publishing
Independent Pubs. Group
Johns Hopkins Univ. Pr.
MyiLibrary
Rittenhouse Bk. Distributors
ebrary, Inc.; *CIP.*

Springer-Verlag New York, Incorporated *See* **Springer**

Springs Ink Publishing *See* **McCaid Paul Books**

SpringTree *Imprint of* **Forest Hill Publishing, LLC**

Sprite Pr., *(978-0-9706654; 978-0-9764295)* 2118 Sycamore Cove Cir., Miamisburg, OH 45343 USA Tel 740-767-2470
E-mail: spritepress@aol.com
Web site: http://www.members.aol.com/spritepress.

Sproing Books *See* **Gripper Products**

Sproles, Clay books *See* **Cats Corner Publishing**

Sprouls, Bridget, *(978-0-692-09142-5; 978-0-692-11034-8)* 219 W. 18th St., SHIP BOTTOM, NJ 08008 USA Tel 609-576-6420
E-mail: BridgetSprouls@gmail.com
Dist(s): **Ingram Content Group.**

Sprouting Peanut Pubs., *(978-0-615-22222-6; 978-0-578-66458-3; 978-0-578-66460-6)* P.O. Box 2606, Gilroy, CA 95021 USA
Web site: http://www.whatsupwillie.com.

Spruce Box *See* **Fun Family Publishing**

Spruce Gulch Pr., *(978-0-9625714; 978-0-9841259)* Orders Addr.: P.O. Box 4347, Rome, NY 13442-4347 USA (SAN 297-3014) Tel 315-337-3626
E-mail: SprGulch@aol.com
Dist(s): **North Country Bks., Inc.**

Spuyten Duyvil Publishing, *(978-0-923389; 978-0-9661242; 978-1-881471; 978-0-9720662; 978-1-933132; 978-1-941550; 978-1-944682; 978-1-947980; 978-1-949966; 978-1-952419)* 223 Bedford Ave. No. 725, Brooklyn, NY 11211 USA (SAN 237-9481) Toll Free: 800-886-5304 (phone/fax)
E-mail: editors@spuytenduyvil.net
Web site: http://www.spuytenduyvil.net
Dist(s): **SPD-Small Pr. Distribution.**

SpyGirls Pr., *(978-0-9852273; 978-0-9979545)* P.O. Box 1537, Fairfax, VA 22038 USA Tel 571-213-1586
E-mail: melissamahle@verizon.net
Web site: www.anatoliasteppe.com.

Spyrou-Andriotis, Vicky, *(978-0-615-24795-3; 978-0-9821808)* 3919 Old Town Rd., Bridgeport, CT 06606 USA
E-mail: info@vickyandriotis.com
Web site: http://www.vickyandriotis.com.

SQP *Imprint of* **Specialized Quality Pubns.**

Square Circle Pr., LLC *See* **Square Circle Pr. LLC**

Square Circle Pr. LLC, *(978-0-9789066; 978-0-9833897; 978-0-9856926; 978-0-9989670)* P.O. Box 913, Schenectady, NY 12301 USA (SAN 851-9145) Tel 518-432-6657 Do not confuse with Square Circle Press in Corte Madera, CA
E-mail: bookinfo@squarecirclepress.com
Web site: http://www.squarecirclepress.com
Dist(s): **Ingram Content Group**
North Country Bks., Inc.

Square Deal Pr., *(978-0-9754941)* 368 S. McCaslin Blvd., Box 206, Louisville, CO 80027 USA.

Square Fish, *(978-0-312)* 175 Fifth Ave., New York, NY 10010 USA Tel 646-307-5770
E-mail: squarefish.market@hbpub.com
Web site: http://www.squarefishbooks.com
Dist(s): **Children's Plus, Inc.**
Macmillan
Westminster John Knox Pr.

Square Halo Bks., *(978-0-9658798; 978-0-9785097; 978-1-941106)* Orders Addr.: P.O. Box 18954, Baltimore, MD 21206 USA Tel 410-485-6227; Edit Addr.: 4310 Southern Ave., Baltimore, MD 21206 USA
E-mail: square_halo@yahoo.com; ned@squarehalobooks.com
Web site: http://www.squarehalobooks.com
Dist(s): **Baker & Taylor Publisher Services (BTPS).**

Square One Pubs., *(978-0-9664202; 978-0-7570; 978-0-9792746)* 115 Herricks Rd., Garden City Park, NY 11040 USA Tel 516-535-2010; Fax: 516-535-2014; *Imprints:* Vital Health Publishing (Vital Hlth)
E-mail: sq1info@aol.com
Web site: http://squareonepublishers.com
Dist(s): **Athena Productions, Inc.**

Square Tree *See* **Blast Cafe**

Squarey Head, Inc., *(978-0-9742003)* 6362 W. Cross Dr., Littleton, CO 80123 USA Tel 303-798-1877; Fax: 303-794-4639.

Squid Works, *(978-0-9755041; 978-0-9972813)* Orders Addr.: 2132 E. 97th Dr., Thornton, CO 80229 USA
E-mail: squidworkscomics@gmail.com
Web site: http://www.squidworkscomics.com
Dist(s): **Mascot Bks., Inc.**

Squires Publishing, *(978-0-9816048)* 7224 S. Yates Blvd., Suite 3N, Chicago, IL 60649 USA Tel 773-667-0039
E-mail: tanyacloud@comcast.net.

SRA/McGraw-Hill, *(978-0-07; 978-0-383)* Div. of The McGraw-Hill Education Group, Orders Addr.: 220 E. Daniel Dale Rd., DeSoto, TX 75115-2490 USA Fax: 972-228-1982; Toll Free: 800-843-8855; Edit Addr.: 8787 Orion Pl., Columbus, OH 43240-4027 USA Tel 614-430-6600; Fax: 614-430-6621; Toll Free: 800-468-5850
E-mail: sra@mcgraw-hill.com
Web site: https://www.sraonline.com
Dist(s): **Libros Sin Fronteras**
Weston Woods Studios, Inc.

SRAtkinson, *(978-0-9964550)* 104 10th St 2E, Hoboken, NJ 07030 USA Tel 435-668-0225
E-mail: savvyatkinson@gmail.com
Web site: sratkinson.com.

SRFPRTY, *(978-1-7342208)* 136 S. Navassa Rd., Leland, NC 28451 USA Tel 910-782-7934
E-mail: justicew095@gmail.com
Web site: FUDGEWILLI.COM.

Sri Ramakrishna Math (IND) *(978-81-7120; 978-81-86465; 978-81-7823) Dist. by* **Vedanta Pr.**

Sroda, George, *(978-0-9604486)* P.O. Box 97, Amherst Junction, WI 54407 USA (SAN 210-8607) Tel 715-824-3868; Fax: 715-824-5344.

SRT Publishing, *(978-0-9771248)* 530 Moon Clinton Rd., Moon Township, PA 15108 USA Tel 412-741-0581; Fax: 412-264-1103
E-mail: merch@silverringthing.com
Web site: http://www.silverringthing.com.

Sruvis Publishing, *(978-0-9889907)* 2219 Pear Blossom, San Antonio, TX 78247 USA Tel 210-219-2156; Fax: 210-494-1994
E-mail: lyndasdavis8@aol.com.

Ssorgsoft, LLC, *(978-0-9765240)* P.O. Box 771192, Orlando, FL 32877 USA.

St. Aidan Pr., Inc., *(978-0-9719230)* 96 Dunlap Dr., Charles Town, WV 25414 USA
E-mail: michael_rabjohns@hotmail.com
Web site: http://www.staidanpress.com.

St. Augustine Academy Pr., *(978-1-936639; 978-1-64051)* 12050 Rambling Rd., Homer Glen, IL 60491 USA Tel 708-645-4691
E-mail: Lbergman2@sbcglobal.net
Web site: www.staugustineacademypress.com.

St. Bernard Publishing, LLC, *(978-0-9741269)* P.O. Box 2218, Bay City, MI 48707-2218 USA Tel 989-892-1348 (phone/fax)
E-mail: bcgirl@charter.net
Web site: http://www.lifeongrannysfarm.com/.

St. Cyr Pr., *(978-1-7339929)* 115 Grove Ave., Albany, NY 12208-3120 USA Tel 518-482-8816
E-mail: aliciastenard@yahoo.com
Web site: aliciastenard.com.

St. Germain, Mark *See* **Three Cups, LLC**

St. Hope Academy, *(978-0-9759548)* Orders Addr.: P.O. Box 5447, Sacramento, CA 95817 USA Tel 916-649-7900; Fax: 916-452-7177; Edit Addr.: 3400 3rd Ave., Sacramento, CA 95817 USA
Web site: http://40acresartgallery.org.

St. John's Pr., *(978-0-9710551; 978-0-615-83132-9; 978-0-9916014)* Orders Addr.: 5318 Torri Park Dr., Cottondale, AL 35453 USA Tel 205-242-4422; Fax: 205-553-9459 Do not confuse with Saint John's Press in Los Angeles, CA
E-mail: charleysix@gmail.com.

St. Martin's Griffin *Imprint of* **St. Martin's Pr.**

St. Martin's Paperbacks *Imprint of* **St. Martin's Pr.**

†St. Martin's Pr., *(978-0-312; 978-0-8050; 978-0-940687; 978-0-9603648; 978-1-55927; 978-1-58063; 978-1-58238; 978-1-4299; 978-1-250)* Div. of Holtzbrinck Pubs., Orders Addr.: 16365 James Madison Hwy., Gordonville, VA 22942 USA Tel 540-672-7600; Fax: 540-672-7540 (customer service); Toll Free Fax: 800-672-2054; Toll Free: 888-330-8477; Edit Addr.: 175 Fifth Ave., 20th Flr., New York, NY 10010 USA (SAN 200-2132) Tel 212-674-5151 (Trade Div.); 212-726-0200 (College Div.); Fax: 212-674-3179 (Trade Div.); 212-686-9491 (College Div.); Toll Free: 800-221-7945 (Trade Div.); 800-470-4767 (College Div.); *Imprints:* Saint Martin's Griffin (St Martin Griffin); Saint Martin's Paperbacks (St Martins Paperbacks); Dunne, Thomas Books (Thomas Dunne); Minotaur Books (Minotaur); Golden Books Adult Publishing Group (Golden Adult); Golden Guides from Saint Martin's Press (Gldn Guides); Priddy Books (Priddy); Wednesday Books (Wednesday Bks); Odd Dot (Odd Dot)
E-mail: webmaster@stmartins.com; enquiries@stmartins.com
Web site: http://www.stmartins.com; http://www.smpcollege.com
Dist(s): **Comag Marketing Group**
Cambridge Univ. Pr.
Children's Plus, Inc.
CreateSpace Independent Publishing Platform
Ediciones Universal
Kaplan Publishing
Libros Sin Fronteras
Macmillan
MyiLibrary
Westminster John Knox Pr.
ebrary, Inc.; *CIP.*

St Mary's Church, *(978-0-9763902)* 429 Central Ave., Sandusky, OH 44870 USA Tel 419-625-7465
Web site: http://www.stmarysandusky.org.

St. Michael's Abbey, *(978-0-9742298)* 19292 El Toro Rd., Silverado, CA 92676-9710 USA
E-mail: fmorbertw@yahoo.com
Web site: http://www.abbeynews.com.

St. Nicholas Pr. *Imprint of* **CrossBearers Publishing**

St. Pauls *Imprint of* **St Pauls/Alba Hse. Pubs.**

St Pauls Pubns. (AUS) *(978-0-909986; 978-0-949080; 978-1-875570; 978-1-876295; 978-1-921032; 978-1-921472; 978-1-921963; 978-1-925494) Dist. by* **St Pauls Alba.**

†St Pauls/Alba Hse. Pubs., *(978-0-8189)* Div. of Society of St. Paul, 2187 Victory Blvd., Staten Island, NY 10314-6603 USA (SAN 201-2405) Tel 718-761-0047; Fax: 718-761-0057; 718-698-8390; Toll Free: 800-343-2522; *Imprints:* Saint Pauls (Saint Pauls)
E-mail: albabooks@aol.com
Web site: http://www.albahouse.org; *CIP.*

St. Roux Pr., *(978-0-9718433)* 308 Montmartre St., Folsom, LA 70437 USA
E-mail: faucheux@msn.com.

Stabenfeldt Inc., *(978-1-933343; 978-1-934983)* Orders Addr.: 225 N. Main St., Bristol, CT 06011 USA Toll Free: 800-410-4145; *Imprints:* PONY (Pny)
Web site: http://www.pony4kids.com.

Stacey Alysson Yoga, *(978-0-692-83320-9; 978-0-692-06023-0; 978-0-692-06025-4; 978-0-692-11213-7; 978-0-692-13589-1)* 234 s gale Dr. #109, BEVERLY HILLS, CA 90211 USA Tel 424-333-6771
E-mail: jeffwcrawford5+LVP0003257@gmail.com; jeffwcrawford5+LVP0003257@gmail.com.

Stacey Publishing (GBR) *(978-1-906768) Dist. by* **Casemate Pubs.**

†Stackpole Bks., *(978-0-8117)* 5067 Ritter Rd., Mechanicsburg, PA 17055 USA (SAN 202-5396) Tel 717-796-0411; Fax: 717-796-0412; Toll Free: 800-732-3669
E-mail: ccraley@stackpolebooks.com
Web site: http://www.stackpolebooks.com/
Dist(s): **MyiLibrary**
National Bk. Network
Rowman & Littlefield Publishers, Inc.; *CIP.*

Stadium Adventure Series *See* **August in Au Train Press**

Staff Development for Educators, *(978-0-9627389; 978-1-884548; 978-1-934026; 978-1-935502; 978-1-63133)* Div. of Highlights for Children, Orders Addr.: P.O. Box 577, Peterborough, NH 03458 USA Tel 603-924-9621; Fax: 603-924-6688; Toll Free Fax: 800-337-9929; Toll Free: 800-321-0401; Edit Addr.: 10 Sharon Rd., Peterborough, NH 03458 USA; *Imprints:* Crystal Springs Books (Crystal Spgs)
E-mail: dfredericks@sde.com
Web site: http://www.sde.com; http://www.crystalsprings.com; http://www.barnesandnoble.com
Dist(s): **Follett School Solutions**
Stenhouse Pubs.

Stafford House, *(978-0-9822587; 978-0-9981070; 978-1-7344786)* P.O. Box 291, Pacific Palisades, CA 90272 USA
Web site: http://www.abcyogaforkids.com; www.kidsyogaday.com.

Stagecast Software, Inc., *(978-1-929721)* 580 College Ave., Palo Alto, CA 94306 USA Tel 650-354-0735; Fax: 650-354-0739; Toll Free: 888-782-4322
E-mail: info@stagecast.com
Web site: http://www.stagecast.com.

Stahl Pubns., *(978-0-9755174)* P.O. Box 201, Ashley, IN 46705-0201 USA.

Staige Productions, *(978-0-9641375)* 290 Orrin St., Winona, MN 55987-2083 USA Tel 507-452-3627.

Stairway Pubns., *(978-0-9740061)* P.O. Box 518, Huntington, NY 11743-0518 USA (SAN 255-3422) Fax: 631-351-2142
E-mail: publisher@stairwaypub.com
Web site: http://www.stairwaypub.com
Dist(s): **Quality Bks., Inc.**

Stairway Publishing, *(978-0-9761953)* 1332 Anacapa St., Suite 200, Santa Barbara, CA 93101 USA; 230 E Pedregosa St., Santa Barbara, CA 93101 (SAN 256-761X) Tel 805-451-5070; Fax: 805-962-1404 Do not Confuse with Shoreline Publishing in Bayside, NY
E-mail: pumoff@seedmackall.com.

Stairwell Bks., *(978-0-9768730; 978-0-9833482; 978-1-939269)* 9 Carleton St., Greenwich, CT 06830 USA
E-mail: rose@stairwellbooks.com; argillott@gmail.com
Web site: http://www.dreamcatchermagsazine.co.uk; http://www.stairwellbooks.co.uk; http://www.stairwellbooks.com.

Stampley, C. D. Enterprises, Inc., *(978-0-915741; 978-1-58087)* Orders Addr.: P.O. Box 33172, Charlotte, NC 28233 USA (SAN 294-1325) Tel 704-333-6631; Fax: 704-336-6932; Edit Addr.: 6100 Orr Rd., Charlotte, NC 28213 USA
E-mail: info@stampley.com; rick@stampley.com
Web site: http://www.stampley.com
Dist(s): **Follett School Solutions**
Giron Bks.

Stance Pubns., *(978-0-615-18108-0; 978-0-9821047)* 4510 Seashore Dr., #A, Newport Beach, CA 92663-2520 USA
E-mail: marcpent@msn.com
Web site: http://www.stancepublications.com
Dist(s): **Ingram Content Group.**

Standard International Print Group Inc., *(978-1-58279; 978-1-888777; 978-1-86091; 978-1-60081)* Orders Addr.: 9723 Acqua Ct. Unit 324, Naples, FL 34113 USA Tel 239-595-5516; Fax: 239-649-5832; Edit Addr.: 2614 Tamiami Trail N., Naples, FL 34103 USA Tel 239-248-5550
E-mail: sales@chefexpressmedia.com; sales@stndpub.com
Web site: https://www.chefexpressmedia.com/; http://stndpub.com/.

Standard Publications, Inc., *(978-0-9709788; 978-0-9722691; 978-1-59462; 978-1-60424; 978-1-60597; 978-1-4385; 978-1-61742)* P.O. Box 3204, Kirkland, WA 98083 USA (SAN 912-9251) Tel 708-669-4643; Fax: 630-214-0564; *Imprints:* Book Jungle (Book Jungle)
E-mail: spi@standardpublications.com
Dist(s): **MyiLibrary.**

†Standard Publishing, *(978-0-7847; 978-0-87239; 978-0-87403; 978-0-933657; 978-1-58170)* 8805 Governors Hill Dr. Ste. 400, Cincinnati, OH 45249-3319 USA (SAN 110-5515) Toll Free Fax: 877-867-5751 (customer service); Toll Free: 800-543-1301; 800-543-1353 (customer service); *Imprints:* Bean Sprouts (Bean Sprouts) Do not confuse with Standard Publishing Corp., Boston, MA
E-mail: customerservice@standardpub.com; trolfes@standardpub.com; dlewis@standardpub.com
Web site: http://www.standardpub.com
Dist(s): **B&H Publishing Group**
Cook, David C.; *CIP.*

Standard Publishing Company *See* **Standard Publishing**

Standing For Christ, Inc., *(978-0-9754834)* P.O. Box 28468, Cleveland, OH 44128 USA Tel 216-299-4523
E-mail: kelvinsfc@yahoo.com
Web site: http://www.standingforchrist.org.

Stanek, Mary Beth, *(978-0-9747556)* 291 Lothrop Rd., Grosse Pointe, MI 48236 USA.

Stanfield, James Co., *(978-1-56304; 978-1-941264)* P.O. Box 41058, Santa Barbara, CA 93140 USA Tel 805-897-1185; Fax: 805-897-1187; Toll Free: 800-421-6534
E-mail: maindesk@stanfield.com
Web site: http://www.stanfield.com.

Stanford Center for Research in Disease Prevention (S C R D P) *See* **Stanford Prevention Research Ctr.**

Stanford Prevention Research Ctr., *(978-1-879552)* Div. of Stanford Univ. Schl. of Medicine, Hoover Pavilion, Rm. N 229 211 Quarry Rd., Stanford, CA 94305-5705 USA Tel 650-723-0003; Fax: 650-498-4828
E-mail: askhprc@med.stanford.edu
Web site: http://hprc.stanford.edu.

Stanger, Robert *See* **Club Pro Products**

Stanley, Donna Lacy, *(978-0-9766894)* 244 Sunset Dr., Waynesboro, VA 22980 USA Tel 540-949-5474
E-mail: dlstanle@yahoo.com.

Stanley Publishing Co., *(978-0-9790350; 978-0-615-55295-8; 978-0-9856495)* 810 Agua Caliente Dr., El Paso, TX 79912-1705 USA (SAN 852-257X)
E-mail: info@stanleypublishing.com
Web site: http://stanleypublishing.com.

Stanley, Shirley, *(978-0-9747318)* Orders Addr.: 1116 20th St. S., No. 216, Birmingham, AL 35205 USA Tel 205-663-6674.

Stansbury Publishing, *(978-0-9708922; 978-0-9766269; 978-1-935807)* Subs. of Heidelberg Graphics, Orders Addr.: 2 Stansbury Ct., Chico, CA 95928 USA
E-mail: spublishing@heidelberggraphics.com
Web site: http://www.heidelberggraphics.com.

Stanton & Harper Bks., *(978-0-9630151)* Orders Addr.: P.O. Box 21585, Greensboro, NC 27420 USA; Edit Addr.: 291 Buckhorn Trail, Reidsville, NC 27320 USA Tel 910-951-1234; Fax: 910-951-9966.

Star Bible & Tract Corp., *(978-0-933672; 978-0-940999; 978-1-56794)* Orders Addr.: P.O. Box 821220, Fort Worth, TX 76182 USA (SAN 203-3518) Tel 817-416-5889; Fax: 817-251-0129; Toll Free: 800-433-7507; Edit Addr.: P.O. Box 821220, N Richlnd Hls, TX 76182-1220 USA (SAN 664-6247)
E-mail: starbible@starbible.com
Web site: http://www.starbible.com
Dist(s): **Twentieth Century Christian Bks.**

Star Bright Bks., Inc., *(978-1-887734; 978-1-932065; 978-1-59572; 978-1-64909)* 13 Landsdowne, Cambridge , MA 02139 USA (SAN 254-5225) Tel 617-354-1300; Fax: 617-354-1399; Toll Free: 800-788-4439
E-mail: info@starbrightbooks.com; r.s.lambert@starbrightbooks.com
Web site: http://www.starbrightbooks.com.

Star Cross'd Destiny *Imprint of* **Bohemian Trash Studios**

Star Dome Publishing, LLC, *(978-0-9766662)* P.O. Box 411300, Melbourne, FL 32941 USA
E-mail: fcavalli@bellsouth.net
Web site: http://www.stardomepublishing.com.

Star Dust Dream, *(978-1-948060)* 4544 Dix, Luna Pier, MI 48157 USA Tel 734-317-7251; 3829 MI ST RD 151, Erie, MI 48133 Tel 734-317-7251
E-mail: mimmi92025@yahoo.com
Web site: prgarcia1.com.

Star Gem Publishing, *(978-0-615-54730-5; 978-0-9978384)* 4101 California Ave #44, Bakersfield, CA 93309 USA Tel 661-932-0573
Dist(s): **CreateSpace Independent Publishing Platform**
Dummy Record Do Not USE!!!!.

Star Light Pr., *(978-1-879817)* 1811 S. First St., Austin, TX 78704-4299 USA Tel 512-441-0588; 512-441-0062 (phone/fax); *Imprints:* Children (Children)
E-mail: info@starlightpress.com
Web site: http://www.starlightpress.com
Dist(s): **Book Wholesalers, Inc.**
iLeon.

Star Pr., The, *(978-0-9676189)* Div. of Indiana Newspapers, Inc., Orders Addr.: P.O. Box 2408, Muncie, IN 47307-0408 USA (SAN 169-2437) Tel 765-213-5799; Fax: 765-213-5703; Toll Free: 800-783-7827; Edit Addr.: 345 S. High St., Muncie, IN 47305 USA
E-mail: rfarmer@thestarpress.com
Web site: http://www.thestarpress.com.

Star Pubns., *(978-0-932356)* 1211 W. 60th Terr., Kansas City, MO 64113 USA (SAN 212-4564) Tel 816-523-8228 Do not confuse with companies with the same name in Rancho Palos Verdes, CA, Orange Park, FL, San Jose, CA, Colorado Springs, CO.

Star Publish LLC, *(978-1-932993; 978-1-935188)*
E-mail: starpublishinfo@gmail.com
Web site: http://www.starpublishllc.com
Dist(s): **Smashwords.**

Star Quest Publishing Phx, *(978-0-9767035)* 3030 E. Shangri-La Rd., Phoenix, AZ 85028 USA Tel 602-621-3431; Fax: 602-926-2484
E-mail: karen@starquestpublishingphx.com
Web site: http://www.starquestpublishing.com.

Publisher Name Index

Star Tribe Publishing, *(978-0-9970554; 978-0-9996387)* 843 N. Calle De Pinos, Palm Springs, CA 92262 USA Tel 925-351-6717
E-mail: authorariellamoon@gmail.com
Web site: http://www.AriellaMoon.com.

Star Write Creations, *(978-0-9743851)* P.O. Box G, Birnamwood, WI 54414 USA Toll Free: 888-999-6609.

Starbell Bks., *(978-0-9747774)* 2507 LaBrecque Dr., Plainfield, IL 60544 USA Tel 815-254-9495
E-mail: starbellbooks@comcast.net
Web site: http://www.starbellbooks.com.

StarBerry *Imprint of* **Astra Publishing Hse.**

Starborne House *See* **Redding, Marion T.**

Starbound Bks. *Imprint of* **Wheatmark, Inc.**

Starbound Publishing Company *See* **Collectors Pr., Inc.**

Starbucks Coffee Co., *(978-0-9726394)* 2401 Utah Ave. S., Seattle, WA 98134 USA Tel 206-447-1575; Toll Free: 800-235-2883
E-mail: info@starbucks.com
Web site: http://www.starbuckscollectibles.com.

Starburns Industries Pr., *(978-0-9889363)* 23720 Canyon Rd, Battle Ground , WA 98604 USA Tel 360-431-4533
E-mail: Sbipress@starburnsind.com
Web site: starburnsindustries.com
Dist(s): **Diamond Comic Distributors, Inc.**
Diamond Bk. Distributors.

StarCastle Publishing *See* **ecEmedia, a Div. of The EC Corp.**

Stardust Books *See* **Stardust Bks.**

Stardust Bks., *(978-0-692-85016-9; 978-0-692-16413-6)* 106 Standing Rock Dr., McMurray, PA 15317 USA Tel 412-736-3253
E-mail: sherri.laughner@gmail.com.

STAReviews *Imprint of* **N&N Publishing Co., Inc.**

Starfall Education, *(978-1-59577)* Starfall Education Foundation, P.O. Box 359, Boulder, CO 80306 USA Toll Free Fax: 800-943-6666; Toll Free: 888-857-8990
Web site: http://www.starfall.com
Dist(s): **Blue Mountain Arts Inc.**

Starfall Publications *See* **Starfall Education**

Starfish Aquatics Institute, *(978-0-9746613; 978-0-578-13105-4; 978-0-578-13448-2; 978-0-578-13449-9)* 10 Ramshorn Ct., Savannah, GA 31411 USA Tel 912-692-1173
E-mail: sara@sai-intl.org; jill@sai-intl.org
Web site: http://www.starfishaquatics.org.

Starfish Bay Publishing Pty Ltd. (AUS) *(978-1-76036) Dist. by* **BTPS.**

Stargazer Publishing Co., *(978-0-9643853; 978-0-9713756; 978-1-933277)* Orders Addr.: P.O. Box 77002, Corona, CA 92877-0100 USA (SAN 298-6566) Tel 951-898-4619; Fax: 951-898-4633; Toll Free: 800-606-7895; Edit Addr.: 958 Stanislaus Dr., Corona, CA 92881 USA Do not confuse with Stargazer Publishing in Neenah, WI
E-mail: stargazer@stargazerpub.com
Web site: http://www.stargazerpub.com.

Stark Productions Inc., *(978-1-936592)* 109 Orange Ave., St. Cloud, FL 34769 USA Tel 407-957-8502 (Tel/Fax) Do not confuse with Stark Productions Inc in OaklandCA
E-mail: stark109@hotmail.com
Web site: www.starkproductioninc.com.

Starks, Shirley *See* **Inspirational Hse. of America**

Starla Enterprises, Inc., *(978-1-938085; 978-0-692-94596-4; 978-0-692-96659-4; 978-0-692-97291-5; 978-0-692-97328-8; 978-0-692-97351-6; 978-0-692-07934-8; 978-0-692-08941-5; 978-0-692-08943-9; 978-0-692-08944-6; 978-0-692-12953-1; 978-0-578-40977-1; 978-0-578-40981-8; 978-0-578-40983-2; 978-0-578-40993-1; 978-0-578-40994-8; 978-0-578-40995-5; 978-0-578-48303-0; 978-0-578-48307-8; 978-0-578-52365-1) 9415 E. Harry St Ste 603, Wichita, KS 67207 USA Tel 316-393-8195*
E-mail: starla@starlakaye.com
Web site: www.starlacriser.com.

Starlight Pubns., *(978-0-9615667; 978-0-9936965-8-9)* 1438 Epping Forest Dr., Atlanta, GA 30319 USA (SAN 695-9644) Tel 404-237-7125.

StarLineage Pubns., *(978-1-885226)* P.O. Box 1630, McCloud, CA 96057-1630 USA Tel 530-964-2496.

Starling Publishing, *(978-0-9857394; 978-0-9976390)* 1011 Paintbrush Ave., Kimberly, ID 83341 USA Tel 435-881-4812
E-mail: amberargyle@yahoo.com.

Starlit Publishing LLC, *(978-0-9792946)* 1750 Powder Springs Rd. Suite 190, Marietta, GA 30064 USA.

Starlog Group, Incorporated *See* **Profile Entertainment, Inc.**

StarProse Corp., *(978-0-9721071)* 17445 Roosevelt Rd., Hemlock, MI 48626 USA
E-mail: webmaster@starprose.com
Web site: http://www.starprose.com.

Starr, Joyce *See* **Dr. Joyce STARR Publishing**

Starry Forest Bks. *Imprint of* **Starry Forest Bks., Inc.**

Starry Forest Bks., Inc., *(978-1-946000; 978-1-946260; 978-1-951784)* 7816 45th Ave., Elmhurst, NY 11373 USA Tel 917-345-2160; *Imprints:* Starry Forest Books (StrryFrstBk)
E-mail: A@aramkim.com
Dist(s): **Two Rivers Distribution.**

Starry Girl Publishing, *(978-0-9960737; 978-0-9986143)* 5553 W. 6th St. No. 2409, Los Angeles, CA 90036 USA Tel 323-931-4038
E-mail: jennifer.farwell@gmail.com
Web site: www.jenniferfarwell.com.

Starry Sky Publishing, *(978-0-9855899; 978-0-9961470; 978-0-9996399)* P.O. Box 419, Tampa, FL 33601 USA Tel 443-838-7228
E-mail: starryskypub@gmail.com.

StarryBks., *(978-0-9882113; 978-0-692-27075-2; 978-0-692-34543-6)* P.O. Box 1788, Yelm, WA 98597 USA Tel 360-894-3592
E-mail: dreamscapes@ywave.com
Dist(s): **CreateSpace Independent Publishing Platform.**

Starscape *Imprint of* **Doherty, Tom Assocs., LLC**

Starseed & Urantian Schools of Melchizedek Publishing *See* **Global Community Communications Publishing**

Starseed Universe Pr., *(978-0-9991251)* 60 Overbrook Dr., Cherry Hill, NJ 08002 USA Tel 609-314-1750
E-mail: stefaniannmilanese@gmail.com.

Starshell Pr., Ltd., *(978-0-9707110)* 210 Ridge Rd., Watchung, NJ 07069 USA Tel 908-755-7050; Fax: 212-983-5271
E-mail: starshellpress@yahoo.com
Web site: http://www.starshellpress.com.

Starshow Pubns., *(978-0-9966665; 978-0-9989245)* 122 Woodland St., BURKESVILLE, KY 42717 USA Tel 6153069481.

Start Publishing LLC, *(978-0-939416; 978-0-9664520; 978-1-57344; 978-1-930486; 978-1-60977; 978-1-936740; 978-1-62558; 978-1-62778; 978-1-62793; 978-1-940550; 978-1-63228; 978-1-63355; 978-1-68146; 978-1-68299; 978-1-63596; 978-1-64506; 978-1-64593; 978-1-951273; 978-1-952438; 978-1-64974) 101 Hudson St. 37th Flr., Ste. 3705, Jersey City, NJ 07302 USA; Imprints:* Salvo Press (SalvoPr); Pyr Books (PyrBks); Cleis Press (CleisPr)
E-mail: weisfeld@start-media.com; start-publishing.com
Web site: http://www.start-publishing.com
Dist(s): **Blackstone Audio, Inc.**
MyiLibrary
National Bk. Network
Red Wheel/Weiser
Simon & Schuster, Inc.
SCB Distributors.

Starter Guides LLC, *(978-0-9995860)* 769 NW 10th St, Miami, FL 33136 USA Tel 520-413-8810
E-mail: info@starterguide.org
Web site: www.starterguide.org.

StarWalk Kids Media *Imprint of* **Isabella Products, Inc.**

Starward Publishing, *(978-0-9862099)* 18552 Ocean Mist Dr, Boca Raton, FL 33498 USA Tel 561-482-9812
E-mail: info@starwardpublishing.com.

Stash Bks. *Imprint of* **C & T Publishing**

State Historical Society of North Dakota, *(978-1-891419; 978-0-9796796; 978-0-9801993)* Orders Addr.: 612 E. Blvd. Ave., Bismarck, ND 58505-0830 USA Tel 701-205-7802; Fax: 701-328-3710
E-mail: nhowe@nd.gov
Web site: http://www.history.nd.gov.

State Historical Society of Wisconsin *See* **Wisconsin Historical Society**

State Hse. Pr., *(978-0-938349; 978-1-880510; 978-1-933337)* S. 14th & Sayles Blvd., Austin, TX 79697 USA (SAN 660-966X); McMurry University, Box 637, Abilene, TX 79697-0637 Tel 325-793-4697; Fax: 325-793-4754 Do not confuse with State House Publishing in Madison, WI
E-mail: ckahl@mcm.edu
Web site: http://www.mcwhiney.org
Dist(s): **Encino Pr.**
Texas A&M Univ. Pr.

State of Growth Publishing Co., *(978-0-9740289)* P.O. Box 38633, Colorado Springs, CO 80937 USA
Web site: http://www.stateofgrowth.com.

State Standards Publishing, LLC, *(978-1-935077; 978-1-935884; 978-1-938813; 978-1-946400)* P.O. Box 68, Athens, GA 30603 USA (SAN 856-292X) Tel 706-621-5225; Fax: 706-621-5226; Toll Free: 866-740-3056; *Imprints:* Everett Press (Everett Pr)
E-mail: jward@statestandardspublishing.com
Web site: http://www.statestandardspublishing.com.

State Street Pr. *Imprint of* **Borders Pr.**

†State Univ. of New York Pr., *(978-0-7914; 978-0-87395; 978-0-88706; 978-1-4384)* Orders Addr.: P.O. Box 960, Herndon, VA 20172-0960 USA (SAN 203-3496) Tel 703-661-1575; Fax: 703-996-1010; Toll Free Fax: 877-204-6074; Toll Free: 877-204-6073 (customer service); Edit Addr.: 22 Corporate Woods Blvd., 3rd Flr., Albany, NY 12211-2504 USA (SAN 658-1730) Tel 518-472-5000; Fax: 518-472-5038; Toll Free: 866-430-7869; *Imprints:* Suny Press (Suny Pr)
E-mail: info@sunypress.edu; suny@presswarehouse.com
Web site: http://www.sunypress.edu
Dist(s): **Books International, Inc.**
CreateSpace Independent Publishing Platform
Ebsco Publishing
Pegasus Pr.
SPD-Small Pr. Distribution
TNT Media Group, Inc.
ebrary, Inc.; *CIP.*

Stationmaster Pr., *(978-0-692-11404-9)* 8907 Center St., Manassas, VA 20110 USA Tel 703-786-7798
E-mail: robbiekirby@yahoo.com
Dist(s): **Independent Pub.**

Staves Creations, *(978-0-9600739; 978-1-7333451; 978-1-951622)* 10745 Cather Ave, LAS VEGAS, NV 89166 USA
Dist(s): **Ingram Content Group.**

Staying Healthy Media, Inc., *(978-0-9763237)* 4409 Summer Grape Rd., Pikesville, MD 21208 USA Tel 410-484-0457
E-mail: healthy@stayinghealthymedia.com
Web site: http://www.stayinghealthymedia.com.

Steam Crow Pr., *(978-0-9774173)* 7233 W. Cottontail Ln., Peoria, AZ 85383 USA
E-mail: sales@steamcrow.com
Web site: http://www.steamcrow.com.

Steam, Karl *See* **Libro Studio LLC**

Steam Passages Pubns., *(978-0-9758584)* 508 Lakeview Ave., Wake Forest, NC 27587 USA
E-mail: sdegaetano@steampassages.com
Web site: http://www.dlrcad.com/book.

STEAM Publishing, LLC, *(978-0-9984337)* 2125 E STANFORD DR, TEMPE, AZ 85283 USA Tel 480-777-2621
E-mail: scolsen.writer@gmail.com.

†Steck-Vaughn, *(978-0-8114; 978-0-8172; 978-0-8393; 978-0-7398; 978-1-4190)* Div. of Houghton Mifflin Harcourt Supplemental Pubs., Orders Addr.: 6277 Sea Harbor Dr., 5th Flr., Orlando, FL 32887 USA Toll Free Fax: 877-578-2638; Toll Free: 888-363-4266; Edit Addr.: 10801 N. Mopac Expressway, Bldg. 3, Austin, TX 78759 USA (SAN 658-1757) Toll Free: 800-531-5015
E-mail: ecare@harcourt.com
Web site: http://www.harcourtachieve.com
Dist(s): **Children's Plus, Inc.**
Follett School Solutions
Houghton Mifflin Harcourt Publishing Co.
Houghton Mifflin Harcourt Supplemental Pubs.; *CIP.*

Stedjee Publishing *See* **Lawe Street Bks.**

Steel Bridge Pr., *(978-0-9764415)* 610 Briarcliff, Bardstown, KY 40004-8941 USA Tel 502-348-7447; Fax: 502-350-1126
E-mail: john@steelbridgepress.com.

Steele, Eugene *See* **E-BookTime LLC**

Steele Studios, *(978-0-9716811)* Orders Addr.: P.O. Box 3093, Glenwood Springs, CO 81602 USA (SAN 254-3230); Edit Addr.: 125 Ctr. Dr., No.18, Glenwood Springs, CO 81601 USA.

Steenblik, Kyle J., *(978-0-692-97391-2)* 36 W. Burton Ln., KAYSVILLE, UT 84037 USA Tel 801-390-9519
E-mail: kyle.j.steenblik@gmail.com
Dist(s): **Ingram Content Group.**

Steerforth Pr., *(978-0-944072; 978-1-58195; 978-1-883642; 978-1-58642)* 45 Lyme Rd. # 208, Hanover, NH 03755-1219 USA; *Imprints:* Campfire (Campf); Pushkin Press (Pushkin P); Elsewhere Editions (ElsewhereEd); Pushkin Children's Books (PushkinChld); Pushkin Collection (PushkinColl)
E-mail: helga@steerforth.com; info@steerforth.com
Web site: http://www.steerforth.com
Dist(s): **Consortium Bk. Sales & Distribution**
MyiLibrary
Penguin Random Hse. Distribution
Penguin Random Hse. LLC
Random Hse., Inc.
Red Wheel/Weiser.

Steich, Brooke, *(978-0-578-54197-6; 978-1-7333882)* 12513 160th Ave SE, Renton, WA 98059 USA Tel 206-351-2474
E-mail: amaia.brooke@gmail.com.

†SteinerBooks, Inc., *(978-0-8334; 978-0-88010; 978-0-89345; 978-0-910142; 978-1-58420; 978-1-85584; 978-0-9701097; 978-0-9831984; 978-1-62148; 978-1-62151; 978-1-938685; 978-0-9969211; 978-1-7324613; 978-1-952166)* Orders Addr.: P.O. Box 960, Herndon, VA 20172-0960 USA Tel 703-661-1594 (orders); Fax: 702-661-1501; Toll Free Fax: 800-277-7947 (orders); Toll Free: 800-856-8664 (orders); Edit Addr.: 610 Main St., Suite 1, Great Barrington, MA 01230 USA Tel 413-528-8233; Fax: 413-528-8826; Fulfillment Addr.: 22883 Quicksilver Dr., Dulles, VA 20166 USA (SAN 253-9519) Tel 703-661-1529; Fax: 703-996-1010; *Imprints:* Bell Pond Books (Bell Pond); Lindisfarne Books (Lindisfarne)
E-mail: service@steinerbooks.org
Web site: http://www.steinerbooks.org
Dist(s): **New Leaf Distributing Co., Inc.**
Red Wheel/Weiser; *CIP.*

Steingart, Nathan Publishing, *(978-0-9769321)* 617 N. Kensington Dr., No. 1, Appleton, WI 54915 USA
E-mail: nathansteingart@new.rr.com
Web site: http://www.santastories.net.

Steinmark, Frances, *(978-0-9789272; 978-0-9977582)* 2374 NW 23rd Rd., Boca Raton, FL 33434-4368 USA
Web site: http://www.fransteinmark.com.

Steinschneider, Bernadetta, *(978-0-9790026)* 205 Georgetown Rd., Weston, CT 06883 USA Tel 203-454-8907; Fax: 203-227-0184
E-mail: swigutb@gmail.com.

Stejskal, Susan M., *(978-0-615-13395-9; 978-0-615-81867-2; 978-0-578-61240-9)* 15095 S. 18th St., Vicksburg, MI 49097 USA.

Stella Bks, Inc., *(978-0-9746932)* P.O. Box 4707, Edwards, CO 81632-4707 USA Tel 970-926-7827 (phone/fax)
E-mail: info@astellabook.com
Dist(s): **Partners/West Book Distributors.**

Stellar Learning, *(978-0-9763833)* P.O. Box 64, Guildrind Ctr, NY 12085-0064 USA
E-mail: admin@stellarlearn.com
Web site: http://www.stellarlearn.com.

Stellar Pubns., *(978-0-9761224)* 3767 Forest Ln., Suite 124 - MBX 1231, Dallas, TX 75244 USA Toll Free: 866-840-4378
E-mail: info@stellarpublishers.com; maymathis@msn.com
Web site: http://www.stellarpublishers.com.

Stellar Publishing, *(978-0-9703041; 978-0-9849660)* Div. of M & M Enterprises, Orders Addr.: 2114 S. Live Oak Pkwy., Wilmington, NC 28403 USA (SAN 860-2298) Tel 910-269-7444
E-mail: info@stellar-publishing.com
Web site: http://www.stellar-publishing.com
Dist(s): **Distributors, The.**

Stellinga, Mark, *(978-0-9762011; 978-0-9796421; 978-0-9817101)* 42 Lancester Pl., Iowa City, IA 52240 USA Tel 319-354-7287
E-mail: mark@writerofbooks.com
Web site: http://www.writerofbooks.com.

Stellium Pr., *(978-1-883376)* P.O. Box 82834, Portland, OR 97282-0834 USA.

Stelting, Kelsie Creative LLC, *(978-0-9998854)* 6211 NW 46th St, Warr Acres, OK 73122 USA Tel 785-340-2216
E-mail: kelsie@kelsiestelting.com
Web site: www.kelsiestelting.com.

Stelucan Pr., *(978-0-9601454)* 2129 State Hwy. 79 S., Wichita Falls, TX 76302 USA (SAN 221-3176).

Stelzer, Shifra, *(978-0-9992231)* 1827 New York Ave, Brooklyn, NY 11210-3941 USA Tel 718-692-2449
E-mail: ceo2.gye@gmail.com
Web site: www.EzequielStelzer.com.

†Stemmer Hse. Pubs., *(978-0-88045; 978-0-916144)* P.O. Box 89, Gilsum, NH 03448 USA (SAN 207-9623) Tel 603-357-0236; Fax: 603-357-2073; *Imprints:* NaturEncyclopedia (Naturencyclop)
E-mail: pbs@pathwaybook.com
Web site: http://stemmer.com
Dist(s): **Pathway Bk. Service;** *CIP.*

Stenhouse Pubs., *(978-1-57110; 978-1-62531)* Div. of Highlights for Children, Orders Addr.: P.O. Box 11020, Portland, ME 04104-7020 USA (SAN 298-1580) Tel 207-253-1600; Fax: 207-253-5121; Toll Free Fax: 800-833-9164; Toll Free: 800-988-9812 (orders)
E-mail: jkilburn@stenhouse.com
Web site: http://www.stenhouse.com
Dist(s): **Ebsco Publishing**
Follett School Solutions
MyiLibrary.

Stensland Bks., *(978-0-9759456)* 6011 S. 102 St., Omaha, NE 68127 USA
E-mail: info@stenslandbooks.com
Web site: http://www.stenslandbooks.com.

Step One Publishing, *(978-0-615-84809-9; 978-0-9913224)* 5521 Scenic Brook Ln., Raleigh, NC 27616 USA Tel 9192107141
Dist(s): **CreateSpace Independent Publishing Platform.**

Stephi /Lee, *(978-0-578-11938-0)* 2884 Blairmont Dr., Danville, VA 24540 USA
Web site: http://www.wheredomyprayersgo.com; http://www.stephileebooks.com.

Stephnie Stewart, Inc., *(978-0-615-43619-7)* P.O. Box 25882, Tamarac, FL 33320 USA
E-mail: stephniestewart@aol.com.

Steps To Literacy, LLC, *(978-0-9728803; 978-1-59564; 978-1-60015; 978-1-60881; 978-1-60923; 978-1-61267; 978-1-62038; 978-1-63395; 978-1-63502; 978-1-68136; 978-1-68288; 978-1-68432; 978-1-64240; 978-1-64241)* Orders Addr.: P.O. Box 6737, Bridgewater, NJ 08807 USA (SAN 858-3005) Toll Free: 800-895-2804
E-mail: sales@stepstoliteracy.com
Web site: http://www.stepstoliteracy.com.

stepup strategies *See* **Stepup Strategies**

Stepup Strategies, *(978-0-9964109; 978-1-947276)* 116 Hazley Ave., Rochelle Park, NJ 07662 USA Tel 561-601-9871
E-mail: trevorscrane@gmail.com.

Sterli Publishing, *(978-0-9790014)* 986 Gable Cove, Collierville, TN 38017 USA (SAN 852-1638) Tel 352-753-4335 (sales office)
E-mail: admin@sterlipublishing.com
Web site: http://www.sterlipublishing.com.

Sterling & Ross Pubs., *(978-0-9766372; 978-0-9779545; 978-0-9787213; 978-0-9814535; 978-0-9814536; 978-0-9821391; 978-0-9821392; 978-0-9827588; 978-1-937802)* 1221 Ave. of the Americas Suite 4200, New York City, NY 10020 USA; *Imprints:* Cambridge House Press (CambridgeHse)
E-mail: contact@sterlingandross.com
Web site: http://www.sterlingandross.com.

Sterling, Bridgette, *(978-0-578-44760-5; 978-0-578-44761-2; 978-0-578-54355-0)* P.O. Box 190821, Hawi, HI 96719 USA Tel 808-731-6751
E-mail: alohasterlings@gmail.com
Dist(s): **Ingram Content Group.**

Sterling Epicure *Imprint of* **Sterling Publishing Co., Inc.**

Sterling Innovation *Imprint of* **Sterling Publishing Co., Inc.**

Sterling Investments I, LLC DBA Twins Magazine, *(978-0-9636745; 978-0-9655442; 978-1-891846)* 30799 Pinetree Rd., #256, Cleveland, OH 44124 USA Tel 855-758-9467; Fax: 855-758-9467; Toll Free: 855-758-9467; *Imprints:* Twins Books (Twins Bks)
E-mail: bill@twinsmagazine.com
Web site: http://www.twinsmagazine.com; http://www.twinsmagazine.com/theBookshelf.shtml.

Sterling Pr., Inc., *(978-0-9637735)* 6811 Old Canton Rd., Apt. 3802, Ridgeland, MS 39157-1248 USA Tel 602-957-9265 Do not confuse with companies with similar names in Bulverde, TX, Chicago, IL, Marysville, WA, Bedford, TX, Kihei,HI.

†Sterling Publishing Co., Inc., *(978-0-8069; 978-1-4027; 978-1-60582; 978-1-4549; 978-1-61837; 978-1-9847)* 1166 Avenue of the Americas, 17th Flr., New York, NY 10036 USA (SAN 211-6324) Tel 212-532-7160 212-213-2495; Toll Free Fax: 800-775-8736 (warehouse); Toll Free: 800-367-9692; 800-542-7567; *Imprints:* Sterling/Main Street (Sterling-Main St); Balloon Books (Balloon Books); Sterling Innovation (SterInnov); Puzzlewright (Puzzlewright); Sterling Epicure (Sterling Epicure); Spark Notes (Spark Notes); Spark Publishing Group (SparkPubng) Do not confuse with companies

with similar names in Falls Church, VA, Fallbrook, CA, Lewisville, TX
E-mail: custservice@sterlingpub.com; tradesales@sterlingpub.com
Web site: http://www.sterlingpublishing.com/
Dist(s): **Booklines Hawaii, Ltd.**
Children's Plus, Inc.
Follett School Solutions
Hachette Bk. Group
MBI Distribution Services/Quayside Distribution
Music Sales Corp.
MyiLibrary
Partners Bk. Distributing, Inc.; *CIP.*

Sterling Test Prep, *(978-0-9892925; 978-0-9977782; 978-1-947556)* 276 Washington St. No. 305, Boston, MA 02108 USA Tel 617-777-5936
E-mail: info@onlinemcatprep.com
Web site: www.onlinemcatprep.com.

Sterling/Main St. *Imprint of* **Sterling Publishing Co., Inc.**

Stern, Frederick *See* **Stern Math, LLC**

Stern Math, LLC, *(978-0-9779132; 978-0-9845392)* 754 N. Hollow Rd., Box 172, Rochester, VT 05767 USA (SAN 850-6027) Tel 212-874-4530
E-mail: sternmath@gmail.com; fredstern@gmail.com; emilyalison@gmail.com
Web site: http://sternmath.com.

Sterner, Hilda, *(978-0-615-22164-9)* P.O. Box 713071, Santee, CA 92072-3071 USA
E-mail: hilda@momsauthenticassyrianrecipes.com
Web site: http://www.momsauthenticassyrianrecipes.com.

Stevans, Andrew, *(978-0-9848340)* 8409 Lee Hwy., Merrifield, VA 22116-0613 USA Tel 703-222-3790
E-mail: alstevans@cox.net.

Steve Diet Goedde, *(978-1-890836)* 2807 W. Sunset Blvd., Los Angeles, CA 90026 USA Tel 323-377-0235
E-mail: stevedg@gmail.com
Web site: http://www.stevedietgoedde.com.

Steveedee Publishing Co,

Stevens, Gareth Incorporated *See* **Stevens, Gareth Publishing LLLP**

†Stevens, Gareth Publishing LLLP, *(978-0-8368; 978-0-918831; 978-1-55532; 978-1-4339)* Orders Addr.: P.O. Box 361640, Strongsville, OH 44136-0140 USA Fax: 877-542-2596; Toll Free: 800-542-2595; Edit Addr.: 111 East 14th St., Suite 349, New York, NY 10003 USA (SAN 696-1592) Toll Free: 877-444-0210; *Imprints*: World Almanac Library (Wrld Almanac Lib); Weekly Reader Leveled Readers (Weekly Read); Gareth Stevens Secondary Library (G S Sec Lib); Gareth Stevens Learning Library (G S Lrning Lib); Gareth Stevens Hi-Lo Must Reads (G S Hi-Lo)
E-mail: customerservice@gspub.com; hollyc@rosen.pub
Web site: http://www.garethstevens.com; http://www.garethstevensclassroom.com
Dist(s): **Bound to Stay Bound Bks.**
Davidson Titles, Inc.
Follett School Solutions
Lectorum Pubns., Inc.; *CIP.*

Stevens Publishing, *(978-0-9632054; 978-1-885529)* Orders Addr.: P.O. Box 160, Kila, MT 59920 USA Tel 406-756-0307; Fax: 406-257-5051; Edit Addr.: 1550 Rogers Ln. Rd., Kila, MT 59920 USA Do not confuse with Stevens Publishing Corp. in Waco, TX.

Stevenson, Ian Author, *(978-0-9984836)* 2221 Eye St. NW, Washington, DC 20037 USA Tel 202-774-4596
E-mail: jim@getstyle.com
Web site: vocabularymoose.com.

Steward & Wise Publishing *See* **Acclaim Pr., Inc.**

Steward, Rebecca, *(978-0-578-58303-7)* 6061 S. Mack Ave., Gilbert, AZ 85298 USA Tel 480-650-0152
E-mail: 4stewsbus@gmail.com.

Stewart, Cathy L, *(978-0-692-06066-7; 978-0-692-06067-4; 978-0-692-06068-1; 978-0-692-06069-8; 978-0-692-06070-4; 978-0-692-06071-1; 978-0-692-06072-8; 978-0-692-06073-5)* 1910 NE Brown Dr, Madras, OR 97741 USA Tel 541-475-9371
E-mail: jimcath24@yahoo.com.

Stewart Education Services, *(978-0-9764154)* 3722 Bagely Ave., No. 19, Los Angeles, CA 90034-4113 USA Tel 310-838-6247; Fax: 310-838-6769
E-mail: info@stewarteducationservices.com
Web site: http://www.stewarteducationservices.com.

Stewart, H. K. Creative Services, Inc., *(978-0-9838992; 978-0-9972312; 978-1-7337964; 978-1-7353167)* 2701 Kavanaugh Blvd. Suite 205, Little Rock, AR 72205 USA Tel 501-664-0500
E-mail: hks@hkstewart.com
Web site: www.hkstewart.com.

Stewart, Mary *See* **Rooster Pubns.**

Stewart, R. J. Bks., *(978-0-9791402; 978-0-9819246; 978-0-9856006)* P.O. Box 239, Berkeley Springs, WV 25411 USA (SAN 852-5382)
E-mail: rjspeak@gmail.com
Web site: http://www.rjstewart.net.

†Stewart, Tabori & Chang, *(978-0-941434; 978-0-941807; 978-1-55670; 978-1-899791; 978-1-58479)* Div. of Harry N. Abrams, Inc., 115 W. 18th St., 5th Flr., New York, NY 10011 USA (SAN 293-4000) Tel 212-519-1200; Fax: 212-519-1210
E-mail: trudi@stcbooks.com
Web site: http://www.abramsbooks.com
Dist(s): **Abrams, Inc.**
Hachette Bk. Group
MyiLibrary
Open Road Integrated Media, Inc.; *CIP.*

Stick & Poke Pr., 89 Arden Rd. 0, BERKELEY, CA 94704 USA Tel 8186790693
E-mail: rcinlala@aol.com
Dist(s): **Ingram Content Group.**

Stickysoft Corp., *(978-0-9740384)* Orders Addr.: P.O. Box 7855, Buffalo Grove, IL 60089 USA Tel 847-229-9999; Fax: 847-808-8777; Toll Free: 800-366-8448; Edit Addr.: 620 Silver Rock Ln., Buffalo Grove, IL 60089 USA
E-mail: euclid@stickysoft.com
Web site: http://www.blackjack678.com.

Still Water Publishing, *(978-0-9740855)* Orders Addr.: 1093 Kiva Cir., Windsor, CO 80550 USA
E-mail: chein8@attbi.com
Web site: http://www.stillwaterpublishing.com.

Stillman, Steve, *(978-0-9740508)* 251 Green St., Shrewsbury, MA 01545-4708 USA.

Stitched Smile Pubns., *(978-0-692-60271-3; 978-0-692-64579-6; 978-0-692-65132-2; 978-0-692-67634-9; 978-1-945263)* 19607 twilight falls ln, Houston, TX 77084 USA Tel 281-902-7502
E-mail: Stitchedsmilepublications@gmail.com
Web site: Www.stitchedsmilepublications.com
Dist(s): **CreateSpace Independent Publishing Platform.**

STL Distribution North America *See* **Send The Light Distribution LLC**

Stockade Bks., *(978-0-9731570; 978-0-9863983; 978-0-9973879)* P.O. Box 30, Woodsville, NH 03785 USA Toll Free: 866-799-4500
E-mail: orders@stockadebooks.com
Web site: http://www.stockadebooks.com.

Stockcero, Inc., *(978-1-934768; 978-1-949938)* 3785 NW 82nd Ave. Suite 302, Doral, FL 33166 USA Tel 305-722-7628; Fax: 305-477-5794
E-mail: pagrest@stockcero.com; stockcero@stockcero.com
Web site: http://www.spanishbookpress.com; http://www.stockcero.com.

Stockwell Publishing, *(978-0-9785594)* 84 State St. Suite 300, Boston, MA 02109 USA Tel 617-290-3039; Fax: 617-720-0761
E-mail: pel.stockwell@lpl.com
Web site: http://www.followthefox.com.

Stogo, Malcolm Assocs., *(978-0-9712703; 978-0-615-28965-6; 978-0-9966586)* 79 Edgewood Ave., West Orange, NJ 07052 USA
Web site: www.icecreamuniversity.org.

Stoica, Dana, *(978-0-615-16913-1; 978-0-578-57564-3; 978-1-7344246)* 1593 Cipres Ct., Camarillo, CA 93010 USA Tel 805-402-6216
E-mail: danastoica7607@gmail.com.

Stoke Bks.,

Stone Acres Publishing Co., *(978-0-9765478; 978-1-937480)* P.O. Box 407, Waverly, PA 18471-0407 USA (SAN 850-0940) Fax: 570-319-1675
E-mail: gmiltony@yahoo.com
Web site: http://www.stoneacrespublishing.com.

Stone & Scott Pubs., *(978-0-9627031; 978-1-891135)* Orders Addr.: P.O. Box 56419, Sherman Oaks, CA 91413-1419 USA (SAN 297-3030) Tel 818-904-9088; Fax: 818-787-1431
E-mail: Friday@StoneandScott.com; BostonLesPaul@adelphia.net
Web site: http://www.stoneandscott.com.

Stone, Anne Publishing, *(978-0-9858811)* 1158 26th St. Suite 440, Santa Monica, CA 90403 USA Tel 310-418-4674; Fax: 310-828-8057
E-mail: JulieK.AnneStone@gmail.com
Web site: www.annestonepublishing.com.

Stone Arch Bks. *Imprint of* **Capstone**

Stone Arrow Bks., *(978-0-9825528)* P.o. Box 221, Draper, UT 84020 USA Tel 801-699-2844
E-mail: komarkris@gmail.com
Dist(s): **Coutts Information Services**
Ingram Content Group
Spring Arbor Distributors, Inc.

Stone Castle Publishing, *(978-0-578-00171-5)* 2602 Skyline Dr., Sedalia, MO 65301 USA
Dist(s): **Lulu Pr., Inc.**

Stone Cottage Bks., *(978-0-9822503)* Orders Addr.: P.O. Box 962497, Riverdale, GA 30296 USA (SAN 857-6734)
E-mail: info@stonecottagebooks.com; orders@stonecottagebooks.com
Web site: http://www.stonecottagebooks.com; http://www.bigandgrown.com; http://www.bigandgrown.com.

Stone Guild Publishing, *(978-1-60532)* P.O. Box 860475, Plano, TX 75086-0475 USA.

Stone Pier Pr., *(978-0-9988623; 978-1-7349011)* P.O. Box 170572, San Francisco, CA 94117 USA Tel 415-484-2821
E-mail: clare@stonepierpress.org
Web site: http://www.stonepierpress.org/
Dist(s): **Chelsea Green Publishing.**

Stone Pine Pr., *(978-0-9728929)* Orders Addr.: P.O. Box 585, Marcola, OR 97454-0585 USA; Edit Addr.: 92985 Marcola Rd., Marcola, OR 97454 USA.

Stone Publishing Co., *(978-1-880991)* Orders Addr.: P.O. Box 711, Mendocino, CA 95460 USA Tel 707-937-0239; Edit Addr.: 10491 Wheeler St., Mendocino, CA 95460 USA.

Stoneback, Paula, *(978-1-7325072)* 1827 Candlewyck Ln, Green Lane, PA 18054-2048 USA Tel 215-803-5000
E-mail: paulastoneback@yahoo.com.

Stonebridge Pubns., *(978-0-9896904; 978-1-940473)* 25036 Meadowdale Ln., Veneta, OR 97487 USA Tel 626-629-0195 Do not confuse with Stonebridge Publications in Chesapeake, VA
E-mail: stonebridgepublications@outlook.com.

Stonechester, Inc., *(978-0-9759014)* 4894 Lone Mountain Rd., No. 311, Las Vegas, NV 89130-2239 USA.

StoneGarden.net Publishing, *(978-0-9765426; 978-1-60076)* 3851 Cottonwood Dr., Danville, CA 94506 USA Tel 925-984-7867
E-mail: theshop@stonegarden.net
Web site: http://www.stonegarden.net.

Stonehorse Publishing, LLC, *(978-0-9764199)* Orders Addr.: 6528 E. 101st St. S., Ste D1 Rm. 296, Tulsa, OK 74133 USA (SAN 256-3797) Toll Free Fax: 888-867-1927; Toll Free: 888-867-1927
E-mail: generalinfo@stonehorsepublishing.com
Web site: http://www.stonehorsepublishing.com
Dist(s): **Educational Distribution Corp.**

StoneHouse Ink, *(978-0-9826078; 978-0-9827705; 978-0-615-52573-0; 978-0-615-52575-4; 978-0-615-53802-0; 978-0-615-54333-8; 978-0-615-54337-6; 978-0-615-54696-4; 978-0-615-54711-4; 978-0-615-54901-9; 978-0-615-56858-4; 978-0-615-56861-4; 978-0-615-56900-0; 978-0-615-57160-7; 978-0-615-57163-8; 978-0-615-57164-5; 978-0-615-57165-2; 978-0-615-57168-3; 978-0-615-57222-2; 978-0-615-57225-3; 978-0-615-57624-4; 978-0-615-58014-2; 978-0-615-61352-9; 978-0-615-61354-3; 978-0-615-61786-2; 978-1-938426; 978-0-615-626) 12235 W. Briarwood Dr, Boise, ID 83713 USA Tel 208-514-6631*
E-mail: Pattersonbooks@hotmail.com; stonehousepress@hotmail.com; StoneHouseMgr@gmail.com
Web site: http://www.stonegateink.com/; http://www.stonehouseink.net
Dist(s): **CreateSpace Independent Publishing Platform**
Smashwords
Wesscott Marketing, Inc.

Stoneledge Pr., *(978-0-615-55922-3; 978-0-9851799)* 251 Wax Myrtle Trail, Kitty Hawk, NC 27949 USA Tel 252-715-3621
E-mail: denine.phillips@charter.net.

StonesThrow Publishing, LLC, *(978-0-9793823)* P.O. Box 1898, Mount Dora, FL 32756 USA Tel 208-610-0431
Web site: http://stonesthrowpublishing.com.

Stonewell Pr., *(978-1-62730)* 965 BIRCHWOOD DR, Salt Lake City, UT 84121 USA Tel 801-269-1523
E-mail: jayparry84121@yahoo.com.

Stoneydale Pr. Publishing Co., *(978-0-912299; 978-1-931291; 978-1-938707)* Orders Addr.: P.O. Box 188, Stevensville, MT 59870 USA Tel 406-777-2729; Fax: 406-777-2521; Toll Free: 800-735-7006; Edit Addr.: 523 Main St., Stevensville, MT 59870 USA (SAN 265-3168)
E-mail: stoneydale@stoneydale.com
Web site: http://www.stoneydale.com
Dist(s): **Partners Bk. Distributing, Inc.**

Stony Meadow Publishing, *(978-0-9787925; 978-0-9834335; 978-0-9850290; 978-0-9885569; 978-0-9894090; 978-0-9962834)* 3412 Imperial Palm Dr., Largo, FL 33771 USA
E-mail: stonymeadowbooks@aol.com; darkmoondigest@gmail.com
Web site: http://www.stonymeadowpublishing.com; http://www.inspiration4songwriters.net; http://www.books4songwriters.com; http://htto://www.darkmoondigest.com.

Stop N Go Fitness, *(978-0-9800091)* 13518 L St., Omaha, NE 68137 USA Fax: 413-669-8870
E-mail: angelinsights@conciergemarketing.com
Web site: http://www.anangeltowatchover.com.

Storer, Mark *See* **Little River Bookshelf**

Storey Books *See* **Storey Publishing, LLC**

†Storey Publishing, LLC, *(978-0-88266; 978-1-58017; 978-0-9674717; 978-1-60342; 978-1-61212; 978-1-63586)* Subs. of Workman Publishing Co., Inc., Orders Addr.: 210 Mass Moca Way, North Adams, MA 01247 USA (SAN 203-4158) Fax: 413-346-2198; Toll Free Fax: 800-865-3429; Toll Free: 800-827-7444; c/o Workman Publishing, 225 Varick St., New York, NY 10014-4381 Tel 212-614-7700; Toll Free Fax: 800-521-1832; Toll Free: 800-722-7202
E-mail: info@storey.com; sales@storey.com
Web site: http://www.storey.com
Dist(s): **MBI Distribution Services/Quayside Distribution**
Open Road Integrated Media, Inc.
Timber Pr., Inc.
Workman Publishing Co., Inc.; *CIP.*

Stori Tyme Huggggs, Inc., *(978-1-890925)* Div. of T.L.B. Publishing, 827 N. Hollywood, #202, Burbank, CA 91505 USA Tel 770-987-5547; 894 Roberts Way, Lawrenceville, GA 30043
E-mail: tenabrown@thejpak.com.

Storie Tree, Inc., The, *(978-0-9679014)* Orders Addr.: P.O. Box 441048, Aurora, CO 80044-1048 USA Tel 303-690-6493; Fax: 303-758-7792; Edit Addr.: 3952 S. Joplin Way, Aurora, CO 80044-1048 USA.

Stories By Mom, *(978-0-692-77347-5; 978-0-692-84555-4; 978-0-692-93774-7; 978-1-7339106)* 2314 E CAPRI AVE, Mesa, AZ 85204 USA Tel 480-293-4860
Web site: www.storiesbymom.com.

Stories From Four Publishing Co., *(978-0-9742288)* 558 N. Nash St., Hortonville, WI 54944 USA Tel 920-779-9995
E-mail: fourinspirations@aol.com
Web site: http://www.storiesfromfour.com.

Stories of My Life, The, *(978-0-9741215)* Div. of Frontsiders Marketing Strategists, P.O. Box 1478, Summerland, CA 93067 USA Tel 805-969-3597
Web site: http://www.thestoriesofmylife.com.

Storiez: Meagan Corrado, *(978-0-9970049; 978-1-7325813)* 4055 Ridge Ave Apt 4404, Philadelphia, PA 19129 USA Tel 267-418-6750
E-mail: storiezguide@gmail.com.

Storm Leaf, *(978-0-9858325)* 6041 S Valdai Way, Aurora, CO 80015 USA Tel 303-408-3838
E-mail: david@stormleaf.com
Web site: www.stormleaf.com.

Storm Moon Pr., LLC, *(978-0-9827008; 978-1-937058; 978-1-62757)* 5705 Fishermans Dr., Bradenton, FL 34209 USA
E-mail: editor@stormmoonpress.com
Web site: http://www.stormmoonpress.com
Dist(s): **Smashwords.**

Storm Mystery Pr., LLC, *(978-0-9987199)* 1212 1st St., Kirkland, WA 98033 USA Tel 425-736-6223; Fax: 425-739-7399
E-mail: dnj2@mac.com
Web site: www.JenniferLHotes.com.

Storm Peak Pr., *(978-0-9641357; 978-1-928990)* 2502 4th Ave N., Seattle, WA 98109-2149 USA.

Storm Praise Publishing, LLC, *(978-0-692-53485-4; 978-0-9995631)* 11700 Mukilteo Speedway Suite 1228-201, Mukilteo, WA 98275 USA Tel 310-968-6441
E-mail: trishabernardo56@gmail.com.

Stormcave, *(978-0-9884512)* 6467 189th St., Chippewa Falls, WI 54729 USA Tel 919-714-0608
E-mail: jenelle@jenelleschmidt.com.

Stormcave Studios *See* **Stormcave**

Storms, Lorraine, *(978-1-7328492)* 106 Mayer St., Reading, PA 19606 USA Tel 610-370-5007
E-mail: lryanstorms@gmail.com
Dist(s): **Ingram Content Group.**

Story and Logic Media Group, *(978-0-615-72436-2; 978-0-615-74806-1; 978-0-9897549; 978-1-941622)* 12386 W. National Rd., New Carlisle, OH 45344 USA Tel 9374783002
E-mail: sharonalavy1@gmail.com
Web site: http://storyandlogic.blogspot.com/
Dist(s): **CreateSpace Independent Publishing Platform.**

Story Direction, *(978-0-9675940)* 39650 Us Hwy. 19 N. Apt. 583, Tarpon Spgs, FL 34689-3950 USA Tel 727-939-8466
E-mail: angelface12@earthlink.net.

Story Merchant, *(978-0-9836058; 978-0-615-65754-7; 978-0-615-65947-3; 978-0-615-65967-1; 978-0-615-65969-5; 978-0-615-66089-9; 978-0-615-66180-3; 978-0-615-67581-7; 978-0-9897154; 978-0-9904216; 978-0-9909436; 978-0-9963689; 978-0-9969908; 978-0-9981628; 978-0-9991621; 978-1-7323411; 978-1-970157; 978-1-7340324) 400 S. Burnside Ave. 11B, Los Angeles, CA 90036 USA Tel 323-932-1685; Fax: 323-932-1220*
E-mail: lisacerasoli@gmail.com; DrK@storymerchant.com
Web site: www.storymerchant.com
Dist(s): **CreateSpace Independent Publishing Platform**
Lulu Pr., Inc.

Story Monsters LLC, *(978-0-9619853; 978-1-877749; 978-1-58985)* Orders Addr.: 4696 W Tyson St, Chandler, AZ 85226 USA (SAN 246-7429) Tel 480-940-8182; Fax: 480-940-8787; Edit Addr.: 4696 W. Tyson St., Chandler, AZ 85226-2903 USA; *Imprints*: Story Monsters Press (MYID_K_STORY M)
E-mail: Linda@storymonsters.com; Patti@storymonsters.com
Web site: http:www.storymonsters.com; http://www.DragonflyBookAwards.com; http://www.AuthorBookings.com
Dist(s): **Quality Bks., Inc.**
Unique Bks., Inc.
ebrary, Inc.

Story Monsters Pr. *Imprint of* **Story Monsters LLC**

Story Night Pr., *(978-0-692-45488-6; 978-0-692-45558-6; 978-0-692-48806-5; 978-0-692-65151-3; 978-0-9986699)* 21 Chestnut St. Apt. 603, Portland, ME 04101 USA Tel 207-761-5801
Dist(s): **CreateSpace Independent Publishing Platform.**

Story of Your Life Publishing Co., The, *(978-0-9771667)* 528 Palisades Dr., No. 711, Pacific Palisades, CA 90272 USA (SAN 256-8241) Tel 310-230-8510.

Story Plant, The, *(978-0-9816087; 978-0-9819568; 978-0-9841905; 978-1-61188)* P.O. Box 4331, Stamford, CT 06907 USA (SAN 856-0234)
Web site: http://www.thestoryplant.com
Dist(s): **MyiLibrary**
National Bk. Network
Open Road Integrated Media, Inc.
Two Rivers Distribution.

Story Pr. Africa *Imprint of* **Catalyst Bk. Pr.**

Story Road Publishing, Inc., *(978-1-939898)* 16564 SW 47th Ter., Miami, FL 33185 USA Tel 818-590-3991
E-mail: zachary@zcbolger.com.

Story Store Collection Publishing, *(978-0-9764798)* 11040 Hickman Rd. # 226, Clive, IA 50325-3740 USA.

Story Stuff, Inc., *(978-1-928811)* P.O. Box 501372, Indianapolis, IN 46250-6372 USA Fax: 317-913-1777
E-mail: jmferrone@storystuff.com
Web site: http://www.storystuff.com.

Story Time Stories That Rhyme, *(978-1-56820)* P.O. Box 416, Denver, CO 80201-0416 USA Tel 303-575-5676; *Imprints*: folder leaf (folder leaf)
E-mail: emailstreet@gmail.com
Web site: http://www.storytimestoriesthatrhyme.net; http://www.storytimestoriesthatrhyme.com/; http://www.storytimestoriesthatrhyme.org; http://www.storiesforschools.com; http://www.kidsrhymenewsletter.com.

Story Weaver Pr., *(978-0-9795580)* 155 Beech St., Frankfort, MI 49635 USA Tel 231-352-8159
E-mail: nedthebanker@sbcglobal.net.

Storybook Acres, *(978-0-9761675)* 4309 Creek Rd., Conneaut, OH 44030 USA (SAN 256-2219) Tel 440-593-2780 (phone/fax) E-mail: storybookacres@adelphia.net Web site: http://storybookacres.org.

StoryBk. Genius, LLC, *(978-0-9910907; 978-1-941434; 978-1-949522; 978-1-952954)* Orders Addr.: 219 Jackson St., Augusta, MO 63332 USA; Edit Addr.: 219 Jackson St., Augusta, MO 63332 USA Tel 314-578-4341 E-mail: nwhartung@gmail.com Web site: http://www.sbgpublishing.com.

Storybook Meadow Publishing, *(978-0-9704621; 978-0-9845236; 978-1-7321629)* 7700 Timbers Trail, Traverse City, MI 49684 USA; *Imprints:* Bower Books (Bower Bks) E-mail: garybower@charter.net Web site: http://www.bowerbooks.com *Dist(s):* **Partners Bk. Distributing, Inc.**

Storybook Pr. & Productions, *(978-1-887683)* 467 Central Park W., Apt. 6E, New York, NY 10025 USA Tel 212-975-2473; 212-749-7178 (phone/fax); Fax: 212-975-2026; Toll Free: 800-779-4341 E-mail: storybookp@aol.com.

Storybook Theatre of Hawaii, *(978-0-9742224)* P.O. Box 820, Hanapepe, HI 96716 USA Web site: http://www.storybook.org.

Storycraft Publishing, *(978-0-9638339)* Orders Addr.: P.O. Box 205, Masonville, CO 80541-0205 USA Tel 970-669-3755 (phone/fax); Edit Addr.: 8600 Firethorn Dr., Loveland, CO 80538 USA E-mail: Vivian@storycraft.com Web site: http://www.storycraft.com *Dist(s):* **Book Wholesalers, Inc.**
Brodart Co.
Follett School Solutions
Quality Bks., Inc.
Unique Bks., Inc.

Storydog, Inc., *(978-0-9722690)* 3510 N. Bell Ave., Chicago, IL 60618 USA (SAN 254-9786) Tel 773-327-1588 Web site: http://www.storydog.com.

StoryGirl Productions, LLC, *(978-0-9762587)* 213 W. Montebello, Phoenix, AZ 85013 USA E-mail: jaime@ding-a-lings.net Web site: http://www.ding-a-lings.net.

Storyman Bks., *(978-1-7322282; 978-0-578-44792-6; 978-0-578-59587-0; 978-0-578-76817-5)* 19601 E 49th St. S., Broken Arrow, OK 74014 USA Tel 978-382-2379 E-mail: davidstoryman@gmail.com Web site: www.healthylivingpublishing.net; www.storymanbooks.com.

StoryMaster Pr., *(978-0-9761179)* 15420 Memorial Dr., Suite M -141, Houston, TX 77079 USA Tel 281-920-0443; Fax: 281-920-1629 E-mail: info@storymasterpress.com Web site: http://www.storymasterpress.com.

StoryRobin Co., *(978-1-937489)* 849 Durshire Way, Sunnyvale, CA 94087 USA Tel 408-905-7543 E-mail: suechen78@gmail.com Web site: www.storyrobin.com.

StoryScapes, *(978-0-9975202; 978-0-9979283)* P.O. Box 116, Sebastopol, CA 95473 USA Tel 707-332-8100 E-mail: erik@permacultureartisans.com Web site: storyscapes.us.

Storytime Ink International, *(978-0-9628769; 978-0-9897371)* P.O. Box 470505, Broadview Heights, OH 44147 USA Tel 440-584-0018; Fax: 270-573-4913; 10001 Gatewood Dr., Brecksville, OH 44141 E-mail: storytimeink@att.net Web site: http://storytimeink.com.

Storytime Pr., Inc., *(978-0-9754942)* 427 W. Main, Suite D, Brighton, MI 48116 USA E-mail: monroestudio@yahoo.com Web site: http://www.michaelglennmonroe.com *Dist(s):* **Ann Arbor Editions LLC.**

Storytime Works, *(978-0-9886984)* 904 Winter Dr., El Paso, TX 79912 USA Tel 915-248-9658 E-mail: storytimeworks@gmail.com Web site: www.storytimeworks.com *Dist(s):* **Greenleaf Book Group.**

StoryTime World Publishing Hse., *(978-0-9792800)* Div. of The Pencil Pro, 202 Rollins Ave., Rockville, MD 20852 USA Tel 301-672-4296 Web site: http://ronirosenthal.com/.

StoryTyme Publishing, *(978-0-9753699)* 7909 Walerga Rd., Suite 112, PMB 178, Antelope, CA 95843 USA (SAN 256-0763) Web site: http://www.storytymepublishing.com.

Stott, Darrel Ministry, *(978-0-9755564)* 1885 Nancy Ave., Central Point, OR 97502-1627 USA Tel 541-840-7171 E-mail: Dstottmin@yahoo.com Web site: www.DarrelStott.com.

Stourbridge Distributors, Inc., *(978-0-9753758)* 812 Ct. St., Honesdale, PA 18431-1965 USA E-mail: rich@stourbridgedist.com Web site: http://www.stourbridgedist.com *Dist(s):* **Phoenix Learning Resources, LLC.**

Stout, William Inc., *(978-0-9712716; 978-0-9743838)* 1468 Loma Vista St., Pasadena, CA 91104-4709 USA Tel 626-798-6490; Fax: 626-798-3756 E-mail: wmstout@altrionet.com Web site: http://www.williamstout.com.

Stowe, Amber, *(978-1-7324237)* 8161 S. Estes St., Littleton, CO 80128 USA Tel 720-357-0398 E-mail: amber.stowe@gmail.com.

STR8*UP Productions *See* **Paved Roads Productions**

Strack, Beth, *(978-0-9898991)* 2594 Hastings Ave., Redwood City, CA 94061 USA Tel 650-368-6158 E-mail: hummingbirdhmmmm@aol.com.

Straight Edge Pr., The, *(978-1-883043)* Subs. of Straight Edge, Inc., 386 Clinton St., Brooklyn, NY 11231-3603 USA (SAN 254-9395) Toll Free: 800-732-3628 E-mail: info@straightedgeinc.com Web site: http://www.straightedgeinc.com.

Straight Forward Technologies, *(978-0-9718515)* P.O. Box 102, Valley Center, KS 67147 USA Tel 316-207-3211; Toll Free Fax: 877-766-8566 E-mail: info@straightforwardtech.com Web site: http://www.bakingwithmommy.com; http://www.straightforwardtech.com; http://www.gardeningwithmommy.com.

Straight From The Heart Publishing, *(978-0-692-78740-3)* 2600 W Ina Rd. Apt 135, Tucson, AZ 85741 USA Tel 310-739-9348 E-mail: Straight From The Heart Publishing jimmydanelli@aol.com.

Straight on till Morningside Prints *Imprint of* **Pitchford, D. L.**

Straight Paths Pr., *(978-0-9759871)* 17450 SW Viking St., Beaverton, OR 97007 USA (SAN 256-1468) Tel 503-259-9764 (phone/fax); Toll Free: 800-348-2346 ext. 23 E-mail: info@straightpathspress.com Web site: http://www.straightpathspress.com.

Strang Communications Company *See* **Charisma Media**

Strange Citizen Press *See* **Leonardoverse Books**

StrangeDays Publishing, *(978-0-9747581)* P.O. Box 587, Merton, WI 53056 USA.

Stranger Comics, *(978-0-578-03139-2; 978-0-578-03140-8; 978-0-578-03141-5; 978-0-578-04111-7; 978-0-578-07612-6; 978-0-578-08000-0; 978-0-578-11087-5; 978-1-939834)* 4121 Redwood Ave. Suite 101, Los Angeles, CA 90066 USA E-mail: sebjones3@gmail.com; stranger@strangercomics.com Web site: http://www.strangercomics.com *Dist(s):* **Ingram Publisher Services.**

Strategic Bk. Publishing *Imprint of* **Strategic Book Publishing & Rights Agency (SBPRA)**

Strategic Book Publishing & Rights Agency (SBPRA), *(978-0-9795935; 978-1-934925; 978-1-60693; 978-1-60911; 978-1-60976; 978-1-61204; 978-1-61897; 978-1-62212; 978-1-62516; 978-1-62857; 978-1-63135; 978-1-63410; 978-1-943204; 978-1-68181; 978-1-946539; 978-1-946540; 978-1-948260; 978-1-948271; 978-1-948858; 978-1-949483; 978-1-950015; 978-1-950860; 978-1-951530; 978-1-952269) 2450 Louisiana St., Houston, TX 77006 USA (SAN 853-8492) Toll Free: 888-808-6187; Imprints:* Eloquent Books (Eloquent Bks); Strategic Book Publishing (Strat Bk) E-mail: payroll@sbpra.net; support@sbpra.net; katie@sbpra.net Web site: http://sbpra.net.

Strategic Destiny, LLC., *(978-0-9982566)* 175-60 Underhill Ave., Fresh Meadows, NY 11365 USA Tel 718-357-0064 E-mail: wyattstrategicdestiny@gmail.com.

Strategic Educational Tools, *(978-0-9842863)* 293 Center St., East Aurora, NY 14052 USA (SAN 858-9666) Tel 716-445-9609.

Strategic Media Group, *(978-0-9824157)* 9800 De Soto Ave., Chatsworth, CA 91311 USA (SAN 858-0979) Web site: http://www.hospitalcritterz.com.

Strategic Partners Press *See* **Strategic Media Group**

Strategic Visions, Inc. *See* **TAOH Inspired Education, LLC**

Strategies Publishing Co., *(978-0-9769662)* Orders Addr.: P.O. Box 5588, Cary, NC 27512 USA Do not confuse with companies with the same or similar name in Sahuarita, AZ, Tampa, FL, New Augusta, MS E-mail: jjohnson0710@yahoo.com; strategiespublishing@nc.rr.com.

Stratford Road Pr., Ltd., *(978-0-9743221; 978-0-9835480; 978-0-9886853)* 128 S. Camden Dr., Suite 201, Beverly Hills, CA 90212-3232 USA Fax: 310-550-8926 E-mail: peasonions@aol.com; peasandonions@gmail.com.

Strathmoor *Imprint of* **Tabby Hse. Bks.**

Strathmoor Pr., *(978-0-9740718)* 1710 Tyler Pkwy., Louisville, KY 40204 USA Tel 502-479-3287.

Stratostream LLC, *(978-0-578-44486-4)* 372 Fifth Ave. 4E, New York, NY 10018 USA Tel 212-772-7109 E-mail: neonissima@gmail.com *Dist(s):* **Ingram Content Group.**

Stratten, Lou, *(978-0-9747173)* Orders Addr.: 3144 S. Barrington Ave. #c, Los Angeles, CA 90066 USA; Edit Addr.: 3144 S. Barrington Ave. Apt. C, Los Angeles, CA 90066-1146 USA.

Stratton Pr., *(978-0-9624813; 978-0-692-86312-1; 978-0-692-86314-5)* Orders Addr.: P.O. Box 22391, San Francisco, CA 94122 USA (SAN 200-3457) E-mail: sashley@strattonpress.com.

Straub, Rick, *(978-0-9793269; 978-0-9842209; 978-0-9913726)* Orders Addr.: 493 Ridgecrest Dr., Blairsville, GA 30512 USA Tel 706-781-6551 E-mail: csddata@windstream.net Web site: http://www.straubpublishing.com/.

Strauberry Studios, *(978-0-9830321)* 11000 NE 10th St. No. 230, Bellevue, WA 98004 USA Tel 425-821-7007 E-mail: susan@strauberrystudios.com Web site: http://www.strauberrystudios.com.

Straus, Jane, *(978-0-9667221)* Orders Addr.: P.O. Box 472, Mill Valley, CA 94942 USA (SAN 253-8202) Toll Free: 800-644-3222 E-mail: jane@grammarbook.com Web site: http://www.grammarbook.com; http://www.thebluebooks.com.

Strauss Consultants, 48 W. 25th St., 11th Flr., New York, NY 10010-2708 USA Toll Free Fax: 888-528-8273; Toll Free: 800-236-7918 E-mail: strausscon@aol.com *Dist(s):* **Smashwords.**

Strauss, Michael L., *(978-0-692-15559-2; 978-0-692-15562-2; 978-0-578-51104-7)* 2275 N. Legion Dr., Signal Hill, CA 90755 USA Tel 310-743-7339 E-mail: michaelstrauss44@yahoo.com *Dist(s):* **Ingram Content Group.**

Strawbery Banke, Incorporated *See* **Strawbery Banke Museum**

Strawbery Banke Museum, *(978-0-9603896)* Orders Addr.: P.O. Box 300, Portsmouth, NH 03802-0300 USA (SAN 221-6515) Tel 603-433-1100; Fax: 603-433-1115; Edit Addr.: 454 Court St., Portsmouth, NH 03802-0300 USA E-mail: deidre@perpublisher.com Web site: http://www.strawberybanke.org *Dist(s):* **Univ. Pr. of New England.**

Stray Dog Pr., LLC, *(978-0-9898831)* 1030 Bowen Creek Rd., Niangua, MO 65713 USA Tel 417-473-1136; *Imprints:* Fun 4 Kids Publishing (Fun four Kids) E-mail: susankeenebooks@gmail.com.

Stray Letter Pr. LLC, The, *(978-0-9996709)* 17487 3rd Cir. S, Burien, WA 98148 USA Tel 253-880-7018; Fax: 253-880-7018 E-mail: LGMoriyama@gmail.com.

Streamline Brands, *(978-0-9855732; 978-0-692-86750-1)* 80 So. Highland Ave. The Holyoke-Manhattan blg, Ossining, NY 10562 USA Tel 914-941-5668 E-mail: jacollen@collenip.com.

Streams Publishing Co., *(978-1-933358)* P.O. Box 260, Sidney, OH 45365-0260 USA Tel 937-492-4586; Fax: 937-492-7633 E-mail: budford@bright.net Web site: http://www.cityreaching.net.

Strebor Bks. *Imprint of* **Strebor Bks.**

Strebor Bks., *(978-0-9674601; 978-0-9711953; 978-1-59309)* 1230 Ave. of the Americas, New York, NY 10020 USA; *Imprints:* Strebor Books (Strebor Imp) *Dist(s):* **Simon & Schuster, Inc.**

Streetside Stories, Inc., *(978-0-9646977; 978-0-9710606)* 3130 20th St. Ste. 311, San Francisco, CA 94110-2700 USA E-mail: contact@streetside.org Web site: http://www.streetside.org.

StreetTalk Publishing Co., *(978-0-9770009)* 187 N. Garfield Ave., Columbus, OH 43203 USA; 1324 Cambrian Ct, Columbus, OH 43220 E-mail: amazingteistreet@gmail.com Web site: www.amazingteistreet.com.

Strelecky, John *See* **Aspen Light Publishing**

Stress Free Kids, *(978-0-9708633; 978-0-9787781; 978-0-9800328; 978-0-9836256; 978-1-937985)* 2561 Chimney Springs Dr, Marietta, GA 30062 USA E-mail: rick@StressFreeKids.com Web site: www.stressfreepublishers.com *Dist(s):* **Ingram Publisher Services**
Ingram Content Group.

Stress Free Publishers *See* **Stress Free Kids**

Strickland, Wilton, *(978-0-9747035)* 618 Pk. Ave., Goldsboro, NC 27530 USA (SAN 255-8114) Tel 919-734-2830 (phone/fax) E-mail: wilton@esn.net Web site: http://www.wiltonstrickland.com.

Striking Presence Pubns., *(978-0-9724935)* Orders Addr.: P.O. Box 475, Moorestown, NJ 08057 USA Tel 609-936-7278; Fax: 609-936-9651; Edit Addr.: 49-13 Quail Ridge Dr., Plainsboro, NJ 08536 USA E-mail: jc@strikingpresence.com Web site: http://www.strikingpresence.com.

String of Beads Pubns., *(978-0-9672012)* 9297 Avignon Pl., West Jordan, UT 84088 USA Fax: 801-566-0406 E-mail: jepp@fiber.net Web site: http://www.stringofbeads.com.

Strive *See* **Staves Creations**

Strong Corner Publishing, LCC, *(978-0-9754755)* 5331 Talavero Pl., Parker, CO 80134-2799 USA E-mail: spencerj@broncos.nfl.com.

Strong, Louise dev, *(978-0-9770950)* P.O. Box 197, Morristown, NY 13664 USA Tel 315-375-4238 E-mail: riverstrong@gisco.net.

Strother, Rosemarie, *(978-0-692-00131-8)* 4880 Coral Wood Dr., Naples, FL 34119 USA Tel 239-353-4919.

Structured Learning LLC, *(978-0-9787800; 978-0-9845881; 978-0-9893690; 978-1-942101)* 27062 Lost Colt, Laguna Hills, CA 92653 USA E-mail: askatechteacher@gmail.com Web site: http://https://askatechteacher.com; http://https://www.structuredlearning.net.

Struggle Against the Odds, *(978-0-9778318)* 3929 Clay Pl., NE, Washington, DC 20019 USA Tel 202-397-5310 (phone/fax) E-mail: satocommunications@rcn.com Web site: http://www.satocommunication.com.

Struminger, Alexander, *(978-0-9915467)* 2985 Shiffletts Mill Rd, Crozet, VA 22932 USA Tel 434-974-7069; *Imprints:* Wren's Nest Productions LLC (WrensNestProd) E-mail: astruminger@gmail.com.

Stryker Illustrations, *(978-0-9821038)* 18011 Biscayne Blvd. Apt. 1901, Aventura, FL 33160-5239 USA Toll Free: 888-710-2513 E-mail: strykercards@bellsouth.net.

Stryker, Laura Kirby, *(978-0-692-98556-4; 978-0-692-98557-1)* 3503 Langdale Dr., High Point, NC 27265 USA Tel 336-869-8377 E-mail: lkstryker@gmail.com.

STS Publishing, *(978-0-9798806)* 1125 E. Second St., Casper, WY 82601 USA Tel 307-577-4227.

Stuart & Weitz Publishing Group *See* **RJ Blackstone Ltd**

Stuart, Jesse Foundation, The, *(978-0-945084; 978-1-931672; 978-1-938471)* 1645 Winchester Ave., Ashland, KY 41101 USA (SAN 245-8845) Web site: http://www.jsfbooks.com.

Stubblefield, Jean A, *(978-0-692-80292-2)* 2716 Inman Bend Rd, Morristown, TN 37814 USA Tel 423-307-3173 E-mail: craigjeanie@bellsouth.net.

Student Pr. Initiative, *(978-1-932948)* 509 W. 121st St., Suite 406, New York, NY 10027 USA Tel 212-678-8339; Fax: 212-678-3746 E-mail: epg10@columbia.edu.

Studio 37 Pubns., *(978-0-615-73166-7; 978-0-615-79740-3; 978-0-615-92329-1; 978-0-578-48087-9)* 3737 NE Alameda St, Portland, OR 97212 USA Tel 503-449-2821 *Dist(s):* **CreateSpace Independent Publishing Platform.**

Studio 403, *(978-0-9633943; 978-1-933129)* 399 Shoreland Dr., Lopez Island, WA 98261-8412 USA Tel 360-468-4347 E-mail: mark@studio403.com Web site: http://www.studio403.com.

Studio 9 Bks. and Music, 162 Margaret St., Plattsburgh, NY 12901 USA Tel 518-298-8595 E-mail: studio9@rdppub.com.

Studio Cherry Publishing, *(978-0-9793360)* 3697 Rt.75, Huntington, WV 25704-9011 USA Tel 304-697-2051 E-mail: studio_cherry@verizon.net.

Studio Egg LLC, *(978-1-951669)* 3841 Third Ave. S., Minneapolis, MN 55409 USA Tel 612-520-1167 E-mail: Studioeggllc@gmail.com Web site: Studioeggllc.com.

Studio Foglio, LLC, *(978-1-889061; 978-1-890856; 978-1-890856-65-6)* 2400 NW 80th St., Suite 129, Seattle, WA 98117-4449 USA (SAN 254-5128) Tel 206-782-8739; Fax: 206-783-3931 E-mail: foglio@studiofoglio.com; savannah@studiofoglio.com; foglio@xxxenophile.com Web site: http://www.studiofoglio.com *Dist(s):* **Berkeley Game Distributors**
Chessex
Cold Cut Comics Distribution
Diamond Comic Distributors, Inc.
Diamond Bk. Distributors
FM International
Rip Off Pr.
Syco Distribution.

Studio Fun International *Imprint of* **Printers Row Publishing Group**

Studio Fun International, *(978-0-276; 978-0-7621; 978-0-88705; 978-0-88850; 978-0-89577; 978-1-57584; 978-1-57619; 978-0-7944)* Subs. of Reader's Digest Assn., Inc., Reader's Digest Rd., Pleasantville, NY 10570-7000 USA (SAN 283-2143) Tel 914-244-4800; Fax: 914-244-4841; *Imprints:* Reader's Digest Children's Books (RD Childrens); Reader's Digest Young Families, Incorporated (RDYF) Web site: http://www.readersdigestkids.com; http://www.studiofun.com/ *Dist(s):* **Children's Plus, Inc.**
Continental Bk. Co., Inc.
MyiLibrary
Simon & Schuster, Inc.
Simon & Schuster Children's Publishing
Simon & Schuster Children's Publishing.

Studio Indiana, *(978-0-9745186)* 430 N. Sewell Rd., Bloomington, IN 47408 USA Tel 812-223-5073 (phone/fax) E-mail: john@studioindiana.com Web site: http://www.studioindiana.com.

Studio Ironcat L.L.C. *See* **International Comics & Entertainment L.L.C.**

Studio Moonfall, *(978-0-9841746; 978-1-942811)* 5605 Sheridan Rd. No. 1172, Kenosha, WI 53141-1172 USA Web site: http://www.fearandsunshine.com; http://www.ratatatgraphics.com *Dist(s):* **Ingram Content Group.**

Studio Mouse LLC, *(978-1-59069)* 353 Main Ave., Norwalk, CT 06851 USA Tel 203-846-2274; Fax: 203-846-1776; Toll Free: 800-228-7839 E-mail: chelsea.shriver@soundprints.com *Dist(s):* **Soundprints.**

Studio Pr., *(978-0-934420)* Orders Addr.: P.O. Box 407, Norfolk, NE 68702-0407 USA (SAN 214-400X) Tel 402-371-5040; Fax: 402-371-9382; Toll Free: 800-228-0629; Edit Addr.: 1500 Square Turn Blvd., Norfolk, NE 68702-0407 USA Do not confuse with companies with the same or similar names in Rome, NY, West Chazy, NY, Soulsbyville, CA, Elkton, MD, Tubac, AZ, Eureka Springs, AR E-mail: contact@marathonpress.com Web site: http://www.marathonpress.com *Dist(s):* **Independent Pubs. Group.**

Studio See *See* **Studio See Publishing, LLC**

Studio See Publishing, LLC, *(978-0-9796974)* P.O. Box 7013, Sheridan, WY 82801 USA Tel 307-673-1207 E-mail: psee@fiberpipe.net Web site: http://www.studiosee.com.

StudioLine Photo *Imprint of* **H&M Systems Software, Inc.**

Studios West Publications *See* **Ritchie Unlimited Pubns.**

Study Ctr. Pr. *Imprint of* **San Francisco Study Ctr.**

Stuff on Paper, *(978-0-578-01210-0; 978-0-578-05355-4; 978-0-578-13881-7)* 21849 Erdahl Ct. NE, Tenstrike, MN 56683 USA *Dist(s):* **Aardvark Global Publishing.**

Stuhl, John, *(978-0-692-99808-3)* 11318 Fords Cove Ln., Farragut, TN 37934 USA Tel 865-414-1639 E-mail: authorjohnstuhl@gmail.com *Dist(s):* **Ingram Content Group.**

Stull, Judy, *(978-0-9765738)* 16401 96th St., Lexington, OK 73051-8208 USA Tel 405-527-7467 E-mail: puppetlady@valornet.com.

Stump, Christopher, *(978-0-692-92741-0)* 5144 Conroy Rd. Unit 1025, Orlando, FL 32811 USA Tel 321-279-8965
E-mail: ChristopherLStump@gmail.com
Dist(s): **Ingram Content Group.**

Stunt Publishing, *(978-0-9745930)* 22287 Mulholland Why, No. 281, Calabasas, CA 91302 USA Tel 818-312-5157
E-mail: stuntpublishing@earthlink.net.

Sturgeon, Cathy, *(978-1-947798)* 3105 Caroline Cres, Suffolk, VA 23435 USA Tel 503-703-6687
E-mail: catherinesturgeon@gmail.com.

Stuttering Foundation of America *See* **Stuttering Foundation, The**

Stuttering Foundation, The, *(978-0-933388; 978-1-930244)* Orders Addr.: P.O. Box 11749, Memphis, TN 38111-0749 USA (SAN 282-3330) Tel 901-452-7343; Fax: 901-452-3931; Toll Free: 800-992-9392
E-mail: stutter@stutteringhelp.org
Web site: http://www.stutteringhelp.org.

Stylewriter Pubns., *(978-0-9718288; 978-0-9721653; 978-0-9729411; 978-0-9748771)* Div. of Stylewriter, Inc., 4395 N. Windsor Dr., Provo, UT 84604-6301 USA Toll Free: 866-802-7888
E-mail: customerservice@spllc.rog
Web site: http://www.spllc.org.

Stylist B. & Creative Endeavors, *(978-0-615-28680-8; 978-0-9907554)* 6961 E. Laverne St., New Orleans, LA 70126 USA Tel 504-237-2464
E-mail: writerstylistb@gmail.com
Web site: www.stylistb.com.

Stylist B. & Stylistic Creations *See* **Stylist B. & Creative Endeavors**

Stylus Publishing, LLC, *(978-1-57922; 978-1-887208; 978-0-9729394; 978-1-62036; 978-1-64267)* Orders Addr.: P.O. Box 605, Herndon, VA 20172-0605 USA; Edit Addr.: 22883 Quicksilver Dr., Sterling, VA 20166-2012 USA (SAN 299-1853) Tel 703-661-1581; Fax: 703-661-1501 Do not confuse with companies with the same name in Sunnyvale, CA, Quakertown, PA
E-mail: stylusmail@presswarehouse.com; jean.westcott@styluspub.com
Web site: http://www.styluspub.com
Dist(s): **ebrary, Inc.**

Subcomission Literature Christiana *See* **Libros Desafio**

Subterranean Pr., *(978-0-9649890; 978-1-892284; 978-1-931081; 978-1-59606; 978-1-64524)* P.O. Box 190106, Burton, MI 48519 USA Tel 810-232-1489; Fax: 810-232-1447 Do not confuse with Subterranean Pr., San Francisco, CA
E-mail: subpress@gmail.com; subpressgeralyn@gmail.com
Web site: http://www.subterraneanpress.com
Dist(s): **Diamond Comic Distributors, Inc.**
Diamond Bk. Distributors.

Subtopian, The *See* **Starburns Industries Pr.**

Success Empowering Techniques, Inc., *(978-0-9753415)* 5500 S. Eastern Ave., Las Vegas, NV 89119 USA Tel 702-893-0042
E-mail: set@setsuccess.com
Web site: http://www.setsuccess.com.

Success for All Foundation, *(978-0-9767850; 978-1-941010)* 300 E. Joppa Rd. 5th Flr., Baltimore, MD 21286 USA Tel 800-548-4998; Fax: 410-324-4458
E-mail: jworrell@successforall.org; tkoromah@successforall.org
Web site: http://www.successforall.org.

Sucharitkul, Somtow *See* **Diplodocus Pr.**

Suckerfish Bks., *(978-0-9764659; 978-1-7332801)* 23700 NW Skyline Blvd., North Plains, OR 97133 USA Tel 503-957-1554
Web site: http://www.suckerfishbooks.com.

Suerth, Renata, *(978-0-9882685)* 349 E. Crescent Ave., Elmhurst, IL 60126 USA Tel 773-793-6830
E-mail: renata98mc@yahoo.com.

Sugar Creek Publishing, *(978-0-9712571)* 4126 N. London Rd., Fairland, IN 46126 USA Tel 727-399-0342.

Sugar Ducky Bks., Inc., *(978-0-9727388)* P.O. Box 56954, Jacksonville, FL 32241-6954 USA (SAN 255-1403)
E-mail: service@sugarduckybooks.com
Web site: http://www.sugarduckybooks.com.

Sugar Goblin LLC, The, *(978-0-9860859)* 2566 Delaware Ave., Sunfish Lake, MN 55118 USA.

Suits, Danial, *(978-0-615-42555-9; 978-0-692-95150-7; 978-0-692-97248-9; 978-0-692-06099-5)* 22660 I-30 Lot 33, Bryant, AR 72022 USA Tel 501-766-6011.

Suk, Amanda, *(978-0-692-19151-4)* 116 W Maple St No. 17, Glendale, CA 91204 USA Tel 314-593-0805
E-mail: amanda.suk@gmail.com.

Sulby Hall Publishing, *(978-0-615-84593-7; 978-0-615-86133-3; 978-0-615-89846-9)* P.O. Box 8687, Malibu, CA 90264 USA Tel 310-457-0439
Dist(s): **CreateSpace Independent Publishing Platform.**

Sullivan, Kayla , *(978-0-578-18078-6)* 2909 Springdale Ln, San Ramon, CA 94583 USA.

Sullivan, Kelley Enterprises, *(978-0-9728556)* c/o L. Leon, KSE, P.O. Box 1843, Lemon Grove, CA 91946-1843 USA
E-mail: ll@mykse.com
Web site: http://www.mykse.com.

Suma de Letras, S.L. (ESP) *(978-84-663; 978-84-95501; 978-84-96463) Dist. by* **Distribks Inc.**

Summa Bks., *(978-0-932423)* P.O. Box 2095, Darien, IL 60561-6895 USA (SAN 687-4096).

Summa Publishing Company *See* **Summa Bks.**

Summer Camp Stories LLC, *(978-0-9863743)* 35 Toilsome Brook Rd., Stamford, CT 06905 USA Tel 203-705-1600
E-mail: elliotsloyer@yahoo.com
Web site: www.summercampstories.com.

Summer Day Publishing, LLC, *(978-0-9768653)* 14747 San Marsala Ct., Tampa, FL 33626 USA Tel 727-224-9874; Fax: 813-926-8215
E-mail: baflorida@aol.com
Web site: http://www.thebreakawaykid.com.

Summer Storm Publishing, LLC, *(978-1-948657)*
E-mail: azettwoch@gmail.com.

Summer Street Pr., *(978-0-9766367; 978-0-9822541)* 460 Summer St., Stamford, CT 06901 USA Tel 203-325-2217; Fax: 203-325-2218 Do not confuse with Summer Street Press in Santa Barbara, CA
E-mail: Cathy@summerstreetpress.com
Web site: http://www.summerstreetpress.com.

Summerbook Co., *(978-1-933055)* 305 Lyndale Dr., Hartsville, SC 29550 USA Tel 843-383-5554 (phone/fax)
E-mail: angela@summerbookcompany.com
Web site: http://www.summerbookcompany.com.

Summerdale Pubs. (GBR) *(978-1-84024; 978-1-873475; 978-1-84953; 978-0-85764; 978-0-85765; 978-1-78372) Dist. by* **HachBkGrp.**

Summerfield Publishing/New Plains Press, *(978-0-9794561; 978-0-9857703; 978-0-9986857; 978-1-7345719)* Orders Addr.: P.O. Box 1946, Auburn, AL 36831-1946 USA (SAN 853-4845) Tel 334-728-2071; Edit Addr.: 833 Choctaw Ave., Auburn, AL 36830 USA
E-mail: summerfield_john@columbusstate.edu; publisher@newplainspress.com
Web site: http://newplainspress.com.

Summerhill Pr., *(978-0-9801861)* P.O. Box 79684, Fort Worth, TX 76179 USA; *Imprints*: Summertime Books (Summertime Bk) Do not confuse with Summerhill Pr., Naperville, IL
E-mail: summerhillpress@charter.net
Web site: http://www.summertimebooks.com.

Summerland Publishing, *(978-0-9794585; 978-0-9794863; 978-0-9795444; 978-0-9824870; 978-0-9837923; 978-0-9891121; 978-0-9893996; 978-0-9905886; 978-0-9963736; 978-0-9986451; 978-0-9995562; 978-1-7329072)* 3181 E. Elgin Dr., Salt Lake City, UT 84109 USA (SAN 853-4497) Tel 307-399-7744
E-mail: summerlandpublishing@gmail.com
Web site: http://www.SummerlandPublishing.com.

Summers, Christine, *(978-0-9987408)* 515 Ruxton Dr., Wilmington, DE 19809 USA Tel 302-545-2367
E-mail: organizedfitnesscoach@gmail.com
Web site: sketchowl.com.

Summerside Lane, *(978-0-9777570)* 179 Highlands Dr., Williston, VT 05495 USA (SAN 850-1793)
Web site: http://www.Summersidelane.com.

Summertime Bks. *Imprint of* **Summerhill Pr.**

Summertime Books *See* **Summerhill Pr.**

Summit Hse. Pubs., *(978-0-9746735; 978-0-9746735-5-4; 978-1-7356699)* Orders Addr.: P.O. Box 15478, Chicago, IL 60615 USA; *Imprints*: Ijiwola Press, Gregory (G Ijiwola Pr)
Web site: http://www.summitpublishers.com; http://thecitylight.org.

Summit Interactive, *(978-1-57458)* Orders Addr.: 302 Albany Ave., Shreveport, LA 71105 USA Tel 318-865-8232; Fax: 318-865-6227; Toll Free: 877-843-0277
E-mail: mhenry@sieducation.com; scavel@sieducation.com; kbriley@sieducation.com
Web site: http://www.sieducation.com; http://www.AscendEdu.com.

Summit Univ. Pr., *(978-0-916766; 978-0-922729; 978-0-9720402; 978-1-932890; 978-1-60988)* Orders Addr.: 63 Summit Way, Gardiner, MT 59030 USA Tel 406-848-9500; Fax: 406-848-9605; Toll Free: 800-245-5445
E-mail: info@summituniversitypress.com
Web site: http://www.summituniversitypress.com
Dist(s): **SCB Distributors.**

Sun Break Publishing, *(978-0-9815557; 978-1-60916)* 1037 NE 65th St., No. 164, Seattle, WA 98115 USA
Web site: http://sunbreakpublishing.com
Dist(s): **Smashwords.**

Sun Cycle Publishing, *(978-0-9794322)* Orders Addr.: 1415 Hwy 85 N Ste 310-439, Fayetteville, GA 30214 USA (SAN 853-4195)
E-mail: suncyclebooks@yahoo.com.

Sun on Earth Bks., *(978-1-883378)* P.O. Box 704, Heathsville, VA 22473 USA Tel 804-435-5195
E-mail: books@sunonearth.com
Web site: http://www.sunonearth.com.

Sun Pubns., *(978-0-9665932; 978-1-931034)* Div. of Success Unleashed, Inc., 300 Carlsbad Village Dr., Suite 108A-7B, Carlsbad, CA 92008 USA (SAN 253-4444) Tel 619-884-7505; Fax: 760-434-7076 Do not confuse with Sun Publications, Charlottesville, VA
E-mail: eagles10@pacbell.net
Dist(s): **Insight Publishing.**

Sun Rose Pubs., *(978-0-9712781)* P.O. Box 2314, East Orange, NJ 07019 USA
E-mail: carolineilo@yahoo.com; eph-llogienboh@worldnet.att.net.

Sun Sings Pubns., *(978-0-9721429; 978-0-9832053)* 4144 Lafayette Pl., Culver City, CA 90232-2818 USA Tel 310-837-1313; Fax: 802-609-2959
E-mail: alan-alanlindgren@hotmail.com.

Sun Sprite Publishing, *(978-0-9745712)* 19 Milton Ave, Cranston, RI 02905 USA Toll Free: 877-883-4798
E-mail: kwanyin@ureach.com
Web site: http://www.mykwanyin.com/sunsprite.html.

Sunbelt Media, Incorporated *See* **Eakin Pr.**

†Sunbelt Pubns., Inc., *(978-0-916251; 978-0-932653; 978-0-9606704; 978-0-9620402; 978-1-941384)* 1250 Fayette St., El Cajon, CA 92020-1511 USA (SAN 630-0790) Tel 619-258-4911; Fax: 619-258-4916; Toll Free: 800-626-6579
E-mail: info@sunbeltpub.com; sales@sunbeltpub.com; dyoung@sunbeltpub.com; mail@sunbeltpub.com
Web site: http://www.sunbeltpub.com; http://www.sunbeltbooks.com; *CIP.*

Sunbird Books *Imprint of* **Phoenix International Publications, Inc.**

Sunbury Press, Inc., *(978-0-9760925; 978-1-934597; 978-1-62006)* PO Box, Boiling Springs, PA 17007-0548 USA Tel 1-855-338-8359
E-mail: orders@sunburypress.com
Web site: http://www.sunburypress.com.

SUNDADMOONMOM, *(978-1-7324860)* 667 Mcvey Ave., Lake Oswego, OR 97034 USA Tel 817-891-4809
E-mail: sundadmoonmom@gmail.com
Web site: sundadmoonmom.com.

Sundance Circle Publishing, *(978-0-9991179)* 540 E. Palm Ave., Burbank, CA 91501 USA Tel 818-679-8616
E-mail: driscoll.kevin1@gmail.com
Web site: www.sundancecircle.com.

Sundance Entertainment, *(978-0-9729847)* P.O. Box 418, New York, NY 10035 USA Tel 646-431-9334.

Sundance Media Group, Inc./VASST, *(978-0-9762380)* P.O. Box 3, Stockton, UT 84071 USA Tel 435-882-8494; Fax: 435-882-8508
E-mail: info@sundancemediagroup.com
Web site: http://www.vasst.com.

SunDance Press *See* **Bk. Pubs. of El Paso**

Sundance/Newbridge Educational Publishing, *(978-0-7608; 978-0-88741; 978-0-940146; 978-1-56784; 978-1-56801; 978-1-58273; 978-1-4007; 978-1-4207)* P.O. Box 740, Northborough, MA 01532 USA (SAN 169-3484) Tel 888-200-2720; Fax: 508-303-2015; Toll Free: 800-343-8204
E-mail: info@sundancepub.com; lroman@sundancepub.com
Web site: http://www.sundancepub.com; http://www.newbridgeonline.com.

Sunday School Board of the Southern Baptist Convention *See* **LifeWay Christian Resources**

Sunday School Publishing Board *See* **Townsend Pr. - Sunday Schl. Publishing Board**

SundaySchoolNetwork.com, *(978-0-9665124)* SA Keith of Creative Imaginations, 438 E. Ilex Dr., Lake Park, FL 33403-2606 USA Tel 561-281-5033
E-mail: info@sundayschoolnetwork.com; orders@SundaySchoolNetwork.com
Web site: http://https://www.sundayschoolnetwork.com; http://www.creativeimaginations.net.

Sundback, Ruth, *(978-0-9776850)* 10430 Perla Bello Ct., Las Vegas, NV 89135 USA (SAN 850-9719)
E-mail: ruthslv@earthlink.net.

Sundie Enterprises, *(978-0-9859811; 978-0-9991261)* P.O. Box 1274, Provo, UT 84603-1274 USA Tel 801-995-9342
E-mail: sundieents@gmail.com.

SunDog Enterprises, *(978-0-9854677)* 119 Persimmon Ridge Rd., Cleveland, SC 29635 USA Tel 864-836-2668
E-mail: gail.mcdiarmid@furman.edu.

Sundog, Ltd., *(978-1-932203; 978-1-59744)* Orders Addr.: 35 W. 92nd St., 5e, New York, NY 10025 USA.

Sunergos Bible Studies, *(978-1-932934)* 2485 Morse Rd., Sebastopol, CA 95472 USA Tel 707-829-2956
E-mail: rich@sunergosbible.org; jan@sunergosbible.org
Web site: http://www.sunergosbible.org.

Sunesis Publishing Co., *(978-0-9716487; 978-1-7327223)* 424 S. Mckinley Maddox Rd., Perry, FL 32347 USA Tel 850-838-3909 (phone/fax); *Imprints*: PathLight Books (PathLight Bks) Do not confuse with Compass Publishing in Savannah, GA
Web site: http://www.sunesispublishing.com.

Sunflower Education, *(978-1-937166)* 15044 Haley Hollow, Austin, TX 78728 USA Tel 512-694-9380
E-mail: cynthia.hannon@gmail.com
Web site: sunflowereducation.net.

Sunflower Pr., *(978-0-9616586; 978-0-9768507; 978-0-9832659)* P.O. Box 750733, Forest Hills, NY 11375 USA (SAN 659-7785) Fax: 718-830-9616
E-mail: order@chutaichi.com.

Sunflower Pr., *(978-0-9896080)* 200 Viridian Dr., Muskegon, MI 49440 USA Tel 347-844-2149
E-mail: edzitron@edzitron.com.

Sunflower Publishing *See* **Growing Field Bks.**

Sunflower Seeds Pr., *(978-0-9743627; 978-0-9830089)* 9470 Hwy 96 W., Franklin, TN 37064 USA
E-mail: bill@rondafriend.com
Web site: http://www.sunflowerseedspress.com; http://www.downonfriendlyacres.com.

Sunflower Univ. Pr., *(978-0-89745)* Subs. of Journal of the West, Inc., 2961 Nevada St., Manhattan, KS 66502-2355 USA (SAN 218-5075) Toll Free: 800-258-1232 (orders)
E-mail: pub@sunflower-univ-press.org
Web site: http://www.sunflower-univ-press.org.

Sungi Bear LLC, *(978-0-692-61262-0; 978-0-692-71225-2; 978-0-9988483)* 87 Forest Hill Rd, West Orange, NJ 07052 USA Tel 973-568-5256; 87 Forest Hill Rd, West Orange, NJ 07052 Tel 973-568-5256.

SunHill Pubs., *(978-0-9673189)* Do not confuse with Hill Publishing in Marina, CA
E-mail: ehill111@comcast.net.

Sunlight Publishing, *(978-0-9818190)* 339 E. Weller St., Ansonia, OH 45303 USA (SAN 924-7130) Tel 937-671-8511; 419-925-4121; *Imprints*: Candy Cane Books (CandyCane).

Sunny & The Chocolate Dog, LLC, *(978-0-9725945)* 5 Palm Row, Saint Augustine, FL 32084 USA Tel 904-808-7144; Fax: 904-808-7142
E-mail: josh@sunnyandthechocolatedog.com
Web site: http://www.sunnyandthechocolatedog.com.

Sunny Bks. *Imprint of* **J B Communications, Inc.**

Sunny Day Publishing, LLC, *(978-0-9825480; 978-0-9903823; 978-0-9978006; 978-1-948613)* 3365 Crestwood Cir., Cuyahoga Falls, OH 44223 USA (SAN 920-8232) Tel 330-414-2760 Do not confuse with Sunny Day Publishing in Richardson, TX
E-mail: sales@sunnydaypublishing.com; stacie@sunnydaypublishing.com
Web site: https://www.sunnydaypublishing.com.

Sunny Future Pr., *(978-0-9754980)* 890 Bruce Dr., Wantagh, NY 11793-1116 USA
E-mail: canivan@optonline.net
Web site: http://www.jc-solarhomes.com.

Sunny Hollow Pr., *(978-0-9755818)* 2517 N. 62nd St., Mesa, AZ 85215 USA Tel 480-830-7634; Toll Free: 800-442-0046
E-mail: rjvb@sunnyhollowpress.com
Web site: http://www.sunnyhollowpress.com.

Sunny Palms Pr., *(978-1-942073; 978-1-951314; 978-1-64778)* P.O. Box 230348, Encinitas, CA 92023 USA Tel 760-902-6502
E-mail: janmoran123@gmail.com.

Sunnycroft Bks., *(978-0-9904320)* 4110 SE Hawthorne Blvd. No. 749, Portland, OR 97214 USA Tel 503-867-3085
E-mail: sunnycroftbooks@gmail.com.

Sunnyfields Publishing, *(978-0-578-06095-8; 978-0-578-06541-0; 978-0-578-06574-8; 978-0-615-75133-7; 978-0-615-76128-2; 978-0-615-76235-7)* 1746 N. Gramercy Pl., No. 15, Los Angeles, CA 90028 USA Tel 323-960-2563
E-mail: Daviddayan666@aol.com.

Sunnyside Pr., *(978-0-9742566)* 902 E. 10th St., Jeffersonville, IN 47130 USA Tel 812-282-8832; Fax: 812-282-4057 Do not confuse with companies with the same or similar name in Saint Johnsville, NY, San Marcos, CA, Washington, DC
E-mail: bprintcenter@cs.com.

Sunphone, Ltd., *(978-0-9652458)* 427 Sippewissett Rd., Falmouth, MA 02540 USA Tel 508-540-6899; Fax: 508-540-8226
E-mail: sunfal@aol.com.

Sunraehealing, *(978-0-9896218; 978-0-9908374)* 3906 Cherrywood Rd., Austin, TX 78722 USA Tel 512-547-2454
E-mail: raedoman@hotmail.com.

SunRaSon Production Co., *(978-0-9677644)* 882 E. 57th St., Brooklyn, NY 11234 USA
E-mail: info@sunrason.com
Web site: http://www.sunrason.com.

Sunray Publishing, *(978-1-934478)* 25123 22nd Ave., Saint Cloud, MN 56301 USA Tel 320-253-8808; Fax: 320-253-9683; Toll Free: 888-253-8808
E-mail: jwindschitl@sunrayprinting.com
Web site: http://www.sunrayprinting.com
Dist(s): **Partners Bk. Distributing, Inc.**

Sunrise Bks., *(978-0-940652)* P.O. Box 7003, Eureka, CA 95502-7003 USA (SAN 665-7893) Do not confuse with with companies with the same name in Lebanon, VA, Lake Bluff, IL
E-mail: Sunrise-2004@sbcglobal.net.

Sunrise Mountain Bks., *(978-0-9842362; 978-1-940728)* Div. of Sunrise Services Distributing, LLC, 13347 W. Tapatio Dr., Boise, ID 83713 USA (SAN 858-8139) Fax: 208-938-8338; *Imprints*: Simple Faith Books (SimpleFaith)
Web site: http://www.sunrisemountainbooks.com; http://www.sunrisedistrib.com; http://www.youcandoitart.com.

Sunrise Publications *See* **Prematurely Yours**

SunRise Publishing, *(978-0-9644552; 978-1-57636)* Orders Addr.: P.O. Box 1001, Orem, UT 84059 USA Tel 801-860-2665; Fax: 801-705-0124; Edit Addr.: P.O. Box 1001, Orem, UT 84059-1001 USA Do not confuse with companies with the same or similar names in Lake Forest, IL, Niagara Falls, NY, Lincoln City, OR, Santa Barbara, CA, Hatfield, PA, Maryland Heights, MD, Austinburg, OH, Inman, SC, Fort Lauderdale, FL, Albuquerque, NM
E-mail: brian@sunrisebooks.com
Web site: http://www.sunrisebooks.com
Dist(s): **Granite Publishing & Distribution Village Marketing.**

Sunrise Selections, *(978-0-9656307)* Orders Addr.: P.O. Box 51602, Provo, UT 84605-1602 USA Tel 801-852-6141; Fax: 801-489-9517; Edit Addr.: 1102 N. Main, Mapleton, UT 84664 USA
E-mail: bbriggs@provo.utah.gov
Web site: http://www.sunrise-selections.com
Dist(s): **Granite Publishing & Distribution.**

SunriseHouse Pubs., *(978-0-9770783)* 5181 Blackpool Rd., Westminster, CA 92683 USA
E-mail: dawn@dawnwilliams.net
Web site: http://www.sunrisehousepublishers.com.

Sunseri, Heather, *(978-0-9887153; 978-1-943165)* P.O. Box 1264, Versailles, KY 40383 USA
E-mail: heather@heathersunseri.com.

Sunset Beach Music, *(978-0-9639279)* P.O. Box 159, Haleiwa, HI 96712 USA
E-mail: msmusic@hula.net.

Sunset Readers Publishing, *(978-0-9749333)* 220 W., 400 N., American Fork, UT 84003-1567 USA
E-mail: beb1@sisna.com
Web site: http://www.bennetthbracken.com.

Sunshine Bks. for Children, *(978-0-9745116)* 8127 E. Weldon Ave., Scottsdale, AZ 85251 USA.

Sunshine Center, Incorporated *See* **Prevention Through Puppetry, Inc.**

Publisher Name Index

Sunshine In My Soul Publishing, *(978-1-68327)* 7380 Park Ridge Blvd. No. 124, San Diego, CA 92120 USA (SAN 990-0969) Tel 619-788-9612
E-mail: admin@speedypublishing.com; bowe@sunshineinmysoulpublishing.com.

Sunshine Publishing, *(978-0-9749844)* 1421 Washington St., Lincoln, NE 68502-2455 USA Do not confuse with companies with the same or similar names in Carthage, NY, Buffalo Grove, IL , Bristol, TN, Columbus, GA, Raleigh, NC, Ft Worth, TX.

Sunshine53 Pr., *(978-0-9855233)* 18008 NW Sylvania Ln., Portland, OR 97229 USA Tel 503-747-2658
E-mail: coryell5150@comcast.net.

SunSprouts *Imprint of* **hand2mind**

Sunstar Publishing *Imprint of* **1st World Publishing, Inc.**

†Sunstone Pr., *(978-0-86534; 978-0-913270; 978-1-61139; 978-1-63293)* Div. of The Sunstone Corporation, Orders Addr.: 239 Johnson St., Santa Fe, NM 87504-2321 USA; Edit Addr.: P.O. Box 2321, Santa Fe, NM 87504-2321 USA (SAN 214-2090) Tel 505-988-4418; Fax: 505-988-1025; Toll Free: 800-243-5644 (Orders Only); *Imprints:* Blackbirch Press, Incorporated (Blackbirch Pr)
E-mail: jsmith@sunstonepress.com
Web site: http://www.sunstonepress.com
Dist(s): **Brodart Co.**
Ingram Content Group
New Leaf Distributing Co., Inc.
Quality Bks., Inc.
Rio Nuevo Pubs.; *CIP.*

Suny Pr. *Imprint of* **State Univ. of New York Pr.**

Super Dentists, The, *(978-0-9798506)* 2226 Otay Lakes Rd., Chula Vista, CA 91915 USA (SAN 854-5650)
Web site: http://www.thesuperdentists.com.

Super Duper Pubns., *(978-1-58650; 978-1-60723)* Div. of Super Duper, Inc., Orders Addr.: P.O. Box 24997, Greenville, SC 29616 USA Tel 864-288-3536; Fax: 864-288-3380; Toll Free: 800-277-8737; Edit Addr.: 5201 Pelham Rd., Greenville, SC 29615-5723 USA
E-mail: lgranger@superduperinc.com
Web site: http://www.superduperinc.com; http://www.handyhandouts.com; http://www.hearbuilder.com; http://www.superduperlearning.com.

Super SandCastle *Imprint of* **ABDO Publishing Co.**

Super Smart Science Stuff, *(978-0-9843848; 978-0-9911472; 978-1-941775)* 5813 Anselm Ct, Austin, TX 78739-7873 USA Tel 512-203-6919; Fax: 512-288-0208
E-mail: april@supersmartsciencestuff.com.

Super Source The *Imprint of* **hand2mind**

SUPERI, LLC. *See* **Superi, LLC.**

Superi, LLC., *(978-0-9970364; 978-0-9974751)* 16038 Eastcape Dr., Webster, TX 77598 USA Tel 832-738-7971
E-mail: cthurmon13@outlook.com
Web site: http://www.superiworld.com.

SuperKids Nutrition Inc., *(978-0-9801148; 978-1-7339692)* 375 S. Grand Oaks Ave., Pasadena, CA 91107 USA (SAN 855-2436) Tel 626-818-6299
E-mail: melissa@superkidsnutrition.com
Web site: http://www.superkidsnutrition.com.

Supreme Art, *(978-1-942912)* 6425 Reseda Blvd., Reseda, CA 91335 USA Tel 818-438-9779
E-mail: info@supremeart.org
Web site: www.supremeArt.org.

Supreme Design, LLC, *(978-0-9816170; 978-1-935721)* P.O. Box 10887, Atlanta, GA 30310 USA Tel 404-759-8799
E-mail: sujandass@ymail.com
Web site: http://www.supremedesignllc.com.

SuProCo, *(978-0-9906567)* 1300 Army Navy Dr. No. 1101, Arlington, VA 22202 USA Tel 703-271-8889
E-mail: SuProCo@aol.com.

Surber, Shawn-Michelle *See* **Mornin' Light Media**

Surface Communications LLC *See* **Books by Kids LLC**

Surfing Group, The, *(978-0-9770730)* Primedia, 236 Avenida Fabricante. Ste. 201, San Clemente, CA 92672-7557 USA
E-mail: ross.garrett@primedia.com.

Surfside Six Publishing, *(978-0-615-32262-9; 978-0-692-87258-1; 978-0-692-04632-6)* P.O. Box 545960, Surfside, FL 33154 USA
Dist(s): **CreateSpace Independent Publishing Platform.**

Sur-Mount Pubs., *(978-0-9673517; 978-0-9740107)* P.O. Box 99396, Emeryville, CA 94662-9396 USA Tel 510-559-8797
E-mail: cs@surmountpublishersincorporated.com; sales@surmountpublishersincorporated.com
Web site: http://www.surmountpublishersincorporated.com.

Suromex, Ediciones, S.A. (MEX) *(978-968-855) Dist. by* **Giron Bks.**

Susaeta Ediciones, S.A. (ESP) *(978-84-305; 978-84-677) Dist. by* **AIMS Intl.**

Susaeta Ediciones, S.A. (ESP) *(978-84-305; 978-84-677) Dist. by* **IPG Chicago.**

Susaeta Ediciones, S.A. (ESP) *(978-84-305; 978-84-677) Dist. by* **Giron Bks.**

Susaeta Ediciones, S.A. (ESP) *(978-84-305; 978-84-677) Dist. by* **Lectorum Pubns.**

Susan Palavics Publishing, *(978-0-692-78458-7)* 51760 Becker Rd., Bigfork, MN 56628 USA Tel 218-743-3458
E-mail: thewildernesslodge1@gmail.com.

Susanna Lagoon Bks. *Imprint of* **J. K. Eckert & Co., Inc.**

Susi B. Marketing, Inc., *(978-0-9773653)* 188 Wentworth St., Charleston, SC 29401 USA Tel 843-822-7676; Fax: 843-958-8444
Web site: http://www.angietheant.com.

Susquehanna Univ. Pr., *(978-0-941664; 978-0-945636; 978-1-57591)* Affil. of Associated Univ. Presses, Orders Addr.: 2010 Eastpark Blvd., Cranbury, NJ 08512 USA Tel 609-655-4770; Fax: 609-655-8366
Web site: http://www.susqu.edu/su_press
Dist(s): **Associated Univ. Presses**
Rowman & Littlefield Publishers, Inc.
ebrary, Inc.

Sussman Sales Co., *(978-0-9755367; 978-1-934211; 978-1-61717; 978-1-68265; 978-1-953038)* 250 E. 54th St. Suite 8A, New York, NY 10022 USA Toll Free Fax: 212-371-8882; Toll Free: 800-350-7180
E-mail: info@sussmansales.com
Web site: http://www.sussmansales.com.

Susy Dorn Productions, LLC, *(978-0-9764010)* P.O. Box 111393, Campbell, CA 95011-1393 USA
Web site: http://www.juguemosenespanol.com.

Sutton, Robin, *(978-0-9755098)* P.O. Box 79174, Saginaw, TX 76179 USA
Web site: http://www.therobinsnestbooks.com.

Suzalooz Pr., *(978-0-9660350)* 139 S. Eighth St., Brooklyn, NY 11211 USA Tel 718-387-3384; Fax: 212-475-4442
E-mail: zhour@inx.net.

Suzeteo Enterprises *See* **Athanatos Publishing Group**

Suzeteo Enterprises *Imprint of* **Athanatos Publishing Group**

Suzuki *Imprint of* **Alfred Publishing Co., Inc.**

Susy & Livy Pubns., *(978-0-9727757)* Orders Addr.: P.O. Box 449, Virginia City, NV 89440 USA Tel 775-847-0454; Fax: 775-847-9010; Edit Addr.: 111 S. C St., Virginia City, NV 89440-0449 USA
E-mail: info@marktwainbooks.com
Web site: http://www.marktwainbooks.com.

Svoboda, David *See* **BooksbyDave Inc.**

Swafford, Bethany, P.O. Box 38, DENVER, IN 46926 USA Tel 765-633-3249
E-mail: bjswaff@gmail.com
Dist(s): **Ingram Content Group.**

†Swallow Pr., *(978-0-8040)* Ohio Univ. Pr., Scott Quadrangle, Athens, OH 45701 USA (SAN 202-5663) Tel 740-593-1158; Fax: 740-593-4536; Toll Free: 800-621-2736
E-mail: arnold@ohio.edu
Web site: http://www.ohio~.edu/oupress/
Dist(s): **Chicago Distribution Ctr.**
Ohio Univ. Pr.
Univ. of Chicago Pr.
ebrary, Inc.; *CIP.*

Swampland Publishing Co., *(978-0-9754785)* P.O. Box 1311, Larose, LA 70373 USA
E-mail: alces@cajunswampland.com.

Swan Creek Pr., *(978-0-9753216; 978-1-7335341)* 3736 Linden Green Dr., Toledo, OH 43614 USA Tel 419-381-0115
E-mail: swancreekpress@buckeye-express.com
Dist(s): **Ingram Content Group.**

Swan-Jones Production, *(978-1-882238)* 8362 San Critobal Dr., Dallas, TX 75218 USA Tel 214-319-7049.

Swannee Rivers *See* **Rivers, Swannee**

Swanson, David, *(978-0-9830830; 978-0-9980859; 978-1-7347837)* 707 Gillespie Ave., Charlottesville, VA 22902 USA Tel 434-296-4228
E-mail: david@davidswanson.org.

SWC Editions *Imprint of* **Wayne, Steven Co.**

Sweden Trade, Inc., *(978-0-9744088)* 9-11 South Blvd. of Presidents, Sarasota, FL 34236 USA; *Imprints:* Sweden Trade Publishing (Sweden Trd Pub)
Web site: http://TheRoadToHappinessBook.com.

Sweden Trade Publishing *Imprint of* **Sweden Trade, Inc.**

Sweet 76 Bakery, *(978-0-615-80672-3)* 8709 58th Ave. SW Apt. D, Lakewood, WA 98499 USA Tel 253-205-1373
E-mail: dineensmith@yahoo.com.

Sweet Cherry Publishing (GBR) *(978-1-78226) Dist. by* **BTPS.**

Sweet Dreams Pr. *Imprint of* **Bier Brothers, Inc.**

Sweet Grin Bks., *(978-0-9905402)* 1305 SE 3rd St., Cape Coral, FL 33990 USA Tel 239-478-0255
E-mail: befranz@yahoo.com.

Sweet, Joanne, *(978-0-9774881)* 228 Westin Hls., New Braunfels, TX 78132-2328 USA.

Sweet, Joanne, *(978-1-936660)* 228 Westin Hills, New Braunfels, TX 78132 USA Tel 830-624-4560
E-mail: store1@jhsweet.com
Web site: www.jhsweet.com.

Sweet Mama Bks., *(978-1-7330254)* 1838 3rd St, Kirkland, WA 98033 USA Tel 206-650-2250
E-mail: courtbcooke@gmail.com
Web site: sweetmamabooks.com.

Sweet Pea Bks., *(978-0-615-21845-8; 978-0-578-01706-8; 978-0-578-03074-6; 978-0-615-38010-0; 978-0-578-11547-4; 978-0-578-11548-1; 978-0-692-39897-5)* 601 Pelham Pwy. N., Suite 614, Bronx, NY 10467 USA (SAN 859-8983) Tel 914-843-1439; 347-341-5612
E-mail: sweetpeabooks@yahoo.com
Web site: http://sweetpeabooks.net.

Sweet Pea Productions, *(978-0-692-21374-2; 978-0-692-24407-4; 978-0-692-24410-4; 978-0-692-29778-0; 978-0-692-35306-6; 978-0-692-66546-6; 978-0-9981098; 978-1-7359187)* 16 lyndhurst Dr., bella vista, AR 72714 USA Tel 4796404312
Web site: www.jennybjones.com
Dist(s): **CreateSpace Independent Publishing Platform.**

Sweet Potato Brown, *(978-0-9788158)* Orders Addr.: 5208 S. Drexel Ave., 2w, Chicago, IL 60615 USA Tel 773-752-3521
E-mail: sofiapenelopebrown@sbcglobal.net
Web site: http://www.at3619.com
Dist(s): **Lulu Pr., Inc.**

Sweet Punkin Pr., *(978-0-9755078)* 43 Riverside Ave., No. 405, Medford, MA 02155-4605 USA Tel 781-389-0693; Fax: 781-396-8052
E-mail: cvenez@aol.com
Web site: http://www.sweetpunkinpress.com.

Sweet Spot Publishing, *(978-0-9907739; 978-0-9863890)* 11370 Twelve Oaks Way, North Palm Beach, FL 33408 USA Tel 561-818-6700
E-mail: d.abis77@gmail.com.

Sweet Success Pr., *(978-0-9700127)* P.O. Box 351564, Westminster, CO 80035-1564 USA
E-mail: Vkrudwig@aol.com
Web site: http://www.members.aol.com/vkrudwig
Dist(s): **Bks. West.**

Sweetbeet Bks., *(978-0-9985362; 978-1-7336109; 978-1-7331539)* P.O. Box 20817, Bethesda, MD 20015 USA
E-mail: almahammonddtc@gmail.com
Web site: http://www.sweetbeetbooks.com.

Sweetbriar Crafts & Pubns., *(978-0-9802015)* 3390 40th St., Mandan, ND 58554 USA Tel 701-663-6941
E-mail: swcandp@gmail.com.

Sweetgrass Bks. *Imprint of* **Farcountry Pr.**

Sweetwater Bks. *Imprint of* **Cedar Fort, Inc./CFI Distribution**

Sweetwater Pr., *(978-1-58173; 978-1-889372; 978-1-60196)* Div. of Books-A-Million, Orders Addr.: 3608 Clairmont Ave., Birmingham, AL 035222 USA Do not confuse with companies with the same name in Ault, CO, Raleigh, NC Miami FL, Little Rock AR .

Sweetwater Stagelines *Imprint of* **Old West Co., The**

Swell Thoughts, *(978-0-9995908)* 5716 Chicago Ave., Minneapolis, MN 55417 USA Tel 612-927-8018
E-mail: swellgaltalks@gmail.com.

Swift Learning Resources, *(978-0-944991; 978-1-56861)* Div. of Swift Printing Corp., 1520 N. State St., Lehi, UT 84043-1079 USA (SAN 245-6737) Toll Free: 800-292-2831
E-mail: swift@swift-net.com
Web site: http://www.swiftlearning.com.

Swingin' Bridge Bks. *Imprint of* **Keystone College Pr.**

Swingset Pr., LLC, *(978-0-9658167; 978-1-930680)* Orders Addr.: P.O. Box 18701, Encino, CA 91416-8701 USA Tel 818-779-1413; Fax: 818-779-1411; Toll Free: 888-543-9366; Edit Addr.: 5987 S. High Dr., Morrison, CO 80465-2608 USA
E-mail: info@swingsetpress.com
Web site: http://www.swingsetpress.com.

Swiss Creek Pubns., *(978-0-9702276)* Orders Addr.: 15565 Swiss Creek Ln., Cupertino, CA 95014-5452 USA Tel 408-741-5809; Fax: 408-741-5231
E-mail: bob@zeidman.net
Web site: http://www.zeidman.net.

Switch Pr. *Imprint of* **Capstone**

Switzer Land Enterprises, *(978-0-9642663)* Orders Addr.: P.O. Box 3800, Estes Park, CO 80517 USA Tel 303-586-4624; Fax: 907-577-0775; Edit Addr.: 1236 Glacier View, Estes Park, CO 80517 USA
E-mail: philalpaca@aol.com.

Sword of the Lord Pubs., *(978-0-87398; 978-1-64942)* Orders Addr.: P.O. Box 1099, Murfreesboro, TN 37133 USA (SAN 203-5642) Tel 615-893-6700; Fax: 615-895-7447
E-mail: cpenland@swordofthelord.com
Web site: http://www.swordbooks.com/; http://www.swordofthelord.com/
Dist(s): **Dake Publishing.**

Sword of the Spirit Publishing, *(978-0-615-20617-2; 978-0-615-20810-7; 978-0-615-21223-4; 978-0-615-21437-5; 978-0-615-22183-0; 978-0-615-22348-3; 978-0-615-24292-7; 978-0-578-01560-6; 978-0-578-03282-5; 978-0-9825870; 978-0-9838836; 978-1-939219)* Orders Addr.: 219 Lakewood Dr., Crossville, TN 38558 USA Tel 931-287-0280
E-mail: scaramouche9999@yahoo.com
Web site: http://www.swordofspirit.net
Dist(s): **Lulu Pr., Inc.**
Send The Light Distribution LLC.

Swordfish Communications, LLC, *(978-0-9741955)* Orders Addr.: 1748 Ohlen Rd. #67, Austin, TX 78757 USA
E-mail: orders@swordfishcommunications.com
Web site: http://www.swordfishcommunications.com.

Sy Publishing, *(978-0-9761613)* 7720 E. Redfield Rd., Suite No. 7, Scottsdale, AZ 85260 USA Tel 480-596-9226; Fax: 480-967-8736
E-mail: devinsper@yahoo.com
Web site: http://www.devinsper.com.

Sybertooth, Inc. (CAN) *(978-0-9688024; 978-0-9739505; 978-0-9810244; 978-0-9864974; 978-1-927592) Dist. by* **LightSource CS.**

Sycuan Pr., *(978-0-9790951)* 5401 Sycuan Rd., El Cajon, CA 92019 USA Tel 619-445-6917; Fax: 619-445-5176
E-mail: jbathke@sycuan.org.

Sydney Pr., LLC, *(978-0-9724577)* Orders Addr.: 2035 Fanning Ct., Leland, NC 28451 USA Tel 910-632-7778
E-mail: buckaloha@gmail.com.

Syentek Books Company, Incorporated *See* **Syentek, Inc.**

Syentek, Inc., *(978-0-914082)* P.O. Box 26588, San Francisco, CA 94126 USA (SAN 202-7534) Tel 415-928-0471.

Sylables, *(978-0-9724394)* 2105 Sheldon Rd., Saint Albans, VT 05478 USA (SAN 255-1500) Tel 802-524-0262
E-mail: sylables@earthlink.net
Web site: http://www.sylables.com.

Syllabets, LLC, *(978-0-9794543)* 3740 30th Ave. S., Suite 307, Grand Forks, ND 58201-5820 USA (SAN 853-4632)
Web site: http://www.syllabets.com.

Syllogism Pr., *(978-0-9638001)* 875 Emory Shield Rd., Murphy, NC 28906 USA Tel 732-290-7901
E-mail: spress@dnet.net.

Sylph Pubns., *(978-0-9673004; 978-0-9760742)* 1248 E. Edison St., W., Tucson, AZ 85719 USA Tel 520-882-3794
E-mail: eliotbooks@aol.com
Web site: http://www.eliotbooks.com.

Sylvan Dell Publishing *See* **Arbordale Publishing**

Sylvan Learning Publishing *Imprint of* **Random Hse. Children's Bks.**

Sylvestre, Gibson Publishing, *(978-0-615-21166-4; 978-0-578-01878-2; 978-0-578-01879-9; 978-0-578-03784-4; 978-0-578-04150-6)* P.O. Box 934741, Margate, FL 33093 USA
E-mail: info@mylifeonpurpose.org
Web site: http://www.mylifeonpurpose.org.

Symmetry Learning Systems, *(978-1-58447)* Div. of Symmetry Research, Inc., 5 Bretton Rd., Dover, MA 02030 USA (SAN 299-7967)
E-mail: info@symmetrylearning.com; prberget@symmetrylearning.com
Web site: http://www.symmetrylearning.com.

Sympathetic Pr., *(978-0-578-12457-5; 978-0-578-54327-7; 978-0-578-64669-5)* 120 State Ave. N.E. No. 134, Olympia, WA 98501 USA Tel 360-943-0929
Dist(s): **SCB Distributors.**

Symtalk, Inc., *(978-1-932770; 978-1-933209)* 875 Montreal Way, Saint Paul, MN 55102-4245 USA Toll Free: 877-796-8255
E-mail: info@symtalk.com
Web site: http://www.symtalk.com.

Symtext Media, *(978-0-9768379)* 21538 N. 65th Ave., Glendale, AZ 85308-6410 USA Tel 623-362-1947
E-mail: fullschedule@symtextmedia.com
Web site: http://www.symtextmedia.com.

Synapse, Edition (JPN) *(978-4-901481; 978-4-931444; 978-4-86166) Dist. by* **Taylor and Fran.**

Synaptic Wammy Works *See* **Loose In The Lab**

Synaxis Pr., *(978-0-911523)* P.O. Box 689, Lynden, WA 98264 USA (SAN 685-4338) Tel 604-826-9336; Fax: 604-820-9758.

Synchrony Hse. Publishing, *(978-0-9993410)* 341 Spring Forest Dr., Simpsonville, SC 29681 USA Tel 864-313-4973
E-mail: elegantredneck@gmail.com.

Syndistar, Inc., *(978-1-56230)* P.O. Box 3027, Hammond, LA 70404-3027 USA (SAN 298-007X) Toll Free: 800-841-9532
E-mail: webmaster@syndistar.com
Web site: http://www.syndistar.com.

SynergEbooks *See* **CamCat Publishing**

Synergetic Pubns., Inc., *(978-0-9632248)* Orders Addr.: P.O. Box 1506, Hendersonville, TN 37075 USA (SAN 297-6129) Tel 615-264-3405; Edit Addr.: 205 Applewood Valley Dr., Hendersonville, TN 37075 USA.

Synergy-Bks. Publishing, *(978-1-936434)* 12702 Woodland Ln., Garden Grove, CA 92840 USA Tel 714-638-4813
E-mail: billw@synergy-books.com
Web site: http://synergy-books.com.

SYP Kids *Imprint of* **Southern Yellow Pine (SYP) Publishing LLC**

†Syracuse Univ. Pr., *(978-0-8156; 978-0-615-28768-3; 978-1-68445)* 621 Skytop Rd., Suite 110, Syracuse, NY 13244-5290 USA (SAN 206-9776) Tel 315-443-5534; Fax: 315-443-5545
E-mail: supress@syr.edu; arpfeiff@syr.edu
Web site: http://www.SyracuseUniversityPress.syr.edu
Dist(s): **Gryphon Hse., Inc.**
Longleaf Services
ebrary, Inc.; *CIP.*

Syren Bk. Co., *(978-0-929636)* Orders Addr.: 5120 Cedar Lake Rd., S., Minneapolis, MN 55416 USA (SAN 249-7719) Tel 763-398-0030; Fax: 763-398-0198; Toll Free: 800-901-3480 Do not confuse with BookMobile in Port Ludlow WA
E-mail: dleeper@bookmobile.com; jogren@bookmobile.com
Web site: http://www.itascabooks.com
Dist(s): **BookMobile**
Itasca Bks.

SYS Publishing, *(978-0-9794871)* P.O. Box 868, Montclair, NJ 07042 USA Tel 973-951-7490; 2142 Blackwolf Run Ln., Raleigh, NC 27604 Toll Free: 800-994-3683
E-mail: SYSPublishing@aol.com
Web site: http://www.sadieshero.com.

Systems Group, Inc., The, *(978-0-9847740)* 4618 Granite Rock Ct., Chantilly, VA 20151 USA Tel 703-378-4193
E-mail: Oliver.Franklin@verizon.net.

Szydlowski, Mary Vigliante, *(978-0-9965622; 978-0-9983869; 978-1-7328815)* 37 Normanside Dr., Albany, NY 12208 USA Tel 518-453-3613
E-mail: maszyd@aol.com
Web site: http://www.maryviglianteszydlowski.com/.

†TAB Bks., Div. of The McGraw-Hill Cos., 11 W. 19th St., New York, NY 10011 USA (SAN 202-568X)
E-mail: bookstore@mcgraw-hill.com; customer.service@mcgraw-hill.com
Web site: http://www.mcgraw-hill.com/; *CIP.*

T. A. S. Enterprises, Incorporated *See* **Lit Torch Publishing**

T & T Roberts Publishing, *(978-0-9723868; 978-0-578-69566-2)* 3105 S. Trenton Cir., Sioux Falls, SD 57103 USA
E-mail: tom.roberts@chssd.org
Web site: http://www.chssd.org/books.

TBM, Inc., *(978-0-9647096)* 280 N. Latah St., Boise, ID 83706 USA Tel 208-853-0555; Fax: 208-383-9010; 9295 Esterbrook, Boise, ID 83703
E-mail: realbows@aol.com
Web site: http://www.tradbow.com.

For full information on wholesalers and distributors, refer to the Wholesaler and Distributor Name Index

TCR Pr., *(978-0-9714465)* P.O. Box 12011, Raleigh, NC 27605 USA
E-mail: newplants@angelfire.com
Web site: http://www.tcrpress.com.

T. E. Publishing, Inc., *(978-0-9722036)* P.O. Box 823, Bath, NY 14810 USA Tel 607-76-1307
E-mail: pcarlton@tepublishing.com.

THINC Corp., *(978-0-9655026)* Orders Addr.: P.O. Box 14, Batesville, MS 38606 USA Tel 601-563-1162; Fax: 601-563-6640; Toll Free: 888-837-7606; Edit Addr.: 150 Hwy. 35 N., Batesville, MS 38606 USA.

TM Photography, Inc., *(978-0-9660144)* 82 King St., Charleston, SC 29401 USA Tel 843-577-3237.

T Pubns. (GBR) *(978-0-9569434) Dist. by* **D C D.**

T.Y.M. Publishing, *(978-0-9641274)* 409 Melville Ave., Palo Alto, CA 94301 USA Tel 415-325-1130.

Tabby Hse. Bks., *(978-0-9627974; 978-1-881539)* Orders Addr.: P.O. Box 544, Mineral, VA 23117 USA Tel 540-895-9093 (phone/fax); Edit Addr.: 12004 Sycamore Shoals Dr. Bumpass, Va 23034, Bumpass, VA 23024 USA; *Imprints:* Strathmoor (Strathmoor)
E-mail: tabbyhouse@gmail.com; publisher@tabbyhouse.com
Web site: http://www.tabbyhouse.com
Dist(s): **Distributors, The.**

Taberah Pr. *Imprint of* **Sonfire Media, LLC**

Table Rock Bks., *(978-0-9726869)* 69 Woodland Ave., Smithfield, RI 02917 USA.

Tabor Pr., *(978-0-9745799)* Orders Addr.: P.O. Box 470842, Brookline Village, MA 02447 USA Tel 617-784-6561; Edit Addr.: 278 Warren St., Brookline, MA 02445 USA
E-mail: ephraim541@hotmail.com.

Tachyon Pubns., *(978-0-9648320; 978-1-892391; 978-1-61696)* 1459 18th St., No. 139, San Francisco, CA 94107 USA Tel 415-285-5615
E-mail: tachyonsf@aol.com
Web site: http://www.tachyonpublications.com/
Dist(s): **Baker & Taylor Publisher Services (BTPS)**
Ebsco Publishing
Firebird Distributing, LLC
Follett School Solutions
Legato Pubs. Group
MyiLibrary
Publishers Group West (PGW)
ebrary, Inc.

Tackett, Melissa, *(978-0-578-45251-7; 978-0-578-45683-6)* 1200 W. Bartlett Ave., Las Vegas, NV 89106 USA Tel 702-824-0210
E-mail: Lyssaann43@gmail.com
Dist(s): **Ingram Content Group.**

Tackett, Viti, *(978-0-9769963)* 85 Pond St., Cabot, AR 72023-3741 USA Toll Free: 877-518-9575.

Tacoma Historical Society, *(978-0-9846234; 978-1-7336181)* P.O. Box 1865, Tacoma, WA 98401 USA Tel 253-472-3738
E-mail: info@tacomahistory.org
Web site: www.tacomahistory.org.

Tadpole Pr. 4 Kids *Imprint of* **Mystic Harbor Pr., LLC**

Tadpole Pr., *(978-1-7328286)* 1802 Centaur Cir., Lafayette, CO 80026 USA Tel 303-668-8812
E-mail: amber@tadpolepress.com
Web site: www.tadpolepress.com.

TAE Nazca Resources, *(978-0-9749745)* P.O. Box 7592, Broomfield, CO 80021 USA
E-mail: anitajg5@aol.com
Web site: http://www.nazcaresources.com
Dist(s): **Mountain Bk. Co.**

Taffey Pop Kids Publishing, *(978-0-9771438)* Div. of Taffey Pop Kids Educational Services LLC, Orders Addr.: 6712 Longmeadow Dr., SACHSE, TX 75048 USA Tel 214-434-9024
E-mail: info@taffeyhpopkids.org
Web site: http://www.taffeypopkids.org.

TAG Publications *See* **Teachers Appreciation Guild**

TAG Publishing, LLC, *(978-1-934606)* Orders Addr.: P.O. Box 8975, Amarillo, TX 79109 USA (SAN 853-9251); Edit Addr.: 2618 Lipscomb, Amarillo, TX 79109 USA Do not confuse with companies with the same name in Hanover, VA, Camerillo. CA
E-mail: deaitra@suddenlink.net
Web site: www.tagbookpublishing.com.

Tagus Pr., Div. of University of Massachusetts Dartmouth, 285 Old Westport Rd., North Dartmouth, MA 02747 USA
Web site: http://www.upne.com/distributed/dist_TPD.html; www.portstudies.umassd.edu
Dist(s): **Chicago Distribution Ctr.**
MyiLibrary
Univ. of Massachusetts Pr.

Tahrike Tarsile Quran, Inc., *(978-0-940368; 978-1-879402; 978-1-952290)* 80-08 51st Ave., Elmhurst, NY 11373 USA (SAN 658-1870) Tel 718-446-6472; Fax: 718-446-4370
E-mail: read@koranusa.org
Web site: http://www.koranusa.org
Dist(s): **BookBaby**
Publishers Group West (PGW).

Tai Chi Chuan Center of New York *See* **Sunflower Pr.**

Taiji Arts Publishing, *(978-0-9728192)* 50 Bates Rd., Hillsborough, CA 94010-7016 USA
E-mail: ben@TaijiArts.com
Web site: http://www.TaijiArts.com
Dist(s): **China Books & Periodicals, Inc.**

Tail Wagging Productions, *(978-0-9752887)* P.O. Box 1357, Brea, CA 92822-1357 USA
E-mail: contact@tailwaggingproductions.us
Web site: http://www.tailwaggingproductions.us.

Tailwind Press, *(978-0-9799473)* 58 Brookshire Dr., Warrenton, VA 20186-3033 USA
E-mail: loribakewell@gmail.com.

Taj Bks. International LLC, *(978-1-62732)* 219 Great Lake Dr., Cary, NC 27519 USA Tel 919-650-1719; *Imprints:* Bellagio Press (BellagioPr)
E-mail: suneel@tajbooks.com
Dist(s): **Casemate Pubs. & Bk. Distributors, LLC**
MyiLibrary.

Takahashi & Black, *(978-0-9723247)* Orders Addr.: 8725 Roswell Rd., Suite 0-129, Atlanta, GA 30350 USA; *Imprints:* PB&J OmniMedia (PB&J)
E-mail: orders@pbjomnimedia.com; credit@pbjomnimedia.com; returns@pbjomnimedia.com; domo@takahashiblack.com
Web site: http://www.pbjomnimedia.com
Dist(s): **Book Wholesalers, Inc.**
Brodart Co.

Takatuka (ESP) *(978-84-936766; 978-84-16003; 978-84-92696) Dist. by* **Lectorum Pubns.**

Take 2 Creative Storywriters, LLC, *(978-0-9982801; 978-1-7344913)* 2377 Gold Meadow Way Suite 100, Gold River, CA 95670 USA
E-mail: contact_us@take2creativestorywriters.com; r.rose@take2creativestorywriters.com; roxyrvt@gmail.com
Web site: www.take2creativestorywriters.com.

Take Charge Books *See* **Take Charge Bks.**

Take Charge Bks., *(978-0-9815818; 978-0-9883866; 978-0-9961589; 978-0-9982658; 978-1-7346068)* 392 Sunny Acre Ln., Brevard, NC 28712 USA Tel 828-883-5695
E-mail: kathleen@kathleenbarnes.com
Web site: http://www.kathleenbarnes.com
Dist(s): **BookBaby.**

Take Five Pubs., *(978-0-930099)* P.O. Box 1094, Arlington, IL 60006 USA (SAN 670-1884) Tel 847-253-4370
E-mail: m.shaughnessy@comcast.net.

Take Heart Press *See* **Skinned Knee Publishing**

Take2CreativeStorywriters *See* **Take 2 Creative Storywriters, LLC**

Takeaway Press *See* **All About Learning Pr.**

Takhar's, Jodi Spilt Milk Collection, *(978-1-886000)* Orders Addr.: P.O. Box 1005, Bemidji, MN 56601 USA Tel 218-759-2089; Fax: 218-759-2088; Edit Addr.: 403 4th St., NW, No. 200, Bemidji, MN 56601 USA.

Taking Grades Publishing Co., *(978-1-934538)* 1110 4th St., Dr., S.E., Conover, NC 28613-1825 USA Tel 866-511-8378; Fax: 828-466-0025; Toll Free: 866-511-8378
E-mail: takinggrades@charter.net
Web site: http://www.takinggrades.com
Dist(s): **Follett School Solutions.**

TakingITGlobal, *(978-0-578-41496-6; 978-0-578-44580-9; 978-0-578-44608-0; 978-0-578-45153-4; 978-0-578-48869-1; 978-0-578-51229-7; 978-0-578-52184-8; 978-0-578-53028-4; 978-0-578-62032-9; 978-0-578-62839-4; 978-0-578-66957-1; 978-0-578-69230-2; 978-0-578-70762-4) 540 President St. 3rd Flr., Brooklyn, NY 11215 USA Tel 416-301-5844*
E-mail: mfurdyk@takingitglobal.org
Web site: http://www.tigweb.org
Dist(s): **Independent Pub.**

Taku Graphics, *(978-0-9717820; 978-0-9772297; 978-0-9801616; 978-0-9823450; 978-0-9846318; 978-0-9899679)* 5763 Glacier Hwy., Juneau, AK 99801 USA Tel 907-780-6310; Fax: 907-780-6314; Toll Free: 800-278-3291
E-mail: adele@takugraphics.com
Web site: htto://www.takugraphics.com.

Talaris Research Institute, *(978-0-9742761; 978-0-615-40953-5)* P.O. Box 45040, Seattle, WA 98145 USA Tel 206-859-5604; Fax: 206-859-5699
E-mail: tinam@talaris.org
Web site: http://www.talaris.org.

Ta-La-Vue Pub., *(978-0-9797521)* 316 Rowan Alley, Apt. 6, Pottstown, PA 19464 USA (SAN 854-2376).

Tale Wag Pr. *Imprint of* **Langson, Bridgett Bell**

Tale Weaver Pr., *(978-0-692-66880-1)* 10942 Canyon Mesa Ln., San Diego, CA 92126 USA Tel 619-200-3836
E-mail: lisadavis92127@gmail.com.

Talented *See* **Cantemos-bilingual bks. and music**

Tales Alive *See* **Words & Music**

Talicor, Inc., *(978-1-57057; 978-0-9674871)* 901 Lincoln Pkwy., Plainwell, MI 49080 USA (SAN 253-0406) Tel 269-685-2345; Fax: 269-685-6789; Toll Free: 800-433-4263
E-mail: webmaster@talicor.com; orders@talicor.com
Web site: http://www.talicor.com.

Taliesin Publishing LLC *See* **Hartwood Publishing Group, LLC, The**

Talisman Pr., *(978-0-9670848)* 7036 Lyndale Cir., Elk Grove, CA 95758 USA Tel 916-683-1749
E-mail: talismanpress@aol.com.

TALK, *(978-0-9741182)* Orders Addr.: P.O. Box 9226, Peoria, IL 61612 USA Tel 309-224-9665; Edit Addr.: 5001 N. Big Hollow Rd., Peoria, IL 61615 USA Tel 309-694-5444
E-mail: dsymo92699@aol.com
Web site: http://www.doristalk.com.

TALKAIDS, Inc., *(978-0-9659046)* Orders Addr.: P.O. Box 112, New York, NY 10113 USA Tel 212-465-2646; Fax: 212-675-7291; Edit Addr.: 305 W. 13th St., 1K, New York, NY 10014 USA
E-mail: talkaids@aol.com.

Talking Crow Publishing, *(978-0-9860287)* P.O. Box 1356, Haines, AK 99827 USA.

Talking Drum Pr., Ltd., *(978-0-9662428)* Div. of Oversoul Theater Collective, Inc., P.O. Box 190028, Roxbury, MA 02119 USA
E-mail: talkingdrumpress@gmail.com.

Talking Drum Press/OTC, Incorporated *See* **Talking Drum Pr., Ltd.**

Talking Hands, Incorporated *See* **Time to Sign, Incorporated**

TalkTools/Innovative Therapists International, *(978-1-932460; 978-0-9979204)* 2209 Mechanic St., Charleston, SC 29405 USA Tel 843-789-3672; Fax: 843-206-0590; Toll Free: 888-529-2879
E-mail: info@talktools.com
Web site: http://www.talktools.com.

Tall Tails Publishing Hse., *(978-0-9823519)* 902 Arlington Box 113, Ada, OK 74820 USA (SAN 857-9288)
E-mail: talltailspublishing@gmail.com
Web site: http://www.talltailspublishing.com.

Tall Tales, *(978-0-9973641; 978-0-9979540; 978-1-947543)* P.O. Box 1262, Lynnwood, WA 98046 USA Tel 425-744-0580
E-mail: kizeliz@gmail.com
Web site: www.kizziejones.com.

Tall Through Bks., *(978-0-9744549)* P.O. Box 6723, Virginia Beach, VA 23456 USA Tel 757-635-6174; Fax: 757-563-8277
E-mail: tallthroughbooks@aol.com
Web site: http://www.tallthroughbooks.com.

Tallfellow Pr., *(978-0-9676061; 978-1-931290)* 9454 Wilshire Blvd. Ste. 550, Beverly Hills, CA 90212-2905 USA
E-mail: Tallfellow@pacbell.net
Web site: http://TallfellowPress.com
Dist(s): **Parklane Publishing**
SCB Distributors.

Tallulah & Bear (GBR) *(978-0-9559752) Dist. by* **LuluCom.**

Talmage Publishing, *(978-0-9773010)* 4820 Strack Rd., Houston, TX 77069 USA (SAN 257-2370) Tel 281-440-1106.

Talonbooks, Ltd. (CAN) *(978-0-88922; 978-1-77201) Dist. by* **Consort Bk Sales.**

Tamaja Pr., *(978-0-9841260; 978-0-9863753)* Div. of Artees / Tamaja, 96 High St. No. 4, West Point, MS 39773 USA; 96 High St. suite 4, West Point, MS 39773
E-mail: tilmon.gloria@yahoo.com; gloriatillman23@yahoo.com; tam3artees@yahoo.com.

Tamara Taylor Edu Publishing LLC, *(978-0-9970313)* P.O. Box PO Box 403, Frisco, TX 75034 USA
E-mail: print@ttayloredupublishing.com.

Tamara's Bks., *(978-0-9909379)* 1844 Colmar Rd., Gwynn Oak, MD 21207 USA Tel 888-503-1575
E-mail: tamarasbooks@aol.com
Web site: tamarasbooks@gmail.com.

Tamarisk Tree Publishing House, *(978-0-578-18030-4; 978-1-948706)* 2208 Collier Dr., Franklin, TN 37064 USA.

Tameme, Inc., *(978-0-9674093)* 199 First St. Suite 335, Los Altos, CA 94022 USA Tel 650-941-2037; Fax: 650-941-5338
E-mail: Sales@tameme.org
Web site: http://www.tameme.org.

Tamerac Publishing, *(978-0-9621292)* 402 Conestoga Dr., Moscow, ID 83843 USA (SAN 250-9466) Tel 208-883-7761
Web site: www.tameracpub.com
Dist(s): **Ingram Content Group.**

Tamerac Publishing Company *See* **Tamerac Publishing**

Tamos Bks., Inc. (CAN) *(978-1-895569) Dist. by* **Sterling.**

TAN Bks., *(978-0-89555; 978-0-911845; 978-0-9675978; 978-1-930873; 978-1-939094)* Div. of Saint Benedict Press, LLC, 13315 Carowinds Blvd Suite Q, Charlotte, NC 28273 USA; *Imprints:* Neumann Press (Neumann NC)
E-mail: rick@tanbooks.com; mara@tanbooks.com
Web site: https://tanbooks.com/; https://neumann.benedictpress.com/
Dist(s): **Baker & Taylor Publisher Services (BTPS)**
Saint Benedict Pr.

Tana Lake Publishing, *(978-0-9651007)* P.O. Box 44595, Fort Washington, MD 20749 USA Tel 301-292-3636; P.O. Box P.O. Box 44595, Fort Washington, MD 20749
E-mail: xnate333@aol.com
Web site: http://www.tanalakepublishing.com
Dist(s): **Evanston Publishing, Inc.**

T&N Children's Publishing, *(978-1-55971; 978-1-58728)* Div. of Rowman & Littlefield Publishing Group, Orders Addr.: 8500 Normandale Lake Blvd., Minneapolis, MN 55437-3813 USA Toll Free: 888-255-9989; Fulfillment Addr.: SDS-12-2462, P.O. Box 86, Minneapolis, MN 55486-2462 USA; *Imprints:* NorthWord Books for Young Readers (NrthWrd Bks); Two-Can Publishing (TCan Pubng)
E-mail: sales@tnkidsbooks.com
Web site: http://www.tnkidsbooks.com
Dist(s): **Follett School Solutions**
National Bk. Network.

Tandora's Box Pr., *(978-0-9627337)* Orders Addr.: P.O. Box 8073, Vallejo, CA 94590 USA
E-mail: barbara@tangrammit.com
Web site: http://www.tangrammit.com.

Tangela Publishing, *(978-0-615-18297-1)* 8093 Miller Cir., Arvada, CO 80005 USA
E-mail: a.newell@comcast.net.

Tangerine Pr. *Imprint of* **Scholastic, Inc.**

Tangerine Tide *Imprint of* **Orange Ocean Pr.**

TangleTown Media Inc., *(978-0-9724022)* 713 Minnehaha Ave. E. Suite 210, Saint Paul, MN 55106 USA (SAN 254-8054)
E-mail: todd.berntson@tangletownmedia.com
Web site: http://www.tangletownmedia.com.

Tanglewood Pr., *(978-0-9749303; 978-1-933718; 978-1-939100)* P.O. Box 3009, Terre Haute, IN 47803 USA Do not confuse with Tanglewood Press in Portland, OR, Raleigh, NC
E-mail: ptierney@tanglewoodbooks.com
Web site: http://www.tanglewoodbooks.com
Dist(s): **Lectorum Pubns., Inc.**
MyiLibrary
Publishers Group West (PGW)
Simon & Schuster, Inc.

Tango Bks. (GBR) *(978-1-85707) Dist. by* **IPG Chicago.**

Tango Latin, *(978-0-9663572)* 325 N. Maple Dr., Beverly Hills, CA 90209 USA Tel 213-381-5820; P.O. Box 16111, Beverly Hills, CA 90209
E-mail: tangomediagroup@yahoo.com.

Tango Publishing International, Incorporated *See* **Tango Latin**

TankerToys, *(978-0-615-16200-3)* 387 C Bergin Dr., Monterey, CA 93940 USA
E-mail: tanker@tankertoys.com
Web site: http://www.tankertoys.com
Dist(s): **Lulu Pr., Inc.**

Tanner, David, *(978-0-9767287; 978-0-578-00817-2)* P.O. Box 140, Avon, CT 06001-0140 USA; 3 David Dr., Simsbury, CT 06070
E-mail: collectiblesodacans@comcast.net
Web site: http://www.collectiblesodacans.com.

Tanner, Matt J., *(978-0-9885253)* 27 Amherst Dr., Basking Ridge, NJ 07920 USA Tel 908-581-9822
E-mail: mtanner07@msn.com.

Tanner, Ralph Assocs., Inc., *(978-0-942078)* P.O. Box 3400, Prescott, AZ 86302-3400 USA (SAN 239-9857).

TanosBooks Publishing, *(978-0-9764666; 978-0-9788520; 978-0-9815522; 978-0-9822543; 978-0-9844865; 978-0-9846540)* 1110 W. 5th St., Coffeyville, KS 67337 USA
Web site: http://www.tanosbookspublishing.com.

Tanser, Julie, *(978-0-692-04586-2; 978-1-7336804; 978-1-7339244)* P.O. Box 26, NY, NY 10116 USA
E-mail: julie82146@gmail.com
Dist(s): **CreateSpace Independent Publishing Platform.**

Tao of Golf *See* **DVTVFilm**

TAOC (AUS) *(978-0-9803455; 978-0-646-46214-1; 978-0-9808435) Dist. by* **Consort Bk Sales.**

TAOH Inspired Education, LLC, *(978-0-9769069)* Orders Addr.: 99 Palatine Rd., Pittsgrove, NJ 08318 USA
E-mail: taohinspirededucation@gmail.com
Web site: http://www.taohinspirededucation.com.

Taos Institute Pubns., *(978-0-9712312; 978-0-9819076; 978-0-9848656; 978-1-938552)* Orders Addr.: 63 Maple Hill Dr., Chagrin Falls, OH 44022 USA Tel 440-338-6733; Edit Addr.: 331 Rogers Ln., Wallingford, PA 19086 USA Toll Free: 888-999-8267
E-mail: info@taosinstitute.net
Web site: http://www.Taosinstitute.net.

Taotime GmbH (CHE) *(978-3-906945; 978-3-9524296; 978-3-033-03088-6) Dist. by* **IPG Chicago.**

Tapestry Productions, *(978-0-692-99114-5; 978-0-578-57750-0)* 6638 river springs dr. s, Salem, OR 97306 USA Tel 503-364-4787; Fax: 503-364-4787
E-mail: deirdradoan@gmail.com.

tapestrypublishing.com, *(978-0-692-86502-6; 978-0-692-91685-8)* 642 Corbin Lake Ct., SANDY SPRINGS, GA 30350 USA Tel 404-512-4542
E-mail: jeffwcrawford5+LVP0003519@gmail.com; jeffwcrawford5+LVP0003519@gmail.com.

Tapis & Assocs., Inc., *(978-0-9729610; 978-0-9741172)* 1950 N. 6900 E., Croydon, UT 84018-9707 USA Tel 801-829-3295; Fax: 509-984-2718
E-mail: info@tapisinc.com
Web site: http://www.tapisinc.com.

Tapper Records Inc., *(978-0-9747465)* P.O. Box 5241, Hollywood, FL 33083-5241 USA Tel 954-483-5093; Fax: 954-961-9049
E-mail: thespeakingsax@juno.com
Web site: http://www.thespeakingsax.com.

Tapper Seminars *See* **Tapper Records Inc.**

Taqwa Images *See* **Early Rise Pubns.**

Tara Publishing (IND) *(978-81-86211; 978-81-906756) Dist. by* **Consort Bk Sales.**

Tarbutton Pr., *(978-0-9714086; 978-1-933094)* 951 Snug Harbor St., Salinas, CA 93906 USA (SAN 254-4989) Tel 831-443-5694
E-mail: info@tarbuttonpress.com
Web site: http://www.tarbuttonpress.com
Dist(s): **CreateSpace Independent Publishing Platform**
Ingram Content Group.

TarcherPerigee *Imprint of* **Penguin Publishing Group**

targa 7 inc, *(978-0-692-84875-3; 978-0-692-84876-0)* 704 1st Ave. N., safety harbor, FL 34695 USA Tel 727-799-4891
E-mail: patriciastewart@tampabay.rr.com
Web site: www.patbrooksbooks.com.

Targum Pr., Inc., *(978-0-944070; 978-1-56871)* 22700 W. Eleven Mile Rd., Southfield, MI 48034 USA (SAN 242-8997) Tel 248-355-2266; Toll Free Fax: 888-298-9992
E-mail: targum@elronet.co.il
Web site: http://www.targum.com
Dist(s): **Feldheim Pubs.**
Lulu Pr., Inc.
SPD-Small Pr. Distribution.

Targum Press USA Incorporated *See* **Menucha Pubs. Inc.**

TARK Classic Fiction *Imprint of* **Arc Manor**

Tarquin Pubns. (GBR) *(978-0-906212; 978-1-899618; 978-1-907550; 978-1-911093) Dist. by* **IPG Chicago.**

Tarver, Monroe, *(978-0-9743568)* 7904 Calibre Crossing Dr. Apt. 205, Charlotte, NC 28227-6781 USA
E-mail: monroetarver@msn.com
Web site: http://www.worldoftarver.com.

TASCHEN (DEU) *(978-3-8228; 978-3-89450; 978-3-8365) Dist. by* **IngramPubServ.**

Taste Life Twice, *(978-0-9898506)* 320 NW Uptown Terr. No. 3B, Portland, OR 97210 USA Tel 805-550-4197
E-mail: mpinard2003@yahoo.com.

Tastica, Suanne Creations Inc., *(978-0-9769348)* 1621 25th St., PMB No. 337, San Pedro, CA 90732 USA.

Tasty Minstrel Games, *(978-0-9841558; 978-1-938146; 978-1-947941; 978-1-951361)* P.O. Box 64794, Tucson, AZ 85728 USA Tel 520-275-8913
E-mail: michael@playtmg.com; daniel@playtmg.com
Web site: http://playtmg.com.

Tate, Hakim, *(978-0-692-88171-2; 978-0-692-15282-9; 978-0-692-15286-7; 978-1-7350772)* 411 Millwoof Dr., capitol heights, MD 20743 USA Tel 202-577-7131
E-mail: hakimtate@gmail.com.

Tate Publishing, Ltd. (GBR) *(978-0-900874; 978-0-905005; 978-1-85437; 978-0-946590; 978-1-84976)* *Dist. by* **HachBkGrp.**

Tate Publishing, Ltd. (GBR) *(978-0-900874; 978-0-905005; 978-1-85437; 978-0-946590; 978-1-84976)* *Dist. by* **Abrams.**

Tathata Inc., *(978-0-578-21228-9)* 1104 Cornell Dr., Yardley, PA 19067 USA Tel 609-558-5696
E-mail: nickfels@gmail.com.

Tattered Essence Publishing LLC, *(978-0-9766130)* P.O. Box 290996, Nashville, TN 37229 USA Tel 615-360-6117
E-mail: info@cinderellasrebellion.com
Web site: http://www.tatteredessence.com.

Tau Publishing *See* **Vesuvius Pr. Inc.**

Tau Publishing *Imprint of* **Vesuvius Pr. Inc.**

†**Taunton Pr., Inc.,** *(978-0-918804; 978-0-942391; 978-1-56158; 978-1-60085; 978-1-62113; 978-1-62710; 978-1-63186; 978-1-64155)* 63 S. Main St., P. O. Box 5506, Newtown, CT 06470-5506 USA (SAN 210-5144) Tel 203-426-8171; Fax: 203-426-7184; Toll Free: 800-477-8727 (orders)
E-mail: tt@taunton.com; cmandarano@taunton.com
Web site: http://www.taunton.com
Dist(s): **Ingram Publisher Services**
Linden Publishing Co., Inc.
Simon & Schuster, Inc.; *CIP.*

Taven Hill Studio, *(978-0-9765321)* 5214n 325w, LaPorte, IN 46350 USA
E-mail: mhill@mc123.com
Web site: http://www.tavenhill.com.

Tavine'ra Publishing, LLC, *(978-0-9713953)* 270 Doug Baker Blvd Suite 700-316, Birmingham, AL 35242 USA Tel 205-218-7678; Toll Free: 888 234-7256
E-mail: tahiera@gmail.com
Web site: www.tahieramoniquebrown.com.

Tawa Productions, *(978-0-9718741)* Orders Addr.: 2186 Buffalo Dr., Grand Junction, CO 81503 USA
E-mail: information@peopal.com
Web site: http://www.poepal.com.

Tawnsy Publishing, *(978-0-9887612)* 1212 N. Wuthering Hills Dr., Janesville, WI 53546 USA Tel 608-754-2024
E-mail: tawnsy@charter.net.

Tayes Bks., *(978-0-9743207)* Orders Addr.: P.O. Box 50973, Fort Myers, FL 33994-0973 USA; Edit Addr.: 813 Dellena Ln., Fort Myers, FL 33905 USA
E-mail: tayesbooks@yahoo.com
Web site: http://www.tayesbooks.com.

Tayler Corp., The, *(978-0-9779074; 978-0-9835746; 978-1-945120)* Orders Addr.: 1066 N. 440 W., Orem, UT 84057 USA Tel 801-426-5714
Web site: http://www.schlockmercenary.com.

Taylor & Francis Group (GBR) *(978-0-389; 978-0-7484; 978-0-85066; 978-0-905273; 978-1-85000; 978-1-85728; 978-1-84142; 978-0-901286; 978-1-902653; 978-0-203; 978-1-904350; 978-1-906540; 978-1-905981; 978-1-907975; 978-1-84872; 978-1-907625; 978-1-907747; 978-1-909662; 978-1-134; 978-1-136; 978-1-910887; 978-1-910526; 978-0-367; 978-0-429; 978-1-000; 978-1-003)* *Dist. by* **Taylor and Fran.**

†**Taylor & Francis Group,** *(978-0-335; 978-0-415; 978-0-8448; 978-0-85066; 978-0-89116; 978-0-903796; 978-0-905273; 978-1-56032; 978-1-85000; 978-1-59169; 978-1-315)* Orders Addr.: 7625 Empire Dr., Florence, KY 41042-2919 USA Toll Free Fax: 800-248-4724; Toll Free: 800-634-7064; 74 Rolark Dr., Scarborough, ON M1R 4G2 Tel 416-299-5388; Fax: 416-299-7531; Toll Free: 877-226-2237; Edit Addr.: 325 Chestnut St., Philadelphia, PA 19106 USA (SAN 241-9246) Tel 215-625-8900; Fax: 215-625-2940; 270 Madison Ave., 4th Flr., New York, NY 10016-0601; *Imprints:* Routledge (RtlgTnF)
Web site: http://www.routledge-ny.com; http://www.crcpress.com; http://www.garlandscience.com; http://www.taylorandfrancis.com
Dist(s): **CRC Pr. LLC**
Ebsco Publishing
LSC Communications Corp.
MyiLibrary
Norton, W. W. & Co., Inc.
Oxford Univ. Pr., Inc.
Pearson Education; *CIP.*

Taylor & Francis, Incorporated *See* **Taylor & Francis Group**

Taylor and Seale Publishing, *(978-0-9846558; 978-0-9887836; 978-1-940224; 978-1-943789; 978-1-950613)* Orders Addr.: 2 Oceans West Blvd. Unit 406, Daytona Beach Shores, FL 32118 USA Tel 386-760-8987
Web site: taylorandsealebooks.com.

Taylor, Ann, *(978-0-9800059)* 4319 Candlewood Ln., Ponce Inlet, FL 32127 USA
E-mail: taboka@aol.com; anntaylor@cfl.rr.com.

Taylor, Dale *See* **Barton Publications**

Taylor, Dorothy Loring, *(978-0-9610640)* R. R. 2, Box 152, Virginia, IL 62691 USA (SAN 265-3567) Tel 217-458-2506.

Taylor Girl LLC *See* **TG8 LLC**

Taylor Productions *Imprint of* **G R M Assocs.**

Taylor Publishing Company *See* **Taylor Trade Publishing**

Taylor Publishing Grp., *(978-0-9762933)* 1605 E. Elizabeth St., Pasadena, CA 91104 USA Tel 626-398-2341
E-mail: tp@finishthetask.org
Web site: http://www.taylorpublishing.info.

Taylor Street Publishing LLC, *(978-0-9892854; 978-0-9911621)* 575 O'Farrell St. Suite 904, San Francisco, CA 94102 USA Tel 415-374-4846
E-mail: timhewtson@gmail.com
Web site: www.taylorstreetbooks.com.

Taylor, Tim P., *(978-0-615-40779-1; 978-0-9830980; 978-0-9859908; 978-0-9890006; 978-1-940359)* 2444 Bedford Cir., Bedford, TX 76021 USA Tel 817-313-4508; *Imprints:* Burkhart Books (BuckhartBks)
E-mail: Revtt007@gmail.com; burkhartbks@gmail.com
Web site: www.burkhartbooks.com
Dist(s): **Amazon Digital Services Inc.**
Whitaker Hse.

†**Taylor Trade Publishing,** *(978-0-87833; 978-0-925190; 978-1-57749; 978-1-58979; 978-1-63076)* Orders Addr.: 15200 NBN Way, Blue Ridge Summit, PA 17214 USA Tel 717-794-3800 (Sales, Customer Service, MIS, Royalties, Inventory Mgmt., Dist., Credit & Collections); Fax: 717-794-3803 (Customer Service &/or orders only); 717-794-3857 (Sales & MIS); 717-794-3856 (Royalties, Inventory Mgmt. & Dist.); Toll Free Fax: 800-338-4550 (Customer Service &/or orders); Toll Free: 800-462-6420 (Customer Service &/or orders); Edit Addr.: 4501 Forbes Blvd., Suite 200, Lanham, MD 20706 USA Tel 301-459-3366; Fax: 301-459-5743 Do not confuse with companies with the same or similar names in Rochester, MI, Bellingham, WA, St. Petersburg, FL, Owatonna, MN, Eureka, CA
Web site: http://www.rlpgbooks.com; http://www.taylortradepublishing.com
Dist(s): **Ebsco Publishing**
Follett School Solutions
MyiLibrary
National Bk. Network
Rowman & Littlefield Publishers, Inc.
Smashwords
ebrary, Inc.; *CIP.*

Taylor, Y. H., *(978-0-9788386)* P.O. Box 9618, Philadelphia, PA 19131-3315 USA.

Taylor-Dth Publishing, *(978-0-9712923; 978-0-9727583; 978-0-9747532; 978-0-9774431; 978-0-9834780; 978-0-9988935)* Orders Addr.: P.O. Box 216, Fairfax, CA 94978 USA Tel 415-299-1087
E-mail: ncardinali@taylor-dth.com
Web site: http://www.taylor-dth.com.

Taylor's Production, *(978-0-9800468)* 126 Willowcrest Dr., Windsor, CT 06095 USA Tel 860-243-3196
E-mail: noproblem11@comcast.net.

TaySysCo Publishing, *(978-0-9773236)* 808 White Ivy Pl. NE, Cedar Rapids, IA 52402 USA
E-mail: taysysco@msn.com
Web site: http://taysysco.com.

TazTales, *(978-0-9742178)* P.O. Box 48031, Oak Park, MI 48237-5731 USA
E-mail: taztales@lycos.com
Web site: http://www.taztales.com.

TBCN Inc., *(978-0-938447)* 1680 Keylake Dr, Suwanee,, GA 30024 USA Tel 470-239-7375
E-mail: Fred@bookfunmagazine.com
Web site: http://www.bookfun.org.

TBG.LLC *See* **Gilliam, T. & Associates, LLC**

Tbooks Publishing Co., *(978-0-9789449)* 324 E. 2nd St., Benicia, CA 94510-3249 USA (SAN 852-0135) Tel 707-342-2280
E-mail: terrie@tbookspublishing.com
Web site: http://tbookspublishing.com.

TBSM Publishing, *(978-0-9860056)* P.O. Box 6314, Traverse City, MI 49686 USA.

T.C. McSears Publishing, *(978-0-9787015)* P.O. Box 341, Linconton, NC 28093 USA
E-mail: tryloc@tryloc.com
Web site: http://www.tryloc.com
Dist(s): **Big Tent Bks.**

TCB-Cafe Publishing, *(978-0-9674898; 978-0-9767682; 978-0-9798640; 978-0-9822200; 978-0-9911208)* Orders Addr.: P.O. Box 471706, San Francisco, CA 94147 USA Tel 415-263-6800
Web site: http://www.cafeandre.com; http://www.tastetv.com
Dist(s): **Quality Bks., Inc.**

TdB Pr. LLC, *(978-0-9740494)* P.O. Box 6348, Altadena, CA 91003-6348 USA (SAN 255-3147)
E-mail: mail@tdbpress.com
Web site: http://www.tdbpress.com.

TDG Communications, Inc., *(978-0-9793584)* 93 Sherman St., Deadwood, SD 57732-5773 USA (SAN 853-2478) Tel 605-722-7111; Fax: 605-722-7112
Web site: http://www.tdgcommunications.com.

TDH Publishing, *(978-0-9704566)* 783 Hunters Trail, Kikomo, IN 46901 USA (SAN 253-4460) Tel 765-457-6445; Fax: 765-459-4116
E-mail: tdhpublishing@insightbb.com; kellnikk@insightbb.com.

TDO Enterprises, *(978-0-9787624)* Orders Addr.: 92 N. Yale St., Nampa, ID 83651-2347 USA (SAN 851-6553)
E-mail: jscott@tdoent.com
Web site: http://www.tdoent.com; http://www.booksbyjeffscott.com.

TDR Brands *See* **TDR Brands Publishing**

TDR Brands Publishing, *(978-0-9907516; 978-0-9988804; 978-1-947574)* 4426 Hugh Howell Rd b No. 515, Tucker, GA 30084 USA Tel 888-353-0899
E-mail: tierradestinyreid@gmail.com
Web site: www.tierradestinyreid.com.

Te Papa Pr. (NZL) *(978-0-909010; 978-0-908953; 978-0-9582371; 978-0-9582432; 978-1-877385; 978-0-9876688; 978-0-9941041; 978-0-9941362; 978-0-9941460; 978-0-9951031; 978-0-9951136; 978-0-9951384; 978-0-9951338)* *Dist. by* **IPG Chicago.**

Tea Party Pr., *(978-0-9749173)* P.O. Box 767425, Atlanta, GA 30076 USA Tel 770-649-4434 Do not confuse with Tea Party Press in Cincinnati, OH
E-mail: paula_taylor@bellsouth.net
Web site: http://www.teapartypress.com.

Tea Time Publishing, *(978-1-7324605)* P.O. Box 143, Troy, MO 63379 USA Tel 636-358-5020
E-mail: TeaTimePublishingllc@gmail.com
Web site: TeaTimePublishing.com.

Tea Time Socials, LLC *Imprint of* **Gunderson, Lisa M.**

Tea with Mrs. B, *(978-0-9863560)* 6703 Lumsden St., McLean, VA 22101 USA Tel 202-448-2930
E-mail: r@czfamily.com
Web site: www.TeawithMrsB.com.

Teach Me Tapes, Inc., *(978-0-934633; 978-1-59972)* P.O. Box 698, Mequon, WI 53092 USA (SAN 693-9309) Tel 262-518-6060; Toll Free: 800-456-4656
E-mail: renee@teachmetapes.com
Web site: http://www.teachmetapes.com
Dist(s): **Ingram Publisher Services.**

TEACH Ministries, *(978-0-9740328)* Orders Addr.: 891 Ted Ln., Elgin, IL 60120 USA
E-mail: marylou@empoweringdiversity.com
Web site: http://www.empoweringdiversity.com/anna.

Teach My Children Pubns., *(978-0-9668891)* 258 Bahia Ln., E., Litchfield Park, AZ 85340-4728 USA Tel 602-935-0386
E-mail: oldbaha@goodnet.com.

Teach Services *See* **TEACH Services, Inc.**

TEACH Services, Inc., *(978-0-945383; 978-1-57258; 978-1-4796)* P.O. Box 954, Ringgold, GA 30736 USA (SAN 246-9863) Tel 706-504-9187; Fax: 866-757-6023; Toll Free: 800-367-1844; 8300 Highway 41, Unit 107, Ringgold, GA 30736 Tel 800-367-1844; Fax: 866-757-6023; *Imprints:* Aspect Book (AspectBk)
E-mail: publisher@teachservices.com
Web site: http://www.teachservices.com; http://www.AspectBooks.com.

Teacher Created Materials, Inc., *(978-0-87673; 978-0-7439; 978-1-4333; 978-1-60401; 978-1-4807; 978-1-4938; 978-1-5164; 978-1-64290; 978-1-64335; 978-1-64406; 978-1-64491; 978-1-0876)* 5301 Oceanus Dr., Huntington Beach, CA 92649 USA (SAN 665-5270) Tel 714-891-2273; Fax: 714-230-7070; Toll Free Fax: 888-877-7606; Toll Free: 800-858-7339
E-mail: sozbat@tcmpub.com; rkarnik@tcmpub.com
Web site: http://www.tcmpub.com; www.teachercreatedmaterials.com
Dist(s): **Children's Plus, Inc.**
Ebsco Publishing
Follett School Solutions
Lectorum Pubns., Inc.
Shell Educational Publishing.

Teacher Created Resources, Inc., *(978-1-55734; 978-1-57690; 978-1-4206; 978-1-4570)* 12621 Western Ave., Garden Grove, CA 92841 USA Tel 714-891-1690; Fax: 800-525-1254; Toll Free: 800-662-4321
E-mail: custserv@teachercreated.com; lvenzon@teachercreated.com
Web site: http://www.teachercreated.com
Dist(s): **Austin & Company, Inc.**
Follett School Solutions
Partners Pubs. Group, Inc.

Teacher Press, Incorporated *See* **Teaching Point, Inc.**

Teachers Appreciation Guild, *(978-0-9752781)* 5320 Pocassett, ARLINGTON, TX 76018 USA Do not confuse with Press On Publishing in Port Huron, MI
E-mail: info@teachersappreciationguild.org
Web site: http://teacchersappreciationguild.org.

†**Teachers College Pr., Teachers College, Columbia Univ.,** *(978-0-8077)* Div. of Teachers College, Columbia University, Orders Addr.: c/o AIDC, P.O. Box 20, Williston, VT 05495-0020 USA (SAN 248-3904) Fax: 802-864-7626; Toll Free: 800-575-6566; Edit Addr.: 1234 Amsterdam Ave., New York, NY 10027 USA (SAN 282-3985) Tel 212-678-3929; Fax: 212-678-4149
E-mail: tcpress@tc.columbia.edu
Web site: http://www.teacherscollegepress.com
Dist(s): **American International Distribution Corp.**
Ebsco Publishing
MyiLibrary; *CIP.*

Teachers College Press, Teachers College, Columbia University *See* **Teachers College Pr., Teachers College, Columbia Univ.**

Teachers' Curriculum Institute, *(978-1-58371; 978-1-934534; 978-1-68468)* 4009 Miranda Ave. Ste. 100, Palo Alto, CA 94304-1227 USA Toll Free: 800-497-6138; P.O. Box 1327, Rancho Cordova, CA 95741 Toll Free: 800-343-6828
E-mail: info@teachtci.com
Web site: http://www.teachtci.com.

Teacher's Discovery, *(978-1-884473; 978-0-7560)* Div. of American Eagle Co., Inc., 2741 Paldan Dr., Auburn Hills, MI 48326 USA (SAN 631-4570) Tel 248-340-7210; Fax: 248-340-7212; Toll Free: 800-832-2437
Web site: http://www.teachersdiscovery-science.com; http://www.teachersdiscovery-english.com; http://www.teachersdiscovery-social studies.com; http://www.teachersdiscovery-foreignlanguage.com; http://www.teachersdiscovery.com
Dist(s): **American Eagle Pubns., Inc.**
Follett School Solutions.

Teacher's Friend Pubns., Inc., *(978-0-943263; 978-1-57882)* Div. of Scholastic, Inc., 2155 Chicago Ave. Ste. 304, Riverside, CA 92507-2209 USA (SAN 668-3177) Toll Free Fax: 800-307-8176; Toll Free: 800-343-9680
E-mail: info@teachersfriend.com
Web site: http://www.teachersfriend.com
Dist(s): **Scholastic, Inc.**

Teachers' Handbooks, *(978-0-9634938)* P.O. Box 2778, San Rafael, CA 94912 USA (SAN 297-8326) Tel 415-461-0871; Fax: 415-461-5357.

Teacher's Treasure *See* **Perfect 4 Preschool**

Teaching & Learning Co., *(978-1-57310)* Div. of Lorenz Corp., 501 E. Third St., Dayton, OH 45401 USA Tel 937-228-6118; Fax: 937-223-2042; Toll Free: 800-444-1144
E-mail: customerservice@teachinglearning.com
Web site: http://www.teachinglearning.com
Dist(s): **Rainbow Horizons Publishing, Inc.**

Teaching Christ's Children Publishing, *(978-0-9855423; 978-0-615-80614-3; 978-0-692-20138-1; 978-0-692-20142-8; 978-0-692-20166-4; 978-0-692-61203-3; 978-1-948476)* 7404 Forrest Ave., Parkville, MD 21234 USA Tel 410-665-2655
E-mail: teachingchristschildren@yahoo.com
Web site: www.teachingchristschildren.com
Dist(s): **CreateSpace Independent Publishing Platform.**

Teaching Point, Inc., *(978-0-9629357; 978-1-931680; 978-1-59657)* Orders Addr.: 6950 Philips Hwy. Ste. 46, Jacksonville, FL 32216-6087 USA Toll Free: 877-494-0550; *Imprints:* Expert Systems for Teachers (Expert Systms Teach)
Web site: http://www.teaching-point.net.

Teaching Resources *Imprint of* **Scholastic, Inc.**

Teaching Strategies *Imprint of* **Scholastic, Inc.**

Teaching Strategies, Incorporated *See* **Teaching Strategies, LLC**

Teaching Strategies, LLC, *(978-0-9602892; 978-1-879537; 978-1-933021; 978-1-60617; 978-1-64553)* 4500 East W. Highway, Suite 300, Bethesda, MD 20814 USA (SAN 222-240X) Tel 301-634-0818; Fax: 301-657-0250; Toll Free: 800-637-3652
E-mail: Matt.M@teachingstrategies.com; jow@teachingstrategies.com; legal@teachingstrategies.com
Web site: http://www.teachingstrategies.com; http://www.EdPro.com; http://www.MindNurture.com
Dist(s): **Delmar Cengage Learning**
Gryphon Hse., Inc.

Teaching That Makes Sense, *(978-0-9972831)* 314 Bolin Forest Dr., Carborro, NC 27510 USA Tel 206-601-2488
E-mail: stevepeha@ttms.org
Web site: www.ttms.org.

Teacup Pr., *(978-1-881817)* Div. of Kettle, Inc., Orders Addr.: P.O. Box 613, Dover Plains, NY 12522-0613 USA; Edit Addr.: Berkshire Rd., Dover Plains, NY 12522-0613 USA Tel 914-832-6401 Do not confuse with Teacup Pr. in Charlotte, NC.

Teahouse of Danger, *(978-0-9801054)* P.O. Box 1361, Tucson, AZ 85702 USA (SAN 855-2193) Toll Free: 877-663-3324
E-mail: teahouseofdanger@gmail.com
Web site: http://www.teahouseofdanger.com.

Team B Creative LLC, *(978-0-9774119; 978-1-937665)* 9864 E. Grand River, Suite 110, No. 244, Brighton, MI 48116 USA
E-mail: mickmorrisinfo@yahoo.com; teambcreative@yahoo.com; karen@teambcreative.com
Web site: http://www.mickmorris.net; http://www.ghostboardposse.com; http://www.mickmorris.com; http://www.totallyunrehearsed.com
Dist(s): **Follett School Solutions**
Partners Bk. Distributing, Inc.

Team Dawg Productions, Inc., *(978-0-9749378)* Orders Addr.: P.O. Box 105, Nesconset, NY 11767 USA Tel 718-926-5984; Edit Addr.: 1 Mayfair Rd., Apt. 1, Nesconset, NY 11767 USA
E-mail: bobby@teamdawg.com
Web site: http://www.teamdawg.com.

Team EEK! *See* **This is RED**

Team Kidz, Inc., *(978-0-9793833; 978-1-7359021)* P.O. Box 2111, Voorhees, NJ 08043-8111 USA Tel 856-768-2181
E-mail: jgkeega@aol.com.

Team Luna Productions, Inc., *(978-0-692-10595-5)* 540 N. Central Ave., Glendale, CA 91203 USA Tel 310-721-2700
E-mail: molly@mollyannluna.com.

Team Reach, Inc., *(978-0-9767610)* 8448 Summit St., Lenexa, KS 66215-5388 USA Fax: 913-312-8872
E-mail: troy@krystal-planet.com; troy@troyhelming.com
Web site: http://www.troyhelming.com; http://www.teamreach.com.

TechArts International LLC, *(978-0-9726326)* 7638 S. Carroll Rd., Indianapolis, IN 46259 USA; P.O. Box 6983, Great Falls, MT 59405.

Technical Data Freeway, Inc., *(978-0-9841600)* P.O. Box 308, Poway, CA 92074 USA.

Technology & Imagination Pr., *(978-0-9798991; 978-1-944273)* 1970 Chalon Glen Ct., Livermore, CA 94550-8206 USA (SAN 854-7068) Tel 925-606-1285; Fax: 925-606-1297
E-mail: books@siliconmap.net.

Technology Education Concepts Inc., *(978-0-9740796; 978-0-9777525)* 32 Commercial St., Concord, NH 03301-5031 USA Tel 603-224-8324; Fax: 603-225-7766; Toll Free: 800-338-2238
E-mail: justyn@tecedu.com
Web site: http://www.tecedu.com.

Tecknl-Corp, Ltd., *(978-0-9724178)* P.O. Box 866, Bettendorf, IA 52722-1955 USA Tel 563-359-4388; Fax: 563-359-4671
E-mail: patrickm@studentsafe.com
Web site: http://www.studentsafe.com.

Tecolote, Ediciones, S.A. de C.V. (MEX) *(978-968-7381)* *Dist. by* **Mariuccia Iaconi Bk Imports.**

Tecolote, Ediciones, S.A. de C.V. (MEX) *(978-968-7381)* *Dist. by* **Lectorum Pubns.**

Tectum B.V.B.A. (BEL) *(978-90-76886; 978-90-79761)* *Dist. by* **InnovativeLog.**

Teddy Bear Pr., Inc., *(978-1-880017)* 5470 Van Ness, Bloomfield Hills, MI 48302 USA Tel 248-851-8607 Do not confuse with Teddy Bear Pr., Las Vegas, NV.

Teddy Traveler Co., *(978-0-9748954)* P.O. Box 3223, Manhattan Beach, CA 90266 USA
Web site: http://www.teddytraveler.com
Dist(s): **Beyda for Bks., LLC.**

Tedesco, James *See* **JBT Publishing**

Teen Town Pr. *Imprint of* **Youngs, Bettie Bks.**

Teen Winners, LLC, *(978-0-9740356)* 19 Quail Run, Berlin, CT 06037 USA Tel 860-829-2067; Fax: 860-829-8067
E-mail: info@teenwinners.com
Web site: http://www.teenwinners.com.

Teens Can Dream LLC *See* **Inspired Imaginations, LLC**

Teeter, Diana, *(978-0-692-88078-4)* 6620 108th St Apt 1L, FOREST HILLS, NY 11375 USA Tel 248-895-9097
E-mail: jeffwcrawford5+LVP0003691@gmail.com; jeffwcrawford5+LVP0003691@gmail.com.

TEG Publishing, *(978-0-9707208; 978-0-9727410)* Orders Addr.: P.O. Box 12737, Tempe, AZ 85284 USA Tel 310-919-3013
E-mail: microlawyers@aol.com; tegpublishing@wwsws.com
Web site: http://www.tegpublishing.com.

Tegen, Katherine Bks *Imprint of* **HarperCollins Pubs.**

Tehabi Bks., *(978-1-887656; 978-1-931688)* 4920 Carroll Canyon Rd., Suite 200, San Diego, CA 92121 USA Tel 858-450-9100; Fax: 858-450-9146; Toll Free: 800-243-7259
E-mail: Emily.Henning@tehabi.com
Web site: http://www.tehabi.com.

Telemachus Pr., LLC, *(978-0-9841083; 978-1-935670; 978-1-937387; 978-1-937698; 978-1-938135; 978-1-938701; 978-1-939337; 978-1-939927; 978-1-940745; 978-1-941536; 978-1-942899; 978-1-945330; 978-1-948046; 978-1-951744)* Orders Addr.: 7551 Ashlord Ct., Dublin, OH 43017 USA (SAN 858-4508) Tel 941-993-5816; 941-993-5987; Fax: 941-296-7873; 7551 Ashlord Ct., Dublin, OH 43017 (SAN 858-4508) Tel 941-993-5816; 941-993-5987; Fax: 941-296-7873
E-mail: Steve.himes@telemachuspress.com
Web site: http://www.telemachuspress.com
Dist(s): **Ingram Content Group**
Smashwords.

Tell Me Pr., LLC, *(978-0-9816453; 978-0-9819835; 978-0-9829421; 978-0-9906453)* 98 Mansfield St., New Haven, CT 06511 USA (SAN 857-8508) Tel 203-562-4215; Fax: 203-562-4225
E-mail: lisa@tellmepress.com
Web site: http://www.tellmepress.com
Dist(s): **Greenleaf Book Group.**

Tell My Story Publishing, LLC, *(978-0-9729363)* Orders Addr.: 898 Mahogany Dr., Kaysville, UT 84037-4409 USA
E-mail: tellmystory@msn.com.

Tell-a-Vision Bks., *(978-0-9727706)* Orders Addr.: P.O. Box 396, Lexington, VA 24450 USA; Edit Addr.: 272 Dogwood Rise, Lexington, VA 24450 USA
Web site: http://www.tell-a-visionbooks.com.

Telling Family Tales, *(978-1-940379)* 12129 S. 2160 W., Riverton, UT 84065 USA Tel 801-787-5673
E-mail: raelyn@tellingfamilytales.com.

Telling Our Stories Pr., *(978-0-9829228; 978-0-9900081)* 185 AJK Blvd., No. 246, Lewisburg, PA 17837 USA Tel 570-795-9550; Fax: 570-246-4091
E-mail: cocoharris@gmail.com
Web site: www.TellingOurStoriesPress.com.

Temenos Pr., *(978-0-9701319)* Orders Addr.: P.O. Box 477, Ashfield, MA 01330 USA Tel 413-625-9148; Edit Addr.: 989 Apple Valley Rd., Ashfield, MA 01330 USA Do not confuse with Temenos Pr., in Cloverdale, CA.

Tempest Bk. Shop, *(978-0-9632484)* Orders Addr.: 5031 Main St., Waitsfield, VT 05673-7111 USA Tel 802-496-2022; Fax: 802-496-3299
E-mail: rayfieldvt@aol.com.

Tempest Pr., *(978-0-9790232)* P.O. Box 3504, New York, NY 10008-3504 USA (SAN 852-2340)
E-mail: info@tempestpress.com
Web site: http://www.tempestpress.com
Dist(s): **Greenfield Distribution, Inc.**

Templar *Imprint of* **Candlewick Pr.**

Temple Care: Body, Mind & Spirit, *(978-0-9773759)* P.O. Box 1221 Ring Bill Loop, Upper Marlboro, MD 20774-7170 USA Tel 301-218-5941; Fax: 719-218-5948
E-mail: templecare@verizon.com.

Temple Street Pr., *(978-0-9896231)* P.O. Box 7071, Halcyon, CA 93421 USA Tel 805-243-8144
E-mail: eva@templestreetpress.com
Web site: http://templestreetpress.com.

†Temple Univ. Pr., *(978-0-87722; 978-1-56639; 978-1-59213; 978-1-4399)* 1601 N. Broad St., Univ. Services Bldg., Rm. 305, Philadelphia, PA 19122-6099 USA (SAN 202-7666) Tel 215-204-3389; Fax: 215-204-4719; Toll Free: 800-447-1656
E-mail: charles.ault@temple.edu
Web site: http://www.temple.edu/tempress
Dist(s): **Chicago Distribution Ctr.**
Ebsco Publishing
Follett School Solutions
Fordham Univ. Pr.
MyiLibrary
Univ. of Chicago Pr.
ebrary, Inc.; *CIP.*

Templeton Foundation Press *See* **Templeton Pr.**

Templeton, Julia, *(978-0-9837367; 978-1-939863)* 601 NW 22nd St., Battle Ground, WA 98604 USA Tel 360-723-0654
E-mail: juliatempleton@comcast.net
Dist(s): **Smashwords.**

Templeton Pr., *(978-1-890151; 978-1-932031; 978-1-59947)* Div. of John Templeton Foundation, 300 Conshohocken State Rd., Conshohocken, PA 19428-3801 USA
E-mail: info@templetonpress.org; lbarrett@templeton.org
Web site: http://www.templetonpress.org
Dist(s): **Chicago Distribution Ctr.**
Ebsco Publishing
MyiLibrary
ebrary, Inc.

Temporal Mechanical Pr., *(978-1-928878)* Div. of Enos Mills Cabin, Orders Addr.: 6760 Hwy. 7, Estes Park, CO 80517-6404 USA Tel 970-586-4706
E-mail: info@enosmills.com
Web site: http://www.enosmills.com.

Tempus (ESP) *(978-84-92567; 978-84-936181) Dist. by* **IPG Chicago.**

Tempus Pr., *(978-0-9620456)* Orders Addr.: P.O. Box 235, Tell City, IN 47586 USA (SAN 248-4609) Fax: 812-547-8144; Edit Addr.: 14904 Senator Way, Carmel, IN 46032-5111 USA (SAN 248-4617)
E-mail: philbalc@psci.net.

Ten Critters Pr., *(978-1-7335506)* 2506 Demere Rd, Saint Simons Island, GA 31522 USA Tel 678-772-9786
E-mail: cturtleatl@yahoo.com
Web site: cturtle.us.

Ten Gallon Pr., *(978-0-615-69261-6; 978-0-9883021; 978-0-9991217)* 2896 Bardy Rd., Santa Rosa, CA 95404 USA Tel 415-713-8386
E-mail: helen@helensedwick.com
Web site: www.tengallonpress.com
Dist(s): **CreateSpace Independent Publishing Platform.**

Ten Minas Publishing, *(978-0-9716786)* P.O. Box 8984, Reston, VA 20195 USA Fax: 703-834-1176
Web site: http://www.crowsofhiddencreek.

Ten Speed Pr. *Imprint of* **Potter/Ten Speed/Harmony/Rodale**

†Ten Speed Pr., *(978-0-89815; 978-0-913668; 978-1-58008; 978-1-60774)* Div. of Crown Publishing Group, Orders Addr.: P.O. Box 7123, Berkeley, CA 94707 USA (SAN 202-7674) Fax: 510-559-1629 (orders); Toll Free: 800-841-2665; 555 Richmond St., W. Suite 405, Box 702, Toronto, ON M5V 3B1 Tel 416-703-7775; Fax: 416-703-9992; *Imprints:* Celestial Arts (CelestialArts); Tricycle Press (TricyclePress)
E-mail: order@tenspeed.com; alan@tenspeed.ca
Web site: http://www.tenspeed.com
Dist(s): **Fujii Assocs.**
MyiLibrary
Penguin Random Hse. LLC
Random Hse., Inc.; *CIP.*

Ten Story Bks., LLC, *(978-0-9916348; 978-1-945131)* P.O. Box 701561, Dallas, TX 75370 USA Tel 972-345-0734
E-mail: info@tenstorybooks.com.

TEN16 Pr. *Imprint of* **Orange Hat Publishing**

Tender Heart Pr., *(978-0-9741401)* 15448 S. Jasper, Bldg. G, Odessa, TX 79766 USA
Web site: http://www.tenderheartpress.com.

Tender Learning Concepts, *(978-0-9708796)* 5362 Rockledge Dr., Buena Pk., CA 90621 USA Tel 714 739 2145; 714-739-2145; Fax: 714-739-0593; Toll Free: 877 886-7091; *Imprints:* TLConcepts, Incorporated (TLCPTS)
E-mail: whm@iqboosters.com
Web site: http://www.iqboosters.com; http://tenderlearning.econgo.com.

Tendril Pr., LLC, *(978-0-9763706; 978-0-9802190; 978-0-9822394; 978-0-9841543; 978-0-9831587; 978-0-9858933)* Orders Addr.: P.O. Box 441110, Aurora, CO 80044 USA Tel 303-696-9227; Fax: 303-873-6766; 2215 S. Oakland Way, Aurora, CO 80014 Tel 720-275-8371 Direct
E-mail: publisher@tendrilpress.com
Web site: http://www.tendrilpress.com
Dist(s): **Brigham Distribution.**

teNeues Publishing Co., *(978-3-570; 978-3-8238; 978-3-929278; 978-3-8327; 978-1-933427; 978-1-60160; 978-1-62325; 978-3-96171)* 7 W. 18th St., New York, NY 10011 USA (SAN 245-176X) Tel 212-627-9090; Fax: 212-627-9511; Toll Free: 800-352-0305; 12 Ferndene Rd., London, SE24 0AQ
E-mail: tnp@teneues-usa.com
Web site: http://www.teneues.com.

Tengan, G. Shay Service Group, *(978-0-9883478)* 2229 Orange Grove Pl., Escondido, CA 92027 USA Tel 760-443-9069
E-mail: stengan@cox.net.

Tenley Circle Pr., *(978-0-9773536)* Orders Addr.: P.O. Box 5625, Washington, DC 20016 USA.

Tennessee Valley Publishing, *(978-1-882194; 978-1-932604)* Orders Addr.: P.O. Box 52527, Knoxville, TN 37950-2527 USA Tel 865-584-5235; Fax: 865-584-0113; Toll Free: 800-762-7079; Edit Addr.: 5227 N. Middlebrook Pike., Knoxville, TN 37921-5963 USA
E-mail: info@tvp1.com
Web site: http://www.tvp1.com
Dist(s): **Chicago Distribution Ctr.**

Tenney, Bob Solutions, LLC, *(978-0-9763485)* 160 Hamburg Mountain Rd., Weaverville, NC 28787-9432 USA
E-mail: bobtenney@earthlink.net
Web site: http://www.tenneypubs.com.

Tensaw Pr., Inc., The, *(978-0-9746444)* 158 S. Jefferson St., Mobile, AL 36602-1119 USA Fax: 251-438-4545
E-mail: tensawpress@aol.com.

Teora USA LLC, *(978-1-59496)* Orders Addr.: 505 Hampton Park Blvd. Ste. G, Capitol Hgts, MD 20743-3862 USA (SAN 256-1220)
E-mail: welcome@teora.com
Web site: http://www.teorausa.com.

Terabyte Pr. LLC, *(978-0-9839877)* 223A S. Durkee Hill Ln., Southbury, CT 06488 USA Tel 203-448-8142
E-mail: cbaileysims@gmail.com.

Teresa E Lavergne, *(978-0-9966237)* 721 W. Main St, New Iberia, LA 70560 USA Tel 337-321-2840
E-mail: teresa@nifreedom.com.

Terminal Pr., LLC, *(978-0-9753683)* 27 June Walk., Long Beach, NY 11561-2884 USA
E-mail: bferrara@terminalpress.com
Web site: http://www.terminalpress.com.

Termino Editorial, *(978-0-930549)* P.O. Box 8905, Cincinnati, OH 45208 USA (SAN 677-5756) Tel 513-891-4621; Fax: 513-791-1756
E-mail: rmadri7239@aol.com
Dist(s): **Ediciones Universal.**

Terra Blue Enterprises, *(978-1-928840)* 310 Lakefront Dr., Wylie, TX 75098 USA Tel 972-332-3880 land line; 469-774-7815 cell phone
E-mail: sheyuli325@yahoo.com; khashahnawaz@gmail.com
Web site: http://www.shwelumaung.org/.

Terra Denuo, Inc., *(978-1-933232)* P.O. Box 485, Rocklin, CA 95677 USA
E-mail: mark@terradenuo.com
Web site: http://www.terradenuo.com.

Terra Linda Publishing, *(978-0-9746710)* 593 Tamarack Dr., San Rafael, CA 94903 USA Tel 415-491-1042
E-mail: rneolson@earthlink.net
Web site: http://www.terralindapublishing.com.

Terra Niños *See* **Solibros**

Terra Nova Press *See* **Across Ocean Bks.**

Terra Nova Publishing Company *See* **Dream Ship Publishing Co.**

Terra Tales, *(978-0-9771804)* 101 Lattice Ln., Collegeville, PA 19426-3374 USA.

Terrapin Pr., *(978-0-9753087)* 2094 Arthur St., Eugene, OR 97405-1519 USA Do not confuse with companies with the same name in Marina del Rey, CA, Aiken, SC.

Terrific Science Pr., *(978-1-883822)* Miami Univ. Middletown, 4200 E. University Blvd., Middletown, OH 45042 USA Fax: 513-727-3328
E-mail: cce@muohio.edu
Web site: http://www.terrificscience.org
Dist(s): **Carolina Biological Supply Co.**
Nasco Math Eighty-Six
Science Kit & Boreal Labs
Teacher's Discovery.

Terrific Twins LLC, *(978-0-9769910)* 659 Kensington Ave., Severna Park, MD 21146 USA Tel 410-647-8923 (phone/fax)
E-mail: carpenterzyla@hotmail.com
Web site: http://terrifictwins.com.

Terry Lowey's Children's Stories, LLC, *(978-0-9792695)* 1325 Airmotive Way, Suite 175, Reno, NV 89502 USA Tel 775-322-1924; Fax: 775-322-1937
Web site: http://www.lifeisamagicaljourney.com.

Tertulia Pubns., *(978-0-9785988)* P.O. Box 2450, Nevada City, CA 95959 USA (SAN 851-0962)
Web site: http://www.tertuliapress.com.

Terumah Publishing, *(978-0-9744277)* Orders Addr.: 5 Pipe Hill Ct., Unit C, Baltimore, MD 21209 USA Tel 410-486-0950
E-mail: info@terumah.com
Web site: http://www.terumah.com.

TESCH, GLORIA *See* **GOLDEN LIBERTY**

Tesoro Publishing, *(978-0-9797419; 978-1-941346)* P.O. Box 528, Fullerton, CA 92836 USA (SAN 854-2279)
E-mail: Info@Tesoropublishing.com
Web site: http://www.TesoroPublishing.com.

Tessellations, *(978-0-9802191; 978-0-9846042; 978-1-938664)* 3913 E. Bronco Tr., Phoenix, AZ 85044-2604 USA Tel 480-763-5440; Fax: 480-763-6948; Toll Free: 800-655-5341
E-mail: tessellations@cox.net
Web site: http://www.tessellations.com
Dist(s): **Parkwest Pubns., Inc.**

Testify Bks., Inc., *(978-0-9725920; 978-1-7320629)* 465 Greenwich St., No. 4, New York, NY 10013 USA
E-mail: extraclip@earthlink.net
Dist(s): **D.A.P./Distributed Art Pubs.**

TESTIMONY PUBLISHERS, LLC. *See* **Testimony Pubs., LLC.**

Testimony Pubs., LLC., *(978-1-7322956; 978-1-7331394)* P.O. Box 2869, Jackson, WY 83001 USA Tel 410-746-5299
E-mail: admin@testimonypublishersllc.online
Web site: www.testimonypublishersllc.online.

Tetoca Pr., *(978-0-9788085)* P.O. Box 337, Puyallup, WA 98371 USA Tel 253-845-1256; 253-845-5090; Toll Free: 888-483-8622
E-mail: thhunter@earthlink.net; tetoca@tetocapress.net
Web site: http://www.tetocapress.net
Dist(s): **Pathway Bk. Service**
Quality Bks., Inc.

Tetrahedron, Incorporated *See* **Tetrahedron Publishing LLC**

Tetrahedron Publishing LLC, *(978-0-923550; 978-0-9609386)* Orders Addr.: c/o Healthy World Distributing, LLC, 206 N. Fourth Ave., Suite 147, Sandpoint, ID 83864 USA Tel 208-265-2575; Fax: 208-265-2775; Toll Free: 888-508-4787; Edit Addr.: P.O. Box 2033, Sandpoint, ID 83864-0906 USA (SAN 260-2717) Toll Free: 888-508-4787 (orders)
E-mail: tetra@tetrahedron.org
Web site: http://www.tetrahedron.org
Dist(s): **New Leaf Distributing Co., Inc.**

Texas A&M AgriLife Extension Service, *(978-0-9672990; 978-0-9721049)* c/o Texas A & M University, 2112 TAMU, College Station, TX 77843-2112 USA Fax: 979-862-1202
E-mail: d-bowen@tamu.edu
Dist(s): **Texas A&M Univ. Pr.**

Texas Bk. Pubs. Assn., *(978-0-87244; 978-0-9717667; 978-0-9798391; 978-0-9903714; 978-1-946182)* Orders Addr.: 11152 Westheimer Rd., #667, Houston, TX 77042 USA Tel 281-438-7500; Fax: 281-438-7501
E-mail: editor@texasbookpublishers.org; publisher@johnhardypublishing.com; sales@johnhardypublishing.com
Web site: http://www.johnmhardy.com; www.texasbookpublishers.org; www.texlanpress.com; www.ironmtnpress.com; http://www.johnhardypublishing.com; http://www.calientexpress.com
Dist(s): **Ingram Content Group.**

†Texas Christian Univ. Pr., *(978-0-87565; 978-0-912646; 978-0-87565-510-9)* P.O. Box 298300, Fort Worth, TX 76129 USA (SAN 202-7690) Tel 817-257-7822; Fax: 817-257-5075
E-mail: j.alter@tcu.edu; s.petty@tcu.edu
Web site: http://www.prs.tcu.edu
Dist(s): **Ebsco Publishing**
MyiLibrary
Texas A&M Univ. Pr.
ebrary, Inc.; *CIP.*

Texas Cooperative Extension *See* **Texas A&M AgriLife Extension Service**

Texas Pride Publishing, *(978-0-9859601; 978-1-7349369)* 6888 Montgomery Dr Unit 4, San Antonio, TX 78239 USA Tel 214-326-4356
E-mail: theamazingcharity@gmail.com
Web site: http://www.charitymarie.com.

†Texas State Historical Assn., *(978-0-87611)* 2-306 Richardson Hall, University Sta., Austin, TX 78712 USA (SAN 202-7704) Tel 512-471-1525; Fax: 512-471-1551; Toll Free: 800-687-8132
Web site: http://www.tshaonline.org
Dist(s): **MyiLibrary**
Texas A&M Univ. Pr.
ebrary, Inc.; *CIP.*

†Texas Tech Univ. Pr., *(978-0-89672; 978-1-68283)* Affil. of Texas Tech Univ., P.O. Box 41037, Lubbock, TX 79409-1037 USA (SAN 218-5989) Tel 806-742-2982; Fax: 806-742-2979; Toll Free: 800-832-4042
E-mail: ttup@ttu.edu; barbara.brannon@ttu.edu
Web site: http://www.ttup.ttu.edu; http://www.ttupress.org
Dist(s): **Chicago Distribution Ctr.**
MyiLibrary; *CIP.*

†Texas Woman's Univ. Pr., *(978-0-9607488; 978-0-9712104)* Orders Addr.: P.O. Box 425858, Denton, TX 76204 USA (SAN 238-4833) Tel 940-898-3123; Fax: 940-898-3127; Edit Addr.: 1200 Frame St., Denton, TX 76205 USA
E-mail: wbenson@twu.edu; *CIP.*

Text 4m Publishing, *(978-0-9779207; 978-0-9795691)* P.O. Box 12586, Milwaukee, WI 53212-0586 USA (SAN 850-6299)
E-mail: info@text4mpublishing.com; teresarae@msn.com
Web site: http://www.text4mpublishing.com.

Text N Tone, Inc., *(978-0-9764429)* 1500 King William Woods Rd., Midlothian, VA 23113-9119 USA
E-mail: mchekel@dslextreme.com.

Text Publishing Co. (AUS) *(978-1-875847; 978-1-876485; 978-1-86372; 978-1-877008; 978-1-920885; 978-1-921145; 978-1-921351; 978-1-921520; 978-1-921656; 978-1-921758; 978-1-921776; 978-1-921799; 978-1-921834; 978-1-921921; 978-1-921922; 978-1-921961; 978-0-85786; 978-1-922079; 978-1-922147; 978-1-922148; 978-1-922182; 978-1-925095; 978-1-922253; 978-1-925240; 978-1-925355; 978-1-925410; 978-1-925498; 978-1-925570; 978-1-925603; 978-1-925626; 978-1-925773; 978-1-925774; 978-1-922268; 978-1-925923; 978-1-922330; 978-1-) Dist. by* **Consort Bk Sales.**

Textbook Pubs., *(978-0-7581; 978-1-60630; 978-1-62583)* Orders Addr.: 17853 Santiago Blvd. Suite 107-133, Villa Park, CA 92861 USA Fax: 951-767-0133
E-mail: reprintservices@gmail.com.

Textbooks On Demand *See* **Reprint Services Corp.**

Textorium Publishing, *(978-0-9988194)* P.O. Box 62385, Virginia Beach, VA 23466 USA Tel 757-270-5590
E-mail: textoriumpublishing@yahoo.com.

Texture Pr., *(978-0-9641837; 978-0-9712061; 978-0-9797573; 978-0-9850081; 978-0-615-69474-0; 978-0-615-71148-5; 978-0-615-71503-2; 978-0-615-75380-5; 978-0-615-77101-4; 978-0-615-78283-6; 978-0-615-81691-3; 978-0-615-82399-7; 978-0-615-85856-2; 978-0-615-87735-8; 978-0-615-90534-1; 978-0-615-95462-2; 978-0-615-95463-9; 978-0-692-21272-1; 978-0-692-30003-9; 978-0-692-30004-6; 978-0-692-31702-0; 978-0-692-35682-1; 978-0-692-35683-8; 978-0-692-36138-2; 978-0-692-39578-3; 978-0-692-40157-6; 978-0-692-52042-) 1108 Westbrooke Terr., Norman, OK 73072 USA Tel 405-314-7730; Fax: 405-310-6617*
E-mail: susan@beyondutopia.com; texturepress@beyondutopia.com
Web site: http://www.texturepress.org; http://beyondutopia.net/texturepress/
Dist(s): **SPD-Small Pr. Distribution.**

TFG, *(978-0-9884132)* P.O. Box 91452, Portland, OR 97291 USA Tel 503-629-5045; Fax: 503-531-9175
E-mail: kimball@kimballfisher.com; info@thefishergroup.com
Web site: www.kimballfisher.com; www.thefishergroup.com.

TFG Pr., *(978-0-9743521; 978-0-9748553)* 244 Madison Ave., No. 254, New York, NY 10016 USA Tel 877-822-2504 do nto confuse with TGF Press in New York, NY.

Publisher Name Index

†TFH Pubns., Inc., *(978-0-7938; 978-0-86622; 978-0-87666; 978-1-85279)* Orders Addr.: One TFH Plaza, Third & Union Aves., Neptune City, NJ 07753 USA (SAN 202-7720) Tel 732-988-8400; Fax: 732-988-5466; Toll Free: 800-631-2188 (outside New Jersey); Edit Addr.: P.O. Box 427, Neptune, NJ 07753 USA (SAN 658-1862)
E-mail: info@tfh.com
Web site: http://www.tfh.com; *CIP.*

TG8 LLC, *(978-0-692-95819-3; 978-0-9997840)* 616 Rosarita Rd, Arlington, TX 76002 USA Tel 214-240-5511; Fax: 214-240-5511
E-mail: kendriatg@gmail.com
Web site: www.jaxandriley.com.

Th1nk Bks. *Imprint of* **NavPress Publishing Group**

Th3rd World Studios, *(978-0-9818694; 978-0-9832161; 978-0-9895744)* 290 Powell Cir., Berlin, MD 21811 USA
Web site: http://www.th3rdworld.com
Dist(s): **Diamond Comic Distributors, Inc.**
Diamond Bk. Distributors.

Thacker Hse. Enterprises, *(978-0-9801919)* 1840 Thacker Ave., Jacksonville, FL 32207 USA Tel 904-398-8332
E-mail: 22dwebb@comcast.net
Web site: http://www.debrawebbrogers.com.

Thalian Bks., *(978-0-9884868; 978-0-9961317)* 271B Heritage Village, Southbury, CT 06488 USA Tel 203-262-1558
E-mail: becklean@gmail.com.

Thames & Hudson, *(978-0-500)* 500 Fifth Ave., New York, NY 10110 USA Tel 212-354-3763; Fax: 212-398-1252; Toll Free: 800-233-4830 (orders)
E-mail: bookinfo@thames.wwnorton.com
Web site: http://www.thamesandhudsonusa.com
Dist(s): **Hachette Bk. Group**
ISD
MyiLibrary
Norton, W. W. & Co., Inc.
Penguin Random Hse. Distribution
Penguin Random Hse. LLC.

Thameside Press *See* **Chrysalis Education**

Thandi's Place, A Billo Communication Company *See* **Youth Popular Culture Institute, Inc.**

Tharpa Pubns. (GBR) *(978-0-948006; 978-1-899996; 978-0-9548790; 978-1-906665; 978-0-9558667; 978-84-15849-24-7) Dist. by* **BTPS.**

That Patchwork Place *Imprint of* **Martingale & Co.**

Thatch, Jaina, *(978-0-692-19830-8; 978-0-578-59280-0)* 111 Huron Ave, Tampa, FL 33606 USA Tel 215-356-7954
E-mail: jaina.thatch@gmail.com.

That's Life, Incorporated *See* **That's Life Publishing, Inc.**

That's Life Publishing, Inc., *(978-0-9722304)* 3431 Thunderbird Rd., No. 200, Phoenix,, AZ 85053 USA Toll Free: 877-896-9500; *Imprints:* ZZ Dogs Press (ZZ Dogs Pr)
Web site: http://www.zzdogs.com.

That's Me Publishing, LLC, *(978-1-933843)* Hc 62 Box 488., Salem, MO 65560-8819 USA
E-mail: mary@thatsmepublishing.com
Web site: http://www.thatsmepublishing.com.

ThatsMyLife Co., *(978-0-9760419)* 5516 Challis View Ln., Charlotte, NC 28226 USA Tel 704-752-0935; Toll Free: 866-752-0935
E-mail: customerservice@thatsmytale.com
Web site: http://www.thatsmytale.com.

The 101 Group, Inc., *(978-0-9772313; 978-0-9817033; 978-0-9848624; 978-1-7340727)* Orders Addr.: W358N5358 Crestview Dr., Oconomowoc, WI 53066 USA; Edit Addr.: P.O. Box 82, Okauchee, WI 53069 USA
Web site: http://www.the101group.com.

Angelic Prince Publishing, The, *(978-0-9985145; 978-1-951428)* P.O. Box 33572, Tulsa, OK 74153 USA Tel 971-246-0160
E-mail: LantzdeContreras@gmail.com
Web site: LantzdeContreras.com.

The Arden Shakespeare *Imprint of* **Bloomsbury Publishing USA**

The Argonauts *See* **Argonauts, The**

The Art of Jessycka Drew, *(978-0-692-85164-7; 978-0-9987596)* 81 Westford St, HAVERHILL, MA 01832 USA.

The Bookworm of Edwards, *(978-0-692-81222-8; 978-0-692-86242-1; 978-0-692-09270-5; 978-0-578-48317-7; 978-0-578-70396-1)* 295 Main Street, C101, EDWARDS, CO 81632 USA Tel 970-926-7323
E-mail: nicole@bookwormofedwards.com; events@bookwormofedwards.com.

The Crown Publishing Group *See* **Crown Publishing Group, The**

The Crowood Press (GBR) *(978-0-7090; 978-0-7091; 978-0-7198; 978-0-85131; 978-0-946284; 978-1-85223; 978-1-86126; 978-1-84797; 978-1-910208; 978-1-78500) Dist. by* **IPG Chicago.**

Dramatic Pen Pr., LLC, The, *(978-0-692-28380-6; 978-0-692-32954-2; 978-0-692-32958-0; 978-0-692-35487-2; 978-0-692-36604-2; 978-0-692-36728-5; 978-0-692-37996-7; 978-0-692-38986-7; 978-0-692-39163-1; 978-0-692-40865-0; 978-0-692-51342-2; 978-0-692-53385-7; 978-0-692-58038-7; 978-0-692-63114-0; 978-1-64157) 322 Cumberland St, Lolo, MT 59847 USA Tel 612-888-3722*
E-mail: susanethomas@juno.com
Web site: www.thedramaticpen.com
Dist(s): **CreateSpace Independent Publishing Platform.**

The Edge *Imprint of* **Sparklesoup LLC**

Beacon Hill Pr. of Kansas City, *(978-0-8341)* Div. of Nazarene Publishing Hse., 2345 Grand Blvd, Ste. 1900, Kansas City, MO 64108 USA (SAN 241-6328) Tel 816-931-1900; Fax: 816-753-4071; Toll Free: 800-877-0700 (orders only)
E-mail: nphdirect@nph.com; orders@nph.com; inquiry@bhillkc.com
Web site: http://www.nph.com; http://www.bhillkc.com
Dist(s): **The Foundry Publishing.**

The Foundry Publishing, *(978-0-8341)* Orders Addr.: 2345 Grand Blvd., Suite 1900, Kansas City, MO 64108 USA (SAN 253-0902) Tel 816-931-1900; Edit Addr.: P.O. Box 419527, Kansas City, MO 64141 USA (SAN 202-9022) Tel 816-931-1900; Fax: 816-531-0923; Toll Free Fax: 800-849-9827; Toll Free: 800-877-0700
E-mail: heather@nph.com
Web site: http://www.bhillkc.com; http://www.nph.com
Dist(s): **LifeWay Christian Resources**
Lorenz Corp., The
Spring Arbor Distributors, Inc.

The Journey, *(978-0-692-78081-7; 978-0-692-78082-4; 978-0-692-18308-3; 978-0-578-43728-6)* 3171 E 129th Ave S., TULSA, OK 74134 USA Tel 918-576-8442.

Laurus Co., Inc., The, *(978-0-9841680; 978-0-9826957; 978-0-9847683; 978-1-938526; 978-1-943523)* P.O. Box 434, Lake Dallas, TX 75065 USA Tel 423-262-8389
E-mail: laurus@thelauruscompany.com; bookstore@thelauruscompany.com; nancywilliams@thelauruscompany.com
Web site: http://www.LaurusCompany.com; http://www.TheLaurusCompany.com; http://www.LaurusBooks.com; http://www.BookShelfDepot.com
Dist(s): **Laurus Co., The**
TLC Distributors.

Old West Co., The, *(978-0-9654341; 978-0-9801743; 978-0-9898004; 978-1-7320075)* Orders Addr.: 5118 Village Trail Dr., San Antonio, TX 78218-3831 USA; *Imprints:* Sweetwater Stagelines (Sweetwtr Stage)
E-mail: kirkwest@sbcglobal.net
Web site: theoldwestcompany.com; celebratethewest.com; lulu.com/spotlight/sweetwater; sweetwaterstagelines.com; aggiebonfireflick.com; http://lulu.com/sweetwater.

The Painted Word, Ltd., *(978-0-9846473; 978-0-692-03494-1)* P.O. Box 4132, Lutherville, MD 21094 USA.

The Publishing Place LLC, *(978-0-9754307; 978-0-9760129; 978-0-9763423; 978-0-9776554; 978-0-9788002; 978-0-9840555; 978-0-9845794; 978-0-9835095; 978-0-9849172)* 2330 Hickory Ridge, Ashland, KY 41101 USA Do not confuse with Avant-garde Publishing Company in Mableton, GA
E-mail: info@avantgardepublishing.com
Web site: http://www.avantgardepublishing.com
Dist(s): **Smashwords.**

The Reading Butterfly, INC., *(978-0-9993336)* 798 Rachel Dr., Franklinville, NJ 08322 USA Tel 609-703-3359; Fax: 856-422-0900
E-mail: gx3@comcast.net.

The Richard Janes Co., *(978-0-692-77834-0)* 12856 Walsh Ave, Los Angeles, CA 90066 USA Tel 310-801-2661
Dist(s): **Independent Pub.**

The Rolling Acorn Pr., *(978-0-692-31870-6; 978-0-692-37782-6; 978-0-692-79386-2; 978-0-692-10389-0; 978-0-692-14774-0)* 4730 Castle Rd, LA CANADA, CA 91011 USA Tel 818-434-2395.

The Svenson Group, Inc. *See* **Svenson Group, Inc., The**

Svenson Group, Inc., The, *(978-1-949436)* 2990 Northfied Dr., Tarpon Springs, FL 34688 USA Tel 727-945-7024
E-mail: svensona@aol.com
Web site: http://thehappyhollisters.com/.

The Tale of Noel: The Holiday Horse Angel, The, *(978-0-692-94230-7; 978-0-692-10176-6; 978-0-578-51603-5; 978-0-578-54889-0)* 14104 225th St., ELKADER, IA 52043 USA Tel 563-329-0806
E-mail: authorkristenhalverson@gmail.com
Dist(s): **Ingram Content Group.**

Vision to Fruition Publishing Hse., The, *(978-0-692-25410-3; 978-0-692-30554-6; 978-0-692-32827-9; 978-0-692-34607-5; 978-0-692-42756-9; 978-0-692-48625-2; 978-0-692-56030-3; 978-0-692-99897-7; 978-1-7327674; 978-1-7339413; 978-0-578-72626-7; 978-1-7358359)* 15912b Crain Hwy Ste. 104, Brandywine, MD 20613 USA Tel 240-343-3563
E-mail: info@vision-fruition.com
Web site: www.vision-fruition.com
Dist(s): **CreateSpace Independent Publishing Platform.**

The Wisdom Pages, Inc., *(978-0-9706482)* Div. of Bullies to Buddies, Inc., 65 Fraser St., Staten Island, NY 10314 USA (SAN 255-1217) Tel 718-983-1333; Fax: 718-983-3851
E-mail: miriam@bullies2buddies.com; izzy@bullies2buddies.com
Web site: http://www.bullies2buddies.com; http://www.thewisdompages.com.

THEAQ LLC, *(978-0-9890723; 978-1-68189)* ; *Imprints:* THEAQ Publishing (THEAQPub)
E-mail: przcook2000@yahoo.com; rzeissler@yahoo.com.

THEAQ Publishing *Imprint of* **THEAQ LLC**

†Theatre Communications Group, Inc., *(978-0-88754; 978-0-913745; 978-0-930452; 978-1-55936; 978-1-84002; 978-1-85459; 978-1-870259; 978-1-899791; 978-1-63670)* 355 Lexington Ave., New York, NY 10017-6603 USA (SAN 210-9387) Tel 212-697-5230; Fax: 212-983-4847
Web site: http://www.tcg.org
Dist(s): **Abraham Assocs. Inc.**
Consortium Bk. Sales & Distribution
MyiLibrary
ebrary, Inc.; *CIP.*

Theatre of Innocence, A, L.L.C., *(978-0-9760283)* 1212 Hull St., No. 1, Louisville, KY 40204 USA.

Theee Hole Punch Publishing, *(978-0-9771678)* P.O. Box 4488, Midlothian, VA 23112 USA
E-mail: threeholepunchpublishing@verizon.net; vzentja9@verizon.net
Web site: http://threeholepunchpublishing.com.

Theisen, Patricia, *(978-0-9793076)* 10520 11th Ave. NW, Seattle, WA 98177 USA
E-mail: ptheisen@gmail.com.

Them Potatoes, *(978-0-9772564)* 7318 21st Ave NW, Seattle, WA 98117-5623 USA (SAN 257-1285)
E-mail: kbrown@thempotatoes.com
Web site: http://www.thempotatoes.com.

Theme Perks Incorporated *See* **Writing Academy Inc.**

TheNetworkAdministrator.com, *(978-0-9744630; 978-1-937485)* Orders Addr.: 201 W. Cottesmore Cir., Longwood, FL 32779 USA
E-mail: douglaschick@thenetworkadministrator.com
Web site: http://www.thenetworkadministrator.com.

Theodore Berlin Publishing, *(978-0-9769196)* Div. of Theodore Berlin LLC, Orders Addr.: 8221 Provident St., Philadelphia, PA 19150 USA Tel 215-327-8212; Fax: 615-704-4422
E-mail: berlintheodore@yahoo.com.

Theophany Pr., *(978-1-7339710)* 2821 Rio Linda Dr., Bakersfield, CA 93305 USA Tel 661-477-6437
E-mail: theophanypress@gmail.com
Web site: jennylynnestes.com.

Theory & Practice *Imprint of* **Scholastic, Inc.**

Theragogy.com, *(978-0-9749862)* 301 1/2 Crescent NE, Grand Rapids, MI 49503 USA
E-mail: drperkins@theragogy.com
Web site: http://www.theragogy.com.

Therapeutae Pr., *(978-0-9675575; 978-1-7335406)* P.O. Box 23542, Flagstaff, AZ 86002 USA
E-mail: nedwolf@rcia.com.

TheWhippetyWood, *(978-0-9897216)* S9305 Slotty Rd., Prairie du Sac, WI 53578 USA Tel 608-544-2242
E-mail: pj.pixie1@gmail.com
Web site: www.theWhippetyWood.com.

Thewordverve, *(978-0-9857157; 978-0-9889264; 978-0-9896979; 978-1-941251; 978-0-9989052; 978-0-9992479; 978-1-948225)* 163 Mountain Vista Blvd., Canton, GA 30115 USA Tel 678-710-4353
E-mail: jan@thewordverve.com
Web site: www.bookswithverve.com; www.thewordverve.com.

Theytus Bks., Ltd. (CAN) *(978-0-919441; 978-1-894778; 978-1-926886) Dist. by* **Orca Bk Pub.**

Thies, Roberta A., *(978-0-692-93363-3; 978-0-578-47690-2)* 5278 Wolfpen Pleasant Hill Rd, MILFORD, OH 45150 USA Tel 513-218-2418
E-mail: thiesbobbi7@gmail.com
Dist(s): **Ingram Content Group.**

Thimble Mouse Publishing, Inc., *(978-0-9794522)* 1619 Saddle Creek Cir., No. 1312, Arlington, TX 76015 USA (SAN 853-4942).

ThingsAsian Pr., *(978-0-9715940; 978-1-934159)* 3230 Scott St., San Francisco, CA 94123 USA Tel 415-921-1316; Fax: 415-921-3432
E-mail: info@thingsasian.com; albert@thingsasian.com
Web site: http://www.thingsasianpress.com; http://www.toasiawithlove.com; http://www.thingsasian.com
Dist(s): **Ingram Publisher Services.**

ThinkerBlox, LLC, *(978-1-7323299; 978-1-7326683)* 1655 Manitoba Dr., Sunnyvale, CA 94087 USA Tel 408-733-8973
E-mail: scurtis@laughingthunder.com.

Thinking Ink Pr., *(978-1-942480)* P.O. Box 1411, Campbell, CA 95009-1411 USA Tel 408-507-1990
E-mail: editorial@thinkinginkpress.com
Web site: www.thinkinginkpress.com.

Thinking Kids *Imprint of* **Carson-Dellosa Publishing, LLC**

Think-Outside-the-Book Publishing, Inc., *(978-0-9770751; 978-0-9896781; 978-0-9985471)* 311 N. Robertson Blvd., Suite 323, Beverly Hills, CA 90211 USA
Web site: http://www.thinkoutsidethebook.com.

Thinkus Pubs., *(978-0-9818449)* Orders Addr.: 13109 SW 43rd St., Davie, FL 33330 USA
E-mail: loriflorido@aol.com
Web site: http://www.Dezzerthebook.com; http://www.HugothePunk.com
Dist(s): **Brodart Co.**
Follet Higher Education Grp
Quality Bks., Inc.

Third Axe Publishing, *(978-0-9765547)* 1150 McFarland, HR 26, Morristown, TN 37814 USA Tel 423-736-0884
E-mail: thirdaxepub@yahoo.com
Web site: http://www.brotherhoodofdwarves.com.

Third Dimension Publishing, *(978-0-9777041)* Div. of Third Dimension Group, Inc., Orders Addr.: P.O. Box 1845, Calhoun, GA 30703-1845 USA Tel 706-602-0398; Fax: 706-625-8712; Edit Addr.: 167 Richardson Rd., Calhoun, GA 30701 USA
E-mail: jeffcompton@msn.com
Web site: http://www.areyouawriter.com; http://www.thirddimensiongroup.com; http://www.thirddimensionpublishing.com.

Third Man Books, *(978-0-9913361; 978-0-9964016; 978-0-9974578; 978-1-7333501; 978-1-7348422)* 623 7th Ave. S., Nashville, TN 37203 USA (SAN 990-0071) Tel 615-720-6758
E-mail: joshua@thirdmanrecords.com
Web site: www.thirdmanrecords.com
Dist(s): **Consortium Bk. Sales & Distribution.**

Third Man Records *See* **Third Man Books**

Third Millennium Pr., *(978-0-9795608; 978-0-9833308)* 1845 Avondale Dr., Baton Rouge, LA 70808-1913 USA (SAN 853-7496) Tel 805-217-3109; Toll Free: 800-891-0390
E-mail: ellenhbrown@gmail.com
Web site: http://www.webofdebt.com; http://www.forbiddenmedicine.org; http://www.ellenbrown.com
Dist(s): **Ingram Content Group.**

Third Millennium Pubns., *(978-1-932657; 978-1-934805; 978-1-947483)* Sci Fi - Arizona, Inc., 1931 E. Libra Dr., Tempe, AZ 85283-5117 USA Tel 602-740-0569
E-mail: mccollum@3mpub.com
Web site: http://www.3mpub.com; http://www.scifi-az.com
Dist(s): **Chicago Distribution Ctr.**

Third Millennium Publishing *Imprint of* **Sci Fi-Arizona, Inc.**

3rd Party Publishing Co., *(978-0-89914)* Div. of Third Party Assocs., Inc., P.O. Box 13306, Oakland, CA 94661-0306 USA (SAN 127-7294) Tel 510-339-2323; Fax: 510-339-6729; Toll Free: 888-339-2323
E-mail: paulmico@tpaserver.com
Web site: http://www.tpaserver.com.

Third Week Bks., *(978-0-9712816; 978-0-9829948)* 1112 W. 66th St., No.1, Richfield, MN 55423-2280 USA Tel 612-990-6011
E-mail: TheBabyReader@yahoo.com
Web site: http://ThirdWeekBooks.com.

Third World Games, Inc., *(978-0-9728526)* P.O. Box 667, Westminster, CA 92684-0667 USA Tel 714-357-2967
E-mail: companyisbn-dir@thirdworldgames.com
Web site: http://www.thirdworldgames.com.

Third World Press, *(978-0-88378)* P.O. Box 19730, Chicago, IL 60619 USA (SAN 202-778X) Tel 773-651-0700; Fax: 773-651-7286
E-mail: TWPress3@aol.com
Web site: http://www.thirdworldpressinc.com
Dist(s): **Austin & Company, Inc.**
Chicago Distribution Ctr.
Ingram Publisher Services.

Third-Career Pr., LLC, *(978-0-9988731)* 212 Magnolia Bluff Dr., COLUMBIA, SC 29229 USA Tel 516-398-2235
E-mail: HalinaSchafer@gmail.com.

Thirsty(?) *Imprint of* **Tyndale Hse. Pubs.**

Thirsty Horse LLC, *(978-0-9723127)* 1220 N. Market St., Suite 606, Wilmington,, DE 19801-2598 USA (SAN 254-7767) Tel 302-428-1222
E-mail: orders@thirsty-horse.com
Web site: http://www.thirsty-horse-media.com.

Thirsty Sponge Publishing Co., *(978-0-9797960)* 898 Southgate Dr., Cookeville, TN 38501 USA.

Thirty-Three Hundred Pr., *(978-0-9646017)* 3300 Mission St., San Francisco, CA 94110 USA Tel 415-826-6886; 300 Vicksburg St., No. 5, San Francisco, CA 94114
Dist(s): **SPD-Small Pr. Distribution.**

This is RED, *(978-0-9767646)* 1 Furnace Rd., Hollidaysburg, PA 16648 USA
E-mail: gimmygum@gimmygum.com
Web site: http://www.gimmygum.com.

This Joy Bks., *(978-0-9821835; 978-0-9834546; 978-0-692-78357-3; 978-1-7323722)* 1111 Loyola Dr., Libertyville, IL 60048 USA Tel 847-401-7668
E-mail: mjvelotta@comcast.net.

This Little Light Productions, *(978-1-7324559)* 28 Balmoral Ct., Aberdeen, NJ 07747 USA Tel 646-320-4089
E-mail: suzvreeland@gmail.com.

Thistle Publishing, *(978-1-879403)* 11985 Cherokee Cir., Shelby Township, MI 48315 USA Tel 586-781-7039; Fax: 586-589-6011
Dist(s): **CreateSpace Independent Publishing Platform.**

Thistledown Pr., Ltd. (CAN) *(978-0-920066; 978-0-920633; 978-1-895449; 978-1-894345; 978-1-897235; 978-1-77187) Dist. by* **IngramPubServ.**

Thistlewood Publishing, *(978-0-9821507; 978-0-9853600)* 92 Wayside Ln., Apalachin, NY 13732 USA
E-mail: gnw@stny.rr.com; gwestover@thistlewoodpublishing.com
Web site: http://www.thistlewoodpublishing.com.

Thomas & Kay, LLC, *(978-0-9729505)* N37w26805 Kopmeier Dr., Pewaukee, WI 53072 USA (SAN 255-7576) Tel 414-581-0449
E-mail: susan@solutionsbysusan.com
Web site: http://www.solutionsbysusan.com.

Thomas & Mercer *Imprint of* **Amazon Publishing**

Thomas & Sons Bks., *(978-0-9758800)* 33 Greenwich Ave., Suite 7L, New York, NY 10014 USA
E-mail: willysthom@rcn.com.

Thomas, Angelo, *(978-0-692-16926-1)* 5505 W. Pages Ln., LOUISVILLE, KY 40258 USA Tel 502-889-6637
E-mail: imangelothomas@gmail.com
Dist(s): **Ingram Content Group.**

Thomas, Brandis, *(978-0-9792526)* P.O. Box 690162, Houston, TX 77269 USA.

†Thomas, Charles C. Pub., Ltd., *(978-0-398)* 2600 S. First St., Springfield, IL 62704 USA (SAN 201-9485) Tel 217-789-8980; Fax: 217-789-9130; Toll Free: 800-258-8980
E-mail: books@ccthomas.com; dmccarty@ccthomas.com; editorial@ccthomas.com
Web site: http://www.ccthomas.com
Dist(s): **Follett School Solutions**
MyiLibrary
ebrary, Inc.; *CIP.*

Thomas, Duerre, *(978-0-9793877; 978-0-9857798)* 23505 Ferndale Ave., Port Charlotte, FL 33980 USA
E-mail: d_jacel@yahoo.com; madpastor1@gmail.com
Web site: http://www.duerrethomas.com.

Thomas Expressions, Incorporated *See* **Thomas Expressions, LLC**

Thomas Expressions, LLC, *(978-0-9713573; 978-0-9771059)* Orders Addr.: 390 S. Tyndall Pkwy.,

#294, Panama City, FL 32404 USA Fax: 850-785-6408; Toll Free: 866-570-5560
E-mail: thomasexpressions@gmail.com
Web site: http://www.thomasexpressions.com; http://www.didyano.com
Dist(s): **Follett School Solutions.**

Thomas, Frederic Inc., *(978-0-9747133; 978-1-933443)* 5621 Strand Blvd. Ste. 301, Naples, FL 34110-7307 USA (SAN 255-8157); *Imprints:* Values to Live By Classic Stories (ValLiveByClass)
E-mail: freimer@fredericthomas.com; bmichalowski@fredericthomas.com
Web site: http://fredericthomas.com; http://www.healthylivingforkids.com; http://www.valuestoliveby.com.

Thomas, L.E., *(978-0-692-75690-4; 978-0-692-77301-7; 978-0-692-77357-4)* 2615 Crosswynd Terr., CUMMING, GA 30040 USA Tel 404-512-5836.

Thomas Max Publishing, *(978-0-9764052; 978-0-9788571; 978-0-9799950; 978-0-9822189; 978-0-9842626; 978-0-9846347; 978-0-9972920)* P.O. Box 250054, Atlanta, GA 30325-1054 USA Tel 404-794-6588
E-mail: LeeC@thomasmax.com; bee.ell.cee@comcast.net
Web site: http://www.thomasmax.com.

Thomas More Publishing, *(978-0-692-75285-2)*.

Thomas Pubns., *(978-0-939631; 978-1-57747)* 3245 Fairfield Rd., Gettysburg, PA 17325 USA (SAN 663-7213) Tel 717-642-6600; Fax: 717-642-5555; Toll Free: 800-840-6782 Do not confuse with companies with the same name in Austin, TX, La Crescenta, CA
E-mail: jim@horsesoldier.com
Web site: http://www.thomaspublications.com.

Thomas, R. E., *(978-0-9761077)* P.O. Box 53091, Houston, TX 77052 USA.

Thomas, Richard Kayeen *See* **MarWel Enterprises, Inc.**

Thomas, Sheldon Wade, *(978-0-9670539)* 1091 Thomas S. Boyland St., Brooklyn, NY 11236 USA Tel 718-495-6002 (phone/fax).

Thomas, Steve Art & Illustration, *(978-0-692-10564-1)* 22040 Iden Ave. N., Forest Lake, MN 55025 USA Tel 651-324-4511
E-mail: artist@stevethomasart.com
Dist(s): **Ingram Content Group.**

Thomas, Thomas C. II, *(978-0-692-80928-0; 978-0-692-84277-5)* 249 Santa Rita Ave., PALO ALTO, CA 94301 USA Tel 917-428-3322.

Thomastar Publishing, *(978-0-615-17087-9)* 14241 NE Wood-Duvall Rd Suite 406, Woodinville, WA 98072 USA Tel 425-703-8807
E-mail: thomastar.publishing@hotmail.com
Dist(s): **Lulu Pr., Inc.**

Thompson, Alyce C. Books, Inc., *(978-0-9746411)* Orders Addr.: 6105 W.master St., Philadelphia, PA 19151-0827 USA; Edit Addr.: P.O. Box 664, Havertown, PA 19083 USA
E-mail: emailalyce8@aol.com; info@alycecthompsonbooksinc.com
Web site: http://alycecthompsonbooksinc.com; http://www.myspace.com/alycecthompson; http://www.myspace.com/alycecthompsonbooksinc
Dist(s): **A & B Distributors & Pubs. Group**
Afrikan World Bk. Distributor
Culture Plus Bk. Distributors
Lushena Bks.

Thompson, Angela Bolden, *(978-0-615-14774-1)* 9501 W. 171st St. Ste. Q, Tinley Park, IL 60487 USA
Web site: http://angelathompson1.tripod.com/
Dist(s): **Lulu Pr., Inc.**

Thompson, Jeniffer, *(978-0-9798551; 978-0-9888882; 978-0-9974413)* 9880 Shadow Rd., La Mesa, CA 91941 USA Tel 619-955-8286; *Imprints:* MCM Publishing (MCMPubng)
E-mail: j@monkeycmedia.com
Web site: http://www.mcmpublishing.com
Dist(s): **Midpoint Trade Bks., Inc.**
Partners Pubs. Group, Inc.

Thompson, Marsha, *(978-0-692-89125-4; 978-0-692-94710-4; 978-0-578-45157-2)* 3130 E Lafayette St., Detroit, MI 48207 USA Tel 407-953-4869
E-mail: mdthomps21@yahoo.com
Web site: www.marshathompsonbooks.com.

Thompson Mill Pr., *(978-0-9883269; 978-0-9971239)* 2110 S. Eagle Rd., No. 368, Newtown, PA 18940 USA
E-mail: bob.regan@thompsonmillpress.com
Web site: http://www.thompsonmillpress.com; http://www.KobeeManatee.com
Dist(s): **Independent Pubs. Group.**

Thompson Original Productions LLC, *(978-0-9799216)* 11997 Youngtree Ct., Bristow, VA 20136 USA (SAN 854-7203)
E-mail: tracyathompson@hotmail.com
Web site: https://www.worldoftheorb.com/; http://www.chickenboybooks.com; www.michaelthompsonbooks.com.

Thomsen, Keith Stuart II, *(978-0-692-55783-9; 978-0-692-79741-9)* 2417 Courtland Ave, HENDERSON, NV 89074 USA Tel 702-610-3662.

Thomson Custom Solutions *See* **CENGAGE Learning Custom Publishing**

Thomson, D.C. & Co., Ltd. (GBR) *(978-0-85116; 978-1-84535) Dist. by* **APG.**

Thomson Delmar Learning *See* **Delmar Cengage Learning**

Thomson ELT, *(978-1-4240; 978-1-4282)* 25 Thomson Pl., 5th Flr., Boston, MA 02210 USA Tel 617-289-7700 Toll Free: 800-237-0053
E-mail: reply@heinle.com
Web site: http://www.elt.thomson.com
Dist(s): **CENGAGE Learning.**

Thomson Gale *See* **Cengage Gale**

Thomson, J P, *(978-0-9754365)* P.O. Box 377, Exton, PA 19341 USA Tel 610-594-1707; Fax: 610-594-1866
E-mail: montanapino@comcast.net.

Thomson Learning *See* **CENGAGE Learning**

Thomson Peterson's *See* **Peterson's**

Thomson South-Western *See* **Cengage South-Western**

Thornapple Farms, LLC, *(978-0-9749728)* 13010 W. Darrow Rd., Vermilion, OH 44089 USA Tel 440-967-2680; Fax: 440-967-2696
E-mail: ashar@hbr.net
Web site: http://www.thornapplefarms.com.

Thorncrown Publishing *Imprint of* **Yorkshire Publishing Group**

†Thorndike Pr., *(978-0-7838; 978-0-7862; 978-0-8161; 978-0-89621; 978-1-56054; 978-1-4104)* Div. of Gale Group, 295 Kennedy Memorial Dr., Waterville, ME 04901 USA Tel 207-859-1053; 207-859-1020; 207-859-1000; Toll Free Fax: 800-558-4676; Toll Free: 800-223-1244 (ext. 15); 800-877-4253 (customer resource ctr.); *Imprints:* Large Print Press (Lrg Print Pr)
E-mail: jamie.knobloch@gale.com; barb.littfield@galegroup.com; Betsy.M.Brown@thomson.com; jamie.knobloch@cengage.com
Web site: http://www.gale.com/thorndike
Dist(s): **Cengage Gale**; *CIP.*

Thornton Publishing, *(978-1-882913)* 1504 Howard St., New Iberia, LA 70560 USA Tel 337-364-2752; Fax: 318-365-0316; Toll Free: 800-551-3076 Do not confuse with companies with the same or similar names in Littleton, CO, Forest Grove, OR, Burley, ID.

Thornton Publishing, Inc., *(978-0-9670242; 978-0-9719597; 978-0-9723309; 978-1-932344; 978-0-9774761; 978-0-9779960; 978-0-9801941; 978-0-9820838; 978-0-9824705; 978-0-9844838; 978-0-9845417; 978-0-9846342; 978-0-9856151; 978-0-9889816)* 17011 Lincoln Ave., No. 408, Parker, CO 80134 USA Tel 303-794-8888; Fax: 720-863-2013; *Imprints:* Profitable Publishing (Profitable Pubng); Books To Believe In (Bks To Believe In) Do not confuse with companies with the same or similar names in New Iberia, LA, Forest Grove, OR, Burley, ID
E-mail: publisher@bookstobelievein.com
Web site: http://bookstobelievein.com; http://www.getting-published.com
Dist(s): **Follett School Solutions.**

Thorogood (GBR) *(978-1-85418) Dist. by* **Stylus Pub VA.**

Thorpe, Betsy Literary Services, *(978-0-9909865; 978-0-9994302; 978-1-7329958)* 824 Stargard Ct., Charlotte, NC 28270 USA Tel 704-840-8471
E-mail: bthorpe@mac.com
Web site: www.betsythorpe.com.

Thorpe, Sandy, *(978-0-9764147)* 20205 NE 3rd Ct., No. 3, N. Miami Beach, FL 33179 USA
E-mail: sthorpe@trekstuff.com.

Thotsup LLC, *(978-0-9883420)* Orders Addr.: 305 NE 6th St. Suite 588, Grants Pass, OR 97526 USA Tel 541-792-0212.

ThoughtRockets, Inc., *(978-0-9766793)* 2033 Ralston Ave., No. 114, Belmont, CA 94002 USA Tel 650-592-3169 (phone/fax)
E-mail: laura@thoughtrockets.com
Web site: http://www.thoughtrockets.com.

Threatt, Cedric L., *(978-0-9720543)* Div. of Ahava Publishing, LLC, 65 Twisted Oak Cir., Odenville, AL 35120 USA
E-mail: cl3tt@windstream.net
Web site: http://www.Ahavapublishing.org.

Three Angels Broadcasting Network, *(978-0-9718083; 978-0-9720888; 978-1-934869; 978-1-942455)* Orders Addr.: P.O. Box 220, West Frankfort, IL 62896 USA Tel 618-627-4651; Edit Addr.: 3391 Charley Good Rd., West Frankfort, IL 62896 USA
Web site: http://www.3abn.org
Dist(s): **Pacific Pr. Publishing Assn.**

Three Bean Pr., *(978-0-9767276; 978-0-9882212; 978-0-9903315)* P.O. Box 301711, Jamaica Plain, MA 02130 USA (SAN 256-5137) Tel 617-584-5759; 617-827-2042
E-mail: seneca@threebeanpress.com
Web site: http://www.threebeanpress.com
Dist(s): **Partners Bk. Distributing, Inc.**

Three Cents Publishing, *(978-0-9746697)* Orders Addr.: 177 Ocean St.: PO Box 339 Brant Rock Ma02020 Usa, Boston, MA 02020 USA.

Three Chucks, *(978-1-7320463)* 216 Juniper Dr., Lancaster, PA 17602 USA Tel 717-471-8278
E-mail: jj@thelandii.com
Web site: www.jjlandis.com.

Three Conditions Pr., *(978-0-9721241)* Drawer H, Baltimore, MD 21228 USA
Web site: http://www.marylandpoetry.org
Dist(s): **Independent Pubs. Group.**

Three Cord Pr., *(978-1-949785)* P.O. Box 260, Mc Lean, VA 22101 USA Tel 202-494-8072
E-mail: jb@jbsimmons.com
Web site: www.threecordpress.com.

Three Crows Media (NZL) *(978-1-927136) Dist. by* **RiverStream.**

Three Cups, LLC, *(978-0-9794563)* 36 S. Pennsylvania St. Suite 190, Indianapolis, IN 46204 USA Tel 317-633-1456
E-mail: trt@hokansoninc.com; Scott@360GroupOnline.com
Web site: http://www.3cupsbook.com
Dist(s): **Ingram Publisher Services.**

Three Danes Publishing LLC, *(978-0-692-30930-8; 978-0-692-35972-3; 978-0-692-41545-0; 978-0-692-43367-6; 978-0-692-54420-4; 978-0-692-59099-7; 978-0-692-63312-0; 978-0-692-74548-9; 978-0-9983036; 978-0-9983037)* 611 Gen MacAuthur Dr, Morgan City, LA 70380 USA Tel 985-507-3401
E-mail: author@dianamariedubois.com
Web site: www.dianamariedubois.com
Dist(s): **CreateSpace Independent Publishing Platform.**

Three Flower Farm Pr., *(978-0-615-67849-8)* 24 Brooks Rd, Wayland, MA 01778 USA Tel 508-653-9307
E-mail: kjlin306@gmail.com.

Three Four Three Publishing Co., *(978-0-9675286)* 3738 Victoria Dr., West Palm Beach, FL 33406 USA Tel 917-407-2270
E-mail: paulnison@mindspring.com
Web site: http://www.rawlife.com.

Three Hermits Pr., *(978-0-9753906)* P.O. Box 99099, Bennington, VT 05201 USA
E-mail: threehermits@mail.com.

Three Kings Publishing, *(978-0-615-66434-7; 978-0-615-67293-9; 978-0-615-68737-7; 978-0-615-82080-4; 978-0-615-83943-1; 978-0-615-84331-5; 978-0-615-84662-0; 978-0-615-85067-2; 978-0-615-89442-3; 978-0-615-89444-7; 978-0-615-89445-4; 978-0-615-89492-8; 978-0-615-89944-2; 978-0-615-89996-1; 978-0-615-91430-5; 978-0-615-94295-7; 978-0-615-99659-2; 978-0-692-44805-2; 978-0-692-54999-5; 978-1-947018) 115 Canterbury Ct., Princeton, KY 42445 USA Tel 270.601.3401*
Dist(s): **CreateSpace Independent Publishing Platform.**

Three Leaf Pr., *(978-0-9835033)* 97 Woodbridge Dr, Colorado Springs, CO 80906 USA Tel 719-352-5828 Do not confuse with Three Leaf Pr. in Grand Haven, MI
E-mail: 3leafpress@gmail.com.

Three Moons Media, *(978-0-9725164; 978-0-9747440; 978-1-933514)* 1610 Valley Brook Ln., Longview, TX 75605-2676 USA
E-mail: marilyn@threemoonsmedia.com
Web site: http://www.threemoonsmedia.com
Dist(s): **CreateSpace Independent Publishing Platform.**

Three Part Harmony LLC, *(978-0-9800577)* Orders Addr.: 538 Eagle Blvd., Kingsland, GA 31548 USA (SAN 855-0972) Tel 386-717-4583; 912-882-7008
E-mail: threepartharmony@earthlink.net.

Three Pebble Pr., LLC, *(978-0-9799289; 978-0-9960219)* 10040 SW 25th Ave., Portland, OR 97219-6325 USA (SAN 854-7777) Tel 503-977-0944
E-mail: info@yogacalm.org
Web site: http://www.threepebblepress.com
Dist(s): **Follett School Solutions**
Independent Pubs. Group
MyiLibrary.

Three Pups Publishing & Creative Studio, *(978-0-692-99090-2; 978-0-692-13000-1)* 5126 Co Rd 40 NE, NEW LONDON, MN 56273 USA Tel 320-354-4103
E-mail: violetdauk@tds.net
Dist(s): **Ingram Content Group.**

Three Ring Circus Publishing Hse., Inc. *Imprint of* **405 Pubns.**

Three River Rambler, *(978-0-615-20131-3)* 422 W. Cumberland Ave., Knoxville, TN 37901 USA Tel 865-524-9411; Fax: 865-546-3717
E-mail: kac@gulfandohio.com
Web site: http://threeriversrambler.com.

Three Rivers Council, BSA, Incorporated *See* **Alchemy Creative, Inc.**

Three Rooms Pr., *(978-0-9840700; 978-0-9835813; 978-0-9884008; 978-0-9895125; 978-1-941110; 978-1-953103)*
E-mail: info@threeroomspress.com
Web site: http://threeroomspress.com
Dist(s): **MyiLibrary**
Publishers Group West (PGW).

Three Sisters Communication, LLC, *(978-0-9771204)* P.O. Box 280, Star, ID 83669-5015 USA (SAN 256-7970)
E-mail: sfunk624@heritagewifi.com.

Three Sisters Pr., *(978-0-9722999)* P.O. Box 17061, Golden, CO 80402 USA Tel 720-231-6540; Fax: 303-561-0626 Do not confuse with Three Sisters Pr., in Washington, DC
E-mail: violeta134@hotmail.com; sjbrehm@comcast.net.

Three Sisters Publishing Hse., Ltd., *(978-0-9785570)* 32104 Cty. Rd., 1, Saint Cloud, MN 56303 USA Tel 320-654-0001.

Three Sixteen Publishing, *(978-1-937212; 978-1-63664)* 17692 Cowan, Suite 200, Irvine, CA 92614 USA Tel 949-756-8400; Fax: 949-756-8484
E-mail: garyk@codra.com; ben@316publishing.com
Web site: www.316publishing.com
Dist(s): **Whitaker Hse.**

Three Socks Publishing, *(978-0-9789631)* 3351 Charlotte, Brighton, MI 48114 USA.

Three Spots Productions, *(978-0-9744509)* 67 Rutz St., Stamford, CT 06906 USA
E-mail: rarruzza@optonline.net; rarruzza@sparkyswalk.com
Web site: http://www.sparkyswalk.com.

Three Trees, Inc., *(978-0-9789426)* P.O. Box 92, Cottleville, MO 63368-6336 USA Tel 636-561-9184; Fax: 636-561-9184
Web site: http://Petalwinkthefairy.com.

Three Willows Pr., *(978-0-9770279)* 4680 S. 1000 W., Rensselaer, IN 47978 USA.

Three Wise Dogs Pr., *(978-1-7323227)* 3212 Storer Ave., Oakland, CA 94619 USA Tel 469-235-3048
E-mail: chrisgray4020@gmail.com
Web site: www.threewisedogspress.com.

Three Wishes Publishing Co., *(978-0-9796380)* 26500 W. Agoura Rd., Suite 102-754, Calabasas, CA 91302 USA Tel 818-878-0902; Fax: 818-878-1805
E-mail: alva710@aol.com
Web site: http://www.alvasachs.com; http://www.threewishespublishing.com.

Three-D Vision Productions *See* **Soul Vision Works Publishing**

Threshold Editions *Imprint of* **Threshold Editions**

Threshold Editions, Div. of Simon & Schuster, 1230 Ave. of the Americas, New York, NY 10020 USA; *Imprints:* Threshold Editions (ThresholdEdit)
Dist(s): **Simon & Schuster, Inc.**

Thriving Churches International *See* **Pastorpreneur Ministries**

Through Their Eyes Bks., *(978-0-692-34424-8; 978-0-692-41922-9)* 5 Grossweiler Ln., Parlin, NJ 08859 USA Tel 732-439-6719
E-mail: info@throughtheireyesbooks.com; info@victoriannephoenix.com
Web site: www.throughtheireyesbooks.com; www.VictoriannePhoenix.com.

Throwback Publishing, *(978-0-9771630)*
Web site: http://www.throwbackpublishing.com.

Thule Ediciones, S. L. (ESP) *(978-84-933734; 978-84-96473) Dist. by* **IPG Chicago.**

Thumb Print Productions, *(978-0-692-97849-8)* 730 Indian springs rd, Georgetown, TX 78633 USA Tel 512-508-2922
E-mail: cat.davis226@gmail.com
Dist(s): **Ingram Content Group.**

Thumbprint Publishing, *(978-0-9741833)* P.O. Box 9972, Cincinnati, OH 45209 USA Tel 513-207-7550 Do not confuse with Thumbprint Publishing in Studio City, CA
E-mail: rdavis_art@fuse.net
Web site: http://www.connectionssp.org/.

Thumbs Up Pr., *(978-0-9772513)* 3731 Reed's Landing Cir., Midlothian, VA 23113 USA Tel 804-320-8331
E-mail: thumbsuppress@earthlink.net.

Thunder Bay Pr. *Imprint of* **Readerlink Distribution Services, LLC**

Thunder Bay Pr. *Imprint of* **Printers Row Publishing Group**

Thunder Bay Pr., *(978-1-882376; 978-1-933272; 978-1-62026)* 4503 S. M-76, West Branch, MI 48661 USA Tel 989-343-5213
E-mail: sspeigel@partners-east.com; thunderbaypressmichigan@gmail.com
Web site: http://www.thunderpressmichigan.com
Dist(s): **Independent Pubs. Group**
Midpoint Trade Bks., Inc.
Partners Bk. Distributing, Inc.

Thunder Child Productions LLC *See* **Thunder Child Productions LLC. dba PuppyDucks Publishing**

Thunder Child Productions LLC. dba PuppyDucks Publishing, *(978-0-9967949)* 18 Old Stage Coach Rd., Newton, NJ 07860 USA
E-mail: rcruz@puppyducks.com
Web site: www.puppyducks.com.

Thunder Enlightening, *(978-0-9832491)* 11 Cherokee Camp Trail No. 20451, JASPER, GA 30143 USA Tel 706-692-2199
E-mail: chrisrumble@gmail.com
Web site: www.chrisrumble.com.

Thunder Mountain Bks., Co., *(978-0-9968565)* 7946 E. 35th Ave, Denver, CO 80238 USA Tel 303-506-1667
E-mail: anthony@aakerr.com
Web site: www.thundermountainbooks.com.

ThunderBolt Pubns., *(978-0-615-16040-5; 978-0-578-00692-5)* 14785 Kay Ln., Atlanta, GA 30306 USA
E-mail: medemach@bellsouth.net
Web site: http://www.kenmedemach.com
Dist(s): **Lulu Pr., Inc.**

Thunderbolt Publishing *See* **We Do Listen Foundation**

ThunderBolt Publishing, *(978-0-9799671)* 113 14th Ave. S., Nampa, ID 83651 USA Tel 208-466-0122; Fax: 208-466-5294
E-mail: arlette@thunder-bolt.com.

ThunderHousePress, *(978-0-9771154)* Div. of ThunderHouse Entertainment, 6709 La Tijera Blvd., No. 141, Los Angeles, CA 90045 USA
E-mail: reggiecook@yahoo.com
Web site: http://www.thunderhousepress.com.

Thundermist Consulting and Research Co., *(978-0-9759494)* P.O. Box 7023, Cumberland, RI 02864-7023 USA
E-mail: book-sales@thundermist.com
Web site: http://www.thundermist.com; http://thundermist.blogspot.com.

ThunderStone Bks., *(978-1-63411)* 6575 Horse Dr., Las Vegas, NV 89131 USA Tel 801-471-9728
E-mail: rachellynchase@msn.com
Web site: www.thunderstonebooks.com.

Thurman Hse., LLC, *(978-1-58989)* 5 Park Ctr. Ct., Suite 300, Owings Mills, MD 21117 USA Tel 410-902-9100; Fax: 410-902-7210
E-mail: thurmanhouse@ottenheimerpub.com.

Thurston, Dorothy Dawn, *(978-0-692-97524-4; 978-0-578-73563-4)* 2255 So Hill Rd No. 14, St. George, UT 84790 USA Tel 435-669-4359
E-mail: dorotthurst@aol.com
Dist(s): **Ingram Content Group.**

THV Pr., *(978-1-7334107)* 2213 Voorhees Ave., Redondo Beach, CA 90278 USA Tel 424-558-0778
E-mail: shawncbaker9@gmail.com
Web site: http://thehorrorvision.com/.

Thynne, Garry R. *See* **Garry & Donna, LLC**

Tia Chucha Pr., *(978-0-9624287; 978-1-882688)* Div. of Guild Complex, Orders Addr.: Northwestern University Press, Chicago Distribution Center, 11030 S. Langley Ave., Chicago, IL 60628 USA Tel 773-296-1108; Fax:

Publisher Name Index

773-528-5452; Edit Addr.: c/o Arts Bridge, 2936 N. Southport, Suite 210, Chicago, IL 60657 USA
E-mail: guildcomplex@earthlink.net
Web site: http://nupress.northwestern.edu/guild
Dist(s): **Chicago Distribution Ctr.**
Northwestern Univ. Pr.
SPD-Small Pr. Distribution.

Tianjin Education Pr.,
Dist(s): **Chinasprout, Inc.**

Tiaanya Literature Pr., (*978-0-9768679; 978-1-60508*) 613 151st St. Pl., NE, Bellevue, WA 98007 USA
E-mail: tianyapress@hotmail.com
Web site: http://www.tianyapress.com.

Tiara Bks. LLC, (*978-0-9729846*) 62 Birchall Dr., Scarsdale, NY 10583-4503 USA Tel 914-723-9133.

Tickle Me Purple, LLC, (*978-0-9990536; 978-1-7341903*) 3120 Stone Arbor Ln., Glen Allen, VA 23059 USA Tel 803-410-0008
E-mail: tmpurple@yahoo.com
Web site: www.ticklemepurple.com.

Tickling Keys, Inc., (*978-0-9724258; 978-1-932802; 978-1-61547*) 13386 Judy Ave., NW, Uniontown, OH 44685 USA Tel 330-715-2875; Fax: 707-220-4510; *Imprints*: Holy Macro! Books (Holy Macro Bks)
E-mail: consult@mrexcel.com; pub@mrexcel.com
Web site: http://www.holymacrobooks.com
Dist(s): **Ebsco Publishing**
Independent Pubs. Group
MyiLibrary
ebrary, Inc.

TICO Publishing, (*978-0-9777688*) 25045 Jaclyn Ave., Moreno Valley, CA 92557 USA (SAN 850-167X) Tel 562-292-0796
E-mail: tijerin@yahoo.com; books@ticopublishing.com.

Tidal Press, Incorporated *See* **Mushgush Pr.**

Tidal Wave Bks., (*978-0-9724770*) 4476 Wedgewood Dr., Pleasant Grove, UT 84062 USA Tel 801-785-5555; Fax: 801-785-9676
E-mail: sgraham@tidalwavebooks.com
Web site: http://www.tidalwavebooks.com
Dist(s): **Send The Light Distribution LLC.**

Tidal Wave Productions *See* **Black, Judith Storyteller**

TidalWave, (*978-1-948724; 978-1-949738*) 1110 SW 170th Ave., No. 203, Beaverton, OR 97006 USA Tel 503-941-5851
E-mail: ddavis@bluewaterprod.com
Web site: tidalwavecomics.com.

Tide-Mark Pr., Ltd, (*978-0-936846; 978-1-55949; 978-1-59490; 978-1-63114*) Orders Addr.: 22 Prestige Park Cir., East Hartford, CT 06108-1917 USA (SAN 222-1802) Tel 860-683-4499; Fax: 860-683-4055; Toll Free: 800-338-2508; Edit Addr.: 22 Prestige Park Cir., East Hartford, CT 06108-1917 USA (SAN 665-794X)
E-mail: carol@tide-press.com
Web site: http://www.tidemarkpress.com
Dist(s): **BookBaby.**

Tiedeman, Leia *See* **Indigo Hse. Publishing, LLC**

TiffanyJ, (*978-0-692-08394-9*) 536 Portchester Dr., COLUMBIA, SC 29203 USA Tel 803-380-8433
E-mail: tiffywill325@gmail.com
Web site: www.iamtiffanyj.com.

Tiffin Pr. of Maine, (*978-0-9646018*) Div. of Tiffin Pr., 110 Jones Point Rd., Brooksville, ME 04617-3570 USA Tel 207-326-0916
E-mail: tiffinpress@yahoo.com; joanmacc45@gmail.com
Dist(s): **Bilingual Pubns. Co., The.**

Tiger Iron Pr., (*978-0-9787263; 978-0-9851745*) Orders Addr.: 4 Hopscotch Ln., Savannah, GA 31411 USA Tel 478-474-2323
E-mail: Sales@TigerIronPress.com
Web site: http://www.TigerIronPress.com; http://Http://www.TI-Holdings.com
Dist(s): **TI-Holdings Distribution Co.**

Tiger Lily Publishing, (*978-1-880883*) Six Swift Ct., Newport Beach, CA 92663 USA Tel 949-645-5907; Toll Free: 800-950-3237 (800-950-DADS)
E-mail: janedrew@home.com.

Tiger Publishing *See* **Tiger Tale Publishing Co.**

Tiger Stripe Publishing, (*978-0-9905895; 978-1-7355729*)
E-mail: jet@tigerstripepub.com.

Tiger Tale Publishing Co., (*978-0-9787533; 978-0-9859579*) 522 N. Grant Ave., Odessa, TX 79761 USA Tel 432-337-8511; Fax: 432-337-1035
E-mail: cynthia.l.clack@gmail.com
Dist(s): **BookBaby.**

Tiger Tales, (*978-1-58925; 978-1-68010; 978-1-944530; 978-1-6643*) ; *Imprints*: 360 Degrees (360 Degrees)
E-mail: barbknight@tigertalesbooks.com
Web site: http://www.tigertalesbooks.com
Dist(s): **Children's Plus, Inc.**
Midpoint National, Inc.
Penguin Random Hse. Distribution
Penguin Random Hse. LLC.

Tiger Tales Pubns., (*978-0-9610576*) 103 Monte Cresta, Oakland, CA 94611 USA (SAN 264-4347) Tel 510-653-8422.

Tigermoth Pubns., (*978-0-9844785*) P.O. Box 4367, Tulsa, OK 74159 USA (SAN 859-4953)
Web site: http://www.tigermothpublications.com.

TIGO & Co., (*978-0-9761167*) P.O. Box 210066, Dallas, TX 75211-0066 USA Tel 214-330-4420
E-mail: thekingskid1982@sbcglobal.net.

Tike Time, Inc., (*978-0-9729093*) Orders Addr.: 872 S. Milwaukee, No. 125, Libertyville, IL 60048 USA (SAN 255-3058)
E-mail: info@tiketime.com
Web site: http://www.tiketime.com.

Tiki Machine, LLC, (*978-0-615-39785-6; 978-0-615-49510-1; 978-0-615-54715-2; 978-0-615-65028-9; 978-0-9894507; 978-0-692-22851-7*) 160 W. Foothill Pkwy. Suite 105 No. 171, Corona, CA 92882 USA Tel 818-237-6325
Web site: www.tikimachine.blogspot.com; www.tikimachine.com.

Tiki Tales, (*978-0-9740582*) P.O. Box 1194, Haiku, HI 96708 USA
Dist(s): **Booklines Hawaii, Ltd.**

Tikva Corp., (*978-0-615-12595-4*) 40 W. 23rd St., New York, NY 10010-5215 USA
E-mail: emilyl@mkugodessa.org.

Tilbury Hse. Pubs., (*978-0-88448; 978-0-937966; 978-1-937644*) 12 Starr St., Thomaston, ME 04861 USA Toll Free: 800-582-1899 (orders)
E-mail: tilbury@tilburyhouse.com; mariellen@tilburyhouse.com
Web site: http://www.tilburyhouse.com
Dist(s): **INscribe Digital**
Lectorum Pubns., Inc.
Norton, W. W. & Co., Inc.
SPD-Small Pr. Distribution
Univ. Pr. of New England.

Tillinger, Theresa D., (*978-0-692-93617-7; 978-0-578-64581-0*) 5426 Old 96, FRANKLIN, TN 37064 USA Tel 203-526-6806
E-mail: Theresa.tillinger@gmail.com
Dist(s): **Ingram Content Group.**

†Timber Pr., Inc., (*978-0-88192; 978-0-917304; 978-0-931146; 978-0-931340; 978-1-60469; 978-1-64326*) Div. of Workman Publishing Co., Inc., 133 SW Second Ave., Suite 450, Portland, OR 97204-3527 USA (SAN 216-082X) Tel 503-227-2878; Fax: 503-227-3070; Toll Free: 800-327-5680; 20 Lonsdale Rd Swavesey, London, NW6 6RD Tel (01954) 232959; Fax: (01954) 206040
E-mail: info@timberpress.co.uk; publicity@timberpress.com
Web site: http://www.timberpress.com
Dist(s): **Ebsco Publishing**
Meredith Bks.
Open Road Integrated Media, Inc.
Workman Publishing Co., Inc.; *CIP.*

Timberwood Pr., (*978-0-9745454*) 112 NW 156th St., Shoreline, WA 98177 USA Tel 206-295-6186
E-mail: kearney@timberwoodpress.com
Web site: http://www.timberwoodpress.com
Dist(s): **Partners Bk. Distributing, Inc.**

Timbuktu Labs, inc., (*978-0-9978958*) 1051 Elkgrove Ave, APT. 2, Venice, CA 90291 USA Tel 415-528-0207; *Imprints*: Rebel Girls (Rebel Girls)
E-mail: francesca@timbuktu.me
Dist(s): **Simon & Schuster, Inc.**

Time & Chance Publishing, (*978-0-9748274*) Orders Addr.: P.O. Box 488, New York, NY 10116 USA Tel 718-370-3655 [phone/fax]
E-mail: tandchpublishing@yahoo.com; timeandchancepublishing@yahoo.com
Dist(s): **Culture Plus Bks.**

Time & We *See* **Liberty Publishing Hse., Inc.**

Time Dancer Press *See* **5 Star Stories, Inc.**

Time Home Entertainment, Incorporated *See* **Time Inc. Bks.**

Time Inc. Bks., (*978-1-883013; 978-1-929049; 978-1-931933; 978-1-932273; 978-1-932994; 978-1-933405; 978-1-933821; 978-1-60320; 978-1-61893; 978-1-68330; 978-1-5478*) Div. of Time, Inc., 1271 Avenue of the Americas, New York, NY 10020-1201 USA (SAN 227-3209); 225 Liberty St., New York, NY 10281; *Imprints*: Real Simple Books (RealSimpleBks); Liberty Street (LibertySt); Southern Living (SouthernLiving)
Dist(s): **Children's Plus, Inc.**
Hachette Bk. Group
Independent Pubs. Group
MyiLibrary
National Bk. Network
Rowman & Littlefield Publishers, Inc.

Time to Organize, (*978-0-9786733*) 1414 Willow Creek Ln., Shoreview, MN 55126 USA Tel 651-717-1284
E-mail: sara@time2organize.net.

Time to Sign, Incorporated, (*978-0-9713666; 978-0-9765364*) Orders Addr.: P.O. Box 110308, Palm Bay, FL 32911 USA Tel 321-723-6997; Fax: 321-723-6896; Edit Addr.: 426 Olsmar St., Palm Bay, FL 32908 USA Do not confuse with Talking Hands, Inc., in Bangor, ME
E-mail: contact@timetosign.com
Web site: http://www.timetosign.com.

Time Warner Book Group *See* **Hachette Bk. Group**

Time Warner Custom Publishing, (*978-1-931722; 978-1-59995*) 1271 Ave. of the Americas, New York, NY 10020 USA Tel 212-522-7381
Dist(s): **Hachette Bk. Group.**

†Timeless Bks., (*978-0-931454; 978-1-932018*) Div. of Assn. for the Development of Human Potential, Orders Addr.: P.O. Box 3543, Spokane, WA 99220-3543 USA (SAN 211-6502) Fax: 509-838-6652; Toll Free: 800-251-9273; P.O. Box 9, Kootenay Bay, BC V0B 1X0 Tel 250-227-9224 (Business Office); Fax: 250-227-9494 (orders); Toll Free: 800-661-8711 (orders) Do not confuse with Timeless Books in Pickerington, OH
E-mail: info@timeless.org; orders@timeless.org; bookstore@timeless.org; Contact@timeless.org
Web site: http://timeless.org
Dist(s): **Lulu Pr., Inc.**
New Leaf Distributing Co., Inc.; *CIP.*

Timeless Voyager Pr., (*978-1-892264*) Orders Addr.: 249 Iris Ave., Goleta, CA 93117 USA; Edit Addr.: P.O. Box 6678, Santa Barbara, CA 93160 USA (SAN 253-9233) Tel 805-455-8895; Fax: 805-683-4456; Toll Free: 800-576-8463
E-mail: bsh@timelessvoyager.com
Web site: http://www.timelessvoyager.com.

Time-Life Education, Inc., (*978-0-7054; 978-0-7370; 978-0-7835; 978-0-8094*) Orders Addr.: P.O. Box 85026, Richmond, VA 23285-5026 USA Toll Free Fax: 800-449-2011; Edit Addr.: 2000 Duke St., Alexandria, VA 22314 USA Tel 703-838-7000; Fax: 703-518-4124; Toll Free: 800-449-2010
E-mail: education@timelifecs.com
Web site: http://www.timelifeedu.com/
Dist(s): **Hachette Bk. Group.**

†Time-Life, Inc., (*978-0-7835; 978-0-8094*) Div. of Time Warner Co., Orders Addr.: Three Center Plaza, Boston, MA 02108-2084 USA Toll Free Fax: 800-308-1083; 800-286-9471; Toll Free: 800-277-8844; 800-759-0190; Edit Addr.: 8280 Willow Oaks Corporate Dr., Fairfax, VA 22031-4511 USA (SAN 202-7836) Toll Free: 800-621-7026
Web site: http://www.timelifeedu.com
Dist(s): **Hachette Bk. Group**
Time-Life Publishing Warehouse
Worldwide Media Service, Inc.; *CIP.*

Timeout LLC, (*978-1-945034*) 531 77th St., West Des Moines, IA 50266 USA Tel 515-371-9710
E-mail: authorerinwatt@gmail.co.

Times Bks. *Imprint of* **Holt, Henry & Co.**

Times Square Church *See* **Petey, Rock & Roo Children's Pubns.**

Time-Together Pr., (*978-1-888384*) Orders Addr.: P.O. Box 11689, Saint Paul, MN 55111 USA Tel 612-827-1639; Fax: 612-823-6404.

T.I.M.M.-E. Co., Inc., (*978-0-9718232*) Div. of NYC Department of Education, 230 E. 25th St, Suite 2E, New York, NY 10010 USA
E-mail: tbellavia@weareallthesameinside.com; tools4tolerance@aol.com
Web site: http://www.weareallthesameinside.com
Dist(s): **Bookazine Co., Inc.**

Timothy Lane Pr., (*978-0-9744751*) 3211 Rosewood Dr., Hattiesburg, MS 39401-4517 USA
Web site: http://www.robynjackson.com.

Timshel Literature, (*978-0-9708317*) P.O. Box 751, Portsmouth, RI 02871 USA Tel 401-835-7156
E-mail: jkatz@timshelarts.com
Web site: http://www.timshelarts.com.

Timtu Ink., (*978-0-9742460*) 11 Via Acuatica, Rancho Santa Margarita, CA 92688-1482 USA (SAN 255-6146); 31441 Santa Margarita Pkwy., Suite A, No. 341, Rancho Santa Margarita, CA 92688
E-mail: timtuink@dslextreme.com
Web site: http://www.dragonopolis.com; http://www.dragonia.net.

Timun Mas, Editorial S.A. (ESP) (*978-84-480; 978-84-7176; 978-84-7722*) *Dist. by* **AIMS Intl.**

Timun Mas, Editorial S.A. (ESP) (*978-84-480; 978-84-7176; 978-84-7722*) *Dist. by* **Lectorum Pubns.**

Tin Hse. Bks., LLC, (*978-0-9773127; 978-0-9776989; 978-0-9794198; 978-0-9802436; 978-0-9820539; 978-0-9825030; 978-0-9825048; 978-0-9825691; 978-1-935639; 978-0-9850469; 978-0-9857869; 978-1-941040; 978-1-947793; 978-1-951142; 978-1-953534*) 2601 NW Thurman St., Portland, OR 97210 USA (SAN 257-2273) Tel 503-219-0622; Fax: 971-222-2548
E-mail: meg@tinhouse.com
Web site: http://www.tinhouse.com
Dist(s): **MyiLibrary**
Norton, W. W. & Co., Inc.
Penguin Random Hse. Distribution
Penguin Random Hse. LLC.

TinBoxPr., (*978-0-9835546*) 550 E. Fourth No. 4f, Cincinnati, OH 45202 USA Tel 513-871-4205
E-mail: info@tinboxpress.com.

Tingley, Megan Bks. *Imprint of* **Little, Brown Bks. for Young Readers**

TINK INK Publishing, (*978-0-9840916*) 6817 W. Lariat Ln., Peoria, AZ 85383 USA Toll Free: 888-829-5117
Web site: http://www.tinkinkpublishing.com.

Tinker Toddlers *Imprint of* **GenBeam LLC**

TinkerToddlers *See* **GenBeam LLC**

Tinkertown Museum, (*978-0-9793124*) Orders Addr.: P.O. Box 303, Sandia Park, NM 87047 USA (SAN 853-1161) Tel 505-281-5233; Edit Addr.: 121 Sandia Crest Rd., Sandia Park, NM 87047-0303 USA
E-mail: tinker4u@tinkertown.com
Web site: http://www.tinkertown.com.

Tino Turtle Travels, LLC, (*978-0-9793158; 978-0-9816297*) 8550 W. Charleston Blvd., Suite 102-398, Las Vegas, NV 89117 USA (SAN 853-0920) Tel 702-499-4477; Toll Free Fax: 800-656-4641
E-mail: info@tinoturtletravels.com
Web site: http://www.tinoturtletravels.com.

Tinsley Phelps, LLC, (*978-1-934195*) 30 Westgate Pkwy. Suite No. 359, Asheville, NC 28806 USA
E-mail: tinsleyphelps@gmail.com
Web site: http://www.tinsleypheps.com.

Tintagel Publications, (*978-0-9743718*) 45 Lapeer St., Lake Orion, MI 48362 USA.

Tintinatie Publishing Hse., (*978-0-9842625; 978-0-9830884; 978-0-9966540*) 32315 Corte Zamora, Temecula, CA 92592 USA Tel 888-998-4684
E-mail: natalie.tinti@tintinatie.com
Web site: http://tintinatiepublishing.com; http://www.sewingafriendship.com
Dist(s): **Ingram Content Group**
Smashwords.

Tiny Owl Publishing Ltd. (GBR) (*978-1-910328*) *Dist. by* **Consort Bk Sales.**

Tiny Stachel Pr., (*978-0-9845318; 978-0-9849146*) 311 W. Seymour St., Philadelphia, PA 19144 USA Tel 215-266-9587
E-mail: TinySatchelPress@gmail.com
Web site: http://www.TinySatchelPress.com
Dist(s): **Two Rivers Distribution.**

Tiny Tortoise Publishing, LLC, (*978-0-9787477*) Orders Addr.: P.O. Box 752123, Las Vegas, NV 89136 USA Tel 702-798-6646.

TinydragonBks., (*978-0-9906401*) 310 Springs Crossing, Canton, GA 30114 USA Tel 678-895-9689
E-mail: triphughes6@gmail.com
Web site: http://tinydragonbooks.wix.com/hornswoggle.

Tip Top Bks., (*978-0-9846830; 978-0-9904899*)
E-mail: karleen@karleent.com
Web site: http://tiptopbooks.us/; http://www.karleent.com/.

Tip-Of-The-Moon Publishing Co., (*978-0-9657047; 978-0-9746372; 978-0-9829121; 978-0-692-93276-6; 978-1-7326618*) Orders Addr.: 175 Crescent Rd., Farmville, VA 23901 USA; Edit Addr.: c/o Francis E. Wood, Jr., Rte. 2, Box 1725, Farmville, VA 23901 USA Tel 434-392-4195; Fax: 434-392-5724
E-mail: fewwords@moonstar.com
Web site: http://www.tipofthemoon.com.

Tisdale, Edward W., (*978-0-9744166*) 3420 SW 1st Pl., Cape Coral, FL 33914 USA.

Tish & Co. LLC, (*978-0-9793419*) 10 Twin Pines Ln. No. 205, Belmont, CA 94002-3889 USA (SAN 853-182X)
Web site: http://www.tishandcompany.com
Dist(s): **Big Tent Bks.**
Music, Bks. & Business, Inc.

Tishomingo Tree Pr., The, (*978-0-9768861; 978-0-9986961*) 606 Bay St., Hattiesburg, MS 39401 USA
E-mail: info@tishomingotree.com
Web site: http://www.tishomingotree.com.

Titan Bks. Ltd. (GBR) (*978-0-907610; 978-1-84023; 978-1-85286; 978-1-900097; 978-1-84576; 978-1-84856; 978-0-85768; 978-1-78116; 978-1-78276; 978-1-78329; 978-1-78585; 978-1-78565; 978-1-78909*) *Dist. by* **Peng Rand Hse.**

Titan Publishing, (*978-0-9770680*) P.O. Box 2457, Glen Allen, VA 23058 USA (SAN 256-6737)
E-mail: sales@titan-media.com
Web site: http://www.titan-media.com.

Titiris Editorial (Mónica Campadabal Gili) (ESP) (*978-84-92636; 978-84-946949*) *Dist. by* **IPG Chicago.**

Titletown Publishing, LLC, (*978-0-9820009; 978-0-9837547; 978-0-9888605; 978-0-9910699; 978-0-9911938*) Orders Addr.: P.O. Box 12093, Green Bay, WI 54304 USA Tel 920-737-8051; Edit Addr.: 1581 Forest Glen Dr., Green Bay, WI 54304 USA
E-mail: tracy.ertl@titletownpublishing.com
Web site: http://www.titletownpublishing.com
Dist(s): **Independent Pubs. Group**
Midpoint Trade Bks., Inc.
MyiLibrary.

Titlewaves Publishing, (*978-1-57077*) 1579 Kuhio Hwy., Suite 104, Kapaa, HI 96746 USA (SAN 152-1357) Tel 808-822-7449; Fax: 808-822-2312; Toll Free: 800-835-0583
E-mail: transform@hshawaii.com
Web site: http://www.bestbookshawaii.com; http://www.writersdirect.com.

Titus Institute of California, (*978-0-9747452*) P.O. Box 77023, Corona, CA 92877 USA
E-mail: titusbooks@titusinstitute.com
Web site: http://www.titusinstitute.com.

Tiville Press *See* **MiraQuest**

Tixlini Scriptorium, Inc., (*978-0-9723720*) 681 Grove St., San Luis Obispo, CA 93401 USA Tel 805-543-3540; Fax: 805-543-5195
E-mail: tixlini@yahoo.com.

Tizbit Books, LLC, (*978-0-9760553*) 304 Rte. 22 W., Springfield, NJ 07081 USA Tel 973-564-7200; Fax: 973-564-8895
E-mail: jill@tizbitbooks.com
Web site: http://www.tizbitbooks.com.

T.J. Publishing, (*978-0-9760811*) 1099 E. Champlain, Suite A, No. 152, Fresno, CA 93720 USA Tel 559-297-5559
E-mail: tjpub@aol.com.

TJ Studios Ltd,
Dist(s): **Baker & Taylor Publisher Services (BTPS)**
Independent Pubs. Group.

TJG Management Publishing Services, Incorporated *See* **Gonsalves, Theresa Joyce**

TJMF Publishing, (*978-0-9759314; 978-0-9789705; 978-0-9801003; 978-0-9829447; 978-0-9910671*) P.O. Box 2923, Clarksville, IN 47131-2923 USA Tel 812-288-7597; Fax: 812-288-1329
E-mail: jimf@dialinn.com
Web site: http://www.tjmfpublishing.com.

TJMF Publishing Daylight Enterprises *See* **TJMF Publishing**

TK Enterprises, (*978-0-9977327; 978-1-7324354*) 5121 Corbina Way, Oxnard, CA 93035 USA Tel 310-591-2779
E-mail: tke@isle.net
Web site: http://www.archieartichoke.com.

Tkac, John Enterprises LLC, (*978-0-9794454*) Orders Addr.: P.O. Box 7813, Delray Beach, FL 33482 USA Tel 954-632-6360; Fax: 561-330-6917; Edit Addr.: 1095 Hibiscus Ln., Delray Beach, FL 33444 USA
E-mail: adstkac@aol.com
Web site: http://www.jtack.com.

TLC, (*978-0-9853560*) 12 W. End Ave., Old Greenwich, CT 06870 USA Tel 203-344-9548
E-mail: tanyalcecc@optonline.net.

TLC Information Services, (*978-0-9771594*) Orders Addr.: P.O. Box 944, Yorktown Heights, NY 10598 USA Tel 914-248-6770; Edit Addr.: 3 Louis Dr., Katonah, NY 10536-3122 USA
E-mail: ifaywanli@yahoo.com
Web site: http://www.mwsearch.com.

TLC Publishing, (*978-0-9721517*) c/o Tiller Lactation Consulting, 5221 Rushbrook Dr., Centreville, VA 20120

USA Tel 703-266-3823 Do not confuse with TLC Publishing in Paonia, CO
E-mail: stiller@breastfeeding101.com
Web site: http://www.breastfeeding101.com.

TLConcepts, Inc. *Imprint of* **Tender Learning Concepts**

TLK Pubns., (*978-0-9752558; 978-0-9970438*) Div. of TLK Enterprise, 762 Heather Ln., Easton, PA 18040 USA Tel 973-906-2814
E-mail: ugochuik@yahoo.com
Web site: http://www.tlkenterprise.com
Dist(s): **Lulu Pr., Inc.**

TLM Publishing Hse., (*978-0-9748829*) P.O. Box 123, Ozark, MO 65721 USA
E-mail: booksellers@tlmpublishinghouse.com
Web site: http://tlmpublishinghouse.com.

TLOV Publishing *Imprint of* **Kaloustian, Varak**

TLS Consulting *See* **TLS Publishing**

TLS Publishing, (*978-0-9716244*) P.O. Box 403, Dobbs Ferry, NY 10522 USA Tel 914-674-2257 Do not confuse with TLS Publishing in Irvine, CA
E-mail: tls@nvbb.net.

TMD Enterprises, (*978-0-9789297; 978-0-9842980*) 76 E. Blvd., Suite 11, Rochester, NY 14610-1536 USA (SAN 851-9617)
E-mail: dbeerse@tmd-enterprises.com
Web site: www.tmd-enterprises.com.

TNJ Ministries, (*978-0-9762770*) 8214 SW 52nd Ln., Gainesville, FL 32608 USA Tel 352-376-8930
E-mail: tnj_ministries@yahoo.com
Web site: http://www.wtswlg.bravehost.com.

TNMG Publishing, (*978-0-9768297*) P.O. Box 1032, Winter Park, FL 32790-1032 USA
Web site: http://www.tnmg.ws.

TNT Bks., (*978-1-885227*) Orders Addr.: 3657 Cree Dr., Salt Lake City, UT 84120-2867 USA
E-mail: twixom@msn.com.

TNT Publishing *See* **Reasor, Teresa J.**

TNT Publishing Co., (*978-0-9800860*) P.O. Box 456, Richmond, CA 94808-9991 USA (SAN 855-1634) Tel 510-334-2533
E-mail: tanithtyler@yahoo.com
Web site: http://tntpublishing.com.

To The Stars.., (*978-1-943272; 978-0-578-43460-5*) 1051 s. coast hwy 101, encinitas, CA 92024 USA Tel 760-645-1045
E-mail: kari@tothestarsinc.com
Web site: www.tothestarsinc.com
Dist(s): **INscribe Digital**
Independent Pubs. Group
Simon & Schuster, Inc.

Toasted Coconut Media LLC, (*978-1-934906*) 200 Second Ave., 4th Flr., Suite 40, New York, NY 10003 USA (SAN 855-4862) Fax: 646-434-1102
E-mail: donuts@toastedcoconutmedia.com; sales@toastedcoconutmedia.com
Web site: http://www.toastedcoconutmedia.com
Dist(s): **Diamond Comic Distributors, Inc.**
Diamond Bk. Distributors.

Toby & Tutter Publishing, (*978-0-9847812*) 817 W. End Ave. No. 5E, New York, NY 10025-5319 USA (SAN 920-6868) Tel 212-663-8416; Fax: 212-663-8715
E-mail: laura@lauradwightphoto.com
Web site: http://www.tobyandtutter.com.

Toby Pr. LLC, The, (*978-1-902881; 978-1-59264; 978-965-301; 978-965-526; 978-1-61329; 978-0-9891520; 978-1-940516; 978-965-7765; 978-965-7760*) Orders Addr.: P.O. Box 8531, New Milford, CT 06776-8531 USA (SAN 253-9985) Fax: 203-830-8512 (questions & orders); Edit Addr.: P.O. Box 4044, Jerusalem, 91040 ISR Tel 972.2.633.0530; Fax: 972.2.673.9948; *Imprints:* Maggid (Maggid)
E-mail: laura@korenpub.com
Web site: http://www.tobypress.com; http://www.korenpub.com.

Todd Communications, (*978-1-57833; 978-1-878100*) 611 E. 12th Ave. Ste. 102, Anchorage, AK 99501-4663 USA (SAN 298-6280)
E-mail: info@toddcom.com
Dist(s): **Chicago Distribution Ctr.**
Ingram Publisher Services
Wizard Works.

Toe The Line, (*978-0-9792820*) 7071 Warner Ave., Suite F-497, Huntington Beach, CA 92647-5495 USA
E-mail: toetheline@earthlink.net
Web site: http://Toetheline.org.

Tofte Literary Enterprises *See* **Creative Quill Publishing, Inc.**

Together in the Harvest Ministries, Incorporated *See* **Together in the Harvest Pubns./Productions**

Together in the Harvest Pubns./Productions, (*978-0-9637090; 978-1-892853*) Div. of Together In The Harvest Ministries, Inc., Orders Addr.: P.O. Box 612288, Dallas, TX 75261 USA Tel 817-849-8773; Fax: 888-800-1509
E-mail: contact@stevehill.org
Web site: http://www.stevehill.org.

Together, Inc., (*978-0-9764572; 978-1-933463*) 3205 Roosevelt St., NE, Saint Anthony, MN 55418 USA Tel 612-706-7836; Fax: 612-789-8008
E-mail: info@togetherinc.com; pesellors@minn.net
Web site: http://www.togetherinc.com.

Toki Productions, (*978-0-9729527*) P.O. Box 88216, Los Angeles, CA 90009-6888 USA
Web site: http://www.betteroffthan.com.

TokoBooks, LLC, (*978-0-9720436; 978-0-692-16778-6; 978-0-578-62519-5*) 1863c Brattleboro Ct., Kettering, OH 45440 USA (SAN 254-573X) Tel 937-231-4193.

Tokyopop Adult *Imprint of* **TOKYOPOP, Inc.**

TOKYOPOP, Inc., (*978-1-892213; 978-1-931514; 978-1-59182; 978-1-59532; 978-1-59816; 978-1-4278*) Div. of Mixx Entertainment, Inc., 9420 Reseda Blvd Suite 555, Northridge, CA 91324 USA Tel 323-920-5967; *Imprints:* TOKYOPOP Manga (Tokyopop Manga); Tokyopop Kids (TokyoKids); Tokyopop Adult (TokyoAdult)
Web site: http://www.tokyopop.com/
Dist(s): **Children's Plus, Inc.**
Diamond Comic Distributors, Inc.
Diamond Bk. Distributors
MyiLibrary.

Tokyopop Kids *Imprint of* **TOKYOPOP, Inc.**

TOKYOPOP Manga *Imprint of* **TOKYOPOP, Inc.**

Tokyopop Press *See* **TOKYOPOP, Inc.**

Tolana Publishing, (*978-0-9773912; 978-1-935208*) Orders Addr.: P.O. Box 719, Teaneck, NJ 07666 USA
E-mail: tolanapub@yahoo.com
Web site: http://www.tolanapublishing.com
Dist(s): **CreateSpace Independent Publishing Platform**
Ingram Content Group.

Toledo Zoo, The, (*978-0-9776974*) P.O. Box 140130, Toledo, OH 43614 USA Tel 419-385-5721; Fax: 419-724-0068
E-mail: tzgift@toledozoo.org
Web site: http://www.toledozoo.org.

Tolerance Project c/o CSS, (*978-1-942649*) P.O. Box 700, Cos Cob, CT 06807 USA Tel 203-861-4000
E-mail: amynewmark@me.com
Dist(s): **Simon & Schuster**
Simon & Schuster, Inc.

Tolstoy Dom Press, LLC *See* **Vernissage Pr., LLC**

Tolwis, (*978-1-944091*) 5211 S Cobble Creek Rd, Murray, UT 84117 USA Tel 972-522-8552
E-mail: gama@gamathewriter.com.

Tom & Susan Allen *See* **Dean's Bks., Inc.**

Tom Bird Retreats, Inc., (*978-1-62747; 978-0-578-43437-7*) 2220 Corral Rd, Sedona, AZ 86336 USA Tel 928-514-1616
E-mail: john@tombird.com
Web site: www.tombird.com.

Tom Bird Seminars, Inc. *See* **Tom Bird Retreats, Inc.**

Tom Icon, (*978-0-9987089; 978-0-9987089-4-2*) 902 Delrey, College Station, TX 77845 USA Tel 361-332-9104
E-mail: izzofzia@gmail.com
Web site: izzofzia.com.

Tomato Enterprises, (*978-0-9617357*) P.O. Box 73892, Davis, CA 95617 USA (SAN 664-0427) Tel 530-750-1832; Fax: 530-759-9741
E-mail: info@tomatoenterprises.com
Web site: http://www.tomatoenterprises.com.

Tomlinson, Lauresa *See* **Young of Heart Publishing**

Tommy Bks. Pubng., (*978-0-9762690*) Div. of C4 Kids, 1220 N. Las Palmas, No. 201, Los Angeles, CA 90038 USA Tel 323-974-8249
E-mail: renegadepic@earthlink.net
Web site: http://www.tommybooks.net
Dist(s): **C4 Kids.**

Tommye-music Corp. DBA Tom eMusic, (*978-1-62321*) 157-17 Willets Point Blvd., Whitestone, NY 11357 USA Tel 718-609-9420
E-mail: office@tommye-music.com.

Tomoka Pr., (*978-0-9657211*) Orders Addr.: 115 Coquina Ave., Ormond Beach, FL 32174 USA Tel 386-677-4219
E-mail: yvonnewpunnett@aol.com
Web site: http://www.tomokapress.com.

Tomorrow's Forefathers, Inc., (*978-0-9719405; 978-1-940793*) Orders Addr.: P.O. Box 11451, Cedar Rapids, IA 52410-1451 USA
E-mail: info@tomorrowsforefathers.com
Web site: http://www.tomorrowsforefathers.com
Dist(s): **Send The Light Distribution LLC.**

TOMY International, Inc., (*978-1-887327; 978-1-890647*) Orders Addr.: 2021 9th St., SE, Dyersville, IA 52040 USA Tel 563-875-5653; Fax: 563-875-5633; Edit Addr.: 1111 W. 22nd St., Oak Brook, IL 60523-1940 USA
E-mail: rcs@rc2corp.com; credit@rc2corp.com
Web site: http://www.learningcurve.com.

Tonepoet Publishing, (*978-0-922224*) 3069 Alamo Dr., Suite 146, Vacaville, CA 95687 USA (SAN 250-3654)
E-mail: tonepoet@jackshiner.com
Web site: http://www.jackshiner.com.

Tongue Untied Publishing, (*978-0-9745783*) Orders Addr.: P.O. Box 822, Jackson, GA 30233 USA; Edit Addr.: 2571 Hwy. 36 E., Jackson, GA 30233 USA
E-mail: maseyree2001@yahoo.com
Web site: http://www.tongueuntiedpublishing.com
Dist(s): **A & B Distributors & Pubs. Group**
Culture Plus Bk. Distributors.

Tony Franklin Cos., The, (*978-0-9714280*) 521 Ridge Rd., Lexington, KY 40503-1229 USA (SAN 254-2145)
E-mail: tlf3c@aol.com; ed@crystalcommunications.biz
Web site: www.thetonyfranklin.com.

Tony Tales, (*978-0-9791362*) 6024 Cottontail Cove, Las Vegas, NV 89130 USA (SAN 852-5285) Tel 702-245-8624; Fax: 702-898-1359
E-mail: barbarites@aol.com
Web site: www.Tony.

Too Fun Publshing, (*978-0-9773317*) P.O. Box 2098, Vashon Island, WA 98070 USA; 1055 SW 178th St., Vashon Island, WA 98070
E-mail: toofunpublishing@gmail.com.

Too Licky LLC, (*978-0-692-88872-8*) 937 Saratoga Dr., JACKSONVILLE, FL 32207 USA Tel 310-927-5345
Dist(s): **Ingram Content Group.**

Toobeez Project-Connect Joint Venture, (*978-0-9765670*) Div. of Connectable Color Tubes, LLC, Orders Addr.: Project Connect JV 1204 Thomas Rd., Wayne, PA 19087 USA Tel 610-975-0102 (phone/fax)
E-mail: jdonahue@toobeez.com
Web site: http://www.toobeez.com; http://www.project-connect.net.

Toodle-oo Innovative Products, (*978-0-9793145*) 2166 E. Wellington Ave., Santa Ana, CA 92701 USA (SAN 853-0890) Tel 714-558-9537
E-mail: w.kawamoto@cox.net; suszanales@adelphia.net
Web site: http://www.makebubblesgrow.com.

Tool Kits For Kids LLC, (*978-0-9819483*) Orders Addr.: P.O. Box 173, Glen Rock, NJ 07452 USA
Web site: http://www.toolkitsforkids.com.

Tools For Young Historians *Imprint of* **BrimWood Pr.**

TOON Books / RAW Junior, LLC, (*978-0-9799238; 978-1-935179; 978-1-943145*) 27 Greene St., New York, NY 10013 USA (SAN 854-7246) Tel 212-226-0146; Fax: 212-343-9296
E-mail: raw.junior@gmail.com
Web site: http://www.toon-books.com
Dist(s): **Children's Plus, Inc.**
Consortium Bk. Sales & Distribution
Diamond Comic Distributors, Inc.
Diamond Bk. Distributors.

Toonhound Studios, LLC, (*978-0-615-37908-1; 978-0-9833944*) 2761 Peach Dr., Little Elm, TX 75068 USA Tel 214-726-2875
E-mail: kurtz@pvponline.com
Web site: http://www.pvponline.com
Dist(s): **Diamond Comic Distributors, Inc.**

Tootle Time Publishing Co., (*978-0-9721706*) Orders Addr.: P.O. Box 62, Cade, LA 70519 USA Tel 337-364-6410; Fax: 337-364-6415; Edit Addr.: 1031 Mary Rd., New Iberia, LA 70560 USA
E-mail: marycelesteclement@yahoo.com.

Tootsiepup Pr., (*978-0-9970290*) 415 Camino de la Tierra, Corrales, NM 87048 USA Tel 505-440-3208
E-mail: liajesse@yahoo.com
Web site: tootsiesvision.org.

TOP *Imprint of* **Top Pubns., Ltd.**

Top5 Co., The, (*978-0-9746760*) Div. of Bucc Wild LLC, Orders Addr.: 785 E. Tibet Rd., Columbus, OH 43211 USA Tel 614-372-3367
E-mail: bzumfelde@hotmail.com.

Top Cat Publishing, (*978-0-9660839; 978-0-615-76812-0; 978-0-615-76816-8; 978-0-615-76817-5; 978-0-692-29330-0*) PO Box 972, Carlsborg, WA 98324 USA
E-mail: literiter@olypen.com
Web site: http://www.prostar.com/web/L-energy
Dist(s): **CreateSpace Independent Publishing Platform.**

Top Choice Pr., LLC., (*978-0-9761396*) 28 Worcester Sq., Unit No. 1, Boston, MA 02118-2943 USA Tel 617-424-9726; Fax: 617-262-0702
E-mail: tberkan@mindspring.com
Web site: http://topchoicebooks.com.

Top Drawer Ink Corp., (*978-0-9884095; 978-0-9861561; 978-1-948331*) Box 21 2659 NE 35th St., Ocala, FL 34479 USA Tel 352-564-1119
E-mail: editor@topdrawerinkcorp.com
Web site: www.topdrawerinkcorp.com.

Top Drawer Publishing, (*978-0-9887519; 978-0-9916564; 978-1-7347780*) 17888 Rd. 320, Springville, CA 93265 USA Tel 559-359-0568
E-mail: D.G.Stebbins@Azmerith.com
Web site: www.Azmerith.com.

Top Five Bks., (*978-0-9789270; 978-0-9852787; 978-1-938938*) 521 Home Ave., Oak Park, IL 60304 USA (SAN 851-9668) Tel 708-663-5133
E-mail: alex@topfivebooks.com
Web site: http://www.topfivebooks.com
Dist(s): **New Shelves Distribution.**

Top Pubns., Ltd., (*978-0-9666366; 978-1-929976; 978-1-935722; 978-1-7333283*) Div. of Top Ventures, Ltd., Orders Addr.: 12221 Merit Dr., Suite 950, Dallas, TX 75251 USA; Edit Addr.: 3100 Independence Pkwy., No. 311-349, Plano, TX 75075-9152 USA Tel 972-960-2240; Fax: 972-233-0713; *Imprints:* TOP (TOP USA)
E-mail: bill@toppub.com
Web site: http://toppub.com.

Top Quality Pubns., (*978-0-9726311*) Orders Addr.: 3925 Americana Dr., Tampa, FL 33634 USA
E-mail: parfisher@yahoo.com
Web site: http://www.topqualitypublications.org.

Top Shelf *Imprint of* **Jawbone Publishing Corp.**

Top Shelf Productions, (*978-1-891830; 978-1-60309*) Orders Addr.: P.O. Box 1282, Marietta, GA 30061 USA; Edit Addr.: 1150 Hungryneck Blvd. Ste C-348, Mount Pleasant, SC 29464 USA
E-mail: chris@topshelfcomix.com; crownelectric54@gmail.com
Web site: http://www.topshelfcomix.com
Dist(s): **Consortium Bk. Sales & Distribution**
Diamond Comic Distributors, Inc.
Diamond Bk. Distributors
Penguin Random Hse. Distribution
Penguin Random Hse. LLC.

Top Shelf Publishing, (*978-0-9770443*) 4124 W. Fremont Rd., Spokane, WA 99224 USA
Web site: http://www.melodramerica.com/html/grammar_keys.html.

Top That! Publishing PLC (GBR) (*978-1-902973; 978-1-84229; 978-1-84510; 978-1-904748; 978-1-905359; 978-1-84666; 978-1-84956; 978-1-78244; 978-1-78445*) *Dist. by* **IPG Chicago.**

Toplink Publishing, (*978-1-946801; 978-0-9991948; 978-1-947620; 978-1-947938; 978-1-948262; 978-1-948556; 978-1-948779; 978-1-948962; 978-1-949169; 978-1-949502; 978-1-949804; 978-1-970066; 978-1-950256; 978-1-950540; 978-1-7330557; 978-1-7330558; 978-1-7330559; 978-1-7330560; 978-1-7330561; 978-1-7331328; 978-1-7331329; 978-1-7331330; 978-1-7331331; 978-1-7331332; 978-1-7333368; 978-1-7333603; 978-1-7334214; 978-1-951464; 978-1-951518; 978-1-7340699; 978-1-7342919; 978-1-7342920*) 2227 Natmore Rd., Kelly, NC 28448 USA Tel 828-483-8791
E-mail: contact@toplinkpublishing.com
Web site: www.toplinkpublishing.com.

TopNotch Pr., (*978-0-930037*) P.O. Box 1185, Merchantville, NJ 08109 USA (SAN 669-7798) Tel 609-364-6902; Fax: 856-488-0291
E-mail: maryann@maryanndiorio.com
Web site: http://www.maryanndiorio.com.

Tor Bks. *Imprint of* **Doherty, Tom Assocs., LLC**

Tor Fantasy *Imprint of* **Doherty, Tom Assocs., LLC**

Tor Romance *Imprint of* **Doherty, Tom Assocs., LLC**

Tor Science Fiction *Imprint of* **Doherty, Tom Assocs., LLC**

Tor Teen *Imprint of* **Doherty, Tom Assocs., LLC**

†Torah Aura Productions, (*978-0-933873; 978-1-891662; 978-1-934527*) 4423 Fruitland Ave., Los Angeles, CA 90058 USA (SAN 692-7025) Fax: 323-585-0327; Toll Free: 800-238-6724
E-mail: jane@torahaura.com
Web site: http://torahaura.com; *CIP.*

Torah Excel, (*978-1-930925*) 6415 N. Sacramento, Chicago, IL 60645 USA Tel 773-743-7915; Fax: 773-508-9874; *Imprints:* Shazak Productions (Shazak Prods)
E-mail: torahxl@megsinet.com
Web site: http://torahxl.com.

Torah Institute of Baltimore, (*978-0-9767505*) 35 Rosewood Ln., Owings Mills, MD 21117-3704 USA Tel 410-654-3500 ext. 3; Fax: 443-394-5999
E-mail: tibexec@comcast.net
Web site: http://www.torahinstitute.org.

Torah Umesorah Pubns., (*978-0-914131; 978-1-878895*) 1090 Coney Island Ave. 3rd Flr., Brooklyn, NY 11230 USA (SAN 218-9992) Tel 718-259-1223; Fax: 718-259-1795.

Torch Flame Media, (*978-0-9988161*) 7162 Beverly Blvd, No. 225, Los Angeles, CA 90036 USA Tel 310-619-4251; Fax: 310-619-4251
E-mail: helena@girlunfiltered.com.

Torch Legacy Pubns., (*978-0-9763487; 978-0-9785333; 978-0-615-26544-5; 978-0-615-30182-2; 978-0-615-30191-4; 978-0-615-37024-8; 978-0-9830141; 978-0-9849441*) P.O. Box 165046, Irving, TX 75016 USA
E-mail: torchlegacypublications@msn.com
Web site: http://www.torchlegacy.com
Dist(s): **Send The Light Distribution LLC**
Smashwords.

Torchflame Bks. *Imprint of* **Light Messages Publishing**

Torchlight Publishing, (*978-1-887089; 978-0-9779785; 978-0-9817273; 978-1-937731*) Orders Addr.: P.O. Box 52, Badger, CA 93603 USA Tel 559-337-2200; Fax: 559-337-2354; Toll Free: 888-867-2458 Do not confuse with Torchlight Publishing in Colorado Springs, CO
E-mail: torchlightpublishing@yahoo.com
Web site: http://www.torchlight.com
Dist(s): **BookMasters**
Independent Pubs. Group.

Torgerson Meadows Publishing, (*978-0-9767116*) 37492 Outpost Rd., NW, Grygla, MN 56727 USA Tel 218-294-6644
E-mail: sstorg@webtv.net
Web site: http://www.taolc.com.

Tornado Creek Pubns., (*978-0-9652219; 978-0-9740881; 978-0-9821529*) P.O. Box 8625, Spokane, WA 99203-8625 USA Tel 509-838-7114; Fax: 509-455-6798; 1308 E. 29th Ave., Spokane, WA 99203 Tel 509-838-7114; Fax: 509-445-6798
E-mail: tcpoffice@comcast.net
Web site: http://www.tornadocreekpublications.com.

Torque Bks. *Imprint of* **Bellwether Media**

Torres, Eliseo & Sons, (*978-0-88303*) P.O. Box 2, Eastchester, NY 10709 USA (SAN 207-0235).

TortoiseBrand Bks., (*978-0-9847107*) 1810 S. El Camino Real Suite B101, Encinitas, CA 92024 USA Tel 760-213-3722 (phone/fax)
E-mail: lovely@AliciaPrevin.com
Web site: www.AliciaPrevin.com.

Tortuga Pr., (*978-1-889910*) Orders Addr.: PMB 181, 2777 Yulupa Ave., Santa Rosa, CA 95405 USA (SAN 299-1756) Tel 707-544-4720; Fax: 707-544-5609; Toll Free: 866-4 TORTUGA
E-mail: info@tortugapress.com
Web site: http://www.tortugapress.com
Dist(s): **Follett School Solutions**
Independent Pubs. Group.

Torty2 Publishing, (*978-0-9996326*) 1372 Trieste Ln., Carpinteria, CA 93013 USA Tel 805-722-7248
E-mail: Torty2@aol.com
Web site: Torty2Publishing.com.

Total 180 Pr., (*978-0-9744118*) Orders Addr.: P.O. Box 984, Monroe, WA 98272 USA Tel 360-794-9129; Edit Addr.: 18578 Rainier View Rd., Monroe, WA 98272 USA
E-mail: susan@howardcorp.com
Web site: http://www.total180.com.

Total Career Resources, (*978-0-615-24214-9; 978-0-9849970*) 2000 Bering Dr., Suite 460, Houston, TX 77057 USA Tel 713-784-3197.

Total Outreach for Christ Ministries, Inc., (*978-0-9745834*) 3411 Asher Ave., Little Rock, AR 72204 USA Tel 501-663-0362; Fax: 501-663-0390
E-mail: tofchristm@aol.com
Web site: http://theonenewman.org.

Total Publishing & Media *Imprint of* **Yorkshire Publishing Group**

Total Recall Learning, Inc., (*978-0-9716238*) 3944 Murphy Canyon Rd., Suite C203, San Diego, CA 92123 USA Tel 858-268-8875; *Imprints:* ExamWise (ExamWise)
E-mail: sales@totalrecallpress.com
Web site: http://www.totalrecalllearning.com
Dist(s): **Baker & Taylor Publisher Services (BTPS).**

Total Wellness *See* **Total Wellness Publishing**

Total Wellness Publishing, *(978-0-9744585)* 14545 Glenoak Pl., Fontana, CA 92337 USA
E-mail: micheleiqbal@netzero.net
Web site: http://www.Totalwellnesspublishing.com; http://www.micheleiqbal.com
Dist(s): **Distributors, The.**

Totally Outdoors Publishing, Inc., *(978-0-9726653)* 7284 Raccoon Rd., Manning, SC 29102 USA
Web site: http://www.totallyoutdoorspublishing.com.

TotalRecall Pubns., *(978-0-9704684; 978-1-59095; 978-1-64883)* Orders Addr.: 1103 Middlecreek, Friendswood, TX 77546 USA Tel 281-992-3131; Edit Addr.: 1103 Middlecreek, Friendswood, TX 77546 USA Tel 281-992-3131
E-mail: Sales@totalrecallpress.com; Bruce@totalrecallpress.com
Web site: http://www.mousegate.com; http://www.totalrecallpress.com
Dist(s): **Ingram Bk. Co.**
Ingram Content Group Inc.
MyiLibrary
ebrary, Inc.

Totem Tales Publishing, *(978-0-9843228)* 219 Salzedo St., Royal Palm Beach, FL 33411 USA Tel 561-537-2522
E-mail: books@totemtales.com; danbodenstein@yahoo.com
Web site: http://www.totemtales.com
Dist(s): **BookBaby.**

Toucan Pr., Inc., *(978-0-9744926)* 307 Sweet Bay Pl., Carrboro, NC 27510-2378 USA.

Toucan Valley Pubns., Inc., *(978-0-9634017; 978-1-884925)* Orders Addr.: P.O. Box 15520, Fremont, CA 94539-2620 USA Tel 510-498-1009; Fax: 510-498-1010; Toll Free Fax: 888-391-6943; Toll Free: 800-236-7946
E-mail: ben@toucanvalley.com; query@toucanvalley.com
Web site: http://www.toucanvalley.com
Dist(s): **Grey Hse. Publishing.**

Touch Books, Incorporated *See* **Minardi Photography**

Touch the Music, *(978-0-9837585)* 110 Konner Ave., Pine Brook, NJ 07058 USA (SAN 860-2794) Tel 973-220-9785
E-mail: Claudia@Touchthemusic.us
Web site: www.Touchthemusic.us.

TouchPoint Pr., *(978-0-615-97340-1; 978-0-615-97374-6; 978-0-615-97375-3; 978-0-615-97554-2; 978-0-615-97555-9; 978-0-615-97556-6; 978-0-615-97884-0; 978-0-615-97885-7; 978-0-615-98003-4; 978-0-615-98400-1; 978-0-615-98753-8; 978-0-615-99258-7; 978-0-615-99410-9; 978-0-692-20053-7; 978-0-692-02416-4; 978-0-692-02417-1; 978-0-692-24865-2; 978-0-692-24920-8; 978-0-692-25104-1; 978-0-692-25653-4; 978-0-692-25669-5; 978-0-692-27195-7; 978-0-692-28049-2; 978-0-692-28145-1; 978-0-692-28149-9; 978-0-692-28179-6;) Orders Addr.: 46-3 Brookland St, Brookland , AR 72401 USA Tel 662-595-4162; Fax: 870-200-6702; Edit Addr.: 46-3 Brookland St., Brookland, AR 72417 USA Tel 662-595-4162; Fax: 870-200-6702*
E-mail: info@touchpointpress.com; media@touchpointpress.com
Web site: http://www.touchpointpress.com
Dist(s): **CreateSpace Independent Publishing Platform.**

TouchSmart Publishing, LLC, *(978-0-9765060; 978-0-9787517)* 167 Old Richmond Rd., Swanzeyti, NH 03446 USA (SAN 256-3835) Tel 603-352-7282; a/o Touchsmart Publishing (Distributor), LLC, 6522 Waldorf Pl., Cincinnati, OH 45230 (SAN 631-8703) Tel 513-225-8765; Fax: 206-666-4856
E-mail: ccardine@touchsmart.net
Web site: http://www.touchsmart.net.

Touchstone *Imprint of* **Touchstone**

Touchstone, *(978-0-7432)* 1230 Avenue of the Americas, New York, NY 10020 USA; *Imprints:* Touchstone (TouchImp)
Dist(s): **Simon & Schuster, Inc.**

Touchstone Center for Children, Incorporated, The *See* **Touchstone Ctr. Pubns.**

Touchstone Ctr. Pubns., *(978-1-929299)* Div. of Touchstone Center for Children, Inc., Orders Addr.: 141 E. 88th St., New York, NY 10028 USA (SAN 265-3664) Tel 212-831-7717
E-mail: rlewis212@aol.com
Web site: http://www.touchstonecenter.net
Dist(s): **State Univ. of New York Pr.**

Touchstone Communications, *(978-0-9790775; 978-0-9973569)* Orders Addr.: P.O. Box 396, Oneonta, NY 13820-0396 USA (SAN 852-3835); 291 Chestnut St., Box 396, Oneonta, NY 13820
E-mail: Touchstonecom@stny.rr.com; bd@bookpublishguide.com
Web site: http://Touchstone-com.com.

Touchstones Discussion Project, *(978-1-878461; 978-1-937742)* PO Box 2329, Annapolis, MD 21404-2329 USA Toll Free: 800-456-6542
Web site: http://www.touchstones.org.

Toure, Khari, *(978-0-692-82465-8)* .

Tower Pr., *(978-0-615-67490-2)* 7211 Brickyard Rd., Potomac, MD 20854 USA Tel 202 944 3810; Fax: 202 944 3826
Dist(s): **CreateSpace Independent Publishing Platform.**

Towers Maguire Publishing *Imprint of* **Local History Co., The**

Town & Country Reprographics, *(978-0-9725808; 978-0-9754383; 978-0-9771894; 978-0-9794860; 978-0-9801439; 978-0-9825067; 978-0-9835219; 978-0-9896702; 978-0-9968302; 978-0-692-16890-5)* 230 N. Main St., Concord, NH 03301 USA (SAN 254-959X)
Web site: http://www.reprographic.com
Dist(s): **Smashwords.**

Towne, Russ, *(978-0-692-56808-8; 978-0-692-56837-8; 978-0-692-57310-5; 978-0-692-57313-6; 978-0-692-57322-8; 978-0-692-57325-9; 978-0-692-57597-0; 978-0-692-57600-7; 978-0-692-57656-4; 978-0-692-57660-1; 978-0-692-57663-2; 978-0-692-60270-6; 978-0-692-70008-2; 978-0-692-70460-8; 978-0-692-70932-0; 978-0-692-72351-7; 978-0-692-74214-3; 978-0-692-77261-4; 978-0-692-80418-6; 978-0-692-80423-0; 978-0-692-81855-8; 978-0-692-90776-4; 978-0-692-94549-0; 978-1-948245; 978-0-578-51700-1) 1114 Bucknam Av, CAMPBELL, CA 95008 USA Tel 408-364-6987.*

Towne Woman Creations, *(978-0-9981499)* 2805 Mowrey Dr., Bloomington, IL 61704 USA Tel 360-485-8078
E-mail: Tammychewe@msn.com.

Townsend, Diana, *(978-0-615-15882-2; 978-0-615-16214-0)* 3432 Briaroaks Dr., Garland, TX 75044 USA Tel 214-703-9718
E-mail: dianatownsend@aol.com
Dist(s): **Lulu Pr., Inc.**

Townsend, J. N. Publishing *Imprint of* **PublishingWorks**

Townsend Pr., *(978-0-944210; 978-1-59194)* 439 Kelly Dr., West Berlin, NJ 08091-9284 USA (SAN 243-0444) Toll Free Fax: 800-225-8894; Toll Free: 800-772-6410
E-mail: townsendcs@aol.com; orderstp@aol.com; emily@townsend.press
Web site: http://www.townsendpress.com.

Townsend Pr. - Sunday Schl. Publishing Board, *(978-0-910683; 978-1-932972; 978-1-939225; 978-1-945356; 978-1-949052)* 330 Charlotte Ave., Nashville, TN 37201-1188 USA (SAN 275-8598) Tel 615-256-2480; Fax: 615-242-4929; Toll Free: 800-359-9398
E-mail: bavant@sspbnbc.com.

Townsends, *(978-0-9997620; 978-0-9998644; 978-1-948837)* P.O. Box 415, Pierceton, IN 46562 USA Tel 574-594-3932
E-mail: jon.townsend1@gmail.com
Web site: townsends.us.

Toy Box Productions, *(978-1-887729; 978-1-932332)* Div. of CRT, Custom Products, Inc., 7532 Hickory Hills Ct., Whites Creek, TN 37189 USA Tel 615-299-0822; 615-876-5490; Fax: 615-876-3931; Toll Free: 800-750-1511
E-mail: leeann@crttoybox.com
Dist(s): **Christian Bk. Distributors.**

Toy Quest, *(978-0-9767325; 978-0-9786246)* Manley, 2229 Barry Ave., Los Angeles, CA 90064-1401 USA.

Toy Rocket Studios, LLC, *(978-0-615-23521-9; 978-0-578-15192-2)* Orders Addr.: 5410 Fallen Timbers Dr., West Chester, OH 45069 USA; Edit Addr.: 814 St.Clair Ave, Hamilton, OH 45015 USA
E-mail: ToyRocketLaunch@gmail.com
Web site: http://www.ToyRocketStudiosLLC.com; http://www.ToyRocketLaunch.com.

Toy Truck Publishing, *(978-0-9764983)* 4602 Lilac Ln., Lake Elmo, MN 55042 USA (SAN 256-3754) Tel 612-716-8383; Fax: 651-275-1279
E-mail: sales@toytruckpublishing.com
Web site: http://www.toytruckpublishing.com.

Toy Vey Toys, *(978-0-615-15195-3; 978-0-615-21091-9; 978-0-578-00861-5; 978-0-9819861; 978-1-935592)* Orders Addr.: 1420 Locust St., No. 10F, Philadelphia, PA 19102 USA (SAN 913-4190) Tel 1-267-847-9018
E-mail: elik@sportschallengenetwork.com
Web site: www.sportschallengenetwork.com.

Toys 'n Things Press *See* **Redleaf Pr.**

TPBMedia, *(978-0-692-95299-3)* 3212 Shoreview, Highland Village, TX 75077 USA Tel 214-995-0229
E-mail: tbevins@verizon.net
Dist(s): **Independent Pub.**

Tpprince Esquire *See* **Tpprince Esquire International**

Tpprince Esquire International, *(978-0-9790110; 978-0-692-22159-4; 978-1-63365)* 7840 Cassia Ct., Saint Louis, MO 63123 USA (SAN 852-2219) Tel 41794299891 (swiss portable); 41218821971 (swiss main office); Cretillon 9, Froideville, ch 1055 Fax: +41218821971
E-mail: dansekarski@gmail.com; tpprince_esq@yahoo.com; dan.sekarski@bluewin.ch; tpprince@tpprince-esquire.com; dan.sekarski@bluewin.ch; sandrinesekarski@bluewin.ch
Web site: http://stores.lulu.com/tpprince_esquire; http://tpprince-esquire.com.

TPRS Publishing, Incorporated *See* **Fluency Matters**

TR Bks., *(978-0-9788969)* 2430 N. Penn Ave., Independence, KS 67301 USA (SAN 851-8882) Tel 620-331-4486; *Imprints:* Exhibit A (Exhibit A).

Tracepaper Bks. Inc., *(978-0-9792728)* 68 Ridgewood Ave., Selden, NY 11784 USA
Web site: http://www.tracepaper.net.

Trachtman, Joseph, *(978-0-9795170)* 5008 Pullman Ave. NE, Seattle, WA 98105 USA.

Traci A Patterson, *(978-0-578-58123-1; 978-0-578-71731-9; 978-0-578-71732-6)*
E-mail: amazinginfluence@gmail.com
Dist(s): **Ingram Content Group.**

Tracks Publishing, *(978-1-884654; 978-1-935937)* 140 Brightwood Ave., Chula Vista, CA 91910 USA Tel 619-476-7125; Fax: 619-476-8173; Toll Free: 800-443-3570
E-mail: tracks@cox.net
Web site: http://www.startupsports.com
Dist(s): **Ebsco Publishing**
Independent Pubs. Group
MyiLibrary
ebrary, Inc.

Tractor Mac Inc., *(978-0-9788496; 978-0-9826870; 978-0-9888329)* 121 Transylvania Rd., Roxbury, CT 06783 USA Tel 860-210-9805; Fax: 260-210-9805
E-mail: bsteers@tractormac.com
Web site: http://tractormac.com.

Tracy, Jean A. *See* **KidsDiscuss.com**

TracyTrends, *(978-0-9708226; 978-0-9814737; 978-0-615-11462-0)* 7710-C Somerset Bay, Indianapolis, IN 46240-3336 USA Toll Free: 800-840-6118
E-mail: tracytrends@aol.com
Web site: http://www.tracytrends.com.

Tradewind Bks. (CAN) *(978-1-896580; 978-1-926890) Dist. by* **Orca Bk Pub.**

Tradition Publishing, *(978-0-9789969)* 1823 Hart Leonard Rd., Cornerville, TN 37047 USA (SAN 852-1603)
Web site: http://www.carouselcarving.com.

Trafalgar Square Bks., *(978-0-943955; 978-1-57076; 978-1-64601)* Orders Addr.: P.O. Box 257, North Pomfret, VT 05053 USA Tel 802-457-1911; Fax: 802-457-1913; Edit Addr.: Howe Hill Rd., North Pomfret, VT 05053 USA
E-mail: mcook@trafalgarbooks.com
Web site: http://www.horseandriderbooks.com; http://www.trafalgarbooks.com/
Dist(s): **Follett School Solutions**
Legato Pubs. Group
MyiLibrary
Publishers Group West (PGW)
Perseus Bks. Group.

Trafalgar Square Publishing, *(978-0-943955; 978-1-57076)* Orders Addr.: P.O. Box 257, North Pomfret, VT 05053-0257 USA (SAN 213-8859) Tel 802-457-1911; Fax: 802-457-1913; Toll Free: 800-423-4525; Edit Addr.: 388 Howe Hill Rd., North Pomfret, VT 05053 USA Tel 802-423-4525; 802-457-1913
E-mail: tsquare@sover.net
Web site: http://www.trafalgarbooks.com; http://www.horseandriderbooks.com
Dist(s): **Independent Pubs. Group**
MyiLibrary.

Trafford Publishing, *(978-1-55212; 978-1-55369; 978-1-55395; 978-1-4120; 978-1-4122; 978-1-4251; 978-1-4269; 978-1-4669; 978-1-4907; 978-1-6987)* 1663 Liberty Dr., Suite 200, Bloomington, IN 47403 USA Tel 812-334-5345; 812-334-5223; 888-232-4444; Fax: 812-339-6554
E-mail: orders@trafford.com; info@trafford.com
Web site: http://www.trafford.com
Dist(s): **Author Solutions, Inc.**
Baker & Taylor Publisher Services (BTPS)
CreateSpace Independent Publishing Platform
DecisionPro, Inc.
Ediciones Universal
Wizard Works
Zondervan.

Trahan, Virginia A. - Author, *(978-0-692-74059-0; 978-0-692-78996-4; 978-0-692-80854-2; 978-0-692-89332-6; 978-0-692-90547-0)* 1649 Sugar Loaf Ln., SAINT AUGUSTINE, FL 32092 USA Tel 904-940-9193; *Imprints:* CVTrahan Publishing, LLC (CVTrahan).

Trail, George (GBR) *(978-0-9559927) Dist. by* **LuluCom.**

Trail Trotter Pr. *Imprint of* **Run to Win, LLC**

Trail Trotters Bk. Ranch, *(978-0-9763209)* 616 N. Aurelius Rd., Mason, MI 48854 USA Tel 517-244-0727
E-mail: rosewoodbouz@aol.com
Web site: http://www.ponypointers.com.

Trails Bks. *Imprint of* **Bower Hse.**

Trails of Discovery, *(978-0-9788926)* 31071 Marbella Vista, San Juan Capistrano, CA 92675 USA.

Train 4 Safety Pr., *(978-0-9987912; 978-1-947690)* 5682 Londonderry Loop NW, bremerton, WA 98312 USA Tel 808-371-2320
E-mail: heather_lynn_beal@yahoo.com
Web site: http://www.train4safety.com.

Training Grounds, *(978-0-9729057)* P.O. Box 5631, Tucson, KY 85703 USA
E-mail: sjrose@plantagriculture.org
Web site: http://www.plantagriculture.org.

Training Solutions, LLC, *(978-0-692-75590-7; 978-0-578-20525-0; 978-0-692-13028-5; 978-0-692-13029-2)* 3928 Ulu Alii St., Kalaheo, HI 96741 USA Tel 508-454-5096; P.O. Box 411387, Kalaheo, HI 96741
E-mail: davene13j@gmail.com
Web site: markjbooks.com.

Train-Up A Child, LLC, *(978-0-9703069)* P.O. Box 1122, Jenks, OK 74037 USA Tel 918-299-8178 (phone/fax)
E-mail: TrainUpStudies@aol.com
Web site: http://www.trainupstudies.com.

Traitor Dachshund, LLC *See* **Minted Prose, LLC**

Trammel, Crystal, *(978-0-9746327)* 133 Montego Dr., Mesquite, TX 75149-1708 USA
E-mail: minc34@hotmail.com.

Tramuntana Editorial (ESP) *(978-84-16578; 978-84-17303; 978-84-939157; 978-84-940213; 978-84-940475; 978-84-941662; 978-84-941825; 978-84-942841; 978-84-942842) Dist. by* **Lectorum Pubns.**

Tranquility Publishing *See* **Tranquility Ranch Publishing**

Tranquility Ranch Publishing, *(978-0-9747425)* 25796 Tranquility Ln., Magnolia, TX 77355 USA
E-mail: gcadwalder@aol.com.

†Transaction Pubs., *(978-0-7658; 978-0-87855; 978-0-88738; 978-1-56000; 978-1-4128)* Div. of Taylor & Francis Group, Orders Addr.: Taylor & Francis Group LLC 7625 Empire Dr., Florence, KY 41042-2919 USA Toll Free Fax: 800-248-4724; Toll Free: 800-634-7064
E-mail: orders@transactionpub.com
Web site: http://www.transactionpub.com
Dist(s): **MyiLibrary**
ebrary, Inc.; *CIP.*

Transaltar Publishing, *(978-0-9771802; 978-0-615-20263-1; 978-0-615-20419-2; 978-0-615-20678-3; 978-0-615-20814-5)* 5517 E St., Sacramento, CA 95819 USA
E-mail: publisher@transaltar.com
Web site: http://www.transaltar.com; http://www.heathbuckmaster.com/
Dist(s): **CreateSpace Independent Publishing Platform**
Lulu Pr., Inc.

Transatlantic Arts, Inc., *(978-0-693)* P.O. Box 6086, Albuquerque, NM 87197 USA (SAN 202-7968) Tel 505-898-2289 Do not confuse with Trans-Atlantic Pubns., Inc., Philadelphia, PA.
E-mail: books@transatlantic.com
Web site: http://www.transatlantic.com/direct
Dist(s): **MyiLibrary.**

Trans-Atlantic Pubns., Inc., 33 Ashley Dr., Schwenksville, PA 19473 USA (SAN 694-0234) Tel 215-717-4655; Fax: 484-919-6486 Do not confuse with Transatlantic Arts, Inc., Albuquerque, NM
E-mail: order@transatlanticpub.com
Web site: http://www.transatlanticpub.com.

Transcontinental Education Inc., *(978-0-692-84805-0; 978-0-692-94946-7)* 11612 Brigit Ct, BOWIE, MD 20720 USA Tel 202-380-7738
E-mail: jeffwcrawford5+LVP0003383@gmail.com; jeffwcrawford5+LVP0003383@gmail.com.

Transcontinental Music Pubns., *(978-0-8074)* Div. of URJ, 633 Third Ave., 6th Flr., New York, NY 10017-6778 USA Tel 212-650-4101; Fax: 212-650-4109
E-mail: tmp@uahc.org
Web site: http://www.eTranscon.com
Dist(s): **Leonard, Hal Corp.**

Transfuzion Publishing *See* **Caliber Comics**

Trans-Galactic Pubns., *(978-0-9616078)* 20 Sunnyside Ave. Suite A134, Mill Valley, CA 94941 USA (SAN 698-0899)
E-mail: transpubls@aol.com.

Transitional Pr., *(978-0-9960369)* 8679 SW 51st St., Cooper City, FL 33328 USA Tel 954-298-8178
E-mail: Mortlaitner@bellsouth.net.

Transmundane Press *See* **Transmundane Pr., LLC**

Transmundane Pr., LLC, *(978-0-692-52614-9; 978-0-9984983; 978-1-948309)* Orders Addr.: 11150 Ana Ln., Guthrie, OK 73044 USA; Edit Addr.: 1332 Elysian Fields Ave, New Orleans, LA 70117 USA Tel 850-774-3366
Dist(s): **CreateSpace Independent Publishing Platform.**

Transworld Publishers Ltd. (GBR) *(978-0-552; 978-0-85752; 978-0-85750) Dist. by* **Children Plus.**

Transworld Publishers Ltd. (GBR) *(978-0-552; 978-0-85752; 978-0-85750) Dist. by* **IPG Chicago.**

Trapper Creek Museum Sluice Box Productions, *(978-0-9718302)* Orders Addr.: P.O. Box 13011, Trapper Creek, AK 99683 USA Tel 907-733-2555; Edit Addr.: Mile 3/4 Petersville Rd., Trapper Creek, AK 99683 USA
E-mail: info@trappercreekmuseum.com
Web site: http://www.trappercreekmuseum.com; http://www.sluiceboxproductions.com.

Trash, Steve Enterprises, *(978-0-9652542)* 975 Old Dirt Rd., Spruce Pine, AL 35585 USA.

Travel 4 Life !, *(978-0-9749441)* 2040 E. 22nd St., Box 911, Fremont, NE 68025 USA Tel 402-727-1559
E-mail: deanjcbs4u@yahoo.com
Web site: http://www.travel4life.org.

Travel America Bks., *(978-0-9795867)* 64 Vanderbilt Ave., Floral Park, NY 11001 USA Tel 516-354-2615
E-mail: shajovin@aol.com.

Travel With Me & See, *(978-0-9600423)* 1518 4th Ave N, Seattle, WA 98109 USA
E-mail: nancy@travelwithmeandsee.com
Web site: www.travelwithmeandsee.com.

TravelBrains, Inc., *(978-0-9705809; 978-1-933763)* 14 Tether Rd, Bedford, NH 03110-5660 USA
Web site: http://www.travelbrains.com.

Travelers' Tales, Incorporated *See* **Travelers' Tales/Solas House, Inc.**

Travelers' Tales/Solas House, Inc., *(978-1-885211; 978-1-932361; 978-1-60952)* 2320 Bowdoin St., Palo Alto, CA 94306 USA
Web site: http://www.travelerstales.com
Dist(s): **Baker & Taylor Publisher Services (BTPS)**
MyiLibrary
Publishers Group West (PGW)
ebrary, Inc.

Traveling Satchel, The, *(978-0-578-18660-3)* 1501 Oakwood Trail, Indianapolis, IN 46260 USA
E-mail: thetravelingsatchel@gmail.com.

Traveling Tales, *(978-0-578-40617-6)* 2526 W Perola Dr., Phoenix, AZ 85085 USA Tel 480-935-3221
E-mail: fin1640@aol.com.

Travis Parker Smith, *(978-1-7335837)* 1616 8th St. NW, Washington, DC 20001 USA Tel 206-465-4419
E-mail: travis.parker.smith@gmail.com.

Trawick, Gary E., *(978-0-615-66181-0)* 202 N. McNeil St., Burgaw, NC 28425 USA Tel 910-602-0993
E-mail: jenningstrawick@hotmail.com.

Traxler Marketing, *(978-0-9971788)* 11152 Westheimer Rd. No. 488, Houston, TX 77042 USA Tel 404-606-2116
E-mail: sonjatraxler@gmail.com.

Traylor, Waverley Publishing, *(978-0-9715068)* Div. of Waverley Traylor Photography, 3407 Longwood Dr.,

Smithfield, VA 23430 USA Tel 757-356-9119 (phone/fax)
E-mail: wlfoto@aol.com.

Tre H Publishing a division of Tre H Music, LLC *See* **Tre H Publishing a division of Tre H Productions, LLC**

Tre H Publishing a division of Tre H Productions, LLC, *(978-0-9987161)* 1615 Elysian St., HOUSTON, TX 77026 USA Tel 713-517-1129; Fax: 713-517-1129
E-mail: mflores@trehmusic.com.

Treadle Pr., *(978-0-935143)* Div. of Binding & Printing Co., Box D, Shepherdstown, WV 25443 USA (SAN 695-2070) Tel 304-876-2557.

Treasure Bay, Inc., *(978-1-891327; 978-1-60115)* 5 Ash Ct., Novato, CA 94949 USA (SAN 859-0958)
E-mail: customerservice@webothread.com; donpanec@comcast.net
Web site: http://www.webothread.com
Dist(s): **Children's Plus, Inc.**

Treasure Chest Books *See* **Rio Nuevo Pubs.**

Treasure Hunt Adventures, Inc., *(978-0-9749809)* P.O. Box 1049, Carmel, NY 10512-9998 USA Tel 845-225-2539
E-mail: info@treasurehuntadventures.com
Web site: http://www.treasurehuntadventures.com.

Treasure Trove, Inc., *(978-0-9760618; 978-0-9772314)* P.O. Box 459, Pound Ridge, NY 10576 USA Fax: 203-801-0099
Web site: http://www.atreasuretrove.com.

Treasured Images, *(978-0-9728770)* P.O. Box 361, Milton, WA 98354-0361 USA
E-mail: snspubs@aol.com.

Treasured Legacies, *(978-0-9819217)* 1589 Althouse Rd., Cochranville, PA 19330 USA Tel 610-593-2053
E-mail: arjoy@epix.net.

Treasures Media Incorporated *See* **BroadStreet Publishing**

Treasures of Glory Ministries, *(978-0-9916112; 978-1-946162)* P.O. Box 23743, San Diego, CA 92193 USA Tel 858-254-1868
E-mail: treasuresofgloryministries@gmail.com.

Treble Heart Bks., *(978-0-9711882; 978-1-931742; 978-1-932695; 978-1-936127; 978-1-938370)* 1284 Overlook Dr., Sierra Vista, AZ 85635-5512 USA (SAN 254-7120) Tel 520-458-5602; Fax: 520-459-0162; *Imprints:* MountainView (MtnView)
Web site: http://www.trebleheartbooks.com
Dist(s): **Smashwords.**

Tree Branch Publishing, *(978-0-9772578)* Orders Addr.: P.O. Box 421004, Summerland Key, FL 33042 USA Tel 305-872-4600; Fax: 305-832-0156; Toll Free: 866-454-6525; Edit Addr.: 19769 Date Palm Dr., Summerland Key, FL 33042 USA
E-mail: info@treeoflifepublishing.com.

Tree Farm Pr., *(978-0-692-18141-6; 978-0-692-18142-3)* 326 N. Cir. Dr., Williamston, MI 48895 USA Tel 517-290-7768
E-mail: lizball@me.com
Dist(s): **Ingram Content Group.**

Tree Musketeers, Inc., *(978-0-9770196)* Orders Addr.: 136 Main St., El Segundo, CA 90245 USA
E-mail: gail@treemusketeers.org
Web site: http://www.treemusketeers.org.

Tree of Life Pr., *(978-0-9727103)* 8422 Woodbrook Dr., Knoxville, TN 37919-8828 USA
E-mail: jana@janaspicka.com
Web site: http://www.janaspicka.com.

Tree Of Life Publishing, *(978-0-9745052)* P.O. Box 421004, Summerland Key, FL 33042 USA Tel 305-744-0330; Fax: 305-744-0320; Toll Free: 866-454-6525; *Imprints:* Peeper & Friends (Peep & Friends)
E-mail: peeper@peeperandfriends.com
Web site: http://www.peeperandfriends.com.

Tree of Life Publishing Hse., *(978-0-9801357; 978-0-9822060)* 730 Gladstone St., La Verne, CA 91750 USA Tel 626-825-5539
E-mail: shaynah@treeoflifepublishinghouse.com
Web site: http://www.treeoflifepublishinghouse.com.

Tree Top Bks., *(978-1-7332492)* 2513 Ferdinand Dr., Knightdale, NC 27545 USA Tel 919-239-0613
E-mail: wearetreetopbooks@gmail.com.

Tree Tunnel Pr., *(978-0-9841037)* P.O. Box 733, Capitola, CA 95010 USA (SAN 931-3931) Tel 831-427-5551; Toll Free: 800-213-1885
E-mail: contact@treetunnelpress.com
Web site: http://www.treetunnelpress.com.

Treecat Publishing, *(978-0-578-44699-8; 978-0-578-50989-1)* 1000 Wilsonville Rd., Newberg, OR 97132 USA Tel 765-662-3574
E-mail: dennis_horine@att.net.

Treehaus Communications, Inc., *(978-0-929496; 978-1-886510)* Orders Addr.: P.O. Box 249, Loveland, OH 45140 USA (SAN 249-5325) Tel 513-683-5716; Fax: 513-683-2882; Toll Free: 800-638-4287; Edit Addr.: 906 W. Loveland Ave., Loveland, OH 45140 USA (SAN 249-5333)
E-mail: treehaus1@fuse.net
Dist(s): **ACTA Pubns.**

TreeHse. Publishing Group, *(978-0-9892079; 978-0-9963901; 978-1-7321391)* Div. of Amphorae Publishing Group, 3963 Flora Pl., St. Louis, MO 63110 USA Tel 314-363-4546
E-mail: kbmakansi@blankslatecommunications.com
Web site: http://www.treehousepublishinggroup.com
Dist(s): **Independent Pubs. Group**
Midpoint Trade Bks., Inc.

Trefry, Deana, *(978-0-9798193)* 587 Essex St., Beverly, MA 01915 USA
E-mail: deanat@comcast.net.

Trembath, Carol Consulting *See* **Lakeside Publishing MI**

Tremendous Leadership *Imprint of* **Tremendous Life Bks.**

Tremendous Life Bks., *(978-0-937539; 978-1-933715; 978-1-936354)* Div. of Life Management Services, Inc., 206 West Allen St., Mechanicsburg, PA 17055-6240 USA (SAN 156-5419) Tel 717-766-9499; Fax: 717-766-6565; Toll Free: 800-233-2665; *Imprints:* Tremendous Leadership (TremendLrdship)
E-mail: JLiller@TremendousLifeBooks.com
Web site: http://www.TremendousLifeBooks.com
Dist(s): **Send The Light Distribution LLC.**

Trend Enterprises, Inc., *(978-1-889319; 978-1-58792; 978-1-60912; 978-1-62807; 978-1-64488)* Orders Addr.: P.O. Box 64073, Saint Paul, MN 55164 USA Tel 651-631-2850; Fax: 651-582-3500; Toll Free Fax: 800-845-4832; Toll Free: 800-328-5540; Edit Addr.: 300 Ninth Ave., SW, New Brighton, MN 55112 USA
Web site: http://www.trendenterprises.com.

Trend Factor Pr., *(978-0-9818669; 978-1-7348534; 978-1-7356943)* 1530 P B Ln. No. M4819, Wichita Falls, TX 76302 USA (SAN 856-7468) Tel 571-723-5645
E-mail: Biz@trendpov.com
Web site: http://www.trendfactorpress.com
Dist(s): **Blu Sky Media Group.**

Trendwood Pr., *(978-1-947865)* 13729 Shirley St, Omaha, NE 68144-1240 USA Tel 402-915-9094
E-mail: danielkenneybooks@gmail.com.

Trenton Creative Enterprises, *(978-0-9754958)* 731 Springdale Dr., Spartanburg, SC 29302 USA
E-mail: trentoncreativeenterprises@charter.net
Web site: http://www.vintagegastonia.com.

Trent's Prints, *(978-0-9728872; 978-0-9762389; 978-0-9773723; 978-1-934035; 978-1-937000)* 3754 Willard Norris Rd., Pace, FL 32571 USA Tel 850-994-1421 Toll Free: 866-275-7124
Web site: http://www.trentsprints.com.

Treorca Pr., *(978-0-9766559)* 1718 W. 102nd St., Chicago, IL 60643-2147 USA
E-mail: joga9@aol.com
Web site: http://www.treorcapress.com.

Tres Canis Publishing Co., *(978-0-9659065)* P.O. Box 163, Nanticoke, PA 18634 USA Tel 570-735-0328
E-mail: rjanosov@verizon.net.

Tres Clavas Pr., *(978-0-615-37077-4; 978-0-9855731)* 626 N. 6th Ave., Tucson, AZ 85705 USA Tel 480-433-0597
E-mail: zaa@dexterandstray.com
Web site: http://dexterandstray.com.

Trevor Romain Company, The *See* **Romain, Trevor Co., The**

Tri House Bks., *(978-0-578-17752-6)* 35211 Buena Mesa, Calimesa, CA 92320 USA
Dist(s): **Outskirts Pr., Inc.**

Tri I Pubns., *(978-0-9793683; 978-0-9821674)* 100 Taylor Pl., Southport, CT 06890 USA Tel 203-254-7631; Fax: 203-254-7826
E-mail: thompson@triist.com; linda@lindasworlds.com
Web site: http://www.triist.com; http://www.lindasworlds.com; http://www.iammyowndragon.com.

TRI LIFE Press *See* **Life Works Pr.**

Tri Valley Children's Publishing, *(978-0-9790962)* 512 Briarwood Ct., Livermore, CA 94551 USA Tel 925-413-0546
E-mail: stephanierutledge@comcast.net.

†**Triad Publishing Co.,** *(978-0-937404)* Imprint of Triad Communications, Inc., Orders Addr.: P.O. Box 13355, Gainesville, FL 32604 USA (SAN 205-4574) Tel 352-373-5800 editorial office; Fax: 352-373-1488 editorial office; Toll Free Fax: 800-854-4947 orders & queries Do not confuse with companies iwth the same or similar name in Tujuga, CA, Sequim, WA, Parker, CO, Marlton, NJ, West Hartford, CT,Raleigh, NC , Sarasota, Fl
E-mail: lorna@triadpublishing.com
Web site: http://www.triadpublishing.com; *CIP.*

Tri-Ad veterans League, Inc., 31 Heath St., Jamaica Plain, MA 02130-1650 USA
E-mail: triadveterans@hotmail.com
Web site: http://www.triadveteransleague.org.

Trialtea USA, LLC, *(978-0-9741482; 978-0-9778295; 978-0-9796067; 978-0-9821418; 978-0-9841136; 978-0-9828388; 978-1-939645; 978-1-68165)* 7955 NW 12th St., Suite 115, Miami, FL 33126 USA Toll Free: 800-210-0344
E-mail: info@trialtea.com
Web site: http://www.trialtea.com
Dist(s): **INscribe Digital**
Independent Pubs. Group.

Triangle Square *Imprint of* **Seven Stories Pr.**

Triarchy Press (GBR) *(978-0-9550081; 978-1-909470; 978-1-911193) Dist. by* **IPG Chicago.**

Tribal Eye Productions, *(978-0-9800272; 978-0-692-78018-3; 978-0-692-95151-4; 978-0-692-95640-3; 978-0-692-16258-3; 978-0-578-49516-3; 978-1-7352003)* P.O. Box 1123, Santa Ynez, CA 93460 USA
E-mail: garyd1123@gmail.com.

Tribute Bks., *(978-0-9765072; 978-0-9795045; 978-0-9814619; 978-0-9822565; 978-0-9837418; 978-0-9857922)* P.O. Box 95, Archbald, PA 18403 USA (SAN 256-4416) Tel 570-876-2416 (phone/fax)
E-mail: info@tribute-books.com
Web site: http://www.tribute-books.com
Dist(s): **Ingram Content Group.**

Tribute Publishing, *(978-0-9906001; 978-0-9982860; 978-0-9998358; 978-1-7337727)* 1624 Marble Falls Dr., Frisco, TX 75034 USA
E-mail: bonnie@TributePublishing.com.

Trice, B.E. Publishing, *(978-0-9631925; 978-1-890885)* 2727 Prytania St., New Orleans, LA 70130 USA Tel 504-895-0111
E-mail: betbooks@aol.com.

Trickle Creek Bks., *(978-0-9640742; 978-1-929432)* Orders Addr.: 500 Andersontown Rd., Mechanicsburg, PA 17055 USA Tel 717-766-2638; Fax: 717-766-1343; Toll Free: 800-353-2791
E-mail: tonialbert@aol.com
Web site: http://www.TrickleCreekBooks.com.

Tricolor Bks., *(978-0-9754641)* P.O. Box 24811, Tempe, AZ 85285 USA
E-mail: tricolorbrian@hotmail.com
Web site: http://www.mountainkingsnake.com.

Tricycle Pr. *Imprint of* **Random Hse. Children's Bks.**

Tricycle Pr. *Imprint of* **Ten Speed Pr.**

Trident, Inc., *(978-1-887801; 978-1-58978)* Orders Addr.: 885 Pierce Butler Rte., Saint Paul, MN 55104 USA; *Imprints:* Atlas Games (Atlas Games)
E-mail: info@atlas-games.com
Web site: http://www.atlas-games.com
Dist(s): **PSI (Publisher Services, Inc.).**

Trident Press International *See* **Standard International Print Group Inc.**

TriEclipse, Inc., *(978-0-9704512; 978-0-9976342)* P.O. Box 7763, Jacksonville, FL 32238 USA Tel 904-778-0372
E-mail: vtaylor4@bellsouth.net
Web site: http://www.trieclipse.com.

Trifolium Bks., Inc. (CAN) *(978-1-55244; 978-1-895579) Dist. by* **Firefly Bks Limited.**

Trigger (GBR) *(978-1-911246; 978-1-912478; 978-1-78956) Dist. by* **IPG Chicago.**

Trigger Memory Co., LLC, *(978-0-9762024; 978-0-9863000; 978-1-7352144)* P.O. Box 361, Pendleton, OR 97801 USA
E-mail: timestalesmj@msn.com
Web site: https://www.timestales.com.

Trigger Memory Systems *See* **Trigger Memory Co., LLC**

Trillas Editorial, S. A. (MEX) *(978-968-24) Dist. by* **Continental Bk.**

Trillas Editorial, S. A. (MEX) *(978-968-24) Dist. by* **Lectorum Pubns.**

Trilogy Christian Publishing, Inc., *(978-1-64088; 978-1-64773)* P.O. Box PO BOX A, Santa Ana, CA 92711 USA Tel 918-494-6868
E-mail: bryan@keymgc.com
Dist(s): **Destiny Image Pubs.**

Trilogy Pubns. LLC, *(978-0-9772799; 978-0-615-80854-3)* Orders Addr.: 560 Sylvan Ave. Suite 1240, Englewood Cliffs, NJ 07632 USA (SAN 257-2044) Tel 201-816-1211; Fax: 201-816-8424
Web site: http://www.trilogypublications.com.

Trine, Greg, *(978-0-578-46407-7; 978-1-7339589)* 3742, Ventura, CA 93003 USA Tel 805-901-2310
E-mail: gjtrine@gmail.com
Web site: www.gregtrine.com.

Trinity Bks., *(978-0-9743669)* P.O. Box 401, Cascade, ID 83611 USA.

Trinity Hills Publishing, Orders Addr.: 855 Penal Rock Rd., Penal, 00000 TTO Tel 868-387-2744
E-mail: markdanielonline@gmail.com.

Trintiy Pr., *(978-0-9822113)* 303 Park Ave., New York, NY 10010 USA
E-mail: yroehker@bookoublishing.com.

†**Trinity Univ. Pr.,** *(978-0-911536; 978-0-939980; 978-0-9651507; 978-1-893271; 978-1-59534)* One Trinity Pl., San Antonio, TX 78212 USA (SAN 205-4590) Tel 210-999-8881; Fax: 210-999-8182; *Imprints:* Maverick Books (MaverickBks) Do not confuse with Trinity University Press in Bannockburn, IL
E-mail: sarah.nawrocki@trinity.edu
Dist(s): **Bilingual Pr./Editorial Bilingue**
MyiLibrary
Publishers Group West (PGW); *CIP.*

Triple A Pr., *(978-0-692-72993-9; 978-0-9991181)* 110 Turnberry Dr., Spartanburg, SC 29306 USA Tel 864-582-7200
E-mail: marjymarj@aol.com.

Triple Ballerina Pr., *(978-1-7328429)* 115 Conifer Ct., MARKLE, IN 46770 USA Tel 260-602-5839
E-mail: BeverlyWitwerAuthor@gmail.com
Web site: thetripletballerinas.com.

Triple Crown Pubns., *(978-0-9702472; 978-0-9747895; 978-0-9762349; 978-0-9767894; 978-0-9778804; 978-0-9799517; 978-0-9820996; 978-0-9825888; 978-0-9832095)* P.O. Box 247378, Columbus, OH 43219 USA (SAN 914-3815) Tel 614-478-9402
E-mail: editor@triplecrownpublications.com
Web site: http://www.triplecrownpublications.com
Dist(s): **Ambassador Bks. & Media**
Brodart Co.
MyiLibrary.

Triple Exposure Publishing, Incorporated *See* **T. E. Publishing, Inc.**

Triple Seven Pr., *(978-0-9710486)* P.O. Box 70552, Las Vegas, NV 89170-0552 USA Do not confuse with Triple Seven International, Gaston, IN
E-mail: wendy@777press.com
Web site: http://www.777press.com.

Triple Tail Publishing *See* **Farcountry Pr.**

Triple Tulip Pr., *(978-0-9754825; 978-0-615-11380-7)* Orders Addr.: P.O. Box 250, Sanbornville, NH 03872 USA Tel 603-522-3398; Fax: 603-218-6502; 2717 Wakefield Rd., Sanbornville, NH 03872 Tel 603-522-3398; Fax: 603-218-6502
E-mail: tripletulip@roadrunner.com
Web site: http://www.tripletulippress.com.

TripleCrown Pubns. *See* **Triple Crown Pubns.**

Tripod Pr., *(978-0-9673265)* P.O. Box 551, Fairfax, CA 94978-0551 USA
E-mail: Tripod@FrankMarrero.com
Web site: http://www.FrankMarrero.com
Dist(s): **Lulu Pr., Inc.**

Tripodi, Pina, *(978-1-7342116)* 1 Elide Rd., Katonah, NY 10536 USA Tel 914-715-3462
E-mail: peacefulbypina@gmail.com
Web site: peacefulbypina.com.

Tripping Light Pr., *(978-0-9795389)* P.O. Box 1107, Wheaton, IL 60189-1107 USA
Web site: http://www.trippinglightpress.com.

Trireme Studios, *(978-1-7321449)* P.O. Box 613, Caneadea, NY 14717 USA Tel 817-516-0018
E-mail: dlee.pe@gmail.com
Web site: triremestudios.com.

Trisar, Inc., *(978-1-886386)* 804 W. Town & Country Rd., Orange, CA 92868-4712 USA.

Mrs. Weisz Bks., *(978-0-9888338; 978-0-9985291; 978-0-9993886)* 636 Elder Ln., Deerfield, IL 60015 USA Tel 847-602-5115
E-mail: erica@trismbooks.com
Web site: www.trismbooks.com
Dist(s): **Independent Pubs. Group.**

TRISTAN Publishing, Inc., *(978-0-931674; 978-0-9726504; 978-1-939881)* 2355 Louisiana Ave N. Ste. 2, Minneapolis, MN 55427-3646 USA Toll Free: 866-545-1383; *Imprints:* Waldman House Press (WaldmanHse)
E-mail: bwaldman@tristanpublishing.com; swaldman@tristanpublishing.com
Web site: http://www.tristanpublishing.com.

Tritium Pr., *(978-0-9761726)* 8690 Aero Dr., No. 339, San Diego, CA 92123 USA
E-mail: tritium@n2.net.

Triumph Bks., *(978-0-9624436; 978-1-57243; 978-1-880141; 978-1-60078; 978-1-61749)* Orders Addr.: 542 S. Dearborn St., Suite 750, Chicago, IL 60605 USA (SAN 852-6826) Tel 312-939-3330; Fax: 312-663-3557; Toll Free: 800-335-5323; Edit Addr.: c/o Kaplan Logistics, 901 Bilter Rd., Aurora, IL 60502 USA
E-mail: Ordering@TriumphBooks.com; J_Martini@triumphbooks.com; s_kaufman@triumphbooks.com; orders@triumphbooks.com; w.swanson@triumphbooks.com
Web site: http://www.triumphbooks.com
Dist(s): **Detroit Free Pr., Inc.**
Independent Pubs. Group
MyiLibrary.

Triumph Publishing, *(978-1-890430)* 10415 219th St., Queens Village, NY 11429-2020 USA Do not confuse with companies with a similar name in Omal, WA, College park, GA.

Triumphant Living Enterprises, Inc., *(978-0-9786681; 978-0-9852789)* Orders Addr.: P.O. Box 691223, Orlando, FL 32869-1223 USA Tel 407-614-5176; Fax: 407-614-5200
E-mail: LHarris@chpublishing.org
Web site: http://www.chpublishing.org; http://www.facebook.com/chpublishing; http://www.twitter.com/ch_publishing; http://lorettafaithharris.com/products/.

Triune Group, Inc., *(978-0-578-45332-3)* 1458 Sumter Dr. SW, Marietta, GA 30064 USA Tel 770-653-0160
E-mail: dickmcbain@gmail.com
Dist(s): **Ingram Content Group.**

Trivium Pubns., *(978-0-9713671)* Orders Addr.: Dept. of Humanities & Human Sciences Point Park Univ., 201 Wood St., Pittsburgh, PA 15222 USA (SAN 254-5152) Tel 716-982-8591
E-mail: bdeanrob@janushead.org
Web site: http://www.janushead.org.

Trivium Pursuit, *(978-0-9743616; 978-1-933228)* 429 Lake Park Blvd., PMB 168, Muscatine, IA 52761 USA Tel 309-537-3641
E-mail: bluedorn@triviumpursuit.com
Web site: http://www.triviumpursuit.com
Dist(s): **Send The Light Distribution LLC.**

Troika Bks. (GBR) *(978-0-9573013; 978-1-909991) Dist. by* **IPG Chicago.**

Trolley (GBR) *(978-0-9542079; 978-0-9542648; 978-1-904563; 978-1-907112) Dist. by* **Dist Art Pubs.**

Trolley Press *See* **Ignite Reality**

Trono-Calderon, Anne, 142 Whitney Ave., Los Gatos, CA 95030 USA Tel 408-677-6877
E-mail: atrocal@gmail.com.

Trotman, Charlie *See* **Iron Circus Comics**

Trotman, Kay L., *(978-0-615-13350-8)* P.O. Box 1501, Lake Elsinore, CA 92531 USA Tel 951-898-6094; Fax: 951-898-6094
E-mail: njeri@mac.com
Web site: www.onsafariwithkay.com.

Troublemaker Publishing, LP, *(978-1-933104)* P.O. Box 608, Spicewood, TX 78669 USA Tel 512-334-7777.

Troublemakers, *(978-0-692-10244-2)* 5130 E Pleasant Run Pkwy N. Dr, Indianapolis, IN 46219 USA Tel 317-354-6474
E-mail: kristinahulvershorn@gmail.com
Web site: www.secretofthetroublemakers.com.

Tru Publishing, *(978-0-9890985; 978-1-941420)* 2939 S Mayflower Way, Boise, ID 83709 USA Tel 612-423-1052; Fax: 888-854-7690
E-mail: Kevin@TruPublishing.com
Web site: www.TruPublishing.com.

truckerkidzPr., *(978-0-9856770)* 121 Overhill Rd., Warwick, RI 02818 USA Tel 401-480-3403
E-mail: ckmellor@cox.net
Web site: http://www.grandpaandthetruck.com.

Trudgian, Sherri *See* **Little Sprout Publishing Hse.**

True Exposures Publishing, Inc., *(978-0-9642595; 978-0-9771762)* Orders Addr.: P.O. Box 5066, Brandon, MS 39047 USA Tel 601-829-1222; Fax: 601-829-1656; Toll Free: 800-323-3398; Edit Addr.: 106 Shenandoah Estates Cir., Brandon, MS 39047 USA
E-mail: trueexposures@bellsouth.net
Web site: http://www.trueexposures.com.

True Friends Bk. Club, LLC, *(978-0-9797165)* 3708 142nd Pl. NE, Bellevue, WA 98007 USA (SAN 854-1833) Tel 425-556-4319
E-mail: laurawreeves@yahoo.com
Web site: http://www.truefriendsbookclub.com.

Publisher Name Index

True Gifts Publishing, *(978-0-9796701)* 14 Clark St., Belmont, MA 02478 USA (SAN 854-056X) Fax: 617-741-4013
Web site: http://truegifts.net.

True Horizon Publishing, *(978-0-9818396)* 12306 Fox Lake Pl., Fairfax, VA 22033 USA Toll Free: 866-601-4106 (phone/fax)
E-mail: montgomerylm@gmail.com
Web site: http://www.truehorizonpublishing.com.

True Light Publishing, *(978-0-9656670)* Orders Addr.: P.O. Box 1284, Boulder, CO 80308-0734 USA Tel 303-447-2547; Fax: 303-443-4373; Edit Addr.: 411 Wild Horse Cir., Boulder, CO 80304-0459 USA Do not confuse with True Light Publishing in Homewood, IL
E-mail: tlpub@ecentral.com; orders@truelightpub.com; amber@truelightmusic.com
Web site: http://www.truelightpub.com; http://www.truelightpublishing.com; http://www.truelightmusic.com
Dist(s): **New Leaf Distributing Co., Inc.**
Gangaji Foundation, The.

True Lightening *Imprint of* **Share & Care Society Inc.**

True Measure, *(978-0-578-42659-4; 978-0-578-42660-0)* 5902 Wishing Well Dr., Port Orange, FL 32127 USA Tel 386-589-2338
E-mail: truemeasureinspections@gmail.com
Dist(s): **Ingram Content Group.**

True North Studio, *(978-0-9845798)* 518 W. 8th St., Traverse City, MI 49684 USA.

True Path Pubs., *(978-0-9830978)* 9620 Smoot Ln., Argyle, TX 76226 USA Tel 817-879-8229
E-mail: ronda@ronda-ray.com.

True Perspective Publishing Hse., *(978-0-9832399; 978-0-9846672; 978-0-9852094; 978-0-9859892; 978-0-9894026; 978-0-9910561; 978-0-9904624; 978-0-9864305; 978-0-9975539; 978-0-9990755; 978-1-7340305; 978-1-7350275; 978-1-7357752)* 2811 Imperial Point Terr., Clermont, FL 34711 USA Tel 407-383-3356; Fax: 352-394-4443
E-mail: seancort3839@yahoo.com
Web site: www.thepowerofperspective.net.

True Vine Publishing Co., *(978-0-9760914; 978-0-9786088; 978-0-9822087; 978-0-9826694; 978-0-9894869; 978-0-9905326; 978-0-9989239; 978-1-7336315; 978-1-7357540)* P.O. Box 280386, Nashville, TN 37202 USA Tel 615-585-0143
E-mail: truevinepublishing@gmail.com
Web site: http://www.truevinepublishing.org.

True You Inc,

Truman Pr., Inc., *(978-0-9637846; 978-0-9798599)* 5 NW. Ave., Fayetteville, AR 72701 USA Tel 479-521-4999; Fax: 479-575-9393; *Imprints:* Hannover House (Hann Hse)
E-mail: hannoverhouse@aol.com
Web site: http://www.HannoverHouse.com
Dist(s): **Follett School Solutions**
National Bk. Network.

Truman State Univ. Pr., *(978-0-943549; 978-1-931112; 978-1-935503; 978-1-61248)* 100 E. Normal Ave., Kirksville, MO 63501-4221 USA (SAN 253-4231) Tel 660-785-7336; Fax: 660-785-4480; Toll Free: 800-916-6802
E-mail: tsup@truman.edu
Web site: http://tsup.truman.edu
Dist(s): **INscribe Digital**
ISD
Longleaf Services
Pennsylvania State Univ. Pr.

Trumpet In Zion Publishing, *(978-0-9716355)* Div. of Spring of Hope Church of God in Christ, P.O. Box 51163, Indian Orchard, MA 01151 USA Tel 413-733-1032; Fax: 413-241-6132; *Imprints:* Solid Rock Books (Solid Rock Bks).

Trumpeter *Imprint of* **Shambhala Pubns., Inc.**

Trunk Up Bks., *(978-1-7342129; 978-1-7349062)* 659 Framingham Ct, Gurnee, IL 60031 USA Tel 815-603-8021
E-mail: vickyweber93@gmail.com.

Truth Bk. Pubs., *(978-0-9778261; 978-0-9794861; 978-0-9815203; 978-1-935298; 978-1-937089; 978-1-940725; 978-1-946598)* 824 Bills Rd., Franklin, IL 62638 USA (SAN 912-2834) Tel 217-243-8880
E-mail: faithprinting77@yahoo.com; truthbookpublishers@yahoo.com
Web site: http://www.faithprinting.net; http://www.itseasywithjesus-printing.com; http://www.truthbookpublishers.com
Dist(s): **BCH Fulfillment & Distribution**
BookBaby
eBooks2go Inc.

Truth For Eternity Ministries, *(978-1-889520)* Div. of Reformed Baptist Church of Grand Rapids, 860 Peachcrest Ct NE, Grand Rapids, MI 49505-6435 USA
E-mail: office@girbc.org
Web site: www.girbc.org.

Truth Pr., *(978-0-692-59377-6; 978-0-9974331)* 306 Hideaway Ln. Central, Hideaway Lakes, TX 75771 USA Tel 903-780-1236
Dist(s): **CreateSpace Independent Publishing Platform.**

Truth Publications, Inc., *(978-0-9620615; 978-1-58427)* Orders Addr.: 220 S. Marion St., Athens, AL 35611 USA Tel 855-492-6657 CEI Bookstore; Fax: 256-232-0913; Edit Addr.: 220 S. Marion St., Athens, AL 35611 USA (SAN 249-4221) Tel 346-216-1707
E-mail: sales@truthpublications.com; lance@truthpublications.com; kyle@truthpublications.com; mark@truthpublications.com
Web site: http://CEIbooks.com; http://www.truthbooks.com/; http://www.ceibooks.com/.

Truth Publishers *See* **Truth Bk. Pubs.**

Truthful Pr. Publishing, *(978-0-9799707)* P.O. Box 240, Statesville, NC 28687 USA Tel 704-287-8378; Fax: 704-878-8972
E-mail: author@daphinerobinson.com
Web site: http://www.daphinerobinson.com.

T.S. Poetry Pr., *(978-0-9845531; 978-0-692-01454-7; 978-0-9898542; 978-1-943120)* 21 Belleview Ave., Ossining, NY 10562 USA Tel 914-944-9036.

Tsaba Hse., *(978-0-9725486; 978-1-933853)* 2252 12th St., Reedly, CA 93654 USA (SAN 254-9441) Tel 559-643-8575; Fax: 559-638-2640
E-mail: ps@tsabahouse.com
Web site: http://www.tsabahouse.com
Dist(s): **Send The Light Distribution LLC.**

T.S.I. Strategies, LLC, *(978-0-9772609)* 140 SE 8th St., Cape Coral, FL 33990 USA Fax: 866-761-4233
E-mail: jim@jamesroach.com
Web site: http://www.producevideos.com.

TSM Publishing Group, LLC *See* **Autumn Publishing Group, LLC**

Tsui Wong-Avery, Sally, *(978-0-9798874; 978-0-9819358; 978-0-9855246)* 2618 W. Canyon Ave., San Diego, CA 92123 USA.

Tu Bks. *Imprint of* **Lee & Low Bks., Inc.**

Tualen (GBR) *(978-0-9556798) Dist. by* **LuluCom.**

Tubbs, Stephen P., *(978-0-9659446; 978-0-9819753)* 1344 Firwood Dr., Pittsburgh, PA 15243-1861 USA Tel 412-279-4866
E-mail: electrpow@aol.com
Web site: http://www.members.aol.com/electrpow/power.htm.

Tubby & Coo's Mid-City Bk. Shop, *(978-1-7322794)* 432 N. Anthony St. Suite 305C, New Orleans, LA 70119 USA (SAN 920-8763) Tel 504-345-8491
E-mail: tubbyandcoos@gmail.com.

Tucker, Peggy *See* **Heritage Publishing**

Tucker, Peter E. *See* **PT Publishing**

Tucker, Terra, *(978-0-9794578)* P.O. Box 2792 Americus Dr, Thompson Station, TN 37179 USA (SAN 853-5027).

Tucson Botanical Gardens, *(978-0-9792253)* 2150 N. Alvernon Way, Tucson, AZ 85712 USA Tel 520-326-9686; Fax: 520-324-0166
E-mail: execdirector@tucsonbotanical.org
Web site: http://www.tucsonbotanical.org.

Tucu Pr., *(978-0-9766572)* Orders Addr.: P.O. Box 447, Bozeman, MT 59771-0447 USA Tel 406-586-5084 (phone/fax); Edit Addr.: 3150 Graf St., No. 8, Bozeman, MT 59715 USA
E-mail: anndiberardinis@msn.com.

Tudor Assocs. Pr., *(978-0-9760939)* P.O. Box 1804, Payson, AZ 85547-1804 USA Tel 928-978-5799
E-mail: press@tudorassociates.com
Web site: http://www.tudorassociates.com.

Tudor Hse. (GBR) *(978-0-9530676) Dist. by* **Orca Bk Pub.**

Tudor Pubs., Inc., *(978-0-936389; 978-0-9778026)* Orders Addr.: P.O. Box 38366, Greensboro, NC 27438 USA; Edit Addr.: 3109 Shady Lawn Dr., Greensboro, NC 27408 USA (SAN 697-3035) Tel 336-288-5395
E-mail: tudorpublishers@triad.rr.com
Dist(s): **Brodart Co.**

Tuesday's Child, *(978-0-9772795)* Orders Addr.: P.O. Box 2512, Cookeville, TN 38502-2512 USA (SAN 257-2060)
E-mail: tuesdayschildpub@charter.net
Web site: http://tuesdayschildpub.com.

Tuggle Publishing, *(978-0-9974722)* 5904 Meadows Dr., Fort Wayne, IN 46804 USA Tel 678-702-2139
E-mail: annieueber@yahoo.com
Web site: tugglepublishing.com.

Tughra Bks. *Imprint of* **Blue Dome, Inc.**

Tulip & Petunia Publishing, *(978-0-692-82983-7)* 3800 Buchtel Blvd #103191, DENVER, CO 80250 USA Tel 720-474-0591
E-mail: jeffwcrawford5+LVP0003235@gmail.com; jeffwcrawford5+LVP0003235@gmail.com.

Tully, Jennifer Cahill, *(978-0-9980531)* 4550 Pearson st, Long Island city, NY 11101 USA Tel 860-810-5216; *Imprints:* Harvest Moon Books (MYID_D_HARVEST)
E-mail: Jncahill@gmail.com.

Tullycrine, LLC, *(978-0-9746554)* P.O. Box 178, Heisson, WA 98622-0178 USA
E-mail: tullycrineinc@aol.com; tullycrinellc@aol.com
Web site: http://www.tullycrine.com; http://www.book.traditionalcats.com.

Tumble Creek Pr., *(978-0-9800660; 978-1-953026)* P.O. Box P.O. Box 12639, Raleigh, NC 27605 USA (SAN 855-1197)
Web site: https://www.danidixonbooks.com; http://www.TUMBLECREEKPRESS.com.

Tumblehome Learning, *(978-0-9850008; 978-0-9897924; 978-0-9907829; 978-1-943431)* P.O. Box 171386, Boston, MA 02117-3225 USA Tel 781-924-5036
E-mail: info@tumblehomelearning.com
Web site: http://www.tumblehomelearning.com
Dist(s): **Independent Pubs. Group.**

Tumbleweed Publishing, *(978-0-9720132)* P.O. Box 194, Valley City, OH 44280 USA Do not confuse with Tumbleweed Publishing Company in Eugene, OR
E-mail: tumbleweedbooks@aol.com.

Tundra Bks. (CAN) *(978-0-88776; 978-0-89541; 978-0-912766; 978-1-77049) Dist. by* **Peng Rand Hse.**

Tundra Bks. (CAN) *(978-0-88776; 978-0-89541; 978-0-912766; 978-1-77049) Dist. by* **Children Plus.**

Tundra Bks. (CAN) *(978-0-88776; 978-0-89541; 978-0-912766; 978-1-77049) Dist. by* **Random.**

Tune, Riley, 10110 Strome Ave. 308, Raleigh, NC 27617 USA Tel 919-438-4780
E-mail: rtune86@gmail.com
Dist(s): **Ingram Content Group.**

Tuned in to Learning, *(978-0-9768881)* P.O. Box 221016, San Diego, CA 92192 USA (SAN 256-5803) Tel 858-453-0590; Fax: 858-777-3626
E-mail: mlazar@coastmusictherapy.com
Web site: http://www.tunedintolearning.com.

Turley, Sandy *See* **Helps4Teachers**

Turman, E., *(978-0-9753042)* 1321 Singingwood Ct., No. 1, Walnut Creek, CA 94595 USA Tel 925-944-5743
E-mail: shihtze1@msn.com.

Turman, Joe Garner, *(978-0-692-14181-6; 978-0-692-14226-4)* 164 Greenfield Ln, Alabaster, AL 35007 USA Tel 205-358-8782
E-mail: joegturman@gmail.com.

Turn the Page Publishing, *(978-0-9832148; 978-1-938501)* Memorial Sta., Upper Montclair, NJ 07043 USA (SAN 860-0864) Tel 973-202-8979
E-mail: rlentin@turnthepagepublishing.com
Web site: www.turnthepagepublishing.com
Dist(s): **Ingram Content Group.**

Turnapaige & Reed Moore, *(978-0-9725231)* P.O. Box 412, Scottsdale, AZ 85252 USA
E-mail: reedmoore@turnapaige.com
Web site: http://www.turnapaige.com.

Turnaround Bk. Publishing Corp., *(978-0-9753028)* 5047 W. Main St., Suite 212, Kalamazoo, MI 49001 USA.

Turnberry Pr., *(978-0-9971477)* 150 Crest Rd., Southern Pines, NC 28387 USA Tel 910-693-9906
E-mail: annieh@microcare.com
Web site: www.AnnabellesReadingCorner.com.

Turner, Barbara, *(978-0-9747019)* P.O. Box 893493, Temecula, CA 92589 USA Tel 951-699-3933
E-mail: adayinsanfrancisco@yahoo.com
Dist(s): **Lulu Pr., Inc.**

Turner, Blaine, *(978-0-615-25688-7; 978-0-578-00165-4; 978-0-578-00497-6; 978-0-578-09035-1; 978-0-578-12843-6; 978-0-578-14952-3)* 26626 Lily Lake Inn Rd., Webster, WI 54893 USA
E-mail: blaine_turner@tsco.org
Dist(s): **Lulu Pr., Inc.**

Turner Publishing Co., *(978-0-89793; 978-0-938021; 978-0-940069; 978-1-56311; 978-1-59652; 978-1-61858; 978-1-62045; 978-1-63026; 978-1-68162; 978-1-68336; 978-1-68442)* 200 4th Ave N. Ste. 950, Nashville, TN 37219-2145 USA; 424 Church St., Suite 2240, Nashville, TN 37209 Tel 615-255-2665; Fax: 615-255-5081; *Imprints:* Hunter House (HunterHse); Gurze Books (GurzeBks) Do not confuse with companies with the same or similar name in Atlanta, GA, Eastchester, NY, Houston, TX
E-mail: editorial@turnerpublishing.com
Web site: http://www.turnerpublishing.com
Dist(s): **Ingram Publisher Services**
MyiLibrary
Partners Bk. Distributing, Inc.

Turner, Rich Photographs, *(978-0-9762410)* 305 Fyffe Ave., Suite 158, Stockton, CA 95203 USA Tel 209-460-1050; Fax: 209-460-1051
E-mail: richt@turnerphoto.com
Web site: http://www.turnerphoto.com.

Turngroup Technologies, LLC, *(978-0-9794377)* 2811 Locust St., Saint Louis, MO 63103-1308 USA
Web site: http://www.hisforhopebooks.com
Dist(s): **Big River Distribution.**

Turning a New Page, *(978-0-9762030; 978-0-692-07658-3)* Orders Addr.: P.O. Box 91603, Tucson, AZ 85752-1603 USA Tel 520-579-7183; Fax: 520-407-6524
E-mail: rick4758@turninganewpage.com
Web site: http://www.turninganewpage.com.

Turning Point LLC, *(978-0-9745745)* 1339 Indiana Ave., Connersville, IN 47331 USA Tel 765-825-9835; 765-265-3207 (Mobile)
E-mail: lsfitzg@aol.com
Web site: http://www.stellarstar.biz.

Turning Point Pubns., LLC, *(978-0-9752742; 978-0-9840986)* Orders Addr.: 2822 Cashwell Dr., No. 233, Goldsboro, NC 27534 USA Tel 615-562-1540 Order books at www.turningpointstore.org Do not confuse with Turning Point Publications in Eureka, CA
E-mail: info@turningpointpublications.com
Web site: http://www.turningpointpublications.com.

Turnstyle, *(978-0-9668541)* Orders Addr.: P.O. Box 810, Portland, IN 47371 USA; Edit Addr.: 1601 W. 100 S., Portland, IN 47371 USA
E-mail: rogdomingo@gmail.com.

Turpin, Jill Lorraine, *(978-0-692-92451-8; 978-1-7320932)* 7311 Dogwood Dr, Fairview, TN 37062 USA Tel 615-509-3115
E-mail: jill.lorraine@gmail.com.

Turquoise Lake *See* **FireFly Lights**

Turquoise Morning Pr., *(978-1-935817; 978-1-937389; 978-1-62237)* PO Box 20, New Holland, OH 43145 USA Tel 859-940-6816
E-mail: kim@turquoisemorning.com; kim.tmpress@gmail.com
Web site: http://www.maddiejames.com
Dist(s): **Draft2Digital**
Smashwords.

Turtle Bks. *Imprint of* **Jason & Nordic Pubs.**

Turtle Bks., *(978-1-890515)* 897 Boston Post Rd., Madison, CT 06443-3155 USA
E-mail: turtlebook@aol.com
Web site: http://www.turtlebooks.com
Dist(s): **Lectorum Pubns., Inc.**

Turtle Gallery Editions, *(978-0-9626935)* P.O. Box 219, Deer Isle, ME 04627-0219 USA Tel 207-348-9977 (phone/fax)
E-mail: person@turtlegallery.com
Web site: http://www.turtlegallery.com.

Turtle Point Pr., *(978-0-9627987; 978-1-885586; 978-1-885983; 978-1-933527; 978-1-885983-51-0; 978-1-7333680)* 233 Broadway, Rm. 946, New York, NY 10279 USA Tel 212-285-1019 (phone/fax)
E-mail: countomega@aol.com
Web site: http://www.turtlepoint.com
Dist(s): **Consortium Bk. Sales & Distribution**
Ingram Content Group
MyiLibrary
SPD-Small Pr. Distribution
Sprout, Inc.

Turtle Pr., *(978-1-880336; 978-1-934903; 978-1-938585; 978-0-9895971)* Orders Addr.: 500 N Washington St No. 1545, Rockville, MD 20849 USA Toll Free: 800-778-8785 (orders only)
E-mail: orders@turtlepress.com; turtlepress@gmail.com
Web site: http://www.turtlepress.com.

Turtle Press Corporation *See* **Turtle Pr.**

Turtle Time Bks., *(978-0-9770957)* P.O. Box 809, San Luis Obispo, CA 93406 USA.

Turtleback, 1000 North Second Ave., Logan, IA 51546-0500 USA.

Turtleback Books *See* **Turtleback Bks. Publishing, Ltd.**

Turtleback Bks. Publishing, Ltd., *(978-1-883385)* Orders Addr.: c/o Martel, P.O. Box 106, Anna Bay, NSW 2316 AUS Tel 0401 843 837; 0423 627 012 Do not confuse with Turtleback Bks., Madison, WI
E-mail: turtlebackbooks@australiamail.com; turtlebackbooks@usa.com
Web site: http://www.turtlebackbooks.net
Dist(s): **Partners/West Book Distributors.**

Tuscarora Publishing Company, *(978-0-9860321)* 3199 Sherman Rd, Mansfield, OH 44903 USA Tel 419-529-5596.

Tush People, The, *(978-0-9722514)* P.O. Box 950100, Mission Hills, CA 91395 USA Tel 661-298-2293; 818-897-1734; Fax: 818-899-4455
E-mail: dfav218@aol.com.

Tutortime4kidz, *(978-0-9986382)* 300 FOXBORO Ct., SAN RAMON, CA 94583 USA Tel 925-413-1071
E-mail: darlenegrimm@sbcglobal.net.

Tuttle Publishing, *(978-0-8048; 978-1-4629)* Orders Addr.: 364 Innovation Dr., North Clarendon, VT 05759 USA (SAN 213-2621) Tel 802-773-8930; Fax: 802-773-6993; Toll Free Fax: 800-329-8885; Toll Free: 800-526-2778; *Imprints:* PeriplusEdition (PeriplEdns)
E-mail: info@tuttlepublishing.com
Web site: http://www.tuttlepublishing.com
Dist(s): **Cheng & Tsui Co.**
MyiLibrary
Publishers Group West (PGW)
Simon & Schuster
Simon & Schuster, Inc.
ebrary, Inc.

Tuva Publishing (TUR) *(978-605-5647) Dist. by* **IPG Chicago.**

Tuvott Publishing, *(978-0-9723974)* P.O. Box 18276, Erlanger, KY 41018 USA (SAN 255-3341) Tel 859-341-6004; Fax: 859-341-6033
E-mail: tuvott@fuse.net
Web site: http://www.trinityunveiled.com
Dist(s): **Book Clearing Hse.**
Spring Arbor Distributors, Inc.

Tuxbury Publishing LLC, *(978-0-9910680; 978-1-942444; 978-1-950155)* PO Box 264, Etna, NH 03750 USA Tel 603-643-2175
E-mail: spinneo@gmail.com.

Tuxedo Blue, LLC, *(978-0-9754056)* Orders Addr.: P.O. Box 2008, Lenox, MA 01240 USA Tel 413-637-2190; Edit Addr.: 455 W. 43rd St., No. 1A, New York, NY 10036 USA Tel 212-262-5113
E-mail: billiamsw@earthlink.net
Web site: http://www.spacenicks.com.

Tuxedo Pr., *(978-0-9774486; 978-1-936161)* 546 E. Springville Rd., Carlisle, PA 17015 USA
E-mail: info@Tuxedo-Press.com
Web site: http://Tuxedo-Press.com.

TV Acres Bks., *(978-0-9794133; 978-0-615-14014-8)* Div. of TV Acres.com, 1965 Broadway St., Saintckport, OH 43787 USA
Web site: http://www.tvacres.com
Dist(s): **CreateSpace Independent Publishing Platform**
Lulu Pr., Inc.

Twain, Mark Media, Inc. Pubs., *(978-1-58037)* 100 E. Main St., Lewistown, MO 63452 USA Tel 573-497-2202; Fax: 573-497-2507
Dist(s): **Carson-Dellosa Publishing, LLC.**

Tweed K LLC, *(978-0-9994843)* 21842 Old Bridge Trail, Boca Raton, FL 33428 USA Tel 561-302-2813
E-mail: foofyoofy@aol.com
Web site: www.spinoculars.com.

Tweener Pr. *Imprint of* **Baker Trittin Pr.**

Twelve Star Pr., *(978-0-9797232)* 1105 2nd Ave. NE, Clarion, IA 50525 USA Tel 515-689-9157
E-mail: duncalfj@goldfieldaccess.net.

Twelve Stones Publishing LLC, *(978-0-9712363; 978-0-692-30050-3; 978-0-692-65064-6; 978-1-7327071)* Orders Addr.: P.O. Box 921, Eufaula, AL 36072 USA Tel 334-687-4491 Do not confuse with Twelve Stones Publishing in Grandville, MI
E-mail: brittbooks@msn.com
Web site: http://www.poemsfromthefast.com
Dist(s): **CreateSpace Independent Publishing Platform.**

Twelve Winters Pr., *(978-0-9895151; 978-0-9861597; 978-0-9987057; 978-1-7331949)* P.O. Box 414, Sherman, IL 62684 USA Tel 217-502-2570; *Imprints:* Shining Hall (ShiningHALL)
E-mail: xii.winters@gmail.com
Web site: twelvewinters.com; shininghall.com.

Twentieth Century Christian Bks., *(978-0-89098)* 2809 Granny White Pike, Nashville, TN 37204 USA (SAN 206-2550) Tel 615-383-3842.

Twenty First Century Bks., *(978-0-9636012; 978-1-893817)* P.O. Box 2001, 507 SCR 528, Breckenridge, CO 80424-2001 USA (SAN 298-248X) Tel 970-453-9293; Fax: 970-453-6692; Toll Free: 877-453-9293 Do not confuse with Twenty First Century Bks., Inc. in New York, NY
E-mail: order_desk03@tfcbooks.com; g.peterson@tfcbooks.com
Web site: http://www.tfcbooks.com; http://www.teslabooks.com
Dist(s): **MyiLibrary.**

Twenty-First Century Bks. *Imprint of* **Lerner Publishing Group**

Twenty-First Century Co., The, *(978-0-933451; 978-1-888264)* 2201 Rockbrook Dr., No. 1916, Lewisville, TX 75067-3830 USA Tel 972-459-6327 (phone/fax)
E-mail: t21cenco@flash.net
Web site: http://www.cleareducation.com.

Twenty-fourth Street Bks, LLC, *(978-0-9726939)* 215 E. 24th St., New York, NY 10010 USA
E-mail: cz@yiddishcat.com
Web site: http://www.yiddishcat.com.

Twenty-Third Pubns./Bayard, *(978-0-89622; 978-1-58595; 978-1-62785)* 1 Montauk Ave. No. 20, New London, CT 06320-4967 USA (SAN 658-2052) Toll Free Fax: 800-572-0788; Toll Free: 800-321-0411
E-mail: kerry.moriarty@bayard-inc.com
Web site: http://www.23rdpublications.com
Dist(s): **Forward Movement Pubns.**

Twenty-Three Publishing, *(978-0-692-25221-5; 978-0-692-25222-2; 978-0-692-25223-9; 978-0-692-25224-6; 978-0-9968131)* 2 Tether Moon Ln., Ladera Ranch, CA 92694 USA Tel 949 254-1011; Fax: (949) 388-0657
E-mail: cookingwithkids@cox.net
Dist(s): **CreateSpace Independent Publishing Platform.**

twhiteart, *(978-0-9639670)* 5290 Meadville St., Excelsior, MN 55331-8792 USA Tel 952-474-2083
E-mail: madonna@twhiteart.com
Web site: http://www.twhiteart.com.

Twianie Roberts Consulting, *(978-0-9718019; 978-0-9815629)* P.O. Box 70236, Rosedale, MD 21237 USA (SAN 855-8787) Fax: 301-965-8249
Web site: http://walkintheworlddc.com/index.html.

Twice As Good Productions, LLC, *(978-0-9960696)* 1105 S. Rio Vista Blvd., Fort Lauderdale, FL 33316 USA Tel 305-778-2775
E-mail: johnathan@twiceasgoodshow.com
Web site: www.twiceasgoodshow.com
Dist(s): **Cookbook Marketplace, The.**

Twiglet The Little Christmas Tree *Imprint of* **PJs Corner**

Twilight Tales, Inc., *(978-0-9711309; 978-0-9779856)* Orders Addr.: 331 Berkshire Terrace, Roselle, IL 60172 USA Tel 630-351-9311 Sales; Edit Addr.: 2339 N. Commonwealth, No. 4C, Chicago, IL 60614 USA (SAN 851-772X) Tel 773-472-8722
E-mail: sales@twilighttales.com
Web site: http://www.twilighttales.com.

Twilight Times Bks., *(978-1-931201; 978-1-933353; 978-1-60619)* Orders Addr.: P.O. Box 3340, Kingsport, TN 376643340 USA; *Imprints:* Paladin Timeless (PalaTimeless)
E-mail: publisher@twilighttimes.com
Web site: http://www.twilighttimesbooks.com
Dist(s): **Book Clearing Hse.**

Twin 20 Publishing, *(978-1-7324014)* 3041 Saint Albans Dr., Los Alamitos, CA 90720 USA Tel 562-824-0760
E-mail: kristina@caseythecontainer.com.

Twin Flame Productions, *(978-1-880765; 978-0-692-24690-0; 978-1-68323)* 70 SW Century Dr. Suite 100-372, Bend, OR 97702 USA (SAN 990-0934); *Imprints:* Harmony House (HarmonyHse)
E-mail: admin@twinflameproductions.us
Web site: https://aingealroseandahonu.com; https://twinflameproductions.us/
Dist(s): **CreateSpace Independent Publishing Platform.**

Twin Guardian Publishing, *(978-0-9858953)* 8821 W. Oklahoma Ave. No. 301, Milwaukee, WI 53227 USA Tel 414-477-5975
E-mail: debh1913@live.com
Web site: www.dperduehenderson.com.

Twin Lights Pubs., Inc., *(978-1-885435; 978-1-934907)* 8 Hale St., Rockport, MA 01966 USA (SAN 257-8867) Tel 978-546-7398; Fax: 978-546-5803; 6 Tide St., Boston, MA 02210
E-mail: info@twinlightspub.com; orders@twinlightspub.com
Web site: http://www.twinlightspub.com
Dist(s): **Strisik, Nancy**
Windhover Performing Arts Ctr.

Twin Monkeys Pr., *(978-0-9768602)* 146 First St., Dunellen, NJ 08812 USA Tel 732-752-3285
E-mail: storytellerjt@optonline.net
Web site: http://www.twinmonkeyspress.com.

Twin Peaks Publishing, Inc., *(978-0-9722259)* 4708 Mountain Vista Ct., Loveland, CO 80537 USA
E-mail: Twinpeakspublish@aol.com
Web site: http://www.bookmasters.com/marktplc/rr00979.htm; http://www.atlasbooks.com/authorspotlight/asdmiller.htm; http://hometown.aol.com/TwinPeaksPublish/TwinPeaks.htm.

Twin Sisters IP, LLC, *(978-0-9632249; 978-1-57583; 978-1-882331; 978-1-59922; 978-1-61938; 978-1-62002; 978-1-62581; 978-1-64033; 978-1-64580)* Orders Addr.: 1653 Merriman Rd. Suite L-1, Akron, OH 44313 USA (SAN 859-8460) Toll Free: 800-248-8946; 800-480-8946
E-mail: doug.kline@twinsisters.com; melissa.chase@twinsisters.com.

Twin Sisters Productions, LLC *See* **Twin Sisters IP, LLC**

Twin Sisters Publishing Co., *(978-0-615-23714-5; 978-0-615-24258-3; 978-0-578-00651-2)* 1805 Breckenridge Dr., Del City, OK 73115 USA Tel 405-882-9606
E-mail: twinsisterspublishing@yahoo.com
Web site: http://www.oklahomawriter/tripod.com
Dist(s): **Lulu Pr., Inc.**

TwinAtaa Studio, *(978-1-889926)* P.O. Box 1162, Stone Mountain, GA 30086 USA Tel 770-469-5138; Fax: 770-469-5139
E-mail: twinataa@twinataa.com; srw@twinataa.com
Web site: http://www.twinataa.com.

TwinAtaa/Sanaa Village Publications *See* **TwinAtaa Studio**

Twinbrook Publishing, *(978-0-9759086)* P.O. Box 355, Bedminster, NJ 07921 USA Tel 908-534-6799
Web site: http://www.pleasantdreaming.com/.

Twinkle Bks., *(978-0-9792992)* 1415 Riverbank St., Lincoln Park, MI 48146-3880 USA (SAN 853-0483) Tel 313-381-2082
E-mail: Treasurecloud@msn.com
Web site: http://Twinkleblink.com.

Twinkle Twinkle Little Bks., *(978-0-9771447)* 131 E. Wilson St., Centre Hall, PA 16828-8703 USA Tel 814-364-2237
E-mail: nicole@twinkletwinklelittlebooks.com
Web site: http://www.twinkletwinklelittlebooks.com.

Twins Bks. *Imprint of* **Sterling Investments I, LLC DBA Twins Magazine**

TwinsBooks, *(978-0-615-35370-8; 978-0-615-60112-0)* 14590 Ludlow St., Oak Park, MI 48237 USA Tel 248-968-2135
E-mail: deanna41969@hotmail.com.

Twisted Key Publishing, LLC, *(978-1-947744)* 165 Bedford Rd., Lincoln, MA 01773 USA Tel 954-864-9405
E-mail: gimjarquin@gmail.com.

Twisted Spice, *(978-0-9893075)* 2873 SW 85th Ave., Miramar, FL 33025 USA Tel 954-391-7520
E-mail: Crimpy79@hotmail.com.

Twisted Tree Pr, *(978-0-9778865)* 1232 Grant Rd, Harlem, GA 30814 USA Tel 706-306-9503
E-mail: twisted_tree_press@hotmail.com.

Twister Publishing Co., *(978-0-9749744)* Orders Addr.: P.O. Box 123, Conover, WI 54519 USA; P.O. Box 123, Conover, WI 54519 Tel 715-479-9417
E-mail: dseltin@gmail.com; dseltin@yahoo.com
Web site: http://www.theministryofpanacea.com.

Two Bear Publishing *See* **Cracker the Crab LLC**

Two Chicks, *(978-0-9899544)* 2063 White Horse Rd, Berwyn, PA 19312 USA Tel 610-408-8688
E-mail: ayfriday@gmail.com.

Two Dogz, *(978-0-9767072)* Orders Addr.: 775 Lefort By Pass Rd., Thibodaux, LA 70301 USA
E-mail: zsagabby@yahoo.com
Web site: http://www.two-dogz.com.

Two Dolphins Publishing Group, *(978-0-615-47819-7; 978-0-9836920)* 28494 Westinghouse Pl. No. 201, Valencia, CA 91355 USA Tel 818-266-8210
E-mail: info@twodolphinspublishing.com
Web site: www.twodolphinspublishing.com; www.wendylewisbooks.com.

Two Girls and a Reading Corner, *(978-0-9994859; 978-1-7329685; 978-1-952879)* 311 Glenwood Dr., Madison, AL 35758 USA Tel 256-658-8794
E-mail: twogirlsandareadingcorner@gmail.com
Web site: www.twogirlsandareadingcorner.com.

Two Harbors Press *Imprint of* **Salem Author Services**

Two Lakes Pr., Inc., *(978-1-59885)* P.O. Box 384, Saint Joseph, MN 56374-0384 USA Tel 616-822-1865
E-mail: s@twolakespress.com
Web site: http://www.twolakespress.com.

Two Lands, *(978-1-933984)* 1631 Lakefield North Ct., Wellington, FL 33414-1066 USA
E-mail: twolandsoffice@yahoo.com.

Two Lines Pr.,
Dist(s): **MyiLibrary**
Publishers Group West (PGW).

Two Lions *Imprint of* **Amazon Publishing**

Two Little Birds Bks., *(978-0-9912935; 978-0-9995569)* 58 Cutts Rd., Kittery, ME 03904 USA Tel 603-828-7343
E-mail: birdie@twolittlebirdsbooks.com
Web site: www.twolittlebirdsbooks.com
Dist(s): **Ingram Publisher Services**
Univ. Pr. of New England.

Two Little Hands Productions LLC, *(978-1-933543; 978-1-936859)* Orders Addr.: 870 E. N. Union Ave., Midvale, UT 84047 USA
E-mail: rose@signingtime.com
Web site: http://www.signingtime.com.

Two Little Pubs., *(978-0-692-76235-6; 978-0-692-79163-9; 978-0-692-82284-5; 978-0-578-51981-4)* 2447 Stately Oaks Dr., Raleigh, NC 27614 USA Tel 803-622-0319
E-mail: globalpartners202@gmail.com.

Two Lives Publishing, *(978-0-9674468)* Orders Addr.: 2500 Painter Ct., Annapolis, MD 21401 USA; Edit Addr.: 2500 Painter Ct., Annapolis, MD 21401 USA
E-mail: bcombs@TwoLives.com
Web site: http://www.TwoLives.com
Dist(s): **Book Wholesalers, Inc.**
Brodart Co.

Two Oaks, LLC, *(978-0-692-92964-3; 978-0-692-92969-8; 978-0-692-93010-6; 978-0-692-93012-0; 978-0-692-10945-8; 978-0-692-10947-2)* 9417 Roosevelt Ave, CARR, CO 80612 USA Tel 970-231-7005
E-mail: monica.yoknis@gmail.com
Dist(s): **Ingram Content Group.**

Two Pens and a Grind Pubns., *(978-0-615-92288-1; 978-0-9978304)* 5915 Quantrell Ave, Alexandria, VA 22312 USA Tel 8509808678; Fax: 7039976332
Dist(s): **CreateSpace Independent Publishing Platform.**

Two Rivers Distribution, Div. of Ingram Content Group, Orders Addr.: 210 American Dr., Jackson, TN 38301 USA Toll Free Fax: 800-351-5073 (Customer Service); Toll Free: 866-400-5351 (Customer Service); 800-343-4499
E-mail: pd_orderentry@ingramcontent.com; ips@ingramcontent.com
Web site: http://www.tworiversdistribution.com/.

Two Saints Publishing, *(978-0-9625782)* 615 Mennonite Church Rd., Kalispell, MT 59901-7753 USA Tel 406-756-1959.

Two Seed Planters Inc., *(978-0-9755789)* 141 Tall Pines Dr., Leesburg, GA 31763-3143 USA
E-mail: twoseedplanters@aol.com
Web site: http://www.twoseedplanters.com.

Two Sees Inc., *(978-0-9983570)* 3811 Streamwood Dr., Hazel Crest, IL 60429 USA Tel 414-764-0206
E-mail: Two_Sees@yahoo.com.

Two Small Fish Pubns., *(978-0-9826582; 978-0-9971972)* 109 W. Market St., Freeburg, PA 17827 USA Tel 570-374-1363
E-mail: brendakhendricks@verizon.net
Web site: http://www.twosmallfish.org.

Two Sons Pr., Inc., *(978-0-9748995)* 14 Red Tail Dr., Highlands Ranch, CO 80126-5001 USA Tel 303-346-3003; Fax: 303-791-2226
E-mail: McAdamfam@aol.com.

Two Sylvias Pr., *(978-0-615-95680-0; 978-0-615-96178-1; 978-0-615-96183-5; 978-0-692-27071-4; 978-0-692-33337-2; 978-0-692-35484-1; 978-0-692-37978-3; 978-0-692-44972-1; 978-0-692-45007-9; 978-0-692-45089-5; 978-0-692-49259-8; 978-0-692-49465-3; 978-0-692-57715-8; 978-0-692-62271-1; 978-0-692-64066-1; 978-0-692-65372-2; 978-0-692-66344-8; 978-0-692-72125-4; 978-0-692-76290-5; 978-0-9986314; 978-1-948767) PO Box 1524, Kingston, WA 98346 USA Tel 3608601213*
Dist(s): **CreateSpace Independent Publishing Platform.**

Two Tired Teachers Connection, Inc., The, *(978-0-9786835)* 151 Michael Ln., Aberdeen, NC 28315 USA (SAN 851-3090) Tel 910-944-8857
E-mail: bevlashley@nc.rr.com
Web site: http://www.twotiredteachers.com.

Two Way Bilingual, Inc., *(978-0-941911)* Cond The Falls, No. 405, Guaynabo, PR 00657 USA (SAN 666-0169).

Two-Can Publishing *Imprint of* **T&N Children's Publishing**

TwoDot *Imprint of* **Globe Pequot Pr., The**

TwoMorrows Publishing, *(978-1-893905; 978-1-60549)* TwoMorrows Inc., 10407 Bedfordtown Dr., Raleigh, NC 27614-8058 USA Tel 919-449-0344; Fax: 919-449-0327
E-mail: twomorrow@aol.com; john@twomorrows.com
Web site: http://www.twomorrows.com
Dist(s): **Diamond Comic Distributors, Inc.**
Diamond Bk. Distributors.

TwoPenny Pubns., *(978-0-9755671)* 205 Rainbow Dr., No. 10503, Livingston, TX 77399-2005 USA
E-mail: samnalice@twopennytravels.com
Web site: http://www.79scenario.com.

Two's Company, *(978-0-9742862)* Div. of Threaded Images, 303 Wrenn Ave., New Paris, OH 45347 USA Tel 937-437-0095; 513-933-9207; Toll Free Fax: 877-217-0700; Toll Free: 800-487-0095
E-mail: sgray6@cinci.rr.com; timages@aol.com
Web site: http://www.twos-company.biz.

Two-Ten Bk. Pr., *(978-0-578-05661-6; 978-0-9827799; 978-0-9884642; 978-0-9896216; 978-1-941208; 978-1-946218)* 5 Gibson Kees Way, Sissonville, WV 25320 USA; P.O. Box 4215, Charleston, WV 25364 Tel 304-419-4169
Web site: http://www.thedarkslayer.com; http://www.thedarkslayer.net
Dist(s): **Smashwords.**

TyBook, *(978-0-9779631)* 5504 Nieman Rd., Shawnee, KS 66203 USA Tel 503-407-1217
E-mail: clayme@claytonpixton.com
Web site: http://www.tybookinc.com.

TYL Publishing, *(978-0-9753902)* 1902 Spillers Ln., Houston, TX 77043 USA Tel 713-647-9501; Fax: 713-647-9410
E-mail: tylnwt@gmail.com
Dist(s): **Partners/West Book Distributors**
Quality Bks., Inc.

Tyler, J. Publishing *See* **Crush Publishing**

Tyler Laws Pr., *(978-0-9992446)* 8344 Golf Links Rd., Oakland, CA 94605 USA Tel 510-423-1172
E-mail: enkaeconsulting@gmail.com.

Tyndale Entertainment *Imprint of* **Tyndale Hse. Pubs.**

Tyndale Espanol *Imprint of* **Tyndale Hse. Pubs.**

†Tyndale Hse. Pubs., *(978-0-8423; 978-1-4143; 978-1-4964)* Orders Addr.: 370 Executive Dr., Carol Stream, IL 60188 USA; Edit Addr.: 351 Executive Dr., Carol Stream, IL 60188 USA (SAN 206-7749) Tel 630-668-8310; Fax: 630-668-3245; Toll Free: 800-323-9400; *Imprints:* Tyndale Kids (Tyndale Kids); Tyndale Entertainment (Tyndale Ent); Thirsty(?) (Thirsty); Tyndale Espanol (Tyndale Espanol); Tyndale Momentum (TyndaleMomentum); Happy Day (HappyDay); Wander (Wander)
E-mail: international@tyndale.com; permission@tyndale.com
Web site: http://www.tyndale.com
Dist(s): **Anchor Distributors**
Brodart Co.
Christian Bk. Distributors
Cokesbury
CreateSpace Independent Publishing Platform
Editorial Unilit
Follett School Solutions
Ingram Entertainment, Inc.
Spring Arbor Distributors, Inc.; *CIP.*

Tyndale Kids *Imprint of* **Tyndale Hse. Pubs.**

Tyndale Momentum *Imprint of* **Tyndale Hse. Pubs.**

Type F, *(978-0-9768733)* P.O. Box 1045, Lodi, CA 95241-1045 USA
E-mail: info@enduranceguide.com
Web site: http://www.enduranceguide.com.

Tyr Publishing, *(978-0-9723473)* P.O. Box 19895, Fountain Hills, AZ 85269-9895 USA (SAN 254-7775) Tel 480-836-4261
E-mail: info@tyrpublishing.com
Web site: http://www.tyrpublishing.com
Dist(s): **Midpoint Trade Bks., Inc.**

Tyson, Sandi *See* **Christiangela Productions**

Tytam Publishing, *(978-0-9758602)* 111 Lincoln Ave., Suite A-9, Newark, NJ 07104-4607 USA
E-mail: Tygoode1@aol.com
Web site: http://www.tygoode.com.

Tzipora Pubns., Inc., *(978-0-9722595; 978-0-578-46157-1)* Orders Addr.: P.O. Box 115, New York, NY 10185 USA Tel 646-476-6115; Toll Free Fax: 775-414-2940
E-mail: ddg1096@gmail.com; tziporapub@msn.com
Web site: https://sites.google.com/view/dina=grossman; http://www.tziporapub.us.

U A H C Press *See* **URJ Pr.**

U H H Hale Kuamo'o Hawaiian Language Center *See* **Hale Kuamo'o Hawaiian Language Ctr. at UHH**

U. S. Capitol Historical Society, *(978-0-916200)* 200 Maryland Ave., NE, Washington, DC 20002 USA (SAN 226-6601) Tel 202-543-8919; Fax: 202-544-8244; Toll Free: 800-887-9318
E-mail: uschs@uschs.org
Web site: http://www.uschs.org
Dist(s): **University of Virginia Pr.**

Ubavie's Gifts, *(978-0-9713589)* 1550 Scenic View Dr., Loudon, TN 37774 USA
Web site: http://www.angelicgift.com.

UBUS Communications Systems, *(978-1-56411)* Div. of Khalifah's Booksellers & Associates, Orders Addr.: 26070 Barhams Hill Rd., Drewryville, VA Southhampton 23844 USA (SAN 630-6748) Tel 434-378-2140; 704-390-0663; *Imprints:* CB Publishing & Design (CB Pubng & Design)
E-mail: khalifah@khabooks.com
Web site: http://www.khabooks.com; http://www.khabooks.com; http://www.blackbooksaward.com; http://www.black-e-books.com; http://www.black-e-books.com
Dist(s): **Khalifah's Booksellers & Assocs.**

Uccello Rosso, *(978-0-9819187)* 328 Windsor St., Reading, PA 19601-2124 USA (SAN 856-955X)
E-mail: mail@uccellorosso.com
Web site: http://uccellorosso.com.

UCLA Center for Labor Research & Education *See* **Center for Labor Research and Education, Univ. of California, Los Angeles**

UFO Photo Archives, *(978-0-934269; 978-0-9608558)* 27341 Stanford St., Hemet, CA 92544 USA (SAN 240-7949) Tel 520-907-0102
Web site: http://www.UFOPhotoArchives.com.

Ufodike, Ekwutosi, *(978-0-9800538)* 3987 Nemours Trail, Kennesaw, GA 30152 USA Tel 404-574-0193
E-mail: tosi.ufodike@ge.com.

UglyTent, *(978-0-9995792)* 1154 Russell St, Ashland, KY 41101 USA Tel 606-232-2346
E-mail: uglytent@gmail.com
Web site: uglytent.com.

U-Impact Publishing LLC, *(978-0-692-38569-2; 978-0-692-38606-4; 978-0-692-39877-7; 978-0-692-45870-9; 978-0-692-49679-4; 978-0-692-49720-3; 978-0-692-50208-2; 978-0-692-52976-8; 978-0-692-57120-0; 978-0-692-57554-3; 978-0-692-65111-7; 978-0-692-65518-4; 978-0-692-65534-4; 978-0-692-69518-0; 978-0-692-72854-3; 978-0-692-72857-4) 38 Ebbtide Ln., Willingboro, NJ 08046 USA Tel 6095262226*
Dist(s): **CreateSpace Independent Publishing Platform.**

Uitti, Daniel, *(978-0-9708430; 978-0-9819478)* Div. of DaSum Company LLC, 223 Buckingham St., Oakville, CT 06779 USA Tel 860-274-9065; Fax: 860-417-0609
E-mail: dan@uitti.net
Web site: http://www.uitti.net/DaSum/.

UK Abrams Bks. for Young Readers,
Dist(s): **Abrams, Inc.**
Hachette Bk. Group.

Ullstein-Taschenbuch-Verlag (DEU) *(978-3-548) Dist. by* **Distribks Inc.**

Ultimacy Pr., *(978-0-9760205)* 11409 Parkside Pl., Bradenton, FL 34202 USA Tel 941-753-6560; Fax: 941-753-6561
E-mail: info@ultimatefinancialadvisor.com
Web site: http://www.ultimatefinancialadvisor.com.

Ultimate Bks., *(978-0-9725953; 978-0-9788430)* 104 Oakhill Key Ct., Valrico, FL 33594 USA Do not confuse with Ultimate Bks., in Glendale, CA
E-mail: info@opynyon.com
Web site: http://www.opynyon.com.

Ultimate Martial Arts CD, The *See* **Black Belt Training**

Ulverscroft Large Print Bks. (GBR) *(978-0-7089; 978-0-85456; 978-1-84395; 978-1-84617; 978-1-4448; 978-1-78541; 978-1-78782) Dist. by* **Ulverscroft US.**

Ulverscroft Large Print Bks., Ltd., *(978-0-7089; 978-1-84617)* Orders Addr.: P.O. Box 1230, West Seneca, NY 14224-1230 USA; Edit Addr.: 950 Union

Rd., West Seneca, NY 14224-3438 USA (SAN 208-3035) Toll Free: 800-955-9659
E-mail: enquiries@ulverscroft.co.uk; sales@ulverscroft.com
Web site: http://www.ulverscroft.co.uk.

Ulysses Pr., *(978-0-915233; 978-1-56975; 978-1-61243; 978-1-64604)* Orders Addr.: P.O. Box 3440, Berkeley, CA 94703-3440 USA (SAN 289-8764) Tel 510-601-8301; Fax: 510-601-8307; Toll Free: 800-377-2542; Edit Addr.: 3286 Adeline St., Suite 1, Berkeley, CA 94703 USA (SAN 289-8772)
E-mail: ulysses@ulyssespress.com
Web site: http://www.ulyssespress.com
Dist(s): **Ingram Publisher Services**
MyiLibrary
Publishers Group West (PGW)
Simon & Schuster, Inc.
Two Rivers Distribution
ebrary, Inc.

Ulyssian Pubns. *Imprint of* **Pine Orchard, Inc.**

Umbrelly Bks., *(978-0-9791127; 978-0-615-14064-3; 978-0-615-14065-0; 978-0-615-15448-0; 978-0-615-20654-7; 978-0-692-53594-3)* P.O. Box 2703, Saratoga, CA 95070-5608 USA
E-mail: umbrelly_books@yahoo.com
Web site: http://www.umbrellybooks.com
Dist(s): **Lulu Pr., Inc.**

UMI *Imprint of* **UMI (Urban Ministries, Inc.)**

UMI (Urban Ministries, Inc.), *(978-0-940955; 978-1-932715; 978-1-934056; 978-1-60352; 978-1-60997; 978-1-63038; 978-1-68353)* 1551 Regency Ct., Calumet City, IL 60409-5448 USA (SAN 665-2247) Fax: 708-868-7105; Toll Free: 800-860-8642; *Imprints*: UMI (UMI)
Web site: http://www.urbanministries.com
Dist(s): **Midpoint Trade Bks., Inc.**

Umina, Lisa M. *See* **Halo Publishing International**

Unaluna Ediciones (ARG) *(978-987-1296) Dist. by* **Lectorum Pubns.**

Unbridled Bks., *(978-1-932961; 978-1-936071; 978-1-60953)* 2000 Wadsworth Blvd., No. 195, Lakewood, CO 80214 USA Toll Free: 888-732-3822 (phone/fax)
E-mail: alexa@unbridledbooks.com; swallace@unbridledbooks.com
Web site: http://www.unbridledbooks.com
Dist(s): **Intrepid Group, Inc., The**
MyiLibrary
Publishers Group West (PGW).

Unchained Spirit Enterprises, *(978-0-9717790; 978-0-615-94962-8; 978-1-7342909)* 5432 Connecticut Ave NW No. 104, Washington, DC 20015 USA Tel 202-830-5115
Dist(s): **CreateSpace Independent Publishing Platform.**

Uncivilized Bks., *(978-0-9846814; 978-0-9889014; 978-1-941250)* 3336 30th Ave. S, Minneapolis, MN 55406 USA Tel 917-495-8637; *Imprints*: odod books (odod bks)
E-mail: chief@uncivilizedbooks.com
Web site: http://www.uncivilizedbooks.com/
Dist(s): **Consortium Bk. Sales & Distribution**
MyiLibrary.

Uncle Dave's Bks., *(978-0-692-68564-8; 978-0-692-84581-3; 978-0-9989598; 978-0-692-18597-1; 978-0-692-19848-3; 978-0-578-41013-5; 978-0-578-46788-7)* 4135 leechburg rd, new kensington, PA 15068 USA Tel 724-833-1289
Web site: www.uncledavesbooks.com; www.uncledavehoward.com
Dist(s): **Independent Pub.**

Uncle Henry Bks., *(978-1-932568)* P.O. Box 41310, Long Beach, CA 90853-1310 USA Tel 562-987-9165; Fax: 562-439-5924
E-mail: unclehenrybooks@aol.com.

Uncle Jim's Publishing, *(978-0-9800764)* Orders Addr.: c/o Potomac Adventist Bookstore, 12004 Cherry Hill Rd., Silver Spring, MD 20904 USA Tel 301-572-0700; Toll Free: 800-325-8492; P.O. Box 410, Chino Valley, AZ 86323 Tel 928-636-9419 (wholesale orders only); Fax: 928-636-1216 (wholesale orders only)
E-mail: soonchin@freezees.com
Web site: http://www.freezees.com; http://www.potomacabc.com.

Under License from Andrews UK *See* **New Publications**

Under the Green Umbrella, *(978-1-929701)* 5808 Westmont Dr., Austin, TX 78731-3836 USA Tel 512-454-2414
E-mail: janesbauld@aol.com
Web site: http://www.uts.cc.utexas.edu/~jbauld.

Underline Publishing LLC, *(978-1-949868)* P.O. Box 420790, Kissimmee, FL 34742 USA Tel 321-203-9874
E-mail: fcstarosa@gmail.com
Web site: www.underlinepublishing.com.

Underlined *Imprint of* **Random Hse. Children's Bks.**

Understanding For Life Ministries, Inc., *(978-0-9714584; 978-0-9721504; 978-0-9749019; 978-0-9797019; 978-0-9822938; 978-0-9833673; 978-0-9850813; 978-0-9904982; 978-0-9970699; 978-1-7343057)* 3665 Kirby Pkwy., Suite 6, Memphis, TN 38115 USA Tel 901-844-3962; Fax: 901-844-3944
E-mail: info@understandingforlife.org
Web site: http://www.understandingforlife.org
Dist(s): **BookBaby.**

Understanding Nutrition PC, *(978-0-9764002; 978-0-9800334)* Orders Addr.: 6240 E. Univ. Blvd., Dallas, TX 75214 USA Tel 214-503-7100
E-mail: jessica@understandingnutrition.com
Web site: http://www.understandingnutrition.com.

Underwood Books, *(978-0-88733; 978-0-934438; 978-1-887424; 978-1-59929)* Orders Addr.: P.O. Box 1919, Nevada City, CA 95945 USA Tel 530-470-9095; Fax: 530-470-9049; Edit Addr.: 12514 Cavanaugh Ln., Navada City, CA 95959 USA
E-mail: tim@underwoodbooks.com; contact@underwoodbooks.com
Web site: http://www.underwoodbooks.com
Dist(s): **Publishers Group West (PGW).**

Unicorn Castle Bks., *(978-0-615-56949-9; 978-0-9890340)* 1110 Pack Rd., White Bluff, TN 37187 USA Tel 615-477-4097; 509-999-4551
E-mail: unicorncastle@bellsouth.net
Web site: http://www.kerrydking.com.

Unicorn Pr., *(978-0-937004)* 3300 Chestnut St., Reading, PA 19605 USA Tel 610-929-8306 Do not confuse with Unicorn Pr. in Northville, MI
E-mail: kthynoll@aol.com
Web site: http://hometown.aol.com/kthynoll.

Uniformology, *(978-0-9815078; 978-1-935344)* 105 Coates Trail, Weatherford, TX 76087 USA Tel 817-629-9205
E-mail: uniformology@mac.com
Web site: http://www.uniformology.com.

Union Creek Communications, Inc., *(978-0-9721404)* P.O. Box 1811, Bryson City, NC 28713 USA Tel 828-488-3596; Fax: 828-488-1018
E-mail: info@researchpaperstation.com
Web site: http://researchpaperstation.com.

Unique Artistic Creations Showcase, *(978-0-9892127; 978-0-9993142)* 4540 60th St., Ste.111, San Diego, CA 92115 USA Tel 619-955-8083
E-mail: ctpetate@gmail.com.

Unique Executive Pubs., *(978-0-9744978)* Div. of Unique Executive.com, 1653 Georgia Hwy. 257, Suite A, Cordele, GA 31015 USA Tel 229-273-8121; Fax: 229-273-7289; *Imprints*: Healthful Living Books (Living Books)
E-mail: harvardg@sowega.net
Web site: http://upublish.uniquexecutive.com.

Uniquely You Resources, *(978-0-9627245; 978-1-888846)* P.O. Box 490, Blue Ridge, GA 30513 USA Tel 706 492 4709; 706-492-5490
E-mail: drmels@myuy.com
Web site: http://www.myuy.com; http://www.uyprofiler.com
Dist(s): **Send The Light Distribution LLC.**

Unisystems, Inc., *(978-0-7666; 978-0-87449; 978-1-56144)* 155 55th St., New York, NY 10022 USA Tel 212-826-0850; Fax: 212-758-4166
Web site: http://www.modernpublishing.com.

†Unitarian Universalist Assn., *(978-0-933840; 978-1-55896; 978-1-946169)* 25 Beacon St., Boston, MA 02108-2800 USA (SAN 225-4840) Tel 617-742-2100; Fax: 617-742-7025; Toll Free: 800-215-9076; *Imprints*: Skinner House Books (Skinner Hse)
Web site: http://www.uua.org
Dist(s): **Red Wheel/Weiser**; *CIP.*

United Bible Societies Association Inc., *(978-1-57697; 978-1-930564; 978-1-931471; 978-1-931952; 978-1-932507; 978-1-933218; 978-1-59877)* 11401 SW 40TH ST Suite 201, MIAMI, FL 33165 USA Tel 305-702-1824; 305-593-0009; Fax: 305-702-1817 Do not confuse with United Bible Societies, New York, NY
E-mail: jhazbun@biblesocieties.org
Web site: http://www.unitedbiblesocieties.org
Dist(s): **American Bible Society.**

United Bible Societies/Americas Service Center *See* **United Bible Societies Association Inc.**

United Christian Fellowship of Chapel Hill, North Carolina *See* **Armour of Light Publishing**

United Comics, *(978-0-9743086)* Div. of Obsidian Entertainment, P.O. Box 401, Milford, CT 06460-0401 USA Toll Free: 800-546-3249 (phone/fax)
E-mail: unitedcomicworks@gmail.com
Web site: http://www.unitedcomicworks.com.

United Educators, Inc., *(978-0-87566)* 900 W. North Shore Dr. Ste. 279, Lake Bluff, IL 60044-2210 USA (SAN 204-8795).

UNITED Hse. Publishing, *(978-1-7327194; 978-1-952840)*
E-mail: info@unitedhousepublishing.com
Web site: http://unitedhousepublishing.com.

United InnoWorks Academy, *(978-0-9771380; 978-1-936478)* 9721 Conestoga Way, Potomac, MD 20854-4711 USA
E-mail: executive@innoworks.org; staff@innoworks.org
Web site: http://www.innoworks.org.

United Nation of Islam, The, *(978-0-9768502)* 1608 N. 13th St., Kansas City, KS 66102 USA Tel 913-342-0758; Fax: 913-342-0340; Toll Free: 800-331-7668
E-mail: unoi@unoi.org
Web site: http://www.unoi.org.

†United Nations Fund for Population Activities, *(978-0-89714; 978-1-61800)* 605 Third Ave, New York, NY 10158 USA (SAN 222-4429) Tel 212-297-4956; Fax: 212-370-0201
Web site: http://www.unfpa.org
Dist(s): **Casemate Pubs. & Bk. Distributors, LLC**
Rowman & Littlefield Publishers, Inc.
United Nations Pubns.; *CIP.*

United Network for Organ Sharing, *(978-1-886651)* Orders Addr.: P.O. Box 2484, Richmond, VA 23218 USA Tel 804-782-4800; Edit Addr.: 700 N. 4th St., Richmond, VA 23219 USA
Web site: http://www.unos.org.

United Optical Publishing Co., *(978-0-9764337)* 9147 Millbranch Rd., Southaven, MS 38671 USA
Web site: http://www.steelguitarbyhughjeffreys.com.

United Research Publishers, *(978-0-9614924; 978-1-887053)* Div. of Solor Products, Inc., 2233 Faraday Ave., Suite G, Carlsbad, CA 92008-7214 USA (SAN 693-5834) Tel 760-930-8937; Fax: 760-930-4291 Do not confuse with United Research, Black Mountain, NC
Web site: http://www.unitedresearchpubs.com.

†United States Government Printing Office, *(978-0-16; 978-0-18)* Orders Addr.: P.O. Box 371954, Pittsburgh, PA 15250-7954 USA (SAN 658-0785) Tel 202-512-1800; Fax: 202-512-2250; Toll Free: 866-512-1800; Edit Addr.: USGPO Stop SSMB, Washington, DC 20401 USA (SAN 206-152X) Tel 202-512-1705 (bibliographic information only); 202-512-2268 (book dealers only); Fax: 202-512-1655; *Imprints*: Defense Department (Defense Dept); Environmental Protection Agency (Envir Protect); Health and Human Services Department (Hlth & Human); Interior Department (Interior Dept); Copyright Office (Copyright Office); Defense Acquisition University (DefenseAcq U); Department of the Army (Dept Army); Federal Emergency Management Agency (F E M A); Food Safety & Inspection Service (F S I S); Forest Service (Forest Service); Joint Committee on Printing (Joint ComPrint); Joint Committee on Taxation (JointCommTaxation); National Defense University (National DefU); National Institute on Alcohol Abuse & Alcoholism (NIAAA); National Marine Fisheries Service (NMFS)
E-mail: orders@gpo.gov; rdavis@gpo.gov; ContactCenter@gpo.gov
Web site: http://bookstore.gpo.gov; https://www.gpo.gov
Dist(s): **Bernan Assocs.**
MyiLibrary
Rowman & Littlefield Publishers, Inc.
Trucatriche
ebrary, Inc.; *CIP.*

United States Judo Federation, Inc., *(978-0-9729790)* P.O. Box 338, Ontario, OR 97914-0338 USA Tel 541-889-8753; Fax: 541-889-5836
E-mail: natofc@usjf.com
Web site: http://www.usjf.com.

United States Power Squadrons, *(978-1-891148; 978-1-938405)* Orders Addr.: P.O. Box 30423, Raleigh, NC 27622 USA Tel 919-821-0281; Fax: 919-836-0813; Toll Free: 888-367-8777; Edit Addr.: 1504 Blue Ridge Rd., Raleigh, NC 27607 USA
Web site: http://www.usps.org.

United States Trotting Association, *(978-0-9793891)* 750 Michigan Ave., Columbus, OH 43215 USA Tel 614-224-2291 Toll Free: 877-800-8782 (ext. 3260)
E-mail: jamie.rucker@ustrotting.com; HRCNews@ustrotting.com
Web site: http://www.ustrotting.com.

United Synagogue of America Bk. Service, *(978-0-8381)* Subs. of United Synagogue of America, 820 2nd Ave., New York, NY 10017-4504 USA (SAN 203-0551)
E-mail: booksvc@uscj.org
Web site: http://www.uscj.org/booksvc.
Dist(s): **Rowman & Littlefield Publishers, Inc.**

United Writers Pr., *(978-0-9725197; 978-0-9760824; 978-1-934216; 978-1-945338; 978-1-952248)* Orders Addr.: 17 Willow Tree Run, Asheville, NC 28803 USA
E-mail: vsharpe@unitedwriterspress.com
Web site: http://www.unitedwriterspress.com.

Unitrust Design, *(978-0-9752775)* P.O. Box 653, Loma Linda, CA 92354 USA
E-mail: unitrustdesign@aol.com
Web site: http://www.unitrustdesign.com.

Unity Books & Multimedia Publishing (Unity School of Christianity) *See* **Unity Schl. of Christianity**

Unity Hse. *Imprint of* **Unity Schl. of Christianity**

Unity Schl. of Christianity, *(978-0-87159)* Orders Addr.: 1901 NW Blue Pkwy., Unity Village, MO 64065-0001 USA (SAN 204-8817) Tel 816-524-3550; 816 251-3571 (ordering); Fax: 816-251-3551; *Imprints*: Unity House (Unity Hse)
E-mail: unity@unityworldhq.org
Web site: http://www.unity.org
Dist(s): **BookBaby**
DeVorss & Co.
New Leaf Distributing Co., Inc.

Univ. of Alberta Pr. (CAN) *(978-0-88864; 978-0-919058; 978-1-55195; 978-1-896445; 978-1-77212) Dist. by* **Wayne St U Pr.**

Univ. of Ottawa Pr./Presses de l'Universite d'Ottawa (CAN) *(978-0-7766; 978-2-7603) Dist. by* **TwoRivers.**

Univ. of Queensland Pr. (AUS) *(978-0-7022; 978-1-875491; 978-0-646-96356-3) Dist. by* **IPG Chicago.**

Univ. of the West Indies Pr. (JAM) *(978-976-640; 978-976-41-0029-4; 978-976-41-0044-7; 978-976-41-0068-3; 978-976-41-0109-3) Dist. by* **U of NC Pr.**

Universal Flag Publishing, *(978-1-933426)* Div. of Universal Flag Cos., 1440 W. Maple Ave., Suite 6B, Lisle, IL 60532 USA Tel 630-245-8500
E-mail: publishing@universalflag.com
Web site: www.universalflag.com.

Universal Handwriting *See* **Universal Publishing**

Universal Life Matters, Incorporated *See* **Quality of Life Publishing Co.**

Universal Marketing Media, Inc., *(978-0-9764272)* Orders Addr.: P.O. Box 7575, Pensacola, FL 32534-0575 USA Toll Free: 877-437-7811
E-mail: sales@universalmarketingmedia.com
Web site: http://www.universalmarketingmedia.com.

Universal Messengers Pubns., *(978-0-9768879)* P.O. Box 9039, Wilmington, DE 19809 USA Tel 302-764-4293; Toll Free: 866-207-9301
E-mail: phdfoxx@msn.com; phdfoxx@verizon.net
Web site: http://mysite.verizon.net/vze0488v.

Universal Politics (Politics & Social Sciences) *Imprint of* **Speedy Publishing LLC**

Universal Pubs., *(978-0-9658564; 978-1-58112; 978-1-59942; 978-1-61233; 978-1-62734)* Orders Addr.: 200 Spectrum Ctr. Dr. Ste 300, Irvine, CA 92618-5004 USA Tel 561-750-4344; Fax: 561-750-6797; Toll Free: 800-636-8329
E-mail: bookorders@upublish.com; bookorders@universal-publishers.com
Web site: http://www.dissertation.com; http://www.universal-publishers.com; http://www.BrownWalker.com.

Universal Publishing, *(978-1-883421; 978-1-931181; 978-1-934732)* Subs. of Gutenberg, Inc., 677 Roosevelt Hwy., Waymart, PA 18472 USA Tel 570-488-9820; Fax: 570-488-9750; Toll Free: 800-940-2270 Do not confuse with companies with the same or similar name in Ecino, CA, Egg Harbor Township, NJ, Gainesville, FL, Newport Beach, CA, Stoughton, MA, Pasadena, CA, Oak Park, IL, Jacksonville, FL
E-mail: tom@upub.net; larry@upub.net
Web site: http://www.upub.net; http://www.universalpublishing.net.

Universal Publishing LLC, *(978-0-9840456)* P.O. Box 99491, Emeryville, CA 94606 USA Tel 510-485-1183
E-mail: universalpublishingllc@gmail.com
Web site: www.universalpublishingllc@gmail.com.

Universal Reference Pubns. *Imprint of* **Grey Hse. Publishing**

Universal Values Media, LLC, *(978-0-9729821; 978-1-60210)* 3800 Powell Ln., No. 823, Falls Church, VA 22041 USA
Web site: http://www.onceandfuturebooks.com.

Universe Publishing, *(978-0-7893; 978-0-87663; 978-1-55550)* Div. of Rizzoli International Pubns., Inc., 300 Park Ave. S., 3rd Flr., New York, NY 10010 USA (SAN 202-537X) Tel 212-387-3400; Fax: 212-387-3444 Do not confuse with similar names in North Hollywood, CA, Englewood, NJ, Mendocino, CA
Dist(s): **Andrews McMeel Publishing**
Ingram Publisher Services
MyiLibrary
Penguin Random Hse. Distribution
Penguin Random Hse. LLC
Random Hse., Inc.
Rizzoli International Pubns., Inc.

Univ. At Buffalo, Child Care Ctr., *(978-0-9712349)* Butler Annex A, 3435 Main St., Buffalo, NY 14214-3011 USA Tel 716-829-2226
E-mail: rorrange@buffalo.edu.

Univ. Editions, *(978-0-9711659; 978-0-615-11379-1; 978-0-692-63610-7; 978-0-578-48615-4)* 1003 W. Centennial Dr., Peoria, IL 61614-2828 USA Tel 309-692-0621; Fax: 309-693-0628 Do not confuse with University Editions in Huntington, WV
E-mail: mikruc@aol.com
Web site: http://www.terrythetractor.com.

Univ. Games, *(978-0-935145; 978-1-57528)* 2030 Harrison St., San Francisco, CA 94110-1310 USA (SAN 695-2321) Tel 415-503-1600; Fax: 415-503-0085
E-mail: info@ugames.com
Web site: http://www.ugames.com.

†Univ. of Alabama Pr., *(978-0-8173)* Orders Addr.: 11030 S. Langley, Chicago, IL 60628 USA Tel 773-702-7000; Toll Free: 800-621-2736; Edit Addr.: P.O. Box 870380, Tuscaloosa, AL 35487-0380 USA (SAN 202-5272) Tel 205-348-5180; Fax: 205-348-9201
Web site: http://www.uapress.ua.edu
Dist(s): **Casemate Academic**
Chicago Distribution Ctr.
Univ. of Chicago Pr.
ebrary, Inc.; *CIP.*

Univ. of Alaska Pr., *(978-0-912006; 978-1-889963; 978-1-60223)* P.O. Box 756240, Fairbanks, AK 99775-6240 USA (SAN 203-3011) Tel 907-474-5831; Fax: 907-474-5502; Toll Free: 888-252-6657
E-mail: fypress@uaf.edu; sue.mitchell@alaska.edu
Web site: http://www.alaska.edu/uapress
Dist(s): **Chicago Distribution Ctr.**
Wizard Works
ebrary, Inc.

Univ. of Arizona, Poetry Ctr., Arizona Board of Regents, *(978-0-9727635)* c/o Univ. of Arizona Poetry Ctr.,, 1216 N. Cherry Ave., Tucson, AZ 85719 USA Tel 520-626-3765; Fax: 520-621-5566
E-mail: poetry@u.arizona.edu
Web site: http://www.poetrycenter.arizona.edu.

†University of Arizona Pr., *(978-0-8165; 978-1-941451)* 355 S. Euclid Ave., Suite 103, Tucson, AZ 85719 USA (SAN 205-468X) Tel 520-621-1441; Fax: 520-621-8899; Toll Free: 800-426-3797 (orders)
E-mail: orders@uapress.arizona.edu
Web site: http://www.uapress.arizona.edu
Dist(s): **Casemate Academic**
Chicago Distribution Ctr.
Continental Bk. Co., Inc.
Many Feathers Bks. & Maps
MyiLibrary
Univ. of Chicago Pr.
Univ of Arizona Critical Languages Program
ebrary, Inc.; *CIP.*

†Univ. of Arkansas Pr., *(978-0-938626; 978-1-55728; 978-1-61075; 978-1-68226)* 105 N. McIlroy Ave., Fayetteville, AR 72701 USA (SAN 239-3972) Tel 479-575-7544; Fax: 479-575-6044; Toll Free: 800-626-0090
E-mail: info@uapress.com
Web site: http://www.uapress.com; http://www.uark.edu/~uaprinfo
Dist(s): **Chicago Distribution Ctr.**
MyiLibrary
Yankee Peddler Bookshop
ebrary, Inc.; *CIP.*

Univ. of California, Berkeley, Lawrence Hall of Science, *(978-0-912511; 978-0-924886; 978-1-931542)* U of CA, Lawrence Hall of Science, Berkeley, CA 94720-5200 USA (SAN 271-9754) Tel 510-642-7771; Fax:

510-643-0309; *Imprints:* GEMS (GEMS); EQUALS (EQUALS)
E-mail: gems@berkeley.edu
Web site: http://www.lhs.berkeley.edu; http://www.lhsgems.org
Dist(s): **Distributors, The.**

†Univ. of California Pr., *(978-0-520; 978-1-7323203)* 155 Grand Ave., Suite 400, Oakland, CA 94612-3758 USA Tel 510-883-8232 (Books & Journals); Fax: 510-836-8910
E-mail: journals@ucpress.edu; orders@cpfsinc.com; askucp@ucpress.edu
Web site: http://www.ucpress.edu
Dist(s): **Ebsco Publishing**
MyiLibrary
Perseus Bks. Group
Ingram Academic
Two Rivers Distribution
ebrary, Inc.; *CIP.*

†Univ. of Chicago Pr., *(978-0-226; 978-0-89065; 978-0-943056; 978-1-892850)* Orders Addr.: 11030 S. Langley Ave., Chicago, IL 60628 USA (SAN 202-5280) Tel 773-702-7000; Fax: 773-702-7212; Toll Free Fax: 800-621-8476 (US & Canada); Toll Free: 800-621-2736 (US & Canada); Edit Addr.: 1427 E. 60th St., Chicago, IL 60637 USA (SAN 202-5299) Tel 773-702-7700; 773-702-7748 (Marketing & Sales); Fax: 773-702-9756
E-mail: general@press.uchicago.edu; kh@press.uchicago.edu; custserv@press.uchicago.rdu; sales@press.uchicago.edu; marketing@press.uchicago.edu; publicity@press.uchicago.edu
Web site: http://www.press.uchicago.edu
Dist(s): **Chicago Distribution Ctr.**
CreateSpace Independent Publishing Platform
Ebsco Publishing
Giron Bks.
ISD
MyiLibrary
Oxford Univ. Pr., Inc.
Open Road Integrated Media, Inc.
TNT Media Group, Inc.
Wiley, John & Sons, Inc.
ebrary, Inc.; *CIP.*

Univ. of Denver, Ctr. for Teaching International Relations Pubns., *(978-0-943804)* 2201 S. Gaylord St., Denver, CO 80208 USA (SAN 241-0877) Tel 303-871-2697; Fax: 303-871-2456
E-mail: ctir-press@du.edu; pubsinfo@du.edu
Web site: http://www.du.edu/ctir
Dist(s): **Ingram Content Group**
Social Studies Schl. Service
Teacher's Discovery.

†Univ. of Georgia, Carl Vinson Institute of Government, *(978-0-89854)* 201 N. Milledge Ave., Athens, GA 30602 USA (SAN 212-8012) Tel 706-542-2736; Fax: 706-542-6239
E-mail: pou@cviog.uga.edu
Web site: http://www.cviog.uga.edu; *CIP.*

†Univ. of Georgia Pr., *(978-0-8203)* Orders Addr.: 4435 Atlanta Hwy. West Dock, Athens, GA 30602 USA; Edit Addr.: Main Library, Third Flr. 320 S. Jackson St., Athens, GA 30602 USA (SAN 203-3054) Fax: 706-542-2558; Toll Free: 800-266-5842
E-mail: books@uga.edu
Web site: http://www.ugapress.org
Dist(s): **Ebsco Publishing**
Longleaf Services
MyiLibrary
ebrary, Inc.; *CIP.*

Univ. of Guam, Micronesian Area Research Ctr., *(978-1-878453; 978-0-9800331; 978-1-935198)* 303 University Dr., UOG Sta., Mangilao, GU 96923 USA Tel 671-735-2150; Fax: 671-734-7403
Web site: http://www.uog.edu/marc
Dist(s): **Univ. of Hawaii Pr.**

†Univ. of Hawaii Pr., *(978-0-8248; 978-0-87022)* Orders Addr.: 2840 Kolowalu St., Honolulu, HI 96822-1888 USA (SAN 202-5353) Tel 808-956-8255; Fax: 808-988-6052; Toll Free Fax: 800-650-7811; Toll Free: 888-847-7377; *Imprints:* Latitude 20 (Latitude Twenty)
E-mail: uhpmkt@hawaii.edu; uhpbooks@hawaii.edu
Web site: http://www.uhpress.hawaii.edu
Dist(s): **Booklines Hawaii, Ltd.**
De Gruyter, Inc.
University of Hawaii Press Agrmt. 2; *CIP.*

†Univ. of Iowa Pr., *(978-0-87745; 978-1-58729; 978-1-60938)* Div. of The University of Iowa, Orders Addr.: c/o Chicago Distribution Ctr. 11030 S. Langley Ave., Chicago, IL 60628 USA Toll Free Fax: 800-621-8476; Toll Free: 800-621-2736; Edit Addr.: 100 Kuhl Hse. 119 W. Park Rd., Iowa City, IA 52242-1000 USA (SAN 203-3070) Tel 319-335-2000; Fax: 319-335-2055 Do not confuse with Univ. of Iowa, Pubns. Dept. at same address
E-mail: uipress@uiowa.edu
Web site: http://www.uiowapress.org
Dist(s): **Chicago Distribution Ctr.**
Ebsco Publishing
Univ. of Chicago Pr.
ebrary, Inc.; *CIP.*

University of Kwazulu-Natal Press (ZAF) *(978-0-86980; 978-1-86840; 978-1-874897; 978-1-86914; 978-1-86914-350-3) Dist. by* **IPG Chicago.**

University of Louisiana at Lafayette *See* **Univ. of Louisiana at Lafayette Pr.**

Univ. of Louisiana at Lafayette Pr., *(978-0-940984; 978-1-887366; 978-1-935754; 978-1-946160)* P.O. Box 43558, Lafayette, LA 70504 USA (SAN 630-9755) Tel 337-482-6027; Fax: 337-482-6028
E-mail: cls@louisiana.edu
Web site: http://www.ulpress.org
Dist(s): **Forest Sales & Distributing Co.**

†Univ. of Michigan Pr., *(978-0-472)* Orders Addr.: c/o Chicago Distribution Center, Perseus Distribution 1094 Flex Dr., Jackson, TN 38301 USA (SAN 282-4884) Toll Free Fax: 800-351-5073; Toll Free: 800-343-4499 , ext. 165; Edit Addr.: 839 Greene St., Ann Arbor, MI 48104-3209 USA Tel 734-764-4388; Fax: 734-615-1540
E-mail: um.press@umich.edu
Web site: http://www.press.umich.edu/
Dist(s): **Chicago Distribution Ctr.**
Ebsco Publishing
MyiLibrary
Palgrave Macmillan
ebrary, Inc.; *CIP.*

†Univ. of Minnesota Pr., *(978-0-8166; 978-1-4529; 978-1-5179)* Affil. of Univ. of Minnesota, 111 Third Ave. S., Suite 290, Minneapolis, MN 55401-2520 USA (SAN 213-2648) Tel 612-627-1970; Fax: 612-627-1980
E-mail: ump@umn.edu
Web site: http://www.upress.umn.edu
Dist(s): **Chicago Distribution Ctr.**
Ebsco Publishing
MyiLibrary
Univ. of Chicago Pr.
ebrary, Inc.; *CIP.*

Univ. of Missouri, Extension, *(978-0-933842)* a/o University of Missouri Extension, 506 Hitt St., 4 Whitten Hall, Columbia, MO 65211-6300 USA Tel 573-882-7216; 573-882-6845; Fax: 573-882-8007; Toll Free: 800-292-0969
E-mail: extpubs@missouri.edu; muextensionweb@missouri.edu; nexus@missouri.edu
Web site: http://https://extension.missouri.edu.

†Univ. of Missouri Pr., *(978-0-8262)* 2910 LeMone Blvd., Columbia, MO 65201 USA (SAN 203-3143) Tel 573-882-7641; Fax: 573-884-4498; Toll Free: 800-828-1894 (orders only)
E-mail: rennerk@umsystem.edu; deandj@umsystem.edu
Web site: http://press.umsystem.edu
Dist(s): **Chicago Distribution Ctr.**
East-West Export Bks.
Ebsco Publishing
Lulu Pr., Inc.
Univ. of Chicago Pr.
ebrary, Inc.; *CIP.*

Univ. of Montana Pr., The, *(978-0-9754009; 978-0-9815760; 978-0-9837259; 978-0-9894031; 978-0-9909748; 978-0-9983438)* Div. of The Univ. of Montana, The University of Montana 32 Campus Dr. Todd Bldg., Lower Level, Missoula, MT 59812-0792 USA (SAN 255-9994) Tel 406-243-2711; Fax: 406-243-2615
E-mail: ken.price@umontana.edu
Web site: http://www.umt.edu/printingandgraphics.com.

†Univ. of Nebraska Pr., *(978-0-8032; 978-1-4962; 978-1-64012)* Orders Addr.: 1111 Lincoln Mall, Lincoln, NE 68588-0630 USA Tel 402-472-3581; 402-472-7702; Fax: 402-472-6214; Toll Free Fax: 800-526-2617; Toll Free: 800-755-1105; Edit Addr.: P.O. Box 880630, Lincoln, NE 68588-0630 USA (SAN 202-5337); *Imprints:* Bison Books (Bison Books)
E-mail: pressmail@unl.edu
Web site: http://www.nebraskapress.unl.edu; http://www.bisonbooks.com
Dist(s): **Casemate Pubs. & Bk. Distributors, LLC**
Continental Bk. Co., Inc.
Ebsco Publishing
Longleaf Services
MyiLibrary
ebrary, Inc.; *CIP.*

Univ. of Nebraska-Lincoln, GPN, *(978-0-7941)* Orders Addr.: P.O. Box 80669, Lincoln, NE 68501-0669 USA (SAN 179-1699) Tel 402-472-2007; Fax: 402-472-4076; Toll Free: 800-228-4630; Edit Addr.: 1800 N. 33rd St., Lincoln, NE 68583 USA
E-mail: gpn@unl.edu
Web site: http://gpn.unl.edu; http://shopgpn.com/.

†Univ. of New Mexico Pr., *(978-0-8263; 978-0-9766839)* Orders Addr.: 1312 Basehart Rd., SE, Albuquerque, NM 87106-4363 USA (SAN 213-9588) Tel 505-277-2346; 505-272-7777 (orders); Toll Free Fax: 800-622-8667; Toll Free: 800-249-7737 (orders)
E-mail: unmpress@unm.edu
Web site: http://www.unmpress.com
Dist(s): **Bks. West**
Casemate Academic
Continental Bk. Co., Inc.
D.A.P./Distributed Art Pubs.
MyiLibrary
Rio Nuevo Pubs.
ebrary, Inc.; *CIP.*

†Univ. of North Carolina Pr., *(978-0-8078; 978-1-4696)* c/o Longleaf Services, 116 S. Boundary St., Chapel Hill, NC 27514-3808 USA (SAN 203-3151) Tel 919-966-3561; Fax: 919-966-3829; Toll Free Fax: 800-272-6817; Toll Free: 800-848-6224
E-mail: uncpress@unc.edu
Web site: http://www.uncpress.unc.edu
Dist(s): **CreateSpace Independent Publishing Platform**
D.A.P./Distributed Art Pubs.
Ebsco Publishing
Longleaf Services
Oxford Univ. Pr., Inc.
ebrary, Inc.; *CIP.*

†Univ. of Notre Dame Pr., *(978-0-268)* Orders Addr.: 11030 S. Langley Ave., Chicago, IL 60628 USA Tel 773-702-7000; Fax: 773-702-7212; Toll Free Fax: 800-621-8476; Toll Free: 800-621-2736; Edit Addr.: 310 Flanner Hall, Notre Dame, IN 46556 USA (SAN 203-3178) Tel 574-631-6346; Fax: 574-631-8148
E-mail: undpress.1@nd.edu
Web site: http://www.undpress.nd.edu
Dist(s): **Ebsco Publishing**
Longleaf Services
Univ. of Chicago Pr.
ebrary, Inc.; *CIP.*

†Univ. of Oklahoma Pr., *(978-0-8061)* Orders Addr.: 2800 Venture Dr., Norman, OK 73069-8218 USA Tel 405-325-2000; Fax: 405-364-5798; Toll Free Fax: 800-735-0476; Toll Free: 800-627-7377
E-mail: presscs@ou.edu
Web site: http://www.oupress.com
Dist(s): **Ebsco Publishing**
Longleaf Services
ebrary, Inc.; *CIP.*

†Univ. of Pennsylvania Pr., *(978-0-8122; 978-1-5128)* Orders Addr.: c/o Hopkins Fullfillment Srvc., Hopkins Fulfillment Service, Baltimore, MD 21211-4370 USA Tel 410-516-6948; Fax: 410-516-6998; Toll Free: 800-537-5487; Edit Addr.: 3905 Spruce St., Philadelphia, PA 19104-4112 USA (SAN 202-5345) Tel 215-898-6261; Fax: 215-898-0404; Toll Free: 800-537-5487 (book orders)
E-mail: custserv@pobox.upenn.edu
Web site: http://www.upenn.edu/pennpress
Dist(s): **De Gruyter, Inc.**
Hopkins Fulfillment Services
MyiLibrary
TNT Media Group, Inc.
Two Rivers Distribution; *CIP.*

Univ. of Phoenix Bookstore, *(978-0-578-52063-6; 978-0-578-52064-3)* a/o University of Phoenix Bookstore, 4615 E. Elwood St., Phoenix, AZ 85040 USA Tel 602-966-7400 Ext. 2124; Fax: 602-920-9030.

†Univ. of Pittsburgh Pr., *(978-0-8229)* 3400 Forbes Ave., Eureka Bldg., Fifth Flr., Pittsburgh, PA 15260 USA (SAN 203-3216) Tel 412-383-2456; Fax: 412-383-2466
E-mail: press@pitt.edu
Web site: http://www.upress.pitt.edu
Dist(s): **Chicago Distribution Ctr.**
ISD
MyiLibrary; *CIP.*

†Univ. of Puerto Rico Pr., *(978-0-8477)* Subs. of Univ. of Puerto Rico, Orders Addr.: P.O. Box 23322, Rio Piedras, PR 00931-3322 USA (SAN 208-1245) Tel 787-250-0435 Administrative Offices; 787-250-8996 Administrative Offices; 787-758-8345 Sales Office and Warehouse; 787-751-8251 Sales Office and Warehouse; 787-934-3400 Sales Office and Warehouse; Fax: 787-753-9116 Administrative Offices; 787-751-8785 Sales/Warehouse, Ordering fax
E-mail: info@laeditorialupr.com
Web site: http://www.laeditorialupr.com
Dist(s): **Ediciones Universal**
Lectorum Pubns., Inc.
Libros Sin Fronteras; *CIP.*

University of Regina Pr. (CAN) *(978-0-88977) Dist. by* **IngramPubServ.**

University of Regina Pr. (CAN) *(978-0-88977) Dist. by* **TwoRivers.**

Univ. of Rhode Island, Sea Grant Pubns. Unit, *(978-0-938412)* Narragansett Bay Campus, Narragansett, RI 02882-1197 USA (SAN 209-0708) Tel 401-874-6800
E-mail: tkennedy@mail.uri.edu
Web site: http://www.seagrant.gso.uri.edu/riseagrant
Dist(s): **Chicago Distribution Ctr.**

Univ. of Scranton Pr., *(978-0-940866; 978-1-58966)* Orders Addr.: c/o Univ. of Scranton Pr., St. Thomas Hall, Linden & Monroe Sts., Scranton, PA 18510 USA Toll Free Fax: 800-941-8804; Toll Free: 800-941-3081; Edit Addr.: Linden & Monroe Sts., Scranton, PA 18510 USA (SAN 288-4067) Tel 570-941-7955; Fax: 570-941-4309
E-mail: richard.rousseau@uofs.edu
Web site: http://www.scrantonpress.com
Dist(s): **Associated Univ. Presses**
Chicago Distribution Ctr.

†Univ. of South Carolina Pr., *(978-0-87249; 978-1-57003; 978-1-61117; 978-1-64336)* Orders Addr.: 718 Devine St., Columbia, SC 29208 USA Tel 803-777-1774; Fax: 803-777-0026; Toll Free Fax: 800-868-0740; Toll Free: 800-768-2500; Edit Addr.: 1600 Hampton St., 5th Flr., Columbia, SC 29208 USA (SAN 203-3224) Tel 803-777-5243; Fax: 803-777-0160; Toll Free Fax: 800-868-0740; Toll Free: 800-768-2500
E-mail: jhaupt@sc.edu
Web site: http://www.sc.edu/uscpress/
Dist(s): **Ebsco Publishing**
MyiLibrary
ebrary, Inc.; *CIP.*

Univ. St. Mary of the Lake, Mundelein Seminary, *(978-0-9774733)* 1000 E. Maple Ave., Mundelein, IL 60060 USA Tel 847-566-6401; Fax: 847-566-7330
E-mail: info@usml.edu
Web site: http://www.usml.edu.

University of Tampa *See* **Univ. of Tampa Pr.**

Univ. of Tampa Pr., *(978-1-879852; 978-1-59732)* 401 W. Kennedy Blvd., Tampa, FL 33606 USA Tel 813-253-6266; Fax: 813-258-7593
E-mail: utpress@ut.edu
Web site: http://utpress.ut.edu.

Univ. of Temecula Pr., Inc., *(978-0-936283)* 42730 De Luz Ave., Murrieta, CA 92562-7214 USA (SAN 697-9793) Tel 951-698-0059; Fax: 951-698-3676; *Imprints:* UTP (UTP)
E-mail: mikeray@utem.com
Web site: http://www.utem.com.

†Univ. of Texas Pr., *(978-0-292; 978-1-4773)* Orders Addr.: P.O. Box 7819, Austin, TX 78713-7819 USA (SAN 212-9876) Tel 512-471-7233; Fax: 512-232-7178; Toll Free: 800-252-3206; Edit Addr.: University of Texas at Austin 2100 Comal, Austin, TX 78722 USA
E-mail: info@utpress.utexas.edu
Web site: http://www.utexas.edu/utpress
Dist(s): **Continental Bk. Co., Inc.**
Ebsco Publishing
Urban Land Institute
ebrary, Inc.; *CIP.*

†Univ. of Utah Pr., *(978-0-87480; 978-1-60781; 978-1-64769)* 295 S. 1500 E., Suite 5400, Salt Lake City, UT 84112-0860 USA (SAN 220-0023) Tel 801-585-0082; Fax: 801-581-3365; Toll Free: 800-773-6672
E-mail: info@upress.utah.edu
Web site: www.uofupress.com
Dist(s): **Casemate Academic**
Chicago Distribution Ctr.
Partners Bk. Distributing, Inc.
Rio Nuevo Pubs.
ebrary, Inc.; *CIP.*

†University of Virginia Pr., *(978-0-8139; 978-0-912759; 978-1-57814)* Orders Addr.: P.O. Box 400318, Charlottesville, VA 22904-4318 USA (SAN 202-5361) Tel 804-924-3468; Fax: 804-982-2655
E-mail: upress@virginia.edu
Web site: http://www.upress.virginia.edu
Dist(s): **Ediciones Universal**
Fordham Univ. Pr.
Longleaf Services
MyiLibrary; *CIP.*

†Univ. of Washington Pr., *(978-0-295; 978-1-902716)* Orders Addr.: P.O. Box 50096, Seattle, WA 98145-5096 USA (SAN 212-2502) Tel 206-543-4050; Fax: 206-543-3932; Toll Free Fax: 800-669-7993; Edit Addr.: P.O. Box 50096, Seattle, WA 98145-5096 USA Toll Free Fax: 800-669-7993; 1126 N. 98th St., Seattle, WA 98103
E-mail: uwpord@u.washington.edu
Web site: http://www.washington.edu/uwpress
Dist(s): **Ebsco Publishing**
Hopkins Fulfillment Services
MyiLibrary
Partners Bk. Distributing, Inc.
Urban Land Institute
ebrary, Inc.; *CIP.*

Univ. of West Florida Foundation, Inc., *(978-0-9659142; 978-0-9798292)* 11000 University Pkwy., Pensacola, FL 32514 USA
E-mail: cmarse@uwf.edu.

†Univ. of Wisconsin Pr., *(978-0-299)* Orders Addr.: c/o Chicago Dist Ctr., 11030 S. Langley Ave., Chicago, IL 60628 USA Tel 773-568-1550; Fax: 773-660-2235; Toll Free Fax: 800-621-8476 (orders only); Toll Free: 800-621-2736 (orders only); Edit Addr.: 1930 Monroe St., 3rd Flr., Madison, WI 53711 USA Tel 608-263-1110; Fax: 608-263-1132
E-mail: uwiscpress@uwpress.wisc.edu
Web site: http://www.wisc.edu/wisconsinpress/
Dist(s): **Chicago Distribution Ctr.**
East-West Export Bks.
Ebsco Publishing
Follett School Solutions
MyiLibrary
ebrary, Inc.; *CIP.*

†Univ. Pr. of America, Inc., *(978-0-7618; 978-0-8191; 978-1-879691)* Member of Rowman & Littlefield Publishing Group, Inc., Orders Addr.: 15200 NBN Way, Blue Ridge Summit, PA 17214-0190 USA Tel 717-794-3800 (Sales, Customer Service, MIS, Royalties, Inventory Mgmt, Dist., Credit & Collections); Fax: 717-794-3803 (Customer Service & orders); 717-794-3857 (Sales & MIS); 717-794-3856 (Royalties, Inventory Mgmt. & Dist.); Toll Free Fax: 800-338-4550 (Customer Service & /or orders); Toll Free: 800-462-6420 (Customer Service &/or orders); Edit Addr.: 4501 Forbes Blvd., Suite 200, Lanham, MD 20706 USA Tel 301-459-3366; Fax: 301-459-5748 Short Discount, please contact rlpgsales@rowman.com
E-mail: custserv@rowman.com
Web site: http://www.univpress.com; http://www.rlpgbooks.com
Dist(s): **CreateSpace Independent Publishing Platform**
Ebsco Publishing
MyiLibrary
National Bk. Network
Rowman & Littlefield Publishers, Inc.
Yale Univ. Pr.
ebrary, Inc.; *CIP.*

Univ. Pr. of Colorado, *(978-0-87081; 978-0-87421; 978-1-60732; 978-1-64642)* Orders Addr.: c/o Utah State University Press, 11030 S. Langley, Chicago, IL 60628 USA (SAN 202-9294) Toll Free: 800-621-2736 CDC; Edit Addr.: 245 Century Cir. Ste 202, Louisville, CO 80027 SUN (SAN 658-0343) Tel 720-406-8849 UPC; 3078 Old Main Hill, Logan, UT 84322 Toll Free: 720-406-8849 USUP
E-mail: beth@upcolorado.com
Web site: http://www.upcolorado.com; http://www.usupress.org
Dist(s): **Bks. West**
Chicago Distribution Ctr.
Ctr. for Literary Publishing, Colorado State Univ.
Ebsco Publishing
Follett School Solutions
MyiLibrary
O'Reilly Media, Inc.
Univ. of Oklahoma Pr.
ebrary, Inc.

†Univ. Pr. of Florida, *(978-0-8130; 978-0-942084; 978-0-9760555; 978-1-61610; 978-1-942852; 978-1-68340)* Orders Addr.: 15 NW 15th St., Gainesville, FL 32611-0279 USA (SAN 207-9275) Tel

352-392-1351; Fax: 352-392-7302; Toll Free Fax: 800-680-1955; Toll Free: 800-226-3822; *Imprints:* Gatorbytes (Gatorbytes)
E-mail: press@upf.com; orders@upf.com
Web site: http://www.upf.com
Dist(s): **Casemate Academic**
Ebsco Publishing
MyiLibrary
Oxford Univ. Pr., Inc.
TNT Media Group, Inc.
ebrary, Inc.; *CIP.*

†**Univ. Pr. of Kentucky,** *(978-0-8131; 978-0-912839; 978-0-916968; 978-1-9859; 978-1-949668; 978-1-949669; 978-1-950564; 978-1-950690)* Orders Addr.: Hopkins Fulfillment Services, Baltimore, MD 21211-4370 USA Tel 800-537-5487; Fax: 410-516-6998; Toll Free: 800-839-6855; Edit Addr.: 663 S. Limestone St., Lexington, KY 40508-4008 USA (SAN 203-3275) Tel 859-257-5200; Fax: 859-323-4981; Toll Free Fax: 800-870-4981
E-mail: twell1@email.uky.edu
Web site: http://www.kentuckypress.com
Dist(s): **Ebsco Publishing**
MyiLibrary
Oxford Univ. Pr., Inc.
Open Road Integrated Media, Inc.
ebrary, Inc.; *CIP.*

†**Univ. Pr. of Mississippi,** *(978-0-87805; 978-1-57806; 978-1-934110; 978-1-60473; 978-1-61703; 978-1-62103; 978-1-62674; 978-1-62846; 978-1-4968)* 3825 Ridgewood Rd., Jackson, MS 39211-6492 USA (SAN 203-1914) Tel 601-432-6205; Fax: 601-432-6217; Toll Free: 800-737-7788 (orders only)
E-mail: kburgess@ihl.state.ms.us; press@mississippi.edu
Web site: http://www.upress.state.ms.us
Dist(s): **CreateSpace Independent Publishing Platform**
East-West Export Bks.
Ebsco Publishing
MyiLibrary
ebrary, Inc.; *CIP.*

†**Univ. Pr. of New England,** *(978-0-87451; 978-0-915032; 978-1-58465; 978-1-61168; 978-1-5126; 978-1-68458)* Orders Addr.: One Court St., Suite 250, Lebanon, NH 03755 USA Tel 603-448-1533 (ext. 255); Fax: 603-448-9429; Toll Free: 800-421-1561; Edit Addr.: 415 South St., Waltham, MA 02453 USA
E-mail: University.Press@Dartmouth.edu
Web site: http://www.upne.com
Dist(s): **Casemate Academic**
Chicago Distribution Ctr.
Hopkins Fulfillment Services
MyiLibrary
Smashwords
ebrary, Inc.; *CIP.*

Univ. Pr. of the Pacific, *(978-0-89875; 978-1-4102)* 4440 NW 73rd Ave., PTY 362, Miami, FL 33166-6437 USA Tel 407-650-2537 (phone/fax)
E-mail: bip@universitypressofthepacific.com
Web site: http://www.universitypressofthepacific.com.

University Publishing Associates, Incorporated *See* **National Film Network LLC**

Univ. Publishing Co., *(978-0-8346)* P.O. Box 80298, Lincoln, NE 68501 USA (SAN 206-0582) Tel 402-476-2761.

University Readers *See* **Cognella, Inc.**

Univ. Science Bks., *(978-0-935702; 978-1-891389; 978-1-938787; 978-1-940380)* 20 Edgehill Rd., Mill Valley, CA 94941-1113 USA (SAN 213-8085); 111 Prospect Pl., South Orange, NJ 07079 Tel 973-378-3900; Fax: 973-378-3925
E-mail: univscibks@igc.org; bjellis@igc.org; deskcopy@uscibooks.com
Web site: http://www.uscibooks.com
Dist(s): **RedShelf.**

UniversityPress.Info *See* **Science Pubs.**

Unland, Denise, *(978-0-9852748; 978-0-9983134; 978-1-949777)* 24954 S. Tryon, Channahon, IL 60410 USA Tel 815-715-4509
E-mail: Artemis279@aol.com.

Unlimited Horizons, *(978-0-9753817)* 427 S. Fraser Dr., Mesa, AZ 85204-2605 USA.

Unlimited Possibilities Publishing, LLC, *(978-0-9724621; 978-0-615-31408-2; 978-0-615-32713-6; 978-0-615-32981-9; 978-0-615-33078-5; 978-0-615-33453-0; 978-0-9826543; 978-0-9828923; 978-0-9834311; 978-1-938442; 978-1-940574)* Orders Addr.: 110 Walter Way., No. 2635, Stockbridge, GA 30281 USA
E-mail: shawnaa@sastyl.com.

Unlimited Potential Publishing, *(978-0-9899212; 978-0-9979879)* 122 Camberley Ct., Columbia, SC 29223 USA Tel 706-399-4916; Fax: 803-865-9271
E-mail: will8149@bellsouth.net
Dist(s): **Ingram Content Group.**

Unlimited Publishing LLC, *(978-0-9677649; 978-1-58832)* P.O. Box 3007, Bloomington, IN 47402 USA Fax: 425-928-5465
E-mail: jaymasp@aol.com; paradoxofthesoul@aol.com
Web site: http://www.unlimitedpublishing.com
Dist(s): **CreateSpace Independent Publishing Platform**
TextStream.

Unlock A Bk. Pubs., LLC, *(978-0-9796456)* 225 S. Bishop, San Angelo, TX 76901 USA
Web site: http://unlockabook.com.

Unlockyourchild *See* **Shrimlife Pr.**

Unmistakably C K C, *(978-0-9742064)* 3244 Kingswood Glen, Decatur, GA 30034 USA Tel 404-244-8113; 404-242-2690; Fax: 678-418-3056
E-mail: info@billyzany.com
Web site: http://www.billyzany.com.

Unseen Gallery, *(978-0-9795206)* Orders Addr.: P.O. Box 6065, Albuquerque, NM 87197 USA Tel 505-232-2161
E-mail: webmaster@unseengallery.com
Web site: http://www.unseengallery.com.

Unshackled Publishing, *(978-0-9708688)* Orders Addr.: P.O. Box 44216, Indianapolis, IN 46244 USA; P.O. Box 44216, Indianapolis, IN 46244
E-mail: lexthewriter@yahoo.com; treks-journey@yahoo.com
Web site: http://www.unshackledpublishing.com; http://www.alexusrhone.com.

Unspeakable Joy Pr., *(978-0-9761538)* Orders Addr.: 499 Adams St., #252, Milton, MA 02186 USA; Edit Addr.: 233 Eliot St., Milton, MA 02186 USA
E-mail: roybue@aol.com; adoptionis@aol.com
Web site: http://www.adoptionis.com.

Unspoken Knowledge Publishing, LLC, *(978-0-9986895)* P.O. Box 3, New Boston, MI 48164 USA Tel 313-570-5492
E-mail: rbey1124@gmail.com
Web site: www.unspokenknowledge.com.

Unspoken Words, *(978-0-9771358)* Orders Addr.: 11224 Mount Overlook, Cleveland, OH 44104 USA; Edit Addr.: 27600 Chardon Rd. Apt. 856, Wickliffe, OH 44092-2781 USA
E-mail: freespirit_publishing@yahoo.com.

Unstoppable Teen, Ltd. (GBR) *(978-0-9553488; 978-1-907189; 978-0-9956079) Dist. by* **Crown Hse.**

Untreed Reads Publishing, LLC, *(978-1-61187; 978-1-945447; 978-1-949135; 978-1-953601)* 506 Kansas St., San Francisco, CA 94107 USA Tel 415-621-0465; Toll Free Fax: 800-318-6037
E-mail: jhartman@untreedreads.com; kdsullivan@untreedreads.com
Web site: http://www.untreedreads.com.

Unveiled Media, LLC, *(978-0-9776385)* P.O. Box 930463, Verona, WI 53593 USA (SAN 257-8093); *Imprints:* Cotton Candy Press (CottonCandy Pr)
Web site: http://www.unveiledmedia.com
Dist(s): **Consortium Bk. Sales & Distribution**
CreateSpace Independent Publishing Platform
Ingram Content Group.

UP *See* **Infobus, Inc.**

Upcentral Publishing, *(978-0-9897466)* 29 Braeside Rd., Baldwinsville, NY 13027 USA Tel 315-720-4684
E-mail: garypluff@yahoo.com.

UPfirst.com Bks., *(978-0-9800222)* Div. of UPfirst.com, 2803 Us Hwy. 41 W. Suite 100, Marquette, MI 49855-2291 USA (SAN 855-0271)
E-mail: michaeleen@upfirst.com
Web site: http://www.upfirst.com.

UPfirst.com Picture Books for Children *See* **UPfirst.com Bks.**

Upheaval Media, Inc., *(978-0-615-19321-2; 978-0-578-03360-0; 978-0-615-36266-3; 978-0-9829610)* 100 Renaissance Ctr. No. 43233, Detroit, MI 48243 USA Tel 313-444-4885
E-mail: ida@upliftinc.org
Web site: http://www.upheavalmedia.net
Dist(s): **Lulu Pr., Inc.**

Upland Avenue Productions, *(978-0-578-10367-9; 978-0-615-92673-5; 978-0-9960401; 978-0-692-53123-5; 978-0-692-53124-2; 978-0-692-53125-9; 978-0-692-53127-3; 978-0-692-54731-1; 978-0-692-77111-2; 978-0-692-80419-3; 978-0-692-85300-9; 978-1-7324167)* 3201 Zafarano Dr. Suite C, No. 541, Santa Fe, NM 87507 USA
Web site: www.uplandavenueproductions.com
Dist(s): **CreateSpace Independent Publishing Platform**
Lulu Pr., Inc.

Upland Public Library Foundation *See* **Citrus Roots - Preserving Citrus Heritage Foundation**

Uplift Pr., *(978-0-9622834)* 295 Lenox Ave., #105, Oakland, CA 94610 USA Do not confuse with Uplift Pr. in Los Angeles, CA.

Upper Deck Co., LLC,The, *(978-1-931860; 978-1-932241; 978-1-932669; 978-1-932825; 978-1-932939; 978-1-933103; 978-1-933252; 978-1-933489; 978-1-59945; 978-1-60806)* 5909 Sea Otter Pl., Carlsbad, CA 92010 USA Tel 760-929-6500; Fax: 760-929-6548; Toll Free: 800-873-7332
Web site: http://www.upperdeck.com
Dist(s): **Diamond Bk. Distributors.**

Upper Room Bks. *Imprint of* **Upper Room Bks.**

Upper Room Bks., *(978-0-8358; 978-0-88177; 978-1-935205)* Div. of The Upper Room, 1908 Grand Ave., Nashville, TN 37212 USA (SAN 203-3364) Tel 615-340-7256; Toll Free: 800-972-0433 (customer service, orders); *Imprints:* Upper Room Books (UpperRmBks); Discipleship Resources (DiscipleshipRes) Do not confuse with Upper Room Education for Parenting, Inc. in Derry, NH
E-mail: jneely@gbod.org; lbruner@gbod.org; atrudel@gbod.org
Web site: http://www.upperroom.org; http://books.upperroom.org; http://bookstore.upperroom.org
Dist(s): **Abingdon Pr.**
Smashwords.

Upper Strata Ink, Incorporated *See* **Crowder, Jack L.**

Upside Down Tree Publishing, *(978-0-9802329)* 1605 N. Grand Ave., Maryville, MO 64468 USA.

Upstart Bks. *Imprint of* **Highsmith Inc.**

Upstart Pr. (NZL) *(978-1-927262; 978-1-927262-02-3; 978-1-927262-53-5; 978-1-988516; 978-1-990003) Dist. by* **IPG Chicago.**

UpTree Publishing, *(978-0-9787248)* P.O. Box 212863, Columbia, SC 29221 USA (SAN 851-447X) Toll Free: 800-905-2157 (phone/fax)
E-mail: sales@uptreepublishing.com; info@uptreepublishing.com
Web site: http://www.uptreepublishing.com.

Upublish.com *See* **Universal Pubs.**

Upword Pr., *(978-0-9654140)* Orders Addr.: P.O. Box 974, Atmore, AL 36504-0974 USA; 1879 Old Bratt Rd., Atmore, AL 36504 Tel 251-609-2918 Do not confuse with Upword Pr., Yelm, WA
Web site: http://www.scattersunshine.com
Dist(s): **American Wholesale Bk. Co.**

Urban Advocacy, *(978-0-9745122)* 917 Columbia Ave. Suite 123, Lancaster, PA 17603 USA Tel 717-490-6148
E-mail: vuuhu02@yahoo.com
Web site: http://www.urbanadvocacy.org.

Urban Edge Publishing Co., *(978-0-9743781)* 16209 Victory Blvd., Suite 207, Van Nuys, CA 91406 USA Tel 818-786-3700; Fax: 818-786-3737
E-mail: willcon@pacbell.net.

Urban, Keith Studios, *(978-0-9815370)* P.O. Box 4572, Wayne, NJ 07474 USA (SAN 855-8280)
Web site: http://www.keithurban.com.

Urban Ministries, Incorporated *See* **UMI (Urban Ministries, Inc.)**

Urban Moon Publishing, *(978-0-9787913; 978-0-9800101)* 931 Monroe Dr., Suite 276, Atlanta, GA 30308 USA Toll Free: 866-205-9228
E-mail: kinglistens@aol.com.

Urban Renaissance *Imprint of* **Kensington Publishing Corp.**

Urban Spirit!, *(978-0-9638127; 978-0-9845359; 978-0-9846480; 978-0-9881958; 978-0-9884572)* 753 Walden Blvd., Atlanta, GA 30349 USA Tel 770-969-7891
E-mail: melbanks2002@yahoo.com; cpickenpack@sbcglobal.net
Web site: http://www.urbanspirit.biz.

Urbane Pubns. Ltd. (GBR) *(978-1-909273; 978-1-910692; 978-1-911129; 978-1-911583; 978-1-911331; 978-1-912666) Dist. by* **BTPS.**

Urbanik, Karen L., *(978-0-9759031)* 2285 Marsh Hawk Ln. Apt. 302, Orange Park, FL 32003-6366 USA.

Ure, Daylene, *(978-0-615-25326-8)* 160 E. 200 S., Washington, UT 84780 USA
Dist(s): **Lulu Pr., Inc.**

Urim Pubns. (ISR) *(978-965-7108; 978-965-524) Dist. by* **Lambda Pubs.**

Urim Pubns. (ISR) *(978-965-7108; 978-965-524) Dist. by* **Coronet Bks.**

†**URJ Pr.,** *(978-0-8074)* 633 Third Ave., New York, NY 10017 USA (SAN 203-3291) Tel 212-650-4120; Fax: 212-650-4119; Toll Free: 888-489-8242
E-mail: press@urj.org
Web site: http://www.urjbooksandmusic.com
Dist(s): **Leonard, Hal Corp.**
MyiLibrary; *CIP.*

URON Entertainment Corp. (CAN) *(978-0-9738652; 978-0-9781386; 978-1-897376; 978-1-926778; 978-1-927925; 978-1-77294) Dist. by* **D C D.**

Urquhart Design, *(978-0-615-35452-1)* 1109 Wandering Oaks Dr., Ormond Beach, FL 32174 USA Tel 386-673-3565
E-mail: urquhartdesign@gmail.com
Web site: http://www.urquhartdesign.com.

Ursu Pubns., *(978-0-9741634)* PMB 429, 5250 Grand Ave., Suite 14, Gurnee, IL 60031-1877 USA
E-mail: info@grandmaursu.com
Web site: http://www.grandmaursu.com.

Urtext, *(978-0-9790573; 978-1-940121)* 39 Longwood Dr., San Rafael, CA 94901-1026 USA (SAN 852-3061).

U.S. Games Systems, Inc., *(978-0-88079; 978-0-913866; 978-1-57281; 978-1-64671)* 179 Ludlow St., Stamford, CT 06902 USA (SAN 158-6483) Tel 203-353-8400; Fax: 203-353-8431; Toll Free: 800-544-2637
E-mail: usgames@aol.com
Web site: http://www.usgamesinc.com
Dist(s): **New Leaf Distributing Co., Inc.**

Usborne *Imprint of* **EDC Publishing**

Usera, Christian, *(978-0-615-14618-8; 978-0-615-14645-4; 978-0-615-31319-1)* 7818 S. Zeno St., Centennial, CO 80016-1849 USA
Dist(s): **Lulu Pr., Inc.**

Utopia Pr., *(978-0-9661060)* 126 1/2 E. Front St., Traverse City, MI 49684 USA Tel 231-922-2234 editorial office
E-mail: pub@fimg.net.

Utopian Dreams Gifts, *(978-0-9997161)* P.O. Box 12, BLACK RIVER FALLS, WI 54615 USA Tel 715-299-4822
E-mail: UTOPIANDREAMSGIFTS@GMAIL.COM
Web site: Www.utopiandreamsgifts.webs.com.

UTP *Imprint of* **Univ. of Temecula Pr., Inc.**

Utterly Global, *(978-0-9891338)* 44 Lenhome Dr., Cranford, NJ 07016 USA Tel 908-272-0631
E-mail: info@antibullyingprograms.com
Web site: www.antibullyingprograms.com.

UWA Publishing (AUS) *(978-0-85564; 978-0-86422; 978-0-909751; 978-1-875560; 978-1-876268; 978-1-920694; 978-0-9802964; 978-0-9802965; 978-1-921401; 978-1-920964; 978-1-74258; 978-0-7316-0213-1; 978-0-7316-1196-6; 978-0-7316-1212-3; 978-0-7316-3945-8; 978-0-646-15226-4; 978-0-646-31692-5; 978-0-646-39116-8; 978-0-646-43446-9; 978-1-76080) Dist. by* **Intl Spec Bk.**

UXL *Imprint of* **Cengage Gale**

Uxor Pr., Inc., *(978-0-932555)* One Blackfield Dr. #174, Tiburon, CA 94920 USA Tel 415-383-8481
E-mail: bobzimmerman@usa.com.

V & R Editorial (ARG) *(978-987-612) Dist. by* **Lectorum Pubns.**

V Bks., *(978-0-9972031)* 7801 NW 37th St., Doral, FL 33166-6503 USA Tel 305-592-0839
E-mail: myarobarts@gmail.com
Web site: https://www.facebook.com/MyaRobartsBooks/.

V M I Publishers *See* **Deep River Bks.**

V V C Publishing *See* **Vic-Vincent Publishing**

Vabella Publishing, *(978-0-9712204; 978-0-9834332; 978-1-938230; 978-1-942766)* Orders Addr.: P.O. Box 1052, Carrollton, GA 30112 USA (SAN 920-1858) Tel 770-328-8355; Edit Addr.: 222 Hampton Way, Carrollton, GA 30116 USA (SAN 860-1682) Tel 770-328-8355
E-mail: belljg@aol.com
Web site: www.vabella.com.

Vacation Spot Publishing, *(978-0-9637688; 978-1-893622)* Orders Addr.: P.O. Box 1723, Lorton, VA 22199-1723 USA Tel 703-684-8142; Fax: 703-684-7955; Toll Free: 800-441-1949; Edit Addr.: 1903 Duffield Ln., Alexandria, VA 22307 USA; *Imprints:* VSP Books (VSP Bks)
E-mail: mail@VSPBooks.com
Web site: http://www.vspbooks.com
Dist(s): **Follett School Solutions.**

Vadeboncoeur, Jim, *(978-0-9724697)* 3809 Laguna Ave., Palo Alto, CA 94306-2629 USA Fax: 650-493-1145
E-mail: images@bpib.com
Web site: http://www.bpib.com/images.htm.

Valenti, Joseph, *(978-0-9700563)* Orders Addr.: P.O. Box 2763 nc highway 731 west, MOUNT GILEAD, NC 27306 USA Tel 914-628-9497; Edit Addr.: 2763 NC Hwy. 731 W., MOUNT GILEAD, NC 27306 USA
E-mail: jvalenti@nerolarp.com
Web site: http://www.nerolarp.com; http://nerolarponline.com.

Valenti, Robert A., *(978-0-9773119)* 3500 Galt Ocean Dr.2401, Fort Lauderdale, FL 33308-6809 USA Tel 954-563-0069; Fax: 954-563-4503
E-mail: rvalenti@bellsouth.net.

Valerie Bendt, *(978-1-885814)* Orders Addr.: 333 W. Rio Vista Ct., Tampa, FL 33604 USA
E-mail: ValerieBendt@verizon.net; ValerieBendt@gmail.com
Web site: http://www.ValerieBendt.com
Dist(s): **Follett School Solutions.**

Valerie Seyforth Clayton, *(978-0-578-60466-4; 978-0-578-63630-6)* 127 Crane Dr., Port St. Joe, FL 32456 USA Tel 850-227-5557
E-mail: vksclayton@gmail.com.

Valiant Entertainment *See* **Valiant Entertainment LLC**

Valiant Entertainment LLC, *(978-0-9796409; 978-1-939346; 978-1-68215)* 424 W. 33rd St., New York, NY 10001 USA Tel 212-972-0361
E-mail: walterb@valiantentertainment.com; inquiries@valiantentertainment.com
Web site: http://www.valiantentertainment.com
Dist(s): **Diamond Comic Distributors, Inc.**
Diamond Bk. Distributors.

Valknut Pr., *(978-0-9837520; 978-1-62411)* 1499 Amberley Dr., Clarksville, TN 37043 USA Tel 931-220-7758
E-mail: juliacrane@zoho.com
Web site: valknutpress.com
Dist(s): **Smashwords.**

Valley Pr., *(978-0-9748447)* P.O. Box 427, Vienna, VA 22183-1427 USA Fax: 703-281-2994 Do not confuse with companies with the same name in Bradenton, FL, Lyndhurst, NJ, GreenBay, WI, Mill Valley, CA.

Valley Publishing *See* **Karosa Publishing**

Values of America Co., *(978-0-9765868)* P.O. Box 1534, Merchantville, NJ 08109 USA Toll Free: 866-467-7304
E-mail: orders@quipman.com
Web site: http://www.quipman.com.

Values to Live By Classic Stories *Imprint of* **Thomas, Frederic Inc.**

Vample, Jessyca Publishing, *(978-0-9969817; 978-1-7323178)* 1013 E Ellet St., Philadelphia, PA 19150 USA Tel 267-334-8423
E-mail: jbvample@yahoo.com.

Van der Westhuizen, Kevin Ministries International, Incorporated *See* **JMC Printing**

van der Zande, Irene, *(978-0-9796191)* P.O. Box 1212, Santa Cruz, CA 95061 USA Tel 831-426-4407 Toll Free: 800-467-6997
E-mail: safety@kidpower.org
Web site: http://www.kidpower.org
Dist(s): **Romeii LLC.**

Van Steenhouse, Andrea L. *See* **Simpler Life Pr.**

Vance Hardy Publishing, *(978-0-578-17187-6)* 2248 Grand Ave, Deland, FL 32720 USA.

Vandalia Pr. *Imprint of* **West Virginia Univ. Pr.**

Vandam Pr., Inc., *(978-0-9702383; 978-1-937010)* P.O. Box 155, Brooklyn, NY 11230 USA Tel 212-969-0286; Fax: 212-858-5720
E-mail: publisher@vandampress.com
Web site: http://www.vandampress.com.

Vandamere Pr., *(978-0-918339)* Subs. of AB Assocs., Orders Addr.: P.O. Box 149, St. Petersburg, FL 33731 USA (SAN 657-3088) Tel 727-556-0950; Fax: 727-556-2560; Toll Free: 800-551-7776
Web site: www.vandamere.com.

V&R Editoras,
Dist(s): **Lectorum Pubns., Inc.**

Vangar Pubs./Baltimore, *(978-1-882788)* 2054 Kabletown Rd, Charles Town, WV 25414 USA Tel 304-728-2829
E-mail: robertgraf@aol.com.

Vanguard Pr., *(978-1-59315)* 425 Madison Ave., 3rd Flr., New York, NY 10017 USA Do not confuse with CDS Books in Paso Robles, CA Durham, NC
Dist(s): **Ebsco Publishing**
Hachette Bk. Group
ebrary, Inc.

Vanguard Productions, (*978-1-887591; 978-1-934331*) 705 Rancho Dr, Mesquite, TX 75149 USA Tel 908-391-0937
E-mail: vanguardpub@att.net
Web site: http://vanguardpublishing.com
Dist(s): **Publishers Group West (PGW).**

Vanir Bks., (*978-0-615-28865-9*) 351 Salem St., No. 2, Glendale, CA 91203 USA Tel 818-669-4070
Web site: http://rickandbobo.com.

Vanishing Horizons, (*978-0-9823445; 978-1-7355602*) Orders Addr.: 1018 Cedarcrest Dr., Pueblo, CO 81005 USA Tel 719-561-0993
E-mail: vanishinghorizons1@me.com
Web site: http://www.vanishinghorizons.com.

Vanissery, Matthew, (*978-0-9759906*) P.O. Box 1056, Guasti, CA 91743-1056 USA; 175 Mountain View Ave., Scotch Plains, NJ 07076 Tel 908-889-7930; Fax: 908-889-6281
E-mail: chemplavil@aol.com.

VanitaBooks, (*978-0-9800162; 978-0-9819714; 978-0-9826366*) 3875 Embassy Pkwy., Suite 250, Akron, OH 44333 USA
Web site: http://www.vanitabooks.com
Dist(s): **Children's Plus, Inc.**
Ingram Publisher Services.

Vansyckle, Elizabeth M., (*978-0-692-82343-9; 978-0-9986754*) 5050 Prosperity Row, Midlothian, TX 76065 USA Tel 214-422-0579
E-mail: bmoreland50@gmail.com; bmoreland50@gmail.com; bmoreland50@gmail.com
Dist(s): **CreateSpace Independent Publishing Platform.**

VanVonderen, Susan, (*978-1-7333107*) 8815 Windsor Terr., Brooklyn Park, MN 55443 USA Tel 651-308-0419
E-mail: Sue1grohs@aol.com.

Vanwell Publishing, Ltd. (CAN) (*978-0-920277; 978-1-55068; 978-1-55125*) *Dist. by* **Casemate Pubs.**

Varas, Reny, (*978-0-9726946*) 918 Cortney Dr., Carpentersville, IL 60110 USA (SAN 255-3333) Tel 847-428-7852; Fax: 847-428-7880
E-mail: lionan2@msn.com.

Variance Author Services, (*978-1-935142*) P.O. Box 612, Cabot, AR 72023-7577 USA (SAN 856-6259) Tel 501-259-6102; *Imprints:* Breakneck Books (Breakneck)
E-mail: tpaulschulte@variancepublishing.com
Web site: http://www.variancepublishing.com
Dist(s): **Bookazine Co., Inc.**
Smashwords.

Variance Publishing, LLC *See* **Variance Author Services**

Varida Publishing & Resources, (*978-1-937046*) P.O. Box 688, Woodinville, WA 98072 USA Tel 425-830-2909
E-mail: president@varida.com
Web site: varida.com.

Vartan, Judith A., (*978-0-692-67697-4; 978-0-9986317; 978-0-578-60674-3*) 14 Atherton Ave., Atherton, CA 94027 USA Tel 650-322-9202.

Vaughan, Christopher, (*978-0-9863101*) 203 Southbrook Pkwy., Kearney, MO 64060 USA Tel 816-728-5718
E-mail: Ljcv125@hotmail.com.

Vaughanworks *Imprint of* **Vaughanworks Publishing**

Vaughanworks Publishing, (*978-0-9771160*) Div. of Vaughanworks, Orders Addr.: P.O. Box 44224, West Allis, WI 53214 USA; *Imprints:* Vaughanworks (Vaughanworks)
E-mail: vaughanworks@sbcglobal.net
Web site: http://www.vaughanworks.com.

Vaughn, Dean Learning Systems, Inc., (*978-0-942168*) 631 Springhouse Ln., Hummelstown, PA 17036 USA (SAN 239-9911) Tel 717-433-7794
E-mail: mathaino@gmail.com
Web site: http://www.deanvaughnlearning.com
Dist(s): **Two Rivers Distribution.**

Vaughn, Jerry T., (*978-0-9772507*) 1921 Ashford Cir., Longmout, CO 80501 USA Tel 303-776-9134
E-mail: vaughn.jc@gmail.com.

Vault Comics *Imprint of* **Creative Mind Energy**

Vecchia Publishing, (*978-0-9860470; 978-1-944906*) 41 Grand Ave., Suite 101, River Edge, NJ 07661 USA.

Vedanta Pr., (*978-0-87481*) Div. of Vedanta Society of Southern California, Orders Addr.: 1946 Vedanta Pl., Hollywood, CA 90068-3996 USA (SAN 202-9340) Tel 323-960-1728 (general manager); 323-960-1727 (orders and customer service); Fax: 323-465-9568 (orders)
E-mail: bob@vedanta.com; vpress@vedanta.com
Web site: http://www.vedanta.com.

Veech, Alyssa, (*978-0-578-41555-0; 978-0-578-41558-1*) 71 Singer Dr., West Seneca, NY 14224 USA Tel 716-472-0403
E-mail: alyssajn18@gmail.com
Dist(s): **Ingram Content Group.**

Vegan Kids Pr., (*978-0-9980358*) 1835 Patricia Dr., Clarksville, TN 37040 USA Tel 916-261-2348
E-mail: kara@vegankidspress.com
Web site: vegankidspress.com.

Vegan Pubs., (*978-1-940184*) 6 Moore Cir., Danvers, MA 01923 USA (SAN 990-0683) Tel 617-872-3623
E-mail: veganpublishers@gmail.com
Web site: www.veganpublishers.com.

Vegas Pub., LLC, A, (*978-0-9968437; 978-0-9969593; 978-0-9985574*) 115 Maple St., Henderson, NV 89015 USA Tel 702-277-8126
E-mail: avegaspublisher@yahoo.com
Web site: avegaspublisher.com.

vegaslocal.com, (*978-0-9752804*) 4329 Talofa Ave., Toluca Lake, CA 91602-2917 USA
E-mail: info@vegaslocal.com
Web site: http://www.vegaslocal.com.

Veillette, Roseanne, (*978-0-9843705; 978-0-9977504*) Orders Addr.: 40 Tutherly Ave., Claremont, NH 03743 USA (SAN 859-2128) Tel 603-372-7390; *Imprints:* Little Paws Press (LittlePaws)
E-mail: roseanneveillette@comcast.net
Web site: http://www.buckandben.com.

Veillette, Sally *See* **Pop the Cork Publishing**

Velazquez de Leon, Mauricio *See* **Duo Pr. LLC**

Velesquious Studios, (*978-0-9754232*) P.O. Box 72, Blakeslee, PA 18610-0072 USA Tel 610-360-8946
E-mail: webmaster@velesquious.com
Web site: http://www.velesquious.com.

Velichko, Vera, (*978-0-9754433*) Orders Addr.: 12671 SE 169th Pl., Renton, WA 98058 USA Tel 253-237-2271; Fax: 253-444-4916; *Imprints:* Language Transformer Books (LangTransforBks)
E-mail: talkinrussian@gmail.com
Web site: http://www.lulu.com/talkinrussian1; http://www.languagetransformer.com/.

Velikanje, Kathryn *See* **Levity Pr.**

Vellum Books *Imprint of* **New Academia Publishing, LLC**

Veloce Publishing Ltd. (GBR) (*978-1-874105; 978-1-901295; 978-1-903706; 978-1-904788; 978-1-84584; 978-1-78711*) *Dist. by* **HachBkGrp.**

VeloPress, (*978-0-9622630; 978-1-884737; 978-1-931382; 978-1-934030*) Div. of Inside Communications, Inc., 1830 N. 55th St., Boulder, CO 80301-2700 USA Tel 303-440-0601; Fax: 303-444-6788; Toll Free: 800-811-4210
E-mail: velopress@7dogs.com
Web site: http://www.velogear.com
Dist(s): **Ingram Publisher Services.**

Velvet Pony Stories, (*978-0-615-26652-7; 978-0-692-80080-5*)
Dist(s): **Independent Pub.**

Velázquez Pr., (*978-1-59495*) Div. of Academic Learning Co., LLC, 9682 Telstar Ave., Suite 110, El Monte, CA 91731-3009 USA (SAN 255-786X) Tel 626-448-3448; Fax: 626-602-3817
E-mail: info@academiclearningcompany.com
Web site: http://www.academiclearningcompany.com.

Vendera Publishing, (*978-0-9749411; 978-1-936307*) 61 Big Pete Rd., Franklin Furnace, OH 45629 USA Tel 740-531-2122; *Imprints:* 711Press (SevenElev)
E-mail: admin@venderapublishing.com
Web site: http://www.venderapublishing.com.

Vengco, Aletha Fulton, (*978-0-578-00613-0; 978-0-578-00778-6; 978-0-578-00890-5; 978-0-578-02728-9*) 2224 O St., Apt. 4, Sacramento, CA 95816 USA
Dist(s): **Lulu Pr., Inc.**

Venture Development Group, (*978-0-9748030*) 1114 Blue Lake Sq., Mountain View, CA 94040-4561 USA Tel 650-967-3403; Fax: 650-965-0320.

Venture Publishing, (*978-0-9761694*) 750 Tabor St., No. 64, Golden, CO 80401 USA Tel 303-239-6531 (phone/fax).

Venture Publishing, Inc., (*978-0-910251; 978-1-892132; 978-1-939476*) 1999 Cato Ave., State College, PA 16801 USA (SAN 240-897X) Tel 814-234-4561; Fax: 814-234-1651 Do not confuse with companies with the same name in Andover, MA, Ho-Ho-Kus, NJ
E-mail: vpublish@venturepublish.com
Web site: http://www.venturepublish.com.

Verb Technology, Inc., (*978-1-887938; 978-1-933057; 978-1-936631*) 782 S. Automall Dr. Unit A, American Fork, UT 84003 USA Tel 801-225-9520; Fax: 801-343-3301; Toll Free: 800-544-7044
E-mail: mjo@soundconcepts.com; jca@soundconcepts.com; jason@soundconcepts.com; vs@soundconcepts.com; edr@soundconcepts.com; jon@verb.tech; carley@verb.tech
Web site: http://www.soundconcepts.com; http://www.verb.tech.

Verbal Images Pr., (*978-0-9625136; 978-1-884281; 978-0-9821982*) 46 Duncott Rd., Fairport, NY 14450-3150 USA
Web site: http://www.verbalimagespress.com
Dist(s): **Gryphon Hse., Inc.**

Veritas Pr., Inc., (*978-1-930710; 978-1-932168; 978-1-936648; 978-1-950271; 978-1-951200*) 1805 Olde Homestead Ln, Lancaster, PA 17601 USA (SAN 255-9617) Tel 717-519-1974; Fax: 717-519-1978; Toll Free: 800-922-5082 Do not confuse with companies with same name in Santa Barbara CA, Santa Monica CA, Bronx NY, Clearwater Fl, Sioux Falls SD, West Hartford CT, West Allis,MI
E-mail: info@veritaspress.com
Web site: http://www.veritaspress.com.

Veritas Publishing, (*978-0-9643261; 978-0-9715007; 978-1-933297; 978-0-9765742; 978-1-933391; 978-1-933885; 978-1-938033; 978-1-7333764*) Orders Addr.: P.O. Box 3516, Sedona, AZ 86340 USA (SAN 254-3613) Tel 928-282-8722; Fax: 928-282-4789 Do not confuse with companies with the same or similar names in Cranbrook, WA, Rockwall, TX, McMinnville, MN, Mountain View, CA, Prescott, AZ
E-mail: veritaspublish@postmark.net; info@veritaspub.com; eventcoordinator@veritaspub.com
Web site: http://www.veritaspub.com
Dist(s): **Baker & Taylor Publisher Services (BTPS)**
DeVorss & Co.
Hay Hse., Inc.
New Leaf Distributing Co., Inc.
Penguin Random Hse. Distribution
Partners Bk. Distributing, Inc.
Penguin Random Hse. LLC.

Veritas Pubns. (IRL) (*978-1-85390; 978-0-901810; 978-0-905092; 978-0-86217; 978-1-84730*) *Dist. by* **Casemate Pubs.**

Verlag Wilhelm Heyne (DEU) (*978-3-453*) *Dist. by* **Distribks Inc.**

Vermont Bookworks, (*978-0-9745931*) 12 Perry Ln., Rutland, VT 05701 USA
E-mail: digbysworld@comcast.net
Web site: http://www.digbysworld.com
Dist(s): **North Country Bks., Inc.**

Vermont Council on the Arts, Incorporated *See* **Vermont Folklife Ctr.**

†Vermont Folklife Ctr., (*978-0-916718; 978-0-692-00433-3*) Orders Addr.: 88 Main St., Middlebury, VT 05753 USA (SAN 208-9092) Tel 802-388-4964; Fax: 802-388-1844
E-mail: bbjorkman@vermontfolklifecenter.org
Web site: http://www.vermontfolklifecenter.org
Dist(s): **Thistle Hill Pubns.**; *CIP.*

†Vermont Life Magazine, (*978-0-936896; 978-1-931389; 978-1-941730*) Div. of State of Vermont, Agency on Development & Community Affairs, 1 National Life Drive, 6th fl, Montpelier, VT 05620-0501 USA (SAN 215-8213) Tel 802-828-3241; Fax: 802-828-3366; Toll Free: 800-455-3399
E-mail: info@vtlife.com; products@vtlife.com; subs@vtlife.com
Web site: http://www.vermontlife.com; http://www.VermontLifeCatalog.com
Dist(s): **Hood, Alan C. & Co., Inc.**
TNT Media Group, Inc.; *CIP.*

Vernacular Pr., (*978-0-9740266*) 197 Grand St. Ste. 2W, New York, NY 10013-3859 USA (SAN 255-3945)
E-mail: hthamann@vernacularpress.com; cvecoli@vernacularpress.com
Web site: http://www.vernacularpress.com.

Verney, Jeff *See* **JRV Publishing**

Vernier Software *See* **Vernier Software & Technology**

Vernier Software & Technology, (*978-0-918731; 978-1-929075; 978-1-948008*) 13979 SW Millikan Way, Beaverton, OR 97005-2886 USA (SAN 293-1753) Tel 503-277-2299; Fax: 503-277-2440
E-mail: info@vernier.com
Web site: http://www.vernier.com.

Vernissage Pr., LLC, (*978-0-9725027*) 2200 Central Ave., Boulder, CO 80301 USA Tel 303-440-8102; Toll Free: 888-849-8697
E-mail: info@vernissagepress.com
Web site: http://www.vernissagepress.com.

Verona (Bk.) Publishing, Inc., (*978-0-9667037; 978-0-9769031*) P.O. Box 24071, Edina, MN 55426 USA
Web site: http://www.veronapublishing.com.

Versait Pr. LLC, (*978-0-9746810*) P.O. Box 644332, Vero Beach, FL 32964-4332 USA
E-mail: info@versaitpress.com
Web site: http://VersaitPress.com.

Versal Editorial Group *See* **Cambridge BrickHouse, Inc.**

Versal Technologies, Inc., (*978-0-9749460*) One Cranberry Hill, Suite 102, Lexington, MA 02421 USA.

Versary Pubns., (*978-0-9641429*) 984 Brownsville Rd., Wernersville, PA 19565 USA Tel 610-693-5920.

Versify *Imprint of* **Houghton Mifflin Harcourt Publishing Co.**

Verso Bks. (GBR) (*978-0-86091; 978-0-902308; 978-1-85984; 978-1-84467; 978-1-78168; 978-1-78478; 978-1-78663*) *Dist. by* **Peng Rand Hse.**

Vertel Publishing *Imprint of* **Nextone Inc.**

Vertical *Imprint of* **Vertical, Inc.**

Vertical *Imprint of* **Kodansha America, Inc.**

Vertical Comics *Imprint of* **Vertical, Inc.**

Vertical Connect Pr., (*978-0-9769087*) 120 N. Magnolia St., Summerville, SC 29483-6836 USA; *Imprints:* Grand Kidz, The (Grand Kidz)
E-mail: kate@verticalconnectpress.com
Web site: http://www.verticalconnectpress.com.

Vertical, Inc., (*978-1-932234; 978-1-934287; 978-1-935654; 978-1-939130; 978-1-941220; 978-1-942993; 978-1-945054; 978-1-947194*) 451 Park Ave. S. 7th Flr., New York, NY 10016 USA; *Imprints:* Vertical (Vrtical); Vertical Comics (Vertical Comics)
E-mail: info@vertical-inc.com
Web site: http://www.vertical-inc.com
Dist(s): **MyiLibrary**
Penguin Random Hse. Distribution
Penguin Random Hse. LLC
Random Hse., Inc.

Vertigo *Imprint of* **DC Comics**

Vertigo Publishing, (*978-0-9764463*) P.O. Box 2683, Dearborn, MI 48123 USA
E-mail: vertigopublish@cs.com
Web site: http://www.vertigopublishing.com.

Verum Publishing, (*978-0-9787476; 978-0-692-10816-1*) 1650 E. gonzales rd No. 187, oxnard, CA 93036 USA Toll Free: 866-600-4840
Web site: http://www.verumpress.com.

Vescori, Laura, (*978-0-9762965*) 28 Fir Tree Dr., Bradford, CT 06405 USA.

Vesper Enterprises, Inc., (*978-0-9663730*) Orders Addr.: P.O. Box 565, Hingham, MA 02043 USA Tel 781-749-5378; Fax: 781-740-2391; Edit Addr.: 102 Central St., Hingham, MA 02043 USA.

Vessel Ministries, (*978-0-9713345; 978-0-9816463; 978-0-615-11148-3*) 1974 E. Mcandrews Rd., Medford, OR 97504-5510 USA
E-mail: vesselmin@cox.net
Dist(s): **Todd Communications.**

Vesta Bks., LLC, (*978-0-9791065*) 3624 Lone Wolf Trail, Saint Augustine, FL 32086-5316 USA.

Vesta Publishing, (*978-1-60481*) 3750 Priority Way S. Dr., Suite 114, Indianapolis, IN 46240 USA
E-mail: customerservice@vestapublishing.com
Web site: http://www.vestapublishing.com.

Vested Owl, (*978-0-9767926*) Div. of IRM, 3217 Wisconsin Ave., NW #5c, Washington, DC 20016 USA
E-mail: nino@irm360.com
Web site: http://www.vestedowl.com; http://www.kit4marketing.com.

Vesuvian Bks., (*978-1-944109; 978-1-64548*) 2817 W. End Ave. Ste. 126-283, Nashville, TN 37203 USA Tel 502-836-1201
E-mail: italia@vesuvianmedia.com
Web site: http://vesuvianbooks.com; http://VesuvianMediaGroup.com
Dist(s): **Independent Pubs. Group**
Pathway Bk. Service.

Vesuvius Pr. Inc., (*978-0-9719921; 978-0-9796766; 978-0-9815190; 978-1-935257; 978-1-61956*) Orders Addr.: 4727 N. 12th St., Phoenix, AZ 85014 USA (SAN 255-2981) Tel 602-651-1873; Fax: 602-651-1875; *Imprints:* Tau Publishing (TauPubng)
E-mail: jeffcampbell@vesuviuspress.com
Web site: http://www.taupublishing.com; http://Amordeus.com; http://http:/WellnessandEducation.com; http://Vesuviuspressincorporated.com; http://VesuviusPress.com.

VG Publishing, (*978-0-9785900*) 51613 Sass Rd., Chesterfield, MI 48047-5935 USA (SAN 851-0482)
Web site: http://www.voyagergroupllc.com.

Via Media, Incorporated *See* **Via Media, Pr.**

Via Media, Pr., (*978-0-9646362*) 3112 James St., San Diego, CA 92106 USA Tel 619-884-6440
E-mail: via_media_press@pacbell.net.

Viaduct Music, (*978-0-9831629*) 711 Broadway E. Apt. 9, Seattle, WA 98102-4680 USA Tel 206-322-3187
E-mail: theramster@gmail.com
Dist(s): **BookBaby.**

Vibatorium LLC, (*978-0-9742495*) 419 N. Larchmont Blvd., No. 3265, Los Angeles, CA 90004 USA Tel 323-460-4441; Fax: 323-935-0225
E-mail: info@backyardwonders.com
Web site: http://www.vibatorium.com; http://www.backyardwonders.com.

Vibrante Pr., (*978-0-935301*) P.O. Box 51853, Albuquerque, NM 87181-1853 USA (SAN 696-2351)
E-mail: Lonnie@vibrante.com
Web site: http://www.vibrante.com.

Vice Press Publishing Company *See* **Ascension Education**

Vicens-Vives, Editorial, S.A. (ESP) (*978-84-316*) *Dist. by* **Lectorum Pubns.**

Vickery Bks., (*978-1-928531*) 3012 Anchor Dr., Ormond Beach, FL 32176-2304 USA
E-mail: kvv145@gte.net.

Vic's Lab, LLC, (*978-1-942178*) P.O. Box 10865, Danville, VA 24543 USA Tel 512-842-7552
E-mail: vicslabpublishing@gmail.com
Web site: VicsLab.com.

Victoria Peace Green, (*978-0-692-85198-2*) 1155 Hillwood Loop, Lincoln, CA 95648 USA Tel 210-273-9012
E-mail: victoriapeace@att.net
Web site: www.victoriapeacegreen.com.

Victoria Tecken, (*978-0-9788850; 978-1-937363*) 1008 N Prairie St, Lake City, MN 55041 USA
E-mail: victoria.tecken@gmail.com
Web site: https://victoriatecken.com/.

Victoria Univ. of Wellington Pr. (NZL) (*978-0-86473; 978-1-77656; 978-1-77656-063-9; 978-1-77656-058-5; 978-1-77656-064-6; 978-1-77656-047-9; 978-1-77656-071-4*) *Dist. by* **IPG Chicago.**

Victor's Crown Publishing, (*978-0-9761188*) 3322 N. 900 E., Ogden, UT 84414 USA Fax: 801-782-3864
E-mail: steve@victorscrown.com
Web site: http://www.victorscrown.com.

Victory Belt Publishing, (*978-0-9777315; 978-0-9815044; 978-0-9825658; 978-1-936608; 978-1-62860*) 32245 Old Ranch Pk. Ln., Auberry, CA 93602 USA (SAN 850-0819) Tel 559-355-4188
Web site: http://www.victorybelt.com
Dist(s): **Simon & Schuster**
Simon & Schuster, Inc.
Tuttle Publishing.

Victory by Any Means Games, (*978-0-9764048; 978-1-935074*) Orders Addr.: P.O. Box 329, Lusk, WY 82225-0329 USA Tel 307-334-3190; Edit Addr.: 315 S. Iron, Lusk, WY 82225-0329 USA
E-mail: tyrel@vbamgames.com
Web site: http://www.vbamgames.com.

Victory Graphics & Media *See* **Yorkshire Publishing Group**

Victory Hse. Pr., (*978-1-935571*) 3836 Tradition Dr., Fort Collins, CO 80526 USA Tel 970-226-1078.

Victory In Grace Ministries, (*978-0-9679145; 978-0-9719262; 978-0-9858764; 978-1-7338976*) 60 Quentin Rd., Lake Zurich, IL 60047 USA Tel 847-438-4494 ext 1071; Fax: 847-438-4232; Toll Free: 800-784-7223
E-mail: feedback@victoryingrace.org
Web site: http://www.victoryingrace.org.

Victory Pr., (*978-0-9753818*) P.O. Box 118, Massillon, OH 44648 USA Do not confuse with companies with the same name in Carlton OR, Chesterfield MO, Monterey CA
E-mail: rabteach2001@aol.com
Web site: http://www.ruthann.faithweb.com.

Victory Publishing Co., (*978-0-9778925*) 3797 N. Ashley Ct., Decatur, IL 62526 USA (SAN 850-4458) Do not confuse with companies with the same or similar name in Hampton, VA, Redwood City, CA, MOunt Pleasant, SC, Inglewood, CA, Banco, VA, Pama, ID, New Orleans, LA, Littleton, CO
E-mail: edmar84@aol.com.

Victory WW 2 Publishing Ltd., (*978-0-9700567*) 18140 Zane St. NW - 200, Elk River, MN 55330 USA (SAN 253-2476) Tel 763-753-5200; Fax: 763-753-2862
E-mail: victorypub@aol.com
Dist(s): **MyiLibrary**
ebrary, Inc.

Vic-Vincent Publishing, (*978-0-9646817*) Div. of Vic-Vincent Corp., Orders Addr.: 362 Gulf Breeze

Publisher Name Index

Pkwy., Suite 151, Gulf Breeze, FL 32561 USA (SAN 257-4039) Tel 850-476-7673; Toll Free: 800-772-3343
E-mail: inventorz@aol.com
Web site: http://www.inventorsfreehelp.com
Dist(s): **Distributors, The.**

Vida Life Publishers International *See* **Vida Pubs.**

Vida Pubs., *(978-0-8297)* 8410 NW 53rd Ter. Ste. 103, Miami, FL 33166-4510 USA Toll Free: 800-843-2548
E-mail: vidapubsales@harpercollins.com
Web site: http://www.editorialvida.com
Dist(s): **Follett School Solutions**
HarperCollins Christian Publishing
Zondervan.

VIDENE Publications *See* **Red Poppy Pr.**

Vidro, Kenneth *See* **Gilbert Square Bks.**

Vidya Bks., *(978-1-878099)* P.O. Box 7788, Berkeley, CA 94707-0788 USA Tel 510-527-9932.

Vidyaranayam, *(978-0-692-71703-5; 978-0-578-47295-9; 978-1-7338088)* 3218 Sharpton Dr., DULUTH, GA 30096 USA Tel 617-899-9122.

Viet Baby, LLC, *(978-0-9776482)* Orders Addr.: P.O. Box 750074, Las Vegas, NV 89136-0074 USA Tel 702-234-5127
E-mail: an@viet-baby.com
Web site: http://www.viet-baby.com.

Vietnamese International Poetry Society, *(978-0-9746300)* Orders Addr.: P.O. Box 246958, Sacramento, CA 95824 USA; Edit Addr.: 3067 Harrison St., NW, Washington, DC 20015 USA.

Viewpoint Pr., *(978-0-943962)* Orders Addr.: P.O. Box 1090, Tehachapi, CA 93581 USA Tel 661-821-5110; Fax: 661-821-7515; Edit Addr.: 785 Tucker Rd., Apt. G400, Tehachapi, CA 93561 USA Do not confuse with companies with the same name in San Diego, CA, Portland, ME
E-mail: joie99@aol.com.

Viewpoints Research Institute, Inc., *(978-0-9743131)* 1209 Grand Central Ave., Glendale, CA 91201 USA
Web site: http://www.viewpointsresearch.org.

Vikasam, *(978-0-615-46456-5)* 23355 N. Empress Dr., Hawthorn Woods, IL 60047 USA Tel 847-815-1978
E-mail: dollysap@gmail.com.

VIKI Publishing, *(978-1-950263)* 5010 Barrenstar Way, San Ramon, CA 94582 USA Tel 408-726-4739
E-mail: vinaykiara@gmail.com
Web site: https://www.vikipublishing.com.

Viking *Imprint of* **Penguin Publishing Group**

Viking Adult *Imprint of* **Penguin Publishing Group**

Viking Books for Young Readers *Imprint of* **Penguin Young Readers Group**

Viking Books for Young Readers *Imprint of* **Penguin Publishing Group**

VILA Group, Inc., The, *(978-0-9635047)* V2947 S. Atlantic Ave., Apt. 1906, Daytona Beach, FL 32118-6029 USA Tel 904-767-8245.

Vilasa Pr., *(978-0-9762809; 978-1-937927)* Orders Addr.: 2835 Long Valley Rd., Santa Ynez, CA 93460 USA (SAN 256-2995) Tel 805-688-6116; Fax: 805-456-3340
E-mail: vilasapress@gmail.com
Web site: http://www.vilasapress.com; http://sandynathan.com
Dist(s): **BookBaby**
Ingram Content Group
Smashwords.

Villa Serena Publishing, *(978-0-9753326)* 15657 Westbrook Rd., Livonia, MI 48154 USA.

Villa Wisteria Pubns., *(978-0-615-52506-8)* 6103 Hoochaneetsa Pl. N., Cochiti Lake, NM 87083 USA Tel 505-465-0361
E-mail: mlpbadarak@villawisteria.com
Web site: http://www.villawisteria.com.

Village Earth Pr. *Imprint of* **Harding Hse. Publishing Sebice Inc.**

Village Monkey LLC, The, *(978-0-9789633)* 7760 McWhorter Rd., Martinsville, IN 46151 USA Tel 765-352-1718
E-mail: zenmonkey@thevillagemonkey.com
Web site: http://www.thevillagemonkey.com.

Village Monkey, The *See* **Village Monkey LLC, The**

Village Museum, *(978-0-9740091)* Orders Addr.: 401 Pinckney St., McClellanville, SC 29458 USA Tel 843-887-3030; Edit Addr.: P.O. Box 595, McClellanville, SC 29458 USA Tel 843-887-3030
Web site: http://www.villagemuseum.com.

Village Publishing, *(978-0-9857741; 978-0-9981196-0-1)* 2924 W.132nd Pl., Gardena, CA 90249 USA Tel 310-922-6562
E-mail: wwilson150@gmail.com.

Village Tales Publishing, *(978-0-9753609; 978-0-9853625; 978-1-945408)* 662 Lookout Point, Lawrenceville, GA 30043 USA
E-mail: publisher@villagetalespublishing.com; villagetalespublishing@yahoo.com; villagetalespub@gmail.com
Web site: http://villagetalespublishing.com; http://www.villagetalespublishing.com.

Villager Bk. Publishing, *(978-1-934643)* Orders Addr.: P.O. Box 222 W. Las Colinas Blvd, Suite 1650, Irving, TX 75039 USA (SAN 854-0969)
E-mail: semerick@villagerdustbunnies.com; jbloom@villagerdustbunnies.com; lrinn@villagerdustbunnies.com; jfox@villagerdustbunnies.com
Web site: http://villagerpublishers.com; http://www.villagerdustbunnies.com.

Villard Bks. *Imprint of* **Random House Publishing Group**

Vilnius Pr., *(978-0-615-80054-7; 978-0-615-80223-7; 978-1-940136)* 152 Ct. St. Suite 2E, Portsmouth, NH 03801 USA Tel 8552607535
Web site: http://vilnius-press.com/
Dist(s): **CreateSpace Independent Publishing Platform.**

Vinay Shankar *See* **VIKI Publishing**

Vincent, Thomas J. Foundation Inc., *(978-0-9759284)* 44-447 Kaneohe Bay Dr., Kaneohe, HI 96744 USA
E-mail: vincentfoundation@yahoo.com.

Vincero Enterprises, *(978-0-9675329)* 490 Marin Oaks Dr., Novato, CA 94949 USA Tel 800-715-1492; Fax: 415-883-4115; Toll Free: 800-715-1492
E-mail: heritage1492@earthlink.net
Web site: http://www.italianheritage.net; http://www.hispaniclatino.net.

Vindof Publishing, *(978-0-9759310)* 410 N. 3rd St., Ft. Atkinson, WI 53538 USA.

Vineyard Publishing, LLC *See* **Ampelon Publishing, LLC**

Vineyard Stories, *(978-0-9771384; 978-0-615-26606-0; 978-0-615-34267-2; 978-0-9827146; 978-0-9849136; 978-0-9915028; 978-0-692-40086-9; 978-0-692-73037-9; 978-0-692-86175-2; 978-0-692-07280-6; 978-0-692-17354-1; 978-0-578-50646-3)* Orders Addr.: RR 1, Box 65-B9, Edgartown, MA 02539 USA Tel 598-221-2338; Fax: 508-627-6909; Edit Addr.: 52 Bold Meadow Rd., Edgartown, MA 02539 USA
Web site: http://www.vineyardstories.com
Dist(s): **Ingram Publisher Services.**

Vinland Pr., *(978-0-9721410)* P.O. Box 927, North Bend, OR 97459 USA Tel 541-751-1566
E-mail: s_coons@charter.net.

Vinland Publishing, *(978-0-9801601; 978-0-9889455)* 661 Tamarron Dr., Grand Jct, CO 81506-4911 USA (SAN 855-3564)
E-mail: jahunsinger@vinlandpublishing.com; info@vinlandpublishing.com
Web site: http://www.vinlandpublishing.com
Dist(s): **Follett School Solutions**
MyiLibrary
ebrary, Inc.

Vinny Tales, *(978-1-7325577)* 98-120 Queens Blvd. Apt. 4A, Rego Park, NY 11374 USA Tel 917-502-7593
E-mail: vinnychen@aol.com.

Vinspire Publishing LLC, *(978-0-9752868; 978-0-9770107; 978-0-9785368; 978-0-9793327; 978-0-9815592; 978-0-9819896; 978-0-9834198; 978-0-9851232; 978-0-9890632; 978-0-9903042; 978-0-9964423; 978-0-9971732; 978-1-7321348; 978-1-7327112; 978-1-7341507)* P.O. Box 1165, Ladson, SC 29456 USA
Web site: http://www.vinspirepublishing.com.

Vintage *Imprint of* **Knopf Doubleday Publishing Group**

Vintage Bird Pr., *(978-0-9994793)* 2140 E. Hackamore St., Mesa, AZ 85213 USA Tel 480-593-4263
E-mail: lauralofgreen@aol.com
Web site: https://vintagebirdpressblog.wordpress.com/about/.

Vintage Espanol *Imprint of* **Knopf Doubleday Publishing Group**

Vintage Romance Publishing, LLC *See* **Vinspire Publishing LLC**

Vintage Wild, *(978-0-9862627; 978-0-9986293; 978-1-7326900)* 10070 n.w. 9 St. Cir. 204, Miami, FL 33172 USA Tel 7863026680.

Vinvatar Publishing, *(978-1-945012; 978-1-63581)* P.O. Box 33, Lawrence, MI 49064 USA Tel 269-487-8184
E-mail: office@vinvatar.com
Web site: www.vinvatar.com.

Violet Bks., *(978-0-615-19128-7)* 306 Edgewater Dr., Anderson, SC 29626 USA
Dist(s): **Lulu Pr., Inc.**

Violette Editions (GBR) *(978-1-900828) Dist. by* **Dist Art Pubs.**

VIP INK Publishing Group, Inc., *(978-0-615-59125-4; 978-0-615-59946-5; 978-0-9886428; 978-0-9911719; 978-0-9861340; 978-0-9965701; 978-0-9970016; 978-0-9978116)* 4623 branch Ct., lithonia, GA 30038 USA
E-mail: AANDE46461@yahoo.com; Lenny@Printhousebooks.com
Web site: http://www.Printhousebooks.com
Dist(s): **Ingram Content Group**
eBookit.com.

VIP Ink Publishing, L.L.C., *(978-1-939670)* 140 Belle Terre Dlvd. Ste. D 211, LaPlace, LA 70068 USA Tel 985-359-2337
E-mail: info@vipinkpublishing.com
Web site: http://www.vipinkpublishing.com.

Viper Comics, *(978-0-9754193; 978-0-9777883; 978-0-9793680; 978-0-9802385; 978-0-9827117; 978-0-9833670)* Div. of Viper Entertainment Inc., 9400 N. MacArthur Blvd., Suite 124-215, Irving, TX 75063 USA Tel 214-638-1400; 469-682-9331; Fax: 817-741-3758
E-mail: jessie@vipercomics.com
Web site: http://www.vipercomics.com
Dist(s): **Diamond Comic Distributors, Inc.**

Vireo Bk., A *Imprint of* **Rare Bird Bks.**

Virginia Museum of Natural History, *(978-0-9625801; 978-1-884549)* 21 Starling Ave., Martinsville, VA 24112-2921 USA
E-mail: dgreytak@vmnh.org.

Virginia Publishing Corp., *(978-0-9631448; 978-1-891442; 978-0-9914806)* P.O. Box 4538, Saint Louis, MO 63108 USA Tel 314-367-6612 (ext. 22); Fax: 314-367-0727 Do not confuse with Virginia Publishing Co. in Lynchburg, VA
E-mail: jfister@westendword.com
Web site: http://www.stl-books.com; http://bluebirdbookpub.com
Dist(s): **Big River Distribution**
Partners Bk. Distributing, Inc.

Virginian Pilot, *(978-0-9648308)* Div. of Landmark Communcations, Inc., 150 W. Brambleton Ave., Norfolk, VA 23501 USA Tel 757-481-4777; Fax: 757-446-2963
E-mail: linda.hollingsworth@pilotonline.com; pam.smithrodden@pilotonline.com
Dist(s): **Parnassus Bk. Distributors.**

VirTru Powers, *(978-0-9778798; 978-0-9779497)* Orders Addr.: P.O. Box 9404, Tavernier, FL 33070 USA; Edit Addr.: 10S073 Clarendon Hills Rd., Willowbrook, IL 60527 USA (SAN 850-492X) Tel 630-986-5262; Fax: 630-986-5262
E-mail: nomorewast@aol.com.

Virtual Baby Nurse LLC, *(978-0-9755180)* P.O. Box 881296, Port Saint Lucie, FL 34988-1296 USA (SAN 256-1239)
Web site: http://www.virtualbabynurse.com.

Virtual Tales *See* **BRP Publishing Group**

Virtual Word Publishing, *(978-0-9787930)* 1660 Cathedral Dr., Margate, FL 33063 USA Tel 954-971-4025; Fax: 954-971-4025
E-mail: diana@virtualwordpublishing.com
Web site: http://www.virtualwordpublishing.com.

Virtualbookworm.com Publishing, Inc., *(978-0-9703682; 978-1-58939; 978-1-60264; 978-1-62137; 978-1-947532; 978-1-949756; 978-1-951985)* P.O. Box 9949, College Station, TX 77842 USA (SAN 852-6575) Toll Free: 877-376-4955 (phone/fax)
E-mail: info@virtualbookworm.com
Web site: http://www.virtualbookworm.com.

Virtue Bks., *(978-0-9746440)* Div. of Virtue Products, Inc., 197 Woodland Pkwy., No. 104-476, San Marcos, CA 92069 USA Tel 760-471-5511; Fax: 760-471-5515; Toll Free: 800-201-5200
E-mail: kenwilcox3@cox.net; ken@virtueproducts.com
Web site: http://www.virtueproducts.com.

Virtue Pr., *(978-0-615-57943-6; 978-0-615-57945-0; 978-0-615-58375-4; 978-0-615-60709-2; 978-0-615-60746-7; 978-0-615-61272-0)* P.O. Box 729, Kamuela, HI 96743 USA Tel 808-250-9235 Do not confuse with Virtue Press in Jacksonville, NC
Dist(s): **CreateSpace Independent Publishing Platform.**

Viselman, Kenn Presents..., *(978-0-9722361)* P.O. Box 195, New York, NY 10113 USA (SAN 254-7783) Tel 212-929-1234
E-mail: viselmanpresents@aol.com.

Visible Ink Pr., *(978-0-7876; 978-0-8103; 978-1-57859)* Orders Addr.: 1094 Flex Dr., Jackson, TN 38301-5070 USA Toll Free Fax: 800-351-5073; Toll Free: 800-343-4499; Edit Addr.: 43311 Joy Rd., Canton, MI 48187-2075 USA (SAN 860-2271) Tel 734-667-3211; Fax: 734-667-4311
E-mail: inquiries@visibleink.com
Web site: http://www.visibleink.com
Dist(s): **Ebsco Publishing**
Follett School Solutions
Legato Pubs. Group
Mint Pubs. Group
MyiLibrary
Publishers Group West (PGW)
Perseus Bks. Group.

Visikid Bks. *Imprint of* **GSVQ Publishing**

Vision *Imprint of* **Grand Central Publishing**

Vision & Voice Publishing LLC, *(978-0-692-77452-6)* 13102 Creek Bridge Ln., Alpharetta, GA 30004 USA Tel 718-598-3076; Fax: 800-387-9075
E-mail: traceyworthen@aol.com.

Vision Bks. LLC, *(978-0-9886402)* 14 Edith Ln., Douglasville, GA 30134 USA
E-mail: visionbooksga@gmail.com
Web site: www.facebook.com/VisionBooksGa.

Vision Chapters Publishing Co., *(978-0-9860169)* 932 Homestead Park Dr., Apex, NC 27502 USA.

Vision Forum, Inc., The, *(978-0-9665233; 978-1-929241; 978-0-9755263; 978-0-9787559; 978-1-934554)* 4719 Blanco Rd., San Antonio, TX 78212 USA Tel 210-340-5250; Fax: 210-340-8577; Toll Free: 800-440-0022
E-mail: orders@visionforum.com
Web site: http://www.visionforum.com
Dist(s): **Send The Light Distribution LLC.**

Vision Harmony Publishing, *(978-0-9748715)* 4195 Chino Hills Pkwy., #393, Chino Hills, CA 91709 USA Tel 951-505-2503; Toll Free Fax: 866-855-1476
E-mail: info@visionharmony.com
Web site: http://www.visionharmony.com.

Vision Pubns., *(978-0-9746161; 978-1-933260)* P.O. Box 71532, Marietta, GA 30007-1532 USA Tel 770-973-9446; Toll Free: 800-862-5264 Do not confuse with companies with the same name in Southfield, MI, Saint Louis, MO, Boise, ID
E-mail: visionpublications@earthlink.net; dvandewalker@earlink.net.

Vision Publishers, Incorporated *See* **Vision Pubs., LLC**

Vision Pubs., LLC, *(978-0-9717054; 978-1-932676; 978-1-63100)* Orders Addr.: P.O. Box 190, Harrisonburg, VA 22803 USA Fax: 540-437-1969; Toll Free: 877-488-0901; Edit Addr.: 755 Cantrell Ave., Suite C, Harrisonburg, VA 22801 USA Do not confuse with Vision Publishers, Fort Lauderdale, FL
E-mail: visionpubl@ntelos.net
Web site: www.vision-publishers.com
Dist(s): **Baker & Taylor Publisher Services (BTPS)**
ebrary, Inc.

Vision Publishing, *(978-0-9651783; 978-0-9762730; 978-0-578-55930-8; 978-0-578-73343-2)* Orders Addr.: P.O. Box 11166, Carson, CA 90746-1166 USA Tel 310-537-0791; Toll Free: 800-478-7925; Edit Addr.: 20123 Harlan Ave., Carson, CA 90746 USA Tel 310-367-0641 Do not confuse with companies with the same name in Sandy, UT, Huntsville, AL, Ramona, CA, Southfield, MI, Griffen, GA, Phoenix, MD, Detroit, MI
E-mail: visionpub@rcn.com
Web site: http://www.visionpublishing.net
Dist(s): **Send The Light Distribution LLC**
Smashwords.

Vision to Fruition Publishing *See* **Vision to Fruition Publishing Hse., The**

Vision Tree, Ltd., The, *(978-1-933334)* 216 Waterbury Cir., Lake Villa, IL 60046 USA (SAN 256-5072) Tel 847-833-2546; Fax: 847-356-3783
E-mail: jo@thevisiontree.com
Web site: http://www.thevisiontree.com.

Vision Unlimited Pr., *(978-0-9746385)* 3832 Radnor Ave., Long Beach, CA 90808 USA Tel 562-537-1397 Do not confuse with Vision Unlimited in Spartanburg, SC
E-mail: joachung@msn.com; susan@newhopegrief.org.

Vision Video, *(978-1-56364)* Orders Addr.: P.O. Box 540, Worcester, PA 19490 USA Tel 610-584-3500; Fax: 610-584-4610; Toll Free: 800-523-0226; Edit Addr.: 2030 Wentz Church Rd., Worcester, PA 19490 USA (SAN 298-7392)
E-mail: info@gatewayfilms.com; info@visionvideo.com
Web site: http://www.gatewayfilms.com
Dist(s): **BJU Pr.**
Christian Bk. Distributors
Follett Media Distribution
Follett School Solutions
Midwest Tape
Spring Arbor Distributors, Inc.
Tapeworm Video Distributor, Inc.

Vision Works Publishing *Imprint of* **Soul Vision Works Publishing**

Vision Your Dreams, *(978-0-615-92446-5; 978-0-9969049)* 67 Curve St. 6, Millis, MA 02054 USA Tel 617-448-2504
E-mail: sandra@visionyourdreams.net
Web site: www.visionyourdreams.com.

Visionary Consulting Services, LLC, *(978-0-692-84351-2; 978-0-692-84352-9; 978-0-692-89967-0)* 9024 PENNINGTON PLACE, MONTGOMERY, AL 36117 USA Tel 334-277-8937
E-mail: jeffwcrawford5+LVP0003343@gmail.com; jeffwcrawford5+LVP0003343@gmail.com.

Visionary Play Pr., *(978-0-615-21946-2; 978-0-615-40324-3)* 5098 Reed Rd., Columbus, OH 43220 USA
Web site: http://www.InspiredFlying.com
Dist(s): **Ingram Content Group.**

VisionQuest Kids *Imprint of* **GSVQ Publishing**

Visions Given Life Publishing Co., *(978-0-9842468)* 1514 Parker Pointe Blvd., Odessa, FL 33556-4022 USA Tel 724-561-9426
E-mail: gdgregdixon@gmail.com.

Visions Of Nature, *(978-0-9656051; 978-0-9749570)* 460 E. 56th St., Suite A, Anchorage, AK 99518 USA Tel 907-561-4062
E-mail: robolson@gci.com
Web site: http://robertolson.com.

Visit to Hawaii, A, *(978-0-9772200)* 445 Kaiolu St., No. 807, Honolulu, HI 55303 USA Tel 808-921-2440
E-mail: hawaiiholm@aol.com
Dist(s): **Booklines Hawaii, Ltd.**

Visor Bks., *(978-0-9771994)* 62 W. Gaslight Pl., The Woodlands, TX 77382 USA (SAN 256-9752)
E-mail: rosszilla@sbcglobal.net
Web site: http://www.visorbooks.com.

Visor Libros (ESP) *(978-84-7522) Dist. by* **AIMS Intl.**

Vista Italia, *(978-0-9820672)* P.O. Box 92, La Mirada, CA 90637 USA (SAN 857-1643).

Vista Press Ventures, Incorporated *See* **Eaglemont Pr.**

Vister Bks., *(978-0-9983337)* 429 Visser Dr., Blackwater, VA 24221 USA Tel 276-346-1650
E-mail: circlevisser@gmail.com.

Visual Education Productions, *(978-1-56918)* 1020 SE Loop 289, Lubbock, TX 79404 USA Tel 806-745-8820; Toll Free: 800-922-9965
E-mail: cev@cevmultimedia.com
Web site: http://www.cevmultimedia.com
Dist(s): **Follett School Solutions.**

Visual Manna, *(978-0-9677386; 978-0-9715970; 978-0-9816093)* Orders Addr.: P.O. Box 553, Salem, MO 65560 USA Tel 573-729-2100; Edit Addr.: 1403 Dent County Rd., 502A, Salem, MO 65560 USA
E-mail: visualmanna@gmail.com.

Visual Velocity, *(978-0-9884679)* 22106 Chesapeake Cir., Commerce Twp., MI 48390 USA Tel 248-345-0789
E-mail: visualvelocityllc@gmail.com.

Vital Health Publishing *Imprint of* **Square One Pubs.**

Vital Link Orange County, *(978-0-9765880)* Orders Addr.: P.O. Box 12064, Costa Mesa, CA 92627 USA Tel 949-646-2520; Fax: 949-646-2523; Edit Addr.: 1701 E. 16th St., Newport Beach, CA 92663 USA
E-mail: kathy@vitallinkoc.org
Web site: http://www.vitallinkoc.org.

Vital Links, *(978-0-9717653)* 6613 Seybold Rd., Suite E, Madison, WI 53719 USA Tel 608-270-5424; Fax: 608-278-9363; Toll Free: 866-829-6331
Web site: http://vitallinks.net.

Vital Narrative Pr., *(978-0-692-38692-7; 978-0-692-39642-1; 978-0-692-39747-3; 978-0-692-40643-4; 978-0-692-40899-5; 978-0-692-46199-0; 978-0-692-46406-9; 978-0-9983364; 978-0-578-44121-4; 978-0-578-46140-3; 978-0-578-46577-7; 978-0-578-59513-9; 978-0-578-64324-3; 978-0-578-64325-0; 978-0-578-71341-0) 1296 Sessions Ct S, Memphis, TN 38119 USA Tel 9196961665; Toll Free: 9196961665*
Dist(s): **CreateSpace Independent Publishing Platform.**

Vitale, Mary Ann, *(978-0-9981359; 978-0-9981359-1-5; 978-1-7341211)* 23550 Hall Rd., Woodhaven, MI 48183 USA Tel 734-675-7946; Fax: 734-675-7946
E-mail: nvitale1@comcast.net.

Vitally Important,
Dist(s): **SPD-Small Pr. Distribution.**

Vitis Vera, LLC, *(978-0-615-73627-3; 978-0-9914009)* 12716 Cross Dale Dr., Huntersville, NC 28078 USA Tel 980-230-9625
E-mail: cwkinser@gmail.com.

Vives, Luis Editorial (Edelvives) (ESP) *(978-84-263; 978-84-140) Dist. by* **Lectorum Pubns.**

VivianLChilds *See* **VLChilds Publishing**

Viz Comics *Imprint of* **Viz Media**

Viz Communications, Incorporated *See* **Viz Media**

Viz Media, *(978-0-929279; 978-1-56931; 978-1-59116; 978-1-4215; 978-1-9747)* Subs. of Shogakukan, Inc., 295 Bay St., San Francisco, CA 94133 USA (SAN 248-8604) Tel 415-546-7073; Fax: 415-546-7086; P.O. Box 77010, San Francisco, CA 94107 Fax: 415-546-7086; *Imprints:* Viz Comics (Viz Comics)
E-mail: scott@viz.com; info@info@viz.com
Web site: http://www.viz.com
Dist(s): **AAA Anime Distribution**
Children's Plus, Inc.
Diamond Comic Distributors, Inc.
Follett School Solutions
Simon & Schuster, Inc.
Simon & Schuster Children's Publishing.

Vizione Productions Inc., *(978-0-9758863)* P.O. Box 54838, Atlanta, GA 30312 USA (SAN 256-1158) Tel 404-538-9424.

VK Pr., LLC, *(978-0-9982754)* 930 Prospect St Unit 206, Indianapolis, IN 46203 USA Tel 317-400-6883
E-mail: vkpressllc@gmail.com.

VK Publishing, Inc., *(978-0-9777171; 978-1-7352931)* 110 N. Milwaukee Ave. Apt.403, Wheeling, IL 60090 USA (SAN 850-0509)
E-mail: vkofman@stellaacademy.com.

VK Publishing, Incorporated *See* **VK Publishing, Inc.**

VL Publishing, *(978-0-692-60457-1; 978-0-692-90618-7)* 10105 Sorrells Creek Ln., Raleigh, NC 27614-7730 USA Tel 919-606-3694
Dist(s): **CreateSpace Independent Publishing Platform.**

VLChilds Publishing, *(978-0-9799896)* Div. of V.L.Childs/UICF, LLC, P.O. Box 9334, Warner Robins, GA 31095 USA
E-mail: vlccreations@yahoo.com
Web site: http://www.vivianlchilds.com.

VMH Publishing, *(978-0-9984553; 978-0-9989653; 978-1-947928)* 3355 Lenox Rd. NE Suite 750, Atlanta, GA 30326 USA Tel 833-842-6657
E-mail: vikki.hankins@gmail.com; info@vikkihankins.net; info@vmhpublishing.com
Web site: http://vikkihankins.net; http://www.vmhpublishing.com.

VMH Vikki M. Hankins Publishing *See* **VMH Publishing**

Vocal Power Inc., *(978-0-934419)* 2123 N. Topanga Canyon Blvd., Topanga, CA 90290 USA (SAN 693-4471) Toll Free: 800-829-7664
E-mail: info@vocalpowerinc.com
Web site: http://www.vocalpowerinc.com
Dist(s): **Alfred Publishing Co., Inc.**

Vocalis, Ltd., *(978-0-9665743; 978-0-9709948; 978-1-932653)* 100 Avalon Cir., Waterbury, CT 06710 USA Tel 203-753-5244; Fax: 203-574-5433
E-mail: vocalis@sbcglobal.net; info@VocalisESL.com
Web site: http://www.vocalisltd.com; http://www.vocalisesl.com; http://www.vocalis.com
Dist(s): **Follett School Solutions**
ebrary, Inc.

Vogel, Robert, *(978-0-9768455)* P.O. Box 551, Chesterton, IN 46304 USA Tel 219-688-5895; Toll Free: 800-815-7685 (phone/fax) Do not confuse with Robert Vogel in South Burlington, VT
E-mail: contact@azarovmemories.com
Web site: http://www.garrythegroundhog.com.

Voice & Vision Pubns., *(978-1-888251)* 902 Fletcher Ave., Indianapolis, IN 46203 USA Tel 317-262-4030; Fax: 317-262-4029
E-mail: voicevision@apostolic.edu.

Voice Connection/Vendera Publishing, The *See* **Vendera Publishing**

Voice of Light Pubns., *(978-0-9785623)* P.O. Box 1437, Fair Oaks, CA 95628 USA (SAN 850-9905) Tel 916-965-3046
E-mail: voiceflight@comcast.net.

Voice of Truths Publishing, *(978-0-9666777; 978-0-9742357; 978-0-9818992; 978-0-9916280)* P.O. Box 34, Donalds, SC 29638-9039 USA
E-mail: publishers@charter.net; robert@voiceoftruths.com
Web site: http://www.voiceoftruths.com.

Voigt, J. M. Incorporated *See* **MindWare Holdings, Inc.**

Volare, LLC *See* **Dividion Group, LLC, The**

†volcano pr., *(978-0-912078; 978-1-884244)* Orders Addr.: P.O. Box 270, Volcano, CA 95689 USA (SAN 220-0015) Tel 209-296-4991; Fax: 209-296-4995; Toll Free: 800-879-9636; Edit Addr.: 21496 National St., Volcano, CA 95689 USA
E-mail: info@volcanopress.com; sales@volcanopress.com; adam@volcanopress.com
Web site: http://www.volcanopress.com
Dist(s): **New Leaf Distributing Co., Inc.**
Quality Bks., Inc.; *CIP.*

Volo *Imprint of* **Hyperion Bks. for Children**

Volunteers of the Colorado Historical Society, *(978-0-9770423)* 1560 Broadway. Ste. 400, Denver, CO 80202-5133 USA
E-mail: angela.caudill@chs.state.co.us.

von Buchwald, Martin Farina, *(978-0-9777266)* 1158 5th Ave., New York, NY 10029 USA Tel 212-348-5580
E-mail: martin@farina.com.

Von Curtis Publishing, *(978-0-9749939)* 1278 Glenneyre, Suite 96, LaGuna Beach, CA 92651 USA Tel 800-459-4007; Fax: 949-497-7163
E-mail: info@beniceorelse.com
Web site: http://www.beniceorelse.com.

von Klan, Laurene, *(978-0-578-00322-1)* 4532 N. Albany, Chicago, IL 60625 USA
E-mail: chicagoriver@hotmail.com
Dist(s): **Lulu Pr., Inc.**

Vook Inc. *See* **Pronoun, Inc.**

Vorndran, Judith Clay, *(978-0-9772439)* 6431 Antoinette Dr., Mentor, OH 44060-3431 USA
E-mail: jclayvorndran05@sbcglobal.net; jclayvorndran@aol.com
Web site: http://www.hometown.aol.com/jclayvorndran/myhomepage.

Vorpal Words, LLC, *(978-0-9881969)* 2840 W Hwy. 101, Wellsville, UT 84339 USA Tel 435-764-7052
E-mail: dcolemanbooks@gmail.com
Web site: www.dcolemanbooks.com.

Voss, Dawn L., *(978-0-615-15324-7; 978-0-615-15581-4)* 481 Hallman St., Berlin, WI 54923 USA
E-mail: wr1t3r@yahoo.com
Dist(s): **Lulu Pr., Inc.**

Vox Dei *Imprint of* **Booktrope**

Voyageur Pr. *Imprint of* **Quarto Publishing Group USA**

VRguy publishing *Imprint of* **LINX Corp.**

VSP Bks. *Imprint of* **Vacation Spot Publishing**

Vulpine Pr., *(978-1-939276; 978-1-910780-18-3)* 4208 Rebecca Ct., Quincy, IL 62305 USA
E-mail: olivia@oliviacunning.com.

WAMY International, Inc., *(978-1-882837)* P.O. Box 8096, Falls Church, VA 22041-8096 USA Tel 703-916-0924; Fax: 703-916-0925.

W & B Pubs., *(978-0-9767732; 978-0-9771971; 978-0-9788985)* Orders Addr.: 9001 Ridge Hill Dr, Kernersville, NC 27284 USA Tel 336-354-7173; 9001 Ridge Hill St., Kernersville, NC 27284
E-mail: argusenterprises@hotmail.com; a-argus@live.com; williamconnor@a-argusbooks.com
Web site: http://www.a-argusbooks.com.

WCS Corp., *(978-0-9639350)* Orders Addr.: P.O. Box 900, Lander, WY 82520 USA Tel 307-332-2881; Fax: 307-332-9332; Toll Free: 800-656-8762.

WGBH Boston Video, *(978-0-9636881; 978-1-57807; 978-1-884738; 978-1-59375)* Orders Addr.: P.O. Box 2284, South Burlington, VT 05407-2284 USA Fax: 802-864-9846; 617-300-1050; Toll Free: 800-255-9424
Web site: http://www.wgbh.org
Dist(s): **Follett School Solutions**
Midwest Tape.

W.J. Fantasy, Inc., *(978-1-56021)* 120 Long Hill Cross Rd., Shelton, CT 06484-6125 USA Toll Free Fax: 800-200-3000; Toll Free: 800-222-7529
E-mail: wjfantasy@erols.com.

WJH Publishing, *(978-0-9674864)* 1445 Ross St., Suite 5400, Dallas, TX 75202-2785 USA Tel 214-978-8520; Fax: 214-978-8526.

W M Books *See* **Sierra Raconteur Publishing**

W M C Publishing *See* **Milestone Pr., Inc.**

W MediaWorks, *(978-0-9981329)* 11124 66th ave, Forest Hills, NY 11375 USA Tel 646-477-8440
Web site: www.wmediaworks.com
Dist(s): **CreateSpace Independent Publishing Platform.**

WP Pr., Inc., *(978-0-9633019; 978-1-884837)* 525 N. Norris Ave., Tucson, AZ 85719-5239 USA.

W Q E D Multimedia, *(978-0-9713080; 978-0-9769936; 978-0-9816697)* 4802 Fifth Ave., Pittsburgh, PA 15213 USA
Web site: http://www.wqed.org.

W Q E D Pittsburgh *See* **W Q E D Multimedia**

W S Publishing, *(978-0-9773520)* 3141 Tiger Run Ct. Suite 102, Carlsbad, CA 92010 USA (SAN 257-3180)
E-mail: elaine@elaineswann.com
Web site: http://www.elaineswann.com.

W. St. James Pr., *(978-0-9672818)* 2683 W. St. James Pkwy., Cleveland Heights, OH 44106 USA Tel 216-932-0290 (phone/fax)
E-mail: marcjaffe@aol.com.

WW West, Inc., *(978-0-9653924; 978-0-9727921; 978-0-9758960)* 20875 Sholes Rd., Bend, OR 97702 USA (SAN 299-2574) Tel 541-385-8911 (phone/fax)
E-mail: wwwest@bendbroadband.com
Web site: http://www.nationalparkspopup.com
Dist(s): **Farcountry Pr.**

W Y Publishing *See* **Bluewood Bks.**

W3 Publishing, *(978-0-9801322)* P.O. Box 1255, Suitland, MD 20752-2075 USA Tel 240-354-7077
E-mail: kellum_ent@verizon.net.

W5YI Group, Incorporated, The *See* **Master Publishing, Inc.**

Wachob, Chuck , *(978-0-578-15467-1)* 311 Rigas Ct, Americas, GA 31709 USA.

Wack, Nancy, *(978-0-615-16634-6)* 600 Fairwick Dr., saint Louis, MO 63129 USA
Dist(s): **Lulu Pr., Inc.**

Wackophoto, *(978-0-9798532)* P.O. Box 14843, Richmond, VA 23221 USA (SAN 854-5529)
E-mail: info@coolingthesouth.com
Web site: http://www.wackophoto.com; http://www.coolingthesouth.com.

Wacky Bee Bks. (GBR) *(978-0-9931109) Dist. by* **IPG Chicago.**

Wacky World Studios LLC, *(978-0-9742997)* 148 E. Douglas Rd., Oldsmar, FL 34677-2939 USA Tel 813-818-8277; Fax: 813-818-8396; Toll Free: 877-429-2259
E-mail: info@wackyworld.tv
Web site: http://www.wackyworld.tv.

Wade & Kayak Fishing Bks., *(978-0-9742253)* 702 Balmoral Ct., Friendswood, TX 77546 USA
E-mail: flyfisher@ev1.net
Web site: http://www.texascoastalfishingbooks.com/pages/1/index.htm.

Wade, John Pub., *(978-0-9623934; 978-1-882425)* Orders Addr.: P.O. Box 303, Phillips, ME 04966 USA Tel 207-639-2501 (phone/fax); 1413 Hwy. 17 S., PMB 154, Surfside Beach, SC 29575 Tel 843-215-1097; Edit Addr.: 193 Weld Rd., Phillips, ME 04966 USA
E-mail: wadecjs@yahoo.com
Web site: http://www.johnwadepublisher.com.

Wade, T.K., *(978-0-692-04547-3; 978-0-692-04699-9)* 3016 Mandy Ln., Morehead City, NC 28557 USA Tel 252-725-1934
E-mail: tkwadeauthor@gmail.com
Dist(s): **Ingram Content Group.**

Wadhams! Pr., *(978-0-9754987)* c/o Cordelia Sand, P.O. Box 264, Essex, NY 12936 USA.

Wading River Bks., LLC., *(978-0-9791463)* P.O. Box 361, Calverton, NY 11933 USA Tel 516-527-6283
E-mail: robert@wrbooks.com
Web site: http://www.wrbooks.com.

†Wadsworth, *(978-0-15; 978-0-314; 978-0-534; 978-0-8185; 978-0-8273; 978-0-942728; 978-1-928916; 978-1-4163; 978-0-495)* Div. of CENGAGE Learning, Orders Addr.: 7625 Empire Dr., Florence, KY 41042-2978 USA (SAN 200-2663) Tel 859 525 2230; Toll Free Fax: 800-487-8488; Toll Free: 800 354 9706; 10650 Toebben Dr., Independence, KY 41051 Toll Free Fax: 800-487-8488; Toll Free: 800-354-9706; Edit Addr.: 10 Davis Dr., Belmont, CA 94002 USA Tel 650 595 2350; Fax: 606 592 9081
Web site: http://www.brookscole.com; http://www.wadsworth.com
Dist(s): **CENGAGE Learning**
Follett School Solutions
MyiLibrary; *CIP.*

Wadsworth Publishing *See* **Wadsworth**

Wagging Tails Publishing *See* **Wagging Tales Publishing**

Wagging Tales Publishing, *(978-0-9715224)* 727 Lincoln Ave., Carbondale, CO 81623 USA.

Wagner Entertainment, *(978-0-9754515)* Orders Addr.: 3640 Loadstone Dr., Sherman Oaks, CA 91403-4558 USA
Web site: http://www.wagnerentertainment.com.

Waide Aaron Riddle, *(978-0-615-24430-3; 978-0-615-24648-2; 978-0-615-33363-2; 978-0-615-38560-0)* P.O. Box 691882, West Hollywood, CA 90069 USA
Web site: http://www.amazon.com/author/waiderriddle
Dist(s): **Left Bank Bks.**
Tattered Cover Bookstore.

Waila Bks., *(978-0-578-42853-6; 978-0-578-43348-6)* 8008 Chapin Rd., Benbrook, TX 76116 USA Tel 541-633-3314
E-mail: dancedamnyou@gmail.com.

WainWave Media, *(978-0-9789319)* P.O. Box 11037, Lexington, KY 40512-1037 USA (SAN 853-6953) Tel 859-294-9033; Fax: 859-233-1999
E-mail: dougwain@earthlink.net
Web site: http://www.waragainstviolence.com.

WainWave Publishing *See* **WainWave Media**

Waiting Room to Heaven *Imprint of* **Bk. Entree(TM)**

Wajsbort, Rochel, *(978-0-9749491)* 1431 E9, Brooklyn, NY 11230 USA Tel 718-339-5070; Fax: 718-998-1615.

Wakefield Connection, The, *(978-0-9703632)* 5201 Kingston Pike, Suite 6-302, Knoxville, TN 37919-5026 USA Tel 304-624-3901
E-mail: richard@wakefieldconnection.com; wendy@wakefieldconnection.com
Web site: http://www.wakefieldconnection.com
Dist(s): **Independent Pubs. Group.**

Waking Lion Press *Imprint of* **Editorium, The**

Wakinglion Studio, *(978-0-9767413)* P.O. Box 624, Bayfield, CO 81122 USA.

Walch Education, *(978-0-8251)* 40 Walch Dr., Portland, ME 04103 USA (SAN 669-6562) Fax: 207-828-8818; Toll Free Fax: 888-991-5755; Toll Free: 800-341-6094
E-mail: customerservice@walch.com
Web site: http://www.walch.com
Dist(s): **Follett School Solutions.**

Walch Publishing *See* **Walch Education**

Walden Pr., *(978-0-692-19471-3)* 1417 Pelican Way, Suisun City, CA 94585 USA Tel 707-372-3389
E-mail: annhamiltonshort@yahoo.com
Dist(s): **Ingram Content Group.**

Waldenhouse Pubs., Inc., *(978-0-9705214; 978-0-9761033; 978-0-9779189; 978-0-9793712; 978-0-9814996; 978-1-935186; 978-1-947589)* 100 Clegg St., Signal Mountain, TN 37377 USA (SAN 856-8111) Toll Free: 888-222-8228
E-mail: karenstone@waldenhouse.com
Web site: http://waldenhouse.com
Dist(s): **eBookit.com.**

Waldman House Pr. *Imprint of* **TRISTAN Publishing, Inc.**

Waldman Publishing Corp., *(978-0-86611; 978-1-59060; 978-1-60340)* P.O. Box 1587, New York, NY 10028-0013 USA (SAN 219-340X)
E-mail: info@waldmanbooks.com
Web site: http://www.waldmanbooks.com/.

Waldon Pond Pr. *Imprint of* **HarperCollins Pubs.**

Waldorf Early Childhood Assn. Of North America, *(978-0-9722238; 978-0-9796232; 978-0-9816159; 978-1-936849)* 285 Hungry Hollow Rd., Chestnut Ridge, NY 10977 USA Tel 845-352-1690
E-mail: mlyons@wardolfearlychildhood.org; publications@waldorfearlychildhood.org.

Waldorf Publications, *(978-0-9623978; 978-1-888365; 978-1-936367; 978-1-943582)* Div. of Research Institute for Waldorf Education, Orders Addr.: Publications Office 38 Main St., Chatham, NY 12037 USA Tel 303-545-9486; Edit Addr.: 575 Quail Cir., Boulder, CO 80304 USA
E-mail: ann_erwin@hotmail.com
Web site: http://www.whywaldorfworks.org; http://www.waldorfeducation.org; http://www.waldorfreasearchinstitute.org
Dist(s): **Midpoint Trade Bks., Inc.**
SteinerBooks, Inc.

Waldorf Publishing, *(978-0-578-19693-0)* 2140 Hall Johnson Rd. 102-345, Grapevine, TX 76051 USA Tel 972-674-3131
E-mail: barbara@waldorfpublishing.com
Web site: http://www.waldorfpublishing.com.

Walford Pr., *(978-0-9787671; 978-0-615-35161-2; 978-0-9826629; 978-0-9826969)* 11693 San Vicente Blvd. Suite 393, Los Angeles, CA 90049 USA (SAN 851-4941) Tel 310-487-3552
E-mail: ericweinsteinl@walfordpress.com; sambabyhead@aol.com
Web site: http://www.walfordpress.com.

Walkabout Publishing, *(978-0-9802086; 978-0-9821799)* P.O. Box 151, Kansasville, WI 53139 USA Tel 262-878-0448
E-mail: publisher@walkaboutpublishing.com
Web site: http://www.walkaboutpublishing.com
Dist(s): **Smashwords.**

†Walker & Co., *(978-0-8027)* 175 Fifth Ave., New York, NY 10010 USA (SAN 202-5213) Tel 646-438-6056; Fax: 212-780-0115 (orders); Toll Free Fax: 800-218-9367; Toll Free: 800-289-2553 (orders); *Imprints:* Bloomsbury USA Childrens (Bloom Child)
Web site: http://www.walkerbooks.com
Dist(s): **Children's Plus, Inc.**
Macmillan
Perfection Learning Corp.
Beeler, Thomas T. Pub.; *CIP.*

Walker Carter Publishing, LLC, *(978-1-947734)* 10945 SW Shad Rd, Terrebonne, OR 97760 USA Tel 402-806-1565
E-mail: carole14@walkercarter.com
Web site: www.walkercarter.com.

Walker, Esther, *(978-0-9716071)* 80-000 Ave. 48, Suite 131, Indio, CA 92201 USA Tel 760-347-4352
E-mail: strwalkr@easyfeed.com.

Walker, Fay Alice *See* **Favortwou Publishing**

Walker Hammond Pubs., *(978-0-615-62598-0; 978-0-615-62907-0; 978-0-615-67413-1; 978-0-615-72769-1; 978-0-692-36508-3; 978-0-692-52624-8; 978-0-692-61809-7; 978-0-9981054)* P.O. Box 192, Emmett, ID 83617 USA Tel 208-365-3733
Dist(s): **CreateSpace Independent Publishing Platform.**

Walker, J.W. Ministries *See* **LightHouse Pr.**

Walker Large Print *Imprint of* **Cengage Gale**

Walker Publishing Company *See* **Walker & Co.**

Walker, Sherry, *(978-0-578-19687-9)* 5280 Timucua Cir., Saint Augustine, FL 32086 USA.

Walking Elk Pubns., *(978-1-59648; 978-0-615-41705-9; 978-0-9881775)* 81 Portsmouth Ave. No. 5, Stratham, NH 03885 USA Tel 603-772-9300; 120 Ledgewood Dr. No. 10, Portsmouth, NH 03801
E-mail: ajkitt@kripara.com.

Walking the Line Pubns., *(978-0-9714540; 978-0-9816247; 978-0-9846299)* 4612 S. Jordan Pkwy., South Jordan, UT 84009 USA
E-mail: kclawson@walkingthelinebooks.com
Web site: http://www.walkingthelinebooks.com.

Walking Tree, Inc., *(978-0-9749832)* P.O. Box 468, Crystal Beach, FL 34681 USA Tel 727-784-5016
E-mail: art@halstowers.com
Web site: http://www.halstowers.com; http://www.lifeblending.com.

Wall, Mary Joanne, *(978-0-9644283)* 601 Ingomar Rd., Pittsburgh, PA 15237-4983 USA Tel 412-364-2598; Fax: 412-314-0862.

Walling, Emma *See* **Emma's Pantry**

Walls Tumbling Down Publishing, *(978-0-9770098)* Manhttanville Station, 871, New York, NY 10027-9998 USA Tel 212-865-6008
E-mail: antonioj365@aol.com
Web site: http://www.hometown.aol.com.

Wallworkshop, The, *(978-1-7328315)* 169 S. 2775 W., West Point, UT 84015 USA Tel 801-493-9655
E-mail: storyboarder@gmail.com
Web site: www.story-monster.com.

wallymeets, *(978-0-9843648)* Div. of wallymeets ltd., Orders Addr.: Hans Memlingdreef 50, LOMMEL, 3920 BEL
Web site: http://wallymeets.com/.

Walnut Springs Bks., *(978-1-933317; 978-1-59992; 978-1-934393; 978-1-935217)* 4110 Highland Dr. Ste. 300, Salt Lake Cty, UT 84124-2676 USA
E-mail: editorial@leatherwoodpress.com
Web site: http://www.leatherwoodpress.com
Dist(s): **Brigham Distribution**
Deseret Bk. Co.
Independent Pubs. Group.

Walnut Street Bks., *(978-1-947597)* 223 E. Walnut St., Lancaster, PA 17602 USA Tel 717-481-7518
E-mail: merlegood7@gmail.com
Dist(s): **Independent Pubs. Group.**

Walrus (FRA) *(978-2-36376) Dist. by* **Firefly Bks Limited.**

Walrus Publishing, Inc., *(978-0-9844857; 978-1-940442)* Div. of Amphorae Publishing Group, 4168 Hartford St.,

Saint Louis, MO 63116 USA (SAN 859-5305) Tel 314-606-7981
E-mail: lisa.miller@walruspublishing.com
Web site: www.walruspublishing.com
Dist(s): **Independent Pubs. Group**
Midpoint Trade Bks., Inc.

Walsh, Joseph, (*978-0-9818019*) P.O. Box 34105, Granada Hills, CA 91394 USA
Web site: http://www.gamblerontheloose.com.

Walt Disney Home Video, 3333 N. Pagosa Ct., Indianapolis, IN 46226 USA Tel 317-890-3030; Fax: 818-560-1930
Web site: http://disney.go.com/DisneyVideos/
Dist(s): **Buena Vista Home Video**
Critics' Choice Video
Follett Media Distribution
Midwest Tape.

Walt Disney Records, (*978-0-7634; 978-1-55723*) Div. of Walt Disney Co., 3333 N. Pagosa Ct., Indianapolis, IN 46226 USA Tel 317-890-3030; Fax: 317-897-4614
Web site: http://disneymusic.disney.go.com/index.html
Dist(s): **Follett School Solutions**
Ingram Publisher Services
Rounder Kids Music Distribution.

Walter Foster *Imprint of* **Quarto Publishing Group USA**

Walter Foster Jr *Imprint of* **Quarto Publishing Group USA**

Water Shoe Pr., (*978-0-9759499*) P.O. Box 928, Langley, WA 98260 USA.

Walter, Wendy D., (*978-0-9857147*) 301 Hillcrest Rd., San Carlos, CA 94070 USA Tel 650-598-0178; *Imprints:* Angry Bicycle (AngryBicycle)
Web site: ambrils-tale.com.

Walterick Pubs., Inc., (*978-0-937396; 978-1-884838*) Orders Addr.: P.O. Box 2216, Kansas City, KS 66110-0216 USA (SAN 211-9366) Tel 913-334-0100; Fax: 913-334-0153; Toll Free: 800-255-4097 (US only); Edit Addr.: 6549 State Ave., Kansas City, KS 66110 USA Toll Free: 800-648-0443 (Canada only).

walters, danna j. author, (*978-0-692-09629-1; 978-0-578-57249-9*) 506 Evergreen Dr., EULESS, TX 76040 USA Tel 817-688-6513
E-mail: dannawalters@yahoo.com
Dist(s): **Ingram Content Group.**

Walters, Jack C., (*978-0-9754658*) 2850 Airport Rd., No. 1, Carson City, NV 89706 USA Tel 775-882-0518
E-mail: waltersjc@charter.net.

Walters, Steve Ministries, (*978-0-9719767*) 3633 Corners Way, Norcross, GA 30092 USA Tel 770-409-1633; Fax: 770-300-9636; *Imprints:* Crowned Warrior Publishing (Crowned Warr)
E-mail: holyspiritinfo@stevewaltersministries.com
Web site: http://www.stevewaltersministries.com.

Waltham Publishing, LLC, (*978-0-9887524; 978-1-942781*) 15709 Brookview Dr., Urbandale, IA 50323 USA Tel 515-986-3626
E-mail: skhealthcomm@yahoo.com.

Waltower Publishing, (*978-0-9905422*) 6405 E. 129th Pl., Grandview, MO 64030 USA Tel 816-695-0541
E-mail: acwaltower@yahoo.com.

Wampum Bks., LLC, (*978-0-9842012*) 115a Pine St., Greenwich, CT 06830 USA (SAN 858-7116) Tel 203-531-8111
E-mail: sgalfas@itoinc.net.

Wan Lee Publishing, (*978-0-9858042*) 2860 Fenton Rd., Hartland, MI 48353 USA Tel 248-408-7103; Fax: 248-889-3647
E-mail: wayne@wanleepublishing.com
Web site: www.wanleepublishing.com.

Wand, Dana Bks., (*978-0-9906659*) 69750 Holmes Rd., Sisters, OR 97759 USA Tel 541-588-6517
E-mail: dwredhatnana@gmail.com.

Wand In Magic, (*978-0-9761921*) P.O. Box 58068, Nashville, TN 37205 USA Fax: 615-269-6820.

W&D Parables, (*978-0-692-16936-0; 978-0-692-17831-7*) 4361 Baychester Ave., Bronx, NY 10466 USA Tel 917-841-3358
E-mail: whernandez4@aol.com.

Wander *Imprint of* **Tyndale Hse. Pubs.**

Wander Twins, The, (*978-0-9985434*) 2803 SE 87th Ave., Portland, OR 97266 USA Tel 707-267-1848
E-mail: wesleynickerman@gmail.com.

Wandering Sage Bookstore & More, LLC *See* **Wandering Sage Pubns., LLC**

Wandering Sage Pubns., LLC, (*978-0-9725230; 978-1-933300*) Orders Addr.: 614 Rivers Bend Estates Dr., Saint Charles, MO 63303 USA Tel 314-623-6647
E-mail: valkpub@yahoo.com
Web site: http://www.wanderingsagebooks.com
Dist(s): **Valkyrie Distribution.**

Wanderlust Publishing, (*978-0-9758933*) P.O. Box 1557, Eastsound, WA 98245-1557 USA
E-mail: info@sabinefinancialservices.com.

WannaBees Media LLC, (*978-0-9767670*) 118 E. 25th St., Suite LL, New York, NY 10010 USA Tel 212-253-9874
E-mail: kdonovan@nvmagazine.com
Web site: http://www.theDobees.com.

Wanniarichchige, Somiruwan, (*978-0-615-17026-8*) 20700 San Jose Hills Rd., Suite 115, Walnut, CA 91789 USA
E-mail: ruwangotu@hotmail.com
Dist(s): **Lulu Pr., Inc.**

WAO Publishing, (*978-1-7339845*) 638 W. Hollyvale St., Azusa, CA 91701 USA Tel 626-733-7409
E-mail: senditomireya@yahoo.com
Web site: hellomireya.com; hellomireya.com/blog.

Waquis *See* **Black Ship Publishing**

War Monkey Pubns., LLC, (*978-1-7323662*) 573 E Heather Rd, Orem, UT 84097 USA Tel 801-680-5425
E-mail: warmonkeypublications@gmail.com
Web site: www.warmonkeypublications.com.

Warbelow, Willy Lou, (*978-0-9618314*) P.O. Box 252, Tok, AK 99780 USA (SAN 667-2639) Tel 907-883-2881.

Warbranch Pr., Inc., (*978-0-9667114; 978-0-692-52275-2*) 329 Warbranch Rd., Central, SC 29630 USA Tel 864-654-6180
E-mail: kspalmer@aol.com; salley.ouellette@gmail.com; jhpalmer42@aol.com
Web site: http://www.warbranchpress.com
Dist(s): **Follett School Solutions**
Partners Bk. Distributing, Inc.

Warburton and Gorman Publishing *See* **BareBones Publishing**

Ward, Amy M., (*978-0-692-05546-5; 978-0-692-11050-8; 978-0-692-18478-3*) 2101 Witcherville Rd., Greenwood, AR 72936 USA Tel 479-459-6928
E-mail: wardsarewriters@gmail.com
Dist(s): **Ingram Content Group.**

Ward Design, LLC DBA Teen Mystery Pr., (*978-0-9894143*) 1656 Hawksway Ct., Westlake Village, CA 91361 USA Tel 818-613-6389
E-mail: teendetectiveskylar@yahoo.com.

Ward, Jason E., (*978-0-9662366*) P.O. Box 719, Bronx, NY 10475 USA Tel 718-379-6285
E-mail: Jason@aiyahlevene.com.

Ward, John H., (*978-0-615-21017-9; 978-0-9834038*) 6606 Deerwood Dr., Crystal Lake, IL 60012 USA.

Warden, Chris, (*978-1-7326741*) 6556 Wandermere Rd., MALIBU, CA 90265 USA Tel 310-457-3757
E-mail: zenwarden@yahoo.com.

Ware Resources, (*978-0-9844685; 978-0-9974404*) 147 Quigley Blvd. PO Box 13192, New Castle, DE 19720-9696 USA.

Warehousing & Fulfillment Specialists, LLC (WFS, LLC), (*978-1-57102; 978-1-58029; 978-1-59093*) 7344 Cockrill Bend Blvd., Nashville, TN 37209-1043 USA Toll Free Fax: 800-510-3650; Toll Free: 800-327-5113; *Imprints:* Eager Minds Press (Eager Minds)
E-mail: vhill@apgbooks.com
Web site: http://www.apgbooks.com
Dist(s): **APG Sales & Distribution Services.**

Warne *Imprint of* **Penguin Young Readers Group**

Warne *Imprint of* **Penguin Publishing Group**

Warne *Imprint of* **Penguin Publishing Group**

Warner Books, Incorporated *See* **Grand Central Publishing**

Warner Bros. Pubns. *Imprint of* **Alfred Publishing Co., Inc.**

Warner Brothers Records, (*978-1-880528*) Div. of Creative Enterprises, 3300 Warner Blvd., Burbank, CA 91505 USA Tel 818-953-3467; Fax: 818-953-3797.

Warner Coaching, Incorporated *See* **She Writes Pr.**

Warner Faith *See* **FaithWords**

†**Warner Pr., Inc.,** (*978-0-87162; 978-1-59317; 978-1-68434*) Orders Addr.: P.O. Box 2499, Anderson, IN 46018-2499 USA (SAN 691-4241) Tel 765-648-2116; Fax: 765-622-9511; Toll Free: 800-848-2464; Edit Addr.: 2902 Enterprise Dr., Anderson, IN 46013 USA (SAN 111-8110) Tel 765-644-7721; Fax: 765-640-8005; Toll Free: 800-741-7721 (orders only)
E-mail: jallison@warnerpress.org; wporders@warnerpress.org; rjackson@warnerpress.org
Web site: http://www.warnerpress.org; http://www.francisasburypress.org
Dist(s): **Anchor Distributors**
Ingram Content Group
OverDrive, Inc.
Potter's House Book Service
SPD-Small Pr. Distribution
Send The Light Distribution LLC
Spring Arbor Distributors, Inc.; *CIP.*

Warner Press Publishers *See* **Warner Pr., Inc.**

Warren Machine Co., (*978-0-9729410; 978-1-934866*) 3 Taylor St., Portland, OR 04102 USA
E-mail: ari.meil@warren-machine.com
Web site: http://www.warren-machine.com.

Warren Publishing, Inc., (*978-1-886057; 978-0-9853094; 978-0-9884170; 978-0-9894814; 978-0-9960506; 978-0-9908136; 978-1-943258; 978-1-7323362; 978-1-7336158; 978-1-7337955; 978-1-7338973; 978-1-7339945; 978-1-7333252; 978-1-7341262; 978-1-7347075; 978-1-7350915; 978-1-7353023; 978-1-7355601; 978-1-7357280; 978-1-7358600) 8145 Ardrey Kell Rd. Suite 207, CHARLOTTE, NC 28277 USA Tel 704-900-0236 Do not confuse with companies with the same or similar name in Indianapolis, IN, Pomona, CA, Washington, DC, Loomis, CA, Roseville, CA, , Chesterfield, VA*
E-mail: warrenpublish@gmail.com
Web site: http://warrenpublishing.net
Dist(s): **BookBaby.**

Warrington Pubns., (*978-0-9889698; 978-0-9890974; 978-0-9984331*) 11100 SE Petrovitsky Apt. A-104, Renton, WA 98055 USA Tel 425-793-9629; *Imprints:* Oceanus Books (Oceanus Bks)
E-mail: WarringtonPress@aol.com
Web site: WarringtonPublications.com.

Warrior Schl. Pr., (*978-0-9715289*) P.O. Box 768, Sonoita, AZ 85637 USA
E-mail: info@warriorschool.com
Web site: http://www.warriorschool.com.

WARTS etc., (*978-0-692-18181-2; 978-0-578-40722-7; 978-0-578-48969-8*) 3108 Taylor Ave., West Point, VA 23181 USA Tel 757-707-0909
E-mail: naysayers@gmail.com
Dist(s): **CreateSpace Independent Publishing Platform**
Ingram Content Group.

Warwick Hse. Publishing, (*978-0-9638455; 978-1-890306; 978-0-9786369; 978-0-9790367; 978-0-9795258; 978-0-9801315; 978-0-9823004; 978-0-9842516; 978-0-9845166; 978-1-936553; 978-0-9978020; 978-0-9994023; 978-1-7349694*) 720 Court St., Lynchburg, VA 24504 USA Tel 434-846-1200
E-mail: whp720@aol.com
Web site: http://www.warwickpublishers.com.

Warwick Publishing (CAN) (*978-1-894020; 978-1-895629; 978-1-894622*) *Dist. by* **TwoRivers.**

Washington Pubs., (*978-0-9715721*) P.O. Box 12517, Tallahassee, FL 32317-2517 USA (SAN 254-2366) Do not confuse with Washington Publishers in Renton, WA
E-mail: info@washingtonpublishers.com
Web site: http://www.washingtonpublishers.com.

†**Washington State Univ. Pr.,** (*978-0-87422; 978-1-63682*) P.O. Box 645910, Pullman, WA 99164-5910 USA (SAN 206-6688) Tel 509-335-3518; Fax: 509-335-8568; Toll Free: 800-354-7360
E-mail: wsupress@wsu.edu; lawton@wsu.edu
Web site: http://wsupress.wsu.edu
Dist(s): **Ebsco Publishing**
MyiLibrary
Partners Bk. Distributing, Inc.
Todd Communications; *CIP.*

Washington University, Gallery of Art *See* **Washington Univ., Mildred Lane Kemper Art Museum**

Washington Univ., Mildred Lane Kemper Art Museum, (*978-0-936316*) Campus Box 1214, 1 Brookings Dr., Saint Louis, MO 63130 USA (SAN 214-4859) Tel 314-935-7460; Fax: 314-935-7282
E-mail: Jane_Neidhardt@wustl.edu
Web site: http://www.kemperartmuseum.wustl.edu
Dist(s): **Chicago Distribution Ctr.**
D.A.P./Distributed Art Pubs.
Univ. of Chicago Pr.

WasiWorks Studio LLC, (*978-0-9845203*) 6109 Piping Rock Rd., Madison, WI 53711 USA Tel 608-239-2526
E-mail: odalo@wasiworks.com
Web site: http://www.wasiworks.com.

Wasteland Pr., (*978-0-9715811; 978-0-9724289; 978-0-9729186; 978-0-9740725; 978-0-9742342; 978-0-9744368; 978-0-9746290; 978-0-9748230; 978-1-932852; 978-1-933265; 978-1-60047; 978-1-68111*) Orders Addr.: 18 Village Plz Pmb 177, Shelbyville, KY 40065 USA; *Imprints:* Curio Creative (curcr)
Dist(s): **Ingram Content Group.**

Watch & Learn, Inc., (*978-1-893907; 978-1-940301*) 1882 Queens Way, Atlanta, GA 30341 USA Tel 404-762-7760; Fax: 770-457-2132; Toll Free: 800-416-7088
E-mail: bc@cvls.com
Web site: http://www.cvls.com
Dist(s): **Music, Bks. & Business, Inc.**

Watch Me Grow Kids, (*978-1-932555*) P.O. Box 4405, Carson, CA 90749 USA (SAN 255-5093) Fax: 310-532-4536
E-mail: panderson@watchmegrowkids.com
Web site: http://www.watchmegrowkids.com.

Watchmaker Publishing *Imprint of* **Wexford College Pr.**

Watchorn Motion, (*978-0-9990474*) 2430 E Dolphin Way, Cottonwood Heights, UT 84121 USA Tel 801-953-9449
E-mail: swatchster@gmail.com.

Water Daughter Publishing, (*978-0-9753089*) Orders Addr.: 108 Academy St., POUGHKEEPSIE, NY 12601 USA Tel 845-397-7157; Toll Free: 888-778-2928
E-mail: omikemi@hotmail.com
Web site: http://www.waterdaughter.com.

†**Water Environment Federation,** (*978-0-943244; 978-1-57278; 978-1-881369*) 601 Wythe St., Alexandria, VA 22314 USA (SAN 217-1406) Tel 703-684-2400; Fax: 703-684-2492; Toll Free: 800-666-0206
E-mail: pubs@wef.org
Web site: http://www.wef.org
Dist(s): **Independent Pubs. Group**; *CIP.*

Water Forest Pr. *Imprint of* **Skyline Pubn.**

Water Lily Pr., Inc., (*978-0-9772168; 978-0-9860394*) 17214 Hillview Ln., Spring, TX 77379 USA
E-mail: hfwynn@outlook.com
Web site: waterlilypress.com.

Water Wave Productions, (*978-0-9987104*) 4640 Waipahee Pl., Honolulu, HI 96821 USA Tel 808-233-9902; Fax: 808-233-9902
E-mail: ikemoto@gmail.com.

WaterBrook Pr. *Imprint of* **Crown Publishing Group, The**

Waterbrook Press *See* **Doubleday Religious Publishing Group, The**

Watercourse, The *See* **Project WET Foundation**

Waterfall Ridge, (*978-0-9725485*) 40497 Cty. Rd. 20, Saint Peter, MN 56082 USA.

Waterford Pr., Inc., (*978-1-62005*) 428 N. 24 St., Phoenix, AZ 85008-6014 USA Tel 602-681-3333
E-mail: jk@waterfordpress.com
Dist(s): **National Bk. Network**
Publishers Group West (PGW).

Waterfront Productions, (*978-0-9759185; 978-0-692-26375-4; 978-0-692-29262-4; 978-0-9976140*) 1751 D W. Howard St. No. 262, Chicago, IL 60626 USA; 1751 D. W. Howard St. No. 262, Chicago, IL 60626
E-mail: jb@johnborowski.com
Web site: http://bloodlinesdocumentary.com/; http://www.hhholmesthefilm.com; http://www.johnborowski.com; http://www.albertfishfilm.com; http://www.panzram.com; http://www.serialkillerculture.com
Dist(s): **MVD Entertainment Group.**

Waterhouse Press LLC, (*978-0-9897684; 978-0-9905056; 978-1-943893; 978-1-947222; 978-1-64263*) P.O. Box 2080, Conway, NH 03818 USA Tel 781-975-6191
E-mail: meredithwild@gmail.com
Dist(s): **Blackstone Audio, Inc.**
CreateSpace Independent Publishing Platform
Ingram Publisher Services
Simon & Schuster
Simon & Schuster, Inc.

Waterhouse Publishing, (*978-0-9764082*) 40 Sheridan Ave., Congers, NY 10920 USA Tel 646-391-6669; Toll Free Fax: 877-260-5758 Do not confuse with Waterhouse Publishing in Scottsdale, AZ
E-mail: dfighter@msn.com
Web site: http://www.devonharris.com.

Watering Can, (*978-0-9759868; 978-0-9826416; 978-0-9984488*) 351 W. 19th St., New York, NY 10011 USA
E-mail: info@wateringcanpress.com
Web site: http://www.wateringcanpress.com.

Watering the Seed Productions *See* **Grace & Mercy Publishing**

Watermark Cruises, (*978-0-9754400*) P.O. Box 3350, Annapolis, MD 21403 USA
Web site: http://www.watermarkcruises.com.

WaterMark, Inc., (*978-1-882077*) 3627 Chalybe Cv, Hoover, AL 35226 USA (SAN 248-2010) Fax: 434-823-1187; Toll Free: 888-490-0100 Do not confuse with Watermark Assocs. in New York, NY or Watermark Pr., Inc. in Wichita, KS
E-mail: amylgary@gmail.com
Web site: http://www.picture-book.com; http://wmibooks.com/.

Watermark Pr., Inc., (*978-0-922820; 978-0-615-53794-8*) 149 N. Broadway, Wichita, KS 67202 USA (SAN 251-4265) Tel 316-263-3007 Do not confuse with companies with similar name in Owings Mill, MD, Seattle, WA.

Watermark Publishing, LLC, (*978-0-9631154; 978-0-9705787; 978-0-9720932; 978-0-9742672; 978-0-9753740; 978-0-9779143; 978-0-9790647; 978-0-9796769; 978-0-9815086; 978-0-9821698; 978-0-9844212; 978-1-935690; 978-1-948011*) Orders Addr.: 1000 Bishop St., Suite 806, Honolulu, HI 96813 USA (SAN 253-7427) Tel 808-587-7766; Fax: 808-521-3461; Toll Free: 866-900-2665 (866-900-BOOK) Do not confuse with confuse with companies with the same or similar names in San Diego, CA, Beverly Hills, CA, Seattle, WA
E-mail: info@bookshawaii.net
Web site: http://www.bookshawaii.net
Dist(s): **Booklines Hawaii, Ltd.**
Islander Group.

Watershed Bks. *Imprint of* **Pelican Ventures, LLC**

Waterside Pr., (*978-0-9627145; 978-1-939116; 978-1-941768; 978-1-943625; 978-1-945390; 978-1-945949; 978-1-947637; 978-1-949001; 978-1-949003; 978-1-951805*) 2055 Oxford Ave., Cardiff-by-the-Sea, CA 92007-1719 USA
Dist(s): **Blackstone Audio, Inc.**
INscribe Digital
Ingram Publisher Services
Midpoint Trade Bks., Inc.
Two Rivers Distribution.

Waterside Productions, Incorporated *See* **Waterside Pr.**

Waterside Publishing, (*978-0-9766801; 978-1-933754*) 2376 Oxford Ave., Cardiff-by-the-Sea, CA 92007 USA
E-mail: admin@waterside.com
Web site: http://www.waterside.com
Dist(s): **Ingram Publisher Services**
Two Rivers Distribution.

Watersprings Media Hse., (*978-0-692-51217-3; 978-0-9988249; 978-1-948877*) PO Box 1284, Olive Branch, MS 38654 USA Tel 662-812-1568
E-mail: athena@waterspringsmedia.com
Dist(s): **Ingram Content Group.**

Waterton Publishing Co., (*978-0-615-68604-2; 978-0-9905249; 978-1-7336233; 978-1-7347632*) 1000 Elmhurst Dr. Unit A, Highlands Ranch, CO 80129 USA
Web site: http://watertonpublishing.com.

Waterwood Publishing Group, (*978-0-9769044*) Orders Addr.: P.O. Box 12540, Charlotte, NC 28220 USA (SAN 257-1072) Tel 704-477-0708
Web site: http://www.waterwoodpublishing.com.

Watkins Media Limited (GBR) (*978-1-900131; 978-1-903296; 978-1-84293; 978-1-904292; 978-1-84483; 978-1-906787; 978-0-85766; 978-1-907486; 978-1-78028; 978-1-84899*) *Dist. by* **Peng Rand Hse.**

Watling St., Ltd. (GBR) (*978-1-904153*) *Dist. by* **IPG Chicago.**

Watling St., Ltd. (GBR) (*978-1-904153*) *Dist. by* **Trafalgar.**

Watosh Publishing, (*978-0-9611954*) P.O. Box 11231, Las Vegas, NV 89111 USA (SAN 286-1976) Tel 702-896-4108
E-mail: gecfly@aol.com
Web site: http://www.watoshpublishing.com; http://www.angietheaviator.com.

Watson, Corinda, (*978-1-7336121*) 651 Picketts Mill Dr., Shreveport, LA 71115 USA Tel 318-455-4761
E-mail: corindawatson@gmail.com
Web site: corindawatson.com
Dist(s): **Ingram Content Group.**

Watson Publishing, (*978-0-615-44576-2; 978-0-473-40077-4*) 8937 S Cornell Ave., Chicago, IL 60617 USA Tel 239-603-3121; Fax: 239-791-1260
E-mail: geraldcwatson@comcast.net.

Watson-Guptill *Imprint of* **Potter/Ten Speed/Harmony/Rodale**

†**Watson-Guptill Pubns., Inc.,** (*978-0-8230; 978-1-60569*) Div. of Crown Publishing Grp., 575 Prospect St., Lakewood, NJ 08701 USA Tel 732-363-5679; Toll Free Fax: 877-227-6564; Edit Addr.: 1745 Broadway # 124, New York, NY 10019-4305 USA (SAN 282-5384)
E-mail: aalexander@watsonguptill.com
Web site: http://www.watsonguptill.com
Dist(s): **Children's Plus, Inc.**
Follett School Solutions
Leonard, Hal Corp.
MyiLibrary
Penguin Random Hse. Distribution
Penguin Random Hse. LLC
Random Hse., Inc.
ebrary, Inc.; *CIP.*

Wattpad Bks. (CAN) *(978-0-9936899; 978-1-989365) Dist. by* **Macmillan.**

Watts, Erika, *(978-0-9980460)* 4277 Buford Cir., Lancaster, SC 29720 USA
E-mail: erikawatts83@gmail.com; dorkymomdoodles@gmail.com
Web site: www.dorkymomdoodles.com.

Watts, Franklin *Imprint of* **Scholastic Library Publishing**

Watts, Katherine (GBR) *(978-0-9556878) Dist. by* **LuluCom.**

Waugh Wright, *(978-0-9989586)* 919 Englewood Ave., Durham, NC 27701 USA Tel 215-715-8549
E-mail: waughwright@gmail.com.

Wave Blue World, A, *(978-0-9824539; 978-1-949518)* 399 W. St., New York, NY 10014 USA
Web site: http://www.awaveblueworld.com
Dist(s): **Diamond Comic Distributors, Inc.**

Wave Publishing, *(978-0-9642359; 978-0-9722430)* Div. of Caroy, Inc., 4 Yawl St., Venice, CA 90292 USA (SAN 298-3788) Tel 310-306-0699; Fax: 310-822-4921 Do not confusw with Wave Publishing in Virginia Beach, VA.

Wave Runner Publishing, *(978-1-7327170)* P.O. Box 7004, Springfield, OR 97475 USA Tel 541-515-1801
E-mail: kswarner@outlook.com.

WaveRider Pr., *(978-0-9968666; 978-1-7356890)* 2129 Central Pk. Ave., Evanston, IL 60201 USA Tel 847-475-4242
E-mail: cleopalex@gmail.com.

Waves of Bliss, *(978-0-9821302)* 6909 VT Rt. 15, Jeffersonville, VT 05464 USA
E-mail: nasrin@nasrinsafai.com
Web site: http://www.wavesofbliss.com.

Wawa Pr. *Imprint of* **Adisoft, Inc.**

Way Out Comics, *(978-0-9742386)* P.O. Box 642218, Los Angeles, CA 90064 USA
E-mail: julieyeh@sbcglobal.net
Web site: http://www.wayoutcomics.com.

Way With Words Publishing Company *See* **W3 Publishing**

WayaMedia, *(978-0-9765700)* 391 Watson Br. Rd., Cullowhee, NC 28723 USA (SAN 256-503X) Do not confuse with PPS Publishing Inc. in Lake in the Hills, IL
Web site: http://www.wayamedia.com.

Wayfarer Pr., LLC, *(978-0-9789965)* P.O. Box 948, Union Lake, MI 48387-0948 USA Do not confuse with Wayfarer Press in Plymouth, NH
E-mail: wayfarerpress@sbcglobal.net
Web site: http://www.wayfarerbooks.com.

Wayland Historical Society, *(978-0-9762756)* Orders Addr.: P.O. Box 56, Wayland, MA 01778 USA Tel 508-358-7959; Edit Addr.: 12 Cochituate Rd., Wayland, MA 01778 USA
E-mail: jane_sciacca@comcast.net
Web site: http://j.w.d.home.comcast.net/whs.

†**Wayne State Univ. Pr.,** *(978-0-8143)* Leonard N. Simons Bldg., 4809 Woodward Ave., Detroit, MI 48201-1309 USA (SAN 202-5221) Tel 313-577-6120; Fax: 313-577-6131; Toll Free: 800-978-7323 (customer orders); *Imprints:* Great Lakes Books (Great Lks Bks)
E-mail: theresa.martinelli@wayne.edu; Kristina.Stonehill@wayne.edu
Web site: http://wsupress.wayne.edu
Dist(s): **East-West Export Bks.**
INscribe Digital
Independent Pubs. Group
ebrary, Inc.; *CIP.*

Wayne, Steven Co., *(978-0-9713154; 978-0-9727696)* 3940 Laurel Canyon Blvd., No. 698, Studio City, CA 91604 USA Tel 323-654-9339; Fax: 323-656-7324; Toll Free: 866-446-1201; *Imprints:* SWC Editions (SWC Editions)
E-mail: wschoenfeld@stevenwaynecompany.com; schoenfeld@swceditions.com
Web site: http://www.stevenwaynecompany.com; http://www.swceditions.com.

Wayside Pubns., *(978-0-9749749)* P.O. Box 318, Goreville, IL 62939 USA (SAN 255-898X)
E-mail: belletrist.1@gmail.com.

Wayside Publishing, *(978-1-877653; 978-1-938026; 978-1-942400; 978-1-944876; 978-1-64159)* Orders Addr.: 262 US Rte 1, Ste 2, Freeport, ME 04032 USA Toll Free: 888-302-2519
E-mail: sales@waysidepublishing.com
Web site: http://www.waysidepublishing.com.

Waystone Pr., *(978-0-9988479; 978-1-7320873; 978-1-951536)* 2603 Jordanville Rd, Jordanville, NY 13361 USA Tel 315-219-0676
E-mail: nkotar@nicholaskotar.com
Web site: waystonepress.com.

Wayward Raven Media, *(978-0-615-77305-6; 978-0-692-29822-0; 978-0-692-91484-7; 978-0-692-91494-6; 978-0-692-94928-3; 978-0-578-54537-0)* 121 Lynnbrook Rd, Fairfield, CT 06825 USA Tel 203-336-9559
Web site: http://waywardraven.com
Dist(s): **CreateSpace Independent Publishing Platform.**

Waywiser Pr., The (GBR) *(978-0-9532841; 978-1-904130; 978-1-911379) Dist. by* **SPD-Small Pr Dist.**

Wayword Pr. Bks., *(978-0-692-79523-1; 978-0-9990515)* 22925 Galaxy Ln., Lake Forest, CA 92630 USA Tel 406-369-0902.

WCI Pr., *(978-0-9745480)* 6161 7th Ave N., St Petersburg, FL 33710-7015 USA
E-mail: clauberfl@aol.com
Web site: http://www.SoccerDreamsBook.com.

WD/GBGM Bks. *Imprint of* **General Board of Global Ministries, The United Methodist Church**

We Do Listen *Imprint of* **We Do Listen Foundation**

We Do Listen Foundation, *(978-0-9715390; 978-0-9826165; 978-0-9910777)* 1750 Ben Franklin Dr. #11g, Sarasota, FL 34236 USA (SAN 254-8119); *Imprints:* We Do Listen (WE DO LISTEN)
E-mail: howardb@wedolisten.com
Web site: http://www.wedolisten.org
Dist(s): **Lerner Publishing Group.**

WE, LLC, *(978-0-9761322; 978-1-7323556)* P.O. Box 120804, Nashville, TN 37212 USA (SAN 256-257X) Tel 615-584-2071; Toll Free: 866-352-9263
E-mail: wanda.scott@live.com
Web site: www.WandaLScott.com.

Wealth of Wisdom LLC, A, *(978-0-9843125; 978-1-941635)* P.O. Box 390038, Keauhou, HI 96739 USA Tel 808-896-3950
Web site: http://www.awealthofwisdom.com.

Wealth Services *See* **Skylar Doreal**

Weapons of Mass Instruction, *(978-0-9766978; 978-0-9769266)* P.O. Box 1299, Freedom, CA 95019 USA Tel 831-728-0600
Web site: http://www.bilingualnation.com.

Weatherhill, Inc. *Imprint of* **Shambhala Pubns., Inc.**

Weatherstock, Inc., *(978-0-9728107)* P.O. Box 31808, Tucson, AZ 85751 USA.

Weaver *Imprint of* **Alpha Omega Pubns., Inc.**

Weaver, Jack R. Company, *(978-0-9773370)* 375 A. Donald Rd., Canton, GA 30114 USA Tel 770-479-1342
E-mail: jackweaver426@tds.net.

Web of Life Children's Bks., *(978-0-9773795; 978-0-9777539; 978-0-9883302; 978-0-9883303; 978-1-970039)* P.O. Box 2726, Berkeley, CA 94702-0726 USA
E-mail: mdunphy@weboflifebooks.com
Web site: http://www.weboflifebooks.com
Dist(s): **Publishers Group West (PGW).**

Web Wise Services, Inc., *(978-0-9748237; 978-1-933404)* 305 Woodstock Rd, Eastlake, OH 44095 USA Tel 440-953-2443; Toll Free: 866-232-7032
Web site: http://www.webwiseseniors.com.

Webb, Dirk E, *(978-0-578-01867-6; 978-0-578-05527-5)* 3367 E. 150 N., Anderson, IN 46012 USA Tel 765-378-7025
E-mail: dirk.webb@comcast.net
Web site: http://lulu.com/dirkwebb
Dist(s): **Lulu Pr., Inc.**

Webb, Genie, *(978-0-692-86133-2; 978-0-692-12959-3)* 1414 W. Lawn Ave, RACINE, WI 53405 USA Tel 262-497-0059
E-mail: jeffwcrawford5+LVP0003504@gmail.com; jeffwcrawford5+LVP0003504@gmail.com.

Webb, Jack, *(978-0-9640275; 978-0-9719906; 978-0-615-99047-7; 978-0-692-69771-9; 978-0-692-86917-8; 978-1-7320522; 978-0-578-49430-2)* Div. of San Diego State Univ. Research Foundation, Orders Addr.: 7618 Stevenson, San Diego, CA 92120 USA Tel 619-723-5371
E-mail: jackwebb1@cox.net
Web site: http://www.bordervoices.com.

Webb Ministries, Inc., *(978-0-9632226)* Orders Addr.: P.O. Box 520729, Longwood, FL 32752-0729 USA Tel 407-834-5233; Fax: 407-332-6277
E-mail: Webbministries@cfl.rr.com
Dist(s): **CreateSpace Independent Publishing Platform**
Spring Arbor Distributors, Inc.

WebbWorks, *(978-0-9791076)* P.O. Box 985, Semmes, AL 36575-0985 USA (SAN 852-4629)
E-mail: duet2sisters@bellsouth.net.

WebCartoons, LLC, *(978-0-9743215)* 3727 W. Magnilia Blvd., Suite No. 141, Burbank, CA 91510 USA Tel 818-620-4256; Fax: 818-598-1842
E-mail: jerryching@earthlink.net
Web site: http://www.thegreatestkingbok.com.

WeBeANS Corp., *(978-0-9740115)* 466 S. Spruce Ave., Galloway, NJ 08205 USA Tel 609-652-5778; Fax: 877-589-3184; Toll Free Fax: 877-589-3184; Toll Free: 888-867-8838
E-mail: john@webeans.net
Web site: http://www.webeans.net.

Webster Henrietta Publishing, *(978-0-9728222)* P.O. Box 50044, Myrtle Beach, SC 29579 USA Tel 843-251-8867; Fax: 843-236-0260
E-mail: mhetzer@websterhenrietta.com
Web site: http://www.websterhenrietta.com.

Webster House Publishing LLC, *(978-1-932635)* 309 Florida Hill Rd., Ridgefield, CT 06877 USA Tel 203-438-0345; Fax: 203-438-0379
E-mail: fred@websterhousepub.com
Web site: http://www.websterhousepub.com.

Webster Pr. LLC, *(978-0-9882261; 978-1-63558)* 57 Woodside Ave., Amherst, MA 01002 USA Tel 413-219-3966; Fax: 413-219-3966
E-mail: alexawh@gmail.com.

Wedding Solutions Publishing, Incorporated *See* **WS Publishing**

Wedgeworth, Anthony G., *(978-0-9859159; 978-0-9989650; 978-0-578-71755-5)* 1014 S. 6th St., Prairie du Chien, WI 53821 USA Tel 563-581-8353
E-mail: AnthonyWedgeworth@hotmail.com
Dist(s): **Ingram Bk. Co.**
Lulu Pr., Inc.
Smashwords.

Wedgeworth, Anthony G., *(978-0-615-20879-4; 978-0-615-25816-4; 978-0-615-26007-5; 978-0-578-00695-6; 978-0-578-03617-5; 978-0-578-04710-2; 978-0-578-05827-6; 978-0-578-06337-9)* Orders Addr.: P.O. Box 621, Monona, IA 52159-0621ed USA; Edit Addr.: 104 N. Anderson St., Monona, IA 52159-0621 USA
E-mail: anthonywedgeworth@hotmail.com; thorlk@alteredcreatures.com
Web site: http://www.anthonywedgeworth.com
Dist(s): **Lulu Pr., Inc.**
Smashwords.

Wednesday Bks. *Imprint of* **St. Martin's Pr.**

WeDream.com, *(978-0-9764351)* P.O. Box 6020, Dillon, CO 80435-6020 USA
E-mail: climbing@wedream.com
Web site: http://www.wedream.com; http://discgolfguides.com.

Wee Creek Pr. LLC, *(978-1-942922)* P.O. Box 51052, casper, WY 82605-1052 USA Tel 307-265-8585; Fax: 307-265-4640
E-mail: weecreekpress@gmail.com
Web site: www.weecreekpress.com.

Wee Read Publishing, *(978-0-9723122)* 2269 Ginger Hill Loop., Lincoln, CA 95648-8719 USA
E-mail: lindamarchus@yahoo.com; vmarchus@hotmail.com
Web site: http://www.weereadpublishing.com.

Weebie Publishing *See* **Susi B. Marketing, Inc.**

Weekly Reader Corp., *(978-0-8374)* Affil. of WRC Media, Orders Addr.: P.O. Box 120023, Stamford, CT 06912-0023 USA (SAN 207-060X) Tel 203-705-3569; Fax: 203-705-3483; Toll Free: 800-446-3355; 3001 Cindel Dr., Delran, NJ 08370 (SAN 207-0618); Edit Addr.: 1 Readers Digest Rd., Pleasantville, NY 10570-7000 USA
E-mail: cpekar@weeklyreader.com
Web site: http://www.weeklyreader.com.

Weekly Reader Leveled Readers *Imprint of* **Stevens, Gareth Publishing LLLP**

Weekly Reader Teacher's Pr *Imprint of* **iUniverse, Inc.**

Weeks, Kermit *See* **KWIP, Inc.**

Weeley Pr., *(978-0-692-84235-5)* 1500 Bay Area Blvd, Suite 324, Houston, TX 77058 USA Tel 832-805-1691; Fax: 832-805-1691
E-mail: phil.roiz@yahoo.com.

Weem, Nadia *See* **Weems, Madia**

Weems, Madia, *(978-0-615-19289-5)* 1343 Stevens Rd. SE, Washington, DC 20020 USA Tel 202-889-5239
E-mail: thewriter1115@yahoo.com.

Weeping Willow Publishing, *(978-0-9789227; 978-1-7322294)* Orders Addr.: 405 Redwater Rd., Wake Village, TX 75501 USA Tel 903-838-9062
E-mail: tomgreer1964@gmail.com
Web site: http://www.tomcgreer.com.

Wegeng, Pam, *(978-0-692-98663-9; 978-0-578-44306-5)* 2312 N Stoneybrook Ct, Wichita, KS 67226 USA Tel 316-636-9167
E-mail: pkwegeng@cox.net
Dist(s): **Ingram Content Group.**

Wehner, Adrienna, *(978-0-9653866)* P.O. Box 6196, San Jose, CA 95150-6196 USA
E-mail: Awehner408@hotmail.com.

Wehr Animations, *(978-0-9748093)* 3890 CloverLeaf Dr., Boulder, CO 80304 USA
Web site: http://www.wehranimations.com.

Wehrley, Susan K. & Associates, Incorporated *See* **Thomas & Kay, LLC**

Weight Loss Buddy, Inc., *(978-0-9754448)* P.O. Box 488, Tenafly, NJ 07670 USA Toll Free: 877-283-3987
Web site: http://www.weightlossbuddy.com.

Weight of Ink, The, *(978-1-7328987)* P.O. Box P.O. Box 143475, FAYETTEVILLE, GA 30214 USA Tel 917-538-1596
E-mail: michael@theweightofink.com
Web site: www.theweightofink.com.

Weightman, Bud, *(978-0-9821035)* PMB#103, 5315 FM 1960 W., Suite B, Houston, TX 77069 USA (SAN 857-247X) Tel 281-444-4950; Fax: 281-966-1769
E-mail: budqsi@isoconsultants.com; piggytales.press@gmail.com
Web site: http://www.piggytalespress.com.

Weigl Pubs., Inc., *(978-1-930954; 978-1-59036; 978-1-60596; 978-1-61690; 978-1-61913; 978-1-62127; 978-1-4896; 978-1-7911)* Orders Addr.: 350 5th Ave. 59th Flr., New York, NY 10118 USA Tel 866-649-3445; Fax: 866-449-3445; 6325 Tenth St., SE, Calgary, AB T2H 2ZP Tel 403-233-7747; Fax: 403-233-7769; *Imprints:* AV2 by Weigl (AVTwo Weigl)
E-mail: editorial3@weigl.com
Web site: http://www.AV2books.com; http://www.weigl.com
Dist(s): **Follett School Solutions.**

Weimer, Brandon Publishing, *(978-0-692-14609-5)* 64 N Cameron St., Saratoga Springs, UT 84045 USA Tel 385-233-7811
E-mail: brandonweimersel@gmail.com
Dist(s): **Ingram Content Group.**

Wei's Publishing Co., *(978-0-9747284)* 116 W. Donald St., South Bend, IN 46613 USA
E-mail: liuwei82@hotmail.com
Web site: http://www.weispublishing.com.

Weiser, Samuel Incorporated *See* **Red Wheel/Weiser**

Weiss, Janet Bruschetti, *(978-0-9747716)* P.O. Box 8411, Longboat Key, FL 34228 USA
E-mail: jentajean@aol.com.

Welt Pr., *(978-0-578-04365-4; 978-0-578-19298-7; 978-0-578-19299-4)* 8819 Lanier Dr., Suite 414, Silver Spring, MD 20910 USA
E-mail: weltpress@gmail.com
Web site: http://LiberalMandate.com.

Welbeck Publishing Group Ltd. (GBR) *(978-1-85906) Dist. by* **TwoRivers.**

Welcome Bks *Imprint of* **Rizzoli International Pubns., Inc.**

Weldon Owen, Inc., *(978-1-875137; 978-1-892374; 978-1-61628; 978-1-68188)* Div. of Bonnier Publishing USA, 1045 Sansome St. Suite 100, San Francisco, CA 94117 USA Tel 415-291-0111 Do not confuse with Weldon Owen Reference, Inc. also at the same address
E-mail: info@weldonowen.com; customer_service@weldonowen.info
Web site: http://www.weldonowen.com/
Dist(s): **Chain Sales Marketing, Inc.**
INscribe Digital
MyiLibrary
Open Road Integrated Media, Inc.
Simon & Schuster, Inc.

Weldon Pubns., Inc., *(978-0-9724175)* 432 Pennsylvania Ave., Waverly, NY 14892 USA
E-mail: weldon@cqservices.com; sales@cqservices.com
Web site: http://www.Marchintotheendlessmountains.com.

Well Fire Pubns., *(978-0-9701912; 978-0-615-11133-9; 978-0-615-11146-9)* Orders Addr.: 100 Markley St., Port Reading, NJ 07064-1897 USA Tel 732-636-2060; Fax: 732-636-2538
E-mail: sherryross@home.com
Web site: http://www.sherryross.com.

WellFire Publications *See* **Well Fire Pubns.**

Wellington, Charles, *(978-0-9972556)* 4681 E. Leonesio Dr., Sun Valley, NV 89433 USA Tel 775-622-0986
E-mail: wellington.charles.2@gmail.com.

Wellington, Monica, *(978-0-578-41810-0)* 243 W. 70th St. No. 7F, New York, NY 10023 USA Tel 212-865-6588
E-mail: monicaaw@earthlink.net
Dist(s): **Ingram Content Group.**

Wellman, Patrick *See* **MrDuz.com**

Wellness & Lifestyle by Mel *See* **Our Blueprint-A Recipe for Wellness**

Wellness, Incorporated *See* **OrganWise Guys Inc., The**

Wellness Institute, Incorporated *See* **Wellness Institute/Self-Help Bks., LLC**

Wellness Institute/Self-Help Bks., LLC, *(978-0-9617202; 978-1-58741)* 515 W. N. St., Pass Christian, MS 39571 USA (SAN 663-382X) Tel 228-452-0770; Fax: 228-452-0775 YES NAME CHANGE CORRECT H DAWLEY
E-mail: publisher@selfhelpbooks.com
Web site: http://www.selfhelpbooks.com.

Wellness pH, *(978-1-933559)* 510 United Cir. Apt B, Greer, SC 29651 USA (SAN 256-6753) Tel 864-395-7866
E-mail: stroblechristine@gmail.com.

Wellness Pubn., *(978-0-9701490; 978-0-9748581; 978-0-9906147)* 624 Marsat Ct., Chula Vista, CA 91911-4646 USA Toll Free: 800-755-4656; *Imprints:* Bayport Press (Bayport Pr) Do not confuse with companies with the same or similar name in Rockport, TX, Omaha, NE, Holland, MI, Ft. Lauderdale, FL, Santa Barbara, CA
E-mail: malan1208@sbcglobal.net; ted@soriano.com
Web site: http://www.drjwallach.com.

Well-Trained Mind Pr., *(978-0-9714129; 978-0-9728603; 978-1-933339; 978-1-942968; 978-1-945841; 978-1-952469)* 18021 The Glebe Ln., Charles City, VA 23030-3828 USA (SAN 254-1726)
E-mail: ptbuff@peacehillpress.net
Web site: http://www.peacehillpress.com
Dist(s): **Norton, W. W. & Co., Inc.**
Penguin Random Hse. Distribution
Penguin Random Hse. LLC.

Welt, Rich & Assocs., *(978-0-9706529)* 8401 Heron Cir., Huntington Beach, CA 92646 USA Tel 866-742-4935
E-mail: richwelt@aol.com
Web site: http://richwelt.com.

Wenner Bks., *(978-1-932958)* 1290 Ave. of the Americas, 2nd Flr., New York, NY 10104 USA Tel 212-484-1696; Fax: 212-484-3433
E-mail: kate.rockland@wennermedia.com.

Wentworth Pr. *Imprint of* **Creative Media Partners, LLC**

We-Publish.com, *(978-1-931335)* 6311 Gulf Freeway #4201, Houston, TX 77023 USA Tel 713-448-0720 phone
E-mail: admin@banmex.com
Web site: http://www.we-publish.com.

Werner, Tamra, *(978-0-692-94041-9; 978-0-692-94042-6; 978-0-692-94044-0; 978-0-578-52434-4; 978-0-578-52436-8)* 38 Crestview Dr., Pittsford, NY 14534 USA Tel 585-749-7043
E-mail: mytopaz39tw@gmail.com
Dist(s): **Ingram Content Group.**

WeShine Pr. Co., *(978-0-9818113)* 12 Lake Mist Dr., Sugar Land, TX 77479 USA
Web site: www.weshinepress.com.

Wesleyan Publishing Hse., *(978-0-89827; 978-1-63257; 978-0-692-88620-5; 978-0-692-92243-9)* Div. of The Wesleyan Church, P.O. Box 50434, Indianapolis, IN 46250-0434 USA (SAN 162-7104) Tel 317-774-3853; Fax: 317-774-3860; Toll Free Fax: 800-788-3535; Toll Free: 800-493-7539 (orders only)
E-mail: wph@wesleyan.org; lebarons@wesleyan.org
Web site: http://www.wesleyan.org/wph
Dist(s): **Faith Alive Christian Resources.**

West 44 Bks. *Imprint of* **Enslow Publishing, LLC**

West Alden Publishing, LLC, *(978-0-9976002)* 208 Biltmore Dr., Colonial Heights, VA 23834 USA Tel 804-520-8866
E-mail: scnorkus@gmail.com.

West Barnstable Pr., *(978-0-9816873; 978-0-9828122; 978-0-9978182; 978-1-7328701)* 21 Meadow Ln., West Barnstable, MA 02668 USA (SAN 856-2490)
Web site: http://www.westbarnstablepress.com.

West Coast Learning Development Center, *(978-0-615-19154-6; 978-0-615-19269-7; 978-0-578-12128-4)* P.O. Box 194, Torrance, CA 90507 USA
E-mail: westcoastlearningdevelopmentcenter@yahoo.com
Web site: http://www.westcoastlearningdevelopmentcenter.org
Dist(s): **R J Communications, LLC.**

West, Dave Corporation *See* **Aztec 5 Publishing**

West End Games *Imprint of* **Purgatory Publishing, Inc.**

Publisher Name Index

West End Games, Inc., (*978-0-87431*) Subs. of Bucci Imports, R.D. 3, Box 2345, Honesdale, PA 18431 USA (SAN 687-8466) Tel 717-253-6990; Fax: 717-253-5104
E-mail: dspweg@hotmail.com
Web site: http://www.westendgames.net.

West Highland Pr., (*978-0-9721486*) P.O. Box 10040, Alexandria, VA 22310 USA
E-mail: westhighlandpress@earthlink.net
Web site: http://www.westhighlandpress.com.

West Margin Pr. *Imprint of* **West Margin Pr.**

West Margin Pr., (*978-0-944197; 978-1-941821; 978-1-943328; 978-1-5131; 978-1-5132; 978-1-5133*) P.O. Box 56118, Portland, OR 97238 USA Tel 503-254-5591; Fax: 503-254-5609; *Imprints:* Alaska Northwest Books (Alaska NW Bks); West Winds Press (West Winds Pr); West Margin Press (West Margin); Graphic Arts Books (Graphic Arts Bks)
Dist(s): **Independent Pubs. Group**
Ingram Publisher Services
MyiLibrary.

West, Mary, (*978-0-578-02740-1*) 733 Avenida Tercera, Apt 109, Clermont, FL 34714 USA
E-mail: sales@hecalledianswered.com
Web site: http://www.hecalledianswered.com
Dist(s): **Lulu Pr., Inc.**

West Ridge Farm Publishing, (*978-0-9845582; 978-0-9892282*) 535 Glendale St., Hampden, MA 01036 USA Tel 413-566-5366
E-mail: luvfisk@yahoo.com; sanj535@charter.net
Web site: http://www.westridgefarmpublishing.com; http://www.angelsclubkids.com.

West Virginia Univ. Pr., (*978-0-937058; 978-1-933202; 978-1-935978; 978-1-938228; 978-1-940425; 978-1-943665; 978-1-946684; 978-1-949199; 978-1-952271*) Orders Addr.: P.O. Box 6295, Morgantown, WV 26506-6295 USA (SAN 205-5163) Tel 304-293-8400; Fax: 304-293-6585; Toll Free: 866-988-7737; *Imprints:* Vandalia Press (Vandalia Pr)
E-mail: fdowney2@wvu.edu
Web site: http://www.wvupress.com
Dist(s): **BookMobile**
Chicago Distribution Ctr.
MyiLibrary
ebrary, Inc.

West Winds Pr. *Imprint of* **West Margin Pr.**

West Woods Pr., (*978-0-9776837*) 3905 Westwood Cir., Flagstaff, AZ 86001 USA (SAN 257-9375)
Web site: http://www.WestWoodsPress.com.

WestBow Pr. *Imprint of* **Author Solutions, Inc.**

WestBow Pr. *Imprint of* **Scholastic, Inc.**

Westchester Publishing, (*978-0-9891504*) 280 Mamaroneck Ave., White Plains, NY 10605 USA Tel 914-761-1894
E-mail: dhampton@newshelves.com.

Westcliffe Pubs. *Imprint of* **Bower Hse.**

Westcom Press *See* **Cathedrall Pr./Encycloware**

Western Images Pubns., Inc., (*978-0-9627600; 978-1-887302*) 2249 Marion St., Denver, CO 80205 USA.

Western Michigan University, New Issues Press *See* **New Issues Poetry & Prose, Western Michigan Univ.**

Western National Parks Assn., (*978-0-911408; 978-1-877856; 978-1-58369*) 12880 N. Vistoso Village Dr., Tucson, AZ 85755 USA (SAN 202-750X) Tel 520-622-1999; Fax: 520-623-9519
E-mail: abby@wnpa.org; derek@wnpa.org
Web site: http://www.wnpa.org
Dist(s): **Canyonlands Pubns.**
Rio Nuevo Pubs.
Sunbelt Pubns., Inc.

Western New York Wares, Inc., (*978-0-9620314; 978-1-879201*) Orders Addr.: P.O. Box 733, Buffalo, NY 14205 USA (SAN 248-6911) Tel 716-832-6088; Edit Addr.: 419 Parkside Ave., Buffalo, NY 14216 USA (SAN 248-692X) Tel 716-832-6088
E-mail: wnywares@gateway.net.

Western Psychological Services, (*978-0-87424*) Div. of Manson Western Corp., 12031 Wilshire Blvd., Los Angeles, CA 90025 USA (SAN 160-8002) Tel 310-478-2061; Fax: 310-478-7838; Toll Free: 800-648-8857
E-mail: weinberg@wpspublish.com
Web site: http://www.wpspublish.com.

Western Reflections Publishing Co., (*978-1-890437; 978-1-932738; 978-1-937851*) Orders Addr.: P.O. Box 1149, Lake City, CO 81235 USA Tel 970-944-0110 Toll Free: 800-993-4490
Web site: http://www.westernreflectionspub.com
Dist(s): **Bks. West**
Hinsdale County Historical Society
Lake City Downtown Improvement and Revitalization Team
Partners/West Book Distributors
Quality Bks., Inc.
Rio Nuevo Pubs.

Westie Pr., (*978-0-578-18653-5; 978-0-578-18956-7*) 26616 Pepperidge Cove, Millsboro, DE 19966 USA
Web site: www.customadultcoloring.com.

Westigan Review Press *See* **Ephemeron Pr.**

†Westminster John Knox Pr., (*978-0-664; 978-0-8042; 978-1-61164; 978-1-947888; 978-1-64698*) Div. of Presbyterian Publishing Corp., Orders Addr.: 100 Witherspoon St., Louisville, KY 40202 USA (SAN 202-9669) Tel 502-569-5052 (outside U.S. for ordering); Fax: 502-569-5113 (outside U.S. for faxed orders); Toll Free Fax: 800-541-5113 (toll-free U.S. faxed orders); Toll Free: 800-227-2872 (customer service); *Imprints:* Flyaway Books (MYID_B_FLYAWAY)
E-mail: orders@wjkbooks.com
Web site: http://www.wjkbooks.com
Dist(s): **Faith Alive Christian Resources**
MyiLibrary
Presbyterian Publishing Corp.; *CIP.*

Weston Priory, (*978-0-9763005*) 58 Priory Hill Rd., Weston, VT 05161-6400 USA Tel 802-824-5409; Fax: 802-824-3573
E-mail: brjohn@westonpriory.org
Web site: http://www.westonpriory.org.

Weston Woods Studios, Inc., (*978-0-7882; 978-0-89719; 978-1-55592; 978-1-56008*) Div. of Scholastic, Inc,, 143 Main St., Norwalk, CT 06851 USA (SAN 630-3838) Tel 203-845-0197; Fax: 203-845-0498; Toll Free: 800-243-5020
E-mail: questions@Scholastic.com
Web site: http://www.scholastic.com/westonwoods
Dist(s): **Findaway World, LLC**
Follett School Solutions.

Westphalia Press, (*978-0-918592; 978-0-944285; 978-1-935907; 978-1-941472; 978-1-941755; 978-1-63391*) 1527 New Hampshire Ave. NW, Washington, DC 20036 USA Tel 202-349-9282
E-mail: dgutierrezs@ipsonet.org
Web site: http://ipsonet.org.

Westphalia Thoroughbreds, LLC, (*978-0-9754103*) 1231 Latigo Ln., Flower Mound, TX 75022 USA Tel 817-368-6981
E-mail: arazielf@yahoo.com
Web site: http://www.westphaliathoroughbreds.com.

Westrim Crafts, (*978-0-9819053*) 7855 Hayvenhurst Ave., Van Nuys, CA 91406 USA Fax: 469-362-8016
E-mail: lisa.groshek@creativityinc.com
Web site: http://www.creativityinc.com.

Westry Wingate Group, Inc., (*978-1-935323*) 2708 Wet Stone Way Unit 108, Charlotte, NC 28208-4794 USA (SAN 857-183X)
E-mail: gabriel@westrywingate.com
Web site: http://www.westrywingate.com.

Westside Bks., (*978-1-934813*) Div. of Marco Bk. Co., 60 Industrial Rd., Lodi, NJ 07644 USA (SAN 855-0166) Tel 973-458-0485; Fax: 973-458-5289; Toll Free: 800-842-4234
Web site: http://www.westside-books.com
Dist(s): **Bks. & Media, Inc.**
Marco Bk. Co.
MyiLibrary.

Westside Press *See* **Wordsmith Pr.**

Westside Studio, (*978-0-9786147*) P.O. Box 703, Trumansburg, NY 14886-0703 USA.

Westview Pr. *Imprint of* **Avalon Publishing**

Westview Publishing Co., Inc., (*978-0-9744322; 978-0-9748730; 978-0-9755646; 978-0-9764940; 978-0-9773179; 978-0-9776207; 978-1-933912; 978-0-9816172; 978-0-692-69338-4*) P.O. Box 210183, Nashville, TN 37221 USA
Web site: http://www.westviewpublishing.com.

Westview Publishing, Incorporated *See* **Westview Publishing Co., Inc.**

WestWind Pr. *Imprint of* **Scott, D.& F. Publishing, Inc.**

Westwood Bks. Publishing, (*978-1-949006; 978-1-64361; 978-0-578-41199-6; 978-0-578-41203-0; 978-0-578-41224-5; 978-0-578-41227-6; 978-0-578-41235-1; 978-1-64803*) 11416 SW Aventino Dr., Port Saint Lucie, FL 90064 USA Tel 888-420-8640
E-mail: admin@westwoodbookspublishing.com
Web site: www.westwoodbookspublishing.com.

Westwood Pr., Inc., (*978-0-936159*) 116 E. 16th St., New York, NY 10003-2112 USA (SAN 696-7183) Tel 212-420-8008 Do not confuse with Westwoods Press, Darien, CT.

Wever Books *See* **Red Engine Pr.**

WeWrite LLC, (*978-1-57635; 978-1-884987*) Orders Addr.: P.O. Box 593, Ben Lomond, CA 95005 USA Tel 831-336-3382; Fax: 831-336-8592; Toll Free: 800-295-9037; Edit Addr.: 11040 Alba Rd., Ben Lomond, CA 95005-9220 USA
E-mail: info@wewrite.net
Web site: http://www.wewrite.net.

Wexford College Pr., (*978-0-9709917; 978-0-9721786; 978-0-9726596*) 401 Merito Pl., Journalism Bldg., Palm Springs, CA 92262 USA; *Imprints:* Watchmaker Publishing (Watchmaker Pub)
E-mail: books@wexfordcollegepress.com
Web site: http://www.wexfordcollegepress.com.

WGH Arts LLC, (*978-0-9776562*) P.O. Box 215, Lisbon, IA 52253-0215 USA
E-mail: bill@wgharts.com
Web site: http://www.wgharts.com.

WHA Publishing, (*978-0-9773228*) P.O. Box 20818, Wickenburg, AZ 85358 USA Tel 520-877-7860; Fax: 520-877-7869
E-mail: jerry@datssoftware.com.

Whale Pr. Bks., (*978-1-7325315*) 30 Jamaicaway, Apt 3, Boston, MA 02130 USA Tel 814-795-2552
E-mail: lukmitchell@gmail.com.

Whale Tale Pr., (*978-0-9824784*) 343 Hertford Cir., Decatur, GA 30030 USA
Web site: http://www.whaletalepress.com.

Whaleback Publishing, (*978-0-9725938*) 4 Captain's Way, Exeter, NH 03833 USA Fax: 603-772-5416; Toll Free: 800-207-2580
Web site: http://www.whalebackpublishing.com.

Whalen Bk. Works Publishing Co., (*978-1-7325126; 978-1-951511*) 338 E. 100 Street, Suite 5A, New York, NY 10029 USA Tel 207-251-1978
E-mail: john@whalenbooks.com
Web site: www.whalenbookworks.com
Dist(s): **Simon & Schuster, Inc.**

Whaler, Norman / Beneath Another Sky Bks., (*978-1-948131*) 2150 Ctr. Ave, Fort Lee, NJ 07024 USA Tel 201-927-0787
E-mail: normwhaler@gmail.com
Web site: normanwhaler.com.

Whale's Jaw Publishing, (*978-0-9740778*) 11 Dennison St., Gloucester, MA 01930 USA Tel 978-281-9684
E-mail: info@whalesjaw.com; chetbrig@comcast.net
Web site: http://www.whalesjaw.com.

Whale's Library, The *See* **Mindsong Math**

What If Pr., (*978-0-9977867*) 2616 Peartree Ln., San Jose, CA 95121 USA Tel 408-460-7316
E-mail: karenlbennett@sbcglobal.net
Web site: karenlynnbennett.com.

What If? Publishing, (*978-0-692-81041-5; 978-0-692-90430-5; 978-0-9995878*) 133 E. 4th St., Loveland, CO 80537 USA Tel 970-667-0292
E-mail: liz@whatifideation.com
Web site: whatifpublishing.com.

What on Earth Bks (GBR) (*978-0-9565936; 978-0-9929249; 978-0-9932847; 978-0-9930199*) *Dist. by* **IngramPubServ.**

What on Earth Books, The Black Barn Wickhurst Farm, Tonbridge Kent, TN11 8PS GBR; 6670 New Nashville Hwy Suite 120, Smyrna, TN 37167
Dist(s): **Ingram Publisher Services.**

What The Flux Media, Incorporated *See* **Ark Watch Holdings LLC**

WhatAboutABoo Productions, (*978-1-7328172*) 31 Olive Ct., Novato, CA 94945 USA Tel 415-235-9322
E-mail: buffypoet@gmail.com
Web site: buffyfordstewart.com.

Whatever is Lovely Publications *See* **Whatever is Lovely Pubns.**

Whatever is Lovely Pubns., (*978-0-615-67198-7; 978-1-948384*) 19 Eagle Rock Rd., Questa, NM 87556 USA Tel 575-404-1840
Dist(s): **CreateSpace Independent Publishing Platform.**

Whatever Publishing, Incorporated *See* **New World Library**

Wheat State Media LLC, (*978-0-9882892*) 21606 W. 52nd St., Shawnee, KS 66226 USA Tel 816-668-8400
E-mail: bhowell@wheatstatemedia.com
Web site: http://www.wheatstatemedia.com
Dist(s): **Anchor Distributors.**

Wheatland Hse. publising, (*978-0-9963659; 978-0-692-13259-3*) 36969 53Rd St., Burlington, WI 53105 USA Tel 262-661-4546
E-mail: kbhumphrey@gmail.com.

Wheatland House publising *See* **Wheatland Hse. publising**

Wheatmark, Inc., (*978-1-58736; 978-1-60494; 978-1-62787*) 2030 E. Speedway Blvd., Suite 106, Tucson, AZ 85719 USA (SAN 253-1054) Tel 520-798-0888; Fax: 520-798-3394; Toll Free: 888-934-0888; *Imprints:* Starbound Books (Starbound Bks); Press Box Books (Pr Box Bks)
E-mail: bookstore@wheatmark.com; atilla@wheatmark.com; sam@wheatmark.com
Web site: http://www.wheatmark.com
Dist(s): **INscribe Digital.**

Wheaton-Smith, Simon, (*978-0-9765286*) 810 W. 6th St., Silver City, NM 88061 USA
E-mail: illustratingshadows@yahoo.com
Web site: http://www.illustratingshadows.com/.

WHEEL Council, Inc., The, (*978-0-9656732; 978-0-9728889*) P.O. Box 22517, Flagstaff, AZ 86002 USA Tel 928-214-0120
E-mail: info@wheelcouncil.org
Web site: http://www.wheelcouncil.org.

Wheeler Publishing, Inc. *Imprint of* **Cengage Gale**

Wheelhouse Publishing, (*978-0-692-56894-1; 978-0-692-56905-4; 978-0-692-56909-2; 978-0-9977493; 978-1-947076*) 33512 SE 126th St., Issaquah, WA 98027 USA Tel 425-899-8174
E-mail: villagiorello@gmail.com
Dist(s): **CreateSpace Independent Publishing Platform.**

When I Grow Up Publishing, Inc., (*978-0-9795117*) 3721 Chelton Rd., Shaker Hts., OH 44120 USA
E-mail: erinn@theblackcrayon.com
Web site: http://www.theblackcrayon.com.

When Miss Bluebird Died, L.L.C., (*978-0-692-92432-7*) P.O. Box 35454, PHOENIX, AZ 85069 USA Tel 831-917-1142
E-mail: jenreich1973@gmail.com
Dist(s): **Ingram Content Group.**

whenpigsjig *See* **Whenpigsjig**

Whenpigsjig, (*978-0-9989924*) 63 S. 1st E., Snowflake, AZ 85937 USA Tel 928-243-1441
E-mail: whenpigsjig@gmail.com.

Where? Pr., Inc., (*978-0-9719144*) Orders Addr.: P.O. Box 154, Paintsville, KY 41240 USA Tel 606-789-9423; Edit Addr.: 830 Robin Ct., Paintsville, KY 41240 USA
E-mail: wherepress@gmail.com
Web site: http://www.wherepress.netfirms.com.

Where-I-Live / Foster Pr., (*978-0-9764893*) 430 91st Ave., NE, Suite 3, Everett, WA 98205 USA Tel 425-334-9317; Fax: 425-334-8155
E-mail: vern@fosterpress.com
Web site: http://www.fosterpress.com.

Whimble Designs, (*978-0-9773523*) 1540/42 Monroe Dr., NE, Atlanta, GA 30324 USA.

WhipperSnapper Bks., (*978-0-9657218*) P.O. Box 3186, Los Altos, CA 94024 USA 925-249-0709 (orders/general); Toll Free: 800-910-4482.

Whipple, Natalie, (*978-0-9911785*) 1937 W. 800 N., Pleasant Grove, UT 84062 USA Tel 801-471-5169
E-mail: nataliewhipple@hotmail.com
Web site: nataliewhipple.com.

Whippoorwill, LLC, (*978-0-9741968*) 9601 Linden St., Overland Park, KS 66207 USA (SAN 255-6553) Tel 913-341-7104; Fax: 913-385-2453
E-mail: schase@mischomeloans.com.

Whipsaw Pr., (*978-0-9899005; 978-0-9970233; 978-1-946910*) 1131 NW Morgan Ln, Grants Pass, OR 97526 USA Tel 541-295-5662; Fax: 866-645-4232
E-mail: frank@frankmorin.org
Web site: www.frankmorin.org.

Whirling Dirvish Publishing, (*978-0-9768870*) 26895 Aliso Creek Rd., Suite B591, Aliso Viejo, CA 92656 USA Tel 949-643-1865; Fax: 949-606-7180; Toll Free: 800-993-1291
E-mail: info@whirlingdirvish.com
Web site: http://www.whirlingdirvish.com/.

Whirlwhim, (*978-0-9800274*) 12930 Ventura Blvd., Studio City, CA 91604 USA
E-mail: whirlwhim@yahoo.com
Web site: http://www.blunderbrothers.com.

Whirlwind Publishing Group, (*978-0-9882643*) 2506 Bridal Wreath Ln., Dallas, TX 75233 USA Tel 858-220-2917
E-mail: lolahawk@hotmail.com
Web site: www.whirlwindpublishinggroup.com
Dist(s): **CreateSpace Independent Publishing Platform.**

Whiskey Creek Pr. *Imprint of* **Whiskey Creek Pr., LLC**

Whiskey Creek Pr., LLC, (*978-1-59374; 978-1-60313; 978-1-61160*) Orders Addr.: 609 Greenwich St. 6th Fl, New York, NY 10014 USA Tel 212-431-5455; Fax: 917-464-6394; *Imprints:* Whiskey Creek Press (Whisk Creek Pr)
E-mail: publishing@start-media.com
Web site: http://www.whiskeycreekpress.com; http://www.whiskeycreekpresstorrid.com
Dist(s): **All Romance Ebooks, LLC**
OverDrive, Inc.
Simon & Schuster, Inc.

Whiskey Creek Restorations, (*978-0-9625756*) 7205 68th Ave., S.W., Elgin, ND 58533 USA Tel 218-354-2253.

Whispering Pine Press, Incorporated *See* **Whispering Pine Pr. International, Inc.**

Whispering Pine Pr. International, Inc., (*978-0-9679368; 978-1-930948; 978-1-59210; 978-1-59434; 978-1-59649; 978-1-59808*) Orders Addr.: P.O. Box 70, Greenacres, WA 99016-0070 USA (SAN 253-200X) Tel 509-928-7888; Fax: 509-922-9949; Edit Addr.: 1710 N. Aladdin Rd., Liberty Lake, WA 99016 USA
E-mail: whisperingpinepress@outlook.com
Web site: http://www.whisperingpinepress.com; http://www.whisperingpinepressbookstore.com.

Whispering Wind Publishing Inc., (*978-0-9721640*) Orders Addr.: 11089 Utica Ct., Westminster, CO 80031-2057 USA Tel 303-717-6442
E-mail: KaKillam@cs.com; publisher@whisperingwind.org
Web site: http://www.whisperingwind.org
Dist(s): **Quality Bks., Inc.**

Whistle Pr., The, (*978-0-9624893*) P.O. Box 1006, Petal, MS 39465-8618 USA Tel 601-544-8486 (phone/fax)
E-mail: contact@whistlepress.com
Web site: www.whistlepress.com.

Whitaker Hse., (*978-0-88368; 978-1-60374; 978-1-62911; 978-1-64123*) Div. of Whitaker Corp., 1030 Hunt Valley Cir., New Kensington, PA 15068 USA (SAN 203-2104) Tel 724-334-7000 Whitaker House/Anchor Distributors; Fax: 724-334-1200 Anchor Distributors; Toll Free Fax: 866-773-7001 Whitaker House; 800-765-1960 Anchor Distributors; Toll Free: 877-793-9800 Whitaker House; 800-444-4484 Whitaker House/Anchor Distributors
E-mail: sales@whitakerhouse.com
Web site: http://www.whitakerhouse.com/; http://www.anchordistributors.com/; http://www.amazon.com/
Dist(s): **Anchor Distributors.**

Whitaker, Thurston Information Services, LLC, (*978-0-9758940; 978-0-9892525*) P.O. Box 271743, West Hartford, CT 06127-1743 USA Tel 860-922-4719
E-mail: gwhit@twisbiz.com
Web site: http://www.thurstonwhitaker.com.

Whitcombe, Renee *See* **Budding Family Publishing**

White Bird Pubns., (*978-0-9828024; 978-1-937690; 978-1-63363*) P.O. Box 90145, Austin, TX 78749 USA
E-mail: whitebirdpublications@gmail.com
Web site: http://www.whitebirdpublications.com.

White Cloud Pr., (*978-1-883991; 978-0-9745245; 978-0-9793840; 978-1-935952; 978-1-940468*) Orders Addr.: P.O. Box 3400, Ashland, OR 97520 USA; Edit Addr.: 300 E. Hersey St., #11, Ashland, OR 97520-6200 USA Fax: 541-482-7708; Toll Free: 800-380-8286 Do not confuse with White Cloud Pr. in Hobbs, NM
Web site: http://www.whitecloudpress.com
Dist(s): **MyiLibrary**
Publishers Group West (PGW).

White Dharma Ltd., (*978-0-9907781*) P.O. Box 390251, Cambridge, MA 02139 USA Tel 617-299-0883
E-mail: whitedharmaltd@gmail.com.

White Dog Pr., Ltd, (*978-0-9741027; 978-0-615-43844-3; 978-0-9855823; 978-0-615-93256-9; 978-0-692-48522-4*) 321 High School Rd., No. 393, Bainbridge Island, WA 98110-2977 USA Tel 206-661-5946
E-mail: whitedogpress@aol.com.

White Dog Studio, (*978-0-9667286; 978-0-9897882*) Orders Addr.: P.O. Box 189, Louisville, TN 37777 USA Tel 865-776-9886; Edit Addr.: 3825 Island Path, Louisville, TN 37777 USA
E-mail: jprince1@mac.com
Web site: http://www.newcooksinamerica.com; www.missjanetsglutenfreeamerica.

White Eagle Publishing Trust (GBR) (*978-0-85487*) *Dist. by* **DeVorss.**

White Falcon Publishing *Imprint of* **White Falcon Publishing**

White Falcon Publishing, (*978-1-943851; 978-1-947293; 978-1-63640*) 4637 Silvertide Dr., Union City, CA 94587 USA Tel 404-771-6653; *Imprints:* White Falcon Publishing (WhiteFalc Pub)
E-mail: whitefalconpublishing@gmail.com.

White Falcon Publishing Platform *See* **White Falcon Publishing**

White Feather Press, LLC, *(978-0-9766083; 978-0-9822487; 978-0-9831751; 978-1-61808)* 579 119th Ave, Martin, MI 49070 USA
E-mail: skipcoryell@hotmail.com
Web site: http://www.whitefeatherpress.com
Dist(s): **Smashwords.**

White Feather Publishing, *(978-0-9740413)* 5595 White Feather Way, Placerville, CA 95667 USA
E-mail: whitefeather@directcom.net.

White Hare Publishing LLC, *(978-0-578-17267-5; 978-0-578-17268-2; 978-0-692-88819-3; 978-0-692-94388-5; 978-0-692-95475-1; 978-0-578-55881-3)* 8660 Fox Ridge Ln., Indianapolis, IN 46256 USA Tel 317-578-8356
E-mail: pbenages.whiteharepub@gmail.com.

White Hat Communications, *(978-0-9653653; 978-1-929109; 978-0-615-62872-1)* Orders Addr.: P.O. Box 5390, Harrisburg, PA 17110-0390 USA Tel 717-238-3787; Fax: 717-238-2090; Edit Addr.: 2793 Old Post Rd., Suite 13, Harrisburg, PA 17110 USA
E-mail: Linda.grobman@paonline.com; lindagrobman@gmail.com
Web site: http://www.whitehatcommunications.com; http://www.socialworker.com
Dist(s): **CreateSpace Independent Publishing Platform**
Smashwords.

White Heat Ltd., *(978-0-9740149; 978-0-9799108)* 901 N. Mcdonald St. Ste. 503, Mckinney, TX 75069-2166 USA
E-mail: info@whiteheatltd.com
Web site: http://www.whiteheatltd.com.

White Horse Bks., *(978-0-9744860; 978-0-9801406)* 1347 Glenmare St., Salt Lake Cty, UT 84105-2707 USA
Web site: http://www.whitehorsebooks.net.

White Horse Flying Pubns., *(978-0-615-28541-2; 978-0-615-41896-4; 978-0-9835647)* 24 N 28th St., Longport, NJ 08403 USA
E-mail: whitehorseflying@comcast.net.

White, Howard Ray, *(978-0-9746875; 978-0-9837192)* Orders Addr.: 6012 Lancelot Dr., Charlotte, NC 28270 USA Tel 704-846-4411 Ask for Howard
E-mail: howardraywhite@gmail.com
Web site: http://www.southernhistorians.org; http://www.amazon.com.

White, James C., *(978-0-9747752)* 7020 E. 28th Ter., Kansas City, MO 64129-1209 USA Do not confuse with James C. White in Ruston, LA
E-mail: jcwhite08@yahoo.com
Web site: http://www.jcwhite08.com.

White Kiser, Dolores, *(978-0-9766648)* 212 Quail Creek Rd., Durant, OK 74701-7543 USA
E-mail: wobblywh@yahoo.com.

White Knight Printing and Publishing, *(978-0-9725916)* 187 E. 670 S., Kamas, UT 84036 USA (SAN 853-3539) Tel 801-955-4504; Fax: 801-955-5324
E-mail: johnmsimmons@whiteknightpublish.com; brigdist@sisna.com; careenlancaster@whiteknightpublish.com
Web site: http://www.brighamdistributing.com; http://www.whiteknightpublish.com
Dist(s): **Brigham Distribution.**

White Line Productions Inc., *(978-0-9729965)* P.O. Box 248411, Coral Gables, FL 33124 USA Tel 305-663-3235
E-mail: lcoll@bewaretheunknown.com
Web site: http://www.bewaretheunknown.com.

White Lion Pr., *(978-0-9615707; 978-1-886942)* 225 E. Fifth St., No. 4D, New York, NY 10003 USA (SAN 695-7919) Tel 212-982-5518; Toll Free: 800-243-9642
Dist(s): **New Leaf Distributing Co., Inc.**

White Mane Kids *Imprint of* **White Mane Publishing Co., Inc.**

White Mane Publishing Co., Inc., *(978-0-942597; 978-1-57249)* Orders Addr.: P.O. Box 708, Shippensburg, PA 17257 USA (SAN 667-1926) Tel 717-532-2237; Fax: 717-532-6110; Toll Free: 888-948-6263; *Imprints:* White Mane Kids (WM Kids)
E-mail: marketing@whitemane.com
Web site: http://www.whitemane.com.

White Media Works, *(978-0-9905386; 978-1-64145)* 16496 Bernardo Ctr. Dr., San Diego, CA 92128 USA Tel 619-922-1579
E-mail: swhite@yinpop.com.

White Oak Creative, *(978-0-9763562)* 26415 W. Stonebriar Way, Channahon, IL 60410-8740 USA Tel 815-922-2890; Fax: 815-521-0042 Do not confuse with White Oak Publishing in Reed Springs, MO; Galena, MO; Sewickley, PA; Portland, OR
E-mail: kashmir37@aol.com.

White Owl Publishing, *(978-1-891691)* P.O. Box 1180, Redding, CA 96001 USA Tel 530-241-1921 Do not confuse with White Owl Publishing, Wellington, KS,
E-mail: editor@whiteowlweb.com
Web site: http://whiteowlweb.com
Dist(s): **Smashwords.**

White Parrot Pr. *Imprint of* **First Steps Publishing**

White Pelican Pr., *(978-0-9625544)* 1805 Cedar Ridge Dr., Austin, TX 78741 USA Tel 512-477-5211 Do not confuse with companies with the same name in Windsor, CO, Sharpsburg, GA.

White Phoenix, *(978-0-9886472)* 405 Litchfield Dr., Moore, SC 29369 USA Tel 847-848-6307
E-mail: ghallium50@yahoo.com.

White Rhino Pr., *(978-0-9704122)* Div. of The Patnaude Corp., Orders Addr.: 6068 Windsor Farm Rd., Summerfield, NC 273589053 USA Tel 336-253-8987; Fax: 336-644-7849
E-mail: joy@patnaude.com.

White Rhino Publishing *See* **White Rhino Pr.**

White, Russ, *(978-0-9742885)* 122 E. Oak Hill Dr., Florence, AL 35633 USA.

White Stag Pr., *(978-0-9792583; 978-0-9828216)* Div. of Publishers Design Group, Inc., P.O. Box 37, Roseville, CA 95678 USA (SAN 852-9353) Tel 916-784-0500; Fax: 916-773-7421; Toll Free: 800-587-6666
E-mail: orders@publishersdesign.com
Web site: http://www.publishersdesign.com.

White Star (ITA) *(978-88-8095; 978-88-544; 978-88-7844; 978-88-540) Dist. by* **Sterling.**

White Star (ITA) *(978-88-8095; 978-88-544; 978-88-7844; 978-88-540) Dist. by* **Random.**

White Star *Imprint of* **Rizzoli International Pubns., Inc.**

White Stone Bks., *(978-1-59379)* P.O. Box 35035, Tulsa, OK 74153 USA Toll Free: 866-253-8622 Do not confuse with White Stone Books in Atlanta, MI
E-mail: amandap@whitestonebooks.com
Web site: http://www.whitestonebooks.com
Dist(s): **Distributors, The**
Harrison House Pubs.

White Stone Publications *See* **Fair Havens Pubns.**

White Stone Publishing *See* **Matisse Studios**

White, T. *See* **twhiteart**

White, Terry, *(978-0-9755835)* P.O. Box 760399, Southfield, MI 48076-0399 USA.

White Tiger Pr. *Imprint of* **Homes for the Homeless Institute, Inc.**

White Tulip Publishing, *(978-0-9746890)* Orders Addr.: P.O. Box 645, Brewster, NY 10509 USA Tel 917-514-7701
E-mail: wtime2write@aol.com
Web site: http://www.whitetulippublishing.com
Dist(s): **Quality Bks., Inc.**

White Turtle Bks., *(978-1-933482)* P.O. Box 2113, North Mankato, MN 56003 USA Tel 605-770-5385
E-mail: info@whiteturtlebooks.com.

White Wolf Publishing, Inc., *(978-0-9627790; 978-1-56504; 978-1-58846)* 2075 W. Park Place Blvd. Ste. G, Stone Mtn, GA 30087-3542 USA (SAN 299-1349) Toll Free: 800-454-9653 Do not confuse with White Wolf Publishing, Cresson, TX
E-mail: dianez@white-wolf.com
Web site: http://www.white-wolf.com
Dist(s): **PSI (Publisher Services, Inc.).**

White Wolf Studio, Inc., *(978-0-9760654)* P.O. Box 490, Windermere, FL 34786 USA Tel 407-909-0889; Fax: 407-876-8462
E-mail: whitewolfstudio@aol.com
Web site: http://www.whitewolfstudio.com.

Whitecap Bks., Ltd. (CAN) *(978-0-920620; 978-0-921061; 978-0-921396; 978-1-55110; 978-1-895099; 978-1-55285; 978-1-77050) Dist. by* **Firefly Bks Limited.**

Whitecap Bks., Ltd. (CAN) *(978-0-920620; 978-0-921061; 978-0-921396; 978-1-55110; 978-1-895099; 978-1-55285; 978-1-77050) Dist. by* **Wizard Works.**

Whitecap Bks., Ltd. (CAN) *(978-0-920620; 978-0-921061; 978-0-921396; 978-1-55110; 978-1-895099; 978-1-55285; 978-1-77050) Dist. by* **IPG Chicago.**

Whitecaps Media, *(978-0-9758577; 978-0-9826353; 978-0-9836825; 978-0-9883628; 978-1-942732)* P.O. Box 680568, Houston, TX 77268-0568 USA
Web site: http://www.whitecapsmedia.com
Dist(s): **Partners Bk. Distributing, Inc.**

Whitedove Pr., *(978-0-9714908; 978-0-615-11118-6; 978-0-615-11600-6)* Orders Addr.: 401 Thornton Rd, Lithia Springs, GA 30112 USA Tel 800-326-2665; Edit Addr.: 2728 Davie Blvd. 226, Fort Lauderdale, FL 33312 USA Tel 954-981-2828; 954-981-2828; 2728 Davie Blvd No. 226, fort Lauderdale, FL 33312 Tel 954-981-2828
E-mail: mail@michelleWhitedove.com
Web site: http://www.michellewhitedove.com
Dist(s): **New Leaf Distributing Co., Inc.**

WhiteFire Printing & Design *See* **WhiteFire Publishing**

WhiteFire Publishing, *(978-0-9765444; 978-0-9834556; 978-1-939023; 978-1-946531)* Div. of WhiteFire Printing & Design, Inc., Orders Addr.: 13607 Bedford Rd., NE, Cumberland, MD 21502 USA (SAN 256-4238) Tel 443-321-3663; Fax: 443-321-3675; *Imprints:* WhiteSpark Publishing (MYID_T_WHITESP)
E-mail: info@whitefire-publishing.com
Web site: http://www.whitefireprinting.com
Dist(s): **eBookit.com.**

Whitegate Books *See* **Wild daisy art**

Whitehead, D. Literature, *(978-0-9972943)* 14854 depot Dr., Neosho, MO 64850 USA Tel 417-389-2773
E-mail: plantatree.doug@gmail.com
Web site: www.whiteheadliterature.com.

Whitehead, Judith, *(978-0-615-23987-3)* 5686 Fieldbrook Dr., East Amherst, NY 14051 USA Tel 716-238-5547
E-mail: juju8451@yahoo.com
Web site: http://myspace.com.

Whitehouse Publishing, *(978-1-933031)* P.O. Box 16, Corning, NY 14830 USA Toll Free: 800-784-0537 Do not confuse with Whitehouse Publishing in Alexandria, VA
E-mail: elizabeth@whitehouse-publishing.com
Web site: http://www.whitehouse-publishing.com.

Whitehouse Publishing, *(978-0-9644171)* 6556 Mckenna Way, Alexandria, VA 22315-5571 USA Do not confuse with Whithouse Publishing in Corning, NY
E-mail: erw192@hotmail.com
Web site: http://users.starpower.net/whitee/bookcover/treasure.html.

Whitepoint Pr., *(978-0-615-51020-0; 978-0-615-51021-7; 978-0-615-51022-4; 978-0-615-74499-5; 978-0-615-77099-4; 978-0-615-79369-6; 978-0-615-84585-2; 978-0-9898971; 978-1-944856)* 1809 S. Meyler St, San Pedro, CA 90731 USA Tel 310-940-1428
Web site: www.whitepointpress.com
Dist(s): **CreateSpace Independent Publishing Platform**
Dummy Record Do Not USE!!!!
Smashwords.

WhiteSpark Publishing *Imprint of* **WhiteFire Publishing**

WhiteWalls, Inc., *(978-0-945323)* Orders Addr.: P.O. Box 8204, Chicago, IL 60647 USA (SAN 246-9952); Edit Addr.: 2845 W. Altgeld, Chicago, IL 60647 USA (SAN 246-9960)
E-mail: aeelms@aol.com
Web site: http://www.whitewalls.org
Dist(s): **Chicago Distribution Ctr.**
SPD-Small Pr. Distribution.

Whiting, James Maxwell, *(978-0-692-94033-4)* 1262 Ruberta Ave., GLENDALE, CA 91201 USA Tel 818-406-3851
E-mail: jjamwfamily@gmail.com
Dist(s): **Ingram Content Group.**

Whitis, Cindy, *(978-0-615-17079-4)* 9018 Imperial Dr., Indianapolis, IN 46239 USA
E-mail: jim.whitis@sbcglobal.net.

Whitline Ink, Inc., *(978-1-930154)* Orders Addr.: P.O. Box 668, Boonville, NC 27011 USA Tel 336-367-6914; Fax: 336-367-6913; Edit Addr.: Hwy. 601 S., Boonville, NC 27011 USA
E-mail: whitlineink@yadtel.net
Dist(s): **Parnassus Bk. Distributors.**

Whitlock Publishing, *(978-0-9770956; 978-1-943115)* 16 High St, Alfred, NY 14802-1303 USA.

†**Whitman, Albert & Co.,** *(978-0-8075)* 250 S. Northwest Hwy. # 320, Park Ridge, IL 60068-4237 USA (SAN 201-2049) Toll Free: 800-255-7675; *Imprints:* AW Teen (AW Teen)
E-mail: mail@awhitmanco.com
Web site: http://www.albertwhitman.com
Dist(s): **Children's Plus, Inc.**
Follett School Solutions
Independent Pubs. Group
MyiLibrary
Open Road Distribution
Perfection Learning Corp.; *CIP.*

Whitman Publishing LLC, *(978-0-937458; 978-1-930849; 978-0-7948)* Div. of Anderson Press Inc., Orders Addr.: 4001 Helton Dr., Florence, AL 35030 USA Tel 256-246-1166; Toll Free: 800-528-3992; Edit Addr.: 3101 Clairmont Rd., NE, Suite C, Atlanta, GA 30329 USA (SAN 253-522X) Tel 404-214-4300; Fax: 404-214-4391; Toll Free: 800-528-3992
E-mail: info@whitmanbooks.com
Web site: http://www.whitmanbooks.com.

†**Whitmore Publishing Co.,** *(978-0-87426)* 1144 Riverview Ln., West Conshohocken, PA 19428-2964 USA (SAN 203-2112)
E-mail: production@whitmorepublishing.com; *CIP.*

Whittet Bks., Ltd. (GBR) *(978-0-905483; 978-1-873580) Dist. by* **Diamond Farm Bk.**

Whlke, Traudl, *(978-1-68377)* 40 Main St., Newark, DE 19711 USA Toll Free: 888-248-4521
E-mail: colinwfscott@gmail.com.

Who Am I Pr., *(978-0-9774174)* 4444 Hazeltine Ave., No. 229, Sherman Oaks, CA 91423 USA Tel 818-501-5908
E-mail: lea@godwhoami.com
Web site: http://www.godwhoami.com.

Who Chains You *See* **Who Chains You Bks.**

Who Chains You Bks., *(978-0-615-19983-2; 978-0-615-21952-3; 978-0-578-01626-9; 978-0-9842897; 978-0-692-71696-0; 978-0-692-74473-4; 978-1-946044)* P.O. Box 581, Amissville, VA 20106 USA Tel 757-474-5474
E-mail: tami@tamiracithayne.com
Web site: http://www.whochainsyou.com
Dist(s): **CreateSpace Independent Publishing Platform.**

Who Would Win?, *(978-0-9852032; 978-0-9863487)* 25 Channel Ctr. St. No. 404, Boston, MA 02210 USA Tel 781-608-0626; Fax: 781-465-7999
E-mail: gpallotta@vzw.blackberry.net
Web site: www.jerrypallotta.com.

Whole Heart Ministries, *(978-1-888692)* Orders Addr.: P.O. Box 3445, Monument, CO 80132-8506 USA; *Imprints:* Whole Heart Press (WholeHeart)
E-mail: whm@wholeheart.org; admin@wholeheart.org
Web site: http://www.wholeheart.org/
Dist(s): **BookBaby.**

Whole Heart Pr. *Imprint of* **Whole Heart Ministries**

Whole Spirit Pr., *(978-1-892857)* 1905 S. Clarkson St., Denver, CO 80210 USA Tel 303-979-5820; 303-246-9554; Fax: 303-979-6151; Toll Free: 877-488-3774
E-mail: sales@wholespiritpress.com
Web site: http://www.wholespiritpress.com.

Whole Systems Support *See* **WiseWoman Pr.**

Wholemovement Pubns., *(978-0-9766773)* Orders Addr.: 4606 N. Elston No. 3, Chicago, IL 60630 USA Tel 773-794-9764
E-mail: bradhs@interaccess.com
Web site: http://www.wholemovement.com.

Wholesome Pr., *(978-1-943449)* 892 Cabaniss Cres, Pensacola, FL 32508 USA
E-mail: hello@wholesome.press
Web site: wholesome.press.

Wholesome Puppy Tales, *(978-0-9762466)* 13432 San Pasqual Rd., Escondido, CA 92025-7834 USA
E-mail: cmodicagraphics@aol.com
Web site: http://www.wholesomepuppytales.com.

Whorl Bks., *(978-0-9778850; 978-0-615-70205-6; 978-0-615-71111-9; 978-0-615-72898-8; 978-0-615-99191-7; 978-0-692-21281-3; 978-0-692-30046-6; 978-0-692-37390-3; 978-0-692-47723-6)* 5658 NW Pioneer Cir., Norman, OK 73072 USA (SAN 850-5713); *Imprints:* Dark Passages (Dark Passages); WhorlBooks Thumbprints (WhorlBks)
E-mail: whorlbooks@gmail.com; marilynahudson@yahoo.com
Web site: http://www.freewebs.com/whorlbooks/
Dist(s): **CreateSpace Independent Publishing Platform.**

WhorlBooks Thumbprints *Imprint of* **Whorl Bks.**

Who's There, Incorporated *See* **KnockKnock LLC**

Who's Who In Sports *Imprint of* **Guidry Assocs., Inc.**

Why Mom Deserves a Diamond, Incorporated *See* **Moon Over Mountains Publishing (M.O.M.)**

Why Not Bks., *(978-0-9849919; 978-0-9962422; 978-0-9978808)* 831 Spruce Ave., Pacific Grove, CA 93950 USA Tel 831-238-1849
E-mail: info@whynotbooks.com; amyherzog@sbcglobal.net
Web site: http://www.bradherzog.com; http://www.whynotbooks.com
Dist(s): **Independent Pubs. Group**
Midpoint Trade Bks., Inc.

Wicked Cow Studios, *(978-0-692-91823-4; 978-0-692-07098-7)* 45 W 21st St., New York, NY 10010 USA Tel 212-699-1888
E-mail: mr@wickedcow.com
Dist(s): **Diamond Comic Distributors, Inc.**

Wicked Stepsister Productions, *(978-0-692-10358-6; 978-0-692-12319-5; 978-0-578-41493-5)* 506 Lee St, Murfreesboro, TN 37130 USA Tel 615-483-3833
E-mail: michelle@iwokeupwell.com.

Wickenburg Healthcare Alliance *See* **WHA Publishing**

Wicker Park Pr., Ltd., *(978-0-9789676; 978-1-936679)* 334 Hawthorn Ave., Glencoe, IL 60022 USA Tel 773-391-1199
E-mail: eric@3ibooks.com
Web site: http://www.wickerparkpress.us.

Wicks, Valerie, *(978-0-615-71556-8; 978-0-9912594)* 831 1/2 Silver Lake Blvd., Los Angeles, CA 90026 USA Tel 678 3613895
Web site: www.sevenspectral.com
Dist(s): **CreateSpace Independent Publishing Platform.**

Wide World Publishing/Tetra, *(978-0-933174; 978-1-884550)* Orders Addr.: P.O. Box 476, San Carlos, CA 94070 USA (SAN 211-1462) Tel 650-593-2839; Fax: 650-595-0802
E-mail: wwpbl@aol.com
Web site: http://www.wideworldpublishing.com
Dist(s): **Booklines Hawaii, Ltd.**
Islander Group
Publishers Group West (PGW).

WideThinker Bks., *(978-0-9728195)* P.O. Box 30144, Philadelphia, PA 19146 USA Tel 215-985-0322; Toll Free: 866-236-1077
E-mail: wtb@widethinker.com
Web site: http://www.widethinkerbooks.com.

WiDo Publishing, *(978-0-9796070; 978-0-9830238; 978-1-937178; 978-1-947966)* Orders Addr.: 840 S W. TEMPLE APT 2, Salt Lake City, UT 84101 USA (SAN 853-8786) Tel 801-935-4357
E-mail: information@widopublishing.com
Web site: http://www.widopublishing.com.

†**Wiener, Markus Pubs., Inc.,** *(978-0-910129; 978-0-945179; 978-1-55876)* 231 Nassau St., Princeton, NJ 08542 USA (SAN 282-5465) Tel 609-921-1141; Fax: 609-921-1140
E-mail: publisher@markuswiener.com
Web site: http://www.markuswiener.com; *CIP.*

Wiese, Michael Productions, *(978-0-941188; 978-1-932907; 978-1-61593)* 6049 37th Ave. NE, Seattle, WA 98115 USA (SAN 237-9716) Tel 206-283-2948; Fax: 206-283-2072; Toll Free: 800-833-5738 (24 hours); 800-379-8808
E-mail: mwpsales@earthlink.net; kenlee@mwp.com
Web site: http://www.mwp.com
Dist(s): **Follett School Solutions**
Ingram Publisher Services
MyiLibrary
Elsevier Science & Technology Bks.

Wiggies, Piggy, *(978-1-939076)* 150 Ocean Pk. Blvd. Ste 418, Santa Monica, CA 90405 USA Tel 310-666-0069
E-mail: emma@emmalouisebooks.com.

Wiggles Pr., *(978-0-9823906; 978-1-935706)* Orders Addr.: 23 Athens St. Suite 2, Cambridge, MA 02138 USA Tel 617-895-7698; 617-981-0285
E-mail: rochelle.thorpe@yahoo.com.

Wighita Pr., *(978-0-9786648)* P.O. Box 30399, Little Rock, AR 72260-0399 USA
E-mail: info@wighitapress.com
Web site: www.wighitapress.com.

Wigu Publishing *Imprint of* **Wigu Publishing**

Wigu Publishing, *(978-1-939973)* 4327 N. Nines Ridge Ln., Boise, ID 83702 USA; *Imprints:* Wigu Publishing (WiguPubng)
E-mail: beressler59@gmail.com
Web site: www.wigupublishing.com; www.whenigrowupbooks.com.

Wigwam Publishing, *(978-0-9721022)* Orders Addr.: P.O. Box 574, Weyauwega, WI 54983 USA; Edit Addr.: 410 S. Harlon St., No. 2, Weyauwega, WI 54983 USA Do not confuse with companies with the same or similar names in Villa Park, IL, Cheyenne, WY.

WigWam Publishing Co., *(978-1-930076)* Orders Addr.: P.O. Box 6992, Villa Park, IL 60181 USA; *Imprints:* New Leaf Books (New Leaf Books) Do not confuse with companies with the same or similar names in Weyauwega, WI, Cheyenne, WY
E-mail: info@newleafbooks.net
Web site: http://www.newleafbooks.net.

Wilander Publishing Co., *(978-0-9628335)* Orders Addr.: P.O. Box 56121, Portland, OR 97238 USA.

Wild About Coloring, *(978-0-692-91040-5; 978-0-692-98064-4)* P.O. Box 94, KEELER, CA 93530 USA Tel 760-608-7245
E-mail: elmirafoley@gmail.com
Dist(s): **Ingram Content Group.**

Wild About Learning, Inc., *(978-0-9789880)* 964 John St., Joliet, IL 60435 USA Tel 815-740-1173; Fax: 815-740-1174
E-mail: info@wildaboutlearning.org
Web site: http://wildaboutlearning.org.

Wild Animal Publishing, *(978-0-9769555)* 246 Meridian St., Westerly, RI 02891 USA
E-mail: sciarrajb@aol.com; keith@wildanimalpublishing.com
Web site: http://www.wildanimalpublishing.com.

Wild Child Publishing, *(978-0-9771314; 978-1-934069; 978-1-935013; 978-1-936222; 978-1-61798)* P.O. Box 4897, Culver City, CA 90231 USA
E-mail: mgbaun@wildchildpublishing.com; mbaun@freyasbower.com
Web site: http://www.wildchildpublishing.com; http://www.freyasbower.com/
Dist(s): **All Romance Ebooks, LLC.**

Wild daisy art, *(978-0-9767570)* The Appletree, P.O. Box 84, Cowley, WY 82420 USA
E-mail: Lyn@wilddaisyart.com
Web site: http://www.appletreedesigns.com.

Wild Earth, *(978-0-9719807)* P.O. Box 407, Charlottesville, VA 22902-0407 USA Tel 434-977-4615 Toll Free: 800-871-5647
Web site: http://www.animalessence.com/.

Wild Flower USA, *(978-0-9646698)* 26614 Oak Ridge Dr., Suite 110, The Woodlands, TX 77380 USA Tel 281-363-2360; Fax: 281-367-4480.

Wild Goose Publishing, *(978-0-9792657; 978-0-9799255)* Orders Addr.: P.O. Box 386, Charlotte, MI 48813 USA
E-mail: wildgoosepub@sbcglobal.net.

Wild Hare Collective, *(978-0-692-90631-6)* 1981 Deep Woods Trail, NASHVILLE, TN 37214 USA Tel 260-908-1908
E-mail: jandra@jandralee.com
Dist(s): **Ingram Content Group.**

Wild Hare Publishing, *(978-0-9772096)* P.O. Box 2144, Ridgeland, MS 39158-2144 USA (SAN 256-9639) Tel 601-853-8120; Fax: 601-853-8121
E-mail: dgibbes@wildharepublishing.com.

Wild Heart Ranch, Inc., *(978-0-9761768)* 1385 Gulf Rd., Suite 102, Point Roberts, WA 98281 USA Toll Free Fax: 866-735-3518; Toll Free: 888-889-9215
E-mail: dawn@wildheartranch.com
Web site: http://www.wildheartranch.com; http://www.iseahorses.com.

Wild Horses Publishing Co., *(978-0-937148; 978-0-9601088)* Orders Addr.: P.O. Box 1373, Los Altos, CA 94022 USA (SAN 211-8289)
E-mail: pwalatka@earthlink.net
Dist(s): **TNT Media Group, Inc.**

Wild Meadow *Imprint of* **Perri, Jessica**

Wild, Meredith *See* **Waterhouse Press LLC**

Wild Mind Creations, *(978-0-615-15138-0)* P.O. Box 1935, Fairview, OR 97024-1806 USA
E-mail: jmm1965mionda_4@msn.com.

Wild Nature Institute, *(978-0-9898182; 978-1-7323234)* PO Box 44, Weaverville, NC 28787 USA Tel 415-763-0348
E-mail: monica@wildnatureinstitute.org
Web site: www.wildnatureinstitute.org.

Wild Plum Woods Bks., *(978-0-9745581)* 39042 Ruann Ct., Zephyrhills, FL 33540 USA.

Wild Roots Pr., *(978-0-9996199)* P.O. Box 733, Narberth, PA 19072 USA Tel 484-844-3803
E-mail: maryam.moss.arts@gmail.com
Web site: www.maryammoss.com.

Wild Rose *Imprint of* **Mayhaven Publishing, Inc.**

Wild Rose Pr., Inc., The, *(978-1-60154; 978-1-61217; 978-1-62830; 978-1-5092)* P.O. Box 708, Adams Basin, NY 14410 USA Tel 585-880-0819
E-mail: info@thewildrosepress.com
Web site: http://www.thewildrosepress.com.

Wild Soccer USA Inc. *See* **Sole Bks.**

Wild Willow Pr., *(978-0-9995444)* 4713 Derbyshire Dr., Antioch, TN 37013 USA Tel 703-786-0948
Dist(s): **CreateSpace Independent Publishing Platform.**

Wilde Art, *(978-0-9974828)* 21807 el Coyote Dr., Sonora, CA 95370 USA Tel 209-533-1261
E-mail: kwilde55@gmail.com
Web site: wilde-art.com.

Wilder Pubns., Corp., *(978-0-9773040; 978-1-934451; 978-1-60459; 978-1-61720; 978-1-62755; 978-1-63384; 978-1-5154)* .

Wilder Publications, Limited *See* **Wilder Pubns., Corp.**

Wilderness Pr. *Imprint of* **AdventureKEEN**

Wilderness Visions Press *See* **Cloudland.net Publishing**

Wildfire Enterprises, *(978-0-9771969)* Orders Addr.: P.O. Box 402, Viola, AR 72583-0402 USA Tel 870-458-3600 (phone/fax); Edit Addr.: P O Box 402, Viola, AR 72583-0402 USA
E-mail: wfenterprises@hotmail.com
Web site: http://www.wildfireenterprises.iceryder.net.

Wildflower Pr., The, *(978-0-9714343; 978-0-9779933)* P.O. Box 4757, Albuquerque, NM 87196-4757 USA Tel 505-296-0691; Fax: 505-296-6124 Do not confuse with companies with the same or similar name in Oceanside, CA ,Phoenix, AZ ,Littleton, CO
E-mail: jspoetry@aol.com
Dist(s): **Smashwords.**

Wildflower Run, *(978-0-9667086)* Orders Addr.: P.O. Box 9656, College Station, TX 77842 USA Tel 979-764-0166
E-mail: atmgold@aol.com
Web site: http://www.aggiegoose.com.

Wildlife Education, Limited *See* **National Wildlife Federation**

Wildlife Tales Publishing, *(978-0-9793207)* Div. of Ark R.A.I.N. Wildlife Sanctuary, Inc., P.O. Box 721, Brownsville, TN 38012-0721 USA Toll Free: 877-352-6657
E-mail: books@wildlifetalespublishing.com
Web site: http://www.wildlifetalespublishing.com.

Wildly Austin, *(978-0-9753990)* P.O. Box 161987, Austin, TX 78716-1987 USA
E-mail: vikki@wildlyaustin.com; vl@intersourcesearch.com
Web site: http://www.wildlyaustin.com.

Wildot Pr., *(978-0-9789043; 978-0-9797933)* 4402 W. Creedance Blvd., Glendale, AZ 85310-3921 USA Tel 623-434-2636
E-mail: wildotpress@cox.net
Web site: http://ww.wildotpress.com.

Wildside Pr., LLC, *(978-0-8095; 978-0-913960; 978-1-880448; 978-1-58715; 978-1-59224; 978-1-4344; 978-1-4794)* Orders Addr.: 9710 Traville Gateway Dr., No. 234, Rockville, MD 20850 USA Tel 301-762-1305; Fax: 301-762-1306
E-mail: customerservice@wildsidepress.com; wildsidepress@gmail.com
Web site: http://www.wildsidepress.com; http://www.weirdtales.net; http://www.wildsidebooks.com
Dist(s): **Diamond Comic Distributors, Inc.**
Diamond Bk. Distributors
MyiLibrary

Wildstone Media, *(978-1-882467)* Orders Addr.: P.O. Box 511580, Saint Louis, MO 63151 USA Tel 314-482-8472; Fax: 314-487-1910; Toll Free: 800-296-1918
E-mail: wildstone@mlc.net
Web site: http://www.wildstonemedia.com
Dist(s): **Anderson News, LLC**
Big River Distribution
BookBaby.

Wildstorm *Imprint of* **DC Comics**

WildWest Publishing, *(978-0-9721800)* P.O. Box 11658, Olympia, WA 98508 USA
E-mail: clamityJan@aol.com
Web site: http://www.CalamityJan.com.

WildWing Pr., *(978-0-9798768; 978-0-9912715; 978-0-9976420; 978-0-9983149)* 3301 Brandywine Ct., Bellingham, WA 98226 USA
E-mail: editor@wildwingpress.com
Web site: http://www.wildwingpress.com
Dist(s): **Outskirts Pr., Inc.**
Smashwords.

Wiley *Imprint of* **Wiley, John & Sons, Inc.**

Wiley, Brandie, *(978-0-692-96976-2)* 5024 Waterford Dr., Fort Worth, TX 76179 USA Tel 682-559-9899
E-mail: brandiewiley@sbcglobal.net
Web site: HomeIsWhereTheAutismIs.com.

Wiley, John & Sons Canada, Ltd, (CAN) *(978-0-471; 978-0-939246) Dist. by* **IngramPubServ.**

†Wiley, John & Sons, Inc., *(978-0-470; 978-0-471; 978-0-7645; 978-0-7821; 978-0-8260; 978-0-87605; 978-0-88422; 978-0-914993; 978-0-937721; 978-0-939246; 978-1-55828; 978-1-56217; 978-1-56561; 978-1-56884; 978-1-57313; 978-1-58245; 978-1-878058; 978-1-118; 978-1-119; 978-1-7994; 978-1-394) Orders Addr.: c/o John Wiley & Sons, Inc., United States Distribution Ctr., 1 Wiley Dr., Somerset, NJ 08875-1272 USA Tel 732-469-4400; Fax: 732-302-2300; Toll Free Fax: 800-597-3299; Toll Free: 800-225-5945 (orders); Edit Addr.: 111 River St., Hoboken, NJ 07030 USA (SAN 200-2272) Tel 201-748-6000; 201-748-6276 (Retail and Wholesale); Fax: 201-748-6088; 201-748-8641 (Retail and Wholesale); Imprints:* Wiley-VCH (Wiley-VCH); Jossey-Bass (Jossey-Bass); For Dummies (For Dummies); Howell Book House (HBH); Capstone (CapstW); Wiley (JWiley); Wiley-Blackwell (WileyBlack)
E-mail: compbks@wiley.com; bookinfo@wiley.com; custserv@wiley.com
Web site: http://www.wiley.com/compbooks; http://www.interscience.wiley.com; http://www.wiley.com
Dist(s): **Casemate Pubs. & Bk. Distributors, LLC**
Ebsco Publishing
Follett School Solutions
Leonard, Hal Corp.
Ingram Publisher Services
Ingram Content Group
Lippincott Williams & Wilkins
MBI Distribution Services/Quayside Distribution
Mastery Education
Mel Bay Pubns., Inc.
MyiLibrary
Pearson Education
TNT Media Group, Inc.
Urban Land Institute
ebrary, Inc.; *CIP.*

Wiley OBrien Worksapce *See* **OBrien, Wiley Workspace**

Wiley-Blackwell *Imprint of* **Wiley, John & Sons, Inc.**

Wiley-VCH *Imprint of* **Wiley, John & Sons, Inc.**

Wilfrid Laurier Univ. Pr. (CAN) *(978-0-88920; 978-0-921821; 978-1-55458; 978-1-77112) Dist. by* **TwoRivers.**

Wilkes Publishing Co., Inc., *(978-0-9747755)* P.O. Box 340, Washington, GA 30673 USA Tel 706-678-2636; Fax: 706-678-3857
E-mail: editor@news-reporter.com
Web site: http://www.news-reporter.com.

Wilkinson, Brittany, *(978-0-692-18822-4)* 12608 Richezza Dr., Venice, FL 34293 USA Tel 941-223-1694
E-mail: beginwithcompassion@yahoo.com
Dist(s): **Ingram Content Group.**

Wilkinson Publishing (AUS) *(978-0-9775457; 978-0-9802818; 978-1-921332; 978-1-921667; 978-1-921804; 978-1-922178; 978-1-925265; 978-1-925642; 978-1-925927) Dist. by* **IPG Chicago.**

Will Hall Bks., *(978-0-9630310; 978-0-9801257)* 611 Oliver Ave., Fayetteville, AR 72701 USA
E-mail: rharriso@uark.edu
Web site: http://www.willhallbooks.com.

Will to Print Pr., *(978-0-9772985)* 234 Hyde St., San Francisco, CA 94102-3324 USA Tel 415-474-0508; Fax: 415-673-1027
E-mail: willtoprintpress@faithfulfools.org
Web site: http://www.faithfulfools.org.

WillGo Pr., *(978-0-9828231)* 2874 Arcade St., Maplewood, MN 55109 USA Tel 651-774-2558
E-mail: gdesigns@comcast.net.

William Askel Art, *(978-0-9752528)* 21665 Wallace Dr., Southfield, MI 48075-7570 USA
E-mail: waksel@provide.net
Web site: http://fieldguidetomonsters.com.

William M. Gaines Agent, INC. *Imprint of* **Diamond Bk. Distributors**

William Morrow Paperbacks *Imprint of* **HarperCollins Pubs.**

William P Castor, *(978-0-578-42824-6)* 135 5th St. Apt. 1, Aspinwall, PA 15215 USA Tel 412-780-2331
E-mail: wpc1027@gmail.com
Dist(s): **Ingram Content Group.**

William Works, Inc., *(978-0-9745244)* P.O. Box 2709, Washington, DC 20013 USA Toll Free: 877-535-2057.

Williams and King Pubs., *(978-0-9983663; 978-0-9998406; 978-1-7332382)* 1112 Climbing Rose Dr., Orlando, FL 32818 USA
E-mail: mwilliams@williamsandkingpublishers.com
Web site: WilliamsAndKingPublishers.com.

Williams, Angela Claudette, *(978-0-615-15833-4; 978-0-615-16052-8; 978-0-615-16098-6; 978-0-615-16138-9; 978-0-615-17571-3; 978-0-615-17889-9)* 3645 Watkins Ridge Ct., Raleigh, NC 27616 USA
E-mail: claudetteexpressions@yahoo.com
Web site: http://www.claudetteexpressions.com
Dist(s): **Lulu Pr., Inc.**

Williams, Aspen *See* **Clair, Aspen**

Williams, Benjamin Publishing, *(978-0-9764945; 978-0-9796180; 978-0-9802398; 978-0-9850233; 978-0-9909650)* 18525 S. Torrence Ave. Suite D3, Lansing, IL 60438 USA Tel 1-888-757-0007
E-mail: ben@bwpublishing.com
Web site: http://www.bwpublishing.com.

Williams, Benny Publishing *See* **Williams, Benjamin Publishing**

Williams, Darnell *See* **Williams, Darnell L. Foundation, The**

Williams, Darnell L. Foundation, The, *(978-0-9747771)* 2402 Magnolia Dr., Harrisburg, PA 17104 USA Tel 717-233-1511
E-mail: WDarn44243@aol.com.

Williams, Dontez *See* **MySheri Enterprises, LLC**

Williams Enterprises, Inc., *(978-0-9755478)* 500 5th Ave., N., Greybull, WY 82426 USA.

Williams, Gary, *(978-0-9743000)* 574 Falcon Fork Way, Jacksonville, FL 32259 USA
Web site: http://www.fbcofmand.org.

Williams, Geoffrey T., *(978-0-9771381; 978-0-9801671)* 3119 Redwood St., San Diego, CA 92104 USA
Web site: http://wildvoices.com
Dist(s): **Audible.com**
Smashwords.

Williams, James E., *(978-0-9746310)* P.O. Box 6921, Atlanta, GA 30315-0921 USA Fax: 404-691-0726.

Williams, Michael, *(978-0-9761503)* 1324 Lake Grove Ln., Desoto, TX 75115-3326 USA.

Williams, Morgan, *(978-0-9762768)* 3243 Cloverwood Dr., Nashville, TN 37214-3428 USA
E-mail: mandj@magiclink.com
Web site: http://www.thestandards.com.

Williams, Rozalia *See* **Hidden Curriculum Education**

Williams, Tempestt, *(978-0-692-94911-5; 978-0-692-12037-8; 978-0-692-12044-6; 978-0-692-14985-0; 978-0-578-51561-8)* 5650 Abbey Dr Apt 2B, Lisle, IL 60532 USA Tel 708-769-9794
E-mail: tempestt.williams@yahoo.com
Dist(s): **Ingram Content Group.**

Williams, Thomas, *(978-0-9763633)* 358 Homestead Rd., NW, Willis, VA 24380 USA Tel 540-789-4295
E-mail: tomwill@swva.net
Web site: http://www.santacares.org.

Williamson County Public Library, *(978-0-9911915; 978-0-9970690)* Williamson Cty. Public Library, Franklin, TN 37064 USA Tel 615-595-1240; *Imprints:* Academy Park Press (AcadParkPr)
E-mail: dgreenwald@williamson-tn.org
Web site: wcpltn.org.

Williamson, Leah, *(978-0-578-43572-5)* 511 Bertrand Dr. Apt. 2102, Lafayette, LA 70506 USA Tel 504-982-6211
E-mail: leahannwilliamson97@gmail.com
Dist(s): **Ingram Content Group.**

Williamspublishing, *(978-0-615-19121-8)* 317 E. Oakgrove, Kalamazoo, MI 49004 USA
E-mail: starowl1@hotmail.clm
Dist(s): **Lulu Pr., Inc.**

Williby-Walker, Debra June, *(978-0-692-70291-8; 978-0-692-85861-5)* 12018 Ingleside Rd., Oakvale, WV 24739 USA Tel 304-396-9105
E-mail: debbeejune@gmail.com.

Willie & Willie, *(978-0-9754126)* P.O. Box 26071, Saint Louis, MO 63136 USA.

Willis, E.B. Bks., *(978-0-9976634)* 209 Braxberry Way, Holly Springs, NC 27540 USA Tel 919-656-5893
E-mail: bethwillis@nc.rr.com
Web site: www.ebwillis.com.

Willis Music Co., *(978-0-87718)* Orders Addr.: P.O. Box 548, Florence, KY 41022-0548 USA (SAN 294-6947) Tel 606-283-2050 859; Fax: 606-283-1784; Toll Free: 800-354-9799; Edit Addr.: 7380 Industrial Rd., Florence, KY 41040 USA
E-mail: willis@willis-music.com; orderdpt@willis-music.com
Web site: http://www.willismusic.com
Dist(s): **Leonard, Hal Corp.**

Willoughby Arts, *(978-1-950285)* 1520 Festival Dr., Houston, TX 77062 USA Tel 713-815-0275
E-mail: trinawilloughby@yahoo.com.

Willow Bend Pr., *(978-0-9896564; 978-1-950019)* P.O. Box PO Box 247, Prosper, TX 75078 USA Tel 972-757-3787
E-mail: susanrutledge@mac.com.

Willow Bend Publishing, *(978-0-9709002; 978-0-9831138; 978-1-7337674)* P.O. Box 304, Goshen, MA 01032 USA Tel 413-230-1514 Do not confuse with Willow Bend Publishing in Lakeland, FL
E-mail: info@willowbendpublishing.com
Web site: http://www.willowbendpublishing.com.

Willow Breeze Publishing, *(978-1-7340039)* P.O. Box 700, Westminster, TX 75485-0700 USA Tel 909-544-1661
E-mail: fff@linkline.com
Web site: www.adogbling.com.

Willow Brook Publishing, *(978-0-9817636)* 19600 W. Shore Dr., Suite 101, Mundelein, IL 60060 USA (SAN 856-4914)
E-mail: Info@willowBrookPublishing.com
Web site: http://www.willowbrook-publishing.com/
Dist(s): **Pathway Bk. Service.**

†Willow Creek Pr., Inc., *(978-0-932558; 978-1-57223; 978-1-59543; 978-1-60755; 978-1-62343; 978-1-68234; 978-1-5492)* Orders Addr.: P.O. Box 147, Minocqua, WI 54548-0147 USA (SAN 255-4038) Tel 715-358-7010; Fax: 715-358-2807; Toll Free: 800-850-9453; P.O. Box 147 / EDI Orders, Minoqua, WI 54548 (SAN 920-8070) Tel 715-358-7010; Fax: 715-358-2807; Edit Addr.: 9931 Hwy 70 W, Minocqua, WI 54548 USA Toll Free: 800-850-9453 Do not confuse with Willowcreek Pr. in Aloha, OR
E-mail: info@willowcrewpress.com; info@wcpretail.com
Web site: http://www.wcpretail.com
Dist(s): **MyiLibrary**
Strauss Consultants
Two Rivers Distribution; *CIP.*

Willow Creel Publishing Co., *(978-0-9729655)* 35 Willow Creek, 820 9th Ave. S., North Myrtle Beach, SC 29582 USA Tel 843-272-1096 Do not confuse with Willow Creek Publishing in Canton, MI, Pine River, MN
E-mail: grayfox.43@att.net
Web site: http://www.chinquawhere.com.

Willow Dance Pubns., *(978-0-9768750)* Orders Addr.: P.O. Box 71, Hillsdale, WY 82060 USA Tel 307-631-0236; Edit Addr.: 1370 CR 142, Hillsdale, WY 82060 USA
E-mail: willowdancepublishing@yahoo.com.

Willow Moon Publisher *See* **Willow Moon Publishing**

Willow Moon Publishing, *(978-1-948256)* 108 Saint Thomas Rd., Lancaster, PA 17601-4829 USA Tel 610-463-6614; Fax: 610-463-6614
E-mail: jodilstapler@gmail.com
Web site: willow-moon-publishing.com; WMPublishing.org; willowmoonpub.com.

Willow Point Press, LLC *See* **Grettler, Kelly**

Willow Publishing, *(978-0-9825212)* 1000 Kinsley Ave., No. 32, Winslow, AZ 86047 USA Toll Free Fax: 800-643-9527.

Willow River Pr. *Imprint of* **Between the Lines Publishing**

Willow Tree Bks. (GBR) *(978-0-9522921) Dist. by* **IPG Chicago.**

Willow Tree Books *See* **Apricot Pr.**

Willow Tree Press *See* **Little Willow Tree Bks.**

Willowgate Pr., *(978-1-930008)* P.O. Box 6529, Holliston, MA 01746 USA (SAN 253-0376); 120 Brook Rd., Port Jefferson, NY 11777-1665
E-mail: willowgatepress@yahoo.com
Web site: http://www.willowgatepress.com.

WillowSpring Downs, *(978-0-9648525; 978-0-9742716)* 1582 N. Falcon, Hillsboro, KS 67063 USA Tel 620-367-8432; Fax: 620-367-8218; Toll Free: 888-551-0973
E-mail: willowspringdowns@juno.com.

WillowTree Pr., L.L.C., *(978-0-9678221; 978-0-9794533; 978-1-937778)* Orders Addr.: P.O. Box 1195, High Ridge, MO 63049 USA Tel 314-740-7791; Edit Addr.: P.O. Box 1195, High Ridge, MO 63049 USA (SAN 253-1178); *Imprints:* Full Circle Press (Full Circle MO)
E-mail: info@willowtreepress.com
Web site: http://www.willowtreepress.com
Dist(s): **Smashwords.**

Willy Waw wees, LLC, *(978-0-9785103)* Orders Addr.: PO Box 390593, Deltona, FL 32739 USA
E-mail: artgallerymeris@aol.com
Web site: http://www.willywawwees.com.

Wilmer, Da'Nall, *(978-0-692-15591-2)* 3211 Fairview Rd., Baltimore, MD 21207 USA Tel 443-421-6939
E-mail: boysinthegood@yahoo.com.

Wilmington Today LLC, *(978-0-9729573; 978-0-9916642)* 1213 Culbreth Dr., Wilmington, NC 28405 USA Tel 910-509-7195
E-mail: hwjones@wilmingtontoday.com
Web site: http://www.wilmingtontoday.com.

Wilshire House of Arkansas *See* **Ozark Publishing**

Wilson & Associates *See* **Gatewood Pr.**

Wilson, Bob, *(978-0-9908537)* 700 E Mesquite Cir. Unit O110, TEMPE, AZ 85281 USA Tel 480-710-0340
E-mail: bobwilson7711@gmail.com.

Wilson, Bob Solutions *See* **Wilson, Bob**

Wilson Boulevard Pr., *(978-0-9979086)* 109 Wilson Blvd, Fairfield, IA 52556 USA Tel 818-321-1921
E-mail: zenbeetleben@gmail.com
Web site: www.wilsonblvdpress.com.

Wilson, Gerrard (IRL) *(978-0-9561553) Dist. by* **LuluCom.**

†**Wilson, H.W.,** *(978-0-8242)* 950 University Ave., Bronx, NY 10452-4224 USA (SAN 203-2961) Tel 718-588-8400; Fax: 718-681-1511 (Outside of the U.S. & Canada); Toll Free: 800-367-6770 ext 2272
E-mail: custserv@hwwilson.com
Web site: http://www.hwwilson.com
Dist(s): **Ebsco Publishing**
Grey Hse. Publishing
MyiLibrary; *CIP.*

Wilson Language Training, *(978-1-56778)* 47 Old Webster Rd., Oxford, MA 01540-2705 USA Toll Free: 800-899-8454.

Wilson Place Comics, *(978-0-9744235)* P.O. Box 435, Oceanside, NY 11572 USA
E-mail: Wilplace@optonline.net
Web site: http://www.wjhc.com
Dist(s): **Brodart Co.**
Diamond Comic Distributors, Inc.
Diamond Bk. Distributors
Follett School Solutions
Mackin Library Media
Midwest Library Service.

Wilson, Rebecca, *(978-0-9760569)* 450 Massachusetts Ave NW Apt. 1004, Washington, DC 20001-6222 USA
E-mail: info@sunfishmanuals.com
Web site: http://www.sunfishmanuals.com.

Wilson, W. Shane, *(978-0-578-00301-6; 978-0-578-00634-5; 978-0-578-00797-7; 978-0-578-01639-9; 978-0-578-02119-5; 978-0-578-02550-6; 978-0-578-03095-1; 978-0-578-03299-3)* 7600 NE 64th Cir., Vancouver, WA 98662 USA Tel 360-521-1584
E-mail: redtimberwolf67@yahoo.com
Web site: http://stores.lulu.com/shanesbooks
Dist(s): **Lulu Pr., Inc.**

Wilson-Barnett Publishing, *(978-1-888840)* P.O. Box 345, Tustin, CA 92781-0345 USA Tel 949-380-5748; Fax: 714-730-6140
E-mail: mrcalc@usa.net.

Wilson-Crawford & Co., *(978-0-9752948)* P.O. Box 809, Island Lake, IL 60042-0809 USA Fax: 847-487-1591
E-mail: freecellmax@aol.com
Web site: http://www.freecellsecrets.com.

Wilson-Jordan, Natashia, *(978-0-578-22011-6; 978-0-578-22204-2)* 4263 Sir Dixon Dr., Fairburn, GA 30213 USA Tel 646-423-1595
E-mail: Natashiawilsonjordan@yahoo.com
Web site: https://schoolisathome.com/.

Wilstonian, *(978-0-9772122)* 3603 Whitaker Dr., Melvindale, MI 48122 USA (SAN 257-0106)
Web site: http://www.wilstonian.com.

Wilt, Lisa, *(978-0-9770053)* Orders Addr.: 1072 Frye Rd., Jeannette, PA 15644-4717 USA
E-mail: thankyoumousie@comcast.net.

Wiltshire Bks., *(978-0-9831685; 978-0-9970240)* 1924 Wiltshire Blvd., Huntington, WV 25701 USA Tel 304-730-0798
E-mail: WiltshireBookLLC@aol.com.

Wimabi Pr., *(978-0-578-02359-5; 978-0-578-03340-2; 978-0-578-05718-7)* 7102 Lakewood Dr., Richmond, VA 23229 USA
E-mail: inquiries@wimabi.com
Web site: http://www.wimabi.com
Dist(s): **Lulu Pr., Inc.**

Win Publishing, LLC, *(978-0-9826865)* 35 E. Main St., Suite 337, Avon, CT 06001 USA Tel 860-651-6859; Fax: 203-413-4409
Dist(s): **Outskirts Pr., Inc.**

Winchester Pr., *(978-0-9745279)* P.O. Box 711, Hollis, NH 03049-0711 USA Tel 603-880-9559 Do not confuse with companies with the same or similar name in Southhampton, NY, Howell, NJ, LaFox, IL.

Wincik, Stephanie *See* **One Horse Pr.**

Wind Pubns., *(978-0-9636545; 978-1-893239; 978-1-936138)* Orders Addr.: 600 Overbrook Dr., Nicholasville, KY 40356 USA
E-mail: books@windpub.com
Web site: http://www.windpub.com.

Windblown Enterprises, *(978-0-9752576)* 12207 243rd Pl NE, Redmond, WA 98053-5685 USA
E-mail: windblowne@msn.com.

Windblown Media, *(978-0-9647292; 978-1-935170; 978-1-61871)* 4680 Calle Norte, Newbury Park, CA 91320 USA Tel 805-498-2484; Fax: 805-499-4260
E-mail: office@windblownmedia.com
Web site: http://www.windblownmedia.com
Dist(s): **Hachette Bk. Group.**

Windcall Enterprises *See* **Windcall Publishing**

Windcall Publishing, *(978-0-9745884; 978-0-9845934; 978-0-9847607)* Div. of Windcall Enterprises, Orders Addr.: 75345 Rd. 317, Venango, NE 69168 USA Tel 308-447-5566 (phone/fax); Fax: 308-447-5566
E-mail: windcall@chase3000.com
Web site: http://www.windcallenterprises.com; http://www.windcallpublishing.com
Dist(s): **Smashwords.**

Windchimes Publishing, *(978-0-9763253)* P.O. Box 1433, Palm City, FL 34991-6433 USA Tel 772-285-5429
E-mail: wchimes@gate.net
Web site: http://www.wchimes.com.

Windfeather Pr., *(978-0-9620122)* 4545 W. Heart Rd., Bismarck, ND 58504-4257 USA (SAN 247-7246); 1203 N. 27th St., Bismarck, ND 58501 (SAN 247-7254) Tel 701-258-5047
Dist(s): **Duebbert, Harold F.**

Windham Pr., *(978-1-62845)* 11240 Plantation Oaks Ln, Lumberton, TX 77657 USA Tel 409-234-4533 Do not confuse with Windham Press in New Rochelle, NY, Miami, FL
E-mail: info@studyguideteam.com.

Windhill Bks. LLC, *(978-0-9844828; 978-1-944734)* 939 Windhill St., Onalaska, WI 54650-2081 USA (SAN 859-5135)
E-mail: jeanna@windhillbooks.com
Web site: http://www.windhillbooks.com.

Windhorse Bks., *(978-0-9973745)* 5429 SW 80 St., Gainesville, FL 32608 USA Tel 352-336-5888
E-mail: barbaragresbach@gmail.com
Web site: windhorsebooks.com.

Winding Road Pubs., *(978-0-615-21989-9; 978-0-578-04819-2; 978-0-578-07274-6; 978-0-578-09900-2; 978-0-578-10413-3; 978-0-578-10703-5; 978-0-578-10929-9; 978-0-578-11074-5; 978-0-578-11693-8; 978-0-578-12821-4; 978-0-578-13843-5)* 2904 Giles St., West Des Moines, IA 50265 USA Tel 515-226-1179
Dist(s): **Lulu Pr., Inc.**

Windjammer Adventure Publishing, *(978-0-9768477; 978-0-615-29130-7; 978-0-615-33790-6; 978-0-615-36411-7; 978-0-615-38745-1; 978-0-9831300; 978-0-9898232; 978-0-9978807; 978-0-9994812; 978-1-7333668)* 289 S. Franklin St., Chagrin Falls, OH 44022-3449 USA Tel 440-247-6610
E-mail: windjammerpub@mac.com
Web site: http://windjammerpublishing.com.

Windmill Bks. *Imprint of* **Rosen Publishing Group, Inc., The**

Windmill Bks. Ltd. (GBR) *(978-1-78121) Dist. by* **Black Rab.**

Windmill Bks., *(978-1-60754; 978-1-62275)* 303 Pk. Ave. S., Suite No. 1280, NEW YORK, NY 10010-3657 USA Tel 646-205-7415
Dist(s): **Rosen Publishing Group, Inc., The.**

Window Bks., *(978-1-889829)* Orders Addr.: 1425 Broadway #513, Seattle, WA 98122 USA Tel 206-351-9993
E-mail: orders@windowbooksonline.com
Web site: http://www.meetmarcadams.com; http://www.windowbooksonline.com.

Window Box Pr. LLC, *(978-0-9793738)* Orders Addr.: 13516 Fillmore Ct., Thornton, CO 80241-1330 USA (SAN 853-2958) Tel 303-255-9432
E-mail: windowboxpress@q.com
Web site: http://windowboxpress.com.

Window Seat Publishing, *(978-0-9721949)* 82 Marlborough Rd., West Hempstead, NY 11552 USA Tel 516-481-5969
E-mail: aferrant@optonline.net.

Windows of Discovery, *(978-0-9785399)* P.O. Box 9085, Spokane, WA 99209-9085 USA
Web site: http://theprofessorstelescope.com.

Windrad Press *See* **Pinwheel Bks.**

WinDruid Publishing, *(978-0-9758943)* Orders Addr.: 220 Walworth Dr., St. Louis, MO 63125-5008 USA; Edit Addr.: P.O. Box 25008, Saint Louis, MO 63125-5008 USA
E-mail: orders@LukeCarter.com; info@windruidpublishing.com; susan@windruidpublishing.com
Web site: http://www.LukeCarter.com; http://www.windruidpublishing.com
Dist(s): **Book Clearing Hse.**
Quality Bks., Inc.

Winds of Happiness, LLC, The, *(978-1-7320905)* 878 Marquette St, Menasha, WI 54952 USA Tel 920-831-3303
E-mail: TFieds5574@gmail.com.

Windsong Publishing Co., *(978-0-9655078)* P.O. Box 588, Rimrock, AZ 86335 USA Do not confuse with companies with the same or similar names in Eugene, OR, San Diego, CA, Staunton, VA, Lake Patagonia, AZ
Dist(s): **New Leaf Distributing Co., Inc.**

Windsor Heights Bks., *(978-0-9753566; 978-1-948204)* Orders Addr.: 8402 Hermosa Dr., Riverside, CA 92504 USA (SAN 255-9935)
E-mail: info@windsorheightsbooks.com
Web site: http://www.windsorheightsbooks.com.

Windsor Heights Publishing *See* **Windsor Heights Bks.**

Windsor Media Enterprises, Inc., *(978-0-9765304; 978-0-9777297; 978-1-934229)* 5412 Wolf St., Longmont, CO 80504-3432 USA Toll Free: 877-947-2665
E-mail: collins@wmebooks.com
Web site: http://www.wmebooks.com.

WindSpirit Publishing, *(978-0-9643407)* Orders Addr.: 220 Compass Ave., Beachwood, NJ 08722-2919 USA Fax: 732-240-7860
E-mail: windspiritpub@earthlink.net
Web site: http://www.windspiritpublishing.net.

Windsurf Publishing LLC, *(978-1-936509)* 14 Ctr. Dr., Old Greenwich, CT 06870 USA Tel 203-698-2975
E-mail: m.lagana@att.net.

Windswept Productions, *(978-0-9764825)* Orders Addr.: P.O. Box 167, Felton, PA 17322-0167 USA Tel 717-244-7700; Edit Addr.: 11525 High Point Rd., Felton, PA 17322 USA
E-mail: wpebs@earthlink.net.

Windtree Pr., *(978-0-615-46251-6; 978-0-9835943; 978-1-940064; 978-1-942368; 978-1-943601; 978-1-944973; 978-1-947983; 978-1-950387; 978-1-952447)* 818 SW 3rd Ave. No. 221-2218, Portland, OR 97204-2405 USA
E-mail: windtree@windtreepress.com
Web site: http://windtreepress.com
Dist(s): **CreateSpace Independent Publishing Platform.**

Windwalker Pr., *(978-0-9993940)* P.O. Box 636, Dayton, WY 82836 USA
E-mail: rendallwriter@gmail.com
Web site: www.jaydinerendall.com; windwalkerpress.com.

Windward Publishing *Imprint of* **Finney Co., Inc.**

Windward Publishing, *(978-0-9758897)* 112 N. St., New Bedford, MA 02740-6513 USA Do not confuse with Windward Publishing in Minneapolis, MN
E-mail: windwardpublish@aol.com; josettefernandes@hotmail.com.

Windy City Pubs., *(978-0-9819505; 978-1-935766; 978-1-941478; 978-1-953294)* 2118 Plum Grove Rd., No. 349, Rolling Meadows, IL 60008 USA Tel 888-673-7126; *Imprints:* Skyscraper Press (children's) (Skyscraper Pr)
E-mail: dawn@windycitypublishers.com
Dist(s): **BookBaby.**

Windy City Publishing *See* **Windy City Pubs.**

Windy Hill Pr., *(978-0-9662983)* Orders Addr.: 22 Hilltop Ave., Barrington, RI 02806 USA Tel 401-247-2707 Do not confuse with Windy Hill Pr., in Menlo Park, CA
E-mail: windyhillpress@cox.net
Web site: http://www.windyhillpress.net.

Windy Hills Press *See* **Old Stone Pr.**

Windy Press International Publishing Hse., LLC, *(978-1-890568)* 29W 424 Tanglewood Ln, Warrenville, IL 60555-2663 USA; P.O. Box 5131, Wheaton, IL 60189-4383 Fax: 630-604-0490; Toll Free Fax: 888-508-5577; *Imprints:* A-BA-BA-HA-LA-MA-HA Publishers (A-BA-BA-HA-LA-MA-HA)
E-mail: interhouse@comcast.net
Web site: http://www.snowqueen.us.

Wineries by County, *(978-0-615-18047-2)* 3373 Silver Rapids Rd., Valley Spgs, CA 95252-9573 USA
E-mail: info@wineriesbycounty.com
Web site: http://www.wineriesbycounty.com.

Winestone *See* **Bed of Angels, Inc.**

Winfield Hse. Pr., *(978-1-7325814)* 610 Gibson Ln., Foster, KY 41043 USA Tel 606-756-2639
E-mail: peter@yourliteraryprose.com.

Winfrey Inc., *(978-0-9818526)* Orders Addr.: 14525 SW. Millikan Way #23515, Beaverton, OR 970052343 USA (SAN 856-7263) Tel 404-993-0532; 228 Pk. Ave. S. #23515, New York, NY 10003; Edit Addr.: 4480 S. Cobb Dr. Ste H Pmb 451, Smyrna, GA 30080 USA
E-mail: info@shakeetawinfrey.com
Web site: http://www.shakeetawinfrey.com
Dist(s): **APG Sales & Distribution Services**
BCH Fulfillment & Distribution
Bella Distribution
Book Hub, Inc.
Bks. Plus, U.S.A.
C & B Bk. Distribution
Cardinal Pubs. Group
Greenleaf Book Group
Independent Pubs. Group
Ingram Content Group
Midpoint Trade Bks., Inc.
Mint Pubs. Group
New Leaf Distributing Co., Inc.
Partners Bk. Distributing, Inc.
Penton Overseas, Inc.
Quality Bks., Inc.
SCB Distributors
SPD-Small Pr. Distribution
Send The Light Distribution LLC
Two Rivers Distribution.

Wing Dam Pr., *(978-0-9758615)* P.O. Box 200, Ferryville, WI 54628 USA Tel 608-734-3292 (phone/fax)
E-mail: nlichter@mwt.net.

Wing Lane Pr., *(978-0-9792430)* 19 Exeter Ln., Morristown, NJ 07960 USA
E-mail: tazni@optonline.net.

Winged Lion Pr. Cooperative, *(978-0-692-69427-5; 978-0-692-99138-1; 978-0-692-08141-9)* 1385 Pinon Dr., Healdsburg, CA 95448 USA Tel 530-757-7576
Dist(s): **CreateSpace Independent Publishing Platform.**

Winged Willow Pr., *(978-0-9664805)* Orders Addr.: P.O. Box 92, Carrboro, NC 27510 USA Tel 919-942-4689; Fax: 919-933-3555
E-mail: info@sudierakusin.com
Web site: http://www.sudierakusin.com
Dist(s): **Parnassus Bk. Distributors.**

Winger Publishing, P.O. Box 20991, Juneau, AK 99802 USA
E-mail: wingerpublishing@gmail.com.

Wings Above, *(978-0-9768403)* 1607 Market St., Galveston, TX 77550 USA Tel 409-750-9176.

Wings ePress, Inc., *(978-1-59088; 978-1-59705; 978-1-61309)* 403 Wallace Crt., Richmond, KY 82225 USA; 3000 N. Rock Rd., Newton, KS 67114 Tel 316-283-0981 Do not confuse with companies with the same or similar name in Northhampton, MA, Union, ME, San Antonio, TX
E-mail: lady0@earthlink.net; wingsbookkeeper@yahoo.com
Web site: http://www.wingsepress.com; http://
Dist(s): **CreateSpace Independent Publishing Platform**
Smashwords.

Wings, Inc., *(978-0-9705018; 978-1-7321457)* 4790 Caughlin Pkwy., Suite 143, Reno, NV 89509 USA
E-mail: glebeck@wingsnv.com
Web site: http://www.wingsnv.com.

Wings Pr., *(978-0-916727; 978-0-930324; 978-1-60940)* 627 E. Guenther, San Antonio, TX 78210 USA (SAN 209-4975) Tel 210-271-7805 Do not confuse with companies with the same or similar name in Northhampton, MA, UNion, ME, Lusk, WY
E-mail: milligan@wingspress.com
Web site: http://www.wingspress.com
Dist(s): **Brodart Co.**
Ebsco Publishing
Follett School Solutions
Independent Pubs. Group
MyiLibrary
SCB Distributors
ebrary, Inc.

Wings Press, Limited *See* **Wings ePress, Inc.**

Wings-on-Disk *Imprint of* **PassionQuest Technologies, LLC**

Wingspan Pr. *Imprint of* **WingSpan Publishing**

WingSpan Publishing, *(978-1-59594; 978-1-63683)* P.O. Box 2085, Livermore, CA 94551 USA Toll Free: 866-735-3782; *Imprints:* Wingspan Press (Wingspan Pr)
Web site: http://www.wingspanpress.com
Dist(s): **BookBaby**
CreateSpace Independent Publishing Platform.

WingSpread Pubs. *Imprint of* **Moody Pubs.**

Wink Publishing, *(978-0-9702572)* P.O. Box 9957, Richmond, VA 23228 USA.

Winkelstein Studios, *(978-0-9824498; 978-0-578-77062-8)* 402 N. Fredericksburg Ave., Margate City, NJ 08402 USA
E-mail: stevenwinkelstein@gmail.com.

Winking Moon Pr., *(978-0-9764175)* 4130 S. Splendor Ct., Gilbert, AZ 85297 USA Do not confuse with Winking Moon Press in Cleveland OH .

Winn, Lynnette, *(978-0-9791884)* 2617 Claudia Dr., Leander, TX 78641 USA (SAN 852-7040)
Web site: http://www.butterpodjerome.com.

Winning Inc. of America, *(978-0-692-89096-7; 978-0-692-89097-4)* 1239 Golf Rd., Benton Harbor, MI 49022 USA Tel 269-934-7213; Fax: 269-934-7213
E-mail: miphilrose@ameritech.net.

Winnow Pr., *(978-0-9764726)* 3505 El Dorado Trail, Suite A, Austin, TX 78739 USA (SAN 256-4017) Tel 512-280-4483
E-mail: publisher@winnowpress.com
Web site: http://winnowpress.com.

Winoca Bks. & Media, *(978-0-9755910; 978-0-9789736; 978-1-935619)* P.O. Box 515, Spur, TX 79370-0515 USA
E-mail: barbaralubbock@gmail.com
Web site: http://www.winocapress.com; http://www.Bookadelphia.com; http://www.winoca.com; http://www.BoldfaceBooks.com.

Winoca Press *See* **Winoca Bks. & Media**

Winslow's Art, *(978-0-9748505)* P.O. Box 2099, Avalon, CA 90704-2099 USA Tel 310-510-1613 (phone/fax)
E-mail: winslow@catalinaisp.com.

Winsor Corporation *See* **Winsor Learning, Inc.**

Winsor Learning, Inc., *(978-1-891602; 978-1-935450)* 3001 Metro Dr. Suite 480, Bloomington, MN 55425 USA Tel 800-321-7585; Fax: 651-222-3969; Toll Free: 800-321-7585
E-mail: info@winsorlearning.com
Web site: http://www.winsorlearning.com.

Winstead Pr., Ltd., *(978-0-940787)* 202 Slice Dr., Stamford, CT 06907 USA (SAN 664-6913) Tel 203-322-4941
E-mail: winstead.press@gte.net.

Winter Goose Publishing, *(978-0-9836764; 978-0-9851548; 978-0-9881845; 978-0-9889049; 978-0-9894792; 978-1-941058; 978-1-952909)* 2701 Del Paso Rd., 130-92, Sacramento, CA 95835 USA Tel 530-771-7058
E-mail: jessica@wintergoosepublishing.com
Web site: http://wintergoosepublishing.com; http://hallwaypublishing.com
Dist(s): **Ingram Content Group.**

Winter Light Bks., Inc., *(978-0-9797372)* 734 Franklin Ave., No. 675, Garden City, NY 11530-4525 USA (SAN 854-2163)
Web site: http://www.winterlightbooks.com; http://www.winterlightbooks.org.

Wintergreen Orchard Hse., *(978-1-933119; 978-1-936035; 978-1-945520)* Div. of Carnegie Communications, 2 Lan Dr., Suite 100, Westford, MA 01886 USA Tel 978-692-9708; Fax: 978-692-2304
E-mail: info@wintergreenorchardhouse.com; cglennon@carnegiecomm.com
Web site: http://www.wintergreenorchardhouse.com.

Wintermantel Group, LLC, The, *(978-0-9767418)* 316 Saddle Back Dr., Saint Louis, MO 63129-3449 USA
Web site: http://www.theangelchildren.com.

Winters Publishing, *(978-0-9625329; 978-1-883651)* Orders Addr.: P.O. Box 501, Greensburg, IN 47240 USA (SAN 298-1645) Tel 812-663-4948 (phone/fax); Toll Free: 800-457-3230; Edit Addr.: 705 E. Washington, Greensburg, IN 47240 USA Do not confuse with Winters Publishing, Wichita, KS
E-mail: tmwinters@juno.com
Web site: http://www.winterspublishing.com
Dist(s): **Partners Bk. Distributing, Inc.**
Partners/West Book Distributors
Send The Light Distribution LLC
Spring Arbor Distributors, Inc.

Winters Publishing Group, *(978-0-9976124; 978-1-947426)* 2448 E. 81st Street, Suite 5900, Tulsa, OK 74137 USA Tel 918-494-6868
E-mail: dboyd@wintersking.com
Dist(s): **Whitaker Hse.**

Winterwolf Publishing, *(978-0-9744831; 978-0-9752711; 978-0-9762471; 978-0-9772632)* Orders Addr.: P.O. Box 1373, Westerville, OH 43086-1373 USA; Edit Addr.: 5446 Highbrook Ct., Westerville, OH 43081 USA
Web site: http://www.winterwolfpublishing.com.

Wipf and Stock *Imprint of* **Wipf & Stock Pubs.**

Wipf & Stock Pubs., *(978-0-9653517; 978-1-55635; 978-1-57910; 978-1-59244; 978-1-59752; 978-1-60608; 978-1-60899; 978-1-61097; 978-1-62032; 978-1-62189; 978-1-62564; 978-1-63087; 978-1-4982; 978-1-5326; 978-1-7252)* Orders Addr.: 199 W 8th Ave Ste 3, Eugene, OR 97401 USA (SAN 990-3038) Tel 541-344-1528; Fax: 541-344-1506; Edit Addr.: 199 W 8th Ave Ste 3, Eugene, OR 97401 USA Tel 541-344-1528; Fax: 541-344-1506; *Imprints:* Resource

Publisher Name Index

Publications (OR) (Resource Pubcns); Wipf and Stock (Wipf and Stock); Slant (Slant)
Web site: http://wipfandstock.com/; http://slantbooks.com; http://stonetablebooks.com/
Dist(s): **CreateSpace Independent Publishing Platform**
Ingram Bk. Co.
MyiLibrary
Spring Arbor Distributors, Inc.

WIPRO, 2 Christie Heights St., Leonia, NJ 07605 USA Tel 201-840-4755.

Wire Rim Bks., *(978-0-9802253; 978-0-615-15357-5; 978-1-935236)* 188 Spring Valley St., Hutto, TX 78634 USA (SAN 913-5960)
E-mail: hmelton@mac.com
Web site: http://www.wirerimbooks.com.

Wisconsin Dept. of Public Instruction, *(978-1-57337)* Orders Addr.: Drawer 179, Milwaukee, WI 53293-0179 USA Tel 608-266-2188; Fax: 608-267-9110; Toll Free: 800-243-8782; Edit Addr.: 125 S. Webster St., Box 7841, Madison, WI 53702 USA
Web site: http://www.dpi.state.wi.us.

†**Wisconsin Historical Society,** *(978-0-87020; 978-1-9766)* 816 State St., Madison, WI 53706 USA (SAN 203-350X) Tel 608-264-6584
E-mail: diane.drexler@wisconsinhistory.org; whspress@wisconsinhistory.org
Web site: http://www.wisconsinhistory.org
Dist(s): **Chicago Distribution Ctr.**
Hoover Institution Pr.
Univ. of Chicago Pr.; *CIP.*

Wisdom Audio-Books *Imprint of* **BloomingFields**

Wisdom Foundation Publishing, *(978-1-932590)* 796 Isenberg St., Suite 19E, Honolulu, HI 96826 USA Tel 808-944-3113; Fax: 808-988-4212
E-mail: wisdomfactors@hawaii.rr.com.

Wisdom Hse. Bks., NC Hwy. 54 W. #325, Carrboro, NC 27510 USA Tel 919-883-4669
E-mail: Ted@wisdomhousebooks.com
Web site: Wisdomhousebooks.com.

†**Wisdom Pubns.,** *(978-0-86171; 978-1-61429; 978-1-949129)* 199 Elm St., Somerville, MA 02144 USA (SAN 246-022X) Tel 617-776-7416 ext 24; Fax: 617-776-7841; Toll Free Fax: 800-338-4550 (orders only); Toll Free: 800-462-6420 (orders only)
E-mail: marketing@wisdompubs.org
Web site: http://www.wisdompubs.org
Dist(s): **MyiLibrary**
Simon & Schuster, Inc.; *CIP.*

Wisdom Tales *Imprint of* **World Wisdom, Inc.**

Wisdom Tree (IND) *(978-81-86685; 978-81-8328) Dist. by* **SCB Distributo.**

Wisdom Tree Records *See* **Rivertree Productions, Inc.**

Wisdon Hse. Bks., *(978-0-9984145; 978-0-9984145-1-5)* 412 Parker Rd.,, Mount Airy, NC 27030 USA Tel 336-786-4922; Fax: 336-786-4922
E-mail: dretjdt1987@gmail.com
Web site: www.wisdomhousebooks.com.

Wise Guides, LLC, *(978-0-9768772; 978-1-935237)* 1924 W. Montrose, PMB No. 206, Chicago, IL 60613 USA Toll Free: 866-262-3842
E-mail: info@wiseguidebooks.com
Web site: http://www.wiseguidebooks.com
Dist(s): **Zagat Survey.**

Wise Media Group, *(978-0-9822907; 978-1-935689; 978-1-62967)* 630 Quintana Rd. Suite 116, Morro Bay, CA 93442 USA
E-mail: support@selfpublish.org
Web site: https://www.50interviews.com; https://www.wisemediagroup.com.

Wise Owl Printing Plus, Incorporated *See* **Deziner Media International**

Wise Pubns. (GBR) *(978-0-7119; 978-0-86001) Dist. by* **Music Sales.**

Wise Words Publications *See* **EPI Bks.**

Wisecracker Press, Inc., *(978-0-9752657)* 2735 April Hill Ln., Dallas, TX 75287 USA
Web site: http://www.wisecrackerpress.com.

Wisehearted Warrior Enterprises, *(978-0-9972797)* 1606 Arrowhead Trail, Neptune Beach, FL 32266 USA Tel 904-307-1941
E-mail: deborajscott@aol.com.

WiseMind Educational Services LLC, *(978-0-692-78691-8; 978-0-692-78692-5; 978-0-692-18164-5)* 1757 Schoolhouse Ct NW, SALEM, OR 97304 USA Tel 541-325-2195.

WiseWoman Pr., *(978-0-945385)* 1521 N. Jantzen Ave., No. 143, Portland, OR 97217 USA (SAN 247-0039) Tel 1-800-603-3005; 1408 NE 65th St., Vancouver, WA 98665 Tel 503 310-0105
E-mail: web@wisewomanpress.com
Web site: http://www.wisewomanpress.com
Dist(s): **DeVorss & Co.**
Lulu Pr., Inc.

Wish Publishing, *(978-1-930546; 978-0-9835754; 978-0-615-74522-0; 978-0-578-59227-5; 978-0-578-67115-4; 978-0-578-67716-3; 978-1-7351459)* P.O. Box 10337, Terre Haute, IN 47801 USA (SAN 253-4320) Fax: 928-447-1836
E-mail: holly@wishpublishing.com
Web site: http://www.wishpublishing.com
Dist(s): **Cardinal Pubs. Group**
Ingram Content Group.

Wish You Were Here *Imprint of* **Sierra Pr.**

Wishful Penny Books *See* **See The Wish**

Wishing Star Children's Bks., *(978-0-615-16077-1; 978-0-615-16078-8; 978-0-615-16079-5)* 12755 Eurels Rd., Southgate, MI 48195 USA Tel 734-754-3168
E-mail: mgrazi@wowway.com
Web site: http://www.wishingstarchildrensbooks.com
Dist(s): **Lulu Pr., Inc.**

Wishing U Well Publishing, *(978-0-9769524)* 1560 Gulf Blvd., Unit 1202, Clearwater, FL 33767 USA.

Wishingstone Enterprises *See* **Wishingstone Publishing**

Wishingstone Publishing, *(978-0-9779701)* 1640 Hartley Ave., Henderson, NV 89052 USA Tel 702-612-7325
E-mail: dapwishingstone@earthlink.net.

Wispvine Publishing, *(978-1-939997)* Orders Addr.: PO BOX 777, Blaine, WA 98231 USA
E-mail: boyce@smboyce.com
Web site: http://smboyce.com.

Witcher Productions, *(978-0-925159; 978-1-55942)* Div. of Marsh Film Enterprises, Inc., P.O. Box 8082, Shawnee Mission, KS 66208 USA Tel 816-523-1059; Fax: 816-333-7421; Toll Free: 800-821-3303 (for orders/customer service only)
E-mail: info@marshmedia.com
Web site: http://www.marshmedia.com
Dist(s): **Follett School Solutions.**

With Little Salt, *(978-0-692-08793-0; 978-0-692-08799-2)* 2778 Kahana St No. C, Wahiawa, HI 96786 USA Tel 808-634-2287
E-mail: withlittlesalt@gmail.com
Dist(s): **Ingram Content Group.**

Witherspoon Pr. *Imprint of* **Curriculum Publishing, Presbyterian Church (U. S. A.)**

Within Reach, Inc., *(978-0-9718864)* P.O. Box 6217, Harrisburg, PA 17112 USA Tel 717-657-8689
E-mail: wreach@epix.net
Web site: http://www.boatingsidekicks.com.

WithinU Life Coaching LLC *See* **A Different Kind of Safari LLC**

Witness Impulse *Imprint of* **HarperCollins Pubs.**

Witness Productions, *(978-0-9627653; 978-1-891390)* Box 34, Church St., Marshall, IN 47859 USA Tel 765-597-2487.

Wits Univ. Pr. (ZAF) *(978-0-85494; 978-1-86814; 978-1-77614) Dist. by* **IngramPubServ.**

Witsil, Grace, *(978-0-578-47323-9)* 806 W. Brumback St., Boise, ID 83702 USA Tel 919-622-7198
E-mail: gwitsil@gmail.com.

Wittman, Natasha, *(978-0-9904091)* 708 Littler Pl., Edmond, OK 73034 USA Tel 405-432-8989
E-mail: natasha2036@gmail.com.

Witty Bit World, Inc., *(978-0-9770548)* 1009 Basil Dr., New Bern, NC 28562 USA
E-mail: deborah@wittybitworld.com
Web site: http://www.wittybitworld.com.

Witty Fools Productions, *(978-0-9745179)* 19 Le Grande Ave., No.14, Greenwich, CT 06830 USA Toll Free: 877-733-0528 (phone/fax)
E-mail: wittyfools@aol.com; flierlp@bww.com
Web site: http://www.wittyfools.com; http://www.prayerlaughterandbroccoli.com.

Witty Publishing, *(978-0-9785571)* 2875 F Northtowne, Box 232, Reno, NV 89512 USA Toll Free: 866-948-8948.

Witwer, Beverly *See* **Triple Ballerina Pr.**

Wiyd, Lewis, *(978-0-9650637)* 47 Glen Park Rd., East Orange, NJ 07017-1813 USA Tel 973-673-0094; Fax: 973-673-0095.

Wizard Academies, LLC, *(978-0-615-18398-5; 978-0-615-18505-7; 978-0-615-18594-1; 978-0-615-18712-9; 978-0-615-18713-6)* 57485 170th St., Ames, IA 50010-9425 USA
E-mail: rivals@interdrama.com
Web site: http://www.interdrama.com/wiz/
Dist(s): **Lulu Pr., Inc.**

Wizard Academy Pr., *(978-0-9714769; 978-1-932226; 978-0-9987523)* 16221 Crystal Hills Dr., Austin, TX 78737 USA Tel 512-295-5700; Fax: 512-295-5701; Toll Free: 800-425-4769
E-mail: publisher@wizardofads.com; sean@wizardofads.com
Web site: http://www.wizardacademypress.com
Dist(s): **BookBaby.**

Wizard Works, *(978-0-9621543; 978-1-890692)* Orders Addr.: P.O. Box 1125, Homer, AK 99603-1125 USA Toll Free: 877-210-2665
E-mail: wizard@xyz.net
Web site: http://www.xyz.net/~wizard.

Wizarding World Pr., *(978-0-9723936)* 8926 N. Greenwood Ave., Suite 133, Niles, IL 60714 USA
E-mail: wizardingworld@waycoolstuffonline.com
Web site: http://www.wizardingworldpress.com
Dist(s): **Children's Plus, Inc.**
SCB Distributors.

Wizard's Mark Pr., *(978-0-9915720)* 27 Ash Street, Dover, NH 03820 USA Tel 603-866-2466
E-mail: kerrydoherty001@gmail.com.

Wizards of the Coast *Imprint of* **Wizards of the Coast**

Wizards of the Coast, *(978-0-7869; 978-1-57530; 978-1-880992; 978-0-7430)* Subs. of Hasbro, Inc., Orders Addr.: P.O. Box 707, Renton, WA 98057-0709 USA Toll Free: 800-821-8028; Edit Addr.: 1801 Lind Ave., SW, Renton, WA 98055 USA (SAN 299-4410) Tel 425-226-6500; *Imprints:* Mirrorstone (Mirrorstone); Wizards of the Coast (Wiz Coast)
E-mail: angella@wizards.com
Web site: http://www.wizards.com
Dist(s): **Children's Plus, Inc.**
Diamond Bk. Distributors
MyiLibrary
Penguin Random Hse. Distribution
PSI (Publisher Services, Inc.)
Penguin Random Hse. LLC
Random Hse., Inc.
Doherty, Tom Assocs., LLC.

WizdomInc, *(978-0-9764829; 978-0-9767958; 978-0-9768053; 978-0-9778512; 978-0-9785170; 978-0-9786574; 978-0-9820173; 978-0-9840885)* 5438 Village Grn, Los Angeles, CA 90016 USA Tel 323-290-9012; Fax: 707-578-4978; Toll Free: 866-607-4510
E-mail: aswan@wizdominc.com
Web site: http://www.wizdominc.com.

WizKids, LLC, *(978-0-9703934; 978-1-931462; 978-1-59041)* Subs. of Topps Europe Ltd., 2002 156th Ave. NE, #300, Bellevue, WA 98007-3827 USA
E-mail: jenny@wizkidsgames.com; customerservice@wizkidsgames.com
Web site: http://www.mageknight.com
Dist(s): **Diamond Bk. Distributors.**

WMG Publishing, *(978-1-56146; 978-0-615-45856-4; 978-0-615-47789-3; 978-0-615-52179-4; 978-0-615-66540-5; 978-0-615-66719-5; 978-0-615-67595-4; 978-0-615-67930-3; 978-0-615-68516-8; 978-0-615-68580-9; 978-0-615-68615-8; 978-0-615-68850-3; 978-0-615-69847-2; 978-0-615-69928-8; 978-0-615-70162-2; 978-0-615-72423-2; 978-0-615-72618-2; 978-0-615-72684-7; 978-0-615-72699-1; 978-0-615-72735-6; 978-0-615-72785-1; 978-0-615-73028-8; 978-0-615-73043-1; 978-0-615-73363-0; 978-0-615-73684-6; 978-0-615-73725-6; 978-0-) P.O. Box 269, Lincoln City, OR 97367 USA Tel 541-614-1400 Do not confuse with WMG Publishing in Riverside, CA*
E-mail: publisher@wmgpublishing.com
Web site: www.wmgpublishing.com
Dist(s): **CreateSpace Independent Publishing Platform.**

Wms-Ashe, Marcella *See* **Allecram Publishing**

WND Bks, Inc., *(978-0-9746701; 978-0-9767269; 978-0-9778984; 978-0-9790451; 978-0-9792671; 978-1-935071; 978-1-936488; 978-1-938067; 978-1-942475; 978-1-944212; 978-1-944229; 978-1-946918; 978-1-7335841; 978-1-952256)* Orders Addr.: 845 Alder Creek, Medford, OR 97504 USA (SAN 255-7304) Tel 541-474-1776; Fax: 541-474-1770; Edit Addr.: 2020 Pennsylvania Ave., NW No. 351, Washington, DC 20006 USA Tel 571-612-8600; Fax: 571-612-8619; *Imprints:* Kids Ahead Books (Kids Ahead); World Ahead Press (World Ahead)
E-mail: marketing@wndbooks.com; gstone@wnd.com
Web site: http://www.wnd.com; http://www.wndbooks.com
Dist(s): **Follett School Solutions**
Independent Pubs. Group
McLemore, Hollern & Assocs.
Midpoint Trade Bks., Inc.
MyiLibrary
Quality Bks., Inc.
REKO
ebrary, Inc.

Wobble Hill Pr., *(978-0-9975892)* 2400 Johnson Ave., Bronx, NY 10463 USA Tel 347-907-2292
E-mail: estherk777@gmail.com
Web site: wobblehillpress.com.

Wobblefoot Ltd., *(978-0-9747149)* 1662 Mars Ave., Lakewood, OH 44107-3825 USA
E-mail: wblft1@sbcglobal.net
Web site: http://wobblefoot.com.

Wobbly Creek, LLC, *(978-1-7322989; 978-1-7331241; 978-1-953870)* 6579 SE 82nd Ave, Newberry, FL 32669 USA Tel 352-472-1992
E-mail: judithabarrettauthor@gmail.com; wcchick@gmail.com
Web site: wobblycreek.com.

Wobbly Creek, LLS *See* **Wobbly Creek, LLC**

Wocto Publishing, *(978-1-934867)* 7486 La Jolla Blvd., Pmb 559, La Jolla, CA 92037 USA (SAN 855-2754) Tel 858-551-5585; Fax: 858-731-4082; Toll Free: 888-551-5010
E-mail: lin@wocto.com; sales@wocto.com
Web site: http://www.wocto.com.

Wohlers Assocs., Inc., *(978-0-9754429; 978-0-9913332)* OakRidge Business Pk., 1511 River Oak Dr., Fort Collins, CO 80525-5537 USA
Web site: http://www.wohlersassociates.com.

Wojcik, Chelsea, *(978-0-692-32646-6; 978-0-692-99191-6)* 3467 Wainscott Pl., WOODBRIDGE, VA 22192 USA Tel 561-389-0033.

Woks Print *Imprint of* **Writers of the Apocalypse, The**

Wold Creative Group, *(978-0-615-24135-7)* 1392 S. 1100 E., Suite 201, Salt Lake City, UT 84105 USA Tel 801-783-4502
Web site: http://www.woldcreative.com
Dist(s): **Lulu Pr., Inc.**

Wold, Kelly, *(978-0-9768944)* 398 Ricketts Rd. Apt. D, Monterey, CA 93940-7420 USA
E-mail: kmwold@hotmail.com.

Wolf Creek Publishing, *(978-0-9768983)* 193 Tenby Chase Dr., Apt. S-233, Delran, NJ 08075 USA
Web site: http://www.photosfromthewild.com.

Wolf Jump Publications, *(978-0-9820440)* 2217 Princess Anne St., Suite 101-1A c/o R.R.R., Fredericksburg, VA 22401 USA
E-mail: rrr@marstel-day.com.

Wolf Pirate Publishing, *(978-0-9798372; 978-0-9822343)* 337 Lost Lake Dr., Divide, CO 80814 USA
E-mail: cmrudy337@gmail.com
Web site: http://www.wolf-pirate.com.

Wolfenden, *(978-0-9642521; 978-0-9786951; 978-0-9973513)* 780-a Redwood Dr., Garberville, CA 95542 USA (SAN 298-4571)
E-mail: dal@asis.com
Web site: http://wolfendenpublishing.com
Dist(s): **Independent Pubs. Group.**

Wolfhound Pr. (IRL) *(978-0-86327; 978-0-905473; 978-0-9503454) Dist. by* **Interlink Pub.**

Wolfhound Pr. (IRL) *(978-0-86327; 978-0-905473; 978-0-9503454) Dist. by* **Irish Amer Bk.**

Wolfhound Pr. (IRL) *(978-0-86327; 978-0-905473; 978-0-9503454) Dist. by* **Irish Bks Media.**

Wolfmont, LLC, *(978-0-9778402; 978-1-60364)* 238 Park Dr., NE, Ranger, GA 30734 USA Fax: 702-543-8386; P.O. Box 205, Ranger, GA 30734; *Imprints:* Honey Locust Press (Honey Locust)
E-mail: tony@wolfmont.com; editor@honeylocustpress.com
Web site: http://www.wolfmont.com; http://www.honeylocustpress.com
Dist(s): **Smashwords.**

Wolfmont Publishing *See* **Wolfmont, LLC**

Wolfpack Publishing, *(978-1-885339; 978-0-9895279; 978-1-62918; 978-1-64119; 978-1-64734)* 6032 Wheat Penny Ave., Las Vegas, NV 89122 USA Tel 702-689-3912; *Imprints:* City Lights Press (City Lights P)
E-mail: admin@wolfpackpublishing.com
Web site: https://wolfpackpublishing.com.

Wolfs Corner Publishing, *(978-0-9779921)* 20 Primrose Ln., Sparta, NJ 07871 USA (SAN 856-4191) Tel 973-579-5305
E-mail: jmd_inc007@hotmail.com
Web site: http://www.wolfscornerpublishing.com.

Wolfy International Corp., *(978-1-7327901)* P.O.BOX 87061, College Park, GA 30337 USA Tel 678-368-1292
E-mail: cyapanther@gmail.com.

Wollaston Pr., *(978-0-9657005)* Div. of Ctr. for Learning Abilities, 4013 Coyte Ct., Marietta, GA 30062 USA Tel 678-318-3518; Fax: 208-474-9521
E-mail: morewords@comcast.net.

Wolsak & Wynn Pubs., Ltd. (CAN) *(978-0-919897; 978-1-894987; 978-1-928088) Dist. by* **IPG Chicago.**

Wolter, Russel II, *(978-0-692-84564-6)* 7200 Carmel Valley Rd., Carmel, CA 93923 USA Tel 831-915-6798
E-mail: rwolterii@yahoo.com
Dist(s): **Independent Pub.**

Woman's Missionary Union, *(978-0-936625; 978-1-62591)* Orders Addr.: c/o Carol Causey, P.O. Box 830010, Birmingham, AL 35283 USA (SAN 699-7015) Tel 205-991-8100; Fax: 205-995-4825; Toll Free: 800-968-7301; Edit Addr.: 100 Missionary Ridge, Birmingham, AL 35242 USA (SAN 699-7023)
E-mail: cwhite@wmu.org
Web site: http://www.wmu.com
Dist(s): **Send The Light Distribution LLC.**

Wombacher, Michael, *(978-0-9713033)* 2412 Valley St., Berkeley, CA 94702-2136 USA
E-mail: michael_wombacher@excite.com
Web site: http://www.doggonegood.org.

Women & Addiction Counseling & Educational Services, *(978-0-9663144)* 43522 Modena Dr., Temecula, CA 92592-9235 USA Tel 951-303-0235 (phone/fax)
E-mail: info@wacespublishing.com
Web site: http://www.wacespublishing.com.

Women in Aviation, International, *(978-0-9749190)* 3647 State Route 503 S., W Alexandria, OH 45381-9354 USA
Web site: http://www.wai.org.

Women's Pr., Ltd., The (GBR) *(978-0-7043) Dist. by* **Trafalgar.**

Wompetias Pr., *(978-0-9961142)* 448 Ocampo Dr., Pacific Palisades, CA 90272 USA Tel 310-454-3970
E-mail: JSharer@gibsondunn.com.

Wonder Chess LLC, *(978-0-9771787)* 2622 10th Ave E., Seattle, WA 98102-3901 USA
E-mail: info@wonderchess.com
Web site: http://www.wonderchess.com.

Wonder Forge, Inc., *(978-0-9797123; 978-0-9819248; 978-1-935595)* 300 E. Pike St., Seattle, WA 98122 USA
E-mail: brant@thewonderforge.com
Web site: http://www.thewonderforge.com.

Wonder Forge LLC, The *See* **Wonder Forge, Inc.**

Wonder Mill Cosmos, *(978-1-949561)* 4013 Egypt Rd., WILLARD, OH 44890 USA Tel 256-318-1259
E-mail: fanning.lee@gmail.com
Web site: www.wondermillcosmos.com.

Wonder Storm Productions, LLC, *(978-0-578-41819-3; 978-0-578-41824-7; 978-0-578-43645-6)* 1321 Cty. Rd. 501, Bayfield, CO 81122 USA Tel 970-769-9638
E-mail: wonderstormproductions@gmail.com
Dist(s): **Ingram Content Group.**

Wonder Toast Arts, Incorporated *See* **WonderToast**

Wonder Workshop, *(978-1-56919)* Div. of Stephens Group, Inc., 1123 Brookstone Blvd., Mount Juliet, TN 37122-3274 USA Toll Free: 800-627-6874.

Wonderbooks Publishing, *(978-0-9773809)* P.O. Box 770741, Orlando, FL 32877 USA (SAN 257-4535)
Web site: http://www.wonderbookspublishing.com.

Wonderful Publishing, *(978-0-9798421)* 150 Brewster Rd., Scarsdale, NY 10583 USA (SAN 854-5006)
Web site: http://www.madelineart.com
Dist(s): **Partners Pubs. Group, Inc.**

Wonderstrand Pr., *(978-0-9818295)* P.O. Box 156, North Eastham, MA 02651-0156 USA (SAN 856-6585)
E-mail: michael@successonyourownterms.com
Web site: http://www.wonderstrandpress.com.

Wonderstruck Bks. *Imprint of* **Crossroad Pr.**

WonderToast, *(978-0-9761606)* Orders Addr.: 3075 E. Bates Ave., Denver, CO 80210 USA Tel 303-330-4770
E-mail: anna@wondertoast.com
Web site: http://www.wondertoast.com.

Wonkybot Press *See* **Wonkybot Publishing**

Wonkybot Publishing, *(978-0-9830463)* 19197 Golden Valley Rd. No. 130, Santa Clarita, CA 91387 USA Tel 424-346-2892
E-mail: stewart@wonkybot.com
Web site: http://www.wonkybot.com.

Wonnacott, Lee Anne, *(978-0-692-91628-5)* 4326 Avenida Lorenzo Apt A, OCEANSIDE, CA 92057 USA Tel 619-708-5913
E-mail: lwonnaco@gmail.com
Dist(s): **Ingram Content Group.**

Wood Designs, Inc., *(978-0-9729454)* P.O. Box 1790, New Waverly, TX 77358-1790 USA Toll Free Fax:

877-612-8306; Toll Free: 877-612-8306; *Imprints:* MomGeek.com (MomGeek.com)
E-mail: sales@pegrack.com
Web site: http://www.flamencoguide.com.

Wood, Ella Sue, *(978-0-9774937)* 3229 Regatta Pointe Ct., Midlothian, VA 23112 USA.

Wood, Katy Lynn, *(978-0-692-88033-3; 978-0-692-88034-0; 978-0-578-66828-4; 978-0-578-66832-1)* 6620 Finecrest Dr., COLORADO SPRINGS, CO 80923 USA Tel 720-822-0598
E-mail: jeffwcrawford5+LVP0003688@gmail.com; jeffwcrawford5+LVP0003688@gmail.com.

Wood Lake Publishing, Inc. (CAN) *(978-0-919599; 978-0-929032; 978-0-929599; 978-1-55145; 978-1-895562; 978-1-77343) Dist. by* **Westminster John Knox.**

Wood, Rachel, *(978-0-9998818)* 219 Chambers Dr., Lincoln, CA 95648 USA Tel 760-362-3356
E-mail: rcwauthor@gmail.com
Web site: rachelcherie.com.

Woodard, Kate, *(978-0-9979221)* 32 Harvard Sq., Woodridge, NY 12789 USA Tel 845-372-3886
E-mail: ladykatethegreat@hotmail.com.

Woodberry International Publishing, *(978-0-615-73339-5; 978-0-615-73423-1; 978-0-9916537)* 3758 Riverchase way, Decatur, GA 30034 USA Tel 4042415864
Dist(s): **CreateSpace Independent Publishing Platform.**

†**Woodbine Hse.,** *(978-0-933149; 978-1-890627; 978-1-60613)* 6510 Bells Mill Rd., Bethesda, MD 20817 USA (SAN 630-4052) Tel 301-897-3570; Fax: 301-897-5838; Toll Free: 800-843-7323
E-mail: info@woodbinehouse.com
Web site: http://www.woodbinehouse.com; *CIP.*

Woodburn Graphics, Inc., *(978-0-9707547)* P.O. Box 490, Terre Haute, ID 47807 USA Tel 812-232-0323; Fax: 812-232-2733; Toll Free: 800-457-0674
E-mail: len@woodburngraphics.com
Web site: http://www.woodburngraphics.com.

Wooded Hill Productions, *(978-1-886635)* Orders Addr.: 7480 Esplin Way, Flagstaff, AZ 86004 USA Tel 928-522-0058 (phone/fax)
E-mail: sig@boloz.com; sigmund.boloz@nau.edu
Web site: http://www.boloz.com.

Wooden Nickel Pr., *(978-0-615-25177-6; 978-0-9882891)* 2189 N. 55th St., Milwaukee, WI 53208 USA
Web site: http://www.woodennickelpress.com.

Wooden Roses Publishing!, *(978-1-7324627)* 1304 New York Ave Apt 5B, Brooklyn, NY 11203 USA Tel 646-707-7588
E-mail: nyeshadavis@gmail.com
Web site: woodenrosespublishing.com.

Wooden Shoe Pr., *(978-0-9762852)* N3566 Cty. Rd., GG, Hancock, WI 54943 USA Do not confuse with Wooden Shoe Press in Philadelphia, PA
E-mail: woodenshoepress@yahoo.com
Web site: http://www.woodenshoepress.com.

WoodenBoat Pubns., *(978-0-937822; 978-1-934982)* P.O. Box 78, Brooklin, ME 04616 USA Tel 207-359-4651; Fax: 207-359-2058; Toll Free: 800-273-7447
E-mail: books@woodenboat.com; wbstore@woodenboat.com
Web site: http://www.woodenboat.com.

Woodfrost Publishing, *(978-1-7320414)* 3944 Brown Bear Trail, Campbell, TX 75422 USA (SAN 990-9966) Tel 903-886-8999
E-mail: canzo2@gmail.com
Web site: davidcanzoneri.com.

Woodglen Publishing LLC, *(978-0-9827951)* P.O. Box 122, Califon, NJ 07830 USA Tel 908-638-5338; Fax: 908-638-0368
E-mail: stephanie@woodglenpublishing.com
Web site: http://www.woodglenpublishing.com.

Woodhall Pr., *(978-0-9975437; 978-1-949116)* 165 Mullen Hill Rd., Windham, CT 06280 USA Tel 919-396-6342
E-mail: woodhallpress@gmail.com
Web site: woodhallpress.com.

Woodland Health Books *See* **Woodland Publishing, Inc.**

Woodland Pr., *(978-0-9755822)* 605 Timber Ln., Lake Forest, IL 60045-3117 USA Tel 847-295-3514; 847-924-0324 Do not confuse with companies with the same name in Minneapolis, MN, Lapeer MI, Salt Lake City, UT.

Woodland Pr., LLC, *(978-0-9724867; 978-0-9793236; 978-0-9824939; 978-0-9829937; 978-0-9852640; 978-0-9912301)* 118 Woodland, Suite 1102, Chapmanville, WV 25508 USA (SAN 254-9999) Tel 304-752-7500; Fax: 304-752-9002 Do not confuse with companies with the same or similar names in Minneapolis, MN, Lapeer, MI, Salt Lake City, UT, Florance, AL, Moscow, ID
E-mail: info@woodlandpress.com; woodlandpresslc@mac.com; fkeithdavis@me.com
Web site: http://www.woodlandpress.com
Dist(s): **New Day Christian Distributors Gifts, Inc.**
Quality Bks., Inc.
West Virginia Book Co., The
Woodland Distribution.

Woodland Publishing, Inc., *(978-0-913923; 978-1-58054; 978-1-885670)* Orders Addr.: 1777 Sun Peak Dr., Park City, UT 84098 USA (SAN 286-9063)
Web site: http://www.woodlandpublishing.com
Dist(s): **Integral Yoga Pubns.**
New Leaf Distributing Co., Inc.
Nutri-Bks. Corp.
Royal Pubns., Inc.

Woodland Scenics, *(978-1-887436)* Div. of Osment Models, Inc., Orders Addr.: P.O. Box 98, Linn Creek, MO 65052 USA Tel 573-346-5555; Toll Free: 800-346-6642; Edit Addr.: 101 E. Valley Dr., Linn Creek, MO 65052 USA
E-mail: sales@woodlandscenics.com.

Woodruff, David Roberts, *(978-0-9716806)* 4075 Carmel View Rd., No.9, San Deigo, CA 92130 USA
E-mail: drbts@att.net.

Woodruff, Paul, *(978-0-9764327)* 58048 Inglewood Ln., Glenwood, IA 51534 USA.

Woods, Candace E., *(978-0-578-55878-3)* 11 Park Pl., New Rochelle, NY 10801 USA Tel 914-646-8481
Dist(s): **CreateSpace Independent Publishing Platform.**

Woods, Emmett L., *(978-0-615-12589-3)* 4016 Monterey Ct., Montgomery, AL 36116 USA Tel 334-288-1380.

Woods, james E, *(978-0-9973324; 978-1-947380)* P.O. Box PO Box 7414, Wilmington, DE 19803 USA Tel 267-446-4433
E-mail: woods2210@elsca.org.

Woods N' Water, Incorporated *See* **Woods N' Water Pr., Inc.**

Woods N' Water Pr., Inc., *(978-0-9707493; 978-0-9722804; 978-0-9769233; 978-0-9795131; 978-0-9820414; 978-0-9828228; 978-0-615-38124-4)* Orders Addr.: P.O. Box 10, South New Berlin, NY 13843 USA (SAN 254-3869) Tel 607-548-4011; Fax: 607-548-4013; Toll Free: 800-652-7527; Edit Addr.: 3312 State Hwy. 8, South New Berlin, NY 13843 USA Tel 607-548-4011; Fax: 607-548-4013; Toll Free: 800-652-7527
E-mail: kate@fiduccia.com
Web site: http://www.woodsnwaterpress.com; http://www.atabooks.com
Dist(s): **Cardinal Pubs. Group.**

Woodstocker Books/Arthur Schwartz & Company, *(978-1-879504)* 15 Meads Mountain Rd., Woodstock, NY 12498-1016 USA (SAN 630-0464) Tel 845-679-4024; Fax: 845-679-4093; Toll Free: 800-669-9080 (orders only)
E-mail: woodstockerbooks@woodstockerbooks.com
Web site: http://www.aschwartzbooks.com
Dist(s): **Antique Collectors' Club**
National Bk. Network.

Woodward, Stephanie Lynn, *(978-0-578-50075-1; 978-0-578-50076-8)* 4080 Riverlook Pkwy SE Unit 102, Marietta, GA 30067 USA Tel 817-637-0952
E-mail: Stephanielynnwoodward@gmail.com; boudreau619@gmail.com
Dist(s): **Ingram Content Group.**

Woolfolk Publications *See* **Gye Nyame Hse.**

Woolley Family Studios, *(978-0-9909391)* 34 Hadley St., Cambridge, MA 02140 USA Tel 310-909-4329
E-mail: jakegpanda@gmail.com
Web site: www.endangeredfiles.com.

Wooster Bk. Co., The, *(978-1-888683; 978-1-59098)* 205 W. Liberty St., Wooster, OH 44691-4831 USA Tel 330-262-1688; Fax: 330-264-9753; Toll Free: 800-982-6651 (800-WUBook-1)
E-mail: mail@woosterbook.com
Web site: http://www.woosterbook.com.

W.O.P. Pr., *(978-0-615-95687-9; 978-0-615-97065-3; 978-0-692-71789-9; 978-0-692-05869-5)* 7237 Mountain Knoll Dr. SE, Caledonia, MI 49508 USA Tel 616-929-0697
E-mail: stephenstromp@gmail.com
Dist(s): **CreateSpace Independent Publishing Platform.**

Wo-Pila Publishing, *(978-1-886340)* Orders Addr.: P.O. Box 8966, Erie, PA 16505-0966 USA Tel 814-868-5331; Fax: 814-868-1711; Toll Free: 888-567-8267; Edit Addr.: 3324 Charlotte St., Erie, PA 16508-2224 USA
E-mail: WopilaPublishing@aol.com
Web site: http://www.MannyTwofeathers.com.

Word Aflame Pr., *(978-0-912315; 978-0-932581; 978-1-56722; 978-0-7577)* Subs. of Pentecostal Publishing Hse., 8855 Dunn Rd., Hazelwood, MO 63042 USA (SAN 212-0046) Tel 314-837-7300; Fax: 314-837-6574
E-mail: pph@upci.org
Web site: http://www.upci.org/pph.

Word Among Us Pr., *(978-0-932085; 978-1-59325)* 7115 Guilford Dr. Suite 100, Frederick, MD 21704 USA (SAN 686-4651) Tel 301-831-1262; Fax: 301-831-1188; Toll Free: 800-775-9673
E-mail: pmm@wall.org
Web site: http://www.wau.org
Dist(s): **Spring Arbor Distributors, Inc.**

Word & Spirit Resources, LLC., *(978-0-9842534; 978-1-936314; 978-1-939570; 978-1-949106)* 9916 S 107th E. Ave, tulsa, OK 74133 USA Tel 918-608-5858; Fax: 918-893-2656
Web site: http://www.wordandspiritresources.com
Dist(s): **Whitaker Hse.**

Word Assocs., Inc., *(978-0-939153; 978-1-57265)* 3226 Robincrest Dr., Northbrook, IL 60062 USA (SAN 679-7792) Tel 847-291-1101; Fax: 847-291-0931
E-mail: microlm@aol.com
Web site: http://www.wordassociates.com.

Word Association Pubs., *(978-1-891231; 978-1-932205; 978-1-59571; 978-1-63385)* 205 Fifth Ave., Tarentum, PA 15084 USA Tel 724-226-4526; Fax: 724-226-3974; Toll Free: 800-827-7903
E-mail: publish@wordassociation.com
Web site: http://www.wordassociation.com
Dist(s): **Chicago Distribution Ctr.**

Word Distribution *See* **Word Entertainment**

Word Entertainment, *(978-0-9644619; 978-1-933876)* 25 Music Sq. W., Nashville, TN 37203 USA Tel 615-726-7900; Toll Free Fax: 800-671-6601; Toll Free: 800-876-9673; *Imprints:* Word Music (Word Music)
E-mail: matt.taylor@wordentertainment.com
Web site: http://www.wordentertainment.com
Dist(s): **Christian Bk. Distributors.**

Word For Word Publishing Co., *(978-1-889732)* 144 Quincy St. Apt. 1, Brooklyn, NY 11216-1393 USA; *Imprints:* A & E Sivells Publications (A & E Sivells Pubns)
E-mail: word4wrd@aol.com.

Word Gift Pubns., *(978-0-9788381)* 6641 Cty. Rd. 912, Joshua, TX 76058 USA (SAN 851-7223)
E-mail: peregrina@wordgift.org
Web site: http://www.wordgift.org.

Word Music *Imprint of* **Word Entertainment**

Word of Life Fellowship, Inc., *(978-1-931235; 978-1-935475)* Orders Addr.: P.O. Box 600, Schroon Lake, NY 12870-0600 USA Fax: 518-494-6312; Toll Free: 888-932-5827; Edit Addr.: 71 Olmstedville Rd., Pottersville, NY 12860 USA Do not confuse with Word of Life Fellowship, Sand Springs, OK
E-mail: timf@wol.org; DReichard@wol.org
Web site: http://www.wol.org.

Word of Mouth Bks. *Imprint of* **KA Productions, LLC**

Word of Mouth Pr., *(978-0-615-24213-2; 978-0-578-03631-1; 978-0-578-05051-5; 978-0-578-05113-0; 978-0-578-12825-2)* 406 Shelby St., Kingsport, TN 37660 USA Tel 423-245-1199
E-mail: electragraphics@earthlink.net.

Word on Da Street Publishing, *(978-0-615-52643-0; 978-0-615-64869-9; 978-0-9885056)* 252 W. Westfield Ave. 252 W. Westfield Ave, Roselle Park, NJ 07204 USA Tel 973-445-1690
E-mail: llperry803@gmail.com.

Word Productions LLC, *(978-0-9728590; 978-0-9765010; 978-0-9827998; 978-0-9909245; 978-0-9978373; 978-1-7356273)* Orders Addr.: P.O. Box 11184, Albuquerque, NM 87192 USA; *Imprints:* Kid-E Books (KID-E Bks)
E-mail: media@wordproductions.org; wordproductions@aol.com
Web site: http://www.wordproductions.org
Dist(s): **Independently Published.**

Word Prostitute, *(978-0-9728465)* 3434 SE 13th Ave., Portland, OR 97202 USA
E-mail: kalabjoster@wordprostitute.com
Web site: http://www.wordprostitute.com.

Word Riot Pr., *(978-0-9728200; 978-0-9779343)* P.O. Box 414, Middletown, NJ 07748 USA
E-mail: editor@wordriot.org
Web site: http://www.wordriot.org
Dist(s): **Pathway Bk. Service.**

Word Seed Publishing, *(978-0-9755232)* 650 NE 2nd St., Hermiston, OR 97838 USA Tel 541-567-0886; Fax: 541-481-7500
E-mail: hashcraftz1@charter.net.

Word Supremacy Pr., *(978-0-9747231)* 910 St., Paul St., No. C, Baltimore, MD 21202 USA Tel 443-414-4600; Fax: 877-504-3140
E-mail: taalam@aol.com
Web site: http://www.taalamacey.com.

Word To The Wise, A, *(978-0-9849321)* 2547 Dug Hill Rd., Brownsboro, AL 35741 USA Tel 256-541-4920
E-mail: edgoad@fastmail.fm.

Word Weaver Bks., Inc., *(978-0-9670600)* 9743 W. Bray Creek St., Star, ID 83669-5815 USA
E-mail: tidegirl32@aol.com
Web site: http://www.wordweaverbooks.com.

Word with You Pr., A, *(978-0-9843064; 978-0-9829094; 978-0-9884646)* 802 S. Tremont St., Oceanside, CA 92054 USA Tel 760-500-5409; 310 E. A St. Suite B, Moscow, ID 83843 Tel 760-500-5409
E-mail: thorn@awordwithyoupress.com
Web site: http://awordwithyoupress.com.

Word Wright International *See* **WordWright.biz, Inc.**

Wordcraft of Oregon, LLC, *(978-1-877655; 978-0-9964371)* P.O. Box 3235, La Grande, OR 97850 USA Do not confuse with Wordcraft, Oakland, CA
E-mail: info@wordcraftoforegon.com
Web site: http://www.wordcraftoforegon.com.

Worden, Robin, *(978-1-7338803)* 2552 Big Oak Rd., Harrison, AR 72601 USA Tel 870-391-6352
E-mail: silvermustang2005@yahoo.com.

WordFire, Incorporated *See* **WordFire Pr.**

WordFire Pr. *Imprint of* **WordFire Pr.**

WordFire Pr., *(978-0-9673548; 978-1-61475; 978-1-68057)* P.O. Box 1840, Monument, CO 80132-1840 USA; *Imprints:* WordFire Press (WrdFire Pr)
E-mail: reb@wordfire.com
Web site: http://wordfire.com; http://wordfirepress.com
Dist(s): **Greenleaf Book Group.**

WordMaster Publishing, *(978-0-9740410)* 4317 W. Farrand Rd., Clio, MI 48420 USA (SAN 255-3325) Tel 810-686-2047; Fax: 810-564-9929
E-mail: wordmasterpub@aol.com.

Wordmeister Pr., *(978-0-9978925; 978-1-7351213)* 1101 Riverside Dr., Owosso, MI 48867 USA Tel 989-723-2084
E-mail: juliewenzlick@gmail.com.

Wordminder Pr., *(978-0-9729103)* Orders Addr.: 1008 Norview Ave., Norfolk, VA 23513-3410 USA Tel 757-853-4775
E-mail: sma@wordminderpress.com; wp@wordminderpress.com
Web site: http://www.wordminderpress.com
Dist(s): **CreateSpace Independent Publishing Platform.**

WordPlay Multimedia, LLC, *(978-0-9755444)* Orders Addr.: P.O. Box 9303, Jacksonville, FL 32208 USA Tel 904-683-8032
E-mail: jjfrederick98@aol.com
Web site: http://www.frederickpreston.com
Dist(s): **A & B Distributors & Pubs. Group.**

Words & Music, *(978-0-9800880; 978-0-615-15540-1)* 13967 Amber Pl., San Diego, CA 92130 USA Do not confuse with Words & Music, Gig Harbor, CA
E-mail: info@talesalive.com
Web site: http://www.talesalive.com.

Words & Pictures Publishing, Inc., *(978-0-9621280)* P.O. Box 61444, Honolulu, HI 96839 USA (SAN 250-9326) Tel 808-955-4742; Fax: 808-951-6541
E-mail: gecko@aloha.net
Web site: http://www.brucehale.com
Dist(s): **Booklines Hawaii, Ltd.**
Sunbelt Pubns., Inc.

Words In The Works, LLC, *(978-0-9910364; 978-0-9972284; 978-1-7320524)* P.O. Box 448, North Salem, NY 10560 USA Tel 914-841-0896; *Imprints:* Crystal Books (Crystal Bks)
E-mail: info@wordsintheworks.com.

Words of Essence Publishing, *(978-0-9768133)* P.O. Box 13182, Durham, NC 27709 USA Tel 919-624-4138
E-mail: godslove232@yahoo.com
Web site: http://www.wordsofessence.com.

Words of Wisdom, *(978-1-947211)* 803 Hadley Ave, Old Hickory, TN 37138 USA Tel 615-448-7304; Fax: 866-350-0669
E-mail: kpruittwow@gmail.com
Web site: www.woweducationalconsulting.com.

words4u, *(978-0-9740419)* P.O. Box 641257, San Francisco, CA 94164-1257 USA
E-mail: info@words4u.com
Web site: http://www.words4u.com.

WordsBright, *(978-1-940229)* 501-I S. Reino Rd, No. 365, Newbury Park, CA 91320 USA Tel 805-413-4525
E-mail: contactus@wordsbright.com
Web site: www.wordsbright.com
Dist(s): **Pathway Bk. Service.**

Wordshed, *(978-0-942684)* 5118 Glendale St., Duluth, MN 55804-1107 USA (SAN 239-6246) Tel 218-525-3266.

Wordsmith Bks., *(978-1-882646)* Orders Addr.: 157 Chris St., Hollidaysburg, PA 16648 USA Tel 814-317-5314 Do not confuse with Wordsmith Bks. in Auburn, AL
E-mail: catalano.tom@gmail.com.

Wordsmith Pr., *(978-1-893972)* 11462 East Ln., Whitmore Lake, MI 48189 USA Tel 810-231-5435
E-mail: info@thewordsmithpress.com
Web site: http://www.thewordsmithpress.com.

Wordsmiths, *(978-0-9632774; 978-1-886061)* 1355 Ferry Rd., Grants Pass, OR 97526 USA Tel 541-476-3080; Fax: 541-474-9756 Do not confuse with the Wordsmiths in Evergreen, CO
E-mail: frodej@chatlink.com
Web site: http://www.jsgrammar.com.

Wordsong *Imprint of* **Boyds Mills Pr.**

Wordsworth Editions, Ltd. (GBR) *(978-1-85326; 978-1-84022; 978-1-84870) Dist. by* **LBMayAssocs.**

WORDSWORTH Publishing Co., *(978-0-9672491; 978-0-9754351)* Orders Addr.: P.O. Box 7132, Santa Rosa, CA 95407 USA Tel 707-829-2316 (phone/fax); Edit Addr.: 2524 S. Edison St., Graton, CA 95444 USA
E-mail: wwinfo@getyourwordsworth.com
Web site: http://www.getyourwordsworth.com.

WordThunder Pubns., *(978-0-9745268; 978-1-59790)* P.O. Box 540931, Merritt Island, FL 32954 USA (SAN 256-3770)
E-mail: books@wordthunder.com
Web site: http://wordthunder.com/books/.

Wordwhittler Bks., *(978-0-9895487)* 3073 Cypress Creek Dr. N., Ponte Vedra Beach, FL 32082 USA Tel 904-285-8531
E-mail: sscalfee@aol.com.

Wordwindow LLC, *(978-0-9774484)* 2125 Jackson Bluff Rd. Apt. V-204, Tallahassee, FL 32304 USA Toll Free: 877-967-3946
Web site: http://www.wordwindow.com.

Wordworker's Shop Publishing, *(978-0-9843239)* 1115 Inman Ave., Suite 337, Edison, NJ 08820-1132 USA
E-mail: wordworker@earthlink.net.

WordWorks Publishing, *(978-0-9831557)* 1081 Rosedale Dr., Atlanta, GA 30306 USA Tel 404-664-5256 Do not confuse with WordWorks Publishing in Austin, TX, Westfield, IN
E-mail: laurelannd@gmail.com
Dist(s): **BookBaby.**

Wordwright Communications, *(978-0-9718838)* 4900 Randall Pkwy. Ste. F, Wilmington, NC 28403-2831 USA Toll Free: 888-235-0248.

WordWright.biz, Inc., *(978-0-9700615; 978-0-9713832; 978-0-9717868; 978-1-932196; 978-1-934335)* P.O. Box 1785, Georgetown, TX 78627 USA Fax: 512-260-3080 (phone/fax); *Imprints:* Legacy (Lgcy TX); One Night Books (One Night Bks)
E-mail: joan@wordwright.biz; snwriter@earthlink.net; jnwriter@aol.com
Web site: http://www.wordwright.biz.

Workhouse Road Productions, *(978-0-615-74249-6; 978-0-615-78551-6; 978-0-692-41154-4; 978-0-692-55532-3; 978-0-692-14674-3)* 1321 S. CLOVERDALE AVE, LOS ANGELES, CA 90019 USA Tel 323-528-7495
E-mail: Bettykbynum@gmail.com
Web site: www.theimagirlcollection.com
Dist(s): **Independent Pubs. Group**
Midpoint Trade Bks., Inc.

Working Parents, LLC, *(978-0-9711040)* P.O. Box 715, Santa Clara, CA 95052-0715 USA Tel 408-554-0280 (phone/fax)
E-mail: info@workingparents.com
Web site: http://www.workingparents.com.

Working Title Publishing, *(978-1-59344; 978-0-9776440)* P.O. Box 384, Lodi, CA 95241 USA
Web site: http://www.workingtitlepublishing.com.

Working Words & Graphics *See* **Lockman, James Consulting**

†**Workman Publishing Co., Inc.,** *(978-0-7611; 978-0-89480; 978-0-911104; 978-1-56305; 978-1-5235)* Orders Addr.: 225 Varick St., New York, NY 10014-4381

Publisher Name Index

USA (SAN 203-2821) Tel 212-254-5900; Fax: 212-254-8098; Toll Free: 800-722-7202
E-mail: info@workman.com
Web site: http://www.workman.com
Dist(s): **Blackstone Audio, Inc.**
Experiment LLC, The
Open Road Integrated Media, Inc.
Storey Publishing, LLC
Timber Pr., Inc.; *CIP.*

World Ahead Media *See* **WND Bks, Inc.**

World Ahead Pr. *Imprint of* **WND Bks, Inc.**

World Almanac Bks. *Imprint of* **Facts On File, Inc.**

World Almanac Library *Imprint of* **Stevens, Gareth Publishing LLLP**

World Audience Pubs., *(978-0-9788086; 978-1-934209; 978-0-9820540; 978-1-935444)* 303 Pk. Ave. S., Suite 1440, New York, NY 10010 USA
E-mail: worldaudience@gmail.com; mstefanstrozier@gmail.com
Web site: http://www.worldaudience.org; http://www.worldaudience.mobi; http://www.worldaudience.co.uk.

World Awake Bks., *(978-0-615-26795-1)* 15508 W. Bell Rd., Suite 101,, Surprise, AZ 85374 USA.

†**World Bank Pubns.,** *(978-0-8213; 978-1-4648)* Orders Addr.: P.O. Box 960, Herndon, VA 20172-0960 USA Toll Free: 800-645-7247; Edit Addr.: 1818 H St., NW, Mail Stop: U11-1104, Washington, DC 20433 USA (SAN 219-0648) Tel 703-661-1580; 202-473-1000 (Head Office); Fax: 202-614-1237
E-mail: books@worldbank.org
Web site: http://www.worldbank.org/publications
Dist(s): **Bernan Assocs.**
Ebsco Publishing
Independent Pubs. Group
MyiLibrary
Oxford Univ. Pr., Inc.
Rowman & Littlefield Publishers, Inc.
ebrary, Inc.; *CIP.*

World Bk., Inc., *(978-0-7166)* Div. of Scott Fetzer Co., 233 N. Michigan, Suite 2000, Chicago, IL 60601 USA (SAN 201-4815) Tel 312-729-5800; Fax: 312-729-5600; 312-729-5614; Toll Free Fax: 800-433-9330 (US orders); 888-690-4002 (Canadian orders); Toll Free: 800-975-3250 (US orders); 800-967-5325; 800-837-5365 (Canadian orders)
Web site: http://www.worldbook.com
Dist(s): **MyiLibrary.**

World CARP, *(978-0-9722946)* 4 W. 43rd St., New York, NY 10036-7408 USA
E-mail: yyk21@worldcarp.org
Web site: http://www.worldcarp.org.

World Cycling Pr., *(978-0-9745842)* 3910 Chapman St., San Diego, CA 92110-5694 USA Tel 619-224-1050; Fax: 619-224-0530
E-mail: team_mallory@hotmail.com.

World Enough Writers, *(978-1-937797)* c/o Lana Ayers, P.O. Box 1808, Kingston, WA 98346 USA Tel 360-881-0880
E-mail: WorldEnoughWriters@yahoo.com
Web site: http://WorldEnoughWriters.com.

World Famous Children's Bks., *(978-0-9725398)* 4455 Torrance Blvd, No. 153, Torrance, CA 90503 USA
Web site: http://www.worldfamouschildrensbooks.com
Dist(s): **Quality Bks., Inc.**

World Forward Foundation, 5090 Easley Rd., Golden, CO 80403 USA Tel 720-545-6350
E-mail: shannon@worldforwardfoundation.org
Dist(s): **Ingram Content Group.**

World Health Organization, *(978-0-11)* Orders Addr.: 49 Sheridan Ave., Albany, NY 12210 USA (SAN 221-6310) Tel 518-436-9686; Fax: 518-436-7433; Edit Addr.: Av Appia, Geneva, 1211 CHE Tel 41-22) 7912111; Fax: 41-22) 7910746
E-mail: publications@who.int
Web site: http://www.who.ch
Dist(s): **Balogh International, Inc.**
Bernan Assocs.
MyiLibrary
Stylus Publishing, LLC
Women Ink.

World Leisure Marketing Ltd (GBR) *(978-1-84006; 978-1-899026) Dist. by* **Midpt Trade.**

World Library Pubns., *(978-0-937690; 978-1-58459; 978-1-64321)* Div. of J. S. Paluch Co., Inc., 3708 River Rd. Suite 400, Franklin Park, IL 60131-2158 USA (SAN 203-0306) Tel 847-233-2767; Toll Free Fax: 888-957-3291; Toll Free: 800-621-5197
E-mail: wlpcs@jspaluch.com
Web site: http://www.wlpmusic.com
Dist(s): **Ingram Publisher Services**
Spring Arbor Distributors, Inc.

World Nouveau, *(978-0-9828865; 978-1-938208)* P.O. Box 571, Torrance, CA 90508 USA Tel 310-776-5510
E-mail: WorldNouveau@Gmail.com
Web site: http://www.WorldNouveau.com.

World of Angels, A, *(978-0-9743964)* 97 Main St., Belfast, ME 04915 USA Tel 207-338-8900
E-mail: aworldofangels@prexar.com
Web site: http://www.aworldofangels.com.

World of Empowerment *See* **Twin Flame Productions**

World of Imagination, *(978-0-9761228)* 200 N. Maryland Ave., Suite 101, Glendale, CA 91206 USA Tel 818-547-5541; Fax: 818-543-1889; Toll Free: 800-266-5255.

World of Learning Publishing *See* **Swift Learning Resources**

World of Reading, Ltd., P.O. Box 13092, Atlanta, GA 30324-0092 USA Tel 404-233-4042; Fax: 404-237-5511; Toll Free: 800-729-3703.

World of Whimsy Productions, LLC, *(978-0-9702675)* 409 N. Pacific Coast Hwy., No. 594, Redondo Beach, CA 90277 USA (SAN 256-1077) Fax: 310-542-9297; Toll Free: 1-888-4-WHIMSY
E-mail: info@worldofwhimsy.com
Web site: http://worldofwhimsy.com.

World Pubns. Group, Inc., *(978-0-7669; 978-0-9640034; 978-1-57215; 978-0-7429; 978-1-4132; 978-1-4279; 978-1-4376; 978-1-4513; 978-1-4643; 978-1-4785)* Orders Addr.: P.O. Box 509, East Bridgewater, MA 02333 USA (SAN 631-7014); *Imprints:* JG Press (JG Pr)
E-mail: sales@wrldpub.net
Web site: http://www.wrldpub.com
Dist(s): **Hachette Bk. Group.**

World Publications, Incorporated *See* **World Pubns. Group, Inc.**

World Quest Learning, *(978-1-933248)* P.O. Box 654, Lewis Center, OH 43035 USA Tel 740-548-3857; Toll Free Fax: 866-722-7521; Toll Free: 866-722-7520
E-mail: info@worldquestlearning.com
Web site: http://www.worldquestlearning.com.

World Thoughts Publishing, Co., *(978-0-9711018)* P.O. Box 3206, Saint Augustine, FL 32084-3206 USA
E-mail: beebes@aug.com
Web site: http://www.energeticawakening.com; http://www.worldthoughts.com.

World Tribune Pr., *(978-0-915678; 978-1-932911; 978-1-935523; 978-1-944604)* Orders Addr.: 8811 Aviation Blvd., Inglewood, CA 90301 USA Tel 310-337-0055; Fax: 310-642-4625; Toll Free: 800-626-1313; Edit Addr.: 606 Wilshire Blvd., Santa Monica, CA 90401 USA (SAN 683-230X) Tel 310-260-8900; Fax: 310-260-8910
E-mail: dmcneill@sgi-usa.org
Dist(s): **PCE International.**

World Wide Distributors, Limited *See* **Island Heritage Publishing**

World Wisdom, Inc., *(978-0-941532; 978-1-933316; 978-1-935493; 978-1-936597; 978-1-937786)* Orders Addr.: P.O. Box 2682, Bloomington, IN 47402-2682 USA (SAN 239-1406) Tel 812-330-3232; Fax: 812-333-1642; Toll Free: 888-992-6651; Edit Addr.: 1501 E. Hillside Dr., Bloomington, IN 47401 USA; *Imprints:* Wisdom Tales (WisdomTales)
Web site: http://www.worldwisdom.com
Dist(s): **Follett School Solutions**
MyiLibrary
National Bk. Network
New Leaf Distributing Co., Inc.
Send The Light Distribution LLC
ebrary, Inc.

Worlds In Ink *See* **Worlds In Ink Publishing, Inc.**

Worlds In Ink Publishing, Inc., *(978-0-9745568)* 4812 Ridgecrest Cir SE, Albuquerque, NM 87108-4435 USA
E-mail: info@WorldsInInk.com
Web site: http://www.WorldsInInk.com.

WorldTrek Publishing, *(978-1-936376)* 121 E. Vermijo, Colorado Springs, CO 80903 USA (SAN 859-7154).

Worldview Publishing, Inc., *(978-1-889995)* 521 Herchel Dr., Tampa, FL 33617 USA Tel 813-985-9344; Fax: 813-985-4505; Toll Free: 800-987-9444 Do not confuse with companies with same or similar names in Tiburon, CA, Colorado Springs, CO
E-mail: drlindahf@aol.com
Web site: http://www.worldviewpub.com.

Worldwide Publishing Group, *(978-0-692-20798-7; 978-0-692-21343-8; 978-0-692-23202-6; 978-0-692-26528-4; 978-0-692-28543-5; 978-0-692-33975-6; 978-0-692-34486-6; 978-0-692-34654-9; 978-0-692-35794-1; 978-0-692-35819-1; 978-0-692-36089-7; 978-0-692-38604-0; 978-0-692-40727-1; 978-0-692-41000-4; 978-0-692-41425-5; 978-0-692-41942-7; 978-0-692-46338-3; 978-0-692-47708-3; 978-0-692-49561-2; 978-0-692-49566-7; 978-0-692-49571-1; 978-0-692-50705-6; 978-0-692-50706-3; 978-0-692-50707-0; 978-0-692-50708-7; 978-0-692-50709-4;) P.O. Box 596, Litchfield, IL 62056 USA Tel 217-851-0361*
E-mail: rwgcontact@yahoo.com
Web site: http://www.worldwidepublishinggroup.com/
Dist(s): **CreateSpace Independent Publishing Platform.**

Worldwide United Publishing *See* **Pearl Publishing, LLC**

Worley, Kayla, *(978-0-578-43153-6; 978-0-578-63097-7; 978-0-578-63253-7)* 7411 N. Delaware Ave., Portland, OR 97217 USA Tel 503-887-5504
E-mail: thisissoyoudonotforget@hotmail.com
Dist(s): **Ingram Content Group.**

Worthen, Olivia, *(978-0-9996833)* 9422 Heather Brae Ct., South Jordan, UT 84095 USA Tel 801-580-1465
E-mail: flower9422@comcast.net.

Worthwhile Bks. *Imprint of* **Idea & Design Works, LLC**

Worthy Kids/Ideals *Imprint of* **Worthy Publishing**

Worthy Media, Incorporated *See* **Worthy Publishing**

Worthy Publishing, 10 Cadillac Dr., Brentwood, TN 37027 USA Tel 615-221-0996; *Imprints:* Museum of the Bible (MOTB)
Dist(s): **Blackstone Audio, Inc.**
Hachette Bk. Group.

Worthy Publishing, *(978-0-8249; 978-0-89542; 978-0-9640955; 978-1-58334; 978-1-887655; 978-0-9794446; 978-0-9796938; 978-1-934770; 978-1-60587; 978-1-935416; 978-1-936034; 978-1-60936; 978-1-61795; 978-1-63326; 978-1-68397; 978-1-945470)* Div. of Worthy Media, Inc., Orders Addr.: One Franklin Park 6100 Tower Cir., Suite 210, Franklin, TN 37067 USA Tel 615-932-7600; *Imprints:* F/S (F/S); Ellie Claire (Ellie Claire); Ideals Publications (IdealsPubns); Museum of the Bible Books (MuseumBible); Worthy Kids/Ideals (WorthyKids) Do not confuse with Worthy Publishing in Birmingham, AL
E-mail: jeana@worthymedia.com; leeannan@worthypublishing.com
Web site: http://worthypublishing.com/
Dist(s): **CreateSpace Independent Publishing Platform**
EMI CMG Distribution
Hachette Bk. Group.

Worthy Shorts, *(978-1-935340; 978-1-937503; 978-1-937504; 978-1-937505; 978-1-937506; 978-1-937507)* P.O. Box 177, Malden on Hudson, NY 12453 USA Tel 845-246-2336; 15 Bostan Rd., Malden on Hudson, NY 12453
Web site: http://www.worthyshorts.com
Dist(s): **Independent Pubs. Group**
Smashwords.

Wowza World LLC,

WowZee Works Inc, *(978-0-9778858)* 2217 Green Mountain Ct., Las Vegas, NV 89135 USA (SAN 850-5128).

WPR Publishing, *(978-1-889379)* 3445 Catalina Dr., Carlsbad, CA 92010 USA Tel 760-645-3455; Fax: 760-434-7476 Do not confuse with WPR Publishing, Dillon, MT
E-mail: kirk@whisler.com
Web site: http://www.WPRbooks.com
Dist(s): **Ingram Content Group.**

WRB Pub., *(978-0-9844198; 978-0-9838832; 978-0-9856762; 978-0-9896247; 978-0-9909040)* 1260 SW 25 LN, Palm City, FL 34990 USA Tel 772-463-0928; Fax: 267-220-1541
E-mail: wrb1174@att.net
Dist(s): **Ingram Publisher Services**
Smashwords.

WRDSMTH Productions, *(978-0-9744562)* Orders Addr.: P.O. Box 1406, Lawton, OK 73502-1406 USA (SAN 255-7282) Tel 580-353-4710; Fax: 580-357-9787; Toll Free: 800-357-9854; Edit Addr.: 130 SW B Ave., Lawton, OK 73501 USA
E-mail: okteller@juno.com
Web site: http://www.stringfigurestore.com.

W.R.E.a.C Havoc Publishing, *(978-0-578-61255-3)* 14643 222nd St., Springfield Gardens, NY 11413 USA Tel 347-262-9882
E-mail: wreachavocwriter@gmail.com
Web site: www.wreachavoconline.com.

Wren Song Pr., *(978-0-9769827)* 233 Poors Mill Rd., Belfast, ME 04915 USA Toll Free: 800-943-7664 Do not confuse with Wren Song Press in Ripton, VT
E-mail: jennifer@jenniferarmstrong.com
Web site: http://www.jenniferarmstrong.com.

Wren's Nest Productions LLC *Imprint of* **Struminger, Alexander**

Wren's Nest Publishing, Inc., *(978-0-9744111)* 177 Rabbit Farm Trail, Advance, NC 27006 USA Tel 336-998-2858
E-mail: rickyp@yadtel.net.

Wright Bk. Publishing, *(978-0-615-23176-1; 978-0-9822822)* 4188 Defoors Farm Dr., Powder Springs, GA 30127 USA
Web site: http://www.wrightbookpublishing.com; http://www.earthsavergirl.com.

Wright Bks., *(978-0-615-19564-3)* 3337 Manning Rd., Indianapolis, IN 46228 USA
E-mail: jbwright37@gmail.com
Web site: http://www.myspace.com/thewidowsjourney.

Wright, Dr. Author O., *(978-0-9679676)* 4524 Portland Ave., S., Minneapolis, MN 55407-3550 USA Tel 612-822-8032
E-mail: Awright@email.usps.gov.

Wright, Gladys, *(978-0-578-46190-8)* 1605 N. Houston School Rd., No. 3103, Lancaster, TX 75134 USA Tel 214-872-0838
E-mail: gladys_fuller@yahoo.com; gladyswrightauthor@yahoo.com
Dist(s): **Ingram Content Group.**

Wright Group/McGraw-Hill, *(978-0-322; 978-0-7802; 978-0-940156; 978-1-55624; 978-1-55911; 978-1-4045)* Div. of Mcgraw-Hill School Education Group, Orders Addr.: P.O. Box 545, Blacklick, OH 43004-0545 USA Tel 614-755-5645; Toll Free: 800-722-4726; 800-442-9685 (customer service)
Web site: http://www.wrightgroup.com/.

Wright, Lacie, *(978-0-615-20657-8; 978-0-615-20658-5)* 413 Acorn Grove Ln. Apt. C, Chesapeake, VA 23320-6561 USA
E-mail: paulndlacie@gmail.com
Dist(s): **Lulu Pr., Inc.**

Wright Publishing, Inc., *(978-0-935087; 978-0-9652368)* Orders Addr.: P.O. Box 1956, Fayetteville, GA 30214 USA Tel 770-460-5525; Fax: 770-460-8998; Edit Addr.: 320 Devilla Trace, Fayetteville, GA 30214 USA (SAN 695-0507) Do not confuse with companies with same or similar name in Los Angeles, CA, Virgina Beach, VA, West Seneca, NY, Torrance, CA, .

Wright, Robert, *(978-0-9763223)* 272 Horse Hill Rd., Ashford, CT 06278 USA.

Wright, Sasha, *(978-0-578-41785-1)* 7829 Magellan Dr., North Charleston, SC 29420 USA Tel 843-343-3106
E-mail: skwright1922@gmail.com
Dist(s): **Ingram Content Group.**

Wright, Willie Etta, *(978-0-9703551)* 403 S. Raddant Rd., Batavia, IL 60510 USA Tel 630-406-1756
E-mail: wilwrite@chicago.avenew.com.

Wright's Way Inc., *(978-0-9767483)* 210 Henderson Dr., Jacksonville, NC 28540 USA Tel 910-989-0000 (phone/fax)
E-mail: sensei@bizec.rr.com
Web site: http://www.wrightskarate.com.

Write As Rain Bks., *(978-0-9897221; 978-1-7331168)* 12131 SE 91st St., Newcastle, WA 98056 USA Tel 425-277-6585
E-mail: martinadalton@comcast.net.

Write Away, *(978-0-615-26181-2)* 242 Hyle Ave., Murfreesboro, TN 37128 USA Tel 615-848-0247.

Write Bloody Publishing, *(978-0-9789989; 978-0-9815213; 978-0-9821488; 978-0-9842515; 978-0-9845031; 978-1-935904; 978-1-938912; 978-1-949342)* 235 E. Broadway, Sixth Flr., No. 609, Long Beach, CA 90802 USA; *Imprints:* Write Fuzzy (Write Fuzzy)
E-mail: writebloody@gmail.com
Web site: http://www.writebloody.com
Dist(s): **SCB Distributors.**

Write Designs, Limited *See* **PricePoint+Publications**

Write Fuzzy *Imprint of* **Write Bloody Publishing**

Write Integrity Pr., *(978-0-9839485; 978-1-938092; 978-1-944120; 978-1-951602)* PO Box 702852, Dallas, TX 75370 USA (SAN 920-0673)
E-mail: writeintegrity@gmail.com; marji.laine@gmail.com
Web site: http://www.writeintegrity.com; http://MarjiLaine.com.

Write 'N Learn *Imprint of* **Zishka Publishing**

Write On!, *(978-0-9753870; 978-0-9825722; 978-0-9890688)* 644 Shadowbrook Dr, Columbia, TN 38401 USA Tel 615-415-9861 Do not confuse with companies with a similar name in Albuquerque, NM, Estes Park, CO
E-mail: writer@yvonneperry.net
Web site: http://weare1inspirit.com/.

Write One Publications *See* **Write One Pubns., Inc.**

Write One Pubns., Inc., *(978-0-9821484)* P.O. Box 20883, Chicago, IL 60620 USA
E-mail: snewell@writeonepublications.com
Web site: http://www.writeonepublications.com.

Write Place, *(978-0-9788507; 978-0-9968644)* 4310 S. Havana, Spokane, WA 99223 USA (SAN 851-7851) Tel 509-448-2901; *Imprints:* Bratcher Publishing (MYID_W_BRATCHE).

Write Place, The, *(978-0-9800084; 978-0-9825974; 978-0-9831961; 978-0-9858077; 978-0-9896710; 978-0-9916528; 978-0-9908419; 978-0-9968250; 978-0-9974659; 978-0-9983058; 978-0-9994887; 978-1-7323526; 978-1-7330085; 978-1-7345829)* 809 W 8th St Suite 2 Ste 2, Pella, 50219-7616 SUN (SAN 854-9761) Tel 641-628-8398
E-mail: sarah@thewriteplace.biz
Web site: http://www.thewriteplace.biz.

Write Way Publishing, *(978-1-885173)* Orders Addr.: P.O. Box 441278, Aurora, CO 80044 USA Tel 303-617-0497; Fax: 303-617-1440; Toll Free: 800-680-1493 Do not confuse with Write Way Publishing, Charleston, WV
E-mail: staff@writewaypub.com; writewy@aol.com
Web site: http://www.writewaypub.com.

Write Way Publishing Co. LLC, *(978-0-9976076; 978-1-946425)* 322 Fox Hollow Dr, Clayton, NC 27527 USA Tel 919-606-2618; *Imprints:* Barnsley Ink (MYID_U_BARNSLE)
E-mail: kevin@writewaypublishingcompany.com; lee@writewaypublishingcompany.com
Web site: writewaypublishingcompany.com.

Write Words, Inc., *(978-0-9706152; 978-1-59431; 978-1-61386)* 2934 Old Rte. 50, Cambridge, MD 21613 USA (SAN 254-0304); *Imprints:* Cambridge Books (CB); Ebooks On The Net (Ebks on the net) Do not confuse with The Write Words Inc., in Arlington, VA
E-mail: arline@mail.com; ArlineChase@comcast.net
Web site: http://www.ebooksonthe.net; http://www.cambridgebooks.us
Dist(s): **CreateSpace Independent Publishing Platform.**

Write World, Inc., *(978-0-9722173)* 3839 McKinney Ave. No. 155-373, Dallas, TX 75204 USA (SAN 254-8445)
E-mail: writeworld@cs.com.

Write Your Way Through Publishing *See* **Urban Moon Publishing**

WriteGirl Pubns., *(978-0-9741251; 978-0-9837081; 978-0-692-88728-8; 978-0-578-49912-3)* 1330 Factory Pl. Unti 104, Los Angeles, CA 90013 USA Tel 213-253-2655
E-mail: info@writegirl.org
Web site: http://www.writegirl.org
Dist(s): **SPD-Small Pr. Distribution.**

WriteLife Publishing *Imprint of* **Boutique of Quality Books Publishing Co., Inc.**

WRITER for HIRE!, *(978-0-9701356; 978-0-9854623; 978-1-950729)* 2425 Lawrenceville Hwy. No. C7, Decatur, GA 30033 USA Tel 404-358-0951 (9am-5pm EST); *Imprints:* Blue Room Books (MYID_O_BLUE RO)
E-mail: angeladurden@msn.com; angeladurden@gmail.com
Web site: https://www.angeladurden-books.com/books.

Writer Stain Publishing, *(978-0-692-86564-4; 978-0-692-95595-6; 978-0-692-99853-3; 978-0-578-44452-9; 978-1-7349652)* 1844 Scenic Dr, Festus, MO 63028 USA Tel 314-218-8085
E-mail: biaggionovels@gmail.com; contact@brettbiaggio.com
Web site: brettbiaggio.com; writersp.com.

Writers Advantage Pr. *Imprint of* **iUniverse, Inc.**

Writers Cafe Pr., The, *(978-1-934284)* 418 S. Brookfield Dr., Lafayette, IN 47905-7299 USA (SAN 852-5498)
E-mail: admin@thewriterscafe.com
Web site: http://www.thewriterscafe.com.

Writers Club Pr. *Imprint of* **iUniverse, Inc.**

Writer's Coffee Shop, The, *(978-1-61213)* P.O. Box 2116, Waxahachie, TX 75168 USA (SAN 860-0112)
E-mail: publishing@thewriterscoffeeshop.com; amhayward@thewriterscoffeeshop.com
Web site: http://www.thewriterscoffeeshop.com; http://ph.thewriterscoffeeshop.com/
Dist(s): **Lulu Pr., Inc.**

Writers' Collective, The, *(978-0-9716734; 978-1-932133; 978-1-59411)* 780 Reservoir Ave., Suite 243, Cranston, RI 02910 USA Toll Free: 800-497-0037
E-mail: factotum@writerscollective.org
Web site: http://www.writerscollective.org
Dist(s): **Midpoint Trade Bks., Inc.**

Writer's Cramp, Inc., *(978-0-9645983)* 711 San Juan Dr., Coral Gables, FL 33143-6224 USA
E-mail: JandyPF@aol.com.

Writers in the Schools (WITS), *(978-0-9747704)* 1523 W. Main, Houston, TX 77006 USA
E-mail: mail@writersintheschools.org
Web site: http://www.writersintheschools.org.

Writer's Ink. Studios, Inc., *(978-0-9704460)* P.O. Box 952, Windermere, FL 34786 USA Tel 407-876-3399; Fax: 270-964-5984; Toll Free: 888-229-9200
E-mail: cat@brownbagbooks.com; writersinkstudios@cfl.rr.com
Web site: http://www.brownbagbooks.com.

Writers Marketplace:Consulting, Critiquing & Publishing, *(978-1-928632)* P.O. Box 21218, Carson City, NV 89721 USA Tel 775-544-0909; Fax: 775-884-3103.

Writers of the Apocalypse, The, *(978-1-944322; 978-0-692-56768-5)* 1117 N Carbon St PMB 208, Marion, IL 62959 USA Tel 618-715-5132; *Imprints:* Woks Print (Woks Print)
E-mail: B00mb00mp0p@apocalypsewriters.com
Web site: http://woksprint.com; http://www.apocalypsewriters.com
Dist(s): **Author's Republic**
BookBaby
CreateSpace Independent Publishing Platform
Ingram Bk. Co.
Smashwords.

Writer of the Round Table Pr., *(978-0-9814545; 978-0-9822206; 978-1-61066; 978-1-937443)* P.O. Box 511, Highland Park, IL 60035-0511 USA (SAN 855-6067)
Web site: www.roundtablecompanies.com; http://www.writersoftheroundtable.com
Dist(s): **Ingram Content Group.**

Writer's Publishing Cooperative *Imprint of* **Beech River Bks.**

Writer's Showcase Pr. *Imprint of* **iUniverse, Inc.**

WritersCorps Bks. *Imprint of* **San Francisco Art Commission, The**

Writing Academy Inc., *(978-0-9729777)* 6488 Currin Dr., Orlando, FL 32835 USA (SAN 852-6435) Tel 407-296-5800; Fax: 407-296-5801
E-mail: salcom@alcorn.com
Web site: http://www.themeperks.com
Dist(s): **Smashwords.**

Writing as a Ghost *See* **Jots & Tittles Publishing**

Writing Bench LLC., The, *(978-0-9818374)* P.O. Box 775037, Saint Louis, MO 63177-5037 USA
E-mail: backwardkingdom@yahoo.com.

Writing Center, The *See* **Full Court Pr.**

Writing etc. *See* **Etcetera Pr. LLC**

Writing for the Lord Ministries, *(978-0-9705902; 978-0-9883038; 978-0-9893188)* 6400 Shannon Ct., Clarksville, MD 21029 USA Tel 410-340-8633
E-mail: pastorkevinwaynejohnson@gmail.com; kgj27@aol.com
Web site: http://www.writingforthelord.com; http://www.thejohnsonleadershipgroup.com
Dist(s): **Ingram Bk. Co.**

Writing The Vision *Imprint of* **Scribe Publishing & Consulting Services, The**

Writing Times Publications *See* **Writing Times Publishing**

Writing Times Publishing, *(978-1-7337375)* Psc 3, Box 2177, APO, AE 96266 USA Tel 512-577-9341
E-mail: writingtimespub@gmail.com.

Writing Wild & Crazy *Imprint of* **Shakalot High Entertainment**

Writing-Right, *(978-0-9772196)* 27 Somerset Dr., Holbrook, NY 11741 USA
E-mail: lori@writing-right.org.

Written and Red, LLC *See* **Baxter The Dog Bks.**

Written & Spoken, *(978-1-7327212)* 7506 Blue Cedar Pl., Chesterfield, VA 23832 USA Tel 301-885-8309
E-mail: longcharlesm@gmail.com.

Written By Clark, Publishing, *(978-0-9795102)* Orders Addr.: P.O. Box 874023, Vancouver, WA 98687 USA Tel 323-447-9676
E-mail: jthomasclark@gmail.com; info@writtenbyclark.com
Web site: http://www.writtenbyclark.com
Dist(s): **Ingram Content Group.**

Written By Jess Publications *See* **Vample, Jessyca Publishing**

Written Expressions Enterprise, Inc., *(978-0-9728674)* 2276 Griffin Way, Suite 105-161, Corona, CA 92879 USA Tel 951-371-0160.

Written Images, Inc., *(978-0-9705721)* 1300 E. Lafayette, Suite 1104, Detroit, MI 48207 USA (SAN 253-7591) Tel 248-356-8310; Fax: 248-356-8311 Do not confuse with Written Image, The in Lancaster, NY
E-mail: writtenimages@aol.com
Web site: http://www.adiaryofjoseph.com.

Written in Black Publishing *See* **WordPlay Multimedia, LLC**

Written World Communications, *(978-0-9829377; 978-1-938679)* Orders Addr.: 4725 Splendid Cir. S., Colorado Springs, CO 80917 USA (SAN 859-9696) Tel 719-947-2181
E-mail: kristinepratt@gmail.com
Web site: http://www.writtenworldcommunications.com/.

WS Publishing, *(978-0-9639654; 978-1-887169; 978-1-934386; 978-1-936061; 978-1-61351)* 7290 Navajo Rd., Suite 207, San Diego, CA 92119 USA Tel 619-589-1919
E-mail: sarah@weddingsolutions.com; info@wspublishinggroup.com
Web site: http://wspublishinggroup.com
Dist(s): **Ingram Publisher Services**
Two Rivers Distribution.

WSB Publishing, Inc., *(978-1-64268)* 5264 Summerlin Commons Way, Fort Myers, FL 33907 USA Tel 850-971-6053
E-mail: w.bader@novumverlag.com.

Wu Li Turtle Corp., *(978-0-9741176)* 3885 S. Decatur Blvd., Suite 2010, Las Vegas, NV 89103 USA Tel 703-864-3769; Fax: 702-920-8118; Toll Free: 888-381-6864
E-mail: rbraye@wuliturtle.com
Web site: http://www.wuliturtle.com.

Wunderlannd Pr., *(978-0-615-62918-6; 978-0-9893166)* 3141 Elmer St., Sarasota, FL 34231 USA Tel 443-742-7039
E-mail: wunderlanndpress@hotmail.com.

Wunderlich, Jordan, *(978-0-578-44066-8; 978-0-578-44242-6)* 280 Hewlett Gulch Rd., Livermore, CO 80536 USA Tel 360-878-0684
E-mail: jwunder@votegoat.net
Dist(s): **Ingram Content Group.**

Wundermill *See* **WunderMill, Inc.**

WunderMill, Inc., *(978-1-943645; 978-1-943978)* 120A N. Salem St., Apex, NC 27502 USA Tel 919-303-3448; Fax: 919-303-3225; *Imprints:* Cornell Lab Publishing Group, The (CornellLab); Persnickety Press (PersnicketyPr)
E-mail: bsockin@cornelllabpg.com
Web site: www.cornelllabpgstore.com
Dist(s): **Baker & Taylor Publisher Services (BTPS)**
Publishers Group West (PGW).

www.margaretmouse.com publishing co., *(978-0-9761326)* Orders Addr.: 41953 20th St., W., Palmdale, CA 93551-0000 USA Please allow four weeks for delivery. Shipments come direct from printer in China. Invoiced at order. Shipping free for all orders over 5000. Dolls are available as well. Please contact me direct at email Lparnold@verizon.net or call US 661-943-0275 with any questions or concerns or special orders.
E-mail: info@margaretmouse.com
Web site: http://www.margaretmouse.com
Dist(s): **Follett School Solutions.**

www.pmptools.com *See* **Project Management Excellence Ctr., Inc., The**

www.underdogpublishing.com, *(978-0-9754420)* 124 Titleist Cir., Savannah, GA 31419 USA; P.O. Box 638, Tybee Island, GA 31328 Tel 912-596-5532
Web site: http://www.underdogpublishing.com.

Wyatt Hse. Publishing, *(978-0-9882209; 978-0-9896119; 978-0-9915798; 978-0-9977422; 978-1-7326049; 978-1-7345398)* 399 Lakeview Dr. W., Mobile, AL 36695 USA Tel 251-421-1296
E-mail: editor@wyattpublishing.com
Web site: www.wyattpublishing.com.

Wyatt Pr., *(978-0-9718161)* 15005 W. 167th Terr., Olathe, KS 66062 USA Tel 913-768-1917; Fax: 913-768-4307.

Wyatt-MacKenzie Publishing, *(978-0-9673025; 978-1-932279; 978-0-9743832; 978-0-9820518; 978-1-936214; 978-1-939288; 978-1-942545; 978-1-948018)* 15115 Hwy. 36, Deadwood, OR 97430-9700 USA (SAN 990-1191) Tel 541-964-3314; Fax: 541-964-3315
E-mail: info@wymacpublishing.com; nancy@wyattmackenzie.com
Web site: http://www.wymacpublishing.com.

Wycliffe Bible Translators, *(978-0-938978)* P.O. Box 628200, Orlando, FL 32862-8200 USA (SAN 211-5484)
Web site: http://www.wycliffe.org.

Wyer Pearce Press *See* **SangFroid Pr.**

Wyland Galleries *See* **Wyland Worldwide, LLC**

Wyland Worldwide, LLC, *(978-0-9631793; 978-1-884840; 978-1-60586)* 6 Mason, Irvine, CA 92618 USA Tel 949-643-7070; Fax: 949-643-7082
E-mail: valeries@wyland.com
Web site: http://www.wyland.com
Dist(s): **Booklines Hawaii, Ltd.**

Wynden *Imprint of* **Canmore Pr.**

Wyoming Historical & Geological Society, *(978-0-937537)* 49 S. Franklin St., Wilkes-Barre, PA 18701 USA (SAN 281-2061) Tel 717-823-6244; Fax: 717-823-9011
E-mail: lchs@epix.net
Web site: http://www.luzernecountyhistory.com.

Wyson, Dan, *(978-0-9771522)* 375 E. Riverside Dr. No. 201, Saint George, UT 84790 USA Tel 435-229-6714 Toll Free: 877-827-0710.

Wysteria, Limited *See* **Wysteria Publishing**

Wysteria Publishing, *(978-0-9651162; 978-0-9677839; 978-1-932412)* P.O. Box 1250, Bellmore, NY 11710 USA Toll Free Fax: 888-434-7979; Toll Free: 888-997-8300
E-mail: wysteria@wysteria.com
Web site: http://www.wysteria.com.

X, Y, & Me LLC, *(978-0-9755028; 978-0-9773441)* 21409 138th St., Webster, IA 52355-9079 USA
E-mail: customerservice@xyandme.com
Web site: http://www.xyandme.com.

Xanadu Metaphysical *See* **Xanadu New Age Products & Services, LLC**

Xanadu New Age Products & Services, LLC, *(978-0-9759752)* Orders Addr.: 1011 S. Lake St., Neenah, WI 54956 USA; Edit Addr.: 1011 S. Lake St., Neenah, WI 54956 USA
E-mail: parisdrake@parisdrake.com
Web site: http://www.parisdrake.com.

XanMaxBks., *(978-0-692-09280-4; 978-1-7326044)* 8842 Southern Orchard Rd N, DAVIE, FL 33328 USA Tel 954-547-4618
E-mail: chalenar@aol.com
Dist(s): **Ingram Content Group.**

xbks publishing, *(978-0-9626458)* c/o Arturo Watlington Station, P.O. Box 568, Saint Thomas, VI 00804 USA
E-mail: llrush@viaccess.net; mail@xbkspublishing.net
Web site: http://www.xbkspublishing.net.

Xbooks *See* **xbks publishing**

Xeno Bks., *(978-1-939096)* 1335N Lave Ave, Pasadena, CA 91104 USA Tel 818-723-3130
E-mail: kromicus@gmail.com
Dist(s): **Chicago Distribution Ctr.**
Ingram Publisher Services.

Xerces Society, The, *(978-0-9744475)* 4828 SE Hawthorne Blvd., Portland, OR 97215 USA Tel 503-232-6639; Fax: 503-233-6794
E-mail: mdshepherd@xerces.org
Web site: http://www.xerces.org.

Xist Classics *Imprint of* **Xist Publishing**

Xist Publishing, *(978-0-615-49153-0; 978-0-9838428; 978-1-62395; 978-1-68195; 978-1-5324)* 16604 Sonora St., Tustin, CA 92782 USA Tel 949-842-5296; 949-478-2568; P.O. Box 61593, Irvine, CA 92692; *Imprints:* Xist Classics (XistClassics)
E-mail: calee@xistpublishing.com; info@xistpublishing.com
Web site: http://xistpublishing.com
Dist(s): **Children's Plus, Inc.**
Follett School Solutions
Ingram Publisher Services
Mackin Educational Resources.

Xlibris, 1663 Liberty Dr., Bloomington, IN 47403 USA Tel 888-795-4274
E-mail: Johnnyline.Jagdon@xlibris.com
Web site: http://www2.xlibris.com/.

Xlibris Corporation *See* **Xlibris Corp.**

Xlibris Corp., *(978-0-7388; 978-0-9663501; 978-1-4010; 978-1-4134; 978-1-59926; 978-1-4257; 978-1-4363; 978-1-4415; 978-1-4500; 978-1-4535; 978-1-4568; 978-1-4628; 978-1-4653; 978-1-4691; 978-1-4771; 978-1-4797; 978-1-4836; 978-1-4931; 978-1-4990; 978-1-5035;-1-5144; 978-1-5245; 978-1-4990-9726-9; 978-1-4990-9725-2; 978-1-4990-9724-5; 978-1-5434; 978-1-9845; 978-1-7960; 978-1-6641) Orders Addr.: 1663 S. Liberty Dr. Suite 200, Bloomington, IN 47403 USA (SAN 299-5522) Tel 812-334-5223; Fax: 812-334-5223; Toll Free: 888-795-4274*
E-mail: info@xlibris.com
Web site: http://www2.xlibris.com
Dist(s): **Author Solutions, Inc.**
Baker & Taylor Publisher Services (BTPS)
CreateSpace Independent Publishing Platform
International Pubns. Service
Lulu Pr., Inc.
Smashwords
TextStream.

Xophix, *(978-0-9754173)* P.O. Box 12081, Scottsdale, AZ 85267 USA Fax: 586-461-1712
E-mail: books@xophix.com
Web site: http://www.xophix.com.

X-treme Reviews *Imprint of* **N&N Publishing Co., Inc.**

Y Linh, *(978-0-9746135)* 6524 San Felipe, No. 110, Houston, TX 77057 USA Tel 713-271-4222
E-mail: ylinhdo@hotmail.com.

Y Lolfa (GBR) *(978-0-86243; 978-0-904864; 978-0-9500178; 978-0-9555272; 978-1-84771; 978-0-9567031; 978-0-9560125; 978-1-78461) Dist. by* **Casemate Pubs.**

Y Lolfa (GBR) *(978-0-86243; 978-0-904864; 978-0-9500178; 978-0-9555272; 978-1-84771; 978-0-9567031; 978-0-9560125; 978-1-78461) Dist. by* **Dufour.**

YA Angst *Imprint of* **Norilana Bks.**

YA Bks., *(978-0-615-72187-3; 978-0-615-79766-3; 978-0-9899934)* 211 Oxford St., Martin, TN 38237 USA Tel 7315875993
Web site: merrybrown.com
Dist(s): **CreateSpace Independent Publishing Platform.**

Yabitoon Bks., *(978-0-578-05342-4)* 1679 Bluffhill Dr., Monterey Park, CA 91754 USA.

Yacos Pubns., *(978-0-9653734)* Orders Addr.: 90-20 169th St., Apt. 4D, Jamaica, NY 11432 USA Tel 718-523-8911 (phone/fax)
E-mail: Drltgrant@yahoo.com
Web site: http://www.yacos.org.

Yad Vashem Pubns. (ISR) *(978-965-308) Dist. by* **Coronet Bks.**

Yadda Yadda Pr., *(978-0-9791387)* 1748 Donwell Dr., South Euclid, OH 44121-3734 USA
E-mail: williamecook@gmail.com
Web site: http://www.yaddayaddapress.com.

Yadeeda.com, *(978-0-9747122)* P.O. Box 38642, Colorado Springs, CO 80937 USA Tel 719-520-5125
E-mail: yadeeda@hotmail.com
Web site: http://www.yadeeda.com.

YALDAH Media, Incorporated *See* **Jewish Girls Unite**

†**Yale Univ. Pr.,** *(978-0-300)* Orders Addr.: c/o Triliteral LLC, 100 Maple Ridge Dr., Cumberland, RI 02864 USA Tel 401-531-2800; Fax: 401-531-2801; Toll Free Fax: 800-406-9145; Toll Free: 800-405-1619; Edit Addr.: 302 Temple St., New Haven, CT 06511 USA (SAN 203-2740) Tel 203-432-0960; Fax: 203-432-0948
E-mail: yupmkt@yale.edu
Web site: http://www.yale.edu/yup/; http://www.yale.edu/yup/index.html
Dist(s): **Casemate Academic**
Cheng & Tsui Co.
De Gruyter, Inc.
Ebsco Publishing
ISD
MyiLibrary
Open Road Integrated Media, Inc.
TriLiteral, LLC
Wiley, John & Sons, Inc.
Yale Univ., Far Eastern Pubns.
ebrary, Inc.; *CIP.*

Yali Bks. *Imprint of* **Yali Publishing LLC**

Yali Books *See* **Yali Publishing LLC**

Yali Publishing LLC, *(978-0-9890615; 978-1-949528)* 43 Longwood Dr, Clifton Park, NY 12065 USA; *Imprints:* Yali Books (MYID_Z_YALI BK)
E-mail: editors@yalibooks.com; sales@yalibooks.com
Web site: www.yalibooks.com.

Yam Hill Publishing, *(978-0-692-50620-2; 978-0-692-83700-9; 978-0-692-84230-0)* 2926 NE Redwood Dr., McMinnville, OR 97128 USA Tel 503-857-5355
Web site: www.jim-gullo.com
Dist(s): **CreateSpace Independent Publishing Platform.**

Yana's Kitchen, *(978-0-9670982)* 5256 Pizzo Ranch Rd., La Canada, CA 91011 USA Tel 818-790-8381 (phone/fax)
E-mail: yana119@yahoo.com
Web site: http://yanasplace.com.

Yang, Jennifer, *(978-0-578-06384-3; 978-0-578-09356-7; 978-0-578-12358-5; 978-0-578-14107-7)* P.O. Box 22204, San Francisco, CA 94122 USA
E-mail: jenniyang@aol.com
Dist(s): **Lulu Pr., Inc.**

Yankee Cowboy, *(978-0-9708530; 978-0-9836149)* P.O. Box 123, Keller, TX 76244 USA Tel 800-557-8166; Toll Free: 800-557-8166
E-mail: publisher@yankeecowboy.com
Web site: http://www.amonplay.com; http://www.watchdognation.com; http://www.davelieber.org.

Yankee Publishing, Inc., *(978-0-89909; 978-1-57198)* Orders Addr.: P.O. Box 520, Dublin, NH 03444 USA Tel 603-563-8111; Fax: 603-563-8252; Edit Addr.: Main St., Dublin, NH 03444 USA; *Imprints:* Old Farmer's Almanac (OldFarmers) Do not confuse with Yankee Publishing, Saint Petersburg, FL
E-mail: almanac@yankeepub.com
Web site: http://www.almanac.com
Dist(s): **Houghton Mifflin Harcourt Publishing Co.**
Houghton Mifflin Harcourt Trade & Reference Pubs.
Hachette Bk. Group
MyiLibrary.

Yarbrough Hse. Publishing, *(978-0-9970132; 978-0-9995800)* 3596 Greensport Rd., Ashville, AL 35953 USA Tel 205-594-5338
E-mail: elizabethl.sorrell@gmail.com
Web site: www.elizabethleesorrell.com.

Yard Dog Pr., *(978-1-893687; 978-0-9824704; 978-1-937105; 978-1-945941)* 710 W. Redbud Ln., Alma, AR 72921 USA Tel 479-632-4693
Web site: http://www.yarddogpress.com
Dist(s): **Smashwords.**

Yari Publishing, *(978-0-578-06838-1)* P.O. Box 142624, Austin, TX 78714-2624 USA.

Yaroslavskaya, Lyudmila, *(978-0-9791248)* 600 W. Diversey Parkaway, Rm. 1410, Chicago, IL 60614 USA.

Yarrow Pr., *(978-0-9741562)* Orders Addr.: P.O. Box 665, Rainelle, WV 25962 USA Tel 304-438-1040 Do not confuse with Yarrow Press in Pelham, NY
E-mail: kate@yarrowpress.com
Web site: http://www.yarrowpress.com.

Yasram Global Industries, LLC, *(978-0-692-36502-1; 978-0-692-56482-0; 978-0-692-79807-2)* 2019 Fox Hill Glenn, Bldg. 18, Apt. 12, Grand Blanc, MI 48439 USA Tel 810-610-1040; Fax: 810-780-4268
Web site: www.keiraandme.info
Dist(s): **CreateSpace Independent Publishing Platform.**

YAV, *(978-0-9790221; 978-1-937449)* Orders Addr.: 1950 Hendersonville Rd. No. 243, Skyland, NC 28776 USA
E-mail: books@yav.com
Web site: http://InterestingWriting.com; http://ScienceOfWriting.com; http://YAVpublications.com.

Yawn Publishing LLC *Imprint of* **Yawn's Bks. & More, Inc.**

Yawn's Bks. & More, Inc., *(978-0-9818673; 978-0-9830190; 978-1-936815; 978-1-940395; 978-1-943529; 978-1-947773)* 2555 Marietta Hwy. Suite 103, Canton, GA 30114 USA (SAN 856-7476) Tel 678-880-1922; Fax: 678-880-1923; *Imprints:* Yawn Publishing LLC (MYID_Y_YAWN PU)
E-mail: fyawn@yawnsbooks.com
Web site: http://www.yawnspublishing.com.

Yay Learner LLC, *(978-0-578-40537-7)* 42993 Lago Stella Pl., Ashburn, VA 20148-7186 USA Tel 571-643-0833
E-mail: yaylearner@gmail.com
Dist(s): **Ingram Content Group.**

YBK Pubs., Inc., *(978-0-9703923; 978-0-9764359; 978-0-9790972; 978-0-9800508; 978-0-9824012; 978-1-936411)* 39 Crosby St. Apt. 2N, New York, NY 10013-3254 USA
E-mail: obarz@ybkpublishers.com
Web site: http://www.ybkpublishers.com.

Ye Hedge Schl., *(978-0-9723239; 978-0-9825521)* Orders Addr.: 24934 478 Ave., Garretson, SD 57030 USA
E-mail: mod61047@alliancecom.net
Web site: http://www.hedgeschool.com.

Ye Olde Font Shoppe, *(978-1-889289)* Orders Addr.: P.O. Box 8328, New Haven, CT 06708 USA Tel 203-575-9385; Edit Addr.: 35 Ferndale, Waterbury, CT 06708 USA Tel 860-870-9741
E-mail: varivas@yahoo.com
Web site: http://www.yeolde.org.

Yearling *Imprint of* **Random Hse. Children's Bks.**

Yehuda, Ben Pr., *(978-0-9769862; 978-0-9789980; 978-1-934730; 978-1-953829)* 122 Ayers Ct. No. 1B, Teaneck, NJ 07666 USA Tel 201-833-5145; Fax: 201-917-1278
E-mail: yudel@benyehudapress.com
Web site: http://www.BenYehudaPress.com.

Yellow Brick Road Publishing, *(978-0-615-24159-3)* 35 Fiske St., No. 1, Waltham, MA 02451 USA.

Yellow Bricks & Rosie Lips, *(978-0-578-66480-4; 978-0-578-66793-5)* 70 Silverwood Dr. 0, NEWPORT NEWS, VA 23608 USA Tel 7572872938
E-mail: gilliamfamily5@live.com.

Yellow City Publishing, *(978-0-9991810; 978-1-7336241; 978-1-7354113)* 109 Wild Plum, Amarillo, TX 79118 USA Tel 806-622-9093
E-mail: vickischoen@outlook.com
Web site: vickischoen.com.

Yellow Daffodil Pr., *(978-0-9824943)* 17939 Chatsworth St., No. 241, Granada Hills, CA 91344 USA
E-mail: mdesannoy@gmail.com.

Yellow Hse. Pr., *(978-0-692-99794-9)* 4223 20th Ave S, Minneapolis, MN 55407 USA Tel 435-513-0057
E-mail: sarahholdenart@gmail.com
Dist(s): **CreateSpace Independent Publishing Platform.**

Yellow Jacket *Imprint of* **Bonnier Publishing USA**

Yellow Sun Bks., *(978-0-692-18165-2; 978-1-7327606)* 2919 S 93RD St., WEST ALLIS, WI 53227 USA Tel 414-232-9871
E-mail: yellowsunbooks@gmail.com
Web site: YellowSunBooks.com.

Yellowstone Association for Natural Science, History & Education, Incorporated *See* **Yellowstone Forever**

Yellowstone Forever, *(978-0-934948)* P.O. Box 117, Yellowstone National Park, WY 82190 USA (SAN 214-4921) Tel 406-848-2454; Fax: 406-848-2453
E-mail: dcollins@yellowstone.org
Web site: http://www.YellowstoneAssociation.org
Dist(s): **Outskirts Pr., Inc.**

Yen Pr. *Imprint of* **Yen Pr. LLC**

Yen Pr. *Imprint of* **Orbit**

Yen Press *See* **Yen Pr. LLC**

Yen Pr. LLC, *(978-0-7595; 978-89-527; 978-1-9753)* Div. of Hachette Book Group, 1290 Avenue of the Americas, New York, NY 10104 USA; *Imprints:* Yen Press (YenOr)
E-mail: customer.service@hbgusa
Web site: http://www.yenpress.com
Dist(s): **Children's Plus, Inc.**
Diamond Comic Distributors, Inc.
Hachette Bk. Group
MyiLibrary.

Yeoman Hse., *(978-0-9754676; 978-0-9822659; 978-0-9852537)* 10 Old Bulgarmarsh Rd., Tiverton, RI 02878 USA Tel 401-816-0061
E-mail: yeomanhouse@cox.net
Dist(s): **Ingram Content Group.**

YES - Your Emergency Safety, *(978-0-9740670)* 1302 W. Adams Ave., Saint Louis, MO 63122 USA Tel 314-822-8895; Fax: 775-458-7717
E-mail: info@youremergencysafety.org
Web site: http://www.youremergencysafety.org.

Yesterday's Classics, *(978-1-59915; 978-1-63334)* Orders Addr.: P.O. Box 3418, Chapel Hill, NC 27515 USA Tel 919-967-3119; Toll Free: 866-497-3729 (phone/fax); Edit Addr.: 1705 Audubon Rd., Chapel Hill, NC 27514 USA
Web site: http://www.yesterdaysclassics.com.

Yestermorrow, Inc., *(978-1-56723)* Orders Addr.: P.O. Box 700, Princess Anne, MD 21853 USA.

Yewtree Pr. LLC, *(978-1-933029)* P.O. Box 110 671, Brooklyn, NY 11211 USA Toll Free: 800-939-7404
E-mail: info@yewtreepress.com
Web site: http://www.yewtreepress.com.

Yhabbut Publishing, *(978-0-9724292)* Orders Addr.: P.O. Box 23032, Seattle, WA 981 USA; Edit Addr.: 2111 15th Ave., S., Suite A, Seattle, WA 98144-4271 USA
E-mail: benthoven@qwest.net
Web site: http://www.1stbooks.com/bookview/20054.

Y-IREAD Publishing, *(978-0-9728549)* Orders Addr.: P.O. Box 33248, Indianapolis, IN 46203 USA Tel 317-294-3423
E-mail: kenyawash@sbcglobal.net.

Yisrael, Sean Publishing Co., *(978-0-9772424)* 11769 Kenn Rd., Cincinnati, OH 45240 USA Tel 513-266-1158
E-mail: syisrael@dps.k12.oh.us.

YNR Media L.L.C., *(978-0-9753262)* 338 Streeter Dr., McCook Lake, SD 57049 USA Tel 310-422-1662.

Yo Puedo Publishing, *(978-0-9714533)* P.O. Box 940895, Houston, TX 77094 USA (SAN 254-3729) Tel 281-496-2015; 866-YO-PUEDO; Fax: 281-558-3773
E-mail: kathryn@yopuedo.com
Web site: http://www.yopuedo.com.

Yofi Bk. Publishing, Inc., *(978-1-931387; 978-1-60046; 978-1-7351868)* 199 Lee Ave. Unit #397, Brooklyn, NY 11211 USA Tel 718-694-9040; Fax: 718-694-9062
E-mail: yofi@yeshivanet.com.

Yoga Life *See* **Love Your Life**

Yoganathan, Anila, *(978-1-7334015)* 3555 Castleridge Dr., Tucker, GA 30084 USA Tel 404-989-5852
E-mail: anilayoganathan@gmail.com
Dist(s): **Ingram Content Group.**

Yogasaurus, *(978-0-9831418)* 137 Dewey Ave., Pittsfield, MA 01201 USA Tel 413-499-1350
E-mail: kenduncanduncan@yahoo.com.

Yoknapatawpha Pr., *(978-0-916242)* P.O. Box 248, Oxford, MS 38655 USA (SAN 213-7593) Tel 601-234-0909 (phone/fax)
E-mail: faulkner@watervalley.net
Web site: http://www.yoknapatawphapress.com.

YOLT Publishing, *(978-0-9982931)* 13518 L St., Omaha, NE 68137 USA Tel 402-884-5995
E-mail: yolt@conciergemarketing.com.

yomitobi, *(978-0-9799470)* 403 Knight Dr., Apt 9, Statesboro, GA 30458 USA
E-mail: yoko_6@hotmail.com
Web site: http://www.yomitobi.com.

Yonay, Shahar, *(978-0-927580; 978-0-9616783)* 126 Dover St., Brooklyn, NY 11235 USA (SAN 661-0544) Tel 718-615-0027.

Yoon-il Auh/Intrepid Pixels, *(978-1-882858)* 820 West End Ave., No. 9E, New York, NY 10025 USA Tel 212-662-6891.

Yoot Pr., *(978-0-9764611)* 17-47 Chandler Dr., Fair Lawn, NJ 07410 USA
Web site: http://www.yootpress.com.

York House Pr., Ltd., *(978-0-9791956; 978-0-9855508)* 1266 E. Main St, suite 700R,, Stamford, CT 06902 USA Tel 203-539-6180; Fax: 914-764-5159
E-mail: pholt@yorkhousepress.com
Dist(s): **Ingram Content Group.**

Yorkshire Publishing Group, *(978-0-88144; 978-1-936750; 978-0-9883786; 978-0-9889281; 978-0-9896518; 978-1-942451; 978-1-946977; 978-1-947247; 978-1-947491; 978-1-947825; 978-1-948282; 978-1-949231; 978-1-950034)* Orders Addr.: 9731 E. 54th St., Tulsa, OK 74147 USA (SAN 260-0285) Tel 918-394-2665; *Imprints:* Thorncrown Publishing (Thorncrown); Total Publishing & Media (Total Pubng)
E-mail: todd.rutherford@yorkshirepublishing.com
Web site: http://www.yorkshirepublishing.com
Dist(s): **BookBaby**
INscribe Digital.

Yorkville Pr., *(978-0-9729427; 978-0-9767442)* Orders Addr.: 1202 Lexington Ave., No. 315, New York, NY 10028 USA (SAN 255-3139) Tel 212-650-9154; Fax: 212-650-9157; 1202 Lexington Ave. # 315, New York, NY 10028 Tel 212-650-9154
E-mail: editors@yorkvillepress.com
Web site: http://www.yorkvillepress.com.

Yoroson Publishing *See* **Young-Robinson, Christine**

Yosemite Association *See* **Yosemite Conservancy**

Yosemite Conservancy, *(978-0-939666; 978-1-930238; 978-1-951179)* Orders Addr.: P.O. Box 230, El Portal, CA 95318 USA (SAN 662-197X) Tel 209-379-2317; Edit Addr.: 5020 El Portal Rd., El Portal, CA 95318 USA
E-mail: nicolegeiger1@gmail.com; jedelbrock@yosemiteconservancy.org; kcoit@yosemiteconservancy.org
Web site: http://www.yosemiteconservancy.org
Dist(s): **MyiLibrary**
Publishers Group West (PGW)
Sunbelt Pubns., Inc.

Yosoy Publishing, *(978-0-9763503)* 4141 Linden Ave, Long Beach, CA 90807 USA Tel 714-271-7667; Fax: 562-989-2031
E-mail: goodbooks@yeomanhouse.com
Web site: http://www.ginaspoems.com; http://www.yosoypublishing.com.

Yost-Haynes, Melissa, *(978-0-9760909)* RR1, 115C, Ravenswood, WV 26164 USA.

You Are Here Bks. *Imprint of* **Bushel & Peck Bks.**

You Can Do It! Productions, *(978-0-9744306)* 106 Paradise Rd., Havana, FL 32333-4236 USA
E-mail: infinipede@juno.com
Web site: http://www.infinipede.com.

You Can Do It! ART Publications *See* **Sunrise Mountain Bks.**

You Come Too Publishing, *(978-0-9816836)* 3138 NW Colonial Dr., Bend, OR 97701 USA Tel 541-317-4912 (phone/fax)
E-mail: imkehoe@msn.com
Web site: http://youcometoo.com
Dist(s): **Smashwords.**

You Publishing Group, *(978-0-9764472)* 2500 S. Lamar Blvd., Austin, TX 78704 USA.

Young Advent Pilgrim's Bookshelf *See* **Barnes Printing**

Young, Beth, *(978-0-9760180)* 124 Chestnut St. Apt. 201, Englewood, OH 45322-1410 USA
E-mail: 369beth@bellsouth.net
Web site: http://www.saintlukespress.com.

Young Createers, *(978-0-9980893)* 4901 E. Kelton Ln, Scottsdale, AZ 85254 USA Tel 480-228-3988
E-mail: lisabenger@hotmail.com
Web site: youngcreateers.com.

Young, Estrell III, *(978-0-692-90306-3; 978-0-692-91185-3)* 2764 Pkwy. Cove, LITHONIA, GA 30058 USA Tel 678-485-8864
E-mail: just.estrell@gmail.com
Dist(s): **Ingram Content Group.**

Young Europe Bks. *Imprint of* **New Europe Bks.**

Young of Heart Publishing, *(978-0-9995608; 978-1-950421)* P.O. Box 2274, McKinleyville, CA 95519 USA Tel 707-839-7061
E-mail: zjavanee@suddenlink.net.

Young Patronesses of the Opera, The, *(978-0-9785364; 978-0-9795725; 978-0-9993895)* P.O. Box 3471616, Miami, FL 33234-7616 USA Tel 305-665-3470; Fax: 305-667-9265
E-mail: education@YPO-Miami.org
Web site: www.ypo-miami.org.

Young Reader's Library *Imprint of* **RNWC Media, LLC**

Young Readers Publications, *(978-0-9789525)* 47 W. Schuyler St., Oswego, NY 13126 USA
E-mail: guntherphotography@hotmail.com
Web site: http://jguntherphotography.com.

Young Scholars Pr., *(978-0-9787138)* 354 1/2 Calle Loma Norte, Santa Fe, NM 87501 USA Tel 505-989-7116; Fax: 505-820-2367
E-mail: MsAnnett1@aol.com
Web site: http://oneworldmanypeople.com.

Young Women Books *See* **Harper Kids Hse.**

Young Women Programming *Imprint of* **Harper Kids Hse.**

Young Writer's Contest Foundation *See* **Miracle Pr.**

Youngheart Music, *(978-0-945267; 978-1-57471)* Affil. of Creative Teaching Pr., Orders Addr.: P.O. Box 2723, Huntington, CA 92647-0723 USA Tel 714-895-5047; Fax: 714-895-5087; Toll Free Fax: 800-229-9929; Toll Free: 800-444-4287; Edit Addr.: 15342 Graham St., Huntington Beach, CA 92649-1111 USA
E-mail: webmaster@creativeteaching.com; rebecca.cleland@creativeteaching.com
Web site: http://www.youngheartmusic.com; http://www.creativeteaching.com
Dist(s): **Creative Teaching Pr., Inc.**
Follett School Solutions
Rounder Kids Music Distribution.

Youngheart Records *See* **Youngheart Music**

Young-Robinson, Christine, *(978-0-9706985)* 1805 Clemson Road, 291333, Columbia, SC 29229 USA
E-mail: miraclewriter4u@aol.com
Web site: http://www.christineyoungrobinson.com.

Youngs, Bettie Bks., *(978-0-9843081; 978-1-936332; 978-0-9836045; 978-0-9882848; 978-1-940784)* Div. of Bettie Youngs Book Publishers, Box 2810 Suite C, Del Mar, CA 92014 USA Tel 702-467-0055; *Imprints:* Kendahl House Press (KendahlHse); Teen Town Press (Teen Town)
E-mail: Bettie@BettieYoungs.com
Web site: http://www.BettieYoungsBooks.com
Dist(s): **Brodart Co.**
Coutts Information Services
Independently Published
Ingram Content Group
Quality Bks., Inc.
SCB Distributors
Smashwords.

Youngs, C. R., *(978-0-9760451)* 11687 Sugar Creek Ave., Mount Carmel, IL 62863 USA
E-mail: ronyoungs@davidbook.com
Web site: http://www.davidbook.com/.

Your Culture Gifts, *(978-0-9797637)* P.O. Box 1245, Ellicott City, MD 21041 USA (SAN 854-3208) Tel 410-461-5799
E-mail: info@yourculturegifts.com
Web site: http://www.yourculturegifts.com.

Your Story Hour Recordings, P.O. Box 511, Medina, OH 44258 USA Tel 216-725-5767; 717 St. Jospeh Dr. #254, Saint Joseph, MI 49085 Tel 269-471-3701
Web site: http://www.yourstoryhour.org.

You're On!, Inc., *(978-0-9760280)* P.O. Box 101071, Fort Worth, TX 76185 USA.

Youth Communication - New York Center, *(978-0-9661256; 978-1-933939; 978-1-935552; 978-1-938970)* 244 W. 27th St., 2nd Flr., New York, NY 10001 USA Tel 212-279-0708 ext. 115; Fax: 212-279-8856
E-mail: khefner@youthcomm.org
Web site: http://www.youthcomm.org
Dist(s): **Follett School Solutions.**

Youth Cultural Publishing Co. (CHN) *(978-957-530; 978-957-574) Dist. by* **Chinasprout.**

Youth Development & Research Fund, *(978-0-9659130)* P.O. Box 2188, Germantown, MD 20875-2188 USA
E-mail: ed@ydrf.com
Web site: http://www.ydrf.com.

Youth Inkwell Publishing, *(978-0-9773451)* 155 S. El Molino Ave., Suite 102, Paadena, CA 91101 USA Tel 626-449-6884; Fax: 626-449-6885
E-mail: info@youthinkwell.org
Web site: http://youthinkwell.org; http://www.youthinkwell.org.

Youth Popular Culture Institute, Inc., *(978-1-887191)* 8906 Fox Park Rd., Clinton, MD 20735 USA Tel 301-877-1525.

Youth Quest Institute, *(978-0-9748994)* 5515 Azalea Trail Ln., Sugar Land, TX 77479 USA
Web site: http://youthquestinstitute.com; http://getagripbooks.com.

Youthleadership.com, *(978-0-9677981)* 5593 Golf Course Dr., Morrison, CO 80465 USA Tel 303-358-1563; Fax: 303-393-9066
E-mail: support@youthleadership.com; mariam@youthleadership.com
Web site: http://www.youthleadership.com.

Youthlight, Inc., *(978-1-889636; 978-1-59850)* Orders Addr.: P.O. Box 115, Chapin, SC 29036 USA (SAN 256-6400) Tel 803-345-1070; Fax: 803-345-0888; Toll Free: 800-209-9774; Edit Addr.: 105 Fairway Pond Dr., Chapin, SC 29036 USA
E-mail: yl@sc.rr.com; yl@youthlightbooks.com
Web site: http://www.youthlight.com; http://www.youthlightbooks.com.

YouthPlays, *(978-1-62088; 978-1-62088-584-0)* 7125 De Longpre Ave. No. 209, Los Angeles, CA 90046 USA Tel 424-703-5315
E-mail: info@youthplays.com
Web site: http://www.youthplays.com.

Ysanti *See* **Lion's Crest Pr.**

Yucca Publishing *Imprint of* **Skyhorse Publishing Co., Inc.**

Yudcovitch, Lorne, *(978-0-9749781)* 6905 S.W. 7th Ave., Portland, OR 97219 USA Tel 503-293-6923
E-mail: yudcovil@pacificu.edu.

Yumcha Studios LLC, *(978-0-9881899)* 33-59 Farrington St., 2nd Flr., Flushing, NY 11354 USA Tel 917-332-8931; Fax: 917-332-8931
E-mail: yenyen@dimsumwarriors.com; colin@dimsumwarriors.com
Web site: www.dimsumwarriors.com
Dist(s): **Diamond Comic Distributors, Inc.**
Diamond Bk. Distributors.

Yunka Publishing, *(978-0-9989640; 978-1-7324236)* 18923 Camillo Ct, Houston, TX 77094 USA Tel 832-725-8787
E-mail: karayaka@msn.com.

YWAM Publishing, *(978-0-927545; 978-0-9615534; 978-1-57658; 978-1-64836)* Div. of Youth With A Mission International, P.O. Box 55787, Seattle, WA 98155 USA (SAN 248-4021)
E-mail: customerservice@ywampublishing.com
Web site: http://www.ywampublishing.com
Dist(s): **christianaudio.**

ZEM Pr., *(978-0-9634168)* 8220 Stone Trail Dr., Bethesda, MD 20817-4556 USA Tel 301-365-4585; Fax: 301-365-4586
E-mail: zem@wbh.com
Web site: http://www.wb4.com.

Z Health Bks. *Imprint of* **New Win Publishing**

Z Pr., *(978-0-615-14380-4)* P.O. Box 6556, Woodland Hills, CA 91365 USA Tel 717-337-9968
E-mail: amy@amyleecoy.com
Dist(s): **Lulu Pr., Inc.**

Z2 Comics, *(978-1-940878)* 527 Madison Ave., NEW YORK, NY 10022 USA Tel 718-440-6576
E-mail: zipcomic@gmail.com
Web site: z2comics.com
Dist(s): **Diamond Comic Distributors, Inc.**
Diamond Bk. Distributors
Simon & Schuster, Inc.

Zaccheus Entertainment Co., *(978-0-692-53734-3; 978-0-9969964; 978-0-9981972; 978-0-9985191; 978-0-9994571; 978-0-9997854)* 136 Morrison Ave., Mt. Prospect, IL 60056 USA Tel 847-894-5574
E-mail: chiefcreta@att.net.

Zach Feuer Gallery, *(978-0-9768533)* 530 W 24th St., New York, NY 10011 USA Tel 212-989-7700
E-mail: zach@zachfeuer.com
Web site: http://www.zachfeuer.com
Dist(s): **D.A.P./Distributed Art Pubs.**

Zach, Jacob, *(978-0-692-93865-2)* 18233 Powers Creek Loop Rd NE, Silverton, OR 97381 USA Tel 541-216-0695
E-mail: jacobhzach@gmail.com.

Zachary James Novels, *(978-0-692-18648-0; 978-0-692-18793-7; 978-0-578-58271-9; 978-0-578-60205-9; 978-0-578-76237-1; 978-0-578-77572-2)* PO BOX 35 200 Rte. 94, BLAIRSTOWN, NJ 07825 USA Tel 9083627751
E-mail: zachjb2000@yahoo.com
Dist(s): **Ingram Content Group.**

Zachmeyer, Mary L., *(978-0-9646864)* 1008 County Road 105., Columbus, TX 78934-1606 USA.

Zack Zombie Publishing *Imprint of* **Herobrine Publishing**

Zadok Supply, LLC, *(978-0-9964727)* 1540 Keller Pkwy. Suite 108 No. 145, keller, TX 76248 USA Tel 800-582-5140; Fax: 800-582-7956
E-mail: info@zadoksupply.com
Web site: www.zadokpublishing.com.

Zadunajsky, Donna M., *(978-0-9842397; 978-1-938037)* Orders Addr.: 17344 S. Parker Rd., Homer Glen, IL 60491 USA (SAN 858-821X) Tel 708-548-9829
E-mail: dmzadunajsky@gmail.com; 72allshookup@gmail.com
Web site: http://www.donnazadunajskymalacina.blogspot.com; http://www.donnazadunajsky.com
Dist(s): **BookBaby**
MyiLibrary
ebrary, Inc.

Zafa Publishing, *(978-0-692-41055-4; 978-0-9967422)* 3918 Glendenning Rd., Downers Grove, IL 60515 USA Tel 630-964-1561
E-mail: mmludwig1@comcast.net.

Zagat Survey, *(978-0-943421; 978-0-9612574; 978-1-57006; 978-1-60478)* 4 Columbus Cir., New York, NY 10019 USA (SAN 289-4777) Tel 212-977-6000; Fax: 212-765-9438; Toll Free: 866-999-0991
E-mail: tradesales@justzagat.com; theinz@zagat.com
Web site: http://www.zagat.com
Dist(s): **Ingram Publisher Services**
Two Rivers Distribution.

Zagorski, Steve, *(978-0-578-05364-6)* Orders Addr.: P.O. Box 50196, Austin, TX 78763 USA Tel 517-789-3259; Edit Addr.: 1009 W. 6th St., Suite 206, Austin, TX 78703 USA
E-mail: swzagorski@gmail.com.

Zaharko, Mary, *(978-0-692-59295-3)* 70 Mohawk Dr., West Hartford, CT 06117 USA Tel 860-463-0700
E-mail: jmintonq@comcast.net.

Zahir Publishing, *(978-0-9741311; 978-0-9786041; 978-0-9831090)* 315 S. Coast Hwy. 101, Suite U8, Encinitas, CA 92024 USA
Web site: http://www.zahirtales.com.

Zahrob Publishing Co., *(978-0-9753641)* Orders Addr.: P.O. Box 5825, Rochester, MN 55903-5825 USA; Edit Addr.: 1445 Valley High Dr., NW, Rochester, MN 55903-5825 USA.

Zaloli, LLC, *(978-0-9857047; 978-0-9897380)* 4065 Sleeping Indian Ln., Colorado Springs, CO 80904 USA Tel 719-685-6505
E-mail: goldflagstudios@gmail.com.

Zander Pubns., *(978-0-578-01907-9; 978-0-578-01908-6; 978-0-578-02012-9; 978-0-578-02076-1; 978-0-578-04264-0; 978-0-578-05322-6; 978-0-578-05695-1; 978-0-9834052)* 2351 Sunset Blvd., Suite 170-433, Rocklin, CA 95765 USA Tel 916-624-1578
E-mail: randall@ips.net; contact@zanderpublications.com
Web site: http://www.zanderpublications.com
Dist(s): **Lulu Pr., Inc.**

zandmsgma Bks., *(978-0-9989583)* 5130 Mayweed Ct, Colorado Springs, CO 80917 USA Tel 719-229-7189
E-mail: rhondaeclark56@gmail.com.

Zaner-Bloser, Inc., *(978-0-7367; 978-0-88085; 978-0-88309; 978-1-4531)* Subs. of Highlights for Children, Orders Addr.: P.O. Box 16764, Columbus, OH 43216-6764 USA (SAN 282-5678) Tel 614-486-0221; Fax: 614-487-2263; Toll Free Fax: 800-992-6087; Toll

Free: 800-421-3018; 1201 Dublin Rd., Columbus, OH 43215-1026
Web site: http://www.zaner-bloser.com/.

Zangadoo Entertainment, *(978-0-9847428)* 14101 19th Dr. SE, Mill Creek, WA 98102 USA Tel 206-234-8123
E-mail: dean@zangadoo.com
Web site: www.zangadoo.com.

Zangadoo LLC *See* **Zangadoo Entertainment**

Zangaro, Brett Michael Biaggio *See* **Writer Stain Publishing**

Zany Angel Projects LLC, *(978-0-9769234)* P.O. Box 1411, New York, NY 10159 USA Tel 212-686-4206.

Zardoz Pr. *Imprint of* **Life Force Bks.**

Zarraonandia, Anne, *(978-0-9741070)* P.O. Box 151435, San Rafael, CA 94915 USA Tel 415-456-4070; Toll Free: 877-892-6974 (phone/fax)
E-mail: annezarra@aol.com
Web site: http://www.cowboyluke.com.

Zarrella, Sharon *See* **Lizzy Anne's Adventures**

Zarriello, Nancy, *(978-0-578-53204-2)* 1266 Ocean Ave., Sea Bright, NJ 07760 USA Tel 732-614-1403
E-mail: nancyzarriello12@gmail.com.

Zarrika, Ltd., *(978-0-9758663; 978-1-934252)* P.O. Box 488, Unionville, PA 19375 USA Fax: 610-486-6501; Toll Free: 888-369-3366
Web site: http://www.zarrika.com.

Zaster Publishing, *(978-0-578-19533-9)* 83 Rosewell Rd., Bedford, NH 03110 USA.

ZC Horses Series of Children's Bks., *(978-0-9721496; 978-0-9791719)* 8 Hokanson Ln., Salmon, ID 83467 USA Tel 208-756-7947
E-mail: zchorses@hotmail.com
Web site: http://www.zchorses.com.

ZCR Pr., *(978-0-9763926)* 4912 Woodman Ave., No. 3, Sherman Oaks, CA 91423 USA (SAN 256-3479) Tel 818-995-3032 (phone/fax)
E-mail: zaldy80@aol.com.

ZE Graphics Inc., *(978-0-692-98225-9; 978-0-692-15431-1; 978-0-692-04205-2; 978-0-578-45948-6; 978-0-578-48184-5; 978-0-578-53757-3; 978-0-578-57939-9)* 125 Radford St. No. 6E, YONKERS, NY 10705 USA Tel 914-457-5446
E-mail: ZEGraphicsinc@gmail.com
Dist(s): **Ingram Content Group.**

Zebra Ginkgo, *(978-0-9891510)* 310 Frieda Ave., Kirkwood, MO 63122 USA Tel 314-292-9452
E-mail: edchen7@zebraginkgo.com
Web site: www.zebraginkgo.com.

Zeezok Publishing *See* **Zeezok Publishing, LLC**

Zeezok Publishing, LLC, *(978-0-9746505; 978-1-933573; 978-1-61006)* P.O. Box 1960, Elyria, OH 44036 USA (SAN 179-4493) Fax: 440-323-9494; Toll Free: 800-749-1681
E-mail: info@zeezok.com
Web site: http://www.zeezok.com.

Zeidman Consulting *See* **Swiss Creek Pubns.**

Zeiger, J. Tod, *(978-1-928672)* 912 Kenilworth Cir., Maryville, TN 37804-5215 USA Tel 423-984-8531.

Zeiger, Jennifer M., *(978-0-692-99474-0; 978-1-7351226)* 7811 S. Blackberry St., Cheney, WA 99004 USA Tel 719-235-8991
E-mail: jennifer.m.zeiger@gmail.com
Dist(s): **Ingram Content Group.**

Zeke & Me Bks., *(978-0-9883042)* 2415 Outlook St., Kalamazoo, MI 49001 USA Tel 269-344-7757
E-mail: sstamm625@gmail.com.

Zellmann Publishing, LLC, *(978-0-9763325)* 420 Springwood Ct., Canton, GA 30115-8287 USA Tel 770-345-7265; Fax: 770-345-7265
E-mail: zellmann@zellmannpublishing.com.

Zelma's Farm, *(978-0-9989774)* 1351 Fulton Rd., E. Corinth, VT 05040 USA Tel 802-439-5126
E-mail: zelmasfarm@gmail.com
Web site: zelmasfarm.com.

Zemek, Alan, *(978-0-9960921)* 1316 LaClair Ave., Pittsburgh, PA 15218 USA Tel 412-508-1491
E-mail: zemeka27@verizon.net.

Zemi Comics, *(978-0-9745825)* SDQ 17, 4440 NW, 73rd Ave., Miami, FL 33166 USA Tel 787-748-4567
E-mail: fans@zemicomics.com
Web site: http://www.zemicomics.com.

Zen Life Bks., *(978-0-578-42420-0; 978-1-7342391)* 782 Trail Ridge Dr., Louisville, CO 80027 USA Tel 209-736-7699
E-mail: alexandermillr@gmail.com
Dist(s): **Independent Pub.**

Zendrera Zariquiey, Editorial (ESP) *(978-84-89675; 978-84-8418)* *Dist. by* **Mariuccia Iaconi Bk Imports.**

Zendrera Zariquiey, Editorial (ESP) *(978-84-89675; 978-84-8418)* *Dist. by* **Lectorum Pubns.**

Zenescope Entertainment, *(978-0-9786874; 978-0-9817550; 978-0-9823630; 978-0-9825826; 978-0-9827507; 978-0-615-40679-4; 978-0-9830404; 978-1-937068; 978-0-9853378; 978-1-939683; 978-1-942275; 978-1-951087)* 433 Caredean Dr Suite C, Horsham, PA 19044 USA (SAN 851-2760); *Imprints*: Silver Dragon Books (SilverDrag)
E-mail: jbrusha@zenscope.com
Web site: http://www.zenescope.com
Dist(s): **Diamond Comic Distributors, Inc.**
Diamond Bk. Distributors.

Zenga Publishing, *(978-0-9765484)* Orders Addr.: P.O. Box 461, Milton, NY 12547 USA
E-mail: mmaniatis@hvc.rr.com
Web site: http://www.agirlscourage.com; http://www.zengapublishing.com.

Zenith Pr. *Imprint of* **Quarto Publishing Group USA**

Zephyr Pr. *Imprint of* **Chicago Review Pr., Inc.**

Zephyr Pr., *(978-0-939010; 978-0-9815521; 978-0-9832970; 978-1-938890)* 50 Kenwood St., No. 2, Brookline, MA 02446 USA (SAN 239-7668) Do not confuse with companies with the same name in New York, NY, Tucson, AZ, Kansas City, MO, Canton, OH
E-mail: editors@zephyrpress.org
Web site: http://www.zephyrpress.org
Dist(s): **Consortium Bk. Sales & Distribution**
MyiLibrary
SPD-Small Pr. Distribution.

Zero To Three Pr., *(978-0-943657; 978-1-934019; 978-1-938558)* Div. of Zero To Three: National Ctr. for Infants, Toddlers & Families, Orders Addr.: P.O. Box 960, Herndon, VA 20172 USA Toll Free: 800-899-4301; Edit Addr.: 1255 23RD St. NW, Suite 350, Washington, DC 20037 USA (SAN 242-5084) Tel 202-638-1144; Fax: 202-638-0851
E-mail: n.guadagno@zerotothree.org; jenniferli@zerotothree.org
Web site: http://www.zerotothree.org.

Zeromayo Studios, LLP, *(978-0-9661985)* Orders Addr.: P.O. Box 417, Haydenville, MA 01039 USA Tel 413-584-9372; Fax: 413-665-2312; Edit Addr.: 16 Market St., Northampton, MA 01060 USA; *Imprints*: Empty Sky (Empty Sky)
E-mail: planetrace@aol.com
Web site: http://www.ninjaturtles.com
Dist(s): **Diamond Comic Distributors, Inc.**

ZeroTo Three: National Center for Instants, Toddlers & Families *See* **Zero To Three Pr.**

Zest Bks. *Imprint of* **Lerner Publishing Group**

Zest Publishing, *(978-0-9758861)* Orders Addr.: P.O. Box 484, Edgar, NE 68935-0484 USA; Edit Addr.: R.R. 1, Edgar, NE 68935-0484 USA Do not confuse with Zest Publishing Company in Southfield, MI.

Zeus Media LLC, *(978-0-9765840)* 12900 Canterbury, Leawood, KS 66209 USA
Web site: http://www.wisdomofzeus.com.

Zeus Sports Florida LLC, *(978-0-9777437)* Orders Addr.: 2312 SE 23rd Rd., Homestead, FL 33035-1900 USA Tel 786-417-9197
E-mail: habbook@msn.com.

ZH, *(978-0-578-41269-6; 978-0-578-62393-1; 978-0-578-73277-0; 978-0-578-77691-0)* 609 Cordova Dept of Dermatology, Davis, CA 95616 USA Tel 555-555-5555
E-mail: spunky1000@aol.com
Dist(s): **Independent Pub.**

JYZ Bks., LLC, *(978-0-9743272; 978-0-9906905)* Orders Addr.: 5816 White Pebble Path, Clarksville, MD 21029 USA (SAN 990-1868) Tel 443-535-2541; Fax: 703-485-2970
E-mail: jianyi.zhang66@gmail.com.

Zhang, Shiyu, *(978-0-692-90983-6)* 888 O'Farrell St APT E509, San Francisco, CA 94109 USA Tel 612-636-7385
E-mail: fishjump_000ya@hotmail.com
Dist(s): **Ingram Content Group.**

Zhera Pubns., *(978-0-9618904)* Orders Addr.: 2605 E. Flora Pl., Denver, CO 80210-6827 USA (SAN 242-231X) Tel 303-753-0384
E-mail: Zhera@msn.com; zhera@msn.com.

Ziert, Paul Assocs., Inc., *(978-0-9666104)* Orders Addr.: P.O. Box 721020, Norman, OK 73070 USA Tel 405-447-9988; Fax: 405-447-5810; Edit Addr.: 3214 Bart Conner Dr., Norman, OK 73072 USA
E-mail: paul@intlgymnast.com; IGDwight@aol.com.

Zig the Pig, *(978-0-9761700)* 815 Poinsettia St., Columbia, SC 29205 USA.

Ziggy Owl Pr., *(978-0-9963747)* 24 Canal St., Medford, MA 02155 USA Tel 781-396-8470
E-mail: johngarp@aol.com.

Ziker, Andrew, *(978-0-9762147)* 1788 E. Indigo St., Gilbert, AZ 85298-3222 USA.

Zilber, Jeremy, *(978-0-9786688)* P.O. Box 5543, Madison, WI 53705 USA
E-mail: jzilber@littledemocrats.net
Web site: http://www.littledemocrats.net.

Zimmerman, W. Frederick *See* **Nimble Bks. LLC**

Zindel Publishing *See* **Graymalkin Media**

Zinka Pr., Inc., *(978-0-9647171)* 1480 Pulaski Ln., Wayne, PA 19087 USA Tel 610-688-2113; Fax: 610-688-0753
E-mail: zinkapress@aol.com
Web site: http://www.zinkapress.com.

Zino Pr. Children's Bks., *(978-1-55933)* Div. of Knowledge Unlimited, Inc., P.O. Box 52, Madison, WI 53701-0052 USA Tel 608-836-6660; Fax: 608-831-1570; Toll Free Fax: 800-618-1570; Toll Free: 800-356-2303
E-mail: madzino@zinopress.com
Web site: http://www.zinopress.com
Dist(s): **Brodart Co.**
Follett School Solutions.

Zion Publishing, *(978-0-9627147; 978-0-9979841; 978-0-9998819; 978-1-7333982; 978-1-7357958)* 1500 Crown Colony Ct., Suite 540, Des Moines, IA 50315 USA Tel 515-282-5940; Toll Free: 800-996-2777 Do not confuse with companies with the same name in Monarch Beach, CA, Vallejo, CA
E-mail: maryenilsen@aol.com
Web site: http://www.zionpublishing.org.

Zion Publishing, *(978-0-9714844)* 17 Harding Ln., Sumiton, AL 35148 USA Tel 205-648-6741
E-mail: driverdm@aol.com.

Zishka Publishing, *(978-1-941691)* 242 B Keyser Ave. PMB 181, Natchitoches, LA 71457 USA Tel 318-228-8614; *Imprints*: Write 'N Learn (Write N Learn)
E-mail: chrism@chrismcmullen.com
Web site: engagenlearn.com.

Zo Publishing, *(978-0-938465)* Orders Addr.: P.O. Box 61335, Honolulu, HI 96839 USA (SAN 660-9864) Tel 808-988-7111; Edit Addr.: 2918 Manoa Rd., Honolulu, HI 96822 USA (SAN 660-9872)
E-mail: dyen@lava.net.

Zoe Life Publishing, *(978-0-9748251; 978-0-9779445; 978-1-934363; 978-1-938807; 978-0-9995405)* P.O. Box 871066, Canton, MI 48187 USA (SAN 256-1735) Tel 734-404-5485; Fax: 734-981-0251; Toll Free: 877-841-3400
E-mail: info@zoelifepub.com
Web site: http://www.zoelifepub.com
Dist(s): **Send The Light Distribution LLC.**

Zolie Zi Empire, *(978-0-692-89897-0; 978-0-692-92967-4)* 200 S. Ryan Dr. #11207, RED OAK, TX 75154 USA Tel 469-892-8816
E-mail: zoliezi@yahoo.com; zoliezi@yahoo.com.

Zonderkidz, *(978-0-310)* Div. of Zondervan, 5300 Patterson Ave., SE, Grand Rapids, MI 49530 USA Tel 1-800-727-3480
E-mail: zprod@zondervan.com
Web site: http://www.zondervan.com
Dist(s): **Children's Plus, Inc.**
Nelson, Thomas Inc.
Zondervan.

†Zondervan, *(978-0-00; 978-0-310; 978-0-937336)* Div. of HarperCollins Christian Publishing, Orders Addr.: c/o Zondervan XNET Ordering Dept., 5249 Corporate Grove, Grand Rapids, MI 49512 USA (SAN 298-9107); Edit Addr.: 5300 Patterson Ave., SE, Grand Rapids, MI 49530 USA (SAN 203-2694) Tel 616-698-6900; Fax: 616-698-3439
Web site: http://www.zondervan.com
Dist(s): **Brilliance Publishing, Inc.**
Children's Plus, Inc.
Ebsco Publishing
Follett School Solutions
HarperCollins Christian Publishing
Send The Light Distribution LLC
Vida Pubs.; *CIP.*

Zondervan bibles *See* **Zondervan Bibles**

Zondervan Bibles, *(978-0-310)* 5300 Patterson Ave., SE, Grand Rapids, MI 49530 USA Tel 800-727-3480
E-mail: zprod@zondervan.com
Web site: http://www.zondervan.com
Dist(s): **Zondervan.**

Zondervan Bks., *(978-0-310)* 5300 Patterson Ave., SE, Grand Rapids, MI 49530 USA Tel 1-800-727-3480
E-mail: zprod@zondervan.com
Web site: http://www.zondervan.com
Dist(s): **HarperCollins Christian Publishing**
Zondervan.

Zondervan Publishing House *See* **Zondervan**

Zonk Galleries *See* **Zonk Galleries and Pubns.**

Zonk Galleries and Pubns., *(978-0-9706537)* 2909 Hansen Rd., Hayward, CA 94541 USA (SAN 254-3443) Tel 510-530-2681
E-mail: davidhoobler@sbcglobal.net
Web site: http://zonktheturtle.com.

Zonneschijn Publishisn, *(978-0-692-10333-3)* 918 Park Ln., Pella, IA 50219 USA Tel 641-780-0714
E-mail: veenstrarosa22@gmail.com.

Zoo Bks. *Imprint of* **National Wildlife Federation**

Zoolook, *(978-0-9656228; 978-0-9830637; 978-0-9883950)* P.O. Box 640806, San Francisco, CA 94164 USA (SAN 254-0398) Tel 415-729-4709
E-mail: ndasilva@zoolook.com
Web site: http://www.zoolook.com; http://www.iriemag.com; http://www.dreadandalive.com; http://www.zoolook.com.

Zoombird Bks., *(978-0-615-32691-7)* Orders Addr.: 2734 Carlsbrook Dr., Oakland, CA 94611 USA Tel 510-530-2737
Web site: http://www.zoombirdbooks.com.

Zoo-phonics, Inc., *(978-0-9617342; 978-1-886441)* Orders Addr.: 20950 Ferretti Rd., Groveland, CA 95321 USA (SAN 663-8589) Tel 209-962-5030; Fax: 209-962-4320; Toll Free: 800-622-8104
E-mail: zoo-info@zoo-phonics.com; shirley@zoo-phonics.com
Web site: http://www.zoo-phonics.com.

Zora, *(978-0-9714039; 978-1-59898)* Orders Addr.: 450 Stedman Pl., Monrovia, CA 91016 USA Tel 626-359-6071
E-mail: emil@zorapubs.com.

Zottola Publishing, Inc., *(978-0-9725880; 978-0-9823907)* Orders Addr.: 4212 Boone Ave. N., New Hope, MN 55428-0001 USA
E-mail: zottolaj@comcast.net
Web site: http://www.zotpub.com.

zReyomi Publishing, *(978-0-9670712)* Div. of Reyomi Global Media Group, Inc., P.O. Box 51928, Durham, NC 27717 USA Tel 919-321-2573; Fax: 919-489-3913
E-mail: drtrevy@me.com
Dist(s): **Bk. Hse., The**
Brodart Co.

Zu Bks., *(978-0-615-15267-7)* 1813 Comet, Altus, OK 73521 USA Tel 580-477-0819
Web site: http://zuopolis.com
Dist(s): **Lulu Pr., Inc.**

Zuber Publishing, *(978-0-9785551)* 52180 Tammy Dr., Granger, IN 46530 USA Tel 574-272-8914
E-mail: admin@zuberpublishing.com
Web site: http://www.zuberpublishing.com
Dist(s): **Distributors, The.**

Zuiho, *(978-0-9743474)* 11628 82nd Ave. NE, Kirkland, WA 98034-3400 USA.

Zuiker Pr., *(978-1-947378; 978-1-7322612)* 16255 Ventura Blvd, Encino, CA 91436 USA Tel 917-847-4156
E-mail: dave@zuikerpress.com
Dist(s): **Simon & Schuster, Inc.**

Zulema Enterprises LLC, *(978-1-881223)* 7715 Yardley Dr., Tamarac, FL 33321 USA Tel 513-659-1753
E-mail: peopleteachers@aol.com
Web site: http://www.zulemabooks.com.

Zulema Enterprises Publishing *See* **Zulema Enterprises LLC**

Zulu Planet Pubs. (ZAF) *(978-1-920070; 978-1-920153)* *Dist. by* **APG.**

Zumaya Embraces *Imprint of* **Zumaya Pubns. LLC**

Zumaya Otherworlds *Imprint of* **Zumaya Pubns. LLC**

Zumaya Pubns. LLC, *(978-1-894869; 978-1-894942; 978-1-55410; 978-1-934135; 978-1-934841; 978-1-936144; 978-1-61271)* Orders Addr.: 3209 S. Interstate 35 APT 1086, Austin, TX 78741-6905 USA Tel 512-537-3145; 512-931-4594; Fax: 512-276-6745; *Imprints*: Zumaya Otherworlds (Zumaya Otherworlds); Zumaya Embraces (Zumaya Embraces); Zumaya Thresholds (ZumThresh)
E-mail: production@zumayapublishing.com; business@zumayapublishing.com
Web site: http://www.zumayapublications.com; http://www.zumayapublishing.com.

Zumaya Thresholds *Imprint of* **Zumaya Pubns. LLC**

Zy Iman Pubng, *(978-0-9779130)* P.O. Box 367, Brooklyn, NY 11221 USA
Web site: http://www.ucanspeakup.com.

Zygote Games LLC, *(978-0-9770419)* 100 Venture Way, Flr. 3, Suite 4, Hadley, MA 01035 USA Tel 413-303-9031; Fax: 253-540-5054
E-mail: orders@zygotegames.com
Web site: http://www.zygotegames.com.

Zyrro, Roggen, *(978-0-9762580)* 5841 Wornall Rd., Kansas City, MO 64113 USA
Web site: http://www.bunsta.com.

ZZ Dogs Pr. *Imprint of* **That's Life Publishing, Inc.**

WHOLESALER & DISTRIBUTOR NAME INDEX

Volume 3

1stBooks Library, *See* **AuthorHouse**

2Learn-English, *(978-0-9627878; 978-1-891077; 978-1-934637)* Div. of Authors & Editors, Orders Addr.: 10736 Jefferson Blvd., No. 604, Culver City, CA 90230-4969 USA Tel 310-251-3931 Arthur Rubin; 310-836-2014 General/Messages; Fax: 310-836-1845
E-mail: info@2learn-english.com
Web site: http://www.2learn-english.com.

3M Sportsman's Video Collection, 3M Ctr., Bldg. 223-4NE-05, Saint Paul, MN 55144-1000 USA (SAN 159-8929) Tel 612-733-7412; Fax: 612-736-7479; Toll Free: 800-940-8273 (orders only).

A & B Books, *See* **A & B Distributors & Pubs. Group**

A & B Distributors & Pubs. Group, *(978-1-881316; 978-1-886433)* Div. of A&B Distributors, 1000 Atlantic Ave., Brooklyn, NY 11238 USA (SAN 630-9216) Tel 718-783-7808; Fax: 718-783-7267; Toll Free: 877-542-6657; 146 Lawrence St., Brooklyn, NY 11201 (SAN 631-385X)
E-mail: maxtay@webspan.net.

A & M Church Supplies, 3535 Bay Rd., Saginaw, MI 48603-2464 USA (SAN 157-0145) Toll Free: 800-345-4694.

A B C-Clio Information Services, *See* **ABC-CLIO, LLC**

A B S Corporation, *See* **Budgetext**

A K J Educational Services, Incorporated, *See* **AKJ Bks.**

AAA Anime Distribution, 4509 Shirley Ave., Unit D, El Mone, CA 91731 USA Tel 626-575-8922
E-mail: vince@aaaanime.com.

Aardvark Global Publishing, *(978-0-9770328; 978-1-933570; 978-1-59971; 978-1-4276)* 9587 S. Grandview Dr., Sandy, UT 84092 USA Do not confuse with Aardvark Global Publishing, Atlanta, GA
E-mail: info@eckohousepublishing.com
Web site: http://eckohousepublishing.com/; http://aardvarkglobalpublishing.com/; http://eckobooks.com.

ABC-CLIO, LLC, *(978-0-275; 978-0-313; 978-0-8371; 978-0-86569; 978-0-87287; 978-0-87436; 978-0-89789; 978-0-89930; 978-0-903450; 978-0-938865; 978-1-56308; 978-1-56720; 978-1-57607; 978-1-85109; 978-1-58683; 978-1-59158; 978-0-9742537; 978-1-59884; 978-1-4408; 978-1-61069) 130 Cremona Dr., Santa Barbara, CA 93117 USA (SAN 301-5467) Tel 805-968-1911; Fax: 805-685-9685; Toll Free: 800-368-6868; P.O. Box 93116, Goleta, CA 93116 (SAN 857-7099)*
E-mail: customerservice@abc-clio.com; service@abc-clio.com; salesuk@abc-clio.com
Web site: http://www.abc-clio.com.

ABC'S Bk. Supply, Inc., 7319 W. Flagler St., Miami, FL 33144 USA Toll Free: 877-383-4240
E-mail: abcbooks@abcbooks.com.

Abdo & Daughters Publishing, *See* **ABDO Publishing Co.**

ABDO Publishing Co., *(978-0-939179; 978-1-56239; 978-1-57765; 978-1-59197; 978-1-59679; 978-1-59928; 978-1-59961; 978-1-60270; 978-1-60453; 978-1-61613; 978-1-61714; 978-1-61758; 978-1-61783; 978-1-61784; 978-1-61785; 978-1-61786; 978-1-61787; 978-1-61478; 978-1-61479; 978-1-61480; 978-1-62401; 978-1-62402; 978-1-62403; 978-1-62968; 978-1-62969; 978-1-62970; 978-1-68076; 978-1-68077; 978-1-68078; 978-1-68079; 978-1-68080; 978-1-5321; 978-1-0982) Div. of ABDO Publishing Group, Orders Addr.: 8000 W. 78th St. Suite 310, Edina, MN 55439 USA (SAN 662-9172) Tel 952-831-2120; Fax: 952-831-1632; Toll Free Fax: 800-862-3480; Toll Free: 800-800-1312*
E-mail: info@abdopublishing.com
Web site: http://www.abdopublishing.com.

Abel Love, Inc., Orders Addr.: P.O. Box 2250, Newport News, VA 23609 USA (SAN 158-4081) Tel 757-877-2939; Toll Free: 800-520-2939; Edit Addr.: 935 Lucas Creek Rd., Newport News, VA 23608 USA Fax: 804-877-2939.

Abingdon Pr., *(978-0-687; 978-1-4267; 978-1-63088; 978-1-5018; 978-1-7910)* Div. of United Methodist Publishing House, Orders Addr.: 2222 Rosa L. Parks Blvd., Nashville, TN 37228 USA Tel 615-749-6409; 615-749-6000; Fax: 615-749-6056; Toll Free: 800-627-1789; Edit Addr.: 201 Eighth Ave., S., Nashville, TN 37202 USA (SAN 699-9956) Tel 615-749-6000; Toll Free Fax: 800-445-8189; Toll Free: 800-672-1789
E-mail: rburgoyne@umpublishing.org; cokes_serv@cokesbury.com
Web site: http://www.abingdonpress.com/; http://www.umph.org.

Abraham Assocs. Inc., 5120-A Cedar Lake Rd., Minneapolis, MN 55416 USA Tel 952-927-7920; Fax: 952-927-8089; Toll Free: 800-701-2489
E-mail: stu@abrahamassociatesinc.com.

Abrams & Co. Pubs., Inc., *(978-0-7664)* Orders Addr.: 61 Mattatuck Heights, Waterbury, CT 06705 USA; Edit Addr.: P.O. Box 10025, Waterbury, CT 06725 USA (SAN 207-7078) Tel 203-756-6562; Fax: 203-756-2895; Toll Free: 800-874-0029
E-mail: custserve@abramsandcompany.com
Web site: http://www.abramsandcompany.com.

Abrams, Harry N. Incorporated, *See* **Abrams, Inc.**

Abrams, Inc., *(978-0-8109; 978-1-4197; 978-1-61769; 978-1-61312; 978-1-68335)* A Subsidiary of La Martinière Groupe, Orders Addr.: The Market Building Third Floor, 72-82 Rosebery Ave., London, EC1R 4RW GBR Tel 020 7713 2060; Fax: 020 7713 2061; Edit Addr.: 115 West 18th St., New York, NY 10011 USA (SAN 200-2434) Tel 212-206-7715; Fax: 212-519-1210
E-mail: webmaster@abramsbooks.com
Web site: http://www.abramsbooks.com.

Abrams Learning Trends, Orders Addr.: 16310 Bratton Ln., Suite 250, Austin, TX 78728 USA Tel 512-735-2863
E-mail: billt@abramslearningtrends.com.

Abyss Distribution, *(978-1-932548)* P.O. Box 48, Middlefield, MA 01243-0048 USA (SAN 630-9925) Tel 413-623-2155; Fax: 413-623-2156; Toll Free: 800-326-0804
E-mail: abyssdist@aol.com
Web site: http://www.azuregreen.om.

Academic Bk. Ctr., Inc., P.O. Box 1320, Lake Oswego, OR 97035-0320 USA (SAN 169-7145) Toll Free: 800-547-7704
E-mail: orders@acbc.com
Web site: http://www.abc.com.

Academic Bk. Services, Inc., 5490 Fulton Industrial Blvd., Atlanta, GA 30336 USA (SAN 631-0591) Tel 404-344-8317; Fax: 404-349-2127.

Academic Studies Pr., *(978-1-934843; 978-1-936235; 978-1-61811; 978-1-64469)* 28 Montfern Ave., Brighton, MA 02135 USA (SAN 855-1766)
E-mail: press@academicstudiespress.com; igor.nemirovsky@academicstudiespress.com
Web site: http://www.academicstudiespress.com.

Academi-Text Medical Wholesalers, P.O. Box 1080, Monroe, MI 48161-6080 USA (SAN 135-2415) Toll Free: 800-552-8398 (out of state)
E-mail: dyourist@academi-text.com.

ACCESS Pubs. Network, 6893 Sullivan Rd., Grawn, MI 49637 USA.

Acorn Alliance, 549 Old North Rd., Kingston, RI 02881-1220 USA Tel 401-783-5480; Fax: 401-284-0959; Fulfillment Addr.: Client Distribution Services 193 Edwards Dr., Jackson, TN 38301 USA Toll Free Fax: 800-351-5073; Toll Free: 800-343-4499
E-mail: moyerbellbooks@yahoo.com
Web site: http://www.moyerbellbooks.com.

ACTA Pubns., *(978-0-87946; 978-0-914070; 978-0-915388)* 5559 Howard St., Skokie, IL 60077-2621 USA (SAN 204-7489) Toll Free Fax: 800-397-0079; Toll Free: 800-397-2282; 4848 N. Clark St., Chicago, IL 60640
E-mail: actapublications@aol.com
Web site: http://www.actapublications.com.

Action Products International, Inc., 344 Cypress Rd., Ocala, FL 34472-3108 USA (SAN 630-8805) Tel 352-687-4961; Toll Free: 800-772-2846
E-mail: sales@apii.com.

Activated Ministries, P.O. Box 462805, Escondido, CA 92046-2805 USA Toll Free: 877-862-3228
E-mail: sales@activatedministries.org.

ACW Pr., *(978-0-9656749; 978-1-892525; 978-1-932124; 978-1-934668)* Orders Addr.: P.O. Box 110390, Nashville, TN 37222 USA Tel 615-834-0450; Toll Free: 800-219-7483; Edit Addr.: 4854 Aster Dr., Nashville, TN 37211 USA
E-mail: regaforder@aol.com.

Adams Bk. Co., Inc., LSC Communications, Attn: Receiving/Ellen Farrell 1 Pierson Parkway, Cranbury, NJ 08512 USA (SAN 107-7171) Tel 718-875-5464; Fax: 718-852-3212; Toll Free: 800-221-0909
E-mail: sales@adamsbook.com
Web site: http://www.adamsbook.com.

Adams News, 1555 W. Galer St., Seattle, WA 98119 USA (SAN 169-8842) Tel 206-284-7617; Fax: 206-284-7599; Toll Free: 800-533-7617.

Adams, Robert Henry Fine Art, *(978-0-9713010)* 2146 W. Sunnyside Ave., Chicago, IL 60625-1626 USA (SAN 159-6918)
E-mail: info@adamsfineart.com
Web site: http://www.adamsfineart.com.

Addicus Bks., *(978-1-886039; 978-1-936374; 978-1-938803; 978-1-940495; 978-1-943886; 978-0-692-67011-8; 978-1-950091)* Orders Addr.: P.O. Box 45327, Omaha, NE 68145 USA Tel 402-330-7493; Fax: 402 330-1707; Toll Free: 800-352-2873; Edit Addr.: 814 N. Franklin St., Chicago, IL 60610 USA
E-mail: addicusbks@aol.com; info@addicusbooks.com
Web site: http://www.AddicusBooks.com.

Addison-Wesley Educational Pubs., Inc., *(978-0-321; 978-0-328; 978-0-673)* Div. of Addison Wesley Longman, Inc., 75 Arlington St., Boston, MA 02116 USA Tel 617-848-7500; Toll Free: 800-447-2226
Web site: http://www.awl.com.

Addison-Wesley Longman, Inc., *(978-0-201; 978-0-321; 978-0-582; 978-0-673; 978-0-8013; 978-0-8053; 978-0-9654123)* Orders Addr.: 200 Old Tappan Rd., Old Tappan, NJ 07675 USA (SAN 299-4739) Toll Free: 800-922-0579; Edit Addr.: 75 Arlington St., Suite 300, Boston, MA 02116 USA (SAN 200-2000) Tel 617-848-7500; Toll Free: 800-447-2226
E-mail: pearsoned@eds.com; orderdeptnj@pearsoned.com
Web site: http://www.awl.com.

Addison-Wesley Publishing Company, Incorporated, *See* **Addison-Wesley Longman, Inc.**

Adelman, Joseph, 530 N. 40th St., Allentown, PA 18104-4558 USA (SAN 285-8002).

Adler, Leo, P.O. Box 10308, Eugene, OR 97440-2308 USA (SAN 169-7021).

Adler's Foreign Bks., Inc., *(978-0-8417)* 915 Foster St., Evanston, IL 60201 USA (SAN 111-3089) Tel 847-864-0664; Fax: 847-864-0804; Toll Free: 800-235-3771
E-mail: info@afb-adlers.com
Web site: http://www.afb-adlers.com.

Advanced Global Distribution Services, 5880 Oberlin Dr., San Diego, CA 32121 USA Toll Free Fax: 800-499-3822; Toll Free: 800-284-3580.

Adventures Unlimited Pr., *(978-0-932813; 978-1-931882; 978-1-935487; 978-1-939149; 978-1-948803)* Orders Addr.: P.O. Box 74, Kempton, IL 60946 USA (SAN 630-1126) Tel 815-253-6390; Fax: 815-253-6300; Edit Addr.: 303 Main St., Kempton, IL 60946 USA (SAN 250-3484)
E-mail: auphq@frontiernet.net
Web site: http://www.adventuresunlimitedpress.com.

Advertising Specialties, Inc., 4920 River Rd., Pascagoula, MS 39567 USA (SAN 108-6316) Tel 601-769-7904
Web site: http://www.advmkt.com; http://www.advantagebooksonline.com.

Advocate Distribution Solutions, Div. of Send The Light Distribution LLC, 100 Biblica Way, Elizabethton, TN 37643 USA Tel 423-767-1100; Fax: 423-547-5199; Toll Free Fax: 800-759-2779; Toll Free: 800-289-2772
Web site: http://www.stl-distribution.com; http://www.advocatedistribution.com.

Affiliated Bk. Distributor, Div. of North Shore Distributors, Inc., 1200 N. Branch St., Chicago, IL 60622 USA (SAN 169-2267).

Africa World Pr., *(978-0-86543; 978-1-59221)* 541 W. Ingham Ave., Suite B, Trenton, NJ 08638 USA (SAN 692-3925) Tel 609-695-3200; Fax: 609-695-6466
E-mail: customerservice@africaworldpressbooks.com
Web site: http://www.africaworldpressbooks.com.

African World Bks., 2217 Pennsylvania Ave., Baltimore, MD 21217 USA (SAN 631-3868) Tel 410-383-2006.

Afrikan World Bk. Distributor, Orders Addr.: P.O. Box 16447, Baltimore, MD 21217 USA; Edit Addr.: 2217 Pennsylvania Ave., Baltimore, MD 21217 USA (SAN 631-2020) Tel 410-383-2006.

Afro-American Bk. Distributor, 2537 Prospect, Houston, TX 77004 USA (SAN 169-8257).

Agencia de Publicaciones de Puerto Rico, GPO Box 4903, San Juan, PR 00936 USA (SAN 169-9296).

Agritech Publishing Group, Inc., Div. of Agritech Corp., 825 W. Samalayuca Dr., Tucson, AZ 85704-3912 USA (SAN 174-612X) Tel 520-544-2542.

AHA, Inc., *(978-0-918545)* P.O. Box 8405, Santa Cruz, CA 95061-8405 USA (SAN 295-5059) Tel 408-458-9119.

AIMS International Bks., Inc., *(978-0-922852)* 7709 Hamilton Ave., Cincinnati, OH 45231-3103 USA (SAN 630-270X) Tel 513-521-5590; Fax: 513-521-5592; Toll Free: 800-733-2067
E-mail: aimsbooks@fuse.net
Web site: http://www.aimsbooks.com.

A-K News Company, *See* **Aramark Magazine & Bk. Co.**

AK Pr. Distribution, *(978-1-873176; 978-1-902593; 978-0-9830597; 978-1-939202)* 370 Ryan Ave, Unit 100, Chico, CA 95973 USA (SAN 298-2234) Tel 510-208-1708; Fax: 510-208-1701
E-mail: akpress@akpress.org
Web site: http://www.akpress.org.

AKJ Bks., 2700 Hollins Ferry Road, Baltimore, MD 21230 USA (SAN 170-5431) Toll Free: 800-922-6066
E-mail: Info@akjbooks.com
Web site: www.akjbooks.com; http://store.akjbooks.com; www.akjebooks.com.

Alabama Bookstore, Orders Addr.: P.O. Box 1279, Tuscaloosa, AL 35401-1626 USA Tel 205-758-4532; Fax: 205-758-5525; Toll Free: 800-382-2665 (orders only)
E-mail: ABS@AlabamaBook.com
Web site: http://www.AlabamaBook.com.

Alamo Square Distributors, P.O. Box 14543, San Francisco, CA 94114 USA Fax: 415-863-7456
E-mail: alamosqdist@earthlink.net.

Alba House, *See* **St Pauls/Alba Hse. Pubs.**

Alexander News Company, *See* **Blue Ridge News Co.**

Alfonsi Enterprises, 8621 Gavinton Ct., Dublin, OH 43017-9615 USA (SAN 169-4227).

Alfred Publishing Co., Inc., *(978-0-7390; 978-0-87487; 978-0-88284; 978-1-58951; 978-1-4574; 978-1-4706)* Orders Addr.: P.O. Box 10003, Van Nuys, CA 91410-0003 USA; Edit Addr.: 123 Dry Rd., Oriskany, NY 13424 USA Tel 315-736-1572; Fax: 315-736-7281
E-mail: customerservice@alfred.com; permissions@alfred.com; submissions@alfred.com
Web site: http://www.alfred.com.

Alibris, *(978-0-9702763)* 1250 45th St., Suite 100, Emeryville, CA 94608 USA Fax: 510-550-6052; Toll Free: 877-254-2747 (877-ALIBRIS, option 1)
E-mail: libraries@alibris.com
Web site: http://www.alibris.com/library.

Alive Books, *See* **Books Alive**

All Electronics Corp., 14928 Oxnard St., Van Nuys, CA 91411 USA.

All Romance Ebooks, LLC, *(978-1-936387; 978-1-943576; 978-1-945193; 978-1-946297)* 6252 Commercial Way No. 145, Weeki Wachee, FL 34613 USA
E-mail: info@allromanceebooks.com.

Allegro New Sound Distribution, Subs. of Allegro Distribution, 20048 NE San Rafael St., Portland, OR 97230-7459 USA.

Allentown News Agency, Inc., Orders Addr.: P.O. Box 446, Allentown, PA 18105 USA; Edit Addr.: 719-723 Liberty St., Allentown, PA 18105 USA (SAN 169-7226) Tel 610-432-4441; Fax: 610-432-2708.

Alliance Bk. Co., P.O. Box 7884, Hilton Head, SC 29938-7884 USA
E-mail: alliancebk@mindspring.com.

Alliance Game Distributors, Centennial Dr., Fort Wayne, IN 46808 USA Tel 260-482-5490 (ext. 253); Fax: 260-471-9539
E-mail: jjh@alliance-games.com
Web site: http://www.alliance-games.com.

Alliance Hse., Inc., *(978-0-9665234)* 220 Ferris Ave., Suite 201, White Plains, NY 10603 USA Tel 914-328-5456; Fax: 914-946-1929
E-mail: alliancehs@aol.com.

Alonso Bk. & Periodical Services, Inc., 2316 2nd St S., Arlington, VA 22204-2010 USA (SAN 170-7035).

Alpen Bks, 4602 Chennault Beach Rd. Ste. B1, Mukilteo, WA 98275-5016 USA.

Alpenbooks, *See* **Alpenbooks Pr. LLC**

Alpenbooks Pr. LLC, *(978-0-9669795)* 4602 Chennault Beach Rd, B1, Mukilteo, WA 98275 USA (SAN 113-5309) Tel 425-415-4560; Fax: 425-493-6381
E-mail: rkoch@alpenbooks.com
Web site: http://www.alpenbooks.com.

Alpha & Omega Distributor, P.O. Box 36640, Colorado Springs, CO 80936-3664 USA (SAN 169-0515).

Alpha Bks., *(978-0-02; 978-0-672; 978-0-7357; 978-0-7897; 978-1-56761; 978-1-57595; 978-0-7431; 978-1-59257; 978-1-61564)* Div. of Pearson Technology Group, 800 E 96th St., 3rd Flr., Indianapolis, IN 46290 USA (SAN 219-6298) Tel 317-581-3500 Toll Free: 800-571-5840 (orders)
Web site: http://www.idiotsguides.com.

Alpine News Distributors, Div. of Mountain States Distributors, 0105 Marand Rd., Glenwood Springs, CO 81601 USA Tel 970-945-2269; Fax: 970-945-2260.

Alta Book Center Publishers, *See* **Alta English Publishers**

Alta English Publishers, *(978-1-878598; 978-1-882483; 978-1-932383)* 1775 E. Palm Canyon Dr. Suite 110-275, Palm Springs, CA 92264 USA (SAN 630-9240) Tel 760-459-2603; Fax: 760-464-0588
E-mail: info@altaenglishpublishers.com
Web site: https://altaenglishpublishers.com; https://altaenglishonline.com.

AMACOM, *(978-0-7612; 978-0-8144)* Div. of Harpercollins Leadership, P.O. Box 141000, Nashville, TN 37214 USA (SAN 201-1670) Toll Free: 800-250-5308
E-mail: pubservice@amanet.org
Web site: http://www.amacombooks.org.

Amarillo Periodical Distributors, P.O. Box 3823, Lubbock, TX 70404 USA (SAN 156-4986) Tel 806-745-6000.

Amato, Frank Pubns., Inc., *(978-0-936608; 978-1-57188; 978-1-878175)* Orders Addr.: P.O. Box 82112, Portland, OR 97282 USA (SAN 214-3372) Tel 503-653-8108; Fax: 503-653-2766; Toll Free: 800-541-9498; Edit Addr.: 4040 SE Wister St., Milwaukie, OR 97222 USA (SAN 858-5741)
E-mail: wholesale@amatobooks.com; Lorraine@amatobooks.com
Web site: http://www.amatobooks.com.

Amazon Digital Services Inc., 440 Terry Ave. N., Seattle, WA 98109 USA.

Amazon.Com, *(978-1-58060)* 1200 12th Ave. S., Suite 1200, Seattle, WA 98144 USA (SAN 179-4205) Tel 206-266-6817; Orders Addr.: P.O. Box 80387, Seattle, WA 98108-0387 USA (SAN 156-143X) Tel 206-622-2335; Fax: 206-622-2405; 1 Centerpoint Blvd., non-carton, New Castle, DE 19720 (SAN 155-3992); 1 Centerpoint Blvd., carton, New Castle, DE 19720 (SAN 156-1405); 520 S. Brandon, non-carton, Seattle, WA 98108 (SAN 152-6642); 520 S. Brandon, carton, Seattle, WA 98108 (SAN 156-1383); 1600 E. Newlands Dr., carton, Fernley, NV 89408 (SAN 156-5982); 1600 E. Newlands Dr., non-carton, Fernley, NV 89408 (SAN 156-6008); Edit Addr.: 520 Pike St., Seattle, WA 98101 USA (SAN 155-3984); P.O. Box 81226, Seattle, WA 98108-1226; 705 Boulder Dr. Carton, Breinigsville, PA 18031
E-mail: catalog-dept@amazon.com
Web site: http://www.amazon.com.

Ambassador Bks. & Media, 42 Chasner St., Hempstead, NY 11550 USA (SAN 120-064X) Tel 516-489-4011; Fax: 516-489-5661; Toll Free: 800-431-8913
E-mail: ambassador@absbook.com
Web site: http://www.absbook.com.

Ambassador Book Service, *See* **Ambassador Bks. & Media**

America Hse. Bk. Pubs., *(978-1-893162; 978-1-58851; 978-1-59129)* Orders Addr.: P.O. Box 151, Frederick, MD 21705-0151 USA; Edit Addr.: 113 E. Church St., Frederick, MD 21701 USA
Web site: http://www.publishamerica.com.

American Assn. for Clinical Chemistry, Inc., *(978-0-915274; 978-1-890883; 978-1-59425)* Orders Addr.: 1850 K St NW Ste. 625, Washington, DC 20006-2215 USA (SAN 214-2813) Toll Free: 800-892-1400
E-mail: info@aacc.org
Web site: http://www.aaccdirect.org.

American Assn. for Vocational Instructional Materials, *(978-0-89606; 978-0-914452)* 220 Smithonia Rd., Winterville, GA 30683 USA (SAN 225-8811) Tel 706-742-5355; Fax: 706-742-7005; Toll Free: 800-228-4689
E-mail: ksseab@aavim.com; sales@aavim.com
Web site: http://www.aavim.com.

American Bible Society, *(978-0-8267; 978-1-58516; 978-1-937628; 978-1-941448; 978-1-941449)* Orders Addr.: 6201 E. 43rd St., Tulsa, OK 74135-6562 USA (SAN 662-7129) Toll Free Fax: 866-570-2877; Edit Addr.: 1865 Broadway, New York, NY 10023-9980 USA (SAN 203-5189) Tel 212-408-1200; Fax: 212-408-1305; 700 Plaza Dr., 2nd Flr., Secaucus, NJ 07094
E-mail: info@americanbible.org
Web site: http://www.bibles.org; http://www.americanbible.org.

American Buddhist Shim Gum Do Assn., Inc., *(978-0-9614427)* 203 Chestnut Hill Ave., Brighton, MA 02135 USA (SAN 113-2873) Tel 617-787-1506; Fax: 617-787-2708
E-mail: marystackhouse@shimgumdo.org
Web site: http://www.shimgumdo.org.

American Business Systems, Inc., 315 Littleton Rd., Chelmsford, MA 01824 USA (SAN 264-8229) Tel 508-250-9600; Fax: 508-250-8027; Toll Free: 800-356-4034.

American Eagle Pubns., Inc., *(978-0-929408)* Orders Addr.: P.O. Box 5111, Sun City West, AZ 85376 USA (SAN 249-2415) Tel 623-556-2925; Fax: 623-556-2926; Toll Free: 866-764-2925; Edit Addr.: 12647 Crystal Lake Dr., Sun City West, AZ 85375 USA
E-mail: custservice@ameaglepubs.com
Web site: http://www.ameaglepubs.com.

American Education Corp., The, *(978-0-87570; 978-1-58636; 978-0-9841672; 978-0-9841972)* 7506 N. Broadway, Suite 505, Oklahoma City, OK 73116-9016 USA (SAN 654-6250) Tel 405-840-6031; Toll Free: 800-222-2811
E-mail: jamesr@amered.com
Web site: http://www.amered.com.

American Educational Computer, Incorporated, *See* **American Education Corp., The**

American Heritage Magazine, 90 Fifth Ave., New York, NY 10011 USA.

American International Distribution Corp., Orders Addr.: 82 Winter Sport Ln., Williston, VT 05495 USA (SAN 631-1083) Tel 802-488-2665; Edit Addr.: 82 Winter Sport Ln., Williston, VT 05495 USA (SAN 630-2238) Toll Free: 800-488-2665
E-mail: jmacon@aidcvt.com
Web site: http://www.aidcvt.com/Specialty/Home.asp.

American Kennel Club Museum of the Dog, *(978-0-9615072)* 1721 S. Mason Rd., Saint Louis, MO 63131 USA (SAN 110-8751) Tel 314-821-3647; Fax: 314-821-7381.

American Library Assn., *(978-0-8389; 978-1-937589)* 50 E. Huron St., Chicago, IL 60611 USA (SAN 201-0062) Tel 312-280-2425; 312-944-8085; Fax: 770-280-4155 (Orders); Toll Free: 800-545-2433; 866-746-7252 (Orders); P.O. Box 932501, Atlanta, GA 31193-2501
E-mail: EditionsMarketing@ala.org
Web site: http://www.ala.org; http://www.alastore.ala.org.

American Magazine Service, *See* **Prebound Periodicals**

American Marketing & Publishing Company, *See* **Christian Publishing Network**

American Mathematical Society, *(978-0-8218; 978-0-8284; 978-0-88385; 978-0-9835005; 978-1-61444; 978-1-4704; 978-1-939512)* Orders Addr.: 201 Charles St., Providence, RI 02904 USA (SAN 250-3263) Tel 401-455-4000; Fax: 401-331-3842; Toll Free: 800-321-4267
E-mail: las@ams.org
Web site: http://www.ams.org.

American Micro Media, 19 N. Broadway, Box 306, Red Hook, NY 12571 USA (SAN 653-9920) Tel 914-758-5567.

American News Company, 325 W. Potter Dr., Anchorage, AK 99518 USA (SAN 168-9274) Tel 907-563-3251; Fax: 907-261-8523 Do not confuse with companies with the same name in Winston-Salem, NC, Elizabeth, NC.

American Overseas Bk. Co., Inc., 550 Walnut St., Norwood, NJ 07648 USA (SAN 169-4863) Tel 201-767-7600; Fax: 201-784-0263
E-mail: books@aobc.com
Web site: http://www.aobc.com.

American Pharmacists Assn., *(978-0-914768; 978-0-917330; 978-1-58212)* 2215 Constitution Ave., NW, Washington, DC 20037-2907 USA (SAN 202-4446) Tel 202-628-4410; Fax: 202-783-2351; Toll Free: 800-878-0729
E-mail: kanderson@aphanet.org
Web site: http://www.pharmacist.com.

American Society of Agronomy, *(978-0-89118)* 5585 Guilford Rd., Fitchburg, WI 53711-5801 USA (SAN 107-5683)
Web site: http://www.agronomy.org.

American Society of Civil Engineers, *(978-0-7844; 978-0-87262)* 1801 Alexander Bell Dr., Reston, VA 20191-4400 USA (SAN 204-7594) Tel 703-295-6300; Fax: 703-295-6211; Toll Free: 800-548-2723
E-mail: pubsful@asce.org
Web site: http://www.asce.org/bookstore.

American Technical Pubs., Inc., *(978-0-8269)* 10100 Orland Pkwy., Orland Park, IL 60467-5756 USA (SAN 206-8141) Toll Free: 800-323-3471
E-mail: service@americantech.net
Web site: http://www.americantech.net.

American West Bks., Orders Addr.: 14190 N. Washington Hwy., Ashland, VA 23005 USA (SAN 920-5233); Edit Addr.: 1254 Commerce Way, Sanger, CA 93657 USA (SAN 630-8570) Toll Free: 800-497-4909 Do not confuse with American West Bks., Albuquerque, NM
E-mail: JBM12@CSUFresno.edu.

American Wholesale Bk. Co., Subs. of Books-A-Million, Orders Addr.: 402 Industrial Ln., Birmingham, AL 35211-4465 USA (SAN 631-7391).

American Wholesale Booksellers Assn., *(978-0-9664715)* 702 S. Michigan St., South Bend, IN 46601 USA Tel 219-232-8500; Fax: 303-265-9292
E-mail: pwalsh@awba.com
Web site: http://www.awba.com.

Americana Publishing, Inc., *(978-1-58807; 978-1-58943)* 195 Us Highway 9. Ste. 204, Englishtown, NJ 07726-8294 USA Toll Free: 888-883-8203; 303 San Mateo Blvd, Ne, Albuquerque, NM 87108
E-mail: editor@americanabooks.com
Web site: http://www.americanabooks.com.

Americana Souvenirs & Gifts, *(978-1-890541)* 206 Hanover St., Gettysburg, PA 17325-1911 USA (SAN 169-7366) Toll Free: 800-692-7436.

America's Cycling Pubns., 6425 Capitol Ave., Suite F, Diamond Springs, CA 95619 USA.

America's Hobby Ctr., 146 W. 22nd St., New York, NY 10011 USA (SAN 111-0403) Tel 212-675-8922.

Ames News Agency, Inc., 2110 E. 13th St., Ames, IA 50010 USA (SAN 169-2550).

Amicus Educational, *See* **Amicus Publishing**

Amicus Publishing, *(978-1-60753; 978-1-68151; 978-1-64549)* P.O. Box 1329, Mankato, MN 56002 USA Tel 507-388-9357; Fax: 507-388-2746
E-mail: anna.erickson@amicuspublishing.us; rglaser@amicuspublishing.us; info@amicuspublishing.us
Web site: http://www.amicuspublishing.us.

Amigos Book Co., Orders Addr.: 5401 Bissonnet, Houston, TX 77081-6605 USA.

Amoskeag News Agency, 92 Allard Dr., Manchester, NH 03102 USA (SAN 169-4537) Tel 603-623-5343.

Analos Magazine, 475 Park Ave. S., New York, NY 10016 USA.

Anchor Distributors, 1030 Hunt Valley Cir., New Kensington, PA 15068 USA (SAN 631-077X) Tel 724-334-7000; Fax: 724-334-1200; Toll Free: 800-444-4484
E-mail: customerservice@anchordistributors.com
Web site: http://www.anchordistributors.com.

Anderson Merchandisers, 421 E. 34th St., Amarillo, TX 79103 USA (SAN 169-8028) Tel 806-376-6251
E-mail: hanleyg@amerch.com.

Anderson News - Tacoma, 9914 32nd Ave., S., Lakewood, WA 98499 USA (SAN 108-1322) Tel 253-581-1940; Fax: 253-584-5941; Toll Free: 800-552-2000 (in Washington).

Anderson News, LLC, 211 Industrial Dr., Roanoke, VA 24019 USA (SAN 168-9223); 6016 Brookvale Ln. Ste. 110B, Knoxville, TN 37919-4003 (SAN 168-9363); 2541 Westcott Blvd., Knoxville, TN 37931 Tel 423-966-7575; 3911 Volunteer Dr., Chattanooga, TN 37416 (SAN 169-7862) Tel 423-894-3945; 6301 Forbing Rd., Little Rock, AR 72219 Tel 501-562-7360; 1185a Commerce Blvd., Midway, FL 32343-6629; 1857 W. Grant Rd., Tucson, AZ 85745-1203; 5184 Sullivan Gardens Pkwy., Kingsport, TN 37660-8104 (SAN 241-6131); 390 Exchange St., Box 1624, New Haven, CT 06506 (SAN 241-6158) Tel 203-777-5545; 5000 Moline St., Denver, CO 80239-2622 Tel 303-321-1111; 1709 N. East St., Flagstaff, AZ 86002 (SAN 168-9290) Tel 520-774-6171; Fax: 520-779-1958; 6016 Brookvale Ln. Ste. 110B, Knoxville, TN 37919-4003; P.O. Box 22968, Chattanooga, TN 37422; P.O. Box 36003, Knoxville, TN 37930-6003; P.O. Box 280077, Memphis, TN 38168-0077; P.O. Box 6660, Pensacola, FL 32503 Do not confuse with Anderson News Company, Pinellas Park, FL.

Anderson-Austin News Co., LLC, 808 Newtown Cir., No. B, Lexington, KY 40511-1230 USA (SAN 169-2836) Tel 606-254-2765; Fax: 606-254-3328.

Andich Brothers News Company, *See* **Tobias News Co.**

Andrews McMeel Publishing, *(978-0-8362; 978-0-939251; 978-1-57939; 978-0-7407; 978-1-4494; 978-1-5248)* Orders Addr.: c/o Simon & Schuster, Inc., 100 Front St., Riverside, NJ 08075 USA Toll Free Fax: 800-943-9831; Toll Free: 800-943-9839 (Customer Service); 800-897-7650 (Credit Dept.); Edit Addr.: 1130 Walnut St., Kansas City, MO 64106-2109 USA (SAN 202-540X) Toll Free: 800-851-8923
Web site: http://www.AndrewsMcMeel.com.

Andrzejewski's Marian Church Supply, *See* **A & M Church Supplies**

Angel City Pr., *(978-1-883318; 978-1-62640)* 2118 Wilshire Blvd., PMB 880, Santa Monica, CA 90403-5784 USA (SAN 298-3370) Tel 310-395-9982; Fax: 310-395-3353; Toll Free: 800-949-8039 (orders)
E-mail: smcauley@angelcitypress.com
Web site: http://www.angelcitypress.com.

Angler's Bk. Supply, 1380 W. Second Ave., Eugene, OR 97402 USA (SAN 631-4546) Tel 541-342-8355; Fax: 541-342-1785; Toll Free: 800-260-3869.

Anglo-American Book Company, Limited (UK), *See* **Crown Hse. Publishing LLC**

Ann Arbor Editions LLC, *(978-1-58726)* 2500 S. State St., Ann Arbor, MI 48104 USA Tel 734-913-1302; Fax: 734-913-1249; 1094 Flex Dr., Jackson, TN 38301
E-mail: ljohnson@aaeditions.com
Web site: http://www.annarbormediagroup.com; http://www.mittenpress.com; http://www.aaeditions.com.

Ann Arbor Media Group, LLC, *See* **Ann Arbor Editions LLC**

answers period, inc., *(978-0-917875)* Orders Addr.: P.O. Box 427, Goliad, TX 77963 USA (SAN 112-6431) Tel 361-645-2268; Toll Free: 800-852-4752
Web site: http://www.answersbook.com.

Anthracite News Company, *See* **Great Northern Distributors, Inc.**

Anthroposophic Press, Incorporated, *See* **SteinerBooks, Inc.**

Antipodes Bks. & Beyond, 9707 Fairway Ave., Silver Spring, MD 20901-3001 USA Tel 301-602-9519; Fax: 301-565-0160
E-mail: Antipode@antipodesbooks.com
Web site: http://www.antipodesbooks.com.

Antiquarian Bookstore, The, 1070 Lafayette Rd., Portsmouth, NH 03801 USA (SAN 158-9938) Tel 603-436-7250.

Antique Collectors' Club, *(978-0-902028; 978-0-907462; 978-1-85149)* Orders Addr.: Eastworks, 116 Pleasant St., Easthampton, MA 01027 USA (SAN 630-7787) Tel 413-529-0861; Fax: 413-529-0862; Toll Free: 800-252-5231 (orders)
E-mail: info@antiquecc.com; sales@antiquecc.com
Web site: http://www.antiquecollectorsclub.com.

AOAC International, *(978-0-935584)* 481 N. Frederick Ave., Suite 500, Gaithersburg, MD 20877-2417 USA (SAN 260-3411) Tel 301-924-7077; Fax: 301-924-7089; Toll Free: 800-379-2622
E-mail: aoac@aoac.org
Web site: http://www.aoac.org.

A-One Bk. Distributors, Inc., 1555 Ocean Ave. Ste. D, Bohemia, NY 11716-1933 USA (SAN 630-7981).

APG Sales & Distribution Services, Div. of Warehousing and Fulfillment Specialists, LLC (WFS, LLC), 7344 Cockrill Bend Blvd., Nashville, TN 37209-1043 USA (SAN 630-818X) Toll Free: 800-327-5113
E-mail: sswift@agpbooks.com
Web site: http://www.apgbooks.com.

APG Sales & Fulfillment, *See* **APG Sales & Distribution Services**

Apollo Bks., *(978-0-938290)* 91 Market St., Wappingers Falls, NY 12590-2333 USA (SAN 170-0928).

Apollo Library Bk. Supplier, 865 Kent Ln., Philadelphia, PA 19115 USA (SAN 159-8031).

Appalachian Bible Co., *(978-1-889049)* Orders Addr.: 522 Princeton Rd., Johnson City, TN 37605 USA (SAN 169-7889) Tel 423-282-9475; Fax: 423-282-9110; Toll Free: 800-289-2772; Edit Addr.: P.O. Box 1573, Johnson City, TN 37601 USA
E-mail: appainc@aol.com.

Appalachian Bk. Distributors, Div. of Send The Light Distribution LLC, Orders Addr.: 100 Biblica Way, Elizabethton, TN 37643-6070 USA Toll Free Fax: 800-759-2779; Edit Addr.: 506 Princeton Rd., Johnson City, TN 37601 USA.

Appalachian, Incorporated, *See* **Appalachian Bible Co.**

Applause Learning Resources, *(978-0-9655052; 978-0-9786746; 978-0-9788527; 978-0-9790091; 978-1-60713)* 85 Fernwood Ln., Roslyn, NY 11576 USA Tel 516-625-1145; Fax: 516-625-7392; Toll Free Fax: 877-365-7484; Toll Free: 800-277-5287
E-mail: info@applauselearning.com
Web site: http://www.applauselearning.com.

Applause Productions, *See* **Applause Learning Resources**

Apple Bk. Co., Div. of Scholastic Bk. Fairs, Inc., Orders Addr.: P.O. Box 217156, Charlotte, NC 28221-0156 USA Tel 704-596-6641; Fax: 704-599-1738; Toll Free: 800-331-1993; Edit Addr.: 5901 N. Northwoods Business Pkwy., Charlotte, NC 28269 USA (SAN 108-4569).

Applewood Bks., *(978-0-918222; 978-1-55709; 978-1-889833; 978-1-933212; 978-1-4290; 978-0-9819430; 978-1-60889; 978-0-9844156; 978-0-9836416; 978-1-938700; 978-0-9882885; 978-1-941216; 978-1-5162; 978-1-944038; 978-1-945187; 978-1-64194)* 1 River Rd., Carlisle, MA 01741-1820 USA (SAN 210-3419) Toll Free: 800-277-5312; 1 Ingram Blvd., La Vergne, TN 37086
E-mail: applewood@awb.com; svec@awb.com
Web site: http://www.awb.com.

Aquarian Concepts Publishing & Distribution, *(978-0-9666593)* Orders Addr.: HC Box 81-L, Payson, AZ 85541 USA (SAN 299-7215) Tel 520-474-0816; Toll Free: 888-539-8069; Edit Addr.: 62 Switchman Ln., Payson, AZ 85541 USA
E-mail: concepts1@cybertrails.com.

Arabic & Islamic Univ. Pr., 4263 Fountain Ave., Los Angeles, CA 90029 USA (SAN 107-6299) Tel 323-665-1000; Fax: 323-665-3107.

Aramark, 18825 67th Ave., NE, Arlington, WA 98223-9656 USA (SAN 631-3507) Tel 360-435-2524; Fax: 360-435-6805 Do not confuse with Aramark, Albuquerque, NM.

Aramark Magazine & Bk. Co., P.O. Box 25489, Oklahoma City, OK 73125 USA (SAN 169-6971) Tel 405-843-9383; Fax: 405-843-0379 Do not confuse with Aramark Magazine & Bk. Services, Inc., Norfolk, VA.

Aramark Magazine & Bk. Services, Inc., P.O. Box 2240, Norfolk, VA 23501 USA (SAN 169-8680) Do not confuse with Aramark Magazine & Book Co., Oklahoma City, OK.

Arbit Bks., Inc., *(978-0-930038)* 8050 N. Port Washington Rd., Milwaukee, WI 53217 USA (SAN 169-913X) Tel 414-352-4404.

Arcadia Publishing, *(978-0-88289; 978-0-910462; 978-0-911116; 978-1-56554; 978-0-7385; 978-1-58973; 978-1-58980; 978-1-59629; 978-1-4396; 978-1-60949; 978-1-4556; 978-1-61423; 978-1-4671; 978-0-578-11080-6; 978-1-62584; 978-1-62585; 978-1-62619; 978-0-578-12310-3;-0-615-91258-5; 978-0-9903765; 978-1-944313; 978-1-5316; 978-1-5402; 978-0-578-19068-6; 978-0-578-59417-0; 978-0-578-59418-7) Orders Addr.: 420 Wando Pk. Blvd., Mount Pleasant, SC 29464 USA (SAN 255-268X) Tel 843-853-2070; Fax: 843-853-0044; Toll Free: 888-313-2665 Do not confuse with Arcadia Publishing in Greenwood Village, CO*
E-mail: sales@arcadiapublishing.com
Web site: http://www.arcadiapublishing.com.

Ardic Bk. Distributors, Inc., 331 High St., 2nd Flr., Burlington, NJ 08016-4411 USA (SAN 170-5415).

Argus International Corp., Subs. of ICS International Group, Skypark Business Pk., P.O. Box 4082, Irvine, CA 92716-4082 USA (SAN 681-9761) Tel 714-552-8494 (phone/fax).

Aries Pr., *(978-0-933646)* P.O. Box 30081, Chicago, IL 60630 USA (SAN 111-9168) Tel 312-725-8300.

Aries Productions, Inc., *(978-0-910035)* Orders Addr.: P.O. Box 29396, Sappington, MO 63126 USA (SAN 669-0009); Edit Addr.: 6935 Tholozan Ave., Saint Louis, MO 63109-1130 USA (SAN 241-2004)
E-mail: uspsisquad@aol.com
Web site: http://ww.ussisquad.com.

Arizona Periodicals, Inc., P.O. Box 5780, Yuma, AZ 85366-5780 USA Tel 520-782-1822.

Arkansas Bk. Co., 1207 E. Second St., Little Rock, AR 72202-2732 USA (SAN 168-9460) Tel 501-375-1184.

Arlington Card Co., Bk. Dept., 140 Gansett Ave., Cranston, RI 02910 USA (SAN 108-5794) Tel 401-942-3188.

Armstrong, J. B. News Agency, *See* **News Group, The**

Arrow, G. H. Co., P.O. Box 676, Bala Cynwyd, PA 19004 USA (SAN 111-3771) Tel 215-227-3211; Fax: 215-221-0631; Toll Free: 800-775-2776.

Arrowhead Magazine Co., Inc., P.O. Box 5947, San Bernardino, CA 92412 USA (SAN 169-0094) Tel 909-799-8294; Fax: 909-799-3774; 1055 Cooley Ave., San Bernardino, CA 92408 (SAN 249-2717) Tel 909-370-4420.

Ars Obscura, *(978-0-9623780)* P.O. Box 4424, Seattle, WA 98104-0424 USA (SAN 113-5368) Tel 206-324-9792.

Art Institute of Chicago, *(978-0-86559)* Orders Addr.: a/o Museum Shop Mail Order Dept., 950 N. North Branch St., Chicago, IL 60622-4276 USA; Edit Addr.: 111 S. Michigan Ave., Chicago, IL 60603-6110 USA (SAN 204-479X) Tel 312-443-3540; Fax: 312-443-1334
Web site: http://www.artic.edu.

Art Media Resources, Inc., *(978-1-878529; 978-1-58886)* 1507 S. Michigan Ave., Chicago, IL 60605 USA (SAN 253-8199) Tel 312-663-5351; Fax: 312-663-5177
E-mail: info@artmediaresources.com
Web site: http://www.artmediaresources.com.

ARVEST, P.O. Box 200248, Denver, CO 80220 USA (SAN 159-8694) Tel 303-388-8486; Fax: 303-355-4213; Toll Free: 800-739-0761
E-mail: copy@concentric.net.

Asia Bk. Corp. of America, *(978-0-940500)* 45-77 157th St., Flushing, NY 11355 USA (SAN 214-493X) Tel 718-762-7204; Fax: 718-460-5030.

ASM International, *(978-0-87170; 978-1-61503; 978-1-62708)* 9639 Kinsman Rd., Materials Park, OH 44073-0002 USA (SAN 204-7586) Tel 440-338-5151; Fax: 440-338-4634; Toll Free: 800-336-5152 Do not confuse with ASM International, Inc., Fort Lauderdale, FL
E-mail: karen.marken@asminternational.org; madrid.tramble@asminternational.org; scott.henry@asminternational.org; sue.sellers@asminternational.org; memberservicecenter@asminternational.org
Web site: http://www.asminternational.org.

ASP Wholesale, c/o A&A Quality Shipping Services 3623 Munster Ave, Unit B, Hayward, CA 94545 USA Tel 510-732-6521 (Voice).

Aspen West Publishing, *(978-0-9615390; 978-1-885348)* P.O. Box 522151, Salt Lake City, UT 84152-2151 USA (SAN 112-7993) Toll Free: 800-222-9133 (orders only)
E-mail: kent@aspenwest.com
Web site: http://www.aspenwest.com.

Assn. of Energy Engineers, Orders Addr.: P.O. Box 1026, Liburn, GA 30048 USA Tel 770-925-9558; Fax: 770-381-9865; Edit Addr.: 4025 Pleasantdale Rd., Suite 420, Atlanta, GA 30340 USA Tel 770-447-5083.

Associated Univ. Presses, *(978-0-8453)* 2010 Eastpark Blvd., Cranbury, NJ 08512 USA (SAN 281-2959) Tel 609-655-4770; Fax: 609-655-8366
E-mail: aup440@aol.com
Web site: http://www.aupresses.com.

Association of Official Analytical Chemists, *See* **AOAC International**

Astran, Inc., 6995 NW 82nd Ave. Ste. 40, Miami, FL 33166-2783 USA (SAN 169-1082) Toll Free: 800-431-4957
E-mail: sales@astranbooks.com
Web site: http://www.astranbooks.com.

ATEXINC, Corp., *(978-0-9702332; 978-1-60405)* Orders Addr.: 17738 Vintage Oak Dr., Glencoe, MO 63038-1478 USA (SAN 631-774X) Toll Free Fax: 866-346-9515 Do not confuse with Atex, Inc., Bedford, MA
E-mail: mail@atexinc.com
Web site: http://www.atexinc.com; http://www.thetextilekit.com; http://www.itextiles.com.

Athelstan Pubns., *(978-0-940753)* Orders Addr.: 5925 Kirby Dr. Suite E. 464, Houston, TX 77005 USA (SAN 663-5318) Tel 713-371-2107; Fax: 713-524-1159
E-mail: info@athel.com; barlow@athel.com
Web site: http://www.athel.com.

Athena Productions, Inc., 5500 Collins Ave., No. 901, Miami Beach, FL 33140 USA Tel 305-868-8482; Fax: 305-868-8891.

Atlas Bks., 2541 Ashland Rd., Ashland, OH 44905 USA.

Atlas News Co., Div. of Hudson News Co., P.O. Box 779, Boylston, MA 01505-0779 USA (SAN 169-3360).

Atlas Publishing Co., *(978-0-930575)* 1464 36th St., Ogden, UT 84403 USA (SAN 110-3873) Tel 801-627-1043.

Attainment Co., Inc., *(978-0-934731; 978-1-57861; 978-1-943148; 978-1-944315; 978-1-64856)* Orders Addr.: P.O. Box 930160, Verona, WI 53593 USA (SAN 694-1656) Tel 608-845-7880; Fax: 608-845-8040; Toll Free: 800-327-4269; Edit Addr.: 504 Commerce Pkwy., Verona, WI 53593 USA (SAN 631-6174)
E-mail: info@attainmentcompany.com; sue@attainmentcompany.com; ameyer@attainmentcompany.com
Web site: http://www.attainmentcompany.com/.

Audible.com, One Washington Pk., Newark, NJ 07102 USA Tel 973-820-0400 (International); Fax: 973-890-2442; Toll Free: 888-283-5051 (USA & Canada)
E-mail: content-requests@audible.com
Web site: http://www.audible.com.

Audio Bk. Co., *(978-0-89926)* 235 Bellefontaine St., Pasadena, CA 91105-2921 USA (SAN 158-1414) Toll Free: 800-423-8273
E-mail: sales@audiobookco.com
Web site: http://www.audiobookco.com.

AudioGO, *(978-0-563; 978-0-7540; 978-0-7927; 978-0-89340; 978-1-55504; 978-1-60283; 978-1-60998; 978-1-62064; 978-1-62460; 978-1-4815; 978-1-4821)* Orders Addr.: c/o Perseus, 1094 Flex Dr., Jackson, TN 38301 USA; Edit Addr.: 42 Whitecap Dr., North Kingstown, RI 02852-7445 USA (SAN 858-7701) Toll Free: 800-621-0182
E-mail: laura.almeida@audiogo.com
Web site: http://www.audiogo.com/us/.

Audubon Prints & Bks., 9720 Spring Ridge Ln., Vienna, VA 22182 USA (SAN 111-820X).

Augsburg Fortress Publishers, Publishing House of The Evangelical Lutheran Church in America, *See* **Augsburg Fortress, Pubs.**

Augsburg Fortress, Pubs., *(978-0-8006; 978-0-8066; 978-1-4514; 978-1-5064)* Orders Addr.: P.O. Box 1209, Minneapolis, MN 55440-1209 USA (SAN 169-4081) Toll Free Fax: 800-722-7766; Toll Free: 800-328-4648 (orders only); Edit Addr.: 510 Marquette 8th Fl., Minneapolis, MN 55402 USA Tel 800-328-4648 800-722-7766
E-mail: customerservice@augsburgfortress.org; info@augsburgfortress.org; subscriptions@augsburgfortress.org; copyright@augsburgfortress.org; international@augsburgfortress.org
Web site: http://www.augsburgfortress.org.

Augusta News Co., 25 Second St., Apt. 124, Hallowell, ME 04347-1481 USA (SAN 169-3026).

Auromere, Inc., *(978-0-89744)* 2621 W. US Hwy. 12, Lodi, CA 95242-9200 USA (SAN 169-0043) Fax: 209-339-3715; Toll Free: 800-735-4691
E-mail: sasp@lodinet.com
Web site: http://www.auromere.com.

Austin & Company, Inc., *(978-0-9657153)* 104 S. Union St., Suite 202, Traverse City, MI 49684 USA (SAN 631-1466) Tel 231-933-4649; Fax: 231-933-4659
E-mail: aandn@aol.com
Web site: http://www.austinandcompanyinc.com.

Austin & Nelson Publishing, *See* **Austin & Company, Inc.**

Austin Management Group, Orders Addr.: P.O. Box 3206, Paducah, KY 42002-3206 USA (SAN 135-3349); Edit Addr.: P.O. Box 300, Paducah, KY 42002-0300 USA (SAN 249-6844).

Author Solutions, Inc., Div. of Penguin Group (USA) Inc., 1663 Liberty Dr., Bloomington, IN 47403 USA Tel 812-334-5223; Toll Free: 877-655-1722
E-mail: sfurr@authorsolutions
Web site: http://www.authorsolutions.com.

AuthorHouse, *(978-1-58500; 978-0-9675669; 978-1-58721; 978-1-58820; 978-0-7596; 978-1-4033; 978-1-4107; 978-1-4140; 978-1-4184; 978-1-4208; 978-1-4259; 978-1-4343; 978-1-4389; 978-1-4490; 978-1-4520; 978-1-61764; 978-1-4567; 978-1-4582; 978-1-4624; 978-1-4633; 978-1-4634; 978-0-9846457; 978-1-4670; 978-1-4678; 978-1-4685; 978-1-4772; 978-1-4817; 978-1-4918; 978-1-4969; 978-1-5049; 978-1-5065; 978-1-5246; 978-1-5462; 978-1-7283; 978-1-6655) Div. of Author Solutions, Inc., 1663 Liberty Dr., Suite 200, Bloomington, IN 47403 USA (SAN 253-7605) Fax: 812-336-5449; Toll Free: 888-519-5121*
E-mail: authorsupport@authorhouse.com; sfurr@authorsolutions.com
Web site: http://www.authorhouse.com.

Authors & Editors, *See* **2Learn-English**

Author's Republic, *(978-1-943499; 978-1-5189; 978-0-9980029)* 2225 Kenmore Ave., Buffalo, NY 14207 USA Tel 905-634-7507
E-mail: michelle@authorsrepublic.com; info@authorsrepublic.com
Web site: www.authorsrepublic.com.

Auto-Bound, Inc., 909 Marina Village Pkwy., No. 67B, Alameda, CA 94501-1048 USA (SAN 170-0782) Tel 510-521-8655; Fax: 510-521-8755; Toll Free: 800-523-5833.

Avanti Enterprises, Inc., P.O. Box 3563, Hinsdale, IL 60522-3563 USA (SAN 158-3727) Toll Free: 800-799-6464.

Avenue Bks., 2270 Porter Way, Stockton, CA 95207-3339 USA (SAN 122-4158).

Avery BookStores, Inc., 516 Asharoken Ave., Northport, NY 11768-1176 USA (SAN 169-510X).

Avian Pubns., *(978-0-910335; 978-0-9585612)* 6380 Monroe St., NE, Minneapolis, MN 55432 USA (SAN 241-2691) Tel 763-571-8902
E-mail: bruce@avianpublications.com
Web site: http://www.avainpublications.com.

Aviation Bk. Co., *(978-0-911720; 978-0-911721; 978-0-916413)* 7201 Perimeter Rd., S., No. C, Seattle, WA 98108-3812 USA (SAN 120-1530) Tel 206-767-5232; Fax: 206-763-3428; Toll Free: 800-423-2708
E-mail: sales@aviationbook.com.

Avonlea Bks., Inc., Orders Addr.: P.O. Box 74, White Plains, NY 10602-0074 USA (SAN 680-4446) Tel 914-946-5923; Fax: 914-761-3119; Toll Free: 800-423-0622
E-mail: avonlea@bushkin.com
Web site: http://www.bushkin.com.

B. P. I. Communications, *See* **VNU**

B T P Distribution, 4135 Northgate Blvd., Suite 5, Sacramento, CA 95834-1226 USA (SAN 631-2489) Tel 916-567-2496; Fax: 916-441-6749.

Baggins Bks., 3560 Meridian St., Bellingham, WA 98225-1731 USA (SAN 156-501X).

Baha'i Distribution Service, *(978-0-87743)* Orders Addr.: P.O. Box 1759, Powder Springs, GA 30127-7522 USA (SAN 213-7496) Toll Free: 800-999-9019; Edit Addr.: 415 Linden Ave., Wilmette, IL 60091 USA Tel 847-251-1854; Fax: 847-251-3652
E-mail: bds@usbnc.org.

Baker & Taylor Bks., *(978-0-8480; 978-1-222; 978-1-223)* A Follett Company, Orders Addr.: Commerce Service Ctr., 251 Mt. Olive Church Rd., Commerce, GA 30599 USA (SAN 169-1503) Tel 404-335-5000; Toll Free: 800-775-1200 (customer service); 800-775-1800 (orders); Reno Service Ctr., 1160 Trademark Dr., Suite 111, Reno, NV 89511 (SAN 169-4464) Tel 775-850-3800; Fax: 775-850-3826 (customer service); Toll Free Fax: 800-775-1700 (orders); Edit Addr.: Bridgewater Service Ctr. 1120 US Hwy. 22, E., Bridgewater, NJ 08807 USA (SAN 169-4901) Toll Free: 800-775-1500 (customer service); Momence Service Ctr., 501W. Gladiolus St., Momence, IL 60954-1799 (SAN 169-2100) Tel 815-472-2444 (international customers); Fax: 815-472-9886 (international customers); Toll Free: 800-775-2300 (customer service, academic libraries)
E-mail: btinfo@btol.com
Web site: http://www.btol.com.

Baker & Taylor Fulfillment, Inc., 2550 W. Tyvola Rd., Suite 370, Charlotte, NC 28217 USA (SAN 760-8772) Tel 704-236-9553
E-mail: johnsod@btol.com.

Baker & Taylor International, 1120 US Hwy. 22 E., Box 6885, Bridgewater, NJ 08807 USA (SAN 200-6804) Tel 908-541-7000; Fax: 908-729-4037.

Baker & Taylor Publisher Services (BTPS), A Follett Company, Orders Addr.: 30 Amberwood Pkwy., Ashland, OH 44805 USA (SAN 631-936X) Fax: 419-281-6883; Toll Free: 800-537-6727; 30 Amberwood Pkwy., Ashland, OH 44805 (SAN 760-9264) Fax: 419-281-6883; Toll Free: 800-537-6727; 30 Amberwood Pkwy., Ashland, OH 44805 (SAN 760-6680) Fax: 419-281-6883; Toll Free: 800-537-6727
E-mail: orders@atlasbooks.com
Web site: http://www.bookmasters.com/.

Baker & Taylor Publishing Group, *See* **Readerlink Distribution Services, LLC**

Baker Bks., *(978-0-8010; 978-0-913686)* Div. of Baker Publishing Group, Orders Addr.: P.O. Box 6287, Grand Rapids, MI 49516-6287 USA (SAN 299-1500) Toll Free Fax: 800-398-3111 (orders only); Toll Free: 800-877-2665 (orders only); Edit Addr.: 6030 E. Fulton, Ada, MI 49301 USA (SAN 201-4041) Tel 616-676-9185; Fax: 616-676-9573
Web site: http://www.bakerpublishinggroup.com.

Baker Book House, Incorporated, *See* **Baker Publishing Group**

Baker Publishing Group, *(978-0-8007; 978-0-8010; 978-1-58743; 978-1-4412; 978-1-4934; 978-1-68196; 978-1-5409)* Orders Addr.: P.O. Box 6287, Grand Rapids, MI 49516-6287 USA Tel 616-676-9573; Toll Free Fax: 800-398-3111 (orders only); Toll Free: 800-877-2665 (orders only); Edit Addr.: 6030 E. Fulton, Ada, MI 49301 USA Tel 616-676-9185; Fax: 616-676-9573; Toll Free Fax: 800-398-3111; Toll Free: 800-877-2665
E-mail: webmaster@bakerpublishinggroup.com
Web site: http://www.bakerbooks.com; http://www.bakerpublishinggroup.com.

Balogh International, Inc., *(978-1-878762; 978-1-891770)* 1911 N. Duncan Rd., Champaign, IL 61822 USA (SAN 297-2344) Tel 217-355-9331; Fax: 217-355-9413
E-mail: balogh@balogh.com
Web site: http://www.balogh.com.

Balogh Scientific Books, *See* **Balogh International, Inc.**

Balzekas Museum of Lithuanian Culture, 6500 S. Pulaski Rd., Chicago, IL 60629 USA (SAN 110-8522) Tel 773-582-6500; Fax: 773-582-5133.

Banner of Truth, The, *(978-0-85151)* Orders Addr.: P.O. Box 621, Carlisle, PA 17013 USA Tel 717-249-5747; Fax: 717-249-0604; Toll Free: 800-263-8085; Edit Addr.: 63 E. Louther St., Carlisle, PA 17013 USA (SAN 112-1553)
E-mail: info@banneroftruth.org
Web site: http://www.banneroftruth.co.uk.

Banta Packaging & Fulfillment, 1071 Willow Spring Rd., Harrisonburg, VA 22801 USA (SAN 631-7731) Tel 540-442-1333; Fax: 540-434-3541; N9234 Lake Park Rd., Appleton, WI 54915 (SAN 631-8290) Tel 920-969-6400; Fax: 920-751-7794
E-mail: jfair@banta.com.

Barbour & Company, Incorporated, *See* **Barbour Publishing, Inc.**

Barbour Publishing, Inc., *(978-0-916441; 978-1-55748; 978-1-57748; 978-1-58660; 978-1-59310; 978-1-59789; 978-1-60260; 978-1-60742; 978-1-61626; 978-1-62029; 978-1-62416; 978-1-62836; 978-1-63058; 978-1-63409; 978-1-944836; 978-1-68322; 978-1-64352; 978-1-63609)* Orders Addr.: P.O. Box 719, Uhrichsville, OH 44683 USA (SAN 295-7094) Fax: 740-922-5948; Toll Free Fax: 800-220-5948; Toll Free: 800-852-8010
E-mail: info@barbourbooks.com
Web site: http://www.barbourbooks.com.

Barnes & Noble Bks.-Imports, *(978-0-389)* 4720 Boston Way, Lanham, MD 20706 USA (SAN 206-7803) Tel 301-459-3366; Toll Free: 800-462-6420.

Barnes & Noble, Inc., *(978-0-7607; 978-0-88029; 978-1-4028; 978-1-4114; 978-1-4351; 978-1-61551; 978-1-61552; 978-1-61553; 978-1-61554; 978-1-61555; 978-1-61556; 978-1-61557; 978-1-61558; 978-1-61559; 978-1-61560; 978-1-61679; 978-1-61680; 978-1-61681; 978-1-61682; 978-1-61683; 978-1-61684; 978-1-61685; 978-1-61686; 978-1-61687; 978-1-61688; 978-1-970008) 76 Ninth Ave., 9th Flr., New York, NY 10011 USA (SAN 141-3651) Tel 212-414-6385; 122 Fifth Ave., New York, NY 10011*
E-mail: smcculloch@bn.com.

Barnes&Noble.com, *(978-1-4005; 978-1-4006)* c/o Merch Accounts Payable/NR Dept., 76 Ninth Ave., 9th Flr., New York, NY 10011 USA (SAN 192-6551) Tel 212-414-6000
Web site: http://www.bn.com.

Basic Crafts Co., 6001 66th Ave., No. 10, Riverdale, MD 20737-1717 USA (SAN 169-5622) Toll Free: 800-847-4127 (outside New York).

Basin News Co., P.O. Box 300, Paducah, KY 42002-0300 USA (SAN 169-2860).

Bassett Printing Corp., *(978-0-9632415)* Orders Addr.: P.O. Box 866, Bassett, VA 24055 USA Fax: 540-629-3416; Toll Free: 800-336-5102 (outside Virginia); Edit Addr.: 101 Main St., Bassett, VA 24055 USA Tel 540-629-2541.

Baum & Beaulieu Assocs., 46 O'Connell Ct., Great River, NY 11749 USA Tel 631-277-3249; Toll Free: 800-923-2444; P.O. Box 582, Great River, NY 11739-0582 Toll Free: 800-923-2444.

Bay News, Inc., 3333 NW 35th Ave., Portland, OR 97210 USA Tel 503-219-3001; Fax: 503-241-1877.

Bayou Bks., 1005 Monroe St., Gretna, LA 70053 USA (SAN 120-1913) Tel 504-368-1171; Toll Free: 800-843-1724.

BBC Audiobooks America, *See* **AudioGO**

BCH Fulfillment & Distribution, 46 Purdy St., Harrison, NY 10528 USA
E-mail: info@bookch.com
Web site: http://www.bookch.com/.

Beagle Bay Bks., *(978-0-9679591; 978-0-9749610)* Div. of Beagle Bay, Inc., 2325 Homestead Pl., Reno, NV 89509-3657 USA
E-mail: info@beaglebay.com
Web site: http://www.beaglebay.com.

Beaver News Co., Inc., 230 W. Washington St., Rensselaer, IN 47978 USA (SAN 630-8864).

Beck's Bk. Store, 4520 N. Broadway, Chicago, IL 60640 USA (SAN 159-8139) Tel 773-784-7963; Fax: 773-784-0066
E-mail: rsvltrd@aol.com
Web site: http://www.aol.members/becks.html.

Beechwood Pubns., Inc., P.O. Box 1158, Kennett Square, PA 19348 USA (SAN 107-5853) Tel 610-444-5991; Fax: 215-566-4178.

Beekman Bks., Inc., *(978-0-8464)* 300 Old All Angels Hill Rd., Wappingers Falls, NY 12590 USA (SAN 170-1622) Tel 845-297-2690; Fax: 845-297-1002
E-mail: manager@beekmanbooks.com
Web site: http://www.beekmanbooks.com.

Beeler, Thomas T. Pub., *(978-1-57490)* Orders Addr.: P.O. Box 310, Rollinsford, NH 03869 USA Toll Free Fax: 888-222-3396; Toll Free: 800-818-7574; Edit Addr.: 710 Main St., Suite 300, Rollinsford, NH 03869 USA Tel 603-749-0392; Fax: 603-749-0395
E-mail: tombeeler@beelerpub.com
Web site: http://www.beelerpub.com.

Before Columbus Foundation, 655 13th St. Ste. 302, Oakland, CA 94612-1225 USA (SAN 159-2955).

Beijing Bk. Co., Inc., 701 E. Linden Ave., Linden, NJ 07036-2495 USA (SAN 169-5673) Tel 908-862-0909; Fax: 908-862-4201.

Bell Magazine, Orders Addr.: P.O. Box 1957, Monterey, CA 93940 USA (SAN 159-7221); Edit Addr.: 3 Justin Ct., Monterey, CA 93940 USA (SAN 169-0353) Tel 408-642-4668.

Bella Distribution, Orders Addr.: P.O. Box 10543, Tallahassee, FL 32302 USA; Edit Addr.: 1041 Aenon Church Rd., Tallahassee, FL 32304 USA Fax: 850-576-3498; Toll Free: 800-533-1973
E-mail: info@belladistribution.com
Web site: http://www.belladistribution.com.

Benchmark LLC, *(978-0-7834; 978-0-929591)* 559 San Ysidro Rd. Suite I, Santa Barbara, CA 93108 USA (SAN 249-7522) Tel 805-565-8911; Toll Free: 888-797-9377
E-mail: bridger@benchmarkmaps.com; teri@benchmarkmaps.com; curtis@benchmarkmaps.com
Web site: http://www.benchmarkmaps.com.

Benjamin News Group, Orders Addr.: 2131 International St., Columbus, OH 43228 USA (SAN 660-9406) Tel 614-777-9768; Fax: 7=614-777-9766; Edit Addr.: 1701 Rankin St., Missoula, MT 59808-1629 USA (SAN 169-4391) Tel 406-721-7801; Fax: 406-721-7802.

Bennett & Curran, Inc., *(978-1-879607)* 1280 Cherryville Rd., Greenwood Vlg, CO 80121-1222 USA
E-mail: Jeff@bennettandcurran.com.

Berkeley Educational Paperbacks, 2480 Bancroft Way, Berkeley, CA 94704 USA (SAN 168-9509) Tel 510-848-7907.

Berkeley Game Distributors, 5850 Hollis St., Emeryville, CA 94608-2016 USA (SAN 631-2934) Toll Free: 800-424-4263; 1164 E. Sandhill Ave., Carson, CA 90746
E-mail: bgdnorth@ix.netcom.com.

Bernan Assocs., *(978-0-400; 978-0-527; 978-0-89059; 978-1-59610; 978-1-59888; 978-1-60175; 978-1-60946; 978-1-63005; 978-1-64143; 978-1-63671)* Div. of Kraus Organization, The, Orders Addr.: 15200 NBN Way, P.O. Box 190, Blue Ridge Summit, PA 17214 USA (SAN 169-3182) Tel 301-459-7666; Fax: 301-459-6988; Toll Free Fax: 800-865-3450; Toll Free: 800-865-3457; Edit Addr.: 4501 Forbes Blvd., Suite 200, Lanham, MD 20706 USA (SAN 760-7253) Tel 301-459-2255; Fax: 301-459-0056; Toll Free: 800-416-4385; 15200 Nbn Way, Blue Ridge Summ, PA 17214
E-mail: query@bernan.com; order@bernan.com; info@bernan.com; jkemp@bernan.com; jculley@rowman.com
Web site: www.rowman.com.

Berrett-Koehler Pubs., Inc., *(978-1-57675; 978-1-58376; 978-1-881052; 978-1-60509; 978-1-60994; 978-1-62656; 978-1-5230)* Orders Addr.: c/o AIDC, P.O. Box 565, Williston, VT 05495 USA Fax: 802-864-7626 (orders); Toll Free: 800-929-2929 (orders); Edit Addr.: 1333 Broadway, Suite 1000, Oakland, CA 94612 USA Tel 510-817-2277; Fax: 415-362-2512
E-mail: bkpub@bkpub.com
Web site: http://www.bkconnection.com.

Bess Pr., Inc., *(978-0-935848; 978-1-57306; 978-1-880188; 978-0-615-50460-5; 978-0-615-56510-1)* 3565 Harding Ave., Honolulu, HI 96816 USA (SAN 239-4111) Tel 808-734-7159; Fax: 808-732-3627
E-mail: kelly@besspress.com
Web site: http://www.besspress.com.

Best Bk. Ctr., Inc., 1016 Ave. Ponce De Leon, San Juan, PR 00926 USA (SAN 132-4403) Tel 809-727-7945; Fax: 809-268-5022.

Best Continental Bk. Co., Inc., P.O. Box 615, Merrifield, VA 22116 USA (SAN 107-3737) Tel 703-280-1400.

Bethany Hse. Pubs., *(978-0-7642; 978-0-87123; 978-1-55661; 978-1-56179; 978-1-57778; 978-1-880089; 978-1-59066)* Div. of Baker Publishing Group, Orders Addr.: P.O. Box 6287, Grand Rapids, MI 49516-6287 USA Toll Free Fax: 800-398-3111 (orders); Toll Free: 800-877-2665 (orders); Edit Addr.: 11400 Hampshire Ave., S., Bloomington, MN 55438-2455 USA (SAN 201-4416) Tel 952-829-2500; Fax: 952-996-1393
E-mail: orders@bakerbooks.com
Web site: http://www.bethanyhouse.com.

Better Homes & Gardens Books, *See* **Meredith Bks.**

Betty Segal, Inc., 1749 Eucalyptus St., Brea, CA 92621 USA Tel 714-529-5359; Fax: 714-529-3882
E-mail: BertySegal@aol.com
Web site: http://www.agoralang.com/trp-bertysegal.html.

Beyda & Associates, Incorporated, *See* **Beyda for Bks., LLC**

Beyda for Bks., LLC, P.O. Box 2535, Montclair, CA 91763-1035 USA (SAN 169-0426) Toll Free: 800-422-3932 (orders only)
E-mail: info@beydaforbooks.com
Web site: http://www.beydaforbooks.com.

B&H Publishing Group, *See* **B&H Publishing Group**

BHB Fullfillment, Div. of Weatherhill, Inc., 41 Monroe Tpke., Trumbull, CT 06611 USA.

BHB International, Incorporated, *See* **Continental Enterprises Group, Inc. (CEG)**

Bibliotech, Inc., P.O. Box 720459, Dallas, TX 75372-0459 USA (SAN 631-8312) Tel 214-221-0002; Fax: 214-221-1794
E-mail: metatron@airmail.net
Web site: http://www.bibliotechincorporated.com.

Biddy Bks., 1235 168 Model Rd., Manchester, TN 37355 USA (SAN 157-8561) Tel 931-728-6967.

Big Kids Productions, Inc., *(978-1-885627)* 2120 Oxford Ave., Austin, TX 78704-4014 USA (SAN 631-340X) Toll Free: 800-477-7811
E-mail: customerservice@bigkidsvideo.com
Web site: http://www.awardvids.com.

Big River Distribution, *(978-0-9795944; 978-0-9823575; 978-0-9845519)* Orders Addr.: 8214 Exchange Way, Saint Louis, MO 63144 USA (SAN 631-9114) Tel 314-918-9800; Fax: 314-918-9804
E-mail: info@bigriverdist.com; randy@bigriverdist.com
Web site: http://www.bigriverdist.com.

Big Tent Bks., *(978-1-60131; 978-0-578-47138-9; 978-0-578-66280-0)* 115 Bluebill Dr., Savannah, GA 31419 USA (SAN 851-1136)
E-mail: admin@dragonpencil.com; admin@bigtentbooks.com
Web site: http://www.bigtentbooks.com.

Bilingual Educational Services, Inc., *(978-0-86624; 978-0-89075)* 2514 S. Grand Ave., Los Angeles, CA 90007 USA (SAN 218-4680) Tel 213-749-6213; Fax: 213-749-1820; Toll Free: 800-448-6032
E-mail: sales@besbooks.com
Web site: http://www.besbooks.com.

Bilingual Pr./Editorial Bilingue, *(978-0-916950; 978-0-927534; 978-1-931010; 978-1-939743)* Orders Addr.: Hispanic Research Ctr. Arizona State Univ. P.O. Box 875303, Tempe, AZ 85287-5303 USA (SAN 208-5526) Fax: 480-965-8309; Toll Free: 800-965-2280; Edit Addr.: Bilingual Review Pr. Administration Bldg. Rm. B-255 Arizona State Univ., Tempe, AZ 85281 USA
E-mail: brp@asu.edu
Web site: http://www.asu.edu/brp.

Bilingual Pubns. Co., The, 270 Lafayette St., New York, NY 10012 USA (SAN 164-8993) Tel 212-431-3500; Fax: 212-431-3567 Do not confuse with Bilingual Pubns., in Denver, CO
E-mail: lindagoodman@juno.com; spanishbks@aol.com.

Birdlegs Christian Apparel, P.O. Box 189, Duluth, GA 30136-0189 USA (SAN 631-3280) Toll Free: 800-545-0790.

BJU Pr., *(978-0-89084; 978-1-57924; 978-1-59166; 978-1-60682; 978-1-62856; 978-1-64626)* 1700 Wade Hampton Blvd., Greenville, SC 29614 USA (SAN 223-7512) Tel 864-242-5731; 864-370-1800 (ext. 4397; Fax: 864-298-0268; Toll Free Fax: 800-525-8398; Toll Free: 800-845-5731
E-mail: bjup@bjup.com
Web site: http://www.bjupress.com.

Bk. Box, Inc., 3126 Purdue Ave., Los Angeles, CA 90066 USA (SAN 243-2285) Tel 310-391-2313.

Bk. Buy Back, 5150 Candlewood St., No. 6, Lakewood, CA 90712 USA (SAN 631-7251) Tel 562-461-9355; Fax: 562-461-9445.

Bk. Co., The, 145 S. Glencoe St., Denver, CO 80222-1152 USA (SAN 200-2809).

Bk. Distribution Ctr., *(978-0-941722)* Div. of Free Islamic Literatures, Inc., Orders Addr.: P.O. Box 35844, Houston, TX 77235 USA (SAN 241-6395); Edit Addr.: P.O. Box 31669, Houston, TX 77231 USA (SAN 226-2770).

Bk. Distribution Ctr., Inc., Orders Addr.: P.O. Box 64631, Virginia Beach, VA 23467-6431 USA (SAN 134-8019) Tel 757-456-0005; Fax: 757-552-0837; Edit Addr.: 5321 Cleveland St., No. 203, Virginia Beach, VA 23462-6552 USA (SAN 169-8672)
E-mail: sales@bookdist.com
Web site: http://www.bookdist.com.

Bk. Dynamics, Inc., *(978-0-9612440)* 18 Kennedy Blvd., East Brunswick, NJ 08816 USA (SAN 169-5649) Tel 732-545-5151; Fax: 732-545-5959; Toll Free: 800-441-4510.

Bk. Express, *(978-0-9612322; 978-1-890308)* Orders Addr.: P.O. Box 1249, Bellflower, CA 90706 USA (SAN 289-1301) Tel 562-865-1226; Edit Addr.: 12122 E. 176th St., Artesia, CA 90701-4013 USA
E-mail: carbks4u@escapenet.net.

Bk. Home, The, 119 E. Dale St., Colorado Springs, CO 80903-4701 USA (SAN 249-3055) Tel 719-634-5885.

Bk. Hse., Inc., The, 208 W. Chicago St., Jonesville, MI 49250-0125 USA (SAN 169-3859) Tel 517-849-2117; Fax: 517-849-9716; Toll Free Fax: 800-858-9716; Toll Free: 800-248-1146
E-mail: bhinfo@thebookhouse.com.

Bk. Hse., The, 9719 Manchester Rd., Saint Louis, MO 63119 USA Toll Free: 800-513-4491.

Bk. Margins, Inc., 7100 Valley Green Rd., Fort Washington, PA 19034-2206 USA (SAN 106-7788) Tel 215-223-5300
E-mail: paul.gross@bookmargins.com
Web site: http://www.bookmargins.com.

Bk. Marketing Plus, 406 Post Oak Rd., Fredericksburg, TX 78624 USA (SAN 630-6543) Tel 830-997-4776; Fax: 830-997-9752; Toll Free: 800-356-2445.

Bk. Mart, The, 1153 E. Hyde Pk., Inglewood, CA 90302 USA (SAN 168-969X).

Bk. Service of Puerto Rico, 102 De Diego, Santurce, PR 00907 USA (SAN 169-9326) Tel 809-728-5000; Fax: 809-726-6131
E-mail: bellbook@coqui.net
Web site: http://home.coqui.net/bellbook.

Bk. Service Unlimited, P.O. Box 31108, Seattle, WA 98103-1108 USA (SAN 169-877X) Toll Free: 800-347-0042.

Bk. Services International, Orders Addr.: P.O. Box 1434-SMS, Fairfield, CT 06430 USA (SAN 157-9541) Tel 203-374-4939; Fax: 203-384-6099; Toll Free: 800-243-2790.

Bk. Shelf, The, 222 Crestview Dr., Fort Dodge, IA 50501-5708 USA (SAN 169-2658).

Bk. Warehouse, 5154 NW 165th St., Hialeah, FL 33014-6335 USA.

Bk. World, 311 Sagamore Pkwy., N., Lafayette, IN 47904 USA (SAN 135-4051) Tel 765-448-1131 Do not confuse with companies with the same or similar name in Sun Lakes, AZ, Roanoke, VA
E-mail: fsjintl@pworld.net.ph.

Bks. & Media, Inc., *(978-0-7848; 978-0-88483; 978-1-55744)* Div. of Marco Bk. Co., Orders Addr.: P.O. Box 695, Lodi, NY 07644 USA (SAN 206-3352) Tel 973-458-8153; Fax: 973-458-5289; Toll Free: 800-901-8150; Edit Addr.: 60 Industrail Rd., Lodi, NJ 07644 USA.

Bks. & Research, Inc., 145 Palisade St. Ste. 389, Dobbs Ferry, NY 10522-1628 USA (SAN 130-1101)
E-mail: brinc@ix.netcom.com
Web site: http://www.books-and-research.com.

Bks. Are Fun, Ltd., *(978-0-9649777; 978-1-58209; 978-1-890409; 978-1-59795; 978-1-60626)* 1 Readers Digest Rd., Pleasantville, NY 10570-7000 USA
E-mail: msmall@booksarefun.com
Web site: http://www.booksarefun.com.

Bks. Plus, U.S.A., 20171 Kelso Rd., Walnut, CA 91789-1922 USA (SAN 630-8473).

Bks. to Grow On, 826 S. Aiken Ave., Pittsburgh, PA 15232 USA (SAN 128-438X); 210 S. Highland Ave., Pittsburgh, PA 15206 Fax: 412-621-5324.

Bks. West, 11111 E. 53rd Ave., Unit D2, Boulder, CO 80239 USA (SAN 631-4724) Tel 303-449-5995; Fax: 303-449-5951; Toll Free: 800-378-4188; 6340 E. 58Th Ave, Commerce City, CO 80022 Do not confuse with Books West, San Diego, CA
E-mail: wnack@rmi.net
Web site: http://www.bookswest.net/.

Black Box Corp., 1000 Park Dr., Lawrence, PA 15055 USA (SAN 277-1985) Tel 412-746-5500; Fax: 412-746-0746.

Black Christian Bk. Distributors, 1169 North Burleson Blvd. Suite 107-246, Burleson, TX 76028 USA.

Black Magazine Agency, 4515 Fleur Dr. Ste. 301, Des Moines, IA 50321-2369 USA (SAN 107-0819) Toll Free: 800-782-9787.

Black Rabbit Bks., *(978-1-58340; 978-1-887068; 978-1-59920; 978-1-77092; 978-1-62310; 978-1-62588; 978-1-68071; 978-1-68072; 978-1-64466)* Orders Addr.: P.O. Box 3263, Mankato, MN 56002 USA (SAN 925-4862); Edit Addr.: 123 S. Broad St., Mankato, MN 56001 USA (SAN 858-902X)
E-mail: jbesel@blackrabbitbooks.com; info@blackrabbitbooks.com
Web site: http://www.blackrabbitbooks.com.

Blackburn News Agency, P.O. Box 1039, Kingsport, TN 37662 USA (SAN 169-7900).

Blackstone Audio Books, Incorporated, *See* **Blackstone Audio, Inc.**

Blackstone Audio, Inc., *(978-0-7861; 978-1-4332; 978-1-4417; 978-1-4551; 978-1-4708; 978-1-4829; 978-1-4830; 978-1-5046; 978-1-5047; 978-1-5384; 978-1-5385; 978-1-9824; 978-1-9825; 978-1-9826; 978-1-7999; 978-1-0940; 978-1-0941; 978-1-6644; 978-1-6645; 978-1-6646; 978-1-6647; 978-1-6650; 978-1-6651; 978-1-6652) 31 Mistletoe Rd., Ashland, OR 97520 USA (SAN 173-2811) Fax: 800-482-9294; Toll Free Fax: 800-482-9294; Toll Free: 800-729-2665*
E-mail: Orders@blackstoneaudio.com; megan.wahrenbrock@blackstoneaudio.com
Web site: http://www.blackstoneaudio.com.

Blackwell, *(978-0-913262; 978-0-916472)* Orders Addr.: 6024 SW Jean Rd., Bldg. G, Lake Oswego, OR 97034 USA (SAN 169-7048) Tel 503-684-1140; Fax: 503-639-2481; Toll Free: 800-547-6426 (in Oregon); Edit Addr.: 100 University Ct., Blackwood, NJ 08012 USA (SAN 169-4596) Tel 856-228-8900; Toll Free: 800-257-7341
Web site: http://www.blackwell.com/.

Blackwell North America, *See* **Blackwell**

Blair, *(978-0-89587; 978-0-910244)* Orders Addr.: 120 Morris St., Durham, NC 27701 USA (SAN 201-4319) Tel 919-560-2738
E-mail: sutton@blairpub.com
Web site: http://www.blairpub.com.

Blair, John F. Pub., *See* **Blair**

Bloomington News Agency, P.O. Box 3757, Bloomington, IL 61702-3757 USA (SAN 169-1732).

Bloomsbury Academic & Professional, *See* **Bloomsbury Academic & Professional**

Bloomsbury Publishing US Trade, Orders Addr.: 16365 James Madison Hwy., Gordonsville, VA 22942 USA.

Bloomsbury Publishing USA, *(978-1-58234; 978-1-59691; 978-1-59990; 978-1-60819; 978-1-84706; 978-1-61963; 978-1-62040; 978-1-62356; 978-1-62892; 978-1-63286; 978-1-5013; 978-1-68119; 978-1-63557; 978-1-5476)* Orders Addr.: 16365 James Madison Hwy., Gordonsville, VA 22942-8501 USA Tel 888-330-8477; Toll Free: 888-330-8477; Edit Addr.: 175 Fifth Ave., Suite 300, New York, NY 10010 USA Toll Free: 888-330-8477; 1385 Broadway, New York, NY 10018 Tel 212-419-5300
E-mail: bloomsbury.kids@bloomsburyusa.com; nathaniel.knaebel@bloomsbury.com; mike.o'connor@bloomsbury.com
Web site: http://www.bloomsburyusa.com.

Blu Sky Media Group, P.O. Box 10069, Murfreesboro, TN 37129-0002 USA
Web site: http://www.bluskymediagroup.com.

Blue Cat, *(978-0-932679; 978-0-936200)* 469 Barbados, Walnut, CA 91789 USA (SAN 214-0322) Tel 909-594-3317.

Blue Mountain Arts Inc., *(978-0-88396; 978-1-58786; 978-1-59842; 978-1-68088)* Orders Addr.: P.O. Box 4549, Boulder, CO 80306 USA (SAN 299-9609) Tel 303-449-0536; Fax: 303-417-6434; 303-417-6496; Toll Free Fax: 800-943-6666; 800-545-8573; Toll Free: 800-525-0642
Web site: http://www.sps.com/.

Blue Mountain Arts (R) by SPS Studios, Incorporated, *See* **Blue Mountain Arts Inc.**

Blue Ridge News Co., 21 Westside Dr., No. B, Asheville, NC 28806-2846 USA (SAN 169-6335).

BMI Educational Services, *(978-0-922443; 978-1-60884; 978-1-60933; 978-1-63071; 978-1-5367)* Orders Addr.: 26 Haypress Rd., Cranbury, NJ 08512 USA (SAN 760-7032); Edit Addr.: P.O. Box 800, Dayton, NJ 08810-0800 USA (SAN 169-4669) Tel 732-329-6991; Fax: 732-329-6994; Toll Free Fax: 800-986-9393 (orders only); Toll Free: 800-222-8100 (orders only)
E-mail: info@bmionline.com
Web site: http://www.bmionline.com/.

Bolchazy-Carducci Pubs., *(978-0-86516; 978-1-61041)* 1570 Baskin Rd., Mundelein, IL 60060-4474 USA (SAN 219-7685) Toll Free: 800-392-6453
E-mail: jcull@bolchazy.com
Web site: http://www.bolchazy.com.

Boley International Subscription Agency, Inc., 1001 Fries Mill Rd., Blackwood, NJ 08012 USA (SAN 159-6225) Tel 609-629-2500.

Bolinda Publishing, Inc., Orders Addr.: 186 S. Long Swamp Rd., Jackson, ME 04921-3154 USA Toll Free Fax: 877-864-8307; Toll Free: 888-235-2019
E-mail: karen@bolinda.com
Web site: http://www.bolinda.com.

Bondcliff Bks., *(978-0-9657475; 978-1-931271)* Orders Addr.: P.O. Box 385, Littleton, NH 03561 USA Toll Free: 800-859-7581; Edit Addr.: 8 Bluejay Ln., Littleton, NH 03561 USA
E-mail: bondclif@ncia.net.

Bonneville News Co., 965 Beardsley Pl., Salt Lake City, UT 84119 USA Tel 801-972-5454; Fax: 801-972-1075; Toll Free: 800-748-5453.

Book Clearing Hse., 46 Purdy St., Harrison, NY 10528 USA (SAN 125-5169) Tel 914-835-0015; Fax: 914-835-0398; Toll Free: 800-431-1579
E-mail: bookch@aol.com.

Book Gallery, *(978-1-878382)* 632 S. Quincy Ave., Apt. 1, Tulsa, OK 74120-4635 USA (SAN 630-9321).

Book Hub, Inc., 903 Pacific Ave., Suite 207A, Santa Cruz, CA 95060 USA Tel 831-466-0145; Fax: 831-515-5955.

Book Publishing Co., *(978-0-913990; 978-1-57067; 978-0-9669317; 978-0-9673108; 978-0-9779183; 978-1-939053)* P.O. Box 99, Summertown, TN 38483 USA (SAN 202-439X) Tel 931-964-3571; Fax: 931-964-3518; Toll Free: 888-260-8458
E-mail: info@bookpubco.com
Web site: http://www.bookpubco.com.

Book Sales, Inc., *(978-0-7628; 978-0-7858; 978-0-89009; 978-1-55521; 978-1-57715; 978-1-4161)* Orders Addr.: 400 1st Ave N. Ste. 300, Minneapolis, MN 55401-1721 USA (SAN 169-488X) Toll Free: 800-526-7257; Edit Addr.: 276 Fifth Ave., Suite 206, New York, NY 10001 USA (SAN 299-4062) Tel 212-779-4972; Fax: 212-779-6058
E-mail: sales@booksalesusa.com
Web site: http://www.booksalesusa.com/.

Book Wholesalers, Inc., *(978-0-7587; 978-1-4046; 978-1-4131; 978-1-4155; 978-1-4156; 978-1-4287)* 1847 Mercer Rd., Lexington, KY 40511-1001 USA (SAN 135-5449) Toll Free: 800-888-4478
E-mail: jcarrico@bwibooks.com; lison@bwibooks.com
Web site: http://www.bwibooks.com.

Bookazine Co., Inc., 75 Hook Rd., Bayonne, NJ 07002 USA (SAN 169-5665) Tel 201-339-7777; Fax: 201-339-7778; Toll Free: 800-221-8112.

Bookazine Company, Incorporated, *See* **Bookazine Co., Inc.**

BookBaby, *(978-1-60984; 978-1-61792; 978-1-61842; 978-1-61927; 978-1-62095; 978-1-62309; 978-1-62488; 978-1-62675; 978-1-4835; 978-1-63192; 978-1-943612; 978-1-68222; 978-1-5439; 978-0-692-95466-9; 978-0-692-11235-9; 978-0-692-11236-6; 978-0-578-41517-8;-1-0983) 7905 N. Rt 130, Pennsauken, NJ 08110 USA Toll Free: 877-961-6878; 7905 N Crescent Blvd, Pennsauken, NJ 08110 Toll Free: 877-961-6878*
E-mail: info@bookbaby.com; support@bookbaby.com; jburton@bookbaby.com; jfoley@bookbaby.com
Web site: http://www.bookbaby.com.

BookHawkers Internet BookSeller, P.O. Box 2094, Wilkes-Barre, PA 18703 USA
Web site: http://www.bookhawkers.com.

Bookhouse, The, 10505 N. May Ave., Oklahoma City, OK 73120-2611 USA (SAN 200-8467) Tel 405-755-0020.

Booklegger, The, *(978-0-936421)* Orders Addr.: P.O. Box 2626, Grass Valley, CA 95945 USA (SAN 697-9548); Edit Addr.: 13100 Grass Valley Ave., Suite D, Grass Valley, CA 95945 USA (SAN 120-6125) Tel 530-272-1556; Fax: 530-272-2133; Toll Free Fax: 800-250-2199; Toll Free: 800-262-1556
E-mail: order@booklegger.com
Web site: http://www.booklegger.com/.

Bookline, Div. of Michiana News Service, Inc., 2232 S. 11th St., Niles, MI 49120 USA (SAN 169-3948) Tel 616-684-3013; Fax: 616-684-8740.

Booklines Hawaii, Ltd., *(978-1-929844; 978-1-58849; 978-1-60274)* Div. of Islander Group, 269 Pali'i St., Mililani, HI 96789 USA (SAN 630-6624) Tel 808-676-0116; Fax: 808-676-0634
E-mail: customerservice@booklines.com
Web site: http://www.booklineshawaii.com.

BookLink, *(978-0-9797436)* 465 Broad Ave., Leonia, NJ 07605-1637 USA (SAN 854-2473) Tel 201-947-3471; Fax: 201-947-6321
E-mail: booklink@es1booklink.com.

BookLink, Inc., 444 Broad St., Camden, SC 29020 USA (SAN 631-5291) Tel 803-432-5169; Fax: 803-424-8418
E-mail: sam@thebooklink.com
Web site: http://www.thebooklink.com.

Bookman Bks., 138 Elena St., Santa Fe, NM 87501 USA (SAN 630-933X) Tel 505-982-5964.

Bookmark, Inc., The, 1445 N. Winchester St., Olathe, KS 66061-5881 USA (SAN 131-4017) Toll Free: 800-642-1288.

Book$mart, Inc., *(978-1-885051)* Div. of Books-A-Million, 602 John Aldridge Dr., Tuscumbia, AL 35674-3002 USA Tel 256-314-4466 Do not confuse with Booksmart in Irondale, AZ
E-mail: brad@roses-4u.com.

BookMasters, 6745 FM 2738, Burleson, TX 76028-1167 USA (SAN 630-8406) Do not confuse with BookMasters Inc., Ashland, OH.

Bookmasters Distribution, *See* **Baker & Taylor Publisher Services (BTPS)**

BookMasters, Inc., *(978-0-917889)* Orders Addr.: P.O. Box 388, Mansfield, OH 44903 USA (SAN 631-3566) Tel 419-281-1802; Fax: 419-281-6883; Toll Free: 800-247-6553; 30 Amberwood Pkwy., Ashland, OH 44805 Tel 419-281-1802; Fax: 419-281-6886
E-mail: info@bookmasters.com; order@bookmaster.com
Web site: http://www.bookmasters.com.

Bookmen, Inc., Orders Addr.: 2300 Louisiana Ave N. # B, Minneapolis, MN 55427-3631 USA (SAN 169-409X) Toll Free Fax: 800-266-5636; Toll Free: 800-328-8411 (customer service)
Web site: http://www.bookmen.com.

BookMobile, Orders Addr.: 5120 Cedar Lake Rd., Saint Louis Park, MN 55416 USA (SAN 760-7245) Fax: 763-398-0198
E-mail: dleeper@bookmobile.com
Web site: http://www.bookmobile.com.

BookPartners, Inc., (*978-0-9622269; 978-1-58151; 978-1-885221*) Orders Addr.: P.O. Box 345, Portland, OR 97205 USA; Edit Addr.: 620 SW Main, Portland, OR 97205 USA Tel 503-225-9900; Fax: 503-225-9901
Web site: http://www.amicapublishing.com.

Books Alive, (*978-0-920470; 978-1-55312*) Div. of Book Publishing Co., Orders Addr.: P.O. Box 99, Summertown, TN 38483 USA (SAN 115-7078) Tel 931-964-3571; Fax: 931-964-3518; Toll Free: 888-260-8458 (orders and customer service)
E-mail: Cynthia@bookpubco.com
Web site: http://www.bookpubco.com.

Books International, Inc., (*978-1-891078*) Orders Addr.: P.O. Box 605, Herndon, VA 20172-0605 USA (SAN 131-761X) Tel 703-661-1500; Fax: 703-661-1501
E-mail: bimail@presswarehouse.com.

Booksellers Order Service, 828 S. Broadway, Tarrytown, NY 10591-5112 USA (SAN 106-5181) Tel 914-591-2665; Fax: 914-591-2720; Toll Free: 800-637-0037.

Booksmith Promotional Co., 100 Paterson Plank Rd., Jersey City, NJ 07307 USA (SAN 664-5364) Tel 201-659-2768; Fax: 201-659-3631.

Booksource, The, (*978-0-7383; 978-0-8335; 978-0-911891; 978-0-9641084; 978-1-886379; 978-1-890760; 978-0-7568; 978-1-4117; 978-1-4178; 978-1-60446; 978-1-4364*) Div. of GL group, Inc., Orders Addr.: 1230 Macklind Ave., Saint Louis, MO 63110-1432 USA (SAN 169-4324) Tel 314-647-0600 Toll Free Fax: 800-647-1923; Toll Free: 800-444-0435
E-mail: khostman@booksource.com; shankins@glgrp.com; gbonebrake@glgrp.com; shankins@booksource.com
Web site: http://www.booksource.com; http://www.goodluckgroup.com/.

BookWorksUSA, 385 Freeport Blvd., Suite 3, Sparks, NV 89431 USA
E-mail: bookworksusa@mac.com.

Bookworld Cos., P.O. Box 2260, Sarasota, FL 34230-2260 USA.

Bookworm, 14 Griffin St., Northport, ME 04849-4446 USA (SAN 170-8074).

Bookworm Bookfairs, P.O. Box 306, Simsbury, CT 06070-0306 USA (SAN 156-5621).

Bookworm, The, 417 Monmouth Dr., Cherry Hill, NJ 08002 USA (SAN 120-9531) Tel 609-667-5884.

Borchardt, G. Inc., 136 E. 57th St., New York, NY 10022 USA (SAN 285-8614) Tel 212-753-5785; Fax: 212-838-6518.

Borders, Inc., 9910 N. By NE Blvd., Bldg. 4, Fishers, IN 46038 USA (SAN 152-5352); Space 497, 1st Level 525 F D Roosevelt Ave. Plaza Las Americas, Hato Rey, PR 00917 (SAN 193-2314); 455 Industrial Blvd., Suite E, La Vergne, TN 37086 (SAN 156-6474); Edit Addr.: 100 Phoenix Dr., Ann Arbor, MI 48108 USA (SAN 152-3546) Tel 734-477-1100; Fulfillment Addr.: a/o Fulfillment Center, 100 Phoenix Dr., Ann Arbor, MI 48108-2202 USA (SAN 197-0917).

Bored Feet Pr., (*978-0-939431*) Orders Addr.: P.O. Box 1832, Mendocino, CA 95460 USA (SAN 661-6992) Tel 707-964-6629; Fax: 707-964-5953; Edit Addr.: 16630 Mitchell Creek Dr., Fort Bragg, CA 95437 USA (SAN 663-3226)
E-mail: Boredft@mcn.org.

Bored Feet Publications, *See* **Bored Feet Pr.**

Bottman Design, Inc., (*978-1-884741*) 1081 S. 300 W., No. A, Salt Lake City, UT 84101 USA (SAN 860-2166) Tel 801-487-1949; Fax: 801-973-6746; Toll Free: 800-365-5564.

Bottom Dog Pr., (*978-0-933087; 978-1-933964; 978-1-947504*) c/o Firelands College, P.O. Box 425, Huron, OH 44839 USA (SAN 689-5492) Tel 419-433-3573; Fax: 419-616-3966
E-mail: LSmithDog@aol.com; lsmithdog@smithdocs.net
Web site: https://www.facebook.com/BottomDogPress/?ref=bookmarks; http://smithdocs.net; http://smithdocs.net/recent_bottom_dog_press_titles.

Bound to Stay Bound Bks., (*978-0-9718238*) 1880 W. Morton Rd., Jacksonville, IL 62650 USA (SAN 169-1996) Toll Free Fax: 800-747-2872; Toll Free: 800-637-6586
Web site: http://www.btsb.com.

Bowers & Merena Galleries, Inc., (*978-0-943161*) Orders Addr.: P.O. Box 1224, Wolfeboro, NH 03894 USA (SAN 168-9746) Tel 603-569-5095; Fax: 603-569-5319; Toll Free: 800-222-5993; Edit Addr.: 18061 Fitch., Irvine, CA 92614-6018 USA (SAN 668-2561).

Bowker LLC, R. R., (*978-0-8352; 978-0-911255; 978-0-641; 978-0-9856945; 978-1-941808*) Subs. of Proquest LLC, Orders Addr.: P.O. Box 32, New Providence, NJ 07974 USA Tel 908-286-1090; Fax: 908-219-0098; Toll Free: 888-269-5372; Edit Addr.: 630 Central Ave., New Providence, NJ 07974 USA (SAN 214-1191); 630 Central Ave., B&T box, New Providence, NJ 07974 (SAN 857-8516)
E-mail: info@bowker.com; pad@bowker.com; customerservice@bowker.com; specialtytitles@bowker.com
Web site: http://www.bowker.com.

Bowling Green State University, Philosophy Documentation Center, *See* **Philosophy Documentation Ctr.**

Boydell & Brewer, Inc., (*978-0-85115; 978-0-85991; 978-0-907239; 978-0-938100; 978-1-57113; 978-1-58046; 978-1-85566; 978-1-870252; 978-1-878822; 978-1-879751; 978-1-900639; 978-1-84384; 978-1-84383; 978-1-64014; 978-1-64825*) Div. of Boydell & Brewer Group, Ltd., Orders Addr.: 668 Mount Hope Ave., Rochester, NY 14620-2731 USA (SAN 013-8479) Tel 585-275-0419; Fax: 585-271-8778
E-mail: boydell@boydellusa.net; boydell@boydell.co.uk
Web site: http://www.boydellandbrewer.com.

Boyds Mills Pr., (*978-1-56397; 978-1-878093; 978-1-886910; 978-1-59078; 978-1-932425; 978-1-62091; 978-1-62979; 978-0-9961172; 978-0-9961173; 978-1-943283; 978-1-68238; 978-1-68329; 978-1-68437; 978-1-64472; 978-1-7922*) Div. of Highlights For Children, Inc., 815 Church St., Honesdale, PA 18431 USA (SAN 852-3177) Tel 570-251-4513; 570-251-4592 Toll Free: 800-490-5111 Admin line; 877-512-8366; 800-874-8817 Cust Svc Columbus, OH
E-mail: admin@boydsmillspress.com; marketing@boydsmillspress.com
Web site: http://www.boydsmillspress.com; http://www.wordsongpoetry.com; http://www.calkinscreekbooks.com; http://www.frontstreetbooks.com.

BPDI, 1000 S. Lynndale Dr., Appleton, WI 54914 USA (SAN 631-6859) Tel 920-830-7897; Fax: 920-830-3857.

Bridge Pubns., Inc., (*978-0-88404; 978-1-57318; 978-1-4031; 978-1-61177; 978-1-4572; 978-1-0789*) Orders Addr.: 5600 E. Olympic Blvd., Commerce, CA 90022 USA (SAN 208-3884) Tel 323-888-6200; Fax: 323-888-6210; Toll Free: 800-722-1733; 800-334-5433; Edit Addr.: 4751_Fountain Ave., Los Angeles, CA 90029 USA
E-mail: annarnow@bridgepub.com; daniellem@bridgepub.com; donarnow@bridgepub.com; purchaser@bridgepub.com
Web site: http://www.bridgepub.com; http://www.clearbodyclearmind.com; http://www.scientology.org; http://www.dianetics.org.

Bridge-Logos Foundation, *See* **Bridge-Logos, Inc.**

Bridge-Logos, Inc., (*978-0-88270; 978-0-912106; 978-0-9841034; 978-1-61036*) Orders Addr.: 14260 W. Newberry Rd, Newberry, FL 32669 USA (SAN 253-5254) Tel 352-727-9324; Toll Free: 800-935-6467 (orders only); 800-631-5802 (orders only)
E-mail: SWooldridge@bridgelogos.com
Web site: http://www.bridgelogos.com.

Brigham Distributing, (*978-0-578-09711-4; 978-0-578-14054-4*) 330 South 150 E., Burley, ID 83318 USA; 110 S 800 W., Brigham City, UT 84302.

Brigham Distribution, 110 S. 800 W., Brigham City, UT 84302 USA (SAN 760-7652) Tel 435-723-6611; Fax: 435-723-6644
E-mail: brigdist@sisna.com.

Brigham, Kay, Orders Addr.: 9500 Old Cutler Rd., Miami, FL 33156 USA Tel 305-666-3844; Fax: 305-661-4843
Web site: http://www.kaybrigham.com.

Brigham Young Univ. Print Services, (*978-0-578-64957-3*) 205 UPB, Provo, UT 84602 USA Tel 801-378-2809; Fax: 801-378-3374
E-mail: denise@upb.byu.edu
Web site: http://www.upb.byu.edu.

Bright Horizons Specialty Distributors, Inc., 206 Riva Ridge Dr., Fairview, NC 28730-9764 USA (SAN 110-4101) Toll Free: 800-437-3959 (orders only).

Bright Sky Publishing, *See* **Night Heron Media**

Brightpoint Literacy, 299 Market St., Saddle Brook, NJ 07663 USA Tel 201-708-6498.

Brill, E. J. U. S. A., Incorporated, *See* **Brill USA, Inc.**

Brill USA, Inc., (*978-0-916846*) Subs. of Brill Academic Publishing Co., The Netherlands, 2 Liberty Square, Eleventh Flr., Boston, MA 02109 USA (SAN 254-6922) Tel 617-263-2323; Fax: 617-263-2324; Toll Free: 800-962-4406
E-mail: cs@brillusa.com; brillonline@brillusa.com
Web site: http://www.brill.nl.

Brilliance Publishing, *See* **Brilliance Publishing, Inc.**

Brilliance Publishing, Inc., (*978-0-930435; 978-1-56100; 978-1-56740; 978-1-58788; 978-1-59086; 978-1-59355; 978-1-59600; 978-1-59710; 978-1-59737; 978-1-4233; 978-1-4418; 978-1-61106; 978-1-4558; 978-1-4692; 978-1-4805; 978-1-4915; 978-1-5012; 978-1-5113; 978-1-5226; 978-1-5318; 978-1-5366; 978-1-5436; 978-1-9786; 978-1-7213; 978-1-7997; 978-1-7135; 978-1-7136; 979-8-9850001) Orders Addr.: P.O. Box 887, Grand Haven, MI 49417 USA (SAN 690-1395) Tel 616-846-5256; Fax: 616-846-0630; Toll Free: 800-648-2312 x330 (phone/fax, retail & library orders); Edit Addr.: 1704 Eaton Dr., Grand Haven, MI 49417 USA (SAN 858-138X) Toll Free: 800-648-2312 x330*
E-mail: sales@brillianceaudio.com; customerservice@brillianceaudio.com; jcraig@brilliancepublishing.com
Web site: http://www.brilliancepublishing.com.

Brisco Pubns., (*978-0-9603576*) P.O. Box 2161, Palos Verdes Peninsula, CA 90274 USA (SAN 133-0268) Tel 310-534-4943; Fax: 310-534-8437.

Bristlecone Publishing Co., 2560 Brookridge Ave., Golden Valley, MN 55422 USA
E-mail: davej@jblcompanies.com.

Brodart Co., (*978-0-87272; 978-1-62844; 978-1-63546; 978-1-64838*) Orders Addr.: 500 Arch St., Williamsport, PA 17705 USA (SAN 169-7684) Tel 570-326-2461 (International); Fax: 570-326-1479; 717-326-2461; 519-759-1144 (Canada); Toll Free Fax: 800-999-6799; Toll Free: 800-233-8467 (US & Canada)
E-mail: bookinfo@brodart.com
Web site: http://www.brodart.com.

Brookes, Paul H. Publishing Company Incorporated, *See* **Brookes Publishing**

Brookes Publishing, (*978-0-933716; 978-1-55766; 978-1-59857; 978-1-68125*) Orders Addr.: P.O. Box 10624, Baltimore, MD 21285-0624 USA (SAN 212-730X) Tel 410-337-9580; Fax: 410-337-8539; Toll Free: 800-638-3775 (customer service/ordering/billing/fulfillment); Edit Addr.: 409 Washington Ave., Suite 500, Baltimore, MD 21204 USA (SAN 666-6485)
E-mail: custserv@brookespublishing.com
Web site: http://www.brookespublishing.com.

Brotherhood of Life, Inc., (*978-0-914732*) P.O. Box 46306, Las Vegas, NV 89114-6306 USA (SAN 111-3674) Fax: 702-319-5577
E-mail: brotherhoodoflife@hotmail.com
Web site: http://www.brotherhoodoflife.com.

Brown Bks., (*978-0-9668452; 978-0-9717197*) Div. of Personal Profiles, Inc., 16200 Dallas Pkwy., Suite 170, Dallas, TX 75248-2616 USA Do not confuse with companies with the same or similar names in Allen, TX, Redway, CA, Montrose, CO, Plano, TX
Web site: http://www.brownbooks.com.

Brown Books Publishing Group, (*978-0-9713265; 978-0-9744597; 978-0-9753907; 978-1-933285; 978-1-934812; 978-1-61254; 978-1-948307*) 16250 Knoll Trail Dr. Ste 205, Dallas, TX 75248 USA Tel 972-381-0009; Fax: 972-248-4336
E-mail: auburn.layman@brownbooks.com
Web site: http://www.brownbooks.com; http://www.thep3press.com.

Brown, David Book Company, The, *See* **Casemate Academic**

Brown Enterprises, Inc., (*978-0-9711451*) P.O. Box 11447, Durham, NC 27703 USA Tel 919-680-2288 Do not confuse with companies with the same or similar names in Pasadena, CA, Bellingham, WA
E-mail: brown.enterprisesinc@verizon.net.

Brunner News Agency, 217 Flanders Ave., P.O. Box 598, Lima, OH 45801 USA (SAN 169-6777) Tel 419-225-5826; Fax: 419-225-5537; Toll Free: 800-998-1727
E-mail: brunnews@aol.com
Web site: http://www.readmoreshallmark.com.

Bryan, R. L., (*978-0-934870*) P.O. Box 368, Columbia, SC 29202 USA Tel 803-779-3560.

Bryant Altman Map, Inc., Endicott St., Bldg. 26, Norwood, MA 02062 USA (SAN 630-2475) Tel 781-762-3339; Fax: 781-769-9080
E-mail: JPG63@aol.com.

Bryant-Altman Book & Map Distributors, *See* **Bryant Altman Map, Inc.**

Buckeye News Co., 6800 W. Central Ave., Suite F, Toledo, OH 43617-1157 USA (SAN 169-6874).

Budget Bk. Service, Inc., Div. of LDAP, Inc., 386 Park Ave. S., Suite 1913, New York, NY 10016-8804 USA (SAN 169-5762) Fax: 212-679-2247.

Budget Marketing, Inc., P.O. Box 1805, Des Moines, IA 50306 USA (SAN 285-8754).

Budgetext, Orders Addr.: P.O. Box 1487, Fayetteville, AR 72702 USA (SAN 111-3321) Tel 501-443-9205; Fax: 501-442-3064; Toll Free: 800-643-3432; Edit Addr.: 1936 N. Shiloh Dr., Fayetteville, AR 72704 USA (SAN 249-3330)
E-mail: wmorgan@absc.com; scaldwell@budgetext.com
Web site: http://www.budgetext.com.

Buena Vista Home Video, (*978-0-7888; 978-1-55890*) Div. of Walt Disney Studios, 500 S. Buena Vista St., Burbank, CA 91521-1120 USA (SAN 249-2342) Tel 818-295-4841; Fax: 818-972-2845; Toll Free: 800-723-4763
Web site: http://www.disney.com.

Burlington News Agency, 382 Hercules Dr., Colchester, VT 05446-5836 USA (SAN 169-8583).

Burns News Agency, P.O. Box 1211, Rochester, NY 14603-1211 USA (SAN 169-5320).

B.W. Bks. on Wings, Orders Addr.: 581 Market St., San Francisco, CA 94105-2847 USA.

BWI, 1340 Ridgeview Dr., Mchenry, IL 60050-7047 USA.

Byeway Bks., (*978-1-85997; 978-1-904586; 978-1-933581; 978-1-934004; 978-1-60176*) 15941 W. 65th St., Shawnee, KS 66217-9342 USA Toll Free Fax: 866-426-3929; Toll Free: 866-429-3929
E-mail: customerservice@byewaybooks.com
Web site: http://www.byewaybooks.com/how_to_order.html.

Byrrd Enterprises, Inc., (*978-1-886715*) 1302 Lafayette Dr., Alexandria, VA 22308 USA (SAN 169-8605) Tel 703-765-5626; Fax: 703-768-4086; Toll Free: 800-628-0901
E-mail: byrrdbooks@aol.com.

C & B Bk. Distribution, 65-77 160th St., Flushing, NY 11365 USA Tel 718-591-4525
Web site: http://www.cbbooksdistribution.com.

C & B Bk. Hse., 21 Oak Ridge Rd., Monroe, CT 06468 USA (SAN 159-8279).

C & H News Co., P.O. Box 2768, Corpus Christi, TX 78403-2768 USA (SAN 169-8249).

C & T Publishing, (*978-0-914881; 978-1-57120; 978-1-60705; 978-1-61745; 978-1-64403*) Orders Addr.: 1651 Challenge Dr., Concord, CA 94520 USA (SAN 289-0720) Tel 925-677-0377; Fax: 925-617-0374; Toll Free: 800-284-1114
E-mail: ctinfo@ctpub.com
Web site: http://www.ctpub.com.

C R C Publications, *See* **Faith Alive Christian Resources**

C4 Kids, Orders Addr.: 1220 N. Las Palmas, No. 201, Los Angeles, CA 90038 USA.

Cadmus Communications, a Cenveo Co., Publisher Services Group 136 Carlin Rd., Conklin, NY 13748 USA Tel 607-762-5555; Fax: 607-762-6774.

Cafepress, 127 Brockmoore Dr., East Amherst, NY 14051 USA.

CafePress.com, (*978-1-4148*) 1850 Gateway Dr. Ste. 300, Foster City, CA 94404-4061 USA Toll Free: 877-809-1659
E-mail: mystore@cafepress.com
Web site: http://www.cafepress.com.

Caldwell Letter Service, 4500 S. Kolin Ave., Chicago, IL 60632 USA.

Calico Subscription Co., P.O. Box 640337, San Jose, CA 95164-0337 USA (SAN 285-9173) Tel 408-432-8700; Fax: 408-432-8813; Toll Free: 800-952-2542.

California Princeton Fulfillment Services, 1445 Lower Ferry Rd., Ewing, NJ 08618 USA (SAN 630-639X) Tel 609-883-1759 ext 536; Toll Free: 800-777-4726
E-mail: donnaw@cpfs.pupress.princeton.edu.

Calliope Bks., (*978-0-9620187*) 2115 Chadbourne Ave., Madison, WI 53705 USA (SAN 247-9370) Tel 608-238-9258 Do not confuse with Calliope Books in Santa Barbara, CA
E-mail: wcoleman@facstaff.wisc.edu; calliopebooks@hotmail.com
Web site: http://www.execpc.com/~calliope.

Calvary Chapel Resources, (*978-0-936728; 978-1-931713; 978-1-932941; 978-1-59751*) Div. of Calvary Chapel Costa Mesa, Orders Addr.: P.O. Box 8000, Costa Mesa, CA 92628 USA (SAN 110-8379) Tel 714-825-9673 Toll Free: 800-272-9673; Edit Addr.: 3232 W. MacArthur Blvd., Santa Ana, CA 92704 USA (SAN 214-2260) Tel 714-825-9673 Toll Free: 800-272-9637
E-mail: cathyr@twft.com
Web site: http://www.twft.com; cccm.com.

Cambium Education, Inc., (*978-0-944584; 978-1-57035; 978-1-59318; 978-1-932282; 978-1-4168; 978-1-60218; 978-1-60697*) 4093 Specialty Pl., Longmont, CO 80504 USA (SAN 243-945X) Tel 303-651-2829; Fax: 303-907-8694; Toll Free: 800-547-6747 (orders only)
E-mail: publishing@sopriswest.com; customerservice@cambiumlearning.com
Web site: http://www.sopriswest.com.

Cambridge Bk. Co., (*978-0-8428*) Div. of Simon & Schuster, Inc., 4350 Equity Dr., Box 249, Columbus, OH 43216 USA (SAN 169-5703) Toll Free: 800-238-5833
Web site: http://www.simonsays.com/.

Cambridge Univ. Pr., (*978-0-521; 978-0-511*) Orders Addr.: 100 Brook Hill Dr., West Nyack, NY 10994-2133 USA (SAN 281-3769) Tel 845-353-7500; Fax: 845-353-4141; Toll Free: 800-872-7423 (orders, returns, credit & accounting); 800-937-9600; Edit Addr.: 32 Avenue of the Americas, New York, NY 10013-2473 USA (SAN 200-206X) Tel 212-924-3900; Fax: 212-691-3239
E-mail: customer_service@cup.org; orders@cup.org; information@cup.org
Web site: http://www.cambridge.org/.

Canyonlands Pubns., (*978-0-9702595*) Orders Addr.: P.O. Box 16175, Bellemont, AZ 86015-6175 USA (SAN 114-3824) Tel 520-779-3888; Fax: 520-779-3778; Toll Free: 800-283-1983; Edit Addr.: 4860 N. Ken Morey, Bellemont, AZ 86015 USA
E-mail: books@infomagic.com.

Cape Cod Scribe, 5 Camelot Ln., Bourne, MA 02532 USA Tel 508-415-1295.

Cape News Co., P.O. Box 568680, Rockledge, FL 32955 USA Tel 407-636-5909.

Capital Business Systems, Div. of Capital Business Service, Orders Addr.: P.O. Box 2088, Napa, CA 94558 USA (SAN 698-3146) Tel 707-252-8844; Fax: 707-252-6368; Edit Addr.: 2033 First St., Napa, CA 94558 USA.

Capital News Co., 961 Palmyra, Jackson, MS 39203 USA Tel 601-355-8341; Fax: 601-352-1343.

Capitol Christian Distribution, Orders Addr.: P.O. Box 5084, Brentwood, TN 37024-5084 USA Tel 800-877-4443
E-mail: ccmgdistribution@umusic.com.

Capitol News Agency, P.O. Box 7886, Richmond, VA 23231 USA (SAN 249-2768); 5203 Hatcher St., Richmond, VA 23231-0271 Tel 804-222-7252.

Capper Pr., 1503 SW 42nd, Topeka, KS 66609 USA (SAN 285-8886) Tel 913-274-4324; Fax: 913-274-4305; Toll Free: 800-678-5779 (ext. 4324).

Capstone, (*978-0-7368; 978-0-929895; 978-1-56065; 978-0-7565; 978-1-4048; 978-1-59889; 978-1-4296; 978-1-934338; 978-1-4342; 978-1-936700; 978-1-937412; 978-1-62065; 978-1-4765; 978-1-62370; 978-1-4795; 978-1-62521; 978-1-4914; 978-1-63079; 978-1-4965; 978-1-4966; 978-1-5157; 978-1-5158; 978-1-68436; 978-1-5435; 978-1-9771; 978-1-68446; 978-1-6639) Div. of Coughlan Companies, LLC, 1905 Lookout Dr., North Mankato, MN 55033 USA Tel 507-385-8215; Fax: 507-388-3752; Orders Addr.: 1710 Roe Crest Dr., North Mankato, MN 56003 USA (SAN 254-1815) Toll Free Fax: 888-262-0705; Toll Free: 800-747-4992; Edit Addr.: 5050 Lincoln Dr Suite 200, Edina, MN 55436 USA Fax: 952-933-2410; Toll Free: 888-517-8977 Do not confuse with Capstone Pr., Inc. in Decatur, IL*
E-mail: customerservice@capstonepub.com
Web site: http://www.capstone-press.com; http://www.capstonepub.com; http://www.capstoneclassroom.com.

Capstone Press, Incorporated, *See* **Capstone**

Cardinal Pubs. Group, 2402 N. Shadeland Ave. Ste. A, Indianapolis, IN 46219-1746 USA (SAN 631-7936)
E-mail: tdoherty@in.net.

Cards Bks. N Things, 1446 St., Rd. 2 West, La Porte, IN 46350 USA (SAN 159-8295).

Carlex, Orders Addr.: 1545 W. Hamlin, Rochester Hills, MI 48309 USA (SAN 631-5615) Tel 810-852-5422; Fax: 810-852-7142.

Carolina Biological Supply Co., (*978-0-89278; 978-1-4350*) 2700 York Rd., Burlington, NC 27215-3398 USA (SAN 249-2784) Tel 336-584-0381; Fax:

910-584-3399; Toll Free Fax: 800-222-7112; Toll Free: 800-334-5551
E-mail: carolina@carolina.com
Web site: http://www.carolina.com.

Carolina Cassette Distributors, Orders Addr.: P.O. Box 429, New Bern, NC 28560 USA (SAN 110-8395) Fax: 919-638-1291; Edit Addr.: 2600 Oaks Rd., New Bern, NC 28560 USA (SAN 659-2155) Tel 919-638-5583.

Carolina News Co., Orders Addr.: P.O. Box 10, Fayetteville, NC 28302 USA; Edit Addr.: 245 Tillinghast St., Fayetteville, NC 28301 USA Tel 910-483-4135.

Carson-Dellosa Publishing Company, Incorporated, *See* **Carson-Dellosa Publishing, LLC**

Carson-Dellosa Publishing, LLC, *(978-0-88724; 978-1-57156; 978-1-57332; 978-1-59441; 978-1-60022; 978-1-60418; 978-1-936022; 978-1-936023; 978-1-936024; 978-0-9823625; 978-0-9823626; 978-0-9823627; 978-0-692-00200-1; 978-1-60996; 978-1-62057; 978-1-62223; 978-1-62399; 978-1-62442; 978-1-62648; 978-1-4838) Orders Addr.: P.O. Box 35665, Greensboro, NC 27425 USA Tel 336-632-0084; Fax: 336-808-3249; Toll Free: 800-321-0943*
Web site: http://www.carsondellosa.com.

Casa Del Libro, Orders Addr.: P.O. Box 3853, La Mesa, CA 91944-3853 USA.

Cascade News, Inc., 1055 Commerce Ave., Longview, WA 98632 USA (SAN 169-8761) Tel 360-425-2450; Fax: 360-425-2451.

Casemate Academic, *(978-0-9774094; 978-1-935488)* Orders Addr.: P.O. Box 511, Oakville, CT 06779 USA (SAN 630-9461) Tel 860-945-9329; Fax: 860-945-9468; Toll Free: 800-791-9354; Edit Addr.: 20 Main St., Oakville, CT 06779 USA
E-mail: queries@dbbconline.com
Web site: http://www.oxbowbooks.com.

Casemate Pubs. & Bk. Distributors, LLC, *(978-0-9711709; 978-1-932033; 978-1-935149; 978-1-61200; 978-1-952715; 978-1-63624)* Orders Addr.: 1950 Lawrence Rd., Havertown, PA 19083 USA; 22883 Quicksilver Dr., Herndon, VA 20166 (SAN 631-9386) Tel 703-661-1500; Edit Addr.: 180 Varick St. Suite 816, New York, NY 10014 USA
E-mail: casemate@casematepublishing.com
Web site: http://www.casematepublishing.com.

Casino Distributors, Orders Addr.: P.O. Box 849, Pleasantville, NJ 08232 USA (SAN 169-457X) Tel 609-646-4165; Fax: 609-645-0152; Edit Addr.: 10 Canale Dr., Pleasantville, NJ 08234 USA (SAN 249-3276).

Casper Magazine Agency, P.O. Box 2340, Casper, WY 82602 USA (SAN 159-8325).

Casscom Media, *(978-1-930034; 978-1-936081; 978-1-62758)* 6000 Industrial Dr., Greenville, TX 75402 USA Tel 903-455-2555; Fax: 903-455-4448; Toll Free: 800-974-1555
E-mail: sue@casscommedia.com; kathy@casscomedia.com
Web site: http://www.casscommedia.com.

Cassette Book Company, *See* **Audio Bk. Co.**

Cassette Communications, Incorporated, *See* **Casscom Media**

Castlebridge Distribution, 115 Bluebill Dr., Savannah, GA 31419 USA Toll Free: 888-300-1961 (phone/fax)
E-mail: orders@castlebridgedistribution.com.

Catholic Bk. Publishing Corp., *(978-0-89942; 978-0-9623410; 978-1-878718; 978-1-933066; 978-1-937913; 978-1-941243; 978-1-947070; 978-1-948843; 978-1-948844; 978-1-953152)* 77 West End Rd., Totowa, NJ 07512-1405 USA (SAN 204-3432) Tel 973-890-2400; Fax: 973-890-2410; Toll Free: 800-892-6657
E-mail: resurpress@aol.com
Web site: http://www.catholicbkpub.com.

Catholic Bookrack Service, 700 E. Elm St., La Grange, IL 60525 USA (SAN 169-2178) Tel 708-482-0044; Fax: 708-482-9644.

Catholic Literary Guild, Inc., 200 Hamilton Ave., White Plains, NY 10601 USA (SAN 285-8908) Tel 914-949-4444.

Catholic Univ. of America Pr., *(978-0-8132; 978-1-949822)* Orders Addr.: c/o Hopkins Fulfillment Services, P.O. Box 50370, Baltimore, MD 21211-4370 USA (SAN 203-6304) Tel 410-516-6953; Fax: 410-516-6998; Toll Free: 800-537-5487; Edit Addr.: 620 Michigan Ave., NE, Washington, DC 20064 USA (SAN 203-6290) Tel 202-319-5052; Fax: 202-319-4985
E-mail: cua-press@cua.edu
Web site: http://cuapress.cua.edu/.

Catweasel Productions, *See* **Ars Obscura**

Cave of the Winds, P.O. Box 826, Manitou Springs, CO 80829 USA Tel 719-685-5444
Web site: http://www.caveofthewinds.com.

Caxton Pr., *(978-0-87004)* Div. of Caxton Printers. Ltd., 312 Main St., Caldwell, ID 83605-3299 USA (SAN 201-9698) Tel 208-459-7421; Fax: 208-459-7450; Toll Free: 800-657-6465
E-mail: publish@caxtonprinters.com; sgipson@caxtonpress.com
Web site: http://www.caxtonpress.com.

Caxton Printers, Limited, *See* **Caxton Pr.**

CBLS Pubs., *(978-1-878907; 978-1-59529)* 119 Brentwood St., Marietta, OH 45750 USA (SAN 169-5517) Tel 740-374-9458; Fax: 740-374-8029
E-mail: cbls@cbls.com
Web site: http://www.cbls.com.

CD Baby, Orders Addr.: 5925 NE 80th Ave., Portland, OR 97218-2891 USA Tel 503-595-3000; Fax: 503-296-2370; Toll Free: 800-289-6923 (CD orders only)
E-mail: cdbaby@cdbaby.com
Web site: http://www.cdbaby.com.

CD Distributing, Inc., P.O. Box 4965, Missoula, MT 59806-4965 USA (SAN 169-4367) Fax: 406-454-0415.

CEC: Council for Exceptional Children, 2900 Crystal Dr., Suite 1000, Arlington, VA 22202-9466 USA
Web site: http://www.cec.sped.org/.

Cedar Fort, Inc./CFI Distribution, *(978-0-88290; 978-0-934126; 978-1-55517; 978-1-59955; 978-1-4621)* 2373 West 700 South, Springville, UT 84663 USA (SAN 170-2858) Tel 801-489-4084; Fax: 801-489-1097; Toll Free: 800-759-2665
E-mail: skybook@cedarfort.com
Web site: http://www.cedarfort.com.

Cedar Graphics, *See* **Igram Pr.**

Cengage Gale, *(978-0-13; 978-0-7876; 978-0-8103; 978-0-936474; 978-1-57302; 978-1-878623; 978-1-59413; 978-1-59414; 978-1-59415; 978-1-4144; 978-1-4205; 978-1-59722; 978-1-4328; 978-1-5358)* Subs. of Cengage Learning, Orders Addr.: P.O. Box 9187, Farmington Hills, MI 48333-9187 USA Toll Free Fax: 800 414 5043; Toll Free: 800 877 4253; Edit Addr.: 27500 Drake Rd., Farmington Hills, MI 48331 USA (SAN 213-4373) Tel 248-699-8495 Toll Free: 800-877-4253; a/o Wheeler Publishing, 295 Kennedy Memorial Dr., Waterville, ME 04901 Toll Free: 800 223 1244
E-mail: gale.salesassistance@thomson.com
Web site: http://www.gale.com.

CENGAGE Learning, Orders Addr.: 10650 Toebben Dr., Independence, KY 41051 USA (SAN 200-2213) Tel 859-525-6620; Fax: 859-525-0978; Toll Free Fax: 800-487-8488; Toll Free: 800-354-9706
Web site: http://www.cengage.com/.

Centennial Pubns., 1400 Ash Dr., Fort Collins, CO 80521 USA (SAN 630-494X) Tel 970-493-2041 Do not confuse with Centennial Pubns., Grand Junction, CO.

Central Arizona Distributing, 4932 W. Pasadena Ave., Glendale, AZ 85301 USA (SAN 170-6128) Tel 602-939-6511.

Central Coast Bks., 1195 Al Sereno Ln., Los Osos, CA 93402-4413 USA Tel 805-534-0307 (phone/fax)
E-mail: ccbooks@charter.net.

Central European Univ. Pr., *(978-1-85866; 978-963-9116; 978-963-9241; 978-963-7326; 978-963-9776; 978-1-61055; 978-615-5053; 978-615-5225; 978-615-5211; 978-963-386)* Orders Addr.: 10335 Kensington Pkwy. Ste. A, Kensington, MD 20895 USA Tel 301-933-0607 All Inquiries & Orders; Toll Free Fax: 301-933-0615 Orders; c/o Books International, Russia Online Bookstore PO Box 558, Kensington, MD 20895; Edit Addr.: Október 6 utca 14, Budapest, 1051 HUN Tel 36-1-327-3000; Fax: 36-1-327-3183
E-mail: books@russia-on-line.com; ceupress@ceu.hu
Web site: http://www.ceupress.com; http://www.Russia-on-line.com.

Central Illinois Periodicals, P.O. Box 3757, Bloomington, IL 61701 USA (SAN 630-8945) Tel 309-829-9405.

Central Kentucky News Distributing Company, *See* **Anderson-Austin News Co., LLC**

Central News of Sandusky, 5716 McCartney Rd., Sandusky, OH 44870-1538 USA (SAN 169-684X).

Central Programs, 802 N. 41st St., Bethany, MO 64424 USA Tel 660-425-7777.

Central South Christian Distribution, 3730 Vulcan Dr., Nashville, TN 37211 USA (SAN 631-2543) Tel 615-833-5960; Toll Free Fax: 800-220-0194; Toll Free: 800-757-0856.

Centralia News Co., 232 E. Broadway, Centralia, IL 62801 USA (SAN 159-8341) Tel 618-532-5601.

CentroLibros de Puerto Rico, Inc., Santa Rosa Unit, Bayamon, PR 00960 USA (SAN 631-1245) Tel 787-275-0460; Fax: 787-275-0360.

Century Bk. Distribution, 814 Boon, Traverse City, MI 49686 USA Tel 231-933-6405 (phone/fax).

Century Pr., *(978-0-9659417)* Div. of Conservatory of American Letters, P.O. Box 298, Thomaston, ME 04861 USA Tel 207-354-0998; Fax: 207-354-8953 Do not confuse with companies with the same name in Arroyo Seco, NM, Oklahoma City, OK
E-mail: cal@americanletters.org
Web site: http://www.americanletters.org.

Ceramic Book & Literature Service, *See* **CBLS Pubs.**

Chain Sales Marketing, Inc., *(978-1-55836)* 149 Madison Ave., Suite 810, New York, NY 10016 USA (SAN 245-1328) Tel 212-696-4230; Fax: 212-696-4391.

Chambers Kingfisher Graham Publishers, Incorporated, *See* **Larousse Kingfisher Chambers, Inc.**

Champaign-Urbana News Agency, Orders Addr.: P.O. Box 793, Champaign, IL 61824 USA (SAN 630-8953) Tel 217-351-7047; Edit Addr.: 503 Kenyon, Champaign, IL 61820 USA.

Charisma Media, *(978-0-88419; 978-0-930525; 978-1-59185; 978-1-59979; 978-1-61638; 978-1-62136; 978-1-62998; 978-1-62999; 978-1-63641)* Div. of Creation House Pr., 600 Rinehart Rd., Lake Mary, FL 32746 USA (SAN 677-5640) Tel 407-333-0600; Fax: 407-333-7100; Toll Free: 800-283-8494
Web site: http://www.charismamedia.com/.

Charlesbridge Publishing, Inc., *(978-0-88106; 978-0-935508; 978-1-57091; 978-1-58089; 978-1-879085; 978-1-60734; 978-0-9822939; 978-0-9823064; 978-1-936140; 978-1-63289; 978-1-64537)* Orders Addr.: c/o Penguin Random House, 400 Hahn Rd., Westminster, MD 21157 USA Toll Free Fax: 800-669-1536; Toll Free: 800-733-3000; Edit Addr.: 85 Main St., Watertown, MA 02472 USA (SAN 240-5474) Tel 617-926-0329; Fax: 617-926-5720; Toll Free Fax: 800-926-5775; Toll Free: 800-225-3214
E-mail: orders@charlesbridge.com
Web site: http://www.charlesbridge.com.

Charlynn Publishing Co., Inc., 4152 E. Fifth St., Tucson, AZ 85711 USA.

Checker Distributors, 400 W. Dussel Dr. Ste. B, Maumee, OH 43537-1636 USA (SAN 631-1431) Toll Free: 800-537-1060.

Chelsea Green Publishing, *(978-0-930031; 978-1-890132; 978-1-931498; 978-1-933392; 978-1-60358; 978-1-64502)* 85 N. Main St., Suite 120, White River Junction, VT 05001 USA
E-mail: info@chelseagreen.com
Web site: http://www.chelseagreen.com.

Cheng & Tsui Co., *(978-0-88727; 978-0-917056; 978-1-62291)* 25 W. St., Boston, MA 02111-1213 USA (SAN 169-3387)
E-mail: service@cheng-tsui.com
Web site: http://www.cheng-tsui.com.

Cherry Lake Publishing, *(978-1-60279; 978-1-61080; 978-1-62431; 978-1-62753; 978-1-63137; 978-1-63188; 978-1-63362; 978-1-63470; 978-1-63471; 978-1-63472; 978-1-5341)* 1215 Overidgeview Ct., Ann Arbor, MI 48103 USA Tel 248-705-2045; 1750 Northway Dr., Suite 101, North Mankato, MN 56003 (SAN 858-9275) Tel 866-918-3956; Toll Free Fax: 866-489-6490; 2395 S. Huron Prkwy Ste. 200, Ann Arbor, MI 48104
E-mail: customerservice@cherrylakepublishing.com; benmondloch@me.com; lois.hume@sleepingbearpress.com
Web site: http://cherrylakepublishing.com; www.sleepingbearpress.com.

Chesbro Music Co., 327 Broadway, Idaho Falls, ID 83403 USA (SAN 631-0850) Tel 208-522-8691.

Chicago Distribution Ctr., Orders Addr.: 11030 S. Langley Ave., Chicago, IL 60628 USA (SAN 630-6047) Tel 773-702-7000 (International); Fax: 773-702-7212 (International); Toll Free Fax: 800-621-8476 (USA/Canada); Toll Free: 800-621-2736 (USA/Canada); 800-621-8471 (credit & collections)
E-mail: custserv@press.uchicago.edu; orders@press.uchicago.edu
Web site: http://www.press.uchicago.edu; http://www.press.uchicago.edu/presswide/cdc/.

Chicago Review Pr., Inc., *(978-0-89733; 978-0-912777; 978-0-913705; 978-0-914090; 978-0-914091; 978-0-915864; 978-1-55652; 978-1-56976; 978-1-61373; 978-1-61374; 978-1-64160)* 814 N. Franklin St., Chicago, IL 60610 USA (SAN 213-5744) Tel 312-337-0747; Toll Free: 800-888-4741 (orders only)
E-mail: frontdesk@chicagoreviewpress.com; orders@ipgbook.com
Web site: http://www.ipgbook.com; http://www.chicagoreviewpress.com.

Chico News Agency, P.O. Box 690, Chico, CA 95927 USA (SAN 168-9533) Tel 530-895-1000; Fax: 530-895-0158.

Children's Bookfair Co., The, 700 E. Grand Ave., Chicago, IL 60611-3472 USA (SAN 630-6705) Tel 312-477-7323; 837 W. Altgeld St., Chicago, IL 60614 (SAN 630-6713).

Children's Plus, Inc., 1387 Dutch Ameican, Beecher, IL 60401 USA Tel 708-946-4100; Fax: 709-946-4199
E-mail: danw@childrensplusinc.com
Web site: http://www.childrensplusinc.com.

Child's World, Inc., The, *(978-0-89565; 978-0-913778; 978-1-56766; 978-1-59296; 978-1-60253; 978-1-60954; 978-1-60973; 978-1-61473; 978-1-62323; 978-1-62687; 978-1-63143; 978-1-63407; 978-1-5038)* 1980 Lookout Dr., Mankato, MN 56003 USA (SAN 858-5385) Tel 507-385-1044; Fax: 888-320-2329; Toll Free Fax: 800-599-7323
E-mail: info@childsworld.com; mary.berendes@childsworld.com; mike.peterson@childsworld.com
Web site: http://www.childsworld.com.

China Books & Periodicals, Inc., *(978-0-8351)* 360 Swift Ave., Suite 48, South San Francisco, CA 94080 USA (SAN 145-0557) Tel 650-872-7718; 650-872-7076; Fax: 650-872-7808
E-mail: chris@chinabooks.com
Web site: http://www.chinabooks.com.

China Cultural Ctr., 3535 Dunn Dr. Apt. 303, Los Angeles, CA 90034-4977 USA (SAN 111-8161).

China House Gallery, China Institute in America, *See* **China Institute Gallery, China Institute in America**

China Institute Gallery, China Institute in America, *(978-0-9654270; 978-0-9774054; 978-0-9893776; 978-0-692-93086-1)* Div. of China Institute in America, 100 Washington St., New York, NY 10006 USA (SAN 110-8743) Tel 212-744-8181; Fax: 212-628-4159
E-mail: gallery@chinainstitute.org
Web site: http://www.chinainstitute.org.

Chinasprout, Inc., *(978-0-9707332; 978-0-9747302; 978-0-9820227; 978-1-945947)* 110 W. 32nd St., Flr. 6, New York, NY 10001-3205 USA Toll Free: 800-644-2611
E-mail: info@chinasprout.com
Web site: http://www.chinasprout.com.

Chinese American Co., 44 Kneeland St., Boston, MA 02111 USA (SAN 159-7248) Fax: 617-451-2318.

Christian Bk. Distributors, Orders Addr.: P.O. Box 7000, Peabody, MA 01961 USA (SAN 630-5458) Tel 978-977-5000; Fax: 978-977-5010
Web site: http://www.christianbook.com.

Christian Literature Crusade, Incorporated, *See* **CLC Pubns.**

Christian Printing Service, 4861 Chino Ave., Chino, CA 91710-5132 USA (SAN 108-2647) Tel 714-871-5200.

Christian Publishing Network, *(978-0-9628406)* P.O. Box 405, Tulsa, OK 74101 USA (SAN 631-2756) Tel 918-296-4673 (918-296-HOPE); Toll Free: 888-688-8125
E-mail: vpsales@olp.net.

christianaudio, *(978-1-59644; 978-1-61045; 978-1-61843; 978-1-63389; 978-1-68366; 978-1-5459)* 6 Business Pk. Rd, Old Saybrook, CT 06475 USA
E-mail: amclaren@tantor.com
Web site: http://christianaudio.com.

Chronicle Bks. LLC, *(978-0-8118; 978-0-87701; 978-0-938491; 978-1-4521; 978-1-7972)* Div. of The McEvoy Group, Orders Addr.: 680 Second St., San Francisco, CA 94107 USA (SAN 202-165X) Tel 415-537-4200; Fax: 415-537-4460; Toll Free Fax: 800-286-9471; Toll Free: 800-759-0190 (orders only); Edit Addr.: 3 Center Plaza, Boston, MA 2108 USA
E-mail: order.desk@hbgusa.com; customer.service@hbgusa.com
Web site: http://www.chroniclebooks.com.

Chulain Publishing Corp., Orders Addr.: 8241 Sweet Water Rd., Lone Tree, CO 80124-3017 USA.

Church Hymnal Corporation, *See* **Church Publishing, Inc.**

Church of Scientology Information Service-Pubns., *(978-0-915598)* c/o Bridge Pubns., Inc., 1414 N. Catalina, Los Angeles, CA 90029 USA (SAN 268-9774).

Church Publishing, Inc., *(978-0-89869; 978-1-59627; 978-1-59628; 978-1-64065)* Orders Addr.: 19 E. 34th St., New York, NY 10016 USA (SAN 857-0140) Tel 212-592-1800; Fax: 212-779-3392; Toll Free: 800-242-1918; Edit Addr.: 19 East 34th st, New York, NY 10016 USA
E-mail: rmasteller@cpg.org; churchpublishingorders@pbd.com; lort@cpg.org; lsimonello@cpg.org
Web site: http://www.churchpublishing.org.

Church Richards Co., 10001 Roosevelt Rd., Westchester, IL 60154 USA (SAN 285-8975) Toll Free: 800-323-0227.

Circa Pubns., Inc., 415 Fifth Ave., Pelham, NY 10803-0408 USA (SAN 169-6122) Tel 914-738-5570; Toll Free: 800-582-5952 (orders only).

Circle Bk. Service, Inc., *(978-0-87397)* P.O. Box 626, Tomball, TX 77377 USA (SAN 158-2526) Tel 281-255-6824; Fax: 281-255-8158; Toll Free: 800-227-1591
E-mail: orders@circlebook.com
Web site: http://www.circlebook.com.

City News Agency, Orders Addr.: P.O. Box 561129, Charlotte, NC 28256-1129 USA (SAN 169-782X); Edit Addr.: P.O. Box 2069, Newark, OH 43055 USA (SAN 169-6947); 220 Cherry Ave., NE, Canton, OH 44702-1198 (SAN 169-6602); 303 E. Lasalle St., South Bend, IN 46617 (SAN 159-9992); 417 S. McKinley, Harrisburg, IL 62946 (SAN 169-1961).

Clarks Out of Town News, 303 S. Andrews Ave., Fort Lauderdale, FL 33301 USA (SAN 159-8384) Tel 954-467-1543.

Class Pubns., Inc., *(978-0-913031)* 71 Bartholomew Ave., Hartford, CT 06106 USA (SAN 283-0302) Tel 860-951-9200.

Classroom Reading Service, P.O. Box 2708, Santa Fe Spgs, CA 90670-0708 USA (SAN 131-3959) Toll Free: 800-422-6657
E-mail: crsbooks@aol.com.

CLC Pubns., *(978-0-87508; 978-1-936143; 978-1-61958)* Div. of CLC Ministries International, Orders Addr.: P.O. Box 1449, Fort Washington, PA 19034-8449 USA Tel 215-542-1242; Fax: 215-542-7580; Toll Free: 800-659-1240; 701 Pennsylvania Ave., Fort Washington, PA 19034 (SAN 169-7358) Tel 215-542-1242; Fax: 215-542-7580; Toll Free: 800-659-1240
E-mail: orders@clcpublications.com; churd@clcpublications.com; dfessenden@clcpublications.com
Web site: http://www.clcusa.org; http://www.clcpublications.com.

CLEARVUE/eav, Inc., 6465 N. Avondale Ave., Chicago, IL 60631-1996 USA (SAN 204-1669) Tel 773-775-9433; Fax: 773-775-9855; Toll Free Fax: 800-444-9855 (24 Hours); Toll Free: 800-253-2788 (8:00 am to 4:30 pm Central Time M-F); P.O. Box 2284, S Burlington, VT 05407-2287
E-mail: custserv@clearvue.com
Web site: http://www.clearvue.com.

Closet Case Bks., P.O. Box 16116, Saint Paul, MN 55116 USA
Web site: http://www.closetcasebooks.com.

Clover Bk. Service, 1220 S. Monroe St., Covingtons, LA 70433-3639 USA (SAN 106-472X) Tel 504-875-0038.

Cobblestone Publishing Co., *(978-0-382; 978-0-942389; 978-0-9607638)* Div. of Cricket Magazine Group, 30 Grove St., Suite C, Peterborough, NH 03458 USA (SAN 237-9937) Tel 603-924-7209; Fax: 603-924-7380; Toll Free: 800-821-0115; P.O. Box 487, Effingham, IL 62401
E-mail: custsvc@cobblestone.mv.com
Web site: http://www.cobblestonepub.com.

Cogan Bks., *(978-0-940688)* P.O. Box 579, Hudson, OH 44236-0579 USA (SAN 168-9649) Toll Free: 800-733-3630.

Cokesbury, 2222 Rosa L. Parks Blvd., Nashville, TN 37228 USA (SAN 200-6863) Tel 615-749-6409; Toll Free: 800-672-1789
Web site: http://www.cokesbury.com.

Cold Cut Comics Distribution, 475-D Stockton Ave., San Jose, CA 95126 USA (SAN 631-6409) Tel 408-293-3844; Fax: 408-293-6645
E-mail: comics@coldcut.com
Web site: http://www.coldcut.com.

Cole, Bill Enterprises, Inc., P.O. Box 60, Randolph, MA 02368-0060 USA (SAN 685-6373) Tel 617-986-2653.

Collector Bks., *(978-0-89145; 978-1-57432; 978-1-60460)* Div. of Schroeder Publishing Co., Inc., Orders Addr.: P.O. Box 3009, Paducah, KY 42003 USA (SAN 157-5368) Tel 270-898-6211; 270-898-7903; Fax: 270-898-8890; 270-898-1173; Toll Free: 800-626-5420 (orders only); Edit Addr.: 5801 Kentucky Dam Rd., Paducah, KY 42003 USA (SAN 200-7479) E-mail: Info@collectorbooks.com; info@AQSquilt.com Web site: http://www.collectorbooks.com; http://www.americanquilter.com/.

College Bk. Co. of California, Inc., 181 W. Orangethorpe Ave. Ste. C, Placentia, CA 92870-6931 USA (SAN 269-0802).

Collegedale Distributors, *See* **Tree of Life Midwest**

Colonial Williamsburg Foundation, *(978-0-87935; 978-0-910412)* P.O. Box 3532, Williamsburg, VA 23187-3532 USA (SAN 128-4630) Fax: 757-565-8999 (orders only); Toll Free: 800-446-9240 (orders only) Web site: http://www.colonialwilliamsburg.com.

Colorado Periodical Distributor, Inc., 1227 Pitkin St., Grand Junction, CO 81502 USA Tel 970-242-3865; Fax: 970-242-3760.

Colorado State University, Center for Literary Publishing, *See* **Ctr. for Literary Publishing, Colorado State Univ.**

Columbia County News Agency, Inc., 49 Bender Blvd., Ghent, NY 12075-3327 USA (SAN 169-5339).

Columbia Univ. Pr., *(978-0-231)* Orders Addr.: 61 W. 62nd St., New York, NY 10023-7015 USA (SAN 212-2480) Toll Free Fax: 800-944-1844; Toll Free: 800-944-8648 x 6240 (orders); Edit Addr.: 61 W. 62nd St., New York, NY 10023 USA (SAN 212-2472) Tel 212-459-0600; Fax: 212-459-3678; 387 Pk. Ave., S., New York, NY 10016; 1094 Flex Dr., Jackson, TN 38301 E-mail: cupbooks@columbia.edu Web site: http://www.columbia.edu/cu/cup.

Comag Marketing Group, 1790 Broadway, Suite 401, New York, NY 10019 USA (SAN 169-5800) Tel 212-841-8365; Fax: 212-977-9401.

Comics Hawaii Distributors, *See* **Hobbies Hawaii Distributors**

Common Ground Distributors, Inc., Orders Addr.: P.O. Box 25249, Asheville, NC 28813-1249 USA Toll Free: 800-654-0626; Edit Addr.: 115 Fairview Rd., Asheville, NC 28803-2307 USA (SAN 113-8006) Tel 828-274-5575; Fax: 828-274-1955 E-mail: orders@comground.com.

Communication Service Corporation, *See* **Gryphon Hse., Inc.**

Communications Technology, Inc., *(978-0-918232)* P.O. Box 209, Rindge, NH 03461 USA (SAN 159-8198) Tel 603-899-6957.

Complete Book & Media Supply, 1200 Toro Grande Dr., Suite 200, Cedar Park, TX 78613 USA Fax: 512-616-0400; 512-616-0410; Toll Free: 800-986-1775 E-mail: books@completebook.com; bradm@completebook.com.

Computer & Technical Bks., 6338 Ranchview Ln., N., Osseo, MN 55311-3924 USA (SAN 630-8120).

Concordia Publishing Hse., *(978-0-570; 978-0-7586)* Subs. of Lutheran Church Missouri Synod, 3558 S. Jefferson Ave., Saint Louis, MO 63118-3968 USA (SAN 202-1781) Tel 314-268-1000; Fax: 314-268-1360; Toll Free Fax: 800-490-9889 (orders only); Toll Free: 800-325-3040 (orders only); 800-325-0191 E-mail: cphorder@cph.org Web site: http://www.cph.org.

Conde Nast Pubns., Inc., *(978-1-878494)* Four Times Sq., 20th Flr., New York, NY 10036 USA (SAN 285-905X) Tel 212-880-8800; Fax: 212-880-8289.

Connecticut River Pr., *(978-0-9706573)* 111 Holmes Rd., Newington, CT 06111 USA Tel 860-666-1200; 203-254-0147; Fax: 860-594-6037 E-mail: wolftalk@ziplink.net.

Consortium Bk. Sales & Distribution, Div. of Ingram Content Group, Orders Addr.: 1094 Flex Dr., Jackson, TN 38301-5070 USA; Edit Addr.: 34 13th Ave NE, Suite 100, Minneapolis, MN 55413-1007 USA (SAN 200-6049) Toll Free: 800-283-3572 (orders) E-mail: info@cbsd.com Web site: http://www.cbsd.com/.

ConsuLogic Consulting Services, 276 Longhouse Ln., Slingerlands, NY 12159-3012 USA Tel 518-452-9228; Fax: 518-452-9216.

Contemporary Arts Pr., *(978-0-931818)* Div. of La Mamelle, Inc., P.O. Box 3123, San Francisco, CA 94119-3123 USA (SAN 170-5423) Tel 415-282-0286.

Continental Bk. Co., Inc., *(978-0-9626800)* Eastern Div., 80-00 Cooper Ave., Bldg. No. 29, Glendale, NY 11385 USA (SAN 169-5436) Tel 718-326-0560; Fax: 718-326-4276; Toll Free: 800-364-0350; Western Div., 625 E. 70th Ave., No. 5, Denver, CO 80229 (SAN 630-2882) Tel 303-289-1761; Fax: 303-289-1764 E-mail: hola@continentalbook.com; esl@continentalbook.com; bonjour@continentalbook.com; tag@continentalbook.com Web site: http://www.continentalbook.com.

Continental Enterprises Group, Inc. (CEG), Orders Addr.: 108 Red Row St., Easley, SC 29640-2820 USA (SAN 631-0915) E-mail: ContactUs@centerprisesgrp.com.

Continental Sales, 213 W. Main St., Barrington, IL 60010-0010 USA Tel 847-381-6530.

Cook, David C., *(978-0-7814; 978-0-88207; 978-0-89191; 978-0-89693; 978-0-912692; 978-1-55513; 978-1-56476; 978-1-4347)* 4050 Lee Vance View, Colorado Springs, CO 80918 USA (SAN 206-0981) Tel 719-536-0100; Fax: 719-536-3244; Toll Free: 800-708-5550; 800-323-7543 (Customer Service) E-mail: wendi.lord@davidccook.com Web site: http://www.davidcook.com.

Cook, David C. Publishing Company, *See* **Cook, David C.**

Cookbook Marketplace, The, P.O. Box 305142, Nashville, TN 37230 USA (SAN 631-4201) Tel 615-391-2656; Toll Free: 800-358-0560.

Coos Bay Distributors, 131 N. Schoneman St., Coos Bay, OR 97420 USA (SAN 169-7064) Tel 541-888-5912.

Copper Island News, 1010 Wright St., Marquette, MI 49855-1834 USA (SAN 169-3824).

Copyright Clearance Ctr., Inc., 222 Rosewood Dr, Danvers, MA 01923 USA Tel 978-750-8400; Fax: 978-750-4343 Web site: http://www.copyright.com.

Cornell Univ. Pr., *(978-0-8014; 978-0-87546; 978-1-5017)* Orders Addr.: P.O. Box 6525, Ithaca, NY 14851 USA (SAN 281-5680) Tel 607-277-2211; Toll Free Fax: 800-688-2877; Toll Free: 800-666-2211; Edit Addr.: Sage House, 512 E. State St., Ithaca, NY 14851 USA (SAN 202-1862) Tel 607-277-2338 E-mail: cupressinfo@cornell.edu; orders@nbninternational.com; cupress-sales@cornell.edu Web site: http://www.cornellpress.cornell.edu.

Cornerstone Publishing & Distribution, Inc., *(978-1-929281)* P.O. Box 490, Bountiful, UT 84011-0490 USA Tel 801-295-9451; Fax: 801-295-0196; Toll Free: 800-453-0812 E-mail: rrhopkins@utah-inter.net.

Coronet Bks., *(978-0-89563)* 33 Ashley Dr., Schwenksville, PA 19473 USA (SAN 210-6043) Tel 484-919-6486; Fax: 215-717-4655 Do not confuse with Coronet Bks. & Pubns., Eagle Point, OR E-mail: ronsmolin@earthlink.net; order@coronetbooks.com Web site: http://www.coronetbooks.com.

Country News Distributors, Div. of Bakers, Inc., P.O. Box 1258, Brattleboro, VT 05302-1258 USA (SAN 169-8575).

Countryside Bks., *(978-0-88453)* 2430 Estancia Blvd. Ste. 100, Clearwater, FL 33761-2644 USA (SAN 107-4415).

Coutts Information Services, Div. of ProQuest LLC, Orders Addr.: 7309 Innovation BLVD, Fort Wayne, IN 46818 USA (SAN 920-6779); Edit Addr.: 7309 Innovation BLVD, Fort Wayne, IN 46818 USA (SAN 169-5401) Toll Free: 800-263-1686.

Coutts Library Service, Incorporated, *See* **Coutts Information Services**

Cove Distributors, 6325 Erdman Ave., Baltimore, MD 21205 USA (SAN 158-9814) Toll Free: 800-622-5656 (Orders).

Cowley Distributing, Inc., 732 Heisinger Rd., Jefferson City, MO 65109 USA (SAN 169-426X) Tel 573-636-6511; Fax: 573-636-6262; Toll Free: 800-346-5950 (orders).

Cox Subscriptions, Inc., 201 Village Rd., Shallotte, NC 28470 USA (SAN 107-0061) Tel 800-571-9554; Fax: 877-755-6274; Toll Free: 800-553-8088 E-mail: dknox@wtcox.com Web site: http://www.wtcox.com.

CQ Products, 507 Industrial St., Waverly, IA 50677 USA (SAN 631-5216) Tel 319-352-2086; Fax: 319-352-5338 E-mail: gifts@cqproducts.com Web site: http://www.cqproducts.com.

Crabtree Publishing, *(978-0-937070)* P.O. Box 3451, Federal Way, WA 98063 USA (SAN 214-3615) Tel 253-925-9300; 59Th Flr., New York, NY 10118 Do not confuse with Crabtree Publishing Co. in New York, NY.

Cram, George F. Co., Inc., *(978-0-87448)* 301 S. LaSalle St., P.O. Box 426, Indianapolis, IN 46201 USA (SAN 204-2630) Tel 317-635-5564; Fax: 317-635-2720; Toll Free: 800-227-4199 E-mail: cram-services@iquest.net.

Cranbury International, Orders Addr.: 7 Clarendon Ave., Suite 2, Montpelier, VT 05602 USA.

CRC Pr. LLC, *(978-0-8493; 978-0-87762; 978-0-87819; 978-0-935184; 978-1-56676; 978-1-57491; 978-1-58488; 978-1-58716; 978-1-4200; 978-1-4398; 978-1-4665; 978-1-4822; 978-1-4987; 978-1-351)* Subs. of Taylor & Francis, Inc., Orders Addr.: 6000 Broken Sound Pkwy., NW, Ste. 300, Boca Raton, FL 33487 USA Tel 800-272-7737 Toll Free Fax: 800-374-3401; Edit Addr.: 270 Madison Ave., New York, NY 10016 USA E-mail: orders@crcpress.com; Theresa.Gutierrez@taylorandfrancis.com Web site: http://www.crcpress.com; http://www.taylorandfrancis.com.

CreateSpace Independent Publishing Platform, *(978-1-58898; 978-1-5423; 978-1-59109; 978-1-59456; 978-1-59457; 978-1-4196; 978-1-4348; 978-1-4382; 978-1-4392; 978-1-4404; 978-1-4414; 978-1-4421; 978-1-61550; 978-1-4486; 978-1-4495; 978-1-4499; 978-1-4505; 978-1-4515; 978-1-4528; 978-1-4536; 978-1-4537; 978-1-4538; 978-1-4563; 978-1-4564; 978-1-4565; 978-1-61789; 978-1-4609; 978-1-4610; 978-1-4611; 978-1-61396; 978-1-61397; 978-1-4635; 978-1-4636; 978-1-4637; 978-1-4662; 978-1-4663; 978-1-4664; 978-1-61914; 978-1-61915; 978-1-61916; 978) Orders Addr.: 4900 LaCross Rd., North Charleston, SC 29406 USA (SAN 255-2132) Tel 843-225-4700 (Ask for ordering department); Fax: 843-577-7506; Toll Free: 866-308-6235; 4900 LaCross Rd., North Charleston, SC 29406* E-mail: info@createspace.com Web site: http://www.createspace.com.

Creative Co., The, *(978-0-87191; 978-0-88682; 978-0-89812; 978-1-56660; 978-1-56846; 978-1-58341; 978-1-60818; 978-1-62832; 978-1-68277; 978-1-64000; 978-1-64026)* 123 S. Broad St., Mankato, MN 56001 USA Tel 507-388-6273; Fax: 507-388-4797; Toll Free: 800-445-6209 Do not confuse with The Creative Co., Lawrenceburg, IN E-mail: info@thecreativecompany.us; kate.riggs@thecreativecompany.us Web site: http://www.thecreativecompany.us.

Creative Homeowner, *(978-0-932944; 978-1-58011; 978-1-880029)* Div. of Courier Corporation, 24 Park Way, Upper Saddle River, NJ 07458-9960 USA (SAN 213-6627) Tel 201-934-7100; Fax: 201-934-8971; Toll Free: 800-631-7795 E-mail: info@creativehomeowner.com Web site: http://www.creativehomeowner.com.

Creative Teaching Pr., Inc., *(978-0-88160; 978-0-916119; 978-1-57471; 978-1-59198; 978-1-60689; 978-1-61601; 978-1-62186; 978-1-63445; 978-1-68310; 978-1-64474)* Orders Addr.: P.O. Box 2723, Huntington Beach, CA 92647-0723 USA Tel 714-895-5047; Fax: 714-895-6547; Toll Free Fax: 800-444-4287; Edit Addr.: 6262 Katella Ave., Cypress, CA 90630 USA (SAN 294-9180) Tel 714-895-5047; Toll Free Fax: 800-229-9929; Toll Free: 800-444-4287 E-mail: toni.gardner@creativeteaching.com; webmaster@creativeteaching.com; we.listen@creativeteaching.com; emond.ling@creativeteaching.com Web site: http://www.creativeteaching.com; http://www.thelearningworks.com; http://www.learntoreadkidsclub.com.

Crescent Imports & Pubns., *(978-0-933127)* P.O. Box 7827, Ann Arbor, MI 48107-7827 USA (SAN 111-3976) Tel 734-665-3492; Fax: 734-677-1717; Toll Free: 800-521-9744 E-mail: crescentus@aol.com Web site: http://www.crescentimports.com.

Crescent International, Inc., 2238 Otranto Rd., Charleston, SC 29418 USA (SAN 110-0777) Tel 803-797-6363; Fax: 803-797-6367.

Critics' Choice, *See* **Critics' Choice Video**

Critics' Choice Video, *(978-1-932566; 978-1-933240)* 900 N. Rohlwing Rd., Itasca, IL 60143 USA Tel 630-775-3300; Fax: 603-775-3340 E-mail: rterry@ccvideo.com Web site: http://www.ccvideo.com.

Cromland, 964 Marcon Blvd, Suite 190, Allentown, PA 18109 USA (SAN 254-6736) Tel 610-266-6610; Fax: 610-266-8987; Toll Free: 800-944-5554 (U.S. & Canada) Web site: http://www.cromland.com.

CrossLife Expressions, *(978-0-9636049; 978-1-57838)* Div. of Exchanged Life Ministries, Inc., 10610 E. Bethany Dr., Suite A, Aurora, CO 80014 USA (SAN 169-0590) Tel 303-750-0440; Fax: 303-750-1228; Toll Free: 800-750-6818 E-mail: info@crosslifebooks.com Web site: http://www.crosslifebooks.com.

Crowley Distributors, *See* **Sunburst Bks., Inc., Distributor of Florida Bks.**

Crowley, Inc., 16120 U.S. Hwy. 19 N., Suite 220, Clearwater, FL 34624-6862 USA (SAN 285-9130) Tel 813-531-5889.

Crown Agents Service, Ltd., 3100 Massachusetts Ave., NW, Washington, DC 20008 USA (SAN 285-919X).

Crown Hse. Publishing LLC, *(978-1-899836; 978-1-904424; 978-1-84590; 978-0-9823573; 978-1-935810; 978-1-78135; 978-1-78583)* Orders Addr.: P.O. Box 2223, Williston, VT 05495 USA Fax: 802-864-7626; Toll Free: 877-925-1213; Edit Addr.: Crown Bldg., Bancyfelin, Carmarthen, Dyfed SA33 5ND GBR Tel 01267 211345; 01267 211880; Fax: 01267 211882; 81 Brook Hills Dr., White Plains, NY 10605 Tel 914-946-3517; Toll Free: 866-272-8497 E-mail: books@crownhouse.co.uk; info@CHPUS.com Web site: http://www.crownhouse.co.uk/; http://www.CHPUS.com; http://www.crownhousepublishing.com.

CSS Publishing Co., *(978-0-7880; 978-0-89536; 978-1-55673; 978-0-615-84860-0)* Orders Addr.: 5450 N. Dixie Hwy., Lima, OH 45807-9559 USA Tel 800-241-4056; 419-227-1818; Fax: 419-228-9184; Toll Free: 800-241-4056 Customer Service; 800-537-1030 Orders; Edit Addr.: P.O. Box 4503, Lima, OH 45802-4503 USA (SAN 207-0707) Tel 419-227-1818; Fax: 419-228-9184; Toll Free: 800-537-1030 (Orders); 800-241-4056 (Customer Service) Do not confuse with CSS Publishing in Tularosa, NM E-mail: editor@csspub.com; csr@csspub.com; info@csspub.com; orders@csspub.com Web site: http://www.csspub.com.

Ctr. for Literary Publishing, Colorado State Univ., *(978-1-885635)* Center for Literary Publishing, Department of English, Colorado State University, Fort Collins, CO 80523 USA Tel 970-491-5449; Fax: 970-491-0283 E-mail: creview@colostate.edu Web site: http://coloradoreview.colostate.edu/.

Cultural Hispana/Ameriketako Liburuak, Orders Addr.: P.O. Box 7729, Silver Spring, MD 20907 USA (SAN 159-2823); Edit Addr.: 1413 Crestridge Dr., Silver Spring, MD 20910 USA (SAN 249-3063) Tel 301-585-0134 E-mail: mokordo@erols.com Web site: http://www.coloquio.com/libros.html.

Culture Plus Bk. Distributors, 44 Willoughby St., Brooklyn, NY 11201-5200 USA.

Culture Plus Bks., 209 N. La Brea Ave., Inglewood, CA 90301-1247 USA (SAN 631-3876).

CUP Services, 750 Cascadilla St., Ithaca, NY 14851 USA (SAN 630-6519) Tel 607-277-2211; Fax: 607-277-6292; Toll Free: 800-666-2211.

Curran Assocs., Inc., *(978-1-60423; 978-1-60560; 978-1-61567; 978-1-61738; 978-1-61782; 978-1-61839; 978-1-62276; 978-1-62748; 978-1-62993; 978-1-63266; 978-1-63439; 978-1-5108; 978-1-7138)* 57 Morehouse Ln., Red Hook, NY 12571 USA Tel 845-758-0400; Fax: 845-758-2633 E-mail: curran@proceedings.com Web site: http://www.proceedings.com.

Curreri, Michelle Morrow, 3 Eagle Ln., Beverly, MA 01915 USA Tel 978-921-8020; Fax: 978-921-7577 E-mail: michelle@curreriworldsvs.net.

Curtis, Ralph Books, *See* **Curtis, Ralph Publishing**

Curtis, Ralph Publishing, *(978-0-88359)* P.O. Box 349, Sanibel, FL 33957 USA (SAN 121-1323) Tel 239-454-0010; Fax: 239-395-2727; Toll Free: 888-454-0011 E-mail: rcurtisbks@yahoo.com Web site: http://www.ralphcurtisbooks.com.

CustomFlix Labs, Inc., *(978-0-9774415)* 100 Enterprise Way Ste. A200, Scotts Valley, CA 95066-3266 USA.

Cybernetics Technology Corp., *(978-0-923458)* 1370 Port Washington Blvd., Port Washington, NY 11050-2628 USA (SAN 295-933X) Tel 516-883-7676.

Cypress Bk. Co., Inc., *(978-0-934643)* Subs. of China International Bk. Trading Corp., 360 Swift Ave. Ste. 42, S San Fran, CA 94080-6220 USA (SAN 112-1162) Toll Free: 800-383-1688 E-mail: sales@cypressbook.com; info@cypressbook.com; cypbook@pacbell.net Web site: http://www.cypressbook.com.

Cypress Hse., *(978-1-879384; 978-0-9987854)* 155 Cypress St., Fort Bragg, CA 95437 USA (SAN 297-9004) Tel 707-964-9520; Fax: 707-964-7531; Toll Free: 800-773-7782 E-mail: cypresshouse@cypresshouse.com; forms@cypresshouse.com Web site: http://www.cypresshouse.com.

D & H News Co., Inc., 79 Albany Post Rd., Montrose, NY 10548 USA (SAN 169-5533) Tel 914-737-3152.

D & J Bk. Distributors, *(978-1-883080)* 229-21B Merrick Blvd., Laurelton, NY 11413 USA (SAN 630-5091) Tel 718-949-5400; Fax: 718-949-6161; Toll Free: 800-446-4707.

D K Publishing, Incorporated, *See* **Dorling Kindersley Publishing, Inc.**

Daedalus Bks., 9645 Gerwig Ln., Columbia, MD 21046-1520 USA (SAN 158-9202) Tel 410-309-2700 E-mail: tstock@daedalus-books.com; custserv@daedalus-books.com Web site: http://www.daedalus-books.com.

Dahlstrom, Carol Field Inc., *(978-0-9679764; 978-0-9768446)* 7952 NE. Berwick Dr., Ankeny, IA 50021 USA Tel 515-964-1777; Fax: 515-964-1788 E-mail: braveink@aol.com Web site: http://www.braveink.com.

Dake Bible Sales, *See* **Dake Publishing**

Dake Publishing, *(978-0-9655968; 978-1-55829)* Orders Addr.: P.O. Box 1050, Lawrenceville, GA 30046 USA (SAN 212-0828) Tel 770-963-1611; Fax: 770-963-7700; Toll Free: 800-241-1239; Edit Addr.: 764 Martins Chapel Rd., Lawrenceville, GA 30246 USA (SAN 243-2684) E-mail: derrick@dake.com Web site: http://www.dake.com.

Dakota News, Inc., 221 Petro Ave., Box 1310, Sioux Falls, SD 57101 USA (SAN 169-7854) Tel 605-336-3000; Fax: 605-336-7279; Toll Free: 800-658-5498.

Dakota West Bks., P.O. Box 9324, Rapid City, SD 57701 USA (SAN 630-351X) Tel 605-348-1075; Fax: 605-348-0615.

Danforth Bk. Distribution, Orders Addr.: 3220 228th St., S. E., Bothell, WA 98021 USA Tel 206-351-5872 E-mail: Danfothbookdist@gmail.com.

D.A.P./Distributed Art Pubs., *(978-1-881616; 978-1-891024; 978-1-933045; 978-1-935202; 978-1-938922; 978-1-942884; 978-1-63681)* Orders Addr.: 75 Broad St., Suite 630, New York, NY 10004 USA (SAN 630-6446) Tel 212-627-1999; Fax: 212-627-9484; Toll Free Fax: 800-478-3128; Toll Free: 800-338-2665 E-mail: dap@dapinc.com Web site: http://www.artbook.com/.

Darr Subscription Agency, P.O. Box 575, Louisburg, KS 66053-0575 USA (SAN 285-9149) Toll Free: 800-850-3741 E-mail: lgriff@midusa.net.

David, Jonathan Pubs., Inc., *(978-0-8246)* 68-22 Eliot Ave., Middle Village, NY 11379 USA (SAN 169-5274) Tel 718-456-8611; Fax: 718-894-2818 E-mail: jondavpub@aol.com Web site: http://www.jdbooks.com.

Davidson Titles, Inc., *(978-1-884756)* Orders Addr.: 2345 Dr. F.E. Wright Dr., Jackson, TN 38303 USA; Edit Addr.: P.O. Box 3538, Jackson, TN 38303-3538 USA (SAN 255-9129) Tel 731-988-5333; Fax: 731-988-5080; Toll Free Fax: 800-787-7935; Toll Free: 800-433-3903 Do not confuse with companies of the same name in Sugar Hill NH, Windsor CT, Redmond & Kirkland WA, Newark NJ, Fairfield & Reddick FL, East Lansing MI, Rocklin CA, Tolono IL, Missoula MT, Ann Arbor MI, Half Moon Bay CA E-mail: brian@davidsontitles.com Web site: http://www.davidsontitles.com.

Davis/Books Distribution, 215 W. Main, Cambridge City, IN 47357 USA Tel 765-478-5773.

Dawson Subscription Service, *See* **Faxon Illinois Service Ctr.**

Day School Magazine Service, P.O. Box 262, Brooklyn, NY 11219 USA (SAN 285-9157) Tel 718-871-1486; Fax: 718-435-2342 E-mail: Elciv@juno.com.

De Gruyter, Inc., *(978-0-89925; 978-1-56445; 978-1-934078; 978-1-61451; 978-1-5015; 978-1-5473; 978-1-5474)* Subs. of Walter de Gruyter & GmbH & Co. KG, Orders Addr.: P.O. Box 960, Herndon, VA 20172-0960 USA Tel 703-661-1589; Fax: 703-661-1501; Toll Free: 800-208-8144; Edit Addr.: 121 High St., Third Flr., Boston, MA 02110 USA Tel 857-284-7073; Fax: 857-284-7358 E-mail: info@deGruyterny.com; kruehle@degruyterny.com; USinfo@degruyter.com; info@degruyter.com Web site: http://www.degruyter.com; http://www.mouton-publishers.com; http://www.mouton-online.com; www.degruyter.com.

De Gruyter, Walter Incorporated, *See* **De Gruyter, Inc.**
De Vore Group/Carla Bks. & More, Orders Addr.: P.O. Box 10276, San Juan, PR 00922 USA (SAN 159-8309) Tel 809-721-7645; Fax: 809-722-9216; Edit Addr.: 1409 Ave. Ponce De Leon, San Juan, PR 00907-4023 USA (SAN 249-2776).
Dearborn Financial Publishing, Inc., *(978-0-7931; 978-0-88462; 978-0-913864; 978-0-936894; 978-1-57410)* 30 South Wacker Dr., Chicago, IL 60606-1719 USA (SAN 201-3622) Tel 312-836-4400 ext 282429; Fax: 312-836-1021
Web site: http://www.dearborn.com.
Dearborn Trade, A Kaplan Professional Company, *See* **Kaplan Publishing**
DeBoer, Bernhard Inc., 113 E. Centre St., Nutley, NJ 07110 USA (SAN 282-1990) Tel 973-667-9300; Fax: 973-667-0086
E-mail: stout@javanet.com
Web site: http://www.javanet.com/-stout/pannus.
DecisionPro, Inc., 2452 General Potter Hwy., Centre Hall, PA 16828-9022 USA.
DeHoff Christian Bookstore, *(978-1-933965)* 749 N. W. Broad St., Murfreesboro, TN 37129-3797 USA (SAN 184-4202) Tel 615-893-8322; Fax: 615-896-7447; Toll Free: 800-695-5385
E-mail: dehoff@bellsouth.net; fakesb@yahoo.com
Web site: http://www.dehoffbooks.com.
Dehoff Publications, *See* **DeHoff Christian Bookstore**
Delmar Cengage Learning, *(978-0-314; 978-0-7668; 978-0-7693; 978-0-8273; 978-0-87350; 978-0-916032; 978-0-944132; 978-0-9653629; 978-1-56253; 978-1-56593; 978-1-56930; 978-1-4018; 978-1-4180; 978-1-4283; 978-1-4354; 978-1-7319)* Div. of Cengage Learning, Orders Addr.: c/o Thomson Learning Order Fulfilment, P.O. Box 6904, Florence, KY 41022 USA Toll Free Fax: 800 487 8488; Toll Free: 800 347 7707; c/o Thomson Delmar Learning Clinical Health Care Series, P.O. Box 3419, Scranton, PA 18505-0419 Fax: 570-347-9072; Toll Free: 888-427-5800; Edit Addr.: P.O. Box 15015, Albany, NY 12212-5015 USA (SAN 206-7544) Tel 518-348-2300; Fax: 518-373-6345; Toll Free: 800-998-7498; 5 Maxwell Dr., Clifton Park, NY 12065- (SAN 658-0440) Tel 518-348-2300; Fax: 518-881-1256; Toll Free: 800-998-7498
E-mail: matthew.grover@thomson.com; clinicalmanuals@thomson.com
Web site: http://www.delmarlearning.com; http://www.clinicalmanuals.com/.
Delmar News Agency, Inc., P.O. Box 7169, Newark, DE 19714-7169 USA (SAN 169-0892) Tel 302-455-9922; Toll Free: 800-441-7025.
DeLong Subscription Agency, P.O. Box 806, Lafayette, IN 47902 USA (SAN 285-9246) Toll Free: 800-992-2092.
Delphi Distribution Inc., Orders Addr.: 1263 SW Blvd., Kansas City, KS 66103 USA (SAN 760-7989) Tel 913-362-7400; Fax: 913-362-7401
E-mail: kent@delphidistribution.com; linda@midpt.com.
Delta Education, Incorporated, *See* **Delta Education, LLC**
Delta Education, LLC, *(978-0-87504; 978-1-58356; 978-1-59242; 978-1-59821; 978-1-60395; 978-1-60902; 978-1-62571; 978-1-64011)* 80 Northwest Blvd., Nashua, NH 03063 USA (SAN 630-1711) Toll Free: 800-442-5444
E-mail: ngosselin@delta-edu.com
Web site: http://www.delta-education.com.
Delta Systems Company, Inc., *(978-0-937354; 978-1-887744; 978-1-932748; 978-1-934960; 978-1-936299; 978-1-936402; 978-1-62167)* Orders Addr.: 1400 Miller Pkwy., McHenry, IL 60050-7030 USA (SAN 220-0457) Tel 815-363-3582; Fax: 815-363-2948; Toll Free Fax: 800-909-9901; Toll Free: 800-323-8270
E-mail: d.patchin@DeltaPublishing.com; L.Bruell@DeltaPublishing.com; j.patchin@deltapublishing.com
Web site: http://www.deltapublishing.com; http://www.raventreepress.com.
Deltiologists of America, *(978-0-913782)* P.O. Box 8, Norwood, PA 19074 USA (SAN 170-3072) Tel 610-485-8572.
Derstine, Roy Bk. Co., 14 Birch Rd., Kinnelon, NJ 07405 USA (SAN 130-822X) Tel 973-838-1109.
DeRu's Fine Arts, *(978-0-939370)* 9100 E. Artesia Blvd., Bellflower, CA 90706 USA (SAN 159-3862) Tel 562-920-1312; Fax: 562-920-3077
E-mail: derusgal@aol.com
Web site: http://www.derusfinearts.com.
Deseret Bk. Co., *(978-0-87579; 978-0-87747; 978-1-57345; 978-1-59038; 978-1-60641; 978-1-60907; 978-1-60908; 978-1-62972; 978-1-64933)* Div. of Deseret Management Corp., P.O. Box 30178, Salt Lake City, UT 84130 USA (SAN 150-763X) Tel 801-517-3165 (Wholesale Dept.); 801-534-1515; Fax: 801-517-3338; Toll Free: 800-453-3876
E-mail: wholesale@deseretbook.com; dbwhsale@deseretbook.com
Web site: http://www.deseretbook.com; http://www.shadowmountain.com.
Destiny Image Pubs., *(978-0-7684; 978-0-914903; 978-1-56043; 978-0-9716036)* 167 Walnut Bottom Rd., Shippensburg, PA 17257 USA (SAN 253-4339) Tel 717-532-3040; Fax: 717-532-9291; Toll Free: 800-722-6774
E-mail: dnj@destinyimage.com
Web site: http://www.destinyimage.com.
Detroit Free Pr., Inc., *(978-0-937247; 978-0-9605692)* Div. of Gannett, 615 W. Lafayette Blvd., Detroit, MI 48226 USA (SAN 239-6998) Tel 313-223-4575; Fax: 313-222-5982; Toll Free: 800-678-6400
E-mail: ajhartley@freepress.com; ldelves@freepress.com
Web site: http://www.freep.com.
Devin-Adair Pubs., Inc., *(978-0-8159)* P.O. Box A, Old Greenwich, CT 06870 USA (SAN 112-062X) Tel 203-531-7755; Fax: 718-359-8568.
DeVorss & Co., *(978-0-87516)* Orders Addr.: P.O. Box 1389, Camarillo, CA 93011-1389 USA (SAN 168-9886) Tel 805-322-9010; Fax: 805-322-9011; Toll Free: 800-843-5743; Edit Addr.: 553 Constitution Ave., Camarillo, CA 93012-8510 USA
E-mail: service@devorss.com
Web site: http://www.devorss.com.
Diamond Bk. Distributors, *(978-1-64031)* Div. of Diamond Comic Distributors, Inc., Orders Addr.: 1966 Greenspring Dr., Suite 300, Timonium, MD 21093 USA (SAN 110-9502) Tel 410-560-7100; Fax: 410-560-2583; Toll Free: 800-452-6642
E-mail: books@diamondbookdistributors.com
Web site: http://www.diamondcomics.com; http://www.diamondbookdistributors.com/.
Diamond Book Distributors Inc., *See* **Diamond Comic Distributors, Inc.**
Diamond Comic Distributors, Inc., *(978-1-59396; 978-1-60584)* 1966 Greenspring Dr., Suite 300, Timonium, MD 21093 USA Tel 410-560-7100; Fax: 410-560-2583; Toll Free: 800-452-6642
E-mail: books@diamondbookdistributors.com
Web site: http://www.diamondbookdistributors.com/.
Diamond Distributors, Inc., Orders Addr.: 1966 Greenspring Dr., Suite 300, Timonium, MD 21093 USA Tel 410-560-7100.
Digital Manga Distribution, *See* **Digital Manga Publishing**
Digital Manga Publishing, *(978-1-56970)* Div. of Digital Manga, Inc., 1487 W. 178th St. Ste. 300, Gardena, CA 90248-3253 USA (SAN 111-817X) Toll Free: 866-897-7300
E-mail: contact@emanga.com
Web site: http://www.dmpbooks.com/.
Dillon Bk., Subs. of Harold Dillon, Inc., 460 S. Marion Pkwy., Apt. 851B, Denver, CO 80209-2508 USA (SAN 169-0493) Tel 303-442-5323; Toll Free: 800-525-0842.
Discount Bk. Distributors, 1854 Wallace School Rd., No. E, Charleston, SC 29407-4822 USA (SAN 107-2250) Tel 843-556-6582.
Disney Publishing Worldwide, *(978-1-892309; 978-1-931580; 978-1-4231; 978-1-4847; 978-1-368; 978-1-368-01377-2)* Subs. of Walt Disney Productions, 44 S. Broadway, 10th Flr., White Plains, NY 10601 USA Tel 914-288-4316; 1101 Flower St., Glendale, CA 91201
Web site: http://www.disney.go.com; http://www.hyperionbooksforchildren.com; books.disney.com.
Distribooks, Inc., Div. of MED, Inc., 8124 N. Ridgeway, Skokie, IL 60076 USA (SAN 630-9763) Tel 847-676-1596; Fax: 847-676-1195
E-mail: info@distribooks.com.
Distribuidora Escolar, Inc., 2250 SW 99th Ave., Miami, FL 00165-7569 USA (SAN 169-1104).
Distribuidora Norma, Inc., *(978-1-881700; 978-1-935164)* Div. of Carvajal International, Orders Addr.: P.O. Box 195040, San Juan, PR 00919-5040 USA Tel 787-788-5050; Fax: 787-788-7161; Edit Addr.: Carretera 869 Km 1.5 Barrio Palmas Royal Industrial, Catano, PR 00962 USA
Web site: http://www.norma.com.
Distribuidora Plaza Mayor, 1500 Ave. Ponce de Leon Local 2 El Cinco, San Juan, PR 1 USA.
Distribution Solutions Group, 1120 Rte. 22 E., Bridgewater, NJ 08807-0885 USA Toll Free: 866-374-4748.
Distributors International, Div. of Dennis-Landman Pubs., 1150 18th St., Santa Monica, CA 90403 USA (SAN 129-8089) Tel 310-828-0680
E-mail: info@moviecraft.com
Web site: http://www.moviecraft.com.
Distributors, The, *(978-0-942520)* 702 S. Michigan, South Bend, IN 46601 USA (SAN 169-2488) Tel 574-232-8500; Fax: 312-803-0887; Toll Free: 800-348-5200
E-mail: info@thedistributors.com
Web site: http://thedistributors.com/.
Diversion Books, *See* **Diversion Publishing Corp.**
Diversion Publishing Corp., *(978-0-9845151; 978-0-9829050; 978-0-9833371; 978-0-9838395; 978-0-9839885; 978-1-938120; 978-1-62681; 978-1-68230; 978-1-63576)* 443 Park Avenue S., Ste. 1008, New York, NY 10016 USA (SAN 990-6304) Tel 212-675-5556; 212-961-6390
E-mail: info@diversionbooks.com; charles@efit.com
Web site: http://www.diversionbooks.com.
Divine, Inc., *(978-0-87305)* 1600 Providence Hwy., Walpole, MA 02081-2553 USA (SAN 159-8619) Toll Free: 800-766-0039
E-mail: pubservices@faxon.com; helpdesk@faxon.com
Web site: http://www.faxon.com.
Dixie News Co., P.O. Box 561129, Charlotte, NC 28256-1129 USA (SAN 169-636X) Tel 704-376-0140; Fax: 704-335-8604; Toll Free: 800-532-1045.
DKE Toys, *(978-0-9915790)* 8568 Walnut Dr., Los Angeles, CA 90046 USA Tel 323-656-3262
E-mail: dkelemer@aol.com
Web site: dketoys.com.
Docustar, 1325 Glendale-Milford Rd., Cincinnati, OH 45215 USA Tel 513-772-5400; Fax: 513-772-5410.
Dog Museum, The, *See* **American Kennel Club Museum of the Dog**
Doherty, Tom Assocs., LLC, *(978-0-312; 978-0-7653; 978-0-8125)* Div. of Holtzbrinck Publishers, Orders Addr.: 16365 James Madison Hwy., Gordonsville, VA 22942-8501 USA Toll Free Fax: 800-672-2054; Toll Free: 888-330-8477; Edit Addr.: 175 Fifth Ave., New York, NY 10010 USA Tel 212-674-5151; Fax: 540-672-7540 (customer service)
E-mail: inquiries@tor.com
Web site: http://www.tor.com/.
Donars Spanish Bks., P.O. Box 808, Lafayette, CO 80026 USA (SAN 108-1586) Tel 303-666-9175; Toll Free: 800-552-3316
E-mail: donars@prolynx.com.
Dorling Kindersley Publishing, Inc., *(978-0-7894; 978-1-56458; 978-1-879431; 978-0-7566; 978-1-4654)* Div. of Penguin Publishing Group, 375 Hudson St., 2nd Flr., New York, NY 10014 USA (SAN 253-0791) Tel 212-213-4800; Fax: 212-213-5240; Toll Free: 877-342-5357 (orders only)
E-mail: Annemarie.Cancienne@dk.com; customer.service@dk.com
Web site: http://www.dk.com.
Dot Gibson Distribution, Div. of Dot Gibson Pubns., P.O. Box 117, Waycross, GA 31502 USA Tel 912-285-2848.
Dover Pubns., Inc., *(978-0-486; 978-1-60660)* Div. of Courier Corporation, 31 E. Second St., Mineola, NY 11501 USA (SAN 201-338X) Tel 516-294-7000; Fax: 516-873-1401 (orders only); Toll Free: 800-223-3130 (orders only)
E-mail: rights@doverpublications.com
Web site: http://www.doverdirect.com; http://www.doverpublications.com.
Downtown Bk. Ctr., Inc., *(978-0-941010)* 247 SE First St., Suites 236-237, Miami, FL 33131 USA (SAN 169-1112) Tel 305-377-9941
E-mail: raxdown@aol.com.
Draft2Digital, *(978-1-4977; 978-1-4989; 978-1-5014; 978-1-5022; 978-1-5070; 978-1-5130; 978-1-5163; 978-1-5199; 978-1-5242; 978-1-5337; 978-1-5365; 978-1-5401; 978-1-386; 978-1-393; 978-0-578-64452-3)* 5629 SE 67th St., Oklahoma City, OK 73135 USA Fax: 866-358-6413; Toll Free Fax: 866-358-6413; Toll Free: 866-336-5099; 9400 N. Broadway Ext. Ste. 410, Oklahoma City, OK 73114 Tel 866-336-5099
E-mail: support@draft2digital.com
Web site: www.draft2digital.com.
Dreams in Action Distribution, P.O. Box 1894, Sedona, AZ 86339 USA Tel 928-204-1560; 70 Yucca St., Sedona, AZ 86351
E-mail: sales@dreamsinaction.us; pamela@deamsinaction.us.
Drown News Agency, P.O. Box 2080, Folsom, CA 95763-2080 USA (SAN 169-0450).
Duebbert, Harold F., P.O.B. 629 E. Adolphus Ave., Fergus Falls, MN 56537 USA Tel 218-736-4312.
Dufour Editions, Inc., *(978-0-8023)* Orders Addr.: P.O. Box 7, Chester Springs, PA 19425-0007 USA (SAN 201-341X) Tel 610-458-5005; Fax: 610-458-7103; Toll Free: 800-869-5677
E-mail: info@dufoureditions.com
Web site: http://www.dufoureditions.com.
Dumont, Charles Son, Inc., *(978-1-61727)* 1085 Dumont Cir. PO Box 1017, Voorhees, NJ 08043 USA (SAN 631-0842) Tel 856-346-9100; Fax: 856-346-3452; Toll Free: 800-257-8283
E-mail: info@dumontmusic.com
Web site: http://www.dumontmusic.com.
Durst, Sanford J., *(978-0-915262; 978-0-942666; 978-1-886720)* 106 Woodcleft Ave., Freeport, NY 11520 USA (SAN 211-6987) Tel 516-867-3333; Fax: 516-867-3397
E-mail: sjdbooks@verizon.net.
Duval News Co., Orders Addr.: P.O. Box 61297, Jacksonville, FL 32203 USA (SAN 169-1015); Edit Addr.: 5638 Commonwealth Ave., Jacksonville, FL 32205 USA (SAN 249-2865) Tel 904-783-2350.
Duval-Bibb Publishing Co., *(978-0-937713)* Div. of Mareeco Enterprises, Inc., Orders Addr.: P.O. Box 24168, Tampa, FL 33623-4168 USA (SAN 111-8641) Tel 813-281-0091; Fax: 813-282-0220; 1808 B St. NW, Suite 140, Auburn, WA 98001 Toll Free Fax: 800-548-1169; Toll Free: 800-518-3541
E-mail: reese.cop@gte.net
Web site: http://lonepinepublishing.com/ordering.
E Learn Aid, Orders Addr.: P.O. Box 39545, Los Angeles, CA 90039-0545 USA Fax: 323-665-8875.
E M C Publishing, *See* **EMC/Paradigm Publishing**
Eagle Business Systems, *(978-0-928210)* P.O. Box 1240, El Toro, CA 92630-1240 USA (SAN 285-7510) Tel 714-859-9622.
Eagle Feather Trading Post, Inc., 168 W. 12th St., Ogden, UT 84404 USA (SAN 630-8996) Tel 801-393-3991; Fax: 801-745-0903; Toll Free: 800-547-3364 (orders only).
Eaglecrafts, Orders Addr.: 168 W. 12th St., Ogden, UT 84404 USA (SAN 630-6381) Tel 801-393-3991; Fax: 801-745-0903; Toll Free: 800-547-3364 (orders only)
E-mail: porsturbo@aol.com.
EAL Enterprises, Inc., Div. of Ambassador Bk. Service, 42 Chasner St., Hempstead, NY 11550 USA (SAN 169-6645) Toll Free: 800-431-8913.
East Kentucky News, Inc., 416 Teays Rd., Paintsville, KY 41240 USA (SAN 169-2879) Tel 606-789-8169.
East Texas Distributing, 7171 Grand Blvd., Houston, TX 77054 USA (SAN 169-8265) Tel 713-748-2520; Fax: 713-748-2504.
Eastern Bk. Co., Orders Addr.: P.O. Box 4540, Portland, ME 04112-4540 USA Fax: 207-774-0331; Toll Free Fax: 800-214-3895; Toll Free: 800-937-0331; Edit Addr.: 55 Bradley Dr., Westbrook, ME 04092-2013 USA (SAN 169-3050)
E-mail: info@ebc.com
Web site: http://www.ebc.com.
Eastern National, *(978-0-915992; 978-1-888213; 978-1-59091)* 470 Maryland Dr., Suite 1, Fort Washington, PA 19034 USA (SAN 630-4044)
E-mail: erich@Easternnational.org
Web site: http://www.easternnational.org.
Eastern National Park & Monument Association, *See* **Eastern National**
Eastern News Distributors, Subs. of Hearst Corp., 250 W. 55th St., New York, NY 10019 USA (SAN 169-5738) Tel 212-649-4484; Fax: 212-265-6239; Toll Free: 800-221-3148; 1 Media Way, 12406 Rte. 250, Milan, OH 44846-9705 (SAN 200-7711); 227 W. Trade St., Charlotte, NC 28202 (SAN 631-600X) Tel 704-348-8427
E-mail: enews@hearst.com.
Eastern Subscription Agency, 231 Moria Ct., Aston, PA 19014-1264 USA (SAN 285-9467).
Easton News Co., 2601 Dearborn St., Easton, PA 18042 USA (SAN 169-7315).
Eastview Editions, *(978-0-89860)* P.O. Box 247, Bernardsville, NJ 07924 USA (SAN 169-4952) Tel 908-204-0535.
East-West Export Bks., c/o Univ. of Hawaii Pr., 2840 Kolowalu St., Honolulu, HI 96822 USA Tel 808-956-8830; Fax: 808-988-6052
E-mail: royden@hawaii.edu
Web site: http://eastwestexportbooks.wordpress.com.
Eastwind Bks. & Arts, Inc., 1435-A Stockton St., San Francisco, CA 94133 USA (SAN 127-3159) Tel 415-772-5888; Fax: 415-772-5885
E-mail: info@eastwindsf.com
Web site: http://www.eastwindsf.com.
Eau Claire News Co., Inc., 8100 Partridge Rd., Eau Claire, WI 54703-9646 USA (SAN 169-9059) Tel 715-835-5437.
eBookit.com, *(978-1-4566)* Div. of Archieboy Holdings, LLC, 365 Boston Post Rd., No. 311, Sudbury, MA 01776 USA
Web site: http://www.ebookit.com.
eBooks2go, *See* **eBooks2go Inc**
eBooks2go Inc, *(978-1-61813; 978-1-5457)* 1111 N. Plaza Dr., Ste. 300, Schaumburg, IL 60173 USA Tel 847-598-1150
E-mail: ram@ebooks2go.net
Web site: http://www.gantecpublishing.com; http://www.ebooks2go.com/.
ebrary, Inc., Div. of Proquest LLC, 318 Cambridge Ave., Palo Alto, CA 94306 USA (SAN 760-7741) Tel 650-475-8700; Fax: 650-475-8881
E-mail: info@ebrary.com
Web site: http://www.ebrary.com.
ebrary.com, *See* **ebrary, Inc.**
EBS, Inc. Bk. Service, 290 Broadway, Lynbrook, NY 11563 USA (SAN 169-5487) Tel 516-593-1195; Fax: 516-596-2911.
EBSCO Media, *(978-1-885860)* Div. of EBSCO Industries, Inc., 801 Fifth Ave., S., Birmingham, AL 35233 USA Tel 205-323-1508; Fax: 205-226-8400; Toll Free: 800-765-0852
Web site: http://www.ebsco.com.
Ebsco Publishing, *(978-1-882248; 978-0-585; 978-1-4175; 978-1-4237; 978-1-4294; 978-1-4298; 978-1-4356; 978-1-4416; 978-1-4619)* Orders Addr.: 10 Estes St., Ipswich, MA 01938 USA (SAN 253-9497) Tel 978-356-6500; 800-653-2726; Fax: 978-356-6565
E-mail: information@ebscohost.com
Web site: http://www.ebscohost.com.
EBSCO Subscription Services, 5724 Hwy. 280 E., Birmingham, AL 35242-6818 USA (SAN 285-9394) Tel 205-991-6000; Fax: 205-991-1479
E-mail: jacomo@ebsco.com
Web site: http://www.ebsco.com.
Ecompass Business Ctr., 3125 Wellner Dr. NE, Rochester, MN 55906 USA Tel 507-280-0787.
Economical Wholesale Co., 6 King Philip Rd., Worcester, MA 01606 USA (SAN 169-3646).
EDC Publishing, *(978-0-7460; 978-0-86020; 978-0-88110; 978-1-58086; 978-0-7945; 978-1-60130)* Orders Addr.: P.O. Box 470663, Tulsa, OK 74147-0663 USA (SAN 658-0505); Edit Addr.: 10302 E. 55th Pl., Tulsa, OK 74146-6515 USA (SAN 107-5322) Tel 918-622-4522; Fax: 918-665-7919; Toll Free Fax: 800-747-4509; Toll Free: 800-475-4522
E-mail: edc@edcpub.com
Web site: http://www.edcpub.com.
Ediciones del Norte, *(978-0-910061)* P.O. Box 5130, Hanover, NH 03755 USA (SAN 241-2993).
Ediciones Enlace de PR, Inc., *(978-0-9904869)* 159 Calle Las Flores, San Juan, PR 00911-2223 USA Tel 787-725-7252; Fax: 787-725-7231
E-mail: info@edenlacepr.com; gramirez@edenlacepr.com
Web site: www.edenlacepr.com.
Ediciones Universal, *(978-0-89729; 978-1-59388)* Orders Addr.: P.O. Box 450353, Miami, FL 33245-0353 USA (SAN 658-0548); Edit Addr.: 3090 SW Eighth St., Miami, FL 33135 USA (SAN 207-2203) Tel 305-642-3355; Fax: 305-642-7978
E-mail: marta@ediciones.com; ediciones@ediciones.com
Web site: http://www.ediciones.com.
Editorial Betania, *See* **Grupo Nelson**
Editorial Cernuda, Inc., 1040 27th Ave., SW, Miami, FL 33135 USA (SAN 158-8850) Tel 305-264-9400.
Editorial Cultural, Inc., *(978-1-56758; 978-84-399)* Orders Addr.: P.O. Box 21056, San Juan, PR 00928 USA; Edit Addr.: Calle Robles, No. 51, San Juan, PR 00928 USA
E-mail: angiev@editorialculturalpr.com; alamo48@gmail.com
Web site: http://www.editorialculturalpr.com.
Editorial Unilit, *(978-0-7899; 978-0-945792; 978-1-56063)* Div. of Spanish Hse., Inc., 1360 NW 88th Ave., Miami,

FL 33172-3093 USA (SAN 247-5979) Tel 305-592-6136; Fax: 305-592-0087; Toll Free: 800-767-7726
E-mail: sales1@unidial.com
Web site: http://www.editorialunilit.com/.

Educa Vision Inc., *(978-1-881839; 978-1-58432; 978-1-62632; 978-1-64382)* 7550 NW 47th Ave., Coconut Creek, FL 33073 USA (SAN 760-873X) Tel 954-968-7433; Fax: 954-970-0330
E-mail: educa@aol.com
Web site: http://www.educavision.com; http://www.educabrazil.org; http://www.caribbeanstudiespress.com; www.educalanguage.com.

Education Guide, Inc., *(978-0-914880)* P.O. Box 421, Randolph, MA 02368 USA (SAN 201-4580) Tel 617-376-0066; Fax: 617-376-0067.

Educational Audio Visual, Incorporated, *See* **CLEARVUE/eav, Inc.**

Educational Bk. Distributors, P.O. Box 2510, Novato, CA 94948 USA (SAN 158-2259) Tel 415-883-3530; Fax: 415-883-4280; Toll Free: 800-761-5501
E-mail: PblshrSvcs@aol.com.

Educational Development Corporation, *See* **EDC Publishing**

Educational Distribution Corp., 10302 E. 55th Pl., Tulsa, OK 74146 USA Tel 918-622-4522.

Educational Media Corp., *(978-0-932796; 978-1-930572)* Orders Addr.: 1443 Old York Rd., Wartminster, PA 18974 USA Fax: 215-956-9041; Toll Free: 800-448-2197; Edit Addr.: 4256 Central Ave. NE, Minneapolis, MN 55421-2920 USA (SAN 212-4203) Tel 763-781-0088; Fax: 763-781-7753; Toll Free: 800-966-3382
E-mail: emedia@educationalmedia.com
Web site: http://www.educationalmedia.com.

Educational Record Ctr., Inc., 3233 Burnt Mill Dr., Suite 100, Wilmington, NC 28403-2698 USA (SAN 630-592X) Tel 910-251-1235; Fax: 910-343-0311; Toll Free Fax: 888-438-1637; Toll Free: 800-438-1637
E-mail: info@erc-inc.com
Web site: http://www.erc-inc.com.

Educational Resources, 1550 Executive Dr., Elgin, IL 60123 USA (SAN 631-5674) Tel 847-888-8300; Toll Free: 800-624-2926 Do not confuse with companies with same or similar name in Shawnee Mission, Columbia, SC, Saint Paul, MN
E-mail: gmhardeman@aol.com.

Educational Showcase, 3571 Newgate Dr., Troy, MI 48084-1042 USA Toll Free: 800-213-3671.

Edumate-Educational Materials, Inc., P.O. Box 711174, San Diego, CA 92171-1174 USA (SAN 630-2955)
E-mail: GusBus@aol.com.

Edu-Tech Corp., The, 65 Bailey Rd., Fairfield, CT 06432 USA (SAN 157-5392) Tel 203-374-4212; Fax: 203-374-8050; Toll Free: 800-338-5463
E-mail: edutcorp@aoc.com.

Edward Weston Graphic, Incorporated, *See* **Weston, Edward Fine Arts**

El Qui-Jote Bk., Inc., 12651 Monarch, Houston, TX 77047 USA (SAN 107-8666) Tel 713-433-3388.

Elder's Bk. Store, 2115 Elliston Pl., Nashville, TN 37203 USA (SAN 112-6091) Tel 615-327-1867.

Elkins, C. J., 400 S. Beverly Dr. Suite 214, Beverly Hills, CA 90212 USA Toll Free: 800-769-2120
E-mail: sitare@aol.com; sitare@zwallet.com.

Ellis News Co., Affil. of L-S Distributors, 130 E. Grand Ave., South San Francisco, CA 94080 USA (SAN 169-0183) Tel 415-873-2094; Fax: 415-873-4222; Toll Free: 800-654-7040 (orders only).

ELS Educational Services, *(978-0-87789; 978-0-89285; 978-0-89318)* Orders Addr.: 200 Old Tappan Rd., Old Tappan, NJ 07675 USA; Edit Addr.: 1357 Second St., Santa Monica, CA 90401-1102 USA (SAN 281-6326).

Elsevier, *(978-0-444; 978-0-7204; 978-0-916086; 978-1-85617; 978-1-59278; 978-0-08; 978-1-4831; 978-1-4832; 978-1-4933)* Orders Addr.: P.O. Box 945, New York, NY 10159-0945 USA (SAN 251-2564) Toll Free: 888-437-4636; P.O. Box 28430, Saint Louis, MO 63146-0930 Toll Free Fax: 800-535-9935; Toll Free: 800-460-3110 (Outside US); 800-545-2522; Edit Addr.: 360 Park Ave S. Flr. 11, New York, NY 10010-1710 USA (SAN 200-2051); 525 B St., Suite 1800, San Diego, CA 92101-4475 Tel 800-894-3434; 1-619-231-6616
E-mail: usinfo-f@elsevier.com; custserv@elsevier.com; d.gomez@elsevier.com
Web site: http://www.elsevier.com.

Elsevier - Health Sciences Div., *(978-0-323; 978-0-443; 978-0-444; 978-0-7020; 978-0-7216; 978-0-7234; 978-0-7236; 978-0-7506; 978-0-8016; 978-0-8151; 978-0-920513; 978-0-932883; 978-1-55664; 978-1-56053; 978-1-898507; 978-1-932141; 978-1-4160; 978-1-4377; 978-1-4557)* Subs. of Elsevier Science, Orders Addr.: a/o Customer Service, 3251 Riverport Ln., Maryland Heights, MO 63043 USA Tel 314-453-7010; Fax: 314-447-8030; Toll Free Fax: 800-535-9935; Toll Free: 800-545-2522; 800-460-3110 (Customers Outside US); 1799 Highway 50, Linn, MO 65051 (SAN 200-2280); Edit Addr.: 1600 John F. Kennedy Blvd., Suite 1800, Philadelphia, PA 19103-2899 USA Tel 215-239-3900; Fax: 215-239-3990; Toll Free: 800-523-4069
E-mail: usbkinfo@elsevier.com
Web site: http://www.elsevier.com; http://www.us.elsevierhealth.com/.

Elsevier Science, *See* **Elsevier**

Elsevier Science - Health Sciences Division, *See* **Elsevier - Health Sciences Div.**

Elsevier Science & Technology Bks., Orders Addr.: P.O. Box 28430, Saint Louis, MO 63146-0930 USA Toll Free Fax: 800-535-9935; Toll Free: 800-545-2522; 800-460-3110 (Customers Outside US); Edit Addr.: 525 B St., Suite 1900, San Diego, CA 92101 USA Toll Free: 1-800-894-3434; 200 Wheeler Rd., 6th Flr., Burlington, MA 01803 Tel 781-313-4700
E-mail: bookstore.orders@elsevier.com
Web site: http://www.elsevier.com/; http://www.syngress.com.

EMC/Paradigm Publishing, *(978-0-7638; 978-0-8219; 978-0-88436; 978-0-912022; 978-1-56118; 978-1-5338)* Div. of EMC Corp., 875 Montreal Way, Saint Paul, MN 55102 USA (SAN 201-3800) Toll Free Fax: 800-328-4564; Toll Free: 800-328-1452
E-mail: publish@emcp.com; educate@emcp.com
Web site: http://www.emcp.com.

Emerald Bk. Co., *(978-1-934572; 978-1-937110)* Div. of Greenleaf Bk. Group, 4425 Mo Pac Expy., Suite 600, Austin, TX 78735 USA.

Emery-Pratt Co., Orders Addr.: 1966 W. M 21, Owosso, MI 48867-1397 USA (SAN 170-1401) Tel 989-723-5291; Fax: 989-723-4677; Toll Free Fax: 800-523-6379; Toll Free: 800-762-5683 (library orders only); 800-248-3887 (customer service only) Distributor to Libraries & Hospitals
E-mail: custserv@emery-pratt.com
Web site: http://www.emery-pratt.com.

Empire Comics, 375 Stone Rd., Rochester, NY 14616 USA (SAN 110-943X) Tel 716-442-0371; Fax: 716-442-7807
E-mail: empires@frontiernet.net.

Empire News of Jamestown, Foot Ave. & Extension St., Box 2029, Sta. A, Jamestown, NY 14702 USA (SAN 169-5371).

Empire Publishing Service, *(978-1-58690)* P.O. Box 1344, Studio City, CA 91614-0344 USA (SAN 630-5687) Tel 818-784-8918
E-mail: empirepubsvc@att.net.

Empire State News Corp., Orders Addr.: P.O. Box 1167, Buffalo, NY 14240-1167 USA Tel 716-681-1100; Fax: 716-681-1120; Toll Free: 800-414-6247; Edit Addr.: 316 Forestview Dr., Buffalo, NY 14221-1461 USA (SAN 169-5177)
Web site: http://www.esnc.com.

Empowerment Technologies, *See* **Empowerment Technologies/Neuro-Semantics Publns.**

Empowerment Technologies/Neuro-Semantics Publns., *(978-1-890001; 978-1-899836)* Orders Addr.: P.O. Box 8, Clifton, CO 81520 USA Tel 970-523-5790; Fax: 970-523-5790; Edit Addr.: P.O. Box 9231, Grand Junction, CO 81501 USA Tel 970-523-7877
E-mail: meta@acsol.net
Web site: http://www.neurosemantics.com.

Encino Pr., *(978-0-88426)* 510 Baylor St., Austin, TX 78703 USA (SAN 201-3843) Tel 512-476-6821; Fax: 512-476-9393.

Encyclopaedia Britannica, Inc., *(978-0-7826; 978-0-8347; 978-0-85229; 978-0-87827; 978-1-59339; 978-1-60835; 978-1-61535; 978-0-9823819; 978-0-9823820; 978-0-9823821; 978-0-9823822; 978-0-9823823; 978-0-9823824; 978-1-62513; 978-1-68382)* 325 N. La Salle St., Chicago, IL 60654 USA (SAN 204-1464) Toll Free Fax: 800-344-9624 (fax orders); Toll Free: 800-323-1229; 800-621-3900 (orders); 2nd Flr., Unity Wharf Mill St., London, SE1 2BH Tel 020 7500 7800; Fax: 020 7500 7878
E-mail: enquiries@britannica.co.uk; contact@eb.com
Web site: http://www.eb.com; http://www.britannica.co.uk.

Enfield Publishing & Distribution Co., Inc., *(978-0-9656184; 978-1-893598)* Orders Addr.: P.O. Box 699, Enfield, NH 03748 USA Tel 603-632-7377; Fax: 603-632-5611; Edit Addr.: 234 May St., Enfield, NH 03748 USA
E-mail: info@enfieldbooks.com
Web site: http://www.enfielddistribution.com; http://www.enfieldbooks.com.

Entrepreneur Media Inc/Entrepreneur Pr., *(978-0-916378; 978-1-55571; 978-1-891984; 978-1-932156; 978-1-932531; 978-1-59918; 978-1-61308; 978-1-64201)* 18061 Fitch, Irvine, CA 92614 USA Tel 949-622-7106; Fax: 949-622-7106; Toll Free: 800-864-6864
E-mail: vcampos@entrepreneur.com
Web site: http://www.entrepreneur.com; http://www.entrepreneurpress.com.

Entrepreneur Press, *See* **Entrepreneur Media Inc/Entrepreneur Pr.**

Entrepreneur Start a Business Store, 9114 River Look Ln., Fair Oaks, CA 95628-6565 USA (SAN 133-1485) Fax: 916-863-0361.

Epic Book Promotions, 914 Nolan Way, Chula Vista, CA 91911-2408 USA Tel 619-498-8547; Fax: 619-498-8540
E-mail: gvjack@pacbell.net.

Epicenter Pr., Inc., *(978-0-945397; 978-0-9708493; 978-0-9724944; 978-0-9745014; 978-0-9790470; 978-1-60381; 978-0-9800825; 978-1-935347; 978-1-941890)* Orders Addr.: 6524 NE 181st St., No. 2, Kenmore, WA 98028 USA (SAN 246-9405) Do not confuse with companies with similar names in Kanehoe, HI, Long Beach, CA, Oakland, CA
E-mail: info@epicenterpress.com; phil@epicenterpress.com; aubrey@epicenterpress.com
Web site: http://www.epicenterpress.com.

E-Pros DG, 32 N. Goodwin Ave., Elmsford, NY 10523 USA Toll Free: 866-377-6700
E-mail: sales@e-pros.ws.

Epson Mid-Atlantic, Subs. of Epson America, Inc., 8 Neshaminy Interplex, Suite 319, Trerose, PA 19053 USA (SAN 285-7243) Tel 215-245-2180.

Equinox, Ltd., 1307 Park Ave., Williamsport, PA 17701 USA.

Eriksson Enterprises, 126 Sunset Dr., Farmington, UT 84025-3426 USA (SAN 110-5892).

Erlbaum, Lawrence Assocs., Inc., *(978-0-8058; 978-0-86377; 978-0-89859; 978-1-880393; 978-1-4106)* 270 Madison Ave. Flr. 4, New York, NY 10016-0601 USA (SAN 213-960X) Toll Free: 800-926-6579 (orders only)
E-mail: orders@erlbaum.com
Web site: http://www.erlbaum.com.

ETA hand2mind, *See* **hand2mind**

ETD KroMar Temple, P.O. Box 535695, Grand Prairie, TX 75053-5625 USA (SAN 169-8435) Tel 254-778-5261; Fax: 254-778-5267.

European Bk. Co., Inc., 925 Larkin St., San Francisco, CA 94109 USA (SAN 169-0191) Tel 415-474-0626; Fax: 415-474-0630; Toll Free: 877-746-3666
E-mail: info@europeanbook.com.

European Press Service - PBD America Wholesalers, 30 Edison Dr., Wayne, NJ 07470-4713 USA (SAN 630-7825).

Evans Bk. Distribution & Pubs., Inc., *(978-0-9654884; 978-1-56684)* 895 W. 1700 S., Salt Lake City, UT 84104 USA.

Evans Book, *See* **Evans Bk. Distribution & Pubs., Inc.**

Evanston Publishing, Inc., *(978-1-879260)* 4824 Brownsboro Ctr. Arcade, Louisville, KY 40207-2342 USA Tel 502-899-1919; Fax: 502-896-0246; Toll Free: 800-594-5190
E-mail: EvanstonPB@aol.com; info@evanstonpublishing.com
Web site: http://www.EvanstonPublishing.com.

Everbind/Marco Book Company, *See* **Marco Bk. Co.**

Excaliber Publishing Co., *(978-1-881353)* 7954 W. Bury Ave., San Diego, CA 92126 USA (SAN 297-6412) Tel 619-695-3091; Fax: 619-695-3095.

Exciting Times, 17430C Crenshaw Blvd., Torrance, CA 90504 USA (SAN 114-4642) Tel 310-515-2676; Fax: 310-515-1382.

Executive Books, *See* **Tremendous Life Bks.**

Experiment LLC, The, *(978-1-61519)* 260 Fifth Ave., Suite 3 S., New York, NY 10001-6425 USA (SAN 857-961X)
E-mail: info@theexperimentpublishing.com
Web site: http://www.theexperimentpublishing.com.

Exploration Films, P.O. Box 1069, Monument, CO 80132 USA Tel 719-481-4599; Fax: 719-481-1399; Toll Free: 800-964-0439
E-mail: jolene@explorationfilms.com
Web site: http://www.explorationfilms.com.

Explorations, 360 Interlocken Blvd., Suite 300, Broomfield, CO 80021 USA Toll Free Fax: 800-456-1139; Toll Free: 800-720-2114
E-mail: customerservice@gaiam.com
Web site: http://www.gaiam.com.

Express Media, *(978-0-9723163)* 127 Rankin Rd., Columbia, MS 37202 USA Tel 615-360-6400
Web site: http://www.authorsexpress.com.

Faber & Faber, Inc., *(978-0-571)* Affil. of Farrar, Straus & Giroux, LLC, Orders Addr.: c/o Van Holtzbrinck Publishing Services, 16365 James Madison Hwy., Gordonsville, VA 22942 USA Fax: 540-572-7540; Toll Free: 888-330-8477; Edit Addr.: 19 Union Sq., W, New York, NY 10003-3304 USA (SAN 218-7256) Tel 212-741-6900; Fax: 212-633-9385
E-mail: sales@fsgbooks.com
Web site: http://www.fsgbooks.com.

Facts On File, Inc., *(978-0-8160; 978-0-87196; 978-1-60413; 978-1-4381; 978-1-61753)* Orders Addr.: 132 W. 31st St., 17th Flr., New York, NY 10001-2006 USA (SAN 201-4696) Tel 212-967-8800; 212-896-4296 (customer service); Fax: 917-339-0325; 917-339-0323; Toll Free Fax: 800-678-3633; Toll Free: 800-322-8755
E-mail: custserv@factsonfile.com; Sales@ChelseaHouse.com
Web site: http://www.factsonfile.com; http://www.fergpubco.com; http://www.chelseahouse.com.

Fairfield Bk. Service Co., 150 Margherita Lawn, Stratford, CT 06615 USA (SAN 131-0976) Tel 203-375-7607.

Faith Alive Christian Resources, *(978-0-930265; 978-0-933140; 978-1-56212; 978-1-59255; 978-1-62025)* 2850 Kalamazoo Ave., SE, Grand Rapids, MI 49560 USA (SAN 212-727X) Tel 616-224-0784; Fax: 616-224-0834; Toll Free Fax: 888-642-8606; Toll Free: 800-333-8300; P.O. Box 5070, Burlington, ON L7R 3Y8 Toll Free Fax: 888-642-8606; Toll Free: 800-333-8300
E-mail: sales@faithaliveresources.org
Web site: http://www.faithaliveresources.org.

Falk Bks. Inc., W.E., 7491 N. Federal Hwy., PMB 267, Boca Raton, FL 33487 USA.

Falk, W. E., *See* **Falk Bks. Inc., W.E.**

Fall River News Co., Inc., 144 Robeson St., Fall River, MA 02720-4925 USA (SAN 169-3425) Tel 508-679-5266.

Familius LLC, *(978-1-938301; 978-1-939629; 978-1-942672; 978-1-942934; 978-1-944822; 978-1-945547; 978-1-64170)* 1254 Commerce Way, Sanger, CA 93657 USA (SAN 990-1515) Tel 801-552-7298; 559-876-2170
E-mail: christopher@familius.com
Web site: www.familius.com.

Family History World, P.O. Box 129, Tremonton, UT 84337 USA (SAN 159-673X) Fax: 801-250-6727; Toll Free: 800-377-6058
E-mail: genealogy@utahlinx.com
Web site: http://www.genealogical-institute.com.

Family Reading Service, 1601 N. Slappey Blvd., Albany, GA 31701-1431 USA (SAN 169-1376).

Fantaco Pubns., *(978-0-938782)* Affil. of Fantaco Enterprises, Inc., Orders Addr.: 1313 W. Gate Drive, Unit 408, Leland, NC 28451 USA; Edit Addr.: 1313 W. Gate Drive, Unit 408, Leland, NC 28451 USA (SAN 158-5134)
E-mail: sanchez.kaz@gmail.com; bluecheer1@yahoo.com
Web site: www.fantaco.net.

Far West Bk. Service, 3515 NE Hassalo, Portland, OR 97232 USA (SAN 107-6760) Tel 503-234-7664; Fax: 503-231-0573; Toll Free: 800-964-9378.

Farcountry Pr., *(978-0-938314; 978-1-56037; 978-1-59152)* Orders Addr.: P.O. Box 5630, Helena, MT 59604 USA (SAN 220-0732) Tel 406-422-1263; Fax: 406-443-5480; Toll Free: 800-821-3874; 2750 Broadwater, Helena, MT 59602
E-mail: books@farcountrypress.com
Web site: http://www.farcountrypress.com.

Farrar, Straus & Giroux, *(978-0-374)* Div. of Holtzbrinck Publishers, Orders Addr.: c/o Holtzbrinck Publishers, 16365 James Madison Hwy., Gordonsville, VA 22942 USA Toll Free Fax: 800-672-2054; Toll Free: 888-330-8477; Edit Addr.: 18 W. 18th St., New York, NY 10011-4607 USA (SAN 206-782X)
E-mail: sales@fsgee.com; fsg.editorial@fsgee.com
Web site: http://www.fsgbooks.com/.

Faxon Company, The, *See* **Divine, Inc.**

Faxon Illinois Service Ctr., Affil. of Dawson Holdings PLC, 1600 Providence Hwy., Walpole, MA 02081-2553 USA (SAN 286-0147) Toll Free: 800-852-7404
E-mail: postmaster@dawson.com; sandy.nordman@dawson.com
Web site: http://www.faxon.com.

Fayette County News Agency, Orders Addr.: P.O. Box 993, Uniontown, PA 15401 USA Tel 724-437-1181; Edit Addr.: Cherry Tree Square 42 Matthew Dr., Uniontown, PA 15401 USA (SAN 169-765X).

FEC News Distributing, 2201 Fourth Ave., N., Lake Worth, FL 33461-3835 USA (SAN 169-1341) Tel 407-547-3000; Fax: 407-547-3080.

Feldheim, Philipp Incorporated, *See* **Feldheim Pubs.**

Feldheim Pubs., *(978-0-87306; 978-1-58330; 978-1-59826; 978-1-68025)* 208 Airport Executive Park., Nanuet, NY 10954-5262 USA (SAN 106-6307) Toll Free: 800-237-7149
E-mail: sales@feldheim.com; eli@feldheim.com
Web site: http://www.feldheim.com.

Fell, Frederick Pubs., Inc., *(978-0-8119; 978-0-88391; 978-0-936320)* Orders Addr.: 1403 Shoreline Way, Hollywood, FL 33019-5007 USA (SAN 215-0670)
Web site: http://www.fellpub.com.

Fennell, Reginald F. Subscription Service, 1002 W. Michigan Ave., Jackson, MI 49202 USA (SAN 159-6071) Tel 517-782-3132; Fax: 517-782-1109.

FEP, A Booksource Co., 1230 Macklind Ave., Saint Louis, MO 63110 USA (SAN 169-1317) Tel 314-647-0600; Fax: 314-647-6850; Toll Free: 800-444-0435
Web site: http://www.booksource.com.

Fiddlecase Bks., HC 63 Box 104, East Alstead, NH 03602 USA (SAN 200-7495) Tel 603-835-7889.

Fiesta Bk. Co., *(978-0-88473)* P.O. Box 490641, Key Biscayne, FL 33149 USA (SAN 201-8470) Tel 305-858-4843.

Fiesta Publishing Corporation, *See* **Fiesta Bk. Co.**

Films for the Humanities & Sciences, *See* **Films Media Group**

Films Media Group, *(978-0-7365; 978-0-89113; 978-1-56950; 978-1-4213; 978-1-60467)* Div. of Infobase Learning, Orders Addr.: 132 W. 31st St., 17th Flr., New York, NY 10001 USA (SAN 653-2705) Toll Free Fax: 800-678-3633; Toll Free: 800-322-8755
E-mail: mgallo@infobaselearning.com
Web site: http://www.films.com.

Findaway World, LLC, *(978-1-59895; 978-1-60252; 978-1-60514; 978-1-60640; 978-1-60775; 978-1-60812; 978-1-60847; 978-1-61545; 978-1-61574; 978-1-61587; 978-1-61637; 978-1-61657; 978-1-61707; 978-1-4676; 978-1-5094; 978-1-9871; 978-1-0942; 978-1-6622; 978-1-6649)* 31999 Aurora Rd., Solon, OH 44139 USA (SAN 853-8778) Tel 440-893-0808 x108
Web site: http://www.findawayworld.com; http://www.playawaydigital.com.

Fine Assocs., One Farragut Sq., S., Washington, DC 20006 USA (SAN 169-0914) Tel 202-628-2609.

Finn News Agency, Inc., 4415 State Rd. 327, Auburn, IN 46706-9542 USA (SAN 169-2356).

Finney Co., Inc., *(978-0-89317; 978-0-912486; 978-0-933855; 978-0-9617767; 978-0-9639705; 978-1-880654; 978-1-893272)* Orders Addr.: 8075 215th St. W., Lakeville, MN 55044 USA (SAN 206-412X) Tel 952-469-6699; Fax: 952-469-1968; Toll Free Fax: 800-330-6232; Toll Free: 800-846-7027
E-mail: feedback@finneyco.com
Web site: http://www.finneyco.com; http://www.ecopress.com; http://www.pogopress.com; http://www.astragalpress.com.

Fire Protection Publications, *See* **IFSTA**

Firebird Distributing, LLC, 1945 P St., Eureka, CA 95501-3007 USA (SAN 631-1229) Toll Free: 800-353-3575
E-mail: sales@firebirddistributing.com
Web site: http://www.firebirddistributing.com.

Firebrand Technologies, 44 Merrimac St., Newburyport, MA 01950 USA.

Firefly Bks., Ltd., *(978-0-920668; 978-1-55209; 978-1-895565; 978-1-896284; 978-1-55297; 978-1-55407)* Orders Addr.: c/o Frontier Distributing, 1000 Young St., Suite 160, Tonawanda, NY 14150 USA (SAN 630-611X) Tel 203-222-9700; Toll Free Fax: 800-565-6034; Toll Free: 800-387-5085; Edit Addr.: 8514 Long Canyon Dr., Austin, TX 78730-2813 USA
E-mail: service@fireflybooks.com
Web site: http://www.fireflybooks.com/.

Firenze Pr., *(978-0-9711236)* Orders Addr.: P.O. Box 6892, Wyomissing, PA 19610-0892 USA (SAN 254-315X); Edit Addr.: 612 Museum Rd., Reading, PA 19610-0892

USA Tel 610-374-7048 Do not confuse with Leonardo Pr., Camden, ME
E-mail: hailejohnjr@msn.com; HaileJohnJr@msn.com; InkPenCJH@msn.com
Web site: http://caroljhaile.com.

Fischer, Carl LLC, (978-0-8258) Orders Addr.: 588 N. Gulph Rd. Ste. B, Kng Of Prussa, PA 19406-2831 USA Toll Free: 800-762-2328; Edit Addr.: 65 Bleeker St., New York, NY 10012-2420 USA (SAN 107-4245) Tel 212-772-0900; Fax: 212-477-6996; Toll Free: 800-762-2328
E-mail: cf-info@carlfischer.com
Web site: http://www.carlfischer.com.

Fish, Enrica Medical Bks., 1208 W. Minnehaha Pkwy., Minneapolis, MN 55419-1163 USA (SAN 157-8588) Toll Free: 800-728-8398.

Fisher King Bks., 316 Mid Valley Ctr., #194, Carmel, CA 93923 USA Tel 831-238-7799; Toll Free: 800-228-9316 (Canada & US).

Flannery Co., 16430 Beaver Rd., Adelanto, CA 92301-3904 USA (SAN 168-9754) Toll Free: 800-456-3400.

Flannery, J. F. Company, *See* **Flannery Co.**

Fleming, Robert Hull Museum, (978-0-934658) Div. of Univ. of Vermont, Univ. of Vermont, 61 Colchester Ave., Burlington, VT 05405 USA (SAN 110-8824) Tel 802-656-0750; Fax: 802-656-8059
Web site: www.upne.com.

Flora & Fauna Bks., P.O. Box 15718, Gainesville, FL 32604 USA (SAN 133-1221) Tel 352-373-5630; Fax: 352-373-3249
E-mail: ffbks@aol.com
Web site: http://www.ffbooks.com.

Florida Academic Pr., (978-1-890357) P.O. Box 540, Gainesville, FL 32602-0540 USA (SAN 299-3643) Tel 352-332-5104; Fax: 352-331-6003
E-mail: fapress@worldnet.att.net.

Florida Classics Library, (978-0-912451) P.O. Drawer 1657, Port Salerno, FL 34992-1657 USA (SAN 265-2404) Tel 561-546-9380 (orders); Fax: 561-546-7545 (orders).

Florida Schl. Bk. Depository, 1125 N. Ellis Rd., Jacksonville, FL 32236 USA (SAN 161-8423) Tel 904-781-7191; Fax: 904-781-3486; Toll Free: 800-447-7957
Web site: http://www.fsbd.com.

Flury & Co., 322 First Ave S., Seattle, WA 98104 USA (SAN 107-5748) Tel 206-587-0260.

FM International, P.O. Box 91, Waunakee, WI 53597-0091 USA.

Fodor's Travel Guides, *See* **Fodor's Travel Pubns.**

Fodor's Travel Pubns., Div. of Random Hse., Information Group, Orders Addr.: 400 Hahn Rd., Westminster, MD 21157 USA Tel 410-848-1900; Toll Free: 800-726-0600; Edit Addr.: 1745 Broadway, New York, NY 10019 USA Tel 212-782-9000
Web site: http://www.fodors.com.

Follet Higher Education Grp, P.O. Box 3488, Oak Brook, IL 60522-3488 USA Tel 630-279-0123.

Follett Audiovisual Resources, *See* **Follett Media Distribution**

Follett Library Resources, *See* **Follett School Solutions**

Follett Media Distribution, 1847 Mercer Rd., Lexington, KY 40511-1001 USA (SAN 631-7316) Toll Free: 888-281-1216.

Follett School Solutions, (978-0-329; 978-0-88153; 978-0-924917; 978-1-4898; 978-1-5160; 978-1-5181; 978-1-5379; 978-1-5444; 978-1-5490; 978-1-7254; 978-1-7137) Div. of the Follett Corp., Orders Addr.: a/o McHenry Warehouse, 1340 Ridgeview Dr., McHenry, IL 60050 USA (SAN 169-1902) Toll Free: 888-511-5114; a/o Patti Hall: R & R Bindery Services, 499 Rachel Rd., Girard, IL 62640 (SAN 155-8412) Tel 815-759-1700; 160 Dulty's Lane, Suite 300, Burlington Township, NJ 08016 (SAN 991-1006); 2801 Alft Lane, Unit 100, Elgin, IL 60124 (SAN 991-1014); 2430 E. Arbrook Blvd, Suite 300, Arlington, TX 76014 (SAN 991-1022); a/o Formerly FES, 1433 Internationale Pkwy. DOCK Door 30, Woodridge, IL 60517 (SAN 631-7901) Tel 630-972-5600; Fax: 630-972-4673; Toll Free: 800-621-4272; a/o Russell Henning (Formerly FSC), 1391 Corporate Dr., McHenry, IL 60050-7041 (SAN 298-587X) Fax: 815-344-8774; 26682 Almond Avenue, Bldg 1, Suite 100, Redlands, CA 92374 (SAN 991-1030); a/o Formerly FLR, 1340 Ridgeview Dr., Suite EDI, McHenry, IL 60050-0000 (SAN 760-7164); 3057 Tradeport Drive, Suite 100, Orlando, FL 32824 (SAN 991-1049)
Web site: http://www.follett.com.

Fondo de Cultura Economica USA, 2293 Verus St., San Diego, CA 92154 USA (SAN 860-1380) Tel 619-429-0455; Fax: 619-651-9684; Toll Free: 800-532-3872
E-mail: orders@fceusa.com; drazo@fceusa.com; fondosales@fceusa.com
Web site: http://www.fceusa.com.

Fordham Univ. Pr., (978-0-8232; 978-1-5315) Joseph A. Martino Hall 45 Columbus Ave., New York, NY 10023 USA (SAN 201-6516) Tel 718-817-4795; Fax: 718-817-4785
E-mail: kasweeney@fordham.edu
Web site: http://www.fordhampress.com.

Forest Hse. Publishing Co., Inc., (978-1-56674; 978-1-878363) P.O. Box 738, Lake Forest, IL 60045 USA Tel 847-295-8287; Fax: 847-295-8201; Toll Free: 800-394-7323.

Forest Sales & Distributing Co., (978-0-9712183) 139 Jean Marie St., Reserve, LA 70084 USA (SAN 157-5511) Toll Free: 800-347-2106
E-mail: tbooks2@juno.com.

Forsa Editores, (978-1-881714) Orders Addr.: P.O. Box 11249, San Juan, PR 00922-1249 USA Tel 787-707-1792; Fax: 787-707-1797; Toll Free: 888-225-8984; Edit Addr.: No. 1594 J.T. Pinero Ave., Caparra Heights, PR 00920 USA
E-mail: forsa@forsaeditores.com
Web site: http://www.forsaeditores.com.

Forsyth Travel Library, Inc., (978-0-9614539) 1750 E. 131st St., P.O. Box 480800, Kansas City, MO 64148-0800 USA (SAN 169-2755) Tel 816-942-9050; Fax: 816-942-6969; Toll Free: 800-367-7984 (orders only)
E-mail: forsyth@gvi.net
Web site: http://www.forsyth.com.

Forward Movement Pubns., (978-0-88028) 300 West Fourth St., Cincinnati, OH 45202 USA (SAN 208-3841) Tel 513-721-6659; Fax: 513-721-0729; Toll Free: 800-543-1813 (orders only)
E-mail: Orders@forwarddaybyday.com
Web site: http://www.forwardmovement.org.

Foster, Walter Publishing, Incorporated, *See* **Quarto Publishing Group USA**

Four Winds Trading Co., (978-0-9672383) 6355 Joyce Dr., Golden, CO 80403-7568 USA (SAN 631-1989) Toll Free: 800-456-5444
E-mail: Paul@Fourwinds-trading.com; sales@fourwinds-trading.com
Web site: http://www.fourwinds-trading.com.

Fox Chapel Publishing Co., Inc., (978-0-932944; 978-1-56523; 978-1-57421; 978-1-58011; 978-1-880029; 978-1-85974; 978-1-903366; 978-0-9777004; 978-1-905523; 978-1-60765; 978-1-906853; 978-1-4971; 978-1-4972; 978-1-5048; 978-1-908397; 978-1-910456; 978-1-64124; 978-1-64178) Orders Addr.: 1970 Broad St., East Petersburg, PA 17520 USA (SAN 920-8887) Tel 717-560-4703; Fax: 717-560-4702; Toll Free Fax: 888-369-2885; Toll Free: 800-457-9112 (orders); Edit Addr.: 903 Square St., Mount Joy, PA 17552 USA Fax: 888-369-2885; Toll Free: 1-800-457-9112
E-mail: sales@carvingworld.com; alan@foxchapelpublishing.com; Younger@foxchapelpublishing.com; sales@foxchapelpublishing.com
Web site: http://www.foxchapelpublishing.com/; http://www.scrollsawer.com/; http://www.carvingworld.com; http://www.foxchapelpublishing.com; www.d-originals.com.

Franklin Bk. Co., Inc., P.O. Box 451, Newtown Sq, PA 19073-0451 USA (SAN 121-4160)
E-mail: service@franklinbook.com
Web site: http://www.franklinbook.com.

Franklin Readers Service, P.O. Box 662, Dunn Loring, VA 22027-0662 USA (SAN 285-9599).

Franklin Square Overseas, 17-19 Washington St., Tenafly, NJ 07670-2084 USA (SAN 285-9637) Tel 201-569-2500; Fax: 201-569-5141
E-mail: esstn@ebsco.com.

Freeman Family Ministries, Orders Addr.: P.O. Box 593, Waldo, FL 32694 USA Tel 352-468-2785
E-mail: freemanfamily9@msn.com.

Freihofer, A. G., 175 Fifth Ave., New York, NY 10010 USA (SAN 285-9602) Tel 272-460-7500; Fax: 272-473-6272.

French & European Pubns., Inc., (978-0-320; 978-0-7859; 978-0-8288; 978-1-5479) 425 E. 58th St., Suite 27D, New York, NY 10022-2379 USA (SAN 206-8109) Fax: 212-265-1094
E-mail: livresny@gmail.com; frenchbookstore@aol.com
Web site: http://www.frencheuropean.com.

Fresno Bk. Fairs, 1030 Bonita Ave., La Verne, CA 91750 USA (SAN 630-6225) Tel 909-593-0697; 1650 W. Orange Grove Ave., Pomona, CA 91768-2153 (SAN 299-2434)
Web site: http://www.mrsnelsons.com.

Friendly Hills Fellowship, *See* **Health and Growth Assocs.**

Fris News Co., 194 River Ave., Holland, MI 49423 USA (SAN 159-8643).

Frontline Communications, *See* **YWAM Publishing**

FRP Cookbook Marketplace, *See* **Cookbook Marketplace, The**

Fujii Assocs., 1400 W. 47th St. Ste. 4, La Grange, IL 60525-6148 USA (SAN 631-5305).

Fulcrum Publishing, (978-0-912347; 978-1-55591; 978-1-56373; 978-1-936218; 978-1-938486; 978-1-68275) Orders Addr.: 4690 Table Mountain Dr. Suite 100, Golden, CO 80403 USA (SAN 200-2825) Toll Free Fax: 800-726-7112; Toll Free: 800-992-2908
E-mail: info@fulcrumbooks.com
Web site: http://www.fulcrumbooks.com.

Fulmont News Co., Affil. of Rubin Periodical Group, P.O. Box 1211, Rochester, NY 14603-1211 USA (SAN 169-5029) Tel 518-843-2421.

Fultz News Agency, 2008 Woodbrook, Denton, TX 76205 USA (SAN 169-8168).

Futech Educational Products, Inc., (978-0-9627001; 978-1-889192) 2999 N. 44th St., Suite 225, Phoenix, AZ 85018-7248 USA Tel 602-808-8765; Fax: 602-278-5667; Toll Free: 800-597-6278.

G A M Printers & Grace Christian Bookstore, *See* **GAM Pubn.**

Gabriel Resources, Orders Addr.: P.O. Box 1047, Waynesboro, GA 30830 USA Tel 706-554-1594; Fax: 706-554-7444; Toll Free: 800-732-6657 (8MORE-BOOKS); Edit Addr.: 129 Mobilization Dr., Waynesboro, GA 30830 USA.

Galda Library Services, Inc., 33 Richdale Ave., Cambridge, MA 02140 USA (SAN 630-5806) Tel 617-864-8232.

Gale Virtual Reference Library, 27500 Drake Rd., Farmington Hills, MI 48331 USA Toll Free: 800-877-4253
Web site: http://www.gale.cengage.com/servlet/GvrlMS?msg=ma.

Galesburg News Agency, Inc., Five E. Simmons St., Galesburg, IL 61401 USA (SAN 169-1945).

Galveston News Agency, P.O. Box 7608, San Antonio, TX 78207-0608 USA (SAN 169-8230).

GAM Pubn., P.O. Box 25, Sterling, VA 20167 USA (SAN 158-7218) Tel 703-450-4121; Fax: 703-450-5311.

Gamboge International, Inc., 18 Brittany Ave., Trumbull, CT 06611 USA (SAN 631-046X) Tel 203-261-2130; Fax: 203-452-0180
E-mail: gamboge@pcaet.com.

Gangaji Foundation, The, (978-0-9632194; 978-1-887984) P.O. Box 716, Ashland, OR 97520-0024 USA Toll Free: 800-267-9205
E-mail: order@Gangaji.org; info@gangaji.org
Web site: http://www.gangaji.org.

Gannon Distributing Co., (978-0-88307) 100 La Salle Cir., No. A, Santa Fe, NM 87505-6916 USA (SAN 201-5889).

Gardner's Book Service, *See* **Gardner's Bk. Service**

Garrett Educational Corp., (978-0-944483; 978-1-56074) Orders Addr.: P.O. Box 1588, Ada, OK 74820 USA (SAN 169-6955) Tel 580-332-6884; Fax: 580-332-1560; Toll Free: 800-654-9366; Edit Addr.: 130 E. 13th St., Ada, OK 74820 USA (SAN 243-2722)
E-mail: mail@garrettbooks.com
Web site: http://www.garrettbooks.com.

Gasman News Agency, 2211 Third Ave., S., Escanaba, MI 49829 USA (SAN 169-3794).

Gatewood Pr., (978-0-9710427) P.O. Box 356, Johnson City, TX 78636 USA Tel 832-723-7313 Do not confuse with Wilson & Associates, Gig Harbor, WA
E-mail: alvincoog@me.com.

Gaunt, Inc., (978-0-912004; 978-1-56169; 978-1-60449) 3011 Gulf Dr., Holmes Beach, FL 34217-2199 USA (SAN 202-9413) Tel 941-778-5211; Fax: 941-778-5252
E-mail: info@gaunt.com; sales@gaunt.com
Web site: http://www.gaunt.com.

Gaunt, William W. & Sons, Incorporated, *See* **Gaunt, Inc.**

GBGM Service Ctr., P.O. Box 691328, Cincinnati, OH 45269 USA.

Gefen Bks., (978-0-86343) 11 Edison Pl., Springfield, NJ 07081 USA (SAN 856-8065)
E-mail: gefenny@gefenpublishing.com
Web site: http://www.gefenpublishing.com.

Gem Guides Bk. Co., (978-0-935182; 978-0-937799; 978-1-889786) Orders Addr.: 1275 W. 9th St., Upland, CA 91786 USA (SAN 221-1637) Tel 626-855-1611; Fax: 626-855-1610
E-mail: info@gemguidesbooks.com
Web site: http://www.gemguidesbooks.com.

Gemini Enterprises, P.O. Box 8251, Stockton, CA 95208 USA (SAN 128-1402).

Genealogical Sources, Unlimited, (978-0-913857) 407 Ascot Ct., Knoxville, TN 37923-5807 USA (SAN 170-8058) Tel 865-690-7831.

Genealogy Digest, 960 N. 400 E., North Salt Lake, UT 84054-1920 USA (SAN 110-389X); 420 S. 425 W., Bountiful, UT 84010 (SAN 243-2439).

General Medical Pubs., (978-0-935236) P.O. Box 210, Venice, CA 90294-0210 USA (SAN 215-689X) Tel 310-392-4911.

Generic Computer Products, Inc., (978-0-918611) P.O. Box 790, Marquette, MI 49855 USA (SAN 284-8856) Tel 906-226-7600; Fax: 906-226-8309.

GenPop Bks., (978-0-9823594; 978-0-9985126) Orders Addr.: P.O. Box 189, Grafton, VT 05146 USA
Web site: http://www.genpopbooks.com.

Geographia Map Co., Inc., (978-0-88433) 75 Moore St., Hackensack, NJ 07601-7107 USA (SAN 132-5566).

Gerold International Booksellers, Inc., 35-23 Utopia Pkwy., Flushing, NY 11358 USA (SAN 129-959X) Tel 718-358-4741; Fax: 718-358-3688.

Gibbs Smith, Publisher, (978-0-87905; 978-0-941711; 978-1-58685; 978-1-4236) Orders Addr.: P.O. Box 667, Layton, UT 84041 USA (SAN 201-9906) Tel 801-544-9800; Fax: 801-544-5582; Toll Free Fax: 800-213-3023 (orders); Toll Free: 800-748-5439 (orders); 800-835-4993 (Customer Service order only); Edit Addr.: 1877 E. Gentile St., Layton, UT 84040 USA Tel 801-544-9800; Fax: 801-546-8853
E-mail: info@gibbs-smith.com; tradeorders@gibbs-smith.com
Web site: http://www.gibbs-smith.com.

Gibson, Dot Pubns., (978-0-941162) Orders Addr.: P.O. Box 117, Waycross, GA 31502-0117 USA (SAN 200-4143) Tel 912-285-2848; Fax: 912-285-0349; Toll Free: 800-336-8095; Edit Addr.: 383 Bonneyman Rd., Blackshear, GA 31516 USA (SAN 200-9676)
E-mail: info@dotgibson.com
Web site: http://www.dotgibson.com.

Gilmore-Howard, P.O. Box 1268, Arlington, TX 76004-1268 USA (SAN 157-485X).

Giron Bks., (978-0-9741393; 978-0-9915442) 2141 W. 21st St., Chicago, IL 60608-2608 USA Tel 773-847-3000; Fax: 773-847-9197; Toll Free: 800-405-4276
E-mail: juanmanuel@gironbooks.com
Web site: http://www.gironbooks.com.

G-Jo Institute/DeerHaven Hills, (978-0-916878) P.O. Box 1460, Columbus, NC 28722-1460 USA (SAN 111-0004)
E-mail: officesupport@g-jo.com
Web site: http://www.g-jo.com.

G-Jo Institute/Falkyn, Incorporated, *See* **G-Jo Institute/DeerHaven Hills**

GL Services, 4588 Interstate Dr., Cincinnati, OH 45246 USA Tel 805-677-6815.

Global Bk. Distributors, P.O. Box 192629, Dallas, TX 75219 USA.

Global Engineering Documents-Latin America, 3909 NE 163rd St., Suite 110, North Miami Beach, FL 33160 USA (SAN 630-7868) Tel 305-944-1099; Fax: 305-944-1028
E-mail: global.csa@ihs.com.

Global Info Centres, *See* **Global Engineering Documents-Latin America**

Global Publishing Associates, Inc., *See* **Jobson, Oliver H.**

Globe Pequot Pr., The, (978-0-7627; 978-0-87106; 978-0-88742; 978-0-914788; 978-0-933469; 978-0-934802; 978-0-941130; 978-1-56440; 978-1-57034; 978-1-57392; 978-1-58574; 978-1-59228; 978-1-59921; 978-1-4779; 978-1-4930) Orders Addr.: P.O. Box 480, Guilford, CT 06437-0480 USA (SAN 201-9892) Tel 888-249-7586; Toll Free Fax: 800-820-2329 (in Connecticut); Toll Free: 800-243-0495 (24 hours); 800-336-8334; Edit Addr.: 246 Goose Ln., Guilford, CT 06437 USA Tel 203-458-4500; Fax: 203-458-4600; Toll Free Fax: 800-336-8334
E-mail: info@globepequot.com
Web site: http://www.globepequot.com.

Gluesing & Gluesing, (978-0-9631357) 10301 Bren Rd W. Ste. 165, Hopkins, MN 55343-9129 USA (SAN 630-0022) Toll Free: 800-747-0227.

GOBI Library Solutionis from EBSCO, 999 Maple St., Contocook, NH 03229 USA Tel 603-746-3102; Toll Free: 800-258-3774
Web site: http://www.gobi.ebsco.com.

Goldberg, Louis Library Bk. Supplier, 45 Belvidere St., Nazareth, PA 18064 USA (SAN 169-7536) Tel 610-759-9458; Fax: 610-759-8134.

Goldenrod Music, Inc., 1310 Turner Rd., Lansing, MI 48906-4342 USA (SAN 630-5962) Tel 517-484-1777
E-mail: music@goldenrod.com
Web site: http://www.goldenrod.com.

Goldenrod/Horizon Distribution, *See* **Goldenrod Music, Inc.**

Goldman, S. Otzar Hasefarim, Inc., 125 Ditmas Ave., Brooklyn, NY 11218 USA (SAN 169-5770) Tel 718-972-6200; Fax: 718-972-6204; Toll Free: 800-972-6201.

Good Bk. Publishing Co., (978-1-881212) P.O. Box 837, Kihei, HI 96753-0837 USA (SAN 297-9578) Tel 808-874-4876 (phone/fax)
E-mail: dickb@dickb.com
Web site: http://www.dickb.com/index.shtml.

Good News Magazine Distributors, 6332 Saunders St., Rego Park, NY 11374-2031 USA (SAN 113-7271) Toll Free: 800-624-7257.

Gopher News Co., 9000 10th Ave N., Minneapolis, MN 55427-4322 USA (SAN 169-4138).

Gopher News Company, *See* **St. Marie's Gopher News Co.**

Gospel Light Pubns., (978-0-8307) Orders Addr.: 1957 Eastman Ave., Ventura, CA 93003 USA (SAN 299-0873) Tel 805-644-9721; Fax: 805-289-0200; Toll Free: 800-446-7735 (orders only) Do not confuse with companies with similar names in Brooklyn, NY, Delight, AR
E-mail: info@gospellight.com; kyleloffelmacher@gospellight.com
Web site: http://www.gospellight.com.

Gospel Mission, Inc., (978-1-62813) Orders Addr.: P.O. Box 318, Choteau, MT 59422 USA (SAN 170-3196) Tel 406-466-2311; Edit Addr.: 316 First St., NW, Choteau, MT 59422 USA (SAN 243-2455).

Gospel Publishing Hse., (978-0-88243; 978-1-60731) Div. of General Council of the Assemblies of God, 1445 N. Boonville Ave., Springfield, MO 65802-1894 USA (SAN 206-8826) Tel 417-862-2781; Fax: 417-862-5881; Toll Free Fax: 800-328-0294; Toll Free: 800-641-4310 (orders only)
E-mail: webmaster@gph.com
Web site: http://www.gospelpublishing.com.

Goyescas Corp. of Florida, P.O. Box 524207, Miami, FL 33152-4207 USA (SAN 169-1120).

Graham Services, Inc., 180 James Dr., E., Saint Rose, LA 70087-9481 USA (SAN 169-2895) Tel 504-467-5863; Fax: 504-464-6196; Toll Free: 800-457-7323 (in Los Angeles only)
E-mail: gsi@aol.com.

Grand Central Publishing, (978-0-445; 978-0-446; 978-0-7595; 978-1-4555; 978-1-5387; 978-1-5460) Orders Addr.: c/o Little Brown & Co., 3 Center Plaza, Boston, MA 02108-2084 USA Toll Free Fax: 800-286-9471; Toll Free: 800-759-0190; Edit Addr.: 237 Park Ave., New York, NY 10017 USA (SAN 281-8892) Fax: 800-331-1664; Toll Free Fax: 800-759-0190; 1290 Avenue of the Americas, New York, NY 10104
E-mail: renee.supriano@twbg.com; customer.service@hbgusa.com
Web site: http://www.hbgusa.com.

Granite Publishing & Distribution, (978-1-890558; 978-1-930980; 978-1-932280; 978-1-59936) 868 N. 1430 W., Orem, UT 84057 USA (SAN 631-0605) Tel 801-229-9023; Fax: 801-229-1924; Toll Free: 800-574-5779 Do not confuse with companies with same or similar names in Madison, WI, Columbus, NC
E-mail: granite@granitepublishing.biz; gregg@granitepublishing.biz
Web site: http://granitepublishing.biz.

Great American Book Fairs, *See* **Scholastic Bk. Fairs**

Great Lakes Reader's Service, Inc., Orders Addr.: P.O. Box 1078, Detroit, MI 48231 USA (SAN 285-9912) Tel 313-965-4577; Fax: 313-965-2445.

Great Northern Distributors, Inc., 634 South Ave., Rochester, NY 14620-1316 USA (SAN 169-7676) Tel 717-342-8159.

Greathall Productions, Inc., (978-1-882513; 978-1-940916) Orders Addr.: P.O. Box 5061, Charlottesville, VA 22905-5061 USA Tel 434-296-4288; Fax: 434-296-4490; Toll Free: 800-477-6234
E-mail: greathall@greathall.com
Web site: http://www.greathall.com.

Green Dragon Bks., (978-0-89334; 978-1-62386) 2875 S. Ocean Blvd. Ste 200, Palm Beach, FL 33480 USA

(SAN 658-0882) Toll Free Fax: 888-874-8844; Toll Free: 800-874-8844 Do not confuse with Humanics ErgoSystems, Inc., Reseda, CA
E-mail: info@greendragonbooks.com
Web site: http://www.greendragonbooks.com; http://www.humanicslearning.com; http://www.humanicsdealer.com.

Green Gate Bks., 6700 W. Chicago St., Chandler, AZ 85226 USA (SAN 169-6785) Tel 480-961-5176; Fax: 480-961-5256; Toll Free: 800-228-3816
E-mail: ggb@wcoil.com
Web site: http://www.greengatebooks.com.

Greenfield Distribution, Inc., Orders Addr.: c/o IDS, 400 Bedford St., Suite 322, Manchester, NH 03101 USA Tel 413-772-2976; Edit Addr.: 20 Blaine St., Manchester, NH 03102 USA
E-mail: Findikzade1@aol.com; Gdibooks@aol.com
Web site: http://www.gdibooks.com.

Greenleaf Book Group, *(978-0-9665319; 978-1-929774; 978-0-9790842; 978-1-60832; 978-1-61486; 978-1-62634)* Orders Addr.: 4005-B Banister Ln., Austin, TX 78704 USA Tel 512-891-6100; Fax: 512-891-6150; Toll Free: 800-932-5420; Edit Addr.: P.O. Box 91869, Austin, TX 78709 USA
E-mail: tanya@greenleafbookgroup.com
Web site: http://www.greenleafbookgroup.com.

Grey Hse. Publishing, *(978-0-939300; 978-1-891482; 978-1-930956; 978-1-59237; 978-1-61925; 978-1-68217; 978-1-64265)* 4919 Rte. 22 PO Box 56, Amenia, NY 12501 USA Tel 518-789-8700; Fax: 518-789-0556; Toll Free: 800-562-2139; 4919 Rte. 22 PO Box 56, Amenia, NY 12501 Tel 518-789-8700; Fax: 518-789-0556; Toll Free: 800-562-2139; 4919 Rte. 22 PO Box 56, Amenia, NY 12501 Tel 518-789-8700; Fax: 518-789-0556; Toll Free: 800-562-2139
E-mail: books@greyhouse.com
Web site: http://www.greyhouse.com.

Grey Owl Indian Craft Co., Inc., 132-05 Merrick Blvd., P.O. Box 468, Jamaica, NY 11434 USA (SAN 132-9979) Tel 718-341-4000.

Grolier Americana, 1111 Crandon Blvd., Apt. C501, Key Biscayne, FL 33149-2734 USA (SAN 108-1764) Tel 305-551-6711.

Grupo Nelson, *(978-0-8499; 978-0-88113; 978-0-89922; 978-1-60255)* Div. of Thomas Nelson, Inc., 501 Nelson Pl., Nashville, TN 37217 USA (SAN 240-6349) Tel 615-889-9000; Fax: 615-883-9376; Toll Free: 800-251-4000
Web site: http://www.editorialcaribe.com.

Gryphon Hse., Inc., *(978-0-87659; 978-0-917505; 978-1-58904; 978-1-63650)* Orders Addr.: 6848 Leon's Way, Lewisville, NC 27023 USA (SAN 169-3190) Tel 800-638-0928; Fax: 800-638-7576; Toll Free: 800-638-0928
E-mail: info@ghbooks.com
Web site: http://www.gryphonhouse.com.

GSG & Assocs., *(978-0-945001; 978-1-933355)* Orders Addr.: P.O. Box 590, San Pedro, CA 90733 USA (SAN 245-7792) Tel 310-548-3455; Fax: 310-548-5802; Edit Addr.: 831 S. Palos Vereds St., San Pedro, CA 90731 USA
E-mail: gsgbooks@earthlink.net.

Guardian Bk. Co., P.O. Box 202, Ottawa Lake, MI 49267-0202 USA (SAN 163-7355).

Gulf States Book Fairs, *See* **Gulf States Educational Bks.**

Gulf States Educational Bks., Orders Addr.: 368 Laurel Dr., Satsuma, AL 36572 USA (SAN 158-7870) Toll Free: 800-533-1189.

Gumdrop Bks., Div. of Central Programs, Inc., Orders Addr.: P.O. Box 505, Bethany, MO 64424 USA (SAN 631-4988) Tel 660-425-3923; Fax: 660-425-3970; Toll Free: 800-821-7199; Edit Addr.: P.O. Box 505, Bethany, MO 64424-0505 USA (SAN 131-0860)
E-mail: wecare@gumdropbooks.com
Web site: http://www.gumdropbooks.com.

H & H Distribution, 1634 Stilesgate, Grand Rapids, MI 49508 USA Tel 616-248-7990; Fax: 616-248-0016.

Hachette Bk. Group, *(978-0-446; 978-1-60286; 978-1-60941; 978-1-61113; 978-1-61969; 978-1-4789; 978-1-64732)* Div. of Hachette Group Livre, Orders Addr.: 3 Center Plaza, Boston, MA 02108 USA (SAN 852-5463) Tel 617-263-1828; Toll Free Fax: 800-286-9471; Toll Free: 800-759-0190; Edit Addr.: P.O. Box 2146, Johannesburg, 2196 ZAF Tel 2711 783-7565; Fax: 2711 883-6866
Web site: http://www.hachettebookgroup.com.

Hagerstown News Distributors, *See* **Mid-States Distributors**

Haitiana Pubns., Inc., *(978-0-944987)* 3740 81st St. Apt. B3, Jackson Hts, NY 11372-6947 USA (SAN 245-7059)
E-mail: haitiana@idt.net
Web site: http://www.idtnet/haitiana/.com.

Halalco Bks., 108 E. Fairfax St., Falls Church, VA 22046 USA
E-mail: halalco@halalco.com.

Hale, Robert & Co., Inc., 1803 132nd Ave., NE, Suite 4, Bellevue, WA 98005 USA (SAN 200-6995) Tel 425-881-5212; Fax: 425-881-0731; Toll Free: 800-733-5330.

Half Halt Pr., *(978-0-939481)* Orders Addr.: P.O. Box 67, Boonsboro, MD 21713-0067 USA (SAN 663-270X) Tel 301-733-7119; Fax: 301-733-7408
E-mail: mail@halfhaltpress.com
Web site: http://www.halfhaltpress.com.

Ham Radio's Bookstore, *See* **Radio Bookstore**

Hamakor Judaica, Inc., 7777 Merrimac Ave., Niles, IL 60714 USA (SAN 169-1791) Tel 847-966-4040; Fax: 847-966-4033; Toll Free: 800-552-4088.

Hamel, Bernard H. Spanish Bk. Corp., 10977 Santa Monica Blvd., Los Angeles, CA 90025 USA (SAN 111-8862) Tel 310-475-0453; Fax: 310-473-6132
E-mail: spanish@primenet.com
Web site: http://www.BernardHamel.com; http://www.SpanishBooksUSA.com.

Hamilton News Co., Ltd., 41 Hamilton Ln., Glenmont, NY 12077 USA (SAN 169-5312) Tel 518-463-1135; Fax: 518-463-3154.

Hammond, Incorporated, *See* **Hammond World Atlas Corp.**

Hammond Publishing Co., Inc., *(978-1-883882)* P.O. Box 279, G7166 N. Saginaw St., Mount Morris, MI 48458 USA (SAN 185-142X) Tel 810-686-8881; Fax: 810-686-0561; Toll Free: 800-521-3440 (orders only)
E-mail: hammondpub@juno.com.

Hammond World Atlas Corp., *(978-0-7230; 978-0-8437)* Subs. of Langenscheidt Pubs., Inc., 193 Morris Ave., Springfield, NJ 07081-1211 USA (SAN 202-2702)
E-mail: rstrung@americanmap.com
Web site: http://www.Hammondmap.com.

Hamon, Gerard Incorporated, *See* **Lafayette Bks.**

Hancock Hse. Pubs., *(978-0-88839; 978-0-919654; 978-1-55205)* No. 104- 4550 Birch Bay-Lynden Rd, Blaine, WA 98230-9436 USA (SAN 665-7079) Tel 604-538-1114; Fax: 604-538-2262; Toll Free Fax: 800-983-2262; Toll Free: 800-938-1114; 19313 Zero Ave., Surrey, BC V3S 9R9 (SAN 115-3730)
E-mail: sales@hancockhouse.com
Web site: http://www.hancockhouse.com.

hand2mind, *(978-0-7406; 978-0-914040; 978-0-923832; 978-0-938587; 978-1-57162; 978-1-57452; 978-1-63406)* 500 Greenview Ct., Vernon Hills, IL 60061 USA (SAN 285-7553) Tel 847-816-5050; Fax: 847-816-5066; Toll Free: 800-445-5985
E-mail: info@hand2mind.com
Web site: http://www.hand2mind.com.

Handleman, 500 Kirts Blvd., Troy, MI 48084-5225 USA (SAN 106-4886).

Handler News Agency, P.O. Box 27007, Omaha, NE 68127-0007 USA (SAN 169-4405).

Hansen Hse., 1842 West Ave., Miami Beach, FL 33139 USA (SAN 200-7908) Tel 305-532-5461; Toll Free: 800-327-8202.

Harcourt Achieve, *See* **Houghton Mifflin Harcourt Supplemental Pubs.**

Harcourt Brace & Company, *See* **Harcourt Trade Pubs.**

Harcourt Trade Pubs., *(978-0-15)* Div. of Houghton Mifflin Harcourt Trade & Reference Pubs., Orders Addr.: 6277 Sea Harbor Dr., Orlando, FL 32887 USA (SAN 200-285X) Tel 619-699-6707; Toll Free Fax: 800-235-0256; Toll Free: 800-543-1918 (trade orders, inquiries, claims); Edit Addr.: 15 E. 26th St., New York, NY 10010 USA Tel 212-592-1000; Fax: 212-592-1011; 525 B St., Suite 1900, San Diego, CA 92101-4495 (SAN 200-2736) Tel 619-231-6616
E-mail: andrewporter@harcourt.com
Web site: http://www.HarcourtBooks.com.

Harness, Miller, 750 Route 73 S. Ste. 110, Marlton, NJ 08053-4142 USA (SAN 169-5789) Toll Free: 800-526-6310.

HarperCollins Christian Publishing, Div. of HarperCollins Publishers, Orders Addr.: P.O. Box 141000, Nashville, TN 37214 USA Toll Free: 800-251-4000; Edit Addr.: 3900 Sparks Dr. SE, Grand Rapids, MI 49546 USA Toll Free: 800-226-1122
Web site: http://www.harpercollinschristian.com/.

HarperCollins Pubs., *(978-0-00; 978-0-06; 978-0-380; 978-0-688; 978-0-690; 978-0-694; 978-0-87795; 978-1-55710)* Div. of News Corp., Orders Addr.: 1000 Keystone Industrial Pk., Scranton, PA 18512-4621 USA (SAN 215-3742) Tel 570-941-1500; Toll Free Fax: 800-822-4090; Toll Free: 800-242-7737 (orders only); Edit Addr.: 10 E. 53rd St., New York, NY 10022-5299 USA (SAN 200-2086) Tel 212-207-7000
Web site: http://www.harpercollins.com; http://www.harpercollinschildrens.com.

Harrisburg News Co., 980 Briarsdale Rd., Harrisburg, PA 17109 USA (SAN 169-7420) Tel 717-561-8377; Fax: 717-561-1466
E-mail: jmurphy@harrisburgnewsco.com
Web site: http://www.harrisburgnewsco.com.

Harrison House, Incorporated, *See* **Harrison House Pubs.**

Harrison House Pubs., *(978-0-89274; 978-1-57794; 978-1-60683; 978-1-68031)* Orders Addr.: P.O. Box 35035, Tulsa, OK 74153 USA (SAN 208-676X) Tel 918-523-5700; Toll Free Fax: 800-830-5688; Toll Free: 800-888-4126; Edit Addr.: 7498 E. 46th Pl., Tulsa, OK 74145 USA Tel 918-523-5700; Toll Free Fax: 800-830-5688; Toll Free: 800-888-4126
E-mail: smckee@norimediagroup.com; jinori@norimediagroup.com; lisad@harrisonhouse.com; juliew@harrisonhouse.com
Web site: http://www.harrisonhouse.com.

Harry-Young Pubn. Services Agency, Inc., 6261 Manchester Blvd., Buena Park, CA 90621-2259 USA (SAN 110-8832).

Harvard Assocs., Inc., *(978-0-924346)* 10 Holworthy St., Cambridge, MA 02138 USA (SAN 170-2939) Tel 617-492-0660; Fax: 617-492-4610; Toll Free: 800-774-5646
E-mail: info@harvassoc.com
Web site: http://www.harvassoc.com.

Harvard Business Review Pr., *(978-0-87584; 978-1-57851; 978-1-59139; 978-1-4221; 978-1-62527; 978-1-63369; 978-1-64782)* 60 Harvard Way, Boston, MA 02163 USA (SAN 202-277X) Tel 617-783-7400; 617 495 6181; Fax: 617-783-7492; Toll Free: 888-500-1016 6-19-01 faxed 2nd prefix app, charge, KC
E-mail: corpcustserv@hbsp.harvard.edu
Web site: http://www.hbsp.harvard.edu; http://www.harvardbusinessonline.com.

Harvard Business School Press, *See* **Harvard Business Review Pr.**

Harvard Univ. Art Museums Shop, 32 Quincy St., Cambridge, MA 02138 USA (SAN 111-3372) Tel 617-495-8286; Fax: 617-495-9985
E-mail: appleyar@fas.harvard.edu
Web site: http://www.artmuseums.harvard.edu.

Harvard Univ. Pr., *(978-0-674; 978-0-916724; 978-0-935617)* Orders Addr.: c/o Triliteral LLC, 100 Maple Ridge Dr., Cumberland, RI 02864 USA Tel 401-531-2800; Fax: 401-531-2801; Toll Free Fax: 800-406-9145; Toll Free: 800-405-1619; 800-448-2242; Edit Addr.: 79 Garden St., Cambridge, MA 02138 USA (SAN 200-2043) Tel 617-495-2600; Fax: 617-495-5898
E-mail: contact_hup@harvard.edu
Web site: http://www.hup.harvard.edu.

Harvest Distributors, *See* **ARVEST**

Hastings Bks., *(978-0-940846)* 116 N. Wayne Ave., Wayne, PA 19087 USA (SAN 205-048X).

Haven Distributors, 5456 N. Damen Ave., Chicago, IL 60625 USA.

Hawaiian Magazine Distributor, 3375 Koapaka St., No. D180, Honolulu, HI 96819-1865 USA (SAN 169-1619).

Hay Hse., Inc., *(978-0-937611; 978-0-945923; 978-1-56170; 978-1-891751; 978-1-58825; 978-1-4019)* Orders Addr.: P.O. Box 5100, Carlsbad, CA 92018-5100 USA (SAN 630-477X) Tel 760-431-7695 ext 112; Fax: 760-431-6948; Toll Free Fax: 800-650-5115 (orders only); Toll Free: 800-654-5126 (orders only); 2776 Loker Ave. W, Carlsbad, CA 92010 (SAN 257-3024) Tel 800-654-5126; Fax: 800-650-5115; 2776 Loker Ave. W., Carlsbad, CA 92010
E-mail: kjohnson@hayhouse.com; pcrowe@hayhouse.com
Web site: http://www.hayhouse.com.

Hazelden, *(978-0-89486; 978-0-89638; 978-0-935908; 978-0-942421; 978-1-56246; 978-1-56838; 978-1-59285; 978-1-61649; 978-1-63634)* 15251 Pleasant Valley Rd., P.o. Box 176, Center City, MN 55012-0176 USA (SAN 209-4010) Fax: 651-213-4044; Toll Free: 800-328-9000; P.O. Box 176, RW4, Center City, MN 55012 Tel 651-213-4000; Toll Free: 800-328-9000
E-mail: bosterbauer@hazelden.org
Web site: http://www.hazelden.org.

Hazelden Publishing & Educational Services, *See* **Hazelden**

Health and Growth Assocs., *(978-0-9630266)* Orders Addr.: 28195 Fairview Ave., Hemet, CA 92544 USA Tel 951-927-1768; Fax: 951-927-1548
E-mail: flloomis@earthlink.net.

Health Communications, Inc., *(978-0-932194; 978-1-55874; 978-0-7573; 978-0-9910732)* Orders Addr.: 3201 SW 15th St., Deerfield Beach, FL 33442-8190 USA (SAN 212-100X) Tel 954-360-0909; Fax: 954-360-0034; Toll Free: 800-441-5569 Do not confuse with Health Communications, Inc., Edison, NJ
E-mail: terip@hcibooks.com; lorig@hcibooks.com
Web site: http://www.hcibooks.com.

Hearst Distribution Group, Incorporated, Book Division, *See* **Comag Marketing Group**

Heartland Bk. Co., 10195 N. Lake Ave., Olathe, KS 66061 USA (SAN 631-2497) Tel 913-829-1784.

Heffernan Audio Visual, Orders Addr.: P.O. Box 5906, San Antonio, TX 78201-0906 USA Tel 210-732-4333; Fax: 210-732-5906; Edit Addr.: 435 Isom Rd. Ste. 210, San Antonio, TX 78216-5144 USA (SAN 166-8722)
E-mail: sales@heffernanav.com
Web site: http://www.heffernanav.com.

Heffernan School Supply, *See* **Heffernan Audio Visual**

Heinecken & Assoc., Ltd., 1733 N. Mohawk, Chicago, IL 60614 USA Toll Free Fax: 800-947-5694; Toll Free: 800-449-0138.

.Heinemann-Raintree, *See* **Heinemann-Raintree**

Heinemann-Raintree, *(978-0-431; 978-1-57572; 978-1-58810; 978-1-4034; 978-1-4109; 978-1-4329; 978-1-4846)* Div. of Capstone, Orders Addr.: 1710 Roe Crest Dr., North Mankato, MN 56003 USA; Halley Court Freepost PO Box 1125, Oxford, OX2 8YY.

Heirloom Bible Pubs., *(978-0-9817263)* Orders Addr.: P.O. Box 118, Wichita, KS 67201-0118 USA (SAN 630-2793) Fax: 316-267-1850; Toll Free: 800-676-2448; Edit Addr.: 9020 E. 35th St. N., Wichita, KS 67226-2017 USA.

Helix, 310 S. Racine St., Chicago, IL 60607 USA (SAN 111-915X) Tel 312-421-6000; Fax: 312-421-1586.

Hemed Books, Incorporated, *See* **Lambda Pubs., Inc.**

Hendrick-Long Publishing Co., *(978-0-937460; 978-1-885777)* Orders Addr.: 10635 Tower Oaks, Suite D, Houston, TX 77070 USA (SAN 281-7756) Toll Free: 800-544-3770; Edit Addr.: 10635 Tower Oaks Blvd., Houston, TX 77070-5927 USA (SAN 281-7748)
E-mail: hendrick-long@worldnet.att.net
Web site: http://www.hendricklongpublishing.com.

Herald Pr., *(978-0-8361; 978-1-5138)* Div. of MennoMedia, Inc., Orders Addr.: 1251 Virginia Ave., Harrisonburg, VA 22802 USA (SAN 202-2915) Fax: 1-316-283-0454; Toll Free: 1-800-245-7894; 800-631-6535 (Canada only) Do not confuse with Herald Pr., Charlotte, NC
E-mail: info@mennomedia.org
Web site: http://www.mennomedia.org.

Herald Publishing Hse., *(978-0-8309)* Orders Addr.: P.O. Box 390, Independence, MO 64051-0390 USA Tel 816-521-3015; Fax: 816-521-3066 (customer services); Toll Free: 800-767-8181; Edit Addr.: 1001W. Walnut St., Independence, MO 64051-0390 USA (SAN 111-7556) Tel 816-257-0200
E-mail: sales@HeraldHouse.org
Web site: http://www.heraldhouse.org.

Heritage Bookstore, Orders Addr.: P.O. Box 6007, Springfield, MO 65801-6007 USA (SAN 111-7696).

Hertzberg-New Method Inc., 617 E. Vandalia Rd., Ebooks, Jacksonville, IL 62650 USA (SAN 780-0479) Tel 217-243-5451.

Hervey's Booklink & Cookbook Warehouse, P.O. Box 831870, Richardson, TX 75083 USA (SAN 630-9747).

Hesteria Records & Publishing Co., 124 Hagar Ct., Santa Cruz, CA 95064 USA Tel 831-459-2575; Fax: 831-457-2917
E-mail: alissa@aainnovators.com
Web site: http://www.aainnovators.com.

Hi Jolly Library Service, 150 N. Gay St., Susanville, CA 96130-3902 USA (SAN 133-5944).

Hibel, Edna Studio, P.O. Box 9967, Riviera Beach, FL 33419 USA (SAN 111-1574) Tel 561-848-9640; Toll Free: 800-275-3426.

Hicks News Agency, Incorporated, *See* **NEWSouth Distributors**

High Peak Bks., *(978-1-884709)* Orders Addr.: P.O. Box 703, Wilson, WY 83014 USA (SAN 299-4232); Edit Addr.: 355 N. Bar Y Rd., Jackson, WY 83011 USA Tel 307-739-0147 Do not confuse with High Peak Pr. in Schenectady, NY.

Hill City News Agency, Inc., 3228 Odd Fellow Rd., Lynchburg, VA 24501 USA (SAN 169-8656) Tel 804-845-4231; Fax: 804-845-0864.

Hillsboro News, Orders Addr.: P.O. Box 25738, Tampa, FL 33622-5738 USA Tel 813-622-8087; Edit Addr.: 7002 Parke E. Blvd., Tampa, FL 33610 USA.

Himber Bks., Div. of F. C. Himber & Son's, Inc., 1380 W. Second Ave., Eugene, OR 97402 USA Tel 541-686-8003; Toll Free: 800-888-5904.

Himber, F. C., *See* **Himber Bks.**

Hinrichs, E. Louis, P.O. Box 1090, Lompoc, CA 93438-1090 USA (SAN 133-1493) Tel 805-736-7512
E-mail: booklompoc@aol.com.

Hinsdale County Historical Society, P.O. Box 353 130 N. Silver St., Lake City, CO 81235 USA Tel 970-944-2050.

Historic Aviation Bks., 121 Fifth Ave., Suite 300, New Brighton, MN 55112 USA (SAN 129-5284) Tel 651-635-0100; Fax: 651-635-0700.

Historic Cherry Hill, *(978-0-943366)* 523 1/2 S. Pearl St., Albany, NY 12202 USA (SAN 110-8859) Tel 518-434-4791; Fax: 518-434-4806.

Hobbies Hawaii Distributors, 4420 Lawehana St., No. 3, Honolulu, HI 96818 USA (SAN 630-8619) Tel 808-423-0265; Fax: 808-423-1635.

Holiday Enterprises, Inc., 3328 US Hwy. 123, Rochester Bldg., Greenville, SC 29611 USA (SAN 169-779X) Tel 864-220-3161; Fax: 864-295-9757.

Holt, Henry & Co., *(978-0-03; 978-0-8050)* Div. of Holtzbrinck Publishers, Orders Addr.: 16365 James Madison Hwy., Gordonsville, VA 22942-8501 USA Toll Free Fax: 800-672-2054; Toll Free: 888-330-8477; Edit Addr.: 115 W. 18th St., 5th Flr., New York, NY 10011 USA (SAN 200-6472) Tel 212-886-9200; Fax: 540-672-7540 (customer service)
E-mail: info@hholt.com
Web site: http://www.henryholt.com.

Holtzbrinck Publishers, *See* **Macmillan**

Holyoke News Co., Inc., 720 Main St., P.O. Box 990, Holyoke, MA 01041 USA (SAN 169-3468) Tel 413-534-4537; Fax: 413-538-7161; Toll Free: 800-628-8372
E-mail: sales@holyoke-news.com.

Homestead Book Co., *(978-0-930180)* Orders Addr.: P.O. Box 31608, Seattle, WA 98103 USA (SAN 662-037X); Edit Addr.: 6101 22nd Ave., NW, Seattle, WA 98107 USA (SAN 169-8796) Tel 206-782-4532; Fax: 206-784-9328; Toll Free: 800-426-6777 (orders only)
E-mail: info@homesteadbook.com
Web site: http://www.homesteadbook.com.

Homestead Book, Incorporated, *See* **Homestead Book Co.**

Hood, Alan C. & Co., Inc., *(978-0-911469)* P.O. Box 775, Chambersburg, PA 17201 USA (SAN 270-8221) Tel 717-267-0867; Fax: 717-267-0572; Toll Free Fax: 888-844-9433; 4501 Forbes Blvd., Lanham, MD 20706
E-mail: hoodbooks@pa.net
Web site: http://www.hoodbooks.com.

Hoover Institution Pr., *(978-0-8179)* Stanford Univ., Stanford, CA 94305-6010 USA (SAN 202-3024) Tel 650-723-3373; Fax: 650-723-8626; Toll Free: 800-935-2882
E-mail: scott.harrison@stanford.edu
Web site: http://www.hooverpress.org.

Hopkins Fulfillment Services, P.O. Box 50370, Baltimore, MD 21211-4370 USA Fax: 410-516-6998; Toll Free: 800-537-5487.

Hotho & Co., P.O. Box 9738, Fort Worth, TX 76147-2738 USA (SAN 169-8192).

Houghton Mifflin Company, *See* **Houghton Mifflin Harcourt Publishing Co.**

Houghton Mifflin Company Trade & Reference Division, *See* **Houghton Mifflin Harcourt Trade & Reference Pubs.**

Houghton Mifflin Harcourt Publishing Co., *(978-0-395; 978-0-87466; 978-0-9631591; 978-1-57630; 978-1-881527; 978-0-618; 978-0-544; 978-0-547; 978-1-328; 978-0-358)* Orders Addr.: 9205 Southpark Ctr. Loop, Orlando, FL 32819 USA Toll Free: 800-225-3362; Edit Addr.: 222 Berkeley St., Boston, MA 02116 USA (SAN 215-3793) Tel 617-351-5000; 125 High St., Boston, MA 02110
Web site: http://www.hmco.com.

Houghton Mifflin Harcourt Supplemental Pubs., *(978-1-60032; 978-1-60277)* 10801 N. Mopac Expressway, Bldg. 3, Austin, TX 78759 USA
Web site: www.harcourtachieve.com.

Houghton Mifflin Harcourt Trade & Reference Pubs., *(978-0-395; 978-0-89919; 978-0-618)* Orders Addr.: 9205 Southpark Ctr. Loop, Orlando, FL 32819 USA Tel 978-661-1300; Toll Free: 800-225-3362; Edit Addr.: 222

Wholesaler & Distributor Name Index

Berkeley St., Boston, MA 02116 USA (SAN 200-2388) Tel 617-351-5000; Fax: 617-227-5409; 215 Park Ave S., 12th Flr., New York, NY 10003-1621
E-mail: trade_sub_rights@hmco.com
Web site: http://www.hmco.com/; http://www.houghtonmifflinbooks.com.

Houston Paperback Distributor, 4114 Gairloch Ln., Houston, TX 77025-2912 USA (SAN 169-8273).

Hovel Audio, Incorporated, *See* **christianaudio**

How-2 Bks., P.O. Box 5793, Denver, CO 80217 USA (SAN 631-1369) Tel 303-778-8383; Toll Free: 800-279-7323.

HPK Educational Resource Ctr., *(978-0-89895)* Div. of H. P. Koppelmann, Inc., 140 Van Block Ave., Hartford, CT 06141 USA (SAN 169-071X) Tel 860-549-6210; Toll Free: 800-243-7724.

Hubbard, P.O. Box 100, Defiance, OH 43512 USA (SAN 169-6726) Tel 419-784-4455; Fax: 419-782-1662; Toll Free: 800-582-0657
E-mail: hubbard@bright.net.

Hudson County News Co., 1305 Paterson Plank Rd., North Bergen, NJ 07047 USA (SAN 169-4782) Tel 201-867-3600.

Hudson Hills Pr. LLC, *(978-0-933920; 978-0-9646042; 978-1-55595)* Orders Addr.: P.O. Box 205, Manchester, VT 05254 USA; Edit Addr.: 74-2 Union St., Manchester, VT 05254 USA (SAN 213-0815) Tel 802-362-6450; Fax: 802-362-6459
E-mail: artbooks@hudsonhills.com
Web site: http://www.hudsonhills.com/.

Hudson Hills Press, Incorporated, *See* **Hudson Hills Pr. LLC**

Hudson Valley News Distributors, P.O. Box 1236, Newburgh, NY 12550 USA (SAN 169-6084) Tel 914-562-3399; Fax: 914-562-6010.

Humanics Publishing Group, *See* **Green Dragon Bks.**

Hyperion Pr., *(978-0-7868; 978-1-56282; 978-1-4013)* Div. of Disney Bk. Publishing, Inc., A Walt Disney Co., Orders Addr.: c/o HarperCollins Publishers, 1000 Keystone Industrial Park, Scranton, PA 18512-4621 USA Toll Free: 800-242-7737; Edit Addr.: 114 Fifth Ave., New York, NY 110011 USA Tel 917-661-2000
Web site: http://www.hyperionbooks.com.

i. b. d., Ltd., *(978-0-88431)* 24 Hudson St., Kinderhook, NY 12106 USA (SAN 630-7779) Tel 518-758-1755; Fax: 518-758-6702
E-mail: lankhof@ibdltd.com
Web site: http://www.ibdltd.com.

I S H K, *(978-0-86304; 978-0-900860; 978-1-883536; 978-1-933779; 978-1-942698; 978-1-944493; 978-1-946270; 978-1-948013; 978-1-949358; 978-1-953292)* Div. of Institute for the Study of Human Knowledge, Orders Addr.: P.O. Box 400541, Cambridge, MA 02140 USA (SAN 226-4536) Tel 617-497-4124; Fax: 617-500-0268; Toll Free Fax: 800-223-4200; Toll Free: 800-222-4745; Edit Addr.: Ishk-hoopoe 171 Main St. #140, Los Altos, CA 94022 USA Tel 650-948-9428
E-mail: ishkbooks@aol.com; ishkadm@aol.com
Web site: http://www.ishk.net; http://www.hoopoebooks.com.

Iaconi, Mariuccia Bk. Imports, *(978-0-9628720)* P.O. Box 77023, San Francisco, CA 94107-0023 USA (SAN 161-1364) Toll Free: 800-955-9577
E-mail: mibibook@ixnetcom.com
Web site: http://www.mibibook.com.

ICG Muse, Inc., 420 W. 42nd St. Apt. 35B, New York, NY 10036-6863 USA (SAN 631-7200).

Icon Distribution, 3325 Donnell Dr., Forestville, MD 20747 USA.

ID International Bk. Service, 126 Old Ridgefield Rd., Wilton, CT 06897-3017 USA (SAN 630-8074) Tel 203-834-2272; Fax: 203-762-9725
E-mail: orders@idintl.com.

Idaho News Agency, 2710 Julia St., Coeur D'Alene, ID 83814 USA (SAN 169-1651) Tel 208-664-3444.

Ideal Foreign Bks., Inc., 132-10 Hillside Ave., Richmond Hill, NY 11418 USA (SAN 169-6173) Tel 718-297-7477; Fax: 718-297-7645; Toll Free: 800-284-2490 (orders only).

IFSTA, *(978-0-87939; 978-1-56916)* Orders Addr.: c/o Oklahoma State Univ., Fire Protection Pubns., 930 N. Willis, Stillwater, OK 74078-8045 USA Tel 405-744-5723; Fax: 405-744-8204; Toll Free: 800-654-4055 (orders only)
Web site: http://www.ifsta.org/.

Ignatius Pr., *(978-0-89870; 978-1-58617; 978-1-62164; 978-1-68149; 978-1-64229)* Orders Addr.: P.O. Box 1339, Fort Collins, CO 80522-1339 USA (SAN 855-3556) Tel 970-221-3920; Fax: 970-221-3964; Toll Free Fax: 800-278-3566; Toll Free: 877-320-9276 (bookstore orders); 800-651-1531 (credit card orders, no minimum, individual orders); 1915 Astor Rd. Sycamore, Sycamore, IL 60178 (SAN 991-4595); 1915 Astor Rd., Sycamore, IL 60178 (SAN 991-4609); Edit Addr.: 1348 10th Ave., San Francisco, CA 94122 USA (SAN 214-3887) Toll Free: 800-651-1531
E-mail: info@ignatius.com
Web site: http://www.ignatius.com.

Igram Pr., *(978-0-911119; 978-1-930279)* 311 Parsons Dr., Hiawatha, IA 52233 USA (SAN 263-1709) Tel 319-393-3600; Fax: 319-393-3934; Toll Free: 800-393-2399
E-mail: clabarr@cedargraphicsinc.com.

Illinois News Service, *See* **News Group - Illinois, The**

Ilmhouse Inc., P.O. Box 74, Haverford, PA 19041-0074 USA
E-mail: admin@ilmhouse.com
Web site: http://www.ilmhouse.com.

Image Processing Software, Inc., *(978-0-924507)* 6409 Appalachian Way, Madison, WI 53705 USA (SAN 265-5977) Tel 608-233-5033; 4414 Regent St., Madison, WI 53705 (SAN 249-3020).

Impact Photographics, *(978-0-918327; 978-1-56540; 978-1-60068)* 4961 Windplay Dr., Eldorado Hills, CA 95630 USA (SAN 657-3126) Tel 916-939-9333; Fax: 916-939-9334; Toll Free: 800-950-0110
E-mail: juliem@impactphotographics.com
Web site: http://www.impactphotographics.com.

Imperial News Co., Inc., 5131 Post Rd., Dublin, OH 43017-1160 USA (SAN 169-5509) Fax: 516-752-8515.

Imported Bks., Orders Addr.: St., Dallas, TX 75208 USA (SAN 169-8095) Tel 214-941-6497.

In Between Bks., *(978-0-935430; 978-0-9802007)* P.O. Box 790, Sausalito, CA 94966 USA (SAN 213-6236) Tel 415-383-8447; Fax: 415-381-1938; 415-381-3513
E-mail: inbetweenbooks@atthebutterflytree.com; karla@inbetweenbooks.com; juno@inbetweenbooks.com
Web site: http://www.atthebutterflytree.com.

Incor Periodicals, 32150 Hwy. 34, Tangent, OR 97389-9704 USA (SAN 169-7072) Tel 541-926-8889; Fax: 541-926-9553.

Independent Magazine Co., 2970 N. Ontario St., Burbank, CA 91504-2016 USA (SAN 159-8783).

Independent Pub., *(978-1-4243; 978-1-59975; 978-1-60402; 978-1-60461; 978-1-60530; 978-1-60585; 978-1-60643; 978-1-60702; 978-1-60725; 978-1-60743; 978-1-61539; 978-1-61584; 978-1-61623; 978-1-61658; 978-1-4507; 978-1-4675; 978-1-4951; 978-0-9927847; 978-1-5323;-1-5323-0640-2; 978-1-7923) Div. of Bar Code Graphics, 875 N. Michigan Ave., Suite 2650, Chicago, IL 60615 USA Fax: 312-595-0725; Toll Free: 800-662-0701; 65 E. Wacker Pl., 18th Flr., Chicago, IL 60601 Tel 312-595-0600; Toll Free: 800-662-0703 Do not confuse with Independent Publishers in Bountiful, UT*
E-mail: pubserv@barcode-us.com
Web site: http://www.publisherservices-us.com; http://www.isbn-us.com.

Independent Pubs. Group, *(978-1-4956)* Subs. of Chicago Review Pr., 814 N. Franklin, Chicago, IL 60610 USA (SAN 201-2936) Tel 312-337-0747; Fax: 312-337-5985; Toll Free: 800-888-4741
E-mail: frontdesk@ipgbook.com
Web site: http://www.ipgbook.com; http://www.trafalgarsquarepublishing.com.

Independently published, *See* **Independently Published**

Indiana Periodicals, Inc., 2120 S. Meridian St., Indianapolis, IN 46225 USA (SAN 169-2380) Tel 317-786-1488; Fax: 317-782-4999.

Indiana Univ. Pr., *(978-0-253; 978-0-86196)* 601 N. Morton St., Bloomington, IN 47404-3797 USA (SAN 202-5647) Fax: 812-855-7931; Toll Free: 800-842-6796
E-mail: iuporder@indiana.edu
Web site: http://www.iupress.indiana.edu.

Indig, Stanley M. Specialty Pubn., *(978-0-945815; 978-1-57767)* 2173 E. 38th St., Brooklyn, NY 11234 USA (SAN 248-0719) Tel 718-692-0648; Fax: 718-677-9542
E-mail: indigpublishing@yahoo.com; indigpublishing@aol.com
Web site: http://www.indigpublishing.com.

Infobase Learning, *(978-0-8160)* 132 West 31st St., 17th Flr., New York, NY 10001 USA.

Infobase Publishing Company, *See* **Infobase Learning**

Ingenix, Incorporated, *See* **OptumInsight, Inc.**

Ingham Publishing, Inc., *(978-0-9611804; 978-1-891130)* Orders Addr.: P.O. Box 12642, Saint Petersburg, FL 33733-2642 USA Tel 813-343-4811; Fax: 813-381-2807; Edit Addr.: 5650 First Ave., N., Saint Petersburg, FL 33710 USA (SAN 112-8930)
E-mail: ftreflex@concentric.net.

Ingram Academic, Div. of Ingram Content Group, Orders Addr.: c/o Perseus Books Group, 210 American Dr., Jackson, TN 38301 USA Toll Free Fax: 800-351-5073; Toll Free: 800-343-4499; c/o Publishers Group Canada, 76 Stafford St., Unit 300, Toronto, ON M6J 2S1 Tel 416-934-9900; Fax: 416-934-1410; Toll Free Fax: 800-565-3770; Toll Free: 800-663-5714
E-mail: academicorders@perseusbooks.com; client.info@perseusbooks.com
Web site: http://www.perseusacademic.com.

Ingram Bk. Co., *(978-1-61522; 978-1-60894)* Subs. of Ingram Industries, Inc., Orders Addr.: 1 Ingram Blvd., P.O. Box 3006, La Vergne, TN 37086-1986 USA (SAN 169-7978) Tel 615-213-5000; Fax: 615-213-3976 (Electronic Orders); Toll Free Fax: 800-285-3296 (fax inquiry US & Canada); 800-876-0186 (orders); 877-663-5367 (Canadian orders); Toll Free: 800-937-8000 (orders only); 800-937-8200 (customer service US & Canada); 800-289-0687 (Canadian orders only customer service); 800-234-6737 (electronic orders US & Canada)) Do not confuse with Ingram Pr., Sacramento, CA
E-mail: flashback@ingrambook.com; customerservice@ingrambook.com; ics-sales@ingrambook.com
Web site: http://www.ingrambook.com.

Ingram Content Group, Orders Addr.: 1246 Heil Quaker Blvd., LaVergne, TN 37086 USA (SAN 179-6976) Tel 615-213-4595; Fax: 615-213-4426; 860 Nestle Way - LSI Lightning Source, Breingsville, PA 18031 (SAN 920-4288); 4260 Port Union Rd. No. 100 - LSI Lightning Source, Fairfield, OH 45011 (SAN 920-4296); 150 Fieldcrest Ave - IBC Ingram Book - IBC, Edison, NJ 08837 (SAN 920-430X) Tel 615-413-4476; 4260 Port Union Rd. No. 100 - IBC Ingram Book - IBC, Fairfield, OH 45011 (SAN 920-4318); 150 Fieldcrest Ave - IPS Ingram Publisher Services, Edison, NJ 08837 (SAN 920-4431); 4260 Port Union Rd. No 100 - IPS Ingram Publisher Services, Fairfield, OH 45011 (SAN 920-444X); 860 Nestle Way - IBC, Breinigsville, PA 18031 (SAN 920-6264); 860 Nestle Way-IPS, Breinigsville, PA 18031 (SAN 920-6272); 3145 S. Northpointe Dr. - LSI N. Pointe Business Pk., Fresno, CA 93725 (SAN 920-6280); 3145 S Northpointe Dr - IPS, Fresno, CA 93725 (SAN 920-7937); 3145 S Northpointe Dr - IBC, Fresno, CA 93725 (SAN 920-7945); 210 American Dr. - IPS, Jackson, TN 3383017716 (SAN 991-1243) Tel 731-265-5943; 193 Edwards Dr. - LSI, Jackson , TN 3383017716 (SAN 991-1812)
E-mail: terri.jones@lightningsource.com.

Ingram Content Group Inc., Sub. of Ingram Industries Inc., 1 Ingram Blvd., La Vergne, TN 37086 USA Tel 615-793-5000; Toll Free: 800-937-8000 (option 3)
E-mail: inquiry@ingramcontent.com; customerservice@ingramcontent.com
Web site: http://www.ingramcontent.com.

Ingram Entertainment, Inc., Two Ingram Blvd. (Corp. Headquarters), La Vergne, TN 37089-7006 USA (SAN 630-6780) Tel 615-287-4000; Fax: 615-287-4995; Toll Free: 800-759-5000; 12000 Ridgemont Dr., Urbandale, IA 50323-2317 (SAN 630-6950); 26391 Curtiss Wright Pkwy. Ste. 106, Cleveland, OH 44143-4401 (SAN 630-6896) Toll Free: 800-621-1333; 15002 Sommermeyer, Houston, TX 77041-5333 (SAN 630-7000) Tel 713-937-3600; Fax: 713-466-4316; 382 E. Lies Rd., Carol Stream, IL 60188-9418 (SAN 630-690X) Toll Free: 800-621-1333; 7911 NE 33rd Dr., Suite 270, Portland, OR 97211-1920 (SAN 630-7116) Tel 503-281-2673; Fax: 503-284-6046; 23 Monte Vista Ave., Larkspur, CA 94939-2120 (SAN 630-6993) Toll Free: 800-621-1333; 2611 S. Roosevelt, Suite 102, Tempe, AZ 85282-2017 (SAN 630-7094) Tel 602-966-6691; Fax: 602-894-0329; 4703 Fulton Industrial Blvd., Atlanta, GA 30336-2017 (SAN 630-6845) Tel 404-691-6280; Fax: 404-696-3944; 400 Airport Executive Pk., Spring Valley, NY 10977-7404 (SAN 630-7078) Tel 914-425-3191; Fax: 914-425-7521; 7949 Woodley Blvd., Van Nuys, CA 91406 (SAN 630-7183) Tel 818-375-5027; Fax: 818-375-5001; 1293 Heil Quaker Blvd., Suite B, P.O. Box 7006, La Vergne, TN 37086-7006 (SAN 630-7051) Fax: 615-793-6196; Toll Free: 800-688-3110; 3675 Crestwood Pkwy NW Ste. 105, Duluth, GA 30096-5045 (SAN 630-6853) Toll Free: 800-876-0832; 3114 S. 24th St., Kansas City, KS 66106-4709 (SAN 630-7027) Tel 913-362-0391; Fax: 913-362-0605; Toll Free: 800-621-1333; 6635 NE 59th Pl., Portland, OR 97218-2709 (SAN 630-7124) Tel 503-284-3313; Fax: 503-284-3876; Toll Free: 800-876-0834; 7319 Innovation Blvd., Fort Wayne, IN 46818-1371 (SAN 630-6985) Fax: 219-489-8850; Toll Free: 800-759-5588; 8779 Greenwood Pl., Savage, MD 20763 (SAN 630-7019) Tel 301-490-1166; Fax: 301-490-0031; Toll Free: 800-621-1333; 1521 W. Copans Rd., Suite 105, Pompano Beach, FL 33064 (SAN 630-7108) Tel 954-971-5412; Fax: 954-971-3113; Toll Free: 800-888-3876; 20435 E. Business Pkwy., Walnut, CA 91789-2999 (SAN 630-7191) Tel 714-594-6569; Fax: 714-595-0735; Toll Free: 800-759-4422; 2 Ingram Blvd., La Vergne, TN 37086-3638 (SAN 630-6837) Toll Free: 800-621-1333; 1349 Charwood Rd., Hanover, MD 21076-3114 (SAN 630-6861) Tel 410-850-9191; Fax: 410-850-9229; 110 Shawmut Rd., Canton, MA 02021-1412 (SAN 630-687X) Tel 617-575-9585; Fax: 617-575-9586; 100 Dobbs Ln., Suite 206, Cherry Hill, NJ 08034-1435 (SAN 630-6888) Tel 609-428-8668; Fax: 609-428-8536; Toll Free: 800-288-7565; 11235 Knott Ave., Suite C, Cypress, CA 90630-5401 (SAN 630-6918) Tel 714-373-8855; Fax: 714-373-8858; Toll Free: 800-759-4422; 1430 Bradley Ln., No. 102, Carrollton, TX 75007-4855 (SAN 630-6926) Tel 214-245-6088; Fax: 214-323-3890; Toll Free: 800-621-1333; 2259 Merritt Dr., Garland, TX 75041-6138 (SAN 630-6934) Tel 214-840-6621; Fax: 214-840-3357; Toll Free: 800-727-0688; 10990 E. 55th Ave., Denver, CO 80239-2007 (SAN 630-6942) Tel 303-371-8372; Fax: 303-373-4583; 35245 Schoolcraft, Livonia, MI 48150-1209 (SAN 630-6969) Tel 313-422-9955; Fax: 313-422-1171; 3540 NW 56th St., Fort Lauderdale, FL 33309-2260 (SAN 630-6977) Tel 305-733-7440; Fax: 305-735-7752; 6733 S. Sepulveda, Suite 108, Los Angeles, CA 90045-1525 (SAN 630-7035) Tel 213-410-4067; Fax: 213-410-0919; Toll Free: 800-759-4422; 9549 Penn Ave S. Ste. 200, Minneapolis, MN 55431-2565 (SAN 630-7043) Toll Free: 800-825-3112; 25 Branca Rd., East Rutherford, NJ 07073-2121 (SAN 630-706X) Tel 201-933-9797; Fax: 201-933-5139; Toll Free: 800-621-1333; 5576 Inland Empire Blvd, Bldg. G, Suite A, Ontario, CA 91764-5117 (SAN 630-7086) Tel 714-948-7998; Fax: 714-948-9778; Freeport Ctr., Bldg. H-12 N., P.O. Box 1387, Clearfield, UT 84016-1387 (SAN 630-7132) Tel 801-775-0555; Fax: 801-773-8172; 2700 Merchantile Dr., Suite 100, Rancho Cordova, CA 95742-6574 (SAN 630-7140) Tel 916-638-8090; Fax: 916-638-8021; Toll Free: 800-866-1568; 4660 Viewridge Ave., Suite B, San Diego, CA 92123-1638 (SAN 630-7159) Tel 619-569-9816; Fax: 619-569-1542; Toll Free: 800-365-5229; 6411 S. 216th, Bldg. F, Kent, WA 98032-1392 (SAN 630-7167) Tel 206-395-3515; Fax: 206-395-0650; 445 W. Freedom Ave., Orange, CA 92865 (SAN 630-7175) Tel 714-282-1232; Fax: 714-282-2245; 201 Ingram Dr., Roseburg, OR 97470; 12600 SE Hwy. 212, Bldg. B, Clackamas, OR 97015-9081 Tel 615-287-4000
Web site: http://www.ingramentertainment.com.

Ingram Publisher Services, Orders Addr.: Customer Services, Box 512 1 Ingram Blvd., LaVergne, TN 37086 USA Toll Free Fax: 800-838-1149; Edit Addr.: 1 Ingram Blvd., LaVergne, TN 37086 USA (SAN 631-8630) Tel 615-793-5000; Fax: 615-213-5811
E-mail: customer.service@ingrampublisherservices.com; Publisher@ingrampublisherservices.com; Retailer@ingrampublisherservices.com
Web site: http://www.ingrampublisherservices.com.

Ingram Software, Subs. of Ingram Distribution Group, Inc., 1759 Wehrle, Williamsville, NY 14221 USA (SAN 285-760X) Toll Free: 800-828-7250; 900 W. Walnut Ave., Compton, CA 90220 (SAN 285-7073).

INgrooves, *See* **INscribe Digital**

Inland Empire Periodicals, *See* **Incor Periodicals**

Inner Traditions International, Ltd., *(978-0-89281; 978-0-905249; 978-1-899171; 978-0-906191; 978-0-9504268; 978-1-84409; 978-1-59477; 978-1-62055; 978-1-64411)* Orders Addr.: P.O. Box 388, Rochester, VT 05767-0388 USA Tel 802-767-3174; Fax: 802-767-3726; Toll Free Fax: 800-246-8648; Edit Addr.: One Park St., Rochester, VT 05767 USA (SAN 208-6948) Tel 802-767-3174; Fax: 802-767-3726
E-mail: customerservice@innertraditions.com; info@innertraditions.com
Web site: http://www.innertraditions.com.

Innovative Logistics, Orders Addr.: 575 Prospect St., Lakewood, NJ 08701 USA (SAN 760-6532) Tel 732-534-7001; 732-363-5679; Fax: 732-363-0338
E-mail: innlogorders@innlog.net
Web site: http://www.innlog.net.

INscribe Digital, *(978-1-61750; 978-1-62517)* Div. of Independent Publishers Group, 55 Francisco St. Suite 710, San Francsico, CA 94105 USA
E-mail: digitalpublishing@ingrooves.com
Web site: http://www.INscribeDigital.com.

Insight Guides, *(978-0-88729; 978-1-58573)* 46-35 54th Rd., Maspeth, NY 11378 USA Tel 718-784-0055; Fax: 718-784-1246
E-mail: customerservice@americanmap.com
Web site: http://www.americanmap.com.

Insight Publishing, *(978-0-9663550)* Orders Addr.: P.O. Box 32383, Jacksonville, FL 32237 USA Tel 904-262-9975; Fax: 904-262-3220; Edit Addr.: 5417 Autumnbrook Trail, N., Jacksonville, FL 32258 USA Do not confuse with companies with the same name in Yreka, CA, Parker, CO, Woodbridge, VA, Salt Lake City, UT, Tulsa, OK
E-mail: 102502.2561@compuserve.com.

Instant Pub., *(978-1-59196; 978-1-59872; 978-1-60458; 978-1-61422)* Orders Addr.: P.O. Box 985, Collierville, TN 38027 USA Tel 901-853-7070; Fax: 901-853-6196; Toll Free: 800-259-2592; Edit Addr.: 410 Hwy. 72 W., Collierville, TN 38017 USA
Web site: http://www.instantpublisher.com.

Instantpublisher.com, *See* **Instant Pub.**

Institute for Healthcare Advancement, *(978-0-9701245; 978-0-9720148; 978-0-9835976; 978-1-940874)* Orders Addr.: 501 S. Idaho St. Ste. 300, La Habra, CA 90631-6047 USA (SAN 860-3456) Tel 562-690-4001; Fax: 562-690-8988; Toll Free: 800-434-4633
E-mail: ESilvis@iha4health.org
Web site: http://www.iha4health.org; http://www.ihahealthliteracy.org.

Integral Yoga Pubns., *(978-0-932040; 978-1-938477)* Satchidananda Ashram-Yogaville, 108 Yogaville Way, Buckingham, VA 23921 USA (SAN 285-0338) Tel 434-969-3121 ex 102; Fax: 434-969-1303; Toll Free: 800-262-1008 (orders)
Web site: http://www.yogaville.org.

Interlink Publishing Group, Inc., *(978-0-940793; 978-1-56656; 978-1-62371)* 46 Crosby St., Northampton, MA 01060-1804 USA (SAN 664-8908) Tel 413-582-7054; Fax: 413-582-6731; Toll Free: 800-238-5465
E-mail: info@interlinkbooks.com; editor@interlinkbooks.com
Web site: http://www.interlinkbooks.com.

InterMountain Periodical Distributors, *See* **Majic Enterprises**

International Bk. Ctr., Inc., *(978-0-86685; 978-0-917062)* 2007 Laurel Dr., P.O. Box 295, Troy, MI 48099 USA (SAN 169-4014) Tel 248-879-7920; 586-254-7230; Fax: 586-254-7230
E-mail: ibc@ibcbooks.com
Web site: http://www.ibcbooks.com.

International Magazine Service, Div. of Periodical Pubs. Service Bureau, 1 N. Superior St., Sandusky, OH 44870 USA (SAN 285-9955) Tel 419-626-0623.

International Networking Assn., 4130 Citrus Ave., Suite 5, Rocklin, CA 95677 USA (SAN 631-1857).

International Periodical Distributors, 674 Via de la Valle, Suite 204, Solana Beach, CA 92075 USA (SAN 250-5290) Tel 619-481-5928; Toll Free: 800-999-1170; 800-228-5144 (in Canada).

International Pubns. Service, *(978-0-8002)* Div. of Taylor & Francis, Inc., Orders Addr.: 325 Chestnut St., 8th Flr., Levittown, PA 19057-4700 USA Fax: 215-785-5515; Toll Free: 800-821-8312.

International Readers League, Div. of Periodical Pubs. Service Bureau, 1 N. Superior St., Sandusky, OH 44870 USA (SAN 285-9971) Tel 419-626-0633.

International Service Co., International Service Bldg., 333 Fourth Ave., Indialantic, FL 32903-4295 USA (SAN 169-5134) Tel 407-724-1443 (phone/fax).

International Specialized Book Services, *See* **ISBS Publisher Services**

International Thomson Computer Pr., *(978-1-85032)* Orders Addr.: 7625 Empire Dr., Florence, KY 41042-2978 USA Tel 606-525-6600; Fax: 606-525-7778; Toll Free: 800-842-3636; Edit Addr.: 20 Park Plaza, 13th Flr., Boston, MA 02116 USA Fax: 617-695-1615
E-mail: itcp@itp.thomson.com
Web site: http://www.itcpmedia.com.

Internet Systems, Inc., Subs. of Internet Systems, Inc., 20250 Century Blvd., Germantown, MD 20874 USA (SAN 129-9611) Tel 301-540-5100; Fax: 301-540-5522; Toll Free: 800-638-8725
Web site: http://www.pwl.com/Internet.

Interstate Distributors, 150 Blackstone River Rd. Ste. 4, Worcester, MA 01607-1455 USA (SAN 170-4885) Toll Free: 800-365-6430.

Interstate Periodical Distributors, 201 E. Badger Rd., Madison, WI 53713 USA (SAN 169-9105) Tel 608-277-2407; Fax: 608-277-2410; Toll Free: 800-752-3131.

Intertech Bk. Services, Inc., 25971 Sarazen Dr., South Riding, VA 20152-1741 USA (SAN 630-5253).

InterVarsity Pr., (*978-0-8308; 978-0-87784; 978-1-5140*) Div. of InterVarsity Christian Fellowship of the USA, Orders Addr.: P.O. Box 1400, Downers Grove, IL 60515 USA (SAN 202-7089) Tel 630-734-4000; Fax: 630-734-4200; Toll Free: 800-843-7225 (other depts.); 800-843-9487 (orders); 800-843-1019 (customer service); 800-873-0143 (electronic ordering)
E-mail: email@ivpress.com
Web site: http://www.ivpress.com.

Intrepid Group, Inc., The, 1331 Red Cedar Cir., Fort Collins, CO 80524 USA (SAN 631-5429) Tel 970-493-3793; Fax: 970-493-8781
E-mail: intrepid@frii.com.

Iowa & Illinois News, 8645 Northwest Blvd., Davenport, IA 52806-6418 USA (SAN 169-2607).

Irish American Bk. Co., Subs. of Roberts Rinehart Pubs., Inc., P.O. Box 666, Niwot, CO 80544-0666 USA Tel 303-652-2710; Fax: 303-652-2689; Toll Free: 800-452-7115
E-mail: irishbooks@aol.com
Web site: http://www.irishvillage.com.

Irish Bks. & Media, Inc., (*978-0-937702*) Orders Addr.: 2904 41st Ave S., Minneapolis, MN 55406-1814 USA (SAN 111-8870) Toll Free: 800-229-3505 Do not confuse with Irish Bks. in New York, NY
E-mail: Irishbook@aol.com
Web site: http://www.irishbook.com.

Ironside International Pubs., Inc., (*978-0-935554*) Orders Addr.: P.O. Box 1050, Lorton, VA 22199-1050 USA (SAN 206-2380) Tel 703-493-9120; Fax: 703-493-9424; Edit Addr.: P.O. Box 1050, Lorton, VA 22199-1050 USA (SAN 663-656X)
E-mail: info@ironsidepub.com.

ISBS Publisher Services, 920 NE 58th Ave., Suite 300, Portland, OR 97213-3786 USA (SAN 169-7129) Tel 503-287-3093; Fax: 503-280-8832; Toll Free: 800-944-6190
E-mail: info@isbs.com
Web site: http://www.isbs.com.

ISD, 70 Enterprise Dr., Suite 2, Bristol, CT 06010 USA Tel 860-584-6546; Fax: 860-540-1001
E-mail: orders@isdistribution.com
Web site: https://www.isdistribution.com/.

Islamic Bk. Service, 1209 Cleburne, Hoston, TX 77004 USA (SAN 169-2453) Tel 713-528-1440; Fax: 713-528-1085.

Island Heritage Publishing, (*978-0-89610; 978-0-931548; 978-1-59700*) Div. of The Madden Corp., 94-411 Koaki St., Waipahu, HI 96797 USA (SAN 211-1403) Tel 808-564-8800; Fax: 808-564-8888; Toll Free: 800-468-2800
E-mail: ihorders@welcometotheislands.com
Web site: http://www.welcometotheislands.com.

Islander Group, 269 Pali'i St., Mililani, HI 96789 USA Tel 808-676-0116
E-mail: customerservice@islandergroup.com
Web site: https://www.islandergroup.com/.

Israel Book Shop, *See* **Israel Bookshop Pubns.**

Israel Bookshop Pubns., (*978-0-9670705; 978-1-931681; 978-1-60091*) 501 Prospect St., No. 97, Lakewood, NJ 08701 USA Tel 732-901-3009; Fax: 732-901-4012; Toll Free: 888-536-7427
E-mail: sales@israelbookshoppublications.com
Web site: http://www.israelbookshoppublications.com.

Itasca Bks., (*978-0-9767054*) Orders Addr.: 5120 Cedar Lake Rd. S., Minneapolis, MN 55416 USA (SAN 855-3823) Tel 952-345-4488; Fax: 952-920-0541; Toll Free: 800-901-3480
E-mail: mjung@itascabooks.com
Web site: http://www.itascabooks.com.

iUniverse, Inc., (*978-0-9665514; 978-1-58348; 978-0-9668591; 978-1-893652; 978-0-595; 978-0-9795279; 978-1-60528; 978-1-4401; 978-1-936236; 978-1-4502; 978-1-4620; 978-1-4697; 978-1-4759; 978-1-4917; 978-1-5320; 978-1-6632*) Orders Addr.: 1663 Liberty Dr., Suite 300, Bloomington, IN 47403 USA (SAN 254-9425) Toll Free: 800-288-4677
Web site: http://www.iUniverse.com; http://iuniverse.com; www.balboapress.com.

iUniverse.com, Incorporated, *See* **iUniverse, Inc.**

J & H Bks., 6300 Wilshire Blvd., No. 130, Los Angeles, CA 90048 USA (SAN 631-8118) Tel 323-497-1089; Fax: 626-336-5700
E-mail: wcjiao@lycos.com.

J & J Bk. Sales, 24871 Pylos Way, Mission Viejo, CA 92691-4668 USA (SAN 253-8075)
E-mail: jacki@hydrasystems.com
Web site: http://www.divanet.com/matilda.

J & L Bk. Co., Orders Addr.: P.O. Box 13100, Spokane, WA 99213 USA (SAN 129-6817) Fax: 509-534-0152; 509-534-7713; Toll Free: 800-288-9756; Edit Addr.: 1710 Trent, Spokane, WA 99220 USA (SAN 243-2145).

J & N Creations, LLC, 48 First St., N., Sauk Centre, MN 56304 USA Tel 320-352-6260.

Jacobob Pr. Distributing, 11035 Ridge Forest Ct., Saint Louis, MO 63126 USA.

JAGCO & Associates Inc., Orders Addr.: 596 Indian Trail Rd. South #227, Indian Trail, NC 28079 USA Tel 802-223-6565.

Jalmar Pr., (*978-0-915190; 978-0-935266; 978-1-880396; 978-1-931061*) Subs. of B. L. Winch & Assocs., P.O. Box 370, Fawnskin, CA 92333-0370 USA (SAN 113-3640) Toll Free: 800-662-9662 (orders)
E-mail: jalmarpress@att.net
Web site: http://jalmarpress.com.

James & Law Co., Orders Addr.: P.O. Box 2468, Clarksburg, WV 26302-2468 USA (SAN 169-894X); Edit Addr.: Middletown Mall I-79 & U. S. 250, Fairmont, WV 26554 USA (SAN 169-8966) Tel 304-624-7401.

James Trading Group, Limited, The, 13 Highview Ave., Orangeburg, NY 10962-2125 USA Toll Free: 800-541-5004
E-mail: sales@thejamestradinggroup.com.

Janway, 11 Academy Rd., Cogan Station, PA 17728 USA (SAN 108-3708) Tel 717-494-1239; Fax: 717-494-1350; Toll Free: 800-877-5242.

Jawbone Publishing Corp., (*978-0-9702959; 978-1-59094*) 1540 Happy Valley Cir., Newnan, GA 30263-4035 USA (SAN 253-5335)
E-mail: marketing@jawbonepublishing.com
Web site: http://www.jawbonepublishing.com.

Jeanies Classics, (*978-0-9609672*) Orders Addr.: 2123 Oxford St., Rockford, IL 61103 USA (SAN 271-7409); Edit Addr.: 2123 Oxford St., Rockford, IL 61103 USA (SAN 271-7395) Tel 815-968-4544.

Jean's Dulcimer Shop & Crying Creek Pubs., P.O. Box 8, Hwy. 32, Cosby, TN 37722 USA (SAN 249-9282) Tel 423-487-5543.

Jech Distributors, 674 Via De La Valle, No. 204, Solana Beach, CA 92075-2462 USA (SAN 107-0258) Tel 619-452-7251.

Jellyroll Productions, *See* **Osborne Enterprises Publishing**

Jenkins Group, Inc., (*978-1-890587; 978-0-9860224*) 121 E. Front St., 4th Flr., Traverse City, MI 49684 USA Tel 231-933-0445; Fax: 231-933-0448; 1129 Woodmere Ave., Traverse City, MI 49686
Web site: http://www.bookpublishing.com.

JIST Publishing, (*978-0-942784; 978-1-56370; 978-1-57112; 978-1-59357; 978-1-63332*) Div. of EMC Publishing, 875 Montreal Way, Saint Paul, MN 55102 USA (SAN 240-2351) Tel 651-290-2800 Toll Free Fax: 800-547-8329
E-mail: info@jist.com
Web site: http://www.jist.com.

JIST Works, Incorporated, *See* **JIST Publishing**

JMS Distribution, 2017 San Mateo St., Richmond, CA 94804 USA.

Jobson, Oliver H., (*978-0-9764988*) 12171 SW 123rd Pl., Miami, FL 33186 USA (SAN 256-5463) Tel 954-260-4914
E-mail: ojobson@gmail.com
Web site: http://www.gpaonline.com.

Johns Hopkins Univ. Pr., (*978-0-8018; 978-1-4214*) Div. of Johns Hopkins Univ., Orders Addr.: P.O. Box 50370, Baltimore, MD 21211-4370 USA; Edit Addr.: 2715 N. Charles St., Baltimore, MD 21218-4319 USA (SAN 202-7348) Fax: 410-516-4189; Toll Free: 800-537-5487
E-mail: webmaster@press.jhu.edu
Web site: http://muse.jhu.edu/; http://www.press.jhu.edu/books/.

Johnson News Agency, P.O. Box 9009, Moscow, ID 83843 USA (SAN 169-1678).

Johnson, Walter J. Inc., (*978-0-8472*) 1 New York Plaza 28th Flr., New York, NY 10004-1901 USA (SAN 209-1828).

Jones, Bob University Press, *See* **BJU Pr.**

Joseph Ruzicka, Incorporated, *See* **Southeast Library Bindery, Inc.**

Journey Pubns., LLC, (*978-0-9671696*) 6709 Ave. A, New Orleans, LA 70124 USA; 1441 Canal St. Suite 318, New Orleans, LA 70112 Do not confuse with companies with the same or similar names in Woodstock, NY, Summerland, CA, Savannah, GA, Avon Park, FL, lacey, WA
E-mail: msl3393@yahoo.com; mlewis@simmonswhite.com.

Joyce Media, Inc., (*978-0-917002*) P.O. Box 57, Acton, CA 93510 USA (SAN 208-7197) Tel 805-269-1169; Fax: 805-269-2139
E-mail: joycemed@pacbell.net
Web site: http://joycemedia.com.

JPL Fulfillment, 3883 Linden Ave., Suite E, Wyoming, MI 49548 USA Toll Free: 877-683-6935
E-mail: orders@jplbooks.com
Web site: https://www.jplfulfillment.com/.

Julia Taylor Ebel, P.O. Box 11, Jamestown, NC 27282 USA
E-mail: ebel@northstate.net.

Junior League of Greensboro Pubns., (*978-0-9605788*) 3101 W. Friendly Ave., Greensboro, NC 27408-7801 USA (SAN 112-9597)
E-mail: Jlgso@aol.com.

Just Us Bks., Inc., (*978-0-940975; 978-1-933491*) 395 Pleasant Valley Way Suite B, West Orange, NJ 07052 USA (SAN 664-7413) Tel 973-672-7701
E-mail: justusbook@aol.com
Web site: http://www.justusbooks.com.

K. M. R. Enterprises, (*978-0-9656379*) 5731 Pony Express Trail, Pollock Pines, CA 95726 USA (SAN 299-237X) Tel 530-644-1410.

Kable Media Services, Subs. of AMREP Corp., 505 Park Ave. 7th Fl., New York, NY 10022 USA Tel 212-705-4600; Fax: 212-705-4666; Toll Free: 800-223-6640
E-mail: info@kable.com
Web site: http://www.kable.com/.

Kable News Company, Incorporated, *See* **Kable Media Services**

Kalispell News Agency, P.O. Box 4965, Missoula, MT 59806-4965 USA (SAN 169-4383) Toll Free: 800-955-1266.

Kamkin, Victor, P.O. Box 34583, Bethesda, MD 20827-0583 USA Toll Free: 800-852-6546; 925 Broadway, New York, NY 10010 (SAN 113-7395) Tel 212-673-0776; Fax: 212-673-2473.

Kamkyi Bks., (*978-0-9675031*) Div. of Source International Technology Corp., 939 E. 156th St., Bronx, NY 10455 USA (SAN 630-8392) Tel 718-378-3878 (phone/fax); Toll Free: 888-729-5117
E-mail: source.Intl.Tech@erols.com
Web site: http://www.kamkyibooks.

Kampmann, Kump & Bell, LLC, Orders Addr.: 27 W. 20th St., Suite 1102, New York, NY 10011 USA Tel 212-727-0190; Fax: 212-727-0195
E-mail: midpointny@aol.com.

Kane Miller, (*978-0-916291; 978-1-929132; 978-1-933605; 978-1-935279; 978-1-61067; 978-1-68464*) Div. of EDC Publishing, Orders Addr.: P.O. Box 470663, Tulsa, OK 74146 USA (SAN 295-8945) Tel 800-475-4522; 918-622-4522; Fax: 800-743-5660; Edit Addr.: P.O. Box 8515, La Jolla, CA 92038 USA Tel 858-456-0540
E-mail: info@kanemiller.com
Web site: http://www.kanemiller.com; http://www.edcpub.com.

Kane/Miller#Book Publishers, Incorporated, *See* **Kane Miller**

Kansas City Periodical Distributing, Orders Addr.: P.O. Box 14948, Lenexa, KS 66285-4948 USA (SAN 107-9433); Edit Addr.: 9605 Dice Ln., Lenexa, KS 66215 USA Tel 913-541-8600.

Kansas State Reading Circle, 715 W. Tenth St., C-170, Topeka, KS 66601 USA (SAN 169-2771).

Kaplan Publishing, (*978-0-7931; 978-0-88462; 978-0-913864; 978-0-936894; 978-0-942103; 978-1-57410; 978-1-60714; 978-1-60978; 978-1-61865; 978-1-62523; 978-1-5062*) 395 Hudson St., New York, NY 10014 USA (SAN 211-2280); 395 Hudson St., New City, NY 10014
E-mail: deb.darrock@kaplan.com; shayna.webb@kaplan.com; alexander.noya@kaplan.com
Web site: http://www.kaplanpublishing.com; http://www.kaplanprofessional.com.

Kaybee Montessori, Inc., 157 Lagrange Ave., Rochester, NY 14613-1511 USA (SAN 133-1256) Toll Free: 800-732-9304.

Kazi Pubns., Inc., (*978-0-933511; 978-0-935782; 978-1-56744; 978-1-871031; 978-1-930637*) 3023 W. Belmont Ave., Chicago, IL 60618 USA (SAN 162-3397) Tel 773-267-7001; Fax: 773-267-7002
E-mail: info@kazi.org
Web site: http://www.kazi.org.

Kehot Pubn. Society, (*978-0-8266*) Div. of Merkos L'Inyonei Chinuch, Orders Addr.: 291 Kingston Ave., Brooklyn, NY 11213 USA Tel 718-778-0226; Fax: 718-778-4148; Toll Free: 877-463-7567 (877-4MERKOS); Edit Addr.: 770 Eastern Pkwy., Brooklyn, NY 11213 USA (SAN 220-7060) Tel 718-604-2785
E-mail: orders@kehotonline.com; info@kehot.com
Web site: http://www.kehotonline.com.

Keith Distributors, 1230 Macklind Ave., Saint Louis, MO 63110-1432 USA (SAN 112-6377) Toll Free: 800-373-2366
E-mail: keithsbooks@juno.com.

Kensington Publishing Corp., (*978-0-7860; 978-0-8065; 978-0-8184; 978-0-8217; 978-1-55817; 978-1-57566; 978-0-7582; 978-1-4201; 978-1-59983; 978-1-60183; 978-0-9817144; 978-0-9818905; 978-0-9824170; 978-0-9841132; 978-1-61650; 978-1-61773; 978-1-4967; 978-1-5161; 978-1-63573) 119 W. 40th St., New York, NY 10018 USA Tel 212-407-1500; Fax: 212-935-0699; Toll Free: 800-221-2647; 499 North Canon Dr., Beverly Hills, CA 90210 Tel 310-887-7082*
E-mail: jmclean@kensingtonbooks.com; melley@kensingtonbooks.com
Web site: http://www.kensingtonbooks.com.

Kent News Agency, Inc., P.O. Box 1828, Scottsbluff, NE 69363-1828 USA (SAN 169-4448) Tel 303-286-9694; 308-635-2225; Fax: 308-635-1563; Toll Free: 877-290-4740
E-mail: kentrob@prairieweb.com.

Keramos, P.O. Box 7500, Ann Arbor, MI 48107 USA (SAN 169-3670) Tel 313-439-1261.

Kerem Publishing, (*978-1-889727*) 723 N. Orange Dr., Los Angeles, CA 90038 USA (SAN 299-1209).

Kerhulas News Co., P.O. Box 751, Union, SC 29379 USA (SAN 169-7838).

Ketab Corp., (*978-1-883819; 978-1-59584*) 12701 Van Nuys blvd suite H, PACOIMA, CA 91331 USA (SAN 107-7791) Tel 310-477-7477; Fax: 818-908-1457; Toll Free: 800-367-4726
E-mail: ketab@ketab.com
Web site: http://www.ketab.com.

Key Bk. Service, Inc., (*978-0-934636*) P.O. Box 1434, Fairfield, CT 06430 USA (SAN 169-0671) Tel 203-374-4939; Fax: 203-384-6099.

Keystone Bks. & Media LLC, 12526 Cutten Rd., Suite C, Houston, TX 77066 USA (SAN 990-0160) Tel 281-893-2665; 888-670-2665; Fax: 281-549-2500; Toll Free: 888-670-2665
E-mail: books@keystonebooksmedia.com; matthew@keystonebooksmedia.com
Web site: http://www.keystonebooksmedia.com/.

Khalifah's Booksellers & Assocs., Orders Addr.: 210 East Arrowhead Dr. #2, Charlotte, NC 28213 USA.

Kidsbooks, Inc., 220 Monroe Tpke., No. 560, Monroe, CT 06468-2247 USA (SAN 169-0795).

King Electronics Distributing, 1711 Southeastern Ave., Indianapolis, IN 46201-3990 USA (SAN 107-6795) Tel 317-639-1484; Fax: 317-639-4711.

Kingdom, Inc., P.O. Box 506, Mansfield, PA 16933 USA.

Kinokuniya Bookstores of America Co., Ltd., 1581 Webster St., San Francisco, CA 94115 USA (SAN 121-8441) Tel 415-567-7625; Fax: 415-567-4109.

Kinokuniya Pubns. Service of New York, 1075 Avenue Of The Americas., New York, NY 10018-3701 USA (SAN 157-5414)
E-mail: kinokuniya@kinokuniya.com
Web site: http://www.kinokuniya.com.

Kirkbride, B.B. Bible Co., Inc., (*978-0-88707; 978-0-934854*) P.O. Box 606, Indianapolis, IN 46206-0606 USA (SAN 169-2372) Tel 317-633-1900; Fax: 317-633-1444; Toll Free: 800-428-4385
E-mail: hyperbible@aol.com
Web site: http://www.kirkbride.com.

Kitrick Management Co., Ltd., P.O. Box 15523, Cincinnati, OH 45215 USA (SAN 132-6236) Tel 513-782-2930; Fax: 513-782-2936
E-mail: bachb@aol.com.

Klein's Booklein, Orders Addr.: P.O. Box 968, Fowlerville, MI 48836 USA (SAN 631-3329) Tel 517-223-3964; Fax: 517-223-1314; Toll Free: 800-266-5534; Edit Addr.: One Klein Dr., Fowlerville, MI 48836 USA (SAN 631-3337).

Knopf, Alfred A. Inc., (*978-0-394*) Div. of The Knopf Publishing Group, Orders Addr.: 400 Hahn Rd., Westminster, MD 21157 USA Tel 410-848-1900; Toll Free: 800-726-0600 (orders); Edit Addr.: 1745 Broadway, New York, NY 10019 USA (SAN 202-5825) Tel 212-782-9000; Toll Free: 800-726-0600
E-mail: customerservice@randomhouse.com
Web site: http://www.randomhouse.com/knopf.

Knox, John Press, *See* **Westminster John Knox Pr.**

KOCH Entertainment, LLC, (*978-0-9721700; 978-1-4172*) 740 Broadway, New York, NY 10003 USA Tel 212-353-8800; Fax: 212-505-3095; 22 Harbor Park Dr., Port Washington, NY 11050 Tel 516-484-1000; Fax: 516-484-4746; Toll Free: 800-332-7553
E-mail: nives@kochent.com; videosales@kochent.com
Web site: http://www.kochvision.com; http://www.kochlorberfilms.com; http://www.kochentertainment.com.

Kodansha America, Inc., (*978-0-87011; 978-1-56836; 978-1-935429; 978-1-61262; 978-1-63236; 978-1-64651*) 451 Park Ave S. Flr. 7, New York, NY 10016-7390 USA (SAN 201-0526) Toll Free: 800-451-7556
E-mail: t-sumi@kodansha-usa.com; ka-kolde@kodansha.co.jp
Web site: http://kodanshacomics.com/; www.kodanshausa.com.

Kodansha USA Publishing, *See* **Kodansha America, Inc.**

Koen Pacific, Orders Addr.: P.O. Box 600, Moorestown, NJ 08057-0600 USA (SAN 631-5593) Toll Free: 800-995-4840
E-mail: info@koenpacific.com.

Kraus Reprint, *See* **Periodicals Service Co.**

Kregel Pubns., (*978-0-8254*) Div. of Kregel, Inc., Orders Addr.: P.O. Box 2607, Grand Rapids, MI 49501-2607 USA (SAN 206-9792) Tel 616-451-4775; Fax: 616-451-9330; Toll Free: 800-733-2607; Edit Addr.: 733 Wealthy St., SE., Grand Rapids, MI 49503-5553 USA (SAN 298-9115)
E-mail: kregelbooks@kregel.com; acquisitions@kregel.com
Web site: http://www.kregel.com.

Krullstone Distributing, LLC, 8751 Clayton Cove Rd., Springville, AL 35146 USA
E-mail: charlotte@krullstonepublishing.com
Web site: http://www.krullstonepublishing.com.

KSG Distributing, 1121 W. Flint Meadow Dr., Kaysville, UT 84037 USA.

Kurian, George Reference Bks., (*978-0-914746*) Orders Addr.: P.O. Box 519, Baldwin Place, NY 10505 USA (SAN 203-1981); Edit Addr.: 3689 Campbell Ct., Yorktown Heights, NY 10598 USA (SAN 110-6236) Tel 914-962-3287.

Kurtzman Bk. Sales Co., 17348 W. 12 Mile Rd., Southfield, MI 48076 USA (SAN 114-0787) Tel 248-557-7230; Fax: 248-557-8705; Toll Free: 800-869-0505.

Kuykendall's Pr., Bookstore Div., P.O. Box 627, Athens, AL 35612-0627 USA (SAN 168-9185) Tel 256-232-1754; Toll Free: 800-781-1754.

L I M Productions, LLC, (*978-1-929617*) 3553 Northdale St., NW, Uniontown, OH 44685-8004 USA Toll Free: 877-628-4532
E-mail: customerservice@limproductions.com
Web site: http://www.limproductions.com.

L L Co., (*978-0-937892*) 1647 Manning Ave., Los Angeles, CA 90024 USA (SAN 110-0009) Tel 310-615-0116; Fax: 310-640-6863; Toll Free: 800-473-3699
E-mail: wallacelab@aol.com.

L M C Source, P.O. Box 720400, San Jose, CA 95172-0400 USA (SAN 631-189X) Tel 408-630-0589; Fax: 408-634-1456; Toll Free: 800-873-3043
E-mail: lmcs@pacbell.net
Web site: http://www.csn.net/~davidl/.

L P C Group, c/o CDS, 193 Edwards Dr., Jackson, TN 38305 USA (SAN 630-5644) Fax: 731-423-1973; 731-935-7731; Toll Free Fax: 800-351-5073; Toll Free: 800-343-4499
E-mail: lpc-info@lpcgroup.com
Web site: http://www.lpcgroup.com.

La Belle News Agency, 814 University Blvd., Steubenville, OH 43952 USA (SAN 169-6858) Tel 740-282-9731.

La Cite French Bks., Div. of The La Cite Group, Inc., P.O. Box 64504, Los Angeles, CA 90064-0504 USA (SAN 168-9789)
E-mail: lacite@aol.com.

La Moderna Poesia, Inc., 5739 NW 7th St., Miami, FL 33126-3105 USA (SAN 169-1139).

Lafayette Bks., P.O. Box 758, Mamaroneck, NY 10543-0758 USA (SAN 135-292X) Tel 914-833-0248.

Lake City Downtown Improvement and Revitalization Team, P.O. Box 973 231 N. Silver St., Lake City, CO 81235 USA Tel 970-944-3478
E-mail: ed@lakecitydirt.com.

Lakeport Distributors, Inc., 139 W. 18th St., P.O. Box 6195, Erie, PA 16501 USA (SAN 169-734X).

Lambda Pubs., Inc., (*978-0-915361; 978-1-55774*) 3709 13th Ave., Brooklyn, NY 11218-3622 USA (SAN 291-0640) Tel 718-972-5449; Fax: 718-972-6307 E-mail: judaica@email.msn.com.

Lambert Bk. Hse., Inc., (*978-0-89315*) 4139 Parkway Dr., Florence, AL 35630-6347 USA (SAN 180-5169) Tel 256-764-4098; 256-764-4090; Fax: 256-766-9200; Toll Free: 800-551-8511 E-mail: Info@lambertbookhouse.com Web site: http://www.lambertbookhouse.com.

Landmark Audiobooks, 4865 Sterling Dr., Boulder, CO 80301 USA Fax: 303-443-3775 Web site: http://www.landmarkaudio.com.

Landmark Bk. Co., (*978-0-929194*) 131 Hicks St., Brooklyn, NY 11201-2318 USA (SAN 169-5843).

Lang, Peter Publishing, Inc., (*978-0-8204; 978-1-4331; 978-1-4539; 978-1-4540; 978-1-4541; 978-1-4542; 978-1-63667*) Subs. of Verlag Peter Lang AG (SZ), 80 Broad St. 5th Flr., New York, NY 10004 USA (SAN 241-5534) Tel 212-647-7700; 212-647-7706 (Outside USA); Fax: 212-647-7707; Toll Free: 800-770-5264 E-mail: customerservice@plang.com Web site: http://www.peterlang.com.

Langenscheidt Publishing Group, (*978-0-88729; 978-1-58573*) Subs. of Langenscheidt KG, Orders Addr.: 15 Tyger River Dr., Duncan, SC 29334 USA Fax: 888-773-7979; Toll Free: 800-432-6277; Edit Addr.: 36-36 33rd St., Long Island City, NY 11106 USA Web site: http://www.americanmap.com; http://www.langenscheidt.com.

Larousse Kingfisher Chambers, Inc., (*978-0-7534; 978-1-85697*) 215 Park Ave., S., New York, NY 10003 USA (SAN 297-7540); 181 Ballardvale St., Wilmington, MA 01887.

Las Vegas News Agency, 2312 Silver Bluff Ct., Las Vegas, NV 89134-6092 USA.

Lash Distributors, 7106 Geoffrey Way, Frederick, MD 21704 USA (SAN 169-3131).

Last Gasp Eco-Funnies, Incorporated, *See* **Last Gasp of San Francisco**

Last Gasp of San Francisco, (*978-0-86719*) Orders Addr.: 777 Florida St., San Francisco, CA 94110 USA (SAN 216-8308); Edit Addr.: 777 Florida St., San Francisco, CA 94110-2025 USA (SAN 170-3242) Tel 415-824-6636; Fax: 415-824-1836; Toll Free: 800-366-5121 E-mail: colin@lastgasp.com Web site: http://www.lastgasp.com.

Laster, Larry D. Old & Rare Bks., Prints & Maps, 2416 Maplewood Ave., Winston-Salem, NC 27103 USA (SAN 112-9600) Tel 336-724-7544; Fax: 336-724-9055.

Latcorp, Ltd., 10 Norden Ln., Huntington Station, NY 11746 USA (SAN 159-8910) Tel 516-271-0548; Fax: 516-549-8849.

Latin American Book Source, Inc., 681 Anita St., Suit 102, Chula Vista, CA 91911-4663 USA Web site: http://www.latambooks.com/.

Latin Trading Corp., 539 H St., Chula Vista, CA 91910 USA (SAN 630-2963) Tel 619-427-7867; Fax: 619-476-1817; Toll Free: 800-257-7248 E-mail: info@latintradingbooks.com Web site: http://www.latintradingbooks.com.

Latta, J. S. Incorporated, *See* **Latta's**

Latta's, 1502 Fourth Ave., P.O. Box 2668, Huntington, WV 25726 USA (SAN 169-8982) Fax: 304-525-5038; Toll Free: 800-624-3501.

Laurus Co., The, Orders Addr.: 524 Guinevere Court, McDonough, GA 30252 USA (SAN 858-608X) Tel 678-814-4047; Fax: 678-272-7255; Toll Free: 800-596-7370 E-mail: thelaurusco@charter.net Web site: http://www.thelauruscompany.com.

LD Bks., Inc., (*978-0-9772669; 978-0-9785897; 978-1-939048; 978-1-940281; 978-1-943387*) 8313 NW 68th St., Miami, FL 33166 USA (SAN 631-8088) Tel 305-406-2292; Fax: 305-406-2293 E-mail: vilmac@ldbooks.com; sales@ldbooks.com Web site: http://www.sinlimites.net; http://www.ldbooks.com.

LEA Bk. Distributors (Libros Espana y America), (*978-1-883110*) 170-23 83rd Ave., Jamaica Hills, NY 11432 USA (SAN 170-5407) Tel 718-291-9891; Fax: 718-291-9830 E-mail: leabook@idt.net Web site: http://www.leabooks.com.

Learning Collection, The, 145 S. Glencoe St., Denver, CO 80246-1152 USA (SAN 630-8287).

Learning Connection, The, (*978-1-56831*) Orders Addr.: 4100 Silver Star Rd. Ste. D, Orlando, FL 32808-4618 USA Toll Free: 800-218-8489 Web site: http://www.tlconnection.com.

Learning Services, 2095 Laura St. Ste. H, Springfield, OR 97477-2285 USA Toll Free: 800-877-3278.

Lectorum Pubns., Inc., (*978-0-9625162; 978-1-880507; 978-1-930332; 978-1-933032; 978-1-941802; 978-1-63245; 978-1-64684*) Orders Addr.: 205 Chubb Ave, Lyndhurst, NJ 07071 USA (SAN 990-0802) Tel 201-559-2232; Edit Addr.: 205 Chubb Ave., Lyndhurst, NJ 07071 USA (SAN 860-0597) Tel 201-559-2200; Fax: 201-559-2201; Toll Free Fax: 877-532-8676; Toll Free: 800-345-5946 E-mail: acorrea@lectorum.com Web site: http://www.lectorum.com; http://www.librerialectorum.com.

Lee Bks., (*978-0-939818*) Div. of Lee S. Cole & Assocs., Inc., 524 San Anselmo Ave., No 215, San Anselmo, CA 94960-2614 USA (SAN 110-649X) Tel 415-456-4388; Fax: 415-456-7532; Toll Free: 800-828-3550 Do not confuse with other companies with the same or similar names in Jacksonville, FL, Columbia, SC E-mail: lcs@lsc-associates.com Web site: http://www.lsc-associates.com.

Left Bank Bks., 92 Pike St., Seattle, WA 98101 USA Web site: http://www.leftbankbooks.com.

Left Bank Books Distribution & Publishing, *See* **Left Bank Distribution**

Left Bank Distribution, (*978-0-939306*) 92 Pike St., Seattle, WA 98101-2025 USA (SAN 216-5368) E-mail: leftbank@leftbankbooks.com Web site: http://www.leftbankbooks.com.

Legato Pubs. Group, Orders Addr.: 1700 4th St., Berkeley, CA 94710 USA Toll Free: 800-343-4499 Web site: http://www.legatopublishersgroup.com/.

Leman Pubns., Inc., (*978-0-943721; 978-0-9602970*) Div. of Rodale Pr. Co., Box 4100, 741 Corporate Cir., Suite A, Golden, CO 80401-5622 USA (SAN 213-3415) Fax: 303-277-0370; Toll Free: 800-877-3775.

Leonard, Hal Corp., (*978-0-634; 978-0-7935; 978-0-87910; 978-0-87930; 978-0-88188; 978-0-931340; 978-0-9607350; 978-1-56516; 978-1-57467; 978-1-4234; 978-1-936098; 978-1-61713; 978-1-61774; 978-1-61780; 978-1-4584; 978-1-4768; 978-1-4803; 978-1-62906; 978-1-4950; 978-1-5400; 978-1-7051) Orders Addr.: P.O. Box 13819, Milwaukee, WI 53213-0819 USA Tel 414-774-3630; Fax: 414-774-3259; Toll Free: 800-524-4425; Edit Addr.: 7777 W. Bluemound Rd., Milwaukee, WI 53213 USA (SAN 239-250X) Tel 414-777-3630; Fax: 414-774-4176* E-mail: halinfo@halleonard.com Web site: http://www.halleonard.com.

Leonardo Press, *See* **Firenze Pr.**

Lerner Publishing Group, (*978-0-7613; 978-0-8225; 978-0-87406; 978-0-87614; 978-0-929371; 978-0-930494; 978-1-57505; 978-1-58013; 978-1-58196; 978-1-4677; 978-1-5124; 978-1-5415; 978-1-7284*) Orders Addr.: 1251 Washington Ave. N., Minneapolis, MN 55401 USA (SAN 256-0283) Tel 612-332-3344; Fax: 612-204-9208; Edit Addr.: 241 First Ave., N., Minneapolis, MN 55401 USA (SAN 201-0828) Tel 612-332-3344; Fax: 612-215-6230; Toll Free Fax: 800-332-1132; Toll Free: 800-328-4929 E-mail: info@lernerbooks.com; custserve@lernerbooks.com Web site: http://www.lernerbooks.com; http://www.karben.com.

Levant Distributors, Incorporated, *See* **Levant USA, Inc.**

Levant USA, Inc., 145 Hook Creek Blvd. BLDG B6B3, Valley Stream, NY 11581-2223 USA (SAN 631-1970) E-mail: levantusa@cs.com.

Levine, J. Religious Supplies, Five W. 30th St., New York, NY 10001 USA (SAN 169-5878) Tel 212-695-6888; Fax: 212-643-1044 E-mail: sales@levine.judica.com.

Levy, Charles Company, *See* **Levy Home Entertainment, Ltd.**

Levy Home Entertainment, *See* **Readerlink Distribution Services, LLC**

Levy Home Entertainment, Ltd., Div. of Charles Levy Co., 1420 Kensington Rd. Ste. 300, Oak Brook, IL 60523-2164 USA (SAN 159-835X).

Lewis International, Inc., (*978-0-9666771; 978-1-930983*) 2201 NW 102nd Pl., No. 1, Miami, FL 33172 USA Tel 305-436-7984; Fax: 305-436-7985; Toll Free: 800-259-5962.

Lewis, John W. Enterprises, 168 Perez St., P.O. Box 3375, Santurce, PR 00936 USA (SAN 169-9334) Tel 809-722-0104.

Lexicon Pubns., Inc., P.O. Box 1737, Danbury, CT 06810 USA (SAN 205-664X) Tel 203-796-2540.

Liberation Distributors, (*978-0-89928*) P.O. Box 5341, Chicago, IL 60680 USA (SAN 169-880X) Tel 773-248-3442.

Library & Educational Services, P.O. Box 288, Berrien Springs, MI 49103 USA Tel 269-695-1800; Fax: 616-695-8500 E-mail: libraryanded@juno.com.

Library Bk. Selection Service, P.O. Box 277, Bloomington, IL 61702-0277 USA (SAN 169-1740).

Library Integrated Solutions & Assocs., P.O. Box 6189, Mckinney, TX 75071-5105 USA Web site: http://www.llibs.com.

Library Sales of N.J., (*978-1-888032*) Orders Addr.: P.O. Box 335, Garwood, NJ 07027-0335 USA Tel 908-232-1446; Edit Addr.: 607 S. Chestnut St., Westfield, NJ 07090-1369 USA E-mail: Librarysalesofnj@aol.com.

Library Video Co., (*978-1-4171*) P.O. Box 580, Wynnewood, PA 19096 USA (SAN 631-3205) Fax: 610-645-4050; Toll Free: 800-843-3620 E-mail: cs@libraryvideo.com Web site: http://www.libraryvideo.com.

LibreDigital, 1835-B Kramer Ln. Suite 150, Austin, TX 78758 USA; 18 Soho Sq., London, W1D3QL E-mail: support@libredigital.com.

Libreria Bereana, 1825 San Alejandro, Urb San Ignacio, Rio Piedras, PR 00927-6819 USA (SAN 169-9288) Tel 809-764-6175.

Libreria Distribuidora Universal, 3090 SW 8th St., Miami, FL 33135 USA Tel 305-642-3234.

Libreria Universal, Inc., (*978-1-881375*) Orders Addr.: P.O. Box 1480, Mayaguez, PR 00680 USA; Edit Addr.: 55 N. Post St., Mayaguez, PR 00680 USA Tel 787-832-6041; Fax: 787-832-8477 E-mail: colom@coqui.net; nikkynicole2004@gmail.com.

Libros de Espana y America, *See* **LEA Bk. Distributors (Libros Espana y America)**

Libros Sin Fronteras, P.O. Box 2085, Olympia, WA 98507 USA Tel 360-357-4332; Fax: 360-357-4964 E-mail: info@librossinfronteras.com Web site: http://www.librossinfronteras.com.

LifeWay Christian Resources, (*978-0-7673; 978-0-633; 978-1-4158; 978-1-4300; 978-1-5359; 978-1-0877*) Div. of The Southern Baptist Convention, One Lifeway Plaza, Nashville, TN 37234 USA Tel 615-251-2000; Fax: 615-277-8221 (product info., ordering, order tracking); 615-251-2626 (shipping/transportation); Toll Free Fax: 800-296-4036; Toll Free: 800-458-2772 (product info., ordering); 800-251-3225 E-mail: customerservice@lifeway.com; support.lifeway.com Web site: http://www.lifewaystores.com; http://www.lifeway.com; http://www.bhpublishinggroup.com.

Light & Life Publishing Co., (*978-0-937032; 978-1-880971; 978-1-933654*) Orders Addr.: 4808 Park Glen Rd., Minneapolis, MN 55416 USA (SAN 213-8565) Tel 952-925-3888; Fax: 888-925-3918; Toll Free Fax: 888-925-3918 E-mail: ivy@light-n-life.com Web site: http://www.light-n-life.com.

Light Impressions Corp., (*978-0-87992*) Orders Addr.: P.O. Box 940, Rochester, NY 14603-0940 USA (SAN 169-619X) Toll Free Fax: 800-826-5539; Toll Free: 800-828-6216; Edit Addr.: P.O. Box 22708, Rochester, NY 14692-2708 USA Web site: http://www.lightimpresionsdirect.com.

Light Technology Publishing, *See* **Light Technology Publishing, LLC**

Light Technology Publishing, LLC, (*978-0-929385; 978-1-891824; 978-1-62233*) Orders Addr.: P.O. Box 3540, Flagstaff, AZ 86003 USA (SAN 249-1389) Tel 928-526-1345; Toll Free: 800-450-0985; Edit Addr.: 4030 E. Huntington Dr., Flagstaff, AZ 86004 USA (SAN 990-0101) E-mail: publishing@lighttechnology.net; art@lighttechnology.net; newmedia@lighttechnology.com; jon.campbell@lighttechnology.com Web site: http://www.sedonajournal.com; http://lighttechnology.com.

Lightning Source, LLC, *See* **Ingram Content Group**

Liguori Pubns., (*978-0-7648; 978-0-89243*) One Liguori Dr., Liguori, MO 63057-9999 USA (SAN 202-6783) Tel 636-464-2500; Fax: 636-464-8449; Toll Free Fax: 800-325-9526; Toll Free: 800-325-9521 (orders) E-mail: liguori@liguori.org Web site: http://www.liguori.org.

Likely Story Bookfairs, A, 7210 SW 57th Ave., Suite 207-A, South Miami, FL 33143 USA (SAN 631-1210) Tel 305-668-9183; Fax: 305-667-3323.

Lilly News Agency, P.O. Box 280077, Memphis, TN 38168-0077 USA (SAN 168-9452).

Limerock Bks., Inc., P.O. Box 57, New Canaan, CT 06840 USA (SAN 630-8708) Tel 203-322-5352; Fax: 203-322-2182 Do not confuse with Limerock Books, Thomaston, ME E-mail: limerockbk@aol.com Web site: http://www.netpocus.com/limerock.

Linden Publishing Co., Inc., (*978-0-941936; 978-1-933502; 978-1-61035*) 2006 S. Mary, Fresno, CA 93721 USA (SAN 238-6089) Tel 559-233-6633 (phone/fax); Toll Free: 800-345-4447 (orders only) Do not confuse with Linden Publishing in Avon, NY E-mail: richard@lindenpub.com Web site: http://www.lindenpub.com.

Linden Tree Children's Records & Bks., 265 State St., Los Altos, CA 94022 USA (SAN 131-744X) Tel 415-949-3390; Fax: 415-949-0346.

Linden Tree Children's Records & Books, *See* **Linden Tree Children's Records & Bks.**

Lindsay News & Photo Service, Inc., 868 Lockport Rd., Youngstown, NY 14174-1139 USA (SAN 169-6092).

Ling's International Bks., Orders Addr.: P.O. Box 82684, San Diego, CA 92138 USA (SAN 169-0116) Tel 619-292-8104; Fax: 619-292-8207; Edit Addr.: 3396 Via Cabo Verde., Escondido, CA 92029-7459 USA.

Linx Educational Publishing, Inc., (*978-1-891818; 978-0-9797510*) P.O. Box 50009, Jacksonville Beach, FL 32240 USA Tel 904-241-1861; Fax: 904-241-3279; Toll Free Fax: 888-546-9338; Toll Free: 800-717-5469 E-mail: mimi@lixedu.com; info@linxedu.com Web site: http://www.linxedu.com.

Lippincott Williams & Wilkins, (*978-0-316; 978-0-397; 978-0-683; 978-0-7817; 978-0-8067; 978-0-8121; 978-0-88167; 978-0-89004; 978-0-89313; 978-0-89640; 978-0-911216; 978-1-881063; 978-1-60547; 978-1-60831; 978-1-60929; 978-1-4698*) Orders Addr.: P.O. Box 1620, Hagerstown, MD 21741 USA Fax: 301-223-2400; Toll Free: 800-638-3030; Edit Addr.: 530 Walnut St., Philadelphia, PA 19106-3621 USA (SAN 201-0933) Tel 215-521-8300; Fax: 215-521-8902; Toll Free: 800-638-3030; 351 W. Camden St., Baltimore, MD 21201 Tel 410-528-4000; 410-528-4209; 345 Hudson St., 16th Flr., New York, NY 10014 Tel 212-886-1200; 16522 Hunters Green Pkwy., Hagerstown, MD 21740 Tel 301-223-2300; Fax: 301-223-2398; Toll Free: 800-638-3030 E-mail: custserv@lww.com; orders@lww.com Web site: http://www.lww.com.

Lippincott-Raven Publishers, *See* **Lippincott Williams & Wilkins**

Listen & Live Audio, Inc., (*978-1-885408; 978-1-931953; 978-1-59316*) Orders Addr.: P.O. Box 817, Roseland, NJ 07068 USA Tel 201-558-9000; Fax: 201-558-9800; Toll Free: 800-653-9400; Edit Addr.: 1700 Manhattan Ave., Union City, NJ 07087-5473 USA E-mail: Alfred@Listenandlive.com Web site: http://www.listenandlive.com.

Literal Bk. Distributors: Bks. in Spanish, Orders Addr.: P.O. Box 7113, Langley Park, MD 20787 USA; Edit Addr.: 7705 Georgia Ave. NW, Suite 102, Washington, DC 20012 USA (SAN 113-2784) Tel 202-723-8688; Fax: 202-882-6592; Toll Free: 800-366-8680.

Little Brown & Co., (*978-0-316; 978-0-8212; 978-0-7595*) Div. of Hachette Bk. Group, Orders Addr.: 3 Center Plaza, Boston, MA 02108-2084 USA (SAN 630-7248) Tel 617-227-0730; Toll Free Fax: 800-286-9471; Toll Free: 800-759-0190; Edit Addr.: 237 Park Ave., New York, NY 10017 USA (SAN 200-2205) Tel 212-364-0600; Fax: 212-364-0952 E-mail: customer.service@hbgusa.com Web site: http://www.hachettebookgroup.com.

Little Dania's Juvenile Promotions, Div. of Booksmith Promotional Co., 100 Paterson Plank Rd., Jersey City, NJ 07307 USA (SAN 169-5681) Tel 201-659-2317; Fax: 201-659-3631 E-mail: hochberga@aol.com.

Little Professor Bk. Ctrs., Inc., P.O. Box 3160, Ann Arbor, MI 48106-3160 USA (SAN 144-2503) Toll Free: 800-899-6232.

Llewellyn Pubns., (*978-0-7387; 978-0-87542; 978-1-56718*) Div. of Llewellyn Worldwide, Ltd., Orders Addr.: 2143 Wooddale Dr., Woodbury, MN 55125-2989 USA Tel 651-291-1970; Fax: 651-291-1908; Toll Free: 800-843-6666 E-mail: sales@llewellyn.com Web site: http://www.llewellyn.com; http://www.midnightinkbooks.com.

Llewellyn Worldwide Ltd., Orders Addr.: 2143 Wooddale Dr., Woodbury, MN 55125-2989 USA Tel 651-291-1970; Fax: 651-291-1908 E-mail: sales@llewellyn.com Web site: http://www.llewellyn.com.

Login Fulfillment Services, *See* **L P C Group**

Lone Pine Publishing USA, Orders Addr.: 1808 B St., NW Suite 140, Auburn, WA 98001 USA (SAN 859-0427) Tel 253-394-0400; Fax: 253-394-0405; Toll Free Fax: 800-548-1169; Toll Free: 800-518-3541 E-mail: mikec@lonepinepublishing.com Web site: http://www.lonepinepublishing.com; http://www.companyscoming.com/; http://overtimebooks.com; http://www.folklorepublishing.com/.

Long Beach Bks., Inc., P.O. Box 179, Long Beach, NY 11561-0179 USA (SAN 164-632X) Tel 718-471-5934.

Longleaf Services, Orders Addr.: P.O. Box 8895, Chapel Hill, NC 27515-8895 USA Tel 800-848-6224; Fax: 800-272-6817; 919-962-2704 (24 hours) E-mail: customerservice@longleafservices.org; orders@longleafservices.org Web site: http://www.longleafservices.org/.

Longstreet Pr., Inc., (*978-0-929264; 978-1-56352*) Subs. of Cox Newspapers, Inc., 325 N. Milledge Ave., Athens, GA 30601-3805 USA (SAN 248-7640) E-mail: scottbard@gmail.com.

Looseleaf Law Pubns., Inc., (*978-0-930137; 978-1-889031; 978-1-932777; 978-1-60885*) Orders Addr.: P.O. Box 650042, Fresh Meadows, NY 11365-0042 USA Tel 718-359-5559; Fax: 718-539-0941; Toll Free: 800-647-5547 E-mail: info@looseleaflaw.com; lynette@looseleaflaw.com Web site: http://www.looseleaflaw.com.

Lord's Line, (*978-0-915952*) 1065 Lomita Blvd., No. 434, Harbor City, CA 90710-1944 USA (SAN 169-0051).

Lorenz Corp., The, (*978-0-7877; 978-0-88335; 978-0-89328; 978-1-55863; 978-1-57310; 978-1-885564; 978-1-4291*) 501 E. Third St., Dayton, OH 45401-0802 USA (SAN 208-7413) Tel 937-228-6118; Fax: 937-223-2042; Toll Free: 800-444-1144 E-mail: service@lorenz.com Web site: http://www.lorenz.com.

Los Angeles Mart, The, 1933 S. Broadway, Suite 665, Los Angeles, CA 90007 USA (SAN 168-9797) Tel 213-748-6449; Fax: 714-523-0796.

Lotus Lights Publications, *See* **Lotus Pr.**

Lotus Pr., (*978-0-910261; 978-0-914955; 978-0-940676; 978-0-940985; 978-0-941524; 978-1-60869*) Div. of Lotus Brands, Inc., P.O. Box 325, Twin Lakes, WI 53181 USA (SAN 239-1120) Tel 262-889-2461; Fax: 262-889-8591; Toll Free: 800-824-6396 Do not confuse with companies with the same or similar name in Lotus, CA, Westerville, OH, Bokeelia, FL, Brattleboro, VT, Detroit, MI, Tobyhanna, PA E-mail: lotuspress@lotuspress.com Web site: http://www.lotuspress.com.

Louisville Distributors, *See* **United Magazine**

Louisville News Co., P.O. Box 36, Columbia, KY 42728 USA (SAN 169-281X) Tel 502-384-3444; Fax: 502-384-9324.

LSC Communications Corp., Orders Addr.: 35 W. Wacker Dr., Chicago, IL 60601 USA (SAN 990-0403); Edit Addr.: 4101 Winfield Rd, Warrenville, IL 60555 USA Tel 630-322-6885 E-mail: stephanie.d.boyer@lsccom.com Web site: www.lsccom.com.

Lubrecht & Cramer, Ltd., (*978-0-934454; 978-0-945345*) P.O. Box 3110, Port Jervis, NY 12771-0176 USA; Orders Addr.: 2749 Albany Post Rd., Montgomery, NY 12549 USA (SAN 214-1256) Toll Free: 800-920-9334; Edit Addr.: 350 Fifth Ave., Suite 3304, New York, NY 10118-0069 USA E-mail: lubrecht@frontiernet.net; books@lubrechtcramer.com Web site: http://www.lubrechtcramer.com.

Luciano Bks., 13111 NW Le Jeune, Opa Locka, FL 33054 USA (SAN 631-2829) Tel 305-769-3103.

Ludington News Co., 1600 E. Grand Blvd., Detroit, MI 48211-3195 USA (SAN 169-3751) Tel 313-929-7600.

Lukeman Literary Management, Ltd., (*978-0-9829537; 978-0-9839778; 978-0-9849753; 978-1-939416; 978-1-63291; 978-1-64029; 978-1-0943*) 157 Bedford Ave., Brooklyn, NY 11211 USA Tel 718-599-8988; Fax: 775-264-2189 E-mail: noah@lukeman.com.

Lulu Enterprises Inc., *See* **Lulu Pr., Inc.**

Lulu Pr., Inc., *(978-1-4116; 978-1-84728; 978-1-4303; 978-1-4357; 978-1-60552; 978-0-557; 978-1-4583; 978-1-257; 978-1-105; 978-1-300; 978-1-4834; 978-1-304; 978-1-312; 978-1-326; 978-1-329; 978-1-365; 978-1-5342; 978-0-692-97338-7; 978-0-359; 978-0-578-42336-4; 978-1-68470; 978-1-68471; 978-1-68474; 978-1-716; 978-0-578-73052-3) 627 Davis Dr. Suite 300, Morrisville, NC 27560 USA Tel 919-459-5858 919-447-3198; 26-28 Hammersmith Grove, London, W6 7BA* E-mail: rbraynin@lulu.com; dllamas@lulu.com.

Lushena Bks., *(978-1-930097; 978-1-63182)* 607 Country Club Dr., Unit E, Bensenville, IL 60106 USA (SAN 630-5105) Tel 630-238-8708; Fax: 630-238-8824 E-mail: Lushenabks@yahoo.com Web site: http://www.lushenabks.com/.

Lyrical Liquor Productions, Orders Addr.: 7212 15th Ave., Takoma Park, MD 20912 USA Tel 202-723-1317 E-mail: llp@speakeasypublishing.com.

M & J Bk. Fair Service, 2307 Sherwood Cir., Minneapolis, MN 55431 USA (SAN 169-4030).

M & M News Agency, Orders Addr.: P.O. Box 1129, La Salle, IL 61301 USA (SAN 169-2062) Fax: 815-223-2828; Toll Free: 800-245-6247.

M L E S, *See* **Pathway Bk. Service**

Ma'ayan, *See* **WellSpring Bks.**

MacGregor News Agency, 1733 Industrial Park Dr., Mount Pleasant, MI 48858 USA (SAN 169-3921) Toll Free: 800-626-1982.

Mackin Bk. Co., 615 Travelers Trail W., Burnsville, MN 55337 USA (SAN 631-3442).

Mackin Educational Resources, *(978-1-62170; 978-1-62353)* 3505 CR 42 W., Burnsville, MN 55306 USA Tel 800-245-9540 E-mail: developers@mackin.com Web site: http://www.mackin.com/.

Mackin Library Media, 3505 County Rd. 42 W., Burnsville, MN 55306-3804 USA (SAN 134-8795) Toll Free: 800-245-9540 E-mail: mackin@mackin.com Web site: http://www.mackin.com.

Macmillan, *(978-0-374; 978-1-4668; 978-1-68274)* Div. of Holtzbrinck Publishing, Orders Addr.: 16365 James Madison Hwy., Gordonsville, VA 22942 USA (SAN 631-5011) Tel 540-672-7600; Fax: 540-672-7664; 540-672-7540 (Customer Service); Toll Free Fax: 800-672-2054 (Order Dept.); Toll Free: 888-330-8477; Edit Addr.: 175 Fifth Ave., 20th Flr., New York, NY 10010 USA Tel 212-674-5151; Fax: 212-677-6487; Toll Free Fax: 800-258-2769; Toll Free: 800-488-5233 E-mail: customerservice@mpsvirginia.com Web site: http://www.macmillan.com.

Macmillan USA, *See* **Alpha Bks.**

MacRae's Indian Bk. Distributor, 1605 Cole St., P.O. Box 652, Enumclaw, WA 98022 USA (SAN 157-5473) Tel 360-825-3737.

Madden Corp., The, *(978-1-61710)* 94-411 Koaki St., Waipahu, HI 96797 USA.

Madison Art Center, Incorporated, *See* **Madison Museum of Contemporary Art**

Madison Museum of Contemporary Art, *(978-0-913883)* 222 W. Washington Ave. Ste. 350, Madison, WI 53703-2719 USA E-mail: mac@itis.com Web site: http://www.madisonartcenter.org.

Magazine Distributors, Inc., 15 Sparks St., Plainville, CT 06062 USA (SAN 169-0817).

Magazines, Inc., 1135 Hammond St., Bangor, ME 04401 USA (SAN 169-3034) Tel 207-942-8237; Fax: 207-942-9226; Toll Free: 800-649-9224 (in Maine) E-mail: pam@mint.net.

Mahoning Valley Distributing Agency, Inc., 2556 Rush Blvd., Youngstown, OH 44507 USA Tel 330-788-6162; Fax: 330-788-9046.

Main Trail Productions, P.O. Box 365, Clearwater, MN 55320 USA.

Maine Writers & Pubs. Alliance, *(978-0-9618592)* P.O. Box 9301, Portland, ME 04104-9301 USA (SAN 224-2303).

Majic Enterprises, 2232 S. 11th St., Niles, MI 49120-4410 USA (SAN 169-8508).

Majors, J. A. Co., Orders Addr.: 1401 Lakeway Dr., Lewisville, TX 75057 USA (SAN 169-8117) Tel 972-353-1100; Fax: 972-353-1300; Toll Free: 800-633-1851 E-mail: dallas@majors.com Web site: http://www.majors.com.

Majors Scientific Bks., Inc., P.O. Box 35705, Dallas, TX 75235-0705 USA Toll Free: 800-633-1851 E-mail: dallas@majors.com Web site: http://www.majors.com.

Manchester News Co., Inc., P.O. Box 4838, Manchester, NH 03108-4838 USA (SAN 169-4480).

Manhattan Publishing Co., Div. of U.S. & Europe Bks., Inc., P.O. Box 850, Croton-on-Hudson, NY 10520 USA (SAN 113-7476) Tel 914-271-5194; Fax: 914-271-5856 Web site: http://www.manhattanpublishing.com.

Manitowoc News Agency, 907 S. Eighth St., Manitowoc, WI 54220 USA (SAN 159-9046).

Manning's Bks. & Prints, 580M Crespi Dr., Pacifica, CA 94044 USA (SAN 157-5384) Fax: 650-355-1851 E-mail: manningsbks@aol.com Web site: http://www.printsoldandrare.com.

Many Feathers Bks. & Maps, 2626 W. Indian School Rd., Phoenix, AZ 85017 USA (SAN 158-8877) Tel 602-266-1043; Toll Free: 800-279-7652.

Map Link, *See* **Benchmark LLC**

Maple Press Co., 1000 Strickler Rd., Mount Joy, PA 17552 USA Tel 717-653-5483; Edit Addr.: P.O. Box 2695, York, PA 17406 USA Tel 717-764-5911; Fax: 717-764-4702; 480 Willow Springs Ln., York, PA 17406.

Marangio, Charles F. Distribution, Orders Addr.: P.O. Box 3643, Sonoro, CA 95370 USA (SAN 631-3965) Tel 209-533-0997; Edit Addr.: 659 Sanguinetti Rd., Sonoro, CA 95370 USA (SAN 631-3973).

Marco Bk. Co., *(978-0-9710756; 978-0-9729765)* 60 Industrail Rd., Lodi, NJ 07644 USA Tel 973-458-0485; Fax: 973-458-5289; Toll Free: 800-842-4234 E-mail: everbind5@aol.com.

Marco Bk. Distributors, *(978-0-88298)* 60 Industrial Rd., Lodi, NJ 07644 USA (SAN 169-5142) Tel 973-458-0485; Fax: 973-458-5289; Toll Free: 800-842-4234 Web site: http://www.everbind.com.

MAR*CO Products, Inc., *(978-1-57543; 978-1-884063)* Orders Addr.: 1443 Old York Rd., Warminster, PA 18974 USA Tel 215-956-0313; Fax: 215-956-9041; Toll Free: 800-448-2197 E-mail: csfunk@marcoproducts.com; marcoproducts@comcast.net Web site: http://www.store.yahoo.com/marcoproducts; http://www.marcoproducts.com.

Marcus Wholesale, P.O. Box 1618, R49 E. Hwy. 4, Murphys, CA 95247 USA (SAN 185-0296).

Mardelva News Co., Inc., 8999 Ocean Hwy., Delmar, MD 21875 USA (SAN 169-3247) Tel 410-742-8613; Fax: 410-742-2616.

Marshall Cavendish Corp., *(978-0-7614; 978-0-85685; 978-0-86307; 978-1-85435; 978-1-60870)* Member of Times Publishing Group, 99 White Plains Rd., Tarrytown, NY 10591-9001 USA (SAN 238-437X) Tel 914-332-8888; Fax: 914-332-8882; Toll Free: 800-821-9881 E-mail: mce@marshallcavendish.com Web site: www.MCEducation.us.

Marshall-Mangold Distribution Co., Inc., 4805 Nelson Ave., Baltimore, MD 21215-2507 USA (SAN 169-3115) Toll Free: 800-972-2665.

Marvin Law Bk., 11020 27th Ave., S., Burnsville, MN 55337 USA (SAN 163-898X) Tel 612-644-2236.

Mascot Bks., Inc., *(978-0-9743442; 978-1-932888; 978-1-934878; 978-1-936319; 978-1-937406; 978-1-62086; 978-1-63177; 978-1-68401; 978-1-64307; 978-1-64543)* 620 Herndon Pkwy. Suite 320, Herndon, VA 20170 USA Tel 703-437-3584; Fax: 703-437-3554; Toll Free: 877-862-7568 E-mail: debbie@mascotbooks.com; naren@mascotbooks.com; kristin@mascotbooks.com Web site: http://www.mascotbooks.com.

Master Communications, Inc., *(978-1-888194; 978-1-60480)* 2692 Madison Rd., Suite N1-307 N1-307, Cincinnati, OH 45208 USA (SAN 299-2140) Tel 513-563-3100; Fax: 513-563-3105; Toll Free: 800-765-5885 E-mail: sales@master-comm.com Web site: http://www.worldculturemedia.com; http://www.master-comm.com.

Master Teacher, One Leadership Ln., Manhattan, KS 66505-1207 USA Web site: http://www.masterteacher.com.

Mastery Education, *(978-1-56256; 978-1-58984; 978-1-4138; 978-1-61526; 978-1-61527; 978-1-936025; 978-1-936026; 978-1-936027; 978-1-936028; 978-1-936029; 978-1-936030; 978-1-936031; 978-0-692-00207-0; 978-0-692-00208-7; 978-0-692-00209-4; 978-0-692-00210-0; 978-1-61602; 978-1-61734; 978-1-60979; 978-1-64090) Orders Addr.: P.O. Box 513, Saddle Brook, NJ 07633 USA Tel 201-712-0090; Fax: 201-712-1534; Toll Free: 800-822-1080; Edit Addr.: 299 Market St. Suite 240, Saddle Brook, NJ 07663 USA (SAN 857-9873)* E-mail: solvier@peoplesed.com; sales@peoplesed.com; customersupport@peoplesed.com; editorial@peoplesed.com Web site: http://www.masteryeducation.com/.

Mastery Education Corporation, *See* **Charlesbridge Publishing, Inc.**

Matagiri Sri Aurobindo Ctr., *(978-0-89071)* 2288 Fulton St., No. 310, Berkeley, CA 94704-1449 USA (SAN 169-5541).

Matthews Medical Bk. Co., Orders Addr.: 10 Old Bloomfield Ave., Pine Brook, NJ 07058 USA; 11559 Rock Island Ct., Maryland Heights, MO 63043 (SAN 146-4655) Tel 314-432-1400; Fax: 314-432-7044 E-mail: mlc@mattmccoy.com Web site: http://www.mattmccoy.com.

Maxwell Scientific International, Inc., *(978-0-8277)* Div. of Pergamon Pr., Inc., 1345 Ave. of the Americas, No. 1036C, New York, NY 10105-0302 USA (SAN 169-524X) Tel 914-592-9141.

May, L. B. & Assocs., 3517 Neal Dr., Knoxville, TN 37918 USA Tel 865-922-7490; Fax: 865-922-7492 E-mail: lbmay@aol.com.

MBI Distribution Services/Quayside Distribution, *(978-0-7603; 978-0-87938; 978-0-912612; 978-1-85010)* Div. of MBI Publishing Co. LLC, Orders Addr.: P.O. Box 1, Osceola, WI 54020-0001 USA (SAN 169-9164) Toll Free: 800-458-0454; Edit Addr.: 400 First Ave., N, Suite 300, Minneapolis, MN 55401 USA Toll Free: 800-328-0590 Web site: http://www.motorbooks.com.

MBS Textbook Exchange, Inc., Orders Addr.: 2711 W. Ash St., Columbia, MO 65203-4613 USA (SAN 140-7015) Tel 573-445-2243; Fax: 573-446-5254; Toll Free: 800-325-0929 (orders); 800-325-0530 (customer service); Edit Addr.: 2711 W. Ash St., Columbia, MO 65203 USA E-mail: kyates@mbsbooks.com Web site: http://www.mbsbooks.com.

McCaslin, Boyce, 3 Greenbriar Dr., Saint Louis, MO 63124-1819 USA (SAN 110-8298).

McCoy Church Goods, 1010 Howard Ave., San Mateo, CA 94401 USA (SAN 107-2315) Tel 415-342-0924.

McCrory's Books, *See* **McCrory's Wholesale Bks.**

McCrory's Wholesale Bks., Orders Addr.: P.O. Box 2032, Alexandria, LA 71301 USA (SAN 108-5999); Edit Addr.: 1808 Rapides Ave., Alexandria, LA 71301 USA.

McEvoy Group, The, 680 Second St., San Francisco, CA 94107 USA Tel 415-537-4300 E-mail: info@mcevoygroup.com Web site: http://mcevoygroup.com.

McGraw-Hill Cos., The, *(978-0-07)* 6480 Jimmy Carter Blvd., Norcross, GA 30071-1701 USA (SAN 254-881X) Tel 614-755-5637; Fax: 614-755-5611; Orders Addr.: 860 Taylor Station Rd., Blacklick, OH 43004-0545 USA (SAN 200-254X) Fax: 614-755-5645; Toll Free: 800-722-4726 (orders & customer service); 800-338-3987 (college); 800-525-5003 (subscriptions); 800-352-3566 (books - US/Canada orders); P.O. Box 545, Blacklick, OH 43004-0545 Fax: 614-759-3759; Toll Free: 877-833-5524; a/o General Customer Service, P.O. Box 182604, Columbus, OH 43272 Fax: 614-759-3759; Toll Free: 877-833-5524 E-mail: customer.service@mcgraw-hill.com Web site: http://www.mcgraw-hill.com; http://www.ebooks.mcgraw-hill.com/.

McGraw-Hill Create (TM), *(978-0-390)* Div. of McGraw-Hill Higher Education, 148 Princeton-Hightstown Rd., Hightstown, NJ 08520-1450 USA Tel 609-426-5721; Toll Free: 800-962-9342 Web site: http://www.mhhe.com.

McGraw-Hill Education, *(978-1-259; 978-1-260; 978-1-264; 978-1-265; 978-1-266)* Two Penn Plaza, New York, NY 10121-2298 USA Tel 212-904-2000; a/o The Mcgraw-Hill Companies, 8787 Orion Pl., Columbus, OH 43240 (SAN 256-3908) Tel 614-755-5637; Fax: 614-755-5611; Level 33, 680 George Street, Sydney, NSW 2000 E-mail: customer.service@mcgraw-hill.com Web site: http://www.mheducation.com/custserv.html; http://www.mcgraw-hill.com.

McGraw-Hill Health Professions Division, *See* **McGraw-Hill Medical Publishing Div.**

McGraw-Hill Higher Education, *(978-0-07; 978-1-121)* Orders Addr.: P.O. Box 545, Blacklick, OH 43004-0545 USA Toll Free: 800-338-3987; Edit Addr.: 1333 Burr Ridge Pkwy., 3rd Flr., Burr Ridge, IL 60527 USA E-mail: customer.service@mcgraw-hill.com Web site: http://www.mhhe.com.

McGraw-Hill Medical Publishing Div., *(978-0-07)* Div. of The McGraw-Hill Cos., Orders Addr.: P.O. Box 545, Blacklick, OH 43004-0545 USA Fax: 614-755-5645 (customer service); Toll Free: 800-262-4729 (customer service); 800-722-4726 (bookstores & libraries) E-mail: customerservice@mcgraw-hill.com Web site: http://www.mghmedical.com.

McGraw-Hill Osborne, *(978-0-07; 978-0-88134; 978-0-931988)* Div. of The McGraw-Hill Professional, 160 Spear St. Flr. 7, San Francisco, CA 94105-1544 USA (SAN 274-3450) Toll Free: 800-227-0900 E-mail: customer.service@mcgraw-hill.com Web site: http://www.osborne.com.

McGraw-Hill Primis Custom Publishing, *See* **McGraw-Hill Create (TM)**

McGraw-Hill Professional Publishing, *(978-0-07)* Div. of McGraw-Hill Higher Education, Orders Addr.: P.O. Box 545, Blacklick, OH 43004-0545 USA Fax: 614-755-5645; Toll Free: 800-722-4726; Edit Addr.: 2 Penn Plaza, New York, NY 10121-2298 USA Tel 212-904-2000.

McGraw-Hill Trade, *(978-0-07; 978-0-658; 978-0-8442)* Div. of McGraw-Hill Professional, Orders Addr.: P.O. Box 545, Blacklick, OH 43004-0545 USA Tel 800-722-4726; Fax: 614-755-5645; Edit Addr.: 2 Penn Plaza, New York, NY 10121 USA Tel 212-904-2000 E-mail: Jeffrey_Krames@mcgraw-hill.com Web site: http://www.books.mcgraw-hill.com.

McGraw-Hill US Higher Ed USE, P.O. Box 182605, Columbus, OH 43218 USA.

McGraw-Hill US Higher Ed USE Legacy, P.O. Box 182605, Columbus, OH 43218 USA.

McGraw-Hill/Contemporary, *(978-0-658; 978-0-8092; 978-0-8325; 978-0-8442; 978-0-88499; 978-0-89061; 978-0-913327; 978-0-940279; 978-0-941263; 978-0-9630646; 978-1-56626; 978-1-56943; 978-1-57028)* Div. of McGraw-Hill Higher Education, Orders Addr.: P.O. Box 545, Blacklick, OH 43004-0545 USA Toll Free Fax: 800-998-3103; Toll Free: 800-621-1918; Edit Addr.: 4255 W. Touhy Ave., Lincolnwood, IL 60712 USA (SAN 169-2208) Tel 847-679-5500; Fax: 847-679-2494; Toll Free Fax: 800-998-3103; Toll Free: 800-323-4900 E-mail: ntcpub@tribune.com Web site: http://www.ntc-cb.com.

McKay, David Co., Inc., *(978-0-679; 978-0-88326; 978-0-89440)* Subs. of Random Hse., Inc., Orders Addr.: 400 Hahn Rd., Westminster, MD 21157 USA Tel 410-848-1900; Toll Free: 800-733-3000 (orders only); Edit Addr.: 201 E. 50th St., MD 4-6, New York, NY 10022 USA (SAN 200-240X) Tel 212-751-2600; Fax: 212-872-8026.

McKnight Sales Co., P.O. Box 4138, Pittsburgh, PA 15202 USA (SAN 169-7587) Tel 412-761-4443; Fax: 412-761-0122; Toll Free: 800-208-8078 E-mail: sales@mscmags.com Web site: http://www.mscmags.com.

McLemore, Hollern & Assocs., 3538 Maple Park Dr., Kingwood, TX 77339 USA Tel 281-360-5204.

McMillen Bk. Distributors, 304 Main St., Ames, IA 50010 USA Fax: 515-232-0402; Toll Free: 866-385-2027.

MeadWestvaco, Orders Addr.: 4751 Hempstead Sta., Kettering, OH 45429 USA Tel 937-495-6323 Web site: http://us.meadwestvaco.com.

MediaTech Productions, *(978-0-9702309)* 917 E. Prospect Rd. Unit B, Fort Collins, CO 80525-1364 USA Toll Free: 800-816-7566 Do not confuse with companies with the same or similar name in Chicago, IL E-mail: maury@mediatechproductions.com Web site: http://mediatechproductions.com.

Medical Information Systems, Inc., 2 Seaview Blvd., Port Washington, NY 11050 USA (SAN 242-1720) Tel 516-621-7200 Do not confuse with Medical Information Systems, Inc., Stamford, CT.

Medicina Biologica, 2937 NE Flanders St., Portland, OR 97232 USA (SAN 113-0226) Tel 503-287-6775; Fax: 503-235-3520 E-mail: med_bio@imagina.com.

Mel Bay Pubns., Inc., *(978-0-7866; 978-0-87166; 978-1-56222; 978-1-60974; 978-1-61065; 978-1-61911; 978-1-5134)* 1734 Gilsinn Ln., Fenton, MO 63026 USA (SAN 657-3630) Tel 636-257-3970; Fax: 636-257-5062; Toll Free: 800-863-5229 E-mail: email@melbay.com; sharon@melbay.com Web site: http://www.melbay.com; www.melbaydealers.com.

Melton Book Company, Incorporated, *See* **Nelson Direct**

Mentor Bks., 5318 Lowell Blvd., Denver, CO 80221 USA Fax: 303-975-1936; Toll Free: 800-795-6198 E-mail: blair@mentorbooks.com.

Merced News Co., 1324 Coldwell Ave., Modesto, CA 95350-5702 USA (SAN 168-9894) Tel 209-722-5791.

Mercedes Book Distributors Corporation, *See* **Mercedes Distribution Ctr., Inc.**

Mercedes Distribution Ctr., Inc., Brooklyn Navy Yard, Bldg. No. 3, Brooklyn, NY 11205 USA (SAN 169-5150) Tel 718-534-3000; Fax: 718-935-9647; Toll Free: 800-339-4804 E-mail: contact@mdist.com.

Meredith Bks., *(978-0-696; 978-0-89721; 978-0-917102)* Div. of Meredith Corp., Orders Addr.: 1716 Locust St., LN-110, Des Moines, IA 50309-3023 USA (SAN 202-4055) Tel 515-284-2363; 515-284-2126 (sales); Fax: 515-284-3371; Toll Free: 800-678-8091 Do not confuse with Meredith Pr. in Skaneateles, NY E-mail: John.OBannon@meredith.com Web site: http://www.bhgstore.com.

Merkos Pubns., Div. of Merkos L'Inyonei Chinuch, 291 Kingston Ave., Brooklyn, NY 11213 USA (SAN 631-1040) Tel 718-778-0226; Fax: 718-778-4148.

Merry Thoughts, *(978-0-88230)* 364 Adams St., Bedford Hills, NY 10507 USA (SAN 169-5061) Tel 914-241-0447; Fax: 914-241-0247.

Messianic Jewish Resources International, Orders Addr.: P.O. Box 1539, Fort Lee, NJ 07024-1539 USA Fax: 201-840-7242; Toll Free: 800-410-7367.

Meta Co., LLC, P.O. Box 2667, Columbia, MD 21045 USA.

Metamorphosis Publishing Company, *See* **Metamorphous Pr., Inc.**

Metamorphous Pr., Inc., *(978-0-943920; 978-1-55552)* Orders Addr.: P.O. Box 10616, Portland, OR 97296-0616 USA (SAN 110-8786) Tel 503-228-4972; Fax: 503-223-9117; Toll Free: 800-937-7771 (orders only); Edit Addr.: P.O. Box 10616, Portland, OR 97296-0616 USA E-mail: metabooks@metamodels.com Web site: http://www.metamodels.com.

Metro Systems, 3381 Stevens Creek Blvd., Suite 209, San Jose, CA 95117 USA (SAN 631-1016) Tel 408-247-4050; Fax: 408-247-4236.

Metropolitan News Co., 47-25 34th, Long Island City, NY 11101 USA (SAN 159-9089) Do not confuse with Metropolitan News Co. in Los Angeles, CA.

Mi Lybro, 9775 Marconi Dr., Suite D, San Diego, CA 92154 USA Tel 619-900-7624 E-mail: sales@milybro.com.

Miami Bks., Inc., 17842 State Rd. 9, Miami, FL 33162 USA (SAN 106-8997) Tel 305-652-3231.

Miami Valley News Agency, 2127 Old Troy Pike, Dayton, OH 45404 USA (SAN 169-6718) Fax: 513-233-8544; Toll Free: 800-791-5137.

Michiana News Service, 2232 S. 11th St., Niles, MI 49120 USA (SAN 110-5051) Tel 616-684-3013; Fax: 616-684-8740.

Michigan Church Supply, P.O. Box 279, Mount Morris, MI 48458-0279 USA (SAN 184-413X) Toll Free: 800-521-3440.

Michigan State Univ. Pr., *(978-0-87013; 978-0-937191; 978-1-60917; 978-1-61186; 978-1-938065; 978-1-62895; 978-1-62896; 978-1-941258; 978-0-9967252; 978-1-68430; 978-1-947134; 978-1-948314)* Orders Addr.: 1405 S. Harrison Rd. Suite 25, East Lansing, MI 48823-5245 USA (SAN 202-6295) Tel 517-884-6901; Fax: 517-432-2611; Toll Free: 800-621-2736; 800-621-8476 E-mail: msupress@msupress.org Web site: http://www.msupress.org.

Mickler's Bks., Inc., 61 Alafaya Woods Blvd., No. 197, Oviedo, FL 32765 USA Tel 407-365-8500; Toll Free Fax: 800-726-0585 E-mail: orders@micklers.com Web site: http://www.micklers.com.

Micklers Floridiana, Incorporated, *See* **Mickler's Bks., Inc.**

Microdistributors International, Inc., *(978-0-918025)* Subs. of Medcomp Technologies, Inc., 34 Maple Ave., P.O. Box 8, Armonk, NY 10504 USA (SAN 296-158X) Tel 914-273-6480.

Mid Penn Magazine Agency, 100 Eck Cir., Williamsport, PA 17701 USA (SAN 169-7692).

Mid South Manufacturing Agency, Incorporated, *See* **Mid-South Magazine Agency, Inc.**

Mid-Cal Periodical Distributors, P.O. Box 245230, Sacramento, CA 95824-5230 USA (SAN 169-0078).

Midpoint National, Inc., 1263 Southwest Blvd., Kansas City, MO 66103-1901 USA (SAN 630-9860) Tel 913-831-2233; Fax: 913-362-7401; Toll Free: 800-228-4321.

Midpoint Trade Bks., Inc., *(978-1-940416)* Orders Addr.: 1263 Southwest Blvd., Kansas City, KS 66103 USA (SAN 631-3736) Tel 913-831-2233; Fax: 913-362-7401; Toll Free: 800-742-6139 (consumer orders); Edit Addr.: 27 W. 20th St., No. 1102, New York, NY 10011 USA (SAN 631-1075) Tel 212-727-0190; Fax: 212-727-0195
E-mail: info@midpointtrade.com
Web site: http://www.midpointtrade.com; http://www.midpointtradebooks.com/.

Mid-South Magazine Agency, Inc., P.O. Box 4585, Jackson, MS 39296-4585 USA (SAN 286-0163) Toll Free: 800-748-9444.

Mid-State Periodicals, Inc., P.O. Box 3455, Quincy, IL 62305-3455 USA Tel 217-222-0833; Fax: 217-222-1256.

Mid-States Distributors, P.O. Box 1374, Chambersburg, PA 17201-5374 USA (SAN 169-3166).

Midtown Auto Bks., 212 Burnet Ave., Syracuse, NY 13203 USA (SAN 169-6289).

Midwest European Pubns., 915 Foster St., Evanston, IL 60201 USA (SAN 169-1937) Tel 847-866-6289; Fax: 847-866-6290; Toll Free: 800-380-8919
E-mail: info@mep-eli.com
Web site: http://www.mep-eli.com.

Midwest Library Service, 11443 St. Charles Rock Rd., Bridgeton, MO 63044-2789 USA (SAN 169-4243) Tel 314-739-3100; Fax: 314-739-1326; Toll Free Fax: 800-962-1009; Toll Free: 800-325-8833
E-mail: hudson@midwestls.com.

Midwest Tape, Orders Addr.: P.O. Box 820, Holland, OH 43528-0820 USA (SAN 254-9913) Toll Free Fax: 800-444-6645; Toll Free: 800-875-2785
E-mail: randys@midwesttapes.com
Web site: http://www.midwesttapes.com.

MightyWords, Inc., *(978-1-58895; 978-0-7173; 978-1-4036)* 2850 Walsh Ave., Santa Clara, CA 95051 USA Tel 408-845-0100; Fax: 408-845-0425; Toll Free: 877-328-2724
Web site: http://www.mightywords.com.

Mightywords.com, *See* **MightyWords, Inc.**

Military History Assocs., 407B E. Sixth St., No. 200, Austin, TX 78701-3739 USA (SAN 111-7866).

Miller Educational Materials, *(978-1-934274)* Orders Addr.: P.O. Box 2428, Buena Park, CA 90621 USA Fax: 714-562-0237; Toll Free: 800-636-4375; Edit Addr.: 3294 Cherry Ave., Long Beach, CA 90807-5214 USA (SAN 631-5445)
E-mail: MillerEdu@aol.com
Web site: http://www.millereducational.com.

Miller Trade Bk. Marketing, 363 W. Erie St. Ste. 700E, Chicago, IL 60610-6996 USA (SAN 631-4287)
E-mail: millertrade@sbcglobal.net.

Milligan News Co., Inc., 150 N. Autumn St., San Jose, CA 95110 USA (SAN 169-0272) Tel 408-286-7604; Fax: 408-298-0235; Toll Free: 800-873-2387.

Millmark Education, *(978-1-4334; 978-1-61618)* Orders Addr.: 7272 Wisconsin Ave, Suite 300, Bethesda, MD 20814-2081 USA (SAN 852-4912) Tel 301-941-1974; Fax: 301-656-0183; Edit Addr.: 7272 Wisconsin Ave. Suite 300, Suite 300, Bethesda, MD 20814-2081 USA
E-mail: rachel.moir@millmarkeducation.com; info@millmarkeducation.com
Web site: http://www.millmarkeducation.com/.

Mind Trip Pr., P.O. Box 489, Georgetown, TX 78626 USA Tel 513-428-9278.

Minerva Science Bookseller, Inc., 175 Fifth Ave., New York, NY 10010 USA (SAN 286-0171).

Mint Pubs. Group, Orders Addr.: 62 June Rd., Suite 241, North Salem, NY 10560 USA Tel 914-276-6576; Fax: 914-276-6579; Edit Addr.: 1220 Nicholson Rd., Newmarket, ON I3Y 7VI CAN Toll Free Fax: 800-363-2665; Toll Free: 800-399-6858
E-mail: info@mintpub.com
Web site: http://www.mintpub.com.

Mintright, Inc., *(978-1-4687)* 55 W. 26th St., Suite 36D, New York, NY 10010 USA (SAN 935-4840) Tel 646-368-8090; Fax: 646-368-8099
E-mail: content@mintright.com
Web site: http://mintright.com/.

Mission Resource Ctr., 1221 Profit Dr., Dallas, TX 75247 USA Toll Free: 800-305-9857.

Mississippi Library Media & Supply Co., P.O. Box 108, Brandon, MS 39043-0108 USA (SAN 169-4189) Tel 601-824-1900; Fax: 601-824-1999; Toll Free: 800-257-7566 (in Mississippi).

Mistco, Inc., P.O. Box 694854, Miami, FL 33269 USA (SAN 630-8384) Tel 305-653-2003; Fax: 305-653-2037; Toll Free: 800-552-0446
E-mail: mistco@worldnet.att.net
Web site: http://www.mistco.com.

Mobile News Co., 1118 14th St., Tuscaloosa, AL 35401-3318 USA (SAN 168-924X) Tel 334-479-1435.

Modern Curriculum Pr., *(978-0-7652; 978-0-8136; 978-0-87895)* Div. of Pearson Education, Orders Addr.: P.O. Box 2500, Lebanon, IN 46052-3009 USA (SAN 206-6572) Toll Free: 800-526-9907 (Customer Service)
Web site: http://www.pearsonlearning.com.

Modesto News Co., 1324 Coldwell Ave., Modesto, CA 95350-5702 USA (SAN 168-9908) Tel 209-577-5551.

Montfort Pubns., *(978-0-910984)* Div. of Montfort Missionaries, 26 S. Saxon Ave., Bay Shore, NY 11706-8993 USA (SAN 169-5053) Tel 631-665-0726; Fax: 631-665-4349
E-mail: info@montfortpublications.com
Web site: http://www.montfortmissionaries.com; http://www.montfortmissionaries.org; http://www.montfortpublications.com.

Mook & Blanchard, P.O. Box 4177, La Puente, CA 91747-4177 USA (SAN 168-9703) Toll Free: 800-875-9911
E-mail: mookbook@ix.netcom.com
Web site: http://www.mookandblanchard.com.

Moon Over the Mountain Publishing Company, *See* **Leman Pubns., Inc.**

More, Thomas Assn., 205 W. Monroe St., 5th Flr., Chicago, IL 60606-5097 USA (SAN 169-1880) Tel 312-609-8880; Toll Free: 800-835-8965.

Morlock News Co., Inc., 496 Duanesburg Rd., Schenectady, NY 12306 USA (SAN 169-6246).

Morris Publishing, *(978-0-7392; 978-0-9631249; 978-1-57502; 978-1-885591; 978-0-9863567)* Orders Addr.: P.O. Box 2110, Kearney, NE 68847 USA Fax: 308-237-0263; Toll Free: 800-650-7888 Do not confuse with companies with the same Wesley Chapel, FL, Elkhart, IN
Web site: http://www.morrispublishing.com.

Moshy Brothers, Inc., 127 W. 25th St., New York, NY 10001 USA (SAN 169-5886) Tel 212-255-0613.

Mother Lode Distributing, 17890 Lime Rock Dr., Sonora, CA 95370-8707 USA (SAN 169-0361).

Motorbooks International Wholesalers & Distributors, *See* **MBI Distribution Services/Quayside Distribution**

Mountain Bk. Co., P.O. Box 778, Broomfield, CO 80038-0778 USA Tel 303-436-1982; Fax: 917-386-2769
E-mail: wordguise@aol.com
Web site: http://www.mountainbook.org.

Mountain n' Air Bks., *(978-1-879415)* Div. of Mountain n' Air Sports, Inc., Orders Addr.: P.O. Box 12540, La Crescenta, CA 91224 USA (SAN 630-5598) Tel 818-248-9345; Toll Free Fax: 800-303-5578; Toll Free: 800-446-9696; Edit Addr.: 2947-A Hololulu Ave., La Crescenta, CA 91214 USA (SAN 631-4198)
E-mail: books@mountain-n-air.com
Web site: http://mountain-n-air.com.

Mountain Pr. Publishing Co., Inc., *(978-0-87842)* Orders Addr.: P.O. Box 2399, Missoula, MT 59806-2399 USA (SAN 202-8832) Tel 406-728-1900; Fax: 406-728-1635; Toll Free: 800-234-5308; Edit Addr.: 1301 S. Third West, Missoula, MT 59801 USA (SAN 662-0868)
E-mail: jrimel@mtnpress.com; info@mtnpress.com; anne@mtnpress.com
Web site: http://www.mountain-press.com.

Mountain States News Distributor, P.O. Drawer P, Fort Collins, CO 80522 USA Tel 970-221-2330; Fax: 970-221-1251.

Mouse Works, *(978-0-7364; 978-1-57082)* Div. of Disney Bk. Publishing, Inc., A Walt Disney Co., 114 Fifth Ave., New York, NY 10011 USA (SAN 298-0797) Tel 212-633-4400; Fax: 212-633-4811
Web site: http://www.disneybooks.com.

MPS, 16365 James Madison Hwy., Gordonsville, VA 22942-8501 USA Toll Free Fax: 800-672-2054; Toll Free: 888-330-8477.

Mr. Paperback/Publishers News Co., 6030 Fostoria Ave., Findlay, OH 45840 USA (SAN 169-393X) Tel 419-424-6774; Fax: 419-420-1805; Toll Free: 800-872-0031.

M-S News Co., Inc., P.O. Box 13278, Wichita, KS 67213-0278 USA Fax: 316-267-5405.

Mullare News Agency, Inc., P.O. Box 578, Brockton, MA 02401 USA (SAN 169-3379) Tel 508-580-1000; Fax: 508-586-0968.

Multi-Cultural Bks. & Videos, Inc., *(978-0-9656274)* 30007 John R. Rd., Madison Hts, MI 48071-2526 USA (SAN 760-6796) Toll Free: 800-567-2220
E-mail: service@multiculbv.com
Web site: http://www.multiculbv.com.

Multilingual Bks., Orders Addr.: P.O. Box 440632, Miami, FL 33144 USA (SAN 169-1155) Tel 305-471-9847 Do not confuse with Multilingual Bks., Seattle, WA.

Mumford Library Bks., Inc., 7847 Bayberry Rd., Jacksonville, FL 32256 USA (SAN 156-7721) Fax: 904-730-8913; Toll Free: 800-367-3927.

Mumford Library Book Sales, *See* **Mumford Library Bks., Inc.**

Murr's Library Service, 4045 E. Palm Ln., No. 5, Phoenix, AZ 85008-3116 USA (SAN 107-3222) Fax: 602-273-1217; Toll Free: 888-273-0279.

Music, Bks. & Business, Inc., Orders Addr.: 4305 32nd St W Suite A, Bradenton, FL 34205 USA (SAN 760-5986) Fax: 941-752-8994; Toll Free: 888-876-7716
E-mail: info@musicbooksbusiness.com
Web site: http://www.musicbooksbusiness.com.

Music Design, Inc., 4650 N. Port Washington Rd., Milwaukee, WI 53212 USA (SAN 200-7649) Tel 414-961-8380; Fax: 414-961-8381; Toll Free: 800-862-7232
E-mail: order@musicdesign.com
Web site: http://www.musicdesign.com.

Music in Motion, P.O. Box 869231, Plano, TX 75086-9231 USA (SAN 631-4589) Fax: 972-943-8906; Toll Free Fax: 866-943-8906; Toll Free: 800-445-0649 Do not confuse with Music In Motion, Ithaca, NY
Web site: http://www.musicmotion.com.

Music is Elementary, *(978-0-9721085; 978-0-9910656; 978-0-9966913; 978-0-90589-0)* P.O. Box 24263, Cleveland, OH 44124 USA Tel 440-442-4475; Fax: 440-461-3631; Toll Free: 800-888-7502
E-mail: music@en.com
Web site: http://www.musiciselementary.com.

Music Sales Corp., *(978-0-7119; 978-0-8256; 978-1-84609)* Orders Addr.: 445 Bellvale Rd., P.O. Box 572, Chester, NY 10918 USA (SAN 662-0876) Tel 845-469-2271; Fax: 845-469-7544; Toll Free Fax: 800-345-6842; Toll Free: 800-431-7187; Edit Addr.: 257 Park Ave., S., 20th Flr., New York, NY 10010 USA (SAN 282-0277) Tel 212-254-2100; Fax: 212-254-2103
E-mail: info@musicsales.com
Web site: http://www.musicroom.com; http://www.musicsales.com.

Music Video Distributors, *See* **MVD Entertainment Group**

Musicart West, P.O. Box 1900, Orem, UT 84059-1900 USA (SAN 110-1250) Tel 801-225-0859; Toll Free: 800-950-1900 (orders only).

MVD Entertainment Group, Orders Addr.: 203 Windsor Rd., Limerick, PA 19464 USA (SAN 255-2663) Tel 610-650-8200; Fax: 610-650-9102; Toll Free: 800-888-0486
E-mail: musviddis@aol.com
Web site: http://www.musicvideodistributors.com.

MVP Wholesales, 9301 W. Hwy. 290, No. D, Austin, TX 78736-7817 USA (SAN 630-9550) Tel 512-416-1452; Toll Free: 800-328-7931 (phone/fax).

MyiLibrary, *(978-1-280; 978-1-281; 978-1-282; 978-1-283; 978-1-299; 978-1-306; 978-1-322; 978-1-336)* Div. of Coutts Information Services, 14 Ingram Blvd., La Vergne, TN 37086 USA Tel 615-213-5400; Fax: 615-213-5111
E-mail: wendell.lotz@ingramcontent.com.

myON, 5050 Lincoln Dr., Suite 200, Edina, MN 55436 USA Toll Free: 800-864-3899.

NACSCORP, Incorporated, *See* **.**

Najarian Music Co., Inc., 236 Partridge Ln., Concord, MA 01742-2651 USA (SAN 169-3344).

Napa Book Company, *See* **Napa Children's Bk. Co.**

Napa Children's Bk. Co., 1239 First St., Napa, CA 94559 USA (SAN 122-2732) Tel 707-224-3893; Fax: 707-224-1212.

Nasco Math Eighty-Six, 901 Janesville Ave., Fort Atkinson, WI 53538 USA (SAN 679-7512).

National Academies Pr., *(978-0-309)* Orders Addr.: 8700 Spectrum Dr., Landover, MD 20785 USA; Edit Addr.: 500 Fifth St., NW Lockbox 285, Washington, DC 20001 USA (SAN 202-8891) Tel 202-334-3313; Fax: 202-334-2451; Toll Free: 888-624-7654
E-mail: zjones@nas.edu
Web site: http://www.nap.edu.

National Academy Press, *See* **National Academies Pr.**

National Assn. of the Deaf, *(978-0-913072)* 8630 Fenton St. Ste. 820, Silver Spring, MD 20910-3819 USA (SAN 159-4974)
E-mail: donna.morris@nad.org
Web site: http://www.nad.org.

National Bk. Co., Keystone Industrial Pk., Scranton, PA 18512 USA Tel 717-346-2020; Toll Free: 800-233-4830 Do not confuse with National Book Company, Portland, OR.

National Bk. Network, Div. of Rowman & Littlefield Pubs., Inc., Orders Addr.: 15200 NBN Way, Blue Ridge Summit, PA 17214 USA (SAN 630-0065) Tel 717-794-3800; Fax: 717-794-3828; Toll Free Fax: 800-338-4550 (Customer Service); Toll Free: 800-462-6420 (Customer Service); a/o Les Petriw, 67 Mowat Ave., Suite 241, Toronto, ON M6P 3K3 Tel 416-534-1660; Fax: 416-534-3699
E-mail: custserv@nbnbooks.com
Web site: http://www.nbnbooks.com.

National Catholic Reading Distributor, 997 Macarthur Blvd., Mahwah, NJ 07430 USA (SAN 169-4855) Tel 201-825-7300; Fax: 201-825-8345; Toll Free: 800-218-1903
E-mail: paulistp@pipeline.com.

National Educational Systems, Inc., *(978-1-893493)* P.O. Box 691450, San Antonio, TX 78269-1450 USA Toll Free: 800-442-2604.

National Film Network LLC, *(978-0-8026)* Orders Addr.: 4501 Forbes Blvd., Lanham, MD 20706 USA (SAN 630-1878) Tel 301-459-8020 ext 2066
E-mail: info@nationalfilmnetwork.com
Web site: http://www.nationalfilmnetwork.com.

National Health Federation, Box 688, Monrovia, CA 91016 USA (SAN 227-9266) Tel 626-357-2181; Fax: 818-303-0642
E-mail: nhf@earthlink.net
Web site: http://www.healthfreedom.net.

National Learning Corp., *(978-0-8293; 978-0-8373; 978-1-7318; 978-1-7993)* 212 Michael Dr., Syosset, NY 11791 USA (SAN 206-8869) Tel 516-921-8888; Fax: 516-921-8743; Toll Free: 800-645-6337
E-mail: sales@passbooks.com
Web site: nlcpassbooks@aim.com.

National Magazine Service, Orders Addr.: P.O. Box 834, Mars, PA 16046 USA (SAN 169-7595); Edit Addr.: 535 Linden Way, Pittsburgh, PA 15202 USA Tel 412-898-0001.

National Organization Service, Inc., P.O. Box 2007, Birmingham, AL 35201-2007 USA (SAN 107-1548) Toll Free: 800-747-3032.

National Rifle Assn., *(978-0-935998)* a/o Office of the General Counsel, 11250 Waples Mill Rd., Fairfax, VA 22030 USA (SAN 213-859X) Tel 703-267-1250; Fax: 703-267-3985; Toll Free: 800-672-3888
E-mail: ndowd@nrahq.org.

National Sales, Inc., 1818 W. 2300 South, Salt Lake City, UT 84119 USA (SAN 159-9127) Tel 801-972-2300; Fax: 801-972-2883.

National School Products, 1523 Old Niles Ferry Rd., Maryville, TN 37803 USA
Web site: http://nationalschoolproducts.com/.

National Technical Information Service, U.S. Dept. of Commerce, *(978-0-934213; 978-1-935239)* Orders Addr.: 5285 Port Royal Rd., Springfield, VA 22161 USA (SAN 205-7255) Tel 703-605-6000; Fax: 703-605-6900; Toll Free: 800-553-6847
E-mail: orders@ntis.gov; info@ntis.gov
Web site: http://www.ntis.gov; http://wnc.fedworld.gov.

Native Bks., P.O. Box 37095, Honolulu, HI 96837 USA (SAN 631-1121) Tel 808-845-8949; Fax: 808-847-6637; Toll Free: 800-887-7751.

Natural Math, 309 Silvercliff Trail, Cary, NC 27513 USA
E-mail: reach.out@naturalmath.com.

Naval Institute Pr., *(978-0-87021; 978-1-55750; 978-1-59114; 978-1-61251; 978-1-68247; 978-1-68269)* Orders Addr.: 291 Wood Rd, Annapolis, MD 21402-5034 USA (SAN 662-0930) Tel 410-268-6110; Fax: 410-295-1084; Toll Free: 800-233-8764; Edit Addr.: 291 Wood Rd., Beach Hall, Annapolis, MD 21402-5034 USA (SAN 202-9006)
E-mail: tskord@usni.org; books@usni.org
Web site: http://www.usni.org.

Nazarene Publishing House, *See* **The Foundry Publishing**

Neal-Schuman Pubs., Inc., *(978-0-918212; 978-1-55570)* Div. of American Library Assn., 100 William St., Suite 2004, New York, NY 10038 USA (SAN 210-2455) Tel 212-925-8650; Fax: 212-219-8916; Toll Free Fax: 800-584-2414
E-mail: info@neal-schuman.com
Web site: http://www.neal-schuman.com.

Neeland Media, LLC, 3921 Harvard Rd., Lawrence, KS 66049 USA Tel 913-548-6825.

Neighborhood Periodical Club, Inc., P.O. Box 830, Clementon, NJ 08021-0860 USA (SAN 285-9262).

Nelson Direct, P.O. Box 140300, Nashville, TN 37214 USA (SAN 169-8133) Toll Free: 800-441-0511 (sales); 800-933-9673
E-mail: csalazar@thomasnelson.com
Web site: http://www.nelsondirect.com.

Nelson News, Inc., P.O. Box 27007, Omaha, NE 68127-0007 USA (SAN 169-443X) Tel 402-734-3333; Fax: 402-731-0516.

Nelson, Thomas Inc., *(978-0-529; 978-0-7852; 978-0-8407; 978-0-8499; 978-0-86605; 978-0-88113; 978-0-89840; 978-0-89922; 978-0-918956; 978-0-7180; 978-1-4002; 978-1-4003; 978-1-4016; 978-1-59145; 978-1-4041; 978-1-59554; 978-1-59555; 978-1-4185; 978-1-59951; 978-1-4261; 978-1-60255; 978-1-4845; 978-1-5000; 978-1-5314; 978-1-6623) Div. of HarperCollins Christian Publishing, Orders Addr.: P.O. Box 141000, Nashville, TN 37214-1000 USA (SAN 209-3820) Fax: 615-902-1866; Toll Free: 800-251-4000; Edit Addr.: 501 Nelson Pl., Nashville, TN 37214 USA*
Web site: http://www.harpercollinschristian.com.

Nelson's Bks., *(978-0-9612188)* P.O. Box 2352, Santa Cruz, CA 95063 USA (SAN 289-4858) Tel 831-465-9148.

Ner Tamid Bk. Distributors, P.O. Box 10401, Riviera Beach, FL 33419-0401 USA (SAN 169-135X) Tel 561-686-9095.

Net Productions, 210 Elm Cir., Colorado Springs, CO 80906-3348 USA (SAN 159-9143).

NetLibrary, Incorporated, *See* **Ebsco Publishing**

NetSource Distribution, Orders Addr.: 675 Dutchess Tpke., Poughkeepsie, NY 12603 USA Tel 845-463-1100 x314; Fax: 845-463-0018; Toll Free: 800-724-1100
Web site: http://www.hudsonhousepub.com.

New Alexandrian Bookstore, 110 N Cayuga St., Ithaca, NY 14850-4331 USA (SAN 159-4958) Tel 607-272-1163.

New Concepts Bks. & Tapes Distributors, Orders Addr.: P.O. Box 55068, Houston, TX 77255 USA (SAN 114-2682) Tel 713-465-7736; Fax: 713-465-7106; Toll Free: 800-842-4807; Edit Addr.: 9722 Pine Lake, Houston, TX 77055 USA (SAN 630-7531).

New Day Christian Distributors, *See* **New Day Christian Distributors Gifts, Inc.**

New Day Christian Distributors Gifts, Inc., *(978-0-692-10672-3)* 124 Shivel Dr., Hendersonville, TN 37075 USA (SAN 631-2551) Tel 615-822-3633; Fax: 615-822-5829; Toll Free: 800-251-3633; 126 Shivel Dr., Hendersonville, TN 37075 (SAN 920-6604).

New England Bk. Service, Inc., 7000 Vt Route 17 W., Vergennes, VT 05491-4408 USA (SAN 170-0952) Toll Free: 800-356-5772
E-mail: nebs@together.net.

New England Mobile Bk. Fair, 82 Needham St., P.O. Box 610159, Newton Highlands, MA 02461 USA (SAN 169-3530) Tel 617-527-5817; Fax: 617-527-0113.

New Jersey Bk. Agency, Orders Addr.: P.O. Box 144, Morris Plains, NJ 07950 USA (SAN 106-861X) Tel 973-267-7093; Fax: 973-292-3177; Edit Addr.: 7 Somerset Hills Ct. Apt. D, Bernardsville, NJ 07924-2619 USA (SAN 243-2307).

New Jersey Bks., Inc., 59 Market St., Newark, NJ 07102 USA Tel 973-624-8070; Toll Free: 800-772-3678.

New Leaf Distributing Co., Inc., *(978-0-9627209)* Div. of Al-Wali Corp., 401 Thornton Rd., Lithia Springs, GA 30122-1557 USA (SAN 169-1449) Tel 770-948-7845; Fax: 770-944-2313; Toll Free Fax: 800-326-1066; Toll Free: 800-326-2665
E-mail: santoshk@msn.com; alimt@bellsouth.net
Web site: http://www.NewLeaf-dist.com.

New Leaf Press, Incorporated, *See* **New Leaf Publishing Group**

New Leaf Publishing Group, *(978-0-89051; 978-0-89221; 978-1-61458; 978-1-68344)* P.O. Box 726, Green Forest, AR 72638 USA (SAN 207-9518) Tel 870-438-5288; Fax: 870-438-5120 Toll Free: 800-643-9535; 800-999-3777 Do not confuse with companies with the same or similar name in Los Angeles, CAStone Mountain, GA
E-mail: nlp@nlpg.com
Web site: http://www.nlpg.com; http://www.masterbooks.com.

New Leaf Resources, 2102 Button Ln., Unit 2, Lagrange, KY 40031 USA Toll Free: 800-346-3087
E-mail: info@newleaf-resources.com
Web site: http://www.newleaf-resources.com.

New Life Foundation, *(978-0-911203; 978-1-934162)* P.O. Box 2230, Pine, AZ 85544-2230 USA (SAN 170-3986) Tel 928-476-3224; Fax: 928-476-4743; Toll Free: 800-293-3377 (wholesale only)
E-mail: info@anewlife.org
Web site: http://www.anewlife.org.

New Shelves Distribution, 103 Remsen St., Cohoes, NY 12047 USA Tel 518-391-2300; Fax: 518-391-2365
Web site: http://www.newshelvesdistribution.com.

New Tradition Bks., *(978-0-9728473; 978-1-932420; 978-0-9845418)* 627 Brickle Ridge Rd., Decatur, TN 37322 USA
E-mail: newtraditionbooks@yahoo.com.

New World Library, *(978-0-931432; 978-0-945934; 978-1-57731; 978-1-880032; 978-1-60868)* 14 Pamaron Way, Novato, CA 94949 USA (SAN 211-8777) Tel 415-884-2100; Fax: 415-884-2199; Toll Free: 800-972-6657 (retail orders only) Do not confuse with New World Library Publishing Co., Los Altos, CA
E-mail: escort@nwlib.com
Web site: http://www.newworldlibrary.com.

New World Resource Ctr., P.O. Box 25310, Chicago, IL 60625-0310 USA (SAN 169-1848).

New York Periodical Distributors, P.O. Box 29, Massena, NY 13662-0029 USA (SAN 169-6149).

New York Univ. Pr., *(978-0-8147; 978-1-4798)* Div. of New York Univ., Orders Addr.: 838 Broadway, 3rd Flr., New York, NY 10003-4812 USA (SAN 658-1293) Tel 212-998-2575; Fax: 212-995-3833; Toll Free: 800-996-6987 (ordering)
E-mail: orders@nyupress.org
Web site: http://www.nyupress.org.

Newborn Enterprises, Inc., P.O. Box 1713, Altoona, PA 16603 USA (SAN 169-7242) Tel 814-944-3593; Fax: 814-944-1881; Toll Free: 800-227-0285 (in Pennsylvania).

NewLife Bk. Distributors, 2969 Spalding Dr., Suite 100, Atlanta, GA 30350 USA (SAN 169-121X) Tel 404-207-5280
E-mail: lifebooks@mindspring.com
Web site: http://www.newlifebookdistributors.com.

News Group, 15 N. Spring St., #2, Bloomfield, NJ 07003 USA.

News Group - Illinois, The, 1301 SW Washington St., Peoria, IL 61602 USA (SAN 169-216X) Tel 309-673-4549; Fax: 309-673-8883.

News Group, The, *See* **American News Company**

News Supply Co., 216 S. La Huerta Cir., Carlsbad, NM 88220-9620 USA (SAN 159-9151).

Newsdealers Supply Co., Inc., P.O. Box 3516, Tallahassee, FL 32315-3516 USA.

NEWSouth Distributors, P.O. Box 61297, Jacksonville, FL 32236-1297 USA (SAN 159-8732).

Newsstand Distributors, 155 W. 14th St., Ogden, UT 84404 USA (SAN 169-8494) Fax: 810-621-7336; Toll Free: 800-283-6247; 800-231-4834 (in Utah).

Ng Hing Kee, 648 Jackson St., San Francisco, CA 94133 USA (SAN 107-1084) Tel 415-781-8330; Fax: 415-397-9766.

Niagara Collectibles, 3727 Lower River Rd., Youngstown, NY 14174 USA
E-mail: nansimon@roadrunner.com.

Niagara County News, 70 Nicholls St., Lockport, NY 14094 USA (SAN 169-541X) Tel 716-433-6466.

Night Heron Media, *(978-0-9704729; 978-0-9709987; 978-1-931721; 978-1-933979; 978-1-936474; 978-1-939055; 978-1-942945)* Orders Addr.: 2365 Rice Blvd., Suite 202, Houston, TX 77005 USA Tel 713-533-9300; Fax: 713-528-2432 Do not confuse with Breakaway Bks., Halcottsville, NY
E-mail: info@nightheronmedia.org
Web site: www.nightheronmedia.org.

Noelke, Carl B., 529 Main, Box 563, La Crosse, WI 54602 USA (SAN 111-8315) Tel 608-782-8544.

Nonagon, 1556 Douglas Dr., El Cerrito, CA 94530 USA (SAN 654-0503) Tel 510-237-5290.

Nonetheless Pr., *(978-1-932053)* 20332 W. 98th St., Lenexa, KS 66220-2650 USA Tel 913-254-7266; Fax: 913-393-3245
E-mail: mschutte@nonethelesspress.com
Web site: http://www.nonethelesspress.com; http://www.lookingglasspress.com.

Nor-Cal News Co., 2040 Petaluma Blvd., P.O. Box 2508, Petaluma, CA 94953 USA (SAN 169-0035) Tel 707-763-2606; Fax: 707-763-3905.

Norfolk SPCA, 916 Ballentine Blvd., Norfolk, VA 23504 USA Tel 757-622-3319
Web site: http://www.norfolkspca.com.

North American Bk. Distributors, P.O. Box 510, Hamburg, MI 48139 USA (SAN 630-4680) Tel 810-231-3728.

North Carolina News Co., P.O. Box 1051, Durham, NC 27702-1051 USA Tel 919-682-5779.

North Carolina Schl. Bk. Depository, Inc., P.O. Box 950, Raleigh, NC 27602-0950 USA (SAN 169-6467) Tel 919-833-6615.

North Central Bk. Distributors, N57 W13636 Carmen Ave., Menomonee Falls, WI 53051 USA (SAN 173-5195) Tel 414-781-3299; Fax: 414-781-4432; Toll Free: 800-966-3299.

North Country Bks., Inc., *(978-0-925168; 978-0-932052; 978-0-9601158; 978-1-59531)* 220 Lafayette Street, Utica, NY 13502 USA (SAN 110-828X) Tel 315-735-4877; Fax: (315) 738-4342
E-mail: ncbooks@verizon.net
Web site: http://www.northcountrybooks.com.

North Shore Distributors, 1200 N. Branch, Chicago, IL 60622 USA (SAN 169-2275).

North Shore News Co., Inc., 150 Blossom St., Lynn, MA 01902 USA (SAN 169-3492).

North Star Editions, *(978-0-9848801; 978-0-9886491; 978-1-939967; 978-1-63163; 978-1-63517; 978-1-63583; 978-1-64185; 978-1-64493; 978-1-64494; 978-1-64619; 978-1-952455)* Subs. of Big Timber Media, 1600 Cliff Rd. E, Burnsville, MN 55337 USA (SAN 990-2325) Tel 952-446-7222
E-mail: info@northstareditions.com
Web site: www.fluxnow.com; www.northstareditions.com; www.focusreaders.com.

North Texas Periodicals, Inc., Orders Addr.: P.O. Box 3823, Lubbock, TX 79452 USA Tel 806-745-6000; Fax: 806-745-7028; Edit Addr.: 118 E. 70th St., Lubbock, TX 79404 USA
E-mail: ntp@hts-online.net.

Northern News Co., P.O. Box 467, Petoskey, MI 49770-0467 USA (SAN 169-3964) Toll Free: 800-632-7138 (Michigan only).

Northern Schl. Supply Co., P.O. Box 2627, Fargo, ND 58108 USA (SAN 169-6548) Fax: 800-891-5836.

Northern Sun, 2916 E. Lake St., Minneapolis, MN 55406 USA (SAN 249-9290) Tel 612-729-2001; Fax: 612-729-0149; Toll Free: 800-258-8579
Web site: http://www.northernsun.com/.

Northern Sun Merchandising, *See* **Northern Sun**

North-South Bks., Inc., *(978-0-7358; 978-1-55858; 978-1-58717)* 350 7th Ave. Rm. 1400, New York, NY 10001-5013 USA
E-mail: mnavarro@northsouth.com
Web site: http://www.northsouth.com.

Northwest News, 1560 NE First St., No. 13, Bend, OR 97701 USA (SAN 111-8587) Tel 541-382-6065; 3100 Merriman Rd., Medford, OR 97501 Tel 541-779-5225.

Northwest News Company, Incorporated, *See* **Benjamin News Group**

Northwest Textbook Depository, Orders Addr.: P.O. Box 5608, Portland, OR 97228 USA Toll Free: 800-676-6630; Edit Addr.: 17970 SW McEwan Rd., Portland, OR 97224 USA (SAN 631-4481) Tel 503-639-3193; Fax: 503-639-2559.

Northwestern Univ. Pr., *(978-0-8101)* Orders Addr.: c/o Univ. of Chicago Pr. Distribution Ctr., 11030 S. Langley Ave., Chicago, IL 60628 USA Tel 773-568-1550; Fax: 773-660-2235; Toll Free Fax: 800-621-8476; Toll Free: 800-621-2736; Edit Addr.: 629 Noyes St., Evanston, IL 60208-4210 USA (SAN 202-5787) Tel 847-491-5313; 847-491.2046; Fax: 847-491-8150
E-mail: nupress@northwestern.edu
Web site: http://www.nupress.northwestern.edu.

Norton News Agency, 905 Kelly Ln., Dubuque, IA 52003-8526 USA (SAN 169-2631); 1467 Service Dr., Winona, MN 55987 (SAN 156-4889).

Norton, W. W. & Co., Inc., *(978-0-393; 978-0-88150; 978-0-914378; 978-0-936399; 978-0-942440; 978-1-58157; 978-1-324; 978-1-68268)* Orders Addr.: c/o National Book Company, 800 Keystone Industrial Pk., Scranton, PA 18512 USA (SAN 157-1869) Tel 570-346-2029; Fax: 570-346-1442; Toll Free Fax: 800-458-6515; Toll Free: 800-233-4830; Edit Addr.: 500 Fifth Ave., New York, NY 10110-0017 USA (SAN 202-5795) Tel 212-354-5500; Fax: 212-869-0856; Toll Free: 800-223-2584
Web site: http://www.wwnorton.com.

Notions Marketing, 1500 Buchanan Ave., SW, Grand Rapids, MI 49507-1613 USA.

NTC/Contemporary Publishing Company, *See* **McGraw-Hill/Contemporary**

Nueces News Agency, 5130 Commerce Pkwy., San Antonio, TX 78218-5523 USA (SAN 169-8079).

Nueva Vida Distributors, 4300 Montana Ave., El Paso, TX 79903-4503 USA (SAN 107-8615) Tel 915-565-6215; Fax: 915-565-1722.

Nutri-Bks. Corp., Div. of Royal Pubns., Inc., 790 W. Tennessee Ave., P.O. Box 5793, Denver, CO 80223 USA Tel 303-778-8383; Fax: 303-744-9383; Toll Free: 800-279-2048 (orders only).

Oak Knoll Pr., *(978-0-938768; 978-1-884718; 978-1-58456; 978-1-872116)* 310 Delaware St., New Castle, DE 19720 USA (SAN 216-2776) Tel 302-328-7232; Fax: 302-328-7274; Toll Free: 800-996-2556 Do not confuse with Oak Knoll Press in Hardy, VA
E-mail: oakknoll@oakknoll.com
Web site: http://www.oakknoll.com.

Octagon Pr./ISHK Bk. Service, *See* **I S H K**

Ohio Periodical Distributors, P.O. Box 145449, Cincinnati, OH 45250-5449 USA (SAN 169-6904) Fax: 513-853-6245; Toll Free: 800-777-2216.

Ohio Univ. Pr., *(978-0-8214)* Orders Addr.: 11030 S. Langley Ave., Chicago, IL 60628 USA Tel 773-702-7000; Fax: 773-702-7212; Toll Free Fax: 800-621-8476; Toll Free: 800-621-2736; Edit Addr.: 19 Circle Dr. The Ridges, Athens, OH 45701 USA (SAN 282-0773) Tel 740-593-1154; Fax: 740-593-4536
Web site: https://www.ohioswallow.com/.

Oil City News Co., 112 Innis St., Oil City, PA 16301-2930 USA (SAN 169-7501).

Oleand Pubns., P.O. Box 375, Lyons, WI 53148 USA Tel 262-342-0018 (phone/fax)
E-mail: wings@oleand.com.

Ollis Bk. Corp., Orders Addr.: P.O. Box 258, Steger, IL 60475 USA (SAN 658-1323); Edit Addr.: 28 E. 35th St., Steger, IL 60475 USA (SAN 169-2224) Tel 312-755-5151; Fax: 708-755-5153; Toll Free: 800-323-0343.

Olson, D & Company, *See* **Nelson's Bks.**

Olson News Agency, P.O. Box 129, Ishpeming, MI 49849 USA (SAN 169-3832).

Omega Pubns., Inc., *(978-0-930872; 978-1-941810)* 34 Amity Pl., Amherst, MA 01002-2255 USA (SAN 214-1493) Toll Free: 888-443-7107 (orders only) Do not confuse with companies with the same name in Medford, OR, Indianapolis, IN
E-mail: sufibooks@omegapub.com
Web site: http://www.omegapub.com.

Omnibooks, 456 Vista Del Mar Dr., Aptos, CA 95003-4832 USA (SAN 168-9487) Tel 408-688-4098; Toll Free: 800-626-6671.

Omnibus Pr., *(978-0-7119; 978-0-8256; 978-0-86001; 978-1-84449)* Div. of Music Sales Corp., Orders Addr.: 445 Bellvale Rd., Chester, NY 10918-0572 USA Tel 845-469-4699; Fax: 845-469-7544; Toll Free Fax: 800-345-6842; Toll Free: 800-431-7187; Edit Addr.: 257 Park Ave., S., 20th Flr., New York, NY 10010 USA Tel 212-254-2100; Fax: 212-254-2013 Do not confuse with Omnibus Pr., Menasha, WI
E-mail: info@musicsales.com
Web site: http://www.musicsales.com.

One Small Voice Foundation, P.O. Box 644, Elmhurst, IL 60126 USA Tel 630-620-6634
E-mail: onesmallvoice@earthlink.net
Web site: htp://www.onesmallvoicefoundation.org.

Onondaga News Agency, P.O. Box 6445, Syracuse, NY 13217-6445 USA (SAN 169-6297).

OPA Publishing & Distributing, Orders Addr.: P.O. Box 1764, Chandler, AZ 85244-1764 USA; Edit Addr.: 777 W. Chandler Blvd., Suite 1322, Chandler, AZ 85244-1764 USA.

Open Road Distribution, Div. of Open Road Integrated Media, Inc., 345 Hudson St., Suite 6C, New York, NY 10014 USA Tel 212-691-0900; Fax: 212-691-0901.

Open Road Integrated Media, Inc., *(978-1-58586; 978-0-7592; 978-1-936317; 978-1-4532; 978-1-61756; 978-0-9832929; 978-1-937624; 978-1-937957; 978-1-938582; 978-0-615-65097-5; 978-1-62467; 978-1-4804; 978-1-4976; 978-1-5040)* 180 Varick St. Suite 816, New York, NY 10014 USA Tel 212-691-0900; Fax: 212-691-0901; 345 Hudson St., Suite 6C, New York, NY 10014 Tel 212-691-0900; Fax: 212-691-0901
E-mail: acolvin@openroadmedia.com
Web site: http://www.openroadmedia.com.

Options Unlimited, 550 Swan Creek Ct., Suwanee, GA 30174 USA (SAN 631-3949) Tel 770-237-3282 Do not confuse with Options Unlimited, Inc., Green Bay, WI.

OptumInsight, Inc., *(978-1-56329; 978-1-56337; 978-1-60151; 978-1-62254)* 2525 Lake Park Blvd., West Valley City, UT 84120 USA (SAN 630-5482) Tel 801-982-3000; Toll Free: 800-464-3649 (phone/fax)
E-mail: jeni.smith@ingenix.com; chris.smith@ingenix.com; jean.parkinson@ingenix.com
Web site: http://www.ingenix.com; http://www.IngenixOnline.com.

Orange News Company, *See* **Anderson News, LLC**

Orbit Bks. Corp., 43 Timberline Dr., Poughkeepsie, NY 12603 USA (SAN 169-6157) Tel 914-462-5653; Fax: 914-462-8409.

Orca Bk. Pubs. USA, *(978-0-920501; 978-1-55143; 978-1-55469)* Orders Addr.: P.O. Box 468, Custer, WA 98240-0468 USA (SAN 630-9674) Tel 250-380-1229; Fax: 250-380-1892; Toll Free: 800-210-5277
E-mail: orca@orcabook.com
Web site: http://www.orcabook.com.

O'Reilly & Associates, Incorporated, *See* **O'Reilly Media, Inc.**

O'Reilly Media, Inc., *(978-0-937175; 978-1-56592; 978-3-89721; 978-3-930673; 978-4-900900; 978-0-596; 978-4-87311; 978-1-60033; 978-1-4493; 978-1-4919; 978-1-4920; 978-1-4571; 978-1-0981)* Orders Addr.: 1005 Gravenstein Hwy. N., Sebastopol, CA 95472 USA (SAN 658-5973) Fax: 707-829-0104; Toll Free: 800-998-9938; Edit Addr.: 10 Fawcett St. Ste. 4, Cambridge, MA 02138-1175 USA Toll Free: 800-775-7731; 4 Castle St, Farnham, GU9 7HR Tel 01252 71 17 76; Fax: 01252 73 42 11; c/o Madeleine Fakhoury Editions O'Reilly, 18, rue Seguier, Paris, F-75006 Tel 33 1 40 51 52 30; Fax: 33 1 40 51 52 31; c/o Michelle Chen, SIGMA Building, Suite B809 No. 49 Zhichun Rd. Haidian District, Beijing, 100080 Tel 86-10-88097476; 86-10-88097475; Fax: 86-10-88097463; c/o O'Reilly Verlag, Gerd Miske, Balthasarstr. 81, Köln, D-50670 Tel 49 221 973160 0; Fax: 49 221 973160 8; 1Fl, No. 21, Lane 295 Section 1, Fu-Shing South Rd., Taipei, Tel 886 2 27099669; Fax: 886 2 27038802; Intelligent Plaza Bldg. 1F 26 Banchi 27, Sakamachi, Shinjuku-ku, Tokyo, 160-0002 Tel 81 3 3356 5227; Fax: 81 3 3356 5261
E-mail: order@oreilly.com; information@oreilly.co.uk; nuts@ora.com; isbn-info@oreilly.com
Web site: http://www.oreilly.com; http://www.editions-oreilly.fr; http://oreilly.co.uk; http://oreilly.com.tw; http://www.ora.com; http://www.oreilly.fr/; http://www.oreilly.com.cn/.

Original Pubns., *(978-0-942272)* Subs. of Maximo, Inc., 129 Forest Dr., Jericho, NY 11753-2324 USA (SAN 133-0225) Toll Free: 888-622-8581.

Osborne Enterprises Publishing, *(978-0-932117)* P.O. Box 255, Port Townsend, WA 98368 USA (SAN 242-7567) Tel 360-385-1200; Toll Free: 800-246-3255 (orders only)
E-mail: jpo@olympus.net
Web site: http://www.jerryosborne.com.

Osborne/McGraw-Hill, *See* **McGraw-Hill Osborne**

Osiander Bk. Trade, 7483H Candlewood Rd., Hanover, MD 21076-3102 USA (SAN 130-0970).

Outbooks, Incorporated, *See* **Vistabooks**

Outdoorsman, The, Orders Addr.: P.O. Box 268, Boston, MA 02134 USA (SAN 169-3352).

Outskirts Pr., Inc., *(978-0-9725874; 978-1-932672; 978-1-59800; 978-1-4327; 978-0-615-20388-1; 978-1-4787; 978-1-9772)* 10940 S. Parker Rd. - 515, Parker, CO 80134 USA (SAN 256-5420)
Web site: http://www.OutskirtsPress.com.

Outskirts Press, Incorporation, *See* **Outskirts Pr., Inc.**

OverDrive, Inc., Valley Tech Ctr. 8555 Sweet Valley Dr., Cleveland, OH 44125-4210 USA (SAN 245-0658) Tel 216-573-6886; Fax: 216-573-6888
Web site: http://www.overdrive.com.

OverDrive Systems, Incorporated, *See* **OverDrive, Inc.**

Overmountain Pr., *(978-0-932807; 978-0-9644613; 978-1-57072; 978-1-935692)* P.O. Box 1261, Johnson City, TN 37605 USA (SAN 687-6641) Tel 423-926-2691; Fax: 423-232-1252; Toll Free: 800-992-2691 (orders only)
E-mail: beth@overmtn.com
Web site: http://www.silverdaggermysteries.com; http://www.overmountainpress.com.

Oxford Univ. Pr., Inc., *(978-0-19; 978-0-87893; 978-1-60535)* Orders Addr.: 2001 Evans Rd., Cary, NC 27513 USA (SAN 202-5892) Tel 919-677-0977 (general voice); Fax: 919-677-1303 (customer service); Toll Free: 800-445-9714 (customer service - inquiry); 800-451-7556 (customer service - orders); Edit Addr.: 198 Madison Ave., New York, NY 10016-4314 USA (SAN 202-5884) Tel 212-726-6000 (general voice); Fax: 212-726-6440 (general fax)
E-mail: custserv@oup-usa.org; orders@oup-usa.org
Web site: http://www.oup.com/us.

Oxford University Press USA - OSO, Orders Addr.: 2001 Evans Rd., Cary, NC 27513 USA Toll Free: 800-451-7556.

Oxmoor Hse., Inc., *(978-0-376; 978-0-8487)* Orders Addr.: Leisure Arts 5701 Ranch Dr., Little Rock, AR 72223 USA; Edit Addr.: 2100 Lakeshore Dr., Birmingham, AL 35209 USA Tel 205-445-6000; Fax: 205-445-6078; Toll Free: 800-633-4910
E-mail: allison_lowery@timeinc.com
Web site: http://www.oxmoorhouse.com/.

Ozark Bk. Distributors, 1802 Van Buren Ave., Mountain Home, AR 72653 USA.

Ozark Magazine Distributing, Incorporated, *See* **Ozark News Distributor, Inc.**

Ozark News Agency, Inc., P.O. Box 1150, Fayetteville, AR 72702 USA.

Ozark News Distributor, Inc., 1630 N. Eldon Ave., Springfield, MO 65803 USA (SAN 169-4332) Tel 417-862-9224; Fax: 417-862-6642; Toll Free: 800-743-0380.

P & G Wholesale, P.O. Box 1548, Fargo, ND 58102 USA (SAN 156-4536).

P & R Publishing, *(978-0-87552; 978-1-59638; 978-1-62995)* Orders Addr.: 1102 Marble Hill Rd., Harmony, Phillipsburg, NJ 08865 USA (SAN 658-1463) Tel 908-454-0505; Fax: 908-859-2390; Toll Free: 800-631-0094 Do not confuse with P & R Publishing Co. in Sioux Center, IA
E-mail: tara@prpbooks.com; jesse@prpbooks.com
Web site: http://www.prpbooks.com.

P C I Education, *(978-1-884074; 978-1-58804; 978-1-61975)* 4560 Lockhill-Selma, Suite 100, San Antonio, TX 78265-4270 USA Tel 210-377-1999; Fax: 210-377-1121; Toll Free Fax: 888-259-8284; Toll Free: 800-594-4263
E-mail: lboulet@pcieducation.com
Web site: http://www.pcieducation.com.

P C I Educational Publishing, *See* **P C I Education**

P. D. Music Headquarters, Inc., Orders Addr.: P.O. Box 252, New York, NY 10014 USA (SAN 282-5880) Tel 212-242-5322.

Pacific Island Bks., 2802 E. 132nd Cir., Thornton, CO 80241 USA Fax: 603-368-6628; Toll Free: 888-492-6657 (888-49-BOOKS)
E-mail: pacificbks@aol.com
Web site: http://www.pacificislandbooks.com.

Pacific Learning, Inc., *(978-1-59055; 978-1-60457; 978-1-61391; 978-1-59055-000-7)* Orders Addr.: P.O. Box 2723, Huntington Beach, CA 92647-0723 USA; Edit Addr.: 6262 Katella Ave., Cypress, CA 90630 USA Tel 800-279-0737; Toll Free: 800-279-0737
E-mail: customer.service@pacificlearning.com
Web site: http://www.pacificlearning.com.

Pacific Magazine-Bk. Wholesaler, 1515 NW 51st St., Seattle, WA 98107 USA (SAN 274-3884) Tel 206-789-5333.

Pacific Periodical Services, LLC, *See* **Anderson News - Tacoma**

Pacific Pr. Publishing Assn., *(978-0-8163; 978-1-5180)* P.O. Box 5353, Nampa, ID 83653-5353 USA (SAN 202-8409) Tel 208-465-2500; Fax: 208-465-2531; Toll Free: 800-447-7377
E-mail: donlay@pacificpress.com
Web site: http://www.AdventistBookCenter.com; http://www.pacificpress.com.

Pacific Trade Group, 68-309 Crozier Dr., Waialua, HI 96791 USA (SAN 169-1635) Tel 808-636-2300; Fax: 808-636-2301.

Paladin Pr., *(978-0-87364; 978-1-58160; 978-1-891268; 978-1-61004)* Orders Addr.: c/o Gunbarrel Tech Ctr., 7077 Winchester Cir., Boulder, CO 80301 USA (SAN 662-1066) Tel 303-443-7250; Fax: 303-442-8741; Toll Free: 800-392-2400 (Credit Card Orders Only)
E-mail: sales@paladin-press.com; editorial@paladin-press.com; service@paladin-press.com
Web site: http://www.paladin-press.com; http://www.flying-machines.com; http://www.sycamoreisland.com.

Palari Publishing LLP, *(978-1-928662)* Orders Addr.: P.O. Box 9288, Richmond, VA 23227-0288 USA Tel 804-355-1035; Toll Free Fax: 866-570-6724 (on demand); Toll Free: 866-570-6724
E-mail: dave@palaribooks.com
Web site: http://www.palaribooks.com.

Palgrave, *See* **Palgrave Macmillan**

Palgrave Macmillan, *(978-0-312; 978-0-333; 978-1-4039; 978-0-230; 978-1-4472; 978-1-137; 978-1-349; 978-1-78632)* Orders Addr.: 16365 James Madison Hwy., Gordonsville, VA 22942-8501 USA Toll Free Fax: 800-672-2054; Toll Free: 888-330-8477; Edit Addr.: 175 Fifth Ave., New York, NY 10010 USA Tel 212-982-9300; Fax: 212-777-6359; Toll Free Fax: 800 672-2054 (Customer Service); Toll Free: 800-221-7945; 888-330-8477 (Customer Service)
E-mail: customerservice@vhpsva.com
Web site: http://www.palgrave.com.

PALH, *(978-0-9719458; 978-1-953716)* P.O. Box 5099, Santa Monica, CA 90409 USA
E-mail: palh@aol.com
Web site: http://www.palhbooks.com.

Palmer News Co., Inc., 534 S. Kansas Ave. Ste. 700, Topeka, KS 66603-3429 USA.

Palmer News, Inc., 9605 Dice Ln., Lenexa, KS 66215 USA Tel 913-541-8600; Fax: 913-541-9413 E-mail: palmerco@oni.com.

Palmetto News Co., 200 Sunbelt Ct., Greer, SC 29650-9349 USA.

Pan American Publishing, Inc., *(978-1-889867)* 420 E. Ohio St., Suite 4-F, Chicago, IL 60611-3355 USA (SAN 299-1977) Tel 773-404-7282.

Pan Asia Pubns. (USA), Inc., *(978-1-57227)* 29564 Union City Blvd., Union City, CA 94587 USA (SAN 173-685X) Tel 510-475-1185; Fax: 510-475-1489; Toll Free: 800-909-8088 E-mail: sales@panap.com; hchan@panap.com; info@panap.com Web site: http://www.panap.com; http://www.cjkv.com.

Pan De Vida Distributors, *(978-1-934811)* 5507 Brooks St., Montclair, CA 91763 USA (SAN 631-0753) Tel 909-510-5219; 909-510-5200; Fax: 909-510-5210 Web site: http://www.pandevida.com.

Panamericana Publishing LLC, 12902 SW 133 Ct., Suite D, Miami, FL 33186 USA (SAN 256-1409) Tel 305-278-2648; Fax: 305-436-7264 E-mail: operez@panamericana.com.co Web site: http://panamericanaeditorial.com.

Pantheon Bks., *(978-0-375; 978-0-394; 978-0-676; 978-0-679)* Orders Addr.: 400 Hahn Rd., Westminster, MD 21157 USA Toll Free: 800-733-3000 (orders); Edit Addr.: 299 Park Ave, New York, NY 10171 USA (SAN 202-862X).

Paperback Books, Incorporated, *See* **Bk. Distribution Ctr., Inc.**

Paperbacks for Educators, *(978-0-9702376; 978-1-59721)* 426 W. Front St., Washington, MO 63090 USA (SAN 103-3379) Tel 636-239-1999; Fax: 636-239-4515; Toll Free Fax: 800-514-7323; Toll Free: 800-227-2591 E-mail: paperbacks@usmo.com Web site: http://www.any-book-in-print.com.

Paradise Cay Pubns., *(978-0-939837; 978-1-937196)* P.O. Box 29, Arcata, CA 95518-0029 USA (SAN 663-690X) Tel 707-822-9063; Fax: 707-822-9163; Toll Free: 800-736-4509 (orders only) E-mail: jim@paracay.com Web site: http://www.paracay.com.

Parent Services Project, 79 Belvedere St., Suite 101, San Rafael, CA 94901 USA Tel 415-454-1870 E-mail: family@parentservices.org.

Park Pl., 1601 Rio Grande, Suite 455, Austin, TX 78701 USA Web site: http://www.ed311.com.

Parklane Publishing, *(978-1-59384)* Div. of Book Club of America, 100 Marcus Blvd. Ste. 8, Hauppauge, NY 11788-3749 USA E-mail: lbaumert@bookclubusa.com Web site: http://www.parklanepublishing.com.

Parkwest Pubns., Inc., *(978-0-88186)* P.O. Box 310251, Miami, FL 33231 USA (SAN 264-6846) Tel 305-256-7880; Fax: 305-256-7816 E-mail: parkwest@parkwestpubs.com; info@parkwestpubs.com Web site: http://www.parkwestpubs.com.

Parliament News Co., Inc., P.O. Box 910, Santa Clarita, CA 91380-9010 USA (SAN 168-9924).

Parnassus Bk. Distributors, 200 Academy Way, Columbia, SC 29206-1445 USA (SAN 631-0680) Tel 803-782-7748; Toll Free: 800-782-7760.

Partners Distributing, Orders Addr.: 13089 Root Rd., Columbia Station, OH 44028 USA Tel 216-236-3744.

Pathfinder Pr., *(978-0-87348; 978-0-913460; 978-1-60488)* Orders Addr.: P.O. Box 162767, Atlanta, GA 30321-2767 USA Tel 404-669-0600 (voice mail only); Fax: 707-667-1141; Pathfinder Books/Livres Pathfinder 6362 Fraser St. Suite 264, VANCOUVER, BC V5W 0A1 Tel 888-692-4939; Fax: 888-692-4939; 120 Bethnal Green Rd., London, E2 6DG; P.O. Box 10130,75723, Paris, Cedex 15 FRANCE Tel 014-010-2837; Fax: 014-010-2837; Australia Pathfinder Level 1, 3/281-287 Beamish St., Campsie, NSW, NSW 2194 Tel 029-718-9698; Fax: 029-718-9698; Unit 4, 125 Grafton Rd., Grafton, Auckland, none; Edit Addr.: 306 W. 37th St., 10th Flr., New York, NY 10018 USA (SAN 202-5906) Do not confuse with companies with the same or similar names in Alameda, CA, Battle Ground, WA, Ellicott City, MD, Midland, MI E-mail: pathfinder@pathfinderpress.com; permissions@pathfinderpress.com; orders@pathfinderpress.com Web site: http://www.pathfinderpress.com.

Pathway Bk. Service, Div. of MLES, Inc., Orders Addr.: 4 White Brook Rd., Gilsum, NH 03448 USA (SAN 170-0545) Tel 603-357-0236; Fax: 603-357-2073; Toll Free: 800-345-6665; P.O. Box 89, Gilsum, NH 03448; Edit Addr.: 34 Production Ave., Keene, NH 03431 USA (SAN 991-2657) Tel 603-357-0236 E-mail: pbs@pathwaybook.com Web site: http://www.pathwaybook.com.

Pathway Bks., *(978-0-935538)* P.O. Box 27790, Golden Valley, MN 55427-0790 USA (SAN 213-4241) Tel 612-694-9434; Toll Free: 800-958-3375 (Pin 32) Do not confuse with Pathway Books, Gilsum, NH E-mail: shermjim@aol.com Web site: http://www.caregiver911.com.

Paul & Co. Pubs. Consortium, Inc., Div. of Independent Publishers Group, Orders Addr.: 814 N. Franklin St., Chicago, IL 60610 USA Tel 312-337-0747; Fax: 312-337-5985; Toll Free: 800-888-4741 E-mail: frontdesk@ipgbook.com Web site: http://www.ipgbook.com.

Paulsen, G. Co., 27 Sheep Davis Rd., Pembroke, NH 03275 USA (SAN 169-4499) Tel 603-225-9787.

PBD, Inc., *(978-0-9846038; 978-0-9837260; 978-1-62219)* 1650 Bluegrass Lakes Pkwy., Alpharetta, GA 30004 USA (SAN 126-6039) Tel 770-442-8633; Fax: 770-442-9742 Web site: http://www.pbd.com.

PCE International, 8811 Aviation Blvd., Inglewood, CA 90301 USA Tel 310-337-0055; Fax: 310-642-4625; Toll Free: 800-626-1313.

Peabody Essex Museum, *(978-0-87577; 978-0-88389)* Orders Addr.: East India Sq., Salem, MA 01970 USA Tel 978-745-9500 ext 3047; Fax: 978-740-3622; Toll Free: 800-745-4054 ext 3047 E-mail: wholesale@pem.org Web site: http://www.pem.org.

Pearson Education, *(978-0-13; 978-0-582; 978-0-7686; 978-1-5093)* Orders Addr.: 200 Old Tappan Rd., Old Tappan, NJ 07675 USA (SAN 200-2175) Tel 201-767-5000 (Receptionist); Toll Free Fax: 800-445-6991; Toll Free: 800-428-5331; 800-922-0579; Edit Addr.: One Lake St., Upper Saddle River, NJ 07458 USA Tel 201-236-7000; 201-236-5321; Fax: 201-236-6549; 800 E. 96th St., Suite 300, Indianapolis, IN 46240 Toll Free: 800-571-4580 E-mail: communications@pearsoned.com Web site: http://www.pearsoned.com; www.pearson.com.

Pearson Learning, *(978-0-7652; 978-1-4284)* Div of Pearson Education, Orders Addr.: P.O. Box 2500, Lebanon, IN 46052 USA Toll Free Fax: 800-393-3156; Toll Free: 800-321-3106; Edit Addr.: 1 Lake St., U Saddle Riv, NJ 07458-1813 USA Toll Free: 800-526-9907 (Customer Service) E-mail: jeff.holtsma@pearsonlearning.com Web site: http://www.pearsonlearning.com.

Pearson School, *See* **Savvas Learning Co.**

Pearson Technology Group, One Lake St., Upper Saddle River, NJ 07458 USA.

Pee Dee News Co., 2321 Lawrens Cir., Florence, SC 29501-9408 USA.

Pegasus Pr., *(978-1-889818)* 2641 S. Emerson St., Chandler, AZ 85248-3248 USA Do not confuse with companies with the same name in Vashon Island, WA, San Diego, CA, Kerrville, TX, Lake Forest, IL E-mail: pegpress@hotmail.com Web site: http://www.pegpress.org.

Pegram, Christine, 1901 Upper Cove Terr., Sarasota, FL 33581 USA (SAN 110-0254) Tel 941-921-2467.

Pekin News Agency, 1637 Monroe St., Madison, WI 53711-2021 USA (SAN 169-2151).

Peller, A. W. & Assocs., 210 Sixth Ave., P.O. Box 106, Hawthorne, NJ 07507-0106 USA (SAN 631-1563) Tel 973-423-4666; Fax: 973-423-5569; Toll Free: 800-451-7450 E-mail: awpeller@worldnet.att.net Web site: http://www.awpeller.com.

Pen Notes, Inc., *(978-0-939564)* 10111 NW 24th Pl. Apt. 201, Sunrise, FL 33322-6882 USA (SAN 107-3621) E-mail: pennotes@worldnet.att.net.

Penguin Group (USA) Incorporated, *See* **Penguin Publishing Group**

Penguin Publishing Group, *(978-0-14; 978-0-399; 978-0-425; 978-0-452; 978-0-525; 978-0-698; 978-0-87477; 978-1-58542; 978-1-933438; 978-1-4295; 978-1-934511; 978-1-4362; 978-1-4406; 978-1-101; 978-1-937007)* Orders Addr.: 405 Murray Hill Pkwy., East Rutherford, NJ 07073-2136 USA (SAN 282-5074) Fax: 201-933-2903 (customer service); Toll Free Fax: 800-227-9604; Toll Free: 800-526-0275 (reseller sales); 800-631-8571 (reseller customer service); 800-788-6262 (individual consumer sales); Edit Addr.: 375 Hudson St., New York, NY 10014 USA Tel 212-366-2000; Fax: 212-366-2666; 405 Murray Hill Pkwy., East Rutherford, NJ 07073 (SAN 852-5455) Tel 201-933-9292 E-mail: customer.service@us.penguingroup.com Web site: http://penguingroup.custhelp.com; http://booksellers.penguingroup.com; http://www.penguinputnam.com.

Penguin Random House LLC, *See* **Penguin Random Hse. Distribution**

Penguin Random Hse. Distribution, *(978-0-593; 978-1-101; 978-1-9848)* 375 Hudson St. 3rd Fl., New York, NY 10014 USA.

Penguin Random Hse. LLC, *(978-0-593; 978-1-101; 978-1-9848)* Orders Addr.: 400 Hahn Rd., Westminster, MD 21157 USA Toll Free Fax: 800-659-2436; Toll Free: 800-733-3000; Edit Addr.: 375 Hudson St. 3rd Flr., New York, NY 10014 USA Tel 212-366-2424 E-mail: brittany.wienke@us.penguingroup.com Web site: http://www.PenguinRandomHouse.com.

Peniel Productions, 73 Smith Hill Rd., Monsey, NY 10952-4131 USA (SAN 631-2837).

Pen-Mar News Distributors, *See* **Americana Souvenirs & Gifts**

Penmarch Publishing, 3932 S. Willow Ave., Sioux Falls, SD 57105 USA Toll Free: 800-282-2399.

Penn News Co., 944 Franklin St., Johnstown, PA 15905 USA (SAN 169-7390).

Pennsylvania State Univ. Pr., *(978-0-271; 978-1-64602)* Orders Addr.: 820 N. University Dr., USB-1 Suite C, University Park, PA 16802 USA (SAN 213-5760) Tel 814-865-1327; Fax: 814-863-1408; Toll Free Fax: 877-778-2665 (orders only); Toll Free: 800-326-9180 (orders only) E-mail: http://www.eisenbrauns.org; info@psupress.org; log-ins@press.psu.edu Web site: http://www.psupress.org.

Pentecostal Publishing Hse., *(978-0-912315)* Subs. of United Pentecostal Church International, 8855 Dunn Rd., Hazelwood, MO 63042-2299 USA (SAN 219-3817) Tel 314-837-7300; (314) 837-7300; Fax: 314-837-4503 E-mail: PPHpublish@aol.com.

Penton Overseas, Inc., *(978-0-939001; 978-1-56015; 978-1-59125; 978-1-60379)* 1958 Kellogg Ave., Carlsbad, CA 92008 USA (SAN 631-0826) Tel 760-431-0060; Fax: 760-431-8110; Toll Free: 800-748-5804 E-mail: kellie@pentonoverseas.com; susan@pentonoverseas.com Web site: http://www.pentonoverseas.com.

Peoples Education, *See* **Mastery Education**

Peregrine Outfitters, Orders Addr.: P.O. Box 1500, Williston, VT 05495 USA (SAN 631-1059) Tel 802-860-2977; Fax: 802-860-2978; Toll Free: 800-222-3088; Edit Addr.: 25 Omega Dr., Suite A, Williston, VT 05482 USA.

Perelandra, Ltd., *(978-0-927978; 978-0-9617713)* Orders Addr.: P.O. Box 3603, Warrenton, VA 20188 USA (SAN 665-0198) Tel 540-937-2153; Fax: 540-937-3360; Toll Free: 800-960-8806 E-mail: email@perelandra-ltd.com Web site: http://www.perelandra-ltd.com.

Perfection Form Company, The, *See* **Perfection Learning Corp.**

Perfection Learning Corp., *(978-0-7807; 978-0-7891; 978-0-8124; 978-0-89598; 978-1-56312; 978-0-7569; 978-1-60686; 978-1-61563; 978-1-61383; 978-1-61384; 978-1-62299; 978-1-62359; 978-1-62765; 978-1-62766; 978-1-62974; 978-1-63419; 978-1-68064; 978-1-68065; 978-1-68240; 978-1-5311; 978-1-6903; 978-1-6636) 1000 N. 2nd Ave., Logan, IA 51546 USA (SAN 221-0010) Tel 712-644-2831; Fax: 712-644-2392; Toll Free Fax: 800-543-2745; Toll Free: 800-831-4190* E-mail: orders@perfectionlearning.com Web site: http://www.perfectionlearning.com.

Perfume River Pubns., 1420 2nd Ave., N., Suite 304, Sauk Rapids, MN 56379 USA Tel 320-761-1229.

Periodical Distributors, Incorporated, *See* **North Texas Periodicals, Inc.**

Periodical Marketing Services, 1065 Bloomfield Ave., Clifton, NJ 07012 USA (SAN 250-5304) Tel 201-342-6334.

Periodical Pubs. Service Bureau, One N. Superior St., Sandusky, OH 44870 USA (SAN 285-9351) Tel 419-626-0623.

Periodicals Service Co., *(978-0-527; 978-0-8115; 978-3-262; 978-3-601)* 11 Main St., Germantown, NY 12526 USA (SAN 164-8608) Tel 518-537-4700; Fax: 518-537-5899 E-mail: psc@periodicals.com Web site: http://www.periodicals.com.

Perma-Bound Bks., *(978-0-605; 978-0-7804; 978-0-8000; 978-0-8479)* Div. of Hertzberg-New Method, Inc., 617 E. Vandalia Rd., Jacksonville, IL 62650 USA (SAN 169-202X) Tel 217-243-5451; Fax: 217-243-7505; Toll Free Fax: 800-551-1169; Toll Free: 800-637-6581 (customer service) E-mail: books@permabound.com Web site: http://www.perma-bound.com.

Perrone, Calle 11. #372-A Urb. Hill Brothers, San Juan, PR 00924 USA Tel 787-764-6112; Fax: 787-754-2374 Do not confuse with Perrone in Franklin, TN E-mail: ecruz@perroneimporters.com Web site: http://www.perroneimporters.com.

Perry Enterprises, *(978-0-941518)* 3907 N. Foothill Dr., Provo, UT 84604 USA (SAN 171-0281) Tel 801-226-1002.

Perseus Academic, *See* **Ingram Academic**

Perseus Bks. Group, *(978-0-7382; 978-0-938289; 978-1-58097; 978-1-882810; 978-1-903985; 978-1-78239)* Div. of Hachette Book Group, Orders Addr.: 2465 Central Ave., Suite 200, Boulder, CO 80301-5728 USA Toll Free: 800-343-4499 (customer service); Edit Addr.: 387 Park Ave., S., 12th Flr., New York, NY 10016-8810 USA Tel 212-340-8100; Fax: 212-340-8105 Web site: http://www.perseusbooksgroup.com.

Perseus Distribution, *See* **Two Rivers Distribution**

Perseus-PGW, *See* **Publishers Group West (PGW)**

Peterson Publishing Co., Inc., *(978-0-9709033)* 1660 Commerce Dr., Suite 1, North Mankato, MN 56003 USA Tel 507-625-4803 Do not confuse with Peterson Publishing Co. in Gunnison, CO.

Peterson's, *(978-0-7689; 978-0-87866; 978-1-56079)* Div. of Nelnet, Orders Addr.: P.O. Box 67005, Lawrenceville, NJ 08648-6105 USA (SAN 200-2167); Edit Addr.: 2000 Lenox Dr., 3rd Flr., Lawrenceville, NJ 08648 USA (SAN 297-5661) Tel 609-896-1800; Fax: 609-896-1811; Toll Free: 800-338-3282 X5660;Customer Service E-mail: custsvc@petersons.com Web site: http://www.petersons.com.

Petterson Antiques, 379 Clayton Dr., Charleston, SC 29414-5048 USA (SAN 114-2399).

Philippine American Literary House, *See* **PALH**

Philosophy Documentation Ctr., *(978-0-912632; 978-1-889680; 978-1-63435)* Orders Addr.: P.O. Box 7147, Charlottesville, VA 22906-7147 USA (SAN 218-6586) Tel 434-220-3300; Fax: 434-220-3301; Toll Free: 800-444-2419 E-mail: order@pdcnet.org Web site: http://www.pdcnet.org.

Phoenix Distributors, Orders Addr.: P.O. Box 1589, Blaine, WA 98231 USA Toll Free Fax: 800-298-4422.

Phoenix Learning Resources, LLC, *(978-0-7915)* Orders Addr.: P.O. Box 510, Honesdale, PA 18431 USA (SAN 246-148X) Tel 570-251-6871; Fax: 570-253-3227; Toll Free: 800-228-9345 E-mail: rich@phoenixlr.com Web site: http://www.phoenixlr.com.

Phoenix Rising Pr., *(978-0-9840521; 978-1-936429)* PO BOX 18809, Asheville, NC 28814 USA (SAN 631-838X) E-mail: support@phoenixrisingpress.com; lynnames@lynnames.com Web site: www.lynnames.com; http://www.phoenixrisingpress.com.

Pictorial Histories Distribution, *See* **West Virginia Book Co., The**

Pilgrim Pr., The/United Church Pr., *(978-0-8298)* Div. of United Church Board for Homeland Ministries, 700 Prospect Ave. E., Cleveland, OH 44115-1100 USA Tel 216-736-3848; Fax: 216-736-2207 E-mail: ucpress@ucc.org; pilgrim@ucc.org Web site: http://www.ucpress.com; http://www.pilgrimpress.com.

Pine Orchard, Inc., *(978-0-9645727; 978-1-930580)* Orders Addr.: 2850 Hwy 95 South. P.O. box 9184, Moscow, ID 83843 USA (SAN 253-4258) Tel 208-882-4838; Fax: 208-882-4845; Toll Free: 877-354-7433 E-mail: orders@pineorchard.com; pineorch@pineorchard.com Web site: http://www.pineorchard.com.

Pine Orchard Press, *See* **Pine Orchard, Inc.**

Pioneer Enterprises, W10085 Pike Plain Rd., Dunbar, WI 54119 USA.

Pitsco Education, 1002 E. Adams St., Pittsburg, KS 66762-6050 USA Tel 620-231-0010.

Pittsfield News Co., Inc., 6 Westview Rd., Pittsfield, MA 01201 USA (SAN 124-2768) Tel 413-445-5682; Fax: 413-445-5683.

PixyJack Pr., Inc., *(978-0-9658098; 978-0-9773724; 978-1-936555)* Orders Addr.: P.O. Box 149, Masonville, CO 80541 USA Tel 303-810-2850; Toll Free Fax: 888-273-7499 E-mail: info@pixyjackpress.com Web site: http://www.pixyjackpress.com.

Plains Distribution Service, P.O. Box 931, Moorhead, MN 56561 USA (SAN 169-6556).

Planeta Publishing Corp., *(978-0-9715256; 978-0-9719950; 978-0-9748724; 978-1-933169; 978-0-9795042)* 999 Ponce De Leon Blvd. Ste. 1045, Coral Gables, FL 33134-3047 USA E-mail: mnorman@planetapublishing.com Web site: http://www.planeta.es.

Plank Road Publishing, Orders Addr.: 3540 J N. 126 St., Brookfield, WI 53005 USA Tel 262-790-5210; Fax: 262-781-8818.

Players Pr., Inc., *(978-0-88734)* P.O. Box 1132, Studio City, CA 91614-0132 USA (SAN 239-0213) Tel 818-789-4980 E-mail: Playerspress@att.net.

Plough Publishing Hse., *(978-0-87486; 978-1-63608)* 151 Bowne Dr., Walden, NY 12586 USA (SAN 202-0092) Tel 845-572-3455; Fax: 845-572-3472; Toll Free: 800-521-8011 E-mail: info@plough.com Web site: http://www.plough.com.

Plymouth Press, Limited, *See* **Plymouth Toy & Book**

Plymouth Toy & Book, *(978-1-882663)* 101 Panton Rd., Vergennes, VT 05491 USA Tel 802-877-2150; Fax: 802-877-2116; Toll Free: 800-350-1007 Do not confuse with Plymouth Pr. in Miami Beach, FL E-mail: plymouth@together.net Web site: http://www.plymouthtoyandbook.com.

PMG Bks. Ltd., P.O. Box 7608, San Antonio, TX 78207-0608 USA (SAN 631-3183).

Polk County Historical Assn., c/o UrbanDog Communications, Inc., P.O. Box 25474, Tampa, FL 33622 USA Tel 813-832-4538; Fax: 813-832-1759 E-mail: cbrownfl@earthlink.net.

Polybook Distributors, Orders Addr.: P.O. Box 109, Mount Vernon, NY 10550 USA Tel 914-664-1633; Fax: 904-428-3953; Edit Addr.: 501 Mamaroneck Ave., White Plains, NY 10605 USA (SAN 169-5568) Tel 914-328-6364 E-mail: mainstreetbook@gmail.com.

Pomona Valley News Agency, 10736 Fremont Ave., Ontario, CA 91762 USA (SAN 169-0019) Tel 909-591-3885.

Pop-M Company, *See* **Bk. Margins, Inc.**

Popular Subscription Service, P.O. Box 1566, Terre Haute, IN 47808 USA (SAN 285-9386) Tel 812-466-1258; Fax: 812-466-9443; Toll Free: 800-466-5038 E-mail: info@popularsubscriptionsvc.com Web site: http://www.popularsubscriptionsvc.com.

Portland News Co., Orders Addr.: P.O. Box 6970, Scarborough, ME 04070-6970 USA (SAN 169-3093) Toll Free: 800-639-1708 (in Maine); Edit Addr.: 18 Hutcherson Dr., Gorham, ME 04038-2643 USA.

Potter's House Book Service, *(978-1-928717)* 1658 Columbia Rd., NW, Washington, DC 20009 USA Tel 202-232-5483; Fax: 202-328-7483 E-mail: pottershse@aol.com Web site: http://www.pottershousebooks.com.

Potter's House Church, *See* **Potter's House Book Service**

Powells.com, Orders Addr.: 2720 NW 29th Ave., Portland, OR 97210 USA Tel 800-291-2676 Web site: http://www.powells.com/.

powerHouse Cultural Entertainment, Incorporated, *See* **powerHse. Bks.**

powerHse. Bks., *(978-1-57687; 978-1-64823)* 32 Adams St, Brooklyn, NY 11201 USA (SAN 850-5845) E-mail: info@powerhousebooks.com Web site: http://www.powerhousebooks.com.

Practice Ring, *(978-0-929758)* Div. of Beeman Jorgensen, Inc., 7510 Allisonville Rd., Indianapolis, IN 46250 USA (SAN 630-6144) Tel 317-841-7677; Toll Free: 800-553-5319.

Pratz News Agency, Orders Addr.: P.O. Box 892, Deming, NM 88030 USA (SAN 159-9275).

Prebound Periodicals, 631 SW Jewell Ave., Topeka, KS 66606-1606 USA (SAN 285-8037).

Premier Pubs., Inc., *(978-0-915665)* P.O. Box 330309, Fort Worth, TX 76163 USA (SAN 292-5966) Tel 817-293-7030; Fax: 817-293-3410.

Presbyterian & Reformed Publishing Company, *See* **P & R Publishing**

Presbyterian Publishing Corp., *(978-0-664)* 100 Witherspoon St., Louisville, KY 40202-1396 USA Tel 502-569-5052; Fax: 502-569-8308; Toll Free Fax: 800-541-5113; Toll Free: 800-227-2872
E-mail: rpinotti@presbypub.com; customer_service@presbypub.com
Web site: http://www.ppcbooks.com.

Prestel Publishing, *(978-3-7913)* Orders Addr.: c/o VNU, 575 Prospect St., Lakewood, NJ 08701 USA Tel 732-363-5679; Fax: 732-363-0338; Toll Free Fax: 877-227-6564; Toll Free: 888-463-6110; Edit Addr.: 900 Broadway, Suite 603, New York, NY 10003 USA Tel 212-995-2720; Fax: 212-995-2733
E-mail: sales@prestel-usa.com
Web site: http://www.prestel.com; http://www.die-gestalten.de; http://www.scalo.com.

Princeton Univ. Pr., *(978-0-691)* Orders Addr.: California-Princeton Fulfillment Services, 1445 Lower Ferry Rd., Ewing, NJ 08618 USA Tel 800-777-4726; Fax: 800-999-1958; Edit Addr.: 41 William St., Princeton, NJ 08540 USA (SAN 202-0254) Tel 609-258-4900; Fax: 609-258-6305; 3 Market Place, Woodstock, OX20 1SY Tel (0) 1993 814501; Fax: (0) 1993 814504
E-mail: webmaster@pupress.princeton.edu
Web site: http://www.press.princeton.edu.

Princeton University Press_mupo, 41 William St., Princeton, NJ 08540 USA Tel 609-258-4900; Fax: 609-258-6305.

Print & Ship, 1412 Greenbrier Pkwy., Suite 145-B, Norfolk, VA 23320 USA Tel 757-424-5868.

Printed Matter, Inc., *(978-0-89439)* 195 10th Ave. FRNT, New York, NY 10011-4739 USA (SAN 169-5924)
E-mail: Keith@printedmatter.org; Max@printedmatter.org
Web site: http://www.printedmatter.org.

Productivity, Incorporated, *See* **Productivity Pr.**

Productivity Pr., *(978-0-527; 978-0-915299; 978-1-56327)* Orders Addr.: 7625 Empire Dr., Florence, KY 41042-2919 USA (SAN 290-036X) Toll Free Fax: 800-248-4724; Toll Free: 800-634-7064 (orders).

PRO-ED, Inc., *(978-0-88744; 978-0-89079; 978-0-933014; 978-0-936104; 978-0-944480; 978-1-4164)* Orders Addr.: 8700 Shoal Creek Blvd., Austin, TX 78757-6897 USA (SAN 222-1349) Tel 512-451-3246 Toll Free Fax: 800-397-7633; Toll Free: 800-897-3202; Edit Addr.: P.O. Box 679029, Dallas, TX 75267-9029 USA
E-mail: cheri@proedinc.com
Web site: http://www.proedinc.com.

Professional Book Distributors, Incorporated, *See* **PBD, Inc.**

Professional Media Service Corp., 1160 Trademark Dr., Suite 109, Reno, NV 89511 USA (SAN 630-5776) Toll Free Fax: 800-253-8853; Toll Free: 800-223-7672.

Project Patch, 2404 E. Mill Plain Blvd., Vancouver, WA 98661-4334 USA.

ProQuest Information and Learning, *See* **ProQuest LLC**

ProQuest LLC, *(978-0-14; 978-0-608; 978-0-7837; 978-0-8357; 978-0-88692; 978-0-89093; 978-0-912380; 978-1-55655; 978-0-591; 978-0-9702937; 978-0-599; 978-1-931694; 978-1-59399; 978-0-496; 978-0-542; 978-1-4247; 978-0-9778091; 978-1-60205; 978-1-4345; 978-0-549; 978-1-109; 978-1-124; 978-1-267; 978-1-303; 978-1-321; 978-1-339; 978-1-369; 978-0-355; 978-0-438; 978-1-392; 978-0-578-52671-3; 978-0-578-52672-0; 978-0-578-52673-7; 978-1-7331884; 978-1-7331885; 978-0-578-52675-1; 978-1-0732; 978-1-0739; 978-1-0) 5252 N. Edgewood Dr., Suite 125, Provo, UT 84604 USA Tel 801-765-1737; 789 Eisenhower Pkwy., Ann Arbor, MI 48108 Tel 734-761-4700; Toll Free: 800-521-0600; 7500 Old Georgetown Rd. Suite 1400, Bethesda, MD 20814*
E-mail: sales@csa.com
Web site: http://www.culturegrams.com; http://www.proquest.com/.

Prosperity Publishing Hse., 1405 Autumn Ridge Dr., Durham, NC 27712 USA Tel 919-767-9620.

Provident Music Distribution, 1 Maryland Farms, Brentwood, TN 37027 USA Tel 615-373-3950; Fax: 615-373-0386; Toll Free: 800-333-9000
E-mail: gmiller@pmgsonybmg
Web site: http://www.providentmusic.com.

PSI (Publisher Services, Inc.), 3095 Kingston Ct., Norcross, GA 30071-1231 USA Toll Free: 800-755-9653; 877-578-4774.

Public Lands Interpretive Assn., *(978-1-879343; 978-0-9863666)* 6501 Fourth St., NW, No. 1, Albuquerque, NM 87107-5800 USA (SAN 133-3119) Tel 505-345-9498; Fax: 505-344-1543.

Publication Consultants, *(978-0-9644809; 978-1-888125; 978-1-59433)* 8370 Eleusis Dr., Anchorage, AK 99502 USA Tel 907-349-2424; Fax: 907-349-2426
E-mail: evan@publicationconsultants.com
Web site: http://www.publicationconsultants.com.

Publications Unlimited, 7512 Coconut Dr., Lake Worth, FL 33467-6511 USA (SAN 285-9432) Tel 407-434-4688 Do not confuse with Publications Unlimited in Raleigh, NC.

Publishers Business Service, Inc., P.O. Box 25674, Chicago, IL 60625 USA (SAN 285-9459) Tel 312-561-5552.

Publishers Clearing Hse., 382 Channel Dr., Port Washington, NY 11050 USA (SAN 285-9440) Tel 516-883-5432.

Publishers Continental Sales Corp., 613 Franklin Sq., Michigan City, IN 46360 USA (SAN 285-9475) Tel 219-874-4245; Fax: 219-872-8961.

Publishers' Graphics, L.L.C., *(978-0-9663402; 978-1-930847; 978-1-933556; 978-1-934703; 978-1-935590)* 140 Della Ct., Carol Stream, IL 60188 USA (SAN 990-0241) Toll Free: 888-404-3769
Web site: http://www.pubgraphics.com.

Publishers Group International, Inc., *(978-0-9633653)* 1506 27th St. NW, No. 1, Washington, DC 20007 USA Tel 202-342-0886; Fax: 202-338-1940
E-mail: issbooks@aol.com.

Publishers Group West (PGW), Div. of Ingram Content Group, Orders Addr.: 1094 Flex Dr., Jackson, TN 38301-5070 USA (SAN 631-7715) Tel 731-423-1973; Toll Free Fax: 800-351-5073; Toll Free: 800-343-4499; Edit Addr.: 387 Park Avenue South, New York, NY 10016 USA (SAN 631-760X) Tel 212-340-8100; Fax: 212-340-8195
E-mail: info@pgw.com
Web site: http://www.pgw.com/home.

Publishers Media, *(978-0-934064)* 1447 Valley View Rd., Glendale, CA 91202-1716 USA (SAN 159-6683) Tel 818-548-1998.

Publishers News Company, *See* **Mr. Paperback/Publishers News Co.**

Publishers Services, Orders Addr.: P.O. Box 2510, Novato, CA 94948 USA (SAN 201-3037) Tel 415-883-3530; Fax: 415-883-4280.

Publishers Storage & Shipping, 46 Development Rd., Fitchburg, MA 01420 USA Tel 978-345-2121; 660 S. Mansfield Dr., Ypsilanti, MI 48197 Tel 734-487-9720
Web site: http://www.pssc.com.

Publishers Wholesale Assocs., Inc., Orders Addr.: P.O. Box 2078, Lancaster, PA 17608-2078 USA (SAN 630-7450) Fax: 717-397-9253; Edit Addr.: 231 N. Shippen St., Lancaster, PA 17608 USA.

Puerto Rico Postcard, P.O. Box 79710, Carolina, PR 00984-9710 USA.

Pulley Learning Assocs., 210 Alpine Meadow Rd., Winchester, VA 22602-6701 USA (SAN 133-1434).

Pura Vida Bks., Inc., P.O. Box 2002, Salinas, PR 00751 USA Tel 787-824-3763
E-mail: info@puravidabooks.com.

Purple Unicorn Bks., *(978-0-931998)* 1928 W. Kent Rd., Duluth, MN 55812-1154 USA (SAN 111-0071) Tel 218-525-4781 Do not confuse with Purple Unicorn in Augusta, ME.

Puzzle Piece Pubns., 846 36th Ave., N., Saint Cloud, MN 56303 USA Tel 320-656-5361.

QEP, Inc. Professional Bks., 3273 Independence Pkwy., Plano, TX 75086-4964 USA Toll Free: 800-323-6787.

Quality Bks., Inc., *(978-0-89196)* 1003 W. Pines Rd., Oregon, IL 61061-9680 USA (SAN 169-2127) Tel 815-732-4450; Fax: 815-732-4499; Toll Free: 800-323-4241 (libraries only)
E-mail: info@quality-books.com.

Quality Book Fairs, 5787 Ryan Rd., Medina, OH 44256-8823 USA (SAN 630-7752).

Quality Schl. Plan, Inc., P.O. Box 10203, Des Moines, IA 50381-0001 USA (SAN 285-953X).

Quarto Publishing Group USA, *(978-0-7603; 978-0-86573; 978-0-89738; 978-0-912612; 978-0-929261; 978-0-9640392; 978-1-55832; 978-1-56010; 978-1-888608; 978-1-930604; 978-1-58923; 978-1-59186; 978-1-59233; 978-1-59253; 978-1-60058; 978-1-61673; 978-1-936309; 978-1-61058; 978-1-61059; 978-1-61060; 978-1-937994; 978-1-939581; 978-1-62788; 978-1-63106; 978-1-63159; 978-1-63322; 978-1-942875) Orders Addr.: Retail Order Dept., Quayside Publishing Group 18705 Lake Dr. E., Chanhassen, MN 55317 USA Tel 1-952-936-4700; Fax: 1-952-099-9101; Toll Free: 1-800-328-0590; Edit Addr.: 3 Wrigley Suite A, Irvine, CA 92618-2748 USA (SAN 249-051X) Toll Free: 800-426-0099*
E-mail: rebecca.razo@quartous.com
Web site: https://www.quartoknows.com/division/Quarto-Publishing-Group-USA/.

R & W Distribution, Inc., 87 Bright St., Jersey City, NJ 07302 USA (SAN 169-4723) Tel 201-333-1540; Fax: 201-333-1541
E-mail: rwmag@mail.idt.net.

R. C. Brayshaw, P.O. Box 91, Warner, NH 03278 USA Tel 603-456-3101.

R J Communications, LLC, *(978-0-9700741; 978-1-59664)* 51 E. 42nd St., Suite 1202, New York, NY 10017-5404 USA Tel 212-867-1331; Fax: 212-681-8002; Toll Free: 800-621-2556 (New York)
E-mail: ron@rjcom.com
Web site: http://www.selfpublishing.com; http://www.booksjustbooks.com.

R T R Publishing Company, *See* **Red Toad Road Co.**

Radio Bookstore, P.O. Box 209, Rindge, NH 03461-0209 USA (SAN 111-3496) Tel 603-899-6957 Do not confuse with Radio Bookstore Pr., Bellevue, WA.

Raimond Graphics Inc., Orders Addr.: 360 Sylvan Ave., Englewd Clfs, NJ 07632-2712 USA.

Rainbow Bk. Co., *(978-1-932834; 978-1-60117; 978-1-60447)* 500 E. Main St., Lake Zurich, IL 60047 USA (SAN 920-2935) Tel 800-255-0965; Fax: 847-726-9935 Do not confuse with Rainbow Book Company in Mt. Mourne, NC
E-mail: mike@rainbowbookcompany.com
Web site: http://www.rainbowbookcompany.com.

Rainbow Horizons Publishing, Inc., *(978-1-55319)* Orders Addr.: P.O. Box 19729, San Diego, CA 92159 USA Toll Free Fax: 800-663-3608; Toll Free: 800-663-3609
E-mail: paul@classroomcompletepress.com
Web site: http://www.ccpinteractive.com; http://www.rainbowhorizons.com; http://www.classroomcompletepress.com.

Rainbow Re-Source Ctr., P.O. Box 491, Kewanee, IL 61443 USA (SAN 631-4007) Tel 309-937-3385; Fax: 309-937-3382
E-mail: rainbowres@aol.com.

Rainier News, Inc., 3400-D Industry Dr., E., Fife, WA 98424-1853 USA (SAN 169-8745) Toll Free: 800-843-2995 (in Washington).

RAM Pubns. & Distribution, *(978-0-9630785; 978-0-9703860; 978-0-9897315)* Bergamot Sta., 2525 Michigan Ave., No. A2, Santa Monica, CA 90404 USA (SAN 298-2641) Tel 310-453-0043; Fax: 310-264-4888
E-mail: rampub@gte.net.

Rand McNally, *(978-0-528)* Orders Addr.: 9855 Woods Dr., Skokie, IL 60077-1074 USA Toll Free Fax: 800-934-3479 (Orders); Toll Free: 800-333-0136 (ext. 4771); 800-678-7263 (Orders); 8770 W Bryn Mawr Ave., Chicago, IL 60631 Tel 800-333-0136; Fax: 847-329-6139
E-mail: Education@randmcnally.com
Web site: http://www.randmcnally.com.

Random House Adult Trade Publishing Group, *See* **Random House Publishing Group**

Random House, Incorporated, *See* **Random Hse., Inc.**

Random House Publishing Group, *(978-1-4070)* Orders Addr.: 400 Hahn Rd., Westminster, MD 21157 USA (SAN 852-5579) Tel 410-848-1900; 410-386-7560; Toll Free: 800-726-0600; Edit Addr.: 1745 Broadway, New York, NY 10019 USA Tel 212-751-2600; Fax: 212-572-4949; Toll Free: 800-726-0600
E-mail: lstark@randomhouse.com.

Random Hse. Bks. for Young Readers, *(978-0-375; 978-0-394; 978-0-517; 978-0-679; 978-1-4000)* Orders Addr.: 400 Hahn Rd., Westminster, MD 21157 USA; Edit Addr.: 1540 Broadway, New York, NY 10036 USA.

Random Hse., Inc., *(978-0-307; 978-0-345; 978-0-375; 978-0-385; 978-0-394; 978-0-440; 978-0-449; 978-0-517; 978-0-553; 978-0-593; 978-0-609; 978-0-676; 978-0-679; 978-0-7364; 978-0-7366; 978-0-7615; 978-0-7679; 978-0-7704; 978-0-8041; 978-0-8052; 978-0-8129; 978-0-8230; 978-0-87637; 978-0-87665; 978-0-87788; 978-0-88070; 978-0-913369; 978-0-914629; 978-0-930014; 978-0-945564; 978-1-57082; 978-1-57673; 978-1-57856; 978-1-878867; 978-1-884536; 978-1-885305; 978-1-58836; 978-1-4000; 978-1-59052; 978-1-4159; 978-) Div. of Penguin Random House LLC, Orders Addr.: 400 Hahn Rd., Westminster, MD 21157 USA (SAN 202-5515) Tel 410 848 1900; Toll Free Fax: 800 659 2436; Toll Free: 800 726 0600 (customer service/orders); Edit Addr.: 1745 Broadway, New York, NY 10019 USA (SAN 202-5507) Tel 212 782 9000; Fax: 212 302 7985*
E-mail: customerservice@randomhouse.com
Web site: http://www.randomhouse.com.

Raven West Coast Distribution, 767 W. 18th St., Costa Mesa, CA 92627 USA
E-mail: ken@ravenwcd.com.

Read News Agency, 2501 Greensboro Ave., Tuscaloosa, AL 35401-6520 USA Tel 205-752-3515.

Readerlink Distribution Services, LLC, *(978-0-934429; 978-1-57145; 978-1-59223; 978-1-60710; 978-1-62686; 978-1-68412; 978-1-64517)* 10350 Barnes Canyon Rd. Suite 100, San Diego, CA 92121 USA (SAN 630-8090) Toll Free: 800-284-3580
E-mail: lnordland@readerlink.com
Web site: http://www.silverdolphinbooks.com; http://www.printersrowpublishinggroup.com; http://www.thunderbaybooks.com/; http://www.bathroomreader.com; http://www.readerlink.com.

Reader's Digest Assn., Inc., The, *(978-0-7621; 978-0-89577; 978-0-86438; 978-1-60652)* One Bedford Rd., Pleasantville, NY 10570 USA (SAN 282-2091) Toll Free: 800-463-8820; 800-334-9599; 800-635-5006
Web site: http://www.readersdigest.com; http://www.rd.com.

Reader's Digest Children's Publishing, Incorporated, *See* **Studio Fun International**

Readex Bk. Exchange, Box 1125, Carefree, AZ 85377 USA (SAN 159-9291).

Reading Circle, The, 7858 Industrial Pkwy., Plain City, OH 43064-9468 USA (SAN 169-670X).

Reading Matters, Inc., *(978-1-930654)* 806 Main St., Akron, PA 17501 USA Tel 717-859-5608; Fax: 717-859-3469; Toll Free: 888-255-6665 Do not confuse with companies with the same name in Brookline, MA, Denver, CO
E-mail: office@readingmatters.net
Web site: http://readingmatters.net.

Reading Peddler Bk. Fairs, 10580 3/4 W. Pico Blvd., Los Angeles, CA 90064 USA (SAN 157-9770) Tel 310-559-2665.

Reading's Fun/Books are Fun, Limited, *See* **Bks. Are Fun, Ltd.**

Readmor, Orders Addr.: P.O. Box 7264, Grand Rapids, MI 49508 USA (SAN 169-3875); Edit Addr.: 301 S. Rath Ave., Ludington, MI 49431 USA Tel 231-843-2537.

Readmore Academic Services, Orders Addr.: P.O. Box 1459, Blackwood, NJ 08012 USA (SAN 630-5741) Tel 609-227-1100; Fax: 609-227-8322; Toll Free: 800-645-6595; Edit Addr.: 700 Black Horse Pike, Suite 207, Blackwood, NJ 08012 USA.

Readmore, Inc., 22 Cortlandt St., New York, NY 10007 USA (SAN 159-9313) Tel 212-349-5540; Fax: 212-233-0746; Toll Free: 800-221-3306.

Recorded Bks., Inc., *(978-0-7887; 978-1-55690; 978-1-84197; 978-1-4025; 978-1-4193; 978-1-84505; 978-1-4281; 978-1-4361; 978-1-4407; 978-1-4498; 978-1-4561; 978-1-4618; 978-1-4640; 978-1-4703; 978-1-4906; 978-1-5019; 978-1-9800; 978-1-7050)* Subs. of W. F. Howes Limited, Orders Addr.: 270 Skipjack Rd., Prince Frederick, MD 20678 USA (SAN 111-3984) Fax: 410-535-5499; Toll Free: 800-638-1304; 7257 Pkwy. Dr., Hanover, MD 21076 (SAN 920-7414)
E-mail: thelvey@recordedbooks.com
Web site: http://www.rbdigital.com.

Recorded Books, LLC, *See* **Recorded Bks., Inc.**

Red Sea Pr., *(978-0-932415; 978-1-56902)* Affil. of Africa World Pr., 541 W. Ingham Ave., Suite B, Trenton, NJ 08638 USA (SAN 630-1983) Tel 609-695-3200; Fax: 609-695-6466
E-mail: awprsp@verizon.net
Web site: http://www.africaworldpressbooks.com.

Red Toad Road Co., *(978-1-889287)* Orders Addr.: P.O. Box 642, Havre de Grace, MD 21078 USA Tel 410-939-4092; Fax: 410-939-5614; Edit Addr.: 223 Heather Way, Havre de Grace, MD 21078 USA
E-mail: redtoadroad@aol.com
Web site: http://www.amazon.com/shops/redtoadroad.

Red Wheel/Weiser, *(978-0-87728; 978-0-943233; 978-1-56414; 978-1-57324; 978-1-57863; 978-1-59003; 978-1-60163; 978-1-60925; 978-1-61283; 978-1-61852; 978-1-61940; 978-1-938875; 978-1-63265; 978-1-63341; 978-1-942785; 978-1-64297; 978-0-692-19811-7; 978-1-953650* Div. of Weiser Bks., Orders Addr.: 65 Parker St., Suite 7, Newburyport, MA 01950 USA (SAN 255-8610) Tel 978-465-0504; Fax: 978-465-0243; Toll Free Fax: 877-337-3309; Toll Free: 800-423-7087 (orders only)
E-mail: customerservice@redwheelweiser.com
Web site: http://www.redwheelweiser.com.

RedShelf, Orders Addr.: 500 North Dearborn St., Suite 1200, Chicago, IL 60654 USA Tel 312-878-8586
E-mail: help@virdocs.com
Web site: http://www.redshelf.com/.

Redwing Bk. Co., Orders Addr.: 202 Bendix Dr., Taos, NM 87571 USA Tel 505-758-7758; Fax: 505-758-7768; Toll Free: 800-873-3946 (USA); 888-873-3947 (Canada); Edit Addr.: P.O. Box 470688, Brookline Vlg, MA 02447-0688 USA (SAN 163-3597) Toll Free: 800-873-3946
E-mail: bob@redwingbooks.com
Web site: http://www.redwingbooks.com.

Reference Bk. Ctr., 175 Fifth Ave., New York, NY 10010 USA (SAN 159-9356) Tel 212-677-2160; Fax: 212-533-0826.

Regent Bk. Co., Inc., Orders Addr.: P.O. Box 750, Lodi, NJ 07644-0750 USA Tel 973-574-7600; Fax: 973-574-7605; Toll Free: 800-999-9554; Edit Addr.: 101 E. Main St. BLDG 5, Little Falls, NJ 07424-1659 USA (SAN 169-4715)
E-mail: info@regentbook.com
Web site: http://www.regentbook.com.

REKO, P.O. Box 4005, Joplin, MO 64803 USA Tel 417-626-0402.

Renaissance News, 5232 Clairton Blvd., Pittsburgh, PA 15236 USA Tel 412-881-4848; Fax: 412-881-5422.

Replica Books, *See* **TextStream**

Representaciones Borinquenas, Inc., *(978-0-9727750; 978-0-9755107)* P.O. Box 139, Aguas Buenas, PR 00703-0139 USA Tel 787-309-9047; Fax: 787-780-5835
E-mail: rborinquenas@centennialpr.net.

Reprint Services Corp., *(978-0-7812; 978-0-932051; 978-1-4227)* P.O. Box 130, Murrieta, CA 92564-0130 USA (SAN 686-2640) Fax: 951-699-5065
E-mail: Reprintservices@gmail.com.

Research Bks., Inc., P.O. Box 555, Old Saybrook, CT 06475-0555 USA
E-mail: info@researchbooks.com.

Resource Software International, Inc., *(978-0-87539)* Affil. of Datamatics Management, 330 New Brunswick Ave., Fords, NJ 08863 USA (SAN 264-8628) Tel 732-738-8500; Fax: 732-738-9603; Toll Free: 800-673-0366
E-mail: info@datamaticsinc.com
Web site: http://www.tc-1.com.

Reveal Entertainment, Inc., *(978-0-9712633)* 1250 Petroleum Dr. Ste. B6, Abilene, TX 79602-7957 USA
E-mail: revealgames@aol.com
Web site: http://www.revealgames.com.

Review & Herald Publishing Assn., *(978-0-8127; 978-0-8280)* 55 W. Oak Ridge Dr., Hagerstown, MD 21740 USA (SAN 203-3798) Tel 301-393-3000
E-mail: smulkern@rhpa.org
Web site: http://www.reviewandherald.com/.

Revolution Booksellers, 60 Winter St., Exeter, NH 03833 USA Tel 603-772-7200; Fax: 603-772-7200; Toll Free: 800-738-6603.

Rhinelander News Agency, 314 Courtney, Crescent Lake, WI 54501 USA (SAN 159-9372) Tel 715-362-6397.

Rhino Entertainment Co, A Warner Music Group Co., *(978-0-7379; 978-0-930589; 978-1-56826; 978-0-9797278)* 3400 W. Olive Ave., Burbank, CA 91505 USA (SAN 677-5454) Tel 818-238-6110; Fax: 818-562-9239
E-mail: gladys.sanchez@wmg.com; tracie.bowers@wmg.com
Web site: http://www.rhino.com.

Rhodes News Agency, *See* **Treasure Valley News**

Richardson's Bks., Inc., 2014 Lou Ellen Ln., Houston, TX 77018 USA (SAN 169-829X) Tel 713-688-2244; Fax: 713-688-8420; Toll Free: 800-392-8562.

Richardson's Educators, *See* **Richardson's Bks., Inc.**

Right Start, Inc., 5388 Sterling Center Dr., Suite C, Westlake Village, CA 91361-4687 USA (SAN 631-7022).

Rio Grande Bk. Co., P.O. Box 2795, McAllen, TX 78502-2795 USA (SAN 169-8354).

Rio Nuevo Pubs., (*978-0-918080; 978-1-887896; 978-0-9700750; 978-1-933855; 978-1-940322*) Orders Addr.: P.O. Box 5250, Tucson, AZ 85703-0250 USA (SAN 209-3251) Tel 520-623-9558; Fax: 520-624-5888; Toll Free Fax: 800-715-5888; Toll Free: 800-969-9558; Edit Addr.: 451 N. Bonita Ave., Tucson, AZ 85745 USA Tel 602-623-9558
E-mail: info@rionuevo.com; info@treasurechestbooks.com; suzang@rionuevo.com
Web site: http://www.treasurechestbooks.com; http://www.rionuevo.com/.

Rip Off Pr., (*978-0-89620*) Orders Addr.: P.O. Box 4686, Auburn, CA 95604 USA (SAN 207-7671) Tel 530-885-8183; Toll Free: 800-468-2669
E-mail: authorkatee@gmail.com; mail@ripoffpress.com
Web site: http://www.ripoffpress.com; http://www.kathetodd.com.

Rishor News Co., Inc., 109 Mountain Laurel Dr., Butler, PA 16001-3921 USA (SAN 159-9402).

Rittenhouse Bk. Distributors, (*978-0-87381*) Orders Addr.: P.O. Box 61565, Kng Of Prussa, PA 19406-0965 USA (SAN 213-4454) Toll Free Fax: 800-223-7488; Toll Free: 800-345-6425
E-mail: alan.yockey@rittenhouse.com; joan.townshend@rittenhouse.com
Web site: http://www.rittenhouse.com.

Ritter Bk. Co., 7011 Foster Pl., Downers Grove, IL 60516-3446 USA (SAN 169-1856).

River Canyon Distributing, P.O. Box 70643, Eugene, OR 97401 USA.

River Road Recipes Cookbook, 9523 Fenway Dr., Baton Rouge, LA 70809 USA (SAN 132-7852) Tel 504-924-0300; Fax: 504-927-2547; Toll Free: 800-204-1726.

RiverStream Publishing, (*978-0-9834972; 978-1-62243*) 123 S. Broad St., Mankato, MN 56001 USA Tel 414-378-2480
Web site: https://riverstreampublishing.net.

Rizzoli International Pubns., Inc., (*978-0-8478; 978-0-88363; 978-0-941807; 978-1-932183; 978-1-59962*) Subs. of RCS Rizzoli Editore Corp., 300 Park Ave., S., 3rd Flr., New York, NY 10010 USA (SAN 111-9192) Tel 212-387-3400; Fax: 212-387-3535
Web site: http://www.rizzoliusa.com/.

Roadrunner Library Service, c/o Kerbs, 700 Highview Ave., Glen Ellyn, IL 60137-5504 USA.

Roberts, F.M. Enterprises, (*978-0-912746*) P.O. Box 608, Dana Point, CA 92629-0608 USA (SAN 201-4688) Tel 714-493-1977; Fax: 714-493-7124.

Rockbottom Bks., Pentagon Towers, P.O. Box 398166, Minneapolis, MN 55439 USA (SAN 108-4402) Tel 612-831-2120.

Rockland Catskill, Inc., 26 Church St., Spring Valley, NY 10977 USA (SAN 169-6254) Tel 914-356-1222; Fax: 914-356-8415; Toll Free: 800-966-6247.

Rocky Mount News Agency, Two Great State Ln., Rocky Mount, NC 27801 USA.

Rodale Institute Bookstore, (*978-0-9652477*) 611 Siegfriedale Rd., Kutztown, PA 19530 USA Tel 610-683-6009; Fax: 610-683-8548; Toll Free: 800-832-6285
E-mail: ribooks@fast.net
Web site: http://www.rodaleinstitute.org.

Rogue Valley News Agency, Inc., 550 Airport Rd., Medford, OR 97504-4156 USA (SAN 169-7137).

Rohr, Hans E., 76 State St., Newburyport, MA 01950-6616 USA (SAN 113-8804).

Roig Spanish Bks., 146 W. 29th St., No. 3W, New York, NY 10001-5303 USA (SAN 165-1021) Fax: 212-695-6811.

Romeii LLC, (*978-0-9830484; 978-1-937391*) 1050 Sommers St. N, Hudson, WI 54016 USA Tel 651-204-3753
E-mail: steve@romeii.com
Web site: Romeii.com.

Rosen Publishing Group, Inc., The, (*978-0-8239; 978-1-56696; 978-1-4042; 978-1-59791; 978-1-4358; 978-1-60851; 978-1-60852; 978-1-60853; 978-1-60854; 978-1-61511; 978-1-61512; 978-1-61513; 978-1-61514; 978-1-61530; 978-1-61531; 978-1-61532; 978-1-61533; 978-1-4488; 978-1-4777; 978-1-4824; 978-1-4994; 978-1-68048; 978-1-5081; 978-1-68416; 978-1-5382; 978-1-5383; 978-1-64282; 978-1-64374; 978-1-7253) a/o Dept. C234561, 29 E. 21st St., New York, NY 10010 USA (SAN 203-3720) Tel 212-777-3017; Fax: 212-358-9588; Toll Free Fax: 888-436-4643; Toll Free: 800-237-9932*
E-mail: hollyc@rosenpub.com; info@rosenpub.com; customerservice@rosenpub.com; hollyc@rosen.pub
Web site: http://www.rosenpublishing.com; http://www.rosendigital.com; http://www.rosenclassroom.com.

Rosen Publishing Group, Incorporated, The, *See* **Rosen Publishing Group, Inc., The**

Rosenblum's, *See* **Rosenblum's World of Judaica, Inc.**

Rosenblum's World of Judaica, Inc., 2906 W. Devon Ave., Chicago, IL 60659 USA (SAN 169-1864) Tel 773-262-1700; Fax: 773-262-1930; Toll Free: 800-626-6536.

Rosewood Foundation, The, Orders Addr.: P.O. Box 252, Archer, FL 32618 USA Tel 352-495-2197; Fax: 352-495-8313
E-mail: lizziePRJ@aol.com.

Rounder Kids Music Distribution, Orders Addr.: P.O. Box 516, Montpelier, VT 05602 USA (SAN 630-6675) Tel 802-223-5825; Fax: 802-223-5303; Toll Free: 800-223-6357; Edit Addr.: 80 W. Harvey Farm Rd., Waterbury Ctr, VT 05677-7132 USA
E-mail: Pauls@rounder.com.

Routledge, (*978-0-04; 978-0-413; 978-0-415; 978-0-7100; 978-0-87830; 978-1-317*) Member of Taylor & Frances Group, Orders Addr.: 7625 Empire Dr., Florence, KY 41042 USA Toll Free Fax: 800-248-4724 (orders, customer serv.); Toll Free: 800-634-7064 (orders, customer serv.); Edit Addr.: 270 Madison Ave. # 3, New York, NY 10016-0601 USA (SAN 213-196X)
E-mail: cserve@routledge-ny.com; info@routledge-ny.com
Web site: http://www.routledge-ny.com.

Rowman & Littlefield Publishers, Inc., (*978-0-8476; 978-0-87471; 978-0-9632978; 978-1-56699; 978-1-888052; 978-0-7425; 978-1-931890; 978-1-933494; 978-1-4422; 978-1-936283; 978-1-61281; 978-1-4616; 978-1-4617; 978-1-62093; 978-1-5381; 978-1-68475*) Mem. of Rowman & Littlefield Publishing Group, Inc., Orders Addr.: 15200 NBN Way, Blue Ridge Summit, PA 17214 USA Tel 717-794-3800 (Sales, Customer Service, MIS, Royalties, Inventory; Fax: 717-794-3803 (Customer Service & orders only); 717-794-3857 (Sales & MIS); 717-794-3856 (Royalties, Inventory Mgmt. & Distribution); Toll Free Fax: 800-338-4550 (Customer Service & orders); Toll Free: 800-462-6420 (Customer Service & orders); Edit Addr.: 4501 Forbes Blvd., Suite 200, Lanham, MD 20706 USA Tel 301-459-3366; Fax: 301-459-5749; Toll Free: 800-462-6420 Short Discount, please contact rlpgsales@rowman.com
E-mail: rlpgsales@rowman.com; lweston@rowman.com
Web site: http://www.rowmanlittlefield.com; http://www.rlpgbooks.com/bookseller/index.shtml.

Royal Pubns., Inc., (*978-0-918738*) Orders Addr.: P.O. Box 5793, Denver, CO 80217 USA (SAN 244-7193) Tel 303-778-8383; Toll Free: 800-279-2048 (orders only); Edit Addr.: 790 W. Tennessee Ave., Denver, CO 80223 USA (SAN 169-054X).

Rumpf, Raymond & Son, Orders Addr.: P.O. Box 319, Sellersville, PA 18960 USA (SAN 631-5259).

Rushmore News, Inc., 924 East St. Andrew, Rapid City, SD 57701 USA (SAN 169-7846) Tel 605-342-2617; Fax: 605-342-9091; Toll Free: 800-423-0501
E-mail: afreese911@aol.com.

Russell News Agency, Inc., P.O. Box 158, Sarasota, FL 33578 USA (SAN 169-1287).

Russica Bk. & Art Shop, Inc., 799 Broadway, New York, NY 10003 USA (SAN 165-1072) Tel 212-473-7480; Fax: 212-473-7486.

Rutgers Univ. Pr., (*978-0-8135; 978-1-9788*) 106 Somerset St., Third Flr., New Brunswick, NJ 08901 USA (SAN 253-2115) Tel 848-445-7786
Web site: http://www.rutgersuniversitypress.org.

S & L Sales Co., Inc., Orders Addr.: P.O. Box 2067, Waycross, GA 31502 USA (SAN 107-413X) Tel 912-283-0210; Fax: 912-283-0261; Toll Free: 800-243-3699 (orders only).

S & S News & Greeting, 5304 15th Ave., S., Minneapolis, MN 55417-1812 USA (SAN 159-9453) Tel 612-224-8227; Toll Free: 800-346-9892.

S & W Distributors, Inc., 1600-H E. Wendover Ave., Greensboro, NC 27405 USA.

S. A. V. E. with Victor Hotho, *See* **S.A.V.E. Suzie & Vic Enterprises**

S V E & Churchill Media, (*978-0-7932; 978-0-89290; 978-1-56357*) 6465 N. Avondale Ave., Chicago, IL 60631-1909 USA (SAN 208-3930) Toll Free Fax: 800-624-1678; Toll Free: 800-829-1900
E-mail: custserv@svemedia.com
Web site: http://www.svemedia.com.

SAAN Corp., 189-01 Springfield Ave., Suite 201, Flossmoor, IL 60422 USA (SAN 631-0419) Tel 708-799-5225; Fax: 708-799-8713.

Saddleback Educational Publishing, *See* **Saddleback Educational Publishing, Inc.**

Saddleback Educational Publishing, Inc., (*978-1-56254; 978-1-59905; 978-1-60291; 978-1-61651; 978-1-61247; 978-1-62250; 978-1-62670; 978-1-63078; 978-1-68021; 978-1-64598*) 151 Kalmus Dr., J-1, Costa Mesa, CA 92626-4564 USA (SAN 860-0902) Toll Free Fax: 888-734-4010; Toll Free: 800-637-8715
E-mail: contact@saddleback.com; amchugh@sdlback.com; adormanesh@sdlback.com
Web site: http://www.sdlback.com.

Sadler, Dale, 209 Foster Dr., White House, TN 37188 USA.

Safari Museum Pr., 111 N. Lincoln Ave., Chanute, KS 66720 USA Tel 630-431-2730; Fax: 630-431-3848.

SAGE Pubns., Inc., (*978-0-7619; 978-0-8039; 978-1-4129; 978-1-4522; 978-1-4462; 978-1-4833; 978-1-5063; 978-1-5443; 978-1-0718; 978-1-0719*) 2455 Teller Rd., Thousand Oaks, CA 91360 USA (SAN 204-7217) Tel 800-818-7243; Fax: 800-583-2665; 805-499-0871
E-mail: info@sagepub.com; deborah.vaughn@sagepub.com
Web site: http://www.sagepub.com; http://www.sagepub.co.uk; http://www.pineforge.com; http://sagepub.com.

Sagebrush Pr., (*978-0-930704*) P.O. Box 87, Morongo Valley, CA 92256 USA (SAN 113-387X) Tel 760-363-7398 Do not confuse with companies with same name in Cedarville, CA, Salt Lake City, UT.

Saint Benedict Pr., Div. of Saint Benedict Press, LLC, Orders Addr.: P.O. Box 410487, Charlotte, NC 28241 USA Toll Free: 800-437-5876
Web site: https://books.benedictpress.com/.

Saint George Book Service, Incorporated, *See* **Steiner, Rudolf College Pr./St. George Pubns.**

Saks News, Inc., P.O. Box 1857, Bismarck, ND 58502 USA (SAN 169-653X).

Sams Technical Publishing, LLC, (*978-0-7906; 978-0-578-12070-6*) 9850 E. 30th St., Indianapolis, IN 46229 USA Toll Free Fax: 800-552-3910; Toll Free: 800-428-7267
E-mail: samstech@samswebsite.com
Web site: http://www.samswebsite.com.

San Diego Museum of Art, (*978-0-937108; 978-0-9845555*) Orders Addr.: P.O. Box 122107, San Diego, CA 92112-2107 USA Tel 619-696-1970; Fax: 619-232-9367
E-mail: sward@sdmart.org
Web site: http://www.sdmart.org.

San Francisciana, (*978-0-934715*) P.O. Box 590955, San Francisco, CA 94159 USA (SAN 161-1607) Tel 415-751-7222.

San Val, Incorporated, *See* **Turtleback Bks.**

Sandlapper Publishing Co., Inc., (*978-0-87844*) Orders Addr.: P.O. Box 730, Orangeburg, SC 29115 USA (SAN 203-2678) Toll Free Fax: 800-337-9420 (orders); Toll Free: 800-849-7263 (orders); Edit Addr.: 1281 Amelia St., NE., Orangeburg, SC 29116 USA Tel 803-533-1658; Fax: 803-534-5223
E-mail: agallman1@bellsouth.net
Web site: http://www.sandlapperpublishing.com.

Sandvik Publishing, (*978-1-58048; 978-1-881445*) Div. of Sandviks Bokforlag, Norway, 3729 Knights Rd., Bensalem, PA 19020-2908 USA Toll Free: 800-843-2445
E-mail: Nicole@sandvikpublishing.com; cust-serv@sandvikpublishing.com
Web site: http://www.sandviks.com.

Santa Barbara Botanic Garden, (*978-0-916436*) 1212 Mission Canyon Rd., Santa Barbara, CA 93105 USA (SAN 208-8398) Tel 805-682-4726; Fax: 805-563-0352
E-mail: info@sbbg.org
Web site: http://www.sbbg.org.

Santa Barbara News Agency, 725 S. Kellogg Ave., Goleta, CA 93117-3806 USA (SAN 168-9665) Tel 805-564-5200.

Santa Monica Software, Inc., 30018 Zenith Point Rd., Malibu, CA 90265-4264 USA (SAN 630-6764) Tel 310-457-8381; Fax: 310-395-7635.

Santillana USA Publishing Co., Inc., (*978-0-88272; 978-1-56014; 978-1-58105; 978-1-58986; 978-1-59437; 978-1-59820; 978-1-60396; 978-1-61605; 978-1-61435; 978-1-62263; 978-1-63113; 978-1-68292; 978-1-64101*) Div. of Grupo Santillana, 8333 NW 53rd St. Suite 402, Doral, FL 33166 USA (SAN 205-1133) Tel 617-351-4867; Av. Rio Mixcoac No. 274 Col. Acacias, C.P. 0324 Benito Juarez, Ciudad de Mexico, DF,
E-mail: dminella@vistahigherlearning.com; esanta@santillanausa.com; customerservice@santillanausa.com
Web site: http://www.loqueleo.com/us.

Saphrograph Corp., (*978-0-87557*) 5409 18th Ave., Brooklyn, NY 11204 USA (SAN 110-4128) Tel 718-331-1233; Fax: 718-331-8231
E-mail: saphrograph@verizon.net.

Sathya Sai Bk. Ctr. of America, (*978-1-57836*) 305 W. First St., Tustin, CA 92780 USA (SAN 111-3542) Tel 714-669-0522; Fax: 714-669-9138
Web site: http://www.sathyasaibooks.com.

Satsang Press, *See* **Gangaji Foundation, The**

Savant Bk. Distribution Co., 3107 E 62nd Ave., Spokane, WA 99223-6934 USA (SAN 631-9203) Tel 509-443-7057; Fax: 509-448-2191
E-mail: service@savant-books.com
Web site: http://www.savant-books.com.

S.A.V.E. Suzie & Vic Enterprises, 303 N. Main, P.O. Box 30, Schulenburg, TX 78956 USA (SAN 630-6365) Tel 409-743-4145; Fax: 409-743-4147.

Savvas Learning Co., (*978-1-59896; 978-1-60637*) 75 Arlington St., Boston, MA 02116 USA.

SCB Distributors, Orders Addr.: 15608 S. New Century Dr., Gardena, CA 90248-2129 USA (SAN 630-4818) Tel 310-532-9400; Fax: 310-532-7001; Toll Free: 800-729-6423 (orders only)
E-mail: info@scbdistributors.com
Web site: http://www.scbdistributors.com.

Schiffer Publishing, Ltd., (*978-0-7643; 978-0-87033; 978-0-88740; 978-0-89538; 978-0-916838; 978-0-9787278; 978-1-5073*) Orders Addr.: 4880 Lower Valley Rd., Atglen, PA 19310 USA (SAN 208-8428) Tel 610-593-1777; Fax: 610-593-2002
E-mail: info@schifferbooks.com; karen@schifferbooks.com
Web site: http://www.schifferbooks.com.

Schmul Publishing Co., Inc., (*978-0-88019*) Orders Addr.: P.O. Box 716, Salem, OH 44460-0716 USA (SAN 180-2771) Tel 330-222-2249; Fax: 330-222-0001; Toll Free: 800-772-6657; Edit Addr.: 3583 Newgarden Rd., Salem, OH 44460 USA
E-mail: spchale@valunet.com
Web site: http://www.wesleyanbooks.com.

Schoenhof's Foreign Bks., Inc., (*978-0-87774*) 76a Mount Auburn St., Cambridge, MA 02138-5051 USA (SAN 212-0062)
E-mail: info@schoenhofs.com
Web site: http://www.schoenhofs.com.

Scholar's Bookshelf, (*978-0-678; 978-0-945726; 978-1-60105*) Orders Addr.: 110 Melrick Rd., Cranbury, NJ 08512 USA (SAN 110-8360) Tel 609-395-6933; Fax: 609-395-0755
E-mail: books@scholarsbookshelf.com
Web site: http://www.scholarsbookshelf.com.

Scholastic Bk. Fairs, P.O. Box 958411, Lake Mary, FL 32795-8411 USA (SAN 173-7457) Tel 407-829-2600.

Scholastic, Inc., (*978-0-439; 978-0-590; 978-0-545; 978-1-338*) 557 Broadway, New York, NY 10012-3999 USA (SAN 202-5442) Fax: 212-343-6802; Toll Free: 800-325-6149 (customer service)
E-mail: info@scholastic.com
Web site: http://www.scholastic.com.

Scholium International, Inc., (*978-0-87936*) P.O. Box 1519, Port Washington, NY 11050-0306 USA (SAN 169-5282) Tel 516-767-7171; Fax: 516-944-9824
E-mail: info@scholium.com
Web site: http://www.scholium.com.

School Aid Co., (*978-0-87385*) 911 Colfax Dr., P.O. Box 123, Danville, IL 61832 USA (SAN 158-3719) Tel 217-442-6855; Toll Free: 800-447-2665.

School Aids, 9335 Interline Ave., Baton Rouge, LA 70809-1910 USA (SAN 169-2909) Tel 504-926-4498.

School Bk. Service, 3650 Coral Ridge Dr., Suite 112, Coral Springs, FL 33065-2559 USA (SAN 158-6963) Tel 954-341-7207; Fax: 954-341-7303; Toll Free: 800-228-7361
E-mail: compedge@ix.netcom.com.

School of Metaphysics, 163 Moonvalley Rd., Windyville, MO 65783 USA (SAN 159-5423) Tel 417-345-8411; Fax: 417-345-6668
E-mail: som@som.org
Web site: http://www.som.org.

Schroeder News Company, *See* **Merced News Co.**

Schroeder's Bk. Haven, 104 Michigan Ave., League City, TX 77573 USA (SAN 122-7998) Tel 281-332-5226; Fax: 281-332-1695; Toll Free: 800-894-5032
E-mail: schroedr@interloc.com.

Schulze News Co., 2451 Eastman Ave., Suite 13, Oxnard, CA 93030-5193 USA (SAN 169-0434) Tel 805-642-9759.

Schuylkill News Service, 1801 W. Market St., Pottsville, PA 17901-2001 USA (SAN 159-9518).

Schwartz, Arthur & Company, Incorporated/Woodstocker Books, *See* **Woodstocker Books/Arthur Schwartz & Company**

Schwartz Brothers, Inc., 822 Montgomery Ave., No. 204, Narberth, PA 19072-1937 USA (SAN 285-7529) Fax: 301-459-6418; Toll Free: 800-638-0243.

Science Kit & Boreal Labs, P.O. Box 5003, Tonawanda, NY 14151-5003 USA (SAN 631-2314)
E-mail: sk@sciencekit.com.

Scientific & Medical Pubns. of France, Inc., P.O. Box 3490, New York, NY 10163-3490 USA (SAN 169-5940).

SCPBooks, *See* **Phoenix Rising Pr.**

Seaboard Sub Agency, 215 S. Ott St., Allentown, PA 18104-6147 USA (SAN 285-9718).

Seaburn Bks., P.O. Box 2085, Long Island City, NY 11102 USA (SAN 631-2799) Tel 718-274-7040
E-mail: info@seaburn.com.

Seattle Bk. Co., Orders Addr.: P.O. Box 2222, Poulsbo, WA 98370 USA Tel 206-922-0418; Edit Addr.: 18864 Front St., Suite 200, Poulsbo, WA 98370 USA
E-mail: sales@seattlebookcompany.com.

Selective Bks., Inc., (*978-0-912584*) P.O. Box 1140, Clearwater, FL 34617 USA (SAN 204-577X) Tel 813-447-0100.

Selective Publishers, Incorporated, *See* **Selective Bks., Inc.**

Semler News Agency, Orders Addr.: P.O. Box 350, New Castle, PA 16101 USA (SAN 169-7471); Edit Addr.: P.O. Box 526, Morgantown, WV 26505 USA (SAN 169-8990).

Send The Light Distribution LLC, (*978-0-9835608; 978-1-939900*) Orders Addr.: 129 Mobilization Dr., Waynesboro, GA 30830 USA (SAN 631-8894) Tel 706-554-5827; Toll Free Fax: 877-323-4551; Toll Free: 877-323-4550; 100 Biblica Way, Elizabethton, TN 37643-6070 (SAN 630-7388) Tel 423-547-5131 editorial Toll Free Fax: 800-759-2779
E-mail: Customerservice@stl.org
Web site: http://www.stl-publisherservices.com.

Seneca News Agency, 800 Pre Emption Rd., Geneva, NY 14456-2010 USA (SAN 169-5304).

Sentai Distributors, 8839 Shirley Ave., Northridge, CA 91324 USA (SAN 168-9959) Tel 818-886-3113; Fax: 818-886-0423
Web site: http://www.plasticmodels.com.

Sepher-Hermon Pr., (*978-0-87203*) 1153 45th St., Brooklyn, NY 11219 USA (SAN 169-5959) Tel 718-972-9010; Fax: 718-972-6935.

Serendipity Couriers, Inc., P.O. Box 5897, Vallejo, CA 94591-5897 USA (SAN 169-0329) Toll Free: 800-459-4005 (Bay area only)
E-mail: dipity@14.netcom.com.

Serpent's Tale Natural History Bk. Distributors, Inc., (*978-1-885209*) Orders Addr.: P.O. Box 405, Lanesboro, MN 55949-0405 USA (SAN 630-6101) Tel 507-467-8734; Fax: 507-467-8735
E-mail: zoobooks@acegroup.cc
Web site: http://www.zoobooksales.com.

Service News Co., 1306 N. 23rd St., Wilmington, NC 28406 USA (SAN 169-6491) Tel 910-762-0837; Fax: 910-762-9539; Toll Free: 800-552-8238; P.O. Box 5027, Macon, GA 31208; Pope's Island, Box D-629, New Bedford, MA 02742 (SAN 169-3514).

Seven Locks Pr., (*978-0-929765; 978-0-932020; 978-0-9615964; 978-1-931643; 978-0-9790950; 978-0-9795852; 978-0-9801270; 978-0-9822293; 978-0-9824957*) P.O. Box 25689, Santa Ana, CA 92799-5689 USA (SAN 211-9781) Toll Free: 800-354-5348
E-mail: sevenlocks@aol.com
Web site: http://www.sevenlockspublishing.com.

Seymour, Dale Pubns., (*978-0-201; 978-0-7690; 978-0-86651; 978-1-57232*) Div. of Pearson Learning, Orders Addr.: P.O. Box 2500, Lebanon, OH 43216 USA Toll Free Fax: 800-393-3156; Toll Free: 800-321-3106 (Customer Service); Edit Addr.: 10 Bank St., White Plains, NY 10602-5026 USA (SAN 200-9781) Toll Free Fax: 800-393-3156; Toll Free: 800-237-3142
E-mail: pearson_learning2@prenhall.com
Web site: http://www.pearsonlearning.com; http://www.pearsonlearning.com/rightsPerm.rtf.

Shadow Mountain Publishing, (*978-0-87579; 978-1-57345; 978-1-59038; 978-1-60907*) Div. of Deseret Book Company, P.O. Box 30178, Salt Lake City, UT 84130 USA Tel 801-517-3223
E-mail: info@shadowmountain.com
Web site: http://www.shadowmountain.com.

Shambhala Publications, Incorporated, *See* **Shambhala Pubns., Inc.**

Shambhala Pubns., Inc., *(978-0-8348; 978-0-87773; 978-0-937938; 978-0-9627138; 978-1-55939; 978-1-56957; 978-1-57062; 978-1-930485; 978-1-59030; 978-1-61180; 978-1-64547)* 4720 Walnut St., Boulder, CO 80301 USA (SAN 203-2481) Tel 303-222-9598; 978-829-2599 (international); Toll Free: 888-424-2329 (orders)
E-mail: editors@shambhala.com; support@shambhala.com; customercare@shambhala.com
Web site: http://www.shambhala.com.

Sharon News Agency Co., 527 Silver St., Sharon, PA 16146 USA (SAN 169-7633).

Sharpe, M.E. Inc., *(978-0-7656; 978-0-87332; 978-1-56324)* 80 Business Park Dr., Armonk, NY 10504 USA (SAN 202-7100) Tel 914-273-1800; Fax: 914-273-2106; Toll Free: 800-541-6563
Web site: http://www.mesharpe.com.

Shea Bks., 1563 Solano Ave., Suite 206, Berkeley, CA 94707 USA (SAN 159-9720) Tel 510-528-5201; Fax: 510-528-4987.

Shell Educational Publishing, *(978-1-4258)* 5301 Oceanus Dr., Huntington Beach, CA 92649 USA Tel 714-489-2080; Fax: 714-230-7070; Toll Free: 888-877-7606; 877-777-3450
E-mail: rkarnik@tcmpub.com; LShill@seppub.com
Web site: http://www.seppub.com; http://www.tcmpub.com.

Shelter Pubns., Inc., *(978-0-936070)* Orders Addr.: P.O. Box 279, Bolinas, CA 94924 USA (SAN 122-8463) Tel 415-868-0280; Fax: 415-868-9053; Toll Free: 800-307-0131; Edit Addr.: 285 Dogwood Rd, Bolinas, CA 94924 USA
E-mail: shelter@shelterpub.com
Web site: http://www.shelterpub.com.

Shenanigan Bks., *(978-0-9726614; 978-1-934860)* 84 River Rd., Summit, NJ 07901-1443 USA (SAN 915-7085)
Web site: http://www.shenaniganbooks.com.

Shoppers Guide Pr., 706 N. Fifth, Alpine, TX 79830 USA (SAN 159-9550) Tel 915-837-7426.

Sierra News Co., 2136 Pony Express Ct., Stockton, CA 95215-7946 USA (SAN 169-4472).

Signature Bks., LLC, *(978-0-941214; 978-1-56085)* 564 W. 400 N., Salt Lake City, UT 84116-3411 USA (SAN 217-4391) Tel 801-531-1483; Fax: 801-531-1488; Toll Free: 800-356-5687 (orders only)
E-mail: people@signaturebooks.com
Web site: http://www.signaturebooks.com.

Silky Way, Inc., 1227 38th Ave., San Francisco, CA 94122-1334 USA (SAN 169-3328).

Silver Bow News Distributing Co., Inc., 219 E. Park St., Butte, MT 59701 USA (SAN 169-4359) Tel 406-782-6995.

Silver, Burdett & Ginn, Inc., *(978-0-382; 978-0-663; 978-1-4182)* Orders Addr.: P.O. Box 2500, Lebanon, IN 46052 USA Toll Free Fax: 800-841-8939; Toll Free: 800-552-2259; Edit Addr.: P.O. Box 480, Parsippany, NJ 07054 USA (SAN 204-5982); 108 Wilmot Rd., Suite 380, Midwest Div., Deerfield, IL 60015 (SAN 111-6517) Tel 708-945-1240; 1925 Century Blvd. NE, Suite 14, Southeast Div., Atlanta, GA 30345 (SAN 111-6509); 8445 Freeport Pkwy., Suite 400, South Div., Irving, TX 75063 (SAN 108-0458) Tel 214-915-4200; 2001 The Alameda, West Div., San Jose, CA 95126 (SAN 111-6525) Tel 408-248-6854; 160 Gould St., East Div., Needham Heights, MA 02194-2310; 1900 E. Lake Ave., Glenview, IL 60025
E-mail: customerservice@scottforesman.com
Web site: http://www.scottforesman.com/.

Simon & Schuster, *(978-0-671; 978-0-684; 978-0-689; 978-0-914676; 978-0-7432; 978-1-4165; 978-1-4391; 978-1-4516; 978-1-4767; 978-1-5011; 978-1-9821; 978-1-7214)* Div. of Simon & Schuster, Inc., Orders Addr.: 100 Front St., Riverside, NJ 08075 USA (SAN 200-2442) Toll Free Fax: 800-943-9831; Toll Free: 800-223-2336 (ordering); 800-223-2348 (customer service); Edit Addr.: a/o Subsidiary Rights, 11th Flr., 1230 Avenue of the Americas, New York, NY 10020 USA (SAN 200-2450) Tel 212-698-7000; Fax: 212-698-7007; 212-632-8099 (Rights & Permissions); 212-698-1269 (Pocket Bks. Rights & Permissions); Toll Free: 800-897-7650 (customer financial services); 100 Front St., Riverside, NJ 08075 (SAN 852-5471) Tel 856-824-2115
E-mail: ssonline_feedback@simonsays.com; consumer.customerservice@simonandschuster.com
Web site: http://www.simonsays.com; http://www.oasis.simonandschuster.com; http://www.simonandschuster.com/.

Simon & Schuster Children's Publishing, *(978-0-02; 978-0-671; 978-0-684; 978-0-689; 978-0-7434; 978-1-4169; 978-1-4424; 978-0-85707)* Orders Addr.: 100 Front St., Riverside, NJ 08075 USA Toll Free Fax: 800-943-9831; Toll Free: 800-223-2336; Edit Addr.: a/o Subsidiary Rights, 4th floor, 1230 Avenue of the Americas, New York, NY 10020 USA Tel 212-698-7200; Fax: 212-698-2797 (Rights & Permissions)
Web site: http://www.simonsays.com.

Simon & Schuster, Inc., *(978-0-02; 978-0-671; 978-0-684; 978-0-689; 978-0-88138; 978-0-914676; 978-0-937860; 978-1-55850; 978-1-58062; 978-0-7432; 978-0-7434; 978-0-7435; 978-1-59337; 978-1-4165; 978-1-4169; 978-1-59869; 978-1-60550; 978-1-4391; 978-1-4405; 978-1-4423; 978-1-4424; 978-1-4516; 978-0-85707; 978-1-4814; 978-1-5072; 978-1-5082; 978-1-5344; 978-1-7971) Div. of Viacom Co., Orders Addr.: 100 Front St., Riverside, NJ 08075 USA Toll Free Fax: 800-943-9831; Toll Free: 800-223-2336 (orders); 800-223-2348 (customer service); Edit Addr.: 1230 Ave. of the Americas, New York, NY 10020 USA Tel 212-698-7000*
E-mail: Consumer.CustomerService@simonandschuster.com
Web site: http://www.simonsays.com; http://www.simonandschuster.com.

Simon & Schuster Trade, *See* **Simon & Schuster**

Skandisk, Inc., *(978-0-9615394; 978-1-57534)* 6667 W. Old Shakopee Rd., Suite 109, Bloomington, MN 55438-2622 USA (SAN 695-4405) Tel 952-829-8998; Fax: 952-829-8992; Toll Free: 800-468-2424 (orders)
E-mail: lhamnes@skandisk.com; tomten@skandisk.com
Web site: http://www.skandisk.com.

Sky Oaks Productions, Inc., *(978-0-940296; 978-1-56018)* P.O. Box 1102, Los Gatos, CA 95031 USA (SAN 217-5843) Tel 408-395-7600; Fax: 408-395-8440
E-mail: TRPWorld@aol.com
Web site: http://www.tpr-world.com.

Slatner, Thomas & Co., Inc., 193 Palisade Ave., 3rd Flr., Jersey City, NJ 07306-1112 USA (SAN 130-9862) Tel 201-420-6700; Fax: 201-420-6787.

Slavica Pubs., *(978-0-89357)* c/o Indiana University, 1430 N. Willis Dr., Bloomington, IN 47404 USA (SAN 208-8576) Tel 812-856-4186; Fax: 812-856-4187
E-mail: slavica@indiana.edu
Web site: http://www.slavica.indiana.edu.

Sleeper, Dick Distribution, 18680-B Langensand Rd., Sandy, OR 97055-6426 USA (SAN 631-0273) Tel 503-668-3454; Fax: 503-668-5314; Toll Free: 800-699-9911
E-mail: sleepydick@bigfoot.com.

Sleuth Pubns., Ltd., *(978-0-915341)* 3398 Washington, San Francisco, CA 94118 USA (SAN 130-9374) Tel 415-771-2689.

Small Pr. United, Div. of Independent Pubs. Group, 814 N. Franklin St., Chicago, IL 60610 USA Tel 312-337-0747 (ext. 274)
Web site: http://www.smallpressunited.com.

Small Press Distribution, *See* **SPD-Small Pr. Distribution**

Smashwords, *(978-1-4523; 978-1-4524; 978-1-4580; 978-1-4581; 978-1-4657; 978-1-4658; 978-1-4659; 978-1-4660; 978-1-4661; 978-1-4760; 978-1-4761; 978-1-4762; 978-1-4763; 978-1-4764; 978-1-301; 978-1-310; 978-1-311; 978-1-370; 978-0-463; 978-0-692-04063-8; 978-0-578-41339-6; 978-1-005) 15951 Gatos Blvd., Suite 16, Los Gatos, CA 95032 USA Tel 408-358-1824; ziya gokalp mah. cimen sk. no:1/1 ikitelli koyu, basaksehir-istanbul, 34306 Tel 90 0538 8939727*
E-mail: bill@smashwords.com
Web site: http://www.smashwords.com.

Smith, Gibbs Publisher, *See* **Gibbs Smith, Publisher**

Smith News Agency, 118 S. Mitchell St., Cadillac, MI 49601 USA (SAN 169-3727).

SMMA Distributors, 6609 Brooks Dr., Temple, TX 76502 USA Tel 254-773-4884.

Snyder Magazine Agency, 3050 S. 9th Terr., Kansas City, KS 66103-2629 USA (SAN 285-9750).

Social Studies Schl. Service, *(978-1-56004; 978-1-57596)* Orders Addr.: 10200 Jefferson Blvd., P.O. Box 802, Culver City, CA 90232-0802 USA (SAN 168-9592) Tel 310-839-2436; Fax: 310-839-2249; Toll Free: 800-421-4246
E-mail: access@socialstudies.com
Web site: http://socialstudies.com.

Sociedad Biblica de Puerto Rico, Orders Addr.: P.O. Box 2548, Bayamon, PR 00960-2548 USA; Edit Addr.: Carr. 167, Km 14.7 Bo, Bayamon, PR 00960-2548 USA.

Society for Visual Education, Incorporated, *See* **S V E & Churchill Media**

Sopris West Educational Services, *See* **Cambium Education, Inc.**

Sort Card Co., The, 400 S. Summit View Dr., Fort Collins, CO 80524-1424 USA (SAN 159-9607).

Soundprints, *(978-0-924483; 978-1-56899; 978-1-931465; 978-1-59249; 978-1-60727)* Div. of Trudy Corp., 353 Main Ave., Norwalk, CT 06851 USA Fax: 203-846-1776; Toll Free: 800-228-7839
Web site: http://www.soundprints.com.

Sounds True, Inc., *(978-1-56455; 978-1-59179; 978-1-60407; 978-1-62203; 978-1-68364; 978-1-64963)* Orders Addr.: P.O. Box 8010, Boulder, CO 80306-8010 USA; Edit Addr.: 413 S. Arthur Ave., Louisville, CO 80027 USA (SAN 850-3532) Tel 303-665-3151; Fax: 303-665-5292; Toll Free: 800-333-9185
Web site: http://www.soundstrue.com.

Source Bk. Pubns., *(978-1-887137)* 1814 Franklin St., Suite 820, Oakland, CA 94612 USA Tel 510-839-5471; Fax: 510-547-3245.

Source Bks., *(978-0-940147; 978-0-85650)* Orders Addr.: 204 E. Fourth St., Suite O, Santa Ana, CA 92701 USA (SAN 248-2231) Tel 714-558-8944 (phone/fax); Toll Free: 800-695-4237 Do not confuse with Source Bks., Nashville, TN
E-mail: studio185@earthlink.net.

Source International Technology Corporation, *See* **Kamkyi Bks.**

Sourcebooks, Inc., *(978-0-942061; 978-0-9629162; 978-0-9629803; 978-1-57071; 978-1-57248; 978-1-58182; 978-1-883518; 978-1-887166; 978-1-888952; 978-1-4022; 978-1-932783; 978-1-62047; 978-1-4926; 978-1-7282)* 1935 Brookdale Rd., Suite 139, Naperville, IL 60563 USA (SAN 666-7864) Tel 630-961-3900; Fax: 630-961-2168; Toll Free: 800-727-8866
E-mail: info@sourcebooks.com
Web site: http://www.sourcebooks.com/.

South Asia Bks., *(978-0-8364; 978-0-88386)* P.O. Box 502, Columbia, MO 65205 USA (SAN 207-4044) Tel 573-474-0116; Fax: 573-474-8124
E-mail: sabooks@juno.com
Web site: http://www.southasiabooks.com.

South Atlantic News, Orders Addr.: P.O. Box 61297, Jacksonville, FL 32236-1297 USA; Edit Addr.: 1426 NE Eighth Ave., Ocala, FL 32678 USA.

South Carolina Bookstore, Orders Addr.: P.O. Box 4767, West Columbia, SC 29171 USA (SAN 131-2294) Tel 803-796-8200; Fax: 803-794-6927; Toll Free: 800-845-8200; Edit Addr.: 523 Jasper St., West Columbia, SC 29169 USA (SAN 243-2390).

South Central Bks., Inc., 1106 S. Strong Blvd., McAlester, OK 74501-6952 USA (SAN 108-1144) Tel 405-275-4522; Toll Free: 800-548-9858.

South Eastern Bk. Co., Inc., 3333 Hwy. 641 N., P.O. Box 309, Murray, KY 42071 USA (SAN 630-4869) Tel 270-753-0732; Fax: 270-759-4742; Toll Free Fax: 800-433-6966 (orders); Toll Free: 800-626-3952 (orders)
E-mail: orders@sebook.com
Web site: http://www.sebook.com.

South Louisiana News Company, *See* **Southern Periodicals, Inc.**

Southeast Library Bindery, Inc., P.O. Box 35484, Greensboro, NC 27425-5484 USA (SAN 159-9445) Tel 336-931-0800
E-mail: 70304.3023@compuserve.com
Web site: http://www.webmasters.net/bookbinding/.

Southeast Periodical & Bk. Sales, Inc., 10100 NW 25th St., Box 520155-Biscayne Annex, Miami, FL 33152 USA.

Southeastern Educational Toy & Bk. Distributors, Orders Addr.: 3215 Wellington Court Suite 113, Raleigh, NC 27615 USA (SAN 630-8104) Tel 704-364-6988; Edit Addr.: 4217 Park Rd., Charlotte, NC 28209 USA Tel 704-527-1921; Fax: 704-527-1653.

Southeastern Library Service, Subs. of Haskins Hse., P.O. Box 44, Gainesville, FL 32602-0044 USA (SAN 159-9615) Tel 352-372-3823.

Southern Bk. Service, *(978-0-9663836)* 4360 NW 135th St, Opa Locka, FL 33054 USA (SAN 169-0981) Tel 305-624-4545; Fax: 305-621-0425; Toll Free: 800-766-3254.

Southern Cross Pubns., 1734 W. Roseberry Rd., P.O. Box 717, Donnelly, ID 83615 USA (SAN 110-8549) Tel 208-325-8606; Fax: 208-325-3400
E-mail: scp@cyberhighway.net
Web site: http://www.thoughtlines.com/southerncross/.

Southern Library Bindery Co., 2952 Sidco Dr., Nashville, TN 37204 USA (SAN 169-7986).

Southern Michigan News Co., 2571 Saradan, P.O. Box 908, Jackson, MI 49204 USA (SAN 169-3697) Tel 517-784-7163; Toll Free: 800-248-2213 (in Michigan); 800-828-2140.

Southern Periodicals, Inc., P.O. Box 407, Rayne, LA 70578-0407 USA (SAN 113-2520); 180 James Dr E., Saint Rose, LA 70087-4005.

Southern Tier News Co., P.O. Box 2128, Elmira Heights, NY 14903 USA (SAN 169-5223).

Southern Wisconsin News, 58 Artisan Dr., Edgerton, WI 53534 USA (SAN 169-9121) Tel 608-884-2600; Fax: 608-756-2357
E-mail: ndewar@southernwisconsinnews.com.

Southwest Cookbook Distributors, Orders Addr.: P.O. Box 707, Bonham, TX 75418 USA (SAN 200-4925) Tel 903-583-8898; Fax: 903-583-2522; Toll Free: 800-725-8898 (orders); Edit Addr.: P.O. Box 707, Bonham, TX 75418-0707 USA (SAN 630-8325).

Southwest Natural Cultural Heritage Association, *See* **Public Lands Interpretive Assn.**

Southwest News Co., Box 5465, Tucson, AZ 85704 USA (SAN 159-9631).

Southwestern Bk. Distributors, c/o Kerbs, 700 Highview Ave., Glen Ellyn, IL 60137-5504 USA (SAN 160-2373).

Sovereign News Company, *See* **Trans World News**

Spama, Inc., 78 Lake St., Jersey City, NJ 07306-3407 USA (SAN 169-5967).

Spanish & European Bookstore, Inc., 3102 Wilshire Blvd., Los Angeles, CA 90010 USA Tel 213-739-8899; Fax: 213-739-0087.

Spanish Bookstore-Wholesale, The, 10977 Santa Monica Blvd., Los Angeles, CA 90025-4538 USA (SAN 168-9835) Tel 310-475-0453; Fax: 310-473-6132
E-mail: BernardHamel@SpanishbooksUSA.com
Web site: http://www.BernardHamel.com.

Spanish Hse. Distributors, 1360 NW 88th Ave., Miami, FL 33172-3093 USA (SAN 169-1171) Tel 305-592-6136; Fax: 305-592-0087; Toll Free: 800-767-7726.

Spanish Language Bk. Services, Inc., Orders Addr.: 7855 N.W. 12th St., Suite 211, Miami, FL 33126 USA.

Spanish Pubs., LLC, 8871 SW 129 Terr., Miami, FL 33176 USA Tel 305-233-3365; Fax: 305-251-1310
E-mail: mariela@spanishpublishers.net
Web site: www.spanishpublishers.net.

Spanishtech, Inc., Div. of Editor's Bureau, Ltd., P.O. Box 68, Westport, CT 06881 USA (SAN 289-9620) Tel 203-452-7655.

SPD-Small Pr. Distribution, *(978-0-914068)* 1341 Seventh St., Berkeley, CA 94710-1409 USA (SAN 204-5826) Tel 510-524-1668; Fax: 510-524-0852; Toll Free: 800-869-7553 (orders)
E-mail: orders@spdbooks.org
Web site: http://www.spdbooks.org.

SpeakWare, 2836 Stephen Dr., Richmond, CA 94803 USA Tel 510-222-2455
E-mail: leds@speakware.com
Web site: http://www.speakware.com.

Specialized Bk. Service, Inc., 307 Autumn Ridge Rd., Fairfield, CT 06432-1003 USA (SAN 166-9788) Tel 203-377-6510; Fax: 203-377-4792.

Specialty Bk. Services, 1150 N. San Francisco, Flagstaff, AZ 86001 USA (SAN 130-8114) Tel 520-779-7843.

Specialty Promotions, 4516 S. Vincennes Ave. # 1S, Chicago, IL 60653-3470 USA (SAN 110-9987).

Speech Bin, Inc., The, *(978-0-937857)* 1965 25th Ave., Vero Beach, FL 32960 USA (SAN 630-1657) Tel 772-770-0007; Fax: 772-770-0006
E-mail: info@speechbin.com
Web site: http://www.speechbin.com.

Speedimpex U.S.A., Inc., 35-02 48th Ave., Long Island City, NY 11101-2421 USA (SAN 169-5479) Tel 718-392-7477; Fax: 718-361-0815
E-mail: nsalvatore@speedimpex.com
Web site: http://www.speedimpex.com.

Spencer Museum of Art, *(978-0-913689)* Affil. of Univ. of Kansas, Univ. of Kansas 1301 Mississippi St., Lawrence, KS 66045-7500 USA (SAN 111-347X) Tel 785-864-4710; Fax: 785-864-3112
E-mail: spencerart@ku.edu
Web site: http://www.spencerart.ku.edu.

SPI Bks., *(978-0-944007; 978-1-56171)* 99 Spring St., 3rd Flr., New York, NY 10012 USA Tel 212-431-5011; Fax: 212-431-8646
E-mail: ian@spibooks.com
Web site: http://www.spibooks.com.

Spirit Filled Pr., Inc., *(978-0-9656668)* 2549 Tallavana Trail, Havana, FL 32333 USA Tel 850-539-3843 (phone/fax)
E-mail: 2549@bellsouth.net
Web site: http://www.mindspring.com/~spiritfilled.

Spirit Rising, c/o Nicole Heyward, 1505 Hadley St., Houston, TX 77002 USA Tel 713-772-5175; Fax: 713-772-3034
E-mail: nicole.heyward@musicworldent.com.

Spring Arbor Distributors, Inc., Subs. of Ingram Industries Inc., 4271 Edison Ave., Chino, CA 91710 USA; 7315 Innovation Blvd., Fort Wayne, IN 46818-1371; 201 Ingram Dr., Roseburg, OR 97470-7148; Newbury Rd., East Windsor, CT 06088; 25420 Weakley Rd., Petersburg, VA 23803; 11333 E. 53rd Ave., Denver, CO 80239-2108; Edit Addr.: 1 Ingram Blvd., La Vergne, TN 37086-1976 USA Fax: 615-213-5192; Toll Free: 800-395-4340; 800-395-7234 (customer service)
E-mail: orders@springarbor.com.

Springer, *(978-0-387; 978-0-8176; 978-3-211; 978-3-540; 978-3-7908; 978-4-431; 978-1-85233; 978-1-84628; 978-1-4419; 978-1-4612; 978-1-4613; 978-1-4614; 978-1-4615; 978-1-4684; 978-1-4757; 978-1-4899; 978-1-4939; 978-1-5041; 978-1-0716)* Subs. of Springer Science+Business Media, Orders Addr.: P.O. Box 2485, Secaucus, NJ 07096-2485 USA Tel 201-348-4033; Fax: 201-348-4505; Toll Free: 800-777-4643; Edit Addr.: a/o Springer Nature, 233 Spring St., New York, NY 10013-1578 USA (SAN 203-2228) Tel 212-815-0249; 212-460-1500; Fax: 212-460-1575; Toll Free: 800-777-4643 Thomson Delmar Learning Distributes Blanchard & Loeb Nursing Videos Only
E-mail: Slu@Springer-ny.com; service-ny@springer.com; customerservice@springernature.com.com
Web site: http://www.springeronline.com; http://www.springer.com.

Springer-Verlag New York, Incorporated, *See* **Springer**

Springwater Bks., Orders Addr.: P.O. Box 194, Springwater, NY 14560-0194 USA (SAN 111-8900); Edit Addr.: Main St. & East Ave., Springwater, NY 14560-0194 USA (SAN 243-2412) Tel 716-669-2450.

Sprout, Inc., Orders Addr.: 430 Tenth St., NW, Suite 007, Atlanta, GA 30318 USA Tel 404-892-9600; Fax: 404-881-1383.

Square Deal Records, 303 Higuera St., San Luis Obispo, CA 93401-4209 USA (SAN 170-6799) Tel 805-543-3636; Fax: 805-543-3938; Toll Free: 800-253-4114
E-mail: sdrsslo@aol.com.

SRA/McGraw-Hill, *(978-0-07; 978-0-383)* Div. of The McGraw-Hill Education Group, Orders Addr.: 220 E. Daniel Dale Rd., DeSoto, TX 75115-2490 USA Fax: 972-228-1982; Toll Free: 800-843-8855; Edit Addr.: 8787 Orion Pl., Columbus, OH 43240-4027 USA Tel 614-430-6600; Fax: 614-430-6621; Toll Free: 800-468-5850
E-mail: sra@mcgraw-hill.com
Web site: https://www.sraonline.com.

Sri Aurobindo Association, Incorporated, *See* **Matagiri Sri Aurobindo Ctr.**

St. Marie's Gopher News Co., 9000 Tenth Ave., N., Minneapolis, MN 55427 USA (SAN 169-4103) Tel 612-546-5300; Fax: 612-546-1487.

St. Martin's Pr., *(978-0-312; 978-0-8050; 978-0-940687; 978-0-9603648; 978-1-55927; 978-1-58063; 978-1-58238; 978-1-4299; 978-1-250)* Div. of Holtzbrinck Pubs., Orders Addr.: 16365 James Madison Hwy., Gordonville, VA 22942 USA Tel 540-672-7600; Fax: 540-672-7540 (customer service); Toll Free Fax: 800-672-2054; Toll Free: 888-330-8477; Edit Addr.: 175 Fifth Ave., 20th Flr., New York, NY 10010 USA (SAN 200-2132) Tel 212-674-5151 (Trade Div.); 212-726-0200 (College Div.); Fax: 212-674-3179 (Trade Div.); 212-686-9491 (College Div.); Toll Free: 800-221-7945 (Trade Div.); 800-470-4767 (College Div.)
E-mail: webmaster@stmartins.com; enquiries@stmartins.com
Web site: http://www.stmartins.com; http://www.smpcollege.com.

St. Mary Seminary Bookstore, 28700 Euclid Ave., Wyckliffe, OH 44092 USA (SAN 169-667X) Tel 216-943-7600.

St Pauls/Alba Hse. Pubs., *(978-0-8189)* Div. of Society of St. Paul, 2187 Victory Blvd., Staten Island, NY 10314-6603 USA (SAN 201-2405) Tel 718-761-0047;

Fax: 718-761-0057; 718-698-8390; Toll Free: 800-343-2522
E-mail: albabooks@aol.com
Web site: http://www.albahouse.org.

Stackpole Bks., *(978-0-8117)* 5067 Ritter Rd., Mechanicsburg, PA 17055 USA (SAN 202-5396) Tel 717-796-0411; Fax: 717-796-0412; Toll Free: 800-732-3669
E-mail: ccraley@stackpolebooks.com
Web site: http://www.stackpolebooks.com/.

Star Bright Bks., Inc., *(978-1-887734; 978-1-932065; 978-1-59572; 978-1-64909)* 13 Landsdowne, Cambridge , MA 02139 USA (SAN 254-5225) Tel 617-354-1300; Fax: 617-354-1399; Toll Free: 800-788-4439
E-mail: info@starbrightbooks.com; r.s.lambert@starbrightbooks.com
Web site: http://www.starbrightbooks.com.

StarCrossed Productions, *(978-0-9668483)* 14552 NW., 88 Pl., Miami, FL 33018 USA Tel 305-828-2619 Phone/Fax
E-mail: tinami@msn.com
Web site: http://www.cookiesisters.com.

Starkmann, Inc., 25-u Olympia Ave., Woburn, MA 01801 USA (SAN 126-6128) Tel 781-938-9643; Fax: 781-938 9647
E-mail: biggs@starkmann.co.uk.

Starmaster Co., 6911 Haverhill Dr., Knoxville, TN 37909 USA (SAN 108-1217) Tel 423-588-6661.

StarWalk Kids, 15 Cutter Mill Rd., Suite 242, Great Neck, NY 11021 USA.

State News Agency, 2750 Griffith Rd., Winston Salem, NC 27103-6418 USA (SAN 169-6424).

State Univ. of New York Pr., *(978-0-7914; 978-0-87395; 978-0-88706; 978-1-4384)* Orders Addr.: P.O. Box 960, Herndon, VA 20172-0960 USA (SAN 203-3496) Tel 703-661-1575; Fax: 703-996-1010; Toll Free Fax: 877-204-6074; Toll Free: 877-204-6073 (customer service); Edit Addr.: 22 Corporate Woods Blvd., 3rd Flr., Albany, NY 12211-2504 USA (SAN 658-1730) Tel 518-472-5000; Fax: 518-472-5038; Toll Free: 866-430-7869
E-mail: info@sunypress.edu; suny@presswarehouse.com
Web site: http://www.sunypress.edu.

Steerforth Pr., *(978-0-944072; 978-1-58195; 978-1-883642; 978-1-58642)* 45 Lyme Rd. # 208, Hanover, NH 03755-1219 USA
E-mail: helga@steerforth.com; info@steerforth.com
Web site: http://www.steerforth.com.

Steiner, Rudolf College Pr./St. George Pubns., *(978-0-916786; 978-0-945803; 978-0-9818095)* 9200 Fair Oaks Blvd., Fair Oaks, CA 95628 USA (SAN 208-8371) Tel 916-961-3722; Fax: 916-961-3032
E-mail: claude.julien@steinercollege.edu; cblatch@comcast.net
Web site: http://www.steinercollege.edu.

SteinerBooks, Inc., *(978-0-8334; 978-0-88010; 978-0-89345; 978-0-910142; 978-1-58420; 978-1-85584; 978-0-9701097; 978-0-9831984; 978-1-62148; 978-1-62151; 978-1-938685; 978-0-9969211; 978-1-7324613; 978-1-952166)* Orders Addr.: P.O. Box 960, Herndon, VA 20172-0960 USA Tel 703-661-1594 (orders); Fax: 702-661-1501; Toll Free Fax: 800-277-7947 (orders); Toll Free: 800-856-8664 (orders); Edit Addr.: 610 Main St., Suite 1, Great Barrington, MA 01230 USA Tel 413-528-8233; Fax: 413-528-8826; Fulfillment Addr.: 22883 Quicksilver Dr., Dulles, VA 20166 USA (SAN 253-9519) Tel 703-661-1529; Fax: 703-996-1010
E-mail: service@steinerbooks.org
Web site: http://www.steinerbooks.org.

Stenhouse Pubs., *(978-1-57110; 978-1-62531)* Div. of Highlights for Children, Orders Addr.: P.O. Box 11020, Portland, ME 04104-7020 USA (SAN 298-1580) Tel 207-253-1600; Fax: 207-253-5121; Toll Free Fax: 800-833-9164; Toll Free: 800-988-9812 (orders)
E-mail: jkilburn@stenhouse.com
Web site: http://www.stenhouse.com.

Sterling Publishing Co., Inc., *(978-0-8069; 978-1-4027; 978-1-60582; 978-1-4549; 978-1-61837; 978-1-9847)* 1166 Avenue of the Americas, 17th Flr., New York, NY 10036 USA (SAN 211-6324) Tel 212-532-7160 212-213-2495; Toll Free Fax: 800-775-8736 (warehouse); Toll Free: 800-367-9692; 800-542-7567 Do not confuse with companies with similar names in Falls Church, VA, Fallbrook, CA, Lewisville, TX
E-mail: custservice@sterlingpub.com; tradesales@sterlingpub.com
Web site: http://www.sterlingpublishing.com/.

Steuben Pr., 230 Primrose Ct. #3, Longmont, CO 80501 USA Tel 303-482-2060
E-mail: orders@steubenpress.com.

Stevens, Gareth Incorporated, *See* **Stevens, Gareth Publishing LLLP**

Stevens, Gareth Publishing LLLP, *(978-0-8368; 978-0-918831; 978-1-55532; 978-1-4339)* Orders Addr.: P.O. Box 360140, Strongsville, OH 44136-0140 USA Fax: 877-542-2596; Toll Free: 800-542-2595; Edit Addr.: 111 East 14th St., Suite 349, New York, NY 10003 USA (SAN 696-1592) Toll Free: 877-444-0210
E-mail: customerservice@gspub.com; hollyc@rosen.pub
Web site: http://www.garethstevens.com; http://www.garethstevensclassroom.com.

Stevens International, Orders Addr.: P.O. Box 126, Magnolia, NJ 08049 USA (SAN 631-3612) Tel 856-435-1555; Edit Addr.: 706 N. White Horse Pike, Magnolia, NJ 08049 USA
Web site: http://www.stevenshobby.com.

Stevens, Mark Industries, Div. of Christian World, Inc., 304 N. Meridian Ave., Suite 6, Oklahoma City, OK 73107 USA (SAN 631-127X) Toll Free: 800-654-6760.

STL Distribution North America, *See* **Send The Light Distribution LLC**

Stoneydale Pr. Publishing Co., *(978-0-912299; 978-1-931291; 978-1-938707)* Orders Addr.: P.O. Box 188, Stevensville, MT 59870 USA Tel 406-777-2729; Fax: 406-777-2521; Toll Free: 800-735-7006; Edit Addr.: 523 Main St., Stevensville, MT 59870 USA (SAN 265-3168)
E-mail: stoneydale@stoneydale.com
Web site: http://www.stoneydale.com.

Storey Books, *See* **Storey Publishing, LLC**

Storey Publishing, LLC, *(978-0-88266; 978-1-58017; 978-0-9674717; 978-1-60342; 978-1-61212; 978-1-63586)* Subs. of Workman Publishing Co., Inc., Orders Addr.: 210 Mass Moca Way, North Adams, MA 01247 USA (SAN 203-4158) Fax: 413-346-2198; Toll Free Fax: 800-865-3429; Toll Free: 800-827-7444; c/o Workman Publishing, 225 Varick St., New York, NY 10014-4381 Tel 212-614-7700; Toll Free Fax: 800-521-1832; Toll Free: 800-722-7202
E-mail: info@storey.com; sales@storey.com
Web site: http://www.storey.com.

Strang Communications Company, *See* **Charisma Media**

Strauss Consultants, 48 W. 25th St., 11th Flr., New York, NY 10010-2708 USA Toll Free Fax: 888-528-8273; Toll Free: 800-236-7918
E-mail: strausscon@aol.com.

Streamwood Distribution, P.O. Box 91011, Mobile, AL 36691 USA Tel 334-665-0022; Fax: 334-665-0570.

Strelow, James C., 12588 Ivy Glen Ln., Garden Grove, CA 92841-4563 USA (SAN 132-4144).

Strisik, Nancy, 10 Main St., Rockport, MA 01966 USA Tel 978-546-7653.

Studio 2 Publishing, Inc., *(978-0-9763601; 978-0-9792455; 978-0-9815281; 978-0-9819874; 978-0-9826427; 978-0-9828175; 978-1-937013; 978-1-944413; 978-1-950082)* 2663 Byington Solway Rd., Knoxville, TN 37931 USA Tel 865-212-3797
E-mail: contact@studio2publishing.com
Web site: http://www.studio2publishing.com.

Studio Fun International, *(978-0-276; 978-0-7621; 978-0-88705; 978-0-88850; 978-0-89577; 978-1-57584; 978-1-57619; 978-0-7944)* Subs. of Reader's Digest Assn., Inc., Reader's Digest Rd., Pleasantville, NY 10570-7000 USA (SAN 283-2143) Tel 914-244-4800; Fax: 914-244-4841
Web site: http://www.readersdigestkids.com; http://www.studiofun.com/.

Stylus Publishing, LLC, *(978-1-57922; 978-1-887208; 978-0-9729394; 978-1-62036; 978-1-64267)* Orders Addr.: P.O. Box 605, Herndon, VA 20172-0605 USA; Edit Addr.: 22883 Quicksilver Dr., Sterling, VA 20166-2012 USA (SAN 299-1853) Tel 703-661-1581; Fax: 703-661-1501 Do not confuse with companies with the same name in Sunnyvale, CA, Quakertown, PA
E-mail: stylusmail@presswarehouse.com; jean.westcott@styluspub.com
Web site: http://www.styluspub.com.

Subscription Account, 84 Needham, Newton Highlands, MA 02161 USA (SAN 285-9424).

Subscription Hse., Inc., 209 Harvard St., Suite 407, Brookline, MA 02146-5005 USA (SAN 285-9343).

Subterranean Co., Orders Addr.: P.O. Box 160, Monroe, OR 97456 USA Fax: 541-847-6018
E-mail: subco@clipper.net.

Success Education Assn., Box 175, Roanoke, VA 24002 USA (SAN 159-9690).

Suite 3 Productions, 90 W. 100 N., Suite 13, Provo, UT 84501 USA Tel 801-472 — 6024.

Sun Life, *(978-0-937930)* 2399 Cool Springs Rd., Thaxton, VA 24174 USA (SAN 240-8333) Tel 540-586-4898.

Sunbelt Pubns., Inc., *(978-0-916251; 978-0-932653; 978-0-9606704; 978-0-9620402; 978-1-941384)* 1250 Fayette St., El Cajon, CA 92020-1511 USA (SAN 630-0790) Tel 619-258-4911; Fax: 619-258-4916; Toll Free: 800-626-6579
E-mail: info@sunbeltpub.com; sales@sunbeltpub.com; dyoung@sunbeltpub.com; mail@sunbeltpub.com
Web site: http://www.sunbeltpub.com; http://www.sunbeltbooks.com.

Sunburst Bks., Inc., Distributor of Florida Bks., 700 S. John Rodes Blvd., #D8, West Melbourne, FL 32904 USA Tel 321-409-0225; Fax: 321-728-2742
Web site: http://www.sunburstbooks.com.

Sunburst Communications, Inc., *(978-0-7805; 978-0-911831; 978-1-55636; 978-1-55826)* 400 Columbus Ave., Valhalla, NY 10595-1335 USA (SAN 213-5620) Toll Free: 800-431-1934
E-mail: webmaster@nysunburst.com
Web site: http://www.sunburst.com.

Sunburst Visual Media, *(978-1-59520)* Orders Addr.: P.O. Box 4455, Scottsdale, AZ 85261 USA Toll Free: 800-262-8837; Edit Addr.: P.O. Box 9120, Plainview, NY 11803-9020 USA
Web site: http://www.schoolspecialty.com.

Sunday School Board of the Southern Baptist Convention, *See* **LifeWay Christian Resources**

Sundaykool Bulletins, *(978-1-888824)* Div. of Griffin Publishing Co., 18022 Cowan, Suite 202, Irvine, CA 92614 USA (SAN 631-5046) Toll Free: 800-472-9741
E-mail: griffinbooks@earthlink.net
Web site: http://www.griffinpublishing.com.

Sunshine Harbor, 825 Glen Arden Way, Altamonte Springs, FL 32701 USA (SAN 159-6640) Tel 407-339-0401.

Swedenborg Foundation, Inc., *(978-0-87785)* 320 N. Church St., West Chester, PA 19380 USA (SAN 111-7920) Tel 610-430-3222; Fax: 610-430-7982
E-mail: editor@swedenborg.com
Web site: http://www.swedenborg.com.

Swenson, Jim, 2610 Riverside Ln., NE, Rochester, MN 55901 USA (SAN 285-9505).

Swift News Agency, Orders Addr.: P.O. Box 160, Poncha Springs, CO 81242 USA (SAN 282-3810); Edit Addr.: 338 E. Hwy. 50, Poncha Springs, CO 81242 USA (SAN 169-0639).

Syco Distribution, 9208A Venture Ct., Manassas, VA 20111-4804 USA.

Symmes Systems, *(978-0-916352; 978-0-9907312)* 3977 Briarcliff Rd., NE, Atlanta, GA 30345-2647 USA (SAN 169-1465) Tel 404-876-7260.

Syndistar, Inc., *(978-1-56230)* P.O. Box 3027, Hammond, LA 70404-3027 USA (SAN 298-007X) Toll Free: 800-841-9532
E-mail: webmaster@syndistar.com
Web site: http://www.syndistar.com.

Syracuse Univ. Pr., *(978-0-8156; 978-0-615-28768-3; 978-1-68445)* 621 Skytop Rd., Suite 110, Syracuse, NY 13244-5290 USA (SAN 206-9776) Tel 315-443-5534; Fax: 315-443-5545
E-mail: supress@syr.edu; arpfeiff@syr.edu
Web site: http://www.SyracuseUniversityPress.syr.edu.

T A Bookstore, *See* **Shea Bks.**

Taku Graphics, *(978-0-9717820; 978-0-9772297; 978-0-9801616; 978-0-9823450; 978-0-9846318; 978-0-9899679)* 5763 Glacier Hwy., Juneau, AK 99801 USA Tel 907-780-6310; Fax: 907-780-6314; Toll Free: 800-278-3291
E-mail: adele@takugraphics.com
Web site: htto://www.takugraphics.com.

Tales of Wonder.com, 3037 Summer Oak Pl., Buford, GA 30518 USA (SAN 920-1246) Tel 770-904-2221; 770-904-2221; Toll Free: 866-796-6337
E-mail: service@towdistribution.com; rob@towdistribution.com
Web site: www.talesofwonder.com; http://www.towdistribution.com.

Tallahassee News Co., Inc., 3777 Hartsfield Rd., Tallahassee, FL 32303-1120 USA.

Tapeworm Video Distributor, Inc., 27833 Avenue Hopkins, Unit 6, Valencia, CA 91355-3407 USA (SAN 630-8767) Tel 805-257-4904; Fax: 805-257-4820; Toll Free: 800-367-8437
E-mail: sales@tapeworm.com
Web site: http://www.tapeworm.com.

Tatnuck BookSeller, The, 335 Chandler St., Worcester, MA 01602-3402 USA (SAN 169-3654) Tel 508-756-7644.

Tattered Cover Bookstore, 1628 16th St., Denver, CO 80202-1308 USA (SAN 631-0214) Toll Free: 800-833-9327 (ext. 250)
E-mail: roy@tatteredcover.com.

Taylor & Francis Group, *(978-0-335; 978-0-415; 978-0-8448; 978-0-85066; 978-0-89116; 978-0-903796; 978-0-905273; 978-1-56032; 978-1-85000; 978-1-59169; 978-1-315)* Orders Addr.: 7625 Empire Dr., Florence, KY 41042-2919 USA Toll Free Fax: 800-248-4724; Toll Free: 800-634-7064; 74 Rolark Dr., Scarborough, ON M1R 4G2 Tel 416-299-5388; Fax: 416-299-7531; Toll Free: 877-226-2237; Edit Addr.: 325 Chestnut St., Philadelphia, PA 19106 USA (SAN 241-9246) Tel 215-625-8900; Fax: 215-625-2940; 270 Madison Ave., 4th Flr., New York, NY 10016-0601
Web site: http://www.routledge-ny.com; http://www.crcpress.com; http://www.garlandscience.com; http://www.taylorandfrancis.com.

Taylor & Francis, Incorporated, *See* **Taylor & Francis Group**

TBN Enterprises, *See* **Ironside International Pubs., Inc.**

Teacher Created Materials, Inc., *(978-0-87673; 978-0-7439; 978-1-4333; 978-1-60401; 978-1-4807; 978-1-4938; 978-1-5164; 978-1-64290; 978-1-64335; 978-1-64406; 978-1-64491; 978-1-0876)* 5301 Oceanus Dr., Huntington Beach, CA 92649 USA (SAN 665-5270) Tel 714-891-2273; Fax: 714-230-7070; Toll Free Fax: 888-877-7606; Toll Free: 800-858-7339
E-mail: sozbat@tcmpub.com; rkarnik@tcmpub.com
Web site: http://www.tcmpub.com; www.teachercreatedmaterials.com.

Teacher Created Resources, Inc., *(978-1-55734; 978-1-57690; 978-1-4206; 978-1-4570)* 12621 Western Ave., Garden Grove, CA 92841 USA Tel 714-891-1690; Fax: 800-525-1254; Toll Free: 800-662-4321
E-mail: custserv@teachercreated.com; lvenzon@teachercreated.com
Web site: http://www.teachercreated.com.

Teacher's Discovery, *(978-1-884473; 978-0-7560)* Div. of American Eagle Co., Inc., 2741 Paldan Dr., Auburn Hills, MI 48326 USA (SAN 631-4570) Tel 248-340-7210; Fax: 248-340-7212; Toll Free: 800-832-2437
Web site: http://www.teachersdiscovery-science.com; http://www.teachersdiscovery-english.com; http://www.teachersdiscovery-social studies.com; http://www.teachersdiscovery-foreignlanguage.com; http://www.teachersdiscovery.com.

Technical Bk. Co., P.O. Box 25934, Los Angeles, CA 90025-8994 USA (SAN 168-9851) Toll Free: 800-233-5150.

Techno Mecca, Inc., 4201 Wilshire Blvd., No. 620, Los Angeles, CA 90019 USA (SAN 631-7812) Tel 323-634-1650; Fax: 323-634-1655
E-mail: tjkim@tmecca.com
Web site: http://www.tmecca.com.

Temme Haus Pr., *(978-0-9727036)* 1784 Palm Ave., Stockton, CA 95205 USA (SAN 253-1925) Fax: 209-463-5527
E-mail: temmehans1953@sbcglobal.net.

Temple News Agency, *See* **ETD KroMar Temple**

Tempo Bookstore, 4905 Wisconsin Ave., NW, Washington, DC 20016 USA Tel 202-363-6683; Fax: 202-363-6686
E-mail: Tempobookstore@usa.net; tempobookstore@usa.net.

Ten Speed Pr., *(978-0-89815; 978-0-913668; 978-1-58008; 978-1-60774)* Div. of Crown Publishing Group, Orders Addr.: P.O. Box 7123, Berkeley, CA 94707 USA (SAN 202-7674) Fax: 510-559-1629 (orders); Toll Free: 800-841-2665; 555 Richmond St., W. Suite 405, Box 702, Toronto, ON M5V 3B1 Tel 416-703-7775; Fax: 416-703-9992
E-mail: order@tenspeed.com; alan@tenspeed.ca
Web site: http://www.tenspeed.com.

teNeues Publishing Co., *(978-3-570; 978-3-8238; 978-3-929278; 978-3-8327; 978-1-933427; 978-1-60160; 978-1-62325; 978-3-96171)* 7 W. 18th St., New York, NY 10011 USA (SAN 245-176X) Tel 212-627-9090; Fax: 212-627-9511; Toll Free: 800-352-0305; 12 Ferndene Rd., London, SE24 0AQ
E-mail: tnp@teneues-usa.com
Web site: http://www.teneues.com.

Territory Titles, 22 Camino Real, Sandia Park, NM 87047 USA.

Tesla Bk. Co., *(978-0-914119; 978-0-9603536)* P.O. Box 121873, Chula Vista, CA 91912-6573 USA (SAN 241-8703) Tel 619-585-8487; Toll Free: 800-398-2056
E-mail: bfeuling@teslabook.com.

Teva Nature, 2344 Black Oak Ct., Sarasota, FL 34232 USA (SAN 631-4619) Tel 941-377-7414; Fax: 941-371-6237; Toll Free: 800-924-8382.

Texas A&M Univ. Pr., *(978-0-89096; 978-1-58544; 978-1-60344; 978-1-62349; 978-1-64843)* 4354 TAMU John H. Lindsey Bldg., Lewis St., College Station, TX 77843-4354 USA (SAN 658-1919) Tel 979-458-3975; Fax: 979-847-8752; Toll Free Fax: 888-617-2421 (orders); Toll Free: 800-826-8911 (orders)
E-mail: katie.duelm@tamu.edu
Web site: http://www.tamupress.com.

Texas Art Supply, 2001 Montrose Blvd., Houston, TX 77006 USA (SAN 169-8303) Tel 713-526-5221; Fax: 713-524-7474; Toll Free: 800-888-9278
E-mail: info@texasart.com
Web site: http://www.texasart.com.

Texas Bk. Co., Orders Addr.: 2601 King, Greenville, TX 75401 USA (SAN 103-4308) Tel 903-455-6969; Fax: 903-454-4775; US Naval Academy/TBC, 5th Wing Bancroft Hall/Textbook, 101 Wilson Rd., Anapolis, MD 21402 (SAN 920-8461) Tel 903-455-6969 ext 642; TBC-NWLTC Bookstore-810 8501 Technology Cir. - Unit 810, Greenville, TX 75402 (SAN 920-9050) Tel 903-455-6969; TBC - #820 Sowela Bookstore 3824 Sen. J. Bennett Johnston Ave., Lake Charles, LA 70615 (SAN 920-9069); TBC-Trenholm State Tech. Coll Bookstore-830 8501 Technology Circle-Unit 830, Greenville, TX 75402 (SAN 920-9077) Tel 903-455-6969; TBC-Drake State Tech College Bookstore-831 8501 Technology Circle-Unit 831, Greenville, TX 75402 (SAN 920-9085) Tel 903-455-6969; Edit Addr.: P.O. Box 212, Greenville, TX 75403 USA Fax: 903-454-2442; Toll Free: 800-527-1016
E-mail: monica@texasbook.com; diana@texasbook.com; molson@texasbook.com.

Texas Bookman, The, *(978-1-931040)* 2700 Lone Star Dr., Dallas, TX 75212-6209 USA (SAN 106-875X) Toll Free: 800-566-2665
E-mail: texas.bookman@halfpricebooks.com.

Texas Hill Country Cookbook, P.O. Box 126, Round Mountain, TX 78663 USA (SAN 110-831X) Tel 210-825-3242; Fax: 210-825-3244; Toll Free: 800-231-3553.

Texas Library Bk. Sales, 1408 West Koenig Lane, Austin, TX 78756 USA (SAN 169-8044) Tel 512-452-4140.

Textbooks On Demand, *See* **Reprint Services Corp.**

TextStream, *(978-0-7351)* Div. of Baker & Taylor Bks., Orders Addr.: c/o Baker & Taylor Digital Media Services, 1120 US Hwy., 22 E., Bridgewater, NJ 08807 USA Tel 908-541-7035; Toll Free Fax: 800-648-0541; Toll Free: 800-775-1800; Edit Addr.: P.O. Box 6885, Bridgewater, NJ 08807-0885 USA
E-mail: btinfo@baker-taylor.com
Web site: http://www.baker-taylor.com/textstream.

TFH Pubns., Inc., *(978-0-7938; 978-0-86622; 978-0-87666; 978-1-85279)* Orders Addr.: One TFH Plaza, Third & Union Aves., Neptune City, NJ 07753 USA (SAN 202-7720) Tel 732-988-8400; Fax: 732-988-5466; Toll Free: 800-631-2188 (outside New Jersey); Edit Addr.: P.O. Box 427, Neptune, NJ 07753 USA (SAN 658-1862)
E-mail: info@tfh.com
Web site: http://www.tfh.com.

Thames Bk. Co., 1 Quarry Rd., Mystic, CT 06355-3200 USA (SAN 169-0760).

Tharpa Pubns. USA, *(978-0-9789067; 978-0-9817277; 978-1-61606)* 47 Sweeney Rd., Glen Spey, NY 12737 USA Tel 845-856-5102; Fax: 845-856-2110; Toll Free: 888-741-3475
E-mail: sales.us@tharpa.com
Web site: http://www.tharpa.com.

The Foundry Publishing, *(978-0-8341)* Orders Addr.: 2345 Grand Blvd., Suite 1900, Kansas City, MO 64108 USA (SAN 253-0902) Tel 816-931-1900; Edit Addr.: P.O. Box 419527, Kansas City, MO 64141 USA (SAN 202-9022) Tel 816-931-1900; Fax: 816-531-0923; Toll Free Fax: 800-849-9827; Toll Free: 800-877-0700
E-mail: heather@nph.com
Web site: http://www.bhillkc.com; http://www.nph.com.

Theme Stream, Inc., P.O. Box 142, Broomfield, CT 06002 USA Tel 860-243-5200
Web site: http://www.themestream.com.

Theological Bk. Service, P.O. Box 509, Barnhart, MO 63012 USA (SAN 631-6662) Tel 636-464-2500; Fax: 636-464-8449; Toll Free Fax: 800-325-9526; Toll Free: 877-484-1600
E-mail: tbs@execpc.com
Web site: http://www.theobooks.org.

Thieme Medical Pubs., Inc., *(978-0-86577; 978-0-913258; 978-1-58890; 978-1-60406; 978-1-62623; 978-1-68420)* Subs. of Georg Thieme Verlag Stuttgart,

333 Seventh Ave., 18th Flr., New York, NY 10001 USA (SAN 169-5983) Tel 212-760-0888; Fax: 212-947-1112; Toll Free: 800-782-3488 (orders only)
E-mail: customerservice@thieme.com
Web site: http://www.thieme.com.

Thieme-Stratton, Inc., *See* **Thieme Medical Pubs., Inc.**

Thinkers' Pr., Inc., *(978-0-938650; 978-1-888710)* Orders Addr.: P.O. Box 8, Davenport, IA 52805-0008 USA Tel 319-323-1226; Fax: 319-323-0511; Toll Free: 800-397-7117 (orders only); Edit Addr.: 1524 Leclaire St., Davenport, IA 52803-4428 USA (SAN 162-7759)
E-mail: tpi@chessco.com
Web site: http://www.chessco.com.

Thistle Hill Pubns., *(978-0-9705511)* 477 Thistle Hill Rd., North Pomfret, VT 05053-0307 USA Tel 802-457-2050; Fax: 802-457-3653; Fulfillment Addr.: P.O. Box 428, White River Junction, VT 05001 USA
E-mail: thp@together.net
Web site: http://www.thistlehillpub.com.

Thomas Brothers Maps, *(978-0-88130; 978-1-58174)* Div. of Rand McNally & Co., 17731 Cowan, Irvine, CA 92614 USA (SAN 158-8192) Fax: 949-757-1564; Toll Free: 800-899-6277
Web site: http://www.thomas.com.

Thompson Schl. Bk. Depository, Orders Addr.: P.O. Box 60160, Oklahoma City, OK 73146 USA (SAN 159-9747) Tel 405-525-9458; Fax: 405-524-5443; Edit Addr.: 39 NE 24th St., Oklahoma City, OK 73143 USA.

Thomson Delmar Learning, *See* **Delmar Cengage Learning**

Thomson Gale, *See* **Cengage Gale**

Thomson Learning, *See* **CENGAGE Learning**

Thomson, Linda, P.O. Box 1225, Orem, UT 84059-1225 USA (SAN 110-3881) Tel 801-226-0155; Fax: 801-226-0166; Toll Free: 800-226-0155.

Thomson Peterson's, *See* **Peterson's**

Thomson West, *See* **West**

Thorndike Pr., *(978-0-7838; 978-0-7862; 978-0-8161; 978-0-89621; 978-1-56054; 978-1-4104)* Div. of Gale Group, 295 Kennedy Memorial Dr., Waterville, ME 04901 USA Tel 207-859-1053; 207-859-1020; 207-859-1000; Toll Free Fax: 800-558-4676; Toll Free: 800-223-1244 (ext. 15); 800-877-4253 (customer resource ctr.)
E-mail: jamie.knobloch@gale.com; barb.littfield@galegroup.com; Betsy.M.Brown@thomson.com; jamie.knobloch@cengage.com
Web site: http://www.gale.com/thorndike.

Tiffin News Agency, 34 Kennat Blvd., Tiffin, OH 44883-4604 USA (SAN 169-6866).

Tiger Bk. Distributors, Ltd., 328 S. Jefferson, Chicago, IL 60661 USA (SAN 631-0672) Tel 312-382-1160; Fax: 312-382-0323.

TI-Holdings Distribution Co., 4 Hopscotch Ln., Savannah, GA 31411 USA.

Timber Pr., Inc., *(978-0-88192; 978-0-917304; 978-0-931146; 978-0-931340; 978-1-60469; 978-1-64326)* Div. of Workman Publishing Co., Inc., 133 SW Second Ave., Suite 450, Portland, OR 97204-3527 USA (SAN 216-082X) Tel 503-227-2878; Fax: 503-227-3070; Toll Free: 800-327-5680; 20 Lonsdale Rd Swavesey, London, NW6 6RD Tel (01954) 232959; Fax: (01954) 206040
E-mail: info@timberpress.co.uk; publicity@timberpress.com
Web site: http://www.timberpress.com.

Time Home Entertainment, Incorporated, *See* **Time Inc. Bks.**

Time Inc. Bks., *(978-1-883013; 978-1-929049; 978-1-931933; 978-1-932273; 978-1-932994; 978-1-933405; 978-1-933821; 978-1-60320; 978-1-61893; 978-1-68330; 978-1-5478)* Div. of Time, Inc., 1271 Avenue of the Americas, New York, NY 10020-1201 USA (SAN 227-3209); 225 Liberty St., New York, NY 10281.

Time Warner Book Group, *See* **Hachette Bk. Group**

Time-Life Publishing Warehouse, 5240 W. 76th, Indianapolis, IN 43268-4137 USA (SAN 631-1504) Fax: 717-348-6409; Toll Free: 800-277-8844
Web site: http://www.timelifecs.com; http://www.timelifeedu.com.

TIS, Inc., *(978-0-89917; 978-1-56581; 978-0-7421)* Orders Addr.: P.O. Box 669, Bloomington, IN 47402 USA Tel 812-332-3307; Fax: 812-331-7690; Toll Free: 800-367-4002; Edit Addr.: 5005 N. State Rd. 37 Business, Bloomington, IN 47404 USA.

Titan Bookstore, P.O. Box 34080, Fullerton, CA 92634-9480 USA (SAN 106-4851).

Title Bks., Inc., 3013 Second Ave. S, Birmingham, AL 35233 USA (SAN 168-9207) Tel 205-324-2596.

TLC Distributors, P.O. Box 434, Lake Dallas, TX 75065 USA.

Tobias News Co., 130 18th St., Rock Island, IL 61201 USA (SAN 169-2186) Tel 309-788-7517.

Todd Communications, *(978-1-57833; 978-1-878100)* 611 E. 12th Ave. Ste. 102, Anchorage, AK 99501-4663 USA (SAN 298-6280)
E-mail: info@toddcom.com.

Topical Review Bk Co., Inc., *(978-1-929099; 978-1-939246)* P.O. Box 328, Onsted, MI 49265 USA Tel 517-547-8072; Fax: 517-547-7512
E-mail: topicalrbc@aol.com
Web site: www.topicalrbc.com.

Total Information, Inc., 844 Dewey Ave., Rochester, NY 14613 USA (SAN 123-7373) Tel 716-254-0621.

T.R. Bks., Orders Addr.: P.O. Box 310279, New Braunfels, TX 78131 USA (SAN 630-4885) Tel 830-625-2665; Fax: 830-620-0470; Toll Free: 800-659-4710; Edit Addr.: P.O. Box 310279, New Braunfels, TX 78131-0279 USA
E-mail: trbooks@trbooks.com
Web site: http://www.trbooks.com.

T.R. Trading Co., *See* **T.R. Bks.**

Tracor Technology Resources (TTR), Specialized Bk. Distributors, 1601 Research Blvd., Rockville, MD 20850 USA (SAN 169-3220) Tel 301-251-4970.

Trafalgar Square Publishing, *(978-0-943955; 978-1-57076)* Orders Addr.: P.O. Box 257, North Pomfret, VT 05053-0257 USA (SAN 213-8859) Tel 802-457-1911; Fax: 802-457-1913; Toll Free: 800-423-4525; Edit Addr.: 388 Howe Hill Rd., North Pomfret, VT 05053 USA Tel 802-423-4525; 802-457-1913
E-mail: tsquare@sover.net
Web site: http://www.trafalgarbooks.com; http://www.horseandriderbooks.com.

Trajectory, Inc., *(978-1-62028; 978-1-62665; 978-1-62978; 978-1-63209; 978-1-68100; 978-1-68124)* 50 Doaks Lane, Marblehead, MA 01945 USA Tel 781-476-2100
E-mail: info@trajectory.com; bob@trajectory.com
Web site: http://www.trajectory.com.

Trans World News, 3700 Kelley Ave., Cleveland, OH 44114-4533 USA (SAN 169-6688) Tel 216-391-4800; Fax: 216-391-9911; Toll Free: 800-321-9858.

Transaction Pubs., *(978-0-7658; 978-0-87855; 978-0-88738; 978-1-56000; 978-1-4128)* Div. of Taylor & Francis Group, Orders Addr.: Taylor & Francis Group LLC 7625 Empire Dr., Florence, KY 41042-2919 USA Toll Free Fax: 800-248-4724; Toll Free: 800-634-7064
E-mail: orders@transactionpub.com
Web site: http://www.transactionpub.com.

Transamerican & Export News Co., 12345 World Trade Dr., San Diego, CA 92128-3743 USA (SAN 169-0140).

Trans-Atlantic Pubns., Inc., 33 Ashley Dr., Schwenksville, PA 19473 USA (SAN 694-0234) Tel 215-717-4655; Fax: 484-919-6486 Do not confuse with Transatlantic Arts, Inc., Albuquerque, NM
E-mail: order@transatlanticpub.com
Web site: http://www.transatlanticpub.com.

Traveler Restaurant, 741 Buckley Hwy., Union, CT 06076 USA (SAN 111-8218) Tel 860-684-4920.

Treasure Chest Bks., P.O. Box 5250, Tucson, AZ 85703-0250 USA Tel 520-623-9558; Fax: 520-624-5888; Toll Free Fax: 800-715-5888; Toll Free: 800-969-9558.

Treasure Chest Books, *See* **Rio Nuevo Pubs.**

Treasure Valley News, 4242 S. Eagleson Rd. Ste. 108B, Boise, ID 83705-4985 USA.

Tree Frog Trucking Co., 7983 SE 13th Ave., Portland, OR 97202-6665 USA (SAN 169-7188).

Tree Hse. Distribution, 1007 Perrywill Ave., Salt Lake City, UT 84124-2428 USA (SAN 631-6603) Fax: 801-262-2324; Toll Free: 888-299-7895.

Tree of Life Midwest, P.O. Box 2629, Bloomington, IN 47402-2629 USA (SAN 169-7994) Toll Free: 800-999-4200.

Tremendous Life Bks., *(978-0-937539; 978-1-933715; 978-1-936354)* Div. of Life Management Services, Inc., 206 West Allen St., Mechanicsburg, PA 17055-6240 USA (SAN 156-5419) Tel 717-766-9499; Fax: 717-766-6565; Toll Free: 800-233-2665
E-mail: JLiller@TremendousLifeBooks.com
Web site: http://www.TremendousLifeBooks.com.

Tres Americas Bks., Orders Addr.: 4336 N. Pulaski Rd., Chicago, IL 60641 USA Tel 773-481-9090.

T-Rex Products, 2391 Boswell Rd., Chula Vista, CA 91914-3509 USA.

Triangle News Co., Inc., 3498 Grand Ave., Pittsburgh, PA 15225 USA (SAN 169-7447).

Tri-County News Co., Inc., 1376 W. Main St., Santa Maria, CA 93458 USA (SAN 169-0345) Tel 805-925-6541; Fax: 805-925-3565
E-mail: trico2000@aol.com
Web site: http://tri-countynews.com.

TriLiteral, LLC, 100 Maple Ridge Dr., Cumberland, RI 02864-1796 USA (SAN 631-8126) Tel 401-531-2800; 401-531-2804 (Credit & Collections); 401-658-4226; Fax: 401-531-2801; 401-531-2803 (Credit & Collections); 401-658-4193; Toll Free Fax: 800-406-9145; Toll Free: 800-405-1619
E-mail: rich.swafford@triliteral.org; customer.care@Triliteral.org
Web site: http://www.triliteral.org/.

Triple Tail Publishing, *See* **Farcountry Pr.**

Tri-State News Agency, P.O. Box 778, Johnson City, TN 37601 USA (SAN 169-7897) Tel 423-926-8159; 604 Rolling Hills Dr., Johnson City, TN 37601 (SAN 282-4744).

Tri-State Periodicals, Inc., Orders Addr.: P.O. Box 1110, Evansville, IN 47706-1110 USA Tel 812-867-7416; Edit Addr.: 9844 Heddon Rd., Evansville, IN 47711 USA (SAN 241-7537) Tel 812-867-7419.

Trucatriche, Orders Addr.: 3800 Main St., Suite 8, Chula Vista, CA 91911 USA Tel 619-426-2690; Fax: 619-426-2695
E-mail: info@trucatriche.com
Web site: http://www.trucatriche.com.

Truth Pubns., Orders Addr.: 8105 NW 23rd Ave., Gainesville, FL 32606 USA Tel 352-376-6320; Fax: 352-376-7105 Do not confuse with companies with the same or similar name in Paris, TX, Lombard, IL, Philadelphia, PA, Springfield, MO, Woodstock, MO
E-mail: upgflorida@juno.com.

Tulare County News, 13595 El Nogal Ave., Visalia, CA 93292-9352 USA (SAN 169-0442) Toll Free: 800-479-6006.

Turner Subscription Agency, Subs. of Dawson Holdings PLC, 15 S. West Park., Westwood, MA 02090-1524 USA (SAN 107-7112) Toll Free: 800-847-4201
E-mail: postmaster@dawson.com.

Turtleback Bks., *(978-0-613; 978-0-7857; 978-0-8085; 978-0-8335; 978-0-88103; 978-1-4176; 978-1-4177; 978-1-4178; 978-0-606)* Sub. of GL group, Inc., 1230 Macklind Ave., Saint Louis, MO 63110-1432 USA (SAN 159-947X) Tel 314-644-6100; Fax: 314-647-2845; Toll Free: 800-458-8438
E-mail: info@sanval.com; rheflin@turtleback.com
Web site: http://www.Turtleback.com.

Tuttle Publishing, *(978-0-8048; 978-1-4629)* Orders Addr.: 364 Innovation Dr., North Clarendon, VT 05759 USA (SAN 213-2621) Tel 802-773-8930; Fax: 802-773-6993; Toll Free Fax: 800-329-8885; Toll Free: 800-526-2778
E-mail: info@tuttlepublishing.com
Web site: http://www.tuttlepublishing.com.

Twentieth Century Christian Bks., *(978-0-89098)* 2809 Granny White Pike, Nashville, TN 37204 USA (SAN 206-2550) Tel 615-383-3842.

Twenty First Century Pubns., *(978-0-933278)* Orders Addr.: P.O. Box 702, Fairfield, IA 52556-0702 USA Tel 515-472-5105; Fax: 515-472-8443; Toll Free: 800-593-2665; Edit Addr.: 401 N. Fourth St., Fairfield, IA 52556 USA Do not confuse with Twenty First Century Pubns., Tolland, CT
E-mail: books21st@lisco.com
Web site: http://www.21stbooks.com.

Twenty-First Century Antiques, Orders Addr.: P.O. Box 70, Hatfield, MA 01038 USA (SAN 110-8085); Edit Addr.: 11 1/2 Main St., Hatfield, MA 01038 USA (SAN 243-248X) Tel 413-247-9396.

Twenty-Third Pubns./Bayard, *(978-0-89622; 978-1-58595; 978-1-62785)* 1 Montauk Ave. No. 20, New London, CT 06320-4967 USA (SAN 658-2052) Toll Free Fax: 800-572-0788; Toll Free: 800-321-0411
E-mail: kerry.moriarty@bayard-inc.com
Web site: http://www.23rdpublications.com.

Twin City News Agency, Inc., P.O. Box 466, Lafayette, IN 47902-0466 USA Tel 765-742-1051.

Two Rivers Distribution, Div. of Ingram Content Group, Orders Addr.: 210 American Dr., Jackson, TN 38301 USA Toll Free Fax: 800-351-5073 (Customer Service); Toll Free: 866-400-5351 (Customer Service); 800-343-4499
E-mail: pd_orderentry@ingramcontent.com; ips@ingramcontent.com
Web site: http://www.tworiversdistribution.com/.

Tyndale Hse. Pubs., *(978-0-8423; 978-1-4143; 978-1-4964)* Orders Addr.: 370 Executive Dr., Carol Stream, IL 60188 USA; Edit Addr.: 351 Executive Dr., Carol Stream, IL 60188 USA (SAN 206-7749) Tel 630-668-8310; Fax: 630-668-3245; Toll Free: 800-323-9400
E-mail: international@tyndale.com; permission@tyndale.com
Web site: http://www.tyndale.com.

Ubiquity Distributors, Inc., 607 Degraw St., Brooklyn, NY 11217 USA (SAN 200-7428) Tel 718-875-5491; Fax: 718-875-8047.

Ultra Bks., P.O. Box 945, Oakland, NJ 07436 USA (SAN 112-9074) Tel 201-337-8787.

Ulverscroft Large Print Bks., Ltd., *(978-0-7089; 978-1-84617)* Orders Addr.: P.O. Box 1230, West Seneca, NY 14224-1230 USA; Edit Addr.: 950 Union Rd., West Seneca, NY 14224-3438 USA (SAN 208-3035) Toll Free: 800-955-9659
E-mail: enquiries@ulverscroft.co.uk; sales@ulverscroft.com
Web site: http://www.ulverscroft.co.uk.

Unarius Academy of Science Pubns., *(978-0-932642; 978-0-935097)* Orders Addr.: 145 S. Magnolia Ave., El Cajon, CA 92020-4522 USA (SAN 168-9614) Tel 619-444-7062; Fax: 619-444-9637; Toll Free: 800-475-7062
E-mail: uriel@unarius.org
Web site: http://www.unarius.org.

Underground Railroad, The, 2769 Club House Rd., Mobile, AL 36605-4373 USA (SAN 630-7892) Tel 334-432-8811.

Unifacmanu International Trading Co., Inc., 22 Cross Ridge Rd., Chappaqua, NY 10514 USA (SAN 631-743X)
E-mail: unifacmanu@att.net
Web site: http://www.bookvariety.com.

Unique Bks., Inc., 5010 Kemper Ave., Saint Louis, MO 63139 USA (SAN 630-0472) Tel 314-776-6695; Fax: 314-776-0841; Toll Free: 800-533-5446.

United Magazine, Orders Addr.: P.O. Box 36, Columbia, KY 42728-0036 USA (SAN 169-2852) Tel 502-384-3444; Fax: 502-384-9324; Edit Addr.: 361 Industrial Park Rd., Louisville, KY 42728-0036 USA (SAN 250-3336).

United Methodist Publishing Hse., *(978-1-63088)* 201 Eighth Ave., S., Nashville, TN 37203 USA Tel 615-749-6000; Fax: 615-749-6079; Toll Free Fax: 800-836-7802; Toll Free: 800-672-1789 (orders only)
Web site: http://www.umph.org; http://www.abingdonpress.com.

United Nations Pubns., *(978-0-680; 978-0-89714; 978-92-1; 978-952-9520)* 300 E. 42nd St., 9th Flr., New York, NY 10017 USA (SAN 206-6718) Tel 212-963-8302; 212-963-7680 UN Bookshop; Fax: 212-963-3489; 212-963-4910 UN Bookshop; Toll Free: 800-253-9646 (bookshop orders); 800-553-3210 UN Bookshop
E-mail: publications@un.org
Web site: https://unp.un.org/.

United News Co., Inc., 111 Lake St., P.O. Box 3426, Bakersfield, CA 93305 USA (SAN 169-7579) Tel 805-323-7864.

United Society of Shakers, *(978-0-915836)* 707 Shaker Rd., New Gloucester, ME 04260 USA (SAN 158-619X) Tel 207-926-4597; Fax: 207-926-3559
E-mail: sdlshakers@aol.com
Web site: http://www.shaker.lib.me.us.

United States Government Printing Office, *(978-0-16; 978-0-18)* Orders Addr.: P.O. Box 371954, Pittsburgh, PA 15250-7954 USA (SAN 658-0785) Tel 202-512-1800; Fax: 202-512-2250; Toll Free: 866-512-1800; Edit Addr.: USGPO Stop SSMB, Washington, DC 20401 USA (SAN 206-152X) Tel 202-512-1705 (bibliographic information only); 202-512-2268 (book dealers only); Fax: 202-512-1655
E-mail: orders@gpo.gov; rdavis@gpo.gov; ContactCenter@gpo.gov
Web site: http://bookstore.gpo.gov; https://www.gpo.gov.

United Subscription Service, 527 Third Ave., No. 284, New York, NY 10016-4100 USA (SAN 286-0104).

Univ of Arizona Critical Languages Program, 1230 N. Park Ave., Suite 102, Tucson, AZ 85719 USA.

Univ. of Arkansas Pr., *(978-0-938626; 978-1-55728; 978-1-61075; 978-1-68226)* 105 N. McIlroy Ave., Fayetteville, AR 72701 USA (SAN 239-3972) Tel 479-575-7544; Fax: 479-575-6044; Toll Free: 800-626-0090
E-mail: info@uapress.com
Web site: http://www.uapress.com; http://www.uark.edu/~uaprinfo.

Univ. of California Pr., *(978-0-520; 978-1-7323203)* 155 Grand Ave., Suite 400, Oakland, CA 94612-3758 USA Tel 510-883-8232 (Books & Journals); Fax: 510-836-8910
E-mail: journals@ucpress.edu; orders@cpfsinc.com; askucp@ucpress.edu
Web site: http://www.ucpress.edu.

Univ. of Chicago Pr., *(978-0-226; 978-0-89065; 978-0-943056; 978-1-892850)* Orders Addr.: 11030 S. Langley Ave., Chicago, IL 60628 USA (SAN 202-5280) Tel 773-702-7000; Fax: 773-702-7212; Toll Free Fax: 800-621-8476 (US & Canada); Toll Free: 800-621-2736 (US & Canada); Edit Addr.: 1427 E. 60th St., Chicago, IL 60637 USA (SAN 202-5299) Tel 773-702-7700; 773-702-7748 (Marketing & Sales); Fax: 773-702-9756
E-mail: general@press.uchicago.edu; kh@press.uchicago.edu; custserv@press.uchicago.rdu; sales@press.uchicago.edu; marketing@press.uchicago.edu; publicity@press.uchicago.edu
Web site: http://www.press.uchicago.edu.

Univ. of Hawaii Pr., *(978-0-8248; 978-0-87022)* Orders Addr.: 2840 Kolowalu St., Honolulu, HI 96822-1888 USA (SAN 202-5353) Tel 808-956-8255; Fax: 808-988-6052; Toll Free Fax: 800-650-7811; Toll Free: 888-847-7377
E-mail: uhpmkt@hawaii.edu; uhpbooks@hawaii.edu
Web site: http://www.uhpress.hawaii.edu.

Univ. of Massachusetts Pr., *(978-0-87023; 978-1-55849; 978-1-61376; 978-1-62534)* Orders Addr.: P.O. Box 429, Amherst, MA 01004 USA (SAN 203-3089) Tel 413-545-2217 (editorial); Fax: 413-545-1226; Toll Free Fax: 800-537-5487; P.O. Box 50370, Baltimore, MD 21211 Tel 800-537-5487; Fax: 410-516-6998
E-mail: info@umpress.umass.edu
Web site: http://www.umass.edu/umpress.

Univ. of Missouri Pr., *(978-0-8262)* 2910 LeMone Blvd., Columbia, MO 65201 USA (SAN 203-3143) Tel 573-882-7641; Fax: 573-884-4498; Toll Free: 800-828-1894 (orders only)
E-mail: rennerk@umsystem.edu; deandj@umsystem.edu
Web site: http://press.umsystem.edu.

Univ. of Nebraska Pr., *(978-0-8032; 978-1-4962; 978-1-64012)* Orders Addr.: 1111 Lincoln Mall, Lincoln, NE 68588-0630 USA Tel 402-472-3581; 402-472-7702; Fax: 402-472-6214; Toll Free Fax: 800-526-2617; Toll Free: 800-755-1105; Edit Addr.: P.O. Box 880630, Lincoln, NE 68588-0630 USA (SAN 202-5337)
E-mail: pressmail@unl.edu
Web site: http://www.nebraskapress.unl.edu; http://www.bisonbooks.com.

Univ. of New Mexico Pr., *(978-0-8263; 978-0-9766839)* Orders Addr.: 1312 Basehart Rd., SE, Albuquerque, NM 87106-4363 USA (SAN 213-9588) Tel 505-277-2346; 505-272-7777 (orders); Toll Free Fax: 800-622-8667; Toll Free: 800-249-7737 (orders)
E-mail: unmpress@unm.edu
Web site: http://www.unmpress.com.

Univ. of North Carolina Pr., *(978-0-8078; 978-1-4696)* c/o Longleaf Services, 116 S. Boundary St., Chapel Hill, NC 27514-3808 USA (SAN 203-3151) Tel 919-966-3561; Fax: 919-966-3829; Toll Free Fax: 800-272-6817; Toll Free: 800-848-6224
E-mail: uncpress@unc.edu
Web site: http://www.uncpress.unc.edu.

Univ. of Oklahoma Pr., *(978-0-8061)* Orders Addr.: 2800 Venture Dr., Norman, OK 73069-8218 USA Tel 405-325-2000; Fax: 405-364-5798; Toll Free Fax: 800-735-0476; Toll Free: 800-627-7377
E-mail: presscs@ou.edu
Web site: http://www.oupress.com.

Univ. of Pennsylvania Pr., *(978-0-8122; 978-1-5128)* Orders Addr.: c/o Hopkins Fullfillment Srvc., Hopkins Fulfillment Service, Baltimore, MD 21211-4370 USA Tel 410-516-6948; Fax: 410-516-6998; Toll Free: 800-537-5487; Edit Addr.: 3905 Spruce St., Philadelphia, PA 19104-4112 USA (SAN 202-5345) Tel 215-898-6261; Fax: 215-898-0404; Toll Free: 800-537-5487 (book orders)
E-mail: custserv@pobox.upenn.edu
Web site: http://www.upenn.edu/pennpress.

Univ. of Tennessee Pr., *(978-0-87049; 978-1-57233; 978-1-62190)* Div. of Univ. of Tennessee & Member of Assn. of American Univ. Presses, Orders Addr.: 11030 S. Langley, Chicago, IL 60628 USA Tel 773-568-1550; Toll Free Fax: 800-621-8471; Toll Free: 800-621-2736 (orders only); Edit Addr.: 110 Conference Ctr. Bldg.,

Knoxville, TN 37996-0325 USA (SAN 212-9930) Tel 865-974-3321; Fax: 865-974-3724
E-mail: tpost@utk.edu
Web site: http://www.utpress.org.

Univ. of Texas Pr., *(978-0-292; 978-1-4773)* Orders Addr.: P.O. Box 7819, Austin, TX 78713-7819 USA (SAN 212-9876) Tel 512-471-7233; Fax: 512-232-7178; Toll Free: 800-252-3206; Edit Addr.: University of Texas at Austin 2100 Comal, Austin, TX 78722 USA
E-mail: info@utpress.utexas.edu
Web site: http://www.utexas.edu/utpress.

Univ. of Washington Pr., *(978-0-295; 978-1-902716)* Orders Addr.: P.O. Box 50096, Seattle, WA 98145-5096 USA (SAN 212-2502) Tel 206-543-4050; Fax: 206-543-3932; Toll Free Fax: 800-669-7993; Edit Addr.: P.O. Box 50096, Seattle, WA 98145-5096 USA Toll Free Fax: 800-669-7993; 1126 N. 98th St., Seattle, WA 98103
E-mail: uwpord@u.washington.edu
Web site: http://www.washington.edu/uwpress.

Univ. of Wisconsin Pr., *(978-0-299)* Orders Addr.: c/o Chicago Dist Ctr., 11030 S. Langley Ave., Chicago, IL 60628 USA Tel 773-568-1550; Fax: 773-660-2235; Toll Free Fax: 800-621-8476 (orders only); Toll Free: 800-621-2736 (orders only); Edit Addr.: 1930 Monroe St., 3rd Flr., Madison, WI 53711 USA Tel 608-263-1110; Fax: 608-263-1132
E-mail: uwiscpress@uwpress.wisc.edu
Web site: http://www.wisc.edu/wisconsinpress/.

Univ. Pr. of Florida, *(978-0-8130; 978-0-942084; 978-0-9760555; 978-1-61610; 978-1-942852; 978-1-68340)* Orders Addr.: 15 NW 15th St., Gainesville, FL 32611-0279 USA (SAN 207-9275) Tel 352-392-1351; Fax: 352-392-7302; Toll Free Fax: 800-680-1955; Toll Free: 800-226-3822
E-mail: press@upf.com; orders@upf.com
Web site: http://www.upf.com.

Univ. Pr. of Kentucky, *(978-0-8131; 978-0-912839; 978-0-916968; 978-1-9859; 978-1-949668; 978-1-949669; 978-1-950564; 978-1-950690)* Orders Addr.: Hopkins Fulfillment Services, Baltimore, MD 21211-4370 USA Tel 800-537-5487; Fax: 410-516-6998; Toll Free: 800-839-6855; Edit Addr.: 663 S. Limestone St., Lexington, KY 40508-4008 USA (SAN 203-3275) Tel 859-257-5200; Fax: 859-323-4981; Toll Free Fax: 800-870-4981
E-mail: twell1@email.uky.edu
Web site: http://www.kentuckypress.com.

Univ. Pr. of Mississippi, *(978-0-87805; 978-1-57806; 978-1-934110; 978-1-60473; 978-1-61703; 978-1-62103; 978-1-62674; 978-1-62846; 978-1-4968)* 3825 Ridgewood Rd., Jackson, MS 39211-6492 USA (SAN 203-1914) Tel 601-432-6205; Fax: 601-432-6217; Toll Free: 800-737-7788 (orders only)
E-mail: kburgess@ihl.state.ms.us; press@mississippi.edu
Web site: http://www.upress.state.ms.us.

Univ. Pr. of New England, *(978-0-87451; 978-0-915032; 978-1-58465; 978-1-61168; 978-1-5126; 978-1-68458)* Orders Addr.: One Court St., Suite 250, Lebanon, NH 03755 USA Tel 603-448-1533 (ext. 255); Fax: 603-448-9429; Toll Free: 800-421-1561; Edit Addr.: 415 South St., Waltham, MA 02453 USA
E-mail: University.Press@Dartmouth.edu
Web site: http://www.upne.com.

Univelt, Inc., *(978-0-87703; 978-0-912183)* Orders Addr.: P.O. Box 28130, San Diego, CA 92198 USA; Edit Addr.: 740 Metcalf St., Suite 13, Escondido, CA 92025-1671 USA (SAN 658-2095)
E-mail: sales@univelt.com
Web site: http://www.univelt.com.

Universal Subscription Service, P.O. Box 35445, Houston, TX 77035 USA (SAN 287-4768).

Universe Publishing, *(978-0-7893; 978-0-87663; 978-1-55550)* Div. of Rizzoli International Pubns., Inc., 300 Park Ave. S., 3rd Flr., New York, NY 10010 USA (SAN 202-537X) Tel 212-387-3400; Fax: 212-387-3444 Do not confuse with similar names in North Hollywood, CA, Englewood, NJ, Mendocino, CA.

University Book Service, Orders Addr.: P.O. Box 608, Grove City, OH 43123 USA (SAN 169-6912); Edit Addr.: P.O. Box 607, Grove City, OH 43123-0607 USA (SAN 282-4841) Toll Free: 800-634-4272.

University of Arizona Pr., *(978-0-8165; 978-1-941451)* 355 S. Euclid Ave., Suite 103, Tucson, AZ 85719 USA (SAN 205-468X) Tel 520-621-1441; Fax: 520-621-8899; Toll Free: 800-426-3797 (orders)
E-mail: orders@uapress.arizona.edu
Web site: http://www.uapress.arizona.edu.

University of Hawaii Press Agrmt. 2, Orders Addr.: 2840 Kolowalu St., Honolulu, HI 96822 USA
E-mail: uhpbooks@hawaii.edu.

University of Nevada Pr., *(978-0-87417; 978-1-943859; 978-1-948908; 978-1-64779)* Orders Addr.: Mail Stop 166, Reno, NV 89557 USA (SAN 203-316X) Tel 775-784-6573; Fax: 775-784-6200; Toll Free: 877-682-6657 (orders only)
E-mail: vfontana@unpress.nevada.edu
Web site: http://www.unpress.nevada.edu.

University of Virginia Pr., *(978-0-8139; 978-0-912759; 978-1-57814)* Orders Addr.: P.O. Box 400318, Charlottesville, VA 22904-4318 USA (SAN 202-5361) Tel 804-924-3468; Fax: 804-982-2655
E-mail: upress@virginia.edu
Web site: http://www.upress.virginia.edu.

University Publishing Associates, Incorporated, *See* **National Film Network LLC**

Untreed Reads Publishing, LLC, *(978-1-61187; 978-1-945447; 978-1-949135; 978-1-953601)* 506 Kansas St., San Francisco, CA 94107 USA Tel 415-621-0465; Toll Free Fax: 800-318-6037
E-mail: jhartman@untreedreads.com; kdsullivan@untreedreads.com
Web site: http://www.untreedreads.com.

Upper Access, Inc., *(978-0-942679)* Orders Addr.: 87 Upper Access Rd., Hinesburg, VT 05461 USA (SAN 667-1195) Tel 802-482-2988 main office
E-mail: info@upperaccess.com
Web site: http://www.upperaccess.com.

Urban Land Institute, *(978-0-87420)* 1025 Thomas Jefferson St., NW, Suite 500 W., Washington, DC 20007-5201 USA (SAN 203-3399) Tel 202-624-7000; Fax: 202-624-7140; Toll Free: 800-321-5011
E-mail: bookstore@uli.org
Web site: http://www.uli.org/.

U.S. Games Systems, Inc., *(978-0-88079; 978-0-913866; 978-1-57281; 978-1-64671)* 179 Ludlow St., Stamford, CT 06902 USA (SAN 158-6483) Tel 203-353-8400; Fax: 203-353-8431; Toll Free: 800-544-2637
E-mail: usgames@aol.com
Web site: http://www.usgamesinc.com.

US PubRep, Inc., 5000 Jasmine Dr., Rockville, MD 20853 USA Tel 301-838-9276; Fax: 301-838-9278
E-mail: craigfalk@aya.yale.edu.

Val Publishing, 16 S. Terrace Ave., Mount Vernon, NY 10551 USA (SAN 107-6876) Tel 914-664-7077.

Valentine Publishing Group, Orders Addr.: P.O. Box 902582, Palmdale, CA 93590-2582 USA; Edit Addr.: 18543 Devonshire St., Northridge, CA 91324 USA Tel 818-831-0649; Fax: 818-831-6659
E-mail: sales@vpg.net.

Valiant International Multi-Media Corp., 55 Ruta Ct., South Hackensack, NJ 07606 USA (SAN 652-8813) Tel 201-229-9800; Fax: 201-814-0418.

Valjean Pr., 721 Shadowlawn Ct., Franklin, TN 37069 USA
E-mail: pastorforthemoment@gmail.com.

Valkyrie Distribution, 43 New Hope Ct., Florissant, MO 63033 USA Tel 314-623-6639
E-mail: valkpub@yahoo.com.

Valley Distributors, Inc., 2947 Felton Rd., Norristown, PA 19401 USA (SAN 169-7498) Tel 610-279-7650; Fax: 610-279-9093; Toll Free: 800-355-2665 (orders only).

Valley Media, Inc., 1276 Santa Anita Ct., Woodland, CA 95776 USA Tel 530-661-6600; Fax: 530-661-5472
E-mail: valley@valley-media.com
Web site: http://www.valsat.com.

Valley Record Distributors, *See* **Valley Media, Inc.**

Van Dyke News Agency, 2238 W. Pinedale Ave., Fresno, CA 93711-0453 USA (SAN 169-9630) Tel 209-291-7768; Fax: 209-291-7770.

Van Khoa Bks., 14601 Moran St., Westminster, CA 92683-5629 USA (SAN 110-7534)
E-mail: vankhoa@vinet.com.

Verham News Corp., 75 Main St., West Lebanon, NH 03784 USA (SAN 169-4561) Fax: 603-298-8843.

VHPS Distribution Center, *See* **MPS**

Victory Multimedia, *(978-0-9661850)* Div. of Victory Audio Video Services, Inc., 460 Hindry Ave., Suite D, Inglewood, CA 90301-2045 USA (SAN 631-4112)
E-mail: sbvictory@juno.com.

Vida Life Publishers International, *See* **Vida Pubs.**

Vida Pubs., *(978-0-8297)* 8410 NW 53rd Ter. Ste. 103, Miami, FL 33166-4510 USA Toll Free: 800-843-2548
E-mail: vidapubsales@harpercollins.com
Web site: http://www.editorialvida.com.

Video Project, The, 200 Estates Dr., Ben Lomond, CA 95005-9444 USA Toll Free: 800-475-2638
E-mail: videoproject@videoproject.org
Web site: http://www.videoproject.org.

Vigilante, Richard Bks., *(978-0-9800763; 978-0-9827163)* 7400 Metro Blvd. Suite 217, Minneapolis, MN 55439 USA.

Village Marketing, 145 W. 400 N., Richfield, UT 84701 USA (SAN 631-6751) Toll Free: 800-982-6683.

Vinabind, P.O. Box 340, Steelville, MO 65565 USA (SAN 159-9828).

Vincennes News Agency, P.O. Box 1110, Evansville, IN 47706-1110 USA (SAN 169-2518).

Virginia Periodical Distributors, *See* **Aramark Magazine & Bk. Services, Inc.**

Virginia Pubns., 16 W. Washington St., Lexington, VA 24450 USA Tel 540-462-3993
E-mail: vapublications@rockbridge.net.

Visible Ink Pr., *(978-0-7876; 978-0-8103; 978-1-57859)* Orders Addr.: 1094 Flex Dr., Jackson, TN 38301-5070 USA Toll Free Fax: 800-351-5073; Toll Free: 800-343-4499; Edit Addr.: 43311 Joy Rd., Canton, MI 48187-2075 USA (SAN 860-2271) Tel 734-667-3211; Fax: 734-667-4311
E-mail: inquiries@visibleink.com
Web site: http://www.visibleink.com.

Vision Distributors, *(978-0-9626732)* Div. of Infinite Creations, Inc., Orders Addr.: P.O. Box 9839, Santa Fe, NM 87504 USA Tel 505-986-8221.

Vision Press, *See* **Vision Distributors**

Vision Video, *(978-1-56364)* Orders Addr.: P.O. Box 540, Worcester, PA 19490 USA Tel 610-584-3500; Fax: 610-584-4610; Toll Free: 800-523-0226; Edit Addr.: 2030 Wentz Church Rd., Worcester, PA 19490 USA (SAN 298-7392)
E-mail: info@gatewayfilms.com; info@visionvideo.com
Web site: http://www.gatewayfilms.com.

Vistabooks, *(978-0-89646)* Orders Addr.: 637 Blue Ridge Rd., Silverthorne, CO 80498-8931 USA (SAN 211-0849) Tel 970-468-7673 (phone/fax)
E-mail: vistabooks@compuserve.com
Web site: http://www.vistabooks.com.

Vitality Distributors, 940 NW 51st Pl., Fort Lauderdale, FL 33309 USA (SAN 169-0973) Toll Free: 800-226-8482.

VNU, Div. of Prestel Publishing, 575 Prospect Ave., Lakewood, NJ 08701 USA (SAN 631-7758) Tel 732-363-5679; Fax: 732-363-0338; Toll Free: 888-463-6110.

volcano pr., *(978-0-912078; 978-1-884244)* Orders Addr.: P.O. Box 270, Volcano, CA 95689 USA (SAN 220-0015) Tel 209-296-4991; Fax: 209-296-4995; Toll Free: 800-879-9636; Edit Addr.: 21496 National St., Volcano, CA 95689 USA
E-mail: info@volcanopress.com; sales@volcanopress.com; adam@volcanopress.com
Web site: http://www.volcanopress.com.

VPD, Inc., 150 Parkshore Dr., Folsom, CA 95630-4710 USA (SAN 631-287X) Toll Free: 800-366-2111
Web site: http://www.vpdinc.com/.

Vroman's, A. C., *(978-0-9639197)* 695 E. Colorado Blvd., Pasadena, CA 91101 USA (SAN 169-0027) Tel 626-449-5320; Fax: 626-792-7308.

W5YI Group, Inc., P.O. Box 565101, Dallas, TX 75356 USA.

WA Bk. Service, P.O. Box 514, East Islip, NY 11730-0514 USA (SAN 107-2943).

Wabash Valley News Agency, 2200 N. Curry Pike, No. 2, Bloomington, IN 47404-1486 USA (SAN 169-250X).

Waffle, O. G. Bk. Co. (The Bookhouse), P.O. Box 586, Marion, IA 52302 USA (SAN 112-8817) Tel 319-373-1832.

Waldenbooks Company, Incorporated, *See* **Waldenbooks, Inc.**

Waldenbooks, Inc., *(978-0-681)* Div. of Borders Group, Inc., a/o Calendar Orders, 455 Industrial Blvd., Suite C, LaVergne, TN 37086 USA (SAN 179-3373); Orders Addr.: One Waldenbooks Dr., LaVergne, TN 37096 USA; 11625 Venture, Mira Loma, CA 91752 Tel 951-361-4025; Edit Addr.: 100 Phoenix Dr., Ann Arbor, MI 48108-2202 USA (SAN 200-8858) Tel 734-477-1100
E-mail: customerservice@waldenbooks.com
Web site: http://www.waldenbooks.com; http://www.preferredreader.com.

Walker Art Ctr., *(978-0-935640; 978-1-935963)* Orders Addr.: 1750 Hennepin Ave., Minneapolis, MN 55403 USA (SAN 206-1880) Tel 612-375-7638; Fax: 612-375-7565
E-mail: paul.schumacher@walkerart.org; lisa.middag@walkerart.org.

Wallace's College Bk. Co., P.O. Box 689, Nicholasville, KY 40340-0689 USA (SAN 169-2844) Tel 606-255-0886; Fax: 606-259-9892; Toll Free Fax: 800-433-9329 (orders only); Toll Free: 800-354-9590 (orders only); 800-354-9500
E-mail: orders@wallaces.com.

Walthers, William K. Inc., *(978-0-941952)* 5601 W. Florist Ave., Milwaukee, WI 53201-3039 USA (SAN 238-4868) Tel 414-527-0770; Fax: 414-527-4423; Toll Free: 800-877-7171.

Ware-Pak, Inc., Orders Addr.: 2427 Bond St., University Park, IL 60466 USA Tel 708-534-2600; Fax: 708-534-7803
E-mail: kshay@ware-pak.com
Web site: http://www.ware-pak.com.

Warner Books, Incorporated, *See* **Grand Central Publishing**

Warner Bros. Pubns., *(978-0-7604; 978-0-7692; 978-0-87487; 978-0-89724; 978-0-89898; 978-0-910957; 978-1-55122; 978-1-57623; 978-0-7579)* Div. of AOL Time Warner, 15800 NW 48th Ave., Miami, FL 33014-6422 USA (SAN 203-0586).

Warner Pr., Inc., *(978-0-87162; 978-1-59317; 978-1-68434)* Orders Addr.: P.O. Box 2499, Anderson, IN 46018-2499 USA (SAN 691-4241) Tel 765-648-2116; Fax: 765-622-9511; Toll Free: 800-848-2464; Edit Addr.: 2902 Enterprise Dr., Anderson, IN 46013 USA (SAN 111-8110) Tel 765-644-7721; Fax: 765-640-8005; Toll Free: 800-741-7721 (orders only)
E-mail: jallison@warnerpress.org; wporders@warnerpress.org; rjackson@warnerpress.org
Web site: http://www.warnerpress.org; http://www.francisasburypress.org.

Warner Press Publishers, *See* **Warner Pr., Inc.**

Washington Bk. Distributors, 4930A Eisenhower Ave., Alexandria, VA 22304 USA (SAN 631-0095) Tel 703-212-9113; Fax: 703-212-9114; Toll Free: 800-699-9113
E-mail: zacwbd@prodigy.net
Web site: http://www.washingtonbk.com.

Washington Toy Co., 2163 28th Ave., San Francisco, CA 94116-1732 USA (SAN 107-1718).

Watson, W. R. & Staff, 150 Mariner Green Ct., Corte Madera, CA 94925 USA (SAN 286-0155) Tel 510-524-6156; Fax: 510-526-5023.

Watson-Guptill Pubns., Inc., *(978-0-8230; 978-1-60569)* Div. of Crown Publishing Grp., 575 Prospect St., Lakewood, NJ 08701 USA Tel 732-363-5679; Toll Free Fax: 877-227-6564; Edit Addr.: 1745 Broadway # 124, New York, NY 10019-4305 USA (SAN 282-5384)
E-mail: aalexander@watsonguptill.com
Web site: http://www.watsonguptill.com.

Waverly News Co., 17 State St., Newburyport, MA 01950 USA (SAN 169-3522).

Wayland Audio-Visual, 210 E. 86th St., Suite 405, New York, NY 10028 USA Toll Free: 800-813-1271
E-mail: jm@waylandav.com.

Waymont Bk. Co., 136 Steuben St., Jersey City, NJ 07302 USA (SAN 630-768X) Tel 201-434-4268; Fax: 201-432-1293
E-mail: waymont@worldnet.att.net.

Wayne State Univ. Pr., *(978-0-8143)* Leonard N. Simons Bldg., 4809 Woodward Ave., Detroit, MI 48201-1309 USA (SAN 202-5221) Tel 313-577-6120; Fax: 313-577-6131; Toll Free: 800-978-7323 (customer orders)
E-mail: theresa.martinelli@wayne.edu; Kristina.Stonehill@wayne.edu
Web site: http://wsupress.wayne.edu.

Weiner News Co., 1011 N. Frio, P.O. Box 7608, San Antonio, TX 78207 USA (SAN 169-8427) Tel 210-226-9333; Fax: 210-226-8679.

Weiser, Samuel Incorporated, *See* **Red Wheel/Weiser**

WellSpring Bks., P.O. Box 2765, Woburn, MA 01888-1465 USA (SAN 111-3399) Do not confuse with companies with the same or similar names in Albuquerque, NM, Ukiah, CA, Adelphia, NJ, Woburn, MA, Groton, VT.

Wenatchee News Agency, 434 Rock Island Rd., East Wenatchee, WA 98802-5360 USA (SAN 169-8885) Tel 509-662-3511.

Wesscott Marketing, Inc., *(978-0-9764077)* P.O. Box 26144, Saint Louis Park, MN 55426 USA Fax: 952-541-4905; Toll Free: 800-375-3702.

West, *(978-0-314; 978-0-7620; 978-0-8321; 978-0-8366; 978-0-87632)* Orders Addr.: 610 Opperman Dr., Eagan, MN 55123-1396 USA Tel 657-687-6849; Fax: 651-687-6857; Toll Free: 800-328-2209; 800-328-9378 (Editorial) Do not confuse with The West Group in Prairie Village, KS
E-mail: west.bookstore@thomson.com; customer.service@westgroup.com; janet.linkert@thompson.com
Web site: http://west.thomson.com; http://westacademic.com.

West Music Co., 1212 Fifth St., Coralville, IA 52241 USA Toll Free: 800-397-9378.

West Texas News Co., Orders Addr.: 1214 Barranca, El Paso, TX 79935 USA; Edit Addr.: P.O. Box 26488, El Paso, TX 79926 USA (SAN 169-8184) Tel 915-594-7586; Fax: 915-594-7589.

West Virginia Book Co., The, 1125 Central Ave., Charleston, WV 25302 USA (SAN 920-9956) Tel 304-342-1848; Fax: 304-343-0594; Toll Free: 888-982-7472
E-mail: wvbooks@wvbookco.com.

Western Book Distributors/Booksource, *See* **Western Booksource, Inc.**

Western Booksource, Inc., 4935 Metart Shwayn, Tillamook, OR 97141 USA (SAN 158-4332) Toll Free: 800-825-0100; 230 Fifth Ave., No. 1104, New York, NY 10001 Tel 212-889-9339; Fax: 212-889-9572.

Western International, Inc., *(978-0-9665194)* 2220 Delaware St., Lawrence, KS 66046-3150 USA (SAN 631-1695) Toll Free: 800-634-6737.

Western Library Bks., 560 S. San Vicente Blvd., Los Angeles, CA 90048 USA (SAN 168-9878) Tel 213-653-8880.

Western Merchandisers, 2900 Airport Rd., Denton, TX 76207-2102 USA (SAN 156-4633).

Western Michigan News, *See* **Readmor**

Western Pubns. Service, 2128 Sun Valley Rd., San Marcos, CA 92069 USA (SAN 630-6241) Tel 760-295-2231; Fax: 760-295-3978.

Western Record Sales, 2991 Saint Andrews Rd., Fairfield, CA 94533-7839 USA (SAN 630-6667).

Western Reserve Historical Society, *(978-0-911704; 978-0-9967844)* 10825 East Blvd., Cleveland, OH 44106 USA (SAN 110-8387) Tel 216-721-5722; Fax: 216-721-0645.

Westminster John Knox Pr., *(978-0-664; 978-0-8042; 978-1-61164; 978-1-947888; 978-1-64698)* Div. of Presbyterian Publishing Corp., Orders Addr.: 100 Witherspoon St., Louisville, KY 40202 USA (SAN 202-9669) Tel 502-569-5052 (outside U.S. for ordering); Fax: 502-569-5113 (outside U.S. for faxed orders); Toll Free Fax: 800-541-5113 (toll-free U.S. faxed orders); Toll Free: 800-227-2872 (customer service)
E-mail: orders@wjkbooks.com
Web site: http://www.wjkbooks.com.

Weston, Edward Fine Arts, P.O. Box 3098, Chatsworth, CA 91313-3098 USA (SAN 168-9967) Tel 818-885-1044; Fax: 818-885-1021.

Weston Woods Studios, Inc., *(978-0-7882; 978-0-89719; 978-1-55592; 978-1-56008)* Div. of Scholastic, Inc., 143 Main St., Norwalk, CT 06851 USA (SAN 630-3838) Tel 203-845-0197; Fax: 203-845-0498; Toll Free: 800-243-5020
E-mail: questions@Scholastic.com
Web site: http://www.scholastic.com/westonwoods.

Westwater Bks., *(978-0-916370; 978-1-941406)* Div. of Belknap Photographic Services, Inc., P.O. Box 2560, Evergreen, CO 80437 USA (SAN 208-3698) Tel 303-674-5410; Fax: 303-670-0586; Toll Free: 800-628-1326.

WFiveYI Group, Inc., The, 7101 N. Ridgeway Ave., Lincolnwood, IL 60712 USA Tel 847-763-0916; Fax: 847-763-0918.

Whatever Publishing, Incorporated, *See* **New World Library**

Whitaker Distributors, *See* **Anchor Distributors**

Whitaker Hse., *(978-0-88368; 978-1-60374; 978-1-62911; 978-1-64123)* Div. of Whitaker Corp., 1030 Hunt Valley Cir., New Kensington, PA 15068 USA (SAN 203-2104) Tel 724-334-7000 Whitaker House/Anchor Distributors; Fax: 724-334-1200 Anchor Distributors; Toll Free Fax: 866-773-7001 Whitaker House; 800-765-1960 Anchor Distributors; Toll Free: 877-793-9800 Whitaker House; 800-444-4484 Whitaker House/Anchor Distributors
E-mail: sales@whitakerhouse.com
Web site: http://www.whitakerhouse.com/; http://www.anchordistributors.com/; http://www.amazon.com/.

Whitewing Pr., P.O. Box 1561, Hemphill, TX 75948 USA Tel 409-787-1526
E-mail: books@whitewingpress.com.

Whiting News Co., 1011 Azalea Dr., Munster, IN 46321-3501 USA (SAN 169-2542).

Whitlock & Co., 10001 Roosevelt Rd., Westchester, IL 60153 USA (SAN 285-9645).

Whitman Distribution Co., Orders Addr.: P.O. Box 513, Lebanon, NH 03766 USA (SAN 631-0540) Fax: 603-448-2576; Toll Free: 800-353-3730; Edit Addr.: 10 Water St., Lebanon, NH 03766 USA
E-mail: distribution@whitmancommunications.com.

Whitman Publishing & Distribution Company, *See* **Whitman Distribution Co.**

Wholesale Distributors, P.O. Box 126, Burlington, IA 52601 USA (SAN 145-8051) Tel 319-753-1683; Fax: 319-753-5988; Toll Free: 800-272-1556.

Wickel, W. W. Co., Inc., 520 N. Exchange Ct., Aurora, IL 60504 USA (SAN 135-1230) Tel 630-820-0044; Fax: 630-820-0057; Toll Free: 800-728-0708.

Wicker Park Pr., Ltd., *(978-0-9789676; 978-1-936679)* 334 Hawthorn Ave,, Glencoe, IL 60022 USA Tel 773-391-1199
E-mail: eric@3ibooks.com
Web site: http://www.wickerparkpress.us.

Wilcor International Bk. Dept., 161 Drive In Rd., Frankfort, NY 13340-5238 USA (SAN 107-7023).

Wild Dog Bks., Orders Addr.: Seven Balsa Ct., Sante Fe, NM 87508 USA
E-mail: WildDogBooks@att.net.

Wiley, John & Sons, Inc., *(978-0-470; 978-0-471; 978-0-7645; 978-0-7821; 978-0-8260; 978-0-87605; 978-0-88422; 978-0-914993; 978-0-937721; 978-0-939246; 978-1-55828; 978-1-56217; 978-1-56561; 978-1-56884; 978-1-57313; 978-1-58245; 978-1-878058; 978-1-118; 978-1-119; 978-1-7994; 978-1-394) Orders Addr.: c/o John Wiley & Sons, Inc., United States Distribution Ctr., 1 Wiley Dr., Somerset, NJ 08875-1272 USA Tel 732-469-4400; Fax: 732-302-2300; Toll Free Fax: 800-597-3299; Toll Free: 800-225-5945 (orders); Edit Addr.: 111 River St., Hoboken, NJ 07030 USA (SAN 200-2272) Tel 201-748-6000; 201-748-6276 (Retail and Wholesale); Fax: 201-748-6088; 201-748-8641 (Retail and Wholesale)*
E-mail: compbks@wiley.com; bookinfo@wiley.com; custserv@wiley.com
Web site: http://www.wiley.com/compbooks; http://www.interscience.wiley.com; http://www.wiley.com.

William Thomson, *See* **Thomson, Linda**

Williamson, Darcy, *See* **Southern Cross Pubns.**

Willman Productions, P.O. Box 272345, Fort Collins, CO 80527 USA Tel 970-224-5911; Toll Free: 800-816-7566.

Wilshire Bk. Co., *(978-0-87980)* 9731 Variel Ave., Chatsworth, CA 91311-4315 USA (SAN 168-9932)
E-mail: mpowers@mpowers.com
Web site: http://www.mpowers.com.

Wilson & Associates, *See* **Gatewood Pr.**

Wilson & Sons, P.O. Box 996, Bellevue, WA 98009 USA (SAN 129-0010) Tel 425-392-1965
E-mail: dchief@seanst.com.

Wimmer Companies, The, *See* **Wimmer Cookbooks**

Wimmer Cookbooks, *(978-0-918544; 978-0-939114; 978-1-879958)* 4650 Shelby Air Dr., Memphis, TN 38118 USA Tel 901-362-8900; 800-727-1034; Fax: 901-795-9806; Toll Free Fax: 800-794-9806; Toll Free: 800-727-1034 Do not confuse with Wimmer Cooksbooks in Atlanta, GA
E-mail: wimmer@wimmerco.com
Web site: http://www.wimmerco.com.

Winch, B. L. & Assocs., *(978-0-935266)* P.O. Box 1185, Torrance, CA 90505 USA (SAN 247-2716) Tel 310-816-3085; Fax: 310-816-3092; Toll Free: 800-662-9662 (orders only)
E-mail: czippi@att.net
Web site: http://www.ierc.com.

Windham County News Co., P.O. Box 8127, Brattleboro, VT 05304 USA (SAN 159-9917) Tel 802-254-2373.

Windhover Performing Arts Ctr., 257 Granite St., Rockport, MA 01966 USA Tel 978-546-3611
Web site: http://www.windhover.org.

Wine Appreciation Guild, Ltd., *(978-0-932664; 978-1-891267; 978-1-934259; 978-1-935879)* 360 Swift Ave., Unit 30, South San Francisco, CA 94080-6220 USA (SAN 169-0264) Tel 650-866-3020; Fax: 650-866-3513; Toll Free: 800-242-9462 (orders only)
E-mail: Jim@wineappreciation.com; bryan@wineappreciation.com
Web site: http://www.wineappreciation.com.

Winebaum News, Inc., P.O. Box 1620, Raymond, NH 03077-3620 USA (SAN 169-4529).

Wipf & Stock Pubs., *(978-0-9653517; 978-1-55635; 978-1-57910; 978-1-59244; 978-1-59752; 978-1-60608; 978-1-60899; 978-1-61097; 978-1-62032; 978-1-62189; 978-1-62564; 978-1-63087; 978-1-4982; 978-1-5326; 978-1-7252)* Orders Addr.: 199 W 8th Ave Ste 3, Eugene, OR 97401 USA (SAN 990-3038) Tel 541-344-1528; Fax: 541-344-1506; Edit Addr.: 199 W 8th Ave Ste 3, Eugene, OR 97401 USA Tel 541-344-1528; Fax: 541-344-1506
Web site: http://wipfandstock.com/; http://slantbooks.com; http://stonetablebooks.com/.

WIPRO, 2 Christie Heights St., Leonia, NJ 07605 USA Tel 201-840-4755.

Wisdom Pubns., *(978-0-86171; 978-1-61429; 978-1-949129)* 199 Elm St., Somerville, MA 02144 USA (SAN 246-022X) Tel 617-776-7416 ext 24; Fax: 617-776-7841; Toll Free Fax: 800-338-4550 (orders only); Toll Free: 800-462-6420 (orders only)
E-mail: marketing@wisdompubs.org
Web site: http://www.wisdompubs.org.

Wittenborn Art Bks., *(978-0-8150; 978-0-89648)* Div. of Alan Wofsy Fine Arts, Orders Addr.: 1109 Geary Blvd., San Francisco, CA 94109 USA Tel 415-292-6500; Fax: 415-292-6594; Edit Addr.: P.O. Box 2210, San Francisco, CA 94126 USA Tel 510-482-3677; Toll Free: 800-660-6403
E-mail: editeur@eathlink.net; art-books.com@jps.net
Web site: http://www.art-books.com.

Wizard Works, *(978-0-9621543; 978-1-890692)* Orders Addr.: P.O. Box 1125, Homer, AK 99603-1125 USA Toll Free: 877-210-2665
E-mail: wizard@xyz.net
Web site: http://www.xyz.net/~wizard.

Wolper Sales Agency, Inc., 6 Centre Sq., Suite 302A, Easton, PA 18042-3606 USA (SAN 285-9785) Tel 610-559-9550; Fax: 610-559-9898.

Wolverine Distributing, Inc., *(978-0-941875)* P.O. Box 503, Powell, WY 82435 USA (SAN 666-1211) Tel 307-754-2948; Fax: 307-754-2968; Toll Free: 800-967-1633
E-mail: wolverine@tctwest.net.

Wolverine Gallery, *See* **Wolverine Distributing, Inc.**

Women Ink, 777 United Nations Plaza, New York, NY 10017 USA (SAN 630-8309) Tel 212-687-8633; Fax: 212-661-2704
E-mail: wink@womenink.org
Web site: http://www.womenink.org.

Woodbine Publishing Co., The, 15621 Chemical Ln., No. B, Huntington Beach, CA 92649 USA (SAN 114-4243) Tel 714-894-9080; Fax: 714-894-4949; Toll Free: 800-451-4788
Web site: http://www.safaripress.com.

Woodcrafters Lumber Sales, Inc., 212 NE Sixth Ave., Portland, OR 97232 USA (SAN 112-6075) Tel 503-231-0226; Toll Free: 800-777-3709.

Woodland Distribution, Orders Addr.: 118 Woodland Dr., Chapmanville, WV 25508 USA Tel 304-752-7152; Fax: 304-752-9002.

Woodstocker Books/Arthur Schwartz & Company, *(978-1-879504)* 15 Meads Mountain Rd., Woodstock, NY 12498-1016 USA (SAN 630-0464) Tel 845-679-4024; Fax: 845-679-4093; Toll Free: 800-669-9080 (orders only)
E-mail: woodstockerbooks@woodstockerbooks.com
Web site: http://www.aschwartzbooks.com.

Word Distribution, *See* **Word Entertainment**

Word Entertainment, *(978-0-9644619; 978-1-933876)* 25 Music Sq. W., Nashville, TN 37203 USA Tel 615-726-7900; Toll Free Fax: 800-671-6601; Toll Free: 800-876-9673
E-mail: matt.taylor@wordentertainment.com
Web site: http://www.wordentertainment.com.

Word For Today, The, *See* **Calvary Chapel Resources**

Word of Life Distributors, 2707 W. Olympic Blvd. Ste. 100, Los Angeles, CA 90006-2850 USA (SAN 108-433X) Toll Free: 800-347-7057.

WordWorks Publishing, *(978-1-887913)* Orders Addr.: 207 E. Pine Ridge Dr., Westfield, IN 46074 USA Tel 317-867-1879 (phone/fax) Do not confuse with Wordworks Publishing, Austin, TX
E-mail: joanetta.hendel@comcast.net.

Workamper Bookstore, 201 Hiram Rd., Heber Springs, AR 72543-8747 USA (SAN 631-547X) Tel 501-362-2637; Toll Free: 800-446-5627 (orders only)
Web site: http://www.workamper.com.

Workman Publishing Co., Inc., *(978-0-7611; 978-0-89480; 978-0-911104; 978-1-56305; 978-1-5235)* Orders Addr.: 225 Varick St., New York, NY 10014-4381 USA (SAN 203-2821) Tel 212-254-5900; Fax: 212-254-8098; Toll Free: 800-722-7202
E-mail: info@workman.com
Web site: http://www.workman.com.

World Bank Pubns., *(978-0-8213; 978-1-4648)* Orders Addr.: P.O. Box 960, Herndon, VA 20172-0960 USA Toll Free: 800-645-7247; Edit Addr.: 1818 H St., NW, Mail Stop: U11-1104, Washington, DC 20433 USA (SAN 219-0648) Tel 703-661-1580; 202-473-1000 (Head Office); Fax: 202-614-1237
E-mail: books@worldbank.org
Web site: http://www.worldbank.org/publications.

World of Reading, Ltd., P.O. Box 13092, Atlanta, GA 30324-0092 USA Tel 404-233-4042; Fax: 404-237-5511; Toll Free: 800-729-3703.

World Publications, Incorporated, *See* **World Pubns. Group, Inc.**

World Pubns. Group, Inc., *(978-0-7669; 978-0-9640034; 978-1-57215; 978-0-7429; 978-1-4132; 978-1-4279; 978-1-4376; 978-1-4513; 978-1-4643; 978-1-4785)* Orders Addr.: P.O. Box 509, East Bridgewater, MA 02333 USA (SAN 631-7014)
E-mail: sales@wrldpub.net
Web site: http://www.wrldpub.com.

World Scientific Textbook, Orders Addr.: 27 Warren St., Hackensack, NJ 07601 USA.

World Univ., *(978-0-941902)* P.O. Box 2470, Benson, AZ 85602 USA (SAN 239-7943) Tel 520-586-2985; Fax: 520-586-4764
E-mail: desertsanctuary@theriver.com
Web site: http://worlduniversity.org.

World Wide Distributors, Limited, *See* **Island Heritage Publishing**

World Wide Hunting Books, *See* **Woodbine Publishing Co., The**

World Wide Pubns., *(978-0-89066)* P.O. Box 668089, Charlotte, NC 28266-8089 USA (SAN 159-9941) Toll Free: 800-788-0442.

World Wisdom, Inc., *(978-0-941532; 978-1-933316; 978-1-935493; 978-1-936597; 978-1-937786)* Orders Addr.: P.O. Box 2682, Bloomington, IN 47402-2682 USA (SAN 239-1406) Tel 812-330-3232; Fax: 812-333-1642; Toll Free: 888-992-6651; Edit Addr.: 1501 E. Hillside Dr., Bloomington, IN 47401 USA
Web site: http://www.worldwisdom.com.

Worldwide Media Service, Inc., Affil. of Hudson County News Agency, 30 Montgomery St., Jersey City, NJ 07302-3821 USA (SAN 630-4826) Tel 201-332-7100; Fax: 201-332-0265; Toll Free: 800-345-6478
Web site: http://www.americanmagazine.com.

Wright Bk./Educational, 2195 Owendale Dr., Dayton, OH 45439 USA (SAN 159-9968).

Wright Group/McGraw-Hill, *(978-0-322; 978-0-7802; 978-0-940156; 978-1-55624; 978-1-55911; 978-1-4045)* Div. of Mcgraw-Hill School Education Group, Orders Addr.: P.O. Box 545, Blacklick, OH 43004-0545 USA Tel 614-755-5645; Toll Free: 800-722-4726; 800-442-9685 (customer service)
Web site: http://www.wrightgroup.com/.

Writers & Bks., *(978-0-9618487; 978-0-9863305)* 740 University Ave., Rochester, NY 14607-1259 USA (SAN 156-9678).

Wybel Marketing Group, Orders Addr.: 213 W. Main St., Barrington, IL 60010 USA Tel 847-382-0384.

Wyoming Periodical Distributor, P.O. Box 2340, Casper, WY 82601 USA (SAN 169-9245).

Xlibris Corp., *(978-0-7388; 978-0-9663501; 978-1-4010; 978-1-4134; 978-1-59926; 978-1-4257; 978-1-4363; 978-1-4415; 978-1-4500; 978-1-4535; 978-1-4568; 978-1-4628; 978-1-4653; 978-1-4691; 978-1-4771; 978-1-4797; 978-1-4836; 978-1-4931; 978-1-4990; 978-1-5035;-1-5144; 978-1-5245; 978-1-4990-9726-9; 978-1-4990-9725-2; 978-1-4990-9724-5; 978-1-5434; 978-1-9845; 978-1-7960; 978-1-6641)* Orders Addr.: *1663 S. Liberty Dr. Suite 200, Bloomington, IN 47403 USA (SAN 299-5522) Tel 812-334-5223; Fax: 812-334-5223; Toll Free: 888-795-4274*
E-mail: info@xlibris.com
Web site: http://www2.xlibris.com.

Xlibris Corporation, *See* **Xlibris Corp.**

X-S Bks., Inc., 81 Brookside Ave., Amsterdam, NY 12010-0740 USA (SAN 169-4634).

Yale Univ., Far Eastern Pubns., *(978-0-88710)* 340 Edwards St., Box 208252, New Haven, CT 06520-8252 USA (SAN 219-0710) Tel 203-432-3109; Fax: 203-432-3111
Web site: http://www.yale.edu/fep.

Yale Univ. Pr., *(978-0-300)* Orders Addr.: c/o Triliteral LLC, 100 Maple Ridge Dr., Cumberland, RI 02864 USA Tel 401-531-2800; Fax: 401-531-2801; Toll Free Fax: 800-406-9145; Toll Free: 800-405-1619; Edit Addr.: 302 Temple St., New Haven, CT 06511 USA (SAN 203-2740) Tel 203-432-0960; Fax: 203-432-0948
E-mail: yupmkt@yale.edu
Web site: http://www.yale.edu/yup/; http://www.yale.edu/yup/index.html.

Yankee Bk. Peddler, Inc., 999 Maple St., Contoocook, NH 03229 USA (SAN 169-4510) Tel 603-746-3102; Fax: 603-746-5628; Toll Free: 800-258-3774
E-mail: ybp@office.ybp.com
Web site: http://www.ybp.com.

Yankee Paperback & Textbook Co., P.O. Box 18880, Tucson, AZ 85731 USA (SAN 112-1073) Tel 520-325-7229 (phone/fax); Toll Free: 800-340-2665 (in Arizona, California, Nevada, Colorado, New Mexico and Utah only).

Yankee Paperback Distributors, *See* **Yankee Paperback & Textbook Co.**

Yankee Peddler Bookshop, *(978-0-918426)* 4299 Lake Rd., Williamson, NY 14589-9615 USA (SAN 209-925X)
E-mail: byankeep@rochester.rr.com
Web site: http://www.shoprochester.com//yankeepeddler-abc.

YBP Library Services, *See* **GOBI Library Solutionis from EBSCO**

Ye Olde Genealogie Shoppe, *(978-0-932924; 978-1-878311)* Orders Addr.: P.O. Box 39128, Indianapolis, IN 46239 USA (SAN 200-7010) Tel 317-862-3330; Toll Free: 800-419-0200 (orders)
E-mail: yogs@iquest.net
Web site: http://www.yogs.com.

Yosemite Association, *See* **Yosemite Conservancy**

Yosemite Conservancy, *(978-0-939666; 978-1-930238; 978-1-951179)* Orders Addr.: P.O. Box 230, El Portal, CA 95318 USA (SAN 662-197X) Tel 209-379-2317; Edit Addr.: 5020 El Portal Rd., El Portal, CA 95318 USA
E-mail: nicolegeiger1@gmail.com; jedelbrock@yosemiteconservancy.org; kcoit@yosemiteconservancy.org
Web site: http://www.yosemiteconservancy.org.

Young News, Inc., 1600 E. Grand Blvd., Detroit, MI 48211-3144 USA (SAN 169-3999) Fax: 517-753-7774.

Youthlight, Inc., *(978-1-889636; 978-1-59850)* Orders Addr.: P.O. Box 115, Chapin, SC 29036 USA (SAN 256-6400) Tel 803-345-1070; Fax: 803-345-0888; Toll Free: 800-209-9774; Edit Addr.: 105 Fairway Pond Dr., Chapin, SC 29036 USA
E-mail: yl@sc.rr.com; yl@youthlightbooks.com
Web site: http://www.youthlight.com; http://www.youthlightbooks.com.

Yuma News, Incorporated, *See* **Arizona Periodicals, Inc.**

YWAM Publishing, *(978-0-927545; 978-0-9615534; 978-1-57658; 978-1-64836)* Div. of Youth With A Mission International, P.O. Box 55787, Seattle, WA 98155 USA (SAN 248-4021)
E-mail: customerservice@ywampublishing.com
Web site: http://www.ywampublishing.com.

Zabel, C. & W. Co., Orders Addr.: P.O. Box 953, East Brunswick, NJ 08816-0953 USA (SAN 169-4731) Tel 732-254-1000; Fax: 732-254-0121; Edit Addr.: 76 Pennsbury Way, E Brunswick, NJ 08816-5278 USA (SAN 241-6441).

Zagat Survey, *(978-0-943421; 978-0-9612574; 978-1-57006; 978-1-60478)* 4 Columbus Cir., New York, NY 10019 USA (SAN 289-4777) Tel 212-977-6000; Fax: 212-765-9438; Toll Free: 866-999-0991
E-mail: tradesales@justzagat.com; theinz@zagat.com
Web site: http://www.zagat.com.

Zeitlin Periodicals Co., Inc., 7917 Lark Meadow Ave., Las Vegas, NV 89131-4710 USA (SAN 160-8088).

Zondervan, *(978-0-00; 978-0-310; 978-0-937336)* Div. of HarperCollins Christian Publishing, Orders Addr.: c/o Zondervan XNET Ordering Dept., 5249 Corporate Grove, Grand Rapids, MI 49512 USA (SAN 298-9107); Edit Addr.: 5300 Patterson Ave., SE, Grand Rapids, MI 49530 USA (SAN 203-2694) Tel 616-698-6900; Fax: 616-698-3439
Web site: http://www.zondervan.com.

Zondervan Publishing House, *See* **Zondervan**

Z-Twist Bks., 3312 Woodview Dr., Lafayette, CA 94549 USA Tel 916-570-3839.

Zubal, John T. Inc., *(978-0-939738)* 2969 W. 25th St., Cleveland, OH 44113 USA (SAN 165-5841) Tel 216-241-7640; Fax: 216-241-6966.